CANADIAN ALMANAC & DIRECTORY

RÉPERTOIRE ET ALMANACH CANADIEN

2022

Additional Publications

For more detailed information or to place an order, see the back of the book.

CANADIAN WHO'S WHO 2022

1,200 pages, 8 3/8 x 10 7/8, Hardcover
December 2021
ISBN 978-1-64265-931-3
ISSN 0068-9963

Published for over 100 years, this authoritative annual publication offers access to the top 10,000 notable Canadians in all walks of life, including details such as date and place of birth, education, family details, career information, memberships, creative works, honours, languages, and awards, together with full addresses. Included are outstanding Canadians from business, academia, politics, sports, the arts and sciences, and more, selected because of the positions they hold in Canadian society, or because of the contributions they have made to Canada.

FINANCIAL POST DIRECTORY OF DIRECTORS 2022

Répertoire des administrateurs

1,669 pages, 5 7/8 x 9, Hardcover
75th edition, September 2021
ISBN 978-1-64265-933-7
ISSN 0071-5042

Published biennially and annually since 1931, this comprehensive resource offers readers access to approximately 16,800 executive contacts from Canada's top 1,400 corporations. The directory provides a definitive list of directorships and offices held by noteworthy Canadian business people, as well as details on prominent Canadian companies (both public and private), including company name, contact information and the names of executive officers and directors. Includes all-new front matter and three indexes.

CANADIAN PARLIAMENTARY GUIDE 2021

Guide parlementaire canadien

1,350 pages, 6 x 9, Hardcover
155th edition, March 2021
ISBN 978-1-64265-919-1
ISSN 0315-6168

Published annually since before Confederation, this indispensable guide to government in Canada provides information on federal and provincial governments, with biographical sketches of government members, descriptions of government institutions, and historical text and charts. With significant bilingual sections, the Guide covers elections from Confederation to the present, including the most recent provincial elections.

ASSOCIATIONS CANADA 2021

Associations du Canada

2,192 pages, 8 ½ x 11, Softcover
42nd edition, February 2021
ISBN 978-1-64265-915-3
ISSN 1186-9798

Over 20,000 entries profile Canadian and international organizations active in Canada. Over 2,000 subject classifications index activities, professions and interests served by associations. Includes listings of NGOs, institutes, coalitions, social agencies, federations, foundations, trade unions, fraternal orders, political parties. Fully indexed by subject, acronym, budget, conference, executive name, geographic location, mailing list availability, and registered charitable organization.

FINANCIAL SERVICES CANADA 2021-2022

Services financiers au Canada

1,502 pages, 8 1/2 x 11, Softcover
24th edition, April 2021
ISBN 978-1-64265-917-7
ISSN 1484-2408

This directory of Canadian financial institutions and organizations includes banks and depository institutions, non-depository institutions, investment management firms, financial planners, insurance companies, accountants, major law firms, associations, and financial technology companies. Fully indexed.

LIBRARIES CANADA 2021-2022

Bibliothèques Canada

900 pages, 8 ½ x 11, Softcover
36th edition, July 2021
ISBN 978-1-64265-921-4
ISSN 1920-2849

Libraries Canada offers comprehensive information on Canadian libraries, resource centres, business information centres, professional associations, regional library systems, archives, library schools, government libraries, and library technical programs.

CAREERS & EMPLOYMENT CANADA 2021

Carrières et emploi Canada

970 pages, 8 ½ x 11, Softcover
1st edition, October 2020
ISBN 978-1-61925-713-5

Careers & Employment Canada is a new go-to resource for job-seekers across Canada, with detailed, current information on everything from industry associations to summer job opportunities. Divided into five helpful sections, plus three indexes, this guide contains 10,000 organizations and 20,000 industry contacts to aid in research and jump-start careers in a variety of fields.

CANADIAN ENVIRONMENTAL RESOURCE GUIDE 2020-2021

Guide des ressources environnementales canadiennes

860 pages, 8 ½ x 11, Softcover
24th edition, September 2020
ISBN 978-1-64265-227-7
ISSN 1920-2725

Canada's most complete national listing of environmental organizations, product and service companies and governmental bodies, all indexed and categorized for quick and easy reference. Also included is the Environmental Update, with recent events, maps, rankings, statistics, and trade shows and conferences. The online version features even more content, including associations, special libraries, and federal/provincial government information.

HEALTH GUIDE CANADA 2020-2021

Guide canadien de la santé

1,098 pages, 8 ½ x 11, Softcover
4th edition, June 2020
ISBN: 978-1-64265-239-0

Health Guide Canada contains thousands of ways to deal with the many aspects of chronic or mental health disorders. It includes associations, government agencies, libraries and resource centres, educational facilities, hospitals and publications, as well as disease descriptions, relevant reports, and statistics.

CANNABIS CANADA

Cannabis au Canada

836 pages, 8 ½ x 11, Softcover
1st edition, April 2019
ISBN 978-1-64265-243-7

Cannabis Canada is a one-of-a-kind resource covering all aspects of this growing industry, including a history of cannabis, current reports, trade show listings, regulations, and a wealth of statistics. Company listings include a comprehensive industry buyer's guide, government resources, associations, venture capital and law firms, schools offering cannabis-related courses, and more.

CANADIAN ALMANAC & DIRECTORY

RÉPERTOIRE ET ALMANACH CANADIEN

2022

GREY HOUSE
PUBLISHING
CANADA

175th YEAR

Grey House Publishing Canada
PUBLISHER: Leslie Mackenzie
GENERAL MANAGER: Bryon Moore
MANAGING EDITOR & COMPOSITION: Stuart Paterson
ASSOCIATE EDITORS: Leah Case, Olivia Parsonson

Grey House Publishing
EDITORIAL DIRECTOR: Laura Mars
MARKETING DIRECTOR: Jessica Moody
PRODUCTION MANAGER: Kristen Hayes

Grey House Publishing Canada
411 Queen St. West, 3rd Fl.
Toronto, ON M5V 2A5
866-433-4739
Fax: 416-644-1904
www.greyhouse.ca
e-mail: info@greyhouse.ca

Statistics Canada information is used with the permission of Statistics Canada. Users are forbidden to copy this material and/or redisseminate the data, in an original or modified form, for commercial purposes, without the expressed permission of Statistics Canada. For more information contact: Toll Free: 1-800-263-1136; URL: www.statcan.gc.ca

Grey House Publishing Canada is a wholly owned subsidiary of Grey House Publishing, Inc. USA.

Printed in Canada by Marquis Book Printing

175th edition published 2021
ISBN: 978-1-64265-929-0
ISSN: 0068-8193
Cataloguing in Publication data is available from Library and Archives Canada

PRIME MINISTER · PREMIER MINISTRE

Statement by the Prime Minister of Canada

It is with great pleasure that I join Grey House Publishing Canada in celebrating their 175th edition of the Canadian Almanac and Directory.

Since its establishment in 1847, the Canadian Almanac and Directory has been Canada's leading sourcebook and has been widely distributed to over 120 countries around the world. A combination of textual material, charts, colour photographs and directory listings, the Canadian Almanac and Directory is the most complete source of Canadian information available. For the past 174 years, cultural, professional and financial institutions, legislative, governmental, judicial and educational organizations alike have all greatly benefited from Canada's authoritative sourcebook, making it the number one reference for collected facts and figures about Canada.

Despite challenges faced by the pandemic, I would like to take this opportunity to thank Grey House Publishing Canada for their remarkable work and contributions as our nation's flagship directory on all things Canadian.

Please accept my warmest regards and best wishes for continued success with your next edition!

Ottawa
2021

PRIME MINISTER · PREMIER MINISTRE

Message du Premier ministre du Canada

J'ai le grand plaisir de me joindre à Grey House Publishing Canada pour souligner la parution de la 175ᵉ édition du *Répertoire et almanach canadien*.

Depuis sa création en 1847, le *Répertoire et almanach canadien* est le principal document d'information canadien et est largement distribué dans plus de 120 pays du monde. Combinant de l'information textuelle, des tableaux, des photographies en couleurs et des répertoires, le *Répertoire et almanach canadien* est la source d'information la plus complète sur le Canada. Depuis les 174 dernières années, les institutions culturelles, professionnelles et financières ainsi que les organisations législatives, gouvernementales, judiciaires et scolaires du Canada ont toutes grandement bénéficié de ce document de référence officiel. Ainsi, cet ouvrage est devenu le principal recueil de faits et chiffres au sujet du Canada.

J'aimerais remercier Grey House Publishing Canada pour ses contributions et le travail remarquable qu'elle accomplit avec la publication de ce répertoire phare de la nation canadienne, malgré toutes les difficultés engendrées par la pandémie.

Je vous offre mes plus sincères salutations et vous souhaite beaucoup de succès avec votre nouvelle édition!

Ottawa
2021

First published 175 years ago as *Canadian Mercantile Almanac for 1847,* the *Canadian Almanac & Directory* is now published by Grey House Publishing Canada. The 2022 edition of this significant work includes over 50,000 entries covering hundreds of topics, making this the number one reference for collected facts and figures about Canada.

The *Almanac* continues to be widely used by business professionals, government officials, information specialists, researchers, publishers, and anyone needing current, accessible information on all topics relevant to those who live and work in Canada. This latest edition provides the most comprehensive picture of Canada, from physical attributes to economic and business summaries to leisure and recreation. It combines textual material, charts, colour photographs and directory listings. This 2022 edition includes hundreds more listings and thousands more details than its predecessor. The comprehensiveness and currency of data is unparalleled.

Each of the 17 sections in the *Almanac* includes a detailed Table of Contents, outlining hundreds of subcategories. A *Topical Table of Contents* on the following pages and a comprehensive *Entry Name Index* at the end of the work make navigation of the massive amount of material quick and easy.

Section 1: Almanac comprises 10 major categories, including History, Vital Statistics, Geography, Science, Awards & Honours, Economics and more. Readers will find articles, colour maps and photographs, charts and tables for a fact-filled snapshot of Canada. This resource section, invaluable for residents, politicians, and the business community, includes a detailed Table of Contents for easy access.

DIRECTORY SECTIONS

Section 2: Arts & Culture begins the **Directory Listings** and includes nine categories: Aquaria, Art Galleries, Botanical Gardens, Museums, National Parks, Observatories, Performing Arts, Science Centres and Zoos. Categories are arranged by province and city. All listings include address, phone, fax, website, email, key executives and a brief description.

Section 3: Associations lists thousands of associations and organizations arranged in over 120 topics from Accounting to Youth. Each listing includes valuable descriptions and current contact information. An Association Name Index precedes the listings.

Section 4: Broadcasting begins with Canada's Major Broadcasting Companies, then lists, by Province, all Radio and Television Stations, as well as Cable Companies and Specialty Broadcasters.

Section 5: Business & Finance combines Accounting, Banking, Insurance, and Canada's Major Companies and Stock Exchanges. It includes a separate section for Major Accounting Firms with company descriptions, as well as an Insurance Class Index.

Section 6: Education is arranged by Province, and includes Government Agencies, Districts, Specialized and Independent Schools, University and Technical facilities, many with valuable descriptions.

Section 7: Federal/Provincial Government begins with a Quick Reference Guide to help you find your way around government agencies. The Guide is followed by Federal and Provincial listings, plus information on The Royal Family and Diplomatic and Consular Representatives in Canada and abroad.

Section 8: Municipal Government details all County and Municipal Districts and segregated Major Municipalities. All profiles include date of incorporation, square miles, and population figures. Also included are District Maps and descriptions for all Provinces.

Section 9: Judicial Government provides thorough coverage for Courts in Canada, including Federal and Provincial. Listings are categorized by type of Court and City within each Province, and include presiding judges.

Section 10: Hospitals and Health Care Facilities is an overview of available facilities by Province. Government agencies, hospitals, community health centres, retirement care and mental health facilities, are all arranged alphabetically by city for easy access.

Originairement publié sous le nom « Canadian Mercantile Almanac for 1847 » il y a 175 ans, le *Répertoire et Almanach Canadien* est maintenant publié par Grey House Publishing Canada. L'édition 2022 comprend plus de 50 000 entrées couvrant des centaines de sujets, faisant de ce répertoire l'*Almanach* le plus complet jamais publié sur les faits et données concernant le Canada.

Le *Répertoire et Almanach Canadien* continu d'être largement consulté par les éditeurs, les gens d'affaires, les bureaux gouvernementaux, les spécialistes de l'information, les chercheurs et par tous ceux qui ont besoin d'une information à jour et facilement accessible sur tous les sujets imaginables concernant le travail et la vie au Canada. La présente édition brosse le tableau le mieux documenté qui soit du Canada en un seul volume, comprenant ses attributs physiques et économiques en passant par les activités commerciales, les divertissements et les loisirs qu'on y pratique. Il constitue un amalgame exceptionnel de textes, de chartes, de photographies couleur et de listes de répertoire. Cette édition comprend un plus grand nombre de données, de profils détaillés et des quantités de mises à jour.

Chaque section de l'ouvrage, qui en compte 17, comprend une table des matières détaillée qui définit des centaines de sous-catégories. Une table des matières par sujet sur les pages suivantes et un index nominatif exhaustif à la fin de l'ouvrage simplifient la consultation de la quantité impressionnante d'information offerte et la rendent plus rapide.

Section 1 : Almanach est composée de 10 catégories principales, notamment Histoire, Statistiques essentielles, Géographie, Sciences, Prix et distinctions, Économie. Il contient plus d'articles, de cartes et de photographies couleur, de chartes et de tableaux qui offrent un portrait juste et à jour des faits et données importants sur le Canada. Elle constitue une source unique de renseignements pour tous les citoyens, les politiciens et les communautés d'affaires. Les tables des matières détaillées de chacune des catégories rendent maintenant la consultation plus facile.

RÉPERTOIRES

Section 2 : Arts et Culture comprend neuf matières principales, des galeries d'art aux parcs zoologiques. Les renseignements y sont regroupés par province et par ville. Chaque entrée comprend des données d'identification, dont l'adresse, numéros de téléphone et télécopieur, site Internet, courriel, cadres, ainsi qu'une brève description.

Section 3 : Associations énumère des milliers d'associations et d'organismes classés selon plus de 120 sujets, de l'agriculture aux voyages. Chaque entrée comprend des données d'identification, dont celles de contacts. Un index par nom au début des catégories facilite la recherche.

Section 4 : Radiodiffusion et télédiffusion présente une liste des principales sociétés de radiodiffusion et télédiffusion au pays suivie des listes, par province, des stations de radio et de télévision ainsi que des entreprises de distribution par câble et des émetteurs spécialisés.

Section 5 : Affaires et finance comprend de l'information sur les cabinets comptables, les banques, les compagnies d'assurances, les plus grandes sociétés canadiennes et les bourses. Elle comprend une section distincte pour les principaux cabinets comptables, y compris des descriptions d'entreprise et un index des catégories d'assurance.

Section 6 : Éducation est divisée par province et donne des renseignements sur les agences gouvernementales, les commissions scolaires, les écoles privées et spécialisées, les institutions universitaires, collégiales et techniques. Vous y trouverez également plusieurs autres renseignements d'intérêts en matière d'éducation.

Section 7 : Gouvernement fédéral/provincial commence par un Guide de références rapide qui vous aidera à trouver votre chemin parmi la multitude d'agences gouvernementales répertoriées, suivi de leurs listes au niveau du pays et des provinces. Cette section comprend également les plus récents résultats d'élection. Vous y trouverez de plus de l'information sur la Famille royale ainsi que les représentants diplomatiques et consulaires au Canada et à l'étranger.

Section 8 : Gouvernement municipal fournit de l'information sur les comtés, les municipalités régionales de comté et les principales villes canadiennes. Chaque profil a été revu pour y incorporer la date d'incorporation, la superficie

Section 11: Law Firms includes a separate section of Major Law Firms with descriptions and Senior Partners. Following the Majors are law firms arranged by Province.

Section 12: Libraries begins with Canada's main Library/Archive and Government Departments for Libraries. Provincial listings follow, with Regional Systems listed first, then Public Libraries and Archives.

Section 13: Publishing includes Publishers—Book, Magazine, Newspapers—and Newspapers by Province. Magazine listings are arranged in six major categories, preceded by a Magazine Name Index for easy searching. Details include frequency and circulation figures.

Section 14: Religion starts off with broad information on religious groups, then lists Associations, arranged alphabetically by 37 denominations.

Section 15: Sports provides information on a variety of sports categories, including Associations, and detailed League and Team listings for Baseball, Basketball, Football, Hockey, Lacrosse and Soccer. You'll also find the major sports venues in Canada, from stadiums to racetracks.

Section 16: Transportation offers comprehensive listings for major transportation modes, plus industry Associations, Government Agencies and Airport and Port Authorities.

Section 17: Utilities includes Associations, Government Agencies and Provincial Utility Companies.

Entry Name Index

The *Canadian Almanac & Directory 2022* is also available as part of **Grey House Publishing's Canada's Information Resource Centre (CIRC)** at www.greyhouse.ca where subscribers have full access to this rich database. Trial subscriptions to CIRC are available by calling 866-433-4739.

We acknowledge the valuable contributions of those individuals and organizations that have responded to our information gathering process. Their help and responses to our phone calls and questionnaires are greatly appreciated.

Every effort has been made to assure the accuracy of the information included in this edition of the *Canadian Almanac & Directory*. Do not hesitate to contact the editorial office in Toronto with comments, or if revisions are necessary.

et la population approximative. Comprend également des plans des secteurs ainsi que des descriptions pour toutes les provinces.

Section 9 : Gouvernement - Juridique adresse la liste de tous les tribunaux judiciaires au Canada, tant fédéraux que provinciaux. Les renseignements y sont regroupés par genre de tribunal et par ville, au niveau de chaque province. On y trouve également le nom des juges actuellement en fonction.

Section 10 : Hôpitaux et soins de santé donne une vue d'ensemble des établissements de santé par province. Pour simplifier la consultation, les agences gouvernementales, les hôpitaux, les centres de santé communautaire, les centres de santé mentale et les établissements de soins de longues durées pour personnes âgées sont regroupés par ville, en ordre alphabétique.

Section 11 : Bureaux d'avocats inclue une sous-section détaillant les principaux cabinets d'avocats au Canada et donnant une brève description de ceux-ci et de leurs principaux associés. Vient ensuite, la liste des bureaux d'avocats regroupés par province.

Section 12 : Bibliothèque présente en premier lieu les principales bibliothèques au Canada et les bibliothèques gouvernementales et d'archives. On y trouve ensuite des renseignements sur les bibliothèques, par province, où sont décrits les systèmes régionaux, suivis des principales bibliothèques publiques et d'archives.

Section 13 : Édition fournit de l'information, détaillé par province, sur les éditeurs des livres, magazines et journaux, ainsi que les quotidiens et autres journaux. La nomenclature des magazines est présentée en six catégories précédées d'un index par nom pour faciliter la recherche. Plusieurs données ont été ajoutées dont celles concernant la fréquence de publication et le tirage.

Section 14 : Religion fournit une vaste quantité d'informations sur les groupements religieux, suivie de celles sur les 37 principales confessions.

Section 15 : Sports fournit des principales informations beaucoup des associations et des catégories de sports et des données sur les ligues et équipes de baseball, basketball, football, hockey, lacrosse et soccer. Vous y trouverez aussi des renseignements sur les majeures installations sportives du Canada comprenant les stades et les pistes de course.

Section 16 : Transport comprend des renseignements complets sur les principaux moyens de transport ainsi que les associations du secteur, les organismes gouvernementaux et les autorités aéroportuaires et portuaires.

Section 17 : Services publics regroupe sous un même chapitre les associations, les agences gouvernementales et les entreprises oeuvrant dans les services publics de chaque province.

Index nominatif

Le *Répertoire et almanach canadien 2022* fait partie des vaste données électroniques du **Centre de documentation du Canada (CDC) de Grey House Publishing Canada** (www.greyhouse.ca) auquel les abonnés peuvent avoir accès de leur ordinateur personnel. Vous pouvez obtenir un abonnement d'essai aux données du CDC en composant le 866 433-4739.

Nous tenons à souligner la précieuse contribution des personnes et des organismes qui ont collaboré tout au long de l'année à notre procédé de cueillette d'information; votre aide, vos réponses à notre questionnaire dans les délais impartis et nos appels téléphoniques sont grandement appréciés.

Nous avons mis tous les efforts pour nous assurer de l'exactitude de l'information contenue dans cette édition du *Répertoire et almanach canadien*. N'hésitez pas à communiquer avec le bureau de la rédaction pour faire part de vos commentaires ou si des modifications s'avèrent nécessaires.

Table of Contents

Table des matières

ALMANAC

History

History of Canada

Over the past 400 years, Canada has evolved from a sparsely populated trading post to the tenth-richest sovereign power in the world. It stands alone as the only country to separate from its colonial power through peaceful means.

The political boundary of what is now known as Canada recorded thousands of years of history before European colonization, but was one of the last places on Earth to host human habitation. While modern *Homo sapiens* emerged from the eastern region of Africa 200,000 years ago, most scientists agree that it took another 175,000 years for humans to find their way across the ice bridge that once joined Alaska and Eastern Siberia. The land that now constitutes Canada has seen the longest period of human habitation in the New World: from the original migration 25,000 years ago came all the indigenous cultures of North and South America including the Arctic Inuit, Blackfoot, Cree, Algonquin, Dene, and Iroquois League of Five Nations. Estimates put the number of native peoples in the United States and Canada before European contact at about two million.

Columbus may have been given credit for the "discovery" of America in 1492, but proof exists that Vikings voyaged to Greenland and further west as early as 982 A.D. Archeological evidence points to Norse settlements in Newfoundland at L'Anse aux Meadows dating back to approximately 1000 A.D., making Canada the actual site of the European discovery of North America. The Vikings, however, were not concerned with permanent colonization, only Canadian natural resources. By the time Christopher Columbus arrived, the Norse settlements had been abandoned.

With Christopher Columbus came the European fervour of colonizing the New World. Seeking a way to circumvent the long land trade routes to Asian goods by crossing the Atlantic to what he thought was India, Columbus inadvertently began the Age of Discovery. European powers established colonies, seeking spice, gold, slaves, and new crops, as well as the promotion of Christianity among the native peoples. The earlier colonies, mostly Spanish and Portuguese, were concentrated in South America, Central America, and the Caribbean. England and France, however, turned their attention north. John Cabot, an Italian-born English explorer, is credited as being the first European explorer after the Vikings to set foot in North America. Although this exploration occurred only five years after Columbus's discoveries, it was not until 1605 that permanent settlements were established. Many explorers, including Henry Hudson, still attempted to find the Northwest Passage, a reputed waterway through the New World to Asia. The reasons for this 100-year gap have more to do with European affairs than those of the New World.

Two events slowed the colonization of North America: religious unrest and war in Europe. In 1517, Martin Luther distributed his list of 95 grievances against the Catholic Church by means of a new invention, the printing press. Thus began the Protestant Reformation. This schism was to have far-reaching consequences across all of European history, but in the short term, it created rancorous religious strife. Most of Europe turned inward to deal with unrest and religious crisis. Escalating political conflicts enveloped most of Western Europe for decades, drawing resources away from colonization efforts. The French Wars of Religion, the Italian Wars, and popular uprisings combined with new religious uprisings to turn the attention of Europe away from the New World for more than a century.

France looked to North America as the best possible source of wealth and power and as a relief from war debt. When French explorer Jacques Cartier sailed up the St. Lawrence River in 1534, he claimed the territory for France, and gave it the name it still bears today: Canada. Once fur traders arrived in Eastern Canada in the 1500s, France monopolized the fur trade. While the French made an effort to establish friendly trading relations with the native population, the Iroquois in particular proved openly hostile. Conflicts with local tribes soon convinced the crown that if traders were to make a profit in Canada, a permanent military and civilian presence was essential. King Henry IV sent his royal "hydrographer," Samuel de Champlain to map the region.

In 1605, after exploring the coast of North America as far south as Cape Cod, Champlain established the first permanent French settlement at Port Royal, and in 1608 he founded Quebec City. New France, as it was then called, grew slowly, mainly due to disinterest from the mainland and war with the Iroquois. The settlers survived attacks from native peoples through their alliance with the Algonquin, Montagnais, and Huron peoples. These alliances not only secured their survival, but greatly increased France's control of the fur trade. Europeans had little experience in the thick wilderness of the area, an expertise that the native peoples supplied.

Once again religious tensions in Europe interfered with Canada's settlement and growth. By the mid-seventeenth century, while England's American and Caribbean colonies grew self-sufficient, New France remained underpopulated. The struggling colony drained France's resources. The French crown decided to take action by creating land incentives for emigrants to New France. Only one caveat stood in the way: all settlers must be Roman Catholic, or convert to Roman Catholicism before leaving Europe. This change of policy, undertaken at the urging of the fanatical Catholic Cardinal Richelieu, closest advisor to King Louis XIII, created friction. Previously, French Protestants, especially the persecuted sect known as Huguenots, had fled to New

France to escape religious persecution. Cardinal Richelieu's new edict would have a lasting impact on the religious and political makeup of modern Canada.

In the late seventeenth century, English and French colonies in the New World began to take a stronger foothold. Both nations finally saw a large-scale financial return on their investments, but a war in Europe again infringed on Canada's nascent growth. New France, already in the middle of brutal intertribal warfare with the Algonquins, conflicted with the Iroquois confederacy opposing them. With the War of the Grand Alliance in 1688, which pitted France against almost all of continental Europe, the Iroquois began to receive English weapons as part of government policy. This escalation by the English heightened the already bloody warfare. English armies and their Iroquois allies captured Port Royal, but were turned back from Quebec City, due mainly to a decimation of forces by disease. The war eventually petered out, and a peace was signed in 1697. The Iroquois, however, continued the fight without British help, and eventually suffered a series of major defeats, forcing them to sue for peace four years later.

New France, and thereby Canada, seemed securely in the mother country's domain following the end of the War of the Grand Alliance. However, France's control of the region was not to last. Queen Anne's War, which began only a year after the French peace with the Iroquois, lead England to claim Nova Scotia and Newfoundland, as well as the rights to the land surrounding Hudson Bay. Fighting broke out again three decades later in 1744, in a battle known as King George's War, but neither side was able to enlarge their colonial positions.

By 1754 the long-standing animosity between the English and French seeped into the New World, culminating in the Seven Years War, known in the Americas as the French and Indian War. The causes of the conflict were threefold. The lucrative fur trade, rich fishing grounds, ample lumber, and mineral deposits all promised great wealth to whoever controlled Canada. Secondly, the fiercely anti-Catholic British felt that the Protestant French were heretics, a feeling that was reciprocated by the French. Thirdly, possession of colonies overseas could be used as diplomatic bargaining chips should the war in Europe go badly.

The Seven Years War was the first worldwide war, fought on five continents: North America, South America, Africa, Europe and Asia. More than a million died, and the war resulted in a complete change in the power structure of the New World. Britain gained all of France's colonial possessions in North America, and Canada became a British colony. However, 150 years of French colonization didn't disappear overnight. Even today, French-English relations in Canada can be contentious.

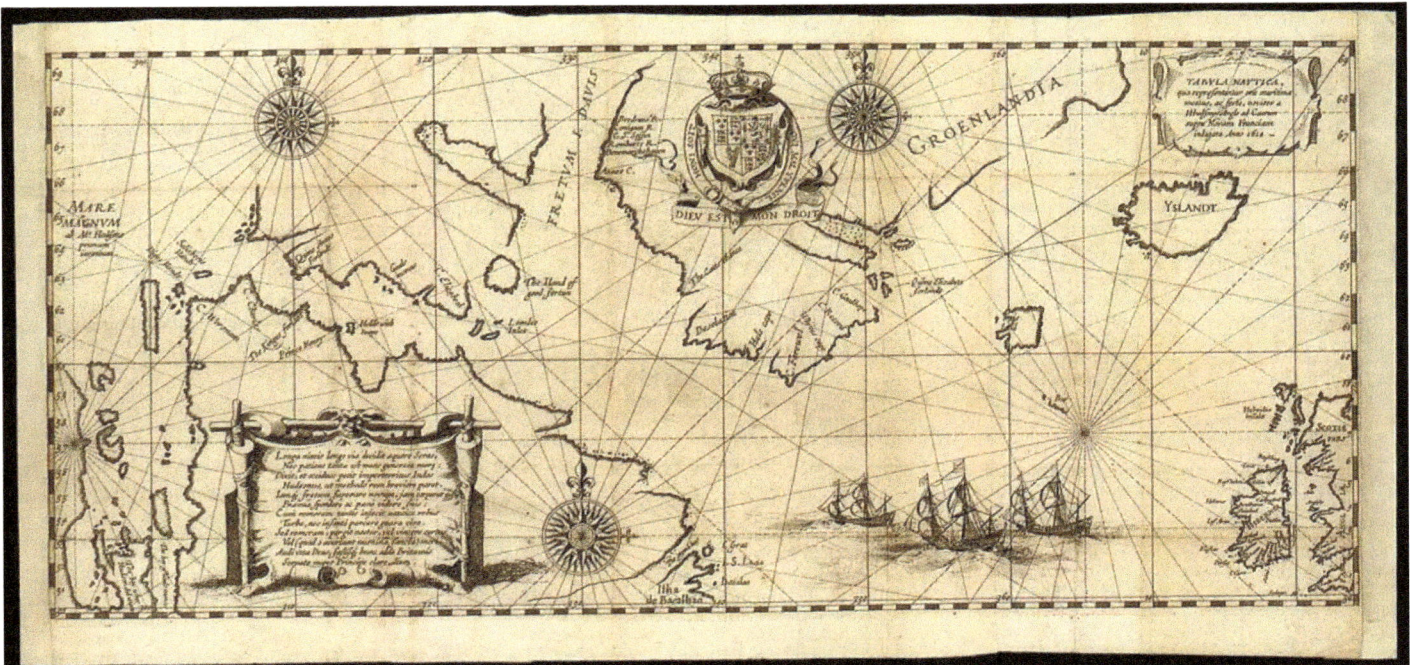

Henry Hudson arrived in Arctic waters in 1610 determined to find the Northwest Passage. He explored Hudson Bay and the mouth of the Bay. His crew mutinied and abandoned him in 1611 and returned to Europe. This map by Dutch cartographer Gerritsz is based on Hudson's discoveries.

Champlain's Map 1632

The British, upon taking control of Canada in 1764, left intact the religious and economic systems already in place, to the relief of the Catholic French colonists. The Quebec Act of 1774 allowed a separate system of French law to continue in Quebec. The British now controlled the entire eastern half of North America, from the eastern seaboard to the Mississippi River. However, George III's mistreatment of the American colonies would soon cause a shift in the balance of power in the New World.

As a base for the British forces, a refuge for fleeing Americans loyal to the British crown, and a source of militia for both the British and American armies, Canada played a large role in the American Revolution. The American army originally attempted to convince Canada to join their revolution but Canadians had just finished rebuilding after the Seven Years War and most did not want no take part in another feud. On June 27, 1775, American troops attacked Quebec and Montreal was taken without a fight. The attack on Quebec City was eventually defeated and in 1776, the American troops evacuated Montreal.

When America gained independence from Britain in 1783, citizens loyal to the British Empire were exiled. Over 35,000 of these loyalists flooded into Nova Scotia. This massive influx prompted the British government to divide Nova Scotia, creating the new colony of New Brunswick. Soon, the loyalists in Quebec were also making demands for their own colony, while the French Canadians were equally determined to have their own elected assembly. In 1791, Quebec was divided into Upper Canada and Lower Canada in order to meet the distinct needs of the English loyalists and the French Canadians.

Tensions between Britain and America remained high in the proceeding decades, and once again a conflict erupted that ensnared Canada. The United States declared war on Britain in 1812 over the arming and supplying of hostile Native American tribes and the forced conscription of American sailors into the British Navy. Canada became one of the primary battlegrounds in this conflict, with the United States planning to seize Canada and use it as leverage against the British. America expected support from the people of Canada, who they assumed were unhappy under English colonial rule. However, many Canadians at that time were children of British loyalists who fled America and saw the United States as invaders and occupiers.

The American army suffered a loss early in the war when they were soundly defeated by General Isaac Brock and his force of Indian allies and local military men at the Battle of Queenston Heights. But the American army did go on to occupy and loot many cities, including York (now Toronto) and Newark (now Niagara-on-the-Lake), eventually controlling much of present day Ontario and Quebec. Ultimately, the American army was driven back, and although the war ended with no real victor, the fact that an attempted American takeover had been thwarted gave Canadians confidence and stimulated national pride.

While Canadians rejected the idea of American invaders on their soil, the political example of the United States resonated throughout the country. Rebellions broke out against the British in 1837. Canadians, angry over the unfair distribution of wealth derived from Canada's natural resources, balked against not being represented in the British government. Based on the opinion of the British that friction between the French and English people was causing conflict in Canada, all of the Canadian colonies were merged together into the United Province of Canada in 1840. In 1849 the United States and the British Empire agreed that the 49th north parallel would be the boundary between the two nations, and the British extended Canada to the western seaboard, encompassing British Columbia.

Canadian independence had been debated in Britain and in Canada almost since the American Revolution. Some advocated violent revolution and total Canadian independence. Others wanted a slower, more gradual autonomy. On July 1st, 1867, the British parliament passed the British North America Act, which established The Dominion of Canada as a separate and self-governing colony. While it was not completely severed from England, especially in matters of foreign policy, domestically, Canada was allowed free reign.

During the next decades, Canada continued to expand westward. With the purchase of two huge northern territories, The North-Western Territory and Rupert's Land, from the Hudson Bay Company, the country more than doubled its size. The sections of Canada west of Ontario housed a large population of French-speaking, Catholic Métis, the children of indigenous people and white settlers. After the sale of Rupert's Land, many settlers from Ontario flooded into the region hoping to claim land.

The Métis became worried that this influx of mostly English Protestant settlers would threaten their rights to language, religion and land. The Métis leader Louis Riel organized the Red River Resistance in 1869 in order to ensure that these rights were guaranteed. The revolt led to the creation of Manitoba, a province with strong laws protecting the Métis, French-speaking people and Catholics. By 1905, the founding provinces of Upper and Lower Canada, New Brunswick, and Nova Scotia were soon joined by British Columbia, Saskatchewan, Prince Edward Island, and Alberta.

The construction of a transcontinental railroad, completed in 1885, spurred Canada's expansion. While the railroad enabled additional settlers to move west into the new provinces, it also pushed the Native people aside. Again rebellion flared, resulting in more bloodshed. The sentiment that the Canadian government didn't heed the concerns of French-speaking Catholic citizens caused a political crisis resulting in the resignation of prime minister Mackenzie Bowell in 1896, when the government tried to ban French as an official language of Manitoba, contrary to the laws of the province.

Both Canada and the United States shared a period of western expansion in the late nineteenth century, based on the prominence of the railroad, the promise of free land and the discovery of mineral deposits. These factors, joined with a large influx of European immigrants, led to Canada becoming the fastest-growing economy in the world between 1896 and 1911. During that time, the Canadian government created the Yukon Territory, a land mass about the size of Germany, Austria and Switzerland combined, then populated by only 8,500 people.

On the verge of the twentieth century, Canada faced the first serious conflict with its colonial power. When Britain entered the Boer War in 1899, most English-speaking Canadians supported bringing South Africa into the fold of the British Empire. French Canadians, however, had little interest in British imperialism, seeing themselves as a separate concern, only nominally part of the Empire. As a compromise, volunteers were allowed to serve in the Boer War, but the Canadian Army stayed uninvolved. The view of French Canada as a separate entity, exacerbated by rebellion and anti-French laws of the past decades, would continue to play out in Canadian politics in years to come.

Arctic regions 1953

Although many French Canadians wanted out from under the British Empire's yoke, the country was still obligated to fall in line with British foreign policy. With the assassination of Archduke Ferdinand on June 28, 1914, Canada was swept into the chaotic system of alliances that created World War I. When Britain declared war on the central powers on August 4th, Canadian troops were called into action. Like most of the allied powers, internal disputes were put aside and support for the war remained high, even among French Canadians. After suffering more than 200,000 dead and wounded casualties out of a population of seven million, support for the war began to wane. By the time the government attempted to introduce conscription in 1917, many Canadians, especially in French Canada, were fiercely anti-war. Despite the popular sentiment, World War I greatly increased the sense of Canadian nationalism and identity, fed by the country's significant role in the largest war mankind had ever known. Massive Canadian casualties in what many Canadians saw as a "British" war also created additional animosity towards the Empire.

World War I radically changed Canada's political landscape. Soldiers returned home from the horrors of the conflict with altered political ideologies. Socialism, communism, trade unionism and other left-wing progressive movements gained traction in the years immediately after the war, as the influx of soldiers returning home caused high unemployment and wage cuts. The Winnipeg General Strike of 1919, the largest of a wave of strikes that swept the country, was violently crushed by police, killing one man and wounding 30. When women's suffrage was enacted nationwide in 1918, the ruling Conservative Party collapsed, partly because of their actions during the strike. The Liberal Party, upon assuming control of the government, enacted many of the original strike committee's demands, including the right to form

unions without government permission. Progressive and socialist parties formed in subsequent years, including the Progressive Party of Canada and the Cooperative Commonwealth Federation.

In 1931, the British Parliament passed the Statute of Westminster, establishing all the colonies and dominions of the British Empire, including Canada, Australia, New Zealand, and Ireland as separate legislative entities. This act allowed these countries to write their own constitutions and removed the power of the British Government to legislate in these areas, effectively making them independent, while still being contained in a worldwide British Commonwealth.

When the American Stock Market crashed on Black Tuesday in 1929, kicking off the Great Depression, the Canadian economy soon felt the effects. By 1933, the Canadian gross national product had dropped 40 percent. Manufacturing and farming suffered the most, with the price of wheat, Canada's main export, cut in half. At its worst point in 1933, 30 percent of Canadians were out of work. Newfoundland, deciding that Canadian government policy was the cause of the economic difficulty, voted to leave the Canadian federation and rejoin the British Empire.

When both the Liberal and Conservative parties were unable to produce any solutions to the crisis, many Canadians began to turn to third parties, such as the socialist Cooperative Commonwealth Federation and the Social Credit Party of Canada. After the Conservative government of R.B. Bennett put unemployed men into work camps to offset the great cost of supporting a huge welfare system, the Workers' Unity League put together a massive protest called the "On to Ottawa Trek" in order to call for improved conditions and benefits. Bennett's attempt to repress the Trek resulted in the Regina Riot, and contributed to his de-

feat in the 1935 election. The new Liberal government did away with the camps and instituted social programs to help lessen the effects of the Depression, but Canada was still severely affected. Almost one-fifth of the population was surviving on government payouts and social support systems. Even after a resurgent boom in Canada's economy, brought on by World War II, these systems remained in place, and continued to evolve.

World War II officially began on September 1, 1939. Canada did not immediately enter the war upon the British declaration as it had in World War I. With its growing independence from England, Canada decided to declare war on its own nine days later. While the Japanese and Nazi onslaught was still in full effect, Canadian supplies and war material were instrumental in keeping Britain from succumbing to German invasion. Once the Allies were in a position to counterattack, Canadian troops were deployed all over the world, and served valiantly in some of the major battles, including the invasion of Sicily and Italy in 1943, the allied landing at Normandy in 1944, the liberation of the Netherlands, and the drive across France and Germany to end the war. However, Canada endured its own share of loss. A predominantly Canadian raid, at Dieppe, France, resulted in more than 3,000 dead, wounded or captured and German U-boats, which prowled Canadian waters, sank many supply ships. In the end, Canada suffered a total of 42,000 casualties.

When the Japanese bombed Pearl Harbor on December 7, 1941, the 22,000 Japanese Canadians then living in British Columbia took the brunt of the resulting pain and anger. The anti-Asian sentiment in the province was further fueled when thousands of Canadians were killed or captured in the Japanese invasion of Hong Kong. In 1942, all people of Japanese descent were sent to internment camps, and after the war, all Japanese

Canadians were deported from British Columbia. It was not until 1949 that they became free to live anywhere in Canada. Japanese Canadians were finally compensated in 1988 for the wrongs that they had suffered during the war.

At the close of World War II, Canada and the United States alone benefited from never having seen fighting on their home soil. Each country was, therefore, in a unique economic position. Due to a revitalized manufacturing sector, the discovery of oil in Alberta, and as the main trading partner to the economic superpower on their southern border, the Canadian economy exploded. This newfound wealth was put into a radical new program of social support. Based upon the centralized welfare state of the late 1930s and early 1940s, as well as many of the policies of the socialist Cooperative Commonwealth Federation, Canadians enjoyed hospital insurance, old-age pensions, veterans' pensions, and family allowance. These progressive social policies convinced Newfoundland to rejoin Canada in a 1949 referendum.

Canada cemented its position in the Cold War with its founding membership in NATO in 1949. The country's fortunes were firmly rooted with the United States. Canada participated in the Korean War, and Canadian troops were stationed in West Germany, on the border of the communist Eastern Bloc. Canada's voting record in the United Nations was not always aligned with the United States, but there is no question that Canada was an American ally pitted against the Soviet Union.

Canada's treatment of its Native peoples has a sad history. As far back as the late 1800s, when the buffalo were hunted almost to extinction and the expansion of the railroad brought more settlers to native territories, First Nations people were treated as second-class citizens. Starvation, assimilation and a crushed rebellion largely put an end to the native resistance movement, but it gained strength again after World War II. Decolonialization and a newfound spirit of democracy was being put forth by the Western powers in their opposition to Soviet tyranny, yet most First Nations people could not vote as late as 1950. In order to vote, First Nations people had to gain suffrage by renouncing their status as "Indians." It was not until 1960 (1969 in Quebec) that all First Nations people were allowed to vote freely.

As Canada entered the 1960s, the government faced growing radicalism and organization among its populace. Quebec nationalism had been growing ever since the British took Canada from the French in 1764. French Canadians saw themselves as a separate nation, and frequently found themselves disagreeing with the policies of the Canadian government. The more radical French Canadian factions felt they were being oppressed, and that their language and culture were under attack. Inspired by revolutions around the world, nationalist and left-wing terrorism began to rise, Canada was not unaffected. The Front de Libération du Québec (FLQ), committed more than 200 bombings, and killed five people in pursuit of an independent Quebec. While violence was rejected by a majority of the population, a genuine desire for independence fueled Québécois protests. When Pierre Elliott Trudeau was elected prime minister in 1968, he declared martial law in Quebec, arresting most members of the FLQ.

While the crisis in Quebec worsened throughout the 1970s, the United States became involved in one of the most controversial conflicts in modern history: the war in Indochina. The Vietnam War resulted in over 1,500,000 dead, and radicalized an entire generation. Canada was no exception. Young people throughout the country protested against what they saw as American imperialism. The Canadian government refused to participate in the war, and granted citizenship to as many as 125,000 American draft dodgers over the course of the conflict. This led to serious friction between the governments of Canada and the US. To this day Vietnam and Canada have a close relationship, and hundreds of thousands of Vietnamese have immigrated to Canada's west coast. The period of the Vietnam War also saw the rise of the New Democratic Party (NDP), the successor to the socialist Cooperative Commonwealth Federation. Since its beginning in 1962, the NDP has altered the balance of Canadian politics, regularly receiving between 10 and 20 percent of the national vote, and often having the ability to form a majority coalition by grouping itself with the winning party. In the 2011 federal election, the NDP had its best result, winning 30 percent of the vote and the role of official opposition for the first time. It has fought for the continuation of Canada's welfare state, a humanitarian foreign policy, and native rights.

Young people across Canada became increasingly involved in politics as a result of the Vietnam War, and this new political awareness allowed the question of Quebec sovereignty to be addressed. The Parti Québécois was formed in 1968 and elected to govern Quebec in 1976, making French the official language of the province in 1977. Finally, the party made good on its biggest promise and introduced a referendum to decide Quebec's fate. The actual referendum simply said that Quebec would "negotiate a new agreement with the rest of Canada, based on the equality of nations; this agreement would enable Quebec to acquire the exclusive power to make its laws, levy its taxes and establish relations abroad - in other words, sovereignty." The fact that the referendum did not advocate full independence, in combination with a full-out public relations assault from the federal government, doomed the referendum.

While Canada became a sovereign entity in 1867, and had its independence increased in 1931, it was not technically a separate nation. Canada could not make amendments to its own constitution and the power of Canada to act directly against the wishes of the British government was in question. In 1982, Trudeau finally sealed Canada's status as its own unique nation by signing the Canada Act and the Charter of Rights and Freedoms. Although still a member of the British Commonwealth, Canada was now free from control by the British parliament.

With Canada's complete independence from Britain, the question of trade with the United States became central to the Canadian economy. The Canada-United States Free Trade Agreement drafted in 1988 set the model for the subsequent North American Free Trade Agreement (NAFTA), which included Canada, the United States, and Mexico. The criticism of the agreement, as well as later free trade agreements, was that by eliminating trade barriers, Canadian consumers and labour unions would be at the mercy of more powerful US corporations. The agreement was a decisive issue in the 1988 elections, with the Liberal Party and NDP in opposition, and the ruling Progressive Conservatives attempting to pass it. A 57 percent majority voted against the Progressive Conservatives, but because they received the most votes for one single party, they were rewarded with the most seats in parliament, and passed the free trade agreement. The agreement entered into force in 1994, and terms were gradually introduced until 2008. Although the general consensus is that NAFTA benefitted the economies of the three member countries, there is debate over its exact impacts, and concern that it actually harmed some industries susceptible to trade competition, particularly in the United States. In 2017, U.S. President Donald Trump began renegotiating the agreement, sparking a process that lasted into 2018. A new deal, the United States-Mexico-Canada Agreement (USMCA), was announced on September 30, 2018.

The Parti Québécois, after failing in its referendum of 1980, had formed a national party, the Bloc Québécois, and doggedly pursued its agenda of an independent Quebec. A second referendum, called in 1995, created an even bigger debate than the referendum of 1980, with massive media campaigns on both sides of the issue. When the vote finally came up, it failed by a slim 54,000 votes, but the issue illustrated a true divide in Quebec. Considering that 86,000 ballots were thrown out as invalid, the question of Quebec independence failed by a razor-thin margin, and the probability of it arising again in the future is still possible.

In 1990, in a small town called Oka, west of Montreal, a First Nations revolt led to the intervention of the Canadian Army and three deaths. While this was far from the first violent conflict between First Nations people and the Canadian government, it has marked a new era of militant native resistance. With more than one million people of Aboriginal descent living in Canada, many native organizations have called for more indigenous control over resources in their lands, resulting in violent conflicts between First Nations people and corporations attempting to mine, fish, or harvest lumber. One effect of these protests was the creation of a new territory, Nunavut, in the far north of Canada in 1999. While the population is less than 35,000, more than 85 percent of its inhabitants claim Inuit status, and the territory has adopted many laws securing their rights and claims to land and resources. In 2014, the Northwest Territories gained control over its land and water resources from the federal government, something for which it had fought for over a decade.

After the crashing of airplanes into the World Trade Center in New York on September 11, 2001, Canada entered the Afghanistan war as part of the International Security Assistance Force in a response to Islamist extremists and stayed to stabilize the country until 2011.

As climate change became more and more a concern, Canada entered into the Kyoto Protocol agreement, an international agreement intended to help reduce greenhouse gases, in 2005. It exited the agreement in 2011, under Stephen Harper, with emissions far over the target rates. The federal Pan-Canadian Framework on Clean Growth and Climate Change was adopted in 2016, under Justin Trudeau, in partnership with the provinces, territories and Indigenous communities. Canada also continues to be involved in various international efforts to stem the effects of climate change.

Today, Canada continues to deal with its internal relations with French-speaking Canadians and indigenous peoples. After the 2015 general election, Trudeau's government sought to repair relations with the country's Indigenous population, launching the National Inquiry into Missing and Murdered Indigenous Women and Girls, revamping the federal Indigenous affairs ministry, and formally apologizing to the survivors of the residential school system, among other initiatives. However, many felt the government should have made more substantive efforts. In 2021, this reckoning with Canada's troubled history intensified after the discovery of over 1,000 unmarked graves on the sites of former residential schools across the country.

As a unified country, it also faces other issues such as participation in peacekeeping missions, drug decriminalization, immigration and control over Arctic seaways. In April 2017, the federal government introduced legislation to legalize recreational cannabis across the country, with legalization eventually coming into effect on October 17, 2018. An agreement was reached whereby the federal government would receive just 25% of the tax revenue generated by cannabis sales, with the remainder going to the provinces and territories, which were given responsibility for the day-to-day logistics of distribution and retail sales. Concerns remained over whether legalization would effectively curb the black market.

Histoire du Canada

Au cours des 400 dernières années, le Canada est passé de simple poste de traite peu peuplé au dixième état souverain le plus riche au monde. Il s'agit de plus du seul pays à s'être séparé pacifiquement de sa puissance coloniale.

Malgré que le grand territoire composant aujourd'hui le Canada avait déjà une histoire vieille de plusieurs millénaires au début de la colonisation européenne, il a néanmoins été un des derniers endroits au monde à accueillir des populations humaines. Alors que l'*Homo Sapiens* moderne aurait émergé dans l'est de l'Afrique il y a 200 000 ans, la majorité des scientifiques conviennent qu'il aura fallu 175 000 années de plus pour que les hommes traversent le pont de glace reliant jadis l'Alaska et l'est de la Sibérie. Sur ce nouveau continent, c'est l'espace que délimitent les frontières canadiennes actuelles qui est habité depuis le plus longtemps; la migration originale qui a eu lieu il y a 25 000 ans est la source des cultures indigènes d'Amérique du Nord et du Sud, incluant les Inuits de l'Arctique, les Pieds-Noirs, les Cris, les Algonquins, les Dénés et la Ligue iroquoise des Cinq-Nations. On estime à environ deux millions le nombre d'Autochtones vivant aux États-Unis et au Canada avant l'arrivée des Européens dans le Nouveau Monde.

Christophe Colomb est peut-être celui à qui l'on attribue la « découverte » de l'Amérique en 1492, mais l'on sait aujourd'hui avec certitudes que les Vikings ont atteint et dépassé le Groenland en 982 apr. J.-C. Des traces archéologiques qui dateraient d'environ 1000 ans indiquent la présence à cette époque de peuples norois à L'Anse aux Meadows, à Terre-Neuve, ce qui ferait du Canada le véritable lieu de découverte de l'Amérique du Nord par les Européens. Les Vikings ne visaient pas toutefois à établir une colonisation permanente, mais étaient plutôt intéressés aux ressources naturelles du Canada. Quand Christophe Colomb foula le sol américain pour la première fois, les installations qui y avaient été construites par les peuples norois étaient abandonnées depuis longtemps déjà.

Le voyage de Christophe Colomb déclencha en Europe une course à la colonisation du Nouveau Monde. En traversant l'Atlantique vers ce qu'il croyait être l'Inde pour trouver une voie alternative aux longues routes de commerce terrestres menant à l'Asie et à ses produits, Christophe Colomb donna sans le vouloir le coup d'envoi à l'Ère des grandes découvertes. Les puissances européennes établirent des colonies à la recherche d'épices, d'or, d'esclaves et de nouvelles cultures, ainsi que pour convertir les peuples autochtones au christianisme. Les premières colonies, principalement espagnoles et portugaises, étaient concentrées en Amérique du Sud, en Amérique Centrale et dans les Caraïbes. L'Angleterre et la France ont plutôt tourné leurs efforts vers le Nord. Jean Cabot, un explorateur anglais d'origine italienne, est considéré comme le premier explorateur européen à avoir mis le pied en Amérique du Nord après les Vikings. Bien que cette exploration eut lieu seulement cinq années après les découvertes de Christophe Colomb, il faudra attendre jusqu'en 1605 pour que des installations permanentes soient établies. À cette époque, beaucoup d'explorateurs, dont Henry Hudson, tentaient encore de trouver le passage du Nord-Ouest, la fameuse voie navigable qui devait relier le Nouveau Monde à l'Asie. Si plus de cent ans se sont écoulés avant ces premières installations permanentes, c'est davantage en raison d'événements se déroulant en Europe que de facteurs attribuables au Nouveau Monde.

Deux événements sont venus ralentir la colonisation de l'Amérique du Nord : l'agitation religieuse et la guerre en Europe. En 1517, Martin Luther diffusa sa liste de 95 griefs contre l'Église catholique en utilisant une invention toute nouvelle, la presse à imprimer. Ainsi débuta la réforme protestante. Ce schisme détournera de façon importante le cours de l'Histoire en Europe, mais à court terme, il suscita surtout un conflit religieux tumultueux. Presque toute l'Europe connut un repli sur soi pour faire face à cette agitation ainsi qu'à cette crise religieuse. Des conflits politiques croissants secouèrent la majeure partie de l'Europe de l'Ouest durant des décennies, accaparant les ressources qui auraient dû être attribuées aux efforts de colonisation. Les guerres de religion en France, les guerres en Italie et les révoltes populaires combinées aux soulèvements religieux ont détourné l'attention de l'Europe du Nouveau Monde pendant plus d'un siècle.

La France voyait l'Amérique du Nord comme la meilleure source de richesse et de puissance possible et souhaitait, en exploitant ces contrées, arriver à alléger ses dettes de guerre. Quand l'explorateur français Jacques Cartier navigua sur le fleuve Saint-Laurent en 1534, il revendiqua le territoire au nom de la France et lui donna le nom qu'il porte encore aujourd'hui : le Canada. Après que les commerçants de fourrure se furent implantés dans l'Est du Canada, la France monopolisa le commerce de la fourrure. Bien que les Français tentèrent d'établir des relations commerciales amicales avec les peuples autochtones, certains d'entre eux, dont les Iroquois, se révélèrent particulièrement hostiles. Les conflits avec les tribus locales ont rapidement fait de convaincre la Couronne que pour assurer la rentabilité du commerce au Canada, une présence militaire et civile permanente était essentielle. Le roi Henri IV dépêcha donc sur place son « hydrographe » Samuel de Champlain pour cartographier la région.

En 1605, après avoir exploré la côte de l'Amérique du Nord jusqu'à Cape Cod, Champlain établira un premier peuplement français à Port-Royal et fondera ensuite la ville de Québec en 1608. La Nouvelle-France, comme on l'appelait à l'époque, se développa lentement, principalement en raison du manque d'intérêt de la mère patrie et de la guerre avec les Iroquois. Les colons survécurent aux attaques des Autochtones grâce à leurs alliances avec les Algonquins, les Montagnais et les Hurons. En plus de garantir la survie des colons, ces alliances permirent à la France d'affermir son contrôle du commerce des fourrures. Les Européens n'avaient aucune notion du milieu sauvage de la région, connaissances que les Autochtones leur procureront.

Une fois de plus, des tensions religieuses en Europe vinrent interférer avec le développement des établissements au Canada. Vers le milieu du dix-septième siècle, alors que les colonies anglaises en Amérique et dans les Caraïbes devenaient autosuffisantes, la Nouvelle-France demeurait sous-peuplée. Cette colonie éprouvait des difficultés et épuisait les ressources de la France. La monarchie française décida de prendre les choses en mains en offrant des primes à ceux qui décideraient d'émigrer en Nouvelle-France. Une seule condition s'imposait : tous les colons en partance devaient être catholiques ou se convertir au catholicisme avant de quitter l'Europe. Ce changement de politique, imposé à la demande du fervent cardinal Richelieu, le conseiller le plus proche du roi Louis XIII, créera de nombreuses frictions. Auparavant, les protestants français, particulièrement la secte persécutée connue sous le nom de Huguenots, s'exilaient souvent en Nouvelle-France pour fuir les persécutions religieuses. Ce nouveau décret du cardinal Richelieu aura un effet durable sur la composition politique et religieuse du Canada moderne.

Vers la fin du dix-septième siècle, les assises des colonies anglaises et françaises du Nouveau Monde commençaient enfin à gagner en solidité. Les deux nations avaient remporté leur mise et leurs colonies dégageaient un bon profit, mais une guerre en Europe devait venir gêner une fois de plus la croissance balbutiante du Canada. La Nouvelle-France, déjà au cœur d'une brutale guerre intertribale avec les Algonquins, entra en conflit avec la confédération iroquoise qui s'opposait à elle. Avec la guerre de Neuf Ans, qui débuta en 1688 et vit la France entrer en conflit avec presque tout le reste de l'Europe, les Iroquois commencèrent à recevoir des armes de la part des Anglais, en accord aux politiques de leur gouvernement. Cette escalade de violence des Anglais envenima cette guerre déjà sanglante. L'armée anglaise et ses alliés iroquois capturèrent Port-Royal, mais furent repoussés de Québec, principalement en raison des maladies qui décimaient les forces. La guerre finit par s'essouffler sur le Continent, et un traité de paix fut signé en 1697. Les Iroquois continueront cependant à se battre sans les Britanniques, mais subiront finalement d'importantes défaites qui les forceront à établir la paix quatre ans plus tard.

La Nouvelle-France (et le Canada par le fait même) semblait bien acquise à la mère patrie à la suite de la conclusion de la guerre de Neuf Ans. Toutefois, le contrôle de la région par la France ne durera pas longtemps. La guerre de Succession d'Espagne, qui commencera un an seulement après la signature du traité de paix entre la France et les Iroquois, permettra à l'Angleterre de prendre possession de la Nouvelle-Écosse et de Terre-Neuve, ainsi que des droits sur la région entourant la baie d'Hudson. Un nouveau conflit, nommé la guerre du roi George, débutera trois décennies plus tard, soit en 1744, mais aucun des deux belligérants ne réussira à élargir alors ses positions coloniales.

En 1754, l'animosité de longue date entre les Anglais et les Français gagnera le Nouveau Monde, avec comme point culminant la guerre de Sept Ans, appelée aussi en Amérique guerre franco-indienne. Trois causes principales étaient à la base de ce conflit. D'abord, le lucratif commerce de la fourrure, l'abondance des poissons, la richesse des forêts et les gisements de minerais étaient tous des sources de fortune pour quiconque contrôlerait le Canada. Ensuite, les Anglais, anticatholiques invétérés, croyaient que les Français étaient des hérétiques, un sentiment qui était d'ailleurs réciproque! Enfin, le contrôle des colonies outre-mer pourrait servir comme monnaie d'échange diplomatique si la guerre en Europe devait se détériorer.

La guerre de Sept Ans fut la première guerre à l'échelle mondiale et qui fit rage sur cinq continents : l'Amérique du Nord, l'Amérique du Sud, l'Afrique, l'Europe et l'Asie. Plus d'un million de personnes perdront la vie et la conclusion de cette guerre changera totalement le partage du pouvoir dans le Nouveau Monde. La Grande-Bretagne obtiendra le contrôle de toutes les colonies françaises en Amérique du Nord, faisant ainsi du Canada une colonie britannique. Toutefois, 150 années de colonisation française ne pouvaient disparaître du jour au lendemain. Encore aujourd'hui, les relations entre Anglais et Français au Canada connaissent leurs tensions et contrariétés.

Les Britanniques, suite à leur prise de contrôle du Canada en 1764, ne touchèrent pas aux systèmes religieux et économiques en place, au grand soulagement des colons catholiques français. L'Acte de Québec de 1774 permit qu'un système indépendant de lois françaises continue au Québec. Les Britanniques contrôlaient maintenant complètement la portion est de l'Amérique du Nord, depuis la rive est du fleuve Mississippi jusqu'à la côte Atlantique. Le mauvais traitement réservé aux colonies américaines par George III viendrait cependant bientôt modifier de nouveau l'équilibre du pouvoir dans le Nouveau Monde.

À titre de base pour les forces britanniques, de refuge pour les Américains loyaux à la monarchie britannique qui étaient en fuite et de source de milice pour les armées britanniques et américaines, le Canada joua un rôle important dans la guerre de l'Indépendance américaine. L'armée américaine tenta à l'origine de convaincre le Canada de prendre part à sa révolution, mais les Canadiens se relevaient à peine de la guerre de Sept Ans, et la majorité d'entre eux ne voulaient pas d'un autre conflit. Le 27 juin 1775, les troupes américaines attaquèrent Québec. Montréal fut pris sans résistance, mais l'attaque sur la ville de Québec se solda par une défaite, et en 1776, les troupes américaines évacuèrent Montréal.

Lorsque l'Amérique gagna son indépendance de la Grande-Bretagne en 1783, les citoyens loyaux à l'Empire britannique durent s'exiler. Plus de 35 000 d'entre eux se rendirent en Nouvelle-Écosse. Cet important mouvement de masse força le gouvernement britannique à diviser la Nouvelle-Écosse, créant ainsi la nouvelle colonie du Nouveau-Brunswick. Peu de temps après, les loyalistes établis au Québec commencèrent à présenter des demandes pour obtenir leur propre colonie, alors que les Canadiens français étaient aussi déterminés à avoir leur propre assemblée d'élus. En 1791, le Québec fut divisé en deux parties, le Haut-Canada et le Bas-Canada, afin de répondre aux exigences des loyalistes anglais et des Canadiens français.

Au cours des décennies qui suivirent, les tensions entre la Grande-Bretagne et l'Amérique demeurèrent vives, et encore une fois, un conflit déchira le Canada. Les États-Unis déclarèrent la guerre à la Grande-Bretagne en 1812 en raison de l'approvisionnement en armes des tribus amérindiennes hostiles et du service militaire obligatoire des marins américains à la marine britannique. Le Canada fut un des champs de bataille principaux de ce conflit puisque les États-Unis avaient planifié s'emparer du Canada et l'utiliser comme monnaie d'échange pour négocier avec les Britanniques. Les Américains s'attendaient à gagner le soutien des Canadiens qu'ils croyaient malheureux sous le contrôle colonial des Anglais. Toutefois, beaucoup de Canadiens, descendants de loyalistes britanniques qui avaient fui l'Amérique, percevaient les États-Unis comme des envahisseurs et des occupants.

L'armée américaine subit une défaite tôt dans le conflit lorsqu'elle fut battue par le général Isaac Brock et ses forces d'alliés indiens et de militaires locaux lors de la bataille de Queenston Heights. L'armée américaine en arriva quand même occuper et à piller un grand nombre de villes, incluant York (aujourd'hui Toronto) et Newark (aujourd'hui Niagra-on-the-Lake), jusqu'à contrôler à un certain moment presque tout le territoire correspondant à l'Ontario et au Québec d'aujourd'hui, mais en fin de compte, l'armée américaine fut repoussée, et bien que la guerre finit sans réel vainqueur, le fait qu'une prise de contrôle américaine fut empêchée donna aux Canadiens un regain de confiance et devint source de fierté nationale.

Même si les Canadiens rejetaient l'idée d'un envahisseur américain sur leur sol, l'exemple politique des États-Unis laissait sa marque à travers le pays. Des rébellions éclatèrent contre les Britanniques en 1837. Les Canadiens, insatisfaits de la distribution inéquitable des richesses tirées des ressources naturelles du Canada, s'insurgeaient de ne pas être représentés au sein du gouvernement britannique. Puisque les Britanniques considéraient que les frictions entre les Français et les Anglais étaient la source des conflits qu'ils vivaient avec le Canada, toutes les colonies canadiennes furent réunies en 1840 sous le nom de la Province du Canada, aussi appelée le Canada-Uni. En 1849, les États-Unis et l'Empire britannique se mirent d'accord pour que le 49e parallèle nord serve de frontière entre les deux nations, et les Britanniques étendirent le Canada jusqu'au au littoral ouest, annexant ainsi la Colombie-Britannique.

C'est pratiquement depuis la guerre d'Indépendance américaine que l'indépendance du Canada fait l'objet de débats en Grande-Bretagne comme au Canada. Certains prônaient une révolution violente et une indépendance canadienne totale. D'autres désiraient suivre un processus vers l'autonomie plus lent et graduel. Le 1er juillet 1867, le Parlement britannique édicta l'Acte de l'Amérique du Nord britannique, qui établit le Dominion du Canada comme une colonie distincte et dotée d'un gouvernement autonome. Sans être complètement détaché de l'Angleterre, particulièrement en ce qui a trait à la politique étrangère, sur le plan de la politique intérieure, le Canada gagnait pleine liberté et souveraineté.

Au cours des décennies suivantes, le Canada continua son expansion vers l'Ouest. Grâce à l'achat de deux énormes territoires au nord, les Territoires du Nord-Ouest et la Terre de Rupert, acquis de la Compagnie de la Baie d'Hudson, le pays doubla pratiquement sa superficie. Beaucoup de francophones et de Métis catholiques, les enfants d'Autochtones et de pionniers, vivaient à l'ouest de l'Ontario. Après la vente de la Terre de Rupert, plusieurs colons ontariens affluèrent dans cette région en espérant réclamer ces terres. Les Métis se mirent à craindre que cette arrivée massive de protestants anglais mette en péril leurs droits linguistiques, religieux et territoriaux. Le chef Métis Louis Riel organisa la Rébellion de la rivière Rouge en 1869 dans le but de garantir la protection de ces droits. Cette révolte mena à la création du Manitoba, une province qui mit en place des lois rigoureuses protégeant les Métis, les francophones et les catholiques. En 1905, la Colombie-Britannique, la Saskatchewan, l'Île-du-Prince-Édouard et l'Alberta furent coup sur coup jointes aux provinces fondatrices du Haut et du Bas-Canada, au Nouveau-Brunswick et à la Nouvelle-Écosse.

La construction d'un chemin de fer transcontinental, complété en 1885, stimula l'expansion du Canada. Ce chemin de fer incita de nouveaux colons à déménager dans l'Ouest pour s'établir dans les nouvelles provinces, mais ces nouveaux arrivants voulurent chasser les Autochtones de leurs terres, ce qui, une fois de plus, fit éclater des rébellions qui finirent en bains de sang. Le sentiment que le gouvernement canadien n'écoutait pas les préoccupations des catholiques francophones engendra une crise politique qui entraîna la démission du premier ministre Mackenzie Bowell en 1896 lorsque le gouvernement tenta de retirer au français son statut de langue officielle au Manitoba, ce qui allait à l'encontre des lois de la province.

Le Canada et les États-Unis connurent une période d'expansion vers l'ouest à la fin du dix-neuvième siècle grâce au développement du chemin de fer, à l'attrait qu'exerçaient ses contrées vierges et à la découverte de gisements de minerais. Ces facteurs, additionnés de l'arrivée massive d'immigrants en provenance d'Europe, permirent au Canada d'être le pays présentant la croissance économique la plus forte entre 1896 et 1911. Durant cette période, le gouvernement canadien créa le Yukon, un territoire dont la superficie se compare à celle de l'Allemagne, l'Autriche et la Suisse combinées, et dont la population se chiffrait à seulement 8 500 habitants à ce moment.

À l'aube du vingtième siècle, le Canada connut son premier conflit d'importance avec sa puissance coloniale. Lorsque la

Grande-Bretagne entra dans la Guerre des Boers en 1889, la majorité des Anglo-canadiens appuyaient l'annexion de l'Afrique du Sud à l'Empire britannique. Les Canadiens français, toutefois, ne s'intéressaient pas vraiment à l'impérialisme britannique, car ils se considéraient comme un cas à part et considéraient qu'ils faisaient partie de l'Empire britannique uniquement pour la forme. En guise de compromis, tous ceux se portant volontaires purent servir dans la Guerre des Boers, mais l'Armée canadienne comme telle ne s'impliqua pas dans ce conflit. Cette vision du Canada français comme une entité à part, vision exacerbée par les rébellions et par les lois anti-françaises des décennies précédentes, continuera de se manifester dans la politique du Canada des années à venir.

Bien qu'un grand nombre de Canadiens français désirait se départir du joug de l'Empire britannique, le pays devait tout de même se plier à la politique étrangère britannique. Avec l'assassinat de l'Archiduc Ferdinand le 28 juin 1914, le Canada fut pris dans le chaotique système d'alliances que suscita la Première Guerre mondiale. Lorsque la Grande-Bretagne déclara la guerre aux puissances centrales le 4 août, les troupes canadiennes furent appelées en renfort. Comme pour la majorité des puissances alliées, les disputes internes furent temporairement mises de côté, et l'appui à la guerre demeura massif, même chez les Canadiens français. Après plus de 200 000 morts et blessés de guerre, sur une population de 7 millions d'habitants, l'effort de guerre commença à s'essouffler. Au moment où le gouvernement tenta d'introduire le service obligatoire en 1917, beaucoup de Canadiens, et principalement des Canadiens français, s'opposèrent farouchement à la guerre. Malgré l'opinion populaire, la Première Guerre mondiale contribua à alimenter le sentiment de nationalisme et d'identité canadienne, surtout grâce au rôle important que joua le Canada dans la guerre la plus importante de l'histoire de l'humanité. Les très nombreuses victimes canadiennes occasionnées par ce conflit que plusieurs considéraient comme une guerre « britannique » vint aussi augmenter le ressentiment accumulé envers l'Empire.

La Première Guerre mondiale changea radicalement le visage politique du Canada. Après les horreurs vécues pendant ce conflit, les soldats rentrèrent chez eux avec de nouvelles idéologies politiques. Le socialisme, le communisme, le syndicalisme et d'autres courants progressistes de gauche gagnèrent en popularité dans les années suivant la guerre, tandis que le retour massif des soldats faisait augmenter le taux de chômage et diminuer les salaires. La grève générale de Winnipeg de 1919, la plus importante d'une série de grèves qui paralysèrent le pays, fut brutalement mise fin par la police, au prix d'un mort et de 30 blessés. Lorsque le Canada accorda le droit de vote aux femmes en 1918, le Parti conservateur en place s'effondra, en partie en raison de ses actions durant la grève. Le Parti libéral, en prenant le contrôle du gouvernement, acquiesça à une bonne partie des demandes originales du comité de grève, incluant le droit de former des syndicats sans la permission du gouvernement. Des partis progressistes et socialistes se formèrent les années suivantes, incluant le Parti progressiste du Canada et la Fédération du Commonwealth coopératif.

En 1931, le Parlement britannique promulgua le Statut de Westminster, qui donna le statut d'entité législative indépendante à toutes les colonies et à tous les dominions de l'Empire britannique, incluant le Canada, l'Australie, la Nouvelle-Zélande et l'Irlande. Cet acte permit à ces pays de rédiger leur propre constitution et supprima le pouvoir législatif qu'avait le gouvernement britannique dans ces régions, assurant ainsi l'indépendance de celles-ci tout en les incluant dans un Commonwealth britannique à l'échelle mondiale.

Lorsque le marché boursier américain connut son krach lors du mardi noir de 1929, événement qui marqua le début de la Grande dépression, l'économie canadienne ne tarda pas à en ressentir les effets. En 1933, le produit national brut canadien connut une baisse de 40 %. Les secteurs manufacturiers et agricoles furent le plus durement touchés, et le prix de blé, le principal produit d'exportation du Canada, chuta de moitié. Au creux de la vague, 30 % des Canadiens étaient sans emploi. Terre-Neuve, affirmant que les politiques du gouvernement canadien étaient la cause de ce creux économique, vota de quitter la Fédération canadienne pour rejoindre l'Empire britannique.

Après que les partis Libéral et Conservateur se soient montrés incapables de trouver des solutions à cette crise, beaucoup de Canadiens se tournèrent vers d'autres partis, comme la Fédération du Commonwealth coopératif et le Parti Crédit Social du Canada. Après que le gouvernement conservateur de R. B. Bennet ait placé des chômeurs dans des camps de travail pour pallier au coût élevé du système d'aide sociale, la Ligue d'unité ouvrière (LUO) organisa une importante manifestation appelée la « Marche sur Ottawa » dans le but d'obtenir des améliorations aux conditions et avantages dans les camps. La tentative de Bennett pour arrêter cette marche provoquera l'émeute de Regina et contribua en fin de compte à sa défaite aux élections de 1935. Le nouveau gouvernement libéral élimina les camps et institua des programmes sociaux pour diminuer les effets de la Dépression, mais ceci n'empêcha pas le Canada d'être fortement touché par cette dernière. Environ un cinquième de la population dépendait des allocations du gouvernement et du soutien des programmes sociaux. Même après le boom de l'économie canadienne causé par la Seconde Guerre mondiale, ces programmes restèrent en place et continuèrent d'évoluer.

La Seconde Guerre mondiale débuta le 1er septembre 1939. Puisque le Canada était de plus en plus indépendant de l'Angleterre, le pays n'entra pas en guerre immédiatement après la déclaration de la Grande-Bretagne comme il l'avait fait lors de la Première Guerre mondiale, mais décida plutôt de déclarer d'elle-même la guerre neuf jours plus tard. Alors que le massacre japonais et nazi était toujours à son comble, le ravitaillement et le matériel de guerre des Canadiens s'avérèrent d'une importance capitale pour permettre à la Grande-Bretagne de résister à l'invasion allemande. Une fois que les Alliés furent en position de contre-attaquer, les troupes canadiennes furent déployées partout dans le monde, et servirent vaillamment dans plusieurs batailles importantes, incluant l'invasion de la Sicile et de l'Italie en 1943, le débarquement allié en Normandie en 1944, la libération des Pays-Bas et la traversée de la France et de l'Allemagne pour mettre fin à la guerre. Un raid majoritairement canadien à Dieppe en France se solda par 3 000 morts, blessés et captifs, et les sous-marins allemands qui infestaient les eaux canadiennes coulèrent un grand nombre de navires de ravitaillement. En tout et partout, la Seconde Guerre mondiale entraînera la mort de 42 000 canadiens.

Lorsque les Japonais bombardèrent Pearl Harbor le 7 décembre 1941, les 22 000 Canadiens d'origine japonaise vivant alors en Colombie-Britannique durent composer avec les conséquences de la douleur et de la colère qui s'ensuivirent. Le sentiment anti-asiatique dans la province fut davantage attisé lorsque des milliers de Canadiens furent tués ou capturés durant l'invasion de Hong Kong par les Japonais. En 1942, toutes les personnes de descendance japonaise furent envoyées dans des camps d'internement, et après la fin de la guerre, tous les Canadiens d'origine japonaise furent déportés de la Colombie-Britannique. Ce n'est qu'en 1949 qu'ils furent libres de vivre n'importe où au Canada. En 1988, les Canadiens d'origine japonaise furent finalement indemnisés pour le tort qu'ils ont dû subir durant la guerre.

À la conclusion de la Seconde Guerre mondiale, le Canada et les États-Unis étaient les deux seuls pays à n'avoir pas eu de combats liés à cette guerre sur leur territoire. Cela permit à ces deux pays de profiter d'un contexte économique unique. Grâce à un secteur manufacturier en pleine relance, à la découverte de pétrole en Alberta et à sa position de partenaire commercial principal de la superpuissance économique juste au sud de la frontière, le Canada vit son économie exploser. Cette nouvelle prospérité favorisa la création d'un programme d'aide sociale radicalement amélioré. Grâce à l'aide sociale centralisée de la fin des années 1930 et du début des années 1940 ainsi qu'aux nombreuses politiques sociales de la Fédération du Commonwealth coopératif, les Canadiens profiteront de l'assurance-hospitalisation, d'un régime de pensions et des allocations familiales. Ces politiques sociales progressistes convainquirent Terre-Neuve de rejoindre le Canada suite à un référendum en 1949.

Le Canada consolida sa position lors de la Guerre froide grâce à son statut de membre fondateur de l'OTAN en 1949. L'économie du pays était directement liée à celle des États-Unis. Le Canada participa à la guerre de Corée, et ses troupes furent postées en Allemagne de l'Ouest, à la frontière du bloc communiste. Le vote canadien aux Nations Unies ne fut pas toujours identique à celui des États-Unis, mais il n'y avait aucun doute que le Canada était un allié des Américains dans sa guerre contre l'Union soviétique.

Le traitement que le Canada réserva à ses peuples autochtones au fil du temps présente une histoire peu reluisante. Si l'on recule à la fin des années 1800, lorsque le bison fut chassé au point d'être presque totalement exterminé et que les chemins de fer amenèrent davantage de colons dans les territoires autochtones, les membres des Premières nations furent traités comme des citoyens de second ordre. La famine, l'assimilation et une rébellion avortée mirent fin à la résistance autochtone, mais celle-ci reprit vigueur après la Seconde Guerre mondiale. La décolonisation et un esprit de démocratie renouvelé étaient mis de l'avant par les puissances occidentales dans leur lutte contre la tyrannie soviétique, mais la majorité des Premières nations n'obtinrent quand même le droit de vote qu'à la fin des années 1950. Pour pouvoir voter, les gens des Premières nations devaient renoncer à leur statut « d'Indien ». Ce n'est qu'en 1960 (1969 au Québec) que les gens des Premières nations obtinrent le droit de voter librement.

Au début des années 1960, le gouvernement canadien dut faire face à une croissance marquée du radicalisme et d'organisations populaires. Le mouvement nationaliste québécois n'avait cessé de prendre de l'ampleur depuis que les Britanniques avaient pris le contrôle du Canada aux dépens des Français en 1764. Les Canadiens français se considéraient comme une nation distincte, et étaient souvent en désaccord avec les politiques gouvernementales canadiennes. Les factions canadiennes-françaises les plus radicales avaient le sentiment d'être opprimées, et que leur langue et leur culture étaient menacées. Inspirés par les révolutions se déroulant partout dans le monde, les groupes de gauche nationalistes ou terroristes se multiplièrent, et le Canada ne fut pas épargné. Le Front de Libération du Québec commit plus de 200 attentats à la bombe, tuant ainsi cinq personnes dans sa quête d'un Québec indépendant. Bien que les actes de violence furent majoritairement condamnés par la population, un profond désir d'indépendance alimentait les protestations des Québécois. Lorsque Pierre Elliott Trudeau fut élu Premier ministre en 1968, il mit le Québec sous la loi martiale et procéda à l'arrestation de plusieurs membres du FLQ.

Pendant que la crise au Québec s'aggravait durant les années 1970, les États-Unis s'engagèrent dans un des conflits les plus controversés de l'histoire moderne : la guerre en Indochine. La guerre du Vietnam entraîna la mort de 1 500 000 personnes et radicalisa une génération entière. Le Canada ne fit pas exception. Les jeunes de tout le pays protestèrent contre ce qu'ils considéraient être l'impérialisme américain. Le gouvernement canadien refusa de participer à cette guerre, et accorda la citoyenneté à plus de 125 000 Américains réfractaires tout au long du conflit. Ceci mena à d'importantes frictions entre les gouvernements canadien et américain. Aujourd'hui encore, le Vietnam et le Canada jouissent d'une relation privilégiée, et des centaines de milliers de Vietnamiens ont immigré sur la côte Ouest du Canada. La guerre du Vietnam coïncida aussi avec l'ascension du Nouveau Parti Démocratique, le successeur de la Fédération du Commonwealth coopératif. Depuis ses débuts en 1962, le NPD changea le visage de la politique canadienne en obtenant régulièrement entre 10 et 20 % des votes et en formant une coalition majoritaire avec le parti vainqueur. Lors des élections fédérales de 2011, le NPD a obtenu son meilleur résultat à ce jour, en récoltant 30 % des voix et le rôle de l'opposition officielle pour la première fois. Il a combattu pour la sauvegarde du programme d'aide sociale du Canada, pour une politique étrangère humanitaire ainsi que pour les droits des Autochtones.

Les jeunes de tous les coins du Canada devinrent de plus en plus impliqués en politique après la guerre du Vietnam, et ce nouvel intérêt marqué pour la politique permit d'aborder la question de la souveraineté du Québec. Le Parti québécois fut formé en 1968, remporta les élections au Québec en 1976 et fit du français la langue officielle de la province en 1977. Finalement, le parti tint sa promesse et instaura un référendum pour décider de l'avenir du Québec. Ce référendum stipulait simplement que le Québec « négocierait une nouvelle entente avec le reste du Canada, entente fondée sur l'égalité des peuples, en vertu de laquelle le Québec aurait obtenu le pouvoir exclusif de faire ses lois, autrement dit, la souveraineté ». Le fait que le référendum ne garantissait pas une indépendance complète, combiné à un assaut du service des relations publiques du gouvernement, fit échouer le référendum.

Bien que le Canada devint une entité souveraine en 1867, et que son indépendance s'est accrue en 1931, techniquement, le pays n'était pas encore tout à fait une nation souveraine. Le Canada n'était pas en mesure d'apporter des amendements à sa propre constitution, et la capacité du Canada d'agir à l'encontre des désirs du gouvernement britannique était encore mise en doute. En 1982, Trudeau confirma le statut de nation souveraine du Canada en signant la loi constitutionnelle et la Charte canadienne des droits et libertés. Bien qu'il était encore membre du Commonwealth britannique, le Canada n'était plus sous le contrôle du parlement britannique.

Suite à l'indépendance complète du Canada par rapport à la Grande-Bretagne, la question du commerce avec les États-Unis devint la principale préoccupation de l'économie canadienne. L'Accord de libre-échange Canada-États-Unis rédigé en 1988 devint un modèle pour l'Accord de libre-échange nord-américain. Cet accord, de même que les accords de libre-échange subséquents, fut critiqué, car on considérait qu'éliminer les barrières commerciales ferait en sorte que les consommateurs canadiens seraient à la merci des puissantes corporations américaines. Cet accord fut au centre des élections de 1988 : le Parti libéral et le NPD s'y opposaient, alors que les progressistes conservateurs tentaient de le faire passer. Une majorité de 57 %

vota contre les progressistes conservateurs, mais puisqu'ils reçurent néanmoins le plus grand nombre de votes pour un unique parti, ils obtinrent une majorité de sièges au parlement et conclurent l'accord de libre-échange. L'entente est entrée en vigueur en 1994 et les modalités ont été mises en place graduellement jusqu'en 2008. Si la majorité s'entend pour dire que l'ALÉNA est avantageux pour l'économie des trois pays membres, on débat encore de ses conséquences exactes; certains s'inquiètent même qu'il soit nocif pour des industries influençables par la concurrence commerciale, particulièrement aux États-Unis. En 2017, le président américain Donald Trump a commencé à renégocier l'accord, un processus qui se poursuit en 2018. Le 30 septembre 2018, une nouvelle entente a été annoncée, soit l'Accord États-Unis-Mexique-Canada (AEUMC).

Le Parti Québécois, suite à l'échec du référendum de 1980, forma un parti politique canadien, le Bloc Québécois, et poursuivit avec acharnement son échéancier pour un Québec indépendant. Un deuxième référendum, en 1995, occasionna un débat encore plus virulent que celui du référendum de 1980, avec des campagnes médiatiques massives de part et d'autres des deux camps. Le jour du scrutin, le référendum échoua par une mince marge de 54 000 votes, un résultat qui mit au jour la division du Québec sur cette question. Considérant que 86 000 bulletins avaient été rejetés comme invalides, le résultat sur la question de l'indépendance du Québec a été si près de la ligne décisive qu'il ne serait pas surprenant qu'un autre referendum ait lieu dans le futur.

En 1990, une révolte amérindienne dans une petite ville baptisée Oka, à l'ouest de Montréal, a mené à l'intervention de l'armée canadienne. Trois personnes moururent au cours de cette crise. Bien qu'il y ait précédemment eu de nombreux conflits violents entre les membres des Premières nations et le gouvernement du Canada, la situation à Oka marqua le début d'une nouvelle ère de résistance active des Autochtones. Comme le Canada compte plus d'un million d'habitants de descendance amérindienne, de nombreuses organisations autochtones ont réclamé un meilleur contrôle des ressources sur leurs terres, ce qui a causé des conflits violents entre les membres des Premières nations et les sociétés exploitant les ressources minières, maritimes ou forestières sur leurs territoires. L'une des conséquences de ces manifestations fut la création d'un nouveau territoire, le Nunavut en 1999, dans les régions de l'extrême nord du pays. Bien que ce territoire compte moins de 35 000 habitants, près de 85 % de sa population y possède le statut d'Inuit, et le territoire a été en mesure d'adopter de nombreuses lois assurant les droits des Inuits et donnant corps à leurs revendications concernant le territoire et ses ressources. En 2014, les Territoires du Nord-Ouest ont pris le contrôle de leurs terres et de leurs ressources aquatiques, préalablement sous juridiction fédérale, résultat d'un combat de plus d'une décennie.

Après l'écrasement des avions d'al-Qaida dans les tours du World Trade Center à New York, le 11 septembre 2001, le Canada s'est engagé dans le conflit en Afghanistan en tant qu'élément de la Force d'assistance à la sécurité internationale en réaction aux extrémistes islamistes; il est resté au pays jusqu'en 2011 afin de l'aider à se stabiliser.

Alors que la question des changements climatiques devenait de plus en plus une source d'inquiétude, le Canada adhère, en 2005, au Protocole de Kyoto, une entente internationale dont l'objectif est de réduire l'émission de gaz à effet de serre. Il s'est retiré de l'entente en 2011, sous la gouverne de Stephen Harper, alors que les émissions excédaient de beaucoup les taux cibles. Le Cadre pancanadien sur la croissance propre et les changements climatiques à portée nationale a été adopté en 2016, sous le gouvernement de Justin Trudeau, en partenariat avec les provinces, territoires et peuples autochtones. Le Canada continue de participer à divers efforts internationaux afin de réduire les effets des changements climatiques.

Aujourd'hui, le Canada doit continuer à gérer ses relations avec le Québec et les membres des Premières nations tout en faisant face à d'autres enjeux, comme la dépénalisation des drogues, l'immigration, sa participation aux missions de maintien de la paix et le contrôle des bras de mer de l'Arctique. Après l'élection générale de 2015, le gouvernement Trudeau a cherché à réparer ses relations avec les peuples autochtones canadiens. Il a ouvert l'Enquête nationale sur les femmes et les filles autochtones disparues et assassinées, il a réorganisé le ministère fédéral des Affaires autochtones et il a présenté des excuses formelles aux survivants du système scolaire résidentiel, entre autres initiatives. Toutefois, plusieurs sont d'avis que le gouvernement aurait dû déployer plus d'efforts. En 2021, cette prise en compte de l'histoire troublante du Canada est devenue plus intense après la découverte de sépultures anonymes sur les lieux d'anciens pensionnats partout au pays.

En avril 2017, le gouvernement fédéral a présenté une législation dans le but de légaliser la consommation de cannabis à des fins récréatives partout au pays; elle devrait entrer en vigueur le 17 octobre 2018. Selon l'entente convenue, le gouvernement fédéral recevrait jusqu'à 25 % des revenus provenant des taxes générées par les ventes de cannabis; le reste sera conservé par les provinces et territoires qui sont responsables de la logistique au jour le jour quant à la distribution et aux ventes au détail. Des préoccupations demeurent à savoir si la légalisation réduira efficacement le recours au marché noir.

National Anthem: O Canada

From "Chapter 5, Statutes of Canada 1980; proclaimed July 1, 1980." Composed by Calixa Lavallée; French lyrics written by Judge Adolphe-Basile Routhier; English lyrics written by Robert Stanley Weir (with some changes incorporated in 1967).

O Canada! Our home and native land!
True patriot love in all thy sons command.
With glowing hearts we see thee rise,
The True North strong and free!
From far and wide, O Canada, We stand on guard for thee.
God keep our land glorious and free!
O Canada, we stand on guard for thee.
O Canada, we stand on guard for thee.

O Canada! Terre de nos aïeux!
Ton front est ceint de fleurons glorieux!
Car ton bras sait porter l'épée, Il sait porter la croix!
Ton histoire est une épopée Des plus brillants exploits.
Et ta valeur, de foi trempée,
Protégera nos foyers et nos droits,
Protégera nos foyers et nos droits.

Note: Private Member's Bill C-210 passed in the House of Commons on June 15, 2016, which changed the second line "in all thy sons command" to "in all of us command," thereby making it gender-neutral. The bill was passed by the Senate on Jan. 31, 2018.

Emblems of Canada

The Beaver
Recognized as a symbol of Canada's sovereignty. Official status as an emblem of Canada as of May 24, 1975.
Maple Tree
Arboreal emblem of Canada, proclaimed April 25, 1996.
Official Colours
Red and white, as proclaimed in 1921.
Official Sports
Hockey (winter); Lacrosse (summer).

Full-colour images of Canadian and provincial flags, coats of arms, floral emblems, and selected honours start on page A-14.

Fathers of Confederation

Three conferences helped to pave the way for Confederation - those held at Charlottetown (September, 1864), Québec City (October, 1864) and London (December, 1866). As all the delegates who were at the Charlottetown conferences were also in attendance at Québec, the following list includes the names of all those who attended one or more of the three conferences. *Hewitt Bernard was John A. Macdonald's private secretary. He served as secretary of both the Québec and London conferences.

DELEGATES TO THE CONFEDERATION CONFERENCES, 1864-1866

LEGEND:
Charlottetown, 1 September, 1864 - C
Québec, 10 October, 1864 - Q
London, 4 December, 1866 - L

CANADA

John A. Macdonald	C	Q	L
George E. Cartier	C	Q	L
Alexander T. Galt	C	Q	L
William McDougall	C	Q	L
Hector L. Langevin	C	Q	L
George Brown	C	Q	
Thomas D'Arcy McGee	C	Q	
Alexander Campbell	C	Q	
Sir Etienne P. Taché		Q	
Oliver Mowat		Q	
J.C. Chapais		Q	
James Cockburn		Q	
W.P. Howland			L

*Hewitt Bernard

NOVA SCOTIA

Charles Tupper	C	Q	L
William A. Henry	C	Q	L
Jonathan McCully	C	Q	L
Adams G. Archibald	C	Q	L
Robert B. Dickey		Q	
J.W. Ritchie			L

NEW BRUNSWICK

Samuel L. Tilley	C	Q	L
J.M. Johnson	C	Q	L
William H. Steeves	C	Q	
E.B. Chandler	C	Q	
John Hamilton Gray	C	Q	
Peter Mitchell		Q	L
Charles Fisher		Q	L
R.D. Wilmot			L

PRINCE EDWARD ISLAND

John Hamilton Gray	C	Q	
Edward Palmer	C	Q	
William H. Pope	C	Q	
A.A. Macdonald	C	Q	
George Coles	C	Q	
T.H. Haviland		Q	
Edward Whelan		Q	

NEWFOUNDLAND

F.B.T. Carter		Q
Ambrose Shea		Q

PARTICIPANTS TO THE FIRST MINISTERS' CONSTITUTIONAL CONFERENCE ON PATRIATION OF THE CONSTITUTION (Held in Ottawa from September 2 to 5, 1981)

- The Right Honourable Pierre Elliott Trudeau, P.C., Q.C., M.P., Prime Minister of Canada;
- The Honourable William G. Davis, Q.C., Premier of Ontario;
- The Honourable René Lévesque, Premier of Québec; The Honourable John M. Buchanan, Q.C., Premier of Nova Scotia;
- The Honourable Richard B. Hatfield, Premier of New Brunswick;
- The Honourable Sterling R. Lyon, Q.C., Premier of Manitoba;
- The Honourable W.R. Bennett, Premier of British Columbia;
- The Honourable J. Angus MacLean, P.C., D.F.C., C.D., Premier of Prince Edward Island; The Honourable Allan Blakeney, Q.C., Premier of Saskatchewan; The Honourable Peter Lougheed, Q.C., Premier of Alberta;
- The Honourable Brian Peckford, Premier of Newfoundland.

Timeline of Canadian History

- 12000 BC Migration of natives across the Bering land bridge
- 2000 BC Inuit arrive in North America
- 1000 Leif Erickson lands on Baffin Island
- 1497 John Cabot reaches Newfoundland
- 1524-1528 Giovanni da Verrazano's voyages; New France named
- 1534-1541 Jacque Cartier explores North America
- 1604 Attempt to settle Acadia by Sieur de Monts and Samuel de Champlain
- 1608 Champlain founds Quebec
- 1610 Henry Hudson's European discovery of Hudson Bay
- 1611 Port-Royal established
- 1621 Nova Scotia granted to Sir William Alexander
- 1627 Company of New France established
- 1628 Kirke brothers raid New France
- 1632 Quebec returned to the French
- 1640s Huron decimated by Iroquois raids and disease
- 1642 Montreal established by Paul de Chomedey de Maisonneuve and Jeanne Mance
- 1663 France regains control of New France
- 1670 Charles II forms the Hudson Bay Company. Fur trade attracts settlers to the Great Lakes area.
- 1689-1697 King William's War
- 1702-1713 Queen Anne's War
- 1713 Treaty of Utrecht cedes Newfoundland and Acadia to Britain; Louisbourg established
- 1744-1748 King George's War
- 1749 Halifax established
- 1755-1762 Acadian deportation
- 1756-1763 Seven Years' War leads to Conquest
- 1759 Quebec City falls to the British
- 1763 Treaty of Paris cedes most of North America to British; Royal Proclamation reformulates British North America
- 1774 Quebec Act extends Quebec's territory and grants limited rights to French
- 1770s-1780s Loyalists arrive in British North America
- 1783 Treaty of Paris; United States victorious in Revolutionary War
- 1784 New Brunswick established by Loyalists
- 1791 Constitutional Act (Canada Act) creates Upper and Lower Canada
- 1793 Alexander Mackenzie crosses the continent and reaches the Pacific Ocean
- 1812 Selkirk grant in Red River (Assiniboia)
- 1812-1814 War of 1812

- 1817 Rush-Bagot Agreement
- 1818 Convention of 1818 creates boundary with the United States at forty-ninth parallel
- 1821 Hudson's Bay Company and North West Company merge
- 1829 Welland Canal opened
- 1832 Rideau Canal completed
- 1837-1838 Rebellions in Lower and Upper Canada
- 1839 Durham's Report; 'Aroostook War'
- 1841 Act of Union creates Canada East and Canada West
- 1846 Oregon Boundary settlement
- 1848-1855 Responsible government established in British North American colonies
- 1849 Annexation Manifesto
- 1854-1866 Reciprocity Treaty with United States
- 1858 British Columbia Colony formed
- 1864 September: Charlottetown Conference; October: Quebec City Conference
- 1867 July 1: Dominion of Canada formed
- 1869-1870 Red River Resistance
- 1870 Manitoba Act
- 1871 British Columbia enters Confederation
- 1872 Dominion Lands Act
- 1873 Prince Edward Island enters Confederation; Supreme Court created
- 1878 National Policy introduced
- 1880 Canada acquires Arctic islands from Britain
- 1885 North-West Rebellion; Canadian Pacific Railway completed
- 1888 Jesuits' Estates Act
- 1890-1897 Manitoba schools controversy
- 1899-1902 South African War (Boer War)
- 1903 Alaska Boundary award
- 1905 Saskatchewan and Alberta join Confederation
- 1909 Boundary Waters Treaty establishes International Joint Commission
- 1910 Naval Service Act creates Canadian navy
- 1911 Reciprocity Agreement with United States rejected
- 1914-1918 World War I
- 1914 War Measures Act passed
- 1917 Battle of Vimy Ridge; Halifax explosion; conscription; Union government formed
- 1917-1920s Canadian National Railway created
- 1918 Women's suffrage for federal elections
- 1919 Winnipeg General Strike
- 1921 Agnes Macphail elected, Canada's first female member of Parliament
- 1923 Halibut Treaty with United States
- 1925-1926 King-Byng controversy

- 1929 U.S. stock market crashes. Drought hits prairies.

- 1931 Statute of Westminster

- 1932 Unemployment Relief Camps organized; Canadian Broadcasting Corporation formed

- 1932-1933 Co-operative Commonwealth Federation established

- 1935 Richard Bedford Bennett's 'New Deal'; On-to-Ottawa Trek

- 1939-1945 World War II (Canada enters war in September 1939)

- 1940 Rowell-Sirois Report on Dominion-Provincial Relations; Ogdensburg Agreement with United States

- 1941 Hyde Park Agreement with United States; Canada declares war on Japan

- 1942 Conscription pledge plebiscite; Dieppe raid

- 1942-1947 Japanese-Canadian relocation

- 1944 Normandy invasion; PC 1003 grants workers the right to collective bargaining

- 1945 Canada joins United Nations as charter member

- 1949 Newfoundland enters Confederation; North Atlantic Treaty Organization (NATO) formed

- 1950-1953 Korean War

- 1951 Massey Commission reports

- 1952 Vincent Massey becomes First Canadian-born governor general

- 1956 Suez Crisis and UN peacekeeping forces organized

- 1957 Hospital Insurance Plan; North American Air Defense Agreement (NORAD) formed

- 1959 St. Lawrence Seaway opens

- 1960s 'Quiet Revolution' in Quebec

- 1961 New Democratic Party (NDP) formed

- 1962 Cuban missile crisis strains Canadian-American relations

- 1965 Canada Assistance Act; Medicare; Canada Pension Plan

- 1967 Expo in Montreal

- 1969 Manhattan incident; Official Languages Act

- 1970 October Crisis

- 1971 National Action Committee on the Status of Women (NAC)

- 1973 Foreign Investment Review Agency (FIRA) created

- 1975 Petro-Can formed; James Bay Agreement between Quebec government, Cree, and Inuit

- 1976 Parti Québécois (PQ) elected in Quebec

- 1977 Bill 101, Charter of the French Language, passed in Quebec

- 1980 National Energy Program; Quebec Referendum on Sovereignty-Association; Canada joins Organization of American States (OAS)

- 1982 Constitution Act passed, including Charter of Rights and Freedoms; Assembly of First Nations formed; Canada agrees to UN Convention on the Law of the Sea

- 1987 Meech Lake Accord; Reform party formed

- 1988 Bill 178 passed in Quebec

- 1989 Free trade agreement with United States implemented

- 1990 Gulf War fought with Canada's participation; Mohawk tensions in Quebec

- 1992 Charlottetown Accord

- 1993 North American Free Trade Agreement (NAFTA) created with United States and Mexico; Bloc Québécois forms official opposition in Canadian Parliament

- 1995 Second Quebec Referendum

- 1997 Canada signs Kyoto Protocol

- 1999 Nunavut, a self-governing territory, established

- 2000 Canadian Alliance formed

- 2001 Canada sends military forces to Afghanistan

- 2003 Conservative Party of Canada (CPC) formed

- 2005 Civil Marriages Act legalizes same-sex marriage

- 2006 Indian Residential Schools Settlement Agreement

- 2008 Economic Recession

- 2010 Vancouver Winter Olympics

- 2014 Formal end to Canada's operations in Afghanistan

- 2016 Federal government launches National Inquiry into Missing and Murdered Indigenous Women and Girls

- 2018 Recreational marijuana becomes legal across the country

- 2020 The COVID-19 pandemic grips the world, including Canada, which passes measures to help support families and businesses; individual provinces adopt health measures to curb the spread of the disease

- 2021 Unmarked graves are discovered on the sites of former residential schools, leading to louder calls for substantive action by the federal government

Chronologie de l'histoire du Canada

- 12 000 av. J.-C. Des peuples en migration traversent le pont continental de Béring

- 2000 av. J.-C. Arrivée des Inuits en Amérique du Nord

- 1000 apr. J.-C. Leif Erickson débarque sur l'Île de Baffin

- 1497 Jean Cabot atteint Terre-Neuve

- 1524-1528 Voyages de Giovanni da Verrazano; la Nouvelle-France obtient son nom

- 1534-1541 Jacques Cartier explore l'Amérique du Nord

- 1604 Le Sieur de Monts et Samuel de Champlain tentent de s'établir en Acadie.

- 1608 Champlain fonde la ville de Québec

- 1610 Découverte européenne de la Baie d'Hudson par Henry Hudson

- 1611 Fondation de Port-Royal

- 1621 La Nouvelle-Écosse est donnée à Sir William Alexander

- 1627 Création de la Compagnie de la Nouvelle-France

- 1628 Les frères Kirke assiègent la Nouvelle-France

- 1632 Québec est remis à la France

- 1640 Les Hurons sont décimés par des attaques d'Iroquois et la maladie

- 1642 Fondation de Montréal par Paul de Chomedey de Maisonneuve et Jeanne Mance

- 1663 La France reprend le contrôle de la Nouvelle-France

- 1670 Le roi Charles II forme la Compagnie de la Baie d'Hudson. Le commerce des fourrures attire des colons vers la région des Grands Lacs.

- 1689-1697 Guerre du roi Guillaume (Guerre de Neuf ans)

- 1770-1780 Arrivée des Loyalistes en Amérique du Nord britannique

- 1702-1713 Guerre de la reine Anne (Deuxième guerre intercoloniale)

- 1713 Traité d'Utrecht cède Terre-Neuve et l'Acadie à l'Angleterre; fondation de Louisbourg

- 1744-1748 Guerre du roi George (Troisième guerre intercoloniale)

- 1749 Fondation de Halifax

- 1755-1762 Déportation des Acadiens

- 1756-1763 La Guerre de Sept ans mène à la conquête de la Nouvelle-France par les Britanniques

- 1759 Chute de la ville de Québec aux mains des Britanniques

- 1763 Le Traité de Paris cède la plus grande partie de l'Amérique du Nord aux Britanniques; la Proclamation royale réorganise l'Amérique du Nord britannique

- 1774 L'Acte de Québec recule les limites du territoire québécois et cède des droits limités aux Français

- 1783 Traité de Paris; les États-Unis remportent la Guerre d'indépendance

- 1784 Les Loyalistes fondent le Nouveau-Brunswick

- 1791 L'Acte constitutionnel créé le Haut et le Bas-Canada

- 1793 Alexander Mackenzie traverse le continent et atteint l'océan Pacifique

- 1812 Selkirk fonde un établissement sur la Rivière Rouge (Assiniboia)

- 1812-1814 Guerre de 1812

- 1817 Accord de Rush-Bagot

- 1818 La Convention de 1818 définit la frontière avec les États-Unis au 49ᵉ parallèle

- 1821 Fusion de la Compagnie de la Baie d'Hudson et de la North West

- 1829 Ouverture du Canal Welland

- 1832 Achèvement du Canal Rideau

- 1837-1838 Rébellions des patriotes dans le Bas et le Haut-Canada

- 1839 Rapport Durham; Guerre d'Aroostook

- 1846 Règlement de la frontière de l'Oregon

- 1848-1855 Établissement d'un gouvernement responsable dans les colonies d'Amérique du Nord britannique

- 1849 Manifeste annexionniste

- 1854-1866 Traité de réciprocité avec les États-Unis

- 1858 Création de la colonie de la Colombie-Britannique

- 1864 septembre : Conférence de Charlottetown; octobre : Conférence de la ville de Québec

- 1867, 1ᵉʳ juillet Création de la Confédération

- 1869-1870 Résistance à Rivière Rouge

- 1870 Acte du Manitoba

- 1871 La Colombie-Britannique intègre la Confédération

- 1872 Acte concernant les terres de la Puissance (*Loi des terres fédérales*)

- 1873 L'Île-du-Prince-Édouard intègre la Confédération; création de la Cour Suprême

- 1878 Introduction d'une Politique nationale

- 1880 Le Canada fait l'acquisition des îles arctiques auprès de l'Angleterre

- 1885 Soulèvement des Métis du Nord-Ouest; le chemin de fer du Canadien Pacifique est complété

- 1888 Règlement final des biens des Jésuites

- 1890-1897 Controverse concernant les écoles du Manitoba (abolition des écoles séparées)

- 1899-1902 Guerre d'Afrique du Sud (Guerre des Boers)

- 1905 La Saskatchewan et l'Alberta intègrent la Confédération

- 1909 Le Traité des eaux limitrophes créa la Commission mixte internationale

- 1910 La *Loi du service naval* établit la Marine canadienne

- 1911 Rejet de l'Accord de réciprocité avec les États-Unis

- 1914-1918 Première Guerre mondiale

- 1914 Adoption de la *Loi sur les mesures de guerre*

- 1917 Bataille de Vimy; explosion à Halifax; conscription; formation d'un gouvernement national

- 1917 aux années 1920 Création du chemin de fer du Canadien National

- 1918 Le droit de vote est accordé aux femmes pour les élections fédérales

- 1919 Grève générale à Winnipeg

- 1921 Élection d'Agnes Macphail, la première députée au Parlement du Canada

- 1923 Signature du Traité du flétan avec les États-Unis

- 1925-1926 Affaire King-Byng

- 1929 Aux États-Unis, le marché s'effondre. La sécheresse fait rage dans les Prairies

- 1931 Statut de Westminster

- 1932 Création de camps de secours pour les chômeurs; fondation de la Canadian Broadcasting Corporation

- 1932-1933 Fondation de la Fédération du Commonwealth coopératif (devenu Nouveau Parti démocratique)

- 1935 *New Deal* (Nouvelle Donne) de Richard Bedford Bennett; marche sur Ottawa

- 1939-1945 Deuxième Guerre mondiale (le Canada entre en guerre en septembre 1939)

- 1940 Publication du Rapport Rowell-Sirois sur les relations fédérales-provinciales; Accord d'Ogdensburg avec les États-Unis

- 1941 Hyde Park Agreement avec les États-Unis; le Canada déclare la guerre au Japon

- 1942 Plébiscite concernant l'engagement à la guerre; raid de Dieppe

- 1942-1947 Déplacement forcé des Canadiens d'origine japonaise

- 1944 Débarquement de Normandie; le C.P. 1003 accorde aux travailleurs le droit à la négociation collective

- 1945 Le Canada intègre les Nations Unies en tant que membre fondateur

- 1949 Terre-Neuve entre dans la Confédération; création de l'Organisation du traité de l'Atlantique Nord (OTAN)

- 1950-1953 Guerre de Corée

- 1951 Publication des rapports de la Commission Massey

- 1952 Vincent Massey devient le premier gouverneur général né au Canada

- 1956 Crise de Suez et organisation des forces de maintien de la paix des Nations Unies

- 1957 Régime d'assurance-hospitalisation; formation de l'Accord de la défense aérienne de l'Amérique du Nord (NORAD)

- 1959 Ouverture des voies maritimes du St-Laurent

- Années 1960 Révolution tranquille au Québec

- 1961 Formation du Nouveau Parti démocratique (NPD)

- 1962 La crise des missiles cubains met à rude épreuve les relations canado-américaines

- 1965 *Loi sur l'aide sociale*; assurance-maladie; régime de retraite du Canada

- 1967 L'Expo 67 bat son plein à Montréal

- 1969 Épisode du Manhattan; *Loi sur les langues officielles*

- 1970 Crise d'octobre

- 1971 Comité d'action national sur le statut de la femme

- 1973 Création de l'Agence d'examen de l'investissement étranger (AEIE)

- 1975 Fondation de Pétro-Canada; Accord de la Baie James entre le gouvernement du Québec, les Cris et les Inuits

- 1976 Élection du Parti Québécois (PQ) au Québec

- 1977 Adoption du projet de loi 101, Charte de la langue française au Québec

- 1980 Programme énergétique national; référendum québécois sur la souveraineté-association; le Canada se joint à l'organisation des États américains (OÉA)

- 1982 Adoption de la Loi constitutionnelle, y compris la Charte des droits et libertés; fondation de l'Assemblée des Premières Nations; le Canada adhère à la Convention des Nations Unies sur le droit de la mer.

- 1987 Accord du Lac Meech; fondation du Parti réformiste du Canada (Reform Party)

- 1988 Adoption du projet de loi 178 au Québec

- 1989 Entrée en vigueur de l'accord de libre-échange entre le Canada et les États-Unis

- 1990 Participation du Canada à la Guerre du Golfe; Crise d'Oka au Québec

- 1992 Accord de Charlottetown

- 1993 Création de l'Accord de libre-échange nord-américain (ALÉNA) avec les États-Unis et le Mexique; le Bloc québécois constitue l'opposition officielle au Parlement canadien

- 1995 Deuxième référendum au Québec

- 1997 Le Canada signe le Protocole de Kyoto

- 1999 Création du Nunavut en tant que territoire autonome

- 2000 Formation de l'Alliance canadienne

- 2001 Le Canada envoie des forces armées en Afghanistan

- 2003 Formation du Parti conservateur du Canada (PCC)

- 2005 La *Loi sur le mariage civil* légalise le mariage des couples du même sexe

- 2006 Accord de règlement sur l'adjudication des pensionnats indiens

- 2008 Récession

- 2010 Jeux olympiques d'hiver à Vancouver

- 2014 Fin officielle de la présence du Canada en Afghanistan

- 2016 Le gouvernement fédéral a lancé l'Enquête nationale sur les femmes et les filles autochtones disparues et assassinées

- 2018 La consommation de marijuana à des fins récréatives devient légale partout au pays

- 2020 La pandémie du COVID-19 frappe le monde, y compris le Canada, qui adopte des mesures pour aider les familles et les entreprises; certaines provinces adoptent des mesures de santé pour freiner la propagation de la maladie

- 2021 De sépultures anonymes sont découvertes sur les lieux d'anciens pensionnats, ce qui nourrit un appel plus fort pour que le gouvernement fédéral accomplisse des gestes importants

THE ROYAL ARMS OF CANADA BY PROCLAMATION OF KING GEORGE V IN 1921

The Royal Arms of Canada were established by proclamation of King George V on 21 November, 1921. On the advice of the Prime Minister of Canada, Her Majesty the Queen approved, on 12 July, 1994, that the arms be augmented with a ribbon bearing the motto of the Order of Canada, DESIDERANTES MELIOREM PATRIAM - "They desire a better country".

This coat of arms was developed by a special committee appointed by Order in Council and is substantially based on a version of the Royal Arms of the United Kingdom, featuring the historic arms of England and Scotland. To this were added the old arms of Royal France and the historic emblem of Ireland, the harp of Tara, thus honouring many of the founding European peoples of modern Canada. To mark these arms as Canadian, the three red maple leaves on a field of white were added.

The supporters, and the crest, above the helmet, are also versions of elements of the Royal Arms of the United Kingdom, including the lion of England and unicorn of Scotland. The lion holds the Union Jack and the unicorn, the banner of Royal France. The crowned lion holding the maple leaf, which is the The Royal Crest of Canada, has, since 1981, also been the official symbol of the Governor General of Canada, the Sovereign's representative.

At the base of the Royal Arms are the floral emblems of the founding nations of Canada, the English Rose, the Scottish Thistle, the French Lily and the Irish Shamrock.

The motto - A MARI USQUE AD MARE - "From sea to sea" - is an extract from the Latin version of verse 8 of the 72nd Psalm - "He shall have dominion also from sea to sea, and from the river unto the ends of the earth."

THE NATIONAL FLAG

The National Flag of Canada, otherwise known as the Canadian Flag, was approved by Parliament and proclaimed by Her Majesty Queen Elizabeth II to be in force as of February 15, 1965. It is described as a red flag of the proportions two by length and one by width, containing in its centre a white square the width of the flag, bearing a single red maple leaf. Red and white are the official colours of Canada, as approved by the proclamation of King George V appointing Arms for Canada in 1921. The Flag is flown on land at all federal government buildings, airports, and military bases within and outside Canada, and may appropriately be flown or displayed by individuals and organizations. The Flag is the proper national colours for all Canadian ships and boats; and it is the flag flown on Canadian Naval vessels.

The Flag is flown daily from sunrise to sunset. However, it is not contrary to etiquette to have the Flag flying at night. No flag, banner or pennant should be flown or displayed above the Canadian Flag. Flags flown together should be approximately the same size and flown from separate staffs at the same height. When flown on a speaker's platform, it should be against the wall or on a flagpole on the left, from the audience's point of view. When used in the body of an auditorium, it should be to the right of the audience. When two or more than three flags are flown together, the Flag should be on the left as seen by spectators in front of the flags. When three flags are flown together, the Canadian Flag should occupy the central position.

A complete set of rules for flying the Canadian Flag can be obtained from the Department of Canadian Heritage.

THE ROYAL UNION FLAG

The Royal Union Flag, generally known as the Union Jack, was approved by Parliament on December 18, 1964 for continued use in Canada as a symbol of Canada's membership in the Commonwealth of Nations and of her allegiance to the Crown. It will, where physical arrangements make it possible, be flown along with the National Flag at federal buildings, airports, and military bases and establishments within Canada on the date of the official observance of the Queen's birthday, the Anniversary of the Statute of Westminster (December 11th), Commonwealth Day (second Monday in March), and on the occasions of Royal visits and certain Commonwealth gatherings in Canada.

QUEEN'S PERSONAL CANADIAN FLAG

In 1962, Her Majesty The Queen adopted a personal flag specifically for use in Canada. The design comprises the Arms of Canada with The Queen's own device in the centre. The device - the initial "E" surmounted by the St. Edward's Crown within a chaplet of roses - is gold on a blue background.

When the Queen is in Canada, this flag is flown, day and night, at any building in which She is in residence. Generally, the flag is also flown behind the saluting base when She conducts troop inspections, on all vehicles in which She travels, and on Her Majesty's Canadian ships (HMCS) when the Queen is aboard.

FLAG OF THE GOVERNOR GENERAL

The Governor General's standard is a blue flag with the crest of the Arms of Canada in its centre. A symbol of the Sovereignty of Canada, the crest is made of a gold lion passant imperially crowned, on a wreath of the official colours of Canada, holding in its right paw a red maple leaf. The standard was approved by Her Majesty The Queen on February 23, 1981. The Governor General's personal standard flies whenever the incumbent is in residence, and takes precedence over all other flags in Canada, except The Queen's.

CANADIAN ARMED FORCES BADGE

The Canadian Armed Forces Badge was sanctioned by Her Majesty Queen Elizabeth II in May 1967. The description is as follows:

Within a wreath of 10 stylized maple leaves Red, a cartouche medium Blue edge Gold, charged with a foul anchor Gold, surmounted by Crusader's Swords in Saltire Silver and blue, pommelled and hilted Gold; and in front an eagle volant affront head to the sinister Gold, the whole ensigned with a Royal Crown proper.

The Canadian Forces Badge replaces the badges of the Royal Canadian Navy, the Canadian Army, and the Royal Canadian Air Force.

ALBERTA

The Arms of the Province of Alberta were granted by Royal Warrant on May 30, 1907. On July 30th, 1980, the Arms were augmented as follows: Crest: Upon a Helm with a Wreath Argent and Gules a Beaver couchant upholding on its back the Royal Crown both proper; Supporters: On the dexter side a Lion Or armed and langued Gules and on the sinister side a Pronghorn Antelope (Antilocapra americana) proper; the Compartment comprising a grassy mount with the Floral Emblem of the said Province of Alberta the Wild Rose (Rosa acicularis) growing therefrom proper; Motto: FORTIS ET LIBER (Strong and Free) to be borne and used together with the Arms upon Seals, Shields, Banners, Flags or otherwise according to the Laws of Arms.

In 1958, the Government of Alberta authorized the design and use of an official flag. A flag bearing the Armorial Ensign on a royal ultramarine blue background was adopted and the Flag Act proclaimed June 1st 1968. Proportions of the flag are two by length and one by width with the Armorial Ensign seven-elevenths of the width of the flag carried in the centre. The flag may be used by citizens of the Province and others in a manner befitting its dignity and importance but no other banner or flag that includes the Armorial Ensign may be assumed or used.

Floral Emblem: Wild Rose (Rosa Acicularis). Chosen in the Floral Emblem Act of 1930.

Provincial Bird: Great horned owl (budo virginianus). Adopted May 3, 1977.

BRITISH COLUMBIA

The shield of British Columbia was granted by Royal Warrant on March 31, 1906. On October 15th, 1987, the shield was augmented by Her Majesty Queen Elizabeth II. The crest and supporters have become part of the provincial Arms through usage. The heraldic description is as follows: Crest: Upon a Helm with a Wreath Argent and Gules the Royal Crest of general purpose of Our Royal Predecessor Queen Victoria differenced for Us and Our Successors in right of British Columbia with the Lion thereof garlanded about the neck with the Provincial Flower that is to say the Pacific Dogwood (Cornus nuttallii) with leaves all proper Mantled Gules doubled Argent; Supporters: On the dexter side a Wapiti Stag (Cervus canadensis) proper and on the sinister side a Bighorn Sheep Ram (Oviscanadensis) Argent armed and unguled Or; Compartment: Beneath the Shield a Scroll entwined with Pacific Dogwood flowers slipped and leaved proper inscribed with the Motto assigned by the said Warrant of Our Royal Predecessor King Edward VII that is to say SPLENDOR SINE OCCASU, (splendour without diminishment).

The flag of British Columbia was authorized by an Order-in-Council of June 27, 1960. The Union Jack symbolizes the province's origins as a British colony, and the crown at its centre represents the sovereign power linking the nations of the Commonwealth. The sun sets over the Pacific Ocean. The original design of the flag was located in 1960 by Hon. W.A.C. Bennett at the College of Arms in London.

Floral emblem: Pacific Dogwood (Cornus Nuttallii, Audubon). Adopted under the Floral Emblem Act, 1956.

Provincial Bird: Steller's jay. Adopted November 19, 1987.

MANITOBA

The Arms of the Province of Manitoba were granted by Royal Warrant on May 10, 1905, augmented by warrant of the Governor General on October 23, 1992. The description is as follows: above the familiar shield of 1905 is a helmet and mantling; above the helmet is the Crest, including the beaver holding a prairie crocus, the province's floral emblem. On the beaver's back is the royal crown. The left supporter is a unicorn wearing a collar bearing a decorative frieze of maple leaves, the collar representing Manitoba's position as Canada's "keystone" province. Hanging from the collar is a wheel of a Red River cart. The right supporter is a white horse, and its collar of bead and bone honours First Peoples. The supporters and the shield rest on a compartment representing the province's rivers and lakes, grain fields and forests, composed of the provincial tree, the white spruce, and seven prairie crocuses. At the base is a Latin translation of the phrase "Glorious and Free."

The flag of the Province of Manitoba was adopted under The Provincial Flag Act, assented to May 11, 1965, and proclaimed into force on May 12, 1966. It incorporates parts of the Royal Armorial Ensigns, namely the Union and Red Ensign; the badge in the fly of the flag is the shield of the arms of the province.

Description: A flag of the proportions two by length and one by width with the Union Jack occupying the upper quarter next the staff and with the shield of the armorial bearings of the province centered in the half farthest from the staff.

Floral Emblem: Pasque Flower, known locally as Prairie Crocus (Anemone Patens). Adopted 1906.

Provincial Bird: Great gray owl. Adopted July 16, 1987.

NEW BRUNSWICK

The Arms of New Brunswick were granted by Royal Warrant on May 26, 1868. The motto SPEM REDUXIT (hope restored) was added by Order-in-Council in 1966. The description is as follows: The upper third of the shield is red and features a gold lion, symbolizing New Brunswick's ties to Britain. The lion is also found in the arms of the Duchy of Brunswick in Germany, the ancestral home of King George III. The lower part of the shield displays an ancient galley with oars in action. It could be interpreted as a reference to the importance of both shipbuilding and seafaring to New Brunswick in those days. It is also based on the design of the province's original great seal which featured a sailing ship on water. The shield is supported by two white-tailed deer wearing collars of Indian wampum. From one is suspended the Royal Union Flag (the Union Jack), from the other the fleur-de-lis to indicate the province's British and French background. The crest consists of an Atlantic Salmon leaping from a coronet of gold maple leaves and bearing St. Edward's Crown on its back. The base, or compartment, is a grassy mound with fiddleheads as well as purple violets, the provincial floral emblem. The motto "Spem Reduxit" is taken from the first great seal of the province and means "Hope restored.".

The flag of New Brunswick, adopted by Proclamation on February 24, 1965, is based on the Arms of the province. The chief and charge occupy the upper one-third of the flag, and the remainder of the armorial bearings occupy the lower two-thirds. The proportion is four by length and two and one half by width.

Floral Emblem: Purple Violet (Viola Cuculata). Adopted by Order-in-Council, December 1, 1936, at the request of the New Brunswick Women's Institute.

Provincial Bird: Black-capped chickadee. Adopted August 1983.

NEWFOUNDLAND & LABRADOR

The Arms of Newfoundland were granted by Royal Letters Patent dated January 1, 1637, by King Charles I. The heraldic description is as follows: Gules, a Cross Argent, in the first and fourth quarters a Lion passant guardant crowned Or, in the second and third quarters an Unicorn passant Argent armed and crined Or, gorged with a Coronet and a Chain affixed thereto reflexed of the last. Crest: on a wreath Or and Gules a Moose passant proper. Supporters: two Savages of the clime armed and apparelled according to their guise when they go to war. The motto reads QUAERITE PRIMEREGNUM DEI (seek ye first the kingdom of God).

The official flag of Newfoundland, adopted in 1980, has primary colours of Red, Gold and Blue, against a White background. The Blue section on the left represents Newfoundland's Commonwealth heritage and the Red and Gold section on the right represents the hopes for the future with the arrow pointing the way. The two triangles represent the mainland and island parts of the province.

Floral Emblem: Purple Pitcher Plant (Sarracenia Purpurea). Adopted June 1954.

Provincial Bird: Atlantic puffin. Adopted 1992.

NORTHWEST TERRITORIES

The Arms of the Northwest Territories were approved by Her Majesty Queen Elizabeth II on February 24, 1956. The crest consists of two gold narwhals guarding a compass rose, symbolic of the magnetic north pole. The white upper third of the shield represents the polar ice pack and is crossed by a wavy blue line portraying the Northwest Passage. The tree line is reflected by a diagonal line separating the red and green segments of the lower portion of the shield: the green symbolizing the forested areas south of the tree line, and the red standing for the barren lands north of it. The important bases of northern wealth, minerals and fur, are represented by gold billets in the green portion and the mask of a white fox in the red.

The official flag of the Northwest Territories was adopted by the Territorial Council on January 1, 1969. Blue panels at either side of the flag represent the lakes and waters of the Territories. The white centre panel, equal in width to the two blue panels combined, symbolizes the ice and snow of the North. In the centre of the white portion is the shield from the Arms of the Territories.

Floral Emblem: Mountain Avens (Dryas Integrifolia). Adopted by the Council on June 7, 1957.

Territorial Bird: Gyrfalcon. Adopted June 1990.

NOVA SCOTIA

The Arms of the Province of Nova Scotia were granted to the Royal Province in 1625 by King Charles I. The complete Armorial Achievement includes the Arms, surmounted by a royal helm with a blue and silver scroll or mantling representing the Royal cloak. Above is the crest of heraldic symbols: two joined hands, one armoured and the other bare, supporting a spray of laurel for peace and thistle for Scotland. On the left is the mythical royal unicorn and on the right a 17th century representation of the North American Indian. The motto reads MUNIT HAEC ET ALTERA VINCIT (one defends and the other conquers). Entwined with the thistle of Scotland at the base is the mayflower, added in 1929, as the floral emblem of Nova Scotia.

The flag of the Province of Nova Scotia is a blue St. Andrew's Cross on a white field, with the Royal Arms of Scotland mounted thereon. The width of the flag is three-quarters of the length.

The flag was originally authorized by Charles I in 1625. In 1929, on petition of Nova Scotia, a Royal Warrant of King George V was issued, revoking the modern Arms and ordering that the original Arms granted by Charles I be borne upon (seals) shields, banners, and otherwise according to the laws of Arms.

Floral Emblem: Trailing Arbutus, also known as Mayflower (Epigaea Repens). Adopted April 1901.

Provincial Bird: Osprey. Adopted Spring, 1994.

NUNAVUT

The dominant colours blue and gold are the ones preferred by the Nunavut Implementation Commissioners to symbolize the riches of the land, sea and sky.

Red is a reference to Canada. In the base of the shield, the inuksuk symbolizes the stone monuments which guide the people on the land and mark sacred and other special places. The qulliq, or Inuit stone lamp, represents light and the warmth of family and the community. Above, the concave arc of five gold circles refers to the life-giving properties of the sun arching above and below the horizon, the unique part of the Nunavut year. The star is the Niqirtsuituq, the North Star and the traditional guide for navigation and more broadly, forever remains unchanged as the leadership of the elders in the community.

In the crest, the iglu represents the traditional life of the people and the means of survival. It also symbolizes the assembled members of the Legislature meeting together for the good of Nunavut; with the Royal Crown symbolizing public government for all the people of Nunavut and the equivalent status of Nunavut with other territories and provinces in Canadian Confederation. The tuktu (caribou) and qilalugaq tugaalik (narwhal) refer to land and sea animals which are part of the rich natural heritage of Nunavut and provide sustenance for people. The compartment at the base is composed of land and sea and features three important species of Arctic wild flowers.

Floral Emblem: Purple Saxifrage (Saxifraga oppositifolia). Adopted May 1, 2000.

Territorial Bird: Rock Ptarmigan.

ONTARIO

The Arms of the Province of Ontario were granted by Royal Warrants on May 26, 1868 (shield), and February 27, 1909 (crest and supporters). The heraldic description is as follows: Vert, a Sprig of three leaves of Maple slipped Or on a Chief Argent the Cross of St. George. Crest: upon a wreath Vert and Or a Bear passant Sable. The supporters are on the dexter side, a Moose, and on the sinister side a Canadian Deer, both proper. The motto reads: UT INCEPIT FIDELIS SIC PERMANET (loyal in the beginning, so it remained).

The flag of the Province of Ontario was adopted under the Flag Act of May 21, 1965. It incorporates parts of the Royal Armorial Ensigns, namely the Union and Red Ensign; the badge in the fly of the flag is the shield of the Arms of the province. The flag is of the proportions two by length and one by width, with the Union Jack occupying the upper quarter next the staff and the shield of the armorial bearings of the province centered in the half farthest from the staff.

Floral Emblem: White Trillium (Trillium Grandiflorum). Adopted March 25, 1937.

Provincial Bird: Common loon. Adopted June 23, 1994.

PRINCE EDWARD ISLAND

The Arms of the Province of Prince Edward Island were granted by Royal Warrant, May 30, 1905. The heraldic description is as follows: Argent on an Island Vert, to the sinister an Oak Tree fructed, to the dexter thereof three Oak saplings sprouting all proper, on a Chief Gules a Lion passant guardant Or. The motto reads: PARVA SUB INGENTI (the small under the protection of the great).

The flag of the Province of Prince Edward Island was authorized by an Act of the Legislative Assembly, March 24, 1964. The design of the flag is that part of the Arms contained within the shield, but is of rectangular shape, with a fringe of alternating red and white. The chief and charge of the Arms occupies the upper one-third of the flag, and the remainder of the Arms occupies the lower two-thirds. The proportions of the flag are six, four and one-quarter in relation to the fly, the hoist and the depth of the fringe.

Floral Emblem: Lady's Slipper (Cypripedium Acaule). Designated as the province's floral emblem by the Legislative Assembly in 1947. A more precise botanical name was included in an amendment to the Floral Emblem Act in 1965.

Provincial Bird: Blue Jay (cyanocitta cristata) was designated as avian emblem by the Provincial Emblems Acts, May 13, 1977.

QUÉBEC

The Arms of the Province of Québec were granted by Queen Victoria, May 26, 1868, and revised by a Provincial Order-in-Council on December 9, 1939. The heraldic description is as follows: Tierced in fess: Azure, three Fleurs-de-lis Or; Gules, a Lion passant guardant Or armed and langued Azure; Or, a Sugar Maple sprig with three leaves Vert veined Or. Surmounted with the Royal Crown. Below the shield a scroll Argent, surrounded by a bordure Azure, inscribed with the motto JE ME SOUVIENS (I remember) Azure.

The official flag of the Province of Québec was adopted by a Provincial Order-in-Council of January 21, 1948. It is a white cross on a sky blue ground, with the fleur-de-lis in an upright position on the blue ground in each of the four quarters. The proportion is six units wide by four units deep.

Floral Emblem: Iris Versicolor. Adopted November 5, 1999.

Provincial Bird: Snowy owl. Adopted December 17, 1987.

SASKATCHEWAN

The complete armorial bearings of the Province of Saskatchewan were granted by Royal Warrant on September 16, 1986, through augmentation of the original shield of arms granted by King Edward VII on August 25, 1906. The heraldic description is as follows: Shield: Vert three Garbs in fesse Or, on a Chief of the last a Lion passant guardant Gules. Crest: Upon a Helm with a Wreath Argent and Gules a Beaver upholding with its back Our Royal Crown and holding in the dexter fore-claws a Western Red Lily (Lilium philadelphicumandinum) slipped all proper Mantled Gules doubled Argent. Supporters: On the dexter side a Lion Or gorged with a Collar of Prairie Indian beadwork proper and dependent therefrom a six-pointed Mullet faceted Argent fimbriated and garnished Or charged with a Maple Leaf Gules and on the sinister side a White tailed deer (Odocoileus virginianus) proper gorged with a like Collar and dependent therefrom a like Mullet charged with a Western Red Lily slipped and leaved proper. Motto: Beneath the Shield a Scroll entwined with Western Red Lilies slipped and leaved proper inscribed with the motto MULTIS E GENTIBUS VIRES (From many peoples strength).

The official flag was dedicated on September 22, 1969, and features the Arms of the province in the upper quarter nearest the staff, with the Western Red Lily, in the half farthest from the staff. The upper green portion represents forests, while the gold symbolizes prairie wheat fields. The basic design was adopted from the prize-winning entry of Anthony Drake of Hodgeville from a province-wide flag design competition.

Floral Emblem: Western Red Lily (Lilium philadelphicum var. andinum). Adopted April 8, 1941.

Provincial Bird: Prairie sharp-tailed grouse. Adopted March 30, 1945.

YUKON

The Arms of the Yukon, granted by Queen Elizabeth II on February 24, 1956, have the following explanation: The wavy white and blue vertical stripe represents the Yukon River and refers also to the rivers and creeks where gold was discovered. The red spire-like forms represent the mountainous country, and the gold discs the mineral resources. The St. George's Cross is in reference to the early explorers and fur traders from Great Britain, and the roundel in vair in the centre of the cross is a symbol for the fur trade. The crest displays a Malamute dog, an animal which has played an important part in the early history of the Yukon.

The Yukon flag, designed by Lynn Lambert, a Haines Junction student, was adopted by Council in 1967. It is divided into thirds: green for forests, white for snow, and blue for water.

The flag consists of three vertical panels, the centre panel being one and one-half times the width of each of the other two panels. The panel adjacent to the mast is coloured green, the centre panel is coloured white and has the Yukon Crest disposed above a symbolic representation of the floral emblem of the territory, epilobium angustifolium, (fireweed), and the panel on the fly is coloured blue. The stem and leaves of the floral emblem are coloured green, and the flowers thereof are coloured red. The Yukon Crest is coloured red and blue, with the Malamute dog coloured black.

Floral Emblem: Fireweed (Epilobium Angustifolium). Adopted November 16, 1957.

Territorial Bird: Common raven. Adopted October 28, 1985.

SYMBOLS OF CANADA

Provinces and Territories	Floral Emblem	Tree	Bird
Alberta	Wild Rose	Lodgepole Pine	Great Horned Owl
British Columbia	Pacific Dogwood	Western Red Cedar	Stellar's Jay
Manitoba	Prairie Crocus	White Spruce	Great Gray Owl
New Brunswick	Purple Violet	Balsam Fir	Black-capped Chickadee
Newfoundland & Labrador	Purple Pitcher Plant	Black Spruce	Atlantic Puffin
Northwest Territories	Mountain Avens	Tamarack Larch	Gyrfalcon
Nova Scotia	Mayflower	Red Spruce	Osprey
Nunavut	Purple Saxifrage		Rock Ptarmigan
Ontario	White Trillium	Eastern White Pine	Loon
Prince Edward Island	Lady's Slipper	Red Oak	Blue Jay
Quebec	Iris Versicolor	Yellow Birch	Snowy Owl
Saskatchewan	Western Red Lily	Paper Birch	Sharp-tailed Grouse
Yukon	Fireweed	Subalpine Fir	Common Raven

Vital Statistics

POPULATION COUNTS, FOR CANADA, PROVINCES AND TERRITORIES, 2016 AND 2011 CENSUSES

Geographic name	Population, 2016	Population, 2011	Population, % change	Population density per kilometre, 2016
Canada	35,151,728	33,476,688	5.0	3.9
Newfoundland and Labrador	519,716	514,536	1.0	1.4
Prince Edward Island	142,907	140,204	1.9	25.1
Nova Scotia	923,598	921,727	0.2	17.4
New Brunswick	747,101	751,171	-0.5	10.5
Quebec	8,164,361	7,903,001	3.3	6.0
Ontario	13,448,494	12,851,821	4.6	14.8
Manitoba	1,278,365	1,208,268	5.8	2.3
Saskatchewan	1,098,352	1,033,381	6.3	1.9
Alberta	4,067,175	3,645,257	11.6	6.4
British Columbia	4,648,055	4,400,057	5.6	5.0
Yukon	35,874	33,897	5.8	0.1
Northwest Territories	41,786	41,462	0.8	0.0
Nunavut	35,944	31,906	12.7	0.0

Source: Adapted from the Statistics Canada publication *Population and Dwelling Count Highlight Tables, 2016 Census* (Catalogue no. 98-402-X2016001). Accessed June 25, 2021.

POPULATION BY SEX AND AGE GROUP, BY PROVINCE AND TERRITORY (NUMBER, BOTH SEXES)

	2011				2016			
	All ages	0 to 14	15 to 64	65 and older	All ages	0 to 14	15 to 64	65 and older
Canada	33,476,685	5,607,345	22,924,285	4,945,055	35,151,725	5,839,570	23,376,525	5,935,630
Newfoundland and Labrador	514,535	76,630	355,805	82,105	519,715	74,445	344,250	101,030
Prince Edward Island	140,205	23,055	94,360	22,785	142,910	22,685	92,510	27,710
Nova Scotia	921,730	138,215	630,140	153,370	923,595	133,830	605,950	183,820
New Brunswick	751,170	113,575	513,960	123,630	747,100	110,495	487,820	148,785
Quebec	7,903,000	1,258,620	5,386,695	1,257,685	8,164,360	1,333,255	5,335,910	1,495,195
Ontario	12,851,820	2,180,775	8,792,725	1,878,325	13,448,495	2,207,970	8,988,865	2,251,655
Manitoba	1,208,270	231,160	804,650	172,450	1,278,365	243,825	835,575	198,965
Saskatchewan	1,033,385	197,860	681,815	153,705	1,098,350	215,685	712,245	170,430
Alberta	3,645,260	684,790	2,554,745	405,725	4,067,175	779,155	2,787,800	500,220
British Columbia	4,400,055	677,365	3,033,975	688,720	4,648,055	691,390	3,107,680	848,985
Yukon	33,900	5,860	24,940	3,090	35,875	6,280	25,340	4,260
Northwest Territories	41,460	9,015	30,055	2,395	41,790	8,875	29,690	3,225
Nunavut	31,905	10,425	20,420	1,060	35,945	11,685	22,895	1,360

Source: Adapted from the Statistics Canada publication *Age and Sex Highlight Tables, 2016 Census* (Catalogue no. 98-402-X2016002). Accessed June 25, 2021.

POPULATION OF CENSUS METROPOLITAN AREAS (2011, 2016)

Geographic name	Total (2016 counts)	Total (2011 counts)	Total (2011 to 2016 % change)
Canada	35,151,730	33,476,685	5.0
St. John's (N.L.)	205,955	196,965	4.6
Halifax (N.S.)	403,390	390,325	3.3
Saint John (N.B.)	126,200	129,055	-2.2
Fredericton (N.B.)	101,760	98,320	3.5
Québec (Que.)	800,295	767,310	4.3
Trois-Rivières (Que.)	156,045	151,775	2.8
Montréal (Que.)	4,098,925	3,934,075	4.2
Ottawa - Gatineau (Ont.)	1,323,780	1,254,920	5.5
Kingston (Ont.)	161,175	159,560	1.0
Peterborough (Ont.)	121,720	118,975	2.3
Toronto (Ont.)	5,928,040	5,583,065	6.2
Hamilton (Ont.)	747,550	721,055	3.7
Guelph (Ont.)	151,985	141,100	7.7
London (Ont.)	494,065	474,785	4.1
Windsor (Ont.)	329,140	319,245	3.1
Barrie (Ont.)	197,060	187,010	5.4
Thunder Bay (Ont.)	121,620	121,595	0.0
Winnipeg (Man.)	778,490	730,015	6.6
Regina (Sask.)	236,490	210,550	11.8
Saskatoon (Sask.)	295,095	262,215	12.5
Calgary (Alta.)	1,392,610	1,214,840	14.6
Edmonton (Alta.)	1,321,425	1,159,875	13.9
Kelowna (B.C.)	194,885	179,840	8.4
Vancouver (B.C.)	2,463,430	2,313,330	6.5
Victoria (B.C.)	367,770	344,615	6.7

Source: Adapted from the Statistics Canada publication *Age and Sex Highlight Tables, 2016 Census* (Catalogue no. 98-402-X2016002). Accessed June 25, 2021.

POPULATION OF CANADA, PROJECTIONS, 2022-2064

IN THOUSANDS

Year	L: low-growth	M1: medium-growth, 1991/1992 to 2010/2011 trends	M2: medium-growth, 1991/1992 to 1999/2000 trends	M3: medium-growth, 1999/2000 to 2002/2003 trends	M4: medium-growth, 2004/2005 to 2007/2008 trends	M5: medium-growth, 2009/2010 to 2010/2011 trends	H: high-growth
				Projection Scenario			
2022	38,322.80	38,694.30	38,694.40	38,694.30	38,694.50	38,693.80	39,133.60
2023	38,615.60	39,102.60	39,102.70	39,102.50	39,102.80	39,101.80	39,665.60
2024	38,897.40	39,509.10	39,509.20	39,509.00	39,509.50	39,508.00	40,206.00
2025	39,168.40	39,913.50	39,913.60	39,913.20	39,913.90	39,912.00	40,754.20
2026	39,428.50	40,315.20	40,315.30	40,314.90	40,315.80	40,313.40	41,309.80
2027	39,677.70	40,713.90	40,714.10	40,713.50	40,714.70	40,711.80	41,872.30
2028	39,915.90	41,109.20	41,109.50	41,108.80	41,110.20	41,106.60	42,441.10
2029	40,143.20	41,500.70	41,501.00	41,500.20	41,501.90	41,497.70	43,015.60
2030	40,359.50	41,888.10	41,888.50	41,887.50	41,889.50	41,884.60	43,595.50
2031	40,564.90	42,271.00	42,271.50	42,270.40	42,272.70	42,267.00	44,180.10
2032	40,759.50	42,649.30	42,649.90	42,648.60	42,651.20	42,644.70	44,769.20
2033	40,943.60	43,022.80	43,023.60	43,022.10	43,024.90	43,017.50	45,362.40
2034	41,117.50	43,391.50	43,392.40	43,390.70	43,393.90	43,385.50	45,959.50
2035	41,281.50	43,755.50	43,756.50	43,754.60	43,758.00	43,748.60	46,560.40
2036	41,436.10	44,114.70	44,115.90	44,113.90	44,117.50	44,106.90	47,165.00
2037	41,581.70	44,469.40	44,470.70	44,468.50	44,472.30	44,460.50	47,773.20
2038	41,718.70	44,819.50	44,821.10	44,818.60	44,822.70	44,809.60	48,384.80
2039	41,847.60	45,165.30	45,167.10	45,164.40	45,168.60	45,154.10	49,000.00
2040	41,968.70	45,506.80	45,508.70	45,505.80	45,510.20	45,494.20	49,618.50
2041	42,082.50	45,843.90	45,846.10	45,843.00	45,847.60	45,829.90	50,240.20
2042	42,189.00	46,176.90	46,179.30	46,175.90	46,180.70	46,161.20	50,865.10
2043	42,288.80	46,505.60	46,508.20	46,504.60	46,509.50	46,488.30	51,493.20
2044	42,388.30	46,831.80	46,834.70	46,830.80	46,835.90	46,812.70	52,117.50
2045	42,484.40	47,156.20	47,159.30	47,155.30	47,160.50	47,135.20	52,746.30
2046	42,577.00	47,479.10	47,482.50	47,478.20	47,483.50	47,456.10	53,380.30
2047	42,666.50	47,800.80	47,804.50	47,799.90	47,805.40	47,775.70	54,019.90
2048	42,752.90	48,121.70	48,125.70	48,120.80	48,126.50	48,094.40	54,665.80
2049	42,836.60	48,442.30	48,446.50	48,441.30	48,447.20	48,412.70	55,319.10
2050	42,917.80	48,763.10	48,767.70	48,762.10	48,768.20	48,731.10	55,980.40
2051	42,996.90	49,084.70	49,089.60	49,083.80	49,090.10	49,050.30	56,650.80
2052	43,074.30	49,407.90	49,413.10	49,406.90	49,413.40	49,370.80	57,331.40
2053	43,150.40	49,733.20	49,738.70	49,732.20	49,738.90	49,693.30	58,023.00
2054	43,225.90	50,061.40	50,067.20	50,060.40	50,067.40	50,018.70	58,726.70
2055	43,301.10	50,393.20	50,399.40	50,392.20	50,399.50	50,347.60	59,443.50
2056	43,376.50	50,729.20	50,735.80	50,728.20	50,735.80	50,680.50	60,174.20
2057	43,452.60	51,070.00	51,076.90	51,069.00	51,076.90	51,018.20	60,919.50
2058	43,529.70	51,416.00	51,423.40	51,415.10	51,423.30	51,360.90	61,680.10
2059	43,608.00	51,767.60	51,775.40	51,766.70	51,775.20	51,709.10	62,456.50
2060	43,687.60	52,125.00	52,133.20	52,124.10	52,133.00	52,063.00	63,249.00
2061	43,768.50	52,488.20	52,496.80	52,487.40	52,496.60	52,422.50	64,057.90
2062	43,850.70	52,857.20	52,866.30	52,856.50	52,866.10	52,787.80	64,883.10
2063	43,934.00	53,231.90	53,241.40	53,231.20	53,241.20	53,158.50	65,724.80
2064	44,018.10	53,611.90	53,622.00	53,611.30	53,621.70	53,534.50	66,582.70

Source: Statistics Canada. *Table 17-10-0057-01 - Projected population, by projection scenario, sex and age group as of July 1 (x 1,000), Canada, provinces and territories, annual (persons).* Accessed June 25, 2021.

People | 2.1

World Development Indicators: Population dynamics

	Population		Average annual population growth %	Population age composition			Dependency ratio		Crude death rate	Crude birth rate
	millions			Ages 0-14 %	Ages 15-64 %	Ages 65+ %	young % of working-age population	old % of working-age population	per 1,000 people	per 1,000 people
	2000	2019	2000-2019	2019	2019	2019	2019	2019	2018	2018
Afghanistan	20.8	38.0	3.2	42	55	3	77	5	6	32
Albania	3.1	2.9	-0.4	17	68	14	25	21	8	12
Algeria	31.0	43.1	1.7	31	63	7	49	10	5	24
American Samoa	0.1	0.1	-0.2	..	..	..	..	..	..	..
Andorra	0.1	0.1	0.9	..	..	..	..	..	4	7
Angola	16.4	31.8	3.5	47	51	2	91	4	8	41
Antigua and Barbuda	0.1	0.1	1.3	22	69	9	32	13	6	15
Argentina	36.9	44.9	1.0	25	64	11	38	18	8	17
Armenia	3.1	3.0	-0.2	21	68	11	31	17	10	14
Aruba	0.1	0.1	0.8	18	68	14	26	21	9	12
Australia	19.2	25.4	1.5	19	65	16	30	25	6	13
Austria	8.0	8.9	0.5	14	67	19	22	29	10	10
Azerbaijan	8.0	10.0	1.2	23	70	6	33	9	6	14
Bahamas, The	0.3	0.4	1.4	22	70	7	31	11	7	14
Bahrain	0.7	1.6	4.8	19	79	3	24	3	2	14
Bangladesh	127.7	163.0	1.3	27	68	5	40	8	6	18
Barbados	0.3	0.3	0.3	17	67	16	26	24	9	11
Belarus	10.0	9.5	-0.3	17	68	15	25	22	13	10
Belgium	10.3	11.5	0.6	17	64	19	27	30	11	10
Belize	0.2	0.4	2.4	30	65	5	45	7	5	21
Benin	6.9	11.8	2.9	42	55	3	77	6	9	36
Bermuda	0.1	0.1	0.2	..	..	..	..	..	8	8
Bhutan	0.6	0.8	1.3	25	69	6	37	9	6	17
Bolivia	8.4	11.5	1.6	31	62	7	49	12	7	22
Bosnia and Herzegovina	3.8	3.3	-0.7	15	68	17	22	25	11	8
Botswana	1.6	2.3	1.8	34	62	4	55	7	6	25
Brazil	174.8	211.0	1.0	21	70	9	30	13	6	14
Brunei Darussalam	0.3	0.4	1.4	23	72	5	31	7	4	15
Bulgaria	8.2	7.0	-0.8	15	64	21	23	33	15	9
Burkina Faso	11.6	20.3	2.9	45	53	2	84	5	8	38
Burundi	6.4	11.5	3.1	45	52	2	87	4	8	39
Cabo Verde	0.4	0.5	1.3	28	67	5	42	7	6	19
Cambodia	12.2	16.5	1.6	31	64	5	48	7	6	22
Cameroon	15.5	25.9	2.7	42	55	3	77	5	9	35
Canada	30.7	37.6	1.1	16	67	18	24	27	8	10
Cayman Islands	0.0	0.1	2.3	..	..	..	..	..	3	10
Central African Republic	3.6	4.7	1.4	44	53	3	82	5	12	35
Chad	8.4	15.9	3.4	47	51	2	92	5	12	42
Channel Islands	0.1	0.2	0.8	15	67	18	22	26	8	10
Chile	15.3	19.0	1.1	19	69	12	28	17	6	12
China	1,262.6	1,397.7	0.5	18	71	11	25	16	7	11
Hong Kong SAR, China	6.7	7.5	0.6	12	70	17	18	25	6	7
Macao SAR, China	0.4	0.6	2.1	14	75	11	19	15	4	11
Colombia	39.6	50.3	1.3	23	69	9	33	13	6	15
Comoros	0.5	0.9	2.4	39	58	3	68	5	7	32
Congo, Dem. Rep.	47.1	86.8	3.2	46	51	3	90	6	9	41
Congo, Rep.	3.1	5.4	2.9	42	56	3	75	5	7	33
Costa Rica	4.0	5.0	1.3	21	69	10	31	14	5	14
Cote d'Ivoire	16.5	25.7	2.4	42	55	3	75	5	10	36
Croatia	4.5	4.1	-0.5	15	65	21	23	32	13	9
Cuba	11.1	11.3	0.1	16	68	16	23	23	9	10
Curacao	0.1	0.2	0.9	18	64	17	29	27	9	11
Cyprus	0.9	1.2	1.3	17	69	14	24	20	7	10
Czech Republic	10.3	10.7	0.2	16	64	20	24	31	11	11
Denmark	5.3	5.8	0.5	16	64	20	26	31	10	11
Djibouti	0.7	1.0	1.6	29	66	5	44	7	7	21
Dominica	0.1	0.1	0.2	..	..	..	..	..	..	..
Dominican Republic	8.5	10.7	1.2	28	65	7	43	11	6	20
Ecuador	12.7	17.4	1.7	28	65	7	43	11	5	20

People | 2.1

World Development Indicators: Population dynamics

	Population		Average annual population growth %	Population age composition			Dependency ratio		Crude death rate	Crude birth rate
				Ages 0-14	Ages 15-64	Ages 65+	young	old		
	millions			%	%	%	% of working-age population	% of working-age population	per 1,000 people	per 1,000 people
	2000	2019	2000-2019	2019	2019	2019	2019	2019	2018	2018
Egypt, Arab Rep.	68.8	100.4	2.0	34	61	5	56	9	6	26
El Salvador	5.9	6.5	0.5	27	65	8	42	13	7	18
Equatorial Guinea	0.6	1.4	4.2	37	61	2	61	4	9	33
Eritrea	2.3	..	..	..	..	..	..	..	7	30
Estonia	1.4	1.3	-0.3	16	64	20	26	31	12	11
Eswatini	1.0	1.1	0.7	38	58	4	65	7	9	26
Ethiopia	66.2	112.1	2.8	40	56	4	72	6	7	32
Faroe Islands	0.0	0.0	0.2	..	..	..	..	..	8	13
Fiji	0.8	0.9	0.5	29	65	6	45	9	8	21
Finland	5.2	5.5	0.3	16	62	22	26	36	10	9
France	60.9	67.1	0.5	18	62	20	29	33	9	11
French Polynesia	0.2	0.3	0.8	23	69	9	33	13	6	15
Gabon	1.2	2.2	3.0	37	59	4	63	6	7	32
Gambia, The	1.3	2.3	3.0	44	53	3	83	5	8	39
Georgia	4.1	3.7	-0.5	20	65	15	31	23	13	13
Germany	82.2	83.1	0.1	14	65	22	21	33	12	10
Ghana	19.3	30.4	2.4	37	60	3	63	5	7	29
Greece	10.8	10.7	0.0	14	64	22	22	34	11	8
Greenland	0.1	0.1	0.0	..	..	..	..	..	9	15
Grenada	0.1	0.1	0.4	24	67	10	36	15	10	16
Guam	0.2	0.2	0.4	24	66	10	37	16	5	17
Guatemala	11.6	16.6	1.9	34	61	5	55	8	5	25
Guinea	8.2	12.8	2.3	43	54	3	81	5	8	36
Guinea-Bissau	1.2	1.9	2.5	42	55	3	77	5	10	35
Guyana	0.7	0.8	0.2	28	65	7	43	10	7	20
Haiti	8.5	11.3	1.5	33	62	5	53	8	9	24
Honduras	6.6	9.7	2.1	31	64	5	49	8	4	22
Hungary	10.2	9.8	-0.2	14	66	20	22	30	13	10
Iceland	0.3	0.4	1.3	20	65	15	30	23	6	12
India	1,056.6	1,366.4	1.4	27	67	6	40	10	7	18
Indonesia	211.5	270.6	1.3	26	68	6	39	9	6	18
Iran, Islamic Rep.	65.6	82.9	1.2	25	69	6	36	9	5	19
Iraq	23.5	39.3	2.7	38	59	3	65	6	5	29
Ireland	3.8	4.9	1.4	21	65	14	33	22	6	13
Isle of Man	0.1	0.1	0.5	..	..	..	..	..	..	..
Israel	6.3	9.1	1.9	28	60	12	47	20	5	21
Italy	56.9	60.3	0.3	13	64	23	21	36	11	7
Jamaica	2.7	2.9	0.6	24	68	9	35	13	8	16
Japan	126.8	126.3	0.0	13	59	28	21	47	11	7
Jordan	5.1	10.1	3.6	34	63	4	54	6	4	22
Kazakhstan	14.9	18.5	1.1	29	63	8	46	12	7	22
Kenya	32.0	52.6	2.6	39	58	2	67	4	5	29
Kiribati	0.1	0.1	1.7	36	60	4	60	7	6	28
Korea, Dem. People's Rep.	22.9	25.7	0.6	20	71	9	28	13	9	14
Korea, Rep.	47.0	51.7	0.5	13	72	15	18	21	6	6
Kosovo	1.7	1.8	0.3	..	..	..	..	..	7	16
Kuwait	2.0	4.2	3.8	22	76	3	29	4	3	14
Kyrgyz Republic	4.9	6.5	1.5	33	63	5	52	7	5	27
Lao PDR	5.3	7.2	1.6	32	64	4	51	7	6	24
Latvia	2.4	1.9	-1.1	16	63	20	26	32	15	10
Lebanon	3.8	6.9	3.0	26	67	7	38	11	4	18
Lesotho	2.0	2.1	0.2	32	63	5	52	8	14	27
Liberia	2.8	4.9	2.9	41	56	3	73	6	8	33
Libya	5.4	6.8	1.2	28	67	4	42	7	5	19
Liechtenstein	0.0	0.0	0.7	..	..	..	..	..	7	10
Lithuania	3.5	2.8	-1.2	15	65	20	23	31	14	10
Luxembourg	0.4	0.6	1.8	16	70	14	22	20	7	10
Madagascar	15.8	27.0	2.8	40	57	3	71	5	6	33
Malawi	11.1	18.6	2.7	43	54	3	81	5	7	34
Malaysia	23.2	31.9	1.7	24	69	7	34	10	5	17
Maldives	0.3	0.5	3.4	20	76	4	26	5	3	14
Mali	10.9	19.7	3.1	47	50	2	94	5	10	42
Malta	0.4	0.5	1.3	14	65	21	22	32	8	9
Marshall Islands	0.1	0.1	0.8	..	..	..	..	..	..	..
Mauritania	2.6	4.5	2.9	40	57	3	70	6	7	34

People | 2.1

World Development Indicators: Population dynamics

	Population		Average annual population growth %	Population age composition			Dependency ratio		Crude death rate	Crude birth rate
				Ages 0-14	Ages 15-64	Ages 65+	young	old		
	millions			%	%	%	% of working-age population	% of working-age population	per 1,000 people	per 1,000 people
	2000	2019	2000-2019	2019	2019	2019	2019	2019	2018	2018
Mauritius	1.2	1.3	0.3	17	71	12	24	17	9	10
Mexico	98.9	127.6	1.3	26	66	7	39	11	6	18
Micronesia, Fed. Sts.	0.1	0.1	0.3	31	64	4	49	7	7	23
Moldova	2.9	2.7	-0.5	16	72	12	22	17	12	10
Monaco	0.0	0.0	1.0	..	..	..	..	..	7	6
Mongolia	2.4	3.2	1.6	31	65	4	47	6	6	24
Montenegro	0.6	0.6	0.1	18	66	15	27	23	11	12
Morocco	28.8	36.5	1.2	27	66	7	41	11	5	19
Mozambique	17.7	30.4	2.8	44	53	3	84	5	9	38
Myanmar	46.7	54.0	0.8	26	68	6	38	9	8	18
Namibia	1.8	2.5	1.7	37	59	4	62	6	8	29
Nepal	23.9	28.6	0.9	30	65	6	46	9	6	20
Netherlands	15.9	17.3	0.4	16	65	20	25	30	9	10
New Caledonia	0.2	0.3	1.6	22	68	9	33	14	6	15
New Zealand	3.9	4.9	1.3	20	64	16	30	25	7	12
Nicaragua	5.1	6.5	1.3	30	65	5	46	8	5	21
Niger	11.3	23.3	3.8	50	48	3	105	5	8	46
Nigeria	122.3	201.0	2.6	44	54	3	82	5	12	38
North Macedonia	2.0	2.1	0.1	16	70	14	24	20	10	11
Northern Mariana Islands	0.1	0.1	0.0	..	..	..	..	..	..	..
Norway	4.5	5.3	0.9	17	65	17	27	26	8	10
Oman	2.3	5.0	4.1	22	75	2	30	3	2	19
Pakistan	142.3	216.6	2.2	35	61	4	58	7	7	28
Palau	0.0	0.0	-0.3	..	..	..	..	..	8	14
Panama	3.0	4.2	1.8	27	65	8	41	13	5	19
Papua New Guinea	5.8	8.8	2.1	35	61	4	58	6	7	27
Paraguay	5.3	7.0	1.5	29	64	7	45	10	5	21
Peru	26.5	32.5	1.1	25	66	8	38	13	6	18
Philippines	78.0	108.1	1.7	30	64	5	47	8	6	21
Poland	38.3	38.0	0.0	15	67	18	23	27	11	10
Portugal	10.3	10.3	0.0	13	64	22	21	35	11	9
Puerto Rico	3.8	3.2	-0.9	16	64	20	25	31	9	7
Qatar	0.6	2.8	8.2	14	85	2	16	2	1	10
Romania	22.4	19.4	-0.8	16	66	19	24	29	14	10
Russian Federation	146.6	144.4	-0.1	18	67	15	27	23	12	12
Rwanda	7.9	12.6	2.4	40	57	3	70	5	5	32
Samoa	0.2	0.2	0.6	38	57	5	66	9	5	24
San Marino	0.0	0.0	1.1	..	..	..	..	..	7	7
Sao Tome and Principe	0.1	0.2	2.2	42	55	3	77	5	5	32
Saudi Arabia	20.7	34.3	2.7	25	72	3	35	5	3	18
Senegal	9.8	16.3	2.7	43	54	3	79	6	6	35
Serbia	7.5	6.9	-0.4	16	66	19	24	29	15	9
Seychelles	0.1	0.1	1.0	24	68	8	35	11	9	17
Sierra Leone	4.6	7.8	2.8	41	56	3	72	5	12	33
Singapore	4.0	5.7	1.8	12	75	12	16	16	5	9
Sint Maarten (Dutch part)	0.0	0.0	1.5	..	..	..	..	..	..	..
Slovak Republic	5.4	5.5	0.1	16	68	16	23	24	10	11
Slovenia	2.0	2.1	0.3	15	65	20	23	31	10	9
Solomon Islands	0.4	0.7	2.5	40	56	4	71	6	4	32
Somalia	8.9	15.4	2.9	46	51	3	91	6	11	42
South Africa	45.0	58.6	1.4	29	66	5	44	8	9	21
South Sudan	6.2	11.1	3.0	42	55	3	76	6	10	35
Spain	40.6	47.1	0.8	15	66	20	22	30	9	8
Sri Lanka	18.8	21.8	0.8	24	65	11	37	17	7	16
St. Kitts and Nevis	0.0	0.1	1.0	..	..	..	..	..	..	..
St. Lucia	0.2	0.2	0.8	18	72	10	25	14	7	12
St. Martin (French part)	0.0	0.0	1.4	..	..	..	..	..	4	15
St. Vincent and the Grenadines	0.1	0.1	0.1	22	68	10	33	14	9	14
Sudan	27.3	42.8	2.4	40	56	4	71	6	7	32
Suriname	0.5	0.6	1.1	27	66	7	41	11	7	19

People | 2.1 World Development Indicators:
Population dynamics

	Population		Average annual population growth %	Population age composition			Dependency ratio		Crude death rate	Crude birth rate
				Ages 0-14	Ages 15-64	Ages 65+	young	old		
	millions			%	%	%	% of working-age population	% of working-age population	per 1,000 people	per 1,000 people
	2000	2019	2000-2019	2019	2019	2019	2019	2019	2018	2018
Sweden	8.9	10.3	0.8	18	62	20	28	32	9	11
Switzerland	7.2	8.6	0.9	15	66	19	23	28	8	10
Syrian Arab Republic	16.4	17.1	0.2	31	64	5	48	7	5	24
Tajikistan	6.2	9.3	2.1	37	60	3	62	5	5	31
Tanzania	33.5	58.0	2.9	44	54	3	82	5	6	37
Thailand	63.0	69.6	0.5	17	71	12	24	18	8	10
Timor-Leste	0.9	1.3	2.0	37	58	4	64	7	6	29
Togo	4.9	8.1	2.6	41	56	3	73	5	8	33
Tonga	0.1	0.1	0.3	35	59	6	59	10	7	24
Trinidad and Tobago	1.3	1.4	0.5	20	69	11	30	16	8	13
Tunisia	9.7	11.7	1.0	24	67	9	36	13	6	18
Turkey	63.2	83.4	1.5	24	67	9	36	13	5	16
Turkmenistan	4.5	5.9	1.4	31	65	5	48	7	7	24
Turks and Caicos Islands	0.0	0.0	3.4	..	..	..	..	..	..	..
Tuvalu	0.0	0.0	1.1	..	..	..	..	..	..	..
Uganda	23.7	44.3	3.3	47	52	2	90	4	7	38
Ukraine	49.2	44.4	-0.5	16	67	17	24	25	15	9
United Arab Emirates	3.1	9.8	6.0	15	84	1	17	1	1	10
United Kingdom	58.9	66.8	0.7	18	64	19	28	29	9	11
United States	282.2	328.2	0.8	19	65	16	28	25	9	12
Uruguay	3.3	3.5	0.2	20	65	15	32	23	9	14
Uzbekistan	24.7	33.6	1.6	29	67	5	43	7	5	23
Vanuatu	0.2	0.3	2.5	39	58	4	67	6	5	30
Venezuela, RB	24.2	28.5	0.9	27	65	8	42	12	7	18
Vietnam	79.9	96.5	1.0	23	69	8	34	11	6	17
Virgin Islands (U.S.)	0.1	0.1	-0.1	19	61	20	32	33	8	13
West Bank and Gaza	2.9	4.7	2.5	39	58	3	66	5	3	29
Yemen, Rep.	17.4	29.2	2.7	39	58	3	68	5	6	30
Zambia	10.4	17.9	2.8	44	53	2	83	4	6	36
Zimbabwe	11.9	14.6	1.1	42	55	3	77	5	8	31
World	**6,114.3**	**7,673.5**	**1.2**	**26**	**65**	**9**	**39**	**14**	**8**	**18**
East Asia & Pacific	2,047.6	2,340.6	0.7	20	69	11	28	16	7	13
Europe & Central Asia	861.3	921.1	0.4	18	65	17	28	25	10	12
Latin America & Caribbean	520.9	646.4	1.1	24	67	9	36	13	6	16
Middle East & North Africa	315.3	456.7	1.9	30	65	5	46	8	5	23
North America	312.9	365.9	0.8	18	65	16	28	25	9	11
South Asia	1,390.9	1,835.8	1.5	28	66	6	42	9	7	19
Sub-Saharan Africa	665.3	1,107.0	2.7	42	55	3	77	5	9	35
Low income	401.8	668.5	2.7	42	55	3	76	6	8	35
Lower middle income	2,155.8	2,913.4	1.6	30	64	6	47	9	7	22
Upper middle income	2,455.3	2,855.9	0.8	21	69	10	31	15	7	14
High income	1,101.5	1,235.9	0.6	16	65	18	25	28	9	10

Most Recent Value (MRV) if data for the specified year or full period are not available; or growth rate is calculated for less than the full period.

About the Data

Population, total

Long definition

Total population is based on the de facto definition of population, which counts all residents regardless of legal status or citizenship. The values shown are midyear estimates.

Source: The World Bank.

BIRTHS, ESTIMATES, BY PROVINCE AND TERRITORY

	2014/2015	2015/2016	2016/2017	2017/2018	2019/2020
	number				
Canada	383,315	383,579	383,187	385,777	374,885
Newfoundland and Labrador	4,466	4,430	4,421	4,344	3,715
Prince Edward Island	1,374	1,397	1,413	1,440	1,353
Nova Scotia	8,523	8,359	8,368	8,475	8,193
New Brunswick	6,693	6,647	6,605	6,581	6,316
Quebec	87,376	86,914	84,642	84,000	84,400
Ontario	139,963	139,924	141,933	145,214	142,739
Manitoba	16,703	16,747	17,089	17,386	16,837
Saskatchewan	15,420	15,518	15,693	15,829	14,435
Alberta	56,333	56,925	56,110	56,329	51,996
British Columbia	44,480	44,699	44,924	44,180	42,996
Yukon	415	450	445	447	483
Northwest Territories	665	708	637	632	576
Nunavut	904	861	907	920	846

Notes:

Period from July 1 to June 30.

The number of births is final up to 2017/2018, updated for 2018/2019 and preliminary for 2019/2020.

Preliminary and updated estimates of births were produced by Demography Division, Statistics Canada. Final data were produced by Health Statistics Division, Statistics Canada. However, before 2011, the final estimates included in this table may differ from the data released by the Health Statistics Division, due to the imputation of certain unknown values (province or territory).

Source: Adapted from Statistics Canada, *Table 17-10-0008-01 – Estimates of the components of demographic growth, annual.* Last modified June 25, 2021. Accessed June 25, 2021.

HEALTH-ADJUSTED LIFE EXPECTANCY IN CANADA

	1994/19995	1998/1999	2001	2005	2009/2010	2015
	years					
Females						
At birth	67.8	70.1	69.8	70.6	71.3	70.5
At 65	13.2	13.8	14.1	14.7	15.2	15.3
Males						
At birth	65	67.4	67.3	68.1	69.3	69
At 65	11.8	12	12.6	13.5	14.2	14.4

Source: Bushnik, Tracey, Michael Tjepkema and Laurent Martel. Statistics Canada. *Health Reports: Health-adjusted life expectancy in Canada, Table A* (catalogue no. 82-003-X). Last modified April 18, 2018. Accessed June 25, 2021.

RANKING, NUMBER AND PERCENTAGE OF DEATH FOR THE 10 LEADING CAUSES OF DEATH, CANADA, 2000, 2018 AND 2019

Cause of death	2000			2018			2019		
	rank	number	percent	rank	number	percent	rank	number	percent
All causes of death	...	218,062	100	...	283,706	100	...	284,082	100
Total, ten leading causes of death	...	175,149	80.3	...	201,598	71	...	200,567	70.6
Malignant neoplasms (cancer)	1	62,672	28.7	1	79,536	28	1	80,152	28.2
Diseases of heart	2	55,070	25.3	2	53,134	18.7	2	52,541	18.5
Accidents	5	8,589	3.9	4	13,290	4.7	3	13,746	4.8
Cerebrovascular diseases (stroke)	3	15,576	7.1	3	13,480	4.8	4	13,660	4.8
Chronic lower respiratory diseases	4	9,813	4.5	5	12,998	4.6	5	12,823	4.5
Diabetes mellitus (diabetes)	6	6,714	3.1	7	6,794	2.4	6	6,912	2.4
Influenza and pneumonia	8	4,966	2.3	6	8,511	3	7	6,893	2.4
Alzheimer's disease	7	5,007	2.3	8	6,429	2.3	8	6,166	2.2
Intentional self-harm (suicide)	9	3,606	1.7	9	3,811	1.3	9	4,012	1.4
Nephritis, nephrotic syndrome and nephrosis	10	3,136	1.4	10	3,615	1.3	10	3,662	1.3
All other causes	...	42,913	20.1	...	82,108	28.9	...	83,515	29.4

... not applicable

Note: The order of the causes of death in this table is based on the ranking of the 10 leading causes of death in 2019.
Source: Adapted from Statistics Canada, *Table 13-10-0394-01 – Leading causes of death, total population, by age group.* Accessed June 25, 2021.

IMMIGRANTS TO CANADA, BY CLASS, 1992 - 2014

Year	Economic	Family	Protected Persons	Others [1]	Total
1992	95,796	101,112	52,345	5,544	254,797
1993	105,653	112,647	30,600	7,751	256,651
1994	102,309	94,193	20,435	7,455	224,392
1995	106,626	77,386	28,093	761	212,866
1996	125,370	68,359	28,478	3,866	226,073
1997	128,350	59,979	24,308	3,400	216,037
1998	97,912	50,896	22,843	2,547	174,198
1999	109,249	55,274	24,397	1,031	189,951
2000	136,287	60,616	30,092	460	227,455
2001	155,718	66,795	27,919	207	250,639
2002	137,863	62,292	25,114	3,780	229,049
2003	121,047	65,120	25,983	9,199	221,349
2004	133,748	62,269	32,687	7,121	235,825
2005	156,312	63,367	35,776	6,786	262,241
2006	138,251	70,517	32,499	10,375	251,642
2007	131,245	66,242	27,954	11,313	236,754
2008	149,071	65,580	21,860	10,736	247,247
2009	153,491	65,208	22,850	10,623	252,172
2010	186,918	60,230	24,697	8,846	280,691
2011	156,118	56,451	27,873	8,305	248,747
2012	160,829	65,018	31,987	...	257,905
2013	148,190	79,698	31,082	...	259,024
2014	165,116	65,451	29,812	...	260,411
%					
1992	37.6	39.7	20.5	2.2	100.0
1993	41.2	43.9	11.9	3.0	100.0
1994	45.6	42.0	9.1	3.3	100.0
1995	50.1	36.4	13.2	0.4	100.0
1996	55.5	30.2	12.6	1.7	100.0
1997	59.4	27.8	11.3	1.6	100.0
1998	56.2	29.2	13.1	1.5	100.0
1999	57.5	29.1	12.8	0.5	100.0
2000	59.9	26.6	13.2	0.2	100.0
2001	62.1	26.6	11.1	0.1	100.0
2002	60.2	27.2	11.0	1.7	100.0
2003	54.7	29.4	11.7	4.2	100.0
2004	56.7	26.4	13.9	3.0	100.0
2005	59.6	24.2	13.6	2.6	100.0
2006	54.9	28.0	12.9	4.1	100.0
2007	55.4	28.0	11.8	4.8	100.0
2008	60.3	26.5	8.8	4.3	100.0
2009	60.9	25.9	9.1	4.2	100.0
2010	66.6	21.5	8.8	3.2	100.0
2011	62.8	22.7	11.2	3.3	100.0
2012	62.4	25.2	12.4	...	100.0
2013	57.2	30.8	12.0	...	100.0
2014	63.4	25.1	11.4	...	100.0

[1] Includes deferred removal order class, post-determination refugee claimant class, temporary resident permit holders, humanitarian and compassionate/public policy cases and unknowns.

... indicates data not available for the given year.

Note: Data available as of September 2015.

Source: Immigration, Refugees and Citizenship Canada.

Source: Adapted from the Statistics Canada publication *Report on the demographic situation in Canada*, Catalogue 91-209-X, http://www.statcan.gc.ca/pub/91-209-x/91-209-x2014001-eng.htm. Accessed June 25, 2021.

NET MIGRATION FOR PROVINCES AND TERRITORIES, 2002-2020

	NL	PEI	NS	NB	QC	ON	MB	SK	AB	BC	YT	NWT	NU
2002-2003	-1,683	165	510	-843	-1,829	637	-2,875	-5,141	11,903	-1,037	149	242	-198
2003-2004	-2,027	144	-772	-760	-822	-6,935	-2,565	-4,521	10,606	7,865	27	-105	-135
2004-2005	-3,710	-139	-3,041	-2,074	-4,963	-11,172	-7,227	-9,515	34,423	8,214	53	-668	-181
2005-2006	-4,342	-639	-3,024	-3,487	-9,411	-17,501	-7,881	-7,083	45,795	8,800	-73	-954	-200
2006-2007	-4,067	-849	-4,126	-2,632	-12,865	-20,047	-5,500	1,549	33,809	15,005	101	-221	-157
2007-2008	-528	-291	-1,794	-908	-11,682	-14,750	-3,703	4,171	15,317	14,643	235	-420	-290
2008-2009	1,877	-536	-751	-237	-7,419	-15,601	-3,111	2,983	13,184	9,995	228	-577	-35
2009-2010	1,558	60	612	571	-3,258	-4,662	-2,412	2,153	-3,271	8,728	325	-351	-53
2010-2011	30	-210	-41	-158	-4,763	-4,007	-3,517	545	8,443	3,421	363	-179	73
2011-2012	545	-618	-2,866	-1,806	-6,915	-10,611	-4,212	1,878	27,652	-2,711	313	-496	-153
2012-2013	495	-901	-3,517	-3,290	-10,431	-13,901	-5,006	392	38,598	-1,868	-94	-482	5
2013-2014	234	-941	-2,571	-3,517	-14,312	-14,564	-6,851	-1,839	35,382	9,475	51	-488	-59
2014-2015	161	-682	-2,311	-2,790	-16,142	-8,695	-6,678	-4,528	21,594	20,379	87	-223	-172
2015-2016	232	30	754	-1,113	-11,118	9,077	-4,881	-4,272	-15,108	26,573	276	-250	-200
2016-2017	-1,430	-444	2,839	434	-8,127	13,382	-5,124	-5,760	-15,559	18,834	577	-375	-135
2017-2018	-2,733	177	3,048	481	-5,693	9,944	-7,148	-8,475	-3,247	13,989	234	-429	-148
2018-2019	-2,597	662	3,632	1,669	-4,128	6,629	-7,351	-9,441	-2.032	13,325	342	-469	-241
2019-2020	-1,469	-462	3,901	963	-1,238	363	-8,689	-11,247	2,183	15,708	219	-309	77

Source: Statistics Canada. *Table 17-10-0008-01 – Estimates of the components of demographic growth, Canada, provinces and territories, annual.* Accessed June 25, 2021.

MOTHER TONGUE

2016 CENSUS (TOP 25)

Language	Total number of people (Canada)
English	20,193,335
French	7,452,075
Mandarin	610,835
Cantonese	594,030
Punjabi (Panjabi)	543,495
Tagalog (Pilipino, Filipino)	510,425
Spanish	495,090
Arabic	486,525
Italian	407,450
German	404,745
Urdu	243,090
Portuguese	237,000
Persian (Farsi)	225,155
Russian	195,920
Polish	191,770
Vietnamese	166,830
Korean	160,455
Tamil	157,125
Hindi	133,925
Gujarati	122,455
Greek	116,460
Ukrainian	110,580
Dutch	104,505
Romanian	100,615
Bengali	80,935

Adapted from the Statistics Canada publication *Proportion of mother tongue responses for various regions in Canada, 2016 Census*. Accessed June 25, 2021.

INDIVIDUALS USING THE INTERNET FROM ANY LOCATION, 2010-2012

	Internet use (%)	
	2010	2012
Canada	78.9	82.5
Newfoundland and Labrador	74.3	78.8
Prince Edward Island	72.9	77.7
Nova Scotia	77.1	79.6
New Brunswick	70.2	76.7
Quebec	72.9	78.1
Ontario	81.4	84.1
Manitoba	73.5	79.9
Saskatchewan	76.3	82.6
Alberta	83.4	85.7
British Columbia	84.4	86.5

Source: Adapted from Statistics Canada, *Table 22-10-0007-01 - Household access to the Internet at home, by household income quartile and geography.* Accessed June 25, 2021.

POSTSECONDARY ENROLMENTS, BY INSTITUTION TYPE AND CLASSIFICATION OF INSTRUCTIONAL PROGRAMS, PRIMARY GROUPING

Classification of Instructional Programs, Primary Grouping (CIP_PG)	2012-2013	2013-2014	2014-2015	2015-2016	2016-2017	2017-2018	2018-2019
Total, instructional programs	2,019,582	2,045,868	2,054,049	2,027,679	2,051,865	2,116,002	2,155,425
University enrolment	1,281,906	1,299,174	1,303,959	1,306,251	1,320,735	1,341,351	1,360,263
College enrolment	737,676	746,691	750,090	721,428	731,130	774,654	795,159
Personal improvement and leisure [0]	25,116	25,665	25,593	22,818	21,177	22,857	24,504
Education [1]	97,428	97,491	96,702	89,631	89,619	89,142	90,516
Visual and performing arts and communications technologies [2]	81,579	81,516	80,649	76,956	77,007	80,097	80,181
Humanities [3]	302,388	291,111	271,659	264,345	258,888	277,038	268,353
Social and behavioural sciences and law [4]	274,029	279,885	278,655	275,436	275,115	275,838	278,022
Business, management and public administration [5]	372,387	379,899	384,288	364,947	373,992	406,458	411,939
Physical and life sciences and technologies [6]	152,403	155,520	156,789	159,564	163,539	171,837	175,284
Mathematics, computer and information sciences [7]	56,979	60,342	65,334	68,808	77,304	88,131	97,164
Architecture, engineering and related technologies [8]	196,539	206,115	215,808	212,622	218,577	230,958	233,463
Agriculture, natural resources and conservation [9]	28,326	28,860	29,484	29,793	31,041	32,373	32,640
Health and related fields[10]	239,175	245,163	251,478	250,971	255,114	265,806	267,576
Personal, protective and transportation services [11]	42,330	42,150	41,889	39,765	39,936	44,433	47,442
Other instructional programs [12]	150,903	152,142	155,715	172,023	170,559	131,034	148,338

Source: Statistics Canada. *Table 37-10-0018-01 - Postsecondary enrolments, by registration status, institution type, sex and student status.* Accessed June 25, 2021.

SELECTED INCIDENT-BASED CRIME STATISTICS, BY DETAILED VIOLATIONS

Violations	Statistics	2015	2016	2017	2018	2019
Total, all violations	Actual incidents	2,118,681	2,161,927	2,213,293	2,269,036	2,438,518
	Rate per 100,000 population	5,934.20	5,987.14	6,057.13	6,122.79	6,487.27
Homicide [110][7, 8]	Actual incidents	609	612	666	651	678
	Rate per 100,000 population	1.71	1.69	1.82	1.76	1.80
Total other violations causing death [120]	Actual incidents	84	108	100	115	108
	Rate per 100,000 population	0.24	0.30	0.27	0.31	0.29
Attempted murder [1210]	Actual incidents	777	786	821	807	865
	Rate per 100,000 population	2.18	2.18	2.25	2.18	2.3
Sexual assault, level 3, aggravated [1310]	Actual incidents	103	112	160	158	125
	Rate per 100,000 population	0.29	0.31	0.44	0.43	0.33
Sexual assault, level 2, weapon or bodily harm [1320]	Actual incidents	379	395	423	459	525
	Rate per 100,000 population	1.06	1.09	1.16	1.24	1.40
Sexual assault, level 1 [1330]	Actual incidents	20,466	21,072	24,157	28,124	30,285
	Rate per 100,000 population	57.32	58.36	66.11	75.89	80.57
Total sexual violations against children [130][9, 10, 11]	Actual incidents	5,256	7,334	8,276	8,660	10,038
	Rate per 100,000 population	14.72	20.31	22.65	23.37	26.70
Assault, level 3, aggravated [1410]	Actual incidents	3,320	3,466	3,584	3,529	3,924
	Rate per 100,000 population	9.30	9.60	9.81	9.52	10.44
Assault, level 2, weapon or bodily harm [1420]	Actual incidents	47,388	49,945	52,140	53,779	59,416
	Rate per 100,000 population	132.73	138.32	142.69	145.12	158.07
Assault, level 1 [1430]	Actual incidents	157,046	159,592	163,279	169,364	187,826
	Rate per 100,000 population	439.87	441.97	446.85	457.01	499.62
Total assaults against a peace officer [135][12, 13]	Actual incidents	9,872	10,406	10,965	11,627	12,132
	Rate per 100,000 population	27.65	28.82	30.01	31.37	32.28
Total other assaults [140]	Actual incidents	2,151	1,863	1,973	2,150	2,226
	Rate per 100,000 population	6.02	5.16	5.40	5.80	5.92
Total firearms, use of, discharge, pointing [150]	Actual incidents	2,358	2,534	2,766	2,809	3,503
	Rate per 100,000 population	6.60	7.02	7.57	7.58	9.32
Total robbery [160][14]	Actual incidents	22,149	21,958	22,831	22,450	23,296
	Rate per 100,000 population	62.04	60.81	62.48	60.58	61.98
Total forcible confinement or kidnapping [510][15]	Actual incidents	3,593	3,775	3,779	3,445	3,695
	Rate per 100,000 population	10.06	10.45	10.34	9.30	9.83
Total abduction [170]	Actual incidents	384	368	321	352	427
	Rate per 100,000 population	1.08	1.02	0.88	0.95	1.14
Extortion [1620]	Actual incidents	3,055	3,075	3,186	4,664	4,174
	Rate per 100,000 population	8.56	8.52	8.72	12.59	11.10
Criminal harassment [1625][16]	Actual incidents	20,038	18,960	19,882	19,576	23,325
	Rate per 100,000 population	56.12	52.51	54.51	52.82	62.05
Total other violent violations [180]	Actual incidents	5,054	5,259	6,327	5,871	7,089
	Rate per 100,000 population	14.16	14.56	17.32	15.84	18.86
Total breaking and entering [210]	Actual incidents	159,630	160,230	159,626	159,812	161,291
	Rate per 100,000 population	447.11	443.73	436.85	431.24	429.09
Total possession of stolen property [211][17, 18]	Actual incidents	19,290	19,691	23,290	23,049	24,614
	Rate per 100,000 population	54.03	54.53	63.74	62.20	65.48
Total trafficking in stolen property [212][17, 18, 19]	Actual incidents	717	847	909	849	1,138
	Rate per 100,000 population	2.01	2.35	2.49	2.29	3.03
Total theft of motor vehicle [220][18]	Actual incidents	78,800	79,055	85,115	86,132	87,066
	Rate per 100,000 population	220.71	218.93	232.93	232.42	231.62
Total theft over $5,000 (non-motor vehicle) [230]	Actual incidents	15,444	15,528	17,265	20,113	21,357
	Rate per 100,000 population	43.26	43.00	47.25	54.27	56.82
Total theft under $5,000 (non-motor vehicle) [240]	Actual incidents	487,176	496,976	505,185	531,312	564,725
	Rate per 100,000 population	1,364.53	1,376.30	1,382.54	1,433.70	1,502.36
Fraud [2160][20]	Actual incidents	94,425	109,630	113,166	129,409	142,140

	Rate per 100,000 population	264.47	303.60	309.70	349.20	378.14
Identity theft [2165][20, 21]	Actual incidents	2,541	3,136	3,295	3,745	4,683
	Rate per 100,000 population	7.12	8.68	9.02	10.11	12.46
Identity fraud [2166][20]	Actual incidents	11,894	14,033	14,344	15,839	19,664
	Rate per 100,000 population	33.31	38.86	29.26	42.74	52.31
Total mischief [250][22]	Actual incidents	274,711	261,655	262,490	258,965	284,579
	Rate per 100,000 population	769.44	724.62	718.36	698.79	757.08
Arson [2110]	Actual incidents	8,967	8,546	8,549	8,000	8,190
	Rate per 100,000 population	25.12	23.67	23.40	21.59	21.79
Counterfeiting [3420][23]	Actual incidents	675	805	939	1,095	1,152
	Rate per 100,000 population	1.89	2.23	2.57	2.95	3.06
Total weapons violations [310]	Actual incidents	14,535	15,240	15,870	16,610	18,622
	Rate per 100,000 population	40.71	42.20	43.43	44.82	49.54
Possession of, or accessing child pornography [3455][6, 10, 24, 25, 26, 27, 28, 29]	Actual incidents	3,424	2,610	1,887	1,777	3,230
	Rate per 100,000 population	9.59	7.23	5.16	4.80	8.59
Total prostitution [320][30]	Actual incidents	150	195	122	110	135
	Rate per 100,000 population	0.42	0.54	0.33	0.30	0.36
Total other violations [340]	Actual incidents	29,115	27,338	27,020	27,934	31,996
	Rate per 100,000 population	81.55	75.71	73.95	75.38	85.12
Impaired operation (alcohol), causing death [9210]	Actual incidents	122	114	101	95	50
	Rate per 100,000 population	0.34	0.32	0.28	0.26	0.13
Impaired operation (drugs), causing death [9215]	Actual incidents	6	11	6	7	10
	Rate per 100,000 population	0.02	0.03	0.02	0.02	0.03
Driving while prohibited [9320]	Actual incidents	6,948	6,664	6,811	7,219	7,556
	Rate per 100,000 population	19.46	18.45	18.64	19.48	20.10

Footnotes:

1. For the period from 1998 to 2017 Incident-based Uniform Crime Reporting Survey (UCR2) data are not available for all respondents. In order to report this level of detail for police services still reporting to the Aggregate Uniform Crime Reporting Survey (UCR) over this time, a process of imputation was applied to derive counts for violations that do not exist on their own in the aggregate survey. For approximately 80% of the aggregate offence codes, there is a 1:1 mapping with a new incident-based violation code. For violations where this was not the case, such as the aggregate other Criminal Code category, it was necessary to estimate (impute) this figure using the distribution of other Criminal Code offences from existing Incident-based UCR2 respondents.

2. During the production of each year's crime statistics, data from the previous year are revised to reflect any updates or changes that have been received from the police services.

3. The methodology for calculating census metropolitan area (CMA) populations was modified in 2003. Starting in 1996, the populations for CMAs have been adjusted to reflect the actual policing boundaries within the CMA and do not reflect the official Statistics Canada population for these CMAs. CMA data are included within province-level data.

4. Police reported statistics may be affected by differences in the way police services deal with minor offences. In some instances, police or municipalities might chose to deal with some minor offences using municipal by-laws or provincial provisions rather than Criminal Code provisions. Counts are based on the most serious violation in the incident.

5. With the release of 2012 data, revised population estimates at the respondent level were applied back to and including 2004. This resulted in boundary changes for the census metropolitan areas (CMA) of Saint John for 2005 to 2011 and for Winnipeg for 2011. Crime data for these years for these respondents have therefore been revised.

6. In 2012, it was discovered that the Montreal Police Service had been incorrectly applying the agreed upon definition for reporting child pornography incidents to the Uniform Crime Reporting Survey (UCR). As such, the number of violations has been revised for the years 2008 to 2011.

7. Homicide data are extracted from the homicide survey database. For further information, refer to: http://www.statcan.gc.ca/imdb-bmdi/3315-eng.htm.

8. In general, the Uniform Crime Reporting Survey (UCR) counts any adult and youth charged for the year in which the charge was laid. The homicide totals, which come from The Homicide Survey, count any adult or youth charged with a homicide that occurred in the reference year, regardless of when the charge was laid.

9. Sexual violations against children is a new crime category with only partial data available prior to 2008. As a result, numbers and rates should not be directly compared to data from previous years.

10. Coming into effect on July 17th, 2015, Bill C-26 increased the maximum penalties for certain sexual offences against children, including failure to comply with orders and probation conditions relating to sexual offences against children. In the Uniform Crime Reporting Survey (UCR), the most serious violation is partially determined by the maximum penalty. As such, changes in maximum penalty may affect the most serious violation in an incident reported by police. Police services are able to utilize these amendments as their Records Management Systems are updated to allow them.

11. Includes Criminal Code violations that specifically concern offences involving child and youth victims. These include sexual interference, invitation to sexual touching, sexual exploitation, making sexually explicit material available to children for the purpose of facilitating sexual offences against children/youth, luring a child via a computer, parent or guardian procuring sexual activity, householder permitting prohibited sexual activity, agreement or arrangement and bestiality in

presence of, or incites, a child. Incidents of child pornography are not included in the category of sexual violations against children. Excludes incidents of sexual assault levels 1, 2 and 3 against children and youth which are counted within those three violation categories. Other sexual offences not involving assault or sexual violations against children are included with "other violent offences".

12. Any reference to Police Officer has been changed to read Peace Officer, as per the Canadian Criminal Code. Peace officer refers to any person employed for the preservation and maintenance of the public peace or for the service or execution of civil process. Examples of a Peace Officer are a mayor, warden, police officer, or bailiff constable. Please see the Canadian Criminal Code for a complete list of designates.

13. In 2009, legislation was introduced to create the offences of assault with a weapon or causing bodily harm to a peace officer (level 2) and aggravated assault to a peace officer (level 3). The introduction of these new codes into the UCR Survey created a system anomaly which resulted in some non-peace officer assaults being coded as peace officer assaults in 2010. Comparisons to 2010 should be made with caution.

14. Robbery counts have been revised for the years 1998 to 2007. This change has resulted in an increase of approximately 12% annually in the number of reported robbery incidents for this time period. Use caution when comparing these data with prior years.

15. Historically police services have reported kidnapping and forcible confinement under a single combined violation code. In 2008 the Incident-based Uniform Crime Reporting Survey (UCR2) introduced separate codes for these violations which police services utilize as their Records Management Systems are updated to allow them. As a result, comparison with previous years should be done with caution.

16. For the period from 1998 to 2007 Incident-based Uniform Crime Reporting Survey (UCR2) data on criminal harassment are not available for all respondents. In order to report this violation for police services still reporting to the aggregate Uniform Crime Reporting Survey (UCR) over this time, a process of imputation was applied to derive counts using the distribution of 'other' Criminal Code offences from existing Incident-based Uniform Crime Reporting Survey (UCR2) respondents.

17. In April 2011, legislation came into effect making it an offence to traffic in property obtained by crime, including possession with intent to traffic property obtained by crime. In addition to creating new Uniform Crime Reporting Survey (UCR) violation codes to capture these offences, the existing UCR violation code pertaining to possession of stolen property was modified. The UCR now separates possession of stolen property into possession of stolen property under $5,000 and possession of stolen property over $5,000 in order to be more in line with the Criminal Code of Canada. As a result of this change, a number of incidents of possession of stolen property under $5,000 are now being reported as secondary offences when they occur in conjunction with more serious offences, leading to a decrease in the number of possession of stolen property incidents reported in 2011.

18. Detailed information of this category is available upon request.

19. In April 2011, legislation came into effect making it an offence to traffic in property obtained by crime, including possession with intent to traffic property obtained by crime. The Uniform Crime Reporting Survey (UCR) introduced two new violations codes to collect this information. They are Trafficking in Stolen Goods over $5,000 (incl. possession with intent to traffic) and Trafficking in Stolen Goods under $5,000 (incl. possession with intent to traffic).

20. In January 2010, the Uniform Crime Reporting Survey (UCR) was modified to create new violation codes for identity fraud and identity theft. Prior to 2010, those offences would have been coded as fraud.

21. In 2013, it was discovered that an error in Quebec's provincial reporting system had incorrectly resulted in a number of thefts being coded as identity thefts in Montreal. As such, the number of incidents of identity theft has been revised for the years 2010 to 2012.

22. In 2014, legislation was introduced to create the offence of Mischief to war memorials (Bill C-217). The offence of mischief in relation to cultural property was also introduced as a result of this legislation. Police services are able to utilise these codes as their Records Management Systems are updated to allow them. As a result, these data may be under-counted and should therefore be interpreted with caution.

23. Counterfeiting counts have been revised for the years 1998 to 2007. This change has resulted in a significant decrease in counterfeiting incidents over this time period. Use with caution when comparing these data with prior years.

24. In 2002, legislative changes were made to include the use of the Internet for the purpose of committing child pornography offences. As such, the percent change in this offence is calculated from 2003 to 2009.

25. Ottawa numbers also include child pornography incidents reported by the National Child Exploitation Coordination Centre of the Royal Canadian Mounted Police (RCMP) which is located in the City of Ottawa. The Centre responds to internet-facilitated sexual abuse cases nationally. Therefore, while the incidents are detected by the RCMP Centre located in Ottawa and appear in Ottawa's crime statistics, the incidents themselves or the offenders are not limited to the city of Ottawa.

26. Due to the complexity of these incidents, the data likely reflect the number of active or closed investigations for the year rather than the total number of incidents reported to police.

27. Historically, police service reported all child pornography offences under a single combined violation code, of which the majority of the offences were possessing child pornography. In early 2016, the Uniform Crime Reporting Survey (UCR) was modified to allow police to report making and distributing child pornography from other child pornography offences (i.e., possession and accessing child pornography). Since police services are able to utilize these codes as their Records Management Systems are updated to allow them, a few were reported in 2015. As a result, these data should therefore be interpreted with caution.

28. The increase in incidents of child pornography between 2014 and 2015 can be in part attributed to a proactive project initiated by the British Columbia Integrated Child Exploitation Unit which recorded Internet Protocol (IP) addresses that were in possession of, and possibly sharing child pornography. As the initiative focused on Victoria in 2015, notable increases in these offences were reported by this jurisdiction.

29. The increase in incidents of child pornography between 2015 and 2016 in Vancouver can be in part attributed to a proactive project initiated by the British Columbia Integrated Child Exploitation Unit which recorded Internet Protocol (IP) addresses that were in possession of, and possibly sharing child pornography. As the initiative focused on Vancouver in 2016, notable increases in these offences were reported by this jurisdiction. As a result, comparison with previous years should be done with caution.

30. Bill C-36 came into effect in December 2014. The new legislation targets "the exploitation that is inherent in prostitution and the risks of violence posed to those who engage in it" (Criminal Code Chapter 25, preamble). New violations classified as "Commodification of sexual activity" under "violations against the person" include: the purchasing of sexual services or communicating for that purpose, receiving a material benefit deriving from the purchase of sexual services, procuring of persons for the purpose of prostitution, and advertising sexual services offered for sale. In addition, a number of other offences related to prostitution continue to be considered non-violent offences and are classified under "Other Criminal Code offences". These include communicating to provide sexual services

for consideration, and; stopping or impeding traffic for the purpose of offering, providing or obtaining sexual services for consideration. At the same time, the survey was amended to classify the violations codes of Parent or guardian procuring sexual activity, and Householder permitting prohibited sexual activity under "violations against the person". The following violations officially expired on December 05, 2014: bawdy house, living off the avails of prostitution of a person under 18, procuring, obtains/communicates with a person under 18 for purpose of sex, and other prostitution. Police services are able to utilize these codes as their Records Management Systems are updated to allow it. As a result, these data should be interpreted with caution.

Source: Statistics Canada. *Table 35-10-0177-01 - Incident-based crime statistics, by detailed violations.* Accessed June 25, 2021.

Geography

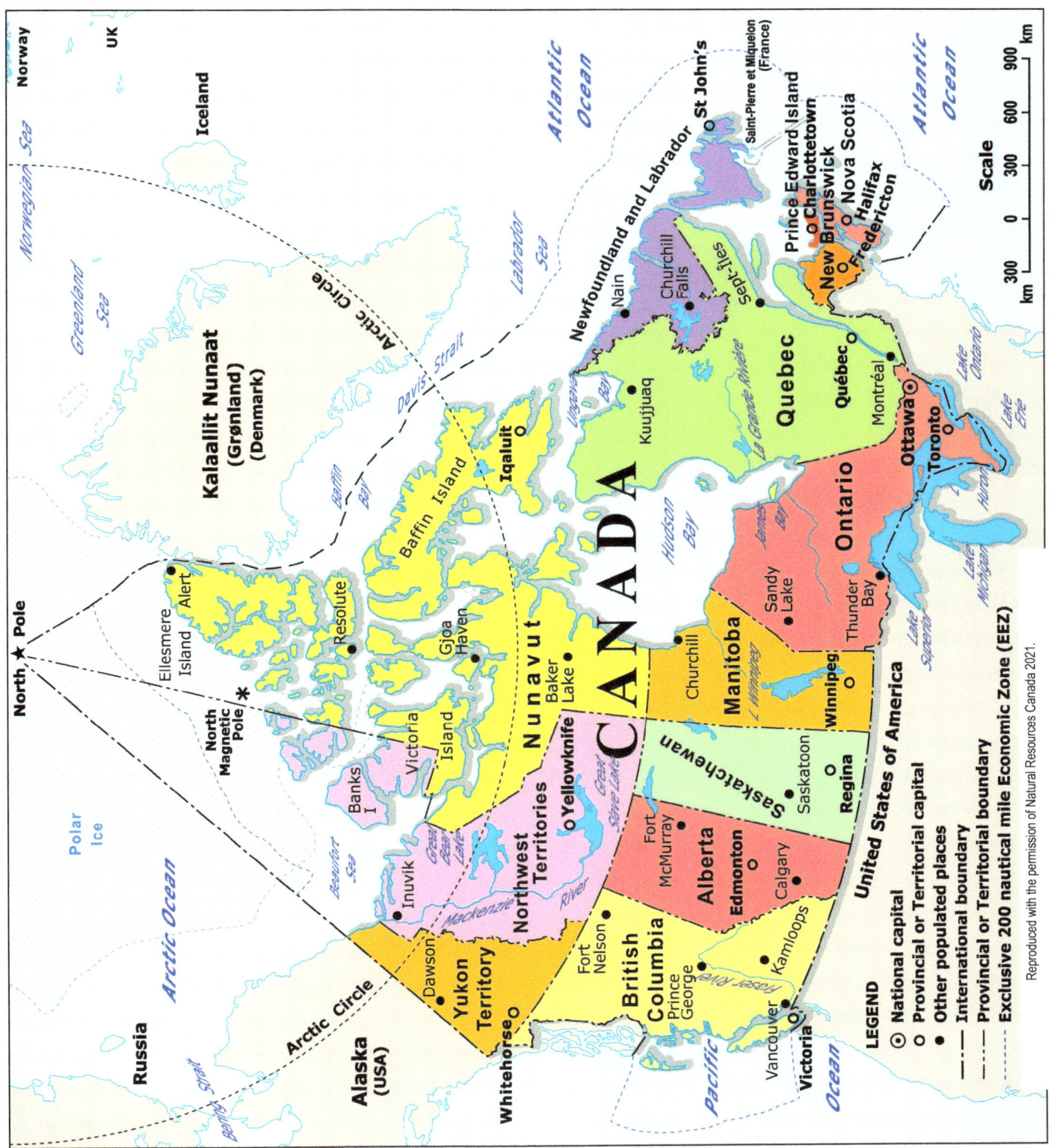

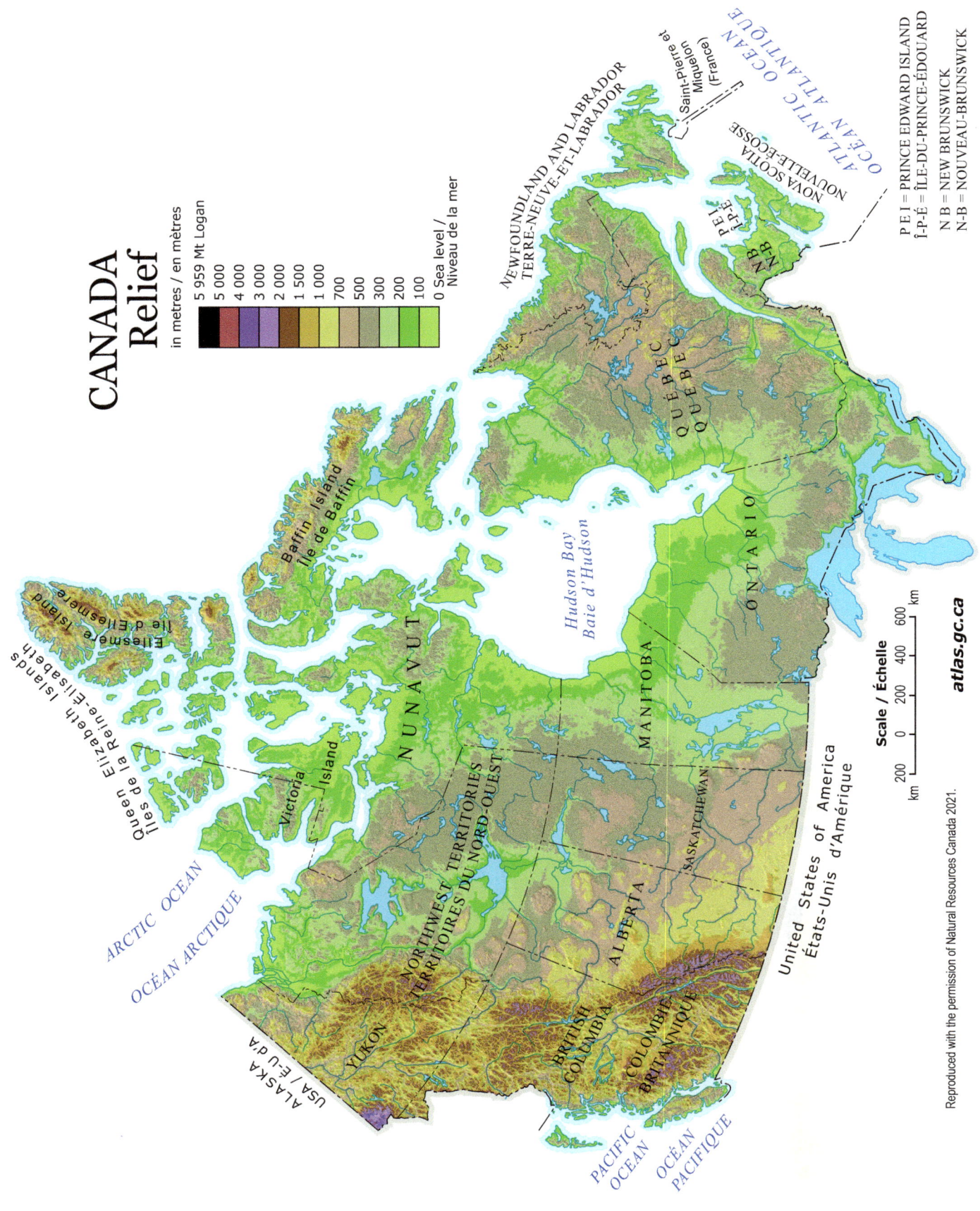

CANADA
Relief

in metres / en mètres

5 959 Mt Logan
5 000
4 000
3 000
2 000
1 500
1 000
700
500
300
200
100
0 Sea level /
Niveau de la mer

NEWFOUNDLAND AND LABRADOR
TERRE-NEUVE-ET-LABRADOR

Saint-Pierre et
Miquelon
(France)

ATLANTIC OCEAN
OCÉAN ATLANTIQUE

NOVA SCOTIA
NOUVELLE-ÉCOSSE

P E I
Î.-P.-É.

N B
N-B

P E I = PRINCE EDWARD ISLAND
Î.-P.-É. = ÎLE-DU-PRINCE-ÉDOUARD

N B = NEW BRUNSWICK
N-B = NOUVEAU-BRUNSWICK

QUÉBEC
QUÉBEC

ONTARIO

MANITOBA

SASKATCHEWAN

ALBERTA

Hudson Bay
Baie d'Hudson

Baffin Island
Île de Baffin

Ellesmere Island
Île d'Ellesmere

Queen Elizabeth Islands
Îles de la Reine-Élisabeth

Victoria Island

NUNAVUT

NORTHWEST TERRITORIES
TERRITOIRES DU NORD-OUEST

ARCTIC OCEAN
OCÉAN ARCTIQUE

YUKON

BRITISH
COLUMBIA
COLOMBIE
BRITANNIQUE

ALASKA / É.-U. d'A.
USA / É.-U. d'A.

United States of America
États-Unis d'Amérique

PACIFIC
OCEAN
OCÉAN
PACIFIQUE

Scale / Échelle

km
600
400
200
0
200
km

atlas.gc.ca

Reproduced with the permission of Natural Resources Canada 2021.

Yoho National Park, BC
© Parks Canada / Zoya Lynch

Rocky Mountain House National Historic Site, AB
© Parks Canada / Michael Moynihan

Grasslands National Park, SK

Courtesy of Tourism Saskatchewan / Chris Hendrickson Photography

Cranberry Portage, Kelsey, MB

Courtesy of Travel Manitoba

Pukaskwa National Park, ON

© Parks Canada / Louis Barnes

Mingan Archipelago National Park Reserve, QC

© Parks Canada / Lévis Landry

Cape Breton Highlands National Park, NS
© Parks Canada / Adam Cornick

Terra Nova National Park, NL
© Parks Canada / Eric Laflamme

Kouchibouguac National Park, NB
© Parks Canada / Nigel Fearon

Prince Edward Island National Park, PE
© Parks Canada / Scott Munn

Ivvavik National Park, YT
© Parks Canada / Louis Barnes

Quttinirpaaq National Park, NU
© Parks Canada / Ryan Bray

Nahanni National Park Reserve, NT
© Parks Canada / Rob Stimpson

LAND AND FRESHWATER AREAS

(IN SQUARE KILOMETRES)

Provinces and Territories	Land	Water	Total Area	Percentage of Canadian Total
Newfoundland and Labrador	373,872	31,340	405,212	4.1
Prince Edward Island	5,660	Not Available	5,660	0.1
Nova Scotia	53,338	1,946	55,284	0.6
New Brunswick	71,450	1,458	72,908	0.7
Quebec	1,365,128	176,928	1,542,056	15.4
Ontario	917,741	158,654	1,076,395	10.8
Manitoba	553,556	94,241	647,797	6.5
Saskatchewan	591,670	59,366	651,036	6.5
Alberta	642,317	19,531	661,848	6.6
British Columbia	925,186	19,549	944,735	9.5
Yukon Territory	474,391	8,052	482,443	4.8
Northwest Territories	1,183,085	163,021	1,346,106	13.5
Nunavut	1,936,113	157,077	2,093,190	21.0
Canada	9,093,507	891,163	9,984,670	100

Reproduced with the permission of Natural Resources Canada.

LARGEST LAKES WHOLLY OR PARTIALLY IN CANADA

Name	Provinces and Territories	Area (square kilometres)
Superior	Ontario (and United States)	82,101 (total); 28,748 in Canada
Huron	Ontario (and United States)	59,569 (total); 36,000 in Canada
Great Bear	Northwest Territories	30,764
Great Slave	Northwest Territories	27,048
Erie	Ontario (and United States)	25,666 (total); 12,768 in Canada
Winnipeg	Manitoba	23,760
Ontario	Ontario (and United States)	19,554 (total); 10,334 in Canada

Reproduced with the permission of Natural Resources Canada.

LONGEST RIVERS IN CANADA

Rank	Name (at outflow)	Length (kilometres)	Outflow	Component Parts
1	Mackenzie	4,241	Beaufort Sea	Mackenzie - Slave - Peace - Findlay
2	Yukon	3,185 (1,143 kilometres in Canada)	Bering Sea	Yukon
3	St. Lawrence	3,058 (small part wholly in U.S.)	Gulf of St. Lawrence	St. Lawrence - Niagara - Detroit - St. Clair - St. Marys - St. Louis
4	Nelson	2,575	Hudson Bay	Nelson - Saskatchewan - South Saskatchewan - Bow
5	Columbia	2,000 (801 kilometres in Canada)	Pacific Ocean	Columbia
6	Churchill	1,609	Hudson Bay	Churchill [of Manitoba and Saskatchewan]
7	Fraser	1,370	Pacific Ocean	Fraser
8	North Saskatchewan	1,287	Saskatchewan River	North Saskatchewan
9	Ottawa	1,271	St. Lawrence River	Ottawa
10	Athabasca	1,231	Slave River	Athabasca
11	Liard	1,115	Mackenzie River	Liard
12	Assiniboine	1,070	Red River (part of Nelson River drainage basin)	Assiniboine

Reproduced with the permission of Natural Resources Canada.

LARGEST ISLANDS OF CANADA

Rank	Name	Provinces and Territories	Area (square kilometres)
1	Baffin (5th largest in the world)	Nunavut	507,451
2	Victoria	Nunavut and Northwest Territories	217,291
3	Ellesmere	Nunavut	196,236
4	Island of Newfoundland	Newfoundland and Labrador	108,860
5	Banks	Northwest Territories	70,028
6	Devon	Nunavut	55,247
7	Axel Heiberg	Nunavut	43,178
8	Melville	Northwest Territories and Nunavut	42,149
9	Southampton	Nunavut	41,214
10	Prince of Wales	Nunavut	33,339
11	Vancouver	British Columbia	31,285

Reproduced with the permission of Natural Resources Canada.

SELECTED WATERFALLS IN CANADA

Name of Waterfall	Vertical Drop (metres)	Location
Della Falls	440	Della Lake, BC
Takakkaw Falls	254	Daly Glacier, BC
Hunlen Falls	253	Atnarko River, BC
Panther Falls	183	Nigel Creek, AB
Helmcken Falls	137	Murtle River, BC
Bridal Veil Falls	122	Bridal Creek, BC
Virginia Falls	90	South Nahanni River, NT
Chute Montmorency	84	Rivière Montmorency, QC
Twin Falls	80	Yoho National Park, BC
Chute Ouiatchouan	79	Rivière Ouiatchouan, QC
Brandywine Falls	61	Brandywine Creek, BC
Niagara Falls (American Falls)	59	(Niagara River, USA)
Niagara Falls (Horseshoe Falls)	57	Niagara River, ON
Wilberforce Falls	49	Hood River, NU
Dog Falls	47	Kaministiquia River, ON
Kakabeka Falls	47	Kaministiquia River, ON
Chute de Shawinigan	46	Rivière Saint-Maurice, QC
Grand Falls	43	Exploits River, NL
Parry Falls	40	Lockhart River, NT
Wawaitin Falls	38	Mattagami River, ON
Elizabeth Falls	34	Fond du Lac River, SK
Aubrey Falls	33	Mississagi River, ON
Alexandra Falls	32	Hay River, NT
Thomas Falls	31	Unknown River, NL
Marengo Falls	30	Marengo Creek, NT
Barrow Falls	27	Barrow River, NU
Pigeon Falls	27	Pigeon River, ON
Scott Falls	27	Unknown River, NL
Tyrrell Falls	26	Lockhart River, NT
High Falls	24	Onaping River, ON
Schist Falls	24	Pukaskwa River, ON
Smoky Falls	24	Mattagami River, ON
Christopher Falls	23	Opasatika River, ON
Chute du Calcaire	22	Rivière Caniapiscau, QC
Chute au Granite	21	Rivière Caniapiscau, QC
Partridge Falls	21	Pigeon River, ON
Steephill Falls	21	Magpie River, ON
Louise Falls	20	Hay River, NT
Muhigan Falls	19	Muhigan River, MB
Big Beaver Falls	18	Kapuskasing River, ON
Chutes aux Schistes	18	Rivière Caniapiscau, QC
Twin Falls	18	Abitibi River, ON
Lady Evelyn Falls	17	Kakisa River, NT
Muskrat Falls	15	Churchill River, NL
Taskinigup Falls	15	Burntwood River, MB
Kazan Falls	14	Kazan River, NU
Rideau Falls	12	Rideau River, ON

Reproduced with the permission of Natural Resources Canada.

HIGHEST POINTS BY PROVINCE AND TERRITORY

Provinces and Territories	Name of Highest Point	Height (metres)
British Columbia	Fairweather Mountain (on Alaska-British Columbia border)	4,663
Alberta	Mount Columbia (on Alberta-British Columbia border)	3,747
Saskatchewan	Cypress Hills	1,392
Manitoba	Baldy Mountain	832
Ontario	Ishpatina Ridge	693
Quebec	Mont D'Iberville (on Quebec-Newfoundland and Labrador boundary; known as Mount Caubvick in Newfoundland and Labrador)	1,652
New Brunswick	Mount Carleton	817
Nova Scotia	White Hill	532
Prince Edward Island	Unnamed hill at 46 degrees 20 minutes North, 63 degrees 25 minutes West	142
Newfoundland and Labrador	Mount Caubvick (on Newfoundland and Labrador-Quebec boundary; known as Mont D'Iberville in Quebec)	1,652
Yukon Territory	Mount Logan (highest point in Canada)	5,959
Northwest Territories	Unnamed peak at 61 degrees 52 minutes North, 127 degrees 42 minutes West	2,773
Nunavut	Barbeau Peak (on Ellesmere Island)	2,616

Reproduced with the permission of Natural Resources Canada.

AVERAGE TEMPERATURE AND PRECIPITATION

	Average daily temperature		Average precipitation
	January	July	Annual
	°C		mm
St. John's	-4.5	15.8	1534.2
Charlottetown	-7.7	18.7	1158.2
Halifax	-5.9	18.8	1396.2
Fredericton	-9.4	19.3	1077.7
Quebec	-12.8	19.3	1189.7
Ottawa	-10.2	21.2	919.5
Toronto	-5.5	21.5	785.9
Winnipeg	-16.4	19.7	521.1
Regina	-14.7	18.9	389.7
Edmonton	-12.1	16.2	446.1
Victoria	4.6	16.9	882.9
Whitehorse	-15.2	14.3	262.3
Yellowknife	-25.6	17	288.6
Iqaluit	-26.9	8.2	403.7

Source: Environment and Climate Change Canada, *Canadian Climate Normals & Averages 1981-2010.*
© Environment and Climate Change Canada.

MILES

KILOMETRES (left axis)

	BANFF	BRANDON	CALGARY	CHARLOTTETOWN	CHICOUTIMI	CORNER BROOK	DAWSON CREEK	EDMONTON	FLIN FLON	FORT SMITH	FREDERICTON	GANDER	GASPÉ	HALIFAX	HAMILTON	JASPER	KENORA	LETHBRIDGE	LONDON	MONCTON	MONTRÉAL	NIAGARA FALLS	NORTH BAY	OTTAWA	PORT AUX BASQUES	PRINCE ALBERT	PRINCE GEORGE	PRINCE RUPERT	QUÉBEC	REGINA	RIVIÈRE-DU-LOUP	ROUYN	SAINT JOHN	ST. JOHN'S	SASKATOON	SAULT STE. MARIE	SEPT-ÎLES	SHERBROOKE	SUMMERSIDE	SYDNEY	THE PAS	THUNDER BAY	TORONTO	VANCOUVER	VICTORIA	WHITEHORSE	WINDSOR	WINNIPEG	YARMOUTH	YELLOWKNIFE
YELLOWKNIFE	1205	1654	1125	4014	3574	4363	751	939	443	3796	4592	566	217	4097	3128	1106	1909	1261	3199	3914	157	3278	3171	2931																							618	1562	2457	910	3055	•
YARMOUTH																																												1400	2011	1677	128	1359	3055	•
WINNIPEG																																												1432	2232	1482	910	•
WINDSOR																																												2514	2377	830	•
WHITEHORSE																																												2963	4014	•
VICTORIA																																												3574	•
VANCOUVER																																												•

Source: National Atlas Service, Natural Resources Canada

Science

Astronomical Calculations

ASTRONOMY IN CANADA

Astronomical research in Canada is carried out in universities, supported by the Natural Sciences and Engineering Research Council (NSERC) of Canada, and by the Canada Foundation for Innovation (CFI), and also in the National Research Council (NRC) — specifically by the Herzberg Institute of Astrophysics (HIA), which operates the following observatories: The Dominion Astrophysical Observatory (DAO) at Victoria, with optical telescopes of 1.8m and 1.2m aperture; and the Dominion Radio Astrophysical Observatory (DRAO) near Penticton, which has a 26m paraboloid and a 7-element array of 9m antennae. The National Research Council also maintains Canada's Time Service in its Institute of National Measurement Standards. The Canadian Astronomy Data Centre (CADC) is housed within HIA.

A number of Canadian universities offer graduate education in astronomy: Victoria, British Columbia (Vancouver), Alberta (Edmonton), Calgary, Saskatchewan (Saskatoon), Manitoba (Winnipeg), Western Ontario (London), Waterloo, McMaster (Hamilton), York (Toronto), Toronto, Queen's (Kingston), Montréal, McGill (Montréal), Laval (Québec), and St. Mary's (Halifax). Most of these have some local facilities for observational and theoretical studies, and all of them have access to national facilities in Canada and elsewhere. Among the major observatories operated by Canadian universities are: a 1.8m infrared telescope opened in 1987 by the University of Calgary; a 1.2m telescope at the University of Western Ontario; a 0.6m telescope now located in, and shared with, Argentina with access through the University of Toronto; and a 1.5m telescope at the Mont Mégantic Observatory operated by the University of Montréal, and Laval University. There is also a Canadian Institute for Theoretical Astrophysics hosted by the University of Toronto. Canadian astronomers established the Association of Canadian Universities for Research in Astronomy (ACURA) to co-ordinate universities' participation in astronomy, especially in the development of large-scale facilities.

Through the National Research Council, Canadian astronomers also have access to excellent international facilities. One of these is the 3.6m Canada-France-Hawaii optical telescope atop Mauna Kea on the island of Hawaii, at an elevation of nearly 4200m. This telescope is shared, both as to cost and operation, by Canada, France, and the state of Hawaii. Canadian astronomers also share (with the Netherlands and the UK) in the operation of the James Clerk Maxwell telescope, a sophisticated millimetre-wave radio telescope at the same site. Canada is also a partner, along with several other countries, in the twin Gemini 8m telescopes, which are in operation in Hawaii and in Chile. Balloon-borne telescopes, Canada's first astronomical satellite MOST (Microvariability and Oscillations of STars), and participation in other space astronomy missions are funded through the Canadian Space Agency, and Canada is a partner in the James Webb Space Telescope, the planned successor to the Hubble Space Telescope. Canada is also a partner in the North American Program in Radio Astronomy, including the Atacama Large Millimetre Array high in the Atacama Desert in Chile.

Astronomical education and outreach are carried out in a wide variety of settings. In the formal education system, astronomy is part of the elementary and secondary school science curriculum in most provinces, and is taught in most universities, most commonly in the form of introductory astronomy courses for non-majors. Canada's planetariums, science centres, and public observatories play a major role in communicating the nature and excitement of astronomy, as do science journalists, and the many professional and amateur astronomers who give public lectures, and organize open houses and star parties.

OBSERVATORIES

Observatories are open to the public as follows:

Burke-Gaffney Observatory: St. Mary's University, Halifax NS B3H 3C3 - 902-420-5633; Info line: 902-496-8257; Fax: 902-496-8218; Email: bgo@ap.smu.ca; URL: www.ap.smu.ca/pr/bgo

Free public tours are held, weather permitting, on the 2nd and 4th Friday of each month, except from June through September when they are usually scheduled every Friday. Tours begin at 7pm between November 1 and March 30 and at either 8pm or later (depending on when it gets dark) between April 1 and October 31. On clear evenings, the 40-cm telescope is used to view the planets, the Moon, or other interesting celestial objects.

There will be no tour on cloudy or rainy nights. Always call the information line two hours befoe the scheduled time to find out if the tour is on or off.

Groups wishing special tours can be accommodated on Monday evenings by reservation.

Canada Science & Technology Museum, Helen Sawyer Hogg Observatory: 2421 Lancaster Rd., Ottawa ON K1G 5A3 - 613-991-3044; Email: contact@IngeniumCanada.org; URL: ingeniumcanada.org/cstm

38-cm refractor (from the former Dominion Observatory). See website for details and special programs.

Canada-France-Hawaii Telescope: CFHT Corporation, #65, 1238 Mamalahoa Hwy., Kamuela HI, 96743 - 808-885-7944; Fax: 808-885-7288; E-mail: info@cfht.hawaii.edu; URL: www.cfht.hawaii.edu

By appointment only.

Climenhaga Observatory: Dept. of Physics & Astronomy, University of Victoria, PO Box 1700, Station CSC, Victoria BC V8W 2Y2 - 250-721-7700; Fax: 250-721-7715; URL: www.uvic.ca/science/physics

Daytime tours are open from the beginning of April until the end of July. The tour includes an entertaining educational presentation, a look through the big, fully automated telescope in the Climenhaga Observatory and weather permitting, an opportunity to search for sunspots using the smaller telescopes on the roof. The tours are free but space is limited. Interested parties are encouraged to book in advance.

Night time viewing sessions are open on Wednesdays from 8 p.m. (or sunset) until 10 p.m. (Oct. - April), and 9 p.m. (or sunset) until 10 p.m. (May - Aug.).

Gordon MacMillan Southam Observatory: H.R. MacMillan Space Centre, 1100 Chestnut St., Vancouver BC V6J 3J9 - 604-738-7827; Fax: 604-736-5665; E-mail: info@spacecentre.ca; URL: www.spacecentre.ca/gordon-southam-observatory

Open Friday and Saturday starting at 8:00 p.m. Admission is by donation. Special events are also accommodated, with a maximum capacity of 30 people, and at a cost of $100 per hour.

Hume Cronyn Memorial Observatory: Dept. of Physics & Astronomy, University of Western Ontario, London ON N6A 3K7 - 519-661-3283; Fax: 519-661-2033; URL: physics.uwo.ca/community/cronyn/index.html

Public Nights run monthly from October through April, and weekly May through August (Saturday evenings, 8:30 p.m.-11:00 p.m.). No reservations needed. Private Exploring the Stars program available through a booking system.

National Research Council Canada, Dominion Astrophysical Observatory: 5071 West Saanich Rd., Victoria BC V9E 2E7 - 250-363-0001; Fax: 250-363-0045; E-mail: NRC.NSIHerzbergAstroInfoISN.CNRC@nrc-cnrc.gc.ca; URL: nrc.canada.ca/en/research-development/nrc-facilities/dominion-astrophysical-observatory-research-facility

Both DOA telescopes are available to qualified researchers through a quarterly peer-reviewed process. The general public should contact the observatory directly.

National Research Council Canada, Dominion Radio Astrophysical Observatory: 717 White Lake Road, PO Box 248, Penticton BC V2A 6J9 - 250-493-2300; Fax: 250-497-2355; E-mail: NRC.DRAO-OFR.CNRC@nrc-cnrc.gc.ca; URL: nrc.canada.ca/en/research-development/nrc-facilities/dominion-radio-astrophysical-observatory-research-facility

Both DOA telescopes are available to qualified researchers through a quarterly peer-reviewed process. The general public should contact the observatory directly. A visitor centre is located on-site at the Dominion Radio Astrophysical Observatory.

Observatoire Astronomique Du Mont Mégantic: 189 route du Parc, Notre-Dame-des-Bois QC J0B 2E0 - 819-888-2645; E-mail: parc.mont-megantic@sepaq.com; URL: omm.craq-astro.ca

The observatory hosts "Festival d'Astronomie Populaire du mont Mégantic" on the weekends in July. For other times of the year, visits including interactive exhibitions, high definition multimedia show, and tours of the observatories can be arranged through AstroLab du Mont Mégantic. See website for details on dates & times.

Rothney Astrophysical Observatory: Dept. of Physics & Astronomy, University of Calgary, SB 605, 2500 University Dr. NW, Calgary AB T2N 1N4 - 403-931-2366; E-mail: rao@phas.ucalgary.ca; URL: science.ucalgary.ca/rothney-observatory

Day and evening programs are available for school groups, which involve a grade appropriate presentation, tour of the observatory and skyviewing. Free drop-in visits to the Interpretive Centre, private tours and school group tours are also available. See website for details. The observatory is located near Priddis, AB, about 30km southwest of the Calgary city centre.

Telus World of Science - RASC Observatory: 11211 - 142 St., Edmonton AB T5M 4A1 - 780-451-3344; Email: info@twose.ca; URL: telusworldofscienceedmonton.ca/explore/experiences/rasc-observatory

Summer hours (July to Labour Day weekend) 1:00 p.m. - 5:00 p.m. and 6:45 p.m. - 10 p.m. 7 days a week. Visit the website for Fall/Winter/Spring hours. Open weather permitting.

University of Alberta Observatory: Dept. of Physics, University of Alberta, Edmonton AB T6G 2E1 - 780-492-5286; Email: stars@ualberta.ca; URL: www.ualberta.ca/physics/outreach/department-of-physics-astronomical-observatory

Open to the public Thursday nights from September through April (closed for final exams and winter holidays), weather permitting. School groups, youth groups and other groups can book a private visit free of charge. Closed in the evenings during summer months. See website for exact hours and details.

University of Saskatchewan Observatory: Dept. of Physics & Engineering Physics, University of Saskatchewan, 116 Science Place, Saskatoon SK S7N 5E2 - 306-966-6396; Email: campus.observatory@usask.ca; URL: artsandscience.usask.ca/physics/facilities/observatory.php

Saturday evening programs year round; times vary. Tours for school and community groups are arranged for Friday evenings (October - March). Special tours may be arranged during the summer months.

University of Toronto, St. George Campus Observatory: Dept. of Astronomy & Astrophysics, University of Toronto, 50 St. George Street, Toronto ON M5S 3H4 - Email: tours@astro.utoronto.ca; URL: www.astro.utoronto.ca/astrotours

Free tours are offered on the first Thursday of every month (excluding January). Tours start at 8 p.m. during winter months and 9 p.m. during summer months. Extra public tours may also be arranged. See website for details.

York University, Allan I. Carswell Observatory: 4700 Keele St., Toronto ON M3J 1P3 - 416-736-2100, ext. 77773 (voice mail); Email: observe@yorku.ca; pdelaney@yorku.ca; URL: observatory.info.yorku.ca

The observatory is open for online viewing Monday nights and public (in-person) viewing on Wednesday nights.

PLANETARY FACT SHEET - METRIC

	MERCURY	VENUS	EARTH	MOON	MARS	JUPITER	SATURN	URANUS	NEPTUNE	PLUTO
Mass (10^{24}kg)	0.33	4.87	5.97	0.073	0.642	1898	568	86.8	102	0.0146
Diameter (km)	4879	12,104	12,756	3475	6792	142,984	120,536	51,118	49,528	2370
Density (kg/m³)	5427	5243	5514	3340	3933	1326	687	1271	1638	2095
Gravity (m/s²)	3.7	8.9	9.8	1.6	3.7	23.1	9	8.7	11	0.7
Escape Velocity (km/s)	4.3	10.4	11.2	2.4	5	59.5	35.5	21.3	23.5	1.3
Rotation Period (hours)	1407.6	-5832.5	23.9	655.7	24.6	9.9	10.7	-17.2	16.1	-153.3
Length of Day (hours)	4222.6	2802	24	708.7	24.7	9.9	10.7	17.2	16.1	153.3
Distance from Sun (10^6 km)	57.9	108.2	149.6	0.384*	227.9	778.6	1433.5	2872.5	4495.1	5906.4
Perihelion (10^6 km)	46	107.5	147.1	0.363*	206.6	740.5	1352.6	2741.3	4444.5	4436.8
Aphelion (10^6 km)	69.8	108.9	152.1	0.406*	249.2	816.6	1514.5	3003.6	4545.7	7375.9
Orbital Period (days)	88	224.7	365.2	27.3	687	4331	10,747	30,589	59,800	90,560
Orbital Velocity (km/s)	47.4	35	29.8	1	24.1	13.1	9.7	6.8	5.4	4.7
Orbital Inclination (degrees)	7	3.4	0	5.1	1.9	1.3	2.5	0.8	1.8	17.2
Orbital Eccentricity	0.205	0.007	0.017	0.055	0.094	0.049	0.057	0.046	0.011	0.244
Obliquity to Orbit (degrees)	0.034	177.4	23.4	6.7	25.2	3.1	26.7	97.8	28.3	122.5
Mean Temperature (C)	167	464	15	-20	-65	-110	-140	-195	-200	-225
Surface Pressure (bars)	0	92	1	0	0.01	Unknown*	Unknown*	Unknown*	Unknown*	0.00001
Number of Moons	0	0	1	0	2	79	62	27	14	5
Ring System?	No	No	No	No	No	Yes	Yes	Yes	Yes	No
Global Magnetic Field?	Yes	No	Yes	No	No	Yes	Yes	Yes	Yes	Unknown
	MERCURY	VENUS	EARTH	MOON	MARS	JUPITER	SATURN	URANUS	NEPTUNE	PLUTO

*The surfaces of Jupiter, Saturn, Uranus, and Neptune are deep in the atmosphere and the location and pressures are not known.

Source: NSSDC/NASA. Last updated October 21, 2019. Accessed October 15, 2021.

PLANETARIUMS

A selection of planetaria with URL, phone number & related information:

ASTROLab du parc national du Mont-Mégantic: 189 route du Parc, Notre-Dame-des-Bois, QC J0B 2E0 - 819-888-2941; Toll Free: 1-800-665-6527; Email: parc.mont-megantic@sepaq.com; astronomie@astrolab.qc.ca; URL: www.astrolab.qc.ca

Cosmic Rhythms multimedia show; on-site lodging.

Doran Planetarium: Laurentian University, 935 Ramsey Lake Rd., Sudbury ON P3E 2C6 - URL: laurentian.ca/planetarium

Largest planetarium in northern Ontario. Shows are available for students, as well as presentations, media lectures and special shows.

The Lockhart Planetarium: University of Manitoba, 500 Dysart Rd., Winnipeg MB R3T 2M8 - 204-474-6202; URL: www.physics.umanitoba.ca/astro

Dome seats 60; open year-round for public groups.

MacMillan Planetarium: H.R. MacMillan Space Centre, 1100 Chestnut St., Vancouver BC V6J 3J9 - 604-738-7827, Fax: 604-736-5665; Email: info@spacecentre.ca; URL: www.spacecentre.ca

Special laser shows in summer, numerous programs for school groups of all ages, teacher packages online.

Manitoba Museum Planetarium: 190 Rupert Ave., Winnipeg MB R3B 0N2 - 204-956-2830; Fax: 204-942-3679; Email: info@manitobamuseum.ca; URL: manitobamuseum.ca/visit/planetarium

First opened in 1968, this planetarium now offers shows featuring pre-recorded sequences and live presenters.

Ontario Science Centre Planetarium: 770 Don Mills Road, North York ON M3C 1T3 - 416-696-1000, Fax:416-696-3166; URL: www.ontariosciencecentre.ca/what-s-on/exhibitions

Toronto's only public permanent planetarium. See website for details.

Planétarium Rio Tinto Alcan Montréal: 4801, av Pierre-De Coubertin, Montréal QC H1V 3V4 - 514-868-3000; URL: espacepourlavie.ca/planetarium

Programs, activity sheets, classroom kits, advanced workshop for teachers & educators.

Royal Ontario Museum Travelling Planetarium: Travelling Programs, Learning Department, Royal Ontario Museum, 100 Queens Park, Toronto ON M5S 2C6 - 416-586-5681; Fax: 416-586-5832; E-mail: travellingprograms@rom.on.ca; URL: www.rom.on.ca

Portable Starlab domes (standard or large) available for any location in Ontario. A ROM astronomy teacher accompanies the large dome.

Science North: 100 Ramsey Lake Road, Sudbury ON P3E 5S9 - 705-522-3701 or toll-free 1-800-461-4898; Fax: 705-522-4954; E-mail: contactus@sciencenorth.ca; URL: www.sciencenorth.ca/planetarium

Digital planetarium with feature films about astronomy and other space topics.

Telus Spark: 220 St. George's Dr. NE, Calgary AB T2E 5T2 - 403-817-6800; E-mail: info@sparkscience.ca; URL: www.sparkscience.ca/dome-theatre

The Planetarium dome offers several programs and multimedia shows.

CALENDAR OF ASTRONOMICAL EVENTS, 2022

Date	EST (h:m)	Event	Date	EST (h:m)	Event
01-Jan	18	Moon at Perigee: 358037 km	20	22:11	LAST QUARTER MOON
02	13:13	NEW MOON	21	04:14	Summer Solstice
03	20:23	Mercury 3.1°N of Moon	21	08	Mars at Perihelion: 1.38130 AU
04	02	Earth at Perihelion: 0.98333 AU	21	08:32	Jupiter 2.7°N of Moon
04	11:50	Saturn 4.2°N of Moon	22	13:08	Mercury 2.8°N of Aldebaran
05	19:09	Jupiter 4.5°N of Moon	22	13:16	Mars 0.9°N of Moon: Occn.
07	06	Mercury at Greatest Elong: 19.2°E	25	02:10	Moon at Ascending Node
08	20	Venus at Inferior Conjunction	26	03:11	Venus 2.7°S of Moon
09	13:11	FIRST QUARTER MOON	27	03:19	Mercury 3.9°S of Moon
12	23:19	Moon at Ascending Node	28	21:52	NEW MOON
12	23	Mercury 3.4°N of Saturn	29	01:08	Moon at Apogee: 406581 km
14	04:27	Moon at Apogee: 405806 km	30	21:45	Venus 4.0°N of Aldebaran
15	18	Mercury at Perihelion	04-Jul	02	Earth at Aphelion: 1.01672 AU
17	18:49	FULL MOON	06	21:14	FIRST QUARTER MOON
23	01	Venus at Perihelion	09	12:28	Moon at Descending Node
23	05	Mercury at Inferior Conjunction	10	17	Mercury at Perihelion
25	08:41	LAST QUARTER MOON	13	04:08	Moon at Perigee: 357264 km
27	01:14	Moon at Descending Node	13	13:37	FULL MOON
29	10:05	Mars 2.4°N of Moon	15	15:16	Saturn 4.0°N of Moon
30	02:09	Moon at Perigee: 362250 km	16	14	Mercury at Superior Conjunction
01-Feb	00:46	NEW MOON	18	19:55	Jupiter 2.2°N of Moon
02	16:08	Jupiter 4.3°N of Moon	20	19:18	LAST QUARTER MOON
04	14	Saturn in Conjunction with Sun	21	11:46	Mars 1.1°S of Moon: Occn.
08	08:50	FIRST QUARTER MOON	22	04:21	Moon at Ascending Node
09	01:12	Moon at Ascending Node	26	05:22	Moon at Apogee: 406276 km
10	21:39	Moon at Apogee: 404897 km	26	09:12	Venus 4.2°S of Moon
16	11:57	FULL MOON	28	12:55	NEW MOON
16	16	Mercury at Greatest Elong: 26.3°W	03-Aug	23:58	Mercury 0.6°N of Regulus
23	01:54	Moon at Descending Node	05	06:06	FIRST QUARTER MOON
23	17:32	LAST QUARTER MOON	05	15:30	Moon at Descending Node
26	17:18	Moon at Perigee: 367787 km	10	12:14	Moon at Perigee: 359830 km
27	04:00	Mars 3.5°N of Moon	11	20:36	FULL MOON
28	15:07	Mercury 3.7°N of Moon	11	22:55	Saturn 3.9°N of Moon
28	18	Mercury at Aphelion	14	12	Saturn at Opposition
28	18:47	Saturn 4.3°N of Moon	15	04:37	Jupiter 1.9°N of Moon
02-Mar	11	Mercury 0.7°S of Saturn	18	05:59	Moon at Ascending Node
02	12:35	NEW MOON	18	23:36	LAST QUARTER MOON
05	08	Jupiter in Conjunction with Sun	19	07:16	Mars 2.7°S of Moon
08	03:22	Moon at Ascending Node	22	16:53	Moon at Apogee: 405419 km
10	05:45	FIRST QUARTER MOON	23	16	Mercury at Aphelion
10	18:05	Moon at Apogee: 404268 km	25	15:58	Venus 4.3°S of Moon
13	06	Neptune in Conjunction with Sun	27	03:17	NEW MOON
15	23	Venus 3.9°N of Mars	27	11	Mercury at Greatest Elong: 27.3°E
18	02:17	FULL MOON	01-Sep	16:21	Moon at Descending Node
20	05	Venus at Greatest Elong: 46.6°W	03	13:08	FIRST QUARTER MOON
20	10:33	Vernal Equinox	04	18	Venus at Perihelion
22	03:12	Moon at Descending Node	06	16:28	Mars 4.2°N of Aldebaran
23	18:28	Moon at Perigee: 369764 km	07	13:17	Moon at Perigee: 364491 km
25	00:37	LAST QUARTER MOON	08	05:31	Saturn 3.9°N of Moon
27	21:54	Mars 4.1°N of Moon	10	04:59	FULL MOON
28	06:43	Saturn 4.4°N of Moon	11	10:11	Jupiter 1.8°N of Moon
28	20	Venus 2.1°N of Saturn	14	09:49	Moon at Ascending Node
30	09:34	Jupiter 3.9°N of Moon	16	16	Neptune at Opposition
01-Apr	01:24	NEW MOON	16	20:41	Mars 3.6°S of Moon
02	18	Mercury at Superior Conjunction	17	16:52	LAST QUARTER MOON
04	08:05	Moon at Ascending Node	19	09:44	Moon at Apogee: 404556 km
04	21	Mars 0.3°S of Saturn	22	20:04	Autumnal Equinox
07	14:11	Moon at Apogee: 404438 km	23	02	Mercury at Inferior Conjunction
09	01:47	FIRST QUARTER MOON	25	16:54	NEW MOON
13	17	Mercury at Perihelion	26	13	Jupiter at Opposition
16	13:55	FULL MOON	28	18:43	Moon at Descending Node
18	09:01	Moon at Descending Node	02-Oct	19:14	FIRST QUARTER MOON
19	10:16	Moon at Perigee: 365143 km	04	12:01	Moon at Perigee: 369335 km
23	06:56	LAST QUARTER MOON	05	10:51	Saturn 4.1°N of Moon
24	15:56	Saturn 4.5°N of Moon	06	16	Mercury at Perihelion
25	17:06	Mars 3.9°N of Moon	08	13:06	Jupiter 2.1°N of Moon
26	20:51	Venus 3.8°N of Moon	08	16	Mercury at Greatest Elong: 18.0°W
27	03:23	Jupiter 3.6°N of Moon	09	15:55	FULL MOON
29	03	Mercury at Greatest Elong: 20.6°E	11	16:49	Moon at Ascending Node

29	14:31	Mercury 1.3°S of Pleiades	14	23:28	Mars 3.6°S of Moon
30	15	Venus 0.2°S of Jupiter	17	05:21	Moon at Apogee: 404330 km
30	15:28	NEW MOON	17	12:15	LAST QUARTER MOON
30	15:41	Partial Solar Eclipse; mag=0.640	22	16	Venus at Superior Conjunction
01-May	14:53	Moon at Ascending Node	25	05:49	NEW MOON
02	09:17	Mercury 1.8°N of Moon	25	06:00	Partial Solar Eclipse; mag=0.862
05	04	Uranus in Conjunction with Sun	26	01:30	Moon at Descending Node
05	07:46	Moon at Apogee: 405287 km	29	09:48	Moon at Perigee: 368289 km
08	19:21	FIRST QUARTER MOON	01-Nov	01:37	FIRST QUARTER MOON
05	10	Venus at Aphelion	01	16:08	Saturn 4.2°N of Moon
15	18:44	Moon at Descending Node	04	15:19	Jupiter 2.4°N of Moon
15	23:11	Total Lunar Eclipse; mag=1.414	08	01:08	Moon at Ascending Node
15	23:14	FULL MOON	08	05:59	Total Lunar Eclipse; mag=1.359
17	10:23	Moon at Perigee: 360298 km	08	06:02	FULL MOON
21	14	Mercury at Inferior Conjunction	08	11	Mercury at Superior Conjunction
21	23:43	Saturn 4.5°N of Moon	09	04	Uranus at Opposition
22	13:43	LAST QUARTER MOON	11	08:43	Mars 2.5°S of Moon
24	14:24	Mars 2.8°N of Moon	14	01:41	Moon at Apogee: 404924 km
24	18:59	Jupiter 3.3°N of Moon	16	08:27	LAST QUARTER MOON
26	21:52	Venus 0.2°N of Moon: Occn.	22	11:23	Moon at Descending Node
28	21:33	Moon at Ascending Node	23	17:57	NEW MOON
29	04	Mars 0.6°S of Jupiter	25	20:30	Moon at Perigee: 362826 km
30	06:30	NEW MOON	28	23:40	Saturn 4.2°N of Moon
01-Jun	20:14	Moon at Apogee: 406191 km	30	09:36	FIRST QUARTER MOON
07	09:48	FIRST QUARTER MOON	01-Dec	19:52	Jupiter 2.5°N of Moon
12	05:02	Moon at Descending Node	05	07:39	Moon at Ascending Node
14	06:52	FULL MOON	07	23:08	FULL MOON
14	18:21	Moon at Perigee: 357434 km	07	23:21	Mars 0.5°S of Moon: Occn.
16	10	Mercury at Greatest Elong: 23.2°W	07	23	Mars at Opposition
18	07:22	Saturn 4.3°N of Moon	11	19:30	Moon at Apogee: 405869 km
			16	03:56	LAST QUARTER MOON
			19	20:36	Moon at Descending Node
			21	10	Mercury at Greatest Elong: 20.1°E
			21	16:48	Winter Solstice
			23	05:17	NEW MOON
			24	03:32	Moon at Perigee: 358270 km
			24	06:29	Venus 3.5°N of Moon
			24	13:31	Mercury 3.8°N of Moon
			26	11:11	Saturn 4.0°N of Moon
			29	02	Mercury 1.4°N of Venus
			29	05:29	Jupiter 2.3°N of Moon
			29	20:21	FIRST QUARTER MOON

Note: Add one hour to the times listed if Daylight Savings Time is in effect.
Source Planetary dates courtesy of Fred Espenak, AstroPixels.com.
Accessed July 16, 2021.

METEOR SHOWER CALENDAR, 2022

Shower	Activity	Peak Night	Radiant	ZHR	Velocity	Parent Object
Quadrantids	Dec. 26 – Jan. 16	Jan. 3-4	15:20 +49.7°	120	25 miles/sec (medium - 40.2km/sec)	2003 EH (Asteroid)
Lyrids	Apr. 15 – Apr. 29	Apr. 21-22	18:04 +34°	18	30 miles/sec (medium - 48.4km/sec)	C/1861 G1 (Thatcher)
Eta Aquariids	Apr. 15 – May 27	May 4-5	22:30 -1°	40	40.7 miles/sec (swift - 65.5km/sec)	1P/Halley
Southern Delta Aquariids	July 18 – Aug. 21	July 29-30	22:42 -16.3°	16	25 miles/sec (medium - 40km/sec)	96P/Machholz?
Alpha Capricornids	July 7 – Aug. 15	July 30-31	20:26 -9.12°	5	14 miles/sec (slow - 22km/sec)	169P/NEAT
Perseids	July 14 – Sept. 1	Aug. 12-13	03:13 +58.0°	100	37 miles/sec (swift - 59km/sec)	109P/Swift-Tuttle
Orionids	Sept. 26 – Nov. 22	Oct. 20-21	06:21 +15.6°	20	41 miles/sec (swift - 66km/sec)	1P/Halley
Southern Taurids	Sept. 28 – Dec. 2	Nov. 4-5	03:35 +14.4°	5	17.2 miles/sec (slow - 27.7km/sec)	2P/Encke
Northern Taurids	Oct. 13 – Dec. 2	Nov. 11-12	03:55 +22.8°	5	18 miles/sec (medium - 30km/sec)	2P/Encke
Leonids	Nov. 3 – Dec. 2	Nov. 17-18	10:17 +21.6°	15	43.5 miles/sec (swift - 70km/sec)	55P/Tempel-Tuttle
Geminids	Nov. 19 – Dec. 24	Dec. 13-14	07:24 +32.3°	150	21 miles/sec (medium - 34km/sec)	3200 Phaethon (asteroid)
Ursids	Dec. 13 – Dec. 24	Dec. 21-22	14:36 +75.3°	10	20.5 miles/sec (medium - 33km/sec)	8P/Tuttle

Source: American Meteor Society.

Telus World of Science - Edmonton: 11211 - 142 St., Edmonton AB T5M 4A1 - 780-451-3344; Email: sim@twose.ca; URL: telusworldofscienceedmonton.ca/educators/mobile-planetarium-rental

Mobile planetarium available. Gift shop, IMAX theatre, science programs & computer lab; observatory operated by RASC volunteers.

W.J. McCallion Planetarium: Dept. of Physics & Astronomy, McMaster University, 1280 Main St. West, Hamilton ON L8S 4M1 - 905-525-9140, ext. 27777; Fax: 905-546-1252; Email: planetarium@physics.mcmaster.ca; URL: www.physics.mcmaster.ca/planetarium

Planetarium has long history of support from RASC Hamilton Centre; first in Ontario open to the public. Public shows are Wednesdays (subject to change on occasion). See website for details.

Many of Canada's professional astronomers, & most of Canada's enthusiastic amateur astronomers are members of the Royal Astronomical Society of Canada (see index) which has 28 Centres across Canada. An extensive list of astronomy clubs in Canada has been published online by SkyNews and can be found at skynews.ca/canadian-astronomy-clubs. Many of these clubs have programs for the general public.

ECLIPSES AND TRANSITS IN 2022

In 2022, there will be four eclipses, two solar and two lunar.

1. A **partial** eclipse of the sun on April 30.

2. A **total** eclipse of the moon on May 16.

3. A **partial** eclipse of the sun on October 25.

4. A **total** eclipse of the moon on November 8.

Source: NASA, eclipse.gsfc.nasa.gov/eclipse.html, accessed July 2, 2021.

METEORS, METEORITES, AND METEOR SHOWERS

A *meteor* or "shooting star" appears momentarily in the sky when a particle from beyond the earth enters the earth's atmosphere at a high velocity. Most visible meteors are caused by particles smaller than a grape or marble, and these small particles are completely vaporized in the atmosphere at a height of about 80 km. A spectacular meteor, known as a *fire-ball*, is caused by a larger body which may fall to the earth's surface in one or more pieces. Particles seen thus to fall, or subsequently found by analysis to be of this nature, are called meteorites.

Meteorites may be divided into two main classes—the irons, which are almost pure nickel-iron, and the stones. Any freshly-fallen meteorite is characterized by a dark, smooth crust caused by the fusion of the outer part.

Meteors may be observed on any clear, moonless night at an average rate of about five an hour. At times *meteor showers* occur, when meteors are seen with much greater frequency and appear to radiate from a particular part of the sky which is called the *radiant*. This is an effect of perspective, the radiant being the vanishing point of the parallel tracks of the meteors. Meteor showers usually repeat themselves annually, and in some cases have been associated with the orbits of comets. When the earth passes through or near the orbit of a comet it can intercept the small particles (meteoroids) which cause meteors. A calendar is provided above showing the principal meteor showers for the northern hemisphere, and the dates on which they should occur in the coming year.

The study of meteors and meteorites adds to our knowledge of the nature and origin of the solar system and also to our knowledge of the earth's outer atmosphere.

MAPS OF THE NIGHT SKY

The maps on the next six pages cover the northern sky. Stars are shown down to a magnitude of 5, i.e. those which are readily apparent to the unaided eye on a reasonably dark night.

The maps are designed for 44°N latitude, but are useful for latitudes several degrees north or south of this. They show the hemisphere of sky visible to an observer at various times of the year. Because the aspect of the night sky changes continuously with both longitude and time, while time zones change discontinuously with both longitude and time of year, it is not possible to state simply when, in general, a particular observer will find that his or her sky fits exactly one of the twelve maps. The month indicated above each map is the time of year when the map will match the sky at 11 pm or 12 am. On any particular night, successive maps will represent the sky as it appears every two hours. For example, at 2 am on a March night, the April map should be used. Just after dinner on a January night, the October map will be appropriate. The centre of each map is the zenith, the point directly overhead; the circumference is the horizon. To identify the stars, hold the map in front of you so that the part of the horizon which you are facing (west, for instance) is downward. (The four letters around the periphery of each map indicate compass directions.)

On the maps, stars forming the usual constellation patterns are linked by straight lines, constellation names being given in upper case letters. The names in lower case are those of first magnitude stars and Polaris, which is near the north celestial pole. Small clusters of dots indicate the positions of bright star clusters, nebulae or galaxies. Although a few of these are just visible to the naked eye, and most can be located in binoculars, a telescope is needed for good views of these objects. A dashed line appears on each of the twelve maps, which is the celestial equator. Coloured dots, each named, show the location of visual planets.

The twelve star charts on the following pages were prepared by Dirk Matussek and are copyright of AstroViewer, 2021.

Sky Map
Toronto - Jan. 15, 2022 11:00 PM EST

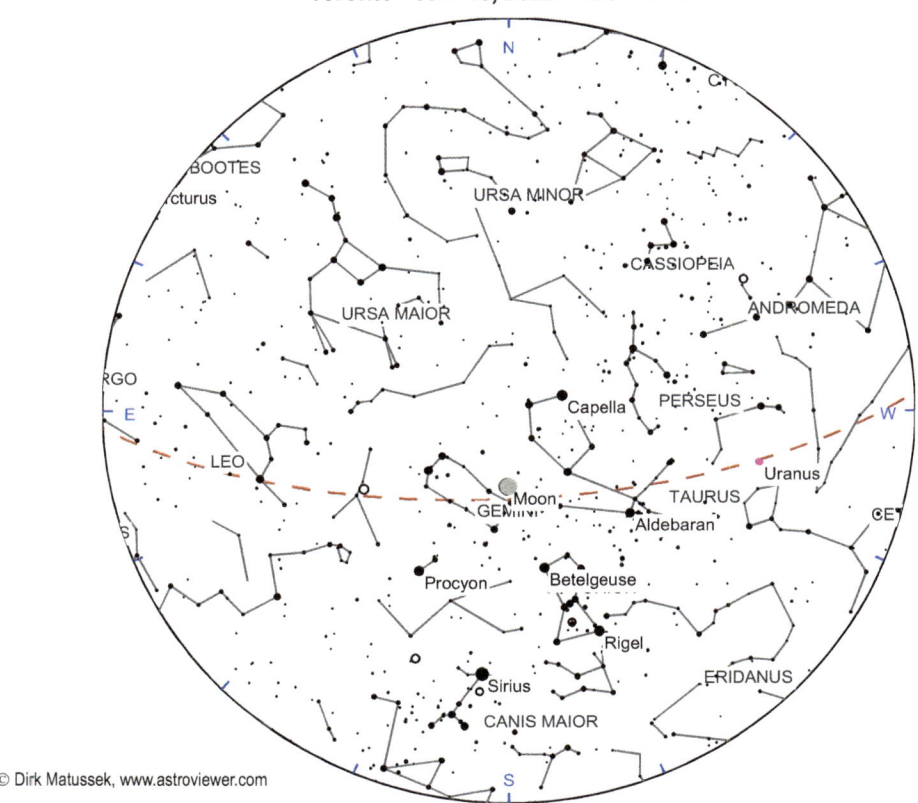

© Dirk Matussek, www.astroviewer.com

Sky Map
Toronto - Feb. 15, 2022 11:00 PM EST

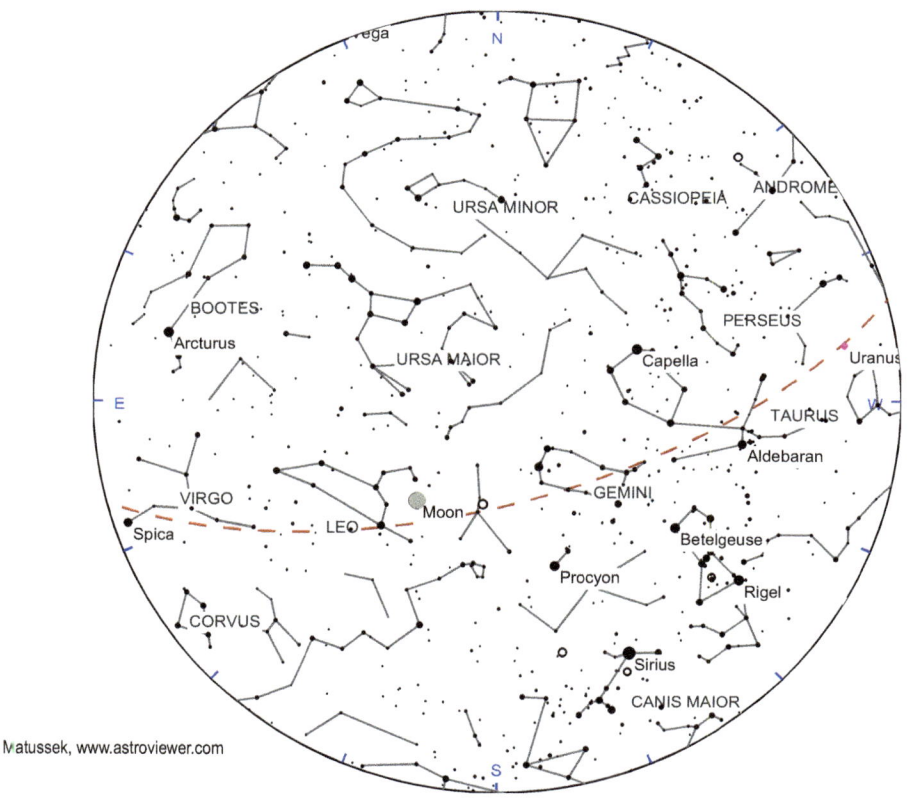

© Dirk Matussek, www.astroviewer.com

Sky Map
Toronto - Mar. 15, 2022 11:00 PM EST

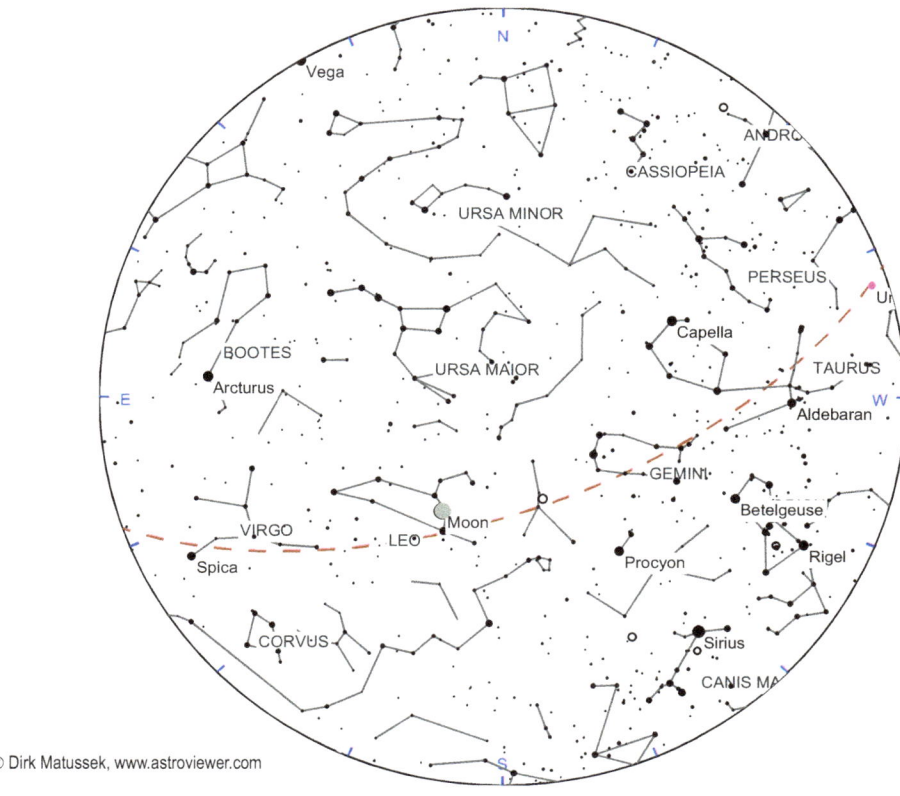

© Dirk Matussek, www.astroviewer.com

Sky Map
Toronto - Apr. 15, 2022 11:00 PM EST

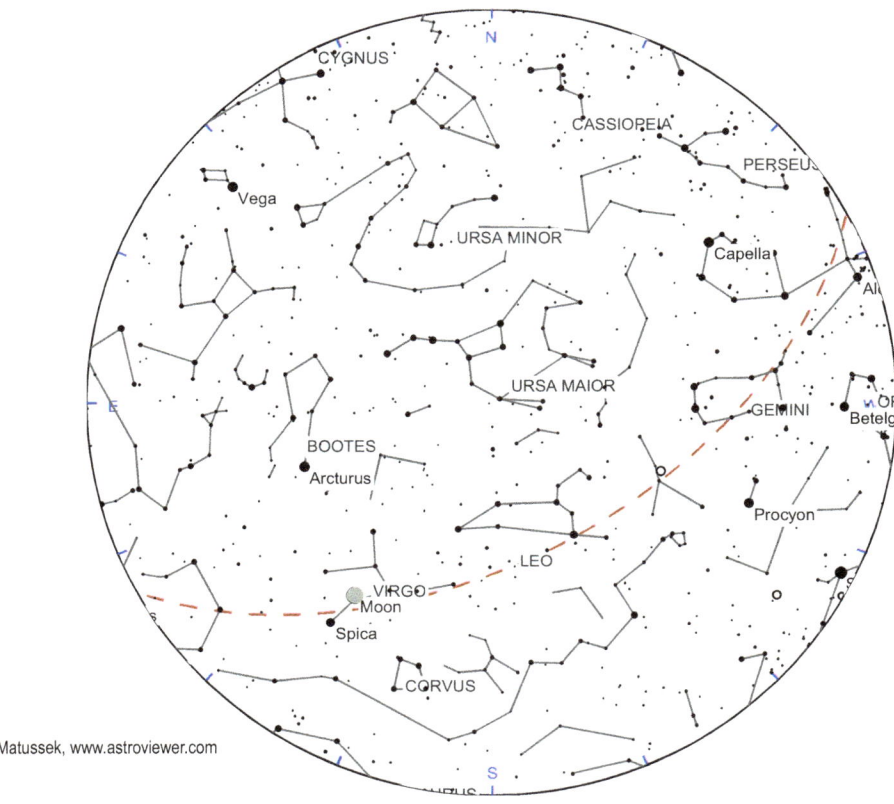

© Dirk Matussek, www.astroviewer.com

Sky Map
Toronto - May 15, 2022 11:00 PM EST

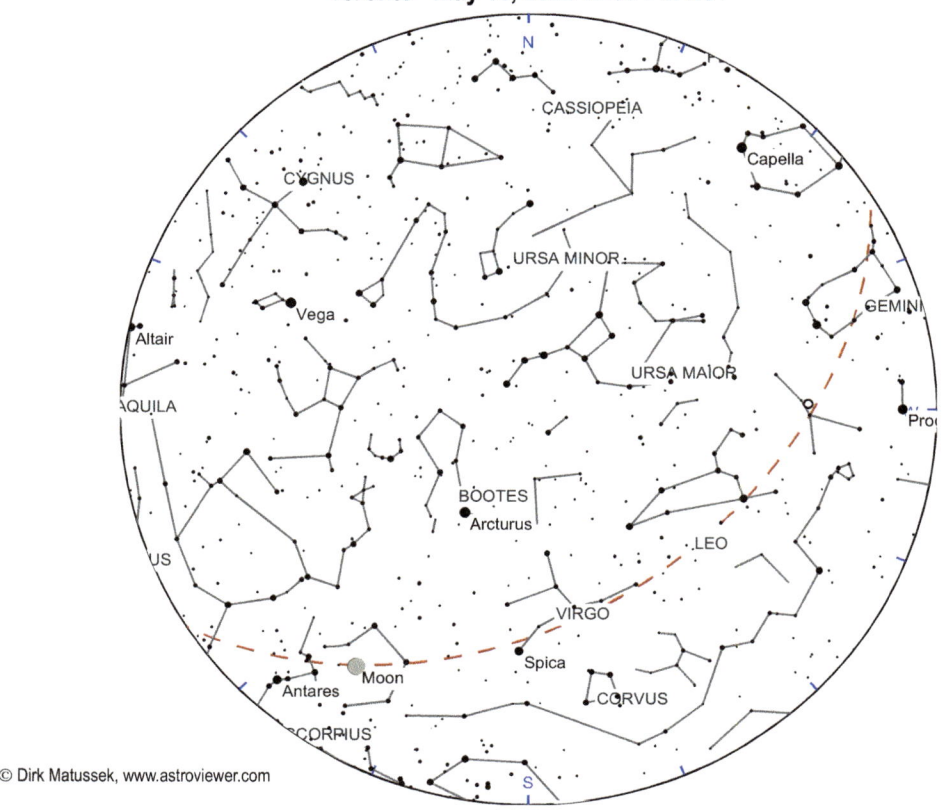

© Dirk Matussek, www.astroviewer.com

Sky Map
Toronto - June 15, 2022 11:00 PM EST

© Dirk Matussek, www.astroviewer.com

Sky Map
Toronto - July 15, 2022 11:00 PM EST

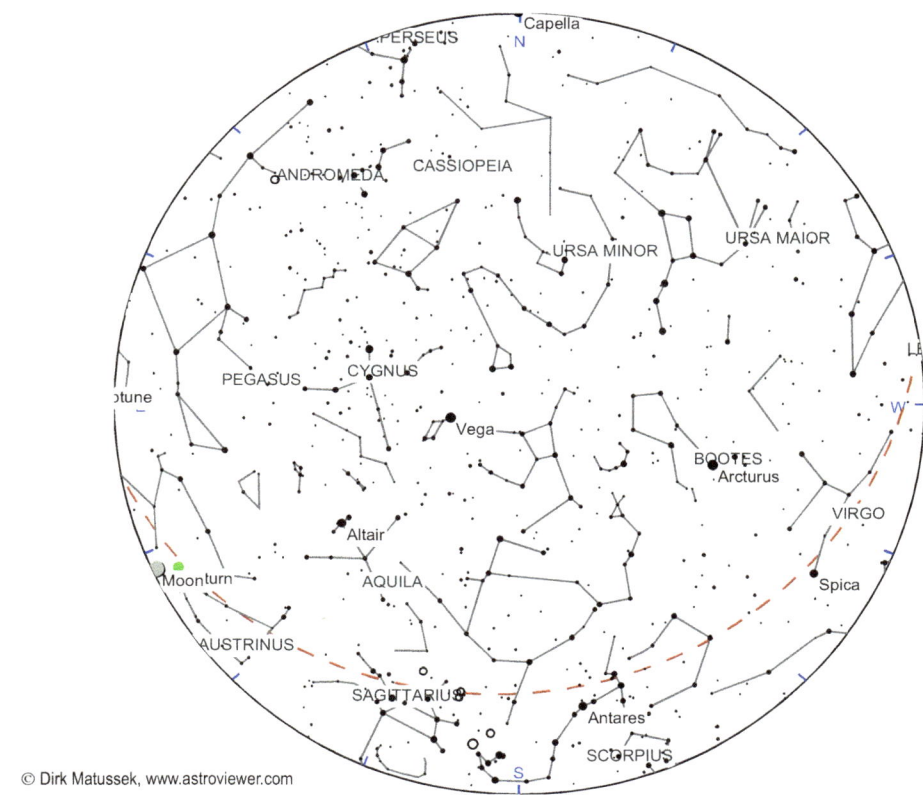

© Dirk Matussek, www.astroviewer.com

Sky Map
Toronto - Aug. 15, 2022 11:00 PM EST

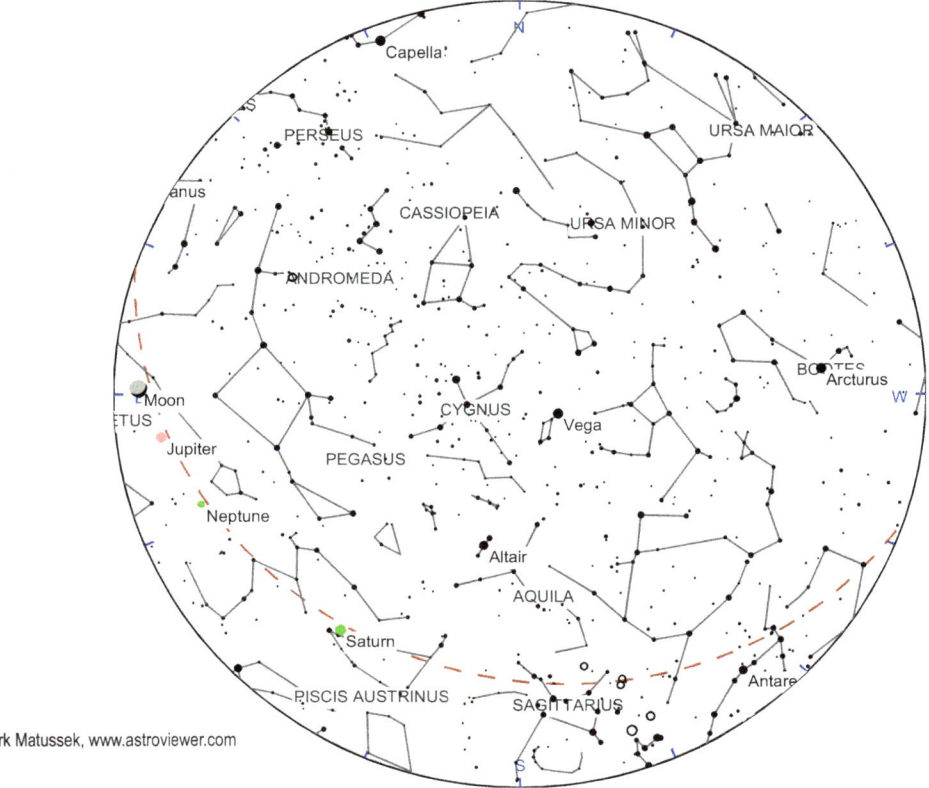

© Dirk Matussek, www.astroviewer.com

Sky Map
Toronto - Sept. 15, 2022 11:00 PM EST

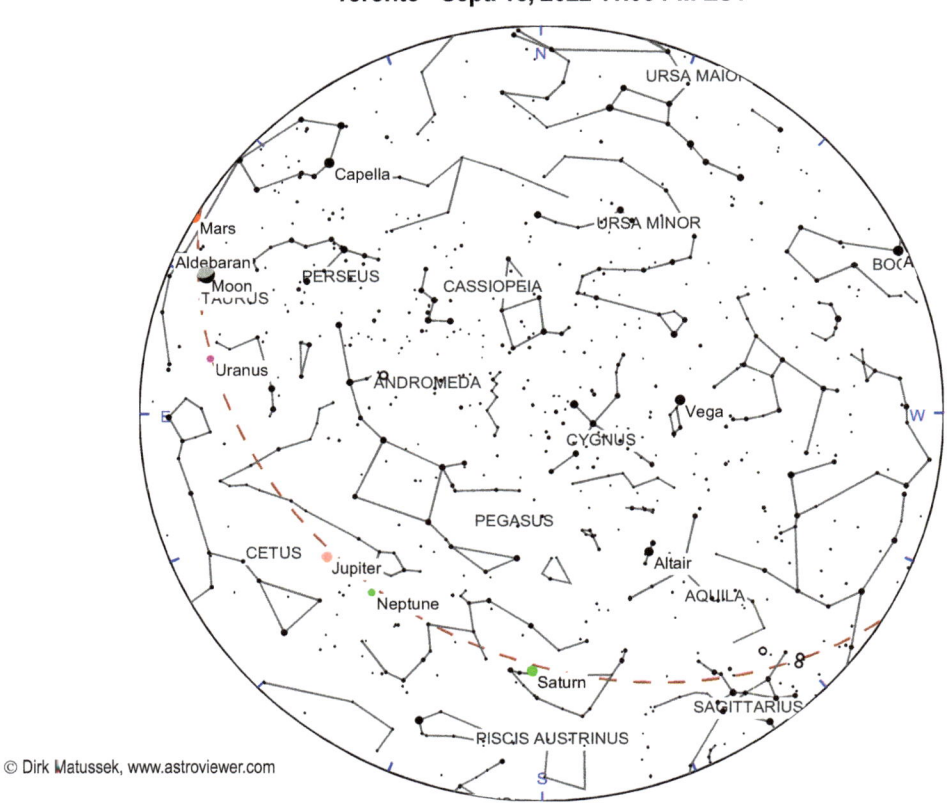

© Dirk Matussek, www.astroviewer.com

Sky Map
Toronto - Oct. 15, 2022 11:00 PM EST

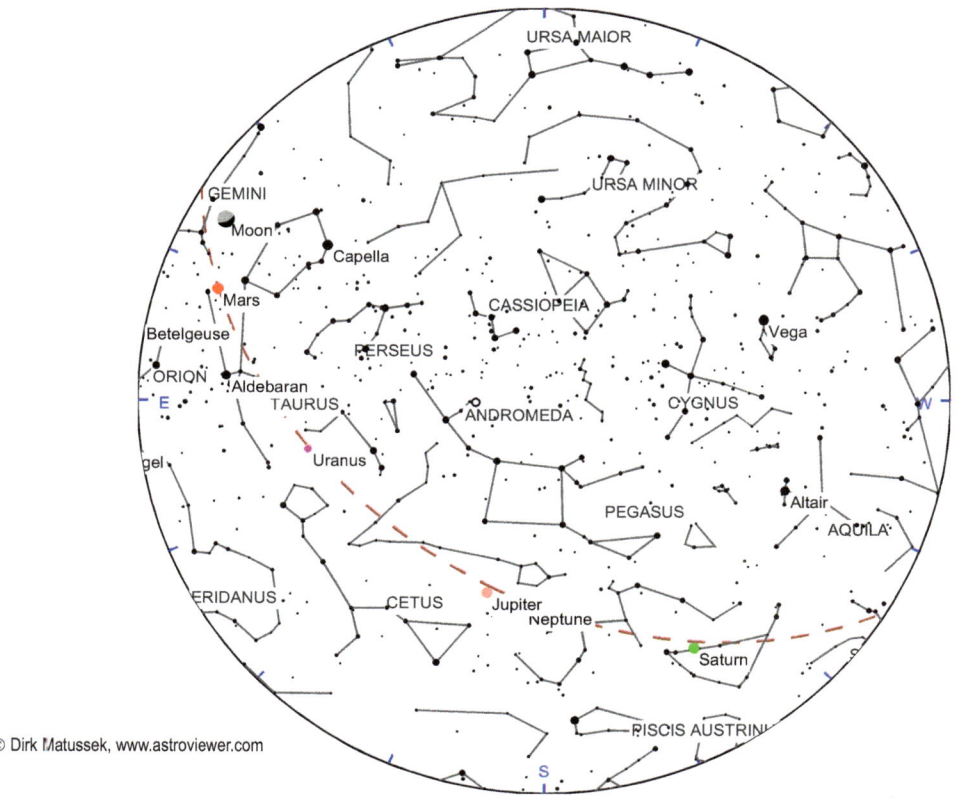

© Dirk Matussek, www.astroviewer.com

Sky Map
Toronto - Nov. 15, 2022 11:00 PM EST

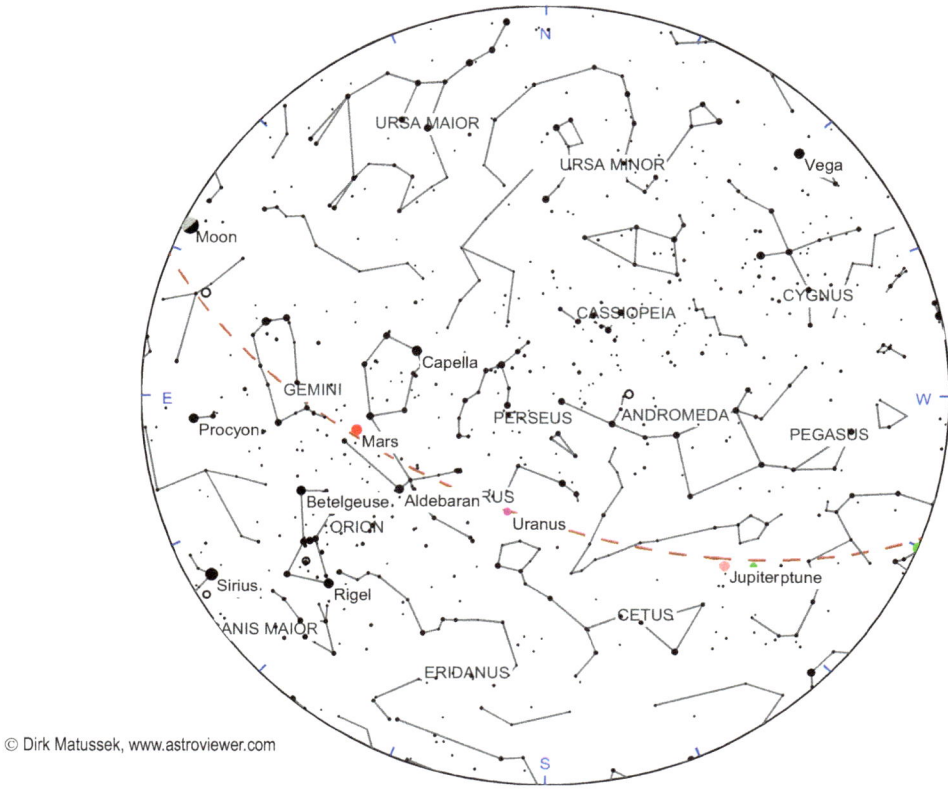

© Dirk Matussek, www.astroviewer.com

Sky Map
Toronto - Dec. 15, 2022 11:00 PM EST

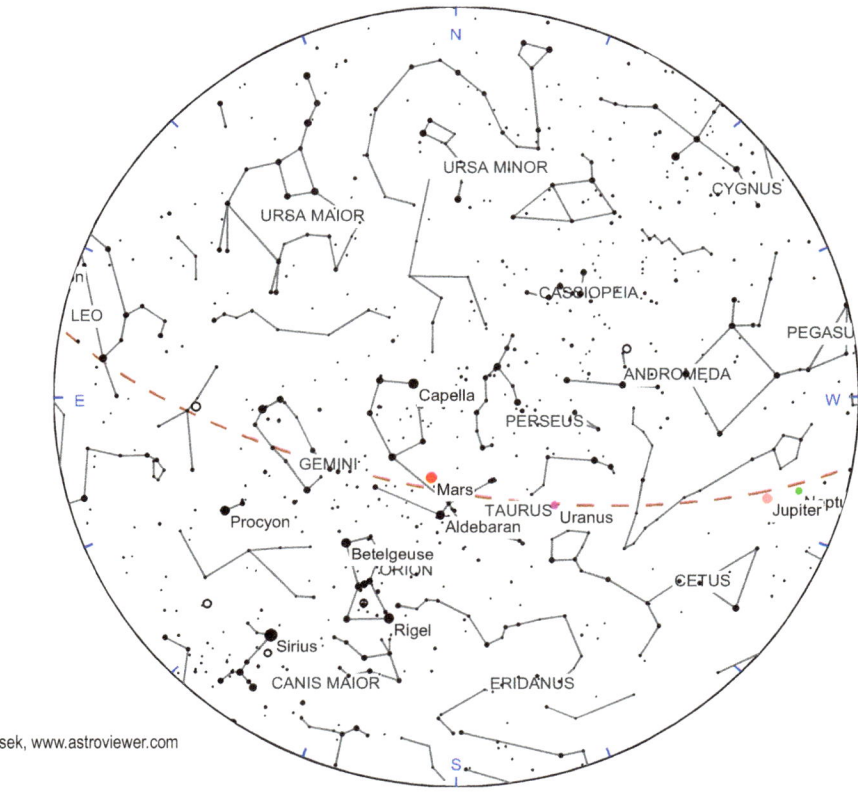

© Dirk Matussek, www.astroviewer.com

AZIMUTHS OF THE POINTS OF RISING AND SETTING OF THE SUN FOR LATITUDES 43°N TO 52°N

IN DEGREES EAST OF NORTH FOR RISING AND WEST OF NORTH FOR SETTING

			43°N	44°N	45°N	46°N	47°N	48°N	49°N	50°N	51°N	52°N
Jan. 2	and	Dec. 11	122	123	124	124	125	126	127	127	128	129
Jan. 10	and	Dec. 3	121	121	122	123	123	124	125	126	127	127
Jan. 16	and	Nov. 27	119	120	120	121	122	122	123	124	125	126
Jan. 21	and	Nov. 22	118	118	119	120	120	121	121	122	123	124
Jan. 25	and	Nov. 17	116	117	117	118	119	119	120	120	121	122
Jan. 29	and	Nov. 14	115	115	116	116	117	118	118	119	119	120
Feb. 2	and	Nov. 10	114	114	114	115	115	116	116	117	118	118
Feb. 5	and	Nov. 6	112	113	113	113	114	114	115	115	116	116
Feb. 9	and	Nov. 3	111	111	111	112	112	113	113	114	114	115
Feb. 12	and	Oct. 31	109	110	110	110	111	111	112	112	113	113
Feb. 15	and	Oct. 28	108	108	109	109	109	110	110	110	111	111
Feb. 18	and	Oct. 25	107	107	107	107	108	108	108	109	109	110
Feb. 20	and	Oct. 22	105	105	106	106	106	106	107	107	108	108
Feb. 23	and	Oct. 19	104	104	104	104	105	105	105	106	106	106
Feb. 26	and	Oct. 17	102	103	103	103	103	104	104	104	104	105
Mar. 1	and	Oct. 14	101	101	101	102	102	102	102	102	103	103
Mar. 3	and	Oct. 11	100	100	100	100	100	100	101	101	101	101
Mar. 6	and	Oct. 9	98	98	98	99	99	99	99	99	100	100
Mar. 8	and	Oct. 6	97	97	97	97	97	97	98	98	98	98
Mar. 11	and	Oct. 4	95	96	96	96	96	96	96	96	96	96
Mar. 13	and	Oct. 1	94	94	94	94	94	94	95	95	95	95
Mar. 16	and	Sept. 28	93	93	93	93	93	93	93	93	93	93
Mar. 18	and	Sept. 26	91	91	91	91	91	92	92	92	92	92
Mar. 21	and	Sept. 23	90	90	90	90	90	90	90	90	90	90
Mar. 23	and	Sept. 21	89	89	89	89	89	88	88	88	88	88
Mar. 26	and	Sept. 18	87	87	87	87	87	87	87	87	87	87
Mar. 28	and	Sept. 16	86	86	86	86	86	86	85	85	85	85
Mar. 31	and	Sept. 13	85	84	84	84	84	84	84	84	84	84
Apr. 3	and	Sept. 10	83	83	83	83	83	83	82	82	82	82
Apr. 5	and	Sept. 8	82	82	82	81	81	81	81	81	80	80
Apr. 8	and	Sept. 5	80	80	80	80	80	80	79	79	79	79
Apr. 11	and	Sept. 2	79	79	79	78	78	78	78	78	77	77
Apr. 13	and	Aug. 30	78	77	77	77	77	76	76	76	76	75
Apr. 16	and	Aug. 28	76	76	76	76	75	75	75	74	74	74
Apr. 19	and	Aug. 25	75	75	74	74	74	73	73	73	72	72
Apr. 22	and	Aug. 22	73	73	73	73	72	72	72	71	71	70
Apr. 25	and	Aug. 19	72	72	71	71	71	70	70	70	69	69
Apr. 28	and	Aug. 16	71	70	70	70	69	69	68	68	67	67
May 1	and	Aug. 12	69	69	69	68	68	67	67	66	66	65
May 5	and	Aug. 9	68	67	67	67	66	66	65	65	64	63
May 8	and	Aug. 5	66	66	66	65	65	64	64	63	62	62
May 12	and	Aug. 2	65	65	64	64	63	62	62	61	61	60
May 16	and	July 28	64	63	63	62	61	61	60	60	59	58
May 21	and	June 24	62	62	61	60	60	59	59	58	57	56
May 26	and	June 19	61	60	60	59	58	58	57	56	55	54
June 1	and	July 12	59	59	58	57	57	56	55	54	53	53
June 10	and	July 3	58	57	56	56	55	54	53	53	52	51

Astronomical Data, U.S. Naval Observatory

LUNAR PHASES FOR 2022
TORONTO (AMERICA/TORONTO) TIME

New Moon	First Quarter	Full Moon	Last Quarter
Jan. 2, Sun 01:35 PM	Jan. 9, Sun 01:13 PM	Jan. 17, Mon 06:51 PM	Jan. 25, Tue 08:42 AM
Feb. 1, Tue 12:49 AM	Feb. 8, Tue 08:51 AM	Feb. 16, Wed 11:59 AM	Feb. 23, Wed 05:34 PM
Mar. 2, Wed 12:38 PM	Mar. 10, Thu 05:46 AM	Mar. 18, Fri 03:20 AM	Mar. 25, Fri 01:39 AM
Apr. 1, Fri 02:27 AM	Apr. 9, Sat 02:48 AM	Apr. 16, Sat 02:57 PM	Apr. 23, Sat 07:58 AM
Apr. 30, Sat 04:30 PM	May 8, Sun 08:22 PM	May 16, Mon 12:15 AM	May 22, Sun 02:44 PM
May 30, Mon 07:32 AM	June 7, Tue 10:49 AM	June 14, Tue 07:52 AM	June 20, Mon 11:11 PM
June 28, Tue 10:53 PM	July 6, Wed 10:14 PM	July 13, Wed 02:38 PM	July 20, Wed 10:19 AM
July 28, Thu 01:55 PM	Aug. 5, Fri 07:07 AM	Aug. 11, Thu 09:36 PM	Aug. 19, Fri 12:36 AM
Aug. 27, Sat 04:16 AM	Sept. 3, Sat 02:08 PM	Sept. 10, Sat 05:58 AM	Sept. 17, Sat 05:52 PM
Sept. 25, Sun 05:54 PM	Oct. 2, Sun 08:15 PM	Oct. 9, Sun 04:54 PM	Oct. 17, Mon 01:16 PM
Oct. 25, Tue 06:48 AM	Nov. 1, Tue 02:38 AM	Nov. 8, Tue 06:02 AM	Nov. 16, Wed 08:29 AM
Nov. 23, Wed 05:57 PM	Nov. 30, Wed 09:38 AM	Dec. 7, Wed 11:09 PM	Dec. 16, Fri 03:59 AM
Dec. 23, Fri 05:17 AM	Dec. 29, Thu 08:22 PM	–	–

Source: https://www.calendar-12.com/moon_phases/2022. Accessed July 2, 2021.

AZIMUTH OF THE SUN AT RISING AND SETTING

Only twice a year, namely about March 21 and September 23, does the sun rise and set more or less exactly in the east and west respectively. It is of interest and sometimes of value to know the position of Sunrise and Sunset at other times. The table above tabulates these in degrees east of north and west of north for Sunrise and Sunset respectively for a selection of latitudes and dates. For latitudes and dates other than those tabulated take simple proportions. See table on previous page.

REFERENCES

The tables and charts in the Canadian Almanac are intended for simple astronomical observations. To make more extensive observations the following are recommended: *The Observer's Handbook* (obtainable from the Royal Astronomical Society of Canada, #203, 4920 Dundas St. West, Toronto, ON M9A 1B7, URL: www.rasc.ca); *Astronomical Phenomena* (obtainable from the U.S. Government Bookstore, URL: bookstore.gpo.gov).

SUGGESTIONS FOR FURTHER READING

There are many excellent astronomy books and materials. Here are some; the books are ones with a Canadian flavour.

Astronomical Society of the Pacific, 390 Ashton Ave., San Francisco CA USA 94112; URL: www.astrosociety.org. Excellent source of astronomical teaching resources, and other useful material; catalogue available. Also publish a free quarterly teachers' newsletter (available on-line).

Astronomy, PO Box 1612, Waukesha WI USA 53187; URL: www.astronomy.com. Popular non-technical monthly magazine for general astronomy readers.

The Backyard Astronomer's Guide, by Terence Dickinson & Alan Dyer. Firefly Books, 4th edition, 2021. URL: www.backyardastronomy.com. The best guide to equipment & techniques.

The Beginner's Observing Guide, by Leo Enright. 6th edition. Royal Astronomical Society of Canada, #203, 4920 Dundas St. West, Toronto, ON M9A 1B7; URL: www.rasc.ca. A simple but serious introduction to the night sky.

The Cold Light of Dawn, by Richard Jarrell. University of Toronto Press, 1988. An authoritative and comprehensive history of Canadian astronomy.

Exploring the Night Sky, by Terence Dickinson. Camden House Publishing, 1987. An award-winning guide, especially for young people.

Looking Up, by Peter Broughton. Dundurn Press, 1993. A history of the Royal Astronomical Society of Canada, illustrated.

Night Sky Almanac: A Month-by-Month Guide to North America's Skies, by Nicole Mortillaro. Firefly Books, annual. Both an introduction to astronomy and a quick-reference book for more experienced sky watchers.

Nightwatch: A Practical Guide to Viewing the Universe, by Terence Dickinson. Firefly Books, 4th revised edition, 2006. Excellent introduction to the night sky.

Sky Atlas 2000.0, by Wil Tirion. Sky Publishing. A popular sky atlas for amateur astronomers.

Sky & Telescope, PO Box 420235, Palm Coast, FL USA 32142-0235; URL: www.skyandtelescope.org. A popular monthly magazine for amateur astronomers.

SkyNews, #203, 4920 Dundas St. West, Toronto, ON M9A 1B7; URL: www.skynews.ca. General astronomy from a Canadian perspective.

SkyWays, by Mary Lou Whitehorne. Royal Astronomical Society of Canada, 2003 (also available in French). A guide for Canadian schoolteachers.

Summer Stargazing, by Terence Dickinson. Firefly Books, 1996. A practical, user-friendly guide.

The Universe and Beyond, by Terence Dickinson. Firefly Books, 5th edition, 2010. Excellent general book on Astronomy.

The Universe at your Fingertips 2.0, edited by Andrew Fraknoi et al. Astronomical Society of the Pacific, 390 Ashton Avenue, San Francisco CA USA 94112. An excellent collection of teaching activities & resources.

The Universe on a T-Shirt, by Dan Falk, Arcade Publishing, 2005 (paperback). An excellent short introduction to our understanding of the universe.

CANADIAN ASTRONOMY WEBSITES

Most astronomical institutions and many of the branches of the Royal Astronomical Society of Canada have websites. They can be accessed from the following key sites:
- Canadian Astronomical Society: www.casca.ca
- Canadian Astronomy Data Centre: www.cadc-ccda.hia-iha.nrc-cnrc.gc.ca
- Canadian Space Agency: www.asc-csa.gc.ca
- Department of Astronomy and Astrophysics, University of Toronto: www.astro.utoronto.ca
- Environment Canada - Astronomy: weather.gc.ca/astro
- Herzberg Institute of Astrophysics: www.nrc-cnrc.gc.ca/eng/rd/nsi
- Royal Astronomical Society of Canada: www.rasc.ca. Local branches of the RASC can be accessed through this site.

CHART OF MAGNETIC DECLINATION

A compass needle, even when unaffected by extraneous magnetic fields, does not in general point due north. The amount and direction by which its direction differs from true north is called magnetic declination or variation. The declination varies with the position of the observer and also varies slowly with time. The above chart gives the values of declination over Canada as of 2000. The chart is © Natural Resources Canada, and was kindly provided by Dr. Larry Newitt, National Geomagnetism Program, Geological Survey of Canada, Natural Resources Canada.

Example: What is the direction of the compass needle at the southern tip of Lake Manitoba?

That location is on the 5° east line; the declination is 5° east; the compass needle points 5° east of the true north.

For more information, see: geomag.nrcan.gc.ca; on the page geomag.nrcan.gc.ca/calc/mdcal-en.php, you can do an online calculation of the magnetic declination for any place at any time.

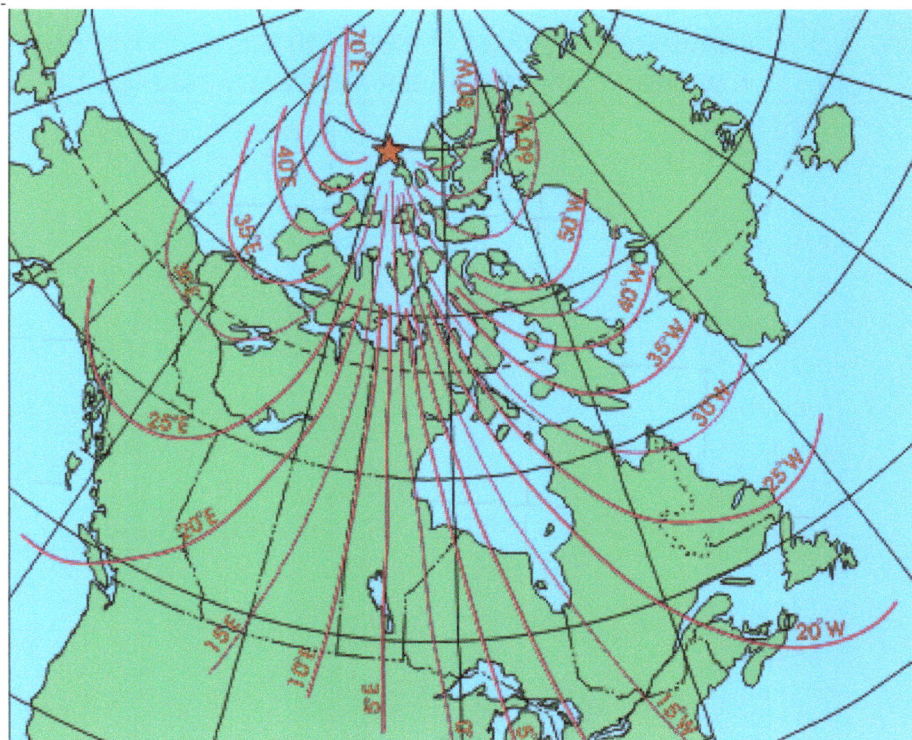

Reproduced with the permission of Natural Resources Canada, courtesy of RETScreen International.

SUNRISE & SUNSET

The following tables show sunrise and sunset times for each month in 2022, using Toronto, Ontario, as the base location. Specifically, these are the coordinates used:

Longitude: -79.370

Latitude: 43.740

Time zone: EST (-5 UTC)

Correction from standard meridian: 17.48 minutes

One hour should be added to the listed times when Daylight Saving Time is in effect.

The tables have been calculated using the National Research Council's Sunrise/Sunset Calculator: nrc.canada.ca/en/research-development/products-services/software-applications/sun-calculator. The calculator can be used to determine sunrise and sunset information in any location in Canada.

Date	Nautical Twilight start	Sunrise	Sunset	Nautical Twilight end	LST, 00:00 EST, hh:mm:ss
1-Jan	6:43	7:51	16:51	18:00	6:25:52
2-Jan	6:43	7:51	16:52	18:01	6:29:48
3-Jan	6:43	7:51	16:53	18:02	6:33:45
4-Jan	6:43	7:51	16:54	18:02	6:37:41
5-Jan	6:43	7:51	16:55	18:03	6:41:38
6-Jan	6:43	7:51	16:56	18:04	6:45:34
7-Jan	6:43	7:51	16:57	18:05	6:49:31
8-Jan	6:43	7:51	16:58	18:06	6:53:27
9-Jan	6:42	7:51	16:59	18:07	6:57:24
10-Jan	6:42	7:50	17:00	18:08	7:01:21
11-Jan	6:42	7:50	17:01	18:09	7:05:17
12-Jan	6:42	7:50	17:03	18:10	7:09:14
13-Jan	6:41	7:49	17:04	18:11	7:13:10
14-Jan	6:41	7:49	17:05	18:12	7:17:07
15-Jan	6:41	7:48	17:06	18:13	7:21:03
16-Jan	6:40	7:48	17:07	18:15	7:25:00
17-Jan	6:40	7:47	17:09	18:16	7:28:56
18-Jan	6:39	7:46	17:10	18:17	7:32:53
19-Jan	6:39	7:46	17:11	18:18	7:36:50
20-Jan	6:38	7:45	17:12	18:19	7:40:46
21-Jan	6:38	7:44	17:14	18:20	7:44:43
22-Jan	6:37	7:44	17:15	18:21	7:48:39
23-Jan	6:37	7:43	17:16	18:23	7:52:36
24-Jan	6:36	7:42	17:18	18:24	7:56:32
25-Jan	6:35	7:41	17:19	18:25	8:00:29
26-Jan	6:34	7:40	17:20	18:26	8:04:25
27-Jan	6:34	7:39	17:22	18:27	8:08:22
28-Jan	6:33	7:38	17:23	18:29	8:12:19
29-Jan	6:32	7:37	17:24	18:30	8:16:15
30-Jan	6:31	7:36	17:26	18:31	8:20:12
31-Jan	6:30	7:35	17:27	18:32	8:24:08

Date	Nautical Twilight start	Sunrise	Sunset	Nautical Twilight end	LST, 00:00 EST, hh:mm:ss
1-Feb	6:29	7:34	17:29	18:33	8:28:05
2-Feb	6:28	7:33	17:30	18:35	8:32:01
3-Feb	6:27	7:32	17:31	18:36	8:35:58
4-Feb	6:26	7:31	17:33	18:37	8:39:54
5-Feb	6:25	7:29	17:34	18:38	8:43:51
6-Feb	6:24	7:28	17:35	18:40	8:47:48
7-Feb	6:23	7:27	17:37	18:41	8:51:44
8-Feb	6:22	7:26	17:38	18:42	8:55:41
9-Feb	6:21	7:24	17:40	18:43	8:59:37
10-Feb	6:19	7:23	17:41	18:45	9:03:34
11-Feb	6:18	7:22	17:42	18:46	9:07:30
12-Feb	6:17	7:20	17:44	18:47	9:11:27
13-Feb	6:16	7:19	17:45	18:48	9:15:23
14-Feb	6:14	7:17	17:46	18:50	9:19:20
15-Feb	6:13	7:16	17:48	18:51	9:23:17
16-Feb	6:12	7:15	17:49	18:52	9:27:13
17-Feb	6:10	7:13	17:50	18:53	9:31:10
18-Feb	6:09	7:12	17:52	18:55	9:35:06
19-Feb	6:07	7:10	17:53	18:56	9:39:03
20-Feb	6:06	7:08	17:54	18:57	9:42:59
21-Feb	6:04	7:07	17:56	18:58	9:46:56
22-Feb	6:03	7:05	17:57	19:00	9:50:52
23-Feb	6:01	7:04	17:58	19:01	9:54:49
24-Feb	6:00	7:02	18:00	19:02	9:58:46
25-Feb	5:58	7:01	18:01	19:03	10:02:42
26-Feb	5:57	6:59	18:02	19:05	10:06:39
27-Feb	5:55	6:57	18:04	19:06	10:10:35
28-Feb	5:54	6:56	18:05	19:07	10:14:32

Date	Nautical Twilight start	Sunrise	Sunset	Nautical Twilight end	LST, 00:00 EST, hh:mm:ss
1-Mar	5:52	6:54	18:06	19:08	10:18:28
2-Mar	5:50	6:52	18:08	19:10	10:22:25
3-Mar	5:49	6:51	18:09	19:11	10:26:21
4-Mar	5:47	6:49	18:10	19:12	10:30:18
5-Mar	5:45	6:47	18:11	19:13	10:34:15
6-Mar	5:44	6:45	18:13	19:15	10:38:11
7-Mar	5:42	6:44	18:14	19:16	10:42:08
8-Mar	5:40	6:42	18:15	19:17	10:46:04
9-Mar	5:38	6:40	18:16	19:18	10:50:01
10-Mar	5:37	6:38	18:18	19:20	10:53:57
11-Mar	5:35	6:37	18:19	19:21	10:57:54
12-Mar	5:33	6:35	18:20	19:22	11:01:50
13-Mar	5:31	6:33	18:21	19:23	11:05:47
14-Mar	5:29	6:31	18:23	19:25	11:09:44
15-Mar	5:28	6:29	18:24	19:26	11:13:40
16-Mar	5:26	6:28	18:25	19:27	11:17:37
17-Mar	5:24	6:26	18:26	19:29	11:21:33
18-Mar	5:22	6:24	18:28	19:30	11:25:30
19-Mar	5:20	6:22	18:29	19:31	11:29:26
20-Mar	5:18	6:20	18:30	19:32	11:33:23
21-Mar	5:16	6:19	18:31	19:34	11:37:19
22-Mar	5:15	6:17	18:32	19:35	11:41:16
23-Mar	5:13	6:15	18:34	19:36	11:45:13
24-Mar	5:11	6:13	18:35	19:38	11:49:09
25-Mar	5:09	6:11	18:36	19:39	11:53:06
26-Mar	5:07	6:10	18:37	19:40	11:57:02
27-Mar	5:05	6:08	18:39	19:42	12:00:59
28-Mar	5:03	6:06	18:40	19:43	12:04:55
29-Mar	5:01	6:04	18:41	19:44	12:08:52
30-Mar	4:59	6:02	18:42	19:45	12:12:48
31-Mar	4:57	6:01	18:43	19:47	12:16:45

Date	Nautical Twilight start	Sunrise	Sunset	Nautical Twilight end	LST, 00:00 EST, hh:mm:ss
1-Apr	4:55	5:59	18:45	19:48	12:20:42
2-Apr	4:54	5:57	18:46	19:50	12:24:38
3-Apr	4:52	5:55	18:47	19:51	12:28:35
4-Apr	4:50	5:54	18:48	19:52	12:32:31
5-Apr	4:48	5:52	18:49	19:54	12:36:28
6-Apr	4:46	5:50	18:51	19:55	12:40:24
7-Apr	4:44	5:48	18:52	19:56	12:44:21
8-Apr	4:42	5:46	18:53	19:58	12:48:17
9-Apr	4:40	5:45	18:54	19:59	12:52:14
10-Apr	4:38	5:43	18:55	20:00	12:56:11
11-Apr	4:36	5:41	18:57	20:02	13:00:07
12-Apr	4:34	5:40	18:58	20:03	13:04:04
13-Apr	4:32	5:38	18:59	20:05	13:08:00
14-Apr	4:30	5:36	19:00	20:06	13:11:57
15-Apr	4:29	5:34	19:01	20:08	13:15:53
16-Apr	4:27	5:33	19:02	20:09	13:19:50
17-Apr	4:25	5:31	19:04	20:10	13:23:46
18-Apr	4:23	5:30	19:05	20:12	13:27:43
19-Apr	4:21	5:28	19:06	20:13	13:31:40
20-Apr	4:19	5:26	19:07	20:15	13:35:36
21-Apr	4:17	5:25	19:08	20:16	13:39:33
22-Apr	4:15	5:23	19:10	20:18	13:43:29
23-Apr	4:14	5:22	19:11	20:19	13:47:26
24-Apr	4:12	5:20	19:12	20:21	13:51:22
25-Apr	4:10	5:18	19:13	20:22	13:55:19
26-Apr	4:08	5:17	19:14	20:24	13:59:15
27-Apr	4:06	5:15	19:16	20:25	14:03:12
28-Apr	4:05	5:14	19:17	20:27	14:07:09
29-Apr	4:03	5:12	19:18	20:28	14:11:05
30-Apr	4:01	5:11	19:19	20:30	14:15:02

Date	Nautical Twilight start	Sunrise	Sunset	Nautical Twilight end	LST, 00:00 EST, hh:mm:ss
1-May	3:59	5:10	19:20	20:31	14:18:58
2-May	3:58	5:08	19:22	20:33	14:22:55
3-May	3:56	5:07	19:23	20:34	14:26:51
4-May	3:54	5:05	19:24	20:35	14:30:48
5-May	3:53	5:04	19:25	20:37	14:34:44
6-May	3:51	5:03	19:26	20:38	14:38:41
7-May	3:49	5:02	19:27	20:40	14:42:38
8-May	3:48	5:00	19:28	20:41	14:46:34
9-May	3:46	4:59	19:30	20:43	14:50:31
10-May	3:45	4:58	19:31	20:44	14:54:27
11-May	3:43	4:57	19:32	20:46	14:58:24
12-May	3:42	4:55	19:33	20:47	15:02:20
13-May	3:40	4:54	19:34	20:49	15:06:17
14-May	3:39	4:53	19:35	20:50	15:10:13
15-May	3:37	4:52	19:36	20:52	15:14:10
16-May	3:36	4:51	19:37	20:53	15:18:07
17-May	3:34	4:50	19:38	20:54	15:22:03
18-May	3:33	4:49	19:40	20:56	15:26:00
19-May	3:32	4:48	19:41	20:57	15:29:56
20-May	3:31	4:47	19:42	20:59	15:33:53
21-May	3:29	4:46	19:43	21:00	15:37:49
22-May	3:28	4:45	19:44	21:01	15:41:46
23-May	3:27	4:45	19:45	21:03	15:45:42
24-May	3:26	4:44	19:46	21:04	15:49:39
25-May	3:25	4:43	19:47	21:05	15:53:36
26-May	3:24	4:42	19:47	21:06	15:57:32
27-May	3:23	4:42	19:48	21:08	16:01:29
28-May	3:22	4:41	19:49	21:09	16:05:25
29-May	3:21	4:40	19:50	21:10	16:09:22
30-May	3:20	4:40	19:51	21:11	16:13:18
31-May	3:19	4:39	19:52	21:12	16:17:15

Date	Nautical Twilight start	Sunrise	Sunset	Nautical Twilight end	LST, 00:00 EST, hh:mm:ss
1-Jun	3:18	4:39	19:53	21:13	16:21:11
2-Jun	3:17	4:38	19:53	21:14	16:25:08
3-Jun	3:17	4:38	19:54	21:15	16:29:05
4-Jun	3:16	4:37	19:55	21:16	16:33:01
5-Jun	3:15	4:37	19:56	21:17	16:36:58
6-Jun	3:15	4:36	19:56	21:18	16:40:54
7-Jun	3:14	4:36	19:57	21:19	16:44:51
8-Jun	3:14	4:36	19:58	21:20	16:48:47
9-Jun	3:13	4:36	19:58	21:21	16:52:44
10-Jun	3:13	4:35	19:59	21:21	16:56:40
11-Jun	3:13	4:35	19:59	21:22	17:00:37
12-Jun	3:12	4:35	20:00	21:23	17:04:34
13-Jun	3:12	4:35	20:00	21:23	17:08:30
14-Jun	3:12	4:35	20:01	21:24	17:12:27
15-Jun	3:12	4:35	20:01	21:24	17:16:23
16-Jun	3:12	4:35	20:02	21:25	17:20:20
17-Jun	3:12	4:35	20:02	21:25	17:24:16
18-Jun	3:12	4:35	20:02	21:26	17:28:13
19-Jun	3:12	4:35	20:03	21:26	17:32:09
20-Jun	3:12	4:36	20:03	21:26	17:36:06
21-Jun	3:12	4:36	20:03	21:26	17:40:03
22-Jun	3:13	4:36	20:03	21:27	17:43:59
23-Jun	3:13	4:36	20:03	21:27	17:47:56
24-Jun	3:13	4:37	20:03	21:27	17:51:52
25-Jun	3:14	4:37	20:03	21:27	17:55:49
26-Jun	3:14	4:37	20:03	21:27	17:59:45
27-Jun	3:15	4:38	20:03	21:27	18:03:42
28-Jun	3:15	4:38	20:03	21:26	18:07:38
29-Jun	3:16	4:39	20:03	21:26	18:11:35
30-Jun	3:16	4:39	20:03	21:26	18:15:32

Date	Nautical Twilight start	Sunrise	Sunset	Nautical Twilight end	LST, 00:00 EST, hh:mm:ss
1-Jul	3:17	4:40	20:03	21:26	18:19:28
2-Jul	3:18	4:40	20:03	21:25	18:23:25
3-Jul	3:18	4:41	20:03	21:25	18:27:21
4-Jul	3:19	4:41	20:02	21:24	18:31:18
5-Jul	3:20	4:42	20:02	21:24	18:35:14
6-Jul	3:21	4:43	20:02	21:23	18:39:11
7-Jul	3:22	4:43	20:01	21:23	18:43:07
8-Jul	3:23	4:44	20:01	21:22	18:47:04
9-Jul	3:24	4:45	20:00	21:21	18:51:01
10-Jul	3:25	4:45	20:00	21:20	18:54:57
11-Jul	3:26	4:46	19:59	21:20	18:58:54
12-Jul	3:27	4:47	19:59	21:19	19:02:50
13-Jul	3:28	4:48	19:58	21:18	19:06:47
14-Jul	3:29	4:49	19:58	21:17	19:10:43
15-Jul	3:30	4:50	19:57	21:16	19:14:40
16-Jul	3:31	4:50	19:56	21:15	19:18:36
17-Jul	3:33	4:51	19:56	21:14	19:22:33
18-Jul	3:34	4:52	19:55	21:13	19:26:30
19-Jul	3:35	4:53	19:54	21:12	19:30:26
20-Jul	3:36	4:54	19:53	21:11	19:34:23
21-Jul	3:38	4:55	19:52	21:09	19:38:19
22-Jul	3:39	4:56	19:51	21:08	19:42:16
23-Jul	3:40	4:57	19:50	21:07	19:46:12
24-Jul	3:42	4:58	19:49	21:06	19:50:09
25-Jul	3:43	4:59	19:48	21:04	19:54:05
26-Jul	3:44	5:00	19:47	21:03	19:58:02
27-Jul	3:46	5:01	19:46	21:01	20:01:59
28-Jul	3:47	5:02	19:45	21:00	20:05:55
29-Jul	3:48	5:03	19:44	20:59	20:09:52
30-Jul	3:50	5:04	19:43	20:57	20:13:48
31-Jul	3:51	5:05	19:42	20:56	20:17:45

Date	Nautical Twilight start	Sunrise	Sunset	Nautical Twilight end	LST, 00:00 EST, hh:mm:ss
1-Aug	3:53	5:06	19:41	20:54	20:21:41
2-Aug	3:54	5:07	19:39	20:52	20:25:38
3-Aug	3:55	5:09	19:38	20:51	20:29:34
4-Aug	3:57	5:10	19:37	20:49	20:33:31
5-Aug	3:58	5:11	19:36	20:48	20:37:28
6-Aug	4:00	5:12	19:34	20:46	20:41:24
7-Aug	4:01	5:13	19:33	20:44	20:45:21
8-Aug	4:03	5:14	19:31	20:43	20:49:17
9-Aug	4:04	5:15	19:30	20:41	20:53:14
10-Aug	4:05	5:16	19:29	20:39	20:57:10
11-Aug	4:07	5:17	19:27	20:37	21:01:07
12-Aug	4:08	5:19	19:26	20:36	21:05:03
13-Aug	4:10	5:20	19:24	20:34	21:09:00
14-Aug	4:11	5:21	19:23	20:32	21:12:57
15-Aug	4:13	5:22	19:21	20:30	21:16:53
16-Aug	4:14	5:23	19:20	20:28	21:20:50
17-Aug	4:15	5:24	19:18	20:27	21:24:46
18-Aug	4:17	5:25	19:17	20:25	21:28:43
19-Aug	4:18	5:26	19:15	20:23	21:32:39
20-Aug	4:20	5:28	19:13	20:21	21:36:36
21-Aug	4:21	5:29	19:12	20:19	21:40:32
22-Aug	4:22	5:30	19:10	20:17	21:44:29
23-Aug	4:24	5:31	19:08	20:15	21:48:26
24-Aug	4:25	5:32	19:07	20:13	21:52:22
25-Aug	4:26	5:33	19:05	20:12	21:56:19
26-Aug	4:28	5:34	19:03	20:10	22:00:15
27-Aug	4:29	5:35	19:02	20:08	22:04:12
28-Aug	4:31	5:37	19:00	20:06	22:08:08
29-Aug	4:32	5:38	18:58	20:04	22:12:05
30-Aug	4:33	5:39	18:57	20:02	22:16:01
31-Aug	4:35	5:40	18:55	20:00	22:19:58

Date	Nautical Twilight start	Sunrise	Sunset	Nautical Twilight end	LST, 00:00 EST, hh:mm:ss
1-Sep	4:36	5:41	18:53	19:58	22:23:55
2-Sep	4:37	5:42	18:51	19:56	22:27:51
3-Sep	4:38	5:43	18:50	19:54	22:31:48
4-Sep	4:40	5:44	18:48	19:52	22:35:44
5-Sep	4:41	5:45	18:46	19:50	22:39:41
6-Sep	4:42	5:47	18:44	19:48	22:43:37
7-Sep	4:44	5:48	18:42	19:46	22:47:34
8-Sep	4:45	5:49	18:41	19:44	22:51:30
9-Sep	4:46	5:50	18:39	19:42	22:55:27
10-Sep	4:47	5:51	18:37	19:40	22:59:24
11-Sep	4:49	5:52	18:35	19:38	23:03:20
12-Sep	4:50	5:53	18:33	19:36	23:07:17
13-Sep	4:51	5:54	18:31	19:34	23:11:13
14-Sep	4:52	5:56	18:30	19:33	23:15:10
15-Sep	4:54	5:57	18:28	19:31	23:19:06
16-Sep	4:55	5:58	18:26	19:29	23:23:03
17-Sep	4:56	5:59	18:24	19:27	23:26:59
18-Sep	4:57	6:00	18:22	19:25	23:30:56
19-Sep	4:59	6:01	18:20	19:23	23:34:53
20-Sep	5:00	6:02	18:19	19:21	23:38:49
21-Sep	5:01	6:04	18:17	19:19	23:42:46
22-Sep	5:02	6:05	18:15	19:17	23:46:42
23-Sep	5:04	6:06	18:13	19:15	23:50:39
24-Sep	5:05	6:07	18:11	19:13	23:54:35
25-Sep	5:06	6:08	18:09	19:11	23:58:32
26-Sep	5:07	6:09	18:08	19:10	0:02:28
27-Sep	5:08	6:10	18:06	19:08	0:06:25
28-Sep	5:10	6:12	18:04	19:06	0:10:22
29-Sep	5:11	6:13	18:02	19:04	0:14:18
30-Sep	5:12	6:14	18:00	19:02	0:18:15

Date	Nautical Twilight start	Sunrise	Sunset	Nautical Twilight end	LST, 00:00 EST, hh:mm:ss
1-Oct	5:13	6:15	17:58	19:00	0:22:11
2-Oct	5:14	6:16	17:57	18:59	0:26:08
3-Oct	5:15	6:17	17:55	18:57	0:30:04
4-Oct	5:17	6:19	17:53	18:55	0:34:01
5-Oct	5:18	6:20	17:51	18:53	0:37:57
6-Oct	5:19	6:21	17:50	18:51	0:41:54
7-Oct	5:20	6:22	17:48	18:50	0:45:51
8-Oct	5:21	6:23	17:46	18:48	0:49:47
9-Oct	5:23	6:25	17:44	18:46	0:53:44
10-Oct	5:24	6:26	17:43	18:44	0:57:40
11-Oct	5:25	6:27	17:41	18:43	1:01:37
12-Oct	5:26	6:28	17:39	18:41	1:05:33
13-Oct	5:27	6:29	17:37	18:39	1:09:30
14-Oct	5:28	6:31	17:36	18:38	1:13:26
15-Oct	5:30	6:32	17:34	18:36	1:17:23
16-Oct	5:31	6:33	17:32	18:35	1:21:20
17-Oct	5:32	6:34	17:31	18:33	1:25:16
18-Oct	5:33	6:36	17:29	18:31	1:29:13
19-Oct	5:34	6:37	17:27	18:30	1:33:09
20-Oct	5:35	6:38	17:26	18:28	1:37:06
21-Oct	5:37	6:39	17:24	18:27	1:41:02
22-Oct	5:38	6:41	17:23	18:25	1:44:59
23-Oct	5:39	6:42	17:21	18:24	1:48:55
24-Oct	5:40	6:43	17:20	18:23	1:52:52
25-Oct	5:41	6:44	17:18	18:21	1:56:49
26-Oct	5:43	6:46	17:17	18:20	2:00:45
27-Oct	5:44	6:47	17:15	18:18	2:04:42
28-Oct	5:45	6:48	17:14	18:17	2:08:38
29-Oct	5:46	6:50	17:12	18:16	2:12:35
30-Oct	5:47	6:51	17:11	18:14	2:16:31
31-Oct	5:49	6:52	17:09	18:13	2:20:28

Date	Nautical Twilight start	Sunrise	Sunset	Nautical Twilight end	LST, 00:00 EST, hh:mm:ss
1-Nov	5:50	6:54	17:08	18:12	2:24:24
2-Nov	5:51	6:55	17:07	18:11	2:28:21
3-Nov	5:52	6:56	17:05	18:10	2:32:18
4-Nov	5:53	6:57	17:04	18:08	2:36:14
5-Nov	5:54	6:59	17:03	18:07	2:40:11
6-Nov	5:56	7:00	17:02	18:06	2:44:07
7-Nov	5:57	7:01	17:01	18:05	2:48:04
8-Nov	5:58	7:03	16:59	18:04	2:52:00
9-Nov	5:59	7:04	16:58	18:03	2:55:57
10-Nov	6:00	7:05	16:57	18:02	2:59:53
11-Nov	6:02	7:07	16:56	18:01	3:03:50
12-Nov	6:03	7:08	16:55	18:00	3:07:47
13-Nov	6:04	7:09	16:54	17:59	3:11:43
14-Nov	6:05	7:11	16:53	17:59	3:15:40
15-Nov	6:06	7:12	16:52	17:58	3:19:36
16-Nov	6:07	7:13	16:51	17:57	3:23:33
17-Nov	6:08	7:15	16:50	17:56	3:27:29
18-Nov	6:10	7:16	16:49	17:55	3:31:26
19-Nov	6:11	7:17	16:48	17:55	3:35:22
20-Nov	6:12	7:18	16:48	17:54	3:39:19
21-Nov	6:13	7:20	16:47	17:54	3:43:16
22-Nov	6:14	7:21	16:46	17:53	3:47:12
23-Nov	6:15	7:22	16:46	17:52	3:51:09
24-Nov	6:16	7:23	16:45	17:52	3:55:05
25-Nov	6:17	7:25	16:44	17:51	3:59:02
26-Nov	6:18	7:26	16:44	17:51	4:02:58
27-Nov	6:19	7:27	16:43	17:51	4:06:55
28-Nov	6:20	7:28	16:43	17:50	4:10:51
29-Nov	6:21	7:29	16:42	17:50	4:14:48
30-Nov	6:22	7:30	16:42	17:50	4:18:45

Date	Nautical Twilight start	Sunrise	Sunset	Nautical Twilight end	LST, 00:00 EST, hh:mm:ss
1-Dec	6:23	7:31	16:42	17:50	4:22:41
2-Dec	6:24	7:33	16:41	17:49	4:26:38
3-Dec	6:25	7:34	16:41	17:49	4:30:34
4-Dec	6:26	7:35	16:41	17:49	4:34:31
5-Dec	6:27	7:36	16:41	17:49	4:38:27
6-Dec	6:28	7:37	16:40	17:49	4:42:24
7-Dec	6:29	7:38	16:40	17:49	4:46:20
8-Dec	6:30	7:39	16:40	17:49	4:50:17
9-Dec	6:31	7:40	16:40	17:49	4:54:14
10-Dec	6:32	7:40	16:40	17:49	4:58:10
11-Dec	6:32	7:41	16:40	17:49	5:02:07
12-Dec	6:33	7:42	16:40	17:49	5:06:03
13-Dec	6:34	7:43	16:40	17:50	5:10:00
14-Dec	6:35	7:44	16:41	17:50	5:13:56
15-Dec	6:35	7:44	16:41	17:50	5:17:53
16-Dec	6:36	7:45	16:41	17:50	5:21:49
17-Dec	6:37	7:46	16:42	17:51	5:25:46
18-Dec	6:37	7:46	16:42	17:51	5:29:43
19-Dec	6:38	7:47	16:42	17:52	5:33:39
20-Dec	6:38	7:48	16:43	17:52	5:37:36
21-Dec	6:39	7:48	16:43	17:52	5:41:32
22-Dec	6:39	7:49	16:44	17:53	5:45:29
23-Dec	6:40	7:49	16:44	17:54	5:49:25
24-Dec	6:40	7:50	16:45	17:54	5:53:22
25-Dec	6:41	7:50	16:45	17:55	5:57:18
26-Dec	6:41	7:50	16:46	17:55	6:01:15
27-Dec	6:41	7:51	16:47	17:56	6:05:12
28-Dec	6:42	7:51	16:48	17:57	6:09:08
29-Dec	6:42	7:51	16:48	17:57	6:13:05
30-Dec	6:42	7:51	16:49	17:58	6:17:01
31-Dec	6:42	7:51	16:50	17:59	6:20:58

TABLE FOR FINDING APPROXIMATE STANDARD TIME OF SUNRISE, SUNSET, MOONRISE, MOONSET, FOR CANADIAN CITIES AND TOWNS

PLACE	Time Zone	FOR SUNRISE OR SUNSET		FOR MOONRISE OR MOONSET	
		Take value for	and apply correction	Take value for	and apply correction
Brandon	C	Winnipeg	+11*m*	50°	+40*m*
Brantford	E	Toronto	+ 4	45	+21
Calgary	M	Winnipeg	+ 8	50	+36
Charlottetown	A	Ottawa	+10	45	+13
Cornwall	E	Ottawa	- 4	45	- 1
Edmonton	M	Winnipeg	+ 6	50	+34
Fredericton	A	Ottawa	+24	45	+27
Gander	N	Vancouver	- 4	50	+ 8
Glace Bay	A	Ottawa	- 3	45	0
Goose Bay	A	Winnipeg	-26	50	- 2
Granby	E	Ottawa	-12	45	- 9
Guelph	E	Toronto	+ 3	45	+21
Halifax	A	Ottawa	+11	45	+14
Hamilton	E	Toronto	+ 2	45	+21
Hull	E	Ottawa	0	45	+ 3
Kapuskasing	E	Vancouver	+17	50	+30
Kingston	E	Toronto	-12	45	+ 6
Kitchener	E	Toronto	+ 4	45	+22
London	E	Toronto	+ 8	45	+25
Medicine Hat	M	Winnipeg	- 4	50	+22
Moncton	A	Ottawa	+16	45	+19
Montréal	E	Ottawa	- 9	45	- 6
Moosonee	E	Winnipeg	- 6	50	+23
Moose Jaw	C	Winnipeg	+34	50	+62
Niagara Falls	E	Toronto	- 1	45	+16
North Bay	E	Ottawa	+14	45	+18
Ottawa	E	Ottawa	0	45	+ 3
Owen Sound	E	Ottawa	+21	45	+24
Penticton	P	Vancouver	-14	50	- 2
Peterborough	E	Toronto	- 4	45	+13
Prince Albert	C	Winnipeg	+36	50	+64
Prince Rupert	P	Winnipeg	+12	50	+40
Québec	E	Ottawa	-18	45	-15
Regina	C	Winnipeg	+30	50	+58
St. Catharines	E	Toronto	0	45	+17
St. Hyacinthe	E	Ottawa	-11	45	- 8
Saint John, NB	A	Ottawa	+22	45	+24
St. John's, NL	N	Vancouver	-11	50	+ 1
Sarnia	E	Toronto	+12	45	+30
Saskatoon	C	Winnipeg	+38	50	+66
Sault Ste. Marie	E	Ottawa	+34	45	+37
Shawinigan	E	Ottawa	-12	45	- 9
Sherbrooke	E	Ottawa	-14	45	-12
Stratford	E	Toronto	+ 6	45	+24
Sudbury	E	Ottawa	+21	45	+24
Sydney	A	Ottawa	- 2	45	+ 1
The Pas	C	Winnipeg	+16	50	+44
Trois-Rivières	E	Ottawa	-12	45	- 9
Thunder Bay	E	Vancouver	+44	50	+57
Timmins	E	Vancouver	+13	50	+25
Toronto	E	Toronto	0	45	+18
Trail	P	Vancouver	-22	50	-10
Truro	A	Ottawa	+10	45	+13
Vancouver	P	Vancouver	0	50	+12
Victoria	P	Vancouver	+2	50	+14
Windsor	E	Toronto	+14	45	+32
Winnipeg	C	Winnipeg	0	50	+28

PROMINENT CANADIAN SCIENTISTS

John F. Allen

Working with Pyotr Leonidovich Kapitsa and Don Misener, Allen discovered the superfluid phase of matter in 1937 at the Royal Society Mond Laboratory in Cambridge, England. A state achieved by a few liquids, such as helium, at extreme temperature where they become able to flow without friction, superfluids are used in high-precision devices, such as gyroscopes, which allow the measurement of some theoretically predicted gravitational effects. Allen along with Harry Jones also discovered the "fountain effect," in which superfluid helium flows up a tube and shoots into the air upon being exposed to a small heat source (the heat source in the original experiment was a flashlight that they were using to look at the apparatus). Allen was born in Winnipeg in 1908 and was professor of physics at St Andrews University, Scotland, from 1947 to 1978, and then emeritus professor until his death in 2001.

Sidney Altman

Born in 1939 in Montreal, the molecular biologist received a Nobel Prize in Chemistry in 1989 for his work with Thomas R. Cech on the catalytic properties of RNA. Their discovery, that ribonucleic acid in living cells is not only a molecule of heredity but also can function as a biocatalyst, affects fundamental aspects of the molecular basis of life. Virtually all chemical reactions taking place in a living cell require catalysts. Such biocatalysts are called enzymes and are determined by hereditary genes. Until the findings of Altman and Cech became known, all enzymes were considered to be proteins. The discovery of catalytic RNA will provide a new tool for gene technology, with potential to create defenses against viral infections. Altman is currently Professor Emeritus of Molecular, Cellular, and Developmental Biology and Professor of Chemistry at Yale University.

Frederick G. Banting

Arthur S. Goss/Library and Archives Canada/PA-123481

A doctor of orthopedic medicine and a decorated World War I veteran, Banting received a Nobel Prize in Medicine in 1923 for his discovery of insulin, a hormone that controls the metabolism of sugar. Early in his medical career, Banting became interested in diabetes, caused by a lack of insulin secreted by the pancreas. Before Banting's work, attempts to supply the missing insulin by feeding patients with fresh pancreas, or extracts of it, had failed. While working with his assistant Charles Best, Banting discovered how to extract insulin from the pancreas before it destroyed itself, thus birthing the first treatment for diabetes sufferers. The Banting and Best Diabetes Centre at the University of Toronto continues the work of the two doctors. The cause of diabetes remains a mystery. Banting was killed in an airplane disaster in 1941 in Newfoundland.

Alexander Graham Bell

Moffett Studio/Library and Archives Canada/C-017335

A Naturalized U.S. citizen, Bell proved himself a Canadian at heart. While he spent winters in the U.S., Bell spent his summers on scientific research in his home in Baddeck, Cape Breton Island. His work with hearing & speech in 1875 birthed his idea of the telephone, which he developed & patented in1876. Bell experimented with the first long distance telephone call between Brantford & Paris, ON, in addition to other scientific experiments on the genetics of sheep breeding, his Silver Draft aircraft, & his hydrofoil speed boat, among others. Bell died of diabetes in 1922, and his grave lies on the summit of Cape Breton's Beinn Bhreagh Mountain overlooking the Bras D'or Lakes of Nova Scotia.

Williard S. Boyle

Boyle's family moved from Nova Scotia to Québec when he was a child. Boyle was homeschooled by his mother until secondary school when he enrolled in Lower Canada College, a Montreal private school. Upon graduation, Boyle joined the Royal Canadian Navy to fight in World War II; however, he became sea-sick & transferred to the Fleet Air Arm of the navy where he completed pilot training. He earned his doctorate in Physics from McGill University in 1950.

Three years later, Boyle joined Bell Laboratories where he contributed to the branch of Solid State Physics or Condensed Matter Physics. His inventions & innovations include the first continuously operating ruby laser & semiconductor lasers. Boyle went on to receive various awards, including his addition into the Science & Engineering Hall of Fame in 2005. In 2009, he received the Nobel Prize in Physics for co-inventing the Charge Coupled Device (CCD), a circuit used in many camcorders & digital cameras as imaging devices & which revolutionized astronomy when used in large telescopes. In 2010, he was recognized as a Companion of the Order of Canada for his lifetime achievements.

Boyle passed away in Wallace, Nova Scotia, in May 2011.

Bertram Brockhouse

Brockhouse was born in 1918 to homesteaders in Alberta and attended a one-room schoolhouse in Vancouver. During the Depression, the impoverished Brockhouses moved to Chicago, where, to help out with family finances, Brockhouse learned how to repair radios, and became involved in the socialist democratic movement. During World War II, he served six years in the Royal Canadian Navy repairing submarine-tracking equipment. At the war's end he attended the University of British Columbia, where he studied physics and mathematics, and received a PhD from the University of Toronto in the budding field of nuclear physics. In 1994 Brockhouse and Clifford G. Shull received a Nobel Prize in Physics for their contributions to the development of neutron scattering techniques for studies of condensed matter. Neutron scattering techniques are used in widely differing areas such as the study of the new ceramic superconductors, catalytic exhaust cleaning, elastic properties of polymers and virus structure.

Brockhouse passed away in Hamilton, Ontario, in October 2003.

Elizabeth Cannon

Born in Charlottetown, PEI, Cannon went to work for Nortech Surveys in Calgary where she utilized her BSc in Geomatics Engineering from the University of Calgary. During the halcyon days of the Global Positioning System (GPS) when it was largely used only by the US military, Cannon worked with the seismic surveying & geomatics company to develop new GPS methodologies. She returned to the University of Calgary to further her study in Geomatics, the science of production & management of spatial information, and won the 1988 Institute of Nagivation (ION) in a student paper competition.

She received her PhD in Geomatics Engineering and served as President and Vice-Chancellor of the University of Calgary from 2010-2018. She also researched the use of the GPS with aircraft positioning and altitude, precision farming, and improvements in precise positioning. She received the Calgary YWCA Women of Distinction Award in 1993, was named one of Canada's Top 40 Under 40 in 1998 and is a Fellow of the Canadian Academy of Engineering and the Royal Society of Canada. Other awards include the Johannes Kepler Award from the U.S. Institute of Navigation, APEGA's Centennial Leadership Award and the Gold Medal Award from Engineers Canada.

John Herbert Chapman

For nearly two decades, Chapman served as scientist, superintendent and deputy chief superintendent in the Ottawa-based Defense Research Telecommunications Establishment, and then as assistant deputy minister for research in the Canadian Department of Communications. In 1966, a government study group appointed Chapman chairman; his report resulted in the redirection of the Canadian space program from scientific to application satellites. He also cooperated with NASA and the European Space Agency to design, develop and establish the Hermes Communications Technology Satellite. These initiatives shaped the Canadian space program. He passed away in Vancouver, B.C., in 1979, the same year he received a posthumous McNaughton Award to add to a list of awards he earned throughout his life.

H.S.M. Coxeter

Coxeter was born and educated in England. Shortly after finishing his doctoral studies at Cambridge University, he spent two years as a research visitor at Princeton University. In 1936 he joined the Faculty of the University of Toronto, where he remained as a mathematics professor until his death in 2003. Coxeter's work was mainly in geometry. In particular he made contributions of major importance in the theory of non-euclidean geometry, group theory, combinatorics, and polytopes or complicated geometric shapes of any number of dimensions that cannot be constructed in the real world but can be described mathematically and can sometimes be drawn. Much of Coxeter's time was devoted to group theory, or ways of measuring symmetry. This concerns the geometry of, for instance, kaleidoscopes and reflections in different planes, now known as Coxeter groups. Coxeter met the artist M.C. Escher, the master of depicting impossible reality, in 1954 and the two became lifelong friends. Coxeter also influenced Buckminster Fuller who used Coxeter's mathematical concepts of symmetry in his architecture. He attributed his long and productive life to vegetarianism and physical fitness.

J.C. Fields

John Charles Fields was born in Hamilton, Ontario, then Upper Canada, in 1863. He graduated with a degree in mathematics from the University of Toronto and was awarded a PhD from Johns Hopkins University in 1887. Dissatisfied with the state of mathematics in North America, Fields left for Europe, where he met the greatest mathematicians of the time, and changed his mathematical interests to algebraic functions. Fields worked tirelessly to raise the stature of mathematics within academic and public circles. He successfully lobbied the Ontario Legislature for an annual research grant of $75,000 for the university and helped establish the National Research Council of Canada, and the Ontario Research Foundation. Fields is best known for establishing what is now known as the Fields Medal, the premier award in mathematics, often called the Nobel Prize in Mathematics. It is awarded every four years to two to four mathematicians, under the age of 40, who have made important contributions to the field.

Sir Sandford Fleming

Library and Archives Canada, Acc. No. 1951-566-1

Fleming was born in Scotland in 1827, and at the age of 17, he emigrated to Ontario, where he was employed as a surveyor and map maker. In 1851 Fleming designed Canada's first postage stamp, which would do much to publicize the beaver as a distinctly Canadian emblem. In 1855 he became the chief engineer of the Northern Railway of Canada, where he instituted the construction of iron bridges instead of wood for safety reasons. Over the next few years he led a team of surveyors and engineers to investigate the first coast-to-coast railway line. Fleming was present in 1885 when the last spike was driven in Craigellachie, British Columbia. After missing a train in 1876 in Ireland because the printed schedule listed p.m. instead of a.m., he proposed Universal Time, a single 24-hour clock for the entire world, located in Greenwich, England, the center of the Earth and not linked to any surface meridian. He urged that standard time zones be used locally, but they were to be subordinate to his single world time. By 1929 all of the major countries of the world had accepted time zones. Fleming was knighted by Queen Victoria In 1897.

John Kenneth Galbraith

The economist's first major book, published in 1952, was *American Capitalism: The Concept of Countervailing Power.* In it he argued that giant firms had replaced small ones to the point where the competitive model no longer applied to much of the American economy. But, he argued, the muscle of large firms was offset by the power of large unions, so that consumers were protected by competing centres of power.

In his best-selling 1958 book *The Affluent Society*, Galbraith contrasted the affluence of the private sector with the squalor of the public sector. Galbraith's main argument is that as society becomes relatively more affluent, so private business must "create" consumer wants through advertising, and while this generates artificial affluence through the production of commercial goods and services, the "public sector" becomes neglected as a result. He proposed significant investment in parks, transportation, education, and other public amenities - what we now call infrastructure - to ameliorate these differences and postpone depression and revolution indefinitely.

Although born in Canada, Galbraith spent most of his life in the United States, namely as a professor at Harvard University. He was active in politics, serving four US presidents and was the US Ambassador to India under Kennedy. He was awarded the Order of Canada in 1997 and two Presidential Medals of Freedom. He died in 2006 at the age of 97.

Biruté Galdikas

Galdikas was born in 1946 in Germany en route to Canada from Lithuania. She grew up in Toronto where she frequented High Park, a home to the wild animals she spent hours observing. She moved to California to complete her undergraduate, Masters & PhD in Anthropology in UCLA & since then has received the PETA Humanitarian Award in 1990, the United Nations Global 500 Award in 1993 and many others. She co-founded and heads the Orangutan Foundation International and is recognized as the world's foremost authority on orangutans and the apes' anthropological connection with humans.

Galdikas is currently a Professor of Anthropology at Simon Fraser University and splits her time between her three homes in Deep Cove, BC; Los Angeles, CA; & Borneo.

William Francis Giauque

Born to American parents on the Canadian side of Niagara Falls, Giauque began his career at the Hooker Electro-Chemical Company in Niagara Falls, NY, as a chemical engineer. Soon after, he received a Ph.D. degree in chemistry with a minor in physics from the University of California, where he became a professor of chemistry in 1934. His principal objective was to demonstrate through a variety of accurate tests that the third law of thermodynamics is a basic natural law. In 1927 he proposed a new method of achieving extremely low temperatures using a process called adiabatic demagnetization. By 1933 he had a working apparatus that obtained a temperature within one-tenth of a degree of absolute zero. In the course of his low-temperature studies of oxygen, Giauque discovered with Herrick L. Johnston the oxygen isotopes of mass 17 and 18 in the Earth's atmosphere. He received the Nobel Prize in Chemistry in 1949.

James Gosling

The father of Java programming language was born in 1955 near Calgary, where he attended university. He received his PhD in Computer Science from Carnegie Mellon University. While at the college he built a multi-processor version of Unix, as well as several compilers and computer mail systems.

From 1984 to 2010, Gosling served Sun Microsystems as Vice President and Fellow. After spending six months at Google, Gosling moved to Liquid Robotics in August 2011, where he served as chief software architect in the creation of robots that explore the bottom of the ocean. In 2017, he announced he was taking a job with Amazon Web Services.

In February 2007, he was named an officer of the Order of Canada.

Gerhard Herzberg

Physicist Herzberg was born in Hamburg, Germany in 1904 but was forced to flee Nazi Germany in 1935, when he settled at the University of Saskatchewan. Herzberg's main contributions have enriched the fields of atomic and molecular spectroscopy for which he won a Nobel Prize in Chemistry in 1971. He and his associates determined the makeup of a large number of diatomic and polyatomic molecules, including the structures of many free radicals difficult to determine in any other way. Herzberg has also applied spectroscopic studies to the identification of certain molecules in planetary atmospheres, in comets, and in interstellar space. Herzberg was elected a Fellow of the Royal Society of Canada in 1939 and of the Royal Society of London in 1951. Herzberg died in 1999.

David Hubel

Hubel, along with Torsten Wiesel, greatly expanded the scientific knowledge of sensory processing, describing how signals from the eye are processed by the brain to generate edge detectors, motion detectors, stereoscopic depth detectors and color detectors, the building blocks of the visual scene. These studies opened the door for the understanding and treatment of childhood cataracts and strabismus. For their work the team was awarded the 1981 Nobel Prize in Physiology or Medicine. Hubel was born to American parents in Windsor, but spent his formative years in Montreal. He died in 2013, in Lincoln, Mass.

Harold Elford Johns

Johns was born in China but grew up in Ontario, where he earned his MA and PhD from the University of Toronto. He was a biophysicist and professor who helped develop the Medical Biophysics Department of the University of Toronto. He invented the cobalt bomb, a nuclear device that birthed the cobalt-60 therapy, which treats cancers located deep within the body that otherwise cannot be reached by other therapies. It has since saved more than 7 million cancer patients. Johns received the 1973 Gairdner International Award and the 1985 W.B. Lewis Award from the Canadian Nuclear Society. He passed away in 1998.

Cecilia Krieger

Krieger was born in Poland but emigrated from Vienna to Toronto in 1920 to escape the persecution of Jews in Europe. Krieger taught at the University of Toronto for three decades after becoming the first woman to earn a Doctorate in Mathematics in Canada in 1930. In honour of Krieger & another woman mathematician, Evelyn Nelson, the Canadian Mathematical Society awarded the CMS Krieger-Nelson Prize Lectureship for Distinguished Research by Women. She passed away in Ontario, in August 1974.

Fernand Labrie

Labrie earned his M.D. in 1962 and Ph.D. in endocrinology in 1966 from the University of Laval. He left his Québec home to study in England with two-time Nobel Prize winner in medicine, Frederick Sanger, and returned in 1969 to found the Laboratory of Molecular Endocrinology at his alma mater. Labrie discovered that castrating hormones from the testes by adding a hormone called GNrH in prostate cancer patients eliminates the need for surgical castration. Next, he discovered that blocking male hormones from the adrenal glands prevents cancer from spreading, thus prolonging life of prostate cancer patients. Labrie also developed medication to prevent the binding of estrogens in the breast and uterus once he discovered that adding estrogen in women was linked to uterine and breast cancer.

Until his death in 2019, Labrie resided in Québec and worked as Director of the Laboratory of Molecular Endocrinology, and CEO and CSO of EndoCeutics, a private pharmaceutical company. Among other awards, he was appointed Fellow of the Royal Society of Canada in 1979 and Officer of the Order of Canada in 1981, and earned the Queen's Golden Jubilee Medal in 2002 and King Faisal International Prize in 2007.

Rudolph Marcus

Born in Montreal in 1923, Marcus received the 1992 Nobel Prize in Chemistry for his theory of electron transfer. The Marcus theory, named after him, provides a thermodynamic and kinetic framework for describing one electron outer-sphere electron transfer. The Marcus theory describes, and makes predictions concerning, such widely differing phenomena as the fixation of light energy by green plants, photochemical production of fuel, chemiluminescence (cold light), the conductivity of electrically conducting polymers, corrosion, the methodology of electrochemical synthesis and analysis, and more.

Marcus developed his theory for what is perhaps the simplest chemical elementary process, the transfer of an electron between two molecules. No chemical bonds are broken in such a reaction, but changes take place in the molecular structure of the reacting molecules and their nearest neighbors. This molecular change enables the electrons to jump between the molecules. He is currently a professor at Caltech and is a member of the International Academy of Quantum Molecular Science.

Sir William Osler

Osler, often dubbed the father of modern medicine, grew up in Ontario, the son of an Anglican minister. After two years at the Toronto School of Medicine, Osler obtained his medical degree in 1872 from McGill University. Upon his death, Osler willed his library to the Montreal university where it forms the nucleus of McGill's Osler Library of the History of Medicine, which opened in 1929. Osler's greatest contribution to medicine was to insist that students learned from seeing and talking to patients and the establishment of the medical residency program. In 1889, Osler accepted the position of Physician-in-Chief at the recently founded Johns Hopkins Hospital in Baltimore where he refined the residency program. He died, at the age of 70, in 1919, during the Spanish influenza epidemic.

Wilder Penfield

The American-born Canadian neurosurgeon studied at Princeton before becoming a Rhodes Scholar at Oxford University where he studied neuropathology, the scientific study of diseases of the nervous system. With his colleague, Herbert Jasper, he invented what is now called the Montreal procedure for treating patients with severe epilepsy by destroying nerve cells in the brain where the seizures originated. Before operat-

ing, he stimulated the brain with electrical probes while the patients were conscious on the operating table and observed their responses. In this way he could more accurately target the areas of the brain responsible, reducing the side-effects of the surgery. His technique enabled him to map the sensory and motor parts of the brain, thus showing their connection to the various limbs and organs of the body. After studying epilepsy in New York, Penfield moved to Montreal where he taught at at McGill University and the Royal Victoria hospital, becoming the city's first neurosurgeon. He eventually became the director of the Montreal Neurological Institute and the associated Montreal Neurological Hospital, which was established with funding from the Rockefeller Foundation. In 1967 he was made a Companion of the Order of Canada. He passed away in 1976, and in 1994 was posthumously inducted into the Canadian Medical Hall of Fame.

John Polanyi

After completing his undergraduate education at Manchester University, Polanyi moved to Canada in 1952 at the age of 23 to work for the for the National Research Council of Canada before moving to the University of Toronto, where he remains to this day. In 1986 Polanyi shared a Nobel Prize in Chemistry with Dudley R. Herschbach and Yuan T. Lee for their research in reaction dynamics, offering much more understanding into how energy disposal in chemical reactions takes place. Polanyi developed the method of infrared chemiluminescence, in which the extremely weak infrared emission from a newly formed molecule is measured and analyzed.

He is currently a University Professor in the Department of Chemistry at the University of Toronto.

Arthur Schawlow

Schawlow grew up in Canada in a deeply religious family and studied at the University of Toronto. After World War II, he studied at Columbia University, spent a decade at Bell Labs, then left to become a professor at Stanford, where he remained as professor emeritus until his retirement in 1996. While at Stanford, he teamed up with Robert Hofstadter, who, like Schawlow, had an autistic child, to help each other find solutions to the condition. Later Schawlow spearheaded an institution to care for people with autism in Paradise, CA, named the Arthur Schawlow Center. Although his research focused on optics, in particular, lasers and their use in spectroscopy, he also pursued investigations in the areas of superconductivity and nuclear resonance. He and Nicolaas Bloembergen shared the 1981 Nobel Prize in Physics by using lasers to study the interactions of electromagnetic radiation with matter. He passed away in 1999.

Myron Scholes

The 1997 winner of the Nobel Memorial Prize in Economics began his early years in Timmins. After the family moved to Hamilton, Scholes attended McMaster University and earned an MBA and PhD from the University of Chicago. He eventually put his name to the Black-Scholes model, which provides the fundamental conceptual framework for valuing options, such as calls or puts, and has become the standard in financial markets globally. All did not go well for Scholes, however. In 2005, Scholes was implicated in the case of Long-Term Capital Holdings v. United States, where he attempted to invest funds from his company, Long-Term Capital Holdings, in an illegal tax shelter in order to avoid having to pay taxes on profits from company investments. It was found that Scholes and his partners were not eligible for US$106 million in tax deductions they had claimed. They were fined more than US$40 million by the IRS. Scholes is currently the Frank E. Buck Professor of Finance, Emeritus, at Stanford Graduate School of Business, and the Chief Investment Strategist at Janus Henderson (formerly Janus Capital Group). He was awarded the 2011 CME Group Fred Arditti Innovation Award for his co-creation of the Black-Scholes options pricing model.

Michael Smith

Born in 1932 in Blackpool, England, Smith attended the University of Manchester and soon after receiving his PhD accepted a fellowship in Vancouver to work on the synthesis of biologically important organo-phosphates. The 1992 Nobel Prize winner in chemistry didn't keep the money he was granted from the award. He gave half of it to researchers working on the genetics of schizophrenia and shared the other half between Science World BC and the Society for Canadian Women in Science and Technology. Smith could afford to be generous. He had made a small fortune in 1988 when he sold his share of Zymogenetics Incorporated, a Seattle-based biotechnology company that he co-founded in 1981. He passed away in 2000.

Andrew Michael Spence

For his work on the dynamics of information flows and market development, Spence and his colleagues George A. Akerlof and

Joseph E. Stiglitz, received the 2001 Nobel Memorial Prize in Economics. In his Job-Market Signaling model, employees convey their respective skills to employers by acquiring a certain degree of education, which is costly to them. Employers will pay higher wages to more educated employees, because they know that the proportion of employees with high abilities is higher among the educated ones, as it is less costly for them to acquire education than it is for employees with low abilities. For the model to work, it is not even necessary for education to have any intrinsic value if it can convey information about the sender (employee) to the recipient (employer) and if the signal is costly.

Spence is currently William R. Berkley Professor in Economics & Business at the NYU Stern School of Business. He grew up in Canada, during and after the war, before leaving for college in the United States.

Henry Taube

For his work on the mechanisms of electron transfer reactions, especially in metal complexes, Taube won the 1983 Nobel Prize in Chemistry. Born in Saskatchewan, Taube has published more than 350 articles and a book as a result of his research. A member of the Stanford University faculty since 1962, Taube was "one of the most creative contemporary workers in inorganic chemistry," according to the Nobel committee who rewarded him for his insights into how electrons are transferred from one molecule to another during chemical reactions. Taube maintained a lifelong interest in oxidation-reduction or redox reactions, in which electrons are lost and gained during a chemical reaction. He died in 2005 at the age of 89 at his home on the Stanford campus.

Richard E. Taylor

Born in 1929 in Medicine Hat, Alberta, Taylor received the 1990 Nobel Prize in Physics for his pioneering investigations concerning deep inelastic scattering of electrons on protons and bound neutrons, which have been of essential importance for the development of the quark model in particle physics. He shared the prize with Jerome Friedman and Henry Kendall. Taylor received his undergraduate degree from the University of Alberta and his PhD from Stanford. He served as Professor Emeritus at the Stanford Linear Accelerator Center until his death in 2018.

William Vickrey

Vickrey was born in Victoria, British Columbia, in 1914. His elementary and secondary education was in Europe and the United States, with graduation from Phillips Andover Academy in 1931. He received a B.S. in mathematics from Yale in 1935, followed by graduate work in economics at Columbia University from 1935 to 1937. A conscientious objector during World War II, he spent part of his alternate service designing a new inheritance tax for Puerto Rico. In 1946 he began his teaching career at Columbia University as a lecturer in economics. An essential part of Vickrey's research focused on the properties of different types of auctions, and how they can best be designed to generate economic efficiency. His work provided the basis for a field of research which has also been extended to practical applications such as auctions of treasury bonds and band spectrum licenses. He received the 1996 Nobel Prize in Economics for his endeavors, and passed away just three days later.

John Tuzo Wilson

The Ottawa-born geologist achieved world-wide acclaim for his contributions to study of plate tectonics, which is the idea that the rigid outer layers of the Earth are broken up into numerous pieces that move independently over the weaker soft zone of the upper mantle. Wilson maintained that the Hawaiian Islands were created as a tectonic plate, extending across much of the Pacific Ocean, shifted slowly over a fixed hotspot, spawning a long series of volcanoes. He also conceived of the transform fault, a major plate boundary where two plates move past each other horizontally, such as the San Andreas Fault. The Wilson cycle of seabed expansion and contraction bears his name. He died in 1993 in Toronto.

CANADA'S ENERGY SOURCES

Canada is endowed with an abundant variety of energy resources. It ranks among top countries in the world for production of oil, natural gas, uranium and coal. Most of the country's energy is derived from hydrocarbons-coal, natural gas, and oil. These are used both as direct fuels and in the production of electricity. The only significant non-hydrocarbon energy sources are hydroelectricity and nuclear power. Canadians are the second-highest per capita consumers of energy in the world, doubling Japan and most of Europe. How will Canada cope with future energy needs and consumption?

Oil and Gas

Canada faces the same oil industry challenges as the rest of the world: recent crude oil prices have been volatile, and geopolitical uncertainty continues to be a threat to supply around the globe. Since 2014 the industry experienced a sharp downturn, but as of 2018 Canada is making a return to profitability thanks to steady global demand and increased production efficiencies. Remaining hurdles include pipeline capacity and difficulty expanding export markets.

Canadian oil sands—a mixture of sand or clay, water, and extremely heavy crude oil—are estimated to contain 1.7 trillion barrels of oil, and based on today's technology, it's believed that 178 billion barrels can be recovered. To put this in perspective, the size of the recoverable resources ranks third to Venezuela and Saudi Arabia. With future developments in technology, more than 300 billion barrels could one day be recovered. The oil sands currently account for approximately 97% of the 3.9 million barrels of oil produced per day in Canada. Conventional oil production in the Western Canada Sedimentary Basin peaked at first in 1973, but took a dramatic upturn in 2003 once major projects became more economically viable. There is call to slow the pace of oil sands development in order to allow for better understanding and assessment of the risks to the environment. This could mean temporarily halting further approvals of projects.

Natural Gas

There has been an ongoing trend on the part of large energy consumers and the general public toward increased use of natural gas as the fuel of choice. This has been particularly noteworthy in the electricity generation industry. Canada is the fourth largest producer and fourth largest exporter of natural gas in the world. Although production of conventional natural gas is declining, production of unconventional natural gas, such as tight gas, is rising as new technologies and methods make wells more economically sound.

Currently the Canadian and the U.S. markets are strongly connected, with 19% of Canadian consumption coming from south of the border. At home, Canadian natural gas supply exceeds consumption, so the surplus is exported to the States in return for importing smaller amounts into Central Canada.

There are also projects underway to allow Canada to export gas overseas by liquefying it (the result being known as liquefied natural gas, or LNG). Prior to 2008, predictions were made that Canada would need to import significant amounts of LNG due to decreasing conventional supplies, with over 40 import terminals planned at one time. However, as unconventional methods arose, especially in the United States with respect to shale gas, Canadian focus turned to the possible export of LNG instead. Currently there are 20 proposed export facilities, 14 of which are to be located in British Columbia. Only one import facility exists, located in Saint John, New Brunswick.

From 2000 to 2013, Canada invested millions of dollars in researching and developing the extraction of gas hydrates, a form of natural gas found in the molecular structure of ice, in Northern provinces and offshore on both coasts. Canadian resource estimates are considered to be larger than the entire world's known coal, oil and gas reserves combined. If there was a viable system available to transport these deposits, hydrates would be as economical as gas, and would also help lessen greenhouse gas emissions since methane is considered cleaner than fossil fuels such as oil and coal. The Canadian government partnered with Japan in researching extraction in the Canadian Arctic, and Japanese researchers successfully produced methane from offshore hydrates, but in 2013 the Canadian government abandoned the project in favour of shale gas and lower-cost conventional natural gas.

Electricity and Coal

The size of Canada's coal resource dwarfs all other energy forms, even the oil sands. Based on current production rates, Canada has a 100-year proven reserve of coal. Currently about 60 percent of Canada's electricity comes from hydro projects, 16 percent from nuclear, 9.5 percent from coal combustion, 8.5 percent from natural gas, and the balance from petroleum and renewables. Coal-based generation became unpopular during the 1980s and 1990s because of its carbon emissions. Canada must develop ways to use coal in a manner that is environmentally acceptable, especially in light of the Paris Agreement adopted in 2015. Until a few years ago, there were two ways to address the challenge of greenhouse gas management: to produce and use energy more efficiently or, to rely increasingly on low-carbon and carbon-free fuels. Unfortunately, energy efficiency and the use of alternative energy may not be enough to stabilize global concentrations of carbon dioxide. Carbon se-

questration offers a third option that could, in tandem with the continued development of clean coal generation technologies, prove affordable, effective and environmentally safe.

Canadian metallurgical coal (coal consumed in making steel) is experiencing a comeback in Alberta and British Columbia, and opportunities for Canadian metallurgical coal are driven by demand in China, India and Brazil. Canadian steam coal (all non-metallurgical coal) production remains consistent with some export growth. Ontario became the first province in Canada to eliminate coal as a source of electrical power, after shutting down the last of its plants in 2014. Steam coal production remains strong in Alberta, Saskatchewan and Nova Scotia.

A number of provinces have introduced or are in the process of introducing plans to address electricity needs by way of new generation and transmission projects. For example, British Columbia Transmission Corp. introduced a $3.2-billion 10-year transmission plan, Alberta Electric System Operator began a $3.5 billion 10-year transmission plan, Saskatchewan agreed to address its aging fleet of coal-fired generators with Carbon Capture and Storage technology, and the Ontario Power Authority moved on its Power System Plan. In November 2016, the federal government announced plans to use the newly created Infrastructure Bank to finance an effort to build clean electricity systems between provinces and territories.

Nuclear Energy

Ontario dominates Canada's nuclear industry, containing most of the country's nuclear power generating capacity. Ontario has 20 reactors, providing about half of the province's electricity. New Brunswick has one reactor, and Quebec did as well, until it was shut down in 2012. Overall, nuclear power provides about 16 percent of Canada's electricity. The cost of nuclear power generation has been dropping over the last decade. This is because declining fuel (including enrichment), operating and maintenance costs, while the plant concerned has been paid for, or at least is being paid off. In general the construction costs of nuclear power plants are significantly higher than for coal- or gas-fired plants because of the need to use special materials, and to incorporate sophisticated safety features and back-up control equipment. These contribute much of the nuclear generation cost, but once the plant is built the cost variables are minor. Canada's nuclear plants, however, are quickly reaching the end of their operating lifespans and are entering the long and costly decommissioning phase.

Canada is one of the world's largest producers of uranium with about one third of world production coming from Saskatchewan mines. The country exports uranium and radioisotopes for medical and industrial purposes. These exports are subject to stringent nuclear non-proliferation policies.

Canada's used reactor fuel is now stored on an interim basis at licensed facilities located where the waste is produced. Like many other countries with nuclear power programs, Canada has yet to decide what to do with this used fuel over the long term. On site storage options are expected to perform well over the near term; however, existing reactor sites were not chosen for their suitability as permanent storage sites. Furthermore, the communities hosting the nuclear reactors have a reasonable expectation that used nuclear fuel will eventually be moved.

Alternative and Renewable Energy

Canadian energy development strategies traditionally focused on low-cost electric power, crude oil, and accessible energy resources. These strategies led to a strong energy industry that has contributed to Canadian prosperity. But today, the world's appetite for cheap energy is counterbalanced by climate change concerns and greenhouse gas emission restrictions. Canada has the potential to become a global leader in renewable energy given its abundant renewable energy resources such as solar, wind, earth, wave, water, tide and biomass. With its large forest and agricultural land base relative to its population, Canada is uniquely positioned to be a world leader in the production and use of biofuels derived from lignocellulose (forestry) biomass, although wind has become the predominant non-hydro renewable source. Renewable energy sources account for 5.2 percent of the total Canadian energy supply today. Utilization of these alternate sources will expand, but they will not become more than small, specialized niche contributors to Canada's energy supply for the foreseeable future.

A study by the Pembina Institute, a sustainable-energy think tank, concluded that smart, targeted investments in a diverse array of energy efficiency and renewable energy solutions over the next 20 years will achieve major cuts in greenhouse gas emissions, accelerate the closure of highly-polluting coal plants and avoid the need for new nuclear investments.

PERPETUAL CALENDAR
(Table for Determining the Weekday of a Given Date)

In the YEAR table, locate the first two figures of the given year (lower left) and the last two figures (upper right) and take the number at the intersection.

With that number, enter the MONTH table, and take the number at the intersection with the given month. Note the special columns for January and February in the case of a bissextile (leap) year.

With that number, enter the DAY OF THE MONTH table. The weekday is found at the intersection with the given day of the month.

Example: 1970 March 7

00	01	02	03	—	04	05
06	07	—	08	09	10	11
—	12	13	14	15	—	16
17	18	19	—	20	21	22
23	—	24	25	26	27	—
28	29	30	31	—	32	33
34	35	—	36	37	38	39
—	40	41	42	43	—	44
45	46	47	—	48	49	50
51	—	52	53	54	55	—
56	57	58	59	—	60	61
62	63	—	64	65	66	67
—	68	69	70	71	—	72
73	74	75	—	76	77	78
79	—	80	81	82	83	—
84	85	86	87	—	88	89
90	91	—	92	93	94	95
—	96	97	98	99		

YEAR

0	7	14	17	21	6	0	1	2	3	4	5
1	8	15 J			5	6	0	1	2	3	4
2	9		18	22	4	5	6	0	1	2	3
3	10				3	4	5	6	0	1	2
4	11	15 G	19	23	2	3	4	5	6	0	1
5	12	16	20	24	1	2	3	4	5	6	0
6	13				0	1	2	3	4	5	6

J: until 1582 October 4 inclusively (Julian Calendar)
G: from 1582 October 15 onwards (Gregorian Calendar)
Example: In the first table, we find 5 at the intersection of 19 and 70.

MONTH	May	Feb. (B) Aug.	Feb. March Nov.	June	Sept. Dec.	Jan. (B) April July	Jan. Oct.
1	2	3	4	5	6	0	1
2	3	4	5	6	0	1	2
3	4	5	6	0	1	2	3
4	5	6	0	1	2	3	4
5	6	0	1	2	3	4	5
6	0	1	2	3	4	5	6
0	1	2	3	4	5	6	0

(B) = Bissextile (leap) year
Example: In the second table, we find 1 at the intersection of 5 and March.

DAY OF MONTH	1 8 15 22 29	2 9 16 23 30	3 10 17 24 31	4 11 18 25	5 12 19 26	6 13 20 27	7 14 21 28
1	Sun.	Mon.	Tue.	Wed.	Thur.	Fri.	Sat.
2	Mon.	Tue.	Wed.	Thur.	Fri.	Sat.	Sun.
3	Tue.	Wed.	Thur.	Fri.	Sat.	Sun.	Mon.
4	Wed.	Thur.	Fri.	Sat.	Sun.	Mon.	Tue.
5	Thur.	Fri.	Sat.	Sun.	Mon.	Tue.	Wed.
6	Fri.	Sat.	Sun.	Mon.	Tue.	Wed.	Thur.
0	Sat.	Sun.	Mon.	Tue.	Wed.	Thur.	Fri.

Example: In the third table, we find *Saturday* at the intersection of 1 and 7.

FIXED AND MOVABLE FESTIVALS AND ANNIVERSARIES

(Gregorian Calendar)	2022			2023			2024			2025			2026		
JANUARY begins on	Sat.			Sun.			Mon.			Wed.			Thu.		
New Year's Day	Sa	Jan.	1	Su	Jan.	1	Mo	Jan.	1	We	Jan.	1	Thu.	Jan.	1
Circumcision	Sa	Jan.	1	Su	Jan.	1	Mo	Jan.	1	We	Jan.	1	Thu.	Jan.	1
Gantan-sai (Shinto New Year)	Sa	Jan.	1	Su	Jan.	1	Mo	Jan.	1	We	Jan.	1	Thu.	Jan.	1
Mary Mother of God	Sa	Jan.	1	Su	Jan.	1	Mo	Jan.	1	We	Jan.	1	Thu.	Jan.	1
Twelfth Night	We	Jan.	5	Th	Jan.	5	Fr	Jan.	5	Su	Jan.	5	Mo	Jan.	5
Epiphany	Th	Jan.	6	Fr	Jan.	6	Sa	Jan.	6	Mo	Jan.	6	Tu	Jan.	6
Maghi	Th	Jan.	13	Fr	Jan.	13	Sa	Jan.	13	Mo	Jan.	13	Tu	Jan.	13
New Year's Day (Orthodox)	Fr	Jan.	14	Sa	Jan.	14	Su	Jan.	14	Tu	Jan.	14	We	Jan.	14
Tu B'shvat	Mo	Jan.	17	Mo	Feb.	6	Th	Jan.	25	Th	Feb.	13	Mo	Feb.	2
FEBRUARY begins on	Tue.			Wed.			Thu.			Sat.			Sun.		
Lunar New Year (Chinese New Year)	Tu	Feb.	1	Su	Jan.	22	Sa	Feb.	10	We	Jan.	29	Tu	Feb.	17
St. Valentine's Day	Mo	Feb.	14	Tu	Feb.	14	We	Feb.	14	Fr	Feb.	14	Sa	Feb.	14
Nirvana	Tu	Feb.	15	We	Feb.	15	Th	Feb.	15	Sa	Feb.	15	Su	Feb.	15
MARCH begins on	Tue.			Wed.			Fri.			Sat.			Sun.		
St. David	Tu	Mar.	1	We	Mar.	1	Fr	Mar.	1	Sa	Mar.	1	Su	Mar.	1
Ash Wednesday	We	Mar.	2	We	Feb.	22	We	Feb.	14	We	Mar.	5	We	Feb.	18
World Day of Prayer	Fr	Mar.	4	Fr	Mar.	3	Fr	Mar.	1	Fr	Mar.	7	Fr	Mar.	6
First Sunday of Lent	Su	Mar.	6	Su	Feb.	26	Su	Feb.	18	Su	Mar.	9	Su	Feb.	22
Daylight Savings Time begins**	Su	Mar.	13	Su	Mar.	12	Su	Mar.	10	Su	Mar.	9	Su	Mar.	8
Purim	Th	Mar.	17	Tu	Mar.	7	Su	Mar.	24	Fr	Mar.	14	Tu	Mar.	3
St. Patrick's Day	Th	Mar.	17	Fr	Mar.	17	Su	Mar.	17	Mo	Mar.	17	Tu	Mar.	17
St. Joseph's Day	Sa	Mar.	19	Su	Mar.	19	Tu	Mar.	19	We	Mar.	19	Th	Mar.	19
Naw Ruz (Baha'i New Year)	Mo	Mar.	21	Tu	Mar.	21	Th	Mar.	21	Fr	Mar.	21	Sa	Mar.	21
Norouz (Persian/Zoroastrian)	Mo	Mar.	21	Tu	Mar.	21	Th	Mar.	21	Fr	Mar.	21	Sa	Mar.	21
Annunciation	Fr	Mar.	25	Sa	Mar.	25	Mo	Mar.	25	Tu	Mar.	25	We	Mar.	25
Khordad Sal (Birth of Prophet Zarathushtra)	Sa	Mar.	26	Su	Mar.	26	Tu	Mar.	26	We	Mar.	26	Th	Mar.	26
APRIL begins on	Fri.			Sat.			Mon.			Tue.			Wed.		
Hindu New Year***	Fr	Apr.	1	We	Mar.	22	Tu	Apr.	9	Sa	Mar.	29	Tu	Apr.	14
First Day of Ramadan*	Su	Apr.	3	Th	Mar.	23	Mo	Mar.	11	Sa	Mar.	1	We	Apr.	18
Palm Sunday (Christian)	Su	Apr.	10	Su	Apr.	2	Su	Mar.	24	Su	Apr.	13	Su	Mar.	29
Baisakhi	Th	Apr.	14	Fr	Apr.	14	Su	Apr.	14	Mo	Apr.	14	Tu	Apr.	14
Good Friday	Fr	Apr.	15	Fr	Apr.	7	Fr	Mar.	29	Fr	Apr.	18	Fr	Apr.	3
First Day of Passover (Pesach)	Sa	Apr.	16	Th	Apr.	6	Tu	Apr.	23	Su	Apr.	13	We	Apr.	1
Easter Sunday	Su	Apr.	17	Su	Apr.	9	Su	Mar.	31	Su	Apr.	20	Su	Apr.	5
First Day of Ridvan	Th	Apr.	21	Fr	Apr.	21	Su	Apr.	21	Mo	Apr.	21	Tu	Apr.	21
St. George's Day	Sa	Apr.	23	Su	Apr.	23	Tu	Apr.	23	We	Apr.	23	Th	Apr.	23
Yom HaSho'ah	Th	Apr.	28	Mo	Apr.	17	Su	May	5	Fr	Apr.	25	Tu	Apr.	14
St. James the Great Day (Orthodox)	Sa	Apr.	30	Su	Apr.	30	Tu	Apr.	30	We	Apr.	30	Th	Apr.	30
MAY begins on	Sun.			Mon.			Wed.			Thu.			Fri.		
Eid al Fitr (Ramadan ends)	Tu	May	3	Sa	Apr	22	We	Apr.	10	Mo	Mar.	31	Fr	Mar.	20
Mother's Day	Su	May	8	Su	May	14	Su	May	12	Su	May	11	Su	May	10
Rogation Sunday	Su	May	22	Su	May	14	Su	May	5	Su	May	26	Su	May	10
Victoria Day	Mo	May	23	Mo	May	22	Mo	May	20	Mo	May	19	Mo	May	18
Ascension Thursday	Th	May	26	Th	May	18	Th	May	9	Th	May	29	Th	May	14
Buddha Day (Visakha Puja)	Fr	May	27	Sa	May	27	Mo	May	27	Tu	May	27	We	May	27
Ascension of Baha'u'llah	Su	May	29	Mo	May	29	We	May	29	Th	May	29	Fr	May	29
Ascension Sunday	Su	May	29	Su	May	21	Su	May	12	Su	June	1	Su	May	17
JUNE begins on	Wed.			Thu.			Sat.			Sun.			Mon.		
Pentecost	Su	June	5	Su	May	28	Su	May	19	Su	June	8	Su	May	24
Pentecost (Whit Sunday)	Su	June	5	Su	May	28	Su	May	19	Su	June	8	Su	May	24
Shavuot	Mo	June	6	Sa	May	27	Th	June	13	Tu	June	3	Sa	May	23
Trinity Sunday	Su	June	12	Su	June	4	Su	May	26	Su	June	15	Su	May	31
Corpus Christi (Thursday)	Th	June	16	Th	June	8	Th	May	30	Th	June	19	Th	June	4
Corpus Christi (Sunday)	Su	June	19	Su	June	11	Su	June	2	Su	June	22	Su	June	7
Father's Day	Su	June	19	Su	June	18	Su	June	16	Su	June	15	Su	June	21
National Indigenous Peoples Day	Tu	June	21	We	June	21	Fr	June	21	Sa	June	21	Su	June	21
Sacred Heart of Jesus	Fr	June	24	Fr	June	16	Fr	June	7	Fr	June	27	Fr	June	12
St-Jean-Baptiste Day	Fr	June	24	Sa	June	24	Mo	June	24	Tu	June	24	We	June	24
Feast of St. Peter and St. Paul	We	June	29	Th	June	29	Sa	June	29	Su	June	29	Mo	June	29
JULY begins on	Fri.			Sat.			Mon.			Tue.			Wed.		
Canada Day	Fr	July	1	Sa	July	1	Mo	July	1	Tu	July	1	We	July	1
Martyrdom of the Bab	Su	July	10	Mo	July	10	We	July	10	Th	July	10	Fr	July	10
St. Benedict Day	Mo	July	11	Tu	July	11	Th	July	11	Fr	July	11	Sa	July	11
Pioneer Day	Su	July	24	Mo	July	24	We	July	24	Th	July	24	Fr	July	24
St. James the Great Day	Mo	July	25	Tu	July	25	Th	July	25	Fr	July	25	Sa	July	25
Islamic New Year	Sa	July	30	We	July	19	Mo	July	8	Fr	June	27	We	June	17
AUGUST begins on	Mon.			Tue.			Thu.			Fri.			Sat.		
Lammas	Mo	Aug.	1	Tu	Aug.	1	Th	Aug.	1	Fr	Aug.	1	Sa	Aug.	1
Tisha B'Av	Sa	Aug.	6	Th	July	27	Tu	Aug.	13	Su	Aug.	3	Th	July	23
Transfiguration	Sa	Aug.	6	Su	Aug.	6	Tu	Aug.	6	We	Aug.	6	Th	Aug.	6
Assumption	Mo	Aug.	15	Tu	Aug.	15	Th	Aug.	15	Fr	Aug.	15	Sa	Aug.	15
SEPTEMBER begins on	Thu.			Fri.			Sun.			Mon.			Tue.		
Labour Day	Mo	Sept.	5	Mo	Sept.	4	Mo	Sept.	2	Mo	Sept.	1	Mo	Sept.	7
Hebrew New Year (Rosh Hashanah)	Mo	Sept.	26	Sa	Sept.	16	Thu.	Oct.	3	Tu	Sept.	23	Sa	Sept.	12
Feast of St. Michael & all Angels	Th	Sept.	29	Fr	Sept.	29	Su	Sept.	29	Mo	Sept.	29	Tu	Sept.	29
OCTOBER begins on	Sat.			Sun.			Tue.			Wed.			Thu.		
St. Francis Day	Tu	Oct.	4	We	Oct.	4	Fr	Oct.	4	Sa	Oct.	4	Su	Oct.	4

Day of Atonement (Yom Kippur)	We	Oct.	5	Mo	Sept.	25	Sa	Oct.	12	We	Oct.	1	Mo	Sept.	21
Mawlid an Nabi	Sa	Oct.	8	We	Sept.	27	Mo	Sept.	16	Fr	Sept.	5	We	Aug.	26
First Day of Feast of Tabernacles (Sukkoth)	Mo	Oct.	10	Sa	Sept.	30	Th	Oct.	17	Tu	Oct.	7	Sa	Sept.	26
Thanksgiving	Mo	Oct.	10	Mo	Oct.	9	Mo	Oct.	14	Mo	Oct.	13	Mo	Oct.	12
Shemini Atzeret	Mo	Oct.	17	Sa	Oct.	7	Th	Oct.	24	Tu	Oct.	14	Sa	Oct.	3
Simchat Torah	Mo	Oct.	17	Sa	Oct.	7	Th	Oct.	24	Tu	Oct.	14	Sa	Oct.	3
Birth of the B'ab	Th	Oct.	20	Fr	Oct.	20	Su	Oct.	20	Mo	Oct.	20	Tu	Oct.	20
Milvian Bridge Day	Fr	Oct.	28	Sa	Oct.	28	Mo	Oct.	28	Tu	Oct.	28	We	Oct.	28
All Hallows Eve	Mo	Oct.	31	Tu	Oct.	31	Th	Oct.	31	Fr	Oct.	31	Sa	Oct.	31
Reformation Day	Mo	Oct.	31	Tu	Oct.	31	Th	Oct.	31	Fr	Oct.	31	Sa	Oct.	31
NOVEMBER begins on	Tue.			Wed.			Fri.			Sat.			Sun.		
All Saints' Day	Tu	Nov.	1	We	Nov.	1	Fr	Nov.	1	Sa	Nov.	1	Su	Nov.	1
All Souls' Day	We	Nov.	2	Th	Nov.	2	Sa	Nov.	2	Su	Nov.	2	Mo	Nov.	2
Daylight Savings Time ends**	Su	Nov.	6	Su	Nov.	5	Su	Nov.	3	Su	Nov.	2	Su	Nov.	1
Remembrance Day	Fr	Nov.	11	Sa	Nov.	11	Mo	Nov.	11	Tu	Nov.	11	We	Nov.	11
Birth of Baha'u'llah	Sa	Nov.	12	Su	Nov.	12	Tu	Nov.	12	We	Nov.	12	Th	Nov.	12
Diwali	Mo	Oct.	24	Mo	Nov.	12	Fr	Nov.	1	Tu	Oct.	21	Su	Nov.	8
Day of Covenant	Sa	Nov.	26	Su	Nov.	26	Tu	Nov.	26	We	Nov.	26	Th	Nov.	26
First Sunday in Advent	Su	Nov.	27	Su	Dec.	3	Su	Dec.	1	Su	Nov.	30	Su	Nov.	29
St. Andrew's Day	We	Nov.	30	Th	Nov.	30	Sa	Nov.	30	Su	Nov.	30	Mo	Nov.	30
DECEMBER begins on	Thu.			Fri.			Sun.			Mon.			Tue.		
Bodhi Day	Th	Dec.	8	Fr	Dec.	8	Su	Dec.	8	Mo	Dec.	8	Tu	Dec.	8
Feast Day (Our Lady of Guadalupe)	Mo	Dec.	12	Tu	Dec.	12	Th	Dec.	12	Fr	Dec.	12	Sa	Dec.	12
First Day in Hanukkah	Mo	Dec.	19	Fr	Dec.	8	Th	Dec.	26	Mo	Dec.	15	Sa	Dec.	5
Christmas Day	Su	Dec.	25	Mo	Dec.	25	We	Dec.	25	Th	Dec.	25	Fr	Dec.	25
Kwanzaa begins on	Mo	Dec.	26	Tu	Dec.	26	Th	Dec.	26	Fr	Dec.	26	Sa	Dec.	26
Zarathosht Diso (Death of Prophet Zarathushtra)	Mo	Dec.	26	Tu	Dec.	26	Th	Dec.	26	Fr	Dec.	26	Sa	Dec.	26
Last Day of Year	Sat.			Sun.			Tue.			Wed.			Thu.		

*These are tabular dates; the festival begins at sunset on the day before. According to Islamic custom, the date is actually set by the direct observation of the new crescent moon.

**All provinces in Canada start Daylight Saving Time on the second Sunday in March and return to standard time on the first Sunday in November, except Saskatchewan, which mostly uses Central Standard Time all year. Areas around Lloydminster are in the Mountain Time zone and change at 2:00 a.m. local time, as in Alberta.

***Different branches of Hinduism celebrate the new year at different times. Jewish holidays begin at sunset the previous evening.

STANDARD HOLIDAYS in Canada include the following: New Year's Day, Good Friday, Victoria Day, Canada Day, Labour Day, Thanksgiving Day, Remembrance Day, Christmas Day, Boxing Day and any other day so proclaimed by the Governor General of Canada, or the Lieutenants Governor of the Provinces.

Additionally, Provincial Holidays include:
ALBERTA: Alberta Family Day (3rd Monday in February), Heritage Day (1st Monday in August)
BRITISH COLUMBIA: British Columbia Family Day (2nd Monday in February), British Columbia Day (1st Monday in August)
MANITOBA: Louis Riel Day (3rd Monday in February), Civic Holiday (1st Monday in August)
NEW BRUNSWICK: New Brunswick Day (1st Monday in August)
NEWFOUNDLAND: Regatta Day/Civic Holiday (1st Wednesday in August, St. John's); following celebrated on nearest Monday: St. Patrick's Day (Mar. 17), St. George's Day (Apr. 23), Discovery Day (June 24), Orangemen's Day (July 12)
NORTHWEST TERRITORIES: National Indigenous Peoples Day (June 21), Civic Holiday (1st Monday in August)
NOVA SCOTIA: Heritage Day (3rd Monday in February), Natal Day (1st Monday in August, varies in Halifax)
NUNAVUT: Nunavut Day (July 9), Civic Holiday (1st Monday in August)
ONTARIO: Family Day (3rd Monday in February), Civic Holiday (1st Monday in August)
PRINCE EDWARD ISLAND: Islanders Day (3rd Monday in February), Natal Day (1st Monday in August)
QUEBEC: Saint-Jean-Baptiste Day / Fête de la Saint-Jean-Baptiste (also known as National Holiday / Fête nationale, June 24)
SASKATCHEWAN: Family Day (3rd Monday in February), Civic Holiday (1st Monday in August)
YUKON: Discovery Day (3rd Monday in August)

THE CALENDAR

The calendar is a method of identifying the passage of time and thereby regulating our civil life and religious observances.

Days, months and years are based on astronomical periods. The day is the time it takes the earth to make one revolution on its axis, the month is associated with the period of orbiting of the moon around the earth, while the year has to do with the orbiting of the earth around the sun.

Many religious ideas and observances have been connected with the changes of the moon, and in ancient times the calendar took account of the moon rather than the seasons. From new moon to new moon is 29.530 days, and from one spring equinox to the next is 365.24219 days. Since the two are incommensurable, the modern calendar disregards the moon, except insofar as our months are roughly equal to a lunation.

The Week

The division of the week is found only among Aryan nations and in nations and regions into which they have penetrated. The day is, for convenience, divided into 24 equal parts and is the period of a single rotation of the earth upon its own axis.

A solar or astronomical day commences at midnight, and is divided into two equal portions of 12 hours each - those before noon being termed (A.M.) those after noon (P.M.).

The Chinese week consists of 5 days, which are named after iron, wood, water, feathers and earth; they divide the day into 12 parts of 2 hours each.

The Anglo-Saxons named the days of the week after the following deities: Sunday, the Sun; Monday, the Moon; Tuesday, Tuesco (God of War); Wednesday, Woden (God of Storms); Thursday, Thor (God of Thunder); Friday, Freya (Goddess of Love); Saturday, Saturn (God of Time).

The word *week* is from Wikon (German); it means change, succession.

The Julian Calendar

When Julius Caesar came to power, the Roman Calendar was hopelessly confused. With the advice of the Alexandrian astronomer Sosigenes, Julius Caesar established the Julian Calendar. The length of the year was taken as 365 1/4 days, and in order to account for the 1/4 day, an extra day was added every fourth year. From 45 B.C. each month has had its present number of days. In the old Roman Calendar which was based on the moon an extra month was inserted to straighten out the difference between 12 lunations 354.37 days, and 355 days, which they called a year. This was inserted when necessary after February 23rd. In the Julian Calendar the extra day was added by repeating the sixth day before the Kalends (1st) of March, whence comes our word bissextile for leap year.

No very significant change was made until the reform by Pope Gregory XIII in A.D. 1582.

The Julian Calendar is known as the "Old Style" whereas the calendar as improved by Pope Gregory is known as the "New Style". The difference between the two is now 13 days.

The Gregorian Calendar

Because the Solar Year is 11 minutes, 12 seconds less than the Julian Year of 365 1/4 days, it followed in course of years that the Julian Calendar became inaccurate by several days, and in 1582 this difference amounted to 10 days. Pope Gregory XIII, at the suggestion of Aloysius Lilus, an astronomer of Naples, determined to rectify this, and devised the Calendar now known as the Gregorian Calendar. He dropped or cancelled these 10 days—October 5th being called October 15th—and made centurial years leap years only once in 4 centuries; so that whilst 1700, 1800 and 1900 were to be ordinary years, 2000 would be a leap year. This modification brought the Gregorian year into such close exactitude with the solar year that there is only a difference of 26 seconds, which amounts to a day in 3,323 years. This is the "New Style". The Gregorian Calendar was adopted in Italy, France, Spain, Portugal and Poland in 1582, by most of the German Roman Catholic states, Holland and Flanders in 1583, Hungary in 1587. The adoption in Switzerland began in 1584 and was not completed till 1812. The German and Dutch Protestant states generally, along with Denmark, adopted it in 1700, British dominions in 1752, Sweden in 1753, Japan in 1873, China in 1912, Bulgaria in 1915, Soviet Russia in 1918, Yugoslavia in 1919, Romania and Greece in 1924, Turkey in 1927. The rules for Easter have not, however, been adopted by those oriental churches that are not subject to the Papacy.

The difference between the two "Styles" will remain 13 days until A.D. 2100.

The Jewish Calendar

The Jewish Calendar from the institution of the Mosaic Law downward was a lunar one, consisting of 12 months. The cycles of religious feasts commencing with the Passover depended not only on the month but on the moon; the 14th of the month of Abid or Nisan was coincident with the full moon; and the new moons themselves were the occasions of regular festivals; the commencement of the month was generally determined by observations of the new moon, but 12 lunar months would make but 354 1/2 days, the years would be short 12 days of the true year and it was necessary that an additional month, Veader, be inserted about every third year.

The modern Jewish Calendar is based on fixed rules and not on observation. A common year may contain 353, 354 or 355 days and the leap year 383, 384 or 385 days. The intercalary month always contains 30 days and is inserted before the month Adar, the name and place of which it takes, Adar itself called second Adar or Veadar. Tishri 1 is the Jewish New Year and it cannot be a Sunday, Wednesday or Friday. Tishri 1 is not necessarily the day of new moon but is governed by a mean new moon which is calculated from the value of a mean lunation. It is complicated as compared with the Gregorian Calendar. The intercalary month is introduced seven times in every 19 years.

The identification of the Jewish months with our own cannot be effected with precision on account of the variations existing between the lunar and solar month.

The Muslim Calendar

The Muslim Calendar is called also the calendar of Hegira (i.e. Migration) and is attributed to the primary migration of Mohammed, the Prophet of Islam, on July 16, 622 A.D. from Mecca, his native city in the land of Hejaz, Arabia, to the city of Medina in the north of the same land. In Medina the Prophet and Founder of the Islamic Faith died and was buried.

Each year consists of 12 lunar months and, since no intercalation is made, the months go round the seasons in between 32 and 33 years.

Far Eastern Calendars

The ancient Chinese calendar is a lunar calendar, divided into 12 months of either 29 or 30 days. It is synchronized with the solar calendar by the addition of extra months as required. The four-day Chinese New Year (Hsin Nien) begins at the first new moon over China after the sun enters Aquarius, and may fall between January 21 and February 19. The calendar runs on a 60-year cycle, and each year has both a number and a name: 2022 (Tiger), 2023 (Rabbit), 2024 (Dragon), 2025 (Snake), 2026 (Horse), 2027 (Sheep), 2028 (Monkey), 2029 (Rooster), 2030 (Dog), and Pig (2031). The three-day Vietnamese New Year (Tet) and the three-to-four-day Korean festival Suhl are set by the same new moon. The Japanese calendar uses the Gregorian date of new year, but with a different epoch.

The Hindu Calendar

The Hindu calendar contains both lunar and solar elements, and is therefore complex. Each lunar month is divided into two halves: the dark half (full moon to new moon) and the bright half (new moon to full moon). For some Hindus (primarily South Indian), the lunar month begins on the day following the new moon; for others (primarily North Indian), it begins on the day following the full moon. Likewise, the calculation of the date of New Year varies. There are some holidays which are set by the solar calendar, as well as several which are set by the lunar calendar.

The Indian Calendar

Various religious groups in India have their own calendars (see The Muslim Calendar, and The Hindu Calendar, above). The Indian civil calendar sets the New Year on March 22 in a common year, and on March 21 in a leap year. The years are reckoned according to the native Saka historical era.

The Zoroastrian Calendar

The Zoroastrian calendar is solar, and consists of 12 months of 30 days; five additional days called "gatha" bring the total days in a year to 365. The calculation of the date of the New Year varies among the various Zoroastrian groups.

The Baha'i Calendar

The Baha'i calendar is astronomically fixed, commencing at the vernal equinox. The calendar is solar, and consists of 19 months of 19 days, with the addition of four or five days to bring the total to 365 or 366.

US Civil Calendar 2022

New Year's Day	Sat. Jan. 1
Martin Luther King Day	Mon. Jan. 17
Presidents' Day	Mon. Feb. 21
Memorial Day	Mon. May 30
Juneteenth	Mon. Jun. 20
Independence Day	Mon. July 4
Labor Day	Mon. Sept. 5
Columbus Day	Mon. Oct. 10
Veterans' Day	Fri. Nov. 11
Thanksgiving Day	Thu. Nov. 24
Christmas Day	Sun. Dec. 25

United Kingdom Civil Calendar 2022

St. David (Wales)	Tue. Mar. 1
Commonwealth Day	Mon. Mar. 14
St. Patrick (Ireland)	Thu. Mar. 17
St. George (England)	Mon. Apr. 25
Early May Bank Holiday	Mon. May 2
Spring Bank Holiday	Thu. Jun. 2
Birthday of Queen Elizabeth II	Sat. Jun. 11
Remembrance Sunday	Sun. Nov. 13
St. Andrew (Scotland)	Wed. Nov. 30

For Canadian holidays and festivals, please see page A-85.

THE SEASONS 2022

Eastern Standard Time
- Spring begins   March 20th   11 h 33 m
- Summer begins   June 21st   5 h 14 m
- Autumn begins   Sept. 22nd   21 h 04 m
- Winter begins   Dec. 21st   16 h 48 m

Eastern Standard Time applies in Ontario and Québec. Newfoundland time is 1 1/2 hours later than Eastern Standard time; in the Maritime Provinces, on Atlantic time, time is 1 hour later; in Manitoba and Saskatchewan, on Central time, time is 1 hour earlier; in Alberta and the western half of Saskatchewan, on Mountain time, time is 2 hours earlier; in B.C., on Pacific time, time is 3 hours earlie

STANDARD TIME

Owing to the great breadth of Canada the difference in solar time in various parts of the country is adjusted by the creation of Standard Time Zones, one hour in width, fixed between arbitrary lines running approximately north and south, 15° of longitude apart, the time observed in each zone being an exact, except for Newfoundland, number of hours slow from Greenwich. Example: When it is 8 a.m. by Pacific Time it is 12 noon by Atlantic Time and 4 p.m. at Greenwich.

There are six zones divided as follows, reckoning from Greenwich:
- *Newfoundland Standard Time:* Newfoundland, excluding most of Labrador, 3 1/2 hours slow.

- *Atlantic Standard Time/60th Meridian Time:* most of Labrador, New Brunswick, Nova Scotia, Prince Edward Island, and those parts of Québec and Northwest Territories east of the 63rd Meridian, 4 hours slow.
- *Eastern Standard Time/75th Meridian Time:* Québec west of the 63rd Meridian and Ontario as far west as the 90th Meridian; Northwest Territories between the 68th and 85th Meridian, 5 hours slow.
- *Central Standard Time/90th Meridian Time:* Ontario west of the 90th Meridian, Manitoba, Saskatchewan and Northwest Territories between the 85th and 102nd Meridian, 6 hours slow.

- *Mountain Standard Time/105th Meridian Time:* Throughout Alberta and in Northwest Territories west of the 102nd Meridian, 7 hours slow.
- *Pacific Standard Time/120th Meridian Time:* Throughout most of British Columbia and in the Yukon, 8 hours slow.

Solar time around the globe varies four minutes with each degree of longitude.

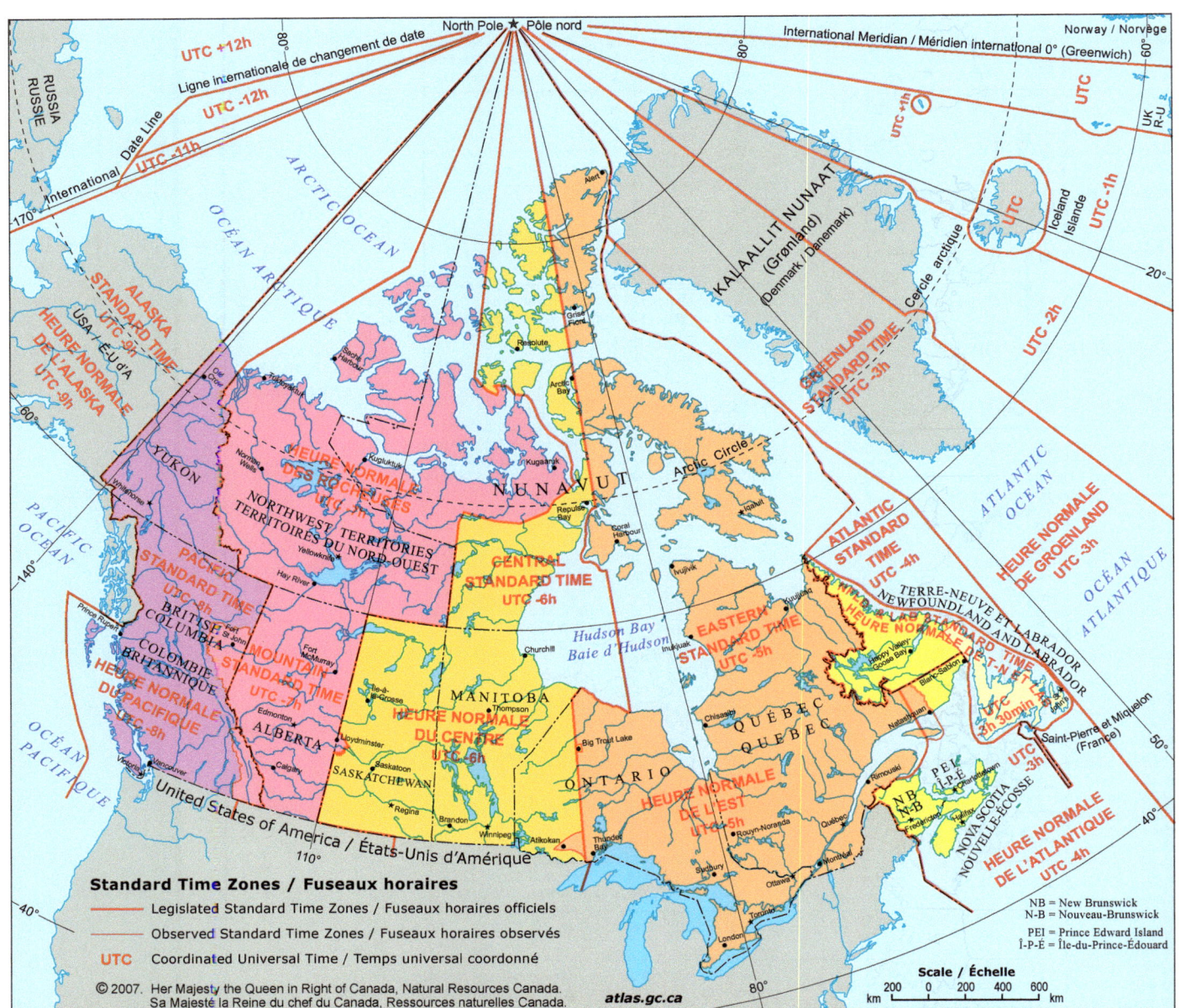

Standard Time Zones / Fuseaux horaires
- Legislated Standard Time Zones / Fuseaux horaires officiels
- Observed Standard Time Zones / Fuseaux horaires observés
- **UTC** Coordinated Universal Time / Temps universel coordonné

NB = New Brunswick
N-B = Nouveau-Brunswick
PEI = Prince Edward Island
Î-P-É = Île-du-Prince-Édouard

Scale / Échelle

© 2007. Her Majesty the Queen in Right of Canada, Natural Resources Canada.
Sa Majesté la Reine du chef du Canada, Ressources naturelles Canada.

atlas.gc.ca

Reproduced with the permission of Natural Resources Canada.

WORLD MAP OF TIME ZONES

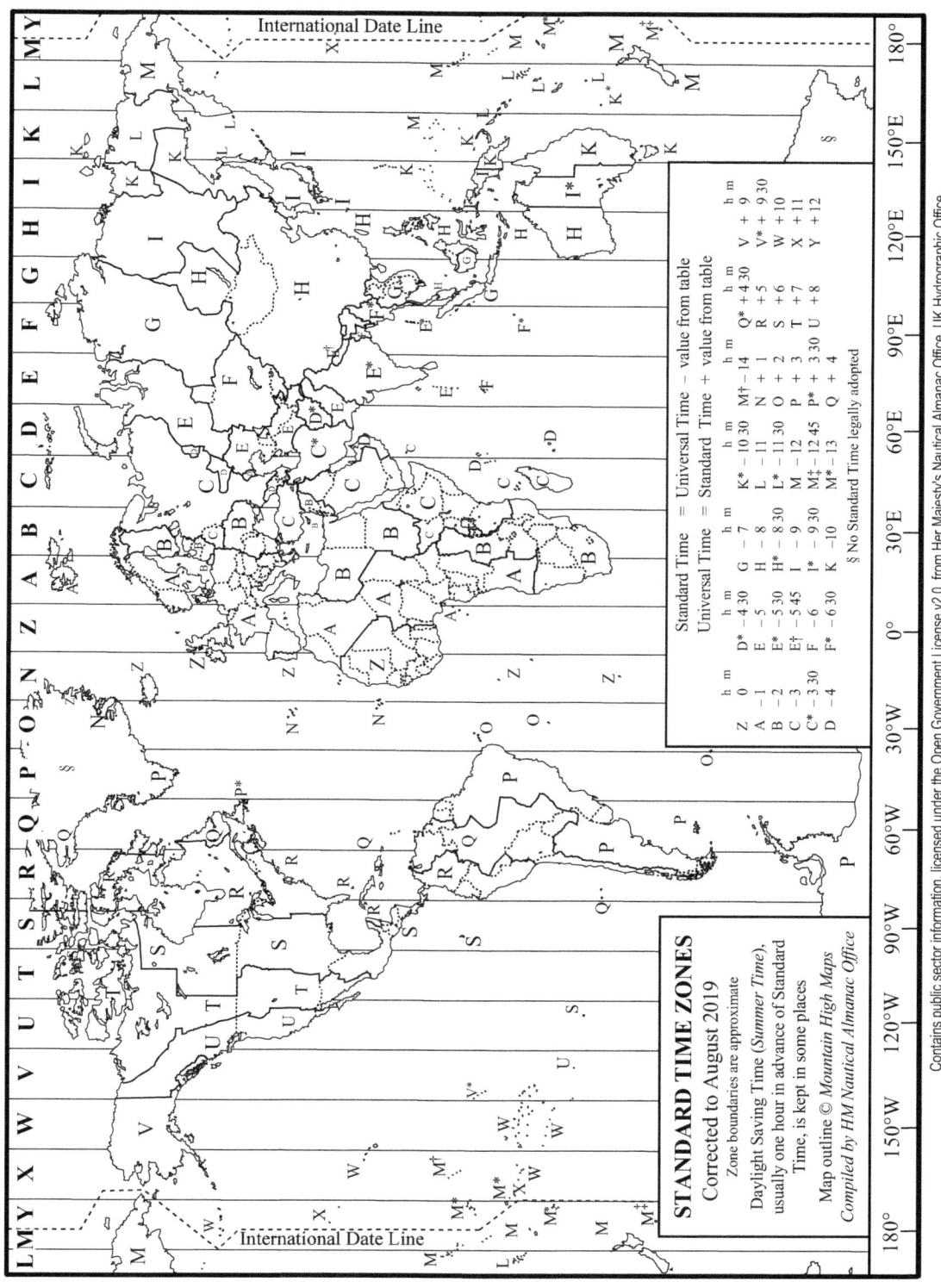

Economics & Finance

Canada's Economy

Since World War II, the growth of Canada's manufacturing, mining and service sectors has transformed the economy of the world's second-largest nation from a largely rural model into one that is primarily industrial and urban. This transformation has been so progressive that Canada has long enjoyed top-level economic status within the G-7, the international grouping of seven leading industrial countries that also includes the United States, the United Kingdom, France, Germany, Italy and Japan.

The 1989 U.S.-Canada Free Trade Agreement and the 1994 North American Free Trade Agreement (which also includes Mexico) spurred a dramatic increase in trade and economic integration of the North American continent. Given its significant natural resources, skilled labor force and modern plants, Canada has benefited tremendously from the free-trade initiatives. As of 2013, some 75.8 percent of Canadian exports are absorbed by Canada's principal trading partner, making it the largest foreign supplier of energy, including oil, gas, uranium and electric power, to the U.S. In 2017, efforts began to revise NAFTA, led by U.S. President Donald Trump. In June 2018, the U.S. imposed tariffs on selected Canadian steel and aluminum products, in the range of 25% and 10% respectively. Canada retaliated by imposing similar tariff rates on a range of U.S. goods. The matter continued to escalate while negotiations took place to construct a new agreement, until September 30, 2018, when the United States-Mexico-Canada Agreement (USMCA) was formally announced.

In general, Canada's overall economy is steady. After the 2008 recession, the economy returned to growth in the third quarter of 2009. Canada is the only G-7 country to have nearly recouped the loss incurred in the recession. The government succeeded in returning to a budgetary surplus by 2015. Canada posted a 5.8 percent unemployment rate in July 2018, down from 6.3 percent in July 2017.

However, like any other allied country from World War II, Canada is now seeing the baby-boom generation pass into retirement, causing the working-age proportion of its population to diminish. As well, there is continuing public debate regarding the rising cost of Canada's world-famous and well-regarded, publicly funded healthcare system.

In the last few decades, Canada's economic model has moved away from being natural-resource dependant to being service-based. While the production of goods remains significant, accounting for a third of the national economy, three out of four citizens are currently employed in service industries. Maintaining the transportation and storage of goods, along with servicing restaurants, shops, entertainment, healthcare, education, defense and government now occupies more Canadians than the actual manufacturing of materials. Canada's gross domestic product, being the balance between consumers' expenditures and income, has shown healthy progress, illustrating a growing demand for big-ticket items including houses, cars, furniture and electronics.

In 2007, the Canadian dollar had reached a 31-year high against the American dollar, achieving one-to-one parity with its neighbour's currency. Later that same year, Bloomberg reported that the dollar was approaching $1.10 U.S., the currency's all-time high since the information-service company began monitoring it in February 1971 (the Bank of Canada only let the currency float in 1970). The Canadian dollar continues to be strong, staying near parity with the U.S., although by July 2015 the dollar sank to $0.76 U.S. — the lowest level since September 2004 — largely due to weaking oil prices. This trend continued into the following years, with the dollar hovering around $0.76 U.S. by the middle of 2016, and a slight gain to $0.80 by August 2017.It continued to hover around that range into 2018, resting at $0.77 by August 2018. August 2019 saw the dollar still in that area, at $0.76. By the summer of 2021, after more than a year dealing with the global COVID-19 pandemic, the Canadian dollar stood at $0.81.

In May 2012, the Royal Canadian Mint halted production of the one-cent piece, with distribution of the penny ending in February 2013. Canadian consumer outlets no longer return pennies with change.

As a major international oil exporter, Canada has benefited from soaring crude prices, although the recent downturn in oil prices, which began in the summer of 2014, had a major impact on the oil industry, including the loss of 35,000 energy industry jobs in Alberta alone by October 2015. In September 2015, Goldman Sachs downgraded its oil forecast, predicting that prices could reach as low as $20 per barrel. Oil sands production was projected in 2008 to expand to reach close to 3.4 million barrels per day by 2017. Indeed, in 2017 the Alberta government forecast that oilsands output would rise from 2.5 million barrels per day in the 2016-17 fiscal year to 3.3 million barrels per day in 2019-20. Data accessed in 2021 showed that this figure was closer to 2.95 million barrels per day in 2019.

The country has profited from the export of nickel, copper, aluminum and zinc, commodities that all sit at or near record highs. Though mineral prices declined from 2012 to 2013, minerals and metals continue to be a major contributor to Canada's economy, with a total value of $40.8 billion in 2017. With commodities and goods-producing industries accounting for approximately 30 percent of Canada's exports, the loonie is finally being viewed around the world as a commodity-based currency and has been bid up accordingly.

Following the recession in 2008, the American housing market saw a decline in lumber prices, hurting British Columbia's forestry industry. However, strong domestic housing starts have boosted the overall production of lumber and other timber products, increasing forestry exports despite U.S. softwood lumber tariffs. The United States is still the largest importer of Canadian lumber, although it took until at least 2015 for softwood lumber levels to return to what they were pre-recession.

In May 2003, the discovery of Bovine Spongiform Encephalopathy (BSE), commonly known as mad-cow disease, in one cow from Alberta caused severe harm to Canada's beef-export market. Compounded by the advent of Severe Acute Respiratory Syndrome (SARS) in the late summer of that same year, Canada's growth forecast dampened from 3.4 percent to 2.3 percent. However, by September 2007, the U.S. Department of Agriculture (USDA) agreed to expand cattle trade with Canada, additionally urging beef-importing nations to eliminate unnecessary barriers erected after the mad-cow scare. By 2016, the U.S. was responsible for 75 percent of all Canadian beef exports. Mainland China & Hong Kong, Japan, Mexico and South Korea were the next-largest importers.

Canada's commercial ocean fisheries have experienced overall production decline, due in part to the 2003 closure of northern cod fishing grounds. The volume of production has been adversely affected by an average rate of 4 percent a year as a result of dwindling resources and problems caused by over-exploitation of some major species. West Coast over-fishing has led to a reduction in the size of the salmon fleet, as well as extensive government intervention in the fishing industry on both coasts. Meanwhile aquaculture, or fish farming, continues to thrive. In particular, Eastern Canada boasts extensive operations, growing predominantly Atlantic salmon and mussels. Other key species include bay and sea scallops, brook trout, oysters, bay quahogs, sea urchins, arctic char, haddock and bar clams, and significant progress has been made in the development of new species such as halibut, sturgeon, abalone and cod. That said, every province in Canada, including the Yukon, runs commercial freshwater aquaculture operations, mostly raising Atlantic salmon,trout, mussels, oysters and clams. British Columbia accounted for 49 percent of total production volume across the country in 2013, followed by Newfoundland and Labrador and Prince Edward Island. As the Canadian freshwater aquaculture industry is young, it is also ideally poised for growth.

Always historically strong, the Canadian stock market has continued to thrive. The Toronto Stock Exchange (TSX) is the country's largest and the world's eighth largest by market capitalization. In addition, the TSX Group is the international leader in the oil and gas sector, boasting more oil and gas sector listings on the Toronto Stock Exchange and TSX Venture Exchange than any other exchange in the world. In 2021, 246 oil and gas companies were listed, with a quoted market value of over $560 billion.

Sourcing from China continues to offer an economically viable solution for Canadian companies. This option to reduce costs while growing wealth in major Chinese cities creates vast new opportunities for Canadian firms, particularly exporters of services. With a small domestic market, the steady expansion of multilateral trade is critical to the structure of the country's economy and the continued prosperity of its citizens. The rapid and ongoing industrialization of China has boosted the world price of Canadian oil, gas, mineral, metal and farm-product exports. Canadian exports to China in 2017 accounted for 4.1 percent of our total, slightly down from 4.4 percent in 2013. However, Canadian sales to Japan have lagged. In 1996, Japan received 4.1 percent of Canada's exports, but only 2.33 percent in 2017.

Since the early 1990s, the focus of Canadian monetary policy on low, stable and predictable inflation has helped to both anchor inflation expectations and reduce the ups and downs in economic activity. Canadians have been able to make spending, saving and investment decisions with greater certainty, knowing that their central bank will hold the line on future inflation and that the economy will be more stable. Low interest rates and greater confidence about the future have encouraged Canadian firms to undertake important restructuring initiatives, stepping up to meet the challenges of sweeping worldwide technological change and intensely competitive global markets.

GROSS DOMESTIC PRODUCT RANKING TABLE 2020

		Economy	$US dollars (millions)
USA	1	United States	20,936,600
CHN	2	China	14,722,731
JPN	3	Japan	5,064,873
DEU	4	Germany	3,806,060
GBR	5	United Kingdom	2,707,744
IND	6	India	2,622,984
FRA	7	France	2,603,004
ITA	8	Italy	1,886,445
CAN	9	Canada	1,643,408
KOR	10	Korea, Rep.	1,630,525
RUS	11	Russian Federation	1,483,498*
BRA	12	Brazil	1,444,733
AUS	13	Australia	1,330,901
ESP	14	Spain	1,281,199
MEX	15	Mexico	1,076,163
IDN	16	Indonesia	1,058,424
NLD	17	Netherlands	912,242
CHE	18	Switzerland	747,969
TUR	19	Turkey	720,101
SAU	20	Saudi Arabia	700,118

*Based on data from official statistics of Ukraine and Russian Federation; by relying on these data, the World Bank does not intend to make any judgment on the legal or other status of the territories concerned or to prejudice the final determination of the parties' claims.

Source: World Development Indicators, The World Bank. "Gross domestic product ranking table," 2021. https://datacatalog.worldbank.org/dataset/gdp-ranking.

YEARLY AVERAGE OF EXCHANGE RATES

Country Pays	Present Value in CAN Currency						
	2020	2019	2018	2017	2016	2015	2014
United States (dollar)	1.3415	1.3269	1.2957	1.2986	1.3248064	1.27871080	1.10446640
European (euro)	1.5298	1.4856	1.5302	1.4650	1.466	1.4182	1.4671
China (renminbi/yuan)	0.1944	0.1922	0.1961	0.1921	0.1995	0.2034	0.1793
United Kingdom (British pound)	1.7199	1.6945	1.7299	1.6720	1.7962116	1.95398400	1.81903120
Switzerland (franc)	1.4294	1.3352	1.3246	1.3189	1.345	1.3286	1.2078
Hong Kong (dollar)	0.1730	0.1693	0.1653	0.1667	0.170665	0.164940	0.142425
Japan (yen)	0.01257	0.01217	0.01174	0.01158	0.01221	0.01056	0.01046
Australia (dollar)	0.9247	0.9228	0.9687	0.9951	0.9852	0.9604	0.9963
New Zealand (dollar)	0.8712	0.8747	0.8973	0.9229	0.9233	0.8933	0.9170
Mexico (peso)	0.06267	0.06894	0.06744	0.06884	0.0711	0.08063	0.08304
South Korea (won)	0.001137	0.001139	0.001178	0.001149	0.001142	0.001129	0.001049
Taiwan (new dollar)	0.04553	0.04294	0.04299	0.04269	0.04109	0.04025	0.03644

Note: All Bank of Canada exchange rates are indicative rates only, obtained from averages of transaction prices and price quotes from financial institutions. The annual average exchange rates are published by 12:30 ET on the last business day of the year. Exchange rates are expressed as 1 unit of the foreign currency converted into Canadian dollars.

Source: Bank of Canada

PRINCIPAL TRADING PARTNERS IN 2020

Imports ($ millions)		Exports ($ millions)	
United States	349,323.5	United States	375,861.5
European Union	60,370.3	European Union	50,092.2
China	49,551.1	China	26,302.8
Mexico	16,930.1	United Kingdom	21,413.8
Switzerland	10,268.7	Japan	12,613.4
Japan	10,010.9	Mexico	6,979.1
United Kingdom	9,402.2	Switzerland	4,897.7
South Korea	7,519	South Korea	4,839.1
Brazil	5,823	India	3,802.8
Hong Kong	4,148.9	Norway	2,609.2
Other Countries	38,004.8	Other Countries	14,426.4
All Countries	561,352.5	All Countries	523,838.5

Source: Statistics Canada. *Table 12-10-0011-01 - International merchandise trade for all countries and by Principal Trading Partners (x 1,000,000)*. Accessed July 5, 2021.

IMPORTS AND EXPORTS FOR CANADA, 2020

Country	EXPORTS ($)	IMPORTS ($)
Afghanistan	13,880,562	5,327,513
Albania	48,435,562	10,142,671
Algeria	616,278,945	41,883,319
American Samoa	1,972,888	694,469
Andorra	752,309	151,643
Angola	141,418,733	51,737
Anguilla	970,347	2,541,531
Antarctica	132,477	68,106
Antigua and Barbuda	9,822,762	144,582
Argentina	241,442,841	695,806,829
Armenia	8,622,686	16,627,110
Aruba	4,204,321	137,414
Australia	2,135,259,558	2,360,127,861
Austria	184,827,820	1,923,435,943
Azerbaijan	7,812,450	883,615
Bahamas	151,267,287	8,021,092
Bahrain	134,151,689	30,436,479
Bangladesh	1,187,587,064	1,579,781,636
Barbados	48,031,778	15,483,681
Belarus (formerly Byelorussia)	15,188,215	23,307,745
Belgium	2,731,450,666	4,353,614,039
Belize	5,858,113	1,629,266
Benin	24,717,576	595,473
Bermuda	70,468,922	515,378
Bhutan	158,222	224,657
Bolivia	16,327,814	256,342,430
Bonaire, Sint Eustatius & Saba	78,760,523	15,854
Bosnia-Hercegovina	4,419,753	12,815,425
Botswana	337,418,928	8,215,156
Bouvet Island	44,092	942
Brazil	2,143,007,315	6,573,840,434
British Indian Ocean Territories	112,974	54,152
British Virgin Islands	4,825,598	902,270
Brunei Darussalam	9,239,360	1,849,885
Bulgaria	245,968,646	318,086,709
Burkina Faso	51,235,040	46,287,437
Burundi	865,988	565,332
Cambodia (Kampuchea)	31,428,950	1,511,096,998
Cameroon	78,314,885	12,791,527
Cape Verde	2,193,520	423,918
Cayman Islands	86,279,155	3,944,597
Central African Republic	209,464	195,632
Chad	9,168,840	136,910
Chile	979,431,289	1,619,884,659
China	25,212,233,296	76,509,045,313
Christmas Island	627,933	453,572
Cocos (Keeling) Islands	257,932	117,422
Colombia	790,954,963	848,782,268
Comoros	1,694,213	800,772
Congo (formerly Brazzaville)	12,590,591	2,893,667
Congo (formerly Zaire)	21,358,158	142,811,290
Cook Islands	5,849	61,930
Costa Rica	159,626,701	568,705,996
Côte-d'Ivoire	65,436,256	337,878,205
Croatia	30,335,473	131,052,422
Cuba	265,122,822	587,578,884
Curacao	12,957,899	666,279
Cyprus	11,372,321	3,333,577
Czech Republic	215,794,330	684,510,395
Denmark	296,320,472	1,385,436,620
Djibouti	5,328,124	479,362
Dominica	3,796,733	305,408
Dominican Republic	252,770,993	671,559,947
Ecuador	394,415,306	242,529,701
Egypt	711,471,177	1,274,628,345
El Salvador	55,026,730	77,553,916
Equatorial Guinea	3,104,509	3,978,077
Eritrea	785,544	40,023
Estonia	25,680,139	116,225,755
Ethiopia	169,728,009	46,998,880
Faeroe Islands	533,924	5,024,828
Falkland Islands	113,313	97,272
Fiji	4,702,757	6,470,325
Finland	662,326,985	999,222,679
France (incl. Monaco, French Antilles)	3,709,336,051	6,475,350,464
French Polynesia	10,206,681	1,032,310
French Southern Territories	13,754	1,182
Gabon	17,461,328	1,006,053
Gambia	3,274,953	262,303
Georgia	29,679,922	21,727,740
Germany	6,368,474,644	17,307,630,115
Ghana	280,623,570	104,884,290
Gibraltar	361,385	6,878
Greece	121,645,207	303,381,617
Greenland	7,169,426	3,012,339
Grenada	7,723,904	1,618,769
Guam	2,362,962	146,155
Guatemala	125,184,214	659,742,147
Guinea	24,396,001	61,247,449
Guinea-Bissau	296,309	25,492
Guyana	29,421,889	417,654,567
Haiti	96,291,361	73,284,175
Heard and McDonald Island	88,779	3,646
Honduras	37,989,404	384,990,091
Hong Kong	1,903,191,405	572,033,958
Hungary	63,326,163	847,361,948
Iceland	68,186,170	83,715,752
India	3,686,249,566	4,970,140,237
Indonesia	1,782,875,696	1,614,569,366
Iran	412,988,086	34,054,251
Iraq	87,817,528	496,017
Ireland	672,340,606	3,199,281,780
Israel	359,919,152	1,253,072,367
Italy (incl. Vatican City State)	3,691,911,935	9,003,642,629
Jamaica	122,176,863	84,906,567
Japan	12,373,150,689	13,534,646,534
Jordan	85,695,221	114,045,224
Kazakhstan	75,948,170	401,075,218
Kenya	102,452,519	29,172,463
Kiribati	443,358	886,003
Korea, North	--	117,897
Korea, South	4,693,131,970	9,569,730,168
Kuwait	96,387,759	277,09
Kyrgyzstan	9,226,117	626,071
Laos	2,554,912	30,266,403
Latvia	158,679,363	61,157,238
Lebanon	70,965,830	38,839,570
Lesotho	150,884	9,001,162
Liberia	5,296,198	24,479,443
Libya	51,569,389	61,611
Lithuania	87,124,420	209,158,347
Luxembourg	123,957,574	171,661,722
Macau (Macao)	55,565,496	16,218,591
Macedonia	5,250,949	17,291,384
Madagascar	11,270,899	118,026,615
Malawi	6,999,613	795,123
Malaysia	768,486,900	3,051,650,235
Maldives	13,310,268	2,630,087
Mali	36,172,350	3,139,102
Malta	273,584,465	33,248,312
Mauritania	28,811,541	776,254,632
Mauritius	7,108,271	11,004,191
Mexico	6,136,024,067	29,882,437,235
Moldova	4,185,772	15,937,105
Mongolia	18,528,824	1,395,601
Montenegro	3,800,425	4,816,981
Montserrat	405,721	167,493
Morocco	609,123,492	389,887,299
Mozambique	86,579,932	32,045,983
Myanmar (Burma)	53,004,025	174,914,150
Namibia	6,570,908	136,840,023
Nauru	39,270	66,636
Nepal	144,493,668	11,027,462
Netherlands	5,410,031,273	3,211,423,685
New Caledonia	23,894,004	356,000
New Zealand	378,425,154	815,077,022
Nicaragua	51,957,070	125,464,565
Niger	10,230,242	168,708,369
Nigeria	716,045,131	657,014,289
Niue	29,475	63,604
Norfolk Island	66,251	220,401
Norway	2,536,651,591	1,177,109,882
Oman (formerly Muscat and Oman)	97,435,495	48,073,562
Pakistan	668,711,889	437,854,922
Panama	129,040,992	15,353,361
Papua New Guinea	14,744,472	6,717,054
Paraguay	15,246,090	10,463,712
Peru	871,732,752	3,664,050,144
Philippines	893,520,467	1,188,295,535
Pitcairn Island	164,754	300,896
Poland	543,171,395	2,053,347,660
Portugal	194,781,616	596,327,707
Qatar	113,485,250	82,676,263
Re-Imports (Canada)	1,357,290	4,011,846,359
Romania	154,728,727	435,170,880
Russia	617,865,431	1,195,540,213
Rwanda	3,127,034	2,380,012
Saint Helena	402,387	97,078
Saint Kitts and Nevis	6,076,956	2,452,138
Saint Lucia	14,098,201	1,008,141
Saint Pierre-Miquelon	17,781,511	6,280,513
Saint Vincent and the Grenadines	12,504,301	113,825
Samoa (Western)	585,266	149,691
Sao Tomé-Principe	33,400	334,550
Saudi Arabia	1,558,686,696	1,675,423,856
Senegal	102,640,378	6,842,305
Serbia	29,372,950	77,846,590
Seychelles	2,444,264	1,101,225
Sierra Leone	8,740,756	3,519,928
Singapore	1,235,559,420	1,179,210,855
Sint Maarten	3,981,452	104,84
Slovakia	34,877,706	660,932,831
Slovenia	104,371,110	237,064,361
Solomon Islands	23,151	192,274
Somalia	3,270,291	432,061
South Africa	312,887,570	1,909,295,843
South Sudan	1,286,474	3,430
Spain	1,409,724,101	3,094,810,797
Sri Lanka	236,924,751	373,598,213
Sudan	70,981,221	699,660
Suriname	22,589,491	16,678,599
Swaziland	1,738,410	5,005,397
Sweden	410,305,395	2,101,007,068
Switzerland	1,798,473,751	5,883,204,229
Syria	38,832,934	3,501,019
Taiwan	1,781,208,391	5,630,177,046
Tajikistan	3,123,857	102,146
Tanzania	36,271,762	37,929,594
Thailand	797,960,062	3,535,105,089
Timor-Leste	150,976	6,455,056
Togo	30,113,020	1,895,785
Tonga	14,850	47,489
Trinidad and Tobago	220,264,664	305,094,916
Tunisia	154,245,600	154,245,600
Turkey	1,125,598,306	1,881,151,217
Turkmenistan	5,364,258	12,460,017
Turks and Caicos Islands	3,491,067	86,215
U.S. Minor Outlying Islands	8,986,451	2,115,676
Uganda	32,406,859	14,767,780
Ukraine	160,473,083	143,993,371
United Arab Emirates	1,769,144,934	249,624,738
United Kingdom	19,910,200,198	7,839,568,045
United States	383,315,240,047	264,362,707,968
Uruguay	65,459,522	117,270,579
Uzbekistan	14,167,483	143,086,135
Vanuatu (New Hebrides)	217,673	44,266
Venezuela	73,538,382	13,083,682
Vietnam	735,182,100	8,162,866,374
Wallis and Futuna Islands	10,375	5,321
Western Sahara	34,142	--
Yemen	8,502,519	675,057
Zambia (Zambi)	10,633,083	107,302,621
Zimbabwe	3,293,029	8,504,592
TOTAL	542,316,171,346	522,331,636,371

Data Source: Statistics Canada & US Census Bureau

Source: "Trade Data Online," retrieved on Industry Canada's website: http://www.ic.gc.ca, Last accessed July 29, 2021. Trade data is subject to revision. Reproduced with the permission of the Minister of Industry, 2021.

RETAIL TRADE, TOTAL SALES AND E-COMMERCE SALES, BY NORTH AMERICAN INDUSTRY CLASSIFICATION SYSTEM (NAICS)

North American Industry Classification System (NAICS)	Sales	2018	2019
Retail trade [44-45]	Total sales (x 1,000)	654,406,918	670,569,328
	E-commerce sales (x 1,000)	22,237,979	28,052,613
	E-commerce as percentage of total sales (percent)	3.4	4.2
	Distribution of E-commerce (percent)	100	100
Motor vehicle and parts dealers [441]	Total sales (x 1,000)	169,953,600	173,557,916
	E-commerce sales (x 1,000)	647,815	846,661
	E-commerce as percentage of total sales (percent)	0.4	0.5
	Distribution of E-commerce (percent)	2.9	3
Furniture and home furnishings stores [442]	Total sales (x 1,000)	19,234,685	19,323,950
	E-commerce sales (x 1,000)	414,656	537,405
	E-commerce as percentage of total sales (percent)	2.2	2.8
	Distribution of E-commerce (percent)	1.9	1.9
Electronics and appliance stores [443]	Total sales (x 1,000)	13,837,459	13,656,482
	E-commerce sales (x 1,000)	1,094,416	1,238,236
	E-commerce as percentage of total sales (percent)	7.9	9.1
	Distribution of E-commerce (percent)	4.9	4.4
Building material and garden equipment and supplies dealers [444]	Total sales (x 1,000)	38,675,378	38,799,718
	E-commerce sales (x 1,000)	516,543	671,495
	E-commerce as percentage of total sales (percent)	1.3	1.7
	Distribution of E-commerce (percent)	2.3	2.4
Food and beverage stores [445]	Total sales (x 1,000)	127,415,941	131,470,445
	E-commerce sales (x 1,000)	629,867	812,193
	E-commerce as percentage of total sales (percent)	0.5	0.6
	Distribution of E-commerce (percent)	2.8	2.9
Health and personal care stores [446]	Total sales (x 1,000)	51,164,630	53,721,041
	E-commerce sales (x 1,000)	735,677	963,974
	E-commerce as percentage of total sales (percent)	1.4	1.8
	Distribution of E-commerce (percent)	3.3	3.4
Gasoline stations [447]	Total sales (x 1,000)	68,728,295	65,008,279
	E-commerce sales (x 1,000)	x	x
	E-commerce as percentage of total sales (percent)	x	x
	Distribution of E-commerce (percent)	x	x
Clothing and clothing accessories stores [448]	Total sales (x 1,000)	35,998,455	36,268,458
	E-commerce sales (x 1,000)	1,595,115	1,850,676
	E-commerce as percentage of total sales (percent)	4.4	5.1
	Distribution of E-commerce (percent)	7.2	6.6
Sporting goods, hobby, book and music stores [451]	Total sales (x 1,000)	13,064,700	12,910,821
	E-commerce sales (x 1,000)	416,010	530,451
	E-commerce as percentage of total sales (percent)	3.2	4.1
	Distribution of E-commerce (percent)	1.9	1.9
General merchandise stores [452]	Total sales (x 1,000)	69,663,061	73,249,950
	E-commerce sales (x 1,000)	278,106	549,368
	E-commerce as percentage of total sales (percent)	0.4	0.7
	Distribution of E-commerce (percent)	1.3	2.0
Miscellaneous store retailers [453]	Total sales (x 1,000)	16,548,130	18,730,270
	E-commerce sales (x 1,000)	1,011,489	1,200,899
	E-commerce as percentage of total sales (percent)	6.1	6.4
	Distribution of E-commerce (percent)	4.5	4.3
Non-store retailers [454]	Total sales (x 1,000)	30,122,583	33,871,998
	E-commerce sales (x 1,000)	14,898,285	18,851,255

	E-commerce as percentage of total sales (percent)	49.5	55.7
	Distribution of E-commerce (percent)	67	67.2
Electronic shopping and mail-order houses [45411]	Total sales (x 1,000)	15,467,471	19,180,953
	E-commerce sales (x 1,000)	13,913,786	17,582,241
	E-commerce as percentage of total sales (percent)	90	91.7
	Distribution of E-commerce (percent)	62.6	62.7

Symbol legend:
x Suppressed to meet the confidentiality requirements of the Statistics Act

Notes:
1. Estimates for the most recent year are preliminary. Preliminary data are subject to revision. Due to rounding, components may not add to total. Scaling may also affect the calculation of ratios.
2. With the release of preliminary estimates, revisions have been made to the previous two years. As a result, caution should be exercised when comparing these data with estimates earlier than the previous two years.

Source: Statistics Canada. *Table 20-10-0065-01 - Retail trade, total sales and e-commerce sales.* Accessed July 5, 2021.

SUPPLY AND DISPOSITION OF REFINED PETROLEUM PRODUCTS
MONTHLY (CUBIC METRES)

Supply and disposition	2018				
	January	February	March	April	May
Net production [1]	10,149,423	9,046,912	9,865,346	7,234,985	7,418,703
Opening Inventory	7,755,263	8,213,213	8,357,529	8,850,120	8,464,361
Closing Inventory	8,213,213	8,357,529	8,850,120	8,464,361	7,328,453
Imports	1,448,729	1,157,752	1,350,393	2,015,796	2,094,022
Exports	2,446,488	2,189,890	2,442,225	2,214,663	2,216,774
Inter-provincial transfers in	2,141,033	1,925,096	2,081,255	1,732,102	2,108,606
Inter-provincial transfers out	2,141,033	1,925,096	2,081,255	1,732,102	2,108,606
Domestic sales[2]	8,466,448	7,915,405	8,519,573	8,222,494	9,400,264

Total refined petroleum products

Notes:
1. Refinery production less inter-product transfers, less the portion of inter-product transfers transferred to petro-chemical feedstocks.
2. Sales by reporting companies, exclusive of exports and sales to other reporting companies, and adjusted for exports and imports by non-reporting companies.

Source: Statistics Canada. *Table 25-10-0044-01 Supply and disposition of refined petroleum products, monthly.* Accessed July 5, 2021.

MANUFACTURERS' SALES, INVENTORIES, ORDERS AND INVENTORY TO SALES RATIOS, BY INDUSTRY
ANNUAL (DOLLARS)

North American Industry Classification System (NAICS)	2016	2017	2018	2019	2020
Manufacturing [31-33]	615,261,591	651,079,681	686,212,785	689,343,893	611,268,611
Food manufacturing [311]	96,531,189	100,104,106	103,601,054	106,368,176	110,039,435
Beverage and tobacco product manufacturing [312]	13,256,972	13,823,629	13,988,565	14,602,631	15,461,722
Textile mills [313]	1,691,531	1,759,913	1,921,598	1,910,041	1,697,740
Textile product mills [314]	1,661,528	1,659,467	1,643,854	1,502,810	1,375,598
Clothing manufacturing [315]	2,276,662	2,431,512	2,788,186	3,076,804	2,456,950
Leather and allied product manufacturing [316]	430,357	365,540	339,992	347,303	267,278
Paper manufacturing [322]	26,140,675	27,658,014	30,568,251	28,228,545	26,988,053
Printing and related support activities [323]	9,171,230	9,344,528	9,480,845	9,207,466	7,780,217
Petroleum and coal product manufacturing [324]	51,716,715	64,180,066	74,221,025	73,653,992	46,356,361
Chemical manufacturing [325]	50,867,613	53,440,288	56,227,080	53,765,721	50,621,111
Plastics and rubber products manufacturing [326]	28,168,595	28,910,456	32,253,656	33,071,061	30,345,783
Wood product manufacturing [321]	29,692,142	32,379,644	34,584,822	29,396,802	34,015,016
Non-metallic mineral product manufacturing [327]	12,860,208	13,759,040	14,588,510	15,233,180	14,707,812
Primary metal manufacturing [331]	44,889,495	49,569,967	51,987,455	49,974,399	44,274,781
Fabricated metal product manufacturing [332]	33,111,832	35,184,326	39,020,178	41,570,922	37,882,716
Machinery manufacturing [333]	32,733,687	37,789,241	40,803,994	42,118,890	37,357,183
Computer and electronic product manufacturing [334]	13,921,236	14,933,779	14,947,551	15,223,065	13,294,640
Electrical equipment, appliance and component manufacturing [335]	10,046,682	11,033,287	11,225,400	11,299,221	10,093,518
Transportation equipment manufacturing [336]	131,140,185	128,071,332	127,213,834	133,228,092	101,624,015
Furniture and related product manufacturing [337]	12,175,362	12,766,278	12,698,852	12,926,627	11,316,391
Miscellaneous manufacturing [339]	12,777,698	11,915,272	12,108,085	12,638,149	13,312,291

Note: North American Industry Classification System (NAICS) 2012.

Source: Statistics Canada. *Table 16-10-0047-01 - Manufacturers' sales, inventories, orders and inventory to sales ratios, by industry (dollars unless otherwise noted) (x 1,000).* Accessed July 5, 2021.

GROWTH STATISTICS: FINANCIAL, CONSOLIDATED GOVERNMENT
QUARTERLY (DOLLARS X 1,000,000)

		Revenue	Total expenditure	Net worth	Net financial worth
2007	Q1	155,883	152,225	-6,846	-646,859
	Q2	162,444	149,513	31,804	-617,588
	Q3	159,565	151,447	87,618	-617,967
	Q4	159,399	154,515	63,073	-635,277
2008	Q1	166,485	164,757	98,937	-649,539
	Q2	162,882	157,700	239,669	-649,539
	Q3	162,340	155,805	315,941	-657,013
	Q4	154,890	164,262	-15,563	-692,835
2009	Q1	159,198	171,549	-102,013	-715,786
	Q2	152,711	166,079	-38,496	-710,504
	Q3	153,076	169,419	19,915	-735,748
	Q4	157,314	175,238	-6,834	-756,738
2010	Q1	162,156	181,941	34,673	-762,520
	Q2	161,925	174,149	-14,647	-792,571
	Q3	155,984	178,215	-6,000	-813,489
	Q4	159,489	183,161	-22,296	-830,822
2011	Q1	169,979	189,953	24,675	-827,064
	Q2	171,807	180,322	11,703	-864,952
	Q3	167,902	182,348	-32,944	-917,423
	Q4	170,239	184,948	-39,882	-937,795
2012	Q1	179,062	192,055	-91,926	-936,371
	Q2	176,278	182,114	-139,908	-977,968
	Q3	172,810	184,949	-59,377	-961,958
	Q4	174,557	188,686	-150,378	-977,748
2013	Q1	183,632	195,759	-94,328	-968,605
	Q2	182,269	184,259	-73,747	-941,570
	Q3	182,882	188,511	19,867	-925,416
	Q4	183,779	191,623	17,777	-918,019
2014	Q1	197,283	195,423	60,516	-916,484
	Q2	191,808	182,937	87,359	-922,654
	Q3	190,228	191,846	116,842	-915,327
	Q4	190,646	195,246	-8,934	-939,593
2015	Q1	201,340	201,977	-98,716	-957,349
	Q2	199,951	193,068	1,790	-919,156
	Q3	195,580	200,215	-39,734	-920,462
	Q4	199,499	201,283	-71,796	-921,254
2016	Q1	209,917	209,257	-75,194	-934,041
	Q2	202,232	199,593	-81,513	-950,722
	Q3	200,150	204,447	-35,868	-945,658
	Q4	202,824	209,155	31,333	-907,121
2017	Q1	216,257	218,528	87,121	-889,504
	Q2	216,798	209,427	93,057	-869,954
	Q3	210,709	214,518	128,214	-833,988
	Q4	212,708	219,484	173,901	-830,869
2018	Q1	229,044	228,903	227,682	-818,693
	Q2	223,286	218,664	239,361	-797,793
	Q3	220,076	224,737	252,001	-789,377
	Q4	222,314	229,865	237,494	-832,177
2019	Q1	240,848	242,076	264,505	-836,401
	Q2	236,310	227,914	231,339	-832,990
	Q3	231,094	236,638	229,067	-835,022
	Q4	233,340	241,696	268,378	-804,149
2020	Q1	245,277	260,213	196,886	-846,686
	Q2	220,162	326,934	29,088	-972,554
	Q3	229,242	298,293	48,740	-1,000,824
	Q4	231,649	279,340	74,463	-1,001,880

Consolidated Government includes federal government, provincial and territorial government, local government, Canada Pension Plan (CPP) and Quebec Pension Plan (QPP).

Includes Aboriginal governments.

Source: Statistics Canada. *Table 10-10-0015-01 – Statement of government operations and balance sheet, government finance statistics (x 1,000,000)*. Accessed July 5, 2021.

GROWTH STATISTICS: FINANCIAL BALANCE OF INTERNATIONAL PAYMENTS

$ MILLIONS

		Canadian Direct Investment Abroad[1,2] (All Countries, $000,000)							Foreign Direct Investment in Canada[1] (All Countries, $000,000)						
		All Industries	Energy and mining[3]	Manufacturing [31-33]	Trade and transportation[4]	Finance and Insurance [52]	Management of companies and enterprises [55]	Other Industries[5]	All Industries	Energy and mining[3]	Manufacturing [31-33]	Trade and transportation[4]	Finance and Insurance [52]	Management of companies and enterprises [55]	Other Industries[5]
2014	Q1	9,727	-2,629	1,400	312	6,948	336	3,360	15,371	4,232	2,843	2,223	874	271	4,928
	Q2	8,773	-413	1,999	-1,174	4,639	4,714	-992	13,369	2,167	6,693	2,592	538	616	763
	Q3	12,780	3,516	1,776	196	-283	-748	8,323	15,775	4,896	3,376	1,757	814	2,379	2,554
	Q4	35,304	8,815	2,129	-744	5,073	18,078	5,580	20,671	8,558	-553	1,158	1,097	11,936	1,452
2015	Q1	18,038	-169	1,038	-42	11,256	2,186	3,771	7,627	2,700	4,009	2,769	-673	-2,375	1,198
	Q2	35,362	3,022	20,528	663	5,887	4,627	635	23,676	9,471	6,660	2,684	2,180	1,519	1,162
	Q3	17,001	-12,351	1,155	1,741	23,256	1,165	2,034	19,030	-10,487	4,759	2,113	945	1,378	20,323
	Q4	16,347	-7,068	2,835	-250	13,700	4,068	3,061	7,997	2,054	-11,256	2,218	-1,884	13,678	3,187
2016	Q1	16,748	2,412	5,033	1,732	6,279	306	986	8,932	362	3,439	2,868	1,401	46	816
	Q2	15,928	767	594	4,327	-1,582	-795	12,616	14,856	1,891	5,504	6,654	3,082	-4,160	1,886
	Q3	28,549	6,882	1,805	11,80	5,893	5,100	-2,932	10,021	258	4,440	-505	1,675	1,517	2,636
	Q4	36,267	9,764	987	4,295	11,566	-2,925	12,579	15,625	8,277	-8,332	3,685	1,127	8,384	2,484
2017	Q1	43,919	-1,190	-1,995	38,213	3,691	2,275	2,924	9,153	1,290	4,731	853	971	757	552
	Q2	20,417	1,017	-751	5,760	11,930	2,032	429	1,806	-11,586	193	5,561	1,363	2,643	3,632
	Q3	17,098	-3,601	650	4,911	4,717	5,725	4,695	12,265	-43	4,764	4,743	1,423	-955	2,333
	Q4	21,209	1,307	1,699	3,265	7,424	899	6,616	8,886	2,334	3,153	1,496	866	183	855
2018	Q1	7,660	337	849	2,992	-94	3,076	500	18,470	3,063	10,014	1,254	1,632	1,095	1,412
	Q2	17,701	2,496	4,091	2,572	4,613	3,020	909	6,781	-973	3,140	1,366	-1,024	1,071	3,201
	Q3	27,548	6,561	1,496	1,624	14,804	-1,291	4,355	11,847	3,880	2,717	2,041	1,457	467	1,285
	Q4	11,368	442	453	10,705	5,612	1,410	-7,255	17,638	-194	1,848	2,971	2,196	575	10,242
2019	Q1	32,462	15,537	973	6,657	6,289	2,092	915	12,444	1,174	8,067	-813	812	159	3,044
	Q2	21,839	2,443	3,011	-948	13,269	2,770	1,095	20,323	13,692	3,086	2,132	2,283	-2,942	2,072
	Q3	18,630	2,199	577	5,658	1,397	8,618	180	16,537	2,354	5,396	-539	2,476	3,278	3,572
	Q4	28,856	-193	-868	2,184	8,717	17,243	1,773	17,859	2,191	1,694	1,858	3,548	8,941	-372
2020	Q1	10,119	3,031	536	596	938	1,185	3,833	11,805	-2,520	3,554	2,592	2,256	5,154	768
	Q2	15,185	1,461	875	-2,662	11,047	2,606	1,859	10,289	-661	136	939	-94	659	9,310
	Q3	21,952	506	1,680	4,561	11,820	1,539	1,846	10,518	-2,168	2,075	3,814	1,903	4,263	630
	Q4	15,020	318	1,997	-889	4,950	2,099	6,545	-291	-1,936	664	2,284	996	-4,448	2,149

Footnotes:
1. In the financial account, a plus sign denotes an increase in investment and a minus sign denotes a decrease in investment.
2. The direct investment flows abroad are classified according to the industrial classification of the Canadian investor company, and not the company abroad that employs this capital.
3. This combines the North American Industry Classification System (NAICS) codes 21 and 22.
4. This combines the North American Industry Classification System (NAICS) codes 41, 44, 45, 48 and 49.
5. This combines the North American Industry Classification System (NAICS) codes 11, 23, 51, 53, 54, 56, 61, 62, 71, 72, 81 and 91.

Source: Statistics Canada. *Table 36-10-0026-01 - Balance of international payments, flows of Canadian direct investment abroad and foreign direct investment in Canada, by North American Industry Classification System (NAICS), quarterly (x 1,000,000).* Accessed July 5, 2021.

GROWTH STATISTICS: MAJOR CANADIAN AIRLINES
ANNUAL SUM (DATA IN THOUSANDS)

	Passengers	Passenger-kilometres	Kilograms of goods	Goods tonne-kilometres (tonne-kilometres)	Hours flown	Turbo fuel consumed (litres)
1997	24,363	62,479,410	449,828	2,058,953	826	3,631,436
1998	24,571	64,426,065	431,150	2,340,594	843	3,855,178
1999	24,047	65,711,146	451,801	2,016,503	904	3,571,445
2000	24,480	68,516,738	407,876	1,934,683	921	3,871,274
2001	23,414	67,018,521	361,834	1,725,325	856	3,678,966
2002	23,430	69,254,337	355,493	1,800,415	806	3,453,486
2003	20,042	59,508,960	298,990	1,419,988	703	2,999,282
2004	28,159	76,122,855	297,246	1,478,716	926	3,660,671
2005	32,091	83,909,440	268,947	1,378,548	981	3,855,953
2006	33,439	88,323,198	265,470	1,425,103	1,010	3,980,077
2007	35,568	93,363,940	242,511	1,301,260	1,078	4,137,528
2008	37,494	96,677,633	218,944	1,260,823	1,119	4,178,965
2009	36,244	93,336,414	195,068	1,169,416	1,077	3,893,014
2010	38,837	102,682,704	253,098	1,510,325	1,155	4,328,366
2011	40,318	107,976,582	249,575	1,519,268	1,215	4,540,715
2012	42,184	112,077,394	254,972	1,593,304	1,239	4,647,021
2013	42,685	114,140,255	251,229	1,594,734	1,243	4,699,769
2014	45,144	123,149,380	274,846	1,731,107	1,274	4,907,146
2015	68,122	171,276,306	..	..	1,985	6,485,495
2016	73,512	188,573,927	..	..	2,043	6,994,641
2017	79,545	208,969,534	..	..	2,160	7,587,721
2018	84,039	223,648,013	..	..	2,270	7,932,156
2019	85,459	228,319,390	..	..	2,277	8,102,149
2020	24,747	59,866,953	..	..	809	2,987,232

.. : data no longer published.

Notes:
1. As of January 2004, major airline data include both WestJet and Air Canada.
2. As of April 2014, Air Canada data include Air Canada rouge.
3. As of January 2015, the major airlines include all Canadian Level I air carriers, which are comprised of Air Canada (including Air Canada rouge), Air Transat, Jazz, Porter, Sunwing and WestJet.
4. As of July 2018, WestJet data include Swoop, WestJet Encore and WestJet Link.
5. From January 2020 until March 2021, inclusive, the major airlines also include Sky Regional Airlines.

Source: Adapted from Statistics Canada, *Table 23-10-0079-01 - Operating and financial statistics for major Canadian airlines, monthly.* Accessed July 5, 2021.

GROWTH STATISTICS: AGRICULTURE
FARM CASH RECEIPTS, ANNUAL (DOLLARS)

	2016	2017	2018	2019	2020
	Dollars				
Total farm cash receipts	60,526,275	61,601,115	62,237,605	66,051,500	72,174,499
Total crop receipts	34,124,481	34,116,692	35,000,311	36,595,938	42,407,744
Wheat, excluding durum	4,476,502	5,066,756	5,657,460	5,388,424	6,162,634
Durum wheat	1,193,272	1,110,013	1,047,953	1,342,393	1,671,784
Oats	461,844	450,960	497,321	634,775	693,626
Barley	701,642	708,256	843,133	949,391	1,080,611
Deferred grain receipts	-2,182,094	-2,100,137	-1,874,734	-1,535,721	-1,911,286
Liquidation of deferred grain receipts	2,021,175	2,192,695	2,077,805	1,867,678	1,553,710
Rye	42,449	34,103	62,051	52,812	64,306
Flaxseed	254,246	216,574	230,166	215,170	305,142
Canola (including rapeseed)	9,242,093	9,917,529	9,300,333	8,613,028	10,247,112
Soybeans	2,904,352	2,714,674	3,053,456	2,515,448	3,082,553
Corn for grain	2,057,989	2,008,720	2,259,974	2,212,671	2,107,003
Fresh potatoes	1,246,952	1,188,520	1,279,952	1,285,062	1,352,569
Cannabis seeds, vegetative plants & flowering tops (incl. leaves)	95,484	189,012	564,077	2,308,824	3,611,338
Fresh vegetables - greenhouse	1,331,163	1,425,900	1,511,251	1,587,417	1,833,876
Fresh vegetables - field	1,704,357	1,741,446	1,775,568	1,857,477	1,830,744
Total fresh fruit	1,074,275	1,088,297	1,142,080	1,185,861	1,174,252
Floriculture, nursery and sod	1,796,474	1,765,867	1,813,740	1,875,644	2,107,843
Unstemmed leaf Tobacco	110,786	134,633	119,394	133,132	68,743
Mustard seeds	127,130	97,094	92,782	79,948	80,487
Sunflower seeds	16,821	9,012	13,867	16,338	27,970
Lentils	2,006,051	1,089,806	702,437	867,159	1,801,257
Canary seeds	71,784	69,400	67,923	89,173	79,423
Dry beans	183,046	204,505	220,836	218,672	321,393
Dry peas	1,461,259	1,023,175	824,736	890,017	1,050,290
Chickpeas	115,353	179,842	70,115	92,818	54,536
Forage and grass seed	116,342	142,225	137,237	139,607	157,867
Hay	517,675	586,487	524,796	586,439	594,746
Maple syrup and other maple products	481,595	496,181	381,032	514,434	555,287
Forest products	61,574	64,013	83,936	81,462	78,327
Miscellaneous crops	211,441	214,407	251,104	261,274	300,259
Ginseng root for medicinal use	239,332	227,904	154,141	131,373	131,853
Christmas trees	77,603	88,391	114,390	137,738	137,490
Total receipts from livestock and livestock products	23,959,646	25,048,524	25,018,787	26,336,321	26,307,402
Cattle	23,959,646	25,048,524	8,140,831	8,465,213	8,247,442
Calves	841,594	889,705	930,923	926,615	845,227
Hogs	4,092,193	4,495,174	4,108,387	4,583,087	4,661,562

Sheep	11,107	13,453	14,760	14,331	20,410
Lambs	169,406	170,573	171,000	174,714	205,384
Unprocessed milk from bovine	6,174,235	6,564,476	6,638,649	6,990,993	7,129,246
Chickens for meat	2,459,432	2,537,771	2,690,829	2,825,896	2,847,664
Turkeys for meat	411,845	384,439	391,787	382,606	366,632
Eggs in shell	1,052,068	1,095,382	1,167,529	1,237,867	1,284,186
Natural honey (except pollen)	185,503	183,102	191,877	184,521	196,450
Raw furs from farm mink & fox	98,450	75,137	97,702	44,224	..
Miscellaneous livestock & livestock products	455,653	477,578	414,296	435,708	433,513
Hatcheries - chicks and poults	54,550	55,594	60,218	70,545	69,685
Total receipts from direct payments	**2,442,148**	**2,435,899**	**2,218,507**	**3,119,241**	**3,459,353**
Crop insurance	1,045,184	1,226,408	893,000	1,408,521	1,704,119
Private hail insurance	276,387	107,574	166,043	245,129	194,855
AgriInvest	297,341	281,386	289,132	261,742	261,982
Agri-Stability	311,025	356,462	339,995	365,519	452,930
Provincial stabilization payments	329,567	222,995	320,967	268,730	408,488
Other payments	182,644	241,074	209,370	569,600	436,979

.. : not available for a specific reference period.

Please see original table online for footnotes.

Source: Statistics Canada Table 32-10-0045-01 - Farm cash receipts, annual (x 1,000). Accessed July 5, 2021.

CONSUMER PRICE INDEX, CANADA
MONTHLY, 2002=100

Products and product groups[3]	2011 Jan.	2012 Jan.	2013 Jan.	2014 Jan.	2015 Jan.	2016 Jan.	2017 Jan.	2018 Jan.	2019 Jan.	2020 Jan.	2021 Jan.
All-items	117.8	120.7	121.3	123.1	124.3	126.8	129.5	131.7	133.6	136.8	138.2
Food[4]	124.9	130.2	131.6	133	139.1	144.6	141.5	144.7	148.7	153.5	155
Shelter[5]	124.5	127.1	127.8	130.5	133.1	134.6	137.8	139.7	143	146.4	148.4
Household operations, furnishings and equipment	109.6	112.2	113.5	114.7	118	120	121.4	122.4	123.3	122.6	124.3
Clothing and footwear	87.9	89.3	87.9	89.2	91.1	90.8	91.1	91.7	92.2	95.8	91.9
Transportation	122.8	127.4	126.7	129.2	122.4	125.1	133	137.2	136.6	143.4	144.9
Gasoline	163.6	174.7	171.6	179.5	131.3	134.1	161.7	174.3	149.6	166.4	160.9
Health and personal care	115.8	118.1	118.5	118.3	120	121.5	123.4	125.1	125.9	128.6	130.3
Recreation, education and reading	102.7	102.6	103.7	104.7	105.6	107.9	111.3	111.8	113.3	113	116.3
Alcoholic beverages and tobacco products	135.2	136.3	138.9	140.9	149.9	154.5	158.7	163.2	170.6	171.4	172.5
All-items excluding food and energy[6]	113.4	115.2	115.9	117.3	119.5	121.6	124.3	126.2	128.6	131	132.8
All-items excluding energy[6]	115.5	117.9	118.7	120.1	122.9	125.6	127.3	129.5	132.2	134.9	136.7
Energy[6]	146	155.5	152.8	160.2	139.5	139	155.8	159.5	148.5	158.6	154.3
Goods[7]	110.5	113.6	112.9	114.2	114	116.6	118.9	120.2	120	123.7	123.8
Services[8]	125	127.8	129.6	131.9	134.7	137	140.2	143.3	147.1	149.7	152.5

Footnotes:

1. The Consumer Price Index (CPI) is not a cost-of-living index. The objective behind a cost-of-living index is to measure changes in expenditures necessary for consumers to maintain a constant standard of living. The idea is that consumers would normally switch between products as the price relationship of goods changes. If, for example, consumers get the same satisfaction from drinking tea as they do from coffee, then it is possible to substitute tea for coffee if the price of tea falls relative to the price of coffee. The cheaper of the interchangeable products may be chosen. We could compute a cost-of-living index for an individual if we had complete information about that person's taste and spending habits. To do this for a large number of people, let alone the total population of Canada, is impossible. For this reason, regularly published price indexes are based on the fixed-basket concept rather than the cost-of-living concept.

2. This table replaces CANSIM table 326-0001 which was archived with the release of April 2007 data.

3. From April 2020 to May 2021, certain sub-indexes and components thereof were imputed using special approaches in either one, or more months. The affected indexes include child care services; housekeeping services; air transportation; personal care services; recreational services; travel tours; spectator entertainment; use of recreational facilities and services; beer served in licensed establishments; wine served in licensed establishments, and liquor served in licensed establishments. The details of these treatments from April 2020 to March 2021 are provided in technical supplements available through the Prices Analytical Series. Starting in April 2021, details and treatments are available upon request by contacting the Consumer Prices Division.

4. The goods and services that make up the Consumer Price Index (CPI) are organized according to a hierarchical structure with the "all-items CPI" as the top level. Eight major components of goods and services make up the "all-items CPI". They are: "food", "shelter", "household operations, furnishings and equipment", "clothing and footwear", "transportation", "health and personal care", "recreation, education and reading", and "alcoholic beverages and tobacco products". These eight components are broken down into a varying number of sub-groups which are in turn broken down into other sub-groups. Indents are used to identify the components that make up each level of aggregation. For example, the eight major components appear with one indent relative to the "all-items CPI" to show that they are combined to obtain the "all-items CPI". NOTE: Some items are recombined outside the main structure of the CPI to obtain special aggregates such as "all-items excluding food and energy", "energy", "goods", "services", or "fresh fruit and vegetables". They are listed after the components of the main structure of the CPI following the last major component entitled "alcoholic beverages and tobacco products".

5. Food includes non-alcoholic beverages.

6. Part of the increase first recorded in the shelter index for Yellowknife for December 2004 inadvertently reflected rent increases that actually occurred earlier. As a result, the change in the shelter index was overstated in December 2004, and was understated in the previous two years. The shelter index series for Yellowknife has been corrected from December 2002. In addition, the Yellowknife All-items Consumer Price Index (CPI) and some Yellowknife special aggregate index series have also changed. Data for Canada and all other provinces and territories were not affected.

7. The special aggregate 'energy' includes: 'electricity', 'natural gas', 'fuel oil and other fuels', 'gasoline', and 'fuel, parts and accessories for recreational vehicles'.

8. Goods are physical or tangible commodities usually classified according to their life span into non-durable goods, semi-durable goods and durable goods. Non-durable goods are those goods that can be used up entirely in less than a year, assuming normal usage. For example, fresh food products, disposable cameras and gasoline are non-durable goods. Semi-durable goods are those goods that may last less than 12 months or greater than 12 months depending on the purpose to which they are put. For example, clothing, footwear and household textiles are semi-durable goods. Durable goods are those goods which may be used repeatedly or continuously over more than a year, assuming normal usage. For example, cars, audio and video equipment and furniture are durable goods.

9. A service in the Consumer Price Index (CPI) is characterized by valuable work performed by an individual or organization on behalf of a consumer, for example, car tune-ups, haircuts and city public transportation. Transactions classified as a service may include the cost of goods by their nature. Examples include food in restaurant food services and materials in clothing repair services.

Source: Statistics Canada. *Table 18-10-0004-01 - Consumer Price Index, monthly, not seasonally adjusted.* Accessed July 5, 2021.

NEW HOUSING PRICE INDEX

	Jan. 2017	Jan. 2018	Jan. 2019	Jan. 2020	Jan. 2021
	201612=100				
Canada	100.1	103.3	103.2	103.4	109
House only	99.9	103.2	102.8	102.6	109.3
Land only	100.4	103.7	104.1	104.8	108.4
Metropolitan areas (house and land)					
St. John's (N.L.)	99.6	99	98.1	97.4	100.7
Charlottetown (P.E.I)	100	100.3E	100.1E	102E	110E
Halifax (N.S.)	100.2	101	101.9	102.9	110.1
Saint John, Moncton, and Fredericton (N.B.)	100.2	101.2	100.9	102.7	104.2
Québec (Que.)	100.2	100.6	100.8	100.9	108.7
Sherbrooke (Que.)	100	99.9	101.2	103.9	104
Trois-Rivières (Que.)	100	100.6	101.4	103.1	108
Montréal (Que.)	100.2	101.8	104.8	111.9	122.1
Ottawa–Gatineau (Que.)	99.8	101.3	102.4	106.2	112.8
Ottawa–Gatineau (Ont.)	100.1	104.8	110.3	119.6	137.9
Oshawa (Ont.)	100	104.9	103.8	103.6	112.4
Toronto (Ont.)	100.2	104.6	103	102.1	106.2
Hamilton (Ont.)	100.6	103.2	103.8	104.4	116.1
St. Catharines–Niagara (Ont.)	100.9	104.5	106.6	107.4	115.7
Kitchener-Cambridge-Waterloo (Ont.)	101	103.6	103.9	107.8	121.8
Guelph (Ont.)	100.4	104.6	105.1	107	114.6
London (Ont.)	100.9	107.8	111.2	114.7	121.2
Windsor (Ont.)	100.7	102.6	105.6	107.8	115.3
Greater Sudbury / Grand Sudbury and Thunder Bay (Ont.)	99.2	99.8	100.9	102.7	106.1
Winnipeg (Man.)	100.3	103.3	104.5	105.3	110.4
Regina (Sask.)	99.8	100.4	97.4	93.8	92.9
Saskatoon (Sask.)	99.9	98.4	97.7	96.4	97.7
Calgary (Alta.)	99.9	100.3	99.2	96.9	97.6
Edmonton (Alta.)	100	99.8	99.3	97.6	98.3
Kelowna (B.C.)	100	103.4	103.2	104	107.6
Vancouver (B.C.)	99.9	108.9	108.6	106	113.1
Victoria (B.C.)	100.4	101.6	102.5	101.8	107.8

.. not available for a specific reference period
E use with caution

Footnotes:
1. This table replaces CANSIM table 327-0046 which was archived with the release of January 2017 data. Data for periods prior to December 2016 were obtained by linking the current New Housing Price Index (NHPI) series, where possible, to indexes in CANSIM table 327-0046.
2. Beginning in December 2016, several changes have been made to the New Housing Price Index (NHPI). The census metropolitan areas (CMAs) of Kelowna, Guelph, Trois-Rivières and Sherbrooke are included in the NHPI basket. Separate indexes are published for the census metropolitan areas (CMAs) of Toronto, Oshawa, Ottawa-Gatineau (Ontario part), Ottawa-Gatineau (Quebec part) and Greater Sudbury. The New Housing Price Index no longer includes Thunder Bay.
3. The index base period, for which the New Housing Price Index (NHPI) equals 100, is December 2016.
4. New Housing price indexes denoted with the data quality indicator "E", should be used with caution.
5. To maintain the accuracy of the index, Saint John, Fredericton and Moncton are published together.
6. The index for Ottawa-Gatineau (Quebec part) begins in December 2016.
7. For historical continuity, the Ottawa-Gatineau (Ontario part) index is linked to the previously combined Ottawa-Gatineau index, which was published until December 2016.
8. The index for Oshawa begins in December 2016.
9. For historical continuity, the Toronto index is linked to the previously combined Toronto and Oshawa index, which was published until December 2016.
10. For historical continuity, the Greater Sudbury index is linked to the previously combined Greater Sudbury and Thunder Bay index, which was published until December 2016. The New Housing Price Index no longer includes Thunder Bay.

Source: Statistics Canada. Table 18-10-0205-01 – New housing price index, monthly. Accessed July 5, 2021.

SURVEY OF HOUSEHOLD SPENDING (SHS), 2017 & 2019
ANNUAL (DOLLARS)

Household expenditures, summary-level categories	2017	2019
Total expenditure	86,479	93,724
Total current consumption	63,944	68,980
Food expenditures	8,968	10,311
Food purchased from stores	6,364	7,536
Food purchased from restaurants	2,604	2,775
Shelter	18,640	20,200
Principal accommodation	16,811	18,371
Rented living quarters	4,038	4,160
Owned living quarters	10,287	11,676
Water, fuel and electricity for principal accommodation	2,486	2,535
Other accommodation	1,829	1,829
Household operations	4,709	5,448
Communications	2,404	2,670
Household furnishings and equipment	2,271	2,486
Household furnishings	973	1,124
Household equipment	1,140	1,218
Household appliances	533	582
Clothing and accessories	3,453	3,344
Transportation	12,721	12,737
Private transportation	11,436	11,258
Public transportation	1,285	1,479
Health care	2,564	2,780
Direct health care costs to household	1,799	1,918
Personal care	1,189	1,384
Recreation	3,979	4,624
Recreation equipment and related services	980	995
Home entertainment equipment and services	203	209
Recreation services	2,184	2,593
Recreational vehicles and associated services	613	826
Education	1,783	1,691
Reading materials and other printed matter	154	165
Tobacco products, alcoholic beverages and cannabis for non-medical use	..	1,785
Tobacco products and alcoholic beverages	1,463t	..
Games of chance	183	186
Miscellaneous expenditures	1,865	1,838
Income taxes	15,144	17,167
Personal insurance payments and pension contributions	5,184	5,297
Gifts of money, support payments and charitable contributions	2,207	2,280

.. not available for a specific reference period
t terminated

Please see data online for footnotes

Source: Statistics Canada. *Table 11-10-0224-01 - Household spending by household type.* Accessed July 5, 2021.

AVERAGE FEMALE AND MALE INCOME, AND FEMALE-TO-MALE INCOME RATIO
ANNUAL, 2019 CONSTANT DOLLARS

	Average income, females (dollars)	Average income, males (dollars)	Female-to-male average income ratio (percent)
1995	29,600[A]	47,000[A]	63
1996	28,900[A]	47,400[A]	61
1997	28,700[A]	47,900[A]	59.9
1998	29,800[A]	49,500[A]	60.2
1999	30,700[A]	50,800[A]	60.4
2000	31,300[A]	52,200[A]	60
2001	32,100[A]	52,800[A]	60.8
2002	32,200[A]	52,600[A]	61.2
2003	32,200[A]	52,300[A]	61.6
2004	32,600[A]	53,300[A]	61.2
2005	33,400[A]	53,100[A]	62.9
2006	34,300[A]	52,800[A]	65
2007	35,500[A]	54,000[A]	65.7
2008	35,600[A]	54,900[A]	64.8
2009	36,800[A]	53,400[A]	68.9
2010	36,600[A]	53,900[A]	67.9
2011	36,600[A]	54,300[A]	67.4
2012	37,200[A]	55,400[A]	67.1
2013	38,100[A]	56,200[A]	67.8
2014	38,100[A]	56,900[A]	67
2015	39,000[A]	56,400[A]	69.1
2016	39,100[A]	55,700[A]	70.2
2017	40,400[A]	57,300[A]	70.5
2018	40,600[A]	57,600[A]	70.5
2019	41,400[A]	56,800[A]	72.9

Footnotes:

1. Data quality indicators are based on the coefficient of variation (CV) and number of observations. Quality indicators indicate the following: A - Excellent (CV between 0% and 2%); B - Very good (CV between 2% and 4%); C - Good (CV between 4% and 8%); D - Acceptable (CV between 8% and 16%); E - Use with caution (1976 to 1992: CV greater than or equal to 16%; 1993 and subsequent years: CV between 16% and 33.3%).
2. Estimates are based on data from the following surveys: the Survey of Consumer Finances (SCF) from 1976 to 1992, a combination of the SCF and the Survey of Labour and Income Dynamics (SLID) from 1993 to 1997, the SLID from 1998 to 2011 and the Canadian Income Survey (CIS) beginning in 2012. For more information, see Statistics Canada, 2015, 'Revisions to 2006 to 2011 income data', Income Research Paper Series, Cat. no. 75F0002MIE - No. 003.
Also, two previous revisions of income data are described in Cotton, Cathy, 2000, 'Bridging Two Surveys: An Integrated Series of Income Data from SCF and SLID 1989-1997', Statistics Canada, Cat. No. 75F0002MIE - No. 002, and Lathe, Heather, 2005, 'Survey of Labour and Income Dynamics: 2003 Historical Revision', Statistics Canada, Cat. No. 75F0002MIE - No. 009.

Source: Adapted from Statistics Canada, *Table 11-10-0239-01 Income of individuals by age group, sex and income source, Canada, provinces and selected census metropolitan areas.* Accessed July 9, 2021.

AVERAGE AFTER-TAX INCOME, 2009-2019
ECONOMIC FAMILIES & PERSONS NOT IN AN ECONOMIC FAMILY, 2019 CONSTANT DOLLARS

	2009	2010	2011	2012	2013	2014	2015	2016	2017	2018	2019
Canada	70,900[A]	70,700[A]	70,800[A]	72,300[A]	73,400[A]	73,800[A]	74,300[A]	74,000[A]	76,100[A]	76,600[A]	77,200[A]
Newfoundland and Labrador	63,500[A]	65,500[A]	67,400[A]	69,100[A]	72,100[A]	72,200[A]	73,200[A]	70,700[A]	69,800[A]	69,800[A]	70,300[A]
Prince Edward Island	61,000[A]	61,400[A]	62,400[A]	61,400[A]	64,500[A]	64,300[A]	64,200[B]	64,100[A]	66,400[A]	67,000[A]	67,200[A]
Nova Scotia	60,500[A]	59,600[A]	60,900[A]	61,800[A]	63,600[A]	63,000[A]	63,100[A]	63,600[A]	63,700[A]	64,100[A]	63,800[A]
New Brunswick	60,600[A]	60,500[A]	62,000[A]	61,800[A]	61,900[A]	62,100[A]	61,600[A]	62,900[A]	64,800[A]	65,900[A]	65,400[A]
Quebec	60,900[A]	60,400[A]	61,300[A]	62,200[A]	62,800[A]	63,100[A]	62,300[A]	64,200[A]	65,100[A]	66,100[A]	68,000[A]
Ontario	75,300[A]	75,900[A]	74,500[A]	76,000[A]	76,800[A]	77,200[A]	78,500[A]	79,100[A]	81,200[A]	81,800[A]	81,700[A]
Manitoba	67,100[A]	67,100[A]	66,400[A]	67,200[A]	69,400[A]	70,000[A]	70,800[A]	70,800[A]	73,200[A]	72,000[A]	71,600[A]
Saskatchewan	71,700[A]	70,700[A]	74,200[A]	74,700[A]	76,100[A]	79,500[B]	77,600[A]	75,900[A]	76,600[A]	74,900[A]	73,400[A]
Alberta	86,200[A]	85,400[A]	86,500[A]	90,500[A]	92,400[A]	93,100[A]	94,300[A]	86,300[A]	89,200[A]	88,700[A]	88,400[A]
British Columbia	70,700[A]	69,700[A]	69,500[A]	70,700[A]	72,900[A]	72,300[A]	72,600[A]	72,500[A]	77,200[A]	77,700[A]	79,700[A]

Footnotes:

1. Data quality indicators are based on the coefficient of variation (CV) and number of observations. Quality indicators indicate the following: A - Excellent (CV between 0% and 2%); B - Very good (CV between 2% and 4%); C - Good (CV between 4% and 8%); D - Acceptable (CV between 8% and 16%); E - Use with caution (1976 to 1992: CV greater than or equal to 16%; 1993 and subsequent years: CV between 16% and 33.3%).
2. Estimates are based on data from the following surveys: the Survey of Consumer Finances (SCF) from 1976 to 1992, a combination of the SCF and the Survey of Labour and Income Dynamics (SLID) from 1993 to 1997, the SLID from 1998 to 2011 and the Canadian Income Survey (CIS) beginning in 2012. For more information, see Statistics Canada, 2015, 'Revisions to 2006 to 2011 income data', Income Research Paper Series, Cat. no. 75F0002MIE - No. 003. Also, two previous revisions of income data are described in Cotton, Cathy, 2000, 'Bridging Two Surveys: An Integrated Series of Income Data from SCF and SLID 1989-1997', Statistics Canada, Cat. No. 75F0002MIE - No. 002, and Lathe, Heather, 2005, 'Survey of Labour and Income Dynamics: 2003 Historical Revision', Statistics Canada, Cat. No. 75F0002MIE - No. 009.
3. Estimates from the Survey of Consumer Finances include income data for persons aged 15 years and over. Estimates from the Survey of Labour and Income Dynamics and the Canadian Income Survey include income data for persons aged 16 years and over.
4. The concept of income covers income received while a resident of Canada or as relevant for income tax purposes in Canada. Market income is the sum of earnings (from employment and net self-employment), net investment income, private retirement income, and the items under other income. It is also called income before taxes and transfers. Total income refers to income from all sources including government transfers and before deduction of federal and provincial income taxes. It may also be called income before tax (but after transfers). After-tax income is total income less income tax. It may also be called income after tax.
5. Estimates for Canada do not include the territories.

Source: Statistics Canada. *Table 11-10-0190-01 - Market income, government transfers, total income, income tax and after-tax income by economic family type.* Accessed July 16, 2021.

CURRENT AND FORTHCOMING MINIMUM HOURLY WAGE RATES FOR EXPERIENCED ADULT WORKERS IN CANADA

Jurisdiction	Effective Date	Wage Rate	Note
Federal[1]	18-Dec-1996		The minimum wage rate applicable in regard to employees under federal jurisdiction is the general adult minimum rate of the province or territory where the employee is usually employed
Federal[1]	29-Dec-2021	$15.00	An employee should be paid at least the federal minimum wage. If the minimum wage of the province or territory where the employee usually works is higher than the federal minimum wage, the employer is to pay the higher minimum wage.
Alberta	01-Oct-2018	$15.00	
British Columbia	01-Jun-2021	$15.20	
Manitoba	01-Oct-2020	$11.90	
Manitoba	01-Oct-2021	$11.95	
New Brunswick	01-Apr-2021	$11.75	
Newfoundland and Labrador	01-Apr-2021	$12.50	
Northwest Territories	01-Apr-2018	$13.46	
Northwest Territories	01-Sep-2021	$15.20	
Nova Scotia	01-Apr-2021	$12.95	
Nunavut	01-Apr-2020	$16.00	Applies to all employees in Nunavut.
Ontario	01-Oct-2020	$14.25	
Ontario	01-Oct-2021	$14.35	
Prince Edward Island	01-Apr-2021	$13.00	
Quebec	01-May-2021	$13.50	
Saskatchewan	01-Oct-2020	$11.45	
Saskatchewan	01-Oct-2021	$11.81	
Yukon	01-Apr-2021	$13.85	

Note: In most jurisdictions, these rates also apply to young workers. More information is available on special rates for young workers under "Current And Forthcoming Minimum Wage Rates in Canada for Young Workers and Specific Occupations".

1. The federal jurisdiction includes labour market sectors coming under federal authority by virtue of the Constitution, such as international and interprovincial transportation, telecommunication and banking.

Source: Title: Current And Forthcoming Minimum Hourly Wage Rates For Experienced Adult Workers. URL: http://srv116.services.gc.ca/dimt-wid/sm-mw/rpt1.aspx?lang=eng. Employment and Social Development Canada, 2017. Reproduced with the permission of the Minister of Employment and Social Development Canada, 2021.

LABOUR FORCE SURVEY ESTIMATES (LFS)
ANNUAL AVERAGE (PERSONS UNLESS OTHERWISE NOTED)

Labour force character- istics	Population[5, 6]	Labour force[7]	Employment[8]	Employment full-time[9]	Employment part-time[10]	Unemploy- ment[11]	Unemploy- ment rate (percent)[12]	Participation rate (percent)[13]	Employment rate (percent)[14]
1999	23,781.50	15,586.00	14,407.50	11,758.40	2,649.20	1,178.50	7.6	65.5	60.6
2000	24,089.70	15,849.30	14,765.70	12,090.60	2,675.00	1,083.70	6.8	65.8	61.3
2001	24,419.40	16,102.00	14,938.20	12,224.80	2,713.40	1,163.80	7.2	65.9	61.2
2002	24,768.60	16,555.80	15,285.90	12,428.40	2,857.50	1,269.90	7.7	66.8	61.7
2003	25,079.90	16,938.70	15,654.70	12,689.20	2,965.50	1,284.00	7.6	67.5	62.4
2004	25,408.10	17,149.00	15,921.80	12,968.20	2,953.50	1,227.20	7.2	67.5	62.7
2005	25,754.70	17,294.30	16,126.70	13,152.70	2,974.00	1,167.60	6.8	67.2	62.6
2006	26,115.50	17,505.80	16,401.50	13,415.20	2,986.30	1,104.30	6.3	67.0	62.8
2007	26,461.70	17,851.90	16,775.00	13,696.40	3,078.60	1,077.00	6.0	67.5	63.4
2008	26,824.40	18,117.60	17,003.90	13,851.10	3,153.00	1,113.80	6.2	67.5	63.4
2009	27,202.50	18,255.70	16,731.90	13,503.30	3,228.60	1,523.80	8.4	67.1	61.5
2010	27,573.60	18,449.70	16,969.60	13,647.10	3,322.40	1,480.10	8.0	66.9	61.5
2011	27,913.30	18,621.70	17,223.80	13,898.20	3,325.60	1,397.90	7.5	66.7	61.7
2012	28,283.30	18,820.40	17,444.30	14,128.60	3,315.70	1,376.20	7.3	66.5	61.7
2013	28,647.20	19,036.50	17,686.40	14,321.30	3,365.20	1,350.00	7.1	66.4	61.8
2014	28,980.60	19,118.90	17,796.50	14,365.60	3,430.90	1,322.30	6.9	66.0	61.4
2015	29,279.80	19,280.50	17,949.20	14,559.60	3,389.60	1,331.30	6.9	65.9	61.3
2016	29,587.00	19,443.00	18,083.10	14,610.90	3,472.20	1,359.80	7.0	65.7	61.1
2017	29,901.75	19,664.19	18,421.20	14,892.37	3,528.85	1,242.99	6.3	65.8	61.6
2018	30,290.42	19,813.40	18,657.71	15,168.18	3,489.54	1,155.66	5.8	65.4	61.6
2019	30,694.75	20,134.43	18,979.17	15,380.19	3,598.97	1,155.29	5.73	65.6	61.8
2020	31,052.60	19,905.33	18,004.51	14,761.86	3,242.65	1,900.82	9.60	64.1	57.9

Footnotes:

1. Fluctuations in economic time series are caused by seasonal, cyclical and irregular movements. A seasonally adjusted series is one from which seasonal movements have been eliminated. Seasonal movements are defined as those which are caused by regular annual events such as climate, holidays, vacation periods and cycles related to crops, production and retail sales associated with Christmas and Easter. It should be noted that the seasonally adjusted series contain irregular as well as longer-term cyclical fluctuations. The seasonal adjustment program is a complicated computer program which differentiates between these seasonal, cyclical and irregular movements in a series over a number of years and, on the basis of past movements, estimates appropriate seasonal factors for current data. On an annual basis, the historic series of seasonally adjusted data are revised in light of the most recent information on changes in seasonality.

2. To ensure respondent confidentiality, estimates below a certain threshold are suppressed. For Canada, Quebec, Ontario, Alberta and British Columbia suppression is applied to all data below 1,500. The threshold level for Newfoundland and Labrador, Nova Scotia, New Brunswick, Manitoba and Saskatchewan is 500, while in Prince Edward Island, estimates under 200 are supressed. For census metropolitan areas (CMAs) and economic regions (ERs), use their respective provincial suppression levels mentioned above. Estimates are based on smaller sample sizes the more detailed the table becomes, which could result in lower data quality.

3. For more information on seasonal adjustment see Seasonally adjusted data - Frequently asked questions.

4. Excluding the territories.

5. Number of persons of working age, 15 years and over. Estimates in thousands, rounded to the nearest hundred.

6. From December 2000 to January 2001, there is a slight level shift in the population series. This is due to the 2015 population rebasing, which was revised back to 2001. This level shift is evident for certain age groups and in two provinces (Manitoba and Saskatchewan). These shifts are minor for labour force estimates and rates.

7. Number of civilian, non-institutionalized persons 15 years of age and over who, during the reference week, were employed or unemployed. Estimates in thousands, rounded to the nearest hundred.

8. Number of persons who, during the reference week, worked for pay or profit, or performed unpaid family work or had a job but were not at work due to own illness or disability, personal or family responsibilities, labour dispute, vacation, or other reason. Those persons on layoff and persons without work but who had a job to start at a definite date in the future are not considered employed. Estimates in thousands, rounded to the nearest hundred.

9. Full-time employment consists of persons who usually work 30 hours or more per week at their main or only job. Estimates in thousands, rounded to the nearest hundred.

10. Part-time employment consists of persons who usually work less than 30 hours per week at their main or only job. Estimates in thousands, rounded to the nearest hundred.

11. Number of persons who, during the reference week, were without work, had looked for work in the past four weeks, and were available for work. Those persons on layoff or who had a new job to start in four weeks or less are considered unemployed. Estimates in thousands, rounded to the nearest hundred.

12. The unemployment rate is the number of unemployed persons expressed as a percentage of the labour force. The unemployment rate for a particular group (age, sex, marital status, etc.) is the number unemployed in that group expressed as a percentage of the labour force for that group. Estimates are percentages, rounded to the nearest tenth.

13. The participation rate is the number of labour force participants expressed as a percentage of the population 15 years of age and over. The participation rate for a particular group (age, sex, marital status, etc.) is the number of labour force participants in that group expressed as a percentage of the population for that group. Estimates are percentages, rounded to the nearest tenth.

14. The employment rate is the number of persons employed expressed as a percentage of the population 15 years of age and over. The employment rate for a particular group (age, sex, marital status, etc.) is the number employed in that group expressed as a percentage of the population for that group. Estimates are percentages, rounded to the nearest tenth.

Source: Statistics Canada. *Table 14-10-0287-01 - Labour force characteristics, monthly, seasonally adjusted and trend-cycle, last 5 months.* Accessed July 16, 2021.

LABOUR FORCE SURVEY ESTIMATES (LFS), BY NATIONAL OCCUPATIONAL CLASSIFICATION (NOC) AND SEX
ANNUAL (PERSONS X 1,000)

National Occupational Classification for Statistics (NOC)[6]	2016	2017	2018	2019	2020
Total, all occupations[8]	19,270.3	19,530.3	19,732.0	20,139.7	19,896.6
Management occupations [0]	1,628.3	1,726.3	1,716.8	1,747.9	1,716
Senior management occupations [00]	52	60.2	55.5	59	51.6
Specialized middle management occupations [01-05]	515.4	572.3	556.2	561.5	609
Middle management occupations in retail and wholesale trade and customer services [06]	540.2	545.4	555.9	554.7	527.1
Middle management occupations in trades, transportation, production and utilities [07-09]	520.7	548.4	549.2	572.7	528.3
Business, finance and administrative occupations [1]	2,948.7	3,010.9	3,056.3	3,110.7	3,182.5
Professional occupations in business and finance [11]	746	772.7	796.9	839.4	915.3
Administrative and financial supervisors and administrative occupations [12]	980.7	1,014.4	985.6	1,053.9	1,027.1
Finance, insurance and related business administrative occupations [13]	227.7	241	255.8	257.2	272.5
Office support occupations [14]	672	662.1	702.2	655.8	654.6
Distribution, tracking and scheduling co-ordination occupations [15]	322.3	320.7	315.8	304.4	313.1
Natural and applied sciences and related occupations [2]	1,434.7	1,453.4	1,506.7	1,597.7	1,705.9
Professional occupations in natural and applied sciences [21]	818	848.1	866	954	1,037.7
Technical occupations related to natural and applied sciences [22]	616.7	605.3	640.6	643.6	668.2
Health occupations [3]	1,345.0	340.3	1,406.8	1,438.5	1,459.3
Professional occupations in nursing [30]	344	1,393.6	348.7	346.1	350.7
Professional occupations in health (except nursing) [31]	310.1	333.4	313.3	316.8	347.6
Technical occupations in health [32]	358.3	376.7	387.5	403.8	406
Assisting occupations in support of health services [34]	332.5	343.2	357.4	371.9	354.9
Occupations in education, law and social, community and government services [4]	2,108.8	2,057.8	2,102.3	2,186.5	2,187.7
Professional occupations in education services [40]	738.8	731.9	766.4	785.2	830.1
Professional occupations in law and social, community and government services [41]	524.4	487.2	500.1	535.4	535.3
Paraprofessional occupations in legal, social, community and education services [42]	474.1	475	459.4	487.6	459.1
Occupations in front-line public protection services [43]	111.7	106.4	108.5	107	109.8
Care providers and educational, legal and public protection support occupations [44]	259.8	585.9	267.8	271.3	253.4
Occupations in art, culture, recreation and sport [5]	574	257.4	580.4	588.7	564.4
Professional occupations in art and culture [51]	189.1	201.4	199.5	199.3	204.8
Technical occupations in art, culture, recreation and sport [52]	384.9	384.6	380.8	389.4	359.6
Sales and service occupations [6]	4,611.7	4,677.4	4,716.8	4,789.6	4,515.6
Retail sales supervisors and specialized sales occupations [62]	597.8	649.6	670.9	671.7	669.9
Service supervisors and specialized service occupations [63]	684.1	673.2	655.4	691.1	624.2
Sales representatives and salespersons – wholesale and retail trade [64]	851.8	841.3	855.5	873.2	818.4
Service representatives and other customer and personal services occupations [65]	849.1	872.8	866.8	887.8	809.8
Sales support occupations [66]	641.2	663.6	648.3	646.5	637.5
Service support and other service occupations, n.e.c. [67]	987.7	976.8	1,019.9	1,019.2	955.9
Trades, transport and equipment operators and related occupations [7]	2,785.9	2,796.8	2,844.9	2,929.8	2,817.3
Industrial, electrical and construction trades [72]	991.2	973.7	955.5	984.2	948.7
Maintenance and equipment operation trades [73]	624.9	622.3	649.3	665.6	636.3
Other installers, repairers and servicers and material handlers [74]	275.8	296.7	306.6	316.2	306.7
Transport and heavy equipment operation and related maintenance occupations [75]	700.4	705.1	742	784.5	747.7
Trades helpers, construction labourers and related occupations [76]	193.6	199.1	191.5	179.3	177.9
Natural resources, agriculture and related production occupations [8]	409.1	412.5	429.9	423.5	413.2
Supervisors and technical occupations in natural resources, agriculture and related production [82]	153.5	151.9	172.5	160.9	153.1
Workers in natural resources, agriculture and related production [84]	128.8	134.5	139.5	145.4	140.3
Harvesting, landscaping and natural resources labourers [86]	126.8	126.1	117.9	117.2	119.8
Occupations in manufacturing and utilities [9]	918.3	913.2	907.9	897.9	853.4
Processing, manufacturing and utilities supervisors and central control operators [92]	206.7	206.5	205.8	203.6	196.5
Processing and manufacturing machine operators and related production workers [94]	331.2	324.7	332.2	317.8	327.4
Assemblers in manufacturing [95]	200.9	202.9	208.8	212.8	188.6
Labourers in processing, manufacturing and utilities [96]	179.5	179.1	161.2	163.6	140.9

Footnotes:
1. To ensure respondent confidentiality, estimates below a certain threshold are suppressed. For Canada, Quebec, Ontario, Alberta and British Columbia suppression is applied to all data below 1,500. The threshold level for Newfoundland and Labrador, Nova Scotia, New Brunswick, Manitoba and Saskatchewan is 500, while in Prince Edward Island, estimates under 200 are suppressed. For census metropolitan areas (CMAs) and economic regions (ERs), use their respective provincial suppression levels mentioned above. Estimates are based on smaller sample sizes the more detailed the table becomes, which could result in lower data quality.
2. For approximate quality indicators of the estimates, see tables 7.1 or 7.2 in the Guide to the Labour Force Survey. For quality indicators of specific data points, contact statcan.labour-travail.statcan@canada.ca.
3. This new table replaces archived table 14-10-0025-01.
4. On April 5, 2019, this table replaced archived table 14-10-0297.
5. Excluding the territories.
6. Occupation estimates are based on the 2016 National Occupational Classification (NOC). Occupation refers to the kind of work persons 15 years of age and over were doing during the reference week, as determined by the kind of work reported and the description of the most important duties of the job. If the individual did not have a job during the reference week, the data relate to the previous job, if that job was held in the past year.
7. Number of persons who, during the reference week, worked for pay or profit, or performed unpaid family work or had a job but were not at work due to own illness or disability, personal or family responsibilities, labour dispute, vacation, or other reason. Those persons on layoff and persons without work but who had a job to start at a definite date in the future are not considered employed. Estimates in thousands, rounded to the nearest hundred.
8. This combines the National Occupational Classification (NOC) codes 00 to 96.

Source: Statistics Canada. Table 14-10-0297-01 Labour force characteristics by occupation, annual (x 1,000). Accessed July 16, 2021.

UNEMPLOYMENT RATES IN CANADA, ANNUAL

Geography	2013	2014	2015	2016	2017	2018	2019	2020
Canada	7.1	6.9	6.9	7.0	6.3	5	5.7	9.5
Newfoundland & Labrador	11.6	11.9	12.8	13.4	14.8	13.1	12.3	14.1
Prince Edward Island	11.6	10.6	10.4	10.7	9.8	8.8	8.8	10.4
Nova Scotia	9.1	9	8.6	8.3	8.4	6.2	7.4	9.8
New Brunswick	10.3	9.9	9.8	9.5	8.1	7.2	8.1	10
Quebec	7.6	7.7	7.6	7.1	6.1	4.9	5.1	8.9
Ontario	7.6	7.3	6.8	6.5	6	4.6	5.6	9.6
Manitoba	5.4	5.4	5.6	6.1	5.4	4.9	5.3	8
Saskatchewan	4.1	3.8	5	6.3	6.3	5.2	5.6	8.4
Alberta	4.6	4.7	6	8.1	7.8	5.7	7	11.4
British Columbia	6.6	6.1	6.2	6	5.1	4.1	4.7	8.9

Note: The unemployment rate is the number of unemployed persons expressed as a percentage of the labour force. The unemployment rate for a particular group (age, sex, marital status, etc.) is the number unemployed in that group expressed as a percentage of the labour force for that group. Estimates are percentages, rounded to the nearest tenth.

Source: Statistics Canada. *Table 14-10-0020-01 Unemployment rate, participation rate and employment rate by educational attainment, annual.* Accessed July 16, 2021.

TOP 15 COUNTRIES VISITED BY CANADIANS, 2014

ONE OR MORE NIGHTS

Country visited	Visits (thousands)	Nights (thousands)	Spending in country (C$ millions)
United States	23,009	233,341	21,195
Mexico	1,900	25,979	2,262
United Kingdom	1,125	13,692	1,353
France	1,019	12,355	1,334
Cuba	844	8,882	780
Dominican Republic	528	6,086	562
Italy	468	5,021	572
Germany	467	4,397	420
China	367	7,526	758
Spain	332	3,846	360
Netherlands	275	2,040	221
Republic of Ireland	271	3,345	332
Hong Kong	236	3,068	284
Bahamas	227	2,153	196
Australia	210	5,179	516

Source: Statistics Canada. *Table 24-10-0037-01 - Travel by Canadians to foreign countries, top 15 countries visited.* Accessed July 16, 2021.

TOURISM DEMAND IN CANADA
QUARTERLY (DOLLARS X 1,000,000)

Expenditures	2020				2021
	Q1	Q2	Q3	Q4	Q1
Tourism expenditures	20,444	6,979	10,798	10,449	10,174
Total tourism commodities	17,406	5,879	9,050	8,752	8,509
Transportation	8,375	1,868	2,938	2,998	2,774
Passenger air transport	4,824	238	565	681	525
Passenger rail transport	46	4	13	11	9
Interurban bus transport	137	23	26	26	26
Vehicle rental	323	107	124	118	118
Vehicle repairs and parts	1,076	549	786	792	781
Vehicle fuel	1,752	880	1,312	1,259	1,202
Other transportation	217	67	112	111	113
Accommodation	3,052	1,174	1,957	1,899	1,891
Food and beverage services	2,880	1,184	1,894	1,680	1,693
Other tourism commodities	3,099	1,653	2,261	2,175	2,151
Recreation and entertainment	1,171	349	648	626	565
Travel agency services	857	287	299	277	243
Pre-trip expenditures	885	967	1,255	1,217	1,288
Convention fees	186	50	59	55	55
Total other commodities	3,038	1,100	1,748	1,697	1,665

Note: 2012 constant prices

Source: Statistics Canada. *Table 36-10-0230-01 Tourism demand in Canada, constant prices (x 1,000,000).* Accessed July 16, 2021.

Exhibitions, Shows & Events

The following list includes Consumer & Trade Shows, Public Events, Conferences & Festivals arranged by category of interest. The addresses given are often the addresses of associations/sponsors. Focus is on events of an ongoing annual or biennial nature. The lists are not complete but are fairly representative of shows held throughout Canada. Users are cautioned that dates or venues may vary, especially with ongoing disruptions from the COVID-19 pandemic.

ABORIGINAL *See* INDIGENOUS

AGRICULTURE *See* FARM BUSINESS/AGRICULTURE

ADVERTISING

AdTechCanada, c/o Brunico Communications Ltd., #100, 366 Adelaide St. West, Toronto ON M5V 1R9 - 416-408-2300; URL: www.brunico.com/conferences

Atomicon, c/o Brunico Communications Ltd., #100, 366 Adelaide St. West, Toronto ON M5V 1R9 - 416-408-2300; URL: atomicon.strategyonline.ca - March

Digimarcon Canada Digital Marketing Conference - URL: digimarconcanada.ca - Event Manager & Conference Host, Aaron Polmeer, Email: aaron@digimarcon.com - Takes place during Techspo Technology Expo - May - Toronto ON

Digital Marketing for Financial Services Summit, c/o Strategy Institute, #401, 401 Richmond St. West, Toronto ON M5V 3A8 - Tollfree: 1-866-298-9343, ext. 200; Email: registrations@strategyinstitute.com; URL: www.financialdigitalmarketing.com - Annual - June - Toronto ON

Dx3 Canada - 416-597-5751, Ext. 221; Email: info@dx3canada.com; URL: dx3canada.com - Exhibiting, Sponsorship & Media Contact, Hifazat 'Faz' Ahmad - Annual show focused on technology, digital marketing & retail - March - Toronto ON

Sign Canada Expo, c/o Sign Association of Canada, #1801, 1 Yonge St., Toronto ON M5E 1W7 - 905-856-0000; Fax: 905-856-0064; Tollfree: 1-877-470-9787; Email: info@sac-ace.ca; URL: www.sac-ace.ca - Sign Association of Canada's national tradeshow - Annual - Oct. - Toronto ON

AIR SHOWS/AVIATION

15 Wing Armed Forces Day, 15 Wing, PO Box 5000, Moose Jaw SK S6H 7Z8 - 306-694-2222; Fax: 306-694-2880; Email: 15wingpao@forces.gc.ca; URL: www.rcaf-arc.forces.gc.ca/en/15-wing/index.page - Static displays, plus ground & aerial demonstrations - Aug., Moose Jaw SK

19 Wing Comox Armed Forces Day & Airshow, 19 Wing, CFB Comox, PO Box 1000, Stn. Forces, Lazo BC V0R 2K0 - 250-339-8211; Fax (Media Information): 250-339-8120; URL: www.rcaf-arc.forces.gc.ca/en/19-wing/index.page - Celebrates Canadian Forces Day - Biennial - July or Aug.

Abbotsford International Airshow, Abbotsford International Airshow Society, 1464 Tower St., Abbotsford BC V2T 6H5 - 604-852-8511; Fax: 604-852-6093; Tollfree: 1-855-852-8511 Email: info@abbotsfordairshow.com; URL: www.abbotsfordairshow.com - Large static display. Six hour flying show. Occurs in conjunction with the Aerospace, Defence and Security Expo (ADSE) - Aug., Abbotsford International Airport, BC

Atlantic Canada International Airshow, Nova Scotia International Air Show Association (NSIASA), 166 Ingram Dr., Fall River NS B2T 1A4 - 902-465-2725; Fax: 902-484-3222; Tollfree: 1-855-465-2725; URL: www.airshowatlantic.ca - Executive Director, Colin Stephenson, Email: colin@airshowatlantic.ca - Aerial displays, including military & civilian aircraft; ground displays - Aug.

Borden Canadian Forces Day & Airshow, CFSTG/Base Borden Public Affairs Officer, Canadian Forces Base Borden, PO Box 1000 Stn. Main, Borden ON L0M 1C0 - 705-424-1200; Email: events@100yearsoffreedom.ca; URL: www.bordenairshow.ca - Military & civilian air demonstration & acrobatic teams; ground displays - June, Canadian Forces Base Borden, Borden ON

Canada Remembers Airshow, 17 Wing Detachment Dundurn, SK; URL: canadaremembersourheroes.ca - Volunteer Director, Brian Swidrovich, Email: b.swid@sasktel.net - Annual - Parade of Veterans; active & static displays - Aug.

Canadian International Airshow, Press Bldg., Exhibition Place, 210 Princes' Blvd., Toronto ON M6K 3C3 - 416-263-3650; Fax: 416-263-3654 ; Email: exhibitors@cias.org; URL: www.cias.org - Annually, three days of the Labour Day Weekend - Best viewed from Canadian National Exhibition grounds - Sept., Over Lake Ontario, Toronto ON

Festival of Flight, Festival of Flight Staff, Parks, Recreation & Tourism, Town of Gander, 100 Elizabeth Dr., Gander NL A1V 1G7 - 709-651-5927; Fax: 709-256-4195 URL: www.gandercanada.com - A celebration of Gander's aviation history - 1st Mon. in Aug.

Lethbridge International Airshow, Lethbridge International Airshow Association, PO Box 1351, Stn. Main, Lethbridge AB T1J 4K1 - 403-380-4245; Fax: 403-380-4998; URL: lethbridgeairshow.ca - July, Lethbridge International Airport, AB

Yukon Sourdough Rendezvous Airshow, Yukon Sourdough Rendezvous Society, 4230 - 4th Ave., Whitehorse YT Y1A 1G7 - 867-667-2148; URL: www.yukonrendezvous.com - Executive Director, Dave Blottner - Annual - Aerial & static displays - Feb., Whitehorse Airport, Whitehorse YT

ANTIQUES

Ancaster Nostalgia Show & Sale, Ontario Collector Shows, PO Box 705, Simcoe ON N3Y 4T2 - 519-426-8875; URL: www.collectorshows.ca - Multiple dates a year

Christie Antique & Vintage Show, 838 Mineral Springs Rd., PO Box 81067, Ancaster ON L9G 4X1 - 905-525-2181; URL: christieshow.ca - Hosted by the Hamilton Conservation Authority - Twice a year: Sat. after Victoria Day, and Sat. after Labour Day

London Nostalgia & Small Antique Show, Ontario Collector Shows, PO Box 705, Simcoe ON N3Y 4T2 - 519-426-8875; URL: www.collectorshows.ca - Oct.

Toronto International Antiquarian Book Fair, c/o Megan Webster, Webster's Fine Books & Maps, 1938 Bloor St. West, PO Box 30009, Toronto ON M6P 4J2 - 416-763-4664; Email: webstermaps@sympatico.ca; URL: www.torontoantiquarianbookfair.com - Annual - Nov.

Toronto Vintage Clothing Show, c/o Affiliated Showsales - 613-521-1970; Email: asi@sympatico.ca; URL: www.torontovintageclothingshow.ca - Annual - Sept.

Woodstock Nostalgia Show & Sale, Ontario Collector Shows, PO Box 705, Simcoe ON N3Y 4T2 - 519-426-8875; URL: www.collectorshows.ca - Multiple dates a year

APPAREL *See* FASHION

ARCHITECTURE *See* CONSTRUCTION

ART/ARTS

***See Also* Crafts; Music; Events**

Art Toronto, Informa Canada, #100, 10 Alcorn Ave., Toronto ON M4V 3A9 - Tollfree: 1-800-663-4173; Email: info@arttoronto.ca; URL: www.arttoronto.ca - Oct.

The Artist Project, Informa Canada, #100, 10 Alcorn Ave., Toronto ON M4V 3A9 - Tollfree: 1-800-663-4173; Email: info@theartistproject.com; URL: www.theartistproject.com - Show Director, Mia Nielsen, Email: mia.nielsen@informa.com - Feb.

Banff Summer Arts Festival, The Banff Centre, PO Box 1020, Banff AB T1L 1H5 - 403-762-6100; Fax: 403-762-6444; Tollfree: 1-800-565-9989; Email: communications@banffcentre.ca; URL: www.banffcentre.ca - President, Janice Price

Bard on the Beach Shakespeare Festival, BMO Theatre Centre, #201, 162 West - 1st. Ave., Vancouver BC V5Y 0H6 - 604-737-0625; Box Office: 604-739-0559; Fax: 604-737-0425; Email: info@bardonthebeach.org; URL: www.bardonthebeach.org - Artistic Director, Christopher Gaze; Executive Director, Claire Sakaki - June - Sept., Vanier Park waterfront, Vancouver BC

Blyth Festival, 423 Queen St., PO Box 10, Blyth ON N0M 1H0 - 519-523-9300; Fax: 519-523-9804; Tollfree: 1-877-862-5984; Email: info@blythfestival.com; URL: www.blythfestival.com - Artistic Director, Gil Garratt, Email:ggarratt@blythfestival.com - June - Sept., Blyth Memorial Community Hall, Blyth ON

Charlottetown Festival, Confederation Centre of the Arts, 145 Richmond St., Charlottetown PE C1A 1J1 - 902-628-1864; Fax: 902-566-4648; Email: info@confederationcentre.com; URL: www.confederationcentre.com/en/theatre.php - CEO, Steve Bellamy - Annual - Musical & dramatic entertainment - June - Sept.

Edmonton International Fringe Theatre Festival, 10330 - 84 Ave., Edmonton AB T6E 2G9 - 780-448-9000; Box Office: 780-409-1910; Fax: 780-431-1893; Email: communications@fringetheatre.ca; URL: fringetheatre.ca - Aug.

Festival Antigonish, Bauer Theatre, St. Francis Xavier University, PO Box 5000, Antigonish NS B2G 2W5 - 902-867-3333; Tollfree: 1-800-563-7529; URL: www.festivalantigonish.com - Artistic Director, Andrea Boyd, Email: aboyd@stfx.ca - July - Sept., Bauer Theatre, Antigonish NS

Lunenburg Craft & Food Festival, Lunenburg War Memorial Arena, c/o Darwin Event Group, P.O. Box 667, #16, 60 Morse Lane, Berwick, NS B0P 1E0 - 902-679-7177; Email: info@darwineventgroup.com; URL: lunenburgcraftandfoodfestival.com - August

Nova Scotia Folk Art Festival, PO Box 1773, Lunenurg NS B0J 2C0 - 902-634-4565; Alt. 902-766-4295; Email: mail@nsfolkartfestival.com; URL: www.nsfolkartfestival.com - Annual. Juried event, featuring an exhibition, workshops, speaker's corner, & sale of work by Nova Scotia folk artists - Aug., Lunenburg Memorial Arena, Lunenburg NS

Ottawa Fringe Theatre, Ottawa Fringe Festival, #100, 2 Daly Ave., Ottawa ON K1N 6E2 - 613-232-6162; Email: info@ottawafringe.com; URL: www.ottawafringe.com

PotashCorp Fringe Theatre & Street Festival, 25th Street Theatre Centre Inc., #209, 220 - 20th St. West, Saskatoon SK S7M 0W9 - 306-664-2239; Fax: 306-955-5852; URL: www.25thstreettheatre.org - Artistic & Executive Director, Anita Smith; Festival Manager, Kodu Manson - Annual - July / Aug., 200+ shows plus 200+ street vendors, Saskatoon SK

Scotiabank Nuit Blanche Toronto, City of Toronto Special Events, Toronto City Hall, West Tower, 100 Queen St. West, 6th Fl., Toronto ON M5H 2N2 - Email: nuitblancheto@toronto.ca; URL: www.toronto.ca/explore-enjoy/festivals-events/nuitblanche

Shakespeare by the Sea, 5799 Charles St., Halifax NS B3K 1K7 - 902-422-0295; Email: info@shakespearebythesea.ca; URL: www.shakespearebythesea.ca

Shakespeare by the Sea Festival, c/o 14 Scott St., St. John's NL A1C 2P7 - 709-691-7287; Email: info@shakespearebytheseafestival.com; URL: shakespearebytheseafestival.com

Shakespeare in High Park, The Canadian Stage Company, 26 Berkeley St., Toronto ON M5A 2W3 - 416-367-8243; Box Office: 416-368-3110; Fax: 416-367-1768; Email: boxoffice@canstage.com; URL: www.canadianstage.com - Artistic Director, Brendan Healy - June-Aug., High Park, Toronto ON

Shakespeare on the Saskatchewan Festival, 205A Pacific Ave., Saskatoon SK S7K 1N9 - 306-653-2300; URL: www.shakespearesask.com - Artistic Producer, Will Brooks - July/Aug.

Shaw Festival, PO Box 774, Niagara-on-the-Lake ON L0S 1J0 - 905-468-2153 ; Fax: 905-468-5438; Tollfree: 1-800-657-1106; URL: www.shawfest.com - Artistic Director, Tim Carroll - Theatre festival with an emphasis on the work of George Bernard Shaw

Stratford Festival, PO Box 520 , Stratford ON N5A 6V2 - 519-273-1600; Tollfree: 1-800-567-1600; URL: www.stratfordfestival.ca - Artistic Director, Antoni Cimolino - Theatre festival with an emphasis on the work of William Shakespeare

Summerworks, #423, 401 Richmond St. West, Toronto ON M5V 3A8 - 416-628-8216; URL: www.summerworks.ca - Artistic & Managing Director, Laura Nanni, Email: laura@summerworks.ca - Aug.

Toronto Fringe Festival, #204, 668 Richmond St. West, Toronto ON M6J 1C5 - 416-966-1062; Email: general@fringetoronto.com; URL: fringetoronto.com - Executive Director, Lucy Eveleigh - July

Toronto Outdoor Art Exhibition, #264, 401 Richmond St. West, Toronto ON M5V 3A8 - 416-408-2754; Email: info@torontooutdoorart.org; URL: www.torontooutdoorart.org - Executive Director, Anahita Azrahimi, Email: anahita@torontooutdoorart.org - Canada's largest outdoor art exhibition, held annually. Award program for participating artists - July, Nathan Phillips Square, Toronto ON

Vancouver Fringe Festival, 1398 Cartwright St., PO Box 203, Vancouver BC V6H 3R8 - 604-257-0350; Email: info@vancouverfringe.com; URL: www.vancouverfringe.com - Interim Executive Director, Sylvia Ceacero, Email: executivedirector@vancouverfringe.com - Annual - Sept.

Winnipeg Fringe Theatre Festival, Manitoba Theatre Centre, 174 Market Ave., Winnipeg MB R3B 0P8 - 204-943-7464; Email: info@winnipegfringe.com; URL: www.winnipegfringe.com - Annual, July

World Stage, Harbourfront Centre, 235 Queens Quay West, Toronto ON M5J 2G8 - 416-973-4600; Email: info@harbourfrontcentre.com; URL: www.harbourfrontcentre.com/worldstage - CEO, Marah Braye - International theatre festival - Harbourfront Centre, Toronto ON

AUTOMOTIVE

Atlantic Truck Show, Master Promotions Ltd., PO Box 565, 48 Broad St., Saint John NB E2L 3Z8 - 506-658-0018; Fax: 506-658-0750; Tollfree: 1-888-454-7469; Email: info@mpltd.ca; URL: www.atlantictruckshow.com - Annual - National Show Manager, Mark Cusack, Email: mcusack@mpltd.ca - June - Coliseum, Moncton NB

Barrie RV Expo, Continuum Productions Inc., 3488 Trelawny Circle, Mississauga ON L5N 6N7 - 905-824-1060; Fax: 905-824-9923; Email: info@continuumevents.ca; URL: www.continuumevents.ca; www.ontariorvshows.com - April

Edmonton Motor Show, Edmonton Expo Centre, Hall C, #C104, 7515 - 118 Ave., Edmonton AB T5B 4X5 - 780-423-2401; Fax: 780-423-2413; URL: www.edmontonmotorshow.com - Show Manager, Eleasha Naso - Annual consumer show - Edmonton Expo Centre

ExpoCam, Newcom Média Québec inc., #100, 6450, rue Notre Dame ouest, Montréal QC H4C 1V4 - 416-614-5817; Tollfree: 1-877-682-7469; URL: www.expocam.ca - Show Manager, Thierry Quagliata, Email: thierry@newcom.ca - Biennial trade & consumer show - April

Grand Prix of Canada, #100, 2170, av Pierre-Dupuy, Montreal QC H3C 3R4 - 514-350-4731; Fax: 514-350-0007; URL: www.gpcanada.ca - Annual international auto racing event - June - Gilles-Villeneuve Circuit, Montréal QC

Halifax RV Show, Master Promotions Ltd., PO Box 565, 48 Broad St., Saint John NB E2L 3Z8 - 506-658-0018; Fax: 506-658-0750; Tollfree: 1-888-454-7469; Email: info@mpltd.ca; URL: www.halifaxrvshow.ca - Annual consumer show - Show Manager, Scott Sprague, Email: ssprague@mpltd.ca - Jan., Halifax NS

Hamilton RV Expo, Continuum Productions Inc., 3488 Trelawny Circle, Mississauga ON L5N 6N7 - 905-824-1060; Fax: 905-824-9923; Email: info@continuumevents.ca; URL: www.continuumevents.ca; www.ontariorvshows.com - Jan.

Honda Indy Toronto, #300A, 370 Queens Quay West, Toronto ON M5V 3J3 - 416-588-7223; Tollfree: 1-877-503-6869; URL: www.hondaindy.com - Annual - July, Toronto ON

Manitoba RV Show, Recreation Vehicle Dealers Association of Manitoba, 31A Eric St., WinnipegMB R2M 5J2 - 204-456-1916; Fax: 204-253-4622; Email: showmanager@manitobarvshow.com; URL: www.manitobarvshow.com - Annual consumer show - March, WinnipegMB

Moncton RV Show, Master Promotions Ltd., PO Box 565, 48 Broad St., Saint John NB E2L 3Z8 - 506-658-0018; Fax: 506-658-0750; Tollfree: 1-888-454-7469; Email: info@mpltd.ca; URL: www.monctonrvshow.ca - Annual consumer show - Show Manager, Scott Sprague, Email: ssprague@mpltd.ca - Feb., Moncton NB

Montréal International Auto Show, 2335, rue Guénette, Montréal QC H4R 2E9 - 514-331-6571; Fax: 514-331-2045; Email: communications@ccqm.qc.ca; URL: www.salonautomontreal.com - Annual consumer show. New cars, light trucks, accessories - Jan. - Palais des Congrès, Montréal QC

Motorama Custom Car & Motorsports Expo, PO Box 370, Brights Grove ON N0N 1C0 - 416-962-7223; Email: info@motoramashow.com; URL: www.motoramashow.com; Annual consumer show - March

Motorcycle & Powersport Atlantic, North Atlantic Fish & Workboat Show, Master Promotions Ltd., PO Box 565, 48 Broad St., Saint John NB E2L 3Z8 - 506-658-0018; Fax: 506-658-0750; Tollfree: 1-888-454-7469; Email: info@mpltd.ca; URL: www.bikeatlantic.ca - Show Manager, Scott Sprague, Email: ssprague@mpltd.ca - Annual - March - Halifax NS

North American International Motorcycle Supershow, PO Box 551, Willow Beach ON L0E 1S0 - 905-722-6766; Fax: 1-888-680-7469; Tollfree: 1-888-661-7469; Email: info@motorcyclesupershow.ca; URL: www.motorcyclesupershow.ca - Director of Sales & Marketing, Booth & Sponsorship, Rick Bloye, Email: rickb@osmmag.com, Jan., International Centre, Toronto ON

RV Exposition & Sale, Recreation Vehicle Dealers Association of Alberta, 10561 - 172 St. NW, Edmonton AB T5S 1P1 - 780-455-8562; Tollfree: 1-888-858-8787; Email: rvda@rvda-alberta.org; URL: www.rvda-alberta.org - Annual consumer show held in Calgary, Edmonton & Red Deer - Feb.

Salon Moto de Montréal, Power Sport Services, #238, 3700, rue Saint-Patrick, Montréal QC H4E 1A1 - 514-375-1974; Fax: 514-221-3725; Tollfree: 1-866-375-1974; URL: www.montrealmotorcycleshow.ca - Director, Bianca Kennedy, Email: bekennedy@powersportservices.ca - Annual consumer show - Feb/March

Toronto Fall Classic Car Auction, Collector Car Productions, Inc., PO Box 1120, 186 Talbot St. West, Blenheim ON N0P 1A0 - 416-923-7500; Fax: 905-248-3353; Email: info@ccpauctions.com; URL: ccpauctions.com - Annual consumer show. Vintage cars, sale of parts & accessories - Oct./Nov. - International Centre, Mississauga ON

Toronto International Motorcycle Springshow - 905-771-0132; Fax: 1-866-355-7256; URL: motorcyclespringshow.com - Vice-President, Sales & Marketing, Peter Derry, Email: peter@motorcyclespringshow.com - March - International Centre, Toronto ON

Toronto Spring Classic Car Auction, Collector Car Productions, Inc., PO Box 1120, 186 Talbot St. West, Blenheim ON N0P 1A0 - 416-923-7500; Fax: 905-248-3353; Email: info@ccpauctions.com; URL: ccpauctions.com - Annual consumer show. Vintage cars, sale of parts & accessories - April - International Centre, Mississauga ON

TRUXPRO, Master Promotions Ltd., PO Box 565, 48 Broad St., Saint John NB E2L 3Z8 - 506-658-0018; Fax: 506-658-0750; Tollfree: 1-888-454-7469; Email: info@mpltd.ca; URL: www.truxpo.com - National Show - Commercial trucking show - Biennial - May

Vancouver Island RV Show & Sale, Recreation Vehicle Dealers Association of British Columbia, #195B, 1151 - 10th Ave. SW, Salmon Arm BC V1E 1T3 - 778-489-5057; Fax: 778-489-5097; Email: info@rvda.bc.ca; URL: www.rvda.bc.ca - Annual consumer show - April, Vancouver BC

BLUEGRASS *See* MUSIC

BOATING

Boat, Fishing & Outdoor Shows, Continuum Productions Inc., 3488 Trelawny Circle, Mississauga ON L5N 6N7 - 905-824-1060; Fax: 905-824-9923; URL: www.ontarioboatshows.com - Consumer show - Feb., London ON & March, Hamilton ON

Halifax International Boat Show, Master Promotions Ltd., PO Box 565, 48 Broad St., Saint John NB E2L 3Z8 - 506-658-0018; Fax: 506-658-0750; Tollfree: 1-888-454-7469; Email: info@mpltd.ca; URL: www.halifaxboatshow.com - Show Manager, Scott Sprague, Email: ssprague@mpltd.ca - Annual - Feb.

Kingston Boat & Recreation Show & Sale, c/o 20/20 Show Productions Inc., PO Box 400, Belle River ON N0R 1A0 - 226-363-0550; Fax: 226-363-0455; URL: ontariotradeshows.com - March

Moncton Boat Show, Master Promotions Ltd., PO Box 565, 48 Broad St., Saint John NB E2L 3Z8 - 506-658-0018; Fax: 506-658-0750; Tollfree: 1-888-454-7469; Email: info@mpltd.ca; URL: www.monctonboatshow.ca - Annual consumer show - Show Manager, Scott Sprague, Email: ssprague@mpltd.ca - March - Moncton Coliseum, Moncton NB

Muskoka In Water Boat & Cottage Show, CanNorth Shows Inc., Phone: 647-344-3122; Toll-Free: 1-855-723-1156; URL: www.muskokashows.com - Contact, Nori Richens, Email: nori@cannorthshows.com

Ottawa Boat Show, Master Promotions Ltd., PO Box 565, 48 Broad St., Saint John NB E2L 3Z8 - 506-658-0018; Fax: 506-658-0750; Tollfree: 1-888-454-7469; Email: info@mpltd.ca; URL: www.ottawaboatshow.ca - Show Manager, Scott Sprague, Email: ssprague@mpltd.ca - Feb. - Ottawa ON

Toronto International Boat Show, Canadian Boat Shows - 905-951-4050; URL: www.torontoboatshow.com - Jan. - Enercare Centre, Exhibition Place, Toronto ON

Victoria Boat & Fishing Show, Canwest Productions Inc., #218, 7710 – 5 St. SE, Calgary AB T2H 2L9 - 403-242-0859; Fax: 403-246-3856; Tollfree: 1-800-626-1538; URL: www.victoriaboatshow.com - Show Director, Kevin Blackburn, Email: kevin@canwestproductions.com - Annual consumer show - Feb. - Pearkes Recreation Centre, Victoria BC

Victoria Classic Boat Festival, c/o Maritime Museum of British Columbia, 634 Humboldt St., Victoria BC V8W 1A4 - Phone: 250-385-4222; URL: www.classicboatfestival.ca - Acting Chair, Stasi Manser - Annually, Labour Day weekend, Victoria BC

BOOKS

International Festival of Authors, 235 Queen's Quay West, Toronto ON M5J 2G8 - 416-973-4760; Fax: 416-954- 4323; Email: info@festivalofauthors.ca; URL: festivalofauthors.ca - Interviews & readings by novelists, poets, playwrights & biographers - Oct. - Harbourfront Centre, Toronto ON

Montréal Book Fair/Salon du livre de Montréal, #430, 300, rue du Saint-Sacrement, Montréal QC H2Y 1X4 - 514-845-2365; Email: slm.info@videotron.ca; URL: www.salondulivredemontreal.com - Executive Director, Olivier Gougeon - Annual consumer show - Nov., Montréal QC

Salon international du Livre de Québec, 26, rue Saint-Pierre, Québec QC G1K 8A3 - 418-692-0010; Fax: 418-692-0029; URL: www.silq.ca - President & CEO, Daniel Gélinas, Email: dgelinas@silq.ca - Annual consumer show - April, Québec QC

The Word on the Street, The Word on the Street Canada, National Office, 147 Liberty St., Toronto ON M6K 3G3 - 416-658-3144; URL: www.thewordonthestreet.ca - Annual celebration of literacy & the printed word; held in Toronto, Halifax, Lethbridge & Saskatoon - Sept.

BRIDAL

BridalExpo - 403-660-0166; Email: info@bridalexpo.ca; URL: bridalexpo.ca - Contact, Lenora Kingcott - Oct., Calgary Telus Convention Centre, Calgary AB

Canada's Bridal Show, #10, 136 Winges Rd., Woodbridge ON L4L 6C4 - 905-264-7000; Fax: 905-264-7300; Email: info@canadasbridalshow.com; URL: www.canadasbridalshow.com - Annual consumer show. Bridal fashion shows, gifts, florists, photography, entertainment, travel - Jan. & Sept., Metro Toronto Convention Centre, Toronto ON

Cannabis Wedding Expo - 720-683-0420; Email: hello@cannabisweddingexpo.com; URL: www.cannabisweddingexpo.com - Expos in the U.S. and Canada - Toronto ON

Modern Bride Wedding Show, #323, 1881 Steeles Ave. West, Toronto ON M3H 0A1 - Toll-Free: 888-222-2860; Email: hello@modernbrideweddingshow.com; URL: modernbrideweddingshow.com - Spring, The International Centre, Toronto ON

National Bridal Show, 3145 Wolfedale Rd., Mississauga ON L5C 3A9 - 905-273-8111; Fax: 905-277-9917; Email: info@nationalbridalshow.com; URL: nationalbridalshow.com - Assistant Show Manager, Laura Jackman, Email: ljackman@starmetrolandmedia.com - Annually, Feb. & Sept.

Vancouver Island Bridal Exhibition, 3319 Savannah Pl., Nanaimo BC V9T 6R9 - 250-244-8449; Fax: 1-877-325-3299; Tollfree: 1-888-501-9696; Email: bridalexhibition@ieginc.ca; URL: www.bridalexhibition.ca

A Wedding Show - URL: aweddingexpo.ca - Sept., Delta Hotel Regina, Regina SK

The Wedding Show - URL: www.theweddingshow.ca - Feb., Hyatt Regency Toronto, Toronto ON

BUSINESS

Business Expo, Greater Nanaimo Chamber of Commerce, 2133 Bowen Rd., Nanaimo BC V9S 1H8 - 250-756-1191; Fax: 250-756-1584; Email: info@nanaimochamber. bc.ca; URL: www.nanaimochamber.bc.ca - CEO, Kim Smythe, Email: ceo@nanaimochamber.bc. - Oct. - Vancouver Island Conference Centre

Canada India International Expo (CIIEXPO) - URL: ciiexpo.ca - Sept.

Canadian SME Business Expo, c/o Cmarketing Inc, #203, 2800 Skymark Ave., Mississauga ON L4W 5A6 - 647-668-5785; 905-206-0055; Email: info@canadiansme.ca; URL: www.smeexpo.ca

Canadian Small Business Women Summer Marketplace - Tollfree: 1-888-526-9366; URL: canadiansmallbusinesswomen.ca - July

CDW Canada's Business Technology Expo (BTEX), #300, 20 Carlson Ct., Toronto ON M9W 7K6; 647-288-5700; URL: www.cdw.ca - May

Franchise Expos, c/o National Event Management Inc., #102, 260 Town Centre Blvd., Markham ON L3R 8H8 - 905-477-2677; Fax: 905-477-7872; Tollfree: 1-800-891-4859; Email: info@nationalevent.com; URL: www.franchiseshowinfo.com

Iranian Canadian Business Expo - 416-450-6840; URL: www.icbe.ca - CEO, Kiu Rezvanifar, Email: kiu@icbe.ca - Nov., Toronto ON

Small Business Calgary Expo, c/o Calgary Chamber of Commerce, #600, 237 - 8th Ave. SE, Calgary, AB T2G 5C3 - 403-750-0400; Email: reception@calgarychamber.com; URL: www.calgarychamber.com

SOHO SME Business Expo, SOHO Business Group, #1, 1680 Lloyd Ave., North Vancouver BC V7P 2N6; 604-929-8250; Tollfree: 1-800-290-7646; URL: soho.ca - Sept./Oct. - Held in Vancouver BC, Calgary AB & Toronto ON

Traders Forum Shows, #200, 96 Bradwick Dr., Concord ON L4K 1K8; 905-760-7694; Fax: 905-738-3557; Tollfree: 1-877-655-6787; Email: info@tradersforum.ca; URL: www.tradersforum.ca - Trade shows for the discount & mass merchandise industry - Aug./Sept. - Held in Toronto ON, Halifax NS & Montreal QC

CARS *See* AUTOMOTIVE

CANNABIS

Atlantic Cannabis Conference & Expo - URL: www.acexpo.ca - Charlottetown PE - May

C-45 Quality Summit - URL: www.c45summit.com - Run by HFC Productions Inc.

Canadian Cannabis Conference - 418-456-6385; Email: pdrapeau@silicycle.com; URL: www.conferencecannabis.ca - Oct.

Canadian Cannabis Expo - URL: www.niagarafalls420expo.com; Email: info@niagarafalls420expo.com - Scotiabank Convention Centre, Niagara Falls ON - April

Canadian Cannabis Summit - 403-608-2661; Email: info@cannabissummit.ca; URL: cannabissummit.ca - Brings together medical professionals, policy makers, and business and community leaders - May-June

Cannabis & Hemp Expo, c/o Canwest Productions, #201, 7710 - 5 St. SE, Calgary, AB T2H 2L9 - 403-242-0859; Fax: 403-246-3856; Tollfree: 1-800-626-1538; URL: cannabishempexpo.com - Expos take place in Calgary and Edmonton

Cannabis Wedding Expo - 720-683-0420; Email: hello@cannabisweddingexpo.com; URL: www.cannabisweddingexpo.com - Expos in the U.S. and Canada - Toronto ON

Expo Cannabis Montréal - 438-800-2020; URL: www.cannabisexpomontreal.com - Contact, Jean-Philippe Turgeon, Email: jpturgeon@nationalevent.com - Palais des congrès - Sept.

Grow Up Cannabis Conference & Expo - Tollfree: 1-866-4769-871; Email: info@growupconference.com; URL: growupconference.com - Niagara Falls ON and Victoria BC

Growing Summit - URL: www.growingsummit.com - Run by HFC Productions Inc.

HempFest Cannabis Expo - URL: www.hempfestcanada.com - Run by HFC Productions Inc. - Calgary AB

The Karma Cup Cannabis Expo, #258, 75 First St., Orangeville ON L9W 5B6 - Email: info@thekarmacup.com; URL: thekarmacup.com - Industry & consumer show - Sept.

Lift & Co. Cannabis Expo - Tollfree: 1-800-681-1593; Email: hello@lift.co; URL: liftexpo.ca - Annual expos held in Toronto ON (May) and Vancouver BC (Jan.)

O'Cannabiz Conference & Expo, 5355 Vail Court, Mississauga ON L5M 6G9 - 905-858-3298; Email: info@ocannabiz.com; URL: ocannabiz.com - Founder & CEO, Neill Dixon, Email: neill@ocannabiz.com - April (Toronto) and Dec. (Vancouver)

CHEMISTRY

Canadian Chemical Engineering Conference, c/o Canadian Society for Chemistry, #400, 222 Queen St., Ottawa ON K1P 5V9 - 613-232-6252; Fax: 613-232-5862; Tollfree: 1-888-542-2242; URL: www.cheminst.ca/conferences - Oct.

Canadian Chemistry Conference & Exhibition, c/o Canadian Society for Chemistry, #400, 222 Queen St., Ottawa ON K1P 5V9 - 613-232-6252; Fax: 613-232-5862; Tollfree: 1-888-542-2242; URL: www.cheminst.ca/conferences - May or June

Canadian Society of Clinical Chemists Conference, CSCC Head Office, #310, 4 Cataraqui St., Kingston ON K7K 1Z7 - 613-531-8899; Tollfree Fax: 1-866-303-0626; Email: office@cscc.ca; URL: www.cscc.ca - July

CHILDREN

Calgary Baby & Tot Show - 403-249-1270; Email: calgarybabyandtot@gmail.com; URL: www.calgarybabyshow.com - Show producer, Kelly Kennedy (KRK Productions Inc.) - Oct. - Calgary AB

Edmonton Mom, Pop & Tots Fair, Family Productions Inc., 4634 - 90A Ave., 2nd Fl., Edmonton AB T6B 2P9 - 780-490-0215 ; Fax: 780-450-3757; Email: info@edmontonshows.com; URL: mpt.edmontonshows.com

International Children's Festival of the Arts, St. Albert Place, 5 St. Anne St., St. Albert AB T8N 3Z9 - 780-459-1600; Email: culture@stalbert.ca; URL: www.childfest.com - Andrea Gammon, Festival Coordinator - Annual - May - The Arden Theatre, St. Albert AB

Nutrien Children's Festival of Saskatchewan, Delta Bessborough Hotel, #400 MacMillan Bldg, 135 - 21st St. East, Saskatoon SK S7K 0B4 - URL: nutrienchildrensfestival.com - Annually, June. Four-day international festival of the performing arts for children

Ottawa Children's Festival, #602, 294 Albert St., Ottawa ON K1P 6E6 - 613-241-0999; Email: contact@ottawachildrensfestival.ca; URL: ottawachildrensfestival.ca - June

Vancouver International Children's Festival 1360 East 3rd Ave., Vancouver BC V5N 5R8 - 604-708-5655; Email: info@childrensfestival.ca; URL: www.childrensfestival.ca - May-June

Winnipeg International Children's Festival, #130, 123 Main St., Winnipeg MB R3C 1A3 - 204-958- 4730; Fax: 204-272-6774; Email: kidsfest@kidsfest.ca; URL: www.kidsfest.ca - Executive Producer, Neal Rempel - Annual - June, Winnipeg MB

CHRISTMAS CRAFTS *See* CRAFTS

COMMUNICATIONS

Canadian CommTech Show & Seminars, Dazzle Me Productions, 25 Forest Rd., Grimsby ON L3M 2J4; 905-309-1914; Fax: 289-235-9867; Tollfree: 1-855-215-1334; Email: info@commtechshow.com; www.commtechshow.com - Annual shows held in Toronto ON and Calgary AB - April & May

Canadian ISP Summit, c/o Canadian Network Operators Consortium, #1105, 20 Eglinton Ave. West - 416-313-2662; Email: info@cnoc.ca; URL: ispsummit.tech - Executive Assistant, Mélanie Vautour, Email: melanie@cnoc.ca - Nov.

Canadian Telecom Summit, c/o Macgregor Communications, P.O. Box 1, Newmarket ON L3Y 4W3 - 1-888-443-6786 ext. 2249; Email: rjirka@macgregorcom.com; URL: www.telecomsummit.com - November

Connection Conference & Gala Awards, c/o Ontario Association of Broadcasters, 5762 Hwy 7 East, PO Box 54040, Markham ON L3P 7Y4 - 905-554-2730; Fax: 905-554-2731; Email: memberservices@oab.ca; URL: oab.ca/conference - Annual, Nov.

COMPUTERS

ACM CHI Conference on Human Factors in Computing Systems - URL: chi2021.acm.org - General Chairs, Yoshifumi Kitamura & Aaron Quigley, Email: generalchairs@chi2021.acm.org

AI/GI/CRV Conference, c/o Pierre Boulanger, Dept. of Computing Science, University of Alberta, Athabasca Hall, #411, Edmonton AB T6G 2E8 - Email: pierreb@cs.ualberta.ca; URL: aigicrv.org - Collaboration of three conferences: Artificial Intelligence, Graphics Interface, & Computer and Robot Vision - May

Canadian Celebration of Women in Computing (CAN-CWiC) - Email: cancwic@gmail.com; URL: www.can-cwic.ca - Annual - Nov.

Canadian Conference on Electrical & Computer Engineering, c/o IEEE Canada, 685 Woodcrest Blvd., London ON N6K 1P8 - 519-472-7842; URL: ccece2021.ieee.ca - Annual - April

International Parallel & Distributed Processing Symposium (IPDPS), c/o IEEE Canada, 685 Woodcrest Blvd., London ON N6K 1P8 - 519-472-7842; Email: info@ipdps.org; URL: www.ipdps.org - May

SecTor Security Education Conference, c/o Informa Tech Canada, Inc., #1018, 6021 Yonge St., Toronto ON M2M 3W2 - 416-977-0330; Email: info@sector.ca; URL: sector.ca - Annual IT security conference - Nov., Metro Toronto Convention Centre, Toronto ON

Western Canada Information Security Conference, ISACA Winnipeg Chapter, #13B, 30 - 360 Main St., Winnipeg MB R3C 3Z8 - Tollfree: 1-844-472-2297, ext. 701; URL: www.wcisc.ca - Annual conference - May - Winnipeg Convention Centre, Winnipeg MB

CONSTRUCTION & BUILDING PRODUCTS

ABSDA Building Supply Expo, c/o Atlantic Building Supply Dealers Association, 70 Englehart St., Dieppe NB E1A 8H3 - 506-858-0700; Fax: 506-859-0064; Email: absda@nbnet.nb.ca; URL: www.absda.ca - Annual trade show - Feb.

Buildex, Informa Canada, #510, 1185 West Georgia St., Vancouver BC V6E 4E6 - 1-877-739-2112; URL: www.buildexcalgary.com - Show Director, Lisa Barnes, Email: lisa.barnes@informa.com

The Buildings Show, Informa Canada, #100, 10 Alcorn Ave., Toronto ON M4V 3A9 - Tollfree: 1-800-663-4173; Email: events@informacanada.com; URL: www.thebuildingsshow.com - Features six shows over three days - Late Nov./early Dec. - Toronto ON

Canadian Concrete Expo, c/o 20/20 Show Productions Inc., PO Box 400, Belle River ON N0R 1A0 - 226-363-0550; Fax: 226-363-0455; URL: canadianconcreteexpo.com - President, Stuart Galloway, Email: stuart@exposition.com - Annual - Feb.

Construct Canada, Informa Canada, #100, 10 Alcorn Ave., Toronto ON M4V 3A9 - Tollfree: 1-800-663-4173; Email: events@informacanada.com; URL: www.constructcanada.com - Annual trade show; part of The Buildings Show. Products, technologies & systems for the design & construction of all building types - Dec. - Metro Toronto Convention Centre, Toronto ON

Contech Expos, Informa Canada, #100, 10 Alcorn Ave., Toronto ON M4V 3A9 - Tollfree: 1-800-663-4173; Email: events@informacanada.com; URL: www.contech.qc.ca/en/tradeshows - Abitibi, Bas-St-Laurent, Montréal, Québec

HomeBuilder & Renovator Expo, Informa Canada, #100, 10 Alcorn Ave., Toronto ON M4V 3A9 - Tollfree: 1-800-663-4173; Email: events@informacanada.com; URL: www.homebuilderexpo.ca - Annual trade show; part of The Buildings Show - Dec. - Metro Toronto Convention Centre, Toronto ON

National Heavy Equipment Show, Master Promotions Ltd., PO Box 565, 48 Broad St., Saint John NB E2L 3Z8 - 506-658-0018; Fax: 506-658-0750; Tollfree: 1-888-454-7469; Email: info@mpltd.ca; URL: www.mpltd.ca - April

The Project Management Conference, Informa Canada, #100, 10 Alcorn Ave., Toronto ON M4V 3A9 - Tollfree: 416-512-0203; Email: events@informacanada.com; URL: www.thepmconference.com - Sept.

World of Concrete Pavilion, Informa Canada, #100, 10 Alcorn Ave., Toronto ON M4V 3A9 - Tollfree: 1-800-663-4173; Email: events@informacanada.com; URL: www.worldofconcretepavilion.com - Part of The Buildings Show - Late Nov./early Dec. - Metro Toronto Convention Centre, Toronto ON

CRAFTS

Art Market, Art Market Productions, P.O. Box 19008, RPO 16, 1153 - 56th St., Delta BC V4L 2P8 - Tollfree: 1-877-929-9933; URL: www.artmarketcraftsale.com - Production Manager, Nichole Windblad - Annual consumer show; art & craft sale - Nov., Calgary AB

Craft East Buyers' Expo, Craft Alliance, Box 3, #15, 1574 Argyle St., Halifax NS B3J 2B3 - Tollfree: 1-855-567-4897; URL: craftalliance.ca/craft-east/details - Director, Bernard Burton, Email: bernard@craftalliance.ca - Annual trade show. Juried craft & giftware products

Beaches Arts & Crafts Show, Signatures Shows Ltd., 113 Murray St., Ottawa ON K1N 5M5 - 613-241-5777; Tollfree: 1-888-773-4444; Email: info@signatures.ca; URL: signatures.ca/beaches-arts-and-crafts - Annual consumer show - June - Toronto ON

Butterdome Craft Show, Signatures Shows Ltd., 113 Murray St., Ottawa ON K1N 5M5 - 613-241-5777; Tollfree: 1-888-773-4444; Email: info@signatures.ca; URL: signatures.ca/butterdome - Spring & Fall - Edmonton

By Hand, Signatures Shows Ltd., 113 Murray St., Ottawa ON K1N 5M5 - 613-241-5777; Tollfree: 1-888-773-4444; Email: info@signatures.ca; URL: signatures.ca/byhand

Christmas at the Forum Crafts Festival, DMS Trade Shows Ltd., PO Box 51064, Halifax NS B3M 4R8; Tollfree: 1-866-995-7469; Tollfree Fax: 1-866-995-7469; Email: info@dmstradeshows.com; URL: www.christmasattheforum.com - Nov. - Halifax NS

Creativ Festival, CanNorth Shows Inc., 19 Marble Arch Cres., Toronto ON MQR 1W8 - 647-344-6700; Tollfree: 1-855-723-1156; URL: csnf.com - Oct. - Toronto ON

Creative Stitches & Crafting Alive, CanNorth Shows Inc. 19 Marble Arch Cres., Toronto ON MQR 1W8 - 647-344-6700; Tollfree: 1-855-723-1156; URL: creativestitchesshow.com - Annual consumer show in Calgary & Edmonton - Sept.

Fall Into Christmas Craft Show, Signatures Shows Ltd., 113 Murray St., Ottawa ON K1N 5M5 - 613-241-5777; Fax: 613-241-5678; Tollfree: 1-888-773-4444; Email: info@signatures.ca; URL: signatures.ca/fall-into-christmas - Oct. - Medicine Hat AB, Lethbridge AB

Festival of Crafts, Signatures Shows Ltd., 113 Murray St., Ottawa ON K1N 5M5 - 613-241-5777; Fax: 613-241-5678; Tollfree: 1-888-773-4444; Email: info@signatures.ca; URL: signatures.ca/festival-of-crafts - Dec. - Calgary AB

Holiday Bazaart, MacKenzie Art Gallery, 3475 Albert St., Regina SK S4S 6X6 - 306-584-4250; Email: info@mackenzieartgallery.ca; URL: mackenzie.art/event/holiday-bazaart - Art show & sale; complete range of crafts - Nov.

Indie Handmade, Signatures Shows Ltd., 113 Murray St., Ottawa ON K1N 5M5 - 613-241-5777; Fax: 613-241-5678; Tollfree: 1-888-773-4444; Email: info@signatures.ca; URL: signatures.ca/indie-handmade - April. & Nov. - St. Albert AB

One of a Kind Christmas Canadian Craft Show & Sale, Informa Canada, #100, 10 Alcorn Ave., Toronto ON M4V 3A9 - Tollfree: 1-800-663-4173; Email: hello@oneofakindshow.com;

URL: www.oneofakindshow.com - Show Director, Janice Leung, Email: janice@oneofakindshow.com - Annual consumer show - Nov./Dec. - Enercare Centre, Exhibition Place, Toronto ON

One of a Kind Springtime Canadian Craft Show & Sale, Informa Canada, #100, 10 Alcorn Ave., Toronto ON M4V 3A9 - Tollfree: 1-800-663-4173; Email: hello@oneofakindshow.com; URL: www.oneofakindshow.com - Show Director, Janice Leung, Email: janice@oneofakindshow.com - Annual consumer show - March - Enercare Centre, Exhibition Place, Toronto ON

Originals Ottawa Christmas Craft Sale, Signatures Shows Ltd., 113 Murray St., Ottawa ON K1N 5M5 - 613-241-5777; Fax: 613-241-5678; Tollfree: 1-888-773-4444; URL: signatures.ca/originals - Dec.

Originals - The Spring Craft Sale, Signatures Shows Ltd., 113 Murray St., Ottawa ON K1N 5M5 - 613-241-5777; Fax: 613-241-5678; Tollfree: 1-888-773-4444; URL: signatures.ca/originals - April

Our Best to You, Signatures Shows Ltd., 113 Murray St., Ottawa ON K1N 5M5 - 613-241-5777; Fax: 613-241-5678; Tollfree: 1-888-773-4444; Email: info@signatures.ca; URL: signatures.ca/our-best-to-you - Red Deer AB, Oct. & Regina SK, Nov.

Pine Tree Potters' Guild Potters Sales, PO Box 28586, Aurora ON L4G 6S6 - 905-727-1278; www.pinetreepotters.ca/sales.html - Spring and Fall sales are held

Signatures Ottawa, Signatures Shows Ltd., 113 Murray St., Ottawa ON K1N 5M5 - 613-241-5777; Fax: 613-241-5678; Tollfree: 1-888-773-4444; Email: info@signatures.ca; URL: signatures.ca/signatures-ottawa - Annual consumer show - Nov., Ottawa ON

Signatures Winnipeg, Signatures Shows Ltd., 113 Murray St., Ottawa ON K1N 5M5 - Fax: 613-241-5678; Tollfree: 1-800-773-4444; Email: info@signatures.ca; URL: signatures.ca/winnipeg - Annual consumer show - Nov., Winnipeg MB

Sundog Arts & Entertainment Faire, c/o Sundog Arts Society, PO Box 7183, Saskatoon SK S7K 4J1 - 306-384-7364; Fax: 306-384-7364; Email: sundoghandcraftfaire@sasktel.net; www.sundoghandcraftfaire.com - Coordinator, Diane Boyko - Juried three-day craft market plus continuous stage acts & gourmet food court. Annually, first weekend of Dec.

Touch of Talent Craft Sale, Signatures Shows Ltd., 113 Murray St., Ottawa ON K1N 5M5 - 613-241-5777; Fax: 613-241-5678; Tollfree: 1-888-773-4444; Email: info@signatures.ca; URL: signatures.ca/touch-of-talent - Sept. - Sherwood Park AB

Victoria Park Craft Fair, c/o Joe Savoie, 67 Otho St., Neguac NB E9G 1M3 - 506-779-5599; 506-779-8908; joe@turnerschristmas.com; URL: victoriaparkcrafts.com - Annually - Aug.

WinterGreen Fine Craft Market, Saskatchewan Craft Council, 813 Broadway Ave., Saskatoon SK S7N 1B5 - 306-653-3616; Fax: 306-244-2711; Tollfree: 1-866-653-3616; Email: saskcraftcouncil@sasktel.net; URL www.saskcraftcouncil.org - Executive Director, Carmen Milenkovic, Email: scc.director@sasktel.net - Annual. Three day Christmas craft market - Nov., Regina SK

DANCE *See* MUSIC

DECORATING *See* HOME SHOWS

DEFENCE/SECURITY

Aerospace, Defence and Security Expo (ADSE), c/o Aerospace Industries Association of Canada, #703, 255 Albert St., Ottawa ON K1P 6A9 - 613-232-4297; URL: www.adse.ca - Held in conjunction with the Abbotsford International Airshow - Aug., Abbotsford BC

Canadian Defence Security & Aerospace Exhibition Atlantic (DEFSEC), 166 Ingram Dr., Fall River NS B2T 1A4 - 902-465-2725; Fax: 902-484-3222 URL: www.defsecatlantic.ca - Executive Director, Colin Stephenson, Email: colin@defsecatlantic.ca - Sept.

Security Canada International Security Conference & Exposition, c/o Canadian Security Association #201, 50 Acacia Ave., Markham ON L3R 0B3, 905-513-0622; Fax: 905-513-0624; Tollfree: 1-800-538-9919; URL: www.securitycanada.com - Director, Trade Shows & Events, Steve Basnett, Email: sbasnett@canasa.org - Shows incude East (April), Alberta (May), Ottawa (May), West (June) Atlantic (Sept.) & Central (Oct.)

ELECTRICAL/ELECTRONICS

Canadian Mobile Audio Expo - URL: cmaexpo.ca - Event Director, Frank Spezzano, Email: frank@cmaexpo.ca - Sheraton Toronto Airport Hotel & Conference Centre, Toronto ON - April

Eptech, Electronic Products & Technology, 80 Valleybrook Dr., Toronto ON M3B 2S9 - 416-442-5600; Fax: 416-510-5134; Email: info@ept.ca; URL: www.ept.ca - Trade show held in various locations. Electronic components, systems

MEET (Mechanical Electical Electronic Technology), Master Promotions Ltd., PO Box 565, Saint John NB E2L 3Z8 - 506-658-0018; Fax: 506-658-0750; Tollfree: 1-888- 454-7469; Email: info@masterpromotions.ca; URL: www.meetshow.ca - Biennial

Techspo Technology Expo - URL: techspo.co - Event Manager & Expo Host, Aaron Polmeer, Email: aaron@techspo.co - Digimarcon Canada takes place as part of this expo - May - Toronto ON

ENVIRONMENT

Canadian Environmental Conference & Tradeshow (CANECT), c/o Envirogate Event Management Inc., #30, 220 Industrial Parkway South, Aurora ON L4G 3V6 - 905-727-4666; URL: canect.net - Sales Contact, Denise Simpson, Email: denise@esemag.com - Annual - May - Toronto ON

Canadian Waste to Resource Conference, #580, 170 Attwell Drive, Etobicoke ON M9W 5Z5 - Email: info@owma.org; URL: www.cw2rc.ca - Annual

Green Living Show, c/o Green Living Enterprises, #307, 70 The Esplanade, Toronto ON M5E 1R2 - 416-360-0044; Email: info@green-living.ca; URL: www.greenlivingshow.ca - April - Toronto ON

National Water & Wastewater Conference, c/o Canadian Water & Wastewater Association, #11, 1010 Polytek Rd., Ottawa ON K1J 9H9 - 613-747-0524; Fax: 613-747-0523; Email: admin@cwwa.ca; URL: www.cwwa.ca - Executive Director, Robert Haller, Email: rhaller@cwwa.ca - Biennial

ETHNIC *See* MULTICULTURAL

EVENTS

***See Also* specific categories for events such as Winter Carnivals, Music Festivals, Rodeos, Exhibitions, etc.**

Ashkenaz: A Festival of New Yiddish Culture, #303, 455 Spadina Ave., Toronto ON M5S 2G8 - 416-979-9901; URL: www.ashkenaz.ca - Managing Director, Samantha Parnes, Email: sam@ashkenaz.ca - Biennial; Aug./Sept.

Billy Barker Days, PO Box 4441, Quesnel BC V2J 3J4 - 250-992-1234; Fax: 250-992-5083; Email: office@billybarkerdays.ca; URL: www.billybarkerdays.ca - July

Creston Valley Blossom Festival, PO Box 329, Creston BC V0B 1G0 - 250-428-4284; Fax: 250-428-9411; Email: info@blossomfestival.ca; URL: www.blossomfestival.ca - May, long weekend

The Canadian Tulip Festival, Canadian Tulip Festival, #203, 1525 Princess Patricia Way, Ottawa ON K1S 5J3, Tollfree: 1-800-668-8547; URL: www.tulipfestival.net - May

The Canadian Gaming Summit, MediaEDGE Communications, #1000, 5255 Yonge St., Toronto ON M2N 6P4 - 416-512-8186; Fax: 416-512-8344; Tollfree: 1-866-216-0860; URL: canadiangamingsummit.com - Director, Show Operations, Brad Moore, Email: bradm@mediaedge.ca

Canmore Highland Games, Three Sisters Scottish Festival Society, PO Box 8102, Canmore AB T1W 2T8 - 403-678-9454; Fax: 403-678-3385; Email: info@canmorehighlandgames.ca; URL: www.canmorehighlandgames.ca - Annually, Labour Day Sunday - Sept., Canmore AB

Calgary Tattoo & Arts Festival, Canwest Productions Inc., #218, 7710 – 5th St. SE, Calgary AB T2H 2L9 - 403-242-0859; Fax: 403-246 -3856; Tollfree: 1-800-626-1538; Email: tattoo@canwestproductions.com; URL: albertatattooshows.com/Calgary - Oct. - Calgary AB

Chocolate Fest, Chocolate Festival, 9 Mark St., St. Stephen NB E3L 1G4 - 506-465-5616; Fax: 506-465- 5610; Email: info@chocolate-fest.ca; URL: www.chocolate-fest.ca

Discovery Days Festival, PO Box 389, Dawson YT Y0B 1G0 - 867-993-5575; Fax: 867-993- 6415; Email: kva@dawson.net; URL: www.dawsoncity.ca - Aug.

Feast of St. Louis, Fortress of Louisbourg Volunteer Association, 259 Park Service Rd., Louisbourg NS B1C 2L2 - 902-733-3548; Fax: 902-733-3046; Email: info@fortressoflouisbourg.ca; URL: www.fortressoflouisbourg.ca - Eighteenth-century celebrations in honour of St. Louis - Aug. - Louisbourg NS

Festival des peches et de aquaculture du Nouveau Brunswick, #200, 1 av Hotel de Ville, Shippagan NB E8S 1M1 - 506-336-8726; Email: festivalshippagan@gmail.com; URL: www.festival.shippagan.com

Icelandic Festival of Manitoba, #107, 94 - 1st Ave., Gimli MB R0C 1B0 - 204-642-7417; Fax: 204-642-9382; Email: info@icelandicfestival.com; URL: www.icelandicfestival.com, Aug. - Gimli MB

Just for Laughs Festival, 2101, boul Saint-Laurent, Montréal QC H2X 2T5 - 514-845-3155; Tollfree: 1-888-244-3155; Email: info@hahaha.com; URL: www.hahaha.com - July

Kitchener-Waterloo Oktoberfest, 17 Benton St., PO Box 1053, Kitchener ON N2G 4G1 - 519-570-4267; Fax: 519-742-3072; Tollfree: 1-888-294-4267; URL: www.oktoberfest.ca - President, Margo Jones - Bavarian festival: foods, entertainment, parades - Annually - Oct.

Manitoba Sunflower Festival, PO Box 1630, Altona MB R0G 0B0 - 204-324-9005; Fax: 204-324-1550; URL: www.manitobasunflowerfestival.ca - Annual, last weekend of July

Northern Manitoba Trappers Festival, Inc., PO Box 475, The Pas MB R9A 1K6 - 204-623-2912; Fax: 204-623- 1974; URL: trappersfestival.ca - World championship sled dog race - Annually - Feb.

Northwest Territorial Days, c/o Battlefords Agricultural Society, PO Box 668, North Battleford SK S9A 2Y9 - 306-445-2024; Fax: 306-445-3352; URL: www.agsociety.com - Aug.

Penticton Peach Festival, PO Box 21003, Cherry Lane Postal Outlet, #165, 2111 Main St., Penticton BC V2A 8K8 - 250-487-9709; Email: peach-festival@hotmail.com; URL: www.peachfest.com - Aug.

Peterborough MusicFest, Del Crary Park, Peterborough ON - Email: info@ptbomusicfest.ca; URL: www.ptbomusicfest.ca - General Manager, Tracey Randall - June to Aug. every Wednesday & Saturday evening

Pictou Lobster Carnival, PO Box 1480, Pictou NS B0K 1H0 - 902-485-5150; URL: pictoulobstercarnival.ca - Annual - July

Québec City Summer Festival, #150, 683, rue Saint-Joseph est, Québec QC G1K 3C1 - 418-523-4540; Fax: 418-523-0194; Tollfree: 1-888-992-5200; Email: infofestival@feq.ca; URL: www.feq.ca - Entertainment in the streets & parks of Old Québec - July

Royal Nova Scotia International Tattoo, #6, 10 Morris Dr., Dartmouth NS B3B 1K8 - 902-420-1114; Tollfree: 1-800-563-1114; Email: info@nstattoo.ca; URL: www.nstattoo.ca - Managing Director & Executive Producer, Jennie King - Annual - June/July

Royal St. John's Regatta, PO Box 214, St. John's NL A1C 5J2 - 709-576-8058; Fax: 709-576-3315; Email: events@stjohnsregatta.com; URL: www.stjohnsregatta.org - North America's oldest continuing sporting event - Aug., St. John's NL

Sam Steele Days, PO Box 115, Cranbrook BC V1C 4H6 - 250-426-4161; Fax: 250-426-3873; URL: www.samsteeledays.org - June

Shediac Lobster Festival, CP 9005, Shediac NB E4P 8W5 - 506-532-1122; Email: info@shediaclobsterfestival.ca; URL: www.shediaclobsterfestival.ca - Annually, first week of July

Steinbach Pioneer Days, c/o Mennonite Heritage Village, 231, PTH 12 North, Steinbach MB R0A 2A0 - 204/326- 9661; URL: www.steinbach.ca

Summerside Lobster Carnival, City Hall, 275 Fitzroy St., Summerside PE C1N 1H9 - 902-432-1298; Email: wyatt.programs@city.summerside.pe.ca; URL: www.summersidelobstercarnival.website - July

Threshermen's Show & Seniors' Festival, PO Box 98, Yorkton SK S3N 2V6 - 306-783-8361; Fax: 306-782- 1027; Email: yorkton@wdm.ca; URL: www.wdm.ca - Annually, Aug.

Toronto Storytelling Festival, The Storytellers School of Toronto, Artscape Wychwood Barns, Studio #173, 601 Christie St., Toronto ON M6G 4C7 - 416-656-2445; Email: admin@storytellingtoronto.org; URL: www.torontostorytellingfestival.ca - Held annually, April

Welland Rose Festival, 30 East Main St., Welland ON L3B 3W3 - 905-732-7673; Email: info@wellandrosefestival.on.ca; URL: www.wellandrosefestival.on.ca - Rose show, lobsterfest, sporting events, juried art show, seniors' events, day in the park, day-on-the-island, craft show, fishing derby, children's events, grand parade - Annual - June

World's Invitational Class A Gold Panning Championships, Taylor Gold Panning Society, District of Taylor, PO Box 300, Taylor BC V0C 2K0 - 250-789-3392; Fax: 250-789-3543; URL: www.districtoftaylor.com - Annually, Aug. long weekend

Yukon Gold-Panning Championships, Klondike Visitors Association, PO Box 389, Dawson YT Y0B 1G0 - 867-993-5575; Fax: 867-993-6415; Email: kva@dawson.net; URL: dawsoncity.ca - On Canada Day - July, Dawson City YT

Yukon River Bathtub Race, Yukon Sourdough Rendezvous Society, 4230 - 4th Ave., Whitehorse YT Y1A 1G7 - 867-667-2148; URL: www.yukonrendezvous.com - Executive Director, Saskrita Shresthra - Longest & hardest bathtub race. Two days, 486 miles, Yukon River - Aug.

Yukon Sourdough Rendezvous, Yukon Sourdough Rendezvous Society, 4230 - 4th Ave., Whitehorse YT Y1A 1G7 - 867-667-2148; URL: www.yukonrendezvous.com - Executive Director, Saskrita Shresthra - Annual - Celebrates the gold rush times. Mad trapper, flour packing, tug-a-truck contests, fiddle show, lip sync & queen contests - Feb.

EXHIBITIONS

See Also Farm Business/Agriculture; Rodeos

Canadian Association of Fairs & Exhibitions Annual Convention, PO Box 21053 (WEPO), Brandon ON R7B 3W8 - 613-233-0012; Tollfree: 1-800-663-1714; Email: info@canadian-fairs.ca; URL: www.canadian-fairs.ca - Nov.

Canadian Lakehead Exhibition, 425 Northern Ave., Thunder Bay ON P7C 2V7 - 807-622-6473; Fax: 807-623-5540; Email: clex@tbaytel.net; URL: www.cle.on.ca - Annually, Aug.

Canadian National Exhibition, Canadian National Exhibition Association, Exhibition Place, 210 Princes' Blvd., Toronto ON M6K 3C3 - 416-263-3330; Fax: 416-263-3838; Email: info@theex.com; URL: www.theex.com - Annual public show - Aug.-Sept.

Comox Valley Exhibition, #201, 580 Duncan Ave., Courtenay BC V9N 2M7 - 250-338-8177; Fax: 250-338-4244; Email: mvokey@frex.ca; URL: www.cvex.ca

New Brunswick Provincial Exhibition, c/o Fredericton Exhibiton Ltd., 361 Smythe St., Fredericton NB E3B 4Y9 - 506-458-8819; Fax: 506-458-9294; URL: www.nbex.ca - Annual - Sept.

Great Northern Exhibition, PO Box 523, Stayner ON L0M 1S0 - 705-444-0308; Fax: 705-446-1972; Email: greatnorthernexhibition@gmail.com; URL: www.greatnorthernex.com - Agricultural Society President, Maureen McLeod, Email: pres@greatnorthernex.com - Sept.

Home Town Fair, Hometown Fair, c/o Moose Jaw Exhibition Co. Ltd., 250 Thatcher Dr. East, Moose Jaw SK S6J 1L7 - 306-692-2723; Fax: 306-692-2762; URL: www.moosejawex.ca - Annual - June

Interior Provincial Exhibition, Interior Provincial Exhibition & Stampede, PO Box 490, Armstrong BC V0E 1B0 - 250-546-9406; Fax: 250-546-6181; Email: info@armstrongipe.com; URL: www.armstrongipe.com - President, Ted Fitchett - Annual consumer agricultural fair & show - Aug.-Sept.

K-Days, 7515 - 118 Ave. NW, Edmonton AB T5B 4X5 - 780-471-7210; Fax: 780-471-8112; Toll-Free: 1-888-800-7275; URL: www.k-days.com - Annual consumer show - July

Lindsay Central Exhibition, 354 Angeline St. South, Lindsay ON K9V 4R2 - 705-324-5551; Fax: 705-324-8111; URL: www.lindsayex.com - Annual consumer agricultural fair & show - Sept.

Markham Agricultural Fair, 10801 McCowan Rd., Markham ON L3P 3J3 - 905-642-3247; Fax: 905-640- 8458; Tollfree: 1-800-450-3557; Email: office@markhamfair.ca; URL: www.markhamfair.ca - Annual consumer show - Sept./Oct.

Medicine Hat Exhibition & Stampede, 2055 - 21st Ave. SE, PO Box 1298, Medicine Hat AB T1A 7N1 - 403-527-1234; Fax: 403-529-6553; Tollfree: 1-888-647-6336; Email: mhstampede@mhstampede.com; URL: www.mhstampede.com - Annual consumer show - July

Miramichi Agricultural Exhibition, PO Box 422, 24 Church St., Miramichi City NB E1N 3A8 - 506-773-5133; Fax: 506-773-6173; URL: maeaca.wordpress.com - Annual consumer show - July

Niagara Regional Exhibition, 1100 Niagara St. North, Welland ON L3C 1M6 - 905-735-6413; Fax: 905-735- 2317; Email: nfo@niagararegionalexhibition.com; URL: www.niagaraex.com - Annual consumer agricultural fair & show - Sept.

Nova Scotia Provincial Exhibition, 73 Ryland Ave., Truro NS B2N 2V5 - 902-893-9222; Fax: 902-897-0069; Email: nspe@eastlink.ca; URL: www.nspe.ca - General Manager, Joe Nicholson - Aug., Bible Hill NS

Pacific National Exhibition, 2901 East Hastings St., Stn Hastings Park, Vancouver BC V5K 5J1 - 604-253- 2311; Fax: 604-251-7753; Email: info@pne.ca; URL: www.pne.ca - President & CEO, Shelley Frost - Agricultural competitions, parade - Annual

Paris Fall Fair, PO Box 124, Paris ON N3L 3E7 - 519-442-2823; Fax: 519-442-5121; Email: info@parisfairgrounds.com; URL: www.parisfairgrounds.com - Annual Labour Day weekend consumer show

Prince Albert Exhibition, Prince Albert Exhibition Association, PO Box 1538, Prince Albert SK S6V 5T1 - 306-764-1711; Fax: 306-764-5246; Email: paex@sasktel.net; URL: www.paexhibition.com - President, Linda Grimard - Annual

Queen City Ex, Evraz Place, PO Box 167, 1700 Elphinstone St., Regina SK S4P 2Z6 - 306-781-9200; Fax: 306-565-3443; Email: info@evrazplace.com; URL: www.evrazplace.com/events/queen-city-ex - July

Red River Exhibition, Red River Exhibition Association, Red River Exhibition Park, 3977 Portage Ave., Winnipeg MB R3K 2E8 - 204-888-6990; Fax: 204-888-6992; Email: info@redriverex.com; URL: www.redriverex.com - Manitoba's largest fair & single-site entertainment event - Annually, 10 days, last two weeks in June

Saint John Ex, PO Box 284, Saint John NB E2L 3Y2 - 506-633-2020; Fax: 506-636-6958; URL: www.exhibitionparksj.com - Annual - Aug.

Saltscapes East Coast Expo, #209, 30 Damascus Rd., Bedford NS B4A 0C1 - 902-464-7258; Fax: 902-464-3755; Tollfree: 1-877-311-5877; URL: saltscapesexpo.com

Threshermen's Reunion & Stampede, Central Canada's Fiddle Festival, PO Box 10, Austin MB R0H 0C0 - 204-637-2354; Email: agmuseum@mymts.net; URL: www.threshermensmb.ca - Annual

Western Nova Scotia Exhibition, PO Box 425, Yarmouth NS B5A 4B3 - 902-742-8222; Email: westernnsexhibition@gmail.com; URL: wnse.ca; President, Mark Firth - Six-day agricultural fair & talent competition - July or Aug., Yarmouth NS

FARM BUSINESS/AGRICULTURE

See Also Exhibitions; Rodeos

CAAR Conference, Canadian Association of Agri-Retailers, #628, 70 Arthur St, Winnipeg MB R3B 1G7 - 204-989-9300; Fax: 204-989-9306; Tollfree: 1-800-463-9323; Email: info@caar.org; URL: www.caar.org

Canada's Farm Progress Show, PO Box 167, Regina SK S4P 2Z6 - 306-781-9200; Fax: 306-565-3443; Email: farmshow@evrazplace.com; URL: www.canadasfarmshow.com - Annual consumer & trade show - June - Regina Evraz Place, Regina SK

Canadian National Hereford Show, c/o Canadian Hereford Association, 5160 Skyline Way NE, Calgary AB T2E 6V1 - 403-275-2662; Fax: 403-295-1333; URL: www.hereford.ca, Nov., Regina SK

Canadian Western Agribition, c/o Public Relations Office, Canadian Western Agribition, PO Box 3535, Regina SK S4P 3J8 - 306-565-0565; Fax: 306-757-9963; Email: cwaquestions@agribition. com; URL: www.agribition.com - CEO, Chris Lane - Annually, Nov.

Chatham-Kent Farm Show, John D. Bradley Centre, 565 Richmond St., Chatham ON N7M 1R2 - 519-997-2911; Email: info@chathamkentfarmshow.com; URL: www.chathamkentfarmshow.com - Owner, Courtney Brochu Email: courtneyb.opsp@gmail.com

Farmfair International, PO Box 1480, Edmonton AB T5J 2N5 - 780-471-7210; Fax: 780-471-8112; Tollfree: 1-888-800-7275; URL: www.farmfairinternational.com - Annual - Nov.

International Potato Technology Expo, Master Promotions Ltd., PO Box 565, Saint John NB E2L 3Z8 - 506-658- 0018; Fax: 506-658-0750; Tollfree: 1-888-454-7469; Email: info@mpltd.ca; URL: www.potatoexpo.ca - Show Manager, Shawn Murphy, Email: smurphy@mpltd.ca - Biennial - Feb.

London Farm Show, Western Fair Association, 316 Rectory St., PO Box 7550, London ON N5Y 5P8 - 519-438- 7203; Tollfree: 1-800-619-4629; Email: contact@westernfairdistrict.com; URL: www.westernfairdistrict.com/london-farm-show - Annual consumer show

Norfolk County Fair & Horse Show, Norfolk County Agricultural Society, 172 South Dr., Simcoe ON N3Y 1G6 - 519-426-7280; Fax: 519-426-7286; URL: www.norfolkcountyfair.com - Annual consumer show

Nova Scotia 4-H Show, c/o NS Dept. of Agriculture, 60 Research Dr., Bible Hill NS B6L 2R2 - 902-843-3990; Fax: 902-843-3989; URL: 4hnovascotia.ca - Annual consumer show, Oct.

Ontario Fruit & Vegetable Convention, #135, 104-155 Main St East, Grimsby ON L3M 1P2 - 905-945-5363; Fax: 905-945-5386; URL: www.ofvc.ca - Manager, Ross Parker, Email: ross@ofvc.ca

Grand Falls Regional Potato Festival, #200, 131 Pleasant St., Grand Falls NB E3Z 1G6 - 506-475-7777; URL: www.grandfallsnb.com/potato-festival - June

Royal Agricultural Winter Fair, Royal Agricultural Winter Fair Association, The Coliseum, National Trade Centre, Exhibition Place, Toronto ON M6K 3C3 - 416-263-3400; Fax: 416-263-3488; Email: info@royalfair.org; URL:

www.royalfair.org - Annual consumer show. World's largest agricultural fair & equestrian event - Nov., Toronto ON

Salon de l'Agriculture, 4770, rue Martineau, Saint-Hyacinthe QC J2R 1V1 - 450-771-1226; Fax: 450-771- 6073; Email: info@salonagr.qc.ca; URL: www.salondelagriculture.com - Annual trade show. Agricultural products - Jan., St-Hyacinthe QC

Western Fair, Western Fair Association, 316 Rectory St., PO Box 7550, London ON N5Y 5P8 - 519-438-7203; Tollfree: 1-800-619-4629; Email: contact@westernfairdistrict.com; URL: www.westernfairdistrict.com - CEO, Hugh Mitchell - Annual consumer show

FASHION

Apparel textile Sourcing Canada - URL: www.appareltextilesourcing.com - Show Director, John Banker, Email: jbanker@manufacturer.com

Luggage, Leathergoods, Handbags & Accessories, PO Box 144, Station A, Toronto ON M9C 4V2 - Fax: 519-624-6408; Tollfree: 1-866-872-2420 ; Email: info@llha.ca; URL: www.llha.ca - Annual trade show - Sept. - International Centre, Mississauga ON

Metro Vancouver, #103, 1951 Glen Dr., Vancouver BC V6A 4J6 - 604-929-8995; Fax: 604-357-1995; Email: info@metroshow.ca; URL: www.metroshow.ca - Trade shows for apparel, footwear, accessories & more - Aug. & Sept.

Trends Apparel, PO Box 66037, Heritage PO, Edmonton AB T6J 6T4 - 780-455-1881; Email: info@trendsapparel.com; URL: trendsapparel.com - Wholesale apparel show - Sept.

FESTIVALS *See* EVENTS; WINTER CARNIVALS

FILM & VIDEO FESTIVALS & SPECIAL EVENTS

Alberta Film & Television Awards, Alberta Media Production Industries Association, #200, 7316 - 101 Ave., Edmonton AB T6A 0J2 - 780-944-0707; Fax: 780-426- 3057; Email: info@ampia.org; URL: www.ampia.org - Executive Director, Bill Evans, Email: bevans@ampia.org - April.

Buffer Festival - Email: support@bufferfestival.com; URL: bufferfestival.com - Online video festival - Toronto ON

Le Carrousel international du film de Rimouski, #204, 133, rue Julien-Réhel, Rimouski QC G5L 9B1 - 418-722-0103; Fax: 418-724-9504; Email: info@carrousel.qc.ca; URL: carrousel.qc.ca - Films for children. Competition, workshops - Sept., Rimouski QC

Cinéfest - The Sudbury International Film Festival, #103, 40 Larch St., Sudbury ON P3E 5M7 - 705-688-1234; Email: cinefest@cinefest.com; URL: www.cinefest.com - Full-length feature festival with over 100 Canadian & international films, animations, shorts, Midnight Madness, documentary & children's film series - Sept., Sudbury ON

Festival du cinéma international en Abitibi-Témiscamingue, 215, av Mercier, Rouyn-Noranda QC J9X 5W8 - 819-762-6212; Fax: 819-762-6212; Email: info@festivalcinema.ca; URL: www.festivalcinema.ca - Features, medium-length & short films. Competition; regional jury award for short or medium-length film; people's choice award for feature & animation - Oct., Rouyn-Noranda QC

Festival du nouveau cinéma de Montréal, 3805, boul Saint-Laurent, Montréal QC H2W 1X9 - 514-282-0004; Fax: 514-282-6664; Email: info@nouveaucinema.ca; URL: www.nouveaucinema.ca - Executive Director, Nicolas Girard Deltruc - New trends in new cinema, video & new media; non-competitive; people's choice award

Festival Vues d'Afrique, Vues d'Afrique, #3100,100, rue Sherbrooke est, Montréal QC H2X 1C3 - 514-284-3322; Fax: 514-845-0631; URL: vuesdafrique.org - Films by & about African & Creole peoples - April, Montréal QC

Film Studies Association of Canada Conference, Film Studies Association of Canada, c/o Ryerson University, Sociology - JOR 306, 350 Victoria St., Toronto ON M5B 2K3; URL: www.filmstudies.ca; Email: membership@filmstudies.ca - - May/June annually, held at a different university each year

Images Festival of Independent Film & Video, #309, 401 Richmond St. West, Toronto ON M5V 3A8 - 416-971-8405; Fax: 416-971-7412; Email: submissions@imagesfestival.com; URL: www.imagesfestival.com - Annual. Independent films & videos. Workshops - April, Toronto ON

Les Rendez-vous du cinéma québécois, 1680, rue Ontario est, Montréal QC H2L 1S7 - 514-526-9635; Fax: 514-526-1955; Email: info@quebeccinema.ca; URL: www.quebeccinema.ca - Restrospective of recent Québec productions - Feb., Montréal QC

Ottawa International Animation Festival, #120, 2 Daly Ave., Ottawa ON K1N 6E2 - 613-232-8769; Fax: 613-232-6315; Email: info@animationfestival.ca; URL: www.animationfestival.ca - Managing Director, Kelly Neall,

Email: kelly@animationfestival.ca - Annual. Animation films & videos. Television animation conference. Workshops & panels - Sept., Ottawa ON

St. John's Women's Film & Video Festival, PO Box 984, Stn. C, St. John's NL A1C 5M3 - 709-754-3141; Fax: 709-754-0049; Email: info@womensfilmfestival.com; URL: www.womensfilmfestival.com - Women's films & videos. Workshops & panels - Oct., St. John's NL

Toronto International Film Festival, Toronto International Film Festival Group, TIFF Bell Lightbox, Reitman Square, 350 King Street West, Toronto ON M5V 3X5 - 416-934-3200; URL: tiff.net - Features & theatrical shorts. Competition. Awards for excellence in Canadian production. People's choice & film critics awards. Symposium, workshops, sales office - Sept., Toronto ON

Toronto Jewish Film Festival, 19 Madison Ave., Toronto ON M5R 2S2 - 416-324-9121; Fax: 416-324-9415; Email: tjff@tjff.ca; URL: tjff.com - Artistic Director, Helen Zukerman

Vancouver International Film Festival, Vancouver International Film Centre, 1181 Seymour St., Vancouver BC V6B 3M7 - 604-685-0260; Fax: 604-688-8221; Email: info@viff.org; URL: www.viff.org - Features medium-length & short films. Competition; juried awards for best western Canadian feature film, best young western Canadian director of a short film, best documentary feature & best film by a new director from Pacific Asia; people's choice award for most popular international film & for most popular Canadian film. - Sept., Vancouver

FISHING/AQUACULTURE

Adams River Sockeye Salmon Run, PO Box 24034, Scotch Creek BC V0E 3L0 - Email: info@salmonsociety.com; URL: www.salmonsociety.com - Oct.

Dieppe Fly Fishing Forum, Master Promotions Ltd., PO Box 565, Saint John NB E2L 3Z8 - 506-658- 0018; Fax: 506-658-0750; Tollfree: 1-888-454-7469; Email: info@mpltd.ca; URL: www.flyfishingforum.ca - Show Manager, Scott Sprague, Email: ssprague@mpltd.ca - Annual - March

Eastern Canadian Fisheries Exposition, Master Promotions Ltd., PO Box 565, Saint John NB E2L 3Z8 - 506-658- 0018; Fax: 506-658-0750; Tollfree: 1-888-454-7469; Email: info@mpltd.ca; URL: www.ecfx.ca - Annual commercial fishing show - Show Manager, Shawn Murphy; Email: smurphy@mpltd.ca - Mariner's Centre, Yarmouth NS

Fish Canada/Workboat Canada, Master Promotions Ltd., PO Box 565, Saint John NB E2L 3Z8 - 506/658- 0018; Fax: 506-658-0750; Tollfree: 1-888-454-7469; Email: info@mpltd.ca; URL: www.fcwc.ca - Show Manager, Shawn Murphy, Email: smurphy@mpltd.ca - Biennial commercial fishing/boat show - Nov., Vancouver BC

Flin Flon Trout Festival, PO Box 751, Flin Flon MB R8A 1N6 - 204-687-5160; URL: www.flinflontroutfestival.com - June, Flin Flon MB

Great Ontario Salmon Derby - 905-361-5246; URL: greatontariosalmonderby.ca - July-Aug.

Nipawin Pike Festival, c/o Town of Nipawin, PO Box 2134, Nipawin SK S0E 1E0 - 306-862-9866; Fax: 306-862-3076; URL: www.facebook.com/NipawinPikeFestival

North Atlantic Fish & Workboat Show, Master Promotions Ltd., PO Box 565, 48 Broad St., Saint John NB E2L 3Z8 - 506-658-0018; Fax: 506-658-0750; Tollfree: 1-888-454-7469; Email: info@mpltd.ca; URL: www.nafish.ca - Show Manager, Shawn Murphy - Biennial - Nov.

Salmon Festival, PO Box 100, Campbellton NB E3N 3G1 - 506-789-2700; Fax: 506-759-7403; Tollfree: 1-888-813-4433; Email: campbellton.salmonfestival@gmail.com; URL: salmon-festival.com - June

FLOWERS/LANDSCAPING/GARDENING

Canada Blooms, 7856 Fifth Line South, Milton ON L9T 2X8; 416-447-8655; Fax: 416-447-1567; Tollfree: 1-800-730-1020; Email: info@canadablooms.com; URL: www.canadablooms.com - March

Orchid Show, Royal Botanical Gardens, 680 Plains Rd. West, Burlington ON L7T 4H4 - 905-527-1158; Fax: 905-577-0375; URL: www.osrbg.ca - March

FOOD & BEVERAGE

See Also Hospitality Industry

Canadian Health Food Association Conferences, #302, 235 Yorkland Blvd., Toronto ON M2J 4Y8 - 905-479-6939; Fax: 905-497-3214; Tollfree: 1-800-661-4510, Tollfree Fax 1-888-2927; Email: info@chfa.ca; URL: www.chfa.ca - Organic & natural products; homeopathy, food supplements & herbs - West, East & Québec conferences - April, Oct. & Feb.

Gluten Free Expo - URL: www.glutenfreeexpo.ca - Vancouver BC

Gourmet Food & Wine Expo, c/o Sun Media, 365 Bloor St. East, 3rd Fl., Toronto ON M4W 3L4 - URL: www.foodandwineexpo.ca - Show Manager, Paul McNair, Email: pmcnair@postmedia.com - Consumer show - Nov. - Metro Toronto Convention Centre, Toronto ON

La Grande Dégustation de Montréal, c/o Association Québécoise des Agences de Vins, Bières & Spiritueux Inc. (AQAVBS), 905, av de Lorimier, Montréal QC K2J 3V9; URL: www.lagrandedegustation.com

Ottawa Wine & Food Festival - 613-523-6356; URL: www.ottawawineandfoodfestival.com - Annual trade & consumer show - Oct./Nov.

Planted Expo - URL: www.plantedlife.com - Vancouver BC, and Toronto ON

SIAL Canada & SET Canada, #901, 2120, rue Sherbrooke Est, Montréal QC H2K 1C3; 438-476-2542; Fax: 514-289-1034; Email: info@sialcanada.com; URL: www.sialcanada.com - International Food & Beverage Tradeshow/National Food Equipment & Technology Tradeshow - April

Toronto Garlic Festival, PO Box 82861 RPO Cabbagetown, 467 Parliament St., Toronto ON M5A 3Y2 - 416-888-7829; URL: www.torontogarlicfestival.ca - Festival Director, Peter McClusky, Email: peterm@TorontoGarlicFestival.ca

FOREST INDUSTRY

DEMO International, Master Promotions Ltd., PO Box 565, 48 Broad St., Saint John NB E2L 3Z8 - 506-658-0018; Fax: 506-658-0750; Tollfree: 1-888-454-7469; Email: info@mpltd.ca; URL: www.demointernational.com - Quadrennial - May

InterSaw, Master Promotions Ltd., PO Box 565, Saint John NB E2L 3Z8 - 506-658-0018; Fax: 506-658-0750; Tollfree: 1-888-454-7469; Email: info@mpltd.ca; URL: www.mpltd.ca - Biennial - Show Manager, Shawn Murphy, Email: smurphy@mpltd.ca - May

FURNITURE See HOME SHOWS

GARDENING See FLOWERS

GIFTS & JEWELLERY

Alberta Gift Fair, c/o Canadian Gift Association, 42 Voyager Ct. South, Toronto ON M9W 5M7 - 416-679-0170; Fax: 416-679-0175; Tollfree: 1-800-611-6100; Email: info@cangift.org; URL: www.cangift.org - Annual trade show. Giftware, stationery, kitchenware, luggage & leathergoods, pottery, china, glass, jewellery - Feb. & Aug.

Expo Prestige, Corporation des bijoutiers du Québec, 868, rue Brisette, Sainte-Julie QC J3E 2B1 - 514-485-3333; Fax: 450-649-8984; Email: info@cbq.qc.ca; URL: www.cbq.qc.ca - août - Palais des Congrès, Montréal QC

Québec Gift Fair/Salon du Cadeau du Québec, c/o Canadian Gift Association, 42 Voyager Ct. South, Toronto ON M9W 5M7 - 416-679-0170; Fax: 416-679-0175; Tollfree: 1-800-611-6100; Email: info@cangift.org; URL: www.cangift.org - Annual trade show. Giftware, stationery, kitchenware, luggage & leathergoods, pottery, china, glass, jewellery - March

Toronto Gift Fair, c/o Canadian Gift Association, 42 Voyager Ct. South, Toronto ON M9W 5M7 - 416-679-0170; Fax: 416-679-0175; Tollfree: 1-800-611-6100; Email: info@cangift.org; URL: www.cangift.org - Annual trade show. Giftware, stationery, kitchenware, luggage & leathergoods, pottery, china, glass, jewellery - Jan., Toronto ON

Vancouver Gift Expo, c/o Smart Shows Inc., PNE Forum Building 2901 East Hastings St., Vancouver BC V5K 5J1; 604-767-0400; Tollfree Fax: 1-888-395-0474; Email: vancouvergiftexpo@shaw.ca; URL: www.vancouvergiftexpo.com - Owner, Smart Shows Inc., Cameron Dix - Annual trade show. Giftwares, housewares, luggage & leathergoods, jewellery - Jan. & Aug.

GRAPHIC ARTS

Design City, #8, 1606 Sedlescomb Dr., Mississauga ON L4X 1M6 - 905-625-7070; Fax: 905-625- 4856; Tollfree: 1-800-331-7408; URL: www.designcityshow.com - Biennial trade show - Nov. - Enercare Centre, Exhibition Place, Toronto ON

Graphics Canada - URL: www.graphicscanada.com - Graphics & printing trade show - Toronto ON

Print World, #8, 1606 Sedlescomb Dr., Mississauga ON L4X 1M6 - 905-625-7070; Fax: 905-625- 4856; Tollfree: 1-800-331-7408; URL: www.printworldshow.com - Biennial trade show - Nov. - Enercare Centre, Exhibition Place, Toronto ON

HAIRDRESSING

Allied Beauty Show, Allied Beauty Association, #26-27, 145 Traders Blvd. East, Mississauga ON L4Z 3L3 - Fax: 905-568-1581; Toll-Free: 800-268-6644; Email: info@abacanada.com; URL: www.abacanada.com - Held in various locations

Maritimes Natural Hair & Beauty Show - 780-292-3293; Email: MaritimesNaturals@gmail.com; URL: www.maritimesnaturals.com - Oct. - Halifax NS

HEALTH & WELLNESS

Activate Fitcon, Ottawa Convention & Event Centre, 200 Coventry Rd., Ottawa ON K1K 4S3; 613-822-7488; URL: www.activatefit.ca

BMO Vancouver Marathon Health & Sports Expo, 1288 Vernon Dr., Vancouver BC V6A 4C9 - 604-872-2928; Fax: 604-872-2928; Email: info@runvan.org; URL: www.bmovanmarathon.ca - April/May - Vancouver Convention Centre, Vancouver BC

e-Health Conference, c/o International Conference Services Ltd., #300, 1201 West Pender St., Vancouver BC V6E 2V2 - 604-681-2153; Fax: 604-681-1049; URL: www.e-healthconference.com - Conference Manager, Jacilyn Edgar, Email: manager@e-healthconference.com - Annual - May

Ottawa Health & Wellness Expo, Shenkman Arts Centre, 245 Centrum Blvd., Ottawa ON K1E 3W8 - 613-837-2883; Email: OttawaHealthandWellnessExpo@gmail.com; URL: www.orleanswellnessexpo.com

The People in Motion Show, Canadian National Show Management, 30 Village Centre PLace, Mississauga ON L4Z 1V9 - 905-361-2677; Fax: 905-361-2679; Tollfree: 1-888-695-2677; URL: www.people-in-motion.com - Show Manager, Sajid Rahman, Email: saj@cnsm.ca - Exhibition for people with disabilities - May - Exhibition Place, Queen Elizabeth Bldg., Toronto ON

Scotiabank Toronto Waterfront Marathon Running, Health & Fitness Expo, 264 The Esplanade, Toronto ON M5A 4J6 - 416-944-2765; Fax: 416-944-8527; URL: wwww.torontowaterfrontmarathon.com

Total Health Show, Total Health Events Inc., #1901, 355 St. Clair Ave. West, Toronto ON M5P 1N5 - 416-924-9800; Fax: 416-924-6404; Tollfree: 1-877-389-0996; URL: www.totalhealthshow.com - April - Metro Toronto Convention Centre, Toronto ON

Whole Life Expo, 356 Dupont St., Toronto ON M5R 1V9 - 416-515-1330; Email: info@wholelifeexpo.ca; URL: www.wholelifecanada.com - Nov. - Metro Toronto Convention Centre, Toronto ON

HEATING, PLUMBING & AIR CONDITIONING

CIPHEX West, c/o Canadian Institute of Plumbing & Heating, #504, 295 The West Mall, Toronto ON M9C 4Z4 - 416-695-0447; 1-800-639-2474; Email: info@ciph.com; URL: www.ciphexwest.ca - Nov., Vancouver BC

CMPX Show, 25 Bradgate Rd. Toronto ON M3B 1J6; 416-444-5225; Tollfree: 1-800-282-0003; Email: cmpx@salshow.com; URL: www.cmpxshow.com - Annual trade show - March - Metro Toronto Convention Centre, Toronto ON

Mécanex/Climatex/Expolectriq/Éclairage (MCEE) - 416-695-0447; Email: mcee@mcee.ca; URL: mcee.ca - Trade show for plumbing, HVACR, hydronics, electrical & lighting - April, Montréal QC

HOBBIES

See Also Crafts

The Gem Expo, 12 Coatsworth Cres., Toronto ON M4C 5P6 - 416-996-2583; Email: info@thegemexpo.com; URL: thegemexpo.com - Spring, Summer & Fall/Winter shows are held - Toronto ON

Gem, Mineral & Fossil Show, Calgary Rock & Lapidary Club, #13, 3650 - 19 St. NE, Calgary AB T2E 6V2 - URL: www.crlc.ca - Show Chair, Shelley Gibbins, Email: sapphire13@shaw.ca - Annual - May

National Postage Stamp & Coin Show, c/o Canadian Stamp News, 600 Ontario St., PO Box 28103, Lakeport PO, St. Catharines ON L2N 7P8 - URL: www.stampandcoinshow.com

Sportcard & Memorabilia Expo, 10 Wynnview Crt., Toronto ON M1N 3K3; Toll-Free: 888-466-7116; E-mail: sales@sportcardexpo.ca; URL: www.sportcardexpo.com

HOME ENTERTAINMENT See ELECTRICAL/ELECTRONICS

HOME SHOWS

Ancaster Lifestyle Home Show, Jenkins Show Productions ON - 905-827-4632; Fax: 905-827-8139; Tollfree: 1-800-465-1073; URL: www.jenkinsshow.com - President, Dave Jenkins, Email: dave@jenkinsshowproductions.com - Annual consumer show - Feb., Ancaster Fairgrounds, Ancaster ON
Atlantic National Home Show, Master Promotions Ltd., PO Box 565, Saint John NB E2L 3Z8 - 506-658-0018; Fax: 506-658-0750; Tollfree: 1-888-454-7469; Email: info@mpltd.ca; URL: www.atlanticnationalhomeshow.ca - Show Manager, Terry Wagner, Email: twagner@mpltd.ca - Annual consumer show - March, Saint John NB
BC Home + Garden Show, Marketplace Events, LLC, #212, 1847 West Broadway, Vancouver BC V6J 1Y6; 604-639-2288 Fax: 604-639-2289; Tollfree: 1-800-633-8332; URL: www.bchomeandgardenshow.com - Annual consumer show - Feb.
Burlington Lifestyle Home Shows, Jenkins Show Productions, ON - 905-827-4632; Fax: 905-827-4632; Tollfree: 1-800-465-1073; URL: www.jenkinsshow.com - President, Dave Jenkins, Email: dave@jenkinsshowproductions.com - Annual consumer show - April & Sept., Burlington ON
Calgary Fall Home Show, Marketplace Events, LLC, Macleod Place II, #602, 5940 Macleod Trail SW, Calgary AB T2H 2G4; 403-253-1177; Fax: 403-253-7878; Tollfree: 1-866-941-0673; URL: www.calgaryhds.com - Annual consumer show - Sept. - BMO Centre, Calgary AB
Canadian Spa & Pool Conference & Expo, Pool & Hot Tub Council of Canada, 5 MacDougall Dr., Brampton ON L6S 3P3 - 905-458-7242; Fax: 905-458-7037; Tollfree: 1-800-879-7066; Email: office@poolcouncil. ca; URL: www.poolandspaexpo.ca - Annual trade & consumer show - Dec. - Toronto Congress Centre, Toronto ON
Chatham-Kent Home & Garden Shows, c/o 20/20 Show Productions Inc., PO Box 400, Belle River ONtario N0R 1A0- 226-363-0550; Fax: 226-363-0455; URL: ontariotradeshows.com - Contact, Stuart Galloway, Email: stuart@exposition.com - Annual - April
Edmonton Fall Home Show, Marketplace Events LLC, Macleod Place II, #602, 5940 Macleod Trail SW, Calgary AB T2H 2G4; 403-253-1177; Fax: 403-253-7878; Tollfree: 1-866-941-0673; URL: www.edmontonhomeandgarden.com - Annual consumer show - Oct. - Edmonton Expo Centre, Edmonton AB
Edmonton Renovation Show, Marketplace Events LLC, Macleod Place II, #602, 5940 Macleod Trail SW Calgary AB T2H 2G4 - 403-253-1177; Fax: 403-253-7878; Tollfree: 1-866-941-0673; URL: www.edmontonrenovationshow.com - Annual consumer show - January
Expo-Habitat de St-Hyacinthe, DBC Communications inc., 655, av Sainte-Anne, Saint-Hyacinthe QC, J2S 5G4 - 450-773-3976; Fax: 450-773-3115; URL: salonexpohabitat.com - Personne ressource, Patrick Desrosiers - Annual consumer show. Home construction & renovation products & services - April - Pavillion de Pionnieres, St-Hyacinthe QC
Fredericton Home Show, Master Promotions Ltd., PO Box 565, Saint John NB E2L 3Z8 - 506-658-0018; Fax: 506-658-0750; Tollfree: 1-888-454-7469; Email: info@mpltd.ca; URL: www.frederictonhomeshow.ca - Senior Show Manager, Terry Wagner, Email: twagner@mpltd.ca - Annual consumer show - April
Greater Niagara Region Home & Garden Show - URL: www.niagarahomeandgardenshow.ca - March - Scotiabank Convention Centre, Niagara Falls ON
Hamilton Spring Home & Garden Show, Continuum Productions Inc., 3488 Trelawny Circle, Mississauga ON L5N 6N7 - 905-824-1060; Fax: 905-824-9923; Email: info@continuumevents.ca; URL: www.ontariohomeshows.com - April
Ideal Whole Home Expo, Master Promotions Ltd., PO Box 565, Saint John NB E2L 3Z8 - 506-658- 0018; Fax: 506-658-0750; Tollfree: 1-888-454-7469; Email: info@mpltd.ca; URL: www.idealwholehomeexpo.ca - Senior Show Manager, Denise Miller, Email: dmiller@mpltd.ca - Annual consumer show - Oct.
Interior Design Show, Informa Canada, #100, 10 Alcorn Ave., Toronto ON M4V 3A9 - Tollfree: 1-800-663-4173; Email: info@interiordesignshow.com; URL: www.interiordesignshow.com - Shows take place in Toronto (Jan.) & Vancouver (Sept.)
Kingston Home & Garden Show, c/o 20/20 Show Productions Inc., PO Box 400, Belle River ON N0R 1A0 - 226-363-0550; Fax: 226-363-0455; URL: ontariotradeshows.com - Contact, Stuart Galloway, Email: stuart@exposition.com
Milton Lifestyle Home Show, Jenkins Show Productions, ON - 905-827-4632; Fax: 905-827-8139; Tollfree: 1-800-465-1073; URL: www.jenkinsshow.com - President, Dave Jenkins, Email: dave@jenkinsshowproductions.com - Annual consumer show - March, Milton Memorial Arena, Milton ON
Mississauga Lifestyle Home Show, Jenkins Show Productions, ON - 905-827-4632; Fax: 905-827-8139; Tollfree: 1-800-465-1073; URL: www.jenkinsshow.com - President, Dave Jenkins, Email: dave@jenkinsshowproductions.com - Annual consumer show - April, Hershey Centre, Mississauga ON
Montréal National Home Show, Expo Media, #210, 370, rue Guy, Montréal QC H3J 1S6 - 514-527-9221; Fax: 514-527-8449; URL: salonnationalhabitation.com
National Home Show, Building Industry & Land Development Association, #100, 20 Upjohn Rd., Toronto ON M3B 2V9 - 416-263-3200; URL: torontohomeshows.com/tbo - Annual consumer show - April - Enercare Centre, Exhibition Place, Toronto ON
Niagara Lifestyle Home Show, Jenkins Show Productions, ON - 905-827-4632; Fax: 905-827-8139; Tollfree: 1-800-465-1073; Email: info@jenkinsshow.com; URL: www.jenkinsshow.com - President, Dave Jenkins - Annual consumer show - April - Seymour-Hannah Sports & Entertainment Centre, St Catharines ON
Nova Scotia Spring Ideal Home Show, Master Promotions Ltd., PO Box 565, Saint John NB E2L 3Z8 - 506-658- 0018; Fax: 506-658-0750; Tollfree: 1-888-454-7469; Email: info@mpltd.ca; URL: www.springideal.ca - Senior Show Manager, Terry Wagner, Email: twagner@mpltd.ca - Annual consumer show - April, Halifax NS
Oakville Lifestyle Home Show, Jenkins Show Productions, ON - 905-827-4632; Fax: 905-827-8139; Tollfree: 1-800-465-1073; URL: www.jenkinsshow.com - President, Dave Jenkins, Email: dave@jenkinsshowproductions.com - Annual consumer show - April
Ottawa Home & Garden Show, Marketplace Events LLC, #210, 370, rue Guy, Montréal QC H3J 1S6 - 613-667-0509; Fax: 514-527-8449; URL: www.ottawahomeshow.com - Annual consumer show - March
PEI Provincial Home Show, Master Promotions Ltd., PO Box 565, Saint John NB E2L 3Z8 - 506-658-0018; Fax: 506-658-0750; Tollfree: 1-888-454-7469; Email: info@mpltd.ca; URL: www.peihomeshow.ca - Show Manager, Terry Wagner, Email: twagner@mpltd.ca - Annual consumer show - March, Charlottetown PE
Red Deer Home Renovation & Design Show, c/o Canadian Homebuilders' Association Central Alberta, #200, 6700 - 76 St., Red Deer AB T4P 4G6 - 403-346-5321; Fax: 403-342-1301; Email: admin@chbacentralalberta.ca; URL: www.reddeerhomeshow.ca - Annual, Oct.
Red Deer Home Show, c/o Canadian Homebuilders' Association Central Alberta, #200, 6700 - 76 St., Red Deer AB T4P 4G6 - 403-346-5321; Fax: 403-342-1301; Email: admin@chbacentralalberta.ca; URL: www.reddeerhomeshow.ca - Annual, Feb./March
Sudbury Home Show, c/o Sudbury & District Homebuilders' Association, 1942 Regent St., Unit C, Sudbury ON P3E 5V5 - 705-671-6099; Fax: 705-671-9590; URL: sudburyhomebuilders.com, March, Sudbury ON
Sunshine Home & Garden Show, Medicine Hat & District Chamber of Commerce, 413 - 6th Ave. SE, Medicine Hat AB T1A 2S7 - 403-527-5214; Fax: 403-527-5182; Email: info@medicinehatchamber.com; URL: www.medicinehatchamber.com - Annual consumer show - Nov.
Truro Home & Outdoor Show, Master Promotions Ltd., PO Box 565, Saint John NB E2L 3Z8 - 506-658-0018; Fax: 506-658-0750; Tollfree: 1-888-454-7469; Email: info@mpltd.ca; URL: www.trurohomeshow.ca - Show Manager, Terry Wagner, Email: twagner@mpltd.ca - Annual consumer show - April
Vancouver Fall Home Show, Marketplace Events, LLC, #212, 1847 West Broadway, Vancouver BC V6J 1Y6 - 604-639-2288, Fax: 604-639-2289; Tollfree: 1-800-633-8332; URL: vancouverfallhomeshow.com - Annual consumer show - Oct.
WinDoor, c/o Fenestration Canada, #240, 65 Overlea Blvd., Toronto ON M4H 1P1 - 613-424-7239; Fax: 1-866-605-0657; Tollfree: 1-888-543-2516; URL: windoorshow.ca - Trade, Windows & doors show, new products & technologies - Nov.
Windsor Home & Garden Show, c/o 20/20 Show Productions Inc., PO Box 400, Belle River ON N0R 1A0 - 226-363-0550; Fax: 226-363-0455; URL: ontariotradeshows.com - President, Stuart Galloway, Email: stuart@exposition.com - Annual - Feb. - University of Windsor, Windsor ON
Winnipeg Renovation Show, Marketplace Events LLC, #212, 1847 West Broadway, Vancouver BC V6J 1Y6 - 604-639-2288; Fax: 604-639-2289; Tollfree: 1-800-633-8332; URL: www.winnipegrenovationshow.com - Exhibit Sales Consultant, Kayla Donaldson, Email: kaylad@mpeshows.com - Annual consumer show - Jan.

HORSES

Arabian & Half-Arabian Championship Horse Show, Canadian Nationals, Arabian Horse Association, Keystone Centre, #1, 1175 - 18th St., Brandon MB R7A 7C5 - 204-726-3500; Fax: 204-727-5552; Tollfree: 877-610-6015; URL: www.arabianhorses.org/CNL - Annual - Aug.
Masters Show Jumping Tournament, Spruce Meadows, 18011 Spruce Meadows Way SW, Calgary AB T2J 5G5 - 403-974-4200; Fax: 403-974-4270; Email: information@sprucemeadows.com; URL: www.sprucemeadows.com - Annual tournament. Includes consumer/trade show Equi-Fair, & the Festival of Nations - Sept.
National Tournament, Spruce Meadows, 18011 Spruce Meadows Way SW, Calgary AB T2J 5G5 - 403-974-4200; Fax: 403-974-4270; Email: information@sprucemeadows.com; URL: www.sprucemeadows.com - Annual tournament featuring riders from around the world, as well as shopping & family activities - June
North American Tournament, Spruce Meadows, 18011 Spruce Meadows Way SW, Calgary AB T2J 5G5 - 403-974-4200; Fax: 403-974-4270; Email: information@sprucemeadows.com; URL: www.sprucemeadows.com - Annual tournament featuring riders from the Americas,as well as shopping & family activities - July

HORTICULTURE *See* FLOWERS

HOSPITALITY INDUSTRY (HOTEL, MOTEL, RESTAURANT)

***See Also* Food & Beverage**

Restaurants Canada Show, Restaurants Canada, 1155 Queen St. West Toronto ON M6J 1J4 - 416-923- 8416; Tollfree: 1-800-387-5649; Email: rcshow@restaurantscanada.org; URL: www.rcshow.com - Annual trade show
Grocery Innovations Canada, Canadian Federation of Independent Grocers, #401, 105 Gordon Baker Rd., Toronto ON M2H 3P8 - 416-492-2311; Fax: 416-492-2347 ; Tollfree: 1-800-661-2344; Email: info@cfig.ca; URL: virtual.groceryinnovations.com; www.cfig.ca - Annual trade show - Oct
Grocery & Specialty Food West, Canadian Federation of Independent Grocers, #401, 105 Gordon Baker Rd., Toronto ON M2H 3P8 - 416-492-2311; Fax: 416-492-2347; Tollfree: 1-800-661-2344; Email: info@cfig.ca; URL: virtual.gsfshow.com; www.cfig.ca - Annual trade show - March - Vancouver Convention Centre, Vancouver BC

INDIGENOUS

First Nations Housing & Infrastructure Forum East, c/o The Canadian Institute, 1329 Bay St., 3rd Fl., Toronto ON M5R 2C4 - 416-927-0718; Tollfree: 1-877-927-7936; Email: fnhousing@canadianinstitute.com; URL: www.canadianinstitute.com - Senior Conference Producer, Desiree Finhert, Email: d.finhert@canadianinstitute.com - Annual
First Nations Housing & Infrastructure East, c/o The Canadian Institute, 1329 Bay St., 3rd Fl., Toronto ON M5R 2C4 - 416-927-0718; Tollfree: 1-877-927-7936; Email: fnhousing@canadianinstitute.com; URL: www.canadianinstitute.com - Senior Conference Producer, Desiree Finhert, Email: d.finhert@canadianinstitute.com - Annual
Indigenous Consultation Atlantic, c/o The Canadian Institute, 1329 Bay St., 3rd Fl., Toronto ON M5R 2C4 - 416-927-0718; Tollfree: 1-877-927-7936; Email: customerservice@canadianinstitute.com; URL: www.canadianinstitute.com - Senior Conference Producer, Desiree Finhert, Email: d.finhert@canadianinstitute.com - Annual
Indigenous Consultation BC, c/o The Canadian Institute, 1329 Bay St., 3rd Fl., Toronto ON M5R 2C4 - 416-927-0718; Tollfree: 1-877-927-7936; Email: customerservice@canadianinstitute.com; URL: www.canadianinstitute.com - Senior Conference Producer, Desiree Finhert, Email: d.finhert@canadianinstitute.com - Annual
Indigenous Consultation Ontario, c/o The Canadian Institute, 1329 Bay St., 3rd Fl., Toronto ON M5R 2C4 - 416-927-0718; Tollfree: 1-877-927-7936; Email: customerservice@canadianinstitute.com; URL:

www.canadianinstitute.com - Senior Conference Producer, Desiree Finhert, Email: d.finhert@canadianinstitute.com - Annual

Indigenous Health Conference, c/o Temerty Faculty of Medicine, University of Toronto, 500 University Ave., 6th Fl., Toronto ON M5G 1V7 - 416-978-2719; Email: facmed.registration@utoronto.ca; URL: www.cpd.utoronto.ca - Dec.

McMaster Indigenous Health Conference, c/o Faculty of Health Sciences, McMaster University, 1200 Main St. West, Hamilton ON L8N 3Z5 - 905-525-9140, ext. 23935; Email: ishs@mcmaster.ca; URL: ishs.mcmaster.ca - Jan./Feb.

National Gathering for Indigenous Education, c/o Indspire #100, 50 Generations Dr., PO Box 5, Six Nations of the Grand River, Ohsweken ON N0A 1M0 - 519-445-3021; Fax: 1-866-433-3159; Tollfree: 1-855-463-7747; education@indspire.ca; URL: indspire.ca

Western Aboriginal Consultation & Engagement, c/o The Canadian Institute, 1329 Bay St., 3rd Fl., Toronto ON M5R 2C4 - 416-927-0718; Tollfree: 1-877-927-7936; Email: fnhousing@canadianinstitute.com; URL: www.canadianinstitute.com - Senior Conference Producer, Desiree Finhert, Email: d.finhert@canadianinstitute.com - Annual

INDUSTRIAL

Advanced Manufacturing Canada, Society of Manufacturing Engineers, #312, 7100 Woodbine Ave., Markham ON L3R 5J2 - 905-752-4444; Tollfree: 1-888-322-7333; Email: canadasales@sme.org; URL: www.advancedmfg.ca - Trade show - Sept.

FABTECH Canada, Society of Manufacturing Engineers, #312, 7100 Woodbine Ave., Markham ON, L3R 5J2 - 905-752-4415; Fax: 905-479-0113; Tollfree: 888.322.7333; URL: canada.fabtechexpo.com - March - Toronto Congress Centre, Toronto ON

Montreal Manufacturing Technology Show, Society of Manufacturing Engineers, #312, 7100 Woodbine Ave., Markham ON, L3R 5J2 - Tollfree: 1-888-322-7333; URL: www.mmts.ca - Biennial trade show - May - Place Bonaventure, Montréal QC

Powder & Bulk Solids Montréal, UBM Canon, #100, 2901 - 28 St., Santa Monica CA, USA, 90405 - 310-445-4200; Fax: 310-996-9499; URL: www.admmontreal.com/en/co-located-shows/powder-and-bulks-montreal.html - Part of the Advanced Design & Manufacturing Expo Montréal - Nov. - Palais des congrès de Montréal, Montréal QC

Powder & Bulk Solids Toronto, UBM Canon, #100, 2901 - 28 St., Santa Monica CA, USA, 90405 - 310-445-4200; Fax: 310-996-9499; URL: www.admtoronto.com/en/show-brands/pbs-toronto.html - Part of the Advanced Design & Manufacturing Expo Toronto - Nov. - Toronto Congress Centre, Toronto ON

Salon industriel Abitibi-Témiscamingue, Les Promotions André Pageau Inc., 6500, boul Pierre Bertrand, Québec QC G2J 1R4 - 418-623-3383; Fax: 418-623-5033; Tollfree: 1-800-387-3383; Email: info@promoapageau.com; URL: www.salonsindustriels.com; www.promoapageau.com - Président, André Pageau, May, Rouyn-Noranda QC

Salon industriel Bas-St-Laurent, Les Promotions André Pageau Inc., 1627, boul Bastien, Québec QC G2K 1H1 - 418-623-3383; Fax: 418-623-5033; Tollfree: 1-800-387- 3383; Email: info@promoapageau.com; URL: www.salonsindustriels.com; www.promoapageau.com - Président, André Pageau, April, Rimouski QC

Salon industriel Centre-du-Québec, Les Promotions André Pageau Inc., 1627, boul Bastien, Québec QC G2K 1H1 - 418-623-3383; Fax: 418-623-5033; Tollfree: 1-800-387- 3383; Email: info@promoapageau.com; URL: www.salonsindustriels.com; www.promoapageau.com - Président, André Pageau, April Drummondville QC

Salon industriel de L'Estrie, Les Promotions André Pageau Inc., 1627, boul Bastien, Québec QC G2K 1H1 - 418-623-3383; Fax: 418-623-5033; Tollfree: 1-800-387- 3383; Email: info@promoapageau.com; URL: www.salonsindustriels.com; www.promoapageau.com - Président, André Pageau, Sept., St-Hyacinthe QC

Salon Industriel de Québec, Les Promotions André Pageau Inc., 1627, boul Bastien, Québec QC G2K 1H1 - 418-623-3383; Fax: 418-623-5033; Tollfree: 1-800-387- 3383; Email: info@promoapageau.com; URL: www.salonsindustriels.com; www.promoapageau.com - Président, André Pageau - Biennial trade show - Oct., Québec QC

Salon Industriel du SAGLAC, Les Promotions André Pageau Inc., 1627, boul Bastien, Québec QC G2K 1H1 - 418-623-3383; Fax: 418-623-5033; Tollfree: 1-800-387-3383;

Email: info@promoapageau. com; URL: www.salonsindustriels.com; www.promoapageau.com - Président, André Pageau - Biennial - May, Chicoutimi QC

Western Manufacturing Technology Show - Edmonton, Society of Manufacturing Engineers, #312, 7100 Woodbine Ave., Markham ON, L3R 5J2 - 905-752-4415; Fax: 905-479-0113; Tollfree: 1-888-322-7333; Email: infocanada@sme.org; URL: wmts.ca - Trade show - June, Edmonton AB

JEWELLERY *See* **GIFTS**

LANDSCAPING *See* **FLOWERS**

LEGAL

Canadian Association of Law Libraries Annual General Meeting, c/o National Office, #200, 411 Richmond St. East, Toronto ON M5A 3S5 - 647-346-8723; Email: office@callacbd.ca; URL: www.callacbd.ca/Conference - Annual - May

CBA Legal Conference, Canadian Bar Association, #500, 865 Carling Ave., Ottawa ON K1S 5S8 - 613-237-2925; 613-237-1988; Fax: 613-237-0185; Tollfree: 1-800-267-8860; Email: pd@cba.org; URL: www.cbalegalconference.org - Aug.

Construction & Infrastructure Law Conference, Canadian Bar Association, #500, 865 Carling Ave., Ottawa ON K1S 5S8 - 613/237-2925; 613-237-1988; Fax: 613-237-0185; Tollfree: 1-800-267-8860; Email: pd@cba.org; URL: www.cbalegalconference.org - April

LEISURE *See* **SPORTS & RECREATION**

LGBTQ+

Black & Blue Festival, c/o BBCM Foundation, 2259, ave Old Orchard, Montréal QC H4A 3A7 - 514-875-7026; Fax: 514-875-9323; Email: information@bbcm.org; URL: bbcm.org - President & Founder, Robert J. Vézina, vp@bbcm.org - Electronic music festival supporting the LGBTQ+ community in Montreal, & people living with HIV/AIDS - Annual

Capital Pride, #2, 403 Bank St., Ottawa ON K2P 1Y6 - 613-680-3033; Email: info@capitalpride.ca; URL: capitalpride.ca - Executive Director, Osmel B. Maynes

Fête arc-en-ciel de Québec, l'Alliance Arc-en-ciel de Québec, #3, 435, rue du Roi, Québec QC G1K 2X1 - 418-809-3383 - URL: arcencielquebec.ca

Halifax Pride, Halifax Pride Committee, PO Box 47027, Halifax NS B3K 5Y2 - Email: info@halifaxpride.com; URL: halifaxpride.com - Executive Director, Adam Reid

Inside Out Film Festival - #219, 401 Richmond St. West, Toronto ON M5V 3A8 - 416-977-6847; Fax: 416-977-8025; URL: www.insideout.ca - Festival featuring films by gay, lesbian, bisexual & trans people - Toronto & Ottawa

Pride Calgary, PO Box 1205, Stn. M, Calgary AB T2P 2K9 - Tollfree Phone/Fax: 1-888-425-2239; URL: www.calgarypride.ca

Pride Festival, Vancouver Pride Society, #304, 1080 Howe St., Vancouver BC V6Z 2T1 - 604-687-0955; Fax: 604-687-0965; Email: info@vancouverpride.ca; URL: vancouverpride.ca

Pride Montréal, #200, 4262, rue Sainte-Catherine est, Montréal QC H2X 1L4 - 514-903-6193; Fax: 514-666-0189; URL: fiertemtl.com - Interim Executive Director, Jean-François Perrier, Email: jfp@fiertemtl.com

Pride Niagara, PO Box 4020, St Catharines ON L2R 3B0 - Email: info@prideniagara.com; URL: prideniagara.com

Pride Toronto, 158 Sterling Rd., Toronto ON M6R 2B7 - Email: office@pridetoronto.com; URL: www.pridetoronto.com - Executive Director, Sherwin Modeste, Email: sherwin@pridetoronto.com - June - Toronto

Pride Winnipeg, PO Box 2101, Stn. Main, Winnipeg MB R3C 3R4 - URL: www.pridewinnipeg.com

Saskatoon Pride, Saskatoon Diversity Network, 320 - 21 St. West, Saskatoon SK S7M 4E6; Email: info@saskatoonpride.ca; URL: saskatoonpride.ca

Victoria Pride, Victoria Pride Society, PO Box 8607, Stn. Main, Victoria BC V8W 3S2 - Email: info@victoriapridesociety.org; URL: victoriapridesociety.org

Whistler Pride & Ski Festival, Alpenglow Productions, 4005 Whistler Way, Whistler BC V0N 1B4 - Tollfree: 1-866-787-1966; Email: info@whistlerpride.com; URL: whistlerpride.com

LOGISTICS

Canada Logistics Conference, c/o CITT, #400, 10 King St. East, Toronto ON M5C 1C3 - 416-363-5696; Fax: 416-363-5698; Email: info@citt.ca; URL: www.citt.ca - Senior Manager, Member Support & Events, Jennifer Traer, Email: jtraer@citt.ca - Oct.

Canadian Crude Logistics Conference, c/o Petroleum Trade Network, #5144, 1200 Frank E Rodgers Blvd. S, Harrison NJ

07029 - 609-331-9120; Email: info@petroleumtradenetwork.com; URL: crude-logistics-conference.com - Conference Director, Alex Leah, Email: alex@petroleumtradenetwork.com - July

Cargo Logistics Canada Expo & Conference, Informa Canada Vancouver Office, #510, 1185 West Georgia St., Vancouver BC V6E 4E6; Tollfree: 1-877-739-2112; Email: info@cargologisticscanada.com; URL: www.cargologisticscanada.com - Feb.

Supply Chain Canada National Conference - URL: www.supplychaincanada.com - President & CEO, Al-Azhar Khalfan, Email: akhalfan@supplychaincanada.com - Oct.

MACHINERY & MANUFACTURING

See Also Industrial

Automation Technology Expo (ATX) Montréal, UBM Canon, #100, 2901 - 28 St., Santa Monica CA, USA, 90405 - 310-445-4200; Fax: 310-996-9499; URL: www.admmontreal.com/en/co-located-shows/atx-montreal.html - Part of the Advanced Design & Manufacturing Expo Montréal - Nov. - Palais des congrès de Montréal, Montréal QC

Automation Technology Expo (ATX) Toronto, UBM Canon, #100, 2901 - 28 St., Santa Monica CA, USA, 90405 - 310-445-4200; Fax: 310-996-9499; URL: admtoronto.com/atx - Part of the Advanced Design & Manufacturing Expo Toronto - Nov. - Toronto Congress Centre, Toronto ON

Atlantic Heavy Equipment Show, Master Promotions Ltd., PO Box 565, Saint John NB E2L 3Z8 - 506-658-0018; Fax: 506-658-0750; Tollfree: 1-888-454-7469; Email: info@mpltd.ca; URL: www.ahes.ca - National Show Manager, Mark Cusack, Email: mcusack@mpltd.ca - Biennial - April - Coliseum, Moncton NB

Canadian Manufacturing Technology Show, Society of Manufacturing Engineers, #312, 7100 Woodbine Ave., Markham ON, L3R 5J2 - Tollfree: 1-888-322-7333; URL: cmts.ca - Director, Canadian Events, Julie Pike, Email: jpike@sme.org - Biennial trade show - Sept., Toronto ON

Design & Manufacturing Montréal, UBM Canon, #100, 2901 - 28 St., Santa Monica CA, USA, 90405 - 310-445-4200; Fax: 310-996-9499; URL: www.admmontreal.com/en/co-located-shows/design-and-manufacturing-montreal.html - Part of the Advanced Design & Manufacturing Expo Montréal - Nov. - Palais des congrès de Montréal, Montréal QC

Design & Manufacturing Toronto, UBM Canon, #100, 2901 - 28 St., Santa Monica CA, USA, 90405 - 310-445-4200; Fax: 310-996-9499; URL: admtoronto.com/dm - Part of the Advanced Design & Manufacturing Expo Toronto - Nov. - Toronto Congress Centre, Toronto ON

Expo Grands Travaux, Master Promotions Ltd., PO Box 565, Saint John NB E2L 3Z8 - 506-658-0018; Fax: 506-658-0750; Tollfree: 1-888-454-7469; Email: info@mpltd.ca; URL: www.expograndstravaux.ca - National Show Manager, Mark Cusack, Email: mcusack@mpltd.ca - April

National Heavy Equipment Show, Master Promotions Ltd., PO Box 565, Saint John NB E2L 3Z8 - 506-658-0018; Fax: 506-658-0750; Tollfree: 1-888-454-7469; Email: info@mpltd.ca; URL: www.nhes.ca - National Show Manager, Mark Cusack, Email: mcusack@mpltd.ca - Biennial - March - International Centre, Toronto ON

Pacific Heavy Equipment Show, Master Promotions Ltd., PO Box 565, Saint John NB E2L 3Z8 - 506-658-0018; Fax: 506-658-0750; Tollfree: 1-888-454-7469; Email: info@mpltd.ca; URL: www.phes.ca - National Show Manager, Mark Cusack, Email: mcusack@mpltd.ca - Biennial - April - Coliseum, Moncton NB

MARIJUANA *See* **CANNABIS**

MARKETING *See* **ADVERTISING**

MATERIALS HANDLING *See* **LOGISTICS**

MEDICAL

Canadian Neurological Sciences Federation Congress, 143N Heritage Square, 8500 Macleod Trail SE, Calgary AB, T2H 2N1 - 403-229-9544; Fax: 403-229-1661; Email: info@intertaskconferences.com - URL: congress.cnsfederation.org

COS Annual Meeting & Exhibition, Canadian Ophthalmological Society, #110, 2733 Lancaster Rd., Ottawa ON K1B 0A9 - 613-729-6779; Fax: 613-729-7209; Email: cos@cos-sco.ca; URL: www.cos-sco.ca - Chief Executive Officer, Elisabeth Fowler, Email: efowler@cos-sco.ca - June

Healthcare Simulation Exposition (SIM Expo), c/o Sim-one - 416-506-1433; URL: www.sim-one.ca - Showcases advancements in healthcare simulation - Annual

MayFest, Ontario Association of the Deaf, 2395 Bayview Ave., Toronto ON M2L 1A2 - 416-413-9191; Fax: 416-413-4822; TTY: 416-513-1893; Email: office@deafontario.ca; URL: www.deafontario.ca - Executive Director, Donald Prong, Email: dprong@deafontario.ca - Latest innovations & access for deaf, deafened & hard of hearing people - May, Toronto ON

Pri-Med Canada, c/o University of Toronto Dept. of Family & Community Medicine, 500 University Ave., 5th Fl., Toronto ON M5G 1V7 - URL: www.pri-med.ca - Three-day continuing medical education event. Formerly known as Primary Care Today - Annual, Toronto ON

MINING & MINERALS

Canadian Mining Expo - 705-264-2251; Fax: 705-264-4401; Tollfree: 1-866-754-9334; URL: canadianminingexpo.com - President, Glenn Dredhart, Email: g.dredhart@canadiantradex.com - Annual - June

CIM Conference & Exhibition, c/o Canadian Institute of Mining, Metallurgy & Petroleum, #1250, 3400, boul de Maisonneuve ouest, Montréal QC H3Z 3C1 - 514-939-2710; Fax: 514-939-2714; Email: cim@cim.org; URL: convention.cim.org - Annual consumers show. Mining industry, equipment & services - April-May

Mines & Minerals Symposia, Ontario Prospectors Association, c/o Gary Clark, 1000 Alloy Dr., Thunder Bay ON P7B 6A5 - 807-622-3284; Fax: 807-622-4156; Tollfree: 1-866-259-3727; Email: gjclark@ontarioprospectors.com; URL: www.ontarioprospectors.com - Annual trade shows & seminars related to regional associations

MOTORCYCLES *See* AUTOMOTIVE

MULTICULTURAL

Canada's National Ukrainian Festival, 17 - 3rd Ave. NE, PO Box 368, Dauphin MB R7N 2V2 - 204-622-4600; Fax: 204-622-4606; Tollfree: 1-877-474-2683; Email: cnuf@mymts.nett; URL: www.cnuf.ca - Annual. Three days of song, dance, music, costume, cuisine, culture - Aug.

Le Festival de l'Escaouette, a/s La Société Saint-Pierre, PO Box 430, Cheticamp NS B0E 1H0 - 902-224-2612; Fax: 902-224-1579; URL: www.cheticamp.ca - Annually. Acadian folklore, traditions, culture - Aug.

Folklorama - Canada's Cultural Celebration, 183 Kennedy St., Winnipeg MB R3C 1S6 - 204-982-6210; Fax: 204-943-1956; Tollfree: 1-800-665-0234; Email: info@folklorama.ca; URL: www.folklorama.ca - Executive Director, Teresa Cotroneo, Email: tcotroneo@folklorama.ca - Annual. Fourteen days. More than forty ethnic pavilions - Aug.

Manitoba Highland Gathering, PO Box 59, Selkirk MB R1A 2B1 - 204-794-6587; URL: www.manitobahighlandgathering.org - President, Joyce Neyedly, Email: joyce@manitobahighlandgathering.org - Annual - July

Mosaic: A Festival of Cultures, Regina Multicultural Council, 2054 Broad St., Regina SK, S4P 1Y3 - 306-757-5990; Email: admin.rmc@sasktel.net; URL: www.reginamulticulturalcouncil.ca - Annual. End of May/early June. Twenty ethno-cultural pavilions

Saskatoon Folkfest, 127B Ave. D North, Saskatoon SK S7L 1M5 - 306-931-0100; Fax: 306-665-3421; Email: info@saskatoonfolkfest.com; URL: www.saskatoonfolkfest.com - Annual. Three days. Twenty or more ethnic pavilions - Aug.

Vesna Festival, PO Box 1592, Saskatoon SK S7K 3R3 - URL: www.vesnafestival.com - Festival Chair, Audrey Smycniuk - Annual Spring celebration. Two days of entertainment, dancing, cultural demonstrations & displays. The World's Largest Ukrainian Cabaret - May

MUSIC

Bal en Blanc - Email: info@balenblanc.com; URL: www.balenblanc.com - One-day electronic music festival - Annual - May, Easter Weekend - Montréal QC

Beaches International Jazz Festival, 1798 Queen St. East, Toronto ON M4L 1G8 - 416-698-2152; Fax: 416-698- 2064; Email: infobeachesjazz@rogers.com; URL: www.beachesjazz.com - Executive Producer, Lido Chilelli - July, Toronto ON

Big Valley Jamboree, 4238 - 37th St., Camrose AB T4V 4L6 - 780-672-0224; Fax: 780-672-0400; Tollfree: 1-888-404-1234; Email: bvj@bigvalleyjamboree. com; URL: www.bigvalleyjamboree.com - Country music - Aug.

Brandon Folk, Music & Arts Festival, PO Box 22091, Brandon MB R7A 6Y9 - Email: brandonfolkfestival@gmail.com; URL: brandonfolkfestival.ca - Annual, last weekend in July

Canada Dance Festival, Canada Dance Festival Society, PO Box 1376, Stn B, Ottawa ON K1P 5R4 - 613-947-7000, ext. 576; Email: info@canadadance.ca; URL: www.canadadance.ca - Biennial - June

Dawson City Music Festival, PO Box 456, Dawson YT Y0B 1G0 - 867-993-5584; Email: info@dcmf.com; URL: www.dcmf.com - Annually, second last weekend in July

Eclipse Festival - Email: info@eclipsefestival.com; URL: www.eclipsefestival.com - Weekend-long electronic music & visual art festival - Biennial - Québec

Edgefest, c/o Edge 102, Corus Quay, 25 Dockside Dr., Toronto ON M5A 0B5 - 416-479-7000; URL: www.edge.ca - July/Aug.

Edmonton International Jazz Festival, Edmonton Jazz Festival Society, 10046 - 116 St., Edmonton AB T5K 1V7 - 780-990-0222; Email: info@edmontonjazz.com; URL: www.edmontonjazz.com - Annual - June

Electric Eclectics, 202 Scotch Mountain Rd., RR#2, Meaford ON N0H 2S0 - 519-378-9899; Email: info@electric-eclectics.com; URL: www.electric-eclectics.com - Three day exprimental music and sound art festival in Meaford ON - Aug.

Electric Island, c/o Platform Entertainment Inc., 1488 Queen St. West, PO Box 90009, Toronto ON M6K 1M4 - 416-479-4276; Email: info@platforment.com; URL: electricisland.to - Two-day electronic music festival - Annual - Sept., Hanlan's Point, Toronto ON

Elora Festival & Singers, 9 Mill St. East, Elora ON N0B 1S0 - 519-846-0331; Tollfree: 1-888-747-7550; Email: info@elorafestival.com; URL: www.elorafestival.com - Choral & contemporary Canadian & international music - July/Aug.

Escapade Music Festival - 613-241-9997, ext. 118; Email: info@escapademf.com; URL: www.escapademf.com - Electronic music festival - Annual - July, usually Canada Day weekend

Evolve Music Festival, 274 Girvan Rd., Clairville NB E4T 2J9 - Email: vending@evolvefestival.com; URL: www.evolvefestival.com - Multi-genre festival promoting sustainable living & environmental awareness - Annual - July

Festival de Lanaudière, 1500, boul Base-de-Roc, Joliette QC J6E 3Z1 - 450-759-7636; Email: festival@lanaudiere.org; URL: www.lanaudiere.org - Largest mostly classical festival in Canada; Annual - June-Aug.

Festival International de Jazz de Montréal, 400, boul Maisonneuve ouest, 9e étage, Montréal QC H3A 1L4 - 514-523-3378; Fax: 514-525-8033; Tollfree: 1-888-299-3378; URL: www.montrealjazzfest.com - Annual. Over 2,000 musicians & 450 shows - June-July, Montréal QC

Le Festival International du Domaine Forget, 5, rang Saint-Antoine, CP 672, Saint-Irénée QC G0T 1V0 - 418-452-8111; Tollfree: 1-888-336-7438; Email: info@domaineforget. com; URL: www.domaineforget.com - June-Aug.

Festival International Nuits d'Afrique de Montréal, c/o Productions Nuits D'Afrique Inc., 4374, boul St-Laurent, 1e étage, Montréal QC H2W 1Z5 - 514-499-9239; Fax: 514-499-9215; Email: info@festivalnuitsdafrique.com; URL: www.festivalnuitsdafrique.com - July

Festival of the Sound, 1 Avenue Rd., PO Box 750, Parry Sound ON P2A 2Z1 - 705-746-2410; Fax: 705-746-2112; Tollfree: 1-866-364-0061; Email: info@festivalofthesound.ca; URL: www.festivalofthesound.ca - Executive Director, Alison Scarrow - July-Aug.

Folk on the Rocks, PO Box 326, Yellowknife NT X1A 2N3 - 867-920-7806; Fax: 867-873-6535; URL: folkontherocks.com - Annual. Two days. Inuit, Dene, other northern & southern folk groups - July

Guelph Jazz Festival, #301, 6 Dublin St. South, Guelph ON N1H 4L5 - 519-763-4952; Email: info@guelphjazzfestival.com; URL: www.guelphjazzfestival.com - Artistic & General Director, Scott Thomson - Sept., Guelph ON

Halifax Jazz Festival, PO Box 33043, Halifax NS B3L 4T6 - 902-492-2225; Fax: 902-420-9943 - Email: info@halifaxjazzfestival.ca; URL: halifaxjazzfestival.ca - Interim Executive Director, Andrea Dawson Thomas, Email: andreathomas@halifaxjazzfestival.ca - July

Harvest Jazz & Blues Festival, 81 Regent St., Fredericton NB E3B 3W3 - 506-454-2583; Tollfree: 1-888-622-5837; Email: info@harvestjazzandblues.com; URL: www.harvestjazzandblues.com - Sept.

Hillside Festival, 341 Woolwich St., Guelph ON N1H 3W4 - 519-763-6396; Fax: 519-763-9514; Email: info@hillsidefestival.ca; URL: www.hillsidefestival.ca

Igloofest, #470, 5455, av De Gaspé, Montréal QC H2T 3B3 - 514-904-1247; Fax: 514-904-2005; Email: info@igloofest.ca; URL: igloofest.ca - CEO & Co-founder, Pascal Lefebvre - Electronic music festival - Annual - Jan.-Feb. - Old Port of Montréal, Montréal QC

International Festival of Baroque Music, International Baroque Music Festival, #2, 28, rue de l'Hôpital, Lameque NB E8T 1C3 - 506-344-3261; Fax: 506-344-3266; Email: baroque@lameque.ca; URL: www.festivalbaroque.com - Early music festival with five productions, last week of July (Northeastern New Brunswick, on Lameque Island)

Kiwanis Music Festival of Greater Toronto, 17 Pinemore Cres., Toronto ON M3A 1W5 - 416-487-5885; Fax: 416-639-5340; Email: office@kiwanismusictoronto.org; URL: kiwanismusictoronto.org - General Manager, Pam Allen, Email: pam@kiwanismusictoronto.org - Feb., Toronto ON

L'OFF Festival de Jazz de Montréal, #305, 1097, rue St-Alexandre, Montréal QC H2J 1P8 - 514-524-0831; Email: info@lofffestivaldejazz.com; URL: www.lofffestivaldejazz.com

Manitoba Electronic Music Exhibition (MEME) - Email: info@memetic.ca; URL: www.memetic.ca - Director, Nathan Zahn - Electronic music festival - Annual - Aug., various locations in Winnipeg MB

Mariposa Folk Festival, Mariposa Folk Foundation, 10 Peter St. South, PO Box 383, Orillia ON L3V 6J8 - 705-326-3655; URL: www.mariposafolk.com

Maritime Fiddle Festival, 50 Caledonia Rd., Dartmouth NS B2X 1K8 - Email: marfiddlefest@ns.sympatico.ca; URL: maritimefiddlefestival.ca - July

Markham Jazz Festival, #281, 4261 A-14, Hwy. #7, Unionville, ON L3R 9W6 - 905-471-5299; URL: www.markhamjazzfestival.com - Executive Director, Christie Day - Aug., Markham ON

Miramichi Folksong Festival, PO Box 13, Miramichi NB E1V 3M2 - 506-623-2150; Fax: 506-623-2261; URL: www.miramichifolksongfestival.com - Aug.

Moose Jaw Band & Choral Festival, PO Box 883, Moose Jaw SK S6H 4P5 - Email: mjbandandchoral@gmail.com; URL: www.mjbandfestival.com - 3,000 musicians, evening concerts. Annual - May, Moose Jaw SK

MUTEK Montréal, 175, rue Roy est, CP 855, succursale Desjardins, Montréal QC H5B 1B9 - 514-871-8646; Fax: 514-871-0447; Email: info@mutek.org; URL: www.mutek.org - Festival of avant-garde electronic music and digital art. Festivals also take place in Mexico City, Barcelona, Tokyo and Buenos Aires - Aug.

Newfoundland & Labrador Folk Festival, c/o Newfoundland and Labrador Folk Arts Society, #206, 223 Duckworth St., St. John's NL A1C 6N1 - 709-576-8508; Fax: 709-757-8500; Tollfree: 1-866-576-8508; Email: office@nlfolk.com; URL: nlfolk.com - Events Coordinator, John Clarke, Email: events@nlfolk.com - Traditional Newfoundland & Labrador music & dance - Aug.

Nova Scotia Bluegrass Oldtime Music Festival, The Downeast Bluegrass & Oldtime Music Society, PO Box 1275, Greenwood NS B0P 1N0 - Tollfree: 1-844-442-2656; URL: www.downeastgrass.com - Annual, last weekend in July

Nova Scotia Kiwanis Music Festival, PO Box 107, 5657 Spring Garden Rd., Halifax NS B3J 3R4 - 902-423-6147; URL: hfxmusicfest.com - Adjudicated music festival & closing concert - Feb., Halifax NS

Open Ears Festival of Music & Sound, PO Box 26011, Stn. College, 250 King St. West, Kitchener ON N2G 1B0; Email: info@openears.ca; URL: www.openears.ca - Musical performances, music in alternative venues, sound poetry, sound installations, & conference activity - June, Kitchener ON

Orford Festival, 3165, Parc Orford Rd., Orford QC J1X 7A2 - 819-843-9871; Tollfree: 1-800-567-6155; URL: www.orford.mu - June-Aug.

Ottawa Bluesfest, 450 Churchill Ave. North, Ottawa ON K1Z 5E2 - 613-247-1188; Fax: 613-247-2220; Tollfree: 1-866-258-3748; URL: www.ottawabluesfest.ca - Executive Director, Mark Monahan - Annual blues music & gospel festival - July

Ottawa Folk Festival (CityFolk), 450 Churchill Ave. North, Ottawa ON K1Z 5E2 - 613-230-8234; URL: cityfolkfestival.com - Sept.

Ottawa International Chamber Music Festival, Ottawa Chamber Music Society, #201, 4 Florence St., Ottawa ON K2P 0W7 - 613-234-8008; Email: info@chamberfest.com; URL: www.chamberfest.com - Artistic Director, Carissa Klopoushak, Email: artistic@chamberfest.com - July-Aug.

Ottawa Jazz Festival, #602, 294 Albert St., Ottawa ON K1P 6E6 - 613-241-2633; Fax: 613-241-5774; URL: ottawajazzfestival.com - Executive Director, Catherine O'Grady, Email: director@ottawajazzfestival.com - June-July

Piknic Électronik Montréal, #470, 5455, av De Gaspé, Montréal QC H2T 3B3 - 514-904-1247; Fax: 514-904-2005; Email: info@piknicelectronik.com; URL: piknicelectronik.com - Electronic music series held every Sunday during the summer

(May-Sept.). Festivals also happen in Dubai, Melbourne & Santiago - Annual

Pembroke Old Time Fiddle & Step Dancing Championships, PO Box 1329, Deep River ON K0J 1P0 - 613-584-3962; URL: bright-ideas-software.com/pembrokefiddle - Labour Day weekend, annually

Regina Folk Festival, #101, 1855 Scarth St., Regina SK S4P 2G9 - 306-757-0308; Email: info@reginafolkfestival.com; URL: www.reginafolkfestival.com - Executive Director, Josh Haugerud - Annual three day folk-based music festival - Aug.

Scotia Festival of Music, 6181 Lady Hammond Rd., Halifax NS B3K 2R9 - 902-429-9467; URL: www.scotiafestival.ns.ca - Artistic & Managing Director, Simon Docking - Chamber music - Annual - May

Shambhala Music Festival, Shambhala Music Festival Ltd., 7790 Hwy. 3 & 6, SalmoBC - 250-352-7623; Email: info@shambhalamusicfestival.com; URL: shambhalamusicfestival.com - Electronic music & arts festival - Annual - Aug., Salmo River Ranch, West Kootenay BC

Shelburne Heritage Music Festival, PO Box 27, Shelburne ON L9V 3L8 - 519-278-0016; Email: fiddleshelburne@yahoo.com; URL: heritagemusicfestival.ca- Aug.

Stan Rogers Folk Festival, PO Box 46, Canso NS B0H 1H0 - Fax: 902-366-2978; Tollfree: 1-888-554-7826; URL: www.stanfest.com

Summerfolk Music & Crafts Festival, c/o Georgian Bay Folk Society, PO Box 521, Owen Sound ON N4K 5R1 - 519-371-2995; Fax: 519-371-2973; Email: gbfs@bmts.com; URL: summerfolk.org

Symphony Under the Sky, Edmonton Symphony Orchestra, 9720 - 102 Ave., Edmonton AB T5J 4B2 - 780-428-1108; Tollfree: 1-800-563-5081; Email: info@winspearcentre.com; URL: www.edmontonsymphony.com - Executive Director, Annemarie Petrov - Aug.-Sept.

Time Festival - URL: embracepresents.com/time-festival - One-day electronic music festival - Biennial - Fort York Garrison Commons, Toronto ON

Toronto Jazz Festival, c/o Toronto Downtown Jazz Society, 82 Bleecker St., Toronto ON M4X 1L8 - 416-928-2033; Fax: 416-928-0533; URL: www.torontojazz.com - Annual - June

Vancouver Folk Music Festival, #230, 275 East 1st Ave., Vancouver BC V5T 1A7 - 604-602-9798; Fax: 604-602-9790; Email: programming@thefestival.bc.ca; URL: www.thefestival.bc.ca - Executive Director, Laurie-Ann Goodwin - Annual festival - July, Vancouver BC

Vancouver International Jazz Festival, c/o Coastal Jazz & Blues Society, 295 West 7th Ave., Vancouver BC V5Y 1L9 - 604-872-5200; Fax: 604-872-5250; Tollfree: 1-888-438-5200; Email: cjbs@coastaljazz.ca; URL: www.coastaljazz.ca - June-July

Vancouver Island Chamber Music Festival, Nanaimo Conservatory of Music, 375 Selby St., Nanaimo BC V9R 2R4 - 250-754-4611; Fax: 250-716-7274; Tollfree: 877-754-4611; Email: registrar@ncmusic.c; URL: www.ncmusic.ca - April

Vancouver Island MusicFest, PO Box 3788, Courtenay BC V9N 7P2 - 250-871-8463; Email: info@islandmusicfest.com; URL: www.islandmusicfest.com - July

Veld Music Festival - Email: info@veldmusicfestival.com; URL: www.veldmusicfestival.com - Two-day electronic music festival - Annual - Aug., Toronto ON

Victoria International JazzFest, c/o Victoria Jazz Society, Harbour Towers Hotel, #202, 345 Quebec St., 2nd Fl., VictoriaBC V8V 1W4 - 250-388-4423; Fax: 250-388-4407; Email: info@jazzvictoria.ca; URL: jazzvictoria.ca

Victoriaville International Festival of New Music, c/o Productions Plateforme Inc., 82, rue Notre-Dame est, CP 460, Victoriaville QC G6P 6T3 - 819-752-7912; Fax: 819-758-4313; Email: info@fimav.qc.ca; URL: www.fimav.qc.ca - General Manager & Artistic Director, Michel Levasseur - 25 concerts in 5 days, musicians from 12 different countries - May

WayHome - Email: info@wayhome.com; URL: wayhome.com - Three-day music & arts festival - Annual - July, Burl's Creek, Oro-Medonte ON

Winnipeg Folk Festival, #203, 211 Bannatyne Ave., Winnipeg MB R3B 3P2 - 204-231-0096; Fax: 204-231-0076; Email: info@winnipegfolkfestival.ca; URL: www.winnipegfolkfestival.ca - Artistic Director, Chris Frayer - Annual - July

Winnipeg Jazz Festival, #007, 100 Arthur St., Winnipeg MB R3B 1H3 - 204-989-4656; Fax: 204-942-1555; Email: info@jazzwinnipeg.com; URL: jazzwinnipeg.com - June

OKTOBERFESTS See **EVENTS**

PACKAGING

PACKEX Montréal, UBM Canon, #100, 2901 - 28 St., Santa Monica CA, USA, 90405 - 310-445-4200; Fax: 310-996-9499; URL: packexmontreal.com - Biennial trade show; part of the

Advanced Design & Manufacturing Expo Montréal - Nov. - Palais des congrès de Montréal, Montréal QC

PACKEX Toronto, UBM Canon, #100, 2901 - 28 St., Santa Monica CA, USA, 90405 - 310-445-4200; Fax: 310-996-9499; URL: packextoronto.packagingdigest.com - Biennial trade show; part of the Advanced Design & Manufacturing Expo Toronto - June - Toronto Congress Centre, Toronto ON

PARANORMAL

Alien Cosmic Expo, 33 Carlson Crt., Toronto ON M9W 6H5 - 519-647-2257; Email: joanne@poweroffreedom.com; URL: aliencosmicexpo.com - June - Crowne Plaza Toronto Airport, Toronto ON

Canadian Haunted Attraction Conference - URL: www.canadahaunts.ca; Email: info@canadahaunts.ca

Shag Harbour UFO Festival, c/o Shag Harbour UFO Museum, 5615 Hwy 3, Shag Harbour NS B0W 3B0 - 902-723-0127; Email: shagharbour@gmail.com - Sept.-Oct.

PARENTS See **CHILDREN**

PETROLEUM

Atlantic Canada Petroleum Show, dmg events (Canada) Inc., #302, 1333 – 8 St. SW, Calgary AB T2R 1M6; 403-209-3555; Fax: 403-245-8649; Fax: 403-245-8649; Tollfree: 1-888-799-2545; URL: atlanticcanadapetroleumshow.com - Director, Marketing & Communications, Paula Arnolds, Email: paulaarnold@eventworx.ca - Annual - June

Global Petroleum Show, dmg events (Canada) Inc., #302, 1333 – 8 St. SW, Calgary AB T2R 1M6 - 403-209-3555; Fax: 403-245-8649; Tollfree: 1-888-799-2545; URL: globalpetroleumshow.com - Operations Director, rebecca Anderson, Email: rebeccaanderson@dmgevents.com - Biennial trade show - Petroleum & natural gas products, services & technology

PETS

Calgary Pet Expo, CanNorth Shows Inc., 821 Bay St., Gravenhurst ON P1P 1G7 - Tollfree: 855-723-1156; Email: info@cannorthshows.com; URL: www.calgarypetexpo.com - Show Manager, Nori Richens, Email: nori@cannorthshows.com - Annual consumer trade show - April

Canadian Pet Expo, PO Box 149, Millgrove ON L0R 1V0 - Tollfree: 1-855-532-3976; Email: info@canadianpetexpo.ca; URL: canadianpetexpo.ca - Annual - Sept. - International Centre, Mississauga ON

Edmonton Pet Expo, Family Productions Inc., 4634 - 90A Ave., 2nd Fl., Edmonton AB T6B 2P9 - 780-490-0215; Fax: 780-450-3757; Email: info@edmontonshows.com; URL: www.petexpo.ca

Exposition Canine, Club Canin de l'Estrie - Email: info@clubcanindelestrie.com; URL: www.clubcanindelestrie.com - Annual - All-breed dog exhibition - Sept.

Salon national des animaux de compagnie (SNAC), C.P. 28530, CSP Verdun, Verdun QC H4G 3L7 - 514-766-6293; Fax: 514-766-0410; URL: www.snac.ca - Annual exhibition for all types of pets - Québec, Montréal & Sherbrooke - Oct., Nov. & April

Spring Canadian Pet Expo, PO Box 149, Millgrove ON L0R 1V0 - Tollfree: 1-855-532-3976; Email: info@canadianpetexpo.ca; URL: canadianpetexpo.ca - Annual - April - International Centre, Mississauga ON

Vancouver Pet Lover Show, PO Box 354, #800, 15355 - 24th Ave., Vancouver BC V4A 2H9 - 604-535-7584; Fax: 604-535-1463; Tollfree: 1-888-960-7584; Email: petlovershow@shaw.ca; URL: www.petlovershow.ca - Show Manager, Nanette Jacques, Email: njacques@shaw.ca - Annual consumer trade show - Feb./March

PHOTOGRAPHY

ProFusion Pro Imaging Expo - 416-365-1778; URL: www.profusionexpo.com - Event Manager, Norma Markham, Email: nmarkham@vistek.ca - Photo & video event for professionals - Annual - Nov. - Toronto ON

PLASTICS & RUBBER

Expoplast, UBM Canon, #100, 2901 - 28 St., Santa Monica CA, USA, 90405 - 310-445-4200; Email: UBMCanonConferences@ubm.com; URL: www.admmontreal.com/en/co-located-shows/expoplast-montreal.html - Part of the Advanced Design & Manufacturing Expo Montréal - Nov., Palais des congrès, Montréal QC

PLAST-EX, UBM Canon, #100, 2901 - #100, 2901 - 28 St., Santa Monica CA, USA, 90405 - 310-445-4200; Email: UBMCanonConferences@ubm.com; URL: www.admtoronto.com/en/show-brands/plastex-toronto.html - Triennial international trade show: plastics machinery, raw materials suppliers, mold makers, processors, fabricators, auxiliary equipment. Part of the Advanced Design & Manufacturing Expo Toronto - May - Toronto Congress Centre, Toronto ON

POPULAR CULTURE

Calgary Comic & Entertainment Expo, BMO Centre, Stampede Park, 20 Roundup Way SE, Calgary AB T2G 2W1 - 403-266-1611; Email: info@calgaryexpo.com; URL: fanexpohq.com/calgaryexpo - April

Comiccon de Québec, 1,000,000 COMIX, 1418 Pierce St., Montréal QC H3H 2S2 - 514-989-9587; URL: www.comicconquebec.com - Oct. - Centre des congrès, Québec

East Coast Comic Expo, 99 Wynwood Dr., Moncton NB E1A 6X4 - URL: www.eastcoastcomicexpo.com - May - Crossman Community Centre, Moncton NB

Edmonton Comic & Entertainment Expo, Edmonton Expo Centre, 7515 - 118 Ave. NW, Edmonton AB T5B 4X5 - 403-554-7368; Email: info@edmontonexpo.com; URL: edmontonexpo.com

Enthusiast Gaming Live Expo - URL: eglx.ca - The International Centre, Mississauga ON

Fan Expo Canada, Informa Canada, #100, 10 Alcorn Ave., Toronto ON M4V 3A9 - Tollfree: 1-800-663-4173; Email: info@fanexpohq.com; URL: fanexpohq.com/fanexpocanada - Show Director, Gilbert Estephan

Fan Expo Vancouver, Informa Canada, #100, 10 Alcorn Ave., Toronto ON M4V 3A9 - Tollfree: 1-800-663-4173 - Email: info@fanexpohq.com; URL: www.fanexpovancouver.com - Show Director, Fiona Standing

Horror-Rama Toronto, 918 Bathurst St., Toronto ON M5R 3G5 - 416-588-6674; Email: info@horrorramacanada.com; URL: www.horrorramacanada.com - Nov.

Montréal Comiccon, 1,000,000 COMIX, 1418 Pierce St., Montréal QC H3H 2S2 - 514-989-9587; URL: www.montrealcomiccon.com - Sept. - Palais des congrès, Montréal

Ottawa Comiccon, 1,000,000 COMIX, 1418 Pierce St., Montréal QC H3H 2S2 - 514-989-9587; URL: www.ottawacomiccon.com

Saskatoon Comic & Entertainment Expo, Prairieland Park, 503 Ruth St W, Saskatoon SK S7J 0S6 - Email: info@saskexpo.com; URL: saskexpo.com

Toronto ComiCon, Informa Canada, #100, 10 Alcorn Ave., Toronto ON M4V 3A9 - Tollfree: 1-800-663-4173; Email: info@fanexpohq.com; URL: fanexpohq.com/comicontoronto - Show Director, Gilbert Estephan

Unplugged Expo, c/o Join Team Unplugged, #102, 40 Wynford Dr., Toronto ON M3C 1J5 - 647-998-9537; Email: info@unpluggedexpo.com; URL: unpluggedexpo.com - Sept.

Vancouver Retro Gaming Expo, Anvil Centre, 777 Columbia St., New Westminster BC V3M 1B6 - 604-515-3830; Email: vancouvergamingexpo.com; URL: www.vancouvergamingexpo.com

REAL ESTATE

Global Property Market Conference, Informa Canada, #100, 10 Alcorn Ave., Toronto ON M4V 3A9 - 416-512-3807; Email: events@informacanada.com; URL: www.realestateforums.com

Informa Canada Apartment Investment Conferences, Informa Canada, #100, 10 Alcorn Ave., Toronto ON M4V 3A9 - 416-512-3807; Email: events@informacanada.com; URL: informaconnect.com - Held in Montréal (Feb.) & Toronto (Sept.)

Informa Canada Real Estate Forums, #100, 10 Alcorn Ave., Toronto ON M4V 3A9 - 416-512-3807; Email: events@informacanada.com; URL: www.realestateforums.com - Held annually in Calgary, Edmonton, Halifax, Montréal, Ottawa, Québec, Saskatchewan, Toronto, Vancouver & Winnipeg

Informa Canada Real Estate Strategy & Leasing Conferences, #100, 10 Alcorn Ave., Toronto ON M4V 3A9 - 416-512-3807; Email: events@informacanada.com; URL: www.realestateforums.com - Held annually in Calgary, Montréal, Toronto & Vancouver

Land & Development Conference, Informa Canada, #100, 10 Alcorn Ave., Toronto ON M4V 3A9 - 416-512-3807; Tollfree: 1-800-660-7083; Email: events@informacanada.com; URL: www.realestateforums.com

Ontario Real Estate Association Conferences, 99 Duncan Mill Rd., Toronto ON M3B 1Z2; 416-445-9910; Fax: 416-445-2644; Tollfree: 1-800-265-6732; Email: info@orea.ca; URL: www.orea.com - Annual trade show - March

PM Springfest, Property Management Exposition & Conference, Informa Canada, #100, 10 Alcorn Ave., Toronto ON M4V 3A9 - 416-512-3807; Email: events@informacanada.com; URL: informaconnect.com/pm-springfest - Part of The Buildings Show; Annual - Dec. - Metro Toronto Convention Centre, South Building, Toronto ON

RealCapital, Informa Canada, #100, 10 Alcorn Ave., Toronto ON M4V 3A9 - 416-512-3807; Email: events@informacanada.com; URL: www.realestateforums.com - Conference on public and private equity and debt financing in the Canadian real estate market - Feb. - Metro Toronto Convention Centre, Toronto ON

RealREIT, Informa Canada, #100, 10 Alcorn Ave., Toronto ON M4V 3A9 - 416-512-3807; Email: events@informacanada.com; URL: www.realestateforums.com - Sept. - Metro Toronto Convention Centre, Toronto ON

RECREATIONAL VEHICLES See AUTOMOTIVE

RODEOS

See Also Exhibitions; Farm Business/Agriculture

Calgary Exhibition & Stampede, PO Box 1060, Stn M, Calgary AB T2P 2K8 - 403-261-0101; Fax: 403-265-7197; Tollfree: 1-800-661-1260; Email: info@calgarystampede.com; URL: www.calgarystampede.com - Annual city-wide festival; agricultural exhibits

CCA Finals Rodeo, Canadian Cowboys Association, PO Box 1027, Regina SK S4P 3B2 - 306-931-2700; Fax: 306-931-2701; Email: canadiancowboys@sasktel.net; URL: canadiancowboys.ca - Annual - Oct., four days

Maple Creek Cowtown Pro-Rodeo, PO Box 428, Maple Creek SK S0N 1N0 - 306-661-8184; URL: www.maplecreek.ca - Annual - June

Williams Lake Stampede, Williams Lake Stampede Association, PO Box 4076, Williams Lake BC V2G 2V2 - 250-392-6585; Fax: 250-398-7701; Tollfree: 1-800-717-6336; Email: info@williamslakestampede.com; URL: www.williamslakestampede.com - July

RVS See AUTOMOTIVE; SPORTS & RECREATION

SEWING See CRAFTS

SEX

The Everything to Do with Sex Show/Taboo Naughty But Nice Sex Show, Canwest Productions Inc., #218, 7710 – 5th St. SE, Calgary AB T2H 2L9 - 403-242-0859; Fax: 403-246-3856; Tollfree: 1-800-626-1538; Email: taboo@canwestproductions.com; URL: tabooshow.com/Toronto - Annual trade show - Calgary, Edmonton, Red Deer, Regina, Toronto, Vancouver

SPORTS & RECREATION

See Also Boating; Automotive, for combined auto/RV shows

Atlantic Outdoor Sports & RV Show, Darwin Event Group, PO Box 667, #16, 60 Morse Lane, Berwick NS B0P 1E0 - 902-679-7177; Fax: 902-678-4436; Tollfree: 1-877-679-7177; Email: info@darwineventgroup.com; URL: www.sportsandrvshow.com - Annual consumer show. Trailer & motor homes, 4x4s, tent trailers, boats, motors, hunting, fishing & camping, tourism & sporting goods - March, Halifax NS

BC Sportsmen's Show, Master Promotions Ltd., PO Box 565, Saint John NB E2L 3Z8 - 506-658-0018; Fax: 506-658-0750; Tollfree: 1-888-454-7469; Email: info@mpltd.ca; URL: www.bcboatandsportsmenshow.ca - Show Manager, Les Trendall, Email: ltrendall@mpltd.ca - Annual consumer show focused on hunting, fishing, boating and more - March

Calgary Boat & Outdoors Show, Master Promotions Ltd., PO Box 565, Saint John NB E2L 3Z8 - 506-658-0018; Fax: 506-658-0750; Tollfree: 1-888-454-7469; Email: info@mpltd.ca; URL: www.calgaryboatandoutdoorshow.ca - Show Manager, Les Trendall, Email: ltrendall@mpltd.ca; Annual consumer show - Feb.

Canadian Power Toboggan Championships, PO Box 22, Beausejour MB R0E 0C0 - 204-268-2049; Fax: 204-268-4209; URL: www.cptcracing.com - Annual - March

Edmonton Boat & Sportsmen's Show, Master Promotions Ltd., PO Box 565, Saint John NB E2L 3Z8 - 506-658-0018; Fax:

506-658-0750; Tollfree: 1-888-454-7469; Email: info@mpltd.ca; URL: www.edmontonboatandsportshow.ca - Show Manager, Les Trendall, Email: ltrendall@mpltd.ca; Annual consumer show - March

Edmonton Ski & Snowboard Show, Family Productions Inc., 4634 - 90A Ave., 2nd Fl., Edmonton AB T6B 2P9 - 780-490-0215; Fax: 780-450-3757; Email: info@edmontonshows.com; URL: powderfest.com

Ironman Canada Triathlon Championship - Email: canada@ironman.com; URL: www.ironman.com - Annual four-day trade expo staged as part of the events prior to the Ironman race - Aug.

London Boat Fishing & Outdoor Show, Western Fair District, 316 Rectory St., London ON N5W 3V9 - 519-438-7203; Tollfree: 800-619-4629; Email: contact@westernfairdistrict.com; URL: www.westernfairdistrict.com/events/london-boat-fishing-outdo or-show - Annual consumer show - Feb.

The Outdoor Adventure Show, c/o National Event Management Inc., #102, 260 Town Centre Blvd., Markham ON L3R 8H8 - 905-477-2677; Fax: 905-477-7872; Tollfree: 1-800-891-4859; Email: info@outdooradventureshow.ca; URL: outdooradventureshow.ca - Toronto, Vancouver, Calgary & Montréal

Salon Plein air, chasse, pêche et camping de Montréal, Canadian National Sportsmen's Shows (1989) Ltd., #330, 8150 boul Métropolitain est, Montréal QC H1K 1A1 - 514-866-5409; Email: lemieux@sportshows.ca; URL: www.salonchassepechepleinair.ca - Show Manager, Shawn Murphy, Email: smurphy@mpltd.ca - Annual consumer show: camping, fishing, hunting, RVs, tourism

Salon Plein air, chasse, pêche et camping de Québec, Canadian National Sportsmen's Shows (1989) Ltd., #330, 8150 boul Métropolitain est, Montréal QC H1K 1A1 - 418-622-8118; Email: lemieux@sportshows.ca; URL: www.salonpleinairquebec.ca - Show Manager, Shawn Murphy, Email: smurphy@mpltd.ca - Annual consumer show: camping, fishing, hunting, RVs, tourism

Toronto International Bicycle Show, #1801, 1 Yonge St., Toronto ON M5E 1W7 - 416-363-1292; Fax: 416-369-0515; URL: www.bicycleshowtoronto.com - Marketing & Sales Manager, Josie Graziosi, Email: josie@telsec.net - Annual consumer show, March; Annual blowout sale, Oct. - Toronto ON

Toronto International Snowmobile, ATV & Powersports Show, 27083 Kennedy Rd., Willow Beach ON L0E 1S0 - 905-722-6766; Tollfree: 1-888-661-7469; Tollfree Fax: 1-888-680-7469; Email: info@torontosnowmobileatvshow.com; URL: www.torontosnowmobileatvshow.com - Director, Sales & Marketing, Booth & Sponsorship, Rick Bloye, Email: rickb@osmmag.com - Annual consumer show, March - Toronto International Centre, Toronto ON

Toronto Ski & Snowboard Show, Canadian National Sportsmen's Shows (1989) Ltd., 30 Village Centre Pl., Mississauga ON L4Z 1V9 - 905-361-2677; Email: info@sportshows.ca; URL: www.torontoskishow.ca - Annual consumer show - Oct. - International Centre, Mississauga ON

Toronto Sportsmen's Show, Canadian National Sportsmen's Shows (1989) Ltd., 30 Village Centre Pl., Mississauga ON L4Z 1V9 - 905-361-2677; Email: info@sportshows.ca; URL: www.torontosportshow.ca - Annual consumer show - Show Manager, Scott Sprague, Email: ssprague@mpltd.ca - March - International Centre, Mississauga ON

The Toronto Star Golf & Travel Show, Metroland Media, 3145 Wolfedale Rd., Mississauga ON L5C 3A9 - Fax: 905-277-9917; URL: www.torontogolfshow.com - General Manager, Lars Melander, Email: lmelander@metroland.com - Annual consumer show - Late Feb./Early March

Vancouver Bike Show, c/o National Event Management Inc., #102, 260 Town Centre Blvd., Markham ON L3R 8H8 - 905-477-2677; Fax: 905-477-7872; Tollfree: 1-800-891-4859; Email: info@nationalevent.com; URL: vancouverbikeshow.com - Show Manager, Seamus McGrath, Email: bikeshow@nationalevent.com

STAMPEDES See RODEOS

THEATRE See ARTS

TOYS & GAMES

Ancaster Collectibles Extravaganza, Ontario Collector Shows, PO Box 705, Simcoe ON N3Y 4T2 - 519-426-8875; URL: www.collectorshows.ca - Dec.

Brantford Model Train Show & Sale, Ontario Collector Shows, PO Box 705, Simcoe ON N3Y 4T2 - 519-426-8875; URL: www.collectorshows.ca

Kitchener Model Train Show & Sale, Ontario Collector Shows, PO Box 705, Simcoe ON N3Y 4T2 - 519-426-8875; URL: www.collectorshows.ca - Nov.

Kitchener Collectibles Expo, Ontario Collector Shows, PO Box 705, Simcoe ON N3Y 4T2 - 519-426-8875; URL: www.collectorshows.ca - Multiple dates a year

Lindsay & District Model Railroaders Model Railway Show, PO Box 452, Lindsay ON K9V 4S5 - Email: allaboard@ldmr.org; URL: www.ldmr.org

London Collectibles Expo, Ontario Collector Shows, PO Box 705, Simcoe ON N3Y 4T2 - 519-426-8875; URL: www.collectorshows.ca - Oct.

Toronto Toy & Doll Collectors' Show, PO Box 217, Grimsby ON L3M 4G3 - 905-945-2775; Email: info@antiquetoys.ca; URL: www.antiquetoys.ca - Contact, Bev Jarvis, Email: bevjarvis@sympatico.ca - Annual antique & collectible childhood memorabilia - Nov., Mississauga ON

Toronto Toy & Nostalgia Auction, Toronto Show Promotions, PO Box 217, Grimsby ON L3M 4G3 - 905-945-2775; Email: info@antiquetoys.ca - Contact, Bev Jarvis, Email: bevjarvis@sympatico.ca - Annual consumer shows/auction - June

Woodstock Model Train Show & Sale, Ontario Collector Shows, PO Box 705, Simcoe ON N3Y 4T2 - 519-426-8875; URL: www.collectorshows.ca - Oct.

Woodstock Toy & Collectibles Expo, Ontario Collector Shows, PO Box 705, Simcoe ON N3Y 4T2 - 519-426-8875; URL: www.collectorshows.ca - Multiple dates a year

TRANSPORTATION

See Also Automotive

Ontario Transportation Expo Conference & Trade Show, #210, 320 North Queen St., Toronto ON M9C 5K4 - 416-229-6622; Email: info@ote.ca; URL: www.ote.ca - Annual conference & trade show. Safety, fuel economy, buses & accessories, computers - International Centre, Mississauga ON - April

Transit Trade Show, Canadian Urban Transit Association, #1401, 55 York St., Toronto ON M5J 1R - 416-365-9800; Fax: 416-365-1295; URL: www.cutaactu.ca - Annual transit industry event, held in conjunction with the CUTA Fall Conference - Nov.

TRAVEL & TOURISM

Canadian Meetings + Events Expo, Newcom Media, #400, 5353 Dundas St. West, Toronto ON M9B 6H8 - 416-614-2200; Fax: 416-614-8861; Email: cmeexpo@newcom.ca; URL: www.cmeexpo.ca - Annual trade show & conference - Oct.

Go Global Expo - 705-742-6869; Email: info@letsgoglobal.ca; URL: www.letsgoglobal.ca - Contact, Jeff Minthorn, Email: jeff@vergemagazine.com - Overseas work, study & volunteering expo

The Ottawa Travel & Vacation Show, Player Expositions Inc., 255 Clemow Ave., Ottawa ON K1S 2B5 - 613-567-6408; Fax: 613-567-2718; URL: www.travelandvacationshow.ca - Annual consumer & trade show - March - Shaw Centre, Ottawa ON

The Ottawa-Gatineau Outdoor & Adventure Travel Show, #107, 2706 Alta Vista Dr., Ottawa ON K1V 7T4 - 613-860-8687; Fax: 613-482-4997; Tollfree: 1-888-228-2918; Email: editor@ottawaoutdoors.ca; URL: www.adventureottawa.ca - Show Owner, Dave Brown

Salon international tourisme voyages, Expo Media, #210, 370, rue Guy, Montréal QC H3J 1S6 - 514-527-9221; Email: info@expomediainc.com; URL: salontourismevoyages.com

Vancouver International Travel Expo - 604-629-0877; Email: socialmedia@vitexpo.ca; URL: www.vitexpo.ca - Sept. - Vancouver Conventon Centre, Vancouver BC

TRUCKS See AUTOMOTIVE

TVS, STEREOS See ELECTRICAL/ELECTRONICS

VIDEO See COMMUNICATIONS

UNIVERSITY/COLLEGE

Student Life Expo, Pumped Inc., #9, 20 Amber St., Markham ON L3R 5P4 - 905-415-3643; Tollfree: 1-877-786-7331 - Email: info@studentlifeexpo.com; URL: studentlifeexpo.com

Study & Go Abroad Fairs, 1484 Doran Rd., North Vancouver BC V7K 1N2 - URL: www.studyandgoabroad.com - Annual. Vancouver, Edmonton, Calgary, Ottawa, Toronto & Halifax

WINTER CARNIVALS

Banff/Lake Louise Winterstart Festival, PO Box 1298, Banff AB T1L 1B3 - 403-762-8421; Fax: 403-762-8163; URL: www.banfflakelouise.com, Nov/Dec.

Carnaval de Québec/Québec Winter Carnival, Carnaval de Québec, 205, boul des Cèdres, Québec QC G1L 1N8 - 418-626-3716; Tollfree: 1-866-422-7628; URL:

www.carnaval.qc.ca - General Manager, Mélanie Raymond,
Email: melanie.raymond@carnaval.qc.ca - Major winter event
Conception Bay South Winterfest, Town of Conception Bay
South, PO Box 14040, Stn. Manuels, 11 Remembrance Sq.,
Conception Bay South NL A1W 3J1 - 709-834-6500, Fax:
709-834-8337; URL: www.conceptionbaysouth.ca - Feb.
Corner Brook Winter Carnival, PO Box 86, Corner Brook NL
A2H 6H6 - 709-632-5343; Fax: 709-632-5344; URL:
www.cornerbrookwintercarnival.ca - annually, 10 days - Feb.
Elliot Lake Winterfest, Lester B. Pearson Civic Centre,
Hwy.#108, Elliot Lake ON P5A 2T1 - 705-848-2084; Fax:
705-848-7121; URL: www.cityofelliotlake.com - Feb.
Fête des Neiges, Parc Jean-Drapeau, circuit
Gilles-Villeneuve, Montréal QC H3C 1A9 - 514-872-6120;
Email: clientele@parcjeandrapeau.com; URL:
www.parcjeandrapeau.com - 6 day major winter event.
Sports, cultural, ice sculptures - Jan.
Hamilton Winterfest, Tourism Hamilton, 28 James St. North, 2nd
Fl., Hamilton ON L8P 4Y5 - 905-546-2666; Fax:
905-546-2667; URL: www.hamiltonwinterfest.ca - Feb.
Jasper in January, Tourism Jasper, PO Box 568, Jasper AB T0E
1E0 - 780-852-6236; URL: www.jasper.travel/january - Jan.
Kapuskasing Winter Carnival, 88 Riverside Dr., Kapuskasing ON
P5N 1B3 - 705-335-2341; URL: kapuskasing.ca - Feb. &
March
Kirkland Lake Winter Carnival, Kirkland Lake Festivals
Committee, PO Box 277, Kirkland Lake ON P2N 3H7 - Email:
klfestivals@hotmail.com; URL: www.klfestivals.com - March
Mount Pearl Frosty Festival, PO Box 838, Mount Pearl NL A1N
3C8 - 709-748-6480; Fax: 709-748-5499; Email:
frostyfestival@live.com; URL: frostyfestival.ca - Feb.
Prince Albert Winter Festival, Email: info@pawinterfestival.com;
URL: princealbertwinterfestival.com - Feb.

Riverview Winter Carnival, 30 Honour House Court, Riverview
NB E1B 3Y9 - 506-387-2020; URL: www.townofriverview.ca -
Feb.
Vernon Winter Carnival, 3401 - 35th Ave., Vernon BC V1T 2T5 -
250-545-2236; Fax: 250-545-0006; Email:
info@vernonwintercarnival.com; URL:
www.vernonwintercarnival.com - Feb.
Winterlude, National Capital Commission, #202, 40 Elgin St.,
Ottawa ON K1P 1C7 - 613-239-5000; Tollfree:
1-800-465-1867; Email: PCH.info-info.PCH@canada.ca;
URL:
www.canada.ca/en/canadian-heritage/campaigns/winterlude -
Major winter festival, first three weekends of February.
Skating on Rideau Canal, international ice & snow sculpture
competitions, musical & figure skating shows, North
America's largest winter playground for kids, various sporting
& social events, fireworks, stage performances & buskers -
Feb.
Winterlude, PO Box 439, Grand Falls-Windsor NL A2A 2J8 -
709-489-0407; URL: grandfallswindsor.com - Director of
Parks and Recreation, Keith Antle, Email:
kantle@townofgfw.com - Feb.

WOMEN

Calgary Woman's Show, The Calgary Woman's Show Ltd.,
#201, 7710 - 5th St. SE, Calgary AB T2H 2L9 -
403-242-0859; Fax: 403-246-3856; Email:
calgarywomansshow@canwestproductions.com; URL:
www.calgarywomansshow.com - Semi-annual consumer
show in April & Oct.; Products & services.
Edmonton Woman's Show, Family Productions Inc., 4634 - 90A
Ave., 2nd Fl., Edmonton AB T6B 2P9 - 780-490-0215; URL:
womanshow.com

National Women's Show, National Event Management Inc.,
#102, 260 Town Centre Blvd., Markham ON L3R 8H8 -
905-477-2677; Tollfree: 1-800-891-4859; Email:
info@nationalevent.com; URL: www.nationalwomenshow.com
- Annual - Toronto, Ottawa, Montréal & Québec

WOOD/WOODWORKING

Canada Woodworking West, Master Promotions Ltd., PO Box
565, Saint John NB E2L 3Z8 - 506-658-0018; Fax:
506-658-0750; Tollfree: 1-888-454-7469; Email:
info@mpltd; URL: www.canadawoodworkingwest.ca -
Annual - Oct.
Canada Woodworking East, Master Promotions Ltd., PO Box
565, Saint John NB E2L 3Z8 - 506-658-0018; Fax:
506-658-0750; Tollfree: 1-888-454-7469; Email:
info@mpltd.ca; URL: www.canadawoodworkingwest.ca -
Annual
Hamilton Woodworking Show, Canadian Warplane Heritage
Museum, 9280 Airport Rd., Hamilton, Ontario L0R 1W0 -
905-779-0422; Email: info@woodshows.com; URL:
www.woodshows.com - Show Manager, Gina Downes, Email:
gina@woodshows.com - Annual - Feb.
Woodworking, Machinery & Supply Expo (WMS), CCI Media,
2240 Country Club Pkwy SE, Cedar Rapids IA USA 52403 -
Tollfree: 1-800-752-6312; Email: wms@heiexpo.com; URL:
www.woodworkingnetwork.com/events-contests/wms -
Annual - International Centre, Mississauga ON
Woodstock Woodworking Show, Woodstock Fairgrounds, 875
Nellis St., Woodstock ON N4S 4C6 - 905-779-0422; Email:
carving@woodshows.com; URL: www.woodshows.com -
Show Manager, Gina Downes, Email: gina@woodshows.com
- Sept-Oct.

Awards & Honours

Canadian Awards

(Including Scholarships, Grants, Bursaries)
Awards are listed under the following categories:

ADVERTISING & PUBLIC RELATIONS

The Advertising & Design Club of Canada
#235, 401 Richmond St. West, Toronto ON M5V 3A8
416-423-4113; Fax: 416-423-3362
Email: info@theadcc.ca; URL: theadcc.ca

The ADCC Awards
Celebrates individuals responsible for achieving excellence. Main categories of awards are: Advertising Broadcast & Print, Graphic Design, Editorial Design, and Interactive Media. Winners receive gold, silver or merit awards.

The Les Usherwood Award
A lifetime achievement award presented in honour of the late Les Usherwood.

The Michael O'Reilly Award
Presented to a talented copywriter in honour of the late Michael O'Reilly.

The Mick Griffin Award
Presented to a talented editor in honour of the late Mick Griffin.

The Scarlet Letter Awards
Celebrates companies for achieving excellence. Four awards are: Agency of the Year, Design Studio of the Year, Interactive Agency of the Year, Production Company of the Year.

The Student Competition
Celebrates the absolute best student work. Categories include: Advertising, Graphic Design, Editorial Design, Interactive Media. Winners receive gold, silver or merit awards.

Association of Canadian Advertisers Inc. / Association canadienne des annonceurs
#1201, 21 St. Clair Ave. East, Toronto ON M4V 1N6
416-964-3805; Fax: 416-964-0771; Toll Free: 1-800-565-0109
Email: communications@acaweb.ca; URL: acaweb.ca

ACA Gold Medal
Established in 1941 to encourage high standards of personal achievement in advertising - for introducing new concepts or techniques, for significantly improving existing practices, or for enhancing the stature of advertising.

Brunico Communications Ltd.
#100, 366 Adelaide St. West, Toronto ON M5V 1R9
416-408-2300; Fax: 416-408-0870
URL: www.brunico.com

AToMiC Awards
Celebrate collaborations in Canada's media and marketing industries. Awards span advertising, technology, media innovation and content categories.

The Marketing Awards
Annual advertising awards offering 40 Gold Awards in the following categories: television/cinema, radio, magazine, newspaper, transit, business press, direct mail, outdoor, point-of-purchase/interior store design, multimedia campaign, non-traditional & public service. Silver Awards, Bronze Awards, & Certificates of Excellence are also awarded. Entries must have run in the previous year & must have been conceived & created by people working in English in the Canadian advertising business. New categories were added in 2011 that include social media, brand content, and experimental and event marketing.

Media Innovation Awards
Recognize individuals who have made breakthrough contributions to the use of media in marketing.

Shopper Innovation Awards
Celebrate innovation in shopper marketing.

The Strategy Awards
Celebrate the best marketing and advertising strategy work being done in Canada.

Canadian Marketing Association / Association canadienne du marketing
#603, 55 University Ave., Toronto ON M5J 2H7
416-391-2362; Fax: 416-441-4062; Toll Free: 1-800-267-8805
Email: info@the-cma.org; URL: www.the-cma.org

CMA Awards
Celebrating the art and science of marketing, CMA's judging breakdown is based equally on Strategy, Creativity and Results. Awards span 6 Disciplines and 9 Categories.

Institute of Communication Agencies / Institut des communications
#3002, 2300 Yonge St., Toronto ON M4P 1E4
416-482-1396; Fax: 416-482-1856; Toll Free: 1-800-567-7422
Email: ica@icacanada.ca; URL: theica.ca; www.effie.org/canada

Effie Canada Awards
Established 1993; Formerly CASSIES, the awards are open to all channels of marketing communications. Eligible submissions must show impressive business results and convincingly prove their success was a result of the advertising.

AGRICULTURE & FARMING

Canadian Society of Animal Science / Société canadienne de science animale
c/o Anita Drabyk, PO Box 674, Pinawa MB R0E 1L0
204-205-0297
Email: csasorscsa@gmail.com; URL: www.asas.org/csas
CSAS offers five awards:

Award for Excellence in Nutrition and Meat Sciences

Award for Technical Innovation in Enhancing Production of Safe Affordable Food
Awarded to a member who has demonstrated excellence in technical innovation, teaching, research or extension in the field of biotechnology, genetics, physiology and animal behavior that has contributed to the production of safe and affordable food.

Canadian Indutries Award in Extension & Public Service
Awarded for outstanding service in technology transfer, leadership, and education in animal production.

Fellowship Award
Awarded to members who have made an outstanding contribution in any field of animal agriculture.

Young Scientist Award
Awarded to a member who has demonstrated excellence in any area of animal and/or poultry science within seven years of obtaining a Ph.D.

International Development Research Centre / Centre de recherches pour le développement international
PO Box 8500, Ottawa ON K1G 3H9
613-236-6163
Email: info@idrc.ca; URL: www.idrc.ca
IDRC offers many competitions and awards for developing-country researchers, institutions, and Canadian researchers. Some awards include:

Bentley Research Fellowship

IDRC Doctoral Research Awards

IDRC International Fellowships

IDRC Research Awards

Provincial Exhibition of Manitoba
1200 - 13th St., #A-1, Brandon MB R7A 4S8
204-726-3590; Fax: 204-725-0202; Toll Free: 1-877-729-0001
Email: info@provincialexhibition.com; URL: www.provincialexhibition.com

Manitoba AG Ex Awards
Prizes given in various categories.

Manitoba Summer Fair Awards
Prizes given in various categories.

Royal Manitoba Winter Fair Awards
Prizes given in various categories for best of show for agricultural products, animals & crops; several equestrian events offer prizes for best in competition.

Royal Agricultural Winter Fair Association / Foire agricole royale d'hiver
The Ricoh Coliseum, Enercare Centre
Exhibition Place, Toronto ON M6K 3C3
416-263-3400; Fax: 416-263-3488
Email: info@royalfair.org; URL: www.royalfair.org

Agricultural Awards
Over 2000 agricultural competitions. Grand Champion is the highest honour in the following categories: dairy, beef, sheep, goats, swine, market livestock, field crops, vegetables, honey & maple, poultry, jams/jellies/pickles, dairy products, square dancing, fiddling, fleece wool, rabbits & eight youth activities.

Breeding Horse Awards
17 sections award prizes in this category.

Hunter and Jumper Horse Awards

Performance Horse Awards
35 divisions & classes offer prizes; Leading International Rider is the highest honour in the horse show.

BROADCASTING & FILM

Academy of Canadian Cinema & Television / Académie canadienne du cinéma et de la télévision
#9, 411 Richmond St. East, Toronto ON M5A 3S5
416-366-2227; Fax: 416-366-8454; Toll Free: 1-800-644-5194
Email: awards@academy.ca; URL: www.academy.ca

Canadian Screen Awards
The Canadian Screen Awards began in 2013 as the result of a merger between the Academy's previous Gemini Awards and Genie Awards. These new awards honour achievement in the fields of Canadian television, film production and digital media.

Alberta Media Production Industries Association
#200, 7316 - 101st Ave., Edmonton AB T6A 0J2
780-944-0707; Fax: 780-426-3057
Email: info@ampia.org; URL: ampia.org

Alberta Film & Television Awards
Awarded annually, the "Rosie Awards", are presented to producers and craftspeople, who reside in Alberta, in recognition of their outstanding film & television works. Awards are given in class categories (ie. Best Documentary, Best Drama, Best Movie, Best Musical etc.) and craft categories (ie. Best Director; Best Screenwriter, Cinematography etc.).

David Billington Award
Awarded to a special individual in recognition of their incomparable dedication and contribution to the growth of Alberta's film and television production industry.

Edmonton Music and Film Prize
Presented in collaboration with Alberta Music and Edmonton Arts Council, the film prize goes to a narrative, documentary or experimental project with special consideration to any filmmakers who have made a unique contribution or outstanding accomplishment in the community. The music prize goes to Edmonton-based musicians or collectives who have released a full-length recording in the past 18 months.

Lifetime Achievement Award

Banff World Media Festival
c/o Brunico Communications Ltd., #100, 366 Adelaide St. West, Toronto ON M5V 1R9
416-408-2300; Fax: 416-408-0870
Email: bwmfcustomercare@brunico.com; URL: banffmediafestival.playbackonline.ca

Banff Rockie Awards
Annual television and digital content awards in the categories of: Documentary and Factual, Arts and Entertainment, Children and Youth; Scripted; Podcasts; Also a grand jury prize, two special jury awards & honorees.

Canadian Ethnic Media Association
24 Tarlton Rd., Toronto ON M5P 2M4
416-488-0048
Email: info@canadianethnicmedia.com; URL: canadianethnicmedia.com

CEMA Awards
Up to nine plaques are offered annually to journalists in print, radio, television, podcast, internet & innovation; awards are given to journalists for excellence in their field; competition is open to all journalists, in any language, whether or not they are members of CEMA; a single award is also given to writers of a published work of fact, fiction or poetry in book form.

Canadian Media Production Association
251 Laurier Ave. West, 11th Fl., Ottawa ON K1P 5J6
613-233-1444; Fax: 613-233-0073; Toll Free: 1-800-656-7440
Email: ottawa@cmpa.ca; URL: cmpa.ca

Indiescreen Awards
Presented to one established and one emerging independent producer of Canadian features being screened at the Toronto International Film Festival.

Canadian Society of Cinematographers
#131, 3085 Kingston Rd., Toronto ON M1M 1P1
416-266-0591
Email: info@csc.ca; URL: www.csc.ca

Canadian Society of Cinematography Awards
15 Awards given annually for various genres and contributions.

Hot Docs Canadian International Documentary Festival
#402, 720 Spadina Ave., Toronto ON M5S 2T9
416-203-2155; Fax: 416-203-0446
Email: info@hotdocs.ca; URL: www.hotdocs.ca

Hot Docs Awards
Recognize outstanding work in documentary film.

Toronto International Film Festival Group
350 King St. West, Toronto ON M5V 3X5
416-599-8433; Toll Free: 1-888-258-8433
Email: customerrelations@tiff.net; URL: www.tiff.net

Best Canadian Feature Film

Best Canadian First Feature Film

Excellence in Canadian Production

FIPRESCI Prize - Special Presentations

FIPRESCI Prize - Discovery
Selected by an international FIPRESCI jury, awarded to a feature film by an emerging filmmaker having its world premiere at the festival.

NETPAC Award
Awarded by the Network for the Promotion of Asian Cinema to spotlight exceptional Asian feature films & promising new talent.

People's Choice Award
Awarded to the best film of the festival, as voted by festival audiences.

People's Choice Documentary Award

People's Choice Midnight Madness Award

Short Cuts Award for Best Canadian Film

Short Cuts Award for Best Film

Toronto Platform Prize

BUSINESS & TRADE

The Caldwell Partners
165 Avenue Rd., 6th Fl., Toronto ON M5R 3S4
416-920-7702; Toll Free: 1-800-292-2973
Email: leaders@caldwell.ca; URL: www.caldwell.ca; www.ceoaward.ca

Canada's Outstanding CEO of the Year
Sponsored by Bennett Jones LLP, this annual award takes into consideration the candidate's leadership, innovation, business achievements, corporate performance, social responsibility, sense of vision & global competitiveness.

Canada's Top 40 Under 40
Established & managed by The Caldwell Partners, celebrates Canadian leaders who have demonstrated remarkable success before the age of 40.

Ernst & Young
Ernst & Young Tower, 100 Adelaide St. West, Toronto ON M5H 0B3
416-864-1234; Fax: 416-864-1174
URL: www.ey.ca

Ernst & Young Entrepreneur of the Year Award
Best entrepreneurs in 5 regions nationwide (Pacific Canada, The Prairies, Ontario, Québec, Atlantic Canada); other awards include Master Entrepreneur, Emerging Entrepreneur, Turnaround Entrepreneur, Young Entrepreneur, Supporter of Entrepreneurship. Awarded annually.

The National Trust for Canada / Fiducie nationale du Canada
190 Bronson Ave., Ottawa, ON K1R 6H4
613-237-1066; Fax: 613-237-5987; Toll Free: 1-866-964-1066
Email: nationaltrust@nationaltrustcanada.ca; URL: nationaltrustcanada.ca

Ecclesiastical Insurance Cornerstone Awards
Recognizes excellence in the regeneration of heritage buildings and sites.

Gabrielle Léger Award for Lifetime Achievement
Founded in 1978, this award is Canada's premier hounour for individual achievement in heritage conservation. It was last awarded in 2016.

Lieutenant Governor's Award for Heritage Conservation
Established in 1979, honours outstanding achievement in heritage conservation at the provincial/territorial level. It was last awarded in 2016.

The Prince of Wales Prize for Municipal Heritage Leadership
Established in 1999, The Prince of Wales agreed to lend his title to this annual award in recognition of the government of a municipality, which has demonstrated a strong and sustained commitment to the conservation of its historic places.

Prix du XXe siècle
This award is presented jointly by the National Trust for Canada and the Royal Architectural Institute of Canada to raise awareness about nationally significant 20th century architecture in Canada. It includes the Award of Excellence and Certificate of Merit.

Excellence Canada
North American Centre, #200, 5700 Yonge St., Toronto, ON M2M 4K2
416-251-7600; Fax: 416-251-9131; Toll Free: 1-800-263-9648
Email: info@excellence.ca; URL: excellence.ca

Canada Awards for Excellence
Previously called the Canada Awards for Business Excellence & established by the Government of Canada in 1984, the awards recognize outstanding continuous achievement in seven key areas: Leadership, Customer Focus, Planning for Improvement, People Focus, Process Optimization, Supplier Focus & Organizational Performance.

Skills/Compétences Canada
#201, 294 Alberta St., Ottawa, ON K1P 6E6
Fax: 613-691-1404; Toll Free: 1-877-754-5226
URL: www.skillscompetencescanada.com

Skills Canada National Competition
Awarded annually; is an Olympic-style skills competition in over 40 skilled trades, technology & leadership contests, representing 6 industry sectors, designed to test skills required in technology & trade occupations; allows students access to newest technologies & communicate with industry experts who serve as mentors
Students compete at the local, regional & provincial levels to win the right to represent their province at the national level.
Gold, silver & bronze medals.

Transportation Association of Canada
#401, 1111 Prince of Wales Dr., Ottawa, ON K2C 3T2
613-736-1350; Fax: 613-736-1395
Email: secretariat@tac-atc.ca; URL: www.tac-atc.ca

Technical Achievement Awards
Awarded to recognize the technical excellence of member endeavours; categories include: Educational Achievement, Environmental Achievement, Road Safety Engineering, Sustainable Urban Transportation.

Volunteer Contribution Awards
Awarded to recognize volunteer contributions; categories include: Distinguished Service, Leadership, Individual Contribution, Committee Excellence.

Young Professional and Student Awards
Awarded to recognize student and young professional contributions; categories include: Young Transportation Professional, Student Paper, Allan Widger Consulting Corporation Grant.

University of Alberta
Alberta School of Business, 11211 Saskatchewan Dr., Edmonton, AB T6G 2M9

URL: www.ualberta.ca/business

Canadian Business Leader Award
Annual award recognizes distinguished professional achievements & contributions to the community.

CITIZENSHIP & BRAVERY

Alberta Order of Excellence
Gayle Stannard, Executive Director
c/o Lieutenant Governor's Office
3rd Fl., Legislature Bldg.
10800 - 97 Ave., Edmonton, AB T5K 2B6
780-449-0517; Fax: 780-417-1085
Email: URL: www.alberta.ca/the-alberta-order-of-excellence.aspx

Alberta Order of Excellence
Established in 1979, the award recognizes those persons who have rendered service of the greatest distinction & of singular excellence for or on behalf of Albertans.

The Canadian Council of the Blind / Le Conseil canadien des aveugles
#100, 20 James St., Ottawa, ON K2P 0T6
613-567-0311; Fax: 613-567-2728; Toll Free: 1-877-304-0968
Email: ccb@ccbnational.net; URL: ccbnational.net

Bursaries
Established at the Paul Menton Centre at Carleton University in Ottawa; eligible blind and vision impaired students across Canada.

Canadian Decorations for Bravery
c/o The Chancellory, Rideau Hall, 1 Sussex Dr., Ottawa, ON K1A 0A1
613-993-8200; Fax: 613-998-8760; Toll Free: 1-800-465-6890
Email: info@gg.ca; URL: www.gg.ca/en/honours/canadian-honours/decorations-bravery

Canadian Decorations for Bravery
Presented by the Governor General, Bravery decorations recognize people who have risked their lives to save or protect others; Three levels - the Cross of Valour, the Star of Courage & the Medal of Bravery - reflect the varying degrees of risk involved in any act of bravery.

The Duke of Edinburgh's International Award
#100, 215 Niagara St., Toronto, ON M6J 2L2
416-203-2282
Email: ontario@dukeofed.org; URL: www.dukeofed.org

The Duke of Edinburgh's International Award - Canada
Established in Canada in 1963 with His Royal Highness Prince Philip as Patron, the award recognizes personal achievement in a voluntary program of activities by young people in the age range of 14-24.
Open to all Canadian youth; young people participate independently or through youth groups, clubs, schools, etc.; program is operated throughout Canada, with divisional offices located in each of the ten provinces.
Award is in the form of a pin & an inscribed certificate representing Gold, Silver, & Bronze levels; Gold awards are presented by Her Excellency The Governor General of Canada, or a member of the Royal Family, at national awards ceremonies.

Indspire
PO Box 5, #100, 50 Generations Dr., Six Nations of the Grand River, Ohsweken, ON N0A 1M0
519-445-3021; Fax: 866-433-3159; Toll Free: 1-855-463-7747
Email: nominations@indspire.ca; URL: indspire.ca

Indspire Awards
The Indspire Awards recognize Indigenous professionals & youth who demonstrate outstanding career achievement. These awards serve to promote self-esteem and pride for Indigenous communities.

Ontario Ministry of Heritage, Sport, Tourism & Culture Industries
Ontario Honours & Awards
438 University Ave. West, 6th Fl., Toronto, ON M5G 2K8
416-314-7526; Fax: 416-314-9000; Toll Free: 1-877-832-8622
URL: www.ontario.ca/page/honours-and-awards

Champion of Diversity Award
Recognizes individuals, groups and employers who help promote immigrant success, economic growth, and inclusion in Ontario; 3 categories: Inclusion and Diversity, Cross-Cultural Understanding, Business Leadership in Immigrant Employment.

David C. Onley Award for Leadership in Accessibility
Recognizes Ontarians who have gone above and beyond to improve accessibility for people with disabilities; 4 categories: Champion, Role Model, Employee, Youth.

Hilary M. Weston Scholarship
Awarded to two graduate-level social work students in the area of mental health. Successful applicants each receive a one-time award of $7,500.

James Bartleman Indigenous Youth Creative Writing Awards
Recognizes up to six Indigenous students for their creative writing talent. Each recipient receives a $2,500 award.

June Callwood Outstanding Achievement Award for Voluntarism
Created in 2007 to commemorate the life of June Callwood CC, O.Ont, LL.D, a Canadian journalist whose life was marked by a strong concern for social justice, especially on issues affecting children and women. This annual award is given to 20 individual volunteers, volunteer groups, businesses and other organizations in recognition of their outstanding contributions to their communities and the province.

Lieutenant Governor's Community Volunteer Award for Students
This award honours one graduating student from each of Ontario's post secondary schools who not only completed the number of volunteer hours required to graduate, but have gone above and beyond.

The Lincoln M. Alexander Award
Recognizes young people who have demonstrated exemplary leadership in eliminating racial discrimination; 2 student awards & 1 community award are offered yearly.

The Ontario Medal for Firefighter Bravery
Established 1976 to recognize acts of superlative courage & bravery performed in the line of duty by members of Ontario's firefighting forces.

The Ontario Medal for Good Citizenship
Established 1973 to recognize people who, through exceptional long-term efforts have made outstanding contributions to the well being of their communities.

The Ontario Medal for Paramedic Bravery
to recognize acts of superlative courage & bravery performed in the line of duty by members of Ontario's paramedic forces.

The Ontario Medal for Police Bravery
Established 1975 to recognize acts of superlative courage & bravery performed in the line of duty by members of Ontario's police forces.

The Ontario Medal for Young Volunteers
Recognizes the outstanding achievements of 10 young volunteers, 15-24 who have made a difference to their communities.

Ontario Senior Achievement Award
Recognizes individuals for significant contributions to their communities after the age of 65. Up to 20 individuals are recognized each year.

Ontario Senior of the Year Award
Given by a municipality to recognize an outstanding senior who, after age 65, enriches the social, cultural or civic life of the community.

The Order of Ontario
Established 1986 to recognize those people who have rendered service of the greatest distinction & of singular excellence in all fields of endeavour benefiting society in Ontario & elsewhere.

Order of British Columbia
Honours & Awards Secretariat, PO Box 9422, Stn Prov Govt, Victoria, BC V8W 9V1
250-387-1616; Fax: 250-356-2814
Email: bchonoursandawards@gov.bc.ca; URL: orderofbc.gov.bc.ca

Order of British Columbia
Established in 1989 to recognize individuals who have served with the greatest distinction & excelled in any field of endeavour benefiting the people of British Columbia or elsewhere.

Order of Manitoba
The Office of the Lieutenant Governor of Manitoba, Legislative Bldg., #235, 450 Broadway, Winnipeg, MB R3C 0V8
204-945-5239
Email: ltgov@leg.gov.mb.ca; URL: www.manitobalg.ca/awards/order-of-manitoba

Order of Manitoba
Established in 1999 to recognize individuals who demonstrate excellence and achievement in any field of endeavour benefitting in an outstanding manner the social, cultural or economic well-being of the province and its residents.

Order of New Brunswick / Ordre du Nouveau-Brunswick
Intergovernmental & International Relations, Office of Protocol
PO Box 6000, #274, 670 King St., Fredericton, NB E3B 5H1
506-453-2671; Fax: 506-453-2995
Email: onb.brunswick@gnb.ca; URL: www2.gnb.ca/content/gnb/en/corporate/promo/order_of_new_brunswick.html

Order of New Brunswick
Established in December, 2000 to recognize individuals who have demonstrated excellence & achievement & who have made outstanding contributions to the social, cultural or economic well-being of New Brunswick & its residents. Maximum of 10 recipients annually

Order of Newfoundland & Labrador
The Order of Newfoundland and Labrador, Chief of Protocol, Government of Newfoundland and Labrador
PO Box 5517, St. John's, NL A1C 5W4
709-729-3670; Fax: 709-729-2234
Email: onl@gov.nl.ca; URL: www.exec.gov.nl.ca/onl

Order of Newfoundland and Labrador
The Order recognizes individuals who demonstrate excellence and achievement in any field benefitting in an exceptional manner the province and its residents. The first investiture occurred in 2004.

Order of the Northwest Territories
Legislative Assembly of the Northwest Territories
PO Box 1320, 4570 - 48th St., Yellowknife, NT X1A 2L9
867-767-9130
URL: www.assembly.gov.nt.ca/node/298113

Order of the Northwest Territories
Established in 2013, the Order is the highest honour awarded to residents of the territory. It recognizes individuals who have excelled in any field of endeavour benefitting the people of the Northwest Territories or elsewhere.

Order of Nova Scotia
Protocol Office, PO Box 1617, Halifax, NS B3J 2Y3
902-424-4463; Fax: 902-424-4309
URL: novascotia.ca/iga/order.asp

Order of Nova Scotia
The Order was established in 2001, and encourages excellence by recognizing citizens of Nova Scotia for outstanding contributions or achievements.

Order of Nunavut
c/o Office of the Clerk of the Legislative Assembly of Nunavut
PO Box 1200, 926 Federal Rd., Iqaluit, NU X0A 0H0
867-975-5000; Fax: 867-975-5191; Toll Free: 1-877-334-7266
Email: submissions@assembly.nu.ca; URL: assembly.nu.ca/order-nunavut

Order of Nunavut
Established in 2010, the Order honours individuals who have provided an outstanding contribution to the cultural, social or economic well-being of the territory.

Order of Prince Edward Island
Legislative Assembly, Province House, PO Box 2000, 197 Richmond St., Charlottetown PE C1A 7N8
902-368-4316; Fax: 902-368-5175
Email: jdholden@assembly.pe.ca; URL: www.assembly.pe.ca/opei

Order of Prince Edward Island
Highest provincial honour that can be bestowed on a resident of the province; it is awarded in public recognition of individual Islanders whose efforts & accomplishments have been exemplary An enameled medallion, which incorporates the Provincial emblem against a blue background worn with a ribbon of rust, green & white. Recipients receive a stylized lapel pin & miniature medal, an official certificate & are entitled to use O.P.E.I. after their names.

The Saskatchewan Order of Merit
Saskatchewan Honours & Awards Program
Protocol Office, #300, 3085 Albert St., Regina, SK S4S 0B1
306-787-8965; Fax: 306-787-1269; Toll Free: 1-877-427-5505
Email: honours@gov.sk.ca; URL: www.saskatchewan.ca/government/heritage-honours-and-awards/saskatchewan-order-of-merit

The Saskatchewan Order of Merit
Established in 1985, this prestigious award recognizes excellence, achievement and contributions to the social, cultural and economic well-being of the province and its residents.

Secrétariat de l'Ordre national du Québec
Ministère du Conseil exécutif, 875, Grande Allée est, Québec, QC G1R 4Y8
418-643-8895; Fax: 418-646-4307
URL: www.ordre-national.gouv.qc.ca

Ordre national du Québec
L'Ordre national du Québec est la plus haute distinction décernée par le gouvernement du Québec. Il a été institué par la Loi sur l'Ordre national du Québec (L.R.Q., c. 0-7.01) sanctionnée le 20 juin 1984 par le Parlement de Québec. L'Ordre national du Québec est composé de personnes à qui le gouvernement a conféré le titre de Grand Officier (G.O.) ou d'Officier (O.Q.) ou de Chevalier de l'Ordre national du Québec (C.Q.). La loi prévoit qu'une nomination puisse être faite à titre posthume. Elle accorde aussi au premier ministre du Québec le privilège exclusif de procéder à des nominations étrangères.

Société Saint-Jean-Baptiste de Montréal
82, rue Sherbrooke ouest, Montréal, QC H2X 1X3
514-843-8851; Fax: 514-844-6369
Email: info@ssjb.com; URL: ssjb.com

Le prix Bene Merenti de Patria
Créé en 1923, la médaille Bene Merenti de Patria souligne les mérites d'un compatriote ayant rendu des services exceptionnels à la patrie.

Le prix Chomedey-de-Maisonneuve - Personnalité montréalaise
Créé en 1983 en l'honneur du fondateur de Montréal. Le prix est remis occasionnellement à une personnalité dont les réalisations contribuent au rayonnement de Montréal.

Le prix Hélène-Pedneault
Créé en 2015, ce prix récompense la promotion des intérêts des femmes.

Le prix Maurice-Champagne - Droits de la personne
Créé en 1998 pour souligner le 50e anniversaire de la proclamation, par l'Organisation des Nations unies, de la Déclaration universelle des droits de l'homme, le prix Maurice-Champagne est attribué à des personnes ou à des institutions qui auront marqué de leur intelligence et de leur courage la défense et l'illustration des droits individuels et collectifs, en particulier ceux inscrits dans la Charte des droits de la personne du Québec, dont Maurice Champagne fut l'artisan.

Le prix Séraphin-Marion - Francophonie hors-Québec
Créé en 1984 en l'honneur d'un professeur franco-ontarien, écrivain et défenseur infatigable des droits des francophones hors-Québec.

Le titre de Patriote de l'année
Créé en 1975, le titre de Patriote de l'année est décerne, en mémoire du mouvement patriote des années 1830, à une personne qui s'est distinguée dans la défense des intérêts du Québec et des luttes démocratiques des peuples.

St. John Ambulance / Ambulance Saint-Jean
#400, 1900 City Park Dr., Ottawa, ON K1J 1A3
613-236-7461; Fax: 613-236-2425; Toll Free: 1-888-840-5646
Email: info@nhq.sja.ca; URL: www.sja.ca

Life-saving Awards of the Order of St. John
Instituted in 1874; At the National level, Gold recognizes those who have saved or attempted to save a life through administering first-aid where a risk to life exists, Silver recognizes those who have saved or attempted to save a life through administering first-aid where no risk to life exists; At the Provincial / Territorial level, a Certificate of Commendation recognizes individuals who helped a casualty to a lesser degree, with or without the application of first aid.

United Nations Association in Canada / Association canadienne pour les Nations-Unies
#400, 30 Metcalfe St., Ottawa, ON K2P 5L4
613-232-5751; Fax: 613-563-2455
Email: info@unac.org; URL: www.unac.org

Global Citizen Award
Established in 2015, the award goes to a Canadian who has contributed significantly to their community, country and world either through short-term benefit or long-term elevation.

Pearson Peace Medal
Established in 1979, the medal is awarded to a Canadian who has contributed significantly to humanitarian causes in the field of international service and understanding.

CULTURE, VISUAL ARTS & ARCHITECTURE

Association des galeries d'art contemporain
Édifice Belgo, #318, 372, rue Sainte-Catherine ouest, Montréal, QC H3B 1A2
514-798-5010
Email: info@agac.ca; URL: www.agac.ca

Prix Louis-Comtois
Créé en 1991 en collaboration avec La Ville de Montréal; Décerné annuellement ce prix qui vient appuyer et promouvoir le travail d'un artiste en mi-carrière qui s'est distingué dans le domaine de l'art contemporain à Montréal depuis les 15 dernières années. Bourse 7500$ et 2 500$ pour organiser une exposition solo.

Prix Pierre-Ayot
Créé en 1996 en collaboration avec La Ville de Montréal; Décerné annuellement ce prix qui souligne la facture exceptionnelle et l'apport original de la production des jeunes artistes en peinture, en estampe, en dessin, en illustration, en photographie ou tout autre médium. Bourse 5000$ et 2 500$ pour organiser une exposition solo.

The Canada Council for the Arts / Conseil des Arts du Canada
PO Box 1047, 150 Elgin St., 2nd Fl., Ottawa, ON K1P 5V8
613-566-4414; Fax: 613-566-4390; Toll Free: 1-800-263-5588
Email: info@canadacouncil.ca; URL: canadacouncil.ca

Bernard Diamant Prize
Awarded to an outstanding Canadian classical singer under 35; Monetary prize of $5,000 to be used to further winner's studies.

Burt Award for First Nations, Métis and Inuit Literature
Awarded annually to English-language Young Adult literary works written by First Nations, Métis or Inuit authors; first prize is valued at $12,000, two honour prizes are valued at $2,000 each. Winners are selected for both English-language and Indigenous-language works.

Canada-Japan Literary Awards
Recognize literary excellence by Canadian writers and translators who write, or translate from Japanese into English or French, a work on Japan, on Japanese themes or on themes that promote mutual understanding between Japan and Canada; Two prizes valued at $10,000 each (one English-language work and one French-language work).

CBC Literary Prizes
A partnership between Canada Council for the Arts, CBC/Radio-Canada, and Air Canada's enRoute magazine; Recognize talented amateur and professional Anglophone writers in three categories: Short Story, Nonfiction and Poetry; 6 winners receive a prize of $6,000 and a writing residency at the Banff Centre as well as publication of the winning work in Air Canada's enRoute magazine and on CBCBooks.ca; $1,000 is awarded to every finalist in each category and publication of their works on CBCBooks.ca.

Coburn Fellowships
Awarded in alternating years to Canadian and Israeli students; Fellowships are intended to cover travel expenses, tuition and accommodation at the University of Tel Aviv or Hebrew University of Jerusalem (for Canadian students) and the University of Toronto (for Israeli students); Two fellowships valued at $20,000 each.

Duke & Duchess of York Prize in Photography
Endowed by the Government of Canada in 1986 on the occasion of Prince Andrew's marriage; $8,000 prize awarded annually to a professional photographer who submits an eligible application to the Explore and Create program; The winner is selected based on the assessment of the grant application.

Eckhardt-Gramatté National Music Competition
A contemporary music competition that rewards the young artists in the categories of piano, voice and strings; First Prize consists of a Canadian tour, a three-week residency at the Casalmaggiore International Music Festival in Italy and $8,000; Second Prize is valued at $3,000; Third Prize at $2,000.

Governor General's Awards in Visual & Media Arts
Granted to artists in recognition of remarkable careers in visual and/or media arts; Up to 8 awards of $25,000 each, one of which is presented as the Saidye Bronfman Award for excellence in the fine crafts, and one of which is given to recognize the outstanding contribution to the visual arts or media arts of an individual or group in a volunteer or professional capacity.

Governor General's Literacy Awards
Recognize the best English-language and French-language book in each of seven categories: Fiction, Literary Non-fiction, Poetry, Drama, Young People's Literature - Text, Young People's Literature - Illustrated Books and Translation (from French to English and vice versa); 14 awards of $25,000 per book is awarded to winners in both languages in the seven categories and $3,000 to each publisher to promote the winning works; $1,000 is awarded per book for the finalists.

Governor General's Medals in Architecture
Up to 12 medals awarded every two years in conjunction with the Royal Architectural Institute of Canada; recognizes excellence in the art of architecture in completed projects by Canadian architects.

Governor General's Performing Arts Awards
Recognize the work of experienced Canadian artists who have made remarkable contributions to the performing arts in Canada in six categories: broadcasting, classical music, dance, film, popular music and theatre; Up to 6 awards valued at $25,000 each.

Healey-Willan Prize
Sponsored by Canada Council and administered by Choral Canada; Awarded biennially for the best performance in the National Competition for Amateur Choirs; Prize valued at $5,000.

Jacqueline Lemieux Prize
Valued at $6,000 and awarded to the most deserving applicants in the Explore and Create Program.

J.B.C. Watkins Award - Architecture
A bequest from the estate of the late John B.C. Watkins; Offered to a Canadian professional architect wishing to pursue postgraduate studies abroad; Priority is given to studies taking place in Denmark, Norway, Sweden or Iceland; Prize is valued at $5,000.

J.B.C. Watkins Award - Music and Theatre
A bequest from the estate of the late John B.C. Watkins; Offered to professional Canadian artists in music and theatre wishing to pursue postgraduate studies abroad; Priority is given to studies taking place in Denmark, Norway, Sweden or Iceland; Prize is valued at $5,000. The award is currently suspended.

Jean A. Chalmers Fund for the Craft
Established with a contribution from the late Mrs. Chalmers in honour of her husband who died in 1985; Assists non-profit visual arts and fine craft organizations and fine crafts professionals in undertaking projects that contribute to an understanding of the fine crafts in Canada; Prize valued at $5,000-$7,000.

Jean-Marie Beaudet Award in Orchestra Conducting
Awarded annually to a young Canadian orchestra conductor; valued at $1,000.

Joan Lowndes Award
Awarded to an independent professional critic or curator in contemporary visual and media arts in recognition of the outstanding quality of their work; Valued at $3,500.

John G. Diefenbaker Award
Awarded annually to a distinguished German researcher in the social sciences and humanities; Funded by an endowment from the Government of Canada; Valued at up to $95,000.

John Hirsch Prize
Awarded to new and developing theatre directors who demonstrate potential for future excellence; one prize each for French and English theatre is awarded every two years; Candidates must be nominated by fellow theatre professionals; Prize valued at $6,000 each.

John Hobday Awards in Arts Management
Two awards are presented each year and allow recipients to enhance their own professional development by taking part in a program, seminar, workshop or mentorship; Prize valued at $10,000 each.

Joseph S. Stauffer Prizes
Awarded to professional Canadian artists with less than 15 years of practice who exhibit strong artistic potential in music, visual arts and literature; Up to 3 awards (one in each category) of $5,000 each.

Jules-Léger Prize for New Chamber Music
Encourages Canadian composers to create avant-garde chamber music and to foster its performance by Canadian chamber groups; Value of the prize is $7,500.

Killam Prizes
The Killam Program offers awards to Canadian scholars working in the humanities, social and health sciences, natural sciences and engineering. Five prizes of $100,000 are awarded each year in recognition of outstanding achievements in these fields.

Killam Research Fellowship
The Killam Program offers release-time awards to Canadian scholars working in the humanities, social and health sciences, natural sciences and engineering; Fellowships are valued at $70,000 a year over two years.

Michael Measures Prize
Awarded to promising young Canadian performers of classical music; Winners are students (between the ages of 16 and 24) of the National Youth Orchestra summer training program; First prize is $25,000, Second prize is $15,000.

Molson Prizes
Two prizes of $50,000 each are awarded annually to distinguished individuals, one in the social sciences / humanities and one in the arts.

Musical Instrument Bank
Professional classical musicians compete for a 3-year loan of 1 of 20 rare musical instruments; Established with a bequest from the Barwick family in 1985.

Peter Dwyer Scholarships
A total of $20,000 is awarded annually to the two most promising students at the National Ballet School ($10,000) and the National Theatre School ($10,000). The schools choose their respective recipients.

Prix de Rome in Architecture - Professional
Established 1987; designed to recognize the work of a Canadians actively engaged in the field of contemporary architecture whose career is well under way & whose personal work shows exceptional talent. Winner is chosen by a peer assessment committee convened by the Canada Council for the Arts; Prize is valued at $50,000.

Prix de Rome - Emerging Practitioners
Awarded to a recent graduate of an accredited Canadian architecture school who demonstrates potential in architectural design. The recipient also has the opportunity to expand their skills with an internship at an architectural firm anywhere in the world; Prize valued at $34,000.

Robert Fleming Prize
Awarded annually to an exceptionally talented young Canadian composer to further their career development; Prize valued at $2,000.

Ronald J. Thom Award for Early Design Achievement
Awarded every two years to a Canadian architect or architectural firm in the early stages of practice and demonstrates both outstanding creative talent & exceptional potential in architectural design; Prize valued at $10,000.

Saidye Bronfman Prize
Funded by the Samuel & Saidye Bronfman Family Foundation; Awarded annually to an exceptional craftsperson for excellence in the fine crafts; Prize is $25,000 and works by the recipient are acquired by the Canadian Museum of History for its permanent collection.

Victor Martyn Lynch-Staunton Awards
Recognize outstanding artistic achievement by Canadian artists in seven disciplines: Dance, Inter-Arts, Media Arts, Music, Theatre, Visual Arts, and Writing and Publishing; Prize is valued at $15,000 each.

Virginia Parker Prize
Awarded to a musician, instrumentalist or classical music conductor who is under 32 years of age and who demonstrates exceptional talent and musicianship; Valued at $25,000.

Walter Carsen Prize for Excellence in the Performing Arts
Awarded annually on a four year cycle (dance, theatre, dance, and music) this prize recognizes the highest level of artistic excellence and career achievement by Canadian artists; Valued at $50,000.

York Wilson Endowment Awards
An award that enables Canadian art museums & public art galleries to purchase original works by living, contemporary Canadian painters & sculptors that would significantly enhance its collection; Valued at $30,000.

Canadian Historical Association / Société historique du Canada
#1912, 130 Albert St., Ottawa, ON K1P 5G4
613-233-7885; Fax: 613-565-5445
Email: cha-shc@cha-shc.ca; URL: cha-shc.ca

Albert B. Corey Prize
Established 1966 and jointly sponsored by the CHA and the American Historical Association; awarded every two years to the best book dealing with the history of Canadian-American relations or the history of both countries.

Best Scholarly Book in Canadian History
Established in 1977; Awarded annually to the best scholarly book in Canadian History; presented at the yearly Governor

General Awards for Excellence in Teaching Canadian History event at Rideau Hall in Ottawa.

Business History Book Prize
Established in 2019; Awarded biennially to books that explore Canadian business history.

Canadian Indigenous History Prize
Awarded to the best book and best article on Aboriginal history.

Canadian Committee on Migration, Ethnicity and Transnationalism Article Prize
Acknowledges scholarly articles and book chapters, in English and French, judged to have made an original, significant, and meritorious contribution to the historical study of migration and ethnicity.

The Canadian Oral History Association Prize
Awarded to an outstanding example of oral history practice.

CCWH-CCHF Book Prize in Women's and Gender History
Awarded every two years to the best book published in the field of women's and gender history by a Canadian author and/or about Canadian history, in either English or French.

CHA Journal Prize
Awarded annually for the best essay published each year in the Journal of the Canadian Historical Association.

CHA Student Prize
Awarded to the best article published in a peer-reviewed journal by a PhD or MA-level student, in either English or French.

Clio Prizes
Awarded annually to meritorious publications or for exceptional contributions by individuals or organizations to regional history.

Eugene A. Forsey Prize
Awarded to the best thesis on labour history.

François-Xavier Garneau Medal
Awarded every five years to honour an outstanding Canadian contribution to historical research.

Hilda Neatby Prizes
Recognizes the best articles of the year on women's history; one awarded for English-language article and another for French-language article.

John Bullen Prize
Awarded to an outstanding PhD thesis on a historical topic submitted in a Canadian university.

The Media and Communication History Committee Prize
Awarded for best article on media and communication history.

Neil Sutherland Article Prize
Awarded biennially to an outstanding work on children's and youth history.

Political History Prizes
Awarded in three categories: Best Book, Best Article (French) and Best Article (English).

Prize for Best article on the history of Sexuality
Recognizes excellence in and encourages the growth of scholarly work in the field of the history of sexuality in Canada.

Public History Prize
Awarded to a project in that advances the field of public history in Canada and achieves high standards of original research, scholarship and presentation.

The Wallace K. Ferguson Prize
Established 1979; awarded annually for outstanding work in a field of history other than Canadian.

The City of Toronto
Toronto Arts & Culture, Cultural Partnerships, City Hall, #9E, 100 Queen St. West, Toronto, ON M5H 2N2
416-392-3831; Fax: 416-696-3645
Email: christopher.jones@toronto.ca; URL: www.toronto.ca/bookawards

Toronto Book Awards
Awarded annually to recognize books of literary / artistic merit that are evocative of Toronto; Winning author is awarded $10,000 and the five finalists are awarded $1,000.

Fondation émile-Nelligan
#202, 100, rue Sherbrooke est, Montréal, QC H2X 1C3
514-278-4657; Fax: 514-278-1948
Email: info@fondation-nelligan.org; URL: www.fondation-nelligan.org

Prix émile-Nelligan
Ce prix annuel date de 1979, année de la création de la Fontation émile-Nelligan. C'est un prix de poésie décerné à des poètes de 35 ans ou moins, pour un recueil publié au cours de l'année; 7 500$

Prix Gilles-Corbeil
Le prix Gilles-Corbeil est un prix de littérature. C'est un prix triennal et is al été décerné pour la première fois en 1990; 100 000$

Prix Ozias-Leduc
Prix triennal en arts visuels (peinture, sculpture, gravure, installations, 'land art'). Décerné à un artiste citoyen du Canada né au Québec ou à un artiste citoyen du Canada ayant sa résidence principale au Québec depuis au moins dix ans; 25 000$

Prix Serge-Garant
Le prix Serge-Garant est un prix de compostiion musicale. C'est un prix triennal qui a été décerné pour le première fois en 1991; 25 000$

The Gershon Iskowitz Foundation
c/o Art Gallery of Ontario, 317 Dundas St. West, Toronto, ON M5T 1G4
URL: iskowitzfoundation.ca/prize; URL: www.ago.net/iskowitz-prize

Gershon Iskowitz Prize
Presented in partnership with the Art Gallery of Ontario to recognize a professional artist on the verge of creating an important body of work or research; Award of $50,000.

Ontario Arts Council / Conseil des arts de l'Ontario
121 Bloor St. East, 7th Fl., Toronto, ON M4W 3M5
416-961-1660; Fax: 416-961-7796; Toll Free: 1-800-387-0058
Email: info@arts.on.ca; URL: www.arts.on.ca

Canadian Music Centre John Adaskin Award
The award supports the Canadian Music Centre in undertaking projects that promote and develop Canadian music in Canadian schools.

Colleen Peterson Songwriting Award
Established in 2003 to honour Colleen Peterson's contribution to Canadian folk and country music; The award supports and promotes the work of an emerging professional singer / songwriter in the genres of roots, traditional, folk and country music; Valued at $1,000.

Heinz Unger Award
Awarded biennially to encourage and highlight the career of a young to mid-career Canadian conductor who has professional experience with an orchestra.

John Hirsch Director's Award
Established in 1989; Awarded triennially to a promising theatre director to further the recipient's professional development; Valued at $5,000.

Leslie Bell Prize for Choral Conducting
Established in 1971; Awarded biennially to support choral conductors in furthering their professional careers and enhancing their choral conducting abilities.

Ontario Arts Council Indigenous Arts Award
Established in 2012; $10,000 awarded annually to a distinguished Indigenous artist. $2,500 awarded to an emerging Indigenous artist.

Oskar Morawetz Award for Excellence in Music Performance
Established in 2007; Awarded biennially to recognize an outstanding Canadian performer or conductor in the field of classical music who has appeared on Canadian concert stages and may have reached a degree of international attention.

Pauline McGibbon Award
Established in 1981; Awarded annually by the Province of Ontario through the Ministry of Culture to a member of Ontario's professional theatre community in the early stages of their career who has displayed a unique talent and a potential for excellence; Valued at $7,000.

Premier's Awards for Excellence in the Arts
Established in 2006; Recognizes the outstanding achievements of artists and arts organizations; The laureate receives an award of $35,000. The laureate also selects a promising new or emerging artist in the same artistic field, who receives an award of $15,000. Five finalists each receive an award of $2,000.

Ontario Arts Foundation / Fondation des Arts de l'Ontario
#1206, 390 Bay St., Toronto, ON M5H 2Y2
416-969-7413; Toll Free: 1-877-386-8029
Email: info@oafdn.ca; URL: ontarioartsfoundation.on.ca

Christina and Louis Quilico Awards
Presented every two years and recognize outstanding young singers, pianists, and composers for voice.

Christopher Dedrick Music Fund
Awarded annually in partnership with the Screen Composers Guild of Canada; Recognizes an Ontario based composer and celebrates and encourage the use of live musicians in the production of media music soundtracks; $1,200.

Ellen Ross Stuart Opening Doors Awards
Established in 2017; Awarded to empower writers in their 20s with some production credits.

Gina Wilkinson Prize for an Emerging Female Director
Awarded annually to offer financial support to the next generation of female theatre directors.

Kathleen McMorrow Music Award
Established in 2015; Recognizes the composition and presentation of Canadian contemporary classical music; Recipients are selected from one of two annual Ontario Arts Council Music Creation Projects deadlines; $7,000.

Laura Ciruls Painting Fund
Established in 2012 by a bequest by Laura; Awarded annually to an artist contributing to the development of painting in Ontario; $5,000.

Louis Applebaum Composers Award
Established 1998 to recognize excellence in composition; $15,000.

Ontario Arts Foundation Artist Educator Award
Presented to an Ontario resident who demonstrates excellence in arts education; $10,000.

Orford String Quartet Fund
Awarded biennially to a Canadian string chamber musician in the early stages of his or her professional career; $3,000.

Paul de Hueck and Norman Walford Career Achievement Awards
Recognize Canadian artists for their contributions and excellence in the areas of keyboard artistry, singing and art photography.

Philip Akin - Black Shoulders Legacy Award
Established in 2020; Five emerging Black Canadian theatre artists are selected annually to receive $5,000 toward training and other opportunities to support artistic growth. See: www.bsla.ca.

Ruth & Sylvia Schwartz Children's Book Awards
Established in 1976; Two awards presented annually: one for picture books, one for young adult / middle readers; 2 at $6,000.

Tim Sims Encouragement Fund Award
Established 1995; Awarded annually to a graduate of the Comedy Writing and Performance program at the Humber College, School of Creative and Performing Arts and to a Conservatory Program Graduate at the Second City Training Program; $2,500.

The Virginia and Myrtle Cooper Award in Costume Design
Established in 2006; Awarded annually to enrich the careers of professional mid-career Canadian costume designers in Ontario through research and travel; $20,000.

William and Mary Corcoran Craft Award
Awarded to students graduating from Sheridan College in the disciplines of glass, textiles, furniture and ceramics; 4 awards of $1,000.

Wuchien Michael Than Fund
Established 2012; Supports the development of theatre arts in Canada, with a particular emphasis on new works by Asian-Canadian playwrights, and the development of emerging talent in the Asian-Canadian theatre community.

Québec Ministère de la culture et des communications
225, Grande Allée est, Québec, QC G1R 5G5
418-380-2363; Fax: 418-380-2364
Email: prixduquebec@mcc.gouv.qc.ca; URL: www.prixduquebec.gouv.qc.ca

Prix Albert-Tessier
La plus haute distinction accordée à une personne pour l'ensemble de son oeuvre et de sa carrière dans le domaine du cinéma; 30 000$

Prix Athanase-David
La plus haute distinction accordée à un écrivain ou une écrivaine pour l'ensemble de son oeuvre; 30 000$

Prix Denise-Pelletier
La plus haute distinction accordée à une personne pour l'ensemble de son oeuvre et de sa carrière dans le domaine des arts de la scène; 30 000$

Prix Ernest-Cormier
La plus haute distinction accordée à une personne pour l'ensemble de son oeuvre et de sa carrière dans les domaines de l'architecture ou du design; 30 000$

Prix Georges-émile-Lapalme
La plus haute distinction accordée à une personne ayant contribué de façon exceptionnelle, par son engagement, son oeuvre ou sa carrière, à la qualité et au rayonnement de la langue française parlée ou écrite au Québec; 30 000$

Prix Gérard-Morisset
Accordé à une personne pour l'ensemble d'une carrière consacrée au patrimoine; 30 000$

Prix Guy-Mauffette
La plus haute distinction accordée à une personne pour l'ensemble de son oeuvre et de sa carrière dans les domaines de la radio ou de la télévision; 30 000$

Prix Paul-émile-Borduas
La plus haute distinction accordée à une personne pour l'ensemble de son oeuvre dans les domaines des arts visuels et des métiers d'art; 30 000$

Royal Architectural Institute of Canada / Institut royal d'architecture du Canada
#330, 55 Murray St., Ottawa, ON K1N 5M3
613-241-3600; Fax: 613-241-5750
Email: info@raic.org; URL: raic.org

Architectural Firm Award
Awarded to recognize excellence from Canadian architectural firms.

Awards of Excellence
These awards are bestowed every two years, recognizing the greatest achievement in several different categories.

Emerging Architect Award
Awarded to honour excellence among young architects in Canada.

Emerging Architectural Practice Award
Awarded to honour excellence and promise from an emerging architectural practice in Canada.

Moriyama RAIC International Prize
Awarded biennially to an architect, team of architects, or architect-led collaboration in recognition of a single work of architecture that is transformative within its societal context and expressive of the values of justice, respect, equality and inclusiveness; $100,000.

National Urban Design Awards
Presented in conjunction with the Canadian Institute of Planners and the Canadian Society of Landscape Architects, as well as with cooperation from Canadian municipalities; the award recognizes individuals, organizations, firms and other projects that contribute to the quality of Canadian city life.

Prix du XXe siècle
Recognizes outstanding and lasting contributions to Canadian architecture, and landmark buildings in the historical context of Canadian Architecture; Celebrates design quality and enduring excellence.

RAIC Gold Medal
Established in 1930; Awarded annually in recognition of an individual whose personal work has demonstrated exceptional excellence in the design and practice of architecture; and/or, whose work related to architecture, has demonstrated exceptional excellence in research or education.

Student Medal
Awarded annually to a student graduating from a professional degree program in each accredited University's School of Architecture in Canada who has achieved the highest level of academic excellence.

The Royal Society of Canada / La Société royale du Canada
Walter House, 282 Somerset St. West, Ottawa, ON K2P 0J6
613-991-6990; Fax: 613-991-6996
Email: info@rsc-src.ca; URL: rsc-src.ca

Alice Wilson Award
Established in 1991; Awarded annually to three women of outstanding academic qualifications studying the Arts and Humanities, Social Sciences or Science, who are entering a career in research at the post-doctoral level.

Centenary Medal
Established 1982; Awarded at irregular intervals in recognition of outstanding contributions to the object of the society & to recognize links to international organizations.

Innis-Gérin Medal
Established in 1966 and awarded biennially to honour a sustained and distinguished contribution to literature of the social sciences.

The J.B. Tyrrell Historical Medal
Established 1927; Awarded biennially for outstanding work in the history of Canada.

Kitty Newman Award
Awarded annually to recognize outstanding contributions from an emerging scholar in the field of philosophy.

Lorne Pierce Medal
Awarded biennially to recognize an achievement in critical or imaginative literature.

Pierre Chauveau Medal
Established in 1951; Awarded biennially to honour a distinguished and significant contribution to knowledge in the humanities in subjects other than Canadian literature and Canadian history.

Rutherford Memorial Medals

Sir John William Dawson Medal
Established 1985; Awarded biennially for important & sustained contributions by one individual in at least two different fields in the general areas of interest of the Society or in a broad domain that transcends the usual disciplinary boundaries.

Ursula Franklin Award in Gender Studies
Established in 1999; Awarded biennially to a Canadian scholar who has made significant contributions in the humanities and social sciences relating to gender issues.

Yvan Allaire Medal
Awarded annually to recognize a meritorious contribution in governance of private and public organisations.

Sobey Art Foundation
c/o National Gallery of Canada
PO Box 427, Stn. A, 380 Sussex Dr., Ottawa, ON K1N 9N4
Email: sobey@gallery.ca; URL: www.gallery.ca/whats-on/sobey-art-award; sobeyartfoundation.com

Sobey Art Award
Awarded every year to an artist 40 years old or younger who has shown their work in a public or commercial art gallery in Canada in the 18 months prior to nomination.
First place: $50,000; Short-listed artists: $10,000; Long-listed artists: $500.

Social Sciences & Humanities Research Council of Canada
PO Box 1610, 350 Albert St., Ottawa, ON K1P 6G4
613-992-0691; Fax: 613-992-1787
Email: webgrant@sshrc-crsh.gc.ca; URL: www.sshrc-crsh.gc.ca
The Social Sciences & Humanities Research Council of Canada offers various funding opportunities under the three programs: Talent, Insight and Connection. Funding is available for Master's and Doctoral students, Postdoctoral researchers, and particularly for research by and with Aboriginal peoples. Additionally, the Council offers the following Impact Awards:

Connection Award
Recognizes an outstanding SSHRC funded initiative to facilitate the flow and exchange of research knowledge within and/or beyond the social sciences and humanities research community; Awarded to an individual or team whose project has created impact in the campus and/or broader community; $50,000.

Gold Medal
Awarded to an individual whose achievements in research have significantly advanced understanding in their respective fields in social sciences and humanities in Canada; The recipient has made ongoing efforts to share the results and impact of their research; $100,000.

Insight Award
Recognizes outstanding achievement arising from a research project funded partially or completely by SSHRC; Awarded to an individual or a team of six people maximum whose project has significantly contributed to knowledge and understanding about people, societies and the world; $50,000.

Partnership Award
Recognizes a SSHRC-funded formal partnership for its outstanding achievement in research; Awarded to a project director in a formal partnership who has demonstrated influence within

and/or beyond the social sciences and humanities research community; $50,000.

Talent Award
Recognizes outstanding achievement by an individual who holds a SSHRC doctoral or postdoctoral fellowship or scholarship and who maintains academic excellence, has a talent for research and knowledge mobilization and has demonstrated leadership; $50,000.

Société Saint-Jean-Baptiste de Montréal
82, rue Sherbrooke ouest, Montréal, QC H2X 1X3
514-843-8851; Fax: 514-844-6369
Email: info@ssjb.com; URL: ssjb.com

Le prix André-Guérin - Cinéma
Créé en 1990; Décerné pour l'excellence dans le cinéma.

Le prix Calixa-Lavallée - Musique
Créé en 1959; Décerné à une personnalité qui s'illustre dans le domaine de la musique.

Le prix Esdras-Minville - Sciences humaine
Créé en 1978 en l'honneur d'Esdras Minville chercheur, professeur et directeur aux HÉC; Décerné à une personnalité canadienne-française qui s'illustre dans le domaine des sciences humaines.

Le prix Hélène-Pedneault - Féminisme
Créé en 2015, ce prix récompense la promotion des intérêts des femmes.

Le prix Louis-Philippe-Hébert - Beaux-Arts
Créé en 1971 en l'honneur du sculpteur Louis-Philippe Hébert; Décerné pour l'excellence dans les beaux-arts.

Le prix Ludger-Duvernay - Littérature
Créé en 1944 en l'honneur de Ludger Duvernay, imprimeur, éditeur, journaliste, politicien et patriote; Décerné à une personne qui s'illustre dans le domaine de la littérature.

Le prix Olivar-Asselin - Journalisme
Créé en 1955; Décerné à une personnalité qui s'illustre dans le domaine du journalisme.

Le prix Victor-Morin - Arts de la scène
Créé en 1962; Décerné à une personnalité canadienne-française qui s'illustre dans le domaine des arts de la scène.

Toronto Arts Council Foundation
#200, 26 Grand Trunk Cres., Toronto, ON M5J 3A9
416-392-6800; Fax: 416-392-6920
Email: michelle@torontoartscouncil.org; URL: torontoartsfoundation.org

Arts for Youth Award
Established in 2007 and awarded annually, the award celebrates an individual, organization or collective that has shown outstanding commitment to engaging Toronto's youth through the arts; winner receives $20,000 and finalists receive $2,000.

Celebration of Cultural Life Awards
Formerly the William Kilbourn Award for the Celebration of Toronto's Cultural Life; Awarded to an individual whose work is a celebration of life through the arts; Winner receives $10,000 and finalists receive $2,000.

Community Arts Award
Awarded annually to an artist or organization that has made a significant contribution in Toronto by collaborating with culturally diverse communities and creating access to arts and culture; Winner receives $10,000.

Emerging Artist Award
Established in 2006 and awarded annually to celebrate the accomplishments and potential of an emerging Toronto artist; award winner receives a $10,00 cash prize, while finalists receive $2,000.

Emerging Jazz Artist Award
Awarded to an outstanding jazz musician to further their career by supporting the pre-production, production, and/or recording of original music composed by the recipient; Winner receives $10,000 and finalists receive $1,000.

Margo Bindhardt and Rita Davies Award
Awarded biennially to an artist, volunteer or administrator whose leadership & vision have had a significant impact on the arts in Toronto; Winner receives $10,000.

Muriel Sherrin Award
Presented to an artist or creator who has made a contribution to the cultural life of Toronto through outstanding achievement in music or dance; The recipient will also have participated in international initiatives, including touring, study abroad & artist exchanges; Awarded biennially; Winner receives $10,000.

Roy Thomson Hall Award
Awarded annually to an individual, ensemble or organization to honour outstanding contributions (creative, performative, administrative, philanthropic) to Toronto's musical life; Winner receives $10,000.

RBC Newcomer Arts Award
Sponsored by RBC; Offered twice each year to newcomer artists in Toronto; Funds range $2,000 to support costs associated with arts projects, professional development and mentorship.

Toronto Arts and Business Award
Presented annually in conjunction with the Toronto Star; Two awards presented: one to a local business that has sponsored the arts for the first time and one to a business that has been a long-time sponsor of the arts.

EDUCATIONAL

Alberta Scholarship Programs
PO Box 28000, Stn Main, Edmonton, AB T5J 4R4
780-427-8640; Fax: 780-427-1288; Toll Free: 1-855-606-2096
Email: scholarships@gov.ab.ca; URL: www.studentaid.alberta.ca/scholarships/alberta-scholarships

Alberta Scholarships Program
Scholarships & awards are available in various fields of study

Black Business & Professional Association
180 Elm St., Toronto, ON M5T 3M4
416-504-4097; Fax: 416-504-7343
Email: info@bbpa.org; URL: bbpa.org

BBPA Legacy Scholarships
Established in the name of Black Canadians who enriched Canada with their contributions in the arts, the professions, science, business, technology, politics and other areas of endeavour; Each scholarship is in the amount of $1,000 - $2,000.

First Generation Scholarships
Awarded to Ontario students whose parents have not participated in post-secondary education studies; Each scholarship is in the amount of $1,000 - $2,000.

Sponsored Scholarships
Funded directly by corporations or individuals; Awards range from $1,000 - $7,000.

Toronto Community Housing / Leaders of Tomorrow Scholarships
Awarded to students from Toronto Community Housing / high priority neighbourhoods in the Greater Toronto Area who are attending an accredited Canadian university or college; Each scholarship is in the amount of $1,000 - $2,000.

Canadian Association of University Business Officers / Association canadienne du personnel administratif universitaire
#315, 350 Albert St., Ottawa, ON K1R 1B1
613-230-6760; Fax: 613-563-7739
Email: caubo-acpau@caubo.ca; URL: www.caubo.ca

CAUBO Quality & Productivity Awards
Designed to recognize, reward and share achievements of administrators in the introduction of new services, improvement in the quality of services provided, and the management of human, financial, and physical resources; Three awards in each of two categories: Open, Themed.
National: first prize $2,500; second prize $1,500; third prize $1,000.

Canadian Mathematical Society / Société mathématique du Canada
#209, 1725 St. Laurent Blvd., Ottawa, ON K1G 3V4
613-733-2662
Email: office@cms.math.ca; URL: cms.math.ca

Canadian Mathematical Olympiad
Annual mathematics competition established to provide an opportunity for students to perform well on the Canadian Open Mathematics Challenge & to complete on a national basis; First Prize winner receives the CMO Cup and $2,000; Second Prize winner receives $1,500; Third Prize winner receives $1,000; Honourable Mentions (up to six) receive $500 each.

Canadian Sociological Association / Société canadienne de sociologie
PO Box 98014, 2126 Burnhamthorpe Rd. West, Mississauga, ON L5L 5V4
416-660-4378
Email: office@csa-scs.ca; URL: www.csa-scs.ca/awards

Best Student Paper Award
Recognizes the best paper among those received for adjudication, written by a graduate student.

Outstanding Graduating Sociology Student
Recognizes top graduating Honours, MA, and PhD students.

Canadian Bureau for International Education
#1550, 220 Laurier Ave. West, Ottawa ON K1P 5Z9
613-237-4820; Fax: 613-237-1073
Email: communication@cbie.ca; URL: cbie.ca

Canadian Francophonie Scholarship Program
Designed to build institutional capacities by training employed nationals from developing countries of La Francophonie; Awarded to qualified candidates who show the greatest aptitude for helping strengthen their institution's capacities when they return to their country.

CHED-CBIE Scholarship for Graduate Studies in Canada
Will bring twenty (20) Filipino scholars to Canada to pursue further studies at Canadian institutions; Prepares these scholars for academic positions, educational leadership, research, policy formulation and teacher training in the Philippines upon completion of the program.

International Atomic Energy Agency Fellowship Program
Since 1987, the program brings fellows to Canada from developing countries to study and train in fields relevant to the development priorities of their home countries.

International Scholarships Program
14 select scholarship components that provide international students and researchers with study and research opportunities in Canada, and that provide Canadian students, researchers and professionals with study and research opportunities abroad.

Libyan-North American Scholarship Program
Facilitate the studies of Libyan graduate and postgraduate students in North America, allowing them to fulfill their academic objectives while addressing the needs of Libyan public institutions, academia and society.

Council of Ontario Universities
#1800, 180 Dundas St. West, Toronto, ON M5G 1Z8
416-979-2165
Email: seniordirectorqa@cou.on.ca; URL: cou.ca

John Charles Polanyi Prizes
Provides up to five prizes annually to researchers in the early stages of their career who have recently started at an Ontario university.
$20,000.

Foundation for Educational Exchange Between Canada & the United States of America
#2015, 350 Albert St., Ottawa, ON K1R 1A4
613-688-5540; Fax: 613-237-2029
Email: info@fulbright.ca; URL: www.fulbright.ca

Canada-US Fulbright Program
To expand research, teaching & study opportunities for Canadian & American faculty & students engaged in the study of Canada, the United States & the relationship between the two countries; based on academic excellence & the merit of the applicant's proposed project, awards given annually for study in a number of different fields. Applicants must relocate from the US to Canada, or Canada to the US.
$20,000 US for graduate students; Varying awards for faculty.

Horatio Alger Association of Canada
#1010, 1410, rue Stanley, Montreal, QC H3A 1P8
Toll Free: 1-844-422-4200
Email: association@horatioalger.org; URL: horatioalger.ca

Horatio Alger Canada Scholarship Program
All disciplines are eligible.
205 scholarships are available at $5,000; 45 Entrance Awards of varying amounts are presented to youth facing significant financial obstacles at select Canadian institutions.

International Development Research Centre / Centre de recherches pour le développement international
PO Box 8500, Ottawa, ON K1G 3H9
613-236-6163
Email: info@idrc.ca; URL: www.idrc.ca

IDRC Research Awards
Awards offered annually to Canadians, permanent residents of Canada and citizens of developing countries pursuing or having completed master's or doctoral studies at a recognized university.

Irving K. Barber B.C. Scholarship Society
#200, 703 Broughton St., Victoria, BC V8W 1E2
778-200-2502; Toll Free: 1-844-478-4645
Email: info@ikbbc.ca; URL: www.ikbbc.ca

Indigenous Student Awards
The Society offers three Award programs for Indigenous students pursuing post-secondary education in BC. Valued from $1,000 to $5,000.

International Scholarships
The Society offers two scholarship programs to assist students who plan to complete some of their course work outside of North America.

Transfer Scholarships
Awarded to students transferring between two BC public-post secondary institutions to continue their education; $5,000.

Women in Technology Scholarships
The Society awards ten scholarships annually to recognize women who are excelling at the study of Computer Science, Engineering or Mathematics at the post-secondary level. At least one of these scholarships is dedicated to a woman of Indigenous ancestry.

The Japan Foundation, Toronto / Kokosai Koryu Kikin Toronto Nihon Bunka Centre
PO Box 130, #300, 2 Bloor St. East, Toronto, ON M4W 1A8
416-966-1600; Fax: 416-966-9773
Email: info@jftor.org; URL: jftor.org

Grant Program for Japanese Studies Projects
Awarded to non-profit organizations to promote Japanese studies overseas by providing grants toward various Japanese studies projects.

Grant Program for Intellectual Exchange Conferences
Awarded to non-profit organizations to partially cover the cost of implementing international intellectual collaborative projects, such as international conferences, to strengthen the ties with Japan.

Japan Foundation Fellowships
Scholars and researchers are provided an opportunity to conduct research or pursue projects in Japan. Term of award is from 21 days to 12 months, depending on category.

The Japan Foundation Scholarships & Programs
The Foundation offers a wide range of programs in more than 180 countries, including the following: exchange of persons (fellowships); support for Japanese-language instruction; support for Japanese studies; support for arts-related exchange; support for media exchange.

Loran Scholars Foundation
#502, 460 Richmond St. West, Toronto, ON M5V 1Y1
416-646-2120; Fax: 416-646-0846; Toll Free: 1-866-544-2673
Email: info@loranscholar.ca; URL: loranscholar.ca

Finalist Award
Given to Loran Award finalists who are not selected as Loran Scholars.
$5,000 awarded to outstanding students from across the country as one-time entrance awards to be used at any accredited Canadian university.

Loran Award
Valued at $100,000 over four years, the award goes to tuition, mentorship, funding for summer internships, annual retreats and orientation expedition at any one of the 25 participating Canadian universities.

Provincial & Territorial Awards
Given to Loran Award semi-finalists; One-time entrance award tenable at any accredited university in Canada at which the recipient gains admission & enrolls in a full-time program of study $2,000 (territory), $5,000 (province).

Indspire
PO Box 5, #100, 50 Generations Dr., Six Nations of the Grand River, Ohsweken, ON N0A 1M0
519-445-3021; Fax: 866-433-3159
Email: education@indspire.ca; URL: indspire.ca

Indspire Bursaries and Scholarships
Designed to assist First Nation, Inuit and Métis students obtain post-secondary education.

Northern Enterprise Fund Inc.
PO Box 220, Beauval, SK S0M 0G0
306-288-2258; Fax: 306-288-4667; Toll Free: 1-800-864-3022
Email: info@nefi.ca; URL: www.nefi.ca

Northern Spirit Scholarship Program
To promote entrepreneurial spirit in Northern Saskatchewan by providing scholarships to students enrolled in courses related to business or based on occupational shortages in the north. Ten $2,500 scholarships are awarded to full-time students who are permanent northern residents of the Northern Administration

District; priority will be given to applicants showing intention of returning to, or remaining in the north.

StudentAid BC
c/o Ministry of Advanced Education, Skills and Training
PO Box 9173, Stn Prov Govt, Victoria, BC V8W 9H7
250-387-6100; Fax: 250-356-9455; Toll Free: 1-800-561-1818
URL: studentaidbc.ca/explore/grants-scholarships

StudentAid BC Grants & Scholarships Program
Scholarships & awards are available in various fields of study.

Universities Canada/Universités Canada
#1710, 350 Albert St., Ottawa, ON K1R 1B1
613-563-1236; Fax: 613-563-9745
Email: info@univcan.ca; URL: www.univcan.ca

Bayer CropScience Scholarship for Future Leaders in Agriculture
Up to 5 scholarships available; $5,000.

C.D. Howe Scholarship Endowment Fund National Engineering Scholarship
Two scholarships of $7,500 available at the bachelor level of an engineering program; one male recipient, one female.

C.D. Howe Scholarship Fund Thunder Bay/Port Arthur Scholarship Program
Scholarships open to all disciplines but students must be residents of Thunder Bay or the former federal constituency of Port Arthur; two at $5,500.

Fessenden-Trott Scholarship
Scholarships open to all disciplines; Recipients must have completed their first year of their first bachelor program; Offered to a different region of Canada each year; four at $9,000.

Frank Knox Memorial Fellowship Program
Awards, plus tuition fees & health insurance for Canadian citizens or permanent residents who have graduated from a AUCC member institution & wish to pursue graduate studies at Harvard; Applications for students currently studying in the US will not be considered.

L'Oréal Canada For Women in Science Research Excellence Fellowships
Two post-doctoral fellowships.

Mattinson Scholarship Program for Students with Disabilities
For students with a permanent disability pursuing undergraduate study, all disciplines; four at $2,000.

Nexen Scholarship
$2,500 for degrees, diplomas or certificates; $750 for apprenticeships.

Queen Elizabeth II Silver Jubilee Endowment Fund for Study in a Second Official Language Award Program
Scholarships open to all disciplines, except translations, for students studying in their second language; three $7,000 (plus travel costs).

Scholarship for Indigenous Students
Available to Canadian students of Indigenous ancestry; three scholarships of $5,000 at the bachelor level; two scholarships of $3,500 at the diploma level.

TD Scholarships for Community Leadership
All disciplines, undergraduate degrees; 20 renewable scholarships for $7,500 living stipend, plus $10,000 for tuition.

Vale Manitoba Operations Scholarship
1 scholarship available to students at the bachelor or diploma level; Recipient must be living in a Manitoba community north of the 52 parallel and be enrolled in a program related to mining engineering, mining technology, geology or surveying.

Yukon Government
PO Box 2703, Whitehorse, YT Y1A 2C6
867-667-5929; Fax: 867-667-8555
Email: sfa@gov.yk.ca; URL: yukon.ca/en/education-and-schools

Yukon Excellence Awards
Awarded to encourage academic achievement in a Yukon secondary school; students are eligible to receive up to $3,000 for 10 awards ($300 per award) to offset post-secondary education and training costs.

ENVIRONMENTAL

Alberta Emerald Foundation
9910 - 103rd St. NW, Edmonton AB T5K 2V7
780-616-1556; Toll Free: 1-800-219-8329
Email: info@emeraldfoundation.ca; URL: emeraldfoundation.ca

Emerald Awards
Awarded to Albertans who have made a significant contribution to the protection or enhancement of the environment. Nominations are open to individual, not-for-profit organizations, business & industry, communities & government, educational institutions & volunteer organizations excelling in environmental achievements.

Atlantic Salmon Federation / Fédération du saumon atlantique
PO Box 5200, St Andrews, NB E5B 3S8
506-529-4581; Fax: 506-529-1028; Toll Free: 1-800-565-5666
Email: savesalmon@asf.ca; URL: www.asf.ca

Lee Wulff Conservation Award
Presented annually to an individual who has made noteworthy, long-term contributions to Atlantic salmon conservation at the regional or national level.

Olin Fellowship
Fellowships offered annually to individuals seeking to improve their knowledge or skills in fields dealing with current problems in biology, management, or conservation of Atlantic salmon & its habitat; the fellowship may be applied toward a wide range of endeavours such as salmon management, graduate study, & research.
Applicants need not be enrolled in a degree program, but must be legal residents of the US or Canada; $1,000-$3,000; ASF member in good standing.

T.B. "Happy" Fraser Award
Presented annually to an individual who has made outstanding long-term contributions to wild Atlantic salmon conservation in Canada. The award reflects efforts on a regional or national level.

Canadian Land Reclamation Association / Association canadienne de réhabilitation des sites dégradés
#202, 5405 - 99th St., Edmonton, AB T6E 3N8
780-437-0044; Fax: 780-413-0076
Email: info@clra.ca; URL: www.clra.ca

Dr. Edward M. Watkin Award
Presented annually to an individual or organization in recognition of outstanding contribution to the CLRA and/or the field of reclamation, through research, field work, teaching or innovation, or distinguished service to the association through active participation & leadership.

Linda Jones Memorial Award
Two $1,000 awards are presented annually to students in a land reclamation related program at a Canadian institution in recognition of academic excellence.

Noranda Land Reclamation Award
Presented annually by the association on behalf of Noranda Mines Inc. in recognition of superior contributions to land reclamation; not restricted to members.

Ontario Chapter Tom Peters Memorial Mine Reclamation Awards
Two awards: one for an industry professional, one for a student.

Canadian Wildlife Federation / Fédération canadienne de la faune
350 Michael Cowpland Dr., Kanata ON K2M 2W1
613-599-9594; Fax: 613-599-4428; Toll Free: 1-800-563-9453
Email: info@cwf-fcf.org; URL: www.cwf-fcf.org

Canadian Conservation Achievement Awards Program:

Doug Clarke Memorial Award
Presented to a CWF affiliate for the most outstanding conservation project completed during the previous year by the affiliate, its clubs or its members.

Past Presidents' Canadian Legislator Award
Presented annually to an elected legislator in recognition of a meaningful contribution to wildlife conservation in Canada.

Robert Bateman Award
Awarded to recognize an individual or group who has furthered the awareness of and/or the appreciation for Canada's wildlife through artistic expression; artistic expression can include: painting, sculpture, photography, choreography, writing, song.

Roderick Haig-Brown Memorial Award
Awarded annually to an individual who has made a significant contribution to furthering the sport of angling &/or conservation & wise use of Canada's recreational fisheries resources.

Roland Michener Conservation Award
A trophy is given annually in recognition of an individual's outstanding achievement in the field of conservation in Canada.

Stan Hodgkiss Outdoorsperson of the Year Award
Presented annually to an outdoorsperson who has demonstrated an active commitment to conservation in Canada.

WILD Educator of the Year Award
Established in 2015 and awarded to any WILD Education instructor who utilizes CWF's education programming to provide innovative experiences for youth that focus on wildlife and conservation.

Wade Luzny Youth Conservation Award
Awarded to a Canadian youth and/or youth group that has participated in a wildlife conservation project or activity.

Youth Mentor Award
Awarded to any individual or group who has made significant contributions in creating or presenting programs that are dedicated toward youth and focus on introducing the importance of conservation, wildlife or habitat.

International Development Research Centre / Centre de recherches pour le développement international
PO Box 8500, 150 Kent St., Ottawa, ON K1G 3H9
613-236-6163; Fax: 613-238-7230
Email: awards@idrc.ca; URL: www.idrc.ca

Climate Change Research Award
One of IDRC's many research awards; Applicants must hold Canadian citizenship or permanent residency status and pursuing or having completed a graduate degree; research proposal is for a doctoral thesis; recipient will conduct research on adaptation to climate change in Latin America and the Caribbean, Asia, and sub-Saharan Africa; Maximum of $15,000 per year.

University of Toronto School of the Environment
University of Toronto, #1016V, 33 Wilcocks St.
Toronto, ON M5S 3E8
416-978-6526; Fax: 416-978-3884
Email: grad.office.env@utoronto.ca; URL: environment.utoronto.ca

Alan H. Weatherley Graduate Fellowship in Environmental Leadership
Awarded to one PhD student enrolled in one of the School of the Environment's Collaborative Specializations; Recipient receives approximately $3,000.

Alexander B. Leman Memorial Award
Awarded to master's and doctoral students enrolled in a Collaborative Specialization at the School of the Environment and the Department of Geography's Program in Planning only; Recipient receives approximately $500.

Arthur and Sonia Labatt Fellowships
Awarded to master's and doctoral students enrolled in the Collaborative Specialization in Environment and Health or Environmental Studies, OR the JD/Certificate Program offered by the Faculty of Law and the School of the Environment; Preference given to students exploring practical based or market place solutions to environmental issues; Approximate value of $5,000.

Beatrice and Arthur Minden Graduate Research Fellowship at the School of the Environment
Awarded to one or more PhD students enrolled one of the School of the Environment's Collaborative Specialization to provide them with support during the research stage of their dissertations; Approximate value of $3,000.

Eric David Baker Krause Graduate Fellowship
Awarded to master's and doctoral students enrolled in the Collaborative Specialization in Environment and Health or Environmental Studies, OR the JD/Certificate Program offered by the Faculty of Law and the School of the Environment; Recipient demonstrates financial need; Approximate value of $500.

George Burwash Langford Award
Awarded to graduate students enrolled in the Collaborative Specialization in Environment and Health or Environmental Studies, OR the JD/Certificate Program offered by the Faculty of Law and the School of the Environment; Approximate value of $500.

John R. Brown Award
Awarded to full-time graduate students enrolled in the Gage Occupational and Environmental Health Unit (Faculty of Medicine); Approximate value of $1,100.

Marjorie Gillespie Bolton and Mabel Gillespie Norris Memorial Scholarship
Awarded to a graduate student at the University of Toronto with demonstrated financial need whose academic focus is in the area of sustainability, environmental justice, biodiversity, and/or conservation; Preference given to a student enrolled in the School of the Environment's graduate programs; Approximate value of $2,000.

Sperrin Chant Award
Awarded to graduate students enrolled in a School of the Environment Collaborative Specialization researching toxicology; Recipient demonstrates academic excellence, strong character and financial need; Value is approximately $1,500.

HEALTH & MEDICAL

Action Canada for Sexual Health & Rights / Fédération canadienne pour la santé sexuelle
#501, 251 Bank St., Ottawa, ON K2P 1X3
613-241-4474
Email: info@actioncanadashr.org; URL:
www.actioncanadashr.org

Helen & Fred Bentley Awards of Excellence
Recognizes the achievements of Action Canada Associate Organizations.

Canadian Association of Medical Radiation Technologists / Association canadienne des technologues en radiation médicale
#1300, 180 Elgin St., Ottawa, ON K2P 2K3
613-234-0012; Fax: 613-234-1097; Toll Free: 1-800-463-9729
Email: awards@camrt.ca; URL: www.camrt.ca

CAMRT Awards
Administers awards for students & registered technologists including: Dr. M. Mallett Student Award, Dr. Petrie Memorial Award, George Reason Memorial Award, E.I. Hood Award, Philips Award.

Canadian Association on Gerontology
c/o Department of Occupational Science & Occupational Therapy, University of Toronto
#160, 500 University Ave., Toronto, ON M5G 1V
Toll Free: 1-855-224-2240
Email: contact@cagacg.ca; URL: www.cagacg.ca

CAG Awards
To recognize individuals who have recently made outstanding contributions to the field of aging and to the CAG.

Canadian Institutes of Health Research
160 Elgin St., 10th Fl.; Address Locator 4809A,
Ottawa, ON K1A 0W9
613-954-1968; Fax: Toll Free: 1-888-603-4178
Email: support-soutien@cihr-irsc.gc.ca; URL: cihr-irsc.gc.ca

CIHR Gold Leaf Prizes
Awarded biennially to an individual or team to recognize excellence in health research and its translation into benefits for Canadians; Each prize has a value of $100,000.

Canadian Nurses Association / Association des infirmières et infirmiers du Canada
50 Driveway, Ottawa, ON K2P 1E2
613-237-2133; Fax: 613-237-3520; Toll Free: 1-800-361-8404
Email: cna@cna-aiic.ca; URL: www.cna-aiic.ca

Jeanne Mance Awards
Established in 1971, this award is named after one of Canada's most inspirational nurses. Awarded every other year, Nurses nominated for this have made significant and innovative contributions to the health of Canadians.

Order of Merit Awards
Established in 2007 and awarded to recognize excellence in clinical nursing practice, nursing administration, nursing education, nursing research and nursing policy.

Canadian Orthopaedic Foundation / Fondation orthopédique du Canada
PO Box 1036, Toronto, ON M5K 1P2
416-410-2341; Fax: 416-352-5078; Toll Free: 1-800-461-3639
Email: mailbox@canorth.org; URL: whenithurtstomove.org

Community Innovation Award
Celebrates community-based surgeons and their research studies dedicated to improving patient care or musculoskeletal health in their community; Two $15,000 awards.

J. Edouard Samson Award
$30,000 awarded for outstanding orthopaedic research over a period of 5+ years at a Canadian centre; research presented at the annual meeting of the Canadian Orthopaedic Research Society.

Canadian Society for Medical Laboratory Science / Société canadienne de science de laboratoire médical
33 Wellington St. North, Hamilton, ON L8R 1M7
905-528-8642; Fax: 905-528-4968; Toll Free: 1-800-263-8277

Email: info@csmls.org; URL: www.csmls.org

Grants, Scholarships, and Awards
To celebrate professional excellence, to help members continue their professional development and to aid students in their education.

Canadian Veterinary Medical Association / Association canadienne des médecins vétérinaires
339 Booth St., Ottawa, ON K1R 7K1
613-236-1162; Fax: 613-236-9681; Toll Free: 1-800-567-2862
Email: admin@cvma-acmv.org; URL:
www.canadianveterinarians.net; www.veterinairesaucanada.net

CVMA Humane Award
Established 1986 to encourage care & well-being of animals; awarded to an individual (veterinarian or non-veterinarian) whose work is judged to have contributed significantly to the welfare & well-being of animals; $1,000 & a plaque awarded.

CVMA Industry Award
Established in 1996; publicly acknowledges and celebrates the role of industry in veterinary medicine; formally recognizes a CVMA member for their contributions to the advancement of veterinary medicine.

CVMA Practice of the Year Award
Established in 2013; recognizes a veterinary practice team for outstanding achievement within their local community; $1,000 and a plaque.

Merck Veterinary Award
Established in 1985 and sponsored by Merck Animal Health; presented to a CVMA member whose work in food and animal production practice, research or science has contributed significantly to the advancement of food animal medicine. Award consists of a plaque and a cash prize of $1,000.

Small Animal Practitioner Award
Established 1987 to encourage progress in the field of small animal medicine & surgery; awarded to a veterinarian whose work in small animal practice, clinical research or basic sciences is judged to have contributed significantly to the advancement of small animal medicine, surgery, or the management of small animal practice, including the advancement of the public's knowledge of the responsibilities of pet ownership; $1,000 & a plaque awarded.

Catholic Health Association of Canada / Association catholique canadienne de la santé
1247 Kilborn Pl., Ottawa, ON K1H 6K9
613-731-7148; Fax: 613-731-7797
Email: info@chac.ca; URL: www.chac.ca

Lifetime Achievement Award
Annually awarded to a leader who has inspired and mentored others in Catholic health care and whose accomplishments, over the course of a career, have strengthened the ministry.

Midcareer Leadership Award
Annually awarded to a young leader in Catholic health care who has demonstrated outstanding leadership in their organization and significant growth as a leader in the ministry.

College of Family Physicians of Canada / Collège des médecins de famille du Canada
2630 Skymark Ave., Mississauga, ON L4W 5A4
905-629-0900; Toll-Free Fax: 1-888-843-2372; Toll Free: 800-387-6197
Email: info@cfpc.ca; URL: www.cfpc.ca, fafm.cfpc.ca

Awards of Recognition
Some of CFPC's most prestigious awards; Includes Awards of Excellence, Early Career Development Awards, Environmental Health Awards, Lifetime Achievement Awards, and more.

Epilepsy Canada / épilepsie Canada
East Tower, #600, 3250 Bloor St. West, Toronto, ON M8X 2X9
647-775-1611; Toll Free: 1-877-734-0873
Email: epilepsy@epilepsy.ca; URL: www.epilepsy.ca

The Jay & Aiden Barker Breakthrough Grant in Clinical & Basic Sciences
$200,000 to be awarded to a single winner, or apportioned to multiple award winners, to conduct investigations that explore the basic mechanisms of epileptic seizures.

The Royal College of Physicians & Surgeons of Canada / Le Collège royal des médecins et chirurgiens du Canada
774 Echo Dr., Ottawa, ON K1S 5N8
613-730-8177; Fax: 613-730-8830; Toll Free: 1-800-668-3740
Email: feedback@royalcollege.ca; URL: www.royalcollege.ca

Royal College Awards
Numerous awards honour the personal achievements of specialist physicians and surgeons across Canada; recognize contributions to the profession, to the Royal College mission and to the health care of citizens in Canada and globally.

The Royal Society of Canada / La Société royale du Canada
Walter House, 282 Somerset St. West, Ottawa, ON K2P 0J6
613-991-6990; Fax: 613-991-6996
Email: info@rsc-src.ca; URL: rsc-src.ca

The McLaughlin Medal
Awarded annually for important research of sustained excellence in any branch of medical science.

JOURNALISM

Atlantic Journalism Awards
46 Swanton Dr., Dartmouth, NS B3W 2C5
902-425-2727; Fax: 902-462-1892
Email: office@ajas.ca; URL: ajas.ca

Atlantic Journalism Awards
Originally a program of the University of King's College School of Journalism established in 1981, is now a non-profit organization to recognize excellence & achievement in work by Atlantic Canadian journalists; covers work in English or French; 23 award categories featuring work published or broadcast in the news media of Atlantic Canada.
Winners in individual categories will receive framed certificate presented at the Awards dinner.

Canadian Association of Journalists / L'Association canadienne des journalistes
PO Box 117, Stn F, Toronto, ON M4Y 2L4
Email: canadianjour@magma.ca; URL: caj.ca

The CAJ Awards Program
Awards presented for excellence in Canadian journalism with a focus on investigative work.

National Magazine Awards Foundation / Fondation nationale des prix du magazine canadien
#1600, 2300 Yonge St., Toronto, ON M4P 1E4
416-939-6200
Email: staff@magazine-awards.com; URL: magazine-awards.com

National Magazine Awards
Awards are presented annually in 29 categories with 2 special awards; Based on the category, the award goes to an individual, an editorial team or a magazine; Written and visual awards have a cash prize of $1,000.

Ontario Newspaper Awards
Email: URL: www.onawards.ca

Ontario Newspaper Awards
An annual celebration of excellence in journalism in Ontario newspapers, excluding those based in Toronto; honours the best journalism produced by reporters, photographers, videographers, graphic artists and editors at three dozen newspapers.

News Media Canada
#200, 37 Front St. East, Toronto, ON M5E 1B3
416-923-3567; Fax: 416-923-7206; Toll Free: 1-877-305-2262
Email: awards@newspaperscanada.ca; URL: nmc-mic.ca; nna-ccj.ca

Edward Goff Penny Memorial Prizes for Young Canadian Journalists
Established in 1991; $1,000 prize awarded in two circulation classes: under 25,000 and 25,000 and over.

National Newspaper Awards / Concours canadien de journalisme
Awards are presented annually in 21 categories: Arts and Entertainment, Beat Reporting, Breaking News, Business, Columns, Editorial Cartooning, Editorials, Explanatory Work, Feature Photo, International, Investigations, Local Reporting, Long Feature, News Photo, Photo Portfolio/Essay, Politics, Presentation, Project of the Year, Short Feature, Sports and Sports Photo; There is also an award for Journalist of the Year.

Société Saint-Jean-Baptiste de Montréal
82, rue Sherbrooke ouest, Montréal, QC H2X 1X3
514-843-8851; Fax: 514-844-6369
Email: info@ssjb.com; URL: ssjb.com

Prix Olivar-Asselin

Established 1955; awarded annually to a French Canadian in recognition of outstanding achievement in journalism in serving the higher interests of the French Canadian people.

LEGAL, GOVERNMENTAL, PUBLIC ADMINISTRATION

Alberta Justice & Solicitor General

John E. Brownlee Bldg., 10365 - 97th St., 10th Fl. South, Edmonton, AB T5J 3W7
780-638-3870
Email: cprj@gov.ab.ca; URL: www.alberta.ca/justice-and-solicitor-general.aspx

Community Justice Awards

Awards highlight the activities & accomplishments of special Albertans who prove that preventing crime is everyone's responsibility; awards are presented to an individual, for youth leadership, business, community program or organization & police member for efforts beyond regular duties that prevent and address crime.

Institute of Public Administration of Canada / Institut d'administration publique du Canada

#401, 1075 Bay St., Toronto, ON M5S 2B1
416-924-8787; Fax: 416-924-4992
URL: www.ipac.ca

Award for Innovative Management

Awarded in recognition of outstanding organizational achievement in the public sector that addresses the wide variety of issues facing society.

Promising New Public Servant Award

Awarded to an emerging leader within the public sector who represents the ideals, values and abilities of sound public administration.

Public Sector Leadership & Excellence Awards

Recognizes organizations that have demonstrated leadership by taking bold steps to improve Canada through advancements in public administration and management.

Vanier Medal

A gold medal is awarded annually as a mark of distinction & exceptional achievement to a person who has shown outstanding leadership in public administration in Canada.

The Professional Institute of the Public Service of Canada / Institut professionnel de la fonction publique du Canada

250 Tremblay Rd., Ottawa, ON K1G 3J8
613-228-6310; Fax: 613-228-9048; Toll Free: 1-800-267-0446
Email: institute_awards@pipsc.ca; URL: pipsc.ca

Gold Medal Awards

Established 1937; the gold medals are presented biennially. Those eligible are scientific, professional, or technical workers or groups of workers employed by the federal, provincial, or municipal government services of Canada who have made a contribution of outstanding importance to national or world well-being in either pure or applied science or in some field outside pure or applied science.

LITERARY ARTS, BOOKS & LIBRARIES

Association des Libraires du Québec

483, boul St-Joseph est, Montréal, QC H2J 1J8
514-526-3349; Fax: 514-526-3340
Email: info@prixdeslibraires.qc.ca; URL: prixdeslibraires.qc.ca

Prix des libraires du Québec

Cette célébration annuelle, organisée par l'Association des libraires du Québec, se veut un hommage aux auteurs, dont l'oeuvre a marqué l'imaginaire des libraires au cours de l'année par son originalité et sa qualité littéraire.

Atlantic Book Awards

c/o Laura Carter, PO Box 36086, Stn Spring Garden, Halifax, NS B3J 3S9
Email: abafcoordinator@gmail.com; URL: atlanticbookawards.ca

Alistair MacLeod Prize for Short Fiction

Awarded to a native or resident Atlantic Canadian for a collection of short fiction in English.

Ann Connor Brimer Award

$2,000 awarded in recognition of outstanding contributions to writing for Atlantic Canadian young people; Alternates between young adult literature (ages 12-17) and children's literature (11 and under) each year; Writer must be residing in Atlantic Canada; $250 awarded to authors of shortlisted titles.

APMA Best Atlantic-Published Book Award

$3,000 awarded to an Atlantic Canadian publisher whose book published in the preceding year best exemplifies excellence and achievement in publishing in Atlantic Canada; $1,000 awarded to the author.

Atlantic Book Award for Scholarly Writing

$1,000 awarded annually to the author(s) of a published book determined to have a significant literary, social and academic impact in the areas of the social sciences and humanities.

Atlantic Book Awards Pioneer Award

A lifetime achievement award presented annually to a trail blazer and ground-breaker who has made a lasting contribution to the development of the literary arts in Atlantic Canada; The recipient can be from the field of publishing, writing, book-selling, literary arts organizations etc.

Dartmouth Book Awards

Two prizes of $2,500 each (one for fiction, one for non-fiction) awarded annually to honor books which have contributed the most to the enjoyment and understanding of Nova Scotia and its people.

Democracy 250 Atlantic Book Award for Historical Writing

$2,000 awarded to an outstanding work of non-fiction that promotes awareness of, and appreciation for, an aspect of the history of the Atlantic Provinces.

Evelyn Richardson Non-Fiction Award

$2,000 awarded to a Nova Scotia writer of non-fiction.

J.M. Abraham Poetry Award

Awarded annually to recognize the best book of poetry written by an Atlantic Canadian.

Lillian Shepherd Memorial Award for Excellence in Illustration

Awarded to an illustrator of a book published in the previous year who: is from or currently residing in Atlantic Canada OR illustrated a book by an Atlantic Canadian writer OR illustrated a book set in Atlantic Canada.

J.M. Abraham Poetry Award

Awarded annually to recognize the best book of poetry written by an Atlantic Canadian.

Margaret and John Savage First Book Award

$2,500 awarded to each an outstanding debut Fiction and Non-Fiction book.

Thomas Raddall Atlantic Fiction Award

Awarded on behalf of the Writers' Federation of Nova Scotia, $25,000 goes to an outstanding Atlantic-region fiction writer.

Book Publishers Association of Alberta

Percy Page Centre, 11759 Groat Rd. NW, 2nd Fl., Edmonton, AB T5M 3K6
780-424-5060; Fax: 780-424-7943
Email: info@bookpublishers.ab.ca; URL: bookpublishers.ab.ca

Alberta Book Awards

To recognize outstanding achievements in Alberta publishing; up to 14 awards are given in the following categories: Trade Fiction, Trade Non Fiction, Speculative Fiction, Scholarly and Academic, Learning, Book Design, Cover Design, Children and Young Adult, Emerging Publisher of the Year and the Robert Kroetsch Award for Poetry.

Lois Hole Award for Editorial Excellence

Established in honour of Lois Hole's dedication to books, libraries, literacy and respect for editors. Awarded to an Alberta book publisher in recognition of outstanding editorial work on books published during the award year.

British Columbia Historical Federation

PO Box 448, Fort Langley, BC V1M 2R7
Email: info@bchistory.ca; URL: www.bchistory.ca

Historical Writing Competition

Recognizes authors whose books have made the most significant contributions to the historical literature of British Columbia; Top prize is the Lieutenant Governor's Medal for Historical Writing, plus a $2,500 cash prize; Awards may also be presented to the runner up ($1,500), second runner up ($500) and/or honorable mentions (certificates).

W. Kaye Lamb Essay Scholarships

Awarded for essays written by students at BC colleges or universities on a topic related to BC history; 2 prizes available: $750 for a student in 1st or 2nd year, $1000 for a student in 3rd or 4th year.

Writing Awards

Established 1983; Honours outstanding contributions by individuals and groups through best article and best website awards.

The Canada Council for the Arts / Conseil des Arts du Canada

150 Elgin St., 2nd Fl., PO Box 1047, Ottawa, ON K1P 5V8
613-566-4414; Fax: 613-566-4390; Toll Free: 1-800-263-5588
Email: info@canadacouncil.ca; URL: canadacouncil.ca

Canada-Japan Literary Awards

Valued at $10,000 each and awarded biennially to both an English language writer & a French language writer; awards are designed to encourage Canadian authors to explore and celebrate Japan, Japanese themes or Japanese-Canadian relations.

Governor-General's Literary Awards

Fourteen $25,000 prizes awarded annually for the best English and French books in seven categories; the publisher of each winning book receives $3,000 to support promotional activities; Finalists receive $1,000.

Joseph S. Stauffer Prizes

Awarded annually to Canadian artists with less than 15 years of practice who exhibit strong artistic potential in music, visual arts and literature; Three prizes of $5,000 (one in each category).

Canadian Authors Association

c/o Book and Periodical Council, #107, 192 Spadina Ave., Toronto, ON M5T 2C2
705-955-0716
Email: apurcell@canadianauthors.org; URL: canadianauthors.org/national

Fred Kerner Book Award

$400 and a one-year membership awarded annually to a Canadian Authors member who has the best overall book published in the previous calendar year.

The Canadian Children's Book Centre

#200, 425 Adelaide St. West, Toronto, ON M5V 3C1
416-975-0010; Fax: 365-214-0108
Email: info@bookcentre.ca; URL: bookcentre.ca

Amy Mathers Teen Book Award

$5,000 awarded annually to recognize excellence in teen / young adult fiction; Eligible books are original works in English, aimed at readers aged 13-18 and written by a Canadian or a Permanent Resident of Canada.

Geoffrey Bilson Award for Historical Fiction

$5,000 awarded annually to recognize excellence in an outstanding work of historical fiction for young people by a Canadian author, published in previous calendar year.

John Spray Mystery Award

$5,000 awarded annually to recognize excellence in the mystery genre; Eligible books are original works in English, aimed at readers 8-18 and written by a Canadian; A mystery book can be a thriller, a crime novel or a whodunit.

Marilyn Baillie Picture Book Award

$20,000 awarded annually to recognize excellence in illustrated picture books; Eligible books are original works in English, aimed at children ages 3-8, written and illustrated by Canadians and first published in Canada; Eligible genres include fiction, non-fiction and poetry.

Monica Hughes Award for Science Fiction and Fantasy

$5,000 awarded annually to recognize excellence in science fiction and fantasy writing for children and teens; Eligible books are original works in English, aimed at readers ages 8-18 and written by a Canadian or a Permanent Resident of Canada.

The Norma Fleck Award for Non-Fiction

$10,000 awarded annually to recognize an outstanding work of non-fiction for young people by a Canadian author.

Prix Harry Black de l'album jeunesse

Sont admissibles au Prix Harry Black de l'album jeunesse, les albums illustrés écrits à l'intention des lecteurs âgés entre trois (3) et huit (8) ans : histoire de tous les jours, documentaire, conte, légende, comptine, poésie, et ne sera accordé qu'aux livres imprimés sur papier.

TD Canadian Children's Literature Award

Two prizes of $30,000 each awarded annually to an English and French book to recognize excellence in children's writing; $20,000 awarded among honour book winners to a maximum of four books each in English and French; $2,500 is awarded to each publisher of the winning books; Eligible books are written in any genre, aimed at children between 0-12, and written and illustrated by Canadians and/or permanent residents.

Canadian Historical Association / Société historique du Canada

#1912, 130 Albert St., Ottawa, ON K1P 5G4
613-233-7885; Fax: 613-567-3110

Email: cha-shc@cha-shc.ca; URL: cha-shc.ca

Albert B. Corey Prize
Established 1966 & jointly sponsored by the CHA & the American Historical Association; awarded every two years to the best book dealing with the history of Canadian-American relations or the history of both countries.

Canadian Indigenous History Prize
Awarded to the best book and best article on Indigenous history.

Canadian Committee on Migration, Ethnicity and Transnationalism Article Prize
Acknowledges scholarly articles and book chapters, in English and French, judged to have made an original, significant and meritorious contribution to the historical study of migration and ethnicity.

CCWH-CCHF Book Prize in Women's and Gender History
Awarded every two years to the best book published in the field of women's and gender history by a Canadian author and/or about Canadian history, in either English or French.

CHA Prize for Best Scholarly Book in Canadian History
Valued at $5,000 and awarded annually to the best scholarly book in Canadian History; presented at the yearly Governor General Awards for Excellence in Teaching Canadian History event at Rideau Hall in Ottawa. Sponsored by Manulife since 2009.

CHA Journal Prize
Awarded annually for the best essay published each year in the Journal of the Canadian Historical Association.

CHA Student Prize
Awarded to the best article published in a peer-reviewed journal by a PhD or MA-level student, in either English or French.

Clio Prizes
Awarded annually to meritorious publications or for exceptional contributions by individuals or organizations to regional history.

Hilda Neatby Prizes
Recognizes the best articles of the year on women's history; one awarded for English-language article and another for French-language article.

Media and Communication History Committee Prize
Awarded for best article on media and communication history.

Political History Prizes
Awarded in three categories: Best Book, Best Article (French) and Best Article (English).

Prize for Best article on the history of Sexuality
Recognizes excellence in and encourages the growth of scholarly work in the field of the history of sexuality in Canada.

Canadian Library Association
#400, 1150 Morrison Dr., Ottawa, ON K2H 8S9
613-232-9625; Fax: 613-563-9895
Email: info@cla.ca; URL: cla.ca/cla-at-work/awards

Amelia Frances Howard-Gibbon Illustrators Medal
Established 1971; $1,000 awarded annually for outstanding illustrations in a children's book published in Canada; the illustrator must be a Canadian or a Canadian permanent resident.

Book of the Year for Children Award
A silver medal awarded annually for an outstanding children's book published in Canada during the calendar year; book must have been written by a Canadian or a permanent resident of Canada.

Young Adult Book Award
$1,000 awarded annually to an author of an outstanding Canadian fiction book which appeals to young adults between the ages of 13 and 18; Eligible books have been published in Canada in the calendar year and authored by a Canadian or permanent resident.

CBC Literary Prizes / Prix Littéraires Radio-Canada
PO Box 500, Stn A, Toronto, ON M5W 1E6
Toll Free: 1-877-888-6788
Email: canadawrites@cbc.ca; URL:
www.cbc.ca/books/literaryprizes

CBC Literary Awards/Prix Littéraires Radio-Canada
Literary competition for original, unpublished works in Canada's two official languages. Awards in three categories: Short Story, Nonfiction and Poetry; Six winners receive $6,000, a writing residency at the Banff Centre, and their winning work published in Air Canada's enRoute magazine and on CBCBooks.ca; Finalists in each category receive $1,000 and publication of their works on cbcbooks.ca; A partnership between CBC/Radio-Canada, the Canada Council for the Arts, and Air Canada's enRoute magazine.

Crime Writers of Canada
Crime Writers of Canada Awards, 716 Thicket Way, Ottawa, ON K4A 3B5
Email: awards@crimewriterscanada.com; URL:
www.crimewriterscanada.com

Arthur Ellis Awards
Established 1984; awarded annually in the following categories: best crime novel (by a previously published novelist), best first crime novel (by a previously unpublished novelist), best crime novella, best crime short story, best French crime book, best young-adult crime book, best crime non-fiction.

Derrick Murdoch Award
Presented to someone who has contributed greatly to the development of crime writing in Canada through their work as writers, editors, producers, publicists and organizers; Awarded biennially, alternating with the Grand Master Award.

Grand Master Award
Presented to a Canadian crime writer with a substantial body of work who has garnered national and international recognition; Awarded biennially, alternating with the Derrick Murdoch Award.

The Unhanged Arthur Award for Best Unpublished Crime Manuscript
$500 awarded annually to the best unpublished first crime novel.

Donner Canadian Foundation
c/o Sherry Naylor, 23 Empire Ave., Toronto, ON M4M 2L3
416-368-8253
Email: sherry@naylorandassociates.com; URL:
donnerbookprize.com

The Donner Prize
Award of $50,000 for the best book on Canadian public policy; five runners-up prizes of $7,500 each.

Fondation Les Forges
CP 335, 1497, rue Laviolette, Trois-Rivières, QC G9A 5G4
819-379-9813; Fax: 819-376-0774
URL: www.fiptr.com

Grand Prix du Festival International de la Poésie
Le Festival International de la Poésie remet une bourse de 15 000$ au lauréat lors de l'ouverture officielle du festival; le candidat doit: être de citoyenneté canadienne et avoir déjà publié trois ouvrages de poésie chez un éditeur reconnu.

Prix Félix-Antoine-Savard de poésie
Décerné annuellement lors des cérémonies d'ouverture du Festival International de la Poésie; vise à honorer, tout en les respectant, la mémoire, l'esprit et l'oeuvre poétique de cet écrivain; une bourse de 250$ y est rattachée et le contenant de 100 feuilles de papier Saint-Gilles sont remis à St-Joseph-de-la-Rive, le jour de l'Action de GrÂce.

Prix Félix-Leclerc de poésie
Créé en octobre 1997, à l'occasion du 10e anniversaire de la mort du poète; décerné tous les 2 ans lors des cérémonies d'ouverture du Festival International de la Poésie; prix de 1 000$

Prix de Poésie Gatien-Lapointe - Jaime-Sabines
bourse de $ 100 000 pesos mexicains remise moitié / moitié au lauréat par le Seminario de Cultura Mexicana et le Festival international de la poésie; Ce concours possède un volet mexicain et un volet québécois; Un poète ne peut remporter qu'une seule fois ce prix.

Freedman & Associates Inc.
121 Richmond St. West, Toronto, ON M5H 2K1
416-868-1500; URL: nbbaward.com
Email: mafreedman@freedmanandassociates.com

National Business Book Award
Established 1985; $30,000 awarded annually to the author of an outstanding book on Canadian business.

The Griffin Trust for Excellence in Poetry
363 Parkridge Cres., Oakville, ON L6M 1A8
905-618-0420
Email: info@griffinpoetryprize.com; URL:
www.griffinpoetryprize.com

The Griffin Prize
Established in 2000, two prizes of $65,000 each awarded annually for collections of poetry published in English during the preceding year; one will go to a living Canadian poet; the other to a living poet or translator from any Canada.

Indigenous Literary Studies Association
Email: indigenouslsa@gmail.com; URL:
www.indigenousliterarystudies.org

Indigenous Voices Awards
Awarded to Indigenous authors of unpublished, published or performed literary art.
$2,000 awarded in each of the following categories: Best Unpublished Prose Piece in English, Best Unpublished Poetic Piece(s) in English, Best Unpublished Prose Piece in French, Best Unpublished Poetic Piece(s) in French, Best Unpublished Piece in (or incorporating significant use of) an Indigenous Language
$5,000 awarded in each of the following categories: Most Significant Book of Prose by an Emerging Indigenous Writer, Most Significant Book of Poetry by an Emerging Indigenous Writer, Most Significant Work in an Alternative Format by an Emerging Indigenous Writer.

International Board on Books for Young People - Canadian Section / Union internationale pour les livres de jeunesse
c/o Canadian Children's Book Centre, #217, 40 Orchard View Blvd., Toronto, ON M4R 1B9
416-975-0010; Fax: 416-975-8970
Email: info@ibby-canada.org; URL: www.ibby-canada.org

Claude Aubry Award
Awarded biennially for distinguished contributions to Canadian children's literature by a librarian, teacher, author, illustrator, publisher, bookseller or editor.

Elizabeth Mrazik-Cleaver Picture Book Award
$1,000 awarded annually for distinguished Canadian picture book illustration.

Frances E. Russell Grant
$1,000 awarded annually to initiate & encourage research in children's literature in Canada.

The League of Canadian Poets
#1519, 2 Carleton St., Toronto, ON M5B 1J3
416-504-1657; Fax: 416-504-0096
Email: info@poets.ca; URL: poets.ca

Gerald Lampert Memorial Award
Established 1979; $2,000 awarded annually for excellence in a first book of poetry, written by a Canadian citizen or landed immigrant, & published in the preceding year.

Jessamy Stursberg Poetry Prize
Awarded to young poets in Canada in the junior category (grades 7-9) and senior category (grades 10-12); first place prize is $400, second place prize is $350 and third place prize is $300.

Pat Lowther Memorial Award
$2,000 awarded annually for excellence in a book of poetry, written by a Canadian female citizen or landed immigrant, & published in the preceding year.

Raymond Souster Award
$2,000 awarded to a book of poetry by a League of Canadian Poets member published in the preceding year.

Sheri-D Wilson Golden Beret Award
$2,000 awarded annually to recognize excellence in spoken word poetry.

The Lionel Gelber Prize
c/o Munk School of Global Affairs and Public Policy, University of Toronto, 315 Bloor St. West, Toronto, ON M5S 0A7
416-946-8450; Fax: 416-946-8877
Email: gelberprize.munk@utoronto.ca; URL:
munkschool.utoronto.ca/gelber

The Lionel Gelber Prize
$15,000 awarded annually in honour of the legacy of Lionel Gelber; Winner is the world's best non-fiction book in English on foreign affairs that seeks to deepen public debate on significant international issues.
Books published in English or English translation, must be copyrighted in the year in which the prize is awarded; books must be published or distributed in Canada; submissions by publishers only.

Literary Translators' Association of Canada / Association des traducteurs et traductrices littéraires du Canada
Concordia University, 1400, boul de Maisonneuve ouest, #LB-631, Montréal, QC H3G 1M8
514-848-2424 ext. 8702; Fax: 514-848-4514
Email: info@attlc-ltac.org; URL: www.attlc-ltac.org

John Glassco Translation Prize
$1,000 and a one-year membership awarded annually for a translator's first work in book-length literary translation into French or English, published in Canada during the previous calendar year.

Manitoba Writers' Guild Inc.
#521, 100 Arthur St., Winnipeg, MB R3E 1H3
204-944-8013; Fax: 204-942-5754; Toll Free: 1-888-637-5802
Email: manitobawritersguild3@gmail.com; URL: www.mbwriter.mb.ca

Manitoba Book Awards:

Alexander Kennedy Isbister Award for Non-Fiction
Presented to the Manitoba writer whose book is judged the best book of adult non-fiction written in English; $3,500.

Carol Shields City of Winnipeg Book Award
To honour books that evoke the special character of & contribute to the appreciation & understanding of the City of Winnipeg; $5,000.

Eileen McTavish Sykes Award for Best First Book
Awarded annually to a Manitoba author whose first professionally published book is deemed the best written.
Must have been written in the previous year; $1,500.

John Hirsch Award for Most Promising Manitoba Writer
Awarded annually to the most promising Manitoba writer working in poetry, fiction, creative non-fiction or drama; $2,500.

Lansdowne Prize for Poetry

Manuela Dias Book Design and Illustration Awards
For the best overall design in Manitoba book publishing in three categories: book design, children's illustration, and general illustration.

Margaret Laurence Award for Fiction
Presented to the Manitoba writer whose book is judged the best book of adult fiction written in English; $3,500.

Mary Scorer Award for Best Book by a Manitoba Publisher
Awarded to the best book published by a Manitoba publisher & written for the trade, bookstore, educational, academic or scholarly market; $1,000.

McNally Robinson Book for Young People Awards
Awarded annually to the writer whose young person's book is judged the best written by a Manitoba author; two categories: children's & young adult; $2,500.

McNally Robinson Book of the Year
To the Manitoba author judged to have written the best book in the calendar year; $5,000.

Michael Van Rooy Award for Genre Fiction

Le Prix littéraire Rue Deschambeault
Biennial award presented to the author whose published book or play is judged to be the best French language work by a Manitoba author; $3,500.

McClelland & Stewart
c/o Penguin Random House Canada. #1400, 320 Front St. West, Toronto, ON M5V 3B6
416-364-4449; Fax: 416-598-7764
Email: jolee@penguinrandomhouse.com; URL: writerstrust.com/Awards/Journey-Prize

The Writers' Trust of Canada/McClelland & Stewart Journey Prize
$10,000 awarded annually to a new & developing writer of distinction for a short story published in a Canadian literary journal. The shortlisted stories are selected from journal submissions & published annually by McClelland & Stewart as The Journey Prize Anthology. Finalists receive $1,000 and the literary journal that published the winning story receives $2,000.
Only submissions from Canadian literary journals are accepted. Stories must have had original publication in the nominating journal during the previous year.

IODE Canada
#219, 40 Orchard View Blvd., Toronto, ON M4R 1B9
416-487-4416; Toll Free: 1-866-827-7428
Email: iodecanada@bellnet.ca; URL: www.iode.ca

IODE Violet Downey Book Award
$5,000 awarded annually to the best English language book containing at least 500 words of text (preferably with Canadian content) in any category, suitable for children aged 13 and under; Eligible book have been written by a Canadian citizen and must have been published in Canada during the preceding calendar year.

IODE Toronto Legacy Fund
c/o IODE Ontario, #9, 45 Frid St., Hamilton, ON L8P 4M3
905-522-9537; Fax: 905-522-3637
Email: iodeontario@gmail.com; URL: www.iodeontario.ca/iode-toronto-legacy

IODE Jean Throope Book Award
Established in 1975; an inscribed scroll & not less than $1,000 awarded annually to the author or illustrator of the best children's book written or illustrated by a Canadian resident in Toronto or surrounding area & published by a Canadian publisher within the preceding 12 months.

Ontario Arts Council / Conseil des arts de l'Ontario
121 Bloor St. East, 7th Fl., Toronto, ON M4W 3M5
416-961-1660; Fax: 416-961-7796; Toll Free: 1-800-387-0058
Email: info@arts.on.ca; URL: www.arts.on.ca

Ruth and Sylvia Schwartz Children's Book Award
Two awards presented annually; $6,000 for best picture book & $6,000 for best young adult/middle reader book; in conjunction with the Ontario Arts Foundation and the Ruth Schwartz Foundation.

Ontario Library Association
2 Toronto St., 3rd Fl., Toronto, ON M5C 2B6
416-363-3388; Fax: 416-941-9581; Toll Free: 1-866-873-9867
Email: info@accessola.com; URL: www.accessola.com

Blue Spruce Award Program
The Blue Spruce Award is a provincial primary reading program which brings recently published Canadian children's picture books to Ontario children ages 4 to 7 in kindergarten through to grade two. Award given out in May every year.

The Evergreen Award Program
The Evergreen Award is OLA's newest addition to the Forest of Reading. It was introduced at Super Conference 2005 for adults of any age. It gives adult library patrons the opportunity to vote for a work of Canadian fiction or non-fiction that they have liked the most.

Red Maple Award Program
The Red Maple Award reading program is offered for the enjoyment of students in Grades 7 and 8. The program, like the Association's Silver Birch Awards reading program, gives students who have read a minimum number of nominated titles the opportunity to vote with a large group of their peers for the nominated title that they feel should win the Red Maple Award each year.

Silver Birch Fiction, Non-Fiction And Express Award Program
The Silver Birch Award is given by students in Grades 3-6 in a spectacular ceremony held annually in May before fifteen hundred of their peers. The children choose winners in Fiction, Non-Fiction and Express when they cast their ballots on the province-wide Voting Day earlier in the same month. It is the most democratic and unbiased process possible when the children make their choice. The program is administered by the Ontario Library Association and run by teacher-librarians and teachers in schools and by children's librarians in public libraries. But the choice belongs to the children. And, in their tens of thousands, they know what they are doing.

White Pine Award Program
The White Pine Award reading program offers high school-aged teens at all grade levels the opportunity to read the best of Canada's recent young adult fiction titles. All of these 10 books for Young Adults on this list are accessible and will allow all readers to be successful participants / voters. As in all of the independent reading programs, a reader only needs to read 5 books out of a list of 10 to qualify for voting. Based on student voting across the province, the most popular book is then selected and author is honoured with the White Pine Award.

Ontario Creates
South Tower, #501, 175 Bloor St. East, Toronto, ON M4W 3R8
416-314-6858; Fax: 416-314-6876
Email: reception@ontariocreates.ca; URL: ontariocreates.ca

Trillium Book Award/Prix Trillium
Awarded annually to one English and one French Ontario author in recognition of excellence; the winning books must have been published within the preceding 12 months; books in English or French in any genre are eligible; winner receives $20,000 & the publisher receives $2,500.

Trillium Book Award for Children's Literature in French Language
Presented biennially (on the year the Book Award for Poetry in French is not offered); $10,000 awarded to the author and $2,000 awarded to the publisher.

Trillium Book Award for Poetry
$10,000 awarded to one English poet and $2,000 to their publisher in recognition of excellence; English language award is present every year to works published in the preceding calendar year; French language award is presented biennially to works published in the previous two calendar years.

PEI Writers' Guild
81 Prince St., Charlottetown, PE C1A 4R3
Email: peiwritersguild@gmail.com; URL: www.peiwritersguild.com

Island Literary Awards
Established in 1987 in recognition of Island writers in five adult categories: Literature for Children, Poetry, Short Story, Creative Non-fiction, Marie Coyoteblanc Award for Indigenous Writing; and four student categories: Early Elementary (Grades 1-3), Late Elementary (Grades 4-6), Junior High (Grades 7-9), Senior High (Grades 10-12).

Prism International
Creative Writing Program, UBC, 1866 Main Mall, #E462, Vancouver, BC V6T 1Z1
604-822-2514; Fax: 604-822-3616
Email: promotions@prismmagazine.ca; URL: prismmagazine.ca

Creative Non-Fiction Contest
$1,500; $600 runner-up; $400 second runner-up.

Earle Birney Prize for Poetry
$500 is awarded annually by the outgoing Poetry Editor to an outstanding poetry contributor published in PRISM international.

The Grouse Grind Lit Prize for V. Short Forms
$500; $150 runner-up; $50 second runner-up.

Jacob Zilber Prize for Short Fiction
$1,500; $600 runner-up; $400 second runner-up.

Pacific Spirit Poetry Prize
$1,500; $600 runner-up; $400 second runner-up.

Prix Aurora Awards
URL: prixaurorawards.ca

Prix Aurora Awards
Awards presented annually for the best in Canadian Science Fiction & Fantasy.

Québec Ministère de la culture et des communications
225, Grande Allée est, Québec, QC G1R 5G5
418-380-2363 ext. 7231; Fax: 418-080-2364
Email: prixduquebec@mcc.gouv.qc.ca; URL: www.prixquebec.gouv.qc.ca

Prix Athanase-David
One of Les Prix du Québec; $30,000 awarded annually to recognize excellence in an author's body of work.

Québec Writers' Federation / Fédération des écrivaines et écrivains du Québec
#3, 1200, av Atwater, Montréal, QC H3Z 1X4
514-933-0878
Email: admin@qwf.org; URL: qwf.org

QWF Literary Prize for Young Writers
Awarded to an emerging writer who is a resident of Quebec and is between 16 and 24 years old at the time of the deadline; Grand prize: $1000; Second prize: $350; Third prize: $150.

QWF Prizes
Established 1988; awards seven annual prizes of $3,000 each to recognize excellence in English writers emerging from Quebec: The A.M. Klein poetry prize, The Hugh MacLennan fiction prize, Mavis Gallant prize for non-fiction, Concordia University First Book Prize; Prix de traduction de la Fondation Cole: anglais-français; The QWF Prize for Children's and Young Adult Literature; The QWF Playwriting Prize.

The Royal Society of Canada / La Société royale du Canada
Walter House, 282 Somerset St. West, Ottawa, ON K2P 0J6
613-991-6990; Fax: 613-991-6996
Email: info@rsc-src.ca; URL: rsc-src.ca

Lorne Pierce Medal
Established in 1926 and awarded to creative or critical literature written in either English or French.

Saskatchewan Book Awards
306-569-1585
Email: director@bookawards.sk.ca; URL: www.bookawards.sk.ca

City of Regina Book Awards

City of Saskatoon and Public Library Saskatoon Book Award

Jennifer Welsh Scholarly Writing Award

Muslims for Peace and Justice Fiction Award

Ministry of Parks, Culture and Sport First Book Award Honouring Brenda MacDonald Riches

Publishing in Education Award

Rasmussen & Co. Indigenous Peoples' Writing Award

Regina Public Library Book of the Year Award

Saskatoon Public Library Indigenous Peoples' Publishing Award

SK Arts Poetry Award Honouring Anne Szumigalski

University of Saskatchewan Non-Fiction Award

Saskatchewan Library Association
#10, 2010 - 7th Ave., Regina, SK S4R 1C2
306-780-9413; Fax: 306-780-9447
Email: slaexdir@sasktel.net; URL: saskla.ca

SLA Frances Morrison Award
Awarded for outstanding service to libraries.

Saskatchewan Writers Guild Inc.
PO Box 3986, #100, 1150 - 8th Ave., Regina, SK S4P 3R9
306-791-7740; Fax: 306-565-8554; Toll Free: 1-800-667-6788
Email: info@skwriter.com; URL: skwriter.com

Cheryl and Henry Kloppenburg Award for Literary Excellence
$10,000 awarded annually to recognize a Saskatchewan writer who has written a substantial body of literary work.

City of Regina Writing Award
$4,500 awarded annually to a Regina writer to reward merit & enable a writer to work on a specific writing project; funded by the City of Regina Arts Commission & administered by the SWG.

John V. Hicks Long Manuscript Awards
Awarded to recognize excellence in unpublished book-length manuscripts of poetry, fiction, and non-fiction by Saskatchewan authors; Each year the competition is open to a different genre.

Scotiabank Giller Prize
416-934-0755
Email: info@scotiabankgillerprize.ca; URL: scotiabankgillerprize.ca

The Giller Prize
$140,000 award to the author of the best Canadian novel or collection of short stories published in English.

Société Saint-Jean-Baptiste de Montréal
82, rue Sherbrooke ouest, Montréal, QC H2X 1X3
514-843-8851; Fax: 514-844-6369
Email: info@ssjb.com; URL: ssjb.com

Prix Ludger-Duvernay
Le prix a été crée en 1944 afin de signaler les mérites d'un compatriote dont la compétence et le rayonnement dans le domaine intellectuel et littéraire servent les intérêts supérieurs de la nation québécoise.

Stephen Leacock Association Inc.
PO Box 854, Orillia, ON L3V 6K8
Email: info@leacock.ca; URL: leacock.ca

The Order of Mariposa
Awarded occasionally to someone who has contributed significantly to humour in Canada, in other than the written word.

Stephen Leacock Memorial Medal
Established 1946 to encourage the writing & publishing of humorous works in Canada; given annually for the best Canadian book of humour published in the preceding year
Winner receives the medal & a cash award of $15,000; Two runners-up receive $3,000 each.

Stephen Leacock Student Humorous Short Story Competition
Awarded to Ontario students for original humorous story or humorous personal essay in English; First place: $1,000; Second place: $700; Third place: $300.

Ville de Montréal
Service du développement culturel
801, rue Brennan, 5e étage, Montréal, QC H3C 0G4
514-872-9090

URL: ville.montreal.qc.ca/culture/grand-prix-du-livre-de-montreal

Grand Prix du livre de Montréal
Le prix est offert par la Ville de Montréal à l'auteur ou aux co-auteurs d'un ouvrage de langue française ou anglaise, pour la facture exceptionnelle et l'apport original de cette publication; le prix consiste en une bourse de 15 000 $, ount admissibles un auteur ou un éditeur qui habite sur le territoire de la Ville de Montréal.

West Coast Book Prize Society
1628 West 75th Ave., 2nd Fl., Vancouver, BC V6P 6G2
778-987-8774
Email: info@bcyukonbookprizes.com; URL: www.bcbookprizes.ca

BC and Yukon Book Prizes:
Established 1985 to a BC publisher or an author or illustrator must have lived in BC or Yukon for the past 12 months or for at least 3 of the past 5 years; $2,000 presented to winning authors, illustrators and publishers in the following categories:

Bill Duthie Booksellers' Choice Prize
Awarded to the author and publisher of the best book in terms of public appeal, initiative, design, production & content; the book must have been published in BC.

Christie Harris Illustrated Children's Literature Prize
Prize shared by author and illustrator.

Dorothy Livesay Poetry Prize
Awarded to the author of the best work of poetry.

Ethel Wilson Fiction Prize
Awarded to the author of the best work of original literary fiction.

Hubert Evans Non-Fiction Prize
Awarded to the author of the best original non-fiction literary work (philosophy, belles lettres, biography, history, etc.).

Jim Deva Prize for Writing That Provokes
Awarded to author(s) or illustrators of an original work in various mediums that challenges or provokes.

Roderick Haig-Brown Regional Prize
Awarded to the author of the book that contributes most to the enjoyment & understanding of BC; the book may deal with any aspect of the province & should epitomize the BC experience.

Sheila A. Egoff Children's Prize
Awarded to the author of the best book for young people aged 16 & under.

Writers Guild of Alberta
11759 Groat Rd., Edmonton, AB T5M 3K6
780-422-8174; Fax: 780-422-2663; Toll Free: 1-800-665-5354
Email: mail@writersguild.ca; URL: writersguild.ca

Alberta Literary Awards
Awarded to recognize outstanding Alberta writing.

City of Calgary W.O. Mitchell Book Prize
Awarded in conjunction with the City of Calgary to honour an outstanding book published the preceding year by Calgary authors; award is worth $5,000.

Golden Pen Award
Awarded to acknowledge the lifetime achievements of outstanding Alberta writers.

Robert Kroetsch City of Edmonton Book Prize
Entries must deal with some aspect of the City of Edmonton or be written by an Edmonton author; award is worth $10,000.

Writers' Federation of Nova Scotia
1113 Marginal Rd., Halifax, NS B3H 4P7
902-423-8116; 902-422-0881
Email: contact@writers.ns.ca; URL: writers.ns.ca

Evelyn Richardson Non-Fiction Award
Award was established in 1978 to recognize outstanding work in non-fiction by a Nova Scotian writer (native or resident); $2,000.

J.M. Abraham Poetry Award (Atlantic Poetry Prize)
$2,000

Nova Scotia Poetry Award
Award was established in 2020 to recognize poetry by a Nova Scotian writer (native or resident) biennially; $500.

Thomas H. Raddall Atlantic Fiction Award
Honours the best fiction writing by an Atlantic Canadian writer; $25,000.

The Writers' Trust of Canada
#600, 460 Richmond St. West, Toronto, ON M5V 1Y1
416-504-8222; Fax: 416-504-9090; Toll Free: 1-877-906-6548
Email: info@writerstrust.com; URL: www.writerstrust.com

Dayne Ogilvie Prize for LGBTQ Emerging Writers
Awarded annually to an emerging writer from the LGBTQ community with an exceptional and promising body of work.
First place: $4,000; Finalists: $250.

Engel Findley Award
Established 1986; awarded annually to a Canadian writer in recognition of an excellent body of work and in hope of future contributions; $25,000.

Hilary Weston Writers' Trust Non-Fiction Prize
Awarded annually to the author of the work of non-fiction published in the previous year that, in the opinion of the judges, shows the best literary merit; First place: $60,000; Finalists: $5,000.

Latner Writers' Trust Poetry Prize
Awarded annually to a Canadian poet in recognition of an excellent body of work and in hope of future contributions; $25,000.

Matt Cohen Award
For a lifetime of distinguished work by a Canadian writer, working in either poetry or prose, writing in either French or English who has dedicated their life to writing as a primary pursuit; $25,000.

RBC Bronwen Wallace Memorial Award
Awarded annually to a Canadian writer under the age of 35 who is not yet published in book form; award alternates each year between poetry & short fiction; First place: $10,000; Finalists: $2,500.

Shaughnessy Cohen Award for Political Writing
Awarded annually to a non-fiction book of outstanding literary merit that covers Canadian political & social issues; First place: $25,000; Finalists: $2,500.

Vicky Metcalf Award for Literature for Young People
Awarded annually to an author of children's literature, either fiction, non-fiction, picture books or poetry, not for a single book, but for a body of work, unless there is no author worthy of the award that year; $25,000.

Writers' Trust Fiction Prize
Awarded annually to the author of the novel or short story collection published in the previous year that shows the best literary merit; First place: $50,000; Finalists: $5,000.

The Writers' Union of Canada
#600, 460 Richmond St. West, Toronto, ON M5V 1Y1
416-703-8982
Email: info@writersunion.ca; URL: www.writersunion.ca

Danuta Gleed Literary Award
Awarded to a Canadian writer for the best first collection of published short stories in the English language; First place: $10,000; Two finalists receive $500 each.

Freedom to Read Award
Recognizes work in support of freedom of expression.

Graeme Gibson Award
Recognizes efforts to improve the circumstances of writers in Canada.

Short Prose Competition for Emerging Writers
$2,500 awarded annually to a Canadian writer for the best piece of unpublished prose of up to 2,500 words in English.

PERFORMING ARTS

Alberta Scholarship Programs
PO Box 28000, Stn Main, Edmonton, AB T5J 4R4
780-427-8640; Fax: 780-427-1288; Toll Free: 1-855-606-2096
Email: scholarships@gov.ab.ca; URL: www.studentaid.alberta.ca/scholarships/alberta-scholarships

Arts Graduate Scholarships
Seven awards of $15,000 at graduate level for study in music, drama, dance & the visual arts.

Association québécoise de l'industrie du disque, du spectacle et de la vidéo
6420, rue Saint-Denis, Montréal, QC H2S 2R7
514-842-5147; Fax: 514-842-7762
Email: info@adisq.com; URL: www.adisq.com

Félix Awards
The event honours the best musical achievement produced in Québec during the past year.

The Banff Centre
PO Box 1020, 107 Tunnel Mountain Dr., Banff, AB T1L 1H5
403-762-6180; Fax: 403-762-6345
Email: arts_info@banffcentre.ca; URL: www.banffcentre.ca

Clifford E. Lee Choreography Award
Established 1978; Awarded annually in recognition of outstanding Canadian choreography; Winner receives a $14,000 cash prize for the commission of a new work and the support of two residencies at the Banff Centre.

The Canada Council for the Arts / Conseil des Arts du Canada

PO Box 1047, 150 Elgin St., 2nd Fl., Ottawa, ON K1P 5V8
613-566-4414; Fax: 613-566-4390; Toll Free: 1-800-263-5588
Email: info@canadacouncil.ca; URL: canadacouncil.ca

Bernard Diamant Prize
$5,000 awarded annually to a professional Canadian classical singer under 35 as an opportunity to pursue their career through further studies.

Eckhardt-Gramatté National Music Competition
Rewards the most talented young artists in the categories of piano, voice and strings; First prize: $8,000; Second prize: $3,000; Third prize: $2,000.

Governor General's Performing Arts Awards
Up to six prizes of $25,000 awarded annually to experienced Canadian artists who have made remarkable contributions to the performing arts in Canada in broadcasting, classical music, dance, film, popular music or theatre.

Healey Willan Prize
$5,000 awarded every two years to the Canadian amateur choir that gives the best performance in terms of musicianship, technique and program in the National Competition for Amateur Choirs.

Jacqueline Lemieux Prize
$6,000 awarded annually to an established dance professional who has made an outstanding contribution to dance in Canada.

J.B.C. Watkins Awards: Music and Theatre
$5,000 awarded annually to professional Canadian artists in music and theatre wishing to pursue postgraduate studies outside Canada, preferably in Denmark, Norway, Sweden or Iceland.

Jean-Marie Beaudet Award in Orchestra Conducting
$1,000 awarded annually to a young Canadian conductor.

John Hirsh Prize
$6,000 each awarded biennially to one English and one French developing theatre director who have demonstrated great potential for future excellence & exciting artistic vision.

Joseph S. Stauffer Prizes
Up to $5,000 awarded annually in each of three categories: literature, music, visual arts; Winners are Canadian artists with less than 15 years of experience who exhibit strong artistic potential.

Jules Léger Prize for New Chamber Music
Established in 1978; annual $7,500 prize designed to encourage Canadian composers to create avant-garde chamber music and to foster its performance by Canadian chamber groups.

Michael Measures Prizes
Recognizes promising Canadian classical music performers aged 16 to 24 who are enrolled in the summer training program of the National Youth Orchestra of Canada; First prize: $25,000; Second prize: $15,000.

Musical Instrument Bank
Created in 1987 as a means of acquiring exceptional instruments to be loaned for three years at a time to established Canadian musicians or gifted young musicians; Collection includes the 1827 McConnel Nicolaus Gagliano cello & the 1717 Windsor-Weinstein Stradivarius violin.

Peter Dwyer Scholarships
Annual scholarships totalling $20,000 awarded to the most promising Canadian students at the National Ballet School & the National Theatre School; each school is awarded $10,000 & chooses the winner on behalf of the Canada Council.

Robert Fleming Prize
The annual $2,000 prize in memory of Robert Fleming is intended to encourage the career development of young composers & is awarded to professional Canadian composers who submit an eligible application to the Explore and Create program.

Victor Martyn Lynch-Staunton Awards
Seven prizes of $15,000 awarded annually to honour outstanding artistic achievement in Dance, Inter-Arts, Media Arts, Music, Theatre, Visual Arts, and Writing and Publishing.

Virginia Parker Award
$25,000 awarded annually to a young Canadian classical musician, instrumentalist, or conductor who demonstrates outstanding talent, musicianship and artistic excellence and who makes a valuable contribution to artistic life in Canada and internationally.

Walter Carsen Prize for Excellence in the Performing Arts
$50,000 awarded annually to a Canadian artist who has demonstrated outstanding excellence in music, theatre, or dance; Prize is presented on a four-year cycle - dance, theatre, dance, music.

Canadian Academy of Recording Arts & Sciences / Académie canadienne des arts et des sciences de l'enregistrement

#211C, 219 Dufferin St., Toronto, ON M6K 3J1
416-485-3135; Fax: 416-485-4978; Toll Free: 1-888-501-3135
Email: info@carasonline.ca; URL: carasonline.ca; junoawards.ca

Juno Awards
Annual awards for: Canadian Hall of Fame Award, Allan Waters Humanitarian Award, Walt Grealis Special Achievement Award, Juno Fan Choice (presented by TD), Single of the Year, International Album of the Year, Album of the Year (sponsored by Music Canada), Francophone Album of the Year, Artist of the Year, Group of the Year, Breakthrough Artist of the Year (sponsored by FACTOR, the Government of Canada, Radio Starmaker Fund and Canada's Private Radio Broadcasters), Breakthrough Group of the Year (sponsored by FACTOR, the Government of Canada, Radio Starmaker Fund and Canada's Private Radio Broadcasters), Instrumental Album of the Year, Songwriter of the Year, Country Album of the Year, Adult Alternative Album of the Year, Alternative Album of the Year (sponsored by Long & McQuade), Rap Recording of the Year, Pop Album of the Year (sponsored by TD), Rock Album of the Year, Vocal Jazz Album of the Year, Jazz Album of the Year: Solo, Jazz Album of the Year: Group, Children's Album of the Year, Classical Album of the Year: Solo or Chamber Ensemble, Classical Album of the Year: Large Ensemble or Soloist(s) with Large Ensemble Accompaniment, Classical Album of the Year: Vocal or Choral Performance, Classical Composition of the Year, Dance Recording of the Year, R&B / Soul Recording of the Year, Reggae Recording of the Year, Contemporary Roots Album of the Year, Traditional Roots Album of the Year, Aboriginal Album of the Year (sponsored by Aboriginal Peoples Television Network), Blues Album of the Year, Contemporary Christian/Gospel Album of the Year, World Music Album of the Year (sponsored by Canada Council for the Arts), Jack Richardson Producer of the Year, Recording Engineer of the Year (sponsored by the Ontario Institute of Audio Recording Technology), Recording Package of the Year, Video of the Year (sponsored by MuchFACT, exclusively funded by Bell Media), Electronic Album of the Year, Heavy Metal Album of the Year, Adult Contemporary Album of the Year.

Canadian Country Music Association / Association de la musique country canadienne

#104, 366 Adelaide St. East, Toronto, ON M5A 3X9
416-947-1331; Fax: 416-947-5924
Email: country@ccma.org; URL: ccma.org

Music Awards
41 awards in 4 categories (Artist, Musician, Radio, Industry) are presented annually to outstanding performers; Honourees have made a significant contribution to country music in the preceding year.

Canadian Theatre Critics Association / Association des critiques de théÃ¢tre du Canada

Email: martinmorrow1@gmail.com; URL: canadiantheatrecritics.ca

The Herbert Whittaker/CTCA Award for Distinguished Contribution to Canadian Theatre
Presented annually to Canadian citizen or permanent resident working in any theatrical discipline who has demonstrated distinguished contribution in playwriting, performance, direction or design; named after Herbert Whittaker Founding Chairman of the CTCA.

Nathan Cohen Award for Excellence in Critical Writing
Two awards presented annually: one for reviews of up 1,000 words and one for longer critical pieces.

Council for Business & the Arts in Canada / Conseil pour le monde des affaires et des arts du Canada

#202, 133 Richmond St. West, Toronto, ON M5H 2L3
416-869-3016; Fax: 416-869-0435
Email: info@businessforthearts.org; URL: www.businessforthearts.org

Arnold Edinborough Award
To recognize a business professional age 40 or under who has demonstrated exemplary leadership and volunteerism in the arts; Winner receives $5,000 to be directed to the arts organization(s) of their choice.

Corporate Champion of the Arts Award
Awarded to a business that has strengthened arts and culture in Canada through long-standing support and commitment.

Community Impact Award
To recognize an arts and business partnership that has enhanced the quality of life and enriched the cultural scene in its community.

Edmund C. Bovey Award
To recognize individual members of the business community who contribute leadership, time, money & expertise to the arts. A sculpture to the winner & $20,000 distributed to the arts in a way specified by the winner.

Peter Herrndorf Arts Leadership Award
To recognize an arts leader who has spent a lifetime dedicated to fostering the arts in Canada by building partnerships with fellow arts executives and institutions; Winner receives $5,000 to be directed to the registered not-for-profit arts organization(s) of their choice.

Dance Ontario Association / Association Ontario Danse

#304, 15 Case Goods Lane, Toronto, ON M5A 3C4
416-204-1083; Fax: 416-204-1085
Email: contact@danceontario.ca; URL: www.danceontario.ca

Dance Ontario Award
Recognizes a lifetime commitment to dance.

Dancer Transition Resource Centre / Centre de ressources et transition pour danseurs

The Lynda Hamilton Centre, #303, 1000 Yonge St., Toronto, ON M4W 2K2
416-595-5655; Fax: 416-595-0009; Toll Free: 1-800-667-0851
Email: nationaloffice@dtrc.ca; URL: dtrc.ca

Anne M. Delicaet Bursary
To help fund tuition, books &/or supplies for applicant in their third year of full-time retraining/grants received from the DTRC Award amount is discretionary.

David Pitblado Memorial Award
Awarded to a former modern dance artist who requires a second year to complete or continue a proposed course of study.

Dr. Stanley E. Greben Award
Awarded to a dancer for a second year of full-time study in a health related field.

Erik Bruhn Memorial Award
Awarded to a dancer in transition who requires a second year to complete or continue a proposed course of study.

Founder's Award
$20,000 awarded every two years to members intending to apply for the FTS-I Grant.

Karen Kain Award
Given to a dancer entering a second or subsequent year of full-time retraining; Award is discretionary.

Lynda Hamilton Award
Awarded annually to a dancer in transition who has completed two years of study & requires a third to complete or continue the proposed course of study; Award amount is discretionary.

Peter F. Bronfman Memorial Award
It is earmarked for a second or third year of retraining & subsistence & may be only awarded for the full amount; $18,000 subsistence & $4,000 for tuition & supplies.

Zella Wolofsky/Doug Wright Bursary
Awarded to a dancer with a degree from a recognized university & who is in second or subsequent year of professional program or doing graduate studies or second degree; Award is discretionary.

East Coast Music Association / Association de la musique de la côte est

#5, 2307 Clifton St., Halifax, NS B3K 4T9
902-423-6770; Fax: 888-519-0346; Toll-Free: 1-800-513-4953
Email: ecma@ecma.com; URL: www.ecma.com

East Coast Music Awards
Annual awards in the following categories: Album of the Year, Song of the Year, Aboriginal Recording of the Year, Blues Recording of the Year, Bucky Adams Memorial Award, Classical Composition of the Year, Classical Recording of the Year, Country Recording of the Year, Electronic Recording of the Year, Folk Recording of the Year, Francophone Recording of the Year, Gospel Recording of the Year, Group Recording of the Year, Indigenous Artist of the Year, Jazz Recording of the Year, Loud Recording of the Year, Pop Recording of the Year, Producer of the Year, R&B / Soul Recording of the Year, Rap / Hip-Hop Recording of the Year, Rising Star Recording of the Year, Rock Recording of the Year, Roots / Traditional Group Recording of the Year, Roots / Traditional Solo Recording of the Year, Solo Re-

cording of the Year, Songwriter of the Year, Traditional Instrumental Recording of the Year, World Recording of the Year, Fans' Choice Entertainer of the Year, Fans' Choice Video of the Year, Event of the Year, Graphic / Media Artist of the Year, Live Sound Engineer of the Year, Management / Manager of the Year, Media Outlet of the Year, Media Person of the Year, Music Merchant of the Year, Studio of the Year, Studio Engineer of the Year, Venue of the Year, Video of the Year.

Elinore & Lou Siminovitch Prize in Theatre
#11D-400, 600 University Ave., Toronto, ON M5G 1X5
Email: info@siminovitchprize.com; URL: siminovitchprize.com

Elinore & Lou Siminovitch Prize
Awarded annually; honours a playwrite, director, or designer who has made a significant contribution through a body of work to the theatre in Canada and whose career is gaining momentum; direction, playwriting & design will be honoured on a three year cycle.
$100,000; the winner will receive an immediate cash prize of $75,000, in addition the honoured artist will be invited to designate $25,000 to a protegé of their choice who is involved in direction, playwriting or design in theatre in Canada or to an institution (theatre or educational facility) that contributes to better & more successful theatre in Canada.

Fondation émile-Nelligan
261, rue Bloomfield, Montréal, QC H2V 3R6
514-278-4657; Fax: 514-278-1943
Email: info@fondation-nelligan.org; URL:
www.fondation-nelligan.org

Prix Serge-Garant
Prix triennal de composition musicale décerné à un compositeur citoyen du Canada né au Québec ou à un compositeur citoyen du Canada ayant sa résidence principale au Québec depuis au moins dix ans; 25 000$

Governor General's Performing Arts Awards Foundation
#400, 280 Metcalfe St., Ottawa, ON K2P 1R7
613-241-5297; Fax: 613-241-4677
Email: awards@ggpaa.ca; URL: ggpaa.ca

Governor General's Performing Arts Awards
Established in 1992; honours six performing artists for their lifetime achievement & contribution to the cultural enrichment of Canada in theatre, dance, classical music, popular music, film, and broadcasting; each recipient is awarded $15,000 & a commemorative medal.

Lifetime Artistic Achievement
$25,000 cash prize contributed by the Canada Council for the Arts and a commemorative medallion struck by the Royal Canadian Mint.

National Arts Centre Award
Recognizes the work of an extraordinary nature by an individual artist or company in the past performance year; $25,000 cash prize from the NAC, a commemorative medallion from the Mint and a specially commissioned work by a Canadian artist.

Ramon John Hnatyshyn Award for Voluntarism in the Performing Arts
Recognizes outstanding service to the performing arts with a commemorative medallion from the Mint and a commissioned work by a Candian artist.

Ontario Arts Council / Conseil des arts de l'Ontario
111 Bloor St. East, 7th Fl., Toronto, ON M4W 3M5
416-961-1660; Fax: 416-961-7796; Toll Free: 1-800-387-0058 ext. 7422
Email: info@arts.on.ca; URL: www.arts.on.ca

Colleen Peterson Songwriting Award
Established in 2003, in honour of Colleen Peterson's contribution to Canadian folk and country music. This annual award was designed to support and promote the work of an emerging professional singer / songwriter in the genres of roots, traditional, folk and country music; $1,000.

Heinz Unger Award
Awarded every two years; Established 1968 to honour the memory of the York Concert Society music director; Presented to an individual a young to mid-career Canadian conductor with professional experience to encourage and highlight their career.

John Adaskin Memorial Fund
Established in memorial of the Canadian Music Centre's first executive secretary; supports a project that encourages the promotion & development of Canadian music in the school system.

John Hirsch Director's Award
Established by a bequest to the Ontario Arts Council from the late John Hirsch; presented every three years to a promising theatre director in Ontario; $5,000.

Leslie Bell Scholarship for Choral Conducting
Established 1973; awarded biennially in competition; the purpose of the award is to help young emerging choral conductors in Ontario further their studies in the choral music field either in Canada or abroad; competition organized by the Ontario Choral Federation.

Pauline McGibbon Award
Annual award alternates between designers, directors & production crafts persons; $7,000.

Premier's Award for Excellence in the Arts
Established in 2006, the Government of Ontario created this award to recognize outstanding achievement in the professional arts by an individual and a group.
Winner receives $35,000 and selects a promising emerging artist in the same artistic field to receive $15,000; Five finalists each receive $2,000.

Tim Sims Encouragement Fund Award
Established in 1995; to be awarded annually to a promising young comedic performer or troupe.

Vida Peene Fund - Orchestra Award
Provides assistance to projects which benefit the orchestra community as a whole.

Québec Ministère de la culture et des communications
225, Grande Allée est, Québec, QC G1R 5G5
418-380-2363 ext. 7231; Fax: 418-080-2364
Email: prixduquebec@mcc.gouv.qc.ca; URL:
www.prixduquebec.gouv.qc.ca

Prix Denise-Pelletier
Prix réservé aux domaines de la chanson, de la musique, de l'art lyrique, du théâtre et de la danse

Québec Ministère des Relations internationales
Édifice Hector-Fabre, 525, boul René-Lévesque est, Québec, QC G1R 5R9
418-649-2300; Fax: 418-649-2656
URL: www.mri.gouv.qc.ca

Prix Rapsat-Lelièvre du disque de chanson
Initialement connu sous le nom Prix Québec/Wallonie-Bruxelles du disque de chanson; vise à encourager le développement et la promotion de la langue française, à stimuler la production et la diffusion de disques francophones.

Société Saint-Jean-Baptiste de Montréal
82, rue Sherbrooke ouest, Montréal, QC H2X 1X3
514-843-8851; Fax: 514-844-6369
Email: info@ssjb.com; URL: ssjb.com

Prix Calixa-Lavallée
Established 1959; awarded annually to a French Canadian in recognition of outstanding achievement in music in serving the higher interests of the French Canadian people.

Toronto Alliance for the Performing Arts
#350, 401 Richmond St. West, Toronto, ON M5V 3A8
416-536-6468; Fax: 416-536-3463
URL: tapa.ca

Dora Mavor Moore Awards
Established 1979; celebrating excellence in Toronto theatre, 50 awards across 7 divisions: General Theatre, Independent Theatre, Musical Theatre, Theatre for Young Audiences, Dance, Opera and Touring.

Western Canadian Music Alliance
#2, Clifton St., Winnipeg, MB R3G 2X6
204-943-8485; Fax: 204-453-1594
URL: breakoutwest.ca

Western Canadian Music Awards
Annual Awards in the following categories: Blues Artist of the Year, BreakOut Artist of the Year, Children's Artist of the Year, Classical Artist / Ensemble of the Year, Classical Composer of the Year, Country Artist of the Year, Electronic / Dance Artist of the Year, Francophone Artist of the Year, Indigenous Artist of the Year, Instrumental Artist of the Year, Jazz Artist of the Year, Metal / Hard Music Artist of the Year, Pop Artist of the Year, Producer of the Year, Rap / Hip-Hop Artist of the Year, Recording of the Year, Rock Artist of the Year, Roots Duo / Group of the Year, Roots Solo Artists of the Year, Songwriter(s) of the Year, Spiritual Artist of the Year, Urban Artist if the Year, Video Director of the

Year, Visual Media Composer of the Year, World Artist of the Year.

Western Canadian Music Industry Awards
Annual awards in the following categories: Audio Engineering Award, Community Excellence Award, Excellence in Visual Design, Impact in Artist Development, Impact in Live Music, Impact in Music Marketing, Heritage Award, Kevin Walters Industry Builder Award.

PUBLIC AFFAIRS

B'nai Brith Canada
15 Hove St., Toronto, ON M3H 4Y8
Toll Free: 1-844-218-2624
Email: info@bnaibrith.ca; URL: www.bnaibrith.ca

Award of Merit & Humanitarian Awards
Established 1981; presented annually at gala events in major communities across Canada.
Selection of honourees based on outstanding achievement in their chosen fields as well as personal commitment to the overall betterment of Canadian society.

Canadian Association on Gerontology / Association canadienne de gérontologie
c/o Dept. of Occupational Science & Therapy, University of Toronto
#160, 500 University Ave., Toronto, ON M5G 1V7
416-978-7977; Fax: 416-978-4771; Toll Free: 1-855-224-2240
Email: contact@cagacg.ca; URL: cagacg.ca

CAG Donald Menzies Bursary
To support post-baccalaureate students registered in a program of study focused on aging or the aged; $1,500.

CAG Margery Boyce Bursary
To support post-baccalaureate students who have made a significant contribution to their community through volunteer activities with or on behalf of seniors & who are registered in a program of study focused on aging or the aged; $500.

Canadian Council of Professional Engineers / Conseil canadien des ingénieurs
#300, 55 Metcalfe St., Ottawa, ON K1P 6L5
613-232-2474; Fax: 613-230-5759; Toll Free: 1-877-408-9273
Email: awards@engineerscanada.ca; URL: engineerscanada.ca

Meritorious Service Award for Community Service
Awarded for exemplary voluntary contribution to a community organization or humanitarian endeavour.

The City of Toronto
Equity, Diversity and Human Rights, City Hall, 100 Queen St. West, Toronto, ON M5H 2N2
416-338-1086
Email: diversity@toronto.ca; URL: www.toronto.ca/civicawards

Access Award for Disability Issues
Established 1982; honours people or organizations that have made or are making a significant or ongoing contribution, beyond legislated requirements, to the well-being & advancement of people with disabilities; the award honours those who are sensitive to the access needs of persons with disabilities when planning structures or programs (this could include consideration of access requirements in the design of new or renovated buildings, a job creation campaign, a transportation system, recreational program, etc.).

Constance E. Hamilton Award on the Status of Women
This award commemorates the Privy Council of Great Britain granting women status as persons in 1929; award is named after the first woman member of City Council; recipients are persons who have made a significant contribution to securing equitable treatment for Toronto women.

Mino Bimaadiziwin Award (Indigenous Award)
Est. 2013, given to a person(s) or organization whose efforts have made or are making a significant or ongoing contribution to the well-being & advancement of the Indigenous community in Toronto.

Pride Award for LGBTQ and Two Spirited Issues
Est. 2003, the Pride Award honours individuals &/or organizations that have made or are making a significant or ongoing contribution to provide protection on the basis of sexual orientation.

William P. Hubbard Race Relations Award
Named for Toronto's first visible minority Member of Council & Acting Mayor, this award honours persons with outstanding achievement & commitment to improving race relations in Toronto; award was presented for the first time in 1990.

Ethics in Action Awards
Kenneth C. Rowe Management Bldg., 6100 University Ave., Halifax, NS B3H 4R2
902-494-7142
Email: ethicsinaction@dal.ca; URL: www.dal.ca/sites/ethicsinaction.html

Ethics in Action Awards
Awards recognize businesses & individuals in business whose actions & decisions have made a positive impact on our communities.

Ontario Ministry of Tourism, Culture & Sport
Ontario Honours & Awards
400 University Ave., 6th Fl., Toronto, ON M7A 2R9
416-314-7526; Fax: 416-314-7743; Toll Free: 1-877-832-8622
URL: www.ontario.ca/page/honours-and-awards

Ontario Senior Achievement Awards
Presented annually to Ontario residents who have made a significant contribution to their communities after reaching 65 years of age; nominations may be made by any individual or organization.

Status of Women Canada
PO Box 8097, Stn T CSC, Ottawa, ON K1P 1H9
613-995-7835; Fax: 819-420-6906
Email: 819-420-6906; URL: cfc-swc.gc.ca

Governor General's Award in Commemoration of Persons Case
Established 1979 to celebrate the 50th anniversary of the "Persons Case" that resulted in women being declared eligible for appointment to the Senate; annual awards recognize contributions by five individuals toward promoting the equality of women in Canada.

SCIENTIFIC, ENGINEERING, TECHNICAL

The Canada Council for the Arts / Conseil des Arts du Canada
PO Box 1047, 150 Elgin St., 2nd Fl., Ottawa, ON K1P 5V8
613-566-4414; Fax: 613-566-4390; Toll Free: 1-800-263-5588
Email: info@canadacouncil.ca; URL: www.canadacouncil.ca

Killam Prizes
Up to five prizes of $100,000 each are given annually to eminent Canadian scholars in recognition of a distinguished career achievement in the natural sciences, health sciences, engineering, social sciences & humanities. Candidates must be nominated by three experts in their field. Chosen by Killam Selection.

Killam Research Fellowships
Fellowships offered on a competitive basis to support specific research projects by distinguished Canadian researchers in any of the following broad fields: humanities, social sciences, natural sciences, health sciences, engineering & studies linking any of the disciplines within these broad fields; provide release time to individual scholars, normally full professors in Canadian universities, who wish to pursue individual research; provides $70,000 a year for two years; application must be made by individuals, not by institutions, universities or organizations

Canadian Aeronautics & Space Institute / Institut aéronautique et spatial du Canada
#104, 350 Terry Fox Drive., Kanata, ON K2K 2W5
613-591-8787; Fax: 613-591-7291
Email: casi@casi.ca; URL: casi.ca

Alouette Award
A trophy awarded for an outstanding achievement in the field of Canadian-led astronautics; The achievement may be either a single outstanding contribution or, in the case of an individual nominee, a sustained high level of performance resulting in several advances in space.

C.D. Howe Award
Established 1966; Awarded to recognize outstanding achievement and sustained excellence in aeronautics and space activities in Canada; Awarded to a professional with at least ten years' experience in Canada.

F.W. (Casey) Baldwin Award
Award is for the best article published in the Canadian Aeronautics and Space Journal during the preceding calendar year.

McCurdy Award
Established 1954; a silver medal & trophy presented annually for outstanding achievement in art, science & engineering relating to aeronautics & space.

Romeo Vachon Award
Established 1969; bronze plaque awarded annually for outstanding contribution of a practical nature to the art, science, & engineering of aeronautics & space in Canada.

Trans-Canada (McKee) Trophy
Canada's oldest aviation award established 1927; presented annually except when no qualified recipient is nominated for outstanding achievement in the field of air operations.

Canadian Institute of Forestry / Institut forestier du Canada
PO Box 99, 6905 HWY. 17 West, Mattawa, ON P0H 1V0
705-744-1715 ext. 585; Fax: 705-744-1716
Email: admin@cif-ifc.org; URL: www.cif-ifc.org

Canadian Forest Management Group Achievement Award
Established 1998; to recognize outstanding achievement by teams in groups of Natural Resource managers, researchers and NGO groups in forest resources related activities in Canada.

Canadian Forestry Achievement Award
Established 1966 & presented annually in recognition of sustained exceptional accomplishments in forestry over a lifetime.

Canadian Forestry Scientific Achievement Award
Established 1980; presented annually in recognition of superior accomplishments in forestry research in Canada.

International Forestry Achievement Award
Established 1980; presented in recognition of outstanding achievement in international forestry.

James M. Kitz Award
Awarded to a person who has made outstanding contributions to the practice of forestry early in their career, including: superior personal accomplishments; outstanding leadership in education, management research or professional association work; promotion of forestry to various audiences; Open to anyone involved in forestry.

James S. Miller Scholarship
Awarded annually to a Northern Ontario student pursuing post-secondary studies in natural resources or a related field.

J. Michael Waldram Memorial Model Forest Fellowship
$1000 awarded annually to Canadian Aboriginal youth in their second year or higher of a degree or diploma program in natural resource management at a Canadian school.

Prince of Wales Award for Sustainable Forestry
Awarded annually to recognize the achievements of an outstanding young forest professional in Canada; Encourages the principles of sustainable forest management policy, planning and practice, sound science based land stewardship, and public outreach and knowledge exchange.

Presidential Award
Presented annually to individuals who have made significant or consistent outstanding contributions to the Institute through advancing the stewardship of Canada's forest resources, demonstrating leadership in forestry, promoting competence among forestry professionals, and raising public awareness of Canadian and international forestry issues.

Schlich Memorial Prize
Schlich medallion and $500 awarded annually to an outstanding student chosen by the university and technical school(s) represented by the Section(s) hosting the CIF annual meeting.

Tree of Life Award
Awarded annually to recognize individuals who have made important contributions to sustainable forest resource management, forest renewal or sustained yield integrated management of the forest and its intrinsic resources; Preference given to members of the institute.

Canadian Institute of Mining, Metallurgy & Petroleum / Institut canadien des mines, de la métallurgie et du pétrole
#1250, 3500, boul de Maisonneuve ouest, Montréal, QC H3Z 3C1
514-939-2710; Fax: 514-939-2714
Email: cim@cim.org; URL: www.cim.org

CIM Awards
The institute administers annually 14 national awards, 7 society and branch awards, and 5 sponsored awards recognizing achievement in mining, metallurgy & petroleum industries.

The Chemical Institute of Canada / Institut de chimie du Canada
#1009, 222 Queen St., Ottawa, ON K1P 5V9
613-232-6252; Fax: 613-232-5862; Toll Free: 1-888-542-2242
Email: info@cheminst.ca; URL: www.cheminst.ca

Canadian Green Chemistry and Engineering Network (CGCEN) Awards
CGCEN is a forum of the Institute; Presents the Canadian Green Chemistry and Engineering Awards to individuals and organizations annually to recognize significant accomplishments and advancements in green chemistry.

Canadian Society for Chemical Engineering (CSChE) Awards
CSChE is a constituent society of the Institute; Presents 7 awards annually to recognize professionals who have made outstanding contributions to chemical engineering.

Canadian Society for Chemical Technology (CSCT) Awards
CSCT is a constituent society of the Institute; Presents the Norman and Marion Bright Memorial Award annually to recognize individuals who have made an outstanding contribution to chemical technology.

Canadian Society for Chemistry (CSC) Awards
CSC is a constituent society of the Institute; Presents 21 awards annually to recognize professionals and students who have made outstanding contributions to the chemical sciences.

Chemical Institute of Canada Awards
The institute administers 9 awards annually to recognize chemists, chemical engineers and chemical technologists for their research and their work in the chemical community.

Chemical Institute of Canada Student Awards
The Institute and its constituent societies offer a variety of students awards and competitions to recognize outstanding contributions by students at all levels at Canadian universities and colleges.

E.W.R. Steacie Memorial Fund / Fondation E.W.R. Steacie
c/o L. Johnston, Secretary, 100 Sussex Dr., Ottawa, ON K1A 0R6
613-990-0736; Fax: 613-954-5242
Email: prixsteacieprize.sims@nrc-cnrc.gc.ca; URL: www.steacieprize.ca

The Steacie Prize
Canada's most prestigious award for young scientists & engineers; named to honour the memory of Edgar William Richard Steacie, a physical chemist & former President of the National Research Council of Canada; established 1963; awarded annually to a young scientist or engineer up to 40 years of age for outstanding scientific work in a Canadian context; winner receives a certificate & $10,000.

The Engineering Institute of Canada / Institut canadien des ingénieurs
PO Box 40140, Ottawa, ON K1V 0W8
613-400-1786;
Email: admin.officer@eic-ici.ca; URL: eic-ici.ca

Sir John Kennedy Medal
Established in 1927 in commemoration of the great services rendered in the field of engineering by Sir John Kennedy, a past president of the EIC; medal is awarded every two years by the council in recognition of outstanding merit in the profession or of noteworthy contributions to the science of engineering or to the benefit of the institute.

Engineers Canada / Ingénieurs Canada
#300, 55 Metcalfe St., Ottawa, ON K1P 6L9
613-232-2474; Fax: 613-230-5759; Toll-Free: 1-877-408-9273
Email: info@engineerscanada.ca; URL: engineerscanada.ca

Award for the Support of Women in the Engineering Profession
Recognizes engineers who, through their engineering and career achievements, have demonstrated noteworthy support for women in the profession and have established a benchmark of engineering excellence.

Gold Medal Award and Gold Medal Student Award
Awarded for exceptional individual achievement & distinction in a field of engineering.

Medal for Distinction in Engineering Education
Awarded for exemplary contribution to engineering teaching at a Canadian University.

Meritorious Service Awards
Two categories: Professional Service and Community Service.

National Award for an Engineering Project or Achievement
Awarded for outstanding engineering projects by a team in which Canadian engineers were part of.

Young Engineer Achievement Award
Awarded for outstanding contribution in a field of engineering by an engineer 36 years of age or younger.

Innovators & Entrepreneurs Foundation
#300, 56 Sparks St., Ottawa, ON K1P 5A9
URL: www.ief-fie.ca

Ernest C. Manning Innovation Awards
Given annually to Canadian innovators who have conceived & developed new concepts, procedures, processes or products of benefit to Canada; awards may be in any area of activity.
One $100,000 Principal Award; one $25,000 Award of Distinction; two $10,000 Innovation prizes; other awards are also presented.

Natural Sciences & Engineering Research Council of Canada / Conseil de recherches en sciences naturelles et en génie
350 Albert St., 16th Fl., Ottawa, ON K1A 1H5
613-995-5992; Fax: 613-992-5337; Toll Free: 1-855-275-2861
URL: www.nserc-crsng.gc.ca

Brockhouse Canada Prize for Interdisciplinary Research in Science and Engineering
Awarded annually to recognize Canadian interdisciplinary research teams who have combined their expertise to produce outstanding and highly significant achievements in the natural sciences and engineering; Achievement must have been made in the last six years.
Winning team receives the prize and a grant of up to $250,000.

E.W.R. Steacie Memorial Fellowships
Awarded to enhance the career development of outstanding & highly promising scientists & engineers who are staff members of Canadian universities; successful fellows are relieved of any teaching & administrative duties, enabling them to devote all their time & energy to research; up to six fellowships are awarded annually for a two-year period; fellowships are held at a Canadian university or affiliated research institution
Fellows receive a grant of $250,000 to be used over two years; $90,000 to be paid to the university by NSERC to cover the cost of replacing the Steacie Fellow's teaching & administrative responsibilities.

Gerhard Herzberg Gold Medal for Science & Engineering
NSERC's highest honour is awarded annually to an individual who has made outstanding & sustained contributions to Canadian research in natural sciences & engineering; the gold medal will be awarded for any activity of exceptional importance & impact that leads to the enhancement of the research enterprise in Canada.
The accomplishments for which the award is given must have been carried out in Canada & achieved over a substantial period of time; persons from any sector (academic, business & industry or government) are eligible; current members of council are not eligible; awardee's performance in relation to the cited achievement must demonstrate an unusually high degree of ability & the application of such qualities as expertise, creativity, imagination, leadership, perseverance & dedication.
Winner receives a medal and $1 million to use for personal university-based research or to direct in some related way, such as the establishment of scholarships or research Chairs in their name at Canadian universities; The monetary award is distributed over a five-year period.

John C. Polanyi Award
Awarded to an individual or team whose research has led to a recent outstanding advance in any NSERC-supported field of the natural sciences or engineering; The research leading to the advance must have been conducted in Canada and funded at least partially by an NSERC grant.
Winner(s) receive a grant of up to $250,000.

Science Promotion Awards
Awarded to honour individuals and groups that promote science to the general public in an inspiring way. Individuals receive $10,000 and groups receive $25,000 to further science promotion activities in Canada.

Synergy Awards for Innovation
Established 1995; Recognize partnerships in natural sciences and engineering research and development between post-secondary institutions and Canadian industry; Award amounts vary.

Prix Galien Canada
#2200, 1250, boul René-Lévesque ouest, Montreal, QC H3B 4W8
514-216-2513
Email: info@prix-galien-canada.com; URL: eng.prix-galien-canada.com

Prix Galien - Innovative Product Award
Awarded to a company that has developed & marketed a drug that has made the most significant contribution to the well-being of the Canadian general public, in terms of efficacy, safety & innovation.

Prix Galien - Research Awards
Awarded to a scientist who is known for their contribution to pharmaceutical research in Canada.

Québec Ministère de l'économie, de la Science et de l'Innovation
Secrétariat des Prix du Québec scientifiques
1150, Grande Allée ouest, Québec, QC G1S 4Y9
514-499-2199, poste 3895; Sans frais: 1-866-680-1884
Email: prixduquebec@economie.gouv.qc.ca; URL: www.prixduquebec.gouv.qc.ca

Prix Armand-Frappier
Décerné pour la création ou le développement d'institutions de recherche, ou pour l'administration et la promotion de recherche.

Prix Léon-Gérin
Accordée à une chercheuse ou un chercheur pour l'ensemble de sa carrière dans l'une des disciplines des sciences humaines et sociales.

Prix Lionel-Boulet
Décerné au une chercheuse ou un chercheur qui s'est distingué par ses inventions, ses innovations scientifiques et technologiques, son leadership dans le développement scientifique et sa contribution à la croissance économique du Québec.

Prix Marie-Andrée-Bertrand
Attribuée à une personne, pour l'ensemble de sa carrière, dont l'envergure et la qualité scientifique des recherches a mené au développement et à la mise en oeuvre d'innovations sociales d'importance conduisant au mieux-être des individus et des collectivités.

Prix Marie-Victorin
Décerné aux chercheurs de sciences exactes et naturelles, les sciences de l'ingénierie et technologiques ainsi que les sciences agricoles.

Prix Relève scientifique
Accordé à un chercheur québécois de 40 ans ou moins se distinguant par l'excellence de ses travaux et démontrant des aptitudes à établir et à maintenir des liens constructifs et durables avec les milieux de la recherche.

Prix Wilder-Penfield
Décerné aux scientifiques dont l'objet de recherche appartient au domaine biomédical.

Royal Astronomical Society of Canada / Société royale d'astronomie du Canada
#203, 4920 Dundas St. West, Toronto, ON M9A 1B7
416-924-7973; Toll Free: 1-888-924-7272
URL: www.rasc.ca

Chant Medal
Established 1940 in appreciation of the great work of the late Prof. C.A. Chant in furthering the interests of astronomy in Canada; silver medal is awarded no more than once a year to an amateur astronomer resident in Canada on the basis of the value of the work carried out in astronomy & closely allied fields of original investigation.

Ken Chilton Prize
Established 1977; plaque awarded annually to an amateur astronomer resident in Canada, in recognition of a significant piece of work carried out or published during the year.

The Plaskett Medal
Presented jointly with CASCA for an outstanding doctoral thesis.

Qilak Award / Prix Qilak
Awarded to recognize Canadian individuals or teams that have made an outstanding contribution to either the public understanding or the informal education of astronomy in Canada.

Simon Newcomb Award
Established 1978; trophy awarded annually for the best article on astronomy, astrophysics or space sciences submitted by a member of the society during the year.

The Royal Canadian Geographical Society / Société géographique royale du Canada
50 Sussex Dr., Ottawa, ON K1M 2K1
613-745-4629; Fax: 613-744-0947; Toll Free: 1-800-267-0824
Email: rcgs@rcgs.org; stieler@rcgs.org; URL: www.rcgs.org

Alex Trebek Medal for Geographic Literacy
Recognizes individuals go above and beyond expectations to heighten geographic literacy. Its name acknowledges the support Alex Trebek has given the Society.

Gold Medal
Established 1972; to recognize a particular achievement of one or more individuals in the field of geography, or a significant national or international event.

Innovation in Geography Teaching Award
Recognizes a Canadian K-12 teacher who is fosters geographic engagement and increases geographic literacy in their students.

Martin Bergmann Medal
Established 2012; Recognizes excellence in Arctic leadership and science.

Massey Medal
Established 1959; awarded annually for outstanding personal achievement in the exploration, development or description of the geography of Canada.

Sir Christopher Ondaatje Medal for Exploration
Established 2013; Recognizes singular achievements and the pursuit of excellence by an outstanding Canadian explorer or a non-Canadian for exploratory achievements within Canada.

The Royal Society of Canada / La Société royale du Canada
Walter House, 282 Somerset St. West, Ottawa, ON K2P 0J6
613-991-6990; Fax: 613-991-6996
Email: info@rsc-src.ca; URL: rsc-src.ca

Bancroft Award
Established 1968; awarded every two years for publication, instruction & research in the earth sciences that have conspicuously contributed to public understanding & appreciation of the subject.

The Flavelle Medal
Established 1924; awarded every two years (since 1966) for an outstanding contribution to biological science during the preceding 10 years or for significant additions to a previous outstanding contribution to biological science.

John L. Synge Award
Established 1986; awarded for outstanding research in any of the branches of mathematics; preference given to candidates under 40.

McLaughlin Medal
Awarded for important research of sustained excellence in any branch of medical sciences.

Miroslaw Romanowski Medal
Established in 1994 and awarded annually to honour significant contributions to the resolution of scientific aspects of environmental problems; award also includes an annual lecture series for the recipient; $3,000.

Rutherford Memorial Medals: Chemistry & Physics
Established 1980; awarded annually for outstanding research, one in chemistry, one in physics; preference given to candidates under 40.

Willet G. Miller Medal
Established 1943; awarded every two years for outstanding research in solid earth sciences and in ocean and atmospheric sciences.

Société Saint-Jean-Baptiste de Montréal
82, rue Sherbrooke ouest, Montréal, QC H2X 1X3
514-843-8851; Fax: 514-844-6369
Email: info@ssjb.com; URL: ssjb.com

Prix Léon-Lortie
Established 1987; awarded for achievement in the area of pure & applied sciences.

Youth Can Innovate
403-466-1348
Email: info@youthcaninnovate.ca; URL: youthcaninnovate.ca

Youth Can Innovate Awards
Sponsored by the Gwyn Morgan & Patricia Trottier Foundation; Recognize 16 projects selected by a team of judges at the annual Canada-Wide Science Fair; Projects are considered on the basis of ingenuity, originality, development and potential social and economic benefits.
Eight senior awards of $1,000, four of these winners are selected to win an additional $7,000; Four intermediate awards of $750; Four junior awards of $500.

SPORTS & RECREATION

Canadian Women and Sport / Femmes et sport au Canada
PO Box 98162, 970 Queen St. East, Toronto, ON M4M 1J0
416-901-0484
Email: info@womenandsport.ca; URL: womenandsport.ca

Women in Sport Encouragement (WISE) Fund
Jointly with Sport Canada; 30 grants annually, valued at $2,500 each awarded to organizations offering or creating opportunities and programming for girls and women in sport.

Canadian Curling Association / Association canadienne de curling
1660 Vimont Ct., Orleans, ON K4A 4J4
613-834-2076; Fax: 613-834-0716; Toll Free: 1-800-550-2875
Email: info@curling.ca; URL: www.curling.ca

Award of Achievement
Commemorative plaque presented in recognition of individuals who have contributed significantly to any aspect of Canadian curling operations.

Ray Kingsmith Award
Awarded to an individual who parallels the level of involvement & commitment exemplified by Ray Kingsmith.

Volunteer of the Year Award
Based on contributions from the previous curling season; national volunteer of the year receives an all-expense paid weekend trip to Tim Hortons Brier where they will be recognized during a playoff game.

Ontario Ministry of Heritage, Sport, Tourism and Culture Industries
438 University Ave., 6th Fl., Toronto, ON M5G 2K8
416-326-9326; Fax: 416-314-7854; Toll-Free: 888-997-9015
Email: internet.feedback.mtour@ontario.ca; URL: www.mtc.gov.on.ca/en/sport/sport/awards.shtml

Ontario Sports Awards
Awards for Athlete of the Year, Para-Athlete of the Year, System Design Excellence, and Leadership in Inclusive Participation.

Physical Health and Education Canada / Éducation physique et santé Canada
2451 Riverside Dr., Ottawa, ON K1H 7X7
613-523-1348; Fax: 613-523-1206; Toll Free: 1-800-663-8708
Email:info@phecanada.ca; URL: phecanada.ca

Dr. Andy Anderson Young Professional Award
Presented annually to one professional age 35 or younger per provincial association that best epitomizes exemplary work on behalf of the physical and health education profession.

Health Promoting Schools Champion Award
Presented once per conference cycle to an individual, group, or organization for their exemplary contribution to the development, promotion, and implementation of Healthy School Communities.

National Award for Teaching Excellence in Health Education
Presented to up to three recipients per conference cycle; Awarded to outstanding Canadian teachers for their work in furthering health education in Canada and who have an exceptional ability to motivate students to participate in a healthy, active lifestyle.

National Award for Teaching Excellence in Physical Education
Presented to up to three recipients per conference cycle; Awarded to outstanding Canadian teachers who have an exceptional ability to motivate students to participate in a lifetime of physical activity, and who further Physical Education in Canada.

North American Society (NAS) Award
Established 1999; Awarded to outstanding professionals within the allied professions of physical and health education, recreation and sport in North America.

PHE Canada Student Award
Awarded to an undergraduate student who exemplifies outstanding leadership in the field of physical and health education or a related discipline.

R. Tait McKenzie Award of Honour
Instituted at the Montreal Convention in 1948, this is the most prestigious award offered; named after the distinguished Canadian physician, sculptor & physical educator Dr. Robert Tait McKenzie; candidate shall have performed distinguished, meritorious service as a recognized leader regionally & nationally in their field.

Société Saint-Jean-Baptiste de Montréal
82, rue Sherbrooke ouest, Montréal, QC H2X 1X3

514-843-8851; Fax: 514-844-6369
Email: info@ssjb.com; URL: ssjb.com

Prix Maurice-Richard
Established 1979; Awarded annually to a French Canadian in recognition of outstanding achievement in sports & athletics in serving the higher interests of the French Canadian people.

Swimming/Natation Canada
307 Gilmour St., Ottawa, ON K2P 0P7
613-260-1348; Fax: 613-260-0804
Email: natloffice@swimming.ca; URL: www.swimming.ca

National Awards
Presented annually in the following categories: Swimmer of the Year (male & female), Coach of the Year, Para-swimmer of the Year (male & female), Para-coach of the Year (male swimmer & female swimmer), Open Water Swimmer of the Year, Open Water Coach of the Year, President's Award, Volunteer Contribution Award, Volunteer of the Year.

Victor Davis Memorial Award
Annual awards from the Victor Davis Memorial Fund assist young Canadian swimmers to continue their training, education & pursuit of excellence at the international level of competition; recipients are determined by the Victor Davis Memorial Fund Awards Committee.

Canadian Honours System

For some years after Confederation, awards were made of a few hereditary honours and some knighthoods and companionships in orders of chivalry, and this policy continued until the end of the First World War.

From 1919 until 1933 no titular honours were granted. There was a brief revival of the defunct honours policy during the Conservative administration of R.B. Bennett, and several distinctions were awarded from 1934 to 1935, but the prohibition was reinstated with the return of the Liberals to office in 1935. Consequently, at the outset of the Second World War, Canadians in the armed services were not entitled to receive awards in the order of chivalry for which other Commonwealth personnel were eligible. A parliamentary committee appointed in 1943 recommended that the ban on nontitular honours be lifted, clearing the way for members of the military and civilians to receive recognition for wartime services.

The hundredth anniversary of Confederation, July 1st, 1967, was the occasion on which the Order of Canada was created as the first component of a distinctly Canadian honours system. More information concerning Orders, Decorations and Medals (as well as various Governor General's awards) may be obtained by writing to: Public Information Directorate, Government House, 1 Sussex Dr., Ottawa ON K1A 0A1.

HERALDRY
Coats-of-arms, flags, badges and other heraldic devices are marks of honour and symbols of identity, authority and, in some cases, sovereignty. Each is granted by the Crown under an exercise of the Sovereign's prerogative to create heraldic honours.

Until June 4, 1988, Canadian corporations and individuals wishing to bear lawful arms petitioned the Sovereign's traditional heraldic officers in London and Edinburgh. On that date, by Royal Letters Patent, the Queen transferred the exercise of her heraldic prerogative, as Queen of Canada, to the Governor General who now heads a new office, the Canadian Heraldic Authority. With the act, heraldry, which has a long history in Canada, has been fully repatriated.

These vice-regal responsibilities are administered by Canadian officers of arms appointed by commission under the Governor General's privy seal: the Herald Chancellor (the Secretary to the Governor General), the Deputy Herald Chancellor (the Deputy Secretary, Chancellery) and the Chief Herald of Canada (Director, Heraldry). He is assisted by three officers of arms: Saint-Laurent, Athabaska, and Fraser heralds, and one officer of arms extraordinary, Dauphin Herald.

New heraldic emblems are granted, and existing ones registered, by the Chief Herald upon receipt of an enabling Warrant from the Herald Chancellor or the Deputy Herald Chancellor acting on behalf of the Governor General. Grants and registrations are made by Letters Patent, documents that set out the Governor General's heraldic responsibilities, describe the emblem granted, and feature a representation of the Governor General's personal arms. To ensure a lasting record, the newly granted and registered emblems are entered in Canada's national armorial, the Public Register of Arms, Flags and Badges of Canada. Since the Authority was created, hundreds of petitions have been received from every part of the country, most for new grants of arms.

Canadian Honours List

ORDER OF CANADA
As mentioned above, the Order of Canada was created July 1, 1967. Her Majesty The Queen is Sovereign of the Order of Canada and the Governor General is, by virtue of that office, Chancellor and Principal Companion. He/She is assisted in the administration of the Order by an Advisory Council which comprises of:
a) the Chief Justice of Canada (Chair)
b) the Clerk of the Privy Council
c) the Deputy Minister, Canadian Heritage
d) the Chair of the Canada Council
e) the President of the Royal Society of Canada
f) the Chair of the Board of the Association of Universities and Colleges of Canada
g) not more than five other members, when considered appropriate by the Governor General, can be appointed for three-year terms.
The Secretary to the Governor General is, by his/her office, Secretary General of the Order.

The Order of Canada is designed to honour Canadian citizens for outstanding achievement and service to the country or to humanity at large and also for distinguished service in particular localities and fields of activity. The Order comprises three levels of membership: Companion, Officer, and Member. Up to 15 Companions may be appointed annually, but the total number of living Companions may not exceed 165. Up to 64 Officers and 136 Members may be appointed annually with no over-all limit.

The Order includes no titles of honour and confers no special privileges, hereditary or otherwise. Awards are made solely on the basis of merit. Members of the Order are entitled to place after their names the letters "C.C." for Companions, "O.C." for Officers, and "C.M." for Members.

Any person or organization may make nominations for appointment to the Order by writing to the Chancellery, Rideau Hall, Ottawa. The Advisory Council submits to the Governor General lists of those nominees who, in the opinion of the Council, are of greatest merit. Appointments to the Order are made by the Sovereign of the Order on the recommendation of the Governor General as Chancellor of the Order, under an instrument sealed with the Seal of the Order.

Non-Canadians whom the Government desires to honour may be accorded honorary membership in the Order.

**Companions of the Order of Canada/
Compagnons de l'Ordre du Canada (C.C.)
(Appointed December 30, 2020)**
Robert Daniel Steadward, C.C., A.O.E., Edmonton, Alta.

(Invested December 16, 2020)
Geoffrey E. Hinton, C.C., Toronto, Ont.

(Appointed November 27, 2020)
Howard Alper, C.C., Ottawa, Ont.
*This is a promotion within the Order
The Honourable Monique Bégin, P.C., C.C., Ottawa, Ont.
*This is a promotion within the Order
Janette Bertrand, C.C., C.Q., Montréal, Que.
*This is a promotion within the Order
Denise Filiatrault, C.C., O.Q., Montréal, Quebec
*This is a promotion within the Order
Tom Jackson, C.C., Calgary, Alta.
*This is a promotion within the Order
Thomas King, C.C., Guelph, Ont.
*This is a promotion within the Order
Phillip James Edwin Peebles, C.C., O.M., Winnipeg, Man., and Princeton, N.J., U.S.A.
Mark Roger Tewksbury, C.C., M.S.M., Calgary, Alta.

**Officers of the Order of Canada/
Officiers de l'Ordre du Canada (O.C.)
(Invested March 29, 2021)**
Joan May Hollobon, O.C., Toronto, Ont.

(Invested March 19, 2021)
Paul Cronin Weiler, O.C., Vancouver, B.C. and Cambridge, Mass., U.S.A

(Invested March 12, 2021)
The Honourable Daniel Hays, P.C., O.C., C.D., Calgary, Alta. and Ottawa, Ont.

(Invested March 5, 2021)
Josef Svoboda, O.C., Toronto, Ont. and Baker Lake, Nunavut

(Invested February 26, 2021)
The Honourable William Alexander Blaikie, P.C., O.C., Winnipeg, Man.

(Appointed December 30, 2020)
John Borrows, O.C., Victoria, B.C.
Helen M. Burt, O.C., Vancouver, B.C.
John Challis, O.C., West Vancouver, B.C.
Elizabeth A. Edwards, O.C., Toronto, Ont.
Peter E. Gilgan, O.C., O.Ont., Toronto, Ont.
J. Edward Johnson, O.C., Montréal, Que.
Daniel Heath Justice, O.C., Halfmoon Bay, B.C.
Vivian McAlister, O.C., London, Ont.
Antony David John Penikett, O.C., Vancouver, B.C.
The Honourable Lynn Smith, O.C., Q.C., Vancouver, B.C.
Daniel John Taylor, O.C., Toronto, Ont.
Yanick Villedieu, O.C., C.Q., Saint-Antoine-de-Tilly, Que.
Lori Jeanne West, O.C., Edmonton, Alta.

(Invested December 16, 2020)
Lorna Wanósts'a7 Williams, O.C., O.B.C., Victoria, B.C.

(Appointed November 27, 2020)
Alice Benjamin, O.C., C.Q., Montréal, Que.
Philip Benjamin Berger, O.C., O.Ont., Toronto, Ont.
Martha Gertrude Muriel Billes, O.C., Calgary, Alta.
The Honourable William Alexander Blaikie, P.C., O.C., Winnipeg, Man.
Jeffery Dahn, O.C., Halifax, N.S.
Jan den Oudsten, O.C., Toronto, Ont.
The Honourable William C. Graham, P.C., O.C., Q.C., Toronto, Ont.
Sandra Kirby, O.C., Winnipeg, Man.
Marcia Vaune Jocelyn Kran, O.C., West Vancouver, B.C.
Eugenia Kumacheva, O.C., Toronto, Ont.
Linda Jane Leith, O.C., Westmount, Que.
Sheldon Levy, O.C., Toronto, Ont.
Claude Meunier, O.C., Montréal, Que.
John E. Peller, O.C., Grimsby, Ont.
The Honourable François Rolland, O.C., Montréal, Que.
Guy Rouleau, O.C., O.Q., Montréal, Que.
John David Runnalls, O.C., Ottawa, Ont.
Sara Seager, O.C., Toronto, Ont. and Concord, Mass., U.S.A.
Elder Doreen Spence, O.C., Calgary, Alta.
Marc Tessier-Lavigne, O.C., Trenton, Ont. and Stanford, Calif., U.S.A.
Yosef Wosk, O.C., O.B.C., Vancouver, B.C.

Members of the Order of Canada/
Membres de l'Ordre du Canada (C.M.)
(Invested May 21, 2021)
Charles Roy Guest, C.M., Calgary, Alta.

(Invested April 8, 2021)
Brigadier-General the Honourable John James Grant, C.M., C.M.M., O.N.S., C.D. (Ret'd), Halifax, N.S.

(Invested March 19, 2021)
Mathew Baldwin, C.M., Edmonton, Alta.

(Invested March 12, 2021)
Robert Dick Richmond, C.M., Toronto, Ont.

(Invested February 5, 2021)
Philip Michael Epstein, C.M., O.Ont., Q.C., Toronto, Ont.

(Appointed December 30, 2020)
Mary S. Aitken, C.M., Toronto, Ont.
Yaprak Baltacioglu, C.M., Ottawa, Ont.
Arthur Frank-Art Bergmann, C.M., Rocky View County, Alta.
Guy Berthiaume, C.M., Laval, Que.
Myer Bick, C.M., Côte Saint-Luc, Que.
Carolle Brabant, C.M., Montréal, Que.
Michael S. W. Bradstreet, C.M., Vittoria, Ont.
John W. Brink, C.M., Edmonton, Alta.
Barbara Elizabeth Butler, C.M., Mahone Bay, N.S.
James Casey, C.M., M.S.M., Charlottetown, P.E.I.
Brian Cherney, C.M., Montréal, Que.
Gina Parvaneh Cody, C.M., North York, Ont.
David Cooper, C.M., Vancouver, B.C.
Michel Cusson, C.M., Montréal, Que.
Rita Davies, C.M., Toronto, Ont.
Serge Demers, C.M., Lac-des-Aigles, Que.
Stanley Louis Dragland, C.M., St. John's, Nfld.
L. David Dubé, C.M., Saskatoon, Sask.
Jacalyn Duffin, C.M., Kingston, Ont.
John Grigsby Geiger, C.M., Toronto, Ont.
Susan R. George Bahl, C.M., Toronto, Ont.
Vivek Goel, C.M., Toronto, Ont.
Gary Gullickson, C.M., Saskatoon, Sask.
John Hartman, C.M., Lafontaine, Ont.
Father James Lassiter Holland, C.M., A.O.E., Edmonton, Alta.
Sally Horsfall Eaton, C.M., C.D., Toronto, Ont.
Raymond Ivany, C.M., O.N.S., Wolfville, N.S.
Michael A. S. Jewett, C.M., Toronto, Ont.

Elder Carolyn King, C.M., Mississaugas of the Credit First Nation, Ont.
Robert Krell, C.M., Vancouver, B.C.
Susan Keiko Langdon, C.M., Toronto, Ont.
Larry J. Macdonald, C.M., Okotoks, Alta.
The Honourable Louise Mailhot, C.M., O.Q., Montréal, Que.
Marilyn McHarg, C.M., O.Ont., Dundas, Ont.
Cheryl Lisa Meeches, C.M., O.M., Long Plain First Nation, Man.
Andrew T. Molson, C.M., Montréal, Que.
Geoffrey Molson, C.M., C.Q., Montréal, Que.
Morris Moscovitch, C.M., Toronto, Ont.
Ginette Noiseux, C.M., Montréal, Que.
Leonard Pennachetti, C.M., Beamsville, Ont.
Lloyd R. Posno, C.M., Mississauga, Ont.
Heather Ross, C.M., Toronto, Ont.
Terry Salman, C.M., West Vancouver, B.C.
Brian Segal, C.M., Toronto, Ont.
Douglas R. Stollery, C.M., Q.C., Edmonton, Alta.
Frances Westley, C.M., New Hamburg, Ont.
Frances Elizabeth Wright, C.M., A.O.E., Calgary, Alta.

(Invested December 16, 2020)
Renaldo Battista, C.M., Montréal, Que.
Omer Chouinard, C.M., Moncton, N.B.
Julie Macfarlane, C.M., Windsor, Ont.
The Honourable Donald H. Oliver, C.M., Q.C., Halifax, N.S. and Ottawa, Ont.

(Appointed November 27, 2020)
Ella Yoelli Amir, C.M., Montréal, Que.
Cristina Amon, C.M., Toronto, Ont.
Ronald Duncan Barr, C.M., Hamilton, Ont.
Christian Barthomeuf, C.M., Frelighsburg, Que.
Chief Darcy Bear, C.M., S.O.M., Whitecap Dakota First Nation, Sask.
B. Lynn Beattie, C.M., Vancouver, B.C.
Yves Beauchamp, C.M., C.Q., Varennes, Que.
Izak Benbasat, C.M., Vancouver, B.C.
Daniel R. Bereskin, C.M., Q.C., Toronto, Ont.
Judy Birdsell, C.M., Calgary, Alta.
Max Blouw, C.M., Victoria, B.C.
Allan Borodin, C.M., Toronto, Ont.
George Brookman, C.M., Calgary, Alta.
Alain Chartrand, C.M., C.Q., Montréal, Que.
Robert Anthony Clark, C.M., Vancouver, B.C.
Ronald Ivan Cohen, C.M., M.B.E., Manotick, Ont.
Liliane Colpron, C.M., Montréal, Que.
Joseph Michael Connors, C.M., Victoria, B.C.
Jean Marc Dalpé, C.M., Montréal, Que.
B. Denham Jolly, C.M., Toronto, Ont.
Sandra Djwa, C.M., Vancouver, B.C.
Michel Doucet, C.M., O.N.B., Q.C., Dieppe, N.B.
James M. Drake, C.M., Toronto, Ont.
Roger Dubois, C.M., Drummondville, Que.
Donald Gordon Duguid, C.M., O.M., Winnipeg, Man.
Hoda ElMaraghy, C.M., O.Ont., Windsor, Ont.
Philip Michael Epstein, C.M., O.Ont., Q.C., Toronto, Ont.
John S. Eyking, C.M., Millville, N.S.
William Fast, C.M., Winnipeg, Man.
Edward Finn, C.M., Ottawa, Ont.
Jackie Flanagan, C.M., Calgary, Alta.
William John Fox, C.M., Toronto, Ont.
The Honourable Joan Fraser, C.M., Montréal, Que.
Timothy Frick, C.M., O.B.C., Pender Island, B.C.
Ross William Glen, C.M., Calgary, Alta.
Robert Godin, C.M., Vaudreuil-sur-le-Lac, Que.
Priscilla Edson Greenwood, C.M., Vancouver, B.C.
David Grimes, C.M., Ottawa, Ont.
Charles Roy Guest, C.M., Calgary, Alta.
Stanley Hamilton, C.M., O.B.C., Vancouver, B.C.
Anthony Olmsted Hendrie, C.M., Nottawa, Ont.
Carol Pearl Herbert, C.M., Vancouver, B.C.
Gordon Hicks, C.M., Uxbridge, Ont.
Jagmohan Humar, C.M., Ottawa, Ont.
Peter Daniel Alexander Jacobs, C.M., Westmount, Que.
The Honourable Janis Guðrún Johnson, C.M., Winnipeg, Man.
Maria Labrecque-Duchesneau, C.M., C.Q., Marieville, Que.
John R. Lacey, C.M., Calgary, Alta.
Elizabeth Langley, C.M., Montréal, Que.
Gérard Raymond Le Chêne, C.M., C.Q., Outremont, Que.
Michele Leering, C.M., Kingston, Ont.
Jacques Légaré, C.M., Montréal, Que.
Elliot Lifson, C.M., Côte Saint-Luc, Que.
William Macdonald, C.M., Toronto, Ont.
Judy Matthews, C.M., Toronto, Ont.
Harvey Andrew McCue (Waubageshig), C.M., Ottawa, Ont.
Brian McFarlane, C.M., Stouffville, Ont.
Lucy Lynn McIntyre, C.M., Calgary, Alta.
John H. McNeill, C.M., Vancouver, B.C.

Sarah Milroy, C.M., Toronto, Ont.
Scott Moir, C.M., Ilderton, Ont.
Menka Nagrani, C.M., Montréal, Que.
Jacques Nantel, C.M., Saint-Placide, Que.
Peggy Nash, C.M., Toronto, Ont.
Glenn O'Farrell, C.M., Toronto, Ont.
Marietta Orlov, C.M. *(deceased)*, Toronto, Ont.
Marc Parent, C.M., Saint-Laurent, Que.
Serge Payette, C.M., C.Q., Saint-Jean-de-l'Île-d'Orléans, Que.
Christina Petrowska Quilico, C.M., Toronto, Ont.
Crystal Pite, C.M., Vancouver, B.C.
Anthony Robin Poole, C.M., South Lancaster, Ont.
Brian Postl, C.M., O.M., Winnipeg, Man.
Tom Radford, C.M., Edmonton, Alta.
The Honourable Allan Michael Rock, P.C., C.M., O.Ont., Q.C., Ottawa, Ont.
Lorio Roy, C.M., Saint-Laurent Nord, N.B.
Vera Schiff, C.M., Toronto, Ont.
Stefan Glenn Sigurdson, C.M., Q.C., West Vancouver, B.C.
Alfred E. Slinkard, C.M., Saskatoon, Sask.
This is an honorary appointment
Lara St. John, C.M., London, Ont. and New York, N.Y. U.S.A.
Dave William Thomas, C.M., St. Catharines, Ont. and Oak Park, Calif., U.S.A.
Tessa Virtue, C.M., London, Ont.
Peter Warrian, C.M., Toronto, Ont.
David P. Wilkinson, C.M., Vancouver, B.C.
Kenneth L. Wilson, C.M., Halifax, N.S.
Roger Wong, C.M., Vancouver, B.C.

ORDER OF MILITARY MERIT
The Order of Military Merit was created on July 1, 1972 to recognize meritorious service and devotion to duty by members of the Canadian Forces. The Order has three grades of membership: Commander (C.M.M.), Officer (O.M.M.) and Member (M.M.M.). The annual number of appointments is limited to one-tenth of one percent of the number of persons in the Canadian Forces in the preceding year.

Commanders of the Order of Military Merit/
Commandeurs de l'Ordre du mérite militaire (C.M.M.)
(Invested July 3, 2019)
Major-General Carl Jean Turenne, C.M.M., M.S.C., C.D., Deputy Commander, Canadian Army, Ottawa, Ont.

(Invested May 27, 2019)
Major-General Frances Jennifer Allen, C.M.M., C.D., Deputy Vice Chief of the Defence Staff, Ottawa, Ont.
This is a promotion within the Order
Rear-Admiral Arthur Gerard McDonald, C.M.M., M.S.M., C.D., Deputy Commander, Royal Canadian Navy, Ottawa, Ont.

(Invested November 6, 2018)
Major General Omer Henry Lavoie, C.M.M., M.S.C., C.D., Commander, 1st Canadian Division Headquarters, Kingston, Ont.

Officers of the the Order of Military Merit/
Officiers de l'Ordre du mérite militaire (O.M.M.)
(Invested July 3, 2019)
Commodore Geneviève Bernatchez, O.M.M., C.D., Judge Advocate General, Ottawa, Ont.
Colonel Joseph Raoul Stéphane Boivin, O.M.M., M.S.C., C.D., 5 Canadian Mechanized Brigade Group Headquarters and Signal Squadron, Courcelette, Que.
Brigadier-General Marie Hélène Lise Bourgon, O.M.M., M.S.C., C.D., Strategic Joint Staff, Ottawa, Ont.
Lieutenant-Colonel Catherine Jocelyne Marchetti, O.M.M., C.D., Office of the Chief Force Development, Ottawa, Ont.
Lieutenant-Colonel Kristopher Robert Purdy, O.M.M., C.D., Canadian Joint Operations Command, Ottawa, Ont.
Colonel Roger Leigh Scott, O.M.M., C.D., Canadian Forces Health Services Group Headquarters, Ottawa, Ont.
Lieutenant-Colonel Eleanor Frances Taylor, O.M.M., M.S.M., C.D., 5th Canadian Division Headquarters, Halifax, N.S.

(Invested May 27, 2019)
Brigadier-General Andrew Michael Downes, O.M.M., C.D., Surgeon General, Ottawa, Ont.
Captain(N) Michael Andrew Hopper, O.M.M., C.D., Her Majesty's Canadian Ship *Carleton*, Ottawa, Ont.
Colonel Iain Stewart Huddleston, O.M.M., C.D., 1 Canadian Air Division Headquarters, Winnipeg, Man.
Brigadier-General Stephen Richardson Kelsey, O.M.M., C.D., Canadian Army Headquarters, Ottawa, Ont.
Colonel Conrad Joseph John Mialkowski, O.M.M., M.S.C., C.D., 2 Canadian Mechanized Brigade Group Headquarters and Signal Squadron, Petawawa, Ont.
Lieutenant-Colonel Kevin Reinhold Morton, O.M.M., M.S.M., C.D., Canadian Special Operations Forces Command, Ottawa, Ont.

Commodore Angus Ian Topshee, O.M.M., M.S.M., C.D., Office of the Deputy Commander North American Aerospace Defense Command, Colorado Springs, CO, U.S.A.

(Invested November 6, 2018)
Lieutenant-Colonel Claire Katherine Bramma, O.M.M., C.D., Mapping and Charting Establishment, Ottawa, Ont.

Brigadier-General Joseph Jean Guy Chapdelaine, O.M.M., C.D., Q.H.C., General Chaplain, Ottawa, Ont.

Lieutenant-Colonel Ryan Glen Deming, O.M.M., C.D., Office of the Chief of the Air Force Staff, Ottawa, Ont.

Colonel Robert Bernard Dundon, O.M.M., C.D., Office of the Director General, Land Equipment Program Management, Ottawa, Ont.

Major Trevor Jain, O.M.M., M.S.M., C.D., 33 Field Ambulance (Halifax), Halifax, N.S.

Captain(N) Marie-France Langlois, O.M.M., C.D., Director, Casualty Support Management, Ottawa, Ont.

Colonel Joseph Bernard Christian Mercier, O.M.M., M.S.M., C.D., 34 Canadian Brigade Group Headquarters, Montréal, Que.

Major Richard Andrew Havelock Nicholson, O.M.M., C.D., The Royal Regiment of Canadian Artillery School, Oromocto, N.B.

Captain(N) Rebecca Louise Patterson, O.M.M., M.S.M., C.D., Canadian Forces Health Services Group Headquarters, Ottawa, Ont.

Colonel Robert Tennant Ritchie, O.M.M., M.S.M., C.D., Canadian Joint Operations Command Headquarters, Ottawa, Ont.

Colonel Josée Diane Marie Robidoux, O.M.M., C.D., 35 Canadian Brigade Group Headquarters, Québec, Que.

Captain(N) Christopher Allan Robinson, O.M.M., C.D., Office of the Director General, Naval Force Development, Ottawa, Ont.

Lieutenant-Colonel Dallas Jay West, O.M.M., C.D., Regional Cadet Support Unit (Northwest), Winnipeg, Man.

Captain(N) Douglas Michael Charles Young, O.M.M., M.S.M., C.D., Maritime Forces Pacific, Joint Task Force Pacific Headquarters, Victoria, B.C.

Members of the Order of Military Merit/
Membres de l'Ordre du mérite militaire (M.M.M.)
(Invested July 3, 2019)
Warrant Officer Charles Barton Ansell, M.M.M., C.D., Royal Military College of Canada, Kingston, Ont.

Warrant Officer Jason Eric Armstrong, M.M.M., C.D., 2 Service Battalion, Petawawa, Ont.

Master Warrant Officer James Matthew Aucoin, M.M.M., C.D., The Royal Regiment of Canadian Artillery School, Oromocto, N.B.

Master Warrant Officer Dean Stanley Burgher, M.M.M., C.D., Real Property Operations Unit (Atlantic), Halifax, N.S.

Chief Petty Officer 1st Class Daniel Eugene Campbell, M.M.M., C.D., Canadian Forces Base Halifax, Halifax, N.S.

Master Warrant Officer Patrick Joseph Noël Crépeau, M.M.M., C.D., 5e Régiment d'artillerie légère du Canada, Courcelette, Que.

Master Warrant Officer Joseph Olivier Richard Descheneaux, M.M.M., C.D., 5 Combat Engineer Regiment, Courcelette, Que.

Warrant Officer Joseph Daniel Steve Desgagné, M.M.M., M.B., C.D., 3rd Battalion, The Royal Canadian Regiment, Petawawa, Ont.

Chief Warrant Officer Joseph Jacques Friolet, M.M.M., M.S.M., C.D., 403 Helicopter Operational Training Squadron, Oromocto, N.B.

Master Warrant Officer Maryse Yolande Nancy Guay, M.M.M., C.D., 35 Canadian Brigade Group Headquarters, Québec, Que.

Chief Warrant Officer Robert Hains, M.M.M., C.D., 2nd Canadian Division Training Centre, Courcelette, Que.

Ranger Linda Marie Kamenawatamin, M.M.M., Bearskin Lake Canadian Ranger Patrol, Bearskin Lake, Ont.

Sergeant Marie-Élaine Michèle Labrèche, M.M.M., C.D., 2nd Canadian Division Headquarters, Montréal, Que.

Petty Officer 1st Class Natasha Tanya Lea Leavitt, M.M.M., C.D., Her Majesty's Canadian Ship Montréal, Halifax, N.S.

Warrant Officer Angel Margaret MacEachern, M.M.M., M.B., C.D., Combat Training Centre Headquarters, Oromocto, N.B.

Chief Warrant Officer David Francis McNeil, M.M.M., C.D., 4th Canadian Division Headquarters, Toronto, Ont.

Petty Officer 2nd Class Pier-Vincent Michaud, M.M.M., M.M.V., C.D., Canadian Special Operations Forces Command, Ottawa, Ont.

Chief Petty Officer 2nd Class John Dwayne Oake, M.M.M., C.D., Canadian Fleet Atlantic Headquarters, Halifax, N.S.

Warrant Officer Suzie Marie Paquin, M.M.M., C.D., 5 Service Battalion, Courcelette, Que.

Chief Warrant Officer Richard Plante, M.M.M., C.D., Canadian Special Operations Forces Command, Ottawa, Ont.

Master Warrant Officer Daniel Robichaud, M.M.M., C.D., 2nd Regiment, Royal Canadian Horse Artillery, Petawawa, Ont.

Chief Petty Officer 1st Class Stanley Jerome Ryan, M.M.M., C.D., Her Majesty's Canadian Ship Montréal, Halifax, N.S.

Warrant Officer Pierre Hugo St-Laurent, M.M.M., C.D., 19 Wing Comox, Lazo, B.C.

Major Timothy Morgan Utton, M.M.M., C.D., Canadian Forces National Counter-Intelligence Unit, Ottawa, Ont.

Master Warrant Officer Ruel Delroy Walker, M.M.M., C.D., 1 Canadian Air Division Headquarters, Winnipeg, Man.

Warrant Officer Casey Todd Welbourn, M.M.M., C.D., 5 Canadian Division Support Base Detachment Aldershot, Aldershot, N.S.

Lieutenant-Commander Kelly Lynne Williamson, M.M.M., C.D., 5th Canadian Division Headquarters, Halifax, N.S.

(Invested May 27, 2019)
Chief Warrant Officer Bruce Edward Ball, M.M.M., C.D., Canadian Special Operations Forces Command, Ottawa, Ont.

Captain Guy Michel Bériau, M.M.M., C.D., Tactics School, oromocto, N.B.

Master Warrant Officer Cordell James Herman Boland, M.M.M., C.D., Lord Strathcona's Horse (Royal Canadians), Edmonton, Alta.

Chief Warrant Officer Jean Gérard Éric Bouffard, M.M.M., C.D., Office of the Chief Force Development, Ottawa, Ont.

Warrant Officer Geoffrey Howard Chin, M.M.M., C.D., 3rd Canadian Division Training Centre, Denwood, Alta.

Captain Blair Ainlie Christie, M.M.M., C.D., Canadian Forces Joint Signal Regiment, Ottawa, Ont.

Master Corporal Mohammed Dibaei-Irani, M.M.M., M.S.M., C.D., Canadian Special Operations Forces Command, Ottawa, Ont.

Sergeant Dustin Gerald Donovan, M.M.M., C.D., 19 Wing Comox, Lazo, B.C.

Master Warrant Officer Robert Allen Englehart, M.M.M., C.D., Lord Strathcona's Horse (Royal Canadians), Edmonton, Alta.

Warrant Officer Charles William Howieson Graham, M.M.M., C.D., Integrated Personnel Support Centre Detachment London, London, Ont.

Sergeant Helen Ruth Hawes, M.M.M., C.D., Canadian Forces School of Communications and Electronics, Kingston, Ont.

Petty Officer 1st Class Leanne Marjorie Hebert, M.M.M., C.D., Her Majesty's Canadian Ship Halifax, Halifax, N.S.

Warrant Officer Christopher Baird Hennebery, M.M.M., C.D., The Royal Westminster Regiment, New Westminster, B.C.

Sergeant Gordon Joseph Hynes, M.M.M., C.D., 424 Transport and Rescue Squadron, Astra, Ont.

Chief Petty Officer 1st Class Joseph François Jean-Claude Sylvain Jaquemot, M.M.M., C.D., Her Majestys Canadian Ship Winnipeg, Victoria, B.C.

Sergeant Andréanne Lise Micheline Joly, M.M.M., C.D., 2nd Battalion, Princess Patricia's Canadian Light Infantry, Shilo, Man.

Chief Petty Officer 2nd Class Chesley Wayne Keeping, M.M.M., C.D., Her Majesty's Canadian Ship Montréal, Halifax, N.S.

Chief Warrant Officer Joseph Roger Dominic Lapointe, M.M.M., C.D., Canadian Forces School of Military Engineering, Oromocto, N.B.

Major Slade Gestur John Lerch, M.M.M., C.D., 3rd Battalion, Princess Patricia's Canadian Light Infantry, Edmonton, Alta.

Sergeant Caroline Marie Linteau, M.M.M., C.D., Joint Personnel Support Unit Detachment Gagetown, Oromocto, N.B.

Master Warrant Officer Jerome Patrick MacMullin, M.M.M., C.D., Joint Personnel Support Unit Detachment Gagetown, Oromocto, N.B.

Master Warrant Officer Duane Lewis May, M.M.M., C.D., 19 Air Maintenance Squadron, Lazo, B.C.

Warrant Officer James Richard McCarron, M.M.M., C.D., Canadian Joint Operations Command Headquarters, Ottawa, Ont.

Sergeant Timothy Charles McLean, M.M.M., C.D., 22 Wing Headquarters, North Bay, Hornell Heights, Ont.

Chief Petty Officer 1st Class Dana Bernice McLellan, M.M.M., C.D., TRINITY, Maritime Operations Support and Intelligence Centre, Halifax, N.S.

Master Warrant Officer David Basil Myers, M.M.M., C.D., 2 Air Movements Squadron, Astra, Ont.

Master Warrant Officer Sarah Ann Powers, M.M.M., C.D., 2 Service Battalion, Petawawa, Ont.

Ranger Ronald Glenn Scott, M.M.M., Snow Lake Canadian Ranger Patrol, Snow Lake, Man.

Master Warrant Officer Martin Sylvestre, M.M.M., C.D., 19 Wing Headquarters, Comox, Lazo, B.C.

Chief Warrant Officer Micheal Brian Talty, M.M.M., C.D., 41 Canadian Brigade Group Headquarters, Calgary, Alta.

Master Warrant Officer Chester William Tingley, M.M.M., C.D., The Royal Canadian Dragoons, Petawawa, Ont.

Chief Petty Officer 2nd Class Joseph André Steve Turgeon, M.M.M., C.D., Her Majesty's Canadian Ship Montréal, Halifax, N.S.

(Invested November 6, 2018)
Ranger Cyril Abbott, M.M.M., C.D., 5th Canadian Ranger Patrol Group, Gander, N.L.

Chief Petty Officer 2nd Class André Lionel Aubry, M.M.M., M.B., C.D., Fleet Maintenance Facility Cape Breton, Victoria, B.C.

Warrant Officer Sean Eldon Benedict, M.M.M., C.D., 3rd Battalion, The Royal Canadian Regiment, Petawawa, Ont.

Chief Petty Officer 1st Class Marc Thomas Bertrand, M.M.M., C.D., Office of the Director General, Compensation and Benefits, Ottawa, Ont.

Lieutenant(N) Randall Milton Binnie, M.M.M., C.D., Canadian Defence Liaison Staff (Washington), Washington, D.C., U.S.A.

Warrant Officer Aaron David Bygrove, M.M.M., M.S.M., C.D., 424 Transport and Rescue Squadron (Trenton), Astra, Ont.

Chief Warrant Officer Claude Rodney Cromwell, M.M.M., C.D., Office of the Director General, Materiel Systems and Supply Chain, Ottawa, Ont.

Chief Petty Officer 1st Class Robert Raymond DeProy, M.M.M., M.B., C.D., Fleet Diving Unit (Pacific), Victoria, B.C.

Warrant Officer Christopher Lee Desjardins, M.M.M., C.D., 2nd Battalion, Princess Patricia's Canadian Light Infantry, Shilo, Man.

Sergeant Michel Doyon, M.M.M., C.D., 400 Tactical Helicopter Squadron, Borden, Ont.

Chief Warrant Officer Desmond Michael Flood, M.M.M., C.D., 407 Long Range Patrol Squadron (Comox), Lazo, B.C.

Warrant Officer Lorilee Ann Flowers, M.M.M., C.D., Combat Training Centre Headquarters, Oromocto, N.B.

Warrant Officer Jason Edward Forth, M.M.M., C.D., Royal Military College Saint-Jean, Richelain, Que.

Warrant Officer Robert Glenn Arthur Fox, M.M.M., C.D., The Princess Louise Fusiliers, Halifax, N.S.

Master Warrant Officer Terry Hans Fraser, M.M.M., C.D., Canadian Forces Logistics Training Centre, Borden, Ont.

Chief Warrant Officer Leslie Darrell Frowen, M.M.M., C.D., 8 Wing Headquarters Trenton, Astra, Ont.

Chief Petty Officer 1st Class Joseph Claude Michel Giguère, M.M.M., C.D., Her Majesty's Canadian Ship Donnacona, Montréal, Que.

Master Warrant Officer Gerrit Ted Gombert, M.M.M., C.D., Canadian Forces Joint Operational Support Group Headquarters, Kingston, Ont.

Master Warrant Officer Raymond Jay Green, M.M.M., C.D., 3rd Battalion, The Royal Canadian Regiment, Petawawa, Ont.

Master Warrant Officer Eileen Elizabeth Hannigan, M.M.M., C.D., Office of the Director General, Compensation and Benefits, Ottawa, Ont.

Master Warrant Officer Michael Henry Hawthorn, M.M.M., C.D., 1st Battalion, The Royal Canadian Regiment, Petawawa, Ont.

Master Warrant Officer Ronald Michael James Heffernan, M.M.M., C.D., Canadian Forces Base Kingston, Kingston, Ont.

Sergeant Lejla Imamovic, M.M.M., C.D., 10th Field Artillery Regiment, Royal Canadian Artillery, Regina, Sask.

Warrant Officer Penny Christina Kennedy, M.M.M., C.D., 5th Canadian Division Support Group Gagetown Personnel Support Services, Oromocto, N.B.

Chief Warrant Officer William Lloyd King, M.M.M., C.D., Canadian Army Headquarters, Ottawa, Ont.

Chief Warrant Officer Blair William Leahy, M.M.M., C.D., Canadian Forces Health Services Group Headquarters, Ottawa, Ont.

Major Marylin Suzanne Lemay, M.M.M., C.D., Office of the Director General, Compensation and Benefits, Ottawa, Ont.

Major James Edward Rene MacInnis, M.M.M., C.D., The Cameron Highlanders of Ottawa (Duke of Edinburgh's Own), Ottawa, Ont.

Master Warrant Officer John Alexander MacKenzie, M.M.M., C.D., Office of the Chief of Staff, Vice Chief of the Defence Staff, Ottawa, Ont.

Warrant Officer Richard John Martin, M.M.M., C.D., Canadian Detachment McChord, Deputy Commander North American Aerospace Defense Command Joint Base Lewis-McChord, Tacoma, WA, U.S.A.

Master Warrant Officer Suzanne Joyce McAdam, M.M.M., C.D., Canadian Forces Health Services Group Headquarters, Ottawa, Ont.

Master Warrant Officer Morris Henry McGarrigle, M.M.M., C.D., 2nd Regiment, Royal Canadian Horse Artillery, Petawawa, Ont.

Master Warrant Officer James Allan McKenzie, M.M.M., C.D., 8 Air Reserve Flight (Trenton), Astra, Ont.

Warrant Officer Michael Melvin, M.M.M., C.D., Office of the Chief of Staff, Vice Chief of the Defence Staff, Level 1 Headquarters, Ottawa, Ont.

ORDER OF CANADA

Companions of the Order of Canada

Members of the Order of Canada

Officers of the Order of Canada

ORDER OF MILITARY MERIT

Officers of the Order of Military Merit

Commanders of the Order of Military Merit

Members of the Order of Military Merit

Major Jennifer Lynn Morrison, M.M.M., C.D., Canadian Forces School of Aerospace Technology and Engineering, Borden, Ont.

Chief Warrant Officer Joseph Paul Rémi Nault, M.M.M., C.D., Canadian Forces Real Property Operations Group, Ottawa, Ont.

Warrant Officer Rebekah Dawn Neville, M.M.M., C.D., 4 Engineer Support Regiment, Courcelette, Que.

Chief Petty Officer 2nd Class Paul Andrew Joseph Parent, M.M.M., C.D., Naval Fleet School (Pacific), Victoria, B.C.

Chief Warrant Officer Joseph Yves Éric Poissant, M.M.M., C.D., 2nd Battalion, Royal 22e Régiment, Québec, Que.

Master Warrant Officer Leonard Andrew Power, M.M.M., C.D., 1 Service Battalion, Edmonton, Alta.

Master Warrant Officer Marie Ginette Isabelle Proulx, M.M.M., C.D., Canadian Manoeuvre Training Centre, Denwood, Alta.

Master Warrant Officer Mark Dennis Riach, M.M.M., C.D., 417 Combat Support Squadron, Cold Lake, Alta.

Master Warrant Officer David Michael Andrew Ridley, M.M.M., C.D., Canadian Forces Military Police Academy, Borden, Ont.

Master Warrant Officer Christopher Allan Rigby, M.M.M., C.D., Office of the Director General, Land Equipment Program Management, Ottawa, Ont.

Chief Warrant Officer Joseph André Daniel Royer, M.M.M., C.D., 1st Battalion, Royal 22e Régiment, Courcelette, Que.

Chief Petty Officer 2nd Class Marie Nathalie Isabelle Scalabrini, M.M.M., C.D., Naval Fleet School (Pacific), Victoria, B.C.

Petty Officer 1st Class Ginette Suzanne Marie Seguin, M.M.M., C.D., Her Majesty's Canadian Ship *Halifax*, Halifax, N.S.

Chief Warrant Officer Mark Thomas Shannon, M.M.M., C.D., 32 Canadian Brigade Group Headquarters, Toronto, Ont.

Chief Petty Officer 2nd Class Stephen James Sheffar, M.M.M., C.D., Her Majesty's Canadian Ship *Calgary*, Victoria, B.C.

Major Derek John Sheridan, M.M.M., C.D., The Ontario Regiment, Royal Canadian Armoured Corps, Oshawa, Ont.

Warrant Officer Stephen Alan Slade, M.M.M., C.D., Royal Canadian Armoured Corps School, Oromocto, N.B.

Sergeant Roxane St. Michael, M.M.M., C.D., 450 Tactical Helicopter Squadron, Petawawa, Ont.

Warrant Officer Joel Kevin Turnbull, M.M.M., C.D., 5th Canadian Division Support Base Gagetown, Detachment Aldershot, Kentville, N.S.

Petty Officer 1st Class Robert Jerome Williams, M.M.M., C.D., Fleet Diving Unit (Atlantic), Shearwater, N.S.

ORDER OF MERIT OF THE POLICE FORCES

In October 2000, Her Majesty The Queen approved the creation of the Order as a means of recognizing conspicuous merit and exceptional service by members and employees of the Canadian police forces whose contributions extend beyond protection of the community. There are three levels of membership - Commander, Officer and Member - that reflect long-term, outstanding service in varying degrees of responsibility. Each level has corresponding nominal letters: C.O.M., O.O.M. and M.O.M.

**Commander of the Order of Merit of the Police Forces/
Commandeur de l'Ordre du mérite des corps policiers
(C.O.M.)**
(Invested October 31, 2019)
Chief Jennifer Evans, C.O.M., Peel Regional Police, Brampton, Ont.
This is a promotion within the Order

**Officers of the the Order of Merit of the Police Forces/
Officiers de l'Ordre du mérite des corps policiers (O.O.M.)**
(Invested October 31, 2019)
Chief Richard M. Bourassa, O.O.M., Moose Jaw Police Service, Sask.
This is a promotion within the Order
Deputy Chief Michael T. Callaghan, O.O.M., Belleville Police Service, Ont.
Chief Murray Cecil Rodd, O.O.M., C.D., Peterborough Police Service, Ont.
This is a promotion within the Order

(Invested January 30, 2019)
Deputy Commissioner Rick Barnum, O.O.M., Ontario Provincial Police, Orillia, Ont.
This is a promotion within the Order

Deputy Commissioner Brenda Butterworth-Carr, O.O.M., Royal Canadian Mounted Police, Surrey, B.C.
This is a promotion within the Order
Chief Constable David Jones, O.O.M., New Westminster Police Department, B.C.
This is a promotion within the Order
Deputy Director Yves Morency, O.O.M., Sûreté du Québec, Montréal, Que.

(Invested November 1, 2018)
Chief Superintendent Jeffery Joseph Adam, O.O.M., Ottawa, Ont.
Assistant Commissioner Barbara Fleury, O.O.M. *(Retired)*, Ottawa, Ont.

**Members of the the Order of Merit of the Police Forces/
Membres de l'Ordre du mérite des corps policiers (M.O.M.)**
(Invested October 31, 2019)
Sergeant Chris Amell, M.O.M., Ontario Provincial Police, Red Lake, Ont.
Chief Joseph Aloysius Boland, M.O.M., Royale Newfoundland Constabulary, St. John's, N.L.
Deputy Chief Kevin Arthur Chalk, M.O.M., Waterloo Regional Police Service, Cambridge, Ont.
Inspector Gordon Frederick Cobey, M.O.M., Royal Canadian Mounted Police, Milton, Ont.
Staff Sergeant Duncan Edward Dixon, M.O.M., Royal Canadian Mounted Police, Milton, Ont.
Inspector Benoit Dubé, M.O.M., Sûreté du Québec, Que.
Superintendent Stephen Eely, M.O.M., Vancouver Police Department, B.C.
Cheif Superintendent John Mark Fisher, M.O.M., Royal Canadian Mounted Police, Winnipeg, Man.
Superintendent Marcelle M. Flamand, M.O.M., Vancouver Police Department, B.C.
Deputy Chief Lee Foreman, M.O.M., Camrose Police Service, Alta.
Superintendent James Ian Hardy, M.O.M.,Calgary Police Service, Alta.

Chief Superintendent Bruce Ian Kirkpatrick, M.O.M., Royal Canadian Mounted Police, Ottawa Ont.

Inspector Eddie Kramer, M.O.M., Royale Canadian Mounted Police, Bagota, Colombia

Chief Superintendent Fernand S. Labelle, M.O.M., Ontario Provincial Police, North Bay, Ont.

Chief Paul A. Ladouceur, M.O.M., Estevan Police Service, Sask.

Inspector Richard Lévesque, M.O.M., Service de police de Trois-Rivières, Que.

Deputy Chief Jeffrey Douglas Littlewood, M.O.M., Chatham-Kent Police Service, Ont.

Superintendent Wade Daniel Lymburner, M.O.M., Royal Canadian Mounted Police, Surrey, B.C.

Chief Bryan Russel MacCulloch, M.O.M., Niagara Regional Police Service, Ont.

Chief David M. MacNeil, M.O.M., Truro Police Service, N.S.

Ms. Cheryl McNeil, M.O.M., Toronto Police Service, Ont.

Inspector Sheri Lynn Meeks, M.O.M., Belleville Police Service, Ont.

Inspector D. Mark Mitchell, M.O.M., Kawartha Lakes Police Service, Ont.

Police Director William Moffat, M.O.M., Naskapi Police Force, Kawawachikamach, Que.

Chief Kent D. Moore, M.O.M., Shelbourne Police Service, Ont.

Superintendent Christopher R.C. Newton, M.O.M., London Police Service, Ont.

Director Robert Pigeon, M.O.M., Service de police de la Ville de Québec, Que.

Superintendent Lorne Edward Pike, M.O.M., Delta Police Department, B.C.

Superintendent Tammy Ann Pozzobon, M.O.M., Calgary Police Service, Alta.

Constable Cynthia L. Provost, M.O.M., Calgary Police Service, Alta.

Superintendent Terrence M. Rocchio, M.O.M., Edmonton Police Service, Alta.

Sergeant Peter Murray Sadler, M.O.M., Vancouver Police Department, B.C.

Inspector Daniel Robert Smith, M.O.M., Peterborough Police Service, Ont.

Superintendemt Chad M. Tawfik, M.O.M., Edmonton Police Service, Alta.

Deputy Chief Constable Colin Watson, M.O.M., Victoria Police Department, B.C.

Chief Peacekeeper Dwayne Zacharie, M.O.M., Kahnawake Peacekeepers, Que.

(Invested January 30, 2019)

Inspector Shawna E. Baher, M.O.M., Royal Canadian Mounted Police, Surrey, B.C.

Superintendent Marc Maurice Bedard, M.O.M., Ontario Provincial Police, Orillia, Ont.

Staff Sergeant Donald Edward Bill, M.O.M., Royal Canadian Mounted Police, St. John's, N.L.

Chief Brent Ivan Blackmore, M.O.M., Woodstock Police Force, N.B.

Superintendent Edward Boettcher, M.O.M., Royal Canadian Mounted Police, Surrey, B.C.

Deputy Director Sylvain Caron, M.O.M., Sûreté du Québec, Montréal, B.C.

Staff Sergeant Diane L. Cockle, M.O.M., Royal Canadian Mounted Police, Surrey, B.C.

Staff Sergeant Stephen T. Conohan, M.O.M., Royal Canadian Mounted Police, St. John's, N.L.

Deputy Chief Paul Cook, M.O.M., Calgary Police Service, Alta.

Chief Superintendent Roseanne DiMarco, M.O.M., Ontario Provincial Police, Orillia, Ont.

Chief Superintendent Bernadine Paulette Freill, M.O.M., Royal Canadian Mounted Police, Surrey, B.C.

Sergeant Luc Gagnon, M.O.M., Sûreté du Québec, Montréal, Que.

Detective Inspector Shawn W. Glassford, M.O.M., Ontario Provincial Police, Orillia, Ont.

Superintendent Marty Lang Kearns, M.O.M., Ontario Provincial Police, Orillia, Ont.

Ann King, M.O.M., Peel Regional Police, Brampton, Ont.

Detective John Phillip Langford, M.O.M., Calgary Police Service, Alta.

Inspector Robyn Dawn MacEachern, M.O.M., Ontario Provincial Police, Orillia, Ont.

Superintendent Paul Russell Mackey, M.O.M., Ontario Provincial Police, Orillia, Ont.

Constable Tad Kenneth Milmine, M.O.M., Calgary Police Service, Alta.

Constable Michelle Mosher, M.O.M., Royal Canadian Mounted Police, Grande Prairie, Alta.

Inspector Wayne O. A. Nichols, M.O.M., Royal Canadian Mounted Police, St. John's, N.L.

Staff Sergeant Thomas Edward Norton, M.O.M., Royal Canadian Mounted Police, Surrey, B.C.

Deputy Chief Satpal Singh Parhar, M.O.M., Calgary Police Service, Alta.

Chief Superintendent Chesley Walter Parsons, M.O.M., Royal Canadian Mounted Police, Ottawa, Ont.

Director Danny W. Paterson, M.O.M., Saint-Jérôme Police Service, Que.

Deputy Chief Robert John Gordon Ritchie, M.O.M., Calgary Police Service, Alta.

Superintendent Manuel Rodrigues, M.O.M., Peel Regional Police, Brampton, Ont.

Sergeant Nancy Rudback, M.O.M., Halifax Regional Police, N.S.

Peter D. Shipley, M.O.M., Ontario Provincial Police, Orillia, Ont.

Inspector Bruce D. Singer, M.O.M., Royal Canadian Mounted Police, St. John's, N.S.

Assistant Commissioner Serge J. J. Therriault, M.O.M., Royal Canadian Mounted Police, Ottawa, Ont.

Superintendent Mark VanZant, M.O.M., Ontario Provincial Police, Orillia, Ont.

Chief Superintendent Ross Arthur White, M.O.M., Royal Canadian Mounted Police, Fredericton, N.B.

Superintendent Brenda Young, M.O.M., Halifax Regional Police, N.S.

Inspector Charles Young, M.O.M., Ontario Provincial Police, Orillia, Ont.

(Invested November 1, 2018)

Sergeant Michael Lamothe, M.O.M., Ottawa, Ont.

MILITARY VALOUR DECORATIONS/DÉCORATIONS DE LA VAILLANCE MILITAIRE

Military Valour Decorations are national honours awarded to recognize acts of valour, self-sacrifice or devotion to duty in the presence of the enemy. The decorations were approved by Her Majesty Queen Elizabeth II in 1993. They consist of the Victoria Cross, the Star of Military Valour and the Medal of Military Valour.

Victoria Cross/La Croix de Victoria (C.V.)
None awarded since last edition.

Star of Military Valour/Étoile de la vaillance militaire (É.V.M.)
None awarded since last edition.

Medal of Military Valour/ Médaille de la vaillance militaire (M.V.M)
None awarded since last edition.

CANADIAN BRAVERY DECORATIONS/DÉCORATIONS CANADIENNES POUR ACTES DE BRAVOURE

The Decorations for Bravery, consisting of the Cross of Valour, the Star of Courage, and the Medal of Bravery, were instituted and created on May 10, 1972. They may be awarded to Canadian citizens or to non-Canadians who have performed an act of bravery in Canada, or outside Canada if the act was in Canada's interest. The Decorations for Bravery may be awarded posthumously.

The Cross of Valour is awarded for acts of the most conspicuous courage in circumstances of extreme peril. The Star of Courage is awarded for acts of conspicuous courage in circumstances of great peril. The Medal of Bravery is awarded for acts of bravery in hazardous circumstances.

Cross of Valour/Croix de Valeur (C.V.)
None awarded since last edition.

Star of Courage/Étoile du courage (S.C.)
(Announced July 1, 2020)

Azzadine Soufiane, S.C. (posthumous), Québec, Que.

(Awarded September 12, 2019)

Constable Ryan Barnett, S.C., Newmarket, Ont.
Constable Nicholas Crowther, S.C., Barrhead, Alta.
Constable Josh McSweeney, S.C., Toronto, Ont.

Medal of Bravery/Médaille de la bravoure (M.B.)
(Awarded September 17, 2021)

Myriam Côté, M.B., Puerto Plata, Dominican Republic
Régis Grégoire, M.B., Gatineau, Que.
Daniel Joseph McKinney, M.B., Gatineau, Que.
John Schuiteboer, M.B., Breckenridge, Que.

(Announced July 1, 2020)

Said Akjour, M.B., Québec, Que.
Hakim Chambaz, M.B., Québec, Que.
Aymen Derbali, M.B., Québec, Que.
Mohamed Khabar, M.B., Québec, Que.
Charlie Brien, M.B., Mitissini, Que.
Debbra Cooper, M.B., Sicamous, B.C.
Kimberly Cossette, M.B., Calgary, Alta.
Myriam Côté, M.B., Montréal, Que.

Amber Dyck, M.B., Morinville, Alta.
Russell Fee, M.B., Calgary, Alta.
Pierre Lessard, M.B., Lac-des-Écorces, Que.
Chris Scott, M.B., Edmonton, Alta.
RCMP Constable David Wynn, M.B. (posthumous), St. Albert, Alta.

(Awarded September 12, 2019)

Constable Rafael Beaulieu, M.B., Saint-Hubert, Que.
Corporal David Brosinsky, M.B., Edmonton, Alta.
Erik Richard Brown, M.B., Koh Tao, Surat Thani, Thailand
Marie-Soleil Côté-Lepage, M.B., Québec, Que.
Stayton Danylowich, M.B. and Wynden Danylowich, M.B., Kelowna, B.C.
Constable Shaun Nicholas De Grandpré, M.B., Roblin, Ont.
Constable Ryan Jeffrey Gillis, M.B., Long Sault, Ont.
*Presented at a previous ceremony
Constable Kyle Josey, M.B., Waverly, N.S.
Sergeant Jérémie Landry, M.B., Cold Lake, Alta.
*Presented at a later date
Constable Bryan David Martell, M.B., Fall River, N.S.
*Presented at a previous ceremony
Rodney Wayne McAlpine, M.B., Barrie, Ont.
Constable Adam Rayner, M.B., Edmonton, Alta.
*Presented at a later date
Michael Tompkins, M.B., Vancouver, B.C.

(Awarded June 13, 2019)

Petty Officer 1st Class Charles Wesley Bressette, M.B., C.D., bedford, N.S.
Master Corporal Jesus Rodrigo Castillo, M.B., Toronto, Ont.
Petty Officer 2nd Class Matthew Compeau, M.B., C.D., Toronto, Ont.
Master Corporal Kashif Dar, M.B., Mississauga, Ont.
Sergeant Andrea Karistinos, M.B., C.D., Bradford, Ont.
Master Seaman Emmanuel Lemieux, M.B., Halifax, N.S.
Leading Seaman Reeves Matheson, M.B., Halifax, N.S.

(Awarded April 25, 2019)

Constable Dru Michael Abernethy, M.B., Rocky Mountain House, Alta.
Juergen Baetzel, M.B., Gray Creek, B.C.
*Presented at a previous ceremony
Michel Denis Bourbonniere, M.B., M.S.M., Winnipeg, Man.
Kaden Clouston, M.B., Calgary, Alta.
*Presented at a later date
Daniel Desrochers, M.B., Thunder Bay, Ont.
Brian Dittmar, M.B., Gore Bay, Ont.
Brant Hannah, M.B., Calgary, Alta.
*Presented at a previous ceremony
Paul Hindson, M.B., Crawford Bay, B.C.
*Presented at a previous ceremony
Tobias MacDonald, M.B., Delta, B.C.
*Presented at a previous ceremony
Don McNeice, M.B., Sandspit, B.C.
Richard Pick, M.B., Sandspit, B.C.
Steve Prior, M.B., Gore Bay, Ont.
Constable Leah Russell, M.B., Fort Vermilion, Alta.
Carol VanRuymbeke, M.B., Crawford Bay, B.C.
Mackenzie Terrance Vatter-Martineau, M.B., Calgary, Alta.

(Awarded March 26, 2019)

Michael Douglas Barkhouse, M.B., Bramber, N.S.
Constable Trevor Joseph Bragnalo, M.B., Stonewall, Man.
Andrew Cartwright, M.B., Banff, Alta.
*Presented at a previous ceremony
Constable Shaun Nicholas De Grandpré, M.B., Cornwall, Ont.
*Presented at a later date
Constable in Training Charlène Desrosiers, M.B., Saint-Roch-de-l'Achigan, Que.
Raymond Doucette, M.B., Saint-Louis-de-Kent, N.B.
Constable Ryan Jeffrey Gillis, M.B., Greely, Ont.
Cameron Robert Gouck, M.B., Niagara Falls, Ont.
Keegan Herries, M.B., Welland, Ont.
Hayley Hesseln, M.B., Saskatoon, Sask.
Rémi Lesage, M.B., Portneuf, Que.
Constable Bryan David Martell, M.B., Fall River, N.L.
*Presented at a previous ceremony
Hussam Mohamed Meshmesha, M.B. (posthumous), Calgary, Alta.
*Received by Yousef Meshmesha
Barry Parks, M.B. (deceased), Almonte, Ont.
*Received by Patricia Paynter Parks
David Pronovost, M.B., Portneuf, Que.
*Presented at a later date
Constable in Training Gabriel Roy-Lacouture, M.B., Longueuil, Que.
Chelsi Sabbe, M.B., Prince George, B.C.
Mohamed Rashed Shaban, M.B., Toronto, Ont.
*Presented at a previous ceremony

Constable Steven Ashley Thompson, M.B., Winnipeg, Man.

(Awarded February 14, 2019)
Constable Shaun De Grandpré, M.B., Cornwall, Ont.
Presented at a later date
Noureddine Fard, M.B., Longueuil, Que.
Constable Michael Gallagher, M.B., Smiths Falls, Ont.
Presented at a later date
Constable Ryan Gillis, M.B., Long Sault, Ont.
Presented at a later date
Constable Daniel King, M.B., Smiths Falls, Ont.
Sergeant Paul Klassen, M.B., Lombardy, Ont.
Constable Bryan David Martell, M.B., Fall River, N.S.
Michael Wassill, M.B. *(posthumous)*, Ottawa, Ont.
Received by Betty-Ann Wassill René Wassill

(Awarded November 5, 2018)
Captain Michael Lawrence Kristy, M.B., C.D. *(Retired)*, Clarksburg, Ont.
Master Corporal Ryan Kristy, M.B., Shiloh, Man.
Petty Officer 2nd Class David LeBlanc, M.B., C.D., Mineville, N.S.

MERITORIOUS SERVICE DECORATIONS/DÉCORATIONS POUR SERVICE MÉRITOIRE

Approved by Her Majesty the Queen on July 10, 1991, the Meritorious Service Decorations were created to honour Canadians & foreigners (military) for commendable actions performed on or after June 11, 1984.

The Meritorious Service Cross (Military Division) is awarded for the performance of a military deed or a military activity in an outstandingly professional manner or of a rare high standard that brings considerable benefit or great honour to the Canadian Forces.

The Meritorious Service Medal (Military Division) is awarded for the performance of a military deed or a military activity in a highly professional manner or of a very high standard that brings benefit or honour to the Canadian Forces.

Meritorious Service Cross/M.S.C. (Military)/
La Croix du service méritoire (militaire)
(Awarded November 12, 2019)
Commander Todd William Bonnar, M.S.C., C.D., Norfolk, V.A., U.S.A.
Brigadier-General Trevor john Cadieu, O.M.M., M.S.C., M.S.M., C.D., Ottawa, Ont.
Sergeant Jeffery Theodore Oshanyk, M.S.C., C.D., Ottawa, Ont.
Brigadier-General Alain Joseph Paul Pelletier, O.M.M., M.S.C., M.S.M., C.D., Headingley, Man.
Susan Jane Pond, M.S.C., Kingsburg, N.S.
Brigadier-General Steven Joseph Russel Whelan, O.M.M., M.S.C., M.S.M., C.D., Ottawa, Ont.

(Awarded June 13, 2019)
Master Corporal John Robert Thomas Archer, M.S.C., C.D., Ottawa, Ont.
Commander Sheldon Roderick Kyle Gillis, M.S.C., C.D., Halifax, N.S.
Corporal Alexandre Nicolas Papineau-Levesque, M.S.C., Pembroke, Ont.

Meritorious Service Medal M.S.M. (Military)/
La Médaille du service méritoire (militaire)
(Awarded November 12, 2019)
Colonel Joseph Antoine Dave Abboud, M.S.C., M.M.V., M.S.M., C.D., Montréal, Que.
Sergeant Gary Barrett, M.S.M., Petawawa, Ont.
Petty Officer 1st Class Jason William Bode, M.S.M., C.D., Victoria, B.C.
Captain(N) Daniel Joseph Jacques Bouchard, M.S.M., C.D., Ottawa, Ont.
Commander Ramona Lynn Burke, M.S.M., C.D., Orléans, Ont.
Chief Warrant Officer Robert Joseph Clarke, M.M.M., M.S.M., C.D., Edmonton, Alta.
Warrant Officer Nicolas Robin Côté, M.S.M., C.D., Kingston, Ont.
Lieutenant-Colonel Sean Martin French, M.S.M., C.D., Ottawa, Ont.
Sergeant Nicholas Shawn Hancock, M.S.M., C.D., Ottawa, Ont.
Commander Jon Jeffrey Hutchinson, M.S.M., C.D., Victoria, B.C.
Chief Petty Officer 1st Class Sylvain Joseph François Jean Claude Jaquemot, M.S.M., C.D., Victoria, B.C.
Colonel Andrew Ronald Jayne, M.S.M., C.D., Ottawa, Ont.
Captain(N) Steve Jorgensen, M.S.M., C.D., Victoria, B.C.
Lieutenant-Colonel Erik Antony Liebert, M.S.M., C.D., Ottawa, Ont.
Major Alan Anderson Lockerby, M.S.M., C.D., Winnipeg, Man.
Major Michael MacKillop, M.M.V., M.S.M., C.D., Calgary, Alta.
Chief Warrant Officer Robert McCann, M.M.M., M.S.M., C.D., Ottawa, Ont.

Lieutenant-Colonel Kristopher Michael Reeves, M.S.M., C.D., Petawawa, Ont.
Commander Michael Scott Shortridge, M.S.M., C.D., Ottawa, Ont.
Commander Michael Edward Thomson, M.S.M., C.D., Borden, Ont.
Major Michael Veitch, M.S.M., C.D., Carleton Place, Ont.
Major Wayne Terrence Wong, M.S.M., C.D., Toronto, Ont.
Master Corporal Alexander Yu, M.S.M., Toronto, Ont.

(Awarded June 13, 2019)
Brigadier-General David James Anderson, O.M.M., M.S.M., C.D., Ottawa, Ont.
Commander Sylvain Elie Jean-Paul Belair, M.S.M., C.D., Victoria, B.C.
Warrant Officer Sean Eldon Benedict, M.S.M., C.D., Pembroke, Ont.
Lieutenant-Colonel George Michael Albert Boyuk, M.S.M., C.D., Ottawa, Ont.
Brigadier-General François Joseph Chagnon, O.M.M., M.S.M., C.D., Ottawa, Ont.
Warrant Officer Danny Carl Compton, M.S.M., C.D., Ottawa, Ont.
Sergeant James Dalebozik, M.S.M., C.D., Ottawa, Ont.
Major Michael Roy Deutsch, M.S.M., C.D., Kingston, N.S.
Lieutenant-Colonel Corey Jason Frederickson, M.S.M., C.D., Ottawa, Ont.
Leading Seaman Steven Edward Galloway, M.S.M., Ottawa, Ont.
Major Tammy Michelle Hiscock, M.S.M., C.D., Bedford, N.S.
Colonel Pierre Huet, M.S.M., C.D., Wainwright, Alta.
Petty Officer 1st Class Joseph Kiraly, M.S.M., C.D., Ottawa, Ont.
Lieutenant-Commander Jason Gary Wade Lorette, M.S.M., Trenton, Ont.
Lieutenant-Colonel Robert Jeffrey Lyttle, M.S.M., C.D., Ottawa, Ont.
Commander Gordon Willis Jacob Noseworthy, M.S.M., C.D., Halifax, N.S.
Chief Warrant Officer Keith Michael Olstad, M.M.M., M.S.M., C.D., Chalk River, Ont.
Colonel Donald Potoczny, M.S.M. (United States Army), Ottawa, Ont.
Lieutenant-Colonel Nickolas Sebastien Roby, M.S.M., C.D., Fredericton, N.B.
Major Carlo Rossi, M.S.M., Ottawa, Ont.
Lieutenant-Colonel Ryan Zane Sexsmith, M.S.M., C.D., Victoria, B.C.
Chief Warrant Officer Thomas Verner, M.M.M., M.S.M., C.D., Petawawa, Ont.

(Awarded November 5, 2018)
Brigadier-General Shane Anthony Brennan, M.S.M., C.D. (Retired), Kemptville, Ont.
Chief Warrant Officer David Edward Hepditch, M.M.M., M.S.M., C.D., Shearwater, N.S.
Commander Jeffrey Lawrence Murray, M.S.C., M.S.M., C.D., Ottawa, Ont.
Lieutenant-Colonel Christopher Lionel Robidoux, M.S.M., C.D., Ottawa, Ont.
Lieutenant-Commander Paul Anthony Smith, M.S.M., C.D., Halifax, N.S.
Chief Petty Officer 1st Class Andrew John Tiffin, M.M.M., M.S.M., C.D. (Retired), Ottawa, Ont.
Major Christopher Wood, M.S.M., C.D., Pembroke, Ont.

Meritorious Service Cross M.S.C. (Civil)/
La Croix du service méritoire (civile)
(Awarded September 17, 2021)
Nahid Aboumansour, C.Q., M.S.C., Montréal, Que.
Tina Boileau, M.S.M., Embrun, Ont.
Jonathan Pitre, M.S.C. (posthumous), Embrun, Ont.

(Awarded February 25, 2021)
Helen Margaret (Peggy) Truscott, M.S.C. (posthumous), Toronto, Ont.
Robin Wettlaufer, M.S.C., Ottawa, Ont.

(Announced July 1, 2020)
Nahid Aboumansour, C.Q., M.S.C., Montréal, Que.
Ian M.F. Arnold, M.S.C., Ottawa, Ont.
Darcy Ataman, M.S.C., Winnipeg, Man.
Robert T. Banno, M.S.C. (deceased), Burnaby, B.C.
Kathryn Blain, M.S.C., Waterloo, Ont.
Sandy Boutin, M.S.C., Montréal, Que.
Michael Andrew Burns, M.S.C., M.S.M., Toronto, Ont.
Franca Damiani Carella, M.S.C. (posthumous), Woodbridge, Ont.
Mackie Greene, M.S.C., Wilson's Beach, N.B.
Joseph Michael Howlett, M.S.C. (posthumous), Wilson's Beach, N.B.
Harry Ing, M.S.C., Deep River, Ont.

Cynthia Lickers-Sage, M.S.C., Toronto, Ont.
Nicole Marcil-Gratton, C.Q., M.S.C. (posthumous), Montréal, Que.
Matthew Pearce, M.S.C., Montréal, Que.
Jonathan Pitre, M.S.C. (posthumous), Embrun, Ont.
Gregory Sadetsky, M.S.C., Montréal, Que.
Byron Smith, M.S.C., Carleton Place, Ont.
Lisa Steele, M.S.C., Toronto, Ont.
Kim Tomczak, M.S.C., Toronto, Ont.
Wanda vanderStoop, M.S.C., Toronto, Ont.
Michèle Vau-Chiagnon, C.Q., M.S.C., Montréal, Que.

(Awarded September 12, 2019)
Jeremy Bryant, M.S.C., Edmonton, Alta.
Aileen Gleason, M.S.C. (deceased), Winnipeg, Man.
Received by Sister Denise Kuyp
Andrew James Allan Hall, M.S.C., Vancouver, B.C.
Sean McCormick, M.S.C., Winnipeg, Man.

(Awarded April 25, 2019)
Lieutenant Colonel Henry Chaim Gourdji, M.S.C., C.D. *(Retired)*, Beaconsfield, Que.
Michael Paterson, M.S.C., Winnipeg, Man.

(Awarded March 26, 2019)
Alex Harvey, M.S.C., Saint-Ferréol-les-Neiges, Que.
Daniel Y. C. Heng, M.S.C., Calgary, Alta.
Dawn Madahbee Leach, M.S.C., Little Current, Ont.

(Awarded February 14, 2019)
Pierre Duval, M.S.C., Cowansville, Que.
François Fassier, M.S.C., Montréal, Que.
Gerald Mitchel Fried, M.S.C., Côte Saint-Luc, Que.
Jean Vincent, M.S.C., Wendake, Que.

(Awarded November 5, 2018)
Kahlil Baker, M.S.C., Bowen Island, B.C.
Samuel Gervais, M.S.C., Montréal, Que.
Richard Howard Gimblett, M.S.C., C.D., Port Hope, Ont.
Laura Howard, M.S.C., Montréal, Que.
Tobias Lütke, M.S.C., Ottawa, Ont.
Brooke van Mossel-Forrester, M.S.C., Montréal, Que.

Meritorious Service Medal M.S.M. (Civil)/
La Médaille du service méritoire (civile)
(Awarded September 17, 2021)
Jeremy Dutcher, M.S.M., Montréal, Que.
Véronique Leduc, M.S.M., Montréal, Que.
Sylvie Rémillard, M.S.M., Saint-Rémi, Que.

(Awarded May 21, 2021)
Art Gruenig, M.S.M., Cranbrook, B.C.

(Awarded February 25, 2021)
Mustafa Alio, M.S.M., Toronto, Ont.
Pierre Allard, M.S.M. (posthumous), Montréal, Que.
Stephen Allen, M.S.M., York, P.E.I.
Roger Augustine, M.S.M., Eel Ground First Nation, N.B.
Yahya Badran, M.S.M., Terrebonne, Que.
Carolyn Elsie Louise Bateman, O.P.E.I., M.S.M., Charlottetown, P.E.I.
Betty Begg-Brooks, M.S.M., Charlottetown, P.E.I.
Elyse Benoît, M.S.M., Gatineau, Que.
Maureen Bianchini-Purvis, M.S.M., Edmonton, Alta.
April Billard, M.S.M., Channel-Port aux Basques, Nfld.
Maryse Bouvette, M.S.M., Gatineau, Que.
Dana Bookman, M.S.M., Toronto, Ont.
Clarence Bourgoin, M.S.M., Saint-Léonard, N.B.
Alan Broadbent, C.M., M.S.M., Toronto, Ont.
William C. Brooks, M.S.M., Lunenburg, N.S.
Scott Bryan, M.S.M., Toronto, Ont.
Didier Calvet, M.S.M., Montréal, Que.
Claude Caron, M.S.M., Longueuil, Que.
Roland Case, M.S.M., Vancouver, B.C.
Stephanie Case, M.S.M., Chamonix, France
Joan Bell Chaisson, M.S.M., Channel-Port aux Basques, Nfld.
Susan Chalmers-Gauvin, M.S.M., Moncton, N.B.
Shannon Christensen, M.S.M., Kelowna, B.C.
Diane Lee Clemons, M.S.M., Mississauga, Ont.
Michael Clemons, O.Ont., M.S.M., Mississauga, Ont.
Jocelyn Dianne Cousineau, M.S.M., Eastern Passage, N.S.
Captain Médric Léo Robert Cousineau, S.C., M.S.M., C.D. (Ret'd), Eastern Passage, N.S.
Isabelle Delisle, M.S.M. (posthumous), Gatineau, Que.
William Di Nardo, M.S.M., Toronto, Ont.
Igor Dobrovolskiy, M.S.M., Moncton, N.B.
Marie-France Dubreuil, M.S.M.., Montréal, Que.
Jeremy Dutcher, M.S.M., Montréal, Que.
Marilyn L. Dyck, M.S.M., Calgary, Alta.
Suzanne Fitzback, M.S.M., Gatineau, Que.
Corey Fleischer, M.S.M., Montréal, Que.
Jean-Martin Fortier, M.S.M., Hemmingford, Que.

CANADIAN BRAVERY DECORATIONS

Star of Courage

Cross of Valor

Medal of Bravery

MERITORIOUS SERVICE DECORATIONS

Meritorious Service Cross
Obverse (Military Version)

Meritorious Service Medal
Reverse (Civil Version)

Serge Fournier, M.S.M.,
  Montréal, Que.
Brother Réjean Gadouas,
  M.S.M., Ottawa, Ont.
Larry Gauthier, M.S.M., Ottawa, Ont.
James Adrian Gehrels, M.S.M. (posthumous), Thunder Bay, Ont.
Robert Gendron, M.S.M., Gatineau, Que.
Isabelle Genest, M.S.M., Québec, Que.
Claude B. Gingras, M.S.M., Ottawa, Ont.
Rick Goodwin, M.S.M., Ottawa, Ont.
Art Gruenig, M.S.M., Cranbrook, B.C.
Mohamed Hage, M.S.M., Montréal, Que.
Joan Elaine Hoffman te Raa, M.S.M. (posthumous), York, P.E.I.
Robert Hughes, M.S.M., Kamloops, B.C.
Colonel Robert Mark Hutchings, M.S.M., C.D., (Ret'd), Kingston, Ont.
Narmin Ismail, M.S.M., Toronto, Ont.
Brent Kaulback, M.S.M., Summerland, B.C.
Tim Kwan, M.S.M., Toronto, Ont.
Martine Laurier, M.S.M., Montréal, Que.
Patrice Lauzon, M.S.M., Montréal, Que.
Pat Lazo, M.S.M., Winnipeg, Man.
Brian Leavitt, M.S.M., Lacombe, Alta.
Robert Lessard, M.S.M., Montréal, Que.
Patricia (Patti) Leigh, O.B.C., M.S.M., West Vancouver, B.C.
Victoria Lennox, M.S.M., Ottawa, Ont.
Kurt D. Lynn, M.S.M. (posthumous), Gores Landing, Ont.
Normand Martin, M.S.M., Montréal, Que.
Todd McDonald, M.S.M., Halifax, N.S.
Bruce McKelvey, M.S.M., Toronto, Ont.
Janet McKelvey, O.Ont., M.S.M., Toronto, Ont.
Steve Mesler, M.S.M., Calgary, Alta.
Jonathan Michaud, M.S.M., Montréal, Que.
Catherine Morissette, M.S.M., Québec, Que.
Julia Ogina, M.S.M., Cambridge Bay, Nunavut
Mathieu Ouellet, M.S.M., Québec, Que.
Leigh Parise, M.S.M., New York, N.Y., U.S.A.
Georges Edward Potvin, M.S.M., Gatineau, Que.

Bassel Ramli, M.S.M., Toronto, Ont.
Eric Rajah, A.O.E., M.S.M., Lacombe, Alta.
Lauren Elizabeth Rathmell, M.S.M., Montréal, Que.
Kelvin Redvers, M.S.M., Deninu K'ue First Nation, N.W.T.
T'áncháy Sarah Judith Redvers, M.S.M., Deninu K'ue First Nation, N.W.T.
Annie Roy, M.S.M., Montréal, Que.
Omar Salaymeh, M.S.M., Toronto, Ont.
Elaine Ruth Maxine Cormier Semkuley, M.S.M., Calgary, Alta.
Myron Semkuley, M.S.M., Calgary, Alta.
Jacques-Denis Simard, M.S.M., Québec, Que.
Jacques Simoneau, M.S.M., Québec, Que.
William J. Simpson, M.S.M., Q.C. (posthumous), Ottawa, Ont.
Christopher Southin, M.S.M., Thessalon, Ont.
Nancy Stevens, M.S.M., Kingston, Ont.
Harry J. Stewart, M.S.M., Thessalon, Ont.
Glenn C. Stronks, M.S.M., Orillia, Ont.
Cyprian Szalankiewicz, M.S.M., Ottawa, Ont.
Brent Tookenay, M.S.M., Fort Frances, Ont.
Marian Walsh, M.S.M., Toronto, Ont.
Ashley Ward, M.S.M., Halifax, N.S.
William Frederick George Williams, M.S.M., Greely, Ont.
Marion Willis, M.S.M., Winnipeg, Man.
Steve Wilson, M.S.M., Winnipeg, Man.
Don Wright, M.S.M., Charlottetown, P.E.I.
Ken Zakem, M.S.M., Charlottetown, P.E.I.

(Announced July 1, 2020)
Adrian Bercovici, M.S.M., Montréal, Que.
Natalie Bercovici, M.S.M., Montréal, Que.
Yves Berthiaume, M.S.M., Hawkesbury, Ont.
Subhas Bhargave, M.S.M., Ottawa, Ont.
Uttra Bhargava, M.S.M., Ottawa, Ont.
Tina Boileau, M.S.M., Embrun, Ont.
Deborrah Sharon Bradwell, M.S.M., Burlington, Ont.
Kenneth Bradwell, M.S.M. (posthumous), Burlington, Ont.

Louise Joanne Foster-Martin, M.S.M., Brampton, Ont.
Todd Alan Halpern, M.S.M., Toronto, Ont.
Jim Hayhurst Sr., M.S.M. (posthumous), Toronto, Ont.
Alexis Kearney Hillyard, M.S.M., Edmonton, Alta.
Mike Hirshbach, M.S.M., Halifax, N.S.
Jacques Janson, M.S.M., Ottawa, Ont.
Superintendent Heinz A.J. Kuck, M.S.M. (Ret'd), North York, Ont.
Véronique Leduc, M.S.M., Montréal, Que.
Gerard Barry Losier, O.N.B., M.S.M., Miramichi, N.B.
Taylor MacGillivray, M.S.M., Halifax, N.S.
Alan Melanson, M.S.M., Annapolis Royal, N.S.
Glori Meldrum, M.S.M., Edmonton, Alta.
James Mercer, M.S.M., Stephenville Crossing, N.L.
Father Fred Monk, M.S.M., Medicine Hat, Alta.
Dean Otto, M.S.M., Nepean, Ont.
Jeanine Otto, M.S.M., Nepean, Ont.
Mavis Ramser, M.S.M., Terrace, B.C.
Ron Ramsey, M.S.M., Terrace, B.C.
Mike Ranta, M.S.M., Killarney, Ont.
Sylvie Rémillard, M.S.M., Saint-Rémi, Que.
Kennith James Skwleqs Robertson, M.S.M., Toronto, Ont.
Catherine Ross, M.S.M., Winnipeg, Man.
Jane Adele Roy, M.S.M., Bedford, N.S.
Jeremie Saunders, M.S.M., Halifax, N.S.
James Scott, M.S.M., Kingsville, Ont.
Ariel Shlien, M.S.M., Montréal, Que.
Ron Shlien, M.S.M., Montréal, Que.
Peter Smyth, M.S.M., Edmonton, Alta.
Brian Matthew Stever, M.S.M., Dartmouth, N.S.
Jean-Pierre Tchang, M.S.M., Saint-Pamphile, Que.
Lanre Tunji-Ajayi, M.S.M., Barrie, Ont.
Sylvana Vilata-Micillo, M.S.M., Montréal, Que.

(Awarded September 12, 2019)
Virginia Elizabeth Edmonds, M.S.M., Tatamagouche, N.S.
Sydney Adam Goldenberg, M.S.M., Toronto, Ont.

*Presented at a previous ceremony
Margaret Louise Hewlett, M.S.M., Richmond, B.C.
Kyle Hill, M.S.M., Toronto, Ont.
*Presented at a previous ceremony
Arlene Lois Kalchman, M.S.M., Toronto, Ont.
Ronald Oscar Linden, M.S.M., Toronto, Ont.
Mark W. Podlasly, M.S.M., Vancouver, B.C.
John Gordon Stewart, M.S.M., Yellowknife, N.W.T.
Nathan T. Tidridge, M.S.M., Waterdown, Ont.
Jennifer Nicole van Wyck, M.S.M., Vancouver, B.C.
Erik Nelson Vu, M.S.M., North Vancouver, B.C.
Bev Woods-Percival, M.S.M. (deceased), Tiny, Ont.
*Received by Bill Percival
Helen Zukerman, M.S.M., Toronto, Ont.

(Awarded June 13, 2019)
Sally F. E. Goddard, M.S.M. and John Timothy Goddard,
    M.S.M., Charlottetown, P.E.I.

(Awarded Aprl 25, 2019)
Katelyn Bateman, M.S.M., Kirkland, Que.
Diana Christina Beaupré, M.S.M., Canterbury, U.K.
Richard Bennett, M.S.M., Dieppe, N.B.
John Raymond Dallaire, M.S.M., Moncton, N.B.
M. David Guttman, M.S.M., Georgetown, Ont.
Robert E. LeBlanc, M.S.M., Moncton, N.B.
Jack A. Moon, M.S.M., Georgetown, Ont.
*Presented at a previous ceremony
Patrick J. O'Brien, M.S.M., Moncton, N.B.
Michelle Sullivan, M.S.M., St. John's, N.L.
Adrian Watkinson, M.S.M., Canterbury, U.K.

(Awarded March 26, 2019)
Caroline Bouchard, M.S.M., Montréal, Que.
J. Gabriel Bran Lopez, M.S.M., Montréal, Que.
Keighobad Esmaeilpour, M.S.M., Burnaby, B.C.
John Morris Fairbrother, M.S.M., Saint-Hyacinthe, Que.
Olivier Farmer, M.S.M., Ville Mont-Royal, Que.
Lison Gagné, M.S.M., Sainte-Thérèse, Que.
Israel Idonije, O.M., M.S.M., Chicago, IL, U.S.A.
Meika McDonald, M.S.M., Fort Smith, N.W.T.
Éric Nadeau, M.S.M., Otterburn Park, Que.
Robb Nash, M.S.M., Winnipeg, Man.
Frances Noronha, O.Ont., M.S.M., M.B.E., Etobicoke, Ont.
Amar (Alex) Sangha, M.S.M., Delta, B.C.

(Awarded February 14, 2019)
Roland Barbier, M.S.M., Terrebonne, Que.
Kathryn Lorna Boesch-Lucking, M.S.M., Port Mouton, N.S.
Sylvain Brosseau, M.S.M., Montréal, Que.
Diane Chênevert, C.Q., M.S.M., Montréal, Que.
Rachel Lapierre, M.S.M., Piedmont, Que.
Monique Nolett-Ille, M.S.M., Odanak, Que.
Gradimir Pankov, M.S.M., Montréal, Que.
Marie Saint Pierre, C.M., C.Q., M.S.M., Montréal, Que.

(Awarded November 5, 2019)
Oleh Michael Antonyshyn, M.S.M., Toronto, Ont.
Monique A. D. Bourassa, M.S.M., Gatineau, Que.
Rachel Corneille Gravel, M.S.M., L'Assomption, Que.
Norman D. Crerar, M.S.M., Vernon, B.C.
Barbara Ellen Crook, M.S.M., Ottawa, Ont.
Daniel George Greenberg, M.S.M., Ottawa, Ont.
Aldo E. J. Del Col, M.S.M., Beaconsfield, Que.
Gilles Desjardins, M.S.M., Gatineau, Que.
Catherine J. Keddy, M.S.M., Carleton Place, Ont.
Paul A. Keddy, M.S.M., Carleton Place, Ont.
Morley Stuart Lymburner, M.S.M., Stouffville, Ont.
Beverley Tosh, M.S.M., Calgary, Alta.

GENERAL SERVICE AWARDS
Rather than creating a new honour for each new Canadian Forces operation as it arises, in July of 2004, Her Majesty the Queen approved the creation of the following:

The General Campaign Star (G.C.S.) recognizes military service in a theatre of operations in the presence of an armed enemy.

The General Service Medal (G.S.M.) acknowledges civilian and military service in direct support of operations in the presence of an armed enemy.

General Campaign Star/Étoile de campagne générale (G.C.S.)
None awarded since last edition.

General Service Medal/Médaille du service général (G.S.M.)
None awarded since last edition.

British & Commonwealth Honours

In earlier times Canadians could receive hereditary titles, knighthoods and other such honours under the British system of honours, and this is still the case with Canadians who pursue ca-

reers in the United Kingdom. Furthermore, the Canadian military system of decorations was based on the British system and many Canadians hold British honours as a result of service in Canadian, British or other Commonwealth forces. While Canada has developed its own honours system, honours are still from time to time granted by the Sovereign to Canadians for, among other things, service to the Commonwealth.

VICTORIA CROSS (V.C.)
The Victoria Cross was founded by Queen Victoria at the close of the Crimean War in 1856, but made retroactive to 1854. It is described as a Maltese cross, made of gun metal, with a Royal Crest in the centre and underneath it an escroll bearing the inscription "For Valour". It is awarded, irrespective of rank, to members of any branch of Her Majesty's services, either in the British Forces or those of any Commonwealth realm, dominion, colony or dependency, the Mercantile Marine, nurses or staffs of hospitals, or to civilians of either sex while serving in either regular or temporary capacity during naval, military, or air force operations. It is awarded only "for most conspicuous bravery or some daring or pre-eminent act of valour or self-sacrifice or extreme devotion to duty in the presence of the enemy." For additional conduct of similar bravery, a Bar is added. The ribbon was formerly red for the Army and blue for the Navy, but it is now red (a dull crimson) for all services. Since June 17th, 1943, the financial responsibility for a stipend to Canadian recipients has been assumed by the Canadian Government. Ninety-six V.C.s have been awarded to Canadians or to foreigners serving in Canadian forces. There are no living Canadian recipients of the Victoria Cross.

GEORGE CROSS (G.C.)
King George VI instituted the George Cross for civilians and members of the services alike, male or female, who performed "acts of the greatest heroism or of the most conspicuous courage in circumstances of extreme danger." This decoration - the second highest Commonwealth award for bravery - is a plain silver cross bearing in the centre a representation of Saint George slaying the dragon and the words: "For Gallantry". The ribbon is garter blue. Eleven Canadians, and a Bermudian serving in the Canadian Forces, have won the G.C. Not all were members of the armed forces. There are no living Canadian recipients of the George Cross.

ALBERT MEDAL (A.M.)
Ernest Alfred Wooding, A.M., R.C.N.V.R. - Queen Elizabeth II requested that all living Albert Medal recipients convert their Albert Medal to a George Cross in honour of her late father King George VI. For some reason Mr. Wooding did not convert his Albert Medal, which he had been awarded for saving two men from an engine room fire on Oct. 13, 1943. He died on Aug. 22, 2017, at the age of 99.

ROYAL HONOURS (COMMONWEALTH)
The Order of Baronets, the lowest Hereditary rank, was instituted in 1611; a Baronet is designated "Sir John Smith, Baronet." The abbreviation Bt. is used in Court Circulars and has been generally adopted in lieu of "Bart." Taking precedence to Baronets are members of The Most Honourable Privy Council, who are addressed "Right Honourable."
The Most Noble Order of the Garter, instituted 1349. - K.G.
The Most Ancient and Most Noble Order of the Thistle, instituted 1687. - K.T.
The Most Honourable Order of the Bath, instituted in 1399, and revived in 1725, is divided into three classes - Knights Grand Cross, G.C.B.; Knights Commanders, K.C.B.; and Companions, C.B.
The Order of Merit, O.M., carries no title.
The Most Distinguished Order of St. Michael and St. George, instituted in 1818, has three classes - Knights Grand Cross, G.C.M.G.; Knights Commanders, K.C.M.G.; Companions, C.M.G.
The Most Eminent Order of the Indian Empire instituted 1877, has three classes - Knights Grand Commanders, G.C.I.E.; Knights Commanders, K.C.I.E.; Companions, C.I.E. (This Order has not been conferred since 1947.)
The Royal Victorian Order, instituted in 1896, has five classes - Knights Grand Cross, G.C.V.O.; Knights Commanders, K.C.V.O.; Commanders, C.V.O., Lieutenants, L.V.O.; Members 4th and 5th classes - M.V.O. Ribbon, blue with red and white edges.
The Most Excellent Order of the British Empire, instituted in 1917, has five classes - Knights (or Dames) Grand Cross, G.B.E.; Knights Commanders, K.B.E.; Dames Commanders, D.B.E.; Commanders, C.B.E.; Officers, O.B.E.; and Members, M.B.E. Ribbon (Military) rose pink, pearl grey edging, vertical pearl stripe in centre; (Civil) rose pink, pearl grey edging, and no central vertical stripe.

Knights Bachelors are gentlemen unconnected with any order who have received the honour of Knighthood, and are entitled to the prefix "Sir". They rank immediately after Knights Commanders of the British Empire.
The Companions of Honour, C.H., instituted in 1917 rank immediately after Knights (Dames) Grand Cross of the Order of the British Empire. Membership is limited and carries no title.
In all Orders of Knighthood the Knights Grand Cross and the Knights Commanders have the prefix "Sir" with the initials of their class following the name. Companions and Members bear no title, but have the letters C.B., C.M.G., L.V.O., M.V.O., as the case may be, attached to their names.
The Garter, the Thistle, The Order of Merit and the Royal Victorian Order are all in the personal bestowal of the Sovereign. Appointments to the other Orders are made by Her Majesty on recommendation of the Prime Ministers of Commonwealth countries who wish to secure such appointments. Premiers of individual Australian states may also make recommendations.

MARQUESS
The Most Hon. the Marquess of Exeter, Michael Anthony Cecil, 8th Marquess
The Most Hon. the Marquess of Ely, Charles John Tottenham, 9th Marquess

EARLS
The Right Hon. the Earl Grey, Philip Kent Grey, 7th Earl
The Right Hon. the Earl of Orkney, Peter St. John, 9th Earl
The Right Hon. the Earl Winterton, Donald David Turnour, 8th Earl

VISCOUNTS
The Right Hon. the Viscount Charlemont, John Dodd Caulfield, 15th Viscount
The Right Hon. the Viscount Galway, John Philip Monckton-Arundell, 13th Viscount
The Right Hon. the Viscount Hardinge, Thomas Henry de Montarville Hardinge, 8th Viscount

OLD CANADIAN TITLE
The title of Baron de Longueuil existed prior to the Treaty of Paris (1763), and was duly recognized by Queen Victoria pursuant to that treaty.

BARONS
The Right Hon. the Lord Beaverbrook, Maxwell William Henry Aitken, 3rd Baron and 3rd Baronet
The Right Hon. the Lord Brain, Michael Cottrell Brain, 3rd Baron
The Right Hon. the Lord Lucas of Chilworth, Simon William Lucas, 3rd Baron
The Right Hon. the Lord Martonmere, John Stephen Robinson, 2nd Baron
The Right Hon. the Lord Morris, Thomas Anthony Salmon Morris, 4th Baron
The Right Hon. the Lord Rodney, John George Brydges Rodney, 11th Baron and 11th Baronet
The Right Hon. the Lord Sanford, James John Mowbray Edmonton Sanford, 3rd Baron
The Right Hon. the Lord Shaughnessy, Charles George Patrick Shaughnessy, 5th Baron
The Right Hon. the Lord Strathcona and Mount Royal, Donald Alexander Smith Howard, 5th Baron
The Right Hon. the Lord Thomson of Fleet David Kenneth Roy Thomson, 3rd Baron
The Right Hon. the Lord Wasserman, Gordon Joshua Wasserman, Life Baron.

BARONETS
Sir Richard Aylmer (16th Bt.)
Sir Christopher Hilaro Barlow (7th Bt.)
Sir James Barlow (4th Bt.)
Sir Benjamin Barrington (8th Bt.)
Sir James Bates (7th Bt)
Sir John Irving Bell, G.B.E. (1st Bt.)
Sir John Lowthian Bell (1st Bt.)
Sir Alexander Boyd (3rd Bt.)
Sir Theodore Jonathan Brinckman (7th Bt.)
Sir James Brunton (4th Bt.)
Sir John Peter Burbidge (7th Bt.)
Sir Richard Butler (4th Bt.)
Sir John Robert Charles Cave-Browne-Cave (17th Bt.)
Sir Bruce Chaytor (9th Bt.)
Sir Peter Chetwynd (10th Bt.)
Sir Richard Charles Davis (4th Bt.)
Sir David Hart Dyke (10th Bt.)
The Revd. Sir Christopher Gibson, Bt., C.P. (4th Bt.)
Sir James Grant-Suttie (9th Bt.)
Sir Philip Grotrian (3rd Bt.)
Sir Charles Gunning C.D., (8th Bt.)

Sir Wayne King (8th Bt.)
Sir Charles Knowles (7th Bt.)
Sir Colpoys Johnson (8th Bt.)
Sir Peter Lambert (11th Bt.)
Sir Richard Latham (3rd Bt.)
Sir John Leeds (9th Bt.)
Sir Alan Keith Mackworth (11th Bt.)
Sir Ian McGregor (8th Bt.)
Sir Roderick McQuhae MacKenzie (12th Bt.)
Sir Allan Morris (11th Bt.)
Sir Christopher Oakes (3rd Bt.)
Sir Matthew Philipson-Stow (6th Bt.)
Sir James Piers (11 Bt.)
Sir Francis Price, Bt. (7th Bt.)
Sir Christopher Robinson (8th Bt.)
Sir John James Michael Laud Robinson (11th Bt.)
Sir Julian Rose (5th Bt.)
Sir James Rugge-Price (10th Bt.)
Sir John Samuel (5th Bt.)
Sir Adrian Sharp (4th Bt.)
Sir Stephen Simeon (9th Bt.)
The Rev. Sir Michael Stonhouse (19th Bt.)
Sir Adrian Stott (4th Bt.)
Sir John Stracey (9th Bt.)
Sir Phillip Stuart (9th Bt.)
Sir Richard Sullivan (9th Bt.)
Sir Allen Synge (9th Bt.)
Sir Eric Touche (3rd Bt.)
Sir Charles Hibbert Tupper (6th Bt.)
Sir Gerald Walsham (6th Bt.)
Sir Ralph Wedgwood (4th Bt.)
Sir Christopher Wells, M.D. (3rd Bt.)
Sir Donald Williams (10th Bt.)

Knight Grand Cross of the Most Honourable Order of the Bath (G.C.B.)

The Order of Merit (O.M.)
The Right Honourable Jean Chrétien, P.C., O.M., C.C.

Knight Grand Cross or Dame Grand Cross of the Most Excellent Order of the British Empire (G.B.E.)
Sir John Irving Bell, G.B.E.

Member of the Order of the Companions of Honour (C.H.)
General John de Chastelain, C.C., C.M.M., C.H., C.D.
Margaret MacMillan, C.H., C.C.
Margaret Atwood, C.H., C.C.

Knight Commander of the Most Distinguished Order of St. Michael and St. George (K.C.M.G.)

Knight Commander of the Royal Victorian Order (K.C.V.O.)

Knight Commander of the Most Excellent Order of the British Empire (K.B.E.)

Knight Commander or Dame Commander of the Most Excellent Order of the British Empire (K.B.E. or D.B.E.)
Dame Clara Furse, D.B.E.
Dame Moya Greene, D.B.E.

KNIGHT BACHELOR
Sir George Bain
Sir Graham Day
Sir Terence Matthews, O.B.E.
Sir Christopher Ondaatje, C.B.E.
Sir Neil Shaw

Companion of the Most Honourable Order of the Bath (C.B.)
Air Vice-Marshal George Brookes, C.B., O.B.E.

Companion of the Most Distinguished Order of St. Michael and St. George (C.M.G.)
Laurent Robert Beaudoin, C.M.G.
H.J. Carmichael, C.M.G.
Edmond Cloutier, C.M.G., B.A., L.Ph.
Donovan Bartley Finn, C.M.G., M.Sc., Ph.D., F.R.S.C., F.C.I.C.
George H. McIvor, C.M.G.
Hector Brown McKinnon, C.C., C.M.G.
William Andrew O'Neil, C.M.G.
Alexander Ross, C.M.G.
Joseph Emile St. Laurent, C.M.G.
Ivor Otterbein Smith, C.M.G., O.B.E.

Companion of the Most Eminent Order of the Indian Empire (C.I.E.)
Maj. Frederick Wernham Gerrard, C.I.E.
Capt. John Ryland, C.I.E., R.C.N.
Maj. Frederick Augustus Berrill Sheppard, C.I.E., O.B.E.

Commander of the Royal Victorian Order (C.V.O.)
Leopold Henry Amyot, C.V.O.
Dr. Michael Jackson, C.V.O., C.D.
The Hon. David C. Lam, C.V.O., C.M., K.St.J., O.B.C.,
    B.A.(Econ.), M.B.A., L.L.D., D.Mil.Sc., D.H.L., D.H.
Veronica Jane Langton, C.V.O.
Judith A. LaRocque, C.V.O.
Kevin Stewart MacLeod, C.V.O.
Cdr. G.J. Manson, C.V.O., C.D., R.C.N.
John Crosbie Perlin, C.V.O.
L.Cdr. Lawrence James Wallace, C.V.O., O.C., O.B.C., R.C.N.V.R.
Stephen Wallace, C.V.O.
W. Galen Weston, C.V.O.
The Honourable Hilary Mary Weston, C.M., C.V.O., O.On.t

Commander of the Order of the British Empire (C.B.E.)
James Pomeroy Anderson, C.B.E.
George Herbert Bowler, C.B.E.
Howard Brown Chase, C.B.E.
Brig. Frederick Graham Coleman, C.B.E.
Air Commodore Barbara Cooper, C.B.E., R.A.F.
Elizabeth Denham, C.B.E.
Conrad Trelawny Fitz-Gerald, C.B.E., M.D.
Gerald Finley, C.B.E.
Charles Gavsie, C.B.E., Q.C.
Brig. Robert James Henderson, C.B.E.
Harold Ferguson Hodgson, C.B.E.
Sandra Horley, C.B.E.
Capt. Francis Deschamps Howie, C.B.E., D.S.O., R.N.
Alexander George Irvine, C.B.E.
Lester Millman Keachie, C.B.E., Q.C.
Allan Collingwood Travers Lewis, C.B.E., Q.C.
Gordon Clapp Lindsay, C.B.E.
John Struthers McNeil, C.B.E.
E.J. Mackie, C.B.E.
Raymond Charles Manning, C.B.E.
Walter Melvill Marshall, C.B.E.
James Matson, C.B.E.
Colin Matthews, C.B.E.
Luke William Pearsall, C.B.E.
Cyril Horace Frederick Pierrepont, C.B.E., E.D.
James Joseph Alexander Ross, C.B.E., C.D.
T.H. Savage, C.B.E.
Lynn Seymour, C.B.E.
Air Vice-Marshal Douglas McCully Smith, C.B.E., C.D.
Brig. Gerald Lucian Morgan Smith, C.B.E., C.D.
William Leonard O'Brien Stallard, C.B.E.
Air Cdre. Stanley Gibson Tackaberry, C.B.E.
Kenneth Wiffin Taylor, O.C., C.B.E.
George Gamlin Thomas, C.B.E.
Lyman Trumbull, C.B.E.

IMPERIAL SERVICE ORDER (I.S.O.)
George Clayton Anderson
Robert Albert Andison
Arthur Barnstead
Avila Bedard
Peter Cooligan
Henri Fortier
Frank Henry French
Arthur Leigh Jolliffe
Edward Jost
Louis MacMillan
Walter Clifton Ronson
David John Scott
Ivan Vallee

ROYAL VICTORIAN CHAIN
Bestows no precedence; currently not held by anyone.

QUEEN ELIZABETH II'S DIAMOND JUBILEE MEDAL
The Diamond Jubilee Medal program closed on February 28, 2013.

Order of Precedence for Orders, Decorations and Medals

The following is the approved order of prededence as of April 2, 1998. The asterisk indicates honours added since that date.

1. The sequence for wearing the insignia of Canadian orders, decorations and medals, and the post-nominal letters associated with such orders, decorations and medals are the following:
Victoria Cross (V.C.)
Cross of Valour (C.V.)

NATIONAL ORDERS
*Order of Merit (O.M.)
Companion of the Order of Canada (C.C.)
Officer of the Order of Canada (O.C.)

Member of the Order of Canada (C.M.)
Commander of the Order of Military Merit (C.M.M.)
*Commander of the Order of Merit of the Police Forces (C.O.M.)
Commander of the Royal Victorian Order (C.V.O.)
Officer of the Order of Military Merit (O.M.M.)
*Officer of the Order of Merit of the Police Forces (O.O.M.)
Lieutenant of the Royal Victorian Order (L.V.O.)
Member of the Order of Military Merit (M.M.M.)
*Member of the Order of Merit of the Police Forces (M.O.M.)
Member of the Royal Victorian Order (M.V.O.)
The Most Venerable Order of the Hospital of St. John of Jerusalem (all grades) (post-nominal letters only for internal use by the Order of St. John)

PROVINCIAL ORDERS
Ordre national du Québec (G.O.Q., O.Q., C.Q.)
Saskatchewan Order of Merit (S.O.M.)
Order of Ontario (O.Ont.)
Order of British Columbia (O.B.C.)
Alberta Order of Excellence (A.O.E.)
Order of Prince Edward Island (O.P.E.I.)
*Order of Manitoba (O.M.)
*Order of New Brunswick (O.N.B.)
*Order of Nova Scotia (O.N.S.)
*Order of Newfoundland & Labrador (O.N.L.)

TERRITORIAL ORDERS
*Order of Nunavut (O.Nu.)
*Order of the Northwest Territories (O.N.W.T.)
*Order of Yukon (O.Y.)

DECORATIONS
Star of Military Valour (S.M.V.)
Star of Courage (S.C.)
Meritorious Service Cross (M.S.C.)
Medal of Military Valour (M.M.V.)
Medal of Bravery (M.B.)
Meritorious Service Medal (M.S.M.)
Royal Victorian Medal (R.V.M.)

MEDALS
*Sacrifice Medal (S.M.)

WAR AND OPERATIONAL SERVICE MEDALS
Korea Medal
Canadian Volunteer Service Medal for Korea
Gulf and Kuwait Medal
Somalia Medal
*South-West Asia Service Medal
*General Campaign Star
    *Allied Force
    *South-West Asia
    *Expedition
*General Service Medal
    *Allied Force
    *South-West Asia
    *Expedition
*Operational Service Medal
    *South-West Asia
    *Sierra Leone
    *Haiti
    *Sudan
    *Humanitas
    *Expedition

SPECIAL SERVICE MEDALS (S.S.M.)
S.S.M. with bars for:
    Pakistan (1989-1990)
    Alert
    Peace/Paix
    NATO/OTAN
    Humanitas
    *Ranger
    *Expedition
*Canadian Peacekeeping Service Medal (C.P.S.M.)

UNITED NATIONS MEDALS
Service (Korea) (1950-54)
Emergency Force (Egypt/Sinai) (1956-67)
Truce Supervision Organization in Palestine (1948-) and Observer Group in Lebanon (1958)
Military Observation Group in India and Pakistan (1948-)
Operation in Congo (1960-64)
Temporary Executive Authority in West New Guinea (1962-63)
Yemen Observation Mission (1963-64)
Force in Cyprus (1964-)
India/Pakistan Observation Misison (1965-66)
Emergency Force Middle East (1973-79)
Disengagement Observation Force Golan Heights (1974-)
Interim Force in Lebanon (1978-)

Military Observation Group in Iran/Iraq (1988-91)
Transition Assistance Group (Namibia) (1989-90)
Observer Group in Central America (1989-92)
Iraq/Kuwait Observer Mission (1991-)
Angola Verification Mission (1988-97)
Mission for the Referendum in Western Sahara (1991-)
Observer Mission in El Salvador (1991-95)
Protection Force (Yugoslavia) (1992-95)
Advance Mission in Cambodia (1991-92)
Transitional Authority in Cambodia (1992-93)
Operation in Somalia (1992-93)
Operation in Mozambique (1992-94)
Observation Mission in Uganda/Rwanda (1993-94)
Assistance Mission in Rwanda (1993-96)
Mission in Haïti (1993-)
Verification of Human Rights and Compliance with the
    Comprehensive Agreement on Human Rights in Guatemala
    (1997-98)
*Mission in the Central African Republic (1998-2000)
*Preventive Deployment Force (Macedonia) (1995-99)
*Mission in Bosnia and Herzegovina (1995-)
*Mission of Observers in Prevlaka (Croatia) (1996-)
*Interim Administration Mission in Kosovo (1999-)
*Observer Mission in Sierra Leone (1999-)
*Mission in East Timor and Transitional Administration in East
    Timor (1999-)
*Mission in the Democratic Republic of the Congo (1999-)
*Mission in Ethiopia and Eritrea (2000-)
*Stabilization Mission in Haiti (2004-)
*Operation in Côte D'Ivoire (2004-)
*Mission in Sudan (2005-)
*Integrated Mission in Timor-Leste (2006-)
*Hybrid Mission with the African Union in Darfur (2007-)
*Mission in the Republic of South Sudan
*Multidimensional Integrated Stabilization Mission in Mali
Special Service (1995-)
*Headquarters

NATO MEDALS
*North Atlantic Treaty Organization (NATO) Medal for the Former
    Yugoslavia (1992-2002)
*NATO Medal for Kosovo (1999-2002)
*NATO Medal for the Former Yugoslav Republic of Macedonia
    (2001-02)
*Article 5 NATO Medal for Operation "Eagle Assist" (2001-02)
*Article 5 NATO Medal for Operation "Active Endeavour"
    (2001-16)
*Non-Article 5 NATO Medal for Operations in the Balkans
    (2003-)
*Non-Article 5 NATO Medal for the NATO Training Mission in
    Iraq (2004-11)
*Non-Article 5 NATO Medal for NATO Logistical Support to the
    African Union Mission in Sudan (2005-2007)
*Non-Article 5 NATO Medal for service on operations and
    activities approved by the North Atlantic Council in relation to
    Africa (2008-)
*Non-Article 5 NATO Medal for Service on NATO Operation
    "Unified Protector - Libya" (2011-)
*Non-Article 5 NATO Medal for Service with NATO in relation to
    Operation "Sea Guardian" (2017-)

INTERNATIONAL COMMISSION AND ORGANIZATION
MEDALS
International Commission for Supervision and Control
    (Indo-China) (1954-74)
International Commission for Control and Supervision (Vietnam)
    (1973)
Multinational Force and Observers (Sinai) (1982-)
European Community Monitor Mission (Yugoslavia) (1991-)
*International Force East Timor (1999-)
*European Security and Defence Policy Service Medal /
    Common Security and Defence Policy Service Medal

POLAR AND VOLUNTEER MEDALS
*Polar Medal
*Sovereign's Medal for Volunteers

COMMEMORATIVE MEDALS
Canadian Centennial Medal (1967)
Queen Elizabeth II's Silver Jubilee Medal (1977)
125th Anniversary of the Confederation of Canada Medal (1992)
*Queen Elizabeth II's Golden Jubilee Medal (2002)
*Queen Elizabeth II's Diamond Jubilee Medal (2012)

LONG SERVICE AND GOOD CONDUCT MEDALS
R.C.M.P. Long Service Medal
Canadian Forces Decoration (C.D.)

EXEMPLARY SERVICE MEDALS
Police Exemplary Service Medal

Corrections Exemplary Service Medal
Fire Services Exemplary Service Medal
Canadian Coast Guard Exemplary Service Medal
Emergency Medical Services Exemplary Service Medal
*Peace Officer Exemplary Service Medal

SPECIAL MEDAL
Queen's Medal for Champion Shot

OTHER MEDALS
Ontario Medal for Good Citizenship (O.M.C.)
Ontario Medal for Police Bravery
Ontario Medal for Firefighters Bravery
Saskatchewan Volunteer Medal (S.V.M.)
Ontario Provincial Police Long Service and Good Conduct Medal
Service Medal of the Most Venerable Order of the Hospital of St.
    John of Jerusalem
Commissionaire Long Service Medal
*Newfoundland and Labrador Bravery Award
*Newfoundland and Labrador Volunteer Service Medal
*British Columbia Fire Services Long Service and Bravery
    Medals
*Commemorative Medal for the Centennial of Saskatchewan
*Alberta Centennial Medal

2. The Bar to the Special Service Medal is worn centred on the
ribbon. If there is more than one Bar, they are spaced evenly on
the ribbon with the most recent uppermost.

3. Commonwealth orders, decorations and medals, the award of
which is approved by the Government of Canada, are worn after
Canadian orders, decorations and medals listed in Section 1, the
precedence in each category being set by the date of
appointment or award.

4. Foreign orders, decorations and medals, the award of which is
approved by the Government of Canada, are worn after those
referred to in Sections 1 and 3, the precedence in each category
being set by the date of appointment or award.

5. Notwithstanding Sections 1, 3 and 4, a person who, prior to 1
June, 1972, was a member of a British Order or the recipient of
a British decoration or medal referred to in this section, may
wear the insignia of the decoration or medal together with the in-
signia of any Canadian order, decoration or medal that the per-
son is entitled to wear, the proper sequence being the following:
Victoria Cross (V.C.)
George Cross (G.C.)
Cross of Valour (C.V.)
Order of Merit (O.M.)
Order of the Companions of Honour (C.H.)
Companion of the Order of Canada (C.C.)
Officer of the Order of Canada (O.C.)
Member of the Order of Canada (C.M.)
Commander of the Order of Military Merit (C.M.M.)
*Commander of the Order of Merit of the Police Forces (C.O.M.)
Companion of the Order of the Bath (C.B.)
Companion of the Order of St. Michael and St. George (C.M.G.)
Commander of the Royal Victorian Order (C.V.O.)
Commander of the Order of the British Empire (C.B.E.)
Distinguished Service Order (D.S.O.)
Officer of the Order of Military Merit (O.M.M.)
*Officer of the Order of Merit of the Police Force (O.O.M.)
Lieutenant of the Royal Victorian Order (L.V.O.)
Officer of the Order of the British Empire (O.B.E.)
Imperial Service Order (I.S.O.)
Member of the Order of Military Merit (M.M.M.)
*Member of the Order of the Police Forces (M.O.M.)
Member of the Royal Victorian Order (M.V.O.)
Member of the Order of the British Empire (M.B.E.)
Member of the Royal Red Cross (R.R.C.)
Distinguished Service Cross (D.S.C.)
Military Cross (M.C.)
Distinguished Flying Cross (D.F.C.)
Air Force Cross (A.F.C.)
Star of Military Valour (S.M.V.)
Star of Courage (S.C.)
Meritorious Service Cross (M.S.C.)
Medal of Military Valour (M.M.V.)
Medal of Bravery (M.B.)
Meritorious Service Medal (M.S.M.)
Associate of the Royal Red Cross (A.R.R.C.)
The Most Venerable Order of St. John of Jerusalem (all grades)
    (post-nominal letters only for internal use by the Order of St.
    John)
Provincial Orders (order of precedence as set out in Section 1)
*Territorial Orders (order of precedence as set out in Section 1)
Distinguished Conduct Medal (D.C.M.)
Conspicuous Gallantry Medal (C.G.M.)
George Medal (G.M.)
Distinguished Service Medal (D.S.M.)

Military Medal (M.M.)
Distinguished Flying Medal (D.F.M.)
Air Force Medal (A.F.M.)
Queen's Gallantry Medal (Q.G.M.)
Royal Victorian Medal (R.V.M.)
British Empire Medal (B.E.M.)

WAR AND OPERATIONAL SERVICE MEDALS
Africa General Service Medal (1902-56)
India General Service Medal (1908-35)
Naval General Service Medal (1915-62)
India General Service Medal (1936-39)
General Service Medal - Army and Air Force (1918-62)
General Service Medal (1962-)
1914 Star
1914-1915 Star
British War Medal (1914-18)
Mercantile Marine War Medal (1914-18)
Victory Medal (1914-18)
Territorial Force War Medal (1914-19)
1939-1945 Star
Atlantic Star
Air Crew Europe Star
*Arctic Star
Africa Star
Pacific Star
Burma Star
Italy Star
France and Germany Star
Defence Medal
Canadian Volunteer Service Medal
Newfoundland Second World War Volunteer Service Medal (see
    Section 6)
War Medal (1939-45)
Korea Medal
Canadian Volunteer Service Medal for Korea
Gulf and Kuwait Medal
Somalia Medal
*South-West Asia Service Medal
*General Campaign Medal
*General Service Medal

SPECIAL SERVICE MEDALS
(The order of precedence is as set out for Special Service
    Medals in Section 1.)

UNITED NATIONS MEDALS
(The order of precedence is as set out for United Nations Medals
    in Section 1.)

INTERNATIONAL COMMISSION MEDALS
(The order of precedence is as set out for International
    Commission and Organization Medals in Section 1.)

POLAR MEDALS
(The order of precedence is by order of date awarded.)

COMMEMORATIVE MEDALS
King George V's Silver Jubilee Medal (1935)
King George VI's Coronation Medal (1937)
Queen Elizabeth II's Coronation Medal (1953)
Canadian Centennial Medal (1967)
Queen Elizabeth II's Silver Jubilee Medal (1977)
125th Anniversary of the Confederation of Canada Medal (1992)
*Queen Elizabeth II's Golden Jubilee Medal (2002)
*Queen Elizabeth II's Diamond Jubilee Medal (2012)

LONG SERVICE AND GOOD CONDUCT MEDALS
Army Long Service and Good Conduct Medal
Naval Long Service and Good Conduct Medal
Air Force Long Service and Good Conduct Medal
RCMP Long Service Medal
Volunteer Officer's Decoration (V.D.)
Volunteer Long Service Medal
Colonial Auxiliary Forces Officer's Decoration (V.D.)
Colonial Auxiliary Forces Long Service Medal
Efficiency Decoration (E.D.)
Efficiency Medal
Naval Volunteer Reserve Decoration (V.R.D.)
Naval Volunteer Reserve Long Service and Good Conduct
    Medal
Air Efficiency Award
Canadian Forces Decoration (C.D.)

EXEMPLARY SERVICE MEDALS
(The order of precedence is as set out for Exemplary Service
    Medals in Section 1.)

SPECIAL MEDAL
Queen's Medal for Champion Shot

OTHER DECORATIONS AND MEDALS
(The order of precedence is as set out for Other Decorations and Medals in Section 1.)

6. The Newfoundland Volunteer War Service Medal has the same precedence as the Canadian Volunteer Service Medal.

7. The insignia of orders, decorations and medals not listed above, as well as foreign awards, the award of which has not been approved by the Government of Canada, shall not be mounted or worn in conjunction with orders, decorations and medals listed in this Directive.

8. The insignia of orders, decorations and medals shall not be worn by anyone other than the recipient of the orders, decorations or medals.

NOTE: Policy regarding the wearing of non-authorized awards
Only the insignia of orders, decorations and medals officially awarded under the authority of the Crown or that the wearing of which has been authorized by the Crown may be worn. Only the actual recipient of an honour can wear its insignia; no family member or any person other than the original recipient may wear the insignia of an order, decoration or medal. Insignia that are purchased or otherwise acquired may be used for display purpose only and cannot be worn on the person in any form or manner.

Abbreviations Indicating Honours and Decorations

A.F.C. - Air Force Cross. Ribbon, wide diagonal stripes of white and red.

A.F.M. - Air Force Medal. Ribbon, narrow diagonal stripes of white and red.

A.M. - Albert Medal, gold (Sea). Ribbon, nine alternate narrow stripes of blue and white.

Albert Medal, gold (Land). Ribbon, nine alternate narrow stripes of red and white.

Albert Medal, bronze (Sea). Ribbon, blue ground with two wide stripes of white.

Albert Medal, bronze (Land). Ribbon, red ground with two wide stripes of white.

B.E.M. - British Empire Medal.

Bt. - Baronet

C.B. - Companion of the Most Honourable Order of the Bath.

C.B.E. - Commander of the Order of the British Empire.

C.C. - Companion of the Order of Canada.

C.D. - Canadian Forces Decoration.

C.G.M. - Conspicuous Gallantry Medal; Navy and Air Force. It carries a cash grant. The Navy Medal ribbon is white with dark blue edges; the Air Force ribbon is light blue with dark blue edges.

C.H. - Member of the Order of the Companions of Honour.

C.I.E. - Companion of the Most Eminent Order of the Indian Empire.

C.M. - Member of the Order of Canada.

C.M.G. - Companion of the Most Distinguished Order of St. Michael and St. George.

C.M.M. - Commander of the Order of Military Merit.

C.P.S.M. - Canadian Peacekeeping Service Medal.

C.S.I. - Companion of the Most Exalted Order of the Star of India.

C.V. - Cross of Valour.

C.V.O. - Commander of the Royal Victorian Order.

D.C.M. - Distinguished Conduct Medal. Ribbon, red ground, dark blue stripe in centre.

D.F.C. - Distinguished Flying Cross. Ribbon, wide diagonal stripes of violet and white.

D.F.M. - Distinguished Flying Medal. Ribbon, narrow diagonal stripes of white and violet.

D.S.C. - Distinguished Service Cross. Ribbon, three broad bands, dark blue, white, dark blue.

D.S.M. - Distinguished Service Medal.

D.S.O. - Companion of the Distinguished Service Order. Instituted 1886. Ribbon, dark red with dark blue stripe at each end.

E.D. - Canadian Efficiency Decoration for Officers of Military Auxiliary Forces.

E.M. - Edward Medal. Posthumous award.

E.M. - Efficiency Medal.

G.B.E. - Knight Grand Cross or Dame Grand Cross of the Most Excellent Order of the British Empire.

G.C. - George Cross.

G.C.B. - Knight Grand Cross of the Most Honourable Order of the Bath.

G.C.I.E. - Knight Grand Commander of the Most Eminent Order of the Indian Empire.

G.C.M.G. - Knight Grand Cross of the Most Distinguished Order of St. Michael and St. George.

G.C.S.I. - Knight Grand Commander of the Most Exalted Order of the Star of India.

G.C.V.O. - Knight Grand Cross of the Royal Victorian Order.

G.M. - George Medal.

I.S.M. - Imperial Service Medal.

I.S.O. - Companion of the Imperial Service Order. Instituted 1902.

K.B.E. - Knight Commander of the Most Excellent Order of the British Empire.

K.C.B. - Knight Commander of the Most Honourable Order of the Bath.

K.C.I.E. - Knight Commander of the Most Eminent Order of the Indian Empire.

K.C.M.G. - Knight Commander of the Most Distinguished Order of St. Michael and St. George.

K.C.S.I. - Knight Commander of the Most Exalted Order of the Star of India.

K.C.V.O. - Knight Commander of the Royal Victorian Order.

K.G. - Knight of the Most Noble Order of the Garter.

K.P. - Knight of the Most Illustrious Order of St. Patrick.

Kt. - Knight Bachelor.

K.T. - Knight of the Most Ancient and Most Noble Order of the Thistle.

L.V.O. - Lieutenant of the Royal Victorian Order.

M.B. - Medal of Bravery.

M.B.E. - Member of the Order of the British Empire.

M.C. - Military Cross. Instituted 1915. Ribbon, white with broad band of blue in centre.

M. du C. - Canada Medal.

M.M. - Military Medal.

M.M.M. - Member of the Order of Military Merit.

M.V.O. - Member of the Royal Victorian Order.

M.S.C. - Meritorious Service Cross.

M.S.M. - Meritorious Service Medal.

O.B.E. - Officer of the Order of the British Empire.

O.C. - Officer of the Order of Canada.

O.M. - Member of the Order of Merit.

O.M.M. - Officer of the Order of Military Merit.

P.C. - Privy Counsellor.

R.R.C. - Royal Red Cross. Instituted 1883. Ribbon, dark blue with narrow band of dark red at each end.

R.V.M. - Royal Victorian Medal.

S.C. - Star of Courage.

S.S.M. - Special Service Medal

U.E. - Unity of Empire. Descendants of United Empire Loyalists.

V.C. - Victoria Cross.

V.D. - Auxiliary Forces (Volunteer) Officers' Decoration.

V.R.D. - Naval Volunteer Reserve Decoration.

Canada's Walk of Fame

Since 1998, Canada's Walk of Fame has helped to celebrate the great depth of talent found in Canadian culture. Here is a list of the inductees honoured by the Walk of Fame, by year.

2021	2020	2019	2018
Banting, Best, Macleod & Collip	Allan Slaight	Will Arnett	Leonard Cohen
Salome Bey		Frank Gehry	Chris Hadfield
Jully Black		Cindy Klassen	Andy Kim
Bruce Cockburn		Mark Messier	Joanne Liu
Roméo Dallaire		Mr. Dressup	Andrea Martin
Laurent Duvernay-Tardif		James Naismith	Jimmy Pattison
Graham Greene		Jim Treliving	Seth Rogen & Evan Goldberg
Bret Hart		Triumph	Tessa Virtue & Scott Moir
Keanu Reeves			
Serena Ryder			
Ajay Virmani			
Damian Warner			

2017	2016	2015	2014
Donovan Bailey	Jeanne Beker	Michael Bublé	Louise Arbour CC GOQ
Stompin' Tom Connors	Corey Hart	Wendy Crewson	The Band
Viola Desmond	Deepa Mehta	Don Cherry & Ron MacLean	Jeff Healey
Anna Paquin	Jason Priestley	Lorne Greene	Rachel McAdams
Ted Rogers	Darryl Sittler	Lawrence Hill	Ryan Reynolds
David Suzuki	Al Waxman	Silken Laumann	Hayley Wickenheiser

2013	2012	2011	2010
Bob Ezrin	Team Canada 1972	Dr. Roberta Bondar	David Clayton-Thomas
Terry Fox	Randy Bachman	Burton Cummings	Nelly Furtado
Victor Garber	Phil Hartman	Daniel Nestor	Doug Henning
Craig Kielburger	Russ Jackson	Sandra Oh	Clara Hughes
Marc Kielburger	Sarah McLachlan	Russell Peters	Eric McCormack
Oscar Peterson	Sonia Rodriguez	Mordecai Richler	Farley Mowat
Christine Sinclair			Sarah Polley
Alan Thicke			

2009	2008	2007	2006
Blue Rodeo	Frances Bay	Johnny Bower	Pamela Anderson
Raymond Burr	James Cameron	Rick Hansen	Jann Arden
Dan and Dean Caten	Kids in the Hall	Jill Hennessy	Crazy Canucks
Kim Cattrall	k.d. lang	Nickelback	Brendan Fraser
Tom Cochrane	Steve Nash	Catherine O'Hara	Robert Goulet
Howie Mandel	Douglas Shearer	Gordon Pinsent	Eugene Levy
Robert Munsch	Norma Shearer	Lloyd Robertson	Paul Shaffer
Chantal Petitclerc	Daria Werbowy		Alex Trebek

2005	2004	2003	2002
Paul Anka	Denys Arcand	Scotty Bowman	Dan Aykroyd
George Chuvalo	Jim Carrey	Toller Cranston	Cirque du Soleil
Michael Cohl	Shirley Douglas	Jim Elder	Alex Colville
Pierre Cossette	John Kay	Linda Evangelista	Timothy Findley
Rex Harrington	Diana Krall	Lynn Johnston	David Foster
Daniel Lanois	Mario Lemieux	Lorne Michaels	Wayne Gretzky
Alanis Morissette	Louis B. Mayer	Mike Myers	Monty Hall
Kiefer Sutherland	Mack Sennett	Luc Plamondon	Ronnie Hawkins
Fay Wray	Helen Shaver	Robbie Robertson	Arthur Hiller
	Jack L. Warner	David Steinberg	Guy Lombardo
		Shania Twain	SCTV
			The Tragically Hip

2001	2000	1999	1998
Kenojuak Ashevak	Maureen Forrester	Juliette Cavazzi	Bryan Adams
Margaret Atwood	Michael J. Fox	David Cronenberg	Pierre Berton
Jean Béliveau	Evelyn Hart	Hume Cronyn	John Candy
Alexander Graham Bell	Gordie Howe	Céline Dion	Glenn Gould
Kurt Browning	William Hutt	Nancy Greene	Norman Jewison
Ferguson Jenkins	Joni Mitchell	Lou Jacobi	Karen Kain
Harry Winston	Ginette Reno	Mary Pickford	Gordon Lightfoot
Jerome	Jean-Paul Riopelle	Maurice Richard	Rich Little
Robert Lepage	Royal Canadian Air Farce	Rush	Anne Murray
Leslie Nielsen	William Shatner	Buffy Sainte-Marie	Bobby Orr
Walter Ostanek	Martin Short	Wayne and Shuster	Christopher Plummer
Ivan Reitman	Donald Sutherland		Barbara Ann Scott
Teresa Stratas	Neil Young		Jacques Villeneuve
Veronica Tennant			
The Guess Who			

Government

Table of Precedence for Canada

1. The Governor General of Canada or the Administrator of the Government of Canada. (Notes 1, 1.1, 2 & 2.1).
2. The Prime Minister of Canada. (Note 3).
3. The Chief Justice of Canada. (Note 4).
4. The Speaker of the Senate.
5. The Speaker of the House of Commons.
6. Ambassadors, High Commissioners, Ministers Plenipotentiary. (Note 5).
7. Members of the Canadian Ministry:
   a. Members of the Cabinet; and
   b. Ministers of State; with relative precedence within sub-categories (a) and (b) governed by the date of their appointment to the Queen's Privy Council for Canada.
8. The Leader of the Opposition. (Subject to Note 3).
9. The Lieutenant Governor of Ontario;
   The Lieutenant Governor of Québec;
   The Lieutenant Governor of Nova Scotia;
   The Lieutenant Governor of New Brunswick;
   The Lieutenant Governor of Manitoba;
   The Lieutenant Governor of British Columbia;
   The Lieutenant Governor of Prince Edward Island;
   The Lieutenant Governor of Saskatchewan;
   The Lieutenant Governor of Alberta;
   The Lieutenant Governor of Newfoundland & Labrador (Note 6).
10. Members of the Queen's Privy Council for Canada, not of the Canadian Ministry, in accordance with the date of their appointment to the Privy Council but with precedence given to those who bear the honorary title "Right Honourable" in accordance with the date of receiving the honorary title.
11. Premiers of the Provinces of Canada in the same order as Lieutenant Governors. (Note 6).
12. The Commissioner of the Northwest Territories; The Commissioner of the Yukon Territory; The Commissioner of Nunavut
13. Premiers of the Territories of Canada in the same order as Commissioners. (Note 7).
14. Representatives of faith communities. (Note 8).
15. Puisne Judges of the Supreme Court of Canada.
16. The Chief Justice and the Associate Chief Justice of the Federal Court of Canada.
17. (a) Chief Justices of the highest court of each Province and Territory; and
    (b) Chief Justices and Associate Chief Justices of the other superior courts of the Provinces and Territories; with precedence within sub-categories (a) and (b) governed by the date of appointment as Chief Justice.
18. (a) Judges of the Federal Court of Canada.
    (b) Puisne Judges of the superior courts of the Provinces and Territories.
    (c) the Chief Judge of the Tax Court of Canada;
    (d) the Associate Chief Judge of the Tax Court of Canada; and
    (e) Judges of the Tax Court of Canada; with precedence within each sub-category governed by date of appointment.
19. Senators of Canada.
20. Members of the House of Commons.
21. Consuls General of countries without diplomatic representation.
22. Clerk of the Privy Council and Secretary to Cabinet.
23. The Chief of the Defence Staff and the Commissioner of the Royal Canadian Mounted Police. (Note 9).
24. Speakers of Legislative Assemblies, within their Provinces and Territory.
25. Members of the Executive Councils, within their Province and Territory.
26. Judges of Provincial and Territorial Courts, within their Province and Territory.
27. Members of Legislative Assemblies, within their Province and Territory.
28. Chairperson of the Canadian Association of Former Parliamentarians.

NOTES

1. The presence of the Sovereign in Canada does not impair or supersede the authority of the Governor General to perform the functions delegated to him under the Letters Patent constituting the office of the Governor General. The Governor General, under all circumstances, should be accorded precedence immediately after the Sovereign.
1.1. In the absence of the Governor General of Canada and the Administrator of the Government of Canada, precedence to be given immediately after the Prime Minister of Canada to

the Lieutenant Governor of the province in which the ceremony or occasion takes place.
2. Precedence to be given immediately after the Chief Justice of Canada to former Governors General, with relative precedence among them governed by the date of their leaving office.
2.1 Precedence to be given immediately after the former Governors General to surviving spouses of deceased former Governors General (applicable only where the spouse was married to the Governor General during the latter's term of office), with relative precedence among them governed by the dates on which the deceased former Governor General left office.
3. Precedence to be given immediately after the surviving spouses of deceased former Governors General referred to in Note 2.1 to former Prime Ministers, with relative precedence among them governed by the dates of their first assumption of office.
4. Precedence to be given immediately after former Prime Ministers to former Chief Justices of Canada, with relative precedence among them governed by the dates of their appointment as Chief Justice of Canada.
5. Precedence among Ambassadors and High Commissioners, who rank equally, to be determined by the date of the presentation of their credentials. Precedence to be given to Chargés d'Affaires immediately after Ministers Plenipotentiary.
6. This provision does not apply to such ceremonies and occasions which are of a provincial nature.
7. This provision does not apply to such ceremonies and occasions which are of a territorial nature.
8. The religious dignitaries will be senior Canadian representatives of faith communities having a significant presence in a relevant jurisdiction. The relevant precedence of the representatives of faith communities is to be governed by the date of their assumption in their present office, their representatives being given the same relative precedence.
9. This precedence to be given to the Chief of the Defence Staff and the Commissioner of the R.C.M.P. on occasions when they have official functions to perform, otherwise they

are to have equal precedence with Deputy Ministers, with their relative position to be determined according to the respective dates of their appointments to office. The relative precedence of Deputy Ministers and other high officials of the public service of Canada is to be determined from time to time by the Minister of Canadian Heritage in consultation with the Prime Minister.

Courtesy of the Department of Canadian Heritage.
© All rights reserved. Table of Precedence for Canada. Reproduced with the permission of the Minister of Canadian Heritage, 2021.

Table of Titles to Be Used in Canada

1. The Governor General of Canada to be styled "Right Honourable" for life and to be styled "His Excellency" and his wife "Her Excellency", or "Her Excellency" and her husband "His Excellency", as the case may be, while in office.
2. The Lieutenant Governor of a Province to be styled "Honourable" for life and to be styled "His Honour" and his wife "Her Honour", or "Her Honour" and her husband "His Honour", as the case may be, while in office.
3. The Prime Minister of Canada to be styled "Right Honourable" for life.
4. The Chief Justice of Canada to be styled "Right Honourable" for life.
5. Privy Councillors of Canada to be styled "Honourable" for life.
6. Senators of Canada to be styled "Honourable" for life.
7. The Speaker of the House of Commons to be styled "Honourable" while in office.
8. The Commissioner of a Territory to be styled "Honourable" while in office.
9. Puisne judges of the Supreme Court of Canada and judges of the Federal Court and of the Tax Court of Canada as well as the judges of the under mentioned Courts in the Provinces and Territories to be styled "Honourable" while in office:

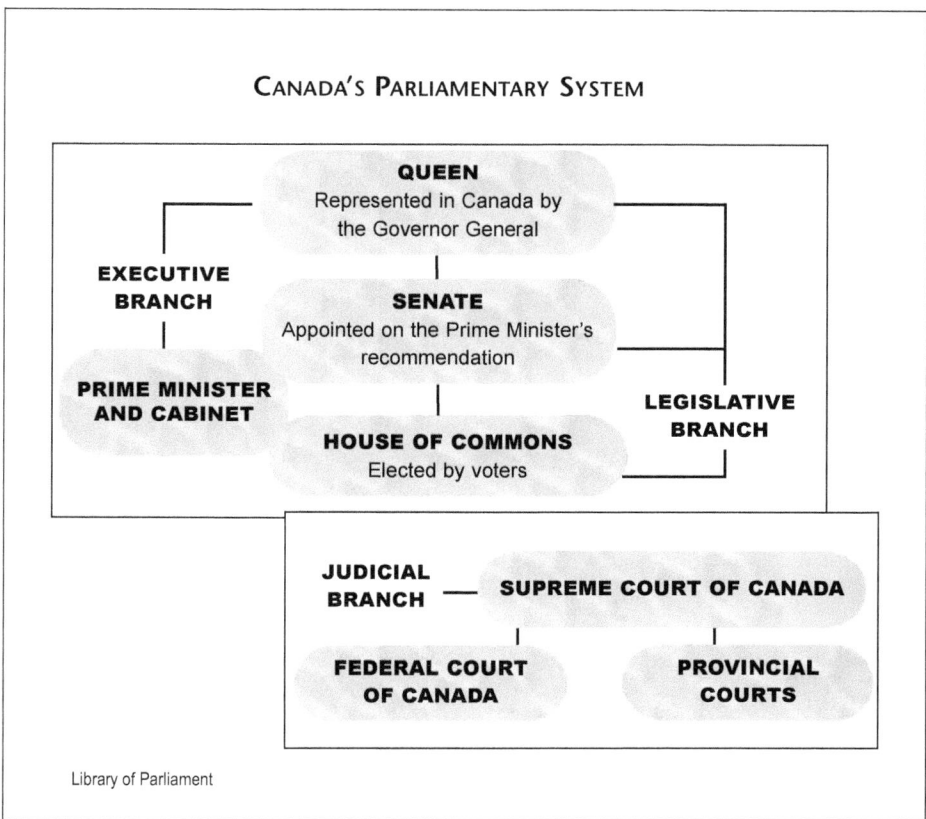

CANADA'S PARLIAMENTARY SYSTEM

Library of Parliament

Parliament as a legislative body functions as an instrument of government within a broader structure that includes the Executive Branch and the Judicial Branch. In the Westminster-based model of parliamentary government, the Executive, comprised of the Prime Minister and the Cabinet, is incorporated into Parliament, while retaining a separate sphere of authority and autonomy. The Judiciary, consisting of the Supreme Court and all the other courts of the land, is the third branch of government that is also independent of either Parliament or the Executive.

Ontario - Court of Appeal and the Ontario Court of Justice (General Division)

Québec - The Court of Appeal and the Superior Court of Québec

Nova Scotia - The Court of Appeal and the Supreme Court of Nova Scotia

New Brunswick - The Court of Appeal and the Court of Queen's Bench of New Brunswick

Manitoba - The Court of Appeal and the Court of Queen's Bench of Manitoba

British Columbia - The Court of Appeal and the Supreme Court of British Columbia

Prince Edward Island - The Supreme Court of Prince Edward Island

Saskatchewan - The Court of Appeal and the Court of Queen's Bench of Saskatchewan

Alberta - The Court of Appeal and the Court of Queen's Bench of Alberta

Newfoundland - The Supreme Court of Newfoundland

Northwest Territories - The Supreme Court of Northwest Territories

Yukon Territory - The Supreme Court of Yukon

Nunavut Territory - The Nunavut Court of Justice

10. Presidents and Speakers of the Legislative Assemblies of the Provinces and Territories to be styled "Honourable" while in office.

11. Members of the Executive Councils of the Provinces and Territories to be styled "Honourable" while in office.

12. Judges of Provincial and Territorial Courts (appointed by the Provincial and Territorial Governments) to be styled "Honourable" while in office.

13. The following are eligible to be granted permission by the Governor General, in the name of Her Majesty The Queen, to retain the title of "Honourable" after they have ceased to hold office: (a) Speakers of the House of Commons; (b) Commissioners of Territories; (c) Judges designated in item 9.

14. The title "Right Honourable" is granted for life to the following eminent Canadian: The Right Honourable Donald F. Mazankowski

GOVERNORS GENERAL OF CANADA SINCE CONFEDERATION

(WITH INSTALLATION DATE)

The Viscount Monck,
G.C.M.G.
July 1, 1867

Lord Lisgar,
G.C.M.G.
February 2, 1869

The Earl of Dufferin,
K.P., G.C.B., G.C.S.I., G.C.M.G.,
G.C.I.E
June 25, 1872

The Marquess of Lorne,
K.T., G.C.M.G., G.C.V.O.
November 25, 1878

The Marquess of Lansdowne,
K.G., G.C.S.I., G.C.M.G., G.C.I.E.
October 23, 1883

Lord Stanley of Preston,
K.G., G.C.B., G.C.V.O.
June 11, 1888

The Earl of Aberdeen,
K.T., G.C.M.G., G.C.V.O.
September 18, 1893

The Earl of Minto,
K.G., G.C.S.I., G.C.M.G., G.C.I.E.
November 12, 1898

The Earl Grey,
G.C.B., G.C.M.G., G.C.V.O.
December 10, 1904

H.R.H. the Duke of Connaught &
Strathearn,
K.G., K.T., K.P., G.M.B., G.C.S.I.,
G.C.M.G., G.C.I.E., G.C.V.O.,
G.B.E., T.D.
October 13, 1911

The Duke of Devonshire,
K.G., G.C.M.G., G.C.V.O., T.D.
November 11, 1916

General Lord Byng of Vimy,
G.C.B., G.C.M.G., M.V.O.
August 11, 1921

The Viscount Willingdon of Ratton,
G.C.S.I., G.C.M.G., G.C.I.E., G.B.E.
October 2, 1926

The Earl of Bessborough,
G.C.M.G.
April 4, 1931

**Lord Tweedsmuir of Elsfield, P.C.,
G.C.M.G., G.C.V.O., C.H.**
Nov. 2, 1935

**Major-General the Earl of Athlone,
K.G., P.C., G.C.B., G.C.M.G., G.C.V.O.,
D.S.O.**
June 21, 1940

**Field Marshal the Rt. Hon. Viscount
Alexander of Tunis,
K.G., P.C., G.C.B., O.M., G.C.M.G.,
C.S.I., D.S.O., M.C., D.C.**
April 12, 1946

**The Rt. Hon. Vincent Massey,
P.C., C.C., C.H., C.D.**
Feb. 28, 1952

**Major-General
the Rt. Hon. Georges-P. Vanier,
P.C., D.S.O., M.C., C.D.**
Sept. 15, 1959

**The Rt. Hon. Roland Michener,
P.C., C.C., C.M.M., O.Ont., C.D.,
Q.C.**
Apr. 17, 1967

**The Rt. Hon. Jules Léger
P.C., C.C., C.M.M., C.D.**
Jan. 14, 1974

**The Rt. Hon.
Edward Richard Schreyer,
P.C., C.C., C.M.M., O.M., C.D.**
Jan. 22, 1979

**The Rt. Hon. Jeanne Sauvé,
P.C., C.C., C.M.M., C.D.**
May 14, 1984

Photo Credit: © Yousuf Karsh. Reproduced with
the permission of the Estate.

**The Rt. Hon.
Ramon John Hnatyshyn,
P.C., C.C., C.M.M., C.D., Q.C.**
Jan. 29, 1990

Photo Credit: © Yousuf Karsh. Reproduced with
the permission of the Estate.

**The Rt. Hon. Roméo LeBlanc,
P.C., C.C., C.M.M., O.N.B., C.D.**
Feb. 8, 1995

Photo Credit: Sgt Christian Coulombe, Rideau Hall
© Her Majesty The Queen in Right of Canada
represented by the
Office of the Secretary to the Governor General
(OSGG), 1998.
Reproduced with permission of the OSGG, 2021.

The Rt. Hon. Adrienne Clarkson, P.C., C.C., C.M.M., C.O.M., C.D.
Oct. 7, 1999

Photo Credit: Andrew MacNaughtan
© Her Majesty The Queen in Right of Canada
represented by the
Office of the Secretary to the Governor General
(OSGG), 1999.
Reproduced with permission of the OSGG, 2021.

The Rt. Hon. Michaëlle Jean, P.C., C.C., C.M.M., C.O.M., C.D.
Sept. 27, 2005

Photo Credit: Sgt Eric Jolin, Rideau Hall
© Her Majesty The Queen in Right of Canada
represented by the
Office of the Secretary to the Governor General
(OSGG), 2006.
Reproduced with permission of the OSGG, 2021.

The Rt. Hon. David Johnston, P.C., C.C., C.M.M., C.O.M., C.D.
Oct. 1, 2010

Photo Credit: Sgt Ronald Duchesne, Rideau Hall
© Her Majesty The Queen in Right of Canada
represented by the
Office of the Secretary to the Governor General
(OSGG), 2015.
Reproduced with permission of the OSGG, 2021.

The Rt. Hon. Julie Payette, C.C., C.M.M., C.O.M., C.Q., C.D.
Oct. 2, 2017

Photo Credit: Sgt Johanie Maheu, Rideau Hall
© Her Majesty The Queen in Right of Canada
represented by the
Office of the Secretary to the Governor General
(OSGG), 2017.
Reproduced with permission of the OSGG, 2021.

The Rt. Hon. Richard Wagner, P.C.,

Administrator of the Government of Canada
Jan. 23, 2021

Photo Credit: Sgt Johanie Maheu, Rideau Hall
© Her Majesty The Queen in Right of Canada
represented by the
Office of the Secretary to the Governor General
(OSGG), 2021.
Reproduced with permission of the OSGG, 2021.

Her Excellency the Rt. Hon. Mary May Simon, C.C., C.M.M., C.O.M., O.Q., C.D.,

Governor General of Canada
July 26, 2021

Photo Credit: Sgt Johanie Maheu, Rideau Hall
© Her Majesty The Queen in Right of Canada
represented by the
Office of the Secretary to the Governor General
(OSGG), 2021.
Reproduced with permission of the OSGG, 2021.

CANADIAN PRIME MINISTERS
(WITH PARTY AFFILIATION AND TIME IN OFFICE)

Rt. Hon. Sir John A. Macdonald
(Conservative)
July 1, 1867 to Nov. 5, 1873
Oct. 17, 1878 to June 6, 189

Photo credit: William James Topley/Library and
Archives Canada/PA-027013

Hon. Alexander MacKenzie
(Liberal)
Nov. 7, 1873 to Oct. 16, 1878

Photo credit: William James Topley/Library and
Archives Canada/PA-026308

Hon. Sir John J. Abbott
(Conservative)
June 16, 1891 to Nov. 24, 1892

Photo credit: William James Topley/Library and
Archives Canada/PA-033933

Rt. Hon. Sir John S. D. Thompson
(Conservative)
Dec. 5, 1892 to Dec. 12, 1894

Photo Credit: Library and Archives Canada/C-000698

Hon. Sir Mackenzie Bowell
(Conservative)
Dec. 21, 1894 to April 27, 1896

Photo Credit: William James Topley/Library and
Archives Canada/PA-027159

Rt. Hon. Sir Charles Tupper
(Conservative)
May 1, 1896 to July 8, 1896

Photo Credit: Library and Archives
Canada/PA-027743

Rt. Hon. Sir Wilrid Laurier
(Liberal)
July 11, 1896 to Oct. 6, 1911

Photo Credit: William James Topley/Library and
Archives Canada/C-001971

Rt. Hon. Sir Robert L. Borden
Oct. 10, 1911 to Oct. 12, 1917
(Conservative Administration)
Oct. 12, 1917 to July 10, 1920
(Unionist Administration)

Photo Credit: William James Topley/Library and
Archives Canada/PA-028121

Rt. Hon. Arthur Meighen
July 10, 1920 to Dec. 29, 1921
(Unionist "National Liberal and
Conservative Party")
June 29, 1926 to Sept. 25, 1926
(Conservative)

Photo Credit: William James Topley/Library and
Archives Canada/PA-026987

Rt. Hon. William Lyon Mackenzie
King
(Liberal)
Dec. 29, 1921 to June 28, 1926
Sept. 25, 1926 to Aug. 6, 1930
Oct. 23, 1935 to Nov. 15, 1948

Photo Credit: Library and Archives
Canada/C-027645

Rt. Hon. Richard Bedford Bennett
(Conservative)
(Became Viscount Bennett, 1941)
Aug. 7, 1930 to Oct. 23, 1935

Photo Credit: Library and Archives Canada/C-000687

Rt. Hon. Louis Stephen St. Laurent
(Liberal)
Nov. 15, 1948 to June 21, 1957

Photo Credit: Library and Archives Canada/C-010461

Rt. Hon. John G. Diefenbaker
(Progressive Conservative)
June 21, 1957 to April 22, 1963

© Estate of Paul Horsdal
Source: Library and Archives Canada/Credit: Paul
Horsdal/The Montreal Star Fonds/PA-130070

Rt. Hon. Lester Bowles Pearson
(Liberal)
April 22, 1963 to April 20, 1968

Photo Credit: Ashley and Crippen Studio/Library
and Archives Canada/PA-126393

Rt. Hon. Pierre Elliott Trudeau
(Liberal)
April 20, 1968 to June 4, 1979
Mar. 3, 1980 to June 30, 1984

© Library and Archives Canada. Reproduced with the
permission of Library and Archives Canada.
Photo Credit: Duncan Cameron/Office of the Prime
Minister Collection/Library and Archives
Canada/C-046600

Rt. Hon. Charles Joseph Clark
(Progressive Conservative)
June 4, 1979 to Mar. 3, 1980

Photo Credit: © House of Commons Collection,
Ottawa

Rt. Hon. John Napier Turner
(Liberal)
June 30, 1984 to Sept. 17, 1984

Photo Credit: With permission of the
Liberal Party of Canada

Rt. Hon. Martin Brian Mulroney
(Progressive Conservative)
Sept 17, 1984 to June 25, 1993

Photo Credit: © Yousuf Karsh. Reproduced with
the permission of the Estate.
Library and Archives Canada/Yousuf Karsh
Collection/Archival Source PA-164231

Rt. Hon. Kim Campbell
(Progressive Conservative)
June 25, 1993 to Nov. 4, 1993

Photo Credit: Denise Grant
Courtesy of the
Office of the Rt. Hon. Kim Campbell

Rt. Hon. Jean Chrétien
(Liberal)
Nov. 4, 1993 to Dec. 11, 2003

Photo Credit: With permission of the
Liberal Party of Canada

Rt. Hon. Paul Edgar Philippe Martin
(Liberal)
Dec. 12, 2003 to Feb. 6, 2006

Photo Credit: With permission of the
Liberal Party of Canada

Rt. Hon. Stephen Joseph Harper
(Conservative)
Feb. 6, 2006 to Nov. 3, 2015

Photo Credit: Jason Ransom
Photo provided by the Privy Council Office
© Her Majesty the Queen in Right of Canada, 2021

Rt. Hon. Justin Pierre James Trudeau
(Liberal)
Nov. 4, 2015 to --

Photo Credit: Adam Scotti
Photo provided by the Office of the Prime Minister
© Her Majesty the Queen in Right of Canada, 2021

PORTRAITS OF PRIME MINISTERS IN THE HOUSE OF COMMONS

Reproduced with the permission of the Curator, House of Commons

Rt. Hon. Sir John Alexander Macdonald
Credit: Henry Sandham
Library and Archives Canada C-025743

Hon. Alexander Mackenzie
Credit: John Wycliffe Lowes Forster
Library and Archives Canada C-116811

Hon. Sir John J. Abbott
Credit: Muli Tang
House of Commons Collection

Rt. Hon. Sir John Thompson
Credit: John Wycliffe Lowes Forster
Library and Archives Canada C-116812

Hon. Sir Mackenzie Bowell
Credit: Joanne Tod
House of Commons Collection

Rt. Hon. Sir Charles Tupper
Credit: Victor A. Long
Library and Archives Canada C-116813

Rt. Hon. Sir Wilfrid Laurier
Credit: John Wentworth Russell
Library and Archives Canada C-116814

Rt. Hon. Sir Robert Borden
Credit: Kenneth Keith Forbes
Library and Archives Canada C-116815

Rt. Hon. Arthur Meighen
Credit: George Ernest Fosbery
Library and Archives Canada C-116816

Rt. Hon. William Lyon Mackenzie King
Credit: Frank O. Salisbury
Library and Archives Canada C-116818

Rt. Hon. Richard Bedford Bennett
Credit: Kenneth Keith Forbes
Library and Archives Canada C-116817

Rt. Hon. Louis St. Laurent
Credit: Audrey Watts McNaughton
Library and Archives Canada C-116819

Rt. Hon. John G. Diefenbaker
Credit: Arthur Edward Cleeve Horne
Library and Archives Canada C-116820

Rt. Hon. Lester Bowles Pearson
Credit: Hugh Seaforth MacKenzie
Library and Archives Canada C-116821

Rt. Hon. Pierre Elliott Trudeau
Credit: Myfanwy Pavelic
House of Commons Collection

Rt. Hon. Charles Joseph Clark
Credit: Patrick Douglass Cox
House of Commons Collection

Rt. Hon. John Napier Turner
Credit: Brenda Bury
House of Commons Collection

Rt. Hon. Brian Mulroney
Credit: Igor Babailov
House of Commons Collection

Rt. Hon. Kim Campbell
Credit: David Goatley
Courtesy of the Office of the Rt. Hon. Kim Campbell

Rt. Hon. Jean Chrétien
Credit: Christian Nicholson
House of Commons Collection

Rt. Hon. Paul Martin
Credit: Paul Wyse
House of Commons Collection

Regulations & Abbreviations

Styles of Address

Styles of Address courtesy of the Department of Canadian Heritage.

The Royal Family/La Famille Royale

THE QUEEN:
Her Majesty The Queen, Buckingham Palace, London SW1A 1AA United Kingdom
Salutation - Your Majesty:
Final Salutation - I remain Your Majesty's faithful and devoted servant,
In Conversation - "Your Majesty" first then "Ma'am"
Note: The Queen's full title is "Her Majesty Queen Elizabeth II, Queen of Canada." Normally one refers to "Her Majesty The Queen" or "The Queen"

LA REINE:
Sa Majesté la Reine, Palais de Buckingham, Londres SW1A 1AA Royaume-Uni
Appel - Majesté,
Salutation - Je prie Votre Majesté d'agréer l'expression de ma très haute considération.
Conversation - ‹‹Majesté››
Remarques: Le titre complet de la Reine est le suivant: ‹‹Sa Majesté la reine Elizabeth II, Reine du Canada›› On parle normalement de ‹‹Sa Majesté›› ou de ‹‹la Reine››

THE PRINCE OF WALES:
His Royal Highness The Prince of Wales, Clarence House, London SW1A 1BA United Kingdom
Salutation - Your Royal Highness:
Final Salutation - Yours very truly,
In Conversation - "Your Royal Highness" first then "Sir"
Note: Although "Prince Charles" and "Charles, Prince of Wales" are often heard informally, they are not used officially.

LE PRINCE DE GALLES:
Son Altesse Royale le prince de Galles, Clarence House, Londres SW1A 1BA Royaume-Uni
Appel - Altesse Royale,
Salutation - Je prie Votre Altesse Royal d'agréer l'expression de ma très haute considération.
Conversation - ‹‹Altesse Royale››
Remarques: On entend souvent « le prince Charles » ou « Charles, le prince de Galles », mais il ne s'agit pas d'appellations officielles.

Government/Gouvernement

GOVERNOR GENERAL OF CANADA:
His/Her Excellency the Right Honourable (full name), C.C., C.M.M., C.O.M., C.D., Governor General of Canada, Rideau Hall, 1 Sussex Dr., Ottawa ON K1A 0A1
Salutation - Excellency:
Final Salutation - Yours truly,
In Conversation - "Your Excellency" or "Excellency" first then "Sir" or "Madam"
Note: The Governor General may have other postnominal letters, such as P.C., Q.C.

GOVERNEUR GÉNÉRAL DU CANADA:
(homme) Son Excellence le très honorable (prénom et nom), C.C., C.M.M., C.O.M., C.D., Gouverneur général du Canada, Rideau Hall, 1, promenade Sussex, Ottawa ON K1A 0A1
(femme) Son Excellence la très honorable (prénom et nom), C.C., C.M.M., C.O.M., C.D., Gouverneure générale du Canada, Rideau Hall, 1, promenade Sussex, Ottawa ON K1A 0A1
Appel - (homme) Excellence,
(femme) Excellence,
Salutation - (homme) Je vous prie d'agréer, Monsieur le Gouverneur général, l'expression de ma très haute considération.
(femme) Je vous prie d'agréer, Madame la Gouverneure générale, l'hommage de mon profond respect.
Conversation - On commence par ‹‹Excellence››. On poursuit avec ‹‹Monsieur›› ou ‹‹Madame››.
Remarques: D'autres initiales peuvent suivre le nom du gouverneur général, comme C.P. et C.R.

LIEUTENANT GOVERNOR OF A PROVINCE:
His/Her Honour the Honourable (full name) Lieutenant Governor of (Province), Address
Salutation - Your Honour or Dear Lieutenant Governor:
Final Salutation - Yours sincerely,
In Conversation - "Your Honour" first then "Sir" or "Madam" or "Mr./Mrs./Ms. (surname)"

Note: The Lieutenant Governor of a province has the title "Honourable" for life; the courtesy title "His/ Her Honour" is used only while in office.

LIEUTENANT-GOUVERNEUR
(homme) Son Honneur l'honorable (prénom et nom) Lieutenant-gouverneur de (province), Adresse
(femme) Son Honneur l'honorable (prénom et nom) Lieutenante-gouverneure de (province), Adresse
Appel - (homme) Monsieur le Lieutenant-Gouverneur,
(femme) Madame la Lieutenante-Gouverneure,
Salutation - (homme) Je vous prie d'agréer, Monsieur le Lieutenant-Gouverneur, l'expression de ma haute considération.
(femme) Je vous prie d'agréer, Madame la Lieutenante-Gouverneure, l'hommage de mes respectueux hommages.
Conversation - On commence par ‹‹Votre Honneur››. On poursuit avec ‹‹Monsieur›› ou ‹‹Madame››
Remarques: Le titre ‹‹honorable›› est accordé à vie au lieutenant-gouverneur; le titre de courtoisie ‹‹Son Honneur›› n'est utilisé que pendant la durée du mandat.

THE PRIME MINISTER OF CANADA:
The Right Honourable (full name), P.C., M.P., Prime Minister of Canada, Langevin Block, Ottawa, ON K1A 0A2
Salutation - Dear Prime Minister, or Prime Minister:
Final Salutation - Yours sincerely,
In Conversation - "Prime Minister" first then "Mr./ Mrs./Ms. (surname)"
Note: While the term "Mr/Madam Prime Minister" is often heard informally, it is not used officially. The Prime Minister may have other post-nominal letters, such as Q.C.

PREMIER MINISTRE DU CANADA
(homme) Le très honorable (prénom et nom), C.P., député Premier Ministre du Canada, Édifice Langevin, Ottawa ON K1A 0A2
(femme) La très honorable (prénom et nom), C.P., députée Première Ministre du Canada, Édifice Langevin, Ottawa ON K1A 0A2
Appel - (homme) Monsieur le Premier Ministre,
(femme) Madame la Première Ministre,
Salutation -
(homme) Je vous prie d'agréer, Monsieur le Premier Ministre, l'expression de ma très haute considération.
(femme) Je vous prie d'agréer, Madame la Première Ministre, l'hommage de mon profond respect.
Conversation - (homme) On commence par ‹‹Monsieur le Premier Ministre››. On poursuit avec ‹‹Monsieur››
(femme) On commence par ‹‹Madame la Première Ministre››. On pousuit avec ‹‹Madame››
Remarques: D'autres initiales peuvent suivre le nom, comme C.R.

THE PREMIER OF A PROVINCE OF CANADA:
The Honourable (full name), M.L.A. or (M.P.P., M.N.A., or M.H.A.), Premier of (Province), Address
Salutation - Dear Premier:
Final Salutation - Yours sincerely,
In Conversation - "Premier" first then "Mr./Mrs./Ms. (surname)"
Note: The title "Honourable" is used only while in office, unless he/she is a member of the Privy Council. While the term "Mr./Madam Premier" is often heard informally, it is not used officially.

LE PREMIER MINISTRE D'UNE PROVINCE
(homme) L'honorable (prénom et nom) M.A.L ou (M.A.N., M.P.P. ou M.C.A) Premier Ministre de (province), Adresse
(femme) L'honorable (prénom et nom) M.A.L ou (M.A.N., M.P.P. ou M.C.A) Première Ministre de (province), Adresse
Appel - (homme) Monsieur le Premier Ministre,
(femme) Madame la Première Ministre,
Salutation - (homme) Je vous prie d'agréer, Monsieur le Premier Ministre, l'expression de ma haute considération.
(femme) Je vous prie d'agréer, Madame la Première Ministre, l'hommage de mon profond respect.
Conversation - On commence par ‹‹Monsieur le Premier Ministre››. On poursuit avec ‹‹Monsieur››
(femme) On commence par ‹‹Madame la Première Ministre››. On poursuit avec ‹‹Madame››
Remarques: Les premiers ministres ne conservent pas le titre ‹‹honorable›› après la fin de leur mandat, à moins qu'ils ne soient membres du Conseil privé.

COMMISSIONER OF A TERRITORY:
The Honourable (full name), Commissioner of (Territory), Address
Salutation - Commissioner (name):
Final Salutation - Yours sincerely,
In Conversation - "Sir" or "Madam" or "Mr./Mrs./ Ms. (surname)"

Note: The Commissioner of a territory has the title "Honourable" only while in office.

COMMISSAIRE DU TERRITOIRE
(homme/femme) L'honorable (prénom et nom) Commissaire du (territoire), Adresse
Appel - (homme) Monsieur le Commissaire,
(femme) Madame la Commissaire,
Salutation - Je vous prie d'agréer, Monsieur le Commissaire, l'expression de ma haute considération.
(femme) Je vous prie d'agréer, Madame la Commissaire, l'expression de mes respectueux hommages.
Conversation - (homme) ‹‹Monsieur››
(femme) ‹‹Madame››
Remarques: Le titre ‹‹honorable›› n'est utilisé que pendant la durée de ses fonctions.

PREMIER OF A TERRITORY:
The Honourable (full name), M.L.A., Premier of (Territory), Address
Salutation - Dear Mr./Mrs./Ms. (surname):
Final Salutation - Yours sincerely,
In Conversation - "Mr./Mrs./Ms. (surname)"
Note: The title "Honourable" is used only while in office, unless he/she is a member of the Privy Council. While the term "Mr./Madam Premier" is often heard informally, it is not used officially.

LE PREMIER MINISTRE D'UN TERRITOIRE
(homme) L'honorable (prénom et nom), M.A.L. Premier ministre du (territoire), Adresse
(femme) L'honorable (prénom et nom), M.A.L. Première Ministre du (territoire), Adresse
Appel - (homme) Monsieur le Premier Ministre,
(femme) Madame la Première Ministre,
Salutation - (homme) Je vous prie d'agréer, Monsieur le Premier Ministre, l'expression de ma haute consideration.
(femme) Je vous prie d'agréer, Madame la Première Ministre, l'hommage de mon profond respect.
Conversation - On commence par ‹‹Monsieur le Premier Ministre››. On poursuit avec ‹‹Monsieur››
(femme) On commence par ‹‹Madame la Première Ministre››. On poursuit avec ‹‹Madame››
Remarques: Les premiers ministres ne conservent pas le titre ‹‹honorable›› après la fin de leur mandat, à moins qu'ils ne soient membres du Conseil privé.

CABINET MINISTERS:
Member of the House of Commons: The Honourable (full name), P.C., M.P., Minister of _____, House of Commons, Ottawa ON K1A 0A6
Salutation - Dear Minister: or Dear Colleague: (between colleagues)
Final Salutation - Yours sincerely,
In Conversation - "Minister" first then "Mr./Mrs./ Ms. (surname)"
For a Senator: Senator the Honourable (full name), P.C., Minister of _____ , The Senate, Ottawa, ON K1A 0A4
Salutation - Dear Minister: or Dear Colleague: (between colleagues)
Final Salutation - Yours sincerely,
In Conversation - "Minister" first then "Mr./Mrs./ Ms. (surname)"

CONSEIL DES MINISTRES DU CANADA
(homme) L'honorable (prénom et nom), C.P. député Ministre de _____, Chambre de communes, Ottawa ON K1A 0A6
(femme) L'honorable (prénom et nom), C.P. députée Ministre de _____, Chambre de communes, Ottawa ON K1A 0A6
Appel - (homme) Monsieur le Ministre, ou Cher collègue, (Entre collègues)
(femme) Madame la Ministre, ou Chère collègue, (Entre collègues)
Salutation - (homme) Je vous prie d'agréer, Monsieur le Ministre, l'expression de ma considération respectueuse.
(femme) Je vous prie d'agréer, Madame la Ministre, l'hommage de mon profond respect.
Conversation - (homme) On commence par ‹‹Monsieur le Ministre››. On poursuit avec ‹‹Monsieur››
(femme) On commence par ‹‹Madame la Ministre››. On poursuit avec ‹‹Madame››
Remarques: Les ministres fédéraux sont membres du Conseil privé de la Reine pour le Canada et conservent le titre ‹‹honorable›› à vie. On place les initiales C.P. après leur nom.

MINISTERS OF STATE:
The Honourable (full name), P.C., M.P., Minister of State (Portfolio), House of Commons, Ottawa ON K1A 0A6
Salutation - Dear Minister of State: or Dear Colleague: (between colleagues)
Final Salutation - Yours sincerely,

In Conversation - "Minister of State" first then "Mr./ Mrs./Ms. (surname)"

Note: Members of the Ministry are members of the Queen's Privy Council for Canada and retain the title "Honourable" for life, using the initials P.C. after their name. While the term "Mr./Madam Minister" is often heard informally, it is not used officially.

MINISTRE D'ÉTAT

(homme) L'honorable (prénom et nom), C.P. député Ministre d'État (Portefeuille), Chambre des communes, Ottawa ON K1A 0A6

(femme) L'honorable (prénom et nom), C.P. députée Ministre d'État (Portefeuille), Chambre des communes, Ottawa ON K1A 0A6

Appel - (homme) Monsieur le Ministre d'État, ou Cher collègue, (Entre collègues)

(femme) Madame la Ministre d'État, ou Chère collègue, (Entre collègues)

Salutation - (homme) Je vous prie d'agréer, Monsieur le Ministre d'État, l'expression de ma considération respectueuse. Ou Je vous prie, cher collègue, de recevoir mes cordiales salutations. (Entre collègues)

(femme) Je vous prie d'agréer, Madame la Ministre d'État, l'hommage de mon profond respect. Ou Je vous prie, chère collègue, de recevoir mes cordiales salutations. (Entre collègues)

Conversation - (homme) On commence par «Monsieur le Ministre d'État». On poursuit avec «Monsieur»

(femme) On commence par «Ministre la Secrétaire d'État». On poursuit avec «Madame»

Remarques: Les ministres d'État sont membres du Conseil privé de la Reine pour le Canada et conservent le titre «honorable» à vie. On place les initiales C.P. après leur nom.

SPEAKER OF THE SENATE:

The Honourable (full name), Senator, Speaker of the Senate, The Senate, Ottawa, ON K1A 0A4

Salutation - Dear Mr./Madam Speaker:

Final Salutation - Yours sincerely,

In Conversation - "Mr. Speaker" or "Madam Speaker"

Note: A senator who is a member of the Canadian Privy Council is addressed as "Senator the Honourable (full name), P.C. " After a Senator retires, he/she retains the title "Honourable" but the salutation is "Dear Sir/ Madam" or "Dear Mr./Mrs./Ms. (name)"

PRÉSIDENT OU PRÉSIDENTE DU SÉNAT

(homme) L'honorable (prénom et nom), sénateur Président du Sénat, Le Sénat, Ottawa ON K1A 0A4

(femme) L'honorable (prénom et nom), sénatrice Présidente du Sénat, Le Sénat, Ottawa ON K1A 0A4

Appel - (homme) Monsieur le Président,

(femme) Madame la Présidente,

Salutation - (homme) Je vous prie d'agréer, Monsieur le Président, l'expression de ma haute considération.

(femme) Je vous prie d'agréer, Madame la Présidente, l'hommage de mon profond respect.

Conversation - (homme) «Monsieur le Président»

(femme) «Madame la Présidente»

Remarques: Dans le cas d'un sénateur ou d'une sénatrice qui est membre du Conseil privé, la formule d'appel à utiliser est «L'honorable (nom), C.P., sénateur(trice)». Après leur retraite, les sénateurs conservent le titre «honorable» mais la formule d'appel devient: «Monsieur/Madame».

SPEAKER OF THE HOUSE OF COMMONS:

The Honourable (full name), M.P., Speaker of the House of Commons, House of Commons, Ottawa, ON K1A 0A6

Salutation - Dear Mr./Madam Speaker:

Final Salutation - Yours sincerely,

In Conversation - "Mr. Speaker" or "Madam Speaker"

PRÉSIDENT OU PRÉSIDENTE DE LA CHAMBRE DES COMMUNES

(homme) L'honorable (prénom et nom) député Président de la Chambre des communes, Chambre des communes, Ottawa ON K1A 0A6

(femme) L'honorable (prénom et nom) députée Présidente de la Chambre des communes, Chambre des communes, Ottawa ON K1A 0A6

Appel - (homme) Monsieur le Président,

(femme) Madame la Présidente,

Salutation - (homme) Je vous prie d'agréer, Monsieur le Président, l'expression de ma haute considération.

(femme) Je vous prie d'agréer, Madame la Présidente, l'hommage de mon profond respect.

Conversation - (homme) «Monsieur le Président»

(femme) «Madame la Présidente»

SENATORS:

The Honourable (full name), Senator, The Senate, Ottawa, ON K1A 0A4

Salutation - Dear Senator (name):

Final Salutation - Yours sincerely,

In Conversation - "Senator (name)"

Note: A senator who is a member of the Queen's Privy Council is addressed as "Senator the Honourable (full name), P.C." After a Senator retires, he/she retains the title "Honourable" for life but the salutation is "Dear Sir/Madam" or "Dear Mr./Mrs./Ms. (name)".

SÉNATEURS:

(homme) L'honorable (prénom et nom) sénateur, Le Sénat, Ottawa ON K1A 0A4

(femme) L'honorable (prénom et nom) sénatrice, Le Sénat, Ottawa ON K1A 0A4

Appel - (homme) Monsieur le Sénateur,

(femme) Madame la Sénatrice,

Salutation - (homme) Je vous prie d'agréer, Monsieur le Sénateur, l'expression de mes meilleurs sentiments.

(femme) Je vous prie d'agréer, Madame la Sénatrice, mes hommages respectueux.

Conversation - (homme) «Monsieur le Sénateur». On poursuit avec «Monsieur»

(femme) «Madame la Sénatrice». On poursuit avec «Madame»

Remarques: Après leur retraite, les sénateurs conservent le titre «honorable», mais la formule d'appel devient: «Monsieur» ou «Madame».

MEMBERS OF THE HOUSE OF COMMONS:

Mr. John Smith, M.P. or The Honourable John Smith, P.C., M.P., House of Commons, Ottawa, ON K1A 0A6

Salutation - Dear Mr./Mrs./Ms. (surname):

Final Salutation - Yours sincerely,

In Conversation - "Mr./Mrs./Ms. (surname)"

Note: The members of the House of Commons who are members of the Queen's Privy Council retain the title "Honourable" for life and use the initials "P.C." after their name. M.P.: Member of the House of Commons. P.C., M.P.: Member of the Privy Council and Member of the House of Commons

DÉPUTÉS FÉDÉRAUX

(homme) Monsieur (prénom et nom), député ou L'honorable (prénom et nom), C.P., député Chambre des communes, Ottawa ON K1A 0A6

(femme) Madame (prénom et nom), députée ou L'honorable (prénom et nom), C.P., députée Chambre des communes, Ottawa ON K1A 0A6

Appel - (homme) Monsieur le Député,

(femme) Madame la Députée,

Salutation - (homme) Je vous prie d'agréer, Monsieur le Député, l'expression de mes meilleurs sentiments.

(femme) Je vous prie d'agréer, Madame la Députée, mes respectueux hommages.

Conversation - (homme) On commence par «Monsieur le Député». On poursuit avec «Monsieur»

(femme) On commence par «Madame la Députée». On poursuit avec «Madame»

Remarques: Les députés qui sont membres du Conseil privé de la Reine pour le Canada ont le «honorable» à vie et portent les initiales «C.P.» après leur nom.

MEMBER OF THE PROVINCIAL/TERRITORIAL CABINET:

The Honourable (full name), M.L.A. or (M.P.P., M.N.A. or M.H.A.), Minister of _____, Address

Salutation - Dear Minister: or Dear Colleague: (between colleagues)

Final Salutation - Yours sincerely,

In Conversation - "Minister" first then "Mr./Mrs./ Ms. (surname)"

Note: A provincial/territorial cabinet minister does not retain the title "Honourable" after tenure of office unless he/she is a member of the Privy Council. M.L.A.: all provinces/territories except for: Ontario (M.P.P.); Québec (M.N.A.); Newfoundland (M.H.A.). While the term "Mr./Madam Minister" is often heard informally, it is not used officially.

MINISTRES PROVINCIAUX/TERRITORIAUX

(homme/femme) L'honorable (prénom et nom), M.A.L. ou (M.A.N., M.P.P. ou M.C.A.) Ministre de _____, Adresse

Appel - (homme) Monsieur le Ministre, ou Cher collègue, (Entre collègues)

(femme) Madame la Ministre, ou Chère collègue, (Entre collègues)

Salutation - (homme) Je vous prie d'agréer, Monsieur le Ministre, l'expression de ma considération respectueuse. Ou Je vous prie, cher collègue, de recevoir mes cordiales salutations. (Entre collègues)

(femme) Je vous prie d'agréer, Madame la Ministre, l'expression de ma considération respectueuse. Ou Je vous prie, chère collègue, de recevoir mes cordiales salutations. (Entre collègues)

Conversation - (homme) On commence par «Monsieur le Ministre». On poursuit avec «Monsieur»

(femme) On commence par «Madame la Ministre». On poursuit avec «Madame»

Remarques: Les ministres provinciaux/territoriaux ne conservent pas le titre «honorable» après la fin de leur mandat à moins qu'ils ne soient membres du Conseil privé des provinces et les territoires, sauf: - l'Ontario (M.P.P.) - le Québec (M.A.N.) - Terre-Neuve (M.C.A.).

MEMBER OF A PROVINCIAL/TERRITORIAL LEGISLATIVE ASSEMBLY:

Mr. John Smith, M.L.A. or (M.P.P., M.N.A., or M.H.A.), Address

Salutation - Dear Mr./Mrs./Ms. (surname),

Final Salutation - Yours sincerely,

In Conversation - "Mr./Mrs./Ms. (surname)"

Note: Members of the Queen's Privy Council retain the title "Honourable" for life and use the initials "P.C." after their name. M.L.A.: all provinces/territories except for: Ontario (M.P.P.); Quebec (M.N.A.); Newfoundland (M.H.A.). P.C., M.L.A.: Member of the Privy Council and Member of the Legislative Assembly

DÉPUTÉS PROVINCIAUX/TERRITORIAUX

(homme) Monsieur (prénom et nom), M.A.L. ou (M.P.P., M.A.N. ou M.C.A.), Adresse

(femme) Madame (prénom et nom), M.A.L. ou (M.P.P., M.A.N. ou M.C.A.), Adresse

Appel - (homme) Monsieur le Député,

(femme) Madame la Députée,

Salutation - (homme) Je vous prie d'agréer, Monsieur le Député, l'expression de mes meilleurs sentiments.

(femme) Je vous prie d'agréer, Madame la Députée, mes respectueux hommages.

Conversation - (homme) «Monsieur»

(femme) «Madame»

Remarques: Les membres du Conseil privé de la Reine conservent le titre «honorable» à vie et placent les initiales C.P. après leur nom. M.A.L.: toutes les provinces et les territoires sauf: - l'Ontario (M.P.P.) - le Québec (M.A.N.) - Terre-Neuve (M.C.A.). C.P., M.A.L.: Membre du Conseil privé et membre de l'Assemblée législative.

MAYOR OF A CITY OR TOWN:

His/Her Worship (full name), Mayor of (name), Address

Salutation - Dear Sir/Madam: or Dear Mr./Madam Mayor:

Final Salutation - Yours sincerely,

In Conversation - "Your Worship" first then "Mayor (surname)"

MAIRE/MAIRESSE

(homme) Son Honneur monsieur (prénom et nom), Maire de (Ville), Adresse

(femme) Son Honneur madame (prénom et nom), Mairesse de (Ville), Adresse Appel - Monsieur le Maire,

(femme) Madame la Mairesse,

Salutation - (homme) Je vous prie d'agréer, Monsieur le Maire, l'expression de mes meilleurs sentiments.

(femme) Je vous prie d'agréer, Madame la Mairesse, mes hommages respectueux.

Conversation - (homme) On commence par «Votre Honneur». On poursuit avec «Monsieur le Maire»

(femme) On commence par «Votre Honneur». On poursuit avec «Madame la Mairesse»

JUDGES/JUGES

CHIEF JUSTICE: The Right Honourable (full name), P.C., Chief Justice of Canada, Supreme Court of Canada, Ottawa, ON K1A 0J1

Salutation - Dear Chief Justice:

Final Salutation - Yours sincerely,

In Conversation - "Mr./Madam Chief Justice" first then "Sir/Madam" or "Mr./Mrs./Ms. (surname)"

JUGE EN CHEF DU CANADA

(homme) Le très honorable (prenom et nom), C.P. Juge en chef du Canada, Cour suprême du Canada, Ottawa ON K1A 0J1

(femme) La très honorable (prenom et nom), C.P. Juge en chef du Canada, Cour suprême du Canada, Ottawa ON K1A 0J1

Appel - (homme) Monsieur le Juge en chef,

(femme) Madame la Juge en chef,

Salutation - (homme) Je vous prie d'agréer, Monsieur le Juge en chef, l'expression de ma très haute considération.

(femme) Je vous prie d'agréer, Madame la Juge en chef, l'hommage de mon profond respect.

Conversation - (homme) On commence par «Monsieur le Juge en chef». On poursuit avec «Monsieur».

(femme) On commence par «Madame la Juge en chef». On poursuit avec «Madame»

JUDGES OF FEDERAL COURTS:

The Honourable (full name), Judge of the (court) of Canada.

Salutation - Dear Mr./Madam Justice (surname):

Final Salutation - Yours sincerely,

In Conversation - "Mr./Madam Justice" first then "Sir/Madam" or simply "Mr./Mrs./Ms. (surname)"

Note: Judges of the Supreme and Federal courts have the title "The Honourable" only while in office.

JUGES DES COURS FÉDÉRALES

L'honorable (prénom et nom), Juge de la (cour) du Canada
Appel - (homme) Monsieur le Juge,
(femme) Madame la Juge,
Salutation - (homme) Je vous prie d'agréer, Monsieur le Juge, l'expression de ma haute considération.
(femme) Je vous prie d'agréer, Madame la Juge, l'expression de ma haute considération.
Conversation - (homme) ‹‹Monsieur le Juge››
(femme) ‹‹Madame la Juge››
et on poursuit avec « Monsieur » ou « Madame », ou simplement « Monsieur (nom) » ou « Madame (nom) ».
Remarques: Les juges de la Cour suprême et des cours fédérales ne portent le titre d'« honorable » que durant leur mandat.

CHIEF JUDGES/JUDGES OF PROVINCIAL/TERRITORIAL COURTS:

The Honourable (full name), Provincial/Territorial Court of _____ , Address
Salutation - Dear Chief Judge/Judge (surname):
Final Salutation - Yours sincerely,
In Conversation - "Judge (surname)"
Note: The Table of Titles to be used in Canada now recognizes the title "Honourable" for provincially/territorially appointed judges. The courtesy title "His/Her Honour" is no longer appropriate given an official title has been granted.

JUGES EN CHEF/JUGES DES COURS PROVINCIALES/TERRITORIALES

L'honorable (prénom et nom), Cour provinciale de _____, Adresse
Appel - (homme) Monsieur le Juge en chef/le Juge,
(femme) Madame la Juge en chef/la Juge,
Salutation -
(homme) Je vous prie d'agréer, Monsieur le Juge en chef/le Juge, l'expression de mon profond respect.
(femme) Je vous prie d'agréer, Madame la Juge en chef//la Juge, l'hommage de mon profond respect.
Conversation - (homme) ‹‹Monsieur le Juge en chef/ le Juge››
(femme) ‹‹Madame la Juge en chef/la Juge››
Remarques: Le tableau des titres pour le Canada reconnaît le titre ‹‹honorable›› aux juges des cours provinciales/territoriales; le titre de courtoisie ‹‹Son Honneur›› n'est plus de mise maintenant qu'un titre officiel est utilisé.

Indigenous Leadership/Les dirigeants autochtones

Note: As there are over 650 Indigenous communities and over 50 Indigenous nations in Canada, each with its own heritage, culture and social system, it cannot be assumed that standard titles or styles of address can relate to all Indigenous Peoples. It is strongly recommended to confirm with the person you are meeting or the community you are visiting how they wish to be addressed.

Remarques: Comme le Canada compte plus de 650 communautés autochtones et une cinquantaine de Nations autochtones ayant chacune son patrimoine, sa culture et sa structure sociale propre, nous ne pouvons présumer des titres ou des formulations à utiliser pour tous les peuples autochtones. Il est fortement recommandé de vérifier les salutations à utiliser auprès de la personne que vous devez rencontrer ou de la communauté que vous devez visiter.

First Nations/Premières Nations

NATIONAL CHIEF OF THE ASSEMBLY OF FIRST NATIONS (AFN):

National Chief (full name), 55 Metcalfe Street, Suite 1600, Ottawa, Ontario K1P 6L5
Salutation - Dear National Chief (surname):
Final Salutation - Yours sincerely,
In Conversation - "National Chief (surname)"

CHEF NATIONAL DE L'ASSEMBLÉE DES PREMIÈRES NATIONS (APN):

Chef national (prénom et nom), 55, rue Metcalfe, bureau 1600 Ottawa (Ontario) K1P 6L5
Appel - Monsieur le Chef national/Madame la Chef national,
Salutation - Je vous prie d'agréer, Monsieur le Chef national/Madame la Chef national, l'expression de mes meilleurs sentiments.
Conversation - ‹‹Monsieur le Chef national›› ou ‹‹Madame la Chef national›› ou ‹‹Chef national (nom)››.

REGIONAL CHIEF:

Regional Chief (full name)
Salutation - Dear Regional Chief (surname):

Final Salutation - Yours sincerely,
In Conversation - "Regional Chief (surname)"

CHEF RÉGIONAL:

Chef régional (prénom et nom)
Appel - Monsieur le Chef régional/Madame la Chef régional,
Salutation - Je vous prie d'agréer, Monsieur le Chef régional/Madame la Chef régional, l'expression de mes meilleurs sentiments.
Conversation - ‹‹Monsieur le Chef régional›› ou ‹‹Madame la Chef régional›› ou ‹‹Chef régional (nom)››.

GRAND CHIEF:

Grand Chief (full name)
Salutation - Dear Grand Chief (surname):
Final Salutation - Yours sincerely,
In Conversation - "Grand Chief (surname)"

GRAND CHEF/GRANDE CHEF:

Grand chef/Grande chef (prénom et nom)
Appel - Grand chef/Grande chef,
Salutation - Je vous prie d'agréer, Grand chef/Grande chef, l'expression de mes meilleurs sentiments.
Conversation - ‹‹Grand chef (nom)›› ou ‹‹Grande chef (nom)››.

CHIEF:

Chief (full name)
Salutation - Dear Chief (surname):
Final Salutation - Yours sincerely,
In Conversation - "Chief (surname)"

CHEF:

Chef (prénom et nom)
Appel - Monsieur le Chef/Madame la Chef,
Salutation - Je vous prie d'agréer, Monsieur le Chef/Madame la Chef, l'expression de mes meilleurs sentiments.
Conversation - ‹‹Monsieur le Chef›› ou ‹‹Madame la Chef››, ou ‹‹Chef (nom)››.

COUNCILLOR:

Councillor (full name)
Salutation - Dear Councillor (surname):
Final Salutation - Yours sincerely,
In Conversation - "Councillor (surname)"

CONSEILLER/CONSEILLÈRE:

Conseiller/conseillère (prénom et nom)
Appel - Monsieur le Conseiller/Madame la Conseillère,
Salutation - Je vous prie d'agréer, Monsieur le Conseiller/Madame la Conseillère, l'expression de mes meilleurs sentiments.
Conversation - ‹‹Monsieur (nom)›› ou ‹‹Madame (nom)››.

Inuit/Inuits

PRESIDENT OF INUIT TAPIRIIT KANATAMI (ITK):

Angajuqqaaq (full name), National Inuit Leader, 75 Albert Street, Suite 1101, Ottawa, Ontario, K1P 5E7
Salutation - Dear Angajuqqaaq (full name):
Final Salutation - Yours sincerely,
In Conversation - "President (surname)"

PRÉSIDENT/PRÉSIDENTE D'INUIT TAPIRIIT KANATAMI (ITK):

Angajuqqaaq (prénom et nom), dirigeant national des Inuits, 75, rue Albert, bureau 1101, Ottawa (Ontario), K1P 5E7
Appel - Angajuqqaaq,
Salutation - Je vous prie d'agréer, Angajuqqaaq, l'expression de mes meilleurs sentiments.
Conversation - ‹‹Monsieur le Président›› ou ‹‹Madame la Présidente››, ou ‹‹Président (nom)›› ou ‹‹Présidente (nom)››

PRESIDENT (REGIONAL):

President (full name)
Salutaion - Dear President (surname):
Final Salutation - Yours sincerely,
In Conversation - "President (surname)"

PRÉSIDENT/PRÉSIDENTE (RÉGIONAL):

Président/Présidente (prénom et nom)
Appel - Monsieur le Président/Madame la Présidente,
Salutation - Je vous prie d'agréer, Monsieur le Président/Madame la Présidente, l'expression de mes meilleurs sentiments.
Conversation - ‹‹Monsieur le Président›› ou ‹‹Madame la Présidente››, ou ‹‹Président (nom)›› ou ‹‹Présidente (nom)››.

CHAIR AND CEO:

Mr./Ms. (full name), Chairman/chairwoman/chairperson of the Board and Chief Executive Officer
Salutation - Dear Mr./Ms. (surname):
Final Salutation - Yours sincerely,
In Conversation - "Mr./Ms. (surname)"

PRÉSIDENT ET DIRECTEUR GÉNÉRAL/PRÉSIDENTE ET DIRECTRICE GÉNÉRALE:

Monsieur/Madame (prénom et nom), Président/Présidente du Conseil d'administration et directeur général/directrice générale
Appel - Monsieur/Madame,
Salutation - Je vous prie d'agréer, Monsieur/Madame, l'expression de mes meilleurs sentiments.
Conversation - ‹‹Monsieur (nom)›› ou ‹‹Madame (nom)››.

Métis Nation/Nation métisse

PRESIDENT OF THE MÉTIS NATIONAL COUNCIL (MNC):

President (full name), #4 – 340, MacLaren Street, Ottawa, Ontario K2P 0M6
Salutation - Dear President (surname):
Final Salutation - Yours sincerely,
In Conversation - "President (surname)"

PRÉSIDENT/PRÉSIDENTE DU RALLIEMENT NATIONAL DES MÉTIS (RNM):

Président/Présidente (prénom et nom), 340, rue MacLaren, bureau 4, Ottawa (Ontario) K2P 0M6
Appel - Monsieur le Président/Madame la Présidente,
Salutation - Je vous prie d'agréer, Monsieur le Président/Madame la Présidente, l'expression de mes meilleurs sentiments.
Conversation - ‹‹Monsieur le Président›› ou ‹‹Madame la Présidente››, ou ‹‹Président (nom)›› ou ‹‹Présidente (nom)››.

PRESIDENT (PROVINCIAL):

President (full name)
Salutation - Dear President (surname):
Final Salutation - Yours sincerely,
In Conversation - "President (surname)"

PRÉSIDENT/PRÉSIDENTE (PROVINCIAL):

Président/Présidente (prénom et nom)
Appel - Monsieur le Président/Madame la Présidente,
Salutation - Je vous prie d'agréer, Monsieur le Président/Madame la Présidente, l'expression de mes meilleurs sentiments.
Conversation - ‹‹Monsieur le Président›› ou ‹‹Madame la Présidente››, ou ‹‹Président (nom)›› ou ‹‹Présidente (nom)››.

Religion

Anglican Church of Canada/ Église anglicane du Canada

PRIMATE:

The Most Reverend (full name), Primate of the Anglican Church of Canada, Address
Salutation - Dear Archbishop (surname):
Final Salutation - Yours sincerely,
In Conversation - "Archbishop"

PRIMAT:

Le révérendissime (prénom et nom), Primate de l'Église anglicane du Canada, Adresse
Appel - Monsieur le Primat,
Salutation - Je vous prie d'agréer, Monsieur le Primat, l'expression de mes sentiments les plus respectueux.
Conversation - ‹‹Monsieur l'Archevêque››

ARCHBISHOP:

The Most Reverend (full name), Archbishop of (name of Diocese), Address
Salutation - Dear Archbishop (surname):
Final Salutation - Yours very truly,
In Conversation - "Archbishop"

ARCHEVÊQUE:

Le révérendissime (prénom et nom), Archevêque de (nom du diocèse), Adresse
Appel - Monsieur l'Archevêque,
Salutation - Je vous prie d'agréer, Monsieur l'Archevêque, l'expression de mes sentiments les plus respectueux.
Conversation - ‹‹Monsieur l'Archevêque››

BISHOP:

The Right Reverend (full name), Bishop of (name of Diocese), Address
Salutation - Dear Bishop (surname):
Final Salutation - Yours very truly,
In Conversation - "Bishop (surname)" or "Bishop"

ÉVÊQUE:

(homme) Le très révérend (prénom et nom), Évêque de (nom du diocèse), Adresse
(femme) La très révérende (prénom et nom), Évêque de (nom du diocèse), Adresse

Appel - (homme) Monsieur l'Évêque,

(femme) Madame l'Évêque,

Salutation - (homme) Je vous prie d'agréer, Monsieur l'Évêque, l'expression de mes sentiments les plus respectueux.

(femme) Je vous prie d'agréer, Madame l'Évêque, l'hommage de mon profond respect.

Conversation - (homme) «Monsieur l'Évêque»

(femme) «Madame l'Évêque»

DEAN:
The Very Reverend (full name), Dean of (name of Cathedral), Address

Salutation - Dear Dean (surname):

Final Salutation - Yours sincerely,

In Conversation - "Dean (surname)" or "Mr./Mrs./Ms. (surname)"

DOYEN:
(homme) Le très révérend (prénom et nom), Doyen de (nom de la cathédrale), Adresse

(femme) La très révérende (prénom et nom), Doyenne de (nom de la cathédrale), Adresse

Appel - (homme) Monsieur le Doyen,

(femme) Madame la Doyenne,

Salutation - (homme) Je vous prie d'agréer, Monsieur le Doyen, l'expression de mes sentiments les plus respectueux.

(femme) Je vous prie d'agréer, Madame la Doyenne, l'hommage de mon profond respect.

Conversation - (homme) «Monsieur le Doyen» ou «Monsieur»

(femme) «Madame la Doyenne» ou «Madame»

ARCHDEACON:
The Venerable (full name), Archdeacon, Address

Salutation - Dear Archdeacon (surname):

Final Salutation - Yours sincerely,

In Conversation - "Archdeacon (surname)"

ARCHIDIACRE:
(homme) Le vénérable (prénom et nom), Archidiacre, Adresse

(femme) La vénérable (prénom et nom), Archidiacre, Adresse

Appel - (homme) Monsieur l'Archidiacre,

(femme) Madame l'Archidiacre,

Salutation - (homme) Je vous prie d'agréer, Monsieur l'Archidacre, l'expression de mes sentiments les plus respectueux.

(femme) Je vous prie d'agréer, Madame l'Archidacre, l'hommage de mon profond respect.

Conversation - (homme) «Monsieur l'Archidiacre»

(femme) «Madame l'Archidiacre»

CANON:
The Reverend Canon (full name), Address

Salutation - Dear Canon (surname):

Final Salutation - Yours sincerely,

In Conversation - "Canon (surname)"

CHANOINE:
(homme) Le chanoine, (prénom et nom), Adresse

(femme) La chanoinesse, (prénom et nom), Adresse

Appel - (homme) Monsieur le Chanoine,

(femme) Madame la Chanoinesse,

Salutation - (homme) Je vous prie d'agréer, Monsieur le Chanoine, l'expression de mes sentiments les plus respectueux.

(femme) Je vous prie d'agréer, Madame La Chanoinesse, l'hommage de mon profond respect.

Conversation - (homme) «Monsieur le Chanoine»

(femme) «Madame la Chanoinesse»

PRIEST:
The Reverend (full name), Address

Salutation - Dear Father (surname) or Dear Mr. (surname): or Dear Mrs./Ms. (surname)

Final Salutation - Yours sincerely,

In Conversation - "Father" or "Father (surname) or "Mrs./Ms. (surname)"

Note: "Reverend" is an adjective which is never used without the full name.

PRÊTRE:
(homme) Le révérend père (prénom et nom), Adresse

(femme) La révérende (prénom et nom), Adresse

Appel - (homme) Monsieur le Curé, Monsieur l'Abbé,

(femme) Madame,

Salutation - (homme) Je vous prie d'agréer, Monsieur le Curé, l'expression de mes sentiments respectueux.

(femme) Je vous prie d'agréer, Madame, l'expression de mes sentiments respectueux.

Conversation - (homme) «Monsieur le Curé/Monsieur l'Abbé»

(femme) « Madame)»

RELIGIOUS:
(man) The Reverend Father (full name), Address

(woman) Reverend Mother (full name)/ Reverend Sister (full name)

Salutation - Dear Father (surname):

Dear Reverend Mother:/ Dear Reverend Sister:

Final Salutation - Yours sincerely,

In Conversation - "Reverend Father", (woman) Reverend Mother (full name)/Reverend Sister (full name)

RELIGIEUX/RELIGIEUSE:
(homme) Le révérend père (prénom et nom), Adresse

(femme) La révérende mère/ soeur (prénom et nom), Adresse

Appel - (homme) Révérend père/Mon père,

(femme) Révérende mère/Ma soeur

Salutation - (homme) Je vous prie d'agréer, Révérend père/Mon père, l'expression de mes sentiments les plus respectueux.

(femme) Je vous prie d'agréer, Révérende mère/ Ma soeur, l'hommage de mon profond respect.

Conversation - (homme) «Révérend père/Mon père»

(femme) «Révérende mère/Ma soeur»

Roman Catholic Church/Église catholique romaine

THE POPE:
His Holiness Pope (name), Apostolic Palace, 00120 Vatican City

Salutation - Your Holiness:

Final Salutation - I have the honour to remain Your Holiness's obedient servant,

In Conversation - "Your Holiness"

LE PAPE:
Sa Sainteté le pape (nom), Palais apostolique, 00120 Cité du Vatican

Appel - Très Saint-Père,

Salutation - Je vous prie d'agréer, Très Saint-Père, l'expression de mon profond respect et de ma très haute considération.

Conversation - «Votre Sainteté» ou «Très Saint- Père»

CARDINAL:
His Eminence (first name) Cardinal (surname), (Additional titles), Address

Salutation - Your Eminence: or Dear Cardinal (surname):

Final Salutation - Yours very truly,

In Conversation - "Your Eminence"

CARDINAL:
Son Éminence le cardinal (prénom et nom), (Titres additionnels), Adresse

Appel - Monsieur le Cardinal,

Salutation - Je vous prie d'agréer, Monsieur le Cardinal, l'expression de mon profond respect.

Conversation - «Éminence»

ARCHBISHOP/BISHOP:
The Most Reverend (full name), Archbishop/Bishop of (name of Diocese), Address

Salutation - Dear Archbishop/Bishop (surname):

Final Salutation - Yours very truly,

In Conversation - "Archbishop/Bishop"

Note: The Holy See accorded the courtesy title "His Excellency" to Roman Catholic Archbishops and Bishops; that title is not recognized by Canadian civil authorities.

ARCHEVÊQUE/ÉVÊQUE:
Monseigneur (prénom et nom), Archevêque ou Évêque de (nom du diocèse), Adresse

Appel - Monseigneur,

Salutation - Je vous prie d'agréer, Monseigneur , l'expression de mes sentiments les plus respectueux.

Conversation - «Monseigneur»

Remarques: Le titre «Son Excellence» est utilisé par le Saint-Siège pour les archevêques et évêques catholiques; il n'est toutefois pas reconnu par les autorités civiles canadiennes.

ABBOT:
The Right Reverend (full name), Abbot of (name of abbey or monastery), Address

Salutation - Right Reverend Father: or Dear Abbott (surname):

Final Salutation - Yours sincerely,

In Conversation - "Father Abbott"

Note: The title of the abbot may be followed by post-nominal letters specific to the abbot's religious order.

ABBÉ:
Le révérend père (prénom et nom), Adresse Appel - Monsieur l'Abbé,

Salutation - Je vous prie d'agréer, Monsieur l'Abbé, l'expression de mes sentiments les plus respectueux.

Conversation - «Monsieur l'Abbé»

Remarques: Le titre de l'abbé peut être suivi d'initiales précisant son ordre religieux.

ABBESS OR PRIORESS:
The Reverend Mother/Mother Superior (full name), Address

Salutation - Dear Mother Superior:

Final Salutation - Yours sincerely,

In Conversation - "Reverent Mother"

Note: The title of the abbess may be followed by post-nominal letters specific to the abbess's religious order.

ABBESSE OU PRIEURE:
La Révérende mère/Mère supérieure (prénom et nom), Adresse

Salutation - Je vous prie d'agréer, Révérende mère/Ma sœur, l'expression de mes sentiments respectueux.

Conversation - «Révérende mère» ou «Ma sœur»

Remarques: Le titre de l'abbesse peut être suivi d'initiales précisant son ordre religieux.

CANON:
The Very Reverend (full name), Address

Salutation - Dear Canon (surname):

Final Salutation - Yours sincerely,

In Conversation - "Canon (surname)"

CHANOINE:
Le chanoine (prénom et nom), Adresse Appel - Monsieur le Chanoine,

Salutation - Je vous prie d'agréer, Monsieur le Chanoine, l'expression de mes sentiments respectueux.

Conversation - «Monsieur le Chanoine»

PRIEST
The Reverend (full name), Address

Salutation - Dear Father:

Final Salutation - Yours sincerely,

In Conversation - "Father" or "Father (surname)"

Note: "Reverend" is an adjective which is never used without the full name.

PRÊTRE:
Le révérend père (prénom et nom), Adresse

Appel - Monsieur le Curé/l'Abbé,

Salutation - Je vous prie d'agréer, Monsieur le Curé, l'expression de mes sentiments respectueux.

Conversation - «Monsieur le Curé/l'Abbé»

SULPICIAN:
Mr. (full name), Address

Salutation - Dear Mr. (surname):

Final Salutation - Yours truly,

In Conversation - "Mr. (surname)"

SULPICIEN:
Monsieur (prénom et nom), Adresse

Appel - Monsieur,

Salutation - Je vous prie d'agréer, Monsieur, l'expression de mes sentiments respectueux.

Conversation - «Monsieur»

RELIGIOUS:
(man) The Reverend Father (full name), Address

(woman) Reverend Mother (full name)/ Reverend Sister (full name)

Salutation - Dear Father (surname):, Dear Reverend Mother:/ Dear Reverend Sister

Final Salutation - Yours sincerely,

In Conversation - "Reverend Father", (woman) Reverend Mother (full name)/ Reverend Sister (full name)

RELIGIEUX/RELIGIEUSE:
(homme) Le révérend père (prénom et nom), Adresse

(femme) La révérende mère/soeur (prénom et nom), Adresse

Appel - (homme) Révérend père/Mon père,

(femme) Révérende mère/Ma soeur,

Salutation - (homme) Je vous prie d'agréer, Révérend père/Mon père, l'expression de mes sentiments respectueux.

(femme) Je vous prie d'agréer, Révérende mère/Ma soeur, l'hommage de mon profond respect.

Conversation - (homme) «Révérend père ou Mon père»

(femme) «Révérende mère/Ma soeur»

Other Religious Denominations/ Autres dénominations:

MODERATOR:
(United Church of Canada and Presbyterian Church in Canada)

A present ordained Moderator: The Right Reverend (full name), Moderator of (name of Church), Address

Salutation - Dear Mr./Mrs./Ms. (surname):

Final Salutation - Yours sincerely,

In Conversation - "Mr./Mrs./Ms. (surname)"

A past ordained Moderator: The Very Reverend (full name), Moderator of (name of Church), Address

Salutation - Dear Mr./Mrs./Ms. (surname):

Final Salutation - Yours sincerely,

In Conversation - "Mr./Mrs./Ms. (surname)"

MODÉRATEURS:
(Église unie du Canada et Église presbytérienne au Canada)
(homme) Le très révérend (prénom et nom), Modérateur de (nom de l'Église), Adresse
(femme) La très révérende (prénom et nom), Modératrice de (nom de l'Église), Adresse
Appel - (homme) Monsieur le Modérateur,
(femme) Madame la Modératrice,
Salutation - (homme) Je vous prie d'agréer, Monsieur le Modérateur, l'expression de mes sentiments respectueux.
(femme) Je vous prie d'agréer, Madame la Modératrice, l'hommage de mon profond respect.
Conversation - (homme) ‹‹Monsieur le Modérateur››
(femme) ‹‹Madame la Modératrice››

MINISTER:
The Reverend (full name), Address
Salutation - Dear Mr./Mrs./Ms. (surname):
Final Salutation - Yours sincerely,
In Conversation - "Mr./Mrs./Ms. (surname)"
Note: "Reverend" is an adjective which is never used without the full name.

MINISTRE:
(homme) Le révérend (prénom et nom), Adresse
(femme) La révérende (prénom et nom), Adresse
Appel - (homme) Monsieur le Pasteur,
(femme) Madame,
Salutation - (homme) Je vous prie d'agréer, Monsieur le Pasteur, l'expression de mes sentiments respectueux.
(femme) Je vous prie d'agréer, Madame, l'hommage de mon profond respect.
Conversation - (homme) ‹‹Monsieur le Pasteur››
(femme) ‹‹Madame››

RABBI:
Rabbi (full name), Address
Salutation - Dear Rabbi (surname):
Final Salutation - Yours sincerely,
In Conversation - "Rabbi (surname)"

RABBIN:
Le rabbin (prénom et nom), Adresse Appel - Monsieur le Rabbin,
Salutation - Je vous prie d'agréer, Monsieur le Rabbin, l'expression de mes sentiments respectueux.
Conversation - ‹‹Monsieur le Rabbin››

Diplomatic/Diplomates

AMBASSADORS/HIGH COMMISSIONERS of foreign countries in Canada:
His/Her Excellency (full name), Ambassador of Canada to (country) /High Commissioner for (country), Address
Salutation - Dear Ambassador/High Commissioner:
Final Salutation - Yours sincerely,
In Conversation - "Your Excellency" or "Excellency"
Note: British High Commissioner and not High Commissioner for Britain

AMBASSADEURS/HAUTS-COMMISSAIRES de pays étrangers au Canada:
(homme) Son Excellence monsieur (prénom et nom), Ambassadeur de (pays)/Haut-Commissaire de (pays), Adresse
(femme) Son Excellence madame (prénom et nom), Ambassadrice de (pays)/Haute-Commissaire de (pays), Adresse
Appel - (homme) Monsieur/l'Ambassadeur/le Haut-Commissaire,
(femme) Madame l'Ambassadrice/la Haute-Commissaire,
Salutation - (homme) Je vous prie d'agréer, Monsieur l'Ambassadeur/le Haut-Commissaire, l'expression de ma haute considération.
(femme) Je vous prie d'agréer, Madame l'Ambassadrice/ la Haute-Commissaire, l'expression de mes respectueux hommages.
Conversation - ‹‹Excellence››

CANADIAN AMBASSADORS/HIGH COMMISSIONERS abroad:
Mr./Mrs. (full name), Ambassador of Canada to (country) /High Commissioner for Canada to (country), Address
Salutation - Dear Ambassador/High Commissioner:
Final Salutation - Yours sincerely,
In Conversation - "Mr./Madam Ambassador/High Commissioner"
Note: When addressed by a Canadian citizen, whether in Canada or abroad, the form used is simply Ambassador or High Commissioner. The title "Excellency" is only used by the government and the citizens of the country to which the person is accredited.

AMBASSADEURS DU CANADA/HAUTS-COMMISSAIRES à l'étranger
(homme) Monsieur (prénom et nom) Ambassadeur du Canada/Haute-commissaire du Canada au (pays), Adresse
(femme) Madame (prénom et nom) l'Ambassadrice du Canada/Haute-commissaire du Canada au (pays), Adresse
Appel - (homme) Monsieur l'Ambassadeur/le Haut-Commissaire,
(femme) Madame l'Ambassadrice/la Haute-Commissaire,
Salutation - (homme) Je vous prie d'agréer, Monsieur l'Ambassadeur/le Haut-commissaire, l'expression de ma haute considération.
(femme) Je vous prie d'agréer, Madame l'Ambassadrice/ la Haute-commissaire, l'expression de mes respectueux hommages.
Conversation - (homme) ‹‹Monsieur l'Ambassadeur/ le Haut-Commissaire››
(femme) ‹‹Madame l'Ambassadrice/la Haut-Commissaire››
Remarques: Si un ambassadeur du Canada ou un haut-commissaire du Canada se trouve au Canada ou à l'étranger, la formule à employer est simplement ‹‹Ambassadeur›› ou ‹‹Haut-commissaire››. Le titre ‹‹Excellence›› n'est pas accordé par un citoyen canadien à un ambassadeur du Canada ou à un haut-commissaire du Canada, mais par le gouvernement et les citoyens du pays auprès duquel l'ambassadeur ou le haut-commissaire est accrédité.

Armed Forces/Forces Armeés

OFFICER RANK:
Brigadier General/Major General/Lieutenant General/General (full name), Address
Salutation - Dear General:
Final Salutation - Yours sincerely,
In Conversation - "General (surname)"
Colonel (full name), Address
Salutation - Dear Colonel:
Final Salutation - Yours sincerely,
In Conversation - "Colonel (surname)"
Lieutenant Colonel (full name), Address
Salutation - Dear Lieutenant Colonel:
Final Salutation - Yours sincerely,
In Conversation - "Lieutenant Colonel (surname)"
Major (full name), Address
Salutation - Dear Major:
Final Salutation - Yours sincerely,
In Conversation - "Major (surname)"
Captain (full name), Address
Salutation - Dear Captain:
Final Salutation - Yours sincerely,
In Conversation - "Captain (surname)"
Lieutenant (full name), Address
Salutation - Dear Lieutenant:
Final Salutation - Yours sincerely,
In Conversation - "Lieutenant (surname)"

AVEC GRADE:
(homme) Le brigadier-général/major-général/lieutenant- général (prénom et nom), Adresse
(femme) La brigadière-générale/majore-générale/lieutenante- générale (prénom et nom), Adresse
Appel - (homme) Général,
(femme) Générale,
Salutation - (homme) Je vous prie d'agréer, Général, l'expression de mes meilleurs sentiments.
(femme) Je vous prie d'agréer, Générale, l'expression de mes hommages respectueux.
Conversation - (homme) ‹‹Général››
(femme) ‹‹Générale››
(homme) Le colonel (prénom et nom), Adresse
(femme) La colonelle (prénom et nom), Adresse
Appel - (homme) Colonel,
(femme) Colonelle,
Salutation - (homme) Je vous prie d'agréer, Colonel, l'expression de mes meilleurs sentiments.
(femme) Je vous prie d'agréer, Colonelle, l'expression de mes hommages respectueux.
Conversation - (homme) ‹‹Colonel››
(femme) ‹‹Colonelle››
(homme) La lieutenant-colonel, (prénom et nom), Adresse
(femme) La lieutenante-colonelle, (prénom et nom), Adresse
Appel - (homme) Lieutenant-Colonel,
(femme) Lieutenante-Colonelle,
Salutation - (homme) Je vous prie d'agréer, Lieutenant- Colonel, l'expression de mes meilleurs sentiments.
(femme) Je vous prie d'agréer, Lieutenante-Colonelle, l'expression de mes meilleurs hommages respectueux.
Conversation - (homme) ‹‹Lieutenant-Colonel››
(femme) ‹‹Lieutenante-Colonelle››
(homme) Le major (prénom et nom), Adresse

(femme) La majore (prénom et nom), Adresse
Appel - (homme) Major,
(femme) Majore,
Salutation - (homme) Je vous prie d'agréer, Major, l'expression de mes meilleurs sentiments.
(femme) Je vous prie d'agréer, Majore, l'expression de mes hommages respectueux.
Conversation - (homme) ‹‹Major››
(femme) ‹‹Majore››
(homme) Le capitaine (prénom et nom), Adresse
(femme) La capitaine (prénom et nom), Adresse
Appel - Capitaine,
Salutation - (homme) Je vous prie d'agréer, Capitaine, l'expression de mes meilleurs sentiments.
(femme) Je vous prie d'agréer, Capitaine, l'expression de mes hommages respectueux.
Conversation - ‹‹Capitaine››
(homme) Le lieutenant (prénom et nom), Adresse
(femme) La lieutenante (prénom et nom), Adresse
Appel - (homme) Lieutenant,
(femme) Lieutenante,
Salutation - (homme) Je vous prie d'agréer, Lieutenant, l'expression de mes meilleurs sentiments.
(femme) Je vous prie d'agréer, Lieutenante, l'expression de mes hommages respectueux.
Conversation - (homme) ‹‹Lieutenant››
(femme) ‹‹Lieutenante››

NCO and other ranks:
Chief Warrant Officer (full name)
Salutation - Dear Chief Warrant Officer (surname)
Final Salutation - Yours sincerely,
In Conversation - "Mr./Mrs./Ms. (surname)"
Master Warrant Officer (full name)
Salutation - Dear Master Warrant Officer (surname):
Final Salutation - Yours sincerely,
In Conversation - "Mr./Mrs./Ms. (surname)"
Warrant Officer (full name)
Salutation - Dear Warrant Officer (surname) or Warrant (surname):
Final Salutation - Yours sincerely,
In Conversation - "Mr./Mrs./Ms. (surname)"
Sergeant (full name)
Salutation - Dear Sergeant (surname):
Final Salutation - Yours sincerely,
In Conversation - "Mr./Mrs./Ms. (surname)"
Corporal (full name)
Salutation - Dear Corporal (surname):
Final Salutation - Yours sincerely,
In Conversation - "Mr./Mrs./Ms. (surname)"
Private (full name)
Salutation - Dear Private (surname):
Final Salutation - Yours sincerely,
In Conversation - "Mr./Mrs./Ms. (surname)"

SOUS OFFICIERS ET AUTRES GRADES:
(homme) L'adjudant-chef (prénom et nom)
(femme) L'adjudante-chef (prénom et nom)
Appel - (homme) Adjudant-chef,
(femme) Adjudante-chef,
Salutation - (homme) Je vous prie d'agréer, Adjudant-chef, l'expression de mes meilleurs sentiments.
(femme) Je vous prie d'agréer, Adjudante-chef, l'expression de mes hommages respectueux.
Conversation - Le qualificatif du grade ‹‹Monsieur/ Madame/Mademoiselle››
(homme) L'adjudant-maître (prénom et nom)
(femme) L'adjudante-maîtresse (prénom et nom)
Appel - (homme) Adjudant-maître,
(femme) Adjudante-maîtresse,
Salutation - (homme) Je vous prie d'agréer, Adjudant-maître, l'expression de mes meilleurs hommages respectueux.
(femme) Je vous prie d'agréer, Adjudantemaîtresse, l'expression de mes hommages respectueux.
Conversation - Le qualificatif du grade ‹‹Monsieur/ Madame/Mademoiselle››
(homme) L'adjudant (prénom et nom)
(femme) L'adjudante (prénom et nom)
Appel - (homme) Adjudant,
(femme) Adjudante,
Salutation - (homme) Je vous prie d'agréer, Adjudant, l'expression de mes meilleurs sentiments.
(femme) Je vous prie d'agréer, Adjudante, l'expression de mes hommages respectueux.
Conversation - Le qualificatif du grade ‹‹Monsieur/ Madame/Mademoiselle››
(homme) Le sergent (prénom et nom)
(femme) La sergente (prénom et nom)
Appel - (homme) Sergent,
(femme) Sergente,
Salutation - (homme) Je vous prie d'agréer, Sergent, l'expression de mes meilleurs sentiments.

(femme) Je vous prie d'agréer, Sergente, l'expression de mes hommages respectueux.
Conversation - Le qualificatif du grade «Monsieur/ Madame/Mademoiselle»

(homme) Le caporal (prénom et nom)
(femme) La caporale (prénom et nom)
   Appel - (homme) Caporal,
   (femme) Caporale,
   Salutation - (homme) Je vous prie d'agréer, Caporal, l'expression de mes meilleurs sentiments.
   (femme) Je vous prie d'agréer, Caporale, l'expression de mes hommages respectueux.
   Conversation - Le qualificatif du grade «Monsieur/ Madame/Mademoiselle»

(homme) Le soldat (prénom et nom)
(femme) La soldate (prénom et nom)
   Appel - Monsieur/Madame/Mademoiselle,
   Salutation - (homme) Je vous prie d'agréer, Monsieur, l'expression de mes meilleurs sentiments.
   (femme) Je vous prie d'agréer, Madame/Mademoiselle, l'expression de mes hommages respectueux.
   Conversation - Le qualificatif du grade «Monsieur/ Madame/Mademoiselle»

Foreign Dignitaries/Les Dignitaires Étrangers

AN EMPEROR/EMPRESS:
His/Her Imperial Majesty (regnal name) or Emperor/Empress of (country), Address
Salutation - Your dignified Majesty:
Final Salutation - I have the honour to remain, Your Imperial Majesty's obedient servant,
In Conversation - "Your Majesty" first then "Sire/Ma'am"

EMPEREUR:
Sa Majesté Impériale (nom de règne) ou Empereur/Impératrice de/du (pays), Adresse Appel - Votre Majesté Impériale
Salutation - Je prie Votre Majesté Impériale de mon profond respect et de ma très haute considération.
Conversation - On commence par «Majesté». On poursuit avec «Sire/Madame»

A KING:
His Majesty (regnal name) or King of (country), Address
Salutation - Your Majesty:
Final Salutation - I have the honour to remain, Your Majesty's obedient servant,
In Conversation - "Your Majesty" first then "Sire"

UN ROI:
Sa Majesté (nom de règne) ou Roi de/du (pays), Adresse Appel - Majesté/Sire,
Salutation - Je prie Votre Majesté d'agréer l'hommage de mon profond respect et de ma très haute considération.
Conversation - On commence par «Majesté». On poursuit avec «Sire»

A QUEEN:
Her Majesty (regnal name) or Queen of (country), Address

Salutation - Your Majesty:
Final Salutation - I have the honour to remain, Your Majesty's obedient servant,
In Conversation - "Your Majesty" first then "Ma'am"

UNE REINE:
Sa Majesté (nom de règne) ou Reine de/du (pays), Adresse Appel - Majesté/Madame
Salutation - Je vous prie d'agréer Madame, l'hommage de mon profond respect et de ma très haute considération.
Conversation - On commence par «Majesté». On poursuit avec «Madame»

A PRESIDENT OF A REPUBLIC:
His/Her Excellency (full name), President of the Republic of (country), Address
Salutation - Excellency:
Final Salutation - Yours sincerely
In Conversation - "Excellency" first then "President" or "Sir/Madam"

UN PRÉSIDENT DE RÉPUBLIQUE:
(homme) Son Excellence monsieur (prénom et nom) Président de la République (nom), Adresse
(femme) Son Excellence madame (prénom et nom) Présidente de la République (nom), Adresse
Appel - (homme) Monsieur le Président,
(femme) Madame la Présidente,
Salutation - (homme) Je vous prie d'agréer Monsieur le Président, l'expression de ma très haute considération.
(femme) Je vous prie d'agréer Madame la Présidente, l'hommage de mon profond respect.
Conversation - (homme) On commence par «Excellence». On poursuit avec «Monsieur le Président» ou «Monsieur»
(femme) On commence par «Excellence». On poursuit avec «Madame la Présidente» ou «Madame»

THE PRESIDENT OF THE UNITED STATES:
His/Her Excellency the Honourable (full name), President of the United States, The White House, Washington, D.C.
Salutation - Dear Mr./Madam President:
Final Salutation - Yours sincerely,
In Conversation - "Mr./Madam President" or "Excellency" first then "Sir/Madam"

PRÉSIDENT DES ÉTATS-UNIS D'AMÉRIQUE:
Son Excellence l'honorable (prénom et nom) Président/Présidente de États-Unis d'Amérique, The White House, Washington D.C.
Appel - Monsieur le Président/Madame la Présidente,
Salutation - Je vous prie d'agréer, Monsieur le Président/Madame la Présidente, l'expression de ma très haute considération.
Conversation - On commence par «Monsieur le Président/Madame la Présidente» ou «Excellence». On poursuit avec «Monsieur» ou «Madame».

A PRIME MINISTER:
His/Her Excellency (full name), Prime Minister of (name), Address

Salutation - Dear Prime Minister:
Final Salutation - Yours sincerely,
In Conversation - "Prime Minister" or "Excellency" first then "Sir/Madam" or "Mr./Mrs./Ms. (surname)"

PREMIER MINISTRE:
(homme) Son Excellence monsieur (prénom et nom) Premier Ministre de _____, Adresse
(femme) Son Excellence madame (prénom et nom) Première Ministre de _____, Adresse
Appel - (homme) Monsieur le Premier Ministre,
(femme) Madame la Première Ministre,
Salutation - (homme) Je vous prie d'agréer Monsieur le Premier Ministre, l'expression de ma haute considération.
(femme) Je vous prie d'agréer Madame la Première Ministre, l'hommage de mon profond respect.
Conversation - (homme) On commence par «Monsieur le Premier Ministre» ou «Excellence». On poursuit par «Monsieur»
(femme) On commence par «Madame la Première Ministre» ou «Excellence». On poursuit par «Madame»

Others/Autres

LAWYERS/NOTARIES:
Mr./Mrs./Ms. (full name) or Mr./Mrs./Ms., Q.C.
Salutation - Dear Mr./Mrs./Ms. (surname):
Final Salutation - Yours sincerely,
In Conversation - "Mr./Mrs./Ms. (surname)"

AVOCATS/NOTAIRES:
Me (prénom et nom) Appel - Maître,
Salutation - Je vous prie d'agréer, Maître, l'expression de mes meilleurs sentiments.
Conversation - «Maître»

AIDE-DE-CAMP:
Military: (according to rank; See Armed Forces) Civilian (according to their title), Mr./Mrs./Ms. (full name)
Salutation - Dear Mr./Mrs./Ms. (surname):
Final Salutation - Yours sincerely,
In Conversation - "Mr./Mrs./Ms. (surname)"
Note: Post nominals "A. de C." have been authorized for Aides-de-camps to the Governor General and Lieutenant Governors.
Militaire: (selon le grade; voir la rubrique «Forces armées») Civil (selon le titre), Monsieur/Madame/Mademoiselle (prénom et nom) Appel - Monsieur/Madame/Mademoiselle,
Salutation - Je vous prie d'agréer, Monsieur/Madame/ Mademoiselle, l'expression de mes sentiments les meilleurs.
Conversation - «Monsieur/Madame/Mademoiselle» Remarque: Les initiales «A. de C.» sont autorisées pour les aides de camp du Gouverneur général et des lieutenants-gouverneurs.

Abbreviations

Indicating Academic, Ecclesiastical and other Degrees, membership in Societies and Institutions, military ranks, etc., appearing in the Canadian Almanac and Directory.

AACCA . . . . Associate of Association of Certified Accountants & Corporate Accountants (British)
AACI . . . . Accredited Appraiser Canadian Institute
AAE . . . . Associate of Accountants' & Executives' Corp. of Canada
AAGO . . . . — of the American Guild of Organists
AASA . . . . — of the Alberta Society of Artists
AB . . . . Bachelor of Arts, American (Artium Baccalaureus)
AC . . . . "Advanced Certification" Canadian Association of Medical Radiation Technologists
ACA . . . . Associate of Institute of Chartered Accountants (Eng.)
ACAM . . . . Associate Certified Administrative Manager
ACCO . . . . — of Canadian College of Organists
AccSCRP. . . . . — of Canadian Public Relations Society Inc.
ACD . . . . Archaeologiae Christianae Doctor
ACGI . . . . Associate of the City & Guilds of London Institute
ACIC . . . . — of Canadian Institute of Chemistry
ACInstM . . . . — of the Institute of Marketing
ACIS . . . . — of Chartered Institute of Secretaries (British)
ACSM . . . . — of Cambourne School of Mines
Adm. . . . . Admiral
Adm. A. Pl.Fin. . . . . Administrateur agréé en planification financière
AFC . . . . Accredited Financial Counsellor
AFRAS (AFRAeS) . . . . . Fellow of the Royal Aeronautical Society
Ag de l'U (Paris) . . . . . . Honorary Professor of University of Paris (Agrégé de l'Université Paris)
Ag. de Phil. . . . . Professor of Philosophy (Agrégé en Philosophie Louvain)
AGSM . . . . Associate of the Guildhall School of Music (British)
AIC . . . . — of the Institute of Chemistry (British)
AICB . . . . Associate of the Institute of Canadian Bankers
AIIC . . . . — of the Insurance Institute of Canada
AKC . . . . — of King's College (London)
ALCM . . . . — of London (Canada) Conservatory of Music
ALS . . . . Commissioned Alberta Land Surveyor
AM . . . . Master of Arts (Artium Magister)
AMEIC . . . . Associate Member of the Engineering Institute of Canada
AMICE . . . . — Member of the Institution of Civil Engineers (British)
AMIEE . . . . — Member of the Institute of Electrical Engineers
AMIMechE . . . . — Member of the Institution of Mechanical Engineers (British)
A.Mus. . . . . — of Music
APA . . . . — Member of the Institute of Accredited Public Accountants (British)
APHA . . . . — Member of the Public Health Association (British)
APR . . . . Accredited Member of the Canadian Public Relations Society
ARA . . . . Associate of the Royal Academy (honorary)
ARCD . . . . — of the Royal College of Dancing
ARCM . . . . — of the Royal College of Music
ARCO . . . . — of the Royal College of Organists (Canadian)
ARCS (A.R.C.Sc.) . . . . . — of the Royal College of Science
ARCT . . . . — of the Royal Conservatory of Music of Toronto
ARCVS . . . . — of the Royal College of Veterinary Surgeons
ARDIO . . . . — of Registered Interior Designers of Ontario
ARDS . . . . — of the Royal Drawing Society (London, Eng.)
ARIBA . . . . — of the Royal Institute of British Architects
ARIC . . . . — of the Royal Institute of Chemistry
ARSH . . . . — of the Royal Society of Health
ARSM . . . . — of the Royal School of Mines
ARSM . . . . — of the Royal School of Music
AScT . . . . Applied Science Technologist
Assoc. Inst. M.M. . . . . . . Associate of the Institute of Mining and Metallurgy (British)
ATCL . . . . — of Trinity College, London (Eng.)
ATCM. . . . . — of the Toronto Conservatory of Music
A.Th. . . . . — in Theology
BA . . . . Bachelor of Arts
BAA . . . . — of Applied Arts
B.Acc. . . . . — of Accountancy
B.Adm. (B.Admin.) . . . . . — of Administration
B.Adm.Pub. . . . . — Baccalauréat spécialisé en administration publique
BAeE (BAeroE) . . . . Bachelor of Aeronautical Engineering
BAI . . . . — of Engineering (U. of Dublin)
BALS . . . . — of Arts in Library Science
BAO . . . . — of Obstetrics
B.Arch. . . . . — in Architecture
BAS (B.A.Sc.) . . . . — of Applied Science
BASM. . . . . — of Arts, Master of Science
B.A.Theo. . . . . — of Arts in Theology
BBA . . . . — of Business Administration
BCD . . . . Bachelier en Chirurgie Dentale
BCE . . . . Bachelor of Civil Engineering
B.Ch. (ChB) . . . . — in Surgery (British)

BChE . . . . — in Chemical Engineering (American)
BCL . . . . — of Civil Law (or Canon Law)
B.Com. (B. Comm.) . . . . — of Commerce
B.Comp.Sc. . . . . — of Computer Science
BD . . . . — of Divinity
BDC . . . . Bachelier en droit canonique
B.Des. . . . . Bachelor of Design
BDS . . . . — of Dental Surgery (British)
BE (B.Eng.) . . . . — of Engineering
B.Ed. (BEAD) . . . . — of Education
BEDS . . . . — of Environmental Design Studies
BEE . . . . — of Electrical Engineering (American)
B. en Ph. . . . . Bachelier en Philosophie
B. en Sc. Com. . . . . — en Science Commerciale
BES . . . . Bachelor of Environmental Sciences (or Studies)
B ès A . . . . Bachelier ès Arts
B ès L . . . . — ès Lettres
B. ès Sc. . . . . — ès Science
B. ès Sc. App. . . . . — ès Science Appliquée
BF . . . . Bachelor of Forestry (American)
BFA . . . . — of Fine Arts
B.Gen. . . . . Brigadier-General
BHE (B.H.Ec.) . . . . Bachelor of Home Economics
B.H.Sc. . . . . — of Household Science
BJ . . . . — of Journalism
BJC . . . . — in Canon Law
BL . . . . — in Literature (or of Laws)
BLA . . . . — of Landscape Architecture
B.Litt. . . . . — of Literature (American & British)
BLS . . . . — of Library Science
BM . . . . — of Medicine
B.Mus. . . . . — of Music
BMV . . . . Bachelier en Médecine Vetérinaire
BN . . . . Bachelor of Nursing
B.N.Sc. . . . . — of Nursing Science
B. Paed. (Péd.) . . . . — of Pedagogy
BPA . . . . — of Public Administration
BPE . . . . — of Physical Education
B.Ph. (B.Phil.) . . . . — of Philosophy
BPHE . . . . — of Physical & Health Education
B.Ps. . . . . Baccalauréat en Psychologie
Br. . . . . Brother
BS . . . . Bachelor of Science (or of Surgery) (American)
BSA . . . . — of Science in Agriculture (or in Accounting, or in Administration)
B.Sc. . . . . — of Science
BScA . . . . Bachelier ès science appliquées
BScB . . . . — en Bibliothéconomie
B.Sc.(CE) . . . . Bachelor of Science in Civil Engineering
B.Sc.Com. . . . . — of Commercial Science
B.Sc.Dom. . . . . Baccalauréat en Sciences Domestiques
BScF (BSF) . . . . Bachelor of Science in Forestry
BScFE . . . . — of Science in Forestry Engineering
BScH . . . . Bachelier en Sciences Hospitalières
BScN . . . . Bachelor of Science in Nursing
B.Sc.(Nurs.) . . . . — of Science in Nursing
B.Sc.(Occ.Ther.) . . . . . . — of Science in Occupational Therapy
B.Sc.(OT) . . . . — of Science in Occupational Therapy
B.Sc.Phm.(BSP) . . . . . . — of Science in Pharmacy
B.Sc.Soc. . . . . — of Social Science
BSCE . . . . — of Science in Civil Engineering
B.S.Ed. . . . . — of Science in Education
BSEE . . . . — of Science in Electrical Engineering
BSN . . . . — of Science in Nursing
BSS . . . . — of Social Sciences
BSW . . . . — of Social Work (or Welfare)
B.Tech. . . . . — of Technology
B.Th. . . . . — of Theology
BTS . . . . — of Technological Science (Edinburgh)
B.V.Sc. . . . . — of Veterinary Science
CA . . . . Chartered Accountant
C. Adm., F.P. . . . . Chartered Administrator in Financial Planning
CAAP . . . . Certified Advertising Agency Practitioner
CAE . . . . — Association Executive
CAE/c.a.é. . . . . Chartered Account Executive
CAM . . . . Certified Administrative Manager
CAP . . . . Certificat d'Aptitude Pedagogique
Capt. (or Capt.(N)) . . . . Captain (or Captain (Naval))
CBE . . . . Commander, Order of the British Empire
CBV . . . . Chartered Business Valuator
CC . . . . Chartered Cartographer

CC	Companion, Order of Canada
CD	Canadian Forces Decoration
Cdr.	Commander
CE	Civil Engineer
CEA	Certified Environmental Administrator
CEA	Certified Environmental Auditor
CEBS	Certified Employee Benefit Specialist
Cer.E.	Ceramic Engineer
Cert. Bus. Admin.	Doctor of Applied Science Diploma Business Administration
CES	Certificat d'Études Secondaires (La Sorbonne)
CFA	Chartered Financial Analyst
CFP	Chartered Financial Planner
CGA	Certified General Accountant
CHA	Certified Housing Administrator
Chan.	Chanoine (Canon)
Ch.E.	Chartered Executive
CHE	Certified Health Executive
Chem. Ing.	Ingénieur Chimiste Diplomé (Swiss Fed. Inst. Technology)
CHFC	Chartered Financial Consultant
CIF	Canadian Institute of Forestry
CIM	Certificate in Management
CIM	Certified Industrial Manager
CIM	Certified Investment Manager
CIS&P	Canadian Inst. of Surveying & Photogrammetry
CLA	Canadian Library Association
CLS	Canada Land Surveyor
CLU	Chartered Life Underwriter
CM	Master in Medicine (British)
CM	Member, Order of Canada
CMA	Certified Management Accountant (or Canadian Medical Association or Canadian Management Association)
CMC	Certified Management Consultant
CmdO	Commissioned Officer
Cmdre.	Commodore
CMM	Certified Municipal Manager (Ontario)
CMM	Commander, Order of Military Merit
COM	Commander of the Order of Merit (Police Forces)
Col.	Colonel
CPA	Chartered Professional Accountant (formerly Certified Public Accountant)
CPC	— Personnel Consultant
CPM	Certificate in Personnel Management
CPPMA	— in Public Personnel Management Association
CPPO	Certified Public Purchasing Officer
CPP	— Professional Purchaser
CR (c.r.)	Conseiller de la Reine (Queen's Counsel)
CRA	Canadian Residential Appraiser
CSC	Canadian Securities Course
CSR	Chartered Stenographic Reporter
CTC	Certified Travel Counsellor
C.Tech.	— Technician
CWO	Chief Warrant Officer
DA	Doctor of Arts (honorary)
DA	— of Archaeology (Laval)
D.Arch.	— of Architecture
D.A.Sc.	— in Applied Sciences
DC	— of Chiropractic
DCD	Docteur en Chirurgie Dentale
D.Ch.	Doctor of Surgery (British)
DChE	— of Chemical Engineering (American)
DCL	— of Civil Law (or Canon Law)
DD	— of Divinity
DDC	Doctorat Droit Canonique
D. de l'Un.	— Docteur de l'Université
DDS	Doctor of Dental Surgery (British)
DDT	— of Drugless Therapy
D.Ed.	— of Education
D.Eng.	— of Engineering
D. en Méd. Vet.	Docteur en Médecine Vetérinaire
D. en Ph.	— en Philosophie
D ès L	— ès Lettres (Doctor of Letters)
D. ès Sc. App.	Doctor of Applied Science
DF	— of Forestry (American)
DFA	— of Fine Arts (often honorary)
D.F.Sc.	— of Financial Science (Laval)
DIC	Diploma of Membership of Imperial College of Science & Technology (British)
Dip. Bact.	— in Bacteriology
Dip d'É	Diplome d'Études
Dip de l'U (P)	Diploma of the U. of Paris
Dip. d'É. Sup. or DipES	Diplome d'Études Supérieures, Paris

Dip. Ing.	Diploma in Engineering
Dipl. Bus. Admin.	Diploma Business Administration
D.Jour	Doctor of Journalism
D. Lit. (D. Litt.)	— of Letters (or Literature)
DLO	Diploma in Laryngology & Otology
DLS	Dominion Land Surveyor (or Doctor of Library Science)
DM	Doctorat Médecine
DMD	Doctor of Dental Medicine
D.Ms.	— in Missionology
D.Mus.	Doctorat en Musique
DMR (D or T)	Diploma in Medical Radiology (Royal Coll. of Surgeons, London)
DMT	— in Tropical Medicine
DMT & H (Eng.)	— in Tropical Medicine & Hygiene
D.N.S (D.N.Sc.)	Doctor of Nursing Science
DO	— of Osteopathy
Doct.Arch.	— of Christian Archaeology (Pontifical Institute, Rome)
D.Paed. (Péd.)	— of Paedagogy
DPE	Diploma in Physical Education
D.Ph. (D.Phil. or PhD)	Doctor of Philosophy
D.P.Ec.	— of Political Economy
DPH	— (or Diploma) in Public Health
D.Ps. (D.Psy.)	— of Psychologie
D.P.Sc.	— of Political Science
D.Psych.	— (or Diploma) in Psychiatry
DPT	— of Physio-Therapy
Dr.	Doctor
DR	Doctor of Radiology
Dr.Com.Sc.	— of Commercial Science
Dr de l'U (P)	— of the U. of Paris
Dr. ès Lettres	— of Letters (History of Literature)
Dr. jur.	— of Law (Dr. Juris)
Dr. rer. pol.	— of Political Economy (Dr. Rerum Politicarum) (Docteur des Sciences Politiques)
DSA (DScA)	Docteur ès science appliqués
D.Sc.	Doctor of Science
D.Sc.Mil.	— of Military Science
DSL	— of Sacred Letters
D.Sc.Com.	— of Commercial Science
D.Sc.Fin.	— of Financial Science
D.Sc.Nat.	— in Natural Science
D.Sc.Soc.	— of Social Science
D.Th.	— of Theology
DVM (DMV)	— of Veterinary Medicine
D.V.Sc.	— of Veterinary Science
E.C.E.	Early Childhood Educator
EdD	Doctor of Education
EdM	Master of Education (Harvard)
EE	Electrical Engineer
EM	Mining Engineer
ETCM	Graduate of Eastern Townships Conservatory of Music
FAAO	Fellow of the American Academy of Optometry
F.A.A.O.Dip.	Diplomatic Fellow of the American Academy of Optometry
FACD	Fellow of the American College of Dentists
FACO	— of the American College of Organists
FACP	— of the American College of Physicians
FACR	— of the American College of Radiology
FACS	— of the American College of Surgeons
FAE	— of the Accountants' & Executives' Corp. of Canada
FAGS	— of the American Geographical Society
FAIA	— of the American Institute of Actuaries
	— of the American Institute of Architects
FAIA	Association of International Accountants
FAOU	Fellow of the American Ornithologists Union
FAPHA	— of the American Public Health Association
FAPS	— of the American Physical Society
FAS	— of the Actuarial Society
FBA	— of the British Academy (honorary)
FBOA	— of British Association of Optometrists
FCA	— of the Institute of Chartered Accountants (British)
FCAM	— of the Certified Administrative Manager
FCBA	— of Canadian Bankers' Association
FCCA	— of the Association of Certified Accountants
FCCO	— of the Canadian College of Organists
FCCT	— of the Canadian College of Teachers
FCCUI	— of the Canadian Credit Union Institute
FCGI	— of the City & Guilds of London Institute
FCI	— of the Canadian Credit Institute
FCIC	— of the Chemical Institute of Canada
FCII	— of the Chartered Insurance Institute (British)
FCIS.	— of the Chartered Institute of Secretaries (British)

FCOG	— of the College of Obstetricians & Gynaecologists (British)
FCAMRT	— of Canadian Association of Medical Radiation Technologists
FCIA.	— of the Canadian Institute of Actuaries
FCMA.	— of the Society of Management Accountants of Canada
FCSI.	— of the Canadian Securities Institute
FCTC	— of the Canadian Institute of Travel Counsellors
FCUIC	— of the Credit Union Institute of Canada
FE	Forest Engineer
FEIC	Fellow of the Engineering Institute of Canada
FFA	— of the Faculty of Actuaries (Scotland)
FFR	— of the Faculty of Radiologists (British)
FGS	— of the Geological Society (British)
FGSA	— of the Geological Society of America
FIA.	— of the Institute of Actuaries (British)
FIC.	— of the Institute of Chemistry
FICB.	— of the Institute of Canadian Bankers
FICE.	— of the Institution of Civil Engineers
FIEE.	— of the Institution of Electrical Engineers
FIIC	— of the Insurance Institute of Canada
FIL.	— of the Institute of Linguists (British)
FLA	— of the Library Association (England)
FMA	Financial Management Advisor
FMSA.	— of the Mineralogical Society of America
Fr.	Father
FRAI	Fellow of the Royal Anthropological Institute
FRAIC	— of the Royal Architectural Institute of Canada
FRAM.	— of the Royal Academy of Music
FRAS.	— of the Royal Astronomical Society
FRCCO	— of the Royal Canadian College of Organists
FRCM	— of the Royal College of Music
FRCO.	— of the Royal College of Organists
FRCOG	— of the Royal College of Obstetricians & Gynaecologists
FRCP.	— of the Royal College of Physicians of London
FRCP(C)	— of the Royal College of Physicians of Canada
FRCP(E)	— of the Royal College of Physicians of Edinburgh
FRCP(I)	— of the Royal College of Physicians of Ireland
FRCP(Glas)	— of the Royal College of Physicians of Glasgow
FRCS	— of the Royal College of Surgeons of England
FRCS(C)	— of the Royal College of Surgeons of Canada
FRCS(E)	— of the Royal College of Surgeons of Edinburgh
FRCS(I)	— of the Royal College of Surgeons of Ireland
FRCS(Glas)	— of the Royal College of Surgeons of Glasgow
FRGS.	— of the Royal Geographical Society
FRHistS	— of the Royal Historical Society
FRHortS	— of the Royal Horticultural Society
FRIBA	— of the Royal Institute of British Architects
FRIC	— of the Royal Institute of Chemistry
FRICS	— of the Royal Institution of Chartered Surveyors
FRMCM	— of Royal Manchester College of Music
FRMS (FRMetS)	— of the Royal Meteorological Society
FRS.	— of the Royal Society (honorary)
FRSA	— of the Royal Society of Arts
FRSC.	— of the Royal Society of Canada
FRSE.	— of the Royal Society of Edinburgh
FRSH.	— of the Royal Society of Health
FRSL	— of the Royal Society of Literature
FSA	— of the Society of Actuaries (or of Antiquaries) (honorary)
FSMAC	— of the Society of Management Accountants of Canada
FSS	— of the Royal Statistical Society
FTCL	— of Trinity College of Music (London)
FZS	— of the Zoological Society (British)
Gen.	General
GJ	Graduate Jeweller
HARCVS	Honorary Associate of Royal College of Veterinary Surgeons
IA	Investment Advisor
IC	Investment Counsellor
IngETP	Diplome de l'École Spéciale des Travaux Publiques
JCB	Bachelor of Canon Law
JCD	Doctor of Canon Law (or of Civil Law)
JCL	Licentiate in Canon Law (Juris Canonici Licentiatus)
JD	Doctor of Jurisprudence
JDS	— of Jurisdical Science
Jr.	Junior
JUL	Licentiate of Law in Utroque (both Civil & Canon Law)
JurM	Master of Jurisprudence
Jur. utr. Dr.	Juris utriusque doctor, Equiv. to LL.D.
LAB	Licentiate of the Assoc. Bd. of Royal Schools of Music (London, Eng.)
L.Cdr.	Lieutenant-Commander
LCL	Licentiate in Canon Law
LCMI	— of the Cost & Management Institute

L.Col.	Lieutenant-Colonel
LDC	Licencié ès Droit Canonique
LDS	Licentiate in Dental Surgery (British)
L ès L	Licencié ès Lettres
L. ès Sc.	— ès Sciences
L.Gen.	Lieutenant-General
LGSM	Licentiate of the Guildhall School of Music & Drama (London, Eng.)
LittD	Doctor of Letters (or Literature)
LittL	Licence ès Lettres
Litt.M.	Master of Letters (or Literature)
LJC	Licentiatus Juris Canonici
LL	License in Civil Law
LLB	Bachelor of Laws (Legum Baccalaureus)
LLD	Doctor of Laws (usually honorary)
LLL	Licence en droit
LLM	Master of Law
L. Mus.	Licentiate in Music
LMUS.	— in Music of the Univ. of Saskatchewan
L Mus TCL	— in General Musicianship of Trinity College, London
L.Péd.	Licence en Pédagogie
L.Ph.	— en Philosophie
L.Psych.	Licencié en Psychologie
LRAM	Licentiate of the Royal Academy of Music (London)
LRCM.	— of the Royal College of Music (London)
LRCP.	— of the Royal College of Physicians
LRCS	— of the Royal College of Surgeons
LRCT	— of the Royal Conservatory of Toronto
LRE	— in Religious Education
LRSM.	— of the Royal Schools of Music (London)
LS	Land Surveyor
LSA	Licentiate in Agricultural Science
L.Sc.Com.	— in Commercial Science
LScO	Licence en optométrie
L.S.Sc.	Licentiate in Sacred Scriptures
L.Sc.Soc.	Licence in Social Science
LST	Licentiate in Sacred Theology
Lt. (or Lt(N))	Lieutenant (or Lieutenant (Naval))
LTCL	Licentiate of Trinity College of Music (London)
LTCM	— of the Toronto Conservatory of Music
L.Th	Licentiate in Theology
M.	Monsieur
MA	Master of Arts
M.Acc.	— of Accountancy
MACF	Membre de l'Académie canadiennefrançaise
MAeE	Master of Aeronautical Engineering
MAIEE	Member of American Institute of Electrical Engineers
MAIME	— of American Institute of Mining Engineers
Maj.	Major
MALS	Master of Arts in Library Science
MAP	Maîtrise en administration publique
M.Arch.	Master of Architecture
MAS.	— of Archival Studies
M.A.Sc. (MAS)	— of Applied Science
MASCE	Member of the American Society of Civil Engineers
MASME	— of the American Society of Mechanical Engineers
MAust IM	— of the Australian Institute of Mining & Metallurgy
MB	Bachelor of Medicine (British)
MBA	Master in Business Administration
MCE.	— of Civil Engineering
M.Ch. (ChM)	— of Surgery (British)
MChE.	— of Chemical Engineering (American)
MCI	Member of the Credit Institute
MCIC	— of the Chemical Institute of Canada
MCIF	— of the Canadian Institute of Forestry
MCIM.	— of the Canadian Institute of Mining
MCIMM	— of the Canadian Institute of Mining & Metallurgy
MCInstM	— of the Canadian Institute of Marketing
MCL	Master of Civil Law
M.Com.	— of Commerce
M.Comp.	— of Canon Law
M.Comp.Sc.	— of Computer Science
MD	Doctor of Medicine
MDC	Master of Canon Law
MDCM	Doctor of Medicine & Master of Surgery
M.Des.	Master of Design
M.Div.	— of Divinity
MDS	— of Dental Surgery (British)
MDV	Doctor of Veterinary Medicine
Me	Maître
ME	Master of Mechanical Engineering

M.Ed. (M.A.Ed.)	— of Education
MEDS	— of Environmental Design Studies
MEE	— of Electrical Engineering (American)
MEIC	Member of the Engineering Institute of Canada
M.Eng.	Master of Engineering
MF	— of Forestry
MFA	— of Fine Arts
M.Gen.	Major-General
Mgr.	Monsignor (or Manager or Monseigneur)
MHA	Master of Health (or Hospital) Administration
MHE (M.H.Ec.)	— of Home Economics
MICE	Member of the Institution of Civil Engineers (British)
MICIA	— of Industrial, Commercial & Institutional Accountants
MIEE	— of the Institution of Electrical Engineers (British)
MIMM	— of the Institute of Mining & Metallurgy (British)
MINA	— of the Institute of Naval Architects
MIRE	— of the Institute of Radio Engineers
M.I.St.	— of Information Studies
MJ	— of Journalism
M.Litt.	— of Letters (or Literature)
MLIS	— of Library & Information Science
MLS	— of Library Science (or Licentiate in Medieval Studies)
MM (M.Mus.)	— of Music
MMM	Member, Order of Military Merit
MOM	Member of the Order of Merit (Police Forces)
MN (M.Nurs.)	Master of Nursing
MP	— of Planning
MP	Member of Parliament
MPE	Master of Physical Education
M.Ph. (M.Phil.)	— of Philosophy
MPM	— of Pest Management
MPP	Member of Provincial Parliament
M.Ps. (M.Psy.)	Master of Psychology
MRAIC	Member of the Royal Architectural Institute of Canada
MRCOG	— of the Royal College of Obstetricians & Gynaecologists
MRCP	— of the Royal College of Physicians
MRCP(E)	— of the Royal College of Physicians of Edinburgh
MRCP(I)	— of the Royal College of Physicians of Ireland
MRCP(Glas).	— of the Royal College of Physicians of Glasgow
MRCS	— of the Royal College of Surgeons
MRCS(E)	— of the Royal College of Surgeons of Edinburgh
MRCVS	— of the Royal College of Veterinary Surgeons
MRM	Master of Resource Management
MRSC	Member of the Royal Society of Canada
MRSH	— of the Royal Society of Health
MRST	— of the Royal Society of Teachers
MS	Master of Surgery (British)
MSA	— of Science in Agriculture
M.Sc.	— of Science
MScA	— of Applied Science
MSCE	— of Science in Civil Engineering
MScF	— of Science in Forestry
M.Sc.(Med.)	— of Science in Medicine
MScN (MSN)	— of Science in Nursing
M.Sc.Phm.	— of Science in Pharmacy
M.Sc.Soc.	— in Social Sciences
M.S.Ed.	— of Science in Education
M.S.Litt.	— of Sacred Letters
MSPE	McGill School of Physical Education
MSRC	Membre Société Royale du Canada
MSS	Master of Social Science
MSW	— of Social Work
MTCI	Member of Trust Companies Institute
M.U.Dr.	Medecinae Universae Doctor (Prague) (Dentistry & Medicine)
MUP	Master of Planning
MURP	— of Urban & Rural Planning
Mus. Bac. (Mus.B.)	Bachelor of Music
Mus. Doc. (Mus.D.)	Doctor of Music
Mus. G. Paed.	Musicae Graduatus Paedagogus (Graduate Teacher in Music)
MusM	Master of Music
MV	Médécin Vétérinaire
M.V.Sc.	Master of Veterinary Science
NDA	National Diploma in Agriculture (Royal Ag. Soc. of Engineering)
NDD	National Diploma in Dairying (Scotland)
NP	Notary Public
OA	Officier d'Académie (France)
OC	Order of Canada
OD	Doctor of Optometry
OIP	Officier de l'Instruction Publique
OLS	Ontario Land Surveyor
OMM	Officer, Order of Military Merit
OOM	Officer of the Order of Merit (Police Forces)
OSA	Ontario Society of Artists
PC	Privy Councillor
PD	Doctor of Parapsychology
PE	Professional Engineer
P.Eng.	Registered Professional Engineer
PFC	Planificateur Financier Certifié
PFP	Personal Financial Planner
PhB	Bachelor of Philosophy
PhC	Philosopher of Chiropractic
PhD	Doctor of Philosophy
PhTD	Physical Therapy Doctor
PhL	Licentiate in Philosophy
PLS	Professional Legal Secretary
P.Mgr.	— Manager
PP	— Purchaser
PPB	— Public Buyer
Prof.	Professor
PTIC	Patent & Trade Mark Institute of Canada
QAA	Qualified Administrative Assistant
QC	Queen's Counsel
QLS	Québec Land Surveyor
RA	Royal Academy (honorary)
R.Adm.	Rear-Admiral
RAM	Royal Academy of Music (Budapest)
RAS	Royal Aeronautical Society
RBA	Royal Society of British Artists
RCA	Royal Canadian Academy of Arts
RCAM	Royal College & Academy of Music (Budapest)
RCM	Royal Conservatory of Music (Leipzig)
RE	Royal Engineers
REBC	Registered Employee Benefits Consultant
Rev.	Reverend
RFP	Registered Financial Planner
RHU	Registered Health Underwriter
RMS	Royal Society of Miniature Painters
RMT	Registered Music Teacher
RN	— Nurse
ROI	Royal Institute of Oil Painters
RP	Member of the Royal Society of Portrait Painters
RP	Révérend Père (Reverend Father)
RPA	Registered Professional Accountant
R.P.Bio.	— Professional Biologist
R.P.Dt.	— Professional Dietitian
RPF	— Professional Forester
RRL	— Record Librarian
RSH	Royal Society of Health
RSW	Registered Specification Writer
RT	— Technician of the Cdn. Association of Medical Radiation Technologists
SC	Senior Counsel (Eire) equivalent of Q.C.
ScD	Doctorat ès Sciences
ScL	Licence ès Sciences
Sc Soc B	Bachelier Science Sociale
Sc Soc D	Doctor of Social Science
Sc Soc L	License in Social Science
SFC	Specialist in Financial Counselling
SJ	Society of Jesus
SLS	Saskatchewan Land Surveyor
S.Lt.	Sub-Lieutenant
SM	Master of Science
Sr.	Senior
Sr.	Sister
SSB	Bachelier en Science Sacrée
SSC	Sculptors' Society of Canada
SSL	Licentiate in Sacred Scripture
STB (SThB)	Bachelor of Sacred Theology
STD (SThD)	Doctor of Sacred Theology
STL (SThL)	Sacrae Theologiae Licentiatus (Licentiate in Sacred Theology)
STM	Master of Sacred Theology
TCL	Trinity College, London
TMMG	Teacher, Massage & Medical Gymnastics
ThD	Doctor of Theology
V.Adm.	Vice-Admiral
VG	Vicar-General
VS	Veterinary Surgeon

Business & Shipping Abbreviations

As shipping terms vary in different countries, insurance or shipping agents should be consulted.

a/c	Account
Ad val.	Ad valorem
avoir	Avoirdupois
bbl.	Barrel
B/L.	Bill of Lading
b.m.	Board Measure
B.O.	Buyer's Option
B/P.	Bills Payable
B/R.	Bills Receivable
B/S.	Bill of Sale
c.	Hundred
C or Cent.	Centigrade
cf.	Compare
C. and F.	Cost & Freight
Cie	Compagnie
c.i.f.	Cost insurance & freight
C.L.	Car Load (of freight)
Co.	Company
C.O.D.	Cash on Delivery
C. of F.	Cost of Freight
Cr.	Credit
C.W.O.	Cash with Order
Cwt.	Hundredweight
D/A.	Documents Attached, also Deposit Account
Dis. (Disct.)	Discount
Dl. (or Tl.)	Double (or triple) first class
D.O.A.	Deliver Documents on Acceptance of Draft
D.O.P.	Deliver Documents on Payment of Draft
Dr.	Debit
D.V.	God willing (Deo volente)
e.g.	For example (exempli gratia)
E.&O.E.	Errors & omissions excepted
Est. Wt.	Estimated Weight
et seq.	And the following (et sequens)
Ex. Div.	Without Dividend
Ex-Warehouse	Purchaser pays carriage charges & assumes risks from seller's warehouse
F.	Fahrenheit
F.a.a.	Free of Average (marine insurance)
F.A.S.	Free Alongside (Seller assumes risks & delivers goods to alongside of steamer free of carriage charges)
F.O.B.	Free on Board (Purchaser pays carriage charges & assumes risks from point specified)
F.P.A.	Free of Particular Average (Insured can recover only for a total loss, subject to other conditions of the contract)
Franco.	Pre-paid free of expense to point specified
G.A.	General Average (All owners of cargo & vessel share in any loss arising from expense incurred to preserve ship & contents from greater loss)
gm.	Grammes

gr. . . . . Grain; grains, or gross
ibid. . . . . In the same place (ibidem)
i.e. . . . . That is (id est)
Inc. . . . . Incorporated
Int. . . . . Interest
K.D. . . . . Knocked down
lb. (libra) . . . . . . Pound
L/C. . . . . Letter of Credit
L.C.L. . . . . Less than Car Load (of freight)
Limited; Ltd. . . . . Limited Liability (Shareholders are "limited" in liability to the amount of their subscribed stock in certain companies)
L.P. . . . . List Price
M. . . . . Thousand (Mille)
MS., MSS. . . . . . Manuscript(s)
N.E.S. (N.O.P.) . . Not Otherwise Provided For (Customs)
N.O.S. . . . . Not Otherwise Specified
N.S.F. . . . . Not Sufficient Funds (re cheques)
Nstd. . . . . Nested
O.K. . . . . Correct
op. cit. . . . . In the work quoted (opere citato)
O.R. . . . . At Owner's Risk
O.R.B. . . . . At Owner's Risk of Breakage
oz. . . . . Ounce
P.A. . . . . Particular Average (As used in Marine Insurance, means damage to the goods caused by perils insured against & named in the contract. This form is often written with a Franchise Clause, & means there will be no claim unless the loss exceeds the percentage named)
P/A. . . . . Power of Attorney
P & D. . . . . Pick Up & Deliver
pp. . . . . Pages
Pro forma . . . . . . As a Matter of Form
P.S. . . . . Postscript
q.v. . . . . Which see (quod vide)
R.R. . . . . Rural Route (Postal delivery)
S.B. . . . . Shipping Bill
s.s. . . . . Steamship
s/o . . . . Ship's Option, weight or measurement
S.U. . . . . Set Up (meaning article is complete)
T.B.L. . . . . Through Bill of Lading
Tare . . . . Weight of Container (Deducting tare from "gross weight" gives "net weight")
Ton . . . . 2,000 (short ton) or 2,240 (long ton) lbs. avoirdupois. A cubic ton in marine freight = 40 cubic feet
Ton wt/M. . . . . . . Ton, weight or measurement (ship's option)
vide . . . . See
viz . . . . Namely; to wit (videlicet)

Border Services, Customs Regulations for Canadians Returning from Abroad

Note: The Canada Border Services Agency (CBSA) operates as an agency under the Public Safety portfolio, and its mission is to ensure the security and prosperity of Canada by managing the access of people and goods to and from Canada. With a workforce of approximately 14,000 public servants, the Canada Border Services Agency (CBSA) provides services at 1,200 points across Canada and 39 locations abroad. At over 100 land border crossings and 13 international airports, it operates on a 24/7 basis. It administers more than 90 acts and regulations on behalf of other Government of Canada departments and agencies, and international agreements.

It integrates several key functions previously spread among three organizations: the Customs program from the Canada Customs Revenue Agency, the Intelligence, Interdiction and Enforcement program from Citizenship and Immigration Canada, and the Import Inspection at Ports of Entry program from the Canadian Food Inspection Agency.

If you have information about suspicious cross-border activity, please call the CBSA Border Watch tollfree line at 1-888-502-9060.

Canadians returning to Canada may bring any amount of goods into the country subject to duties and any provincial or territorial assessments, with the exception of restricted items. This applies even if you do not qualify for a personal exemption. The term duty can include Goods and Services. Duties represent duty, excise taxes and the Goods & Services Tax (GST) or Harmonized Sales Tax (HST). In addition to duties, provincial and territorial taxes (PST) are assessed if an agreement has been signed between the federal government and a province or territory whereby the federal government collects the PST, levies and fees on their behalf.

Goods included in personal exemptions must be for personal or household use, souvenirs or gifts. Goods brought in for commercial use, or on behalf of another person do not qualify and are subject to full duties.

On your return to Canada, you must declare to the Canada Border Services Agency (CBSA) all goods acquired (purchases, gifts, awards, prizes, and purchases made at Canadian or foreign duty-free shops and still in your possession) and repairs or modifications you made to your vehicle, vessel or aircraft while outside Canada.

Personal Exemptions

To qualify for personal exemptions you must be:

- Canadian resident returning from a trip abroad;
- former resident of Canada returning to live in Canada; or
- temporary resident of Canada.

Children and infants qualify for personal exemptions as long as the goods are for the use of the child or infant. The parent or guardian makes the customs declaration for the child.

Personal exemptions are applicable after the following minimum absences:

1. After an absence of 24 hours but less than 48 hours: up to a value of $200 (Canadian) in total (with the exception of tobacco products and alcoholic beverages) any number of times a year. If the value of the goods exceeds $200, you pay duties and PST on the full value (exemption cannot be claimed). The goods must accompany you on your return to Canada.

2. After an absence of 48 hours but less than seven days: up to $800 (Canadian) in total any number of times in a year. The goods must accompany you on your return to Canada.

3. After an absence of seven days or more: up to $800 (Canadian) any number of times in a year. You may have to make a written declaration. Goods you claim under this exemption may follow you by mail or other means, with the exception of alcoholic beverages and tobacco products. You require a Form E24, Personal Exemption Customs Declaration, which is to be completed at the time of arrival and can be obtained from a customs officer. To claim your goods when they arrive, present your copy of the E24 to the CBSA for clearance. Goods must be claimed within 40 days of their arrival in Canada; duties and taxes are then payable, along with a Canada Post Corporation processing fee. You may pay the duties and then apply to the CBSA for a refund (if the personal exemption applies) or refuse delivery; following a review that determines if the goods are eligible for free importation, the goods will be released to you without an assessment.

Persons residing outside Canada for part of the year are considered to be residents of Canada and are entitled to the above personal exemptions.

Exemptions cannot be transferred to another person or combined with another person's personal exemption. You cannot combine a 24-hour ($200) or 48-hour ($800) or the seven-day ($800) exemption when claiming an exemption, nor can you carry over an unused portion of an exemption for another period of absence.

Tobacco & Alcohol

Tobacco products and alcoholic beverages must accompany you in your hand or checked luggage and may be included in the 48-hour ($800) or the seven-day ($800) exemptions, but not in the 24-hour ($200) exemption. You must meet the age requirements set by the province or territory where you enter Canada. In addition the following conditions apply:

1. You may bring in up to 200 cigarettes, 50 cigars or cigarillos, 200 tobacco sticks **and** 200 grams of manufactured tobacco. Duties must be paid on anything above this allowance, plus any applicable provincial or territorial limits or assessments.

If you include cigarettes, tobacco sticks, or manufactured tobacco in your personal allowance, only a partial exemption will apply. You will have to pay a special duty on these products **unless** they are marked "DUTY-PAID CANADA — DROIT ACQUITTÉ." You will find Canadian-made products sold at a duty-free shop marked this way. You can speed up your clearance by having your tobacco products available for inspection when you arrive.

2. You may include up to 1.5 litres of wine, or 1.14 litres (40 ounces) of liquor, or a total of 1.14 litres (40 ounces), or 24 x 335 ml (12-ounce) cans or bottles (8.5 litres) of beer or ale. Wine coolers are classified as wine; beer coolers are classified as beer. Beer or wine that contains 0.5% alcohol by volume or less is not classified as an alcoholic beverage, so no quantity limits apply. You may bring in more than this allowance of alcohol anywhere in Canada (with the exception of the Northwest Territories and Nunavut) as long as the quantities are within the limits set by the province or territory. If bringing in more than the free allowance, you must pay customs and provincial/territorial assessments. For more information, check with the appropriate provincial/ territorial liquor control agency prior to leaving Canada.

Cannabis

Despite the legalization of recreational cannabis in Canada on October 17, 2018, it remains illegal to transport cannabis across the Canadian border, no matter what amount you are carrying, and regardless of whether you have medical authorization, or if you are coming from or travelling to a location where cannabis is legal. If you enter Canada with cannabis, you must declare it to Canada Border Services or risk arrest and prosecution.

If you travel to any country carrying cannabis, regardless of whether it's legal there, you could face criminal penalties both there and in Canada. Travellers should be aware that countries may refuse entry if you have ever consumed cannabis or other prohibited substances. Even Canadians travelling to the U.S. for purposes related to the cannabis industry may be denied entry. Though cannabis is legal in some states, it remains illegal federally. The Canadian government cannot intervene if you are refused entry by another country.

However, you may travel within Canada with 30 grams as per personal possession laws, provided the cannabis is in a legal form. You may also consume cannabis before boarding a flight, but it is up to the airline's discretion whether to admit you if they deem you to be too intoxicated.

It is worth noting that occasions do arise where domestic flights are required to divert to a U.S. airport. In that event, you are solely responsible for the outcome should you be denied entry for possession of cannabis.

Gifts

While abroad, you may send gifts duty- and tax-free to recipients in Canada. To qualify, the gift must be valued at $60 CAN or less and cannot be an alcoholic beverage, tobacco product, or advertising material. Gifts in excess of $60 CAN require duty payment by the recipient on the excess amount. Gifts that accompany you on your return to Canada must be included in your personal exemption, while gifts you send from abroad are not included. Some conditions apply - for additional information, contact the CBSA Border Information Service (BIS) at one of the numbers listed at the end of this section.

Prizes & Awards

In most cases, you pay regular duties on prizes or awards received outside Canada. Contact the BIS line for more information.

Paying Duties

Duties may be paid by cash or travellers' cheques. Personal cheques are also acceptable (for amounts of $2,500 or less and with proper identification); VISA, American Express and MasterCard are accepted at most border services locations and Debit Cards at many locations.

For information on duty rates for particular items, contact the BIS line.

NAFTA Special Duty Rate

Goods qualify for a lower U.S. duty rate under NAFTA if they are:

- for personal use
- marked as made in the U.S., Canada or Mexico
- not marked or labelled to indicate they were made anywhere other than in the U.S., Canada or Mexico

If you do not qualify for a personal exemption, or if you exceed your exemption limit, you will have to pay GST or HST over and above applicable duties or taxes on the portion not eligible under your exemption. The rates vary according to the goods, their country of origin, and the country from which you are importing them.

For information on goods eligible for the special duty rate under NAFTA, contact your nearest CBSA office and ask for a copy of Memorandum D11-4-13, Rules of Origin for Casual Goods Under Free Trade Agreements.

Regular Duty Rates

If you do not qualify for a personal exemption, or you exceed your exemption limit, you will pay GST or HST over and above all duties, taxes, and assessments that apply on the portion not eligible under your exemption. The rates vary according to the goods, their country of origin, and the country from which you are importing them. You may also have to pay provincial sales tax if you live in a province where we have an agreement to collect the tax and you return from your trip through your province.

World Trade Organization (WTO) Agreement

The duty on a wide range of products originating in non-NAFTA countries has been eliminated or will be reduced to zero within the next few years. NAFTA goods also qualify for the WTO rate, so if the rate on the goods you are importing is lower under WTO than under NAFTA, the lower rate will automatically be applied.

Value for Duty/Foreign Sales Tax

Value for duty is the amount used to calculate duty and is generally the price you paid for the item. Foreign sales tax is included in the price and forms part of the value of the item.

Some foreign governments will refund sales tax to you if you export the items you bought. If this is the case, you do not include the amount of the foreign sales tax that was or will be refunded to you.

Declaration

When returning to Canada by commercial aircraft, a Canada Border Services Agency (CBSA) declaration card is distributed for completion before arrival. At select airports, travellers may use a kiosk to confirm their identity and complete and on-screen declaration. Cards are also used at some locations for people arriving by train, vessel or bus. If arriving by a private vehicle (e.g., automobile), you must make an oral declaration unless you are claiming goods that preceded or will follow your arrival in Canada as part of your $800 exemption. If this is the case, ask the border services officer for Form E24, Personal Exemption Customs Declaration. You will need your copy of this form to claim your goods. Otherwise, you may have to pay regular duty on them.

CBSA officers are legally entitled to examine luggage; you are responsible for opening, unpacking and repacking the luggage. Retain receipts of purchases and repairs made to verify length of stay and value of goods or repairs. Failure to declare or a false declaration may result in the seizure of goods. Penalties range from 25% to 80% of the value of the seized goods. Vehicles used to transport unlawfully imported goods may also be seized, with a penalty imposed before the vehicle can be returned. Commodities such as alcohol and tobacco are seized and not returned.

Currency and Monetary Instruments

If you are importing or exporting monetary instruments equal to or greater than CAN$10,000 (or its equivalent in a foreign currency), whether in cash or other monetary instruments, you must report it to the CBSA when you arrive or before you leave Canada. For more information, ask for a copy of the publication called "Crossing the Border with $10,000 or More?" or select "Publications" on the CBSA Web site at www.cbsa-asfc.gc.ca.

Restrictions

Firearms: Contact the Canadian Firearms Program at: 506-624-6626, Toll-Free Phone: 1-800-731-4000, Fax: 613-993-0260, Email: cfp-pcaf@rcmp-grc.gc.ca; URL: www.rcmp-grc.gc.ca/cfp-pcaf.

Replica firearms are designed or intended to resemble a firearm with near precision. They are classified as prohibited devices and you cannot import them into Canada.

Mace or pepper spray that is used for the purpose of injuring, immobilizing or otherwise incapacitating any person is considered a prohibited weapon. You cannot import it into Canada. Aerosol or similar dispensers that contain substances capable of repelling or subduing animals are not considered weapons if the label of the container specifically indicates that they are for use against animals.

Explosives, fireworks, certain types of ammunition: You require written authorization and permits. Contact Chief Inspector of Explosives Regulatory Division, Natural Resources Canada, 580 Booth St., 10th Fl., Ottawa ON K1A 0G1, 613-948-5200, Fax: 613-948-5195, Email: ERDmms@nrcan.gc.ca.

Vehicles: Vehicles must meet the requirements of the CBSA, Transport Canada and the Canadian Food Inspection Agency before they can be imported. Transport Canada defines a vehicle as any vehicle that is capable of being driven or drawn on roads, by any means other than muscular power exclusively, but does not run exclusively on rails. It considers trailers such as recreational, camping, boat, horse and stock trailers as vehicles, as well as woodchippers, generators and any other equipment mounted on rims and tires.

CBSA import restrictions apply to most used or second- hand vehicles that are not manufactured in the current year. Transport Canada requirements apply to vehicles that are less than fifteen years old. All imported vehicles less than fifteen years old must comply with Canadian federal safety and emission standards. The person importing the vehicle is responsible for ensuring it meets the Canadian safety standards.

If you have acquired a vehicle from the United States, you must contact the Transport Canada's Registrar of Imported Vehicle (RIV) before you import your vehicle, to ensure that it is admissible for importation and can be modified to meet the Canadian standards after you import it.

Registrar of Imported Vehicles: Telephone: 1-888-848-8240 (toll free in Canada, the United States and Mexico); 416-626-6812 (from all other countries), Fax: 1-888-346-8235, Website: www.riv.ca.

Import restrictions apply to most used or secondhand cars, generally from countries other than the United States. Under NAFTA, restrictions do not apply to vehicles imported from the U.S., however, not all vehicles that are manufactured for sale in the U.S. can be imported because they do not meet the Transport Canada requirements; special duty rates, as outlined above, apply. Excise tax and GST continue to apply in the usual way. Under NAFTA, customs restrictions continued to apply to vehicles imported from Mexico until 2009, after which time you are able to import vehicles ten years or older. The age restriction will drop every second year until the restriction is dropped altogether in 2019.

In most instances, Canadian residents are not allowed to import vehicles into Canada that have been purchased or obtained in countries other than the United States. If you have acquired a vehicle from a country other than the United States, before importing it, contact: Transport Canada, Motor Vehicle Safety, Place de Ville, Tower C, 330 Sparks St., Ottawa ON K1A 0N5, 800-333-0371 (toll free from Canada and the U.S.), Email: mvs-sa@tc.gc.ca, Website: www.tc.gc.ca.

Your vehicle may be subject to provincial or territorial sales tax; contact your provincial or territorial department of motor vehicles for information. In addition, you may need to meet some requirements in the country which the vehicle is being exported.

Import Controls: Importations of certain goods are controlled. You may need a permit to import, even for personal and household use. For information, visit: Export & Import Controls, Foreign Affairs, Trade & Development, Website: www.international.gc.ca/controls-controles.

Meat, dairy products, wheat, barley, and their products: Complex requirements and restrictions exist; importation of certain meat and dairy products from certain U.S. states is allowed. All meat and meat products have to be identified as products of the United States. Limits exist for amounts or dollar value in certain foodstuffs you can import for personal use; if above those limits, duty ranges from 150 to 300% and you may also require an agri-cultural inspection certificate. For more information, contact the CBSA BIS line.

Agricultural products: Restrictions exist on live animals and animal products, meat and poultry products, dairy products, egg and egg products, honey and fresh fruits and vegetables, seeds and grains, animal feeds, plant and plant products, forestry products, soil and fertilizers, pest control products, biological products. For information on these products, refer to the Automated Import Reference System (AIRS) on the CFIA Website at www.inspection.gc.ca or call the CBSA BIS line.

Cultural property: Antiquities or cultural objects of significance in the country of origin cannot be imported into Canada. For information, contact Secretariat to the Canadian Cultural Property Export Review Board, Canadian Heritage, 25 Eddy St., 9th Fl., Gatineau, QC K1A 0M5, 819-997-7761, Fax: 613-997-7757, Email: PCH.secretariatdelacommission-reviewboardsecretariat.PCH@canada.ca.

Endangered species: Canada has signed an international agreement restricting the sale, trade or movement of endangered animals, birds, reptiles, fish, insects and certain forms of plant life; the restrictions also apply to their parts or products made from their parts. Before you bring back any of these products, you should contact CITES Administrator, Canadian Wildlife Service, Environment & Climate Change Canada, Ottawa ON K1A 0H3, 1-800-668-6767 (toll-free number in Canada), 819-938-4119 (local calls and from all other countries).

Appeals

If you disagree with the amount of duty and taxes that you had to pay, please ask to speak with the superintendent on duty. A consultation can often resolve the issue quickly and without cost. If you are still not satisfied, CBSA officers can tell you how to make a formal appeal. If you do not declare goods, or if you falsely declare them, the CBSA can seize the goods. This means that you may lose the goods permanently, or that you may have to pay a penalty to get them back.

If you do not declare tobacco products and alcoholic beverages at the time of importation, they will be permanently seized.

Depending on the type of goods and the circumstances involved, the CBSA may impose a penalty that ranges from 25% to 80% of the value of the seized goods.

In addition, the *Customs Act* provides CBSA officers with the authority to seize all vehicles that were used unlawfully to import goods. When this happens, a penalty will be imposed, which you will have to pay before the vehicle is returned.

If goods have been seized and you disagree with the action taken, you must notify the CBSA in writing within 90 days of the seizure date of your intention to appeal. You should send your appeal to the CBSA Office where the seizure took place. You can find more information about this process on the front of your seizure receipt form.

In addition to the activities mentioned above, designated CBSA officers may arrest for a criminal offence under the *Criminal Code* or any other Act of Parliament. This includes the offences of impaired driving, outstanding arrest warrants, stolen property, and abductions/kidnappings. If you are arrested, you may be compelled to attend court in Canada. You should note that all persons arrested in Canada are protected by, and will be treated in accordance with, the *Canadian Charter of Rights and Freedoms.*

A record of infractions is kept in the CBSA computer system. If you have an infraction record, you may have to undergo a more detailed examination on future trips.

Precautions

Carry proper identification.

Traveling with Children

Border services officers are on alert for children who need protection. Children under the age of 18 are classified as minors and are subject to the same entry requirements as any other visitor to Canada.

Border officers will conduct a more detailed examination of minors entering Canada without proper identification or those traveling in the company of adults other than their parents or legal guardian(s). This additional scrutiny helps ensure the safety of the children.

Minors traveling alone must have proof of citizenship and a letter from both parents detailing the length of stay, providing the parents' telephone number and authorizing the person waiting for them to take care of them while they are in Canada.

If you are traveling with minors, you must carry proper identification for each child such as a birth certificate, passport, citizenship card, permanent resident card or Certificate of Indian Status.

If you are a parent traveling alone with your child, it is recommended that you have a letter of authorization from your spouse. If you are divorced or separated, you should carry with you copies of the legal custody agreements for your children. If you are traveling with minors and you are not their parent/guardian, you should have written permission from the parent/guardian authorizing the trip. The letter should include addresses and telephone numbers of where the parents or guardian can be reached and identify a person who can confirm that the children are not being abducted or taken against their will. Some travellers have the consent letter notarized to further support its authenticity.

If you are traveling with a group of vehicles, make sure you arrive at the border in the same vehicle as your children, to avoid any confusion.

Identification of Articles for Temporary Exportation

CBSA offices offer a free identification program for valuables; a list of your valuables (excluding jewellery) and their serial numbers on a wallet-sized form will show border services officers that the items were previously purchased in Canada or that you lawfully imported them prior to your current time abroad. In the case of jewellery, carry an appraisal of the item(s) from a gemmologist, jeweller or insurance agent, together with a signed and dated photograph and a written declaration that the items in the photograph are those described in the appraisal report. If previously imported, carry a copy of the customs receipt.

If you take any item outside Canada and modify it, it is considered to be a new item and its full value will need to be declared. Similarly, under Canadian law, any repairs or modifications to a vehicle that increase its value, improve its condition or modify it while abroad may require that you pay duties on its full value on your return to Canada. This does not apply to incidental repairs to keep the car in operational condition while abroad, although you may be required to pay duties on the repairs and parts. A special provision is available that waives duties payable in such cases. Contact the CBSA for information.

Additional Information

If you have any other questions, contact the Border Information Service (BIS) line. This is a 24-hour telephone service that automatically answers all incoming calls and provides general border services information. If you call during regular business hours (8:00 a.m. to 4:00 p.m. local time, Monday to Friday, except holidays), you can speak directly to an agent by pressing "0" at any time.

Calls inside Canada:

English Enquiries: 1-800-461-9999 (toll-free in Canada)
French Enquiries: 1-800-959-2036 (toll-free in Canada)

TTY: 866-335-3237

Out-of-Canada callers can reach BIS by calling:

Western

English: . . . . . . 204-983-3500 (long-distance charges will apply)

Eastern

English: . . . . . . 506-636-5064 (long-distance charges will apply)

Website: www.cbsa-asfc.gc.ca

Election Regulations

According to the Canada Elections Act, and subject to certain exceptions, the general rule as to the franchise of electors at a federal election is that every person is qualified as an elector if such person

(a) is of the full age of 18 years on election day;

(b) is a Canadian citizen.

Among persons disqualified are certain officials charged with administering the elections, and, individuals who have lost their right to vote for a specified period for the commission of an election-related offence.

Writs for an election (general or by-election) are issued at least 36 days before the date fixed for election day.

Similar qualifications apply in the Provinces and Territories, although for provincial and territorial elections there is usually a residence requirement of either six or twelve months before the date of the issue of the writ of election. The age requirement is 18 years.

To contact election officers see "Elections" under the Government Quick Reference Guide in Section 7.

Elections Canada - 613-993-2975; Toll Free in Canada and the U.S.: 1-800-463-6868; Toll Free in Mexico: 001-800-514-6868; TTY: 1-800-361-8935; Fax: 1-888-524-1444; URL: www.elections.ca.

Liquor, Gaming & Cannabis Regulations

For Liquor, Gaming and Cannabis Control Board contact information, see "Liquor Control" or "Cannabis Control" in the Government Quick Reference Guide, in Section 7.

Alberta

The Alberta Gaming & Liquor Commission has the following mandates:
- Ensure integrity, transparency, disclosure, public consultation & accountability in Alberta's gaming & liquor industries;
- Administer the Alberta Lottery Fund with full public disclosure & continue to support communities & charitable organizations;
- License, regulate & monitor liquor & gaming activities, as well as certain aspects of tobacco sales;
- Implement & account for specific lottery fund programs administered by Alberta Gaming;
- Develop & communicate provincial gaming & liquor policy;
- Oversee distribution of cannabis, private retailers, and the province's online cannabis store.

Alberta Gaming & Liquor Commission, 50 Corriveau Ave., St. Albert AB T8N 3T5 - 780-447-8600; Toll Free: 1-800-272-8876; Fax: 780-447-8989; URL: www.aglc.ca

British Columbia

The Liquor & Cannabis Regulation Branch is responsible for issuing licences to:
- pubs, bars, lounges, stadiums, nightclubs & restaurants to sell liquor by the glass, & cold beer & wine stores to sell liquor by the bottle
- breweries, distilleries & wineries to manufacture liquor, &
- UBrews/UVins to sell their customers the ingredients, equipment & advice they need to make their own beer, wine cider or coolers
- private cannabis retail stores
In addition, the branch:
- regulates both Serving It Right: The Responsible Beverage Service Program & Special Occasion Licences for the events such as community celebrations, weddings or banquets
- educates those who hold liquor and cannabis licences (called licensees) about the laws & rules that may affect them inspects licensed establishments, &
- takes enforcement action when licensees do not follow the *Liquor Control & Licensing Act* or the *Cannabis Control & Licensing Act*, Regulations, &/or the specific terms & conditions of their licences

British Columbia Liquor & Cannabis Regulation Branch, PO Box 9292, Stn Prov Govt, Victoria BC V8W 9J8; street address: 400-645 Tyee Rd., Victoria BC V9A 6X5, 250-952-5787; Fax: 250-952-7066; Toll Free: 1-866-209-2111; Email: lclb.lclb@gov.bc.ca; URL: www2.gov.bc.ca/gov/content/employment-business/business/liquor-regulation-licensing

Manitoba

The Liquor, Gaming and Cannabis Authority of Manitoba is the regulator for liquor, gaming and cannabis in the province, as of 2018. The LGCA was renamed following the legalization of recreational cannabis, and was previously known as The Liquor and Gaming Authority of Manitoba. It was originally created as a result of a merger between the Manitoba Liquor Control Commission and the Manitoba Gaming Control Commission in 2014.

Persons over the age of 18 years and who are not otherwise prohibited may purchase and consume spirits, wine and beer in premises licensed by Manitoba Liquor & Lotteries - a Crown corporation that distributes and sells liquor. Further, those persons may purchase from an MBLL liquor mart, liquor vendor or specialty wine store for consumption in a residence.

Beer may also be purchased from beer vendor depots located in most hotels throughout the province.

Parents dining with their children may purchase alcoholic beverages for the latter, for consumption with meals, only in licensed restaurants, dining rooms, cocktail lounges or cabarets.

Beverage rooms and cocktail rooms must be vacated within 30 minutes after the hour at which sale of liquor must cease.

The LGCA is also responsible for licensing cannabis stores and distributors. Individuals over the age of 19 may purchase recreational cannabis.

Liquor, Gaming & Cannabis Authority of Manitoba, 1055 Milt Stegall Dr., Winnipeg, MB R3G 0Z6 - 204-927-5300; Fax: 204-927-5385; Tollfree: 1-800-782-0363; URL: lgcamb.ca

Manitoba Liquor & Lotteries, 830 Empress St., Winnipeg MB R3G 3H3 - 204-957-2500; Toll-Free: 1-800-265-3912; Fax: 204-284-3500; URL: www.liquormarts.ca; www.mbll.ca

New Brunswick

Intoxicating liquor is sold in sealed packages at Liquor Stores and agency stores. Where a permit and/or a license has been obtained, liquor may be sold by the glass in dining rooms, restaurants, taverns, cabarets, lounges, beverage rooms, and clubs. The age of majority is 19.

As of 2018, New Brunswick Liquor Corp. also oversees the subsidiary Cannabis NB, which operates retail cannabis stores as well as online sales.

New Brunswick Liquor Corp., PO Box 20787, 170 Wilsey Rd., Fredericton NB E3B 5B8 - 506-452-6826; Fax: 506-462-2024; URL: www.anbl.com

Cannabis NB - Toll-Free: 1-833-821-2195; URL: www.cannabis-nb.com

Newfoundland & Labrador

The importation, manufacture, and sale of alcoholic beverages through Retail Liquor outlets is the responsibility of the Newfoundland Labrador Liquor Corp.

The Newfoundland Labrador Liquor Corporation is also responsible for the issuing of all licenses, including those to manufacture and to sell packaged beer, and enforcement of regulations including, but not limited, to the following:
- All liquor sold upon licensed premises shall be consumed thereon.
- All liquor served in licensed premises shall be dispensed from the original container in which the liquor is purchased from or under the authority of the Liquor Corp.
- The drinking age in Newfoundland is 19 years.

Cannabis NL is the division of the Newfoundland Labrador Liquor Corporation responsible for the regulation and sale of non-medical Cannabis.

Newfoundland Labrador Liquor Corp., PO Box 8750, Stn A, 90 Kenmount Rd., St. John's NL A1B 3V1 - 709-724-1100; Fax: 709-754-0321; Email: info@nlliquor.com; URL: www.nlliquor.com

Cannabis NL - Toll-Free: 1-844-757-5986; Email: info@shopcannabisnl.com; URL: shopcannabisnl.com

Northwest Territories

The *Northwest Territories Act,* Chapter 331 of the Revised Statutes of Canada, 1952, authorizes the Commissioner in Council of the Northwest Territories to make acts respecting intoxicants.

The Liquor Licensing Board, established under Part I of the *Liquor Act,* controls the conduct of licensees and operation of licensed premises; grants, renews and transfers licenses and, after a hearing, may cancel or suspend licenses. There are presently twelve types of licenses issued by the Board. Part I also provides for plebiscites to be held concerning new liquor license applications and also concerning restriction or prohibition in a community. The Board maintains an online database of licenses and Board decisions, and provides an online newsletter to keep license and permit holders up to date.

Part II of the *Liquor Act* establishes a Liquor Commission, which expanded to include cannabis at the time of legalization. The Minister responsible for this Part may designate his powers to the Liquor and Cannabis Commission to operate liquor stores and to purchase, sell and distribute liquor in the Northwest Territories through a network of seven retail outlets and one warehouse. It likewise operates an online cannabis store, and authorizes select physical vendors to sell cannabis.

Cananbis is regulated under the *Cannabis Legalization and Regulation Implementation Act* and the *Cannabis Products Act.* The former controls the sale and distribution, minimum age for purchase and consumption, drug-impaired driving, workplace safety, public smoking of cannabis and more, while the latter allows for the establishment of private cannabis retailers across the territory.

Northwest Territories Liquor Licensing Board, #204, 31 Capital Dr., Hay River NT X0E 1G2 - 867-874-8715; Fax: 867-874-8722; Tollfree: 1-800-351-7770; Email: LLBinfo@gov.nt.ca; URL: www.fin.gov.nt.ca/en/services/nwt-liquor-licensing-board

Northwest Territories Liquor and Cannabis Commission, #201, 31 Capital Dr., Hay River NT X0E 1G2 - 867-874-8700; Fax: 867-874-8720; URL: www.ntlcc.ca

Nova Scotia

- All liquor is sold through government-run NSLC stores.
- Generally local option vote applies.
- Eating establishment liquor licenses, lounges, clubs and cabarets serve spirits, draught beer, bottled beer and wine.
- The legal minimum drinking age is 19 years.
- Cannabis is also sold through select NSLC stores and online.

Nova Scotia Liquor Corporation, Bayers Lake Business Park, 93 Chain Lake Dr., Halifax NS B35 1A3 - 1-800-567-5874; URL: www.mynslc.com

Nunavut

Liquor and cannabis management is overseen by the Department of Finance within the Government of Nunavut. The oversight bodies are the Nunavut Liquor and Cannabis Commission and the Nunavut Liquor and Cannabis Board.

The Nunavut Liquor and Cannabis Commission is responsible for, as first receiver, the purchasing, storage and distribution of alcohol and cannabis products within the Nunavut Territory.

The Nunavut Liquor and Cannabis Board deals with the issuance of liquor licenses, liquor permits, inspection and enforcement under the *Nunavut Liquor Act.*

Communities in Nunavut are empowered and are enabled to establish their own liquor controls through the *Nunavut Liquor Act.* They are prohibited, restricted (variety) and unrestricted (only Liquor Act applies). The age of majority in Nunavut is 19.

Cannabis is regulated in the territory through the *Cannabis Act* and the *Cannabis Statutes Amendments Act,* which allow the government to license establishments, seek community consultations before opening stores or lounges, and regulate home cultivation.

Nunavut Liquor and Cannabis Commission - URL: www.gov.nu.ca/finance/information/nunavut-liquor-commission

Nunavut Liquor and Cannabis Licensing Board, PO Box 1000, Stn. 330, Iqaluit, NU X0A 0H0 - 876-975-5875; 867-975-5805; Email: nllb@gov.nu.ca; URL: www.gov.nu.ca/finance/information/about-nunavut-liquor-licensing-board

Ontario

In accordance with the provisions of the *Liquor Control Act* of Ontario, the Liquor Control Board buys wine, spirits and beer from all over the world for distribution and sale to Ontario consumers and licensed establishments. To provide this service, the LCBO operates five major regional storage and distribution centres which supply more than 1,100 retail stores.

In the interests of consumer protection, the LCBO also regularly tests all alcoholic beverages sold in Ontario. This "quality control" testing ensures that all products carried by LCBO stores, Ontario winery stores and Brewers Retail (Beer Store) outlets comply with the standards required under the Federal *Food & Drug Act* and Regulations.

In 2016, the LCBO introduced an online shopping option.

The Alcohol and Gaming Commission of Ontario (AGCO) is a Provincial agency that was established on February 23, 1998 after legislation was tabled to merge the Liquor Licence Board of Ontario (LLBO) with the Gaming Control Commission (GCC). The AGCO is responsible for administering the *Liquor Licence Act,* the *Gaming Control Act, 1992,* and the *Wine Content Act.* The AGCO conducts hearings as required: to determine the eligibility for liquor licences or gaming registration; to determine the eligibility for, or the revocation of liquor licences in public interest cases; and, in disciplinary cases involving liquor licensees or gaming registrants.

Liquor-related responsibilities include: licensing of public places which serve beverage alcohol for on-premises consumption; licensing of Ontario liquor manufacturers and the sales representatives of foreign manufacturers; promoting moderation and the responsible use of beverage alcohol.

Gaming-related responsibilities include: regulating charitable and casino gambling in Ontario; ensuring that games of chance are conducted fairly in compliance with the *Gaming Control Act,* regulations, and the terms and conditions that are imposed with charity gaming licences; ensuring that the people and the companies involved in casino and charitable gaming satisfy high standards of honesty, integrity and financial responsibility; registering commercial suppliers and gaming assistants of charitable gaming events and administering the issuance of charity gaming licences in partnership with municipalities.

Cannabis in Ontario is regulated under the *Cannabis, Smoke-Free Ontario, and Road Safety Statute Law Amendment Act, 2017.* Upon legalization, non-medical cannabis became available online through the government-run Ontario Cannabis Store (OCS). Plans were then established to operate a system of private physical retail outlets by April 2019, in addition to the online OCS platform.

Liquor Control Board of Ontario, #1100, 1 Yonge St., Toronto, ON M5E 1E5 - 416-365-5900; Toll-Free: 1-800-668-5226; TTY: 1-800-361-3291; URL: www.lcbo.com

Alcohol and Gaming Commission of Ontario, #200-300, 90 Sheppard Ave. E., Toronto ON M2N 0A4; Enquiries: 416-326-8700, or 1-800-522-2876 (toll-free in Ontario); Fax: 416-326-5555; Email: customer.service@agco.ca; URL: www.agco.on.ca

Ontario Cannabis Store - Toll-Free: 1-888-910-0627; URL: ocs.ca; helloocs.ca

Prince Edward Island

Beverage alcohol sealed packages may be purchased at Prince Edward Island Liquor Control Commission (PEI Liquor) stores throughout the Province by any person 19 or older who is not otherwise disqualified.

Spirits by the glass, and beer and wine by the open bottle or glass, may be purchased in dining rooms, lounges, clubs and military canteens licensed by the Commission.

Cannabis sales are overseen by the Prince Edward Island Cannabis Management Corporation and the Prince Edward Island Liquor Control Commission. Apart from online sales, four physical locations are maintained: Charlottetown, Summerside, Montague, and in the West Prince region.

Prince Edward Island Liquor Control Commission, 3 Garfield St., PO Box 967, Charlottetown, PE C1A 7M4 - 902-368-5710; Fax: 902-368-5735; URL: liquorpei.com

Prince Edward Island Cannabis Management Corporation, 85 Belvedere Ave., Charlottetown, PE C1A 6B2 - 902-368-5551; Email: infopeicmc@peicannabiscorp.com; URL: peicannabiscorp.com

Québec

Spirits and wines are sold by Québec Liquor Corporation (Société des alcools du Québec) stores only.

Spirits, beer and wine may be sold to the public by restaurants, bars and clubs under permit for consumption on the premises. Taverns may sell beer and cider. Pubs may sell beer, draught wine and cider.

A licensed grocery store may sell beer and certain designated wines and the product must not be consumed on the premises.

Persons under the age of 18 years old cannot be admitted into bars, pubs and taverns and at no time may alcoholic beverages be sold to them in other establishments.

The Québec Cannabis Society (Société québécoise du cannabis (SQDC)), a subsidiary of the Québec Liquor Corporation, was created in 2018 to oversee the sale of non-medical cannabis.

Société des Alcools du Québec, 905 av De Lorimier, Montréal QC H2K 3V9 - 514-254-2020, or 1-866-873-2020; Email: info@saq.com; URL: www.saq.com

Société québécoise du cannabis, 7355, rue Notre-Dame est, Montréal QC H1N 3S7 - 514-504-7732; Toll-Free: 1-888-551-2161; URL: www.sqdc.ca

Saskatchewan

The Saskatchewan Liquor & Gaming Authority, a Treasury Board Crown corporation, regulates liquor and gaming activities and conducts and manages gaming in the Saskatchewan Indian Gaming Authority Casinos and the Video Lottery Terminals throughout the province. It is responsible for the control, sale and distribution of liquor in the province, and also licenses and regulates bingos, raffles, casinos, and breakopen tickets.

The minimum drinking age is 19.

The Authority also oversees cannabis retail permits.

Saskatchewan Liquor & Gaming Authority, PO Box 5054, 2500 Victoria Ave., Regina SK S4P 3M3 - 306-787-5563; Toll-Free: 1-800-667-7565; www.saskliquor.com; www.slga.com

Yukon Territory

The *Yukon Act,* Chapter Y-2 of the Revised Statutes of Canada, 1970, authorizes the Commissioner in Executive Council, Yukon Territory, to make acts respecting intoxicants.

By virtue of Chapter 105 cited as the *Liquor Act,* established the laws governing the importation, distributing, licensing and retailing of alcoholic beverages in Yukon.

The formation of the Yukon Liquor Corporation by means of amendments to the *Liquor Act* came into force on April 1st, 1977. The separation as a Corporate entity resulted in increased responsibility and full accountability in all areas except major government policy.

The five members of the Board of Directors are appointed by the Commissioner in executive council to hold office at pleasure.

The President and Chief Executive Officer of the Corporation, is charged with the general direction, supervision and control of the Corporation and the administration of the Act.

The Corporation oversees private cannabis retail licenses, as well as operating an online store. As with alcohol, no one under the age of 19 may purchase the substance.

Yukon Liquor Corp., 9031 Quartz Road, Whitehorse YT Y1A 4P9 - 867-667-5245; Fax: 867-393-6306; Toll-free: 1-800-661-0408, ext. 5245; Email: yukon.liquor@gov.yk.ca; URL: www.ylc.yk.ca

Legal Age of Consent to Sexual Activity

Age of Consent, under the *Tackling Violent Crime Act, 2008*:

Raises the age at which youths can consent to non-exploitative sexual activity from 14 to 16 years of age;

Maintains the existing age of protection of 18 years for exploitative sexual activity (i.e. sexual activity involving prostitution, pornography, or a relationship of trust, authority or dependency or that is otherwise exploitative); and

Includes a close-in-age exception which permits 14- and 15-year old youths to engage in consensual, non-exploitative sexual activity with a partner who is less than five years older. An exception also exists for 12- and 13-year old youths, whereby persons of those ages can consent to non-exploitative sexual activity with another young person who is less than two years older.

Marriage Regulations

Divorce Act in Canada
Divorce grounds in Canada, under the *Divorce Act, 1985:*

Breakdown of marriage, established by:
- Spouses intentionally living separate and apart at least one year with the idea that the marriage is over, or

Since the marriage, either spouse has:
- Committed adultery, or
- Treated the other spouse with physical or mental cruelty rendering continued cohabitation intolerable.

Alberta
Marriageable age:
- Without parental consent: 18 years
- With parental consent: 16 years
- No one younger than 16 years of age may marry

Blood Test: not required
Waiting Period: None. Marriage Licence is valid immediately & is valid for 3 months (from date of issuance).
Licence fee: $50 + agent
Civic Marriage ceremony fee: uncapped

British Columbia
Marriageable age:
- Without parental consent: 19 years
- With parental consent: 16 to 18 years
- A court order of consent: under 16 years

Blood test: not required
Waiting period for licence: none
Marriage Licence: $100
Civil Marriage Ceremony: $75

Manitoba
Marriageable age:
- Without parental consent: 18 years

- With parental consent: 16 years (Persons under 16 years of age can be married only with the consent of a judge of the Family Court.)

Blood test: not required
Waiting period for licence: none
Waiting period after issuance of licence: 24 hours (This may be waived in exceptional circumstances by person performing ceremony.)
Licence fee: $100. Licence valid for 3 months (from date of issuance).

New Brunswick
Marriageable age:
- Without parental consent: 18 years
- With parental consent: under 18 years
- Under 16 years: a declaration of a Judge of the Court of Queen's Bench that the proposed marriage may take place is necessary.

Blood test: not required
Waiting period for licence: none
Licence fee: $115. Licence valid for 3 months (from date of issuance).

Newfoundland & Labrador
Marriageable age:
- Greater than or equal to 19 years: without parental consent
- Greater than or equal to 18 years: without parental consent in certain circumstances
- Greater than or equal to 16 years and less than 19 years: with the applicable parental, guardian or Director of Child Welfare consent (Consent may be dispensed within exceptional cases.)
- Less than 16 years: where by reason of pregnancy a judge issues a licence

Blood test: not required
Licence fee: $100. Licence valid for 30 days (from date of issuance).

Northwest Territories
Marriageable age:
- Without parental consent: 19 years
- Under the age of 19 years and declares via statutory declaration that:
  ◦ (a) that no person has lawful custody of the minor; or
  ◦ (b) that any person who has lawful custody of the minor not a resident of the Territories & that the minor has been a resident of the Territories for not less than 12 months immediately preceding the date of the declaration; or
  ◦ (c) that any person who has lawful custody of the minor is unable to consent by reason of disability; or
  ◦ (d) that the minor has, for not less than six months immediately preceding the date of the declaration, withdrawn from the charge of the persons who have lawful custody of the minor & that the minor has not returned to such charge
- With parental consent: 15 years, or under 15 years & pregnant

Blood test: not required
Waiting period for licence: none
Licence fee: $60

Nova Scotia
Marriageable age:
- Without parental consent: 19 years or over
- With parental consent, or if a widow, widower, or divorcee: 16 years
- With court order: under 16 years

Blood test: not required
Waiting period for licence: 5 days
Licence fee: $132.70

Nunavut
Marriageable age:
- Without parental consent: 19 years
- At least 18 years of age

Blood test: not required
Waiting period for licence: none
Licence fee: $25

Ontario
Marriageable age:
- Without parental consent: 18 years
- With parental consent: 16 years

Blood test: not required
Waiting period after issuance of licence: none
Licence fee: $125-$140

Fee for solemnization of marriage by judge or justice of the peace: $75

Purchased marriage licence must be used within 3 months.

Prince Edward Island

Marriageable age:
- Without parental consent: 18 years
- With parental consent: under 18 years

Other requirements: birth certificates and Social Insurance Numbers; in the case of a widow or widower, death certificate; in the case of a divorced person, certified copy of the Decree Absolute or Certificate of Divorce

Waiting period for licence: none

Licence fee: $100. License valid for 3 months from date of issuance.

Québec

Marriageable age:
- Minimum age: 16 years (ref.: art. 373, Code Civil du Québec)
- Moreover, a minor (under 18 years of age) must have the authorization of his or her parent(s) or tutor to get married.

Blood test: not required

Waiting period for licence: none

Fee for civil marriage: $268

Saskatchewan

Marriageable age:
- Without parental consent: 18 years
- With parental consent: 16 to 17 years
- With parental and court consent: under 16 years

Blood test: not required

Licence fee: $60

Yukon Territory

Marriageable age:
- Without parental consent: 19 years (In the case of an 18 year old person who has lived apart from his parents/ guardians for at least 6 months & received no financial aid from them during that time, no consent is needed.)
- With parental consent: under 19 years.
- With a Supreme Court Order: between the ages of 15 to 19 years

A certificate of divorce or death must be produced if previously married

Blood test: not required

Waiting period for licence: none

Waiting period after issuance of licence: 24 hours

Licence fee: $20. Licence valid for 3 months (from date of issuance).

Postal Information

Services and rates quoted are subject to change. For complete and up-to-date information you may: consult a local Canada Post retail outlet; call 1-800-267-1177, TTY 1-800-267-2797; or refer to the Canada Post website at www.canadapost.ca. For refunds, or to make a claim, call 1-888-550-6333. For Postal Code information (fees apply) call 1-900-565-2633 (English) or 1-900-565-2634 (French).

Direct Marketing & Transaction Mail

LETTERMAIL™ SERVICE RATES FOR DELIVERY IN CANADA*

Includes letters, postcards, greeting cards and business correspondence.

Standard Lettermail™ service:

Up to 30g (Single Stamp(s))	$1.07
Up to 30g (Booklet/Coils/Other)	$0.92
Over 30g up to 50g	$1.30

Medium Lettermail™ has been discontinued as of 2014.

Other Lettermail™ Incl. Non-Standard & Oversize:

Up to 100g	$1.94
Over 100g up to 200g	$3.19
Over 200g up to 300g	$4.44
Over 300g up to 400g	$5.09
Over 400g up to 500g	$5.47
Retail Registered	$9.75

New pricing as of January 13, 2020.

For Standard Items, the maximum dimensions are 245 mm (length) x 156 mm (width). Rates apply to all letters with any dimension greater than 140 mm (length) x 90 mm (width) x 0.18 mm (thickness), but not greater than 380 mm (length) x 270 mm (width) x 20 mm (thickness). Maximum weight for Standard items is 50 g and for Other Lettermail™ service is 500g. Items with any dimension exceeding the maximum dimension for Other (Non-standard and Oversize) mail items or exceeding 500g must be paid at parcel rates. Incentive Rates are available for customers whose mailing meets volume and mail preparation requirements. For details, please contact a Canada Post representative. Canada Post is committed to consistently deliver Lettermail™ mail as follows: two business days within the same metropolitan area/community; three business days within the same province; four business days between provinces (some exceptions apply).

Distribution Services

PRIORITY™ SERVICE

Priority™ is Canada Post's fastest service for time-sensitive documents and parcels with next business day delivery* between major urban centres. Delivery times are guaranteed, and delivery and tracking information is available online at canadapost.ca/track. Signature collection is offered at no extra charge.

XPRESSPOST™ SERVICE

Xpresspost™ is a fast and cost-effective delivery service for documents and parcels within Canada, with next-day and 2 day delivery.* All items are tracked, delivery times are guaranteed, and delivery status is available online at canadapost.ca/track.

EXPEDITED PARCEL™ SERVICE

Expedited Parcel™ is a cost-effective ground service for items shipped within Canada. Delivery times are next day for local, up to 3 days for regional and up to 7 days for national.* All items are tracked, delivery times are guaranteed, and delivery status is available online at canadapost.ca/track.

REGULAR PARCEL™ SERVICE

Regular Parcel™ service is the most economical ground delivery service for items shipped within Canada. Delivery timeframe is 2 days for local delivery, up to 5 five days for regional and up to 9 days for national.* A tracking number is provided and delivery status is available online at canadapost.ca/track.

Delivery standards are for items sent between most major urban centres and depend on origin and destination. Delivery standards are in business days. Find the specific delivery standard from your postal code at canadapost.ca/deliverytool.

AIR STAGE SERVICE (LESS THAN 5 ITEMS)

Canada Post services many remote communities where the only access to the community is by air; these communities are called Air Stage Offices. At these offices, mail needs to be airlifted in and out for more than 6 months of the year.

CANADIAN FORCES MAIL SERVICE

Canadian Forces Mail is mail sent to or by Canadian Forces personnel, their dependents and the civilians attached to the Canadian Forces served through the Canadian Forces Post Office (CFPO) or the Fleet Mail Office (FMO).

The rate charged for domestic mail is applicable for mail sent to Canadian Forces personnel providing it is sent through a CFPO or an FMO.

All parcels must include an International Customs Declaration form (CP72) and are subject to customs inspection in the country of destination. Oversize parcels and parcels over 20 kg are not acceptable.

COLLECT ON DELIVERY (COD)

Collect on Delivery (COD) is available for parcel shipments within Canada, for an additional fee. Before the item is delivered, the addressee or the addressee's representative must pay the COD amount as specified by the shipper on the Collect on Delivery form/shipping label. After collection, the COD funds are submitted to the shipper by cheque or electronic fund transfer.

DEFICIENT POSTAGE FEE

Unpaid or shortpaid mail is mail for which the postage or fees have not been paid or have been partially paid. Lettermail™ and Parcelmail items are returned to the sender for the collection of the postage.

When there is no return address on the item, the item is forwarded to the addressee for the collection of the postage plus an administrative charge. All postage due charges must be paid before delivery.

DO NOT FORWARD SERVICE

Do Not Forward is a service for Lettermail™ items, mailed in Canada for delivery in Canada. If mail cannot be delivered as addressed because the addressee has a Mail Forwarding service in place, it will be returned to the sender rather than forwarded to the addressee.

GOVERNMENT MAIL FREE OF POSTAGE

Canada Post provides free mailing privileges to the following:
1. Governor General or Secretary to the Governor General;
2. Speaker or Clerk of the Senate or House of Commons;
3. Parliamentary Librarian or Associate Parliamentary Librarian;
4. Members of the Senate;
5. Members of the House of Commons.
6. Conflict of Interest and Ethics Commissioner or Senate Ethics Officer
7. Director of the Parliamentary Protective Service
8. The Parliamentary Budget Officer

In addition, anyone mailing an item to the above in Canada receives free postage. As a general rule, only Lettermail™ items, Publications Mail™ items, Personalized Mail™ and items up to 500g and Neighbourhood Mail (printed matter only) are acceptable. Parcels and add-on services are not acceptable as part of this service. As long as the letters M.P. appear on the mailing, it can be sent free of postage.

FLEXDELIVERY™

FlexDelivery™ is an exclusive Canada Post service that allows customers to have their parcels sent directly to a post office of their choice – near work, home or anywhere in Canada. The service is convenient, secure and free of charge. To access FlexDelivery™, customers can complete their online registration at canadapost.ca/flexdelivery and choose their preferred post office locations.

COLLECTION OF THE GOODS AND SERVICES TAX/HARMONIZED SALES TAX (GST/HST)

The GST/HST is a value added consumption tax administered by the Federal Government. By law, businesses must charge GST/HST on most goods and services provided.

Most postal services and products are subject to the GST/HST, such as stamps, Advance Purchase Products, all add-on options (e.g., Insurance, Trace Mail, COD), optional Postal Box rentals, and postage meter fill ups.

There are certain items sold by Canada Post that are not taxable such as Postal Money Orders, the fee on a Money Order and the exchange on a Money Order. The provincial and territorial governments of Alberta, Manitoba, Northwest Territories, Saskatchewan and Yukon are exempt from paying the GST/HST.

Mail addressed to foreign destinations requiring total shipping charges of $5 or more (single item or a cumulative purchase) and products ordered from and shipped directly by Canada Post to a foreign destination, such as Philatelic and Retail products, are not subject to the GST/HST. The GST/HST is calculated on the total taxable purchased and rounded up or down to the nearest cent.

HOLD MAIL

Canada Post's Hold Mail service securely stores your mail when you are away from your home or business. Delivery resumes the day following the service's end date. The service can be purchased online in a few easy steps or at a post office.

The Hold Mail service's set-up fee includes two weeks of service for residential purchases, and one week of service for commercial purchases. Service can be extended in weekly increments with applicable fees.

MIGRATORY GAME BIRD HUNTING PERMITS

Prior to and during the migratory game bird hunting season, hunting permits can be purchased from a select postal outlet. The rules, regulations and fees pertaining to these permits are provided to the outlets by the Federal body (Environment & Climate Change Canada) responsible for these permits.

LIABILITY COVERAGE

Priority™, Xpresspost™ and Expedited Parcel™ services include up to $100 Liability Coverage against loss or damage. The first $100 of Liability Coverage must be purchased for the Regular Parcel service. Additional Liability Coverage is available in increments of $100, up to $5,000 for most items within Canada, including prepaid products and labels. With the exception of the Priority service that offers the Signature option at no extra charge, the purchase of the Signature option is mandatory for additional Liability Coverage with all other services. The availability and limits of Liability Coverage may vary according to the nature of the items being shipped and the service used.

LIBRARY BOOKS

Library Materials is a service accessible to recognized public libraries, university libraries, or other libraries maintained by

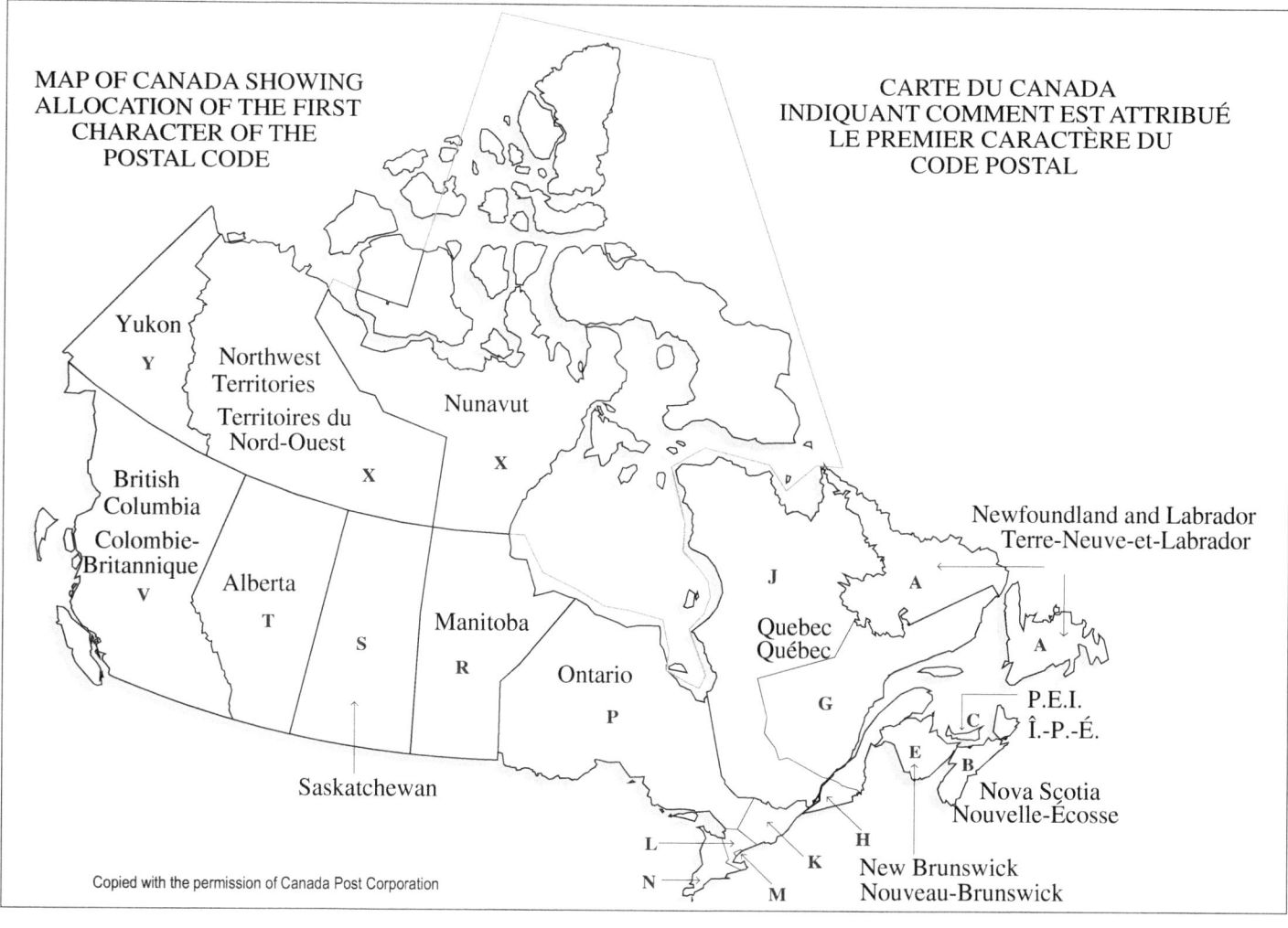

MAP OF CANADA SHOWING ALLOCATION OF THE FIRST CHARACTER OF THE POSTAL CODE

CARTE DU CANADA INDIQUANT COMMENT EST ATTRIBUÉ LE PREMIER CARACTÈRE DU CODE POSTAL

Copied with the permission of Canada Post Corporation

non-profit organizations or associations and which are for public use in Canada. It is available for eligible library materials that are mailed by a library to its patrons or to a borrowing library for use by their patrons.

Library Materials may consist of books, magazines, records, CDs, CD-ROMs, audiocassettes, videocassettes, DVDs and other audiovisual materials and other similar library materials. The library must complete a Library Materials Service Application Form and be authorized by the Canadian Urban Libraries Council (CULC) to use this service. The maximum weight per shipment is 5kg. Rates are based on a per item cost plus weight and destination. Postage paid by the library at the time of mailing covers both the outgoing and the return postage.

LITERATURE FOR THE BLIND

Literature for the Blind is a service available free of charge from Canada Post allowing blind persons and recognized institutions for the blind to mail free of postage specific items used by blind persons.

Admissible items in Canada include items impressed in Braille or similar raised type, plates for printing literature for the blind, tapes, records and CDs posted by the blind in Canada for delivery in Canada and recording tapes, records, CDs and special writing paper intended solely for the use of the blind-when mailed by or addressed to a recognized institution for the blind. These items are subject to the conditions and restrictions as set out in the Material for the Use of the Blind Regulations. The maximum weight in Canada is 7kg.

MAILING LISTS

Some Canadians may object to receiving Personalized Mail™ items and would like their name removed from all mailing lists. Canadians are advised to contact the sender of the Personalized Mail™ items to request that his or her name be removed from their mailing list.

If any recipient of this type of mail wishes to have all stopped, the customer should write to the following addresses asking them to have their members delete his or her name from their mailing lists.

In Canada:
Canadian Marketing Association
Do Not Mail Service
#607, 1 Concorde Gate, Toronto ON M3C 3N6
416-391-2362; Fax: 416-441-4062; E-mail: info@the-cma.org;
URL: www.the-cma.org/consumers/do-not-mail

In the United States:
Direct Marketing Association
DMAchoice™ Mail Preference Service
1615 L St., Washington DC 20036, USA.
212-768-7277, ext. 1888; URL: www.dmachoice.org

PHILATELIC PRODUCTS

Canada Post offers stamp collectors, ranging from those who've just discovered an interest in stamps to the most learned philatelist, a complete range of collectible products. Stamps and collectibles are available at your local post office, online at canadapost.ca/shop, by phone at 1-800-565-4362 (Canada/US) or 902-863-6550 (all other countries) or by mail at Philatelic Customer Service, PO Box 90022, Canada Post Place, 2701 Riverside Drive, Ottawa, ON, K1V 1J8.

POSTAL BOXES/CONTAINERS/BAG SERVICE/GENERAL DELIVERY/COMMUNITY MAILBOXES

A postal box is a numbered compartment in a post office that is kept locked, and to which the boxholder and postal employee have access.

The container/bag service is a service whereby containers or bags are assigned to a customer for the delivery of mail, either because postal boxes are not available or because the size of the postal boxes cannot accommodate the volume of mail addressed to this particular customer.

The General Delivery service at post offices is offered to the travelling public, customers with no fixed address within the letter carrier delivery area, or to anyone who cannot receive their mail from the normal delivery modes.

MONEY ORDERS

A Money Order is a secured cashable document, guaranteed by Canada Post, which is used to transfer funds anywhere in Canada and to countries with whom Canada Post has an active agreement. The service guarantee offers a refund of lost or destroyed money orders upon enquiry from the purchaser. Some conditions apply.

Postal money orders can be purchased by consumers and businesses, and constitute a guaranteed payment. They can be used for financial or retail transactions. Postal money orders may be purchased in Canadian or U.S funds. The maximum value of a single postal money order is $999.99 (Canadian and U.S. dollars). A separate fee applies to each additional Money Order purchased.

PROHIBITED MAIL

Prohibited Mail is defined as any mail which is prohibited by law or may contain products or substances that could harm postal employees or damage other mail or postal equipment.

The mail service cannot be used for criminal activities or for the transportation of dangerous goods. Animals and plants are generally not acceptable except under certain well-defined conditions in Canada. Prohibitions and restrictions on mail sent to the USA and to international destinations exist and are wide-ranging.

MAIL FORWARDING FOR TEMPORARY RELOCATION

Canada Post provides a secure and affordable mail redirection service that allows all individuals across Canada to have their mail forwarded to their new home or a temporary address. All individuals with residential requests must allow at least 3 business days before services start, and 10 business days for commercial requests.

CHANGE OF ADDRESS (MOVER SERVICE)

When individuals are permanently moving (not planning to return to their old address), a Canada Post Change of Address mover service can be purchased to ensure that all their important mail follows them to their new address. The most convenient way to purchase a mover service is through a secure online application at canadapost.ca. The online registration feature offers self-service capabilities with immediate insight to all transaction details that are included in the automated confirmation email that is sent after the registration has been completed. Individuals can also purchase this service at their nearest Canada Post location.

Mail can be redirected from any Canadian address to any other address in Canada, the USA and most international destinations. The service is available for a twelve-month period.

MAIL FORWARDING SERVICE

Whether you are moving or temporarily relocating to a new home or office, Canada Post's Mail Forwarding service allows individuals and businesses to forward mail from an original address to an alternate address anywhere in Canada, the U.S. or an international location. The service can be purchased online or at a post office at least 3 business days before its start date for residential requests and 10 business days before its start date for business requests.

UNDELIVERABLE MAIL

Undeliverable Mail is mail that fails delivery and does not bear a return address. Mail is considered undeliverable if:

1. The address is incomplete or does not exist
2. The addressee has moved and not purchased a Mail Forwarding service (or their service has expired)
3. It is refused by the addressee
4. It is refused by the addressee, bears a return address, & is refused by the sender
5. The addressee refuses to pay postage due charges
6. It is prohibited by law
7. It is an item found loose in the mail
8. It is an empty wrapper or carton.

PROOF OF DELIVERY/HARD COPY SIGNATURE - REGISTERED MAIL

A hard copy of the signature can be obtained at a later date, if required, by calling 1-888-550-6333. There is a fee for this service. The Signature Copy will be sent via Lettermail™ service or Fax within three business days of your request.

Other Services

SELECTED RATES TO THE UNITED STATES (its Territories & Possessions):

LETTER-POST*

Weight Steps:

Up to 30g	$1.30
Over 30g up to 50g	$1.94
Up to 100g	$3.19
Over 100g up to 200g	$5.57
Over 200g up to 500g	$11.14

New pricing as of January 13, 2020.

USA Incentive Letterpost offers Canadian mailers postage savings linked to volume, and quality of mail preparation. For information on USA and International Letter-Post rates, please contact Canada Post Customer Service at 1-866-757-5480.

REGISTERED MAIL SERVICE

Available from Xpresspost™ USA for airmail Letter-post items. Fees to the USA can be calculated online, plus the applicable postage.

ADVICE OF RECEIPT

The Advice of Receipt (AR) service provides mailers with the actual signature of the addressee. An Advice of Receipt card is purchased at the time of mailing. The addressee's signature is obtained on the AR card and returned to the sender, thus providing the mailer with a Delivery Confirmation.

SELECTED INTERNATIONAL RATES

All countries except the USA, its Territories and Possessions, Canadian Forces post offices and Fleet Mail Offices.

LETTER-POST*

Up to 30g	$2.71
Over 30g up to 50g	$3.88
Up to 100g	$6.39
Over 100g to 200g	$11.14
Over 200g to 500g	$22.28

New pricing as of January 13, 2020

General Information

PROVINCIAL SYMBOLS

Standard two-letter postal abbreviations for the provinces and territories are as follows:

Alberta	AB
British Columbia	BC
Manitoba	MB
New Brunswick	NB
Newfoundland & Labrador	NL
Northwest Territories	NT
Nova Scotia	NS
Nunavut	NU
Ontario	ON
Prince Edward Island	PE
Québec	QC
Saskatchewan	SK
Yukon Territory	YT

STAMP & COLLECTOR SERVICES

Canada Post offers a wide selection of postage stamps, stationery, supplies and philatelic products such as Official First Day Covers, annual souvenir collections and commemorative stamp packs. Products are available at your local post office, online at canadapost.ca/shop, by phone at 1-800-565-4362 (Canada/US) or 902-863-6550 (all other countries) or by mail at Philatelic Customer Service, PO Box 90022, Canada Post Place, 2701 Riverside Drive, Ottawa ON, K1V 1J8.

CUSTOMER SERVICE

Further information on Canada Post's products and services can be obtained through your local postal outlets, postal directory, your local customer service representative, or by calling one of the following numbers:

Toll Free (Canada)	1-800-267-1177
(8 a.m. to 6 p.m. local time)	
Outside of Canada	416-979-8822
Hearing Impaired with TTY-Teletyping	1-800-267-2797

Customers may also contact Canada Post via the Internet: www.canadapost.ca or mail: Canada Post Corporation, 2701 Riverside Dr., Ottawa ON K1A 0B1.

Weights & Measures

THE INTERNATIONAL SYSTEM OF UNITS (SI) (BASE & DERIVED UNITS)

With the permission of Canadian Standards Association, (operating as "CSA Group"), 178 Rexdale Blvd., Toronto, ON, M9W 1R3, material is reproduced from CSA Group's withdrawn standard Z234.1-00 (R2011) - Metric Practice Guide. This material is not the complete and official position of CSA Group on the referenced subject, which is represented solely by the Standard in its entirety. While use of the material has been authorized, CSA Group is not responsible for the manner in which the data is presented, nor for any representations and interpretations. No further reproduction is permitted. For more information or to purchase standard(s) from CSA Group, please visit https://store.csa.org/ or call 1-800-463-6727.

SI BASE UNITS

The International System of Units includes two classes of units: seven base units, and derived units. The base units are seven precisely defined units used internationally for transactions, teaching and scientific research.

Quantity	Unit name	Unit symbol
length	metre	m
mass	kilogram	kg
time	second	s
electric current	ampere	A
thermodynamic temperature	kelvin	K
amount of substance	mole	mol
luminous intensity	candela	cd

Source: Table 1, **CAN/CSA Z234.1-00 (R2011) - Metric Practice Guide**.
©2000 Canadian Standards Association

SI PREFIXES

SI Prefixes and their symbols given in this table are used to form names and symbols of decimal multiples or sub-multiples of SI units.

Prefix	Symbol	Multiplying factor	
yotta	Y		10^{24}
zetta	Z		10^{21}
exa	E		10^{18}
peta	P		10^{15}
tera	T		10^{12}
giga	G		10^{9}
mega	M		10^{6}
kilo	k	1000	10^{3}
hecto	h	100	10^{2}
deca	da	10	10^{1}
deci	d	0.1	10^{-1}
centi	c	0.01	10^{-2}
milli	m	0.001	10^{-3}
micro	μ		10^{-6}
nano	n		10^{-9}
pico	p		10^{-12}
femto	f		10^{-15}
atto	a		10^{-18}
zepto	z		10^{-21}
yocto	y		10^{-24}

Source: Table 4, **CAN/CSA Z234.1-00 (R2011) - Metric Practice Guide**.
©2000 Canadian Standards Association

SI DERIVED UNITS WITH SPECIAL NAMES

Name	Symbol	Typical formula	In base units	Quantity
becquerel	Bq	s^{-1}	s^{-1}	activity (referred to a radionuclide)
coulomb	C	$s \cdot A$	$s \cdot A$	quantity of electricity, electric charge
degree Celsius	°C	K	K	Celsius temperature *
farad	F	C/V	$m^{-2} \cdot kg^{-1} \cdot s^{4} \cdot A^{2}$	capacitance
gray	Gy	J/kg	$m^{2} \cdot s^{-2}$	absorbed dose, kerma, specific energy (imparted)
henry	H	Wb/A	$m^{2} \cdot kg \cdot s^{-2} \cdot A^{-2}$	inductance
hertz	Hz	s^{-1}	s^{-1}	frequency
joule	J	$N \cdot m$	$m^{2} \cdot kg \cdot s^{-2}$	energy, work, quantity of heat
katal	kat	mol/s^{-1}	mol/s^{-1}	catalytic activity
lumen	lm	$cd \cdot sr$	Cd	luminous flux
lux	lx	lm/m^{2}	$m^{-2} \cdot cd$	illuminance
newton	N	$m \cdot kg/s^{2}$	$m \cdot kg \cdot s^{-2}$	force
ohm	Ω	V/A	$m^{2} \cdot kg \cdot s^{-3} \cdot A^{-2}$	electric resistance
pascal	Pa	N/m^{2}	$m^{-1} \cdot kg \cdot s^{-2}$	pressure, stress
radian	rad	m/m	$m \cdot m^{-1} = 1$	plane angle
siemens	S	A/V	$m^{-2} \cdot kg^{-1} \cdot s^{3} \cdot A^{2}$	electric conductance
sievert	Sv	J/kg	$m^{2} \cdot s^{-2}$	dose equivalent, dose equivalent index
steradian	sr	m^{2}/m^{2}	$m^{2} \cdot m^{-2} = 1$	solid angle
tesla	T	Wb/m^{2}	$kg \cdot s^{-2} \cdot A^{-1}$	magnetic flux density
volt	V	W/A	$m^{2} \cdot kg \cdot s^{-3} \cdot A^{-1}$	electric potential, potential difference, electromotive force
watt	W	J/s	$m^{2} \cdot kg \cdot s^{-3}$	power, radiant flux
weber	Wb	$V \cdot s$	$m^{2} \cdot kg \cdot s^{-2} \cdot A^{-1}$	magnetic flux

*Celsius temperature scale (once called centigrade, a name abandoned in 1948 to avoid confusion with "centigrad", associated with the centesimal system of angular measurement) is the commonly used scale, except for certain scientific and technological purposes where the thermodynamic temperature scale is preferred. Note the use of upper case C for Celsius.

Source: Table 2, **CAN/CSA Z234.1-00 (R2011) - Metric Practice Guide**.
©2000 Canadian Standards Association

EXAMPLES OF SI DERIVED UNITS WITHOUT SPECIAL NAMES

Unit Name	Typical formula	In base units	Typical quantity
ampere per metre	A/m	$A \cdot m^{-1}$	magnetic field strength
ampere per square metre	A/m²	$A \cdot m^{-2}$	current density
candela per square metre	cd/m²	$cd \cdot m^{-2}$	luminance
coulomb per cubic metre	C/m³	$m^{-3} \cdot s \cdot A$	electric charge density
coulomb per kilogram	C/kg	$A \cdot s \cdot kg^{-1}$	exposure (X or y rays)
coulomb per square metre	C/m²	$m^{-2} \cdot s \cdot A$	electric flux density
cubic metre	m³	m^3	volume
cubic metre per kilogram	m³/kg	$m^3 \cdot kg^{-1}$	specific volume
farad per metre	F/m	$m^{-3} \cdot kg^{-1} \cdot s^4 \cdot A^2$	permittivity
gray per second	Gy/s	$m^2 \cdot s^{-3}$	absorbed dose rate
henry per metre	H/m	$m \cdot kg \cdot s^{-2} \cdot A^{-2}$	permeability
joule per cubic metre	J/m³	$m^{-1} \cdot kg \cdot s^{-2}$	energy density
joule per kelvin	J/K	$m^2 \cdot kg \cdot s^{-2} \cdot K^{-1}$	heat capacity, entropy
joule per kilogram	J/kg	$m^2 \cdot s^{-2}$	specific energy
joule per kilogram kelvin	J/(kg·K)	$m^2 \cdot s^{-2} \cdot K^{-1}$	specific heat capacity
joule per mole	J/mol	$m^2 \cdot kg \cdot s^{-2} \cdot mol^{-1}$	molar energy
joule per mole kelvin	J/(mol·K)	$m^2 \cdot kg \cdot s^{-2} \cdot K^{-1} \cdot mol^{-1}$	molar entropy
kilogram per cubic metre	kg/m³	$kg \cdot m^{-3}$	density
metre per second	m/s	$m \cdot s^{-1}$	linear speed
metre per second squared	m/s²	m/s^2	linear acceleration
mole per cubic metre	mol/m³	$mol \cdot m^{-3}$	concentration
newton metre	N·m	$m^2 \cdot kg \cdot s^{-2}$	moment of force
newton per metre	N/m	$kg \cdot s^{-2}$	surface tension
pascal second	Pa·s	$m^{-1} \cdot kg \cdot s^{-1}$	viscosity
radian per second	rad/s	s^{-1}	angular velocity
radian per second squared	rad/s²	s^{-2}	angular acceleration
reciprocal metre	m⁻¹	m^{-1}	wavenumber
square metre	m²	m^2	area
square metre per second	m²/s	$m^2 \cdot s^{-1}$	kinematic viscosity
volt per metre	V/m	$m \cdot kg \cdot s^{-3} \cdot A^{-1}$	electric field strength
watt per metre kelvin	W/(m·K)	$m \cdot kg \cdot s^{-3} \cdot K^{-1}$	thermal conductivity
watt per square metre	W/m²	$kg \cdot s^{-3}$	heat flux density
watt per steradian	W/sr	$m^2 \cdot kg \cdot s^{-3}$	radiant intensity

Source: Table 3, **CAN/CSA Z234.1-00 (R2011) - Metric Practice Guide**.
©2000 Canadian Standards Association

UNITS THAT ARE USED WITH THE SI

Quantity	Unit name	Unit symbol	Definition (Note 1)	See Note
time	minute	min	1 min = **60** s	2
	hour	h	1 h = **3600** s	2
	day	d	1 d = **86 400** s	2
	year	a	See conversion table	2
plane angle	degree	°	1 ° = (π/**180**) rad	3
	minute	'	1 ' = (π/**10 800**) rad	3
	second	"	1 " = (π/**648 000**) rad	3
	revolution	r	1 r = **2** π rad	3
length	nautical mile	M	1 nautical mile = **1852** m	5
speed	knot	kn	1 nautical mile per hour 1 kn = (**1852/3600**) m/s	6
area	hectare	ha	1 ha = **1** hm² = **10 000** m²	7
volume	litre	L	1 L = **1** dm³	
mass	metric ton or tone	t	1 t = **1000** kg = **1** Mg	8
linear density	tex	tex	1 tex = **1 x 10⁻⁶** kg/m	9
pressure	millibar	mbar	1 mbar = **100** Pa	10
energy	electronvolt	eV	*	11
mass of an atom	unified atomic mass unit	u	*	12
length	astronomical unit	ua		13
	parsec	pc	*	14

*The values for these units must be obtained by experiment and are therefore not known exactly.

1. Conversion factors that are exact are shown in boldface type throughout this Table.

2. These symbols are used only in the sense of duration of time and not for expressing the time of day. See also CSA Standard CAN/CSA-Z234.4.

3. As an exception to Clause 4.6.2, no space is left between these symbols and the last digit of a numerical value. The unit "degree", with its decimal subdivisions, is used when the unit "radian" is not suitable.

4. The designations revolution per minute (r/min) and revolution per second (r/s) are widely used in connection with rotating machinery.

Source: Table 6, **CAN/CSA Z234.1-00 (R2011) - Metric Practice Guide**.
©2000 Canadian Standards Association

5. The nautical mile is a special unit employed for marine and aerial navigation to express distances. There is no universally recognized symbol for the nautical mile; M has been recommended by the International Hydrographic Organization. The conventional value given above was adopted by the First International Extraordinary Hydrographic Conference, Monaco, 1929, under the name "International nautical mile".

6. There is no universally recognized symbol for the knot; kn has been recommended by the International Hydrographic Organization.

7. Because of the need for a unit of similar magnitude to the acre, the hectare will continue to be recognized as a unit for use in surveying and agriculture.

8. Care must be taken in the interpretation of the word "tonne" when it occurs in French text of Canadian origin, where the meaning may be a "ton of 2000 pounds".

9. The tex is used only in the textile industry.

10. Pressure and stress should be expressed in pascals. The millibar may continue to be used, but only for international meteorological work. One millibar is equal to one hectopascal.

11. One electronvolt is the kinetic energy acquired by an electron in passing through a potential difference of 1 V in vacuum; 1 eV . 0.160 217 733 aJ.

12. The unified atomic mass unit is equal to the fraction 1/12 of the mass of an atom of the nuclide 12C; 1 u . 1.660 540 2 yg.

13. The astronomical unit of distance is the length of the radius of the unperturbed circular orbit of a body of negligible mass moving around the sun with a sidereal angular velocity of 0.017 202 098 950 radian per day of 86 400 ephemeris seconds. In the system of astronomical constants of the International Astronomical Union, the value adopted for it is 1 ua = 149.597 870 Gm.

14. 1 parsec (pc) is the distance at which 1 astronomical unit subtends an angle of 1 second of arc; thus 1 pc . 206 265 ua . 30.857 Pm.

CONVERSION OF UNITS TO THE INTERNATIONAL SYSTEM OF UNITS

Area
1 acre	= 0.404 685 6 ha
1 arpent (French measure)	= 0.341 889 4 ha
1 circular mil	= 506.707 5 µm²
1 hectare	= **1** hm²
1 legal subdivision (40 acres)	= 0.161 874 2 km²
1 perch (French measure)	= 34.188 94 m²
1 rood (1210 square yards)	= 0.101 171 4 ha
1 section (1 mile square, 640 acres)	= 2.589 988 km²
1 square foot	= **929.030 4** cm²
1 square foot (French measure)	= 1 055.214 cm²
1 square inch	= **645.16** mm²
1 square mile	= 2.589 988 km²
1 square rod	= 25.292 85 m²
1 square yard	= 0.836 127 4 m²

Energy
1 British thermal unit (Btu) (International Table)*	= 1.055 056 kJ
1 British thermal unit (Btu) (mean)*	= 1.055 87 kJ
1 British thermal unit (Btu) (thermochemical)*	= 1.054 35 kJ
1 British thermal unit (Btu) (39°F)*†	= 1.059 67 kJ
1 British thermal unit (Btu) (59°F, 15 °C)*	= 1.054 80 kJ
1 British thermal unit (Btu) (60.5°F)*	= 1.054 615 kJ
1 Calorie (dietetic)	= 4.185 5 kJ
1 calorie (International Table)	= **4.186 8** J
1 calorie (thermochemical)	= **4.184** J
1 calorie (15 °C)†§	= 4.185 5 J
1 electronvolt	= 0.160 217 7 aJ
1 erg	= **0.1** µJ
1 foot poundal	= 42.140 11 mJ
1 foot pound-force	= 1.355 818 J
1 horsepower hour	= 2.684 520 MJ

1 kilowatt hour	= **3.6** MJ
1 quad	= 1.055 EJ
1 therm	= 105.506 MJ
1 ton (nuclear equivalent of TNT)	= 4.2 GJ
1 watt hour	= **3.6** kJ
1 watt second	= **1** J

Force
1 dyne	= **10** µN
1 kilogram-force	= **9.806 65** N
1 kilopond	= **9.806 65** N
1 kip (thousand pounds force)	= 4.448 222 kN
1 ounce-force	= 0.278 013 9 N
1 poundal	= 0.138 255 0 N
1 pound-force	= 4.448 222 N
1 ton-force	= 8.896 443 kN
1 ton-force (UK)	= 9.964 016 kN

Length
1 ångström	= **0.1** nm
1 arpent (French measure)	= 58.471 31 m
1 astronomical unit	= 149.597 870 Gm
1 chain (66 feet)	= **20.116 8** m
1 ell (45 inches)	= **1.143** m
1 fathom	= **1.828 8** m
1 fermi	= **1** fm
1 foot	= **0.304 8** m
1 foot (French measure)	= 0.324 840 6 m
1 foot (US survey, limited usage)	= 0.304 800 6 m
1 furlong	= **0.201 168** km
1 inch	= **25.4** mm
1 league (International nautical)	= **5.556** km

1 league (UK nautical)	= **5.559 552** km
1 league (US)	= **4.828 032** km
1 light year	= 9.460 528 Pm
1 link (1/100 chain)	= **0.201 168** m
1 microinch	= **25.4** nm
1 micron	= **1** µm
1 mil (0.001 inch)	= **25.4** µm
1 mile	= **1.609 344** km
1 mile (International nautical)	= **1.852** km
1 mile (UK nautical)	= **1.853 184** km
1 parsec	= 30.856 78 Pm
1 perch	= **5.029 2** m
1 perch (French measure)	= **5.847 130 8** m
1 pica (printer's)	= 4.217 518 mm
1 point (Didot)	= 0.375 972 9 mm
1 point (paper or card thickness)	= **25.4** µm
1 point (pica)	= 0.351 459 8 mm
1 pole	= **5.029 2** m
1 rod	= **5.029 2** m
1 X unit	= 100.2 fm
1 yard	= **0.914 4** m

Mass
1 carat	= **200** mg
1 cental (100 lb)	= **45.359 237** kg
1 coal tub (100 lb, Newfoundland)	= **45.359 237** kg
1 drachm (apothecary)	= 3.887 935 g
1 dram (troy or apothecary, US)	= 3.887 935 g
1 dram (avoirdupois)	= 1.771 845 g
1 gamma	= **1** µg
1 grain	= **64.798 91** mg
1 hundredweight (100 lb)	= **45.359 237** kg

1 hundredweight (long) (112 lb, UK)	= 50.802 35 kg
1 metric carat	= **200** mg
1 ounce (avoirdupois)	= 28.349 523 g
1 ounce (troy or apothecary)	= **31.103 476 8** g
1 pennyweight	= 1.555 174 g
1 pound (avoirdupois)	= **0.453 592 37** kg
1 pound (troy or apothecary)	= **373.241 721 6** g
1 quarter (28 lb, UK)	= 12.700 58 kg
1 scruple (apothecary, 20 grains)	= 1.295 978 g
1 slug	= 14.593 90 kg
1 stone (14 lb, UK)	= 6.350 293 kg
1 ton (long, 2240 lb, UK)	= **1.016 046 908 8** Mg
1 ton (short, 2000 lb)	= **0.907 184 74** Mg
1 unified atomic mass	= 1.660 540 yg

Power - General

1 Btu (IT) per hour	= 0.293 071 1 W
1 Btu (thermochemical) per hour	= 0.292 875 1 W
1 Btu (thermochemical) per minute	= 17.572 50 W
1 Btu (thermochemical) per second	= 1.054 350 kW
1 foot pound-force per hour	= 0.376 616 1 mW
1 foot pound-force per minute	= 22.596 97 mW
1 foot pound-force per second	= 1.355 818 W
1 horsepower (boiler)	= 9.809 50 kW
1 horsepower (electric)	= **746** W
1 horsepower (metric, *cheval vapeur*)	= **735.498 75** W
1 horsepower (water)	= 746.043 W
1 horsepower (550 ft·lbf/s)	= 745.699 9 W
1 ton of refrigeration (12 000 Btu/h)	= 3514 W

Pressure or Stress (Force per Unit Area)

1 atmosphere, standard (= 760 torr)	= 101.325 kPa
1 atmosphere, technical (= 1 kgf/cm²)	= **98.066 5** kPa
1 bar	= 100 kPa
1 foot of water (39.2°F, 4 °C)	= 2.988 98 kPa
1 inch of mercury (0 °C)	= 3.386 39 kPa
1 inch of mercury (60°F)	= 3.376 85 kPa
1 inch of mercury (68°F, 20 °C)	= 3.374 11 kPa
1 inch of water (conventional)	= 249.088 9 Pa
1 inch of water (39.2°F, 4 °C)	= 249.082 Pa
1 inch of water (60°F)	= 248.843 Pa
1 inch of water (68°F, 20 °C)	= 248.641 Pa
1 ksi (1000 lbf/in2)	= 6.894 757 MPa
1 mm mercury (0 °C)	= 133.322 4 Pa
1 poundal per square foot	= 1.488 164 Pa
1 pound-force per square foot	= 47.880 26 Pa
1 pound-force per square inch (psi)	= 6.894 757 kPa
1 ton-force per square inch	= 13.789 514 MPa
1 ton-force (UK) per square inch	= 15.444 3 MPa
1 torr	= 133.322 4 Pa

Temperature – Scales

Celsius temperature	= temperature in kelvins − 273.15
Fahrenheit temperature	= **1.8** (Celsius temperature) + **32**
Fahrenheit temperature	= **1.8** (temperature in kelvins) − **459.67**
Rankine temperature	= **1.8** (temperature in kelvins)

Time

1 day	= **86.4** ks
1 day (sidereal)	= 86.164 09 ks
1 hour	= **3.6** ks

1 hour (sidereal)	= 3.590 17 ks
1 minute	= **60** s
1 minute (sidereal)	= 59.836 17 s
1 second (sidereal)	= 0.997 269 6 s
1 Svedberg unit	= **0.1** ps
1 year (365 days)	= **31.536** Ms
1 year (sidereal)	= 31.558 150 Ms
1 year (tropical)	= 31.556 930 Ms
year 1900, tropical, January day 0, hour 12 (ephemeris)	= 31.556 926 Ms

Velocity (Speed)

1 foot per hour	= 84.666 67 µm/s
	= **304.8** mm/h
1 foot per minute	= **5.08** mm/s
	= **304.8** mm/min
1 foot per second	= **304.8** mm/s
1 inch per minute	= **25.4** mm/min
1 inch per second	= **25.4** mm/s
1 knot (International)	= **1.852** km/h
	= 0.514 444 4 m/s
1 knot (UK)	= **1.853 184** km/h
1 mile per hour	= **0.447 04** m/s
	= **1.609 344** km/h
1 mile per minute	= **26.822 4** m/s

Volume - General

1 acre foot	= 1233.482 m³
1 barrel (oil, 42 US gallons)	= 0.158 987 3 m³
1 barrel (US dry, 7056 in³)	= 0.115 627 1 m³
1 barrel (US dry, cranberries, 5826 in³)	= 95.471 03 dm³
1 barrel (UK, 36 gallons)	= 0.163 659 2 m³
1 board foot*	= 2.359 737 dm³
1 bushel	= 36.368 72 dm³
1 bushel (US dry, 2150.42 in³)	= 35.239 07 dm³
1 cord (128 ft³)†	= 3.624 556 m³
1 cubic foot	= 28.316 85 dm³
1 cubic inch	= **16.387 064** cm³
1 cubic yard	= 0.764 554 9 m³
1 cunit (100 ft³ solid wood)	= 2.831 685 m³
1 cup‡	= **250** cm³
1 demiard	= 0.284 130 6 dm³
1 drop (1/100 teaspoon)‡	= **0.05** cm³
1 fluid dram	= 3.551 633 cm³
1 fluid dram (US measure)	= 3.696 691 cm³
1 fluid ounce	= 28.413 062 cm³
1 fluid ounce (US)	= 29.573 53 cm³
1 gallon§	= **4.546 09** dm³
1 gallon (US)	= **3.785 411 784** dm³
1 gill	= 0.142 065 dm³
1 herring barrel	= 145.474 9 dm³
1 herring tub	= **72.737 44** dm³
1 hogshead	= 245.488 9 dm³
1 lambda	= **1** mm³
1 minim	= 59.193 9 mm³
1 minim (US)	= 61.611 52 mm³
1 peck	= 9.092 180 dm³
1 peck (US dry)	= 8.809 768 dm³
1 Petrograd standard (165 ft3, sawn timber)	= 4.672 280 m³
1 pint	= 0.568 261 2 dm³
1 pint (US dry)	= 0.550 610 5 dm³
1 pint (US liquid)	= 0.473 176 5 dm³
1 quart	= 1.136 522 dm³

1 quart (US dry)	= 1.101 221 dm³
1 quart (US liquid)	= 0.946 352 9 dm³
1 salt cart	= 490.977 7 dm³
1 salt tub	= **81.829 62** dm³
1 sand barrel	= **81.829 62** dm³
1 tablespoon‡	= **15** cm³
1 teaspoon‡	= **5** cm³
1 ton (register)	= 2.831 685 m³

Measures Having Former Household Usage

1 cup (8 fluid ounces)	= 227 cm³
1 cup (US, 8 US fluid ounces)	= 237 cm³
1 cup (UK, 10 fluid ounces)	= 284 cm³
1 tablespoon (1/2 fluid ounce)	= 14.21 cm³
1 tablespoon (UK, 5/8 fluid ounce)	= 17.8 cm³
1 tablespoon (US, 1/2 US fluid ounce)	= 14.8 cm³
1 teaspoon (1/6 fluid ounce)	= 4.74 cm³
1 teaspoon (UK, 5/24 fluid ounce)	= 5.92 cm³
1 teaspoon (US, 1/6 US fluid ounce)	= 4.93 cm³

Note that 1 cm³ = 1 mL.

Notes

Energy

*To convert from British thermal units (Btu) to the SI requires knowledge of which Btu is used, in order that the correct factor may be applied. The Btu is defined as the energy required to heat 1 lb of water through 1°F; however, because the specific heat of water varies with temperature, it is necessary to identify the particular Btu. This is done by specifying the midpoint of the range used, eg, the Btu (60.5°F) was determined over the range 60–61°F. The value for the Btu (60.5°F), 1.054 615 kJ, is the value that has been adopted for use in the Canadian petroleum and natural gas industry. The value recognized by ISO is 1.0545 kJ.

†Based on CIPM value.

‡Based on US National Bureau of Standards value.

§The values for the 15 °C calorie have been determined experimentally. The value generally used in North America, 4.1858 J, was determined at the US National Bureau of Standards in 1939. There is another value, 4.1855 J, which is a weighted average of several data; this value was adopted by CIPM in March 1950.

For further details, refer to CIPM, P.-V. 2e série, tome 22, Annexe 1, "Table 1950 des valeurs les plus précises que l'on peut tirer des expériences faites sur la chaleur spécifique de l'eau entre 0° et 100 °C".

Volume – General

*The board foot is nominally 1 × 12 × 12 = 144 in³. However, the actual volume of wood is about 2/3 of the nominal quantity.

†This applies to stacked wood, comprising wood, bark, and airspace, to a total volume of 128 ft³.

‡Rational metric values.

§Also referred to as the "imperial gallon".

Source: "9. Conversion Factors," **CAN/CSA Z234.1-00 (R2011) - Metric Practice Guide.**
©2000 Canadian Standards Association

SECTION 2
ARTS & CULTURE

Many of the following categories are also represented in Section 3: Associations.

Art Galleries

National Art Galleries

National Gallery of Canada / Musée des beaux-arts du Canada
PO Box 427 A, 380 Sussex Dr.,
Ottawa, ON K1N 9N4

Tel: 613-990-1985; *Fax:* 613-990-8075
Toll-Free: 800-319-2787
info@gallery.ca
www.gallery.ca
www.instagram.com/natgallerycan
twitter.com/natgallerycan
www.facebook .com/nationalgallerycanada
Other contact information: TDD: 613-990-0777
Year Founded: 1880 The permanent collection of the National Gallery of Canada comprises of paintings, sculptures, prints, drawings, photographs, as well as film & video art from Canadian, European, American & Asian artists. The Gallery also displays the collection from the Canadian Museum of Contemporary Photography. Special exhibitions as well as permanent installations of the gallery's collections are on display. The gallery also sends its exhibitions on tour across the country & participates in international exhibitions. Online showcases are also available for select material.
Sasha Suda, Director & CEO
David Lowe, Chief Operating Officer
Kitty Scott, Chief Curator
Isabelle Corriveau, Director, Exhibitions & Outreach
Stephen Gritt, Director, Conservation & Technical Research

Alberta

Provincial Art Galleries

Art Gallery of Alberta (AGA)
2 Sir Winston Churchill Sq.,
Edmonton, AB T5J 2C1

Tel: 780-422-6223
info@youraga.ca
www.youraga.ca
www.instagram.com/youraga
twitter.com/yourAGA
www.facebook.com/artgall eryofalberta
Year Founded: 1924 The Art Gallery collections include: Canadian, international, contemporary & historical paintings, sculpture, photography, video & graphic art. Research fields include: Western Canadian art, historical and contemporary art, paintings, sculpture, photography, & graphics.There are also a number of fun & engaging activities to be a part of, including: guided tours, lectures, films, gallery talks, art rental & sales gallery, studio art classes for children & adults, program workshops & seminars.
Catherine Crowston, Executive Director & Chief Curator
Pat St. Arnaud, Head, Finance & Administration
Dara Armsden, Head, Education & Learning
Janette Hubka, Head, Enterprise & Engagement

Local Art Galleries

Banff: Canada House Gallery
201 Bear St.,
Banff, AB T1L 1B5

Toll-Free: 800-419-1298
info@canadahouse.com
canadahouse.com
instagram.com/ch_gallery
twitter.com/ch_gallery
www.facebook.com/CanadaHouseGallery
Year Founded: 1974 Paintings & sculptures by Canadian & Inuit artists.
Barbara Pelham, Owner
Eric Pelham, Owner

Banff: Mountain Galleries at the Fairmont
Fairmont Banff Springs
PO Box 898, 405 Spray Ave.,
Banff, AB T1L 1A9

Tel: 403-760-2382*Toll-Free:* 888-310-9726
banff@mountaingalleries.com
www.mountaingalleries.com
www.instagram.com/mountaingalleries
twitter.com/MntGalleries
www.faceb ook.com/mountaingalleries
Year Founded: 1992 Exhibits work by Canadian artists
Wendy Wacko, Founder & Executive Director
Elizabeth Peacock, Co-Director

Banff: Walter Phillips Gallery (WPG)
The Banff Centre, PO Box 1020 14, 107 Tunnel Mountain Dr.,
Banff, AB T1L 1H5

Tel: 403-762-6281
walter_phillips_gallery@banffcentre.ca
www.banffcentre .ca/walter-phillips-gallery
www.instagram.com/walterphillipsgallery
www.facebook.com/walterphillipsg allery
Year Founded: 1976 Contemporary, national & international fine arts; open year round
Peta Rake, Curator

Brocket: Oldman River Cultural Centre
PO Box 70,
Brocket, AB T0K 0H0

Tel: 403-965-3939

Aboriginal history

Calgary: ARCHEloft Gallery
#200, 1209 - 1 St. SW,
Calgary, AB T2R 0V3

Tel: 403-532-7800
info@archeloft.com
www.endeavorarts.com
twitter.com/archeloft; www.instagram.com/archeloft
twitter.com/endeavorarts
www.facebook.com/ endeavorarts
Year Founded: 2010 ARCHEloft is an art space dedicated to hosting workshops and events. Some services offered include lasercutting, 3D printing, corporate team building, event catering and screen printing.
Maria Hoover, Lab Manager

Calgary: Contemporary Calgary
#900 105, 12 Ave. SE,
Calgary, AB T2P 1A1

Tel: 403-770-1350
info@contemporarycalgary.com
www.contemporarycalgary.com
www.instagram.com/contemporarycalgary
twitter.com/C_Calgary
www.facebo ok.com/contemporary.yyc
Non-profit public gallery, exhibiting works by contemporary Canadian artists; travelling exhibitions & education programs.
Pierre Arpin, Director & CEO
Erin O'Connor, Managing Director

Calgary: Esker Foundation Contemporary Art Gallery
1011 - 9 Ave. SE,
Calgary, AB T2G 0H7

Tel: 403-930-2490
info@eskerfoundation.com
eskerfoundation.com
instagram.com/eskerfoundation
twitter.com/eskercalgary
Year Founded: 2012 Contemporary work by international artists.
Naomi Potter, Director & Curator
Shauna Thompson, Curator

Calgary: Gainsborough Galleries
441 - 5 Ave. SW,
Calgary, AB T2P 0L6

Tel: 403-262-3715; *Fax:* 403-262-3743
Toll-Free: 866-425-5373
art@gainsboroughgalleries.com
www.gainsboroughgallerie s.com
www.instagram.com/gainsboroughgalleries
twitter.com/GainsboroughG
www.facebook.com/gainsboroughgalleries
Year Founded: 1923 Representational & impressionistic work by Canadian & international artists.

Calgary: Gerry Thomas Art Gallery
602 - 11 Ave. SW,
Calgary, AB T2R 1M7

Tel: 403-265-1630
info@gtgallery.com
www.gerrythomasgallery.com
www.instagram.com/gerrythomasgallery
twitter.com/gtgallery
www.facebo ok.com/gerry.thomas.gallery
Celebrates Canadian works of art.
Gerry Thomas, Owner

Calgary: Gibson Fine Art
628 - 11 Ave. SW,
Calgary, AB T2R 0E2

Tel: 403-244-2000; *Fax:* 403-244-2036
info@gibsonfineart.ca
www.gibsonfineart.ca
www.instagram.com/gibsonfineart
twitter.com/GibsonFineArt
www.facebook .com/Gibsonfineart
Year Founded: 1970 Work by new & established artists, with over 50% of the collection coming from Albertan artists.
Patti Dibski, Owner

Calgary: Illingworth Kerr Gallery (IKG)
Alberta College of Art & Design, 1407 - 14 Ave. NW,
Calgary, AB T2N 4R3

Tel: 403-284-7633
www.ikg.acad.ca
Year Founded: 1958 Contemporary art exhibitions, publications, lectures, screenings & related events
Lorenzo Fusi, Curator

Calgary: Latitude Art Gallery
708 - 11 Ave. SW,
Calgary, AB T2R 0E4

Tel: 403-262-9598
www.latitudeartgallery.com
twitter.com/LatitudeArtYYC
www.facebook.com/LatitudeArtGallery
Year Founded: 2007 Celebrates contemporary Canadian artwork

Calgary: Loch Gallery
Calgary
1516 - 4th St. SW,
Calgary, AB T2R 0Y4

Tel: 403-209-8542
www.lochgallery.com
www.instagram.com/loch_gallery
twitter.com/lochgallery
www.facebook.com/lochgallery
Year Founded: 2006 Work by Canadian & European artists both contemporary & historical.

Winnipeg: Ukrainian Museum of Canada (UMC)
Manitoba Branch
1175 Main St.,
Winnipeg, MB R2W 3S4

Tel: 204-582-1018
www.htuomc.org/museum.html
Year Founded: 1950 Open July - Aug., or by appointment the rest of the year.

Calgary: Marion Nicoll Gallery (MNG)
Alberta College of Art + Design, 1407 - 14th Ave. NW,
Calgary, AB T2N 4R3

mng.acadsa@auarts.ca
www.acad.ca/mng.html
Student-run gallery for students attending the Alberta College of Art & Design.

Calgary: Planet Art Gallery
#1451 - 14 St. SW,
Calgary, AB T3C 1C8

Tel: 403-619-0976
planetartinc@gmail.com
www.planetartgallery.ca
www.facebook.com/planetartgallery
Year Founded: 2010
Janice Mather, Owner
Marcus Z, Owner

Calgary: Stephen Lowe Art Gallery
Bow Valley Square III, #251, 255 - 5th Ave. SW,
Calgary, AB T2P 3G6

Tel: 403-261-1602; *Fax:* 403-261-2981
stephenloweartgallery@shaw.ca
www.stephenloweartgallery.ca
www.facebook com/stephenloweartgallery
Year Founded: 1970 Stephen Lowe Art Gallery offers fine art by Canadian artists. Works include oil paintings, blown glass, ceramics and sculpture. Additional services include consulting, financing, art delivery and installation and more. Hours: M-Sa 10:00-5:00.
Anna Lam, Director

Calgary: Stride Gallery
1006 MacLeod Trail SE,
Calgary, AB T2G 2M7
Tel: 403-262-8507; Fax: 403-269-5220
info@stride.ab.ca
www.instagram.com/stridegallery
twitter.com/stridegallery
www.facebook.com/stridegallery
Year Founded: 1985 This non-profit gallery, is an artist run
centre that promotes experimentation & community involvement.
Shelley Ouellet, President
Diane Colwell, Vice-President
Nicole Kelly Westman, Director, director@stride.ab.ca

Calgary: Wallace Galleries
500 - 5 Ave. SW,
Calgary, AB T2P 3L5
Tel: 403-262-8050; Fax: 403-264-7112
Toll-Free: 877-962-8050
info@wallacegalleries.com
www.wallacegalleries.com
www.instagram.com/wallacegalleries
twitter.com/WallaceGallery
www.facebook.com/wallacegalleries
Year Founded: 1986 Exhibits visual artwork by artists in all
stages of their careers.
Colette Hubner, Director

Calgary: Webster Galleries Inc.
812 - 11 Ave. SW,
Calgary, AB T2R 0E5
Tel: 403-263-6500; Fax: 403-263-6501
info@webstergalleries.com
www.webstergalleries.com
www.instagram.com/webstergalleries
twitter.com/WebsterArt
www.facebook.com/WebsterGalleriesInc
Year Founded: 1979 Canadian artwork
John Webster, Owner
Lorraine Webster, Owner

Camrose: Candler Art Gallery
5002 - 50 St.,
Camrose, AB T4V 1R2
Tel: 780-672-8401 Toll-Free: 888-672-8401
candler@syban.net
www.candlerartgallery.com
Year Founded: 1978 This gallery celebrates the work of
Canadian artists from the Camrose area.

Cochrane: Rustica Gallery
PO Box 1267, 123 - 2 Ave. West,
Cochrane, AB T4C 2B9
Tel: 403-851-5181; Fax: 403-241-0263
rons@rusticagallery.com

Edmonton: Fine Arts Building Gallery
University of Alberta, 112 St. & 89 Ave.,
Edmonton, AB T6G 2C9
Tel: 780-492-2081
bbrennan@ualberta.ca
www.artdesign.ualberta.ca/en/FAB_Gallery
www.facebook.com/FABgallery
Work by students, faculty, staff & professional artists.

Edmonton: Front Gallery
10402 - 124th St.,
Edmonton, AB T5N 1RS
Tel: 780-488-2952
info@thefrontgallery.com
thefrontgallery.com
www.instagram.com/thefrontgallery
twitter.com/thefrontgallery
www.facebook.com/frontgallery
Also provides picture framing services.

Edmonton: Latitude 53
10242 - 106 St.,
Edmonton, AB T5J 1H7
Tel: 780-423-5353
info@latitude53.org
www.latitude53.org
twitter.com/Latitude53
www.facebook.com/Latitude53
Year Founded: 1973 Contemporary artistic projects,
experimental cultural development; performance art; literary
projects; interdisciplinary art
Max Amerongen, President
Michelle Schultz, Executive Director, director@latitude53.org

Edmonton: West End Gallery
10337 - 124 St.,
Edmonton, AB T5N 1R1
Tel: 780-488-4892 Toll-Free: 855-488-4892
art@westendgalleryltd.com
www.westendgalleryltd.com
www.instagram.com/westendgallery
twitter.com/westendgallery
www.facebook ook.com/westendgalleryltd
Year Founded: 1975 Fine art gallery representing Canadian
paintings & sculpture; the largest representation of glass artists
in Canada.
Dan Hudon, Director

Foothills: Leighton Art Centre
282027-144 St. West,
Foothills, AB T1S 0Y4
Tel: 403-931-3633
info@leightoncentre.org
www.leightoncentre.org
www.facebook.com/leightonartcentre
Year Founded: 1974 A.C. Leighton's paintings, as well as those
by other prominent Alberta artists; programs for children &
adults; open year round
Melissa Cole, Chair
Christina Cuthbertson, Executive Director,
christinac@leightoncentre.org
Lindsay Corbet, Manager, Exhibitions, Events & Volunteers,
lindsayc@leightoncentre.org

Grande Prairie: The Art Gallery of Grande Prairie
#103, 9839 - 103 Ave.,
Grande Prairie, AB T8V 6M7
Tel: 780-532-8111; Fax: 780-539-9522
info@aggp.ca
www.aggp.ca
twitter.com/artgalleryofgp
www.facebook.com/ArtGalleryofGP
Public art gallery. The gallery's collection currently stands at
approximately 600 works of art, almost exclusively created in
Alberta in the mid to late 20th Century.
Nick Radujko, Chair, chair@aggp.ca
Terry Gorgichuk, Vice-Chair
Pam Balderton, Director
Jeff Erbach, Executive Director

Jasper: Mountain Galleries at the Fairmount
Fairmont Jasper Park Lodge
PO Box 1651, 1 Old Londge Rd.,
Jasper, AB T0E 1E0
Tel: 780-852-5378 Toll-Free: 888-310-9726
jasper@mountaingalleries.com
www.mountaingalleries.com
www.instagram.com/mountaingalleries
twitter.com/MntGalleries
www.faceb ook.com/mountaingalleries
Exhibits work by Canadian artists.
Wendy Wacko, Founder & Executive Director
Elizabeth Peacock, Co-Director

Lethbridge: Southern Alberta Art Gallery (SAAG)
601 - 3 Ave. South,
Lethbridge, AB T1J 0H4
Tel: 403-327-8770
info@saag.ca
www.saag.ca
twitter.com/THESAAG
www.facebook.com/southernalbertaartgallery
Fosters the work of contemporary visual artists who challenge
the boundaries of their discipline & advance their work in a
larger public realm
Adam Whitford, Interim Curator

Lethbridge: University of Lethbridge Art Gallery
W600, Centre for the Arts, 4401 University Dr.,
Lethbridge, AB T1K 3M4
Tel: 403-329-2666
www.uleth.ca/artgallery
www.instagram.com/ulethartgallery
twitter.com/ulethartgallery
www.faceb ook.com/ulethartgallery
Features rotating exhibits from the University of Lethbridge art
collection
Josephine Mills, Director & Curator, 403-329-2690,
josephine.mills@uleth.ca

Okotoks: Okotoks Art Gallery (OAG)
53 North Railway St.,
Okotoks, AB T1S 1K1
Tel: 403-938-3204
www.okotoks.ca

Year Founded: 1981 The art gallery serves the Town of Okotoks
& the Foothills region, promoting art & visual culture.

St Albert: Art Gallery of St. Albert (AGSA)
19 Perron St.,
St Albert, AB T8N 1E5
Tel: 780-460-4310; Fax: 780-460-9537
ahfgallery@artsheritage.ca
artgalleryofstalbert.ca
pinterest.com/artgallerysa
twitter.com/artgallerystalb
www.facebook.co m/ArtsAndHeritageStAlbert
Hours of operation: Tu-F 1:00-5:00, Sa 10:00-5:00.
Emily Baker, Curator, 780-651-5745,
exhibitions@artsandheritage.ca

British Columbia

Provincial Art Galleries

Vancouver Art Gallery
750 Hornby St.,
Vancouver, BC V6Z 2H7
Tel: 604-662-4700
customerservice@vanartgallery.bc.ca
www.vanartgallery. bc.ca
www.instagram.com/vanartgallery
twitter.com/VanArtGallery
www.facebook.com/VancouverArtGallery
Other contact information: 604-662-4700 ext. 2503
Year Founded: 1931 Largest gallery in western Canada;
presents major exhibitions from contemporary art to historical
masters; founded in 1931, has over 7,800 works in its collection,
41,400 sq. ft. of exhibition space & is located in the former
provincial courthouse in downtown Vancouver; collection
includes acclaimed Canadian artists such as Douglas Coupland,
Janet Cardiff & George Bures Miller
Anthony Kiendl, CEO & Director
Marie Dickens, Chief Operating Officer
Diana Freundl, Interim Chief Curator
Larah Luna, Director, Marketing & Communications,
604-662-4700, lluna@vanartgallery.bc.ca
Debra Nesbitt, Director, Human Resources
Melissa Karmen Lee, Director, Education & Public Programs
Elain Evans, Chief Development Officer

Local Art Galleries

Abbotsford: Kariton Art Gallery
2387 Ware St.,
Abbotsford, BC V2T 6Z6
Tel: 604-852-9358
info@abbotsfordartscouncil.com
abbotsfordartscouncil.com
www.instagram.com/abbotsfordartscouncil
twitter.com/AbbyArtsCouncil
ww w.facebook.com/AbbotsfordArtsCouncil
Work by local artists. Operated by the Abbotsford Arts Council
Aaron Levy, President, Abbotsford Arts Council
Will Davis, Executive Director, Abbotsford Arts Council,
will@abbotsfordartscouncil.com

Agassiz: Ruby Creek Art Gallery
58611 Lougheed Hwy.,
Agassiz, BC V0M 1A2
Tel: 604-796-0740; Fax: 604-796-9289
info@rubycreekartgallery.com
rubycreekartgallery.com
www.instagram.com/rubycreekart
twitter.com/RubyCreekArt
www.facebook.com/RubyCreekArtGallery
Northwest First Nations artwork

Brackendale: Brackendale Art Gallery Theatre
Teahouse
PO Box 100, 41950 Government Rd.,
Brackendale, BC V0N 1H0
Tel: 604-898-3333
www.brackendaleartgallery.com
www.facebook.com/139533814492
The gallery also serves food, holds concerts, presents theatre
productions, hosts workshops with artists, & more.

Burnaby: Burnaby Art Gallery
6344 Deer Lake Ave.,
Burnaby, BC V5G 2J3
Tel: 604-297-4422; Fax: 604-205-7339
gallery@burnaby.ca
www.burnabygallery.ca
www.instagram.com/bbyartgallery
twitter.com/BurnabyArtGall
www.faceboo k.com/BurnabyArtGallery

Services include educational programs for children, adults & seniors; community projects & exhibitions in libraries & recreational centres; school programs support the exhibitions & take works of art into the schools.
Ellen van Eijnsbergen, Director & Curator

Burnaby: The Simon Fraser University Gallery
Burnaby Campus
Simon Fraser University, 8888 University Dr.,
Burnaby, BC V5A 1S6
Tel: 778-782-4266
sfugallery@sfu.ca
www.sfu.ca/gallery
www.instagram.com/sfugalleries
twitter.com/SFU_Gallery
www.facebook.com/SFUGalleries
Year Founded: 1970 Hosts six or seven exhibitions a year, both historical & contemporary, covering the full range of media; serves the SFU community directly by providing an occasional platform for student, staff & faculty work to be shown; The Gallery also administers the Teck Gallery at the SFU Vancouver Campus, a small space used to show work that deals with social & environmental issues
Melanie O'Brian, Director, 778-782-4990, melanie_obrian@sfu.ca
Amy Kazymerchyk, Curator, 778-782-9685, amy_kazymerchyk@sfu.ca

Campbell River: Campbell River Art Gallery
Parent: Campbell River & District Public Art Gallery
1235 Shopper's Row,
Campbell River, BC V9W 2C7
Tel: 250-287-2261
admin@crartgallery.ca
www.crartgallery.ca
Contemporary work from both local & visiting artists; classes, lectures & workshops throughout the year
Sara Lopez Assu, Executive Director, director@crartgallery.ca
Jenelle Pasiechnik, Curator, curator@crartgallery.ca

Castlegar: Kootenay Gallery of Art, History & Science
120 Heritage Way,
Castlegar, BC V1N 4M5
Tel: 250-365-3337
kootenaygallery@telus.net
www.kootenaygallery.com
Exhibits on art, history & science, from international to local sources; offers workshops, performances, lectures & classes; gift shop. Hours: Mar-Nov: Tu-Sa 10:00-5:00; Dec: M-Su 10:00-5:00.
Audrey Maxwell-Polovnikof, Chair
Valentine Field, Executive Director
Maggie Shirley, Curator

Courtenay: Comox Valley Art Gallery
580 Duncan Ave.,
Courtenay, BC V9N 2M7
Tel: 250-338-6211
contact@comoxvalleyartgallery.com
www.comoxvalleyartgallery.com
www.instagram.com/comoxvalleyartgallery
www.facebook.com/comoxvalleyartgallery
The Comox Valley Art Gallery features contemporary art by regional, national, & international artists. Open Th-Sa 10:00-5:00.
Jasmin Badrin, President
Glen Sanford, Executive Director
Angela Somerset, Program Director & Co-Curator
Denise Lawson, Co-Curator

Dawson Creek: Dawson Creek Art Gallery
Parent: South Peace Arts Society
816 Alaska Ave.,
Dawson Creek, BC V1G 4T6
Tel: 250-782-2601; *Fax:* 250-782-8801
artadmin@dcartgallery.ca
www.dcartgallery.ca
www.facebook.com/DawsonCreekArtGallery
Managed by the South Peace Art Society. Open year round
Kit Fast, Curator, curator@dcartgallery.ca

Gibsons: Gibsons Public Art Gallery (GPAG)
431 Marine Dr.,
Gibsons, BC V0N 1V0
Tel: 604-886-0531
info@gpag.ca
www.gpag.ca
instagram.com/gpagart
twitter.com/GPAGart
www.facebook.com/316757548359391
Year Founded: 2003 Gibsons Public Art Gallery hosts mothly exhibitions and special events to showcase art in various forms,

with an emphasis on works by Sunshine Coast Artists. GPAG also offers lectures, screenings, workshops and seminars, as well as art classes for adults and children. Gallery hours are as follows: M 11:00-4:00; Th-Su 11:00-4:00.
Stewart Stinson, President
Joan Fallis, Treasurer
Pat Bean, Director
Michael Aze, Gallery Manager
Andrea Coates, Social Media

Golden: Kicking Horse Culture: Art Gallery of Golden
PO Box 228, 516 9 Ave. N,
Golden, BC V0A 1A0
Tel: 250-344-6186
kickinghorseculture.ca/art-gallery-of-golden
www.youtube.com/user/khcgdac
twitter.com/goldenculture
www.facebook.com/khculture
Open M-Sa 10:00-6:00.
Bill Usher, Executive Director

Grand Forks: Grand Forks & District Art & Heritage Centre
PO Box 2140, 524 Central Ave.,
Grand Forks, BC V0H 1H0
Tel: 250-442-2211; *Fax:* 250-442-0099
communications@g2gf.ca
www.gallery2grandforks.ca
Historical & contemporary works by established & emerging regional, national & international artists
Tim van Wijk, Director & Curator, tvanwijk@g2gf.ca

Kamloops: Kamloops Art Gallery
#101 465 Victoria St.,
Kamloops, BC V2C 2A9
Tel: 250-377-2400; *Fax:* 250-828-0662
kamloopsartgallery@kag.bc.ca
www.kag.bc.ca
twitter.com/artsinkamloops
www.facebook.com/KamloopsArtsGallery
Year Founded: 1978 Changing exhibits of contemporary & historical art; permanent collection of Canadian art. Hours: M-W, F-Sa 10:00-5:00. Th 10:00-9:00.
Manju Singh, President
Rob Wilson, Vice-President
Margaret Chrumka, Executive Director, 250-377-2412, mchrumka@kag.bc.ca
Charo Neville, Curator, 250-377-2410, cneville@kag.bc.ca

Kaslo: Langham Cultural Centre
Parent: The Langham Cultural Society
447 A Ave.,
Kaslo, BC V0G 1M0
Tel: 250-353-2661; *Fax:* 250-353-2671
langham@netidea.com
www.thelangham.ca
www.facebook.com/thelangham
Year Founded: 1975 Art exhibits; theatre; music; workshops; The Japanese Canadian Museum. Open Th-Su 1:00-4:00
John Cathro, President
Marianne Hobden, Vice-President
Paul Grace-Campbell, Executive Director
Seathra Bell, Curator

Kelowna: Alternator Centre for Contemporary Art
#103 421 Cawston Ave.,
Kelowna, BC V1Y 6Z1
Tel: 250-868-2298
info@alternatorcentre.com
www.instagram.com/the_alternator
twitter.com/alternatortweet
www.facebook.com/AlternatorArt
Year Founded: 1989 Work by emerging local & national artists.
Lorna McParland, Artistic & Administrative Director, lorna@alternatorcentre.com

Kelowna: Kelowna Art Gallery
1315 Water St.,
Kelowna, BC V1Y 9R3
Tel: 250-762-2226; *Fax:* 250-762-9875
info@kelownaartgallery.com
www.kelownaartgallery.com
www.instagram.com/kelownaartgallery
twitter.com/kelownaart
www.facebook.com/KelownaArtGallery
Year Founded: 1976 Historical & contemporary fine art; extensive education programs; open year round
Joanna Wrzesniewski, President
Paul Mitchell, Vice-President
Nataley Nagy, Executive Director, nataley@kelownaartgallery.com

Kelowna: Sopa Fine Arts
2934 Pandosy St.,
Kelowna, BC V1Y 1V9
Tel: 250-763-5088
info@sopafinearts.com
www.sopafinearts.com
www.instagram.com/sopafinearts
twitter.com/SopaFineArts
www.facebook.com/106624962755286
Year Founded: 2005 Contemporary art with an emphasis on abstract work.

Kelowna: Tutt Street Gallery
#9 3045 Tutt St.,
Kelowna, BC V1Y 2H4
Tel: 250-861-4992; *Fax:* 250-861-4992
info@tuttartgalleries.com
www.tuttartgalleries.ca
twitter.com/tuttstga llery
www.facebook.com/TuttStreetGallery
Canadian oil & acrylic paintings.
Martina Kral, Owner

Koksilah: Hill's Native Art
5209 Trans-Canada Hwy.,
Koksilah, BC V0R 2C0
Tel: 250-746-6731
www.hills.ca
www.facebook.com/HillsNativeArt
First Nations artwork

Ladysmith: Ladysmith Waterfront Gallery
PO Box 2370, 610 Oyster Bay Dr.,
Ladysmith, BC V9G 1B8
Tel: 250-245-1252
info@ladysmithwaterfrontgallery.com
www.ladysmithwaterfrontgallery.com
www.instagram.com/explore/locations/311356604
www.facebook.com/ladysmithwaterfrontgallery
Year Founded: 2007 The Ladysmith Waterfront Gallery exhibits contemporary art, photography, design and crafts. The gallery also offers classes and workshops. Types of art exhibited include paintings, photography, sculpture, glass art, jewelry, prints, carvings and more. Gallery hours are Monday to Sunday, 11:00 to 4:00pm.
Gail Ralphs, Vice President, admin@ladysmithwaterfrontgallery.com
Claudia Lohmann, Director
Leona Petrak, Curator
Betty Peebles, Treasurer
Susan Derby, Secretary, art@ladysmithwaterfrontgallery.com

Lake Country: Lake Country Art Gallery
10356A Bottom Wood Lake Rd.,
Lake Country, BC V4V 1T9
Tel: 250-766-1299
lakecountryartgallery@shaw.ca
www.lakecountryartgallery.ca
instagram.com/lakecountryartgallery
twitter.com/LakeCountryArtG
www.facebook.com/Lakecountryartgallery
Year Founded: 2010 Lake Country Art Gallery exhibits art, as well as providing presentations, performances, classes and workshops for the public. Hours are Wednesday to Sunday, 10:00 to 4:00.
Petrina McNeill, Gallery Manager
Wanda Lock, Gallery Curator

Maple Ridge: Maple Ridge Art Gallery Society
11944 Haney Pl.,
Maple Ridge, BC V2X 6G1
Tel: 604-476-2787; *Fax:* 604-476-2187
info@mract.org
www.theactmapleridge.org
www.instagram.com/actartgallery
twitter.com/mapleridgeact
www.facebook.com/mapleridgeact
Exhibition of local, amateur & professional artists; art rental program for patrons
Dawn Flanagan, President
Laura Butler, Vice-President
Curtis Pendleton, Executive Director, 604-476-2780, curtisp@mract.org

Nakusp: Bonnington Arts Centre
6th Ave. & 4th St. NW,
Nakusp, BC V0G 1R0
Tel: 250-265-4087
AlacNak@columbiacable.net
www.nakusp.com/municipal-services/culture/bonnington-arts-centre
Located in Nakusp Elementary School. Open Sept.-June.

Nanaimo: Hill's Native Art
76 Bastion St.,
Nanaimo, BC V9R 3A1
Tel: 250-755-7873
info@hillsnativeart.com
www.hills.ca
www.facebook.co m/HillsNativeArt
First Nations artwork

Nanaimo: Nanaimo Art Gallery
Vancouver Island University, Nanaimo Campus, 150
Commercial St.,
Nanaimo, BC V9R 5G6
Tel: 250-754-1750
www.nanaimogallery.ca
www.instagram.com/nanaimo_art_gallery
twitter.com/NanaimoArt
www.faceb ook.com/nanaimoartgallery
Celebrating art on the west coast; art central & sales program;
gift shop full of elegant & eclectic gifts; inspiring & thought
provoking exhibitions
Deborah Giunio-Zorkin, President BSc., MA.
Sarah E. Lane, Vice-President
Julie Bevan, Executive Director
Jesse Birch, Curator

New Westminster: Amelia Douglas Gallery
Douglas College, 700 Royal Ave., 4th Fl. North,
New Westminster, BC V3M 5Z5
Tel: 604-527-5723
artsevents@douglascollege.ca
www.douglascollege.ca
www.facebook.com/AmeliaDouglasGallery
Year Founded: 1992 A non-profit organization run by members
of the Arts Exhibition Committee at Douglas College; mandate is
to feature new & established BC artists & to enhance the
educational offerings of the College

North Vancouver: Heffel Gallery Limited
2247 Granville St.,
North Vancouver, BC V7V 0A2
Tel: 604-732-6505; Fax: 604-732-4245
Toll-Free: 800-528-9608
mail@heffel.com
www.heffel.com/gallery/Gallery_V_E.asp x
www.instagram.com/heffelauction
twitter.com/heffelauction
Fine art auction house.
David Kenneth John Heffel, President
Robert Campbell Scott Heffel, Vice-President,
robert@heffel.com
Martin A. Burian, Chief Financial Officer, martin@heffel.com

North Vancouver: The Polygon Gallery
101 Carrie Cates Ct.,
North Vancouver, BC V7M 3J4
Tel: 604-986-1351
info@thepolygon.ca
www.presentationhousegallery.org
www.instagram.com/thepolygongallery
twitter.com/_ThePolygon
www.faceb ook.com/thepolygongallery
Year Founded: 1976 Celebrates & preserves North Vancouver's
social, industrial & cultural history. Operated by the British
Columbia Photography & Media Arts Society. Hours: W-Su
12:00-5:00
Iain Mant, President
Paula Palyga, Vice-Chair
Reid Shier, Director & Curator

North Vancouver: Seymour Art Gallery
4360 Gallant Ave.,
North Vancouver, BC V7G 1L2
Tel: 604-924-1378
info@seymourartgallery.com
seymourartgallery.com
twitter.com/seymourgallery
www.facebook.com/seym ourartgallery
Open year round
Svetlana Bardos, President
Vanessa Black, Curator

Osoyoos: Oliver Art Gallery
8302 Main St.,
Osoyoos, BC V0H 1V3
Tel: 778-437-2238
office@okanaganartgallery.ca
www.okanaganartgallery.ca/contact.html
www.instagram.com/okanaganartgallery
twitter.com/okanagangallery
www.f acebook.com/okanaganartgallery
Year Founded: 2011 Exhibits work by artists in South Okanagan

Sandra Albo, Vice-President
Sue Whittaker, Curator

Osoyoos: Osoyoos Art Gallery
8713 Main St.,
Osoyoos, BC V0H 1V0
Tel: 250-495-2800
osoyoosartgallery@gmail.com
www.osoyoosarts.com/groups/osoyoos-art-gallery
www.facebook.com/OsoyoosA rtsCouncil
Open year round
Dianne Hughes, Managing Director

Penticton: Penticton Art Gallery
199 Marina Way,
Penticton, BC V2A 1H5
Tel: 250-493-2928; Fax: 250-493-3992
info@pentictonartgallery.com
www.pentictonartgallery.com
www.instagram.com/pentictonartgallery
twitter.com/pentartgallery
www.facebook.com/pentictonartgallery
Year Founded: 1972 The Penticton Art Gallery offers in-house &
touring exhibitions from local, regional & national sources.
Rodney N. Penway, President & Treasurer
Paul Crawford, Director & Curator,
curator@pentictonartgallery.com

Port Alberni: Rollin Art Centre
3061 Eighth Ave.,
Port Alberni, BC V9Y 2K5
Tel: 250-724-3412
communityarts@shaw.ca
www.alberniarts.com
www.instagram.com/rollinartcentre
www.facebook.com/CommunityArtsCouncilO fTheAlberniValley
Fine arts gallery, gift shop, classroom & gardens.
Melissa Martin, Executive Director, admincac@shawcable.com

Prince George: Two Rivers Gallery
Parent: Prince George Regional Art Gallery Association
Prince George Art Gallery Association, 725 Canada Games
Way,
Prince George, BC V2L 5T1
Tel: 250-614-7800; Fax: 250-563-3211
www.tworiversartgallery.com
www.instagram.com/tworiversgallery
twitter.com/tworiversart
www.faceb ook.com/tworiversart
Year Founded: 1949 The Two Rivers Gallery is a centre for
visual art in Prince George & the central interior of British
Columbia, Canada. It seeks to encourage lifelong learning
through the arts, create an environment for artistic & cultural
expression & provide opportunities through participation &
exhibition.
Cori Ramsay, President
Steve Reynolds, Vice-President
Carolyn Holmes, Managing Director,
carolyn@tworiversgallery.ca
George Harris, Curator, george@tworiversgallery.ca

Qualicum Beach: The Old School House Arts Centre
(TOSH)
122 Fern Rd. West,
Qualicum Beach, BC V9K 1T2
Tel: 250-752-6133
qbtosh@shaw.ca
www.theoldschoolhouse.org
twitter.com/theoshcafe
www.facebook.com/1912 school
Twelve resident artists; 3 exhibition galleries; concert series;
classrooms; gift shop
Corinne James, Executive Director

Quesnel: Quesnel Art Gallery
Quesnel Recreation Centre, 500 North Star Rd.,
Quesnel, BC V2J 5P6
Tel: 250-991-4014
quesnelartgallery@gmail.com
www.quesnelartgallery.com
twitter.com/quartgallery
www.facebook.com/qu esnelartgallery
Quesnel Art Gallery showcases works by local Cariboo artists in
BC, with additional contributions by international artists. Its
collections include landscape paintings, interpretive sculptures
and more. Gallery is open Tuesday to Saturday, 10:00 to 4:00.
Amy Quarry, Volunteer, amy@smalltownlove.com

Richmond: Richmond Art Gallery
7700 Minoru Gate,
Richmond, BC V6Y 1R8
Tel: 604-247-8363
gallery@richmond.ca
www.richmondartgallery.org
www.youtube.com/user/RichmondArtGallery
www.facebook.com/RichmondArtGall eryBC
Year Founded: 1980 Presents a diverse program of exhibitions,
workshops, lectures & special events, as well as outreach
programs which focus on contemporary art & art issues
Jas Lally, President
Shaun Dacey, Director
Nan Capogna, Curator

Salt Spring Island: Blue Horse Folk Art Gallery
175 North View Dr.,
Salt Spring Island, BC V8K 1A9
Tel: 250-537-0754
bluehorsefolkart@gmail.com
www.bluehorse.ca
www.facebook.com/BlueHorseFolkArt
Year Founded: 1994 Wooden animal carvings by Paul Burke &
raku vases & lamps by Anna Gustafson.
Paul Burke, Owner & Artist
Anna Gustafson, Owner & Artist

Salt Spring Island: Gallery 8
Grace Point Square, #3104 115 Fulford Ganges Rd.,
Salt Spring Island, BC V8K 2T9
Tel: 250-537-8822; Fax: 250-537-8822
Toll-Free: 866-537-8822
art@gallery8saltspring.com
www.artgallery8.com
www.instagram.com/gallery_8
Work by local & national contemporary artists
Andrea Gruber, Regional Director
Timea Junghaus, Curator

Sidney: Peninsula Gallery
2506 Beacon Ave.,
Sidney, BC V8L 1Y2
Tel: 250-655-1722 Toll-Free: 877-787-1896
info@pengal.com
www.pengal.com
Year Founded: 1986 This gallery celebrates local & national
artists.
Ying Tang, Owner

Smithers: Smithers Art Gallery
Central Park Building, PO Box 122, 1425 Main St.,
Smithers, BC V0J 2N0
Tel: 250-847-3898
info@smithersart.org
www.smithersart.org
www.instagram.com/smithersartgallery
twitter.com/smithersart
www.faceb ook.com/smithersartgallery
Year Founded: 1971 Public gallery, admission by donation;
monthly exhibition rotation; workshops & artcamps for young &
old, all artisan levels & mediums; call for a current listing
Lauren Bell, President, director2@smithersart.org
Susan Smith, Vice-President, director8@smithersart.org

Surrey: Arnold Mikelson Mind & Matter Gallery
13743 16th Ave.,
Surrey, BC V4A 1P7
Tel: 604-536-6460
www.mindandmatterart.com
twitter.com/MikelsonGallery
Year Founded: 1966 Wood sculptures of the late Arnold
Mikelson.
Mary Mikelson, Owner & Director, mary@mindandmatterart.com

Surrey: Surrey Art Gallery
Surrey Arts Centre, 13750 - 88 Ave.,
Surrey, BC V3W 3L1
Tel: 604-501-5566
artgallery@surrey.ca
www.surrey.ca/culture-recreation/1615.aspx
www.instagram.com/surreyartgal
twitter.com/SurreyArtGal
www.facebook.c om/surreyartgallery
Year Founded: 1975 Promotes contemporary BC & Canadian
artists; exhibitions & public programs encourage community
appreciation of contemporary visual art; open year round
Liane Davison, Manager, Visual & Community Art,
604-501-5197, ljdavison@surrey.ca
Jordan Strom, Curator, Exhibitions & Collections, 604-592-6986,
artgallery@surrey.ca

Terrace: Terrace Art Gallery
Terrace Public Library, 4610 Park Ave.,
Terrace, BC V8G 1V6

Tel: 250-638-8884
coordinator@terraceartgallery.com
www.facebook.com/TerraceArtGallery
Year Founded: 1981 Terrace Art Gallery exhibits visual arts.
Gallery hours are as follows: T-F 12:00-4:00pm; Sa
12:00-5:00pm; Su 1:00-5:00pm.
Bob Park, Chair
Chris Stone, Vice-Chair
Ann Kantakis, Treasurer, Membership
Denise McGillivray, Director, Policies & Procedures
Laura McGregor, Gallery Coordinator

Vancouver: AHVA Gallery
Audain Art Centre, University of British Columbia, #1001
6398 University Blvd.,
Vancouver, BC V6T 1Z2

Tel: 604-822-4563
ahva.gallery@ubc.ca
gallery.ahva.ubc.ca
twitter.com/ubcahva
www.facebook.com/ahva.ubc.ca
Features student & faculty artwork.
Scott Watson, Director

Vancouver: Art Works
1536 Venable St.,
Vancouver, BC V5L 2G9

Tel: 604-688-3301; Fax: 604-683-4552
Toll-Free: 800-663-0341
info@artworksbc.com
www.instagram.com/artworks.gallery
twitter.com/ArtWorksBC
www.facebook.com/ArtWorksVan
Year Founded: 1986 This gallery displays modern &
contemporary art pieces. The gallery celebratres the works of
Canadian artists & highlights the work of British Columbia's best
artists.

Vancouver: Artspeak Gallery
233 Carrall St.,
Vancouver, BC V6B 2J2

Tel: 604-688-0051
info@artspeak.ca
artspeak.ca
www.instagram.com/artspeakartspeak
twitter.com/artspeakgallery
www.facebook.com/ArtspeakGallery
Year Founded: 1986 A non-profit artist-run centre for
contemporary art & writing.
Bopha Chhay, Director & Curator

Vancouver: Bau-Xi Gallery
3045 Granville St.,
Vancouver, BC V6H 3J9

Tel: 604-733-7011
info@bau-xi.com
Www.bau-xi.com
www.instagram.com/bauxigallery
twitter.com/BauXiGallery
www.facebook.c om/BauXiGallery
Year Founded: 1965 Bau-Xi Gallery exhibits work by Canadian
artists on the West Coast. Bau-Xi is a member of the Art Dealers
Association of Canada, and has branches in Toronto and
Seattle. Types of art exhibited include photography, paintings
and sculpture. Hours: M-Sa 10:00-5:30; Su 11:00-5:30.
Xisa Huang, Owner
Riko Nakasone, Director

Vancouver: Bill Reid Gallery of Northwest Coast Art
639 Hornby St.,
Vancouver, BC V6C 2G3

info@billreidgallery.ca
www.billreidgallery.ca
www.instagram.com/billreidgallery
twitter.com/billreidgallery
www.face book.com/billreidgallery
Other contact information: Visitor Services: 604-682-3455 ext.
221
Year Founded: 2008 Contemporary work by Aboriginal artists of
the Northwest Coast.

Vancouver: Centre A
PO Box 88363 Chinatown, 268 Keefer St.,
Vancouver, BC V6A 1X6

Tel: 604-683-8326; Fax: 604-683-8632
info@centrea.org
centrea.org
instagram.com/centre_a
twitter.com/centrea
www.facebook.com/CentreAGal lery
Year Founded: 1999 Contemporary Asian visual art.
April Liu, President
Kevin Harding, Vice-President
Tyler Russell, Executive Director & Curator

Vancouver: Chali-Rosso Art Gallery
549 Howe St.,
Vancouver, BC V6C 2C2

Tel: 604-733-3594
gallery@chalirosso.com
www.chalirosso.com
www.instagram.com/chalirossoartgallery
twitter.com/chalirosso
www.face book.com/chalirosso
Year Founded: 2005 Chali-Rosso Art Gallery exhibits the
artworks of renowned European artists such as Pablo Picasso,
Salvador Dali, Marc Chagall and more. Gallery hours are as
follows: M-Sa 10:00-6:00pm; Su 12:00am-5:00pm.
Susanna Strem, Contact, gallery@chalirosso.com

Vancouver: Charles H. Scott Gallery
Emily Carr University of Art + Design, 1399 Johnston St.,
Vancouver, BC V6H 3R9

Tel: 604-844-3809
www.canadianart.ca/galleries/charles-h-scott-gallery
Year Founded: 1980 A public art gallery specializing in
contemporary art. Open seven days a week.
Cate Rimmer, Curator

Vancouver: Circle Craft Gallery
Net Loft Building, #1, 1666 Johnston St.,
Vancouver, BC V6H 3S2

Tel: 604-669-8021
info@circlecraft.net
www.circlecraft.net
www.instagram.com/circlecraft
www.facebook.com/CircleCraft
Year Founded: 1973 Features over 200 works of BC artists
Wendy Van Riesen, President

Vancouver: Coastal Peoples Fine Arts Gallery
332 Water St.,
Vancouver, BC V6B 1B6

Tel: 604-684-9222
info@coastalpeoples.com
www.coastalpeoples.com
Year Founded: 1996 Exhibits work by Northwest Coast First
Nations & Inuit.

Vancouver: Contemporary Art Gallery (CAG)
555 Nelson St.,
Vancouver, BC V6B 6R5

Tel: 604-681-2700; Fax: 604-683-2710
contact@contemporaryartgallery.ca
www.contemporaryartgallery.ca
twitte r.com/CAGVancouver
www.facebook.com/CAGVancouver
Year Founded: 1971 Promotes knowledge & understanding of
contemporary visual art through: exhibitions that address current
issues in contemporary art; educational programs in the form of
artist & curator talks, student tours, high school projects, public
symposia; publications; visiting artist/curator programs;
information & resource services; The City of Vancouver Art
Collection of 3,000 works of art
David Brown, President
Matthew Hyland, Executive Director
Julia Lamare, Associate Curator

Vancouver: Equinox Gallery
525 Great Northern Way,
Vancouver, BC V5T 1E1

Tel: 604-736-2405
info@equinoxgallery.com
www.equinoxgallery.com
www.instagram.com/equinoxgallery
twitter.com/equinoxgallery
Year Founded: 1972
Andy Sylvester, Curator

Vancouver: Gallery Gachet
9 West Hastings St.,
Vancouver, BC V6B 1G4

Tel: 604-687-2468
contact@gachet.org
gachet.org
www.facebook.com/gallerygachet
Gallery Gachet is an artist-run public gallery in Vancouver's
Downtown Eastside. Open W-Sa 12:00-5:00.
Manuel Axel Strain, Programming Coordinator,
programassociate@gachet.org

Vancouver: Gordon Smith Gallery of Canadian Art
2121 Lonsdale Ave.,
Vancouver, BC V7M 2K6

Tel: 604-998-8563
admin@smithfoundation.ca
www.gordonsmithgallery.ca
www.instagram.com/artists_for_kids
twitter.com/GSmithGallery
www.faceb ook.com/Gordon.Smith.Gallery
Exhibits work by Canadian artists

Vancouver: grunt gallery
#116, 350 East 2nd Ave.,
Vancouver, BC V5T 4R8

Tel: 604-875-9516
grunt.ca
www.youtube.com/user/gruntgallery1
twitter.com/gruntgallery
www.facebo ok.com/gruntgallery
Year Founded: 1984 Artist-run centre furthering contemporary
art through exhibitions, performances, artist talks, publications, &
other projects. Open Tu-Sa, 12-5
Vanessa Kwan, Program Director, vanessakwan@grunt.ca
Meagan Kus, Operations Director, meagan@grunt.ca
Whess Harman, Curator, whess@grunt.ca

Vancouver: Hill's Native Art
120 East Broadway,
Vancouver, BC V5T 1V9

Tel: 604-685-4249
www.hills.ca
www.facebook.com/HillsNativeArt
First Nations artwork

Vancouver: Ian Tan Gallery
2342 Granville St.,
Vancouver, BC V6H 3G3

Tel: 604-738-1077
info@iantangallery.com
www.iantangallery.com
www.instagram.com/iantangallery
twitter.com/iantangallery
www.facebook .com/iantangallery
Year Founded: 1999 Exhibits contemporary work by Canadian
artists, with an emphasis on west coast art.
Julie Lepper, Director

Vancouver: Kurbatoff Gallery
2435 Granville St.,
Vancouver, BC V6H 3G5

Tel: 604-736-5444
art@kurbatoffgallery.com
kurbatoffgallery.com
kurbatoffgallery.tumblr.com
twitter.com/kurbatoffg
www.facebook.com/pages/247016175341630
Year Founded: 2002 Kurbatoff Gallery promotes contemporary
Canadian artists at all stages of their careers. Collections include
paintings and sculptures. Gallery hours are as follows: T-Sa
10:30-5:30; Su 12:00-5:00.
Konstantin Kurbatoff, Owner
Elena Kurbatoff, Director

Vancouver: LeSoleil Fine Art Gallery
100-535 Howe St.,
Vancouver, BC V6C 2Z4

Tel: 604-565-2424
art@lesoleilfineart.com
www.lesoleilfineart.com
twitter.com/lesoleilfineart
www.facebook.com/l esoleilfineartgallery
Year Founded: 1996 This gallery celebrates French
impressionists, modern-day contemporary artists as well as 20th
century artists & Old Masters.

Vancouver: Marion Scott Gallery/Kardosh Projects
2423 Granville St.,
Vancouver, BC V6H 3G5

Tel: 604-685-1934; *Fax:* 604-685-1890
art@marionscottgallery.com
www.marionscottgallery.com
www.instagram.com/marion_scott_gallery
www.facebook.com/marionscottgallery
Established in 1975, & one of the leading galleries dealing with
Canadian Inuit art
Robert Kardosh, Director/Curator,
robert@marionscottgallery.com

Vancouver: Morris & Helen Belkin Art Gallery
University of British Columbia, 1825 Main Mall,
Vancouver, BC V6T 1Z2

Tel: 604-822-2759
belkin.gallery@ubc.ca
belkin.ubc.ca
www.youtube.com/user/belkinartgallery
www.facebook.com/BelkinArtGallery
Year Founded: 1948 Specializes in exhibiting contemporary work
by national & international artists; programming includes
exhibitions, artists' talks, publications & collaborative projects
with other galleries/organizations; masters program in Critical
Curatorial Studies; archival collections focus on Vancouver
Canadian avant garde in 1960s-70s
Lorna Brown, Acting Director/Curator, lorna.brown@ubc.ca

Vancouver: RendezVous Art Gallery
323 Howe St.,
Vancouver, BC V6C 3N2

Tel: 604-687-7466
info@rendezvousartgallery.com
www.rendezvousartgallery.com
Work by Canadian artists.

Vancouver: Rennie Collection at Wing Sang Building
51 East Pender St.,
Vancouver, BC V6A 1S9

renniecollection.org
www.instagram.com/renniecollect
twitter.com/renniecollect
Exhibits work of 200 artists.
Bob Rennie, Founder

Vancouver: Stewart Stephenson Fine Art Gallery
1063 Hamilton St.,
Vancouver, BC V6B 5T4

Tel: 604-893-7841 *Toll-Free:* 877-278-7100
info@stewartstephenson.com
stewartstephenson.com
www.instagram.com/stewart_stephenson
www.facebook.com/StewartStephensonFineArt
Year Founded: 2011 Stewart Stephenson Fine Art Gallery
exhibits large-scale abstract artwork by artist Stewart
Stephenson. Stephenson's most recent collection focuses on
celebrity, social and media culture.
Stewart Stephenson, Owner & Artist
Saba Orouji, Art Consultant

Vancouver: Trench Contemporary Art Gallery
148 Alexander St.,
Vancouver, BC V6A 2S5

Tel: 604-681-2577
info@trenchgallery.com
twitter.com/TrenchGallery
www.facebook.com/TrenchGallery

Vancouver: VIVO Media Arts Centre
2625 Kaslo St.,
Vancouver, BC V5M 3G9

Tel: 604-872-8337; *Fax:* 604-876-1185
info@vivomediaarts.com
vivomediaarts.com
www.instagram.com/vivomediaarts
twitter.com/VIVOMediaArts
www.facebook.com/vivomediaarts
Year Founded: 1973 VIVO is vancouver's oldest media arts
access centre, specializing in video production, exhibition &
distribution. Open Tu-Sa 11:00-6:00, & M by appointment.
Kate Lingley, Chair
Mariane Bourcheix-Laporte, Director
Frans Van De Ven, Director

Vancouver: Western Front
303 8 Ave. East,
Vancouver, BC V5T 1S1

Tel: 604-876-9343; *Fax:* 604-876-4099
front.bc.ca
www.instagram.com/western_front
twitter.com/western_front

Year Founded: 1973 An artist-run centre dedicated to
contemporary art & new music. The centre is open Tu-Sa
12:00-5:00.
Shelly Rosenblum, President
Carol Sawyer, Vice-President
Caitlin Jones, Executive Director

Vancouver: Wickaninnish Gallery
The Net Loft, #14 1666 Johnston St.,
Vancouver, BC V6H 3S2

Tel: 604-681-1057; *Fax:* 604-331-1066
wickgallery@gmail.com
www.wickaninnishgallery.com
Year Founded: 1987 Native-owned art gallery & boutique.
Patricia Rivard, Owner & Founder

Vernon: Vernon Public Art Gallery (VPAG)
3228 31st Ave.,
Vernon, BC V1T 2H3

Tel: 250-545-3173
info@vernonpublicartgallery.com
www.vernonpublicartgallery.com
www.instagram.com/vernonpublicartgallery
twitter.com/VernonAGallery
www.facebook.com/vernonpublicartgallery
Year Founded: 1945 Community programming; local, regional,
national & international exhibitions; gift shop; art & video rentals;
group tours
Dauna Kennedy-Grant, Executive Director,
dauna@vernonpublicartgallery.com
Lobos Culen, Curator, curator@vernonpublicartgallery.com

Victoria: Alcheringa Gallery
621 Fort St.,
Victoria, BC V8W 1G1

Tel: 250-383-8224; *Fax:* 250-383-9399
alcheringa@islandnet.com
www.alcheringa-gallery.com
twitter.com/alcher ingag
Work by Aboriginal artists from the Northwest Coast of Canada,
Papua New Guinea & Australia.
Elaine Monds, Director & Founder

Victoria: Art Gallery of Greater Victoria
1040 Moss St.,
Victoria, BC V8V 4P1

Tel: 250-384-4171; *Fax:* 250-361-3995
aggv.ca
www.instagram.com/artgalleryvic
twitter.com/artgalleryvic
www.facebook.com/artgalleryvictoria
Year Founded: 1951 Canadian works of arts from 1860 to the
present; work of Emily Carr; extensive collection of Asian art.
John Tupper, Director, jtupper@aggv.ca

Victoria: The Avenue Gallery
2184 Oak Bay Ave.,
Victoria, BC V8R 1G3

Tel: 250-598-2184 *Toll-Free:* 844-598-2184
info@theavenuegallery.com
theavenuegallery.com
www.instagram.com/theavenuegallery
twitter.com/galleryavenue
www.facebook.com/theavenuegallery
Year Founded: 2002 Exhibits paintings, sculptures, glass art &
jewellery.
Heather Wheeler, Owner

Victoria: Open Space
510 Fort St.,
Victoria, BC V8W 1E6

Tel: 250-383-8833
openspace@openspace.ca
www.openspace.ca
www.instagram.com/openspacevic
twitter.com/openspacevic
www.facebook.com/openspace.victoria
Year Founded: 1972 An artist-run centre dedicated to exploring
the boundaries of contemporary art & media in all forms. Hours
of Operation: Tu-Sa 12:00-5:00.
Kegan McFadden, Executive Director, director@openspace.ca

Victoria: Red Art Gallery
Victoria, BC

Tel: 250-881-0462
redartgallery.ca
www.facebook.com/pages/158074164265760
Year Founded: 2010 The Red Art Gallery sells and exhibits
original artwork. Pieces include figurative and abstract paintings
and mixed media works.
Bobb Hamilton, Director, 250-881-0462, bobb@redartgallery.ca

Victoria: Victoria Emerging Art Gallery (VEAG)
1016 Fort St.,
Victoria, BC V8V 3K4

Tel: 778-430-5585
info@victoriaemergingart.com
www.victoriaemergingart.com
Celebrates emerging artists from Vancouver

Victoria: Xchanges Gallery & Studios
2333 Government St.,
Victoria, BC V8T 4P4

Tel: 250-382-0442
www.xchangesgallery.org
www.facebook.com/Xchanges.Gallery
Year Founded: 1967 Celebrates the Victoria arts community.
Kate Seymour, President

Wells: Island Mountain Gallery
PO Box 65, 2323 Pooley St.,
Wells, BC V0K 2R0

Tel: 250-994-3466; *Fax:* 250-994-3433
Toll-Free: 800-442-2787
info@imarts.com
www.imarts.com
www.instagram.com/islandmountainarts
twitter.com/ima_arts
www.facebook .com/islandmountainarts
Year Founded: 1977 Provides visual, literary & performing arts
instruction; presents contemporary art exhibitions; concert venue
in summer; also holds workshops
Emma Jarrett, President
Kim Freeman, Vice-President
Julie Fowler, Executive Director, media@imarts.com

West Vancouver: Ferry Building Gallery
1414 Argyle Ave.,
West Vancouver, BC V7T 1C2

Tel: 604-925-7290
gallery@westvancouver.ca
ferrybuildinggallery.com
www.facebook.com/ferrybuildinggallery
Year Founded: 1989 Work by new & established artists who are
former & current residents of the North Shore area.

Whistler: Adele Campbell Fine Art Gallery
4090 Whistler Way,
Whistler, BC V0N 1B4

Tel: 604-938-0887
art@adelecampbell.com
www.adelecampbell.com
instagram.com/adelecampbellart
twitter.com/Whistlerart
Exhibits work by emerging & established Canadian artists.
Elizabeth Harris, Owner

Whistler: Mountain Galleries at the Fairmount
Fairmont Chateau Whistler
4599 Chateau Blvd.,
Whistler, BC V0N 1B4

604-935-1862 *Toll-Free:* 888-310-9726
whistler@mountaingalleries.com
www.mountaingalleries.com
www.instagram.com/mountaingalleries
twitter.com/MntGalleries
www.facebook.com/mountaingalleries
Exhibits work by Canadian artists.
Wendy Wacko, Founder & Executive Director
Elizabeth Peacock, Co-Director

Whistler: Whistler Contemporary Gallery
4293 Mountain Sq.,
Whistler, BC V0N 1B4

Tel: 604-938-3001; *Fax:* 604-938-3113
info@whistlerart.com
www.whistlerart.com
www.pinterest.com/WhistlerFineArt
twitter.com/whistlerfineart
www.face book.com/248419491849863
Year Founded: 1992 Whistler Contemporary Gallery represents
artists at various stages of their careers. They welcome
figurative, abstract and landscape styles. The gallery is open
daily.
Jeanine Messeguer, Director
Stephanie Young, Art Consultant

Williams Lake: Station House Gallery & Gift Shop
1 Mackenzie Ave. North,
Williams Lake, BC V2G 1N4

Tel: 250-392-6113
manager@stationhousegallery.com
www.stationhousegallery.com
twitter.com/stationhouseg
www.facebook.com /stationhousegallery
Year Founded: 1981 Monthly exhibitions; gift shop.
Kathryn Steen, President
Diane Toop, Executive Director

Manitoba
Provincial Art Galleries

The Winnipeg Art Gallery (WAG)
300 Memorial Blvd.,
Winnipeg, MB R3C 1V1

Tel: 204-786-6641
inquiries@wag.ca
wag.ca
www.instagram.com/wag_ca
twitter.com/wag_ca
www.facebook.com/wag.ca
Year Founded: 1912 The WAG is Western Canada's oldest civic
art gallery. With over 23,000 works in its collection, the WAG
features 9 galleries of contemporary & historical works (fine arts,
decorative arts & photography) by Manitoban, Canadian &
international artists. A highlight is the Gort Collection of Northern
Gothic & Renaissance paintings & altar panels.
Stephen Borys, Director & CEO, director-ceo@wag.ca
Maxine Bock, Executive Officer, executive-officer@wag.ca
Bill Elliott, Deputy Director & Chief Financial Officer,
belliott@wag.ca
Radovan Radulovic, Head, Museum Services,
visitor-museum-services-head@wag.ca

Local Art Galleries

Brandon: The Art Gallery of Southwestern Manitoba
(AGSM) / Le Musé D'art du Sud-ouest du Manitoba
#2, 710 Rosser Ave.,
Brandon, MB R7A 0K9

Tel: 204-727-1036; *Fax:* 204-726-8139
info@agsm.ca
www.agsm.ca
instagram.com/meetartagsm
twitter.com/TheAGSM
www.facebook.com/groups/ artgalleryswm
Year Founded: 1907 Contemporary Manitoban art;
approximately 16 exhibitions a year; open year round
Danielle Adriaansen, Chair
Deirdre Chisholm, Executive Director, director@agsm.ca
Lucie Lederhender, Curator, curator@agsm.ca

Charleswood: Pavilion Gallery Museum
Assiniboine Park, 55 Pavilion Cres.,
Charleswood, MB R3P 2N6

Tel: 204-927-6002; *Fax:* 204-927-7200
info@assiniboinepark.ca
www.travelmanitoba.com/listings/pavilion-gallery -museum/6716
Year Founded: 1930 The gallery museum features a large
collection of works by Ivan Eyre, Clarence Tillenius & Walter J.
Phillips, all renowned Manitoba artists. Open May-Sept.

Flin Flon: Northern Visual Arts Centre
177 Green St.,
Flin Flon, MB R8A 0G5

Tel: 204-686-4237
norvacentre@gmail.com
www.norvacentre.com
twitter.com/NorvaCentre
www.facebook.com/NorvaCent re
Year Founded: 2010 Gallery specializing in a variety of art forms,
includign pottery & painting. Visitors can watch artists at work.

Winnipeg: aceartinc.
208 Princess St.,
Winnipeg, MB R3B 1L4

Tel: 204-944-9763
www.aceart.org
instagram.com/aceartinc
twitter.com/aceartinc
aceartinc. is an artist-run centre dedicated to the development,
exhibition & dissemination of contemporary art by cultural
producers; dedicated to cultural diversity
Allison Yearwood, Chair
Tani Miki, Director, Finance & Administration, tani@aceart.org
Brianna Wentz, Director, Special Projects Coordination,
brianna@aceart.org

Winnipeg: Birchwood Art Gallery
1068 Pembina Hwy.,
Winnipeg, MB R3T 1Z8

Tel: 204-888-5840*Toll-Free:* 800-822-5840
sales@birchwoodartgallery.com
www.birchwoodartgallery.com
www.facebook .com/birchwoodartgallerywpg
Year Founded: 1993

Winnipeg: Centre culturel franco-manitobain (CCFM)
340, boul Provencher,
Winnipeg, MB R2H 0G7

Tel: 204-233-8972; *Fax:* 204-233-3324
reception@ccfm.mb.ca
www.ccfm.mb.ca
twitter.com/CCFManitoba
www.fa cebook.com/CCFManitoba
Year Founded: 1974 Le Centre culturel franco-manitobain a un
rôle de premier plan comme maison de la culture et carrefour de
la vie culturelle et artistique en français à Winnipeg et au
Manitoba/The Centre culturel franco-manitobain is the focal point
of French cultural life in Winnipeg & Manitoba
Ginette Lavack, Directrice générale, glavack@ccfm.mb.ca

Winnipeg: Loch Gallery
Winnipeg
306 St. Mary's Rd.,
Winnipeg, MB R2H 1J8

Tel: 204-791-2239
winnipeg@lochgallery.com
www.lochgallery.com
www.instagram.com/loch_gallery
twitter.com/lochgallery
www.facebook.co m/lochgallery
Year Founded: 1972 Work by Canadian & European artists both
contemporary & historical.

Winnipeg: Plug In ICA Gallery
460 Portage Ave.,
Winnipeg, MB R3C 0E8

Tel: 204-942-1043
info@plugin.org
www.plugin.org
plug-in-ica.tumblr.com
www.facebook.com/pluginica
This gallery is centred on analysing & exploring society's issues
through the use of multidisciplinary art forms.
Sotirios Kotoulas, President
Julie Nagam, Vice-President
Jenifer Papararo, Executive Director

Winnipeg: School of Art Gallery
ARTlab, School of Art, University of Manitoba, #255, 180
Dafoe Rd.,
Winnipeg, MB R3T 2N2

Tel: 204-474-9322
gallery@umanitoba.ca
umanitoba.ca/schools/art
Year Founded: 1965 The gallery exhibits & collects
contemporary & historical art, & includes the FitzGerald Study
Collection, featuring papers, drawings & watercolours of L.L.
Fitzgerald. Open year round.

Winnipeg: University of Winnipeg Fine Art Collection &
Gallery 1C03
515 Portage Ave.,
Winnipeg, MB R3B 2E9

Tel: 204-786-7811
www.uwinnipeg.ca/index/artgallery-index
gallery1c03.blogspot.ca
twitter.com/1c03
www.facebook.com/gallery1c03
Year Founded: 1986 19th & 20th century paintings, drawings,
prints, photographs & sculptures; open year round; offers
exhibitions, talks, panel discussions, screenings & other public
programming

Winnipeg: Urban Shaman: Contemporary Aboriginal Art
(US)
203-290 McDermot Ave.,
Winnipeg, MB R3B 0T2

Tel: 204-942-2674; *Fax:* 204-942-2674
info@urbanshaman.org
urbanshaman.org
Exhibits contemporary work by First Nations, Métis & Inuit
artists.
Diana Warren, Director, daina@urbanshaman.org

New Brunswick
Provincial Art Galleries

Owens Art Gallery
Mount Allison University, 61 York St.,
Sackville, NB E4L 1E1

Tel: 506-364-2574
owens@mta.ca
www.mta.ca/owens
twitter.com/owensartgallery
www.facebook.com/owensartgallery
Year Founded: 1895 Permanent collection of over 2500 works,
dating from the 18th century; 30 exhibitions yearly
Emily Falvey, Director & Curator, 506-364-2576,
efalvey@mta.ca

Local Art Galleries

Campbellton: Galerie Restigouche Gallery
39 Andrew St.,
Campbellton, NB E3N 3H1

Tel: 506-753-5750
galerie.restigouche@gmail.com
www.facebook.com/galerierestigouchegallery
Year Founded: 1975

Edmundston: Galerie Colline
195, boul Hébert,
Edmundston, NB E3V 2S8

Tél: 506-737-5282
www.galeriecolline.com
www.facebook.com/galerie.colline
Fondée en: 1968 Trente ans d'expositions d'artistes amateurs &
professionnels qui ont aidé à favoriser une appréciation de l'art
dans la communauté.
Jacques Paul Couturier, Présidente & Vice Chancelier

Fredericton: Beaverbrook Art Gallery / La galerie d'art
Beaverbrook
PO Box 605, 703 Queen St.,
Fredericton, NB E3B 1C4

Tel: 506-458-2028; *Fax:* 506-459-7450
emailbag@beaverbrookartgallery.org
www.beaverbrookartgallery.org
twitt er.com/BeaverbrookAG
www.facebook.com/BeaverbrookArtGallery
Year Founded: 1959 Atlantic Canadian art & historical British art;
open year round
Tom Smart, Director & CEO, 506-458-2030,
tsmart@beaverbrookartgallery.org
Terry Graff, Chief Curator

Fredericton: Connexion ARC
Charlotte Street Arts Centre, 732 Charlotte St.,
Fredericton, NB E3B 1M5

Tel: 506-478-4484
info@connexionarc.org
www.connexionarc.org
www.instagram.com/connexion.arc
twitter.com/connexionarc
www.facebook. com/ConnexionArtistRunCentre
Artist-run centre, non-profit & non commercial; gallery exists for
the purpose of exhibiting, supporting & promoting the
development & understanding of all forms of contemporary art
practice of local, national & international significance.
Christina Lovegrove Thomson, President
Kasie Wilcox, Executive Director

Fredericton: Gallery 78
796 Queen St.,
Fredericton, NB E3B 1C6

Tel: 506-454-5192; *Fax:* 506-443-0199
Toll-Free: 888-883-8322
art@gallery78.com
www.gallery78.com
www.instagram.com/gallery78official
twitter.com/Gallery78
www.facebook.com/Gallery78.ca
Year Founded: 1976 Exhibits visual art, with a focus on work by
Atlantic Canadians & artists from New Brunswick.
Inge Pataki, Founder

Fredericton: New Brunswick Art Bank
20 McGloin St.,
Fredericton, NB E3A 5T8

collection.art.nb@gnb.ca
www2.gnb.ca
Year Founded: 1968 The Art Bank has over 700 works of art by
250 New Brunswick artists in its collection. The art is accessible
to the public through the Bank's loans program, & the Bank
purchases art biannually through its acquisitions program. The

exhibition program allows the work to be displayed publicly both in New Brunswick & elsewhere.

Fredericton: UNB Art Centre
Memorial Hall, University of New Brunswick, PO Box 4400, 9 Bailey Dr.,
Fredericton, NB E3B 5A3

Tel: 506-453-4623
artcntr@unb.ca
www.unb.ca/cel/enrichment/art-centre/index.html
www.instagram.com/discoverunb
twitter.com/UNB
www.facebook.com/uofnb
Historical & contemporary exhibitions; interpretive programs; Atlantic art collection
Marie Maltais, Director

Moncton: Atelier IMAGO
Centre Culturel Aberdeen, 140 Botsford St.,
Moncton, NB E1C 4X5

Tel: 506-388-1431
atelierestampeimago@gmail.com
www.atelierimago.com
www.facebook.com/AtelierImagoInc
Year Founded: 1986 Artist-run not-for-profit printmaking studio.

Moncton: Galerie d'art Louise-et-Reuben-Cohen
Campus de Moncton, Université de Moncton, 405 Universitén Ave.,
Moncton, NB E1A 3E9

Tél: 506-858-4687
nisk.imbeault@umoncton.ca
www.umoncton.ca/umcm-ga
twitter.com/galeriedartlrc
Fondée en: 1964 La Galerie a pour mission encourager la créativité des artistes acadiens/acadiennes & collectioner & documenter les oeuvres d'art; centre de documentation; programmation.
Nisk Imbeault, Directrice & Conservatrice, 506-858-4687, nisk.imbeault@umoncton.ca

Moncton: Galerie Sans Nom Coop Ltée (GSN)
Centre Culturel Aberdeen, 140 Botsford St.,
Moncton, NB E1C 4X5

Tél: 506-854-5381
direction@galeriesansnom.org
www.galeriesansnom.org
www.instagram.com/galeriesansnom
twitter.com/GalerieSansNom
www.facebo ok.com/galeriesansnomorg
Fondée en: 1977 Galerie Sans Nom (GSN) est à but non lucratif centre géré par des artistes engagés dans la promotion, la production & l'exposition d'art contemporain. GSN est un lieu d'expression créative de la communauté artistique & agissant comme un moyen de communication essentiel, fournit une impulsion à l'innovation & la créativité.
Paul Édouard Bourque, Président
Annie France Noël, Directrice

Saint John: Saint John Arts Centre (SJAC)
20 Peel Plaza,
Saint John, NB E2L 3G6

Tel: 506-633-4870
www.sjartscentre.ca
twitter.com/SJArtsCentre
www.facebook.com/SaintJohnArtsCentre
First municipally funded art gallery in Atlantic Canada; features monthly exhibitions of local & regional art works
Andrew Kierstead, Executive Director, director@sjartscentre.ca

St Andrews: Sunbury Shores Arts & Nature Centre
139 Water St.,
St Andrews, NB E5B 1A7

Tel: 506-529-3386
info@sunburyshores.org
www.sunburyshores.org
www.facebook.com/sunburyshores
Year Founded: 1964 Provides facilities for the study, practice & appreciation of the art, crafts & environmental sciences; stresses the aesthetic appreciation of nature & the importance of its use
Joel Mason, Artistic Director

Newfoundland & Labrador
Local Art Galleries

Corner Brook: Grenfell Art Gallery
Fine Arts Bldg., Memorial University of Newfoundland, 20 University Dr.,
Corner Brook, NL A2H 5G4

Tel: 709-637-6209
gallery@grenfell.mun.ca
www.grenfellartgallery.ca
www.instagram.com/grenfellartgallery
twitter.com/grenfellgallery
www.f acebook.com/GrenfellArtGallery
Contemporary art; Hours of Operation: Tu-F 11-4

St. John's: Eastern Edge Art Gallery
72 Harbour Dr.,
St. John's, NL A1C 6K1

Tel: 709-739-1882; *Fax:* 709-739-1866
easternedgegallery@gmail.com
www.easternedge.ca
twitter.com/easternedg e
www.facebook.com/easternedgeart
Year Founded: 1984 Not-for-profit, artist-run centre dedicated to exhibiting contemporary art in diverse media; exhibitions include work by Newfoundland artists & artists from the rest of Canada
Philippa Jones, Executive Director, director@easternedge.ca
Daniel Rumbolt, Operations Manager

Tors Cove: Five Island Art Gallery
7 Cove Rd.,
Tors Cove, NL A0A 4A0

Tel: 709-334-3645*Toll-Free:* 866-876-3645
fiveislandgallery@nf.aibn.com
www.newfoundlandlabrador.com
twitter.com /fiveislandart
Work by local artists including paintings, sculptures & rugs.

Twillingate: Ted Stuckless Fine Arts & Driftwood Gallery
124 Main St.,
Twillingate, NL A0G 4M0

Tel: 709-884-2568
tedstucklessart@gmail.com
www.tedstuckless.com
Pencil sketches, paintings & other artwork.

Northwest Territories
Territorial Art Galleries

Gallery of the Midnight Sun
5005 Bryson Dr.,
Yellowknife, NT X1A 2A3

Tel: 867-873-8064
gallerymidnightsun@theedge.ca
www.nwtarts.com/organization-profile/gallery-midnight-sun
www.facebook.c om/nwtarts
Year Founded: 1989 NWT's largest selection of Inuit & Dene arts & crafts

Nova Scotia
Provincial Art Galleries

Art Gallery of Nova Scotia (AGNS)
341 Main St.,
Yarmouth, NS B5A 1E7

Tel: 902-749-2248; *Fax:* 902-749-2255
angela.collier@novascotia.ca
www.artgalleryofnovascotia.ca/visit-yarmout h
www.instagram.com/artgalleryns
twitter.com/ArtGalleryNS
www.facebook.com/ArtGalleryNS
Year Founded: 2006 This is Atlantic Canada's largest art museum, with locations in Halifax and Yarmouth. The Gallery's permanent collection has over 17,000 pieces. It is also a centre for visual arts education.
Nancy Nobel, Director & CEO, 902-424-8075, Nancy.Noble@novascotia.ca
Sarah Fillmore, Chief Curator & Deputy Director, Programs, sarah.fillmore@novascotia.ca

Art Gallery of Nova Scotia Halifax (AGNS)
1723 Hollis St.,
Halifax, NS B5A 1E7

Tel: 902-424-5280; *Fax:* 902-424-7359
info.agns@novascotia.ca
www.artgalleryofnovascotia.ca
www.instagram.com/artgalleryns
twitter.com/ArtGalleryNS
www.facebook.com/ArtGalleryNS

Year Founded: 1908 Housed in the historic Dominion Building, which was built in 1865, the Art Gallery of Nova Scotia has over 17,000 pieces of art. These collections consist of a wide range of artwork that include Inuit stone carvings, Nova Scotian folk art & classical portraits.
Nancy Noble, Director & CEO, 902-424-8075, nancy.noble@novascotia.ca
Sarah Fillmore, Chief Curator & Deputy Director, Programs, sarah.fillmore@novascotia.ca

Local Art Galleries

Antigonish: St. Francis Xavier Art Gallery
Bloomfield Centre,
Antigonish, NS B2G 2W5

Tel: 902-867-2303; *Fax:* 902-867-5115
gallery@stfx.ca
sites.stfx.ca/artgallery
www.facebook.com/StfxArtGalle ry
Year Founded: 1976 Exhibits work by Nova Scotia artists

Chéticamp: Les Trois Pignon
c/o La Société St-Pierre, CP 430,
Chéticamp, NS B0E 1H0

Tél: 902-224-2642; *Téléc:* 902-224-1579
info@lestroispignons.com
www.lestroispignons.com
twitter.com/LesTroisP ignons
www.facebook.com/lestroispignons
Fondée en: 1947 Les tapisseries du Dr. Elizabeth LeFort ainsi que d'autres tapis historiques de la région; le musée d'antiquité à Marguerite Gallant est attaché sur la Galerie aussi que centre généalogique
Lisette Aucoin-Bourgeois, Directrice générale, dg@lestroispignons.com

Halifax: Anna Leonowens Gallery
1891 Granville St.,
Halifax, NS B3J 3L6

Tel: 902-494-8223
annaleonowens@nscad.ca
www.alg.nscad.ca
www.instagram.com/annaleonowensgallery
www.facebook.com/AnnaLeonowensGal lery
Year Founded: 1968 Work primarily by students of the school.
Melanie Colosimo, Director, 902-494-8184, mcolosimo@nscad.ca

Halifax: Centre for Art Tapes
2238 Maitland St.,
Halifax, NS B3K 2Z9

info@cfat.ca
cfat.ca
twitter.com/CentreforArtTap
www.facebook.com/centre4arttapes
Year Founded: 1979 An artist-run centre that facilitates & supports emerging, intermediate & established artists working with electronic media, such as video, audio & new media; strives to provide production facilities, ongoing programming & training to a diverse membership whose creative abilities contribute to social & artistic goals
Tori Fleming, Executive Director, tori@cfat.ca
Jesse Mitchell, Coordinator, Programming, jesse@cfat.ca

Halifax: Centre for Craft Nova Scotia
#140, 1061 & 1096 Marginal Rd.,
Halifax, NS B3H 4P7

Tel: 902-424-2522
centre.admin@craftnovascotia.ca
craft-design.ns.ca
www.instagram.com/centreforcraft
twitter.com/NSCraftStudios
www.facebo ok.com/centreforcraft
Other contact information: Studio: 902-492-2524
Year Founded: 1991 Develops & promotes crafts & design in Nova Scotia; includes the Mary E. Black Gallery, a craft showroom, an info. centre, & 5 studios; open year round
Emily Blair Wareham, Director

Halifax: Eye Level Gallery
2482 Maynard St.,
Halifax, NS B3K 1K4

Tel: 902-425-6412
eyelevel.appointlet.com
www.eyelevelgallery.ca
twitter.com/EyeLevelGallery
www.facebook.com/EY ELEVEL.arc
Year Founded: 1974 Not-for-profit organization dedicated to presenting, developing, & promoting contemporary art.
Carrie Allison Payiw, Co-Chair
Amanda Shore, Co-Chair
Sally Wolchyn-Raab, Artistic Director, director@eyelevel.art

Halifax: The Khyber Centre for the Arts / Le Khybre
Parent: Khyber Arts Society
1880 Hollis St.,
Halifax, NS B3J 1W6

Tel: 902-422-9668
info@khyber.ca
www.khyber.ca
www.facebook.com/khybercentre/
Year Founded: 1995 Apart from art exhibitions, the Khyber offers concerts, an educational program for kids, lectures, & fund-raising events.
Daniel Joyce, Artistic Director, director@khyber.ca

Halifax: MSVU Art Gallery, Mount Saint Vincent University
166 Bedford Hwy.,
Halifax, NS B3M 2J6

Tel: 902-457-6160
art.gallery@msvu.ca
msvuart.ca
twitter.com/msvuartgallery
www.facebook.com/MSVUArtGallery
Year Founded: 1971 Open daily except Mondays; exhibition program emphasizes women as cultural subjects & producers, new Nova Scotia artists, & themes relevant to the university's academic programs; admission free
Laura Ritchie, Director, laura.ritchie@msvu.ca
David Dahms, Gallery Technician, david.dahms@msvuart.ca
Claire Dykhuis, Coordinator, Education & Outreach,
claire.dykhuis@msvu.ca

Halifax: Port Loggia Gallery
1107 Marginal Rd.,
Halifax, NS B3H 4P8

Tel: 902-442-8769
www.canadianart.ca/galleries/port-loggia-gallery
Work by undergraduate & graduate students.

Halifax: Saint Mary's University Art Gallery
923 Robie St.,
Halifax, NS B3H 3C3

Tel: 902-420-5445
gallery@smu.ca
www.smu.ca/campus-life/art-gallery.html
www.facebook.com/SMUartGallery
Year Founded: 1971 Contemporary visual arts by artists within & outside the region; lectures, publications & performing arts program; permanent collection of over 1,800 works
Pam Corell, Assistant Curator, pam.corell@smu.ca

Lunenburg: Lunenburg Art Gallery (LAG)
PO Box 1418,
Lunenburg, NS B0J 2C0

Tel: 902-640-4044
info@lunenburgartsociety.ca
www.lunenburgartgallery.com
twitter.com/art_lag
www.facebook.com/Lunen burgArtGallery
Year Founded: 1972 The gallery promotes the works of local, provincial & international artists, sponsors workshops & raises funds; houses the Meldrum collection by the late Earl Bailly; month-long solo exhibitions & ongoing Members Gallery; open seasonally: Mar.-Oct., Tu-Sa 10:00-5:00 & Su 1:00-5:00.
Wendy Muise, President, president@lunenburgartsociety.ca
James Gray, Treasurer, treasurer@lunenburgartsociety.ca

Sydney: Cape Breton University Art Gallery
1250 Grand Lake Rd.,
Sydney, NS B1P 6L2

Tel: 902-563-1342
art_gallery@cbu.ca
www.cbu.ca/community/art-gallery
www.instagram.com/cbuartgallery
www.facebook.com/CBUArtGallery1
First & only full-time public art gallery on Cape Breton Island; acquires & presents art with emphasis on contemporary Canadian works & the artistic traditions of Cape Breton Island; offers educational & research facilities; a major cultural resource within the educational & research context of the university

Wolfville: Acadia University Art Gallery
10 Highland Ave.,
Wolfville, NS B4P 2R6

Tel: 902-585-1373
artgallery@acadiau.ca
gallery.acadiau.ca
www.instagram.com/AcadiaGallery
twitter.com/AcadiaGallery
www.facebook .com/artgallery.acadiauniversity
Year Founded: 1978 The University Gallery serves both as a public gallery & as a teaching facility within Acadia's Faculty of Arts. Its purpose in the community & on the campus is to enrich

visual experience through showcasing original works of historical or contemporary importance. The Gallery looks after Acadia's collection of art.
Laurie Dalton, Director/Curator

Ontario

Provincial Art Galleries

Art Gallery of Hamilton (AGH)
123 King St. West,
Hamilton, ON L8P 4S8

Tel: 905-527-6610; *Fax:* 905-577-6940
info@artgalleryofhamilton.com
www.artgalleryofhamilton.com
www.instagram.com/at_theagh
twitter.com/TheAGH
www.facebook.com/artgalleryofhamilton
Year Founded: 1914 Collection of 8,000 art objects; holds one of Canada's most comprehensive collections of Canadian historical, modern & contemporary art; British, American & European works
Shelley Falconer, President & CEO, 905-527-6610, shelley@artgalleryofhamilton.com
Greg Dawe, Chief Preparator, 905-527-6610, greg@artgalleryofhamilton.com
Tobi Bruce, Senior Curator & Director, Exhibitions & Collections, 905-527-6610, tobi@artgalleryofhamilton.com
Tor Lukasik-Foss, Director, Programs & Education, 905-527-6610, tor@artgalleryofhamilton.com
Cindy M.Carson, Director CFRE, Partnerships & Development, 905-527-6610, cindy@artgalleryofhamilton.com

Art Gallery of Ontario (AGO) / Musée des beaux-arts de l'Ontario
317 Dundas St. West,
Toronto, ON M5T 1G4

Tel: 416-979-6648*Toll-Free:* 877-225-4246
www.ago.ca
www.instagram.com/agotoronto
twitter.com/agotoronto
www.facebook.com/AGOToronto
Other contact information: Donations: 416-979-6619
Year Founded: 1918 The AGO, located in the heart of Toronto, has an expansive art collection that includes European Old Masters, Group of Seven, & Canadian & international contemporary works. The Gallery also displays the world's largest public collection of sculptures created by Henry Moore.
Stephan Jost, Michael & Sonja Koerner Director & CEO
Rocco Saverino, Chief Financial Officer
Julian Cox, Deputy Director & Chief Curator
Lisa Clements, Chief, Communications & Brand
Christy Thompson, Chief, Exhibitions & Collections
Mike Mahoney, Executive Director, Corporate Special Projects

Art Gallery of Windsor (AGW)
401 Riverside Dr. West,
Windsor, ON N9A 7J1

Tel: 519-977-0013
visit@agw.ca
www.agw.ca
www.instagram.com/agw401
twitter.com/AGW401
www.facebook.com/agw401
Year Founded: 1943 One of the larger, non-government run galleries in Ontario; focus is on Canadian art in an international context; permanent collection of 2,500 paintings & sculptures; resource centre & gift shop.
Jennifer Matotek, Executive Director

Government of Ontario Art Collection
134 Ian Macdonald Blvd.,
Toronto, ON M7A 2C5

Tel: 416-327-1600
reference@ontario.ca
www.archives.gov.on.ca/en/goac/index.aspx
The Government of Ontario's art collection is spread throughout ministry & government offices around Toronto, although many of the works are featured in the Legislative Building. In all, the collection comprises around 2,500 pieces.

McMichael Canadian Art Collection
10365 Islington Ave.,
Kleinburg, ON L0J 1C0

Tel: 905-893-1121*Toll-Free:* 888-213-1121
info@mcmichael.com
www.mcmichael.com
www.instagram.com/mcmichaelgallery
twitter.com/mcacgallery
www.faceboo k.com/mcmichaelgallery
Year Founded: 1965 The collection features works of art created by First Nations & Inuit artists, the artists of the Group of Seven

& their contemporaries, & other artists who have contributed to the development of Canadian art. Comprehensive education programs at kindergarten, elementary & secondary school levels; guided group tours by appt.; extension & temporary exhibition programs. Programs are also available for adults.
Andy Pringle, Chair, Board of Trustees
Doug McDonald, Chair, McMichael Canadian Art Foundation Board
Ian Dejardin, Executive Director

Local Art Galleries

Amherstburg: Gibson Gallery
140 Richmond St.,
Amherstburg, ON N9V 1G4

Tel: 519-736-2826
office@gibsonartgallery.com
www.gibsonartgallery.com
twitter.com/ARTamherstburg
www.facebook.com/G ibsonGallery
Year Founded: 1975 Gibson Gallery features works by local artists, photographers and stitchers. The gallery also offers arts and crafts classes for kids and adults, as well as a number of creative guilds. Hours of operation are Thursday to Sunday, 11:00 to 5:00.
Bonnie Deslippe, Office Administrator

Aurora: Aurora Cultural Centre
22 Church St.,
Aurora, ON L4G 1G4

Tel: 905-713-1818
info@auroraculturalcentre.ca
www.auroraculturalcentre.ca
www.instagram.com/auroraculturalcentre
twitter.com/auroraculture
www.f acebook.com/AuroraCulturalCentre
Year Founded: 2010 The centre exhibits visual artwork, holds concerts & provides art classes for the Aurora community.
Laura Schembri, Executive Director

Bancroft: The Art Gallery of Bancroft (AGB)
PO Box 398, 10 Flint Ave.,
Bancroft, ON K0L 1C0

Tel: 613-332-1542
artgalleryofbancroft@gmail.com
www.artgallerybancroft.ca
www.facebook.com/artbancroft
Local & other Ontario artists; gift shop for area artists only; open year round

Barrie: MacLaren Art Centre
37 Mulcaster St.,
Barrie, ON L4M 3M2

Tel: 705-721-9696
maclaren@maclarenart.com
www.maclarenart.com
twitter.com/MacLarenArt
www.facebook.com/maclarena rt
Year Founded: 1986 Open Tu-F 10:00-5:00, Sa 10:00-4:00
Lisa Daniels, Executive Director

Bloomfield: OENO Gallery
2274 County Rd #1,
Bloomfield, ON K0K 1G0

Tel: 613-393-2216; *Fax:* 613-393-2215
info@oenogallery.com
oenogallery.com
www.youtube.com/user/oenogallery
twitter.com/OenoGallery
www.facebook. com/29363322998
Year Founded: 2004 OENO exhibits artwork by mid-career and senior Canadian artists. The gallery is a member of Art Dealers Association of Canada, and is open Monday to Sunday, 10:00 to 5:00pm.
Carlyn Moulton, Owner & Curator
Sandra Goldie, Director
John MacDonald, Art Consultant
Dana Charles, Logistics & Communications Director

Bowmanville: Visual Arts Centre of Clarington (VAC)
PO Box 52, 143 Simpson Ave.,
Bowmanville, ON L1C 3K8

Tel: 905-623-5831
communications@vac.ca
www.vac.ca
www.instagram.com/visualartscentre
twitter.com/c_vac
www.facebook.com/ visualartscentre.clarington
A non-profit visual arts gallery
Mary Anne Slemon, President
Anna McQuaid, Vice-President

Dionne Powlenzuk, Executive Director, 905-623-5831, director@vac.ca
Sandy Saad, Curator, 905-623-5831, curator@vac.ca

Bracebridge: Chapel Gallery
c/o Muskoka Arts & Crafts Inc., PO Box 376,
Bracebridge, ON P1L 1T7
Tel: 705-645-5501; *Fax:* 705-645-0385
info@muskokaartsandcrafts.com
www.muskokaartsandcrafts.com/Chapel_Galler
y/chapel_gallery.htm
Year Founded: 1989 The Chapel Gallery has been the home of
Muskoka Arts & Crafts since the fall of 1989. The Gallery hosts
various lectures and workshops offered to members and the
public.
Shanandoah Kidd, President
Elene J. Freer, Executive Director

Brampton: Beaux-Arts Brampton
70 Main St. North,
Brampton, ON L6V 2B2
Tel: 905-454-5677 *Toll-Free:* 866-339-7779
beauxart1@bellnet.ca
beaux-artsbrampton.com
www.instagram.com/beauxartsbrampton
twitter.com/beauxartsbab
www.faceb ook.com/BeauxArtsBrampton
This centre celebrates the work of new & experienced
multi-media & visual artists as well as photographers.
Vanessa Scott, President
Erica Philips, Vice-President
Regan Hayward, Executive Director,
regan@beauxartsbrampton.org

Brampton: Peel Art Gallery, Museum & Archives
(PAMA)
Peel Heritage Complex, 9 Wellington St. East,
Brampton, ON L6W 1Y1
Tel: 905-791-4055; *Fax:* 905-451-4931
infopama@peelregion.ca
pama.peelregion.ca
www.facebook.com/visitPAMA
Year Founded: 1968 Located within a cluster of 19th century
buildings; features the works of local artists in Peel &
contemporary art from across Canada; collection of over 1,500
works consists of contemporary & historic Canadian works with
a special emphasis on artists from Peel.
Sharona Adamowicz-Clements, Curator

Brantford: Glenhyrst Art Gallery of Brant
20 Ava Rd.,
Brantford, ON N3T 5G9
Tel: 519-756-5932
info@glenhyrst.ca
www.glenhyrst.ca
www.facebook.com/ Glenhyrst
Year Founded: 1986 Permanent collection comprises
contemporary works on paper & paintings by Robert Reginald
Whale & his descendants; offers a rotating schedule of art
exhibitions, an art rental & sales showroom, giftshop & a variety
of classes & programmes
Leslie Barker, President, board@glenhyrst.ca
Matthew Ryan Smith, Curator & Head, Collections,
curator@glenhyrst.ca

Bright's Grove: Gallery in the Grove
PO Box 339, 2618 Hamilton Park Rd.,
Bright's Grove, ON N0N 1C0
Tel: 519-869-4643
info@galleryinthegrove.com
www.galleryinthegrove.com
The gallery is housed on the second floor of the historic
Faethorne House, circa 1875. Open M-Th 11:00-5:00, Sa
11:00-3:00.

Brockville: Marianne van Silfhout Gallery
Brockville Campus, St. Lawrence College, 2288 Parkedale
Ave.,
Brockville, ON K6V 5X3
Tel: 613-345-0660
www.stlawrencecollege.ca
Located at the front atrium of the Brockville campus; operating
hours: Tuesday to Friday 10 am to 8 pm, Monday and Saturday
10 am to 4 pm.

Burlington: Art Gallery of Burlington (AGB)
1333 Lakeshore Rd.,
Burlington, ON L7S 1A9
Tel: 905-632-7796; *Fax:* 905-632-0278
info@artgalleryofburlington.com
artgalleryofburlington.com
www.linkedin.com/company/burlington-art-centre
twitter.com/ArtGallBurl
www.facebook.com/ArtGallBurl
Year Founded: 1978 Exhibitions of regional & nationally
recognized Canadian artists; a permanent collection of
contemporary Canadian ceramic art & a gallery shop, art rental
& sales & studios; open daily

Cambridge: Idea Exchange
Queen's Square, 1 North Square,
Cambridge, ON N1S 2K6
Tel: 519-621-0460; *Fax:* 519-621-2080
ideaexchange.org
twitter.com/IdeaXchng
www.facebook.com/IdeaXchng
Exhibitions offered at 6 locations within Cambridge reflect a
range of local & international developments in contemporary &
historical visual arts & architecture; collection of contemporary
Canadian fibre art; studio courses for all ages; concerts
Marcie Bronson, Director & Curator,
mbronson@ideaexchange.org

Chatham: Thames Art Gallery (TAG)
Chatham Cultural Centre, 75 William St. North,
Chatham, ON N7M 4L4
Tel: 519-360-1998
ckartgallery@chatham-kent.ca
www.tagartspace.com
twitter.com/TAG_CK
www.facebook.com/tagck
Year Founded: 1975 Historical & contemporary artwork by local,
national & international artists; hosts 12-15 exhibitions a year;
guided tours available with advanced bookings; art lectures &
workshops for children & adults; open daily 1-5; admission by
donation
Phil Vanderwall, Director/Curator

Cobourg: Art Gallery of Northumberland
Victoria Hall, 55 King St. West, 3rd Fl.,
Cobourg, ON K9A 2M2
Tel: 905-372-0333
www.artgalleryofnorthumberland.com
twitter.com/ArtGofN
www.facebook.com/ArtGalleryOfNorthumberland
Year Founded: 1960 Maintains a permanent collection of more
than 600 works of art; changing exhibitions are displayed
throughout the year; lectures; education trips; workshops &
special events
Michael Maynard, President & Chair
Olinda Casimiro, Executive Director, ocasimiro@agncobourg.ca

Colborne: Colborne Art Gallery
PO Box 903, 51 King St. East,
Colborne, ON K0K 1S0
Tel: 905-355-1798
info@thecolborneartgallery.ca
www.thecolborneartgallery.ca
www.facebook.com/159525184113252
Year Founded: 1997 Colborne Art Gallery welcomes
independent artists such as photographers, painters, sculptors,
printmakers and mixed media artists to exhibit their work. Gallery
hours are Thursday to Sunday 12:00-4:00.
Judith Hawkins, Membership Chair

Curve Lake Indian Reserve: Whetung Ojibwa Centre
875 County Rd. 22,
Curve Lake Indian Reserve, ON K0L 1R0
Tel: 705-657-3661
info@whetung.com
www.whetung.com
www.facebook.com/WhetungOjibwaCentre
Year Founded: 1966 Craft centre & art gallery; authentic works
by Indian artists from across Canada.
Michael Whetung, Owner, mwhetung@whetung.com

Dundas: The Carnegie Gallery
Andrew Carnegie Library, 10 King St. West,
Dundas, ON L9H 1T7
Tel: 905-627-4265
carnegie@carnegiegallery.org
www.carnegiegallery.org
twitter.com/carnegiegallery
www.facebook.com/c arnegiegallery
Year Founded: 1980 This is an artist run, non-profit gallery
located in the town of Dundas.
Pam Norman, Chair

Marla Panko, Curator, info@carnegiegallery.org

Durham: Durham Art Gallery
PO Box 1021, 250 George St. E.,
Durham, ON N0G 1R0
Tel: 519-369-3692
info@durhamart.on.ca
www.durhamart.on.ca
www.facebook.com/Durham.Art.Gallery
The gallery features 6 exhibits by established artists & 6 exhibits
from emerging arts from Durham & surrounding areas per year.
They also are involved with festivals, lectures & performances.
Jaclyn Quaresma, Executive Director & Curator

Fergus: Wellington Artists' Gallery & Art Centre
6142 Wellington Rd. 29,
Fergus, ON N1M 2W5
Tel: 519-843-6303
wellingtonartistsgallery@outlook.com
www.wellingtonart istsgallery.ca
twitter.com/WAGArtFergus
www.facebook.com/2143039285842 09
Year Founded: 2006 Wellington Artists' Gallery and Art Centre
exhibits art such as paintings, mixed media art, crafts, pottery &
carvings and more. The gallery is open from May to November,
Wednesday to Sunday, 11:00 to 5:00pm.
Emery Dawson, Co-Owner
John McGill, Chairperson, 519-843-8850,
johnsmcgill@outlook.com

Fort Erie: Mewinzha Archaeology Gallery
Parent: Fort Erie Museum Services
100 Queen St.,
Fort Erie, ON L2A 3S6
Tel: 905-894-5322
www.museum.forterie.ca
Native tools, weapons & contemporary artwork; a joint project
between the Buffalo-Fort Erie Public Bridge Authority, the Town
of Fort Erie, Fort Erie Museum Services & the Fort Erie Native
Friendship Centre

Goderich: Elizabeth's Art Gallery
54 Courthouse Sq.,
Goderich, ON N7A 1M5
Tel: 519-524-4080
artinfo@elizabeths.ca
www.elizabeths.ca
www.youtube.com/user/ArtAwhile
twitter.com/ArtAwhile
www.facebook.com/203810526308209
Other contact information: www.pinterest.com/artawhile;
www.instagram.com/artawhile
Year Founded: 1992 Elizabeth's Art Gallery exhibits work by
artist Elizabeth Van den Broeck as well as by other artists.
Works include original paintings, fine crafts and jewellery. The
gallery also offers services such as printing, framing, art supplies
and a camera club. Hours: M-Sa 10:00-5:00
Elizabeth Van den Broeck, Owner

Grimsby: Grimsby Public Art Gallery
18 Carnegie Lane,
Grimsby, ON L3M 1Y1
Tel: 905-945-3246
www.grimsby.ca
www.instagram.com/theGPAG
twitter.com/thegpag
www.facebook.com/thegpag
Year Founded: 1975 Permanent collection of 1,000+ works;
contemporary exhibitions & programmes year round

Guelph: Art Gallery of Guelph
358 Gordon St.,
Guelph, ON N1G 1Y1
Tel: 519-837-0010
info@artgalleryofguelph.ca
artgalleryofguelph.ca
Year Founded: 1980 Established in 1978 as the former
Macdonald Stewart Art Centre, the AGG operates today with
three sponsors: the University of Guelph, City of Guelph and the
Upper Grand District School Board. Its collection holds of over
10,000 Canadian and international works.
Shauna McCabe, Executive Director,
smccabe@artgalleryofguelph.ca

Haileybury: Temiskaming Art Gallery / Galerie d'Art du
Temaiskaming
PO Box 1090,
Haileybury, ON P0J 1K0
Tel: 705-672-3706
info@temiskamingartgallery.ca
www.temiskamingartgallery.ca
twitter.com/TemisArtGallery

Public gallery; open year round
Melissa La Porte, Executive Director & Curator

Haliburton: Ethel Curry Gallery
PO Box 242, 94 Maple Ave.,
Haliburton, ON K0M 1S0

Tel: 705-457-9687
wayne@theethelcurrygallery.com
www.instagram.com/ethelcurrygallery
www.facebook.com/TheEthelCurryGaller y
This gallery displays the work of Ontario artists, who have been inspired by nature.
Wayne Hooks, Owner
Tiffany Howe, Curator

Haliburton: Rails End Gallery & Arts Centre
23 York St.,
Haliburton, ON K0M 1S0

Tel: 705-457-2330
info@railsendgallery.com
www.railsendgallery.com
twitter.com/RailsEnd
www.facebook.com/railsend
Year Founded: 1980 Located in Haliburton's landmark rail station, the gallery features contemporary Canadian art, craft and music by regional Artists.

Hamilton: McMaster Museum of Art (MMA)
Alvin A. Lee Building, McMaster University, 1280 Main St. West,
Hamilton, ON L8S 4L6

Tel: 905-525-9140; Fax: 905-527-4548
museum@mcmaster.ca
museum.mcmaster.ca
www.youtube.com/McMasterMuseum
twitter.com/macmuseum
www.facebook.com/ mcmastermuseum
Year Founded: 1967 Historical, modern & contemporary art.
Carol Podedworny, Director & Chief Curator, 905-525-9140, podedwo@mcmaster.ca

Hamilton: Nathaniel Hughson Art Gallery
27 John St. North,
Hamilton, ON L8R 1H1

Tel: 905-923-1192
info@nathanielhughsongallery.com
nathanielhughsongallery.com
twitter.com/NHGonJohn
www.facebook.com/Nat hanielHughsonGallery
Year Founded: 2012 The Nathaniel Hughson Art Gallery represents artists in their early to mid careers. The store hours are M-F 9:00-5:00; Sa 12:00-6:00. They also offer space rental for private dinners, receptions and small performances.
Daniel Banko, Owner & Principal, dan@bankomedia.com

Huntsville: Eclipse Art Gallery
1235 Deerhurst Dr.,
Huntsville, ON P1H 1A9

Tel: 705-789-8803
info@eclipsegallery.ca
www.eclipseartgallery.ca
www.instagram.com/eclipseartgallery
twitter.com/EclipseArt
www.faceboo k.com/EclipseArtDesign
Exhibits work by emerging & established Canadian artists.

Ingersoll: Ingersoll Creative Arts Centre
PO Box 384, 125 Centennial Lane,
Ingersoll, ON N5C 3V3

Tel: 519-485-4691
creative.arts@on.aibn.com
creativeartscentre.com
www.instagram.com/ingersollcreativeartscentre
twitter.com/_icac
www.fa cebook.com/ingersollcreativeartscentre
The centre aims to provide members of the community with the opportunity for creative expression & development, specifically in the following areas: fine arts, pottery, quilting, rug hooking, & fibre arts. The centre also hosts exhibitions a gallery. Office hours: M-F 9:00-12:00 & 1:00-4:00; Gallery hours: F-Su 2:00-4:00.

Jordan Village: Jordan Art Gallery
3836 Main St.,
Jordan Village, ON L0R 1S0

Tel: 905-562-6680
info@jordanartgallery.com
www.jordanartgallery.com
www.facebook.com/JordanArtGallery
Year Founded: 2001 Jordan Art Gallery exhibits original work by artists in the Niagara area. Collections include works made in

glass, wood, steel, fibre art, raku and more. Gallery hours are as follows: Su-Th 10:00-5:00; F-Sa 10:00-6:00.
Mori McCrae, Artist & Co-Owner
Jan Yates, Artist & Co-Owner
George Langbroek, Artist & Co-Owner

Kanata: Kanata Civic Art Gallery
2500 Campeau Dr.,
Kanata, ON K2K 2W3

Tel: 613-580-2424
info@kanatagallery.ca
www.kanatagallery.ca
www.instagram.com/kanatagallery
twitter.com/kanatagallery
www.facebook .com/KanataGallery
Other contact information: Blog: kanatagallery.blogspot.ca
Kanata Civic Art Gallery exhibits and sells original works of art by its members. Operating hours are as follows: W-F 1:00-8:00pm; Sa 10:00-5:00; Su 1:00-5:00. Summer hours: Tu-Th 1:00-7:00pm.

Kingston: Agnes Etherington Art Centre (AEAC) /
Centre d'art Agnes Etherington
Queen's University, 36 University Ave.,
Kingston, ON K7L 3N6

Tel: 613-533-2190; Fax: 613-533-6765
aeac@queensu.ca
agnes.queensu.ca
twitter.com/aeartcentre
www.facebook.com/aeartcentre
Year Founded: 1957 Contemporary & historical art collections & exhibitions; gallery shop, art rental & sales gallery, facility rentals; open year round
Emelie Chhangur, Director

Kingston: Modern Fuel Artist-Run Centre
#305 370 King St. West,
Kingston, ON K7K 2X4

Tel: 613-548-4883
info@modernfuel.org
www.modernfuel.org
www.instagram.com/modernfuelarc
twitter.com/ModernFuelARC
www.facebook .com/ModernFuel
Year Founded: 1977 Exhibits visual, time-based & interdisciplinary art.
Kelley Bolen, President
Chris Ball, Director

Kitchener: Homer Watson House & Gallery
1754 Old Mill Rd.,
Kitchener, ON N2P 1H7

Tel: 519-748-4377
marketing@homerwatson.on.ca
www.homerwatson.on.ca
www.instagram.com/homerwatsonhouse
www.facebook.com/HomerRWatson
Year Founded: 1980 Hours: Tu-Su 12:00-4:30
Tabatha Watson, Director & Curator

Kitchener: Kitchener-Waterloo Art Gallery (KWAG)
101 Queen St. North,
Kitchener, ON N2H 6P7

Tel: 519-579-5860
mail@kwag.on.ca
www.kwag.ca
www.youtube.com/user/kwagadmin
twitter.com/kwartgallery
www.facebook.c om/kwartgallerypage
Year Founded: 1956 Open year round; Monday - Wednesday, Friday: 9:30-5:00; Thursday: 9:30-9:00; Saturday: 10:00-5:00; Sunday 1:00-5:00.
Shirley Madill, Exective Director, smadill@kwag.on.ca

Leamington: Leamington Art Centre (LAC)
72 Talbot St. West,
Leamington, ON N8H 1M4

Tel: 519-326-2711
info@leamingtonartscentre.com
www.leamingtonartscentre.com
ca.linkedin.com/pub/leamington-arts-centre/65/602/716/
twitter.com/leami ngton_arts
www.facebook.com/leamingtonartscentre
Other contact information: Art Supply Store:
shop@leamingtonartscentre.com
Year Founded: 1971 The Leamington Arts Centre, run by the South Essex Arts Association, is a charitable, not-for-profit organization. Its purpose is to serve the community through arts & culture. The Leamington Arts Centre includes a main gallery, which exhibits the work of local artists.
Mike Thibodeau, Chair
Chad Riley, Director & Curator M.F.A.

London: Art Gallery of Lambeth
2454 Main St.,
London, ON N6P 1P9

Tel: 519-652-5556
info@artgalleryoflambeth.com
www.artgalleryoflambeth.com
twitter.com/aglartstudio
www.facebook.com/ ArtGalleryOfLambeth
Work by local artists, as well as events & educational programming.
Vivian Tserotas, Curator
Brenda Colley, Curator

London: McIntosh Gallery
1151 Richmond St.,
London, ON N6A 3K7

Tel: 519-661-3181
mcintoshgallery@uwo.ca
www.mcintoshgallery.ca
twitter.com/McIntoshGallery
www.facebook.com/Mc IntoshGallery
Year Founded: 1942 Exhibitions featuring local, national, & international artists working in various media; exhibitions change every 6 weeks & are accompanied by art-related videos, films & lectures; art collection & gallery's records, some artist archives & periodical library available as resources to students for research purposes; open 6 days/week
James Patten, Director, jpatten2@uwo.ca
Helen Gregory, Curator, celliots@uwo.ca
Brian Lambert, Collections Manager, blamber3@uwo.ca

London: Michael Gibson Gallery
157 Carling St.,
London, ON N6A 1H5

Tel: 519-439-0451 Toll-Free: 866-644-2766
info@gibsongallery.com
www.gibsongallery.com
www.instagram.com/michaelgibsongallery
twitter.com/gibsongallery
www.f acebook.com/michaelgibsongallery
Year Founded: 1984 Contemporary Canadian & international art
Michael Gibson, President, michael@gibsongallery.com
Jennie Kraehling, Associate Director, info@gibsongallery.com

Minden: Agnes Jamieson Gallery
Minden Hills Cultural Centre, 7 Milne St.,
Minden, ON K0M 2K0

Tel: 705-286-1260
admin@mindenhills.ca
mindenhills.ca
Year Founded: 1981 The collection mostly consists of work by Andre Lapine.
Laurie Carmount, Curator

Mississauga: Art Gallery of Mississauga (AGM)
300 City Centre Dr.,
Mississauga, ON L5B 3C1

Tel: 905-896-5088
www.artgalleryofmississauga.com
twitter.com/artgallerymiss
www.facebook.com/ArtGalleryofMississauga
A public art gallery providing state of the art exhibitions by local, national & international artists
Anna Gulbindki, Executive Direcor
Mandy Salter, Director/Curator

Mississauga: Blackwood Gallery
University of Toronto Mississauga, 3359 Mississauga Rd. North,
Mississauga, ON L5L 1C6

Tel: 905-828-3789
blackwood.gallery@utoronto.ca
www.blackwoodgallery.ca
twitter.com/the_Blackwood
www.facebook.com/Bla ckwoodGallery
Year Founded: 1992 Visitors can experience art as the practice of experimenting, questioning, discovering, dismantling, rebuilding, amplifying, imagining, conjuring.
Christine Shaw, Director & Curator
Sasa Rajsic, Exhibition Coordinator

Mississauga: Harbour Gallery
1697 Lakeshore Rd. West,
Mississauga, ON L5J 1J4

Tel: 905-822-5495
inforequest@harbourgallery.com
www.harbourgallery.com
www.instagram.com/harbourgallery
Rotating collection of over 30 accredited Canadian artists in a variety of mediums.

Mississauga: Visual Arts Mississauga
4170 Riverwood Park Lane,
Mississauga, ON L5C 2S7

Tel: 905-277-4313
info@visualartsmississauga.com
www.visualartsmississauga.com
instagram.com/visualartsmississauga
twitter.com/VisualArtsMiss
www.fac ebook.com/vamriverwood
Visual Arts Mississauga offers art exhibition space, as well as classes, workshops & art camps.
Annis Karpenko, Executive Director,
execdirector@visualartsmississauga.com

Niagara Falls: Niagara Falls Art Gallery (NFAG)
8058 Oakwood Dr.,
Niagara Falls, ON L2E 6S5

Tel: 905-356-1514; *Fax:* 905-356-3039
info@niagarafallsartgallery.com
www.niagarafallsartgallery.ca
www.instagram.com/niagarafallsartgallery
twitter.com/nf_art_gallery
www.facebook.com/NiagaraFallsArtGallery
Year Founded: 1979 The Niagara Falls Art Gallery houses the William Kurelek Art Collection. The gallery offers programs such as art, yoga, and dance classes. It also has two subsidiary organizations: Niagara Children's Museum and Art Gallery of Welland. Open hours are Sept-June: Su-F by appointment; Sa 12:00-4:00. July-Aug: M-F 12:00-4:00.
Barbara Buetter, President
John Burtniak, Vice President
Jill Hampson, Treasurer
Debra Attenborough, Executive Director,
deb@niagarafallsartgallery.ca
David Gilbert, Director

North Bay: W.K.P. Kennedy Gallery
150 Main St. East,
North Bay, ON P1B 1A8

Tel: 705-474-1944
info@kennedygallery.org
www.kennedygallery.org
www.instagram.com/kennedygallery
www.facebook.com/KennedyGallery
A changing program of historical & contemporary visual art.
Alix Voz, Director & Curator

North Bay: White Water Gallery (WWG)
PO Box 1491,
North Bay, ON P1B 8K6

info@whitewatergallery.com
whitewatergallery.com
www.instagram.com/white_water_gallery
twitter.com/wwgnorthbay
www.face book.com/whitewater.gallery
Year Founded: 1974 Artist-run centre for contemporary art
Rihkee Strapp, Executive Director

Oakville: In2art Gallery
350 Lakeshore Rd. East,
Oakville, ON L6J 1J6

Tel: 905-582-6739
www.in2artgallery.com
www.instagram.com/in2artgallery
twitter.com/In2artOakville
This gallery celebrates urban, contemporary artwork which range from paintings, photography, etching & multimedia.
Susan Hoeltke, Co-Owner
Kelly McDonagh, Co-Owner

Oakville: Oakville Galleries
1306 Lakeshore Rd. East,
Oakville, ON L6J 1L6

Tel: 905-844-4402; *Fax:* 905-844-7968
info@oakvillegalleries.com
www.oakvillegalleries.com
twitter.com/Oakvl leGallries
www.facebook.com/OakvilleGalleries
Year Founded: 1974 Contemporary art gallery with 2 exhibition spaces: Oakville Galleries at Centennial Square, 120 Navy St. & Oakville Galleries in Gairloch Gardens, 1306 Lakeshore Rd. East
Sally Frater, Executive Director
Frances Loeffler, Curator

Ohsweken: Two Turtle Iroquois Fine Art Gallery
c/o Arnold Jacobs,
Ohsweken, ON N0A 1M0

Tel: 289-253-8545
twoturtleartgallery@live.ca
www.twoturtle.ca

Year Founded: 1985 Showcasing the art of the Hodenosaunee & Arnold Jacobs.
Arnold Aron Jacobs, Owner

Orillia: Orillia Museum of Art & History (OMAH)
30 Peter St. South,
Orillia, ON L3V 5A9

Tel: 705-326-2159
visitors@orilliamuseum.org
www.orilliamuseum.org
twitter.com/OrilliaMuseum
www.facebook.com/orill iamuseum
Year Founded: 1999 Public art gallery & museum; gift shop; open Tu-Su.
Ninette Gyorody, Executive Director,
executivedirector@orilliamuseum.org

Oshawa: The Robert McLaughlin Gallery (RMG)
Civic Centre, 72 Queen St.,
Oshawa, ON L1H 3Z3

Tel: 905-576-3000
communications@rmg.on.ca
www.rmg.on.ca
www.youtube.com/RMGOshawa
twitter.com/theRMG
www.facebook.com/TheRMG
Year Founded: 1967 Permanent exhibitions include masterpieces of Canadian Art: Emily Carr, members of the Group of Seven, Painters Eleven
Lauren Gould, CEO, lgould@rmg.on.ca
Leila Timmins, Senior Curator, ltimmins@rmg.on.ca

Ottawa: Carleton University Art Gallery (CUAG)
Carleton University, St. Patrick's Bldg., 1125 Colonel By Dr.,
Ottawa, ON K1S 5B6

Tel: 613-520-2120
cuag.ca
www.youtube.com/user/CUArtGallery
twitter.com/CUArtGallery
www.faceboo k.com/carleton.university.art.gallery
Year Founded: 1992 27,000 works in contemporary Canadian art; European prints & drawings from the 16th to 19th centuries; Inuit prints & sculpture.
Sandra Dyck, Director, sandra.dyck@carleton.ca

Ottawa: Gallery 101
280 Catherine St.,
Ottawa, ON K1R 3T5

Tel: 613-230-2799
office@g101.ca
www.g101.ca
Year Founded: 1979 A non-profit artist operated centre dedicated to the professional presentation & circulation of visual & media arts; solo & curated group exhibitions by local Canadian & international contemporary artists
Laura Margita, Director/Curator, director@g101.ca

Ottawa: Heffel Gallery Ottawa
451 Daly Ave.,
Ottawa, ON K1N 6H6

Tel: 613-230-6505; *Fax:* 613-230-6505
Toll-Free: 888-818-6505
ottawa@heffel.com
www.heffel.com
Fine art auction house, headquartered in Vancouver, BC.
Andrew J.H. Gibbs, Ottawa Representative

Ottawa: Koyman Galleries
1771 St. Laurent Blvd.,
Ottawa, ON K1G 3V4

Tel: 613-526-1562; *Fax:* 613-521-8056
Toll-Free: 877-526-1562
information@koymangalleries.com
www.koymangalleries.co m
www.instagram.com/koymangalleries
twitter.com/KoymanGalleries
www.facebook.com/KoymanGalleries
Year Founded: 1965 Work by established & up & coming Canadian artists

Ottawa: Orange Art Gallery
290 City Centre Ave.,
Ottawa, ON K1R 7R7

Tel: 613-761-1500
orangeartgallery@bellnet.ca
www.orangeartgallery.ca
twitter.com/orangeartgalery
www.facebook.com/O AGOTTAWA
Year Founded: 2010 Orange Art Gallery exhibits work by contemporary artists in the Ottawa & surrounding areas. The gallery also offers venue rentals for weddings, private parties,

fundraisers and corporate events. Hours of operation are as follows: W 11:00-5:00pm; Th 11:00-9:00pm; F-Su 11:00-5:00pm.
Ingrid Hollander, Owner & Director

Ottawa: Ottawa Art Gallery (OAG) / La Galerie d'art d'Ottawa
Arts Court, 50 MacKenzie King Bridge,
Ottawa, ON K1N 0C5

Tel: 613-233-8699; *Fax:* 613-569-7660
info@oaggao.ca
www.oaggao.ca
www.instagram.com/ottawaartgallery
twitter.com/OttawaArtG
www.facebook .com/ottawaartgallery
Year Founded: 1988 The gallery's programs include exhibits, lectures, tours & publications.
Alexandra Badzak, Director & CEO, 613-233-8699,
abadzak@oaggao.ca
Susan Mok, Chief Financial Officer, 613-233-8699,
smok@oaggao.ca
Michelle Gewurtz, Curator, 613-233-8699,
mgewurtz@oaggao.ca

Owen Sound: Tom Thomson Art Gallery (TTAG)
840 - 1st Ave. West,
Owen Sound, ON N4K 4K4

Tel: 519-376-1932
tomthomson.org
www.youtube.com/user/TomThomsonArtGallery
twitter.com/TheTomThomson
ww w.facebook.com/tomthomsonartgallery
Year Founded: 1967 Public art gallery featuring an extensive collection of Canadian art, historical & contemporary, with a focus on Thomson & the Group of Seven; full range of educational activities including lectures, workshops, & tours; gallery shop
Aidan Ware, Director & Chief Curator, aware@tomthomson.org

Peterborough: Art Gallery of Peterborough
250 Crescent St.,
Peterborough, ON K9J 2G1

Tel: 705-743-9179; *Fax:* 705-743-8168
Toll-Free: 855-738-3755
www.agp.on.ca
twitter.com/AGPtbo_
www.facebook.com/A GPtbo
Year Founded: 1979 Public art gallery with changing exhibitions
Jennifer Moon, President
Celeste Scopelites, Director
Fynn Leitch, Curator

Peterborough: Artspace
PO Box 1748, #3, 378 Aylmer St. North,
Peterborough, ON K9J 7X6

Tel: 705-748-3883
gallery@artspace-arc.org
www.artspace-arc.org
www.instagram.com/artspaceptbo
twitter.com/artspaceptbo
www.facebook.c om/artspaceptbo.arc
Year Founded: 1974 Committed to supporting the growth & development of contemporary artists & related-art practices; dedicated to artistic freedom & exploration
Lucas Cabral, Artistic Director & Curator,
lucas@artspace-arc.org

Queenston: RiverBrink Art Museum
116 Queenston St.,
Queenston, ON L0S 1J0

Tel: 905-262-4510
manager@riverbrink.org
riverbrink.org
twitter.com/RiverBrinkArt
www.facebook.com/RiverBrinkAr t
Year Founded: 1981 RiverBrink Art Museum interprets Niagara and Canadian heritage and culture.
Denis Greenall, President
Debra Antoncic, Director/Curator, dantoncic@riverbrink.org
Morgan Chin-Yee, Programming & Assistant Curator,
mchinyee@riverbrink.org

St Catharines: TAG Art Gallery
214 King St.,
St Catharines, ON L2R 3J9

Tel: 905-682-5072 *Toll-Free:* 877-682-5072
info@tagartgallery.ca
www.tagartgallery.ca
instagram.com/tag_artgallery
twitter.com/TAG_ArtGallery
www.facebook.c om/194823673869376

TAG Art Gallery exhibits Canadian contemporary and fine art, sculpture, jewellery and historical lithographs. Hours are Wednesday to Saturday, 12:00 to 6:00.
Tom Goldspink, Owner

St Thomas: St Thomas-Elgin Public Art Centre
301 Talbot St.,
St Thomas, ON N5P 1B5

Tel: 519-631-4040
info@stepac.ca
www.stepac.ca
twitter.com/STEPACDOTCA
www.facebook.com/stepacdotca
Year Founded: 1970 Promotion of visual arts by a permanent collection of over 800 artworks, exhibitions by current artists, & a variety of art education programs; volunteers & new members welcome; facility rental available; open Tu-Sa 12-4pm.
Laura Woermke, Executive Director/Curator

Sarnia: Judith & Norman Alix Art Gallery
147 Lochiel St.,
Sarnia, ON N7T 0B4

Tel: 519-336-8127; *Fax:* 519-336-8128
gallery.info@county-lambton.on.ca
www.jnaag.ca
twitter.com/GalleryLamb ton
www.facebook.com/gallery.lambton
Year Founded: 1961 Exhibitions of contemporary art, featuring some of the best artists working in Ontario today, many with national & international reputations; collection contains paintings by the Group of Seven, & others, which are important to Canadian art history & are considered national treasures; wide range of changing exhibitions; tours for adults & school groups
Sonya Blazek, Curator/Supervisor, 519-336-8127

Sault Ste Marie: Art Gallery of Algoma
10 East St.,
Sault Ste Marie, ON P6A 3C3

Tel: 705-949-9067
galleryinfo@artgalleryofalgoma.com
www.artgalleryofalgoma.com
www.youtube.com/channel/UCgO-xHc5pCq_we0swCkRwAg
twitter.com/ArtAlgoma
www.facebook.com/ArtGalleryofAlgoma
Year Founded: 1975 Dedicated to cultivating & advancing the awareness of visual arts in Sault Ste Marie & the district of Algoma; open year round
Mark A. Lepore, President, mlepore@artgalleryofalgoma.com
Jasmina Jovanovic, Executive Director & Chief Curator, jasmina@artgalleryofalgoma.com

Simcoe: Norfolk Arts Centre
21 Lynnwood Ave.,
Simcoe, ON N3Y 2V7

Tel: 519-428-0540
norfolkartscentre@norfolkcounty.ca
www.norfolkartscentre.ca
twitter.com/NorfolkArts
www.facebook.com/Norf olkArtsCentre
Norfolk county's only arts centre, located in downtown Simcoe; programming includes exhibitions, kids studio, adult art workshops, Lynnwood's Film Simcoe, annual drive-thru art gallery exhibition

Southampton: Southampton Art Gallery
201 High St.,
Southampton, ON N0H 2L0

Tel: 519-797-5068*Toll-Free:* 800-806-8838
info@southamptonart.com
www.southamptonart.com
www.facebook.com/southa mpton.art
Exhibits handmade work by local artists
David Park, President
Gayle Slinger, Vice-President
Emily Laur, Program Manager

Stouffville: Latcham Art Centre
2 Park Dr.,
Stouffville, ON L4A 4K1

Tel: 905-640-8954
www.latchamartcentre.ca
www.instagram.com/latchamartcentre
twitter.com/LatchamArt
www.facebook.com/LatchamArtCentre
Year Founded: 1979 Latcham Art Centre hosts 5-6 curated exhibitions each year.
Margaret Wallace, Chief Executive Officer, margaret.wallace@wsplibrary.ca
Alexandra Hardstone, Curator, curator@latchamartcentre.ca

Stratford: Gallery Stratford
54 Romeo St. South,
Stratford, ON N5A 4S9

Tel: 519-271-5271
www.gallerystratford.on.ca
www.linkedin.com/company/gallery-stratford
twitter.com/GalleryStrat
www.facebook.com/GalleryStratford
Year Founded: 1967 A non-profit, public art gallery open year round; contemporary, historical, local, national & international artists are highlighted annually in the heritage building; offers educational programs, workshops & fundraisers
Angela Brayham, Director & Curator, abrayham@gallerystratford.on.ca

Sudbury: Art Gallery of Sudbury / Galerie d'art de Sudbury
251 John St.,
Sudbury, ON P3E 1P9

Tel: 705-675-4871
artgalleryofsudbury.myshopify.com
twitter.com/ArtSudbury
www.facebook.com/artsudbury
Year Founded: 1967 Historical & contemporary Canadian art
Demetra Christakos, Director, 705-675-4871

Sutton: Georgina Arts Centre & Gallery
PO Box 1455, 149 High St.,
Sutton, ON L0E 1R0

Tel: 905-722-9587
reception@gacag.com
www.gacag.com
www.instagram.com/georginaarts
twitter.com/georginaarts
www.facebook.com/GACAG
Bill Major, Chair
Grant Peckford, Executive Director
Ewa Chwojko, Curator

Thornhill: Gallery M Contemporary
7039 Yonge St.,
Thornhill, ON L3T 2A6

Tel: 905-597-7937
info@gallerym.ca
twitter.com/gallerym_to
www.facebook.com/gallerycontemporary
Year Founded: 2013 Gallery M Contemporary is an art gallery with a focus on showcasing unconventional pieces by emerging and established artists. Hours of operation are W-F 1:00-6:00; and Sa 10:00-4:00.
Janet Park, Director

Thunder Bay: Ahnisnabae Art Gallery
18 Ct. St. South,
Thunder Bay, ON P7B 2W3

Tel: 807-577-2656; *Fax:* 807-577-2656
www.ahnisnabae-art.com
twitter.com/ahnisart
Year Founded: 1997 This gallery celebrates Ahnisnabae culture.
Louise Thomas, Owner, louisethomas@ahnisnabae-art.com

Thunder Bay: Thunder Bay Art Gallery
1080 Keewatin St.,
Thunder Bay, ON P7B 6T7

Tel: 807-577-6427; *Fax:* 807-577-3781
info@theag.ca
https://theag.ca
www.instagram.com/thunderbayartgallery
twitter.com/THEAG33
www.faceboo k.com/thunderbayAG
Year Founded: 1976 Collection & exhibition of contemporary First Nations art, regional & international exhibits
Christine Bates, Chair

Toronto: Abbozzo Gallery
#128, 401 Richmond St. West,
Toronto, ON M5V 3A8

Tel: 416-260-2220*Toll-Free:* 866-844-4481
mail@abbozzogallery.com
abbozzogallery.com
Year Founded: 1993 Abbozzo Gallery represents regional, Canadian & international artists, showcasing original paintings, prints, works on paper & sculpture. Also provides home consultation, framing design, delivery, installation & appraisal services.
Ineke Zigrossi, Director & Consultant, ineke@abbozzogallery.com
Margaret Kirwin, Associate Director, mail@abbozzogallery.com

Toronto: Annex Art Centre
1075 Bathurst St.,
Toronto, ON M5R 3G8

Tel: 416-433-8373
annexartcentre@gmail.com
annexartcentre.com
instagram.com/annexartcentre
www.facebook.com/AnnexArtCentre
Art gallery & teaching studio located in Toronto's Annex, offering visual art & drama for kids, teens, & adults.

Toronto: Art Gallery of York University (AGYU)
Accolade East Bldg., 4700 Keele St.,
Toronto, ON M3J 1P3

Tel: 416-736-5169
agyu@yorku.ca
agyu.art
www.facebook.com/ArtGalleryofYorkUniversity
Devoted to the presentation of innovative contemporary art; aims to situate Canadian art within an international context & to introduce Canadian audiences to important artists working abroad
Felicia Mings, Curator

Toronto: The Art Gallery, Neilson Park Creative Centre
56 Neilson Dr.,
Toronto, ON M9C 1V7

Tel: 416-622-5294
info@neilsonparkcreativecentre.com
www.neilsonparkcreativecentre.com
www.facebook.com/NPCCArts
Provides a community focus for creative visual arts; variety of exhibitions with strong emphasis on local & contemporary artists
Petra Nyendick, Executive Director, petra@neilsonparkcreativecentre.com
Alonso Rodriguez, Coordinator, Programs, programs@neilsonparkcreativecentre.com

Toronto: Art Metropole
163 Sterling Rd., Unit 135,
Toronto, ON M6R 2B2

Tel: 416-703-4400
info@artmetropole.com
www.artmetropole.com
twitter.com/ArtMetropole
www.facebook.com/artmetr opole
Year Founded: 1974 Specializes in contemporary art in multiple formats; offers artists' products for sale on premises & through web site as well as publishes, promotes, exhibits & distributes artists' products in various formats
Corinn Gerber, Director

Toronto: The Art Museum
Hart House, University of Toronto, 7 Hart House Circle,
Toronto, ON M5S 3H3

Tel: 416-978-1838
artmuseum@utoronto.ca
artmuseum.utoronto.ca
Year Founded: 1982 The Art Museum is comprised of the Justina M. Barnicke Gallery and the University of Toronto Art Centre. Building on the two galleries' distinguished histories, the Art Museum organizes and presents an intensive year-round program of exhibitions and events.
Barbara Fischer, Executive Director/Chief Curator, barbara.fischer@utoronto.ca
Sarah Robayo Sheridan, Curator, s.robayosheridan@utoronto.ca

Toronto: Baffin Inuit Art Gallery
120 Portland St.,
Toronto, ON M5V 2N5

Tel: 416-931-3540*Toll-Free:* 877-326-9700
info@baffininuitart.com
www.baffininuitart.com
www.facebook.com/inuita rtofcanada
Year Founded: 1987 Baffin Inuit Art Galleries preserve & exhibit art created by First Nations people from Cape Dorset on Baffin Island. The gallery has two locations; one in Montreal and the other in Toronto.
Jacques Bandet, President

Toronto: Bezpala Brown Gallery
21 Yorkville Ave.,
Toronto, ON M4W 1L1

Tel: 416-907-6875
info@bezpalabrown.com
www.bezpalabrowngallery.com
www.pinterest.com/bezpalab
twitter.com/bezpalabrown
www.facebook.com/1 45366415531583
Year Founded: 2010 Bezpala Brown Fine Art is a gallery that exhibits Canadian & International emerging artists. Its art

collection includes sculptures, paintings, drawings, photographs, print and other media. The gallery hours are Monday to Sunday, 10:30am to 10:30pm.
Darrell Brown, President, dbrown@bezpalabrown.com
Mila Bezpala-Brown, Gallery Director, mila@bezpalabrown.com
Sashka Avanyan, Gallery Assistant & Research Manager, sashka@bezpalabrown.com
Marina Dessiatkina, Art Council Advisor, marina@bezpalabrown.com

Toronto: The Bluffs Gallery
Parent: Scarborough Arts
Scarborough Arts, 1859 Kingston Rd.,
Toronto, ON M1N 1T3
Tel: 416-698-7322
hello@scarborougharts.com
www.scarborougharts.com
www.youtube.com/scarborougharts
twitter.com/scararts
www.facebook.com/ scarborougharts
Year Founded: 1979 The Bluffs Gallery is dedicated to the exhibition & sale of artwork by Scarborough Arts members. The Gallery offers solo & group exhibitions of all arts media, special events, workshops, & city-wide programs to promote the arts. Open Monday - Saturday; Closed on long weekends.
Suman Roy, Chair
Emily Peltier, Program Director

Toronto: Canadian Fine Arts (CFA)
80 Scollard St.,
Toronto, ON M5R 1G2
Tel: 416-544-8806
info@canadianfinearts.com
www.canadianfinearts.com
twitter.com/CFA_88Scollard
Artwork by historical Canadian masters.

Toronto: Cedar Ridge Creative Centre
225 Confederation Dr.,
Toronto, ON M1G 1B2
Tel: 416-396-4026
crcc@toronto.ca
www.toronto.ca/culture/cedar_ridge/index.htm
www.facebook.com/cedarridge creativecentre
Year Founded: 1844 An arts hub housed in a 1912 mansion. Art exhibitions are featured in the ground floor gallery from Sept.-June.

Toronto: Christopher Cutts Gallery
21 Morrow Ave.,
Toronto, ON M6R 2H9
Tel: 416-532-5566; Fax: 416-532-7272
info@cuttsgallery.com
www.cuttsgallery.com
twitter.com/@cuttsgallery
www.facebook.com/cuttsgallery
Year Founded: 1986 The Christopher Cutts Gallery exhibits art by well known Canadian & International artists. Gallery hours of operation are Tuesday to Saturday, 10:00 to 6:00pm.
Christopher Cutts, Director & Owner

Toronto: Coldstream Fine Art
#208, 80 Spadina Ave.,
Toronto, ON M5V 2J4
Tel: 647-401-6469
info@coldstreamfineart.com
www.coldstreamfineart.com
www.instagram.com/coldstreamfineart
twitter.com/ColdstreamFA
www.faceb ook.com/coldstreamfineart
Kariv Oretsky, Director

Toronto: The Commons @ 401
#440, 401 Richmond St. West,
Toronto, ON M5V 3A8
Tel: 416-351-1317
info@vtape.org
www.vtape.org
Year Founded: 2017 Shared-use gallery, screening room & event space, with joint programming from V Tape, imagineNATIVE Film + Media Arts Festival, FADO Performance Art Centre, Toronto Reel Asian International Film Festival & South Asian Visual Arts Centre (SAVAC).

Toronto: Corkin Gallery
7 Tank House Lane,
Toronto, ON M5A 3C4
Tel: 416-979-1980
info@corkingallery.com
www.corkingallery.com
instagram.com/corkin_gallery
twitter.com/corkingallery
www.facebook.co m/corkingallery
Year Founded: 1978 Eclectic works by contemporary artists in all media
Jane Corkin, Owner

Toronto: Darren Gallery
346 Margueretta St,
Toronto, ON M6H 3S5
Tel: 647-494-9633
info@darrengallery.com
darrengallery.com
www.pinterest.com/darrengallery
twitter.com/DarrenGalleryTO
www.faceb ook.com/darrengalleryTO
Darren Gallery is an art gallery in Toronto that hosts art viewing events. Their art includes painting, sculpture, video and photography. The gallery is open Thursday to Sunday, 12 to 6pm.

Toronto: DISH GALLERY + STUDIO
#112, 15 Case Goods Lane,
Toronto, ON M5A 3C4
Tel: 416-700-3474
www.dishgalleryandstudio.com
www.instagram.com/dishstudio
twitter.com/susan_card
www.facebook.com/p ages/274760405892264
Year Founded: 2006 DISH GALLERY + STUDIO exhibits handmade sculptures & pottery. Additional services offered include art workshops. Gallery hours are Wednesday to Sunday, 12:00 to 5:00pm.
Susan Card, Ceramic Designer, susan.l.card@gmail.com

Toronto: Doris McCarthy Gallery
University of Toronto, 1265 Military Trail,
Toronto, ON M1C 1A4
Tel: 416-287-7007
dmg@utsc.utoronto.ca
www.utsc.utoronto.ca/dmg
www.instagram.com/DMG_UTSC
twitter.com/DMG_UTSC
www.facebook.com/Doris McCarthyGallery
The gallery seeks to display works in all media forms by contemporary Canadian & international artists. Open W-F 10:00-4:00, Sa 12:00-5:00.
Ann MacDonald, Director & Curator, amacdonald@utsc.utoronto.ca

Toronto: Eric Arthur Gallery
University of Toronto, 230 College St., Main Fl.,
Toronto, ON M5T 1R2
Tel: 416-978-5038
enquiry@daniels.utoronto.ca
www.daniels.utoronto.ca
www.instagram.com/uoftdaniels
twitter.com/UofTDaniels
www.facebook.com /UofTDaniels
Year Founded: 2001 Architecture, landscape & urban design exhibits.

Toronto: Etobicoke Civic Centre Art Gallery
399 The West Mall,
Toronto, ON M9C 2Y2
Tel: 416-394-8628
eccartgallery@toronto.ca
www.toronto.ca
The gallery hosts monthly exhibits & juried art shows.

Toronto: Feheley Fine Arts
65 George St.,
Toronto, ON M5A 4L8
Tel: 416-323-1373; Fax: 647-361-7667
Toll-Free: 877-904-9114
gallery@feheleyfinearts.com
feheleyfinearts.com
www.youtube.com/user/FeheleyFineArts
twitter.com/FeheleyFineArts
www.facebook.com/FeheleyFineArts
Year Founded: 1961 The gallery exhibits Inuit artwork, both traditional and contemporary. Their collections include sculptures, paintings and drawings. The gallery also offers services such as art appraisal, collection management, research, and display and exhibition advice. Feheley Fine Arts is

a member of the Art Dealers Association of Canada, and is open from Tuesday to Saturday, 11:00am to 6:00pm.
Brad van der Zanden, Manager, Gallery

Toronto: Gallery 44 (G44)
#120, 401 Richmond St. West,
Toronto, ON M5V 3A8
Tel: 416-979-3941
info@gallery44.org
gallery44.org
gallery44.tumblr.com; vimeo.com/gallery44
twitter.com/Gallery44
www.facebook.com/gallery44.org
Year Founded: 1979 G44 is a a charitable, non-profit, artist-run centre supporting contemporary photography & lens-based media.
Noa Bronstein, Executive Director, 416-979-3941
Meera Margaret Singh, Curator, Education & Community Outreach, 416-979-3941
Leila Timmins, Curator, Exhibitions & Public Programs, 416-979-3941
Aidan Cowling, Head, Communications & Development, 416-979-3941
Darren Rigo, Head, Membership & Facilities, 416-979-3941

Toronto: Gallery Arcturus
80 Gerrard St. East,
Toronto, ON M5B 1G6
Tel: 416-977-1077
ob-art@arcturus.ca
www.arcturus.ca
www.youtube.com/user/GalleryArcturus
twitter.com/GalleryArcturus
www.facebook.com/GalleryArcturus
Contemporary art gallery.

Toronto: Gallery at NeXt
#102B, 219 Dufferin St.,
Toronto, ON M6K 3J1
Tel: 416-646-0460
instagram.com/galleryatnext
twitter.com/GalleryatNext
This gallery specializes in showcasing contemporary art, sculpture and photography.
Alexandre Legault, Co-Owner
Jonathan Girard, Co-Owner

Toronto: Gallery Indigena
46 Gristmill Lane,
Toronto, ON M5A 3C4
Tel: 416-366-3000 Toll-Free: 888-238-5442
toronto@galleryindigena.com
www.galleryindigena.com
Year Founded: 1981 Contemporary Inuit art
Leila Zandi, Managing Director

Toronto: Gallery TPW
170 St. Helenes Ave.,
Toronto, ON M6H 4A1
Tel: 416-645-1066
info@gallerytpw.ca
gallerytpw.ca
twitter.com/GalleryTPW
www.facebook.com/GalleryTPW.Toronto
Year Founded: 1977 Contemporary photography by Canadian & international artists.
Noa Bronstein, Executive Director, noa@gallerytpw.ca
Annie Wong, Curator, Programming, annie@gallerytpw.ca

Toronto: Gerrard Art Space (GAS)
1475 Gerrard St. East,
Toronto, ON M4L 2A1
Tel: 416-778-0923
gerrardartspace@gmail.com
gerrardartspace.com
gerrardartspace.blogspot.ca
twitter.com/gerrardartspace
www.facebook.com/gerrardartspace
Gerrard Art Space is an organization dedicated to supporting the creation and promotion of various art forms, including visual arts, performance, poetry, spoken word and film. The space offers programming such as workshops, classes and shows. GAS is open Wednesday to Sunday, 2 to 7pm.

Toronto: Harbourfront Centre
235 Queens Quay West,
Toronto, ON M5J 2G8
Tel: 416-973-4600; Fax: 416-973-6055
info@harbourfrontcentre.com
www.harbourfrontcentre.com
Contemporary art at Toronto's Harbourfront.

Toronto: Heffel Gallery Inc.
13 Hazelton Ave.,
Toronto, ON M5R 2E1

Tel: 416-961-6505; *Fax:* 416-961-4245
Toll-Free: 888-818-6505
mail@heffel.com
www.heffel.com
Year Founded: 2002 Fine art auction house, headquartered in Vancouver, BC.
David K.J. Heffel, President
Patsy-Kim Heffel, Director, Toronto Office

Toronto: InterAccess Electronic Media Arts Centre (I/A)
#1 950 Dupont St.,
Toronto, ON M6H 1Z2

Tel: 416-532-0597
info@interaccess.org
www.interaccess.org
www.instagram.com/interaccessTO
twitter.com/InterAccessTO
www.facebook.com/InterAccessTO
Year Founded: 1982 Technological media arts exhibitions.
Laura Berazadi, Executive Director

Toronto: Joseph D. Carrier Art Gallery
Columbus Centre, 901 Lawrence Ave. West,
Toronto, ON M6A 1C3

Tel: 416-789-7011
www.villacharities.com
Year Founded: 1987 Third largest public art gallery in Toronto; features contemporary photography, painting, sculpture, & design.

Toronto: Koffler Gallery/Koffler Centre of the Arts
Artscaoe Youngplace, #104-105, 180 Shaw St.,
Toronto, ON M6J 2W5

Tel: 647-925-0643
info@kofflerarts.org
kofflerarts.org
twitter.com/Kof flerArts
www.facebook.com/KofflerArts
Year Founded: 1977 The Koffler Gallery maintains a year-round exhibition program of contemporary art; programming emphasizes new work by mid-career & more senior Canadian artists, & within this context, work of special interest to the Jewish community
Mona Filip, Curator/Director, Koffler Gallery,
mfilip@kofflerarts.org
Karen Tisch, Executive Director, ktisch@kofflerarts.org

Toronto: KUMF Gallery
145 Evans Ave.,
Toronto, ON M8Z 5X8

Tel: 416-766-6802
info@kumfgallery.com
kumfgallery.com
www.facebook.co m/kumfartgallery
Year Founded: 1975 Exhibits work of by artists of Ukranian descent.
Yurij Klufas, Chair & President

Toronto: Le Labo
277, 401 Richmond St. West,
Toronto, ON M5V 3A8

Tel: 647-352-4411
info@lelabo.ca
www.lelabo.ca
www.instagram.com/lelaboart
twitter.com/lelaboArt
www.facebook.com/lel aboArt
Year Founded: 2004 Le Labo is a Toronto-based organization that produces & hosts French media arts projects.
Dyana Ouvrard, Executive Director

Toronto: Larry Wayne Richards Project Gallery
John H. Daniels Faculty of Architecture, University of Toronto, 1 Spadina Cres.,
Toronto, ON M5S 2J5

Tel: 416-978-5038
www.daniels.utoronto.ca
Year Founded: 2001 Ongoing & recently completed student projects.

Toronto: Liss Gallery
112 Cumberland St.,
Toronto, ON M5R 1A6

Tel: 416-787-9872; *Fax:* 416-787-6843
info@lissgallery.com
www.lissgallery.com
www.instagram.com/lissgallery
twitter.com/LissGallery
www.facebook.com /LissGallery

Year Founded: 1983 Liss Gallery features contemporary fine art in the forms of paintings, photographs, sculptures and prints. The gallary also offers services such as art rental & leasing, appraisals and custom framing. Hours of operation are T-F 10:00-6:00; Sa 11:00-6:00. Appointments can be made for other days of the week.
Brian Liss, President, 416-787-9872, brianliss@lissgallery.com
David Reed, Art Gallery Director, 416-787-9872,
davidreed@lissgallery.com

Toronto: Loch Gallery
Toronto
16 Hazelton Ave.,
Toronto, ON M5R 2E2

Tel: 416-964-9050
www.lochgallery.com
www.instagram.com/loch_gallery
twitter.com/lochgallery
www.facebook.com/lochgallery
Year Founded: 2003 Work by Canadian & European artists both contemporary & historical.
Alan Loch, Manager

Toronto: The Market Gallery
St. Lawrence Market, 95 Front St. East, 2nd Fl.,
Toronto, ON M5E 1C2

Tel: 416-392-7604
marketgallery@toronto.ca
www.toronto.ca
www.facebook.com/TorontoMarketGallery
Year Founded: 1979 A focus on the art & history of Toronto

Toronto: Mercer Union, A Centre for Contemporary Visual Art
1286 Bloor St. West,
Toronto, ON M6H 1N9

Tel: 416-536-1519; *Fax:* 416-536-2955
office@mercerunion.org
www.mercerunion.org
www.facebook.com/1238236576 40991
Year Founded: 1979 An artist-run centre dedicated to the existence of contemporary art; provides a forum for the production & exhibition of Canadian & international conceptually & aesthetically engaging art & related cultural practices; pursues primary concerns through critical activities that include exhibitions, lectures, screenings, performances, publications, events & special projects; non-profit, charitable organization.
Julia Paoli, Director & Curator

Toronto: MJG Gallery
Toronto, ON

Tel: 416-319-9844
mjggallery.com
www.instagram.com/mjggallery
twitter.com/mjggallery
www.facebook.com/2 38062092892271
www.pinterest.com/markaloo
Other contact information: www.markaloo
Year Founded: 2011 MJG Gallery showcases original artwork by Toronto artists. The artist-owner of the gallery, Mark Gleberzon, also offers consultations for private and corporate purchases.
Mark Gleberzon, Owner, 416-923-4031, markaloo@yahoo.com

Toronto: Museum of Contemporary Art (MOCA)
158 Sterling Rd.,
Toronto, ON M6R 2B7

Tel: 416-530-2500
info@moca.ca
www.moca.ca
Year Founded: 1999 Contemporary artists' works, including traditional & new media
Kathleen Bartels, Executive Director/CEO
November Paynters, Artistic Director

Toronto: Navillus Gallery
110 Davenport Rd.,
Toronto, ON M5R 3R3

Tel: 416-921-6467
inquire@navillusgallery.com
www.navillusgallery.com
navillusgallery.tumblr.com
twitter.com/navillusgallery
Year Founded: 2011 Navillus Gallery promotes artwork by emerging and mid-career artists, with a focus on paintings and photography. They also offer services such as consultation & advisory, custom framing, delivery & installation and more. Gallery hours are Tuesday to Saturday, 10:00 to 6:00pm.
Mckenzie Sullivan, Gallery Associate, 416-921-6467

Toronto: Norman Felix Gallery
2275 Lakeshore Blvd.,
Toronto, ON M8V 3Y3

Tel: 416-366-6676; *Fax:* 416-366-6686
art@normanfelix.com
www.normanfelix.com
www.instagram.com/normanfelixgallery
twitter.com/normanfelixart
www.fa cebook.com/normanfelixgallery
Year Founded: 2006 Contemporary visual work by new & established artists.
Erin Bittschwan, Director

Toronto: Ocon Wagner Gallery
196 Davenport Rd.,
Toronto, ON M5R 1J2

Tel: 416-962-0438; *Fax:* 416-962-1581
www.odonwagnergallery.com
twitter.com/owgallery
www.facebook.com/odonw agnergallery
Year Founded: 1969 Fine art gallery featuring masterpieces of past & present; sale & purchase of quality paintings, restoration, appraisal, consultation & framing services
Odon Wagner, Director, odon@odonwagnergallery.com

Toronto: Olga Korper Gallery Inc.
17 Morrow Ave.,
Toronto, ON M6R 2H9

Tel: 416-538-8220
info@olgakorpergallery.com
www.olgakorpergallery.com
www.instagram.com/olgakorpergallery
twitter.com/OlgaKorper
www.facebook.com/olgakorpergallery
Year Founded: 1973 The gallery exists to exhibit & promote Canadian & international contemporary art
Shelli Cassidy-McIntosh, Executive Director,
shelli@olgakorpergallery.com
Olga Korper, Cwner

Toronto: Onsite [at] OCAD University
Creative City Campus, 199 Richmond St. W,
Toronto, ON M5V 0H4

Tel: 416-977-6000
onsite@ocadu.ca
www.ocadu.ca/onsite
www.instagram.com/onsite_at_ocadu
twitter.com/ONSITEatOCADU
www.facebo ok.com/OnsiteOCADU
Year Founded: 2007 Onsite Gallery is OCAD University's professional art gallery. It promotes various kinds of arts, such as design, visual arts and digital media. The gallery is open Monday to Friday, 9:00 to 5:00pm.
Lisa Smith, Curator, 416-977-6000, ldsmith@ocadu.ca
Linda Columbus, Programs Assistant, 416-977-6000,
lcolumbus@ocadu.ca

Toronto: Open Studio
#104, 401 Richmond St. West,
Toronto, ON M5V 3A8

Tel: 416-504-8238
www.openstudio.on.ca
www.instagram.com/openstudio_toronto
twitter.com/openstudioTO
www.face book.com/OpenStudioPrintmakingCentre
An artist-run centre that seeks to produce, preserve & promote contemporary printmaking practice.
Lee Petrie, Chair
Jennifer Bhogal, Executive Director, jennifer@openstudio.ca
Astrid Ho, Manager, Print Sales & Archive, sales@openstudio.ca

Toronto: Pentimento Fine Art Gallery
1164 Queen St. East,
Toronto, ON M4M 1L4

Tel: 416-406-6772
rockinrolland@sympatico.ca
pentimentogallery.blogspot.ca
Year Founded: 2006 Pentimento Fine Art Gallery exhibits art by comtemporary Canadians at all stages in their careers. Additional services offered include private viewings, commissions and installation. Gallery hours are Wednesday to Sunday, 12:00 to 6:00pm.

Toronto: The Power Plant Contemporary Art Gallery at Harbourfront Centre
231 Queens Quay West,
Toronto, ON M5J 2G8

Tel: 416-973-4949
info@thepowerplant.org
www.thepowerplant.org
twitter.com/ThePowerPlantTO

Year Founded: 1987 Exclusively promotes Canadian contemporary art through exhibitions, publications & public programming.
Jacques Bernier, President
Gaëtane Verna, Director

Toronto: Prefix Institute of Contemporary Art
#124, 401 Richmond St. West,
Toronto, ON M5V 3A8

Tel: 416-591-0357
info@prefix.ca
www.prefix.ca
www.facebook.com/Prefix-Institute-of-Contemporary-Art-361120 10008

Year Founded: 1999 Public art gallery & publishing house
Barbara Astman, President
Scott McLeod, Acting Director & Curator
Alysha Rajkumar, Gallery Manager

Toronto: Project Gallery
1109 Queen St. East,
Toronto, ON M4M 1K7

Tel: 416-315-1192
info@projectgallerytoronto.com
projectgallerytoronto.com
www.instagram.com/explore/locations/103361090
twitter.com/ProjectGallery T
www.facebook.com/Projectgallerytoronto

Year Founded: 2013 Project gallery is a gallery and studio in Toronto, exhibiting a critical selection of contemporary art. Operating hours are Wednesday to Sunday, 12:00 to 5:00pm.
Devan Patel, Gallery Director & Co-Owner, 416-315-1192, devan@projectgallerytoronto.com
Alex Buchanan, Gallery Manager & Co-Owner, 416-890-5051, alex@projectgallerytoronto.com
Callen Schaub, Gallery Associate & Co-Owner, 647-377-1677, cal@projectgallerytoronto.com

Toronto: Propeller Centre for the Visual Arts
30 Abell St.,
Toronto, ON M6J 0A9

Tel: 416-504-7142
gallery@propellerctr.com
propellerctr.com
twitter.com/propellerto
www.facebook.com/PropellerTO

Year Founded: 1997 Propeller Centre for the Visual Arts is an artist-run gallery providing programming to support artists in community building, networking, and forming partnerships. Galley hours are W-Sa 12:00-6:00pm; Su 12:00-5:00pm.
Nathan Heuvingh, Gallery Director, gallery@propellerctr.com
David Griffin, Co-Chair
Frances Patella, Co-Chair
Sharron Forrest, Secretary
Nancy Newton, Treasurer
Heather Gentleman, Selection Chair
Anthony Saad, Programming Chair

Toronto: Red Head Gallery
#115, 401 Richmond St. West,
Toronto, ON M5V 3A8

info@redheadgallery.org
www.redheadgallery.org
instagram.com/redheadgallery; vimeo.com/redheadgallery
twitter.com/redheadgallery

Year Founded: 1990 The Red Head Gallery is an artists' cooperative committed to exhibiting the work of established & emerging artists. Since its inception the gallery has hosted more than 100 artists & produced over 200 exhibitions.
Jennifer Vong, Gallery Administrator

Toronto: Ryerson Image Centre (RIC)
33 Gould St.,
Toronto, ON M5B 1W1

Tel: 416-979-5164
ric@ryerson.ca
www.ryersonimagecentre.ca
www.instagram.com/ricgallery
www.facebook.com/RICgallery
www.facebook.com/r yersonimagecentre

Year Founded: 2012 Contemporary Canadian & international artwork.
Bonnie Rubenstein, Curator

Toronto: A Space Gallery
#110, 401 Richmond St. West,
Toronto, ON M5V 3A8

Tel: 416-979-9633; Fax: 416-979-9683
info@aspacegallery.org
www.aspacegallery.org
www.facebook.com/A-Space- Gallery-130666663707397

Year Founded: 1971 A Space has a thirty year history of multi-disciplinary artist-run activity. The organizations' mandate encompasses the investigation, presentation & interpretation of contemporary art forms, different disciplines & theories. A Space maintains a politically engaged issue oriented programming that is inclusive of a wide range of media, disciplines & views.
Rebecca McGowan, Executive Director
Vicky Moufawad-Paul, Director & Curator

Toronto: Stephen Bulger Gallery
1026 Queen St. West,
Toronto, ON M6J 1H6

Tel: 416-504-0575; Fax: 416-504-8929
info@bulgergallery.com
www.bulgergallery.com
www.instagram.com/stephenbulgergallery
twitter.com/BulgerGallery
www.f acebook.com/BulgerGallery
Other contact information: Blog: bulgergallery.blogspot.ca

Year Founded: 1994 Stephen Bulger gallery exhibits photography from Canadian & international artists. Its founder, Stephen Bulger, was also the co-founder of CONTACT, Toronto's photography festival that has been around for 20 years. The gallery is open Tuesday to Saturday, 11:00 to 6:00.
Stephen Bulger, President

Toronto: Susan Hobbs Gallery
137 Tecumseth St.,
Toronto, ON M6J 2H2

Tel: 416-504-3699; Fax: 416-504-8064
info@susanhobbs.com
www.susanhobbs.com
www.facebook.com/SusanHobbsGall ery

Year Founded: 1993 Exhibition & sales of contemporary Canadian art; artists represented include Ian Carr-Harris, Magdalen Celestino, Robin Collyer, Max Dean, Brian Groombridge, Scott Lyall, Arnaud Maggs, Liz Magor, Sandra Meigs, Colette Whiten, Robert Wiens, Shirley Wiitasalo, & Kevin Yates

Toronto: Tangled Art Gallery (TAG)
#122, 401 Richmond St. West,
Toronto, ON M5V 3A8

Tel: 647-725-5064
info@tangledarts.org
tangledarts.org
vimeo.com/tangledarts; www.instagram.com/tangled_arts
twitter.com/TangledArtsTO
www.facebook.com/tangledartanddisability

Year Founded: 2002 A registered charitable organization providing opportunities for artists with disabilities; formerly known as Abilities Arts Festival.
Barak adé Soleil, Artistic Director
Katie McMillan, Interim Executive Director
Sean Lee, Curator in Residence
Kristina McMullin, Coordinator, Communication & Design

Toronto: Telephone Booth Gallery
Toronto, ON

Tel: 647-270-7903
www.telephoneboothgallery.ca
twitter.com/TBoothGallery
www.facebook.com/138897496155128

Year Founded: 2010 Telephone Booth Gallery serves clients online. The gallery specializes in contemporary Canadian & international art, with a focus on materials and process-oriented works.
Sharlene Rankin, Gallery Director, sharlene@telephoneboothgallery.ca

Toronto: The TELL
#133, 401 Richmond St. West,
Toronto, ON M5V 3A8

Tel: 647-896-3358
www.401richmond.com/tenant/the-tell
www.facebook.com/t hetelltoronto

The TELL is a creative environment hosting events, education, installations & performances. The constantly evolving collection includes art, installations, objects, books & modern & vintage instruments that guests can interact with.
Roger Sader, Director, roger.s@zero11zero.com

Toronto: Thompson Landry Gallery
Stone Distillery
32 Distillery Lane,
Toronto, ON M5A 3C4

Tel: 416-364-4955
info@thompsonlandry.com
www.thompsonlandry.com
www.instagram.com/thompsonlandrygallery
twitter.com/ThompsonLandry

Year Founded: 2006 Work by Quebec artists

Toronto: Thompson Landry Gallery
The Cooperage
6 Trinity St.,
Toronto, ON M5A 3C4

Tel: 416-364-4955Toll-Free: 416-364-4866
info@thompsonlandry.com
www.thompsonlandry.com
www.instagram.com/thompsonlandrygallery
twitter.com/ThompsonLandry

Year Founded: 2009 Work by Quebec artists

Toronto: Twist Gallery
1100 Queen St. West,
Toronto, ON M6J 1H9

Tel: 416-588-2222
nadia@twistgallery.ca
www.twistgallery.ca
www.instagram.com/twistgallery
twitter.com/TwistGallery
www.facebook.c om/TwistGallery

Year Founded: 2010 This gallery creates a welcoming environment for visitors to socialize & view various artwork.
Nadia Kakridonis, Director, nadia@twistgallery.ca

Toronto: University of Toronto Art Centre
University College, 15 King's College Circle,
Toronto, ON M5S 3H7

Tel: 416-978-1838
www.utac.utoronto.ca
twitter.com/utac
www.facebook.com/UofTArtCentre

Year Founded: 1996 Housing galleries with selections from university collections as well as a schedule of changing exhibitions

Toronto: Urban Gallery
400 Queen St. East,
Toronto, ON M5A 1T3

Tel: 647-460-1278
urbangalleryart1@gmail.com
urbangallery.ca
www.pinterest.com/urbangallery400
www.facebook.com/329901097131926

Year Founded: 2012 Urban Gallery provides rental space to showcase Canadian artists and host shows. Gallery hours are as follows: M-F 12:00-5:00pm; Th 12:00-8:00pm; Sa 1:00-5:00pm.
Calvin Hambrook, Gallery Manager
Allen Shugar, Curator

Toronto: Urbanspace Gallery
401 Richmond St. West, Ground Fl.,
Toronto, ON M5V 3A8

Tel: 416-595-5900
info@urbanspacegallery.ca
www.urbanspacegallery.ca
www.instagram.com/urbanspaceTO
twitter.com/urbanspaceTO
www.facebook.c om/urbanspacegallery
Other contact information: After Hours Emergency Phone: 647-668-5511

The gallery examines cities & urban life, with a focus on Toronto.Themes include community, public space, housing, transportation, planning, governance, diversity, sustainability & citizenship.

Toronto: TD Gallery of Indigenous Art
79 Wellington St. West,
Toronto, ON M5J 2Z9

art.td.com

Year Founded: 1987 Open daily.

Toronto: V Tape
#452, 401 Richmond St. West,
Toronto, ON M5V 3A8

Tel: 416-351-1317; Fax: 416-351-1509
info@vtape.org
www.vtape.org

V Tape houses a collection of Canadian video art projects with over 5,000 tapes & other works.

Toronto: Wellington Street Art Gallery
270 Wellington St. West,
Toronto, ON M5V 3P5

Tel: 647-352-3453
wellington.street.art.gallery@gmail.com
www.wellingtonstreetartgallery.c a
www.facebook.com/111931708886789

Year Founded: 2011 Wellington Street Art Gallery features Canadian contemporary & abstract art.

Toronto: Wil Kucey Gallery
1183 Dundas St. West,
Toronto, ON M6J 1X3

Tel: 416-532-8467
info@wilkuceygallery.ca
www.wilkuceygallery.ca
www.instagram.com/wil.kucey.gallery
twitter.com/kilwucey
www.facebook.com/Wilkuceygallery
Other contact information: Blog:
wilkuceygallery.blogspot.ca/2017
Year Founded: 2003 Wil Kucey Gallery specializes in
showcasing the works of new & mid-career artists. They are also
dealers of contemporary and historical fine art. Some additional
services offered by them include advisory services on the
purchasing of art. Operating hours are Wednesday to Saturday,
11 to 6pm.
Wil Kucey, Director, wil@wilkuceygallery.ca
Vinna Ly, Gallery Manager, vinna@wilkuceygallery.ca

Toronto: Yumart Gallery
401 Richmond St. West, #B12,
Toronto, ON M5V 3AB

info@yumart.ca
yumart.ca
twitter.com/yumartgallery
www.facebook.com/yumartgallery
Year Founded: 2013 Primarily showcases contemporary
Canadian paintings, but paper works including illustration,
printmaking, digital collage & mixed media are also featured.
Yvonne Whelan, Curator

Toronto: YYZ Artists' Outlet
#140, 401 Richmond St. West,
Toronto, ON M5V 3A8

Tel: 416-598-4546; Fax: 416-598-2282
yyz@yyzartistsoutlet.org
www.yyzartistsoutlet.org
twitter.com/YYZ_YYZB OOKS
www.facebook.com/yyzartistsoutlet
Other contact information: YYZBOOKS: www.yyzbooks.com
Year Founded: 1979 YYZ is dedicated to the support of work by
contemporary artists working in all media, & to the provision of a
venue for the exhibition of this work through on-going programs
in both visual & time-based arts - video, film & performance. Also
runs the YYZBOOKS alternative press.
Sarah Jane Gorlitz, Chair, bod@yyzartistsoutlet.org
Ana Barajas, Director, abarajas@yyzartistsoutlet.org

Unionville: Varley Art Gallery of Markham
216 Main St.,
Unionville, ON L3R 2H1

Tel: 905-477-9511
varley@markham.ca
www.varleygallery.ca
www.instagram.com/varleyartgallery
twitter.com/VarleyGallery
www.faceb ook.com/VarleyGallery
Named after Frederick Varley, a member of the Group of Seven;
the Varley offers exhibition space to regional & national artists
Anik Glaude, Curator, aglaude@markham.ca

Waterloo: Canadian Clay & Glass Gallery / Galerie
Canadienne de la Céramique et du Verre
25 Caroline St. North,
Waterloo, ON N2L 2Y5

Tel: 519-746-1882
info@theclayandglass.ca
www.theclayandglass.ca
twitter.com/cdnclayandglass
www.facebook.com/th eclayandglass
Exhibits contemporary artworks executed in clay, glass, stained
glass & enamel for public education & enjoyment
Rebecca Fernandez Short, Chair
Denis Longchamps, Executive Director & Chief Curator,
director@theclayandglass.ca
Peter Flannery, Curator, peter@theclayandglass.ca

Waterloo: Robert Langen Art Gallery (RLAG)
Wilfrid Laurier University, 75 University Ave. West,
Waterloo, ON N2L 3C5

library.wlu.ca
www.facebook.com/RobertLangenArtGallery
Other contact information: Phone: 519-884-0710 x3801
Year Founded: 1989 The University's visual arts centre; provides
knowledge, stewardship, appreciation & enjoyment of Canadian
art & culture to members of the Laurier community & the
community at large
Suzanne Luke, Curator, 519-884-0710, sluke@wlu.ca

Waterloo: University of Waterloo Art Gallery (UWAG)
University of Waterloo, 200 University Ave. West.,
Waterloo, ON N2L 3G1

uwag.uwaterloo.ca
www.instagram.com/uwartgallery
www.facebook.com/uwag.waterloo
Other contact information: Office Phone: 519-888-4567 ext.
36741
Year Founded: 1964 Produces exhibitions of contemporary
Canadian art in all media; holds a collection of contemporary
Canadian art since 1960; open Tue. - Sat. during academic year
at two sites: Modern Languages Building & the main gallery in
East Campus Hall
Ivan Jurakic, Director/Curator, ijurakic@uwaterloo.ca

Whitby: The Station Gallery
1450 Henry St.,
Whitby, ON L1N 0A8

Tel: 905-668-4185
art@stationgallery.ca
www.whitbystationgallery.com
www.linkedin.com/company/station-gallery
twitter.com/stationgallery
ww w.facebook.com/stationgallery
Year Founded: 1970 The gallery's Permanent Collection
exceeds 300 original prints, paintings, sculpture, & mixed media
works.
Vidal Chavannes, Chair
Kerri King, CEO
Olexander Wlasenko, Curator

Windsor: Artcite Inc.
109 University Ave. West,
Windsor, ON N9A 5P4

Tel: 519-977-6564; Fax: 519-977-6564
info@artcite.ca
www.artcite.ca
www.instagram.com/artciteinc
twitter.com/artcite
www.facebook.com/Artc iteInc
Year Founded: 1982 Artcite is Windsor's only artist-run centre
exclusively dedicated to presenting contemporary &
experimental art forms. The gallery is open W-Sa 12:00-5:00, or
by appointment; the office is open Tu-Sa 12:00-5:00.
Kewy Janisse, President
Garth Rennie, Vice-President
David McNamara, Director

Woodstock: Woodstock Art Gallery (WAG)
PO Box 1539,
Woodstock, ON N4S 0A7

Fax: 519-539-2564
www.cityofwoodstock.ca
Other contact information: Phone: 519-539-6761 ext. 2801
Year Founded: 1967 Features contemporary & historical
exhibitions; wide range of classes & workshops for adults &
children; focuses on local painter Florence Carlyle through an
extensive permanent collection & family artifacts
Mary Reid, Director/Curator

Prince Edward Island

Provincial Art Galleries

Confederation Centre of the Arts / Le Centre des arts
de la Confédération
145 Richmond St.,
Charlottetown, PE C1A 1J1

Tel: 902-566-1267 Toll-Free: 800-565-0278
info@confederationcentre.com
www.confederationcentre.com
www.instagram.com/confedcentre
twitter.com/ConfedCentre
www.facebook.com/ConfedCentre
Year Founded: 1964 This is a cultural centre that honours
Canada's past and present through the visual arts, musical
theatre and interactive programs. The centre was established to
commemorate the historic 1864 Charlottetown Conference.
Steve Bellamy, CEO, 902-628-6131,
sbellamy@confederationcentre.com
Kelly Dawson, Chief Operations Officer, 902-628-6133,
kdawson@confederationcentre.com

Local Art Galleries

Charlottetown: Lorimer Gallery
82 Great George St.,
Charlottetown, PE C1A 4K4

Tel: 902-892-1953
www.lorimergallery.com
www.instagram.com/lorimer_gallery
twitter.com/LorimerGallery
www.faceb ook.com/Lorimergallery
This gallery celebrates the work of Canadian art, with a focus on
Inuit artwork.
Brian Lorimer, Owner

Quebec

Provincial Art Galleries

Musée d'art contemporain de Montréal (MACM)
185 rue Sainte-Catherine Ouest,
Montréal, QC H2X 3X5

Tél: 514-847-6226
info@macm.org
www.macm.org
www.instagram.com/macmontreal
twitter.com/macmtl
www.facebook.com/macm ontreal
Fondée en: 1964 A une collection de plus de 6000 oeuvres
datant de 1939 par des artistes du Québec, du Canada & du
monde entier; un centre de référence est disponible pour la
recherche; divers spectacles, conférences & des programmes
éducatifs sont proposés par le musée tout au long de l'année.
Alexandre Taillefer, Président, Conseil d'administration
John Zeppetelli, Directeur et Gonservateur en Chef

Musée des beaux-arts de Montréal (MBAM) /
Montreal Museum of Fine Arts (MMFA)
CP 3000 H, 1380 rue Sherbrooke O,
Montréal, QC H3G 1J5

Tél: 514-285-2000 Ligne sans frais: 800-899-6873
musee@mbamtl.org
www.mbam.qc.ca
www.instagram.com/mbamtl
twitter.com/mbamtl
www.facebook.com/mbamtl
Fondée en: 1860 Le musée abrite une collection encyclopédique
qui comprend l'art canadien, art contemporain, art européen,
arts décoratifs, cultures antiques & archéologie
méditerranéenne; depuis 2007, le musée a reçu des collections
du Musée Marc-Aurèle Fortin(maintenant définitivement fermé);
l'accès à la collection permanente est gratuit.
Stéphan Aquin, Directeur & Conservateur en chef

Musée national des beaux-arts du Québec (MNBAQ)
/ National Museum of Fine Arts of Quebec
179 Grande allée ouest,
Québec, QC G1R 2H1

Tél: 418-643-2150 Ligne sans frais: 866-220-2150
info@mnba.qc.ca
www.mnbaq.org/en
www.instagram.com/mnbaq
twitter.com/mnbaq
www.facebook.com/mnbaq
Fondée en: 1933 Le musée, situé sur les plaines d'Abraham,
abrite des collections de l'art des 17eme, 18eme, et 19eme
siècles, en plus d'une collection d'art contemporain. Diverses
expositions temporaires sont également organisées. Le musée
propose également une bibliothèque, une librairie, & des jeux
éducatifs.
Jean-Luc Murray, Directeur-général

Local Art Galleries

Alma: Langage Plus
CP 2157, 555, rue Collard,
Alma, QC G8B 5W1

Tél: 418-668-6635
info@langageplus.com
www.langageplus.com
www.facebook.com/LangagePlus
Fondée en: 1979 Langage Plus est un centre d'art actuel où la
recherche et la création donnent lieu à une programmation
diversifiée d'expositions, de résidences, d'événements et
d'activités éducatives.
Audrey Turcotte, Présidente
Mariane Tremblay, Directrice, residences@langageplus.com

Amos: Centre d'exposition d'Amos
222, 1e av est,
Amos, QC J9T 1H3

Tél: 819-732-6070
www.ville.amos.qc.ca

L'art actuel et traditionnel; les sciences et l'histoire

Baie-Saint-Paul: Musée d'art contemporain de Baie-Saint-Paul
23, rue Ambroise-Fafand,
Baie-Saint-Paul, QC G3Z 2J2

Tél: 418-435-3681
info@macbsp.com
www.macbsp.com
www.facebook.com/macbsp

Fondée en: 1992 Le musée est consacré à la présentation de l'art contemporain au Québec.
Mathieu Simard, Président
Martin Ouellet, Directeur général, martin.ouellet@macbsp.com

Beaconsfield: Chase Art Gallery
450 Beaconsfield Blvd.,
Beaconsfield, QC H9W 4B9

Tel: 514-426-3700; *Fax:* 514-426-2820
info@chaseartgallery.com
www.chaseartgallery.com
twitter.com/ChaseArtG allery
www.facebook.com/chaseartgallery

This gallery celebrates new artists as well as seasoned Canadian &international artists.

Bromont: Galerie Artêria / Artêria Gallery
625, rue Shefford,
Bromont, QC J2L 1C2

Tel: 450-919-3133
hello@arteriagallery.com
www.arteriagallery.com
www.instagram.com/arteriagallery
www.facebook.com/Arteriagallery

Year Founded: 2005 Illustration visuelle contemporaine par des artistes nouveaux & établis
Geneviève Lévesque, Director
Mr. Christian Dorey, Curator

Carleton-sur-Mer: Centre d'Artistes Vaste et Vague
774, boul Perron,
Carleton-sur-Mer, QC G0C 1J0

Tél: 418-364-3123
www.vasteetvague.ca
www.youtube.com/user/Vasteetvague
twitter.com/vasteetvague
www.facebook.com/vasteetvague

Fondée en: 1990 Centre de production et de diffusion en art actuel et contemporain Expositions, résidences d'artiste, atelier de production, production d'événements majeurs (Symposium)
Maryse Goudreau, Présidente
Anjuna Langevin, Directrice générale,
direction@vasteetvague.ca

Chicoutimi: Espace Virtuel
534, rue Jacques-Cartier est,
Chicoutimi, QC G7H 1Z6

Tél: 418-543-2744
information@centrebang.ca
www.centrebang.ca
www.facebook.com/centrebang

Fondée en: 1958 Heures d'opération: mercredi au vendredi 10h à 17h
Sébastien Harvey, Co-Directeur,
sebastien.harvey@centrebang.ca
Patrick Moisan, Co-Directeur, patrick.moisan@centrebang.ca

Drummondville: Maison des arts Desjardins Drummondville
175, rue Ringuet,
Drummondville, QC J2C 2P7
Tél: 819-477-5412*Ligne sans frais:* 800-265-5412
billetterie@artsdrummondville.com
www.artsdrummondville.com
www.youtube.com/drspectacles
twitter.com/artsdrummond
www.facebook.com/maisondesarts

Fondée en: 2011 Ouverte toute l'année
Catherine Lafranchise, Directrice,
clafranchise@artsdrummondville.com

Gatineau: AXENÉO7
80, rue Hanson,
Gatineau, QC J8Y 3M5

Tél: 819-771-2122
axeneo7@axeneo7.qc.ca
www.axeneo7.qc.ca
twitter.com/axeneo7
www.facebook.com/AXENEO7

Fondée en: 1983 Dispose de trois galeries d'exposition ainsi que d'une résidence d'artiste avec un espace d'atelier.

Jean-Michel Quirion, Directeur

Gatineau: Centre d'exposition Art-Image et espace Odyssée Maison de la Culture de Gatineau
855, boul de la Gappe,
Gatineau, QC J8T 8H9

Tél: 819-243-2325
artimage@gatineau.ca
www.gatineau.ca/artimage
fr-ca.facebook.com/artimageespaceodyssee

Fondée en: 1992 Pour améliorer la communication entre les domaines artistiques et le grand public
Vickie Séguin, Coordonnatrice des espaces d'exposition

Gatineau: Centre d'exposition l'Imagier
9, rue Front,
Gatineau, QC J9H 4W8

Tél: 819-684-1445
info@limagier.qc.ca
www.limagier.qc.ca
www.facebook.com/Imagier

L'Imagier est un organisme sans but lucratif qui a pour mission de susciter un intérêt pour l'art contemporain et de promouvoir l'activité artistique.
Leonore-Namkha Beschi, Directrice, direction@limagier.qc.ca

Gatineau: Galerie Montcalm
Maison du Citoyen, 25, rue Laurier, 1er étage,
Gatineau, QC J8X 3Y9

Tél: 819-595-7488
info.gm.epd@gatineau.ca
www.gatineau.ca

Fondée en: 1980 La galerie accueille 6 expositions par an d'art visuel local et international.

Jonquière: Centre national d'exposition (CNE)
CP 605, 4160, rue du Vieux Pont,
Jonquière, QC G7X 7W4

Tél: 418-546-2177; *Téléc:* 418-546-2180
info@centrenalexposition.com
www.centrenalexposition.com

Présente des expositions d'ouvres d'artistes professionnels et plusieurs expositions itinérantes; démontre la richesse des collections du Québec et d'autres musées canadiens et internationaux; visites guidées, ateliers, démonstrations et trousses éducatives disponibles.
Manon Guérin, Directrice générale,
mguerin@centrenalexposition.com

Kamouraska: Centre d'art de Kamouraska
111, av Morel,
Kamouraska, QC G0L 1M0

Tél: 418-492-9458
info@kamouraska.org
www.kamouraska.org
www.instagram.com/centre.dart.de.kamouraska
twitter.com/c_art_k
www.fa cebook.com/centre.dart.de.kamouraska

Fondée en: 1988 Le centre accueille des expositions, ainsi que des ateliers & des conférences.

Laval: Salle Alfred Pellan, Maison des arts de Laval
1395, boul de la Concorde ouest,
Laval, QC H7N 5W1

Tél: 450-662-4440
maisondesarts@laval.ca
www.ville.laval.qc.ca
www.facebook.com/maisondesartsdelaval

Arts visuels à caractère contemporain

Lennoxville: Foreman Art Gallery of Bishop's University / Galerie d'art Foreman de l'Université Bishop's
Bishop's University, 2600 College St.,
Lennoxville, QC J1M 1Z7

Tel: 819-822-9600
gallery@ubishops.ca
www.foreman.ubishops.ca
twitter.com/ForemanArtGal
www.facebook.com/for emanartgallery

Year Founded: 1998 To serve as a forum for the presentation & examination of the visual arts through the programming of contemporary & historical exhibitions as well as lecture series , workshops & films; open Tu-Sa 12:00-5:00, evenings when Centennial Theatre open; admission free
Gentiane Bélanger, Director/Curator, gbelange@ubishops.ca

Longueuil: Plein sud, centre d'exposition en art actuel à Longueuil
#D-0626, 150, rue de Gentilly Est,
Longueuil, QC J4H 4A9

Tél: 450-679-2966
plein-sud@plein-sud.org
www.plein-sud.org
www.facebook.com/PleinSudcentreexposition

Fondée en: 1985 Diffuse la production d'artistes professionnels dont les recherches s'inscrivent en art actuel; présente des expositions temporaires et offre des activités qui visent à familiariser le public avec les différentes avenues proposées par cet art
Hélène Poirier, Directrice générale et éditrice,
hpoirier@plein-sud.org
Ariane De Blois, Directrice artistique, adeblois@plein-sud.org

Matane: Galerie d'art de Matane
520, av Saint-Jérôme,
Matane, QC G4W 3B5

Tél: 418-562-8661; *Téléc:* 418-562-6675
info@espacef.org
www.espacef.org

Présenter environ 8 expositions d'artistiques du Québec, du Canada et de l'étranger

Mont-Laurier: Centre d'exposition Mont-Laurier
CP 334,
Mont-Laurier, QC J9L 3N7

Tél: 819-623-2441
reception@expomontlaurier.ca
www.expomontlaurier.ca
fr-ca.facebook.com/472445632795269

Fondée en: 1977 Le Centre d'exposition de Mont-Laurier est une institution muséale dont la mission est la diffusion, l'éducation et l'action culturelle en arts visuels et en patrimoine
Marie-Annick Larochelle, Directrice générale

Montréal: Artothèque
5720, rue St-André,
Montréal, QC H2S 2K1

Tél: 514-278-8181
info@artotheque.ca
www.artotheque.ca
www.instagram.com/artotheque
www.facebook.com/artothequemontreal

Montréal: La Centrale (Galerie Powerhouse)
4296, boul Saint-Laurent,
Montréal, QC H2W 1Z3

Tél: 514-871-0268
info@lacentrale.org
www.lacentrale.org
twitter.com/lacentralemtl
www.facebook.com/lacentra legaleriepowerhouse

Fondée en: 1973 Centre d'artistes autogéré qui se consacre à la présentation de l'art contemporain des femmes
Mattia Zylak, Coordonnatrice, Administration,
administration@lacentrale.org
Julia Piccolo, Coordonnatrice, Communications,
communication@lacentrale.org
Jessica Côté, Coordonnatrice, Développement,
developpement@lacentrale.org

Montréal: Centre international d'art contemporain de Montréal (CIAC)
1-3651, av Laval,
Montréal, QC H2X 3E1

Tél: 514-288-0811
www.ciac.ca
www.instagram.com/ciac_mtl
www.facebook.com/ciacmontreal

Centre international d'art contemporain de Montréal est un bureau pour l'art contemporain, la production d'expositions de la Biennale de Montréal, un magazine d'art électronique, publications, et événements.
Claude Gosselin, Directeur général et artistique,
claude.gosselin@ciac.ca

Montréal: Galerie de l'UQAM
Université du Québec à Montréal, #J-R120, 1400, rue Berri,
Pavillon Judith-Jasmin,
Montréal, QC H3C 3P8

Tél: 514-987-6150
www.galerie.uqam.ca
twitter.com/galeriedeluqam
www.facebook.com/galerie.uqam

Fondée en: 1975 La collection comprend surtout du travail contemporain d'artistes québécois. Heures: Ma-S 12h-18h. L'entrée est gratuite.
Louise Déry, Directrice, dery.louise@uqam.ca

Montréal: Galerie Heffel Québec Ltée
1840, rue Sherbrooke Ouest,
Montréal, QC H3H 1E4
Tél: 514-939-6505; *Téléc:* 514-939-1100
Ligne sans frais: 866-939-6505
montreal@heffel.com
www.heffel.com
Beaux-arts maison de vente aux enchères, dont le siège est à Vancouver, en Colombie-Britannique.
1 Tania Poggione, Directrice

Montréal: Galerie Visual Voice / Visual Voice Art Gallery
Édifice Belgo, 372, rue Ste-Catherine ouest,
Montréal, QC H3B 1A2
Tel: 514-878-3663
info@visualvoicegallery.com
www.visualvoicegallery.com
www.flickr.com/photos/visualvoicegallery
twitter.com/VisualVoiceMtl
ww w.facebook.com/visualvoicegallery
Year Founded: 2007 Oeuvres d'artistes contemporains
Bettina Forget, Owner & Manager

Montréal: La Guilde / Canadian Guild of Crafts
1356, rue Sherbrooke ouest,
Montréal, QC H3G 1J1
Tél: 514-849-6091*Ligne sans frais:* 866-477-6091
https://laguilde.com
www.facebook.com/LaGuildeMTL
Sculptures et artefacts d'art inuit et de l'art des Premières Nations; produits de métiers d'art canadien; gravures
Michelle Joannette, Directrice

Montréal: Leonard & Bina Ellen Art Gallery / Galerie Leonard et Bina Ellen
Concordia University, #LB-165, 1455 boul de Maisonneuve ouest,
Montréal, QC H3G 1M8
Tel: 514-848-2424
ellen.artgallery@concordia.ca
ellengallery.concordia.ca
twitter.com/ellengallery
www.facebook.com/el lengallery
Year Founded: 1966 Committed to researching, collecting & interpreting Canadian art; programming centres on exhibitions that help advance knowledge in the visual arts; in keeping with Concordia's academic mission, the Gallery is committed to the enhancement of the University's educational programmes & cultural environment
Michèle Thériault, Director, michele.theriault@concordia.ca

Montréal: Musée des maîtres d'art du Québec (MUMAQ)
615, av Sainte-Croix,
Montréal, QC H4L 3X6
Tél: 514-747-7367; *Téléc:* 514-747-8892
info@mumaq.com
www.mumaq.com
www.youtube.com/user/MuseeMAQ
twitter.com/museemaq
www.facebook.com/Mu seeMetiersdartQuebec
Fondée en: 1977 Chefs d'oeuvres de grands maîtres et pièces exceptionnelles d'artisans anonymes présentent un panorama de la culture traditionnelle québécoise dans une église néo-gothique de 1867
Perrette Subtil, Directrice générale, p.subtil@mumaq.com
Murielle Gagnon, Conservatrice, m.gagnon@mumaq.com

Montréal: OBORO
#301, 4001, rue Berri,
Montréal, QC H2L 4H2
Tél: 514-844-3250
oboro@oboro.net
www.oboro.net
www.instagram.com/oboro4001
www.facebook.com/oboro4001
Fondée en: 1984 Art, des pratiques contemporaines et des nouveaux médias
Marianne Breton, Directrice générale
Tamar Tembeck, Directrice artistique
Yuras Mourog, Directeur Administratif

Montréal: Segal Centre for Performing Arts
5170, ch de la Côte-Ste-Catherine,
Montréal, QC H3W 1M7
Tel: 514-739-2301
info@segalcentre.org
www.segalcentre.org
www.youtube.com/user/SegalCentre
twitter.com/segalcentre
www.facebook. com/segalcentre

A performing arts centre, staging productions involving theatre, music, dance and cinema. The Segal Centre for the Performing Arts also holds workshops involving these categories.
Elliot Lifson, President
Myer Bick, Vice-President
Lisa Rubin, Artistic & Executive Director
Barry Taggart, Director, Finance & Operations
Jon Rondeau, General Manager

Montréal: Yves Laroche Galerie d'Art
6355, boul Ste-Laurent,
Montréal, QC H2S 3C3
Tel: 514-393-1999
info@yveslaroche.com
www.yveslaroche.com
twitter.com/ylgallery
Year Founded: 1991 Exhibits work of underground graffiti, tattoo, comic, pop, illustration & surrealist artists.

Mont-Saint-Hilaire: Musée des beaux-arts de Mont-Saint-Hilaire
150, rue du Centre-Civique,
Mont-Saint-Hilaire, QC J3H 5Z5
Tél: 450-536-3033
reception@mbamsh.qc.ca
www.mbamsh.qc.ca
www.facebook.com/museeartsainthilaire
Fondée en: 1995 Favorise le travail d'artistes locaux Ozias Leduc, Paul-Émile Borduas et Jordi Benet; des ouvres d'artistes contemporains
André Michel, Directeur général par interim, direction@mbamsh.com

Pointe-Claire: La Galerie d'art Stewart Hall Art Gallery
Centre culturel de Pointe-Claire Stewart Hall, 176, ch Bord-du-Lac,
Pointe-Claire, QC H9S 4J7
Tél: 514-630-1254
www.ville.pointe-claire.qc.ca
Fondée en: 1963 Open year round; exhibitions from local, national & international sources; paintings, photographs, sculptures, graphics & theme exhibitions; free admission; wheelchair access

Pointe-Claire: Viva Vida Art Gallery
278 Lakeshore Dr.,
Pointe-Claire, QC H9S 4K9
Tel: 514-694-1110
info@vivavidaartgallery.com
www.vivavidaartgallery.com
twitter.com/vivavidagallery
www.facebook.co m/vivavidaartgallery
This gallery celebrates contemporary art in all its forms.
Nedia El Khouri, Owner & Curator

Québec: VU centre de diffusion et de production de la photographie
523, Saint-Vallier est,
Québec, QC G1K 3P9
Tél: 418-640-2558
info@vuphoto.org
www.vuphoto.org
www.facebook.com/CentreVU
Fondée en: 1981 VU se consacre à la promotion et au développement de la photographie d'auteur. Son mandat vise principalement le soutien aux activités de recherche et de création en photographie à travers des expositions, des résidences d'artistes, des publications et des événements spéciaux. VU offre un accès privilégié à une vaste gamme d'équipements de production en photographie argentique et numérique
Jacynthe Carrier, Codirectrice, direction@vuphoto.org
Anne-Marie Proulx, Codirectrice, artistique@vuphoto.org

Rouyn-Noranda: Musé d'art de Rouyn-Noranda
201, av Dallaire,
Rouyn-Noranda, QC J9X 4T5
Tél: 819-762-6600
museema.org
Contribue à la vitalité des expressions artistiques dans le grand territoire de l'ouest-nord du Québec. Avec une collection de près de 1,000 ouvres et une programmation artistique multidisciplinaire axée sur la recherche et l'excellence, le MA fixe dans l'imaginaire collectif une identité nordique forte et singulière.
Virginia Pesemapeo Bordeleau, Présidente
Jean-Jacques Lachapelle, Directeur général

Sainte-Hénédine: Centre d'art Révérend Louis-Napoléon-Fiset
109, rue Principale,
Sainte-Hénédine, QC G0S 2R0
Tél: 418-935-3543
info@centrelouisnapoleonfiset.ca
centrelouisnapoleonfiset.ca
www.instagram.com/louisnapoleonfiset
twitter.com/calnpf
www.facebook.c om/calnpf
Sculptures sur bois; scènes d'époque; orfèverie; broderie; hangar à dîme

Saint-Hyacinthe: Expression, Centre d'exposition de Saint-Hyacinthe
495, rue Saint-Simon,
Saint-Hyacinthe, QC J2S 5C3
Tél: 450-773-4209
expression@expression.qc.ca
www.expression.qc.ca
www.facebook.com/ExpressionCentreDexpositionDeSaint Hyacinthe
Fondée en: 1985 Une institution muséale dont la mission est de promouvoir et de diffuser l'art contemporain et actuel. Depuis 1985, Expression présente au public, dans une salle magnifique et spacieuse, des expositions réputées pour leur qualité artistique. A ces expositions, s'ajoutent un service d'animation, des conférences et des publications. De plus, Expression insère ponctuellement des activités satellites
Marcel Blouin, Direction générale et artistique

Saint-Jean-Port-Joli: Maison-musée Médard-Bourgault
322, av de Gaspé ouest,
Saint-Jean-Port-Joli, QC G0R 3G0
Tél: 418-598-3880
mmbcontact@gmail.com
medardbourgault.org
Fondée en: 1980 Le musée est la maison de l'artiste Médard Bourgault. La maison affiche son ouvre et possessions et est ouvert au public pendant l'été.

Saint-Léonard: Galerie Port-Maurice
8420, boul Lacordaire,
Saint-Léonard, QC H1R 3G5
www.facebook.com/bibliothequedesaintleonard
Fondée en: 1979 Crée en 1979; sensibilise la population aux différents courants contemporains d'arts visuels

La Sarre: Centre d'art Rotary
195, rue Principale,
La Sarre, QC J9Z 1Y3
Tél: 819-332-2824
www.ville.lasarre.qc.ca
Le centre d'art abrite les ouvres d'artistes locaux et internationaux. Il offre également des programmes d'éducation artistique.
Véronique Trudel, Responsable du Centre d'art Rotary, vtrudel@ville.lasarre.qc.ca

Shawinigan: Centre d'exposition Léo-Ayotte
c/o Corporation culturelle de Shawinigan, 2100, boul Des Hêtres,
Shawinigan, QC G9N 8R8
Tél: 819-539-1888
info@cultureshawinigan.ca
https://leo-ayotte.ca/
Le centre accueille des expositions et offre des programmes d'éducation artistique
Bryan Perreault, Directeur général et artistique, dga@cultureshawinigan.ca
Isabelle Gingras, Responsable des programmes éducatifs, igingras@cultureshawinigan.ca

Sherbrooke: Galerie d'art du Centre culturel de l'Université de Sherbrooke
2500, boul de l'Université,
Sherbrooke, QC J1K 2R1
Tél: 819-820-1000
galerie@usherbrooke.ca
www.centrecultureludes.ca
www.facebook.com/galerieUdeS
Fondée en: 1964 Abrite l'art contemporain
Caroline Loncol Daigneault, Conservatrice & Directrice artistique

Sherbrooke: Musée des beaux-arts de Sherbrooke
241, rue Dufferin,
Sherbrooke, QC J1H 4M3

Tél: 819-821-2115
accueil@mbas.qc.ca
mbas.qc.ca
instagram.com/mbasherbrooke
twitter.com/MBASherbrooke
www.facebook.com /MBASherbrooke
Fondée en: 1982 Plusieurs expositions temporaires ainsi que la
collection du Musée, notamment les oeuvres de Frederick
Simpson Coburn et la collection Luc LaRochelle
Maude Charland-Lallier, Director/Curator, direction@mbas.qc.ca

St-Georges: Centre d'Art de St-Georges
Centre culturel Marie-Fitzbach, 250, 18e rue ouest,
St-Georges, QC G5Y 4S9

Tél: 418-226-2271
ccmf@saint-georges.ca
https://ccmf.saint-georges.ca
www.facebook.com/fitzbach
Fondée en: 1992 Situé au coeur de l'arrondissement historique
de Ville de Saint-Georges, le centre culturel Marie-Fitzbach
rassemble en ses murs divers organismes dédiés à la culture et
au patrimoine tels : la bibliothèque municipale, le Centre d'art et
d'exposition, Artistes et artisans de Beauce, la Société historique
Sartigan ainsi que la Société de généalogie de Beauce.

Trois-Rivières: Galerie d'art du Parc
CP 871, 864, rue des Ursulines,
Trois-Rivières, QC G9A 5J9

Tél: 819-374-2355
galerie@galeriedartduparc.qc.ca
www.galeriedartduparc.qc.ca
www.facebook.com/galeriedartduparc
Dessins, peintures, sculptures, timbres, photos, vidéos et
expositions techniques mixtes; exposition permanente sur
l'histoire du Manoir de Tonnancour.
Christiane Simoneau, Directrice générale

Valcourt: Centre culturel Yvonne L. Bombardier
1002, av J.-A.-Bombardier,
Valcourt, QC J0E 2L0

Tél: 450-532-2250
ccylb@fjab.qc.ca
www.centreculturelbombardier.com
www.facebook.com/CentreCulturelBombardi er
Le centre culturel abrite les arts visuels, ainsi que d'une
bibliothèque et diverses activités artistiques

Val-d'Or: Centre d'exposition de Val-d'Or (CEVD)
600, 7e rue,
Val-d'Or, QC J9P 3P3

Tél: 819-825-0942
www.expovd.ca
www.facebook.com/centredexpositiondevaldor
Fondée en: 1978 Le centre expose des peintures, sculptures,
photographies, vidéos d'artistes locaux. Il accueille également
des activités éducatives, des ateliers et des conférences.
Ginette Vézina, Présidente
Carmelle Adam, Directrice, direction.voart@ville.valdor.qc.ca

Verdun: Centre culturel de Verdun
5955, rue Bannantyne,
Verdun, QC H4H 1H6

Tél: 514-765-7170

Year Founded: 1967

Westmount: Han Art
4209 rue Ste-Catherine,
Westmount, QC H3Z 1P6

Tél: 514-876-9278
info@hanartgallery.com
www.hanartgallery.com
www.instagram.com/hanartgallery
Year Founded: 1995 This gallery celebrates Canadian & Chinese
contemporary & modern art as well as Italian & transavantgarde
art.
Andrew Lui, Art Director

Saskatchewan
Provincial Art Galleries

MacKenzie Art Gallery (MAG)
3475 Albert St.,
Regina, SK S4S 6X6

Tel: 306-584-4250; *Fax:* 306-569-8191
info@mackenzieartgallery.ca
mackenzie.art
www.instagram.com/mackenzie.art.gallery
twitter.com/AtTheMAG
www.faceb ook.com/MacKenzieArtGallery
Year Founded: 1953 Historical & contemporary Canadian,
American & European works; special emphasis on western
Canadian art; works on paper, contemporary photography, major
touring exhibits; facilities include learning centre, studios,
theatre, gift shop; sculpture court; outdoor sculpture garden.
John G. Hampton, Executive Director & CEO, 306-584-4250,
jhampton@mackenzie.art
Jackie Martin, Director, Finance & Operations, 306-584-4250,
jmartin@mackenzie.art
Timothy Long, Head Curator, 306-584-4250,
tlong@mackenzie.art

Local Art Galleries

Assiniboia: Shurniak Art Gallery
PO Box 1178, 122-3rd Ave West,
Assiniboia, SK S0H 0B0

Tel: 306-642-5292; *Fax:* 306-642-4541
info@shurniakartgallery.com
shurniakartgallery.com
www.facebook.com/16 5582726956688
Year Founded: 2005 Shurniak Art Gallery showcases original
Canadian and international art. Hours are Tuesday to Saturday,
10:00 to 4:30pm.
William Shurniak, Founder & President
Gail Mergen, General Manager & Assistant Curator
Sandra Peutert, Receptionist & Assistant to Founder
Jared Williams, Building & Grounds Manager

North Battleford: Allen Sapp Gallery
PO Box 460, 1 Railway Ave. East,
North Battleford, SK S9A 2Y6

Tel: 306-445-1760; *Fax:* 306-445-1694
www.allensapp.com
www.facebook.com/AllenSappGallery
Year Founded: 1989 Cree art & interpretive centre; open year
round
Leah Garven, Curator/Manager, lgarven@cityofnb.ca

North Battleford: The Chapel Gallery
North Battleford Galleries, 891 - 99th St.,
North Battleford, SK S9A 2Y6

Tel: 306-445-1760
galleriesofnb@cityofnb.ca
www.chapelgallery.ca
www.facebook.com/North-Battleford-Galleries-4221975
77865936
Exhibition of local to international artists, permanent collection of
the city of North Battleford

Prince Albert: Grace Campbell Gallery
John M. Cuelenaere Public Library, 125 - 12 St. East,
Prince Albert, SK S6V 1B7

Tel: 306-763-8496; *Fax:* 306-763-3816
Year Founded: 1973 Local, provincial & national exhibitions; no
permanent collection

Prince Albert: Mann Art Gallery
142 - 12th St. West,
Prince Albert, SK S6V 3B5

Tel: 306-763-7080
reception@mannartgallery.ca
mannartgallery.ca
The gallery specializes in contemporary art, & seeks to promote
artistic creation & appreciation in the region. Hours of operation:
Tu-F 10:00-5:00; Sa 12:00-5:00
Marcus Miller, Director/Curator, curator@mannartgallery.ca

Regina: Art Gallery of Regina
Neil Balkwill Civic Arts Centre, 2420 Elphinstone St.,
Regina, SK S4P 3C8

Tel: 306-522-5940
info@artgalleryofregina.ca
www.artgalleryofregina.ca
www.instagram.com/artgalleryofregina
twitter.com/agr_regina
www.faceb ok.com/228399860562366
Year Founded: 1974 The gallery focuses on contemporary art,
especially works by Saskatchewan artists.
Jess Richter, Director

Sandee Moore, Curator, Exhibitions & Programming

Regina: Assiniboia Gallery
2266 Smith St.,
Regina, SK S4P 2P4

Tel: 306-522-0997 *Toll-Free:* 866-378-0997
info@assiniboia.com
www.assiniboia.com
instagram.com/assiniboiaart
twitter.com/ArtYouCanBuy
www.facebook.com/ AssiniboiaGallery
Year Founded: 1977 Displays visual work from emerging &
established artists.
Mary Weimer, Owner
Jeremy Weimer

Regina: Dunlop Art Gallery
Regina Public Library, 2311 - 12th Ave.,
Regina, SK S4P 0N3

Tel: 306-777-6000
www.reginalibrary.ca/dunlop-art-gallery
Year Founded: 1964 Permanent art collection of contemporary &
historical significance by Saskatchewan artists; open year round

Regina: Slate Fine Art Gallery
2078 Halifax St.,
Regina, SK S4P 1T7

Tel: 306-775-0300
slate@sasktel.net
slategallery.ca
www.instagram.com/slategallery
twitter.com/slatefineart
Year Founded: 2013 Displays visual work from emerging &
established artists.
Kimberly Fyfe, Contact
Gina Fafard, Contact

Saskatoon: A.K.A. Gallery
424 - 20th St. West,
Saskatoon, SK S7M 0X4

Tel: 306-491-6102
gallerycoordinator@akaartistrun.com
www.akaartistrun.c om
www.instagram.com/aka_artist_run
www.facebook.com/akaartistrun
Year Founded: 1971 Artist-run centre; membership open to all

Saskatoon: The Gallery/art placement inc,
228 3rd Ave. South,
Saskatoon, SK S7K 1L9

Tel: 306-664-3931; *Fax:* 306-933-2521
gallery@artplacement.com
www.artplacement.com
Year Founded: 1978 Work by mid-career & experienced artists
from Saskatchewan.
Levi Nicholat, Director & Curator, 306-664-3385,
manager@artplacement.com

Saskatoon: Gordon Snelgrove Art Gallery
Room 191 Murray Bldg., University of Saskatchewan, 3
Campus Dr.,
Saskatoon, SK S7N 5A4

Tel: 306-966-4208
www.usask.ca/snelgrove
vimeo.com/gordonsnelgrove/albums
twitter.com/gordonsnelgrove
www.faceb ook.com/groups/gordonsnelgrove
The gallery, managed by the Univ. of Sask. department of Art &
Art History, supports program & course instruction, student
shows & exhibitions, & community outreach.

Saskatoon: St. Thomas More Art Gallery
St. Thomas More College, 1437 College Dr.,
Saskatoon, SK S7N 0W6

www.stmcollege.ca
www.youtube.com/stm1936
twitter.com/stm1936
www.facebook.com/stmcolleg e
Year Founded: 1964 Located on the 2nd floor of the College,
next to the Library. Exhibitions from Sept. through April, featuring
local & regional artists with a university level studio background
or extensive formal training. Submissions accepted year round.

Saskatoon: U of S Art Galleries
University of Saskatchewan, Peter MacKinnon Bldg., 107
Administration Pl.,
Saskatoon, SK S7N 5A2

www.art.usask.ca
Year Founded: 1991 The University of Saskatchewan Art
Galleries collection includes: College Art Galleries 1 and 2,
Kenderine Art Gallery, Gordon Snelgrove Gallery, and the
USask Art Collection.

Jake Moore, Director, 306-966-2618, jake.moore@usask.ca
Leah Taylor, Curator, Exhibits, 306-966-4571,
leah.taylor@usask.ca
Blair Barbeau, Registrar, 306-966-4571,
blair.barbeau@usask.ca

Swift Current: Art Gallery of Swift Current (AGSC)
411 Hebert St. East,
Swift Current, SK S9H 1M5
Tel: 306-778-2736; *Fax:* 306-773-8769
k.houghtaling@swiftcurrent.ca
www.artgalleryofswiftcurrent.org
www.fac ebook.com/ArtGalleryofSwiftCurrent
Year Founded: 1974 Non-profit public art gallery & national
standard art museum offering exhibitions of provincial, national &
international artwork; provides access to & education in visual
art culture for Southwest Saskatchewan
Kim Houghtaling, Director & Curator,
k.houghtaling@swiftcurrent.ca

Watrous: Gallery on 3rd
PO Box 63,
Watrous, SK S0K 4T0
Tel: 306-946-3856; *Fax:* 306-946-1333
cbaschak@gmail.com
saskmuseums.org
The gallery features local artists, as well as traveling art shows.
Open year-round, W-Sa 1:00-4:00.

Weyburn: Allie Griffin Art Gallery (AGAG)
45 Bison Ave.,
Weyburn, SK S4H 0H9
Tel: 306-848-3922
weyburnartscouncil@weyburn.ca
Year Founded: 1964 Features touring exhibitions from the
Mendel Art Gallery, the Mackenzie Art Gallery, the
Saskatchewan Craft Council, the Saskatchewan Arts Board
through OSAC, and many locally curated shows. The exhibitions
feature the work of well-known as well as emerging
Saskatchewan artists.

Yorkton: Godfrey Dean Art Gallery
Yorkton Arts Council, 49 Smith St. East,
Yorkton, SK S3N 0H4
Tel: 306-786-2992
www.deangallery.ca
twitter.com/deangallery
www.facebook.com/GodfreyDeanArtGallery
Year Founded: 1981 Devoted to the exhibition of visual art that
reflects contemporary issues relevant to the Yorkton region;
classes & special events programming.
Jeff Morton, Director/Curator, director@godfreydeanartgallery.ca

Yukon Territory
Territorial Art Galleries

Yukon Arts Centre (YAC)
PO Box 16, 300 University Dr.,
Whitehorse, YT Y1A 5X9
Tel: 867-667-8574
gallery@yac.ca
www.yukonartscentre.com
www.instagram.com/yukonarts
twitter.com/YukonArtsCentre
www.facebook.c om/YukonArtsCentre
The Yukon Arts Centre is a non-profit charitable organization &
the territory's premier venue for performing & visual arts. The
Gallery hosts 10-14 contemporary art exhibitions per year.
Emphasis is placed on professional Yukon artists & exhibitions
of national importance to the Yukon. The Theatre is a 428-seat
proscenium theatre.
Casey Prescott, CEO, 867-667-8577, casey.prescott@yac.ca

Local Art Galleries

Pelly Crossing: Big Jonathan House
PO Box 40, Klondike Hwy. 2,
Pelly Crossing, YT Y0B 1P0
Tel: 867-537-3150; *Fax:* 867-537-3902
www.yukonmuseums.ca/cultural/jonathan/jonathan.html
Big Jonathan House is a cultural centre for the Selkirk First
Nations people, featuring works by local artists, as well as locally
made clothing, baskets, & traditional items. A video presentaion
called "Fort Selkirk: Voices of the People" reveals the history of
the region & its people. Open May-Sept., daily 9:00-7:00.

Aquaria
British Columbia
Local Aquaria

Sidney: Shaw Centre for the Salish Sea
Port Sidney Marina, 9811 Seaport Pl.,
Sidney, BC V8L 4X3
Tel: 250-665-7511
info@salishseacentre.org
www.salishseacentre.org
www.instagram.com/salishseacentre
twitter.com/SalishSeaCentre
www.face book.com/salishseacentre
Year Founded: 2009 The Centre displays over 3,500 live marine
animals, a marine mammal artifact exhibit, & a Coast Salish art
display. Open daily, Fall & Winter: 10:00-4:30; Spring & Summer:
10:00-5:00
Pauline Finn, Executive Director, 250-665-7511,
pauline.finn@salishseacentre.org

Vancouver: Vancouver Aquarium
845 Avison Way,
Vancouver, BC V6B 3E2
Tel: 604-659-3400
visitorexperience@ocean.org
www.vanaqua.org
www.instagram.com/vanaqua
twitter.com/vanaqua
www.facebook.com/vanaqua
Year Founded: 1956 The largest aquarium in Canada & one of
the five largest in North America; a self-sufficient, non-profit
organization, the Aquarium is internationally recognized for
display & interpretation excellence & was the first facility to
incorporate professional Naturalists into the galleries to
complement interpretive graphics; research projects extend
world wide & it is internationally recognized for its success. Open
daily 9:30-6:00
Lasse Gustavsson, President & CEO
Clint Wright, Vice-President and Executive Director

New Brunswick
Local Aquaria

St Andrews: Huntsman Marine Science Centre (HMSC)
1 Lower Campus Rd.,
St Andrews, NB E5B 2L7
Tel: 506-529-1200
huntsman@huntsmanmarine.ca
www.huntsmanmarine.ca
www.instagram.com/huntsmanmarine
www.facebook.com/huntsmanmarine
Year Founded: 1969 Public aquarium/museum with local flora &
fauna, & the Atlantic Reference Centre which houses a
zoological & botanical museum reference collection; research &
teaching in marine sciences & coastal biology; marine education
courses for elementary, high school & university groups;
aquaculture research & development facilities
Chris Bridger, Executive Director

Shippagan: Aquarium et Centre marin du
Nouveau-Brunswick (ACM)
100, rue de l'Aquarium,
Shippagan, NB E8S 1H9
info@aquariumnb.ca
www.aquariumnb.ca
L'Aquarium et le Centre marin du Nouveau-Brunswick est le plus
grand aquarium public du Canada atlantique. 31 étangs
d'exposition; 1 réservoir tactile extérieur; L'Attraction vedette est
une famille de phoque communs; Présentation audio-visuelle;
Bassin touchez-y; Ouvert de juin au sept 10 h à 18 h

Newfoundland & Labrador
Local Aquaria

St. John's: The Suncor Energy Fluvarium
5 Nagle's Pl.,
St. John's, NL A1B 2Z2
Tel: 709-754-3474; *Fax:* 709-754-5947
info@fluvarium.ca
www.fluvarium.ca
twitter.com/Fluvarium
www.facebook.com/Fluvarium
Other contact information: Alternate Phone: 709-722-3825
Year Founded: 1990 Delivers an environmental education
program to over 10,000 school children annually; houses
interactive fresh water exhibits & nine underwater viewing
windows into Nagle's Hill Brook.
Stephanie Korab, Chair

Shantille Butler, Executive Director

Ontario
Local Aquaria

Niagara Falls: Marineland of Canada Inc.
7657 Portage Rd.,
Niagara Falls, ON L2E 6X8
Tel: 905-356-9565
www.marineland.ca
www.instagram.com/marinelandofcanada
www.facebook.com/MarinelandofCanada
Year Founded: 1961 Interactive marina & amusement park;
facility for animal & marine mammal care, where guests can
learn about animals through a mix of entertainment & education.
Contains the largest whale habitat in the world. Open May - Oct.

Toronto: Ripley's Aquarium of Canada
288 Bremner Blvd.,
Toronto, ON M5V 3L9
Tel: 647-351-3474
TGServices@ripleysaquariumofcanada.com
www.ripleyaquar ium.com/canada
instagram.com/RipleysAquaCA
twitter.com/RipleysAquaCA
www.facebook.com/RipleysAquariumCanada
Year Founded: 2013 Ripley's Aquarium of Canada has more
than 5.7 million litres (1.5 million gallons) of water depicting
marine & freshwater habitats from around the world. There are
more than 13,500 underwater creatures, including a 2.84 million
litre (750,000 gallon) Shark Lagoon. The aquarium also offers an
extensive Education and Conservation program, touch exhibits &
dive shows. Open daily 9:00-11:00
Peter Doyle, General Manager

Prince Edward Island
Local Aquaria

Stanley Bridge: Carr's Wildlife Museum
32 Campbellton Rd.,
Stanley Bridge, PE C0B 1M0
Tel: 902-886-3355
oysterbar@carrspei.ca
www.carrspei.ca
twitter.com/CarrsPEI
www.facebook.com/CarrsPEI
The aquarium features live fish, the World of Butterflies display,
& over 700 mounted birds. Also featured are the histories of
Malpeque oysters, Irish moss, & shellfish industries. Carr's
Oyster Bar & Restaurant is located on-site.

Quebec
Local Aquaria

Les Escoumins: Marine Environment Discovery Centre
41, rue des Pilotes,
Les Escoumins, QC G0T 1K0
pc.infossl@canada.ca
www.pc.gc.ca/fr/amnc-nmca/qc/saguenay/Centre-Decouverte-du
-Milieu-Marin
Marine interpretation site featuring live collections & an
amphitheatre; located in Saguenay-St. Lawrence Marine Park.
Discovery activities & tours available. Open June-Sept daily
9:00-6:00; Sept-Oct Fri-Sun 9:00-5:00

Monte-Joli: Parc de la rivière Mitis (CISA)
300, av du Sanatorim,
Monte-Joli, QC G5H 1V7
Tél: 418-775-7987
info@parcregionalrivieremitis.org
www.parcmitis.com
www.facebook.com/parcregionalrivieremitis
Fondée en: 2002 Le Parc de la rivière Mitis est un site
écotouriste qui éduque les gens sur la préservation du
patrimonie naturel & culturel. Chemins au cour des expositions
muséales nature. Ouvert juin-août tous les jours, de 9 h à 17 h.
Martin Reid, Président
Guadalupe Fernandez Nieto, Biologiste en chef

Québec: Aquarium du Québec
1675, av des Hôtels,
Québec, QC G1W 4S3
Tél: 418-659-5264; *Téléc:* 418-646-9238
Ligne sans frais: 866-659-5264
aquarium@sepaq.com
www.sepaq.com/ct/paq
instagram.com/aquariumduqc
twitter.com/AquariumduQC
www.facebook.com/aquariumduquebec

Fondée en: 1959 Un parc de 16 hectares englobant les aspects de l'écosystème du nord & la vie marine. Observer & d'interagir avec plus de 10.000 échantillons frais & d'eau salée poissons, les reptiles, les amphibiens, les invertébrés, ainsi que les mammifères marins comme le morse de l'Atlantique & du Pacifique, les phoques & les ours polaires. Horaire d'hiver: tous les jours 10 h à 16 h; horaire d'été: tous les jours 9 h à 17 h.

Sainte-Anne-des-Monts: Exploramer, la mer à découvrir / Exploramer: Discovering the Sea
1, rue du Quai,
Sainte-Anne-des-Monts, QC G4V 2B6

Tél: 418-763-2500
info@exploramer.qc.ca
www.exploramer.qc.ca
www.instagram.com/exploramer
twitter.com/Exploramer
www.facebook.com/E xploramer
Exploramer, la mer à découvrir est une institution muséale reconnue par le Ministère de la culture, des communications & de la condition féminine & a pour mission de sensibiliser le public à la préservation & à la préservation& à la reconnaissance du milieu marin du Saint-Laurent dans l'environnement. Cette mission est poursuivie à travers les activités de scientifiques amusantes & engageantes musée & parc aquarium.
Gilles Thériault, Président, conseil d'administration
Sandra Gauthier, Directrice générale,
sandra.gauthier@exploramer.qc.ca

Saskatchewan

Local Aquaria

Fort Qu'appelle: Fish Culture Station
PO Box 190,
Fort Qu'appelle, SK S0G 1S0

Tel: 306-332-3200
rbirns.swam@sasktel.net
www.facebook.com/SaskFishHatchery
Year Founded: 1915 The Fort Qu'Appelle Fish Culture Station is the only fish hatchery in Saskatchewan hatching & stocking fish to enhance public angling opportunities. Tours available May-Sept. Open 9:00-12:00, 1:00-4:00, free admission.

Botanical Gardens

Alberta

Local Botanical Gardens

Brooks: Golden Prairie Arboretum & CDCS Grounds
Alberta Agriculture & Rural Development, 301 Horticulture Station Rd. East,
Brooks, AB T1R 1E6

Tel: 403-362-1350; *Fax:* 403-362-1306
www.bgci.org/garden.php
Collection of deciduous trees & shrubs
Christine Murray, Director
Shelley Barkley, Curator & Information Officer,
shelley.barkley@gov.ab.ca

Calgary: University of Calgary Herbarium
Dept. of Biological Sciences, 2500 University Dr. NW,
Calgary, AB T2N 1N4
science.ucalgary.ca/about/faculty-office/collections-room/herbari um
twit ter.com/uofc_herbarium
Calgary's Herbarium has been providing indispensable botanical resources for teaching, research & industry for over 40 years. With an extensive collection of land plants from Alberta & around the world, the herbarium is dedicated to the collection, preservation & documentation of past & present plant biodiversity.
Dr. Jana Vamosi, Director, Associate Professor Ph.D,
jvamosi@@ucalgary.ca
Bonnie Smith, Curator, smib@ucalgary.ca

Edmonton: Muttart Conservatory
9626 - 96A St. NW,
Edmonton, AB T6C 4L8

Tel: 780-442-5311
muttartquestions@edmonton.ca
www.muttartconservatory.ca
www.facebook.com/muttart.conservatory1
Year Founded: 1976 Four pyramids house; flora of different world climatic zones, including arid, temperate, & tropical; Show Pyramid features 6 different floral shows per year; orchid greenhouse; outdoor trail gardens in summer; M-W, F-Sun 10:00-5:00; Thu 10:00-9:00

Edmonton: University of Alberta Vascular Plant Herbarium (ALTA)
Dept. of Biological Sciences, University of Alberta, 116 St. & 85 Ave.,
Edmonton, AB T6G 2R3

Tel: 780-492-8611
altavp@ualberta.ca
www.ualberta.ca/museums/museum-collections/vascular-plant-h erbarium
Year Founded: 1912 The Vascular Plant Herbarium is a research & teaching resource for the study of evolution, diversity, distribution & ecology of cordilleran, prairie, arctic & alpine plants. It is the largest herbaria of its kind in Alberta, & the third largest in Western Canada; holds more than 120,000 specimens.
Jocelyn Hall, Curator, 780-492-8611, jocelyn.hall@ualberta.ca

Lethbridge: Nikka Yuko Japanese Garden
c/o Lethbridge & District Japanese Garden Society, PO Box 751, 9 Ave S & Mayor Magrath Dr.,
Lethbridge, AB T1J 3Z6

Tel: 403-328-3511; *Fax:* 403-328-0511
info@nikkayuko.com
www.nikkayuko.com
www.instagram.com/nikkayuko
twitter.com/NikkaYuko
www.facebook.com/nik kayuko
Year Founded: 1967 The Nikka Yuko Japanese Garden is a mature four acre garden providing a quiet, serene place for the appreciation of nature & the discovery of inner peace. Includes a dry rock garden, a mountain & a waterfall, streams & bridges, ponds & islands & a flat prarie garden.
Brad Hembroff, President
Colin Hirano, Vice-President
Timothy Koba, Treasurer

Parkland County: University of Alberta Botanic Garden
51227 AB-60,
Parkland County, AB T7Y 1C5

Tel: 780-492-3050
uabg.info@ualberta.ca
www.botanicgarden.ualberta.ca
www.instagram.com/uabotanicgarden
twitter.com/UABotanicGarden
www.face book.com/UABotanicGarden
Year Founded: 1959 240 acres; native & alpine plants, ecological reserves, Kurimoto Japanese Garden & Orchid House; Tropical Showhouse; Native Peoples Garden; open May-Oct
Carl Charest, Interim General Manager

Trochu: Trochu Arboretum & Gardens
c/o Trochu Arboretum Society, PO Box 340, 622 North Road, Trochu, AB T0M 2C0

Tel: 403-588-8600; *Fax:* 403-442-2528
www.town.trochu.ab.ca/trochu-arboretum-gardens
www.facebook.com/trochu.a rboretum
Year Founded: 1989 Trees, shrubs, flowers grown & exhibited for scientific & educational enjoyment. Site is available for group photos & weddings.

British Columbia

Local Botanical Gardens

Brentwood Bay: The Butchart Gardens Ltd.
800 Benvenuto Ave.,
Brentwood Bay, BC V8M 1J8

Tel: 250-652-4422 *Toll-Free:* 866-652-4422
www.butchartgardens.com
www.instagram.com/thebutchartgardens
twitter.com/butchartgardens
www.f acebook.com/butchartgardens
Year Founded: 1904 55 acres of manicured gardens on a 130 acre private estate; open year-round

Burnaby: Simon Fraser University Arboretum
Dept. of Biological Sciences, Simon Fraser University, 8888 University Dr.,
Burnaby, BC V5A 1S6

Tel: 778-782-4475; *Fax:* 778-782-3496
bisc-chr@sfu.ca
www.bgci.org/garden.php
Year Founded: 1967
Felix Breden, Director & Chair, Dept. of Biological Sciences
Leslie Dodd, Curator & Greenhouse Technician

Kimberley: Cominco Gardens
290 Rossland Blvd.,
Kimberley, BC V1A 2R6

Tel: 250-427-2293
www.tourismkimberley.com/attractions/cominco-gardens

With a stunning view of the valley & surrounded by natural trees, Cominco Gardens is a 5 hectare property that boasts over 45,000 flowers annually & is free to visit.

North Vancouver: Park & Tilford Gardens
333 Brookbank Ave.,
North Vancouver, BC V7J 3S8

Tel: 604-513-8880
service@clikfix.com
www.parkandtilford.com
Other contact information: Alt. URL: parkandtilfordfogs.ca
Year Founded: 1957 8 themed public gardens; free admission; open dawn to dusk
Ann Pentland, President, Friends of the Garden Society,
annpentland@shaw.ca

Vancouver: Bloedel Conservatory
4600 Cambie St.,
Vancouver, BC V5Y 2M4

Tel: 604-257-8584
www.vancouver.ca/bloedel
www.instagram.com/bloedel_conservatory
twitter.com/bloedelconserv
www.facebook.com/bloedelconservatory
Year Founded: 1969 Canada's largest single-structure tropical conservatory featuring over 500 species in simulated rain-forest, subtropic & desert environments; also features free-flying tropical birds & a Japanese Koi fish collection. May-Aug 10:00-8:00 Sept-Apr 10:00-5:00

Vancouver: Dr. Sun Yat-Sen Classical Chinese Garden
578 Carrall St.,
Vancouver, BC V6B 5K2

Tel: 604-662-3207
vancouverchinesegarden.com
www.instagram.com/vancouverchinesegarden
twitter.com/vangarden
www.fac ebook.com/vancouverchinesegarden
Year Founded: 1986 The first authentic, full-scale, classical Chinese garden built outside China; museum, garden & cultural attraction
Stella Boyland, Chair
Terry Yung, Vice Chair

Vancouver: Nitobe Memorial Garden
c/o UBC Botanical Garden, 6804 SW Marine Dr.,
Vancouver, BC V6T 1Z4

Tel: 604-822-4208; *Fax:* 604-822-2016
garden.info@ubc.ca
https://botanicalgarden.ubc.ca/visit/nitobe-memorial- garden/
Year Founded: 1916 Authentic Japanese tea & stroll garden; cherry blossoms; Japanese Irises, Japanese Maples; Koi; lanterns & much more
Ryo Sugiyama, Curator

Vancouver: UBC Botanical Garden
University of British Columbia, 6804 SW Marine Dr.,
Vancouver, BC V6T 1Z4

Tel: 604-822-4208; *Fax:* 604-822-2016
garden.info@ubc.ca
www.botanicalgarden.ubc.ca
www.instagram.com/ubcgarden
twitter.com/UBCgarden
www.facebook.com/UBC garden
Year Founded: 1916 Living museum of plants in 110 acres of BC coastal native forest; over 10,000 assorted trees, shrubs, flowers; divided into various components
Ryo Sugiyama, Curator

Vancouver: VanDusen Botanical Garden
5251 Oak St.,
Vancouver, BC V6M 4H1

Tel: 604-257-8666
www.vandusengarden.org
www.instagram.com/vandusengarden
twitter.com/vandusengdn
www.facebook.com/vandusenbotanicalgarden
Other contact information: 24-Hour Information Line: 604-257-8335
Year Founded: 1975 22-hectare garden comprised of over 255,000 plants. Open year-round.
Stephen Sharpiro, Executive Director, 604-257-8625
Ema Tanaka, Garden Director, Vancouver Park Board, 604-718-6218

Victoria: Government House Gardens
1401 Rockland Ave.,
Victoria, BC V8S 1V9

Tel: 250-387-2080
ghinfo@gov.bc.ca
www.ltgov.bc.ca/gardens
Other contact information: Alt. URL: www.fghgs.ca

The gardens are open to the public, & walking tours for groups are offered through the Friends of the Government House Gardens Society. There are nearly thirty individual gardens at the site. Open daily.

Victoria: Horticultural Center of the Pacific (HCP)
Pacific Horitcultural College, 505 Quayle Rd.,
Victoria, BC V6E 2J7
Tel: 250-479-3210
www.hcp.ca
www.instagram.com/hcpgardens
twitter.com/hcpgardens
www.facebook.com/H CPGardens
Year Founded: 1979 Manages 103 acres to demonstrate sound gardening practices using the diversity of plants that can be grown in this area, to preserve natural plant & animal habitat, & to provide a unique environment for preparing students for careers in horticulture. Relies on public funding, local businesses, & its own fundraising activities to support these activities. Nov-Mar 10:00-4:00; Daily 9:00-5:00
Ed Chwyl, Chair, Board of Directors

Victoria: Royal Roads Botanical Garden
c/o Royal Roads University, 2005 Sooke Rd.,
Victoria, BC V9B 5Y2
Tel: 250-391-2666*Toll-Free:* 866-241-0674
www.hatleypark.ca
Japanese, Italian, & Rose formal gardens; 15km of walking & hiking trails through old-growth forest; a protected migratory bird sanctuary; a historic First Nations' site; a spectacular view of the Juan de Fuca Strait.

Manitoba
Local Botanical Gardens

Boissevain: International Peace Garden
PO Box 419,
Boissevain, MB R0K 0E0
Tel: 204-534-2510*Toll-Free:* 888-432-6733
admin@peacegarden.com
www.peacegarden.com
Year Founded: 1932 2300-acre park located on the North Dakota & Manitoba boarders; tribute to peace & friendship between the people of Canada & the United States of America; maintains extensive gardens containing a wide variety of shrubs, perennials, & annual plants; interpretative centre, picnic sites, hiking trails, International music camp, Royal Canadian Legion sports camp, & 9/11 Memorial Site. W-Sun 10:00-4:00
Marshall McCullough, President
Dorothy Dobbie, Vice-President
Tim Chapman, CEO

Leaf Rapids: Leaf Rapids National Exhibition Centre
PO Box 340,
Leaf Rapids, MB R0B 1W0
Tel: 204-473-2436; *Fax:* 204-473-2566
The Exhibition Centre features traveling displays & local & regional artists exhibits. Each year, two to four live performances are offered for youth & adults.

Morden: Morden Arboretum
Morden Research Centre, Agriculture & Agri-Food Canada,
PO Box 3001, 100 - 101, Rte. 100,
Morden, MB R6M 1Y5
Tel: 204-822-4471; *Fax:* 204-983-4604
www.bgci.org/garden.php
Year Founded: 1924 A federal government research centre; variety of programs including breeding & development of trees, shrubs, roses & herbaceous perennials; improvement & agronomic research programs carried out on linseed flax, field peas & dry edible beans
Scott Duguid, Director, scott.duguid@agr.gc.ca

Winnipeg: Assiniboine Park
55 Pavilion Cres.,
Winnipeg, MB R3P 2N6
Tel: 204-927-6000
info@assiniboinepark.ca
www.assiniboinepark.ca
www.instagram.com/assiniboineparkzoo
twitter.com/assiniboinepark
www.f acebook.com/assiniboineparkzoo
Year Founded: 1909 Includes Assiniboine Park Zoo, Assiniboine Park Conservatory, Leo Mol Sculpture Garden, Pavillion Art Gallery, Qualico Family Centre, Assiniboine Forest Natural Area
Hartley Richardson, Chair
Margaret Redmond, President & CEO

Winnipeg: Living Prairie Museum Interpretive Centre
2795 Ness Ave.,
Winnipeg, MB R3J 3S4
Tel: 204-832-0167
friendsofLPM@gmail.com
www.winnipeg.ca/livingprairie
www.instagram.com/livingprairiemuseum
twitter.com/LivingPrairie
www.fa cebook.com/LivingPrairieMuseum
Other contact information: www.friendsoflivingprairie.org
Year Founded: 1968 30 acre tall grass prairie preserve; interpretive centre; open May- Jun on Sundays; July-Aug open daily

New Brunswick
Local Botanical Gardens

Edmundston: New Brunswick Botanical Garden (NBBG) / Jardin botanique du Nouveau-Brunswick
PO Box 1629, 15 Main St.,
Edmundston, NB E7B 1A3
Tel: 506-737-4444
info@jardinNBgarden.com
jardinnbgarden.com/en
twitter.com/jardinNBgarden
www.facebook.com/jard inNBgarden
Year Founded: 1993 7 hectares; over 50,000 plants; interactive workshops. May-Jun, Sept 9:00-5:00; Jul-Aug 9:00-8:00
Josée Landry, Executive Director

Fredericton: Fredericton Botanic Garden / Le Jardin Botanique de Fredericton
10 Cameron Ct.,
Fredericton, NB E3B 2R9
Tel: 506-452-9269
fredbotanicgarden@gmail.com
www.frederictonbotanicgarden.com
twitter.com/FredBotGarden
www.faceboo k.com/FrederictonBotanicGarden
Year Founded: 1989 Provides recreational opportunities to the public by means of walks, interpretive trails & beautiful displays of flowers & foilage.
Stephen Heard, President

St Andrews: Kingsbrae Garden
220 King St.,
St Andrews, NB E5B 1Y8
Tel: 506-529-3335; *Fax:* 506-529-4875
Toll-Free: 866-566-8687
kgoffice@kingsbraegarden.com
www.kingsbraegarden.com
twitter.com/KingsbraeGarden
www.facebook.com/Kingsbrae.Garden
Year Founded: 1998 27 acres; over 2,500 species of perennials as well as a wide variety of trees & shrubs.
John Flemer, Founder
Lucinda Flemer, Founder

Newfoundland & Labrador
Local Botanical Gardens

St. John's: The Memorial University of Newfoundland Botanical Garden (MUN)
Memorial University of Newfoundland, 306 Mount Scio Rd.,
St. John's, NL A1C 5S7
Tel: 709-864-8590; *Fax:* 709-864-8596
garden@mun.ca
www.mun.ca/botgarden
www.instagram.com/mun_botanical_garden
twitter.com/munbotgarden
www.fa cebook.com/MUNBotanicalGarden
Year Founded: 1977 The Garden has been developed to display plants native to the province & cultivated plants suitable to the local climate & to provide access to a number of habitats through a system of trails.
Kim Shipp, Garden Director B.A, M.A, 709-864-3326,
kshipp@mun.ca

Nova Scotia
Local Botanical Gardens

Annapolis Royal: Annapolis Royal Historic Gardens
441 St. George St.,
Annapolis Royal, NS B0S 1A0
Tel: 902-532-7018
marketing@historicgardens.com
www.historicgardens.com
www.youtube.com/historicgardens
twitter.com/Historicgardens
www.facebo ok.com/historic.gardens
Year Founded: 1605 Historically themed areas tell the story of Nova Scotia settlement from an agricultural & horticultural perspective, showcasing gardening methods, designs & materials representing more than four hundred years of local history. May-Jun, Sept-Oct 9:00-5:00; Jul-Aug 9:00-8:00

Halifax: Halifax Public Gardens
PO Box 36013, 5665 Spring Garden Rd.,
Halifax, NS B3J 3S9
infohalifaxpublicgardens@gmail.com
www.halifaxpublicgardens.ca
www.flickr.com/groups/halifaxpublicgardens
twitter.com/HfxPublicGarden
Year Founded: 1867 In true Victorian fashion, the Gardens boast ornate fountains, a bandstand, statues, urns & a magnificent wrought iron entrance. Also among their treasures are over 140 different species of trees, including unusual or rare species & some centenarians.

Wolfville: E.C. Smith Herbarium
K.C. Irving Environmental Science Centre, Acadia University, 32 University Ave.,
Wolfville, NS B4P 2P8
Tel: 902-778-0852
alain.belliveau@acadiau.ca
www.herbarium.acadiau.ca
www.facebook.com/ECSmithHerbarium
The herbarium contains over 200,000 specimens, & is the first herbarium in Canada to have a digital database containing images of the collection.
Dr. Allison Walker, Director, 902-585-1333,
allison.walker@acadiau.ca
Alain Belliveau, Collections Manager, 902-585-1335,
alain.belliveau@acadiau.ca

Wolfville: Harriet Irving Botanical Gardens
Acadia University, 32 University Ave.,
Wolfville, NS B4P 2R6
botanicalgardens@acadiau.ca
botanicalgardens.acadiau.ca
twitter.com/irvingcentre
www.facebook.com/HarrietIrvingBotanicalGardens
Year Founded: 2002 A six-acre Botanical Garden on the campus of Acadia University dedicated to showcasing the native flora of the Acadian Forest Region. Open daily 8:00-10:00
Marcel Falkenham, Director, Facilities, 902-585-1839,
marcel.falkenham@acadiau.ca

Ontario
Local Botanical Gardens

Burlington: Centre for Canadian Historical Horticultural Studies (CCHHS)
c/o Royal Botanical Gardens, 680 Plains Rd. West,
Burlington, ON L7T 4H4
Tel: 905-527-1158
dgalbraith@rbg.ca
www.facebook.com/centreforcanadianhistorichorticulturalstudies
Year Founded: 1979 Horticultural & nursery trade catalogues constitute the largest collection within the centre. The catalogue collection includes approximately 30,000 items & is actively growing.
Nancy Rowland, CEO

Burlington: Royal Botanical Gardens (RBG)
680 Plains Rd. West,
Burlington, ON L7T 4H4
Tel: 905-527-1158*Toll-Free:* 800-694-4769
www.rbg.ca
www.instagram.com/rbgcanada
twitter.com/RBGCanada
www.facebook.com/RoyalBotanicalGardens
Year Founded: 1932 A living museum which serves local, regional & global communities while developing & promoting public understanding of the relationship between the plant world, humanity & the rest of nature. Approximately 1,100 hectares of land: 120 cultivated hectares, while the rest remains a managed

natural area including marshlands & walking trails. Open Daily
10:00-8:00
Nancy Rowland, CEO

Guelph: The Arboretum
University of Guelph, College Ave E,
Guelph, ON N1G 2W1

arbor@uoguelph.ca
www.uoguelph.ca/arboretum
www.instagram.com/uogarboretum
www.twitter.com/uogarboretum
www.faceb ok.com/uogarboretum
Other contact information: Phone: 519-824-4120 ext. 52113
Year Founded: 1971 Environmental education & research
activities; plant collections; formal gardens; recreational
workshops; dinner theatre; meeting & banquet facilities. M-F
8:30-4:30
Justine Richardson, Director

Kingsville: Colasanti's Tropical Gardens
1550 Rd. 3 East,
Kingsville, ON N9Y 2E5

Tel: 519-326-3287
tropical@colasanti.com
www. colasanti.com
www.instagram.com/colasanti_farms
twitter.com/colasantifarms
www.faceb ook.com/colasantistropicalgardens
Year Founded: 1941 Colasanti's Tropical Gardens features over
3.5 acres of tropical greenhouses. It is open 363 days each year.
Attractions include exotic plants, animals, indoor miniature golf,
children's rides, an indoor playground, an arcade, a restaurant,
plus home decor & collectables. M-Th 8:00-5:00; F-Sun
8:00-6:00

London: Sherwood Fox Arboretum
University of Western Ontario, 1151 Richmond St,
London, ON N6A 5B7

www.uwo.ca/biology/research/biology_facilities/arboretum.html
Year Founded: 1981 The Sherwood Fox Arboretum
encompasses all the planted trees & shrubs in the manicured
areas on campus at Western. It represents a diversity of woody
plants hardy in temperate regions throughout the northern
hemisphere.
Dr. R. Greg Thorn, Curator, Western Herbarium, 519-661-2111,
rgthorn@uwo.ca

Niagara Falls: Niagara Parks Botanical Gardens & School of Horticulture
2565 Niagara Pkwy.,
Niagara Falls, ON L2E 2S7

Toll-Free: 877-642-7275
www.niagaraparks.com/visit/nature-garden/botanical-gardens-2
www.instagram.com/niagaraparks
twitter.com/niagaraparks
www.facebook.com/niagaraparks
Year Founded: 1936 The Niagara Parks Botanical Gardens
presents visitors with 99 acres of beautifully maintained gardens
& our world-famous rose garden featuring over 2,400 roses. This
section of the parkland is also the home to the Niagara Parks
School of Horticulture, an institution that provides unique
practical training to horticulture students on the grounds of the
Botanical Gardens. Open 6:00-9:00

North Bay: North Bay Heritage Gardeners
Nipissing Botanical Gardens
Parent: Heritage North Bay
100 Ferguson St.,
North Bay, ON P1B 1W8

Tel: 705-476-2323
heritage.gardeners@heritagenorthbay.com
www.northbayheritagegardeners.co m
www.instagram.com/NBHGardeners
twitter.com/NBHGardeners
www.facebook.com/NBHGardeners
A volunteer gardening organization that maintains & enhances
the ornamental gardens along the waterfront; focus on
horticultural & environmental education. T-Sa 10:00-5:00
Jade Scognamillo, Executive Director

Oshawa: The Oshawa Valley Botanical Gardens (OVBG)
50 Centre St. South,
Oshawa, ON L1H 3Z7

Tel: 905-436-3311; *Fax:* 905-436-5642
Toll-Free: 800-667-4292
service@oshawa.ca
www.oshawa.ca/things-to-do/oshawa-va
lley-botanical-gardens.asp
Year Founded: 2001 Includes parks, trails & 11 planned garden
districts; playground; wedding location. Apr 1st-Oct 31st
6:00-10:00, Nov 1st-Mar 31st 6:00-6:00

Ottawa: Central Experimental Farm
72, c/o Friends of the Farm,
Ottawa, ON K1A 0C6

Tel: 613-230-3276
info@friendsofthefarm.ca
friendsofthefarm.ca
www.instagram.com/friendsofthefarmottawa
twitter.com/fcefottawa
www.fa cebook.com/FCEFOttawa
Year Founded: 1886 Arboretum; Ornamental garden; Tropical
greenhouse; houses many diverse research programs

Ridgetown: J.J. Neilson Arboretum
Ridgetown College University of Guelph, 120 Main St. East,
Ridgetown, ON N0P 2C0

Tel: 519-674-1500
www.ridgetownc.com/aboutus/arboretum.cfm
Year Founded: 1986 Includes upwards of 500 taxa., including
Carolinian trees & shrubs, & collections of Viburnum &
Dogwood, along with perennial & annual displays, & theme
landscape areas. Free admission; open every day; staff
available M-F 8:30-4:30.

Sault Ste. Marie: Great Lakes Forestry Centre Arboretum (GLFC)
Canadian Forest Service, PO Box 490, 1219 Queen St. East,
Sault Ste. Marie, ON P6A 2E5

Tel: 705-949-9461; *Fax:* 705-541-5700
www.cfs.nrcan.gc.ca/centres/read/glfc
Two hectares of natural land & forest featuring a wide array of
trees collected & labelled by species. One of five research
centres within the Canadian Forest Service.
Danny Galarneau, Director General

Thunder Bay: Centennial Botanical Conservatory
c/o City Parks Division, 1601 Dease St.,
Thunder Bay, ON P7C 5H4

www.thunderbay.ca/en/recreation/conservatory.aspx
Year Founded: 1967 Tropical arboretum featuring exotic flowers,
trees, shrubs & other plants from around the world in a
year-round tropical setting. Free admission. M-Sun 10:00-4:00

Thunder Bay: Soroptimist International Friendship Gardens
Parks Division, Victoriaville Civic Centre, 102 Legion Track Dr,
Thunder Bay, ON P7C 5K4

www.thunderbay.ca/en/recreation/city-parks.aspx
Year Founded: 1967 Soroptimist International Friendship Garden
was created by Canadians of varied ethnic origins as a
centennial gift to Canada & the community. Individual gardens
have been planned, designed, constructed, & financed by the
respective groups; Each group has created a garden typical of
their culture & homeland.

Toronto: Allan Gardens Conservatory
160 Gerrard St. East,
Toronto, ON M5A 2P2

parks@toronto.ca
www.toronto.ca/data/parks/prd/facilities/complex/41/index.html
www.faceb ook.com/AllanGardensTO
Year Founded: 1879 Permanent plant collection of tropical &
sub-tropical plants; seasonal plant displays; open daily
10:00-5:00

Toronto: Edwards Gardens
755 Lawrence Ave. East,
Toronto, ON M3C 1P2

Tel: 416-397-1341
torontobotanicalgarden.ca/get-gardening/public-gardens/edward
s-gardens
w ww.facebook.com/TorontoBotanicalGarden
Year Founded: 1956 Edwards Gardens is a former Estate
garden turned public park, featuring a wide variety of plants &
flowers, as well as rock gardens, a greenhouse, wooden arch
bridges, a waterwheel, fountains & walking trails. The Toronto
Botanical Gardens (TBG) is also housed here.

Toronto: Humber Arboretum & Centre for Urban Ecology
205 Humber College Blvd.,
Toronto, ON M9W 5L7

Tel: 416-675-5009
arboretum@humber.ca
humber.ca/arboretum
www.instagram.com/humberarb
twitter.com/HumberArb
www.facebook.com/HumberArb
Year Founded: 1977 100 hectares of ornamental gardens &
green space on the west branch of the Humber River; also
on-site is the educational Centre for Urban Ecology. Open 7
days a week during daylight hours.

Alexandra Link, Director

Toronto: Toronto Botanical Gardens (TBG)
777 Lawrence Ave. East,
Toronto, ON M3C 1P2

Tel: 416-397-1341
info@torontobotanicalgarden.ca
torontobotanicalgarden.ca
www.instagram.com/tbg_canada
twitter.com/TBG_Canada
www.facebook.com/T orontoBotanicalGarden
Year Founded: 1956 Located within the Edwards Gardens public
park, the Toronto Botanical Gardens features 17 themed
gardens on four acres of land. The TBG offers garden tours, day
camps, field trips, a horticultural library, rental facilities, gift shop
& seasonal café.
David McIsaac, CEO, 416-397-1484,
ceo@torontobotanicalgarden.ca
Rochelle Strauss, Director, Education, 416-397-1355,
education@torontobotanicalgarden.ca

Toronto: Toronto Sculpture Garden
115 King St. East,
Toronto, ON M5C 1G6

Tel: 416-515-9658
tclf.org/landscapes/toronto-sculpture-garden
Year Founded: 1981 Toronto Sculpture Garden is the site of
innovative contemporary sculpture installations. This small urban
park serves as a testing ground for artists to experiment with
public space & address issues of architectural scale, materials &
context. Open daily.
Catherine Dean, Officer, Public Art, 416-395-0249,
catherine.dean@toronto.ca

Wilsonville: Whistling Gardens Ltd.
698 Concession 3 Townsend,
Wilsonville, ON N0E 1Z0

Tel: 519-443-5773; *Fax:* 519-443-4141
info@whistlinggardens.ca
www.whistlinggardens.ca
www.instagram.com/whistlinggardens
twitter.com/WhistlingG
www.facebook .com/Whistling.Gardens
Year Founded: 2012 The gardens total 20 acres & are home to
over 4,000 different plants.
Darren Heimbecker, Owner

Windsor: Fogolar Furlan Botanic Garden
Fogolar Furlan Gardens, 1800 North Service Rd.,
Windsor, ON N8W 1Y3

Tel: 519-966-2230; *Fax:* 519-966-2237
info@fogolar.com
www.bgci.org/garden.php
Specializes in weddings & many other events.

Windsor: Jackson Park
Queen Elizabeth II Garden
c/o Parks & Forestry Dept., 125 Tecumseh Rd. E,
Windsor, ON N8X 2P7

parkrec@city.windsor.on.ca
www.citywindsor.ca
More than 10,000 plants; World War II Air Force Monument;
sports park

Quebec

Local Botanical Gardens

Grand-Métis: Jardin de Métis / Reford Gardens
200, rte 132,
Grand-Métis, QC G0J 1Z0

Tél: 418-775-2222; *Téléc:* 418-775-6201
info@jardinsdemetis.com
www.jardinsdemetis.com
www.instagram.com/jardinsdemetis
twitter.com/jardinsdemetis
www.faceb ook.com/JardinsdeMetis
Quelque 3 000 espèces & variétés de plantes sont réparties
dans une quinzaine de jardins. Des oeuvres d'art contemporain
parsèment le parcours & s'intègrent avec harmonie aux jardins
historiques. Les Jardins de Métis sont administrés par Les Amis
des Jardins de Métis, corporation à but non lucratif reconnue
comme organisme de bienfaisance.
Frédérick Boucher, Chef exécutif, 418-896-9286
Alexander Redford, Directeur, 418-775-2222

Montréal: Jardin botanique de Montréal / Montréal Botanical Garden
4101, rue Sherbrooke est,
Montréal, QC H1X 2B2

Tél: 514-863-3000
www.espacepourlavie.ca/jardin-botanique
www.instagram.com/espacepourlavie
twitter.com/espacepourlavie
www.face book.com/Espacepourlavie
Collection de 22000 espèces de plantes & variétés, 10 serres d'exposition & 30 jardins thématiques du monde entier; insectarium; couvre 75 hectares. L-J, D 9:00-18:00, V-S 9:00-19:00
René Pronovost, Directeur

Québec: Jardin botanique Roger-Van den Hende
Pavillon de L'Envirotron, Université Laval, local 1227, 2480, boul Hochelaga,
Québec, QC G1V 0A6

Tél: 418-656-2046; *Téléc:* 418-656-3515
jardin@fsaa.ulaval.ca
www.jardin.ulaval.ca
www.instagram.com/jardin_rvdh
www.facebook.com/Jardinuniversitaire.Quebe c
Fondée en: 1978 Plus de 4000 espèces qui sont disposées dans l'ordre de la famille botanique. En période estivale, le jardin est ouvert entre 8 h et 20 h les sept jours de la semaine. L'entrée est gratuite.

Sainte-Anne-de-Bellevue: Morgan Arboretum
Macdonald Campus, McGill University, PO Box 186, 150 Pine St.,
Sainte-Anne-de-Bellevue, QC H9X 3V9

Tel: 514-398-7811
morgan.arboretum@mcgill.ca
www.morganarboretum.org
twitter.com/MorganArboretum
www.facebook.com/F riendsofMorganArboretum
Year Founded: 1945 245 hectares; an expanse of natural woodland containing examples of most of Quebec's native trees; supports 18 collections of trees & shrubs, from across the world. Open daily 9:00-4:00
Dr. Jim Fyles, Academic Director

Saskatchewan

Local Botanical Gardens

Saskatoon: Patterson Garden Arboretum
Dept. of Plant Sciences, University of Saskatchewan, 51 Campus Dr.,
Saskatoon, SK S7N 5A8

Tel: 306-966-5855; *Fax:* 306-966-5015
patterson-arboretum.usask.ca
Year Founded: 1966 Patterson Garden Arboretum is one of the last remaining Prairie Regional Trials for Woody Ornamentals sites, dedicated to Dr. Cecil Patterson in 1969.
Jackie Bantle, Manager, Greenhouse & Horticulture Facility, 306-966-5864, jackie.bantle@usask.ca
Alan Weninger, Arborist

Saskatoon: W.P. Fraser Herbarium Saskatchewan (SASK)
Agriculture Building, University of Saskatchewan, 51 Campus Dr.,
Saskatoon, SK S7N 5A8

Tel: 496-966-4968; *Fax:* 306-966-5015
sask.herbarium@usask.ca
www.herbarium.usask.ca
Year Founded: 1961 The herbarium houses 180,000 specimens, the largest collection in Saskatchewan. Open by permission only.
Dr. Hugo Cota-Sánchez, Curator, hugo.cota@usask.ca

Museums

National Museums

Bank of Canada Museum / Musée de la Banque du Canada
30 Bank St.,
Ottawa, ON K1A 0G9

Tel: 613-782-8914 *Toll-Free:* 800-303-1282
museum-musee@bankofcanada.ca
www.bankofcanadamuseum.ca
www.instagram.com/bocmuseum
twitter.com/BoCMuseum
www.facebook.com/BoCMuseum
Year Founded: 1980 The most complete collection of Canadian notes & coins in the world, plus representative collections of world coins & paper money, including whales' teeth, glass pearls, elephant-hair bracelets, shells & copper axes.
Patricia Measures, Conservator & Manager

Canada Agriculture and Food Museum (CAFM) / Musée de l'agriculture du Canada
901 Prince of Wales Dr.,
Ottawa, ON K2C 3K1

Tel: 613-991-3044 *Toll-Free:* 866-442-4416
contact@ingeniumcanada.org
ingeniumcanada.org/cafm
www.instagram.com/AgFoodMuseum
twitter.com/AgMuseum
www.facebook.com/A gMuseum
Other contact information: TTY: 613-991-0607; Phone, Media: 613-410-5943
The Canada Agriculture & Food Museum is a demonstration farm & research station, which features animal barns, the Dominion Arboretum, ornamental gardens & special exhibitions. It is part of the Ingenium brand, which consists of two other museums, including: The Canada Aviation & Space Museum & the Canada Science & Technology Museum.
Kerry-Leigh Burchill, Director General

Canada Aviation and Space Museum (CASM) / Musée de l'aviation et de l'espace du Canada
11 Aviation Pkwy.,
Ottawa, ON K1K 2X5

Tel: 613-991-3044 *Toll-Free:* 866-442-4416
contact@ingeniumcanada.org
ingeniumcanada.org/aviation
www.instagram.com/avspacemuseum
twitter.com/avspacemuseum
www.facebook.com/AvSpaceMuseum
Year Founded: 1960 The Canada Aviation & Space Museum, collects, preserves, & displays aviation-related objects from the past & present, which include collections from the pioneer era & from periods of war & peace.
Chris Kitzan, Director General

Canada Science & Technology Museum (CSTM) / Société du Musée des Sciences et de la technologie du Canada
PO Box 9724 T, 1867 St. Laurent Blvd.,
Ottawa, ON K1G 5A3

Tel: 613-991-3044; *Fax:* 613-993-7923
Toll-Free: 866-442-4416
contact@ingeniumcanada.org
ingeniumcanada.org/scitech
www.instagram.com/scitechmuseum
twitter.com/SciTechMuseum
www.facebook.com/SciTechMuseum
Year Founded: 1967 Exhibits at the Canada Science & Technology Museum include astronomy, space, marine & land transportation, communications, computer technology, & domestic technology displays. The library of the Canada Science & Technology Museum contains material that centres on the history & development of science & technology, with an emphasis on Canada. This museum is part of Ingenium Corporation.
Lisa Leblanc, Director General

Canadian Museum of History / Musée canadien de l'histoire
100 Laurier St.,
Gatineau, QC K1A 0M8

Tel: 819-776-7000 *Toll-Free:* 800-555-5621
www.historymuseum.ca
www.instagram.com/canmushistory
twitter.com/CanMusHistory
www.facebook .com/CanMusHistory
Other contact information: TTY: 819-776-7003
Year Founded: 1856 Conducts research in Canadian studies, & collects, preserves & displays objects which reflect Canada's cultural heritage. Its activities extend across the country through field research programs, publications & loans to various groups & institutions. Visitors can see permanent & changing exhibitions, public programs & film & theatre programs. The museum is a Crown corporation that manages three museums including: the Canadian War Museum, the Canadian Museum of History & the Virtual Museum of New France.
Henry Kim, President & CEO

Canadian Museum of Immigration at Pier 21
1055 Marginal Rd.,
Halifax, NS B3H 4P7

Tel: 902-425-7770; *Fax:* 902-423-4045
Toll-Free: 855-526-4721
info@pier21.ca
www.pier21.ca
www.instagram.com/pier21_quai21
twitter.com/pier21
www.facebook.com/Ca nadianMuseumofImmigration
Year Founded: 2011 The Canadian Museum of Immigration at Pier 21 details the country's immigration history through personal stories, with an emphasis on the Pier 21 site. Pier 21 was the gateway for about one million immigrants (between 1928 & 1971) & for soldiers leaving Canada during WWII. The museum is Atlantic Canada's only National Museum.
Marie Chapman, Chief Executive Officer, 902-425-7770, mchapman@pier21.ca
Kendall Blunden, Chief Financial Officer, 902-425-7770, kblunden@pier21.ca
Fiona Valverde, Vice-President, Development, 902-425-7770, fvalverde@pier21.ca
Jennifer Sutherland, Vice-President, Marketing, Communications & Partnerships, 902-425-7770, jsutherland@pier21.ca

Canadian Museum of Nature / Musée canadien de la nature
Victoria Memorial Museum Building, PO Box 3443 D, 240 McLeod St.,
Ottawa, ON K2P 2R1

Tel: 613-566-4700 *Toll-Free:* 800-263-4433
www.nature.ca
www.instagram.com/museumofnature
twitter.com/MuseumofNature
www.facebook.com/canadianmuseumofnature
Other contact information: TTY: 613-566-4770; 1-866-600-8801
Year Founded: 1912 The museum focuses on the natural sciences & Canada's natural history. It features eight permanent galleries namely; the Fossil Gallery, the Earth Gallery, the Mammal Gallery, the Water Gallery, the Bird Gallery, Nature Live, the Stone Wall Gallery, Landscapes of Canada Gardens & The Canada Goose Arctic Gallery.
Meg Beckel, President & CEO
Ikram Zouari, Chief Financial Officer
Ailsa Barry, Vice-President, Experience & Engagement
Charles Bloom, Vice-President, Corporate Services
Jeffery Saarela, Vice-President, Research & Collections

Canadian War Museum (CWM) / Musée canadien de la guerre
1 Vimy Pl.,
Ottawa, ON K1A 0M8

Tel: 819-776-7000 *Toll-Free:* 800-555-5621
www.warmuseum.ca
www.instagram.com/canwarmuseum
twitter.com/CanWarMuseum
www.facebook.com/warmuseum
Other contact information: TTY: 819-776-7003
Year Founded: 1880 The Canadian War Museum displays exhibitions which focus on improving our understanding of the human experience of war & armed conflict. The galleries illustrate defining moments in Canadian military history.
Caroline Dromaguet, Acting President & CEO
Dr. Peter MacLeod, Director, Research

Hockey Hall of Fame (HHOF) / Le Temple de la Renommée du Hockey
Brookfield Place, 30 Yonge St.,
Toronto, ON M5E 1X8

Tel: 416-360-7765
info@hhof.com
www.hhof.com
www.youtube.com/user/HockeyHallFame
twitter.com/HockeyHallFame
www.fac ebook.com/HockeyHallFame
Year Founded: 1943 The museum holds artifacts, memorabilia, films & photos, displayed in multimedia exhibits. Also on site is the D.K. (Doc) Seaman Hockey Resource Centre, which stores a vast archive. The museum offers a variety of educational programs, & visitors can enjoy interactive games. This is the home of the Stanley Cup.
Jeff Denomme, President & Chief Executive Officer, jdenomme@hhof.com
Phil Pritchard, Vice-President, Resource Centre, ppritchard@hhof.com
Craig Baines, Vice-President, Development & Building Operations, cbaines@hhof.com
Peter Jagla, Vice-President, Marketing & Attraction Services, pjagla@hhof.com
Kelly Masse, Director, Corporate & Media Relations, kmasse@hhof.com

Alberta
Provincial Museums

Glenbow Museum
130 - 9 Ave. SE,
Calgary, AB T2G 0P3

Tel: 403-268-4100; *Fax:* 403-265-9769
info@glenbow.org
www.glenbow.org
www.instagram.com/glenbowmuseum
twitter.com/Glenbow
www.facebook.com/g lenbowmuseum

Year Founded: 1966 Glenbow documents the settlement of western Canada, with exhibits that trace the lives & traditions of native peoples, the development of the railway, ranching, farming & growing up in the West. A large art gallery highlights historical & contemporary art from Glenbow's own collections as well as from national & international collections.
Nicholas R. Bell, President & CEO

The Military Museums of Calgary (TMM)
4520 Crowchild Trail SW,
Calgary, AB T2T 5J4

Tel: 403-410-2340
www.themilitarymuseums.ca
www.instagram.com/tmm_yyc
twitter.com/tmm_yyc
www.facebook.com/The-Military-Museums

Year Founded: 1990 The Military Museums features the following museums: Air Force Museum of Alberta; Army Museum of Alberta; Lord Strathcona's Horse (Royal Canadians) Museum; Princess Patricia's Canadian Light Infantry Museum & Archives; The Calgary Highlanders Regimental Museum & Archives; The King's Own Calgary Regiment (Royal Canadian Armoured Corps) Museum; & The University of Calgary Military Museums Library & Archives. The Military Museums also contain art & exhibit space, an Education Centre for students, & an Archival Reading Room.
Dave Peabody, Museum Manager, 403-410-2340, director@themilitarymuseums.ca

Royal Alberta Museum (RAM)
9810 - 103 Ave. NW,
Edmonton, AB T5J 0G2

www.royalalbertamuseum.ca
www.instagram.com/royal_alberta_museum
twitter.com/RoyalAlberta
www.fa cebook.com/RoyalAlbertaMuseum

Year Founded: 1967 Major collections & exhibits of Alberta's natural & human history, including habitat groups, geology, palaeontology, archaeology, & western Canadian history & the Syncrude Gallery of Aboriginal Culture; feature exhibitions, museum shop, café, films, lectures, live demonstrations & cultural performances; special programs for schools & other groups; & discovery room.
Alwynne Beaudoin, Acting Executive Director, 825-468-6170
Jayne Custance, Director, Business Operations, 825-468-6126
Oksana Gowin, Head, Marketing & Communications, 825-468-6127

Royal Tyrrell Museum
PO Box 7500, 1500 Dinosaur Trail,
Drumheller, AB T0J 0Y0

Tel: 403-823-7707 *Toll-Free:* 888-440-4240
tyrrell.info@gov.ab.ca
www.tyrrellmuseum.com
www.instagram.com/royaltyrrell
www.instagram.com/royaltyrrell
www.facebook.c om/RoyalTyrrellMuseum

Year Founded: 1985 Located in Midland Provincial Park, on Hwy #838 in Drumheller, the Royal Tyrrell Museum is situated in one of the richest fossil locations in the world. The Museum is dedicated exclusively to palaeontology & showcases Alberta's abundant, diverse fossil record, & features more than 800 fossils & 35 dinosaur skeletons on display. Other highlights include dioramas, interactive exhibits, computer stations & a mini-theatre, special events & programming, as well as a gift shop & cafeteria.
Lisa Making, Executive Director, 403-820-6244, lisa.making@gov.ab.ca
Craig Scott, Preservation & Research Director Ph.D., 403-820-6219, craig.scott@gov.ab.ca
Jason Martin, Operations & Finance Director, 403-820-6223, jason.martin@gov.ab.ca
Becky Kowalchuk, Executive Assistant, 403-820-6202, becky.kowalchuk@gov.ab.ca

Local Museums

Airdrie: Nose Creek Valley Museum
1701 Main St. SW,
Airdrie, AB T4B 1C5

Tel: 403-948-6685
ncvm@telus.net
www.nosecreekvalleymuseum.com
www.facebook.com/NCVMuseum

Nose Creek Valley Museum offers the history of Airdrie & the surrounding region. Visitors will learn about the geology & natural history of the area, the First Nations & pioneers, farming, antique automobiles, & military history. A Canadian Pacific caboose is also on display. The museum is open year-round.
Laurie Harvey, Curator

Alberta Beach: Alberta Beach & District Museum
PO Box 68, 5000 - 47 Ave.,
Alberta Beach, AB T0E 0A0

Tel: 780-924-2140; *Fax:* 780-924-2053
abmuseum@xplornet.ca
www.albertabeachmuseum.com

History of the Lac Ste Anne area; open every day July & Aug., except Tuesdays

Alix: Alix Wagon Wheel Museum
4912 - 50th St.,
Alix, AB T0C 0B0

Tel: 403-747-2584
alixmuseum@gmail.com
https://alixwagonwheelmuseum.ca
www.facebook.com/alixmuseum

Local history and artifacts; souvenir shop. Open year round, but by appointment from Oct. through May.
Donna Peterson, President

Alliance: Alliance & District Museum
Parent: Alliance & District Museum Society
PO Box 101,
Alliance, AB T0B 0A0

Tel: 780-879-2333

Local history; pioneer & farming artifacts; early log cabin & blacksmith shop on-site; doll collection; Norman Johnston room.

Andrew: Andrew & District Local History Museum
5313 - 50 Ave.,
Andrew, AB T0B 0C0

Local artifacts & records; open year round

Banff: Banff Park Museum National Historic Site
91 Banff Ave.,
Banff, AB T1L 1K2

Tel: 403-762-1558
www.pc.gc.ca
twitter.com/banffnp
www.facebook.com/BanffNP

Year Founded: 1903 The Banff Park Museum is a natural history museum, showcasing a collection of 5,000 specimens. The park also features an outdoor activities for children.

Banff: Buffalo Nations Luxton Museum
PO Box 850,
Banff, AB T1L 1A8

Tel: 403-762-2388
buffalonations@telus.net
buffalonationsmuseum.com
twitter.com/buffalonations
www.facebook.com/B uffaloNationsLuxtonMuseum

Year Founded: 1952 The Buffalo Nations Luxton Museum depicts the cultures & traditions of the First Nations people of the Plains. Artifacts date back over 100 years.

Banff: Luxton Historic Home
Parent: Eleanor Luxton Historical Foundation
PO Box 1480,
Banff, AB T1L 1B4

Tel: 403-762-2105
luxton@webarmour.ca
www.luxtonfoundation.org

The house was once owned by one of Banff's prominent pioneer families, the Luxtons. Now the museum holds a collection featuring native artifacts, antiques, costumes, & unique international items. Open F-Su & holiday mondays May-Sept. 11:00-3:00.

Banff: Whyte Museum of the Canadian Rockies
111 Bear St.,
Banff, AB T1L 1A3

Tel: 403-762-2291
info@whyte.org
www.whyte.org

Visitors to the Whyte Museum discover the history, art, & social & cultural past of the Canadian Rockies. Guided tours are provided of the heritage gallery, the art gallery, heritage homes, the Luxton home & garden, & historic Banff. The Archives & Library, located at the museum, collects books, journals, maps, newspaper clippings, microforms, textual records, photographs, & audio-visual materials related to the Canadian Rockies.
Marino DiManno, Chair
Donald Watkins, Vice Chair

Barrhead: Barrhead Centennial Museum
5629 - 49th St.,
Barrhead, AB T7N 1K9

Tel: 780-674-5203
barrheadcentennialmuseum@gmail.com
barrheadcentennial.wixsite.com
www.instagram.com/barrheadcentennial
www.facebook.com/barrheadcentennial museum

Year Founded: 1967 The Barrhead Centennial Museum is operated by the Barrhead & District Historical Society. Exhibits at the Barrhead Centennial Museum & Visitor Information Center include Barrhead settlers' furniture, pioneer farm equipment, & tools. The complete local newspaper is also available at the museum, plus a large collection of African artifacts. The museum is open from the Victoria Day weekend in May to the Labour Day weekend in September.

Beaverlodge: South Peace Centennial Museum
PO Box 493,
Beaverlodge, AB T0H 0C0

southpeacemuseum.com

Year Founded: 1967 Pioneer equipment & buildings; open mid-May - Sept. 1

Bellevue: Bellevue Underground Mine
Parent: Crowsnest Pass Ecomuseum Trust Society
PO Box 519,
Bellevue, AB T0K 0E0

Tel: 403-564-4700; *Fax:* 403-564-4711
info@bellevuemine.org
www.bellevueundergroundmine.org
twitter.com/Bell evueMine

Guided tours through a mine originally used from 1903-1961. Open May-Sept., daily 10:00-6:30 & Oct.-Apr., M-F 9:00-5:00

Bentley: Bentley Museum
PO Box 620,
Bentley, AB T0C 0J0

Tel: 403-748-2455; *Fax:* 403-748-4537
bentleymuseum@shaw.ca

The museum depicts the lives of early settlers through exhibits housed in a 1924 farmhouse & separate agricultural buildings. Summer Hours: M-W & Sa 9:00-5:00, Su 2:00-5:00. Winter Hours: Open W morning, or by request.

Big Valley: Big Valley Creation Science Museum (BVCSM)
PO Box 340,
Big Valley, AB T0J 0G0

Tel: 403-876-2100
info@bvcsm.com
www.bvcsm.com

Year Founded: 2008 The museum seeks to "refute the lie of evolution" through its exhibits, which include fossils & a large model of Noah's ark.

Big Valley: Big Valley Museum
PO Box 342,
Big Valley, AB T0J 0G0

Tel: 403-741-5522
bvhistoricsociety@gmail.com
bvhistoricsociety.wix.com/bvhs

The museum includes a number of sites: a garage featuring artifacts & antique vehicles & machinery; St. Edmund's Church; former Alberta Wheat Pool grain elevator; two antique railway baggage cars featuring thousands of artifacts; & a section of the CNR station, featuring local memorabilia. Open May-Sept., 10:00-6:00; open by request the rest of the year.

Bowden: Bowden Pioneer Museum
Parent: Bowden Historical Society
2201 - 19th Ave.,
Bowden, AB T0M 0K0

Tel: 403-224-2122
bhs@shawbiz.ca
www.bowden.ca/p/bowden-pioneer-museum-

Year Founded: 1967 Governed by the Bowden Historical Society, the Bowden Pioneer Museum is located in the old Bowden curling rink. The museum contains the following artifacts & exhibits: The Bob Hoare Photography Exhibit; The Eastern Star Exhibit; The Irene M. Wood Avon Collection, The Women of Aspenland Lives & Works; a hardware & general store display; military artifacts; geological collections, decorative arts, such as musical instruments; fine arts of First Nations & European origins; & human hisotry artifacts, such as religious objects, household items, & sports equipment. The museum also conducts research services. It is open from the long weekend in May to September.

Breton: Breton & District Historical Museum
Breton Elementary School, 4711 - 52st St.,
Breton, AB T0C 0P0

Tel: 780-696-2551
bretonmuse@yahoo.com
www.village.breton.ab.ca/history.html
Year Founded: 1989 The museum focuses on the history of black prisoners who emigrated to Canada during the early 1900s, becomming pioneers as they established their own community in central Alberta.
Allan Goddard, Contact

Brooks: Brooks & District Museum & Historical Society
568 Sutherland Dr. East,
Brooks, AB T1R 1C7

Tel: 403-362-5073; Fax: 403-362-5085
museum@xplornet.com
www.brooksmuseum.ca
Year Founded: 1974 Local history; open May-Sept., daily 9:00-5:00; weekly March-May.

Brownvale: Brownvale North Peace Agricultural Museum
PO Box 186,
Brownvale, AB T0H 0L0

Tel: 780-597-3934
The Brownvale North Peace Agricultural Museum features artifacts such as historic farm machinery, horse-powered equipment & construction equipment. The museum is open during July & August.

Calgary: Air Force Museum of Alberta (AFMA)
Parent: The Military Museums of Calgary
4520 Crowchild Trail SW,
Calgary, AB T2T 5J4

Tel: 403-410-2340; Fax: 403-410-2359
moradmin@telusplanet.net
www.themilitarymuseums.ca/gallery-airforce
The Air Force Museum of Alberta tells the story of Canada's Air Force through artifacts, models, interactive displays, & films.
Alison Mercer, Curator, 403-410-2340,
alison@themilitarymuseums.ca

Calgary: Army Museum of Alberta (AMA)
Parent: The Military Museums of Calgary
4520 Crowchild Trail SW,
Calgary, AB T2T 5J4

Tel: 403-410-2340; Fax: 403-410-2359
moradmin@telusplanet.net
www.themilitarymuseums.ca/gallery-army
The Army Museum of Alberta exhibits the province's army heritage from 1885 to the present. A major exhibit is The Fall of '44, which commemorates the efforts of Canadian troops during the last years of the Second World War.
Rory M. Cory, Senior Curator,
seniorcurator@themilitarymuseums.ca

Calgary: Calgary Chinese Cultural Centre
197 - 1st St. SW,
Calgary, AB T2P 4M4

Tel: 403-262-5071; Fax: 403-232-6387
info@culturalcentre.ca
www.culturalcentre.ca
Year Founded: 1992 The Calgary Chinese Cultural Centre promotes Chinese heritage, history & culture, as well as cultural diversity.
Victor Mah, Chair
Jake Louie, Vice-Chair
Tony Wong, President
Leonard Chow-Wah, Chief Financial Officer & Executive Vice-President

Calgary: The Calgary Highlanders Museum & Archives
Parent: The Military Museums of Calgary
4520 Crowchild Trail SW,
Calgary, AB T2T 5J4

Tel: 403-410-2340; Fax: 403-410-2359
museum@calgaryhighlanders.com
www.calgaryhighlanders.com
A history & recollection of the Calgary Highlanders.
Captain Peter Boyle, Curator CD, AdeC
Sergeant Dennis Russell, Curator CD
Mike Henry, Archivist

Calgary: Canada's Sports Hall of Fame (CSHOF) / Panthéon des Sports Canadiens
169 Canada Olympic Rd. SW,
Calgary, AB T3B 6B7

Tel: 403-776-1040
info@cshof.ca
www.sportshall.ca
instagram.com/cansportshall
twitter.com/CANsportshall
www.facebook.com/CANsportshall
Year Founded: 1955 Canada's Sports Hall of Fame tells the stories of Canadian amateur & professional athletes, as well as sport builders who have made outstanding achievements thoughout sports history. Includes 12 galleries, artifacts, interactive exhibits, theatres, sport challenges & lessons.
Marnie Krell, Director, Communications & Marketing,
mkrell@cshof.ca
Janice Smith, Director, Exhibits & Programs, jsmith@cshof.ca

Calgary: Fort Calgary
Parent: Fort Calgary Preservation Society
750 - 9 Ave. SE,
Calgary, AB T2G 5E1

Tel: 403-290-1875
info@fortcalgary.com
www.fortcalgary.com
instagram.com/fortcalgary
twitter.com/fortcalgary
www.facebook.com/fortcalgary
40-acre park; interpretive centre; 1875 fort reconstruction project; guided tours; open year round
Naomi Grattan, President & CEO, ngrattan@fortcalgary.com

Calgary: The Grain Academy & Museum
Plus 15, BMO Centre, 20 Roundup Way SE,
Calgary, AB T2G 2W1

Tel: 403-263-4594
grainacademy@nucleus.com
www.grainacademy.com
twitter.com/grainacademy
www.facebook.com/G rainAcademyMuseum
Year Founded: 1981 Centre devoted to preserving the history of early pioneers in the prairies and the evolution of the grain industry. Exhibits include videos, a working grain elevator demonstration, samples of products and other displays.
Jim Anderson, Operations Manager

Calgary: Hangar Flight Museum
4629 McCall Way NE,
Calgary, AB T2E 8A5

Tel: 403-250-3752; Fax: 403-250-8399
info@thehangarmuseum.ca
thehangarmuseum.ca
www.instagram.com/thehangarmuseum
twitter.com/thehangarmuseum
www.face book.com/TheHangarMuseum
Year Founded: 1985 With over 20 historical aircrafts on display, guests can explore Canadian achievements in aviation & space. Aircraft engines, extensive aviation library & interactive exhibits; educational programs & tours; gift shop; meeting/function room rentals. Open year round.
Brian Desjardin, Executive Director,
ExecDir@thehangarmuseum.ca

Calgary: Heritage Park Historical Village
1900 Heritage Dr. SW,
Calgary, AB T2V 2X3

Tel: 403-268-8500; Fax: 403-268-8500
info@heritagepark.ca
www.heritagepark.ca
twitter.com/HeritageParkYYC
www.facebook.com/HeritageParkYYC
Year Founded: 1964 Billed as a living history museum, the expansive site offers a wide range of exhibits and activities, most notably the exploration of a village of historical, "old west" buildings replete with antiques, artifacts and costumed guides. Gasoline Alley Museum focuses on the history of the automobile. There is a steam train, antique midway and Haskayne Mercantile Block of shops. Open May - Sept.
Lindsey Galloway, President/CEO

Calgary: The King's Own Calgary Regiment (RCAC) Museum
Parent: The Military Museums of Calgary
4520 Crowchild Trail SW,
Calgary, AB T2T 5J4

Tel: 403-410-2340
www.kingsown.ca
Depicts the history of the four regiments of Calgary; art gallery; open all year. Artifacts & pictures of regimental "family tree"; permanent displays of the 50th Battalion C.E.F. which deature

The Deadly Sniper; Cpl. Henry Norwest; M.M. Vimy; Pte. John George Pattison V.C.; non-permanent active militial Dieppel The Prisoner of War Room; Sicily, Italy, including the Kingsmill Bridge & the Battle of Cassino. Special film & military documentaties in the Amoco Theatre.

Calgary: Lord Strathcona's Horse (Royal Canadians) Regimental Museum
Parent: The Military Museums of Calgary
4520 Crowchild Trail SW,
Calgary, AB T2T 5J4

Tel: 403-410-2340; Fax: 403-410-2359
museum@strathconas.ca
www.strathconas.ca/strathcona-museum
www.faceboo k.com/Strathconas
Other contact information: Alt. email: archives@strathconas.ca
Year Founded: 1990 Museum relates the history of the Regiment from 1900 to present. The collection holds many artifacts yet undisplayed. The Archives store photographs, records, documents & diaries and research is conducted for personal & professional institutions. Open year round.

Calgary: Lougheed House
Parent: Lougheed House Conservation Society
707 - 13th Ave. SW,
Calgary, AB T2R 0K8

Tel: 403-244-6333; Fax: 403-244-6354
info@lougheedhouse.com
www.lougheedhouse.com
lougheedhouse.blogspot.ca
twitter.com/lougheedhouse
www.facebook.com/1 05991712783670
Lougheed House was built in 1891 & was originally known was Beaulieu, & is a National Historic Site. Visitors can tour the building, eat lunch in the on-site restaurant, & visit the gift shop. The house is open W-F 11:00-4:00, Sa & Su 10:00-4:00.
Kirstin Evenden, Executive Director,
kirstinevenden@lougheedhouse.com
Cassandra Cummings, Curator,
cassandra@lougheedhouse.com
Cathy Olson, General Manager,
cathyolson@lougheedhouse.com

Calgary: Naval Museum of Alberta (NMA)
Parent: The Military Museums of Calgary
4520 Crowchild Trail SW,
Calgary, AB T2T 5J4

Tel: 403-410-2340; Fax: 403-410-2359
moradmin@telusplanet.net
www.themilitarymuseums.ca/gallery-navy
Year Founded: 1988 Collection includes one each of the 3 naval aircraft (fighter planes) used by RCN; naval armament including guns, torpedos, anti-submarine equipment, clothing etc.
Bruce Connolly, Curator, bruce@themilitarymuseums.ca

Calgary: The Nickle Arts Museum
University of Calgary, 2500 University Dr. NW,
Calgary, AB T2N 1N4

nickle.ucalgary.ca
twitter.com/nicklegalleries
www.facebook.com/NickleGalleries
Founded in 1979 through a donation from Sam Nickle & a Province of Alberta grant; champions contemporary Canadian art, numismatics & Oriental carpets; changing exhibitions & programs.
Christine Sowiak, Chief Curator, 403-220-6098,
cfsowiak@ucalgary.ca

Calgary: Princess Patricia's Canadian Light Infantry Regimental Museum & Archives (PPCLI)
Parent: The Military Museums of Calgary
4520 Crowchild Trail S.W.,
Calgary, AB T2T 5J4

Tel: 403-410-2340
ppcli.museumgm@gmail.com
www.ppcli.com
www.facebook.com/ppcli
Princess Patricia's Canadian Light Infantry Regimental Museum & Archives collects & preserves items that cover the dates from 1914, when Princess Patricia's Canadian Light Infantry was founded, to the present day. The Infantry is known for its service in both World Wars, Korea, & Afghanistan, & during other operations for the United Nations & NATO. Holdings include war journals, photographs, training manuals, cartographic materials, & audio-visual resources, especially related to the Princess Patricia's Canadian Light Infantry, & to the Canadian Army in general. The museum is open year-round.
Sgt. Nate Blackmore, General Manager, 403-410-2340

Calgary: University of Calgary, Museum of Zoology
Biological Sciences Bldg., 2500 University Dr. NW,
Calgary, AB T2N 1N4

science.ucalgary.ca

Teaching museum used for zoology & ecology courses; also
services the Archaeology, Geology, & Art departments, as well
as Inglewood Bird Sanctuary & the Alberta Science Centre.

Calgary: Youthlink Calgary: Calgary Police Service
Interpretive Centre
5111 - 47th St. NE,
Calgary, AB T3J 3R2

Tel: 403-428-4530; Fax: 403-974-0508
youthlink@calgarypolice.ca
www.youthlinkcagary.ca
www.youtube.com/youthlinkcgy
twitter.com/YouthLinkCGY
www.facebook.com/YouthLinkCGY

Interactive exhibits & programs educate youth about life, crime,
& law enforcement.
Joan Shilling, Chair

Calgary: YouthLink Calgary: The Calgary Police
Interpretive Centre
5111 - 47th St. NE,
Calgary, AB T3J 3R2

Tel: 403-428-4566
info@youthlinkcalgary.com
www.youthlinkcalgary.com
www.youtube.com/youthlinkcgy
twitter.com/YouthLinkCGY
www.facebook.com/YouthLinkCGY

Year Founded: 1995 The purpose of YouthLink is to education
young people about the role of police in society, & the
consequences of crime, through exhibits & programs.
Tara Robinson, Executive Director,
tara.robinson@calgarypolice.ca

Camrose: Camrose & District Museum
4522 - 53 St.,
Camrose, AB T4V 4E3

Tel: 780-672-9949
www.camrose.ca

Year Founded: 1967 Buildings on the museum grounds include a
pioneer home, The Likeness School, the St. Dunstan's Church, a
firehall, the local newspaper building, a blacksmith shop, the
Mona Sparling Building, the Oldtimers Hut, & the R.C.M.P.
Machine Building. The musuem is open from Victoria Day
weekend to Labour Day weekend. Appointments may be
arranged at other times of the year.

Canmore: Canmore Museum & Geoscience Centre
Civic Centre, PO Box 8849, 902B - 7th Ave.,
Canmore, AB T1W 3K1

Tel: 403-678-2462
info@canmoremuseum.com
www.cmags.org
twitter.com/Canmoremuseum
www.facebook.com/canmoremuseum

The Canmore Museum & Geoscience Centre features historical
artifacts, geological collections, & information about the heritage
of Canmore & the surrounding mountainous area. The museum
also operates the 1893 North West Mounted Police Barracks,
which is situated on 609 Main Street.
Ron Ulrich, Executive Director, director@canmoremuseum.com

Cardston: Card Pioneer Home & Museum
337 Main St.,
Cardston, AB T0K 0K0

Tel: 403-653-3366

C.O. Card Home & Museum is a Provincial Historic Site. It
features the log cabin built by Charles Ora Card, who was the
founder of Cardston. The museum is open during July & August.
During the off season, appointments may be arranged.

Cardston: Courthouse Museum
89 - 3rd Ave. West,
Cardston, AB T0K 0K0

www.cardstonhistoricalsocety.org

The Courthouse is a Provincial Historic Site, which was
constructed in 1907 from local sandstone. Court artifacts are on
display, including the witness stand, judge's bench, & orginal jail
cells. The musuem is open during July & August. During the off
season, appointments may be arranged.

Cardston: Remington Carriage Museum
623 Main St.,
Cardston, AB T0K 0K0

Tel: 403-653-5139
info@RemingtonCarriageMuseum.com
remingtoncarriagemuseum.ca
www.facebook.com/RemingtonCarriageMuseum1

Year Founded: 1993 The Remington Carriage Museum features
the largest collection of horse-drawn vehicles in North America,
such as carriages, sleighs, & wagons. The facility also contains
a working stable, a carriage factory, & a restoration shop.
Educational programs are offered. The museum is open
year-round.

Caroline: Caroline Wheels of Time Museum
Parent: Community Historical Society of Caroline
PO Box 535,
Caroline, AB T0M 0M0

Tel: 403-722-3884
wheels3884@gmail.com
www.carolinemuseum.ca

Year Founded: 1991 The museum operates five historic
buildings, including a country store, a school, & a trapper's
cabin. Open May-Sept., 12:00-6:00

Carstairs: Carstairs Heritage Centre
Parent: Carstairs & District Historical Society
PO Box 1067, 1138 Nanton St.,
Carstairs, AB T0M 0N0

Tel: 403-337-3710
carstairsmuseum@icloud.com
www.carstairs.ca/en/visitingcarstairs/museum.asp

Year Founded: 1988 The main collection is housed in the hall of
Knox Presbyterian Church (1901), and is a registered historic
site. Amongst a collection of over 4,000 artifacts includes church
records; pictures & artifacts of local life from early settlement to
present; archives; a new library research room and a new farm
implement display building. In the summer, the museum also
serves as the town's visitor information centre.
Betty Ayers, Curator
Robert Disney, President

Castor: Castor & District Museum
PO Box 864,
Castor, AB T0C 0X0

Tel: 403-882-3271

Year Founded: 1978 Local history, including a 1910 Alberta
Pacific Grain Elevator & collection of restored railcars. Open
March-Nov., Th, Sa & Su 2:00-4:00.

Claresholm: Appaloosa Horse Club of Canada
Museum & Archives
Parent: ApHCC Museum & Archive Society
PO Box 940, 4189 - 3rd St. SE,
Claresholm, AB T0L 0T0

Tel: 403-625-3326; Fax: 403-625-2274
registry@appaloosa.ca
www.appaloosa.ca/museum.html

History of the Appaloosa horse
Donna Wyatt, Museum Liaison, dmwyatt@live.com

Claresholm: Claresholm Museum
5115 - 2nd St. East,
Claresholm, AB T0L 0T0

Tel: 403-625-1742
museum@townofclaresholm.com
www.claresholm.com
www.instagram.com/claresholmmuseum
twitter.com/claresholmuseum
www.facebook.com/claresholmmuseum
Other contact information: Information Centre, Phone:
403-625-3131

Year Founded: 1969 Local history museum in the old Sandstone
Railway Station; Claresholm was home to Louise C. McKinney, a
social activist for the cause of women's welfare and legal status,
and the first woman parliamentarian in the British Empire; open
daily May-Sept; admission by donation

Cochrane: Cochrane Ranche Historic Site
PO Box 1522,
Cochrane, AB T0L 0W0

Tel: 403-851-2535
rec.culture@cochrane.ca
www.cochrane.ca/704/Discover-the-Ranche

Located off Hwy #22, north of downtown Cochrane, The
Cochrane Ranche is Alberta's first large-scale livestock ranch.
Open May 15 - Labour Day; hiking & picnic areas open year
round.

Cold Lake: Cold Lake Air Force Museum
PO Box 5770 Forces,
Cold Lake, AB T9M 2C6

Tel: 780-594-3546
clafm@telus.net
www.facebook.com/pages/Cold-Lake-Museums/343764180120

Coleman: Crowsnest Museum
Parent: Crowsnest Historical Society
7701 - 18 Ave.,
Coleman, AB T0K 0M0

Tel: 403-563-5434
cnmuseum@shaw.ca
www.crowsnestmuseum.ca

Year Founded: 1985 Over 25,000 artifacts on display interpreting
the history of the Crowsnest Pass & its people; themed galleries
include pioneers, underground mining, general store/blacksmith
shop, Legends of Prohibition, Gushul Studio. Veterans' exhibit,
wildlife diorama; open year round

Crowsnest Pass: The Frank Slide Interpretive Centre
(FSIC)
PO Box 959 Blairmore,
Crowsnest Pass, AB T0K 0E0

Tel: 403-562-7388; Fax: 403-562-8635
frankslideinfo@gov.ab.ca
www.history.alberta.ca/frankslide/
www.facebook.com/FrankSlideInterpretiveCentre
Other contact information: In Alberta, toll free 310-0000

Site of the 1903 rockslide avalanche; visual presentation "In the
Mountain's Shadow" shown daily; open year-round.

Crowsnest Pass: Leitch Collieries Provincial Historic
Site
Crowsnest Pass, AB

Tel: 403-564-4211
FrankSlideInfo@gov.ab.ca
https://leitchcollieries.ca

Ruin of coal mining operation; staffed May 15 - Labour Day;
located off Hwy. #3 in Crowsnest Pass, AB.

DeBolt: DeBolt & District Pioneer Museum
404 Virginia Ave.,
DeBolt, AB T0H 1B0

Tel: 780-957-3955
deboltmuseum@gmail.com
http://spiritofthepeace.ca/
www.facebook.com/197729256911960

Year Founded: 1975 The museum comprises 8 heritage
buildings with displays: in Hubert Memorial Park on Viriginia
Ave., in the community church & Legion Hall; collections include
the Bickell Fossil Collection. Open summer.

Delburne: Anthony Henday Museum
2603 - 20 St.,
Delburne, AB T0M 0V0

Tel: 403-749-2711

Housed in the former CNR train station; water tank tower,
caboose, machine shed & pioneer cabin replica on site; depicts
history of Delburne & district with emphasis on agriculture,
households & coal mining.

Dewberry: Dewberry Valley Museum
PO Box 30,
Dewberry, AB T0B 1G0

Tel: 403-847-3053
dewberry@hmsinet.ca
www.villageofdewberry.ca/museum.html

Year Founded: 1974 History of the Dewberry Valley area,
including prehistoric, fur trade, Riel Rebellion, & pioneer artifacts;
also features a pioneer log cabin.
Phillip Porter, Curator

Didsbury: Didsbury & District Museum
Parent: Didsbury & District Historical Society
PO Box 1175, 2110 - 21st Ave.,
Didsbury, AB T0M 0W0

Tel: 403-335-9295
ddhs@telusplanet.net
www.didsburymuseum.com
www.facebook.com/166327316875568

Year Founded: 1978 The Didsbury and District Museum tells the
story of the founding, settlement and development of Disbury
Albeta and the surrounding area from the late 1800s to the
present.

Donalda: Donalda & District Museum
PO Box 179,
Donalda, AB T0B 1H0

Tel: 403-883-2100
info@donaldamuseum.com
www.donaldamuseum.com
www.facebook.com/donaldamuseum

Over 850 lamps; Whitford Collection of Métis artifacts from the
late 1800s; native tools; artifacts; open during the summer
season, 10-5

Drayton Valley: Drayton Valley & District Historical Society Museum
Parent: Drayton Valley & District Historical Society
PO Box 5099, 6009 - 43rd Ave.,
Drayton Valley, AB T7A 1R3

Tel: 780-542-4908
www.draytonvalley.ca/museum
Other contact information: Alt. Phone: 780-542-5482
The museum is dedicated to the preservation of local history in-and-around Drayton Valley. The museum is run by the Drayton Valley Historical Society.
Charlie Miner, Contact

Drumheller: Homestead Antique Museum
901 North Dinosaur Trail,
Drumheller, AB T0J 0Y1

Tel: 403-823-2600
Year Founded: 1965 Situated in the Canadian Badlands, the Homestead Pioneer Museum presents exhibits from the Drumheller Valley, including farm machinery & tools, vehicles, & a 1919 house. The museum is open from mid May to mid October.

East Coulee: Atlas Coal Mine National Historic Site
PO Box 521, 110 Century Ave.,
East Coulee, AB T0J 1B0

Tel: 403-822-2220; *Fax:* 403-822-2225
info@atlascoalmine.ab.ca
www.atlascoalmine.ab.ca
www.youtube.com/user/atlascoalmine
www.facebook.com/184631621585939
Year Founded: 1989 Located in the Canadian Badlands, the Atlas Coal Mine National Historic Site offers tours & educational programs. Visitors can go underground, explore the last wooden tipple in Canada, see the blacksmith shop, & ride an authentic mine locomotive. The site is open from the beginning of May to mid-October.

East Coulee: East Coulee School Museum (ECSM)
PO Box 514,
East Coulee, AB T0J 1B0

Tel: 403-822-3970
www.ecsmuseum.ca
www.facebook.com/ecspringfest
Open year round

Edmonton: Alberta Aviation Museum
11410 Kingsway Ave. NW,
Edmonton, AB T5G 0X4

Tel: 780-451-1175; *Fax:* 780-451-1607
info@albertaaviationmuseum.com
www.albertaaviationmuseum.com
twitter.c om/AbAvMuseum
www.facebook.com/abavmuseum/
The museum tells & interprets the story of aviation & its importance to Edmonton & Northern Alberta. Its displays & exhibits allow visitors to embrace the spirit of those involved in early aviation endeavours that helped Edmonton establish its title as "Gateway to the North." On site can be found: flight simulator & an aircraft restoration area; activities for children, guided tours, and special events; and space rentals, with theatre projection & sound system. Open year-round.

Edmonton: Alberta Railway Museum
24215 - 34th St.,
Edmonton, AB T5Y 6B4

Tel: 780-472-6229
www.albertarailwaymuseum.com
twitter.com/abrailwaymuseum
www.facebook.com/AlbertaRailwayMuseum
Year Founded: 1968 The Alberta Railway Museum features over sixty railway cars & locomotives, interpretive displays, a Morse telegraph demonstration, tours, & train rides on selected long weekends. The museum is open on weekends only from Victoria Day (the long weekend in May) to Labour Day (the long weekend in September).
Stephen Yakimets, Special Bookings, 780-441-5917

Edmonton: Calgary & Edmonton (1891) Railway Museum
Parent: Junior League of Edmonton
10447 - 86th Ave.,
Edmonton, AB T6E 2M4

Tel: 780-433-9739
admin@jledmonton.org
a62312.wix.com/canderailwaymuseum
www.twitter.com/TheCandEStation
www.facebook.com/CandERailwayStation
Year Founded: 1982 Visitors to the Calgary & Edmonton (1891) Railway Museum can see a replica railway station, which served the area from 1891 to 1907. Train & station artifacts are on display, including a working telegraph service. The museum is

open from June to August. At other times, appointments may be arranged.

Edmonton: College & Association of Registered Nurses of Alberta Museum & Archives (CARNA)
CARNA Provincial Office, 11620 - 168 St.,
Edmonton, AB T5M 4A6

Tel: 780-453-0534; *Fax:* 780-482-4459
lmychajlunow@nurses.ab.ca
www.nurses.ab.ca
Items related to the founding & development of the AARN (now known as CARNA), as well as the early history of professional nursing in Alberta. Collection includes caps, pins, uniforms, yearbooks, original diplomas & photographs from early days of nurses' education in Alberta to present; scrapbooks, uniforms & military medals (WWI & WWII) from the Nursing Sisters Association; and records of various nursing interest groups.

Edmonton: Edmonton Power Historical Foundation Museum (EPHF)
PO Box 31121 Namao,
Edmonton, AB T5Z 2P3

Tel: 780-471-4285
www.ephf.ca/museum
www.youtube.com/channel/UChvlzsR_U5DVnxGtxZqLHAw
The museum seeks to relate Alberta's electrical power industry to the general public, including hands-on activities & games for kids. The website also features a Online Museum with pictures & descriptions of items from the physical collection. Open once in May, twice in July & once in September; open to groups by appointment.

Edmonton: Edmonton Public Schools Archives & Museum
McKay Avenue School, 10425 - 99 Ave. NW,
Edmonton, AB T5K 0E5

Tel: 780-422-1970
archivesmuseum@epsb.ca
archivesmuseum.epsb.ca
www.instagram.com/historic_mckay_avenue_school
twitter.com/EPSB_McKay
Located in historic McKay Ave. School, site of the first session of the Alberta Legislature; 1905 restored brick building & features the restored 1906 legislative Chamber; holdings include Edmonton Public School Board District #7 & individual school records from 1885 to present

Edmonton: Edmonton Radial Railway Society
Strathcona Streetcar Barn, PO Box 76057 Southgate,
Edmonton, AB T6H 5Y7

Tel: 780-437-7721
info@edmonton-radial-railway.ab.ca
edmonton-radial-railway.ab.ca
twitter.com/yegstreetcar
www.facebook.co m/edmontonstreetcar
Vintage 3 km streetcar ride from Strathcona to downtown Edmonton along former CPR right of way & across the High Level Bridge; restored streetcar rides for visitors to Fort Edmonton Park

Edmonton: Fort Edmonton Park
7000 - 143 St. SW,
Edmonton, AB T6H 4P3

www.fortedmontonpark.ca
www.instagram.com/fortedmontonpark
twitter.com/fortedpark
www.facebook .com/fortedmontonpark
Canada's largest living history park; a complete 1846 fur-trading fort & 1885, 1905 & 1920 costumed interpreters; steam train & street car; giftshops & restaurants; fully operational hotel on site

Edmonton: John Janzen Nature Centre
PO Box 2359, 7000 - 143 St.,
Edmonton, AB T5J 2R7

Tel: 780-442-5311
attractions@edmonton.ca
www.edmonton.ca
www.facebook.com/JohnJanzenNatureCentre
Year Founded: 1976 Nature appreciation programming.

Edmonton: John Walter Museum
9180 Walterdale Hill NW,
Edmonton, AB T6E 2V3

attractionsexperiences@edmonton.ca
www.edmonton.ca/johnwalter
www.facebook.com/johnwaltermuseum
The museum consists of houses from 1874, 1886, & 1901. A variety of group programs are available. John Walter Museum is open from mid March to mid December.

Edmonton: The Loyal Edmonton Regiment Military Museum
Prince of Wales Armouries Heritage Centre, #118, 10440 - 108 Ave.,
Edmonton, AB T5H 3Z9

Tel: 780-421-9943; *Fax:* 780-421-9943
info@lermuseum.org
www.lermuseum.org
twitter.com/49bnlermus
www.face book.com/203117963074315
Military museum focusing on history of The Loyal Edmonton Regiment & other military service branches from Northern Alberta.
Kathleen Haggarty, Collections Manager

Edmonton: Rutherford House Provincial Historic Site
11153 Saskatchewan Dr.,
Edmonton, AB T6G 2S1

Tel: 780-427-3995
Rutherford.House@gov.ab.ca
rutherfordhouse.ca
Home of Alberta's first premier; gift shop, tea room, tours & special events; open year round

Edmonton: Ukrainian Canadian Archives & Museum of Alberta (UCAMA)
9543 - 110 Ave. NW,
Edmonton, AB T5H 1H3

www.facebook.com/ucama.museum
Year Founded: 1972 The Ukrainian Canadian Archives & Museum of Alberta is dedicated to preserving Ukrainian-Canadian history & culture. Collections include Ukrainian-Canadian military memorabilia such as uniforms, textiles made by Ukrainian pioneers in Alberta, as well as ecclesiastical artifacts.

Edmonton: Ukrainian Catholic Women's League of Canada Arts & Crafts Museum (UCWLC)
8907 - 156 Ave.,
Edmonton, AB T5Z 3B8

PresidentNatlucwlc@gmail.com
www.ucwlc.ca
Open by appt.
Barbara Hlus, President

Edmonton: Ukrainian Cultural Heritage Museum
Edmonton, AB T6G 2P8

Tel: 780-662-3640; *Fax:* 780-662-3273
uchv@gov.ab.ca
www.history.alberta.ca/ukrainianvillage/default.aspx
1899 Ukrainian settlement; traditional Ukrainian arts & crafts; open Jun-Sep & by appointment.
David Makowsky, Director, 780-662-3855,
david.makowsky@gov.ab.ca
Becky Dahl, Curator, 780-662-3855, becky.dahl@gov.ab.ca

Edmonton: University of Alberta Dental Museum
Edmonton, AB T6G 2N8

Tel: 780-492-3427
Collection of antique dental instruments & furniture as well as a natural history collection of animal skulls & fossil hominid models. Although the collection still exists, the museum is currently inactive, as the School of Dentistry moved to a location that could not accommodate the collection.
Dr. Loren Kline, Curator, lkline@ualberta.ca

Edmonton: University of Alberta Museum of Paleontology
Department of Earth & Atmospheric Science
University of Alberta - B-01 Earth Sciences Building,
Edmonton, AB T6G 2E3

Tel: 780-492-3265; *Fax:* 780-492-2030
eas.inquiries@ualberta.ca
easweb.eas.ualberta.ca/page/Paleontology_Museu m
twitter.com/UofA_EAS
www.facebook.com/UofAEarthandAtmosphericScience sDepartment
The museum presents the history of life over the course of geological time, starting with PreCambrian stromatolites & ending with Pleistocene megafauna; open during business hours Mon.-Thu.

Edmonton: University of Alberta Museum of Zoology (UAMZ)
#Z1011, Biological Sciences Bldg., University of Alberta,
Edmonton, AB T6G 2E9

Tel: 780-492-4622
www.biology.ualberta.ca/uamz.hp/uamz.html
Open year round
Cindy Paszkowski, Curator, Amphibian, Reptile and Ornithology Collections, cindy.paszkowski@ualberta.ca

Edmonton: University of Alberta Museums
3-20 Rutherford South,
Edmonton, AB T6G 2J4

Tel: 780-492-5834
museums@ualberta.ca
www.museums.ualberta.ca
twitter.com/UAlbertaMuseums
www.facebook.com/u albertamuseums
Museum services & expertise are provided to more than 35 teaching & research collections at the University; human history, fine art, natural & applied science collections, public programs, educational outreach & other community service programs offered
Frannie Blondheim, Associate Director/Interim Director,
frannie.blondheim@ualberta.ca
Nadia Kurd, Curator, Univ. of Alberta Art Collection,
kurd@ualberta.ca

Edmonton: Victoria School Archives & Museum
10210 - 108 Ave.,
Edmonton, AB T5H 1A8

Tel: 780-492-8715
Year Founded: 1995 Artifacts that relate to the school from 1903 to present; student & teacher records from 1911; books, playbills, posters, uniforms, photos, sweaters; the museum's collection is temporarily in storage while staff search for a new home.

Edson: Galloway Station Museum & Travel Centre
223 - 55 St.,
Edson, AB T7E 1L5

Tel: 780-723-5696
manager@gallowaystationmuseum.com
gallowaystationmuseum.com
The Galloway railway station was originally a Canadian Northern Type C station built in 1911. It was donated by CN to the Edson and District Historical Society in 1975 and officially opened to the public in 1981.
Jim Gomumka, President, gomjb@telus.net

Edson: Red Brick Arts Centre & Museum
4818 - 7 Ave.,
Edson, AB T7E 1K8

Tel: 780-723-3582
echored@telus.net
www.redbrickartscentre.com
www.facebook.com/RedBrickArtsCentre
Year Founded: 1987 Art gallery, theatre, school room museum, dance studio & gift shop

Etzikom: Etzikom Museum & Historic Windmill Centre
PO Box 585,
Etzikom, AB T0K 0W0

Tel: 403-666-3737; *Fax:* 403-666-2002
Canadian national historic windmill centre; open May long weekend - Sept. long weekend Mon-Sat 10-5, Sun. 12-6

Forestburg: Forestburg & District Museum
Parent: Forestburg Historical Society
4703 - 50 St.,
Forestburg, AB T0B 1N0

Tel: 780-582-2298
www.forestburg.ca/content/museum
The building the museum is housed in was built in 1927 and was the former Masonic Temple; it is now a registered historical resource and has been restored by the Forestburg Historical Society. The Forestburg Historical Society also maintains the Diplomat Mine Museum.
Ryan Hunting, President, 780-582-3758,
ryan.hunting@persona.ca
Gordon Lunty, Treasurer, 780-582-4285, glunty@persona.ca
Michael Jahns, Director, 780-582-3553

Fort Chipewyan: Fort Chipewyan Bicentennial Museum
PO Box 203, 109 Mackenzie Ave.,
Fort Chipewyan, AB T0P 1B0

Tel: 780-697-3844; *Fax:* 780-697-2389
www.rmwb.ca/Visiting/Arts-and-Heritage/Fort-Chipewyan-Bicent
ennial-Museum
Year Founded: 1991 The museum is a replica of the Hudson's Bay Store. Opened by the Fort Chipewyan Historical Society in 1990, it was built to commemorate Fort Chipewyan's 200th birthday in 1988. The museum's displays and exhibits, along with a growing collection of artifacts, an archive for papers, photos and slides and a small reference library, depict Fort Chipewyan's past. The museum operates culture classes and participates in community events. Fort Chipewyan is the oldest inhabited settlement in Alberta.

Fort MacLeod: The Fort Museum
219 Jerry Potts Blvd.,
Fort MacLeod, AB T0L 0Z0

Tel: 403-553-4703 *Toll-Free:* 866-273-6841
info@nwmpmuseum.com
www.nwmpmuseum.com
twitter.com/thefortmuseum
www .facebook.com/fortmuseum
Tells the story of the arrival of the NWMP into Western Canada, & the Natives & Pioneers of that time

Fort MacLeod: Head-Smashed-In Buffalo Jump
275068 Secondary Hwy 785,
Fort MacLeod, AB

Tel: 403-553-2731
info.hsibj@gov.ab.ca
www.head-smashed-in.com
Year Founded: 1987 Designated a UNESCO World Heritage Site in 1981, this jump is a testimony to the hunting customs of native peoples, particularly the Blackfoot, for thousands of years. The Interpretive Centre, blending into a sandstone cliff, explores the lives of the Blackfoot peoples from the geography of the region to the family life and ceremonies. Open Daily 10-5, throughout the Summer

Fort McMurray: Fort McMurray Oil Sands Discovery Centre
515 MacKenzie Blvd.,
Fort McMurray, AB T9H 4X3

Tel: 780-743-7167
osdc@gov.ab.ca
history.alberta.ca/oilsands
Open year round

Fort McMurray: Heritage Park
Parent: Fort McMurray Historical Society
1 Tolen Dr.,
Fort McMurray, AB T9H 1G7

Tel: 780-791-7575; *Fax:* 780-791-5180
heritage@fortmcmurrayhistory.com
www.fortmcmurrayhistory.com
twitter.c om/McMurrayHistory
www.facebook.com/260650299824
Year Founded: 1974 The park is a village of 17 historic buildings, including a trapper's cabin & a Catholic Mission, designed to celebrate the history of Ft. McMurray & the region. On site are 2 railway cars. Exhibits cover the logging, fishing & trapping industries. There is an extensive archive of photographs and historical documents.
Roseann Davidson, Executive Director, 780-791-7575

Fort Saskatchewan: Fort Heritage Precinct
10006 - 100 Ave.,
Fort Saskatchewan, AB T8L 0J3

Tel: 780-998-1783
museumprograms@fortsask.ca
fortheritageprecinct.ca
www.instagram.com/fortheritageprecinct
twitter.com/FortPrecinct
www.fa cebook.com/fortheritageprecinct
Year Founded: 1970

Girouxville: Musée Girouxville Museum
5015 - 50 St.,
Girouxville, AB T0H 1S0

Tel: 780-323-4252
girouxvl@serbernet.com
girouxville.ca/museum
Year Founded: 1969 Located in the heart of Girouxville, museum offers visitors a glimpse back into a time when pioneers first settled in the Smoky River Region; more than 6,000 pieces on display; collections includes: Religion, Native history, Natural history, Pioneer life, Hunting & Trapping, Transportation, Fur trade, Domestic history, Communications, Agriculture, Photography, Education, Geology & Palaeontology

Grande Prairie: Grande Prairie Museum
10329 - 101 Ave.,
Grande Prairie, AB T8V 6V3

Tel: 780-830-7090
culture@cityofgp.com
www.cityofgp.com
www.facebook.com/GPMuseum
Dinosaur bones; arrowheads; wildlife exhibits; pioneer artifacts; heritage village; archives; open daily, closed on holidays

Grande Prairie: The Heritage Discovery Centre (HDC)
Centre 2000, 11330 - 106 St., Lower Level,
Grande Prairie, AB T8V 7X9

Tel: 780-532-5790; *Fax:* 780-532-8039
culture@cityofgp.com
www.culture.cityofgp.com
twitter.com/GPMuseum
w ww.facebook.com/GPMuseum
Located at Centre 2000 in the Tourist Information Bldg., includes a main exhibit gallery, a Rotary Learning Theatre & the Kin Gallery. Also includes dinosaur exhibit, survivor games, mini-theatres and hands-on displays. Open year-round.
Kathy Pfau, Contact, 780-532-5790, kpfau@cityofgp.com

Grouard: Native Cultural Arts Museum
62 Mission St.,
Grouard, AB T0G 1C0

Tel: 780-751-3306; *Fax:* 780-751-3308
Toll-Free: 866-652-3456
www.northernlakescollege.ca/content.aspx?id=2472
Year Founded: 1976 Cultural & arts collections of the Woodland Cree & Métis People of northern Alberta. Summer hours: July-Aug., M-Sa 10:00-4:00; Winter hours: Sept.-May, Tu-Th 10:00-4:00; closed in Jan. May-June by appointment only.

Hanna: Hanna Museum & Pioneer Village
Parent: Hanna & District Historical Society
502 Pioneer Trail,
Hanna, AB T0J 1P0

Tel: 403-854-4244
hannamuseum1912@gmail.com
www.hanna.ca
Historic buildings at the pioneer village include a ranch house, a one room schoolhouse, a store, a church, a hospital, a dental office, & a power mill. Archives are also available for research. The museum & pioneer village is open from June to August, & in May & September by appointment.

High Prairie: High Prairie & District Museum & Historical Society
5301 - 49 St.,
High Prairie, AB T0G 1E0

Tel: 780-523-2601
www.highprairiemuseum.com
www.facebook.com/highprairiemuseum
Year Founded: 1967 The museum preserves the history of High Prairie & surrounding area by conserving artifacts used by homesteaders from the early 1900s. Stories of the settlers are also archived. Programs offered to children include butter-making, bread-making and sewing lessons. Open year round, with summer & winter hrs.

High River: Museum of the Highwood
406 - 1st St. SW,
High River, AB T1V 1M5

Tel: 403-652-7156
info@museumofthehighwood.com
www.museumofthehighwood.com
twitter.com/MuseumHighwood
www.facebook.co m/MuseumoftheHighwood
The museum, located inside a former CPR station, is home to thousands of photographs of High River area; open year round, M - Su.

Hinton: Alberta Forest Service Museum
1176 Switzer Dr.,
Hinton, AB T7V 2B7

Tel: 780-865-8200
Established to preserve a history of forestry in the province of Alberta; displays reflect work performed by the early rangers & provide an appreciation of their accomplishments achieved without benefit of modern transportation, tools & technology; "compact disk" guided tour; ranger headquarters cabin built in 1922; open daily; weekends by appt

Holden: Holden Historical Society Museum
PO Box 32,
Holden, AB T0B 2C0

Tel: 780-688-3593; *Fax:* 780-688-3928
holdenmuseum@gmail.com
The collection is of the local farming community with objects pertaining to pioneer life. Open Wed., Fri., & Sun. in summer, 2-4

Innisfail: Innisfail & District Historical Village
Parent: Innisfail & District Historical Society
PO Box 6042,
Innisfail, AB T4G 1S7

Tel: 403-227-2906; *Fax:* 403-227-2901
idhs@telus.net
www.innisfailhistory.ca

Year Founded: 1970 Promote the preservation, interpretation, enjoyment of the history of Innisfail & District; village is made up of seventeen buildings on two acres of land; farm machinary and picnic area.

Irvine: Prairie Memories Museum
PO Box 215,
Irvine, AB T0J 1V0
Tel: 403-834-3923; *Fax:* 403-834-3923
Local history; open June 30 - Sept.

Jasper: Jasper Yellowhead Museum & Archives (JYHS)
400 Bonhomme St.,
Jasper, AB T0E 1E0
Tel: 780-852-3013
manager@jaspermuseum.org
www.jaspermuseum.org
twitter.com/jaspermuseum
www.facebook.com/1235617 47657136
Year Founded: 1963 The Jasper Yellowhead Museum & Archives collects, preserves, & exhibits artifacts & documents related to the human history of Jasper National Park & the Yellowhead corridor. Displays in the historical gallery tell the story of the fur trade, the railway, & early tourism. The area has been designated as part of a World Heritage Site. The Jasper Yellowhead Museum & Archives is open year-round. Visits to the archives are by appointment only. Open daily from Jun - Sept. and Th - Su from Oct - May.

Kingman: Kingman Regional School Museum & Tea House
PO Box 97,
Kingman, AB T0B 2M0
Tel: 780-672-8220
Other contact information: Alternate Phone: 780-672-6969
Country school building from 1938.

Lamont County: Ukrainian Cultural Heritage Village
Lamont County, AB
Tel: 780-662-3640
uchv@gov.ab.ca
www.ukrainianvillage.ca
www.facebook.com/ukrainianvillage.ca
The provincial historic site presents Ukrainian settlement in east central Alberta between 1892 & 1930. The Ukrainian Cultural Heritage Village has over 30 historic buildings for visitors to explore, including a grain elevator, a budei (a sod hut), & three churches of Eastern Byzantine Rite. The village is open from the May long weekend to Labour Day. School groups may book a tour at other times of the year.

Leduc: Dr. Woods House Museum
4801 - 49 Ave.,
Leduc, AB T9E 7G6
Tel: 780-986-1517
woodsmuseum@telus.net
www.woodsmuseum.com
Restored 1920s house with attached garage & medical wing

Lethbridge: Fort Whoop-Up National Historic Site
PO Box 1074,
Lethbridge, AB T1J 4A2
info@fortwhoopup.com
fortwhoopup.com
twitter.com/FortWhoopUp
www.facebook.com/WhoopUp
Located in Indian Battle Park, west end of 3rd Ave. As an Interpretive Centre, "the Fort" has been reconstructed & interpreted to be the norotirious whiskey fort: as such is has electronic displays, historical sights & sounds to pay tribute to & commentorate the legacy of the NMMP, Aboriginal People, & pioneers that shaped Western Canada. Open year round.

Lethbridge: Galt Historic Railway Park
c/o Great Canadian Plains Railway Society, PO Box 1013,
Lethbridge, AB T1J 4A2
Tel: 403-756-2220
gcprs@telus.net
galtrailway.com
www.facebook.com/103478453113008
Year Founded: 1998 Exhibits include a variety of items related to rail travel in the late 1800s.
Ray Oldenburger, President, 403-756-3313

Lethbridge: Sir Alexander Galt Museum & Archives
502 - 1 St. South,
Lethbridge, AB T1J 1Y4
Tel: 403-320-3954*Toll-Free:* 866-320-3898
info@galtmuseum.com
www.galtmuseum.com
www.flickr.com/photos/galtmuseum
twitter.com/GaltMuseum
www.facebook.com/GaltMuseum
Year Founded: 1967 The human history of Lethbridge & southern Alberta in 5 galleries & an outdoor courtyard; free admission
Aimee Benoit, Curator, 403-320-3907,
aimee.benoit@galtmuseum.com
Darrin J. Martens, CEO/Executive Director, 403-329-7300,
darrin.martens@galtmuseum.com

Longview: Bar U Ranch National Historic Site
PO Box 168, Township Rd. 17B & Township Rd. 17A,
Longview, AB T0L 1H0
Tel: 403-395-3044*Toll-Free:* 888-773-8888
baru.info@pc.gc.ca
www.pc.gc.ca/en/lhn-nhs/ab/baru
With 35 buildings & structures, the Bar U Ranch commemorates the history of ranching in Canada. The Ranch is open from late May to the end of September. Visits can be arranged during the off season.

Lougheed: Iron Creek Museum
5001 Harvey St.,
Lougheed, AB T0B 2V0
Tel: 780-385-5856
ironcreekmuseum@gmail.com
www.facebook.com/ironcreekmuseum
Two one-room schoolhouses; church; blacksmith & shoe repair shop; log hall housing artifacts & farm machinery

Magrath: Magrath Museum
37 North 1st St. West,
Magrath, AB T0K 1J0
Tel: 403-758-6618
magrathmuseum@gmail.com
www.magrathmuseum.org
www.youtube.com/user/magrathmuseum
twitter.com/MagrathMuseum
www.faceb ook.com/146547325418743
Local history & pioneer artifacts; open May-Aug., M-F 9:00-5:30.

Mallaig: Mallaig & District Museum
PO Box 211,
Mallaig, AB T0A 2K0
Tel: 780-726-2614; *Fax:* 780-635-3757
mallaigmuseum@hotmail.com
The museum's exhibits are housed in a replica 1920 log schoolhouse & a 1931 church. Open Tu-F 10:00-4:00.

Manning: Battle River Pioneer Museum
PO Box 574,
Manning, AB T0H 2M0
Tel: 780-836-2180; *Fax:* 780-836-2180
www.manning.govoffice.com
Other contact information: Alternate Phone: 780-836-2374
Artifacts from pioneer life; 1,500 year-old arrowhead; albino moose; open May-Sept., daily 1:00-6:00; open 10:00 am in July & Aug.

Markerville: Historic Markerville Creamery
Parent: Stephan G. Stephansson Icelandic Society
114 Creamery Way,
Markerville, AB T0M 1M0
Tel: 403-728-3006; *Fax:* 403-728-3225
Toll-Free: 877-728-3007
admin@historicmarkerville.com
www.historicmarkerville. com
twitter.com/Markerville
www.facebook.com/Historic.Markerville
Creamery museum restored to 1930s profiles Icelandic settlement of central Alberta; "Kaffistofa" features Icelandic menu

Medicine Hat: Esplanade Arts & Heritage Centre
401 - 1st St. SE,
Medicine Hat, AB T1A 8W2
Tel: 403-502-8580
esplanade@medicinthat.ca
www.esplanade.ca
pinterest.com/esplanadeag
twitter.com/Esplanade
www.facebook.com/MedHatEsplanade
Museum: Permanent Gallery featuring the history of Medicine Hat & area using pieces from vast collection, including pioneer home funishings, Victorian period artifacts, archaeological artifacts, military, sporting & Native artifacts, business & industry equipment, clothing & more; Archives: database of manuscripts, extensive black & white photographic collection, genealogical information & more.

Medicine Hat: Medicine Hat Clay Industries National Historic District
713 Medalta Ave. SE,
Medicine Hat, AB T1A 3K9
Tel: 403-529-1070
info@medalta.org
www.medalta.org
twitter.com/medalta
www.facebook.com/112945865394219
The 150-acre Historic Clay District preserves the history of the region's pottery industry. With working, circular kilns and original factory, it is living museum. The Medalta International Artists in Residence (MIAIR) program hosts contemporary ceramic artists. An interactive clay area and education programs are available for children.

Millet: Millet & District Museum & Archives
PO Box 178,
Millet, AB T0C 1Z0
Tel: 780-387-5558
info@milletmuseum.ca
www.milletmuseum.ca
twitter.com/MilletMuseum
www.facebook.com/22109293 1274232
Year Founded: 1985 Exhibits incude archives on local history, home settings from 1900-1950 and portraits of over 200 local veterans of World Wars I, II. Building also houses the Millet Visitor Information Centre; open year round.
Tracey Leavitt, Executive Director/Curator

Mirror: Mirror & District Museum
4910 - 53 St.,
Mirror, AB T0B 3C0
Tel: 403-788-3828
Settler & railway artifacts are presented at the Mirror & District Museum. The museum is open from mid June to the beginning of September. Appointments may be arranged at other times.

Morinville: Musée Morinville Museum
PO Box 3252, 10010 - 101 St.,
Morinville, AB T8R 1S2
Tel: 780-572-5585; *Fax:* 780-572-5586
morinvillemuseum@shaw.ca
museemorinvillemuseum.com
Local history; designated a Provincial Historic Site; open W-Sa 12:00-5:00.
Sheila Houle, President
Donna Garrett, Museum Attendant

Mundare: Basilian Fathers Museum
PO Box 386, 5335 Sawchuk St.,
Mundare, AB T0B 3H0
Tel: 780-764-3887
www.basilianmuseum.ca
Ukrainian culture & religion

Nanton: Bomber Command Museum of Canada
PO Box 1051,
Nanton, AB T0L 1R0
Tel: 403-646-2270; *Fax:* 403-646-2214
office@bombercommandmuseum.ca
www.bombercommandmuseum.ca
twitter.com/B CMofCanada
www.facebook.com/101722206538665
Other contact information: Library & Archives:
library@bombercommandmuseum.ca
Year Founded: 1986 The Bomber Command Museum of Canada honours persons associated with Bomber Command during World War II. It also commemorates the operations of the British Commonwealth Air Training Plan.
Bob Evans, Curator, curator@bombercommandmuseum.ca
Robert Pedersen, President

Newell County: Brooks Aqueduct National & Provincial Historic Site
c/o Alberta Historic Sites & Museum, 142 Range Rd.,
Newell County, AB T1R 1C5
Tel: 780-431-2321
brooksaqueduct.ca
The Brooks Aqueduct is located 8 km southeast of Brooks, Alberta. The structure was completed in 1914 by the irrigation division of the Canadian Pacific Railway. It has been preserved by the Government of Alberta, Environment Canada, the Prairie Farm Rehabilitation Administration, & the Eastern Irrigation District. The interpretive center at the aqueduct is open from May 15th to Labour Day, 10:00-5:00.

Nobleford: Nobleford Area Museum
PO Box 505,
Nobleford, AB T0L 1S0

Tel: 403-824-3909
www.facebook.com/157129377662576
Year Founded: 1989 The museum replicates the manufacturing process of the Noble Blade, invented by Charles Noble. Open July & Aug., M-Sa 10:00-4:00, or by appointment.

Okotoks: Okotoks Museum & Archives (OMA)
Heritage House, 49 North Railway St.,
Okotoks, AB T1S 1K1

Tel: 403-938-8969; *Fax: 403-938-8963*
culture@okotoks.ca
www.okotoks.ca
Year Founded: 2000 Local history; the online archives allows users to search the Archive's photographic collection. Summer hours: M-Sa 10:00-5:00, Su & holidays 12:00-5:00.

Olds: Mountain View Museum & Archives
Parent: Olds Historical Society
PO Box 3882, 5038 - 50 St.,
Olds, AB T4H 1P6

Tel: 403-556-8464
mountainviewmuseum@gmail.com
www.oldsmuseum.ca
twitter.com/mvmuseum_olds
www.facebook.com/Mountain-
View-Museum-Olds-646167382075285
Year Founded: 1972 The Olds Historical Society preserves artifacts, textual documents, & photographs, which depict the history & heritage of Olds & its surrounding area. Items are displayed & research services are available at the Mountain View Museum & Archives, which is located in the 1920 Olds AGT building. The museum is open from Monday to Friday. Guided tours & educational programs are offered.

Onoway: Onoway Museum
Parent: Onoway & District Historical Guild
c/o Onoway & District Historical Guild, PO Box 1368,
Onoway, AB T0E 1V0

Tel: 780-967-1015
info3@onowaymuseum.ca
www.onowaymuseum.ca
www.facebook.com/OnowayMuseum
Other contact information: Appointment Phone: 780-967-5263
Year Founded: 2007 Housed in an old schoolhouse, the museum presents artifacts of local Onoway life from the community's early years. Opening hours: May - Aug. Tu-Sa 10:00-3:00 or by appointment.

Oyen: Crossroads Museum
312 - 1st Ave. East,
Oyen, AB T0J 2J0

Tel: 403-664-2330
OyenMuseum@outlook.com
oyencrossroadsmuseum.org
www.facebook.com/OyenMuseum
Buildings include a period house (1918); cook car; blacksmith shop; tractor & truck building; a 120x40 Quonset; 1912 schoolhouse; former community hall; "teepee" type building containing archaeological artifacts; season May-Aug., 9:00-12:00 & 1:00-5:00.

Paradise Valley: Climb Thru Time Museum
Paradise Valley, AB

Tel: 780-745-2412
www.facebook.com/ClimbThruTimeMuseum
Other contact information: Alternate Phone: 780-745-2150
The museum is located inside the Paradise Valley grain elevator, & features objects & art portraying agricultural life in Western Canada.

Patricia: Dinosaur Provincial Park
PO Box 60,
Patricia, AB T0J 2K0

Tel: 403-378-4342
albertaparks.ca/dinosaur.aspx
www.facebook.com/AlbertaParksDinosaur
Year Founded: 1955 Some of the most extensive dinosaur fossil fields in the world are found here; the area's badlands & cottonwood river habitat are the other significant features that resulted in the park's designation as a UNESCO World Heritage Site in 1979; also includes the Royal Tyrrell Museum of Palaeontology Field Station, located within the park.
Donna Martin, Contact, donna.martin@gov.ab.ca

Peace River: Peace River Museum, Archives, & Mackenzie Centre
10302 - 99 St.,
Peace River, AB T8S 1K1

Tel: 780-624-4261
museum@peaceriver.ca
www.peaceriver.ca/visitors/museum
Displays include: Sir Alexander Mackenzie, fur trade, town of Peace River

Picture Butte: Prairie Acres Museum
PO Box 768,
Picture Butte, AB T0K 1V0

Tel: 403-329-1201
The museum's collection includes antique automobiles, machinery, tractors, combines, & small antique items.

Pincher Creek: Heritage Acres Farm Museum
PO Box 2496,
Pincher Creek, AB T0K 1W0

Tel: 403-627-2082
heritageacres.org
Year Founded: 1988 The museum seeks to preserve & promote the agricultural history of Southern Alberta from 1880-1960. In its collection it has a grain elevator, antique cars, Doukhobor barn, church, model railway, log house, general store, sawmill, & school. Open May-Sept., 9:00-5:00.

Pincher Creek: Kootenai Brown Pioneer Village
PO Box 1226, 1037 Bev McLachlin Dr.,
Pincher Creek, AB T0K 1W0

Tel: 403-627-3684
mail.kbpv@gmail.com
www.kootenaibrown.org
Year Founded: 1966 Open year round

Plamondon: Plamondon & District Museum
10013 - 98 Ave.,
Plamondon, AB T0A 2T0

Tel: 780-798-3193
www.facebook.com/PlamondonMuseum
Operated by the Plamondon & District Museum Society, the Plamondon & District Museum features local cultural artifacts from early pioneers. The museum is open from June to August.

Ponoka: Fort Ostell Museum
Parent: Fort Ostell Museum Society
5320 - 54 St.,
Ponoka, AB T4J 1L8

Tel: 403-783-5224
fom01@telus.net
www.fortostellmuseum.com
www.facebook.com/fortostellmuseum
Year Founded: 1967 The museum collects artifacts from the surrounding area which help to tell the story of this area's past. It also serves as a research tool for many residents wanting to know specific details about the area or historical events. It's the intention of the museum to care for and to display as many artifacts as possible, thus making them viewable to the public through the gallery and through temporary exhibits.

Raymond: Raymond Pioneer Museum
Parent: Raymond & District Historical Society
10 Broadway North,
Raymond, AB T0K 2S0

Tel: 403-752-4799
raymondhistory.ca
www.facebook.com/RaymondHistory
Other contact information: After-hours Phone: 403-752-0060
Year Founded: 1989 The museum's collection details the founding of the town of Raymond, mostly through photographs & text.

Red Deer: Alberta Sports Hall of Fame & Museum (ASHFM)
102 - 4200 Hwy. 2,
Red Deer, AB T4N 1E3

Tel: 403-341-8614; *Fax: 403-341-8619*
info@ashfm.ca
ashfm.ca
twitter.com/ASHFM1
www.facebook.com/ashfm.ca
Year Founded: 1957 Preserves artifacts & archival material that are significant in Alberta's sporting history; 7 Honoured Members are inducted into the Sports Hall of Fame each year, plus 3 award recipients. Interactive multisport virtual game system & a curriculum based education program, a theatre and boardroom rental available.
Donna Hately, Managing Director

Red Deer: Kerry Wood Nature Centre
6300 - 45 Ave.,
Red Deer, AB T4N 3M4

Tel: 403-346-2010; *Fax: 403-347-2550*
general@waskasoopark.ca
www.waskasoopark.ca
www.youtube.com/user/NatureCentre
twitter.com/naturecentre
Year Founded: 1986 Central Alberta's year-round home of entertaining & informative nature activities & exhibits; gateway to Gaetz Lakes Sanctuary; features art gallery, bookshop, A/V theatre, meeting rooms, children's Discovery Room & exhibits; extensive programs, courses, field trips for all ages; open daily except Christmas; admission by donation
Jim Robertson, Executive Director,
jim.robertson@waskasoopark.ca

Red Deer: Norwegian Laft Hus Society & Museum
4402 - 47th Ave.,
Red Deer, AB T4N 6T4

Tel: 403-347-2055
norwegianlafthus@gmail.com
www.norwegianlafthussociety.ca
instagram.com/lafthus
twitter.com/Laft_Hus
www.facebook.com/lafthus
Norwegian-style log house with a sod roof, located in downtown Red Deer. Open year-round; Winter hours: W 9:00-3:00; Summer hours: Tu-Sa 10:00-4:00, Su 12:00-4:00.

Red Deer: Red Deer Museum & Art Gallery
4525 - 47A Ave.,
Red Deer, AB T4N 6Z6

Tel: 587-797-4040
museum@reddeermuseum.com
www.reddeermuseum.com
twitter.com/RedDeerMuseum
www.facebook.com/RedDeerMuseumandArtGallery
Year Founded: 1978 The Red Deer Museum & Art Gallery tells the story of the people, history, & culture of central Alberta, through its collections, exhibitions, & programs. The museum's more than 85,000 objects include clothing & First Nations & Inuit art. A library on the site houses artifact books, catalogues, & other printed material.
Lorna Johnson, Executive Director BFA, M.ED,
lorna.johnson@reddeer.ca
Melanie Berndt, Coordinator, Collections,
melanie.berndt@reddeermuseum.com

Red Deer: Stephansson House Provincial Historic Site
2230 Twp Rd. 371,
Red Deer, AB T4G 0M9

Tel: 403-728-3929
stephansson.house@gov.ab.ca
stephanssonhouse.ca
Icelandic poet's pioneer home; open May 15 - Labour Day; located 7 km. north of Markerville off Hwy. 592 or 781

Red Deer: Sunnybrook Farm Museum
4701 - 30th St.,
Red Deer, AB T4N 5H7

Tel: 403-340-3511; *Fax: 403-340-3574*
sbfs@shaw.ca
www.sunnybrookfarmmuseum.ca
twitter.com/sbfmuseum
www.facebook.com/sunnybrookfarmAB/
The museum celebrates the early days of farming in Alberta, as the farm itself dates back to the turn of the century. Summer hours: May-Sept., daily 10:00-4:00; off-season hours: M-F 1:00-4:00, or by appointment.
Ian Warwick, Executive Director, 403-340-3511, sbfs@shaw.ca
Nicole Parson-Admussen, Collections & Interpretation Coordinator, Interpretive Program

Redcliff: Redcliff Historical & Museum Society
2 - 3rd St. NE,
Redcliff, AB T0J 2P0

Tel: 403-548-6260
redcliff.museum@gmail.com
www.facebook.com/RedcliffMuseum
Exhibits showing the commercial & recreational aspect of Redcliff citizens; extensive drug store, domestic, school, toy & organizational exhibits; history of past industries with manufactured artifacts; weekly newpaper on microfilm 1910-1939; open May-Aug., Tue.-Sat., Sun., Oct.-Apr. by appt.

Rimbey: PasKaPoo Historic Park & Smithson International Truck Museum
Parent: Rimbey Historical Society
PO Box 813,
Rimbey, AB T0C 2J0

Tel: 403-843-2004
paskapoo@telus.net
www.paskapoopark.com

Year Founded: 1990 The park offers two museum buildings & ten historic buildings; included in the park is the Truck Museum, which features 19 refurbished International trucks, as well as farm machinery, a police car, an ambulance, vintage photographs, & more.

Rochfort: Lac Ste-Anne Historical Society Pioneer Museum
57115 Range Rd. 80,
Rochfort, AB T0E 1Y0

Tel: 780-785-2816
www.facebook.com/rochfortbridgepioneermuseum

Rocky Mountain House: Nordegg Heritage Museum/Brazeau Collieries Mine Site
Parent: Nordegg Historical Society
c/o Nordegg Historical Society, PO Box 550,
Rocky Mountain House, AB T4T 1A4

Tel: 403-845-4444
administrator@nordegghistoricalsociety.org
www.nordegghistoricalsociety. org
Other contact information: Museum Phone: 403-721-2625
The museum holds aritfacts pertaining to local history & coal mining at the Brazeau Collieries. The mine site, which is a both a Provincial & National Historic Site, is open for guided tours. The museum is open May-Sept., daily 9:00-5:00; the mine tour season is May-Sept.; site tours are held at 10:00 am, & technical tours are held at 1:00 pm, July-Aug.
Tom Clark, President
Rick Emmons, Director, Planning
Amanda Rodriguez, Coordinator, Heritage

Rocky Mountain House: Rocky Mountain House National Historic Site of Canada
Comp. 6, Site 127, RR#4,
Rocky Mountain House, AB T4T 2A4

Tel: 403-845-2412
pc.rockyinfo.pc@canada.ca
www.pc.gc.ca/rockymountainhouse
Site of four fur trading posts dating back to 1799; Commemorates the fur trade & the role of Native peoples in the fur trade & western exploration (David Thompson); Over 500 acres; Hiking trails, displays, herd of bisons; Exhibits; 3/4 size playfort; Eight trailside listening stations; Heritage demonstrations & presentations; Open Victoria Day weekend - Labour Day

Rosebud: Rosebud Centennial & District Museum
Parent: Rosebud Historical Society
PO Box 601, 117 Main St.,
Rosebud, AB T0J 2T0

Tel: 403-677-2601
rosebud.museum@gmail.com
www.rosebud.ca/museum_home.htm
Year Founded: 1967 A collection of pioneer tools, etc. that have been donated to the museum; open year round
Peter Lauridsen, Secretary, Rosebud Historical Society

St. Albert: Father Lacombe Chapel - Provincial Historic Site / La Chapelle du Père Lacombe
5 St. Vital Ave.,
St. Albert, AB T8N 1K1

Tel: 780-431-2321
www.history.alberta.ca/fatherlacombe
Year Founded: 1983 Alberta's oldest building; Located on St. Vital Ave., St. Albert; open May 15 - Labour Day
Olga Fowler, Contact, olga.fowler@gov.ab.ca

St Albert: Little White School
2 Madonna Dr.,
St Albert, AB T8N 2M2

Tel: 780-459-4404
museum@artsheritage.ca
museeheritage.ca

Call ahead to book a visit.

St Albert: Musée Heritage Museum
Parent: Arts & Heritage St. Albert
St. Albert Place, 5 St. Anne St.,
St Albert, AB T8N 3Z9

Tel: 780-459-1528; *Fax:* 780-459-1232
museum@artsheritage.ca
museeheritage.ca
museeheritagemuseum.blogspot.ca
twitter.com/artsandheritage
www.facebo ok.com/ArtsAndHeritageStAlbert
The museum presents the history of St. Albert through various exhibits & programs, in an effort to preserve the community's history. It also manages St. Albert's Heritage Sites: Little White School, St. Albert Grain Elevator Park, & River Lot 24. Hours of operation: Tu-Sa 10:00-5:00, Su 1:00-5:00.
Shari Strachan, Director, sharis@artsandheritage.ca
Joanne White, Curator, joannew@artsheritage.ca
Vinothaan Vipulanantharajah, Archivist,
vinov@artsandheritage.ca

St Albert: Musée Héritage Museum & Archives
St. Albert Place, 5 St. Anne St.,
St Albert, AB T8N 3Z9

Tel: 780-459-1528; *Fax:* 780-459-1232
museum@artsheritage.ca
museeheritage.ca
www.youtube.com/channel/UCa3LaEOwZPzvBBLTtACkt2g
twitter.com/artsandheri tage
www.facebook.com/ArtsAndHeritageStAlbert
History of St. Albert & surrounding area
Shari Strachan, Director, sharis@artsandheritage.ca
Joanne White, Curator, 780-459-1528,
curatormhm@artsandheritage.ca
Vinothaan Vipulanantharajah, Archivist, 780-459-1528,
vinov@artsheritage.ca

St Albert: St. Albert Grain Elevator Park
4 Meadowview Dr.,
St Albert, AB T8N 2R9

Tel: 780-419-7354
museum@artsheritage.ca
museeheritage.ca
Open May-Sept., W-Su 10:00-5:00.

St Paul: Fort George & Buckingham House Provincial Historic Site (FGBH)
6015 Twp Rd. 565,
St Paul, AB

Tel: 780-724-2611
fort.george@gov.ab.ca
www.history.alberta.ca/fortgeorge/default.aspx
Archaeological remains of 2 fur trade forts; interpretive centre & gift shop; open May 15 - Labour Day; located 13 km SE of Elk Point on Hwy. 646

St Paul: Musée St. Paul Museum
PO Box 639, 5409 - 50 Ave.,
St Paul, AB T0A 3A0

Tel: 780-645-5562
stpaulmuseum.ca
Other contact information: Off-Season Phone: 780-645-4401
Relever l'histoire de la communauté de Saint-Paul; expositions; cours d'histoire aux élèves; projets spéciaux.

St Paul: Musée St. Paul Museum
PO Box 410,
St Paul, AB T0A 3A0

Tel: 780-645-5562
www.town.stpaul.ab.ca
The museum is located on the same site as People's Museum of St. Paul & District.

St Paul: People's Museum of St. Paul & District
Parent: Peoples Museum Society of St. Paul & District
PO Box 410,
St Paul, AB T0A 3A0

Tel: 780-645-5562; *Fax:* 780-645-5273
www.town.stpaul.ab.ca
Local agricultural history; part of the same complex as Musée St. Paul Museum.

Sedgewick: Sedgewick Archives Gallery & Museum
PO Box 508, 4813 - 47 St.,
Sedgewick, AB T0B 4C0

Tel: 780-384-3741
sedgewickmuseum@persona.ca
Year Founded: 1989 Housed in the 1906 "Merchants Bank," the museum contains a collection of cameras, jewellery and china. Displays are changed to fit the seasons and special holidays. The Goose Creek School (1912-1957) was moved to the museum as a "hands on" exhibit, with the original Waterman-Waterbury heater and blackboard, plus other large

artifacts. Open year round with special events on RObbie Burns Day, St. Patrick's Day, Norwegian Independence Day and Christmas.

Sherwood Park: Strathcona County Museum & Archives
913 Ash St.,
Sherwood Park, AB T8A 2G3

Tel: 780-467-8189
www.strathconacountymuseum.ca
www.youtube.com/user/strathconacountymuse
twitter.com/strathcomuseum
w ww.facebook.com/StrathconaCountyMuseumArchives
Year Founded: 1997 Local history; open year round
Monroe Kinloch, President

Siksika: Siksika Nation Museum
PO Box 1730,
Siksika, AB T0J 3W0

Tel: 403-734-5361; *Fax:* 403-264-9659

Smoky Lake: Victoria Settlement Provincial Historic Site
58161 Range Rd 171A,
Smoky Lake, AB

Tel: 780-656-2333
VictoriaSettlement@gov.ab.ca
www.history.alberta.ca/victoria
www.facebook.com/Vic.Settlement
Located 10 km south of Smoky Lake on Hwy. 855, 6 km east along Victoria Trail; Hudson Bay Company post & settlement; open May 15-Labour Day

Spirit River: Spirit River & District Museum
Parent: Spirit River Settlement Historical Society
PO Box 221,
Spirit River, AB T0H 3G0

Tel: 780-864-2180; *Fax:* 780-864-2199
contact@spiritrivermuseum.com
Local history; open May-Sept., M-Su 10:00-5:00; Oct.-Apr., M-F 10:00-4:00

Spruce View: Danish Canadian National Museum & Gardens
PO Box 92,
Spruce View, AB T0M 1V0

Tel: 403-728-0019; *Fax:* 403-728-0020
Toll-Free: 888-443-4114
info@stepintothesaga.com
thedanishcanadianmuseum.com
twitter.com/danishcanadians
www.facebook.com/theDanishCanadianMuseum
Year Founded: 2002 The museum's exhibits celebrate the contribution of Danish immigrants to Canada. The grounds also offer paths, hiking trails, picnic spots, & a man-made lake. Open May-Sept.
Faye Kjearsgaard, Curator, curator@danishcanadians.com

Spruce View: Dickson Store Museum
PO Box 146,
Spruce View, AB T0M 1V0

Tel: 403-728-3355; *Fax:* 403-728-3351
dicksonstoremuseum@gmail.com
www.dicksonstoremuseum.com
dicksonstoremuseum.blogspot.ca
www.facebook.com/dicksonstoremuseum1
Year Founded: 1991 A general store circa the 1930s, staffed by costumed interpreters who recreate the store's operations for visitors. Open May-Sept., M-Sa 10:00-5:30, Su 12:30-5:30

Stettler: Stettler Town & Country Museum
6502 - 44th Ave.,
Stettler, AB T0C 2L0

Tel: 403-742-4534
info@stettlermuseum.com
stettlermuseum.com
A village replica housing artifacts from the local & surrounding areas; includes a courthouse, schools, church, CN station, pioneer homes & barns, agricultural items as well as a local sports museum; also an original Estonian Grist mill & log cabin of the early twenties constructed by early Estonian pioneers; situated on 10 acres in SW Stettler; open daily May-Sept. or by appt.

Stony Plain: Multicultural Heritage Centre
PO Box 2188, 5411 - 51 St.,
Stony Plain, AB T7Z 1X7

Tel: 780-963-2777
info@multicentre.org
multicentre.org
twitter.com/Mul tiCentre
www.facebook.com/MultiCentreAB

The Heritage Centre includes restored buildings including a 1925 high school, a settler's cabin, & a homestead's kitchen. This living history museum offers entertainment & weekend demos. Open M-Su 9:00-4:00.
Melissa Hartley, Executive Director

Stony Plain: Stony Plain & Parkland Pioneer Museum Society
5120 - 41 Ave.,
Stony Plain, AB T7Z 1L5
Tel: 780-963-1234; *Fax:* 780-968-5564
info@pioneermuseum.ca
www.pioneermuseum.ca
Year Founded: 1992 Open year round.

Strome: Sodbuster Archives Museum
5029 - 50th St.,
Strome, AB T0B 4H0
museumsa86@gmail.com
www.sodbustersarchivesmuseum.com
Shows the development of the West & of the Strome & district community from 1900 to the 1950s

Sundre: Sundre & District Pioneer Village Museum
211 - 1st Ave. SW,
Sundre, AB T0M 1X0
Tel: 403-638-3233; *Fax:* 403-638-3295
sundremuseum@telus.net
www.sundremuseum.com
twitter.com/sundremuseum
www.facebook.com/sundremuseum
Year Founded: 1968 Home to artifacts that represent the history of the Sundre community; wildlife museum is adjacent; open year long.

Taber: Taber Irrigation Impact Museum
4702 - 50 St.,
Taber, AB T1G 2B6
Tel: 403-223-5708; *Fax:* 403-223-0529
www.facebook.com/569300306428531
Open year-round, closed in Aug.

Thorhild: Thorhild Museum
Parent: Thorhild & District Historical Society
c/o Thorhild & District Municipal Library, PO Box 658,
Thorhild, AB T0A 3A0
Tel: 780-398-3502; *Fax:* 780-398-3504
www.thorhildlibrary.ab.ca/Museum
Local history; housed in the town library; open year-round.

Three Hills: Kneehill Historical Museum
PO Box 653,
Three Hills, AB T0M 2A0
Tel: 403-443-2092; *Fax:* 403-443-7941
khsmuseum@gmail.com
www.unlockthepast.ca/places/Kneehill-Historical-Muse um_8285
Local history; collection housed in three historic buildings; open May-Sept., M-Sa 9:00-4:30, Su 1:00-4:30.

Tofield: Beaverhill Lake Nature Centre & Tofield Museum
5020 - 48th Ave.,
Tofield, AB T0B 4J0

Year Founded: 1985 The Beaverhill Lake Nature Centre presents information about Beaverhill Lake & its wildlife. The lake is a federally recognized bird sanctuary. Located in the Beaverhill Lake Nature Centre facility is the Tofield Museum. The museum features the history of the community since 1882.

Trochu: Trochu & District Museum
Parent: Trochu & District Historical Society
315 Arena Ave.,
Trochu, AB T0M 2C0
Tel: 403-442-2220
trochumuseum@gmail.com
www.town.trochu.ab.ca/culture-tourism/trochu-museum
Displays on the early pioneers including a kitchen, blacksmith shop, general store, schools, coal mining & an extensive collection of WW I & II pictures & uniforms; open May to Aug.

Tsuut'ina Nation: Tsuu T'ina Culture Museum
62 Old Agency Rd.,
Tsuut'ina Nation, AB T2W 3C4
Tel: 403-238-2677
cultural@tsuutina.com
tsuutinamuseum.com
Year Founded: 1983 Located on Sarcee (Tsuu T'ina) Reserve, the museum features artifacts such as headdresses from around 1938 & a model tipi.

Two Hills: Two Hills & District Historical Museum
PO Box 566,
Two Hills, AB T0B 4K0
Tel: 403-657-2461
Houses 4,000 artifacts pertaining to the area; collection of steamers, automobiles, farm equipment, farm tools, early household artifacts, buildings, railways caboose, etc.

Valhalla Centre: Melsness Mercantile Café & Museum
Parent: Valhalla Heritage Society
PO Box 52,
Valhalla Centre, AB T0H 3M0
Tel: 780-356-3535
vhs@gpnet.ca
www.valhallaheritagesociety.ca
Provincial historic site; museum displays, deli café, gift shop

Vegreville: Vegreville Regional Museum
PO Box 328,
Vegreville, AB T9C 1R3
Tel: 780-632-7650
museum@digitalweb.net
www.vegreville.com/visiting/what-to-see-and-do/regional-museum
Located on the site of the solonetzic soils research station of Agriculture Canada, The Vegreville Regional Museum depicts the history of Vegreville & its agricultural & business development. A special collection is The Right Honourable Donald Mazankowski, P.C. Collection. Mazankowski was the former Deputy Prime Minister of Canada. The regional museum also houses the Vegreville & District Sports Hall of Fame. The museum is open year-round.

Vermilion: Vermilion Heritage Museum
5310 - 50 Ave.,
Vermilion, AB T9X 1L1
Tel: 780-853-6211
History of Vermilion, AB; located in the forme S.R.P. Cooper School.

Viking: Viking Historical Museum
PO Box 106, 5108 - 61st Ave.,
Viking, AB T0B 4N0
Tel: 780-336-3066
Displays various facets of pioneer life; includes 1907 school, 1903 log store, 1938 church & 1919 farm house; open summer; May 15 - Thanksgiving

Vulcan: Vulcan & District Museum
Parent: Vulcan & District Historical Society
232 Centre St.,
Vulcan, AB T0L 2B0
Tel: 403-485-2768
www.vdhs.vulcancountyhistory.com
The museum's collection emphasizes agriculture, communications, medical history & education. Open July & Aug., Tu-Sa 10:00-12:00, 12:45-4:30. Off season by appointment.

Wainwright: Wainwright & District Museum
Parent: Battle River Historical Society
1001 - 1st Ave.,
Wainwright, AB T9W 1S9
Tel: 780-842-3115
wainwrightmuseum@gmail.com
www.instagram.com/wainwrightmuseum
twitter.com/WainwrightMuse
www.face book.com/WainwrightMuseum
Year Founded: 1984 Open year round

Wainwright: Wainwright Rail Park
Parent: Wainwright Railway Preservation Society
c/o Wainwright Railway Preservation Society, PO Box 2972,
Wainwright, AB T9W 1S8
Tel: 780-842-3138
info@railpark.org
www.railpark.org
www.facebook.com/ 131026620265329
Year Founded: 1995 The Society collects & preserves items relating to Canadian National Railways in the Wainwright area. The park is open May-Sept., 10:00-4:00.

Warner: Devil's Coulee Dinosaur Heritage Museum
PO Box 156,
Warner, AB T0K 2L0
Tel: 403-642-2118; *Fax:* 403-642-3660
dinoegg@telusplanet.net
www.devilscoulee.com
Dinosaur eggs; local fossils; local history

Westlock: Canadian Tractor Museum
Parent: Westlock & District Tractor Museum Foundation
PO Box 5414, 9704 - 96 Ave.,
Westlock, AB T7P 2P5
Tel: 780-349-3353
canadiantractormuseum@telus.net
www.canadiantractormuseum.ca
www.facebook.com/732971786755110
Year Founded: 1999 The museum features over 200 restored antique tractors, as well as steam engines.

Westlock: Westlock Pioneer Museum
Parent: Westlock & District Historical Society
c/o Westlock & District Historical Society, PO Box 5806,
Westlock, AB T7P 2P6
Tel: 780-349-4849 *Toll-Free:* 866-349-4445
info@westlock.ca
westlockmuseum.com
www.youtube.com/user/westlockmusem/videos
www.facebook.com/1375256362730 05
Other contact information: Off-Season Phone: 780-349-4444; Alt. E-mail: westlockmuseum@yahoo.ca
Year Founded: 1962 Local history; open May-Sept.; off-season by appointment.

Wetaskiwin: Alberta Central Railway Museum
Wetaskiwin, AB T9A 1W9
Tel: 780-352-2257
www.abcentralrailway.com
Year Founded: 1981 Collection of early heavy weight cars from the passenger era, as well as fright equipment, cabooses, freight cars, and a snowplow. They also house the second oldest standing grain elevator in Alberta built by the Alberta Grain Company in 1906. Located southeast of Westaskiwin. Open from Victoria Day until Labour Day.

Wetaskiwin: Canada's Aviation Hall of Fame (CAHF) / Panthéon de l'Aviation du Canada
PO Box 6090,
Wetaskiwin, AB T9A 2G1
Tel: 780-312-2084
info@cahf.ca
www.cahf.ca
www.youtube.com/user/cahf1973
Year Founded: 1973 Canada's Aviation Hall of Fame collects, preserves, & exhibits material related to individuals & organizations that have made outstanding contributions to aviation & aerospace in Canada. Open Tu-Th, 9:00-4:00.
Rod Sheridan, Chair
David Wright, Chair, Operations
Aja Davis, Executive Director/Curator

Wetaskiwin: Reynolds-Alberta Museum
6426 - 40 Ave.,
Wetaskiwin, AB T9A 2G1
Tel: 780-312-2065
reynoldsalbertamuseum@gov.ab.ca
reynoldsmuseum.ca
www.youtube.com/user/ReynoldsABMuseum
twitter.com/friendsofram
www.fac ebook.com/reynoldsmuseum
Year Founded: 1992 The museum houses more than 5,000 artifacts, around 100 of which are on display. The collections are organized by the following themes: Transportation, Aviation, Agriculture, & Industry. The core collection of 1,500 items was donated by the late Stan Reynolds between 1982 & 1986, & continued to donate items until his death in 2012.

Wetaskiwin: Wetaskiwin & District Heritage Museum
5007 - 50th Ave.,
Wetaskiwin, AB T9A 0S3
Tel: 780-352-0227; *Fax:* 780-352-0226
wdhm@persona.ca
www.wetaskiwinmuseum.com
twitter.com/HeritageMuseum1
www.facebook.com/wetaskiwinmuseum
Year Founded: 1986 The Wetaskiwin & District Heritage Museum presents the history of Westaskiwin, Alberta & the surrounding area, from dinosaur fossils, to First Nations' history, to the war years. Visitors can also learn about life on a Hutterite colony. A resource library is part of the museum. The museum is open year-round.
Kathy Lund, President
Karen Aberle, Executive Director & Chief Curator

British Columbia

Provincial Museums

Museum of Anthropology (MOA)
University of British Columbia, 6393 Northwest Marine Dr.,
Vancouver, BC V6T 1Z2

Tel: 604-822-5087
info@moa.ubc.ca
www.moa.ubc.ca
www.instagram.com/moa_ubc
twitter.com/MOA_UBC
www.facebook.com/MOAUBC

Year Founded: 1947 The Museum of Anthropology displays art & objects from around the world & its collections emphasize First Nations cultures of the Northwestern Coast. The museum's awarding-winning concrete & glass buidling was designed by the Canadian architect, Arthur Erickson.
Anthony Shelton, Director, anthony.shelton@ubc.ca

Museum of Vancouver (MOV)
1100 Chestnut St.,
Vancouver, BC V6J 3J9

Tel: 604-736-4431; Fax: 604-736-5417
guestservices@museumofvancouver.ca
www.museumofvancouver.ca
www.instagram.com/museumofvan
twitter.com/museumofvan
www.facebook.com/MuseumofVancouver

Year Founded: 1894 The Museum of Vancouver offers permanent displays, exhibitions, & educational programs about the human, cultural & natural history of the city of Vancouver & the surrounding area. The Local History Lab & the Archaeology Education Centre contribute to the museum's school programs. The museum is open year-round.
Mauro Vescera, Chief Executive Officer M.A., B.A., 604-730-5323, mvescera@museumofvancouver.ca
Greg Fruno, Director, Operations & Visitor Experience, 604-730-5302, gfruno@museumofvancouver.ca
Viviane Gosselin, Director, Collections & Exhibitions, 604-730-5318, vgosselin@museumofvancouver.ca
Alex Orlovskyy, Director, Finance, 604-730-5306, aorlovskyy@museumofvancouver.ca

The Royal BC Museum Corporation
675 Belleville St.,
Victoria, BC V8W 9W2

Tel: 250-356-7226 Toll-Free: 888-447-7977
reception@royalbcmuseum.bc.ca
www.royalbcmuseum.bc.ca
www.instagram.com/royalbcmuseum
twitter.com/RoyalBCMuseum
www.facebook.com/RoyalBCMuseum

Year Founded: 1886 The RBCM specializes in the natural & human history of British Columbia.
Daniel Muzyka, Chief Executive Officer
Mischelle van Thiel, Deputy CEO & Vice Pres., Inclusion & Community Engagement
Melissa Sands, Chief Financial Officer CPA, CA
David Alexander, Vice Pres., Collections & Research
Erika Stenson, Vice Pres., Museum Operations

Local Museums

108 Mile Ranch: 108 Mile House Heritage Site & Museum
100 Mile House & District Historical Society, PO Box 225,
Hwy. 97,
108 Mile Ranch, BC V0K 2Z0

Tel: 250-791-5288
heritagesite108@gmail.com
historical.ca

The 108 Mile Heritage Site is a collection of buildings dating from the mid-1800s to the mid-twentieth century which chonicle the Cariboo gold rush of the 1860s.
Ulli Vogler, President

108 Mile Ranch: 108 Mile Ranch Heritage Site
Parent: 100 Mile & District Historical Society
PO Box 225,
108 Mile Ranch, BC V0K 2Z0

historical@bcinternet.net
www.historical.bc.ca/main.html

The 108 Mile Ranch Heritage Site comprises 11 historical buildings dating from the Gold Rush era; largest log barn in Canada; open May long weekend to Labour Day

Abbotsford: Fraser Valley Antique Farm Machinery Association
Abbotsford, BC

Tel: 604-746-4880
2011website@pioneercorner.com
pioneercorner.com

To collect & restore to working condition antique farm & household machinery; displays annually at Agrifair; maintains the Pioneer Barn, where visitors welcome to building any time of year except December; call for appt.
Ed Steinke, President
Jerry Gosling, Treasurer, 604-864-2916

Abbotsford: Trethewey House Heritage Site
Parent: MSA Museum Society
2313 Ware St.,
Abbotsford, BC V2S 3C6

Tel: 604-853-0313; Fax: 866-373-2771
info@tretheweyhouse.ca
www.tretheweyhouse.ca
www.flickr.com/photos/msamuseum
twitter.com/TretheweyHouse
www.faceboo k.com/TretheweyHeritageSite

Exhibits include historical photographs of the region, in addition to an array of artifacts from local home life & businesses, particularly the lumber industry. Tours available Mon-Fri.
Gerry Borden, President
Christina Reid, Collections & Operations Manager, 604-853-0313, creid@tretheweyhouse.ca

Agassiz: Agassiz-Harrison Museum & Visitor Information Centre
PO Box 313,
Agassiz, BC V0M 1A0

Tel: 604-796-3545
agassizharrisonmuseum@shawbiz.ca
www.agassizharrisonmuseum.org
twitter.com/AgassizMuseum
www.facebook.c om/110299242344218

Year Founded: 1986 The museum presents local & Canadian Pacific Railway history, & is housed in a CPR station, circa 1893. Hours of operation: M-Sa 10:00-4:00, Su 1:00-4:00; May-Oct. M-F 8:30-4:00.
Joan Vogstad, President
Judy Pickard, Museum Staff Contact, jpickard.ahmuseum@shawbiz.ca

Alert Bay: Alert Bay Public Library & Museum
PO Box 440, 116 Fir St.,
Alert Bay, BC V0N 1A0

Tel: 250-974-5721
abplb@island.net
alertbay.bc.libraries.coop

Ethnographic material; artifacts related to the fishing industry, local history; gift shop
Joyce Wilby, Managing Librarian & Archivist

Alert Bay: U'mista Cultural Centre
Parent: U'mista Cultural Society
c/o U'mista Cultural Society, PO Box 253, 1 Front St.,
Alert Bay, BC V0N 1A0

Tel: 250-974-5403; Fax: 250-974-5499
Toll-Free: 800-690-8222
info@umista.ca
www.umista.ca
pinterest.com/umistacentre
twitter.com/UmistaCentre
www.facebook.com/U mista.Cultural.Society

Year Founded: 1980 Kwakwaka'wakw masks depicting the Potlatch ceremony; traditional & contemporary arts & crafts. Open Sept-Jun Tue-Sat 9:00-5:00; Jul-Sept daily 9:00-5:00.

Armstrong: Armstrong Spallumcheen Museum & Arts Society
3415 Pleasant Valley Rd.,
Armstrong, BC V0E 1B0

Tel: 250-546-8318
armstrongspallmuseumart.com

Year Founded: 1974 The Armstrong Spallumcheen Museum & Arts Society features a museum, archives, & an art gallery. Visitors are educated about the history of the local region. Genealogy & art workshops are conducted.
Lark Lindholm, Administrator

Ashcroft: Ashcroft Museum & Archives
PO Box 129,
Ashcroft, BC V0K 1A0

Tel: 250-453-9161; Fax: 250-453-9664
admin@ashcroftbc.ca
www.ashcroftbc.ca

Year Founded: 1935 History of the Southern Cariboo region, & the farming & ranching communities of Hat Creek Valley. Open 5 days a week, Apr.-Nov.; open 7 days a week July & Aug. Admission by donation. Located at the corner of Brink & Fourth streets in Ashcroft.

Atlin: Atlin Historical Museum
PO Box 111,
Atlin, BC V0W 1A0

www.atlinhistoricalsociety.com

First Nations artifacts; gold mining artifacts; photo collections. Open May 15 - Labour Day; closed on Mondays.

Bamfield: Bamfield Community Museum & Archive
Parent: Bamfield Community School Association
240 Nuthatch Rd.,
Bamfield, BC V0R 1B0

Tel: 250-728-1220; Fax: 250-728-1220
bcsa.ct@gmail.com
bamfieldcommunity.ca

Local history; collection built from community donations; open M-F 9:00-4:30.

Barkerville: Barkerville Historic Town
Parent: Barkerville Heritage Trust
PO Box 19, 14301 Hwy 26 E.,
Barkerville, BC V0K 1B0

Tel: 250-994-3332; Fax: 250-994-3435
Toll-Free: 888-994-3332
barkerville@barkerville.ca
www.barkerville.ca
instagram.com/barkervillebc; youtube.com/user/BarkervilleTV
twitter.com/BarkervilleBC
www.facebook. com/barkervillebc
Other contact information: Info Email:
barkerville@gems8.gov.bc.ca

Year Founded: 1862 Restored Cariboo Gold Rush town; Blessing's Grave; Richfield Court House. Open year round.
Ed Coleman, CEO, ed.coleman@barkerville.ca
Don Bassermann, Chair

Barriere: North Thompson Museum
Parent: Barriere & District Heritage Society
PO Box 228, 343 Lilley Rd.,
Barriere, BC V0E 1E0

Tel: 250-672-5583
info@barrieremuseum.ca

Year Founded: 1987 Local history; open seasonally.
Shirley Kristensen, Vice-President

Bella Coola: Bella Coola Valley Museum (BCVM)
PO Box 726, 269 Hwy. 20,
Bella Coola, BC V0T 1C0

Tel: 250-799-5767
info@bellacoolamuseum.ca
www.bellacoolamuseum.ca

Year Founded: 1963 Owned & operated by the Bella Coola Valley Museum Society, the Bella Coola Valley Museum depicts the human history of the Bella Coola Valley. Exhibits present the history of the area from European contact to 1955. The museum's historic building is open from June to September. School presentations can be arranged at other times of the year. The British Columbia Central Coast Archives is open year-round, from Tuesday to Thursday.

Bowen Island: Bowen Island Museum & Archives
PO Box 97,
Bowen Island, BC V0N 1G0

Tel: 604-947-2655
bihistorians@telus.net
bowenhistory.ca
twitter.com/BowenMuseum
www.facebook.com/bowen.Island. Museum.Archives

Year Founded: 1967 Local history displayed through two exhibits & the archival collection. Open daily in the summer, 10:00-4:00, Sept.-Apr. Su-W 11:00-3:00.
Cathy Bayly, Curator, curator@bowenislandmuseum.ca

Bralorne: Bralorne Pioneer Museum
3767 Lilooet Pioneer Rd. 40,
Bralorne, BC V0K 1P0

Tel: 250-238-2349
bralornepioneermuseum@gmail.com
www.facebook.com/bralornepioneermuseum

Year Founded: 1977 Bralorne Pioneer Museum depicts the history of a community which is known as the home of the Bralorne Mine. Collection includes mining artifacts & historical information about the local Bridge River Valley area. Open Fri-Mon 10:00-4:00

Britannia Beach: Britannia Mine Museum (BCMM)
150 Copper Dr.,
Britannia Beach, BC V0N 1J0
Tel: 604-896-2233; Fax: 604-896-2260
Toll-Free: 800-896-4044
company.store@bcmm.ca
www.britanniaminemuseum.ca
www.youtube.com/BritanniaMineMuseum
twitter.com/britanniamine
www.facebook.com/BritanniaMineMuseum
Year Founded: 1971 Governed by the Britannia Beach Historical Society, the British Columbia Museum of Mining preserves the material & social history of mining in British Columbia.
Cheryl Hendrickson, Executive Director
Deron Johnston, Site Manager

Burnaby: Burnaby Village Museum & Carousel
6501 Deer Lake Ave.,
Burnaby, BC V5G 3T6
Tel: 604-297-4565; Fax: 604-297-4557
bvm@burnaby.ca
www.burnabyvillagemuseum.ca
instagram.com/burnabyvillage
twitter.com/bbyvillage
www.facebook.com/BurnabyVillageMuseum
Other contact information: Phone, Schools: 604-297-4558;
Phone, Rentals: 604-297-4552
Year Founded: 1971 The Burnaby Village Museum consists of heritage & replica buildings from the 1920s as well as a carousel.

Burnaby: Canadiana Costume Society of British Columbia & Western Canada
6501 Deer Lake Ave.,
Burnaby, BC V5G 3T6
Tel: 604-293-6520
www.facebook.com/203038403236068
Year Founded: 1976 The Canadiana Costume Society of British Columbia & Western Canada collects, conserves, researches, & displays British Columbia's costume heritage. The collection dates from the late 1700s to the 1980s.

Burnaby: Nikkei National Museum & Cultural Centre (NNMCC)
6688 Southoaks Cres.,
Burnaby, BC V5E 4M7
Tel: 604-777-7000; Fax: 604-777-7001
info@nikkeiplace.org
centre.nikkeiplace.org
twitter.com/nikkeimuse
w ww.facebook.com/NNMCC
Year Founded: 2000 The complex houses a Japanese-Canadian cultural centre, the museum, a community centre & a Japanese-Canadian garden. Centre hours: Tu-F 10:00-9:30, Sa 9:00-5:00, Su 10:00-5:00; Museum hours: Tu-Sa 11:00-5:00.
Roger Lemire, Executive Director, 604-777-7000, rlemire@nikkeiplace.org
Sherri Kajiwara, Director & Curator, 604-777-7000, skajiwara[at]nikkeiplace.org
Robert T.Banno, Director

Burnaby: Simon Fraser University Museum of Archaeology & Ethnology
Simon Fraser University, 8888 University Dr.,
Burnaby, BC V5A 1S6
Tel: 778-782-3325; Fax: 778-782-5666
www.sfu.ca/archaeology/museum.html
youtube.com/channel/UCpdGua66pgA6a9PJ5dP4zCA
www.facebook.com/SFUMAE
Year Founded: 1965 Collects, reseraches & exhibits artifacts from British Columbia.
Dr. Barbara J. Winter, Curator, bwinter@sfu.ca

Burns Lake: Lakes District Museum Society
PO Box 266, 540 16 Hwy,
Burns Lake, BC V0J 1E0
Tel: 250-692-7450
Year Founded: 1978 Artifacts, archival records & historical reference material relation to the cultural & economical history of the area.

Cache Creek: Historic Hat Creek Ranch
PO Box 878,
Cache Creek, BC V0K 1H0
Tel: 250-457-9722; Fax: 250-457-9311
Toll-Free: 800-782-0922
contact@hatcreekranch.com
www.hatcreekranch.com
plus.google.com/112771217543072452676
twitter.com/hatcreekranch
www.facebook.com/hatcreekranch

Year Founded: 1984 Offering a blend of cultures, on site are an 1860 roadhouse with gold rush era artifacts and a traditional kekuli, or pit house, used as a winter home by people of the Shuswap Nation. Costumed guides explain the life of area's history & culture and visitors can experience firsthand a stagecoach ride. Other activities include gold panning and archery. There are a gift shop, food services, as well as cabins & campground facilities. Open daily, May to Sept.

Campbell River: Campbell River Maritime Heritage Centre
Parent: Maritime Heritage Society
PO Box 483,
Campbell River, BC V9W 5C1
Tel: 250-286-3161; Fax: 250-286-3162
info@maritimeheritagecentre.ca
www.maritimeheritagecentre.ca
www.faceb ook.com/221432144123
Year Founded: 1998 The Maritime Heritage Centre seeks to educate visitors about the mhistory of the Campbell River area, & to preserve marine documents & artifacts. Open M-Su 10:00-4:00.
Marv Everett, President
Trish Whiteside, Operations Manager

Campbell River: Haig-Brown Heritage House
Parent: Museum at Campbell River
2250 Campbell River Rd.,
Campbell River, BC V9W 4N7
Tel: 250-286-6646; Fax: 250-286-0109
haig.brown@crmuseum.ca
www.haig-brown.bc.ca
haig-brownhouse.blogspot.ca
Operated by the Museum at Campbell River, the Haig-Brown House is a historic building that offers bed & breakfast accomodation, & can be rented for private functions.

Campbell River: Museum at Campbell River (CRMuseum)
PO Box 70 A,
Campbell River, BC V9W 4Z9
Tel: 250-287-3103; Fax: 250-286-0109
general.inquiries@crmuseum.ca
www.crmuseum.ca
twitter.com/CRMuseum
w ww.facebook.com/100483307218
Year Founded: 1958 Exhibits include First Nations ceremonial masks & regalia, coastal logging, fishing history & settler development; archives & research centre; gift shop; open year-round.
Sandra Parrish, Executive Director, sandra.parrish@crmuseum.ca
Megan Purcell, Manager, Collections, megan.purcell@crmuseum.ca
Beth Boyce, Curator & Manager, Education, beth.boyce@crmuseum.ca

Castlegar: Castlegar & District Heritage Society
400 - 13th Ave.,
Castlegar, BC V1N 1G2
Tel: 250-365-6440
stationmuseum@shaw.ca
www.stationmuseum.ca
The Society operates the Zuckerberg Island park & the CPR Museum, housed in a 99 year old station. Includes newspaper archives, a gift shop featuring local artisans, special events & programming.

Cedarvale: Meanskinisht Museum
PO Box 183,
Cedarvale, BC V0J 2A0
Tel: 250-849-5732
Houses the history & remnants of ancient village of Gitlusec, Meanskinisht village & Cedarvale. Open by appt.
Mary G. Dalen, Director

Chase: Chase & District Museum & Archives Society
1042 Shuswap Ave.,
Chase, BC V0E 1M0
Tel: 250-679-8847
info@chasemuseum.ca
www.chasemuseum.ca
www.facebook.com/125651564125503
Year Founded: 1984 Housed in the Blessed Sacrament Catholic Church, built in 1910.

Chemainus: Chemainus Valley Museum
Parent: Chemainus Valley Historical Society
c/o Chemainus Valley Historical Society, PO Box 172, 9799 Water Wheel Cres.,
Chemainus, BC V0R 1K0
Tel: 250-246-2445
cvhs@telus.net
www.chemainusvalleymuseum.ca
Local history; Hours of operation: daily 9:00-4:00.

Chetwynd: Little Prairie Heritage Museum
Parent: Little Prairie Heritage Society
PO Box 1777, 5633 Westgate Rd,
Chetwynd, BC V0C 1J0
Tel: 250-788-1943
heritagemuseumchetwynd@gmail.com
www.facebook.com/lpheritagemuseum
Other contact information: Alternate phone: 250-401-3362
Local history

Chilliwack: Canadian Military Education Centre Museum
PO Box 2123 Main, 45540 Petawawa Rd.,
Chilliwack, BC V2R 1A5
www.cmedcentre.org
The CMEC is a Non Profit Museum Society. They are a member of the Organization Of Military Museums and a recognized Military Museum by the DND. Operated by a group of volunteers, the museum functions by public donations and the support of the City of Chilliwack.
Dan Jahn, Contact, 604-467-1988, danjahn@cmedcentre.org

Chilliwack: Chilliwack Museum & Archives
45820 Spadina Ave.,
Chilliwack, BC V2P 1T3
Tel: 604-795-5210; Fax: 604-795-5291
info@chilliwackmuseum.ca
www.youtube.com/user/ChilliwackMuseum;
instagram.com/chwkmuseum
twitter.com/CHWKMuseum
www.facebook.com/ChilliwackMuseumArchive
Year Founded: 1958 The culture, heritage, human & natural history of Chilliwack. Special exhibits; programming; gift shop. Open year round.
Matthew Francis, Executive Director, matthew@chilliwackmuseum.ca
Jane Lemke, Curator, jane@chilliwackmuseum.ca

Clinton: Clinton Museum
Parent: South Cariboo Historical Museum Society
PO Box 217, 1419 Cariboo Hwy,
Clinton, BC V0K 1K0
Tel: 250-459-2442; Fax: 250-459-0058
info@clintonmuseumbc.org
www.clintonmuseumbc.org
www.facebook.com/clin tonmuseum
Other contact information: Clinton Village Office Phone:
250-459-2261
Year Founded: 1956 Local history. Open May-Oct Wed-Sun 10:00-6:00

Comox: Comox Air Force Museum (CAFM)
PO Box 1000 Forces, 11 Military Row,
Comox, BC V0R 2K0
Tel: 250-339-8162; Fax: 250-339-8162
cafm.info@gmail.com
comoxairforcemuseum.ca
www.youtube.com/user/WatchCAFM
www.facebook.com/ComoxAirForceMuseum
Year Founded: 1987 History of CFB Comox & West Coast aviation. Open Tue-Sun 10:00-4:00
Capt. Lynn Barley, Director

Comox: Comox Archives & Museum Society
1729 Comox Ave.,
Comox, BC V9M 3M2
Tel: 250-339-2885
info@comoxmuseum.ca
www.comoxmuseum.ca
Local history; open Tu-Sa 10:00-4:00, Su 1:00-4:00.
Pam Moughton, Chair

Comox: Filberg Heritage Lodge & Park
Parent: Filberg Heritage Lodge & Park Association
c/o Filberg Heritage Lodge & Park Association, 61 Filberg Rd.,
Comox, BC V9M 2S7
Tel: 250-339-2715
info@filberg.com
filberg.com
www.facebook.com/FHLPA

The park features nine acres of landscaped grounds, on which sit a number of heritage buildings. Former Comox Logging Company President Robert Filberg once owned the land.
Mo MacKendrick, Chair
Eden Lindsay-Bodie, Administrator

Coquitlam: Mackin House Museum
Parent: Coquitlam Heritage Society
1116 Brunette Ave.,
Coquitlam, BC V3K 1G2

Tel: 604-516-6151
www.coquitlamheritage.ca
www.instagram.com/coquitlam_heritage
twitter.com/Coq_Heritage
www.face book.com/mackinhousemuseum
An historic house that serves as a museum, tourist information stop & administrative offices for the Coquitlam Heritage Society. Open year-round, M-F 11:00-5:00, Sa 12:00-4:00.
Candrina Bailey, Executive Director

Courtenay: Courtenay & District Museum & Palaeontology Centre
207 - 4th St.,
Courtenay, BC V9N 1G7

Tel: 250-334-0686; *Fax:* 250-338-0619
museum@island.net
www.courtenaymuseum.ca
www.youtube.com/user/courtenaymuseum
twitter.com/courtenaymuseum
www.f acebook.com/103653546358656
Other contact information: Alt. E-mails:
info@courtenaymuseum.ca; archives@island.net
Year Founded: 1961 Natural history of the Comox Valley region, including marine fossils; includes archives; open year round.
Deborah Griffiths, Executive Director

Cowichan Bay: Cowichan Bay Maritime Centre
Parent: Cowichan Wooden Boat Society
PO Box 22, 1761 Cowichan Bay Rd.,
Cowichan Bay, BC V0R 1NO

Tel: 250-746-4955
cwbs@classicboats.org
www.classicboats.org
www.facebook.com/100396373389938
Exhibits housed in unique pods designed to reflect the surrounding landscape & reveal the rich maritime history of Cowichan Bay. Offers classic wooden boat building programs & undertakes restoration projects.
Ion Barnes, President
Sharon McLeod, Manager

Cranbrook: Aasland Museum Taxidermy
3700 Collinson Rd.,
Cranbrook, BC V1C 7B8

Tel: 250-426-3566; *Fax:* 250-426-3574
Small natural history museum displaying mounted birds & animals. School groups, handicapped, adult groups & individual visitors welcome. Open Mon-Fri 8:00-6:00. Free admission.
Joyce Aasland, Proprietor

Cranbrook: Canadian Museum of Rail Travel
PO Box 400, 57 Van Horne St.,
Cranbrook, BC V1C 4H9

Tel: 250-489-3918; *Fax:* 250-489-5744
mail@trainsdeluxe.com
www.trainsdeluxe.com
The Canadian Museum of Rail Travel depicts the story of rail travel in Canada through the collection, restoration & display of historic rail equipment from various eras. The museum features a large historic railcar collection. Other sights include the Royal Alexandra Hall, an 1898 railway freight shed & a wooden railway water tower.
Garry W. Anderson, Executive Director
Brian Dees, Office Manager

Creston: Creston & District Museum
219 Devon St.,
Creston, BC V0B 1G3

Tel: 250-428-9262
crestonmuseum@telus.net
www.crestonmuseum.ca
twitter.com/CrestonMuseum
www.facebook.com/Cresto nMuseum
Year Founded: 1982 Local history of Creston Valley. Guided tours, permanent & temporary exhibits. Open daily 10:00-5:00
Lou Knafla, President

Crofton: Old Crofton School Museum Society
PO Box 49, 1507 Joan St.,
Crofton, BC V0R 1R0

Tel: 250-246-9731; *Fax:* 250-246-2456
History of old schools, Crofton & area. Open June-Sept.

Cumberland: Cumberland Museum & Archives
PO Box 258, 2680 Dunsmuir Ave.,
Cumberland, BC V0R 1S0

Tel: 250-336-2445
info@cumberlandmuseum.ca
www.cumberlandmuseum.ca
www.facebook.com/cumberlandbc.museum
Year Founded: 1981 Local history. Open Jun-Dec
Michelle Willard, Executive Director,
director@cumberlandmuseum.ca

Dawson Creek: Dawson Creek Station Museum
Parent: South Peace Historical Society
900 Alaska Ave.,
Dawson Creek, BC V1G 4T6

Tel: 250-782-9595
info@tourismdawsoncreek.com
Includes the Northern Alberta Railway & the Natural History Gallery. Open year round

Dawson Creek: Walter Wright Pioneer Village
1901 Alaska Ave.,
Dawson Creek, BC V1G 1P7

Tel: 250-782-2590
www.mile0park.ca/pioneer-village
www.facebook.com/362278520475336
The Walter Wright Pioneer Village presents life in Dawson Creek, before the construction of the Alaska Highway. Historic buildings include the Pouce Coupe School, the W.O. Harper General Store & the St. Paul's Anglican Church. Located in Mile 0 Park.

Delta: Delta Museum & Archives
4918 Delta St.,
Delta, BC V4K 2V2

Tel: 604-946-2850; *Fax:* 604-946-5791
info@dmasociety.org
dmasociety.org
www.facebook.com/DeltaMuseumAndArch ivesSociety
Other contact information: Delta Archives phone: 604-952-3832
Year Founded: 1969 1912 heritage building; archives; exhibitions on pioneer homelife, village life, farming, fishing, First Nations archeology, basketry.
Gabrielle Martin, Executive Director, gmartin@deltamuseum.ca
Darryl MacKenzie, Curator, dmackenzie@deltamuseum.ca

Denman Island: Denman Island Museum
PO Box 28, 1111 Northwest Rd.,
Denman Island, BC V0R 1T0

Tel: 250-335-3196
www.denmanisland.com/denman/museum.htm
Collection houses Northwest Coast artifacts from the Salish; natural history specimens; European settlement items; photographs & maps; administered by the Denman Island Seniors & Museum Society.
Christine Oliver, President

Duncan: British Columbia Forest Discovery Centre
2892 Drinkwater Rd.,
Duncan, BC V9L 6C2

Tel: 250-715-1113
info.bcfdc@shawlink.ca
bcforestdiscoverycentre.ca
www.facebook.com/bcforestdiscoverycentre
Year Founded: 1965 The BC Forest Discovery Centre is a 100-acre, open air museum, which features forest & marsh trails, logging artifacts, & heritage buildings.
Alf Carter, President
Chris Gale, General Manager, cgale.bcfdc@shaw.ca

Duncan: Cowichan Valley Museum
PO Box 1014, 130 Canada Ave,
Duncan, BC V9L 3Y2

Tel: 250-746-6612; *Fax:* 250-746-6612
cvmuseum.archives@shaw.ca
www.cowichanvalleymuseum.bc.ca
www.facebook.com/cowichanvalleymuseum
Local history & artifacts. Open year round.

Duncan: Fairbridge Chapel Heritage Society
4791 Fairbridge Dr.,
Duncan, BC V9L 6N9

Tel: 250-746-7519
fairbridgechapel.com
Year Founded: 1987 The Society protects & maintains the Fairbridge Chapel, a provincial heritage site, & provides guided tours on request.
Ron Smith, Secretary-Treasurer, rgwsmiths@hotmail.com

Enderby: Enderby & District Museum Society
PO Box 367, 901 George St.,
Enderby, BC V0E 1V0

Tel: 250-838-7170
enderbymuseum@gmail.com
www.enderbymuseum.ca
www.twitter.com/enderbymuseum
www.facebook.com/en derbymuseum
Year Founded: 1973 Hours: Tu-Sa 10:00am-4:00pm
Naomi Fournier, Curator/Administrator

Fernie: Fernie & District Historical Society Museum
PO Box 1527, 491 2nd Ave,
Fernie, BC V0B 1M0

Tel: 250-423-7016
www.ferniemuseum.com
Year Founded: 1979 Local history. Open daily 10:00-5:30
Dave O'Haire, President, president@ferniemuseum.com
Ron Ulrich, Director & Curator, director@ferniemuseum.com

Fort Langley: British Columbia Farm Museum
PO Box 279,
Fort Langley, BC V1M 2R6

Tel: 604-888-2273
info@bcfma.com
www.bcfma.com
twitter.com/FarmBC
www.facebook.com/bcfma
British Columbia Farm Machinery & Agricultural Museum Association presents the history of farming in British Columbia. Displays include horse drawn carriages & wagons, steam, gas & diesel powered grinders & tractors, an 1890s sawmill, a blacksmith shop & British Columbia's first crop duster, the Tiger Moth airplane. The museum is open seven days a week from April 1st to Thanksgiving Day.

Fort Langley: Fort Langley National Historic Site of Canada (FLNHSC) / Lieu historique national du Canada Fort-Langley
PO Box 129, 23433 Mavis Ave.,
Fort Langley, BC V1M 2R5

Tel: 604-513-4777; *Fax:* 604-513-4798
fort.langley@pc.gc.ca
www.pc.gc.ca/lhn-nhs/bc/langley.aspx
www.faceboo k.com/FortLangleyNHS
Interactive displays & activities. 19th century Hudson's Bay Co. trading post. Open year round 10:00-5:00

Fort Langley: Langley Centennial Museum & National Exhibition Centre
PO Box 800, 9135 King St.,
Fort Langley, BC V1M 2S2

Tel: 604-532-3536
museum@tol.ca
museum.tol.ca
Year Founded: 1958 Art, history & science exhibits. Open Mon-Sat 10:00-4:45, Sun 1:00-4:45

Fort Nelson: Fort Nelson Heritage Museum
PO Box 716,
Fort Nelson, BC V0C 1R0

Tel: 250-774-3536
info@fortnelsonmuseum.ca
www.fortnelsonmuseum.ca
Artifacts related to the construction of the Alaska Highway; open mid-May - mid-Sept.

Fort St. James: Fort St. James National Historic Site of Canada
PO Box 1148,
Fort St. James, BC V0J 1P0

Tel: 250-996-7191; *Fax:* 250-996-8566
stjames@pc.gc.ca
www.pc.gc.ca/lhn-nhs/bc/stjames/index.aspx
The Fort St James National Historic Site offers a large collection of original wooden buildings representing the fur trade in Canada. The following buildings are located at the site: Fur WareHouse (1888-1889); Fish Cache (1889); Men's House (1884); Trade Store & Office (1884); Murray House (1883-1884); Dairy (1884); & Wharf & Tramway (1894-1914). The Historic Site is open daily from 9:00 to 5:00, from the long weekend in May to the end of September.
Bob Grill, Site Manager, bob.grill@pc.gc.ca

Fort St. John: Fort St. John North Peace Museum
9323 - 100 St.,
Fort St. John, BC V1J 4N4

Tel: 250-787-0430
fsjnpmuseum@fsjmail.com
www.fsjmuseum.com
www.facebook.com/102713059806910
Local history. Mon-Sat 9:00-5:00

Heather Sjoblom, Curator & Manager

Fort Steele: Fort Steele Heritage Town
9851 Hwy. 93/95,
Fort Steele, BC V0B 1N0
Tel: 250-417-6000; *Fax:* 250-489-2624
info@FortSteele.bc.ca
fortsteele.ca
twitter.com/fortsteele
www.faceb ook.com/fortsteeleheritagetown
Year Founded: 1961 Restored 1890s mining boom town of the
East Kootenay. Activities vary by season. Open year round.
Jessica VanOostwaard, Curator,
Jessica.VanOostwaard@FortSteele.bc.ca

Fraser Lake: Fraser Lake Museum
PO Box 430, 30 Carrier Cres.,
Fraser Lake, BC V0J 1S0
Tel: 250-699-8844
www.fraserlake.ca
Open summer

Gabriola Island: Gabriola Museum
Parent: Gabriola Historical & Museum Society
PO Box 213,
Gabriola Island, BC V0R 1X0
Tel: 250-247-9987
info@gabriolamuseum.org
www.gabriolamuseum.org
Year Founded: 1996 Through its museum, the Historical Society
presents the history of the island through displays, exhibits,
lectures, presentations, & tours.
Diane Cornish, President
Janet Stobbs, Director/Archivist

Gibsons: Sunshine Coast Museum & Archives (SCMA)
PO Box 766, 716 Winn Rd.,
Gibsons, BC V0N 1V0
Tel: 604-886-8232
scm_a@dccnet.com
www.sunshinecoastmuseum.ca
A regional museum located on the Sunshine Coast of British
Columbia, aimings to present the history of the Coast and its
inhabitants, with the help of two floors of exhibits, a resource
room, a reference library and extensive archives. The museum
hosts collaborative workshops, film screenings and events
related to the exhibits and community issues. Open year round;
closed Sun. & Mon.

Golden: Golden & District Museum
PO Box 992, 1302 - 11 Ave. South,
Golden, BC V0A 1H0
Tel: 250-344-5169; *Fax:* 250-344-5169
museum.golden@gmail.com
www.goldenbcmuseum.com
www.facebook.com/150197 378373720
Year Founded: 1974 The history of the Canadian Pacific
Railways Swiss Guides & their families. Open Mon-Fri
10:00-5:00
Robert Munro, President

Grand Forks: Boundary Museum
6145 Reservoir Rd.,
Grand Forks, BC V0H 1H0
Tel: 250-442-3737
boundarymuse@shaw.ca
www.boundarymuseum.com
Year Founded: 1958 The Boundary Museum is situated in a
former schoolhouse, which was built in 1929 by the Christian
Communities of Universal Brotherhood Doukhobors. The
grounds of the restored schoolhouse feature a fruit drying facility
& a bread oven which were also built by the society.
Cher Wyers, Manager

Grand Forks: Mountain View Doukhobor Museum
PO Box 1235, 3655 Hardy Mountain Rd.,
Grand Forks, BC V0H 1H0
Tel: 250-442-8855

Granisle: Granisle Museum & Information Centre
PO Box 128,
Granisle, BC V0J 1W0
Tel: 250-697-2428; *Fax:* 250-697-2568
infocentre@villageofgranisle.ca
The log house museum contains artifacts from pioneer days &
earlier.

Greenwood: Greenwood Museum & Visitor Centre
PO Box 399, 214 South Copper Ave.,
Greenwood, BC V0H 1J0
Tel: 250-445-6355; *Fax:* 250-445-6355
www.greenwoodmuseum.com

Year Founded: 1967 Mining, forestry, ranching & the internment
of Japanese Canadians. Open year round.

Groundbirch: Bruce Groner Museum
PO Box 124,
Groundbirch, BC V0C 1T0

Open summer

Harrison Mills: Kilby Historic Site
PO Box 55, 215 Kilby Rd.,
Harrison Mills, BC V0M 1L0
Tel: 604-796-9576; *Fax:* 604-796-9592
info@kilby.ca
kilby.ca
www.youtube.com/user/kilbyhistoricsite
www.facebook.com/KilbyHistoricSit e
Year Founded: 1972 Includes farm, café, general store & gift
shop. Open Apr-Dec

Hazelton: 'Ksan Historical Village & Museum
PO Box 440,
Hazelton, BC V0J 1Y0
Tel: 250-842-5544; *Fax:* 250-842-6533
Toll-Free: 877-842-5518
ksan@ksan.org
www.ksan.org
Year Founded: 1960 Replica Gitxkan Indian Village; museum
has approx. 600 items on display, including ceremonial artifacts,
hunting and fishing tools, masks and shaman's regalia; open
year round

Hazelton: Hazelton Pioneer Museum & Archives
PO Box 323, 4255 Government St.,
Hazelton, BC V0J 1Y0
Tel: 250-842-5961; *Fax:* 250-842-2176
hazlib@bulkley.net
hazelton.bclibrary.ca/services
The museum is located in the Hazelton District Public Library, &
houses artifacts pertaining to local history.

Hope: Hope Museum
PO Box 370, 919 Water Ave.,
Hope, BC V0X 1L0
Tel: 604-869-2021
vc@hope.bc.ca
hopebc.ca/museum
Year Founded: 1979 A variety of exhibits dedicated to the district
of Hope & its history.
Inge Wilson, Manager

Hudson's Hope: Hudson's Hope Museum & Historical
Society
PO Box 98, 9510 Beattie Dr.,
Hudson's Hope, BC V0C 1V0
Tel: 250-783-5735; *Fax:* 250-783-5770
hhmuseum@gmail.com
www.hudsonshopemuseum.com
twitter.com/hhmuseum
ww w.facebook.com/124162084280248
Other contact information: Alt. E-mail: hhmuseum@pris.ca
Hudson's Bay Company store of 1942; archives; fossil collection;
Aboriginal display; North West & Hudson's Bay Company
artifacts; North West Mounted Police, trapping, coal mining, gold
mining, pioneer, logging & World War memorabilia &
photographic history of W.A.C. Bennett dam. Open year round.

Invermere: Windermere Valley Museum & Archives
PO Box 2315, 222 - 6th Ave.,
Invermere, BC V0A 1K0
Tel: 250-342-9769
wvmuseum@shaw.ca
www.windermerevalleymuseum.ca
www.facebook.com/WindermereValleyMuseum
Local history. Open Mon-Fri 10:00-4:00 during summer hours;
open Tue 12:00-4:00 during spring & fall hours

Kamloops: Kamloops Museum & Archives
207 Seymour St.,
Kamloops, BC V2C 2E7
Tel: 250-828-3576; *Fax:* 250-828-3760
museum@kamloops.ca
www.kamloops.ca/museum
instagram.com/kamloopsmuseum
twitter.com/kamloopsmuseum
www.facebook.c om/kamloopsmuseum
Year Founded: 1937 Local history. Open Tue-Sat 9:30-4:30

Kamloops: Rocky Mountain Rangers Museum &
Archives
JR Vicars Armoury, PO Box 3250, 1221 McGill Rd.,
Kamloops, BC V2C 6K7
Tel: 250-372-9535
Year Founded: 1984 Collection includes artifacts, records,
documents & other materials from the history of The Rocky
Mountain Rangers.

Kamloops: Secwepemc Museum & Heritage Park
(SCES)
Parent: Secwepemc Cultural Education Society
200-330 Chief Alex Thomas Way,
Kamloops, BC V2H 1H1
Tel: 250-828-9749; *Fax:* 250-372-8833
museum@kib.ca
www.secwepemcmuseum.com
Exhibits artifacts, photographs & histories of the Secwepemc
people. Museum open year round Mon-Sat 8:00-4:00
Daniel Saul, Museum Manager, dsaul@kib.ca

Kamloops: Shuswap Lake Provincial Park Nature
House
1210 McGill Rd,
Kamloops, BC V2C 6N6
Tel: 250-955-0861
shuswaplakepark@gmail.com
Natural history

Kaslo: Kaslo Village Hall
PO Box 576, 312 Fourth St.,
Kaslo, BC V0G 1M0
Tel: 250-353-2311; *Fax:* 250-353-7767
admin@kaslo.ca
www.kaslo.ca
One of only two wooden municipal buildings left in Canada still
used as a seat of government; designated National Historic Site;
open Mon-Fri
Neil Smith, CAO, cao@kaslo.ca

Kaslo: S.S. Moyie National Historic Site
Parent: Kootenay Lake Historical Society
PO Box 537, 324 Front St.,
Kaslo, BC V0G 1M0
Tel: 250-353-2525; *Fax:* 250-353-2525
archives@klhs.bc.ca
www.klhs.bc.ca
www.facebook.com/kaslovisitorscente r
The oldest intact passenger sternwheeler in the world; operated
by the Kootenay Lake Historical Society. Open daily mid-May to
mid-Oct.
John Addison, President

Kelowna: Benvoulin Heritage Park & Benvoulin
Heritage Church
Parent: Central Okanagan Heritage Society
c/o Central Okanagan Heritage Society, 1060 Cameron Ave.,
Kelowna, BC V1Y 8V3
Tel: 250-861-7188
cohs@telus.net
www.okheritagesociety.com
The Benvoulin Church was built in 1892 in the Gothic Revival
style. The pioneer church was restored by the Central Okanagan
Heritage Society, which owns & operates Benvoulin Heritage
Park.
Janice Henry, Executive Director, Central Okanagan Heritage
Society

Kelowna: British Columbia Orchard Industry Museum
Parent: Kelowna Museums
1304 Ellis St.,
Kelowna, BC V1Y 1Z8
Tel: 778-478-0347
www.kelownamuseums.ca/museums/the-bc-orchard-industry-mu
seum
Year Founded: 1989 The BC Orchard Industry Museum is
located in the historic, restored Laurel Packinghouse. The
museum features exhibits about the Okanagan Valley's orchard
industry, including picking, processeing, packing, preserving, &
marketing. The BC Wine Museum & VQA Wine Shop is also at
this location. The museum is open year round.

Kelowna: British Columbia Wine Museum & VQA Wine
Shop
Parent: Kelowna Museums
1304 Ellis St.,
Kelowna, BC V1Y 1Z8
Tel: 250-868-0441
www.kelownamuseums.ca/museums/the-bc-wine-museum-vqa-
wine-shop

The museum aims to bring Okanagan wine heritage, as well as the broader history of BC wine, to the public. The VQA Wine Shop carries wine from over 90 BC wineries. The museum & shop are at the same location as the British Columbia Orchard Industry Museum. Open year round.

Kelowna: Central Okanagan Heritage Society
1060 Cameron Ave.,
Kelowna, BC V1Y 8V3
Tel: 250-861-7188
cohs@telus.net
www.okheritagesociety.com
www.facebook.com/OkHeritageSociety
Year Founded: 1982 The Society promotes & participates in the preservation of the Central Okanagan region's natural, cultural & horticultural heritage; operates the Guisachan Heritage Park, the Benvoulin Heritage Park & Brent's Grist Mill Park.
Janice Henry, Executive Director

Kelowna: Central Okanagan Sports Hall of Fame & Museum
Parent: Kelowna Museums
c/o Kelowna Museums, 470 Queensway Ave.,
Kelowna, BC V1Y 6S7
Tel: 250-763-2417
www.kelownamuseums.ca/museums/the-central-okanagan-sport s-hall-of-fame
Located at the Capri Mall on Gordon Drive. Open year round.

Kelowna: Father Pandosy Mission
3685 Benvoulin Rd.,
Kelowna, BC V1W 4M7
Tel: 250-860-8369
www.okanaganhistoricalsociety.org/pandosy_mission.html
Oblate Mission, 1859
Tracy Satin, President, Okanagan Historical Society,
okheritagehistory@gmail.com

Kelowna: Kelowna Museums
Okanagan Heritage Museum
Parent: Kelowna Museums Society
470 Queensway Ave.,
Kelowna, BC V1Y 6S7
Tel: 250-763-2417
www.kelownamuseum.ca
youtube.com/user/KelownaMuseums;
instagram.com/kelowna_museums
twitter.com/kelownamuseums
www.facebook. com/260810793981037
One society comprised of 5 museums. This location also houses the Kelowna Public Archives.
Carol Zuckerman, President
Linda Digby, Executive Director, 778-478-0346,
ldigby@kelownamuseums.ca

Kelowna: Okanagan Military Museum
Parent: Kelowna Museums
1424 Ellis St.,
Kelowna, BC V1Y 2A5
Tel: 250-763-9292
www.kelownamuseums.ca/museums/the-okanagan-military-mus eum
Other contact information: Alt. URL: www.okmilmuseum.ca
The museum is dedicated to preserving the military heritage of Okanagan Valley residents. The collection includes small arms, uniforms, insignia, badges, & equipment. Open year round.
Keith Boehmer, Manager, Operations,
KBoehmer@KelownaMuseums.ca

Keremeos: Keremeos Museum
Parent: South Similkameen Museum Society
PO Box 135, 604 - 6th Ave.,
Keremeos, BC V0X 1N0
Tel: 250-499-2499
info@keremeosmuseum.ca
www.keremeosmuseum.ca
Year Founded: 1972 Restored gaol-house with B.C. provincial police displays & pioneer artifacts. Open July-Sept 9:00-5:00
Rob Showell, President
Francis Peck, Appointed Historian

Keremeos: The Old Grist Mill & Gardens at Keremeos
2691 Upper Bench Rd., SS#4,
Keremeos, BC V0X 1N4
Tel: 250-499-2888
info@oldgristmill.ca
www.oldgristmill.ca
instagram.com/old_grist_mill; pinterest.com/oldgristmill
twitter.com/old_grist_mill
www.facebook.com /oldgristmill
Designated British Columbia Heritage Site includes flour mill, workshops & performances.

Kimberley: Kimberley Heritage Musuem
105 Spokane St.,
Kimberley, BC V1A 2E5
Tel: 250-427-7510
kdhs@shawbiz.ca
kimberleyheritagemuseum.blogspot.com
www.facebook.com/263618083650062
Year Founded: 1980 Early Kimberley History. Open year round.
Marie Stang, Curator

Kitimat: Kitimat Museum & Archives
293 City Centre,
Kitimat, BC V8C 1T6
Tel: 250-632-8950; *Fax:* 250-632-7429
info@kitimatmuseum.ca
www.kitimatmuseum.ca
instagram.com/kitimatmuseum
www.facebook.com/161440070544293
Year Founded: 1969 Community & natural history, homesteader & Haida histories, Kemano-Kitimat Project history; temporary exhibitions. Open year round Mon-Sat 10:00-5:00.
Louise Avery, Curator, 250-632-8951,
lavery@kitimatmuseum.ca

Lake Cowichan: Kaatza Station Museum & Archives
PO Box 135, 125 South Shore Rd.,
Lake Cowichan, BC V0R 2G0
Tel: 250-749-6142
kaatzamuseum@shaw.ca
www.kaatzastationmuseum.ca
www.facebook.com/KaatzaStationMuseum
Year Founded: 1983 Open year round
Barbara Simkins, Curator/Manager

Langley: Canadian Museum of Flight (CMF)
Hangar 3, Langley Airport, 5333 - 216th St.,
Langley, BC V2Y 2N3
Tel: 604-532-0035; *Fax:* 604-532-0056
info@canadianflight.org
www.canadianflight.org
www.youtube.com/user/CanadianFlight
twitter.com/CanadianFlight
www.fac ebook.com/CanadianMuseumOfFlight
Year Founded: 1977 The Canadian Museum of Flight restores, preserves, & displays Canada's aviation heritage. The museum & restoration site features more than twenty-five aircraft, such as a World War II Handley Page Hampden & a T-33 Silver Star. The Millennium Kids Room is a "hands-on" facility for young visitors.
Bruce Bakker, President
Mike Sattler, General Manager

Laxgalts'ap: Nisga'a Museum
PO Box 300, 810 Highway Dr,
Laxgalts'ap, BC V0J 1X0
Tel: 250-633-3050
nisgaamuseum@nisgaa.net
nisgaamuseum.ca
Year Founded: 2011 Artifacts that represent the Nisga'a society & culture.

Lillooet: Lillooet District Historical Society & Museum
PO Box 441, 790 Main St.,
Lillooet, BC V0K 1V0
Tel: 250-256-4308; *Fax:* 250-256-0043
lillmuseum@cablelan.net
lillooetbc.ca/Arts,-Culture-Community/Historical -Sites.aspx
www.facebook.com/125437187488516
Includes First Nations artifacts, Gold Rush era relics & Visitor Centre.

Lytton: Lytton Museum & Archives
PO Box 640, 420 Fraser St.,
Lytton, BC V0K 1Z0
Tel: 250-455-2254
curator@lyttonmuseum.ca
lyttonmuseum.ca
Year Founded: 1995 Built by the Canadian National Railway as a residence in 1942, the museum is filled with local artifacts and archives, including pieces formally used at the C.N. station. Open July & August, and when volunteers are available throughout the rest of the year.
Dorothy V. Dodge, Curator

Mackenzie: Mackenzie & District Museum
Parent: Mackenzie & District Museum Society
Ernie Bodin Community Centre, PO Box 340, 86 Centennial Dr.,
Mackenzie, BC V0J 2C0
Tel: 250-997-3021
museum@mackbc.com
www.mackenziemuseum.ca
www.facebook.com/mackenziemuseum
Other contact information: Virtual Museum:
www.settlerseffects.ca
Year Founded: 1991 Showcases the heritage & people of Mackenzie & the Northern Rocky Mountain Trench. Open Tue-Sat Jul-Aug 9:00-5:00, Winter 10:00-2:00

Maple Ridge: Haney House Museum
Parent: Maple Ridge Historical Society
11612 - 224th St.,
Maple Ridge, BC V2X 5Z7
Tel: 604-463-1377
mapleridgemuseum.org/haney-house-museum
Year Founded: 1981 Haney House was the residence of pioneer Thomas Haney, who came to Maple Ridge, British Columbia in 1876. Guided tours are available year-round.

Maple Ridge: Maple Ridge Museum & Archives
Parent: Maple Ridge Historical Society
22520 - 116th Ave.,
Maple Ridge, BC V2X 0S4
Tel: 604-463-5311
mrmuseum@gmail.com
www.mapleridgemuseum.org
instagram.com/mapleridgemuseum
twitter.com/MRMArchives
www.facebook.co m/mapleridgemuseum
Year Founded: 1984 Features First Nations prehistory, history of settlement & families of Maple Ridge & a model railway diorama of the Port Haney area.
Erica Williams, President
Val Patenaude, Executive Director
Allison White, Museums Curator

Mayne Island: Mayne Island Museum
424 Fernhill Rd.,
Mayne Island, BC V0N 2J2
Tel: 250-539-3004
writeus@mayneisland.com
www.mayneisland.com/maynehistory.html
History of Mayne Island.

McBride: Valley Museum & Archives
PO Box 775, 241 Dominion St.,
McBride, BC V0J 2E0
Tel: 250-569-2749
curator@valleymuseum.ca
www.valleymuseum.ca/index.html
Other contact information: Alternate E-mail:
webmaster@valleymuseum.ca
Year Founded: 1985 New exhibits & displays every few weeks on a variety of subjects.

Merritt: Nicola Valley Museum & Archives
PO Box 1262, 1675 Tutill Court,
Merritt, BC V1K 1B8
Tel: 250-378-4145; *Fax:* 250-378-4145
nvma@uniserve.com
www.nicolavalleymuseum.org
www.facebook.com/NVMuseum
Year Founded: 1976 The museum houses an extensive collection of artifacts & photographs of various aspects of Nicola Valley's history, transportation, sports, mining, ranching as well as archives. Open year round.
Barbara Watson, Office Manager

Midway: Kettle River Museum
Parent: Kettle River Museum Society
907 Hwy. 3,
Midway, BC V0H 1M0
Tel: 250-449-2614
kettlerivermuseum@shaw.ca
kettlerivermuseum.weebly.com
www.facebook.com/pages/Kettle-River-Museum/
224641084317690
Year Founded: 1976 Includes original station house, restored 1900s CPR Station, artifacts yard, caboose & section house that commemorates the steam railway era of Southern British Columbia & the British Columbia Provincial Police. Open May-Sept.

Mission: Fraser River Heritage Park
PO Box 3341, 7494 Mary St.,
Mission, BC V2V 6Y9
Tel: 604-826-0277; Fax: 604-826-0333
mhaadmin@telus.net
mission.ca/fraser-river-heritage-park
www.facebook.com/FraserRiverHeritagePark
Other contact information: Alternate phone: 604-820-5368
Original site of St. Mary's Mission & Indian Residential School.
Park features foundations of Mission.

Mission: Mission District Historical Society & Museum
PO Box 3522, 33201 - 2nd Ave.,
Mission, BC V2V 4L1
Tel: 604-826-1011
info@missionmuseum.com
www.missionmuseum.com
instagram.com/missionmuseum
twitter.com/mission_museum
www.facebook.co m/missionmuseum
Year Founded: 1972 Permanent exhibits include Sto:lo First
Nations display, the history of settlement with pioneers, rails,
rivers, & items from business and home life, notably period
1920s rooms. Also featured are items from Mission's old
Chinatown. Open Thu-Fri 10:00-4:00, Sat 10:00-1:00
Hazel Godley, Manager

Mission: Xá:ytem Longhouse Interpretive Centre
Parent: Sto:lo Heritage Trust Society
c/o Sto:lo Heritage Trust Society, 35087 Lougheed Hwy.,
Mission, BC V2V 6T1
Tel: 604-820-9725; Fax: 604-820-9735
On the coast of British Columbia, Xá:ytem has been an
important Salish spiritual site. Today, Xá:ytem is a National
Historic Site, where visitors discover a traditional Salish cedar
longhouse & two pit houses. The site is open year-round.

Naksup: Arrow Lakes Historical Society
PO Box 819,
Naksup, BC V0G 1R0
Tel: 250-265-0110
alhs1234@telus.net
alhs-archives.com
Other contact information: Appointment Phone: 250-265-3323
The society stores archival material for the Arrow Lakes & Trout
Lake regions.

Nanaimo: The Bastion
c/o Nanaimo Museum, 94 Front St.,
Nanaimo, BC V9R 5H7
Tel: 250-753-1821
info@nanaimomuseum.ca
www.nanaimomuseum.ca
Year Founded: 1853 Former Hudson's Bay Company building.
Daily cannon firing ceremony. Open daily May-Sept 10:00-3:00

Nanaimo: Museum of Natural History
Vancouver Island University, Nanaimo Campus, 900 Fifth
St.,
Nanaimo, BC V9R 5S5
Tel: 250-753-3245
info@viu.ca
www.scitech.viu.ca/museum-natural-history
Year Founded: 1976 The museum supports student, faculty, &
external research. It is open in the summer by appointment only.

Nanaimo: Nanaimo District Museum (NDM)
100 Museum Way,
Nanaimo, BC V9R 5J8
Tel: 250-753-1821
info@nanaimomuseum.ca
www.nanaimomuseum.ca
twitter.com/nanaimomuseum
www.facebook.com/Nanaim oMuseum
Year Founded: 1964 Local history & development. Open year
round 10:00-5:00
John Manning, President
Debbie Trueman, General Manager,
debbie@nanaimomuseum.ca

Nanaimo: Vancouver Island Military Museum
Parent: Vancouver Island Military Museum Society
100 Cameron Rd.,
Nanaimo, BC V9R 0C8
Tel: 250-753-3814
oic@vimms.ca
www.vimms.ca
www.facebook.com/vimmsnanaimo
Year Founded: 1986 The museum is entirely staffed by
volunteers & seeks to collect, conserve & display artifacts
related to the Canadian armed forces.
Roger Bird, President

Brian McFadden, Vice-President, 250-756-6182

Naramata: Naramata Heritage Museum
PO Box 95, 224 Robinson Ave.,
Naramata, BC V0H 1N0
Tel: 250-496-5572
contact@naramatamuseum.com
naramatamuseum.com
Year Founded: 1997 Local history; 3 permanent displays. Open
Fri-Sun 2:00-4:00

Nelson: Touchstones Nelson: Museum of Art & History
502 Vernon St.,
Nelson, BC V1L 4E7
Tel: 250-352-9813
info@touchstonesnelson.ca
www.touchstonesnelson.ca
www.flickr.com/photos/touchstonesnelson
www.facebook.com/62908084663
Year Founded: 1955 The museum displays the history & culture
of Nelson, British Columbia. Archives & an art gallery are also
part of the museum. It is open year round.
Leah Best, Executive Director, director@touchstonesnelson.ca
Laura Fortier, Collections Manager & Archivist,
collections@touchstonesnelson.ca
Jessica Demers, Curator, exhibitions@touchstonesnelson.ca
Rod Taylor, Curator, rod@touchstonesnelson.ca
Alex Dudley, Visitor Services Manager,
shop@touchstonesnelson.ca
Linda Sawchyn, Executive Assistant / Volunteer and
Membership Coordinator, linda@touchstonesnelson.ca

New Denver: Sandon Historical Society Museum &
Visitors' Centre
Parent: Sandon Historical Society
PO Box 52,
New Denver, BC V0G 1S0
Tel: 250-358-7920
www.sandonmuseum.ca
Heritage photographs, artifacts, guided tours & archives of
Sandon.
Dan Nicholson, President, 250-358-7215

New Denver: Silvery Slocan Historical Museum
Parent: Silvery Slocan Historical Society
PO Box 301, 202 - 6th Ave.,
New Denver, BC V0G 1S0
Tel: 250-358-2201; Fax: 250-358-7251
silveryslocanhs@gmail.com
sshsnd.blogspot.ca/p/blog-page.html
www.face book.com/SilverySlocan
Other contact information: Alternate URL:
slocanvalley.com/listing/silvery-slocan-museum
Cultural & economic history of the Slocan Lake area. Open
Jun-Oct

New Westminster: Canadian Lacrosse Hall of Fame
Museum
Parent: Canadian Lacrosse Association
PO Box 308, 65 East 6th Ave.,
New Westminster, BC V3L 4G6
info@canadianlacrossehalloffame.com
www.canadianlacrossehalloffame.com
instagram.com/lacrossehall
twitter.com/CanLaxHall
www.facebook.com/clh of
Year Founded: 1965 Inductees to the Canadian Lacrosse Hall of
Fame are featured in the following categories: builders, box
players, field players, veteran players, & teams.

New Westminster: New Westminster Museum &
Archives
777 Columbia St.,
New Westminster, BC V3M 1B6
Tel: 604-527-4640
museum@newwestcity.ca
www.nwpr.bc.ca
www.facebook.co m/NWMuseumandArchives
Year Founded: 1950 The New Westminster Museum, with more
than 30,000 items in its collection, depicts the history of British
Columbia's first capital. The New Westminster Archives, which
contains 13,000 archival items, preserves the documentary
heritage of the city from its time as a Royal Engineers'
settlement camp. Irving House is an 1865 colonial period house.
Guided tours are given of the home.

New Westminster: The Royal Westminster Regiment
Historical Society & Museum
The Armoury, 530 Queens Ave.,
New Westminster, BC V3L 1K3
Tel: 604-526-5116; Fax: 604-666-4042
rwestmrrmuseum@gmail.com
www.royal-westies-assn.ca/museum.html
Permanent collection of military artifacts & memorabilia from the
experience of The Royal Westminster Regiment & its
antecedents. Open Tue & Thu 11:00-3:00
Brig. Gen. Herb E. Hamm, Contact C.D., (Ret'd)

New Westminster: Samson V Maritime Museum
880 Quayside Dr.,
New Westminster, BC V3M 6T8
Tel: 604-527-4640
museum@newwestcity.ca
www.newwestpcr.ca
A restored sternwheel snagpuller, moored on the Fraser River at
the Westminster Quay Market; history of the vessel, educational
programming

North Vancouver: Deep Cove Heritage Society
4360 Gallant Rd.,
North Vancouver, BC V7G 1L2
Tel: 604-929-5744
info@deepcoveheritage.com
deepcoveheritage.com
www.facebook.com/deepcoveheritage
Year Founded: 1985 The Society provides archival documents
on Deep Cove's history, as well as an organized walking tour of
the area, highlighting many historical sites that helped shape the
community.

North Vancouver: Lynn Canyon Ecology Centre
3663 Park Rd.,
North Vancouver, BC V7J 3G3
Tel: 604-990-3755
ecocentre@dnv.org
www.dnv.org/ecology
twitter.com/ecologycentre
www.facebook.com/LynnCan yonEcologyCentre
Year Founded: 1971 Exhibits featuring local ecosystems, natural
history, local & global environmental concerns as well as animal,
human & plant galleries. Open year round.

North Vancouver: North Vancouver Museum &
Archives (NVMA)
Community History Centre, 3203 Institute Rd.,
North Vancouver, BC V7K 3E5
Tel: 604-990-3700; Fax: 604-987-5688
nvmac@dnv.org
www.northvanmuseum.ca
twitter.com/NorthVanMuseum
www.f acebook.com/NorthVancouverMuseumArchives
Celebrates & preserves North Vancouver's social, industrial &
cultural history; WWII shipbuilding; P.G.E. Railway; logging;
Archives Reading Room & Archives Collection
Nancy L. Kirkpatrick, Director, kirkpatrickn@dnv.org

North Vancouver: Pacific Great Eastern (PGE) Railway
Station
107 Carrie Cates Ct.,
North Vancouver, BC V7M 3J4
www.facebook.com/800217229990484
Restored station building with railway exhibits

Okanagan: Lake Country Museum
11255 Okanagan Centre Rd. West,
Okanagan, BC V4V 2J7
Tel: 250-766-0111
lcmuseum@shaw.ca
www.lakecountrymuseum.com
www.facebook.com/lakecountrymuseum
Year Founded: 1985 Open year round
Dr. Duane Thomson, President, duane.thomson@shaw.ca
Shannon Jorgenson, Manager, slgca@shaw.ca
Dan Bruce, Curator, caballero@shaw.ca
Laura Neame, Archivist, lauraneame@gmail.com

Okanagan Falls: Okanagan Falls Heritage House &
Museum
Okanagan Falls Heritage & Museum Society, PO Box 323,
1145 Main St.,
Okanagan Falls, BC V0H 1R0
Tel: 250-497-7047
okhs25@telus.net
www3.telus.net/okmuseum
Local history & artifacts.
Marla K. Wilson, President

Oliver: Oliver & District Heritage Society Museum & Archives
PO Box 847, 9728 356th Ave.,
Oliver, BC V0H 1T0

Tel: 250-498-4027; Fax: 250-498-4027
info@oliverheritage.ca
www.oliverheritage.ca
www.facebook.com/OliverHe ritageS
Year Founded: 1980 Local history; Museum open Th-Sa
10:00-4:00 from June-Aug. Archives open W-F 10:00-4:00 from
June-Aug.
Pamela Woolner, Community Heritage Manager

Osoyoos: Nk'Mip Desert Cultural Centre
1000 Rancher Creek Rd.,
Osoyoos, BC V0H 1V6

Tel: 250-495-7901; Fax: 250-495-7912
Toll-Free: 888-495-8555
marketing@oib.ca
www.nkmipdesert.com
www.flickr.com/photos/nkmipdesert
twitter.com/NkmipDesert
www.facebook.com/NkmipDCC
Year Founded: 2006 The centre houses indoor & outdoor
cultural & nature exhibits & provides guided desert trail walks by
interpreters.

Osoyoos: Osoyoos & District Museum & Archives
Parent: Osoyoos Museum Society
PO Box 791, 19 Park Pl.,
Osoyoos, BC V0H 1V0

Tel: 250-495-2582
info@osoyoosmuseum.ca
osoyoosmuseum.ca
Year Founded: 1963 Local history; open Sept.-May, Tu-F
11:00-3:00; June, Tu-Sa 11:00-3:00; July & Aug., M-Sa
10:00-4:00.
Mat Hassen, President
Kara Burton, Manager, 250-689-2353

Osoyoos: Osoyoos Desert Society & Osoyoos Desert
Centre
PO Box 123,
Osoyoos, BC V0H 1V0

Tel: 250-495-2470 Toll-Free: 877-899-0897
mail@desert.org
www.desert.org
Year Founded: 1991 The Osoyoos Desert Society operates the
Osoyoos Desert Centre, which is an interpetive centre with
hands-on exhibits & a 1.5 km elevated wooden walkway that
allows visitors to explore the desert, either with a guided or
self-guided tour. The Desert Centre is open annually from April
through October.
Denise Eastlick, Executive Director

Parksville: Parksville Museum & Archives
1245 East Island Hwy.,
Parksville, BC V9P 2E5

Tel: 250-248-6966
www.parksvillemuseum.ca
www.pinterest.com/parksvillepast
twitter.com/ParksvillePast
www.facebo ok.com/parksvillemuseum
Operated by the Parksville & District Historical Society. Open
mid-May - Sept. 30.
Nikki Gervais, Curator

Pemberton: Pemberton & District Museum & Archives
Society
PO Box 267, 7455 Prospect St.,
Pemberton, BC V0N 2L0

Tel: 604-894-5504
info@pembertonmuseum.org
www.pembertonmuseum.org
www.facebook.com/PembertonDistrictMuseum
Year Founded: 1982 Three heritage buildings decorated with
artifacts depicting local history dating back to 1850s. Open daily
10:00-5:00
George Henry, President
Niki Madigan, Curator

Penticton: Penticton Museum
785 Main St.,
Penticton, BC V2A 5E3

Tel: 250-490-2451; Fax: 250-490-2442
museum@city.penticton.bc.ca
www.pentictonmuseum.com
www.youtube.com/user/OkanaganSteamfest
www.facebook.com/108559494129
Year Founded: 1954 Local history. The museum is open Tu-Sa
10:00-5:00; the archives are open Wed-Fri 10:00-5:00.
Dennis Oomen, Manager/Curator

Chandra Wong, Museum Assistant

Penticton: S.S. Sicamous Inland Marine Museum
Parent: Historic Okanagan Lake Steamships
1099 Lakeshore Dr. West,
Penticton, BC V2A 1B7

Tel: 250-492-0403; Fax: 250-490-0492
Toll-Free: 866-492-0403
info@sssicamous.ca
www.sssicamous.ca
twitter.com/sss icamous
www.facebook.com/sssicamous
Year Founded: 1998 The 1914 steamship that houses the
museum is a Provincial Heritage site. The museum is in the
process of restoring another steamship, the S.S. Naramata.
Hours of Operation: June-Aug, daily 10:00-8:00.

Pitt Meadows: Pitt Meadows Museum & Archives
12294 Harris Rd.,
Pitt Meadows, BC V3Y 2E9

Tel: 604-465-4322
pittmeadowsmuseum@telus.net
www.pittmeadowsmuseum.com
www.flickr.com/photos/pittmeadowsmuseum
twitter.com/PittMeadowsmuse
www.facebook.com/pittmeadowsmuse
Year Founded: 1997 The Pitt Meadows Museum & The
Hoffmann & Son machine shop both relate the pioneer &
agricultural history of the community. Open year round.

Port Alberni: Alberni Valley Museum
4255 Wallace St.,
Port Alberni, BC V9Y 3Y6

Tel: 250-723-2181
info@alberniheritage.com
www.alberniheritage.com
www.facebook.com/143084405755239
Year Founded: 1971 History & culture of Alberni Valley & West
Coast of Vancouver Island; exhibits include aboriginal artifacts,
particularly the Nuu chah Nulth basketry; clothing and textiles;
household implements and tools; agricultural equipment; local
memorabilia; and 17,000 historic photographs available for
research purposes or reproduction on request. Open year round

Port Alberni: McLean Mill National Historic Site
Parent: Alberni District Museum & Historical Society
5633 Smith Rd.,
Port Alberni, BC V9Y 7L5

Tel: 250-723-1376 Toll-Free: 855-866-1376
info@alberniheritage.com
www.alberniheritage.com/mclean-mill/welcome-mcl
ean-steam-sawmill
www.facebook.com/106253281318
Year Founded: 1989 Operated by R.B. McLean & his three sons
from 1926 to 1965, the site commemorates the history of logging
& saw milling in British Columbia. As well as the steam sawmill,
typical remote coastal lumber camp buildings are being restored.
A resident troupe of interpretive actors called the Tin Pants
Theatre Company perform original stage shows & offer guided
tours. There is also a cafe & gift shop.

Port Clements: Port Clements Museum
PO Box 417, 45 Bayview Dr.,
Port Clements, BC V0T 1R0

Tel: 250-557-4576
ljhein@telus.net
www.portclementsmuseum.ca
www.facebook.com/175359227203
Other contact information: Alternate URL:
lovehaidagwaii.com/businesses/port-clements-museum
Year Founded: 1987 The Port Clements Museum contains
artifacts of pioneer life on the Queen Charlotte Islands, including
information & photographs about the logging, farming, fishing, &
mining industries as well as early machinery from the logging
industry. Open year round.

Port Coquitlam: PoCo Heritage Museum & Archives
2248 McAllister Ave.,
Port Coquitlam, BC V3C 2A9

Tel: 604-927-8403
info@pocoheritage.org
www.pocoheritage.org
twitter.com/pocoheritage
www.facebook.com/pocoher itage
Year Founded: 1988 Members of the Society create exhibits &
displays at the Display Centre, Port Coquitlam City Hall & the
Terry Fox Library, showcasing their collection of photographs,
collectables, antiques, maps & First Nations artifacts. The
Society opened a Heritage Centre in 2013.
Linda Sliworsky, President
Brian Hubbard, Director

Port Edward: North Pacific Cannery Historic Site &
Museum
1889 Skeena Dr.,
Port Edward, BC V0V 1G0

Tel: 250-628-3538; Fax: 250-628-3540
info@northpacificcannery.ca
www.northpacificcannery.ca
www.facebook.co m/NorthPacificCannery
Year Founded: 1889 National historic site; oldest & most intact
salmon cannery village in BC. Guided tours, gift shop, café;
open May-Sept.
Laurie Davie, General Manager,
manager@northpacificcannery.ca

Port Hardy: Port Hardy Museum & Archives
Parent: Port Hardy Heritage Society
**c/o Port Hardy Heritage Society, PO Box 2126, 7110 Market
St.,**
Port Hardy, BC V0N 2P0

Tel: 250-949-8143
info@porthardymuseum.com
porthardymuseum.com
The Port Hardy Museum & Archives houses geological & First
Nations displays, natural & settlers' history & local industry.
Open year round.

Port McNeill: Port McNeill Museum
351 Shelley Cres.,
Port McNeill, BC V0N 2R0

Tel: 250-956-9898
Hornsby steam tractor located at Seven Hills Golf Course

Port Moody: Port Moody Station Museum
2734 Murray St.,
Port Moody, BC V3H 1X2

Tel: 604-939-1648
info@portmoodymuseum.org
www.portmoodymuseum.org
www.flickr.com/photos/55316408@N00
twitter.com/pmmuseum
www.facebook.c om/Portmoodyheritagesociety
Year Founded: 1983 Exhibits & programs about the heritage of
Port Moody & the surrounding area. Open year round.
David Ritcey, President
Jim Millar, Executive Director, jim@portmoodymuseum.org

Pouce Coupe: Pouce Coupe Museum
PO Box 293, 5006 49 Ave.,
Pouce Coupe, BC V0C 2C0

Tel: 250-786-5555; Fax: 250-786-5555
admin@poucecoupe.ca
www.poucecoupe.ca/content/museum
www.facebook.com/ VillageofPouceCoupe
Other contact information: Winter Phone: 250-786-5794
Year Founded: 1932 Pioneer artifacts & archives. Open
May-Aug daily 8:00-5:00
Joe Tremblay, President

Powell River: Powell River Historical Museum &
Archives
PO Box 42, 4798 Marine Ave.,
Powell River, BC V8A 4Z5

Tel: 604-485-2222; Fax: 604-485-2327
info@powellrivermuseum.ca
www.powellrivermuseum.ca
www.facebook.com/PR HMuseum
Exhibits include the local First Nation culture, logging at the
Powell River Mill, local culture & the war years. Open year
round.
Lee Coulter, President
Nikita Johnston, Collections Manager

Powell River: Townsite Heritage Society of Powell
River
6211 Walnut St.,
Powell River, BC V8A 4K2

Tel: 604-483-3901; Fax: 604-483-3991
thetownsite@shaw.ca
www.powellrivertownsite.com
Year Founded: 1992 The Society seeks to preserve local history
through education, by providing workshops, restoration projects,
guided tours, as well as hosting a research centre.

Prince George: The Exploration Place at the Fraser-Fort George Regional Museum (FFGRM)
PO Box 1779, 333 Becott Pl.,
Prince George, BC V2L 4V7
Tel: 250-562-1612; Fax: 250-562-6395
Toll-Free: 866-562-1612
info@theexplorationplace.com
www.theexplorationplace.c om
instagram.com/theexplorationplace
twitter.com/ExplorationPG
www.facebook.com/TheExplorationPlace
Children's gallery; hands-on Explorations Gallery of Science & Natural History; History Hall of regional development; photo archives; motion simulator ride; Nature Exchange; Sports Hall of Fame Gallery with interactive sports machine. Open year round.
Tracy Calogheros, CEO,
tracy.calogheros@theexplorationplace.com
Katherine Scouten, President
Alyssa Tobin, Curator, alyssa.tobin@theexplorationplace.com

Prince George: Huble Homestead/Giscome Portage Heritage Society
#202, 1685 - 3rd Ave.,
Prince George, BC V2L 3G5
Tel: 250-564-7033; Fax: 250-564-7040
admin@hublehomestead.ca
www.hublehomestead.ca
www.facebook.com/hubleho mestead
Year Founded: 1984 A living heritage site with over one dozen historic buildings

Prince George: The Railway & Forestry Museum, Prince George & Region
850 River Rd.,
Prince George, BC V2L 5S8
Tel: 250-563-7351
trains@pgrfm.bc.ca
www.pgrfm.bc.ca
twitter.com/pgrai lmuseum
www.facebook.com/railwayandforestrymuseum
A wide variety of artifacts including historic buildings, locomotives, logging machinery, communication devices & fire department equipment. Open year round.

Prince Rupert: Kwinitsa Station Railway Museum
PO Box 669,
Prince Rupert, BC V8J 3S1
Tel: 250-624-3207; Fax: 250-627-8009
museumofnorthernbc.com/exhibits/kwinitsa-railway-museum
Depicts the life of early station agents & linemen who worked the Grand Trunk Railway as well as the development of Prince Rupert. Located at the Prince Rupert waterfront next to Rotary Waterfront Park.

Prince Rupert: Museum of Northern British Columbia
PO Box 669, 100 - 1st Ave. West,
Prince Rupert, BC V8J 3S1
Tel: 250-624-3207; Fax: 250-627-8009
www.museumofnorthernbc.com
Exhibits artifacts depicting 12,000 years of human & natural history of the Northwest Coast of BC.

Prince Rupert: Prince Rupert Fire Museum Society
200 - 1st Ave. West,
Prince Rupert, BC V8J 1A8
Tel: 250-624-2211; Fax: 250-624-3407
shirts@citytel.net
www.princerupertlibrary.ca/fire
Fire service artifacts including a restored 1958 American LaFrance pumper truck & a 1925 R.E.O. Speedwagon fire truck.

Princeton: Princeton & District Museum & Archives Society
PO Box 281,
Princeton, BC V0X 1W0
Tel: 250-295-7588
princetonmuseum@gmail.com
www.princetonmuseum.org
twitter.com/PrincetonMuseum
www.facebook.com/p rincetonmuseum
Year Founded: 1958 The museum's collection features fossils & mining artifacts, as well as Aboriginal, Chinese, & pioneer items. Archives collected include records of Princeton & surrounding area organizations, land assessment rolls, court information, photographs, historical newspapers, postcards, posters, & personal papers.
Robin Lowe-Irwin, Operations Manager, 250-295-7588

Qualicum Beach: Qualicum Beach Museum
Parent: Qualicum Beach Historical & Museum Society
587 Beach Rd.,
Qualicum Beach, BC V9K 1K7
Tel: 250-752-5533; Fax: 250-752-0111
qbmuseum@shaw.ca
www.qbmuseum.ca
www.facebook.com/Qualicum-Beach-Museu m-411367768880517
Year Founded: 1984 Local, oral & natural history. Open Jun-Sept Tue-Sat 10:00-4:00; Oct-May Tue-Thu 1:00-4:00
Chris Lemphers, President
Netanja Waddell, Museum Manager, qbmuseum@shaw.ca

Quathiaski Cove: Nuyumbalees Cultural Centre
Parent: Nuyumbalees Society
PO Box 8, 34 Weway Rd,
Quathiaski Cove, BC V0P 1N0
Tel: 250-285-3733; Fax: 250-285-3753
info@nuyumbalees.com
www.museumatcapemudge.com
twitter.com/132765133452990
www.facebook.com/132765133452990
Year Founded: 1979 Potlatch collection of Kwakwaka'wakw (Kwagiulth) ceremonial artifacts.
Jodi Simkin, Executive Director,
executivedirector@nuyumbalees.com

Queen Charlotte: Gitwangak Battle Hill National Historic Site
c/o Gwaii Haanas Field Unit, Parks Canada, PO Box 37,
Queen Charlotte, BC V0T 1S0
Tel: 250-559-8818; Fax: 250-559-8366
Toll-Free: 877-559-8818
gwaii.haanas@pc.gc.ca
www.pc.gc.ca/eng/lhn-nhs/bc/gitw angak/index.aspx
Other contact information: TTY: 250-559-8139
Commemorates the culture of the Tsimshian people & their history. Self-guiding trails available.

Quesnel: Cottonwood House Historic Site
241 Kinchant St.,
Quesnel, BC V2J 2R3
Tel: 250-992-2071; Fax: 250-992-6830
cottonwoodhouse@sd28.bc.ca
cottonwoodhouse.ca
twitter.com/cottonwoodh
www.facebook.com/cottonwood.house
Year Founded: 1963 A Provincial Historic Site that trains secondary & post-secondary students in the areas of tourism & agriculture. The house is open to the public, & visitors can explore the site, farm, & nearby trail system, as well as stay overnight in one of the site's cabin accommodations. Open May-Sept., daily 7:00-4:00.
Bill Edwards, Manager, Operations, edwardsb404@hotmail.com

Quesnel: Quesnel & District Museum & Archives (QDMA)
705 Carson Ave.,
Quesnel, BC V2J 2B6
Tel: 250-992-9580
www.quesnelmuseum.ca
www.facebook.com/350659608390264
Year Founded: 1963 Artifacts & archival items include Chinese artifacts, pioneer items, medical instruments, World War II letters from service men & women, & photographs from Quesnel & the surrounding area. Open year round.
Elizabeth Hunter, Manager, Museum & Heritage,
ehunter@quesnel.ca

Revelstoke: Revelstoke Court House
PO Box 380, 1123 - 2nd St. West,
Revelstoke, BC V0E 2S0
Tel: 250-837-6981; Fax: 250-837-4669
Courthouse built in 1913; no tours & no collections

Revelstoke: Revelstoke Firefighters Museum
PO Box 1908, 227 West 4th St.,
Revelstoke, BC V0E 2S0
Tel: 250-837-2884
Revelstokemuseum@telus.net
www.cityofrevelstoke.com/96/Museum
The museum exhibits artifacts depicting the history of firefighting in Revelstoke.

Revelstoke: Revelstoke Museum & Archives
PO Box 1908, 315 - 1st St. West,
Revelstoke, BC V0E 2S0
Tel: 250-837-3067; Fax: 250-837-3094
info@revelstokemuseum.ca
www.revelstokemuseum.ca
revelstokemuseum.blogspot.ca
twitter.com/revmuseum
www.facebook.com/14 4528853796
Year Founded: 1962 Local history. The museum organizes exhibits, programs, heritage walks, & cemetery tours. The archives, consisting of photographs, newspapers, assessment rolls, & records of local businesses & organizations. Open Mon-Sat 10:00-6:00, Sun 11:00-5:00

Revelstoke: Revelstoke Railway Museum (RRM)
Parent: The Revelstoke Heritage Railway Society
PO Box 3018, 719 Track St. West,
Revelstoke, BC V0E 2S0
Tel: 250-837-6060; Fax: 250-837-3732
Toll-Free: 877-837-6060
railway@telus.net
www.railwaymuseum.com
twitter.com/ rail_museum
www.facebook.com/revelstokerailwaymuseum
Displays the history of the Canadian Pacific Railway in the Columbia Mountains as well as the role the railway & its workers have played in building Canada. Includes artifacts, photographs, a locomotive, artwork, railways tools & CPR china & silverware. Open May-Oct daily 9:00-5:00

Revelstoke: Rogers Pass National Historic Site
Mount Revelstoke & Glacier National Parks, PO Box 350,
9520 Trans-Canada Hwy.,
Revelstoke, BC V0E 2S0
Tel: 250-837-7500; Fax: 250-837-7536
revglacier.reception@pc.gc.ca
www.pc.gc.ca/eng/lhn-nhs/bc/rogers/index.a spx
Other contact information: TTY: 866-787-6221
Natural & human history of Mount Revelstoke & Glacier National Park.

Revelstoke: Three Valley Gap Heritage Ghost Town & Railway Round House
PO Box 860,
Revelstoke, BC V0E 2S0
Tel: 250-837-2109; Fax: 250-837-5220
Toll-Free: 888-667-2109
hello@3valley.com
www.3valleyroundhouse.com
Guided tours of historic town of late 1800s; open mid April - mid Oct.

Richmond: 12 (Vancouver) Service Battalion Museum
The Sherman Armoury, 5500 No. 4 Rd.,
Richmond, BC V6X 3L5
Tel: 604-238-2320; Fax: 604-238-2302
12svcbnmuseum.org
Year Founded: 1990 An accredited Canadian Forces museum; military artifacts, with particular emphasis on the 12 Service Battalion & it's predecessor corps; small reference library of military-related materials; open Tue. - Fri. by appointment.

Richmond: Britannia Heritage Shipyard
Parent: Britannia Heritage Shipyard Society
Britannia Heritage Shipyard Site Office, 5180 Westwater Dr.,
Richmond, BC V7E 6P3
Tel: 604-238-8038
bhssprograms@gmail.com
britanniashipyard.ca
www.instagram.com/britanniashipyard/
twitter.com/bhshipsociety
www.fac ebook.com/BritanniaHeritageShipyardSociety/
Britannia Heritage Shipyard is a National Historic Site, which depicts Canada's west coast marine history. It is an example of a village which served the fishing industry and many buildings date back to 1885. The Britannia Heritage Shipyard Society works to preserve the history of commercial boat building in Steveston. The shipyard is open from the beginning of May to the end of September. From Oct. to Apr., the shipyard is open on weekends.

Richmond: Gulf of Georgia Cannery National Historic Site
Parent: Gulf of Georgia Cannery Society
12138 - 4th Ave.,
Richmond, BC V7E 3J1

Tel: 604-664-9009
gog.info@pc.gc.ca
www.gulfofgeorgiacannery.com
www.flickr.com/groups/gulfofgeorgiacannery
twitter.com/gogcannery
www. facebook.com/GulfofGeorgiaCannery
Year Founded: 1986 History of the west coast fishing industry.
Rebecca Clarke, Executive Director, rebecca.clarke@pc.gc.ca

Richmond: Richmond Museum
7700 Minoru Gate,
Richmond, BC V6Y 1R9

Tel: 604-247-8300; *Fax:* 604-247-8341
museum@richmond.ca
www.richmond.ca
www.facebook.com/143214483190
The mission of the Richmond Musuem is to collect, research,
document, preserve, exhibit, & interpret items of significance to
the history of the community.
Connie Baxter, Supervisor, Museum & Heritage Services
Rebecca Forrest, Curator, Collections
Emily Ooi, Coordinator, Educational Programs

Richmond: Steveston Museum
3811 Moncton St.,
Richmond, BC V7C 3A0

Tel: 604-271-6868
www.steveston.bc.ca/online/museum.html
Year Founded: 1976 History of the building as well as of the
village. Open year round Mon-Sat 9:30-5:00.

Rose Prairie: Doig River First Nation Cultural Centre
c/o Band Office, Indian Reserve 206, PO Box 56,
Rose Prairie, BC V0C 2H0

Tel: 250-827-3776; *Fax:* 250-827-3778
Year Founded: 2003 The centre houses a museum,
administrative space, gathering space, health care offices, a
gym, & rodeo grounds.

Rossland: Rossland Historical Museum
Parent: Rossland Museum & Archives Association
c/o Rossland Museum & Archives Association, PO Box 26,
1100 Hwy. 3B,
Rossland, BC V0G 1Y0

Tel: 250-362-7722 *Toll-Free:* 888-448-7444
rosslandmuseum@netidea.com
www.rosslandmuseum.ca
instagram.com/rosslandmuseum
twitter.com/rosslandmuseum
www.facebook.c om/rosslandmuseum
Year Founded: 1955 Local pioneer, industrial, skiing, cultural,
natural & mining history. Open daily 10:00-6:00
Libby Martin, President, president@rosslandmuseum.ca
Michael Ramsey, Vice President,
vice-president@rosslandmuseum.ca

Saanichton: Log Cabin Museum & Archives
Parent: Saanich Pioneer Society
c/o Saanich Pioneer Society, 7910 Polo Park Cres.,
Saanichton, BC V8M 2J4

Tel: 250-658-8347
info@saanichpioneersociety.org
www.saanichpioneersociety.org
Artifacts & archives from the early days of the Saanich Peninsula
pioneer families; operates in the log cabin built for this purpose
in 1933

Saanichton: Saanich Historical Artifacts Society
(SHAS)
7321 Lochside Dr.,
Saanichton, BC V8M 1W4

Tel: 250-652-5522
shas@shas.ca
shas.ca

Year Founded: 1969 Collects & preserves artifacts from
Saanich's rural past, including household & industrial objects,
working steam engines, tractors & other agricultural machinery.
Chapel, schoolhouse & other buildings on site. Open year round.

Salmo: Salmo Museum
100 - 4th St.,
Salmo, BC V0G 1Z0

Tel: 250-357-2200; *Fax:* 250-357-2596
salmomus@telus.net
www.salmovillage.ca
Administered by the Salmo Arts & Museum Society; local
histories, photographs, mining/logging/farming artifacts;

household objects & clothing; tours; educational programming;
annual Heritage Tea & annual Dinner Evening; admission by
donation; open May-Sept.

Salmon Arm: R.J. Haney Heritage Village & Museum
(SAM)
Parent: Salmon Arm Museum & Heritage Association
PO Box 1642, 751 Hwy. 97B NE,
Salmon Arm, BC V1E 4P7

Tel: 250-832-5243; *Fax:* 250-832-5291
info@salmonarmmuseum.org
www.salmonarmmuseum.org
twitter.com/HaneyHeri tage
www.facebook.com/Haneyheritage
Other contact information: Archives phone: 250-832-5289;
E-mail: archives@salmonarmmuseum.org
40-acre parcel of land with a municipally designated heritage
home; 10 relocated, replicated & restored buildings from the
village depict thematic displays on the history of Salmon Arm; 2
km nature trail; majority of collection housed in Salmon Arm
Museum; Ernie Doe Archives Room also on site, with 111 linear
feet of records dating from turn of 20th century; Museum open
May-June & Sept.-Oct. W-Su, 10-5, July-Aug. M-Su 10-5.
Archives open all year round, W & Th, 10-4.
Susan Mackie, General Manager
Deborah Chapman, Curator

Sechelt: Téms Swiya Museum
PO Box 740,
Sechelt, BC V0N 3A0

Tel: 604-885-2273; *Fax:* 604-885-3490

Shawnigan Lake: Shawnigan Lake Museum
PO Box 331, 1775 Shawnigan Lake-Mill Bay Rd.,
Shawnigan Lake, BC V0R 2W0

Tel: 250-743-8675
info@shawniganlakemuseum.com
www.shawniganlakemuseum.com
www.instagram.com/shawniganlakemuseum
twitter.com/shawniganmuseum
www. facebook.com/ShawniganLakeMuseum
Year Founded: 1977 Local history, featuring information on the
Kinsol Trestle, the Esquimalt-Nanaimo railway & artist E.J.
Hughes.
Marcy Green, Board Chair
Lori Treloar, Executive Director
Sally Davies, Director

Sicamous: Sicamous & District Museum & Historical
Society
PO Box 944, 446 Main St.,
Sicamous, BC V0E 2V0

Tel: 250-836-5260
info@sicamousmuseum.ca
www.sicamousmuseum.ca
www.facebook.com/1431943780413600
Year Founded: 1981 History of Sicamous & the Eagle Valley
displayed through photographs, artifacts, digital media & texts.
Open May-Sept Tue-Sat 12:00-4:00.
Gordon Mackie, President
Reid Finlayson, Director

Sidney: A.N.A.F. Vets Sidney No. 302 Museum Unit
9831 - 4th St.,
Sidney, BC V8L 3S3

Tel: 250-656-3777; *Fax:* 250-656-6410
www.unit302.ca
Other contact information: Office Phone: 250-656-2051
Military artifacts

Sidney: British Columbia Aviation Museum
1910 Norseman Rd.,
Sidney, BC V8L 5V5

Tel: 250-655-3300; *Fax:* 250-655-1611
inquiries@bcam.net
www.bcam.net
Located beside Victoria International Airport, the British
Columbia Aviation Museum preserves & displays aircraft &
aviation artifacts, with an emphasis on the history of aviation in
British Columbia. Aircraft on display include the Avro Anson MK
II, the Eastman E2 Sea Rover, & the Bristol Bolingbroke MK IV.
The museum is open year-round.

Sidney: Sidney Museum & Archives
Parent: Society of Saanich Peninsula Museums
2423 Beacon Ave.,
Sidney, BC V8L 1X5

Tel: 250-655-6355
info@sidneymuseum.ca
www.sidneymuseum.ca
twitter.com/sidneymuseum
www.facebook.com/SidneyMu seumArchives

Year Founded: 1971 The museum's collection features over
6,000 items related to the history of Sidney & North Saanich.
Museum open daily 10:00-4:00; archives open M-Sa 10:00-3:00.
Richard Novek, President
Margaret Hutchison, Vice-President
Barbara Gilbert, Director
Peter Garnham, Executive Director

Silverton: Silverton Outdoor Mining Exhibit
PO Box 69,
Silverton, BC V0G 1S0

Tel: 250-358-2485; *Fax:* 250-358-2485

Skidegate: Haida Heritage Centre at Kaay Llnagaay
Second Beach Rd.,
Skidegate, BC V0T 1S1

Tel: 250-559-7885; *Fax:* 250-559-7886
info@haidaheritagecentre.com
www.haidaheritagecentre.com

Michaela McGuire, Contact

Smithers: Adams Igloo Wildlife Museum
11955 Hwy. 16 W,
Smithers, BC V0J 2N2

Tel: 250-847-3188
Display of animals & birds native to British Columbia.

Smithers: Bulkley Valley Museum
PO Box 2615, 1425 Main St.,
Smithers, BC V0J 2N0

Tel: 250-847-5322
www.bvmuseum.com
Year Founded: 1976 The Bulkley Valley Museum's collection
showcases the social & technological development of the
Bulkley Valley. Exhibits include the Bulkley Valley First Nations,
the Grand Trunk Pacific Railway in Smithers, & the forestry &
mining industries in the area. The museum, operated under the
Bulkley Valley Historical & Museum Society, is open year-round.

Sooke: Sooke Region Museum, Gallery, Historic
Cottage & Lighthouse
PO Box 774,
Sooke, BC V9Z 1H7

Tel: 250-642-6351; *Fax:* 250-642-7089
Toll-Free: 866-888-4748
info@sookeregionmuseum.com
www.sookeregionmuseum.com
twitter.com/SookeRegionMuse
www.facebook.com/118482471530145
Extensive archive and significant collection of photographs from
Sooke's past. Artifacts include a restored steam engine yarder,
blacksmith shop, and a rotating lighthouse light.
Lee Boyko, Executive Director

Squamish: West Coast Railway Heritage Park
Parent: West Coast Railway Association
39645 Government Rd.,
Squamish, BC V8B 0B6

Tel: 604-898-9336 *Toll-Free:* 800-722-1233
info@wcra.org
www.wcra.org
www.youtube.com/WCRailway
twitter.com/WCRailway
www.facebook.com/wcrhp
Other contact information: Alt. Phone: 604-524-1011
The mission of the West Coast Railway Association is the
collection & preservation of British Columbia's railway heritage.
Visitors to the West Coast Railway Heritage Park have the
opportunity to view authentic railway equipment, including
seventy locomotives & cars. The site also features the 1914
Pacific Great Eastern carshop & a railway station, built to 1915
Pacific Great Eastern plans. The heritage park is open
year-round.

Stewart: Stewart Historical Museum
PO Box 402, 703 Brightwell St.,
Stewart, BC V0T 1W0

Tel: 250-636-2229
stewartbcmuseum@gmail.com
districtofstewart.com/discover-stewart/heritage
Other contact information: Alternate Email:
info@stewartbcmuseum.ca
Year Founded: 1976 Artifacts, archives & historical records
about the history of the Stewart, Hyder & Premier areas. Open
May-Aug 10:00-4:00; Open Sept-Apr by appointment.

Summerland: Kettle Valley Steam Railway (KVSR)
Parent: Kettle Valley Railway Society
PO Box 1288, 18404 Bathville Rd.,
Summerland, BC V0H 1Z2

Tel: 250-494-8422
reservation@kettlevalleyrail.org
www.kettlevalleyrail.org
www.facebook.com/kettlevalleysteamrailway
The Kettle Valley Steam Railway operates on ten miles of
preservedhistoric land & visitors can ride in a passenger coach
or open-air car. Please see the website for schedule details.
Doug Clayton, President

Summerland: Summerland Museum & Heritage Society
PO Box 1491, 9521 Wharton St.,
Summerland, BC V0H 1Z0

Tel: 250-494-9395; Fax: 250-494-9326
info@summerlandmuseum.org
www.summerlandmuseum.org
www.facebook.com/su mmerlandmuseum
Collections & displays devoted to Summerland's history. Open
year round.
Alex Weller, Curator, info@summerlandmuseum.org

Surrey: Historic Stewart Farmhouse
13723 Crescent Rd.,
Surrey, BC V4P 1J4

Tel: 604-592-6956; Fax: 604-591-4789
www.surrey.ca/culture-recreation/2875.aspx
twitter.com/StewartFarm1
This restored Victorian farmhouse was originally built in 1894
and features a parlor, dining room and kitchen with working
wood-burning stove. Also on site are a circa-1900 pole barn
which used to house 6 draft horses and other animals, as well as
a fully loaded hay wagon. A team of staff and volunteers tend the
heritage gardens of period flowers, vegetables and herbs, and to
the orchards with trees of apple, pear and plum. Tours and
school programs are also available.

Surrey: Surrey Museum
17710 - 56A Ave.,
Surrey, BC V3S 5H8

Tel: 604-592-6956; Fax: 604-592-6957
www.surrey.ca/culture-recreation/2372.aspx
twitter.com/ASurreyMuseum
Local history collections; includes textile studio, childrens gallery
& cenotaph.

Tahsis: Tahsis Heritage Museum
c/o Village of Tahsis Municipal Office, PO Box 219, 977
South Naquinna Dr.,
Tahsis, BC V0P 1X0

Tel: 250-934-6425
reception@villageoftahsis.com
www.villageoftahsis.com/history-heritage.php
Year Founded: 2000 Local history; open seasonally, or by
appointment in the off-season.

Taylor: Jack Lynn Memorial Museum
10508 105 Ave.,
Taylor, BC V0C 2K0

Tel: 250-620-3304
Open daily Jul-Aug, anually; Sep-June by appointment only.
Small museum run by volunteers; features artifacts, photos &
paper archives.

Telkwa: Telkwa Museum
PO Box 595,
Telkwa, BC V0J 2X0

Tel: 250-846-9656
Open from June - Aug.
Doug Boersema, Contact, dboersema@bulkley.net

Terrace: Heritage Park Museum
PO Box 512, 4702 Kerby Ave.,
Terrace, BC V8G 4B5

Tel: 250-635-4546; Fax: 250-635-4536
curator@heritageparkmuseum.com
heritageparkmuseum.com
instagram.com/terracemuseum
twitter.com/TerraceMuseum
www.facebook.com/heritageparkmuseum
Contains historic log cabins depicting the history of the pioneers
in the region. Guided tours offered; Open daily May - Aug
10:00-6:00.
Kelsey Wiebe, Curator

Trail: Trail Museum
Parent: Trail Historical Society
PO Box 405, 1051 Victoria St.,
Trail, BC V1R 4L7

Tel: 250-364-0829; Fax: 250-364-0830
history@trail.ca
www.trailhistory.com
www.facebook.com/167796571913162 5
Arifacts, photographs & historical items relating the history of
Trail. Open Jun-Aug Mon-Fri 1:00-4:30 or by appointment.

Valemount: Valemount Museum & Archives
Parent: Valemount Historic Society
PO Box 850, 1090 Main St.,
Valemount, BC V0E 2Z0

Tel: 250-566-4177; Fax: 250-566-4244
administrator@valemountmuseum.ca
www.valemountmuseum.ca
www.facebook.c om/ValemountMuseum
Other contact information: Alternate Email:
info@valemountmuseum.ca
Year Founded: 1992 Local history. Exhibits include information
about trapping, the railroad, early settlers, the Japanese
internment camps & art displays. Open May-Sept

Van Anda: Texada Island Historical Society, Museum &
Archives
PO Box 53,
Van Anda, BC V0N 3K0

Tel: 604-486-7109
info@texadaheritagesociety.com
www.texadaheritagesociety.com
Local history; open July-Sept., Th-Su 11:00-3:00; open rest of
the year W 10:00-12:00.

Vancouver: 15th Field Artillery Regiment Museum &
Archives Society
Bessborough Armoury, 2025 W 11th Ave.,
Vancouver, BC V6J 2C7

Tel: 604-666-4370; Fax: 604-666-4083
Equipment of artillery units from Vancouver area. Open year
round

Vancouver: Beaty Biodiversity Museum
University of British Columbia, 2212 Main Mall,
Vancouver, BC V6T 1Z4

Tel: 604-827-4955; Fax: 604-822-0686
info@beatymuseum.ubc.ca
www.beatymuseum.ubc.ca
www.youtube.com/user/beatymuseum
twitter.com/beatymuseum
www.facebook. com/BeatyMuseum
Year Founded: 2010 The museum is divided into six different
collections: Cowan Tetrapod Collection, The Herbarium, Spencer
Entomological Collection, The Fish Museum, Marine
Invertebrate Collection & Fossil Collection.
Eric B. Taylor, Director, 604-822-9152, etaylor@zoology.ubc.ca

Vancouver: British Columbia Golf Museum & Hall of
Fame
Parent: BC Golf House Society
University Golf Club, 2545 Blanca St.,
Vancouver, BC V6R 4N1

Tel: 604-222-4653
office@bcgolfhouse.com
www.bcgolfhouse.com
twitter.com/BCGolfHouse
www.facebook.com/BCGolfHou se
Year Founded: 1986 The BC Golf Museum & Hall of Fame
collects, preserves, & displays the history of golf & golfers in
British Columbia. A collection of golf clubs dates back to 1790.
The reference library houses a collection of over 5,000 books,
plus player biographies & tournament records. The museum is
open year round.

Vancouver: British Columbia Medical Association
Medical Museum
c/o British Columbia Medical Association Archives
Department, #115, 1665 West Broadway,
Vancouver, BC V6J 5A4

museum@bcma.bc.ca
www.bcmamedicalmuseum.org
Other contact information: Alternate URL:
museum@doctorsofbc.ca
Year Founded: 1962 The BCMA Medical Museum holdings
include instruments & other equipment used by physicians in
British Columbia throughout the past 150 years.

Vancouver: British Columbia Sports Hall of Fame &
Museum
Gate A, BC Place Stadium, 777 Pacific Blvd. S,
Vancouver, BC V6B 4Y8

Tel: 604-687-5520; Fax: 604-687-5510
sportsinfo@bcsportshalloffame.com
www.bcsportshalloffame.com
www.youtube.com/user/BCSportsHallofFame
twitter.com/BCSportsHall
www.facebook.com/bcsportshall
Year Founded: 1966 The BC Sports Hall of Fame & Museum
contains interactive displays about British Columbia's
world-class athletes. The Hall of Fame & Museum also features
galleries devoted to Terry Fox & Rick Hansen, a Greg Moore
gallery, & a participation gallery.
Allison Mailer, Executive Director,
allison.mailer@bcsportshalloffame.com
Jason Beck, Curator, jason.beck@bcsportshalloffame.com

Vancouver: Cowan Vertebrate Museum
Parent: Beaty Biodiversity Museum
Beaty Biodiversity Museum, Univ. of British Columbia, 2212
Main Mall,
Vancouver, BC V6T 1Z4

Tel: 604-822-4665
vertmus@zoology.ubc.ca
www.zoology.ubc.ca/~vertmus
Natural history collection with bird, mammal & herpetological
specimens; part of the Beaty Biodiversity Museum; open year
round, by appt.
Dr. Darren Irwin, Director

Vancouver: Deeley Motorcycle Exhibition
1875 Boundary Rd.,
Vancouver, BC V5M 3Y7

Tel: 604-293-2221; Fax: 604-909-6232
info@deeleymotorcycleexhibition.ca
www.deeleymotorcycleexhibition.ca
instagram.com/deeleyexhibition
www.facebook.com/deeleymotorcycleexhibition
Display of over 250 classic & antique motorcycles. Open daily.
Naomi Deildal, Manager

Vancouver: Jewish Museum & Archives of British
Columbia
Peretz Centre for Secular Jewish Culture, 6184 Ash St.,
Vancouver, BC V5Z 3N4

Tel: 604-257-5199
info@jewishmuseum.ca
www.jewishmuseum.ca
www.instagram.com/jewishmuseumbc
twitter.com/JMA_BC
www.facebook.com/J ewishBC
Other contact information: Alt. URL: www.peretz-centre.org
Year Founded: 1971 The museum's administrative offices are
located at the Peretz Centre & are open to researchers &
volunteers by appointment only. Museum exhibits & displays are
located in various venues throughout the year; please see the
website for current listings. The museum also has a virtual
component accessible through their website.
Perry Seidelman, President

Vancouver: Old Hastings Mill Store Museum
1575 Alma Rd.,
Vancouver, BC V6R 3P3

Tel: 604-734-1212
www.hastings-mill-museum.ca
www.facebook.com/OldHastingsMillStoreMuseum
Year Founded: 1919 Considered the oldest building in
Vancouver; owned by The Native Daughters of British Columbia
Post No. 1; houses artifacts pertaining to the pioneers of the city
& Native peoples; open June 15 - Sept. 15, Tu-Su 1-4;
weekends in winter months, closed Dec. & Jan.

Vancouver: The Pacific Museum of the Earth
Earth, Ocean & Atmospheric Sciences, University of British
Columbia, 6339 Stores Rd.,
Vancouver, BC V6T 1Z4

pme@eos.ubc.ca
www.eos.ubc.ca/resources/museum
plus.google.com/110390493423212082809
twitter.com/UBCPME
www.facebook.com/PacificMuseumoftheEarth
Year Founded: 1925 Includes mounted dinosaur, insects in
amber, wide variety of fossils & minerals
Kirsten Hodge, Curator

Vancouver: Roedde House Museum
Parent: Roedde House Preservation Society
1415 Barclay St.,
Vancouver, BC V6G 1J6

Tel: 604-684-7040
info@roeddehouse.org
www.roeddehouse.org
www.youtube.com/user/roeddehouse
twitter.com/RoeddeHouse
www.facebook. com/RoeddeHouseMuseum
Year Founded: 1990 Roedde House is a late-Victorian home,
built in 1893. Today, the house reflects the life of an immigrant,
middle class family around 1900. The museum provides guided
tours & educational & cultural programs. Hours: Seasonal hours
may vary, contact for details. Open for Tea & Tour Su 1:00-4:00.
Regular hours Tu - Sa 11:00 - 4:00
Anthony Norfolk, President, anorfolk@uniserve.com
Matthew Thiesen, Vice President
Susan Erb, Secretary, dserb@shaw.ca
Josh Philipchalk, Treasurer, nikhilaprakash@hotmail.com
Sheila Giffen, Museum Manager, 604-684-7040,
info@roeddehouse.org

Vancouver: St. Roch National Historic Site
Parent: Vancouver Maritime Museum
c/o Vancouver Maritime Museum, 1095 Ogden Ave.,
Vancouver, BC V6J 1A3

Tel: 604-257-8300; *Fax:* 604-737-2621
info@vancouvermaritimemuseum.com
www.vancouvermaritimemuseum.com
www.instagram.com/vanmaritime/
twitter.com/vanmaritime
www.facebook.co m/vanmaritime
Exhibit focused on the St. Roch Arctic patrol vessel, the first ship
to sail the Northwest Passage from west to east. Also contains
1944 RCMP memorabilia. Part of the Vancouver Maritime
Museum.
Simon Robinson, Executive Director,
director@vancouvermaritimemuseum.com

Vancouver: Seaforth Highlanders Regimental Museum
Seaforth Armoury, 1650 Burrard St.,
Vancouver, BC V6J 3G4

Tel: 604-225-2520
seaforthhighlanders.ca/organization/seaforth-museum
www.youtube.com/SeaforthsofCanada
twitter.com/seaforth100
www.facebook .com/172606082834734
Year Founded: 1972 Artifacts pertaining to the Seaforth
Highlanders of Canada & affiliated regiments
Jim Purdy, Curator, Seaforth.curator@gmail.com

Vancouver: Vancouver Holocaust Education Centre
(VHEC)
Parent: Vancouver Holocaust Centre Society
#50, 950 - 41st Ave. W,
Vancouver, BC V5Z 2N7

Tel: 604-264-0499; *Fax:* 604-264-0497
info@vhec.org
www.vhec.org
twitter.com/VHolocaustCntr
www.facebook.c om/140874547755
Other contact information: Library: library@vhec.org
Year Founded: 1994 The Vancouver Holocaust Education Centre
is a teaching museum which provides Holocaust based
anti-racism education. It aims to promote human rights,
genocide awareness & social justice. The causes &
consequences of discrimination, racism, & antisemitism are
explored. The centre includes a museum collection, archives, a
library & a resource centre. The education centre is also
engaged in a survivor testimony project. School programs &
outreach speakers are available. Exhibits are not recommended
for children under the age of ten. The education centre is open
year-round.
Nina Krieger, Executive Director
Adara Goldberg, Education Director
Shannon LaBelle, Librarian
Elizabeth Shaffer, Archivist
Gisi Levitt, Coordinator, Suvivior Services

Vancouver: Vancouver Maritime Museum (VMM)
1905 Ogden Ave.,
Vancouver, BC V6J 1A3

Tel: 604-257-8300; *Fax:* 604-737-2621
info@vancouvermaritimemuseum.com
www.vancouvermaritimemuseum.com
www.flickr.com/photos/84985836@N03
twitter.com/vanmaritime
www.facebook.com/vanmaritime
Year Founded: 1959 Includes National Historic Site St. Roch,
RCMP Schooner. Closed Mondays.

Ken Burton, Executive Director, 604-257-8301,
director@vancouvermaritimemuseum.com
Duncan MacLeod, Curator MA, 604-257-8307,
collections@vancouvermaritimemuseum.com

Vancouver: Vancouver Naval Museum & Heritage
Society
PO Box 91399 West,
Vancouver, BC V7V 3P1

Tel: 604-913-3363
Depicts the history of the Royal Canadian Navy since its
inception: uniforms, medals & decorations, 3D artifacts, pictorial
displays, including naval library & archives

Vancouver: Vancouver Police Museum
Parent: Vancouver Police Historical Society
240 East Cordova St.,
Vancouver, BC V6A 1L3

Tel: 604-665-3346
info@vancouverpolicemuseum.ca
www.vancouverpolicemuseum.ca
instagram.com/policemuseum
twitter.com/policemuseum
www.facebook.com/P oliceMuseum
Year Founded: 1986 Located in the historic City Morgue &
Coroner's Court in Vancouver, the Vancouver Police Museum
presents a collection of artifacts, papers, photographs, &
published materials related to the history of the Vancouver Police
Department. The museum is open year-round.
Kristin Hardie, Curator

Vanderhoof: Vanderhoof Community Museum & O.K.
Cafe
Parent: Nechako Valley Historical Society
PO Box 1515, 478 1st St.,
Vanderhoof, BC V0J 3A0

Tel: 250-567-2991; *Fax:* 250-567-2331
curator@vanderhoofmuseum.ca
www.vanderhoofmuseum.com/VCM_Museum.html
1920's heritage village & community museum with restaurant
café serving old-fashioned food.
Chelsea Thorne, Curator, curator@vanderhoofmuseum.ca

Vavenby: Michif Métis Museum
Parent: Michif Historical & Cultural Preservation Society
c/o Michif Historical & Cultural Preservation Society, PO
Box 126,
Vavenby, BC V0E 3A0

Tel: 250-676-0096; *Fax:* 250-676-0069
metismuseum@yahoo.com
www.michifmetismuseum.org
The museum seeks to preserve Michif Métis culture; it is the only
museum in British Columbia of its kind.
Dale R. Haggerty, President & Curator
Thomas Lalonde, Vice-President

Vernon: Greater Vernon Museum & Archives
3009 - 32 Ave.,
Vernon, BC V1T 2L8

Tel: 250-542-3142; *Fax:* 250-542-5358
mail@vernonmuseum.ca
www.vernonmuseum.ca
www.facebook.com/vernonmuseum
Open year round
Ron Candy, Director & Curator, rcandy@vernonmuseum.ca
Barbara Bell, Archivist, archives@vernonmuseum.ca

Vernon: O'Keefe Ranch
PO Box 955, 9380 Hwy. 97,
Vernon, BC V1T 6M8

Tel: 250-542-7868
info@okeeferanch.ca
www.okeeferanch.ca
twitter.com/okeeferanchca
www.facebook.com/Historic OkeefeRanch
Year Founded: 1867 Founded in 1867, the O'Keefe Ranch
operated when thousands of cattle grazed in the Okanagan,
Thompson, & Cariboo regions. Today, Historic O'Keefe Ranch
depicts the story of early ranching in British Columbia. The ranch
offers an informative & entertaining school program. Each
summer the ranch hosts a Cowboy Festival.
Glen Taylor, Manager, manager@okeeferanch.ca

Victoria: Canadian Forces Base Esquimalt Naval &
Military Museum
Canadian Forces Base Esquimalt, PO Box 17000 Forces,
Victoria, BC V9A 7N2

Tel: 250-363-4312; *Fax:* 250-363-4252
info@navalandmilitarymuseum.org
www.navalandmilitarymuseum.org
Other contact information: Alternate Phone: 250-363-5655

The CFB Esquimalt Naval & Military Museum collects,
preserves, & displays the history of naval presence on the
Canadian west coast. In addition, the history of the military on
southern Vancouver Island is also depicted. The musuem
features an archive & research library. Reproductions of
photographs in the archive are available.

Victoria: The Canadian Scottish Regiment (Princess
Mary's) Regimental Museum
Bay Street Armoury, 715 Bay St.,
Victoria, BC V8T 1R1

Tel: 250-363-3818; *Fax:* 250-363-3593
cscotrmuseum@shaw.ca
www.canadianscottishregiment.ca
Year Founded: 1980 Items of historical significance to the
regiment. Open year round.

Victoria: Craigdarroch Castle
1050 Joan Cres.,
Victoria, BC V8S 3L5

Tel: 250-592-5323; *Fax:* 250-592-1099
info@thecastle.ca
www.thecastle.ca
twitter.com/craigdarroch
www.fac ebook.com/craigdarrochcastle
Historic house museum, built in 1890 by Robert Dunsmuir, a
wealthy coal baron; 39 rooms, 87 stairs to tower, Victorian era
furnishings, woodwork, stained glass
John Hughes, Executive Director
Bruce Davies, Curator

Victoria: Craigflower Manor & Schoolhouse National
Historic Sites of Canada
Parent: The Land Conservancy
110 Island Hwy.,
Victoria, BC V9B 1M5

Tel: 250-356-1432; *Fax:* 250-356-2842
The farm & schoolhouse are part of a Hudson's Bay Company
complex built in 1853.

Victoria: Emily Carr House
207 Government St.,
Victoria, BC V8V 2K8

Tel: 250-383-5843
info@emilycarr.com
www.emilycarr.com
twitter.com/Emi lyCarrHouse
www.facebook.com/164231946928850
Birthplace of Emily Carr; People's Gallery; open May-Oct. &
Dec. or by appointment
Jan Ross, Curator

Victoria: Fort Rodd Hill & Fisgard Lighthouse National
Historic Sites
603 Fort Rodd Hill Rd.,
Victoria, BC V9C 2W8

Tel: 250-478-5849; *Fax:* 250-478-2816
fort.rodd@pc.gc.ca
www.fortroddhill.com
Turn of the century coastal defence gun batteries & first
permanent lighthouse (1860) on Canada's west coast; open
daily year-round, except Christmas

Victoria: Hatley Park National Historic Site
Hatley Park Museum
2005 Sooke Rd.,
Victoria, BC V9B 5Y2

Tel: 250-391-2666; *Fax:* 250-391-2620
Toll-Free: 866-241-0674
info@hatleypark.ca
www.hatleypark.ca
Year Founded: 1999 The museum is located in the basement of
Hatley Castle & features two rooms of artifacts, photos, replicas
& reconstructions, & local history.
Bonnie Nelson, Director, Campus Services

Victoria: Helmcken House
Parent: Royal BC Museum Corp.
Royal BC Museum, 675 Belleville St.,
Victoria, BC V8W 9W2

Tel: 250-356-7226 *Toll-Free:* 888-447-7977
reception@royalbcmuseum.bc.ca
www.royalbcmuseum.bc.ca
www.flickr.com/photos/36463010@N05
twitter.com/RoyalBCMuseum
www.faceb ook.com/RoyalBCMuseum
Home of Dr. John Sebastian Helmcken built in 1852; medical &
domestic collections; managed by the Royal BC Museum

Victoria: Lt. General Ashton Armoury Museum
724 Vanalman Ave.,
Victoria, BC V8Z 3B5

Tel: 250-363-8346; Fax: 250-363-8326
Army service support

Victoria: Maritime Museum of British Columbia (MMBC)
28 Bastion Sq.,
Victoria, BC V8W 1H9

Tel: 250-385-4222; Fax: 250-382-2869
info@mmbc.bc.ca
www.mmbc.bc.ca
www.youtube.com/user/maritimemuseumvic
twitter.com/MaritimeMusBC
www.f acebook.com/maritimemuseumofbc
Year Founded: 1954 This extensive museum of 3 floors covers
the history of marine navigation on the BC coast from First
Nation cultures through to European explorers & territorial
tussles. Interactive displays include a mock-up of a ship's deck
complete with climbable crow's nest & ratlines. The 2nd floor
offers model ships for viewing, while the 3rd floor houses a
library. Open all year, with winter & summer hours.
Anissa Paulsen, Curator/Collections Manager,
apaulsen@mmbc.bc.ca
Jillan Valpy, Volunteer Coordinator, jvalpy@mmbc.bc.ca

Victoria: Metchosin School Museum
Parent: Metchosin Museum Society
4475 Happy Valley Rd.,
Victoria, BC V9C 3Z3

metchosinmuseum.ca
Year Founded: 1972 School, household & agricultural exhibits &
archives pertaining to the school & area. Open April-Oct Sat-Sun
1:30-4:30.

Victoria: Museum & Archives of 5 (BC) Regiment,
Royal Canadian Artillery
The Armoury, #305, 715 Bay St.,
Victoria, BC V8T 1R1

Tel: 250-363-8270
www.5thartilleryregiment.ca
Year Founded: 1996 The Museum & Archives of 5 (BC)
Regiment depicts the history of coast artillery & associated units.
Displays date from 1861 to the present. Examples of artifacts
include a rifled muzzle loading gun & a vintage cannon. An
archives & reference library are also available for research. The
museum is open year-round on Tuesday nights. For visits
outside regular hours, please call 250-363-8270 or
250-363-3626.

Victoria: Point Ellice House & Gardens
Parent: Point Ellice House Preservation Society
2616 Pleasant St.,
Victoria, BC V8T 4V3

Tel: 250-380-6506; Fax: 250-381-2238
Info@PointElliceHouse.com
www.pointellicehouse.ca
twitter.com/ElliceHo use
www.facebook.com/PointElliceHouse
Contains period rooms of the O'Reilly family's original
furnishings. Open May-Sept.

Victoria: St. Ann's Academy National Historic Site
PO Box 9188, 835 Humboldt St.,
Victoria, BC V8V 9V1

Tel: 250-953-8829
stanns.academy@gov.bc.ca
www.stannsacademy.com
The restored 1920s-era building services as office space for
BC's Ministry of Advanced Education, as well as housing an
Interpretive Centre for visitors. Winter hours: Sept.-May, Th-Su
1:00-4:00; Summer hours: May-Sept., daily 10:00-4:00.

Victoria: Victoria Police Historical Society
850 Caledonia Ave.,
Victoria, BC V8T 5J8

Tel: 250-995-7654
History of the Victoria police, est. 1858; exhibits include 1921
"Commerce" Patrol Wagon, 1938 UL Harley Davidson
motorcycle & sidecar, 1940 Dodge police car

Wells: Wells Museum
Parent: Wells Historical Society
PO Box 244,
Wells, BC V0K 2R0

Tel: 250-994-3422
museum@wellsbc.come
www.wellsmuseum.ca
Wells Museum is located within the Island Mountain Mine office,
which was built during the 1930s when Wells was established as
a company town for the Cariboo Gold-Quartz Mine. The
museum features displays about the mining history in the area. It

is open from May to September. The museum's website, Mining
the Motherlode, features a digital collection of historical
information & photographs.

West Kelowna: Westbank Museum
2376 Dobbin Rd.,
West Kelowna, BC V4T 2H9

Tel: 250-768-0110
info@westbankmuseum.com
www.westbankmuseum.com
twitter.com/WestbankHistory
Year Founded: 1978 Local history; also houses the West
Kelowna Visitor Centre; open Mon-Sun 9:00-6:00.
Carol Zuckerman, President
Lorne Sisley, Vice-President
Howard Hisdal, Director
Linda Digby, Executive Director

West Vancouver: West Vancouver Museum
680 - 17th St.,
West Vancouver, BC V7V 3T2

Tel: 604-925-7295
wvmuseum@westvancouver.ca
www.westvancouvermuseum.ca
twitter.com/westvanmuseum
www.facebook.com/ wvmuseum
The West Vancouver Museum offers exhibitions & educational
programs to increase awareness of the history, culture & art of
the West Vancouver region & the country. The museum is open
year-round.
Darrin Morrison, Curator, 604-925-7296,
dmorrison@westvancouver.ca
Carol Howie, Coordinator, Collections, 604-925-7294,
chowie@westvancouver.ca
Isaac Vanderhorst, Coordinator, Education, 604-925-7297,
ivanderhorst@westvancouver.ca

Whistler: Whistler Museum & Archives
4333 Main St.,
Whistler, BC V0N 1B4

Tel: 604-932-2019; Fax: 604-932-2077
info@whistlermuseum.org
www.whistlermuseum.org
instagram.com/whistlermuseum
twitter.com/WhistlerMuseum
www.facebook.c om/WhistlerMuseum
Year Founded: 1987 The museum celebrates the history of the
Whistler community. Open daily 11:00-5:00.
John Hetherington, President
Colin Pitt- Taylor, Vice-President
Bradley Nichols, Executive Director & Curator

White Rock: White Rock Museum & Archives
14970 Marine Dr.,
White Rock, BC V4B 1C4

Tel: 604-541-2221; Fax: 604-541-2223
shop@whiterockmuseum.ca
www.whiterock.museum.bc.ca
twitter.com/WhiteRo ckMuseum
www.facebook.com/whiterockmuseumandarchives
Collections include artifacts relating to the history & families of
White Rock, documentation relating to the civic, political &
business life of the community, objects relating to the Great
Northern Railway & rail history of the area, & natural history
objects of the locality.
Colleen Kerr, President
Kate Petrusa, Curator, curator@whiterockmuseum.ca
Karinn Bjerke-Lisle, Executive Director, 604-541-2251,
director@whiterockmuseum.ca

Williams Lake: Museum of the Cariboo-Chilcotin
113 North 4th Ave.,
Williams Lake, BC V2G 2C8

Tel: 250-392-7404; Fax: 250-392-7404
mccwl@uniserve.com
cowboy-museum.com
Displays focusing on the ranching & rodeo history of the Cariboo
Chilcotin area; home of the BC Cowboy Hall of Fame; Shuswap
First Nation, Chinese & Chilcotin materials; open June-Aug.,
Mon.-Sat. 10-4; Sept.-May, Tues.-Sat. 11-4

Yale: Historic Yale Museum
Parent: Yale & District Historical Society
PO Box 74, 31187 Douglas St.,
Yale, BC V0K 2S0

Tel: 604-863-2324
info@historicyale.ca
historicyale.ca
instagram.com/historicyale
twitter.com/HistoricYale
www.facebook.com/HistoricYale

Exhibits include First Nations, Gold Rush, Railway Era & local
history. Open daily Apr-Oct 10:00-5:00

Ymir: Ymir Arts & Museum Society
7306 - 3 Ave.,
Ymir, BC V0G 2K0

Tel: 250-357-9262
ymirartsandmuseumsociety@hotmail.com
www.ymirbc.com/ya ms
The Ymir Arts & Museum Society preserves the Ymir
Schoolhouse, where arts & culture in Ymir are promoted.
Located in the West Kootenays of British Columbia, Ymir was an
active mining town in the late 1800s.
Robyn Balaski, Contact, rainspirit13@hotmail.com

Manitoba

Provincial Museums

The Manitoba Museum / Le Musée du Manitoba
190 Rupert Ave.,
Winnipeg, MB R3B 0N2

Tel: 204-956-2830
info@manitobamuseum.ca
www.manitobamuseum.ca
www.instagram.com/manitobamuseum
www.facebo ok.com/ManitobaMuseum
Year Founded: 1965 Nine permanent galleries & Alloway Hall
which houses temporary & travelling exhibitions. Permanent
galleries include: Earth History, Grasslands, Urban,
Arctic-Subarctic & Boreal Forest. Other galleries include:
Hudson's Bay Company Gallery & The Parklands Gallery. The
Planetarium provides programs for the general public & school
groups in the Star Theatre, including feature presentations on
astronomy, science facts & science fiction, as well as present
day space programs & technology. The Science Gallery allows
visitors to test various scientific principles through 100 hands-on
exhibits.
Dorota Blumczynska, Chief Executive Officer
David Sierhuis, Director of Finance & Operations

Local Museums

Alonsa: Alex Robertson Museum
6 Church Ave.,
Alonsa, MB R0H 0A0

Tel: 204-767-2101; Fax: 204-767-2044
www.travelmanitoba.com/listings/alex-robertson-museum/6806
Local history; Antique guns, pioneer tools & artifacts, 1939 fire
engine. Open May-Sep Sun 1:00-5:00

Angusville: Angusville & District Museum
235 Main St.,
Angusville, MB R0J 0A0

Local history. Located inside the former rural municipality
building.

Anola: Anola & District Museum
PO Box 153, 725 Weiser Cres.,
Anola, MB R0E 0A0

Tel: 204-866-2922
www.facebook.com/1346906872059063
Artifacts & buildings from the early days of the area.

Arborg: Arborg & District Multicultural Heritage Village
PO Box 4007,
Arborg, MB R0C 0A0

Tel: 204-376-5653
admhv4007@gmail.com
www.arborgheritagevillage.ca
www.facebook.com/228744913909942
Year Founded: 1999 A museum & interpretive centre specializing
in the multicultural history of rural life in the pre-1930s Interlake
region. Structures from the former Winnipeg Beach Ukrainian
Homestead are now housed here. Open May-Sep Mon-Sat
10:00-4:00, Sun 12:00-4:00
Pat Eyolfson, Association Contact, 204-376-5079

Ashern: Ashern Pioneer Museum
PO Box 642, 26 - 1st St. South,
Ashern, MB R0C 0E0

Tel: 204-768-3051; Fax: 204-768-3051
lifeash@mts.net
Other contact information: Phone, appointments: 204-768-2394
The Ashern Museum features the St Michael's Anglican Church,
the CNR station, the Ashern Post Office, the Hoffman Log
House, the Darwin School House, & Ashern's first Rural
Municipality of Siglunes Office. Artifacts include a threshing
machine, tractor, bailer, & plow.

Austin: Manitoba Agricultural Museum
PO Box 10,
Austin, MB R0H 0C0

Tel: 204-637-2354; Fax: 204-637-2395
www.ag-museum.mb.ca
twitter.com/manitobaag
www.facebook.com/mbagmuseum
Year Founded: 1953 Located 3 km south of Hwys. 1 & 34, the site boasts Canada's largest collection of vintage agricultural equipment from 1900 on. There is also a pioneer village with over 20 buildings from log cabins to mills & mansions. The Manitoba Amateur Radio Museum is also housed on site. Events include the annual Thresherman's Reunion & Stampede last week in July. Open daily 9:00-5:00, May 12 - Oct. 5.

Austin: Manitoba Amateur Radio Museum Inc. (MARM)
PO Box 10,
Austin, MB R0H 0C0

Tel: 204-637-2354
info@ag-museum.mb.ca
www.marminc.ca
Located on the grounds of the Manitoba Agricultural Museum, Hwy. #34 in Austin; Canada's only amateur radio museum; home of amateur radio station VE4ARM/VE4MTR.
Dave Snydal, Curator & Secretary-Treasurer, 204-728-2463, dsnydal@mts.net

Beausejour: Pioneer Village Museum
Parent: Broken Beau Historical Society
PO Box 310, 7th St. & Park Ave.,
Beausejour, MB R0E 0C0

Tel: 204-268-5535
PioneerVillageMuseum@gmail.com
www.pioneervillagemuseum.ca
www.facebook.com/BrokenBeauPioneervillagemus eum
Year Founded: 1967 Pioneer village with artifacts depicting the lifestyle of early pioneers & the area.

Belmont: Belmont & District Museum
PO Box 69, 202 - 5th St.,
Belmont, MB R0K 0C0

Tel: 204-528-3300
Other contact information: Phone, Off-season: 204-537-2405;
204-537-2474; 204-537-2604
The Belmont & District Museum features a CNR caboose & displays of medical equipment, sports memorabilia, military uniforms, & printing equipment for the Belmont News. Open Jul-Aug & by appointment at other times of the year.

Belmont: Evergreen Firearms Museum Inc.
PO Box 57,
Belmont, MB R0K 0C0

Tel: 204-537-2647
Military & non-military historical firearms; open year round

Binscarth: Binscarth & District Gordon Orr Memorial Museum
PO Box 239, 162 - 2nd Ave.,
Binscarth, MB R0J 0G0

Tel: 204-532-2217; Fax: 204-532-2012
binscarthmuseum@outlook.com
www.binscarthmb.com/museum.htm
The Binscarth & District Gordon Orr Memorial Museum contains displays such as Native artifacts, a chapel, a general store, a school room & large agricultural machinery. The museum is open June through Aug.

Birtle: Birdtail Country Museum
PO Box 508, 738 Main St.,
Birtle, MB R0M 0C0

Tel: 204-842-3363
Year Founded: 1983 The Birdtail Country Museum is housed in the former Union Bank Building in Birtle. Contains artifacts from pioneer days in the Birtle area. The museum also holds local newspapers on microfilm. Open May-Aug

Boissevain: Beckoning Hills Museum
PO Box 389, 425 Mill Rd. South,
Boissevain, MB R0K 0E0

Tel: 204-534-6544
bhmuseum@mts.net
www.boissevain.ca/visitors/beckoninghills.htm
Other contact information: Alt. Phones: 204-534-6813;
204-534-8506
The Beckoning Hills Museum presents historical displays from Boissevain & the surrounding area. Exhibits include pioneer household items, agricultural tools & implements, native artifacts, & military items. The museum is open from June until September. Appointments can be arranged at other times of the year.

Boissevain: Irvin Goodon International Wildlife Museum
c/o Turtle Mountain Community Development Corporation,
PO Box 368,
Boissevain, MB R0K 0E0

Tel: 204-534-6662
tmcdc@boissevain.ca
www.boissevain.ca/visitors/goodonwildlifemuseum.htm
The museum features over 300 mounted animals in natural scenes, with full descriptions of each creature.

Boissevain: Moncur Gallery
Irvin Goodon Wildlife Museum, PO Box 1241, 298 Mountain St.,
Boissevain, MB R0K 0E0

Tel: 204-534-2433; Fax: 204-534-6478
info@moncurgallery.org
www.moncurgallery.org
Year Founded: 1986 Gallery showcases an extensive collection of ancient artifacts portraying the earliest history of the Turtle Mountain & surrounding prairie area in southwestern Manitoba. Exhibits include lifestyle artifacts of nomadic peoples which predate the written record, such as ceremonial items, food preparation utensils & tools. Open daily 10:00-6:00, May-Sept., or by appointment during the off-season.
Phyllis Hallett, Chair

Brandon: Chapman Museum
PO Box 43, RR#2,
Brandon, MB R7A 5Y2

Year Founded: 1967 Village-type museum setting with 16 historic buildings, among them the Roseville Church, Harrow School, Pendennis Rail Station, Robinville School, & various shops; guided tours; special needs facilities & wheelchair access; picnic area; open during the summer, free admission or donations appreciated.

Brandon: Commonwealth Air Training Plan Museum
PO Box 3, Group 520, RR#5,
Brandon, MB R7A 5Y5

Tel: 204-727-2444; Fax: 204-725-2334
airmuseum@inetlink.ca
www.airmuseum.ca
Canada's only air museum dedicated to those who trained & fought for the British Commmonwealth during WWII; artifacts include photographs, uniforms & clothing, personal papers, logbooks, station magazines, tools, equipment, trade badges, & medals; display of training aircraft
Stephen Hayter, Executive Director

Brandon: Daly House Museum & Steve Magnacca Research Centre
122 18th St.,
Brandon, MB R7A 5A4

Tel: 204-727-1722; Fax: 204-727-1722
dalymuseum@wcgwave.ca
www.dalyhousemuseum.ca
twitter.com/DalyHouseMuse um
www.facebook.com/dalyhouse/^rf=203513976372165
Home of Brandon's first mayor. Includes grocery store, garden & archives. Open Sep-Jun Tue-Sat 10:00-4:00; Jul-Aug Mon-Sat 10:00-4:00, Sun 1:00-4:00
Eileen Trott, Curator

Brandon: Manitoba Agricultural Hall of Fame
1129 Queens Ave.,
Brandon, MB R7A 7C5

Tel: 204-728-3736; Fax: 204-726-6260
info@manitobaaghalloffame.com
www.manitobaaghalloffame.com
Recognizing those who have made an outstanding contribution to Manitoba agriculture and to a better way of life for farm families; plaques are located at the Keystone Centre in Brandon (1175 - 18th St.). Open daily.
Bill Anderson, President
Patricia Bailey, Executive Director

Brandon: XII Manitoba Dragoons/26 Field Regiment Museum
Brandon Armoury, 1116 Victoria Ave.,
Brandon, MB R7A 1B2

Tel: 204-725-4579; Fax: 204-725-1766
26fdregCurator@wcgwave.ca
www.12mbdragoons.com
www.facebook.com/369782 049790739
Year Founded: 1979 The museum has a wide range of military memorabilia and artifacts on display, including photos, uniforms and equipment; small research library; archival materials; regimental button collection; open Tuesdays throughout the year
Mr. Ed McArthur, Curator, 204-726-3498,
26fdregCurator@wcgwave.ca
Gord Sim, Researcher, 204-727-7691

Carberry: Carberry Plains Museum
PO Box 1072, 520 4th Ave.,
Carberry, MB R0K 0H0

Tel: 204-834-6609
www.townofcarberry.ca/carberry-plains-museum
The Carberry Plains Museum reflects early prairie life through its collections from former residents, including sports memorabilia & paintings. Open Jul-Aug daily 1:00-6:00; Jun-Sep by appointment only.

Carberry: The Seton Centre
PO Box 508, 116 Main St.,
Carberry, MB R0K 0H0

Tel: 204-834-2509
etseton@mymts.net
www.thesetoncentre.ca
www.facebook.com/TheSetonCentre
Other contact information: Alternate Email:
setoncentre1946@gmail.com
Life & work of Ernest Thompson Seton. Open Jun-Aug Mon-Sat 9:00-5:00
Cheryl Orr-Hood, Chair, 204-834-2056

Carberry: Spruce Woods Provincial Heritage Park
c/o Manitoba Conservation, PO Box 900,
Carberry, MB R0K 0H0

Tel: 204-834-8800
www.manitobaparks.com
Other contact information: Alternate phone: 204-827-8850
Northwest Co. fur-trading artifacts

Carman: Dufferin Historical Museum
PO Box 1646,
Carman, MB R0G 0J0

Tel: 204-745-3597
info@dufferinhistoricalmuseum.ca
www.dufferinhistoricalmuseum.ca
An early 20th century home. Open Mid-June - Sept.
Trish Aubin, President, 204-745-6790

Carman: Heaman's Antique Autorama
PO Box 105,
Carman, MB R0G 0J0

Tel: 204-745-2981
Early Canadian & American automobiles dating back to 1902. Visits by appointment only.

Cartwright: Heritage Village Museums
Parent: Cartwright/Roblin Historical Society
PO Box 9,
Cartwright, MB R0K 0L0

Tel: 204-529-2363
www.cartwrightroblin.ca/node/97
This is a collection of historic buildings representing village life in pioneer days. The Blacksmith Museum is a fully restored, functional smithy. Todds Shoe Repairs has authentic cobbling equipment. Badger Creek Museum conserves artifacts of rural family life. There is also a schoolhouse, post office & telephone office.

CFB Shilo: The RCA Museum; Canada's National Artillery Museum / Le Musée national de l'Artillerie du Canada; Le Musée de l'ARC
N-118, Patricia Road,
CFB Shilo, MB R0K 2A0

Tel: 204-765-3000
RCAMuseum@intern.mil.ca
www.rcamuseum.com
twitter.com/TheRCAMuseum
www.facebook.com/1460996254 88939
Three permanent galleries, one temporary exhibits gallery; archives; library; kit shop; 109 major pieces of equipment; largest collection of Canadian military-pattern vehicles; open year round. Winter hours: M - F 10:00 - 5:00. Summer hours: M - Su 10:00 - 5:00.

Churchill: Eskimo Museum
PO Box 10, 242 Laverendrye Ave.,
Churchill, MB R0B 0E0

Tel: 204-675-2030; Fax: 204-675-2140
www.attractionscanada.com/manitoba/churchill/Eskimo-museum
.asp
History & life of Eskimos & the Inuit. Includes art work, tools, ivory & carvings.
Lorraine Brandson, Curator

Churchill: Manitoba North National Historic Sites
PO Box 127, 1 Mantayo Seepee Meskanow,
Churchill, MB R0B 0E0
Tel: 204-675-8863; Fax: 204-675-2026
Toll-Free: 888-773-8888
mannorth.nhs@pc.gc.ca
www.pc.gc.ca/eng/lhn-nhs/mb/prin ce/index.aspx
Guided tours are offered to Prince of Wales Fort, Cape Merry
Battery, Sloop Cove & York Factory by contacting the Parks
Canada Visitor Centre in Churchill which houses exhibits
introducing the history of the Hudson's Bay Company & the fur
trade of the 1700s. Open year round.

Cranberry Portage: Cranberry Portage Heritage
Museum
PO Box 310, 20 Portage Rd. West,
Cranberry Portage, MB R0B 0H0
cphmuseum@gmail.com
www.cpmuseum.ca
Year Founded: 2001 Local history.
Richard G.Gibbons, President, r.cgibbons@mymts.net
Dale Streamer, Vice-President, 204-472-3222,
dstreamer@hotmail.com
Mary-Ann Playford, Curator, cphmuseum@gmail.com

Crystal City: Crystal City Community Printing Museum
PO Box 302, 218 Broadway St. South,
Crystal City, MB R0K 0N0
Tel: 204-873-2095
www.crystalcitymb.ca/community/tourism.html
Operational newspaper print shop. Open year round Mon-Fri
tours by request
Jim Martin, Contact, 204-873-2095, jimmartin2012@hotmail.com
Mike Webber, Contact, 204-873-2374
Bill Sandercock, Contact, 204-873-2659

Darlingford: Darlingford School Heritage Museum
c/o Darlingford School Heritage Fund, PO Box 67, 197
Bradburn St.,
Darlingford, MB R0G 0L0
Tel: 204-822-6882
School built in 1910; open by appointment

Dauphin: Cross of Freedom Inc.
PO Box 183,
Dauphin, MB R7N 2V1
Tel: 204-638-9641
The history & culture of Ukrainian pioneers; Cross of Freedom
site of first Ukrainian Catholic Divine Liturgy & first Ukrainian
Catholic Church St. Michael's, the oldest such church in Canada
& dedicated as an Heritage site building in 2000; monuments
include a large granite cross, bronze bust of Rev. Nestor
Dmytriw, a grotto & monument of the first Ukrainian Catholic
Bishop in Canada, Bishop Nyky
Kay Slobodzian, Contact

Dauphin: Dauphin Rail Museum
101 - 1 Ave. NW,
Dauphin, MB R7N 1G8
Tel: 204-622-3216
dauphinrailmuseum@dauphin.ca
www.tourismdauphin.ca/heritage/dauphin-rail-museum-cnr-statio
n
The museum is housed in a CNR railway station circa 1912 &
features artifacts, pictures & archival material about the history
of rail travel in Dauphin.
Derm English, President, 204-638-1410
Robert Gilmore, Vice-President, 204-638-8383

Dauphin: Fort Dauphin Museum
PO Box 181, 140 Jackson St.,
Dauphin, MB R7N 2V1
Tel: 204-638-6630; Fax: 204-629-2327
fortdphn@mymts.net
fortdauphinmuseum.wordpress.com
twitter.com/FortDau phin
www.facebook.com/fortdphn
Local history, fur trade & pioneer history & artifacts. Includes
trapper's cabin, blacksmith, trading post, & the Parkland
Archaeological Laboratory. Open May-Jun, Sep Mon-Fri
9:00-5:00; Jul-Aug Sat 9:00-5:00; Oct-Apr by appointment only.

Dauphin: Trembowla Cross of Freedom Museum
20-26 Tuxedo Dr.,
Dauphin, MB R7N 0A1
Tel: 204-638-9641
www.tourismdauphin.ca/heritage/trembowla-cross-of-freedom
Other contact information: Alternate Phone: 204-638-9047
History of early Ukrainian settlement in the Dauphin area. Open
June-Aug., or by appointment.

Dugald: Cook's Creek Heritage Museum
PO Box 10, 68148 Hwy 212,
Dugald, MB R0E 0K0
Tel: 204-444-4448; Fax: 204-444-4224
info@cchm.ca
www.cchm.ca
www.facebook.com/124965140914084
Other contact information: Off-Season Contact Liz:
204-444-3247
Year Founded: 1968 Manitoba's pioneers from the Eastern
European Slavic countries. Open May-Aug 10:00-5:00

Elgin: Elgin & District Historical Museum Inc.
PO Box 102,
Elgin, MB R0K 0T0
Tel: 204-769-2147; Fax: 204-769-2002
elgin.historical.museum@gmail.com
www.museumsmanitoba.com
Year Founded: 1995 Local history; open by appointment only.

Elkhorn: Manitoba Antique Automobile Museum
PO Box 477,
Elkhorn, MB R0M 0N0
Tel: 204-845-2161; Fax: 204-845-2312
www.mbautomuseum.com
www.facebook.com/ManitobaAntiqueAutomoblieMuseum
Year Founded: 1961 Donated to the community by local farmer,
Isaac "Ike" Clarkson, the collection began with a hand-restored
1909 Hupmobile to a sizeable array of vintage automobiles. The
site also includes exhibits of agricultural machinery and
household articles. Open May - Sept., 9:00-6:00.

Eriksdale: Eriksdale Museum
PO Box 71,
Eriksdale, MB R0C 0W0
Tel: 204-739-5322; Fax: 204-739-2140
www.eriksdale.com/profile
Other contact information: Alt. Phone: 204-739-2140
Open mid-May - Sept., excluding Thurs. & Sun.

Ethelbert: Ethelbert & District Museum
35 Railway Ave. North,
Ethelbert, MB R0L 0T0
Tel: 204-742-8860
ethelbertmuseum@gmail.com
ethelbertmuseum.googlepages.com
The museum's collections pertain to the pioneer history of the
area, featuring a kitchen, sewing room, nursery, bedroom, &
school room. Open July & Aug., all other times by appointment
only.
Merv Harrison, Chair
Peter Rehaluk, Vice-Chair

Flin Flon: Flin Flon Station Museum
CN Building, PO Box 160, Highway 10,
Flin Flon, MB R8A 1M6
Tel: 204-687-2946
www.cityofflinflon.ca
Household artifacts from the late 1920s; mining; open Victoria
Day - Labour Day

Foxwarren: Foxwarren Historical Society Inc.
PO Box 85,
Foxwarren, MB R0J 0R0
Tel: 204-847-4031
foxwarrenmuseum@outlook.com
www.foxwarrenmuseum.wixsite.com/foxwarrenmuseum
www.instagram.com/foxwarrenmuseum
www.facebook.com/foxwarrenmuseum
Local history.

Gardenton: Ukrainian Museum & Village Society
PO Box 88,
Gardenton, MB R0A 0M0
Tel: 204-425-3702
www.manta.com/ic/mt68lck/ca/ukrainian-museum-village-society
-inc
Clothing & many articles from the early settlers; an exhibit of
churches & photos of early pioneer life; clay thatched roof house
& a one-room school; picnic facilities; tours & meals upon
request
Harry Hawryshko, President
Kelvin Chubaty, Director

Gilbert Plains: Gilbert Plains & District Historical
Society Inc.
PO Box 662, MB-5,
Gilbert Plains, MB R0L 0X0
Tel: 204-548-2326
www.gilbertplains.com/p/heritage
Sites managed by the Gilbert Plains & District Historical Society
include the Nygrych Pioneer Homestead, Beef Ring, Gilbert

Plains Museum & Tourist Information Centre & the ELdon
Cemetery & Mausoleum.

Gimli: New Iceland Heritage Museum
The Waterfront Centre, #108, 94 - 1st Ave.,
Gimli, MB R0C 1B1
Tel: 204-642-4001; Fax: 204-642-9382
nihm@mts.net
www.nihm.ca
instagram.com/nihmgimli
www.facebook.com/263641135716
Year Founded: 1974 The New Iceland Heritage Museum
preserves & interprets the history of New Iceland, Lake
Winnipeg & its fishing industry. Open daily 10:00-4:00
Tammy Axelsson, Executive Director

Gladstone: Gladstone District Museum Inc.
PO Box 651, #49, 6th St.,
Gladstone, MB R0J 0T0
Tel: 204-385-2551
www.gladstone.ca
www.facebook.com/gladstonemuseum
Other contact information: Alt. Phone: 204-385-2979
Local pioneer artifacts; open Tues.-Sun.

Glenboro: Burrough of the Gleann Museum
Parent: Glenboro Community Development Corporation
PO Box 385, 237 Broadway St.,
Glenboro, MB R0K 0X0
Tel: 204-827-2105; Fax: 204-827-2444
glenboro.com/visiting/museum
Other contact information: Alt Phone: 204-827-2444
Antiques & memorabilia related to the history of Glenboro.

Grandview: The Watson Crossley Community Museum
PO Box 396, 405 Railway Ave. North,
Grandview, MB R0L 0Y0
Tel: 204-546-2667; Fax: 204-546-3368
www.grandviewmanitoba.com
Year Founded: 1973 Facility includes museum display of local
area pioneer artifacts, antique farm machinery, tractors &
automobiles. Also includes a pioneer homestead building (1896),
pioneer house (1918), rural one-room schoolhouse & a pioneer
Ukrainian Orthodox church. Open daily June-Sept & year round
by appt.

Haines Junction: Da Ku (Our House)
PO Box 5310, 280 Alaksa Hwy.,
Haines Junction, MB Y0B 1L0
Tel: 867-634-3300; Fax: 867-634-2162
daku@cafn.ca
www.yukonmuseums.ca/cultural/da-ku/da-ku.html
The centre is owned & operated by the Champagne & Aishihik
First Nations, & features cultural displays, heritage resource
centre, classroom space, language lab, & more.
Steve Smith, Chief, Champagne and Aishihik First Nations,
867-634-4200, ssmith@cafn.ca
Fran Asp, Executive Director, Champagne and Aishihik First
Nations, 867-456-6880, fasp@cafn.ca
Rob Fendrick, Chief Financial Officer, Champagne and Aishihik
First Nations, 867-456-6879, rfendrick@cafn.ca

Hamiota: Hamiota Pioneer Club Museum
Hamiota Municipal Park, PO Box 279, 7th St. South,
Hamiota, MB R0M 0T0
Tel: 204-764-2552
www.hamiota.com/hc_museum.html
Year Founded: 1962 History of the settlement & development of
the area as well as its native cultre, geology & wildlife. Open by
appointment & for special events.
Ken Smith, Contact

Hartney: Hart-Cam Museum
PO Box 399, 310 Poplar St.,
Hartney, MB R0M 0X0
Tel: 204-858-2127
hartney@mts.net
www.hartney.ca/main.asp^id_menu=62&parent_id=57
Year Founded: 1999 Artifacts from Aboriginal to post-settlement
times.
Pat Phillips, Contact
Eleanor Vandusen, Contact, 204-858-2064

Headingley: Jim's Vintage Garages
5353 Portage Ave.,
Headingley, MB R4H 1J9
Tel: 204-889-3132; Fax: 204-831-0816
robnowosad@shaw.ca
www.jimsvintagegarages.ca
www.facebook.com/JimsVint ageGarages
Year Founded: 2005 The museum's collection features
automotive & petroleum industry memorabilia collected &

donated to the Rural Municipality of Headingley by a couple of long-time residents. Hours of Operation: May-Sept., M-Sa 10:00-5:00, Su 12:00-5:00; Sept.-Apr. by appointment.

Inglis: Inglis Grain Elevators National Historic Site
Parent: Inglis Area Heritage Committee
PO Box 81,
Inglis, MB R0J 0X0

Tel: 204-564-2243; *Fax:* 204-564-2617
iahc@mts.net
www.ingliselevators.com
www.instagram.com/ingliselevators
twitter.com/ingliselevators
www.face book.com/ingliselevators
Year Founded: 1996 The site represents the development of Canada's grain industry from 1900-1930. Open summer, M-Sa 10:00-6:00, Su 12:00-6:00; off-season, F-Sa 10:00-6:00, Su 12:00-6:00.

Inglis: St. Elijah Pioneer Museum
Inglis, MB R0J 0X0

Tel: 204-564-2228
info@stelijahpioneermuseum.ca
www.stelijahpioneermuseum.ca
twitter.com/stelijahmuseum
www.facebook.c om/133664709977119
Other contact information: Tours: tour@stelijahpioneermuseum.ca
Year Founded: 1979 Commemorates Romanian & Ukrainian pioneers who immigrated to Canada. Includes the Paulencu Pioneer House, the St. Elijah Pioneer Church & the Pioneer Cemetery.

Killarney: J.A.V. David Museum
PO Box 584, 414 William St.,
Killarney, MB R0K 1G0

Tel: 204-523-7325
javdavidmuseum@outlook.com
www.facebook.com/javdavidmuseumatkillarneymb
Museum of artifacts, clothing & memorabilia associated with Killarney & area history. Open Jun-Aug Tue-Sat 10:00-5:00, other times by appointment.

Lac du Bonnet: Lac du Bonnet & District Historical Society
PO Box 658,
Lac du Bonnet, MB R0E 1A0

Tel: 204-345-2726
ldbhistorical.ca
Year Founded: 1988 Preserves the history of Lac du Bonnet. Leon Clegg, President, leon.clegg@gmail.com

Ladywood: Atelier Ladywood Museum
PO Box 14, RR#3,
Ladywood, MB R0E 0C0

Year Founded: 1991 Atelier Ladywood Museum features the former H. Gabel's General Store, with items from the 1930s to the 1950s.

Lundar: Lundar Museum Society
PO Box 265,
Lundar, MB R0C 1Y0

Tel: 204-739-0147
Features the CNR station, Mary Hill School, former Notre Dame Church & pioneer artifacts. Open Jun-Sept; located at Railway & Main St.

Lynn Lake: Lynn Lake Mining Town Museum
PO Box 100, 460 Cobalt Pl.,
Lynn Lake, MB R0B 0W0

Tel: 204-356-8302

Open May 24 - Aug. 31
Neil Campbell, Contact

McCreary: Satterthwaite Log Cabin
PO Box 251,
McCreary, MB R0J 1B0

Tel: 204-835-2341; *Fax:* 204-835-2658
www.gov.mb.ca/chc/hrb/mun/m106.html
Year Founded: 1995 A restored 1800s log cabin that shows pioneer building methods & offers visitors a recreated pioneer garden, memorial plaques & a rest area.

Melita: Antler River Historical Society Museum
PO Box 67, 71 Ash St.,
Melita, MB R0M 1L0

Tel: 204-522-3103
www.facebook.com/melitamuseum
Other contact information: Alternate Phones: 204-522-3438;
204-522-3825

Year Founded: 1972 Local history. Open Jul-Aug 1:00-5:00 & by appointment

Miami: Miami Museum
PO Box 153, 3rd St. & Kerby Ave,
Miami, MB R0G 1H0

Tel: 204-435-2305; *Fax:* 204-435-2534
Fossils; souvenirs of WWI & WWII; wedding dresses from 1896-1900

Miniota: Miniota Municipal Museum Inc.
PO Box 189, 110 Steuart Ave.,
Miniota, MB R0M 1M0

Tel: 204-567-3690; *Fax:* 204-567-3807
Archeological and paleontological specimens, pioneer & Aboriginal artifacts.

Minnedosa: Minnedosa Heritage Museum
100 Heritage Park Cres.,
Minnedosa, MB R0J 1E0

Tel: 204-867-3542
minnedosamuseum@gmail.com
www.minnedosa.com/visiting/things-to-do/museum-heritage-villa ge
Other contact information: Off-Season Phone: 204-867-3816
Local history includes Cadurcis House, Hunterville Church, Havelock School, McManus Trappers' Cabin, Munro Blacksmith Shop, Minnedosa Power House, Hopkins Log Barn & operating windmill & waterwheel. Open Jul-Sep 10:00-4:00; group tours available by appointment year round.

Moosehorn: Moosehorn Heritage Museum Inc.
PO Box 28, Railway Ave. & 1st St. North,
Moosehorn, MB R0C 2E0

Tel: 204-768-3788
www.grahamdale.ca
Local pioneer history & artifacts, replica of St. Thomas Lutheran Church, Buztynski Heritage House & a variety of equipment. Open Jul-Sep Tue-Sat 10:00-4:00

Morden: Canadian Fossil Discovery Centre (CFDC)
111B Gilmour St.,
Morden, MB R6M 1N9

Tel: 204-822-3406; *Fax:* 204-272-3303
info@discoverfossils.com
www.discoverfossils.com
www.youtube.com/cdnfossildiscovery
twitter.com/discoverfossils
www.fac ebook.com/bruce.mosasaur
Housing an extensive collection of marine reptile fossils, the galleries of the Canadian Fossil Discovery Centre interpret life in the Western Interior Seaway during the cretaceous period. The museum is open year round.
Peter Cantelon, Executive Director, peter@discoverfossils.com

Morden: Manitoba Baseball Hall of Fame (MBHOF)
111C Gilmour St.,
Morden, MB R6M 1M9

Tel: 204-822-4636
mbbbhof@mts.net
www.mbhof.ca
www.instagram.com/baseballhall
www.facebook.com/manitobabaseballhalloffa me
Year Founded: 1997 The Hall of Fame also includes a museum where visitors can explore the history of baseball in Manitoba. Open daily 8:00-9:00.
Morris Mott, Chair, 204-726-5167, mott@brandonu.ca
Dan Giesbrecht, Vice-Chairman, 204-822-4989, dangiesbrecht48@gmail.com

Morris: Morris & District Centennial Museum
PO Box 344, 6370 Lord Selkirk Hwy,
Morris, MB R0G 1K0

Tel: 204-746-2169
mormus@mts.net
townofmorris.ca/morris-district-centennial-museum
Exhibits artifacts which depict local history & pioneer life in the Red River Valley.

Neepawa: Beautiful Plains Museum
91 Hamilton St. West,
Neepawa, MB R0J 1H0

Tel: 204-476-3896
www.neepawa.ca
Other contact information: Virtual Museum:
www.neepawa.ca/museum/front.htm
Year Founded: 1976 The Beautiful Plains Museum features the following attractions: a military room; costume rooms; a medical hall; jewellery & general store displays; a post office exhibit; a local history room; office equipment; farm & home tools; information about local lodges; sports memorabilia; information about the local Ukranian Polish culture; & a chapel room, which depicts the history of religious settlement in the Neepawa area. The museum is house in the CNR station, which was built in 1902. Neepawa's Beautiful Plains Museum is open from Victoria Day to Labour Day.

Neepawa: The Margaret Laurence Home
312 First Ave.,
Neepawa, MB R0J 1H0

Tel: 204-476-3612
Year Founded: 1987 Birthplace of Margaret Laurence; includes research area, meeting room & modern artwork; open daily in summer, other times by appt.

Notre Dame de Lourdes: Pioneers & Chanoinesses Museum / Musée des Pionniers & des Chanoinessess
PO Box 186, 55 Rogers St.,
Notre Dame de Lourdes, MB R0G 1M0

Tel: 204-248-7220
museend@mts.net
joiedevivremanitoba.com
www.facebook.com/393246174125139
The Pioneers & Chanoinesses Museum houses artifacts of the pioneers & Chanoinesses in the community. Open year round Mon-Fri 8:30-4:00

Nutimik Lake: Whiteshell Natural History Museum
Whiteshell Provincial Park, PR 307,
Nutimik Lake, MB R0E 1Y0

Tel: 204-369-3157
ParkInterpretation@gov.mb.ca
www.gov.mb.ca/conservation/parks/act_interp/centres/wnhm
Other contact information: Museum (summer only):
204-248-2846
Year Founded: 1960 Located in the Whiteshell Provincial Park, the natural history museum contains informative displays about the wildlife in the park, the boreal forest, sturgeon & the Winnipeg River, petroforms, & the Aboriginal people. The Whiteshell Natural History Museum, located in a log building at Nutimik Lake, is open from the long weekend in May to the long weekend in September.

The Pas: Charlebois Heritage Museum
108 First St. West,
The Pas, MB R9A 1K4

Tel: 204-623-6152
archives@keepas.ca
www.museumsmanitoba.com/en/find-a-museum-by-name/details /18
History & information about Bishop Charlebois, housed in a chapel built in 1897.

The Pas: The Sam Waller Museum
PO Box 185, 306 Fischer Ave.,
The Pas, MB R9A 1K4

Tel: 204-623-3802; *Fax:* 204-623-5506
samwallermuseum@mts.net
www.samwallermuseum.ca
Permanent collection comprises some 70,000 items of natural history specimens, historical artifacts, books & other library materials, photographs & negatives, fine art objects, & archival resources of the Town of The Pas; temporary exhibits; special events & programming. Open daily 1:00 - 5:00. Jul - Aug 10:00 - 5:00.
Sharain Jones, Director
Joanna Munholland, Curator and Archivist

Pilot Mound: Marringhurst Pioneer Park Museum
217 Beveridge Ave,
Pilot Mound, MB R0G 1P0

Tel: 204-825-2334
Schoolhouse with original furnishings; open year round

Pilot Mound: Pilot Mound Museum
Pilot Mound Millennium Complex, 213 Lorne Ave.,
Pilot Mound, MB R0G 1P0

Pioneer household & agricultural items; natural history artifacts; open year round

Plum Coulee: Plum Coulee & District Museum
277 Main Ave.,
Plum Coulee, MB R0G 1R0

Tel: 204-829-3419; *Fax:* 204-829-3436
pcoulee@mts.net
www.townofplumcoulee.com/tourism
Artifacts & photographs portray the Ukrainian, Mennonite, Jewish, & Ukrainian pioneer history of Plum Coulee & the surrounding area. The Plum Coulee & District Museum is open during the summer, or by appointment.

Portage la Prairie: The Fort-La-Reine Museum & Pioneer Village
PO Box 744, 2652 Saskatchewan Ave. East,
Portage la Prairie, MB R1N 3Z9
Tel: 204-857-3259; *Fax:* 204-239-4917
info@fortlareinemuseum.com
www.fortlareinemuseum.com
instagram.com/fortlareine
twitter.com/fortlareine
www.facebook.com/fortlareinemuseum
Year Founded: 1967 Depicts native & pioneer life in the 1800s & includes a fort, trading post, village store, country church, schoolhouse, print shop, fire hall, stable, trapper's cabin & several heritage homes. Also includes an 1882 official private railcar of Sir William Van Horne. Open Mon-Sat 10:00-5:00, Sun 12:00-5:00
Tracey Turner, Executive Director/Curator,
manager@fortlareinemuseum.ca

Rapid City: Rapid City Museum & Cultural Centre
PO Box 271, 4th Ave.,
Rapid City, MB R0K 1W0
Tel: 204-826-2732
rapidcitymuseum@gmail.com
sites.google.com/site/rapidcitymuseum/home
Cundy watch display; Frederick Philip Grove display; old school building; old Rapid City Reporter building with press & back copies; open July & Aug., other times by appt.
Lenny DeSchutter, Chair, sedynnel@gmail.com

Reston: Reston & District Museum
PO Box 280, 102 9th St.,
Reston, MB R0M 1X0
Tel: 204-877-3641; *Fax:* 204-877-3659
Local artifacts & archival material. Open Jul-Aug Tue-Sat 12:00-6:00

Riverton: Hecla Island Heritage Home Museum
c/o Manitoba Conservation,
Riverton, MB R0C 2R0
Tel: 204-279-2056
gov.mb.ca/sd/parks/act_interp/centres/hecla.html
Depiction of the life of an Icelandic family from 1920-1940s.

La Riviere: Archibald Historical Museum
PO Box 97,
La Riviere, MB R0G 1A0
Tel: 204-242-2825
Other contact information: Alternate Phones: 204-242-2554; 204-242-2235
1878 log house furnished as it was during Nellie McClung's residency plus large frame home (furnished) where she lived. Also La Rivière C.P.R. Station & more. Open mid-May - Labour Day, closed Wed-Thu unless by appt.

RM of Blanshard: The Clack Family Heritage Museum
RM of Blanshard, MB R0K 1X0
Tel: 204-328-5240
riversdaly.ca/attractions
Other contact information: Alt. Phone: 204-764-2726
Antique cars, tractors, trucks & farm implements; Victorian china & clothing; railway, RCMP military & native artifacts; open June-Sept.; guided tours available.
Vernon J. "Tim" Clack, Contact

Roblin: Keystone Pioneers Museum Inc.
PO Box 10,
Roblin, MB R0L 1P0
Tel: 204-937-2979
keystonemuseum@gmail.com
kpmroblinmb.webs.com
www.facebook.com/189524247747064
Agricultural equipment & artifacts; Elaschuk House; Makaroff Church; Sawmill; themed rooms. Open May-Aug Mon-Thu 1:00-5:00
Richard Wileman, President, 204-773-6634
Marilyn Simpson, Secretary & Treasurer, 204-937-4914

Roland: Roland 4-H Museum
72 Third St.,
Roland, MB R0G 1T0
Tel: 204-343-2061
info@roland4hmuseum.ca
www.roland4hmuseum.ca
www.instagram.com/national4h
History of the 4-H club in Roland, MB. Open July & Aug., M-F 1:00-4:00.

Rossburn: Rossburn Museum
c/o Town of Rossburn, PO Box 70, 43 Main St. North,
Rossburn, MB R0J 1V0
Tel: 204-859-2828
rossburn.ca/visiting/culture-heritage/
Other contact information: Alt Phone: 204-859-0051S
The Rossburn Museum features rooms representing a pioneer kitchen, a classroom, a hospital room, a print shop & a hairdressing salon. The museum also displays a miniature Ukrainian village, plus Ukrainian artifacts.

St Andrews: Lower Fort Garry National Historic Site of Canada
5925 Hwy. 9,
St Andrews, MB R1A 4A8
Tel: 204-785-6050; *Fax:* 204-482-5887
Toll-Free: 888-773-8888
lfg.info@pc.gc.ca
pc.gc.ca/en/lhn-nhs/mb/fortgarry
Other contact information: TTY: 866-787-6221
1830s stone Hudson's Bay Co. fort; costumed interpreters, visitor centre, gift store, restaurant. Open May-Sep

Saint-Boniface: Le Musée de Saint-Boniface Museum
494 Taché Ave,
Saint-Boniface, MB R2H 2B2
Tel: 204-237-4500; *Fax:* 204-986-7964
info@msbm.mb.ca
msbm.mb.ca
instagram.com/museeestbonifacemuseum;
pinterest.com/museeestbmuseum
twitter.com/msbm_mb_ca
www.facebook.com/msbm.mb.ca
Year Founded: 1967 Artifacts related to the French-Canadian and Métis heritage of Western Canada. Thematic exhibitions; More than 30,000 historical and ethnological objects in the collection. Open Mon-Wed, Fri-Sat 10:00-4:00, Thu 9:00-9:00
Vania Gagnon, Directeur, vgagnon@msbm.mb.ca
Pierrette Boily, Conservatrice, pboily@msbm.mb.ca

St Claude: Manitoba Dairy Museum
Parent: St. Claude Historical Society
164 Jobin Ave.,
St Claude, MB R0G 1Z0
Tel: 204-379-2156
shstclaude@gmail.com
www.facebook.com/manitoba.dairy.museum
Artifacts from settlers, Pioneer museum, chapel, county school & a variety of dairy artifacts & equipment. Demonstrations available. Open daily 10:00-5:00

Sainte-Anne-des-chênes: Musée Pointe des Chênes
208, av Centrale,
Sainte-Anne-des-chênes, MB R5H 1C9
Tél: 204-422-5639; *Téléc:* 204-422-5514
Situé dans un parc à côté de la Villa Youville; vieux musée présente des objets de pionniers de la région. Sa collection comprend près de 2000 items historiques utilisés par les premiers résidents métis et canadiens-français de la Pointe-des-Chênes qui ont servi à ouvrir et à coloniser le pays.

Ste-Geneviève: Site Historique Monseigneur Taché / Monseigneur Taché Historic Site
98, rue Saltel,
Ste-Geneviève, MB R0E 1S0
Tél: 204-853-7509; *Téléc:* 204-422-8508
www.gov.mb.ca/chc/hrb/mun/m027.html
Fondée en: 1989 This restored church reflects French culture of rural Manitoba during the 17th & 18th centuries.
Diane Dornez-Laxdal, Présidente

St Joseph: Musée St-Joseph Museum Inc.
PO Box 34, 25 Brais Blvd.,
St Joseph, MB R0G 2C0
Tel: 204-737-2244
museestjoseph@gmail.com
museestjoseph.ca
www.youtube.com/channel/UC_z6SB6v_1rAf_r6Djm60mA
www.facebook.com/MuseeS tJosephMuseum
Year Founded: 1977 Domestic & agricultural artifacts; the oldest timber house in southern Manitoba; antique tractors; pioneer village.

St. Malo: Le Musée Pionnier St Malo
CP 705, 8 Beach Rd,
St. Malo, MB R0A 1T0
Tél: 204-347-5396
stmalomuseum@gmail.com
www.iadorestmalo.ca/musee-st-malo-museum
Représentation de la vie des premiers colons
Florence Beaudry, Contact, 204-427-2922

Saint-Pierre-Jolys: Musée de St-Pierre-Jolys / St-Pierre-Jolys Museum
CP 321, 432 rue Joubert,
Saint-Pierre-Jolys, MB R0A 1V0
Tél: 204-433-7002
museestpierrejolys@live.ca
www.museeestpierrejolys.ca
www.facebook.com/MuseeDeStPierreJolysMuseum
Autre numéros: Alt. Phone: 204-792-6149
Le musée est un ancien couvent et sert à se rappeler le patrimoine et les contributions des religieuses au développement du village de Saint-Pierre-Jolys; on retrouve aussi la Maison Goulet, et un cabane à sucre.

Selkirk: Marine Museum of Manitoba (Selkirk) Inc.
PO Box 7, 490 Eveline St.,
Selkirk, MB R1A 2B1
Tel: 204-482-7761
marinemuseum@mymts.net
www.marinemuseum.ca
www.facebook.com/286895044784
Year Founded: 1973 The museum gathers and restores marine vessels related to Manitoba's Lake Winnipeg and the Red River from about 1850 to the present. Storehouses of artifacts and records are located aboard historic vessels, including the S.S. Keenora and the C.G.S. Bradbury. Open May - Sept.; school/group tours available.

Selkirk: St. Andrews' Rectory National Historic Site
374 River Rd.,
Selkirk, MB R1A 2Y1
Tel: 204-339-6396; *Fax:* 204-482-5887
standrewsmuseum@hotmail.ca
www.standrewsrectory.ca
instagram.com/starectory
twitter.com/starectory
www.facebook.com/STARe ctory
Pioneer life; features exhibits about Red River architecture, the roles of the Church Missionary Society & the Church of England in the Red River Settlement. Open Jun-Sep Tue-Sun

Shoal Lake: Clegg Carriage Museum
c/o Prairie Mountain Regional Museums Collection Inc., PO Box 568,
Shoal Lake, MB R0J 1Z0
Tel: 204-759-2245; *Fax:* 204-759-2245
Located 3 miles south of Hwy #24 in Arrow River; collection of 90 completely restored horse-drawn vehicles, including a WW1 ambulance, a covered wagon, peddlar's wagon & hearse

Shoal Lake: Prairie Mountain Regional Museum
PO Box 568, Hwy. 16,
Shoal Lake, MB R0J 1Z0
Tel: 204-759-2245
www.pmrm.ca
This Museum celebrates the local history of Prairie Mountain as well & showcases a collection of about 90 historical carriages.

Shoal Lake: Shoal Lake Police & Pioneer Museum
PO Box 233, 201 - 1 Ave.,
Shoal Lake, MB R0J 1Z0
Tel: 204-759-2429; *Fax:* 204-759-2704
Other contact information: Summer phone: 204-759-3326
Houses a collection of North West Mounted Police & Royal Canadian Mounted Police displays; official Museum for the Mounted Police in Manitoba; open Jun-Sep by summer staff, other times by appt.; school talks & presentations available

Snowflake: Star Mound School Museum
Snowflake, MB R0G 2K0
Tel: 204-873-2600
One-room country school features textbooks & records. Open daily Apr-Oct

Souris: Hillcrest Museum
16 Crescent Ave. West,
Souris, MB R0K 2C0
Tel: 204-483-2008
www.sourismanitoba.com/hillcrest-museum.html
Year Founded: 1967 Includes agricultural museum, CPR caboose, aboriginal artifacts, mounted butterflies & vintage fire engine. Open daily Jul-Sep

Souris: The Plum - 1883 Souris Heritage Church Museum
Parent: Souris & District Heritage Club Inc.
PO Box 1305, 142-1st St. South,
Souris, MB R0K 2C0
Tel: 204-483-3643
suzan@mts.net
www.theplum.weebly.com
Other contact information: Off-Season Phone: 204-483-2643

Housed in St. Luke's Anglican Church, circa 1883, the museum's collection focuses on local art & history. Open July-Sept., 11:00-7:00.

Sprague: Sprague & District Historical Museum
PO Box 123, 5 Rosebay St.,
Sprague, MB R0A 1Z0

Tel: 204-437-2210
www.mhs.mb.ca/docs/sites/spraguemuseum.shtml
www.facebook.com/Spraguemus eum
Local & military history.

Springfield: Aunt Margaret's Museum of Childhood Inc.
212 Cooks Creek,
Springfield, MB R0E 0R0

Aunt Margaret's Museum of Childhood includes a collection of antique furniture & artifacts.

Steinbach: Mennonite Heritage Village (Canada) Inc.
231 Hwy. 12 N,
Steinbach, MB R5G 1T8

Tel: 204-326-9661; *Fax:* 204-326-5046
Toll-Free: 866-280-8741
info@mhv.ca
www.mennoniteheritagevillage.com
instagram.com/mhvillage
twitter.com/MHVSteinbach
www.facebook.com/MHVSteinbach
Includes J.J. Reimer Historical Library & Archives; historical village with traditional housebarns, semlin, blacksmith shop, printery, general store, operating windmill, farm fields, exihibition gallery; livery barn restaurant serving ethnic Mennonite food; library. Open May-Oct
Barry Dyck, Executive Director, barryd@mhv.ca
Andrea Dyck, Curator, andread@mhv.ca
Anne Toews, Program Director, annet@mhv.ca

Stonewall: Stonewall Quarry Park
PO Box 250, 166 Main St,
Stonewall, MB R0C 2Z0

Tel: 204-467-7980; *Fax:* 204-467-7985
stoneqp@stonewall.ca
stonewallquarrypark.ca
www.facebook.com/quarrypar kheritageartscentre
Exhibits pertain to the limestone quarries & their role in the development of the community of Stonewall.

Strathclair: The Strathclair Museum Association
PO Box 383, 33 Main St.,
Strathclair, MB R0J 2C0

Tel: 204-720-6041
info@strathclairmuseum.com
strathclairmuseum.com
Year Founded: 1972 In a restored CPR station and residence, the museum contains material relating to the district, which includes geneaology and information on Lord Elphinstone; replica blacksmith shop and machine shed; Open July & August or by appt.

Swan River: Swan Valley Historical Museum & Archives
PO Box 2078, 10 Hwy. N,
Swan River, MB R0L 1Z0

Tel: 204-734-3585
www.facebook.com/SwanValleyHistoricalMuseum
Year Founded: 1972 History of Swan River Valley. Open May-Sep Mon-Fri 9:00-5:00, Sat-Sun 1:00-5:00

Teulon: Teulon & District Museum
Green Acres Park, PO Box 197, 145 7 Ave SE,
Teulon, MB R0C 3B0

Tel: 204-886-2216
www.teulon.ca
Site includes a log house, a caboose, two schoolhouses, a small church, a large machine shed, old shoe shop, the Dr. Hunter Home, 1918 Ford car, doll house with over 300 dolls; open Jun-Aug Tue-Fri 9:00-4:00; Sat-Sun 1:00-4:00

Thompson: Heritage North Museum
162 Princeton Dr.,
Thompson, MB R8N 2A4

Tel: 204-677-2216
hnmuseum@mts.net
www.heritagenorthmuseum.ca
Year Founded: 1990 The museum preserves the heritage & history of Thompson & area, where in 1956 nickel was discovered. One of the log buildings displays a taxidermy array of animals native to the region, hides, furs and fossils, while the other building focuses on the mining industry. There is a gift shop.
Tanna Teneycke, Executive Director

Greg Scott, President

Treherne: Treherne Museum
183 Vanzile St.,
Treherne, MB R0G 2V0

Tel: 204-723-2621
trehernemuseum@gmail.com
www.treherne.ca
Year Founded: 1978 A period house museum, furnished by items from the early 20th century. Open May-Jun Mon-Fri 8:30-4:30; Jul-Aug Mon-Fri 9:00-5:00, Sat 1:00-5:00

Virden: Currahee Military Museum
PO Box 729, River Valley Road North,
Virden, MB R0M 2C0

Tel: 204-748-1461
Open by appt. only year round.
John Hipwell, President, john@wolverinesupplies.com

Virden: River Valley School Museum
PO Box 2048, 297 3 Ave S,
Virden, MB R0M 2C0

Tel: 204-748-3920
Other contact information: Alternate phone: 204-748-1461
Country school furnishings & library 1896-1955

Virden: Virden Pioneer Home Museum Inc.
PO Box 2001, 390 King St. West,
Virden, MB R0M 2C0

Tel: 204-748-1659; *Fax:* 204-748-2501
virden_pioneer_home@mymts.net
virdenpioneerhome.wixsite.com/museum
instagram.com/virden_pioneer_home
twitter.com/virdenpioneers
www.facebook.com/505286296220783
Year Founded: 1970 Lives of early settlers with over 11,000 artifacts. Open May-Jun Tue-Sat & Jul-Aug Mon-Sat 10:00-5:30

Wabowden: Wabowden Historical Museum
PO Box 219, 2 Fleming Dr.,
Wabowden, MB R0B 1S0

The Wabowden Historical Museum preserves & displays artifacts from Wabowden & the surrounding region, such as mining, logging, fishing, & trapping items. Open Jul-Sep

Wasagaming: Riding Mountain Historical Society & Pinewood Museum
PO Box 578,
Wasagaming, MB R0J 1N0

Tel: 204-848-2810
Records & preserves the history of humans in the Riding Mountain National Park; open daily 2-5pm in July & Aug.

Wasagaming: Riding Mountain National Park (RMNPC) / Parc national du Canada du Mont-Riding
133 Wasagaming Dr.,
Wasagaming, MB R0J 2H0

Tel: 204-848-7275; *Fax:* 204-848-2596
rmnp.info@pc.gc.ca
www.pc.gc.ca/ridingmountain
twitter.com/RidingNP
www.facebook.com/RidingNP
Other contact information: TTY: 1-866-787-6221; Friends of RMNP: 204-848-4037
The Riding Mountain National Park of Canada covers 3,000 km2 of the Manitoba prairie & escarpment. The park provides a variety of school & interpretation programs. The Visitor Centre is open from mid May to mid October.
Marjorie Huculak, Partnering and Engagement Officer, 204-848-7256, marjorie.huculak@pc.gc.ca

Waskada: Waskada Museum
c/o Village of Waskada, PO Box 27, 43 Railway Ave.,
Waskada, MB R0M 2E0

Tel: 204-673-2503
waskadamuseum@mail.com
www.waskada.org/visitors/museum
Other contact information: Appointments: 204-673-2557
Year Founded: 1970 The Waskada Museum features the following buildings: the 1914 Anglican Church, the 1906 Union (Royal) Bank, a 1927 blacksmith shop, the 1896 Menota country school, a vehicle display building, & a display building. The museum is open during July & August.

Wawanesa: Sipiweske Museum
102 4th St.,
Wawanesa, MB R0K 2G0

Tel: 204-824-2289; *Fax:* 204-824-2244
wacomcon@mts.net

Memorabilia from pioneers, Nellie McClung, Native people & 1903 insurance company. Open Jul-Aug by appointment other times

Whitemouth: Whitemouth Municipal Museum
PO Box 294, Henderson Ave. & 1st St.,
Whitemouth, MB R0E 2G0

Tel: 204-348-2675
whitemouthmuseum@gmail.com
bovoril.wixsite.com/whitemouthmuseum
www.facebook.com/WhitemouthMunicipa lMuseum
Year Founded: 1975 Museum depicting the different ways of life in the area. Artifacts housed in six buildings & two pole sheds; cairn honouring Dr. Charlotte Ross (The Iron Rose), first female to practice medicine in Manitoba; turn of the century house; 1905 Anglican Church; CPR Caboose. Open Jul-Sep

Winkler: Pembina Threshermen's Museum Inc.
PO Box 1103,
Winkler, MB R6W 4B2

Tel: 204-325-7497; *Fax:* 204-331-3733
info@threshermensmuseum.com
www.threshermensmuseum.com
www.facebook.co m/PembinaThreshermensMuseum
Year Founded: 1968 The Pembina Threshermen's Museum preserves the area's agricultural & Mennonite heritage. The grounds of the museum feature several heritage buildings, such as the 1909 Pomeroy School, the 1905-1906 Morden CPR Sation, an 1885 log house, plus a sawmill, windmill, blacksmith shop, barbershop, & post office. Open May-Sep Mon-Fri 10:00-5:00, Sat-Sun 1:00-5:00

Winnipeg: Air Force Heritage Museum & Air Park / Le Musée du patrimoine de la force aérienne et du parc aérien
PO Box 17000 Forces,
Winnipeg, MB R3J 3Y5

Tel: 204-833-2500; *Fax:* 204-833-2512
The museum, located in the Billy Bishop building, is part of a complex that consists of an outdoor air park showcasing 14 aircraft. The air park is open year round. Museum is open daily Mon-Fri throughout the summer from 8:00-4:00 by appointment. Guided tours, with services in English and French; wheelchair accessible; food service and restrooms. Located on Air Force Way, north off Ness Ave. on Sharp Blvd.

Winnipeg: Anthropology Museum
University of Winnipeg, 515 Portage Ave.,
Winnipeg, MB R3B 2E9

Tel: 204-786-9282; *Fax:* 204-771-4134
www.uwinnipeg.ca/index/anthropology-museum
Collections include artifacts from the categories of Archaeology, Cultural Anthropology & Ethnography, & Biological Anthropology.
Val McKinley, Curator, v.mckinley@uwinnipeg.ca

Winnipeg: Canadian Museum for Human Rights (CMHR)
85 Israel Asper Way,
Winnipeg, MB R3C 0L5

Tel: 204-289-2000 *Toll-Free:* 877-877-6037
info@humanrights.ca
humanrights.ca
www.youtube.com/humanrightsmuseum
twitter.com/cmhr_news
www.facebook.c om/canadianmuseumforhumanrights
Other contact information: TTY: 204-289-2050
Year Founded: 2014
Isha Khan, President & Chief Executive Officer

Winnipeg: Costume Museum of Canada
#301, 250 McDermot Ave.,
Winnipeg, MB R3B 0s5

Tel: 204-989-0072
costumemuseumcanada@gmail.com
www.costumemuseumcanada.com
www.facebook.com/94897456640
Over 35,000 artifacts spanning over 400 years; collection of costumes, textiles & related accessories. The museum is currently closed, but seeking support to continue their efforts.
Maralyn MacKay Hussain, President

Winnipeg: The Ed Leith Cretaceous Menagerie
Wallace Building, University of Manitoba, 125 Dysart Rd.,
Winnipeg, MB R3T 2N2

Tel: 204-474-9371
umanitoba.ca/geoscience/cretaceousmenagerie
The Menagerie displays four complete skeletal replicas of creatures from the Cretaceous Period. Open M-F 8:30-4:30.

Winnipeg: The Fire Fighters Museum of Winnipeg
56 Maple St.,
Winnipeg, MB R3B 0Y8
Tel: 204-942-4817; Fax: 204-885-1306
firemuseum@gatewest.net
www.winnipegfiremuseum.ca
www.facebook.com/WFH SMuseum
The museum's collections cover every aspect of Winnipeg's fire service. Call the museum for their hours of operation.

Winnipeg: Fort Garry Horse Museum & Archives
c/o McGregor Armoury, 551 Machray Ave.,
Winnipeg, MB R2W 1A8
Tel: 204-586-6298; Fax: 204-582-0370
www.fortgarryhorse.ca
www.facebook.com/104479622936633
Depicts the history of the Fort Garry Horse from 1912 to present; Open Tuesday evenings 7:30-10:00; other times by appt.

Winnipeg: FortWhyte Alive
1961 McCreary Rd.,
Winnipeg, MB R3P 2K9
Tel: 204-989-8355; Fax: 204-895-4700
info@fortwhyte.org
www.fortwhyte.org
instagram.com/fortwhytealive; pinterest.com/fortwhytealive
twitter.com/fortwhytealive
www.facebook.com/FortWhyteAlive
Year Founded: 1966 Nature centre & wildlife refuge; 74 hectares of lakes; educational programs & events. Open Mon-Fri 9:00-5:00, Sat-Sun 10:00-5:00
Bill Elliott, President & CEO, welliott@fortwhyte.org

Winnipeg: Historical Museum of St. James-Assiniboia
Parent: Historical Museum Association of St. James-Assiniboia
3180 Portage Ave.,
Winnipeg, MB R3K 0Y5
Tel: 204-888-8706; Fax: 204-949-3454
Red River frame house with period pieces, exhibits from the local area & parishes & farming, pioneer, blacksmith & transportation displays. Open May-Sep daily 10:00-5:00; Sep-May Mon-Fri 10:00-5:00

Winnipeg: Ivan Franko Museum
595 Pritchard Ave,
Winnipeg, MB R2W 2K4
Tel: 204-589-4397; Fax: 204-589-3404
ult-wpg.ca/ivan-franko-museum
History of Ivan Franko, Ukrainian poet, novelist, & social activist; ceramics, woodcarving, glassware, embroidery, & weaving; open year-round.

Winnipeg: Jewish Heritage Centre of Western Canada Inc.
Asper Jewish Community Campus, #C140, 123 Doncaster St.,
Winnipeg, MB R3N 2B2
Tel: 204-477-7460; Fax: 204-477-7465
jewishheritage@jhcwc.org
www.jhcwc.org
www.facebook.com/JewishHeritage Centre
The centre includes a library & archive collection; a Holocaust resource & education centre; artifact exhibitions & seasonal visiting exhibits. Open M-Th 9:00-4:00.
Ilana Abrams, General Manager, 204-478-8590
Stan Carbone, Director of Programs & Exhibits, 204-477-7467

Winnipeg: La Maison Gabrielle-Roy
CP 133, 375, rue Deschambault,
Winnipeg, MB R2H 3B4
Tél: 204-231-3853; Télec: 204-231-3910
info@maisongabrielleroy.mb.ca
www.maisongabrielleroy.mb.ca
twitter.com /maisongabroy
www.facebook.com/LaMaisonGabrielleRoy
Fondée en: 2003 Honore le travail de Gabrielle Ray.
Laurent Gimenez, Président
Lucienne Châteauneuf, Directeur, 204 231-3853

Winnipeg: Manitoba Children's Museum
45 Forks Market Rd.,
Winnipeg, MB R3C 4T6
Tel: 204-924-4000; Fax: 204-956-2122
general@childrensmuseum.com
www.childrensmuseum.com
pinterest.com/mcminwinnipeg
twitter.com/mcminwinnipeg
Year Founded: 1983 Catering to children, the site includes such hands-on exhibits as a 1950s train station with CNR diesel locomotive. Open daily, year round.
Sara Hancheruk, Executive Director

Winnipeg: Manitoba Crafts Museum & Library (MCML)
1045-190 Rupert Ave.,
Winnipeg, MB R3C 1S6
Tel: 204-487-6117; Fax: 204-487-6117
info@mcml.ca
www.mcml.ca
pinterest.com/mcraftsml; instagram.com/infomcml
twitter.com/infomcml
www.facebook.com/258347936 251
Year Founded: 1986 The museum's collection focuses on the development of Canadian, particularly Manitoban, crafts since the 1920s. The library houses about 2,500 titles pertaining to crafts, including scrapbooks & design patterns as well as over 10,000 artifacts.
Andrea Reichert, Curator, curator@mcml.ca

Winnipeg: Manitoba Electrical Museum & Education Centre
PO Box 815, 680 Harrow St.,
Winnipeg, MB R3C 2P4
Tel: 204-360-7905
www.hydro.mb.ca/corporate/history/electrical_museum.shtml
Year Founded: 1971 The museum explores the history of hydroelectrical development in Manitoba from the 1870 to today. Exhibits include archival photographs, documents & electrical artifacts, such as vintage household appliances & an electric streetcar. In the lower level of the museum is an interactive section with Hazard Hamlet where children can learn about potentially hazardous situations if electricity is not used properly.

Winnipeg: Manitoba Military Aviation Museum
PO Box 17000, 186 Air Force Way,
Winnipeg, MB R3J 3Y7
www.aviationmuseum.eu/Blogvorm/manitoba-military-aviation-m
useum
The museum is dedicated to preserving Manitoba aviation heritage through its collection & exhibits. Open Tu-F, 1:00-5:00.

Winnipeg: Manitoba Sports Hall of Fame & Museum Inc. (MSHOF)
Parent: Sport Manitoba
Sport for Life Centre, 145 Pacific Ave.,
Winnipeg, MB R3B 2Z6
Tel: 204-925-5736; Fax: 204-925-5916
halloffame@sportmanitoba.ca
www.sportmanitoba.ca/hall-of-fame
www.youtube.com/user/sportmanitoba
twitter.com/SportManitoba
www.facebook.com/sportmb
Year Founded: 1993 The museum honours those who have contributed significantly to Manitoba's rich sports history. The exhibits use various memorabilia & photos to cover such sports as basketball, baseball, curling, football, golf, hockey & the Winter Olympics. Open Tue-Sat 10:00-4:00
Rick D. Brownlee, Sport Heritage Manager
Andrea Reichert, Collections Manager, 204-925-5935,
andrea.reichert@sportmanitoba.ca

Winnipeg: Naval Museum of Manitoba
HMCS Chippawa Bldg., 1 Navy Way,
Winnipeg, MB R3C 4J7
Tel: 204-943-7745; Fax: 204-947-9533
curator@naval-museum.mb.ca
naval-museum.mb.ca
The museum honours Manitoba's contributions to the Canadian Navy. Open to visitors on Wednesdays from 9:00 to 3:00; also open Sundays 1:00 to 4:00 in the summer.

Winnipeg: Ogniwo Polish Museum Society Inc.
1417 Main St.,
Winnipeg, MB R2W 3V3
Tel: 204-586-5070
info@polishmuseum.com
www.polishmuseum.com
twitter.com/Ogniwo
www.facebook.com/1204092847117 55
Year Founded: 1985 Artifacts related to Polish immigrants, history, culture, traditions & folklore in Canada. Open year round

Winnipeg: Queen's Own Cameron Highlanders of Canada Regimental Museum
Minto Armoury, 969 St. Matthew's Ave.,
Winnipeg, MB R3G 0J7
Tel: 204-786-4330
hodonnell@draega.net
thequeensowncameronhighlandersofcanada.net
Military museum featuring regimental dress, equipment & archives from 1910 to present.

Winnipeg: Riel House National Historic Site of Canada / Parc historique national du Canada de la Maison-Riel
c/o Lower Fort Garry National Historic Site, 330 River Rd.,
Winnipeg, MB R2M 3Z8
Tel: 204-983-6757
riel.info@pc.gc.ca
pc.gc.ca/en/lhn-nhs/mb/riel
Other contact information: TTY: 1-866-787-6221
Riel family home, depicts life of Métis family in St. Vital during the 1880s. Open May-Jun Mon-Fri 9:00-5:00; Jul-Sep Fri-Wed 10:00-5:00, Thu 1:00-8:00

Winnipeg: Robert B. Ferguson Museum of Mineralogy
Wallace Building, University of Manitoba, 125 Dysart Rd.,
Winnipeg, MB R3T 2M7
Tel: 204-474-9371
www.umanitoba.ca
Year Founded: 1918 The museum's collection includes mineral specimens & research papers.

Winnipeg: Ross House Museum
Joe Zuken Heritage Park, 140 Meade St. North,
Winnipeg, MB R2W 3K5
Tel: 204-943-3958
rosshouse@mhs.mb.ca
www.mhs.mb.ca
twitter.com/RossHo useMuseum
www.facebook.com/groups/107918235910933
Other contact information: Fall/Winter Phone: 204-947-0559
Ross House was the first post office in western Canada. It is now a museum, owned by the City of Winnipeg & operated by the Manitoba Historical Society. The museum depicts the operation of early postal service & the life of the Ross family around 1850. Ross House is open from the beginning of June to the end of August. Schools & large groups may arrange appointments at other times of the year.
Victor Sawelo, Museum Manager

Winnipeg: Royal Aviation Museum of Western Canada / Musée de l'aviation de l'ouest du Canada
Hangar T-2, 958 Ferry Rd.,
Winnipeg, MB R3H 0Y8
Tel: 204-786-5503; Fax: 204-775-4761
Info@RoyalAviationMuseum.com
www.wcam.mb.ca
twitter.com/historyofflight
The Western Canada Aviation Museum's recovery & restoration department works to prepare aircraft for display. The museum features sights such as Canada's first helicopter, bushplanes, historic military jets, & commercial aircraft. The museum also contains an aviation reference library, with collections of books, magazines, manuals, photographs, drawings, & audio-visual materials. The library is open to the public by appointment. The museum is open year-round.

Winnipeg: Royal Canadian Mint - Winnipeg Facility
520 Lagimodière Blvd.,
Winnipeg, MB R2J 3E7
Tel: 204-983-6429; Fax: 204-255-5203
Toll-Free: 877-974-6468
info@rcmint.ca
www.mint.ca
www.youtube.com/user/canadianmint
twitter.com/CanadianMint
www.faceboo k.com/RoyalCanadianMint
Tours of the mint available year round; call for reservations.
Winter hours: Tu - Sa 9:00 - 4:00. Summer hours: M - Su 9:00 - 4:00.

Winnipeg: Royal Winnipeg Rifles Regimental Museum
Minto Armoury, #109, 969 St. Matthews Ave.,
Winnipeg, MB R3G 0J7
Tel: 204-786-4300
www.royalwinnipegrifles.com
Year Founded: 1970 Collects & preserves the history of the Regiment, & also houses displays relevant to the Winnipeg Light Infantry & the Winnipeg Grenadiers; military artifacts & memorabilia, pictures, books & other documents; open Tu 3:00 - 9:00. Tours can be arranged by appointment
Gerry Woodman, Operations Manager, 204-895-2588, gerrywoodman@live.com

Winnipeg: St. Norbert Provincial Heritage Park
PO Box 30, 200 Saulteaux Cres.,
Winnipeg, MB R3J 3W3
Tel: 204-945-4236
www.gov.mb.ca/conservation/parks/popular_parks/central/norber t_info.html
Other contact information: Off season: 204-945-7665
Illustrates how a natural landscape used for hunting, fishing & camping by Aboriginal peoples evolved into a French-speaking Métis settlement, then a French-Canadian agricultural

community of the pre-World War I period; guided tours of restored Turenne & Bohémier houses; open daily May long weekend to Labour Day weekend.

Winnipeg: St. Vital Museum
Parent: St. Vital Historical Society Inc.
600 St. Mary's Rd.,
Winnipeg, MB R2M 3L5

Tel: 204-255-2864
info@svhs.ca
www.svhs.ca
www.youtube.com/user/stvitalmuseum
twitter.com/SVHistoricalSoc
www.fac ebook.com/stvitalmuseum
Year Founded: 2008 Educational centre, bringing "the history of St. Vital" to the community by way of shows & displays; museum holds artifacts
Bob Holliday, President
John Dempster, Resident Historian

Winnipeg: St. Volodymyr Ukrainian Catholic Museum
Parent: Ukrainian Catholic Archeparchy of Winnipeg
233 Scotia St.,
Winnipeg, MB R2V 1V7

www.mh.mb.ca/docs/sites/stvolodymyrmuseum.shtml
Year Founded: 1967 Ukrainian religious & cultural collection.

Winnipeg: Sandilands Forest Discovery Centre
Parent: Manitoba Forestry Association
c/o Manitoba Forestry Association, 900 Corydon Ave.,
Winnipeg, MB R3M 0Y4

Tel: 204-453-3182; *Fax:* 204-477-5765
sandilands.mfa@gmail.com
www.thinktrees.org/Sandilands_Forest_Discovery_ Centre.aspx
www.facebook.com/229261507091158
Year Founded: 1957 Information on biodiversity, forest ecology, sustainable management of forest resources, fire prevention & management. Includes nature trails, museum, fire tower, picnic area, educational programming, commemorative tree planting.
Dave Wotton, President
Patricia Pohrebniuk, Executive Director, Manitoba Forestry Association

Winnipeg: Seven Oaks House Museum
50 Mac St.,
Winnipeg, MB R2V 4Z9

Tel: 204-339-7429
sohmuseum@gmail.com
www.mhs.mb.ca/docs/sites/sevenoakshousemuseum
www.facebook.com/SevenOaks HouseMuseum
Year Founded: 1958 Seven Oaks House is a log residence, which was built between 1851 & 1853. It has been restored to reflect life during the Red River settlement in the 19th century. The museum is open from mid-May to Labour Day.

Winnipeg: Stewart Hay Memorial Museum
Duff Roblin Bldg., Dept. of Zoology, University of Manitoba,
Winnipeg, MB R3T 2N2

Tel: 204-474-9245; *Fax:* 204-474-7588
Mounted & study specimens of mammals, birds, fish, reptiles, amphibians, crustaceans, mollusks & other invertebrates; casts of fossils; open year round

Winnipeg: Transcona Historical Museum
141 Regent Ave. W,
Winnipeg, MB R2C 1R1

Tel: 204-222-0423; *Fax:* 204-222-0208
info@transconamuseum.mb.ca
www.transconamuseum.mb.ca
www.youtube.com/user/TransconaMuseum
twitter.com/transconamuseum
www.facebook.com/transconamuseum
The Transcona Museum was established in 1967 as Transcona's Centennial Project for the 100th anniversary of Canadian Confederation. The primary function of the museum's collection is to document the growth and development of Transcoma and the surrounding Springfield district through the collection, preservation and interpretation of artifacts and archival materials. The museum has accumulated over 45,000 objects of historical and natural significance, including photographs, rare books, reference files, natural history (including an 8,000 specimen lepidoptera collection), First Nations cultural artifacts, Euro-Canadian cultural artifacts & a clothing & textile collection.
Alanna Horejda, Curator
Jennifer Maxwell, Assistant Curator

Winnipeg: Ukrainian Cultural & Educational Centre
184 Alexander Ave. East,
Winnipeg, MB R3B 0L6

Tel: 204-942-0218
ucec@mymts.net
www.ukrainianwinnipeg.ca/oseredok
oseredok.blogspot.ca
www.facebook.com/oseredok
Library, art gallery, museum & archival collections about the history of Ukrainians in Canada & the Ukraine. Open Mon-Sat 10:00-4:00

Winnipeg: University of Winnipeg Geography Museum
515 Portage Ave.,
Winnipeg, MB R3B 2E9

Tel: 204-786-9485; *Fax:* 204-774-4134
geography@uwinnipeg.ca
geograph.uwinnipeg.ca/facilities.htm
Teaching & reference collection of rocks, minerals & fossils, with a Manitoba focus; open year round
Kim Monson, Curator, k.monson@uwinnipeg.ca

Winnipeg: UVAN Historical Museum & Archives
456 Main St.,
Winnipeg, MB R3B 1B6

Tel: 204-942-5861
Historical, ethnological & archival material

Winnipeg: The Wallis-Roughley Museum of Entomology
Dept. of Entomology, University of Manitoba, 12 Dafoe Rd,
Winnipeg, MB R3T 2N2

Tel: 204-474-9257; *Fax:* 204-474-7628
head_entomo@umanitoba.ca
www.wallisroughley.ca
250,000 species of insects
Dr. Rob Currie, Department Head Ph.D.,
rob_currie@umanitoba.ca
Dr. Jason Gibbs, Curator, jason.gibbs@umanitoba.ca

Winnipeg: Winnipeg Police Museum
Parent: Winnipeg Police Museum & Historical Society Inc.
Winnipeg Police Headquarters, 245 Smith St.,
Winnipeg, MB R3C 1K1

Tel: 204-986-3976
wps-museum@winnipeg.ca
www.winnipeg.ca/police/Museum
Year Founded: 1974 The Winnipeg Police Museum exhibits items related to the Winnipeg Police Force, which formed in 1874. Objects on display include early handcuffs,& identification cameras, & a jail cell which was built in 1911. There are also exhibits surrounding the 1919 Winnipeg General Strike & Earle "The Strangler" Nelson. Located at the Winnipeg Police Academy, the Winnipeg Police Museum is open daily. Conducted group tours can be arranged.

Winnipeg: Winnipeg Railway Museum
PO Box 48, 123 Main St.,
Winnipeg, MB R3C 1A3

Tel: 204-942-4632
wpgrail@mts.net
www.wpgrailwaymuseum.com
The museum contains artifacts, trains & train-related vehicles & equipment. Open year-round, M & Th 9:00-12:00.

Winnipegosis: Medd House Museum
Parent: Winnipegosis Historical Society Inc.
c/o Winnipegosis Historical Society Inc., PO Box 336,
Winnipegosis, MB R0L 2G0

Tel: 204-656-4318
winnipegosismuseum@yahoo.ca
www.winnipegosis.org
Other contact information: Alternate Phone: 204-656-4273
Historic house once owned by a local Winnipegosis doctor, Dr. Medd.

Winnipegosis: Winnipegosis Museum (WHS)
Parent: Winnipegosis Historical Society Inc.
c/o Winnipegosis Historical Society Inc., PO Box 336, 62 Jubilee Ave E,
Winnipegosis, MB R0L 2G0

Tel: 204-656-4273
winnipegosismuseum@yahoo.ca
www.winnipegosis.org
Housed in former CNR Railway Station. Depicts the lifestyle of early immigrants. Includes 65-foot freighter, the "Myrtle M", artifacts, CNR historical material, War Memorial items & native handiwork.

Woodlands: Woodlands Pioneer Museum
PO Box 206,
Woodlands, MB R0C 3H0

Tel: 204-383-5691
www.rmwoodlands.info/page.php?id=56
Other contact information: Alternate Phones: 204-383-5919; 204-383-5589
School houses, church, log house & other buildings with pioneer artifacts; located of Hwy 6; open Jul-Aug.

New Brunswick

Provincial Museums

Kings Landing Historical Settlement / Village historique de Kings Landing
5804 Rte 102,
Prince William, NB E6K 0A5

Tel: 506-363-4999
www.kingslanding.nb.ca
www.instagram.com/kingslandingnb
twitter.com/kingslandingnb
www.facebo ok.com/KingsLandingNB
Year Founded: 1960's Historical settlement on the St. John River with more than 100 costumed interpreters depicting rural life from 1790-1910; 65,000 artifacts.
Mary Baruth, Chief Executive Officer, 506-363-4957, Fax: 506-476-3106, mary.baruth@gnb.ca

Musée Acadien
Campus de Moncton, Université de Moncton, 405 Université Ave., Local 134,
Moncton, NB E1A 3E9

Tél: 506-858-4088
maum@umoncton.ca
www.umoncton.ca/umcm-maum
www.instagram.com/museeacadien
twitter.com/macadien
www.facebook.com/M usee.acadien
Fondée en: 1886 Le plus ancien musée acadien au monde est fondé par le père Camille Lefebvre. La collection dépasse 35,000 objets & photographies & représente tous les aspects de la vie acadienne. Exposition permanente; expositions temporaires; expositions virtuelles.
Jeanne-Marie Cormier, Conservatrice

New Brunswick Museum (NBM) / Musée du Nouveau-Brunswick
277 Douglas Ave.,
Saint John, NB E2K 1E5

Tel: 506-643-2300*Toll-Free:* 888-268-9595
NBM-MNB@nbm-mnb.ca
www.nbm-mnb.ca
www.instagram.com/nbm_mnb
twitter.com/nbmmnb
www.facebook.com/nbmmnb
Year Founded: 1842 Collections at the provincial museum of New Brunswick depict human history as well as marine life. They also include collections centred on technology. And there is a wide range of printed works as well as fine & decorative arts. Other works include those that focus on botany, zoology & geology. A full range of exhibitions & programs are offered daily.
Bernard Riordon, CEO, 506-643-2351
Alfredo Justo, Head Ph.D., Botany & Mycology, 506-643-3443

Local Museums

Aulac: Fort Beauséjour National Historic Site
111 Fort Beauséjour Rd.,
Aulac, NB E4L 2W5

Tel: 506-364-5080; *Fax:* 506-536-4399
fort.beausejour@pc.gc.ca
www.pc.gc.ca/lhn-nhs/nb/beausejour/index_E.asp
twitter.com/nhsnb
Year Founded: 1751 Built in 1751 by the French; star-shaped fort overlooking the Bay of Fundy. Features such activites as kite flying, bird watching and scavenger hunts.

Bartibog Bridge: MacDonald Farm Historic Site
600 Rte. 11,
Bartibog Bridge, NB E1V 7G1

Tel: 506-778-6085
info@macdonaldfarm.ca
www.macdonaldfarm.ca
www.facebook.com/441360032574933
Year Founded: 1970 Constructed by Scottish settler, Lt. Col. Alexander MacDonald of Bartibog, between 1815 & 1820 in Georgian style, the site includes a barn, 4 outbuildings, as well as a wharf & boat house. Costumed guides demonstrate cooking, crafts & care of animals. The site is operated by the Highland Society of New Brunswick.

Bathurst: Musee de la Guerre / Memorial War Museum
Légion Royale Canadienne, Herman J.Good V.C. Branche
18, 575, av St-Peter,
Bathurst, NB E2A 2Y5

Tél: 506-546-3135

Bathurst: Nepisiquit Centennial Museum & Cultural Centre
Parent: Bathurst Heritage Trust Commission Inc.
360 Douglas Ave.,
Bathurst, NB E2A 4S6

Tel: 506-546-9449; Fax: 506-545-7050
bhtc@nb.aibn.com
bathurstheritage.ca
www.facebook.com/BathurstHeritage MuseeBathurst
Year Founded: 2003 The Centre houses the Bathurst Heritage Museum, Nepisiguit Genealogy/Archives, & Multicultural Association of the Chaleur Region.

Bayfield: Cape Jourimain Nature Centre
5039 rte. 16,
Bayfield, NB E4M 3Z8

Tel: 506-538-2220; Fax: 506-538-2226
Toll-Free: 866-538-2220
www.capejourimain.ca
twitter.com/CJNC_CINCJ
www.face book.com/CapeJourimain
Year Founded: 2001 The Centre contains a lighthouse (c.1870), observation tower, exhibit hall & art gallery.
Susan Purdy, President

Bertrand: Village Historique Acadien
PO Box 5626, 5 rue de Pont,
Bertrand, NB E1W OE1

Tel: 506-726-2600Toll-Free: 877-721-2200
villageha@gnb.ca
www.villagehistoriqueacadien.com
www.facebook.com/vil lagehistoriqueacadien
This is a reconstrcuted village that reflects the history & way of life of Acadians between 1770 & 1949.
Sylvain Godin, Directeur général, sylvain.godin2@gnb.ca

Boiestown: Central New Brunswick Woodmen's Museum Inc.
6342 Rte. 8,
Boiestown, NB E6A 1Z5

Tel: 506-369-7214; Fax: 506-369-9081
woodmen@nb.aibn.com
www.woodmensmuseum.com
www.facebook.com/WoodmensMu seum
Year Founded: 1979 Sixteen exhibit buildings; depicts life of Central New Brunswick lumberjack & culture of Miramichi people
Bernice Price, Executive Director

Bouctouche: Musée de Kent
150, ch du Couvent,
Bouctouche, NB E4S 3C1

Tél: 506-743-5005
admin@museedekent.ca
www.museedekent.ca
www.facebook.com/museedekent
Fondée en: 1880 Formerly known as the Convent of the Immaculate Conception boarding school, c.1880.
Pierre Cormier, President
Normand Cormier, Vice-President

Caraquet: Éco-Musée de l'huître / Oyster Museum
675, boul Saint-Pierre ouest,
Caraquet, NB E1W 1A2

Tel: 506-727-3226
rmne.ca/eco-musee-huitre

Caraquet: Musée Acadien de Caraquet / Acadian Museum of Caraquet
15, boul St-Pierre Est,
Caraquet, NB E1W 1B6

Tél: 506-726-2682; Téléc: 506-726-2660
museecaraquet.ca
Fondée en: 1963 Favorise l'histoire et la culture des Acadiens de la Péninsule acadienne en utilisant sa propre collection ainsi que d'autres collections et archives régionales. Ouvrir Juin-Sept

Clair: Société historique de Clair Inc.
724, rue Principale,
Clair, NB E7A 2H4

Tel: 506-992-3637
sochclair@nb.aibn.com
Museum & historic site guided tours; Beaux-arts, Historie humaine; visites guidées; summer hours: M - Su 9:30 - 6:00; off season hours by appointment

Connors: Pioneer Historical Connors Museum
3614 Rte. 205,
Connors, NB E7A 1S3

Tel: 506-992-2500
Items used in general store; blacksmith shop; Victorian mansion

Dalhousie: Musée Restigouche Regional Museum
115 George St.,
Dalhousie, NB E8C 1R6

Tel: 506-684-7490; Fax: 506-684-7490
gurrm@nbnet.nb.ca
www.restimuse.org/dalhousie.html
www.facebook.com/re stigoucheregionalmuseum
Year Founded: 1967 Local history museum, archives, & gallery.

Doaktown: Atlantic Salmon Museum
263 Main St.,
Doaktown, NB E9C 1A9

Tel: 506-365-7787
museum@nbnet.nb.ca
www.atlanticsalmonmuseum.com
www.facebook.com/AtlanticSalmonMuseum
Year Founded: 1982 Through interpretive displays & the an aquarium, the Atlantic Salmon Museum shows the history of the life of the Atlanic salmon, as well as the cultural & economic value of the Atlantic salmon to the Miramichi River & New Brunswick. Conservation is also emphasized. The museum is open from June to October. Appointments for rentals can be made during other times.

Doaktown: Doak House Historic Site
386 Main St.,
Doaktown, NB E9C 1E4

Tel: 506-365-2026
museum@nbnet.nb.ca
www.facebook.com/DoakHistoricSite
Open end of June - early Sept.

Dorchester: Westmorland Historical Society Inc.
Dorchester Heritage Properties Committee
4974 Main St.,
Dorchester, NB E4K 2Z1

Tel: 506-379-6633
keillorhouse@nb.aibn.com
www.keillorhousemuseum.com
Home to the The Keillor House Museum, St. James Textile Museum, The Bell Inn, The Payzant & Card Building, Sir Pierre-Amand Landry House, & St. James Presbyterian Church Museum.

Edmundston: Musée historique du Madawaska
c/o Campus d'Edmundston, Université de Moncton, 165, boul Hébert,
Edmundston, NB E3V 2S8

Tél: 506-737-5282; Téléc: 506-737-5373
musee@umce.ca
www.umoncton.ca/umce-mhm
twitter.com/UMCE_UMoncton
www .facebook.com/UdeMEdmundston
Histoire locale et la Galerie Colline. Ouvrir lundi au jeudi 10h à 17h, samedi et dimanche 13h à 17h.
Christian Michaud, Responsable, 506-737-5050

Florenceville-Bristol: Shogomoc Historical Railway Site
9189 Main St.,
Florenceville-Bristol, NB E7L 2Y3

Tel: 506-392-6763
tourism@florencevillebristol.ca
www.tourismnewbrunswick.ca/Products/S/ShogomocRailwaySite.aspx
Restored 1914 CPR railway station featuring three renovated train cars; open May-Aug., Mon.-Sat.

Fredericton: 'School Days' Museum
PO Box 752,
Fredericton, NB E3B 5R6

Tel: 506-459-3738; Fax: 506-459-3738
sdmuseum@nb.sympatico.ca
museum.nbta.ca
NB's educational heritage from 19th century; located in Justice Bldg. ANNEX, off Queen St.; artifacts pertaining to NB schools & teacher training
Harry Palmer, President, hspalmer@nb.sympatico.ca

Fredericton: Brydone Jack Observatory Museum
University of New Brunswick, PO Box 4400,
Fredericton, NB E3B 5A3

Tel: 506-453-4723
The first astronomical observatory in Canada, built in 1851. The building is now a National Historic Site & a museum on the campus of the University of New Brunswick. It houses tools & equipment used by Dr. William Brydone Jack, who was a professor of mathematics, natural philosophy, & astronomy.

Fredericton: Fredericton Region Museum / Musée de la région de Fredericton
Parent: York Sunbury Historical Society
PO Box 1312 A, 571 Queen St.,
Fredericton, NB E3B 5C8

Tel: 506-455-6041; Fax: 506-458-8741
info@frederictonregionmuseum.com
www.frederictonregionmuseum.com
www.youtube.com/user/ysmuseum
twitter.com/FredMuseum
www.facebook.com/ FrederictonRegionMuseum
Year Founded: 1934 Local history. Home to the Coleman Frog & New Brunswick's oldest manmade artifact. Open year round.
Ruth Murgatroyd, Executive Director

Fredericton: Guard House & Soldiers' Barracks
c/o Fredericton Tourism, PO Box 130, 11 Carleton St.,
Fredericton, NB E3B 4Y7

Tel: 506-460-2041; Fax: 506-460-2474
Toll-Free: 888-888-4768
www.tourismfredericton.ca
Historic military buildings 1828-1866

Fredericton: New Brunswick Sports Hall of Fame Inc. / Temple de la renommée sportive du Nouveau-Brunswick
PO Box 6000, 503 Queen St.,
Fredericton, NB E3B 5H1

Tel: 506-453-3747
nbsportshalloffame@gnb.ca
www.nbsportshalloffame.nb.ca
twitter.com/NBSHF
www.facebook.com/NBSpor tsHallofFame
Open year round, hours vary; recognizes, collects, preserves, exhibits & promotes New Brunswick's sports heroes & sports heritage.

Fredericton: Old Government House
PO Box 6000,
Fredericton, NB E3B 5H1

Tel: 506-453-2505
www.gnb.ca/lg/ogh/index-e.asp
Constructed from 1826 to 1828, Government House was the residence of New Brunswick's Governors & Lieutenant-Governors. Government House also served as a school for hearing impaired students, a military barracks during World War I, a hospital for returning soldiers, & an RCMP headquarters. The House has been open to the public since 1999, featuring restored rooms, exhibits, & bilingual tours during the summer. Government House still contains the Lieutenant-Governor's office & residence.

Fredericton: Wulastook Museums Inc.
PO Box 700,
Fredericton, NB E3B 5B4

Tel: 506-451-7777; Fax: 506-451-1029

Fredericton Junction: Currie House
110 Currie Lane,
Fredericton Junction, NB E0G 1T0

Tel: 506-368-2818
www.facebook.com/CurrieHouseMuseum
Museum with displays of antiques and artifacts, history of area and local families. Large picnic area, nature trails through woods and by river.

Gagetown: Queens County Heritage
69 Front St.,
Gagetown, NB E5M 1A4

Tel: 506-488-2483; Fax: 504-488-2483
info@queenscountyheritage.com
www.queenscountyheritage.com
twitter.com/QCHeritage
www.facebook.com/QCHeritage
The Tilley House was the home of Sir Leonard Tilley, a Father of Confederation. The museum within it contains furnishings of the Loyalist & Victorian periods, plus historical exhibits. It is open from mid-June to mid-Sept.

Grand Falls: Grand Falls Museum / Musée de Grand-Sault
68 Madawaska Rd.,
Grand Falls, NB E3Y 1C6

Tel: 506-473-5265
Local artifacts; Extensive collection of church records, genealogies, etc.; Open mid-June to end of Aug. or by appt.

Grand Manan: Grand Manan Art Gallery
21 Cedar St.,
Grand Manan, NB E5G 2C3

Tel: 506-662-3662
info@grandmananartgallery.ca
www.grandmananartgallery.ca
Artwork by local & visiting artists with a connection to Grand
Manan Island; open daily June-Sept.

Grand Manan: Grand Manan Museum
1141 Rte. 776,
Grand Manan, NB E5G 4E9

Tel: 506-662-3524; *Fax:* 506-662-3009
gmadmin@grandmananmuseum.ca
www.grandmananmuseum.ca
twitter.com/GMMuse um
www.facebook.com/pages/Grand-Manan-Museum/11481146193
8351
Open June - Sept.; in winter by appt.

Grand Manan: Swallowtail Lightstation
Parent: Swallowtail Keepers Society
50 Lighthouse Rd.,
Grand Manan, NB E5G 2A2

Tel: 506-662-8316 *Toll-Free:* 888-525-1655
swallowtail.lighthouse@gmail.com
www.swallowtaillighthouse.com/index.htm l
swallowtailkeepers.blogspot.com
twitter.com/SwallowtailGM
www.facebook.com/SwallowtailLighthouse
Year Founded: 1859 The Lightstation was established in 1860,
renovated in 1980 & is still active today. It is one of the few
remaining wooden lighthouses in Canada.

Grand-Anse: Musée des Cultures Fondatrices /
Museum of Founding Cultures
184, rue Acadie,
Grand-Anse, NB E8N 1A6

Tél: 506-732-3003; *Téléc:* 506-732-5491
info@museedescultures.ca
www.museedescultures.ca/index.html
www.facebo ok.com/190968550939951
Fondée en: 1985 Le seul musée nord-américain dédié à la
papauté. Ouvert de mi-Juin à fin Août.

Hampton: Kings County Museum
Parent: Kings County Historical & Archival Society Inc.
27 Centennial Rd.,
Hampton, NB E5N 6N3

Tel: 506-832-6009
kingscm@nbnet.nb.ca
www.kingscountymuseum.com
twitter.com/KingsCountyHS
www.facebook.com/4 34926949879214
Year Founded: 1968 Artifacts include textiles, clothing,
steamships, guns, glassware, military, royalty, art & archival
material; Kings County jail

Harvey: Mary's Point Bird Sanctuary
415 Mary's Point Road,
Harvey, NB E4H 2M9

Tel: 506-459-4209; *Fax:* 506-459-4209
www.fundy-biosphere.ca/en/amazing-places/mary-s-point.html
www.facebook. com/naturenb
Located in the Shepody National Wildlife Area & administered by
both Nature NB & Environment Canada's Canadian Wildlife
Service, these wetlands protect large numbers of shorebird
species. The Interpretation Centre educates the public on the
shorebirds' habitats & their hemispheric migrations over the Bay
of Fundy region.

Hillsborough: Hon. William Henry Steeves House
40 Mill St.,
Hillsborough, NB E4H 2Z8

Tel: 506-734-3102
steevesmuseum@nb.aibn.com
www.steeveshousemuseum.ca
instagram.com/SteevesHouseMuseum
www.facebook.com/249068845106673
Year Founded: 1971 Operated by Heritage Hillsborough Inc.;
birthplace of William Henry Steeves, a Father of Confederation;
open every day July 1 to Labour Day

Hillsborough: New Brunswick Railway Museum
2847 Main St.,
Hillsborough, NB E4H 2X7

Tel: 506-734-3195
nbrailway@nb.aibn.com
www.nbrm.ca
Year Founded: 1984 Dedicated to preserving the history of train
travel in New Brunswick, the museum has on site an extensive
collection of full-sized railway cars. This is the province's only
operating railway museum, with excursion trains 4 days a week
along the Petitcodiac River & southeastern New Brunswick.
Displays of equipment & artifacts highlight the local & area
railway history. There is a gift shop. Open daily, June - Sept.

Hopewell Cape: Albert County Museum
Parent: Albert County Historical Society Inc.
3940 Rte. 114,
Hopewell Cape, NB E4H 3J8

Tel: 506-734-2003; *Fax:* 506-734-3291
albertcountymuseum@nb.aibn.com
www.albertcountymuseum.ca
twitter.com/A lbertCoMuseum
www.facebook.com/albertcountymuseum
The museum is located in the UNESCO Fundy Biosphere
Reserve. Visitors can experience early life in Albert County & the
Shepody Bay region by visiting the original Shire Town buildings,
circa 1845. The site also features the former County Jail
complete with cells, displays & collections relating to the early
history of the area, & the County Courthouse. The museum also
has a 20-seat theatre that shows a documentary film on R.B.
Bennett, Canada's 11th Prime Minister. Displays include
shipbuilding & farming. Other features include a gift shop,
meeting rooms & a research resources room.
Donald Alward, Manager & Curator

Kingston: John Fisher Memorial Museum
Parent: Kingston Peninsula Heritage Inc.
Macdonald Consolidated School, 874 Rte. 845,
Kingston, NB E5N 1V3

Tel: 506-763-2101
jfmmuseum@nb.aibn.com
www.kingstonnb.ca/JFMM
Open Jun-Aug Tue-Sat 9:00-4:30

McAdam: McAdam Railway Station
Parent: McAdam Historical Restoration Commission
146 Saunders Rd.,
McAdam, NB E6J 1L2

Tel: 506-784-2293
villageofmcadam@nb.aibn.ca
www.mcadamstation.ca
www.facebook.com/McAdamRailwayStation
Year Founded: 1900 The McAdam Railway Station is both a
national & provincial historic site, as well as a heritage railway
station. The museum offers guided tours, catered meals,
conference facilities & a visitors centre.

Memramcook: Monument Lefebvre National Historic
Site / Lieu historique national du Monument-Lefebvre
Parent: Société du Monument-Lefebvre
480, rue Centrale,
Memramcook, NB E4K 3S6

Tel: 506-758-9808; *Fax:* 506-758-9813
monument@nbnet.nb.ca
www.pc.gc.ca/lhn-nhs/nb/lefebvre/index_e.asp
twit ter.com/nhsnb
Other contact information: Alt. URL: www.monumentlefebvre.ca
Year Founded: 1982 Located in the Monument LeFebvre
building, in cooperation with Parks Canada, the centre focuses
on the survival of the Acadian people from 1755 to present.
Shows are performed in the theatre. There is a gift shop with a
variety of Acadian products. Guided tours are offered.
Claude Boudreau, Executive Director

Memramcook: Société historique de la Vallée de
Memramcook inc.
612, rue Centrale,
Memramcook, NB E4K 3S7

Tél: 506-758-0087; *Téléc:* 506-758-0087
shvm@shvm.ca
shvm.ca
This museum celebrates the history of the Memramcook Valley.
There is a collection of artifacts and photographs that reflect the
early life of the people of Memramcook.
Edmond Babineau, Présidente fondateur

Minto: Minto Museum & Information Centre
187 Main St.,
Minto, NB E4B 3N4

Tel: 506-327-3383
www.villageofminto.ca/attractions/minto-museum-and-informatio
n-centre
Local history. Includes renovated caboose, antiques, railway &
coal-mining artifacts. Open Jun-Sept

Minto: New Brunswick Internment Camp Heritage
Museum
#1, 420 Pleasant Dr.,
Minto, NB E4B 2T3

Tel: 506-327-3573; *Fax:* 506-328-6008
nbinternmentcampmuseum.ca
Artifacts & model of the Ripples Internment Camp
Ed Caissie, Project Coordinator, 506-450-9666,
edmuseum62@hotmail.com

Miramichi: Beaubears Island Interpretive Centre &
Museum
Parent: Friends of Beaubears Island Inc.
35 St. Patrick's Dr.,
Miramichi, NB E1N 4P6

Tel: 506-622-8526
info@beaubearsisland.ca
www.beaubearsisland.com
twitter.com/beaubearsisland
www.facebook.com/b eaubearsisland
The interpretive centre is a living museum with actors portraying
shipbuilders, fur traders & the Marquis Charles Deschamps de
Boishebert. The Friends of Beaubears Island oversee the
Boishébert National Historic Site of Canada & the Beaubears
Island Shipbuilding National Historic Site of Canada & J.Leonard
O'Brien Memorial.

Miramichi: St. Michael's Museum
PO Box 368, 10 Howard St.,
Miramichi, NB E1N 3A7

Tel: 506-778-5152
mmuseum@nbnet.nb.ca
saintmichaelsmuseum.com
Miramichi history & extensive civil & church records for most
denominations; geneology; tours in June-Aug.

Miramichi: W.S. Loggie Cultural Centre
222 Wellington St.,
Miramichi, NB E1N 1M9

Tel: 506-773-7645
www.facebook.com/loggiehouse
Other contact information: Alternate phone: 506-773-4996
History of the Loggie family, artifacts from the 18th century
Victorian home, & WWI artifacts. Open daily Jul-Aug 10:00-6:00

Moncton: Free Meeting House
Parent: Moncton Museum
20 Mountain Rd.,
Moncton, NB E1C 2J8

Tel: 506-856-4383; *Fax:* 506-389-5904
info@resurgo.ca
resurgo.ca

Moncton: Lutz Mountain Heritage Museum
Lutz Mountain Heritage Foundation, 3143 Mountain Rd.,
Moncton, NB E1G 2X1

Tel: 506-384-7719
lutzmtnheritage@rogers.com
www.lutzmtnheritage.ca
Year Founded: 1975 Operates a heritage museum &
genealogical research facility; open mid-June to mid-Sept.,
Mon.-Sat., other times by appointment.

Moncton: Moncton Museum / Musée de Moncton
20 Mountain Rd.,
Moncton, NB E1C 2J8

Tel: 506-856-4383; *Fax:* 506-856-4355
info@resurgo.ca
resurgo.ca
Year Founded: 1974 The permanent exhibits showcase
Moncton's history from the time of the Micmacs to the period
preceding the Deportation of Acadians, when agriculture was
Moncton's primary economic engine, to the golden shipbuilding
years & the railway era. There are also temporary & travelling
exhibits. A research library & educational programs are offered.
Open year round. The museum also operates the Free Meeting
House & Thomas Williams House.

Moncton: Thomas Williams House
Parent: Moncton Museum
103 Park St.,
Moncton, NB E1C 2B2

Tel: 506-857-0590
info.museum@moncton.ca
www.tourismnewbrunswick.ca/Products/T/The-Thomas-Williams
-House.aspx
Other contact information: Off-Season: 506-856-4383
This is the home of Thomas Williams, the treasurer for the
Intercolonial Railway in the 1800's. This is a municipal heritage
site in Moncton & was built in 1883. It features special events &
the Verandah Tearoom.

New Denmark: New Denmark Memorial Museum
Parent: New Denmark Historical Society
6 Main Rd.,
New Denmark, NB E7G 2B7

Tel: 506-553-6724
www.tourismnewbrunswick.ca/Products/N/New-Denmark-Memor
ial-Museum.aspx
New Denmark Memorial Museum honours the Danish
immigrants who settled in the New Denmark area of New
Brunswick in 1872. Exhibits include books, china, & farm
machinery, tools & portraits. Open Jun-Aug.

Oromocto: Canadian Military Engineers Museum
Canadian Forces School of Military Engineering, CFB / ASG
Gagetown, #J-10, Mitchell Bldg.,
Oromocto, NB E2V 4J5

Tel: 506-422-2000; *Fax:* 506-422-1220
cmemuseum@forces.gc.ca (Museum Staff)
www.cmemuseum.ca
Other contact information: E-mail, Research Inquiries:
cme.research@sympatico.ca
Year Founded: 1957 Displays at the Canadian Military Engineers
Museum date back before the 1800s, with drawings, plans, &
photographs of forts built by engineers, such as the Citadel in
Nova Scotia. Displays also depict trench life during World War I.
Weapons & uniforms from World War II, artifacts from the
Korean War, & a United Nations display are also part of the
museum. A research library houses photographs, reference
books, training manuals, & personal diaries. The museum is
open year round.
Col. John Tattersall, Chair
Maj. Joe Gale, Museum Executive Officer
CWO Blaine Thurston, Vice-President, History & Heritage
Sgt John Wilt, Curator & Treasurer

Oromocto: Fort Hughes Military Blockhouse
62 Miramichi Rd.,
Oromocto, NB E2V 1S2

Tel: 506-357-4400; *Fax:* 506-357-2266
recreation@oromocto.ca
www.oromocto.ca
Located in Sir Douglas Hazen Park, 1 Wharf Rd., Oromocto, NB.

Oromocto: New Brunswick Military History Museum
(NBMHM) / Museum Musée d'histoire militaire du
nouveau brunswick
Bldg. A-5, PO Box 17000 Forces,
Oromocto, NB E2V 4J5

Tel: 506-422-1304
info@nbmilitaryhistorymuseum.ca
nbmilitaryhistorymuseum.ca
twitter.com/nbmhm
www.facebook.com/16600767 6795263
Year Founded: 1973 The museum presents exhibits about the
Canadian Army, the Royal Canadian Navy, & the Royal
Canadian Air Force, the Canadian Armed Forces pre-1800 &
New Brunswick military history & artifacts. Open Mon-Fri
8:00-4:00, Sat-Sun by appointment.

Paquetville: Salon de la renommée de Paquetville et
village natal d'Edith Butler
1094, rue du Parc,
Paquetville, NB E8R 1J4

Tel: 506-764-2500
rmne.ca/salon-de-la-renommee-de-paquetville-et-village-natal-d-
edith-butle r

Petitcodiac: Maritime Motorsports Hall of Fame
5 Hooper Lane,
Petitcodiac, NB E4Z 0B4

Tel: 506-756-2110
maritimemotorsports@gmail.com
www.maritimemotorsporthalloffame.com
twitter.com/MMHallOfFame
www.face book.com/185591104855616
The Hall also features a museum showcasing the heritage of
maritime motorsports. Open Mon.-Sat., Sun. by appointment
until June.
Ernest McLean, President
Winona McLean, Managing Director

Petitcodiac: Petitcodiac War Museum
Legion Building, University of New Brunswick, 18 Kay St.,
Petitcodiac, NB E4Z 4K6

Tel: 506-756-7461
wrmuseum@nb.aibn.ca
www.villageofpetitcodiac.com
www.facebook.com/PetitcodiacWarMuseum
The museum commemorates soliders from Petitcodiac who
served in WWI, WWII, the Korean War & on peace keeping
missions.

Petit-Rocher: New Brunswick Mining & Mineral
Interpretation Centre (CIMMNB) / Centre d'interprétation
des mines & minerais du Nouveau-Brunswick
397, rue Principale,
Petit-Rocher, NB E8J 1L9

Tel: 506-542-2672
petit-rocher@nb.aibn.com
The Mining & Mineral Interpretation Centre features exhibitions
about the mining heritage of New Brunswick, plus a simulation of
an underground descent.

Plaster Rock: Plaster Rock Museum & Information
Centre
159 Main St.,
Plaster Rock, NB E7G 2H2

Tel: 506-356-6077
Plaster Rock Museum & Information Centre features exhibits
about the community's past, including the lumbering & farming
activities in Plaster Rock & the surrounding region.

Rexton: Bonar Law Common
31 Bonar Law Ave.,
Rexton, NB E4W 1V6

Tel: 506-523-7615 *Toll-Free:* 877-731-7007
bonarlawcommon@nb.aibn.com
www.bonarlawcommon.com
www.youtube.com/BonarLawCommons
www.facebook.com/bonar.common
Other contact information: Off-season Phone: 506-523-6921
Birthplace of the Right Honourable Andrew Bonar Law
(1858-1923), who was the only Prime Minister of Britain born
outside the British Isles. Also located in the Common is the
Richibucto River Historical Society Museum.

Rexton: Richibucto River Historical Society Museum
(RRHS)
Parent: Richibucto River Historical Society
Bonar Law Common, 31 Bonar Law Ave.,
Rexton, NB E4W 1V6

Tel: 506-523-7615 *Toll-Free:* 877-731-7007
bonarlawcommon@nb.aibn.com
www.bonarlawcommon.com/RRHS.html
www.youtube.com/BonarLawCommons
www.facebook.com/bonar.common
Other contact information: Off-season Phone: 506-523-6921
The museum documents local Rexton history.

Riverside-Albert: Old Bank Museum
Parent: Albert County Heritage Trust
c/o Albert County Heritage Trust, 5985 Rte. 114,
Riverside-Albert, NB E4H 4B8

Tel: 506-882-2015
mynewbrunswick.ca/old-bank-museum
Other contact information: Off-Season Phone: 506-882-2100
Historic bank building now a museum & information centre.

Sackville: Boultenhouse Heritage Centre
Parent: Tantramar Heritage Trust, Inc.
PO Box 3554, 29 Queen's Rd.,
Sackville, NB E4L 4G4

Tel: 506-536-2541; *Fax:* 506-536-2537
tantramarheritage@nb.aibn.com
www.heritage.tantramar.com/ththeritagecent re.html
twitter.com/TrustTantramar
www.heritage.tantramar.com
Former home of the shipwright, Christopher Boultenhouse; built
in 1842; site also houses the Tantramar Heritage Trust office.
Karen Valanne, Executive Director, 506-536-2541,
tantramarheritage@gmail.com

Sackville: Campbell Carriage Factory Museum
Parent: Tantramar Heritage Trust, Inc.
PO Box 3554, 19 Church St.,
Sackville, NB E4L 1H5

Tel: 506-536-2541
tantramarheritage@nb.aibn.com
www.heritage.tantramar.com/thtcampbell.html
twitter.com/TrustTantramar
www.heritage.tantramar.com
Other contact information: Off-season phone: 506-536-2541
19th century industrial site featuring a carriage factory &
blacksmith shop.
Karen Valanne, Executive Director, 506-536-2541,
tantramarheritage@gmail.com

Sackville: Struts Gallery & Faucet Media Arts Centre
7 Lorne St.,
Sackville, NB E4L 3Z6

Tel: 506-536-1211
info@strutsgallery.ca
www.strutsgallery.ca
twitter.com/strutsgallery
www.facebook.com/133378 256676635
Year Founded: 1982 An artist-run centre dedicated to presenting
regional & national contemporary artist initiated activities.
Expositions, performances, demonstrations, workshops &
symposia. Open Mon-Sat 1:00-5:00

Saint John: Barbour's General Store
Parent: G.E. Barbour Inc.
10 Market Sq.,
Saint John, NB E2L 4Z6

www.facebook.com/208036962572426
Year Founded: 1967 Artifacts housed at Barbour's General Store
include authentic grocery items, pharmaceutical items, cooking
utensils, china, farm implements, & yard goods. The restored
nineteenth-century country general stored is open from mid-June
to mid-September.

Saint John: Loyalist House Museum
120 Union St.,
Saint John, NB E2L 1A3

Tel: 506-652-3590
info@loyalisthouse.com
www.loyalisthouse.com
Year Founded: 1960 Operated by the New Brunswick Historical
Society as a national historic site. Original furniture still on
display. This buiding is one of the few surviving buildings of the
Great Saint John Fire in 1877. Open May-Sept

Saint John: Saint Croix Island International Historic Site
/ Lieu historique international de l'Ile-Sainte-Croix
Carleton Martello Tower, 454 Whipple St.,
Saint John, NB E2M 2R3

Tel: 506-636-4011; *Fax:* 506-636-4574
info.martello@pc.gc.ca
www.pc.gc.ca/en/lhn-nhs/nb/stcroix
twitter.com/ nhsnb
Other contact information: TTY: 506-887-6015
Year Founded: 1984 Located on Rte. 127 Bayside, with a view of
Saint Croix Island; site of Pierre Dugua's first attempt to found a
settlement in North America; viewing deck & self-guided
interpretive trail; picnic area. The site is also a U.S. National
Monument (www.nps.gov/sacr).

Saint John: Saint John Firefighters Museum
24 Sydney St.,
Saint John, NB E2L 2L3

Tel: 506-633-1840
The museum is the site of the No. 2 Engine house, built in 1840;
a collection of firefighting artifacts & photographs; includes an
entire room dedicated to the Great Saint John Fire of 1877, an
authentic hand pump, a 1956 LaFrance Fire Engine, a Junior
Firefighters play room & much more.

Saint John: Saint John Jewish Historical Museum
91 Leinster St.,
Saint John, NB E2L 1J2

Tel: 506-633-1833; *Fax:* 506-642-9926
sjjhm@nbnet.nb.ca
jewishmuseumsj.com
www.facebook.com/118753971549220
Year Founded: 1986 Housed in the same building with the
Shaarei Zedek Synagogue, the museum collects, displays &
preserves articles related specifically to the Saint John Jewish
community; provides a research facility for genealogists,
historians & religious scholars; 7 display areas; Jewish education
outreach kits, membership program
Katherine Biggs-Craft, Curator

Saint John: Saint John Sports Hall of Fame
Leisure Services, 171 Adelaide St.,
Saint John, NB E2K 1W9

Tel: 506-658-2908
www.saintjohn.ca
Located in Harbour Station

Saint John: St. Andrews Blockhouse National Historic
Site
454 Whipple St.,
Saint John, NB E2M 2R3

Tel: 506-529-4270; *Fax:* 506-636-4574
fundy.info@pc.gc.ca
www.pc.gc.ca/lhn-nhs/nb/standrews/index.aspx
Other contact information: Off-season Tel: 506-636-4011

Blockhouse built for border defence during the War of 1812; contains elements of the oldest blockhouse in New Brunswick; located at 23 Joe's Point Rd., St. Andrews NB E5B 2J7

St Andrews: Atlantic Reference Centre (ARC)
1 Lower Campus Rd.,
St Andrews, NB E5B 2L7
Tel: 506-529-1200
arc@sta.dfo.ca
www.mar.dfo-mpo.gc.ca/e0011886
www.instagram.com/fundydiscoveryaquarium
twitter.com/@FundyAquarium
The ARC acts as a museum, biodiversity centre, laboratory & provider of scientific services. It is a joint project between Department of Fisheries & Oceans, St. Andrews Biological Station & the Huntsman Marine Science Centre (HMSC).
Gerhard Pohle, Curator ARC, 506-529-1203, gpohle@huntsmanmarine.ca

St Andrews: Ross Memorial Museum / Musée mémorial Ross
188 Montague St.,
St Andrews, NB E5B 1J2
Tel: 506-529-5124; *Fax:* 506-529-5183
rossmuse@nb.aibn.com
www.rossmemorialmuseum.ca
Year Founded: 1824 Decorative arts museum in one of St. Andrews' finest early houses; open daily from Jun. - Sept.

St Andrews: Sheriff Andrews House
PO Box 6000, 63 King St.,
St Andrews, NB E3B 1X6
Tel: 506-529-5080; *Fax:* 506-453-2416
town@townofstandrews.ca
www.tourismnewbrunswick.ca/Products/S/SheriffAnd
rewsHouse.aspx
Other contact information: Off-season: 506-529-5120
Guided tours are offered through this 19th century home.

Saint-Jacques: Antique Automobile Museum
35 Main St.,
Saint-Jacques, NB E7B 1V6
Tel: 506-737-2637
Vintage cars, fire truck, farm tractor & carriages. Open June-Sept.

St Martins: Quaco Museum & Library
Parent: Quaco Historical & Library Society
236 Main St.,
St Martins, NB E5R 1B8
Tel: 506-833-4740; *Fax:* 506-833-2008
www.quaco.ca/QuacoMuseum.htm
Year Founded: 1978 Displays the history & heritage of the Quaco-St. Martins area with a specific focus on the shipbuilding heritage of the region. Archives available for historical & genealogical research. Museum & archives open June-Sept, other times by apppointment.
Jacqueline Bartlett, President, president@quaco.ca
Eric Bartlett, Manager, 506-833-4499,
quaco.museum@bellaliant.com

St Stephen: Charlotte County Museum Inc.
443 Milltown Blvd.,
St Stephen, NB E3L 1J9
Tel: 506-466-3295; *Fax:* 506-466-6606
charlottecountymuseum@gmail.com
www.facebook.com/CharlotteCountyMuseum
Year Founded: 1977 Exhibits reflect the immigration of early settlers. Collection includes early Chinese porcelain, hand-crafted articles, quilts, samplers; costumes, early tools & furniture. Displays includes lumbering & shipbuilding, past industries, kitchen artifacts, school room, & tool shed. Open Jun-Aug
Irene Ritch, Executive Director

St Stephen: The Chocolate Museum
73 Milltown Blvd.,
St Stephen, NB E3L 1G5
Tel: 506-466-7848; *Fax:* 506-466-7701
chocolate.museum@nb.aibn.com
www.chocolatemuseum.ca
www.facebook.com/t hechocolatemuseum
Year Founded: 1999 History of local chocolate company Ganong Bros., Limited. Open Mon-Fri 10:00-4:00; Sat-Sun 11:00-3:00.

Shippagan: Société historique Nicolas-Denys (SHND)
218, boul J.D. Gauthier,
Shippagan, NB E8S 1P6
Tél: 506-336-3461; *Téléc:* 506-336-3603
shnd@umoncton.ca
www.umoncton.ca/umcs-bibliotheque/node/6
www.facebook .com/187957724571999

Fondée en: 1969 Heures d'ouvertures et les différentes coordonnées comment nous joindre pour le centre de documentation: mardi au jeudi de 9 h 00 à 12 h et de 13 h à 16 h, mercredi soir de 19 à 21 h.
Philippe Basque, Président
Nathalie M. Lanteigne, Responsable

St-Isidore: St-Isidore Museum Inc. / Musée de Saint Isidore Inc.
3942, boul des Fondateurs,
St-Isidore, NB E8M 1C2
Tel: 506-358-6003
villasti@nb.aibn.com
Exhibits depict agricultural & forestry background of the region; open in July & Aug., Thu.-Sun.

Sussex: 8th Hussars Regimental Museum
66 Broad St.,
Sussex, NB E4E 5S2
Tel: 506-433-5226
hussarssussex@nb.aibn.com
8chassociation.com/Museum.html
www.facebook.com/8thHussarsMuseum
Other contact information: Alt. E-mail:
Info.8thhussars@yahoo.ca
The museum, located in the historical Sussex train station, houses 16 displays, including those about the Boer War, WWI & WWII.
Don Bourque, President
Jake Douthwaite, Vice-President
Tom McLaughlan, Vice-President
Rick Cosman, Director

Sussex: Agricultural Museum of New Brunswick
28 Perry St.,
Sussex, NB E4E 2N7
Tel: 506-433-6799
info@agriculturalmuseumofnb.com
www.agriculturalmuseumofnb.com
www.facebook.com/469958723016450
Year Founded: 1986 The museum houses agricultural equipment, military memorabilia, furniture & housewares. Open Jun-Sept Tue-Sat 9:00-5:00, Sun 12;00-5:00

Tabusintac: Tabusintac Centennial Memorial Library & Museum
4490 Rte. 11,
Tabusintac, NB E9H 1J3
Tel: 506-779-1918
gsavoy@nbnet.nb.ca
www.discovermiramichi.com/tabusintac-centennial-memorial-libr
ary-museum
www.facebook.com/TabusintacLibraryMuseum
Other contact information: Alternate Email:
tabusintaclibrarym@nb.aliant.net
Houses historical artifacts & memorabilia from the Tabusintac area. Also features a craft shop.

Tracadie-Sheila: Musée Historique de Tracadie Inc.
#399, 222, rue du Couvent,
Tracadie-Sheila, NB E1X 1E1
Tel: 506-393-6366; *Fax:* 506-395-6355
museehi.sb.sympatico.ca
www.musee-tracadie.ca
instagram.com/museetracadie
twitter.com/mhdetracadie
www.facebook.com/
Museehistoriquedetracadiehistoricalmuseum
Year Founded: 1968 Ce qu'il soit le seul au Canada à présenter un aperçu de ce que pouvait être une léproserie à l'époque du 19e siècle. Aussi l'histoire de Tracadie, des objets datant de plusieurs siècles avant l'arrivée des colons blancs, et des articles relatifs à la vie des Acadiens. L-V 9:00h-17:00h; Sa-D 12:00h-17:00h

Welshpool: Roosevelt Campobello International Park / Parc international Roosevelt de Campobello
459 Rte. 774,
Welshpool, NB E5E 1A4
Tel: 506-752-2922; *Fax:* 506-752-6000
Toll-Free: 877-851-6663
info@fdr.net
www.fdr.net
www.youtube.com/user/RooseveltCampobello
twitter.com/FDRCampobello
www .facebook.com/Roosevelt.Campobello
The Roosevelt Campobello International Park, located on Campobello Island in New Brunswick's Bay of Fundy, features the 34-room summer residence of Franklin D. Roosevelt & his wife Eleanor. Guided tours are given of the home. The park also contains the Edmund S. Muskie Visitor Center, where visitors learn the story of the former president of the United States,

through displays & a film. The Roosevelt Cottage & Visitor Centre are open from mid May to mid October. The park is open year-round, & is administered by a commission of six members & six alternates, with equal representation from both Canada & the United States.

Woodstock: Old Carleton County Court House
Parent: Carleton County Historical Society
c/o Carleton County Historical Society, 128 Connell St.,
Woodstock, NB E7M 1L5
Tel: 506-328-9706
cchs@nb.aibn.com
www.cchs-nb.ca
Year Founded: 1986 Local history & artifacts. Guided tours are available during the summer & by appointment.
John Thompson, President

Newfoundland & Labrador

Provincial Museums

The Rooms
PO Box 1800 C, 9 Bonaventure Ave.,
St. John's, NL A1C 5P9
Tel: 709-757-8000; *Fax:* 709-757-8017
information@therooms.ca
www.therooms.ca
www.instagram.com/therooms_nl
twitter.com/TheRooms_NL
www.facebook.com /TheRoomsNL
Other contact information: Archives: 709-757-8030; Museum:
709-757-8020; Gallery: 709-757-8040
Year Founded: 2005 The Rooms consists of the Newfoundland & Labrador Provincial Archives, Art Gallery, & Museum. The Archives collects records of the Government of Newfoundland & Labrador, as well as records from private sources which have value to the history of the province. Permanent exhibits at the museum depict Newfoundland & Labrador's early people, as well as Fort Townsend, the home of British soldiers &, since 1870, the Royal Newfoundland Constabulary. One level of the museum is dedicated to the birds of Newfoundland & Labrador. The Rooms Provincial Art Gallery presents more than 7,000 historical & contemporary works.
Anne Chafe, CEO, annechafe@therooms.ca

Local Museums

L'Anse Au Loup: Labrador Straits Museum
PO Box 281,
L'Anse Au Loup, NL A0K 3L0
Tel: 709-927-5600
webmaster@labradorstraitsmuseum.ca
www.labradorstraitsmuseum.ca
Other contact information: Alternate phone: 709-927-5077
Year Founded: 1978 Local history with a focus on domestic life & the role of women in communities.

Baie Verte: Baie Verte Peninsula Miners' Museum
PO Box 122, 319 Rte. 410,
Baie Verte, NL A0K 1B0
Tel: 709-532-8090; *Fax:* 709-532-4166
baievertepeda@nf.aibn.com
manl.nf.ca/index.php/component/mtree/baie-vert
e-miners-museum.html?Itemid=
Year Founded: 1975 The Miners' Museum presents a replica of life & work during the mining years on the Baie Verte Peninsula. Open year round.

Bonavista: Bonavista Historical Society Museum
Building 2, Ryan Premises National Historic Site, PO Box 295,
Bonavista, NL A0C 1B0
Tel: 709-468-2920; *Fax:* 709-468-2495
manl.nf.ca/index.php/newfoundland-labrador-museums/bonavist
a-museum.html
Year Founded: 1969 The collection reflects local life in the late 19th century in one of Newfoundland's inshore fishing communities. The musuem also holds a collection of medical artifacts from the early 20th century. Open Jun-Oct daily 10:00-6:00

Botwood: Botwood Heritage Centre
PO Box 490,
Botwood, NL A0H 1E0
Tel: 709-257-4612; *Fax:* 709-257-3330
botwoodheritage@hotmail.com
town.botwood.nl.ca
The Botwood Heritage Centre depicts the time of the Beothuk, the European exploration era in the Exploits Valley, & the early railway & shipping period of Abitibi.

Burin: Burin Heritage House
33 Seaview Dr.,
Burin, NL A0E 1E0

Tel: 709-891-2217; Fax: 709-891-2358
burinheritagemuseums@nf.aibn.com
www.townofburin.com/tourism
The Burin Heritage House features artifacts related to the history of Burin, including artwork & the tidal wave. Open May-Oct.

Carbonear: Baccalieu Trail Heritage Corporation (BTHC)
4 Pikes Ln,
Carbonear, NL A1Y 1A7

Tel: 709-596-1906; Fax: 709-596-2121
contact@baccalieudigs.ca
www.baccalieudigs.ca
Year Founded: 1993 The corporation preserves, protects, & promotes the heritage of the Baccalieu Trail Region, which consists of approximately seventy communities along 240 km of coastline on Newfoundland & Labrador's Avalon Peninsula. Since 1994 the BTHC has een conducting an ongoing program of archaeological survey, excavating and interpretation in the region. Important sites include: Cupids Cove Plantation Provincial Historic Site, Didldo Island/Anderson's Cove, New Perlican, Russell's Point and Winterton.

Carbonear: Carbonear C.N. Railway Station
PO Box 999, 223 Water St.,
Carbonear, NL A1Y 1C5

Tel: 709-596-0714; Fax: 709-596-5021
www.carbonear.ca
The Carbonear Railway Station is one of Newfoundland & Labrador's Resgistered Heritage Structures. Operated by the Carbonear Heritage Society, the station contains railway artifacts, exhibits about the history of Carbonear, genealogical information, & a tourist information centre. Open from Jun-Sept. Appointments may be arranged during the off season.

Cow Head: Dr. Henry N. Payne Community Museum
Conservation & Heritage Inc., 143 Main St.,
Cow Head, NL A0K 2A0

Tel: 709-243-2023
cowheadheritage@gmail.com
www.facebook.com/149833015034340
Restored theme home; artifacts tell story of Dr. Henry N. Payne & cultural heritage of area; gift shop. Located at the northern tip of Gros Morne National Park.

Cupids: Cupids Legacy Centre
PO Box 210, 368 Seaforest Dr.,
Cupids, NL A0A 2B0

Tel: 709-528-1610
info@cupidslegacycentre.ca
www.cupidslegacycentre.ca
twitter.com/CupidsLegacy
www.facebook.com/Cu pidsLegacy
Year Founded: 2010 Built to commemorate the 400th anniversary of the first English settlement in Canada. Houses exhibits that illuminate the rich historical and cultural background of Cupids and the Conception Bay North area; contains more than 160,000 artifacts, an archaeologists field labratory, a full-service reception hall, a Family History Resource Centre, a rooftop Faerie Garden and a museum shop. Open seasonally, seven days a week.
Linda Kane, Curator

Deer Lake: Roy Whalen Heritage Museum
44 Trans Canada Hwy.,
Deer Lake, NL A8A 2E4

Tel: 709-635-4440; Fax: 709-635-5103
www.town.deerlake.nf.ca
www.facebook.com/Valley.Crafts.Roy.Whalen.Museum
Year Founded: 1988 The museum preserves the local history with displays related to logging, agriculture and the settlers' lives in the Humber Valley. Open May-Dec.

Ferryland: Historic Ferryland Museum
PO Box 7, Baltimore Dr.,
Ferryland, NL A0A 2H0

Tel: 709-432-2711
historicferrylanmuseum1@gmail.com
manl.nf.ca/index.php/component/mtree/avalon/ferryland-museum.html
Exhibits depicting community life & Ferryland's role in colonization of North America. Open Jun-Sept 10:00-4:00, Sun 1:00-4:00

Flatrock: Flat Rock Museum
c/o Town Council of Flatrock, 663 Windgap Rd.,
Flatrock, NL A1K 1C7

Tel: 709-437-6312; Fax: 709-437-6311
townofflatrock.com/flatrock-museum

Year Founded: 1988 Artifacts and photographs of life in Flatrock, fishing & farming industry & St. Michael's Church. Open Jul-Aug Mon-Fri 9:00-4:00.

Fogo: Bleak House Museum
#32, 36 North Shore Rd.,
Fogo, NL A0G 2B0

Tel: 709-266-2487; Fax: 709-266-1323
recreation@townoffogoisland.ca
Other contact information: Alternative Phone: 709-266-2237
Year Founded: 1988 Bleak House was built around 1816 for the Slade family, who were involved in the Fogo Island fish trade. The home features items that belonged to owners of the home, plus artifacts that depict the history of Fogo. Open Jul-Sept.

Forteau: Point Amour Lighthouse Provincial Historic Site
Parent: Labrador Straits Historical Development Corporation
c/o Labrador Straits Historical Development Corporation, PO Box 112,
Forteau, NL A0K 2P0

Tel: 709-927-5825; Fax: 709-656-3150
Toll-Free: 800-563-6353
lshdc@labradorstraits.net
www.pointamourlighthouse.ca
www.facebook.com/ProvincialHistoricSites.NL
Other contact information: Alt. Phone: 709-931-2013
Consisting of several buildings, the Point Amour Light station dates back to the 1850s. The Provincial Historic Site in Newfoundland & Labrador has been restored, & now features displays that depict the maritime history of the Labrador Straits. An interpretive trail at the site takes visitors to the site of the HMS Raleigh & HMS Lily shipwrecks. The site is open from mid May to the beginning of October.
Bonnie Goudie, Executive Director
Kim Shipp, Contact, kimshipp@gov.nl.ca

Gander: North Atlantic Aviation Museum
Parent: North Atlantic Aviation Museum Association
135 Trans Canada Hwy.,
Gander, NL A1V 1P6

Tel: 709-256-2923; Fax: 709-256-8561
info@northatlanticaviationmuseum.com
www.northatlanticaviationmuseum.com
twitter.com/NAAMGANDER
www.facebook.com/NAAMGander
Year Founded: 1986 The North Atlantic Aviation Museum depicts important aviation moments over the North Atlantic, from the war years to commercial flying. The focus is upon Gander's involvement in aviation history. The Museum features six aircraft.
Bob Briggs, President
Carl Squires, Vice-President
Jonathan Waterman, Secretary
Sandra Seaward, Executive Director

Grand Bank: Provincial Seamen's Museum (PSM)
Parent: The Rooms
PO Box 1109, 54 Marine Dr.,
Grand Bank, NL A0E 1W0

Tel: 709-832-1484
psminfo@therooms.ca
www.therooms.ca/museums#Provincial
www.facebook.com/provincialseamensmus eum
Year Founded: 1971 Artifacts pertaining to the people of Newfoundland & Labrador & their lives on sea & land dating back to the 1800s. Open Apr-Oct Mon-Sat 9:00-4:30, Sun & holidays 12:00-4:30

Grand Falls-Windsor: Logger's Life Provincial Museum
c/o Provincial Bldg., Cromer Ave.,
Grand Falls-Windsor, NL A2A 1W9

Tel: 709-486-0492
mmpminfo@therooms.ca
www.therooms.ca/museum/loggers_life_museum.asp
Other contact information: Off-Season Phone: 709-757-8023
Logging exhibit is a replica of 1920s logging camp; displays tools & clothing representative of that era; located west of Grand Falls-Windsor on Trans Canada Hwy.

Grand Falls-Windsor: Mary March Provincial Museum
c/o Provincial Building, 24 St. Catherine St.,
Grand Falls-Windsor, NL A2A 1X3

Tel: 709-292-4522
conniepenton@therooms.ca
www.therooms.ca/museums#Mary
www.facebook.com/marymarchprovincialmuseum
Year Founded: 1988 The Mary March Museum traces the Aboriginal, European, natural & geological history of the Central Newfoundland Region. Open Apr-Oct 9:00-4:30, Sun & holidays 12:00-4:30

Happy Valley-Goose Bay: Northern Lights Military Museum
Northern Lights Bldg., 170 Hamilton River Rd.,
Happy Valley-Goose Bay, NL A0P 1E0

Tel: 709-896-5939
Includes a trappers's exhibit, a life-like brook, animals, & O Gauge Lionel toy trains.

Harbour Brenton: St. Bartholomew's Church
c/o Mt. Arlington Hts., 25,
Harbour Brenton, NL A0H 1P0

Tel: 709-228-2583
www.facebook.com/1558745601031046
Other contact information: Alternate phone: 709-885-2225
Church built in 1930 by parishoners

Harbour Grace: Conception Bay Museum
PO Box 298, 1 Water St.,
Harbour Grace, NL A0A 2M0

Tel: 709-596-5465; Fax: 709-596-5465
conceptionbaymuseum@outlook.com
conceptionbaymuseum.wordpress.com
instagram.com/conceptionbaymuseum
twitter.com/cbmuseum1870
www.facebook.com/conceptionbaymuseum
Year Founded: 1970 Local history. Includes an aviation room, pirate room, fishing room, World War exhibit & a Period Setting room. Open daily 10:00-5:00

Hopedale: Moravian Mission Museum
Parent: Agvituk Historical Society
Moravian Mission House, PO Box 12,
Hopedale, NL A0P 1G0

Tel: 709-933-3777; Fax: 709-933-3746
manl.nf.ca/index.php/newfoundland-labrador-museums/moravian-mission-museum
Collection includes archaeology artifacts from 1500-2000 years ago, items related to Labrador Inuit & European medical supplies, furniture & utensils. Tours available daily 8:30-8:00

Lewisporte: By The Bay Museum & Craft Shop
235 Main Rd.,
Lewisporte, NL A0G 3A0

Tel: 709-535-1911
bythebayshop@bellaliant.com
www.facebook.com/lporteHeritageCentre
Year Founded: 1872 Exhibits at the Bye The Bay Museum show the history of Lewisporte & its surrounding region, including Beothuk artifacts, the shipbuilding & logging industries & World War I & World War II. Owned & operated by the Lewisporte Area Development Association, the museum is open from the end of May to the end of August.

Marystown: Marystown Heritage Museum Corporation
PO Box 688, 242 Ville Marie Dr.,
Marystown, NL A0E 2M0

Tel: 709-279-1462; Fax: 709-279-5116
marystownmuseum@hotmail.com
manl.nf.ca/index.php/component/mtree/eastern
/marystown-heritage-museum.html
Other contact information: Off season phone: 709-279-2463
The museum exhibits include everyday artifacts from the town's historic past.

Moreton's Harbour: Moreton's Harbour Community Museum
6A Main Rd.,
Moreton's Harbour, NL A0G 3H0

Tel: 709-684-2353
Other contact information: Alt. Phone: 709-684-2351
The museum features various artifacts, including agricultural implements & equipment used during the inshore fishery. Archives include census records, diaries, & school minute books. The community museum is open from mid June to the beginning of September. Tours may be arranged during the off season.

Mount Pearl: Admiralty House Communications Museum
365 Old Placentia Rd,
Mount Pearl, NL A1N 0G7

Tel: 709-748-1124
admiraltyhouse@mountpearl.ca
www.admiraltymuseum.ca
www.facebook.com/AdmiraltyHouse
Exhibits focus on local history, wireless communication history & the tragedy of the S.S Florizel. Open Jul-Aug daily 9:00-5:00; Sept-Jun Mon-Fri 10:00-4:00

Musgrave Harbour: Fisherman's Museum
PO Box 159,
Musgrave Harbour, NL A0G 3J0
Tel: 709-655-2589; *Fax:* 709-655-2064
bantinghti@nf.aibn.com
www.musgraveharbour.com/museum.html
Year Founded: 1910 Ship models, engines, photographs,
accounts of local shipwrecks. Open from the third week of June
until labour day weekend.
Mitzi Abbott, Contact

Newtown: Barbour Living Heritage Village
PO Box 135,
Newtown, NL A0G 3L0
Tel: 709-536-3220; *Fax:* 709-536-3150
barboursite@nf.aibn.com
www.barbour-site.com
www.facebook.com/34990249 8362983
A historic fishing village, featuring a schoolhouse, sealing
interpretation centre, fisherman's stage, theatre, & art gallery.
Open Jun-Sept
Roberta Vincent Bungay, President
Judy Stagg, Executive Director

North West River: Labrador Heritage Museum
Parent: Labrador Heritage Society
c/o Labrador Heritage Society, PO Box 99,
North West River, NL A0P 1M0
Tel: 709-497-8858; *Fax:* 709-497-8228
info@labradorheritagemuseum.ca
www.labradorheritagemuseum.ca
Other contact information: Craft Shop Phone: 709-497-8282
Exhibit includes arifacts & infomation about the Hudson Bay
Company store, trapping, exploration of Labrador & the
International Grenfell Association in North West River. Open
Jun-Sept daily 9:00-5:00

Old Perlican: Howard House of Artifacts
PO Box 100,
Old Perlican, NL A0A 3G0
Tel: 709-587-2022
Artifacts represent the 1890s & 1900-1945; collection of
Newfoundland homemade furniture of the 1930s. Open daily

Placentia: O'Reilly House Museum
Parent: Placentia Area Historical Society
c/o Placentia Area Historical Society, PO Box 233, 48 Orcan
Dr.,
Placentia, NL A0B 2Y0
Tel: 709-227-5568
www.placentiahistory.ca
Year Founded: 1989 The Victorian home displays royal relics &
period artifacts from Placentia' past. Open daily.
Tom O'Keefe, President, 709-227-0322,
tokeefe@personainternet.com

Placentia Bay: Castle Hill National Historic Site of
Canada
PO Box 10 Jerseyside, Route 100,
Placentia Bay, NL A0B 2G0
Tel: 709-227-2401; *Fax:* 709-227-2452
castle.hill@pc.gc.ca
www.pc.gc.ca/eng/lhn-nhs/nl/castlehill/index.aspx
17th & 18th century remains of French & English fortifications.
Picnic areas & hiking trails; special events & programming;
Visitor Centre with gift shop. Open Jun-Sept daily 10:00-6:00

Port au Choix: Port au Choix National Historic Park
Site
PO Box 140,
Port au Choix, NL A0K 4C0
Tel: 709-861-3522; *Fax:* 709-861-3827
site@pc.gc.ca
pc.gc.ca/en/lhn-nhs/nl/portauchoix
Commemorates area's rich aboriginal history dating back 5400
years. Visitors can view artifacts & exhibits on the four
prehistoric cultures that occupied area; walking trails,
archaeological sites, lighthouse & fossils. Open Jun-Oct daily
9:00-5:00

Port au Port: Our Lady of Mercy Museum
PO Box 330,
Port au Port, NL A0N 1T0
Tel: 709-648-2632
Former rectory now holds artifacts from the Bay St. George
area; open May - Sept.

Port aux Basques: Gulf Museum
c/o South West Coast Historical Society, PO Box 1299, 118
Main St.,
Port aux Basques, NL A0M 1C0
Tel: 709-695-7560; *Fax:* 709-956-2170

Local history, nautical items & astrolabes found in a shipwreck.
Open Jul-Sept daily 9:00-9:00.

Port aux Basques: Port aux Basques Railway Heritage
Centre
PO Box 1229, 1 Trans Canada Hwy,
Port aux Basques, NL A0M 1C0
Tel: 709-695-3688
pabmuseum@gmail.com
www.portauxbasques.ca/tourism/railway_heritage_center.php
Other contact information: Alt. Phone: 709-694-4862
The Port aux Basques Railway Heritage Centre depicts the
significance of the railway to Newfoundland's history. In the late
1890s, Port aux Basques became the western terminus of the
Newfoundland Railway, where the railway schedule connected
with steamers. Open from June to October, the heritage centre
features the train station & various rail cars.

Port de Grave: Fishermen's Museum, Porter House &
School
Port de Grave, NL A0A 3J0
Tel: 709-786-3912
hermanporter@personainternet.com
Year Founded: 1979 Museum contains artifacts depicting life &
times of Newfoundland fishermen. Porter House is a traditional
fisherman's house restored to early 1900s; Hibbs' Hole
Schoolhouse, a restored one-room school.

Port Union: Port Union Museum
PO Box 98,
Port Union, NL A0C 2J0
Tel: 709-469-2728
Other contact information: Alternate Phone: 709-469-2159
History of Sir Willam F. Coaker, the Fishermen's Protective
Union, the town of Port Union & the Reid Newfoundland Railway.

Pouch Cove: Pouch Cove Museum
Town Hall, PO Box 59, 660 Main Rd.,
Pouch Cove, NL A0A 3L0
Tel: 709-335-2848; *Fax:* 709-335-2840
info@pouchcove.ca
pouchcove.ca/our-museum
Local history. Open year round
Barbara Tilley, Town Manager, info@pouchcove.ca

Red Bay: Red Bay National Historic Site of Canada
PO Box 103,
Red Bay, NL A0K 4K0
Tel: 709-920-2142; *Fax:* 709-920-2144
redbay.info@pc.gc.ca
www.pc.gc.ca/lhn-nhs/nl/redbay/natcul/basque.aspx
The Visitor Centre features discoveries from a marine
archaeology project in the Red Bay area. Visitors learn about
Labrador's 16th century history, through displays of original
artifacts recovered from archaeological excavations, plus
reproductions. Open Jun-Oct

Rocky Harbour: Gros Morne National Park Visitor
Reception Centre
PO Box 130,
Rocky Harbour, NL A0K 4N0
Tel: 709-458-2417; *Fax:* 709-458-2059
grosmorner.info@pc.gc.ca
www.pc.gc.ca/eng/pn-np/nl/grosmorne/index.aspx
Other contact information: TTY: 709-772-4564
Gros Morne discovery centre looks at the forces of nature while
the centre looks at geology, plant & animal life, marine story &
human history. It is located on the south side of Bonne Bay, one
hour from Deer Airport & the Trans Canada Highway. Open
May-Oct

St. Anthony: Grenfell House Museum
Parent: Grenfell Historic Properties
PO Box 93, 4 Maravel Rd.,
St. Anthony, NL A0K 4S0
Tel: 709-454-4010; *Fax:* 709-454-4047
info@grenfell-properties.com
www.grenfell-properties.com/about_grenfell_house.php
Other contact information: Alternate Email:
manager@grenfell-properes.com
Year Founded: 1998 Dr. Wilfred Grenfell's former home restored
circa 1920. Seasonal Hours: M-F 9:00-6:00pm; Off-Season
Hours: M-F 9:00-5:00

St. John's: Anglican Cathedral of St. John the Baptist
Museum & Archives
PO Box 23112, 16 Church Hill,
St. John's, NL A1C 3Z9
Tel: 709-726-5677; *Fax:* 709-726-2053
angcathedral@nf.aibn.com
www.stjohnsanglicancathedral.org

Year Founded: 1699 The parish is the oldest non-Roman
Catholic religious foundation in Canada. Includes pictures,
artifacts, records, documents & books related to the history of
the Cathedral & Parish.

St. John's: Beothuk Interpretation Centre Provincial
Historic Site
Provincial Historic Sites, Dept. of Tourism, Culture &
Recreation, PO Box 8700,
St. John's, NL A1B 4J6
Tel: 709-729-0592; *Fax:* 709-729-7989
Toll-Free: 800-563-6353
info@seethesites.ca
www.seethesites.ca/the-sites/beoth uk-interpretation-centre.aspx
Year Founded: 1981 The Beothuk site at Boyd's Cove dates
back to the late 17th & early 18th centuries. The site features the
archaeological remains of Beothuk life, including their house pits.
Visitors can learn about these extinct people at the interpretive
centre, where several artifacts from the site are displayed & on
the interpretive trail. The centre is open from mid June to mid
October.
Kim Shipp, Historic Sites Officer

St. John's: Cape Bonavista Lighthouse Provincial
Historic Site
Provincial Historic Sites, Dept. of Tourism, Culture &
Recreation, PO Box 8700,
St. John's, NL A1B 4J6
Tel: 709-729-0592; *Fax:* 709-729-7989
Toll-Free: 800-563-6353
info@seethesites.ca
www.seethesites.ca/the-sites/cape- bonavista-lighthouse.aspx
Year Founded: 1970 The Cape Bonavista Lighthouse was built
in 1843. The site features guided tours & a walking trail. The
lighthouse is open May-Oct.
Kim Shipp, Historic Sites Officer

St. John's: Cape Spear National Historic Site of
Canada / Lieu historique national du Canada du
Cap-Spear
PO Box 1268, 1914-1930 Black Head Rd.,
St. John's, NL A1A 1J0
Tel: 709-772-5367; *Fax:* 709-772-6302
cape.spear@pc.gc.ca
www.pc.gc.ca/eng/lhn-nhs/nl/spear/index.aspx
Year Founded: 1983 Visitors can view displays about the history
of lighthouses & lightkeeping. The grounds are open year round
& the lighthouse, Visitor Interpretation Centre & the Heritage Gift
Shop are open May-Oct.

St. John's: Commissariat House Provincial Historic Site
Provincial Historic Sites, Dept. of Tourism, Culture &
Recreation, PO Box 8700,
St. John's, NL A1B 4J6
Tel: 709-729-0592; *Fax:* 709-729-7989
Toll-Free: 800-563-6353
info@seethesites.ca
www.seethesites.ca/the-sites/the-c ommissariat.aspx
Year Founded: 1818 This building, one of the oldest buildings in
Newfoundland, was built especially for the Commissariat to
supply the city's garrison and has been restored back to the
1830's era complete with tradtionally dressed maids and clerks
to help answer questions.
Kim Shipp, Historic Sites Officer

St. John's: Heart's Content Cable Station Provincial
Historic Site, Heart's Content NF
Provincial Historic Sites, Dept. of Tourism, Culture &
Recreation, PO Box 8700,
St. John's, NL A1B 4J6
Tel: 709-729-0592; *Fax:* 709-729-7989
Toll-Free: 800-563-6353
info@seethesites.ca
www.seethesites.ca/the-sites/heart 's-content-cable-station.aspx
www.facebook.com/ProvincialHistoricSites.N L
Year Founded: 1974 Located on Hwy. 80, this cable station
marks the first successful transatlantic telegraph cable landing in
1866. Displays focus on the history of cable, with equipment and
instrumentation on exhibit. Open May-Oct., 10:00-5:30 daily.
Kim Shipp, Historic Sites Officer

St. John's: Hiscock House Provincial Historic Site
Provincial Historic Sites, Dept. of Tourism, Culture &
Recreation, PO Box 8700,
St. John's, NL A1B 4J6
Tel: 709-729-0592; *Fax:* 709-729-7989
Toll-Free: 800-563-6353
info@seethesites.ca
www.seethesites.ca/the-sites/trini ty-historic-sites/hiscock-house.aspx
www.facebook.com/ProvincialHistoric Sites.NL

Year Founded: 1982 Owned solely by the Hiscock family until it was reborn as a museum, the house has been restored to its 1910 style. Located on Church St., it is open late spring to early autumn, 10:00-5:30 daily.
Kim Shipp, Historic Sites Officer

St. John's: James J. O'Mara Pharmacy Museum
Parent: Newfoundland & Labrador Pharmacy Board
Apothecary Hall, 488 Water St.,
St. John's, NL A1E 1B3

Tel: 709-753-5877; *Fax:* 709-753-8615
inforx@nlpb.ca
www.nlpb.ca/for-the-public/james-j-omara-pharmacy-museum
www.facebook.com/139035376271594
Includes antique drug store fixtures, equipment used by pharmacists & patent medicines.

St. John's: Mockbeggar Plantation Provincial Historic Site
Provincial Historic Sites, Dept. of Tourism, Culture & Recreation, PO Box 8700, Roper St.,
St. John's, NL A0C 1B0

Tel: 709-729-0592; *Fax:* 709-729-7989
Toll-Free: 800-563-6353
info@seethesites.ca
www.seethesites.ca/the-sites/mockbeggar-plantation.aspx
www.facebook.com/ProvincialHistoricSites.NL
Year Founded: 1990 The museum is restored to the 1939 period. Other buildings include a carpenter shop, fish store & cod-liver oil factory from the 18th century.
Kim Shipp, Historic Sites Officer

St. John's: Quidi Vidi Battery Provincial Historic Site
PO Box 8700,
St. John's, NL A1B 4J6

Tel: 709-729-2977
rnchs.ca/tattoo/qvb2.html
The site is now restored to the era of 1812, when it was used to ward off a possible American attack. The Quidi Vidi Battery is located on Cuckhold's Cove Road in Quidi Vidi Village, Newfoundland & Labrador. Tours are available from guides dressed in period costumes, from late June until September.

St. John's: Royal Newfoundland Constabulary Historical Society Archives & Museum (RNCHS)
Royal Newfoundland Constabulary Bldg., PO Box 7247, 1 Fort Townshed,
St. John's, NL A1C 2G2

Tel: 709-729-8000; *Fax:* 709-729-8214
contactrnc@rnc.gov.nl.ca
www.rnchs.ca
Other contact information: Alternate URL:
ngb.chebucto.org/Research/royal.shtml
Collects & preserves early police records, audio tapes of oral history interviews & photographs. Researchers may contact the office of the Chief of Police, indicating their area of interest, to arrange for access to the archives. Open year round.
Hon. Edward Roberts, Chair

St. John's: The Royal St. John's Regatta Museum
PO Box 214,
St. John's, NL A1C 5J2

Tel: 709-576-8921; *Fax:* 709-576-3315
general@stjohnsregatta.com
www.stjohnsregatta.com
www.youtube.com/user/regattacommittee
twitter.com/StJohnsRegatta
www.facebook.com/royalstjohnsregatta
The long history of rowing competition in St. John's, dating back to the early 1800s, is depicted at the Regatta Museum, through photographs, trophies, & other memorabilia. Please contact the Regatta Museum to arrange an appointment to visit.
Paul Rogers, President
Chris Neary, Vice-President

St. John's: St. Thomas' Church Museum
8 Military Rd.,
St. John's, NL A1C 2C4

Tel: 709-576-6632; *Fax:* 709-737-0472
office@st-thomaschurch.com
www.st-thomaschurch.com
Museum located in the basement; church c. 1836

St. John's: Signal Hill National Historic Site of Canada / Lieu historique national du Canada de Signal Hill
PO Box 1268,
St. John's, NL A1C 5M9

Tel: 709-772-5367; *Fax:* 709-772-6302
signal.hill@pc.gc.ca
www.pc.gc.ca/lhn-nhs/nl/signalhill/index.aspx
In 1901, Signal Hill was the reception point of the first transatlantic wireless signal. From the 18th century to World War

II, Signal Hill was also the site of harbour defence for St. John's, Newfoundland. Today, visitors can tour the Visitor Interpretation Centre & visit Cabot Tower to view the Marconi exhibit. The site is open year-round.

St Lawrence: St. Lawrence Miner's Memorial Museum
PO Box 326, Route 220,
St Lawrence, NL A0E 2V0

Tel: 709-873-2222; *Fax:* 709-873-3352
www.townofstlawrence.com/museum.php
Showcases the reality of a miner's life through photographs, clothing & equipment displays.

St. Lunaire-Griquet: L'Anse aux Meadows National Historic Site
PO Box 70,
St. Lunaire-Griquet, NL A0K 2X0

Tel: 709-623-2608; *Fax:* 709-623-2028
viking.lam@pc.gc.ca
www.pc.gc.ca/eng/lhn-nhs/nl/meadows/index.aspx
Includes tours of the replicas of the Norse sod buildings, exhibits about Viking lifestyle & the archaeological discovery of the site, artifacts & blacksmith & weaving demonstrations. Open May-Oct

---

Salvage: Salvage Fishermens' Museum
General Delivery, 52 Mountain View Rd.,
Salvage, NL A0G 3X0

Tel: 709-677-2659
salvage.fishermensmuseum@gmail.com
manl.nf.ca/index.php/newfoundland-labrador-museums/salvage-fishermens-museu
Other contact information: Alternate phone: 709-677-2414
Collection of fishing & domestic artifacts relates to the history & cultural life of Salvage, from the late 19th century to the present. Open daily, Jun-Sept

---

Springdale: Harvey Grant Heritage Centre
50 Main St.,
Springdale, NL A0J 1T0

Tel: 709-637-3439; *Fax:* 709-673-4969
manl.nf.ca/index.php/newfoundland-labrador-museums/central
Year Founded: 1981 Artifacts related to Springdale & the life of Harvey Grant. Open Jun-Aug 11:00-8:00

Torbay: Torbay Museum
PO Box 1160, 1288 Torbay Rd.,
Torbay, NL A1K 1K4

Tel: 709-437-6532
www.torbay.ca/things-to-do/museum
www.facebook.com/TorbayMuseum
Year Founded: 1988 Includes over 2000 artifacts & exhibits about local, religious & military history, fishing, farming, domestic life, & women's work. The collection is dedicated to the preservation and promotion of the Torbay heritage.
Contessa Small, Curator, csmall@torbay.ca

Trepassey: Trepassey Area Museum
PO Box 63, Main Rd.,
Trepassey, NL A0A 4B0

Tel: 709-438-2044
Features artifacts from Amelia Earhart's flight & the community. Open Jul-Aug.

Trinity: Cooperage
Parent: Trinity Historical Society
PO Box 8,
Trinity, NL A0C 2S0

Tel: 709-464-3599
info@trinityhistoricalsociety.com
www.trinityhistoricalsociety.com/cooperage.htm
www.facebook.com/19321685 0915
Year Founded: 2008 Functional living history museum where a working cooper demonstrates the 17th century craft; built in 2007 from an artists rendering of an actual cooperage from that era. The site is open daily from mid-May to mid-October.

Trinity: Court House, Gaol & General Building
Parent: Trinity Historical Society
PO Box 8,
Trinity, NL A0C 2S0

Tel: 709-464-3599
info@trinityhistoricalsociety.com
www.trinityhistoricalsociety.com/court_house_gaol.htm
www.facebook.com/1 93216850915
Year Founded: 2010 Constructed in 1903, the structure is similar to other government buildings of the day; in addition to the court and jail, the building housed the police constable and his family, the Customs House, the Magistrate's Office and the Post & Telegraph Office. The building has been undergoing renovations since 2010.

Trinity: Fort Point Military Site
Parent: Trinity Historical Society
PO Box 8,
Trinity, NL A0C 2S0

Tel: 709-464-3599; *Fax:* 709-464-3599
info@trinityhistoricalsociety.com
www.trinityhistoricalsociety.com/fort_ point.html
twitter.com/historictrinity
www.facebook.com/thsoc
Year Founded: 1744 The site details the history of the fort, c.1746, which was captured by the French in 1762, then rebuilt by the British in 1780, during the American Revolution. Other local history is also explored, such as the salt cod trade, lighthouse keepers & shipwrecks. The site is open daily from mid-May to mid-October.

Trinity: Green Family Forge
Parent: Trinity Historical Society
PO Box 8,
Trinity, NL A0C 2S0

Tel: 709-464-3599
info@trinityhistoricalsociety.com
www.trinityhistoricalsociety.com/green_family_forge.htm
www.facebook.com /193216850915
Year Founded: 1991 Forge originating from between 1895-1900; was restored and opened as a museum in 1991, blacksmith demonstrations located on site. Oopen daily mid-May to mid-Oct.

Trinity: Lester-Garland Premises Provincial Historic Site
Parent: Trinity Historical Society
PO Box 8,
Trinity, NL A0C 2S0

Tel: 709-464-3599
info@trinityhistoricalsociety.com
www.trinityhistoricalsociety.com/lestergarland_house.htm
www.facebook.co m/193216850915
The site serves as an example of the mercantile buissness that existed in Newfoundland and the "Truck System" of the late 18th and 19th centuries. The restored building consists of authentic and reconstructed office furniture c. 1820 in the counting house, while the store section has been restored to the 1910 period with artifacts and reproductions from that time period. Located on West St., Trinity following Rtes. 230 or 239; open daily June - Sept.

Trinity: Trinity Interpretation Centre
PO Box 6, West St,
Trinity, NL A0C 2S0

Tel: 709-464-2064; *Fax:* 709-464-7989
Toll-Free: 800-563-6353
trinity@nf.aibn.com
www.townoftrinity.com
Other contact information: Off Season: 709-729-0592
Once a family home, the building was relocated to the present site in 1991. The centre is operated by the Department of Tourism, Culture and Recreation as an exhibit and information centre on Trinity and the surrounding area.
Gerry Osmond, Manager, Provincial Historic Sites, 709-729-7212, gerryosmond@gov.nl.ca
Joan Kane, Site Supervisor

Trinity: Trinity Museum
Parent: Trinity Historical Society
PO Box 8,
Trinity, NL A0C 2S0

Tel: 709-464-3599
info@trinityhistoricalsociety.com
www.trinityhistoricalsociety.com/trinity_museum.htm
www.facebook.com/193 216850915
Year Founded: 1967 The collection reflects the history of Trinity, & includes fishing, boat building, commercial, & domestic items. The site also features a fire engine shed, which displays an 1811 fire pump. Open Jun-Oct & by appointment at other times during the year.

Twillingate: Durrell Museum & Crafts
PO Box 83, 17 Museum Rd.,
Twillingate, NL A0G 4M0

Tel: 709-884-5537
www.visittwillingate.com/durrellmuseum
www.facebook.co m/DurrellMuseum
Other contact information: Alternate Phone: 709-884-2780
Exhibits include artifacts from WWI & WWII, the fishing industry, mounted polar bear & life in the late 1800s. Open May-Sept.
Lloyd Bulgin, President, lebulgin@hotmail.com

Twillingate: Twillingate Museum & Craft Shop
PO Box 369,
Twillingate, NL A0G 4M0

Tel: 709-884-2825
info@tmacs.ca
www.tmacs.ca
Year Founded: 1973 Twillingate Museum is located in the former
Anglican Church Rectory. Furnishings in the museum reflect the
Victorian era. Exhibits include Inuit, Dorset, & Beothuk First
Nations artifacts. Archives include photographs, family histories,
& cemetery data. Open May-Oct.
Linda Blondin, Contact

Wesleyville: Bonavista North Museum & Gallery
PO Box 257,
Wesleyville, NL A0G 4R0

Tel: 709-536-2110; Fax: 709-536-3039
museum@nf.aibn.com
www.bonavistanorth.blogspot.com
twitter.com/Bonavis taNorth
www.facebook.com/368789463136218
The Bonavista North Museum & Gallery contains photographs,
artifacts, & artwork from the local area. The museum is open
daily Jul-Aug. Appointments can be arranged during the off
season.

Northwest Territories

Territorial Museums

Prince of Wales Northern Heritage Centre (PWNHC)
c/o Government of NWT, PO Box 1320, 4750 48th St.,
Yellowknife, NT X1A 2L9

Tel: 867-767-9347; Fax: 867-873-0205
pwnhc@gov.nt.ca
www.pwnhc.ca
www.instagram.com/northernheritage
twitter.com/nrthrnheritage
www.face book.com/pwnhc
Year Founded: 1979 Located on the shores of Frame Lake, the
Prince of Wales Northern Heritage Centre is open year-round.
Visitors to the centre will discover various exhibits about the
people, places, & natural history of the Northwest Territories.
Sarah Carr-Locke, Director, 867-767-9347,
sarah_carr-locke@gov.nt.ca
Vacant, Manager, Finance, 867-767-9347
Vacant, Curator, Collections, 867-767-9347
Rosalie Scott, Senior Conservator, 867-767-9347,
rosalie_scott@gov.nt.ca

Local Museums

Colville Lake: Colville Lake Museum & Gallery
PO Box 54,
Colville Lake, NT X0E 1L0

Tel: 867-709-2500
spectacularnwt.com/attraction/colville-lake-museum
Museum houses ethnographic artifacts, art gallery & archives;
discovery centre; guided tours; gift shop; part of Colville Lake
Lodge.

Fort Good Hope: Dene Museum & Archives
General Delivery,
Fort Good Hope, NT X0E 0H0

Tel: 403-598-2331
The museum's collection includes photographs of area elders &
residents, oral history tapes, written materials (including
transcripts of tapes), & printed material.

Fort Smith: Northern Life Museum & Cultural Centre
(NLMCC)
PO Box 420, 110 King St.,
Fort Smith, NT X0E 0P0

Tel: 867-872-2859; Fax: 867-872-5808
info@nlmcc.ca
www.nlmcc.ca
twitter.com/NorthernLifeMus
www.facebook.com/NLMCC
Year Founded: 1972 Collection, preservation & presentation of
northern native & early white settlement history. Artifacts include
clothing, pioneer & trade items, & work of the Inuit, Inuvialuit,
Dene & Metis. Open Mon-Fri
Daniel Stewart, Manager
Rachel Dell, Curator

Hay River: Hay River Heritage Centre
69-102nd Ave.,
Hay River, NT X0E 0R9

Tel: 867-874-3872
The museum has collections in human history, natural sciences,
the arts & an archive of photos, maps, prints & drawings, &
manuscripts.

Holman: Holman Museum
PO Box 162,
Holman, NT X0E 0S0

Tel: 867-396-3804; Fax: 867-396-3054
The museum's collection features Inuit artifacts from the Holman
area.

Norman Wells: Norman Wells Historical Centre
Parent: Norman Wells Historical Society
PO Box 145, 23 Mackenzie Dr.,
Norman Wells, NT X0E 0V0

Tel: 867-587-2415; Fax: 867-587-2469
canol.trail@theedge.nw.ca
www.normanwellsmuseum.com
www.facebook.com/N ormanWellsHistoricalSociety
Year Founded: 1989 Dene cultural artifacts; geological history;
WWI & Canol Project interpretation; Great Bear Lake &
MacKenzie River explorers; local archives. Open year round
Sarah Colbeck, Manager/Curator

Nova Scotia

Provincial Museums

Fisheries Museum of the Atlantic
Lunenburg Waterfront, PO Box 1363, 68 Bluenose Dr.,
Lunenburg, NS B0J 2C0

fisheriesmuseum.novascotia.ca
www.instagram.com/fisheriesmuseum
twitter.com/FisheriesMuseum
www.face book.com/FisheriesMuseumoftheAtlantic
Year Founded: 1967 Part of the Nova Scotia Museum; features
historic buildings with 3 floors of exhibits & activities: Millenium
Aquarium; Bluenose Memorabilia; Fishermen's Memorial Room;
August Gales 1926-1927; Bank Fishery Gallery; Rum Running;
life in fishing communities; Hall of Inshore Fisheries; fisherman's
store; Marine Engine Room, whales, boat shop; schooner
Theresa E. Connor; side trawler Cape Sable; part of the Nova
Scotia Museum.
Adrian Morrison, Curator, Collections & Research,
adrian.morrison@novascotia.ca

**Maritime Museum of the Atlantic / Musée Maritime
d'Atlantique**
1675 Lower Water St.,
Halifax, NS B3J 1S3

Tel: 902-424-7490
maritimemuseum.novascotia.ca
www.youtube.com/user/NovaScotiaMuseum n s_mma
twitter.com/ns_mma
www.facebook. com/maritimemuseum
Year Founded: 1982 Marine history branch of the Nova Scotia
Museum; on waterfront; marine artifacts, memorabilia from the
Titanic, Halifax explosion exhibit, restored ship chandlery,
extensive small craft collection; library & gift shop; Vessel CSS
Acadia at museum wharf.
Kim Reinhardt, General Manager, 902-424-6440,
kim.reinhardt@novascotia.ca
Roger Marsters, Curator, Marine History, 902-424-6442,
roger.marsters@novascotia.ca

Nova Scotia Museum (NSM)
NS Communities, Culture & Heritage
1747 Brunswick St., 3rd Fl.,
Halifax, NS B3J 2R5

Tel: 902-424-2170; Fax: 902-424-0560
museum@novascotia.ca
museum.novascotia.ca
www.instagram.com/novascotiamuseum
twitter.com/ns_museum
www.facebook. com/novascotiamuseum
Year Founded: 1868 The Nova Scotia Museum family includes
28 museums across the province, including Nova Scotia
Museum of Natural History and Maritime Museum of the
Atlantic.The museum oversees over 2oo historic buildings, which
house collections of approximately 1 million artifacts and
specimens. The museum is part of the Nova Scotia Department
of Communities, Culture and Heritage.
Stephanie Smith, Executive Director, Archives, Libraries &
Museums, 902-424-7344

Local Museums

Amherst: Cumberland County Museum & Archives
150 Church St.,
Amherst, NS B4H 3C4

Tel: 902-667-2561
www.cumberlandcountymuseum.com
Year Founded: 1973 Exhibits & archives on the natural, social &
industrial heritage of Cumberland County; located in the 1838
heritage home of Robert Barry Dickey, a Father of
Confederation; the archives houses genealogical & other

material; fine art collection by County artists; well maintained
gardens surround the museum. Open year round.
Natasha Richard, Manager/Curator

Amherst: Nova Scotia Highlanders Regimental
Museum
Col. James Layton Ralson Armoury, 36 Acadia St.,
Amherst, NS B4H 3L6

Tel: 902-661-6797; Fax: 902-667-6551
nshmuseum@eastlink.ca
nshighlanders.fav.cc
Exhibits military artifacts such as uniforms, badges & vehicles.
C.W.O. (Ret'd) Ray Coulson, Curator C.D.

Annapolis Royal: Fort Anne National Historic Site /
Lieu historique national du Fort-Anne
PO Box 9,
Annapolis Royal, NS B0S 1A0

Tel: 902-532-2397; Fax: 902-532-2232
information@pc.gc.ca
www.pc.gc.ca/eng/lhn-nhs/ns/fortanne/index.aspx
Other contact information: Off-Season Phone: 902-532-2321
Year Founded: 1917 French & English period fortifications,
1629-1854; exhibits; open daily 9:00 - 5:30, July and August.
Hours are Tu - Sa 9:00 - 5:30 during June and September.

Annapolis Royal: O'Dell House Museum
Parent: Annapolis Heritage Society
PO Box 503, 136 Saint George St.,
Annapolis Royal, NS B0S 1A0

Tel: 902-532-7754; Fax: 902-532-0700
annapolisheritage@gmail.com
www.annapolisheritagesociety.com/museums/ode ll.html
www.annapolisroyalheritage.blogspot.com
twitter.com/odellmuseum
The museum is housed in a stagecoach inn & tavern from
around 1869 that is the former home of Nova Scotia Pony
Express rider, Corey O'Dell & his family. Among the displays are
items from Annapolis Royal's ship-building & sea-faring history.
The Annapolis Heritage Society's Genealogy Centre's Archives
& Collections Centre is also located at O'Dell House Museum.
The Centre contains local histories, vital statistics for Annapolis
& Digby counties, deeds, & church, cemetery & probate records.
Jane DeWolfe, Chair, Annapolis Heritage Society

Annapolis Royal: Port-Royal National Historic Site of
Canada / Lieu historique national de Port-Royal
PO Box 9,
Annapolis Royal, NS B0S 1A0

Tel: 902-532-2898; Fax: 902-532-2232
information@pc.gc.ca
www.pc.gc.ca/lhn-nhs/ns/portroyal/index.aspx
Other contact information: Off-season Phone: 902-532-2321
(mid-Oct. to mid-May)
The national historic site on the coast of Nova Scotia is a
reconstruction of early 17th-century buildings. The buildings
represent a French colony from the era. The site features
costumed interpreters & demonstrations to reflect life in one of
the earliest settlements in North America.

Annapolis Royal: Sinclair Inn Museum
Parent: Annapolis Heritage Society
230 Lower St. George St.,
Annapolis Royal, NS B0S 1A0

Tel: 902-532-0996
www.annapolisheritagesociety.com/museums/sinclair.html
Other contact information: Off-season Phone: 902-532-7754
Built in the early 1700s, this National Historic Site is the earliest
surviving Acadian building in Canada.

Antigonish: Antigonish Heritage Museum
20 East Main St.,
Antigonish, NS B2G 2E9

Tel: 902-863-6160
antheritage@parl.ns.ca
www.parl.ns.ca/aheritage
twitter.com/antheritage
www.facebook.com/Anti gonishHeritageMuseum
Local history. Open year round.
Allan Armsworty, Chair
Jocelyn Gillis, Curator

Arichat: Lenoir Forge Museum
PO Box 223, 708 Veterans Memorial Dr.,
Arichat, NS B0E 1A0

Tel: 902-226-9364; Fax: 902-226-1919
islemadamehistoricalsociety@gmail.com
imhs.ca/le-noir-forge-museum
Community museum; local artifacts & houses a working forge.
Open June Mon-Fri 10:00-5:00; Jul-Aug Tue-Sat 10:00-5:00,
Sun 1:00-5:00

Baddeck: Alexander Graham Bell National Historic Site of Canada / Lieu historique national Alexander-Graham-Bell du Canada
PO Box 159, 559 Chebucto Street,
Baddeck, NS B0E 1B0

Tel: 902-295-2069; *Fax:* 902-295-3496
information@pc.gc.ca
www.pc.gc.ca/lhn-nhs/ns/grahambell/index.aspx
twitter.com/ParksCanada_NS
www.facebook.com/AGBNHS

Presents Dr. Bell's life & work, with emphasis on his accomplishments in Baddeck; open year round; Nov. 1 - Apr. 30 site visits by arrangement. The site is located on Chebucto St. (Rte 205), on the eastern edge of Baddeck.

Baddeck: Canso Islands National Historic Site / Iles-Canso Lieux historiques
PO Box 159,
Baddeck, NS B0E 1B0

Tel: 902-295-2069; *Fax:* 902-295-3496
information@pc.gc.ca
www.pc.gc.ca/eng/lhn-nhs/ns/canso/index.aspx
www. facebook.com/cansoislands

Other contact information: Summer Phone: 902-366-3136
The Canso Islands were a fishing base for the French during the 16th & 17th centuries. The British used the fishing port during the first half of the 18th century. The Islands were the scene of several battles between the French & English & the Mi'kmaq. In 1744, the Canso settlement was destroyed by the French. The visitor centre & interpretive trail are open from June 1st to September 15th.

Baddeck: Marconi National Historic Site of Canada / Lieu historique national Marconi du Canada
c/o Alexander Graham Bell National Historic Site, PO Box 159,
Baddeck, NS B0E 1B0

Tel: 902-295-2069; *Fax:* 902-295-3496
information@pc.qc.ca
www.pc.gc.ca/lhn-nhs/ns/marconi.aspx
www.facebook .com/MarconiNHS

Other contact information: Summer Phone: 902-842-2530
The site marks where Guglielmo Marconi initiated the age of global communications in 1902 by transmitting the first wireless message across the Atlantic Ocean. Visitors can see the Wireless Hall of Fame and walk to the original transmission station. Open June 1 - Sept.

Balmoral Mills: Balmoral Grist Mill
544 Peter Macdonald Rd.,
Balmoral Mills, NS B0K 1V0

Tel: 902-657-3016; *Fax:* 902-657-2606
balmoralgristmill.novascotia.ca
Operational 19th century mill. Open Jun-Oct daily.
Darrell Burke, Site Manager, 902-657-3017, burked@gov.ns.ca

Barrington: Barrington Woolen Mill Museum
Parent: Cape Sable Historical Society
2368 Hwy. 3,
Barrington, NS B0W 1E0

Tel: 902-637-2185
woolenmill.novascotia.ca
Year Founded: 1968 A preserved wool mill from the 1800s; part of the Nova Scotia Museum; open June-Sept.

Barrington: Cape Sable Historical Society Centre
Old Court House, Barrington Head, PO Box 67, 2401 Hwy. 3,
Barrington, NS B0W 1E0

Tel: 902-637-2185
barmuseumcomplex@eastlink.ca
www.capesablehistoricalsociety.com
Year Founded: 1937 The Cape Sable Historical Society illustrates the history of Shelburne & Yarmouth Counties by collecting historical documents, genealogical records, & other items, & preserving historical sites. Open daily Jun-Sep

Barrington: Old Meeting House Museum
2408 Hwy. 3,
Barrington, NS B0W 1E0

Tel: 902-637-2185
meetinghouse.novascotia.ca
A preserved New England-style meeting house c.1765; part of the Nova Scotia Museum group. Open June - Sept.

Bedford: Atlantic Canada Aviation Museum (ACAM) / Musée D'aviation des provinces Atlantique
PO Box 44006, 1658 Bedford Hwy.,
Bedford, NS B4A 3X5

Tel: 902-873-3773
info@atlanticcanadaaviation.com
www.atlanticcanadaaviation.com
atlanticcanadaaviationmuseum.wordpress.com
www.facebook.com/ACAMMuseum

Other contact information: Off season phone: 902-446-7606
Year Founded: 1977 The Atlantic Canada Aviation Museum preserves the aviation heritage of Atlantic Canada. The aircraft collection includes the Bell 47-J-2 Ranger Helicopter, the CF-5A Freedom Fighter, a Harvard Mk II, & a CF-104 Starfighter. The museum is open from mid-May to mid-October. At other times, tours can be arranged.
Michael White, Public Affairs Officer, 902-446-7606

Bedford: Scott Manor House
Parent: Fort Sackville Foundation
15 Fort Sackville Rd.,
Bedford, NS B4A 2G6

Tel: 902-832-2336
www.scottmanorhouse.ca
The house dates from 1749 & was still a private residence until 1992. It is the only full two and a half storey, gambrel-roofed colonial structure in Nova Scotia and is a registered Provincial and Municipal Heritage Property. The former Fort Sackville is located nearby & the Manor House contains artifacts excavated from that site.

Berwick: Apple Capital Interpretive Centre
Parent: Apple Capital Museum Society
PO Box 730, 173 Commercial St.,
Berwick, NS B0P 1E0

Tel: 902-538-9229
berwickvic@hotmail.com
www.acmuseum.ednet.ns.ca

Other contact information: Off-season: 902-538-4016
Artifacts & information relating to the apple industry of Berwick & District.

Bridgetown: James House Museum
PO Box 645, 12 Queen St.,
Bridgetown, NS B0S 1C0

Tel: 902-665-4530
www.jameshousemuseum.com
www.instagram.com/bridgetownahs
twitter.com/bridgetownahs
www.facebook.com/jameshousemuseum1835

Other contact information: Genealogy contact: 902-825-1287
Year Founded: 1979 James House was built in 1835 by Richard James, a member of the British Army who served in England & India. The house was donated to the Bridgetown & Area Historical Society. It became a Provincial Heritage Building, & now operates as the museum for the town of Bridgetown. James House features the Memorial Military Museum, which is sponsored by the Royal Canadian Legion, Branch 33. The museum is open from June to August daily or by appointment from September to May.

Bridgewater: DesBrisay Museum & Exhibition Centre
130 Jubilee Rd.,
Bridgewater, NS B4V 3X9

Tel: 902-543-4033; *Fax:* 902-543-4713
museum@bridgewater.ca
www.desbrisaymuseum.ca
www.youtube.com/desbrisaybridgewater
www.facebook.com/190907454254694
Year Founded: 1902 Local history & art. Open year round.
Barbara Thompson, Director,
barbara.thompson@bridgewater.ca
Linda Bedford, Curator, linda.bedford@bridgewater.ca

Bridgewater: Wile Carding Mill Museum
c/o DesBrisay Museum, 242 Victoria Rd.,
Bridgewater, NS B4V 3X9

Tel: 902-543-8233; *Fax:* 902-543-4713
wilemill@bridgewater.ca
cardingmill.novascotia.ca
www.facebook.com/447 062668657408
Year Founded: 1974 Last surviving plant of a 19th-century water-powered industrial park. Open Jun-Sep daily

Canso: Whitman House Museum & Tourist Bureau
Parent: Canso Historical Society
c/o Canso Historical Society, PO Box 128, 1297 Union St.,
Canso, NS B0H 1H0

Tel: 902-366-2170; *Fax:* 902-366-3093
tgis@atcon.com
whitmania.com/whitmanhousemuseum.htm

Year Founded: 1975 Whitman House was built in 1885. The first resident was C.H. Whitman, a Baptist minister. The operation of the Whitman House Museum is now overseen by the Canso Historical Society. Exhibits at the Whitman House Museum depict the history of the town of Canso & eastern Guysborough County, & Canso Harbour. The museum is open from June 1st to September 30th. At other times of the year, appointments may be arranged.
Martha Kavanaugh, Curator, 902-366-2170
Joseph Walsh, Society Chairperson, 902-366-2329

Cape North: North Highlands Community Museum & Culture Centre
29263 The Cabot Trail,
Cape North, NS B0C 1G0

Tel: 902-383-2579
nhco2579@gmail.com
www.northhighlandsmuseum.ca
www.youtube.com/user/nhcmuseum
twitter.com/NHCmuseum
www.facebook.com/ northhighlandscommunitymuseum
The history & culture of northern Cape Breton Island is displayed through artifacts & documents. The collection includes maritime artifacts, such as shipwreck booty, schoolroom materials, doctor's instruments & farming tools. Open Jun-Oct daily
Ron Nickel, Co-Chair
Ken Murray, Co-Chair
Meghan Dudley, Manager

Cape Sabler Island: Archelaus Smith Museum & Historical Society
PO Box 190, 915 Hwy 330,
Cape Sabler Island, NS B0W 1P0

Tel: 902-745-2642
archsmithmuseum@gmail.com
www.archelaus.org
www.facebook.com/ArchelausSmithMuseum
Portrays the history of Cape Sable Island including fishing techniques & gear, boat displays, shipwrecks, lives of sea captains, items from old kitchens, paintings by local artists, geneological & other historical records.
Blanche O'Connell, President,
blancherossoconnell@hotmail.com

Centreville: Charles Macdonald Concrete House Museum
19 Saxon St.,
Centreville, NS B0P 1J0

Tel: 902-678-3177
info@concretehouse.ca
www.concretehouse.ca
House originally belonging to Nova Scotian artist Charles Macdonald, now converted into a museum, art gallery & sculpture garden. Open daily in season.

Cherry Brook: Black Cultural Centre for Nova Scotia (BCC)
10 Cherry Brook Rd,
Cherry Brook, NS B2Z 1A8

Tel: 902-434-6223; *Fax:* 902-434-2306
Toll-Free: 800-465-0767
contact@bccns.com
www.bccns.com
www.youtube.com/user/bccnsvideo
twitter.com/BCC_NS
www.facebook.com/18 8265867860941
Year Founded: 1983 Programs at the cultural education centre have include guided tours, music, plays, workshops, & lectures. Winter hours: by appointment. Summer hours: Tu - F 10:00 - 4:00, Sa - M 12:00 - 3:00.
Russell Grosse, Executive Director
Rielle Williams, Cultural Tour Developer

Chester: Chester Train Station
Parent: Chester Municipal Heritage Society
PO Box 628, 133 Central St.,
Chester, NS B0J 1J0

Tel: 902-275-3842
www.chesterbound.com/heritage.htm
www.facebook.com/180126828677505
The site contains a visitor information centre, Train Station Gallery, Forman Hawboldt exhibit & Explore Oak Island display. Oak Island is located on the south shore of Nova Scotia, and is the home of the so-called "Money Pit," which has been the site of treasure hunting for over 200 years.
Carol Nauss, Chair, Chester Municipal Heritage Society
Danny Hennigar, Contact, Oak Island

Chester: Lordly Estate Municipal Museum
Parent: Chester Municipal Heritage Society
PO Box 628, 133 Central St.,
Chester, NS B0J 1J0

Tel: 902-275-3842
lordlyhouse@ns.aliantzinc.ca
www.chester-municipal-heritage-society.ca
www.youtube.com/user/lordlymuseum
www.facebook.com/lordlyhousemuseum/
Other contact information: After-hours Phone: 902-275-3826
The Georgian house was built c.1806 & was the first municipal building of Municipality in the District of Chester. Chester Municipal Heritage Society also operates the Chester Train Station.
Roberta Harrington, Contact

Church Point: Musée Église Sainte-Marie Museum
PO Box 28, 1713 Hwy. 1,
Church Point, NS B0W 1M0

Tel: 902-769-2378; *Fax:* 902-769-0048
www.museeeglisesaintemariemuseum.ca
Largest wooden church in North America. Open May-Oct daily

Clementsport: Old St. Edward's Anglican Loyalist Church Museum
PO Box 171, 34 Old Post Rd.,
Clementsport, NS B0S 1E0

Tel: 902-638-8081
www.facebook.com/555674361203912
Original Loyalist, Old St. Edward's Anglican Church & Cemetery
Wayne Linda, Contact, wayne.linda@eastlink.ca

Cole Harbour: Cole Harbour Heritage Farm Museum
Parent: Cole Harbour Royal Heritage Society
471 Poplar Dr.,
Cole Harbour, NS B2W 4L2

Tel: 902-434-0222
farm.museum@ns.aliantzinc.ca
www.coleharbourfarmmuseum.ca
twitter.com/coleharbourfarm
www.facebook.com/ColeHarbourHeritageFarmMuseum
A community museum dedicated to preserving and interpreting Cole Harbour's agricultural past. It is owned and operated by the Cole Harbour Rural Heritage Society and is open daily from May 15 - Oct. 15, or by appointment.
Elizabeth Corser, Volunteer

Dartmouth: Dartmouth Heritage Museum
Parent: Dartmouth Heritage Museum Society
26 Newcastle St.,
Dartmouth, NS B2Y 3M5

Tel: 902-464-2300; *Fax:* 902-464-8210
info@dartmouthmuseum.ca
www.dartmouthheritagemuseum.ca
www.facebook.com/205574426126756
The museum was established in 1967 as a Canadian Centennial Project by the City of Dartmouth. Although the Halifax Regional Municipality now owns the collection and both Historic Houses, the Dartmouth Museum Society continues to develp, manage, promote, operate and administer the properties and the collections. The two locations are Evergreen House & Quaker House.
Bonnie Elliott, Executive Director, 902-464-2916,
elliottb@bellaliant.com
Crystal Martin, Curator, 902-464-2916, martinc@bellaliant.com

Debert: Debert Military Museum
Parent: Debert Military History Society (DMHS)
PO Box 154, 35 Acadia Ave.,
Debert, NS B0M 1G0

Tel: 902-662-2860
debert.museum@ns.sympatico.ca
debertmilitaryhistorysociety.weebly.com
Military exhibits. Open May-Aug Tue-Sun 10:00-4:00; Sept Fri-Sun 1:00-4:00.
Michael Taylor, President, 902-662-3875

Denmark: Sutherland Steam Mill Museum
Parent: Nova Scotia Museum
c/o Balmoral Grist Mill, 3169 Denmark Station Rd.,
Denmark, NS B0K 1V0

Tel: 902-657-3365; *Fax:* 902-657-2606
sutherlandsteammill.novascotia.ca
Restored steam woodworking mill. Open daily Jun-Sep
Darrell Burke, Site Manager, 902-657-3017, burked@gov.ns.ca

Digby: Admiral Digby Museum
PO Box 1644, 95 Montague Row,
Digby, NS B0V 1A0

Tel: 902-245-6322
admuseum@ns.sympatico.ca
admiraldigbymuseum.ca
Other contact information: Geneology E-mail:
adgen1@ns.aliantzinc.ca
Museum is housed in a Georgian-style home & is named for Rear Admiral Robert Digby. On display are period rooms, furnishings & artifacts relating to the history of Digby; costumes; Marine Room with charts, ship models, & navigational equipment; photographs; online gift shop; online archives which include family registers & other items of interest to genealogical & historical researchers. Open mid-June - mid-Oct.; two days a week in winter
Gail Hersey, President

East Lake Ainslie: MacDonald House Museum
Parent: Lake Ainslie Historical Society
3458 Hwy. 395,
East Lake Ainslie, NS B0E 3M0

Tel: 902-258-3317
lahistorical@seasidehighspeed.com
www.seasidehighspeed.com/~p.maclean
The site contains the MacDonald House Museum, Glenmore School & Display Barn. Open all year from Tuesday - Sunday.

Englishtown: Great Hall of The Clans, Highland Pioneers Museum
Parent: The Gaelic College
PO Box 80, 51779 Cabot Trail,
Englishtown, NS B0C 1H0

Tel: 902-295-3411; *Fax:* 902-295-2912
info@gaeliccollege.edu
www.gaeliccollege.edu
www.youtube.com/user/gaeliccollege
twitter.com/GaelicCollege
www.faceb ook.com/gaeliccollege
Open daily June - Sept.

Glace Bay: Cape Breton Miners' Museum
PO Box 310, 17 Museum St.,
Glace Bay, NS B1A 5T8

Tel: 902-849-4522
www.minersmuseum.com
twitter.com/CBMinersMuseum
www.facebook.com/CapeBretonMinersMuseumGB
The Cape Breton Miners' Museum tells the story of the area's history of coal mining. Visitors may tour the Ocean Deeps Colliery, which is a coal mine situated beneath the museum building. Exhibits include coal mining equipment. Research inquiries will be responded to by museum staff. The museum also features the Men of the Deeps Theatre.

Glace Bay: Glace Bay Heritage Museum
Parent: Glace Bay Heritage Museum Society
14 McKeen St.,
Glace Bay, NS B1A 5B9

Tel: 902-842-5345
office@oldtownhallglacebay.ca
www.oldtownhallglacebay.ca
www.facebook.com/367848499982
Located in Glace Bay's Old Town Hall; the museum creates temporary theme-based exhibits dedicated to the town's founding industries: coal mining and fishing. Open April - December.

Grand Pre: Grand-Pré National Historic Site of Canada
2205 Grand-Pré Rd.,
Grand Pre, NS B0P 1M0

Tel: 902-542-3631
info@visitgrandpre.ca
www.grand-pre.com
www.facebook.com/DestinationGrandPre
Year Founded: 1997 Bilingual guides interpret history of the Acadians; open daily May 1 - Oct. 30; entrance fee
Victor Tétrault, Executive Director

Granville Ferry: North Hills Museum
Parent: Annapolis Heritage Society
PO Box 503, 5065 Granville Rd.,
Granville Ferry, NS B0S 1A1

Tel: 902-532-2168
northhills.novascotia.ca
Late 18th-century farmhouse which serves as the setting for the collection of Georgian furniture, ceramics, glass, silver & paintings of former owner Robert Patterson. Open Jun-Oct daily

Greenwood: Greenwood Military Aviation Museum (GMAM)
PO Box 786, 1 Ward Rd.,
Greenwood, NS B0P 1N0

Tel: 902-765-1494; *Fax:* 902-765-1261
wingmuseum@bellaliant.com
www.gmam.ca
twitter.com/gmamuseum
www.face book.com/GMAM.CA
Year Founded: 1995 The museum contains permanent and temporary exhibits that chronicle its beginnings as an RAF Station in 1942, to its present day status as the largest airbase in Atlantic Canada.
Robert Johnson, General Manager, 902-765-1492, Fax: 902-765-1261, robert.johnson9@forces.gc.ca
Bryan Nelson, Curator, 902-765-1492, Fax: 902-765-1261, dndwingmuseum@bellaliant.com

Guysborough: Old Court House Museum & Information Centre
Parent: Guysborough Historical Society
c/o Guysborough Historical Society, PO Box 232,
Guysborough, NS B0H 1N0

Tel: 902-533-4008
guysborough.historical@ns.sympatico.ca
www.guysborough historicalsociety.ca
Open June - Oct.
Sandra Grant, Curator

Halifax: Africville National Historic Site
Parent: Africville Genealogy Society
Halifax, NS

www.africville.ca
www.facebook.com/africville
Accessible year round
Irvine Carvery, President, Africville Genealogy Society,
irvine@africville.ca

Halifax: Army Museum Halifax Citadel
Cavalier Bldg., Halifax Citadel National Historic Site, PO Box 9080 A,
Halifax, NS B3K 5M7

Tel: 902-422-5979; *Fax:* 902-426-4228
armymuseum@ns.aliantzinc.ca
www.armymuseumhalifax.ca/
twitter.com/army museumhfx
www.facebook.com/155451351199603
Year Founded: 1953 The Army Museum preserves & promotes the military heritage of Atlantic Canada. Displays, including uniforms, decorations, weapons & firearms, are related to the British, Canadian Regular Force & Militia. The museum is open from May to Oct.

Halifax: Halifax Citadel National Historic Site of Canada
PO Box 9080 A,
Halifax, NS B3K 5M7

Tel: 902-426-5080; *Fax:* 902-426-4228
halifax.citadel@pc.gc.ca
www.pc.gc.ca/eng/lhn-nhs/ns/halifax/index.aspx
twitter.com/ParksCanada_NS
www.facebook.com/ParksCanada
The Citadel was completed in 1856 & was the fourth in a series of British forts on the site. Now the Citadel serves as a national landmark commemorating Halifax's role as a key naval station in the British Empire. The historic site features a living history program with the 78th Highlanders & the precision of the Royal Artillery.

Halifax: HMCS Sackville
PO Box 99000 Forces,
Halifax, NS B3K 5X5

Tel: 902-429-2132; *Fax:* 902-427-1346
execdir@canadasnavalmemorial.ca
canadasnavalmemorial.ca
vimeo.com/user7544880
twitter.com/HMCSSACKVILLE1
www.facebook.com/254372034574664
Other contact information: Winter Phone: 902-427-2837
Year Founded: 1985 Canada's Naval Memorial; WWII corvette museum; HMCS Dockyard
Commodore (Ret'd) Bruce Belliveau, Chair,
chair@canadasnavalmemorial.ca
LCdr. (Ret'd) Jim Reddy, Director/Commanding Officer,
co@canadasnavalmemorial.ca
Doug Thomas, Executive Director,
execdir@canadasnavalmemorial.ca

Halifax: Maritime Command Museum / Musée du Commandement Maritime
Admiralty House, PO Box 99000 Forces, 2729 Gottingen St, Halifax, NS B3K 5X5
Tel: 902-721-8250; Fax: 902-721-8541
marcommuseum@forces.gc.ca
Year Founded: 1974 Displays representing facets of the Canadian Military. The collection consists of a research library, uniforms, model ships, medals, badges, ships' bells & other memorabilia associated with naval life. Open year round

Halifax: Museum of Natural History (MNH)
1747 Summer St., Halifax, NS B3H 3A6
Tel: 902-424-7353; Fax: 902-424-0747
naturalhistory.novascotia.ca
www.instagram.com/mnhnovascotia/
twitter.com/MNH_Naturalists
www.facebook.com/mnhnovascotia
Other contact information: Collections, Fax: 902-424-0560
Part of the Nova Scotia Museum group, the Museum of Natural history features galleries on archeology, geology, mammals, aquatic life & more. It also has a collection of live animals native to Nova Scotia, including 90-year-old Gus the Tortoise, who originally comes from Florida.
Calum Ewing, Director, Nova Scotia Museum, 902-424-7715
John Kemp, Manager, Museum of Natural History, 902-424-6515
Jeff Gray, Curator, Marketing & Communications, 902-424-6511, grayjr@gov.ns.ca

Halifax: Nova Scotia Sport Hall of Fame (NSSHF)
#446, 1800 Argyle St., Halifax, NS B3J 3N8
Tel: 902-421-1266; Fax: 902-425-1148
sporthalloffame@eastlink.ca
www.novascotiasporthalloffame.com
www.linkedin.com/company/nova-scotia-sport-hall-of-fame
twitter.com/NSSHF
www.facebook.com/116064731766960
The Hall of Fame honours Nova Scotians who have made an impact on sports during the past 100 years. Inductees are added to the Hall of Fame each year, during The Hall of Fame Induction Night.
Bill Robinson, Chief Executive Officer, bill@nsshf.com
Shane Mailman, Manager, Programs & Facility, shane@nsshf.com
Karolyn Sevcik, Manager, Administration & Special Events, karolyn@nsshf.com

Halifax: Prince of Wales Tower National Historic Site of Canada
c/o Halifax Citadel National Historic Site, PO Box 9080 A, Halifax, NS B3K 5M7
Tel: 902-426-5080; Fax: 902-426-4228
halifax.citadel@pc.gc.ca
www.pc.gc.ca/lhn-nhs/ns/prince/index.aspx
The Prince of Wales Tower was built in 1796 & 1797. Its purpose was to protect the British from French attack. Over 200 years later, visitors will discover exhibits which show the tower's history. The Tower is open from the beginning of July to the end of August.

Halifax: Thomas McCulloch Museum
Biology Dept., Life Science Centre, Dalhousie University, 1355 Oxford St. Rm 827, Halifax, NS B3H 4J1
Tel: 902-494-3515; Fax: 902-494-3736
dal.ca/faculty/science/biology/research/facilities
Year Founded: 1883 Collection of mounted birds, artifacts, Lorenzen ceramic mushrooms, shells & insects; marine & freshwater aquaria; occasional temporary exhibits. Open weekdays

Halifax: York Redoubt National Historic Site of Canada
c/o Halifax Citadel National Historic Site, PO Box 9080 A, Halifax, NS B3K 5M7
Tel: 902-426-5080; Fax: 902-426-4228
halifax.citadel@pc.gc.ca
www.pc.gc.ca/lhn-nhs/ns/york/index.aspx
York Redoubt was established in 1793 to defend the Halifax Harbour. Today, it is a National Historic Site of Canada, which is part of the Halifax Defence Complex. The site is open year-round.

Hantsport: Churchill House & Marine Memorial Room
c/o Hantsport & Area Historical Society, PO Box 525, Hantsport, NS B0P 1P0
Tel: 902-684-3461
hantsportareahistoricalsociety@gmail.com
nsgna.ednet.ns.ca/hantsport/ChurchillHouse.html

Located at 6 Main St., Hantsport; open daily July - Sept., or by appt.; classic Victorian architecture; documents local shipbuilding history

Harbourview, Port Hood: Chestico Museum & Historical Society
PO Box 144, 8095 Rte. 19, Harbourview, Port Hood, NS B0E 2W0
Tel: 902-787-2244
chesticoplace.com
twitter.com/chesticomuseum
www.facebook.com/106197469418363
Year Founded: 1986 Located in Harbourview, the museum houses artifacts from the local community; house histories, historical events, people of the Port Hood area; a gift shop, tea room and special programming.
Susan Mallette, Director

La Have: LaHave Islands Marine Museum
PO Box 69, 100 LaHave Islands Rd., La Have, NS B0R 1C0
Tel: 902-688-2973
limms@auracom.com
www.lahaveislandsmarinemuseum.ca
www.facebook.com/LaHave.Islands.Marine. Museum
Historical artifacts & information about the history of in-shore fisheries & local life. Open Jun-Sep
Douglas Berrigan, President
Kathy Sullivan, Curator

Inverness: Inverness Miners Museum
Parent: Inverness Historical Society
PO Box 598, 62 Lower Railway St., Inverness, NS B0E 1N0
Tel: 902-258-3291
www.inverness-ns.ca/inverness-miners-museum.html
Exhibits work that illustrates mining history & the life of miners. Open Jun-Oct 10:00-6:00
Terry MacDonald, Curator, 902-258-2877

Iona: Highland Village Museum / An Clachan Gàidhealach
4119 Hwy. 223, Iona, NS B2C 1A3
Tel: 902-725-2272; Fax: 902-725-2227
Toll-Free: 866-442-3542
highlandvillage@gov.ns.ca
highlandvillage.novascotia.ca
instagram.com/highland_village;
youtube.com/NSHighlandVillage
twitter.com/highlandv
www.facebook.com/highlandvillagemusuem
Year Founded: 1959 The museum's mission is to collect & preserve the Gaelic heritage of Nova Scotia, with a focus on advancing the language. Included on site are: interpretation centre & museum, carding mill, 1880-1900 frame house, schoolhouse, forge, country store, barn, frame house (1830-1875), log cabin, stone (black) house, outdoor performance centre. There is also an extensive database of genealogical information. The museum is open June - Oct., 9:30-5:30 daily. Part of the Nova Scotia Museum.
Rodney Chaisson, Director, rodney.chaisson@novascotia.ca

Jeddore Oyster Pond: Fisherman's Life Museum
58 Navy Pool Loop, Jeddore Oyster Pond, NS B0J 1P0
Tel: 902-889-2053
fishermanslife.novascotia.ca
In a restored house that used to belong to an early 20th century fishing family, the musuem depicts the ways of life in rural Nova Scotia at the turn of the 19th century. A part of the Nova Scotia Museum group; open daily June 1 - Oct. 15.
Martha Monk, Site Manager, monkma@gov.ns.ca

Kentville: Blair House Museum
c/o N.S. Fruit Growers' Association, Kentville Agricultural Centre, 32 Main St., Kentville, NS B4N 1J5
Tel: 902-678-1093; Fax: 902-678-1567
www.nsapples.com/museumb.htm
Year Founded: 1981 The Blair House Museum was opened by the Nova Scotia Fruit Growers' Association. The purpose of the museum is the preservation & presentation of the history of the apple growing industry. The Agriculture Canada wing of the museum displays past & present research conducted at the station. The museum is located in a building constructed in 1911, which was the residence of the research station's first superintendent, Dr. William Saxby Blair.
Dela Erith, Executive Director, Nova Scotia Fruit Growers' Association, derith@nsapples.com
Marjo Balknap, Services Coordinator, mbelknap@nsapples.com
Teresa Rooney, Bookkeeper, trooney@nsapples.com

Kentville: Kings County Museum
Parent: Kings Historical Society
37 Cornwallis St., Kentville, NS B4N 2E2
Tel: 902-678-6237; Fax: 902-678-2764
info@kingscountymuseum.ca
kingscountymuseum.ca
www.facebook.com/kingscountymuseum
Year Founded: 1980 Cultural & natural history of Kings County. Exhibits include courtroom, Victorian Parlour, & New England Planters. Open Apr-Dec
Bria Stokesbury, Curator, curator@okcm.ca

LaHave: Fort Point Museum
Parent: Lunenburg County Historical Society
c/o Lunenburg County Historical Society, PO Box 99, LaHave, NS B0R 1C0
Tel: 902-688-1632; Fax: 902-688-1632
geoffbiddulph@eastlink.ca
www.fortpointmuseum.com
fortpointmuseum.wordpress.com
twitter.com/fortpointmuseum
www.facebook.com/fort.point.5
Year Founded: 1974 Fort Point, in the village of LaHave, is the site of the First Capital of New France. Today, this site is known as Fort Point, a National Historic Site and home of Fort Point Museum and Lighthouse. This community museum is operated by the Lunenburg County Historical Society.

Lake Charlotte: Memory Lane Heritage Village
Parent: Lake Charlotte Area Heritage Society
5435 Clam Harbour Rd., Lake Charlotte, NS B0J 1Y0
Tel: 902-845-1937 Toll-Free: 877-287-0697
info@heritagevillage.ca
heritagevillage.ca
twitter.com/MemoryLane_News
www.facebook.com/heritagevillage
Living history village including 16 buildings, meant to show visitors what life in rural Nova Scotia during the 1940s, including life during and after WWII, would have been like.
Thea Wilson-Hammond, Executive Director, admin@heritagevillage.ca

Liverpool: Hank Snow Home Town Museum
PO Box 1419, 148 Bristol Ave., Liverpool, NS B0T 1K0
Tel: 902-354-4675; Fax: 902-354-5199
Toll-Free: 888-450-5525
info@hanksnow.com
www.hanksnow.com
twitter.com/HankSnowMuseum
www.facebook.com/198142203553851
Year Founded: 1996 A tribute to Hank Snow, legendary country/folk singer from "down east." The displays include a plethora of photos and memorabilia, from his guitar strings to his iconic toupées to his yellow 1947 Cadillac. The centre also houses the Nova Scotia Country Music Hall of Fame. Open year round.
Kelly Inglis, Manager, 902-354-4675, info@hanksnow.com

Liverpool: Perkins House Museum
PO Box 1078, 105 Main St., Liverpool, NS B0T 1K0
Tel: 902-354-4058
perkinshouse.novascotia.ca
Connecticut style cottage built by merchant & diarist Simeon Perkins in 1766. Open daily Jun-Oct

Liverpool: Queens County Museum
PO Box 1078, 109 Main St., Liverpool, NS B0T 1K0
Tel: 902-354-4058; Fax: 902-354-2050
www.queenscountymuseum.ca
www.facebook.com/205294966183248
Year Founded: 1980 The Queens County Museum depicts the cultural history of Nova Scotia's Queens County. The south shore of the province has a strong history related to the Mi'kmaq culture, fishing & the forest. Programs are available for schools & the public.
Linda Rafuse, Director, 902-354-4058, Fax: 902-354-2050, linda.a.rafuse@novascotia.ca
Kathy Stitt, Administrative Assistant, 902-354-4058, Fax: 902-354-2050, kathleen.stitt@novascotia.ca

Lockeport: Little School Museum
PO Box 189, 29 Locke St, Lockeport, NS B0T 1L0
Tel: 902-875-7768; Fax: 902-656-2935
townoflockeport@ns.sympatico.ca
www.lockeport.ns.ca

Replica of a former school room & a marine room; historical artifacts of local area.

Louisbourg: Fortress of Louisbourg National Historic Site / Forteresse-de-Louisbourg, Lieu historique national
259 Park Service Rd.,
Louisbourg, NS B1C 2L2
Tel: 902-733-3552; *Fax:* 902-733-2362
louisbourg.info@pc.gc.ca
www.pc.gc.ca/eng/lhn-nhs/ns/louisbourg/index.as px
twitter.com/ParksCanada_NS
www.facebook.com/FortressOfLouisbourgNHS

Louisbourg: Sydney & Louisburg Railway Museum
7330 Main St.,
Louisbourg, NS B1C 1P5
Tel: 902-733-2720; *Fax:* 902-733-2214
Year Founded: 1972 Exhibits include railroad artifacts, models, photographs & other documentation; an extensive model of the town's coal-to-ship transfer; and a large quilt display and vintage passenger cares, including Nova Scotia's oldest passenger coach. Visitor Information Centre on site.

Lower Sackville: Fultz House Museum
Parent: Fultz Corner Restoration Society
PO Box 124, 33 Sackville Dr.,
Lower Sackville, NS B4C 2S8
Tel: 902-865-3794; *Fax:* 902-865-6940
fultz.house@ns.sympatico.ca
www.fultzhouse.ca
www.facebook.com/FultzHo use
Year Founded: 1982 1860s home which belonged to the Fultz family of Sackville, NS; contains artifacts & photographs from the Sackville area; blacksmith shop & cooperage shop from 1800s. Open Jul-Aug daily 10:00-5:00

Lower Selma: The Lower Selma Museum & Heritage Cemetery
Parent: East Hants Historical Society
6971 Hwy. 215,
Lower Selma, NS B0N 1T0
Tel: 902-261-2293
hantshistorical@gmail.com
ehhs.weebly.com
www.facebook.com/241534932553607
Year Founded: 1981 The East Hants Historical Society is an all volunteer non-profit organization devoted to the promotion and preservation of history within East Hants. The Society offers regular programs of historial interest and operates a seasonal museum in Lower Selma - The Lower Selma Museum and Heritage Cemetery. The museum is a designated Municipal Heritage Property and a repository for documents, photos and other artifacts pertaining to East Hants. It also houses a small research library.
Nancy Doane, Committee Co-Chair, East Hants Historical Society, 902-632-2504, nancy@doane.ca
Doug Lynch, Committee Co-Chair, 902-297-2057, dglynch@fivefires.com
Olive Terris, Treasurer

Lower Wedgeport: Wedgeport Sport Tuna Fishing Museum & Interpretive Centre / Musée de la pêche sportive au thon et Centre d'interprétation
Parent: L'Association du musée de Wedgeport
PO Box 488,
Lower Wedgeport, NS B0W 2B0
Tel: 902-663-4345; *Fax:* 902-663-2075
tuna_museum@hotmail.com
www.wedgeporttunamuseum.com
Year Founded: 1996 The museum preserves artifacts, photos, literature & archives from Wedgeport's tuna sport-fishing history.
Raymond Doucette, President
Gwen LeBlanc, Vice President
Ellen Cottreau, Secretary
Kerri Pothier, Treasurer

Lower West Pubnico: Le Village historique acadien de la Nouvelle-Écosse / Historic Acadian Village of Nova Scotia
CP 70,
Lower West Pubnico, NS B0W 2C0
Tél: 902-762-2530; *Téléc:* 902-762-2543
Ligne sans frais: 888-381-8999
villagehistorique@ns.aliantzinc.ca
levillage.novascotia.ca
Fondée en: 1999 Un village historique vivant dédié à la préservation et mettre en valeur la façon de vie des Acadiens d'autrefois; partie du musée de la Nouvelle-Écosse; ouvert juin à octobre.
Roger W. d'Entremont, Directeur général,
roger@ns.aliantzinc.ca

Lunenburg: Knaut-Rhuland House Museum
Parent: Lunenburg Heritage Society
PO Box 674, 125 Pelham St.,
Lunenburg, NS B0J 2C0
Tel: 902-634-3498
lunenburgheritagesociety@hotmail.com
www.lunenburgheri tagesociety.ca/krhouse.htm
twitter.com/lunenburghs
www.facebook.com/lu nenburg.heritage.9
Living history museum depicting the early history of Lunenburg; designated Canadian National Historic Site & Heritage Property of both Nova Scotia & the Town of Lunenburg.

Mabou: An Drochaid
Parent: Mabou Gaelic & Historical Society
PO Box 175, 11513 Hwy 19,
Mabou, NS B0E 1X0
Tel: 902-945-2311
mghs1975@gmail.com
www.facebook.com/AnDrochaid
Housed in an old general store; a centre for arts & crafts, genealogical & historical records, & research.
Rodney MacDonald, Contact

Mahone Bay: Mahone Bay Settlers Museum
PO Box 583, 578 Main St,
Mahone Bay, NS B0J 2E0
Tel: 902-624-6263
info@mahonebaymuseum.com
www.settlersmuseum.ns.ca
instagram.com/MahoneBayMuseum
twitter.com/MahoneBayMuseum
www.facebook .com/MahoneBayMuseum
Year Founded: 1979 Local history. Open May-Sep daily
Anne Palfreyman, Chair
Lyne Allain, Manager & Curator

Main-à-Dieu: Coastal Discovery Centre
Parent: Main-A-Dieu Community Development Association
2886 Louis-Main-à-Dieu Rd.,
Main-à-Dieu, NS B1C 1X5
Tel: 902-733-2258; *Fax:* 902-733-2653
office.meda@gmail.com
www.coastaldiscoverycentre.ca
The Coastal Discovery Centre contains the Main-à-Dieu Fishermen's Museum, as well as The Big Wave Cafe, a library and a centre that provides weekly community activies. Open year-round.

Maitland: Lawrence House Museum
Parent: Nova Scotia Museum
8660 Hwy. 215, RR #1,
Maitland, NS B0N 1T0
Tel: 902-261-2628
lawrencehouse.novascotia.ca
Home of William D. Lawrence features photographs & family heirlooms. Open Jun-Sep Tue-Sat

Malagash: Malagash Salt Miners' Museum
1926 North Shore Rd.,
Malagash, NS B0K 1E0
Tel: 902-257-2407
malagash_museum@live.ca
www.facebook.com/www.malagashsaltminemuseum.ca
Details the history of Canada's first salt mine, which operated from 1918-1959.

Maplewood: Parkdale-Maplewood Community Museum
3005 Barss Corner Rd.,
Maplewood, NS B0R 1A0
Tel: 902-644-2893; *Fax:* 902-644-3422
p-mcm@hotmail.com
parkdale.ednet.ns.ca
www.facebook.com/94020106181
Local history. Open May-Sep
Sandy Hagell, Chair
Donna Wentzell Arenburg, Curator, 902-644-3421

Middleton: Annapolis Valley Macdonald Museum
Parent: Annapolis Valley Historical Society
PO Box 925, 21 School St,
Middleton, NS B0S 1P0
Tel: 902-825-6116; *Fax:* 902-825-0531
macdonald.museum@ns.sympatico.ca
macdonaldmuseum.ca
www.facebook.c om/AnnapolisValleyMacdonaldMuseum
Features antique clocks & pocket watches, Art Gallery featuring local artists, historical artifacts, household items, tools, recreated classroom & general store, research library & gift shop. Open year round

Millbrook: Millbrook Cultural & Heritage Centre
65 Treaty Hall,
Millbrook, NS B6L 1W3
Tel: 902-843-3493; *Fax:* 902-893-3013
www.millbrookheritage.ca/
www.flickr.com/photos/glooscapheritagecenre/
twitter.com/GlooscapCentre
www.facebook.com/millbrookheritagecentre/
The museum is dedicated to preserving the heritage of the Mi'kmaq people through programs & exhibits; features a 40-foot statue of the legendary Glooscap.
Heather Stevens, Operations Supervisor & Senior Heritage Interpreter

Milton: Milton Blacksmith Shop Museum
351 West St,
Milton, NS B0T 1P0
Tel: 902-356-3113
miltonblacksmithshop@gmail.com
www.facebook.com/170660393085645
Managed by the Milton Heritage Society, the museum is a 1903 smithy, complete with forge, ox sling & original workbenches, as well as a wide array of tools of the trade; also large display of photographs of historical Milton, NS.

Minudie: Amos Seaman School Museum
Parent: The Minudie Heritage Association
5558 Barronsfield Rd.,
Minudie, NS B0L 1G0
Tel: 902-251-2289
minudieheritage@gmail.com
Photographs & documents relating to Amos "King" Seaman, who was a merchant & industrialist in the 18th century; museum housed in a one-room schoolhouse. Walking tour of the area available.

Mount Uniacke: Uniacke Estate Museum Park
Parent: Nova Scotia Museum
758 Hwy. 1,
Mount Uniacke, NS B0N 1Z0
Tel: 902-866-0032; *Fax:* 902-866-2560
uniacke.novascotia.ca
instagram.com/uniackeestatemuseum
twitter.com/uniackeestate
www.facebo ok.com/uniackeestate
Features a country mansion from 1816, nature & hiking trails, portraits & personal belongings of Richard John Uniacke, Nova Scotia's Attorney General. Open daily
Winfried Viebahn, Site Manager, VIEBAHWI@gov.ns.ca

Musquodoboit Harbour: Musquodoboit Railway Museum
Parent: Nova Scotia Railway Heritage Society (NSRHS)
7895 Main St.,
Musquodoboit Harbour, NS B0J 2L0
Tel: 902-889-2689
www.novascotiarailwayheritage.com/musquodoboit.htm
Artifacts, photographs & maps of Nova Scotia's Railways. Open Jun-Sep daily

New Glasgow: Carmichael Stewart House Museum
Parent: Pictou County Historical Society
86 Temperance St.,
New Glasgow, NS B2H 3A7
Tel: 902-752-5583
carmich@eastlink.ca
carmichael-stewart-house.business.site
www.facebook.com/224779827 547853
Year Founded: 1965 Exhibits items belonging to the Carmichael Stewart family as well as historical pieces from the area. Open Mon-Fri 9:00-4:30
Lynn MacLean, President

New Ross: Ross Farm Museum
4568 Hwy 12,
New Ross, NS B0J 2M0
Tel: 902-689-2210; *Fax:* 902-689-2264
Toll-Free: 877-689-2210
rossfarm@novascotia.ca
rossfarm.novascotia.ca
instagram.com/rossfarmmuseum;
youtube.com/user/RossFarmMuseum
twitter.com/RossFarmMuseum
www.facebo ok.com/RossFarmMuseum
Year Founded: 1969 Ross family farm 1817; includes a working blacksmith, stave mill & original workshop. Open daily
Lisa Wolfe, Director, lisa.wolfe@novascotia.ca

North East Margaree: Margaree Salmon Museum
60 East Big Intervale Rd.,
North East Margaree, NS B0E 2H0

Tel: 902-248-2848
margareesalmonmuseum@gmail.com
www.margareens.com/margaree_salmon.html
Year Founded: 1965 Exhibits relate to salmon angling on the Margaree River. Located in a former schoolhouse; includes collections of fishing tackle, photos & memorabilia of famous anglers. Open June-Oct.
Frances Hart, Curator

North Sydney: North Sydney Heritage Museum
Parent: North Sydney Historical Society
PO Box 163, 309 Commerical St.,
North Sydney, NS B2A 1C3

Tel: 902-794-2524
roberthillman2@gmail.com
Year Founded: 1985 The museum showcases Cape Breton's oldest incorporated town, housing exhibits, photographs, artifacts, original documents and the history of the people and politics that make up North Sydney. Areas devoted to communications, police and fire departments and Dutch Heritage are also located on site.

Orangedale: Orangedale Railway Museum
Parent: Orangedale Station Association
1428 Orangedale Rd.,
Orangedale, NS B0E 2K0

Tel: 902-756-3384; *Fax:* 902-756-2547
orangedale.station@gmail.com
www.novascotiarailwayheritage.com/orangedal e.htm
Open June - Sept.; railway station built in 1911
Jay Underwood, President, jp.underwood@ns.sympatico.ca

Parrsboro: Fundy Geological Museum
162 Two Islands Rd.,
Parrsboro, NS B0M 1S0

Tel: 902-254-3814; *Fax:* 902-254-3666
Toll-Free: 866-856-9466
fundygeological.novascotia.ca
twitter.com/FundyGeo
w ww.facebook.com/120369588016683
The museum includes an exhibition gallery, lab space, a multi-purpose room, gift shop and administration offices.
Dr. Tim Fedak, Director/Curator, tim.fedak@novascotia.ca
Leisa Babineau, Administrator, leisa.babineau@novascotia.ca
Pat Welton, Coordinator of Public Programs,
patricia.welton@novascotia.ca
Sandra Tanner, Visitor's Services Coordinator,
sandra.tanner@novascotia.ca
Ivan Richard, Maintenance Supervisor,
ivan.richardson@novascotia.ca
Regan Maloney, Fossil Lab Manager,
regan.maloney@novascotia.ca

Parrsboro: Ottawa House By-the-Sea Museum
PO Box 98, 1155 Whitehall Rd.,
Parrsboro, NS B0M 1S0

Tel: 902-254-2376
ottawa.house@ns.sympatico.ca
www.ottawahousemuseum.ca
Housed in a building over 200 years old that once belonged to Sir Charles Tupper, who was Premier of Nova Scotia in the 1870s, a Father of Confederation & Prime Minister of Canada. The museum's collection contains photographs, artifacts, documents & furnishings from many of the building's owners.
Susan Clarke, Facility Manager

Pictou: McCulloch House Museum
100 Haliburton Rd.,
Pictou, NS B0K 1H0

Tel: 902-485-4563
mccullochhouse.novascotia.ca
Year Founded: 1972 Home to Rev. Dr. McCulloch, the founder of Pictou Academy & first president of Dalhousie University. The exhibits reflect the life & times of Scottish immigrants & their influence on today's Nova Scotia. Open Jun-Sep

Pictou: Northumberland Fisheries Museum & Pictou Lobster Hatchery (NFMHA)
71 Front St.,
Pictou, NS B0K 1H0

Tel: 902-485-8925; *Fax:* 902-485-6586
www.northumberlandfisheriesmuseum.com
twitter.com/lobsterhatchery
www. facebook.com/1311163863589998
Year Founded: 1978 The Northumberland Fisheries Museum contains many artifacts related to the area's fishing industry and people, including: an original fisherman's bunkhouse, the "Silver Buller" vessel, and a collection of over 80 photos dating from 1900-1950. Periodic demonstrations are presented throughout the season. Children's programs and lobstery hathery lab; tours available.
Michelle Davey, Business Coordinator, 902-485-4972,
nfm-business@ns.aliantzinc.ca
Pearl Joyce, Outreach Coordinator
Lois Kitchen, Exhibit Coordinator
Linda Laybolt, Research Coordinator

Port Grenville: Age of Sail Heritage Museum
Parent: Greville Bay Shipbuilding Museum Society
8334 Hwy. 209,
Port Grenville, NS B0M 1T0

Tel: 902-348-2030
gbsmsageofsail@yahoo.com
www.ageofsailmuseum.ca
www.facebook.com/ageofsailmuseum/
The Grenville Bay Shipbuilding Museum Society is dedicated to the preservation and conservation of the lumbering and shipbuilding history of the Parrsboro Shore; primarily by collecting artifacts and archives relevant to the local history and its communities. Open May - Oct.
Oralee O'Byrne, Curator, 902-254-2079

Port Hastings: Port Hastings Museum & Archives
24 Rte. 19,
Port Hastings, NS B9A 1M1

Tel: 902-625-1295
porthastingsmuseum@gmail.com
www.porthastingsmuseum.ca
www.facebook.com/PortHastingsMuseum
Located in 100-year-old Cape Breton house; displays include pioneer artifacts, photographic displays & exhibits on construction of causeway; railroads, ferries & model ship displays; genealogical records available
Bob MacEachern, President

Pubnico-Ouest: Musée des Acadiens des Pubnicos et Centre de recherche
CP 92,
Pubnico-Ouest, NS B0W 3S0

Tél: 902-762-3380; *Téléc:* 902-762-0726
musee.acadien@ns.sympatico.ca
www.museeacadien.ca
www.facebook.com/101 935276541461
Le Musée: #898, autoroute 335; consacré au patrimoine des Acadiens/Acadiennes de Pubnico-Ouest; articles de maison; documents; photographies; archives; potager traditionnel; boutique de souvenirs.
Elaine Surette, Président

Riverport: Ovens Natural Park & Museum
PO Box 38, 326 Ovens Rd.,
Riverport, NS B0J 2W0

Tel: 902-766-4621
info@ovenspark.com
www.ovenspark.com
ovenspark.tumblr.com
www.facebook.com/ovensnaturalpark
Year Founded: 1987 Ovens Natural Park is a reserve of coastal forest, featuring the sea caves or "Ovens". The area became known internationally during th 1861 gold rush. The Gold Rush Museum contains artifacts from that era.

St Peters: Nicolas Denys Museum
PO Box 204, 46 Denys St.,
St Peters, NS B0E 3B0

Tel: 902-535-2379
nicolasdenysmuseum@gmail.com
www.facebook.com/NicolasDenysMuseum
Year Founded: 1967 Micmac, Acadien, Scottish & Irish artifacts as well as a reference library. Open Jun-Sep
Judy Madden, Curator, judy_madden80@hotmail.ca

Shag Harbour: Chapel Hill Museum & Observation Tower
Parent: Chapel Hill Historical Society
PO Box 46, 5492 Hwy. 3,
Shag Harbour, NS B0W 3B0

Tel: 902-723-1313
chapelhillns@gmail.com
Located in a former Baptist Church, the museum features various displays related to the local area including tools for ship-building, genealogical research materials and various fishing exhibits. From the observation tower, all four local lighthouses can be viewed. Open June 1 - Sept. 15 daily; during the off season, by appointment only.
Douglas Shand, President, Chapel Hill Historical Society, 902-723-2949, shawimm@ns.sympatico.ca
Veronica Hopkins, Vice President/Treasurer, Chapel Hill Historical Society, vhopkins@ns.sympatico.ca

Shag Harbour: Shag Harbour Incident Society Museum
PO Box 53, 5615 Nova Scotia Trunk 3,
Shag Harbour, NS B0W 3B0

Tel: 902-723-0127
shagharbour@gmail.com
www.shagharbourincident.wordpress.com
twitter.com/ShagHarbour1967
www.facebook.com/shagharbourUFO
Year Founded: 2007 The museum displays memorabilia, TV programs & other material related to the documented 1967 crash of a UFO in the Gulf of Maine, near Shag Harbour. The museum also details local history unrelated to the crash. Open M-F 10:00-5:00, Sa 12:00-5:00, Su 1:00-5:00; also open by appointment.
Laurie Wickens, President

Shearwater: Shearwater Aviation Museum
PO Box 5000 Main, 12 Wing,
Shearwater, NS B0J 3A0

Tel: 902-720-1083; *Fax:* 902-720-2037
info@shearwateraviationmuseum.ns.ca
www.shearwateraviationmuseum.ns.ca
twitter.com/YAWmuseum
www.facebook.com/shearwateraviationmuseum
Year Founded: 1978 Maritime military aviation artifacts.

Sheet Harbour: MacPhee House Community Museum
22404 Main St.,
Sheet Harbour, NS B0J 3B0

Tel: 902-885-2092
macpheehouse@gmail.com
www.facebook.com/macpheehouse
The museum is situated in a house that's over 100 years old, housing a collection of artifacts. In its history the house has served as a private home, post office, grocery store & rooming house. Open daily June - Sept.

Shelburne: The Dory Shop Museum
Parent: Shelburne Historical Society
PO Box 39, 11 Dock St.,
Shelburne, NS B0T 1W0

Tel: 902-875-3219; *Fax:* 902-875-4141
doryshop.novascotia.ca
Restored dory factory. Open Jun-Oct; dories still built to order

Shelburne: Ross-Thomson House & Store Museum
Parent: Shelburne Historical Society
9 Charlotte Ln.,
Shelburne, NS B0T 1W0

Tel: 902-875-3219; *Fax:* 902-875-4141
rossthomson.novascotia.ca
Located on Charlotte St. in Shelburne. Site contains a 1785 Loyalist house & garden, an 18th-century store & chandlery, a 19th-century military room complete with artifacts. Operated by the Shelburne Historical Society and part of the Nova Scotia Museum group; open June 1 - Oct. 15.

Shelburne: Shelburne County Museum
Parent: Shelburne Historical Society
PO Box 39, 20 Dock St.,
Shelburne, NS B0T 1W0

Tel: 902-875-3219; *Fax:* 902-875-4141
shelburne.museum@ns.sympatico.ca
www.shelburnemuseums.com
www.facebook .com/364893103570881
Museum focusing on the cultural & economic history of the Shelburne area from 1783. Contains model ships, antique tools, portraits, costumes and maps, as well as Canada's oldest fire pumper.

Sherbrooke: St. Mary's River Association Education & Interpretive Centre (SMRA)
PO Box 179, 8404 Hwy. 7,
Sherbrooke, NS B0J 3C0

Tel: 902-522-2099; *Fax:* 902-522-2241
stmarysriver@ns.sympatico.ca
www.stmarysriverassociation.com/eandicentre .html
Year Founded: 2001 Artifacts & educational information relating to salmon fishing on the St. Mary's river; open daily.

Sherbrooke: Sherbrooke Village
Parent: Historic Sherbrooke Village Development
Society
42 Main St.,
Sherbrooke, NS B0J 3C0

Tel: 902-522-2400; *Fax:* 902-522-2974
Toll-Free: 888-743-7845
svillage@gov.ns.ca
sherbrookevillage.novascotia.ca
www.youtube.com/user/sherbrookevillage
twitter.com/Sherbrooke_NS
www.facebook.com/sherbrookevillage
Historic village with 25 original buildings; includes pottery shop,
blacksmith, woodturner shop & printery. Open daily Jun-Sep
Michelle MacArthur, Chair
Mark Sajatovich, Executive Director, sajatomc@gov.ns.ca

Smith's Cove: Old Temperance Hall Museum
590 Hwy. 1,
Smith's Cove, NS B0S 1S0

Tel: 902-245-4665
smithscovemuseum@gmail.com
Exhibits of the 19th and 20th century pertaining to the local
community including the earliest inhabitants, the Mi'kmaq;
history of the Sons of Temperance.

Springhill: The Anne Murray Centre
PO Box 610, 36 Main St.,
Springhill, NS B0M 1X0

Tel: 902-597-8614; *Fax:* 902-597-2001
amcentre@eastlink.ca
www.annemurraycentre.com
twitter.com/AnneMurrayCe ntr
www.facebook.com/amcentre
Year Founded: 1989 Pays tribute to the achievements of singer
Anne Murray, who was born in Springhill, Nova Scotia; open May
- Oct., otherwise by appointment or by chance.

Springhill: Springhill Miner's Museum
145 Black River Rd.,
Springhill, NS B0M 1X0

Tel: 902-597-3449
springhillminersmuseum@hotmail.com
novascotia.com/see-do/attractions/tour-a-mine-springhill-miners-
museum/131 7
www.facebook.com/SpringhillMinersMuseum
Tours of the Springhill coal mine. Museum features artifacts of
local history & its industrial heritage. Open daily

Starr's Point: Prescott House
1633 Starr's Point Rd.,
Starr's Point, NS B0P 1T0

Tel: 902-542-3984
nancy.morton@novascotia.ca
prescotthouse.novascotia.ca
www.facebook.com/PrescottHouseMuseum
Georgian home of Charles Ramage Prescott. Displays portraits,
oriental carpets & antique furnishings. Open Jun-Sep
Diana Baldwin, Contact, diana.baldwin@novascotia.ca

Stellarton: Museum of Industry
147 North Foord St.,
Stellarton, NS B0K 1S0

Tel: 902-755-5425; *Fax:* 902-755-7045
industry@novascotia.ca
museumofindustry.novascotia.ca
twitter.com/ns_m oi
www.facebook.com/MuseumofIndustry
Chronicles the impact of industrialization on the people,
economy & landscape of Nova Scotia; features Canada's oldest
steam locomotives, a historic model railway layout, a belt-driven
working machine shop & a collection of Nova Scotia's Trenton
glass. Open year round.
Debra McNabb, Director
Erika Smith, Curator, Collections
Andrew Phillips, Curator, Education & Public Programming

Sydney: Cape Breton Centre for Heritage & Science
225 George St.,
Sydney, NS B1P 1J5

Tel: 902-539-1572
oldsydneysociety@ns.aliantzinc.ca
www.oldsydney.com/cape-breton-centre-for-heritage-science
www.facebook.c om/197073480392754
Social & natural history of Cape Brenton County. One of the 3
Old Sydney Society family of museums. Open Jun-Aug

Sydney: Cossit House Museum
Parent: Old Sydney Society
c/o Cape Breton Centre for Heritage & Science, 225 George
St.,
Sydney, NS B1P 4P4

Tel: 902-539-7973
cossithouse.novascotia.ca
One of the oldest buildings on Cape Breton Island, c.1787; part
of the Nova Scotia Museum.

Sydney: Jost House Musuem
54 Charlotte St.,
Sydney, NS B1P 6T7

Tel: 902-539-0366; *Fax:* 902-539-7998
www.facebook.com/230720683606240
House originally owned by a prominant merchant c.1786 and
was bought by Thomas Jost in 1836. Today the house is filled
with Victorian artifacts with each room featuring a different
theme.

Sydney: Whitney Pier Historical Society Museum
Parent: Whitney Pier Historical Society
88 Mount Pleasant St.,
Sydney, NS B1N 2G1

Tel: 902-562-8454
wphs@syd.eastlink.ca
Year Founded: 1988 A community museum that aims to honour
its population and their diverse cultural roots. The collection
includes photographs, scrapbooks and newspaper clippins, as
well as artifacts from daily life, the steel plant and the war years.
Open June - August.
Simon Gillis, Vice-President, 902-564-4248
Sandra Dunn, Treasurer, 902-562-8454

Sydney Mines: Sydney Mines Heritage Museum, Cape
Breton Fossil Centre & Sydney Mines Sports Museum
Parent: Sydney Mines Heritage Society
159 Legatto St.,
Sydney Mines, NS B1V 5S6

Tel: 902-544-0992
smheritage@ns.aliantzinc.ca
sydneyminesheritage.ca
The Heritage Museum is located in the historic Sydney Mines
Train Station & contains local artifacts, including photographs,
pottery & memorabilia. The Cape Breton Fossil Centre
showcases fossils, mostly of plants, that come from the Sydney
Coalfields. The Sports Museum contains photographs &
memorabilia relating to Sydney Mines' sporting history.

Tatamagouche: Anna Swan Museum
PO Box 402, 39 Creamery Sq.,
Tatamagouche, NS B0K 1V0

Tel: 902-657-3449
info@tatamagoucheheritagecentre.ca
tatamagoucheheritagecentre.ca/anna-swan.html
Artifacts from the life of Nova Scotia giantess Anna Swan.

Tatamagouche: Margaret Fawcett Norrie Heritage
Centre at Creamery Square
39 Creamery Rd.,
Tatamagouche, NS B0K 1V0

Tel: 902-657-3500; *Fax:* 902-657-0240
cs.heritage@ns.aliantzinc.caa
www.creamerysquare.ca
twitter.com/creame rysquare
www.facebook.com/129652823882556
The Heritage Centre contains the following: Creamery Museum,
Sunrise Trail Museum, Anna Swan Museum & the Brule Fossil
Museum.

Truro: Colchester Historeum
Parent: Colchester Historical Society
PO Box 412, 29 Young St,
Truro, NS B2N 5C5

Tel: 902-895-6284; *Fax:* 902-895-9530
colchesterhistoreum.ca
twitter.com/Col_Historeum
www.facebook.com/colc hesterhistoreum
Other contact information: Archives Phone: 902-895-9530
Year Founded: 1976 Museum & archive devoted to preserving
the history of Colchester County. Open year round.
Margaret Mulrooney, Curator, curator@colchesterhistoreum.ca
Nan Harvey, Archivist, 902-895-9530,
archivist@colchesterhistoreum.ca

Truro: The Little White Schoolhouse
PO Box 25005, 20 Arthur St.,
Truro, NS B2N 5N2

Tel: 902-895-5170
littlewhiteschoolhousemuseum@bellaliant.com
littlewhiteschool.ca
www.f acebook.com/littlewhiteschoolhousemuseum
Year Founded: 1982 Original Riverton School; commemorates
schoolhouses in Nova Scotia from Confederation to the 1950s;
contains books, photographs & artifacts; Open Jun-Aug Mon-Fri
10:00-5:00; Tue 9:00-12:00 or by appointment.

Tupperville: Tupperville School Museum
2663 Hwy. 201,
Tupperville, NS B0S 1C0

Tel: 902-665-2579; *Fax:* 902-665-4875
tuppervillemuseum@gmail.com
Year Founded: 1972 One room school with book collection,
scrapbooks, photographs & furniture. Open Jun-Aug
Jane Barkhouse, Contact, 902-665-2129

Wallace: Wallace & Area Museum
Parent: Wallace & Area Museum Society
PO Box 179,
Wallace, NS B0K 1Y0

Tel: 902-257-2191; *Fax:* 902-257-2191
wallacemuseum@ns.aliantzinc.ca
www.wallaceandareamuseum.com
www.facebo ok.com/120610681314312
Year Founded: 1983 The museum collect, preserves, & displays
the history of Wallace & the surrounding region. Artifacts include
nineteenth century marine charts & maps, the United Empire
Loyalist grant, pre-Confederation letters, & items about
shipbuilding in Wallace & the Wallace sandstone quarries. Open
year round.
Doris Purdy, President
Warren Hebb, Vice-President
David Dewar, Curator
Doug Perry, Secretary

Waverley: Waverley Heritage Museum
2463 Rocky Lake Dr.,
Waverley, NS B2R 1S1

Tel: 902-861-1463
waverleyheritagemuseum@gmail.com
waverleycommunity.ca/?page_id=1789
www.facebook.com/waverleyheritagemuse um
Local history of the community during its development.

West Bay: Marble Mountain Library & Museum
RR#1,
West Bay, NS B0E 3K0

Tel: 902-756-2638

West Chezzetcook: Acadian House Museum
Parent: L'Acadie de Chezzetcook
PO Box 18, 79 Hill Rd.,
West Chezzetcook, NS B0J 1N0

Tel: 902-827-5992
info.acadiedechezzetcook@gmail.com
www.acadiedechezzetcook.ca/en/historical-site/museum
www.facebook.com/LA
cadie-de-Chezzetcook-245386768810556
Local Acadian history & way of life. Open Jul-Aug Tue-Sun
10:00-4:30.

Windsor: Fort Edward National Historic Site / Lieu
historique national du Fort Édouard
Parent: West Hants Historical Society
67 Fort Edward St.,
Windsor, NS B0N 2T0

Tel: 902-798-2639; *Fax:* 902-532-2232
information@pc.gc.ca
www.pc.gc.ca/en/lhn-nhs/ns/edward
twitter.com/Par ksCanada_NS
Built in 1750 by Major Charles Lawrence, this Fort protected the
route from Halifax to the Annapolis Valley & remains one of Nova
Scotia's oldest buildings.

Windsor: Haliburton House Museum
Parent: Nova Scotia Museum
PO Box 2683, 414 Clifton Ave.,
Windsor, NS B0N 2T0

Tel: 902-798-2915
haliburtonhouse.novascotia.ca
www.facebook.com/HaliburtonShandHouseMuseums
Year Founded: 1940 Former home of author Thomas Chandler
Haliburton includes antiques, trails, orchard & memorabilia.
Open Jun-Sep daily

Windsor: Shand House Museum
389 Avon St.,
Windsor, NS B0N 2T0
Tel: 902-798-8213; *Fax:* 902-798-5619
shandhouse.novascotia.ca
www.facebook.com/HaliburtonShandHouseMuseums
Historic family home c.1890; Open Jun-Oct

Windsor: West Hants Historical Society Museum
Parent: West Hants Historical Society
PO Box 2335, 281 King St.,
Windsor, NS B0N 2T0
Tel: 902-798-4706
whhs@ns.aliantzinc.ca
westhantshistoricalsociety.ca
twitter.com/WHHSWindsor
www.facebook.com/141349919273121
Artifacts related to the history of Hants County in Nova Scotia
are collected & preserved by the West Hants Historical Society &
displayed at its museum. Visitors will find information about the
Mi'kmaq, the Acadians, the Loyalists, the Great Windsor Fire of
1897 & the local shipbuilding industry. The society also operates
a genealogy department. The museum is open five days a week
from mid June to the end of August, & one day a week from
September to June. Summer tours are available of the Fort
Edward Blockhouse. Appointments may be arranged for times
when the museum is closed.

Wolfville: Randall House Museum
Parent: Wolfville Historical Society
259 Main St.,
Wolfville, NS B4P 1C6
Tel: 902-542-9775
randallhouse@outlook.ca
www.wolfvillehs.ednet.ns.ca
www.instagram.com/randallhousens/
twitter.com/RandallHouseNS
www.faceb ook.com/WolfvilleHistoricalSociety/
The Randall House Museum is situated in an historic farmhouse,
from around 1800, and is owned & operated by the Wolfville
Historical Society. The museum reflects life in Wolfville & the
surrounding area during the 18th & 19th centuries. On display
are furniture, clothing, china & a collection of Victorian greeting
cards. A library is located in The Randall House for persons
researching local history & genealogy.
Anthony J. Harding, President
Heather Watts, Archivist, 902-542-0307

Yarmouth: Firefighters' Museum of Nova Scotia
Nova Scotia Museum Complex, 451 Main St.,
Yarmouth, NS B5A 1G9
Tel: 902-742-5525
firefightersmuseum.novascotia.ca
www.instagram.com/firefighters_museum_of_ns/
twitter.com/FFmuseumofNS
www.facebook.com/FirefightersMuseumOfNS
The museum focuses on the history of firefighting in Nova Scotia
through the use of photographs, stories and thousands of
artifacts. Collection of vintage firefighting equipment, including
trucks, on site. A part of the Nova Scotia Museum group.
David Darby, Curator

Yarmouth: Yarmouth County Museum & Archives
Parent: Yarmouth County Historical Society
22 Collins St.,
Yarmouth, NS B5A 3C8
Tel: 902-742-5539; *Fax:* 902-749-1120
ycmuseum@eastlink.ca
yarmouthcountymuseum.ca
instagram.com/yarmouthmuseum
www.facebook.com/92402018979
Year Founded: 1969 Artifacts of Yarmouth County's heritage.
Includes ship portrait collection, costume collléction, musical
instruments & an M.V Bluenose exhibit. Open year round
Nadine Gates, Director/Curator, ycmuseum@eastlink.ca
Lisette Gaudet, Archivist, ycarchives@eastlink.ca

Nunavut
Local Museums

Baker Lake: Inuit Heritage Centre
PO Box 149,
Baker Lake, NU X0C 0A0
Tel: 867-793-2598; *Fax:* 867-793-2315
Year Founded: 1998 The Centre's goal is to preserve, protect &
promote Inuit culture through a collection of Inuit artifacts & a
teaching room where elders can record oral histories & teach
youth about traditional ways of life. Open year-round.

Cambridge Bay: Kitikmeot Heritage Society (KHS)
PO Box 2160,
Cambridge Bay, NU X0B 0C0
Tel: 867-983-3009; *Fax:* 867-983-3397
heritage@qiniq.com
www.kitikmeotheritage.ca
Located in the May Hakongak Community Library & Cultural
Centre, the KHS strives to preserve the history, culture &
language of the people of the Kitikmeot region. The collection
includes oral histories as told by elders & archeological artifacts.
Kim Crockatt, President, kimcr@netkaster.ca
Pamela Gross, Executive Director
Darren Keith, Senior Researcher, dkeith@cgocable.ca

Iqaluit: Nunatta Sunakkutaangit Museum
PO Box 1900, 212 Sinaa St,
Iqaluit, NU X0A 0H0
Tel: 867-979-5537; *Fax:* 867-979-4533
museum@nunanet.com
Year Founded: 1969 Collections on Inuit culture & history from
the Baffin region, including historical & archeological artifacts,
tools, clothing, & equipment as well as arts & crafts; also
maintains a collection of archival photographs, publications &
documents for exhibition & research purposes.

Pangnirtung: Sipalaseequtt Museum Society
Angmarlik Visitor Centre, PO Box 227,
Pangnirtung, NU X0A 0R0
Tel: 867-473-8737
Inuit artifacts; whaling history in Cumberland Sound Baffin
Island; Elders' meetings; craft production; tours

Sanikiluaq: Najuqsivik Community Museum
General Delivery,
Sanikiluaq, NU X0A 0W0
Tel: 867-266-8400; *Fax:* 867-266-8175
najuqsivik@yahoo.ca
www.najuqsivik.com
The museum provides hands-on cultural activities during limited
hours in July & Aug. The museum is operated by the Najuqsivik
Society, which also operates a daycare, custom frameshop, and
a variety of local production and crafts related businesses,
including: polar bear rug making, archaeological & lost wax
casting, fishskin doll production, coffee mug artwork, garment
screening, an upholstery shop, a community access program,
and a TV & radio station.

Ontario
Provincial Museums

Royal Ontario Museum (ROM)
Visitor Services Department, 100 Queen's Park,
Toronto, ON M5S 2C6
Tel: 416-586-8000
info@rom.on.ca
www.rom.on.ca
www.instagram.com/romtoronto
twitter.com/ROMtoronto
www.facebook.com/r oyalontariomuseum
Year Founded: 1912 The Royal Ontario Museum (ROM) is
Canada's largest museum, an internationally renowned facility &
popular public attraction. Created in 1912, the ROM has an
unusually broad dual mandate of collecting & preserving in the
areas of natural history & human cultures & communicating its
research to the world. Today, the ROM holds in excess of 6
million objects in its collections, which include galleries of art,
archaeology & science.
Josh Basseches, Director & CEO
Dan Wright, Deputy Director & Chief Financial Officer
Lynda Hartigan, Deputy Director, Collections & Research
Chen Shen, Vice-President, Art & Culture

Local Museums

Ailsa Craig: Donald Hughes Annex Museum
Parent: North Middlesex Historical Society
169 George St.,
Ailsa Craig, ON N0M 1A0
Tel: 519-517-0105
northmiddlesexhs@gmail.com
Local history. Open Mon-Sat 1:00-4:00
Ron Walker, Contact, 519-854-7734

Algonquin Highlands: Stanhope Heritage Discovery
Museum
1123 North Shore Rd.,
Algonquin Highlands, ON K0M 1J1
Tel: 705-489-2379
info@stanhopemuseum.on.ca
www.stanhopemuseum.on.ca
www.facebook.com/pages/Stanhope-Museum/23440667 2514

Year Founded: 1996 Local pioneer history. Open Jun-Sept
Tue-Thu, Sat 11:00-2:00
Betty Moffat, Chair, 705-489-3021

Alliston: Museum on the Boyne
250 Fletcher Cres.,
Alliston, ON L9R 1A1
Tel: 705-435-3900; *Fax:* 705-434-3006
boynemuseum@newtecumseth.ca
www.motb.ca
Community museum displaying household, agricultural &
industrial artifacts from the 1840's to present; site features
1850's log cabin, 1858 English barn & 1914 fair building. Open
Jun-Aug Tue-Sun, Sept-May Mon-Fri 10:00-3:30.

Almonte: Mill of Kintail Conservation Area
Parent: Mississippi Valley Conservation
2854 Ramsay Concession 8,
Almonte, ON K0A 1A0
Tel: 613-259-3610
info@mvc.on.ca
www.mvc.on.ca/conservation-areas/mill-of-kintail
twitter.com/MVC5
www. facebook.com/1744197192507 47
Kintail Museum, housed in a heritage grist mill, is a collection &
a conservation site on the Indian River in Lanark County. The
museum showcases the life & works of Robert Tait McKenzie &
the largest collection of McKenzie's sculptures & memorabilia in
Canada.

Almonte: Mississippi Valley Textile Museum (MVTM)
PO Box 784, 3 Rosamond St. East,
Almonte, ON K0A 1A0
Tel: 613-256-3754
mvtm.ca
twitter.com/MVTextileMuseum
www.facebook.com/MVTextileMuseum
Year Founded: 1985 Museum is a National Historic Site; located
in the annex of the former Rosamond Woolen Company
constructed in 1867; houses information on the early mills & their
owners, displays of period offices, artifacts & machinery related
to the beginnings of the textile industry.
Michael Rikley-Lancaster, Executive Director & Curator,
curator@mvtm.ca

Ameliasburg: Ameliasburgh Historical Museum
517 County Rd. 19,
Ameliasburg, ON K0K 1A0
Tel: 613-968-9678
amelmuseum@pecounty.on.ca
pecounty.on.ca/government/community_development/museums/
ameliasburgh.php
Year Founded: 1968 Household items, quilts, crafts, agricultural
machinery & tools & a 1910 Goldie Corlis engine with an 18-foot
flywheel in a village setting.
Jennifer Lyons, Head Curator, Museums of Prince Edward
County, 613-476-3833, Fax: 613-471-2050,
museums@pecounty.on.ca
Janice Hubbs, Site Curator

Ameliasburg: Quinte Educational Museum & Archives,
Inc.
PO Box 14, 13 Coleman St.,
Ameliasburg, ON K0K 1A0
Tel: 613-966-5501
info@qema1978.com
www.qema1978.com
The history of education in Prince Edward County & Ontario is
preserved at the Quinte Educational Museum & Archives,
through educational artifacts & archival material.
Lynda Sommer, President, lyndasommer@qema1978.com

Amherstburg: Amherstburg Freedom Museum
277 King St.,
Amherstburg, ON N9V 2C7
Tel: 519-736-5433
www.amherstburgfreedom.org
www.facebook.com/AmherstburgFreedom
The Museum allows visitors to experience Black history through
the Taylor Log Cabin, a home of escaped slaves from the United
States, the Nazrey African Methodist Episcopal Church & a
Cultural Centre.
Terran Fader, Curator & Administrator

Amherstburg: Fort Malden National Historic Site of
Canada (FMNHS) / Lieu historique national du Canada
du Fort-Malden
PO Box 38, 100 Laird Ave.,
Amherstburg, ON N9V 2Z2
Tel: 519-736-5416; *Fax:* 519-736-6603
ont.fort-malden@pc.gc.ca
www.parkscanada.gc.ca/malden
www.facebook.com/FortMaldenNHS
Year Founded: 1796 Riverfront site includes original earthworks,
a restored soldier's barrack & a museum. Open daily Jun-Sept
10:00-5:00

Amherstburg: Park House Museum
Kings Navy Yard, 214 Dalhousie St.,
Amherstburg, ON N9V 1W4
Tel: 519-736-2511; *Fax:* 519-736-2511
parkhousemuseum.com
Built during the 1790s by a family of Loyalists, Park House is an
example of Pièce sur Pièce log construction. The Park House
Museum is open year-round to display items of historical
significance to the town of Amherstburg & the surrounding area.
During the summer, tinsmithing is demonstrated in the
pensioner's cottage.
Stephanie Pouget, Curator, curator@parkhousemuseum.com

Ancaster: Dundas Valley Trail Centre
c/o Hamilton Conservation Authority, PO Box 81067,
Ancaster, ON L9G 4X1
Tel: 905-627-1233; *Fax:* 905-648-4622
dvalley@conservationhamilton.ca
www.conservationhamilton.ca/dundas-valle y
www.youtube.com/user/HamiltonConservation
twitter.com/Hamilton_CA
www.facebook.com/HamiltonConservation
Centre is a replica of an 1800-era train station. Displays exhibits
on the Niagara Escarpment, local cultural heritage & trail
etiquette governing the valley's extensive, multi-use trail
network; bird watching, cycling & historical tours available.
Carissa Bishop, Superintendent, Dundas Valley Conservation
Area, Carissa.Bishop@conservationhamilton.ca
Karen Laur, Contact, Trail Centre

Ancaster: Fieldcote Memorial Park & Museum
64 Sulphur Springs Rd.,
Ancaster, ON L9G 1L8
Tel: 905-648-8144; *Fax:* 905-648-4857
fieldcote@hamilton.ca
www.hamilton.ca
Collection, preservation & exhibition of local history; landscaped
gardens & walking trails. Open year round Tue-Sun 1:00-5:00

Appin: Ekfrid Community Museum
48 Wellington St.,
Appin, ON N0L 1A0
Tel: 519-287-2015
Located in the former Appin Post Office & Orange Hall; artifacts
from late 1800s; open May-Aug., weekends by request

Appleton: North Lanark Regional Museum
Parent: North Lanark Historical Society
PO Box 218, 647 River Rd.,
Appleton, ON K0A 1A0
Tel: 613-257-8503
appletonmuseum@hotmail.com
northlanarkregionalmuseum.com
Year Founded: 1971 Local history including artifacts,
photographs, documents & books. Open Mon-Fri 10:00-4:00
Doreen Wilson, Manager, 613-256-2866

Arnprior: Arnprior & District Museum / Musée d'Arnprior
et Région
35 Madawaska St.,
Arnprior, ON K7S 1R6
Tel: 613-623-4902
www.arnpriormuseum.org
www.youtube.com/user/ArnpriorMuseum
www.facebook.com/220198278002242
The Arnprior & District Museum features local artifacts &
photographs, a 1928 fire engine, a lumbering exhibit, & an early
19th century canon. Open Mon-Sat.
Janet Carlile, Curator, jcarlile@arnprior.ca

Astra: National Air Force Museum of Canada
8Wing/CFB Trenton, PO Box 1000, 220 RCAF Rd.,
Astra, ON K0K 2W0
Tel: 613-965-7223; *Fax:* 613-965-7352
Toll-Free: 866-701-7223
publicrelations@airforcemuseum.ca
airforcemuseum.ca
twitter.com/nafmcanada
www.facebook.com/nafmcanada

Year Founded: 1984 Museum dedicated to the airmen &
airwomen who served in Canada's Air Force. Features daily
viewing of the restoration of the world's only fully restored Halifax
bomber aircraft. Open daily May-Sep 10:00-5:00; Oct-Apr
Wed-Sun 10:00-5:00
Chris Colton, Executive Director, 613-965-2208,
director@airforcemuseum.ca
Kevin Windsor, Curator, 613-965-3521,
curator@airforcemuseum.ca

Atikokan: Atikokan Centennial Museum & Historical
Park
PO Box 849,
Atikokan, ON P0T 1C0
Tel: 807-597-6585; *Fax:* 807-597-6585
acmuseum@bellnet.ca
www.facebook.com/27862016983
Restored logging engine & train; mining & logging exhibits;
Steep Rock & Caland Iron Ore Mines; local archival & art
collections
Lois Fenton, Museum Curator

Aurora: Aurora Historical Society & Hillary House,
National Historic Site
15372 Yonge St.,
Aurora, ON L4G 1N8
Tel: 905-727-8991
aurorahs.ca
www.facebook.com/HillaryHouseNHS
Year Founded: 1963 Heritage artifacts held by the Aurora
Historical Society date back over 200 years. The collections are
related to the history of Aurora & to Hillary House. Hillary House,
the Koffler Museum of Medicine, contains a significant collection
of medical instruments.
Erika Mazanik, Curator

Aurora: Hillary House, the Koffler Museum of Medicine
Parent: Aurora Historical Society
15372 Yonge St.,
Aurora, ON L4G 1N8
Tel: 905-727-8991
www.hillaryhouse.ca
www.facebook.com/HillaryHouseNHS
Exhibits include medicial instruments, books, papers, household
furnishings & equipment dating from the early 19th century. The
museum is a National Historic Site. Open May-Aug 9:30-4:30
daily; Sept-Apr by appointment only.

Aylmer: Aylmer-Malahide Museum & Archives (AMMA)
14 East St.,
Aylmer, ON N5H 1W2
Tel: 519-773-9723
aylmermuseum@amtelecom.net
www.amtelecom.net/~aylmermuseum
twitter.com/AylmerMuseum
www.facebook. com/AylmerMalahideMuseumArchives
Year Founded: 1977 The Aylmer & District Museum Association
preserves & promotes the history of Aylmer & Malahide. Open
Jun-Aug Sat 11:00-4:00; Mar-Nov Mon-Fri 10:00-5:00
Jacquie Jeffery, Chair
Amanda Vanden Wyngaert, Curator

Aylmer: Gay Lea Dairy Heritage Museum
Parent: Gay Lea Foods Co-operative Limited
48075 Jamestown Line, RR#2,
Aylmer, ON N5H 2R2
Tel: 888-773-2955
museum@gayleafoods.com
www.dairyheritagemuseum.ca
twitter.com/DairyMuseum
www.facebook.com/ww w.dairyheritagemuseum.ca
Artifacts that dairy farmers would have used previous to the
development of modern technology. Workshops & events
available. Open May-Aug Wed-Sun 9:00-5:00; Sept Sat
9:00-5:00.

Aylmer: Ontario Police College Museum
PO Box 1190, 10716 Hacienda Rd.,
Aylmer, ON N5H 2T2
Tel: 519-773-5361; *Fax:* 519-773-5762
Year Founded: 1962 Small display of police related items
including speed measuring devices, breath collection & testing
equipment, handcuffs & batons, police uniforms & hats, First
Nations Police display & Forensics Investigative display.

Azilda: Rayside-Balfour Museum
Azilda Public Library, 120 Staint Agnes St.,
Azilda, ON P0M 1B0
Tel: 705-692-4448
www.sudburymuseums.ca

The museum houses artifacts related to the history of Azilda &
Chelmford. Open Sept-June, M 10:00-2:00, Tu-Th 3:00-8:00, Sa
10:00-2:00.

Baden: Castle Kilbride National Historic Site
60 Snyder's Rd. West,
Baden, ON N3A 1A1
Tel: 519-634-8444; *Fax:* 519-634-5035
Toll-Free: 800-469-5576
www.castlekilbride.ca
www.facebook.com/castlekilbride
Year Founded: 1877 A restored 1877 mansion originally built by
industrialist James Livingston, now a National Historic Site.
Open Tu-F 10:00-4:00, Sa-Su 1:00-4:00.

Baden: Wilmot Heritage Fire Brigades
10 Bell Dr.,
Baden, ON N3A 4J8
Tel: 519-634-8153
wilmotfiremuseum@gmail.com
www.wilmotfiremuseum.com
Year Founded: 1996 Local & national firefighting artifacts

Bala: Bala's Museum
PO Box 14, 1024 Maple Ave.,
Bala, ON P0C 1A0
Tel: 705-762-5876 *Toll-Free:* 888-579-7739
balamus@muskoka.com
bala.net/museum
www.facebook.com/BalasMuseumWithMe
moriesOfLucyMaudMontgomery
Year Founded: 1992 The museum's collection features items
related to Lucy Maud Montgomery. Spring hours: May-June, Sa
11:00-4:00; Summer hours: June-Sept., Tu-Sa 11:00-4:00; Fall
hours: Sept.-Oct., Sa 11:00-4:00.

Bancroft: Bancroft Mineral Museum
8 Hastings Heritage Way,
Bancroft, ON K0L 1C0
Tel: 613-332-1513; *Fax:* 613-332-2119
Toll-Free: 888-443-9999
The Bancroft Mineral Museum is a natural science museum
which features mineral specimens collected from the local area.
Open year round.

Bancroft: North Hastings Heritage Museum
PO Box 239, 28 C Station St.,
Bancroft, ON K0L 1C0
Tel: 613-332-1884
nhhmuseum@nexicom.net
bancroftheritagemuseum.ca
Local history including artifacts from Victorian costumes, mineral
collections, agricultural tools & early doctors & dentistry
equipment. Open Tue-Sat 10:00-5:00

Barrie: Grey & Simcoe Foresters Regimental Museum
c/o Barrie Armoury, 37 Parkside Dr.,
Barrie, ON L4N 1W8
Tel: 705-737-5559
gsfmus@csolve.net
thegreyandsimcoeforesters.org
Grey & Simcoe Foresters Regiment artifacts on display include:
period uniforms, medals, field gear, & official recognitions &
documentation.
Peter Litster, Curator

Bath: Bath Museum of Loyalist County
The Old Town Hall, 434 Main St.,
Bath, ON K0H 1G0
Tel: 613-352-7716
Thebathmuseum@gmail.com
www.bathmuseumontario.com
Year Founded: 1936 Local history, including aboriginal artifacts;
open May-Sept., W-Su 10:00-4:00.

Bath: United Empire Loyalist Heritage Centre & Park
Parent: Bay of Quinte Br., United Empire Loyalist
Association of Canada
54 Adolphustown Park Rd.,
Bath, ON K0H 1G0
Tel: 613-373-2196 *Toll-Free:* 877-384-1784
library@uel.ca
www.uel.ca
The United Empire Loyalist Heritage Centre houses the H.C.
Burleigh Archives, a library & museum. The Heritage Centre is
owned & operated by the Bay of Quinte Branch of the United
Empire Loyalist Association of Canada. It is open from Apr-Oct &
by appointment at other times of the year.
Brian Tackaberry, Bay of Quinte Branch Vice-President, United
Empire Loyalist Association, 1784@uel.ca

Beachville: Beachville District Museum
PO Box 220, 584367 Beachville Rd,
Beachville, ON N0J 1A0

Tel: 519-423-6497; *Fax:* 519-423-6935
bmchin@execulink.com
www.beachvilledistrictmuseum.com
www.facebook.com/ 1025550934142072
Year Founded: 1992 The Beachville District Museum features
artifacts from the local history of Beachville. Open year round.

Beamsville: Jordan Historical Museum
4996 Beam St.,
Beamsville, ON L0R 1B0

Tel: 905-563-2799
museum@lincoln.ca
www.lincoln.ca/content/jordan-historical-museum
Local history & artifacts. Open May-Aug Mon 8:30-4:30, Tue-Sat
10:00-5:00; Sept-May Mon-Fri 8:30-4:30, Sat 1:00-4:00
Sylvia Beben, Manager, 905-563-2799, sbeben@lincoln.ca

Beaverton: Beaver River Museum
PO Box 314, 284 Simcoe St.,
Beaverton, ON L0K 1A0

Tel: 705-426-9641
bte.hist.soc@bellnet.ca
www.btehs.com
The Beaver River Museum consists of the Old Stone Jail, a
settlers' log house (c.1850), a brick house (c.1900), meeting
place & gift shop. Open May-Sept.
Heather Salzman, Curator
Ken Alsop, Archivist

Belleville: Belleville Public Library & John M. Parrott Art
Gallery
254 Pinnacle St.,
Belleville, ON K8N 3B1

Tel: 613-968-6731
gallery@bellevillelibrary.com
bellevillelibrary.com/johnmparrottartgallerys9.php
twitter.com/Bellvill ePL
Year Founded: 1973 The gallery is located on the third floor of
the public library. The gallery is open Tu, W & F 9:30-5:00, Th
9:30-8:00 & Sa 9:30-5:30.
Trevor Pross, CEO, 613-968-6731, tpross@bellevillelibrary.ca

Belleville: Belleville Scout-Guide Museum
350 Dundas St. West,
Belleville, ON K8P 1B3

Tel: 613-966-2740
www3.sympatico.ca/pandj
www.youtube.com/user/ScoutsAgonquinte
Year Founded: 1975 Scout & guide memorabilia; 25,000 items;
open by appointment only
Paul Deryaw, Curator, pandj@sympatico.ca
David Bentley, Historian & Archivist

Belleville: Glanmore National Historic Site
257 Bridge St. East,
Belleville, ON K8N 1P4

Tel: 613-962-2329; *Fax:* 613-962-6340
glanmore.ca
twitter.com/glanmorehns
www.facebook.com/GlanmoreNHS
The restored Victoria home of the Phillips-Burrows-Faulkner
families; original & period furnishings displayed in principal
rooms; paintings & decorative art from the Couldery Collection
on permanent exhibit; lamps from the Paul Lamp Collection, as
well as other exhibits; special exhibits/events held throughout the
year
Rona Rustige, Curator

Belleville: Hastings & Prince Edward Regiment Military
Museum
The Armoury, 187 Pinnacle St.,
Belleville, ON K8N 3A5

Tel: 613-966-2125; *Fax:* 613-966-2110
www.theregiment.ca/hpmuseum.html
Open year round.

Blind River: Timber Village Museum
PO Box 628, 180 Leacock St.,
Blind River, ON P0R 1B0

Tel: 705-356-7544
museum@blindriver.ca
www.blindriver.ca/art_culture/timber_village_museum
www.facebook.com/263 036348216
Other contact information: Year round: 705-356-2251
Year Founded: 1967 Ariftacts from the McFadden Lumber
Company, medical instruments, sports memorabilia & an art
gallery which exhibits works of contemporary local artists &
artisans. Open year round.

Bobcaygeon: The Boyd Museum
PO Box 1221, 21 Canal East,
Bobcaygeon, ON K0M 1A0

Tel: 705-738-9482; *Fax:* 705-738-0918
info@theboydmuseum.com
www.theboydmuseum.com
The museum shows, through artifacts & archival material, how
the Boyd family helped develop the Bobcaygeon & Kawartha
Lakes region. Open May, June & Sept., Sa 11:00-3:00, Su
1:00-3:00; July & Aug., W-Su 10:00-4:00.

Bobcaygeon: Kawartha Settlers' Village
PO Box 755, 85 Dunn St.,
Bobcaygeon, ON K0M 1A0

Tel: 705-738-6163
info@settlersvillage.org
settlersvillage.org
instagram.com/kawarthasettlersvillage
twitter.com/KSVillage
www.facebo ok.com/kawartha.settlersvillage
Over 20 historic homes & buildings collected on a former
Kawartha farm. Open daily May-Sept 10:00-4:00
Al Ingram, President
Maureen Lytle, General Manager,
maureen.lytle@settlersvillage.org

Borden: Base Borden Military Museum
Canadian Forces Base Borden, 27 Ram St.,
Borden, ON L0M 1C0

Tel: 705-423-3531; *Fax:* 705-423-3623
www.cg.cfpsa.ca
The Base Borden Military Museum consists of several buildings
& a memorial park. It features the history of CFB Borden, with a
collection of armoured vehicles, artillery pieces, trucks, & aircraft
from World War I, World War II, & the present. Base Borden also
displays the Avro 504 K aircraft, a Tiger Moth, a Silver Star, & a
Tutor aircraft.

Bothwell: Fairfield Museum
14878 Longwoods Rd., RR#5,
Bothwell, ON N0P 1C0

Tel: 519-692-4397
fairfield.museum@sympatico.ca
www.friendsoffairfieldmuseum.ca
Site of Moravian Delaware mission, est. 1792, destroyed 1813
by US soldiers; artifacts from burnt village
Chris Aldred, Curator, 519-692-4397

Bowmanville: Bowmanville Museum
Parent: Clarington Museums & Archives
37 Silver St.,
Bowmanville, ON L1C 3C4

Tel: 905-623-2734
www.claringtonmuseums.com
Restored as a period home to reflect the lifestyle of a wealthy
merchant family.

Bowmanville: Clarington Museums & Archives
Municipality of Clarington, 62 Temperance St.,
Bowmanville, ON L1C 3A8

Tel: 905-623-2734
info@claringtonmuseums.com
www.claringtonmuseums.com
claringtonmuseumsandarchives.blogspot.ca
twitter.com/ClarMuseum
www.fa cebook.com/110074875701103
Comprised of Bowmanville Museum, Clarke Museum, Sarah
Jane Williams Heritage Centre; depicts the early urban & rural
roots of the Municipality of Clarington; special collections
including Dominion Pianos & Organs; one of the largest doll
collections in Canada
Michael Adams, Executive Director,
madams@claringtonmuseums.com

Bowmanville: Sarah Jane Williams Heritage Centre
Parent: Clarington Museums & Archives
62 Temperance St.,
Bowmanville, ON L1C 3A8

Tel: 905-623-2734; *Fax:* 905-623-5684
www.claringtonmuseums.com/sarah-jane-williams-heritage-centr
e
Houses the majority of the Clarington Museums & Archives'
collection. Open Mon-Wed, Fri-Sat 10:00-4:00, Thu 10:00-8:00.
Free admission.

Bracebridge: Woodchester Villa
15 King St.,
Bracebridge, ON P1L 1T7

Tel: 705-645-5264; *Fax:* 705-645-7525
KBall@bracebridge.ca
www.octagonalhouse.com

Woodchester Villa is an octagonal house museum, which dates
back to 1882. The house is designated as a historic site, under
the Ontario Heritage Act. Woodchester Villa is open from
Canada Day to Labour Day.

Brampton: Lorne Scots Regimental Museum
2 Chapel St.,
Brampton, ON L6W 2H1

Tel: 519-833-9008
www.lornesmuseum.ca
History of various wars.
Maj. (Ret'd) Richard E. Ruggle, Chair, shepherd@kw.igs.net
Maj. (Ret'd) Tom Graham, Curator, tom069@sympatico.ca

Brantford: Bell Homestead National Historic Site
94 Tutela Heights Rd.,
Brantford, ON N3T 1A1

Tel: 519-756-6220; *Fax:* 519-759-5975
bellhomestead@brantford.ca
www.bellhomestead.ca
www.facebook.com/BellH omestead
Displays at the Bell Homestead National Historic Site depict the
household of Alexander Graham Bell, the invention of the
telephone, & the origins of Canadian telephone operations.
Brian Wood, Curator

Brantford: Brant Museum & Archives
Parent: Brant Historical Society
c/o Brant Historical Society, 57 Charlotte St.,
Brantford, ON N3T 2W6

Tel: 519-752-2483; *Fax:* 519-752-1931
information@brantmuseums.ca
www.brantmuseum.ca
www.youtube.com/user/branthistorical
twitter.com/branthistorical
www.f acebook.com/BrantHistoricalSociety
Local history. Features photographs, diaries, letters, & maps in
the archive collection. Open year round.
Chelsea Carss, Curator

Brantford: Canadian Military Heritage Museum
347 Greenwich St.,
Brantford, ON N3S 7X4

Tel: 519-759-1313
cmhm@execulink.com
www.canadianmilitaryheritagemuseum.ca
A privately owned & operated museum displaying artifacts from
Canada's military history. Hours of Operation: March & Apr.,
F-Su 10:00-4:00; May-Sept., Tu-Su 10:00-4:00; Oct. & Nov.,
F-Su 10:00-4:00.
Richard Shaver, Chair

Brantford: Myrtleville House Museum
Parent: Brant Historical Society
34 Myrtleville Dr.,
Brantford, ON N3V 1C2

Tel: 519-752-3216
information@brantmuseums.ca
www.brantmuseums.ca
One of the oldest homes in Brant County (1837); the museum
also promotes interactive learning & provide hands-on activities
to aid students in explore the heritage of the county. Open
year-round M-F 9:00-4:00
Tim Philp, President

Brantford: Personal Computer Museum
13 Alma St.,
Brantford, ON N3R 2G1

Tel: 226-227-5898
sbolton@bfree.on.ca
www.pcmuseum.ca
twitter.com/vint agepc
www.facebook.com/personalcomputermuseum
Year Founded: 2005 Exhibits the history of personal computers,
software & related magazines & books.
Syd Bolton, Contact, sbolton@bfree.on.ca

Brantford: Woodland Cultural Centre
PO Box 1506, 184 Mohawk St.,
Brantford, ON N3S 2X2

Tel: 519-759-2650; *Fax:* 519-759-8912
Toll-Free: 866-412-2202
www.woodland-centre.on.ca
www.youtube.com/user/woodlandcc1972
twitter.com/woodlandcc
www.facebo ok.com/WoodlandCulturalCentre
Year Founded: 1972 Houses a First Nations art gallery as well
as a museum with historical documents, artifacts & visual art.
Open Mon-Fri 9:00-4:00, Sat 10:00-5:00

Brighton: Presqu'ile Provincial Park
328 Presqu'ile Pkwy.,
Brighton, ON K0K 1H0

Tel: 613-475-4324
www.ontarioparks.com/park/presquile
pinterest.com/ontarioparks/presqu-ile;
instagram.com/presquilepp
twitter.com/PresquilePP
www.facebook.com/Pre squilePP
Year Founded: 1922 One of Ontario's oldest provincial parks;
includes displays & programs of early history of the area,
working lighthouse, camping sites & Nature Centre. Open year
round.

Brighton: Proctor House Museum
Parent: Save Our Heritage Organization
PO Box 578, 96 Young St.,
Brighton, ON K0K 1H0

Tel: 613-475-2144
info@proctorhousemuseum.ca
proctorhousemuseum.ca
www.facebook.com/proctorhousemuseum
Living museum: 1860s gentleman's home, completely furnished.

Brockville: Brockville Museum
5 Henry St.,
Brockville, ON K6V 6M4

Tel: 613-342-4397; Fax: 613-342-7345
museum@brockville.com
www.brockvillemuseum.com
www.facebook.com/586855 381324643
Year Founded: 1981 Brockville history & artifacts.
Natalie Wood, Director/Curator

Brockville: Fulford Place
Parent: Ontario Heritage Trust
287 King St. East,
Brockville, ON K6V 1E1

Tel: 613-498-3003; Fax: 613-498-1050
fulford@heritagetrust.on.ca
www.heritagetrust.on.ca/Fulford-Place/Home.a spx
Year Founded: 1993 Historic Edwardian mansion with seasonal
art exhibits.
Pamela Peacock, Contact

Brooke-Alvinston: A.W. Campbell House Museum
8477 Shiloh Line,
Brooke-Alvinston, ON N0N 1A0

Tel: 519-245-3710
www.scrca.on.ca
www.facebook.com/196653253699385
Other contact information: In-season phone: 519-847-5357
The museum is located in the A.W. Campbell Conservation
Area, R.R.#2 Alvinston, ON, off Nauvoo Rd. A typical 1890s
southwestern Ontario rural home comprises the museum, & the
conservation area also includes a campground & walking trails.
Brian McDougall, General Manager, St. Clair Conservation,
bmcdougall@scrca.on.ca

Bruce Mines: Bruce Mines Museum
Hwy. 17,
Bruce Mines, ON P0R 1C0

Tel: 705-206-9642
bmd.historicalsociety@gmail.com
www.facebook.com/522714371178738
Year Founded: 1961 Situated in a church built in 1894, the Bruce
Mines Museum features pioneer items such as an 1876 slot
machine, a Victorian doll house, & a Yakaboo canoe.

Burlington: Ireland House at Oakridge Farm
2168 Guelph Line,
Burlington, ON L7P 5A8

Tel: 905-332-9888; Fax: 905-332-1714
Toll-Free: 800-374-2099
www.museumsofburlington.com/ireland-house
Home of Joseph Ireland, built between 1835 & 1837; open year
round
Barbara Teatero, Director, Museums

Burlington: Joseph Brant Museum
1240 North Shore Blvd. East,
Burlington, ON L7S 1C5

Tel: 905-634-3556; Fax: 905-634-4498
Toll-Free: 888-748-5386
www.museumsofburlington.com/joseph-brant
vimeo.com/museumsofburlington
twitter.com/BurlingtonMuse
www.facebook.com/pages/Museums-of-Burlington/14389272142
Year Founded: 1942 The museum is a replica of the original
1800 home of Mohawk, Captain Joseph Brant,
"Thayendanegea"; exhibits relating to indigenous culture, with
emphasis on the Iroquois; history of Burlington; historical

costume exhibit, one of Ontario's finest collection of Victorian
clothing & accessories; open year round.
Barbara Teatero, Director of Museums

Caledonia: Edinburgh Square Heritage & Cultural
Centre
PO Box 2056, 80 Caithness St. East,
Caledonia, ON N3W 2G6

Tel: 905-765-3134; Fax: 905-765-3009
esquare.centre@haldimandcounty.on.ca
www.haldimandcounty.on.ca/residents .aspx?id=64
Artifacts relating to the history of Caledonia. Displays include an
original 1857 jail cell & the gypsum mining industry. Includes
reference library. Open Mon-Fri 10:00-4:30, Sat 11:00-3:00
Anne Unyi, Curator

Callander: Callander Bay Heritage Museum
PO Box 100, 107 Lansdowne St.,
Callander, ON P0H 1H0

Tel: 705-752-2282; Fax: 705-752-3116
museum@callander.ca
www.mycallander.ca/museum
www.facebook.com/4031686 0327
The museum contains exhibits about Dr. Allan R. Dafoe & the
Dionne quintuplets. The Alex Dufrense Gallery features the work
of local artists. The museum also houses local genealogical
sources & historical records for research.
Carol Pretty, Curator, cpretty@callander.ca

Cambridge: Cambridge Sports Hall of Fame
444 Hespeler Rd.,
Cambridge, ON N1R 8J6

Tel: 519-653-7071
info@cambridgeshf.ca
cambridgesportshalloffame.ca
Year Founded: 1997 The Hall of Fame seeks to celebrate the
sporting history of Cambridge through text, images, &
memorabilia, as well as annually inducting athletes, teams &
builders.
Gary Hedges, Chair
Jim Cox, Curator & Archivist

Cambridge: The Fashion History Museum
75 Queen St. East,
Cambridge, ON N3C 2B1

Tel: 519-654-0009
info@FashionHistoryMuseum.com
www.fashionhistorymuseum.com
www.instagram.com/fashionhistorymuseum
twitter.com/FashionHistoryM
www .facebook.com/fashionhistorymuseum
Year Founded: 2004 The museum's collection features over
8,000 garments & accessorie from the 1660s to the present. The
museum currently lacks a permanent home, but creates
travelling exhibitions & engages in research.
Kenn Norman, Chair
Jonathan Walford, Curator
Kenn Norman, Co-Founder

Cambridge: Valens Log Cabin Museum
1691 Regional Rd 97, RR#6,
Cambridge, ON N1R 5S7

Tel: 905-525-2183
C. 1836 restored homestead.

Campbellford: Campbellford-Seymour Heritage Centre
Campbellford-Seymour Heritage Society, PO Box 1294, 113
Front St. North,
Campbellford, ON K0L 1L0

Tel: 705-653-2634
csheritage@persona.ca
www.csheritage.org
Year Founded: 1989 The Campbellford-Seymour Heritage
Centre is the home of the Campbellford-Seymour Heritage
Society. The Society preserves & communicates the history of
Campbellford / Seymour, maintains local archives, & assists with
genealogical research.
Anne Linton, Secretary
Ian McCulloch, President

Cannington: Cannington Historical Museum
c/o Cannington & Area Historical Society, PO Box 196, 21
Laidlaw St. South,
Cannington, ON L0E 1E0

Tel: 705-432-3136
canningtonhistoricalsociety@hotmail.ca
www.canningtonh istoricalsociety.ca
Located in Cannington's MacLeod Park on Peace Street, the
Cannington Historical Museum features log homes (circa 1827 &
1857), an 1871 Canadian Northern Railway station, a 1929
Canadian National Railway caboose, the 1934 Derryville (LOL)

Hall, & a driving shed. The museum is open from Victoria Day to
Labour Day, or by appointment.
Ted Foster, President

Capreol: Northern Ontario Railroad Museum & Heritage
Centre (NORMHC)
26 Bloor St.,
Capreol, ON P0M 1H0

Tel: 705-858-5050; Fax: 705-858-4539
info@normhc.ca
www.normhc.ca
www.facebook.com/normhc67
Year Founded: 1993 Lumber, mining & railroad exhibits. Open
daily May-Sep 10:00-4:00
Brian Yensen, President
Stu Thomas, Vice President

Carleton Place: Carleton Place & Beckwith Heritage
Museum & Gardens
Parent: C.P. & Beckwith Historical Society
267 Edmund St.,
Carleton Place, ON K7C 3E8

Tel: 613-253-7013
cpbheritagemuseum@bellnet.ca
cpbheritagemuseum.ca
www.facebook.com/173158069407762
Year Founded: 1872 Local history of Carleton Place & Beckwith
Township. Open year round.
Jennifer Irwin, Manager

Carp: Diefenbunker Museum / Musée canadien de la
Guerre froide
PO Box 466, 3929 Carp Rd.,
Carp, ON K0A 1L0

Tel: 613-839-0007
www.diefenbunker.ca
pinterest.com/diefenbunker
twitter.com/Diefenbunker
www.facebook.com/diefenbunker
Other contact information: diefenbunker.wordpress.com
The museum is housed in a once secret Cold War era bunker,
which was meant to shelter members of the government in the
event of a nuclear attack. The bunker is now a National Historic
Site of Canada. The museum seeks to preserve the history of
Canada's involvement in the Cold War & to create interest in the
Cold War in general. Open daily 11:00-4:00.
Bernard Proulx, President
Mitchell Besner, Vice-President
David Loye, Director

Cayuga: Haldimand County Museum & Archives
PO Box 38, 8 Echo St.,
Cayuga, ON N0A 1E0

Tel: 905-772-5880; Fax: 905-772-1725
museum.archives@haldimandcounty.on.ca
www.haldimandcounty.on.ca/resident s.aspx?id=150
www.facebook.com/128909910457566
Temporary & permanent exhibits; 1835 log cabin on site;
regional & genealogical archives. Open Mon-Fri 10:00-4:30, Sat
10:00-3:00
Karen E. Richardson, Curator

Cayuga: Ruthven Park
PO Box 610, 243 Haldimand Hwy #54,
Cayuga, ON N0A 1E0

Tel: 905-772-0560; Fax: 905-772-0561
Toll-Free: 877-705-7275
info@ruthvenpark.ca
ruthvenparknationalhistoricsite.co m
www.pinterest.com/RuthvenPark_NHS
twitter.com/RuthvenPark_NHS
www.facebook.com/RuthvenParkNHS
A national historic site representing Canadian landscapes &
houses one of the three Haldimand Bird Observatory Banding
Stations.

Chapleau: Chapleau Centennial Museum
PO Box 129, 94 Monk St.,
Chapleau, ON P0M 1K0

Tel: 705-864-1122; Fax: 705-864-2138
www.chapleau.ca/en/visit/museumsteamengine.asp
Year Founded: 1967 Exhibits dedicated to the township's
railroading past & historical figures. Includes tourist information
centre, mineral collection, mounted animals, material related to
Chapleau & area.

Chatham: Chatham Railroad Museum
PO Box 434, 2 McLean St.,
Chatham, ON N7M 5K5

Tel: 519-352-3097
crms@mnsi.net
www.chathamrailroadmuseum.ca
www.facebook.com/195849387130379
Located in a CN baggage car built in 1955. Contains early
railroad equipment, several model trains & other memorabilia.
Open May through Labour Day, with group tours available all
year round.

Chatham: Chatham-Kent Historical Society
177 King St. East,
Chatham, ON N7M 3N1

Tel: 519-352-3565
info@ckblackhistoricalsociety.org
www.ckblackhistoricalsociety.org
https://www.facebook.com/CKBHS
Year Founded: 1992 The society offers guided tours of heritage
sites around the Essex & Kent areas of Southern Ontario, as
well as a Heritage Room featuring displays & archival material.
Lucille Cooper, Founder

Chatham: Chatham-Kent Museum
Parent: The Cultural Centre
Chatham Cultural Centre, 75 William St. North,
Chatham, ON N7M 4L4
Tel: 519-360-1998; *Fax:* 519-354-4170
Toll-Free: 800-714-7497
ckcccmuseum@chatham-kent.ca
www.chatham-kent.ca
twit ter.com/culturalcentre1
www.facebook.com/231501020233902
Local history museum & archives. Features a retrospective of
Chatham-Kent during first half of 20th century; special
exhibitions gallery with changing displays throughout year. Open
daily
Stephanie Saunders, Curator

Chatham: Milner Heritage House
59 William St. North,
Chatham, ON N7M 4L4
Tel: 519-360-1998; *Fax:* 519-354-4170
ckcccmuseum@chatham-kent.ca
www.chatham-kent.ca/milnerheritagehouse
ww w.facebook.com/231501020233902
Year Founded: 1943 Milner Heritage House depicts the turn-of-the-century
lifestyle of Robert Milner,a successful, local industrialist and
carriage maker. Also features award-winning artwork by Robert's
wife Emma, the Rev. Sandys bird collection & the MacPhail
exotic animal collection. Affiliated with the Chatham-Kent
Museum (The Cultural Centre)
Stephanie Saunders, Curator

Cheltenham: The Great War Flying Museum
c/o Brampton Flying Club, PO Box 27, 13691 McLaughlin
Rd., RR#1,
Cheltenham, ON L7C 3L7
Tel: 905-838-4936
info@greatwarflyingmuseum.com
www.greatwarflyingmuseum.com
www.youtube.com/TheGWFM
www.facebook.com/186888438015885
Volunteer group builds, maintains & flies WWI replica fighter
aircraft; artifacts from WWI; located at the Brampton Airport
Nat McHaffie, Curator

Chesterville: Chesterville Historical Society
PO Box 693, 14 Victoria St.,
Chesterville, ON K0C 1H0
Tel: 613-448-9130
www.northdundas.com/tourism/chesterville-heritage-centre
www.facebook.co m/ChestervilleDHS
Year Founded: 1984 The centre is housed in an 1867 building, &
features a collection of artifacts on local history.
Jill Metcalfe, President, 613-448-9130,
chestervillehistoricalsociety@gmail.com

Clinton: School on Wheels Railcar Museum
Sloman Memorial Park, PO Box 488, 76 Victoria Terrace,
Clinton, ON N0M 1L0
Tel: 519-482-3997
cnrschoolonwheels@gmail.com
www.schoolcar.ca
www.facebook.com/151143751653755
Year Founded: 1982 A former railway school that both children &
adults attended in Northern Ontario between 1926 & 1965 now
used as a museum.
Margaret Sloman, Curator

Cloyne: Cloyne Pioneer Museum & Archives
Parent: The Cloyne & District Historical Society
PO Box 228, 14235 Hwy. 41,
Cloyne, ON K0H 1K0
Tel: 613-336-8619
pioneerinfo@mazinaw.on.ca
pioneer.mazinaw.on.ca
www.flickr.com/photos/cdhs
www.facebook.com/1462641087369572
Artifacts from the pioneer days of the area including tools,
clothing, kitchen & other households effects, glass bottles, flat
irons, photos & old catalogues; genealogical archive. Open daily
Jun-Sep 10:00-4:00

Cobalt: The Bunker Military Museum
PO Box 848, 24 Prospect Ave.,
Cobalt, ON P0J 1C0
Tel: 705-679-5191; *Fax:* 705-679-5050
bunkermilitarymuseum@gmail.com
www.bunkermilitarymuseum.ca
www.faceboo k.com/bunkermilitarymuseum
Year Founded: 1990 The museum consists of the private military
memorabilia collection of Cobalt resident Jim Jones & is housed
in the Bilsky Block, in Cobalt.
Brit Griffin, Chair

Cobalt: Cobalt Mining Museum
PO Box 215, 24 Silver St.,
Cobalt, ON P0J 1C0
Tel: 705-679-8301
cobaltminingmuseum@gmail.com
cobalt.ca/visitors/museums
Year Founded: 1953 The museum preserves the world's largest
collection of native silver ore, mining & prospecting equipment &
artifacts, & fluorescent rock. Other displays highlight the early
cultural & social life of Cobalt. Underground tours of the Colonial
Adit can be arranged. Open daily 9:30-4:30

Cobourg: Cobourg Museum Foundation (CMF)
c/o Cobourg Museum Foundation, 141 Orr St.,
Cobourg, ON K9A 0J6
Tel: 905-373-7222
info@cobourgmuseum.ca
northumberlandheritage.ca
pinterest.com/CobourgMuseum
twitter.com/CobourgMuseum
Year Founded: 1999 The centre is housed in an old barracks
building; the site also includes an 1860's workman's cottage. It is
a non-profit charity & is managed by volunteers.
Joan Chalovich, Chair

Cobourg: Marie Dressler House
PO Box 673, 212 King St. West,
Cobourg, ON K9A 2N1
dresslermuseum@gmail.com
www.mariedressler.ca
Other contact information: Alternate URL:
www.dresslermuseum.ca
Local history & birthplace of actress Marie Dressler. Open
Mon-Fri 9:00-5:00
Rick Miller, President & Chair, Marie Dressler Foundation Board

Cochrane: Cochrane Railway & Pioneer Museum
PO Box 490, 210 Railway St.,
Cochrane, ON P0L 1C0
Tel: 705-272-4361; *Fax:* 705-272-6068
Located across from the train station in Cochrane; railway
artifacts & memorabilia, photographs & display.

Coldwater: Coldwater Canadiana Heritage Museum
PO Box 125, 1474 Woodrow Rd.,
Coldwater, ON L0K 1E0
Tel: 705-955-1930
www.coldwatermuseum.com
www.facebook.com/581207571912813
1840s log house & other buildings; open May - Oct.
Wayne Scott, Director/Curator

Collingwood: Bygone Days Heritage Village
879 Sixth St.,
Collingwood, ON L9Y 3Y9
Tel: 705-441-5109
www.bygonedaysheritagevillage.ca
Year Founded: 1972 The village features 30 buildings that date
from the mid-1800s, as well as costumed interpreters who walk
about the village. Open June-Oct., weekends 10:00-5:00.
Adara Bull, Contact, adarabull@yahoo.ca

Collingwood: The Collingwood Museum
PO Box 556, 45 St. Paul St.,
Collingwood, ON L9Y 4B2
Tel: 705-445-4811
www.collingwood.ca/museum
www.facebook.com/collingwoodmuseum
Large collection relating to history of Collingwood & area;
exhibits showcasing shipping & shipbuilding & early history.
Archival materials & special events & activities throughout the
year.
Susan Warner, Supervisor, Station & Museum,
swarner@collingwood.ca

Comber: Comber & District Historical Society Museum
10405 Hwy. 77,
Comber, ON N0P 1J0
Tel: 519-687-3400
combermuseum1.wix.com/comber-museum
www.facebook.com/2 90834654327344
Pioneer articles & agricultural items; admission by donation;
open Thu-Mon.
Mark McKinlay, Contact, markmckinlay@xplornet.com

Combermere: Madonna House Pioneer Museum
Madonna House Apostolate, 2888 Dafoe Rd., RR#2,
Combermere, ON K0J 1L0
Tel: 613-756-3713; *Fax:* 613-756-0211
combermere@madonnahouse.org
www.madonnahouse.org
www.youtube.com/MadonnaHouseCanada
twitter.com/madonnahouse
www.faceboo k.com/MadonnaHouse
Year Founded: 1967 History of early settlers in the area; located
in century-old barn
Fr. David May, Director General
Mark Schlingerman, Director General
Susanne Stubbs, Director General

Commanda: Commanda Museum
4077 Hwy. 522,
Commanda, ON P0H 1J0
Tel: 705-729-2113
rvlunn@gmail.com
www.commandamuseum.ca
www.facebook.com/commandageneralstoremuseum
Complete with original shelves, counter & floor from the 1870s;
features artifacts from 1870s - 1930s as well as a gift shops
which features work from the region; tea room. Open Jul-Sept
Wed-Sat 11:00-4:00

Copper Cliff: Copper Cliff Museum
26 Balsam St.,
Copper Cliff, ON P0M 1N0
Tel: 705-674-4455
curator@greatersudbury.ca
www.sudburymuseums.ca
Year Founded: 1901 Contains artifacts pertaining to the lifestyle
of residents of a mining community, photographs & documents
leading back to establishment of Copper Cliff.

Cornwall: Cornwall Community Museum
160 Water St. W,
Cornwall, ON K6H 5T5
Tel: 613-936-0280
cornwallcommunitymuseum@gmail.com
cornwallcommunitymuseum. wordpress.com
twitter.com/CornwallCMuseum
www. facebook.com/CornwallCommunityMuseum
Loyalist & local history archives, local domestic manufacturing.
Open year round Wed-Sun
Ian Bowering, Curator, 613-936-0842, ian10@bellnet.ca

Cornwall: Cornwall Community Museum in the Wood
House
Parent: Stormont, Dundas & Glengarry Historical
Society
PO Box 773, 160 Water St. West,
Cornwall, ON K6H 5T5
Tel: 613-963-0280
cornwallhistory@outlook.com
cornwallcommunitymuseum.wordpress.com
twitter.com/cornwallcmuseum
www. facebook.com/CornwallCommunityMuseum
Local history. Open Wed-Sun 10:00-4:00
Jeffrey Crooke, President, 613-537-2075
Ian Bowering, Curator, 613-936-0842, ian10bellnet.ca

Cornwall: Musée historique des Soeurs de l'Assomption de la Sainte Vierge
3213 Johnston Ave.,
Cornwall, ON K6K 1H4

Tél: 819-293-4560
suecar77@gmail.com
www.sasv.ca

costumes religieux; peintures; meubles; instruments de musique; sculptures; objets liturgiques.

Cornwall: Stormont, Dundas & Glengarry Highlanders Regimental Museum
505 - 4th St. East,
Cornwall, ON K6H 2J7

Tel: 613-936-9124; *Fax:* 613-993-8147
Open year round.

Cornwall Island: Ronathahon:ni Cultural Centre
RR#3,
Cornwall Island, ON K6H 5R7

Tel: 613-932-9452; *Fax:* 613-932-0092
Iroquois, Cree & Ojibwa artifacts.

Cumberland: Cumberland Heritage Village Museum
2940 Old Montreal Rd.,
Cumberland, ON K4C 1E6

Tel: 613-833-3059
cumberlandmuseum@ottawa.ca
www.ottawa.ca/museums
www.facebook.com/cumberlandmuseum
Representation of a rural village in the Lower Ottawa Valley, with artifacts related to period of 1880-1935; open year round

Deep River: Canadian Clock Museum
PO Box 1684, 60 James St.,
Deep River, ON K0J 1P0

Tel: 613-584-9687
enquiries@canclockmuseum.ca
www.canclockmuseum.ca
Year Founded: 2000 Clock seller & manufacturer history. Open Jun-Aug daily 10:00-4:00; Sept-May Tue-Sat 10:00-4:00

Delhi: Delhi Ontario Tobacco Museum & Heritage Centre
200 Talbot Rd.,
Delhi, ON N4B 2A2

Tel: 519-582-0278; *Fax:* 519-582-0122
delhi.museum@norfolkcounty.ca
www.delhimuseum.ca
www.facebook.com/2208 43701442455
Year Founded: 1979 Exhibits on tobacco, ginseng and alternate crops grown in Norfolk County. Also features tobacco-related machinery, local history & multicultural exhibits. Open year round

Delta: The Old Stone Mill, National Historic Site (DMS)
Parent: The Delta Mill Society
PO Box 172, 46 King St.,
Delta, ON K0E 1G0

Tel: 613-928-2584
info@deltamill.org
www.deltamill.org
www.facebook.co m/DeltaMill
The oldest surviving automatic stone grist mill in Ontario; showcases milling technology & 1800s industrial heritage. Artifacts include buhr millstones, 48 inch Swain turbines, roller mills. Open May-Sept

Dorset: Dorset Heritage Museum
PO Box 111, 1040 Main St.,
Dorset, ON P0A 1E0

Tel: 705-766-0323
dhm@muskoka.com
www.dorsetheritagemuseum.ca
Year Founded: 2001 Local history of the early pioneers of the Dorset area; open May-July, Sa & Su 10:00-4:00; July-Oct. W-Sa 10:00-4:00.
Kerry Lock, Chair

Dresden: Uncle Tom's Cabin Historic Site (UTCHS)
29251 Uncle Tom's Rd.,
Dresden, ON N0P 1M0

Tel: 519-683-2978; *Fax:* 519-683-1256
utchs@heritagetrust.on.ca
www.heritagetrust.on.ca/Uncle-Tom-s-Cabin-Historic-Site/home.aspx
www.facebook.com/2082286122579633
Uncle Tom's Cabin educates visitors about fugitive slaves in the Dresden area. The site focuses on the life of the Reverend Josiah Henson; The grounds feature the Josiah Henson Interpretive Centre, the North Star Theatre, the Underground Railroad Freedom Gallery, the Harris House, a smokehouse, a sawmill, the Josiah Henson House, a pioneer church, & the Henson Family Cemetery. Open May-Oct

Drumbo: Drumbo & District Museum
Parent: Drumbo & District Heritage Society
42 Centre St.,
Drumbo, ON N0J 1G0

Tel: 519-463-5233
DDHS1995Drumbo@yahoo.ca
ddhs1995.wordpress.com
Year Founded: 2012 Local history of Drumbo & the surrounding district. Open Tue 9:30-4:30; Jul-Aug Sun 10:00-4:00

Dryden: Dryden & District Museum
15 Van Horne Ave.,
Dryden, ON P8N 2A5

Tel: 807-223-4671; *Fax:* 807-223-7354
lgardner@dryden.ca
www.dryden.ca/city_services/museum
www.facebook.com /42558327650
First Nations & pioneer artifacts; minerals; archival material
Leah Gardner, Curator, lgardner@dryden.ca

Dundas: Dundas Museum & Archives
Parent: Dundas Historical Society Museum
139 Park St. West,
Dundas, ON L9H 1X8

Tel: 905-627-7412; *Fax:* 905-627-4872
mail@dundasmuseum.ca
www.dundasmuseum.ca
youtube.com/user/DundasMuseum
twitter.com/DundasMuseum
www.facebook.co m/DundasMuseum
Celebrates & preserves the story of the Dundas community; museum features true to life displays, & a diversified collection of exhibits reflecting the varied occupations & activities of those who have contributed to the development of the community.
Open Tue-Sat
Kevin Puddister, Curator, kpuddister@dundasmuseum.ca

Dundas: Griffin House National Historic Site
733 Mineral Springs Rd.,
Dundas, ON L9H 5E3

Tel: 905-648-8144
griffinhouse@hamilton.ca
www.museumsontario.ca/museum/Griffin-House
Year Founded: 1827 The house commemorates the determination of black men & women who journeyed to Canada via the Underground Railroad. Open July-Sept., Su 1:00-4:00.

Dunvegan: The Glengarry Pioneer Museum (GPM)
1645 County Rd. 30, RR#1,
Dunvegan, ON K0C 1J0

Tel: 613-527-5230
info@glengarrypioneermuseum.ca
www.glengarrypioneermuseum.ca
www.facebook.com/171844766199518
1840 log inn; miniature cheese factory; 1869 municipal hall; carriage shed & log barn; blacksmith shop

Ear Falls: Ear Falls District Museum
PO Box 309,
Ear Falls, ON P0V 1T0

Tel: 807-222-3624
Dedicated to the history of exploration, transportation, & the settlement of the area.

Egmondville: The Van Egmond House
Parent: The Van Egmond Foundation
80 Kippen Rd.,
Egmondville, ON N0K 1G0

Tel: 519-522-0413
dminhinn@gmail.com
thevanegmondfoundation.shutterfly.com
www.facebook.com/vanegmondhouse
Restored & furnished Georgian county-manor house dating to the mid-19th century with antiques indicitive of the time. Exhibits pioneer life, local history & the Van Egmond family.

Elgin: Jones Falls Defensible Lockmaster's House & Blacksmith Shop
PO Box 10, 182 Lock Rd.,
Elgin, ON K0G 1E0

Tel: 613-507-3185
Fully functioning blacksmith shop from 1843.

Elgin: Lockmaster's House Museum
c/o Chaffey's Lock and Area Heritage Society, PO Box 162,
Elgin, ON K0G 1E0

Tel: 613-359-5022; *Fax:* 613-359-6376
muffet@rideau.net
www.rideau-info.com/lockhouse/museum.html

Year Founded: 1982 Exhibits centered around the economic and social life of Chaffey's Lock & Area Heritage Society, the history of the house & Chaffey's Lock. Open daily June-Sept 9:00-4:30.
Gay Henniger, Contact, Chaffey's Lock and Area Heritage Society, ghenniger@live.ca

Elk Lake: Elk Lake Heritage Museum
c/o Corporation of Township of James, 575 Main St.,
Elk Lake, ON P0J 1G0

Tel: 705-678-2237
History of area, in particular, mining, lumbering & agriculture.

Elliot Lake: Elliot Lake Nuclear & Mining Museum
Lester B. Pearson Civic Centre, Hwy. 108,
Elliot Lake, ON P5A 2T1

Tel: 705-848-2287
Mining heritage; northern home of the Canadian Mining Hall of Fame; Dr. Franc Joubin Mineral Collection; open Sept-Jun Mon-Fri; Jul-Aug daily

Emeryville: Maidstone Bicentennial Museum
Parent: Maidstone & District Historical Society
1093 Puce Rd., RR#3,
Emeryville, ON N8M 2X7

Tel: 519-727-3766
stonegbb@cogeco.ca
Year Founded: 1984 Contains artifacts from the former Maidstone Township; the New Heritage Gardens feature native plants, trees, & shrubs.

Emo: Rainy River District Women's Institute Museum
PO Box 511, 21 Tyrell St.,
Emo, ON P0W 1E0

Tel: 807-482-2007; *Fax:* 807-482-2556
Pioneer museum & artifacts. Open mid May-Oct; other times by appointment

Englehart: Englehart & Area Historical Museum
PO Box 444, 67 - 6th Ave.,
Englehart, ON P0J 1H0

Tel: 705-544-2400; *Fax:* 705-544-8737
englehartandareamuseum@ntl.sympatico.ca
www.englehart.ca/node/25
www.f acebook.com/groups/207859746036914
Exhibits show how settlement along the Temiskaming & Northern Ontario railway created town of Englehart & brought homesteaders to the claybelt's rural communites. Open May-Oct Wed-Sun 10:00-4:00

Essex: Essex Railway Station
Parent: Heritage Essex Inc.
87 Station St.,
Essex, ON N8M 2C5

Tel: 519-776-9800; *Fax:* 519-776-7241
heritageessex@bellnet.ca
www.essexrailwaystation.ca
A restored stone railway station from 1887. Also on site are a heritage gardens area & two antique railcars.
Tony Malkowski, President

Exeter: Arkona Lions Museum & Information Centre
Parent: Ausable Bayfield Conservation
c/o Ausable Bayfield Conservation Authority, 71108 Morrison Line, RR#3,
Exeter, ON N0M 1S5

Tel: 519-235-2610; *Fax:* 519-235-1963
Toll-Free: 888-286-2610
www.abca.on.ca
www.youtube.com/user/TheAusable
twitter.com/LandWaterNews
www.facebook .com/1630061137621184
Arkona Lions Museum & Information Centre features local First Nations artifacts, Devonian era fossils, minerals, & semi-precious stone.
Brian Horner, General Manager, bhorner@abca.on.ca

Fenelon Falls: Fenelon Falls Museum
PO Box 179, 50 Oak St.,
Fenelon Falls, ON K0M 1N0

Tel: 705-887-1044
curator@maryboro.ca
www.maryboro.ca
Open daily June 15 - Labour Day; weekends only May 20-June 15 & Labour Day to Thanksgiving
Ali Scott, Curator

Fenelon Falls: Horseless Carriage Museum
1427 Kawartha Lakes County Rd. 8,
Fenelon Falls, ON K0M 1N0

Tel: 705-738-9576
info@horselesscarriage.net
www.horselesscarriage.net
www.youtube.com/user/lauracbennett
The museum is privately owned & operated, & specializes in early transportation & mechanical antiquities. Please call for an appointment.
Richard Bennett, Curator

Fergus: Wellington County Museum & Archives
0536 Wellington Rd. 18,
Fergus, ON N1M 2W3

Tel: 519-846-0916; *Fax:* 519-846-9630
Toll-Free: 800-663-0750
www.wellington.ca/en/museum.asp
Other contact information: Museum: 519-846-0916, ext. 5221
The Wellington County Museum reflects the history of Wellington County people. The museum is housed in the former House of Industry & Refuge. Permanent exhibits include a World War I military exhibit, a pioneer log cabin, a 1920s kitchen, & textiles. The archives feature historical & genealogical records which date back to the first settlement in Wellington County. The Couling Collection consists of architectural information.
Susan Dunlop, Curator
Karen Wagner, Archivist
Patty Whan, Conservator

Flesherton: South Grey Museum & Historical Library
PO Box 299, 40 Sydenham St.,
Flesherton, ON N0C 1E0

Tel: 519-924-2843
museum@greyhighlands.ca
www.southgreymuseum.ca
www.facebook.com/240275574222
Open Tues. - Sat. end of June - Labour Day, or by appt; Open Thurs. - Sat. Labour Day - June.
Kate Russell, Curator/Manager, 519-924-2843

Forest: Forest-Lambton Museum
8 Main St. North,
Forest, ON N0N 1J0

Tel: 519-786-3239
museum.forest@gmail.com
www.facebook.com/240210859331349
Local artifacts including doll collection; flax industry; early telephone equipment; Grand Truck Railroad; First Nation's Artifacts; pictures & documents from the 1800s

Foresters Falls: Ross Museum
Parent: Whitewater Historical Society
2022 Foresters Falls Rd.,
Foresters Falls, ON K0J 1V0

Tel: 613-646-2622
info@rossmuseum.ca
www.rossmuseum.ca
Year Founded: 1995 Local history. Open May-Sept

Fort Erie: Fort Erie Railroad Museum
Parent: Fort Erie Museum Services
400 Central Ave.,
Fort Erie, ON L2A 3T6

Tel: 905-894-5322
www.museum.forterie.ca/railroad.html
Includes Steam engine #6218, caboose & 2 train stations; open daily Victoria Day - Labour Day; open weekends until Thanksgiving
Jane Davies, Curator BA

Fort Erie: Old Fort Erie
350 Lakeshore Rd.,
Fort Erie, ON L2A 1B1

Tel: 905-871-0540
www.niagaraparks.com/old-fort-erie
Collection of military equipment housed in a reconstructed fort. Re=enactments, daily tours & demonstrations avaialble. Open May-Oct.

Fort Frances: Fort Frances Museum & Cultural Centre
259 Scott St.,
Fort Frances, ON P9A 1G8

Tel: 807-274-7891
ffmuseum@fort-frances.com
www.fort-frances.com/museum
www.facebook.com/FortFrancesMuseum
The community museum is housed in an 1898 schoolhouse. The exhibits of the Fort Frances Museum & Cultural Centre reflect the development of Fort Frances & the Rainy River District from pre-contact to present day.
Sherry George, Contact

Frankville: Maple Sugar House & Museum
41 Leacock Rd., RR#1,
Frankville, ON K0E 1H0

Tel: 613-275-2893 *Toll-Free:* 877-440-7887
mail@gibbonsmaple.com
www.rideau-info.com/gibbons
The House produces & sells maple syrup, maple sugar, maple butter & other maple products. As well, there displays from the past and present of maple syrup making equipment. Tours are offered.

Gananoque: Arthur Child Heritage Museum
Parent: Historic Thousand Islands Village Foundation
125 Water St.,
Gananoque, ON K7G 3E3

Tel: 613-382-2535; *Fax:* 613-382-2912
Toll-Free: 877-217-7391
ivillage@cogeco.net
www.1000islandsheritagemuseum.com
twitter.com/GanHeritage
www.facebook.com/ArthurChildHeritageMuseum
Year Founded: 1995 The museum building was once the main station for the Thousand Islands Railway; now it is the centrepiece of the Historic Thousand Islands Village complex.
Open daily 10:00-6:00.
Joanne van Dreumel, Executive Director
Deborah McGee, Finance Officer

Georgetown: Halton Hills Sports Museum & Resource Centre (HHSM)
Gordon Alcott Heritage Hall, Mold-Masters SportsPlex, 221 Guelph St.,
Georgetown, ON L7G 4A8

Tel: 905-873-1360
info.hhsm@bell.net
www.hhsm.ca
Year Founded: 2009 The museum commemorates the history of sports in the Halton Hills communities.
Finn Poulstrup, Chair
Steve Foreman, Vice-Chair
Bruce Andrews, Director
Pat Graham, Director
Dave Kentner, Director
Rod Pasma, Director
Mark Rowe, Director
Ron Stiel, Director

Gloucester: Gloucester Museum & Historical Society
4550B Bank St.,
Gloucester, ON K1T 3W6

Tel: 613-822-2076
www.gloucesterhistory.com
Domestic ware; agricultural implements; Gloucester History Society archives; City of Gloucester archives

Goderich: Huron County Museum & Historic Gaol
110 North St.,
Goderich, ON N7A 2T8

Tel: 519-524-2686; *Fax:* 519-524-1922
museum@huroncounty.ca
www.huroncountymuseum.ca
instagram.com/huroncountymuseum
twitter.com/hcmuseum
www.facebook.com/ huroncountymuseum
Year Founded: 1951 Local history including transportation, military, agriculture & early settlement. Open year round

Gore Bay: Gore Bay Museum
12 Dawson St.,
Gore Bay, ON P0P 1H0

Tel: 705-282-2040 *Toll-Free:* 887-732-955
gorebaymuseum@gmail.com
www.gorebaymuseum.com
Various artifacts & art exhibits as well as a marine museum.
Open June Tue-Sat 10:00-4:00; Jul-Oct Mon-Sat 10:00-4:00, Sun 2:00-4:00

Gore Bay: Western Manitoulin Island Historical Society Museum
PO Box 298, 12 Dawson St.,
Gore Bay, ON P0P 1H0

Tel: 705-282-2420
Canadian 19th century artifacts, including historical & documentary art. Open Mar-Nov

Gormley: Whitchurch-Stouffville Museum & Community Centre
14732 Woodbine Ave.,
Gormley, ON L0H 1G0

Tel: 905-727-8954; *Fax:* 905-727-1282
Toll-Free: 888-290-0337
www.townofws.ca/en/explore/museum.asp

Year Founded: 1971 The museum is located in the hamlet of Vandorf & includes the Bogarttown Schoolhouse, a restored 1850 log cabin, the Brown House, barn, & the Vandorf Public School; special events & programming, tours, craft workshops, & research material. Open year round.

Gowganda: Gowganda & Area Museum
General Delivery,
Gowganda, ON P0J 1J0

Tel: 705-624-3171
Silver mining displays; log cabin; research library & resource centre; open mid-May - mid-Sept.

Grafton: Barnum House Museum
PO Box 161, 10568 Country Rd. 2,
Grafton, ON K0K 2G0

Tel: 905-349-2656
barnum@heritagetrust.on.ca
www.heritagetrust.on.ca
Owned by the Ontario Heritage Trust, Barnum House was built in 1819. The home is an example of Neo-Classical architecture. The decor of Barnum House reflects an Upper Canada home between 1820 & 1840. Barnum House Museum is open from June to Labour Day.

Grand Bend: Lambton Heritage Museum
10035 Museum Rd, RR#2,
Grand Bend, ON N0M 1T0

Tel: 519-243-2600; *Fax:* 519-243-2646
heritage.museum@county-lambton.on.ca
www.lambtonmuseums.ca/heritage
tw itter.com/HeritageLambton
www.facebook.com/lambtonheritagemuseum
Year Founded: 1978 Extensive collection of pressed glass & Currier & Ives prints; features history of Sarnia-Lambton area including large collection of agricultural implements.

Gravenhurst: Bethune Memorial House National Historic Site
235 John St. North,
Gravenhurst, ON P1P 1G4

Tel: 705-687-4261; *Fax:* 705-687-4935
ont-bethune@pch.gc.ca
www.pc.gc.ca/bethune
At the Bethune Memorial House National Historic Site, the life & achievements of Dr. Henry Norman Bethune are commemorated. Dr. Bethune is recognized for his time in China, where he served as a surgeon & a teacher. Open from Jun-Oct

Gravenhurst: Muskoka Boat & Heritage Centre
275 Steamship Bay Rd.,
Gravenhurst, ON P1P 1Z9

Tel: 705-687-2115
realmuskoka.com
www.youtube.com/user/muskokasteamships
twitter.com/RMSSegwun
www.faceb ook.com/MuskokaSteamships
The Muskoka Boat & Heritage Centre presents the history of boat-building, Muskoka's steamship era, & life on the water in Muskoka. At the site is a large in water collection of antique boats. The RMS Segwun is the oldest operating steamship in North America. Open year round.

Gravenhurst: Muskoka Rails Museum
150-1 Second St.,
Gravenhurst, ON P1P 1H4

Tel: 705-646-9711
www.muskokarailsmuseum.com
Dedicated to showcasing the history of Canadian rail travel, with an emphasis on the Muskoka area. Guided historical tours of the area are available.

Grimsby: Grimsby Museum
PO Box 244, 6 Murray St.,
Grimsby, ON L3M 4G5

Tel: 905-945-5292; *Fax:* 905-945-0715
www.grimsby.ca/residents/cultural-facilities/museum
twitter.com/GrimsbyM useum
www.facebook.com/GriMuseum
Year Founded: 1984 The museum interprets the history of Grimsby from prehistoric times. The Gallery of the Forty explores the settlement of the United Empire Loyalists in 1787. The Grimsby museum provides educational programs, as well as local history & genealogical information. Open year round.
Janet Cannon, Director & Curator

Guelph: C.A.V. Barker Museum of Canadian Veterinary History
Ontario Veterinary College, University of Guelph, 50 Stone Rd.,
Guelph, ON N1G 2W1

Tel: 519-823-8800; *Fax:* 519-837-3230
www.museumsontario.ca/museum/C-A-V—Barker-Museum-of-Canadi
The museum details the history of the Ontario Veterinary College, as well as Canadian veterinary medicine in general & holds more than 10,000 items in its collection. The museum is open by appointment only.
Lisa Cox, Curator

Guelph: Guelph Civic Museum
52 Norfolk St.,
Guelph, ON N1H 4H8

Tel: 519-836-1221
guelphmuseums.ca
twitter.com/guelphmuseums
www.facebook.com/guelphmuseums
Year Founded: 1967 The museum is housed in a c. 1850 limestone building and features over 30,000 artifacts and 4,000 photos relating to the history of Guelph and area; special events and programming for children.
Tammy Adkin, Manager, Tammy.Adkin@guelph.ca
Bev Dietrich, Curator, 519-822-1260, bev.dietrich@guelph.ca

Guelph: Hammond Museum of Radio
595 Southgate Dr.,
Guelph, ON N1G 3W6

Tel: 519-822-2441
webweaver@hammondmuseumofradio.org
www.hammondmuseumofradio.org
The museum's collection includes hundreds of radios; open M-F 9:00-5:00, & weekends by request.
Nori Irwin-Hahn, Curator, curator@hammondmuseumofradio.org

Guelph: McCrae House
108 Water St.,
Guelph, ON N1G 1A6

Tel: 519-836-1482
museum@guelph.ca
guelphmuseums.ca
twitter.com/guelph museums
www.facebook.com/109822192370415
Year Founded: 1968 The house, built in 1858, is the 1872 birthplace of John McCrae, author of "In Flanders Fields", & a National Historic Site. Exhibitions interpret McCrae's life & times, & an award-winning historic garden is maintained by volunteers. Activities include garden teas, the Poppy Push, Teddy Bear Picnic & Canada Day celebration.
Bev Dietrich, Curator, 519-822-1260, bev.dietrich@guelph.ca

Haileybury: Haileybury Heritage Museum
PO Box 911, 575 Main St.,
Haileybury, ON P0J 1K0

Tel: 705-672-1922; *Fax:* 705-672-2551
hhmuseum@hotmail.ca
www.alexand.ca
Haileybury Heritage Museum is focused on one of Canada's ten worst natural disasters, the Great Fire of 1922 which destroyed 90 percent of the Town of Haileybury & communities in 18 surrounding townships in South Temiskaming; features a restored 1904 Toronto Railway Company streetcar (used as housing after the '22 fire); a 1922 Ruggles Fire Pumper; & the tugboat M.V. Beauchene.

Haliburton: Haliburton Highlands Museum
66 Museum Rd.,
Haliburton, ON K0M 1S0

Tel: 705-457-2760
info@haliburtonhighlandsmuseum.com
haliburtonhighlandsmuseum.com
twitter.com/HH_Museum
www.facebook.com/4 98191436905810
Year Founded: 1968 Local, lumbering & agricultural history. Open year round. Hours: Summer: Tue-Sun 10:00-5:00; Spring/Fall: Tue-Sat 10:00-5:00; Winter: Sat-Sun 10:00-5:00
Kate Butler, Director
Steve Hill, Curator

Halton Hills: Canadian Motorsport Hall of Fame & Museum (CMHF)
Parent: Canadian Motorsport Heritage Foundation
8220 - 5th Line,
Halton Hills, ON L7G 4S6

Tel: 905-876-2454
archives@cmhf.ca
www.cmhf.ca
www.instagram.com/CMHFofficial
twitter.com/CMHFofficial
www.facebook.c om/CanadianMotorsportHallOfFame
Year Founded: 1993 The CMHF seeks to honour & recognize the Canadians who have made a contribution to the area of motorsports. The CMHF is currently looking for a new location.
Dr. Hugh Scully, Chairman
John Magill, Vice-Chair

Hamilton: Canadian Football Hall of Fame & Museum
58 Jackson St. West,
Hamilton, ON L8P 1L4

Tel: 905-528-7566; *Fax:* 905-528-9781
info@cfhof.ca
www.cfhof.ca
www.youtube.com/user/CFHOFandM
twitter.com/CFHOF
www.facebook.com/CFHO FandM
Year Founded: 1962 The Canadian Football Hall of Fame & Museum features exhibits which depict the history of the game at all levels. A special section is dedicated to the Hall of Famers.
Mark DeNobile, Executive Director, mark@cfhof.ca
Dave Marler, Chair
Christopher Alfred, Curator, chris@cfhof.ca

Hamilton: Dundurn National Historic Site
610 York Blvd.,
Hamilton, ON L8R 3H1

Tel: 905-546-2872; *Fax:* 905-546-2875
dundurn@hamilton.ca
www.dundurncastle.com
Restored home of Sir Allan MacNab, one of Canada's first premiers. Depiction of mid-19th century life in over 40 rooms. Open year round Tue-Sun 12:00-4:00

Hamilton: Hamilton & Scourge National Historic Site
c/o Hamilton Museum of Steam & Technology, 900 Woodward Ave.,
Hamilton, ON L8H 7N2

Tel: 905-546-4797; *Fax:* 905-546-4798
www.hamilton-scourge.hamilton.ca
Research files on the Hamilton & Scourge, armed merchant schooners from the War of 1812, which capsized & lie in water off Port Dalhousie.
Michael McAllister, Curator, michael.mcallister@hamilton.ca

Hamilton: Hamilton Children's Museum
1072 Main St. East,
Hamilton, ON L8M 1N6

Tel: 905-546-4848; *Fax:* 905-546-4851
childrensmuseum@hamilton.ca
hamilton.ca/attractions/hamilton-civic-museu ms/hamilton-childrens-museum
Year Founded: 1978 This is an interactive, hands-on learning centre that offers children the opportunity to explore a wide variety of themes from the natural sciences & the arts. Open Oct-Mar Wed-Sat 9:30-3:30, Sun 11:00-4:00; Apr-Sep Tue-Sat 9:30-3:30

Hamilton: Hamilton Military Museum / Le musée militaire de Hamilton
610 York Blvd.,
Hamilton, ON L8R 3H1

Tel: 905-546-2872; *Fax:* 905-546-2875
military@hamilton.ca
hamilton.ca/attractions/hamilton-civic-museums/hami lton-military-museum
Uniforms, weapons & lifestyle from War of 1812, Rebellion of 1837-38, the Victorian era, Boer War, & WWI. Open year round Tue-Sun 12:00-4:00

Hamilton: Hamilton Museum of Mental Health Care
Level 2, Block B, St. Joseph's Healthcare Hamilton, West 5th Campus, 100 West 5th St.,
Hamilton, ON L9C 0E3

Tel: 905-522-1155
museumpc@stjoes.ca
www.stjoes.ca
Exhibits that showcase photographs, documents & artifacts from mental health care practices from the early years of the hospital. Open Mon, Wed, Fri 10:00-2:00
Katrina Peredun, Museum Coordinator, kperedun@stjoes.ca
Sharlene Wilson, Volunteer Coordinator, 905-552-1155, swilson@stjoes.ca

Hamilton: Hamilton Museum of Steam & Technology
900 Woodward Ave.,
Hamilton, ON L8H 7N2

Tel: 905-546-4797
steammuseum@hamilton.ca
www.hamilton.ca
The facility is a Civil & Power Engineering Landmark & a National Historic Site. It contains two steam engines that pumped water to Hamilton more than 140 years ago. Open year round Tue-Sun 12:00-4:00.

Hamilton: Hamilton Psychiatric Hospital Museum
c/o St. Joseph's Healthcare Hamilton, 100 West 5th St.,
Hamilton, ON L8N 3K7

Tel: 905-388-2511
museumpc@stjoes.ca
www.stjosham.on.ca
Other contact information: Alt. Phone: 905-522-1155 ext. 35512
With a variety of artifacts & photographs, the museum preserves the history of psychiatric care & treatment in Ontario with an emphasis on events at the Hamilton Psychiatric Hospital & in the regions it serves.
Katrina Peredun, Museum Coordinator, kperedun@stjoes.ca

Hamilton: Hermitage Gatehouse Museum
Sulphur Springs Rd.,
Hamilton, ON L9G 1L8

Tel: 905-525-2181
nature@conservationhamilton.ca
www.conservationhamilton.ca
Displays various artifacts from the family that formerly owned Hermitage Gatehouse as well as items that are relevant to the area.

Hamilton: HMCS Haida National Historic Site of Canada
57 Discovery Dr.,
Hamilton, ON L8L 8K4

Tel: 905-526-6742; *Fax:* 905-526-9734
haida.Info@pc.gc.ca
www.pc.gc.ca/lhn-nhs/on/haida.aspx
Commissioned in 1943 & dubbed "the fightingest ship in the Royal Canadian Navy," HMCS Haida saw service in WWII & the Korean War. Canada's most famous warship & the last of the Tribal Class destroyers left in the world is berthed at Hamilton.

Hamilton: Royal Hamilton Light Infantry Heritage Museum
John Weir Foote VC Armoury, 200 James St. North,
Hamilton, ON L8R 2L1

Tel: 905-528-2945
museumcurator@rhli.ca
www.rhli.ca/museum/museum.html
Military artifacts from 1830 to present, with specific reference to the Royal Hamilton Light Infantry; library
Stan Overy, Curator, 905-573-2002, museumcurator@rhli.ca

Hamilton: Whitehern Historic House & Garden
41 Jackson St. West,
Hamilton, ON L8P 1L3

Tel: 905-546-2018; *Fax:* 905-546-4933
whitehern@hamilton.ca
www.whitehern.ca/whitehern.php
Former home of the McQuesten family from 1852 - 1968; period rooms feature original furnishings.

Hamilton: Workers Arts & Heritage Centre (WA&HC)
51 Stuart St.,
Hamilton, ON L8L 1B5

Tel: 905-522-3003
wahc@wahc-museum.ca
www.wahc-museum.ca
twitter.com/WAHC
www.facebook.com/WorkersArtsandHer itageCentre
Year Founded: 1991 Located at Hamilton's former Custom House, which was built in 1860, the Workers Arts & Heritage Centre celebrates the history & culture of all working people in Canada. Exhibits include the labour movement in the Hamilton area, a history of office work, & the history of life on the shop floor, which explores Canada's early industrial days to the rise of automation in the workplace. The museum is open year-round.
Florencia Berinstein, Executive Director, florencia@wahc-museum.ca
Katherine Roy, Coordinator, Development, katherine@wahc-museum.ca
Brian Kelly, Coordinator, Facilities, brian@wahc-museum.ca
Andrew Lochhead, Coordinator, Program, andrew@wahc-museum.ca

Harrow: John R. Park Homestead
915 County Rd. 50 E RR#1,
Harrow, ON N0R 1G0

Tel: 519-738-2029
jrph@erca.org
erca.org/conservation-areas-events/conservation-areas/john-r-p
ark-homestea d
Living history museum. Open year round.

Hornell Heights: Canadian Forces Museum of
Aerospace Defence
Canadian Forces Base North Bay, 22 Wing,
Hornell Heights, ON P0H 1P0

Tel: 705-494-2011
aerospace.defence@live.ca
www.aerospacedefence.ca

Huntsville: Muskoka Heritage Place
88 Brunel Rd.,
Huntsville, ON P1H 1R1

Tel: 705-789-7576
www.muskokaheritageplace.org
twitter.com/muskokamuseum
www.facebook.com/MuskokaHeritagePlace
Other contact information: TTY: 705-789-1768
Muskoka Heritage Place contains the following: Muskoka
Museum, Muskoka Pioneer Village & the Portage Flyer Train.

Ignace: Ignace Heritage Centre
Ignace Public Library, PO Box 480, 36 Main St.,
Ignace, ON P0T 1T0

Tel: 807-934-2280; *Fax:* 807-934-6452
ceoignacelibrary@gmail.com
olsn.ca/ignace/?id=heritage.asp&label=heritag e&lang=en
www.facebook.com/218910864872499
Local history & artifacts relating to early life & people, fur trade,
railroads, logging, mining & road & air transportation. Open
Wed-Sat

Ingersoll: Ingersoll Cheese & Agricultural Museum
c/o Town of Ingersoll, 290 Harris St, Hwy. 119,
Ingersoll, ON N5C 2V5

Tel: 519-485-5510
curator@ingersoll.ca
ingersoll.ca/visitors/cheese-and-agricultural-museum/events-exhi
bits
twi tter.com/ingersollmuse1
www.facebook.com/IngersollCheeseMuseum
Includes cheese factory, blacksmith shop, barn, community
museum & Ingersoll Sports Hall of Fame. Open year round
Mon-Fri 10:00-5:00. Open daily in summer.
Scott Gillies, Curator

Ingersoll: Oxford County Museum School
PO Box 232, 290 Harris St.,
Ingersoll, ON N5C 3K5

Tel: 519-926-0206
info@museumschool.ca
www.museumschool.ca
Now located in the Ingersoll Cheese & Agricultural Museum, in a
replica rural schoolhouse; collection & archives located at the
Ingersoll Town Hall

Iron Bridge: Iron Bridge Historical Museum
PO Box 460, 1 James St.,
Iron Bridge, ON P0R 1H0

Tel: 705-843-2033; *Fax:* 705-843-2035
huronshores.ca/pointsofinterest/iron-bridge-historical-museum
Year Founded: 1974 Local history & pioneer artifacts. Includes
log house & farmers market. Open Jun-Sep daily 9:00-5:00

Iroquois: Carman House Museum
PO Box 472, 5895 Carman Rd,
Iroquois, ON K0E 1K0

Tel: 613-652-4808; *Fax:* 613-652-4636
www.facebook.com/CarmanHouseMuseum
Other contact information: Alternate phone: 163-543-3556
Carman House is a United Empire Loyalist home, which was
built in 1815. It is a living history museum, which reflects life in
1835. Open Jun-Sep

Iroquois Falls: Iroquois Falls Pioneer Museum
PO Box 448, 245 Devonshire Ave.,
Iroquois Falls, ON P0K 1E0

Tel: 705-258-3730; *Fax:* 705-258-3730
ifpioneermuseum@outlook.com
iroquoisfallschamber.com/page/pioneer_museum
www.facebook.com/557678680916361
Year Founded: 1970 Local history, the arrival of the first
Europeans in Iroquois Falls, the settlement of Iroquois Falls,
pioneer life, artifacts & photographs. Open May-Sep

Denis Charette, President & Curator,
d_charette2006@hotmail.com

Kagawong: Old Mill Heritage Centre & Post Office
Museum
PO Box 34, 15 Old Mill Rd.,
Kagawong, ON P0P 1J0

Tel: 705-282-1442
oldmillheritage@billingstwp.ca
www.kagawongmuseum.ca
www.facebook.com/KagawongMuseum
Year Founded: 2007 Local history
Rick Nelson, Curator
Dianne Fraser, Chair

Kakabeka Falls: Hymers Museum
RR#1,
Kakabeka Falls, ON P0T 1W0

Tel: 807-577-4787
www.facebook.com/HymersMuseum
Local history. Displays include mining, farming, logging, school
rooms, & a church.
Linda Turk, Contact, lindat@tbaytel.net

Kapuskasing: Ron Morel Memorial Museum
88 Riverside Dr.,
Kapuskasing, ON P5N 1B3

Tel: 705-337-4274; *Fax:* 705-337-1741
mci390.wix.com/ron-morel-museum
Museum is housed in two railway cars & a caboose headed by
steam locomotive 5107. One railway car is devoted to trains &
railway history, with a large working HO-gauge model. the
Heritage Caravan with its clay sculptures depict Northern
Ontario history. Open daily from early June to Labour Day
Julie Latimer, Curator, 705-337-4474

Kars: Swords & Ploughshares Museum
7500 Reeve Craig Rd. North, RR#1,
Kars, ON K0A 2E0

Tel: 613-489-3447; *Fax:* 613-489-1166
swords@calnan.com
www.calnan.com/swords
Year Founded: 1995 Military artifacts from 1914-present.
Includes agricultural machinery & implements. Open May-Oct &
by appointment.

Keene: Hope Water-Powered Saw Mill
c/o Otonabee Region Conservation Authority, 3414 Hope
Mill Rd,
Keene, ON K9H 7M9

Tel: 705-745-5791
hopemill.ca
twitter.com/thehopemill
www.facebook.com /hopemill.ca
Year Founded: 1966 The saw-powered Hope Mill has been
restored to its original charm and is fully functional.
Demonstrations & tours are offered. A collection of 19th-century
carpentry tools, as well as larger pieces of equipment (lathe,
planer, drill-press), are on exhibit.
Robert Rehder, Restoration Team Leader,
rrehder@sympatico.ca
Kathryn Campbell, Contact, kcampbell@trentu.ca

Keene: Lang Grist Mill
Lang Pioneer Village Museum, 104 Lang Rd,
Keene, ON K0L 2G0

Tel: 705-745-5791; *Fax:* 705-295-6644
Fully operational water-powered grist mill located on the west
bank of the Indian River at Lang Pioneer Village
(Otonabee-South Monaghan Township-County of Peterborough).

Keene: Lang Pioneer Village
c/o County of Peterborough, Attn: Lang Pioneer Village
Museum, 104 Lang Rd.,
Keene, ON K0L 2G0

Tel: 705-295-6694; *Fax:* 705-295-6644
Toll-Free: 866-289-5264
info@langpioneervillage.ca
langpioneervillage.ca
linkedin.com/in/lang-pioneer-village-museum-5470aa56
twitter.com/LangPioneer
www.facebook.com/langpioneervillage
Year Founded: 1967 Living history museum from 1800-1900;
over 25 restored buildings with costumed interpreters. Open
year round

Kenora: Lake of the Woods Museum
PO Box 497, 300 Main St. South,
Kenora, ON P9N 3X5

Tel: 807-467-2105; *Fax:* 807-467-2109
museum@kmts.ca
www.lakeofthewoodsmuseum.ca
www.facebook.com/LakeOfTheW oodsMuseum
Year Founded: 1964 Collection of more than 20,000 articles;
displays feature native & pioneer artifacts, natural history,
minerals, textiles, pictorial & archival material illustrating local
history. Open Sep-Jun Tue-Sat 10:00-5:00; Jul-Aug daily
10:00-5:00
Rita Boutette, Chair
Lori Nelson, Director

Keswick: Georgina Military Museum (GMM)
26061 Woodbine Ave.,
Keswick, ON L4P 3E9

Tel: 905-989-9900
frontdesk@georginamilitarymuseum.ca
www.georginamilita rymuseum.ca
www.facebook.com/georginamilitarymuseum
The museum is dedicated to teaching the public about the
involvement of Canadians in wartime conflicts throughout history.
Open Sa & Su 10:00-4:00.
Sid Giddings, President
Martin Connell, Vice-President
Ron Serkes, Vice-President

Keswick: Georgina Pioneer Village & Archives
Parent: Georgina Historical Society
26557 Civic Centre Rd., RR#2,
Keswick, ON L4P 3G1

Tel: 905-476-4305; *Fax:* 905-476-7492
curator@georgina.ca
www.georginapioneervillage.ca
www.flickr.com/photos/georginapioneervillage
twitter.com/GeorginaHistory
www.facebook.com/georginapioneervillage
Year Founded: 1975 Late 19th century historic village. Includes
schoolhouse, blacksmith shop, train station, apothecary &
genealogical archives. Open Jun-Aug, Wed-Sun 10:00-5:00 or
by appt.
Melissa D. Matt, Cultural Services Representative

Killarney: Killarney Centennial Museum
29 Commissioners St.,
Killarney, ON P0M 2A0

Tel: 705-287-2424; *Fax:* 705-287-2660
www.municipality.killarney.on.ca
Year Founded: 1967 The museum preserves historical artifacts
from the time of the fur trade to the present. Collection includes
household items, objects from local commercial fishing, logging,
mining & tourism industries, & photographs. Open Jun-Sep.

King City: King Township Museum
2920 King Rd.,
King City, ON L7B 1L6

Tel: 905-833-2331
kingmuseum@king.ca
www.king.ca
www.facebook.com/KingTownshipMuseum
Year Founded: 1982 Local history & artifacts including tools,
clothing, books & household items. Open Tue-Sat 10:00-4:00

Kingston: Bellevue House National Historic Site
(BHNHS)
35 Centre St.,
Kingston, ON K7L 4E5

Tel: 613-545-8666; *Fax:* 613-545-8721
bellevue.house@pc.gc.ca
www.pc.gc.ca/lhn-nhs/on/bellevue/index_e.asp
Built in the early 1840s, Bellevue House was the home of Sir
John A. Macdonald. The site is closed Nov-Mar, but groups may
make reservations.

Kingston: Canada's Penitentiary Museum (CPM) /
Musée pénitentiaire du Canada
PO Box 1174, 555 King St.,
Kingston, ON K7L 4Y8

Tel: 613-530-3122; *Fax:* 613-536-4815
fpm@cogeco.net
www.penitentiarymuseum.ca
twitter.com/CSCmuseum
www.f acebook.com/381003918638580
To preserve & interpret the past & contemporary experiences of
the people & places associated with the history of corrections in
Canada.
Dave St. Onge, Curator

Kingston: Cataraqui Archaeological Research Foundation / Kingston Archaeological Centre (CARF)
611 Princess St.,
Kingston, ON K7L 1E1

Tel: 613-542-3483
www.carf.info/archaeological-centre
twitter.com/carfki ngston
www.facebook.com/Kingstonarchaeologicalcentre
Year Founded: 1986 The Foundation was established to oversee the excavation of Fort Frontenac & to collect & preserve artifacts from the site. It is now involved in numerous archaeological projects at sites in Eastern Ontario, & operates the Kingston Archaeological Centre; educational programming & research collection. Open Mon-Fri 9:30-4:00.
Kip Parker, Executive Director
Ashley Mendes, Curator

Kingston: City of Kingston Fire Department Museum
271 Brock St.,
Kingston, ON K7L 1S5

Antique firefighting equipment, photographs & models

Kingston: Fort Henry
1 Fort Henry Dr.,
Kingston, ON K7K 5G8

Tel: 613-542-7388 *Toll-Free:* 800-437-2233
getaway@parks.on.ca
www.forthenry.com
twitter.com/FortHenry
www.face book.com/forthenry1832
The Citadel of Upper Canada, brought to life by the Fort Henry Guard; restaurant; gift stores; children's muster parades; festivals, events, historic dining
Darren Dalgleish, General Manager & CEO, St. Lawrence Parks Commission

Kingston: Frontenac County Schools Museum (FCSM)
PO Box 2146, 414 Regent St.,
Kingston, ON K7L 5J9

Tel: 613-544-9113
fcschoolsmuseum@gmail.com
www.fcsmuseum.com
www.facebook.com/SchoolsMuseum
This community museum & archives has a geographical focus on Frontenac County & the City of Kingston, with a heritage schoolroom, a late 19th 20th century archival collection & public elementary school records. Public programming includes costumed interpretive tours, educational programs & research assistance.

Kingston: Kingston Mills Blockhouse
573 Kingston Mills Rd.,
Kingston, ON K7L 4V3

Tel: 613-283-5170
Military lifestyle of Canadian soliders in 1839.

Kingston: Kingston Scout Museum (KSM)
PO Box 2259, 644 MacDonnell St.,
Kingston, ON K7K 4X2

Tel: 613-329-3456
www.kingstonmuseums.ca/kingston-scout-museum
Scouting memorabilia; open by appointment only.

Kingston: MacLachlan Woodworking Museum
2993 Hwy. 2 East,
Kingston, ON K7L 4V1

Tel: 613-542-0543
woodworkingmuseum.ca
twitter.com/maclachlanwood
www.facebook.com/maclachlanwood
Year Founded: 1967 Exhibits include tools & lifestyles of 19th century tradespeople; hands-on workshops, educational programs & demonstrations are offered. The gift shop stocks handmade wooden kitchenware, linen, toys & wooden ornaments.
Tom Riddolls, Curator, triddolls@cityofkingston.ca

Kingston: Marine Museum of the Great Lakes at Kingston
55 Ontario St.,
Kingston, ON K7L 2Y2

Tel: 613-542-2261; *Fax:* 613-542-0043
marmus@marmuseum.ca
www.marmuseum.ca
twitter.com/MMGLK
Year Founded: 1976 The museum showcases an original pumping station & steam engines built in 1891. Exhibits include the history of boat building, as well as Kingston's maritime history on the Great Lakes. An Eco Gallery focuses on environmental issues related to the Great Lakes. At dock is the Alexander Henry, a icebreaking ship built in 1959.

Doug Cowie, Museum Manager, manager@marmuseum.ca
Sandrena Raymond, Curator, curator@marmuseum.ca

Kingston: Military Communications & Electronics Museum
PO Box 17000 Forces, 95 Craftsman Blvd. Hwy 2,
Kingston, ON K7K 7B4

Tel: 613-541-4675; *Fax:* 613-540-8111
www.c-and-e-museum.org
Year Founded: 1963 Preserves & inteprets the Communications & Electronics Branch military history. Provides group & individual tours, responds to research requests & is available to provide expert artifact appraisals. Open May-Sep 11:00-5:00
Karen Young, Manager, 613-541-4211,
Karen.Young@forces.gc.ca
Annette Gillis, Curator, Artifacts & Research Inquiries, 613-541-5130, gillis.ae@forces.gc.ca

Kingston: Miller Museum of Mineralogy & Geology
Miller Hall, Queen's University, 36 Union St.,
Kingston, ON K7L 3N6

Tel: 613-533-6767; *Fax:* 613-533-6592
geol.queensu.ca/museum
Year Founded: 1931 Collection of rocks, minerals & fossils from around the world. Open Mon-Fri 8:30-4:30
Mark Badham, Curator, badham@queensu.ca

Kingston: Murney Tower Museum
Parent: Kingston Historical Society
c/o Kingston Historical Society, PO Box 54, 1421 King St W,
Kingston, ON K7L 4V6

Tel: 613-507-5181
kingstonhs@gmail.com
www.kingstonhistoricalsociety.com/murney-tower
instagram.com/murneytower
twitter.com/murneytower
www.facebook.com/Mur
neyTowerMuseum/?rf=108334745858091
Other contact information: Alternate Email:
murneytower@gmail.com
Tower, built in 1846, now houses military, agricultural, Aboriginal & early settlers' artifacts. Open daily May-Sep 10:00-5:00
Peter Gower, President, Kingston Historical Society
Graeme Watson, Chair, Murney Tower Committee

Kingston: Museum of Health Care
Ann Baillie Bldg. National Historic Site, 32 George St.,
Kingston, ON K7L 2V7

Tel: 613-548-2419
museum@kgh.kari.net
www.museumofhealthcare.ca
www.youtube.com/user/MuseumOfHealthCare
twitter.com/MuseumofHealth
www .facebook.com/MuseumofHealthCare
Year Founded: 1904 The museum, located in an early 1900s residence for student nurses, tells the story of the evolution of health care in Canada. Open May-Aug., Tu-Su 10:00-4:00.
Hugh Gorwill, Chair & President
Dr. James Low, Founder
Dr. Pamela Peacock, Curator

Kingston: Original Hockey Hall of Fame & Museum
Invista Centre, PO Box 82, 1350 Gardiners Rd., 2nd Fl.,
Kingston, ON K7L 4V6

Tel: 613-507-1943
info@originalhockeyhalloffame.com
www.originalhockeyhalloffame.com
www.facebook.com/207141552735961
Year Founded: 1943 Includes Don Cherry exhibit, Original Six Collection & a variety of artifacts. Open Thu-Sun 12:00-6:00
Mark Potter, President, mpotter1@cogeco.ca
Larry Paquette, Vice-President, ihhof@kos.net

Kingston: Princess of Wales' Own Regiment Military Museum
The Armouries, 100 Montreal St.,
Kingston, ON K7K 3E8

Tel: 613-532-1027
pwormuseum@hotmail.com
pwormuseum.ca
Year Founded: 1969 Open year round.
Stuart MacDonald, Curator

Kingston: Pump House Steam Museum
23 Ontario St.,
Kingston, ON K7L 2Y2

Tel: 613-544-7867
steammuseum.ca
twitter.com/PumpMuseum
www.facebook.com/pumphousemuseum
Former pumping station with artifacts relating to steam power; operating steam & pump engines

Gordon Robinson, Curator, grobinson2@cityofkingston.ca

Kingston: The Royal Military College Museum / Le musée du Collège militaire royal du Canada
PO Box 17000 Forces,
Kingston, ON K7K 7B4

Tel: 613-541-6000; *Fax:* 613-542-3565
www.rmc.ca/cam/mus
Year Founded: 1962 Housed in the Fort Frederick Martello Tower on the College grounds; holdings relate to the history of the College, the achievements of its ex-cadets & to the history of the Royal Navy Dockyard which once occupied the site; amongst the Museum's possessions is the Douglas Arms Collection; open daily last Sat. in June - Labour Day
Lena Beliveau, Curator

Kingsville: Canadian Transportation Museum & Heritage Village (CTMHV)
6155 Arner Townline,
Kingsville, ON N9Y 2E5

Tel: 519-776-6909; *Fax:* 519-776-8321
info@ctmhv.com
www.ctmhv.com
Year Founded: 1954 Located on County Road #23 in Kingsville, Ontario, the Canadian Transportation Museum collects, restores, & exhibits modes of transportation from the mid 1800s to 1992. Displays include horse drawn carts, fire trucks, & Ford Model Ts. The Heritage Village contains buildings, such as a one room schoolhouse, a train station, a log home, & a general store.

Kingsville: Jack Miner Bird Sanctuary & Museum
360 Rd. 3 West,
Kingsville, ON N9Y 2E5

Tel: 519-733-4034
www.jackminer.com
twitter.com/JM_Sanctuary
www.facebook.com/JackMinerMigratoryBirdSanctuar y
Year Founded: 1904 In addition to the sanctuary & grounds, the museum includes memorabilia, wildlife prints, medals, manuscripts & newspaper clippings, books, a bust of Jack Miner & letter from friend Henry Ford, & baseball bats from Ty Cobb.
Mary E. Baruth, Executive Director

Kingsville: Kingsville Historical Park
145 Division St. South,
Kingsville, ON N9Y 1P5

Tel: 519-733-2803
khpi@mnsi.net
khpi.mnsi.net
Year Founded: 2000 A military museum that exhibits artifacts from the United Empire Loyalists & Essex County citizens regarding their contribution to various wars. Open Mon-Tue, Thu-Sat 9:00-4:00

Kingsville: The Windsor Wood Carving Museum
Elford United Church, 6155 County Rd. 23,
Kingsville, ON N9Y 2E5

Tel: 519-776-7056
Year Founded: 1996 Located in Windsor's Central Library, the museum holds a collection of wood carvings from around the world.

Kirby: Clarke Museum
Parent: Clarington Museums & Archives
7086 Old Kirby School Rd.,
Kirby, ON L0B 1M0

Tel: 905-983-9243
info@claringtonmuseums.com
www.claringtonmuseums.com/clarke-museum
Exhibits early pioneer life in the Clarke township.

Kirkland Lake: Museum of Northern History at the Sir Harry Oakes Chateau
2 Chateau Dr.,
Kirkland Lake, ON P2N 3M7

Tel: 705-568-8800
museum@tkl.ca
www.museumkl.com
instagram.com/mnhchateau
twitter.com/MNHChateau
www.facebook.com/museu mkl
Year Founded: 1967 The Chateau, built by Sir Henry Oakes, has been preserved as a museum exhibit and & a space to preserve northern history. Open Sep-May Tue-Sat; May-Sep Mon-Sat

Kitchener: Doon Heritage Village
Parent: Waterloo Region Museum
10 Huron Rd.,
Kitchener, ON N2P 2R7

Tel: 519-748-1914; *Fax:* 519-748-0009
WaterlooRegionMuseum@regionofwaterloo.ca
www.waterlooregionmuseum.com
www.youtube.com/user/WaterlooRegionMuseum
twitter.com/WRegionMuseum
www.facebook.com/WaterlooRegionMuseum
Other contact information: TTY: 519-575-4608
Turn of the century living history village; open daily May - Dec.
Thomas A. Reitz, Curator/Manager, 519-748-1914,
TReitz@regionofwaterloo.ca

Kitchener: Joseph Schneider Haus Museum
466 Queen St. South,
Kitchener, ON N2G 1W7

Tel: 519-742-7752; *Fax:* 519-742-0089
jsh@regionofwaterloo.ca
www.schneiderhaus.ca
instagram.com/jschneiderhaus
twitter.com/JSchneiderHaus
www.facebook.c om/SchneiderHausNationalHistoricSite
Other contact information: TTY: 519-575-4608
Year Founded: 1981 Living history museum. Traces back to the
Schneider family, one of the first group of Pennsylvania German
Mennonites in the area. Open Jul-Sep Mon-Sat 10:00-5:00
Adele Hempel, Manager & Curator, 519-748-1914

Kitchener: THEMUSEUM
10 King St. West,
Kitchener, ON N2G 1A3

Tel: 519-749-9387; *Fax:* 519-749-8612
info@THEMUSEUM.ca
www.themuseum.ca
www.youtube.com/THEMUSEUMtv
twitter.com/THEMUSEUM
www.facebook.com/THE MUSEUMKitchener
Year Founded: 2003 Interactive cultural museum. Open daily
Frank Boutzis, President
Linda Fabi, Vice President

Kitchener: Waterloo Region Museum
10 Huron Rd.,
Kitchener, ON N2P 2R7

Tel: 519-748-1914; *Fax:* 519-748-0009
WaterlooRegionMuseum@regionofwaterloo.ca
www.waterlooregionmuseum.com
instagram.com/wregionmuseum
twitter.com/WRegionMuseum
www.facebook.com/WaterlooRegionMuseum
Other contact information: TTY: 519-575-4608
Local history. Also home to the Doon Heritage Village. Open
Jan-Apr, Sept-Dec Mon-Fri 9:30-5:00, Sat-Sun 11:00-5:00;
May-Sept Mon-Sun 9:30-5:00.
Adele Hempel, Manager & Curator, 519-748-1914

Kitchener: Woodside National Historic Site of Canada /
Lieu historique national de Woodside
528 Wellington St. North,
Kitchener, ON N2H 5L5

Tel: 519-571-5684; *Fax:* 519-571-5686
Toll-Free: 888-773-8888
ont-woodside@pc.gc.ca
www.pc.gc.ca/lhn-nhs/on/woodside /index.aspx
Woodside National Historic Site was the childhood home of
Canada's longest-serving Prime Minister William Lyon
Mackenzie King. Today, the house is restored to the Victorian
era of the 1890s. Open May-Dec

Komoka: Komoka Railway Museum Inc.
131 Queen St.,
Komoka, ON N0L 1R0

Tel: 519-657-1912
station-master@komokarailmuseum.ca
www.komokarailmuseum.ca
Year Founded: 1978 Restored railroad station; site includes
1913 Shay logging locomotive, 1939 CN baggage car, 1972
caboose & a collection of CN maintenance jiggers. Open Jul-Dec

Lakefield: Christ Church Community Museum
c/o St. John the Baptist Anglican Church, PO Box 217, 62
Queen St.,
Lakefield, ON K0L 2H0

Tel: 705-652-8302
stjohnslakefield.ca
History of Lakefield, & the Strickland family, The Bill Twist
Collection, Lakefield's literary history, & artifacts & displays of
Christ Church. Open 1:00-4:00 daily

Lanark: Lanark & District Museum
c/o The Corporation of the Township of Lanark Highlands,
PO Box 340, 75 George St.,
Lanark, ON K0G 1K0

Tel: 613-259-2575
lanarkanddistrictmuseum@gmail.com
www.lanarkcountymuseums.ca
twitter.com/LandMuseum
www.facebook.com/La narkDistrictMuseum
Other contact information: Alt. URL:
lanarkanddistrictmuseum.blogspot.ca
Year Founded: 1977 Open weekends, mid-May to mid-Oct.

Latchford: House of Memories
PO Box 82, 78 Trans-Canada Hwy,
Latchford, ON P0J 1N0

Tel: 705-676-2416
Year Founded: 1967 Local artifacts from 1900-1940, WWI &
WWII items, natural history exhibits, lumbering & blacksmith
tools.

Leamington: Point Pelee National Park of Canada,
Visitor Centre, DeLaurier Historical House, & Trail / Parc
national du Canada de la Pointe-Pelée
407 Monarch Lane, RR#1,
Leamington, ON N8H 3V4

Tel: 519-322-2365; *Fax:* 519-322-1277
Toll-Free: 888-773-8888
pelee.info@pc.gc.ca
www.pc.gc.ca./pelee
www.youtube.com/user/ParksCanadaAgency
twitter.com/PointPeleeNP
www.facebook.com/ParksCanada
Other contact information: TTY: 1-866-787-6221
Point Pelee National Park features the DeLaurier Historical
House. The homestead & barn depict the park's human &
cultural heritage. The Visitor Centre houses exhibits, a children's
discovery room, & theatre programs about the area's natural &
cultural heritage.

Limehouse: Canadian Military Studies Museum
RR#1,
Limehouse, ON L0P 1H0

Tel: 905-877-6522
The Canadian Military Studies Museum features artifacts from
the mid-17th century, the Boer War, World War I, & World War II,
to the Korean & Vietnam Wars.

Lincoln: Ball's Falls Centre for Conservation
3292 - 6th Ave.,
Lincoln, ON L0R 1S0

Tel: 905-562-5235; *Fax:* 905-788-1121
info@ballsfalls.ca
npca.ca/conservation-areas/balls-falls
www.facebook .com/BallsFalls
Other contact information: Wordpress: ballsfalls.wordpress.com
Year Founded: 2008 The Ball's Falls Centre for Conservation
offers information about the Niagara Peninsula's history, the
natural history of the Twenty Valley & its watershed, & the
Niagara Escarpment Biosphere Reserve. Historical homes, a
mill, & a church are available for touring. Open daily

Lindsay: Olde Gaol Museum
Parent: Victoria County Historical Society
50 Victoria Ave. North,
Lindsay, ON K9V 4G3

Tel: 705-324-3404
info@oldegaolmuseum.ca
www.oldegaolmuseum.cam
www.linkedin.com/company/olde-gaol-museum
www.facebook.com/OldeGaolMuseu m.VCHS
The Lindsay Jail, built in 1863, was historically known as the
County Gaol. The Victoria County Historical Society collects,
preserves, & exhibits the history of the County of Victoria.

Little Current: Centennial Museum of Sheguiandah
10862 Hwy. 6,
Little Current, ON P0P 1K0

Tel: 705-368-2367
museum@townofnemi.on.ca
www.manitoulin-island.com/museums/centennial_museum.html
Year Founded: 1967 Pioneer culture & history on Manitoulin
Island. Fall hours: Tu - Sa 9:00 - 4:30. Summer hours: M - W, F -
Su 9:00 - 4:30; Th 9:00 - 8:00.
Heidi Ferguson, Curator

London: Banting House National Historic Site
Parent: Canadian Diabetes Association
442 Adelaide St. North,
London, ON N6B 3H8

Tel: 519-673-1752; *Fax:* 519-660-8992
banting@diabetes.ca
www.diabetes.ca/about-us/who/banting-house
twitter .com/BantingHouse
www.facebook.com/BantingHouseNHS
Other contact information: Alt URL:
bantinghousenhsc.wordpress.com
Year Founded: 1984 The hosue where Dr. F.G. Banting, the
co-discoverer of insulin, once lived. Open Tu-Sa 12:00-4:00.
Grant Maltman, Curator

London: Canadian Medical Hall of Fame
267 Dundas St.,
London, ON N6A 1H2

Tel: 519-488-2003; *Fax:* 519-488-2999
cmhf@cdnmedhall.org
www.cdnmedhall.org
www.instagram.com/cdnmedhallfame
twitter.com/CdnMedHallFame
www.facebo ok.com/cdnmedhall
Year Founded: 1994 The Hall features a portrait gallery, featured
exhibits, a wall fo quotations, a stamp display refelcting the
history of Canadian health care, & a media theatre. Open M-F
8:30-4:30, Sa 10:00-5:00, Su 10:00-5:00 (May-Sept. only).
Bryce Taylor, Chair
Lissa Foster, Executive Director, lfoster@cdnmedhall.org
Debbie Ash, Finance Officer, dash@cdnmedhall.org

London: Eldon House
481 Ridout St. North,
London, ON N6A 5H4

Tel: 519-661-5169
info@eldonhouse.ca
www.eldonhouse.ca
www.facebook.co m/EldonHouseHeritageMuseum
Year Founded: 1961 House of the Harris family from 1834-1959
Maureen Spencer Golovchenko, Chair
Tara Whittmann, Curator, wittmann@eldonhouse.ca

London: Fanshawe Pioneer Village (FPV)
2609 Fanshawe Park Rd. East,
London, ON N5X 4A1

Tel: 519-457-1296
info@fanshawepioneervillage.ca
www.fanshawepioneervillage.ca
Costumed interpreters demonstrate life in mid-1800s to early
1900s rural Ontario crossroads community
Sheila Johnson, Executive Director,
sjohnson@fanshawepioneervillage.ca
Shanna Dunlop, Curator, sdunlop@fanshawepioneervillage.ca

London: First Hussars Museum
"A" Block, Wolseley Barracks, 701 Oxford St. East,
London, ON N5Y 4T7

1hmuseum@sympatico.ca
www.firsthussars.ca/museum.html
www.youtube.com/user/firsthussarstv
twitter.com/1stHussars
www.facebook.com/groups/2374582807
Follows the history of the 1st Hussars from 1856 until today;
includes material on the Boer War, the Great War & WWII;
located at 1 Dundas St., London, ON.
Alastair Neely, Curator

London: Forest City Gallery (FCG)
258 Richmond St.,
London, ON N6B 2H7

Tel: 519-434-5875
info@forestcitygallery.com
www.forestcitygallery.com
www.instagram.com/forestcitygallery
twitter.com/ForestCityGlry
www.fac ebook.com/forestcitygallery
Other contact information: Blog: www.fcgintern.blogspot.ca
Year Founded: 1973 An artist-run centre dedicated to
showcasing national & international artists working in
visual/media arts, performance, literature, & music. Open W-Sa
12:00-5:00.
Ruth Skinner, President, board@forestcitygallery.com
Jenna Faye Powell, Director

London: Grosvenor Lodge
Parent: Heritage London Foundation
1017 Western Rd.,
London, ON N6G 1G5
Tel: 519-645-2845; *Fax:* 519-645-0981
info@grosvenorlodge.com
grosvenorlodge.ca
www.facebook.com/grosvenorlo dge
Year Founded: 1981 1853 estate; operates as London Regional Resource Centre for Heritage & the Environment. Venue for meetings, seminars & social events; library & display areas open to public. Open Mon-Fri 9:00-4:30

London: Guy Lombardo Music Centre
205 Wonderland Rd. South,
London, ON N6K 3T3
Tel: 519-473-9003
seventyeights@aol.com
www.guylombardomusic.com/museum.html
Memorabilia relating to bandleader & his band, the Royal Canadians, including original recordings & videotapes.
Doug Flood, Director, 519-652-3417, seventyeights@aol.com

London: Jet Aircraft Museum (JAM)
2465 Aviation Lane Unit #2,
London, ON N5V 3Z9
Tel: 519-453-7000
info@jetaircraftmuseum.ca
www.jetaircraftmuseum.ca
www.youtube.com/user/JetAircraftMuseum
twitter.com/_JAM_News
www.faceb ook.com/JetAircraftMuseum
Year Founded: 2009 Modern Royal Canadian Air Force history.
Open Thu-Sat 10:00-4:00
Scott Ellinor, President, president@jetaircraftmuseum.ca

London: London Regional Children's Museum
21 Wharncliffe Rd. South,
London, ON N6J 4G5
Tel: 519-434-5726
info@londonchildrensmuseum.ca
www.londonchildrensmuseum.ca
pinterest.com/LDNchildrensmus
twitter.com/children_museum
www.facebook .com/LondonChildrensMuseum
Year Founded: 1975 Hands-on, interactive museum features ten themed galleries, school programs, day camps, workshops & birthday parties. Open Mon-Thu, Sat-Sun 10:00-5:00, Fri 10:00-8:00
Natalie Spoozak, President
Amanda Conlon, Executive Director, amanda@londonchildrensmuseum.ca

London: Museum London
421 Ridout St. North,
London, ON N6A 5H4
Tel: 519-661-0333; *Fax:* 519-661-2559
www.museumlondon.ca
plus.google.com/u/0/109986306694279488979
twitter.com/MuseumLondon
www .facebook.com/MuseumLondon
Operates Eldon House; exhibits include family life, historical & contemporary art & historical artifacts from the London area from 1834 to 1960
Brian Meehan, Executive Director
Cydna Mercer, Head of Administration
Melanie Townsend, Head of Exhibitions & Collections

London: Museum of Ontario Archaeology (MOA)
Lawson-Jury Bldg., University of Western Ontario, 1600
Attawandaron Rd.,
London, ON N6G 3M6
Tel: 519-473-1360; *Fax:* 519-850-2363
info@archaeologymuseum.ca
www.archaeologymuseum.ca
instagram.com/museontarch
twitter.com/MuseOntArch
www.facebook.com/Arc haeologyMuseum
Year Founded: 1981 Archaeological & ethnographical collection; Lawson archaeological site. Open Sep-Apr Tue-Sun & May-Aug daily 10:00-4:30
Ronald F. Williamson, President
Dr. Rhonda Bathurst, Executive Director, rhonda@archaeologymuseum.ca
Nicole Aszalos, Curator, nicole@archaeologymuseum.ca

London: The Royal Canadian Regiment Museum
Wolseley Barracks, 701 Oxford St. East,
London, ON N5Y 4T7
Tel: 519-660-5275
info@thercrmuseum.ca
www.thercrmuseum.ca
twitter.com/RCRMuseum
www.facebook.com/RCRMuseum
To serve as a training medium to teach regimental history; to preserve regimental history through the collection of documents, pictures, books & artifacts with emphasis on the RCR; to serve as a place of military interest for the public & Canadian Forces personnel; to provide research facilities for the study of Canadian military history.
Georgiana Stanciu, Curator

London: Secrets of Radar Museum
PO Box 24033, 2155-B Crumlin Side Rd.,
London, ON N5V 3Z9
Tel: 519-691-5922
info@secretsofradar.com
secretsofradar.com
www.facebook.com/SecretsofRadar
Year Founded: 2001 Exhibits artifacts that were used by radar mechanics, operators, teachers, trainers, physicists & researchers during WWII.

London: Spirit of Flight Aviation Museum
Parent: 427 Wing Association
2155 Crumlin Side Rd.,
London, ON N5V 3Z9
Tel: 519-455-0430
museum@427wing.com
www.427wing.com/museum
www.linkedin.com/company#3167726^trk=NUS_DIG_CMPY-fol
www.facebook.com/4 27winglondon
Other contact information: General Inquiries: info427wing.com
Civilian & military aviation history, artifacts & documents.
Michael Adams, Executive Director & Curator, michaeladamstv@gmail.com

Lucan: Donnelly Homestead
34937 Roman Line, RR#3,
Lucan, ON N0M 2J0
Tel: 519-227-1244
www.quadro.net/~donnelly
Historical on-site tours given on the original Donnelly property by current owner; artifacts & photographs; tours preferably by appt., year-round; private residence
J. Robert Salts, Owner, rsalts@quadro.net

Lucan: Lucan Area Heritage & Donnelly Museum
PO Box 427, 171 Main St.,
Lucan, ON N0M 2J0
Tel: 519-227-0756
lucanheritage@donnellymuseum.com
www.donnellymuseum.com
twitter.com/LucanHeritage
www.facebook.com/luca ndonnellymuseum
Year Founded: 1995 Exhibits dedicated to local history, Wilberforce Colony & the Donnelly family. Open holiday Mondays, Tue-Sun 11:00-4:00

Madoc: O'Hara Mill Homestead & Conservation Area
PO Box 56, 638 Mill Rd.,
Madoc, ON K0K 2K0
Tel: 613-473-2084
info@ohara-mill.org
www.ohara-mill.org
www.facebook.com/OHaraMillHomesteadAndConservationAre a
Year Founded: 1965 Attractions include O'Hara House, a log house, a saw mill, & a one room log schoolhouse. O'Hara House is restored to represent the Victorian era around 1840. The saw mill is a rare working English Gate or Reciprocating Frame saw mill. Grounds are open daily all year. Buildings are open May-Oct

Magnetawan: Magnetawan Historical Museum
PO Box 70, Hwy. 520,
Magnetawan, ON P0A 1P0
Tel: 705-387-3308
www.magnetawan.com/index.php/living/heritage-center
Other contact information: Alternate Phone: 705-387-3357
Restored plant & turbine that supplied first electricity for village; Artifacts commemorating the logging & farming history of the area. Open Jul-Aug daily 11:00-5:00

Manitowaning: Assiginack Museum Heritage Complex
125 Arthur St.,
Manitowaning, ON P0P 1N0
Tel: 705-859-3905
AssiginackMuseumCurator@gmail.com
www.assiginack.ca/assiginack-museum-heritage-complex
The Assiginack Museum & Heritage Park is a community & marine museum. Includes collection of glassware, porcelain & pottery. Visitors can see a pioneer home & school, a 19th century grist mill, & the Great Lakes steamship, S.S. Norisle.
Open from Jun-Sep
Kelsey Maguire, Curator

Manotick: Watson's Mill
PO Box 145, 5525 Dickinson St.,
Manotick, ON K4M 1A3
Tel: 613-692-6455
manager@watsonsmill.com
www.watsonsmill.com
twitter.com/watsonsmill
www.facebook.com/WatsonsMi llManotick
Year Founded: 1860 Operated by Watson's Mill Manotick Incorporated; 19th century working gristmill, built 1860; gift shop; tours; picnic area; live interpretation, gossip tours
Karlis Adamsons, President, Board of Directors

Marathon: Marathon District Museum
PO Box 728, 25 Stevens Ave,
Marathon, ON P0T 2E0
Tel: 807-229-8175
marathonmuseum@gmail.com
marathondistrictmuseum.weebly.com
Displaying information on the Gold Mines, Port Coldwell, Marathon's history, The Mill, Logging Camps & the D.C. Everest.

Markham: Markham Museum & Historic Village
9350 Markham Rd Hwy 48,
Markham, ON L3P 3J3
Tel: 905-305-5970; *Fax:* 905-305-5971
museuminfo@markham.ca
www.markham.ca/wps/portal/Markham/RecreationCultur e/MarkhamMuseum
Buildings, vehicles, furnishing & agricultural & industrial equipment that relate to Markham Township's history, from native presence to the 20th century. Open Mon-Fri 10:00-5:00, Sat-Sun 12:00-5:00

Markham: York Region District School Board Museum & Archives (YRDSB)
21 Renfrew Dr.,
Markham, ON L3R 8H3
Tel: 905-470-6119; *Fax:* 905-470-1783
museum@yrdsb.ca
www.yrdsb.ca/schools/museum/Pages/default.aspx
www.youtube.com/user/YRDSBMedia
twitter.com/YRDSB
The museum & archives collects & preserves material related to the development of education in what is now known as York Region. Open year-round with reduced hours in the summer.
Janet Emonson, Curator, jan.emonson@yrdsb.edu.on.ca

Marten River: Marten River Provincial Park Logging Museum
c/o Marten River Provincial Park, 2860 Hwy. 11 N,
Marten River, ON P0H 1T0
Tel: 705-892-2200; *Fax:* 705-892-2147
pinterest.com/ontarioparks/marten-river
Artifacts for early logging era in Northern Ontario.

Massey: Massey Area Museum (MAM)
150 Sable St.,
Massey, ON P0P 1P0
Tel: 705-865-2266
info@masseyareamuseum.com
www.masseyareamuseum.com
www.facebook.com/121143151263273
Year Founded: 1967 The museum details logging history, as well as Aboriginal, Fort LaCloche, mining, farming, & early settler history. Model rooms, a chapel, a general store, & Massey's first horse-drawn fire engine are also featured. There is also an historical & genealogical research centre, which includes records of the Township of Sables-Spanish River's ten cemeteries.

Matheson: Thelma Miles Historical Museum
374 Hough Rd.,
Matheson, ON P0K 1N0
Tel: 705-273-2325
History of the communities of Val Gagné, Shillington, Wavel, Ramore, Holtyre & Matheson from 1900-1945

Mattawa: Mattawa & District Museum
PO Box 9, 285 1st St.,
Mattawa, ON P0H 1V0
Tel: 705-744-5495
MattawaMuseum@gmail.comom
mattawamuseum.com
Year Founded: 1976 Local history. Open Thu-Mon 10:00-4:00

Mattawa: Voyageur Heritage Centre
Samuel de Champlain Provincial Park, PO Box 147,
Mattawa, ON P0H 1V0
Tel: 705-744-2276
www.ontarioparks.com/park/samueldechamplain
The Voyageur Heritage Centre tells the story of the Mattawa
River & the lives of the voyageurs. The centre features one of
the largest reproduced birch bark canoes.

Maxville: Glengarry Sports Hall of Fame
35 Fair St.,
Maxville, ON K0C 1A0
Tel: 613-527-1044
glenhalloffame@bellnet.ca
www.glengarrysports.com
www.facebook.com/121512007937959
Year Founded: 1978
William Hinse-MacCulloch, Curator

Meaford: Meaford Museum
111 Bayfield St.,
Meaford, ON N4L 1N4
Tel: 519-538-5974; *Fax:* 519-538-5974
meafordmuseum@meaford.ca
meaford.ca/meaford-museum.html
Year Founded: 1961 Local history, families, businesses &
Research Room. Open Sep-May Tue-Fri 11:00-3:00; Jun-Aug
daily 11:00-3:00
Jody Seeley, Services Coordinator, jseeley@meaford.ca

Meldrum Bay: Mississagi Strait Lighthouse Museum
Hwy 540,
Meldrum Bay, ON
Tel: 705-783-6014
info@themississagilighthouse.com
www.themississagilighthouse.com
www.facebook.com/116354762988
Other contact information: Alternate Email: w.madd@yahoo.ca
Lighthouse built in 1873, includes artifacts related to seafaring &
fishing; keeper's house features 19th-century furnishings; open
mid-May - Sept. Located at the western tip of Manitoulin Island,
near the village of Meldrum Bay.
Mary Eadie, Manager

Meldrum Bay: The Net Shed Museum
Water St.,
Meldrum Bay, ON
Tel: 705-282-2040
meldrumbaymarina.ca/netshed/index.html
www.facebook.co m/517808374965274
Other contact information: Alternate phone: 705-283-3267
Artifacts of pioneer fishing, lumbering & farming; display of
nursing in WWII. Open Jun-Aug Tue-Sat 11:00-5:00, Sun
11:00-4:00

Merrickville: The Blockhouse Museum
Parent: Merrickville & District Historical Society
PO Box 294,
Merrickville, ON K0G 1N0
Tel: 613-269-4034
info@merrickvillehistory.org
www.merrickvillehistory.org/museum.html
Built as a defence for the Rideau Canal built in 1830. Contains
local pioneer artifacts.

Middleville: Middleville & District Museum
2130 Concession Rd. 6D,
Middleville, ON K0G 1K0
Tel: 613-259-5462
middlevillemuseum@gmail.com
www.middlevillemuseum.blogspot.ca
www.facebook.com/186945718019189
Year Founded: 1974 Local pioneer artifacts including items for
the maple syrup, cheese & lumbering industries. Open Fri-Sun &
holiday Mondays 11:00-3:00 May-Thanksgiving

Midland: Huronia Museum
PO Box 638, 549 Little Lake Park,
Midland, ON L4R 4P4
Tel: 705-526-2844; *Fax:* 705-527-6622
info@huroniamuseum.com
www.huroniamuseum.com
www.flickr.com/photos/huroniamuseum
twitter.com/HuroniaMuseum
www.face book.com/huroniamuseum
Canada's first recreated Native village with a replica of a
pre-contact village, lookout tower, wigwam & longhouse.
Extensive exhibits on regional history, art gallery, archives &
Mundys Bay Store as well as a large selection of native &
historical books. Open Oct-May Mon-Fri 9:00-5:00; May-Oct
daily 9:00-5:00
John French, Chair

Midland: Martyrs' Shrine
PO Box 7, 16163 Hwy. 12 West,
Midland, ON L4R 4K6
Tel: 705-526-3788*Toll-Free:* 855-526-3788
info@martyrs-shrine.com
www.martyrs-shrine.com
twitter.com/martyrsshri ne1
www.facebook.com/204667312903160
Year Founded: 1926 Built in 1926 in tribute to the Jesuit
missionaries who laboured among the Huron, 1625-50, & to the
eight who were martyred, the interior of this church with its
wooden walls & canoe-like ceiling celebrates the melding of
historical cultures. Open daily May-Oct; tours & talks given on
request.
Fr. Bernie Carroll, Director

Midland: Sainte-Marie among the Hurons /
Sainte-Marie-au-Pays-des-Hurons
16164 Hwy. 12 East,
Midland, ON L4R 4K8
Tel: 705-526-7838; *Fax:* 705-526-9193
www.saintemarieamongthehurons.on.ca
Other contact information: TTY: 705-528-7697
During the 17th century, Sainte-Marie served as the fortress &
headquarters for the French Jesuit mission to the Huron nation.
Based upon archaeological & historical research, Sainte-Marie
was recreated on its original site. Special programs & courses
are offered about the first European community in Ontario. Open
Apr-Oct
Will Baird, General Manager, Huronia Historical Parks

Milford: Mariners Park Museum
2065 County Rd. 13,
Milford, ON K0K 2P0
Tel: 613-476-8392
marinersmuseum@pecounty.on.ca
pecounty.on.ca/government/community_development/museums/
mariners.php
www .facebook.com/museumspec
Year Founded: 1967 Indoor & outdoor exhibits as well as
displays of various artifacts from marine activity in the area,
including treasures from diving expeditions, as well as pieces
related to local fishing, ship building, ice harvesting & rum
running days. The False Duck Lighthouse has become a
memorial to the County's sailors.
Jennifer Lyons, Head Curator, Museums of Prince Edward
County, 613-476-3833, museums@pecounty.on.ca
Diane Denyes-Wenn, Site Curator, 613-476-8392

Miller Lake: Cabot Head Lightstation Museum & Visitor
Centre
806 Cabot Head Rd.,
Miller Lake, ON N0H 1Z0
Tel: 519-795-7780
www.cabothead.ca
www.facebook.com/CabotHead
Local history and artifacts.

Milton: Country Heritage Park
PO Box 38, 8560 Tremaine Rd.,
Milton, ON L9T 2Y3
Toll-Free: 888-681-2497
www.countryheritagepark.com
pinterest.com/countryherpark
twitter.com/countryherpark
www.facebook.c om/CountryHeritagePark
Display of machinery & tools related to all aspects of agricultural
industry in Ontario

Milton: Halton County Radial Railway (HCRR)
c/o Ontario Electric Railway Historical Association Inc., PO
Box 578, 13629 Guelph Line,
Milton, ON L9T 5A2
Tel: 519-856-9802; *Fax:* 519-856-1399
streetcar@hcry.org
www.hcry.org
twitter.com/streetcarmuseum
Operating streetcar & electric railway museum

Milton: Halton Region Museum
Kelso Conservation Area, 5181 Kelso Rd., RR#3,
Milton, ON L9T 2X7
Tel: 905-875-2200; *Fax:* 905-876-4322
Toll-Free: 866-442-5866
museum@halton.ca
www.halton.ca/museum
www.facebook.c om/HaltonRegionMuseum
Year Founded: 1962 Focusing on Halton's natural & cultural
heritage, the main exhibits are located in Alexander Barn & in
the Visitor Centre on the main floor. Both Heritage &
Environmental Programmes are offered. The Reference Library
stores various regional, historical records available for research
purposes. Open year round.

Milton: Waldie Blacksmith Shop
16 James St.,
Milton, ON L9T 2P4
Tel: 905-875-4156
info@miltonhistoricalsociety.ca
www.miltonhistoricalsociety.ca
twitter.com/miltonhistsoc
Administered by the Milton Historical Society; open mid-March to
Dec., Wed & Sat.
Mandy Sedgwick, President, Milton Historical Society

Mindemoya: Pioneer Museum
PO Box 320, 2207 Hwy. 551,
Mindemoya, ON P0P 1S0
Tel: 705-377-4045
www.centralmanitoulin.ca
www.facebook.com/CMHistoricalSociety
Other contact information: Alt Phone: 705-377-4045
The museum features a log cabin, workshop & blacksmith shop,
frame barn, farm equipment, & reinactments of pioneer life.
Open July & Aug., M-F 1:00-4:00, or by appointment.
Ted Taylor, President, 705-377-5649, tedeve@amtelecom.net
Linda Farquhar, Vice-President, 705-377-6691,
biglakelin@amtelecom.net

Minden: The Minden Hills Museum & Heritage Village
Minden Hills Cultural Centre, 174-176 Bobcaygeon Rd.,
Minden, ON K0M 2K0
Tel: 705-286-3154
museum@mindenhills.ca
mindenhills.ca/community-centre
Other contact information: Alternate Email:
mcoleman@mindenhills.ca
Year Founded: 1984 Local history & pioneer village. Open
May-Oct Tue-Sat 10:00-4:00
Laurie Carmount, Gallery Curator, 705-286-3763,
gallery@mindenhills.ca

Minesing: Simcoe County Museum
1151 Hwy. 26,
Minesing, ON L0L 1Y2
Tel: 705-728-3721; *Fax:* 705-728-9130
museum@simcoe.ca
museum.simcoe.ca
www.youtube.com/countyofsimcoe
twitter.com/simcoecountymus
www.facebo ok.com/simcoecountymuseum
Year Founded: 1928 Local history, including a replica of Barrie's
main street from th turn of the 20th century. Open daily,
9:00-4:30 Mon-Sat, Sun 1:00-4:00

Mississauga: Benares Historic House & Visitor Centre
1507 Clarkson Rd. North,
Mississauga, ON L5J 2W8
Tel: 905-822-2347
www.mississauga.ca/portal/discover/benareshistorichouse
Year Founded: 1995 Owned & operated by the City of
Mississauga, Community Services Department, the Benares
Historic House is a Georgian style home, which was built in
1857. The home has been restored to reflect the early 20th
century & displays original artifacts from the Harris family &
home. The Benares House is believed to be the inspiration for
Mazo de la Roche's Jalna novels.

Mississauga: Bradley House Museum
1620 Orr Rd.,
Mississauga, ON L5J 4T2

Tel: 905-615-4860
museums@mississauga.ca
culture.mississauga.ca/venu/bradley-museum
Year Founded: 1967 The museum grounds feature an early 19th century home known as The Anchorage, a farmhouse which was built in 1830, & a log cabin. Open year round.

Mississauga: Lithuanian Museum/Archives of Canada (LMAC)
Parent: Lithuanian Canadian Community
2185 Stavebank Rd.,
Mississauga, ON L5C 1T3

Tel: 416-533-3292
info@klb.org
www.klb.org/muziejusEN.html
Year Founded: 1989 To collect, display, organize & preserve documents, photographs, fine art, textiles, memorabilia, souvenirs of community events, uniforms, medals, coins, maps, flags, videos, audio tapes & rare books or periodicals which pertain to Lithuania & Lithuanian Canadians; small lending library

Mississauga: Old Britannia Schoolhouse
Friends of the Schoolhouse, 5576 Hurontario St.,
Mississauga, ON L5R 1C6

Tel: 905-890-1010
chair@britanniaschoolhousefriends.org
www.britanniasch oolhousefriends.org
The building is a one-room schoolhouse built in 1852. Today, modern school children are given the chance to role-play what it would have been like to attend the school in the 1800s. The building is open to visitors on the second Sunday of each month & space is also available for special functions.

Mississauga: Slovak Canadian Heritage Museum (SCHM)
5255 Thornwood Dr.,
Mississauga, ON L4Z 3J3

slovakmuseum@gmail.com
www.slovakcanadianheritagemuseum.ca
Artifacts relating to Slovak culture in the context of Canadian society
Margaret Dvorsky, President & Curator

Mississippi Mills: J.H. Naismith Museum & Hall of Fame
c/o Dr. James Naismith Foundation, 2854 Ramsay
Concession 8 RR#1,
Mississippi Mills, ON K0A 1A0

Tel: 613-256-3610
museum@naismithbasketballfoundation.com
naismithbasketballfoundation.com
Artifacts related to life of Dr. James Naismith, originator of game of basketball, as well as Canadian Basketball Hall of Fame exhibits & archives.

Mooretown: Moore Museum
94 Moore Line,
Mooretown, ON N0N 1M0

Tel: 519-867-2020
www.mooremuseum.ca
Year Founded: 1975 Open year round; Jan. - Feb. by appt.
Laurie Mason, Curator

Morpeth: Rondeau Provincial Park Visitor Centre
18050 Rondeau Park Rd.,
Morpeth, ON N0P 1X0

Tel: 519-674-1750
rondeau@ontario.ca
rondeauprovincialpark.ca/about-rondeau-park
instagram.com/rondeau_pp
twitter.com/Rondeau_PP
www.facebook.com/11267 6132080713
Hiking trails, summer & winter recreational opportunities & over 200 campsites. Herbarium, egg, mammal, insect, archaeological, photographic & bird collection. Open year round.
Brady Watterworth, President, Friends of Rondeau

Morrisburg: Upper Canada Village
13740 County Rd. 2,
Morrisburg, ON K0C 1X0

Tel: 613-543-4328 *Toll-Free:* 800-437-2233
getaway@parks.on.ca
www.uppercanadavillage.com
twitter.com/UpperCanada Vill
www.facebook.com/100502250000481
Upper Canada Village features more than forty heritage buildings. The village depicts daily life in the 1860s through

demonstrations, talks, & hands-on activities. The site also has a library & research facility. Open May-Oct

Mount Brydges: Ska-Nah-Doht Iroquoian Village & Museum
8348 Longwoods Rd.,
Mount Brydges, ON N0L 1W0

Tel: 519-264-2420; *Fax:* 519-264-1562
info@ltvca.ca
www.lowerthames-conservation.on.ca
Year Founded: 1973 This recreated Iroquoian village of 1,000 years ago has 18 outdoor exhibits including a palisade with maze & longhouses; museum in resource centre; displays on nature & conservation; trails, wetland boardwalks & picnic areas. There are hands on exhibits and an archaeological collection.

Mount Hope: Canadian Warplane Heritage Museum (CWHM)
9280 Airport Rd.,
Mount Hope, ON L0R 1W0

Tel: 905-679-4183; *Fax:* 905-679-4186
Toll-Free: 877-347-3359
museum@warplane.com
www.warplane.com
www.youtube.com/user/CWHMuseum
twitter.com/CWHM
www.facebook.com/CanadianWarplaneHeritageMuseum
Year Founded: 1971 The museum is dedicated to the acquisition & preservation of aircraft flown by Canadians from WWII to the present, & the collection of related aviation artifacts & memorabilia; library & archival resources; meeting room & hangar rental; special events & programming; group tours available. Open daily 9:00-5:00 year round.
David G. Rohrer, President & Chief Executive Officer, 905-679-4183
Erin Napier, Curator, 905-679-4183, erin@warplane.com

Mulmur: Dufferin County Museum & Archives (DCMA)
936029 Airport Rd.,
Mulmur, ON L9V 0L3

Tel: 705-435-1881; *Fax:* 705-435-9876
Toll-Free: 877-941-7787
info@dufferinmuseum.com
www.dufferinmuseum.com
twitt er.com/DufferinMuseum
www.facebook.com/DufferinCountyMuseum
Two log structures; CPR flagging station; historic church; changing exhibits; archives
Sarah Robinson, Curator, srobinson@dufferinmuseum.com

Napanee: Allan Macpherson House
180 Elizabeth St.,
Napanee, ON K7R 1B5

Tel: 613-354-3027
www.macphersonhouse.ca
www.facebook.com/200934956626534
Year Founded: 1967 1826 mansion of Allan Macpherson, one of Napanee's leading citizens; reflects the taste, public & private activities of an entrepreneurial Scottish immigrant. Open May-Dec. School programs; bridal party rentals; children's summer activity days; annual whiskey tasting.

Napanee: Lennox & Addington County Museum & Archives
97 Thomas St. East,
Napanee, ON K7R 4B9

Tel: 613-354-3027
nmuseum@lennox-addington.on.ca
www.lennox-addington.on.ca
Other contact information: Archives E-mail:
archives@lennox-addington.on.ca
Located in former County jail (1864); genealogy & historical research centre, county's origins, Loyalist settlement & development from 1784 to present, displays & extensive archives; open year round
Jane Foster, Manager, jfoster@lennox-addington.on.ca
Shelley Respondek, Archivist,
srespondek@lennox-addington.on.ca

Napanee: Old Hay Bay Church
2365 South Shore Rd.,
Napanee, ON K7R 3K7

Tel: 613-767-3100
kathystaples0@gmail.com
www.oldhaybaychurch.ca
www.facebook.com/OHBC1792
A National Historic Site, Old Hay Bay Church was erected in 1792. The church is the oldest Methodist building in Canada. Open May-Oct

Nepean: Fairfields Heritage House
3080 Richmond Rd.,
Nepean, ON K2B 7J5

Tel: 613-726-2652
museums@ottawa.ca
ottawa.ca/en/residents/arts-heritage-and-culture/museums-and-h istoric-site s
Other contact information: Alternate URL:
www.nepeanmuseum.ca/content/fairfields-0
19th century gothic revival farmhouse & local history.
Emily Greenlaw, Contact, emily.greenlaw@ottawa.ca

Nepean: Nepean Museum Inc. / Musée de Nepean
16 Rowley Ave.,
Nepean, ON K2G 1L9

Tel: 613-580-9638; *Fax:* 613-723-7936
museums@ottawa.ca
www.nepeanmuseum.ca
twitter.com/NepeanMuseum
www.f acebook.com/NepeanMuseum
Year Founded: 1983 Housed in the first Nepean Library, the museum displays historical objects related to Nepean's past & present. Nepean Museum contains two meeting rooms.

New Liskeard: Little Claybelt Homesteaders Museum
PO Box 1718, 883356 Hwy. 65 E,
New Liskeard, ON P0J 1P0

Tel: 705-647-9575
lchmuse@gmail.com
claybeltmuseum.ca
www.facebook.com /480542642108942
Year Founded: 1974 Exhibits the geological origin of Little Claybelt, pioneer activities, historical documents, artifacts & agricultural implements & pioneer family histories. Open during summer months.

Newmarket: Elman W. Campbell Museum
134 Main St. S,
Newmarket, ON L3Y 3Y7

Tel: 905-953-5314; *Fax:* 905-898-2083
Exhibits trace the development of Newmarket from the time of the first settlers. Open Tue-Sat.

Niagara Falls: Battle Ground Hotel Museum
6151 Lundy's Lane,
Niagara Falls, ON L2G 1T4

Tel: 905-358-5082
nfhmuseum@niagarafalls.ca
niagarafallsmuseums.ca/visit/battle-ground-hotel-museum.aspx
www.instagram.com/niagarafallsmuseums
twitter.com/nfmuseums
www.facebo ok.com/battlegroundhotelmuseum
The museum is located on the site of the Lundy's Lane Battlefield, is housed in a restored 1850s tavern & showcases artifacts related to the War of 1812. Open May-Aug., F-Su 11:00-5:00.
Dino Fazio, Co-Chair, Niagara Falls Arts, Culture & Museum Committee
Laura Moffat, Co-Chair, Niagara Falls Arts, Culture & Museum Committee

Niagara Falls: Daredevil Gallery
6170 Fallsview Blvd.,
Niagara Falls, ON L2G 7T8

Tel: 905-358-3611; *Fax:* 905-358-3613
Toll-Free: 866-405-4629
info@imaxniagara.com
imaxniagara.com/daredevil-exhibit
Collection of original daredevil barrels found in Niagara Falls

Niagara Falls: Guinness World Records Museum
4943 Clifton Hill,
Niagara Falls, ON L2G 3N5

Tel: 905-356-2299
falls.com/guinnessworldrecords
Interactive displays of human achievements, models of the extraordinary & games trivia. Open year round

Niagara Falls: Louis Tussaud's Waxworks
4983 Clifton Hill,
Niagara Falls, ON L2G 3N4

Tel: 905-374-6601
www.ripleys.com/niagarafalls/wax
Year Founded: 1953 Museum displays wax models of famous & infamous people, such as artists, musicians, celebrities, politicians & religious & historical figures. Open year-round.

Niagara Falls: Movieland Wax Museum of the Stars
4950 Clifton Hill,
Niagara Falls, ON L2G 3N4

Tel: 905-358-3061
www.cliftonhill.com/attractions/movieland-wax-museum-stars

Wax figures of movie, television & music celebrities. Includes House of Horrors & Fun Factory gift shop. Open year round

Niagara Falls: Niagara Falls History Museum
5810 Ferry St.,
Niagara Falls, ON L2G 1S9
Tel: 905-358-5082
nfhmuseum@niagarafalls.ca
www.niagarafallsmuseum.ca
plus.google.com/NiagarafallsmuseumsCanada
twitter.com/nfmuseums
www.facebook.com/nfmuseums
Year Founded: 1961 Exhibits include a significant collection of War of 1812 artifacts, as well as historic prints of Niagara Falls. The Museum also houses a variety of artifacts relating to all aspects of the founding & development of the City of Niagara Falls.
Clark Bernat, Manager

Niagara Falls: Niagara Military Museum
5049 Victoria Ave.,
Niagara Falls, ON L2E 4E2
Tel: 905-358-1949
niamilmuseum@gmail.com
www.niagaramilitarymuseum.ca
www.facebook.com/Niagara.Military.Museum.the.armoury
Year Founded: 2012 Military artifacts & local history of Niagara. Open Wed-Sat 11:00-4:00. Free admission.

Niagara Falls: Niagara Scouting Museum
4377 Fourth Ave.,
Niagara Falls, ON L2E 4N1
Tel: 905-354-6864
www.wj55.org
Collection contains scouting badges, uniforms, items from the 8th World Jamboree in 1955 & other items; open by appointment only.
Ted Claxton, Co-Chair, 519-998-8616
Anthony Roberts, Co-Chair, 905-354-6864

Niagara Falls: Ripley's Believe It or Not! Museum
4960 Clifton Hill,
Niagara Falls, ON L2G 3N4
Tel: 905-356-2238
nfalls@ripleys.com
ripleysniagara.com
ripleysniagara.tumblr.com
twitter.com/ripleysniagara
Year Founded: 1963 Ripley's Believe It or Not! in Niagara Falls presents strange & bizarre exhibits. The museum is open year-round.

Niagara Falls: Willoughby Historical Museum
9935 Niagara Pkwy.,
Niagara Falls, ON L2E 6S6
Tel: 905-295-4036; Fax: 905-295-4036
niagarafallsmuseums.ca/visit/willoughby-historical-museum.aspx
The Willoughby Historical Museum collects, preserves, interprets, & displays items related to Ontario's former Township of Willoughby, the Village of Chippawa, & the surrounding region. Artifacts include household objects, school materials, toys, telephones, & a functioning magneto switchboard. The museum is open year-round. Tours & research can be arranged by phoning the museum.

Niagara-on-the-Lake: Fort George National Historic Site of Canada
c/o Parks Canada National Office, 51 Queens Parade,
Niagara-on-the-Lake, ON L0S 1J0
Tel: 905-468-6614; Fax: 905-468-4638
Toll-Free: 888-773-8888
ont-niagara@pc.gc.ca
www.pc.gc.ca/en/lhn-nhs/on/fortge orge
twitter.com/fofg
www.facebook.com/friendsoffortgeorge
Other contact information: Friends of Fort George URL:
www.friendsoffortgeorge.ca
Reconstructed fort built in 1799; musket demonstrations. Open Apr-Dec

Niagara-on-the-Lake: McFarland House
15927 Niagara Pkwy.,
Niagara-on-the-Lake, ON L0S 1J0
Tel: 905-468-3322
mcfarland@niagaraparks.com
www.niagaraparks.com/niagara-falls-attractions/mcfarland-house
.html
Year Founded: 1959 Built in 1800 & home to John McFarland & his family for 150 years, the house served as a hospital for both the British & American wounded during the War of 1812. Restored by the Niagara Parks Commission in period style, there are also traditional grounds & the McFarland Tea Garden

to enjoy refreshments. Nature trails can be accessed from the park.

Niagara-on-the-Lake: Niagara Apothecary
5 Queen St.,
Niagara-on-the-Lake, ON L0S 1J0
Tel: 905-468-3845 Toll-Free: 800-220-1921
niagaraapothecary@ocpinfo.com
www.niagaraapothecary.ca
The Niagara Apothecary depicts an 1869 pharmacy. Artifacts include the Harvey bottles & jars, mortars & pestles, a 19th century leech jar, & tools. Open May-Oct daily 12:00-6:00

Niagara-on-the-Lake: Niagara Fire Museum
2 Anderson Lane,
Niagara-on-the-Lake, ON L0S 1J0
Tel: 905-468-7279
Fire-fighting equipment dating back 140 years. Not open to the public.

Niagara-on-the-Lake: Niagara Historical Society & Museum
PO Box 208, 43 Castlereagh St.,
Niagara-on-the-Lake, ON L0S 1J0
Tel: 905-468-3912; Fax: 905-468-1728
contact@niagarahistorical.museum
www.niagarahistorical.museum
Year Founded: 1895 Ontario's first purpose-built museum; artifacts from Niagara's social & military history
Sarah Kaufman, Managing Director

Nipigon: Nipigon Museum
40 Front St.,
Nipigon, ON P0T 2J0
Tel: 807-887-0356
nipigonmuseum@gmail.com
nipigon.net/visitors/nipigon-historical-museum
nipigonmuseumtheblog.blogspot.ca
www.facebook.com/128774150545422
Local history & artifacts relating to local lumbering & fur trading, rocks, minerals, & bottles. Open summer 11:00-8:00
Betty Brill, Curator

Nipissing: Nipissing Township Museum
4363 Highway 654,
Nipissing, ON P0H 1W0
Tel: 705-724-2938
nipissing.museum@hotmail.ca
nipissingtownship.com/web/^page_id=20
www.facebook.com/217430341633800
Housed in a former Anglican log church built in late 1800s. Displays tools, items from the local lumber industry, clothing & photos pertaining to families who first settled in the area. Open summer Wed-Sun 10:00-4:30
Tracy Butler, Curator
Liz Smith, Contact, 705-724-6943

North Bay: Dionne Quints Museum
c/o North Bay & District Chamber of Commerce, 1375
Seymour St.,
North Bay, ON P1B 9V6
Tel: 705-472-8480; Fax: 705-472-8027
Toll-Free: 888-249-8998
museum@northbaychamber.com
www.northbaychamber.com/tou rism/museum
The Quints Museum is a not for profit institution dedicated to the Dionne Quintuplets. Artifacts from the Quints's early years include baby buggies, baby dresses, books, newspaper and magazine articles, artisitic reproductions, postcards.
Kimberly Lyon, Director

North Bay: Discovery North Bay Museum
Parent: Heritage North Bay
100 Ferguson St.,
North Bay, ON P1B 1W8
Tel: 705-476-2323
www.discoverynorthbay.com
twitter.com/discoverynbay
www.facebook.com/discovery.n.bay
10,000 domestic & business objects related to the settlement & development of the local region. Open year round
Naomi Rupke, Director/Curator,
naomi.rupke@heritagenorthbay.com

North Buxton: Buxton National Historic Site & Museum
21975 A.D. Shadd Rd.,
North Buxton, ON N0P 1Y0
Tel: 519-352-4799
buxton@ciaccess.com
www.buxtonmuseum.com
www.facebook.com/168126086579515

Year Founded: 1967 The site is a memorial to the Elgin Settlement, which was the last stop on the Underground Railroad for many fugitives of the American system of slavery in the pre-Civil War years. The Raleigh (Buxton) Schoolhouse of 1861 & a settlement cabin from 1854 are now part of the museum. The museum preserves the artifacts of the original settlers of the Elgin Settlement & their descendants.
Shannon Prince, Curator

Norwich: The Norwich & District Museum & Archives
Parent: Norwich & District Historical Society
89 Stover St. North,
Norwich, ON N0J 1P0
Tel: 519-863-3101; Fax: 519-863-3638
norwichdhs@execulink.com
www.norwichdhs.ca
twitter.com/norwichdhs
ww w.facebook.com/archives@norwichdhs.ca
Other contact information: Archives e-mail:
archives@norwichdhs.ca
1889 Quaker meeting house; archives & genealogical library; blacksmith shop; CN station; restored Lossing house; dairy & agricultural barns; windmill & stump; Quaker school house

Oakville: Canadian Golf Hall of Fame & Museum (CGHF)
Glen Abbey Golf Club, 1333 Dorval Dr.,
Oakville, ON L6M 4X7
Tel: 905-849-9700
cghf@golfcanada.ca
www.rcga.org/cghf
Year Founded: 1971 The Canadian Golf Hall of Fame & Museum tells the history of golf in Canada. The Hall of Fame honours amateur & professional golfers & builders of the sport, who have made extraordinary contributions to the game in Canada. The archives & library collects photographs & documents, as well as golf publications about the game, golf courses & golfers. The museum also arranges travelling exhibitions. Open year round.
Karen Hewson, Managing Director, Membership & Heritage Services, khewson@golfcanada.ca
Meggan Gardner, Curator, mgardner@golfcanada.ca

Oakville: Oakville Museum at Erchless Estate
8 Navy St.,
Oakville, ON L6J 2Y5
Tel: 905-338-4400
oakvillemuseum@oakville.ca
www.oakville.ca/museum
twitter.com/oakville_museum
www.facebook.com/oa kvillemuseum
The Oakville Museum at Erchless Estate features the following historical buildings: Erchless Estate (c. 1858), The Custom House & Toronto Bank (c. 1856), & The Old Post Office (c. 1835). The Thomas Museum is operated by the Oakville Historical Society.
Bill Nesbitt, Museum Supervisor
Carolyn Cross, Curator, Collections
Susan Crane, Learning and Community Development Officer, Learning & Community Development

Oakville: Spruce Lane Farm House
Bronte Provincial Park, 1219 Burloak Dr.,
Oakville, ON L6M 4J7
Tel: 905-827-6911
bcppfriends@gmail.com
www.brontecreek.org
A living history museum located in Bronte Provincial Park.

Odessa: Historic Babcock Mill
100 Bridge St.,
Odessa, ON K0H 2H0
Tel: 613-386-7363
www.loyalisttownship.ca
Restored, fully operational water-powered 1856 mill

Ohsweken: Chiefswood National Historic Site
PO Box 640, 1037 Hwy. 54,
Ohsweken, ON N0A 1M0
Tel: 519-752-5005; Fax: 519-758-0768
chiefswood@sixnations.ca
www.chiefswood.com
www.youtube.com/user/Chiefswood
twitter.com/epaulinejohnson
www.facebo ok.com/epauline.johnson
The site is the location of the Chiefswood Museum, birthplace & childhood home of poet Emily Pauline Johnson (Tekahionwake); educational programming; tours; gift shop; "The Homing Bee" newsletter. Open Tues-Sun 10:00-3:00 May-Oct. Open by appointment Oct-May.

Oil Springs: Oil Museum of Canada
PO Box 16, 2423 Kelly Rd.,
Oil Springs, ON N0N 1P0
Tel: 519-834-2840; *Fax:* 519-834-2840
oil.museum@county-lambton.on.ca
www.lambtonmuseums.ca/oil
www.facebook .com/OilMuseumofCanada
Situated in Oil Springs, Ontario, The Oil Museum of Canada preserves the site of the first commercial oil well in North America. Visitors learn the story of Canadian oil pioneers, through petroleum industry artifacts, working exhibits & photographs. Visitors can also see original oil wells, which continue to produce oil.

Orillia: OPP Museum / Musée de l'OPP
777 Memorial Ave.,
Orillia, ON L3V 7V3
Tel: 705-329-6889; *Fax:* 705-329-6618
opp.museum@ontario.ca
www.opp.ca/museum
Exhibits artifacts used throughout the history of the Ontario Provincial Police. Open year round Mon-Fri 8:30-4:30. Free admission
Chris Johnstone, Curator, christine.johnstone@ontario.ca

Orillia: Stephen Leacock Museum
PO Box 625, 50 Museum Dr.,
Orillia, ON L3V 6K5
Tel: 705-329-1908; *Fax:* 705-326-5578
admin@leacockmuseum.com
orillia.ca/en/visitorillia/leacock-museum-and-na
tional-historic-site.asp
www.facebook.com/1040441929 64809
The home of Canadian author Stephen Leacock. Open daily 10:00-4:00
Jenny Martynyshyn, Administrative Coordinator, 705-329-1908

Oshawa: Canadian Automotive Museum
99 Simcoe St. South,
Oshawa, ON L1G 4G7
Tel: 905-576-1222; *Fax:* 905-576-1223
info@canadianautomotemuseum.com
www.canadianautomotivemuseum.com
instagram.com/canadianautomotivemuseum
twitter.com/CanAutoMuse
www.facebook.com/CanadianAutomotiveMuseum
Other contact information: Alternate Email:
camuseum@bellnet.ca
Year Founded: 1961 The Canadian Automotive Museum depicts the history & future plans of the Canadian automotive industry. More than sixty vehicles dating from 1898-1981 on display. Items related to the era of the vehicles are also displayed. Open daily
Denis Bigioni, President
Alexander Gates, Executive Director & Curator

Oshawa: Ontario Regiment (RCAC) Museum
Col. R.S. McLaughlin Armoury, 53 Simcoe St. North,
Oshawa, ON L1G 4R9
Tel: 905-728-6199
info@ontrmuseum.ca
www.ontrmuseum.ca
www.facebook.co m/Ontario.Regiment.Museum
Operational military vehicles
David Mountenay, President, president@ontrmuseum.ca
Earl Wotten, Curator, president@ontrmuseum.ca

Oshawa: Oshawa Community Museum & Archives (OCMA)
Parent: Oshawa Historical Society
Guy House, 1450 Simcoe St. South,
Oshawa, ON L1H 8S8
Tel: 905-436-7624
info@oshawamuseum.org
www.oshawamuseum.org
twitter.com/oshawamuseum
www.facebook.com/OshawaM useum
Preserves Oshawa's history from the earliest First Nation occupation to WWII. Includes Henry House c. 1849, Robinson House c. 1846, Guy House c. 1835, & Drive Shed. Open Sep-Jun Tue-Fri 8:00-4:00, Sun 12;00-4:00; Jul-Aug Mon-Fri 8:00-4:00, Sat-Sun 12:00-4:00
Merle Cole, President, Oshawa Historical Society
Melissa Cole, Curator

Oshawa: Parkwood National Historic Site, The R.S. McLaughlin Estate
270 Simcoe St. North,
Oshawa, ON L1G 4T5
Tel: 905-433-4311
info@parkwoodestate.com
www.parkwoodestate.com
www.youtube.com/user/ParkwoodEstate
twitter.com/ParkwoodEstate
www.fac ebook.com/194658330590548
Year Founded: 1989 Built between 1915 & 1917, Parkwood was the grand estate of R. Samuel McLaughlin, who was the founder of General Motors of Canada. The McLaughlin family lived at the home from 1917 to 1972. Today, it is furnished to reflect the 1920s & 1930s. The National Historic Site is open year-round.
Nancy Shaw, President
Diana Kirk, Vice-President
William Smith, Comptroller

Ottawa: The Billings Estate National Historical Site / Lieu historique national du domaine Billings
2100 Cabot St.,
Ottawa, ON K1H 6K1
Tel: 613-247-4830; *Fax:* 613-247-4832
museums@ottawa.ca
www.ottawa.ca/museums
www.facebook.com/billingsestat e
Home & property of Braddish & Lamira Billings, two of Ottawa's earliest settlers, c. 1828; exhibits highlight 5 generations of family & community history
Brahm Lewandowski, Museum Administrator

Ottawa: Bytown Museum / Musée Bytown
PO Box 523 B, 1 Canal Lane,
Ottawa, ON K1P 5P6
Tel: 613-234-4570; *Fax:* 613-234-4846
info@bytownmuseum.ca
www.bytownmuseum.ca
www.facebook.com/bytown
Bytown Museum is situated in the oldest stone building in Ottawa, which was a treasury & storehouse during the construction of the Rideau Canal. Within the museum, the history of Bytown & the nation's capital is traced. The museum is open Apr-Nov & during March Break. From Dec-Mar the museum is open by appointment only.
Tom Caldwell, President
Robin Etherington, Executive Director,
robinetherington@bytownmuseum.ca

Ottawa: Cameron Highlanders of Ottawa Regimental Museum
Cartier Sq. Drill Hall, 2 Queen Elizabeth Dr.,
Ottawa, ON K2P 2H9
Tel: 613-990-3507
www.camerons.ca
www.facebook.com/cameronhighlandersofottawa
The Regimental Museum contains memorabilia of the Cameron Highlanders of Ottawa. It is open one evening each week.

Ottawa: The Canadian Museum of Scouting
1345 Baseline Rd.,
Ottawa, ON K2C 0A7
Tel: 613-224-5131 *Toll-Free:* 888-855-3336
museum@scouts.ca
www.scouts.ca
twitter.com/scoutscanada
www.facebook .com/scoutscanada
Year Founded: 1907 Scouting artifacts & historical memorabilia (Canada/UK/World); Open by appointment only
Gord Kelly, Contact

Ottawa: Governor General's Foot Guards Regimental Museum
Drill Hall, Cartier Sq., 2 Queen Elizabeth Dr.,
Ottawa, ON K1A 0K2
Tel: 613-233-6979
footguards.ca
Regimental museum; brief history of regiment from 1872 to present by way of artifacts
Martin J. Lane, Curator CD, martinlane@rogers.com

Ottawa: Laurier House National Historic Site
335 Laurier Ave. East,
Ottawa, ON K1N 6R4
Tel: 613-992-8142; *Fax:* 613-947-4851
Toll-Free: 888-773-8888
laurier-house@pc.gc.ca
pc.gc.ca/en/lhn-nhs/on/laurier
Residence of Sir Wilfrid Laurier & the Right Honourable William Lyon MacKenzie King, built in 1878. Includes personal items & artwork.

Ottawa: Muséoparc Vanier Museopark
300, av des Pères Blancs,
Ottawa, ON K1L 7L5
Tel: 613-842-9871
info@museoparc.ca
www.museoparc.ca
www.instagram.com/museoparc
twitter.com/museoparc
www.facebook.com/MuseoparcVanier
Year Founded: 2006 Dedicated to preserving the heritage of the Quartier Vanier French-speaking community in Ottawa
Jean Malavoy, Executive Director, 613-842-9523,
direction@museoparc.ca
Janik Labossière, Curator & Program Manager,
recherche@museoparc.ca

Ottawa: Pinhey's Point Historic Site
270 Pinhey's Point Rd. Dunrobin,
Ottawa, ON K0A 1T0
Tel: 613-832-4347
museums@ottawa.ca
www.ottawa.ca/pinheyspoint
www.facebook.com/pinheyspoint
Former home of Hamnett Kirkes Pinhey, a British settler & prominent individual in Upper Canada. Open May - September.

Ottawa: Skate Canada Hall of Fame & Museum
PO Box 15, 261-1200 St. Laurent Blvd.,
Ottawa, ON K1K 3B8
Tel: 613-747-1007; *Fax:* 613-748-5718
Toll-Free: 888-747-2372
info@skatecanada.ca
www.skatecanada.ca
Year Founded: 1990 Photographs, videos, trophies & other materials significant to figure skating in Canada. Collection is available by appointment.

Ottawa: Workers' History Museum (WHM) / Musée de l'histoire ouvrière
PO Box 4461 E, 251 Bank St. 2nd Fl.,
Ottawa, ON K2P 1X3
Tel: 613-566-3448
info@workershistorymuseum.ca
workershistorymuseum.ca
www.youtube.com/user/WorkersHistoryMuseum
twitter.com/WorkersHistory
w ww.facebook.com/WHM.MHO
Year Founded: 2011 Labour history in the National Capital Region & Ottawa Valley.
Arthur Carkner, President
Paul Harrison, Vice President

Owen Sound: Billy Bishop Home & Museum
948 - 3rd Ave. West,
Owen Sound, ON N4K 4P6
Tel: 519-371-0031
info@billybishop.org
www.billybishop.org
twitter.com/BillyBishopHero
www.facebook.com/Billy BishopHomeMuseum
Year Founded: 1987 The museum, housed in the former home of Air Marshal William Avery Bishop & serves to preserve Canada's aviation history. Hours of Operation: Regular, Tu-F 11:00-5:00, Sa & Su 12:00-5:00; May-Oct., M-Sa 10:00-5:00, Su 12:00-5:00; Holidays 12:00-4:00.
Gloria Habart, Board Chair
Dave Alexander, Vice-Chair
John Totton, Director

Owen Sound: Grey Roots Museum & Archives
102599 Grey Rd. 18, RR#4,
Owen Sound, ON N4K 5N6
Tel: 519-376-3690; *Fax:* 519-376-4654
Toll-Free: 877-473-9766
info@greyroots.com
www.greyroots.com
twitter.com/gre yrootsmuseum
www.facebook.com/grey.roots
Year Founded: 1955 Collects, preserves, restores, documents, interprets & displays the material culture of Grey County & the city of Owen Sound, c. 1815 - present; research, interpretive programs, tours; gift shop
Petal Furness, Manager, 519-376-3690,
petal.furness@greyroots.com

Paris: Paris Museum
Syl Apps Community Centre, 51 William St.,
Paris, ON N3L 1L2

Tel: 519-442-9295
info@theparismuseum.com
theparismuseum.com
youtube.com/user/TheParisMuseum
twitter.com/TheParisMuseum
www.faceboo k.com/TheParisMuseum
Local history
Cate Breaugh, Chairperson

Parry Sound: West Parry Sound District Museum (WPSDM)
17 George St.,
Parry Sound, ON P2A 2X4
Tel: 705-746-5365; *Fax:* 705-746-8775
info@museumontowerhill.com
museumontowerhill.com
www.facebook.com/TheM useumonTowerHill
Year Founded: 1983 Situated in Tower Hill Park, the West Parry Sound District Museum displays items related to the First Nations, settlement, logging, shipping, agriculture, recreation, & natural history. The museum is open year-round.
Nadine Hammond, Curator/Manager

Pelee Island: Pelee Island Heritage Centre
1073 West Shore Rd.,
Pelee Island, ON N0R 1M0
Tel: 519-724-2291
peleeislandhc@gmail.com
www.peleeislandmuseum.ca
twitter.com/Pelee_Heritage
www.facebook.com/P eleeIslandHeritageCentre
The Island's natural heritage & human history displayed through rare flora & fauna exhibits, early navigation displays, local shipwreck information & historical events & places.

Pembroke: 42nd Field Regiment (Lanark and Renfrew Scottish) RCA Regimental Museum
177 Victoria St.,
Pembroke, ON K8A 4K2
Tel: 613-588-6166
Free admission; open year round, by appointment only.

Pembroke: Champlain Trail Museum & Pioneer Village
1032 Pembroke St. East,
Pembroke, ON K8A 6Z2
Tel: 613-735-0517; *Fax:* 613-629-5067
pembrokemuseum@nrtco.net
www.champlaintrailmuseum.ca
Economic, political & social history of upper Ottawa Valley & Renfrew County; archival & genealogical material

Penetanguishene: Discovery Harbour / Havre de la Découverte
93 Jury Dr.,
Penetanguishene, ON L9M 1G1
Tel: 705-549-8064; *Fax:* 705-549-4858
www.discoveryharbour.on.ca
Other contact information: TTY: 705-528-7697
Ontario's leading Marine Heritage Site; orginally built as a military base with its roots tracing back to the War of 1812. Tours, interactive daily activies in the summer. Open weekdays May-Jul; open daily Jul-Sept

Penetanguishene: Penetanguishene Centennial Museum & Archives
13 Burke St.,
Penetanguishene, ON L9M 1C1
Tel: 705-549-2150; *Fax:* 705-549-7542
info@pencenmuseum.com
www.pencenmuseum.com
www.facebook.com/1787791345 28
Penetanguishene's museum is housed in the former C. Beck Lumber Office & General Store which was built in 1875. The location also features a Genealogy & History Research Center & Archives, which houses the Georgian Bay Heritage League Collection with more than 500 genealogical files & local history books. Penetanguishene Centennial Museum & Archives is open year-round.
Nicole Jackson, Curator, njackson@pencenmuseum.com
Janice Gadsdon, Curatorial Assistant, jgadsdon@pencenmuseum.com

Perth: The Perth Museum
11 Gore St. East,
Perth, ON K7H 1H9
Tel: 613-267-1947
www.perth.ca/content/perth-museummatheson-house

Year Founded: 1967 1840 stone home of Senator Matheson; open year round; National Historic Site; 2 galleries; historic gardens
Karen Rennie, Contact

Petawawa: Canadian Airborne Forces Collection / Musée des Forces aéroportées canadiennes
Garrison Petawawa Military Museums, PO Box 9999 Main,
63 Colborne Rd.,
Petawawa, ON K8H 2X3
Tel: 613-588-6238
info@petawawamuseums.org
http://petawawamuseums.org
The Canadian Airborne Forces Museum preserves & honours the memory of airborne forces that served Canada since World War II. Their history is presented through historical artifacts, dioramas, videos, & a large screen mini-theatre. The museum is a member of the following organizations: the Organization of Military Museums of Canada, the Canadian Museums Association, the Ontario Museums Association, the Ottawa Valley Tourist Association, & the Renfrew County Museums Network. The Canadian Airborne Forces Museum is open year-round.

Petawawa: Canadian Forces Base Petawawa Military Museum
Canadian Forces Base Petawawa, PO Box 9999 Main, 63 Colborne Rd.,
Petawawa, ON K8H 2X3
Tel: 613-588-6238
info@petawawamuseums.com
www.petawawamuseums.com
The Canadian Forces Base Petawawa Military Museum collects, preserves, & interprets items related to the history of individuals & units of CFB Petawawa since 1905. Museum staff also assist with research requests. Open daily 11:00-4:00.

Petawawa: Petawawa Heritage Village
Parent: Petawawa Heritage Society
176 Civic Centre Rd.,
Petawawa, ON K8H 3B5
Tel: 613-633-6287
www.petawawaheritagevillage.com
twitter.com/kitchisibi
www.facebook.com/PHV1999
Year Founded: 2005 Local history & the settlement era of early Canada.
Ann McIntyre, President, Petawawa Historical Society, 613-687-5054, annmcintyre21@gmail.com

Peterborough: The Canadian Canoe Museum
910 Monaghan Rd.,
Peterborough, ON K9J 5K4
Tel: 705-748-9153; *Fax:* 705-748-0616
Toll-Free: 866-342-2663
info@canoemuseum.ca
www.canoemuseum.ca
canoemuseum.wordpress.com;
pinterest.com/cndncanoemuseum
twitter.com/CndnCanoeMuseum
www.facebook.com/CndnCanoeMuseum
Year Founded: 1997 Collection of over 600 canoes, paddled watercrafts & kayaks, plus related artifacts. Open year round
John Ronson, Chair
Jeremy Ward, Curator, jeremy.ward@canoemuseum.ca
Carolyn Hyslop, General Manager,
carolyn.hyslop@canoemuseum.ca

Peterborough: Hutchison House Museum
Parent: Peterborough Historical Society
270 Brock St.,
Peterborough, ON K9H 2P9
Tel: 705-743-9710
info@hutchisonhouse.ca
www.hutchisonhouse.ca
www.facebook.com/HutchisonHouse
Year Founded: 1978 Living history museum owned & operated by the Peterborough Historical Society. Includes doctor's study, Victorian parlour, period gardens & the Sir Sandford Fleming room. Open Jun-Sep Tue-Fri 10:00-4:00, Sat-Sun 11:00-4:00; Sep-May Mon-Fri 10:00-4:00

Peterborough: Peterborough Museum & Archives
Ashburnham Memorial Park, PO Box 143, 300 Hunter St. East,
Peterborough, ON K9J 6Y5
Tel: 705-743-5180; *Fax:* 705-743-2614
www.peterboroughmuseumandarchives.ca
www.youtube.com/channel/UCSARKb_GQSRs5DEI5pSCvgg
twitter.com/OntheHill3
www.facebook.com/112608310308

The heritage & culture of Peterborough & the surrounding area is preserved at Peterborough Museum & Archives. The Museum houses archaeological collections, technological artifacts, & military collections. The Archives holds over 2,000 fonds, including personal letters, maps, photographs, association records, early Peterborough Examiner newspapers, & the early records of Peterborough County Court. Open year round. Appointments are required to visit the Archives.
Kim Reid, Curator

Peterborough: Trent-Severn Waterway National Historic Site of Canada, Lock 21 - Peterborough Lift Lock
PO Box 567, 2155 Ashburnham Dr,
Peterborough, ON K9J 6Z6
Tel: 705-750-4900; *Fax:* 705-742-9644
Toll-Free: 888-773-8888
Ont.Trentsevern@pc.gc.ca
www.pc.gc.ca/en/lhn-nhs/on/tr entsevern
twitter.com/TrentSevernNHS
www.facebook.com/TrentSevernNHS
Other contact information: Teletypewriter (TTY): 705-750-4949
Opened in 1904, the Peterborough Lift Lock is the highest hydraulic lift lock in the world. Located next to Lock 21 is the Peterborough Lift Lock Visitor Centre, which contains exhibits & films. The Peterborough Lift Lock Visitor Centre is open during the navigation season.

Petrolia: Petrolia Discovery
PO Box 1480, 4281 Discovery Line,
Petrolia, ON N0N 1R0
Tel: 519-381-5979
petdisc@xcelco.on.ca
petroliadiscovery.com
www.facebook.com/ThePetroliaDiscoveryFoundationInc
Petrolia Discovery depicts the history of the pioneer oil men of Lambton County, Ontario. The museum is located at an oilfield which was established in the 1870s. This 19th century oilfield has been restored & is still operational. Petrolia Discovery is open from Victoria Day until Labour Day. School & educational tours may be arranged after the summer season.

Pickering: Pickering Museum Village
c/o City of Pickering, 2365 6th Concession Rd,
Pickering, ON L1V 6K7
Tel: 905-683-8401; *Fax:* 905-686-4079
Toll-Free: 866-683-2760
www.pickering.ca/en/pickering-museum-village.aspx
youtube.com/user/PickeringMuse; pinterest.com/pickeringmuse
twitter.com/pickeringmuse
www.facebook.com /pickeringmuse
Other contact information: TTY: 905-420-1739
Year Founded: 1961 The Pickering Museum Village features fifteen restored heritage buildings, including a schoolhouse, churches, blacksmith shop, houses, & barns. Open Jun-Sep

Picton: Macaulay Heritage Park
35 Church St.,
Picton, ON K0K 2T0
Tel: 613-476-3833; *Fax:* 613-476-8356
pecounty.on.ca/government/community_development/museums/
macaulay.php
www .facebook.com/museumspec
Year Founded: 1973 The site encompasses the 1830 Macaulay House, home of the Rev. William Macaulay, carriage house, heritage gardens & former St. Mary Magdalene Church and cemetary; open May-Sep Tue-Sun 1:00-4:30; Jul-Aug 10:00-4:30
Jennifer Lyons, Head Curator, Museums of Prince Edward County, 613-476-2148

Picton: Rose House Museum
3333 County Rd. 8,
Picton, ON K0K 2T0
Tel: 613-476-5439
museums@pecounty.on.ca
pecounty.on.ca/government/community_development/museums/
rose_house.php
w ww.facebook.com/museumspec
1804 original homestead; home to five generations of the Rose family; living history depicting life in 1800s; guided tours
Jennifer Lyons, Head Curator, Museums of Prince Edward County, 613-476-3833, Fax: 613-476-8356
Diane Denyes-Wenn, Site Curator

Port Burwell: Port Burwell Marine Museum & Historic Lighthouse
20 Pitt St.,
Port Burwell, ON N0J 1T0
Tel: 519-874-4807
www.bayham.on.ca/pages/museums
Local history, lighthouse lenses & artifacts.

Port Carling: Muskoka Lakes Museum
PO Box 432, 100 Joseph St.,
Port Carling, ON P0B 1J0

Tel: 705-765-5367
info@mlmuseum.com
www.mlmuseum.com
instagram.com/muskokalakesmuseum
twitter.com/mlmuseum
www.facebook.com/MuskokaLakesMuseum
Year Founded: 1964 Log home from 1875; artifacts of early
settlers & lumber industry; displays related to boat building &
water transportation; archives of Muskoka region; open May-Oct
Wed-Sat 10:00-4:00, Sun 12:00-4:00

Port Colborne: Port Colborne Historical & Marine
Museum & Heritage Village
PO Box 572, 280 King St.,
Port Colborne, ON L3K 5X8

Tel: 905-834-7604; Fax: 905-834-6198
museum@portcolborne.ca
portcolborne.ca/page/museum
The Port Colborne Historical & Marine Museum depicts the
history of Port Colborne & the Welland Canala. The museum
features heritage buidings, such as an 1869 home & carriage
house, a log schoolhouse, & an 1850 marine blacksmith shop. A
reproduction of the parapet of Port Colborne's Lighthouse
contains ship models & marine artifacts. Open May-Dec
Stephanie Powell Baswick, Director & Curator
Michelle Mason, Assistant Curator,
michellemason@portcolborne.ca
Michelle Vosburgh, Technician, Heritage Research,
archives@portcolborne.ca

Port Dover: Port Dover Harbour Museum
PO Box 1298, 44 Harbour St.,
Port Dover, ON N0A 1N0

Tel: 519-583-2660
portdover.museum@norfolkcounty.ca
www.portdovermuseum.ca
www.facebook.com/340416399319352
The Port Dover Harbour Museum tells the story of Port Dover's
fishing industry, ship building, Lake Erie shipwrecks, rum
running, & other parts of lakeside life. The museum is open year
round.
Angela Wallace, Curator/Director

Port Hope: Canadian Fire Fighters Museum
PO Box 325, 95 Mill St. South,
Port Hope, ON L1A 3W3

Tel: 905-885-8985; Fax: 905-885-8985
info@firemuseumcanada.com
www.firemuseumcanada.com
www.facebook.com/FireMuseumCanada
Year Founded: 1985 The museum's collection represents the
history of firefighting in Canada, including vehicles, gear, fire
alarms, & photos. Open daily, except Wednesdays, May-Oct.,
10:00-4:00.

Port Hope: Dorothy's House Museum
Parent: Port Hope & District Historical Society
PO Box 116, 3632 Ganaraska Rd.,
Port Hope, ON L1A 3V9

Tel: 905-885-2981
info@porthopehistorical.ca
www.porthopehistorical.ca
Other contact information: Alt. Phone: 905-885-2814
Artifacts from the Port Hope & Hope Township area; house built
around 1869; barn; driveshed; open May - Aug.
Tim Austin, President
Stephen Austin, Vice-President

Port Perry: Scugog Shores Heritage Centre & Archives
1655 Reach St.,
Port Perry, ON L9L 1P2

Tel: 905-985-8698; Fax: 905-985-2697
www.scugogshoresmuseum.com
twitter.com/ScugogMuseum
www.facebook.com/ScugogMuseum
Formerly housed in the Scugog Shores Museum Village, the
Scugog Heritage Centre & Archives is now located in the
Scugog Area & is accessible to the public. Galleries showcase
local history & First Nations history, as well as rotating art shows
& travelling exhibits.
Shannon Kelly, Curator

Port Perry: Scugog Shores Museum Village
16210 Island Rd.,
Port Perry, ON L9L 1B4

Tel: 905-985-8698; Fax: 905-985-2697
www.scugogshoresmuseum.com
twitter.com/ScugogMuseum
www.facebook.com/300750283308118

Historic village, comprising a log cabin, Lee House, blacksmith &
woodright shops, print shop, school, church, barns, heritage
flower, herb & dye plant gardens, & Ojibway Heritage
Interpretive Lands; special events & programming, themed
artifact kits for rent, tours, building rentals
Shannon Kelly, Curator, Township of Scucog

Prescott: Fort Wellington National Historic Site of
Canada
PO Box 479, 370 Vankoughnet St.,
Prescott, ON K0E 1T0

Tel: 613-925-2896; Fax: 613-925-1536
ont-wellington@pc.gc.ca
www.pc.gc.ca/lhn-nhs/on/wellington/index.aspx
Other contact information: TTY: 613-925-2896
Displays exhibits related to the War of 1812 & the Upper Canada
Rebellion. The site is open May-Sept. During the off-season,
groups of ten or more may make an appointment.

Prescott: The Forwarders' Museum
201 Water St.,
Prescott, ON K0E 1T0

Tel: 613-925-1861
www.prescott.ca
Forwarding trade; St Lawrence River & local history; open
June-Labour Day

Prescott: Stockade Barracks & Hospital Museum
PO Box 446, 356 East St.,
Prescott, ON K0E 1T0

Tel: 613-925-4894
www.museumsontario.ca/museum/Stockade-Barracks-and-Hosp
ital
The oldest military building in Ontario.

Queenston: Brock's Monument National Historic Site
Parent: Friends of Fort George
14184 Niagara Pkwy.,
Queenston, ON L0S 1P0

Tel: 905-262-4759
www.friendsoffortgeorge.ca
twitter.com/fofg
www.facebook.com/102031676507960
A 185-foot-high monument to Major-General Sir Isaac Brock,
situated on the Queenston Heights battlefield.

Queenston: Laura Secord Homestead
29 Queenston St.,
Queenston, ON L0S 1L0

Tel: 905-262-4851
www.niagaraparks.com/heritage-trail/laura-secord-homestead.ht
ml
www.face book.com/FriendsofLauraSecord
History of Laura Secord, the Homestead & the local area. Open
May-Sept.
Caroline McCormick, President, Friends of Laura Secord

Queenston: Mackenzie Printery & Newspaper Museum
Parent: Niagara Parks Commission
1 Queenston St.,
Queenston, ON L0S 1L0

Tel: 905-262-5676
printer@mackenzieprintery.org
mackenzieprintery.wordpress.com
Year Founded: 1991 Printing history, technology & its influence
on society.
Ron Schroder, Chairman

Red Lake: Red Lake Regional Heritage Centre
(RLRHC)
PO Box 64, 51A Hwy. 105,
Red Lake, ON P0V 2M0

Tel: 807-727-3006
heritage@redlake.ca
www.redlakemuseum.com
www.facebook.com/redlakeheritagecentre
Year Founded: 2005 Aboriginal, fur trade, gold mining, &
immigration history. Open year round.
John Frostiak, Chair
Trevor Osmond, Director
Lisa Hughes, Curator

Renfrew: McDougall Mill Museum
Parent: The Renfrew & District Historical & Museum
Society
PO Box 554, 65 Arthur Ave.,
Renfrew, ON K7V 3S1

www.renfrewmuseum.ca
Year Founded: 1969 Housed in a stone, 1855 grist mill built on
the Bonnechere River by Hudson's Bay Company agent, John
Lorne McDougall, the museum displays 3 floors of artifacts,
including early appliances from Renfrew's industrial days. There

are also exhibits of military articles, Victorian clothing & a
wedding dress gallery.

Renfrew: The NHA/NHL Birthplace Museum
249 Raglan St. South,
Renfrew, ON K7V 1R3

Tel: 343-361-0202
info@nhanhl.ca
www.nhanhl.ca
www.facebook.com/375277432568370
Year Founded: 2002 The museum details the history of the
National Hockey Association & the National Hockey League,
starting with the influence of hockey enthusiast & founder of the
Town of Renfrew, M.J. O'Brien.
Bob Barker, Chair
Ray Dunbar, Executive Director

Richards Landing: Fort St. Joseph National Historic
Site of Canada
PO Box 220,
Richards Landing, ON P0R 1J0

Tel: 705-246-2664; Fax: 705-246-1796
fortstjoseph-info@pc.gc.ca
www.pc.gc.ca/lhn-nhs/on/stjoseph/index_e.asp
Ruins of a fort erected after 1796 to serve as a fur trade centre;
artifacts from excavation of site

Richards Landing: St. Joseph Island Museum
Complex
RR#2,
Richards Landing, ON P0R 1J0

Tel: 705-246-2672
info@stjoemuseum.com
stjoemuseum.com
Year Founded: 1963 Six artifact buildings represent the pioneer
era (1820-1880) & the settlement era after the Homestead Act of
1868; over 6,000 artifacts; farming, lumbering, maple syruping &
early navigation displays; 2 schools, a church, a store, a barn,
an 1880 log cabin & a general store
Carrie Kennedy-Uusitalo, Curator

Richmond Hill: Canadian Museum of Hindu Civilization
(CMOHC)
8640 Yonge St.,
Richmond Hill, ON L4C 6Z4

Tel: 905-764-5516
curator@cmohc.com
www.cmohc.com
The museum is the first of its kind in North America & celebrates
Hinduism's contributions to philosophy, the arts & science.
Shylee Someshwar, Chair, 647-866-0959, cmohc@csican.com
Dr. Budhendra Doobay, Chair

Richmond Hill: Richmond Hill Heritage Centre
19 Church St. North,
Richmond Hill, ON L4C 3E6

Tel: 905-737-1818
maggie.mackenzie@richmondhill.ca
richmondhill.ca/en/find-or-learn-about/Richmond-Hill-Heritage-C
entre.aspx
Year Founded: 1997 The Centre offers historic galleries &
exhibits, as well as an archive of material related to the history of
Richmond Hill. Visitors can also take the Museum of the Streets
self-guided tour of the Richmond Hill area.

Ridgetown: Ridge House Museum
PO Box 550, 53 Erie St. South,
Ridgetown, ON N0P 2C0

Tel: 519-674-2223 Toll-Free: 800-714-7497
ckridgehouse@chatham-kent.ca
www.chatham-kent.ca/RidgeHouseMuseum
Year Founded: 1975 The Ridge Hose Museum depicts the life of
a middle class family in Ridgetown around 1875. Interactive
tours & interpretive programs are provided. Open daily from Mar -
Dec.
Lydia Burggraaf, Curator, 519-647-2223,
lydiab@chatham-kent.ca

Ridgeway: Fort Erie Historical Museum
Parent: Fort Erie Museum Services
402 Ridge Rd.,
Ridgeway, ON L0S 1N0

Tel: 905-894-5322
www.town.forterie.ca/pages/FortErieHistoricalMuseum
Exhibits on archaelogy, genealogy, Fenian Raids, local history &
archives; open year-round Sun.-Fri.; daily in July & Aug.
Jane Davies, Curator

Ridgeway: Ridgeway Battlefield National Historic Site
Parent: Fort Erie Museum Services
3388 Garrison Rd.,
Ridgeway, ON L0S 1N0

Tel: 905-871-1600
www.museum.forterie.ca/battlefield.html
The Ridgeway Battlefield national historic site marks the location where in 1866 Irish-American soldiers, known as Fenians, fought Canadian forces in an attempt to gain Ireland's independence of England. Fort Erie Museum Services maintains the original cabin at the battle site, where visitors can see a visual account of the Battle of Ridgeway.
Jane Davies, Museum Administrator BA, Fort Erie Museum Services

Rockton: Westfield Heritage Village (WHV)
1049 Kirkwall Rd.,
Rockton, ON L0R 1X0

Tel: 519-621-8851
westfield@speedway.ca
westfieldheritage.ca
The Heritage Village presents more than thirty-five historical & reproduction buildings. The site also features Ontario's oldest log cabin & a T.H. & B. steam locomotive.
Rondalyn Brown, Manager,
Rondalyn.Brown@conservationhamilton.ca

Russell: Keith M. Boyd Museum
PO Box 307, 1150 Concession St.,
Russell, ON K4R 1E1

Tel: 613-445-3849
info@russellmuseum.ca
www.russellmuseum.ca
Year Founded: 1989 Local history & artifacts from the village of Russell.
Dorothy Kinkaid, Curator
Judy James, Chair, 613-445-5690

St Catharines: Morningstar Mill
2714 Decew Rd.,
St Catharines, ON L2R 6P7

Tel: 905-688-6050
info@morningstarmill.ca
www.morningstarmill.ca
www.facebook.com/morningstar.mill
Year Founded: 1962 Museum site is made up of a number of buildings: the water-powered gristmill (built in 1872 & known as Morningstar Mill), the turbine shed, the millers house, the icehouse, sawmill & the barn which houses the blacksmith shop & carpentry shop. School tours are welcome. Admission by donation.

St Catharines: St. Catharines Museum
PO Box 3012, 1932 Welland Canals Pkwy.,
St Catharines, ON L2R 7C2

Tel: 905-984-8880; Fax: 905-984-6910
Toll-Free: 800-305-5134
museum@stcatharines.ca
www.stcatharines.ca/en/St-Catha rines-Museum.asp
twitter.com/StCMuseum
www.facebook.com/StCatharinesMu seum
Other contact information: TTY: 905-688-4889
Year Founded: 1965 Major collection of artifact, archival & art material related to the history of St. Catharines & the Welland Canal; collections include Girl Guides, Fred Pattison Aviation Collection (BCATP), St. Lawrence Seaway, family papers, marine photographs, Ferranti-Packard & the DeCew Falls Waterworks Collection; guided tours; summer camps, edu-fun camps; guest speakers; tours & special events
Kathleen Powell, Curator & Supervisor, Historical Services, 905-984-8880, kpowell@stcatharines.ca

St George: Adelaide Hunter Hoodless Homestead
PO Box 209, 359 Blue Lake Rd.,
St George, ON N0E 1N0

Tel: 519-448-1130
info@adelaidehoodless.ca
www.adelaidehoodless.ca
instagram.com/user/addiehoodless;
youtube.com/user/homestead1857
twitter.com/AddieHoodless
www.facebook.com/adelaidehoodless
Other contact information: Alternate Email:
curator@adelaidehoodles.ca
Year Founded: 1959 Birthplace of Adelaide Hunter Hoodless, an educational reformer, one of Canada's early feminists and a co-founder of organizations promoting the cause of women's well-being. The homestead includes Unter family artifacts, picnic facilities & grounds that can be rented for gatherings & other special occasions. Guided tours, & school programs available. Open year round.

St George: St. George Museum & Archives
Parent: South Dumfries Historical Society
c/o South Dumfries Historical Society, PO Box 472, 36 Main St. South,
St George, ON N0E 1N0

Tel: 519-448-3265
info@southdumfrieshistory.ca
southdumfrieshistory.ca
Local history

St Jacobs: The Maple Syrup Museum
Country Mill, 1441 King St. North, 3rd Fl.,
St Jacobs, ON N0B 2N0

Tel: 519-664-1232
www.stjacobs.com
History of maple syrup production; artifacts; photographs

St Marys: Canadian Baseball Hall of Fame & Museum
PO Box 1838, 386 Church St. East,
St Marys, ON N4X 1C2

Tel: 519-284-1838; Fax: 519-284-1234
Toll-Free: 877-250-2255
baseball@baseballhalloffame.ca
baseballhalloffame.ca
www.youtube.com/user/CanadianHallofFame
twitter.com/CDNBaseballHOF
www.facebook.com/cdnbaseballhof
Year Founded: 1983 Commemorates the accomplishments of Canadian baseball teams & players. Open year round
Scott Crawford, Director, Operations,
scott@baseballhalloffame.ca

St Marys: St Marys Museum
PO Box 998, 177 Church St. South,
St Marys, ON N4X 1B6

Tel: 519-284-3556
museum@town.stmarys.on.ca
www.stmarysmuseum.ca
www.facebook.com/stmarysmuseum
Changing exhibits; seasonal activities; research facilities for genealogy & area history in 1850s limestone house
Amy Cubberley, Curator & Archives Assistant
Trisha McKibbin, Manager, Museum & Archives

St Thomas: Elgin County Museum
450 Sunset Dr.,
St Thomas, ON N5R 5V1

Tel: 519-631-1460; Fax: 519-631-9209
www.elgincounty.ca/museum
twitter.com/ecpmcounty
www.facebook.com/7508 66584990608
Year Founded: 1957 History of Elgin County; changing exhibits in gallery, workshops & special events
Mike Baker, Curator, 519-631-1460
Georgia Sifton, Assistant, 519-631-1460

St. Thomas: Elgin County Railway Museum
225 Wellington St.,
St. Thomas, ON N5R 2S6

Tel: 519-637-6284
thedispatcher@ecrm5700.org
ecrm5700.org
www.instagram.com/elgincountyrailwaymuseum
twitter.com/ecrailwaymuseum
www.facebook.com/ecrm5700
Year Founded: 1988 The museum seeks to preserve the heritage of the St. Thomas & Elgin County railroad, & to educate the public on the railroad's contributions to the community. Open May-Sept., Tu-Su 10:00-4:00.
Jeremy Locke, President
Blaine Skirtschak, Vice-President
Dawn Miskelly, Executive Director

St Thomas: The Elgin Military Museum
30 Talbot St.,
St Thomas, ON N5P 1A3

Tel: 519-633-7641
curator@elginmilitarymuseum.ca
elginmilitarymuseum.ca
www.facebook.com/ElginMMuseum
Year Founded: 1982 Military history & veterans from Elgin County as well as an archive collection with military documents & publications.

Sarnia: Discovery House Museum
PO Box 134, 475 Christina St N,
Sarnia, ON N7T 5W3

Tel: 519-332-1556; Fax: 519-383-8042
centre@ebtech.net
Other contact information: Alt Phone: 519-383-8472
Local railroad & marine heritage.

Sarnia: Stones 'N Bones Museum
233 North Christina St.,
Sarnia, ON N7T 5V1

Tel: 519-336-2100
stonesnbones@cogeco.net
www.stonesnbones.ca
www.facebook.com/StonesnBonesMuseum
The collection includes fossils, mounted wildlife, minerals, stones & RCMP memorabilia. Open holiday Mondays, Wed-Sun 10:00-5:00

Sault Ste Marie: Canadian Bushplane Heritage Centre (CBHC)
50 Pim St.,
Sault Ste Marie, ON P6A 3G4

Tel: 705-945-6242; Fax: 705-942-8947
Toll-Free: 877-287-4752
retail@bushplane.com
www.bushplane.com
pinterest.com/strokeguy/canadian-bushplane-heritage-centre
twitter.com/BushplaneCentre
www.facebook.com/bushplane.museum
Year Founded: 1987 The centre celebrates the heritage of bushplanes & forest fire protection in Canada through hands-on displays, including flight simulators. Open May-Oct., daily 9:00-6:00; daily 10:00-4:00 during the rest of the year.
Mike Delfre, Executive Director, 705-945-6242,
director@bushplane.com
Todd Fleet, Curator, 705-945-6242, display@bushplane.com

Sault Ste Marie: Ermatinger-Clergue National Historic Site
c/o Historic Sites Board, PO Box 580, 800 Bay St.,
Sault Ste Marie, ON P6A 5N1

Tel: 705-759-5443; Fax: 705-541-7023
old.stone.house@cityssm.on.ca
www.ermatingerclerguenationalhistoricsite. ca
www.facebook.com/ErmatingerClergue
Features Interactive Heritage Discovery Centre, 1814 stone houses, historic crop gardens, recreated rooms, exhibits & period furnishings.
Kathryn Fisher, Curator

Sault Ste Marie: St. Mary's River Marine Heritage Centre
PO Box 23099 Mall,
Sault Ste Marie, ON P6A 6W6

Tel: 705-256-7447
gjsmed@shaw.ca
www.norgoma.org
Year Founded: 1981 An 188-foot passenger ship & packet freighter built in 1950. Open Jun-Oct.
Louis Muio, President
Gordon Smedley, Chairman

Sault Ste Marie: Sault Ste Marie Canal National Historic Site
1 Canal Dr.,
Sault Ste Marie, ON P6A 6W4

Tel: 705-941-6262; Fax: 705-941-6206
info-saultcanal@pc.gc.ca
www.parkscanada.gc.ca/sault
Operates a recreational lock between May-Oct & offers school programming & guided tours. Open May-Oct

Sault Ste Marie: Sault Ste Marie Museum
690 Queen St. East,
Sault Ste Marie, ON P6A 2A4

Tel: 705-759-7278; Fax: 705-759-3058
saultmuseum@gmail.com
www.saultmuseum.com
www.youtube.com/user/saultmuseum
www.facebook.com/143320129039949
Maintained by the Sault St. Marie & 49th Field Regiment R.C.A. Historical Society; the museum collects & preserves artifacts & archival material illustrating the history of Sault Ste Marie & area

Selkirk: Cottonwood Mansion Museum
Parent: Cottonwood Mansion Preservation Foundation
PO Box 56, 740 Haldimand Rd.,
Selkirk, ON N0A 1P0

Tel: 905-776-2538
cottonwoodmansion@gmail.com
www.cottonwoodmansion.ca
twitter.com/cottonwood1870
www.facebook.com/c ottonwood.mansion
A restored mansion, circa 1870. Open May-Sept., Th & Sa 11:00-3:00.
Richard Hoover, President
Catherine Berry Stidesen, Vice-President

Selkirk: Wilson MacDonald Memorial School Museum
3513 Rainham Rd.,
Selkirk, ON N0A 1P0
Tel: 905-776-3319; *Fax:* 905-776-0683
wmacdonald.museum@haldimandcounty.on.ca
www.haldimandcounty.on.ca
Wilson MacDonald Memorial School Museum presents the story
of poet Wilson Pugsley MacDonald, rural education, & Selkirk,
Ontario & its surrounding area. Archival research is available for
a fee. Open Mar-Dec
Dana B. Stavinga, Curator

Shakespeare: Fryfogel Tavern
Parent: Perth County Historical Foundation
Perth County Historical Foundation, 1931 Perth Line 34,
Shakespeare, ON N0B 2P0
Tel: 519-271-1178
perthhistorical@yahoo.ca
www.stratfordperthheritage.ca/tavern.html
www.facebook.com/1486958485552 54
Year Founded: 1990 Stagecoach stop & resting place 1844-45;
history of Perth County's settlers; open by appt.
Eric Adams, Chair, 519-273-1955
David Hastie, Vice-Chair, 519-275-2866

Sharon: Sharon Temple National Historic Site &
Museum
18974 Leslie St.,
Sharon, ON L0G 1V0
Tel: 905-478-2389
info@sharontemple.ca
www.sharontemple.ca
The Sharon Temple National Historic Site features nine historic
buildings. The centerpiece of the site is the Temple of the
Children of Peace, which was completed in 1832. Open
May-Oct. Group & scholars may make appointments at other
times of the year.

Simcoe: Eva Brook Donly Museum & Archives
Parent: Norfolk Historical Society
109 Norfolk St. South,
Simcoe, ON N3Y 2W3
Tel: 519-426-1583; *Fax:* 519-426-1584
office@norfolklore.com
www.norfolklore.com
twitter.com/museumnorfolk
www.facebook.com/evabrookdonly
Other contact information: Archive/Genealogy E-mail:
genealogy@norfolklore.com
Year Founded: 1942 The Museum & Archives feature
information about the people, heritage, art & history of Norfolk
County. Museum displays artifacts from the first inhabitants.
Archives include family histories, documents, records, &
phototgraphs.
Keitha Davis, President, Norfolk Historical Society
Helen Bartens, Curator & Marager, curator@norfolklore.com

Sioux Lookout: Sioux Lookout Community Museum
PO Box 158, 25 5th Ave.,
Sioux Lookout, ON P8T 1A4
Tel: 807-737-2700
museum@siouxlookout.ca
www.siouxlookoutmuseum.ca
Year Founded: 1967 First Nations artifacts; pioneer artifacts
related to logging, mining, aviation & the Canadian National
Railway. Open Mon, Wed-Thu, Sat 12:00-4:00
Stu Finn, Coordinator, 807-737-2700

Smiths Falls: Heritage House Museum / Musée de la
maison du patrimoine
PO Box 695, 11 Old Slys Rd.,
Smiths Falls, ON K7A 4T6
Tel: 613-283-6311
heritagehouse@smithsfalls.ca
www.smithsfalls.ca/heritagehouse
Year Founded: 1981 Built in 1860-1861 by Joshua Bates, the
house is located near the Rideau River & displays 7 rooms,
including kitchen, parlor & bedroom, all restored to Victorian
style. Workshops & programs for children are offered. Tours
available; open year round.
Carol Miller, Curator, cmiller@smithsfalls.ca

Smiths Falls: Industrial Heritage Complex Merrickville
Lockstation
c/o Rideau Canal Office, 34A Beckwith St. South,
Smiths Falls, ON K7A 2A8
Tel: 613-283-5170
19th century construction on Rideau Canal & equipment used to
build it. Open May-Oct daily 9:00-3:00

Smiths Falls: Rideau Canal National Historic Site of
Canada
34 Beckwith St. South,
Smiths Falls, ON K7A 2B3
Tel: 613-283-5170; *Fax:* 613-283-0677
Toll-Free: 888-773-8888
RideauCanal-info@pc.gc.ca
www.pc.gc.ca/lhn-nhs/on/ride au/index.aspx
twitter.com/RideauCanalNHS
www.facebook.com/RideauCanalN HS
Other contact information: TTY: 1-866-787-6221
The historic Rideau Canal is operated by Parks Canada in an
effort to preserve the canal's historic features as well as to
provide a navigable waterway for boaters.

Smiths Falls: Smiths Falls Railway Museum of Eastern
Ontario
PO Box 962, 90 William St. West,
Smiths Falls, ON, K7A 5A5
Tel: 613-283-5696
info@rmeo.org
rmeo.org
twitter.com/RMEOsmithsfalls
www.facebook.com/RMEOsmithsfalls
Collection includes rolling stock and inspection vehicles as well
as over 10,000 artifacts, archival & library materials. Open daily
10:00-5:00

Sombra: Sombra Museum Cultural Centre
3470 St. Clair Parkway,
Sombra, ON N0P 2H0
Tel: 519-892-3982
sombramuseum@hotmail.com
sombramuseum.webs.com
twitter.com/SombraMuseum
www.facebook.com/Sombra Museum
Year Founded: 1959 Local historical artifacts housed in 1880
Victorian frame home. Includes the Marine Room with nautical
equipment, log cabin & The Bury Home. Features photos,
records, letters, newspapers, reference collection & family
archives. Open Jun-Sep
Shelley Lucier, Curator, shelley.lucier@county-lambton.on.ca

South Baymouth: Little Schoolhouse & Museum South
Baymouth
113 Church St.,
South Baymouth, ON P0P 1Z0
Tel: 705-859-3663; *Fax:* 705-859-3663
sbmuseum@volnetmmp.net
www.manitoulin-island.com/museums/little_schoolho use.htm
Displays the history of Tehkummah Township, Michael's Bay &
its fishing history through artifacts & pictures. Open daily
May-Oct 9:30-4:30

Southampton: Bruce County Museum & Cultural
Centre
33 Victoria St. North,
Southampton, ON N0H 2L0
Tel: 519-797-2080; *Fax:* 519-797-2191
Toll-Free: 866-318-8889
museum@brucecounty.on.ca
www.brucemuseum.ca
twitter.com/brucemuseum
www.facebook.com/BruceCountyMuseum
Year Founded: 1955 A variety of exhibits about the history of
Bruce County, temporary exhibits, archives, programs & events.
Open Mon-Sat 10:00-5:00, Sun 1:00-5:00.

Stirling: Hastings County Museum of Agricultural
Heritage
PO Box 174, 437 West Front St.,
Stirling, ON K0K 3E0
Tel: 613-395-0015
info@agmuseum.ca
farmtownpark.ca
www.facebook.com/farmtownpark
Year Founded: 1986 Agricultural history & lifestyle in rural
Ontario. Open May-Sep 10:00-4:00
Margaret Grotek, Contact

Stittsville: Goulbourn Museum
2064 Huntley Rd.,
Stittsville, ON K2S 1B8
Tel: 613-831-2393
info@goulbournmuseum.ca
goulbournmuseum.ca
instagram.com/goulbourn_museum;
pinterest.com/goulbournmuseum
twitter.com/GoulbournMuseum
www.facebook .com/GoulbournMuseum

Year Founded: 1990 Collection housed in 1873 Township Hall &
1961 Clerk's Building. Displays about family farms & rural
schools, exhibit of military service from 1812 & early settlers.
Open year round Wed-Sun 1:00-4:00
Kathryn Jamieson, Curator/Manager,
kathryn@goulbournmuseum.ca

Stoney Creek: Battlefield House Museum & Park
PO Box 66561, 77 King St. West,
Stoney Creek, ON L8G 5E5
Tel: 905-662-8458; *Fax:* 905-546-4141
battlefield@hamilton.ca
www.battlefieldhouse.ca
As a living history museum, the Battlefield House Museum &
Park is the site of a military re-enactment of the Battle of Stoney
Creek. Open Jul-Sep

Stoney Creek: Erland Lee (Museum) Home
Parent: Federated Women's Institutes of Ontario (FWIO)
552 Ridge Rd.,
Stoney Creek, ON L8J 2Y6
Tel: 905-662-2691
erlandleehome@fwio.on.ca
www.fwio.on.ca/erland
Year Founded: 1972 Birthplace of the Women's Institutes.
Features artifacts from a Victorian lifestyle. Tours available
Thu-Sun 10:30-4:00

Stoney Creek: Ingledale House
c/o Hamilton Region Conservation Authority, Fifty Point
Conservation Area,
Stoney Creek, ON
Tel: 905-643-2103
fiftypt@conservationhamilton.ca
conservationhamilton.ca/ingledale-house-2
c. 1812 home of Inglehart family

Stratford: Brocksden Country School Museum
2830 Perth Line 37, R.R.#1,
Stratford, ON N5A 6S2
Tel: 519-271-0499; *Fax:* 519-271-1978
Year Founded: 1969 The school which opened in 1853 presents
a living history program for classes. Open May 15 - September
15 by appointment.
Wilma McCaig, Secretary, 519-271-0499

Stratford: Stratford Perth Museum
Parent: Stratford Perth Museum Association
4275 Huron Rd. RR# 5,
Stratford, ON N5A 6S6
Tel: 519-393-5311; *Fax:* 519-393-5318
www.stratfordperthmuseum.ca
www.instagram.com/stratfordperthmuseum
twitter.com/StratPerthMuse
www. facebook.com/StratfordPerthMuseum
Year Founded: 1997 Local history
John Kastner, General Manager, 519-393-5312,
johnkastner@stratfordperthmuseum.ca

Strathroy: Museum Strathroy-Caradoc
34 Frank St.,
Strathroy, ON N7G 2R4
Tel: 519-245-0492; *Fax:* 519-245-1073
www.strathroymuseum.ca
www.youtube.com/user/strathroymuseum
twitter.com/strathroymuseum
www.f acebook.com/museumstrathroycaradoc
Open year-round; medical theme room; military display; 1930s
electric kitchen; printing shop; archival material
Andrew Meyer, Curator & Manager, Community Development,
agmeyer@strathroy-caradoc.ca
Crystal Loyst, Coordinator, Collections & Research,
cloyst@strathroy-caradoc.ca

Stratton: Kay-Nah-Chi-Wah-Nung Historical Centre
Parent: Rainy River First Nations
PO Box 100, Shaw Rd.,
Stratton, ON P0W 1E0
Tel: 807-483-1163; *Fax:* 807-483-1263
mounds.rrfn@bellnet.ca
www.manitoumounds.com
Year Founded: 1969 The Manitou Mounds are the centre's focal
point. The Mounds are sacred First Nations ground & were
integral to the continent-wide aboriginal trading network. Visitors
can explore the site on nature trails & also learn about the area's
history in the visitors centre.

Sturgeon Falls: Musée Sturgeon River House Museum
250, ch Fort Rd.,
Sturgeon Falls, ON P2B 2N7

Tél: 705-753-4716
admin@sturgeonriverhouse.com
www.sturgeonriverhouse.com
Le musée se trouve sur un site de la Compagnie de la Baie d'Hudson; l'exposition traite de fourrure et les animaux de la région.

Sudbury: Anderson Farm Museum
Parent: Anderson Farm Museum Heritage Society
PO Box 6400, 550 Regional Rd 24,
Sudbury, ON P3Y 1M9

Tel: 705-671-2489
museums@greatersudbury.ca
sudburymuseums.ca/index.cfm?app=w_vmuseum&lang=en&cur
rID=1372&parID=1371
Local history. Includes the Anderson family farmhouse & dairies.
Open Jul-Aug daily 10;00-4:00; May-Jun, Sep-Oct Mon-Fri
10:00-4:00 by appontment only

Sudbury: Centre franco-ontarien de folklore (CFOF) /
The Franco-Ontarian Center for Folklore
Université de Sudbury, 935, ch du Lac Ramsay,
Sudbury, ON P3E 2C6

Tél: 705-675-8986; Téléc: 705-675-5809
cfof@cfof.on.ca
www.cfof.on.ca
twitter.com/LeCFOF
www.facebook.com/C FOFSudbury
Fondée en: 1972 A pour mission de mettre en valeur le folklore et le patrimoine franco-ontarien; musée; activités éducatives; bibliothèque; archives; publications; magasin virtuel
François Hastir, Président

Sudbury: Flour Mill Museum
245 Staint Charles St.,
Sudbury, ON P3C 2Z3

Tel: 705-674-4455
www.sudburymuseums.ca
Year Founded: 1974 The museum is made out of two buildings: a heritage house built in 1902 & a log cabin built in 1983 to celebrate Sudbury's centennial. Open July & Aug., W-Su 10:00-4:00.

Sudbury: Greater Sudbury Heritage Museums
Greater Sudbury Public Library, 74 MacKenzie St.,
Sudbury, ON P3C 4X8

Tel: 705-692-4448
www.sudburymuseums.ca
www.facebook.com/SudburyMuseums
Greater Sudbury Heritage Museums is the collective name for the following four heritage sites located in & around Sudbury: Anderson Farm Museum, Copper Cliff Museum, Flour Mill Museum, & Rayside-Balfour Museum. The Greater Sudbury Virtual Museum is the online collection of photos, videos, archives, & more hosted on www.sudburymuseums.ca.

Sudbury: Irish Regiment of Canada Regimental Museum
Sudbury Armoury, 333 Riverside Dr.,
Sudbury, ON P3E 1H5

Tel: 705-669-2300

Sudbury: Sudbury Region Police Museum
190 Brady St.,
Sudbury, ON P3E 1C7

Tel: 705-675-9171; Fax: 705-674-7090
museum@gsps.ca
www.gsps.ca/en/yourpolice/Museum.asp
www.facebook.com/1 30223547044054
Displays artifacts, documents & photographs about the history and development of law enforcement in Sudbury. Open Mon-Fri 8:00-4:00
Heather Lewis, Vice Chair

Sutton West: Eildon Hall Sibbald Memorial Museum
Sibbald Point Provincial Park, 26071 York Rd. 18,
Sutton West, ON L0E 1R0

Tel: 905-722-8061
Year Founded: 1835 Situated by the shore of Lake Simcoe, Eildon Hall was the Sibbald family home. Open Jul-Sept 1:00 - 4:00.

Tavistock: Tavistock & District Historical Society
PO Box 280, 37 Maria St.,
Tavistock, ON N0B 2R0

Tel: 519-655-3342
info@tavistockhistory.ca
www.tavistockhistory.ca
Other contact information: Alt. Phone: 519-655-9915

Local history

Teeterville: Teeterville Pioneer Museum
194 Teeter St.,
Teeterville, ON N0E 1S0

Tel: 519-443-4400; Fax: 519-428-3069
teeterville.museum@norfolkcounty.ca
teetervillemuseum.ca
www.facebook. com/teetervillemuseum
Year Founded: 1967 Features historical buildings & Windham artifacts. Open Jun-Sep Thu-Sat 10:00-4:30
Jodie Keene, Coordinator, jodie.keene@norfolkcounty.ca

Thorold: Thorold Museum
Parent: Thorold & Beaverdams Historical Society
Lock 7 Viewing Complex, 50 Chapel St. South,
Thorold, ON L2V 2C7

Tel: 289-479-1037
thorold.museum@gmail.com
www.facebook.com/tbhsmuseum
Local history. Open daily 9:00-5:00
Randy Barnes, President, 905-984-4435

Thunder Bay: Centennial Park 1910 Logging Camp & Museum
c/o City of Thunder Bay Parks Division, 111 Syndicate Ave. South,
Thunder Bay, ON P7E 6S4

Tel: 807-625-2941; Fax: 807-625-3588
Toll-Free: 888-711-5094
www.thunderbay.ca/parks
Full scale replica of a 1910 logging camp re-creates the early history of Northern Ontario's forest industry. Open year round; logging camp and museum open Jun-Sep 8:00-8:00. Muskeg Express logging train; Winter sleigh rides; craft shop; picnic area; trails

Thunder Bay: Definitely Superior Art Gallery
PO Box 21015 Grandview Mall, 250 Park Ave.,
Thunder Bay, ON P7B 8A7

Tel: 807-344-3814
defsup@tbaytel.net
www.definitelysuperior.com
twitter.com/DefSup
www.facebook.com/defsup
An artist-run centre for contemporary arts, hosting exhibitions as well as workshops, lectures, film & video screenings, performance, music & literary events. Open Tu-Sa 12:00-6:00.
Peter Wragg, President
David Karasiewicz, Executive Director

Thunder Bay: Duke Hunt Museum
3218 Rosslyn Rd.,
Thunder Bay, ON P7C 5N5

Tel: 807-939-1262
www.oliverpaipoonge.ca
Year Founded: 1952 Reflecting the history of the Municipality of Oliver/Paipoonge & area during the late 1800s & early 1900s. Collection of pioneer material and farm machinery, old school room, kitchen and bedroom displays. Hours: May 1 - Aug 31 Tu-Su 1:00 - 5:00, or by appointment.
Lois Garrity, Curator & Director

Thunder Bay: Fort William Historical Park (FWHP)
1350 King Rd.,
Thunder Bay, ON P7K 1L7

Tel: 807-577-8461; Fax: 807-473-2327
info@fwhp.ca
www.fwhp.ca
www.youtube.com/user/FortWilliamHistPark
twitter.com/FWHPtweets
www.fa cebook.com/fortwilliamhistoricalpark
Year Founded: 1973 A living history site that depicts the fur trade activities of the North West Company in the early 1800s; 42 reconstructed buildings on a 225-acre site. Open year round
Sergio Buonocore, General Manager

Thunder Bay: Northwestern Ontario Sports Hall of Fame
219 May St. South,
Thunder Bay, ON P7E 1B5

Tel: 807-622-2852; Fax: 807-622-2736
nwosport@tbaytel.net
www.nwosportshalloffame.com
twitter.com/nwosports
www.facebook.com/105561449476479
Year Founded: 1978 The Hall's mission is to preserve and honour Northwestern Ontario's sports heritage, with displays, photos, archival material, artifacts and other documentation on over 200 athletes; reference library; educational programming. Open all year, Tu - Sa 12:00 - 5:00.
Diane Imrie, Executive Director

Thunder Bay: Thunder Bay Military Museum
The Armoury, 317 Park Ave.,
Thunder Bay, ON P7B 1C7

Tel: 807-343-5175
army.ca/inf/lssrmus.php
Georg Hoegel Art Collection - paintings & drawings done by Mr. Hoegel when he was a prisoner of war in Canada from 1941-1946; other military art; tri-service collection, representing all three services, rotated regularly; open 4 afternoons, 2 evenings & by request
L.Col./Dr. T.M.S. Kaipio, President C.D., Ph.D.
Myles G. Penny, Curator C.D., B.A., B.Ed., pennym@air.on.ca

Thunder Bay: Thunder Bay Museum
Parent: Thunder Bay Historical Museum Society
425 East Donald St.,
Thunder Bay, ON P7E 5V1

Tel: 807-623-0801
info@thunderbaymuseum.com
www.thunderbaymuseum.com
www.pinterest.com/tbaymuseum
twitter.com/tbaymuseum
www.facebook.com/T hunderbaymuseum
A museum, historical society & archives for Thunder Bay & Northwestern Ontario
Dr. Tory Tronrud, Curator, director@thunderbaymuseum.com
Nick Sottile, Chief Administrative Officer,
cao@thunderbaymuseum.com

Tillsonburg: Annandale National Historic Museum
30 Tillson Ave.,
Tillsonburg, ON N4G 2Z8

Tel: 519-842-2294; Fax: 519-842-5355
www.tillsonburg.ca/en/Annandale-National-Historic-Site.aspx^_m
id_=104570
www.facebook.com/AnnandaleNHS
Annandale House is restored to the 1880's period. Features the Pratt Gallery with changing exhibits & artifacts. Open year round
Patricia Phelps, Curator, pphelps@tillsonburg.ca

Tillsonburg: Backus Heritage Conservation Area & Village (BHCA)
c/o Long Point Region Conservation Authority, 4 Elm St.,
Tillsonburg, ON N4G 0C4

Tel: 519-586-2201
conservation@lprca.on.ca
www.lprca.on.ca/NHW.htm
Other contact information: Phone, Administration Office:
519-842-4242; Fax: 519-842-7123
Owned & operated by the Long Point Region Conservation Authority, the Backus Heritage Conservation Area features a conservation education centre & a heritage village. The village consists of restored & reconstructed buildings, including the John C. Backhouse Mill, the Teeterville Baptist Church, the Vittoria Carriage Shop, & the Forbes Barn. The history of the Long Point Region Watershed is depicted through exhibits & artifacts.

Timmins: Timmins Museum: National Exhibition Centre / Musée de Timmins: Centre national d'exposition
325 2nd Ave,
Timmins, ON P4N 1B3

Tel: 705-360-2617; Fax: 705-360-2693
museum@timmins.ca
www.timminsmuseum.ca
twitter.com/TimminsMNEC
www.f acebook.com/TimminsMNEC
Year Founded: 1975 Preserves, presents & studies the history of Timmins Ontario including art displays, mineral specimens, artifacts & archival records.
Karen Bachmann, Director/Curator,
karen.bachmann@timmins.ca

Tobermory: The Peninsula & St. Edmunds Township Museum
PO Box 250, 7072 Highway #6,
Tobermory, ON N0H 2R0

Tel: 519-373-7032
Year Founded: 1967 Housed in the former St. Edmunds Settlement School (ca. 1898), the museum's holdings include land deeds & registers, photographs & exhibits on lumbering, fishing & hunting activities; the upper floor of the museum is dedicated to area marine history and includes maps, tools & relics from shipwrecks. Located south of Tobermory Harbour, on the east side of Hwy 6. Open Sat-Sun May-Oct; weekdays Jul-Sep

Toronto: 48th Highlanders Museum
73 Simcoe St.,
Toronto, ON M5J 1W9

Tel: 416-596-1382
geordie48@sympatico.ca
www.48highlanders.com/04_03.html
www.instagram.com/48highlanders
Year Founded: 1959 The museum seeks to collect, preserve, & present the legacy of the 48th Highlanders of Canada. Open year-round, W & Th 10:00-3:00.

Toronto: Aga Khan Museum (BCHCC)
77 Wynford Dr.,
Toronto, ON M3C 1K1

information@agakhanmuseum.org
www.agakhanmuseum.org
twitter.com/agakhanmuseum
www.facebook.com/agakhanmuseumtoronto
Year Founded: 2014 The Aga Khan Museum in Toronto, Canada offers visitors a window into worlds unknown or unfamiliar: the artistic, intellectual, and scientific heritage of Islamic civilizations across the centuries from the Iberian Peninsula to China.
His Highness the Aga Khan, Chair
Henry Kim, Director & CEO

Toronto: Applewood: The Shaver Homestead
450 The West Mall,
Toronto, ON M9C 1E9

Tel: 416-622-4124
www.applewoodshaverhouse.ca
www.facebook.com/ApplewoodShaverHouse
The homestead is an historic building that now offers space for meetings, weddings & parties. Open M-F 10:00-5:00, Sa & Su by appointment.

Toronto: The Bata Shoe Museum (BSM)
327 Bloor St. West,
Toronto, ON M5S 1W7

Tel: 416-979-7799
www.batashoemuseum.ca
pinterest.com/batashoemuseum;
instagram.com/batashoemuseum
twitter.com/batashoemuseum
www.facebook.com/batashoemuseum
Other contact information: Blog:
astepintothebatashoemuseum.blogspot.ca
Explores footwear in the social & cultural life of humankind from ancient times to the present. Includes 4 galleries as well as changing exhibits. Open year round.
Elizabeth Semmelhack, Senior Curator,
elizabeth@batashoemuseum.ca

Toronto: Beth Tzedec Reuben & Helene Dennis Museum
c/o Beth Tzedec Synagogue, 1700 Bathurst St.,
Toronto, ON M5P 3K3

Tel: 416-781-3514; Fax: 416-781-0150
www.beth-tzedec.org/page/museum
Year Founded: 1965 The museum features a major Judaica collection, including Jewish art & history from ancient times to the present. Appointments may be made for tours. Hours are M, W, Th 11:00 - 1:00, 2:00 - 5:00 and Su 11:00 - 2:00. Closed on Jewish holidays and weekends in July and August.
Dorion Liebgott, Curator, 416-781-3514,
dliebgott@beth-tzedec.org

Toronto: Black Creek Pioneer Village
1000 Murray Ross Pkwy.,
Toronto, ON M3J 2P3

Tel: 416-736-1733
bcpvinfo@trca.on.ca
www.blackcreek.ca
www.flickr.com/groups/blackcreekpioneervillage
twitter.com/blackcreeknew s
www.facebook.com/BlackCreekPioneerVillage
Operated by the Toronto & Region Conservation Authority (TRCA), Black Creek Pioneer Village is a living history experience, which spans over 30 acres. It exemplifies a small south central Ontario community between the 1790s & the 1860s. Demonstrations & special activities depict rural life. Black Creek Village also features the historic Black Creek Historic Brewery. Open May-Dec
Wendy Rowney, Supervisor, Historic Programs,
wrowney@trca.on.ca

Toronto: Cabbagetown Regent Park Community Museum
Residence House, Riverdale Farm, 201 Winchester St.,
Toronto, ON M4X 1B8

Tel: 416-392-6794
farm@toronto.ca
www.crpmuseum.com

Year Founded: 2004 The museum collects, preserves, & displays the history of the Cabbagetown & Regent Park neighbourhoods in Toronto. Open year-round, Sa & Su 11:00-4:00.

Toronto: Campbell House
160 Queen St. West,
Toronto, ON M5H 3H3

Tel: 416-597-0227; Fax: 416-597-0750
info@campbellhousemuseum.ca
www.campbellhousemuseum.ca
twitter.com/Cam pbellHouseTO
www.facebook.com/campbellhouseTO
Built in 1822, the Campbell House is the oldest remaining building from the original town of York. The Sir William Campbell Foundation operates the museum. Special programs are available for groups. Open Jun-Sep Tue-Fri 9:30-4:30, Sat-Sun 12:00-4:30
Liz Driver, Director & Curator

Toronto: Canadian Advertising Museum (CAM)
3199 Lakeshore Blvd. West,
Toronto, ON M8V 1K8

Tel: 416-675-6622; Fax: 416-251-3797
info@canadianadvertisingmuseum.com
www.canadianadvertisingmuseum.com
t witter.com/cam_tweets
www.facebook.com/canadianadvertisingmuseum
The museum seeks to preserve Canadian business & culture through advertising, both online & in their physical collection.

Toronto: Canadian Air & Space Museum (TAM)
Parc Downsview Park, PO Box 1, 65 Carl Hall Rd. North York,
Toronto, ON M3K 2E1

Tel: 416-638-6078 Toll-Free: 866-585-2227
casm@casmuseum.org
www.casmuseum.org
www.youtube.com/user/CASMuseum
twitter.com/CASMuseum
www.facebook.com/ casmuseum
Year Founded: 1997 The museum focuses on the history of aviation & the aviation industry in the Toronto region, with a collection that consists of artifacts including a full-scale metal replica of the AVRO Arrow aircraft. The museum is temporarily closed to the public, but it's website is still in use.
Ian McDougall, Chair
Brian Keaveney, Curator, bkeaveney@casmuseum.org

Toronto: Canadian Broadcasting Corporation Museum & Graham Spry Theatre
PO Box 500 A, 250 Front St. West,
Toronto, ON M5W 1E6

Tel: 416-205-5574
www.cbc.ca/museum
Year Founded: 1936 The CBC Museum presents the story of CBC's broadcasting history.

Toronto: The Canadian Business Hall of Fame / Le Temple de la renommée de l'entreprise canadienne
Parent: Junior Achievement of Canada Foundation
#218, 1 Eva Rd.,
Toronto, ON M9C 4Z5

Tel: 416-622-4602; Fax: 416-622-6861
Toll-Free: 800-265-0699
cbhf.ca
Year Founded: 1979 Lifetime achievements of Canada's business leaders.
Aliya Ansari, Vice President, 647-430-2091,
aansari@jacanada.org

Toronto: Canadian Language Museum / Musée Canadien des Langues
Glendon Gallery, Glendon College, 2275 Bayview Ave,
Toronto, ON M4N 3M6

Tel: 647-785-1012
langmuse@chass.utoronto.ca
www.languagemuseum.ca
instagram.com/canlangmuseum
twitter.com/CanLangMuseum
www.facebook.com /clm.mcl
Year Founded: 2011 Designs travelling exhibits about Canadian English, French & Inuit languages in order to promote the languages spoken in Canada & their role in developing this country.
Elaine Gold, Chair

Toronto: Canadian Sculpture Centre
Parent: Sculptors Society of Canada
500 Church St.,
Toronto, ON M4Y 2C8

Tel: 647-435-5858
gallery@cansculpt.org
cansculpt.org
The Sculptors Society of Canada hosts a sculpture gallery on Church St. in Toronto that displays temporary exhibits.
Judi Michelle Young, President
Richard McNeill, Vice-President

Toronto: Canadian Transit Heritage Foundation (CTHF)
PO Box 30, 260 Adelaide St. East,
Toronto, ON M5A 1N1

info@transitheritage.ca
www.transitheritage.ca
www.facebook.com/CanadianTransitHeritageFoundation
The Foundation collects & preserves items relating to transit in Canada, including a small collection of old transit busses. No formal museum exists yet, but a public access program is in the works.
Chris Prentice, President
Gordon Nevison, Vice-President

Toronto: Casa Loma
1 Austin Terrace,
Toronto, ON M5R 1X8

Tel: 416-923-1171; Fax: 416-923-5734
info@casaloma.org
www.casaloma.org
www.instagram.com/Casalomatoronto
twitter.com/casalomatoronto
Year Founded: 1937 Owned by the City of Toronto & operated by The Kiwanis Club of Casa Loma, Casa Loma is the former home of Sir Henry Pellatt, a Canadian financier, industrialist, & military man. The decorated castle contains an 800 foot tunnel, secret passages, towers, & stables. A self-guided audio tour is available in eight languages.
Nick Di Donato, Chief Executive Officer

Toronto: Chinese Cultural Centre of Greater Toronto (CCC)
5183 Sheppard Ave. East,
Toronto, ON M1B 5Z5

Tel: 416-292-9293
twitter.com/chinculturalctr
Year Founded: 1998 The cultural centre contains a collection of Chinese artifacts, as well as a library, art gallery, theatre, exhibition hall, classrooms & offices.
Dr. Ming-Tat Cheung, President

Toronto: Colborne Lodge
c/o Museum Services, Metro Hall, 55 John St., 8th Fl.,
Toronto, ON M5V 3C6

Tel: 416-392-6916
clodge@toronto.ca
www.toronto.ca/museums/colbornelodge
twitter.com/ColborneLodgeTO
www.f acebook.com/colbornelodge
Site of the 19th century home of High Park founders, John & Jemmina Howard; contains many of their original furnishings, watercolours of early Toronto, & other artifacts; coach house, tomb & restored gardens on the property; special events & programming; party room rentals; located at the south end of High Park, Colborne Lodge Dr., just north of the Queensway. Open year round.
Bob Webber, Contact, bwebber@toronto.ca

Toronto: Dance Collection Danse (DCD)
#301, 149 Church St.,
Toronto, ON M5B 1Y4

Tel: 416-365-3233; Fax: 416-365-3169
Toll-Free: 800-665-5320
talk@dcd.ca
www.dcd.ca
www.instagram.com/dancecollectiondanse
twitter.com/DanceCollection
www .facebook.com/DanceCollectionDanse1
Dance Collection Danse is an archive of Canadian dance history. The organization also runs an online store & produces exhibitions relating to dance history in Canada.
Miriam Adams, Co-Founder & Director
Amy Bowring, Director, Collections & Research

Toronto: Design Exchange (DX)
PO Box 18 TD Centre, 234 Bay St.,
Toronto, ON M5K 1B2

Tel: 416-363-6121; *Fax:* 416-368-0684
info@dx.org
www.dx.org
www.flickr.com/photos/thedesignexchange
twitter.com/designexchange
www .facebook.com/DesignExchange
The DX is the only museum in Canada dedicated to preserving design heritage. The museum is housed in the old Toronto Stock Exchange building in downtown Toronto. Hours of Operation: M-Sa 10:00-5:00, Su 12:00-5:00.
Shauna Levy, President, 416-727-7315, shauna@dx.org

Toronto: The Enoch Turner Schoolhouse (1848)
106 Trinity St.,
Toronto, ON M5A 3C6

Tel: 416-392-6227
info@enochturnerschoolhouse.ca
www.enochturnerschoolhouse.ca
twitter.com/Enoch_Turner_SH
One of Toronto's oldest institutions & the city's first free school
P. Lynne Kurylo, Chair

Toronto: Fort York National Historic Site
250 Fort York Blvd.,
Toronto, ON M5V 3K9

Tel: 416-392-6907; *Fax:* 416-392-6917
fortyork@toronto.ca
www.toronto.ca/museums/fortyork
twitter.com/fortyo rk
www.facebook.com/fortyork
Other contact information: Alternate URL: www.fortyork.ca
Year Founded: 1934 Built by Lieutenant-Governor John Graves Simcoe as a garrison in 1793, Fort York was purchased by the City of Toronto in 1909 & restored as a museum in 1934. Its fortified walls contain the largest collection of original War of 1812 buildings in Canada. Some of the restored interiors reflect the life of the garrison community, while others serve as exhibit space for artifacts on a military theme. The site offers seasonal guided tours as well as musket, drill & music demonstrations.
David O'Hara, Manager

Toronto: Gardiner Museum of Ceramic Art
111 Queen's Park,
Toronto, ON M5S 2C7

Tel: 416-586-8080; *Fax:* 416-586-8085
mail@gardinermuseum.on.ca
www.gardinermuseum.on.ca
www.youtube.com/user/gardinermuseum
twitter.com/gardinermuseum
www.fac ebook.com/16720993289
Containing 3,000+ historical & contemporary pieces, the Gardiner Museum is North America's premier specialized ceramic museum; gift shop; Gail Brooker Ceramic Research Library; Gardiner Bistro; permanent & special exhibits; studio spaces & ceramic courses; talks, book launches, films & other programs.
Kelvin Browne, Executive Director & CEO

Toronto: Gibson House Museum
5176 Yonge St.,
Toronto, ON M2N 5P6

Tel: 416-395-7432
gibsonhouse@toronto.ca
www.toronto.ca
twitter.com/GibsonMuseumTO
www.facebook.com/gibsonmuseu m
Gibson House, built in 1851, was the home of Scottish immigrant David Gibson and his family. Provides exhibits, events, heritage garden, board game nights, community quilt groups & childrens programs. Open year round
Dorie Billich, Curator

Toronto: Historic Zion Schoolhouse
1091 Finch Ave. East,
Toronto, ON M2J 2X3

Tel: 416-395-7435
zionschool@toronto.ca
www.toronto.ca
twitter.com/Zio nSchoolhouse
www.facebook.com/zionschoolhouse
Year Founded: 1869 A City of Toronto Museum, the Zion Schoolhouse offers modern students a roleplaying experience into the lives of children circa 1910.

Toronto: L Space Gallery
Lakeshore Campus, Humber College, Rm #L1002 19 Colonel Samuel Smith Park Dr,
Toronto, ON M8V 4B6

Tel: 416-675-6622
galleries@humber.ca
www.humbergalleries.ca/galleries/l-space
instagram.com/HumberGalleries
twitter.com/HumberGalleries
www.facebook .com/HumberGalleries
Year Founded: 2012 Work by students & local artists. Open Mon-Fri 10:00-5:00
Ashley Watson, Curator, ashley.watson@humber.ca

Toronto: Lambton House
4066 Old Dundas St.,
Toronto, ON M6S 2R6

Tel: 416-767-5472
postmaster@lambtonhouse.org
www.lambtonhouse.org
twitter.com/LambtonHouse
www.facebook.com/Lambton House
Year Founded: 2012 The last remaining building from the Village of Lambton Mills.

Toronto: Mackenzie House
82 Bond St.,
Toronto, ON M5B 1X2

Tel: 416-392-6915
machouse@toronto.ca
www.toronto.ca/museums/mackenziehouse
twitter.com/MackenzieHouse
www.f acebook.com/mackenziehouse
Year Founded: 1950 The final home of Toronto's first mayor, William Lyon Mackenzie who gained notoriety during the 1837 Upper Canada Rebellion, this 1858 Georgian rowhouse has been refurnished in period style and also showcases a print shop.

Toronto: Montgomery's Inn
4709 Dundas St. West,
Toronto, ON M9A 1A8

Tel: 416-394-8113; *Fax:* 416-394-6027
montinn@toronto.ca
www.montgomerysinn.com
twitter.com/MontINNTO
www.facebook.com/montgomerysinn
Year Founded: 1975 Built in 1830, the restored inn reflects life in 1847. Its library holds photographs, artifacts, and archival materials documenting the history of Etobicoke; tearoom; gift shop; seasonal programs; community theatre and music; workshops

Toronto: The Morris & Sally Justein Heritage Museum
Baycrest Hospital, 3560 Bathurst St., North York,
Toronto, ON M6A 2X8

Tel: 416-785-2500; *Fax:* 416-785-2378
czita@baycrest.org
www.baycrest.org/Baycrest/Living-at-Baycrest/Amenitie s/Museum
The Morris & Sally Justein Heritage Museum displays Judaica exhibits. The historical & cultural Judaica exhibits & permanent collections are designed for Baycrest Hospital & Home's elderly clients.
Nicole Lancovitz, Museum Curator

Toronto: MZTV Museum of Television
64 Jefferson Ave.,
Toronto, ON M6K 1Y4

Tel: 416-599-7339
mztv@mztv.com
www.mztv.com
www.facebook.com/239799029379279
The museum seeks to protect & preserve television sets & related technologies, as well as books, magazines, original papers, discs, toys & ephemera of television; interactive 3D gallery; museum; e-gallery online at website; guided tours Tues - Fri.

Toronto: National Presbyterian Museum
415 Broadview Ave.,
Toronto, ON M4K 2M9

Tel: 416-469-1345
museum@presbyterian.ca
www.presbyterianmuseum.ca
twitter.com/PresbyterianMu1
Year Founded: 2002 The museum is dedicated to preserving the history of the Presbyterian Church in Canada.

Toronto: Osborne Collection of Early Children's Books
Lillian H. Smith Branch, Toronto Public Library, 239 College St., 4th Fl.,
Toronto, ON M5T 1R5

Tel: 416-393-7753
www.torontopubliclibrary.ca/osborne
The collection of historic children's books includes the following: The Osborne Collection; The Lillian H. Smith Collection; The Canadian Collection; & The Jean Thomson Collection of Original Art.

Toronto: Parliament Interpretive Centre
265 Front St. East,
Toronto, ON M5A 1G1

Tel: 416-212-8897
programs@heritagetrust.on.ca
Year Founded: 2012 Exhibits the history of the site as well as the War of 1812.

Toronto: The Queen's Own Rifles of Canada Regimental Museum
Casa Loma, 1 Austin Terrace,
Toronto, ON M5R 1X8

Tel: 416-605-9159
museum@qormuseum.org
qormuseum.org
instagram.com/qormuseum; pinterest.com/qormuseum
twitter.com/qormuseum
www.facebook.com/qormuseum
Year Founded: 1956 Display artifacts pertinent to the history of the regiment from 1860 to the present. Open year round 9:30-5:00
Dorit Leo, Curator, dleo@casaloma.org

Toronto: Queen's York Rangers Regimental Museum
Fort York Armoury, 660 Fleet St. West,
Toronto, ON M5V 1A9

Tel: 416-203-4622; *Fax:* 416-203-4650
qyrang.ca/about/history
Traces the history of the Queen's York Rangers, an active reconnaissance unit of the Army Reserve; Displays include the Seven Year's War, the American Revolution & settlement of Upper Canada, the campaigns of 19th century & two world wars.
L.Col. Diane Kruger, Curator,
qyrangcentralregistry@intern.mil.ca

Toronto: Redpath Sugar Museum
95 Queen's Quay East,
Toronto, ON M5E 1A3

Tel: 416-366-3561 *Toll-Free:* 800-267-1517
Consumer-Canada@redpathsugar.com
www.redpathsugars.com
www.youtube.com/redpathsugar
twitter.com/actsofsweetness
www.facebook.com/redpathsugar
Year Founded: 1979 The Redpath Sugar Museum displays the history of sugar production & refining, models of transportation that bring sugar to the refinery, as well as the story of the Redpath family. The museum offers a program for schools.
Richard Feltoe, Curator & Corporate Archivist,
Richard.Feltoe@asr-group.com

Toronto: Royal Canadian Military Institute Museum (RCMI)
426 University Ave.,
Toronto, ON M5G 1S9

Tel: 416-597-0286; *Fax:* 416-597-6919
Toll-Free: 800-585-1072
info@rcmi.org
www.rcmi.org
twitter.com/rcmiHQ
Artifacts related to Canadians' participation in the military; library open to researchers & members; open year round
Gregory Loughton, Curator, gregory.loughton@rcmi.org

Toronto: The Royal Regiment of Canada Museum
Fort York Armoury, 660 Fleet St.,
Toronto, ON M5V 1A9

Tel: 416-755-1727
Year Founded: 1996 Military artifacts, dating from 1862, of the The Royal Regiment of Canada, & predecessors: the 10th Royal Grenadiers (Toronto Regiment), & the 3rd, 123rd, 124th, 204th & 58th Battalions; archives; school tours by appointment. Located next to the Royals' WO's & Sergeants' Mess on the 2nd floor, at the east end of Fort York Armoury.

Toronto: St. Mark's Coptic Museum
41 Glendinning Ave.,
Toronto, ON M1W 3E2

Tel: 416-494-4449
stmarkmuseum@yahoo.com
www.stmarkstoronto.ca

Year Founded: 2000 The only Coptic museum outside of Egypt; collection contains artwork & artifacts

Toronto: The Salvation Army Museum
2 Overlea Blvd.,
Toronto, ON M4H 1P4

Tel: 416-285-4344
heritage_centre@can.salvationarmy.org
salvationist.ca/ about/history/museum-archives
Open to public & gives a pictorial outline of Salvation Army history, particularly as it pertains to Canada & Bermuda, through the use of artifacts, photographs & special techniques. Open Mon-Fri 8:00-3:30

Toronto: Sarah & Chaim Neuberger Holocaust Education Centre
UJA Federation of Greater Toronto, Lipa Green Centre, Sherman Campus, 4600 Bathurst St.,
Toronto, ON M2R 3V2

Tel: 416-631-5689
neuberger@ujafed.org
www.holocaustcentre.com
neubergerhec.tumblr.com
twitter.com/holocaust_ed
www.facebook.com/HoloCentre
The centre is dedicated to educating the public about the Holocaust & creating dialogue about civil society through programs, exhibitions, an on-site museum, & library. Open M-Th 9:00-4:30, F 9:00-1:00, or by appointment.
Shael Rosenbaum, Chair
Mira Goldfarb, Executive Director
Dara Soloman, Executive Director
Carson Phillips, Managing Director

Toronto: Scadding Cabin
Parent: York Pioneeer & Historical Society
c/o York Pioneer & Historical Society, PO Box 45026, 2482 Yonge St.,
Toronto, ON M4P 3E3

Tel: 416-219-2454
yorkpioneers@gmail.com
www.yorkpioneers.org/cabin.html
Built for John Scadding, clerk to Lieutenant-Governor John Graves Simcoe, the cabin is Toronto's oldest dwelling. Located at Exhibition Place, southeast of 25 British Columbia Rd.; wooden house, built in late 1700s, contains furniture which belonged to John Graves Simcoe; open late Aug.-Labour Day (during CNE)

Toronto: Scarborough Historical Museum
1007 Brimley Rd.,
Toronto, ON M1P 3E8

Tel: 416-338-8807
shm@toronto.ca
www.toronto.ca/scarboroughmuseum
twitter.com/ScarbMuseum
www.facebook. com/scarboroughmuseum
History of Scarborough's development & early settlement. Includes Cornell House, McCowan Log House, Kennedy Gallery & Hough Carriage Works. Open year round

Toronto: Sesquicentennial Museum & Archives
263 McCaul St.,
Toronto, ON M5T 1W7

Tel: 416-397-3680; *Fax:* 416-397-3685
greg.mckinon@tdsb.on.ca
pubhist.info.yorku.ca/institution/sesquicentenni
al-museum-and-archives
Preserves the history, artifacts, documents & art of the Toronto District School Board & its schools. Open Mon-Fri 8:30-4:30

Toronto: Spadina Museum: Historic House & Gardens
285 Spadina Rd.,
Toronto, ON M5R 2V5

Tel: 416-392-6910
spadina@toronto.ca
www.toronto.ca/museums/spadina
twitter.com/SpadinaMuseum
www.facebook. com/spadinamuseum
Year Founded: 1984 1866 mansion contains four generations of décor, reflecting art movements such as Art Nouveau
Karen Edwards, Administrator

Toronto: Taras H. Shevchenko Museum
1614 Bloor St. West,
Toronto, ON M6P 1A7

Tel: 416-534-8662; *Fax:* 416-535-1063
shevchenkomuseum@bellnet.ca
www.infoukes.com/shevchenkomuseum
www.face book.com/ShevchenkoMuseum
The museum is dedicated to the art, life and literary legacy of Ukraine's renowned poet, Taras Schevchenko; the Toronto site is

the only Shevchenko museum in the Americas. Library; art exhibits; Ukrainian folk art and handicrafts. Open year round.

Toronto: Textile Museum of Canada
55 Centre Ave.,
Toronto, ON M5G 2H5

Tel: 416-599-5321
info@textilemuseum.ca
www.textilemuseum.ca
twitter.com/tmctoronto
www.facebook.com/textilemu seumofcanada
Year Founded: 1975 Unique exhibitions & programming; focus on the traditions & aesthetics of historic & contemporary textiles
Shauna McCabe, Executive Director, 416-599-5321,
smccabe@textilemuseum.ca

Toronto: Theatre Museum Canada (TMC)
#309, 15 Case Goods Lane,
Toronto, ON M5A 3C4

Tel: 416-413-7847; *Fax:* 416-923-0226
www.theatremuseumcanada.ca
www.youtube.com/theatremuseumcanada
twitter.com/TheatreMuseumC
www.fac ebook.com/TheatreMuseumCanada
Year Founded: 1982 While no physical location yet exists, the Theatre Museum Canada's collection consists of memorabilia & artifacts that document the history of Canadian theatre.
Michael Wallace, Executive Director,
mwallace@theatremuseumcanada.ca

Toronto: Todmorden Mills Heritage Museum & Art Centre
67 Pottery Rd.,
Toronto, ON M4K 2B8

Tel: 416-396-2819
todmorden@toronto.ca
www.toronto.ca/culture/museums/todmorden.htm
twitter.com/TodmordenMills
www.facebook.com/TodmordenMills
Depicts early industry in Toronto; new papermill galleries & theatre feature frequent exhibitions & is available for rental

Toronto: Toronto Police Museum & Discovery Centre
40 College St.,
Toronto, ON M5G 2J3

Tel: 416-808-7020
museum@torontopolice.on.ca
www.torontopolice.on.ca/museum
Interactive displays; collection includes uniforms, badges, communication & transportation equipment; high profile crimes; open year round

Toronto: Toronto Railway Museum
Parent: Toronto Railway Historical Association
255 Bremner Blvd. Unit #15,
Toronto, ON M5V 3M9

Tel: 416-214-9229
info@torontorailwaymuseum.com
www.torontorailwaymuseum.com
pinterest.com/TOrailwayMuseum
twitter.com/TORailwayMuseum
www.facebook .com/TORailwayMuseum
Year Founded: 2010 Toronto & Ontario railway history. Open May-Jun, Sept-Oct Sat-Sun 12:00-5:00; Jun-Sept daily 12:00-5:00.

Toronto: Toronto Scottish Regiment Museum
70 Birmingham St.,
Toronto, ON M8V 3W6

Tel: 416-635-4250
tsrpd.com/regiment/museum.html
Year Founded: 1984 Military artifacts. Available for viewing by appointment.
Tim Stewart, Curator

Toronto: Toronto's First Post Office (TFPO)
Parent: Town of York Historical Society
260 Adelaide St. East,
Toronto, ON M5A 1N1

Tel: 416-865-1833; *Fax:* 416-865-9414
tfpo@total.net
www.townofyork.com
instagram.com/tos1stpo
twitter.com/tos1stpo
www.facebook.com/TOs1stPO
Year Founded: 1983 Canada's only surviving pre-1851 Post Office; restored as a museum & full postal service operation. Open daily
Janet Walters, Curator & Director

Tweed: Tweed & Area Heritage Centre
PO Box 665, 40 Victoria St. North,
Tweed, ON K0K 3J0

Tel: 613-478-3989; *Fax:* 613-478-6457
tweedheritageinfo@on.aibn.com
www.facebook.com/tweed.heritagecentre
Year Founded: 1988 An information centre, art gallery, museum, archives & genealogical research centre; local arts & crafts promotional centre.
Evan Morton, Curator, 613-478-3989, Fax: 613-478-6457,
tweedheritageinfo@on.aibn.com

Uxbridge: Thomas Foster Memorial Temple
9449 Concession Rd. 7,
Uxbridge, ON L0C 1C0

Tel: 905-640-3966
www.fostermemorial.com
www.facebook.com/foster.memorial
Built by former mayor of Toronto, Thomas Foster, in 1935/36 as a memorial to his wife, unique in the design of Byzantine architecture; holds tours on the 1st & 2nd Sun., June-Sept.; special concerts throughout the year, with special program in Oct.

Uxbridge: Uxbridge Historical Centre
PO Box 1301, 7230 Concession Rd. 6,
Uxbridge, ON L9P 1R2

Tel: 905-852-5854
museum@town.uxbridge.on.ca
www.uxbridgehistoricalcentre.com
instagram.com/uxbridgehistoricalcentre
twitter.com/UxbridgeMuseum
www. facebook.com/uxbridgehistoricalcentre
Year Founded: 1972 Archives & displays of artifacts & photos about the heritage of the Uxbridge area. Includes Quaker Trail, displays of famous Canadians & 8 heritage buildings on site. Open Mar-May, Oct-Nov daily 8:30-4:30; Jun-Sep Wed-Sun 9:00-5:00
Nancy Marr, Curator

Vankleek Hill: Musée Vankleek Hill Museum
PO Box 537, 95 Main St. East,
Vankleek Hill, ON K0B 1R0

Tel: 613-678-2323
info@vankleek.ca
www.vankleek.ca
www.facebook.com/vankleekhillmuseum
Year Founded: 1997 Local history
J. Denis Seguin, President
Harvey LeRoy, Vice President

Vaughan: The Soccer Hall of Fame & Museum
7601 Martin Grove Rd.,
Vaughan, ON L4L 9E4

Tel: 905-264-9390
museum@thesoccerhalloffame.ca
thesoccerhalloffame.ca
www.facebook.com/SoccerHallofFame
Year Founded: 1997 Archives relating to Canadian soccer history
Steve Reed, President
Nick Bontis, Vice-President

Vernon: Osgoode Township Historical Society & Museum
PO Box 74, 7814 Lawrence St.,
Vernon, ON K0A 3J0

Tel: 613-821-4062; *Fax:* 613-821-3140
manager@osgoodemuseum.ca
www.osgoodemuseum.ca
twitter.com/OsgoodeMuseu m
www.facebook.com/125725207465630
The Osgoode Township Historical Society & Museum preserves the development of the Township of Osgoode, situated south of Ottawa, Ontario. Artifacts include indigenous Native & pioneer articles & documents, such as historic furniture & clothing, & agricultural tools & equipment. The Museum is open Tuesdays to Saturdays.
Robin Cushnie, Museum Manager,
manager@osgoodemuseum.ca

Vienna: Edison Museum of Vienna
14 Snow St.,
Vienna, ON N0J 1Z0

Tel: 519-874-4999
Other contact information: Off season phone: 519-866-5521
Artifacts that belonged to relatives of Thomas Edison who lived in Vienna. Open mid-May to Labour Day.

Virgil: Lincoln & Welland Regiment Museum (LWRM)
504 Line 2 Rd.,
Virgil, ON L0S 1T0

Tel: 905-468-0888
lwrm@lwmuseum.ca
www.lwmuseum.ca
www.youtube.com/channel/UCgc0DqUQAP71KeyAw1uf-Pw
twitter.com/lwmuseum
www.facebook.com/NiagaraMilitaryHeritageCentre
Year Founded: 2001 Exhibits include the origins & heritage of the Lincoln & Welland Regiment.

Wallaceburg: Wallaceburg & District Museum
505 King St.,
Wallaceburg, ON N8A 1J1

Tel: 519-627-8962
curator@kent.net
www.kent.net#wallaceburg-museum/index.html
instagram.com/wallaceburg_district_museum
twitter.com/W_burgMuseum
www.facebook.com/Wallaceburg-Museum-299325500526177
Year Founded: 1984 Local history. Open Tue-Sat 10:00-4:00

Wallacetown: Backus-Page House Museum
PO Box 26, 29424 Lakeview Line,
Wallacetown, ON N0L 2M0

Tel: 519-762-3072
info@backuspagehouse.ca
www.backuspagehouse.ca
twitter.com/BackusPageHouse
www.facebook.com/ba ckuspagehouse
Year Founded: 1994 A living history museum featuring costumed interpreters & period artifacts. May-Oct., Tu-F 10:00-4:30, Sa & Su 12:00-4:30; open year-round by appointment.
Lori Milos-Ivanski, Curator

Wasaga Beach: Nancy Island Historic Site
c/o Wasaga Beach Provincial Park, 119 Mosley St.,
Wasaga Beach, ON L9Z 2V9

Tel: 705-429-2516; Fax: 705-429-7983
www.wasagabeachpark.com/Activities-Events/Nancy-Island-Historic-Site.html
nancyislandblog.wordpress.com
twitter.com/FriendsofNancy
Artifacts from the British schooner "Nancy" from the War of 1812; replica of Upper Lakes lighthouse. Open May-Jun Sat-Sun 10:00-5:00; Jun-Sep daily 10:00-5:00; Sep-Oct Sat-Sun 10:00-5:00
John Fisher, Superintendent, Wasaga Beach Provincial Park

Waterford: Waterford Heritage & Agricultural Museum
159 Nichol St.,
Waterford, ON N0E 1Y0

Tel: 519-443-4211
www.waterfordmuseum.ca
www.facebook.com/147540755302855
History of the Waterford & Townsend area; includes unique collection of agricultural equipment representative of southern Ontario
Melissa Collver, Curator & Director, melissa.collver@norfolkcounty.ca
James Christison, Museum Assistant, james.christison@norfolkcounty.ca

Waterloo: Brubacher House Museum
c/o University of Waterloo, North Campus,
Waterloo, ON N2L 3G6

Tel: 519-886-3855
bhouse@uwaterloo.ca
uwaterloo.ca
Built in 1850, the Brubacher House was later purchased by the University of Waterloo. The home's interior was rebuilt to reflect a Pennsylvania German Mennonite home from the 1850 to 1890 era. Many of the furnishings in the Brubacher House, collected from local Mennonite families, also reflect the time period. Operated by Conrad Grebel University College & the Mennonite Historical Society of Ontario, the House is open from the beginning of May to the end of October.

Waterloo: City of Waterloo Museum
Conestoga Mall, 550 King St. North,
Waterloo, ON N2J 4A8

Tel: 519-885-8828; Fax: 519-885-6455
www.waterloo.ca/en/living/CityofWaterlooMuseum.asp
Other contact information: TTY: 1-866-786-3941
Local history & permanent collection comprised of artifacts that relate to the Seagram family & the Seagram Distillery.

Waterloo: Earth Sciences Museum
Centre for Environmental & Information Technology,
University of Waterloo, 200 University Ave. West,
Waterloo, ON N2L 3G1

Tel: 519-888-4567
earthmuseum@uwaterloo.ca
uwaterloo.ca/earth-sciences-museum
twitter.com/EarthSciMuseum
Year Founded: 1967 Exhibits include dinosaurs, mining tunnel, fossils, gems, minerals & a 60-tonne rock garden. Open Mon-Fri 8:30-4:30
Corina McDonald, Curator, corina.mcdonald@uwaterloo.ca

Waterloo: Elliott Avedon Virtual Museum & Archive of Games
University of Waterloo, 200 University Avenue West,
Waterloo, ON N2L 3G1

Tel: 519-888-4567
www.gamesmuseum.uwaterloo.ca
Year Founded: 1971 Specializes in the collection, presentation & display of games, both Canadian & international collections; researchers act as a resource for archiving related materials related to games & also provide research facilities & expertise to persons interested in pursuing the study of Games. The physical collection was relocated to the Canadian Museum of Civilization in 2009; the University of Waterloo currently maintains information about the collection on its website as a virtual museum.

Waterloo: Museum of Visual Science & Optometry
School of Optometry & Vision Science, University of
Waterloo, 200 Columbia St. West,
Waterloo, ON N2L 3G1

Tel: 519-888-4567; Fax: 519-725-0784
jfleet@uwaterloo.ca
optometry.uwaterloo.ca/museum-of-vision-science
Antique spectacles & eye examining equipment galleries; historical documents & books. Open Mon-Fri 8:30-5:00
Paul Lofthouse, Curator, plofthou@uwaterloo.ca

Wawa: Lake Superior Provincial Park Visitor Centre
PO Box 267,
Wawa, ON P0S 1K0

Tel: 705-856-2284; Fax: 705-856-1333
info@lakesuperiorpark.ca
www.lakesuperiorpark.ca
Open from May - Oct., this interpretive centre includes information on the Lake Superior Provincial Park's natural & cultural features & the area's recreational opportunities

Welland: Welland Historical Museum
140 King St.,
Welland, ON L3B 3J3

Tel: 905-732-2215; Fax: 905-732-9169
wellandhistoricalmuseum@cogeco.net
www.wellandmuseum.ca
instagram.com/wellandmuseum;
linkedin.com/company/welland-museum
twitter.com/WellandMuseum
www.face book.com/212024838829918
History of Welland including the Welland Canal & its industries. Includes childrens galleries & WWI interactive display. Open Tue-Sat 10:00-4:00
Nora Reid, Executive Director, nr.wm@cogeco.net
Penny Morningstar, Curator, pm.wm@cogeco.net

Wellington: Wellington Heritage Museum
290 Main St.,
Wellington, ON K0K 3L0

Tel: 613-399-5015
wellmuseum@pecounty.on.ca
pecounty.on.ca/government/community_development/museums/wellington.php
The local history collection of the Wellington Heritage Museum is housed within a Quaker Meeting House, which was built in 1885. The museum features a tribute to the Society of Friends, who helped develop the county. A special collection is the Douglas A. Crawford Canning Industry Collection. Wellington Heritage Museum is open from May to mid October.
Jennifer Lyons, Head Curator, Museums of Prince Edward County, 613-476-3833, museums@pecounty.on.ca

Westport: Rideau District Museum
29 Bedford St.,
Westport, ON K0G 1X0

rdmuseum@kingston.net
www.rideaudistrictmuseum.webs.com
Year Founded: 1961 Housed in 1850s blacksmith & carriage shop with forges & bellows intact & showing many artifacts from the local district, including a 9-foot tall 19th-century statue of Sally Grant, the Blind Lady of Justice

White Lake: Waba Cottage Museum & Gardens
24 Museum Rd.,
White Lake, ON K0A 3L0

Tel: 613-623-8853 Toll-Free: 800-957-4621
garden_visit@sympatico.ca
www3.sympatico.ca/jsktyrrell/museum.html
www .facebook.com/WabaCottageMuseumGardens
Year Founded: 1967 Situated in an 8-acre park amongst heritage buildings; includes log schoolhouse, church & a variety of flower gardens. Open Jul-Sep daily 9:30-4:30; May-Jun Sat-Sun

White River: White River Heritage Museum
PO Box 583, 200 Elgin St.,
White River, ON P0M 3G0

Tel: 807-822-2657
heritagemuseum@bellnet.ca
heritagemuseumwhiteriver.ca
www.facebook.com/whiteriverheritagemuseum
Local history & Winnie the Pooh exhibit. Open Mon-Fri 9:00-5:00

Whitney: Algonquin Visitor Centre, Algonquin Logging Museum & Algonquin Art Centre
PO Box 219,
Whitney, ON K0J 2M0

Tel: 613-637-2828; Fax: 613-637-2138
www.algonquinpark.on.ca
www.youtube.com/user/FOAPAlgonquinPark
twitter.com/AlgonquinPark
www.f acebook.com/TheFriendsofAlgonquinPark
Other contact information: Park Information: 705-633-5572
Visitor Centre contains exhibits on the Park's natural & human history, restaurant, & bookstore. Logging Museum presents the history of logging from 1830's to current times; exhibits include a recreated Camboose camp & a steam powered amphibious tug. Art Centre has indoor & outdoor galleries & offers art activities. Open daily 9:00-5:00 from late June until Thanksgiving.
Rick Stronks, Chief Park Naturalist

Williamstown: Bethune-Thompson House
19730 John St.,
Williamstown, ON K0C 2J0

Tel: 613-347-7192
Year Founded: 1977 The house was first built in 1784 by an early settler to the Williamstown area & is now a National Historic Site.

Williamstown: The Nor'Westers & Loyalist Museum
PO Box 69, 19651 John St. (County Rd. 17),
Williamstown, ON K0C 2J0

Tel: 613-347-3547
gnlmuseum@gmail.com
www.glengarrynorwestersandloyalistmuseum.ca
twitter.com/NorWestLoyalist
www.facebook.com/GlengarryNorwestersandLoyalistMuseum
Year Founded: 1967 History of the United Empire Loyalist migration & the heritage of Glengarry Country. Open May-Sep Wed-Mon 10:00-5:00; Sep-Oct Sat-Sun 10:00-4:00
Ken MacDonald, President
Keleigh Goodfellow, Curator

Windsor: Ojibway Nature Centre
5200 Matchette Rd.,
Windsor, ON N9C 4E8

Tel: 519-966-5852
ojibway@citywindsor.ca
www.ojibway.ca
twitter.com/OjibwayPark
The Ojibway Nature Centre presents displays about the natural history & ecology of the Ojibway Prairie Complex. Includes a live exhibit area featuring the Eastern Fox Snake & the Eastern Massasauga Rattlesnake. Lessons & tours available. Open 10:00-5:00 daily

Windsor: Serbian Heritage Museum of Windsor (SHM)
6770 Tecumseh Rd. East,
Windsor, ON N8T 1E6

Tel: 519-944-4884
info@serbianheritagemuseum.com
www.serbianheritagemuseum.com
www.youtube.com/user/shmuseum
www.facebook.com/shmuseum
Year Founded: 1987 Artifacts & archival material of Serbian people in Windsor dating back to 1920s; tours, educational programming & lectures; gift shop; open year round

Windsor: Willistead Manor
1899 Niagara St.,
Windsor, ON N8Y 1K3

Tel: 519-253-2365; Fax: 519-253-5101
willistead@citywindsor.ca
citywindsor.ca/residents/Culture/Willistead-Ma
nor/Pages/Willistead-Manor.as
36-room mansion built in 1906; viewing by appt. Available for
special events.

Windsor: Windsor's Community Museum
254 Pitt St. West,
Windsor, ON N9A 5L5

Tel: 519-253-1812; Fax: 519-253-0919
wmuseum@city.windsor.on.ca
www.citywindsor.ca/residents/Culture/Windsors
-Community-Museum
Year Founded: 1958 The Museum includes the François Baby
House on Pitt St. W., & the Duff-Baby Interpretation Centre,
located at 221 Mill St.; changing exhibits on the history of the
Windsor region; houses over 15,000 artifacts, paintings,
drawings, prints & photos, maps, newspapers & books, & a large
archival collection. Open year round.

Wingham: North Huron District Museum
PO Box 1522, 273 Josephine St.,
Wingham, ON N0G 2W0

Tel: 519-357-1096; Fax: 519-357-1110
nhmuseum@northhuron.ca
www.northhuron.ca/visitors.php^area=THINGS&cid=4&aid=10
Exhibits featuring the history of North Huron's writers, painters,
businesses, farmers & people; Special exhibit & garden
dedicated to Alice Munro.

Woodstock: Woodstock Museum National Historic Site
Museum Square, 466 Dundas St.,
Woodstock, ON N4S 1C4

Tel: 519-537-8411; Fax: 519-537-7235
museum@city.woodstock.on.ca
www.woodstockmuseum.ca
The Woodstock Museum National Historic Site exhibits the local
history of Woodstock from 10,000 B.C. to 2001. At the former
Town Hall & Market House, which was built in 1853, visitors can
see the 1879 Council Chambers & the 1889 Grand Hall. The
museum contains a research room, with books & vertical files. It
is open to the public by appointment only. School education
programs are available, by phoning 519-539-1382, extension
2903. The museum is open year-round.
Karen Houston, Curator, khouston@city.woodstock.on.ca

Prince Edward Island

Provincial Museums

Prince Edward Island Museum & Heritage
Foundation / L'Ile-du-Prince-Édouard Musée et la
Fondation du patrimoine
2 Kent St.,
Charlottetown, PE C1A 1M6

Tel: 902-368-6600; Fax: 902-368-6608
mhpei@gov.pe.ca
www.peimuseum.com
www.flickr.com/photos/pei_museum
twitter.com/PEIMUSEUM
www.facebook.co m/PEIMuseum
The organization is the operator of seven provincial museums &
heritage sites across Prince Edward Island. Sites include the
Elmira Railway Museum, Basin Head Fisheries Museum, Orwell
Corner Historic Village & Agricultural Museum, Beaconsfield
Historic House, Eptek Art & Culture Centre, The Acadian
Museum of Prince Edward Island, & Green Park Shipbuilding
Museum & Yeo House. The Prince Edward Island Museum &
Heritage Foundation also has the responsibility for the provincial
collection of over 90,000 artifacts.
Matthew McRae, Executive Director

Local Museums

Alberton: Alberton Museum
PO Box 515, 457 Church St.,
Alberton, PE C0B 1B0

Tel: 902-853-4048; Fax: 902-853-3190
ahf@isn.net
www.townofalberton.ca/history/museum.htm
Year Founded: 1964 Genealogy resources on area families; old
photo collection; history of the fox industry; Micmac Indian
displays; displays of antique furniture, glassware, textiles & toys.
Open Jun-Sept.

Belfast: Point Prim Lighthouse
2147 Point Prim Rd.,
Belfast, PE C0A 1A0

Tel: 902-659-2768
pointprimlighthouse@gmail.com
pointprimlighthouse.com
The oldest lighthouse in PEI, built in 1845; now serves as a
museum featuring historical displays & artifacts. Open mid-June
through mid-Sept., with guided tours offered in July & Aug.

Bideford: Bideford Parsonage Museum
Parent: West Country Historical Society Inc.
784 Bideford Rd. Rte. 166,
Bideford, PE C0B 1J0

Tel: 902-831-3133
bpm.bideford@pei.sympatico.ca
www.bidefordparsonagemuseum.com
Owned & operated by the West Country Historical Society Inc.;
Lucy Maud Montgomery boarded at the home from 1894-95.

Bonshaw: Car Life Museum Inc.
18191 Trans Canada Hwy.,
Bonshaw, PE C0A 1C0

Tel: 902-675-3555
https://www.facebook.com/CarLifeMuseum/
The Car Life Museum features restored cars which date back to
1898. The museum also houses farm machinery from the early
1800s & the early 1900s. Open from June to September.
Doris MacKay, Contact

Cavendish: Ripley's Believe It or Not! Museum
PO Box 860, 8863 Cavendish Rd.,
Cavendish, PE C0A 1N0

Tel: 877-963-3939; Fax: 902-963-3949
cavendishentertainment.com
Displays of human & animal oddities. Open May-Sep
Thom McMillan, Contact, thom.mac@pei.aibn.com

Charlottetown: Ardgowan National Historic Site
2 Palmers Lane,
Charlottetown, PE C1A 5V8

Tel: 902-566-7050 Toll-Free: 888-773-8888
pnipe.peinp@pc.gc.ca
www.pc.gc.ca/eng/lhn-nhs/pe/ardgowan/index.aspx
t witter.com/ParksCanadaPEI
www.facebook.com/PEInationalpark
Restored house originally belonging to William Henry Pope, one
of the Fathers of Confederation at the time of the Charlottetown
Conference of 1864. The house and two-fectare property were
acquired by the federal government in 1967 and were then
restored to their 1860s appearance. The interior now houses
Parks Canada administrative offices and not open for public
tours, although the maintained period gardens welcome visitors.
Accessible Mon. - Fri. 8:30am - 4:30pm.

Charlottetown: Green Gables Heritage Place
8679 Route 6,
Charlottetown, PE C0A 1M0

Tel: 902-963-7874; Fax: 902-963-7869
Toll-Free: 888-773-8888
greengables.info@pc.gc.ca
www.pc.gc.ca/en/lhn-nhs/pe/g reengables
twitter.com/ParksCanadaPEI
www.facebook.com/PEInationalpark
Dedicated to Anne of Green Gables, a fictional but nonetheless,
famous character created by Lucy Maud Montgomery for her
book series "Anne of Green Gables". Open May 1 - Oct. 31

Charlottetown: PEI Sports Hall of Fame & Museum Inc.
40 Enman Cres.,
Charlottetown, PE C1A 1E6

Tel: 902-393-5474
peisportshall@gmail.com
www.peisportshalloffame.ca
twitter.com/PEISportsHall
www.facebook.com/ 210800825622110
Year Founded: 1968 The Sports Hall of Fame recognizes and
pays tribute to athletes and builders of sport who have brought
special honour to the province; collects artifacts, photographs
and other memorabilia depicting the history of sport in PEI.
Paul H. Schurman, Chair, phbjschurman@islandtelecom.com
Dave Holland, Media, dholland@newscap.ca
Doug Johnston, Director at Large,
dougjohnston@pei.sympatico.ca
Clair Sweet, Director at Large, clairsweet1951@gmail.com
Nick Murray, Special Advisor, njmurray100@gmail.com

Charlottetown: Port-la-Joye-Fort Amherst National
Historic Site of Canada
c/o Parks Canada, 2 Palmer's Lane,
Charlottetown, PE C1A 5V8

Tel: 902-566-7626; Fax: 902-566-8295
pljfa.info@pc.gc.ca
www.pc.gc.ca/lhn-nhs/pe/amherst/activ.aspx
Other contact information: Summer Phone: 902-675-2220
Visitors to the Port-la-Joye-Fort Amherst National Historic Site of
Canada learn the history of the Mi'kmaq of Prince Edward
Island. Interpretive services are available in July & August.
Guided tours are offered in both English & French. The grounds
are open from June to October.

Charlottetown: Prince Edward Island Regiment
(RCAC) Museum
Queen Charlotte Armouries, PO Box 1480,
Charlottetown, PE C1A 7N1

Tel: 902-368-0108; Fax: 902-368-3034
www.facebook.com/107780305912036

Charlottetown: Province House National Historic Site
of Canada
c/o Parks Canada, 165 Richmind St.,
Charlottetown, PE C1A 1J1

Tel: 902-566-7050; Fax: 902-566-8295
pnipe.peinp@pc.gc.ca
www.pc.gc.ca/eng/lhn-nhs/pe/provincehouse/index.asp x
Includes Confederation Chamber, site of historic discussions
regarding union of the BNA colonies; remains of the Legislative
Bldg. for PEI; open year round

Charlottetown: Spoke Wheel Car Museum
RR#3,
Charlottetown, PE C1A 7J7

Antique automobiles

Hunter River: Farmers' Bank of Rustico Museum &
Doucet House
c/o Friends of the Farmer's Bank, PO Box 5654, RR#3,
Hunter River, PE C0A 1N0

Tel: 902-963-3168
farmers@pei.aibn.com
www.farmersbank.ca
twitter.com/farmersbankpei
www.facebook.com/2192368 21451017
Other contact information: Off-season: 902-963-2194;
info@farmersbank.ca
Rustico is the oldest Acadian settlement in PEI. The site houses
exhibits and activities such as: banking artifacts, from the
precursor to the Credit Union movement in North America; the
early Acadian Doucet House, one of the oldest houses in the
province; library, fishing, natural history, and bread oven baking
exhibits.
J.D. MacDonald, President

Kensington: Anne of Green Gables Museum at Silver
Bush
5 Gerald McCarville Dr.,
Kensington, PE C0B 1M0

Tel: 902-886-2884 Toll-Free: 800-665-2663
info@annemuseum.com
www.annemuseum.com
Open May - Thanksgiving

Kensington: The Keir Memorial Museum
2214 Rte. 20,
Kensington, PE C0B 1M0

Tel: 902-836-3054
kmmuseum@bellaliant.com
www.malpequebay.ca/keirmuseum.htm
Open July - Sept.

Kensington: Veteran's Memorial Military Museum
PO Box 182, 88 Victoria St. W,
Kensington, PE C0B 1M0

Tel: 902-836-3600
Contains a collection of military memorabilia mostly from WWI,
WWII & the Korean War.
Fred Thibeau, Manager

Miminegash: Irish Moss Interpretive Centre & Museum
Rte. 14,
Miminegash, PE C0B 1S0

Tel: 902-882-4313
Details the history of Irish moss harvesting through photographs
& artifacts; visitors can sample dishes made from Irish moss,
such as seeweed pie.

Montague: Garden of the Gulf Museum
PO Box 1237, 564 Main St.,
Montague, PE C0A 1R0

Tel: 902-838-2467
ggmuseum@eastlink.ca
www.montaguemuseumpei.ca
Other contact information: Genealogy/Research Centre:
902-838-1523; genealogy2015@eastlink.ca
Year Founded: 1958 The museum houses more than 5,000
artifacts, with an archives and storage facility. Operations were
suspended in summer 2016 due to staffing issues and the board
of directors is currently exploring other options.
Donna Collings, Curator

Montague: Roma at Three Rivers / Roma à Trois
Rivières
Three Rivers Roma Inc., 505 Roma Point Rd.,
Montague, PE C0A 1R0

Tel: 902-838-3413
roma1732@gmail.com
www.roma3rivers.com; www.romapei.com
twitter.com/Roma_3_Rivers
www.facebook.com/RomaAtThreeRivers
A national historic site depicting the settlement and international
trading post established in 1732 by Jean Pierre Roma.
Interactive programs such as the Pioneer Festival and Heritage
Lunches occur at the site. Open daily June to late September.
Marlo Dodge, Site Manager, 902-838-3413,
roma1732@gmail.com

O'Leary: Canadian Potato Museum
1 Dewar Ln,
O'Leary, PE C0B 1V0

Tel: 902-859-2039 Toll-Free: 844-849-1470
info@canadianpotatomuseum.com
www.canadianpotatomuseum.info
www.facebook.com/groups/138711350502
Other contact information: Off Season: 800-565-3457
The history of the potato industry is depicted at the Canadian
Potato Museum. Visitors will see a collection of machinery &
farm implements related to growing & harvesting potatoes. The
museum also includes the Potato Hall of Fame & a 14-foot-high
potato sculpture. Open from mid-May to mid-October.
Donna Rowley, Manager, 902-853-2312

Summerside: Bishop's Machine Shop Museum
Parent: Wyatt Heritage Properties
PO Box 1510, 101 Water St.,
Summerside, PE C1N 4K4

Tel: 902-432-1296; Fax: 902-432-1328
culturesummerside.com/bishops-machine-shop-museum
www.youtube.com/user/culturesummerside
twitter.com/culturesside
www.facebook.com/CultureSummerside
Historical machine shop complete with lathes & machining tools.
Open daily Monday - Saturday in July and August.
Lori Ellis, Manager, Heritage & Cultural Properties,
lori.ellis@city.summerside.pe.ca

Summerside: International Fox Museum & Hall of
Fame Inc.
286 Fitzroy St.,
Summerside, PE C1N 1J2

Tel: 902-436-0177
toxpei@isn.net
Located at historic Holman Homestead & Gardens; museum
tells the story of the PEI silver fox industry heyday between 1894
& WWII
Julie Simmons, Contact

Summerside: Lefurgey Cultural Centre
Parent: Wyatt Heritage Properties
PO Box 1510, 205 Prince St.,
Summerside, PE C1N 4K4

Tel: 902-432-1327; Fax: 902-432-1328
culturesummerside.com/lefurgey-cultural-center
www.youtube.com/user/culturesummerside
twitter.com/culturesside
www.facebook.com/CultureSummerside
An 1867 shipbuilder's home, now dedicated to arts education;
operated by Wyatt Heritage Properties.
Lori Ellis, Manager, Heritage & Cultural Properties,
lori.ellis@city.summerside.pe.ca

Summerside: MacNaught History Centre & Archives
Parent: Wyatt Heritage Properties
PO Box 1510, 75 Spring St.,
Summerside, PE C1N 4K4

Tel: 902-432-1296; Fax: 902-432-1328
culturesummerside.com/macnaught-history-centre
www.youtube.com/user/culturesummerside
twitter.com/culturesside
www.facebook.com/CultureSummerside
Other contact information: Alt. URL: www.peiancestry.com
Administrative headquarters for Wyatt Heritage Properties,
featuring exhibits on local Summerside history.
Lori Ellis, Manager, Heritage & Cultural Properties,
lori.ellis@city.summerside.pe.ca

Summerside: Wyatt Historic House Museum
Parent: Wyatt Heritage Properties
PO Box 1510, 85 Spring St.,
Summerside, PE C1N 4K4

Tel: 902-432-1296; Fax: 902-432-1328
culturesummerside.com/wyatt-historic-house-museum
www.youtube.com/user/culturesummerside
twitter.com/culturesside
www.facebook.com/CultureSummerside
Restored 1867 house of Wanda Lefurgey Wyatt, operated by
Wyatt Heritage Properties. Open Monday - Saturday in July and
August.
Lori Ellis, Manager, Heritage & Cultural Properties,
lori.ellis@city.summerside.pe.ca

Tignish: Tignish Cultural Centre
103 School St.,
Tignish, PE C0B 2B0

Tel: 902-882-7363
www.tignish.com
Local history

Vernon Bridge: Sir Andrew Macphail Homestead
Sir Andrew Macphail Foundation, 271 McPhail Park Rd.,
Vernon Bridge, PE C0A 2E0

Tel: 902-651-2789
macphailhomestead@pei.aibn.com
www.macphailhomestead.ca
An educational facility & interpretive centre dedicated to
honouring Sir Andrew Macphail; Tea Room, walking trails and
gallery located on site. The Homestead is open to the public July
1 - Sept. 30.
Mary Elliott, Site Manager

Wellington: The Bottle Houses / Les Maisons de
Bouteilles
6891 Route 11, Boite 53,
Wellington, PE C0B 2E0

Tel: 902-854-2987
maisonsbouteille@eastlink.ca
www.bottlehouses.com
Other contact information: Off Season: 902-854-2254
Three buildings made of over 25,000 vari-coloured bottles; the in
sides are lit in a variety of colours. Located in Cape Egmont;
flower gardens, giftshop and bilingual services on site.
Réjeanne Arsenault, Owner & Operator

West Point: West Point Inn & Museum
Lot 8, 364 Cedar Dunes Park Rd.,
West Point, PE C0B 1V0

Tel: 902-859-3605 Toll-Free: 800-764-6854
westpointlighthouse1@gmail.com
westpointharmony.ca/inn_and_museum
twitter.com/WestPointPEI
www.facebook.com/westpointlighthouse/
Year Founded: 1983 The West Point Development Corporation
restored the historic West Point Lighthouse in 1987, partially
converting the lighthouse into an inn. The lighthouse itself was
built in 1875 & had a keeper until 1963. The museum houses an
extensive collection of lighthouse information, memorabilia and
artifacts that tell the story of the community, the Lightkeepers
and the history of PEI's maritime beacons. Today, the lighthouse
continues to operate as a navigational aid. The museum is open
daily from June - September.

Wood Islands: Wood Islands Lighthouse
173 Lighthouse Rd.,
Wood Islands, PE C0A 1B0

Tel: 902-962-3110
lightkeepers@woodislandslighthouse.com
www.woodislandslighthouse.com
The restored 1876 lighthouse is an interpretive museum with 10
themed rooms & historical displays.
Kris Rollins, Contact, 902-962-3498
Bev Stewart, Contact, 902-962-3110

**Canadian Centre for Architecture (CCA) / Centre
canadien d'architecture**
1920 Baile St.,
Montreal, QC H3H 2S6

Tel: 514-939-7026
info@cca.qc.ca
www.instagram.com/canadiancentreforarchitecture
twitter.com/ccawire
ww w.facebook.com/cca.conversation
Year Founded: 1979 The Canadian Centre for Architecture is a
museum & an international research centre. The Centre raises
awareness of the role of architecture, cultivates design
innovation, & promotes scholarly research.
Bruce Kuwabara, Chair, Board of Trustees
Pierre-André Themens, Vice-Chair, Board of Trustees

**McCord Museum of Canadian History / Musée
McCord**
690 Sherbrooke St. West,
Montreal, QC H3A 1E9

Tel: 514-861-6701
info.mccord@mccord-stewart.ca
www.mccord-museum.qc.ca
www.instagram.com/museemccord
twitter.com/MuseeMcCord
www.facebook.com/museemccord
Year Founded: 1921 The museum started with the collections of
David Ross McCord & a building from McGill University. It
conserves a variety of objects reflecting the social history &
material culture of Montreal, Quebec & Canada. Exhibits include
over 1,440,000 pieces that range from paintings, costumes &
decorative arts, to archives of texts & photographs.
Suzanne Sauvage, President & CEO
Martine Couillard, Senior Officer, Government & Institutional
Relations
Nathalie Lévesque, Executive Director, McCord Museum
Foundation
Pascale Grignon, Director, Marketing, Communications & Visitor
Experience
Philip Leduc, Director, Operations

Musée de l'Amerique francophone (MAF)
2 côte de la Fabrique,
Québec, QC G1R 3V6

Tél: 418-643-2158 Ligne sans frais: 866-710-8031
renseignements@mcq.org
www.mcq.org/fr/informations/maf
www.facebook.co m/MCQchapelle
Le plus ancien musée au Canada; la collection regroupe des
instruments d'enseignement des sciences, monnaies anciennes,
médailles, collections de minéralogie, de géologie, de
numismatique, de zoologie, de botanique, de fossiles, livres
anciens, & de peintures; expositions et activités; centre de
référence.
Stéphan La Roche, Directeur général

**Musée de la civilisation (MCQ) / Museum of
Civilization**
CP 155 B, 85 rue Dalhousie,
Québec, QC G1K 8R2

Tél: 418-643-2158 Ligne sans frais: 866-710-8031
renseignements@mcq.org
www.mcq.org
www.instagram.com/mcqorg
twitter.com/mcqorg
www.facebook.com/mcqorg
Fondée en: 1988 Le musée a la plus grand collection
ethnographique de l'historie du Québec & se distingue par sa
muséologie novatrice; activités éducatives & culturelles; ateliers
& visites. Musées de la civilisation comprend quatre principaux
constituants: Musée de la civilisation, Musée de l'Amérique
francophone, Musée de la place Royale, Maison historique
Chevalier & CNCEC.
Stéphan La Roche, Directeur général

Pointe-à-Callière
350 Place Royale,
Montréal, QC H2Y 3Y5

Tél: 514-872-9150
info@pacmusee.qc.ca
www.pacmusee.qc.ca
www.instagram.com/pointeacalliere
twitter.com/PointeaCalliere
www.face book.com/pointeacalliere
Fondée en: 1992 Le Musée de'archéologie & d'histoire de
Montréal est situé sur le si où en 1642, une messe célébrait la
fondation de Montréal. Pointe-à-Callière était aussi

l'emplacement d'une maison construite en 1688 par le troisième gouverneur de Montréal, Chevalier Louis Hector de Callière. Le site présente des vestiges architecturaux & le musée abrite des centaines d'objets.
Daniel Desjardins, Président
Francine Lelièvre, Directeur Exécutif

Local Museums

Alma: L'Odyssée des Bâtisseurs
1671, av du Pont nord,
Alma, QC G8B 5G2
Tél: 418-668-2606; *Téléc:* 418-668-5851
Ligne sans frais: 866-668-2606
info@odyseedesbatisseurs.com
www.odyseedesbatisseurs.com
www.facebook.com/OdysseeDesBatisseurs
Fondée en: 2004 Axé sur l'importance de l'eau au coeur du développement, le parc thématique L'Odyssée des Bâtisseurs vous invite à visiter des expositions vivantes, admirer un panorama naturel et industriel extraordinaire et vivre une expérience multimédia 360 saisissante à l'intérieur d'un ancien château d'eau.
Alexandre Garon, Directeur générale

Angliers: Site historique T.E Draper/Chantier de Gédéon
Parent: Les Promoteurs d'Angliers inc.
CP 82, 11, rue T.E Draper,
Angliers, QC J0Z 1A0
Tél: 819-949-4431; *Téléc:* 819-949-4431
tedraper@tlb.sympatico.ca
www.tedraper.ca
L'exposition du musée au T.E. Draper comprend une visite guidée du bateau; Chantier Gédéon. Ouvrir Juin-Sep
Cathy Fraser, Contact, tedraper@hotmail.com

Authier: École du Rang II d'Authier
269, rang II,
Authier, QC J0Z 1C0
Tél: 819-782-3289; *Téléc:* 819-782-2421
Ligne sans frais: 866-336-3289
info@ecoledurang2.com
www.ecoledurang2.com
www.faceb ook.com/172772349545122
Fondée en: 1983 Représente les écoles de rang qui ont meublé le paysage rural du Québec dans les années quarantes

La Baie: Musée de la Défense aérienne de Bagotville / Bagotville Air Defense Museum
CP 567 Main, 6513 ch St Anicet,
La Baie, QC G7B 3N8
Tél: 418-677-7159; *Téléc:* 418-677-4104
museebagotville@forces.gc.ca
www.museebagotville.ca/fr
www.facebook.co m/museedefenseaerienne
Fondée en: 1997 Le musée présente une collection d'uniformes & les avions qui ont été employés par l'armée de l'air canadienne. Il est ouvert chaque jour du juin au sept, du 9h à 17h.
Marie-Josée Duchesne, Curator, 418-677-4000, marie-josee.duchesne@forces.gc.ca

Batiscan: Vieux presbytère de Batiscan
340, rue Principale,
Batiscan, QC G0X 1A0
Tél: 418-362-2051; *Téléc:* 418-362-1373
communication@presbytere-batiscan.com
www.recitsquifontjaser.com
www.f acebook.com/vieuxpresbyterebatiscan
Ce presbytère a été construit en 1816, et il a remplacé le presbytère précédent, qui été construit en 1696; l'attraction offre un aperçu de la vie quotidienne du père Fréchette et de sa gouverante Adeline, les deux habitant du presbytère de l'époque; exposition temporaire à chaque année; sentier ornithologique; aire de repos et de pique-nique; boutique souvenir.

Beauharnois: Pointe-du-Buisson/Musée québécois d'archéologie
Parent: Société d'archéologie préhistorique du Québec
333, rue Émond,
Beauharnois, QC J6N 0E3
Tel: 450-429-7857; *Fax:* 450-429-5921
administration@pointedubuisson.com
twitter.com /PointeDuBuisson
www.facebook.com/pointedubuisson.museequecoisdarcheol ogie
Year Founded: 1986 Site archéologique; objets préhistoriques qui forment une collection qui est reconnu dans le monde scientifique comme l'un des plus importants dans le nord-est du

continent; recherche, l'éducation de sensibilisation; plus de deux millions d'objets et fragments d'objets et écofacts qui marquent SW Québec.
Caroline Nantel, Directrice générale, direction@pointedubuisson.com

Beaumont: Moulin de Beaumont
2, rte du Fleuve,
Beaumont, QC G0R 1C0
Tél: 418-833-1867
Moulin à farine de 1821

Beaupré: Musée de Sainte-Anne-de-Beaupré
9803, boul Sainte-Anne,
Beaupré, QC G0A 3C0
Tél: 418-827-6873
www.quoifaireaquebec.com/attraits-touristiques/musee-de-sainte -anne
Le musée retrace l'histoire d'un pèlerinage & rend hommage à la Vierge Marie; expositions permanentes & temporaires; visites guidées; jardins; magasin; Sanctuaire.

Berthierville: Chapelle des Cuthbert de Berthier
461, rue de Bienville,
Berthierville, QC J0K 1A0
Tél: 450-836-7336
www.lachapelledescuthbert.com
twitter.com/bit_berthier
Autre numéros: hors saison: 450-836-8158
Fondée en: 1958 La plus ancien templé protestant au Québec; expositions, visites commentées; pique-nique sur place; ouverte tous les journs, du juin au fête du Travil, 10h-18h

Berthierville: Musée Gilles-Villeneuve
960, av Gilles-Villeneuve,
Berthierville, QC J0K 1A0
Tél: 450-836-2714; *Téléc:* 450-836-3067
Ligne sans frais: 800-639-0103
info@museegillesvilleneuve.com
www.museegillesvilleneuve.com
www.facebook.com/MuseeGillesVilleneuveMuse um
Fondée en: 1988 Le mandat du musée est de prepétuer la mémoire de Gilles Villeneuve, le grand coureur automobile du F1; voitures, photographies, Galerie M. Trudel.
Alain Bellehumeur, Président et directeur général

Blanc-Sablon: Musée Monseigneur Scheffer
Église Notre-Dame-de-Lourdes, 1, rue Deslauriers,
Blanc-Sablon, QC G0G 1W0
Tél: 418-461-2000
www.tourismecote-nord.com/recherche
Ce musée commémore la vie du vicaire apostolique de Schefferville-Labrador, Monseigneur Scheffer.

Bonaventure: Musée acadien du Québec à Bonaventure
95, av Port Royal,
Bonaventure, QC G0C 1E0
Tél: 418-534-4000; *Téléc:* 418-534-4105
reception@museeacadien.com
www.museeacadien.com
www.twitter.com/museea cadien
www.facebook.com/museeacadienduquebec

Boucherville: Maison Louis-Hippolyte Lafontaine
314, boul Marie-Victorin,
Boucherville, QC J4B 1X1
Tél: 514-449-8347
maison.lh.lafontaine@videotron.ca
Expose des objets de la vie de Louis-Hippolyte La Fontaine et l'histoire de Boucherville.

Cascapédia-Saint-Jules: Musée de la rivière Cascapédia / The Cascapedia River Museum
275, rte 299,
Cascapédia-Saint-Jules, QC G0C 1T0
Tél: 418-392-5079; *Téléc:* 418-392-5070
cascapedia_museum@globetrotter.net
www.cascapedia.org
Le musée raconte l'histoire de la région autour de la rivière Cascapédia, la pêche au saumon, et le patrimoine gaspésien; boutique.

Causapscal: Maison Dr. Joseph-Frenette
3, rue Frenette,
Causapscal, QC G0J 1J0
Tél: 418-756-5999; *Téléc:* 418-756-3344
faucus@causapscal.quebec
www.maisondrjosephfrenette.ca
Joseph Frenette était un médecin de campagne. Il a consacré sa vie à soigner les malades et les blessés, aux femmes enceintes et aux enfants et à sauver des vies. Cette exposition

dévoile les détails de sa vie familiale et professionnelle ainsi que le rôle essentiel de ce médecin de campagne dans l'histoire de Québec.
Carole Bernier, directrice

Causapscal: Site historique Matamajaw
53 C, rue Saint-Jacques sud,
Causapscal, QC G0J 1J0
Tél: 418-756-5999; *Téléc:* 418-756-3344
matamajaw@causapscal.quebec
www.sitehistoriquematamajaw.com
twitter.co m/SMatamajaw
www.facebook.com/Matamajaw
Ancien lieu de villégiature de Sir John A. McDonald et de Lord Mount Stephen, le Matamajaw Salmon Club a attiré les membres de la haute société anglaise, américaine et canadienne durant la fin du 19e et au début du 20e siècle. Le Site Matamajaw est le seul ancien établissement privé accessible au public en Amérique du Nord.

Chambly: Lieu historique du Fort-Chambly
2, rue Richelieu,
Chambly, QC J3L 2B9
Tél: 514-658-1585; *Téléc:* 514-658-7216
Ligne sans frais: 888-773-8888
information@pc.gc.ca
www.pc.gc.ca/en/lhn-nhs/qc/fortchambly
Autre numéros: TTY: 1-866-787-6221
Présente l'histoire et les coutumes de la Nouvelle-France de 1665-1760; expositions; activités.

Chambord: Village Historique de Val-Jalbert / Historical Village of Val-Jalbert
95, rue St-Georges,
Chambord, QC G0W 1G0
Tél: 418-275-3132; *Téléc:* 418-275-5875
Ligne sans frais: 888-675-3132
valjalbert@valjalbert.com
www.valjalbert.com
www.youtube.com/user/valjalbert1901
www.facebook.com/426543094744
Partiellement restauré ville morte; créée par l'ouverture d'une usine de pâtes et papiers 1901; au fil des années par la ville a prospéré et plusieurs services et les bâtiments ont été ajoutés, notamment une gare, couvent, hôtel et un magasin général; le 13 août 1927, la plante arrêté obligeant les travailleurs à quitter Val-Jalbert; aujourd'hui, il est un patrimoine historique, industriel et religieux.
Dany Bouchard, Directeur général, dbouchard@valjalbert.com

Château-Richer: Centre d'interpretation de la Côte-de-Beaupré
CP 40, 7976, av Royale,
Château-Richer, QC G0A 1N0
Tél: 418-824-3677
info@auxtroiscouvents.org
www.histoire-cotedebeaupre.org
www.facebook.com/centredinterpretationdel acotedebeaupre
Fondée en: 1984 Rend hommage à la culture, la géographie, l'histoire et le patrimoine de la région; activités éducatives; programme d'enseignement complémentaire; ouvert tous les jours, 9h30-16h30.

Château-Richer: Musée de l'Abeille
8862, boul Sainte-Anne,
Château-Richer, QC G0A 1N0
Tél: 418-824-4411; *Téléc:* 418-824-4422
info@naturoney.com
www.naturoney.com/fr/halte-miel
Centre d'interpretation; l'exposition Des Abeilles; visites guidées; informations sur le miel; boutique.
Redmond Hayes, President

Chelsea: Mackenzie King Estate / Domaine Mackenzie-King
c/o Gatineau Park Visitor Centre, 33 Scott Rd.,
Chelsea, QC J9B 1R5
Tel: 819-827-2020 *Toll-Free:* 800-465-1867
info@ncc-ccn.ca
www.canadascapital.gc.ca/places-to-visit/mackenzie-king- estate
Other contact information: TTY: 1-866-661-3530
Located in Gatineau Park; open daily from mid-May to the end of Oct.

Chicoutimi: Centre historique des Soeurs de Notre-Dame du Bon-Conseil de Chicoutimi
700, rue Racine est,
Chicoutimi, QC G7H 1V2
Tél: 418-543-4861; *Téléc:* 418-543-7194
centrehistorique@sndbc.qc.ca
www.centrehistoriquesndbc.com

L'objectif de ce centre est de sensibiliser le patrimoine culturel, educatif & religieux de la Congrégation des Soeurs de Notre-Dame du Bon Conseil & de redonner de l'intérêt à la foundatrice du centre, Mère Françoise Simard.

Chicoutimi: La Pulperie de Chicoutimi / Musée régional
300, rue Dubuc,
Chicoutimi, QC G7J 4M1
Tél: 418-698-3100; Télec: 418-698-3158
Ligne sans frais: 877-998-3100
info@pulperie.com
www.youtube.com/user/PulperieChicoutimi
www.facebook.com/PulperiedeChicoutimi
Collection de plus de 26 000 ojets et oeuvres; Arthur-Villeneuve maison; expositions d'art et d'ethnologie; vestiges restaurés des anciennes installations de la Compagnie de pulpe de Chicoutimi; parc.
Jacques Fortin, Directeur général

Claybank: Claybank Brick Plant Historical Museum & National Historic Site
Parent: Claybank Brick Plant Historical Society
PO Box 2-5,
Claybank, S0H 0W0
Tel: 306-868-4774; Fax: 306-868-4854
claybank@sasktel.net
claybank.sasktelwebsite.net
The museum is a well-preserved brick plant dating from 1914, & has been designated a National Historic Site. Visitors can also explore the surrounding Massold Clay Canyons area, & hike on a variety of nature trails. Open May-Aug., daily 10:00-12:00 & 1:00-5:00, or by appointment.

Coaticook: Beaulne Museum / Musée Beaulne
96, rue de L'Union,
Coaticook, QC J1A 1Y9
Tél: 819-849-6560; Fax: 819-849-9519
info@museebeaulne.qc.ca
www.museebeaulne.qc.ca
Year Founded: 1964 Beaulne Museum depicts the history & achievements of the local Norton family, who were known for manufacturing railway jacks & their philanthropy. The museum is located in Château Arthur Osmore Norton, a Victorian-style mansion which was built in 1912. Beaulne Museum is open year-round from Tuesday to Sunday.
François Thierry Toé, Director

Cookshire-Eaton: Compton County Historical Museum Society / Société d'histoire du musée du comté Compton
374 Rte 253,
Cookshire-Eaton, QC J0B 1M0
Tél: 819-875-5256; Fax: 819-875-3182
mus.eatoncorner@gmail.com
www.townshipsheritage.com
Year Founded: 1959 Housed in a former Congregationalist Church built in 1842, this is a non-profit community organization. It's collections include pieces that reflect the everday lives and culture of the descendants from the Eastern Township region.

Coteau-du-Lac: Lieu historique national du Canada de Coteau-du-Lac / Coteau-du-Lac National Historic Site of Canada
308A, ch du Fleuve,
Coteau-du-Lac, QC J0P 1B0
Tél: 450-763-5631; Télec: 450-763-1654
Ligne sans frais: 888-773-8888
information@pc.gc.ca
www.pc.gc.ca/fra/lhn-nhs/qc/coteaudulac/index.aspx
Autre numéros: ATS: 1-866-787-6221
Exposition et activités: le site stratégique de Coteau-du-Lac, le Blockhaus, coin de famille, circuit nature, jardin archéologique, reconstitution militaire, marché champêtre.

Cowansville: Musée Bruck
225, rue Principale,
Cowansville, QC J2K 1J4
Tél: 450-263-6101; Télec: 450-266-7547
museebruck@ville.cowansville.qc.ca
www.ville.cowansville.qc.ca/fr
This is an arts museum & displays a permanent collection by Bruck-Lee, which consists of over 75 pieces of art. The museum also celebrates the work of local artists by hosting a number of temporary visal arts exhibitions. The building used to be the Eastern Townships Bank & was built in 1874.

Desbiens: Centre d'histoire et d'archéologie de la Métabetchouane
243, rue Hébert,
Desbiens, QC G0W 1N0
Tél: 418-346-5341
lepostedetraite@gmail.com
www.lepostedetraite.com
www.facebook.com/postedetraitemetabetchouan
Fondée en: 1995 Site historique et archéologique; il y a existé depuis environ 5,000 ans; poste de traite; salle de découverte; animation; exposition thématique; 20 juin - sept. ou par réservation

La Doré: Le Moulin des Pionniers de La Doré
4205, ch des Peupliers,
La Doré, QC G8J 1E4
Tél: 418-256-8242; Télec: 418-256-3539
Ligne sans frais: 866-272-2842
moulindespionniers@live.ca
moulindespionniers.com
Moulin à scie à pouvoir hydraulique, toujours à l'oeuvre depuis 1889; Maison de Marie, une des plus anciennes maisons de La Doré, avec un potager et une grange-étable; petite ferme avec des animaux; camp qui abrite un restaurant et un bar; auberge "La Nuit Boréale"; sentiers pédestres; tour d'observation; expositions; programmation.
Rodrigue Tremblay, Président
Guylaine Lapointe, Directrice générale,
guylainemoulin@hotmail.com

Dorval: Musée d'histoire et du patrimoine de Dorval / The Dorval Museum of Local History and Heritage
1850, ch Bord-du-Lac,
Dorval, QC H9S 2E6
Tél: 514-633-4314
musee@ville.dorval.qc.ca
www.ville.dorval.qc.ca
www.facebook.com/museedorvalmuseum
Fondée en: 2002 This museum celebrates the local history & heritage of Dorval. It is situated in the historic coach house of the Forest & Stream Club, which was built in 1874.

Drummondville: Musée populaire de la photo
400 rue, Hériot,
Drummondville, QC J2B 1B3
Tél: 819-474-5782
museedelaphoto@gmail.com
www.museedelaphoto.info
www.instagram.com/museedelaphoto
This museum pays homeage to the history of photography & celebrates the technical & aesthetic aspects of the art form.
Jocelyn Gagné, Président
Michel Doyon, Vice-Président
Jonathan-Hugues Potvin, directeur général

Drummondville: Le Village Québecois d'Antan
1425, rue Montplaisir,
Drummondville, QC J2C 0M2
Tél: 819-478-1441; Télec: 819-478-8155
Ligne sans frais: 877-710-0267
renseignements@villagequebecois.com
www.villagequebecois.com
www.twitter.com/villageqcantan
www.facebook.c om/villagequebecois
Fondée en: 1977 Village touristique historique fracno-canadien-français illustrant la période entre 1810-1910; le village est ouvrir du juin à septembre
Eric Verreault, Directeur général

Forestville: Petite Anglicane
CP 147,
Forestville, QC G0T 1E0
Tél: 418-587-2109; Télec: 418-587-6212
Archéologie locale, les gardes-feu, les remèdes d'autrefois, la vie domestique, nos pionniers, l'histoire de Forestville en photos; expositions temporaires; visites guidées

Gaspé: Manoir Le Boutillier, lieu historique national du Canada
CP 37, 578, boul Griffon,
Gaspé, QC G4X 6A4
Tél: 418-892-5150
manoir.leboutillier@lanseaugriffon.ca
manoirleboutilli er.ca
www.pinterest.com/1850manoir
www.facebook.com/manoirleboutillier1
L'exposition portraits de famille met en lumière la généalogie de John Le Boutillier. Boutique de Métiers d'arts; Salon de thé

Gaspé: Musée de la Gaspésie
80, boul de Gaspé,
Gaspé, QC G4X 1A9
Tél: 418-368-1534; Télec: 418-368-1535
info@museedelagaspesie.ca
www.museedelagaspesie.ca
www.youtube.com/user/musee1534
twitter.com/MG1534
www.facebook.com/pages/Musée-de-la-Gaspésie/11072457562
4365
Fondée en: 1962 Le musée favoriser la connaissance et l'appréciation de l'histoire et du patrimoine gaspésiens; activités de conservation et de recherche; collections y compris les disciplines de l'ethnologie, l'histoire, les beaux-arts, les sciences naturelles, l'archéologie; archives; boutique; programmation.
Nathalie Spooner, Directrice générale,
direction@museedelagaspesie.ca

Gaspé: Parc national du Canada Forillon / Forillon National Park of Canada
122, boul Gaspé,
Gaspé, QC G4X 1A9
Tél: 418-368-5505; Télec: 418-368-6837
Ligne sans frais: 888-787-6221
information@pc.gc.ca
www.pc.gc.ca/pn-np/qc/forillon.aspx
twitter.com/ForillonNP
www.facebook.com/ForillonNP
Autre numéros: ATS: 1-866-787-6221

Gaspé: Parc national du Canada Forillon
1238 boul de Forillon,
Gaspé, QC G4X 6T9
Tél: 418-368-5505; Télec: 418-368-6837
Ligne sans frais: 888-773-8888
information@pc.gc.ca
www.pc.gc.ca/pn-np/qc/forillon.aspx
twitter.com/ForillonNP
www.facebook.c om/ForillonNP
Autre numéros: ATS: 1-866-787-6221
Magasin au centre du village, de l'époque 1920, autrefois la propriété de la compagnie de pêche "William Hyman & Sons," au Parc national du Canada Forillon; animation en costumes; programmation; visites guidées.

Gatineau: Musée de l'Auberge Symmes / Symmes Inn Museum
PO Box 311, 1, rue Front,
Gatineau, QC J9H 5E6
Tél: 819-682-0291; Fax: 819-682-6594
symmesreception@gmail.com
www.symmes.ca
twitter.com/CharlesSymmes
ww w.facebook.com/museesymmesmuseum
Year Founded: 1831 Histoire régionale de Gatineau
Gilles Laroche, President & Treasurer
Roger Blanchette, Vice-President
Ron Loyer, Director

Godbout: Musée amérindien et inuit de Godbout
134, ch Pascal-Comeau,
Godbout, QC G0H 1G0
Tél: 418-568-7306

Granby: Centre d'interpretation de la Nature du Lac Boivin (CINLB)
700, rue Drummond,
Granby, QC J2H 0K6
Tél: 450-375-3861; Télec: 450-375-3736
info@cinlb.org
www.cinlb.org
www.facebook.com/cinlb.org
Fondée en: 1980 Sa mission est de conserver le terre, la faune & la flore de la région & de protéger ceux qui vivent sur la terre.
Mario Fortin, Directeur général
Yvon Lalumière, président
Michel Aubé, vice-président

Grandes-Bergeronnes: Centre D'Interpretation Archéo
498, rue de la Mer,
Grandes-Bergeronnes, QC G0T 1G0
Tél: 418-232-6286; Télec: 418-232-6695
Ligne sans frais: 866-832-6286
archeo95@bellnet.ca
www.archeotopo.com
L'histoire de la région de La Haute-Côte-Nord; exposition interactive retrace la vie des tribus amérindiennes dans la région; jeux didactiques; ateliers pour les enfants & les jeunes; excursions; spectacle multimédia; boutique.

Grandes-Bergeronnes: Centre d'interprétation et d'observation de Cap-de-Bon-Désir
13, ch du Cap de Bon Désir,
Grandes-Bergeronnes, QC G0T 1G0

Tél: 418-232-6751; *Téléc:* 418-235-4192
Ligne sans frais: 888-773-8888
information@pc.gc.ca
www.pc.gc.ca/fr/amnc-nmca/qc/saguenay/Cap-de-Bon-Desir
Autre numéros: hors saison: 418-235-4703
Promontoire naturel pour l'observation des mammifères marins; guides-interprètes; salle d'exposition, phare. Ouvert mi-juin-mi-octobre.

Guérin: Musée de Guérin
932, rue Principale Nord,
Guérin, QC J0Z 2E0

Tél: 819-784-7014
musee-guerin@tlb.sympatico.ca
www.museedeguerin.com
Le Musée de Guérin offre deux expositions permanentes: "Autour du clocher" et "Le Réveil rural" qui retracent la vie religieuse et agricole des années 1940-50. Situé à la "Terre de la Fabrique", concédée au début de la paroisse, le site du musée comprend encore un lieu du culte et la ferme de Monsieur le Curé

Harrington Harbour: Centre d'interprétation de la maison Rowsell / Rowsell House Interpretation Center
Parent: Association touristique de Harrington Harbour
CP 147, 1, place Harding,
Harrington Harbour, QC G0G 1N0

Tél: 418-795-3131
hhtourism2010@gmail.com
www.harringtonharbour.ca/culture.html
www.facebook.com/RowsellHouse
This house celebrates the culture & heritage of Harrington & the Lower North Shore. Local residents display their works in this 100 year-old house.

Havre-Aubert: Musée de la Mer
1023 chemin de la Grâve,
Havre-Aubert, QC G4T 9C8

Tél: 418-937-5711; *Téléc:* 418-937-2449
info@museedelamer-im.com
www.museedelamer-im.com
www.facebook.com/2694 77289781053
L'histoire des Îles-de-la-Madeleine, l'évolution de la navigation, l'histoire de la pêche; collections de roches, de minéraux, de coquillages; photos et objets marins. Ouvert à l'année.
Alice Pierre, Directeur Général

Inukjuak: Musée Daniel Weetaluktuk / Daniel Weetaluktuk Commemorative Museum
c/o Institut culturel Avataq,
Inukjuak, QC J0M 1M0

Tél: 819-254-8277; *Téléc:* 819-254-8148
Ligne sans frais: 866-897-2287
museum@nvinukjuak.ca
www.avataq.qc.ca
Autre numéros: Tél: 819 254-8939
Fondée en: 1992 Le centre contribue à la protection & à la diffusion de la culture des Inuits d'Inukjuak & du Nunavik; collection de plus de 400 objets anciens & contemporains présentés dans leur contexte culturel d'origine; oeuvres d'art, vêtements traditionnels, artefacts; exposition permanente; expositions temporaires.

Inverness: Musée du Bronze d'Inverness
1760, chemin Dublin,
Inverness, QC G0S 1K0

Tél: 418-453-2101; *Téléc:* 418-453-7711
info@museedubronze.com
www.museedubronze.com
www.youtube.com/user/museedubronze
www.facebook.com/museedubronze
Dédié à la recherche, au développement à la diffusion, à la production, à l'interprétation & l'éducation de l'art du bronze; fonderie; ateliers; visites guidées; jardin; programmation.

L'Islet-sur-Mer: Musée maritime du Québec
55, ch des Pionniers est,
L'Islet-sur-Mer, QC G0R 2B0

Tél: 418-247-5001
info@mmq.qc.ca
www.mmq.qc.ca
www.youtube.com/user/museemaritimequebec
www.facebook.com/MuseeMaritimeQ cCapitaineJEBernier
Fondée en: 1968 Le musée a pour mission la sauvegarde, l'étude, et la mise en valeur du patrimoine maritime se rattachant au fleuve Saint-Laurent, et de la porte des Grands Lacs; la conservation des navires historiques; expositions permanentes: "Gens du pays, gens du fleuve", "Capt.

Joseph-Elzéar Bernier", "Ilititaa...Bernier, ses hommes et les Inuits", et "Pirates ou corsaires?"; boutique; visites guidées; accessible aux personnes à mobilité réduite.
Marie-Ôve Brisson, Directrice

Jonquière: Centre d'histoire Sir-William-Price / Sir William Price History Centre
CP 2314, 1994, rue Price,
Jonquière, QC G7X 7X8

Tél: 418-695-7278; *Téléc:* 418-695-7172
info@sirwilliamprice.com
www.sirwilliamprice.com
www.facebook.com/cent redhistoiresirwilliamprice
This centre celebrates the history of the Saguenay-Lac-Saint-Jean region as well as the legacy of Sir William Price, whose historic company was directly responsible for the development & economic prosperity of the town.

Kahnawake: Musée Kateri Tekakwitha
Mission Saint-François-Xavier, PO Box 70, 1 River Rd.,
Kahnawake, QC J0L 1B0

Tel: 450-632-6030; *Fax:* 450-632-6031
saintkaterishrine@yahoo.ca
katerishrine.net
www.facebook.com/ShrineofSaintKateriTekakwitha
www.twitter.com/stkaterir cdsb
www.facebook.com/ShrineofSaintKateriTekakwitha
Religious & ethnic artifacts dating back to the 17th century; historical mission buildings (rectory 1717, church 1845) contain Blessed Kateri's tomb (1656-1680) & precious works of art including the Deerfield Bell (17th - 19th cent.); Kahnawake is a native Mohawk reservation

Kamouraska: Musée régional de Kamouraska
Place de l'église, 69, av Morel,
Kamouraska, QC G0L 1M0

Tél: 418-492-9783; *Téléc:* 418-492-9783
museekam@videotron.ca
www.museedekamouraska.com
www.twitter.com/museek amouraska
www.facebook.com/museeregionaldekamouraska
Fondée en: 1977 Le musée remplit fidèlement sa mission de protection, conservation et diffusion le riche patrimoine historique et culturel de Kamouraska.
Yvette Raymond, Directrice générale

Knowlton: Brome County Historical Museum
PO Box 690, 130 Chemin Lakeside,
Knowlton, QC J0E 1V0

Tel: 450-243-6782
bchs@endirect.qc.ca
bromemuseum.com
Year Founded: 1898 Managed by the Brome County Historical Society, the Brome County Museum presents the history of Brome County & the surrounding region. The museum's grounds feature an old fire hall from 1904, an academy building from 1854, & the Brome County Court House from 1858-1859. The court house contains the archives of the Brome County Historical Society. The museum is open from mid May to mid September. The archives are open year round.
Donald Gray-Donald, President
Peter G. White, Vice-President
Cari Ensio, Curator

Lac-Drolet: Maison du Granit
301, rte du Morne,
Lac-Drolet, QC G0Y 1C0

Tél: 819-549-2566
info@maisondugranit.ca
www.maisondugranit.ca
www.facebook.com/lamaisondugranit
A pour mission de collecter & de diffuser l'histoire de l'industrie du granit & de ses artisans & les tailleurs de pierre; exposition permanente; expositions thématiques; visites guidées; jardin panoramique.
Michel Fortin, directeur général

Lachine: Centre historique des Soeurs de Sainte-Anne
1280, boul Saint-Joseph,
Lachine, QC H8S 2M8

Tél: 514-637-4616
musee@ssacong.org
www.ssacong.org/musee
Fondée en: 1918 Musée communautaire de la Congrégation des Soeurs de Sainte-Anne. Le musée a pour mission de faire découvrir la vie des Soeurs de Sainte-Anne marquée par les lieux et les époques où elles ont évolué; ouvert toute l'année.
Murielle Gagnon, Directrice, murielle.gagnon@bellnet.ca

Lachine: Musée de Lachine
1, ch du Musée,
Lachine, QC H8S 4L9

Tél: 514-634-3478; *Téléc:* 514-637-6784
museedelachine@lachine.ca
lachine.ville.montreal.qc.ca/musee
Comprend Maison LeBer-LeMoyne et la Dépendance, les anciens bâtiments complets sur l'île de Montréal ainsi que le Benoît-Verdickt Pavillion, un centre d'exposition d'art contemporain; le Pavillon de l'Entrepôt présente des expositions pluridisciplinaires et multiculturelles; programme d'éducation disponibles pour les visiteurs d'âge scolaire ainsi que d'autres; ouvert au public d'avril à novembre
Marc Pitre, Directeur

Lasalle: Moulin Fleming, centre d'interprétation historique
9675, boul LaSalle,
Lasalle, QC H8R 4A8

Tél: 514-367-6439; *Téléc:* 514-367-6606
ville.montreal.qc.ca/lasalle
Fondée en: 1991 Ouvert mai - sept.

Laval: Centre d'interprétation de l'eau (C.I.EAU) / Water Interpretation Center
12, rue Hotte,
Laval, QC H7L 2R3

Tél: 450-963-6463
info@cieau.qc.ca
www.cieau.qc.ca
twitter.com/CIEAU_Laval
www.facebook.com/C.I.EAU
Ce centre est dédié à la sensibilisation à l'utilisation durable de l'eau & à la conservation de l'eau.
Marie-Eve Le Scelleur, directrice générale, 450-963-6464, melescelleur@cieau.qc.ca

Laval: Musée Armand-Frappier, Centre d'interprétation des biosciences
531, boul des Prairies,
Laval, QC H7V 1B7

Tél: 450-686-5641; *Téléc:* 450-686-5391
musee-afrappier@iaf.inrs.ca
www.musee-afrappier.qc.ca/fr
www.youtube.com/user/bcarmandfrappier
www.facebook.com/BiocentreArmandFrappie
Le musée offre des activités pour favoriser la compréhension d'enjeux scientifiques reliés à la santé humaine, animale & environnementale; le travail du Dr Armand Frappier, un microbiologiste est affiché.
Guylaine Archambault, Directrice Générale, 450-686-5641, Fax: 450-686-5665, guylaine.archambault@iaf.inrs.ca

Laval: Musée écologique - (C.J.N.) Vanier
3995, boul Lévesque,
Laval, QC H7E 2R3

Lavaltrie: Maison Rosalie-Cadron
1997, rue Notre-Dame,
Lavaltrie, QC J5T 1S6

Tél: 450-586-2727
info@maisonrosaliecadron.org
www.maisonrosaliecadron.org
www.facebook.com/Maison.Rosalie
Fondée en: 1790 Cette maison célèbre la vie de Rosalie Cadron-Jetté, qui était le foudateur des Soeurs de la Miséricorde. Elle était mère de onze enfants a consacré sa vie à aider les mères dans le besoin.
Michelle Picard, présidente du conseil d'administration, 450-586-1575
Sophie Lemercier, directrice, 450-586-2727

Lévis: Maison Alphonse-Desjardins
6, rue du Mont-Marie,
Lévis, QC G6V 1V9

Tél: 418-835-2090; *Téléc:* 418-835-9173
Ligne sans frais: 866-835-8444
info@maisonalphonsedesjardins.com
www.desjardins.com
www.facebook.com/MaisonAlphonseDesjardins
La maison de style néo-gothique a été construite en 1883 pour Alphonse Desjardins, fondateur des caisses populaires. C'est là que Desjardins a conçu un grand projet coopératif qui a débuté en 1901.

Lévis: Musée du College de Lévis
9, rue Mgr Gosselin,
Lévis, QC G6V 5K1

Tél: 418-837-8600
Fermé au public, ouvert sur demande

Lévis: Musée Le Régiment de la Chaudière
Manège militaire de Lévis, 10, rue de l'Arsenal,
Lévis, QC G6V 4P7
Tél: 418-835-0340*Ligne sans frais:* 877-748-3783

Longueuil: Musée Marie-Rose Durocher
80, rue St-Charles est,
Longueuil, QC J4H 1A9
Tél: 450-651-8104
centremarierose@yahoo.ca
www.snjm.org
Le Centre Marie-Rose est ouvert au public; le musée présente des expositions à caractère religieux et historique de la vie de Marie-Rose Durocher, fondatrice de la Congrégation des Soeurs des Saints Noms de Jésus et de Marie; collection de tableaux et d'artefacts.

Malartic: Musée minéralogique de l'Abitibi-Témiscamingue
650, rue de la Paix,
Malartic, QC J0Y 1Z0
Tél: 819-757-4677; *Télec:* 819-757-4140
info@museemalartic.qc.ca
www.museemalartic.qc.ca
Expositions de roches rares

La Malbaie: Musée de Charlevoix
10, ch du Hâvre,
La Malbaie, QC G5A 2Y8
Tél: 418-665-4411; *Télec:* 418-665-4560
info@museedecharlevoix.qc.ca
museedecharlevoix.qc.ca
twitter.com/Musee Charlevoix
www.facebook.com/MuseeDeCharlevoix
Fondée en: 1975 Principaux domaines d'intérêt: l'ethnohistoire et folklorique art; art textuel; arts décoratifs; beaux-arts; histoire
Raymond Lavoie, Président
Annie Breton, Directrice générale, directiongenerale@bellnet.ca

Maniwaki: Centre d'interprétation, Maniwaki
8, rue Comeau,
Maniwaki, QC J9E 2R8
Tél: 819-449-7999; *Télec:* 819-449-5102
info@ci-chateaulogue.qc.ca
www.ci-chateaulogue.qc.ca/en/index.shtml
Le Château Logue; centre d'interprétation; expositions y compris l'histoire des grands feux de forêts au Québec, la déforestation, la protection des forêts; visites gratuites et randonnées gratuites; tour d'observation.
François Ledoux, Directeur

La Martre: Corporation du Centre d'interprétation archéologique de la Gaspésie
6, rue des Fermières,
La Martre, QC G0E 2H0
Tél: 418-288-1318; *Télec:* 418-288-1318
ci_archeologie_gaspésie@hotmail.com
Interprète sur la préhistoire gaspésienne dont l'accent est mis sur la période paléoindienne récente; exposition et sentier d'interprétation

Mashteuiatsh: Musée amérindien de Mashteuiatsh / The Native Museum of Mashteuiatsh
1787, rue Amishk,
Mashteuiatsh, QC G0W 2H0
Tél: 418-275-4842; *Télec:* 418-275-7494
Ligne sans frais: 800-875-4842
reservation@cultureilnu.ca
www.cultureilnu.ca
www.facebook.com/musee.demashteuiatsh
Dédié à la protection du patrimoine & à la promotion de la communauté parmi les indigènes, la population générale; expositions permanentes & temporaires; programmes éducatifs.
Jean-Denis Gill, Directeur, direction.museeilnu@cgocable.ca

Matane: Musée du Vieux-Phare
#300, 235, av Saint-Jerome,
Matane, QC G4W 3A7
Tél: 418-562-1065; *Télec:* 418-562-1917
cldtourisme@globetrotter.net

Melbourne: Richmond County Historical Society Museum (RCHS)
1296 Rte. 243,
Melbourne, QC J0B 2B0
Tel: 819-826-1332
www.richmondcountyhistoricalsociety.com
To research & preserve historical facts in the Richmond County area; museum refurbished as a typical home of the late 1800s; archives centre
Esther Healy, Archivist, e-dhealy@sympatico.ca

Métabetchouan-Lac-à-la-Croix: Centre d'interprétation de l'agriculture et de la ruralité / Interpretation Center for Agriculture and Rurality
281, rue St-Louis,
Métabetchouan-Lac-à-la-Croix, QC G8G 2C8
Tél: 418-349-3633; *Télec:* 418-349-5013
Ligne sans frais: 877-611-3633
ciar@cgocable.ca
www.ciar-lacalacroix.qc.ca
www.facebook.com/CIAR.lacalacroix
Fondée en: 1976 Situé au coeur d'une plaine agricole, le CIAR est un site désigné pour découvrir la richesse du patrimoine agricole du Saguenay-Lac-Saint-Jean. A travers l'exposition Gens de la terre, découvrez 150 ans d'histoire, us & coutumes des ancêtres, qui ont bâti le paysage actuel. Labyrinthe dans un Champ de Maïs; ferme pédagogique; camp d'établissement (1868); programmes éducatifs.

Middle Bay: Centre d'interprétation de Middle Bay
Parent: Fondation pour le développement du tourisme de Bonne-Espérance
Middle Bay, QC G0G 1Z0
Tél: 418-461-3597
info@middlebay9000.com
www.tourismebassecotenord.com
Ce centre célèbre l'histoire et le patrimoine de Middle Bay vieux de 9,000 ans.
Melva Flynn, President

Mont Saint-Hilaire: Centre de la nature Mont Saint-Hilaire
422, ch des Moulins,
Mont Saint-Hilaire, QC J3G 4S6
Tél: 450-467-1755; *Télec:* 450-467-8015
Ligne sans frais: 866-382-2962
info@centrenature.qc.ca
www.centrenature.qc.ca
www.twitter.com/centrenaturemsh
www.facebook.com/CNMSH
Sa mission est d'assurer l'intégrité du patrimoine naturel de la région de Saint-Hilaire; fournit un lien avec la nature; une gamme d'activités éducatives et culturelles, favorise la conservation de l'environnement naturel de la région; offre un réseau de 24 km de sentiers; trottoir de bois accessible aux personnes à mobilité réduite.
Kees Vanderheyden, Directeur

Montebello: Lieu historique national du Canada du Manoir-Papineau / Manoir-Papineau National Historic Site of Canada
500, rue Notre-Dame,
Montebello, QC J0V 1L0
Tél: 819-423-6965; *Télec:* 819-423-6455
Ligne sans frais: 888-773-8888
manoir.papineau@pc.gc.ca
www.pc.gc.ca/en/lhn-nhs/qc/manoirpapineau
Autre numéros: TTY: 1-866-787-6221
La maison de la famille Papineau (1848-1850); plus de 800 objets, meubles, vêtements, oeuvres d'art, livres et documents; fresques de Napoléon Bourassa; Concerts d'Amédée; jardin.

Montmagny: Musée de l'accordéon
301, boul Taché est,
Montmagny, QC G5V 1C5
Tél: 418-248-7927; *Télec:* 418-248-1596
accordeon@montmagny.com
accordeonmontmagny.com
Fondée en: 1992 Centre de recherche et de collecte des accordéons.

Montréal: Basilique Notre-Dame de Montréal
110, rue Notre-Dame ouest,
Montréal, QC H2Y 1T2
Tél: 514-842-2925; *Télec:* 514-842-3370
info@basiliquenddm.org
www.basiliquenotredame.ca/fr
www.instagram.com/basiliquenddm
twitter.com/BasiliqueD
Fondée en: 1989 Construite entre 1824 & 1829, la basilique accueille des centaines de milliers de visiteurs chaque année; réputée pour la richesse de son intérieur decoratif: vitrail, éléments architecturaux et oeuvres d'art; visites individuelles/ en groupe; visites scolaires; services religieux; accueille des concerts; location de chambre; boutique.
Yoland Tremblay, Directeur général

Montréal: Biodôme de Montréal
4777, av Pierre-De Coubertin,
Montréal, QC H1V 1B3
Tél: 514-868-3000
www.espacepourlavie.ca/en
www.youtube.com/Espacepourlavie
twitter.com/espacepourlavie
www.facebo ok.com/Espacepourlavie
Le Biodôme recrée des Écosystèmes des Amériques: forêt tropicale, forêt laurentienne, Saint-Laurent marin, monde polaire.

Montréal: The Black Watch of Canada Museum
2067 rue Bleury,
Montréal, QC H3A 2K2
Tel: 514-496-1686; *Fax:* 514-496-2758
museum@blackwatchcanada.com
www.blackwatchcanada.com
twitter.com/bwrhc
www.facebook.com/blackwatchcanada
Uniforms, photographs & artifacts from early 1860s to present; open Tue. evenings, 7-9 pm & by appt.

Montréal: Canadian Grenadier Guards Regimental Museum
4171, av Esplanade,
Montréal, QC H2W 1S9
Tel: 514-496-1984

Montréal: Centre d'exposition de l'Université de Montréal
2940 ch Côte-Ste-Catherine,
Montréal, QC H3T 1B9
Tél: 514-343-6111; *Télec:* 514-343-2183
informations@expo.umontreal.ca
www.expo.umontreal.ca/expositions/en_cour s.htm
twitter.com/ExpoUdeM
www.facebook.com/CentreExpoUdeM
Centre d'exposition multidisciplinaire. Comprend: collection herbier Marie-Victorin; collection du département d'anthropologie; collection du Laboratoire de recherche sur les musiques du monde; oeuvres d'art; design industriel
Bruno Viens, Directeur, 514-343-6111
Sophie Banville, Adjointe administrative, 514-343-6111
Patrick Mailloux, Coordonnateur des expositions et de la collection, 514-343-6111

Montréal: Centre d'histoire de Montréal (CHM)
335, Place d'Youville,
Montréal, QC H2Y 3T1
Tél: 514-872-3207; *Télec:* 514-872-9645
chm@ville.montreal.qc.ca
ville.montreal.qc.ca
www.instagram.com/chmmtl
www.facebook.com/chmmtl
Fondée en: 1983 This city museum is located in an old firehall. Here Montreal's story is told through exhibits, models, sets, videos & 8,000 photographs from 1642 to the present day.
Jean-François Leclerc, Director
Catherine Charlebois, Muséologue

Montréal: Chapelle Notre-Dame-de-Bon-Secours/Musée Marguerite Bourgeoys
400, rue Saint-Paul est,
Montréal, QC H2Y 1H4
Tél: 514-282-8670; *Télec:* 514-282-8672
info@marguerite-bourgeoys.com
www.marguerite-bourgeoys.com
twitter.com/margbourg
www.facebook.com/margueritebourgeoys
Fondée en: 1998 Chapelle, musée d'histoire, et site archéologique; programmation diversifiée, visites guidées, boutique, location des salles.

Montréal: Cité Historia
10897, rue du Pont,
Montréal, QC H2B 2N5
Tél: 514-850-4222; *Télec:* 514-850-0607
info@citehistoria.qc.ca
pinterest.com/citehistoria
twitter.com/cite_historia
Maison du Pressoir; site des moulins

Montréal: Écomusée du fier monde
2050, rue Amherst St.,
Montréal, QC H2L 3L8
Tél: 514-528-8444; *Téléc:* 514-528-8686
info@ecomusee.qc.ca
www.ecomusee.qc.ca
twitter.com/ecomuseeefm
twitter.com/EcomuseeEFM
www.facebook.com/Ecomu seedufiermonde
Fondée en: 1980 Highlights the history of the Centre-Sud
heritage, which is a mircososm of the industrial revoltuion which
took place in Canada during the latter half of the 19th century.
René Binette, Director, direction@ecomusee.qc.ca

Montréal: The Edward Bronfman Museum
450, av Kensington,
Montréal, QC H3Y 3A2
Tel: 514-937-9474; *Fax:* 514-937-2067
admin@theshaar.org
www.shaarhashomayim.org/museum
Antique artwork & texts; congregation documents &
memorabilia; ceremonial objects; open daily; special tours by
appointment
Penni Kolb, Executive Director, pkolb@theshaar.org

Montréal: Insectarium de Montréal / Montreal
Insectarium
4581, rue Sherbrooke est,
Montréal, QC H1X 2B2
Tél: 514-868-3000
www.espacepourlavie.ca
www.instagram.com/espacepourlavie
twitter.com/espacepourlavie
ww.facebook.com/Espacepourlavie
Autre numéros: 514-872-0663
Largest insectarium in North America; 140,000 scientific
specimens collection; 20,000 exhibition collection (including
4,000 on public display); about 100 species of arthropods; live
collection.

Montréal: Lieu historique national de Sir
George-Etienne Cartier / Sir George-Étienne Cartier
National Historic Site
458, rue Notre-Dame est,
Montréal, QC H2Y 1C8
Tel: 514-283-2282; *Fax:* 514-283-5560
Toll-Free: 888-773-8888
information@pc.gc.ca
www.pc.gc.ca/lhn-nhs/qc/etienneca rtier.aspx
Other contact information: ATS: 1-866-558-2950
Year Founded: 1985 Commemorates the life and
accomplishments of Sir George-Étienne Cartier; Cartier family
homes; performances and re-enactments that vary depending
on season; Open June - December

Montréal: Le lieu historique national du Commerce de
la fourrure à Lachine / The Fur Trade at Lachine
National Historic Site
1255, boul Saint-Joseph, Lachine Borough,
Montréal, QC H8S 2M2
Tél: 514-637-7433 *Ligne sans frais:* 888-733-8888
information@pc.gc.ca
www.pc.gc.ca/lhn-nhs/qc/lachine.aspx
www.instagram.com/parks.canada
www.twitter.com/parkscanada
www.faceboo k.com/NHSinQC
Autre numéros: TTY: 1-866-787-6221; Off season phone:
514-283-2282
A bord d'un bateau, découvrez le point de départ des grands
explorateurs du continent nord-américain; programmes et
activités; exposition le commerce des fourrures; visites
thématiques.

Montréal: Maison de Mère d'Youville
138, rue Saint-Pierre,
Montréal, QC H2Y 2L7
Tél: 514-842-9411; *Téléc:* 514-842-0142
asscong@sgm.qc.ca
www.sgm.qc.ca
Fondée en: 1981 Ancien couvent des Soeurs Grises; l'hospice
et le couvent restauré en 1981; la chapelle mise en valeur en
1991; les anciens magasins-entrepôts rénovés; par rendez-vous.

Montréal: Maison Saint-Gabriel
2146, Place Dublin, Pointe-Sainte-Charles,
Montréal, QC H3K 2A2
Tél: 514-935-8136; *Téléc:* 514-935-5692
mjrcip@globetrotter.net
www.maisonsaint-gabriel.qc.ca/en/index.php
www.instagram.com/maisonsaintgabriel
www.facebook.com/MaisonStGabriel

Fondée en: 1966 La Maison est la maison d'accueil des Filles du
Roy et pendant 300 ans, la maison de ferme de la Congrégation
de Notre-Dame; un exemple de l'architecture du Régime
français; expositions qui expliquent le rôle de Marguerite
Bourgeoys et la vie à la colonie de l'Ile de Montréal pendant le
17e siècle; jardin; visites guidées.
Madeleine Juneau, Directrice générale

Montréal: The Montréal Holocaust Memorial Centre
(MHMC) / Le Centre commémoratif de l'Holocauste à
Montréal
Cummings House, 5151, ch. de la Côte-Sainte-Catherine,
Montréal, QC H3W 1M6
Tel: 514-345-2605; *Fax:* 514-344-2651
info@museeholocauste.ca
www.museeholocauste.ca/en
www.twitter.com/Muse eHolocauste
Year Founded: 1979 To collect, research & preserve historical,
cultural & ethnographic material related to Jewish communities
in Europe & North Africa which fell under Nazi rule.
Alice Herscovitch, Executive Director

Montréal: Musée de BMO Banque de Montréal / BMO
Bank of Montreal Museum
129, rue St-Jacques, #D,
Montréal, QC H2Y 1L6
Tél: 514-877-6810; *Téléc:* 514-877-7341
Le bureau de la Caisse de la plus ancienne institution bancaire
du Canada est recréé; ouvert toute année (fermé les jours non
bancaires); , visite gratuite de l'auto-guidée.
Yolaine Toussaint, Archivist, yolaine.toussaint@bmo.com

Montréal: Musée de L'Oratoire Saint-Joseph du
Mont-Royal / Museum of Saint Joseph's Oratory of
Mount-Royal
3800 Queen Mary Rd.,
Montréal, QC H3V 1H6
Tél: 514-733-8211; *Téléc:* 514-733-9735
Ligne sans frais: 877-672-8647
info@osj.qc.ca
www.saint-joseph.org/en/culture/oratory-museum
twitter.com/osjmr
www.f acebook.com/osaintjoseph
Fondée en: 1904 Le musée se consacre à l'art chrétien et à
l'histoire et le patrimoine québécoise; expositions thématiques.
L'Oratoire mise en valeur la vie et l'oeuvre de frère André; visites
commentées; boutique; bibliothèque/archives/centre de
recherche.

Montréal: Musée des Hospitalières de l'Hôtel-Dieu de
Montréal
201, av des Pins ouest,
Montréal, QC H2W 1R5
Tél: 514-849-2919; *Téléc:* 514-849-4199
museehospitalieres@bellnet.ca
www.museedeshospitalieres.qc.ca
twitter. com/mhospitalieres
www.facebook.com/museedeshospitalieres
Fondée en: 1992 Le musée présent l'histoire des Hospitalières
de Saint-Joseph & les Hospitalières de l'Hôtel-Dieu; expositions
permanentes; programmation & activités; boutique; salles de
conférence à louer; 20 000 objets; archives.

Montréal: Musée des Ondes Émile Berliner
1001, rue Lenoire,
Montréal, QC H4C 2Z6
Tél: 514-932-9663
www.moeb.ca
www.instagram.com/moeb_mtl
Fondée en: 1996 Émile Berliner a inventé le gramophone, le
disque horizontal, & la matrice pour imprimer les disques. Le
musée compte plus de 30 000 objets & est dédié à l'histoire des
vagues; les archives; activités.

Montréal: Musée des Soeurs de Miséricorde /
Misericordia Sisters Museum
12435, av de la Miséricorde,
Montréal, QC H4J 2G3
Tel: 514-332-0550
museemisericorde@yahoo.ca
www.museemisericorde.org
www.pinterest.ca/museesm
www.facebook.com/musee.misericorde
Soins de santé & services sociaux; sage-femmerie; Hôpital de la
Miséricorde de Montréal; crèche de la Miséricorde; comprendre
les problèmes des femmes entourant la santé mentale.

Montréal: Musée du Château Ramezay / Château
Ramezay Museum
280, rue Notre-Dame est,
Montréal, QC H2Y 1C5
Tél: 514-861-3708; *Téléc:* 514-861-8317
info@chateauramezay.qc.ca
www.chateauramezay.qc.ca
twitter.com/chateau ramezay
www.facebook.com/Chateau.Ramezay
Fondée en: 1895 Le musée est consacré à la conservation, et la
mise en valeur d'une collection axée sur l'histoire de Montréal et
du Québec; plus de 25 000 objets, oeuvres d'art, artefacts
ethnologiques et archéologiques, objets numismatiques;
photographies; meubles; costumes; bibliothèque; jardin;
boutique; café.
André J. Delisle, Directeur général/Conservateur

Montréal: Musée du Château-Dufresne
2929, av Jeanne-d'Arc,
Montréal, QC H1W 3W2
Tél: 514-259-9201
info@chateaudufresne.com
www.chateaudufresne.com
twitter.com/chateaudufresne
www.facebook.com/d ufresneninchen
Le Château, construit entre 1915 et 1918 pour servir de
résidence aux frères, Oscar & Marius Dufresne, met en pratique
les principes du style Beaux-Arts. Programmation culturelle;
visites guidées; expositions; salles à louer pour réceptions.

Montréal: Musée du Cinéma/Cinémathèque
québécoise
335, boul de Maisonneuve est,
Montréal, QC H2X 1K1
Tél: 514-842-9763; *Téléc:* 514-842-1816
info@cinematheque.qc.ca
www.cinematheque.qc.ca
instagram.com/cinemathequeqc
twitter.com/cinemathequeqc
www.facebook.c om/cinematheque.quebecoise
Fondée en: 1963 L'objectif de la Cinémathèque est de préserver
et documenter le patrimoine cinématographique et télévisuel
national et international.
Christian Pitchen, Chair
Dominique Dugas, Vice-Chair
Félize Frappier, Vice-Chair
Marcel Jean, Executive Director

Montréal: Musee du Corps des Magasins Militaires /
Royal Canadian Ordnance Corps Museum
CP 4000, 6560 Hochelaga St.,
Montréal, QC H3C 3R9
Tél: 514-252-2241; *Téléc:* 514-252-2273
An accredited military museum of the Department of National
Defence, the Royal Canadian Ordnance Corps Museum depicts
the historical mission of the Royal Canadian Ordnance Corps, &
other pre-unification support elements of the Canadian Army, the
RCAF, & the RCN. These service elements united in 1968 to
create the Logistics Branch of the Canadian Forces. The
collection of the RCOC Museum is housed in a 1943 building,
which originally served as Longue-Pointe Garrison's St-Barbara
Catholic & Protestant chapels.
Andrew Gregory, Curator Ph.D, agregory17@cogeco.ca

Montréal: Musée du costume et du textile du Québec
385, rue de la commune Est,
Montréal, QC H2Y 1J3
Tél: 514-419-2300; *Téléc:* 514-419-2330
info@mctq.org
mctq.org
twitter.com/MCTQ_MTL
www.facebook.com/1119280 18835551
Fondée en: 1979 Le musée se consacre à la recherche, la
conservation, l'éducation, l'éducation, et la diffusion; expositions de costume,
textiles, et de la fibre; boutique.
Jean-Claude Poitras, Président
Joanne Watkins, Directrice générale, joanne.watkins@mctq.org

Montréal: Musee du Sault-au-Récollet
Parent: Cité Historia
10865, rue du Pressoir,
Montréal, QC H2B 2L1
Tél: 514-280-6783
info@citehistoria.qc.ca
pinterest.com/citehistoria
twitter.com/cite_historia

Maison historique

Montréal: Musée Édouard-Dubeau
Cliniques dentaires, Université de Montréal, CP 6123
Centre-ville,
Montréal, QC H3C 3J7
Tél: 514-343-6750; Téléc: 514-343-2233
musee@medent.umontreal.ca
www.expo.umontreal.ca/collections/dentaire.htm
Affiche des formes primitives d'outils de dentisterie moderne.

Montréal: Musée régimentaire les Fusiliers Mont-Royal
3721, av Henri-Julien,
Montréal, QC H2X 3H4
Tél: 514-283-7444; Téléc: 514-496-5086
museo@lesfusiliersmont-royal.com
lesfusiliersmont-royal.com
twitter.co m/museefmr
www.facebook.com/museeregimentaire.fusiliersmontroyal
Fondée en: 1977

Montréal: Le Musée Stewart au Fort de l'Ile
Sainte-Hélène / The Stewart Museum at the Fort Ile
Sainte-Hélène
British Military Depot, St. Helen's Island, Parc
Jean-Drapeau, 20 ch. du Tour de l'Isle,
Montréal, QC H3C 0K7
Tél: 514-861-6701; Téléc: 514-284-2211
info.stewart@mccord-stewart.ca
www.stewart-museum.org/en
www.youtube.com/user/museestewart
twitter.com/museestewart
www.faceboo k.com/MuseeStewartMuseum
Fondée en: 1955 Ceci est un fort historique, et il a été construit
pour défendre le Canada de invasion américaine dans les
années 1820.
Suzanne Sauvage, President & CEO, 514-861-6701
Sylvie Dauphin, Curator, 514-861-6701

Montréal: Museum of Jewish Montreal / Musée du
Montréal juif
4040 St. Laurent Blvd #R01,
Montréal, QC H2W 1Y8
Tel: 514-840-9300Toll-Free: 888-405-8645
info@mimj.ca
imjm.ca
instagram.com/museemtljuif
twitter.com/musee_mtl_juif
www.facebook.com /museedumontrealjuif
Year Founded: 2010 History of the Montreal Jewish community.
Open Tue-Wed, Fri-Sat 10:00-5:00, Thu 10:00-6:00
Zev Moses, Executive Director, zev@imjm.ca

Montréal: Phonothèque québécoise, Musée du son
335, boul de Maisonneuve est,
Montréal, QC H2X 1K1
Tél: 514-282-0703; Téléc: 514-282-0019
phono@bellnet.ca
www.phonotheque.org
Histoire des archives sonores, de l'industrie du disque, etc.
History of sound archives, sound recording & radio industry.

Montréal: Redpath Museum
McGill University, 859 Sherbrooke St. West,
Montréal, QC H3A 2K6
Tel: 514-398-4086; Fax: 514-398-3185
redpath.museum@mcgill.ca
www.mcgill.ca/redpath
pinterest.com/redpathmuseum
twitter.com/RedpathMuseum
www.facebook.com /308943939115940
Year Founded: 1882 Extensive collections in paleontonlogy,
mineralogy, zoology & ethnology; family workshop series
"Discovery Workshop"
Dr. David M. Green, Director/Curator B.Sc., M.Sc., Ph.D.,
Vertebrates, david.m.green@mcgill.ca
Virginie Millien, Asst. Prof./Chief Curator Ph.D., D.E.A.,
Paleontology & Zoology, virginie.millien@mcgill.ca

Mont-Saint-Grégoire: Centre d'interprétation du milieu
écologique du Haut-Richelieu
16, ch du Sous Bois,
Mont-Saint-Grégoire, QC J0J 1K0
Tél: 450-346-0406
services@cimehautrichelieu.qc.ca
www.cimehautrichelieu.qc.ca
A pour mission la conservation du Mont-Saint-Grégoire, &
d'autres sites naturels dans la région du Haut-Richelieu
Renée Gagnon, Directice générale,
r.gagnon@cimehautrichelieu.qc.ca

Mont-Saint-Hilaire: Maison amérindienne
510, Montée des Trente,
Mont-Saint-Hilaire, QC J3H 2R8
Tél: 450-464-2500; Téléc: 450-464-0071
info@maisonamerindienne.com
www.facebook.co m/lamaison.amerindienne
Un lieu célébration culturelle & d'échanges culturel à travers une
gamme d'activités, d'expositions, d'histoires, de légends & de
conférences; expositions, environnementales & gastronomiques;
érablière.

New Richmond: Gaspesian British Heritage Village
351 Blvd. Perron,
New Richmond, QC G0C 2B0
Tel: 418-392-7000
aleblanc@villenewrichmond.com
www.villenewrichmond.com
British heritage in Gaspé from 1760 to 1900s.
Stephane Cyr, Director General, Ville de New Richmond,
418-392-7000, scyr@villenewrichmond.com
Ann-Julie LeBlanc, Recreation & Tourism Director, Ville de New
Richmond, aleblanc@villenewrichmond.com

Nicolet: Musée des religions du monde
900, boul Louis-Fréchette,
Nicolet, QC J3T 1V5
Tél: 819-293-6148; Téléc: 819-293-4161
musee@museedesreligions.qc.ca
www.museedesreligions.qc.ca/home
twitter .com/museereligions
www.facebook.com/museedesreligionsdumonde
Fondée en: 1986 Le musée se dedie à l'histoire des rites
religieux du bouddhisme, de l'hindouisme, de l'islam, du
judaïsme & du christianisme; boutique; programmation et
activités; les installations muséales sont adaptées aux
personnes à mobilité réduite.
Jean-François Royal, Directeur, 819-293-6148, jfroyal@mdrm.ca

Notre-Dame-de-l'Ile-Perrot: Parc historique
Pointe-du-Moulin
2500, boul Don-Quichotte,
Notre-Dame-de-l'Ile-Perrot, QC J7V 7P2
Tél: 514-453-5936; Téléc: 514-453-8744
info@pointedumoulin.com
www.pointedumoulin.com
Fondée en: 1979
Ani Kataroyan, Directrice générale

Notre-Dame-du-Nord: Centre thématique fossilifère du
lac Témiscamingue / Lake Timiskaming Fossil Centre
5, rue Principale,
Notre-Dame-du-Nord, QC J0Z 3B0
Tél: 819-723-2500; Téléc: 819-723-2369
musee@fossiles.qc.ca
www.fossiles.qc.ca
www.facebook.com/Fossilarium
Fondée en: 1997 A pour mission de mettre en valeur la période
Orodovicien-Silurien dans la région; recherche; expositions;
boutique.

Nouvelle: Musée d'histoire naturelle du parc de
Miguasha
231, rte Miguasha ouest,
Nouvelle, QC G0C 2E0
Tél: 418-794-2475; Téléc: 418-794-2033
parc.miguasha@sepaq.com
maritime.musees.qc.ca/en/museums/miguasha/index. php
www.facebook.com/parcnationaldemiguasha
Protège et affiche le site de fossiles à la Gaspésie

Odanak: Musée des Abénakis
Société historique d'Odanak, 108, Waban-Aki,
Odanak, QC J0G 1H0
Tél: 450-568-2600; Téléc: 450-568-5959
info@museedesabenakis.ca
www.museedesabenakis.ca
twitter.com/MuseeAben akis
www.facebook.com/musee.desabenakis
Fondée en: 1962 Ouvert en 1962 & entièrement rénové en
2005; le premier musée amérindien au Québec. Au coeur d'un
site historique; Spectacle multimédias, expositions, belvédères;
église catholique; chapelle; aire de pique-nique.

Oujé-Bougoumou: Aanischaaukamikw Cree Cultural
Institute
PO Box 1168, 205 Opemiska Meskino,
Oujé-Bougoumou, QC G0W 3C0
Tel: 418-745-2444; Fax: 418-745-2324
info@creeculture.ca
www.creeculturalinstitute.ca
twitter.com/CreeCultu re
www.facebook.com/210316972365081
Year Founded: 2010 The centre serves as museum, archive,
library & teaching centre. The museum collection includes
traditional Cree artifacts.
Sarah Pashagumskum, Executive Director,
sarah.pash@creeculture.ca

Pabos Mills: Centre d'interprétation du Parc du Bourg
de Pabos
75, rue de la Plage,
Pabos Mills, QC G0C 2J0
Tél: 418-689-6043; Téléc: 418-689-4240
bourg@globetrotter.net
www.lebourgdepabos.com
Promouvoir l'histoire de la seule seigneurie de la
Nouvelle-France à exploiter commercialement la pêche; ouvert
tous le jours, juin-septembre.

Paspébiac: Site historique du
Banc-de-Pêche-de-Paspébiac
CP 430, 76, rue du Banc,
Paspébiac, QC G0C 2K0
Tél: 418-752-6229; Téléc: 418-752-6408
shbp@globetrotter.net
www.shbp.ca
twitter.com/shbppaspebiac
www.face book.com/sitedepaspebiac
Sea heritage & traditional trades; tours; gift shop; restaurant;
open June - Oct.
Thomas Martens, Directeur général, shbp@globetrotter.net

Percé: Centre d'interprétation, Bonaventure
CP 310, 4, rue du Quai,
Percé, QC G0C 2L0
Tél: 418-782-2240; Téléc: 418-782-2241
parc.ibrperce@sepaq.com
www.sepaq.com/pq/bon
www.instagram.com/parc_ibrperce
www.facebook.com/PNIBRP
L'objectif est de protéger un refuge d'oiseaux migrateurs, et le
patrimoine historique de la région.
Rémi Plourde, directeur général

Percé: Musée Le Chafaud
145, rte 132,
Percé, QC G0C 2L0
Tél: 418-782-5100; Téléc: 418-782-5565
www.musee-chafaud.com
Expose l'art qui a été inspiré par Percé, la pointe de la péninsule
gaspésienne.

Péribonka: Musée Louis-Hémon
700, rte Maria-Chapdelaine,
Péribonka, QC G0W 2G0
Tél: 418-374-2177; Téléc: 418-374-2516
museelh@destination.ca
www.museelh.ca
Expositions qui illustrent l'histoire de la MRC de
Maria-Chapdelaine.

Plaisance: Centre d'interprétation du patrimoine de
Plaisance
Parent: Corporation North Nation Mills Inc.
276, rue Desjardins,
Plaisance, QC J0V 1S0
Tél: 819-427-6400
info@cipplaisance.qc.ca
www.chutesplaisance.ca
www.facebook.com/patrimoineplaisance
Claire Leblanc, président
Daniel Cloutier, vice-président
Pierre Bernier, directeur général

La Pocatière: Musée François-Pilote
100, 4e av,
La Pocatière, QC G0R 1Z0
Tél: 418-856-3145; Téléc: 418-856-5611
info@mqaa.ca
www.facebook.com/musee.qaa
Paroissé rurale du passe; chambres reconstruites de maisons;
bureaux de professionnels & d'artisans, une collection de
sciences naturelles, agriculture & sciences pures, éducation

agricole; des expositions; programmes scolaires; rampe d'acces & ascenseur disponible.
Luc St-Amand, Directeur général

Pointe-à-la-Croix: Battle of the Restigouche National Historic Site of Canada
PO Box 359, 40 boul Perron,
Pointe-à-la-Croix, QC G0C 1L0
Tel: 418-788-5676; *Fax:* 418-788-5895
information@pc.gc.ca
www.pc.gc.ca/en/lhn-nhs/qc/ristigouche
Other contact information: TTY: 1-866-787-6221
Located at the mouth of the Restigouche River, the Battle of the Restigouche National Historic Site is the scene of the last naval battle between France & England for possession of North America in 1760. Visitors to the site can see the vestiges of the vessel, The Machault, as well as several artifacts from the wreck. The national historic site is open daily from June to mid-October.

Pointe-Claire: Canadian Ski Museum & Canadian Ski Hall of Fame (CSMus) / Musée canadien du ski et Temple de la renommée du ski canadien
317, ch du Bord-du-Lac,
Pointe-Claire, QC H9S 4L6
Tel: 514-429-8444
info@skimuseum.ca
www.linkedin.com/groups/Canadian-Ski-Hall-Fame-Museum-417 4287
www.facebo ok.com/59397511258
The Canadian Ski Museum & Canadian Ski Hall of Fame preserves Canadian skiing history & celebrates Canadian skiing & snowboarding traditions & achievements. The Hall of Fame honours Canada's accomplished skiers, snowboarders, coaches, officials, & builders of the sport.
Stephen Finestone, Chair

La Prairie: Société d'histoire de la Prairie de la Magdeleine (SHLM)
249, rue Sainte-Marie,
La Prairie, QC J5R 1G1
Tél: 450-659-1393
info@shlm.info
shlm.info
Fondée en: 1972 La société historique actif dans les domaines de la généalogie, de la recherche historique et visites guidées.
Stéphane Tremblay, Président
Johanne Doyle, Coordinatrice

Québec: La Citadelle de Québec & Le Musée du Royal 22e Régiment
La Citadelle, 1 Côte de la Citadelle,
Québec, QC G1R 3R2
Tél: 418-694-2815; *Téléc:* 418-694-2853
information@lacitadelle.qc.ca
www.lacitadelle.qc.ca
www.youtube.com/user/museeroyal
www.facebook.com/CitadelleQuebec
Fondée en: 1980 Située sur le Cap Diamant, La Citadelle est un site du patrimoine mondial de l'UNESCO, et la résidence officielle du Royal 22e Régiment. Le musée offre des visites guidées, activités, et collections d'artefacts militaires (médailles, insignes, uniformes et textiles, armes).
Dany Hamel, Directeur, d.hamel@lacitadelle.qc.ca

Québec: Commission des Champs-de-Bataille nationaux / National Battlefields Commission
390, av de Bernières,
Québec, QC G1R 2L7
Tél: 418-648-3506; *Téléc:* 418-648-3638
information@ccbn-nbc.gc.ca
www.ccbn-nbc.gc.ca
Les Plaines d'Abraham; Parc des Braves; Maison de la découverte des plaines d'Abraham; Exposition multimédia Odyssée Canada; Tours Martello; Souper mystère de 1814 à la tour Martello 2; Bus d'Abraham: tour guidé des plaines d'Abraham, Maison patrimoniale Louis S.-St-Laurent, Kiosque Edwin-Bélanger, Jardin Jeanne d'Arc

Québec: Lieu historique national du Canada Cartier-Brébeuf / Cartier-Brébeuf National Historic Site of Canada
CP 10 B, 175, rue de l'Espinay,
Québec, QC G1K 7A1
Tél: 418-648-7016; *Téléc:* 418-648-7931
Ligne sans frais: 888-773-8888
information@pc.gc.ca
www.pc.gc.ca/en/lhn-nhs/qc/cartierbrebeuf
www.instagram.com/parks.canada
twitter.com/ParksCanada
www.facebook.co m/qcparkscanada
Autre numéros: TTY: 418-648-7931
Commémore la rencontre de Jacques Cartier et des Iroquoïs de Saint-Laurent.

Québec: Lieu historique national du Canada de la Grosse-Ile-et-le-Mémorial-des-Irlandais / Grosse-Ile & the Irish Memorial National Historic Site of Canada
Grosse-Ile, Saint-Antoide-l'Isle-aux-Grues,
Québec, QC G0R 1P0
Tél: 418-234-8841 *Ligne sans frais:* 888-773-8888
information@pc.gc.ca
www.pc.gc.ca/en/lhn-nhs/qc/grosseile
www.youtube.com/parcscanada
twitter.com/parcscanada
www.facebook.com/ParcsCanada
Autre numéros: ATS: 1-866-787-6221
Commémore l'importance de l'immigration au Canada, plus particulièrement via la porte d'entrée de Québec, & les événements tragiques vécus par les immigrants irlandais en ce lieu, notamment l'épidémie de typhus de 1847.

Québec: Lieu historique national du Canada des Fortifications-de-Québec / Fortifications of Québec National Historic Site of Canada
2, rue d'Auteuil,
Québec, QC G1R 5C2
Tél: 418-648-7016; *Téléc:* 418-648-7931
Ligne sans frais: 888-773-8888
information@pc.gc.ca
www.pc.gc.ca/en/lhn-nhs/qc/fortifications
www.instagram.com/parks.canada
twitter.com/ParksCanada
www.facebook.co m/qcfortifications
Autre numéros: TTY: 1-866-787-6221
Trésor de l'UNESCO; la Citadelle et ses environs, terrasse Dufferin, Château Frontenac; visites guidées.

Québec: Lieu historique national du Canada des Forts-de-Lévis
41, ch du Gouvernement,
Québec, QC G1K 7R3
Tél: 418-835-5182; *Téléc:* 418-948-9119
Ligne sans frais: 888-773-8888
information@pc.gc.ca
www.pc.gc.ca/fra/lhn-nhs/qc/levis/index.aspx
Autre numéros: ATS: 1-866-787-6221

Québec: Maison Hamel-Bruneau
CP 700, 2608, ch Saint-Louis,
Québec, QC G1R 4S9
Tél: 418-641-6280
patrimoineste foysillery@ville.quebec.qc.ca
www.maisonsdupatrimoine.com
www.facebook.com/MaisonsDuPatrimoine
Construit vers 1857; maison historique; a un centre de diffusion; programmation thématique variée; concerts; activités; jardins, aire de pique-nique.

Québec: Maison Henry-Stuart
82, Grande Allée ouest,
Québec, QC G1R 2G6
Tél: 418-647-4347
info@maisonhenrystuart.qc.ca
www.maisonhenrystuart.qc.ca
Construite en 1849, la maison représente un exemple d'un type d'habitation courant aux 19e siècle à Québec; collection d'objets, meubles; visites thématiques; jardin.
Pierre B. Landry, Directeur général

Québec: Moulin des Jésuites / Jesuit mill
7960, boul Henri-Bourassa,
Québec, QC G1H 3G3
Tél: 418-624-7720; *Téléc:* 418-624-7519
direction@moulindesjesuites.org
www.moulindesjesuites.org
Fondée en: 1742 Ce moulin est l'un des rares moulins à eau de la ville de Québec. Il a été construit par les jésuites en 1742 & fonctionne maintenant comme un centre d'interprétation. La

fabrication du pain & d'autres activités familiales sont offertes sur le site.
Joanne Timmons, Directrice générale

Québec: Musée Bon-Pasteur
14, rue Couillard,
Québec, QC G1R 3S9
Tél: 418-694-0243; *Téléc:* 418-694-6233
info@museebonpasteur.com
www.museebonpasteur.com
Fondée en: 1992 L'histoire de la Congrégation des Servantes du Coeur Immaculé de Marie (Soeurs du Bon-Pasteur de Québec); condition féminine au XIXe siècle; meubles et peintures d'époque; visites personnalisées en français et en anglais (portugais sur demande)
Claudette Ledet, Directrice

Québec: Musée de géologie
Pavillon Adrien-Pouliot, Université Laval, 1065, av de la Médecine,
Québec, QC G1V 0A6
Tél: 418-656-2131; *Téléc:* 418-656-7339
www.musee-geologie.ulaval.ca
Possède la plus ancienne collection géologique du Québec.
Olivier Rabeau, Conservateur, olivier.rabeau@ggl.ulaval.ca

Québec: Musée de la place Royale
Parent: Musée de la civilisation
27, rue Notre-Dame,
Québec, QC G1K 4E9
Tél: 418-646-3167 *Ligne sans frais:* 866-710-8031
mcqweb@mcq.org
www.mcq.org/fr/cipr
Fondée en: 1999 Site historique; le Centre est situé au premier établissement français permanent en Amérique; expositions, visites commentées, animations historiques, espace découverte, activités éducatives, ateliers.

Québec: Musée de la santé mentale Lucienne-Maheux / Lucienne-Maheux Mental Health Museum
2601, ch de la Canardière,
Québec, QC G1J 2G3
Tél: 418-663-5000; *Téléc:* 1974
musee@institutsmq.qc.ca
www.cityseeker.com/quebec-city/841787-musée-luci enne-maheux
Documents d'archives; photographies anciennes; meubles & objets d'époque; équipements médicaux; oeuvres d'art

Québec: Musée des Augustines de l'Hôtel-Dieu de Québec
32, rue Charlevoix,
Québec, QC G1R 5C4
Tél: 418-692-2492; *Téléc:* 418-692-2668
www.augustines.org
Fondée en: 1958 Tableaux canadiens et européens, meubles, vaisselle, broderies, instruments médicaux. Le musée est en réaménagement et est fermée jusqu'en 2011.

Québec: Musée des Ursulines de Québec
12, rue Donnacona,
Québec, QC G1R 3Y7
Tél: 418-694-0694; *Téléc:* 418-694-0136
info@poleculturedesursulines.ca
www.poleculturedesursulines.ca
Le musée met en valeur la collection pédagogique des Ursulines du Québec; documents; instruments de musique; objets scientifiques; spécimens; photographies; broderies; tableaux.

Québec: Musée les Voltigeurs de Québec
835, boul Pierre-Bertrand,
Québec, QC G1M 2E7
Tel: 418-648-4422; *Fax:* 418-648-3040
info@voltigeursdequebec.net
voltigeursdequebec.net/musee.html
www.youtube.com/voltigeursdequebec
twitter.com/voltigeurs
Year Founded: 1964 Expose des objets militaires et des véhicules.
Raymond Falardeau, Conservateur du musée
L'adjudant-chef (r) Éric Godbout, Directeur des projets

Québec: Musée Naval de Québec / Naval Museum of Québec
170, rue Dalhousie,
Québec, QC G1K 8M7
Tél: 418-694-5387; *Téléc:* 418-694-5550
info@museenavaldequebec.com
museenavaldequebec.com
www.youtube.com/user/MuseeNavaldeQuebec
twitter.com/museenaval
www.facebook.com/mnq.nmq

Fondée en: 1995 Le musée a pour mission de préserver l'histoire navale du Saint-Laurent & de la Réserve navale du Canada.
André Kirouac, Directeur chez

Québec: Site patrimonial du Parc-de-L'Artillerie
2, rue d'Auteuil,
Québec, QC G1R 5C2

Tél: 418-648-7016; *Téléc:* 418-648-7931
Ligne sans frais: 888-773-8888
information@pc.gc.ca
www.pc.gc.ca/en/lhn-nhs/qc/fortifications
Autre numéros: TTY: 1-866-787-6221
Ce site commémore le passé militaire du Québec. Cela nous rappelle w Lorsque les régimes française et britannique on aidé à défendre la colonie.

Québec: Villa Bagatelle
1563, ch St-Louis,
Québec, QC G1S 1G1

Tél: 418-654-0259; *Téléc:* 418-654-0991
www.quebecregion.com

Centre d'exposition et de jardin.

Richmond: Centre d'interprétation de l'ardoise
5, rue Belmont,
Richmond, QC J0B 2B0

Tél: 819-826-3313
info@centreardoise.ca
www.centreardoise.ca
www.facebook.com/centreardoise
Fondée en: 1992 Sa mission est de promouvoir le patrimoine de la vallée de Saint-Françcois; le centre est abrité dans une église presbytérienne construite en 1889, ayant un toit en ardoise.

Rimouski: Musée régional de Rimouski
35, rue Saint-Germain ouest,
Rimouski, QC G5L 4B4

Tél: 418-724-2272; *Téléc:* 418-725-4433
info@museerimouski.qc.ca
www.museerimouski.qc.ca
www.instagram.com/museeregionalderimouski
twitter.com/museederimouski
www.facebook.com/museerimouski
Autre numéros: Alt. E-mail: mrdr@globetrotter.net
Le musée, abrité dans la plus ancienne église en pierre de la région, présente des collections thématiques sur l'art contemporain, histoire et science; artefacts; guides d'interprétation; activités.
Francine Périnet, Directeur général,
direction@museerimouski.qc.ca

Rimouski: Site historique de la Maison Lamontagne
707, boul du Rivage,
Rimouski, QC G5L 7L3

Tél: 418-722-4038
maisonlamontagne@globetrotter.net
www.maisonlamontagne.com/accueil.asp
www.instagram.com/maisonlamontagne
www.facebook.com/sitehistoriquemaison lamontagne
La maison Lamontagne de Rimouski est une monument historique de Quebec. Il représente un type d'architecture qui était commun en Nouvelle-France au milieu des années 1800.

Rimouski: Site historique maritime de la Pointe-au-Père
1000 rue du Phare,
Rimouski, QC G5M 1L8

Tél: 418-724-6214; *Téléc:* 418-721-0815
info@shmp.qc.ca
www.shmp.qc.ca
www.instagram.com/shmp.qc.ca
twitter.com/SHMP_officiel
www.facebook.co m/SitehistoriquePointeauPere
Fondée en: 1980 Le musée regroupe les artefacts du navire l'Empress of Ireland, et met en valeur le Phare-de-Pointe-au-Père et le sous-marin ONONDAGA, désarmé par la Défense nationale en 2000.

Rivière Saint-Paul: Musée Whiteley Museum
302 Boul. Bonne Esperance,
Rivière Saint-Paul, QC G0G 2P0

Tél: 418-379-2211
info@whiteleymuseum.com
www.whiteleymuseum.com
www.facebook.com/whiteleymuseum
This museum explores the maritime heritage & culture of the Bonne Espérance Island. It also pays tribute to William Henry Whiteley, who invented the cod-trap & in so doing, radically changed the cod fishing industry in Atlantic Canada.

Rivière-du-Loup: Musée du Bas-St-Laurent
300, rue St-Pierre,
Rivière-du-Loup, QC G5R 3V3

Tél: 418-862-7547; *Téléc:* 418-862-3019
musee@mbsl.qc.ca
www.mbsl.qc.ca
Fondée en: 1975 Consacré à la photographie ethnologique, art moderne, & à l'éducation; conservation, recherche & diffusion; plus de 2,000 objets ethnologiques & plus de 300 objets d'art; plus de 125,000 photographies anciennes; expositions itinérantes; publications; boutique; location de salle.
Mélanie Girard, Directeur général

Rivière-Éternite: Centre de découverte et de services Le Béluga / Beluga Discovery and Visitors Center
Parc National du Saguenay, 91, rue Notre-Dame,
Rivière-Éternite, QC G0V 1P0

Tél: 418-272-1556; *Téléc:* 418-272-3438
Ligne sans frais: 800-665-6527
parc.saguenay@sepaq.com
www.sepaq.com/pq/sag/fr/interpretation.html
Exposition permanente "Baie des bélugas"; l'histoire & l'importance de protéger le béluga dans son milieu naturel; activités de découverte.

Rivière-Éternite: Centre de découverte et de services le Fjord du Saguenay
Parc National du Saguenay, 91, rue Notre-Dame,
Rivière-Éternite, QC G0P 1P0

Tél: 418-272-1556; *Téléc:* 418-272-3438
parc.saguenay@sepaq.com
www.sepaq.com/pq/sag
Découvrez les secrets du fjord region; exposition permanente

Rouyn-Noranda: La Maison Dumulon
CP 242, 191, av du Lac,
Rouyn-Noranda, QC J9X 5C3

Tél: 819-797-7125; *Téléc:* 819-797-7109
maison.dumulon@rouyn-noranda.ca
www.facebook.com/maisondumulon
Fondée en: 1980 La maison de la famille Dumulon est une reconstitution fidèle du bâtiment d'origine; visites guidées; animation; activités spéciales; location de salle; boutique. L'église orthodoxe russe Saint-Georges est administrée par la Corporation de La maison Dumulon.

Saguenay: Musée du Fjord
3346, boul de la Grande-Baie sud,
Saguenay, QC G7G 1G2

Tél: 418-697-5077; *Téléc:* 418-697-5079
Ligne sans frais: 866-697-5077
info@museedufjord.com
www.museedufjord.com
www.youtube.com/user/museedufjord
twitter.com/Musee_du_Fjord
www.faceb ook.com/118098813663
Fondée en: 1983 Voué à la préservation & à la mise en valeur du patrimoine historique, naturel et artistique du territoire du Saguenay; expositions permanentes; expositions temporaires thématiques; la programmation; artefacts historiques; photographies; documents.
Guylaine Simard, Directrice générale

Saint-André-Avellin: Musée des Pionniers de Saint-André-Avellin
20, rue Bourgeois,
Saint-André-Avellin, QC J0V 1W0

Tél: 819-983-2624
www.museedespionniers.qc.ca
Relate la vie rurale des 19e & 20e siècles; meubles, objets, outils & machines en expositions; livres du XIXe siècle; photographies.
Raymond Whissell, Président
Ginette Labrosse-Lafleur, Secrétaire-archiviste

Saint-André-d'Argenteuil: Musée régional d'Argenteuil / Caserne-de-Carillon - Lieu historique national du Canada (MRA)
44, rte du Long-Sault,
Saint-André-d'Argenteuil, QC J0V 1X0

Tél: 450-537-3861; *Téléc:* 450-537-1983
info@museearg.com
www.museeregionaldargenteuil.ca
twitter.com/mrargent euil
www.facebook.com/184512031562388
Fondée en: 1938 Expositions historiques: 8 salles d'exposition; Le musée est installé dans l'ancienne Caserne-de-Carillon.
Luc Grondin, Président
Lyne St-Jacques, Directrice

Saint-Constant: Exporail: Musée ferroviaire canadien / Exporail: Canadian Railway Museum
Parent: Association canadienne d'histoire ferroviaire
110, rue St-Pierre,
Saint-Constant, QC J5A 1G7

Tél: 450-632-2410; *Téléc:* 450-638-1563
info@exporail.org
www.exporail.org
www.youtube.com/user/Exporail110
twitter.com/Exporail
www.facebook.com /Exporail
Fondée en: 1961 La plus grande collection au Canada de matériel ferroviaire (150 véhicules, un plateau tournant, 2 gares, un nouveau pavillon d'exposition).
Nadine Cloutier, Directrice, Opérations et gestion des bénévoles, nadine.cloutier@exporail.org

Saint-Denis-de-la-Bouteillerie: Maison Chapais
2, rte 132 est,
Saint-Denis-de-la-Bouteillerie, QC G0L 2R0

Tél: 418-498-2353; *Téléc:* 418-498-4070
infos@maisonchapais.com
www.maisonchapais.com
twitter.com/MaisonChapai s
www.facebook.com/213524838684198
Fondée en: 1990 Monument historique daté de 1834; trois étages et diverses dépendances; réservations préférables pour les groupes; visites guidées de la maison et ses jardins oubliés; galerie-boutique offre cadeaux et souvenirs, livres.

Sainte-Famille: Maison de nos Aïeux
Parent: La Fondation François-Lamy
2485, ch Royal,
Sainte-Famille, QC G0A 3P0

Tél: 418-829-0330
info@fondationfrancoislamy.com
www.maisondrouin.com/fr/maison-de-nos-aieux
www.facebook.com/Maisondenos Aieux
La Fondation François-Lamy se consacre à la préservation du patrimoine de l'île d'Orléans & de Sainte-Famille.

Sainte-Famille: Maison Drouin
Parent: La Fondation François-Lamy
2958, ch Royal,
Sainte-Famille, QC G0A 3P0

Tél: 418-829-0330
info@fondationfrancoislamy.com
www.maisondrouin.com/fr/maison-drouin
www.facebook.com/MaisonDrouin
La Fondation François-Lamy se consacre à la préservation du patrimoine de l'île d'Orléans & de Sainte-Famille.

Sainte-Marie: Maison J.A. Vachon
383, rue de la Coopérative,
Sainte-Marie, QC G6E 3X5

Tél: 418-387-4052; *Téléc:* 418-387-2652
Ligne sans frais: 866-387-4052
maisonjavachon@globetrotter.net
www.vachon.com/en/history/maison

Saint-Eustache: Maison de la Culture et du Patrimoine
235, rue Saint-Eustache,
Saint-Eustache, QC J7R 2L8

Tél: 450-974-5170; *Téléc:* 450-974-2632
Fondée en: 2005 Expose des objets qui mettent en valeur l'histoire de la ville

Saint-Eustache: Moulin Légaré / Légaré Mill
232, rue St-Eustache,
Saint-Eustache, QC J7R 2L7

Tél: 450-974-5400; *Téléc:* 450-974-2632
www.corporationdumoulinlegare.com
Fondée en: 1975 Ce moulin à farine construit en 1762 n'a jamais cessé de travailler une fois depuis son achèvement. Le meunier y produit du blé et de farine de sarrasin avec les meules d'origine et la farine est vendue sur place. Les activités sont disponibles pour les étudiants.
Mélanie Séguin, Directrice, 450-974-5001,
mseguin@corporationdumoulinlegare.com

Saint-Hyacinthe: Musée du Centre Élisabeth-Bergeron
2545 rue Dessaulles,
Saint-Hyacinthe, QC J2S 0K2

Tél: 450-780-1800
ceb@sjsh.org
www.sjsh.org
www.youtube.com/user/SoeursSaintJoseph
twitter.com/sjsh_org
www.faceb ok.com/SJSH.org
Présente la vie & l'œuvre de la fondatrice des Soeurs de Saint-Joseph-de-Saint-Hyacinthe; l'histoire d'une communauté de religieuses enseignantes, fondée en terre Maskoutaine;

quatre salles d'exposition, visite commentée comprenant une présentation audiovisuelle, un arrêt au tombeau de la vénérable Élisabeth Bergeron ainsi qu'à la chapelle; ouvert tous les jours.

Saint-Hyacinthe: Musée du séminaire de Saint-Hyacinthe
650, rue Girouard est,
Saint-Hyacinthe, QC J2S 7B7
Tél: 450-774-8977; *Téléc:* 450-774-7101
Musée des sciences naturelles, de l'archéologie, de l'ethnologie, patrimoine religieux et des ouvres d'art

Saint-Hyacinthe: Société du patrimoine religieux du diocèse de Saint-Hyacinthe
650, rue Girouard est,
Saint-Hyacinthe, QC J2S 2Y2
Tél: 450-261-0593; *Téléc:* 450-252-3018
www.prah.org
Fondée en: 1995 Le diocèse de Saint-Hyacinthe présente une collection virtuelle d'objets religieux. Ces objets reflètent l'héritage des couvents, des monastères, des églises et des presbytères.
Chanoine Denis Lépine, Président
Soeur Angèle Vaneau, Vice-Président
Anick Chandonnet, Directrice

Saint-Jean-Port-Joli: Musée de la mémoire vivante / Museum of living memory
710, av de Gaspé ouest,
Saint-Jean-Port-Joli, QC G0R 3G0
Tél: 418-358-0518; *Téléc:* 418-358-0519
information@memoirevivante.org
www.memoirevivante.org
www.youtube.com/user/museememoirevivante
twitter.com/Memoire_vivante
www.facebook.com/MuseeMemoireVivante
Ce musée reflète le mode de vie du manoir seigneurial d'Aubert de Gaspé.
Edwin Bourget, président
Louise Bourgeois, vice-président

Saint-Jean-Port-Joli: Musée de sculpture sur bois des Anciens Canadiens
332, av de Gaspé ouest,
Saint-Jean-Port-Joli, QC G0R 3G0
Tél: 418-598-3392; *Téléc:* 418-598-3329
info@museedesancienscanadiens.com
www.museedesancienscanadiens.com
Collection de plus de 250 sculptures originales, et un vidéo sur la sculpture sur bois et sur neige. Le musée est ouvert du mai jusqu'au novembre.

Saint-Jean-sur-Richelieu: Musée Du Fort St-Jean
15, rue Jacques-Cartier nord,
Saint-Jean-sur-Richelieu, QC J3B 8R8
Tél: 450-358-6500; *Téléc:* 450-358-6909
info@museedufortsaintjean.ca
www.museedufortsaintjean.ca
Fondée en: 1965 Expose des objets militaires et des véhicules
Col. (ret.) Pierre Cadotte, Président O.M.M., M.S.M., C.D.
Eric Ruel, Conservateur

Saint-Jean-sur-Richelieu: Musée du Haut-Richelieu
182, rue Jacques-Cartier nord,
Saint-Jean-sur-Richelieu, QC J3B 7W3
Tél: 450-347-0649; *Téléc:* 450-347-9994
info@museeduhaut-richelieu.com
www.museeduhaut-richelieu.com
www.youtube.com/user/MuseeHR
twitter.com/musee_hr
www.facebook.com/MuseeduHautRichelieu
Fondée en: 1971 L'histoire du Haut-Richelieu; matériel ethnographique et des photographies prises Joseph-Laurent Pinsonneault.

Saint-Jérôme: Musée d'art contemporain des Laurentides (MACL)
101, Place du Curé-Labelle,
Saint-Jérôme, QC J7Z 1X6
Tél: 450-432-7171; *Téléc:* 450-432-8171
musee@museelaurentides.ca
www.museelaurentides.ca
www.instagram.com/maclaurentides
twitter.com/MACLaurentides
www.facebook.com/MACLaurentides
Ce musée célèbre les arts visuels & fournit une plate-forme pour les artistes florissants et professionnels.
Serge Tessier, président du conseil d'administration

Saint-Jérôme: Société d'histoire de la Rivière-du-Nord (SHRN)
CP 206, 101, Place du Curé-Labelle,
Saint-Jérôme, QC J7Z 1X6
Tél: 450-436-1512; *Téléc:* 450-436-1211
courriel@shrn.org
www.shrn.org
wwww.facebook.com/SocietedhistoireRDN
Cette Société se concentre sur la préservation du patrimoine archivistique de la Rivière-du-Nord.

Saint-Joseph-de-Beauce: Musée Marius-Barbeau
139, rue Sainte-Christine,
Saint-Joseph-de-Beauce, QC G0S 2V0
Tél: 418-397-4039; *Téléc:* 418-397-6151
info@museemariusbarbeau.com
www.museemariusbarbeau.com
twitter.com/Mus eeMBarbeau
www.facebook.com/MuseeMariusBarbeau
La mission du musée est la conservation, la recherche et le développement; l'accent est mis sur le patrimoine historique et ethnologique de la Beauce.

Saint-Joseph-de-la-Rive: Musée maritime de Charlevoix
305, rue de l'Église,
Saint-Joseph-de-la-Rive, QC G0A 3Y0
Tél: 418-635-1131
expom@charlevoix.net
www.museemaritime.com
www.facebook.com/MuseeMaritimeCharlevoix
Conserve le patrimoine maritime est les goélettes qui ont naviguées sur le Saint-Laurent; bâtiment thématique central, scierie, atelier & magasin maritime historique; exposition sur l'astroblème; les archives; boutique.
André Simard Simard, Direction générale

Saint-Joseph-de-la-Rive: Papeterie Saint-Gilles
CP 40,
Saint-Joseph-de-la-Rive, QC G0A 3Y0
Tél: 418-635-2430; *Téléc:* 418-635-2613
Ligne sans frais: 866-635-2430
papier@papeteriesaintgilles.com
www.papeteriesaintgilles.com
Papier fait à la main, 100% coton, sans acide et chiné de pétales de fleurs de la région, selon des techniques traditionnelles datant du XVIIe siècle

Saint-Prime: Musée du fromage cheddar
148, av Albert-Perron,
Saint-Prime, QC G8J 1L4
Tél: 418-251-4922; *Téléc:* 418-251-1172
Ligne sans frais: 888-251-4922
cheddar@bellnet.ca
www.museecheddar.org
www.facebook .com/MuseeDuFromageCheddar
L'ancienne Fromagerie Perron est la seule survivante de son genre au Québec. Aujourd'hui il fournit des informations sur la production traditionnell de fromage cheddar; visites guidées; boutique de souvenirs, vente de fromage; casiers verrouillés pour bicyclettes; ouverte au public juin - sept. & sur réservation pour le reste de l'année.
Diane Hudon, Directrice générale

Salaberry-de-Valleyfield: Écomusée des Deux-Rives
75, rue St-Jean-Baptiste,
Salaberry-de-Valleyfield, QC J6T 1Z6
Tél: 450-370-4855; *Téléc:* 450-370-4861
info@museedesdeuxrives.com

Sept-îles: Musée régional de la Côte-Nord (MRCN)
500, boul Laure,
Sept-îles, QC G4R 1X7
Tél: 418-968-2070; *Téléc:* 418-968-8323
mrcn@mrcn.qc.ca
www.museeregionalcotenord.ca/mrcn
Fondée en: 1976 Beaux-Arts; archéologie; photographie; sciences naturelles; ethnologie
Christian Marcotte, directeur général,
christian.marcotte@mrcn.qc.ca

Sept-Iles: Musée Shaputuan / Shaputuan Museum
290, boul des Montagnais,
Sept-Iles, QC G4R 5R2
Tél: 418-962-4000
A pour mission de perpétuer la culture des Innus; le musée s'engage a acquérir, étudier et promouvoir la culture; expositions; activités.

Shawinigan: Cité de l'Énergie
CP 156,
Shawinigan, QC G9N 6T9
Tél: 819-536-8516; *Téléc:* 819-536-2982
Ligne sans frais: 866-900-2483
infocite@citedelenergie.com
www.citedelenergie.com
www.youtube.com/user/CiteEnergie
twitter.com/citedelenergie
www.facebo ok.com/CiteEnergie
Fondée en: 1997 Centre de sciences, expositions, spectacle multimédia, tour d'observation Hydro-Québec

Shawinigan-Sud: Église Notre-Dame-de-la-Présentation
825, 2e Avenue,
Shawinigan-Sud, QC G9P 1E1
Tél: 819-536-3652; *Téléc:* 819-536-4170
eglisendp@cgocable.ca
www.oziasleducenmauricie.com
www.facebook.com/Oz iasLeducenMauricie
Fondée en: 1977 Lieu historique national du Canada; protection et mise en valeur des oeuvres de Leduc dans l'église

Sherbrooke: Centre culturel et du patrimoine Uplands / Uplands Cultural & Heritage Centre
Parent: Société d'histoire et de musée Lennoxville-Ascot
9, rue Speid,
Sherbrooke, QC J1M 1R9
Tél: 819-564-0409; *Téléc:* 819-564-8951
uplands@uplands.ca
uplands.ca
www.facebook.com/uplandslahms
Oeuvres d'artistes locaux et régionaux; des ateliers; thé à l'anglaise; des activités & des concerts; importante collection d'antiquités
Melanie Cutting, président
Pauline Farrugia, vice-président & trésorier
Nancy Robert, Directrice

Sherbrooke: Musée de la nature et des sciences de Sherbrooke / Sherbrooke Museum of Nature & Science
225, rue Frontenac,
Sherbrooke, QC J1H 1K1
Tél: 819-564-3200; *Téléc:* 819-564-0287
Ligne sans frais: 877-434-3200
info@naturesciences.qc.ca
www.naturesciences.qc.ca
twitter.com/naturesciences
www.facebook.com/n aturesciencessherbrooke
Fondée en: 1879 Situé dans une ancienne usine de textile, le Musée renferme une collection de près de 100 000 objets dont 65 000 en sciences naturelles; expositions; théâtre d'objets intéractifs sur la fonction du cerveau; services d'animation et d'éducation et une salle multifonctionnelle disponible en location.
Michelle Bélanger, Directrice générale

Sherbrooke: Musée Régimentaire des Fusiliers de Sherbrooke
64, rue Belvédère sud,
Sherbrooke, QC J1H 4B4
Tél: 819-564-5940; *Téléc:* 819-564-5641
musee.fusdesher@videotron.ca
www.fusiliersdesherbrooke.ca

Attirail militaire

Sherbrooke: La Société d'histoire de Sherbrooke
275, rue Dufferin,
Sherbrooke, QC J1H 4M5
Tél: 819-821-5406; *Téléc:* 819-821-5417
info@histoiresherbrooke.com
www.histoiresherbrooke.com
plus.google.com/111475291093887610216/
www.facebook.com/22243800789
Fondée en: 1927 A pour mission de préserver le patrimoine local, et promouvoir l'histoire de Sherbrooke et les Cantons-de-l'Est
Michael Harnois, Directeur général,
michel.harnois@histoiresherbrooke.com
Karine Savary, Archiviste,
karine.savary@histoiresherbrooke.com

Sorel-Tracy: Biophare
6, rue Staint-Pierre,
Sorel-Tracy, QC J3P 3S2
Tél: 450-780-5740; *Téléc:* 450-780-5734
Ligne sans frais: 877-780-5740
info@biophare.com
www.biophare.com
www.facebook.com/Biophare.observatoire

Fondée en: 1995 Consacre a la préservation de la reserve de biosphère du lac Saint-Pierre; présente une exposition permanente "l'observatoire du lac Saint-Pierre"; musée, boutique, location de salle.
Marc Mineau, Directeur général, 450-780-5740

Stanbridge East: Missisquoi Museum / Musée Missisquoi
2 rue River,
Stanbridge East, QC J0J 2H0
Tel: 450-248-3153; *Fax:* 450-248-0420
info@missisquoimuseum.ca
www.museemissisquoi.ca
Year Founded: 1964 Museum building is a three-story, red brick house in Cornell Mill, which was built in 1830. Exhibitions include Missisquoi County Archives that explore the historic development of the county. Other buildings on site are the Walbridge Barn and Hodge's General Store.
Pamela Realffe, Executive Secretary,
prealffe@missisquoimuseum.ca
Heather Darch, Curator, hdarch@missisquoimuseum.ca
Judy Antle, Archivist, jantle@missisquoimuseum.ca

Stanstead: Stanstead Historical Society / Société Historique de Stanstead
535, rue Dufferin,
Stanstead, QC J0B 3E0
Tel: 819-876-7322; *Fax:* 819-876-7936
info@colbycurtis.ca
www.colbycurtis.ca/stanstead-historical-society
www.instagram.com/colbycurtismuseum
www.facebook.com/MuseeColbyCurtis
Other contact information: Archives E-mail:
archives@colbycurtis.ca
Year Founded: 1929 Operates the Colby Curtis Museum & Carrollcroft Property
Chloë Southam, Director & Curator, chloe@colbycurtis.ca

St-Lin-Laurentides: Lieu historique national du Canada de Sir-Wilfrid-Laurier / Sir Wilfrid Laurier National Historic Site of Canada
945, 12e av,
St-Lin-Laurentides, QC J5M 2W4
Tél: 450-439-3702; *Téléc:* 450-439-5721
Ligne sans frais: 888-787-8888
information@pc.gc.ca
www.pc.gc.ca/fra/lhn-nhs/qc/wilfridlaurier/index.aspx
Autre numéros: ATS: 1-866-787-6221
Centre d'interprétation; exposition présente la vie et l'oeuvre de Sir Wilfrid Laurier.

St-Paul-de-l'Ile-aux-Noix: Lieu historique national du Canada du Fort-Lennox / Fort Lennox National Historic Site of Canada
1, 61e Avenue,
St-Paul-de-l'Ile-aux-Noix, QC J0J 1G0
Tél: 450-291-5700; *Téléc:* 450-291-4389
Ligne sans frais: 888-773-8888
information@pc.gc.ca
www.pc.gc.ca/fra/lhn-nhs/qc/lennox/index.aspx
Autre numéros: ATS: 1-866-787-6221
Visites guidées; activités; caserne, poudrière, corps de garde, et prison; expositions: "Ces messieurs les officiers", et "Le fort Lennox, Oeuvre des ingénieurs royaux".

Sutton: Eberdt Museum of Communications
30A, rue Principale sud,
Sutton, QC J0E 2K0
Tél: 514-891-9560
mchs@aide-internet.org
www.facebook.com/museedesutton
This museum celebrates the history of the town of Sutton, in the Eastern Townships of Quebec. There are over 1,200 artifacts.

Sutton: Musée des communications et d'histoire de Sutton
32, rue Principale sud,
Sutton, QC J0E 2K0
Tél: 450-538-2883
www.facebook.com/224180200996688
Expose des objets ayant à voir avec l'histoire de la ville de Sutton et de l'histoire du comté de Brome-Missisquoi.

Tadoussac: Centre d'interprétation des mammifères marins (CIMM)
108, rue de la Cale-Sèche,
Tadoussac, QC G0T 2A0
Tél: 418-235-4701
info@gremm.org
www.gremm.org
twitter.com/GREMM_
www.facebook.com/GREMM1985
Sa mission est la conservation du milieu marin & la recherche scientifique des mammifères marins de Saint-Laurent.
Robert Michaud, Directeur scientifique & Président

Tadoussac: La maison des Dunes
750, ch du Moulin Baude,
Tadoussac, QC G0T 2A0
Tél: 418-235-4238/*Ligne sans frais:* 800-665-6527
Maison faisant partie du patrimoine local, transformée en centre d'interprétation; exposition permanente; présentations, par des naturalistes, sur le phénomène des dunes de sable

Tadoussac: La Petite chapelle de Tadoussac
165, rue du Bord de L'Eau,
Tadoussac, QC G0T 2A0
Tél: 418-235-4324
www.chapelledetadoussac.com
Ce bâtiment commémoré l'activité missionnaire jésuite du Nouveau France. C'est la plus vieille église en bois du Québec et du Canada et elle est inscrite sur la liste des sites hisotériques nationaux.

Tadoussac: Poste de Traite Chauvin Trading Post
157, rue du Bord-de-l'Eau,
Tadoussac, QC G0T 2A0
Tél: 418-235-4657
culture@tadoussac.com
Réplique du premier poste de traite des fourrures du 17e siècle; présente des objets se rapportant à la vie des autochtones et les produits d'échange; dégustation de phoque tous les dimanches

Témiscouata-sur-le-Lac: Fort Ingall Site Historique
Parent: Société d'Histoire et d'Archéologie du Témiscouata
81, rue Caldwell,
Témiscouata-sur-le-Lac, QC G0L 1E0
Tél: 418-854-2375; *Téléc:* 418-854-6477
Ligne sans frais: 866-242-2437
info@fortingall.ca
www.fortingall.ca
www.facebook.com/fortingall
Expositions, animations et visites guidées
Raymonde Gratton, présidente du conseil d'administration

Terrebonne: Site historique de l'île-des-Moulins / Historic site of Ile-des-Moulins
866, rue St-Pierre,
Terrebonne, QC J6W 1E5
Tél: 450-471-0619; *Téléc:* 450-471-8311
info@iledesmoulins.com
www.iledesmoulins.qc.ca
www.instagram.com/idmsodect
twitter.com/IDM_SODECT
www.facebook.com/il edesmoulins
Bureau seigneurial; le Moulin neuf; le Moulin à scie et le Moulin à farine; la Boulangerie

Tête-à-la-Baleine: Centre d'interprétation de l'île Providence et Musée Jos Hébert
Parent: Association touristique de Tête-à-la-Baleine
Tête-à-la-Baleine, QC G0G 2W0
Tél: 418-242-2015
www.tourismlowernorthshore.com/attractions.asp
This site celebrates the life of one of the region's iconic locals, Joseph Hebert. The house is a replica of his last house & commemorates his legacy. As the Lower North's first mail carrier, Joseph was dedicated to delivering news to distant villages, making his way by dogsled.

Thetford Mines: Musée minéralogique et minier de Thetford Mines
711, boul Frontenac ouest,
Thetford Mines, QC G6G 7Y8
Tél: 418-335-2123; *Téléc:* 418-335-5605
Ligne sans frais: 855-335-2123
service.client@museemineralogique.com
www.museemineralogique.com
www.instagram.com/museethetford
www.facebook.com/museemineralogique
Fondée en: 1976 Présente l'histoire géologique, minière & social de la région de L'Amiante; expositions; activités educatives; excursions

Virginie Bizier, directrice générale,
v.bizier@museemineralogique.com

Trois-Pistoles: Parc de l'aventure basque en Amérique (PABA)
66, rue du Parc,
Trois-Pistoles, QC G0L 4K0
Tél: 418-851-1556
info@aventurebasque.ca
www.aventurebasque.ca
www.facebook.com/Aventurebasque
Fondée en: 1996

Trois-Rivières: Boréalis - Centre d'histoire de l'industrie papetière
CP 368, 200, av des Draveurs,
Trois-Rivières, QC G9A 5H3
Tél: 819-372-4633; *Téléc:* 819-374-1900
borealis@v3r.net
www.borealis3r.ca
www.youtube.com/user/borealis3r
www.facebook.com/borealis3r
Boréalis s'engage à vous faire découvrir l'histoire de l'industriepapière du québécoise; activités; groupes scolaires & adultes; ouvert tous les jours 10h-18h, du 26 mai au 30 septembre & sur réservation pour les groupes
Valérie Bourgeois, Directrice

Trois-Rivières: Lieu historique national du Canada des Forges-du-Saint-Maurice / Forges du Saint-Maurice National Historic Site
10 000, boul des Forges,
Trois-Rivières, QC G9C 1B1
Tél: 819-378-5116; *Téléc:* 819-378-0887
Ligne sans frais: 888-773-8888
information@pc.gc.ca
www.pc.gc.ca/en/lhn-nhs/qc/saintmaurice
Autre numéros: Off season phone: 514-283-2282; Off season fax: 514-238-5560
A 20 minutes de Trois-Rivières, commémore l'établissement de la plus grande communauté industrielle du Canada; ouvert de mi-mai à mi-octobre; réservation de groupes.

Trois-Rivières: Musée des Filles de Jésus / Museum of the Daughters of Jesus
1193, boul Saint-Louis,
Trois-Rivières, QC G8Z 2M8
Tél: 819-376-3741; *Téléc:* 819-376-8107
fjtrmuse@infoteck.qc.ca
www.musee-fdj.com
www.facebook.com/pg/musee.je sus/posts
Fondée en: 1834 Ce musée est dédié à la conservation du patrimoine de la Congrégation des Filles de Jésus. Il y a trois expositions principlaes qui impliquent une visite d'une chapelle néo-gothique.

Trois-Rivières: Musée des Ursulines de Trois-Rivières
734, rue des Ursulines,
Trois-Rivières, QC G9A 5B5
Tél: 819-375-7922; *Téléc:* 819-375-0238
info@musee-ursulines.qc.ca
www.musee-ursulines.qc.ca
twitter.com/musee ursulines
www.facebook.com/musee.desursulines
Autre numéros: Alt. URL: www.ursulines-uc.com
Conserve et met en valeur l'histoire des Ursulines dès 1697; expositions thématiques, visites guidées, galerie d'art.

Trois-Rivières: Musée militaire de Trois-Rivières
574, rue St-François-Xavier,
Trois-Rivières, QC G9A 1R6
Tél: 819-371-5290
museemilitaire@cgocable.ca
www.12rbc.ca
www.instagram.com/tourismetr
Musée & manège militaire; exposition retraçant l'histoire du régiment; salles d'armes; collections d'uniformes, pièces d'équipements, armes blanches & armes à feu en usage dans les Forces canadiennes.

Trois-Rivières: Musée Pierre Boucher
858, rue Laviolette,
Trois-Rivières, QC G9A 5S3
Tél: 819-376-4459; *Téléc:* 819-378-0607
museepierre-boucher@ssj.qc.ca
www.museepierreboucher.com
Musée fondé en 1920 par Mgr Albert Tessier pour protéger et sauvegarder le patrimoine local et régional; art contemporain (québecois et canadien); un programme d'animation adapté pour les groupes scolaires et les groupes d'adultes est centré sur les expositions temporaires, consacrées aux artistes contemporains

et aux collections du musée; le musée est ouvert gratuitement du mardi au dimanche

Trois-Rivières: Musée québécois de culture populaire / Museum of Quebec Folk Culture
200, rue Laviolette,
Trois-Rivières, QC G9A 6L5
Tél: 819-372-0406; Téléc: 819-372-9907
info@culturepop.qc.ca
www.culturepop.qc.ca
www.youtube.com/user/museeculturepop
twitter.com/Museeculturepop
www.f acebook.com/culturepop
Fondée en: 2001 Le Musée propose six expositions audacieuses, non conventionnelles et empreintes de plaisir à la manière des Québécois; reliée au Musée, la Vieille prison de Trois-Rivières, offre une visite-expérience, guidée par des ex-détenus. Heures: 24 juin à la fête du Travail: L-D 10h-18h; Automne, hiver, printemps: Ma-D 10h-17h
Yvon Noël, Directrice, ynoel@culturepop.qc.ca

Ulverton: Moulin à laine d'Ulverton / Ulverton Woolen Mills
210, ch Porter,
Ulverton, QC J0B 2B0
Tél: 819-826-3157; Téléc: 819-826-6266
moulin@moulin.ca
www.moulin.ca
twitter.com/Moulinalaine
www.facebook .com/UlvertonWoolenMills
Fondée en: 1982 Initie aux méthodes artisanales et industrielles de production et de traitement de la laine

Upton: Musée Saint-Éphrem
351, rue Monseigneur-Desmarais,
Upton, QC J0H 2E0
Tél: 450-549-4533; Téléc: 450-549-4563
info@museestephrem.com
museestephrem.com
Ce musée est dédié à la restauration de l'intérêt pour l'ère religieuse du Québec durant les 19e et 20e siècles.
Pierre Bernard, président

Valcourt: Musée J. Armand Bombardier
1001, av J.A. Bombardier,
Valcourt, QC J0E 2L0
Tél: 450-532-5300; Téléc: 450-532-2260
info@museebombardier.com
www.museebombardier.com
www.youtube.com/MuseeJAB
www.facebook.com/MuseeBombardier
Fondée en: 1971 Le musée présente la vie et l'oeuvre de Joseph-Armand Bombardier, mécanicien, inventeur et entrepreneur; retrace l'évolution de l'industrie de la motoneige; expositions; activités.

Val-d'Or: La Cité de l'Or
Parent: La Corporation du Village minier de Bourlamaque
CP 212, 90, Perreault av,
Val-d'Or, QC J9P 4P3
Tél: 819-825-1274; Téléc: 819-825-9853
Ligne sans frais: 855-825-1274
courrier@citedelor.com
www.citedelor.com/fr-ca/index.php
www.facebook.com/citedelor
Fondée en: 1995 Site historique du patrimoine minier; visites guidées à la seule mine d'or du Québec; accessible à 91 mètre sous terre; expositions; boutique; par réservation.

Vaudreuil-Dorion: Centre d'histoire La Presqu'île
431, av St-Charles,
Vaudreuil-Dorion, QC J7V 2N3
Tél: 450-424-5627; Téléc: 450-424-5675
info@chlapresquile.qc.ca
www.chlapresquile.qc.ca
This center is dedicated to preserving the heritage of the Vaudreil-Soulanges region.
Pierre Marchand, président du conseil d'administration
Jean-Luc Brazeau, Archiviste

Vaudreuil-Dorion: Musée régional de Vaudreuil-Soulanges (MRVS)
431, av St-Charles,
Vaudreuil-Dorion, QC J7V 2N3
Tél: 450-455-2092; Téléc: 450-455-6782
Ligne sans frais: 877-455-2092
info@mrvs.qc.ca
www.mrvs.qc.ca
www.facebook.com/Cyprienne.la.souris
Fondée en: 1953 Exposition permanente et expositions temporaires; collections spéciales; ethnologie et histoire;

collection d'ouvres d'art; visites du patrimoine; centre de documentation en généalogie et histoire régionale; visites guidées, activités, ateliers, programmation; location de chambres; boutique; café.
Daniel Bissonnette, Directeur générale

Victoriaville: Musée Laurier
16, rue Laurier ouest,
Victoriaville, QC G6P 6P3
Tél: 819-357-8655; Téléc: 819-357-8655
info@museelaurier.com
museelaurier.com
www.facebook.com/musee.laurier
Fondée en: 1929 Résidence de Sir Wilfrid Laurier, ancien premier ministre du Canada, et sa femme Lady Laurier; maintenant la propriété de la Société du Musée Laurier; collection d'objets d'art et de meubles, sculpture et oeuvres en art contemporain.
Richard Pedneault, Directeur/Conservateur

Ville-Marie: Lieu historique national du Canada du Fort-Témiscamingue / Fort Témiscamingue National Historic Site of Canada
834, ch du Vieux-Fort,
Ville-Marie, QC J9V 1H4
Tél: 819-629-3222 Ligne sans frais: 888-773-8888
information@pc.gc.ca
www.pc.gc.ca/en/lhn-nhs/qc/temiscamingue
Autre numéros: TTY: 1-866-787-6221; Off season phone: 514-283-2282
Fondée en: 1679 Commémmore l'histoire des Algonquins & de ce poste de traite situé dans le détroit du Témiscamingue.

Westmount: Aron Museum
Temple emanu-el-beth sholom, 4100 Sherbrooke St. West,
Westmount, QC H3Z 1A5
Tél: 514-937-3575; Fax: 514-937-7058
www.templemontreal.ca/programming/museum-gallery
twitter.com/templemontr eal
www.facebook.com/TempleEmanuElBethSholom
Contains over 300 Jewish, ceremonial pieces of art.
Shellie Ettinger, Executive Director, 514-937-3575

Westmount: Royal Montreal Regiment Museum
4625, rue Ste-Catherine ouest,
Westmount, QC H3Z 1S4
Tél: 514-496-2003; Fax: 514-496-5085
royalmontrealregiment.com
twitter.com/rmtlr
www.facebook.com/royalmont realregiment

Windsor: Parc histoique de la Poudrière de Windsor / Windsor Powder Mill Historical Park
342, rue St-Georges,
Windsor, QC J1S 2Z5
Tél: 819-845-5284
poudriere@villedewindsor.qc.ca
www.poudriere-windsor.qc.ca
www.facebook.com/195123797205009
Fondée en 1864, dans la foulée de la guerre de session, la Poudrière de Windsor s'est investie dans la fabrication de poudre noire, un composé essentiel des explosifs. Jusqu'en 1922, la ville de Windsor a vécu au rythme de cette industrie dangereuse. On peut maintenant découvrir les secrets, le comment et le pourquoi de cette industrie via une toute nouvelle exposition permanente et la visite guidé

Saskatchewan

Provincial Museums

Royal Saskatchewan Museum (RSM)
2445 Albert St.,
Regina, SK S4P 4W7
Tel: 306-787-2815
info@royalsaskmuseum.ca
www.royalsaskmuseum.ca
www.instagram.com/royalsaskmuseum
twitter.com/royalsaskmuseum
www.face book.com/Royal.Saskatchewan.Museum
Year Founded: 1906 Saskatchewan's natural & human history; archaeology; entomology; botany; natural history; paleontology; geology. Life Sciences Gallery; Earth Sciences Gallery; First Nations Gallery; Paleo Pit interactive gallery for children; Megamunch, a half-size robotic Tyrannosaurus rex. Publication of informational booklets & nature notes, giftshop, research library.
Peter Menzies, Director, 306-787-2813, peter.menzies@gov.sk.ca
Victoria Kablys, Museum Conservator, 306-787-2667, victoria.kablys@gov.sk.ca

Western Development Museum (WDM)
Curatorial Centre
2610 Lorne Ave.,
Saskatoon, SK S7J 0S6
Tel: 306-931-1910; Fax: 306-934-0525
saskatoon@wdm.ca
www.wdm.ca
www.instagram.com/wdm.ca
twitter.com/wdmtweets
www.facebook.com/wdm.mu seum
The Western Development Museum preserves Saskatchewan's collective heritage in order to raise awareness of & generate interest in the cultural & economic development of western Canada. The Curatorial Centre in Saskatoon coordinates services for the museum's branches in Moose Jaw, North Battleford, Saskatoon, & Yorkton. Tours of the Curatorial Centre may be arranged through the education & extension staff.
Joan Kanigan, Chief Executive Officer, jkanigan@wdm.ca
Jason Wall, Manager, Saskatoon Western Development Museum
Elizabeth Scott, Curator, escott@wdm.ca

Local Museums

Abernethy: Abernethy Nature-Heritage Museum
PO Box 125, Main St.,
Abernethy, SK S0A 0A0
Tel: 306-333-2202
anhm@sasktel.net
www.facebook.com/AbernethyNatureHeritageMuseum
Other contact information: Alt. Phones: 306-333-2102; 306-333-2125
Heritage & antique artifacts with a core exhibit of more than 300 wildlife specimens mounted by the late Ralph Stueck (1897-1979); video presentation of Stueck's "talking goose" & other folklore; activities/hands-on displays for children; small art gallery and a 1930s classroom. Open daily May - Sept. Wheelchair accessible.

Abernethy: Motherwell Homestead National Historic Site
Autoroute 22,
Abernethy, SK S0A 0A0
Tel: 306-333-2116; Fax: 306-333-2210
Toll-Free: 888-772-8888
motherwell.homestead@pc.gc.ca
www.pc.gc.ca/en/lhn-nhs/ sk/motherwell
twitter.com/parkscanada_sk
www.facebook.com/saskNHS
Year Founded: 1983 The site includes Lanark Place, the farmstead estate of pioneer farmer & politician W.R. Motherwell, who had a significant influence on the development of scientific agriculture in Western Canada. The homestead depicts the lifestyles, costumes & architecture of the early 20th century, with costumed guides. Open Victoria Day - Labour Day.

Alameda: Alameda & District Heritage Museum
PO Box 195,
Alameda, SK S0C 0A0
Tel: 306-483-5099
Open Wed. July-Aug., or by appointment.

Allan: Allan Community Heritage Society & Museum
326 Main St.,
Allan, SK S0K 0C0
Tel: 306-257-3511; Fax: 306-257-4249
allanskmuseum@sasktel.net
www.facebook.com/AllanSKMuseum
Other contact information: Alternate Phone: 306-257-3634
Year Founded: 2005

Arborfield: Dickson Hardie Interpretive Centre at Pasquia Regional Park
PO Box 339,
Arborfield, SK S0E 0A0
Tel: 306-768-3239; Fax: 306-769-8307
pasquia1@xplornet.ca
www.pasquia.com
The museum features fossil castings of archaeological finds from around the Carrot River, & pieces from throughout the region collected by locals. Open May-Sept.

Arcola: Arcola Museum
PO Box 354, 520 Railway Ave,
Arcola, SK S0C 0G0
Tel: 306-455-2379
www.townofarcola.ca/^page_id=124
Other contact information: Alternate phone: 306-455-2566
Artifacts of local history include clothing, tools, & machinery.
Open Jul-Aug Fri 2:00-4:00

Assiniboia: Assiniboia & District Museum
PO Box 1211, 506 - 3rd Ave. West,
Assiniboia, SK S0H 0B0

Tel: 306-642-5353; Fax: 306-642-5622
assini.museum@sasktel.net
southcentralmuseums.ca/assiniboia.html
www.facebook.com/173848239361722
The Assiniboia & District Museum features vintage cars from 1916 to 1964, a grain elevator, a Pole Shed with agricultural machinery, a school room & a military display. The museum is open seven days a week during July & August, & Monday to Friday from September to June.

Avonlea: Avonlea Heritage Museum
PO Box 401, 219 Railway Ave.,
Avonlea, SK S0H 0C0

Tel: 306-868-2101
www.avonleamuseum.ca
www.facebook.com/avonleamuseum
Year Founded: 1980 The Avonlea Heritage Museum displays artifacts which depict the history of native people, pioneers, & ranchers in the area as well as local history & archaeological findings. Open Jun-Sep daily
Richard Geisler, President
Joyce Holland, Secretary

Batoche: Batoche National Historic Site
PO Box Hwy. 225,
Batoche, SK S0K 3R0

Tel: 306-423-6227; Fax: 306-423-5400
Toll-Free: 888-773-8888
batoche.info@pc.gc.ca
www.pc.gc.ca/en/lhn-nhs/sk/batoche
twitter.com/hashtag/batoche
www.facebook.com/friendsbatoche
Other contact information: TTD: 306-423-5540
The Batoche National Historic Site of Canada, on the banks of the South Saskatchewan River, is the scene of the last battlefield in the Northwest Rebellion of 1885. The site displays the remains & several restored buildings of the village of Batoche. The life of the Métis at Batoche between 1860 & 1900 is depicted. The site is open from May to September.

Battleford: Fort Battleford National Historic Site
PO Box 70,
Battleford, SK S0M 0E0

Tel: 306-937-2621; Fax: 306-937-3370
battleford.info@pc.gc.ca
pc.gc.ca/en/lhn-nhs/sk/battleford
twitter.com/parkscanada_sk
www.facebook.com/saskNHS
Other contact information: TTY: 306-937-3199
Year Founded: 1876 The site features camping grounds, year round special events and learning opportunities for children, as well as access to other museums in the area. Open three days a week May - Jun; seven days a week from Jul - Sept, 10:00 - 4:00.

Battleford: Fred Light Museum
PO Box 40, 11 - 20th St. East,
Battleford, SK S0M 0E0

Tel: 306-937-7111
flmuseum@battleford.ca
fredlightmuseum.webs.com
www.facebook.com/fredlightmuseum
Year Founded: 1980 Themed rooms, pioneer artifacts, gun collection, military artifacts. Open May-Aug.
Bernadette Leslie, Manager

Battleford: Saskatchewan Baseball Hall of Fame & Museum
PO Box 1388, 292 - 22nd St. West,
Battleford, SK S9A 0E0

Tel: 306-446-1983; Fax: 306-446-0509
saskbaseballmuseum@sasktel.net
Year Founded: 1983 Displays memorabilia and artifacts pertaining to the history of baseball in Saskatchewan. Has over 3,000 artifacts, in addition to 6,000 items of archival nature such as pictures, books & magazines. Also the home of what is claimed to be "Canada's largest baseball bat." Open year round, M - F 9:00 - 4:00.
Mike Ramage, Executive Director, 306-780-9237, Fax: 306-352-3669, mramage@sasktel.net

Beauval: Frazer's Museum
PO Box 64,
Beauval, SK S0M 0G0

www.sicc.sk.ca/archive/saskindian/a01win19.htm
Year Founded: 1969 First Nations owned and operated museum displaying first nation & pioneer artifacts, including articles from Hudson's Bay Company, missionaries & Métis people.
John G. Frazer, Owner

Mathilda Frazer, Owner

Bengough: Bengough & District Museum
190 - 1st Ave. West,
Bengough, SK S0C 0K0

Tel: 306-268-2909
www.southcentralmuseums.ca/bengough.html
Other contact information: Alternate Phone: 306-268-2927
Local history; open daily from July-Aug., & by appointment Sept.-May.

Big River: Big River Memorial Museum
PO Box 834, Third Ave. North,
Big River, SK S0J 0E0

Tel: 306-469-2112
The Big River Memorial Museum contains items from fishing & logging in the area.

Biggar: Biggar Museum & Gallery
PO Box 1598, 105 - 3rd Ave. West,
Biggar, SK S0K 0M0

Tel: 306-948-3451; Fax: 306-948-3478
biggarmuseum@sasktel.net
biggarmuseum.webs.com
www.facebook.com/Biggar Museum
Year Founded: 1972 The museum collects historical artifacts from the settlement of the town of Biggar & the surrounding district. Among it collections are a general store display & a reconstruction of the Biggar train station. Biggar Museum & Gallery is open year round, M - F in the winter, and M - Sa in the summer, 9:00 - 5:00.
Anne Livingston, Executive Director

Birch Hills: Birch Hills & District Historical Society
PO Box 693,
Birch Hills, SK S0J 0G0

Tel: 306-749-2262
bhmuseum@yahoo.ca
birchhills.ca/recreation/museum.html
The museum's collection contains restored agricultural machines, a memorial wall, & a lending library of over 200 Saskatchewan history books. Buildings on-site include a log barn, a milk house, & a CPR station. Open year round, W 2:00-4:00, also by appointment.

Blaine Lake: General Store Memories, Museum & Antiques
PO Box 457,
Blaine Lake, SK S0J 0J0

Tel: 306-226-4646
12-40andbeyond.com
The General Store contains antiques on the first floor & a museum preserving local history on the second floor.
Bill Nemish, Contact
Vivian Nemish, Contact

Bonnyville: Bonnyville & District Museum
Parent: Bonnyville & District Historical Society
4401 - 54 Ave.,
Bonnyville, SK T9N 2H4

Tel: 780-826-4925
bvmuseum@mcsnet.ca
bonnyvillemuseum.ca
Year Founded: 1991 The museum features 250,000 artifacts pertaining to local history.
Germaine Prybysh, Manager/Curator

Borden: Borden & District Historical Museum
PO Box 5,
Borden, SK S0K 0N0

Tel: 306-997-4517
Year Founded: 1990 Artifacts housed in a one-room schoolhouse & former Masonic Lodge; site also includes a replica of the Diefenbaker homestead, as well as a butcher shop & barber shop. Open June-Sept., or by appointment.

Briercrest: Briercrest & District Museum
PO Box 216,
Briercrest, SK S0H 0K0

Tel: 306-799-4951
briercrestmuseum.ca
Year Founded: 1987 The Briercrest & District Museum houses collections from the Briercrest area's earliest settlers & their descendants. Examples of the museum's artifacts include household items & small farm equipment. Open by appointment.
Marge Cleave, Curator
Georgina Gadd, Curator
Chuck Alton, Chair

Broadview: Broadview Historical Museum
PO Box 556, 10th Ave. North,
Broadview, SK S0G 0K0

Tel: 306-696-3244
broadviewmuseum@hotmail.com
broadviewmuseum.weebly.com
Year Founded: 1972 Articles related to Broadview's history are collected & displayed. Visitors can see the Highland School, a blacksmith shop, a post office, a sod house, a log home & a Canadian Pacific Railway station & caboose. Broadview Historical Museum is open from the beginning of June to the end of Aug. 12:00 - 5:00 from F - Su.

Cabri: Cabri & District Museum
PO Box 467, 202 Centre St.,
Cabri, SK S0N 0J0

Tel: 306-587-2300
townofcabri@sasktel.net
www.cabri.ca/cabri-district-museum
Displays include artifacts from World War I & World War II, First Nations, & household & farm items. The museum is open from May to Sept.

Cadillac: Cadillac Historic Museum
Centre St.,
Cadillac, SK S0N 0K0

Tel: 306-785-4512
Other contact information: Alt Phone: 306-785-2042
Housed in a 1914 church with restored siding and roof, the museum features household articles & early 20th century tools; clothing; fire-fighting equipment; a quilt exhibit and demonstrations. Open upon request.
Luanne Hancock, Contact

Canora: CN Station House Museum
PO Box 717,
Canora, SK S0A 0L0

Tel: 306-563-4591
cdo.canora@sasktel.net
The museum contains CN & pioneer artifacts, & is housed in the oldest Class 2 station left in Saskatchewan. Part of the museum is being integrated into the town's new Visitor Centre. Open July-Sept., daily 10:00-4:00.

Canwood: Canwood Museum
PO Box 511, 635 - 3rd Ave. East,
Canwood, SK S0J 0K0

Tel: 306-468-2659
Year Founded: 1971 Canwood Museum is a community museum located in an old schoolhouse. Displays include farm artifacts, clothing, & pictures. There is a miniature golf course on site.

Carlyle: Rusty Relics Museum Inc.
PO Box 840, 306 Railway Ave W,
Carlyle, SK S0C 0R0

Tel: 306-453-2266
rustyrelicmuseum@sasktel.net
Other contact information: Alternate Phone: 306-453-2363
A museum of pioneer life in Saskatchewan. Artifacts relating to Carlyle area displayed in a 1910 CN railway station. Includes a 1943 CPR caboose, a CN Motor car, CN tool shed with railway tools, furnished 1905 one-room country school, agricultural machinery & old church. Ope Jun-Sep

Choiceland: Choiceland Historical Society
PO Box 234,
Choiceland, SK S0J 0M0

Tel: 306-428-2850
choiceland.ca/museum.html
Local & military history. Open May-Sept., F 1:00-4:00

Climax: Climax Community Museum
PO Box 59,
Climax, SK S0N 0N0

Tel: 306-293-2051
The Climax Community Museum chronicles the history of Climax and its surrounding area, featuring a pioneer collection with tools & farm machinery; military, hospital & sports equipment; and a community archive. Open May to Aug daily 10:00 - 12:00, 1:00 - 5:00 or by appointment.

Consul: Consul Museum
PO Box 144,
Consul, SK S0N 0P0

Tel: 306-299-4493
consulmuseum@gmail.com
www.consulmuseum.ca
Year Founded: 2005 The Consul Museum is the first Saskatchewan museum to exist solely as a website. The site contains pictures, videos, & stories of local history.

Coronach: Coronach District Museum
240 - 1st. St. West,
Coronach, SK S0H 0Z0

Tel: 306-267-4403
rm11@sasktel.net
www.southcentralmuseums.ca/coronach.html
Other contact information: For Appointments: 306-267-5704
The museum consists of historical displays, records, photos &
artifacts representing the lives of pioneers of the area. Open Jul
- Aug, Su - M from 1:00 - 4:00, or by appointment.
Helen Foley, Contact, 306-267-4403

Craik: Craik Oral History Museum
PO Box 144,
Craik, SK S0G 0V0

Tel: 306-734-2751
Local history; collection contains photographs, slides, videos,
documents & record books, & 600 hours of audio cassette
recordings. Open Jan.-Dec., or by appointment.

Craik: Prairie Pioneer Museum
PO Box 157, 541 Parks Rd.,
Craik, SK S0G 0V0

Tel: 306-734-2249
Year Founded: 1966 The pioneer way of life in Craik & rural
Saskatchewan is portrayed at the Prairie Pioneer Museum.
Buildings include two rural schools & a heritage house, which
was built in 1906. Artifacts, such as household furnishings &
medical & veterinary instruments, are on display. The museum is
open during the summer & is accessible year-round by request.

Creighton: Royal Northwest Mounted Police Post
Museum
216 Creighton Ave.,
Creighton, SK S0P 0A0

Tel: 306-688-3538
creightontourism@sasktel.net
www.townofcreighton.ca/museum.html
A reconstruction of the original Royal Northwest Mounted Police
Post in Beaver City, circa 1915. Located at the Creighton
Recreation Culture & Tourism Centre. Open May-Sept.

Cudworth: Cudworth Museum
PO Box 69,
Cudworth, SK S0K 1B0

Tel: 306-256-3492; Fax: 306-256-3515
town.cudworth@sasktel.net
Year Founded: 2004 Local history; former CN station.

Cupar: Cupar & District Heritage Museum
PO Box 164, 307 Aberdeen St.,
Cupar, SK S0G 0Y0

Tel: 306-723-4253
shirley.pain@uregina.ca
www.townofcupar.com/pages/museum.php
cuparmuseum.blogspot.ca
twitter.com/cuparmuseum
Year Founded: 1995 Housed in two buildings: an old Masonic
Hall & a curling rink; open May - Sept. or by appt.

Cut Knife: Clayton McLain Memorial Museum (CMMM)
PO Box 8, 101 Hill St.,
Cut Knife, SK S0M 0N0

Tel: 306-398-2345
cmmmcutknife@gmail.com
www.cmmmcutknife.ca
cmmmcutknife.blogspot.com
Located in Tomahawk Park, site of the world's largest tomahawk.
The site focuses on local history, including First Nation history &
the Battle of Cut Knife Hill. Houses the McLain family collection;
archives including personal papers, photographs, and a
complete collection of the local newspaper; as well as other
educational programming and research services. Open
June-Sept.

Denare Beach: Northern Gateway Museum
PO Box 70, Moody Dr.,
Denare Beach, SK S0P 0B0

Tel: 306-362-2141
ngmdenarebeach@gmail.com
www.northerngatewaymuseum.com
Year Founded: 1957 The Northern Gateway Museum houses
artifacts from fur trade excavations, First Nations life, gold rush
activities, & mining operations. Archives include architectural
records, photographs, & films. Open Jun-Aug daily

Dinsmore: Yester-Years Community Museum
PO Box 216, 100 Railway Ave,
Dinsmore, SK S0L 0T0

Tel: 306-846-2220
Other contact information: Alternate phone: 306-846-4613

Features the main museum, blacksmith shop, butter & post
office buildings.

Dodsland: Dodsland & District Museum
PO Box 171, Main St. & 1st Ave,
Dodsland, SK S0L 0V0

Tel: 306-356-2228
Local history; museum depicts different aspects of life such as a
hospital, school, store & barber shop. Open May-Nov Tu & Th
1:30-4:30, or by appointment.

Duck Lake: Duck Lake Regional Interpretive Centre
(DLRIC)
PO Box 328, Hwy. 11 (Louis Riel Trail),
Duck Lake, SK S0K 1J0

Tel: 306-467-2057 Toll-Free: 866-467-2057
duckmuf@sasktel.net
www.dlric.org
Year Founded: 1959 Frontier of First Nation, Métis & Pioneer
Society, 1870-1905. Museum contains artifact & art galleries, a
theatre, gift shop, 24m viewing tower and conference facilities.
Open daily May - Sept 10:00 - 5:30 or by appointment.

Duck Lake: Fort Carlton Provincial Park
212 Hwy.,
Duck Lake, SK S0K 0W0

Tel: 306-467-5215 Toll-Free: 800-205-7070
fortcarlton@gov.sk.ca
Located 26 km. west of Duck Lake on Hwy. 212, the site
contains a reconstructed Hudson's Bay Company fur trade post,
guided tours, picnic grounds, hiking and camping. Open May -
Sept.

Dysart: Dysart & District Museum
PO Box 327,
Dysart, SK S0G 1H0

Tel: 306-432-2255
Other contact information: Alternate Phone: 306-432-2100
Local history; replicas of area country schools; Wall of Honour
war memorial; open June-Sept., Th & Sa 1:30-4:00.

Eastend: Eastend Historical Museum & Cultural Centre
Inc. (EHMCCI)
306 Red Coat Drive,
Eastend, SK S0N 0T0

Tel: 306-295-3375
eastendhistoricalmuseum.com
www.facebook.com/EastendHistoricalMuseum
The EHMCCI is a community organization whose missions is to
preserve and promote the history of Southwest Saskatchewan.
The centre includes a Tie Rail Ranch House, a blacksmith shop,
an operating 1903 Cae Steam Engine, a 1927 Federal Truck & a
stage coach. The LaRose Building contains 1500 artifacts. The
Centre also serves as a Tourist Information Centre and as a
community resource to its cultural activities. Open daily May -
Labour Day; by appointment in the winter.
Shelly Parker, President
Glen Duke, Treasurer
Doreen Stewart, Secretary

Eastend: T.rex Discovery Centre
PO Box 460, 1 T-rex Dr.,
Eastend, SK S0N 0T0

Tel: 306-295-4009
trex.centre@gov.sk.ca
www.royalsaskmuseum.ca/trex
www.youtube.com/user/trexcentre
www.facebook.com/trexcentre
The T.rex Discovery Centre is home to Scotty, the largest & most
complete fossilized skeleton of a Tyrannosaurus rex in Canada.
The Royal Saskatchewan Museum Fossil Research Station is
also located on-site.
Tim Tokaryk, Curator of Vertebrate Palaeontology,
306-295-4701, Fax: 306-295-4702, Tim.Tokaryk@gov.sk.ca

Eatonia: Eatonia Heritage Park
PO Box 189,
Eatonia, SK S0L 0Y0

Tel: 306-967-2251
eatonia@yourlink.ca
Municipal Heritage Property featuring a train caboose &
wood-frame railway station & house from the early 1900s.

Edam: Harry S. Washbrook Museum
PO Box 182, 2nd Ave.,
Edam, SK S0M 0V0

Tel: 306-397-2260
Local pioneer & First Nations artifacts

Elbow: Elbow Museum
PO Box 207, Saskatchewan St.,
Elbow, SK S0H 1J0

Tel: 306-854-2290; Fax: 306-854-2229
elbow@sasktel.net
www.facebook.com/439097509605236
The Elbow Museum is housed in an old schoolhouse and its
primary attraction is the "Sod Shack" which is a symbol of the
past, giving visitors a glimpse of how thousands of settlers lived
when they homesteaded to the Canadian prairies in the early
1900s. Open daily May - Sept. or by appointment.

Elrose: Elrose Museum
Parent: Elrose Heritage Society
PO Box 556, 102 - 4th Ave.,
Elrose, SK S0L 0Z0

Tel: 306-378-2889
elrosemuseum@hotmail.com
www.facebook.com/pages/Elrose-Museum/382380058543349
Furniture, Canadian military uniforms & items, arcaeology
collection of First Nations artifacts & artwork. Open May-Sep
Carolyn Andreas, President

Esterhazy: Esterhazy Community Museum
PO Box 1744,
Esterhazy, SK S0A 0X0

Tel: 306-745-2245; Fax: 306-745-5406
museum.esterhazy@sasktel.net
The Esyerhazy Museum features general antiques, pioneer
artifacts, a firearms collection, local photos and memorabilia, a
country store and a doctor's room. Also includes a room of
painted murals by local artist Jocelyn Duchek, depicting the
development of Esterhazy. A tourist information booth is located
on the site as well. Open May - Oct. or by appointment.

Esterhazy: Kaposvar Historic Site
PO Box 371,
Esterhazy, SK S0A 0X0

Tel: 306-745-2715
1907 church & rectory, artifacts from the early Hungarian
settlement

Estevan: Estevan Art Gallery & Museum
118 - 4th St.,
Estevan, SK S4A 0T4

Tel: 306-634-7644; Fax: 306-634-2490
eagm@sasktel.net
www.estevanartgallery.org/
www.instagram.com/estevanartgallery/
www.facebook.com/EstevanArtGalleryA ndMuseum/
North West Mounted Police Wood End Post Histoical Site serves
to collect, preserve, research, exhibit & interpret objects that
best illustrate the arrival of the NWMP to the Estevan area in
1874. Priority is given to objects associated with the NWMP,
important events, periods, episodes and personalities in Esteven
and surrounding area. Open year-round.
Amber Anderson, Director/Curator, eagm@sasktel.net
Karly Garnier, Educator, galleryed@sasktel.net
Sarah Durham, Curator of Collections, office.eagm@sasktel.net

Eston: Prairie West Historical Centre & Society
PO Box 910, 946 2nd St SE,
Eston, SK S0L 1A0

Tel: 306-962-3772
emljacobson@sasktel.net
Other contact information: Alternate Phones: 206-962-2559;
306-962-4578
Local history museum & art gallery; wildflower garden

Foam Lake: Foam Lake Museum
PO Box 1041, 113 Bray Ave. West,
Foam Lake, SK S0A 1A0

Tel: 306-272-4292
foamlake.com/foam-lake-museum
The museum is housed in an historic brick building c. 1925 and
contains many artifacts relevant to the history of Foam Lake and
surrounding areas. In addition, there is the "Douglas House," a
two-storey home built in 1915 that contains many of its original
features, including an oak staircase and hardwood floors. Fresh
bread baked in a "piche" clay oven during the summer months.
Ruth Gushulak, President, 306-272-3360

Fort Qu'appelle: Fort Qu'Appelle Museum
PO Box 1093, 198 Bay Ave. North,
Fort Qu'appelle, SK S0G 1S0

Tel: 306-332-4503
www.fortquappelle.com/town-office/history
Located beside Qu'Appelle River on the site of the original
trading post and fort. Open June - Aug. Lebret Museum located
at the corner of Pl. de L'Eglise & St. Joseph Ave (306-332-4597).
Open May - Sept.
Lynn Anderson, President

Frenchman Butte: Frenchman Butte Museum
PO Box 114,
Frenchman Butte, SK S0M 0W0

Tel: 306-344-4478
info@frenchmanbuttemuseum.ca
www.frenchmanbuttemuseum.ca
www.facebook.com/frenchmanbuttemuseum
Other contact information: Off season: 306-825-2246
Year Founded: 1979 The Frenchman Butte Museum was
founded in 1979 in an attempt to preserve and pass on the
history of the area, and currently consists of nine restored
buildings situated around their own street in the community. The
museum is based on a collection of guns, arrowheads and other
pioneer artifacts. Open daily July - Sept. and by appointment in
the winter.
Rudy Buchta, Contact, 306-825-2029

Frobisher: Frobisher Threshermen's Museum
PO Box 194, 515 - 5th St.,
Frobisher, SK S0C 0Y0

Displays steam engines, wooden threshing separators, gas &
diesel tractors, ploughshares, household items & photographs.

Glaslyn: Glaslyn & District Museum
PO Box 363,
Glaslyn, SK S0M 0Y0

Tel: 306-342-7993
Museum contains artifacts from the 1800's, housed in a restored
CNR station house circa 1926; CNR water tank & caboose also
on-site; taxidermy articles, including a rare two-headed calf.

Glen Ewen: Glen Ewen Community Antique Centre
Sports Grounds, PO Box 87,
Glen Ewen, SK S0C 1C0

Tel: 306-925-2048
The Centre features a collection of antique cars including a 1910
Ford & a 1937 Packard; also showcases guns, dishes &
household articles from the early 1900s. Open seasonally or by
request.

Glenavon: Glenavon Museum
PO Box 246,
Glenavon, SK S0G 1Y0

Tel: 306-429-2011; Fax: 306-429-2260
www.glenavonsk.ca
Open July & Aug., Tue & Th 1:00-4:00.

Goodsoil: Goodsoil Historical Museum
PO Box 370, 401 Main St.,
Goodsoil, SK S0M 1A0

Tel: 306-238-4565; Fax: 306-238-4991
schamber@sasktel.net
Other contact information: Alt. Phone: 306-238-7776
Year Founded: 1977 Museum housed in a natural stone school
building built in 1945. Contains pioneer items, bank and hospital
displays, a trapper's shack, a school room, the smallest chapel
in Saskatchewan and 1950s and 1960s themed rooms. Erna's
Doll House with over 2200 dolls also located on site. Open June
- Aug.
Alex Schamber, President, 306-238-4565,
schamber@sasktel.net
Rudy Leiter, Secretary

Gravelbourg: Gravelbourg & District Museum
300 Main St.,
Gravelbourg, SK S0H 1X0

Tel: 306-648-2332
louis.stringer@sasktel.net
www.southcentralmuseums.ca/gravelbourg.html
This museum provides a history of the Gravelbourg region &
contains the medical collection from Dr. Antoine Soucy as well
as artwork by Charles Maillard.
Louis Stringer, Chair, Board of Trustees

Grenfell: Grenfell Museum
PO Box 1156, 711 Wolseley Ave.,
Grenfell, SK S0G 2B0

Tel: 306-697-2839
veljon@sasktel.net
Year Founded: 1973 Museum located in a restored 1904 Queen
Anne turreted house that originally belonged to Mr. & Mrs.
Edward Fitz-Gerald, the editor and publisher of Grenfell's first
local newspaper. The museum contains furniture & tools of
bygone days, as well as a military display. Open Jun - Aug, F -
Su and by appointment.

Gull Lake: Gull Lake Museum
3570 Rutland Ave.,
Gull Lake, SK S0N 1A0

Tel: 306-672-4377
gulllakesk.ca/museum.htm

The museum site features artifacts housed in three buildings: a
vintage house, an old country schoolhouse, & a pole structure
with farm-related items.

Hague: Saskatchewan River Valley Museum
PO Box 630, 307 E Railway St.,
Hague, SK S0K 1X0

Tel: 306-225-2112; Fax: 306-225-4642
rivervalleymuseum@sasktel.net
Other contact information: Alternate phone: 306-225-4511
Approx. 6,000 artifacts, including First Nations & Mennonite;
original European house/barn; country school; Mennonite
church; horse-drawn farming machinery, blacksmith tools,
pre-1950 furniture & appliances. Open May-Oct

Harris: Harris Museum
PO Box 131, 204 Railway Ave.,
Harris, SK S0L 1K0

Tel: 306-656-2002
www.saskmuseums.org/museums/detail/harris-museum
www.facebook.com/harris districtmuseum
Other contact information: Alt. Phone 306-656-2172
The volunteer operated Harris Museum features local history &
archives, plus a C.N. Water Tower & a gas engine water pump.
The museum is open from May to Sept., or by appointment.

Hazenmore: Heritage Hazenmore Museum
PO Box 55, 3 E St,
Hazenmore, SK S0N 1C0

Tel: 306-264-5100; Fax: 306-264-3218
Community church & museum.

Hepburn: Hepburn Museum of Wheat
PO Box 69,
Hepburn, SK S0K 1Z0

Tel: 306-947-4351
Other contact information: Alternate Phone: 306-947-2042
Museum collection housed in an original grain elevator. Open
Sat. in the summer.

Herbert: Herbert CPR Train Station Museum
Parent: Herbert Heritage Association
625 Railway Ave.,
Herbert, SK S0H 2A0

Tel: 306-784-3411
www.townofherbert.com/herbert_train_station.html
Year Founded: 1986 The museum's collection is housed in a
restored CPR station circa 1910, with a caboose on-site. Open
June-Sept.
Frances Schwartz, President
Doreen Schroeder, Manager

Herschel: Ancient Echoes Interpretive Centre
PO Box 40,
Herschel, SK S0L 1L0

Tel: 306-377-2045
ancientechoes@sasktel.net
www.ancientechoes.ca
www.facebook.com/herschelancientechoes
Year Founded: 1994 The Centre contains local artifacts,
including petroglyph rock carvings & the remains of a Pleisosaur.

Hodgeville: Country Craft Shoppe & Homestead
Museum
PO Box 264, 102 - 1st St. West,
Hodgeville, SK S0H 2B0

Tel: 306-677-2693; Fax: 306-677-2707
History of Hodgeville & eight rooms depicting an early
homestead; crafts, gifts & tearoom.

Hudson Bay: Al Mazur Memorial Heritage Park
PO Box 37,
Hudson Bay, SK S0E 0Y0

Tel: 306-865-2180
1910heritage@sasktel.net
www.townofhudsonbay.com/default.aspx?page=80
Year Founded: 1984 Local history; artifacts housed in original
buildings; 16-acre museum park; located at the junction of Hwy.
3 & 9; open May-Sept., daily 9:00-5:00

Hudson Bay: Hudson Bay Museum
Parent: Hudson Bay & District Cultural Society
c/o Hudson Bay & District Cultural Society, PO Box 931, 512
Churchill St.,
Hudson Bay, SK S0E 0Y0

Tel: 306-865-2170
hbmuseum@hotmail.com
www.townofhudsonbay.com/default.aspx?page=84
Displays of various rooms that depict life in the 1950s in the
Hudson Bay area; open June Fri-Sat 1:00-5:00; Jul-Aug Tue-Sat
1:00-5:00

Humboldt: Humboldt & District Museum & Gallery
PO Box 2349, 602 Main St.,
Humboldt, SK S0K 2A0

Tel: 306-682-5226; Fax: 306-682-1430
humboldt.museum@sasktel.net
www.youtube.com/channel/UCvmWCuqMil5iut7hA8YJEtQ
twitter.com/Hum_Muse_in gs
www.facebook.com/120057151339718
www.humboldtmuseum.ca
Year Founded: 1982 Focus on the Humboldt Telegraph Station
of 1878, as well as the settlement of Humboldt & district, & the
spiritual influence of St. Peter's Abbey; housed in a 1912 post
office building
Jennifer Hoesgen, Curator

Imperial: Nels Berggren Museum
PO Box 125,
Imperial, SK S0G 2J0

Tel: 306-963-2033
Lamps, clocks, sewing machines, musical instruments, & art.

Indian Head: Bell Barn Society of Indian Head
PO Box 1882,
Indian Head, SK S0G 2K0

Tel: 306-695-2355
bellbarn.ca
Year Founded: 2006 The society helps preserve the Bell Barn, a
125-year-old structure that once belonged to the Qu'Appelle
Valley Farming Company. Open May-Sept., daily 10:00-4:00, or
by appointment.
Kay Dixon, Chair
Jerry Willerth, Barn Boss, 306-695-2086, gdwillerth@sasktel.net
Connie Billett, Secretary, 306-695-3456, cbillett@sasktel.net

Indian Head: Indian Head Museum
PO Box 566, 610 Otterloo St.,
Indian Head, SK S0G 2K0

Tel: 306-695-2234
www.townofindianhead.com/our-history/history-resources.html
www.facebook .com/IndianHeadMuseum
1907 two-storey fire hall displaying artifacts of local pioneer
days; also 1926 one room school, 1883 Bell Farm Cottage;
replica of 1930s one-bay village garage; farm implements

Ituna: Ituna & District Museum
Ituna Branch, Parkland Regional Library, PO Box 730, 518 -
5th Ave. East,
Ituna, SK S0A 1N0

Tel: 306-795-2941; Fax: 306-795-3330
mkspilchuk@sasktel.net
www.saskmuseums.org/museums/detail/ituna-district -museum
Other contact information: Alternate Phones: 306-795-3458;
306-795-2484
Local history including Ukrainian & aboriginal artifacts.

Kamsack: Kamsack & District Museum
PO Box 991, Queen Elizabeth Boul.,
Kamsack, SK S0A 1S0

Tel: 306-542-4415
kphm@gmail.com
Other contact information: Alt. Phone: 306-542-3055
The former Power Building is a Municipal Heritage Property
featuring a one-story industrial building constructed of brick,
which now serves as the museum. Exhibits focus on both First
Nations & European history; featuring one of the original diesel
engines that generated the town's electricity until 1958; rooms
furnished in the style of a typical 1920s pioneer dwelling. Open
May - Sept.; car show & shine mid-June.

Kelliher: Kelliher & District Heritage Museum Inc.
PO Box 111, 116 Centre St.,
Kelliher, SK S0A 1V0

Tel: 306-322-2232
www.saskmuseums.org/museums/detail/rose-valley-district-herit
age-museum-in c
One of the oldest buildings in Kelliher; now contains a collection
of local artifacts; open Sundays; hosts school tours

Kenosee Lake: Cannington Manor Provincial Park
PO Box 220,
Kenosee Lake, SK S0C 2S0

Tel: 306-739-5251; Fax: 306-577-2622
manor.cannington@gov.sk.ca
www.saskparks.net/CanningtonManor
Other contact information: Phone, Off Season: 306-577-2600
Year Founded: 1882 In the late 1800s, partners in the Moose
Mountain Trading Company established the village of
Cannington Manor. Buildings from this village have been
reconstructed or restored for visitors. Buildings at the site include
a Land Titles Office, a bachelor's cabin, a Moose Mountain
Trading Company store, a carpenter's shop, a blacksmith shop,

a flour mill, & the Mitre Hotel. Cannington Manor is open from Victoria Day to Labour Day.

Kerrobert: Kerrobert & District Museum
PO Box 452,
Kerrobert, SK S0L 1R0

Tel: 306-834-5277
Other contact information: Alternate Phone: 306-834-2991
Replica of the first tent store & pioneer furniture.
Darren Obritsch, President, 306-834-2934
Bobbi Hebron, Secretary, 306-834-2409

Kincaid: Kincaid Museum
PO Box 177, 14 Railway Ave. West,
Kincaid, SK

Tel: 306-264-3910; *Fax:* 306-264-3277
villageofkincaid@sasktel.net
Local historical material that celebrates the early people of Saskatchewan.

Kindersley: Kindersley & District Plains Museum
PO Box 599, 903 - 11th Ave. East,
Kindersley, SK S0L 1S0

Tel: 306-463-6620
kindersleymuseum@sasktel.net
www.saskmuseums.org
www.facebook.com/KDPMuseum
Wide collection of early farm machinery & tools, household items, education items & items from school & churches; fire hall & fire truck; military display, a general store, post office & print shop; an archaeological display; open May to Sept.
Bill Warrington, Chairman, Kindersley and District Plains Museum Board
Mark Scholz, President

Kinistino: Kinistino & District Pioneer Museum Inc.
510 Main St.,
Kinistino, SK S0J 1H0

Tel: 306-864-2461
townofkinistino@sasktel.net
www.canspark.ca/kin/kinistino-district-pioneer-museum
Displays of artifacts from fur trade & pioneer times; oldest purely agricultural settlement in Saskatchewan.

Kipling: Kipling & District Historical Society
PO Box 414,
Kipling, SK S0G 2S0

Tel: 306-736-8254

Kisbey: Kisbey Museum
PO Box 117,
Kisbey, SK S0C 1L0

Tel: 306-462-2162
Detailed history & pictures of Kisbey's namesake, R. Claude Kisbey; 1,000+ objects; open Thu. through July & Aug. & by request

Kronau: Kronau Heritage Society
Parent: Kronau Bethlehem Heritage Society Inc.
PO Box 1,
Kronau, SK S0G 2T0

Tel: 306-781-3082; *Fax:* 306-781-2267
4efarms@sasktel.net
www.facebook.com/pages/Kronau-Heritage-Society/24828
8010817
The museum collection is housed in the restored Kronau Lutheran Church building, circa 1912. Open May-Sept., Wed.-Su 10:00-4:00.

Kyle: Kyle & District Museum
PO Box 543,
Kyle, SK S0L 1T0

Tel: 304-375-2525; *Fax:* 206-375-2534
Local history; collection housed in former Tuberose Red Cross outpost hospital; artifacts include World War I & II items, machinery & vehicles, fossils, & items relating to Wooly Mammoth remains found in 1964.
Bill Stepple, Contact, 306-375-2336

Lancer: Lancer Centennial Museum
PO Box 3,
Lancer, SK S0N 1G0

Tel: 306-689-2925
Open June-Sept.

Langenburg: Langenburg Homestead Museum
PO Box 864,
Langenburg, SK S0A 2A0

Tel: 306-743-2432; *Fax:* 306-743-2625
Local history; open June-Aug.
Kay Klopstock, Contact, 306-743-2625

Langham: Langham & District Heritage Village & Museum
PO Box 516, 3rd Ave. Railway St.,
Langham, SK S0K 2L0

Tel: 306-283-4342; *Fax:* 306-283-4772
www.saskmuseums.org/museums/detail/langham-district-heritag
e-village-museu m
www.facebook.com/pg/LanghamAndDistrictHeritageVillageMuse
um
Year Founded: 1993 Preserves & exhibits artifacts illustrating the history & culture of Langham & area; special events & programming. Open May long weekend to Sept. 30, Wed. 9-12 & Sat. 9-3, or by appointment.

Lanigan: Lanigan & District Heritage Centre
PO Box 424, 75 Railway Ave.,
Lanigan, SK S0K 2M0

Tel: 306-365-2569; *Fax:* 306-365-2960
lanigan.dist.heritage@sasktel.net
www.saskmuseums.org/museums/detail/lan
igan-district-heritage-centre
www.facebook.com/Laniganheritagecentre
The Lanigan & District Heritage Association's mission is to preserve the Lanigan CPR Station, where the Centre is currently housed; includes a museum, tourism information, agricultural interpretive display, potash exposition, caboose, recreation & coffee area & storage. Located at 75 Railway Ave., Lanigan. Open June 1 to Labour Day.

Lashburn: Lashburn Centennial Museum
PO Box 275,
Lashburn, SK S0M 1H0

Tel: 306-285-4145
lashburncentennialmuseum@gmail.com
Other contact information: Town Office: 306-285-3533
Vetern's Gallery with artifacts from the Boer War to Korean War; 1908 Gully School; artifacts of the Barr Colony settlers; log cabin & blacksmith shop; open July & Aug.

Leross: Kellross Heritage Museum
PO Box 10, 2nd Ave.,
Leross, SK S0A 1V0

Tel: 306-675-4423
rm247@sasktel.net
This museum preserves the history of the Kellross area. Open from June to Sept. or by appointment. There are four main buildings that comprise this museum. They include a one-room country school house, a school built in 1907, an RM office built in 1910 & the George Volman museum.

Leroy: Leroy & District Heritage Museum
PO Box 47,
Leroy, SK S0K 2P0

Tel: 306-286-3464
Open July & Aug.

Lloydminster: Lloydminster Cultural & Science Centre (LCSC)
4207 - 44th St.,
Lloydminster, SK S9V 0Z8

Tel: 780-874-3720
www.lloydminster.ca/index.aspx?nid=400
instagram.com/yourlcsc
www.facebook.com/LloydCSC
Located at Highway 16 & 45th Avenue, the Barr Colony Heritage Cultural Centre consists of an antique museum, the Imhoff art collection, the OTS Heavy Oil Science Centre, & the Fuchs wildlife exhibit. The Richard Larsen Museum presents antiques of the Barr Colonists. Artifacts include funiture & agricultural equipment. Visitors can also see Lloydminster's first church, a log cabin, a filling station, & a 1906 schoolhouse. The centre is open year-round.

Loon Lake: Steele Narrows Provincial Historic Park
PO Box 39,
Loon Lake, SK S0M 1L0

Tel: 306-837-7410; *Fax:* 306-837-2415
makwalake@gov.sk.ca
www.saskparks.net/SteeleNarrows
The park rests on the site of the last battle of the 1885 North West Rebellion. The battle is depicted on interpretive panels located at the top of a hill overlooking the park. The burial ground containing the remains of the Cree killed in the battle is located across the road.

Lucky Lake: Lucky Lake Museum
PO Box 268,
Lucky Lake, SK S0L 1Z0

Tel: 306-858-2641

Lumsden: Lumsden Heritage Museum
PO Box 91, 50 Qu'Appelle Dr. W,
Lumsden, SK S0G 3C0

Tel: 306-731-2905
The museum consists of five pioneer buildings, a machine shed, a livery stable, & a blacksmith shop. Four of the pioneer buildings contain artifacts depicting the district's early history.

Luseland: Luseland & Districts Museum
PO Box 8,
Luseland, SK S0L 2A0

Tel: 306-372-4258
Other contact information: Alternate Phone: 306-372-4331
Year Founded: 1990 Hours: May - Oct Sa 1:00-4:00 or open upon request

Macklin: Macklin & District Museum
PO Box 444, Herald St.,
Macklin, SK S0L 2C0

Tel: 306-753-9419
pneufarm@hotmail.com
www.saskmuseums.org/museums/detail/macklin-district-museu
m
Year Founded: 1922 Built in 1919 by Frank Shaw, the town's first bank manager, the house later became a hospital during the 1920s. Open Tu, Th & F in the summer.

Macrorie: Macrorie Museum
PO Box 177,
Macrorie, SK S0L 2E0

Tel: 306-243-4327
www.macrorie.com/04-history.html
Other contact information: Alternate Phones: 306-243-4507;
306-243-4207
Consists of 3 sites: an old post office, insurance office, & living quarters which depict the local farming area; an old brick school, heritage site; a caboose & jigger; open Mon. in July & Aug. 2-4, or by appt.

Maidstone: Maidstone & District Historical & Cultural Society Inc.
PO Box 250,
Maidstone, SK S0M 1M0

Tel: 306-893-2890
May - Sept.

Main Centre: Main Centre Heritage Museum
PO Box 105,
Main Centre, SK S0H 2V0

Tel: 306-784-2903
Local history & early pioneering artifacts; school & church history; Herbert Ferry Crossing display; open by appointment year round

Maple Creek: Fort Walsh National Historic Site
PO Box 278,
Maple Creek, SK S0N 1N0

Tel: 306-662-2645; *Fax:* 306-662-2711
fort.walsh@pc.gc.ca
www.pc.gc.ca/eng/lhn-nhs/sk/walsh/index.aspx
Other contact information: TTY: 306-662-3124
NWMP fort & Cypress Hills Massacre site; open mid May - Sept. 1.

Maple Creek: Jasper Cultural & Historical Centre
PO Box 1504, 311 Jasper St.,
Maple Creek, SK S0N 1N0

Tel: 306-662-2434; *Fax:* 306-662-4359
jasper.centre@sasktel.net
www.jaspercentre.ca
www.facebook.com/jasperc ulturalandhistoricalcentre
This centre focuses on the history of the Maple Creek area, particularly the early life & settlement of the region. The centre consists of 13 rooms, each with a distinct theme. Open Mon.-Fri. in winter; daily in summer.
Heather Wickstrom, Manager/Curator, 306-332-2434,
jasper.centre@sasktel.net

Maple Creek: St. Victor Petroglyph Provincial Historic Park
c/o Cypress Hills Interprovincial Park, PO Box 850,
Maple Creek, SK S0N 1N0

Tel: 306-662-5411
CypressHills@gov.sk.ca
stvictor.sasktelwebsite.net
Other contact information: Alt. URL: www.saskparks.net/St.Victor
The St. Victor Petroglyphs are an enduring mystery; their origin & purpose is unknown, yet they provide a clue as to who populated the plains in the era pre-dating written records. The petroglyphs are best viewed in the early morning on a clear day; an interpretive panel & reproduction of a few of the petroglyphs

are provided for visitors at the site, which is located south of St. Victor. Admission is free.

Maple Creek: Southwest Saskatchewan Oldtimers Museum
PO Box 1540, 218 Jasper St.,
Maple Creek, SK S0N 1N0
Tel: 306-662-2474; Fax: 206-662-2711
oldtimers@sasktel.net
Ranching, First Nations, NWMP, firearms; open May 20 to Sept. 30

Maple Creek: Wood Mountain Post Provincial Park
c/o Cypress Hills Interprovincial Park, PO Box 850,
Maple Creek, SK S0N 1N0
Tel: 306-662-5411; Fax: 306-662-5482
cypresshills@gov.sk.ca
www.saskparks.net
The post was an important site for the North-West Mounted Police around the turn of the century, where the local detachment patrolled the Canada-USA border. Visitors to the park will find two reconstructed buildings with displays inside, & staff hosting guided tours. Open June-Aug., daily 10:00-5:00.

Maryfield: Maryfield Museum
PO Box 262,
Maryfield, SK S0G 3K0
Tel: 306-646-2201
Clocks, tools, record players, telephones

McCord: McCord & District Museum
PO Box 82, Main St.,
McCord, SK S0H 2T0
Tel: 306-478-2522
ba.wilson@xplornet.com
www.southcentralmuseums.ca/mccord.html
Other contact information: Alt. Phone: 306-478-2559
Year Founded: 1973 Museum is housed in a 1928 CPR railway station & exibits include historical items from households & businesses in the area. Of note is an actual caboose on tracks beside the museum. A companion museum is the 1913 church at the opposite end of the street which displays religious articles from various churches in the region.

Meadow Lake: Meadow Lake Museum
PO Box 1028,
Meadow Lake, SK S0M 2M0
Tel: 306-234-2455
meadowlakemuseum@outlook.com
meadowlakenow.com/community-group/meadow-lake-and-distric t-museum
www.fa cebook.com/796553457063868
The Meadow Lake Museum features items of interest from local pioneers' lives, and a look at the development of forestry in the area. Tourist Informatio nCentre located on the same site. Open May - Sept.
Cecil Midgett, Contact, 306-234-2455

Melfort: Melfort & District Museum
PO Box 3222, 401 Melfort St. West,
Melfort, SK S0E 1A0
Tel: 306-752-5870; Fax: 306-752-5556
melfort.museum2@sasktel.net
www.melfortmuseum.org
twitter.com/MelfortM useum
www.facebook.com/melfortmuseum/
Year Founded: 1973 Community museum showing casing the history of Melfort and its surrounding area. Includes archives and agricultural machinery displays. Open year-round.
Gailmarie Anderson, Curator, 306-752-5870,
melfort.museum@sasktel.net
Peggy Hause, Assistant Curator, 306-752-5870,
melfort.museum2@sasktel.net

Melville: Melville Heritage Museum Inc.
PO Box 2528, 100 Heritage Dr.,
Melville, SK S0A 2P0
Tel: 306-728-2070; Fax: 306-728-2038
melmus@sasktel.net
Regional museum, located in the former Luther Academy (1913-1926); artifacts & histories of local, provincial & national interest; includes chapel, library, Grand Trunk Pacific/CNR & Military; over 100 original B & W framed photographs depict Melville's first quarter century; gift shop; murals; limited wheelchair access

Melville: Melville Railway Museum
PO Box 2863,
Melville, SK S0A 2P0
Tel: 306-728-3722
Year Founded: 1986 Former CNR steam locomotive #5114; a J-4-5 class 4-6-2 built in 1919; also former Grand Trunk Pacific

station from Duff, Saskatchewan containing artifacts including exhibits of communications equipment, from telegraphs, and telephones. There are also records from the Grand Trunk Railway and CNR, including employee records
Jennifer Mann, Tourism Manager, 306-728-3722, Fax: 306-728-2443, jmann@melville.ca

Midale: Souris Valley Antique Association
PO Box 352,
Midale, SK S0C 1S0
Tel: 306-458-2374
Other contact information: Alternate Phones: 306-458-2409;
306-458-2476
Year Founded: 1966 The association runs a 33-acre Heritage Village consisting of two pioneer houses, a barn, blacksmith shop, church, service station & rural school. Open June-Sept.

Middle Lake: Middle Lake Museum
PO Box 157,
Middle Lake, SK S0K 2X0

Pioneer artifacts

Milden: Milden Community Museum
PO Box 218,
Milden, SK S0L 2L0
Tel: 306-935-4511
A community museum holding local artifacts including those of an old-time school, hospital & bedroom; open July-Aug.

Moose Jaw: 15 Wing Military Aviation Museum
PO Box 5000, 15 Wing Moose Jaw,
Moose Jaw, SK S6H 7Z8
Tel: 306-694-2222; Fax: 306-694-2813
15wingpao@forces.gc.ca
www.cg.cfpsa.com/cg-pc/moosejaw

Moose Jaw: Moose Jaw Museum & Art Gallery
461 Langdon Cres.,
Moose Jaw, SK S6H 0X6
Tel: 306-692-4471; Fax: 306-694-8016
educator.mjmag@sasktel.net
www.mjmag.ca
www.facebook.com/mjmag
Year Founded: 1966 The building houses art, history & science exhibits, with a wide range of human history artifacts with strong representation of First Nations beadwork, women's clothing & clothing-related artifacts from 1880 onward. The Learning Centre offers programs for school children and art classes for all ages. Open year round; admission by donation.
Jennifer McRorie, Curatorial Director,
curator.mjmag@sasktel.net
Joan Maier, Administrative Director,
manager.mjmag@sasktel.net
Christy Schweiger, Education Coordinator,
educator.mjmag@sasktel.net

Moose Jaw: Sukanen Ship Pioneer Village & Museum
PO Box 2071,
Moose Jaw, SK S6H 7T2
Tel: 306-693-7315
office@sukanenshipmuseum.ca
www.sukanenshipmuseum.ca
twitter.com/sukanenship
www.facebook.com/1091 38739128897
The Sukanen Ship Pioneer Village & Museum is dedicated to the preservation, restoration & display of artifacts reflecting the history of Saskatchewan. The site contains the Sukanen Ship, the Diefenbaker Homestead and the Pioneer Village. Open mid-May to mid-Sept.

Moose Jaw: Western Development Museum (WDM) Moose Jaw Branch
50 Diefenbaker Dr.,
Moose Jaw, SK S6J 1L9
Tel: 306-693-5989; Fax: 306-691-0511
moosejaw@wdm.ca
www.wdm.ca/mj.html
www.facebook.com/skwdm
Moose Jaw is one of four exhibit branches of Saskatchewan's Western Development Museum. The other branches are located in North Battleford, Saskatoon, & Yorkton. The Moose Jaw Western Development Museum displays the history of transportation, from the canoe to the railway. The museum also features the Snowbirds Gallery, which presents Canadian military aerobatic flight history.
Katherine Fitton, Manager, kfitton@wdm.ca
David Samson, Museum Technician, dsamson@wdm.ca
James Herrem, Supervisor, Maintenance, jherrem@wdm.ca
Shirley Stenko, Officer, Museum Operations, sstenko@wdm.ca

Moosomin: Jamieson Museum
PO Box 236, 306 Gertie St.,
Moosomin, SK S0G 3N0
Tel: 306-435-3156
Pre-1900 house, church, military collection; open May - Oct.

Moosomin: Moosomin Regional Museum
PO Box 1654,
Moosomin, SK S0G 3N0
Tel: 306-435-7604
Open July & Aug.

Morse: Morse Museum & Cultural Centre
PO Box 308,
Morse, SK S0H 3C0
Tel: 306-629-3230
morsemuseum@sasktel.net
sites.google.com/site/morsemuseum1
www.facebook.com/8511642284
Year Founded: 1980 Former school, built in 1912; open year round.

Mortlach: Mortlach Museum & Drop In Centre
PO Box 163,
Mortlach, SK S0H 3E0
Tel: 306-355-2268
Other contact information: Chair, Phone: 306-355-2214
Located in the town's old fire hall; pioneer & aboriginal artifacts; replica courthouse & jail cell; open year-round, M-F, or by appointment.

Mossbank: Mossbank & District Museum Inc.
PO Box 172, 517 Main St.,
Mossbank, SK S0H 3G0
Tel: 306-354-2811
mossbank.ca/museum
www.facebook.com/MossbankDistrictMusum
A community history museum dedicated to the history of No. 2 Bombing & Gunnery School which was located three miles east of Mossbank during WWII. The site also contains the Ambroz Blacksmith Shop, which is now classified as provincial heritage property.
Roy Tollefson, President
Don Smith, Contact, 306-354-2491

Naicam: Naicam Museum
PO Box 93,
Naicam, SK S0K 2Z0
Tel: 306-874-2280
www.townofnaicam.ca/museum.htm
History & archives of Naicam & District in Heritage building (pioneer school)

Neilburg: Manitou Pioneers Museum
PO Box 336,
Neilburg, SK S0M 2C0
Tel: 306-823-4264
The museum features the largest collection of arrowheads & stone hammers in Saskatchewan, as well as salt & pepper shakers, & lamps. Open July & Aug., or by appointment.

Nipawin: Nipawin & District Living Forestry Museum
PO Box 1917, Old Hwy. 35 W,
Nipawin, SK S0E 1E0
Tel: 306-862-9299
www.nipawin.com/forestrymuseum.php
Situated on 14 acres; open May - Aug.

Nokomis: Nokomis District Museum & Heritage Co-op
PO Box 417,
Nokomis, SK S0G 3R0
Tel: 306-528-2979
Displays & artifacts of early days & local history; open June 1 - Labour Day daily 10-5

North Battleford: Western Development Museum (WDM)
North Battleford Branch
PO Box 183, Hwys 16 & 40,
North Battleford, SK S9A 2Y1
Tel: 306-445-8033; Fax: 306-445-7211
nbattleford@wdm.ca
www.wdm.ca/nb.html
www.facebook.com/skwdm
North Battleford is one of four exhibit branches of Saskatchewan's Western Development Museum. The other branches are located in Moose Jaw, Saskatoon, & Yorkton. The North Battleford Western Development Museum provides visitors with the opportunity to explore a Heritage Farm & Village. Sights include a Wheat Pool grain elevator, a 1910 Case 110 tractor, A Co-op store, homes, & churches. The museum is located at the intersection of Highways 16 & 40.

Joyce Smith, Manager, jsmith@wdm.ca
Cheryl Stewart-Rahm, Coordinator, Programs & Volunteer,
cstewart@wdm.ca
David Gilbert, Museum Technician, dgilbert@wdm.ca

Ogema: Deep South Pioneer Museum (DSPM)
510 Government Rd.,
Ogema, SK S0C 1Y0

Tel: 306-459-7909
deepsouthpioneermuseum@gmail.com
www.deepsouthpioneermuseum.ca
Year Founded: 1977 28 buildings dipicting early pioneer life in
Saskatchewan. Open May-Oct., Sa-Su 1:00-5:00, or by
appointment.

Outlook: Outlook & District Heritage Museum & Gallery
PO Box 1095,
Outlook, SK S0L 2N0

Tel: 306-867-8285
Located in a former railway station, the Outlook & District
Heritage Museum & Gallery is open from June to August.
Exhibits include a caboose & an old jail cell. The Museum also
keeps copies of the local newspaper, entitled "The Outlook",
dating back to 1910.

Oxbow: Ralph Allen Memorial Museum
PO Box 911, 802 Railway Ave.,
Oxbow, SK S0C 2B0

Tel: 306-483-5177
ralphallenmemorialmuseum@outlook.com
www.facebook.com/ RalphAllenMuseumOxbow

Paynton: Bresaylor Heritage Museum
PO Box 33, Main St.,
Paynton, SK S0M 2J0

Tel: 306-895-4813
velmaf@sasktel.net
The Bresaylor Heritage Museum collects artifacts from the
Bresaylor & Paynton area. Items date back to 1882, when the
earliest residents settled in Bresaylor. The museum also holds
the Joe Sayers Collection. The museum is open in July &
August, & at other times of the year by appointment.

Pelly: Fort Pelly-Livingstone Museum
PO Box 217, 1st Ave. South,
Pelly, SK S0A 2Z0

Tel: 306-595-2116; *Fax:* 306-595-4574
pellymuseum@gmail.com
www.pelly.ca/museum.html
Other contact information: Alt. Phone: 306-595-4429
The museum is located in the old high school in the Village of
Pelly and was the first seat of NWT and the NWMP, Fort
Livingstone. The museum features a range of artifacts from the
village's early days as well as scale models of both Fort Pelly
and Fort Linvingstone. Open May - Aug.

Perdue: Perdue Museum
PO Box 243,
Perdue, SK S0K 3C0

Tel: 306-237-9161

Plenty: Plenty & District Museum
PO Box 118,
Plenty, SK S0L 2R0

Tel: 306-377-4727
Other contact information: Alt. Phone: 306-932-4707
Situated in a 1911 building, which once served as Plenty's post
office & hardware store, the Plenty & District Museum depicts
pioneer life in the community & surrounding area. Other displays
include information on military history, area archaeology & sports
history & memorabilia. Farming equipment is featured in a
separate building. Open July & Aug.

Ponteix: Notukeu Heritage Museum
PO Box 603,
Ponteix, SK S0N 1Z0

Tel: 306-625-3340; *Fax:* 306-625-3965
auvergnois@sasktel.net
The museum's collection includes fossils, Paleo-Indian artifacts,
& the collection of amateur archaeologist Henri Liboiron.

Porcupine Plain: Porcupine Plain & District Museum
PO Box 171, 137 Windsor Ave.,
Porcupine Plain, SK S0E 1H0

Tel: 306-278-2317
www.porcupineplain.com
Other contact information: Alternate Phone: 306-278-2073
Year Founded: 1968 The Porcupine Plain & District Museum
features local pioneer artifacts, such as antique machinery &
clothing. The museum also houses a bird displat, with birds from
the Porcupine Plain & Somme area. The soldier settlement
consists of a log home, a schoolhouse, & a church. The

Porcupine Plain & District Museum is open from the beginning of
July to the Labour Day weekend in September. At other times,
tours may be arranged.

Prairie River: Prairie River Museum
PO Box 86,
Prairie River, SK S0E 1J0

Tel: 306-889-4248
prairierivermuseum@yourlink.ca
Railway, agriculture, lumbering, trapping, First Nations artifacts.
Located in an old CN railway station. Open Jan.-Dec., or by
appointment.

Preeceville: Preeceville & District Heritage Museum
PO Box 511,
Preeceville, SK S0A 3B0

Tel: 306-547-2774
www.townofpreeceville.ca/default.aspx?page=52
www.facebook.com/142550417 4354539
Year Founded: 1985 Local history

Prelate: Blumenfeld & District Heritage Site
PO Box 220,
Prelate, SK S0N 2B0

Tel: 306-673-2200; *Fax:* 306-673-2635
The museum's collection includes the history of St. Peter & St.
Paul Blumenfeld Church, as well as other churches in the area,
& artifacts of early pioneers.

Prelate: St. Angela's Museum & Archives
PO Box 220, 201 - 3rd Ave.,
Prelate, SK S0N 2B0

Tel: 306-673-2200; *Fax:* 306-673-2635
stangela.acad01@sk.sympatico.ca
To preserve valuable history of pioneer Saskatchewan & of the
pioneer Ursulines of St. Angela's Convent Academy at Prelate
Saskatchewan; collection tells story of Ursuline life & apostolate
that were used in chapel, classroom & other departments

Prince Albert: Cumberland House Provincial Historic
Park
Prince Albert Park Area, PO Box 3003,
Prince Albert, SK S6V 6G1

Tel: 306-953-3571
cumberlandhousehistpark@gov.sk.ca
Site of the first Hudson's Bay Company post.

Prince Albert: Diefenbaker House Museum
Parent: Prince Albert Historical Society
246 - 19th St. West,
Prince Albert, SK S6V 8A9

Tel: 306-764-2992
historypa@citypa.com
historypa.com/hours_and_dates/the_diefenbaker_house_museu
m.html
Other contact information: Off Season: 306-953-4863
Residence of John G. Diefenbaker prior to becoming Prime
Minister of Canada; museum furnished as it was in Mr.
Diefenbaker's day. Also includes artifacts, documents and
photographic displays of his life & associations in Prince Albert.
Administered by the Prince Albert Historical Society; open daily
May - Sept.
James Benson, Manager

Prince Albert: Evolution of Education Museum
3700 2nd Ave. West & Marquis Rd.,
Prince Albert, SK S0J 3H0

Tel: 306-764-2992
historypa@citypa.com
www.historypa.com
twitter.com/historypa
www.facebook.com/PrinceAlbertH istoricalSociety
Year Founded: 1963 Housed in the original Claytonville
one-room rural school & features a class-room setting, plus
displays of many early educational materials & artifacts.
Administered by the Prince Albert Historical Society.

Prince Albert: Prince Albert Historical Museum
Parent: Prince Albert Historical Society
10 River St. E,
Prince Albert, SK S6V 8A9

Tel: 306-764-2992
historypa@citypa.com
historypa.com/hours_and_dates/the_historical_museum.html
twitter.com/his torypa
www.facebook.com/PrinceAlbertHistoricalSociety
Located in the "Central Fire Hall," a municipal heritage building
built in 1912. The building houses the Society's main office,
archive, volunteer activities area, exhibits and artifact storage.
James Benson, Manager

Prince Albert: Rotary Museum of Police & Corrections
3700 2nd Ave. West & Marquis Rd.,
Prince Albert, SK S6V 8A9

Tel: 306-764-2992
historypa@citypa.com
historypa.com
twitter.com/histo rypa
www.facebook.com/PrinceAlbertHistoricalSociety
Other contact information: alt. phone 306-922-3313
Housed in the guardhouse of the Prince Albert division of the
NorthWest Mounted Police & Royal Northwest Mounted police;
features artifacts, equipment & uniforms from the RCMP, Prince
Albert City Police, the Provincial Correctional Service & the
Correctional Service of Canada, as well as from the
Saskatchewan Provincial Police; administered by the Prince
Albert Historical Society

Prud'homme: Prud'homme Museum
PO Box 38,
Prud'homme, SK S0K 3K0

Tel: 306-654-2001; *Fax:* 306-654-2007
voprud@sasktel.net
www.prudhommevillage.com
Open year-round.

Punnichy: Punnichy & District Museum
PO Box 396,
Punnichy, SK S0A 3C0

Tel: 306-835-2887
Local history; open July & Aug., Tu & Th 2:00-4:00, or by
appointment.

Radville: Radville CN Station/Firefighters Museum
c/o Tourism Radville, PO Box 253,
Radville, SK S0C 2G0

Tel: 306-869-3237
Open by appointment only.

Raymore: Raymore Pioneer Museum Inc.
PO Box 453,
Raymore, SK S0A 3J0

Tel: 306-476-2180
Collection of local pioneer artifacts

Regina: Alex Youck School Museum
1600 - 4th Ave.,
Regina, SK S4R 8C8

Tel: 306-791-8200
Open by appt. only

Regina: Civic Museum of Regina
1375 Broad St.,
Regina, SK S4R 7V1

Tel: 306-780-9435
www.civicmuseumofregina.com
www.facebook.com/CMofRegina/
Year Founded: 1960 Regina Plains Museum is the civic history
museum of the city. It is open year-round.
Shari Sokochoff, Executive Director
Rose Schmidlechner, Administrative Assistant, Communications

Regina: Government House Museum & Heritage
Property (GH)
4607 Dewdney Ave.,
Regina, SK S4T 1B7

Tel: 306-787-5773; *Fax:* 306-787-5714
governmenthouse@gov.sk.ca
www.governmenthouse.gov.sk.ca
twitter.com/Go vt_House
www.facebook.com/governmenthouse
Year Founded: 1980 Former residence of the Lieutenant
Governor of the Northwest Territories & the Province of
Saskatchewan

Regina: RCMP Heritage Centre
5907 Dewdney Ave.,
Regina, SK S4T 0P4

Tel: 306-522-7333; *Fax:* 306-522-7340
Toll-Free: 866-567-7267
info@rcmphc.com
www.rcmpheritagecentre.com
twitter.c om/RCMP_HC
www.facebook.com/RCMPHC
Year Founded: 2007 The complete history of the RCMP is told
through exhibits, multimedia, & programs.
Tracy Fahlman, Chair
Al Nicholson, CEO

Regina: Saskatchewan African Canadian Heritage Museum Inc.
PO Box 1171,
Regina, SK S4P 3B4

Tel: 306-545-8824; *Fax:* 306-543-6181
info@sachm.org
www.sachm.org
SACHM is a virtual museum dedicated to preserving the history of people of African ancestry who lived & currently live in Saskatchewan.
Muna DeCiman, Chair

Regina: Saskatchewan Military Museum
The Armouries, 1600 Elphinstone St.,
Regina, SK S4T 3N1

Tel: 306-347-9349
saskatchewanmilitarymuseum@hotmail.ca
www.saskatchewan militarymuseum.com
pinterest.com/saskmilmuseum
twitter.com/SaskMilMuseum
www.facebook.com/SaskMilitaryMuseum
Collects & preserves Saskatchewan's military history from 1885 to the present; artifacts, uniforms, badges & medals, vehicles, ammunition; photos, archival material & paintings; open M, Th 7:00 - 9:00 or by appointment.
Kristian Peachey, Board President
Maj. (Ret'd) C. Keith Inches, Curator

Regina: Saskatchewan Pharmacy Museum
Parent: Saskatchewan Pharmacy Museum Society
4010 Pasqua St.,
Regina, SK S4S 7B9

Tel: 306-359-7277; *Fax:* 306-352-6770
info@saskatchewanpharmacymuseum.ca
www.saskatchewanpharmacymuseum.ca
t witter.com/skpharmmuseum
www.facebook.com/saskatchewanpharmacymuseum
Collection & preservation of pharmacy artifacts, documentation of pharmacy history.

Regina: Saskatchewan Sports Hall of Fame & Museum
2205 Victoria Ave.,
Regina, SK S4P 0S4

Tel: 306-780-9232
sasksportshalloffame.com
twitter.com/SaskSportsHF
www.facebook.com/SaskSportsHF
Year Founded: 1966 3,000 sq. ft. of exhibit space celebrating the sport heritage of Saskatchewan; open year round with extended summer hours
Sheila Kelly, Executive Director, skelly@sshfm.com

Regina Beach: Lakeside Heritage Museum
PO Box 102,
Regina Beach, SK S0G 4C0

Tel: 306-729-2671
Located beside the Cultural Centre, near South Shore School; open May-Sept., Su.

Regina Beach: Last Mountain House Provincial Historic Park
PO Box 215,
Regina Beach, SK S0G 4C0

Tel: 306-725-5203; *Fax:* 306-725-5207
www.saskparks.net/LastMountainHouse
Other contact information: July & Aug., Phone: 306-731-4409
The Last Mountain House dates from 1869, & was used by the Hudson's Bay Company as a winter outpost for its Fort Qu'Appelle fur trade operation. The museum is a reconstruction, featuring three buildings, a privy, & an ice house. Open July-Sept., Th-Su.
John Currie, Contact, john.currie@gov.sk.ca

Riverhurst: F.T. Hill Museum
PO Box 201, 324 Teck St.,
Riverhurst, SK S0H 3P0

Tel: 306-353-2220
villageofriverhurst@sasktel.net
Year Founded: 1963 Gun collection, aboriginal artifacts, pioneer items; open June 15 - Aug. 31 & by appt.

Rocanville: Rocanville & District Museum
PO Box 490, 220 Qu'Appelle Ave.,
Rocanville, SK S0A 3L0

Tel: 306-645-2113; *Fax:* 306-645-2087
rocanvillemuseum@gmail.com
www.rocanville.ca/museum.php
twitter.com/ro canvillemuse
www.facebook.com/RocanvilleMuseum
The Rocanville & District Museum showcases a CPR station, a church, a schoolhouse, a blacksmith shop, & a Masonic Lodge.

The museum is open during July & August, & by appointment at other times of the year.

La Ronge: Mistasinihk Place Interpretive Centre
c/o Saskatchewan Family Foundation, PO Box 5000, La Ronge Ave.,
La Ronge, SK S0J 1L0

Tel: 306-425-4350
Aboriginal artifacts, artwork by northern artists, displays about northern industries & activites

Rose Valley: Rose Valley & District Heritage Museum
PO Box 123, 115 Centre St.,
Rose Valley, SK S0E 1M0

Tel: 306-322-4642
Museum with artifacts from area 1900 to present; open July & Aug., Mon.-Fri.; off season viewing available by request

Rosetown: Rosetown & District Museum
PO Box 37, 605 Colwell Rd. E,
Rosetown, SK S0L 2V0

Tel: 306-882-2199
rdmuseum@sasktel.net
Natural history specimens, photographs, handicrafts

Rosthern: Mennonite Heritage Museum
PO Box 116,
Rosthern, SK S0K 3R0

Tel: 306-232-4415
Museum housed in school, artifacts from 1800 to present, collection of World Wheat champion; open May to Sept.

St Brieux: Musée St. Brieux Museum
CP 224, 300, ch Barbier,
St Brieux, SK S0K 3V0

Tél: 306-275-2123
Documentation au sujet de la vie des pionniers, de leurs origines, des missions environnantes et de l'église catholique pré-Vatican II; des tournées en français ou en anglais sont offertes

St Victor: Le Beau Village Museum
PO Box 58,
St Victor, SK S0H 3T0

Tel: 306-642-3215; *Fax:* 306-642-3215
Religious & pioneer artifacts; open by appointment only.

St Walburg: St. Walburg & District Historical Museum
PO Box 368,
St Walburg, SK S0M 2T0

Tel: 306-248-3232
Local exhibits from pioneer days to 1945

Saltcoats: Saltcoats Museum
PO Box 309,
Saltcoats, SK S0A 3R0

Tel: 306-744-2977
Local history; open July & Aug., or by appointment.

Saskatoon: Children's Discovery Museum on the Saskatchewan
Market Mall, #116, 2325 Preston Ave.,
Saskatoon, SK S7J 2G2

Tel: 306-683-2555
discovery@museumforkids.sk.ca
www.museumforkids.sk.ca
www.facebook.com/museumforkids.sk.ca
Year Founded: 2009 The museum provides hands-on exhibits & programs to children ten & under, in an effort to promote creativity, curiosity, & a love of learning.
Erica Bird, President

Saskatoon: Diefenbaker Canada Centre
University of Saskatchewan, 101 Diefenbaker Pl.,
Saskatoon, SK S7N 5B8

Tel: 306-966-8384; *Fax:* 306-966-1967
dief.centre@usask.ca
www.usask.ca/diefenbaker
www.instagram.com/diefcentre
twitter.com/diefcentre
www.facebook.com/d iefenbakercentre
Year Founded: 1980 The Diefenbaker Canada Centre includes a museum, archives, & research centre. The centre houses artifacts, such as a personal library, papers, & memorabilia which were bequeathed to the University of Saskatchewan by former prime minister of Canada, John G. Diefenbaker. The archives features collections of press clippings, photographs, & documents related to Diefenbaker's life & Canadian history.
Teresa Carlson, Curator & Collections Manager, 306-966-8383, teresa.carlson@usask.ca
Teresa Ann DeMong, Manager, 306-966-8382, teresa.demong@usask.ca

Saskatoon: Gabriel Dumont Institute of Native Studies & Applied Research (GDI)
The Virtual Museum of Métis History & Culture
c/o Saskatoon Publishing Office, #2, 604 - 22nd St. West,
Saskatoon, SK S7M 5W1

Tel: 306-934-4941; *Fax:* 306-244-0252
general@gdi.gdins.org
www.metismuseum.com
twitter.com/gdins_org
www. facebook.com/gabrieldumontinstitute
Other contact information: Alt. URL: www.gdins.org
Year Founded: 1980 A joint project between GDI & Saskatchewan Department of Learning, the Department of Canadian Heritage's Canadian Culture Online Program, the Canada Council for the Arts, SaskCulture, the Government of Canada, & the University of Saskatchewan Division of Media & Technology; the virtual museum provides users with a comprehensive study of Métis history & culture, including many primary documents such as oral history interviews, photos, & other archival materials.
Darren R. Préfontaine, Project Leader

Saskatoon: Marr Residence
326 - 11th St. East,
Saskatoon, SK S7N 0E7

Tel: 306-652-1201
themarr.ca
Year Founded: 1982 The oldest building in Saskatchewan (built in 1884) that's still on its original site, now designated a heritage site by the City of Saskatoon.

Saskatoon: Meewasin Valley Authority
402 Third Ave. South,
Saskatoon, SK S7K 3G5

Tel: 306-665-6887; *Fax:* 306-665-6117
meewasin@meewasin.com
www.meewasin.com
www.instagram.com/meewasinvalley
twitter.com/meewasin
www.facebook.com /Meewasin
Year Founded: 1979 Conservation agency for the South Saskatchewan River
Colin Tennent, Chair, Meewasin Board of Directors
Andrea Lafond, CEO

Saskatoon: Musée Ukraina Museum Inc. (MUM)
PO Box 26072,
Saskatoon, SK S7K 8C1

Tel: 306-244-4212
ukrainamuseum@sasktel.net
www.mumsaskatoon.com
Year Founded: 1955 The museum's goal is to collect & preserve Ukranian cultural heritage, & make it available to the public.

Saskatoon: Museum of Antiquities
#116, College Bldg., University of Saskatchewan, 107 Administration Pl.,
Saskatoon, SK S7N 5A2

Tel: 306-966-7818; *Fax:* 306-966-1954
museum_antiquities@usask.ca
www.artsandscience.usask.ca/antiquities
www.instagram.com/mofantiquities
twitter.com/MofAntiquities
www.facebook.com/usaskantiquities
Year Founded: 1974 A collection of Eastern, Egyptian, Greek, Roman & Medieval sculpture in full scale replica as well as original works & coinage.
Tracene Harvey, Director & Curator, 306-966-7818, tracene.harvey@usask.ca

Saskatoon: Museum of Natural Sciences
Biology & Geological Sciences
University of Saskatchewan, 112/114 Science Pl.,
Saskatoon, SK S7N 5E2

Tel: 306-966-4399; *Fax:* 306-966-4461
biology.dept@usask.ca
www.artsandscience.usask.ca/museumofnaturalscience s
www.youtube.com/user/artsandscienceUofS
www.facebook.com/Arts.Scienc e.UofS
Designed to show evolution through time beginning with marine invertebrates & ending with evolution of animals; displays of living plants & animals correspond to fossils & create an integrated learning experience; free self-guided tours year-round; brochures downloaded from website
Dr. P. Bonham-Smith, Head, Biology, peta.bonhams@usask.ca
Dr. B. Pratt, Geology, brian.pratt@usask.ca

Saskatoon: Royal Canadian Legion Artifacts Room
The Royal Canadian Legion, Nutana Branch, 3021 Louise St.,
Saskatoon, SK S7J 3L1

Tel: 306-374-6303; Fax: 306-374-3233
nutana.legion@sasktel.net
www.museum.nutanalegion.ca
www.pinterest.com/nutanamuseum
twitter.com/MuseumWar
www.facebook.com/613019275419606
The collection is located in the basement of the Legion building, & features a variety of military memorabilia. Open Th 9:00 AM - 10:30 AM or by appointment
Shirley Timpson, Manager, stimpson@sasktel.net

Saskatoon: Saskatchewan Railway Museum
Parent: Saskatchewan Railroad Historical Association
PO Box 21117,
Saskatoon, SK S7H 5N9

Tel: 306-382-9855
srha@saskrailmuseum.org
www.saskrailmuseum.org
www.facebook.com/SaskatchewanRailwayMuseum
Year Founded: 1990 The museum site features locomotives, cabooses, a sleeping car, & streetcars that visitors can board. Visitors can also ride the museum's "speeder."

Saskatoon: Ukrainian Museum of Canada (UMC)
Parent: Ukrainian Women's Association of Canada
910 Spadina Cres. East,
Saskatoon, SK S7K 3H5

Tel: 306-244-3800; Fax: 306-652-7620
ukrmuse@sasktel.net
www.umc.sk.ca
Year Founded: 1936 The Ukrainian Museum preserves & encourages Ukrainian folk arts in Canada. The permanent gallery tells the story of Ukrainian immigration to Canada with displays of folk arts, including costumes, embroideries, weaving, ceramics, & Easter eggs. The museum's collection of textiles is one of the largest of its kind in North America.
Sonia Korpus, President
Janet C.P. Danyliuk, Director & CEO

Saskatoon: Wanuskewin Heritage Park
Penner Rd., RR#4,
Saskatoon, SK S7K 3J7

Tel: 306-931-6767; Fax: 306-931-4522
www.wanuskewin.com
twitter.com/wanuskewin_park
www.facebook.com/Wanuskewin
The Wanuskewin Heritage Park represents the life of the Northern Plains First Nations people. Visitors will find tipi rings, bison kill sites, a medicine wheel & pottery fragments. The 116 hectare park operates under the leadership & guidance of First Nations people. It is open year-round.

Saskatoon: Western Development Museum (WDM)
Saskatoon Branch
2610 Lorne Ave.,
Saskatoon, SK S7J 0S6

Tel: 306-931-1910; Fax: 306-934-0525
saskatoon@wdm.ca
www.wdm.ca/stoon.html
www.facebook.com/skwdm
Saskatoon is one of four exhibit branches of Saskatchewan's Western Development Museum. The other branches are located in Moose Jaw, North Battleford, & Yorkton. The Saskatoon Western Development Museum presents a 1910 Boomtown. Visitors can explore more than thirty buildings, including a blacksmith shop & a general store. The museum is also home to the Saskatchewan Agricultural Hall of Fame.
Jason Wall, Manager, jwall@wdm.ca
Scott Whiting, Coordinator, Education & Public Programs, swhiting@wdm.ca
Dean Fey, Museum Technician, dfey@wdm.ca

Sceptre: Great Sandhills Museum & Interpretive Centre
Parent: Great Sandhills Historical Society
PO Box 29, Hwy. 32,
Sceptre, SK S0N 2H0

Tel: 306-623-4345; Fax: 306-623-4612
gshs@sasktel.net
www.greatsandhillsmuseum.com
Dedicated to collecting, displaying & preserving the heritage of the "Great Sandhills" District in SW Saskatchewan through natural history specimens.

Scout Lake: St. Mary's Historical Society of Maxstone
PO Box 33, 15km South of Assiniboia,
Scout Lake, SK S0H 3V0

Tel: 306-642-4079
louis.stringer@sasktel.net
www.southcentralmuseums.ca/maxstone.html
Other contact information: Alternate Phone: 306-642-3150
Heritage site includes old church (1917) & graveyard, old school; open year round, by appt. only

Semans: Semans & District Museum
PO Box 205,
Semans, SK S0A 3S0

Tel: 306-524-2020
Year Founded: 1983 The museum is housed in an old school-turned-Oddfellows Hall. The collection contains artifacts & archives on local history. The museum is located on the corner of Main Street & 4th Ave.; open June-Sept.

Shaunavon: Grand Coteau Heritage & Cultural Centre
PO Box 966, 440 Centre St.,
Shaunavon, SK S0N 2M0

Tel: 306-297-3882; Fax: 306-297-3668
gchcc@sasktel.net
www.shaunavon.com
Natural history museum, heritage museum, art gallery, public library; open year-round
Wendy Thienes, Director
Kelly Attrell, Collections Manager

Shell Lake: Shell Lake Museum
PO Box 280,
Shell Lake, SK S0J 2G0

Tel: 306-427-2275
village.sl@sasktel.net
www.tourismsaskatchewan.com/listings/789/shell-lake-museum
The Shell Lake Museum is located in the historic station house & contains relics from 1900-1950. The site also features a log house. It is open on weekends during the summer.

Shellbrook: Shellbrook & Districts Museum
PO Box 40,
Shellbrook, SK S0J 2E0

Tel: 306-747-4949; Fax: 306-747-3111
Open year-round.

Spalding: Reynold Rapp Museum
PO Box 308,
Spalding, SK S0K 4C0

Tel: 306-872-2276
www.facebook.com/spaldingmuseum
Year Founded: 1972 Housed in Reynold Rapp M.P.'s family home

Spiritwood: Spiritwood & District Museum
PO Box 34,
Spiritwood, SK S0J 2M0

Tel: 306-883-2828
townofspiritwood.ca/museum
www.facebook.com/SpiritwoodAndDistrictMuseum
Local history, with an emphasis on agriculture & vintage machinery & vehicles. Open year-round by appointment.
Auralia Wasden, Contact, awasden@sasktel.net
Geraldine Lavoie, Contact, 306-883-8891,
geraldinemarie65@hotmail.com

Spy Hill: Spy Hill Museum
PO Box 268,
Spy Hill, SK S0A 3W0

Tel: 306-534-4462; Fax: 306-534-2227
Year Founded: 1954 The museum has three buildings depicting the history of Spy Hill, from prehistoric days to the present. Open July & Aug., M, Tu, Th-Su 2:00-4:00.

Spy Hill: Wolverine Hobby & Historical Society Inc.
PO Box 191,
Spy Hill, SK S0A 3W0

Tel: 306-534-2200
Three buildings, former country school, former retail outlet & Lutheran church; touring/visiting on request

Star City: Star City Heritage Museum
PO Box 38, 217 - 5th St.,
Star City, SK S0E 1P0

Tel: 306-863-2282
lcronk@sasktel.net
www.saskmuseums.org/museums/detail/star-city-heritage-museum
Year Founded: 1970 Star City's Heritage Museum presents World War I & World War II memorabilia, personal & household items, & farm equipment. The museum is open from June to August & by appointment during the off season.

Stoughton: Stoughton & District Museum
PO Box 492, 327 Main St.,
Stoughton, SK S0G 4T0

Tel: 306-457-2413
stoughtontown@sasktel.net
Pioneer items; open July to Sept.

Strasbourg: Strasbourg & District Museum
PO Box 369,
Strasbourg, SK S0G 4V0

Tel: 306-725-3443
townofstrasbourg.ca/museum
www.facebook.com/StrasbourgAndDistrictMuseum
Year Founded: 1971 Pioneer & First Nations artifacts, mounted animals & birds.
Ingrid Youck, Curator

Sturgis: Sturgis Station House Museum
PO Box 255, 306 Railway Ave. SE,
Sturgis, SK S0A 4A0

Tel: 306-548-5565; Fax: 306-548-2948
sturgismuseumsk@sasktel.net
www.saskmuseums.org/museums/detail/sturgis-station-house-museum
www.facebook.com/SturgisStationhouseMuseum
Aboriginal & early settlers artifacts; open May-Aug.

Swift Current: Doc's Town Heritage Village
Parent: Swift Current Agricultural & Exhibition Association
Kinetic Exhibition Park, PO Box 146, 1700 17th Ave. SE,
Swift Current, SK S9H 3V5

Tel: 306-773-2944; Fax: 306-773-7015
kineticpark@swiftcurrent.ca
www.swiftcurrentex.com
twitter.com/SCAGEX
www.facebook.com/DocsTownHeritageVillage
A reconstructed town depicting Saskatchewan life in the early 1900s.

Swift Current: Swift Current Museum
44 Robert St. West,
Swift Current, SK S9H 4M9

Tel: 306-778-2775; Fax: 306-778-4818
www.swiftcurrent.ca
www.facebook.com/SwiftCurrentMuseum
Year Founded: 1949 The museum hosts a featured exhibit on how human activities impact the environment, as well as temporary exhibits throughout the year. The museum also houses the Swift Current & district archives. Open year-round, M-F, 8:00-5:00.
Lloyd Begley, Contact, l.begley@swiftcurrent.ca

Tisdale: Tisdale & District Museum
PO Box 1528,
Tisdale, SK S0E 1T0

Tel: 306-873-4999
tmuseum@hotmail.com
www.facebook.com/TisdaleAndDistrictMuseum
Year Founded: 1986 The museum features vintage cars, the history of Tisdale bee farming, & artifacts from a historic shoot-out between the Provincial Police & four Russian Bolsheviks. Open May-Sept., 9:00-6:00.

Turtleford: Turtleford & District Museum
PO Box 43,
Turtleford, SK S0M 2Y0

Tel: 306-845-2433
dmbleakney@littleloon.ca
townofturtleford.ca
Local history, science & technology; located in Lions Park, south of Turtleford; open May-Sept daily.

Unity: Unity & District Heritage Museum
Unity Regional Park, PO Box 852,
Unity, SK S0K 4L0

Tel: 306-228-4464; Fax: 306-228-2149
unitymuseum@outlook.com
unitymuseum.wixsite.com/unitysk
The Unity & District Heritage Museum has 30 buildings and momuments, including a 1909 CP Rail Station, the 1908 St. Thomas Anglican Church, the 1926 St. Swarthmore United Church, restored schools, an original home of Unity, a blacksmith shop & a harness shop. The museum is open from mid-May to October.

Vanguard: Vanguard Centennial Museum
PO Box 208, Hwy 43, Dominion St. South,
Vanguard, SK S0N 2V0

Tel: 306-582-2244; Fax: 306-582-2010
vanguardmuseum@sasktel.net

This museum celebrates the history of the early settlers of Vanguard.

Verigin: National Doukhobor Heritage Village (NDHV)
PO Box 99,
Verigin, SK S0A 4H0

Tel: 306-542-4441
ndhv@yourlink.ca
www.ndhv.ca

Year Founded: 1980 The Village is a National & Provincial Historical Site, depicting the life of the Russian Doukhobor people who immigrated to Canada in the late 1800s. The Village features 12 buildings, a gift shop, & an on-site picnic area. Open May-Sept., daily 10:00-6:00.

Verwood: Verwood Community Museum
PO Box 213,
Verwood, SK S0H 4G0

Tel: 306-642-5767
Pioneer articles housed in former church built in 1916

Wadena: Wadena & District Museum & Nature Centre
302 Main St. South,
Wadena, SK S0A 4J0

Tel: 306-338-3454; Fax: 306-338-3804
wadena.museum@sasktel.net
www.townofwadena.com/242/Museum
www.facebook.com/pages/Wadena-Museum
Year Founded: 1985 Relics & artifacts of early settlers from Wadena; 1904 CNR station house; 1907 rural school; open June - Aug., Tue.-Sun.
Amber Mayer, Curator

Wakaw: Wakaw Heritage Society Museum
PO Box 520, 315 - 1 St. S,
Wakaw, SK S0K 4P0

Tel: 306-233-4296
Year Founded: 1983 Collections associated with pioneer life, Replica of the former prime minister's law office, located in Wakaw from 1918-1925
Isabelle McCulloch, Chair, 306-233-4843

Waskesiu Lake: Waskesiu Heritage Museum
928 Waskesiu Dr.,
Waskesiu Lake, SK S0J 2Y0

waskesiuheritagemuseum@hotmail.com
waskesiuheritagemuseum.org
Year Founded: 2005 Located in Prince Albert National Park, in the Friends of the Park Bookstore; open May & June, Sa-Su 10:00-6:00, July & Aug., daily, 10:00-6:00.

Watson: Watson & District Heritage Museum
PO Box 736,
Watson, SK S0K 4V0

Tel: 306-287-3783
The museum is housed in a National Heritage Site building, originally belonging to the Canadian Bank of Commerce, circa 1907. 2,000 artifacts are on display, including farm machinery, tools, ladies' fashion, & sports memorabilia. Open June-Aug., Tu-Sa 10:00-5:00.

Wawota: Wawota & District Museum
PO Box 179, 101 Main St.,
Wawota, SK S0G 5A0

Tel: 306-739-2110
wawota.com/live-and-work/wawota-district-museum/
Year Founded: 1980 The Wawota & District Museum consists of four buildings: a 4-room pioneer home, a trapper's cabin, a schoolhouse and the town's first firehall. The museum also features early movie theatre equipment from the Royal Theatre, which once operated in town. High Tea is served every Friday afternoon in July & August. Open during July & August, & by appointment at other times.

Weyburn: Soo Line Historical Museum
PO Box 1016, 411 Industrial Lane,
Weyburn, SK S4H 2L2

Tel: 306-842-2922
slhm@sasktel.net
www.southcentralmuseums.ca/sooline.html
www.facebook.com/118758801502753
Year Founded: 1960 The Soo Line Historical Museum houses many displays consisting of artifacts used by Weyburn and area pioneers. Features: the largest private collection of silver in the world; the Saskatchewan Mental Hospital, Weyburn memorabilia and the Weyburn & District Archives.
Jacquie Mallory, Curator

Weyburn: Turner Curling Museum
PO Box 370, 327 Mergens St. NW,
Weyburn, SK S4H 2K6

Tel: 306-848-3218
www.weyburn.ca
The museum was established by the late Don Turner & his wife Elva Turner; collection includes curling stones, brooms, clothing, pins, crests & books from around the world; tours available; open by appointment.

Weyburn: Weyburn & Area Heritage Village
PO Box 370,
Weyburn, SK S4H 2K6

Tel: 306-842-6377
www.weyburn.net/attractions.html
Reproduction of a village community from the early 1900s; open May-Aug., daily 1:00-8:00.

White Fox: White Fox Museum
PO Box 399,
White Fox, SK S0J 3B0

Trapper's cabin, tool & harness shop, pioneer items; open June-Sept.

Whitewood: Whitewood Historical Museum
PO Box 752, 603 North Railway,
Whitewood, SK S0G 5C0

Tel: 306-735-2380
Other contact information: Alternate Phone: 306-735-2210
The museum consists of 5 buildings, including a pioneer school room & home, military display, Hungarian, French, Finnish & Swedish collections; open July - Aug.

Wilcox: Athol Murray College of Notre Dame Archives & Museum
Archives & Museum
PO Box 100, 49 Main St.,
Wilcox, SK S0G 5E0

Tel: 306-732-1275
g.scheibel@notredame.ca
www.notredame.ca/page/about/archives-museum
The Athol Murray College of Notre Dame Archives & Museum collects & preserves items that tell the story of Père Athol Murray & the history of the Athol Murray College of Notre Dame. The archives & museum features Père Athol Murray's collection of Rare Books, the Rex Beach Repository, the Parthenon Frieze, the Nicholas de Grandmaison Art Portrait collection, sculptures, & stained glass windows.
Gerry Scheibel, Archivist

Wilkie: Wilkie & District Museum
PO Box 868, 209 - 1 St. E,
Wilkie, SK S0K 4W0

Tel: 306-843-2717
wilkiemuseum@gmail.com
Open summer; by appt. the rest of the year

Willow Bunch: McGillis House
16 Edouard Beaupré St.,
Willow Bunch, SK S0H 4K0

Tel: 306-473-2450; Fax: 306-473-2312
www.willowbunch.ca/visiting/attractions.html
Located in St. Victor's regional park, McGillis House was built in 1890. Artifacts in the home include Métis items, kerosene lanterns, early saddles & bridles, & a feathered buffalo skull. The House is located 18km from Williow Bunch.

Willow Bunch: Willow Bunch Museum
Parent: Willow Bunch Museum & Heritage Society
PO Box 157, 16 Édouard Beaupré St.,
Willow Bunch, SK S0H 4K0

Tel: 306-473-2806
wbmuseum@sasktel.net
www.willowbunch.ca/museum
Other contact information: Alt Phone: 306-640-7785;
306-640-8150
Year Founded: 1972 The Willow Bunch Museum is located in a Convent school which was built in 1914 by the Sisters of the Cross. One attraction is the display about Edouard Beaupré, an eight foot, three inch tall circus performer who was born in Willow Bunch in 1881. The museum is open from mid-May to mid-September. Tours may be arranged during the off-season.
Doris O'Reilly, Director

Wolseley: Wolseley & District Museum
PO Box 218,
Wolseley, SK S0G 5H0

Tel: 306-698-2360
Local history of the Wolseley including decorative arts, furnishings, household objects, & maps.

Wood Mountain: Wood Mountain Rodeo Ranch Museum
PO Box 53,
Wood Mountain, SK S0H 4L0

Tel: 306-266-4953
www.woodmountain.ca/RodRanc.html
Other contact information: Phone, Tour Bookings: 306-266-2000
Located in the Wood Mountain Regional Park, Wood Mountain Rodeo Ranch Museum offers a glimpse into the life of ranchers & cowboys who arrived in the area in the 1880s. Exhibits include the history of the Wood Mountain Stampede, which is the oldest continuous rodeo in Canada. An extensive archival collection is also housed at the museum. Open May - Sept.
Lois Todd, Museum Contact

Wynyard: Frank Cameron Museum
PO Box 734,
Wynyard, SK S0A 4T0

Tel: 306-554-3661
recreation.wynyard@sasktel.net
Local history; houses in a country schoolhouse; open May-Aug.

Wynyard: Wynyard & District Museum
Parent: Wynyard & District Museum Society
c/o Town of Wynyard, PO Box 220,
Wynyard, SK S0A 4T0

Tel: 306-554-2123; Fax: 306-554-3224
www.facebook.com/875423055807635
CPR hand car, household accesories, farm implements, WWI materials

Yorkton: Western Development Museum (WDM)
Yorkton Branch
PO Box 98, Hwy. 16 A West,
Yorkton, SK S3N 2V6

Tel: 306-783-8361; Fax: 306-782-1027
yorkton@wdm.ca
www.wdm.ca/yk.html
www.facebook.com/skwdm
Yorkton is one of four exhibit branches of Saskatchewan's Western Development Museum. The other branches are located in Moose Jaw, North Battleford, & Saskatoon. The Yorkton Western Development Museum presents the times when immigrants settled in western Canada, including the English, Ukrainians, Doukhobors, Germans, Swedes, & Icelanders.
Susan Mandziuk, Manager, smandziuk@wdm.ca
Carla Madsen, Coordinator, Education & Public Programs, cmadsen@wdm.ca

Yukon Territory

Territorial Museums

MacBride Museum of Yukon History
1124 Front St.,
Whitehorse, YT Y1A 1A4

Tel: 867-667-2709
frontdesk@macbridemuseum.com
www.macbridemuseum.com
www.instagram.com/macbride_museum
twitter.com/MacBrideMuseum
www.faceb ook.com/MacBrideMuseum
Year Founded: 1952 The Yukon Historical Society acquired the unoccupied Government Telegraph Office built in 1900, & in the 1960s opened it to the public as a museum to house the growing collection of cultural & natural history: Yukon heritage from pre-history to present. Exhibits include archeological & paleontological specimens; ethnographic artifacts, historic artifacts, photographs & archival materials; large industrial & transportation artifacts. There are also outdoor displays & two heritage buildings.
Erik Nielsen, Chair
Jo-Ann Waugh, Vice-Chair
Patricia Cunning, Executive Director, pcunning@macbridemuseum.com

Local Museums

Burwash Landing: Kluane Museum of Natural History
PO Box 45,
Burwash Landing, YT Y0B 1V0

Tel: 867-841-5561; Fax: 867-841-5605
kluanemus@yknet.ca
kluanemuseum.ca
Wildlife displays, native clothing, tools & handicrafts. Open May-Sep daily

Carmacks: Tagé Cho Hudän Interpretive Centre
PO Box 135, Klondike Hwy.,
Carmacks, YT Y0B 1C0

Tel: 867-863-5831; *Fax:* 867-863-5710
tagechohudan@northwestel.net
www.yukonmuseums.ca/cultural/tagecho/tagech o.html
Other contact information: Alternate Fax: 867-863-5831
The centre's collection includes traditional boats, stone & bone tools, & traditional clothing. Visitors can also explore the outside area, which features a walking trail & a mammoth snare diorama. Open May-Sept., daily 9:00-6:00; off-season by appointment.

Dawson: Dänojà Zho Cultural Centre
PO Box 599, 1131 Front St.,
Dawson, YT Y0B 1G0

Tel: 867-993-7100
cultural.centre@trondek.ca
www.trondekheritage.com/danoja-zho
twitter.com/ShadhalaAsheyi
www.face book.com/DanojaZhoCulturalCentre
The centre presents Tr'ondëk Hwëch'in heritage through galleries, exhibits, & walking tours. Operated by the Tr'ondëk Hwëch'in First Nation Heritage Department.
Steve Smith, Chief, Champagne and Aishihik First Nations, 867-634-4200, ssmith@cafn.ca
Fran Asp, Executive Director, Champagne and Aishihik First Nations, 867-456-6880, fasp@cafn.ca
Rob Fendrick, Chief Financial Officer, Champagne and Aishihik First Nations, 867-456-6879, rfendrick@cafn.ca

Dawson City: Dawson City Museum
PO Box 303, 959 - 5th Ave.,
Dawson City, YT Y0B 1G0

Tel: 867-993-5291; *Fax:* 867-993-5839
info@dawsonmuseum.ca
www.dawsonmuseum.ca
twitter.com/dcmuseum
www.fa cebook.com/DawsonCityMuseum
Year Founded: 1959 Three main galleries include objects & photographs which tell the story of the Klondike era through the Gold Rush; native history.
Alex Somerville, Executive Director, asomerville@dawsonmuseum.ca

Dawson City: Klondike Institute of Art & Culture (KIAC)
Odd Fellows Hall, PO Box 8000, 902 Second Ave.,
Dawson City, YT Y0B 1G0

Tel: 867-993-5005; *Fax:* 867-993-5838
kiac@kiac.ca
kiac.ca
twitter.com/kiactweets
www.facebook.com/7329752 7596
Operated by the Dawson City Arts Society, the KIAC hosts arts & culture-related courses, presentations, festivals & exhibitions.
Karen DuBois, Executive Director, kdubois@kiac.ca
Tara Rudnickas, Gallery Director, Gallery/Residence, gallery@kiac.ca
Dan Sokolowski, Arts Residence Coordinator, Dawson City International Short Film Festival, filmfest@kiac.ca

Dawson City: Klondike National Historic Sites
PO Box 390,
Dawson City, YT Y0B 1G0

Tel: 867-993-7200; *Fax:* 867-993-7203
dawson.info@pc.gc.ca
www.pc.gc.ca/en/lhn-nhs/yt/klondike/decouvrir-disco ver/dawson
Historic buildings; artifacts; documents; related to Klondike history, Yukon Consolidated Gold Corp. & the Dawson Daily News

Faro: Campbell Regional Interpretive Centre
PO Box 580,
Faro, YT Y0B 1K0

Tel: 867-994-2728
admin-faro@faroyukon.ca
www.yukonmuseums.ca/interp/campbell/campbell.html
The centre is housed in a log building & offers visitors information on the area's tourist destinations, hiking trails & heritage sites. The centre also features displays on the area's history, geology & wildlife. Hours of Operation: May, daily 9:00-5:00; June-Aug., daily 8:00-6:00; Sept., daily 9:00-5:00.

Haines Junction: Kluane National Park
PO Box 5495, 119 Logan Pl.,
Haines Junction, YT Y0B 1L0

Tel: 867-634-7207; *Fax:* 867-634-7208
kluane.info@pc.gc.ca
www.pc.gc.ca/kluane
Other contact information: Administration Phone: 867-634-7250;
Conservation Phone: 867-634-7279

Natural & cultural history of Kluane National Park & Reserve of Canada. Rafting, fishing, biking, hiking & other activities available.

Keno City: Keno City Mining Museum
PO Box 17, Main St.,
Keno City, YT Y0B 1M0

Tel: 867-995-3103; *Fax:* 867-995-3103
kenomuseum@northwestel.net
www.yukonmuseums.ca/museum/keno/keno.html
History of mining of gold & silver in the early 1900s. Features tools, equipment, photographs & other artifacts. Open May-Sept daily 10:00-6:00

Mayo: Binet House
PO Box 160,
Mayo, YT Y0B 1M0

Tel: 867-996-2926; *Fax:* 867-996-2907
mayo@northwestel.net
www.yukonmuseums.ca/interp/binet/binet.html
Other contact information: Off-Season Phone: 867-996-2317
A restored heritage building with displays on area history, early medical equipment, wildlife, & geology; open May-Sept.

Old Crow: John Tizya Centre
PO Box 94,
Old Crow, YT Y0B 1N0

Tel: 867-667-3910
vuntut.info@pc.gc.ca
www.pc.gc.ca/en/pn-np/yt/vuntut
Situated in the only Yukon community north of the Arctic Circle, the centre presents Vuntut Gwitchin's culture, oral history, & surrounding landscape. Open year-round, weekdays 9:00-12:00, 1:00-4:30.

Teslin: George Johnston Tlingit Indian Museum
PO Box 146, Km 1294 Mile 804, Alaska Hwy,
Teslin, YT Y0A 1B0

Tel: 867-390-2550; *Fax:* 867-390-8810
manager.teslinhms@gmail.com
www.gjmuseum.yk.net
Exhibits & artifacts honoring the life of George Johnston, the Inland Tlingit & Teslin Lake residents. Includes theatre, gift shop & summer programs. Open Jun-Aug

Teslin: Teslin Tlingit Heritage Centre
PO Box 133,
Teslin, YT Y0A 1B0

Tel: 867-390-2532
admin@ttc-teslin.com
www.ttc-teslin.com/heritage-centre.html
www.facebook.com/teslintlingitco uncil
Visitors to the centre can explore the Tlingit people's day-to-day life; the centre's collection includes traditional masks & artifacts. Open June-Sept., daily 9:00-5:00; off-season by appointment.

Whitehorse: Copperbelt Railway & Mining Museum
Parent: Miles Canyon Historic Railway Society
c/o Miles Canyon Historic Railway Society, 1127 First Ave.,
Whitehorse, YT Y1A 0G5

Tel: 867-667-6355
copperbelt@yukonrails.com
www.yukonrails.com/museum
twitter.com/MCHRSYukon
www.facebook.com/MCHR SYukon
The museum site features a working railway, station museum, & picnic area; open May-Sept.

Whitehorse: Fort Selkirk
c/o Tourism & Culture, Cultural Services Branch, PO Box 2703,
Whitehorse, YT Y1A 2C6

Tel: 867-667-5386; *Fax:* 867-667-8023
museevirtuel-virtualmuseum.ca/sgc-cms/expositions-exhibitions/f ort_selkirk
Living cultural heritage site. Depicts the history of trade & settlement in the north. Open May-Sept

Whitehorse: Kwanlin Dün Cultural Centre
1171 Front St.,
Whitehorse, YT Y1A 0G9

Tel: 867-456-5322
info@kdcc.ca
www.kwanlinduncult(uralcentre.com
twitter.com/KDCulture
www.facebook.co m/KwanlinDunCulturalCentre
The centre seeks to benefit the Kwanlin Dün people by reviving & preserving their culture, heritage, & way of life. Visitors can experience Kwanlin Dün culture through programs, exhibits, & events. Open June-Sept., M-F 9:00-5:00, Sa-Su 10:00-4:00.
Heather McIntyre, Executive Director, heather@kdcc.ca

Whitehorse: Old Log Church Museum
PO Box 31461, 3rd Ave. & Elliot St.,
Whitehorse, YT Y1A 6K8

Tel: 867-668-2555; *Fax:* 867-667-6258
logchurch@klondiker.com
www.oldlogchurchmuseum.ca
twitter.com/oldlogch urch
www.facebook.com/oldlogchurchmuseum
Year Founded: 1962 Early pioneers & missionaries & the history of the church. Open Mon-Sat 10:00-5:00, Sun 12:00-4:00

Whitehorse: Yukon Beringia Interpretive Centre
PO Box 2703,
Whitehorse, YT Y1A 2C6

Tel: 867-667-8855; *Fax:* 867-667-8854
beringia@gov.yk.ca
www.beringia.com
www.facebook.com/126598970843
Beringia was an ancient place, situated between two continents on the edge of the Arctic. The land connection between Siberia & Alaska was part of the larger area known as Beringia. The land of ice was home to huge mammals, such as woolly mammoths & scimitar cats, & the first people of North America. The Yukon Beringia Interpretive Centre is open from May to September. During the winter, it is open on Sundays, or by appointment.

Whitehorse: Yukon Historical & Museums Association
Donnenworth House, 3126 - 3rd Ave.,
Whitehorse, YT Y1A 1E7

Tel: 867-667-4704; *Fax:* 867-667-4506
info@heritageyukon.ca
www.yukonmuseums.ca/interp/yhma/yhma.html
twitte r.com/Yukonheritage
www.facebook.com/Yukonheritage
The Association offers visitors a 45-minute walking tour of Whitehorse's heritage sites. Donnenworth House features a photographic display depicting various heritage sites around the Yukon. The website offers downloadable audio walking tours.
Sally Robinson, President, Yukon Historical & Museums Association
Katie Newman, Vice-President, Yukon Historical & Museums Association
Lianne Maitland, Executive Director, Yukon Historical & Museums Association

Whitehorse: Yukon Transportation Museum
30 Electra Cres.,
Whitehorse, YT Y1A 6E6

Tel: 867-668-4792; *Fax:* 867-633-5547
info@goytim.ca
goytm.ca
instagram.com/go_ytm
twitter.com/go_ytm
www.facebook.com/YukonTransportationMuseum
Year Founded: 1995 Transportation displays depicting the first commercial aircraft in the Yukon, construction of the Alaska Highway, the White Pass & Yukon Route Railway. Open year round
Hugh Kitchen, President
Casey Mclaughlin, Executive Director

National Parks & Outdoor Education Centres

Alberta

Banff: Banff National Park
Banff, AB T1L 1K2

Tel: 403-762-1550
pc.banff-vrc.pc@canada.ca
banffnationalpark.com
twitter.com/banffnp
www.facebook.com/BanffNP
Other contact information:
www.pc.gc.ca/eng/pn-np/ab/banff/index.aspx
Year Founded: 1885 Banff National Park was Canada's first national park. It spans 6,641 square kilometres (2,564 square miles) of valleys, mountains, glaciers, forests, meadows, & rivers. Banff Visitor Centre: June - Sept, 9:00-7:00, Oct - May, 9:00 - 5:00

Fort Saskatchewan: Elk Island National Park
1 - 54401 Range Road 203,
Fort Saskatchewan, AB T8L 0V3

Tel: 780-922-5790; *Fax:* 780-992-2951
Toll-Free: 888-773-8888
pc.pnelkisland-elkislandnp.pc@canada.ca
www.pc.gc.ca/p n-np/ab/elkisland
Year Founded: 1913 Elk Island National Park of Canada protects the aspen parkland, which is one of the most endangered

habitats in Canada. The park is home to herds of plains bison, wood bison, moose, deer, & elk. The park is also home to over 250 species of birds. Hours: Campground Reservations; Administration Building open year round, 8:00-4:00; Park open daily

Jasper: Jasper National Park of Canada
PO Box 10,
Jasper, AB T0E 1E0
Tel: 780-852-6176
pc.jasperinfo.pc@canada.ca
www.pc.gc.ca/en/pn-np/ab/jasper
www.youtube.com/ParksCanadaAgency
twitter.com/JasperNP
www.facebook.co m/JasperNP
Year Founded: 1907 Jasper is the largest & most northerly Canadian rocky mountain national park; part of a World Heritage Site. The park is comprised of carefully protected ecosystems, & includes destinations such as Sunwapta Falls, Mount Edith Cavell, Athabasca Glacier, Miette Hotsprings, & 1,000-plus kilometres of trails.

Waterton Park: Waterton Lakes National Park of Canada
PO Box 200,
Waterton Park, AB T0K 2M0
Tel: 403-859-5133; *Fax:* 403-859-5152
pc.watertoninfo.pc@canada.ca
www.pc.gc.ca/eng/pn-np/ab/waterton/index.as px
twitter.com/watertonlakesnp
www.facebook.com/WatertonLakesNP
Year Founded: 1895 Waterton Lakes National Park helps protect the unique physical, biological & cultural resources found in one of the narrowest places in the Rocky Mountains. Upper Waterton Lake is the deepest lake in the Canadian Rockies. In 1932, the park was joined with Montana's Glacier National Park to form the Waterton-Glacier International Peace Park. Campsites & Parkways May-Sept. Park open year round

British Columbia

Field: Yoho National Park of Canada
Visitor Centre, Trans-Canada Hwy,
Field, BC V0A 1G0
Tel: 250-343-6783*Toll-Free:* 888-773-8888
pc.yohoinfo-infoyoho.pc@canada.ca
www.pc.gc.ca/en/pn-np/bc/yoho/index.a spx
twitter.com/YohoNP
www.facebook.com/YohoNP
Year Founded: 1886 Yoho National Park is situated on the western slopes of the Canadian Rocky Mountains. 'Yoho' is a Cree experession of awe & wonder, given to the park because of its immense rock walls, waterfalls, & mountain peaks. Parklands are open year round; Visitor Centre open only Spring-Fall.

Queen Charlotte: Gwaii Haanas National Park Reserve & Haida Heritage Site
PO Box 37,
Queen Charlotte, BC V0T 1S0
Tel: 250-559-8818*Toll-Free:* 877-559-8818
pc.gwaiihaanas.pc@canada.ca
www.pc.gc.ca/en/pn-np/bc/gwaiihaanas
www.f acebook.com/GwaiiHaanas
Gwaii Haanas National Park is jointly managed by the Government of Canada & the Council of the Haida Nation through an agreement signed in 1993. Boating; kayaking; hiking. Open year round

Radium Hot Springs: Kootenay National Park of Canada
PO Box 220, 7556 Main St. East,
Radium Hot Springs, BC V0A 1M0
Tel: 250-347-9505*Toll-Free:* 888-773-8888
pc.kootenayinfo-infokootenay.pc@canada.ca
www.pc.gc.ca/en/pn-np/bc/koot enay/index.aspx
twitter.com/KootenayNP
www.facebook.com/KootenayNP
Year Founded: 1920 Kootenay National Park represents the south-western region of the Canadian Rocky Mountains. The park contains such diverse landscapes as glaciers-topped mountains & semi-arid grasslands. Parklands are open year round; the Kootenay National Park Visitor Centre is open May-Oct 9:00-5:00.

Revelstoke: Glacier National Park of Canada
PO Box 350, 9520 Trans-Canada Hwy,
Revelstoke, BC V0E 2S0
Tel: 250-837-7500
pc.mrg.information.pc@canada.ca
www.pc.gc.ca/en/pn-np/bc/glacier
www.facebook.com/MRGnationalparks

Year Founded: 1886 Glacier National Park of Canada protects part of the Columbia Mountains Natural Region in British Columbia's interior, which includes stands of old-growth cedar & hemlock, & habitat for endangered species such as mountain caribou, mountain goat, & grizzly bear. Also located in the park is The Rogers Pass National Historic Site, which commemorates the construction of the country's first major national transportation route.

Revelstoke: Mount Revelstoke National Park of Canada
PO Box 350,
Revelstoke, BC V0E 2S0
Tel: 250-837-7500
pc.mrg.information.pc@canada.ca
www.pc.gc.ca/eng/pn-np/bc/revelstoke/index.aspx
www.facebook.com/MRGnati onalparks
Year Founded: 1914 Mount Revelstoke National Park showcases western Canada's dramatic mountain landscapes & dense rainforests. Hiking trails take visitors through various landscapes, including Western Red Cedars & jungle-like wetland. Park open year round. Revelstoke Office is open year-round, M-F 8:00-8:30.

Sidney: Gulf Islands National Park Reserve of Canada
2220 Harbour Rd.,
Sidney, BC V8L 2P6
Tel: 250-654-4000*Toll-Free:* 866-944-1744
pc.gulfinfo.pc@canada.ca
www.pc.gc.ca/en/pn-np/bc/gulf/
twitter.com/Gu lfIslandsNPR
www.facebook.com/GulfIslandsNPR
Year Founded: 2003 Gulf Islands National Park Reserve protects part of British Columbia's southern Gulf Islands archipelago. These islands represent the Strait of Georgia Lowlands, which is one of the most ecologically sensitive regions in southern Canada. Includes fifteen islands, many islets & reefs, & around twenty-six square kilometres of marine areas. Hours of Operation: May 15 to September 30. Camping offer is limited from October 1 to May 14.

Ucluelet: Pacific Rim National Park Reserve of Canada (PRNPR)
2040 Pacific Rim Hwy.,
Ucluelet, BC V0R 3A0
Tel: 250-726-4212
pc.pacrim.pc@canada.ca
www.pc.gc.ca/en/pn-np/bc/pacificrim/index.aspx
twitter.com/pacificrimNP R
www.facebook.com/PacificRimNPR
Year Founded: 1970 Pacific Rim National Park Reserve of Canada is backed by the Insular Mountains Range of Vancouver Island, & faces the Pacific Ocean. Pacific Rim presents the rich natural and cultural heritage of Canada's west coast & the history of the Nuu-chah-nulth First Nations, as well as that of European explorers & settlers. Open year round.

Manitoba

Churchill: Wapusk National Park of Canada
PO Box 127,
Churchill, MB R0B 0E0
Tel: 204-675-8863*Toll-Free:* 888-773-8888
pc.manitoba.pc@canada.ca
www.pc.gc.ca/en/pn-np/mb/wapusk/index.aspx
Year Founded: 1996 Wapusk National Park of Canada is home to one of the world's largest polar bear maternity denning areas ("Wapusk" is a Cree word meaning "White Bear"). The park encompasses the Hudson James Lowlands region, bordering on Hudson Bay & lies on the transition area between boreal forest & Arctic tundra. Access to the park is via licensed tour operator from Churchill.

Onanole: Riding Mountain National Park of Canada
PO Box 299, 133 Wasagaming Dr.,
Onanole, MB R0J 1N0
Tel: 204-848-7275; *Fax:* 204-848-2596
pc.info-riding@canada.ca
www.pc.gc.ca/en/pn-np/mb/riding/index.aspx
t witter.com/RidingNP
www.facebook.com/RidingNP
Year Founded: 1933 Riding Mountain forms part of the Manitoba Escarpmet & protects a variety of wildlife & vegetation. The park features many hiking trails & Agassiz Tower, which offers visitors a panoramic view of the prairies to the north. Administration Office M-F 8:00-12:00, 12:30-4:00; Visitor Centre, Spring & Fall Th-M 9:30-5:00, Summer 9:30-8:00.

New Brunswick

Alma: Fundy National Park of Canada
PO Box 1001,
Alma, NB E4H 1B4
Tel: 506-887-6000; *Fax:* 506-887-6008
Toll-Free: 888-773-8888
pc.fundy.pc@canada.ca
www.pc.gc.ca/eng/pn-np/nb/fundy/ index.aspx
www.facebook.com/FundyNP
Other contact information: TDD: 506-887-6015
Year Founded: 1948 Fundy National Park of Canada protects some of the only remaining wilderness in southern New Brunswick, including the Caledonia Highlands & Bay of Fundy. Inland, visitors can explore forests & stream valleys. Vistor Reception Centre open daily

Kouchibouguac: Kouchibouguac National Park of Canada
186 Rte. 117,
Kouchibouguac, NB E4X 2P1
Tel: 506-876-2443; *Fax:* 506-876-4802
Toll-Free: 888-773-8888
pc.kouchibouguac.pc@canada.ca
www.pc.gc.ca/en/pn-np/n b/kouchibouguac/index.aspx
twitter.com/KouchibouguacNP
www.facebook.co m/KouchibouguacNP
Other contact information: TDD: 866-787-6221
Year Founded: 1969 Kouchibouguac National Park of Canada is a Canadian Heritage protected area, & is one of only two wilderness national parks in New Brunswick. The landscape is characteristic of the Maritime Plain Natural Region in which it is located, including such features as bogs, salt marshes, tidal rivers, lagoons & forests. The name Kouchibouguac is of Mi'kmaq origin & means "river of the long tides." Visitors can enjoy hiking, cycling, canoeing, kayaking, swimming, camping, bird watching, & cross country skiing, snowshoeing, & tobogganing in winter.

Newfoundland & Labrador

Glovertown: Terra Nova National Park of Canada
Glovertown, NL A0G 2L0
Tel: 709-533-2801
pc.infopnterra-nova-terranovanpinfo.pc@canada.ca
www.pc.gc.ca/eng/pn-np/ nl/terranova/index.aspx
www.facebook.com/TerraNovaNP
Year Founded: 1957 Terra Nova National Park of Canada encompasses the North Atlantic Ocean & the boreal forest of Eastern Newfoundland. The park's landscape varies from cliffs & inlets to forested hills, bogs, & ponds. Visitors can also explore the remnants of sawmills & past human cultures found within the park. Hours of Operation: May-Oct.

Nain: Torngat Mountains National Park of Canada
PO Box 471,
Nain, NL A0P 1L0
Tel: 709-922-1290*Toll-Free:* 888-922-1290
pc.infopntorngats-torngatsnpinfo.pc@canada.ca
www.pc.gc.ca/en/pn-np/nl/ torngats/index.aspx
Other contact information: French Phone: 709-458-2417
Year Founded: 2008 The Torngat Mountains National Park of Canada protects an area of Arctic wilderness, featuring the highest peaks in eastern North America, small glaciers, fjords, river valleys & rugged coastal landscapes. This land has been home to the Inuit & their ancestors for thousands of years. Park office hours: M-F 8:00-4:30. The park is a remote wilderness with no on-site facilities or road access. As a result, visitors are encouraged to come in late winter & early spring & summer.

Rocky Harbour: Akami-uapishku-KakKasuak-Mealy Mountains National Park Reserve
Rocky Harbour, NL A0K 4N0
Tel: 709-896-2394
pc.mealys.pc@canada.ca
www.pc.gc.ca/en/pn-np/nl/mealy
Year Founded: 2015 Akami-Uapishk-KakKasuak-Mealy Mountains National Park Reserve is Canada's newest national park and will protect cultural landscapes of importance to Innu, Inuit, & other people in the region.

Rocky Harbour: Gros Morne National Park of Canada
PO Box 130,
Rocky Harbour, NL A0K 4N0
Tel: 709-458-2417
pc.grosmorne.pc@canada.ca
www.pc.gc.ca/en/pn-np/nl/grosmorne
www.facebook.com/GrosMorneNP
Other contact information: Emergency Line: 877-852-3100
Year Founded: 1973 Gros Morne National Park of Canada was inscribed a UNESCO World Heritage Site in 1987. Visitors can hike through mountains or camp by the sea. Boat tours,

waterfalls beaches, & nearby fishing villages can all be explored. Park Headquaters: M-F 8:00-12:00, 1:00-4:30; Visitor Centre: May-June 9:00-5:00, June-Sept. 8:00-8:00, Sept-Oct. 9:00-5:00.

Northwest Territories

Fort Simpson: Nahanni National Park Reserve of Canada
PO Box 348, 10002 100 St,
Fort Simpson, NT X0E 0N0

Tel: 867-695-7750
nahanni.info@pc.gc.ca
www.pc.gc.ca/en/pn-np/nt/nahanni
Year Founded: 1972 Nahanni National Park Reserve of Canada protects a portion of the Mackenzie Mountains Natural Region. A key feature of the park is the South Nahanni River, and the park's diverse landscape is home to many species of birds, fish & mammals. The Ford Simpson visitor centre features displays on the history, culture & geography of the area. The park was inscribed on UNESCO's World Heritage List in 1978. Winter: M-F 8:30-12:00, 1:00-5:00; Summer: daily 8:30-12:00, 1:00-5:00

Fort Smith: Wood Buffalo National Park of Canada
PO Box 750,
Fort Smith, NT X0E 0P0

Tel: 867-872-7960
pc.woodbuffaloinfo-infowoodbuffalo.pc@canada.ca
www.pc.gc.ca/pn-np/nt/wo odbuffalo.aspx
Other contact information: 24-Hour Hotline: 867-872-7962
Year Founded: 1922 Wood Buffalo National Park is Canada's largest national park & one of the largest in the world. It was established to protect the last herds of bison in northern Canada, & today it protects an example of Canada's Northern Boreal Plains. Park is open year round; Fort Smith Visitor Reception Centre open seven days a week in the summer, and M-F in the winter; Fort Chipewyan Visitor Reception Centre open M-F with most weekends open in summer as well.

Inuvik: Ivvavik National Park of Canada
c/o Western Arctic Field Unit, 81 Kingmingya Rd,
Inuvik, NT X0E 0T0

Tel: 867-777-8800; *Fax:* 867-777-8820
pc.infoinuvik-inuvikinfo.pc@canada.ca
www.pc.gc.ca/eng/pn-np/yt/ivvavik/index.aspx
Year Founded: 1984 Ivvavik National Park of Canada is the first national park in Canada to be created as a result of an aboriginal land claim agreement. The park protects a portion of the calving grounds of the Porcupine caribou herd and represents the Northern Yukon and Mackenzie Delta natural regions. Park is open year round

Paulatuk: Tuktut Nogait National Park of Canada
PO Box 91,
Paulatuk, NT X0E 1N0

Tel: 867-580-3233
pc.infoinuvik-inuvikinfo.pc@canada.ca
www.pc.gc.ca/eng /pn-np/nt/tuktutnogait/index.aspx
Year Founded: 1998 The park is located 170 kilometres north of the arctic circle & is home to the Bluenose West caribou herd, as well as wolves, grizzly bears, muskoxen, arctic char & a variety of migratory birds. The Inuvialuit continue to practice traditional harvesting and are also active as interpretive guides within the park today. Open year round

Sachs Harbour: Aulavik National Park of Canada
PO Box 29,
Sachs Harbour, NT X0E 0Z0

Tel: 867-777-8800; *Fax:* 867-777-8820
pc.infoinuvik-inuvikinfo.pc@canada.ca
www.pc.gc.ca/eng/pn-np/nt/aulavik/ index.aspx
Year Founded: 1992 Aulavik National Park protects more than 12,000 square kilometres of arctic lowlands on the north end of Banks Island. At the heart of the park lies the Thomsen River, one of Canada's most northerly navigable waterways. The park is home to the endangered Peary caribou and the highest density of muskoxen in the world. Open year round.

Tulita: Nááts'ihch'oh National Park Reserve of Canada
c/o Parks Canada Agency, PO Box 157,
Tulita, NT X0E 0K0

Toll-Free: 867-588-4884
pc.tulitainfo-infotulita.pc@canada.ca
www.pc.gc.ca/eng/pn-np/nt/naatsihc hoh
Year Founded: 2012 Canada's newest national park. Canoeing; hiking; open year round
Jonah Mitchell, Superintendent

Nova Scotia

Halifax: Sable Island National Park Reserve of Canada
1869 Upper Water Street,
Halifax, NS B3J 1S9

Tel: 902-426-1500
pc.sable.pc@canada.ca
www.pc.gc.ca/eng/pn-np/ns/sable/index.aspx
Year Founded: 2013 Sable Island is Canada's newest National Park. Parks Canada & Environment Canada operate a research post called Main Station, which serves as the hub of all island activities & programs. The island features a landscape devoid of trees & an abundance of protected wildlife, including the free-roaming Sable Island horses, as well as Harbour & Grey seals. Visitors can access the island from Jun-Oct, must register in advance. Visitor access is by charter plane & boat only, & visitors are responsible for their own travel arrangements to & from the island.

Ingonish Beach: Cape Breton Highlands National Park of Canada
37639 Cabot Trail,
Ingonish Beach, NS B0C 1L0

Tel: 902-224-2306; *Fax:* 902-285-2866
pc.cbinfo.cb@canada.ca
www.pc.gc.ca/pn-np/ns/cbreton
twitter.com/Parks Canada_NS
www.facebook.com/CBHNP
Year Founded: 1936 Cape Breton Highlands National Park of Canada is home to the Cabot Trail & offers visitors scenery, wildlife, & human history stretching back to the last Ice Age. Hours of Operation: park is open year round; Visitor Centre Spring 9:00-5:00, Summer 8:30-7:00, Fall 9:00-5:00.

Maitland Bridge, Annapolis County: Kejimkujik National Park & National Historic Site of Canada
3005 Kemjimkujik Main Pkwy,
Maitland Bridge, Annapolis County, NS B0T 1B0

Tel: 902-682-2772
pc.kejimkujik.pc@canada.ca
www.pc.gc.ca/eng/pn-np/ns/kejimkujik
twitter.com/ParksCanada_NS
www.fa cebook.com/Kejimkujik
Other contact information: Phone from January to Mid-May: 902-682-2770
Year Founded: 1967 Kejimkujik is the sole inland national park in the Maritimes, featuring lakes & rivers, woodlands, & a variety of wildlife. Visitors can explore historic canoe routes, portages, & hiking trails in the park.

Nunavut

Iqaluit: Quttinirpaaq National Park of Canada
PO Box 278,
Iqaluit, NU X0A 0H0

Tel: 867-975-4673; *Fax:* 867-975-4674
Toll-Free: 888-773-8888
pc.infonunavut-nunavutinfo.pc@canada.ca
www.pc.gc.ca/e ng/pn-np/nu/quttinirpaaq/index.aspx
Year Founded: 1988 Quttinirpaaq National Park's artic terrain includes ice caps, glaciers, rugged peaks, tundra & a rare thermal oasis. The Tanquary Fiord Camp is only staffed during the summer field season. Parks Canada Office in Iqaluit is open M-F 8:30-12:00, 1:00-5:00 year round.

Iqaluit: Qausuittuq National Park
PO Box 278,
Iqaluit, NU X0A 0H0

Tel: 867-975-4673 *Toll-Free:* 888-773-8888
www.pc.gc.ca/en/pn-np/nu/qausuittuq
Year Founded: 2015 Qausuittuq National Park is Canada's 45th national park & protects the endangered Peary caribou & their habitat. Traditional hunting & fishing area. Park open Jun-Sep, Visitor Services M-F 8:30-5:00

Naujaat: Ukkusiksalik National Park of Canada
PO Box 220,
Naujaat, NU X0C 0H0

Tel: 867-462-4500; *Fax:* 867-462-4095
Toll-Free: 888-773-8888
pc.infonunavut-nunavutinfo.pc@canada.ca
www.pc.gc.ca/e ng/pn-np/nu/ukkusiksalik
twitter.com/ParksCanNunavut
www.facebook.com/ ParksCanadaNunavut
Year Founded: 2003 The park grounds are used for hiking, camping, boating & traditional Inuit use. The office is open all year, M-F 8:30-5:00. The park does not have any facilities or services.

Pangnirtung: Auyuittuq National Park of Canada
PO Box 353,
Pangnirtung, NU X0A 0R0

Tel: 867-473-2500 *Toll-Free:* 888-773-8888
pc.infonunavut-nunavutinfo.pc@canada.ca
www.pc.gc.ca/eng/pn-np/nu/auyuittuq/index.aspx
Year Founded: 1976 Auyuittuq National Park of Canada protects 19,089 km2 of terrain. Auyuittuq is an Inuktitut word meaning "land that never melts." The park is located in the eastern Arctic on southern Baffin Island, & includes the highest peaks of the Canadian Shield, the Penny Ice Cap, coastal fiords, & Akshayuk Pass, which was a traditional corridor used by the Inuit for thousands of years. Hours of Operation: Visitor Centre open year-round, M-F 8:30-12:00, 1:00-5:00. Summer hours posted in June.

Pond Inlet: Sirmilik National Park of Canada
PO Box 300,
Pond Inlet, NU X0A 0S0

Tel: 867-899-8092; *Fax:* 867-899-8104
pc.infopnsirmilik-sirmiliknpinfo.pc@canada.ca
www.pc.gc.ca/eng/pn-np/nu/ sirmilik/contact.aspx
Year Founded: 2001 Sirmilik National Park represents the Northern Eastern Arctic Lowlands Natural Region & portions of the Lancaster Sound Marine Region. The park features wilderness hiking & camping, & a prominent seabird colony near of Baillarge Bay. Administration & Visitor Centre: M-F 8:30-12:00, 1:00-5:00. All visitors must register, attend orientation & report for post-trip de-briefing.

Ontario

Heron Bay: Pukaskwa National Park of Canada
Hwy 627,
Heron Bay, ON P0T 1R0

Tel: 807-229-0801
pc.pukaskwaont.pc@canada.ca
www.pc.gc.ca/en/pn-np/on/pukaskwa
twitter.com/PukaskwaNP
www.facebook. com/PukaskwaNP
Year Founded: 1978 Pukaskwa National Park is the only wilderness national park in Ontario, & protects 1878 square km of boreal forest & Lake Superior shoreline. Hours of Operation: Administration Office M-F 8:30-4:30 year-round. Visitor Centre: Jul-Aug Sun-Th 9:00-4:00, Fri-Sa 9:00-8:00

Leamington: Point Pelee National Park of Canada
1118 Point Pelee Drive,
Leamington, ON N8H 3V4

Tel: 519-322-2365 *Toll-Free:* 888-773-8888
pc.pelee.info.pc@canada.ca
www.pc.gc.ca/eng/pn-np/on/pelee/index.aspx
twitter.com/PointPeleeNP
www.facebook.com/PointPeleeNP
Year Founded: 1918 Point Pelee National Park is located at the southern tip of Canada, 50 km (30 miles) south-east of Windsor, Ontario. It is one of Canada's smallest national parks, but features picnic areas & a Visitor Centre, as well as the famous Tip, & Marsh Boardwalk. April-May 6:00-10:00, May 5:00-10:00, May-Sept 6:00-10:00, Sept- Apr 7:00-7:00.

Mallorytown: Thousand Islands National Park
1121 Thousand Islands Pkwy,
Mallorytown, ON K0E 1R0

Tel: 613-923-5261 *Toll-Free:* 888-773-8888
ont-ti@pc.gc.ca
www.pc.gc.ca/en/pn-np/on/1000
twitter.com/tinationalpa rk
www.facebook.com/TINationalPark
Year Founded: 1904 Thousand Islands National Park works to promote sustainable recreation while protecting the land & wildlife; hiking trail, interpretive programs, exhibits, & activities for the whole family available at the Visitor Centre. Visitor Centre: May-Sept & weekends & holidays 10:00-4:00. Administration Office: M-F 8:00-4:30 year round

Midland: Georgian Bay Islands National Park of Canada
PO Box 9, 901 Wye Valley Rd,
Midland, ON L4R 4K6

Tel: 705-527-7200; *Fax:* 705-526-5939
Toll-Free: 877-737-3783
pc.info.gbi-ibg.pc@canada.ca
www.pc.gc.ca/eng/pn-np/on /georg/index.aspx
twitter.com/GBINP
Year Founded: 1929 Georgian Bay Islands National Park of Canada protects the Canadian Shield, including the Honey Harbour area to Twelve Mile Bay in southern Georgian Bay. The islands are accessible by boat only. Beausoleil, the largest island, offers tent camping, overnight & day docking, heritage education programs, & hiking trails. Midland administration office

open year-round, 8:00-4:00; Cedar Spring Welcome Centre open Su-Th 9:30-5:00, F 9:00-7:00, Sa 9:00-6:00.

Tobermory: Bruce Peninsula National Park of Canada
PO Box 189, 120 Chi sin tib dek Rd,
Tobermory, ON N0H 2R0
Tel: 519-596-2233*Toll-Free:* 888-773-8888
pc.bruce-fathomfive.pc@canada.ca
www.pc.gc.ca/eng/pn-np/on/bruce/index.a spx
twitter.com/BrucePNP
www.facebook.com/BrucePeninsulaNP
Year Founded: 1987 Bruce Peninsula National Park of Canada is located inside a World Biosphere Reserve. The cliffs of the park are inhabited by thousand-year-old cedar trees, & the park is comprised of habitats ranging from alvars to forests & lakes. The ecosystem is the largest remaining chunk of natural habitat in southern Ontario. Administration Office, M-F 8:00-4:30; Visitor Centre: Spring & Fall 9:00-5:00, Summer 8:00-8:00

Toronto: Rouge National Urban Park
1749 Meadowvale Rd,
Toronto, ON M1B 5W8
Tel: 416-264-2020
pc.rouge.pc@canada.ca
www.pc.gc.ca/en/pn-np/on/rouge
Year Founded: 2015 As Canada's first national urban park, Rouge National Urban Park is home to over 1,700 species of plants & animals, some of the last remaining working farms in the Greater Toronto Area, rare Carolinian ecosystems, Toronto's only campground, & some of Canada's oldest known Indigenous sites. Park open year round

Prince Edward Island

Charlottetown: Prince Edward Island National Park of Canada
2 Palmers Lane,
Charlottetown, PE C1A 5V8
Tel: 902-672-6350
pc.pnipe-peinp.pc@canada.ca
www.pc.gc.ca/en/pn-np/pe/pei-ipe
twitter.com/ParksCanadaPEI
www.facebo ok.com/PEInationalpark
Year Founded: 1937 The landscape of Prince Edward Island National Park of Canada includes sand dunes, barrier islands & sand pits, beaches, sandstone cliffs, wetlands, & forests. Various plants & animals call these habitats home, including the endangered Piping Plover. The Park also features Green Gables & Dalvay-by-the-Sea National Historic Site. Park open May-Oct

Quebec

Gaspé: Forillon National Park of Canada
122 Gaspé Blvd.,
Gaspé, QC G4X 0B1
Tel: 418-368-5505*Toll-Free:* 888-773-8888
pc.information.pc@canada.ca
www.pc.gc.ca/en/pn-np/qc/forillon
twitter. com/ForillonNP
www.facebook.com/ForillonNP
Year Founded: 1970 Forillon National Park of Canada is located at the farthest point of the Gaspé Peninsula. It protects a portion of the Notre-Dame & Mégantic mountain regions, & elements of the Gulf of St. Lawrence marine region. Present in the park are ten different rock formations, colonies of seabirds, & arctic-alpine plants. The Grande-Grave National Heritage Site is located within the park & reveals the way of life of fishing families in the region. Park open Jun-Oct

Havre-Saint-Pierre: Mingan Archipelago National Park Reserve of Canada
1340 de la Digue St.,
Havre-Saint-Pierre, QC G0G 1P0
Tel: 418-538-3285*Toll-Free:* 888-773-8888
pc.information.pc@canada.ca
www.pc.gc.ca/eng/pn-np/qc/mingan/index.aspx
twitter.com/MinganNPR
www.facebook.com/MinganNPR
Year Founded: 1984 The Mingan Archipelago National Park Reserve of Canada is situated along the North Shore of the Gulf of St. Lawrence, & is comprised of about forty limestone islands, & and over 1,000 islets & reefs. This park is home to the largest concentration of monoliths in Canada. Havre-Saint-Pierre Reception & Interpretation Center & Longue-Pointe-de-Mingan Reception & Interpretation Centre open June-Sept.

Shawinigan: La Mauricie National Park of Canada / Parc National du Canada de la Mauricie
Administration Office, 702, 5 rue de la Pointe,
Shawinigan, QC G9N 1E9
Tel: 819-538-3232; *Fax:* 819-536-3661
Toll-Free: 888-773-8888
pc.information.pc@canada.ca
www.pc.gc.ca/en/pn-np/qc/m auricie
www.facebook.com/MauricieNP
Year Founded: 1970 La Mauricie National Park of Canada covers an area of 536 km2, protecting a sample of the southernmost part of the Canadian Shield. Canoeing; camping; cycling; hiking; recreational fishing. Park open Summer May-Oct, Winter Dec-Mar

Saskatchewan

Val Marie: Grasslands National Park of Canada
PO Box 150,
Val Marie, SK S0N 2T0
Tel: 306-476-2018; *Fax:* 306-298-2042
pc.infopnprairies-grasslandsnpinfo.pc@canada.ca
www.pc.gc.ca/eng/pn-np/s k/grasslands/index.aspx
twitter.com/parkscanada_sk
www.facebook.com/gr asslandsNP
Other contact information: TTY: 1-866-787-6221; West Block
Visitor Centre: 1-877-345-2257
Year Founded: 1981 Grasslands is the first national park of Canada to preserve a section of the mixed prairie grasslands. Visitor activities include guided hikes, interpretive trails, bird watching, & nature photography. Parklands are open year round. Visitor Centre: May-Oct

Waskesiu Lake: Prince Albert National Park
Northern Prairies Field Unit, PO Box 100,
Waskesiu Lake, SK S0J 2Y0
Tel: 306-663-4522*Toll-Free:* 888-773-8888
pc.princealbertinfo.pc@canada.ca
pc.gc.ca/en/pn-np/sk/princealbert
www .facebook.com/175220649199551
Year Founded: 1927 Protecting part of the boreal forest, Prince Albert National Park features the cabin of conservationist Grey Owl, a white pelican nesting colony, & a free-range herd of plains bison. Visitors to the park can participate in interpretive programs & special events. The park is open year-round, & the Interpretive Centre is open from the end of Jun-Sep

Yukon Territory

Haines Junction: Kluane National Park & Reserve of Canada
PO Box 5495,
Haines Junction, YT Y0B 1L0
Tel: 867-634-7207
pc.kluaneinfo.pc@canada.ca
www.pc.gc.ca/en/pn-np/yt/kluane
twitter.com/ParksCanYukon
www.facebook .com/ParksCanadaYukon
Year Founded: 1972 Kluane National Park & Reserve of Canada covers an area of 21,980 km2, & features mountains including Mount Logan, Canada's highest peak, icefields, & valleys that are home to a variety of plant & wildlife species.

Old Crow: Vuntut National Park of Canada
PO Box 19,
Old Crow, YT Y0B 1N0
Tel: 867-667-3910
pc.vuntutinfo.pc@canada.ca
www.pc.gc.ca/eng/pn-np/yt/vuntut/index.aspx
twitter.com/ParksCanYukon
www.facebook.com/ParksCanadaYukon
Year Founded: 1995 Vuntut National Park was established after negotiations through the Vuntut Gwitchin First Nation's Final Land Claims Agreement, between the Vuntut Gwitchin of Old Crow & the Government of Canada & the Yukon. The park protects the northern part of the Vuntut Gwitchin First Nation Traditional Territory. Park is open year round with no services available.

Observatories

Alberta

Edmonton: University of Alberta Observatory Physics
University of Alberta, 4-181 Centennial Center for Interdisciplinary Science,
Edmonton, AB T6G 2J1
Tel: 780-492-5286; *Fax:* 780-492-0714
stars@ualberta.ca
www.uab.ca/observatory
twitter.com/UofAObservatory
www.facebook.com/UofAObservatory
Campus Observatory has permanently mounted 12 & 14 inch telescopes & an exhibit area; facility used for undergraduate instruction & public observing during academic year; admission is free.
Mauricio Sacchi, Chair, 780-492-1060, msacchi@ualberta.ca

Foothills: Rothney Astrophysical Observatory (RAO) Physics & Astronomy
University of Calgary, 210 Avenue W, Hwy 22 S,
Foothills, AB T0L 1W0
Tel: 403-931-2366
rao@phas.ucalgary.ca
www.ucalgary.ca/rao
twitter.com/RAOastronomy
facebook.com/rothney.obse rvatory
Other contact information: 385
Year Founded: 1972 The RAO is used as both a research & teaching facility & is home to a collection of telescopes. It is also an astronomy resource for school children, teachers & community groups.
Phil Langill, Director, pplangil@ucalgary.ca

British Columbia

Kaleden: Dominion Radio Astrophysical Observatory (DRAO)
717 White Lake Rd,
Kaleden, BC V0H 1K0
Tel: 250-497-2300
NRC.DRAO-OFR.CNRC@nrc-cnrc.gc.ca
nrc.canada.ca
Year Founded: 1960 DRAO is an internationally known facility for science & technology research related to radio astronomy. Site is open for self-guided tours year round M-Fri 08:30-5:00

Kamloops: Thompson Rivers University Observatory
900 McGill Rd.,
Kamloops, BC V2C 0C8
physics@tru.ca
www.tru.ca/science/programs/physics/observatory.html
twitter.com/TRUObse rvatory
Year Founded: 2005 Features an outdoor observation platform and a 6 metre dome housing a reflector telescope on an equatorial mount with a Gemini GoTo positioning system.
George Weremczuk, Chair, Physics & Geology Department, 250-828-5448, taylor@tgweremczuk@tru.ca

Kamuela: Canada-France-Hawaii Telescope (CFHT)
c/o CFHT Corporation, 65-1238 Mamalahoa Hwy.,
Kamuela, Hawaii 96743 USA
Tel: 808-885-7944; *Fax:* 808-885-7288
info@cfht.hawaii.edu
www.cfht.hawaii.edu
twitter.com/CFHTelescope
ww w.facebook.com/cfhtelescope
Other contact information: FTP: ftp.cfht.hawaii.edu
Year Founded: 1979 The CFH observatory hosts a world-class, 3.6 meter optical/infrared telescope. The observatory is located atop the summit of Mauna Kea, a 4,200 meter, dormant volcano located on the island of Hawaii. By appointment only.
Doug Simons, Executive Director, simons@cfht.hawaii.edu

Vancouver: Gordon MacMillan Southam Observatory (GSO)
Parent: H.R. MacMillan Space Centre
1100 Chestnut St.,
Vancouver, BC V6J 3J9
Tel: 604-738-7827; *Fax:* 604-736-5665
info@spacecentre.ca
www.spacecentre.ca/gordon-southam-observatory
www.youtube.com/user/MacMillanSpaceCentre
twitter.com/AskAnAstronomer
www.facebook.com/MacMillanSpaceCentre
Year Founded: 1968 Part of the H.R. MacMillan Space Centre. Open daily 10:00-5:00; Evening Shows Fri-Sat 7:30-9:00; Observatory Fri-Sat 8:00-12:00.
Jonathan Burke, Chair

Raylene Marchand, Executive Director
Samaneh Badiei, Director, Finance

Victoria: Climenhaga Observatory
Physics & Astronomy
**University of Victoria, PO Box 1700 CSC, 3800 Finnerty Rd.,
Victoria, BC V8P 5C2**

Tel: 250-721-7211
observatory@uvic.ca
www.uvic.ca
www.facebook.com/uvicobservatory

Victoria: Dominion Astrophysical Observatory / Centre
de l'Univers - Centre d'interprétation en astronomie
**5071 West Saanich Rd.,
Victoria, BC V9E 2E7**

Tel: 250-363-3638
info@centreoftheuniverse.org
centreoftheuniverse.org
Year Founded: 1918 This centre is a national historic site of
Canada. The telescopes are available to both qualified Canadian
& non-Canadian researchers.
James Di Francesco, Director PhD

Manitoba

Glenlea: Glenlea Astronomical Observatory (GAO)
**Glenlea Research Station, University of Manitoba, 1290
Research Station Rd,
Glenlea, MB R0G 0S0**
www.physics.umanitoba.ca/astro/?page_id=6
This facility is used primarily for undergraduate teaching &
observing sessions for first year astronomy classes at the
University of Manitoba. Equiped with the 40cm Evans'
Telescope.

Winnipeg: The Lockhart Planetarium
Physics & Astronomy
**University of Manitoba, 210 Dysart Rd.,
Winnipeg, MB R3T 2M8**

Tel: 204-474-6202
physics.umanitoba.ca
www.physics.umanitoba.ca/astro
www.instagram.com/lockhart_planetarium
Year Founded: 1964 Planetarium theatre; display area;
astronomy reference library
Danielle Pahud, Director, Danielle.Pahud@umanitoba.ca

Winnipeg: Manitoba Planetarium
Parent: The Manitoba Museum
**190 Rupert Ave.,
Winnipeg, MB R3B 0N2**

Tel: 204-956-2830
info@manitobamuseum.ca
manitobamuseum.ca/main/visit/planetarium
Year Founded: 1968 A 287 seat space theatre equipped with
Zeiss MkV star projector, which is capable of reproducing the
night sky as seen from any location on Earth;complimented with
advanced video project & multimedia projectors; shows &
programs change throughout the year.
Scott Young, Manager, Planetarium & Science Gallery

New Brunswick

Sackville: Mount Allison Gemini Observatory (MAGO)
Physics Dept.
**Mount Allison University, 67 York St.,
Sackville, NB E4L 1E6**

Tel: 506-364-2592
gemini@mta.ca
www.mta.ca/gemini
Year Founded: 2008 Mount Allison Gemini Observatory is a
dual-dome astronomical observational observatory used
extensively by the physics department for hands-on astronomy
classes, as well as being open to the public for special viewing
nights & activities.

Newfoundland & Labrador

Corner Brook: Grenfell Campus Observatory
**Arts & Science Extension, Grenfell Campus, Memorial
University, 20 University Dr.,
Corner Brook, NL A2H 5G4**

Tel: 709-639-2397
observatory@grenfell.mun.ca
www.grenfell.mun.ca/observatory
twitter.com/grenfellobs
www.facebook.c om/grenfellobservatory
Year Founded: 2012 Grenfell Campus Observatory is home to a
number of advanced telescopes used to observe & decode the
mysteries of the sky.

Nova Scotia

Halifax: Burke-Gaffney Observatory (BGO)
Astronomy & Physics
**Saint Mary's University,
Halifax, NS B3H 1C3**

Tel: 902-420-5633; Fax: 902-496-8218
bgo@ap.smu.ca
www.ap.smu.ca/pr/bgo
twitter.com/smubgobs
www.facebook .com/bgobs
Other contact information: Info Line: 902-496-8257
Year Founded: 1972 The Burke-Gaffney Observatory at St.
Mary's University is the first Facebook-controlled observatory in
the world. Free public tours held on the 2nd & 4th Fri. of each
month at 7:00 (Nov.-Mar.) or 9:00 or 10:00 (Apr.-Oct.), weather
permitting; Mon. evening group tours by arrangement.
Dave Lane, Director, Astronomy & Physics, 902-420-5640,
dlane@ap.smu.ca

Halifax: Halifax Planetarium
Department of Physics & Atmospheric Science
**Sir James Dunn Bldg., Dalhousie University, PO Box 15000,
6310 Coburg Rd.,
Halifax, NS B3H 4R2**
www.astronomynovascotia.ca/index.php/planetarium
twitter.com/AstronomyNS
Currently running shows every two weeks on Thursday
evenings. Shows also available for group classes & organized
groups.
Stephen Payne, Administrator

Ontario

Cranton: Elginfield Observatory
Physics & Astronomy
**University of Western Ontario, 7601-7999 Observatory Dr.,
Cranton, ON N0M 1V0**

Tel: 519-661-2111
https://physics.uwo.ca/
Year Founded: 1969 The telescope is no longer in regular use,
however the observatory site serves as a home to research
projects.

Hamilton: W.J. McCallion Planetarium
Dept. of Physics & Astronomy
**Burke Science Bldg B149, McMaster University, 1280 Main
St. West,
Hamilton, ON L8S 4L8**

Tel: 905-525-9140; Fax: 905-546-1252
planetarium@physics.mcmaster.ca
www.physics.mcmaster.ca/planetarium
The McCallion Planetarium was the first in Ontario to offer
publicshowings, with the original projector having been
purchased in 1949.
Graeme Luke, Chair & Professor, Physics & Astronomy

Kingston: Queen's Observatory
Physics, Engineering Physics & Astronomy
**Ellis Hall, Queen's University, 58 University Ave.,
Kingston, ON K7L 3N6**

Tel: 613-533-2711
queensobservatory@gmail.com
http://observatory.phy.queensu.ca/
The Queen's Observatory is a non-profit facility run by the
Queen's University Astronomy Research Group & the Queen's
Physics Department. The Queen's Observatory has been
providing access to the campus & community through its student
training & public programs. Available for school & public tours.
Open houses are held the 2nd Saturday of each month.

London: Hume Cronyn Memorial Observatory
Physics & Astronomy
**University of Western Ontario, 1151 Richmond St.,
London, ON N6A 3K7**

Tel: 519-661-3283; Fax: 519-661-2033
cronyn@uwo.ca
physics.uwo.ca/about_us/outreach/cronyn/index.html
twitt er.com/westernuCRONYN
www.facebook.com/westernuCronyn
Year Founded: 1940 The observatory houses a 25 cm refactor
currently used for teaching & visitor programs. Public Nights: Sat
May-Aug 8:30-11:00, open fall & winter once a month 7:00-9:00.
Jan Cami, Coordinator, 519-661-2111, jcami@uwo.ca

Ottawa: Kessler Observatory
**Carlton University, 1125 Colonel By Dr.,
Ottawa, ON K1S 5B6**

observatory@physics.carleton.ca
research.physics.carleton.ca/observatory
Year Founded: 1980 The Observatory is primarily used for
instructional purposes in support of the Physics Department's

two planetary & stellar astronomy courses. Observing sessions
will be held regularly in the Fall.
Dr. Heather Logan, Chair, Physics, 613-520-2600,
physchair@physics.carleton.ca

Pembroke: Algonquin Radio Observatory (ARO)
Parent: Thoth Technology Inc.
**Achray Rd, RR#6,
Pembroke, ON K8A 6W7**

Tel: 905-713-2884
info@thothx.com
http://thothx.com/aro
Year Founded: 1959 The Algonquin Radio Observatory is a radio
observatory that contains a collection of instruments designed
for research in several phases of radio astronomy. Summer
resort also available.

Richmond Hill: David Dunlap Observatory (DDO)
Parent: Metrus Development Inc.
**Observatory Hill, 123 Hillsview Dr.,
Richmond Hill, ON L4C 1T3**

Tel: 905-771-8800
www.richmondhill.ca/en/david-dunlap-observatory.aspx
twitter.com/Dunlap_ Obs
Year Founded: 1935 The observatory was sold to Metrus
Development in 2008, & is now part of the Observatory Hill site.
Public programs are scheduled throughout the summer, &
Viewing Nights are held most Saturday nights for the public to
drop in & use the facilities.

St Catharines: Niagara Community Observatory (NCO)
**c/o Brock University, 1812 Sir Isaac Brock Way,
St Catharines, ON L2S 3A1**

Tel: 905-688-5550
www.brocku.ca/niagara-community-observatory
twitter.com/BrockNCO
The Niagara Community Observatory is a public-policy
think-tank working in partnership with the Niagara community to
foster, produce & disseminate research on current & emerging
issues.
Dr. Charles Conteh, Director PhD, 905-688-5550,
cconteh@brocku.ca

Staples: Hallam Observatory
**c/o Royal Astronomical Society of Canada - Windsor Center,
3989 South Middle Rd.,
Staples, ON N0P 2J0**

www.rascwindsor.com
www.facebook.com/hallamobservatory
The Hallam Observatory grounds are private property. Other
than the private group observing sessions the site is closed to
the public.

Sudbury: Doran Planetarium
**Laurentian University, 935 Ramsey Lake Rd.,
Sudbury, ON P3E 2C6**

laurentian.ca/planetarium
www.instagram.com/planetariumdoran
www.facebook.com/doranplanetarium
Year Founded: 1968 The Doran Planetarium is the largest
planetarium in Northern Ontario. Various astronomy
presentations for groups of all ages available in English &
French.
Paul-Émile Legault, Director, 705-675-1151,
plegault@laurentian.ca

Thunder Bay: David Thompson Astronomical
Observatory (DTAO)
**c/o Fort William Historical Park, 1350 King Rd.,
Thunder Bay, ON P7K 1L7**

Tel: 807-473-2344
reservations@fwhp.ca
www.fwhp.ca/observatory
The largest telescope in central Canada; workshops & lectures;
solar viewing; interactive exhibits; education programs; celestial
events.
Sergio Buonocore, General Manager

Toronto: Allan I. Observatory
**446 Petrie Science Building, York University, 4700 Keele St.,
Toronto, ON M3J 1P3**

observe@yorku.ca
www.observatory.info.yorku.ca
twitter.com/yorkobservatory
www.facebook.com/AllanICarswellObs
Other contact information: Phone: 416-736-2100 ext. 77773
A hands-on teaching facility in support of all undergraduate &
graduate astronomy courses at York University that also
encourages public interest. Tours also available.
Paul Delaney, Director & Senior Lecturer M.Sc, Astophysics &
Astronomy, pdelaney@yorku.ca

Toronto: University of Toronto Planetarium
Astronomy Bldg., 50 St. George St.,
Toronto, ON M5S 3H4

www.universe.utoronto.ca
Other contact information: General inquiries:
outreach@dunlap.utoronto.ca.
Shows are presented live by an astronomer in the University of
Toronto's 25-seat star theatre, which is equipped with a new 4K
digital projector & sophisticated planetarium software. Also
available for group shows.

Waterloo: Gustav Bakos Observatory
Physics & Astronomy
Physics Bldg., University of Waterloo, 200 University Ave.
West,
Waterloo, ON N2L 3G1

bservatory@uwaterloo.ca
uwaterloo.ca/physics-astronomy/community-outreach/gustav-ba
kos-observatory
Open for public tours on the 1st Wednesday of every month, free
of charge.

Quebec

Champlain: Observatoire du Cégep de Trois-Rivières
300, rte Sainte-Marie,
Champlain, QC G0X 1C0

Tél: 819-295-3043
observatoire@cegeptr.qc.ca
www.cegeptr.qc.ca/observatoire
www.instagram.com/cegeptr
www.twitter.com/cegeptr
www.facebook.com/obs ervatoire
Fondée en: 1980 Ouvert 25 juin au 30 août du mardi au samedi.

Laval: Observatoire astronomique de Laval
Parent: Club des Astronomes Amateurs de Laval
825, av du Parc,
Laval, QC H7E 2T7

www.astronomielaval.org
twitter.com/ObsDeLaval
www.facebook.com/ObservatoireLaval
Ouvert du 1er mai au 31 octobre.
Jean-Marc Richard, Directeur de l'observatoire

Montréal: Observatoire du Mont-Mégantic (OMM)
Parent: Centre de recherche en astrophysique du
Québec
Département de physique, Université de Montréal, CP 6128
Centre-Ville, C.P. 6128, Succ. Centre-Ville,
Montréal, QC H3C 3J7

Tél: 514-343-6667; *Téléc:* 514-343-2071
omm.craq-astro.ca
www.pinterest.ca/ommofficiel
twitter.com/OMM_Officiel
www.facebook.com/OMMastro
Fondée en: 1978 L'observatoire est situé au sommet du mont
Mégantic dans les Cantons de l'est, à une altitude de 1111m.
L'observatoire est le plus important centre de recherche en
astronomie & astrophysique au Canada.
René Doyon, Directeur, 514-343-6111, Fax: 514-343-2071,
doyon@astro.umontreal.ca

Notre-Dame-des-Bois: Astrolab du Parc National du
Mont Mégantic
189, rte du Parc,
Notre-Dame-des-Bois, QC J0B 2E0

Tél: 819-888-2941; *Téléc:* 819-888-2943
Ligne sans frais: 800-665-6527
parc.mont-megantic@sepaq.com
www.astrolab.qc.ca
www.facebook.com/MontMegantic
Fondée en: 1996 Situé dans le décor exceptionnel du parc
national du Mont-Mégantic, l'ASTROLab est un centre d'activités
en astronomie dédié au public. Deux observatoires publics, de
nombreux télescopes & instruments d'observation permettent de
découvrir les splendeurs de l'espace & de l'Univers.
Dany Gareau, Director, 819-888-2941,
gareau.dany@sepaq.com

Saint-Elzéar-de-Beauce: Observatoire du Mont
Cosmos
750, rang du Haut Sainte-Anne,
Saint-Elzéar-de-Beauce, QC G0S 2J2

Tél: 418-476-7830
info@montcosmos.com
www.montcosmos.com
Fondée en: 1995 Conférences astronomiques; ateliers
scientifiques destinés aux jeunes du primaire & du secondaire; la
lumière s'éclate & plus d'activités sur le site même de
l'observatoire.

Sherbrooke: Bishop's University Astronomical
Observatory
2600 College St.,
Sherbrooke, QC J1M 1Z7

observ@ubishops.ca
https://physics.ubishops.ca/observatory
www.face book.com/ubishopsobservatory
Other contact information: Phone: 819-822-9600 ext. 2228
The observatory is used for educational purposes & is open to
the public for tours & stellar evenings.

Saskatchewan

Saskatoon: University of Saskatchewan Observatory
Physics & Engineering Physics
University of Saskatchewan, 108 Wiggins Rd,
Saskatoon, SK S7N 5E6

campus.observatory@usask.ca
artsandscience.usask.ca/physics/facilities/observatory.php
twitter.com/uofaobservatory
www.facebook.com/usaskobservatory
Open every Saturday evening after dark for public viewing
through the telescope; admission is free

Yukon Territory

Watson Lake: Northern Lights Centre (NLC)
PO Box 590,
Watson Lake, YT Y0A 1C0

Tel: 867-536-7827; *Fax:* 867-536-2823
nlc@northwestel.net
www.northernlightscentre.ca
Year Founded: 1996 The NLC presents the aurora borealis
phenomenon & explains the science behind it through displays &
a video broadcast in the centre's domed theatre during the
summer. In the winter visitors can experience the real northern
lights.

Performing Arts - Dance

International

**Border Boosters Square & Round Dance
Association (BBSRDA)**

Tel: 514-631-3679
www.squaredance.qc.ca
To promote square & round dancing in the Québec, eastern
Ontario & northern New York area
Reina Ruben, President

The Royal Scottish Country Dance Society (RSCDS)
12 Coates Cres., Edinburgh EH3 7AF United Kingdom

info@rscds.org
www.rscds.org
www.youtube.com/user/TheRSCDS
To preserve & further the practice of traditional Scottish Country
Dancing; To provide or assist in providing special education or
instruction in the practice of Scottish Country Dances
Lorna Ogilvie, Chair
Clare MacGregor, Office Manager

Alberta

Alberta Ballet Company
141 - 18th Ave. SW, Calgary AB T2S 0B8

Tel: 403-245-4222
info@albertaballet.com
www.albertaballet.com
www.youtube.com/user/AlbertaBallet
To enrich & bring beauty to people's lives through creating,
performing & teaching ballet
Chris George, President & CEO
Christopher Anderson, Co-Artistic Director
Jean Grand-Maître, Co-Artistic Director

Alberta Dance Alliance (ADA)
Percy Page Centre, 11759 Groat Rd., 2nd Fl., Edmonton AB
T5M 3K6

Tel: 780-422-8107; *Fax:* 780-422-2663
Toll-Free: 888-422-8107
info@abdancealliance.ab.ca
www.abdancealliance.ab.ca
www.youtube.com/user/AlbertaDanceAlliance
To foster & promote the appreciation & practice of dance in
Alberta, through administrative, technical & informative services,
programs, advocacy & special events; To support professional
development through consultation in grant research, preparation
& production
Nova Andrews, President
Bobbi Westman, Executive Director

Alberta Square & Round Dance Federation
PO Box 114, Holden AB T0B 2C0

Tel: 780-688-2380
squaredance.ab.ca
To promote square dancing, round dancing & clogging in Alberta
Brenda Ryder, Co-President
Bud Sedman, Co-President

Brian Webb Dance Co.
PO Box 53092, Stn. Glenora, Edmonton AB T5N 48A

Tel: 780-452-3282
bwdancecompany@gmail.com
bwdc.ca
www.instagram.com/brianwebbdanceco
To produce & present contemporary dance; To build new works
through collaboration
Leanne Reeb, President
Brian Webb, Artistic Director

Catalyst Theatre Society of Alberta
9828 - 101A Ave., Edmonton AB T5J 3C6

Tel: 780-431-1750
catalysttheatre.ca
www.youtube.com/user/catalystart
To create & present original Canadian work that explores new
possibilities for theatre
Jonathan Christenson, Artistic Director
Lana Michelle Hughes, Managing Director

Decidedly Jazz Danceworks (DJD)
111 - 12th Ave. SE, Calgary AB T2G 0Z9

Tel: 403-245-3533; *Fax:* 403-245-3584
djd@decidedlyjazz.com
www.decidedlyjazz.com
www.youtube.com/user/decidedlyjazz
To create concert jazz dance that sustains the spirit & traditions
of jazz; To mix groove, African roots, rhythm, improvisation,
interplay with musicians & soul; To offer a season of
performances, touring & jazz classes
Kimberley Cooper, Artistic Director
Kathi Sundstrom, Executive Director

Footprints Dance Project Society of Alberta
AB

Tel: 587-228-5440
calgaryfootprintsdance@gmail.com
footprintsdance.com
www.youtube.com/CalgaryFootprints
To ensure children & youth facing barriers have opportunities to
explore & enjoy the arts
Nicole Pemberton, Artistic Producer

Springboard Dance Collective Calgary Society
205 - 8th Ave. SE, 2nd Fl., Calgary AB T2G 0K9

Tel: 403-265-3230
info@springboardperformance.com
springboardperformance.com
To produce, create & perform intellectually & sensually
stimulating modern dance
Nicole Mion, Artistic Director & Curator

Sun Ergos, A Company of Theatre & Dance
130 Sunset Way, Priddis AB T0L 1W0

Tel: 403-931-1527; *Fax:* 403-931-1534
Toll-Free: 800-743-3351
waltermoke@sunergos.com
www.sunergos.com
www.youtube.com/user/sunergostheatre
To witness, maintain & develop the ethnocultural roots of theatre
& dance, without prejudice of race, creed, sex or cultural
background, to celebrate the differences & recognize the
similarities among all peoples; To provide the best possible
theatre & dance within the urban & rural communities, nationally
& internationally
Robert Greenwood, Artistic & Managing Director
Dana Luebke, Artistic & Production Director

Vinok Worldance
11727 Kingsway, Edmonton AB T5G 3A1

Tel: 780-454-3739
www.vinok.ca
To present music & dances of the world to audiences all across
Canada; To reflect world dance as a way of celebrating life &
expressing through dance, music, song & improvisation
Leanne Koziak, Artistic Director

British Columbia

British Columbia Square & Round Dance Federation
BC

Toll-Free: 800-335-9433
info@squaredance.bc.ca
squaredance.bc.ca
To provide healthy recreation at the community level for an affordable cost
Jean Wood, President

Canadian Alliance of Dance Artists, West Chapter (CADA/West)
PO Box 88029, Stn. Chinatown, Vancouver BC V6A 4A4
Tel: 604-724-8824
office@cadawest.org
cadawest.org
To act as a unified voice for professional dance artists in British Columbia; To advance the socioeconomic status & working conditions of professional dance artists; To enable dance artists to attain their potential; To foster excellence in dance
Olivia C. Davies, Chair
Jessica Wadsworth, Executive Director

The Dance Centre Society (TDC)
Scotiabank Dance Centre, 677 Davie St., Level 6, Vancouver BC V6B 2G6
Tel: 604-606-6400; *Toll-Free:* 877-649-3010
info@thedancecentre.ca
thedancecentre.ca
www.youtube.com/c/dancecentre
To raise the profile of dance in BC; To serve as a focal point & advocate for issues & concerns affecting the entire dance community; To coordinate the resources & activities of this wide ranging community
Mirna Zagar, Executive Director
Nazanin Oghanian, Coordinator, Membership & Outreach

EDAM Performing Arts Society (EDAM)
303 East 8th Ave., Vancouver BC V5T 1S1
Tel: 604-876-9559
info@edamdance.org
www.edamdance.org
To explore new directions in dance & the performing arts
Peter Bingham, Artistic Director
Julia Carr, General Manager

Goh Ballet Vancouver Society
2345 Main St., Vancouver BC V5T 3C9
Tel: 604-872-4014; *Fax:* 604-872-4011
admin@gohballet.com
www.gohballet.com
www.youtube.com/user/GohBallet
To prepare aspiring dancers for professional careers by providing rigorous training in the vocabulary & artistry of classical ballet
Chan Hon Goh, Director

Kinesis Dance Society
Scotia Bank Dance Centre, 677 Davie St., Level 6, Vancouver BC V6B 2G6
Tel: 604-684-7844; *Fax:* 604-684-7834
admin@kinesisdance.org
www.kinesisdance.org
To contribute new & provocative works of contemporary dance to the local, national & international dance scene; To educate through workshops & cultural exchanges & to collaborate with other media, such as film, video & theatre
Paras Terezakis, Artistic Director
Carline Dolmazon, Administrator

Mascall Dance Society
211 Keefer St., Vancouver BC V6A 2T9
operations@mascalldance.ca
www.mascalldance.ca
To provide a forum for research, creation, performance, education, documentation & dissemination of contemporary dance & related disciplines
Jennifer Mascall, Artistic Director

Pacific Ballet British Columbia
601 Smithe St., Vancouver BC V6G 5G1
Tel: 604-732-5003; *Fax:* 604-732-4417
info@balletbc.com
balletbc.com
www.youtube.com/c/BalletBCVancouver
To commission & perform a balanced repertoire rooted in classical technique, which encompasses the best new ballets & late 20th century classics
Branislav Henselmann, Executive Director
Emily Molnar, Artistic Director

Vancouver Moving Theatre Society (VMT)
PO Box 88270, Stn. Chinatown, 418 Main St., Vancouver BC V6A 4A4
Tel: 604-628-5672
vancouvermovingtheatre@shaw.ca
vancouvermovingtheatre.com
To develop a new form of interdisciplinary art influenced by the Pacific Rim culture of Vancouver; To present services & products to affirm the importance of art in questions of healing, humanity & the soul
Savannah Walling, Artistic Director
Terry Hunter, Executive Director

Manitoba

Canadian Square & Round Dance Society (CSRDS)
c/o Lorraine Kozera, #467, 2701 Scotia St., Winnipeg MB R2V 5A5
info@squaredance.ca
csrds.ca
To link information about Canadian square & round dancing associations together in order to promote awareness, inspire activity & to offer information
Laurie Illsley, President
Lorraine Kozera, Secretary

Contemporary Dancers Inc.
#204, 211 Bannatyne Ave., Winnipeg MB R3B 3P2
Tel: 204-452-0229
communications@winnipegscontemporarydancers.ca
www.winnipegscontemporarydancers.ca
vimeo.com/wpgcontemps
To create a place on the local, national & international arts landscape that enables vital intersections, linkages & exchange among dance creators, dance interpreters, spectators and communities
Jolene Bailie, Artistic Director

Dance Manitoba Inc.
#1836, 201 Portage Ave., Winnipeg MB R3B 3K6
Tel: 204-794-1094
dancemanitobainc@gmail.com
www.dancemb.org
To promote the development of dance through festivals, workshops & showcases
Claire Marshall, President
Wendy Bobby, Executive Director

Manitoba Square & Round Dance Federation
MB
squaredancemb.com
To promote & govern square, round, clog & line dancing in Manitoba
Del Marks, Co-President
Yvonne Marks, Co-President

Royal Winnipeg Ballet (RWB)
380 Graham Ave., Winnipeg MB R3C 4K2
Tel: 204-956-0183; *Fax:* 204-943-1994
Toll-Free: 800-667-4792
customerservice@rwb.org
www.rwb.org
www.instagram.com/rwballet
To enrich the human experience by teaching, creating & performing outstanding dance
Don Leitch, Chair
André Lewis, Artistic Director & CEO

New Brunswick

Federation of Dance Clubs of New Brunswick (FDCNB)
c/o President, 55 Christopher Dr., Burton NB E2V 3H4
Tel: 506-446-9640
squaredancenb.ca
To serve as New Brunswick's family of dancers, expounding the virtues of dance-related recreational activity in every region of the province, actively involved with training, teaching, instructing, informing & assisting others to learn more about dance-related ideas
Geraldine Lefebvre, Co-President
Michel Lefebvre, Co-President

Les Productions DansEncorps Inc.
Centre Culturel Aberdeen, #14, 140, rue Botsford, Moncton NB E1C 4X5
Tél: 506-855-0998
info@dansencorps.ca
www.dansencorps.ca
De contribuer au développement des arts au Nouveau-Brunswick
Chantal Cadieux, Directrice artistique

Nova Scotia

Amethyst Scottish Dancers of Nova Scotia
NS
amethystdancersns@gmail.com
amethystscottishdancersns.ca
www.instagram.com/amethyst_dancers
To enrich Nova Scotia's Scottish culture through traditional & modern dance performances
Meg Grandmaison, Artistic Director

Dance Nova Scotia
1113 Marginal Rd., Halifax NS B3H 4P7
Tel: 902-422-1749; *Fax:* 902-422-0881
office@dancens.ca
www.dancens.ca
To promote, stimulate & encourage the development of dance as a cultural, educational, healthy & social activity for all ages, abilities & backgrounds
Cliff Le Jeune, Executive Director
Lynn Graham, Administrative Officer

Square & Round Dance Federation of Nova Scotia
NS
www.chebucto.ns.ca
To provide liaison between clubs & the provincial government; To suggest guidelines & provide an organizational framework for operating & coordinating activities of member clubs; To encourage cooperation in advertising, promoting & operating Square & Round Dance classes throughout the province of Nova Scotia; To support & supplement the work of the Association of Nova Scotia Square & Round Dance Teachers

Ontario

Atelier Theatre Society (OA)
St. Lawrence Hall, 157 King St. East, 4th Fl., Toronto ON M5C 1G9
Tel: 416-703-3767; *Fax:* 416-703-4895
opera.atelier@operaatelier.com
www.operaatelier.com
www.youtube.com/user/OperaAtelier
To produce opera, ballet & drama from the 17th & 18th centuries; To educate and instruct young performers
Alexandra Skoczylas, Executive Director
Jeannette Lajeunesse Zingg, Co-Artistic Director & Choreographer
Marshall Pynkoski, Co-Artistic Director & Director
David Fallis, Resident Music Director

Ballet Creole
#124, 1 Wiltshire Ave., Toronto ON M6N 2V7
info@balletcreole.org
balletcreole.org
To preserve & promote traditional & contemporary African & Caribbean dance styles; To build a dance legacy in Canada; To bring cultures together through entertainment, as well as education, accessibility & archival projects
Rhea Howley, President
Patrick Parson, Artistic Director

Ballet Jörgen Canada
c/o Bldg. C, Casa Loma Campus, George Brown College, #126, 160 Kendal Ave., Toronto ON M5R 1M3
Tel: 416-961-4725; *Fax:* 416-415-2865
info@balletjorgen.ca
www.balletjorgen.ca
To operate exclusively as a charitable organization to administer & employ its property, assets & rights for the purpose of raising the public's awareness of ballet as an art form by establishing, maintaining & operating a ballet company; To advance knowledge & increase public recognition of ballet by developing a repertoire of original dance productions for performance, film & video for the benefit of the community at large; To advance artistic appreciation & education of the general public of choreography as a distinctive art form by commissioning & making available to the public presentations by a variety of choreographers
Bengt Jörgen, Artistic Director & CEO

Canada Dance Festival Society
476 Parliament St., Toronto ON M4X 1P2
Tel: 613-947-7000
cdffdc@nac-cna.ca
www.canadadance.ca
To present diverse dance performances; To provide community networking & audience development
Jeanne Holmes, Artistic Director

Canadian Alliance of Dance Artists, East Chapter (CADA/East)
476 Parliament St., 2nd Fl., Toronto ON M4X 1P2
Tel: 416-657-2276
office@cada-on.ca
cadaontario.camp8.org
To advance the socioeconomic status & working conditions of professional dance artists in Ontario; To support the professional & artistic development of Ontario's dance artists
Ashley Bomberry, Administrative Director

Canadian Children's Dance Theatre (CCDT)
509 Parliament St., Toronto ON M4X 1P3
Tel: 416-924-5657; *Fax:* 416-924-4141
info@ccdt.ca
www.ccdt.org
To promote dance theatre to young people
Deborah Lundmark, Artistic Director & Resident Choreographer
Michael de Coninck Smith, Managing Director & Tour Manager

Canadian Dance Teachers' Association (CDTA) / Association canadienne des professeurs de danse
#38, 6033 Shawson Dr., Mississauga ON L5T 1H8
Tel: 905-564-2139; *Fax:* 905-564-2211
office@cdtaont.com
cdtaont.com
To advance education in the field of dance & maintain throughout Canada an organization of qualified dance teachers; To promote friendship & the exchange of ideas & information among the dance teachers of Canada; To provide an organization to represent Canadian dance teachers internationally
Christine Campbell, President

Dance Ontario Association / Association Ontario Danse
The Distillery District, #304, 15 Case Goods Lane, Toronto ON M5A 3C4
Tel: 416-204-1083; *Fax:* 416-204-1085
contact@danceontario.ca
www.danceontario.ca
To support the advancement of all forms of dance; To offer a unified voice on dance issues
Samara Thompson, Chair
Jennifer Watkins, Vice-Chair
Amy Hampton, Executive Director
Julie McLachlan, Coordinator, Membership

Dance Umbrella of Ontario (DUO)
410 Jarvis St., 2nd Fl., Toronto ON M4Y 2G6
Tel: 416-504-6429
duo@danceumbrella.net
danceumbrella.net
www.instagram.com/danceumbrellaofontario
To assist & support professional dance creators in Ontario dance centres
Robert Sauvey, Executive Director

Dancemakers
#301, 15 Case Goods Lane, Toronto ON M5A 3C4
Tel: 416-367-1800
info@dancemakers.org
dancemakers.org
To bring dance of challenging physicality & emotional impact to audiences by drawing on the diverse talents & individual strengths of its artists; To develop & support works which both provoke & entertain
Brodie Stevenson, President
Desirée Leverenz, Interim General Manager

Dancer Transition Resource Centre (DTRC) / Centre de ressources et transition pour danseurs (CRTD)
The Lynda Hamilton Centre, #303, 1000 Yonge St., Toronto ON M4W 2K2
Tel: 416-595-5655; *Fax:* 416-595-0009
Toll-Free: 800-667-0851
nationaloffice@dtrc.ca
dtrc.ca
www.youtube.com/user/DancerTransition
TO help dancers make necessary transitions into, within & from professional performing; To provide resources for the dance community & the public, offering seminars, education materials & other information
Monique Rabideau, Chair
Kristian Clarke, Executive Director

Fujiwara Dance Inventions
509 Parliament St., 2nd Fl., Toronto ON M4X 1P3
Tel: 416-593-8455
info@fujiwaradance.com
www.fujiwaradance.com

To create, perform, & teach dance; To use dance to move & change people, as well as encounter the complexity of humanity
Denise Fujiwara, Artistic Director

Gina Lori Riley Dance Enterprises
Windsor ON
www.ginaloririleydanceenterprises.com
To advance art through the development of new work, the presentation of contemporary dance & the presentation & promotion of community education
Gina Lori Riley, Artistic Director

National Ballet of Canada
Walter Carsen Centre, 470 Queens Quay West, Toronto ON M5V 3K4
Tel: 416-345-9686; *Fax:* 416-345-8323
info@national.ballet.ca
national.ballet.ca
www.youtube.com/user/nationalballetcanada
Karen Kain, Artistic Director
Barry Hughson, Executive Director
David Briskin, Music Director & Principal Conductor

Ontario Folk Dance Association (OFDA)
Toronto ON
ontariofolkdancers@gmail.com
ofda.ca
To promote the practice of international folk arts & dance; To prepare, collect & disseminate information & material relating to folk arts & dance

Ontario Square & Round Dance Federation (OSRDF)
88 Foxhollow Cres., London ON N6G 3R2
Tel: 519-472-1596
squaredance.on.ca
To coordinate square, round, clog & line dancing throughout Ontario
Dan Roy, President

Royal Academy of Dance Canada
#601, 1210 Sheppard Ave. East, Toronto ON M2K 1E3
Tel: 416-489-2813; *Toll-Free:* 888-709-0895
info@radcanada.org
ca.royalacademyofdance.org
To provide dance education & training
Clarke MacIntosh, National Director

Toronto & District Square & Round Dance Association
ON
www.td-dance.ca
To promote, encourage & foster wider knowledge of square & round dancing; To provide for mutual exchange of philosophy & material pertaining to square & round dancing between callers, teachers & leaders; To improve quality of square & round dancing; To encourage use of standards of uniformity relating to square & round dancing
Howard Lander, Co-President
Jean Lander, Co-President

Toronto Dance Theatre (TDT)
80 Winchester St., Toronto ON M4X 1B2
Tel: 416-967-1365
info@tdt.org
tdt.org
www.instagram.com/tdtwinch
To develop Canadian dance works of art; To perform nationally & internationally; To explore new ideas in choreographic expression while embracing the fresh & vital aspects of inherited traditions
Jessica Whitford, Managing Director
Andrew Tay, Artistic Director

Québec

Ballet West / Ballet Ouest
#218, 269, boul St-Jean, Montréal QC H9R 3J1
Tel: 514-783-1245
reception@balletouest.com
balletouest.com
vimeo.com/balletouestdemontreal
To provide a milieu that encourages young dancers to express themselves through dance & to move from amateur to professional status; To educate & develop audiences; To present an alternative view to counteract the mass culture that is being fed to our youth
Claude Caron, Artistic Director

Les Ballets Jazz de Montréal (BJM)
1210, rue Sherbrooke est, Montréal QC H2L 1L9
Tél: 514-982-6771; *Téléc:* 514-982-9145
info@bjmdanse.ca
www.bjmdanse.ca
www.youtube.com/c/LesBalletsJazzdeMontréal
Crée, produit et diffuse à l'échelle nationale et internationale des spectacles de danse contemporaine; offre à ses danseurs un entraînement professionnel; permet aux chorégraphes invités et aux danseurs de développer leur propre recherche; génère un répertoire exclusif et conserve l'esprit novateur qui anime la compagnie de puis sa création
Marie-Joëlle Tremblay, Directrice générale
Jeremy Raia, Directeur artistique répertoire par intérim

Le Carré des Lombes
#401, 2022, rue Sherbrooke est, Montréal QC H2K 1B9
Tél: 514-287-9339
info@lecarredeslombes.com
www.lecarredeslombes.com
Diffuser des spectacles de danse; promouvoir la danse comme discipline artistique
Danièle Desnoyers, Directrice artistique et chorégraphe

Cercle d'expression artistique Nyata Nyata / Nyata Nyata Circle of Artistic Expression
4374, boul St-Laurent, 2e étage, Montréal QC H2W 1Z5
Tél: 514-849-9781; *Ligne sans frais:* 877-692-8208
info@nyata-nyata.org
www.nyata-nyata.org
Pour créer musical et l'art chorégraphique dans le but de développer l'art de la danse et les compétences des artistes
Zab Maboungou, Directrice artistique

Compagnie Marie Chouinard
4499, av de l'esplanade, Montréal QC H2W 1T2
Tél: 514-843-9036; *Téléc:* 514-843-7616
info@mariechouinard.com
www.mariechouinard.com
www.youtube.com/user/MarieChouinard
Pour être dédié à des interprétations modernes et uniques de la danse, nouvelle chorégraphie artistique, et l'expression à travers les mouvements du corps humain
Marie Chouinard, Directrice générale et artistique

Danse-Cité inc
#426, 3680, rue Jeanne-Mance, Montréal QC H2X 2K5
Tél: 514-525-3595
info@danse-cite.org
www.danse-cite.org
www.youtube.com/user/DANSECITE
Création et production de spectacles de danse contemporain
Sophie Corriveau, Directrice générale et artistique

Fédération des loisirs-danse du Québec (FLDQ)
c/o CPDDSQ, 1307, rue Legendre est, Montréal QC H2M 1H3
Tél: 514-214-9481; *Téléc:* 514-251-8038
www.cpddsq.ca
De promouvoir et développer la danse sous toutes ses formes

Les Grands Ballets Canadiens (GBCM)
#500, 1435, rue de Bleury, Montréal QC H3A 2H7
Tél: 514-849-0269
info@grandsballets.com
grandsballets.com
www.youtube.com/user/LesGrandsBallets
Maintenir la tradition du ballet classique et élargir le champ d'expression de cette forme artistique par la création; faire connaître et apprécier la danse à tous les publics grâce à la qualité de nos presentations et de nos productions
Maurice Côté, Président
Marc Lalonde, Directeur général
Ivan Cavallari, Directeur artistique

Louise Bédard Danse
#301, 2022, rue Sherbrooke est, Montréal QC H2K 1B9
Tél: 514-982-4580
infos@lbdanse.org
www.lbdanse.org
vimeo.com/lbdanse
De poursuivre les activités modernes création de danse, de sensibilisation d'éducation, et en offrant des créations chorégraphiques originales pour le grand public
Louise Bédard, Directrice artistique et générale

Lucie Grégoire Danse
#302, 4416 boul St-Laurent, Montréal QC HW2 1Z5
Tél: 514-278-1620
infos@luciegregoiredanse.ca
www.luciegregoiredanse.ca
Lucie Grégoire, Directrice artistique

Margie Gillis Dance Foundation / Fondation de danse Margie Gillis
#304, 1908, rue Panet, Montréal QC H2L 3A2

Tel: 514-845-3115
info@margiegillis.org
margiegillis.org

To reach as large a public as possible with a dance program of physical & emotional integrity; To make the audience aware of the potential of their own lives
Margie Gillis, Artistic Director

Montréal Danse
#109, 372, rue Sainte-Catherine ouest, Montréal QC H3B 1A2

Tél: 514-871-4005
questions@montrealdanse.com
montrealdanse.com

Se voue à la création de vibrantes oeuvres chorégraphiques avec le concours de plusieurs chorégraphes nationaux et internationaux
Kathy Casey, Directrice artistique

O Vertigo Danse
175, rue Sainte-Catherine ouest, Montréal QC H2X 1Z8

Tél: 514-251-9177; *Téléc:* 514-251-7358
info@overtigo.com
overtigo.com

Se consacre à la création en nouvelle danse et la diffusion des oeuvres de la fondatrice et directrice artistique de la compagnie
Ginette Laurin, Directrice générale

Regroupement québécois de la danse (RQD)
#440, 3680, rue Jeanne-Mance, Montréal QC H2X 2K5

Tél: 514-849-4003; *Téléc:* 514-849-3288
info@quebecdanse.org
quebecdanse.org
www.youtube.com/user/quebecdanse

Promouvoir, encourager et soutenir le développement artistique, social et économique des danseurs, chorégraphes et de tout intervenant professionnel de la communauté de la danse au Québec
Fabienne Cabado, Directrice générale

Saskatchewan

Dance Saskatchewan Inc.
309 Fairmont Dr., Saskatoon SK S7M 5G7

Tel: 306-931-8480; *Fax:* 306-244-1520
Toll-Free: 800-667-8480
office@dancesask.com
www.dancesask.com

To support & enhance the development of all dance forms; To promote dance in Saskatchewan; To represent & educate about dance; To encourage a passion for dance; To create a viable, unified organization which represents & advocates dance interests; To foster free expression of cultural identity through dance; To establish an active environment which focuses on job creation, performance & cultural diversity within a central dance facility
Kathy Bond, President

Saskatchewan Square & Round Dance Federation (SSRDF)
SK

sksquaredance.ca

To guide & promote Square & Round Dancing & Clogging throughout the province as recreation for people of all ages & in all walks of life to enjoy
Donna Barber, Co-President
Dwayne Barber, Co-President

Performing Arts - Music

International

Barbershop Harmony Society
110 - 7th Ave. North, Nashville TN 37203-3704 USA

Tel: 615-823-3993; *Fax:* 615-313-7620
Toll-Free: 800-876-7464
customerservice@barbershop.org
www.barbershop.org
www.youtube.com/user/BarbershopHarmony38

To celebrate barbershop quartets; To promote & encourage vocal harmony & good fellowship among its members through the formation of local chapters & districts; To encourage & promote the education of its members & the public in music appreciation
Marty Monson, CEO & Executive Director
Erik Dove, Chief Financial Officer & COO
Holly J. Kellar, Chief Marketing Officer

Alberta

Alberta Band Association (ABA)
5708 - 72nd St., Edmonton AB T6B 3J4

Tel: 780-800-0482; *Toll-Free:* 877-687-4239
info@albertabandassociation.com
www.albertabands.com

To promote & develop the musical, educational & cultural values of bands & band music in Alberta
Brent Pierce, President

Alberta Music Industry Association (AMIA)
#304, 9804 Jasper Ave., Edmonton AB T5J 0C5

Tel: 780-428-3372
info@albertamusic.org
www.albertamusic.org
www.youtube.com/user/AlbertaMusic1

To help music professionals succeed by providing professional development, education, mentoring & training opportunities; To lobby government agencies in support of the music industry; To conduct fundraising & sponsorship activities
Carly Klassen, Executive Director

Calgary Opera Association
Mamdani Opera Centre, 1315 - 7th St. SW, Calgary AB T2R 1A5

Tel: 403-262-7286
info@calgaryopera.com
calgaryopera.com
www.youtube.com/user/CalgaryOpera

To enrich the cultural life of the community by celebrating musical art through the performance of professional opera
Heather Kitchen, General Director & CEO
Mark Morash, Interim Music Director

Calgary Philharmonic Society (CPO)
Arts Commons, 205 - 8th Ave. SE, 2nd Fl., Calgary AB T2G 0K9

Tel: 403-571-0270; *Fax:* 403-294-7424
info@calgaryphil.com
calgaryphil.com
www.youtube.com/c/CalgaryPhilharmonic

To provide audience with a rich, diverse & unequalled symphonic musical experience which earns broad community support
Paul Dornian, President & CEO

Calgary Youth Orchestra Society
Mount Royal University Conservatory, 4825 Mount Royal Gate SW, Calgary AB T3E 6K6

Tel: 403-440-5978; *Fax:* 403-440-6594
cyo@mtroyal.ca
www.calgaryyouthorchestra.org

To provide the best possible musical experience for the talented young musicians of the Calgary region, in an art form that is considered one of the highest forms of expression
Edmond Agopian, Director

Choir Alberta Association
5708 - 72nd St. NW, Edmonton AB T6B 3J4

Tel: 780-488-7464; *Fax:* 780-488-6403
Toll-Free: 855-723-6397
info@choiralberta.ca
www.choiralberta.ca

To promote choral music within the communities of Alberta; To gain support for choral music through public policy
Julie Freedman Smith, President
Brendan Lord, Executive Director

Crowsnest Pass Symphony
Crowsnest Pass AB T0K 0E0

To provide a vehicle for young people to learn & perform music; To give amateur adult musicians the opportunity to play classical music recreationally
Debbie Goldstein, Conductor

Edmonton Jazz Society (EJS)
11 Tommy Banks Way, Edmonton AB T6E 2M2

info@yardbirdsuitejazz.com
yardbirdsuite.com
www.instagram.com/yardbirdsuiteyeg

To present, promote & develop the performance of live jazz music in the city of Edmonton
Francis Remedios, President

Edmonton Opera Association
15230 - 128th Ave., Edmonton AB T5V 1A8

Tel: 780-424-4040; *Fax:* 780-429-0600
edmopera@edmontonopera.com
www.edmontonopera.com
www.youtube.com/c/EdmontonOpera1

To develop & promote opera as a dynamic & progressive art form; To attract & challenge audiences & artists through a creative program of opera production & education
Cindy Neufeld, President
Richard Cook, Interim General Director
Mel Kirby, Artistic Director

Edmonton Symphony Orchestra (ESO)
4 Sir Winston Churchill Sq., Edmonton AB T5J 4X8

Tel: 780-428-1108
edmontonsymphony@gmail.com
www.winspearcentre.com
www.youtube.com/c/edmontonsymphony

To foster appreciation & enjoyment of live, professional orchestral music through presenting concert performances, educational & community programs

Edmonton Youth Orchestra Association (EYO)
PO Box 66041, Stn. Heritage, Edmonton AB T6J 6T4

Tel: 780-569-5290
eyo@shaw.ca
www.eyso.com

To provide young musicians with the opportunity to develop their orchestral skills & increase their knowledge & appreciation of music, while enriching the cultural life of the community through concerts & benefit performances
Michael Massey, Music Director

The Festival Chorus
c/o Arts Commons, 205 - 8th Ave. SE, Calgary AB T2G 0K9

Tel: 403-294-7400
info@thefestivalchorus.com
www.thefestivalchorus.com

To present choral music & concert presentations for the community
Mel Kirby, Artistic Director

Lethbridge Symphony Association (LSO)
PO Box 1101, Lethbridge AB T1J 4A2

Tel: 403-328-6808
hello@lethbridgesymphony.org
www.lethbridgesymphony.org

To promote the orchestra & provide memorable musical experiences for their audiences
Vicki Hegedus, Executive Director
Glenn Klassen, Music Director

Prairie Saengerbund Choir Association
4823 Claret St. NW, Calgary AB T2L 1B9

Tel: 403-284-3731; *Fax:* 403-284-1470

To share, enhance, encourage & celebrate German musical heritage

Red Deer Symphony Orchestra Association
5205 - 48th Ave., Red Deer AB T4N 6S5

Tel: 403-340-2948
info@rdso.ca
www.rdso.ca
www.instagram.com/reddeersymphony

To provide nationally-recognized, quality symphonic music to central Alberta; To encourage an appreciation for the performance and development of symphonic music in central Alberta
Jamie L. Smith, President
Claude Lapalme, Music Director

Youth Singers of Calgary (YSC)
1371 Hastings Cres. SE, Calgary AB T2G 4C8

Tel: 403-234-9549
yscadmin@youthsingers.org
www.youthsingers.org
www.youtube.com/c/YouthSingersCalgary

To deliver a local choral music education program for children, teens & adults; To foster a lifelong interest in the performing arts through music, singing, dancing & acting
Megan Emmett, Chief Executive Officer
Tricia Penner, Artistic Director

British Columbia

British Columbia Youth Music Society
PO Box 26064, Stn. Central, Richmond BC V6Y 3V3

Tel: 604-365-3584
admin@rdyo.ca
www.rdyo.ca

To sponsor & operate the Richmond Delta Youth Orchestra; To encourage young musicians to excel through education & performance; To provide a comprehensive & balanced musical education as a member of an ensemble; To promote an understanding & appreciation of orchestral music in the community at large
Sarah Xie, President

Stephen Robb, Music Director

Canadian Federation of Music Teachers' Associations (CFMTA) / Fédération canadienne des associations des professeurs de musique (FCAPM)
PO Box 814 Summerland, 13409 Hermiston Dr., Summerland BC V0H 1Z0

Tel: 250-328-2198
admin@cfmta.org
www.cfmta.org

To promote high musical & academic qualifications among members
Amy Boyes, Public Relations
Laureen Kells, President
Dina Pollock, Communications

Chilliwack Symphony Orchestra & Chorus (CSO)
PO Box 521, Stn. Main, Chilliwack BC V2P 7V5

Tel: 604-795-0521
chilliwacksymphony@gmail.com
www.chilliwacksymphony.com

To perform orchestral music to the residents of Chilliwack & surrounding communities
Bevin van Liempt, President
Paula DeWit, Music Director

Fraser Valley Symphony Society (FVS)
Abbotsford BC

Tel: 604-744-9110
info@fraservalleysymphony.org
www.fraservalleysymphony.org

Linda Jensen, President
Lindsay Mellor, Music Director

Friends of Chamber Music
PO Box 38046, RPO King Edward Mall, Vancouver BC V5Z 4L9

friendsofchambermusic.ca
www.youtube.com/user/FCMVancouver

To present the best in chamber music

Greater Victoria Youth Orchestra (GVYO)
1611 Quadra St., Victoria BC V8W 2L5

Tel: 250-360-1121; *Fax:* 250-381-3573
gvyorchestra@gmail.com
www.gvyo.org

To affirm & nourish the love of music in young people; To foster musical development of orchestra members; To serve as musical resource to the community at large
Yariv Aloni, Music Director

Kamloops Symphony (KSO)
#6, 510 Lorne St., Kamloops BC V2C 1W3

Tel: 250-372-5000
info@kamloopssymphony.com
www.kamloopssymphony.com
www.instagram.com/kamsymphony

To operate & promote a symphony orchestra for the Kamloops region
Daniel Mills, Executive Director
Dina Gilbert, Music Director

Music BC Industry Association (PMIA)
#201B, 196 West 3rd Ave., Vancouver BC v5y 1e9

info@musicbc.org
musicbc.org
www.instagram.com/music_bc

To address key issues; To implement positive change by presenting a strong voice to government, business & community; To enhance the profile of the BC music industry in the international marketplace; To promote communication; To stimulate activity & employment
Lindsay MacPherson, Executive Director
Jimmy Leitch, Program Manager
Kentya Kurban, Coordinator, Community Engagement

Okanagan Symphony Society
PO Box 20238, Kelowna BC V1Y 9H2

Tel: 250-763-7544
admin@okanagansymphony.com
okanagansymphony.com

To provide the communities of the Okanagan Valley with an orchestra that is committed to excellence in the performance of classical music
Geraldine Parent, Executive Director
Rosemary Thomson, Music Director

Pacific Opera Victoria Association (POV)
925 Balmoral Rd., Victoria BC V8T 1A7

Tel: 250-382-1641
info@pacificopera.ca
pacificopera.ca

To create a dynamic operatic experience, & to inspire audiences, artists & community
Ian Rye, Chief Executive Officer
Timothy Vernon, Artistic Director

Prince George Symphony Orchestra Society (PGSO)
2880 - 15th Ave., Prince George BC V2M 1T1

Tel: 250-562-0800
admin@pgso.com
www.pgso.com
www.youtube.com/user/pgsymphony

To provide symphonic music for Prince George & region consistent with Prince George Symphony Orchestra artistic policy that facilitates artistic development of its players; To foster & facilitate positive community image & financial responsiblity so that a wide spectrum of musical experiences is offered to players & audiences alike
Roy Stewart, President
Ken Hall, Executive Director
Michael Hall, Music Director

Richmond Community Orchestra & Chorus Association
#130, 10691 Shellbridge Way, Richmond BC V6X 2W8

Tel: 604-276-2747; *Fax:* 604-270-3644
roca@roca.ca
www.roca.ca
www.youtube.com/c/RocaCamusicians

To build community connections and enrich the Richmond cultural scene by performing orchestral & choral music; To nurture musical talent and provide community service
Bernie Barrett, President

Sooke Philharmonic Society
PO Box 767, Sooke BC V9Z 1H7

Tel: 250-419-3569
sookephilharmonic@gmail.com
www.sookephil.ca

To promote & enhance the appreciation of music; To support & nurture musical talent in the community
Yariv Aloni, Music Director

Surrey Symphony Society (SSS)
PO Box 39083, Stn. Panorama, #100, 15157 - 56th Ave., Surrey BC V3S 9A0

Tel: 604-825-1896
gm@surreysymphony.com
surreyyouthorchestra.com

To expand an appreciation of orchestral music among young musicians & to share this with the community through public performance
Sue Anderlini, President

University of British Columbia Symphony Orchestra
c/o School of Music, University of British Columbia, 6361 Memorial Rd., Vancouver BC V6T 1Z2

Tel: 604-822-3113; *Fax:* 604-822-4884
music.ubc.ca/symphony-orchestra

To perform symphonic works from the 18th, 19th & 20th centuries
Jonathan Girard, Director

Vancouver Island Symphony
PO Box 661, Nanaimo BC V9R 5L9

Tel: 250-754-0177
info@vancouverislandsymphony.com
www.vancouverislandsymphony.com

To promote & present orchestra music in the Central Vancouver Island Region
Margot Holmes, Executive Director
Pierre Simard, Artistic Director

Vancouver New Music Society (VNM)
837 Davie St., Vancouver BC V6Z 1B7

Tel: 604-633-0861
info@newmusic.org
newmusic.org
www.youtube.com/c/VancouverNewMusic

To foster connections in the community to bring new music to a wider audience; To commission & premiere new work by Canadian composers; To produce music-theatre & electroacoustic music; To explore the interaction of contemporary music with other disciplines
Allison MacDonald, President
Giorgio Magnanensi, Artistic Director

Vancouver Opera Association (VOA)
1945 McLean Dr., Vancouver BC V5N 3J7

Tel: 604-682-2871; *Fax:* 604-682-3981
online@vancouveropera.ca
www.vancouveropera.ca
www.youtube.com/user/vancouveropera

To share the power of opera with all who are open to receiving it, through superior performances & meaningful education programs for all ages
Tom Wright, General Director

Vancouver Philharmonic Society
PO Box 27503, Stn. Oakridge, Vancouver BC V5Z 4M4

vancouver.philharmonic@gmail.com
www.vanphil.ca

To provide non-professional musicians with an opportunity to perform orchestral music with a full symphony orchestra; To train aspiring professional conductors & musicians; To inspire & entertain the Vancouver community through performance
Jin Zhang, Music Director

Vancouver Society for Early Music
1254 - 7th Ave. West, Vancouver BC V6H 1B6

Tel: 604-732-1610; *Fax:* 604-732-1602
www.earlymusic.bc.ca

To foster increased understanding & appreciation of early music by providing educational programs, high quality concerts at reasonable prices featuring both local & internationally acclaimed musicians & by providing informative publications
Fran Watters, President
Suzie LeBlanc, Artistic & Executive Director

Vancouver Symphony Society (VSO)
#500, 833 Seymour St., Vancouver BC V6B 0G4

Tel: 604-876-3434; *Fax:* 604-684-9264
customerservice@vancouversymphony.ca
www.vancouversymphony.ca
www.youtube.com/c/VancouverSymphonyOrchestra

To provide stewardship for the Vancouver Symphony Orchestra to achieve recognition as one of Canada's highest quality symphony orchestras; To perform at all times with artistic distinction & thereby enrich BC's quality of life; To expand the enjoyment & appreciation of the finest orchestral music of the past & present
Angela Elster, President & CEO
Otto Tausk, Music Director

Vancouver Youth Symphony Orchestra Society (VYSO)
3214 - 10th Ave. West, Vancouver BC V6K 2L2

Tel: 604-737-0714
vyso.com

To provide orchestral training & experience to music students in Greater Vancouver & the Lower Mainland from beginner to advanced level career student; To contribute to the cultural landscape of the local & provincial community by offering education & support to school & community groups
Roger Cole, Artistic Director
Holly Littleford, Executive Director

Victoria Symphony Society
#610, 620 View St., Victoria BC V8W 1J6

Tel: 250-385-9771; *Fax:* 250-385-7767
boxoffice@victoriasymphony.ca
victoriasymphony.ca

To advance musical culture; To advance musical education among younger members of community; To encourage, foster & promote performance of Canadian & other contemporary musicians
Matthew White, Chief Executive Officer
Christian Kluxen, Music Director

Manitoba

Brandon University School of Music Orchestra
Queen Elizabeth II Music Bldg., 270 - 18th St., Brandon MB R7A 6A9

music@brandonu.ca
www.brandonu.ca/music/ensembles/orchestra

Leanne Zacharias, Director

Canadian Band Association (CBA) / Association canadienne des harmonies
131 Rouge Rd., Winnipeg MB R3K 1J5

Tel: 204-663-1226
www.canadianband.org

To promote & develop the musical educational & cultural values of band & band music in Canada
Scott Harrison, President
John Balsille, Executive Director

Manitoba Band Association
204 Arnold Ave., Winnipeg MB R3L 0W5

Tel: 204-663-1226
mbband@shaw.ca
www.mbband.org

To promote growth & development of bands in Manitoba
Chloé Plamondon, President

Chelsey Hiebert, Executive Director

Manitoba Chamber Orchestra (MCO)
Portage Place, 393 Portage Ave., #Y300, Winnipeg MB R3B 3H6

Tel: 204-783-7377; *Fax:* 204-783-7383
info@themco.ca
www.manitobachamberorchestra.org
www.youtube.com/c/ManitobaChamberOrchestra
To perform chamber orchestra repertoire with emphasis on premiering new Canadian works & Canadian soloists
Anne Manson, Music Director

Manitoba Music
#1, 376 Donald St., Winnipeg MB R3B 2J2

info@manitobamusic.com
www.manitobamusic.com
www.youtube.com/user/musicmanitoba
To develop & sustain the Manitoba music community & industry to their fullest potential
Sean McManus, Executive Director

Manitoba Opera Association Inc.
#1060, 555 Main St., Winnipeg MB R3B 1C3

Tel: 204-942-7479; *Fax:* 204-949-0377
mbopera@mbopera.ca
mbopera.ca
www.youtube.com/c/ManitobaOperaTV
To present & develop appreciation for art of opera in Manitoba; To assist in development of Canadian talent, with emphasis on Manitobans
Larry Desrochers, General Director & CEO

Western Canadian Music Alliance (WCMA)
#2, 600 Clifton St., Winnipeg MB R3G 2X6

Tel: 204-943-8485
info@breakoutwest.ca
breakoutwest.ca
www.youtube.com/user/BreakOutWest
To unite the music industry associations of Manitoba, Alberta, Yukon & Saskatchewan to develop the infrastructure of the independent music industry in Western Canada
Robyn Stewart, Executive Director

Winnipeg Symphony Orchestra Inc. (WSO)
555 Main St., Winnipeg MB R3B 1C3

Tel: 204-949-3999; *Fax:* 204-956-4271
wso.ca
www.youtube.com/WinnipegSymphony
To perform a wide variety of orchestral music including classical, contemporary, pop & children's music in Manitoba & Northwestern Ontario; To enrich the cultural landscape by engaging with the community
Angela Birdsell, Executive Director
Daniel Raiskin, Music Director

Winnipeg Youth Orchestras
PO Box 273, Winnipeg MB R3C 2G9

Tel: 204-805-9961
admin@winnipegyouthorchestras.ca
winnipegyouthorchestras.ca
To enable young musicians from Winnipeg to expand their musical abilities while playing in an ensemble setting
Gwen Hoebigd, President
Margaret Fjeldsted, Administrator

New Brunswick

Music / Musique NB (MNB)
PO Box 1638, Moncton NB E1C 4X9

Tel: 506-383-4662
contact@musicnb.org
www.musicnb.org
www.instagram.com/musicmusiquenb
To support musicians, managers & businesses involved in the music industry in New Brunswick
Jean Surette, Executive Director

Symphony New Brunswick / Symphonie Nouveau-Brunswick
Brunswick Square, 39 King St., Level III, Saint John NB E2L 4W3

Tel: 506-634-8379
symphony@nbnet.nb.ca
symphonynb.com
To present high-quality, live orchestral & chamber music from all periods; To promote the appreciation of music through educational activities in New Brunswick

Newfoundland and Labrador

CALOS Youth Orchestras Inc.
NL

calos.office@gmail.com
calosmusic.ca
To encourage and develop the musical abilities of young musicians; To play high quality orchestral music
Amanda Joseph, Executive Director
Grant Etchegary, Artistic Director

MusicNL
186 Duckworth St., St. John's NL A1C 1G5

Tel: 709-754-2574
info@musicnl.ca
www.musicnl.ca
www.youtube.com/c/MusicNL709
To promote, encourage & develop the music from Newfoundland & Labrador, in all its forms, whether written, recorded or in live performances
Rhonda Tulk-Lane, Executive Director

Newfoundland Symphony Orchestra Association (NSO)
PO Box 23125, St. John's NL A1B 4J9

Tel: 709-722-4441
nso@nsomusic.ca
nsomusic.ca
www.youtube.com/c/NewfoundlandSymphonyOrchestra
To foster & promote in all age groups of the general public of the province an interest in & an appreciation of music; To provide the province with a symphony orchestra of the highest possible standard; To provide professional musicians, highly skilled amateur players & talented students with the opportunity of performing
Hugh Donnan, Chief Executive Officer
Marc David, Music Director

Northwest Territories

Aurora Fiddle Society
PO Box 2071, Yellowknife NT X1A 2P6

aurorafiddle@gmail.com
aurorafiddle.com
To present, promote & develop fiddle music in Yellowknife & the Great Slave region
Christine Wenman, President

Music NWT
PO Box 127, Yellowknife NT X1A 2N1

info@musicnwt.ca
musicnwt.ca
To bring together musicians, offers workshops & other resources, & provides networking opportunities
Ted McLeod, President

Nova Scotia

African Nova Scotian Music Association (ANSMA)
Halifax NS

Tel: 902-404-3036
info@ansma.ca
www.ansma.ca
To develop, promote & enhance African Nova Scotia music locally, nationally & internationally

Canadian Society for Traditional Music (CSTM) / Société canadienne pour les traditions musicales (SCTM)
c/o Jeffrey van den Scott, Dept. of History, Memorial Univ., 230 Elizabeth Ave., Sydney NS A1C 5S7

info@cstm-sctm.ca
cstm-sctm.ca
To study & promote musical traditions of all cultures; To reflect the interests of members of the music community
Marcia Ostashewski, President
Jeffrey van den Scott, Treasurer
Jeanette Gallant, Secretary

Chebucto Orchestral Society of Nova Scotia
Halifax NS

info@chebuctosymphony.ca
www.chebuctosymphony.ca
To provide an opportunity for amateur musicians to perform the great symphonic works & to bring classical music to local audiences
Peter Oleskevich, Musical Director

Deep Roots Music Cooperative
466A Main St., Wolfville NS B4P 1E2

Tel: 902-542-7668
office@deeprootsmusic.ca
deeprootsmusic.ca

To develop year-round musical programs culminating in an annual festival; To encourage meaningful connections between cultures, community groups, artists & audiences
Peter Mowat, President

East Coast Music Association (ECMA) / Association de la musique de la côte est
#802, 1800 Argyle St., Halifax NS B3J 3N8

Tel: 902-423-6770; *Toll-Free:* 800-513-4953
ecma@ecma.com
www.ecma.com
To develop, foster, promote & celebrate East Coast music locally & globally
Andy McLean, Chief Executive Officer

Music Nova Scotia
2169 Gottingen St., Halifax NS B3K 3B5

Tel: 902-423-6271; *Fax:* 902-423-8841
Toll-Free: 888-343-6426
info@musicnovascotia.ca
musicnovascotia.ca
www.youtube.com/user/MusicNS
To encourage the creation, development, growth & promotion of Nova Scotia's music industry
Darryl Smith, Manager, Membership, Education & Investment Program
Grace Russell, Manager, Marketing, Communications & Events

Nova Scotia Band Association
#210, 721 Windmill Rd., Dartmouth NS B3B 0J7

nsband@accesswave.ca
novascotiabandassociation.com
To support & promote the development of bands throughout the province of Nova Scotia through communication, coordination, program development, advocacy & lobbying at the provincial level
Steve Hartlen, President
Hope Gendron, Executive Director

Nova Scotia Youth Orchestra (NYSO)
#301, 5657 Spring Garden Rd., Halifax NS B3J 3R4

symphonynovascotia.ca/nsyo
To provide young musicians with the finest orchestral training; To provide live orchestral music to audiences in Nova Scotia
Jack Chen, General Manager
Greg Burton, Artistic Advisor

Scotia Chamber Players
6181 Lady Hammond Rd., Halifax NS B3K 2R9

Tel: 902-429-9467; *Fax:* 902-425-6785
admin@scotiafestival.com
www.scotiafestival.ns.ca
www.youtube.com/user/scotiafestival
To enhance the quality of music by producing an annual festival of world-class chamber music in study & performance for the benefit of musicians, students & audiences
Simon Docking, Managing and Artistic Director

Symphony Nova Scotia Society (SNS)
Park Lane Mall, #301, 5657 Spring Garden Rd., Halifax NS B3J 3R4

Tel: 902-421-1300; *Fax:* 902-422-1209
info@symphonyns.ca
symphonynovascotia.ca
www.youtube.com/user/SymphonyNovaScotia
To enhance the quality of life of the citizens of Nova Scotia through high quality, professionally performed orchestral music
Christopher Wilkinson, Chief Executive Officer
Holly Mathieson, Music Director

Ontario

Alliance for Canadian New Music Projects (ACNMP) / Alliance pour des projets de musique canadienne nouvelle
20 St Joseph St., Toronto ON M4Y 1J9

Tel: 647-794-4804
info@acnmp.ca
www.acnmp.ca
To provide young musicians with an opportunity to celebrate & enjoy the music of their own time & country through the organization's syllabus & its festival, Contemporary Showcase
Stephanie Chua, General Manager

Association for Opera in Canada
#6286, 2100 Bloor St. West, Toronto ON M6S 5A5

Tel: 416-591-7222
www.opera.ca
To advance the interests of Canada's opera community; To create greater opportunity for opera audiences and professionals alike
Michael Hidetoshi Mori, Chair

Christina Loewen, Executive Director

Association of Canadian Choral Communities (ACCC) / Association des communautés chorales canadiennes
#500, 59 Adelaide St. East, Toronto ON M5C 1k6
Tel: 647-606-2467
info@choralcanada.org
www.choralcanada.org
To promote choral music, particularly Canadian works, in schools, post-secondary institutions, churches & communities throughout Canada; To support and encourage participation in all levels of choral music through training & resources
Laurier Fagnan, President
Meghan Hila, Executive Director

Bach Elgar Choral Society
86 Homewood Ave., Hamilton ON L8P 2M4
Tel: 905-527-5995; *Fax:* 905-527-0555
bachelgar@gmail.com
bachelgar.com
www.instagram.com/bachelgarchoir
To provide choral music of excellent quality & broad-based appeal to the community; To act as a cultural & educational resource
Alexander Cann, Artistic Director

Brantford Symphony Orchestra Association Inc.
PO Box 24012, 185 King George Rd., Brantford ON N3R 7X3
Tel: 519-759-8781; *Fax:* 519-759-0842
administrator@brantfordsymphony.ca
www.brantfordsymphony.ca
To provide symphonic experiences & give people of all ages opportunities for musical appreciation & education
Maureen Wills, Co-Chair
Joann Alho, Co-Chair
Aida Steenkist, Office Administrator

Burlington Symphony Orchestra
#300, 1100 Burloak Dr., Burlington ON L7L 6B2
Tel: 905-320-4697
info@burlingtonsymphony.ca
www.burlingtonsymphony.ca
www.instagram.com/burlingtonsymphonyorchestra
To enrich the cultural life of the Hamilton & surrounding area by maintaining a full-size community symphony orchestra; To perform a wide repertoire of symphonic music, including works by Canadian composers; To make great symphonic music accessible to a larger public by offering attractive concert programs at affordable prices
Anda Protopopescu, President
Denis Mastromonaco, Music Director

Canadian Academy of Recording Arts & Sciences (CARAS) / Académie canadienne des arts et des sciences de l'enregistrement (ACASE)
#211C, 219 Dufferin St., Toronto ON M6K 3J1
Tel: 416-485-3135; *Fax:* 416-485-4978
Toll-Free: 888-440-5866
info@carasonline.org
carasonline.ca
To promote Canadian artists and music; To identify & reward the achievements of Canadian artists
Mark Cohon, Chair
Allan Reid, President & CEO, CARAS, The JUNO Awards & MusiCounts
Meghan McCabe, Director, Communications

Canadian Association for the Advancement of Music & the Arts (CAAMA)
1525 Trotwood Ave., Mississauga ON L5G 3Z8
info@caama.org
www.caama.org
To further the independent music industry, in Canada & abroad; To ensure that laws regarding the music industry are favourable to members
Patti Jannetta, President

Canadian Association of Music Therapists (CAMT) / Association canadienne des musicothérapeutes (AMC)
#5, 1124 Gainsborough Rd., London ON N6H 5N1
Fax: 519-641-0431
Toll-Free: 800-996-2268
info@musictherapy.ca
www.musictherapy.ca
To promote excellence in music therapy practice & education in Canadian clinical, educational & community settings
Kiki Chang, President, president@musictherapy.ca

Canadian Band Association (Ontario) Inc.
3 Vianney Ave., Toronto ON M1L 4V5
info@cba-ontario.ca
cba-ontario.ca
To support community, professional & military bands in Ontario
Joseph Resendes, President

Canadian Bureau for the Advancement of Music (CBAM)
22372 Talbot Line, Rodney ON N0L 2C0
Tel: 647-352-4015
admin@cbam.ca
www.cbam.ca
To promote music (piano) education program for elementary school students
Pamela Hetherington, President

Canadian Children's Opera Company (CCOC)
227 Front St. East, Toronto ON M5A 1E8
Tel: 416-366-0467
info@canadianchildrensopera.com
www.canadianchildrensopera.com
www.youtube.com/c/CanadianChildrensOperaCompany1
To be the foremost children's operatic chorus in Canada; To achieve international recognition
Katherine Semcesen, Executive Director

Canadian Country Music Association (CCMA)
#104, 366 Adelaide St. East, Toronto ON M5A 3X9
Tel: 416-947-1331
country@ccma.org
ccma.org
www.youtube.com/c/CCMAOfficial
To promote & recognize Canadian country music
Tracy Martin, President

Canadian Independent Music Association (CIMA)
30 St Patrick St., 2nd Fl., Toronto ON M5T 3A3
Tel: 416-485-3152
www.cimamusic.ca
To lobby governments for support & copyright reform; To raise the profile of Canadian music abroad by promoting the industry at international events
Stuart Johnston, President
Trisha Carter, Senior Manager, Business Development
Jenia Schukov, Officer, Communications & Programming

Canadian League of Composers / La Ligue canadienne de compositeurs
Chalmers House, 20 St Joseph St., Toronto ON M4Y 1J9
Tel: 416-964-1364; *Toll-Free:* 877-964-1364
info@composition.org
composition.org
To represent the interests of composers & to monitor & influence the conditions that affect their livelihood & public image
Sophie Dupuis, President
Kathryn Knowles, General Manager

Canadian Music Centre (CMC) / Centre de musique canadienne
20 St Joseph St., Toronto ON M4Y 1J9
Tel: 416-961-6601
info@cmccanada.org
cmccanada.org
www.youtube.com/user/CanadianMusicCentre
To stimulate the awareness, appreciation & performance of Canadian music
Glenn Hodgins, President & CEO
Ana-Maria Lipoczi, Manager, Music Services

Canadian Opera Company (COC) / Compagnie d'opéra canadienne
227 Front St. East, Toronto ON M5A 1E8
Tel: 416-363-6671; *Fax:* 416-363-5584
info@coc.ca
www.coc.ca
www.youtube.com/user/CanadianOpera
To produce opera of the highest international standard while attracting growing public support & participation in opera through increased accessibility & education; To attract, develop & promote young Canadian singers, musicians, stage directors, conductors, designers, technical personnel & administrators; To encourage Canadian librettists & composers to compose new works
Alexander Neef, General Director
Johannes Debus, Music Director

Canadian Sinfonietta Youth Orchestra (CSYO)
47 Proctor Ave., Toronto ON L3T 1L9
Tel: 647-812-0839
csyo.ca

To provide young musicians with quality orchestral experience to further their musical development
Tak-Ng Lai, Music Director

Canadian University Music Society / Société de musique des universités canadiennes
#202, 10 Morrow Ave., Toronto ON M6R 2J1
Tel: 416-538-1650; *Fax:* 416-489-1713
office@muscan.org
muscan.org
To stimulate research, musical performance & composition; To improve instructional methods in university teaching; To provide a forum to exchange views on common problems, scholarly research in music & other matters of professional concern; To advise on new university programs & monitor existing programs
Stephanie Lind, President

Cathedral Bluffs Symphony Orchestra Inc. (CBSO)
PO Box 51074, 18 Eglinton Sq., Toronto ON M1L 2K2
Tel: 416-879-5566
info@cathedralbluffs.com
cathedralbluffs.com
To provide residents of Greater Toronto with an opportunity to hear classical symphonic music performed by a live orchestra; To provide both skilled and amateur musicians with an opportunity to perform
Tim Hendrickson, President
Peggy Wong, Orchestra Manager

Choirs Ontario
230 St Clair Ave. West, Toronto ON M4V 1R5
Tel: 416-923-1144; *Fax:* 416-929-0415
Toll-Free: 866-935-1144
info@choirsontario.org
choirsontario.org
To promote choral singing in communities, schools, universities & places of worship throughout Ontario
Mark Vuorinen, President

Conservatory Canada
#101, 201 Queens Ave., London ON N6A 1J1
Tel: 519-433-3147; *Toll-Free:* 800-461-5367
officeadmin@conservatorycanada.ca
conservatorycanada.ca
To promote achievement in music through a comprehensive program of study, evaluation & recognition for teachers & students; To foster the development of musical talent & potential
Derek Oger, Executive Director

Counterpoint Community Orchestra (CCO)
PO Box 75134, 20 Bloor St. East, Toronto ON M4W 3T3
info@ccorchestra.org
ccorchestra.org
To foster pride as a LGBT positive orchestra; To perform for the community & promote equality within Toronto
Andrew Chung, Music Director

Deep River Symphony Orchestra (DRSO)
PO Box 398, Deep River ON K0J 1P0
Tel: 613-584-4264
drsoemail@gmail.com
www.drso.ca
To promote the development & enjoyment of music in the Upper Ottawa Valley
Jane Craig, President
Peter Morris, Music Director

Dundas Valley Orchestra
29 Park St. West, Hamilton ON L9H 1X3
dundasvalleyorchestra.ca
To play orchestral music for residents of Hamilton & area
Laura M. Thomas, Music Director

Durham Chamber Orchestra
Whitby ON
info@durhamchamberorchestra.com
www.durhamchamberorchestra.com
Sandy Weeks, President & Treasurer
Carlos Bastidas, Music Director

Durham Youth Orchestra (DYO)
168 Gladstone Ave., Oshawa ON L1J 4E7
dyomusic.com
To nurture the artistic growth of young musicians through orchestral performance; To positively contribute to the musical landscape of Durham Region
John Beaton, Music Director

Esprit Orchestra
#511, 174 Spadina Ave., Toronto ON M5T 2C2
Tel: 416-815-7887; *Fax:* 416-815-7337
info@espritorchestra.com
www.youtube.com/user/EspritOrchestra
To present "new music" programs & collaborative arts events; To act as an example for new music groups to develop similar programs which strengthen the new music community as a whole
Margaret Logan, President
Alex Pauk, Music Director

Etobicoke Philharmonic Orchestra (EPO)
PO Box 60002, 1500 Islington Ave., Toronto ON M9A 5G2
Tel: 416-239-5665
info@eporchestra.ca
www.eporchestra.ca
To provide an opportunity for trained amateur musicians to perform together & become acquainted with an orchestral repertoire; To provide the community with symphonic music, competently performed in a local setting; To assist serious music students in their studies through performance experience & a scholarship program
Judy Gargaro, President

Foundation Assisting Canadian Talent on Recordings (FACTOR)
247 Spadina Ave., 3rd Fl., Toronto ON M5T 3A8
Tel: 416-696-2215
general.info@factor.ca
www.factor.ca
www.youtube.com/user/FACTORfunded
To provide financial assistance for production of sound recordings, videos, syndicated radio programs & international tour support; English-language counterpart of Musicaction
Duncan McKie, President & CEO
Phil Gumbley, Director, Operations

Georgian Bay Symphony (GBS)
PO Box 133, 994 - 3rd Ave. East, Owen Sound ON N4K 5P1
Tel: 519-372-0212
gbs@bmts.com
www.georgianbaysymphony.ca
To enhance appreciation of music which includes growth & development of regional orchestra
Nancy A. MacDonald, President
François Koh, Music Director

Guelph Symphony Orchestra (GSO)
35 Woolwich St., Guelph ON N1H 3V1
Tel: 519-820-4111
info@guelphsymphony.com
www.guelphsymphony.com
To provide symphonic performances to audiences in Guelph & surrounding area
Catherine Molina, General Manager

Hamilton Philharmonic Orchestra (HPO)
10 MacNab St. South, Hamilton ON L8P 4Y3
Tel: 905-526-1677
communications@hpo.org
hpo.org
www.youtube.com/c/HamiltonPhilharmonic
To provide artistically excellent music to patrons; To educate music students of all ages
Kim Varian, Executive Director
Gemma New, Music Director
Neil Spaulding, Manager, Operations & Personnel

Hamilton Philharmonic Youth Orchestra (HPYO)
Hamilton ON
Tel: 905-526-1677
info@hpyo.com
hpyo.com
To provide young people with the joy & discipline of orchestral music & perform regular concerts to enrich the cultural landscape of Hamilton & area
Courtney Prizrenac, General Manager
Gemma New, Artistic Advisor

Hart House Orchestra
University of Toronto, 7 Hart House Circle, Toronto ON M5S 3H3
www.harthouseorchestra.ca
Henry Janzen, Music Director

Huronia Symphony Orchestra (HSO)
PO Box 904, Stn. Main, Barrie ON L4M 4Y6
Tel: 705-721-4752
office@huroniasymphony.ca
www.huroniasymphony.ca

To operate & support a symphony orchestra in Simcoe County; To provide symphonic music for people of the area as well as an opportunity for children & youth to receive instruction in orchestral music
Oliver Balaburski, Artistic Director & Conductor

International Symphony Orchestra (ISO)
143 North Christina St., Sarnia ON N7T 5T8
Tel: 519-337-7775
info@theiso.org
www.theiso.org
To provide cultural enrichment within the community by providing high calibre choral & symphonic performances; To reinforce strong commitment to youth music education and initiatives
John Coury, President
Anthony Wing, Executive Director
Douglas Bianchi, Music Director & Conductor
Troiano David, Choral Director

La Jeunesse Youth Orchestra (LJYO)
ON
info@ljyo.ca
www.ljyo.ca
To provide young musicians from the Port Hope area with the enriching experience of performing a wide range of symphonic music
Virginia Dakers, President
Laurie Mitchell, Music Director

Kingston Symphony Association (KSA)
PO Box 1616, #206, 11 Princess St., Kingston ON K7L 5C8
Tel: 613-546-9729; *Fax:* 613-546-8580
info@kingstonsymphony.on.ca
www.kingstonsymphony.on.ca
www.youtube.com/user/Kingstonsymphony
To maintain & produce professional orchestral & symphonic music in the Kingston area
Andrea Haughton, General Manager
Evan Mitchell, Music Director

Kingston Youth Orchestra
c/o Kingston Symphony Association, PO Box 1616, #206, 11 Princess St., Kingston ON K7L 5C8
Tel: 613-546-9729
www.kingstonsymphony.ca
Hugh Johnston, Music Director
Susan Johnston, General Manager

Kitchener-Waterloo Chamber Orchestra (KWCO)
F-168 Lexington Ct., Waterloo ON N2J 4R9
info@kwchamberorchestra.ca
kwchamberorchestra.ca
To present lesser-known orchestral music from the 18th & 19th century to the residents of the Kitchener-Waterloo area
Matthew Jones, Music Director

Kitchener-Waterloo Symphony Orchestra Association Inc. (KWSOA)
36 King St. West, Kitchener ON N2G 1A3
Tel: 519-745-4711; *Fax:* 519-745-4474
Toll-Free: 888-745-4717
info@kwsymphony.on.ca
kwsymphony.on.ca
www.youtube.com/user/kwsymphony
To cultivate the tradition of live performance through the presentation of classical orchestral & popular music for the edification, enrichment, education & excitement of our community & beyond
Andrew Bennett, Executive Director
Andrei Feher, Music Director

Kitchener-Waterloo Symphony Youth Orchestra (KWSYO)
36 King St. West, Kitchener ON N2G 1A3
Tel: 519-745-4711; *Fax:* 519-745-4474
Toll-Free: 888-745-4717
info@kwsymphony.on.ca
kwsymphony.ca
Barbara Kaplanek, Manager, Education & Community Programs, Youth Orchestra & Schools
Matthew Jones, Youth Orchestra Conductor

Kiwanis Music Festival Association of Greater Toronto
17 Pinemore Cres., Toronto ON M3A 1W5
Tel: 416-487-5885
office@kiwanismusictoronto.org
kiwanismusictoronto.org
To bring together various choirs in music competitions
Pam Allen, General Manager
Martha Gregory, Artistic Director

Korean-Canadian Symphony Orchestra (KGSO)
#203, 3333 Bayview Ave., Toronto ON M2K 1G4
Tel: 416-737-0521
meetkcso@gmail.com
kcso.ca
To provide concerts to people in the GTA & to promote Korean-Canadian musicians
Sharon Lee, Music Director

London Community Orchestra (LCO)
#815, 520 Wellington St., London ON N6A 3R2
info@lco-on.ca
lco-on.ca
To give concerts & to sponsor local young artists as soloists
Leonard Ingrao, Artistic Director

London Youth Symphony (LYS)
London ON
londonyouthsymphony@gmail.com
www.londonyouthsymphony.net
To provide the region's most talented young musicians with the opportunity to build self-discipline, confidence & team spirit within an outstanding symphonic environment that offers professional directorship & coaching
Len Ingrao, Artistic Director

Mariposa Folk Foundation
PO Box 383, Orillia ON L3V 6J8
Tel: 705-326-3655
officemanager@mariposafolk.com
mariposafolk.com
www.youtube.com/mariposafolk
To promote & preserve folk arts in Canada through song, story, dance & craft
Pam Carter, President

Mooredale Youth Concert Orchestra
c/o Mooredale House, 146 Crescent Rd., Toronto ON M4W 1V2
Tel: 416-922-3714
www.mooredaleconcerts.com/youth-orchestras
To give serious young musicians an opportunity to prepare & perform orchestral selections at a high standard
Christina A. Cavanagh, Managing Director

Music Canada
85 Mowat Ave., Toronto ON M6K 3E3
Tel: 416-967-7272
info@musiccanada.com
musiccanada.com
www.instagram.com/music_canada
To develop & promote high ethical standards in the creation, manufacture & marketing of sound recordings
Patrick Rogers, President
Jackie Dean, Chief Operating Officer
Quentin Burgess, Director, Communications
Erica Meekes, Director, Public Relations & Events

Music for Young Children (MYC) / Musique pour jeunes enfants
#7, 1240 Teron Rd., Kanata ON K2K 2B5
Tel: 613-592-7565; *Fax:* 613-592-8632
Toll-Free: 800-561-1692
myc@myc.com
www.myc.com
www.instagram.com/myc_musicforyoungchildren
To develop, deliver, & support comprehensive entry level music education programs of the finest quality
Olivia Riddell, President & International Director
Riddell David, Chief Operating Officer

Music Managers Forum Canada
1731 Lawrence Ave. East, Toronto ON M1R 2X7
Tel: 416-462-9160
info@mmfcanada.ca
mmfcanada.ca
www.instagram.com/mmfcanada
To be a source of information for Canadian musicians, artists & managers
Meg Symsyk, President
Amie Therrien, Director, Operations

National Academy Orchestra (NAO)
301 Bay St. South, Hamilton ON L8P 3J7
Tel: 905-525-7664; *Fax:* 905-526-9934
Toll-Free: 888-475-9377
nationalacademyorchestra.com
To professionally train emerging young Canadian musicians through education, rehearsal & public performance
Boris Brott, Musical Director

National Shevchenko Musical Ensemble Guild of Canada
626 Bathurst St., Toronto ON M5S 2R1
Tel: 416-533-2725
info@shevchenkomusic.com
www.shevchenkomusic.com
To provide instruction in vocal, instrumental & dance for youth & adults by maintaining the Shevchenko Musical Ensemble & Shevchenko School of Dance & Music; To perpetuate Ukrainian cultural traditions & share this with others in multicultural communities

National Youth Orchestra Association of Canada
#500, 59 Adelaide St. East, Toronto ON M5C 1K6
Tel: 416-532-4470; *Fax:* 416-532-6879
Toll-Free: 888-532-4470
info@nyoc.org
nyoc.org
www.youtube.com/user/NYOConjc
To provide comprehensive training for Canada's best young classical musicians
Barbara Smith, President & CEO

Niagara Youth Orchestra Association
#148, 12-111 - 4th Ave., St Catharines ON L2S 3P5
Tel: 905-323-5892
music@niagarayouthorchestra.org
niagarayouthorchestra.org
To foster an interest & understanding of orchestral music in the youth of the Niagara Region

Northumberland Orchestra Society (NOC)
PO Box 1012, Cobourg ON K9A 4W4
Tel: 905-376-3021
www.northumberlandmusic.ca
To perform orchestral & choral music to the Northumberland area; To encourage young local musicians through inclusion & education
John Kraus, Music Director & Conductor

Oakville Chamber Orchestra (OCO)
PO Box 76036, 1500 Upper Middle Rd. West, Oakville ON L6M 3H5
Tel: 905-483-6787
mail@oakvillechamber.org
oakvillechamber.org
www.youtube.com/user/oakvillemusic
To enrich the cultural landscape of Oakville by performing chamber music concerts, developing local amateur musicians & promoting Canadian soloists
Andrew Cripps, President
Charles Demuynck, Music Director

Oakville Symphony Orchestra (OSO)
#310, 200 North Service Rd. West, Oakville ON L6M 2Y1
Tel: 905-338-1462; *Fax:* 905-338-7954
office@oakvillesymphony.com
www.oakvillesymphony.com
To bring audiences a variety of music for all ages & to contribute to the cultural growth of the community
Bianca Chambers, Executive Director
Roberto De Clara, Artistic & Music Director

Oakville Symphony Youth Orchestra (OSYO)
PO Box 86068, Oakville ON L6H 5V6
Tel: 289-815-0018
office@osyo.ca
osyo.ca
To inspire, encourage & challenge young musicians to build their musical skills through the experience of various forms of orchestral music; To create an enjoyable environment that promotes teamwork, leadership & community involvement
Colin Clarke, Music Director

Ontario Band Association
c/o Andria Kilbride, 106 Little Rouge Circle, Stouffville ON L4A 0G2
membership@onband.ca
www.onband.ca
To promote & develop musical, educational & cultural values of bands in Ontario by sponsoring annual band & solo instrument competition, composition competition, original works
Lynn Tucker, President

Ontario Philharmonic (OP)
18 Simcoe St. South, Oshawa ON L1H 4G2
Tel: 905-579-6711; *Toll-Free:* 844-858-6711
contact@ontariophil.ca
www.ontariophil.ca
To bring fine orchestral music to residents of Durham Region, Toronto, & the GTA
Laura Vaillancourt, Executive Director

Marco Parisotto, Music Director

Orchestra Toronto (OT)
5040 Yonge St., Toronto ON M2N 6R8
Tel: 416-467-7142
info@orchestratoronto.ca
orchestratoronto.ca
To provide affordable family entertainment, music education & full repertoire in all its programs
Jennie Worden, Executive Director
Michael Newnham, Music Director

Orchestras Canada (OC) / Orchestres Canada
PO Box 2386, Peterborough ON K9J 2Y8
Tel: 416-366-8834; *Toll-Free:* 877-809-7288
info@oc.ca
oc.ca
To strengthen Canada's orchestral community through leadership in advocacy, education & professional development
Katherine Carleton, Executive Director
Sarah Thomson, Administrator
Krista Wodelet, Administrator, Job Board & Inventory of Orchestra Music Libraries

Orchestras Mississauga
Living Arts Centre, 4141 Living Arts Dr., 2nd Fl., Mississauga ON L5B 4B8
Tel: 905-615-4405; *Fax:* 905-615-4402
info@mississaugasymphony.ca
www.mississaugasymphony.ca
www.youtube.com/user/MississaugaSymph
To perform & promote orchestral music; To ensure its accessibility to all segments of the community
Denis Mastromonaco, Music Director
Eileen Keown, Executive Director

Orillia Youth Symphony Orchestra (OYSO)
Orillia ON
orilliayouthsymphonyorchestra@gmail.com
www.oyso.ca
To offer youth 6-24 years of age to play in a symphonic orchestra; To participate in community events

Ottawa Chamber Orchestra (OCO)
Ottawa ON
info@ottawachamberorchestra.com
www.ottawachamberorchestra.com
To share masterpieces of symphonic music with audiences from Ottawa & surrounding area
Donnie Deacon, Musical Director

Ottawa Symphony Orchestra (OSO) / Orchestre symphonique d'Ottawa
#202, 4 Florence St., Ottawa ON K2P 0W7
Tel: 613-231-7802
info@ottawasymphony.com
ottawasymphony.com
To develop the highest possible artistic level of performance of symphonic repertoire among local musicians, local & Canadian soloists, Canadian music, partnership opportunities for performance with other local performing arts organizations, educational outreach opportunities for young audiences & young performers
Sarah Devlin, Executive Director

Ottawa Youth Orchestra Academy (OYO) / L'Orchestre des jeunes d'Ottawa
#38, 2450 Lancaster Rd., Ottawa ON K1B 5N3
Tel: 613-233-9318; *Fax:* 613-233-5038
administrator@oyoa-aojo.ca
www.oyoa-aojo.ca
To provide high-quality orchestral training to youth in the Ottawa region
Donnie Deacon, Conductor

Pembroke Symphony Orchestra
401 Isabella St., Pembroke ON K8A 5N6
pembrokesymphonyorchestra@gmail.com
To provide members with the opportunity to perform classical & modern music in an orchestral setting; To share orchestral music with the listening public

Peterborough Symphony Orchestra (PSO)
PO Box 1135, Peterborough ON K9J 7H4
Tel: 705-742-1992
info@thepso.org
www.thepso.org
To perform & develop excellence in symphonic music that will enrich, stimulate & attract the widest possible audience by presenting quality orchestral music to the people of Peterborough & beyond
Deanna Guttman, Executive Director

Michael Newnham, Music Director

Quinte Symphony
c/o Quinte Arts Council, PO Box 22113, Belleville ON K8N 2Z5
Tel: 613-962-7430
tqs.greatmusic@gmail.com
thequintesymphony.com
To enrich the Quinte community by actively promoting an appreciation of Classical & Canadian orchestral music
Dan Tremblay, Music Director

Radio Starmaker Fund
#302, 372 Bay St., Toronto ON M5H 2W9
Tel: 416-597-6622; *Toll-Free:* 888-256-2211
www.starmaker.ca
To provide funding for Canadian musicians, bands & labels that have achieved a proven "track record" with previous work
Chip Sutherland, Executive Director

Royal Canadian College of Organists (RCCO) / Collège royal canadien des organistes (CRCO)
#414, 15 Case Goods Lane, Toronto ON M5A 3C4
Tel: 416-929-6400
info@rcco.ca
www.rcco.ca
To promote a high standard of organ playing, choral directing, church music & composition; To hold examinations in organ playing, choir directing, theory & general knowledge of music; To encourage recitals; To increase the understanding among church musicisans, authorities & the public of matters relating to church music
Elizabeth Shannon, Executive Director

Royal Conservatory Orchestra (RCO)
273 Bloor St. West, Toronto ON M5S 1W2
Tel: 416-408-2824; *Fax:* 416-408-5025
www.rcmusic.ca
To develop individuals' potential through leadership in music & the arts

Sault Ste Marie Symphony Association
Sault Ste Marie ON
info@saultsymphony.com
www.saultsymphony.ca
To promote symphonic music in Sault Ste Marie, Ontario & the surrounding region
Louis St.Pierre, President
John Wilkinson, Artistic Director

Scarborough Philharmonic Orchestra (SPO)
#209, 3007 Kingston Rd., Toronto ON M1M 1P1
Tel: 416-482-7761
spo@spo.ca
www.spo.ca
www.youtube.com/user/SPOGreatMusic
To enrich the cultural life of Scarborough, through the promotion & presentation of high calibre musical performances; To develop a strong & financially viable organization
Devin Scott, Executive Director
Ronald Royer, Music Director

Screen Composers Guild of Canada (SCGC)
41 Valleybrook Dr., Toronto ON M3B 2S6
Tel: 416-410-5076; *Fax:* 416-410-4516
Toll-Free: 866-657-1117
info@screencomposers.ca
screencomposers.ca
www.instagram.com/screencomposers
To improve the status & quality of music as it applies to film / tv / new media through education & the professional development of its members & the producing community; To represent & communicate the interests of its members to the music & film / tv / new media industries as well as other institutions; To collaborate with trade & industry associations with common interests; To represent all Canadian composers within the certified territories & producer entities detailed in our certification under the Canadian Status of the Artist Act, as the exclusive organization for collective negotiations
Tonya Dedrick, Managing Director

Songwriters Association of Canada (SAC) / Association des auteurs-compositeurs canadiens
41 Valleybrook Dr., Toronto ON M3B 2S6
Tel: 416-961-1588; *Fax:* 416-961-2040
Toll-Free: 866-456-7664
sac@songwriters.ca
www.songwriters.ca
www.youtube.com/user/SongwritersCanada
To protect & develop the creative & business environments for songwriters in Canada & around the world
Zoë Cunningham, Executive Director

Soundstreams Canada Concerts / Concerts Soundstreams du Canada
20 St Joseph St., Toronto ON M4Y 1J9
Tel: 416-504-1282; *Fax:* 416-504-1285
info@soundstreams.ca
soundstreams.ca
www.instagram.com/soundstreams
To foster & promote the development of 20th century music & music by Canadian composers, through the sponsorship of concerts, musical theatre works for young audiences, festivals & special events, recording projects, the commissioning of new works by Canadian composers & touring of Canadian artists
Lawrence Cherney, Artistic Director
Menon Dwarka, Executive Director

Sudbury Symphony Orchestra Association Inc. (SSO) / Orchestre symphonique de Sudbury inc
#403, 96 Larch St., Sudbury ON P3E 1C1
Tel: 705-673-1280; *Fax:* 705-673-1434
info@sudburysymphony.com
sudburysymphony.com
www.youtube.com/user/SudburySymphony
To provide the opportunity for a broad spectrum of the public in the Sudbury Region & surrounding area to attend a stimulating program of concerts; To maintain an environment & organization which encourages artistic responsibility & commitment; To attract & maintain private & public funding in order to achieve accessibility & continuity through financial stability; To increase the awareness & appreciation of music in the community; To provide a vehicle for the participation in & ongoing development of the performance of orchestral music; To increase the awareness, appreciation & performance of Canadian music in the community
Mélanie Léonard, Music Director

Sudbury Youth Orchestra Inc. (SYO)
c/o Jamie Arrowsmith, Music Program, Cambrian College, 1400 Barrydowne Rd., Sudbury ON P3A 3V8
Tel: 705-566-8101
sudburyyouthorch@gmail.com
www.sudburyyouthorchestra.ca
To foster an appreciation of orchestral music; To create opportunities for orchestral performance; To provide access to education & training in an orchestral setting for the youth of Sudbury & area
Jamie Arrowsmith, Music Director

Tafelmusik
Trinity-St. Paul's Centre, PO Box 14, 427 Bloor St. West, Toronto ON M5S 1X7
Tel: 416-964-9562; *Fax:* 416-964-2782
info@tafelmusik.org
www.tafelmusik.org
www.youtube.com/user/tafelmusik1979
Bringing baroque music to Toronto & the world, through concerts, recordings, & a music education programme
Carol Kehoe, Managing Director
Elisa Citterio, Music Director

Thunder Bay Symphony Orchestra Association (TBSO)
PO Box 29192, Thunder Bay ON P7B 6P9
Tel: 807-474-2284; *Fax:* 807-622-1927
info@tbso.ca
tbso.ca
To maintain & nurture a professional, regional orchestra of artistic integrity & excellence; To offer a variety of programs to enrich & encourage the widest possible audience; To support the development of local young musicians
Linda Penner, President
Paul Haas, Music Director

Timmins Symphony Orchestra
35 Pine St. South, Timmins ON P4N 7N2
Tel: 705-267-1006
info@timminssymphony.com
www.timminssymphony.com
Paul Pigeau, President
Joshua Wood, Music Director

Toronto Downtown Jazz Society
Toronto ON
torontojazz.com
To produce the Toronto Downtown Jazz Festival, as well as many other events & programs to further develop jazz talent & audience appreciation; To promote community involvement, artistic excellence & outstanding production standards
Howard Kerbel, Chief Executive Officer
Josh Grossman, Artistic Director

The Toronto Mendelssohn Choir
#3, 596 St Clair Ave. West, Toronto ON M6C 1A6
Tel: 416-598-0422
admin@tmchoir.org
www.tmchoir.org
www.youtube.com/user/TOMendelssohnChoir
To give Canadian audiences the experience of choral music
Anna Kajtár, Executive Director

Toronto Sinfonietta Concert Association
#848, 24 Southport St., Toronto ON M6S 4Z1
tosinfonietta@gmail.com
torontosinfonietta.com
Matthew Jaskiewicz, Music Director

The Toronto Symphony
#500, 145 Wellington St. West, Toronto ON M5J 1H8
Tel: 416-598-3375; *Fax:* 416-598-9522
Toll-Free: 855-593-7769
contactus@tso.ca
www.tso.ca
www.youtube.com/user/TorontoSymphony
To present concerts of both established & new music at the highest artistic standard possible, while recognizing audiences' needs; To play a role in the development of future musicians & audiences
Matthew Loden, Chief Executive Officer
Gustavo Gimeno, Music Director

Toronto Symphony Youth Orchestra (TSYO)
212 King St. West, 6th Fl., Toronto ON M5H 1K5
Tel: 416-593-7769; *Fax:* 416-977-2912
www.tso.ca/learn-connect/toronto-symphony-youth-orchestra
To provide a high-level orchestral experience for young musicians aged 22 & under; To encourage significant achievement for participants through education & performance
Rachel Malach, Vice-President & General Manager
Simon Rivard, Conductor

University of Toronto Symphony Orchestra (UTSO)
Faculty of Music, University of Toronto, 80 Queen's Park Cres., Toronto ON M5S 2C5
Tel: 416-978-3750; *Fax:* 416-946-3353
performance.music@utoronto.ca
music.utoronto.ca
Uri Mayer, Conductor

Western University Symphony Orchestra
Faculty of Music, Western University, Lambton Dr., London ON N6A 3K7
Tel: 519-661-2111
music@uwo.ca
music.uwo.ca

Wilfrid Laurier University Symphony Orchestra
Faculty of Music, 75 University Ave. West, Waterloo ON N2L 3C5
www.wlu.ca/academics/faculties/faculty-of-music
To train music students to be musicians with solid knowledge of music theory & history & competent performers
Kira Omelchenko, Conductor

Windsor Symphony Society
121 University Ave. West, Windsor ON N9A 5P4
Tel: 519-973-1238
www.windsorsymphony.com
www.youtube.com/c/WindsorSymphonyOrchestra
To enrich community life & serve as an educational resource through high quality live performance of orchestral music
Sheila Wisdom, Executive Director
Robert Franz, Music Director

York Symphony Orchestra Inc.
ON
yorksymphonyorchestra@hotmail.com
yorksymphony.ca
To provide musical enjoyment for audiences & musicians, with the goal of being recognized & supported throughout York Region
Denis Mastromonaco, Music Director

Music PEI
PO Box 2371, Charlottetown PE C1A 8C1
Tel: 902-894-6734; *Fax:* 902-894-4404
music@musicpei.com
www.musicpei.com
www.instagram.com/musicpei
To promote, foster & develop artists & the music industry in PEI
Rob Oakie, Executive Director

Prince Edward Island Symphony Society (PEISO)
PO Box 185, Charlottetown PE C1A 7K4
Tel: 902-892-4333
admin@peisymphony.com
www.peisymphony.com
To establish & promote symphonic music; To further & foster appreciation of musical education; To promote the welfare of musicians; To give & arrange performances, entertainments & concerts; To employ teachers & instructors to inform the public & awaken interest
Bruce Craig, President
Mark Shapiro, Music Director

Académie de musique du Québec (AMQ)
5, rue Lakeside, Montréal QC H9C 1H6
Tél: 514-528-1961
prixdeurope@videotron.ca
www.prixdeurope.ca/lacademie.html
Promouvoir le goût et l'avancement de la musique au Québec, aux professeurs oeuvrant dans le secteur privé et soucieux à la fois d'autonomie et d'encadrement, aux élèves qui désirent une reconnaissance officielle de leur travail
Lise Boucher, Présidente

Alliance chorale du Québec (ACQ)
#302, 2, rue Sainte-Catherine est, Montréal QC H2X 1K4
Tél: 514-252-3020; *Téléc:* 514-252-3222
Ligne sans frais: 888-924-6387
info@chorales.ca
www.chorales.ca
Regrouper des chorales de tous styles et de tous niveaux; donner des moyens de mieux chanter; promouvoir et développer le chant choral au Québec
Roxanne Croteau, Directrice générale

Association des orchestres de jeunes de la Montérégie (AOJM)
CP 36573, 58, rue Victoria, Saint-Lambert QC J4P 3S8
Tél: 450-923-3733
courrier@aojm.org
www.aojm.org
De promouvoir le développement et la formation de jeunes musiciens
Jean-Claude Paré, Président

Association québécoise de l'industrie du disque, du spectacle et de la vidéo (ADISQ)
6420, rue Saint-Denis, Montréal QC H2S 2R7
Tél: 514-842-5147; *Téléc:* 514-842-7762
info@adisq.com
www.adisq.com
www.instagram.com/adisq
Promouvoir les intérêts des producteurs de disques, spectacles et vidéos
Philippe Archambault, Président
Solange Drouin, Directrice générale et Vice-présidente, Affaires publiques

CAMMAC
85, rue Cammac, Harrington QC J8G 2T2
Tel: 819-687-3938; *Fax:* 819-687-3323
Toll-Free: 888-622-8755
communications@cammac.ca
cammac.ca
www.youtube.com/user/CAMMACMusicCentre
To create opportunities for musicians of all levels & ages to play music in a non-competitive environment
Susan King, President
Cynthia Bonenfant, Executive Director
Guylaine Lemaire, Artistic Director

Canadian New Music Network (CNMN) / Réseau canadien pour les musiques nouvelles (RCMN)
#200, 1085, Côte du Beaver Hall, Montréal QC H2Z 1S5
admin@reseaumusiquesnouvelles.ca
www.newmusicnetwork.ca
To improve communication, understanding & knowledge within the new music community; To represent the community in Canadian society, by working with the media, Canadian government & arts organizations
Juliet Palmer, President
Terri Hron, Executive Director

Chants Libres, compagnie lyrique de création
#303, 1908, rue Panet, Montréal QC H2L 3A2
Tél: 514-841-2642
creation@chantslibres.org
chantslibres.org
www.youtube.com/user/chantslibres

Réunir des créateurs de toutes les disciplines (musique, théâtre, arts plastiques, arts électroniques, vidéo etc.) autour d'un point commun: la voix
Marilyn Carnier, Directeur général
Pauline Vaillancourt, Directrice artistique

Concours de musique du Canada inc. (CMC) / Canadian Music Competitions Inc.
69, rue Sherbrooke ouest, Montréal QC H2X 1X2
Tél: 514-284-5398; *Téléc:* 514-284-6828
Ligne sans frais: 877-879-1959
info@cmcnational.com
www.cmcnational.com
Faire participer a une véritable expérience nationale de musique, en étroite collaboration avec les institutions et les professeurs de musique du pays, les plus doués de nos jeunes musiciennes et musiciens canadiens; réunir les jeunes interprètes canadiens, de les soutenir dans leur apprentissage de la musique classique et d'encourager le dépassement de soi, la discipline et la persévérance
Marie-Claude Matton, Directrice générale

Ensemble contemporain de Montréal (ECM+)
3890, rue Clark, Montréal QC H2W 1W6
Tél: 514-524-0173; *Téléc:* 514-524-0179
info@ecm.qc.ca
ecm.qc.ca
Promouvoir la création de la musique canadienne par la performance, la formation et le recherche multidisciplinaire
Véronique Lacroix, Directrice artistique
Natalie Watanabe, Directrice générale

Ensemble vocal Ganymède
CP 476, Succ. C, Montréal QC H2L 4K4
Tél: 514-528-6302
contacter@evganymede.com
www.evganymede.com
Présenter le répertoire classique de la voix masculine;
D'introduire dans l'imagerie populaire une autre vision de la communauté gaie
Yvan Sabourin, Directeur

Fédération des harmonies et des orchestres symphoniques du Québec (FHOSQ)
4545, av Pierre-de Coubertin, Montréal QC H1V 0B2
Tél: 514-252-3026; *Ligne sans frais:* 833-252-3026
info@fhosq.org
fhosq.org
www.instagram.com/fhosq
Contribuer au développement et à l'amélioration des harmonies en tant que loisir éducatif et culturel
Gabrielle Ayotte, Directrice générale

Jeunesses Musicales du Canada (JMC) / Jeunesses Musicales of Canada (JMC)
305, av du Mont-Royal est, Montréal QC H2T 1P8
Tél: 514-845-4108; *Fax:* 514-845-8241
Toll-Free: 877-377-7951
info@jmcanada.ca
www.jmcanada.ca
www.youtube.com/c/jeunessesmusicalescanada
To promote Canadian musical artists & develop audiences
Danièle LeBlanc, Directeur général et artistique
Claudia Morissette, Directrice, Artistic Operations

Ladies' Morning Musical Club (LMMC) / Les Matinées de musique de chambre
#260, 1980, rue Sherbrooke ouest, Montréal QC H3H 1E8
Tel: 514-932-6796
info@lmmc.ca
www.lmmc.ca
Constance V. Pathy, President
Rosemary Neville, Secretary-Treasurer

Musicaction
#2, 4385, rue Saint-Hubert, Montréal QC H2J 2X1
Tél: 514-861-8444; *Téléc:* 514-861-4423
Ligne sans frais: 800-861-5561
info@musicaction.ca
musicaction.ca
Développement de la musique vocale francophone au Canada
Pierre Rodrigue, Président
Louise Chenail, Directrice générale

L'Opéra de Montréal (ODM) / Montréal Opera
260, boul de Maisonneuve ouest, Montréal QC H2X 1Y9
Tél: 514-985-2222
info@operademontreal.com
www.operademontreal.com
www.youtube.com/user/OperadeMtl
Afin de présenter des productions d'opéra de comparable qualité et originalité à ceux observés dans les plus grands opéras du monde; cherche la contribution du personnel de création de niveaux local et national; ainsi que d'inviter les meilleurs artistes de l'étranger; soutient l'émergence de nouveaux talents opéra canadienne
patrick Corrigan, Directeur général
Michel Beaulac, Directeur artistique
Louis Bouchard, Directeur technique
Pierre Vachon, Directeur, Communications, communauté et éducation

Opéra de Québec
1220, av Taché, Québec QC G1R 3B4
info@operadequebec.com
operadequebec.com
www.youtube.com/c/OpéradeQuébec
Produire des spectacles d'opéra professionnels à Québec
Daniel Turp, Président
Jean-François Lapointe, Directeur artistique

Orchestre classique de Montréal (OCM)
5459, av Earnscliffe, Montréal QC H3X 2P8
Tél: 514-487-5190
info@orchestre.ca
orchestre.ca
Boris Brott, Directeur artistique
Taras Kulish, Directeur général

Orchestre de chambre de Montréal (OCM) / Montréal Chamber Orchestra (MCO)
5821, av de l'Esplanade, Montréal QC H2T 3A2
Tél: 514-871-1224
info@mco-ocm.qc.ca
www.mco-ocm.qc.ca
Se consacrer au répertoire pour ensemble de chambre & oeuvres canadiennes
Wanda Kaluzny, Directrice artistique

Orchestre Métropolitain
#401, 486, rue Sainte-Catherine, Montréal QC H3B 1A6
Tél: 514-598-0870
info@orchestremetropolitain.com
orchestremetropolitain.com
www.youtube.com/c/OrchestreMétropolitainmontreal
Apporter la musique classique à la communauté métropolitaine de Montréal
Abe Adham, Directeur général
Yannick Nézet-Séguin, Directeur artistique

Orchestre symphonique de Laval
#203, 3235, boul Saint-Martin est, Laval QC H7E 5G8
Tél: 450-978-3666
info@osl.ca
www.osl.qc.ca
www.youtube.com/c/OSLaval
Diffuser la musique classique et symphonique
Sarah Belleville, Directrice générale
Alain Trudel, Directeur artistique

Orchestre symphonique de Longueuil
156, boul Churchill, Greenfield Park QC J4V 2M3
Tél: 450-466-6661
info@osdl.ca
osdl.ca
Assurer la diffusion du grand répertoire classique et la promotion de l'excellence musicale en Montérégie
Michel Vallée, Directeur général par intérim
Alexandre Da Costa, Directeur artistique

Orchestre symphonique de Montréal
1600, rue Saint-Urbain, Montréal QC H2X 0S1
Tél: 514-840-7400; *Téléc:* 514-842-0728
Ligne sans frais: 888-842-9951
servicealaclientele@osm.ca
www.youtube.com/c/OrchestresymphoniquedeMontréal
De diffuser, au plus large public, le répertoire mondial de la musique symphonique et les artistes de niveau international; assumer son rôle social & institutionnel
Madeleine Careau, Chef de la direction
Rafael Payare, Directeur musical

Orchestre symphonique de Québec
#250, 437, Grande Allée est, Québec QC G1R 2J5
Tél: 418-643-8486
info@osq.org
www.osq.org
www.youtube.com/c/OrchestresymphoniquedeQuébec
Interpréter le répertoire symphonique; être le principal moteur de l'activité musicale de la région
Astrid Chouinard, Présidente-directrice générale
Fabien Gabel, Directeur musical

Orchestre symphonique de Sherbrooke (OSS) / Sherbrooke Symphony Orchestra
135, rue Don Bosco nord, Sherbrooke QC J1L 1E5
Tél: 819-821-0227
info@osssherbrooke.com
osssherbrooke.com
www.youtube.com/c/OrchestresymphoniquedeSherbrooke
Faire connaître la musique symphonique de la région et permettre aux musiciens de la région de jouer dans un orchestre professionnel
Nicolas Bélanger, Directeur Général
Stéphane Laforest, Directeur artistique

Orchestre symphonique de Trois-Rivières (OSTR)
CP 1281, Trois-Rivières QC G9A 5K8
Tél: 819-373-5340; *Téléc:* 819-373-6693
administration@ostr.ca
www.ostr.ca
www.youtube.com/user/OSTRofficiel
Poursuivre l'atteinte des objectifs inhérents à ses axes de développement: éducation, implication dans son milieu, diffusion de musique symphonique, création musicale et diffusion de nouveaux produits
Natalie Rousseau, Directrice générale
Jean-Claude Picard, Directeur artistique

Orchestre symphonique des jeunes de Montréal (OSJM) / Montréal Youth Symphonic Orchestra
CP 83566, Succ. Garnier, Montréal QC H2J 4E9
Tél: 514-645-0311
osjmontreal@gmail.com
www.osjm.org
www.youtube.com/user/osjmontreal
Présenter le jeune musicien de talent à un auditoire et lui fournir une expérience formative sous la supervision d'artistes reconnus; encourager et soutenir le choix d'une carrière musicale qui peut mener à un grand orchestre; promouvoir un intérêt dans les concerts et développer un soutien plus diversifié dans les activités de l'orchestre; fournir à l'entreprise privée l'occasion de participer plus activement dans une activité culturelle d'envergure et l'aider à faire apprécier son rôle dans la communauté
Anne-Marie Desbiens, Directrice générale
Louis Lavigueur, Directeur artistique

Orchestre symphonique des jeunes de Sherbrooke
CP 1536, Succ. Place de la Cité, Sherbrooke QC J1H 5M4
Tél: 819-566-1888
www.osjs.ca
Fournir aux jeunes musiciens et musiciens de Sherbrooke et de la région un milieu où ils pourront apprendre à faire de la musique d'ensemble, développer la maîtrise de leur instrument et perfectionner leur art dans un contexte de vie collective particulièrement enrichissante
Félix Ste-Marie, Directeur musicale

Orchestre symphonique des jeunes du West Island (OSJWI) / West Island Youth Symphony Orchestra (WIYSO)
CP 1028, Succ. Pointe-Claire, Montréal QC H9S 4H9
Tél: 514-834-9025
info@osjwi.qc.ca
www.osjwi.qc.ca
Permettre aux jeunes de 8-25 ans de jouer dans un orchestre regroupant tous les instruments sous la direction d'un chef professionnel
Michel Joron, Président
Jean Ai Seow, Directrice musicale
Jean-Pascal Hamelin, Directeur artistique

Orchestre symphonique des jeunes Philippe-Filion
2100, boul des Hêtres, Shawinigan QC G9N 8R8
Tél: 819-539-6000
info@aosjpf.ca
www.aosjpf.ca
Formation orchestrale spécialisé pour jeunes musiciens

Orchestre symphonique du Saguenay-Lac-St-Jean (OSSLSJ)
202, rue Jacques-Cartier est, Chicoutimi QC G7H 6R8
Tél: 418-545-3409
info@lorchestre.org
lorchestre.org
www.instagram.com/orchestre_slsj
Produire et diffuser des concerts professionnels à travers tout le Saguenay-Saint-Jean en regard des enjeux financiers et des structures d'accueil existantes. Ses qualités artistiques et administratives en constante évolution lui permettent d'exercer un leadership au sein des organismes musicaux régionaux, basé sur un partenariat serré avec le milieu, au service du développement de sa discipline et de sa communauté

Jean-Michel Malouf, Directeur artisique

Société chorale de Saint-Lambert / St. Lambert Choral Society
CP 36546, Saint-Lambert QC J4P 3S8
Tél: 450-878-0200
info.choeur.scsl@gmail.com
choralesaintlambert.com
De promouvoir et de recueillir une appréciation pour la musique chorale
Xavier Brossard-Ménard, Directeur artistique

Société des Mélomanes de l'Abitibi-Témiscamingue
CP 2305, Rouyn-Noranda QC J9X 5A9
Tél: 819-762-0043
info@osrat.ca
osrat.ca
Diffusion de la musique classique et integration de la relève
Jacques Marchand, Directeur artistique

Société du Palais Montcalm
Bureau des arts et de la culture, 995, Place D'Youville, Québec QC G1R 3P1
Tél: 418-641-6220; Téléc: 418-691-5171
Ligne sans frais: 877-641-6040
info@palaismontcalm.ca
www.palaismontcalm.ca
Pour faire fonctionner un centre de culture et de promouvoir les arts
Sylvie Roberge, Directrice générale
Claudie Lapointe, Directrice, Communications et du marketing

Société Pro Musica Inc. / Pro Musica Society Inc.
#2, 4672, rue Saint-Denis, Montréal QC H2J 2L3
Tél: 514-845-0532
concerts@promusica.qc.ca
promusica.qc.ca
Promouvoir et présenter à Montréal la plus belle musique de chambre par les meilleurs interprètes d'ici et d'ailleurs; dans la série TOPAZE, promouvoir et offrir aux jeunes familles de meilleures conditions pour assister aux concerts avec un atelier d'animation musicale pour les enfants

Saskatchewan

Regina Symphony Orchestra (RSO)
2424 College Ave., Regina SK S4P 1C8
Tel: 306-791-6395; Fax: 306-586-2133
info@reginasymphony.com
reginasymphony.com
To promote & enhance the performance & enjoyment of live orchestral music in Regina & southern Saskatchewan & contribute to the cultural life of the city, province & nation
Mike Forrester, Executive Director
Gordon Gerrard, Music Director

Saskatchewan Band Association (SBA)
2205 Victoria Ave., Yorkton SK S4P 0S4
Tel: 306-993-9729
info@saskband.org
www.saskband.org
To promote & support instrumental music in Saskatchewan; To act as a voice on issues that affect bands in Saskatchewan
Suzanne Gorman, Chief Executive Officer

Saskatchewan Orchestral Association, Inc. (SOA)
4647 Pasqua St., Regina SK S4S 6B9
Tel: 306-529-7366
info@saskorchestras.com
www.saskorchestras.com
To enhance the quality of life in Saskatchewan by helping to develop a thriving orchestral community
Adrian Casas, President
Elaine Kaloustian, Executive Director

Saskatchewan Recording Industry Association (SRIA)
1831 College Ave., 3rd Fl., Regina SK S4P 4V5
Tel: 306-347-0676; Toll-Free: 800-347-0676
info@saskmusic.org
www.saskmusic.org
To develop & promote the music & sound recording industry of Saskatchewan
Mike Dawson, Executive Director

Saskatoon Symphony Society (SSO)
602B - 51st St., Saskatoon SK S7K 7K3
Tel: 306-665-6414
office@saskatoonsymphony.org
saskatoonsymphony.org
www.youtube.com/c/SaskatoonSymphonyOrchestra

To promote, encourage & support symphonic & classical music in Saskatoon & elsewhere in Saskatchewan
Mark Turner, Executive Director
Eric Paetkau, Music Director

Saskatoon Youth Orchestra (SYO)
PO Box 21108, Saskatoon SK S7H 5N9
Tel: 306-955-6336
info@syo.ca
syo.ca
www.instagram.com/syoplayers
To provide young musicians in the Saskatoon area with an opportunity to improve their playing skills in a full orchestral ensemble; To enrich the cultural landscape of the city of Saskatoon & the province of Saskatchewan at large
Paul Sinkewicz, Executive Director
Richard Carnegie, Music Director
Bernadette Wilson, Strings Music Director

South Saskatchewan Youth Orchestra (SSYO)
PO Box 868, Lumsden SK S0G 3C0
Tel: 306-761-2576
info@ssyo.ca
www.ssyo.ca
To provide orchestral training to young musicians in Southern Saskatchewan
Alan Denike, Music Director

Yukon Territory

Jazz Yukon
PO Box 31307, Whitehorse YT Y1A 5P7
Tel: 867-334-2789
info@jazzyukon.ca
www.jazzyukon.ca
To promote & present jazz in the Yukon through an annual integrated program of live jazz presentations & jazz education outreach

Music Yukon
#416, 108 Elliott St., Whitehorse YT Y1A 6C4
Tel: 867-456-8742
office@musicyukon.com
musicyukon.com
To promote the Yukon music industry
Allyn Walton, Acting President
K. Scott Maynard, Executive Director

Performing Arts - Theatre

Alberta

Alberta Playwrights' Network (APN)
#2, 1709 - 8th Ave. NE, Calgary AB T2E 0S9
Tel: 403-269-8564; Toll-Free: 800-268-8564
www.albertaplaywrights.com
To foster playwriting in Alberta
Trevor Rueger, Executive Director

Evergreen Theatre Society
#2, 1709 - 8th Ave. SE, Calgary AB T2E 0S9
Tel: 403-228-1384
info@evergreentheatre.com
www.evergreentheatre.com
To create innovative, entertaining, accessible & educational theatre for a healthy & sustainable future
Valmai Goggin, President
Sean Fraser, Executive Director

New West Theatre Society
#111, 210A - 12A St. North, Lethbridge AB T1H 2J1
Tel: 403-381-9378
info@newwesttheatre.com
www.newwesttheatre.com
To provide Lethbridge & surrounding region with a broad-based & diverse program of professional quality theatrical, musical & dramatic performances
Kelly Reay, Artistic Director
Sheri Becker, General Manager

Theatre Alberta Society
Percy Page Centre, 11759 Groat Rd., 3rd Fl., Edmonton AB T5M 3K6
Tel: 780-422-8162; Fax: 780-422-2663
Toll-Free: 888-422-8160
theatreab@theatrealberta.com
www.theatrealberta.com
To encourage the growth of theatre in Alberta through high quality support & training opportunities to theatre professionals, educators & community theatre practitioners
Keri Mitchell, Executive Director

Theatre Calgary
220 - 9th Ave. SE, Calgary AB T2G 5C4
Tel: 403-294-7440
info@theatrecalgary.com
www.theatrecalgary.com
www.youtube.com/user/TheatreCalgary
To produce classical & modern theatre for Calgary audiences
Craig Senyk, Chair
Maya Choldin, Executive Director
Stafford Arima, Artistic Director

Theatre Network (1975) Society
8529 Gateway Blvd., Edmonton AB T6E 6P3
Tel: 780-453-2440
info@theatrenetwork.ca
theatrenetwork.ca
www.youtube.com/user/TheatreNetworkEdm
To promote original regional drama
Bradley Moss, Artistic & Executive Director

British Columbia

Bard on the Beach Theatre Society
#201, 162 West 1st Ave., Vancouver BC V57 0H6
Tel: 604-737-0625; Fax: 604-737-0425
info@bardonthebeach.org
bardonthebeach.org
www.youtube.com/user/bardonthebeachfest
To provide Vancouver residents & visitors with affordable, accessible Shakespearean productions of high quality
Christopher Gaze, Artistic Director
Claire Sakaki, Executive Director

British Columbia Drama Association
Old Courthouse Cultural Centre, 7 Seymour St. West, Kamloops BC V2C 1E4
Tel: 778-471-5620; Fax: 778-471-5639
Toll-Free: 888-202-2913
info@theatrebc.org
theatrebc.org
To promote the development of theatre in BC & Canada through a wide range of programs, services, activities, competitions, festivals & events
Douglas Perri, President

First Pacific Theatre Society
1440 West 12th Ave., Vancouver BC V6H 1M8
Tel: 604-731-5483
info@pacifictheatre.org
pacifictheatre.org
www.instagram.com/pacifictheatre
To produce high quality theatre; To operate with artistic, spiritual, relational & financial integrity
Jennifer Milley, Executive Director
Kaitlin Williams, Artistic Director

Greater Vancouver Professional Theatre Alliance (GVPTA)
#308, 237 Keefer St., Vancouver BC V6A 1X6
Tel: 604-608-6799
info@gvpta.ca
www.gvpta.ca
To promote live theatre & foster a thriving environment for the continued growth & development of theatre in Greater Vancouver
Kenji Maeda, Executive Director

Intrepid Theatre Co. Society
#2, 1609 Blanshard St., Victoria BC V8W 2J5
Tel: 250-383-2663
www.intrepidtheatre.com
To educate & enhance the public's awareness & aesthetic appreciation of contemporary & progressive styles of modern theatre by encouraging, developing & producing new or experimental works for public performance; by coordinating & producing the annual Fringe Theatre Festival in Victoria
Sammie Gough, Producer
Justine Shore, Managing Director

Playwrights Theatre Centre (PTC)
1422 William St., Vancouver BC V5L 2P7
Tel: 604-685-6228
plays@playwrightstheatre.com
www.playwrightstheatre.com
www.instagram.com/ptcplaywrights
To develop new Canadian plays; To provide support to experienced, emerging, & aspiring playwrights from across the country through dramaturgy, workshops, writers' groups & other programs
Natasha McEwen, President
Heidi Taylor, Artistic & Executive Director

Théâtre la Seizième
#266, 1555 - 7th Ave. West, Vancouver BC V6J 1S1
Tél: 604-736-2616
info@seizieme.ca
www.seizieme.ca
vimeo.com/seizieme
Promouvoir le théâtre professionnel francophone en
Colombie-Britannique
Esther Duquette, Directrice générale et artistique

Theatre Terrific Society (TTS)
#430, 111 West Hastings St., Vancouver BC V6B 1H4
Tel: 604-222-4020; *Fax:* 604-669-2662
info@theatreterrific.ca
www.theatreterrific.ca
To provide theatrical opportunities to people with disabilities
Susanna Uchatius, Artistic Director

Vancouver Fringe Theatre Society (VFTS)
PO Box 203, 1398 Cartwright St., Vancouver BC V6H 3R8
Tel: 604-257-0350
info@vancouverfringe.com
www.vancouverfringe.com
To promoting interest in the arts in Vancouver; To nurture &
support artists
Claudia Sjoberg, President
Sylvia Ceacero, Interim Executive Director

Vancouver TheatreSports League (VTSL)
1515 Anderson St., Vancouver BC V6H 3R5
www.vtsl.com
To challenge & inspire the community by growing & exploring
exceptional improv-based work

Western Canada Theatre Company Society (WCT)
PO Box 329, Kamloops BC V2C 5K9
Tel: 250-372-3216; *Fax:* 250-374-7099
www.wctlive.ca
www.youtube.com/user/wctkamloops
To provide the regional community with challenging professional
theatre; To entertain, educate, enrich & interact with the cultural
mosaic of its community; To promote & assist the performing
arts through the provision of educational, theatrical & artistic
opportunities & services & through the management & operation
of facilities
Evan Klassen, Managing Director
James MacDonald, Artistic Director

Manitoba

Cercle Molière Inc.
340, boul Provencher, Winnipeg MB R2H 0G7
Tél: 204-233-8053; *Téléc:* 204-233-2373
info@cerclemoliere.com
www.cerclemoliere.com
Présenter des spectacles de théâtre en français au Manitoba
Geneviève Pelletier, Directrice artistique et générale

Manitoba Association of Playwrights (MAP)
#503, 100 Arthur St., Winnipeg MB R3B 1H3
Tel: 204-942-8941
mbplay@mts.net
mbplays.ca
To provide support for playwrights in Manitoba through the
operation of programs for emerging & established playwrights
Ann Hodges, President
Brian Drader, Executive Director

Prairie Theatre Exchange (PTE)
**Portage Place, 393 Portage Ave., 3rd Fl., #Y300, Winnipeg
MB R3B 3H6**
Tel: 204-942-7291; *Fax:* 204-942-1774
www.pte.mb.ca
www.instagram.com/prairie_theatre
To operate a professional theatre of high calibre for the
entertainment & edification of a broad spectrum of people; To
operate a school to encourage appreciation of theatre & to
provide accessible, high quality, innovative drama education; To
support the development of new plays; To foster theatre
arts-related endeavours of others through use of our facilities &
expertise; To manage one or more community theatre arts
centres
Jane Helbrecht, President
Lisa Li, Managing Director
Thomas Morgan Jones, Artistic Director
Jenna Khan, Director, Communications

Royal Manitoba Theatre Centre (MTC)
174 Market Ave., Winnipeg MB R3B 0P8
Tel: 204-956-1340; *Fax:* 204-947-3741
royalmtc.ca
www.youtube.com/user/MTCWinnipeg

To study, practice & promote all aspects of the dramatic arts,
with particular emphasis on professional production
John Guttormson, Chair
Camilla Holland, Executive Director
Kelly Thornton, Artistic Director

New Brunswick

La Cooperative de théâtre l'Escaouette Ltee
170, rue Botsford, Moncton NB E1C 4X6
Tél: 506-855-0001; *Téléc:* 506-855-0010
escaouette@nb.aibn.com
www.escaouette.com
www.youtube.com/c/escaouette
Pour effectuer productions acadiennes theatrical originaux
Marcia Babineau, Direction artistique & codirection générale

Theatre New Brunswick (TNB)
55 Whitting Rd., Fredericton NB E3B 5Y5
Tel: 506-460-1381; *Fax:* 506-453-9315
info@tnb.nb.ca
www.tnb.nb.ca
www.youtube.com/user/theatreNB
To provide live professional theatre to the people of New
Brunswick by touring & performing in nine centres throughout
the province; To entertain by providing quality theatre & acting
as a theatrical resource for playwrights, actors & young people
interested in the field
Natasha MacLellan, Artistic Director

Théâtre populaire d'Acadie (TPA)
#302, 220, boul St-Pierre ouest, Caraquet NB E1W 1A5
Tél: 506-727-0920
tpa@tpacadie.ca
tpacadie.ca
www.youtube.com/user/tpacadie1
Créer, produire, diffuser et faire rayonner le théâtre d'ici et
d'ailleurs
Allain Roy, Directeur artistique

Newfoundland and Labrador

Theatre Newfoundland Labrador
PO Box 655, Corner Brook NL A2H 6G1
Tel: 709-639-7238; *Fax:* 709-639-1006
www.theatrenewfoundland.com
To create & produce professional theatre which reflects the lives
& diversity of the audiences on the province's west coast,
extending to Labrador & across the island of Newfoundland
Jeff Pitcher, Artistic Director

Nova Scotia

Neptune Theatre Foundation
1593 Argyle St., Halifax NS B3J 2B2
Tel: 902-429-7070; *Toll-Free:* 800-565-7345
info@neptunetheatre.com
www.neptunetheatre.com
www.youtube.com/c/NeptuneTheatreHFX
To pursue theatrical excellence with artistic vision; To develop
local & Canadian artistic talent; To encourage the youth of our
community to develop a life-long interest in live theatre
Jeremy Webb, Artistic Director
Lisa Bugden, General Manager

Theatre Nova Scotia (TNS)
1113 Marginal Rd., Halifax NS B3H 4P7
Tel: 902-425-3876; *Fax:* 902-422-0881
theatrens@theatrens.ca
www.theatrens.ca
To provide services, training & resources to professional &
amateur theatre community throughout Nova Scotia
Colleen MacIsaac, Co-Chair
Chris O'Neill, Co-Chair
Cat MacKeigan, Executive Director

Two Planks & a Passion Theatre Company (TP&aP)
PO Box 190, 555 Ross Creek Rd., Canning NS B0P 1H0
Tel: 902-582-3073; *Fax:* 902-582-7943
mail@twoplanks.ca
www.artscentre.ca/twoplanks.html
To develop & present high quality, professional theatre both
regionally & nationally which reflects Canadian life, with strong
roles for women; To develop & build an artistic centre in
Canning, NS, accessible to both the local community & to artists
of all disciplines & residencies
Ken Schwartz, Artistic Director

Ontario

Actors' Fund of Canada
#301, 1000 Yonge St., Toronto ON M4W 2K2
Tel: 416-975-0304; *Fax:* 416-975-0306
Toll-Free: 877-399-8392
contact@afchelps.ca
afchelps.ca
www.youtube.com/user/ActorsFundofCanada
To provide encouragement & short-term financial aid to help
entertainment industry workers maintain their health, housing &
ability to work after an illness, injury or sudden unemployment
David Hope, Executive Director

Buddies in Bad Times Theatre
12 Alexander St., Toronto ON M4Y 1B4
Tel: 416-975-9130; *Fax:* 416-975-9293
buddiesinbadtimes.com
www.youtube.com/user/BIBTTV
To promote gay, lesbian & queer theatrical expression
Shawn Daudlin, Managing Director

The Canadian Stage Corporation
26 Berkeley St., Toronto ON M5A 2W3
Tel: 416-367-8243; *Fax:* 416-367-1768
www.canadianstage.com
www.youtube.com/user/canadianstage
To develop, produce & export the best in Canadian &
international contemporary theatre
Monica Esteves, Executive Director
Brendan Healy, Artistic Director

Canadian Theatre Critics Association (CTCA) /
Association des critiques de théâtre du Canada
ON
www.canadiantheatrecritics.ca
To promote excellence in theatre criticism; to encourage the
dissemination of information on theatre on a national level; to
encourage the awareness & development of Canadian theatre
nationally & internationally through theatre criticism in all the
media; to promote & encourage excellence in Canadian theatre
through national awards; to improve the status & working
conditions of theatre critics
Carly Maga, President
Steve Fisher, Secretary & Treasurer

Compagnie vox théâtre
10 Patro St., Ottawa ON K1N 8B1
Tél: 613-241-1090
info@voxtheatre.ca
voxtheatre.ca
Avec son travail de création, ses productions de théâtre chanté,
ses accueils de spectacle pluridisciplinaires et ses tournées, la
compagnie Vox Théâtre présente une programation complète
pour les enfants et leur propose aussi des activités de formation
Alain Lauzon, Président
Pier Rodier, Direction artistique et générale

Harbourfront Centre
235 Queens Quay West, Toronto ON M5J 2G8
Tel: 416-973-4600; *Fax:* 416-973-6055
info@harbourfrontcentre.com
www.harbourfrontcentre.com
www.youtube.com/c/HarbourfrontCentreToronto
To nurture the growth of new cultural expression; To stimulte
Canadian & international interchange; To provide a dynamic,
accessible environment for the public to experience the marvels
of the creative imagination
John Clark, Executive Director
Medhi Walerski, Artistic Director

National Arts Service Organization
#350, 401 Richmond St. West, Toronto ON M5V 3A8
Tel: 416-907-5829
adc@designers.ca
www.designers.ca
www.instagram.com/associateddesignersofcanada
To promote, pursue & protect the interests & needs of theatrical
designers working in Canada
Ken MacKenzie, President
Simon Rossiter, Treasurer
Gail Packwood, Executive Director
Louise Plunkett, General Manager

Native Earth Performing Arts Inc. (NEPA)
#250, 585 Dundas St. East, Toronto ON M5A 2B7
Tel: 416-531-1402
office@nativeearth.ca
www.nativeearth.ca
To enable Native actors, writers, designers, directors &
technicians to work together to produce quality theatre that is
vital to their development as artists & their identity as Native

people; To encourage the use of theatre as form of communication within the Native community, including the use of the Native languages
Keith Barker, Artistic Director
Isaac Thomas, Managing Director

Ontario Puppetry Association (OPA)
c/o Stephanie Filippi, 51 Park Ave., St Catharines ON L2P 1R2
www.ontariopuppetryassociation.com
To promote recognition of puppetry as art; To distribute information on all aspects; To assist in eventual formation of national puppet theatre

Playwrights Guild of Canada (PGC)
St. Matthew's Clubhouse, 450 Broadview Ave., Toronto ON M4K 2N1
Tel: 416-703-0201
info@playwrightsguild.ca
playwrightsguild.ca
To encourage Canadian playwriting; To publish, promote & distribute Canadian plays; To provide current information of Canadian plays & their authors; To offer copyright protection; To promote the study & appreciation of Canadian plays; To safeguard freedom of expression on the stage
Rebecca Burton, Manager, Membership & Contracts
Idl Djafer, Office Manager

Professional Association of Canadian Theatres (PACT)
Artscape Distillery Studios, #201, 15 Case Goods Lane, Toronto ON M5A 3C4
Tel: 416-595-6455; *Fax:* 416-595-6450
Toll-Free: 800-263-7228
info@pact.ca
www.pact.ca
To gain recognition & support for professional theatre in Canada; To support the development of Canadian theatre companies by sharing resources & knowledge; To develop working standards & relationships with theatre professionals through their associations; To inform & connect theatres across Canada through a communications network; To act as a major force in influencing cultural policy at all levels of government
Boomer Stacey, Executive Director
Mirette Shoeir, Manager, Membership & Communications

Shaw Festival Theatre, Canada
PO Box 774, 10 Queen's Parade, Niagara-on-the-Lake ON L0S 1J0
Tel: 905-468-2153; *Fax:* 905-468-5438
Toll-Free: 800-657-1106
www.shawfest.com
www.youtube.com/user/TheShawFestival
To create intellectually challenging & entertaining theatre at an affordable price
Tim Carroll, Artistic Director
Tim Jennings, Executive Director

Tarragon Theatre
30 Bridgman Ave., Toronto ON M5R 1X3
Tel: 416-531-1827
patronservices@tarragontheatre.com
www.tarragontheatre.com
To develop & produce new Canadian plays
Elaine Stavro, President
Mike Payette, Artistic Director
Andrea Vagianos, Managing Director

Théâtre Action (TA)
269 Montfort St., #G, Ottawa ON K1L 5P1
Tél: 613-745-2322
communications@theatreaction.ca
theatreaction.ca
Oeuvrer au developpement du théâtre franco-ontarien
Marie Eve Chassé, Directrice générale
Sarah Anne LaCombe, Directrice, Communications et des partenariats

Théâtre de la Vieille 17
204 King Edward Ave., Ottawa ON K1N 7L7
Tél: 613-241-8562
communications@vieille17.ca
www.vieille17.ca
vimeo.com/user8318968
Créer et diffuser des spectacles pour la jeunesse et pour les adultes à l'échelle régionale, nationale et internationale
France Boily, Directrice administrative et générale
Geneviève Pineault, Directrice artistique

Théâtre du Nouvel-Ontario (TNO)
21 Lasalle Blvd., Sudbury ON P3A 6B1
Tél: 705-525-5606
tno@letno.ca
letno.ca
www.youtube.com/user/TheatreNouvelOntario
Dédié à la création, à la dramaturgie franco-ontarienne et à l'accueil d'oeuvres principalement canadiennes
Marie-Pierre Proulx, Directrice artistique

Théâtre du Trillium
333 King Edward Ave., Ottawa ON K1N 7M5
Tél: 613-789-7643
info@letrillium.com
letrillium.com
www.youtube.com/user/theatredutrillium
Pour effectuer des productions théâtrales contemporaines
Pierre Antoine Lafon Simard, Directeur artistique

Théâtre français de Toronto
#610, 21 College St., Toronto ON M5G 2B3
Tél: 416-534-7303
info@theatrefrancais.com
theatrefrancais.com
www.youtube.com/user/LeTheatreFrancaisTfT
Contribue au développement culturel et pédagogique de la communauté de Toronto
Karine Ricard, Directeur artistique
Ghislain Caron, Directeur général

Théâtre la Catapulte
269 Montfort St., Ottawa ON K1L 5P1
Tél: 613-562-0851; *Téléc:* 613-562-0631
communications@catapulte.ca
catapulte.ca
Création, de production et de diffusion enracinée en Ontario français, proposant aux adolescents et au grand public des expériences théâtrales audacieuses et éclectiques nourries par la fougue de la relève et par des artistes établis; Productions une diffusion importante dans la région d'Ottawa-Gatineau et dans l'ensemble du Canada tout en cultivant sa relation avec ses publics
Danielle Le Saux-Farmer, Directrice artistique et générale

Toronto Alliance for the Performing Arts (TAPA)
#350, 401 Richmond St. West, Toronto ON M5V 3A8
Tel: 416-536-6468; *Fax:* 416-536-3463
info@tapa.ca
tapa.ca
To foster greater respect & support for the arts by advocating on behalf of Canadian theatre & dance, representing all cultural backgrounds, to government, supporters, & the general public; To provide services which enhance the artistic, technical & administrative development of members
Jacoba Knaapen, Executive Director
Theresa Gerrow, Manager, Membership & Sponsorship

Young People's Theatre (YPT)
165 Front St. East, Toronto ON M5A 3Z4
Tel: 416-862-2222
online@youngpeoplestheatre.ca
www.youngpeoplestheatre.ca
www.youtube.com/user/YoungPeoplesTheatre
To make a positive impact on the intellectual, social, & emotional development of young people; To produce plays for young audiences; To operate a year-round drama school for youth
Nancy J. Webster, Executive Director
Allen MacInnis, Artistic Director

Québec

Association québécoise des marionnettistes (AQM)
30, av Saint-Just, Montréal QC H2V 1X8
Tel: 514-270-2717
info@aqm.ca
aqm.ca
Représenter ses membres et créer un terrain propice aux échanges, aux actions communes et à la réflexion sur la pratique de l'art de la marionnette
Maude Gareau, Présidente
Vincent Ranallo, Coordonnateur général

Black Theatre Workshop (BTW)
#432, 3680, rue Jeanne-Mance, Montréal QC H2X 2K5
Tel: 514-932-1104
info@theatrebtw.ca
blacktheatreworkshop.ca
www.youtube.com/c/BlackTheatreWorkshop
To encourage & promote the development of a Black & Canadian theatre, rooted in a literature that reflects the creative will of Black Canadian writers & artists, & the creative collaborations between Black & other artists; To strive to create

a greater cross-cultural understanding by its presence & the intrinsic value of its work
Quincy Armorer, Artistic Director
Adele Benoit, Managing Director

Canadian Institute for Theatre Technology (CITT) / L'Institut Canadien des Technologies Scénographiques (ICTS)
#302, 4529, rue Clark, Montréal QC H2T 2T3
Tel: 514-504-9998; *Fax:* 514-504-9997
Toll-Free: 888-271-3383
info@citt.org
www.citt.org
To work for the betterment of the Canadian live performance community; To promote safe & ethical work practices
Matt Frankish, President
Monique Corbeil, National Coordinator

Centre des auteurs dramatiques (CEAD)
#328, 5445 av de Gaspé, Montréal QC H2T 3B2
Tél: 514-288-3384; *Téléc:* 514-288-7043
cead@cead.qc.ca
www.cead.qc.ca
Promotion et diffusion ici et à l'étranger des textes d'auteurs québécois et d'auteurs franco-canadiens; développement dramaturgique
Alain Jean, Directeur général

Conseil québécois du théâtre (CQT)
#808, 460, rue Sainte-Catherine ouest, Montréal QC H3B 1A7
Tél: 514-954-0270; *Téléc:* 514-954-0165
Ligne sans frais: 866-954-0270
cqt@cqt.qc.ca
www.cqt.ca
Promouvoir et défendre les intérêts du milieu théâtral et le représenter auprès des diverses instances; concerter, animer et informer la communauté théâtrale sur toutes les questions qui touchent la pratique théâtrale; promouvoir et développer le théâtre
Anne Trudel, Présidente
Catherine Voyer-Léger, Directrice générale

Fédération québécoise du théâtre amateur (FQTA)
CP 211, Succ. Saint-Élie-d'Orford, Sherbrooke QC J1R 1A1
Tél: 819-571-9358; *Ligne sans frais:* 877-752-2501
info@fqta.ca
www.fqta.ca
Promouvoir le théâtre amateur en réunissant tous les individus et les groupes de théâtre pour contribuer à l'éducation artistique, esthétique et sociale de la population; établir un contact permanent entre les individus; fournir des occasions d'échange, de travaux, de recherches, de méthodes, de matériel et d'information ayant trait au théâtre
Rénald Pelletier, Président
Yoland Roy, Directeur général

Théâtre des épinettes
Chibougamau QC
Tél: 418-770-7687

Théâtres associés inc. (TAI)
#405, 1908, rue Panet, Montréal QC H2L 3A2
Tél: 514-842-6361; *Téléc:* 514-842-9730
info@theatresassocies.ca
www.theatresassocies.ca
Se faire la voix d'institutions théâtrales francophones québécoises
Marc-Antoine Malo, Président
Jacques Cousineau, Secrétaire général

Théâtres unis enfance jeunesse (TUEJ)
#217, 911, rue Jean-Talon est, Montréal QC H2R 1V5
Tél: 514-380-2337
info@tuej.org
tuej.org
Défendre les intérêts des producteurs dans le domaine du théâtre pour la jeunesse
Joachim Tanguay, Président
Pierre Tremblay, Directeur général

Saskatchewan

Globe Theatre Society
Globe Theatre, Prince Edward Bldg., 1801 Scarth St., Regina SK S4P 2G9
Tel: 306-525-6400; *Fax:* 306-352-4194
Toll-Free: 866-954-5623
onstage@globetheatrelive.com
globetheatrelive.com
To create & produce professional theatre & make it accessible with a view to entertain, educate & challenge
Jennifer Brewin, Artistic Director

Saskatchewan Playwrights Centre Inc. (SPC)
PO Box 31037, RPO Broadway, Saskatoon SK S7H 5S8
sk.playwrights@sasktel.net
www.saskplaywrights.ca
To develop playwrights
Laura Helgert, Chair
James Avramenko, Director, Creative & Operations

Theatre Saskatchewan Inc.
#104, 1102 - 8th Ave., Regina SK S4R 1C9
Tel: 306-352-0797
info@theatresaskatchewan.com
theatresaskatchewan.com
To strive to build a strong foundation for theatre which allows all people in Saskatchewan accessibility to live drama
John Dyck, President
Melissa Biro, Executive Director

La Troupe du Jour (LTDJ)
914 - 20th St. West, Saskatoon SK S7M 0Y4
Tél: 306-244-1040
building@latroupedujour.ca
www.latroupedujour.ca
Développement du théâtre francophone en Saskatchewan
Bruce McKay, Directeur artistique

Science Centres

Alberta

Local Science Centres

Calgary: TELUS Spark
220 St. George's Dr. NE,
Calgary, AB T2E 5T2
Tel: 403-817-6800
info@sparkscience.ca
www.sparkscience.ca
www.instagram.com/telus_spark
twitter.com/telus_spark
www.facebook.com /telusspark
Year Founded: 1967 The new TELUS Spark science centre features a variety of exhibits & installations for people of all ages as well as a HD Digital Dome Theatre. Available for birthday parties, corporate & team building events. Open year round Sun-Fri 10:00-4:00; Sat 10:00-5:00
Mary Anne Moser, President & CEO

Edmonton: TELUS World of Science - Edmonton
11211 - 142 St. NW,
Edmonton, AB T5M 4A1
Tel: 780-451-3344
info@twose.ca
telusworldofscienceedmonton.ca
www.instagram.com/twosedm
twitter.com/twosedm
www.facebook.com/Edmonto nScience
Other contact information: Bookings: 780-451-3344
Year Founded: 1984 The TELUS World of Science - Edmonton is an interactive science centre that features interactive exhibit galleries, Alberta's largest IMAX Theatre showing documentary & Hollywood films, a planetarium & observatory with daily shows, a science demonstration stage, robotics lab & feature gallery hosting world-class exhibitions. Open daily Fri-Sat 9:00-8:00; Sun-Th 9:00-5:00 & 9:00-6:00 in summer
Alan Nursall, President & CEO, 780-452-9100,
anursall@twose.ca

British Columbia

Local Science Centres

Kamloops: BIG Little Science Centre (BLSC)
458 Seymour St.,
Kamloops, BC V2C 5M8
Tel: 250-554-2572
susan@blscs.org
www.blscs.org
www.instagram.com/biglittlescience
twitter.com/BIG_Little_Sci
www.face book.com/BIGLittleScienceCentre
Year Founded: 2000 A child-friendly science centre located in the Happyvale School. Hands-on Exploration Room with over 140 different science exhibits. Weekly interactive shows, science labs, & science related activities. Available for birthday parties, camps, & special events. Open Tue-Sat 10:00-4:00
Gordon Stewart, Executive Director, gord@blscs.org
Susan Hammond, Operator

Vancouver: H.R. MacMillan Space Centre (HRMSC)
1100 Chestnut St.,
Vancouver, BC V6J 3J9
Tel: 604-738-7827; Fax: 604-736-5665
info@spacecentre.ca
www.spacecentre.ca
www.instagram.com/spacecentreyvr
twitter.com/SpaceCentreYVR
www.facebo ok.com/SpaceCentreYVR
Year Founded: 1968 Western Canada's premier earth, space science & astronomy attraction & educational resource. Live demostrations; exhibits; games & shows. Open daily 10:00-5:00
Raylene Marchand, Executive Director

Vancouver: Science World
1455 Quebec St.,
Vancouver, BC V6A 3Z7
Tel: 604-443-7440
info@scienceworld.ca
www.scienceworld.ca
www.instagram.com/scienceworldca
twitter.com/scienceworldca
www.facebo ok.com/scienceworldca
Year Founded: 1977 Hands-on exhibits; demonstrations; Omnimax theatre. Mar-June Mon-Fri 10:00-5:00, Sat-Sun 10:00-6:00; Jul-Sept 10:00-6:00, Th 10:00-8:00
Tracy Redies, President & CEO
Brian Radburn, Vice-President CPA & CA, Corporate Operations

Vernon: Okanagan Science Centre
Polson Park, 2704 Hwy 6,
Vernon, BC V1T 5G5
Tel: 250-545-3644
info@okscience.ca
www.okscience.ca
www.instagram.com/okanaganscience
twitter.com/OkanaganScience
www.face book.com/okanagansciencecentre
Year Founded: 1990 All of the centre's exhibits are based on scientific principals, in an effort to inspire visitors to appreciate the universal nature of science. Hours of Operation: M-F 10:00-5:00, Sa 11:00-5:00.
Dione Chambers, Executive Director

New Brunswick

Local Science Centres

Fredericton: Science East
Parent: Science East Association
668 Brunswick St.,
Fredericton, NB E3B 1H6
Tel: 506-457-2340; Fax: 506-462-7687
science@scienceeast.nb.ca
www.scienceeast.nb.ca
twitter.com/science_ea st
www.facebook.com/ScienceEast
Year Founded: 1994 Science East offers hands-on science & education exhibits & programs. Summer & March Break camp programs; public science shows; birthday parties; workshops. Summer: Mon-Sa 10:00-5:00, Sun 12:00-4:00; Winter: Mon-Fri 12:00-5:00, Sa 10:00-5:00, Sun 12:00-4:00
Guy Robbins, CEO, 506-457-2340,
guy.robbins@scienceeast.nb.ca

Newfoundland & Labrador

Local Science Centres

St. John's: Johnson Geo Centre
175 Signal Hill Rd.,
St. John's, NL A1A 1B2
Tel: 709-864-3200; Fax: 709-864-8065
Toll-Free: 866-868-7625
geocentre@mun.ca
www.geocentre.ca
twitter.com/NLGEOC ENTRE
www.facebook.com/JohnsonGEOCENTRE
Other contact information: Guest Services: 709-864-7997
Year Founded: 2002 The Johnson GEO CENTRE is a geological interpretation centre & a not-for-profit organization. The GEO CENTRE houses exhibit galleries related to our planet & our provincial geology, oil & gas exploration, natural resources, space exploration, & the Titanic disaster. Educational areas; public presentations; hands-on curriculum-based programming for school groups; Open daily 9:30-5:00
Kim Shipp, Director, 709-864-7588, kshipp@mun.ca

Nova Scotia

Local Science Centres

Halifax: Discovery Centre
1215 Lower Water St.,
Halifax, NS B3J 3S8
Tel: 902-492-4422
info@thediscoverycentre.ca
thediscoverycentre.ca
www.instagram.com/THEDISCOVERYCENTRE
twitter.com/DiscoveryCntr
www.fac ebook.com/DiscoveryCentre
Year Founded: 1985 Discovery Centre is an interactive science centre with hands-on exhibits, films, science shows & special events. Interactive exhibits & programs including four galleries, an open atrium, an Innovation Lab, Featured Exhibits & the first Immersive Dome Theatre in the region. Open Mon-Tu,Th-Sun 10:00-5:00, Wed 10:00-8:00
Dov Bercovici, President & CEO, 902-492-4422,
dbercovici@thediscoverycentre.ca

Ontario

Provincial Science Centres

Ontario Science Centre / Centre des sciences de l'Ontario
770 Don Mills Rd.,
Toronto, ON M3C 1T3
Tel: 416-696-1000 Toll-Free: 888-696-1110
contact.centre@OntarioScienceCentre.ca
www.ontariosciencecentre.ca
www.instagram.com/OntarioScienceCentre
twitter.com/ontsciencectr
www.facebook.com/ontariosciencecentre
Year Founded: 1969 Over 800 interactive exhibits on the environment, technology, food, chemistry, communications, sport & space; exhibits, programs, demonstrations, workshops & films for the public; special programs for school groups, children, adults & senior citizens; gift shops & restaurant; Ontario's only IMAX Dome theatre, featuring a 24-metre dome screen with wrap-around sound.
Paul Kortenaar, CEO Ph.D.

Local Science Centres

Sudbury: Science North
100 Ramsey Lake Rd.,
Sudbury, ON P3E 5S9
Tel: 705-522-3701 Toll-Free: 800-461-4898
info@sciencenorth.ca
www.sciencenorth.ca
www.instagram.com/sciencenorth
twitter.com/ScienceNorth
www.facebook.c om/ScienceNorth
Year Founded: 1984 Escape room, IMAX Theatre, planetarium, living butterfly gallery & special exhibits hall; exhibit design & consulting services.
Guy Labine, CEO, labine@sciencenorth.ca
Brenda Tremblay, Chief Operating Officer

Windsor: Canada South Science City
749 Felix Ave.,
Windsor, ON N9C 3K9
Tel: 519-973-3667
info@csssciencecity.com
www.csssciencecity.com
twitter.com/cs_science_city
www.facebook.com/Can adaSouthScienceCity
Year Founded: 2004 A child-friendly science centre that serves the Science & Technology component of the elementary school curriculum, but is also open to the general public. Hours of Operation: Sept.-June, Th, F & Sa 12:00-5:00, Su 1:00-5:00; July & Aug., M-Sa 10:00-5:00; after-hours tours available on request.
William E. Baylis, President Ph.D., baylis@uwindsor.ca

Quebec

Provincial Science Centres

The Montréal Science Centre / Centre des sciences de Montréal
333 de la Commune St. West,
Montréal, QC H2Y 2E2
Tel: 514-496-4724 Toll-Free: 877-496-4724
information@oldportofmontreal.com
www.montrealsciencecentre.com
www.instagram.com/centredessciences
twitter.com/centresciences
www.facebook.com/centredessciences

Year Founded: 2000 Visitors acquire an understanding of science & technology & how it affects daily living; three interactive science exhibition halls; IMAX TELUS Cinema. Montréal Science Centre is managed by the Old Port of Montréal Corporation, which also oversees the Quays of the Old Port of Montréal.
Cybèle Robichaud, Director, Programming

Local Science Centres

Laval: Cosmodôme - Centre des sciences de l'espace et Camp spatial Canada / Cosmodome - Space Science Center and Space Camp Canada
2150, rte des Laurentides,
Laval, QC H7T 2T8
Tél: 450-978-3600*Ligne sans frais:* 800-565-2267
info@cosmodome.org
www.cosmodome.org
www.instagram.com/cosmodome_laval
twitter.com/cosmodomelaval
www.faceb ook.com/cosmodome
Fondée en: 1994 Le Cosmodôme est la seule institution muséale de haut niveau entièrement consacrée à l'astronautique & à l'exploration spatiale au Canada. Les missions virtuelles; exposition permanente; camp spatial; fêtes d'enfants. Sept-Juin L-D 10h-17h; 24 Juin-Sept L-D 9h-17h
Ian Galipeau, Président

Montréal: Biosphère
160, ch Tour-de-L'Isle,
Montréal, QC H3C 4G8
espacepourlavie.ca/propos-de-la-biosphere
Fondée en: 1967 En tant que musée de l'environnement, la Biosphère utilise des expositions interactives & éducatives & des activités animées pour sensibiliser le public aux enjeux environnementaux & les aider à agir pour protéger l'environnement. Jan-Mai J-D 10h-17h; Juin-Sep 10h-17h; Oct-Dec Me-D 10h-17h

Montréal: Planétarium Rio Tinto Alcan / The Rio Tinto Alcan Planetarium
4801, av Pierre-de Coubertin,
Montréal, QC H1V 3V4
Tél: 514-868-3000*Ligne sans frais:* 855-518-4506
espacepourlavie.ca/planetarium
www.youtube.com/Espacepourlavie
twitter.com/espacepourlavie
www.faceb ook.com/Espacepourlavie
Fondée en: 1966 Le Planétarium de Montréal a fermé en 2011 en raison du manque de fonds, mais a été rouverte en 2013 comme le Planétarium Rio Tinto Alcan.

Saint-Louis-du-Ha-Ha: Aster, La Station scientifique du BSL
170 ch Jacques-Pelletier,
Saint-Louis-du-Ha-Ha, QC G0L 3S0
Tél: 418-854-2172; *Téléc:* 418-854-1898
direction@asterbsl.ca
www.asterbsl.ca
www.youtube.com/user/observatoireaster
www.facebook.com/SciencesAster
Fondée en: 1976 Aster est un organisme d'interprétation scientifique, à but non lucratif & situé dans l'Est du Canada. C'est un centre d'interprétation, d'animation & de formation qui suscite l'intérêt pour l'astronomie; l'environnement, la science & la technologie auprès de la clientèle scolaire & du public. Elle valorise également les carrières scientifiques & l'entrepreneurship technologique auprès de ses clientèles.
Stéphane Madore, Directeur

Saskatchewan

Provincial Science Centres

Saskatchewan Science Centre
2903 Powerhouse Dr.,
Regina, SK S4N 0A1
Tel: 306-791-7900
www.sasksciencecentre.com
www.instagram.com/sasksciencecentre
twitter.com/SkScienceCentre
www.facebook.com/SaskScienceCentre
Year Founded: 1989 Interactive science museum featuring hands-on exhibits; Kramer 3D IMAX theatre; stage shows; workshops.
Sandy Baumgartner, Chief Executive Officer
Vandana Jain, Chief Financial Officer

Zoos

Alberta

Calgary: Bow Habitat Station
1440 - 17A St. SE,
Calgary, AB T2G 4T9
Tel: 403-297-6561
bow.habitat@gov.ab.ca
www.bowhabitat.alberta.ca
twitter.com/BowHabitat
www.facebook.com/BowH abitatStation
Year Founded: 2009 Includes a Discovery Centre; the Sam Livingston Fish Hatchery; a trout pond available for fishing; Estate Park Interpretive Wetland. Open May-Oct Tue-Sun 10:00-4:00
Robyn Saude, Managing Director

Calgary: Calgary Zoo, Botanical Garden & Prehistoric Park
210 St. George's Dr. NE,
Calgary, AB T2E 7V6
Tel: 403-232-9300; *Fax:* 403-237-7582
Toll-Free: 800-588-9993
guestrelations@calgaryzoo.com
www.calgaryzoo.com/anima ls/prehistoric-park
www.instagram.com/thecalgaryzoo
twitter.com/calgaryzoo
www.facebook.co m/thecalgaryzoo
Year Founded: 1929 136 acres & 320 acre off-site breeding & conservation facility; educational programs; gift shop; Open year round 9:00-5:00.
Glenn Solomon, Board Chairman
Dr. Clément Lanthier, President & CEO

Calgary: Inglewood Bird Sanctuary
2425 9 Ave. SE,
Calgary, AB T2G 0V7
www.calgary.ca/csps/parks/locations/se-parks/inglewood-bird-sa nctuary.html
Year Founded: 1929 Offers more than 2km. of level trails; more than 270 species of birds, 300 species of plants & several kinds of mammals have been observed; visitor centre; two classrooms for nature-related programs. Free admission.

Edmonton: Edmonton Valley Zoo
PO Box 2359, 13315 Buena Vista Rd.,
Edmonton, AB T5J 2R7
Tel: 780-442-5311
attractions@edmonton.ca
www.edmonton.ca/valleyzoo
instagram.com/edmontonvalleyzoo
www.facebook.com/edmontonvalleyzoo
Year Founded: 1959 Features more than 350 endangered & exotic animals; children's zoo; education facility; camel rides available. Open daily May-Sep 9:00-6:00; Sep-Oct Mon-Fri 9:00-4:00, Sat-Sun 9:00-6:00; Oct-Dec 10:00-4:00.

Lacombe County: Ellis Bird Farm
PO Box 5060,
Lacombe County, AB T4L 1W7
Tel: 403-885-4477
info@ellisbirdfarm.ca
www.ellisbirdfarm.ca
www.youtube.com/user/EllisBirdFarmLacombe
twitter.com/EllisBirdFarm
ww w.facebook.com/EllisBirdFarm
Year Founded: 1982 A working farm & non-profit organization dedicated to the conservation of native cavity-nesting birds. Includes nestboxes; wildlife gardens; tea house. Open holiday Mondays, Tue-Sun 11:00-5:00.
Bob Winchell, Chair

British Columbia

Aldergrove: Greater Vancouver Zoo
5048 - 264th St.,
Aldergrove, BC V4W 1N7
Tel: 604-856-6825
info@gvzoo.com
www.gvzoo.com
instagram.com/greatervancouverzoo
twitter.com/GVZooChat
www.facebook.c om/greatervancouverzoo
Year Founded: 1970 Over 960 animals representing 176 species. Home to the world's only albino black bear & one of North America's largest grizzly bear habitats. Available for birthday parties & weddings. Open daily Apr-Sep 9:00-7:00; Oct-Mar 9:00-4:00.

Brentwood Bay: Victoria Butterfly Gardens
1461 Benvenuto Ave.,
Brentwood Bay, BC V8M 1J5
Tel: 250-652-3822; *Fax:* 250-652-4683
Toll-Free: 877-722-0272
info@butterflygardens.com
www.butterflygardens.com
instagram.com/victoriabutterflygardens
twitter.com/bflygrdns
www.facebook.com/butterfly.gardens
Indoor tropical gardens, fish, birds, butterflies & an insectarium. Open year round.
Ronalea Durrance, General Manager,
ronalea@butterflygardens.com

Creston: Creston Valley Wildlife Management Area (CVWMA)
1874 Wildfire Rd.,
Creston, BC V0B 1G0
Tel: 250-402-6900
www.crestonwildlife.ca
twitter.com/crestonwildlife
www.facebook.com/CrestonWildlife
Year Founded: 1968 17,000-acre wetland habitat with over 300 species of birds, 57 species of mammals & 29 species of fish, reptiles & amphibians. This diverse wildlife resource provides hiking, cycling, canoeing, picnicking, wildlife viewing, hunting, fishing & many other outdoor activities. Open May-Oct
Marc-André Beaucher, Head, Conservation Programs

Kamloops: British Columbia Wildlife Park
9077 Dallas Dr.,
Kamloops, BC V2C 6V1
Tel: 250-573-3242
info@bcwildlife.org
www.bcwildlife.org
www.instagram.com/bcwildlifepark
twitter.com/bcwildlifepark
www.facebo ok.com/BCWildlifePark
Year Founded: 1966 A non-profit organization dedicated to the conservation of BC wildlife through display, interpretation, education, wildlife rehabilitation, endangered species & direct action. Open Jan-Feb Sat-Sun 9:30-4:00; daily Mar-Apr 9:30-4:00; daily May-Oct 9:30-5:00; Oct-Dec Sat-Sun 9:30-4:00.
Glenn Grant, General Manager & Executive Director, 250-573-3242, glenn@bcwildlife.org

Port Hardy: Quatse Salmon Stewardship Centre
Parent: Northern Vancouver Island Salmonid Enhancement Association
8400 Byng Rd.,
Port Hardy, BC V0N 2P0
Tel: 250-902-0336
info@thesalmoncentre.org
www.thesalmoncentre.org
www.facebook.com/quatsesalmon.stewardshipcentre
Other contact information: Alt. email:
manager@quatsehatchery.ca
Year Founded: 1983 The centre features an aquarium & a working salmon hatchery that visitors can observe. All proceeds go towards salmon conservation. Open daily 10:00-5:00.
Grant Anderson, Executive Director

Qualicum Beach: Butterfly World & Gardens
PO Box 36, 1080 Winchester Rd.,
Qualicum Beach, BC V0R 1M0
Tel: 250-248-7026
butterflyworldc@gmail.com
www.butterflyworldcoombs.com
www.instagram.com/butterflyworldcoombs
www.facebook.com/Butterfly.World. Coombs
Year Founded: 1988 The Butterfly World & Gardens is a nature park with tropical gardens, ponds, birds, butterflies & reptiles. Open Jul-Aug Sun-Thu 11:00-4:00, Fri-Sa 10:00-5:00
Shiray Raines, Manager

Richmond: Richmond Nature Park
11851 Westminster Hwy.,
Richmond, BC V6X 1B4
Tel: 604-718-6188
nature@richmond.ca
www.richmond.ca/parks/parks/naturepark/about
Year Founded: 1968 Features trails through bog & forest; more than 100 species of birds, mammals, reptiles & amphibians; seasonal programs & events. Open daily 7:00-sunset. Free admission
Brenda Bartley-Smith, President, Nature Park Society
Kristine Bauder, Coordinator

Vancouver: Stanley Park Ecology Society
Stanley Park Dining Pavilion 2nd Floor, PO Box 5167,
Vancouver, BC V6B 4B2

Tel: 604-257-6908
info@stanleyparkecology.ca
stanleyparkecology.ca
twitter.com/StanleyParkEco
www.facebook.com/Stan leyParkEcology
Year Founded: 1988 Encourages stewardship of the natural
world through education, action & by fostering awareness;
provides public programs for adults & families, school programs,
wildlife information & resources promoting coexistence between
people & their wild neighbours.
Tom McIllfaterick, President
Rita Douglas, Vice-President
Tricia Collingham, Executive Director,
exec@stanleyparkecology.ca

Victoria: Swan Lake Christmas Hill Nature Sanctuary
3873 Swan Lake Rd.,
Victoria, BC V8X 3W1

Tel: 250-479-0211
info@swanlake.bc.ca
www.swanlake.bc.ca
www.instagram.com/swanlakenature
twitter.com/swanlakenature
www.facebo ok.com/SwanLakeChristmasHillNatureSanctuary
Year Founded: 1975 Nature education centre; 125 acres
including marshy lowlands surrounding Swan Lake & the
highlands of Christmas Hill. Open year round Mon-Fri 8:30-4:00;
Sat-Sun 12:00-4:00
Fallon Lindsay, Interim Chair
Cara Gibson, Executive Director

Manitoba

Whitemouth: Alfred Hole Goose Sanctuary & Visitor
Centre (AHGS)
c/o Manitoba Conservation, PO Box 130,
Whitemouth, MB R0E 1R0

Tel: 204-369-3157
parkInterpretation@gov.mb.ca
www.gov.mb.ca/sd/parks/education-and-interpretation/alfredhole.
html
Other contact information: Visitor Centre (Summer only):
204-369-5470
Year Founded: 1939 Visitor Centre provides the history of the
site as well as the biology of Canadian geese. Spring, summer &
fall programs features hands-on activities, guided hikes, school
programming & special events. Free admission

Winnipeg: Assiniboine Park Zoo
2595 Roblin Blvd.,
Winnipeg, MB R3P 2N7

Tel: 204-927-6000
info@assiniboinepark.ca
www.assiniboineparkzoo.ca/zoo
www.instagram.com/assiniboineparkzoo
twitter.com/assiniboinezoo
www.fa cebook.com/assiniboineparkzoo
Year Founded: 1904 Currently has over 2,000 animals of 200
different species. Includes a conservatory, playgrounds, theatre,
scultpure garden, museum & is available for special events. Park
open year round. Zoo open daily 9:00-5:00.
Margaret Redmond, President & CEO, Assiniboine Park
Conservancy

New Brunswick

Moncton: Magnetic Hill Zoo
125 Magic Mountain Rd.,
Moncton, NB E1G 4V7

Tel: 506-877-7720
info.zoo@moncton.ca
www.moncton.ca/magnetichillzoo
www.instagram.com/magnetichillzoodemagnetichill
www.facebook.com/zoodema gnetichillzoo
Year Founded: 1953 The Magnetic Hill Zoo has 625 animals,
including over 77 indigenous and exotic species, & is dedicated
to protecting animals & increasing public awareness of
endangered species. Open Apr-Dec.
Jill Marvin, Director

Newfoundland & Labrador

Holyrood: Salmonier Nature Park
PO Box 190, Salmonier Line,
Holyrood, NL A0A 2R0

Tel: 709-229-7888
www.gov.nl.ca/ffa/wildlife/snp/
www.facebook.com/salmoniernaturepark2018

Year Founded: 1978 A centre for environmental education,
wildlife rehabilitation, research & environmental monitoring.
Open Jun-Sep 10:00-6:00; Sept-Oct 10:00-4:00. Free
admission.
Lanna Campbell, Program Director, Nature Conservancy of
Canada

Nova Scotia

Aylesford: Oaklawn Farm Zoo
997 Ward Rd.,
Aylesford, NS B0P 1C0

Tel: 902-847-9790
www.oaklawnfarmzoo.ca
www.facebook.com/OaklawnFarmZoo
Year Founded: 1984 As the largest zoo in Nova Scotia, Oaklawn
provides an up close experience of the largest collection of big
cats & primates in Eastern Canada. Open daily Apr-Nov
10:00-dusk.

Shubenacadie: Shubenacadie Provincial Wildlife Park
149 Creighton Rd,
Shubenacadie, NS B0N 2H0

WildLifePark@novascotia.ca
www.wildlifepark.novascotia.ca
twitter.c om/shubenacadiesam
www.facebook.com/ShubenacadieWildlifePark
Year Founded: 1954 45 exhibits featuring native & exotic species
in natural enclosures along a 2.3 km walking trail; picnic area &
playground; Open daily May-Oct 9:00-6:30; Oct-May Sat-Sun
9:00-3:00

Ontario

Brantford: Brantford Twin Valley Zoo
84 Langford Church Rd.,
Brantford, ON N3T 5L4

Tel: 519-752-0607; *Fax:* 519-751-0152
twinvalleyzoo@hotmail.com
www.twinvalleyzoo.com
twitter.com/twinvalley zoo
www.facebook.com/twinvalleyzoo
Year Founded: 1991 In addition to animal exhibits, the zoo
features a nature trail, pony rides, picnic areas, petting areas &
an educational animal program. Hours: Apr-Sep daily 9:00-6:00;
Sep-Oct Mon-Fri 10:00-4:00, Sa-Sun 9:00-6:00

Caledonia: Killman Zoo
Parent: Killman's Wildlife Sanctuary
237 Unity Side Rd. East,
Caledonia, ON N3W 2H7

Tel: 905-765-5966
therealkillmanzoo@gmail.com
www.thekillmanzoo.com
www.instagram.com/thekillmanzoo
www.facebook.com/killmanzoo
Year Founded: 1988 Home to one of the largest big cat
collections in Ontario including many rare species of endangered
animals. Open daily 10:00-6:00.
Mark Killman, Owner

Cambridge: Cambridge Butterfly Conservatory
2500 Kossuth Rd.,
Cambridge, ON N3H 4R7

Tel: 519-653-1234
info@cambridgebutterfly.com
www.cambridgebutterfly.com
instagram.com/cambridgebutterflyconservatory
twitter.com/conservatory_
www.facebook.com/CambridgeButterflyConservatory
Year Founded: 2001 Live butterfly conservatory & tropical
garden, also features birds & insects; open daily 10:00-5:00.
Adrienne Brewster, Executive Director & Curator

Elmvale: Elmvale Jungle Zoo
PO Box 3003,
Elmvale, ON L0L 1P0

Tel: 705-322-1112
info@elmvalejunglezoo.com
www.elmvalejunglezoo.com
www.facebook.com/elmvalejunglezoo
Year Founded: 1967 The zoo occupies 25 acres of land with
over 300 animals on-site, including lions, tigers, jaguars,
monkeys, lemurs, giraffes, zebras & more. Open late May -
Thanksgiving.

Hamilton: African Lion Safari & Game Farm
1396 Cooper Rd,
Hamilton, ON N1R 5S2

Tel: 519-623-2620*Toll-Free:* 800-461-9453
admin@lionsafari.com
www.lionsafari.com
www.instagram.com/africanlionsafari
www.facebook.com/AfricanLionSafariCa nada
Year Founded: 1969 African Lion Safari is a Canadian-owned
family business that seeks to entertain guests & act as a
conservation park. Open May-Oct.
Mike Takacs, President

Indian River: Indian River Reptile Zoo & Dinosaur Park
2206 County Rd. 38,
Indian River, ON K0L 2B0

Tel: 705-639-1443
reptilezoo.dinopark@gmail.com
reptilezoo.org
www.youtube.com/user/Indianriverreptilezo
twitter.com/Reptilezoo1
www. facebook.com/indianriverreptile
Year Founded: 1998 Home to over 200 reptiles. Focuses its
resources on the protection of the reptile species. Offers live
animal education demonstrations, hiking trails & nature walks,
paleontological digs & reptile handling courses. Open daily May -
Sep, 10:00-5:00.

Kingsville: Jack Miner Bird Sanctuary
332 Rd. 3 West,
Kingsville, ON N9Y 2E5

Tel: 519-733-4034; *Fax:* 519-733-0932
questions@jackminer.com
www.jackminer.com
instagram.com/Jackminer1865
twitter.com/JM_Sanctuary
www.facebook.com/ JackMinerMigratoryBirdSanctuary
Year Founded: 1931 Centre for the conservation of migrating
Canada geese & wild ducks originating from the waterfowl
refuge management system. Open year-round, free admission.

Midland: Wye Marsh Wildlife Centre
PO Box 100, 16160 Hwy. 12 East,
Midland, ON L4R 4K6

Tel: 705-526-7809; *Fax:* 705-526-3294
info@wyemarsh.com
www.wyemarsh.com
www.instagram.com/wyemarsh
twitter.com/WyeMarsh
www.facebook.com/wyema rshwildlifecentre
Year Founded: 1969 Includes an amphibian & reptile display hall;
education & recreation programs; fully accessible nature centre
& trails; observation tower. Open daily 9:00-5:00.
Mary Ann Milne, Executive Director, 705-526-7809,
mmilne@wyemarsh.com

Morrisburg: Upper Canada Migratory Bird Sanctuary
(UCMBS)
c/o Parks of the St. Lawrence, 13740 County Rd. 2,
Morrisburg, ON K0C 1X0

Toll-Free: 800-437-2233
www.stlawrenceparks.com/bird-sanctuary
www.facebook.com/UpperCanadaBirdS anctuary
Year Founded: 1961 Home to 200 waterfowl, raptor, passerine &
other bird species. Includes nature trails, bird watching,
campground, feeding program & gift shop.
Hollee Kew, General Manager & CEO

Orono: Jungle Cat World Wildlife Park (JCW)
3667 Concession Rd. 6,
Orono, ON L0B 1M0

Tel: 905-983-5016; *Fax:* 905-983-9858
info@junglecatworld.com
www.junglecatworld.com
www.instagram.com/junglecatworld
twitter.com/JungleCatWorld
www.facebo ok.com/JungleCatWorld
Year Founded: 1983 A wildlife park that is home to a variety of
threatened & endangered species & wild felines. Works to
guarentee the survival of wildlife & endangered species by
providing educational programs & environmental socialization.
Open daily 10:00-5:00
Wolfram Klose, President & Owner
Christa Klose, Director & Owner

Oshawa: Oshawa Zoo & Fun Farm
3441 Grandview St. North,
Oshawa, ON L1H 0J5

Tel: 905-655-5236
info@oshawazoo.ca
www.oshawazoo.ca
instagram.com/oshawazoo
twitter.com/OshawaZoo
www.facebook.com/OshawaZooAndFunFarm
Year Founded: 1993 The zoo is home to 40 species of birds as well as domestic & exotic animals including abandonded & orphaned animals. Includes picinic areas, refreshment & animal food kiosk.

Ottawa: Little Ray's Reptile Zoo
2781 Colonial Rd.,
Ottawa, ON K0A 3E0

Tel: 613-822-8924
info@lrnc.ca
raysreptiles.com
www.facebook.com/LittleRaysOttawa
Year Founded: 1995 The zoo also serves as an animal rescue & has a large animal education outreach program. Locations in Hamilton, Nova Scotia, Newfoundland & The U.S.Open Fri-Sun & holiday Mondays.
Lee Parker, Director
Natalie Parker, Curator

Peterborough: Riverview Park & Zoo
Parent: Peterborough Utilities Group
1300 Water St.,
Peterborough, ON K9H 6Z5

Tel: 705-748-9301
info@riverviewparkandzoo.ca
www.instagram.com/riverviewparkandzoo
twitter.com/RiverviewZoo
www.fac ebook.com/riverviewzoo
Other contact information: Main Visitor Entrance Extension: 2304
Year Founded: 1933 The zoo's activities include 27 exhibits & 48 species. It is also home to gardens, trails, a frisbee golf course & a splash pad. Open year round 8:30-dusk.
John Stephenson, President & CEO, Peterborough Utilities Group

St Catharines: Happy Rolph Bird Sanctuary & Children's Petting Farm
c/o St Catharines Recreation & Community Services, 650 Read Rd.,
St Catharines, ON L2R 7K6

Tel: 905-688-5600
www.stcatharines.ca/en/playin/HappyRolphs.asp
A park on the shores of Lake Ontario includes gardens, a petting farm, picnic area & playground facilities.

Stevensville: Safari Niagara
2821 Stevensville Rd.,
Stevensville, ON L0S 1S0

Tel: 905-382-9669; Fax: 905-382-1619
Toll-Free: 866-367-9669
info@safariniagara.com
www.safariniagara.com
instagram.com/safariniagara
twitter.com/SafariNiagara
www.facebook.com /SafariNiagara
Year Founded: 2002 Safari Niagara is home to over 1000 native & exotic mammals, reptiles & birds. Offers educational shows, presentations, rides & tours, shows, picnic areas & an outdoor amphitheatre. Open May 9:00-5:00; Jun-Sep 9:00-6:00; Sep-Oct 9:00-5:00.

Thunder Bay: Chippewa Wildlife Park
Parent: Chippewa Park
c/o Thunder Bay Parks Division, Victoriaville Civic Centre, 2465 City Rd.,
Thunder Bay, ON P7J 1J7

Tel: 807-623-5111
chippewa@tbaytel.net
www.chippewapark.ca
twitter.com/chippewapark
www.facebook.com/chippewa .park
Year Founded: 1921 Includes a campground, widlife park, amusement rides & an elevated walkway for viewing the animals.

Toronto: Friends of High Park Zoo
PO Box 109, 95 Lavinia Ave.,
Toronto, ON M6S 3H9

parks@toronto.ca
www.highparkzoo.ca
www.instagram.com/highparkzoo
twitter.com/highparkzoo
www.facebook.com /HighParkZoo
Year Founded: 1893 Home to a variety of domestic & exotic species including bison, llamas, peacocks, deer, emus & wallabies. Open year round 7:00-dusk. Free admission.
Sarah Doucette, Chair

Toronto: Riverdale Farm
201 Winchester St.,
Toronto, ON M4X 1B8

Tel: 416-392-6794
riverdalefarmsg@gmail.com
www.riverdalefarmtoronto.ca
twitter.com/riverdale_farm
www.facebook.co m/RiverdaleFarmToronto
Year Founded: 1978 Riverdale Farm is a Toronto Parks, Forestry & Recreation Division facility featuring animals & gardens. Open year round 9:00-5:00. Free admission

Toronto: Toronto Zoo
2000 Meadowvale Rd.,
Toronto, ON M1B 5K7

Tel: 416-392-5900
www.torontozoo.com
www.instagram.com/thetorontozoo
twitter.com/thetorontozoo
www.facebook.com/TheTorontoZoo
Year Founded: 1974 The Toronto Zoo is one of Canada's premier zoos, offering interactive education & conservation activities. The zoo has over 5,000 animals representing over 500 species. Open year round.
Paul Ainslie, Chair
Dolf DeJong, CEO

Vaughan: Reptilia
2501 Rutherford Rd.,
Vaughan, ON L4K 2N6

Tel: 905-761-6223
zoo.vaughan@reptilia.org
www.reptilia.org
www.instagram.com/reptiliazoo
twitter.com/ReptiliaCanada
www.facebook.com/ReptiliaZoo
Showcases hundreds of different reptiles & amphibians. Reptile feedings every day, free live theatre shows & zoo keeper tours. Available for birthday parties, camps, education programs & phobia courses. Open Mon-Sun 10:00-6:00; holidays 10:00-5:00.

Woodbridge: Kortright Centre for Conservation
9550 Pine Valley Dr.,
Woodbridge, ON L4L 1A6

Tel: 905-832-2289
vservices@trca.ca
www.kortright.org
www.instagram.com/kortrightcentre
twitter.com/KortrightCentre
www.face book.com/KortrightCentre
Other contact information: Visitor Services Phone: 416-667-6295
Year Founded: 1979 An environmental education & demonstration centre. Offers sustainable energy workshops & programs. Open daily 9:30-4:00

Quebec

Bonaventure: Bioparc de la Gaspésie
123 rue des Vieux Ponts,
Bonaventure, QC G0C 1E0

Tél: 418-534-1997; Téléc: 418-534-1998
Ligne sans frais: 866-534-1997
info@bioparc.ca
www.bioparc.ca
www.youtube.com/user/BioparcGaspesie
twitter.com/BioparcGaspesie
www.facebook.com/BioparcGaspesie
Fondée en: 1998 Les visiteurs découvrent une collection de faune et de flore sauvages indigènes de la région présentés dans leurs écosystèmes respectifs. Disponible pour les fêtes d'enfants, le camp de jour & dormir avec les loups. Ouvert de Juin-Oct tous les 9h à 17h. Ouvert de Juin-Oct tous les 9h à 17h.
Serge Arsenault, Président
Robert Lapointe, Vice-Président
Marie-Josée Bernard, Directrice Générale, 418-534-1997, mjbernard@bioparc.ca

Frampton: Miller Zoo
20, rte Hurley,
Frampton, QC G0R 1M0

Tél: 418-479-2000
info@millerzoo.ca
www.millerzoo.ca
www.instagram.com/miller_zoo
www.facebook.com/MillerZoo
Fondée en: 2013 Un centre de réadaptation pour les animaux sauvages. Favorise le respect & la compréhension de la faune. Les visiteurs peuvent ainsi observer une centaine d'animaux dans leur milieu naturel. Une mini ferme permet également aux petits et grands de nourrir chèvres, ânes et cochons, ainsi qu'une grande variété d'oiseaux. Ouvrir Mai-Sep 9h30-17:00h; Sep-Oct V-D 9h30-17:00h
Émilie Ferland, propriétaire
Clifford Miller, propriétaire

Granby: Zoo de Granby / Granby Zoo
525, rue St-Hubert,
Granby, QC J2G 5P3

Tél: 450-372-9113Ligne sans frais: 877-472-6299
info@parcsafari.com
www.zoodegranby.com
www.youtube.com/user/ZOOdeGRANBYOfficiel
twitter.com/zoodegranby
www.f acebook.com/zoogranby
Fondée en: 1953 Le Zoo de Granby offre aux visiteurs une expérience d'apprentissage; animaux en voie de disparition & exotiques, favorise la conservation & le développement scientifique.
Réal Deslauriers, Président
Marc Filion, Vice-Président
Joëlle Francoeur, Vice-Président
Paul Gosselin, Directeur général et secrétaire exécutif

Saint-Bernard-de Lacolle: Parc Safari Africain
Bureau administratif, 242 Rang Roxham,
Saint-Bernard-de Lacolle, QC J0L 1V0

Tél: 450-247-2727
info@parcsafari.com
www.parcsafari.com
www.instagram.com/parcsafari
twitter.com/ParcSafari
www.facebook.com/P arcSafari
Fondée en: 1972 Le parc s'efforce de protéger & préserver les espèces menacées, tout en offrant aux visiteurs une aventure safari. Le parc abrite 500 animaux de 75 espèces différentes, y compris des éléphants, des rhinocéros, des girafes, des zèbres, des lions, des macaques, des chimpanzés, des tigres blancs & plus. Il comprend aussi un parc aquatique & reptilium.

Sainte-Anne-de-Bellevue: Ecomuseum
21125, ch Sainte-Marie,
Sainte-Anne-de-Bellevue, QC H9X 3Y7

Tél: 514-457-9449
info@ecomuseum.ca
www.zooecomuseum.ca/fr
instagram.com/zooecomuseum
twitter.com/ZooEcomuseum
www.facebook.com/z ooecomuseum
Fondée en: 1988 Plus de 115 espèces d'animaux vivants indigènes de la vallée du St-Laurent au Québec. Ouvert tous les jours 9h-17h
David Rodrigue, Directeur exécutif

Saint-Eustache: Ferme de Reptiles Exotarium
846, ch Fresnière,
Saint-Eustache, QC J7R 0G2

www.exotarium.net
www.facebook.com/Exotarium
Fondée en: 1990 Reptiles rares & menacées d'extinction, les amphibiens & les invertébros.
Hervé Maranda, Directeur & Propriètaire

Saint-Félicien: Zoo Sauvage de Saint-Félicien
Parent: The Centre for Conservation of Boreal Biodiversity inc
2230, boul du Jardin,
Saint-Félicien, QC G8K 2P8

Tél: 418-679-0543Ligne sans frais: 800-667-5687
info@zoosauvage.org
www.zoosauvage.org
www.instagram.com/zoosauvageofficiel
twitter.com/zoostfelicien
www.fac ebook.com/zoosauvage
Fondée en: 1960 Axé sur la conservation de la faune boréale et des animaux nordiques.
Lauraine Gagnon, Directrice générale
Louis Bouchard, Directeur financier

Saint-Joachim: Réserve Nationale de Faune du Cap Tourmente (RNF) / Cap Tourmente National Wildlife Area
570, ch du Cap-Tourmente,
Saint-Joachim, QC G0A 3X0

Tél: 418-827-3776
ec.captourmente.ec@canada.ca
www.quebec-cite.com/en/businesses/cap-tourmente-national-wildlife-area
Autre numéros: Centre d'interprétation: 418-827-4591
Fondée en: 1978 Réserve Nationale de Faune du Cap Tourmente a plus de 305 espèces d'oiseaux. Des activités d'interprétation, un centre d'interprétation & plus de 20 km de sentiers pédestres y sont offerts. Ouvert toute l'année.

Saskatchewan

Moose Jaw: Saskatchewan Burrowing Owl Interpretive Centre (SBOIC)
250 Thatcher Dr. East,
Moose Jaw, SK S6J 1L7

Tel: 306-692-8710; *Fax:* 306-692-2762
sboic@sasktel.net
www.skburrowingowl.ca
www.facebook.com/1179452016309 85

Year Founded: 1997 The centre has displays, a gift store, a travelling education program & a small population of captive burrowing owls. Open daily May-Sep 10:00-5:00
Lori Johnson, Owl Coordinator

Regina: Wascana Waterfowl Park
Wascana Centre, PO Box 7111, 2900 Wascana Dr.,
Regina, SK S4P 3S7

Tel: 306-522-3661; *Fax:* 306-565-2742
wascanainfo@gov.sk.ca
www.wascana.ca/nature-in-wascana/waterfowl-display -ponds
twitter.com/wascanacentre
www.facebook.com/WascanaCentreRegina
Year Founded: 1971 The Wascana Waterfowl Park is a 223 hectare thriving marshland in Regina & is home to increasing wildlife and waterfowl populations.

Saskatoon: Saskatoon Forestry Farm Park & Zoo
1903 Forestry Farm Park Dr.,
Saskatoon, SK S7S 1G9

Tel: 306-975-3382
zoo@saskatoon.ca
saskatoon.ca/parks-recreation-attractions/events-attractions
Year Founded: 1972 The zoo is home to gardens, restored heritage buildings, a playground & over 300 animals. Open Apr-Oct

Yukon Territory

Whitehorse: Yukon Wildlife Preserve
Takini Hot Springs Rd.,
Whitehorse, YT Y1A 7A2

Tel: 867-456-7300; *Fax:* 867-633-2425
info@yukonwildlife.ca
www.yukonwildlife.ca
www.instagram.com/yukonwildlifepreserve
twitter.com/YukonWildlife
www.facebook.com/yukonwildlife
Year Founded: 2004 Exhibits Northern Canadian animals in their natural environment. Open daily May-Oct 9:30-6:00.
Alexandra Tait, President, president@yukonwildlife.ca
Jake Paleczny, Executive Director, 867-456-7313, jake@yukonwildlife.ca

SECTION 3
ASSOCIATIONS

Associations in this section are listed alphabetically by subject. Directly following this page is an Entry Index arranged alphabetically by entry name, regardless of subject. Many subjects are also represented in other sections throughout the book. For example, Section 2: Arts & Culture includes Art Galleries, while this section includes Art Gallery Associations.

A

ABC Life Literacy Canada, 298
Aboriginal Agricultural Education Society of British Columbia, 323
Aboriginal Coalition to End Homelessness, 323
Aboriginal Friendship Centres of Saskatchewan, 323
Aboriginal Head Start Association of British Columbia, 323
Aboriginal Veterans Society of Alberta, 323
Aboriginal Women's Association of Prince Edward Island, 323
Abortion Rights Coalition of Canada, 253
AboutFace, 208
Academy of Canadian Cinema & Television, 238
Academy of Canadian Executive Nurses, 329
Access Copyright, 332
Accreditation Canada, 280
Acoustic Neuroma Association of Canada, 253
Act To End Violence Against Women, 385
Action Canada for Sexual Health & Rights, 351
Action Dignité de Saint-Léonard, 377
Action Patrimoine, 276
Action-Haïti, 362
Active Aging Canada, 360
Active Healthy Kids Canada, 253
Acupuncture Canada, 253
Addictions Foundation of Manitoba, 170
Administrative Sciences Association of Canada, 310
Adoption Council of Ontario, 202
ADR Institute of Canada, 289
Adult Children of Alcoholics, 170
AdvantAge Ontario, 360
The Advertising & Design Club of Canada, 170
Advertising Standards Canada, 171
Advocacy Centre for the Elderly, 360
The Advocates' Society, 300
Advocis, 284
Aéroclub des cantons de l'est, 348
Affected Families of Police Homicide, 201
Affiliation of Multicultural Societies & Service Agencies of BC, 319
African & Caribbean Council on HIV/AIDS in Ontario, 176
African Canadian Social Development Council, 319
African Medical & Research Foundation Canada, 253
AFS Interculture Canada, 286
Aga Khan Foundation Canada, 286
Agence universitaire de la Francophonie, 213
Agincourt Community Services Association, 362
Agricultural Alliance of New Brunswick, 171
Agricultural Manufacturers of Canada, 236
Agricultural Research & Extension Council of Alberta, 171
Agriculture Union, 290
Agri-Food Innovation Council, 171
Aide internationale pour l'enfance, 363
Aide internationale à l'enfance, 362
AIDS Committee of Durham Region, 176
AIDS Committee of North Bay & Area, 176
Air Cadet League of Canada, 317
Air Currency Enhancement Society, 348
Airspace Action on Smoking & Health, 170
Al-Anon Family Groups (Canada), Inc., 170
Alberta Aboriginal Women's Society, 323
Alberta Advantage Party, 336
Alberta Angus Association, 176
Alberta Assessment Consortium, 214
Alberta Association of Academic Libraries, 306

Alberta Association of Agricultural Societies, 171
Alberta Association of Architects, 183
Alberta Association of Family School Liaison Workers, 214
Alberta Association of Landscape Architects, 298
Alberta Association of Library Technicians, 306
Alberta Association of Marriage & Family Therapy, 363
Alberta Association of Midwives, 202
Alberta Association of Optometrists, 253
Alberta Association of Police Governance, 300
Alberta Association of Rehabilitation Centres, 208
Alberta Associations for Bright Children, 202
Alberta Barley Commission, 171
Alberta Building Officials Association, 343
Alberta Camping Association, 348
Alberta Canola Producers Commission, 172
Alberta Chambers of Commerce, 193
Alberta Children's Hospital Foundation, 253
Alberta Civil Liberties Research Centre, 282
Alberta Civil Trial Lawyers' Association, 300
Alberta College & Association of Chiropractors, 253
Alberta College of Combined Laboratory & X-Ray Technologists, 214
Alberta College of Occupational Therapists, 253
Alberta College of Pharmacists, 333
Alberta College of Social Workers, 363
Alberta Construction Association, 189
Alberta Continuing Care Association, 360
Alberta Council on Aging, 361
Alberta Country Vacations Association, 377
Alberta Craft Council, 383
Alberta Dental Association & College, 206
Alberta Easter Seals Society, 208
Alberta Ecotrust Foundation, 229
Alberta Educational Facilities Administrators Association, 214
Alberta Egg Producers' Board, 340
Alberta Environmental Network, 229
Alberta Family Child Care Association, 202
Alberta Family History Society, 276
Alberta Family Mediation Society, 363
Alberta Federation of Agriculture, 172
Alberta Federation of Labour, 290
Alberta Federation of Police Associations, 300
Alberta Fire Chiefs Association, 356
Alberta Fish & Game Association, 229
Alberta Floor Covering Association, 313
Alberta Forest Products Association, 245
Alberta Foundation for the Arts, 184
Alberta Funeral Service Association, 248
Alberta Gerontological Nurses Association, 329
Alberta Historical Resources Foundation, 276
Alberta Home Education Association, 214
Alberta Hospice Palliative Care Association, 254
Alberta Hotel & Lodging Association, 377
Alberta Innovates, 254
Alberta Institute of Agrologists, 172
Alberta Land Surveyors' Association, 375
Alberta Law Foundation, 300
Alberta Liberal Party, 336
Alberta Library Trustees Association, 306
Alberta Media Production Industries Association, 238
Alberta Medical Association, 254
Alberta Men's Wear Agents Association, 238
Alberta Milk, 172
Alberta Motor Association, 185
Alberta Municipal Clerks Association, 250

Alberta Museums Association, 249
Alberta Music Festival Association, 236
Alberta Native Friendship Centres Association, 323
Alberta Occupational Health Nurses Association, 254
Alberta Party, 336
Alberta Professional Planners Institute, 334
Alberta Psychiatric Association, 316
Alberta Public Health Association, 254
Alberta Public Housing Administrators' Association, 281
Alberta Ready Mixed Concrete Association, 189
Alberta Real Estate Association, 343
Alberta Recreation & Parks Association, 348
Alberta Restorative Justice Association, 300
Alberta Roadbuilders & Heavy Construction Association, 189
Alberta Roofing Contractors Association, 189
Alberta Rural Municipal Administrators Association, 250
Alberta Safety Council, 356
Alberta Salers Association, 176
Alberta School Boards Association, 214
Alberta School Councils' Association, 214
Alberta School Learning Commons Council, 306
Alberta Sheep Breeders Association, 176
Alberta Shorthorn Association, 177
Alberta Society for the Prevention of Cruelty to Animals, 179
Alberta Society of Professional Biologists, 358
Alberta Sulphur Research Ltd., 201
Alberta Teachers' Association, 214
Alberta Union of Provincial Employees, 290
Alberta Urban Municipalities Association, 251
Alberta Veterinary Medical Association, 179
Alberta Veterinary Technologist Association, 179
Alberta Water Council, 229
Alberta Water Well Drilling Association, 212
Alberta Weekly Newspapers Association, 341
Alberta West Realtors' Association, 343
Alberta Whitewater Association, 348
Alberta Wilderness Association, 229
Alberta Women's Institutes, 385
Alcoholics Anonymous (GTA Intergroup), 170
Alcooliques Anonymes du Québec, 170
The Alcuin Society, 341
Alfa Romeo Club of Canada, 185
Algoma Kinniwabi Travel Association, 377
ALIGN Association of Community Services, 363
All Terrain Vehicle Association of Nova Scotia, 348
AllerGen NCE Inc., 352
Alliance autochtone du Québec, 323
Alliance des femmes de la francophonie canadienne, 385
Alliance des gais et lesbiennes Laval-Laurentides, 304
Alliance des professeures et professeurs de Montréal, 214
Alliance des radios communautaires du Canada, 187
Alliance du personnel professionnel et technique de la santé et des services sociaux, 290
Alliance for Audited Media, 171
Alliance for Chiropractic, 254
Alliance for Healthier Communities, 280
Alliance Française, 247
Alliance of Canadian Cinema, Television & Radio Artists, 290
Alliance québécoise des techniciens de l'image et du son, 377
Allied Beauty Association, 238
Alliston & District Chamber of Commerce, 193
Almaguin-Nipissing Travel Association, 377

Association des producteurs maraîchers du Québec, 237

Association des professionnels en développement économique du Québec, 213

Association des professionnels en exposition du Québec, 236

Association des professionnels à l'outillage municipal, 205

Association des propriétaires de machinerie lourde du Québec inc., 236

Association des propriétaires du Québec inc., 344

Association des pères gais de Montréal inc., 304

Association des pédiatres du Québec, 256

Association des radiologistes du Québec, 256

Association des radio-oncologues du Québec, 256

Association des restaurateurs du Québec, 355

Association des réalisateurs et réalisatrices du Québec, 239

Association des services de réhabilitation sociale du Québec inc., 363

Association des sexologues du Québec, 256

Association des spécialistes du pneus et Mécanique du Québec, 185

Association des spécialistes en chirurgie plastique et esthétique du Québec, 256

Association des spécialistes en médecine interne du Québec, 256

Association des technologues en agroalimentaire, 172

Association des urologues du Québec, 256

Association des économistes québécois, 213

Association des éleveurs de chevaux Belge du Québec, 177

Association des établissements privés conventionnés - santé services sociaux, 280

Association du Québec pour enfants avec problèmes auditifs, 209

Association d'orthopédie du Québec, 255

Association d'oto-rhino-laryngologie et de chirurgie cervico-faciale du Québec, 255

Association for Bright Children (Ontario), 202

Association for Canadian Studies, 352

Association for Corporate Growth, Toronto Chapter, 193

Association for Image & Information Management International - 1st Canadian Chapter, 283

Association for Literature, Environment, & Culture in Canada, 230

Association for Manitoba Archives, 306

Association for Mineral Exploration British Columbia, 318

Association for Native Development in the Performing & Visual Arts, 324

Association for New Canadians, 204

Association for Operations Management, 313

Association franco-culturelle de Hay River, 205

Association franco-culturelle de Yellowknife, 205

Association francophone des municipalités du Nouveau-Brunswick Inc., 251

Association francophone pour le savoir, 214

Association francophone à l'éducation des services à l'enfance de l'Ontario, 202

Association féminine d'éducation et d'action sociale, 385

Association Hereford du Québec, 177

Association Heritage New Brunswick, 249

Association Hôtellerie Québec, 377

Association internationale des maires francophones - Bureau à Québec, 251

Association internationale pour le partenariat entreprises-ONG - Canada, 363

Association littéraire et artistique internationale Canada, 332

Association minière du Québec, 318

Association médicale du Québec, 256

Association nationale des peintres - locale 99, 290

Association nationale des éditeurs de livres, 341

Association of Administrative Professionals, 310

Association of Alberta Coordinated Action for Recycling Enterprises, 351

Association of Allied Health Professionals: Newfoundland & Labrador (Ind.), 291

Association of Applied Geochemists, 318

Association of Architectural Technologists of Ontario, 183

Association of Atlantic Universities, 214

Association of Battlefords Realtors, 344

Association of Black Law Enforcers, 335

Association of Book Publishers of British Columbia, 341

Association of British Columbia Forest Professionals, 245

Association of British Columbia Land Surveyors, 375

Association of British Columbia Teachers of English as an Additional Language, 214

Association of Canada Lands Surveyors, 375

Association of Canadian Advertisers Inc., 171

Association of Canadian Archivists, 306

Association of Canadian Corporations in Translation & Interpretation, 298

Association of Canadian Deans of Education, 214

Association of Canadian Distillers, 244

Association of Canadian Ergonomists, 358

Association of Canadian Faculties of Dentistry, 214

Association of Canadian Film Craftspeople, 239

Association of Canadian Financial Officers, 291

Association of Canadian Industrial Designers, 286

Association of Canadian Map Libraries & Archives, 306

Association of Canadian Pension Management, 240

Association of Canadian Publishers, 341

Association of Canadian Search, Employment & Staffing Services, 225

Association of Canadian Travel Agencies - Atlantic, 378

Association of Canadian Travel Agents - British Columbia & Yukon, 378

Association of Canadian Universities for Northern Studies, 215

Association of Canadian University Presses, 341

Association of Canadian Women Composers, 385

Association of Commercial & Industrial Contractors of PEI, 190

Association of Condominium Managers of Ontario, 281

Association of Consulting Engineering Companies - Prince Edward Island, 226

Association of Day Care Operators of Ontario, 202

Association of Early Childhood Educators of Alberta, 215, 202

Association of Educational Researchers of Ontario, 215

Association of Engineering Technicians & Technologists of Newfoundland & Labrador, 226

Association of English Language Publishers of Québec, 342

Association of Equipment Manufacturers - Canada, 236

Association of Faculties of Medicine of Canada, 215

Association of Faculties of Pharmacy of Canada, 333

Association of Fundraising Professionals, 310

Association of Home Appliance Manufacturers Canada Council, 313

Association of Independent Corrugated Converters, 313

Association of Independent Schools & Colleges in Alberta, 215

Association of Interior Designers of Nova Scotia, 286

Association of International Customs & Border Agencies, 193

Association of Internet Marketing & Sales, 315

Association of Iroquois & Allied Indians, 324

Association of Legal Court Interpreters & Translators, 300

Association of Local Public Health Agencies, 256

Association of Manitoba Book Publishers, 342

Association of Manitoba Land Surveyors, 375

Association of Manitoba Municipalities, 251

Association of Manitoba Museums, 249

Association of MBAs in Canada, 310

Association of Medical Microbiology & Infectious Disease Canada, 256

Association of Municipal Administrators of New Brunswick, 251

Association of Municipal Administrators, Nova Scotia, 251

Association of Municipal Managers, Clerks & Treasurers of Ontario, 251

Association of Municipalities of Ontario, 251

Association of New Brunswick Land Surveyors, 376

Association of New Brunswick Professional Educators, 291

Association of Newfoundland & Labrador Archives, 307

Association of Newfoundland Land Surveyors, 376

Association of Nova Scotia Land Surveyors, 376

Association of Nova Scotia Museums, 249

Association of Ontario Land Economists, 376

Association of Ontario Land Surveyors, 376

Association of Ontario Midwives, 202

Association of Parliamentary Libraries in Canada, 307

Association of Prince Edward Island Land Surveyors, 376

Association of Prince Edward Island Libraries, 307

Association of Professional Archaeologists, 182

Association of Professional Biology, 358

Association of Professional Canadian Consultants, 283

Association of Professional Economists of British Columbia, 193

Association of Professional Engineers & Geoscientists of Saskatchewan, 226

The Association of Professional Engineers & Geoscientists of the Province of Manitoba, 226

Association of Professional Engineers of Yukon, 227

Association of Professional Executives of the Public Service of Canada, 311

Association of Professional Librarians of New Brunswick, 307

Association of Professional Recruiters of Canada, 225

Association of Public Sector Information Professionals, 251

Association of Regina Realtors, 344

Association of Registered Interior Designers of Ontario, 286

Association of Registered Professional Foresters of New Brunswick, 245

Association of Registrars of the Universities & Colleges of Canada, 215

Association of Saskatchewan Realtors, 344

Association of Science & Engineering Technology Professionals of Alberta, 227

The Association of Social Workers of Northern Canada, 363

Association of Translators & Interpreters of Nova Scotia, 299, 298

Association of Translators, Terminologists & Interpreters of Manitoba, 299

Association of University Forestry Schools of Canada, 215

Association of Visual Language Interpreters of Canada, 299

Association of Workers' Compensation Boards of Canada, 289

Association of Yukon Communities, 251

British Columbia Association of Broadcasters, 188
British Columbia Association of Family Resource Programs, 364
British Columbia Association of Social Workers, 364
British Columbia Broiler Hatching Egg Producers' Association, 340
British Columbia Camping Association, 348
British Columbia Cancer Foundation, 257
British Columbia Career College Association, 215
British Columbia Centre for Ability Association, 257
British Columbia Chamber of Commerce, 193
British Columbia Chiropractic Association, 258
British Columbia Civil Liberties Association, 282
British Columbia College of Nursing Professionals, 329
British Columbia Confederation of Parent Advisory Councils, 215
British Columbia Conservative Party, 336
British Columbia Construction Association, 190
British Columbia Council for Families, 364
British Columbia Courthouse Library Society, 307
British Columbia Cranberry Marketing Commission, 315
British Columbia Dental Association, 206
British Columbia Doctors of Optometry, 258
British Columbia Egg Marketing Board, 315
British Columbia Environment Industry Association, 230
British Columbia Environmental Network, 230
British Columbia Excalibur Party, 336
British Columbia Family Child Care Association, 202
British Columbia Federation of Foster Parent Associations, 364
British Columbia Federation of Labour, 291
British Columbia Fruit Growers' Association, 172
British Columbia Funeral Association, 248
British Columbia Genealogical Society, 276
British Columbia Government & Service Employees' Union, 291
British Columbia Grapegrowers' Association, 172
British Columbia Ground Water Association, 212
British Columbia Hereford Association, 177
British Columbia Historical Federation, 277
British Columbia Hog Marketing Commission, 315
British Columbia Industrial Designer Association, 286
British Columbia Institute of Agrologists, 172
British Columbia Landscape & Nursery Association, 279
British Columbia Law Institute, 301
British Columbia Liberal Party, 336
British Columbia Libertarian Party, 336
British Columbia Library Association, 307
British Columbia Library Trustees' Association, 307
British Columbia Lions Society for Children with Disabilities, 362
British Columbia Lodging & Campgrounds Association, 378
British Columbia Lung Association, 258
British Columbia Lupus Society, 258
British Columbia Marijuana Party, 336
British Columbia Maritime Employers Association, 314
British Columbia Milk Marketing Board, 315
British Columbia Museums Association, 249
British Columbia Native Women's Association, 324
British Columbia Naturopathic Association, 258
British Columbia Northern Real Estate Board, 344
British Columbia Nurses' Union, 329
British Columbia Paint Manufacturers' Association, 313
British Columbia Party, 336
British Columbia Peoples Party, 336
British Columbia Pharmacy Association, 333
British Columbia Police Association, 301
British Columbia Principals & Vice-Principals Association, 215

British Columbia Printing & Imaging Association, 340
British Columbia Provincial Renal Agency, 258
British Columbia Public Interest Advocacy Centre, 301
British Columbia Real Estate Association, 344
British Columbia Recreation & Parks Association, 348
British Columbia Refederation Party, 336
British Columbia Restaurant & Food Services Association, 355
British Columbia Road Builders & Heavy Construction Association, 190
British Columbia Salmon Farmers Association, 243
British Columbia School Trustees Association, 215
British Columbia Science Teachers' Association, 215
British Columbia Seafood Alliance, 243
British Columbia Seniors Living Association, 361
British Columbia Shellfish Growers Association, 243
British Columbia Social Credit Party, 336
British Columbia Society for Male Survivors of Sexual Abuse, 364
British Columbia Society for the Prevention of Cruelty to Animals, 180
British Columbia Society of Landscape Architects, 298
British Columbia Teacher Regulation Branch, 291
British Columbia Teachers of English Language Arts, 216
British Columbia Teachers' Federation, 216
British Columbia Transplant Society, 258
British Columbia Turkey Farms, 340
British Columbia Vegetable Marketing Commission, 315
British Columbia Waterfowl Society, 328
British Columbia Women's Institutes, 385
Broadcast Research Council of Canada, 188
Bronte Historical Society, 299
The Bruce Trail Conservancy, 348
Building Owners & Managers Association - Canada, 344
Building Owners & Managers Association Toronto, 344
Building Supply Industry Association of British Columbia, 190
BullyingCanada Inc., 364
Bureau de coopération interuniversitaire, 216
Burlington Chamber of Commerce, 193
BurlingtonGreen Environmental Association, 230
Bus History Association, Inc., 277
Business & Institutional Furniture Manufacturer's Association, 313
Business Council of British Columbia, 382
Business Council of Canada, 194
Business for the Arts, 184

C

CAA British Columbia, 186
CAA Manitoba, 186
CAA Québec, 186
Caisse Groupe Financier, 240
Calgary Chamber of Commerce, 194
Calgary Exhibition & Stampede, 205
Calgary Health Trust, 258
Calgary Humane Society, 180
Calgary Real Estate Board Cooperative Limited, 344
Cambridge Association of Realtors Inc., 344
Cambridge Chamber of Commerce, 194
Cambridge Tourism, 378
Campaign for Nuclear Phaseout, 230
Campbell River & District Chamber of Commerce, 194
Campbell River & District United Way, 364
Campground Owners Association of Nova Scotia, 348
Camping Association of Nova Scotia & PEI, 348
Camping in Ontario, 378
Camping Québec, 378
Canada - Albania Business Council, 382

Canada Backyard Housing Association, 190
Canada Beyond the Blue, 364
Canada BIM Council Inc., 227
Canada China Business Council, 382
Canada East Equipment Dealers' Association, 236
Canada Employment & Immigration Union, 291
Canada Grains Council, 172
Canada Health Infoway, 258
Canada Media Fund, 352
Canada New Zealand Business Council, 382
Canada Organic Trade Association, 382
Canada Safety Council, 356
Canada Tibet Committee, 282
Canada West Foundation, 213
Canada Without Poverty, 364
Canada World Youth, 286
Canada-Arab Business Council, 382
Canada-ASEAN Business Council, 382
Canada-Finland Chamber of Commerce, 194
CanadaGAP, 244
Canada-India Business Council, 382
Canada-Israel Cultural Foundation, 205
Canada-Sri Lanka Business Council, 382
Canada-UK Foundation, 287
Canada's Accredited Zoos & Aquariums, 180
Canada's Advanced Internet Development Organization, 283
Canada's Aviation Hall of Fame, 187
Canada's History, 277
Canada's National Firearms Association, 348
Canada's Oil Sands Innovation Alliance, 318
Canada's Public Policy Forum, 251
Canadian 4-H Council, 172
Canadian Abilities Foundation, 209
Canadian Aboriginal & Minority Supplier Council, 324
Canadian Aboriginal Veterans & Serving Members Association, 317
Canadian Academic Accounting Association, 169
Canadian Academy of Endodontics, 206
Canadian Accredited Independent Schools, 216
Canadian Acoustical Association, 227
Canadian Actors' Equity Association (CLC), 291
Canadian Advanced Technology Alliance, 227
Canadian Aerophilatelic Society, 348
Canadian Agency for Drugs & Technologies in Health, 258
The Canadian Agency Network, 171
Canadian Agricultural Economics Society, 213
Canadian Agricultural Safety Association, 238
Canadian Agri-Marketing Association, 315
Canadian Agri-Marketing Association (Alberta), 315
Canadian Agri-Marketing Association (Manitoba), 315
Canadian Agri-Marketing Association (Saskatchewan), 315
Canadian AIDS Society, 176
Canadian AIDS Treatment Information Exchange, 176
Canadian Air Cushion Technology Society, 227
Canadian Alliance of Chinese Associations, 205
Canadian Alliance of Physiotherapy Regulators, 258
Canadian Alliance of Student Associations, 216
Canadian Alliance on Mental Illness & Mental Health, 316
Canadian Alliance to End Homelessness, 364
Canadian Anesthesiologists' Society, 258
Canadian Angus Association, 177
Canadian Animal Health Institute, 180
Canadian Anthropology Society, 352
Canadian Anti-Hate Network, 282
Canadian Apparel Federation, 238
Canadian Aquaculture Industry Alliance, 243

Canadian Automobile Association North & East Ontario, 186

Canadian Automobile Association Saskatchewan, 186

Canadian Automobile Association South Central Ontario, 186

Canadian Automobile Dealers' Association, 186

Canadian Automobile Sport Clubs - Ontario Region Inc., 186

Canadian Avalanche Association, 224

Canadian Bankers Association, 241

Canadian Bar Association, 301

Canadian Battlefields Foundation, 317

Canadian Beef, 172

Canadian Beef Breeds Council, 177

Canadian Belgian Horse Association, 177

Canadian Beverage Association, 244

Canadian Biomaterials Society, 328

Canadian Bison Association, 177

Canadian Black Chamber of Commerce, 194

Canadian Blonde d'Aquitaine Association, 177

Canadian Blood Services, 260

Canadian Board Diversity Council, 385

Canadian Board of Marine Underwriters, 284

Canadian Boating Federation, 349

Canadian Bookbinders & Book Artists Guild, 342

Canadian Bookkeepers Association, 169

Canadian Booksellers Association, 342

Canadian Border Collie Association, 177

Canadian Botanical Association, 358

Canadian Bottled Water Association, 244

Canadian Brain Tumour Tissue Bank, 260

Canadian Bridge Federation, 349

Canadian Brown Swiss & Braunvieh Association, 177

Canadian Bureau for International Education, 217

Canadian Call Management Association, 376

Canadian Camping Association, 349

Canadian Cancer Research Alliance, 260

Canadian Cancer Society, 260

Canadian Cancer Society Research Institute, 260

Canadian Cancer Survivor Network, 260

Canadian Cannabis Nurses Association, 260

Canadian Canola Growers Association, 172

Canadian Carbonization Research Association, 352

Canadian Cardiovascular Society, 260

Canadian Career Development Foundation, 364

Canadian Cartographic Association, 376

Canadian Casting Federation, 349

Canadian Cattlemen's Association, 177

Canadian CED Network, 213

Canadian Celiac Association, 260

Canadian Celtic Arts Association, 184

Canadian Centre for Abuse Awareness, 364

Canadian Centre for Architecture, 183

Canadian Centre for Fisheries Innovation, 243

Canadian Centre for Gender & Sexual Diversity, 305

Canadian Centre for Occupational Health & Safety, 356

Canadian Centre for Victims of Torture, 364

Canadian Centre on Substance Use & Addiction, 170

The Canadian Chamber of Commerce, 194

Canadian Charolais Association, 177

Canadian Child Care Federation, 203

Canadian Children's Book Centre, 342

Canadian Chiropractic Association, 260

Canadian Christian Relief & Development Association, 208

Canadian Circulations Audit Board Inc., 342

Canadian Civil Liberties Association, 282

Canadian Coalition Against the Death Penalty, 341

Canadian Coalition for Farm Animals, 180

Canadian Coalition for Genetic Fairness, 260

Canadian Coalition for Nuclear Responsibility, 225

Canadian College & University Food Service Association, 244

Canadian College of Health Leaders, 260

Canadian College of Medical Geneticists, 260

Canadian College of Physicists in Medicine, 359

Canadian Colombian Professional Association, 383

Canadian Commission for UNESCO, 287

Canadian Committee of Byzantinists, 352

Canadian Committee of Graduate Students in Education, 217

Canadian Committee on Cataloguing, 307

Canadian Committee on Labour History, 290

Canadian Committee on MARC, 307

Canadian Communications Foundation, 188

Canadian Community Reinvestment Coalition, 241

Canadian Comparative Literature Association, 299

Canadian Concrete Masonry Producers Association, 190

Canadian Concrete Pipe Association, 190

Canadian Condominium Institute, 281

Canadian Construction Association, 190

Canadian Consumer Specialty Products Association, 201

Canadian Co-operative Wool Growers Ltd., 177

Canadian Copper & Brass Development Association, 319

Canadian Copyright Institute, 332

Canadian Corporate Counsel Association, 301

Canadian Corps Association, 317

The Canadian Corps of Commissionaires, 317

Canadian Correspondence Chess Association, 349

Canadian Corrugated Containerboard Association, 332

Canadian Council for Aboriginal Business, 324

The Canadian Council for Accreditation of Pharmacy Programs, 333

Canadian Council for International Co-operation, 287

The Canadian Council for Public-Private Partnerships, 194

Canadian Council for Refugees, 364

Canadian Council for Small Business & Entrepreneurship, 194

Canadian Council for the Advancement of Education, 217

Canadian Council for the Americas, 383

Canadian Council for the Americas - British Columbia, 383

Canadian Council of Archives, 307

Canadian Council of Cardiovascular Nurses, 329

Canadian Council of Practical Nurse Regulators, 329

Canadian Council of Professional Certification, 311

Canadian Council of Professional Fish Harvesters, 243

Canadian Council of Technicians & Technologists, 227

The Canadian Council of the Blind, 209

Canadian Council on Animal Care, 180

The Canadian Council on Continuing Education in Pharmacy, 333

Canadian Council on International Law, 301

Canadian Council on Invasive Species, 230

Canadian Council on Rehabilitation & Work, 209

Canadian Council on Social Development, 251

Canadian Counselling & Psychotherapy Association, 364

Canadian Craft Brewers Association, 244

Canadian Crafts Federation, 384

Canadian Credit Union Association, 241

Canadian Criminal Justice Association, 301

Canadian Critical Care Society, 260

Canadian Culinary Federation, 355

Canadian Cultural Society of The Deaf, Inc., 209

Canadian Cutting Horse Association, 177

Canadian Deafblind Association (National), 209

Canadian Dental Assistants Association, 206

Canadian Dental Association, 206

Canadian Dental Hygienists Association, 206

Canadian Dermatology Association, 260

Canadian Dexter Cattle Association, 177

Canadian Diamond Drilling Association, 212

Canadian Donkey & Mule Association, 177

The Canadian Doukhobor Society, 320

Canadian Down Syndrome Society, 260

Canadian Dyslexia Association, 260

Canadian Economic Party, 336

Canadian Economics Association, 213

Canadian Education Association, 217

Canadian Educational Researchers' Association, 217

Canadian Electrical Contractors Association, 224

Canadian Electrical Manufacturers Representatives Association, 224

Canadian Environmental Certification Approvals Board, 230

Canadian Environmental Law Association, 230

Canadian Environmental Network, 230

Canadian Environmental Technology Advancement Corporation - West, 230

Canadian Epilepsy Alliance, 260

Canadian ETF Association, 241

Canadian Ethnic Media Association, 320

Canadian Ethnic Studies Association, 320

Canadian Ethnocultural Council, 320

Canadian Evaluation Society, 375

Canadian Executive Service Organization, 311

Canadian Expat Association, 287

Canadian Explosive Technicians' Association, 227

Canadian Explosives Industry Association, 313

Canadian Fabry Association, 260

Canadian Faculties of Agriculture & Veterinary Medicine, 217

Canadian Fallen Firefighters Foundation, 224

Canadian Farm Writers' Federation, 387

Canadian Federal Pilots Association, 291

Canadian Federation for the Humanities & Social Sciences, 353

Canadian Federation of Agriculture, 172

Canadian Federation of Apartment Associations, 281

Canadian Federation of Aromatherapists, 260

The Canadian Federation of Business & Professional Women's Clubs, 385

Canadian Federation of Business School Deans, 217

Canadian Federation of Earth Sciences, 359

Canadian Federation of Friends of Museums, 249

Canadian Federation of Humane Societies, 180

Canadian Federation of Independent Business, 194

Canadian Federation of Independent Grocers, 244

Canadian Federation of Junior Leagues, 362

Canadian Federation of Library Associations, 307

Canadian Federation of Mental Health Nurses, 329

Canadian Federation of Nurses Unions, 291

Canadian Federation of Outfitter Associations, 349

Canadian Federation of Students, 217

Canadian Federation of University Women, 217

Canadian Feed The Children, 364

Canadian Fertility & Andrology Society, 351

Canadian Film Centre, 239

Canadian Film Institute, 239

Canadian Filmmakers Distribution Centre, 239

Canadian Finance & Leasing Association, 241

Canadian Fire Alarm Association, 313

Canadian Fire Safety Association, 356

Canadian Organization for Rare Disorders, 262
Canadian Ornamental Horticulture Alliance, 279
Canadian Ornamental Plant Foundation, 279
Canadian Orthopaedic Association, 262
Canadian Orthopaedic Foundation, 262
Canadian Orthopaedic Nurses Association, 330
Canadian Orthoptic Council, 262
Canadian Out-of-Home Marketing & Measurement Bureau, 171
Canadian Paediatric Society, 262
Canadian Pain Society, 262
Canadian Paint & Coatings Association, 190
Canadian Palomino Horse Association, 178
Canadian Paper Money Society, 349
Canadian Parents for French, 299
Canadian Parks & Recreation Association, 349
Canadian Parks & Wilderness Society, 349
Canadian Partnership Against Cancer, 262
Canadian Payroll Association, 241
Canadian Peace Alliance, 287
Canadian Peacekeeping Veterans Association, 318
Canadian Pediatric Foundation, 262
Canadian Pension & Benefits Institute, 241
Canadian Percheron Association, 178
Canadian Peregrine Foundation, 230
Canadian Pest Management Association, 173
Canadian Pharmacists Association, 333
Canadian Philosophical Association, 353
Canadian Photonic Industry Consortium, 353
Canadian Physicians for Aid & Relief, 287
Canadian Physiological Society, 359
Canadian Physiotherapy Association, 262
Canadian Phytopathological Society, 359
Canadian Picture Pioneers, 239
Canadian PKU and Allied Disorders Inc., 262
Canadian Plowing Organization, 173
Canadian Plywood Association, 246
Canadian Podiatric Medical Association, 262
Canadian Point of Care Ultrasound Society, 262
Canadian Police Association, 335
Canadian Polish Congress, 320
Canadian Political Science Association, 336
Canadian Pork Council, 178
Canadian Postmasters & Assistants Association, 292
Canadian Post-MD Education Registry, 262
Canadian Precast / Prestressed Concrete Institute, 190
Canadian Printing Industries Association, 340
Canadian Printing Ink Manufacturers' Association, 340
Canadian Process Control Association, 236
Canadian Produce Marketing Association, 315
Canadian Professional Association for Transgender Health, 305
Canadian Professional Sales Association, 194
Canadian Progress Club, 362
Canadian Property Tax Association, Inc., 376
Canadian Psychiatric Association, 316
Canadian Psychoanalytic Society, 316
Canadian Psychological Association, 316
Canadian Public Health Association, 263
Canadian Public Health Association - NB/PEI Branch, 263
Canadian Public Health Association - NWT/Nunavut Branch, 263
Canadian Public Relations Society Inc., 311
Canadian Publishers' Council, 342
Canadian Quarter Horse Association, 178
Canadian Quaternary Association, 353
Canadian Quilters' Association, 384
Canadian Race Relations Foundation, 320

Canadian Racing Pigeon Union Inc., 349
Canadian Radiation Protection Association, 356
The Canadian Real Estate Association, 344
Canadian Recreational Vehicle Association, 378
Canadian Red Angus Promotion Society, 178
Canadian Red Cross, 224
Canadian Red Poll Cattle Association, 178
Canadian Remote Sensing Society, 227
Canadian Research Institute for the Advancement of Women, 353
Canadian Retina Society, 263
Canadian Rheumatology Association, 263
Canadian Roofing Contractors' Association, 190
Canadian Rose Society, 279
Canadian School Boards Association, 218
Canadian School Libraries, 308
Canadian Science & Technology Historical Association, 359
Canadian Science Policy Centre, 359
Canadian Search Dog Association, 335
Canadian Securities Administrators, 241
Canadian Securities Institute, 241
Canadian Security Association, 357
Canadian Security Traders Association, Inc., 241
Canadian Seed Growers' Association, 173
Canadian Seed Trade Association, 173
Canadian Senior Pro Rodeo Association, 349
Canadian Sheep Breeders' Association, 178
Canadian Sheep Federation, 178
Canadian Sheet Steel Building Institute, 375
Canadian Shorthorn Association, 178
Canadian Simmental Association, 178
Canadian Skills Training & Employment Coalition, 375
Canadian Slovak League, 320
Canadian Snack Food Association, 244
Canadian Society for Aesthetics, 353
Canadian Society for Analytical Sciences & Spectroscopy, 359
Canadian Society for Bioengineering, 173
Canadian Society for Civil Engineering, 227
Canadian Society for Clinical Investigation, 263
Canadian Society for Education through Art, 218
Canadian Society for Eighteenth-Century Studies, 353
Canadian Society for Engineering Management, 227
Canadian Society for Horticultural Science, 279
Canadian Society for International Health, 263
Canadian Society for Mechanical Engineering, 227
Canadian Society for Medical Laboratory Science, 263
The Canadian Society for Mesopotamian Studies, 184
Canadian Society for Molecular Biosciences, 359
Canadian Society for Pharmaceutical Sciences, 263
Canadian Society for Surgical Oncology, 263
Canadian Society for the History & Philosophy of Science, 359
Canadian Society for the History of Medicine, 263
Canadian Society for the Study of Education, 218
Canadian Society for the Study of Higher Education, 218
Canadian Society for the Study of Names, 277
The Canadian Society for the Weizmann Institute of Science, 359
Canadian Society for Transfusion Medicine, 263
Canadian Society for Vascular Surgery, 263
Canadian Society of Agronomy, 173
Canadian Society of Air Safety Investigators, 357
Canadian Society of Allergy & Clinical Immunology, 263
Canadian Society of Animal Science, 180
Canadian Society of Association Executives, 311
Canadian Society of Cardiac Surgeons, 263
Canadian Society of Celebrants, 263

Canadian Society of Children's Authors, Illustrators & Performers, 387
Canadian Society of Cinematographers, 239
Canadian Society of Clinical Neurophysiologists, 263
Canadian Society of Customs Brokers, 194
Canadian Society of Cytopathology, 263
Canadian Society of Endocrinology & Metabolism, 263
Canadian Society of Environmental Biologists, 230
Canadian Society of Exploration Geophysicists, 359
Canadian Society of Forensic Science, 359
Canadian Society of Gastroenterology Nurses & Associates, 263
Canadian Society of Hand Therapists, 264
Canadian Society of Hospital Pharmacists, 333
Canadian Society of Internal Medicine, 264
Canadian Society of Iranian Engineers & Architects, 227
Canadian Society of Landscape Architects, 298
Canadian Society of Mayflower Descendants, 277
Canadian Society of Microbiologists, 359
Canadian Society of Nephrology, 264
Canadian Society of Nutrition Management, 264
Canadian Society of Otolaryngology - Head & Neck Surgery, 264
Canadian Society of Painters in Water Colour, 384
Canadian Society of Palliative Care Physicians, 264
Canadian Society of Pharmacology & Therapeutics, 359
Canadian Society of Physician Leaders, 311
Canadian Society of Plant Biologists, 359
Canadian Society of Plastic Surgeons, 264
Canadian Society of Presbyterian History, 277
Canadian Society of Respiratory Therapists, 264
Canadian Society of Safety Engineering, Inc., 357
Canadian Society of Soil Science, 359
Canadian Society of Technical Analysts, 195
Canadian Society of Transplantation, 264
Canadian Society of Zoologists, 180
Canadian Sociological Association, 353
Canadian Space Society, 359
Canadian Sphagnum Peat Moss Association, 173
Canadian Spice Association, 244
Canadian Spinal Research Organization, 264
Canadian Sporting Goods Association, 355
Canadian Stamp Dealers' Association, 349
Canadian Standards Association, 375
Canadian Steel Construction Council, 375
Canadian Steel Producers Association, 375
Canadian Student Leadership Association, 311
Canadian Sugar Institute, 244
Canadian Swine Breeders' Association, 178
Canadian Tamils' Chamber of Commerce, 195
Canadian Tarentaise Association, 178
Canadian Tax Foundation, 376
Canadian Taxpayers Federation, 376
Canadian Teachers' Federation, 218
Canadian Technical Asphalt Association, 227
Canadian Test Centre Inc., 218
Canadian Textile Industry Association, 238
Canadian Thoracic Society, 264
Canadian Thoroughbred Horse Society, 178
Canadian Tibetan Association of Ontario, 320
Canadian Tooling & Machining Association, 314
Canadian Tourism Research Institute, 378
Canadian Toy Association / Canadian Toy & Hobby Fair, 314
Canadian Toy Collectors' Society Inc., 349
Canadian Trakehner Horse Society, 179
Canadian Translators, Terminologists & Interpreters Council, 299
Canadian Transplant Association, 264
Canadian Tribute to Human Rights, 282

Chambre immobilière de Saint-Hyacinthe Inc., 345
Chambre immobilière des Laurentides, 345
Chambre immobilière du Grand Montréal, 345
Chambre immobilière du Saguenay-Lac St-Jean Inc., 345
The Champlain Society, 277
Changement intégrité pour notre Québec, 336
The Chartered Governance Institute of Canada, 311
Chartered Professional Accountants Canada, 169
Chartered Professional Accountants of Alberta, 169
Chartered Professional Accountants of British Columbia, 169
Chartered Professional Accountants of Manitoba, 169
Chartered Professional Accountants of Newfoundland & Labrador, 169
Chartered Professional Accountants of Nova Scotia, 169
Chartered Professional Accountants of Ontario, 169
Chartered Professional Accountants of Prince Edward Island, 169
Chartered Professional Accountants of Saskatchewan, 169
Chartered Professional Accountants of the Yukon, 169, 170
Chartered Professionals in Human Resources, 225
Chatham-Kent Chamber of Commerce, 196
Chatham-Kent Real Estate Board, 345
Chemical Institute of Canada, 201
Chess Federation of Canada, 349
Les Chevaliers de Colomb du Québec, 248
Chicken Farmers of Canada, 340
Chicken Farmers of Prince Edward Island, 340
Chiefs of Ontario, 324
Child & Parent Resource Institute, 316
The Child Abuse Survivor Monument Project, 366
Child Care Advocacy Association of Canada, 366
Child Find British Columbia, 203
Child Find Canada Inc., 203
Child Find Newfoundland & Labrador, 203
Child Find Ontario, 203
Child Find PEI Inc., 203
Child Find Saskatchewan Inc., 203
Child Welfare League of Canada, 366
Childhood Cancer Canada Foundation, 265
Children's Healthcare Canada, 280
Children's Hospital Foundation of Manitoba, 265
Children's Hospital Foundation of Saskatchewan, 265
Children's Hospital of Eastern Ontario Foundation, 265
Children's International Summer Villages (Canada) Inc., 287
Children's Mental Health Ontario, 316
Children's Miracle Network, 203
Children's Wish Foundation of Canada, 203
Chilliwack & District Real Estate Board, 345
Chinese Canadian Association of Prince Edward Island, 205
Chinese Canadian National Council, 320
Christian Farmers Federation of Ontario, 173
Christian Heritage Party of British Columbia, 336
Christian Heritage Party of Canada, 337
Christie-Ossington Neighbourhood Centre, 366
Christmas Tree Farmers of Ontario, 246
Chronic Pain Association of Canada, 265
La cinémathèque québécoise, 239
CIO Association of Canada, 311
Cities of New Brunswick Association, 251
Citizen Scientists, 360
Citizens for a Safe Environment, 231
The Citizens Foundation Canada, 366
Citizens Opposed to Paving the Escarpment, 231
Citizens' Environment Watch, 231

Citoyens au pouvoir du Québec, 337
City Farmer - Canada's Office of Urban Agriculture, 279
Civil Air Search & Rescue Association, 224
CIVIX, 203
Clans & Scottish Societies of Canada, 320
Classical Association of Canada, 353
Clean Nova Scotia Foundation, 231
Climb Yukon Association, 349
Clowns sans frontières, 366
Club Optimiste de Rivière-du-Loup inc., 362
Les Clubs 4-H du Québec, 173
Coady International Institute, 287
Coal Association of Canada, 319
Coalition Avenir Québec, 337
Coalition des familles LGBT, 305
Coalition des organismes communautaires québécois de lutte contre le sida, 176
Coalition to Oppose the Arms Trade, 357
CODE, 287
CoDevelopment Canada, 288
Coffee Association of Canada, 244
Colchester-East Hants Public Library Foundation, 308
Collectif des femmes immigrantes du Québec, 204
The College & Association of Registered Nurses of Alberta, 330
College of Alberta Professional Foresters, 246
College of Dental Hygienists of Nova Scotia, 206
College of Dental Surgeons of British Columbia, 207
College of Dental Surgeons of Saskatchewan, 207
College of Dental Technologists of Ontario, 207
College of Dietitians of Alberta, 265
College of Dietitians of British Columbia, 265
College of Dietitians of Manitoba, 265
College of Dietitians of Ontario, 265
College of Family Physicians of Canada, 265
College of Licensed Practical Nurses of Newfoundland & Labrador, 330
College of Midwives of British Columbia, 202
College of Naturopathic Doctors of Alberta, 265
College of Nurses of Ontario, 330
College of Occupational Therapists of British Columbia, 265
College of Pharmacists of British Columbia, 333
College of Pharmacists of Manitoba, 334
College of Physicians & Surgeons of Alberta, 265
College of Physicians & Surgeons of British Columbia, 265
College of Physicians & Surgeons of Manitoba, 265
College of Physicians & Surgeons of New Brunswick, 265
College of Physicians & Surgeons of Newfoundland & Labrador, 265
College of Physicians & Surgeons of Nova Scotia, 265
College of Physicians & Surgeons of Ontario, 266
College of Physicians & Surgeons of Prince Edward Island, 266
College of Physicians & Surgeons of Saskatchewan, 266
College of Registered Nurses of Manitoba, 330
College of Registered Psychiatric Nurses of Manitoba, 330
College of Veterinarians of Ontario, 181
Colleges and Institutes Canada, 218
Colleges Ontario, 218
Collège des médecins du Québec, 265
Le Collège du Savoir, 247
Comité condition féminine Baie-James, 385
Comité des citoyens et citoyennes du quartier Saint-Sauveur, 377

Comité d'action des citoyennes et citoyens de Verdun, 377
Comité d'action Parc Extension, 377
Comité logement de Lacine-Lasalle, 377
Comité logement du Plateau Mont-Royal, 377
Comité logement Rosemont, 377
Comité pour les droits humains en Amérique latine, 366
Comité Syndical Francophone de l'Éducation et de la Formation, 292
Commercial Seed Analysts Association of Canada Inc., 173
Commission canadienne pour la théorie des machines et des mécanismes, 354
Commission de la santé et des services sociaux des Premières Nations du Québec et du Labrador, 324
Commission nationale des parents francophones, 205
Committee of Progressive Pakistani-Canadians, 204
The Commonwealth of Learning, 218
Commonwealth War Graves Commission - Canadian Agency, 318
Communist Party of BC, 337
Communist Party of Canada, 337
Communist Party of Canada (Alberta), 337
Communist Party of Canada (Manitoba), 337
Communist Party of Canada (Marxist-Leninist), 337
Communist Party of Canada (Ontario), 337
Community Action Resource Centre, 366
Community Health Nurses of Canada, 330
Community Legal Education Association (Manitoba) Inc., 302
Community Legal Education Ontario, 302
Community Legal Information Association of Prince Edward Island, 302
Community Living Manitoba, 210
Community Living Ontario, 210
Community Museums Association of Prince Edward Island, 249
Community One Foundation, 305
Community Planning Association of Alberta, 302
Community Social Services Employers' Association, 366
Comox Valley Chamber of Commerce, 197
The Comparative & International Education Society of Canada, 218
Compassion Canada, 288
Compensation Employees' Union (Ind.), 292
Compost Council of Canada, 231
Compute Canada, 204
Concerned Children's Advertisers, 203
Concrete BC, 190
Concrete Canada, 190
Concrete Manitoba, 191
Concrete Ontario, 191
Concrete Sask, 191
Confederacy of Mainland Mi'kmaq, 324
Confederation of Alberta Faculty Associations, 218
Confederation of University Faculty Associations of British Columbia, 219
The Conference Board of Canada, 213
Conference of Defence Associations, 318
Conference of Independent Schools (Ontario), 219
Conflict Resolution Saskatchewan, 366
Confédération des organismes familiaux du Québec, 366
Confédération des syndicats nationaux, 292
Congress of Aboriginal Peoples, 324
Congress of Black Lawyers & Jurists of Québec, 302
Congress of Black Women of Canada, 385
Congress of Union Retirees Canada, 292
Connexions Information Sharing Services, 342

Electrical Contractors Association of New Brunswick, Inc., 224
Electrical Contractors Association of Ontario, 224
Electrical Contractors Association of Saskatchewan, 224
Electronic Cigarette Trade Association, 283
Electronic Frontier Canada Inc., 283
Electronics Import Committee, 383
Elementary Teachers' Federation of Ontario, 219
Elizabeth House, 201
Elsa Wild Animal Appeal of Canada, 231
Embroiderers' Association of Canada, Inc., 384
Empire Club of Canada, 248
Employees' Union of St. Mary's of the Lake Hospital - CNFIU Local 3001, 292
Enfant-Retour Québec, 203
The Engineering Institute of Canada, 228
Engineers Canada, 228
Engineers Nova Scotia, 228
Enviro-Accès Inc., 231
Environment Resources Managament Association, 243
Environmental Careers Organization of Canada, 232
Environmental Education Association of the Yukon, 232
Environmental Health Association of British Columbia, 232
The Environmental Law Centre (Alberta) Society, 232
Environmental Managers Association of British Columbia, 232
Environmental Services Association of Alberta, 232
Environmental Services Association of Nova Scotia, 232
Environnement jeunesse, 232
Epilepsy & Seizure Association of Manitoba, 266
Epilepsy Canada, 266
Epilepsy Ontario, 267
Equitas - International Centre for Human Rights Education, 282
ERS Training & Development Corporation, 388
Esperanto Association of Canada, 299
Les EssentiElles, 247
Estonian Central Council in Canada, 320
Ethiopiaid, 267
European Union Chamber of Commerce in Canada, 197
Evangelical Medical Aid Society Canada, 267
Evergreen, 232
Excellence Canada, 197
Exhibitions Association of Nova Scotia, 237
Experiences Canada, 219
Eye Bank of BC, 267
Eye Bank of Canada - Ontario Division, 267

F

Facility Association, 285
Families Canada, 308
Family & Community Support Services Association of Alberta, 367
Family Enterprise Xchange, 197
Family History Society of Newfoundland & Labrador, 277
Family Mediation Canada, 367
Family Mediation Manitoba, 367
Family Service Canada, 367
Family Service Toronto, 367
Farm & Food Care Ontario, 179
Farmers of North America, 173
Farmers of North America Strategic Agriculture Institute, 173
FaunENord, 232
Federal Association of Security Officials, 357
Federal Liberal Association of Nunavut, 337
Federated Women's Institutes of Canada, 385
Federated Women's Institutes of Ontario, 385
Fédération acadienne de la Nouvelle-Écosse, 247

Fédération autonome du collégial (ind.), 292
Fédération CSN - Construction (CSN), 292
Fédération culturelle canadienne-française, 205
Fédération de la jeunesse canadienne-française inc., 247
Fédération de la santé du Québec - CSQ, 330
Fédération de la santé et des services sociaux, 292
Fédération de l'industrie manufacturière (FIM-CSN), 292
Fédération des agricultrices du Québec, 173
Fédération des associations de familles monoparentales et recomposées du Québec, 367
Fédération des associations de juristes d'expression française de common law, 302
Fédération des aînées et aînés francophones du Canada, 361
Fédération des centres d'action bénévole du Québec, 367
Fédération des comités de parents du Québec inc., 219
La Fédération des commissions scolaires du Québec, 219
Fédération des communautés francophones et acadienne du Canada, 247
Fédération des cégeps, 219
Fédération des employées et employés de services publics inc. (CSN), 292
Fédération des enseignantes et enseignants de cégeps, 292
Fédération des familles et amis de la personne atteinte de maladie mentale, 316
Fédération des femmes du Québec, 385
Fédération des intervenantes en petite enfance du Québec, 292
Fédération des milieux documentaires, 308
La fédération des mouvements personne d'abord du Québec, 210
Fédération des médecins omnipraticiens du Québec, 267
Fédération des médecins résidents du Québec inc. (ind.), 292
Fédération des médecins spécialistes du Québec, 267
Fédération des parents du Manitoba, 219
Fédération des policiers et policières municipaux du Québec (ind.), 292
Fédération des producteurs de bovins du Québec, 174
Fédération des producteurs d'oeufs de consommation du Québec, 340
Fédération des producteurs forestiers du Québec, 246
Fédération des professionnelles et professionnels de l'éducation du Québec, 293
Fédération des professionnèles, 292
Fédération des secrétaires professionnelles du Québec, 311
Fédération des sociétés d'histoire du Québec, 277
Fédération des sociétés d'horticulture et d'écologie du Québec, 279
Fédération des syndicats de l'action collective, 293
Fédération des Syndicats de l'Enseignement, 293
Fédération des travailleurs et travailleuses du Québec - Construction, 293
Fédération des établissements d'enseignement privés, 219
Fédération du commerce (CSN), 293
Fédération du personnel de l'enseignement privé, 293
Fédération du personnel de soutien scolaire (CSQ), 293
Fédération du personnel professionnel des collèges, 293, 219
Fédération du Québec pour le planning des naissances, 352
Federation for Scottish Culture in Nova Scotia, 205
Fédération franco-ténoise, 247
Fédération indépendante des syndicats autonomes, 293

Fédération interdisciplinaire de l'horticulture ornementale du Québec, 279
Fédération interprofessionnelle de la santé du Québec, 331
Fédération nationale des communications (CSN), 293
Fédération nationale des enseignants et des enseignantes du Québec, 219
Federation of Asian Canadian Lawyers, 302
Federation of BC Youth in Care Networks, 201
Federation of British Columbia Naturalists, 328
Federation of British Columbia Writers, 388
Federation of Canada-China Friendship Associations, 320
Federation of Canadian Artists, 184
Federation of Canadian Municipalities, 252
Federation of Canadian Music Festivals, 237
Federation of Canadian Turkish Associations, 321
Federation of Chinese Canadian Professionals (Québec), 321
Federation of Danish Associations in Canada, 321
Federation of Independent School Associations of BC, 219
Federation of Law Reform Agencies of Canada, 302
Federation of Law Societies of Canada, 302
Federation of Medical Regulatory Authorities of Canada, 267
Federation of Medical Women of Canada, 385
Federation of Metro Tenants' Associations, 281
Federation of Music Festivals of Nova Scotia, 237
Federation of New Brunswick Faculty Associations, 219
Federation of Northern Ontario Municipalities, 252
Federation of Ontario Cottagers' Associations, 349
Federation of Ontario Public Libraries, 308
Federation of Prince Edward Island Municipalities Inc., 252
Federation of Saskatchewan Indian Nations, 324
Fédération québécoise de camping et de caravaning inc., 349
Fédération québécoise de l'autisme, 267
Fédération québécoise des chasseurs et pêcheurs, 232
Fédération québécoise des coopératives forestières, 246
Fédération québécoise des directions d'établissements d'enseignement, 220
Fédération Québécoise des Intervenants en Sécurité Incendie, 357
Fédération québécoise des jeux récréatifs, 349
Fédération québécoise des massothérapeutes, 267
Fédération Québécoise des Municipalités, 252
Fédération québécoise des professeures et professeurs d'université, 220
Fédération québécoise des revêtements de sol, 314
Fédération québécoise des sociétés Alzheimer, 267
Fédération québécoise des sociétés de généalogie, 277
Fédération québécoise des échecs, 349
Fédération québécoise du loisir littéraire, 299
Fédération québécoise pour le saumon atlantique, 243
Femmes autochtones du Québec inc., 325
Fenestration Association of BC, 314
Fenestration Canada, 314
Fertility Matters Canada, 352
Fertilizer Canada, 201
Festivals & Events Ontario, 237
Festivals et Événements Québec, 237
Fibrose kystique Québec, 267
FilmOntario, 239
Financial Executives International Canada, 241
Financial Services Commission of Ontario, 285
Finnish Canadian Cultural Federation, 321
Fire Prevention Canada, 357

First Nations Breast Cancer Society, 325
First Nations Confederacy of Cultural Education Centres, 325
First Nations Environmental Network, 232
First Nations Lands Advisory Board, 325
First Nations Lands Management Resource Centre, 325
First Nations SchoolNet, 220
First Nations Summit Society, 325
Fisheries Council of Canada, 243
Fishermen & Scientists Research Society, 243
The 519 Church St. Community Centre, 367
Flavour Manufacturers Association of Canada, 245
Flemingdon Neighbourhood Services, 367
Flin Flon & District Chamber of Commerce, 197
Flowers Canada, 280
Flowers Canada Growers, 280
Fondation de la faune du Québec, 232
La Fondation des Auberges du coeur, 367
Fondation des maladies du coeur du Québec, 267
Fondation des étoiles, 267
Fondation du barreau du Québec, 302
Fondation franco-ontarienne, 205
Fondation Jeunes en Tête, 316
Fondation Mario-Racine, 305
Fondation Papillon, 210
Fondation Paul Gérin-Lajoie, 367
Fondation québécoise du cancer, 267
Fondation Tourisme Jeunesse, 379
Food & Beverage Atlantic, 245
Food Banks Canada, 367
Food Processors of Canada, 245
Food, Health & Consumer Products of Canada, 245
For British Columbia, 337
Force Jeunesse, 389
Foreign Agricultural Resource Management Services, 174
Forest Nova Scotia, 246
Forest Products Association of Canada, 246
Foresters, 248
Forests Ontario, 246
Fort McMurray Realtors Association, 345
Fort McMurray Society for the Prevention of Cruelty to Animals, 181
FortWhyte Alive, 232
Forum for International Trade Training, 288
Foster Parent Support Services Society, 367
Foundation Fighting Blindness, 267
Foundation for Advancing Family Medicine of the College of Family Physicians of Canada, 267
Foundation for Educational Exchange Between Canada & the United States of America, 220
Foundation for Legal Research, 302
Foundation Mères du Monde en Santé, 368
FP Canada, 242
FPInnovations, 354
Fraser Basin Council, 232
The Fraser Institute, 213
Fraser Valley Real Estate Board, 345
Fraternité interprovinciale des ouvriers en électricité (CTC), 293
Fraternité nationale des forestiers et travailleurs d'usine (CTC), 293
Fred Victor Centre, 368
Fredericton Chamber of Commerce, 197
Fredericton Tourism, 379
Freedom Party of Ontario, 337
Frequency Co-ordination System Association, 377
Fresh Outlook Foundation, 232
Friends of Canadian Broadcasting, 188
The Friends of Library & Archives Canada, 308

Friends of Red Hill Valley, 232
Friends of the Earth Canada, 232
Front d'action populaire en réaménagement urbain, 281
Frontiers Foundation, 368
Funeral & Cremation Services Council of Saskatchewan, 249
Funeral Advisory & Memorial Society, 249
Funeral Service Association of Canada, 249
Fur Council of Canada, 249
Fur Institute of Canada, 249
The Fur-Bearers, 249
Fuse Collective, 232
Future Possibilities for Kids, 203
Futurpreneur Canada, 197

G

GAMA International Canada, 285
Garrod Association, 267
Gay Fathers of Toronto, 305
Gem & Mineral Federation of Canada, 250
Genealogical Association of Nova Scotia, 277
Genealogical Institute of The Maritimes, 277
Genetic Aortic Disorders Association Canada, 267
Geneva Centre for Autism, 268
GEOIDE Network, 354
Geological Association of Canada, 360
The Georgian Triangle Tourist Association & Tourist Information Centre, 379
German-Canadian Congress (Manitoba) Inc., 321
Gerontological Nurses Association of British Columbia, 331
Gerontological Nursing Association of Ontario, 331
GI (Gastrointestinal) Society, 268
Girl Guides of Canada, 203
Gitxsan Treaty Office, 325
Glass & Architectural Metals Association, 191
Glaucoma Research Society of Canada, 268
Glendon & District Business Alliance, 197
Global Automakers of Canada, 383
Global Network of Director Institutes, 311
Go Vegan, 337
Goethe-Institut (Toronto), 321
Good Jobs for All Coalition, 368
Goodwill Industries of Alberta, 368
Governance Professionals of Canada, 312
Government Services Union, 293
Governor General's Performing Arts Awards Foundation, 184
Grain Growers of Canada, 174
Grain Services Union (CLC), 293
Grand Council of the Crees, 325
GRAND Society, 368
Grande Prairie & Area Association of Realtors, 345
Grande Prairie & Region United Way, 368
Great Lakes Institute for Environmental Research, 354
The Great Lakes Marine Heritage Foundation, 314
Greater Bathurst Chamber of Commerce, 197
Greater Charlottetown & Area Chamber of Commerce, 197
Greater Kingston Chamber of Commerce, 197
Greater Kitchener & Waterloo Chamber of Commerce, 197
Greater Moncton Chamber of Commerce, 197
Greater Moncton Real Estate Board Inc., 345
Greater Nanaimo Chamber of Commerce, 197
Greater Niagara Chamber of Commerce, 198
Greater Peterborough Chamber of Commerce, 198
Greater Summerside Chamber of Commerce, 198
Greater Vancouver International Film Festival Society, 240

Greater Vancouver Japanese Canadian Citizens' Association, 321
Greater Victoria Chamber of Commerce, 198
Green Action Centre, 232
The Green Party of Alberta, 337
Green Party of Canada, 337
The Green Party of Manitoba, 337
Green Party of New Brunswick, 337
Green Party of Nova Scotia, 337
The Green Party of Ontario, 337
Green Party of Prince Edward Island, 337
Greenbelt Foundation, 232
Greenpeace Canada, 233
Greens of British Columbia, 337
Greenspace Alliance of Canada's Capital, 233
Greenwood Board of Trade, 198
Grimsby & District Chamber of Commerce, 198
GRIS-Mauricie/Centre-du-Québec, 305
The Group Halifax, 386
Group of 78, 288
Groupe CTT Group, 238
Groupe de recherche et d'intervention sociale, 305
Groupe d'économie solidaire du Québec, 368
Groupe export agroalimentaire Québec - Canada, 383
Groupe gai de l'Outaouais, 305
Groupe gai de l'Université Laval, 305
Groupe régional d'intervention social - Québec, 305
Groupement des assureurs automobiles, 285
GS1 Canada, 283
Guelph & District Real Estate Board, 345
Guelph Chamber of Commerce, 198
Guide Outfitters Association of British Columbia, 349
Guild of Industrial, Commercial & Institutional Accountants, 170
Gunn Métis Local Council #55, 325

H

Habitat for Humanity Canada, 368
Halifax Chamber of Commerce, 198
Halifax Library Association, 308
Halifax North West Trails Association, 350
Halifax Regional CAP Association, 377
Halifax-Dartmouth Automobile Dealers' Association, 186
Hamilton Chamber of Commerce, 198
Hamilton Industrial Environmental Association, 233
Hamilton Police Association, 302
Hamilton-Burlington & District Real Estate Board, 345
Harbourfront Community Centre, 368
Harmony Foundation of Canada, 233
Harold Greenberg Fund, 239
Head & Hands, 389
Health Action Network Society, 268
Health Association Nova Scotia, 280
Health Association of African Canadians, 268
Health Employers Association of British Columbia, 280
Health Libraries Association of British Columbia, 308
Health Sciences Association of Alberta, 293
Health Sciences Association of British Columbia, 268
Health Sciences Association of Saskatchewan, 293
Health Sciences Centre Foundation, 268
HealthCareCAN, 281
Heart & Stroke Foundation of Alberta & NWT, 268
Heart & Stroke Foundation of British Columbia & Yukon, 268
Heart & Stroke Foundation of Canada, 268
Heart & Stroke Foundation of Manitoba, 268
Heart & Stroke Foundation of New Brunswick, 268
Heart & Stroke Foundation of Newfoundland & Labrador, 268
Heart & Stroke Foundation of Nova Scotia, 268

International Organization of Securities Commissions, 242

International Organization of Ukrainian Communities: Fourth Wave, 321

International Personnel Management Association - Canada, 312

International Police Association - Canada, 335

International Political Science Association, 337

International Sanitary Supply Association Canada, 314

International Social Service Canada, 368

International Union of Bricklayers & Allied Craftworkers (AFL-CIO/CFL), 294

International Union, United Automobile, Aerospace & Agricultural Implement Workers of America, 294

Inuit Art Foundation, 325

Inuit Tapiriit Kanatami, 325

Investment Funds Institute of Canada, 242

Investment Industry Regulatory Organization of Canada, 242

IODE Canada, 248

Iranian Canadian Congress, 321

Iranian Canadian Legal Professionals, 302

Iranian Women's Organization of Ontario, 321

Iranian-Canadian Association of Immigration Consultants, 283

IRIS Mundial, 269

Irish Canadian Cultural Association of New Brunswick, 321

Islamic Food & Nutrition Council of Canada, 245

The Island Party of Prince Edward Island, 338

Island Technology Professionals, 228

Italian Chamber of Commerce of Ontario, 198

Italian Cultural Institute (Istituto Italiano di Cultura), 321

J

J. Douglas Ferguson Historical Research Foundation, 278

Jack Miner Migratory Bird Foundation, Inc., 328

Jamaica Association of Montréal Inc., 321

Jamaican Canadian Association, 321

Jane Austen Society of North America, 299

Jane Finch Community & Family Centre, 368

Japan Automobile Manufacturers Association of Canada, 186

The Japan Foundation, Toronto, 206

Japanese Canadian Association of Yukon, 321

Jasper Environmental Association, 233

Jazz Festivals Canada, 237

Jersey Canada, 179

Jeunesse Acadienne et Francophone de l'Ile-du-prince-Édouard, 203

Jeunesse Lambda, 305

Jewish Family & Child, 368

Jewish Federations of Canada - UIA, 322

Jewish Genealogical Society of Toronto, 278

Jewish Heritage Centre of Western Canada Inc., 322

The John Howard Society of British Columbia, 341

The John Howard Society of Canada, 341

Joy Smith Foundation Inc., 282

Junior Achievement Canada, 203

Junior Chamber International Canada, 203

Justice for Children & Youth, 203

Juvenile Diabetes Research Foundation Canada, 269

K

Kamloops & District Real Estate Association, 345

Kapuskasing & District Chamber of Commerce, 198

Kawartha Lakes Real Estate Association, 345

Keewatinook Fishers of Lake Winnipeg, 325

Kelowna Chamber of Commerce, 198

Keystone Agricultural Producers, 174

Kidney Cancer Canada Association, 269

Kidney Foundation of Canada, 269

Kids First Parent Association of Canada, 368

Kids Help Phone, 368

Kin Canada, 362

Kin Canada Foundation, 362

Kingston & Area Real Estate Association, 345

Kinsmen Foundation of British Columbia & Yukon, 211

Kiwanis International (Eastern Canada & the Caribbean District), 362

Kiwanis International (Western Canada District), 362

Klondike Visitors Association, 379

Knights of Columbus, 248

Knights of Pythias - Domain of British Columbia, 248

Kootenay Real Estate Board, 345

Kootenay Rockies Tourism, 379

Korea Veterans Association of Canada Inc., Heritage Unit, 318

Korean Canadian Women's Association, 204

L

L'arc-en-ciel littéraire, 298

L'Association de spina-bifida et d'hydrocéphalie du Québec, 255

L'Association du Québec de l'Institut canadien des évaluateurs, 344

L'Association québécoise des centres de la petite enfance, 202

L'Héritage canadien du Québec, 277

L'Institut canadien de Québec, 206

L'Institut d'assurance de dommages du Québec, 285

L'Office de Certification Commerciale du Québec Inc., 199

L'Ordre des comptables professionnels agréés du Québec, 170

L'Ordre des psychologues du Québec, 317

L'Union culturelle des Franco-Ontariennes, 206

Laborers' International Union of North America (AFL-CIO/CLC), 294

Labrador Native Women's Association, 325

LakeCity Employment Services Association, 211

Lakeland United Way, 368

Lakeshore Area Multi-Service Project, 368

Landscape Alberta Nursery Trades Association, 280

Landscape New Brunswick Horticultural Trades Association, 280

Landscape NL Horticultural Association, 280

Landscape Nova Scotia, 280

Landscape Ontario Horticultural Trades Association, 280

Languages Canada, 299

Last Post Fund, 362

Latvian Canadian Cultural Centre, 322

Latvian National Federation in Canada, 322

The Latvian Relief Society of Canada, 322

Law Foundation of British Columbia, 302

Law Foundation of Newfoundland & Labrador, 302

Law Foundation of Nova Scotia, 302

Law Foundation of Ontario, 303

Law Foundation of Prince Edward Island, 303

Law Foundation of Saskatchewan, 303

Law Society of Alberta, 303

Law Society of British Columbia, 303

Law Society of Manitoba, 303

Law Society of New Brunswick, 303

Law Society of Newfoundland & Labrador, 303

Law Society of Nunavut, 303

Law Society of Ontario, 303

Law Society of Prince Edward Island, 303

Law Society of Saskatchewan, 303

Law Society of the Northwest Territories, 303

Law Society of Yukon, 303

League for Human Rights of B'nai Brith Canada, 282

The League of Canadian Poets, 388

League of Ukrainian Canadian Women, 322

League of Ukrainian Canadians, 322

Learning Assistance Teachers' Association of British Columbia, 220

Learning Disabilities Association of Alberta, 220

Learning Disabilities Association of British Columbia, 220

Learning Disabilities Association of Canada, 220

Learning Disabilities Association of Manitoba, 220

Learning Disabilities Association of Newfoundland & Labrador Inc., 220

Learning Disabilities Association of Ontario, 220

Learning Disabilities Association of Prince Edward Island, 220

Learning Disabilities Association of Saskatchewan, 220

Learning Disabilities Association of The Northwest Territories, 220

Learning Disabilities Association of Yukon Territory, 221

Learning Enrichment Foundation, 221

La Leche League Canada, 202

Legal Education Society of Alberta, 303

Legal Information Society of Nova Scotia, 303

Leprosy relief (Canada) Inc., 369

Lethbridge & District Association of Realtors, 345

Lethbridge Chamber of Commerce, 198

Leucan - Association pour les enfants atteints de cancer, 269

The Leukemia & Lymphoma Society of Canada, 269

The Liberal Party of Canada, 338

The Liberal Party of Canada (British Columbia), 338

The Liberal Party of Canada (Manitoba), 338

Liberal Party of Canada (Ontario), 338

Liberal Party of Canada in Alberta, 338

Liberal Party of Newfoundland & Labrador, 338

Liberal Party of Nova Scotia, 338

Liberal Party of Prince Edward Island, 338

The Libertarian Party of Canada, 338

Library Association of Alberta, 308

Library Boards Association of Nova Scotia, 308

Lieutenant Governor's Circle on Mental Health & Addiction, 269

The LifeLine Canada Foundation, 316

Life's Vision Manitoba Inc., 352

Lindsay & District Chamber of Commerce, 198

Literary & Historical Society of Québec, 278

The Literary Press Group of Canada, 342

Literary Translators' Association of Canada, 300

The Lithuanian Canadian Community, 322

Little People of Ontario, 369

Livres Canada Books, 342

Lloydminster & District United Way, 369

Lloydminster Chamber of Commerce, 198

L.M. Montgomery Institute, 300

Local Government Administrators of the Northwest Territories, 252

Local Government Management Association of British Columbia, 252

LOMA Canada, 285

London & St. Thomas Association of Realtors, 346

Luggage, Leathergoods, Handbags & Accessories Association of Canada, 238

Lumber & Building Materials Association of Ontario, 191

Lunenburg Board of Trade, 198

The Lung Association AB & NWT, 269

The Lung Association of Nova Scotia, 269

Lung Health Foundation, 269

Lupus Canada, 269

Lupus Foundation of Ontario, 269

None of the Above Direct Democracy Party, 338
Non-Smokers' Rights Association, 369
North American Broadcasters Association, 188
North American Farmers' Direct Marketing Association, Inc., 315
North American Native Plant Society, 280
North American Recycled Rubber Association, 233
North Atlantic Salmon Conservation Organization, 243
North Bay Real Estate Board, 346
North Grenville Chamber of Commerce, 199
North of Superior Film Association, 239
North of Superior Tourism Association, 379
North Pacific Anadromous Fish Commission, 243
North Pacific Marine Science Organization, 360
North Queens Board of Trade, 199
North Shore Forest Products Marketing Board, 315
North Shore Multicultural Society, 322
North Vancouver Chamber of Commerce, 199
North York Community House, 369
Northeastern Alberta Aboriginal Business Association, 327
Northeastern Ontario Tourism, 379
Northern Alberta Health Libraries Association, 309
Northern British Columbia Tourism Association, 379
Northern Film & Video Industry Association, 239
Northern Frontier Visitors Association, 379
Northern Ontario Party, 338
Northern Rockies Aboriginal Women Society, 327
Northern Rockies Alaska Highway Tourism Association, 379
Northern Territories Federation of Labour, 294
The North-South Institute, 213
Northumberland Hills Association of Realtors, 346
Northumberland United Way, 369
Northwest Atlantic Fisheries Organization, 243
Northwest Ontario Sunset Country Travel Association, 379
Northwest Territories & Nunavut Association of Professional Engineers & Geoscientists, 229
Northwest Territories & Nunavut Chamber of Mines, 319
Northwest Territories & Nunavut Construction Association, 192
Northwest Territories & Nunavut Dental Association, 207
Northwest Territories Archives Council, 309
Northwest Territories Arts Council, 185
Northwest Territories Association of Architects, 183
Northwest Territories Association of Communities, 252
Northwest Territories Association of Landscape Architects, 298
Northwest Territories Association of Provincial Court Judges, 303
Northwest Territories Chamber of Commerce, 199
Northwest Territories Federal Liberal Association, 338
Northwest Territories Library Association, 309
Northwest Territories Medical Association, 271
Northwest Territories Recreation & Parks Association, 350
Northwest Territories Society for the Prevention of Cruelty to Animals, 181
Northwest Territories Teachers' Association, 221
Northwest Territories Tourism, 379
Northwest Territories/Nunavut Council of Friendship Centres, 327
Northwestern Ontario Municipal Association, 252
Nova Scotia & Prince Edward Island Pioneers, 377
Nova Scotia Archaeology Society, 183
Nova Scotia Association for Community Living, 211
Nova Scotia Association of Architects, 183
Nova Scotia Association of Black Social Workers, 369
Nova Scotia Association of Naturopathic Doctors, 271

Nova Scotia Association of Optometrists, 271
Nova Scotia Association of REALTORS, 346
Nova Scotia Automobile Dealers' Association, 186
Nova Scotia Barristers' Society, 304
Nova Scotia College of Chiropractors, 271
Nova Scotia College of Pharmacists, 334
Nova Scotia College of Social Workers, 369
Nova Scotia Construction Labour Relations Association Limited, 192
Nova Scotia Dental Assistants' Association, 207
Nova Scotia Dental Association, 207
Nova Scotia Designer Crafts Council, 384
Nova Scotia Dietetic Association, 271
Nova Scotia Federation of Agriculture, 174
Nova Scotia Federation of Anglers & Hunters, 233
Nova Scotia Federation of Home & School Associations, 221
Nova Scotia Federation of Labour, 294
Nova Scotia Fruit Growers' Association, 174
Nova Scotia Gerontological Nurses Association, 331
Nova Scotia Government & General Employees Union, 294
Nova Scotia Ground Water Association, 212
Nova Scotia Hearing & Speech Centres, 211
Nova Scotia Institute of Agrologists, 174
Nova Scotia Library Association, 309
Nova Scotia Mink Breeders' Association, 179
Nova Scotia Native Women's Society, 327
Nova Scotia Nature Trust, 234
Nova Scotia Nurses' Union, 331
Nova Scotia Progressive Conservative Association, 338
Nova Scotia Real Estate Appraisers Association, 346
Nova Scotia Road Builders Association, 192
Nova Scotia Salmon Association, 243
Nova Scotia School Boards Association, 222
Nova Scotia School Counsellor Association, 222
Nova Scotia Society for the Prevention of Cruelty to Animals, 181
Nova Scotia Teachers Union, 222
Nova Scotia Trails Federation, 350
Nova Scotia Union of Public & Private Employees (CCU), 295
Nova Scotia Veterinary Medical Association, 181
Nova Scotia Wool Marketing Board, 315
Nova Scotian Institute of Science, 360
NSERC Chairs for Women in Science & Engineering, 386
Nuclear Insurance Association of Canada, 285
Numeris, 188
Nunavummi Disabilities Makinnasuaqtiit Society, 211
Nunavut Association of Landscape Architects, 298
Nunavut Employees Union, 295
Nunavut Library Association, 309
Nunavut Teachers' Association, 222
Nunavut Tourism, 379
Nurses Association of New Brunswick, 331

O

Oak Ridges Moraine Foundation, 234
Oakville & Milton Humane Society, 181
The Oakville, Milton & District Real Estate Board, 346
Occupational & Environmental Medical Association of Canada, 271
Occupational First Aid Attendants Association of British Columbia, 225
Office & Professional Employees International Union (AFL-CIO/CLC), 295
Office du tourisme et des congrès de Québec, 379
Okanagan Mainline Real Estate Board, 346
Older Adult Centres' Association of Ontario, 361
The Older Women's Network, 386

On Screen Manitoba, 239
One Parent Families Association of Canada, 369
Ontario Aerospace Council, 187
Ontario Agri Business Association, 174
Ontario Agri-Food Technologies, 174
Ontario Alliance, 338
The Ontario Archaeological Society, 183
Ontario Arts Council, 185
Ontario Association for Family Mediation, 369
Ontario Association for Marriage & Family Therapy, 369
Ontario Association of Architects, 183
Ontario Association of Art Galleries, 250
Ontario Association of Broadcasters, 188
Ontario Association of Cemetery & Funeral Professionals, 249
Ontario Association of Certified Engineering Technicians & Technologists, 229
Ontario Association of Chiefs of Police, 335
Ontario Association of Children's Aid Societies, 369
Ontario Association of Credit Counselling Services, 242
Ontario Association of Deans of Education, 222
Ontario Association of Emergency Managers, 312
Ontario Association of Fire Chiefs, 357
Ontario Association of Interval & Transition Houses, 369
Ontario Association of Landscape Architects, 298
Ontario Association of Library Technicians, 309
Ontario Association of Medical Laboratories, 281
Ontario Association of Naturopathic Doctors, 271
Ontario Association of Optometrists, 271
Ontario Association of Police Services Boards, 304
Ontario Association of Property Standards Officers Inc., 281
Ontario Association of Residents' Councils, 361
Ontario Association of School Business Officials, 222
Ontario Association of Social Workers, 370
Ontario Association of Trading Houses, 383
Ontario Beekeepers' Association, 174
Ontario Black History Society, 278
Ontario Building Officials Association Inc., 346
Ontario Camps Association, 350
Ontario Campus Radio Organization, 188
Ontario Catholic School Trustees' Association, 222
Ontario Centres of Excellence, 354
Ontario Chamber of Commerce, 199
Ontario Chiropractic Association, 271
Ontario Coalition for Abortion Clinics, 352
Ontario Coalition for Better Child Care, 370
Ontario Coalition of Indigenous Peoples, 327
Ontario Coalition of Rape Crisis Centres, 370
Ontario College & University Library Association, 309
Ontario College of Pharmacists, 334
Ontario Community Justice Association, 370
Ontario Community Newspapers Association, 343
Ontario Community Support Association, 370
Ontario Concrete Pipe Association, 192
Ontario Confederation of University Faculty Associations, 222
Ontario Convenience Store Association, 356
Ontario Council for International Cooperation, 288
Ontario Council for University Lifelong Learning, 222
Ontario Council of Agencies Serving Immigrants, 204
Ontario Council of University Libraries, 309
Ontario Council on Graduate Studies, 222
Ontario Crafts Council, 384
Ontario Criminal Justice Association, 304
Ontario Crown Attorneys Association, 304
Ontario Dairy Council, 174
Ontario Dental Assistants Association, 207
Ontario Dental Association, 208

Society of Composers, Authors & Music Publishers of Canada, 333

Society of Graphic Designers of Canada, 341

Society of Kabalarians of Canada, 248

Society of Local Government Managers of Alberta, 253

Society of Motion Picture & Television Engineers, 229

The Society of Notaries Public of British Columbia, 304

Society of Obstetricians & Gynaecologists of Canada, 275

Society of Ontario Nut Growers, 175

The Society of Professional Accountants of Canada, 170

Society of Professional Engineers & Associates, 296

Society of Public Insurance Administrators of Ontario, 286

Society of Rural Physicians of Canada, 275

Society of Toxicology of Canada, 360

Society of Translators & Interpreters of British Columbia, 300

Society of Tribologists & Lubrication Engineers, 229

Society Promoting Environmental Conservation, 235

Société canadienne de la sclérose en plaques (Division du Québec), 275

Société de criminologie du Québec, 304

Société de développement des entreprises culturelles, 206

Société de développement des périodiques culturels québécois, 343

Société de généalogie de Québec, 279

Société de la francophonie manitobaine, 248

Société de l'Acadie du Nouveau-Brunswick, 248

Société de Promotion et de Diffusion des Arts et de la Culture, 185

Société des Auteurs de Radio, Télévision et Cinéma, 296

Société des chefs, cuisiniers et pâtissiers du Québec, 355

Société des musées du Québec, 250

Société généalogique canadienne-française, 279

Société historique de Québec, 279

Société Huntington du Québec, 275

Société nationale de l'Acadie, 206

Société Parkinson du Québec, 275

Société professionnelle des auteurs et des compositeurs du Québec, 388

Société québécoise d'espéranto, 300

Société québécoise pour la défense des animaux, 182

Société québécoise pour la déficience intellectuelle, 212

Société Saint-Jean-Baptiste de Montréal, 206

Société Saint-Thomas-d'Aquin, 248

Société Santé en français, 275

Société Santé et Mieux-être en français du Nouveau-Brunswick, 275

Sollio Groupe Coopératif, 175

Soroptimist Foundation of Canada, 362

SOS Children's Villages Canada, 371

Sous-Traitance Industrielle Québec, 314

South Okanagan Immigrant & Community Services, 323

South Okanagan Real Estate Board, 347

South Western Alberta Teachers' Convention Association, 224

Southeast Environmental Association, 235

Southern Alberta Health Libraries Association, 310

Southern Georgian Bay Association of REALTORS, 347

Southern Ontario Seismic Network, 360

Soy Canada, 245

Special Needs Planning Group, 212

The Speech & Stuttering Institute, 212

Speech-Language & Audiology Canada, 275

Spina Bifida & Hydrocephalus Association of Canada, 275

Spinal Cord Injury Canada, 275

Springtide Resources, 371

Spruce City Wildlife Association, 235

Standardbred Canada, 179

Startup Canada, 242

Statistical Society of Canada, 360

Stem Cell Network, 355

Stephen Leacock Associates, 300

Stop Climate Change, 340

Stratford & District Chamber of Commerce, 200

Stratford Tourism Alliance, 380

Structural Innovation & Monitoring Technologies Resources Centre, 229

Stó:lo Research & Resource Management Centre, 328

Stó:lo Service Agency, 328

Sunbeam Sportscar Owners Club of Canada, 351

Supply Chain Management Association, 312

Supply Chain Management Association - Alberta, 312

Supply Chain Management Association - British Columbia, 312

Supply Chain Management Association - Manitoba, 312

Supply Chain Management Association - Newfoundland & Labrador, 312

Supply Chain Management Association - Nova Scotia, 312, 313

Supply Chain Management Association - Ontario, 313

Supply Chain Management Association - Saskatchewan, 313

Surrey Board of Trade, 356

Sustainable Urban Development Association, 235

Swift Current United Way, 371

Swiss Canadian Chamber of Commerce (Ontario) Inc., 200

Syme-Woolner Neighbourhood & Family Centre, 371

Syndicat de la fonction publique et parapublique du Québec inc. (ind.), 296

Syndicat de professionnelles et professionnels du gouvernement du Québec, 296

Syndicat des Agents Correctionnels du Canada (CSN), 296

Syndicat des agents de la paix en services correctionnels du Québec, 296

Syndicat des agents de maîtrise de TELUS (ind.), 296

Syndicat des employé(e)s de magasins et de bureau de la Société des alcools du Québec (ind.), 296

Syndicat des employés en radio-télédiffusion de Télé-Québec (CSQ), 296

Syndicat des pompiers et pompières du Québec (CTC), 296

Syndicat des professeurs et professeurs de l'Université du Québec à Chicoutimi, 296

Syndicat des professeurs de l'État du Québec (ind.), 296

Syndicat des technicien(ne)s et artisan(e)s du réseau français de Radio-Canada (ind.), 296

Syndicat des technologues en radiologie du Québec, 297

Syndicat des travailleurs de la construction du Québec (CSD), 297

Syndicat du personnel technique et professionnel de la Société des alcools du Québec (ind.), 297

Syndicat interprovincial des ferblantiers et couvreurs, la section locale 2016 à la FTQ-Construction, 297

Syndicat québécois de la construction, 297

T

Table de développement de la production biologique, 175

Tamil Eelam Society of Canada, 204

TD Friends of the Environment Foundation, 235

Tea & Herbal Association of Canada, 245

Teaching Support Staff Union, 297

Teamwork Children's Services International, 208

Technion Canada, 355

TechNova, 229

Tecumseh Community Development Corporation, 328

Telecommunities Canada Inc., 377

TelecomPioneers of Alberta, 377

TelecomPioneers of Canada, 377

Terrazzo Tile & Marble Association of Canada, 193

The Terry Fox Foundation, 275

TESL Canada Federation, 224

TESL Ontario, 224

Teslin Tlingit Council, 328

Thalidomide Victims Association of Canada, 275

Thermal Environmental Comfort Association, 276

Thermal Insulation Association of Canada, 193

Thinktv Inc., 188

Thompson Crisis Centre, 371

Thompson Okanagan Tourism Association, 380

Thompson, Nicola, Cariboo United Way, 371

Thrombosis Canada, 275

Thunder Bay Chamber of Commerce, 200

Thyroid Cancer Canada, 275

Thyroid Foundation of Canada, 275

Tillsonburg District Real Estate Board, 347

Tire & Rubber Association of Canada, 314

Tobacco Harm Reduction Association of Canada, 205

Together We Stand Foundation, 184

Toronto Association for Business Economics Inc., 200

Toronto Community Foundation, 371

Toronto Health Libraries Association, 310

Toronto International Film Festival Inc., 240

Toronto Japanese Association of Commerce & Industry, 314

Toronto Musicians' Association, 297

Toronto Police Association, 336

Toronto Press & Media Club, 343

Toronto Real Estate Board, 347

Tourette Canada, 276

Tourism Burlington, 380

Tourism Calgary, 380

Tourism Cape Breton, 380

Tourism Hamilton, 380

Tourism Industry Association of British Columbia, 380

Tourism Industry Association of Canada, 380

Tourism Industry Association of New Brunswick Inc., 380

Tourism Industry Association of Nova Scotia, 380

Tourism Industry Association of PEI, 380

Tourism Industry Association of the Yukon, 380

Tourism London, 381

Tourism Saint John, 381

Tourism Sarnia Lambton, 381

Tourism Saskatoon, 381

Tourism Simcoe County, 381

Tourism Thunder Bay, 381

Tourism Toronto, 381

Tourism Vancouver/Greater Vancouver Convention & Visitors Bureau, 381

Tourism Victoria/Greater Victoria Visitors & Convention Bureau, 381

Tourism Windsor Essex Pelee Island, 381

Tourisme Abitibi-Témiscamingue, 381

Tourisme Bas-Saint-Laurent, 381

Tourisme Cantons-de-l'Est, 381

Tourisme Centre-du-Québec, 381

Tourisme Chaudière-Appalaches, 381

Tourisme Côte-Nord, 381

Tourisme Gaspésie, 381

Tourisme Îles-de-la-Madeleine, 382

Tourisme Lanaudière, 381
Tourisme Laurentides, 381
Tourisme Laval, 382
Tourisme Mauricie, 382
Tourisme Montréal/Office des congrès et du tourisme du Grand Montréal, 382
Tourisme Montérégie, 382
Townshippers' Association, 206
Trade Facilitation Office Canada, 383
Trail Riders of the Canadian Rockies, 351
La Trame, 306
Trans Canada Trail Foundation, 351
Transition House Association of Nova Scotia, 387
TransParent Canada, 306
Travel & Tourism Research Association (Canada Chapter), 382
Travellers' Aid Society of Toronto, 382
Trillium Automobile Dealers' Association, 187
Trillium Gift of Life Network, 276
Trillium Party of Ontario, 340
Truro & Colchester Chamber of Commerce, 200
Truss Plate Institute of Canada, 314
Tunnelling Association of Canada, 229
Turkey Farmers of Canada, 340
Turkish Community Heritage Centre of Canada, 323
Turner Syndrome Society of Canada, 276
2-Spirited People of the First Nations, 328

U

UJA Federation of Greater Toronto, 323
Ukrainian Canadian Congress, 323
Ukrainian Canadian Research & Documentation Centre, 323
Ukrainian Democratic Youth Association, 323
Ukrainian National Federation of Canada, 323
Ukrainian Self-Reliance League of Canada, 323
Ukrainian War Veterans Association of Canada, 318
Ukrainian Women's Association of Canada, 323
Ukrainian Youth Association of Canada, 323
Underwater Archaeological Society of British Columbia, 183
Underwriters' Laboratories of Canada, 286
UNI Coopération financière, 242
UNIFOR, 297
UniforACL, 297
Union des artistes, 185
Union des Artistes (FIA) - Bureau de Québec, 297
Union des cultivateurs franco-ontariens, 238
Union des municipalités du Québec, 253
Union des producteurs agricoles, 175
Union des écrivaines et écrivains québécois, 388
Union of British Columbia Indian Chiefs, 328
Union of British Columbia Municipalities, 253
Union of Calgary Co-op Employees, 297
Union of Health & Environment Workers, 297
Union of Injured Workers of Ontario, 290
Union of Municipalities of New Brunswick, 253
Union of National Defence Employees, 297
Union of National Employees, 297
Union of Northern Workers, 297
Union of Nova Scotia Indians, 328
Union of Nova Scotia Municipalities, 253
Union of Ontario Indians, 328
Union of Postal Communications Employees, 297
Union of Safety & Justice Employees, 297
Union of Taxation Employees, 297
Union of Veterans' Affairs Employees, 297
Unison Benevolent Fund, 371
UNITE HERE, 297
UNITE HERE Canada, 297

United Brotherhood of Carpenters & Joiners of America (AFL-CIO/CLC), 297
United Conservative Association, 340
United Empire Loyalists' Association of Canada, 279
United Food & Commercial Workers Canada, 297
United Food & Commercial Workers' International Union, 298
United Generations Ontario, 372
United Mine Workers of America (CLC), 298
United Nations Association in Canada, 289
United Native Nations Society, 328
United Nurses of Alberta, 332
United Senior Citizens of Ontario Inc., 362
United Steelworkers of America (AFL-CIO/CLC), 298
United Way Alberta Northwest, 372
United Way Central & Northern Vancouver Island, 372
United Way Elgin-St. Thomas, 372
United Way for the City of Kawartha Lakes, 372
United Way Greater Toronto, 372
United Way Niagara, 372
United Way of Brandon & District Inc., 372
United Way of Burlington & Greater Hamilton, 372
United Way of Calgary & Area, 372
United Way of Cambridge & North Dumfries, 372
United Way of Canada - Centraide Canada, 372
United Way of Cape Breton, 372
United Way of Central Alberta, 372
United Way of Chatham-Kent County, 372
United Way of Cochrane-Timiskaming, 372
United Way of Cumberland County, 372
United Way of Durham Region, 372
United Way of East Kootenay, 372
United Way of Estevan, 372
United Way of Fort McMurray, 372
United Way of Greater Moncton & Southeastern New Brunswick, 372
United Way of Greater Saint John Inc., 372
United Way of Greater Simcoe County, 372
United Way of Guelph, Wellington & Dufferin, 373
United Way of Haldimand-Norfolk, 373
United Way of Halifax Region, 373
United Way of Halton Hills, 373
United Way of Kingston, Frontenac, Lennox & Addington, 373
United Way of Kitchener-Waterloo & Area, 373
United Way of Lanark County, 373
United Way of Leeds & Grenville, 373
United Way of Lethbridge & South Western Alberta, 373
United Way of London & Middlesex, 373
United Way of Milton, 373
United Way of Morden & District Inc., 373
United Way of North Okanagan Columbia Shuswap, 373
United Way of Northern BC, 373
United Way of Oakville, 373
United Way of Oxford, 373
United Way of Perth-Huron, 373
United Way of Peterborough & District, 373
United Way of Pictou County, 373
United Way of Prince Edward Island, 373
United Way of Quinte, 373
United Way of Regina, 373
United Way of Sarnia-Lambton, 374
United Way of Saskatoon & Area, 374
United Way of Sault Ste Marie & District, 374
United Way of South Eastern Alberta, 374
United Way of Stormont, Dundas & Glengarry, 374
United Way of the Alberta Capital Region, 374
United Way of the Central Okanagan & South Okanagan/Similkameen, 374
United Way of the Fraser Valley, 374

United Way of the Lower Mainland, 374
United Way of Trail & District, 374
United Way of Windsor-Essex County, 374
United Way of Winnipeg, 374
United Way/Centraide (Central NB) Inc., 374
United Way/Centraide Ottawa, 374
United Way/Centraide Sudbury & District, 374
United World Colleges, 224
Universities Canada, 224
Unparty: The Consensus-Building Party, 340
Urban Alliance on Race Relations, 323
Urban Development Institute Pacific Region, 335
Urban Municipal Administrators' Association of Saskatchewan, 253
USC Canada, 236

V

Vancouver International Children's Festival, 237
Vancouver Island Party, 340
Vancouver Island Real Estate Board, 347
Vancouver, Coast & Mountains Tourism Region, 382
Vanier Institute of The Family, 374
Vaping Advocacy & Education Project Inc., 283
Vaping Industry Trade Association, 283
Variety - The Children's Charity (Ontario), 362
Variety - The Children's Charity of BC, 362
Variety - The Children's Charity of Manitoba, Tent 58 Inc., 362
Variety Club of Northern Alberta, Tent 63, 362
Variety Club of Southern Alberta, 362
Vaughan Chamber of Commerce, 200
Vecova Centre for Disability Services & Research, 212
Vegetable Growers' Association of Manitoba, 175
Velo Halifax Bicycle Club, 351
Veterans Transition Network, 318
Victims of Violence, 374
Victoria Real Estate Board, 347
Victorian Order of Nurses for Canada, 332
Vides Canada, 289
Vietnamese Canadian Federation, 323
The Vimy Foundation, 279
Vintage Road Racing Association, 351
Vision Institute of Canada, 212
VISION TV, 188
Visual Arts Nova Scotia, 385
Vividata, 171
Vocational Rehabilitation Association of Canada, 276
VOICE for Children Who Are Deaf & Hard of Hearing, 276
Voice of Albertans with Disabilities, 212
Voices: Manitoba's Youth in Care Network, 201
Voie du peuple, 340
Volunteer Canada, 374
Volunteer Grandparents, 374

W

WABC Coaches Inc., 200
The War Amputations of Canada, 374
Warden Woods Community Centre, 374
Water Environment Association of Ontario, 236
Welcome Friend Association, 306
Wellesley & District Board of Trade, 200
Wellington Waterloo Dufferin Health Library Network, 310
West Vancouver Chamber of Commerce, 200
West Vancouver Municipal Employees' Association, 253
Western Association of Broadcast Engineers, 188
Western Association of Broadcasters, 188
Western Ayrshire Club, 179
Western Barley Growers Association, 175
Western Canada Children's Wear Markets, 238

Accounting

Canadian Academic Accounting Association (CAAA) / Association canadienne des professeurs de comptabilité (ACPC)
439 University Ave., 5th Fl., Toronto ON M5G 1Y8
Tel: 416-486-5361; *Fax:* 416-486-6158
admin@caaa.ca
www.caaa.ca
twitter.com/caaa_acpc
To promote excellence in accounting education & research in Canada with particular reference to Canadian post-secondary accounting programs & Canadian issues
Vittoria Fortunato, Manager, Finance & Administration

Canadian Bookkeepers Association
#482, 283 Danforth Ave., Toronto ON M4K 1N2
Fax: 866-804-4617
Toll-Free: 866-451-2204
www.c-b-a.ca
To promote, support, provide for & encourage Canadian bookkeepers; to promote & increase the awareness of Bookkeeping in Canada as a professional discipline; to support national, regional & local networking among Canadian Bookkeepers; to provide information on leading-edge procedures, education & technologies that enhance the industry, as well as, the Canadian bookkeeping professional; to support & encourage responsible & accurate bookkeeping practices throughout Canada
Guy Desmarais, President

Canadian Insurance Accountants Association (CIAA) / Association canadienne des comptables en assurance
#301, 250 Consumers Rd., Toronto ON M2J 4V6
Tel: 416-494-1440
info@ciaa.org
www.ciaa.org
www.linkedin.com/company/canadian-insurance-accountants-association
twitter.com/CIAA_Official
To promote study, research & development of management & insurance accounting
Daniel Singer, CPA, CA, President

Chartered Professional Accountants Canada (CPA) / Comptables professionnels agréés du Canada
277 Wellington St. West, Toronto ON M5V 3H2
Tel: 416-977-3222; *Fax:* 416-977-8585
Toll-Free: 800-268-3793
member.services@cpacanada.ca
www.cpacanada.ca
www.instagram.com/cpa.canada
www.linkedin.com/company/cpa-canada
www.facebook.com/CPACanada
twitter.com/CPAcanada
To foster public confidence in the chartered professional profession; To assist members to excel; To oversee a single, unified professional accounting designation known as CPA (note that some provinces/regions will be represented by a merged CPA body, while others will be represented by the legacy bodies until integration is complete)
Joy Thomas, MBA, FCPA, FCMA, President & CEO
Stephen Anisman, CPA, CMA, Chief Financial Officer
Tashia Batstone, MBA, FCPA, FCA, Senior Vice-President, External Relations & Business Development
Lou Ragagnin, BBA, CPA, CA, Senior Vice-President, Operations
Heather Whyte, MBA, APR, CDMP, Senior Vice-President, Marketing, Communications & Public Affairs
Bruce Ball, FCPA, FCA, CFP, Vice-President, Taxation
Gordon Beal, CPA, CA, M.Ed., Vice-President, Research, Guidance & Support
Nancy Foran, FCPA, FCMA, C.D, Vice-President, International
Stephenie Fox, CPA, CA, Vice-President, Financial Reporting & Assurance Standards Canada
Lorraine Pitt, MBA, CDMP, Vice-President, Marketing, Communications & Public Affairs
Janet Treasure, BA, FCPA, FCMA, Vice-President, Member Development & Support
Michele Wood-Tweel, FCPA, FCA, Vice-President, Regulatory Affairs

Chartered Professional Accountants of Alberta
#800, 444 - 7th Ave. SW, Calgary AB T2P 0X8
Tel: 403-299-1300; *Fax:* 403-299-1339
Toll-Free: 800-232-9406
info@cpaalberta.ca
www.cpaalberta.ca
www.facebook.com/CPAalberta
twitter.com/cpa_ab
To foster public confidence in the Chartered Professional Accountant profession in Alberta by helping members excel through professional development; To promote professional excellence within the CPA profession; To serve as the primary voice for the CPA profession in Alberta
Rachel Miller, FCA, FCPA, Chief Executive Officer
Yuen Ip, Chief Operating Officer
Cindy Priebe, Chief Financial Officer
Joe Hunder, Senior Vice-President, Regulatory
Gordon Turtle, Senior Vice-President, Communications & Business Development

Chartered Professional Accountants of British Columbia (CPABC)
#800, 555 West Hastings St., Vancouver BC V6B 4N6
Tel: 604-872-7222; *Toll-Free:* 800-663-2677
www.bccpa.ca
www.instagram.com/cpabc
www.linkedin.com/company/cpabritishcolumbia
www.facebook.com/cpabc
twitter.com/cpa_bc
To foster public confidence in the Chartered Professional Accountant profession in British Columbia by helping members excel through professional development; To promote professional excellence within the CPA profession; To serve as the primary voice for the CPA profession in British Columbia
Lori Mathison, LLB, FCPA, FCGA, President & Chief Executive Officer
Amy Lam, FCPA, FCA, CFO & Executive Vice-President, Corporate Services
James Midgley, FCPA, FCA, Executive Vice-President, Regulation & Registrar
Jan Sampson, FCPA, FCA, Executive Vice-President, Member & Student Experience

Chartered Professional Accountants of Manitoba (CPAMB)
#1675, 1 Lombard Place, Winnipeg MB R3B 0X3
Tel: 204-943-1538; *Fax:* 204-943-7119
Toll-Free: 800-841-7148
cpamb@cpamb.ca
www.cpamb.ca
www.linkedin.com/company/cpa-manitoba
www.facebook.com/CPAmanitoba
twitter.com/CPAManitoba
To foster public confidence in the Chartered Professional Accountant profession in Manitoba by helping members excel through professional development; To promote professional excellence within the CPA profession; To serve as the primary voice for the CPA profession in Manitoba
Todd Scaletta, FCPA, FCMA, President & CEO
Kathy Zaplitny, CPA, CA, Senior Director, Regulatory Affairs & Member Services
Dianne Laidler, CPA, CMA, Director, Finance

Chartered Professional Accountants of New Brunswick (CPANB) / Comptables professionnels agréés Nouveau-Brunswick
#602, 860 Main St., Moncton NB E1C 1G2
Tel: 506-830-3300; *Fax:* 506-830-3310
info@cpanewbrunswick.ca
www.cpanewbrunswick.ca
www.linkedin.com/company/cpa-new-brunswick-cpa-nouveau-brunswick
www.facebook.com/cpanewbrunswick
twitter.com/CPAnewbrunswick
To foster public confidence in the Chartered Professional Accountant profession in New Brunswick by helping members excel through professional development; To promote professional excellence within the CPA profession; To serve as the primary voice for the CPA profession in New Brunswick
Rock Lefebvre, MBA, FCPA, FCGA, President & Chief Executive Officer
Mylène Lapierre, CPA, CA, CFE, Senior Compliance Officer
Kristen Steeves, CPA, CGA, Senior Manager, Operations
Murielle Cormier, Officer, Admissions & Compliance

Chartered Professional Accountants of Newfoundland & Labrador (CPA NL)
95 Bonaventure Ave., 5th Fl., St. John's NL A1B 2X5
Tel: 709-753-3090; *Fax:* 709-753-3609
info@cpanl.ca
www.cpanl.ca
www.linkedin.com/company/cpa-nl
twitter.com/CPANL
To foster public confidence in the Chartered Professional Accountant profession in Newfoundland & Labrador by helping members excel through professional development; To promote professional excellence within the CPA profession; To serve as the primary voice for the CPA profession in Newfoundland & Labrador
Jason Hillyard, CPA, CGA, Chief Executive Officer

Kim Mayo, CPA, CA, Director, Professional Services & Operations
Kathryn Mercer-Oliver, Director, Regulatory Affairs & Registrar

Chartered Professional Accountants of Nova Scotia
#300, 1871 Hollis St., Halifax NS B3J 0C3
Tel: 902-425-7273; *Fax:* 902-407-2967
info@cpans.ca
www.cpans.ca
www.linkedin.com/company/cpanovascotia
www.facebook.com/CPANovaScotia
twitter.com/CPANovaScotia
To foster public confidence in the Chartered Professional Accountant profession in Nova Scotia by helping members excel through professional development; To promote professional excellence within the CPA profession; To serve as the primary voice for the CPA profession in Nova Scotia
Patricia (Patti) Towler, BA, JD, LLM, CI, President & CEO
Anne Robinson, B.Comm., CPA, C, Registrar & Senior Director, Regulatory Affairs
Amy MacIsaac, CPA, CA, Director, Member Services
Rodney Rodenhiser, B.Comm., CPA, C, Director, Finance & Administration

Chartered Professional Accountants of Ontario
69 Bloor St. East, Toronto ON M4W 1B3
Fax: 416-962-8900
Toll-Free: 800-387-0735
customerservice@cpaontario.ca
www.cpaontario.ca
www.instagram.com/gocpaontario
www.linkedin.com/company/cpa-ontario
www.facebook.com/CPAOntario
twitter.com/CPA_Ontario
To foster public confidence in the Chartered Professional Accountant profession in Ontario by helping members excel through professional development; To promote professional excellence within the CPA profession; To serve as the primary voice for the CPA profession in Ontario
Carol Wilding, FCPA, FCA, President & CEO
Julie Lam, CPA, CA, MBA, I, Executive Vice-President & COO
Elizabeth Cowie, Vice-President & General Counsel
Kelly Gorman, CPA, CA, Vice-President, Regulatory & Standards
Richard Piticco, CPA, CA, Vice-President, Student Services
Craig Smith, Vice-President, Member Services

Chartered Professional Accountants of Prince Edward Island (CPA PEI)
PO Box 301, #600, 97 Queen St., Charlottetown PE C1A 7K7
Tel: 902-894-4290; *Fax:* 902-894-4791
info@cpapei.ca
www.cpapei.ca
To foster public confidence in the Chartered Professional Accountant profession in Prince Edward Island by helping members excel through professional development; To promote professional excellence within the CPA profession; To serve as the primary voice for the CPA profession in Prince Edward Island
Tanya O'Brien, CPA, CA, Chief Executive Officer

Chartered Professional Accountants of Saskatchewan (CPA SK)
#101, 4581 Parliament Ave., Regina SK S4W 0G3
Tel: 306-359-0272; *Fax:* 306-347-8580
Toll-Free: 800-667-3535
info@cpask.ca
www.cpask.ca
To foster public confidence in the Chartered Professional Accountant profession in Saskatchewan by helping members excel through professional development; To promote professional excellence within the CPA profession; To serve as the primary voice for the CPA profession in Saskatchewan
Shelley Thiel, FCPA, FCA, Chief Executive Officer

Chartered Professional Accountants of the Northwest Territories & Nunavut
PO Box 128, Yellowknife NT X1A 2N1
Tel: 867-873-5020; *Fax:* 867-873-4469
admin@cpa-nwt-nu.org
www.cpa-nwt-nu.ca
To foster public confidence in the Chartered Professional Accountant profession in the Northwest Territories & Nunavut by helping members excel through professional development; To promote professional excellence within the CPA profession; To serve as the primary voice for the CPA profession in the Northwest Territories & Nunavut
Marlene Sutton, Executive Director

Chartered Professional Accountants of the Yukon (CPAYT)
c/o Chartered Professional Accountants of British Columbia, #800, 555 West Hastings St., Vancouver BC V6B 4N6
Tel: 604-872-7222; Toll-Free: 800-663-2677
www.bccpa.ca/yukon
www.youtube.com/user/cpabritishcolumbia
www.linkedin.com/company/cpabritishcolumbia
www.facebook.com/cpabc
twitter.com/cpa_bc
To foster public confidence in the Chartered Professional Accountant profession in the Yukon by helping members excel through professional development; To promote professional excellence within the CPA profession; To serve as the primary voice for the CPA profession in the Yukon
Lori Mathison, LL.B., FCPA, FC, President & CEO

Guild of Industrial, Commercial & Institutional Accountants / Guilde des comptables industriels, commerciaux et institutionnels
36 Tandian Ct., Woodbridge ON L4L 8Z9
Tel: 905-264-2713; Fax: 905-264-1043
iciaguild@aol.com
www.guildoficia.ca
To support & promote interest in vocational accountancy; To encourage acceptance of modern accounting methods & procedures
Laura Ballantyne, President

L'Ordre des comptables professionnels agréés du Québec
#800, 5, Place Ville Marie, Montréal QC H3B 2G2
Tél: 514-288-3256; Téléc: 514-843-8375
Ligne sans frais: 800-363-4688
info@cpaquebec.ca
cpaquebec.ca
www.instagram.com/cpaquebec
www.linkedin.com/groups/3996221
www.facebook.com/CPAquebec
twitter.com/CPAquebec
Favoriser la confiance du public dans la profession de comptable professionnel agréé en Québec en aidant ses membres à exceller dans le développement professionnel; Promouvoir l'excellence professionnelle au sein de la profession de CPA; Servir de principale voix pour la profession de CPA en Québec
Geneviève Mottard, CPA, CA, Présidente et chef de la direction
Manon Durivage, FCPA, FCA, Première vice-présidente, Encadrement et développement de la profession
Jean-François Lasnier, FCPA, FCMA, Premier vice-président, Opérations et rayonnement de la profession
Hélène Racine, FCPA, FCA, Vice-président, Accès à la profession et développement professionnel
Mélanie Charbonneau, CPA, CA, Vice-président, Administration, finances et soutien aux membres

Petroleum Accountants Society of Canada (PASC)
PO Box 4520, Stn. C, Calgary AB T2T 5N3
Tel: 403-262-4744; Fax: 403-244-2340
info@petroleumaccountants.com
www.petroleumaccountants.com
www.linkedin.com/groups/3814298
To contribute to the long term success of the Canadian petroleum industry by staying abreast of the constantly changing needs of the industry & striving to satisfy those needs
Paul Puscasu, President
Michelle Willis, Treasurer

The Society of Professional Accountants of Canada (SPAC) / La Société des comptables professionnels du Canada
#1007, 250 Consumers Rd., Toronto ON M2J 4V6
Tel: 416-350-8145; Fax: 416-350-8146
Toll-Free: 877-515-4447
admin@professionalaccountant.org
www.professionalaccountant.org
To provide ongoing education & to set qualifying standards, to ensure the professional competence of its members in the practice of accountancy
Edmund C. De Freitas, President & CEO

Addiction

Addictions Foundation of Manitoba (AFM) / Fondation manitobaine de lutte contre les dépendances
1031 Portage Ave., Winnipeg MB R3G 0R8
Tel: 204-944-6200; Fax: 204-944-7082
Toll-Free: 866-638-2561
execoff@afm.mb.ca
afm.mb.ca
To advance services related to addiction & to collaborate with community members in order to improve quality of life for Manitobans; To provide prevention, education & treatment programs related to addictions to individuals & communities; To conduct research into the negative effects of addictions
Ben Fry, CEO

Adult Children of Alcoholics (ACA)
#505, 5863 Leslie St., Toronto ON M2H 1J8
Tel: 416-631-3614
acatoronto@hotmail.com
www.acatoronto.org
To improve members' lives through the 12 step program

Airspace Action on Smoking & Health
PO Box 18004, 1215C - 56th St., Delta BC V4L 2M4
Tel: 778-899-4832
airspace.bc.ca
www.facebook.com/234024210003649
twitter.com/airspace_bc
To educate non-smokers on the effects that smoking has on them & of their legal right to smoke-free air; To help establish laws to protect the comfort, safety & health of non-smokers; To help reduce the number of future smokers

Al-Anon Family Groups (Canada), Inc. / Groupe familiaux Al-Anon
#900, 275 Slater St., Ottawa ON K1P 5H9
Tel: 613-723-8484
wso@al-anon.ca
www.al-anon.org
www.linkedin.com/company/al-anon-wso
www.facebook.com/AlAnonFamilyGroupsWSO
twitter.com/AlAnon_WSO
To provide support for friends & family members of alcoholics

Alcoholics Anonymous (GTA Intergroup) (AA)
#202, 234 Eglinton Ave. East, Toronto ON M4P 1K5
Tel: 416-487-5591; Fax: 416-928-2521
Toll-Free: 877-404-5591
TTY: 866-831-4657
info@aatoronto.org
www.aatoronto.org

Alcooliques Anonymes du Québec
Bureau des services de la Région 87, 3920, rue Rachel est, Montréal QC H1X 1Z3
Tél: 514-374-3688; Téléc: 514-374-2250
www.aa-quebec.org
Demeurer abstinent et aider d'autres alcooliques à le devenir
Marco L., Président

Canadian Assembly of Narcotics Anonymous (CANA)
PO Box 812, Stn. Edmonton Main, Edmonton AB T5J 2L4
canaacna.org
To help individuals who suffer from the disease of addiction

Canadian Centre on Substance Use & Addiction (CCSA) / Centre canadien sur les dépendances et l'usage de substances (CCLAT)
#500, 75 Albert St., Ottawa ON K1P 5E7
Tel: 613-235-4048; Fax: 613-235-8101
media@ccsa.ca
www.ccsa.ca
www.youtube.com/user/CCSACCLAT
www.linkedin.com/company/canadian-centre-on-substance-abus
e-ccsa-
twitter.com/CCSAcanada
To minimize the harm associated with addictions, including substance abuse & problem gambling
Rita Notarandrea, CEO
Rhowena Martin, Vice-President, Operations & Strategies
Amy Porath, Director, Research
Anne Richer, Director, Finance
Scott Hannant, Interim Director, Public Affairs & Communications
Darlene Pinto, Director, Human Resources
Rebecca Jesseman, Director, Policy

Centre for Addiction & Mental Health (CAMH) / Centre de toxicomanie et de santé mentale
250 College St., Toronto ON M5T 1R8
Tel: 416-535-8501; Toll-Free: 800-463-2338
www.camh.ca
www.youtube.com/camhtv
www.linkedin.com/company/camh
www.facebook.com/CentreforAddictionandMentalHealth
twitter.com/CAMHnews
To provide treatment for & research into substance abuse & mental health issues
Catherine Zahn, President & CEO

Drug Prevention Network of Canada (DPNC)
1695 53A St., Delta BC V4M 3G3
Tel: 778-838-0201
exec@dpnoc.org
www.dpnoc.org
www.drugpreventionnetworkofcanada.blogspot.ca
To advance abstinence-based drug & alcohol treatment recovery programs; To promote, through education & prevention, healthy lifestyles free of drugs; To oppose the legalization of drugs in Canada
Chuck Doucette, President

MADD Canada / Les mères contre l'alcool auvolant
#500, 2010 Winston Park Dr., Oakville ON L6H 5R7
Tel: 905-829-8805; Fax: 905-829-8860
Toll-Free: 800-665-6233
info@madd.ca
www.madd.ca
www.facebook.com/maddcanada.ca
twitter.com/maddcanada
To stop impaired driving & to support victims of this crime
Andrew Murie, CEO
Dawn Regan, COO

Overdose Prevention Society (OPS)
58 East Hastings St., Vancouver BC V6A 1N1
Tel: 778-952-2015
vancityoverdoseprevention.com
www.facebook.com/734627406687532
twitter.com/vancouverops
To prevent fatal drug overdoses in Vancouver; To reduce harm caused by drugs through the provision of peer-based services; To support cannabis use & reduce dependence on powerful opioids; To increase the number of sanctioned safe injection sites; To advocate for improved government response to the opioid crisis
Sarah Blyth, Executive Director

Parent Action on Drugs (PAD)
#121, 7 Hawksdale Rd., Toronto ON M3K 1W3
Tel: 416-395-4970; Toll-Free: 877-265-9279
pad@parentactionondrugs.org
www.parentactionondrugs.org
www.facebook.com/ParentActionOnDrugs
twitter.com/PAD_Ontario
To address issues of substance use among youth through outreach, prevention, education & parent support; enhances the capacity of parents, youth & communities to promote an environment that encourages youth to make informed choices
Joanne Brown, Executive Director

Physicians for a Smoke-Free Canada / Médecins pour un Canada sans fumée
134 Caroline Ave., Ottawa ON K1Y 0S9
Tel: 613-297-3590; Fax: 613-728-9049
psc@nospamsmoke-free.ca
www.smoke-free.ca
To address tobacco issues; To promote reduced smoking & prevent tobacco-caused illness
Atul Kapur, President
James Walker, Secretary-Treasurer

Responsible Gambling Council (Ontario) (RGC(O)) / Le Conseil ontarien pour le jeu responsable
#205, 411 Richmond St. East, Toronto ON M5A 3S5
Tel: 416-499-9800; Fax: 416-499-8260
www.responsiblegambling.org
www.youtube.com/user/RGCouncilCanada
www.linkedin.com/company/responsible-gambling-council
www.facebook.com/ResponsibleGamblingCouncil
twitter.com/RGCouncil
To increase awareness of compulsive gambling among families, community & service club leaders; To support research into the causes & treatment
Hamlin Grange, Chair
Shelley M. White, Chief Executive Officer

Advertising & Marketing

The Advertising & Design Club of Canada (ADCC)
#235, 401 Richmond St. West, Toronto ON M5V 3A8
Tel: 416-423-4113; Fax: 416-423-3362
info@theadcc.ca
www.theadcc.ca
www.facebook.com/TheADCC
twitter.com/TheADCC
To recognize, support & promote creative excellence in the Canadian advertising, publishing & design community
Fidel Pena, President
Dawn Wickstrom, Executive Director

Advertising Standards Canada (ASC) / Les normes canadiennes de la publicité
South Tower, #1801, 175 Bloor St. East, Toronto ON M4W 3R8
Tel: 416-961-6311; *Fax:* 416-961-7904
www.adstandards.com
To ensure the integrity & viability of advertising through industry self-regulation.
Linda J. Nagel, President/CEO

Alliance for Audited Media (AAM)
AAM Canada, PO Box 75066, 20 Bloor St. East, Toronto ON M4W 3T3
Tel: 647-793-7341
auditedmedia.com
www.youtube.com/user/auditedmedia
www.linkedin.com/company/alliance-for-audited-media
www.facebook.com/auditedmedia
twitter.com/auditedmedia
To be the pre-eminent self-regulatory auditing organization, responsible to advertisers, advertising agencies & the media they use, for the verification & dissemination of members' circulation data & other information for the benefit of the advertising marketplace in the United States & Canada
Tom Drouillard, President & Managing Director

Association canadienne des annonceurs inc.
#1250, 505, boul René Lévesque ouest, Montréal QC H2Z 1Y7
Tél: 514-842-6422; *Téléc:* 514-964-0771
Ligne sans frais: 800-565-0109
acaweb.ca
www.linkedin.com/company/association-of-canadian-advertisers
twitter.com/aca_tweets
Pour représenter les intérêts des entreprises de publicité et de marketing au Canada
Ron Lund, Président et chef de la direction

Association des agences de publicité du Québec (AAPQ) / Association of Québec Advertising Agencies
#925, 2015, rue Peel, Montréal QC H3A 1T8
Tél: 514-848-1732; *Téléc:* 514-848-1950
Ligne sans frais: 877-878-1732
aapq@aapq.ca
www.aapq.ca
Promouvoir et défendre les intérêts des agences membres
Dominique Villeneuve, Directrice générale

Association of Canadian Advertisers Inc. (ACA) / Association canadienne des annonceurs
#1008, 95 St. Clair Ave. West, Toronto ON M4V 1N6
Tel: 416-964-3805; *Fax:* 416-964-0771
Toll-Free: 800-565-0109
communications@acaweb.ca
acaweb.ca
www.linkedin.com/company/association-of-canadian-advertisers
twitter.com/ACA_tweets
To promote the common interests of advertisers & to provide expertise, education & information
Ron Lund, President & CEO
Judy Davey, Vice-President, Media Policy & Marketing Capabilities

The Canadian Agency Network (tCAN)
#300, 25 Sheppard Ave. West, Toronto ON M2N 6S6
Tel: 416-221-6984; *Fax:* 416-221-8260
tcan.co
To serve & support its members in every type of marketing & communications endeavour; Focuses on advertising, communications & marketing
Bill Whitehead, Managing Director

Canadian Automatic Merchandising Association (CAMA) / L'Association canadienne d'auto-distribution
Member Services, #304, 2233 Argentia Rd., Mississauga ON L5N 2X7
Tel: 905-826-7695; *Fax:* 905-826-4873
Toll-Free: 888-849-2262
info@vending-cama.com
www.vending-cama.com
www.linkedin.com/groups/8241090
twitter.com/CAMA_Vending
To represent the interests of Vending Operators, Machine Manufacturers, & Product & Service Suppliers in Canada
Chris Stegehuis, President
Marie Saint-Ivany, Executive Director

Canadian Media Directors' Council (CMDC)
175 Bloor St. East, Toronto ON M4W 3R8
www.cmdc.ca
www.instagram.com/cmdccanada
www.facebook.com/canadianmedialeadership
twitter.com/CMDCCanada
To advance media advertising in Canada; To create more efficient processes to execute and administer media transactions by adopting industry-wide standards
Shannon Lewis, President

Canadian Out-of-Home Marketing & Measurement Bureau (COMMB) / Bureau canadien du marketing et de l'évaluation de l'affichage
#605, 111 Peter St., Toronto ON M5V 2H1
Tel: 416-968-3823; *Fax:* 416-968-9396
Toll-Free: 800-866-1189
info@commb.ca
www.commb.ca
www.linkedin.com/company/out-of-home-marketing-association-of-canada
www.facebook.com/commbca
twitter.com/COMMBCA
To provide unbiased quantitative research; To aid members in the research & media measurement processes
Amanda Dorenberg, President

Conseil des directeurs médias du Québec (CDMQ)
#925, 2015, rue Peel, Montréal QC H3A 1T8
Tél: 514-990-1899
www.cdmq.ca
www.facebook.com/170319683021723
Etre un point de convergence d'opinions et d'information, un instrument de défense des intérêts des clients/agences et un outil de promotion et de stimulation de la fonction média
Michèle Savard, Présidente

Institute of Communication Agencies (ICA) / Institut des communications et de la publicité (ICP)
PO Box 2350, #3002, 2300 Yonge St., Toronto ON M4P 1E4
Tel: 416-482-1396; *Fax:* 416-482-1856
Toll-Free: 800-567-7422
ica@icacanada.ca
www.icacanada.ca
www.youtube.com/user/TheICAcanada
www.linkedin.com/company/institute-of-communication-agencies
twitter.com/icacanada
To anticipate, serve & promote the collective interests of ICA members, with regard to defining, developing & helping to maintain the highest possible standards of professional practice
Knox Scott, President & CEO

National Advertising Benevolent Society (NABS) / Société nationale de bienfaisance en publicité
#403, 55 St. Clair Ave. West, Toronto ON M4V 2Y7
Tel: 416-962-0446; *Fax:* 416-962-9149
Toll-Free: 800-661-6227
www.nabs.org
www.youtube.com/user/NABSCan
www.linkedin.com/company/nabs-canada
www.facebook.com/nabsCanada
twitter.com/NABS_Canada
To relieve the suffering of individuals & their families who have derived the majority of their income from advertising
Manuela Yarhi, Executive Director

National Association of Major Mail Users, Inc. (NAMMU) / Association nationale des grands usagers postaux inc. (ANGUP)
Toronto ON
Fax: 416-860-1097
Toll-Free: 877-477-5697
admin@nammu.ca
www.nammu.ca
www.linkedin.com/company/national-association-of-major-mail-users
To work in cooperation with Canada Post to improve cost & service

Promotional Product Professionals of Canada Inc. / Professionnels en produits promotionnels du Canada
#503, 386 Broadway St., Winnipeg MB R3C 3R6
Fax: 877-947-9767
Toll-Free: 866-450-7722
info@pppc.ca
pppc.ca
www.youtube.com/user/pppcinc
www.facebook.com/PPPC.ca
twitter.com/PPPCInc
To advance the promotional products industry; To act as the voice of the predominant advertising medium in Canada

Johnathan Strauss, President & CEO
Victoria Peers, Specialist, Communications
Pam Forsyth, Manager, Accounting
Radhouan Jebeniani, Coordinator, Member Services

Sign Association of Canada (SAC) / Association canadienne de l'enseigne (ACE)
#1801, 1 Yonge St., Toronto ON M5E 1W7
Tel: 905-856-0000; *Fax:* 905-856-0064
Toll-Free: 877-470-9787
sacinfo@signs.org
sac-ace.ca
www.linkedin.com/company/sign-association-of-canada
www.facebook.com/sacace
twitter.com/SACACE
To represent & support association members
Karin S. Eaton, Executive Director

Vividata
#1101, 77 Bloor St. West, Toronto ON M5S 1M2
Tel: 416-961-3205
info@vividata.ca
vividata.ca
www.linkedin.com/company/vividata
twitter.com/VividataCanada
To conduct research on the topics of print readership, non-print media exposure, product usage & lifestyles
Pat A. Pellegrini, President & CEO
Tosha Kirk, Vice-President, Client Services

Agriculture & Farming

Agricultural Alliance of New Brunswick (AANB) / Alliance agricole du Nouveau-Brunswick
2-150 Woodside Lane, Fredericton NB E3C 2R9
Tel: 506-452-8101; *Fax:* 506-452-1085
alliance@fermenbfarm.ca
www.fermenbfarm.ca
To promote & advance the social & economic conditions of those engaged in agricultural pursuits; To formulate & promote agricultural policies to meet changing economic conditions
Josée Albert, Chief Executive Officer
Nicole Arseneau, Office Manager

Agricultural Research & Extension Council of Alberta (ARECA)
#2, 5304 - 50 St., Leduc AB T9E 6Z6
Tel: 780-612-9712; *Fax:* 780-612-9711
www.areca.ab.ca
www.facebook.com/132819060066672
twitter.com/ARECAresearch
To provide agricultural producers with access to field research & new technology, in order to enhance & improve their operations
Janette McDonald, Executive Director

Agri-Food Innovation Council (AIC) / Conseil de l'innovation agroalimentaire
70 George St., 3rd Fl., Ottawa ON K1N 5V9
Tel: 613-232-9459; *Toll-Free:* 866-851-5689
office@aic.ca
www.aic.ca
twitter.com/agfoodinnov
To provide the voice for national knowledge & expertise; To promote the creation, production, & delivery of safe foods & sustainable use of related national resources in Canada & beyond
Serge Buy, Chief Executive Officer
Shannon Hallett, Manager, Finance

Alberta Association of Agricultural Societies (AAAS)
J.G. O'Donoghue Bldg., #108, 7000 - 113th St., Edmonton AB T6H 5T6
Tel: 780-427-2174; *Fax:* 780-422-1613
aaas@gov.ab.ca
www.albertaagsocieties.ca
To preserve & enhance the viability of agricultural societies in Alberta
Tim Carson, Chief Executive Officer

Alberta Barley Commission
#200, 6815 - 8th St. NE, Calgary AB T2E 7H7
Tel: 403-291-9111; *Fax:* 403-291-0190
Toll-Free: 800-265-9111
barleyinfo@albertabarley.com
www.albertabarley.com
www.youtube.com/user/albertabarley
twitter.com/AlbertaBarley
To support barley farmers & help advance the industry
Tom Steve, General Manager

Alberta Canola Producers Commission (ACPC)
Vantage Business Park, 14560 - 116 Ave. NW, Edmonton AB T5M 3E9

Tel: 780-454-0844; *Fax:* 780-451-6933
web@albertacanola.com
www.albertacanola.com
www.youtube.com/albertacanola
www.facebook.com/albertacanola
twitter.com/albertacanola

To provide leadership in a vibrant canola industry for the benefit of Alberta canola producers; to strive to improve the long-term profitability of Alberta canola producers
Ward Toma, General Manager

Alberta Federation of Agriculture
5033 - 52 St., Lacombe AB T4L 2A6

Tel: 403-789-9151; *Fax:* 780-789-9152
Toll-Free: 855-789-9151
info@afaonline.ca
www.afaonline.ca
twitter.com/AlbertaFedAg

To represent its members at the regional, provincial & national level for the benefit of agriculture; To create an atmosphere of cooperation & communication to ensure that areas of common concern among all producers are dealt with to the benefit of agriculture as a whole
Shannon Scofield, Executive Director

Alberta Institute of Agrologists
#1430, 5555 Calgary Trail NW, Edmonton AB T6H 5P9

Tel: 780-435-0606; *Fax:* 780-464-2155
Toll-Free: 855-435-0606
www.albertaagrologists.ca
www.linkedin.com/company/alberta-institute-of-agrologists
twitter.com/ABagrologists

To serve as a regulatory body within the province for matters related to agrology
David Lloyd, CEO & Registrar

Alberta Milk
1303 - 91 St. SW, Edmonton AB T6X 1H1

Tel: 780-453-5942; *Fax:* 780-455-2196
Toll-Free: 877-361-1231
cblatz@albertamilk.com
www.albertamilk.com
www.youtube.com/user/albertamilk
www.linkedin.com/company/alberta-milk
www.facebook.com/MoreAboutMilk
twitter.com/MoreAboutMilk

To promote the sustainability of the dairy industry in Alberta
Tom Kootstra, Chair
Mike Southwood, General Manager
Denise Brattinga, Manager, Finance
Mike Slomp, Manager, Industry & Member Services
Katherine Loughlin, Manager, Marketing, Nutrition & Education
Gerd Andres, Manager, Policy and Transportation

Animal Nutrition Association of Canada (ANAC) / Association de nutrition animale du Canada
#1301, 150 Metcalfe St., Ottawa ON K2P 1P1

Tel: 613-241-6421; *Fax:* 613-241-7970
info@anacan.org
www.anacan.org

To advocate on behalf of the livestock & poultry feed industry with government regulators & policy-makers; To maintain high standards of feed & food safety
Melissa Dumont, Executive Director

Association des jeunes ruraux du Québec (AJRQ)
#105, 555, boul Roland-Therrien, Longueuil QC J4H 4E7

Tel: 819-364-5606
info@ajrq.qc.ca
www.ajrq.qc.ca

Promouvoir la formation auprès de nos membres; soutenir leur sentiment d'appartenance au milieu rural
Valérie Giard, Présidente
Anaïs Thibodeau, Coordonnatrice

Association des technologues en agroalimentaire (ATA) / Agricultural Technologists Association Inc.
3230, rue Sicotte, Saint-Hyacinthe QC J2S 2M2

Tél: 450-778-6504
assotechnologues@gmail.com
www.technologuesagroalimentaire.com

Défendre des intérêts professionnels; promouvoir la profession et le perfectionnement des membres
Patrick Sullivan, Directeur général

Association québécoise des industries de nutrition animale et céréalière (AQINAC)
#100, 4790, rue Martineau, Saint-Hyacinthe QC J2R 1V1

Tel: 450-799-2440; *Téléc:* 450-799-2445
info@aqinac.com
www.aqinac.com
twitter.com/AQINAC

Ôtre le leader dans la défense et la promotion de la production et de la nutrition animales tout en contribuant au développement d'une industrie agroalimentaire moderne et durable
Yvan Lacroix, Président-directeur général
Sébastien Lacroix, Directeur général adjoint

Atlantic Dairy Council (ADC)
PO Box 9410, Stn. A, #700, 6009 Quinpool Rd., Halifax NS B3K 5S3

Tel: 902-425-2445; *Fax:* 902-425-2441
info@adcrecycles.com
www.adcrecycles.com

To maintain good relations among those engaged in dairy processing & distribution industries; to provide opportunities for industry training courses; & to enable united action on any matter concerning the welfare of the dairy trade
John K. Sutherland, Executive Secretary

Barley Council of Canada (BCC)
#200, 6815 - 8 St. NE, Calgary AB T2E 7H7

Toll-Free: 800-265-9111
info@barleycouncil.com
www.barleycanada.com
www.linkedin.com/company/barley-council-of-canada
twitter.com/BarleyCanada

To drive the growth & profitability of the barley industry in Canada; To represent members
Brian Otto, Chair

British Columbia Fruit Growers' Association
880 Vaughan Ave., Kelowna BC V1Y 7E4

Tel: 250-762-5226; *Fax:* 250-861-9089
Toll-Free: 800-619-9022
info@bcfga.com
www.bcfga.com
www.facebook.com/208331935875260

To represent fruit growers' interests in British Columbia
Glen Lucas, General Manager

British Columbia Grapegrowers' Association (BCGA)
PO Box 1138, Penticton BC V2A 6J9

Toll-Free: 877-762-4652
www.grapegrowers.bc.ca

To represent British Columbia's commercial grape producers on agricultural issues & concerns; To advance the interests of grapegrowers in British Columbia

British Columbia Institute of Agrologists (BCIA)
2777 Claude Rd., Victoria BC V9B 3T7

Tel: 250-380-9292; *Fax:* 250-380-9233
Toll-Free: 877-855-9291
admin@bcia.com
www.bcia.com
www.facebook.com/bcinstituteofagrologists

To ensure the professional integrity & competency of members to protect the public interest in the sustainable use of resources; To protect the scientific methods & principles that are the foundation of agrology
JP Ellson, Executive Director

Canada Grains Council (CGC)
#703, 350 Sparks St, Ottawa ON K1R 7S8

Tel: 613-422-0166
office@canadagrainscouncil.ca
canadagrainscouncil.ca

To be the primary networking group for those involved in the grain industry
Cam Dahl, Chair
Rick White, Vice-Chair
Tyler Bjornson, President

Canadian 4-H Council / Conseil des 4-H du Canada
Central Experimental Farm, Bldg. 106, 960 Carling Ave., Ottawa ON K1A 0C6

Tel: 613-759-1013; *Fax:* 613-759-1016
Toll-Free: 844-759-1013
info@4-h-canada.ca
www.4-h-canada.ca
www.instagram.com/4hcanada
www.linkedin.com/company/4hcanada
www.facebook.com/4HCanada
twitter.com/4HCanada

To empower youth to be responsible, caring & contributing leaders that effect positive change in the world around them
Shannon Benner, Chief Executive Officer

Jay Poulton, Director, Marketing & Communications

Canadian Beef
Eastern Office, #210, 2550 Argentia Rd., Mississauga ON L5N 5R1

Tel: 905-821-4900
info@canadabeef.ca
canadabeef.ca
www.youtube.com/user/LoveCDNBeef
www.linkedin.com/company/canada-beef-inc-
www.facebook.com/LoveCDNBeef
twitter.com/canadianbeef

To build consumer demand for beef
Michael Young, President
Ron Glaser, Vice-President, Corporate Affairs
Michele McAdoo, Executive Director, Communications
Joyce Parslow, Executive Director, Consumer Marketing

Canadian Canola Growers Association (CCGA)
#400, 1661 Portage Ave., Winnipeg MB R3J 3T7

Tel: 204-788-0090; *Fax:* 204-788-0039
Toll-Free: 866-745-2256
ccga@ccga.ca
www.ccga.ca

To supprt canola producers by voicing their concerns about national & international issues
Rick White, General Manager
Kelly Green, Director, Communications

Canadian Federation of Agriculture (CFA) / Fédération canadienne de l'agriculture (FCA)
21 Florence St., Ottawa ON K2P 0W6

Tel: 613-236-3633; *Fax:* 613-236-5749
info@canadian-farmers.ca
www.cfa-fca.ca
www.facebook.com/CanadianFederationofAgriculture
twitter.com/CFAFCA

To coordinate the efforts of agricultural producer organizations throughout Canada for the purpose of promoting their common interests through collective action; to promote & advance the social & economic conditions of those engaged in agricultural pursuits; to assist in formulating & promoting national agricultural policies to meet changing national & international conditions
Mary Robinson, President
Errol Halkai, Executive Director
Laurie Karson, Director, Communications

Canadian Foundation for Food & Agricultural Education (CFFAE)
#109, 2020 Lanthier Dr., Ottawa ON K4A 3V4

manager@cffae.ca
cffae.ca

To enhance agriculture & the role it plays in providing Canadians with a safe, affordable, nutritious food supply

Canadian Honey Council (CHC) / Conseil canadien du miel (CCM)
#218, 51519 RR#220, Sherwood Park AB T8E 1H1

Toll-Free: 877-356-8935
chc-ccm@honeycouncil.ca
www.honeycouncil.ca
twitter.com/honeycouncil

To promote, develop & maintain cooperation among all persons, organizations & government personnel involved with Canadian beekeeping industry
Rod Scarlett, Executive Director

Canadian Organic Growers Inc. (COG) / Cultivons Biologique Canada Inc.
#600, 56 Sparks St., Ottawa ON K1P 5B1

Tel: 613-216-0741; *Fax:* 613-236-0743
Toll-Free: 888-375-7383
office@cog.ca
www.cog.ca
www.instagram.com/canadianorganic
www.facebook.com/CanadianOrganic
twitter.com/CanadianOrganic

To conduct research into alternatives to traditional chemical & energy-intensive food growing practices; To provide a resource base & a forum open to all farmers & food growers interested in alternative agriculture; To foster the goals of a decentralized, bio-regionally-based food system; To endorse practices which promote & maintain long-term soil fertility, reduce fossil fuel uses, reduce pollution, recycle wastes & conserve non-renewable resources; To assist the farmer, grower, food processor & consumer, through education & demonstration, in understanding the value of organic foods
Wayne Adams, Executive Director
Catherine Shaw, Director, Marketing & Communications

Canadian Pest Management Association (CPMA) / Association canadienne de la gestion parasitaire (ACGP)
#360, 13 - 3120 Rutherford Rd., Vaughan ON L4K 0B2
Fax: 866-957-7378
Toll-Free: 866-630-2762
cpma@pestworld.org
pestworldcanada.net
To provide pest management information; To act as the voice of the pest management industry throughout Canada; Upholding the association's Code of Ethics
Stan Burton, President

Canadian Plowing Organization
Sunderland ON L0C 1H0
Tel: 905-926-7642
To preserve the art of match plowing in Canada; To promote the efficient operation & use of farm machinery; To promote improved farm productivity & yield efficiency through proper seed bed preparation & soil management
Thomas Murdock, President

Canadian Seed Growers' Association (CSGA) / Association canadienne des producteurs de semences
PO Box 8455, Ottawa ON K1G 3T1
Tel: 613-236-0497; *Fax:* 613-563-7855
seeds@seedgrowers.ca
seedgrowers.ca
twitter.com/Seedgrowers
To advance the Canadian seed industry; To advocate for the use of the seed certification as an integral part of quality & identity assurance programs; To develop & provide seed crop certification standards & regulations
Glyn Chancey, Executive Director

Canadian Seed Trade Association (CSTA) / Association canadienne du commerce des semences (ACCS)
#300, 130 Albert St., Ottawa ON K1P 5G4
Tel: 613-829-9527; *Fax:* 613-829-3530
info@seedinnovation.ca
seedinnovation.ca
www.instagram.com/seedinnovation
www.linkedin.com/company/canadian-seed-trade-association
www.facebook.com/cdnseed
twitter.com/SeedInnovation
To foster an environment conducive to researching, developing, distributing, & trading seed & associated technologies
Tyler McCann, Interim Executive Director

Canadian Society for Bioengineering (CSBE) / Société canadienne de génie agroalimentaire et de bioingénierie (SCGAB)
Dept. of Biosystems Engineering, EITC Bldg., Univ. of Manitoba, 75A Chancellor Circle, #E2-376, Winnipeg MB R3T 5V6
Tel: 780-487-2648
csbe-scgab.ca
To provide expertise in the areas of farm power & machinery, structures & environment, soil & water & electrical power & processing
Chandra Madramootoo, President
John Feddes, Society Manager

Canadian Society of Agronomy (CSA)
PO Box 637, Pinawa MB R0E 1L0
Tel: 204-299-2327
agronomycanada.com
www.facebook.com/AgronomyCanada
twitter.com/AgronomyCanada
To enhance cooperation & coorindation among agronomists; To recognize significant achievements in agronomy; To provide the oppourtunity to report & evaluate information pertinent to agronomy in Canada
Nancy Zubriski, Executive Director

Canadian Sphagnum Peat Moss Association (CSPMA) / Association canadienne Tourbe de Sphaigne
#2208, 13 Mission Ave., St Albert AB T8N 1H6
Tel: 780-460-8280; *Fax:* 780-459-0939
cspma@peatmoss.com
peatmoss.com
To promote the benefits of peat moss to horticulturists & home gardeners throughout North America
Paul Short, President

Canola Council of Canada
#400, 167 Lombard Ave., Winnipeg MB R3B 0T6
Tel: 204-982-2100; *Fax:* 204-942-1841
Toll-Free: 866-834-4378
admin@canolacouncil.org
www.canolacouncil.org
www.youtube.com/c/CanolaCouncil
www.facebook.com/CanolaWatchCCC
twitter.com/canolacouncil
To enhance the Canadian canola industry's ability to profitably produce & supply seed, oil & meal products that offer superior value to customers throughout the world
Jim Everson, President
Émilie Bergeron, Director, Public Affairs
Heidi Dancho, Director, Communications

Certified Organic Associations of British Columbia (COABC)
#202, 3002 - 32nd Ave., Vernon BC V1T 2L7
Tel: 250-260-4429; *Fax:* 250-260-4436
office@certifiedorganic.bc.ca
www.certifiedorganic.bc.ca
To maintain a credible set of organic production & processing standards
Jen Gamble, Administrator

Christian Farmers Federation of Ontario (CFFO)
642 Woolwich St., Guelph ON N1H 3Y2
Tel: 519-837-1620; *Toll-Free:* 855-800-0306
cffomail@christianfarmers.org
www.christianfarmers.org
www.instagram.com/cffont
www.facebook.com/CFFOnt
twitter.com/CFFOnt
To enable members as producers, marketers & citizens by developing both the entrepreneurial & community leadership of members; To promote a family farm & stewardship perspective; To be upfront about the Christian value system that motivates members, in order to make the wisdom of the Christian faith available to farm practice & farm policy
Clarence Nywening, Interim General Manager
Suzanne Armstrong, Director, Research & Policy

Les Clubs 4-H du Québec
#202, 6500 boul Arthur-Sauvé, Laval QC H7R 3X7
Tél: 450-314-1942; *Téléc:* 450-314-1952
info@clubs4h.qc.ca
www.clubs4h.qc.ca
www.facebook.com/LesClubs4HDuQuebec
Développer l'intérêt et les compétences des jeunes relativement à la nature, la forêt et l'environnement par des activités éducatives et de loisir
Andrée Gignac, Directrice

Commercial Seed Analysts Association of Canada Inc. (CSAAC)
5788 L&A Rd., Vernon BC V1B 3PG
Tel: 204-720-0052
www.seedanalysts.ca
To help determine the future of the seed industry; to enhance professionalism through ongoing education; to provide customers with seed analysis services & information
Morgan Webb, President
Krista Erickson, Executive Director

Conseil des industriels laitiers du Québec inc. (CILQ) / Québec Dairy Council Inc.
#307, 2035, av Victoria, Saint-Lambert QC J4S 1H1
Tél: 450-486-7331; *Téléc:* 450-486-7017
cilq@cilq.ca
cilq.ca
Regrouper les entreprises laitières industrielles du Québec qui s'occupent des différentes phases de la transformation, distribution et commercialisation du lait et des produits laitiers; promotion, protection et développement de leurs intérêts économiques, sociaux et professionnels
Charles Langlois, Président-directeur général
Yolaine Villeneuve, Directrice, Affaires publiques & corporatives

CropLife Canada
#1201, 350 Sparks St., Ottawa ON K1R 7S8
Tel: 613-230-9881
www.croplife.ca
www.youtube.com/croplifecanada
twitter.com/croplifecanada
To represent Canada's plant science industry; To foster the development of the industry; To build Canadians' trust & appreciation for plant science innovations
Pierre Petelle, President & CEO
Alan Schlachter, Vice-President, Chemistry
Nadine Sisk, Vice-President, Communications & Member Services
Dennis Prouse, Vice-President, Government Affairs

Russel Hurst, Vice-President, Sustainability & Stewardship
Ian Affleck, Vice-President, Plant Biotechnology
Maria Trainer, Managing Director, Science & Regulatory Affairs, Chemistry
Jennifer Hubert, Director, Plant Biotechnology
Hillary Lutes, Communications Officer

Dairy Farmers of Canada (DFC) / Les Producteurs laitiers du Canada (PLC)
21 Florence St., Ottawa ON K2P 0W6
Tel: 613-236-9997; *Fax:* 613-236-0905
communications@dfc-plc.ca
dairyfarmers.ca
www.youtube.com/user/DairyFarmersofCanada
www.facebook.com/dfcplc
twitter.com/dfc_plc
To coordinate action of dairy producer organizations on all issues of national scope; To collaborate with relevant agencies in elaboration of national policies of interest to Canadian dairy industry
Pierre Lampron, President

Dairy Farmers of Nova Scotia (DFNS)
#100, 4060 Hwy. 236, Lower Truro NS B6L 1J9
Tel: 902-893-6455; *Fax:* 902-897-9768
www.dfns.ca
To provide a regulatory & administrative service to Nova Scotia's dairy producers
Brian Cameron, General Manager

Egg Farmers of Canada (EFC) / Producteurs d'oufs du Canada
21 Florence St., Ottawa ON K2P 0W6
Tel: 613-238-2514
www.eggfarmers.ca
www.instagram.com/eggsoeufs
www.linkedin.com/company/egg-farmers-of-canada
www.facebook.com/eggsoeufs
twitter.com/eggsoeufs
To forcast demand for eggs; To promote eggs nationally; To develop national standards for egg farming
Roger Pelissero, Chair
Tim Lambert, Chief Executive Officer
Judi Bundrock, Chief Marketing & Communications Officer

Éleveurs de porcs du Québec
#120, 555, boul Roland-Therrien, Longueuil QC J4H 4E9
Tél: 450-679-0540; *Téléc:* 450-679-0102
leseleveursdeporcs@upa.qc.ca
www.leseleveursdeporcsduquebec.com
www.youtube.com/user/leporcduquebec
www.facebook.com/Porcduquebec
twitter.com/PorcQc
A l'ordre du jour du Plan agroenvironnemental de la production porcine on trouve; l'application de plans de fertilisation sur toutes les fermes; la diminution des rejets de phosphore et d'azote pour éviter la surfertilisation; la réduction des odeurs; l'utilisation du lisier comme matière fertilisante; mise en place d'actions collectives
David Boissonneault, Président

Farmers of North America (FNA)
320 - 22nd St. East, Saskatoon SK S7K 0H1
Tel: 306-665-2294; *Fax:* 306-651-0444
Toll-Free: 877-362-3276
info@fna.ca
fna.ca
www.linkedin.com/company/farmers-of-north-america
www.facebook.com/FNACanada
twitter.com/fna_canada
To improve farm profitability across Canada
James Mann, President & CEO

Farmers of North America Strategic Agriculture Institute (FNA-SAG)
320 - 22nd St. East, Saskatoon SK S7K 0H1
Tel: 306-665-4529; *Fax:* 306-651-0444
www.fnastag.ca
To identify new methods for farm profitability; To identify policy & regulatory issues affecting profitability; To help advocate for change; To identify areas of needed research
Bob Friesen, Chief Executive Officer
Tooba Sabir, Director, Research

Fédération des agricultrices du Québec (FAQ)
555, boul Roland-Therrien, Longueuil QC J4H 4E7
Tél: 450-679-0540; *Téléc:* 450-463-5228
fed.agricultrices@upa.qc.ca
www.agricultrices.com
www.facebook.com/fed.agricultrices
Valoriser la profession; créer un réseau entre les femmes; avoir une force politique capable de défendre les intérêts des agricultrices; prodiguer de la formation

Fédération des producteurs de bovins du Québec (FPBQ) / Federation of Québec Beef Producers
#305, 555, boul Roland-Therrien, Longueuil QC J4H 4G2
Tél: 450-679-0530; Téléc: 450-442-9348
www.bovin.qc.ca

Regrouper et défendre les intérêts professionnels et économiques des producteurs de bovins du Québec; administrer et appliquer le plan conjoint des producteurs de bovins du Québec
Claude Viel, Président
Guy Gallant, Vice-président

Foreign Agricultural Resource Management Services (FARMS)
#706, 5995 Avebury Rd., Mississauga ON L5R 3P9
Fax: 905-568-4175
Toll-Free: 866-271-0862
www.farmsontario.ca

To facilitate & coordinate requests for foreign seasonal agricultural workers
Ken Forth, President
Sue Williams, General Manager

Grain Growers of Canada (GGC)
#912, 350 Sparks St., Ottawa ON K1R 7S8
Tel: 613-233-9954; Fax: 613-236-3590
office@ggc-pgc.ca
www.ggc-pgc.ca

To supprt policies that allow for a competitive global farming industry
Stephen Vandervalk, President
Janet Krayden, Manager, Public Affairs

Horticulture Nova Scotia (HORT NS)
Kentville Agricultural Centre, 32 Main St., Kentville NS B4N 1J5
Tel: 902-678-9335; Fax: 902-678-1280
info@horticulturens.ca
www.horticulturens.ca
www.facebook.com/horticulture.novascotia
twitter.com/horticultureNS

To enhance collaborative efforts among members which will strengthen & provide leadership to the horticultural industry
Marlene Huntley, Executive Director
Kiki Cliff, Administrative Officer

Inland Terminal Association of Canada (ITAC)
PO Box 283, Elbow SK S0H 1J0
Tel: 306-854-4554
www.inlandterminal.ca

To supprt & promote the interests of people working with inland terminals
Kevin Hursh, Executive Director

International Federation of Agricultural Journalists (IFAJ)
PO Box 250, Ormstown QC J0S 1K0
Toll-Free: 877-782-6456
www.ifaj.org

To give agricultural journalists & communicators opportunities for professional development & international networking
Owen Roberts, President
Steve Werblow, Secretary-General

Keystone Agricultural Producers (KAP)
#601, 386 Broadway Ave., Winnipeg MB R3C 3R6
Tel: 204-697-1140; Fax: 204-697-1109
kap@kap.ca
www.kap.ca
twitter.com/KAP_Manitoba

To be a democratic & effective policy organization, promoting the social, economic & physical well-being of all Manitoban agricultural producers
James Battershill, General Manager

Manitoba Institute of Agrologists (MIA)
#201, 38 Dafoe Ave., Winnipeg MB R3T 2N2
Tel: 204-275-3721; Fax: 888-315-6661
agrologist@mia.mb.ca
www.mia.mb.ca
www.linkedin.com/company/manitoba-institute-of-agrologists

To act in accordance with the Agrologists Act of Manitoba; To regulate the practice of agrology in Manitoba; To ensure the knowledge, competence, & integrity of institute members, in order to protect the public interest; To act as the voice of the agrology profession
Jim Weir, Executive Director & Registrar

Mushrooms Canada (CMGA)
PO Box 100, 60 Elora St. South, Harriston ON N0G 1Z0
Tel: 519-510-8888
www.mushrooms.ca
www.youtube.com/cdnmushroom
www.facebook.com/mushroomscanada
twitter.com/mushroomscanada

To encourage cooperation & communication within the Canadian industry, with various levels of government & with related organizations internationally; To promote mushroom consumption
Ryan Koeslag, Chief Executive Officer

National Farmers Foundation
c/o Glen Koroluk, 595 Goulding St., Winnipeg MB R3G 2S3
nfu@nfu.ca
www.nfu.ca/about/national-farmers-foundation

To stimulate rural / urban cooperation; To fund education & research that will further the progressive farm movement in Canada
Michelle Melnyk, President

National Farmers Union (NFU) / Syndicat national des cultivateurs
2717 Wentz Ave., Saskatoon SK S7K 4B6
Tel: 306-652-9465; Fax: 306-664-6226
nfu@nfu.ca
www.nfu.ca
www.facebook.com/nfuCanada
twitter.com/NFUcanada

To improve economic & social well-being of rural people & rural communities; To ensure family farms are a primary unit of food production
Mara Shaw, Executive Director
Joan Lange, Director, Finance & Administration
Cathy Holtslander, Director, Research & Policy

New Brunswick Institute of Agrologists (NBIA) / L'Institut des agronomes du Nouveau-Brunswick (IANB)
PO Box 3479, Stn. B, Fredericton NB E3B 5H2
Tel: 506-459-5536; Fax: 506-454-7837
www.ianbia.com

To maintain high competency & professional standards for those practicing agrology in New Brunswick; To uphold the NBIA Code of Ethics; To offer advice to the public about agriculture & related areas; To formulate policies & improve the agriculture & food industry
Nicole Williams, President
Susannah Banks, Vice-President
Duncan Fraser, Secretary & Treasurer

Newfoundland & Labrador Federation of Agriculture
PO Box 1045, 308 Brookfield Rd., Mount Pearl NL A1N 3C9
Tel: 709-747-4874; Fax: 709-747-8827
info@nlfa.ca
www.nlfa.ca
www.facebook.com/nlfarms
twitter.com/NLFarms

To act as the united voice of farmers in Newfoundland & Labrador; To improve the agricultural industry in Newfoundland & Labrador; To advance the economic & social conditions of those in the agricultural industry
Paul Connors, Executive Director
Nicole Parrell, Financial Officer

Newfoundland & Labrador Institute of Agrologists (NLIA)
PO Box 978, Mount Pearl NL A1N 3C9
Tel: 709-772-4170
www.aic.ca/agrology/nlia.cfm

Dedicated to the professional aspects of Canadian agriculture.
Gary Bishop, President/Treasurer
Samir Debnath, Registrar

Nova Scotia Federation of Agriculture (NSFA)
Perennia Innovation Park, 60 Research Dr., Bible Hill NS B6L 2R2
Tel: 902-893-2293; Fax: 902-893-7063
info@nsfa-fane.ca
www.nsfa-fane.ca

To act as the voice for the agricultural community in Nova Scotia; To ensure a competitive & sustainable future for agriculture in Nova Scotia; To build financially viable, ecologically sound, & socially responsible farm businesses in the province
Henry Vissers, Executive Director

Nova Scotia Fruit Growers' Association (NSFGA)
Kentville Agricultural Centre, 32 Main St., Kentville NS B4N 1J5
Tel: 902-678-1093; Fax: 902-678-1567
contact@nsapples.com
www.nsfga.com
www.facebook.com/nsfga
twitter.com/nsfga1863

To serve the interests of tree fruit growers in Nova Scotia
C. Andrew Parker, President

Nova Scotia Institute of Agrologists (NSIA)
Annapolis Building, 60 Research Dr., Bible Hill NS B6L 2R2
Tel: 902-897-6742
info@nsagrologists.ca
www.nsagrologists.ca

Carolyn Van Den Heuvel, President

Ontario Agri Business Association (OABA)
#104, 160 Research Lane, Guelph ON N1G 5B2
Tel: 519-822-3004; Fax: 519-822-8862
info@oaba.on.ca
www.oaba.on.ca

To serve & represent firms engaged in the crop inputs, country grain elevator, & feed & farm supply industy, plus related agricultural businesses operating within Ontario
Dave Buttenham, Chief Executive Officer
Darcy Oliphant, President
Dave Bender, Vice-President
Cassandra Loomans, Treasurer

Ontario Agri-Food Technologies (OAFT)
Agri-Technology Commercialization Centre, #200, 120 Research Lane, Guelph ON N1G 0B4
Tel: 519-826-4195; Fax: 519-821-7361
info@oaft.org
www.oaft.org

To generate wealth & sustainability for the Ontario agriculture & food industries by utilizing current technologies
Tyler Whale, President
Andrea Murray, Program Administrator

Ontario Beekeepers' Association (OBA)
490 York Rd., Guelph ON N1E 6V1
Tel: 905-636-0661; Fax: 905-636-0662
info@ontariobee.com
www.ontariobee.com
www.instagram.com/obattp
www.facebook.com/471022232933063
twitter.com/ontariobee

To coordinate & advance the beekeeping industry in Ontario
Bernie Wiehle, President
Adam Ritchie, 1st Vice-President
Ian Grant, 2nd Vice-President

Ontario Dairy Council (ODC)
6533D Mississauga Rd., Mississauga ON L5N 1A6
Tel: 905-542-3620; Fax: 905-542-3624
Toll-Free: 866-542-3620
info@ontariodairies.ca
www.ontariodairies.ca

To represent interests of dairy product processors, marketers & distributors in Ontario
Christina Lewis, President

Ontario Federation of Agriculture (OFA)
200 Hanlon Creek Blvd., Guelph ON N1C 0A1
Tel: 519-821-8883; Fax: 519-821-8810
Toll-Free: 800-668-3276
www.ofa.on.ca
www.youtube.com/user/ontariofarms
www.facebook.com/ontariofarms
twitter.com/ontariofarms

To represent farm families throughout Ontario; To champion the interests of Ontario farmers; To work towards a sustainable future for farmers
Cathy Lennon, General Manager

Ontario Fruit & Vegetable Growers' Association (OFVGA) / L'Association des fruiticulteurs et des maraîchers de l'Ontario
#105, 355 Elmira Rd. North, Guelph ON N1K 1S5
Tel: 519-763-6160; Fax: 519-763-6604
info@ofvga.org
www.ofvga.org
www.facebook.com/ofvga
twitter.com/OntFruitVeg

Dedicated to the advancement of horticulture, working proactively through effective lobbying for the betterment of the industry & producers as a whole through advocacy, research, education, communication & marketing
Jason Verkaik, Chair
John Kelly, Executive Vice President

Ontario Institute of Agrologists (OIA)
Ontario AgriCentre, #108, 100 Stone Rd. West, Guelph ON N1G 5L3
Tel: 519-826-4226; *Fax:* 519-826-4228
Toll-Free: 866-339-7619
www.oia.on.ca
www.linkedin.com/company/ontario-institute-of-agrologists
www.facebook.com/ontarioinstituteofagrologists
To regulate Ontario's Professional Agrologists & ensure that competencies meet a Standard of Practice within a specific scope of agrology
Drew Orosz, President
Terry Kingsmill, Registrar

Ontario Maple Syrup Producers' Association (OMSPA)
275 Country Rd. 44, RR#4, Kemptville ON K0G 1J0
Tel: 613-258-2294; *Fax:* 613-258-0207
Toll-Free: 866-566-2753
admin@ontariomaple.com
www.ontariomaple.com
www.facebook.com/OntarioMapleSyrup
twitter.com/OntMapleSyrup
To promote Ontario maple products through research & education
Rhonda Roantree, Office Administrator

Ontario Plowmen's Association (OPA)
188 Nicklin Rd., Guelph ON N1H 7L5
Tel: 519-767-2928; *Fax:* 519-767-2101
Toll-Free: 800-661-7569
admin@plowingmatch.org
www.plowingmatch.org
www.facebook.com/internationalplowingmatchandruralexpo
To provide leadership to local plowing associations; To advance interest & involvement in agriculture by promoting new technologies, environmental & safety issues; To preserve the history of soil cultivation; To promote rural economic development
Cathy Lasby, Executive Director

Ordre des agronomes du Québec (OAQ)
#450, 1200, av Papineau, Montréal QC H2K 4R5
Tél: 514-596-3833; *Téléc:* 514-596-2974
Ligne sans frais: 800-361-3833
agronome@oaq.qc.ca
www.oaq.qc.ca
Assurer les utilisateurs de services agronomiques et les consommateurs de la compétence, du professionnalisme et de l'engagement des agronomes et ainsi favoriser le mieux-être de la société
Louise Richard, Directrice générale

Prince Edward Island Federation of Agriculture (PEIFA)
#110, 420 University Ave., Charlottetown PE C1A 7Z5
Tel: 902-368-7289; *Fax:* 902-368-7204
www.peifa.ca
www.facebook.com/peifederationofagriculture
To provide a united voice for Island farmers
Robert Godfrey, Executive Director

Prince Edward Island Institute of Agrologists (PEIIA)
PO Box 2712, Charlottetown PE C1A 8C3
info@peiia.ca
www.peiia.ca
www.facebook.com/PEIInstituteofAgrologists
twitter.com/PEIAgrologists
To safeguard the public by ensuring its members are qualified & competent to provide knowledge & advice on agriculture & related areas
Paul MacDonald, Registrar

Prince Edward Island Vegetable Growers Co-op Association
PO Box 1494, 280 Sherwood Rd., Charlottetown PE C1A 7J7
Tel: 902-892-5361; *Fax:* 902-566-2383
peiveg@eastlink.ca
Don Read, Manager

Les producteurs de lait du Québec (PLQ)
#415, 555, boul Roland-Therrien, Longueuil QC J4H 4G3
Tél: 450-679-0530; *Téléc:* 450-679-5899
plq@lait.qc.ca
lait.org
www.youtube.com/user/FPLQ
www.facebook.com/ProdLaitQc
twitter.com/ProdLaitQc
Défense et promotion des intérêts professionnels et sociaux des producteurs de lait et mise en marché du lait de la ferme
Geneviève Rainville, Directrice générale

Québec Farmers' Association (QFA)
#255, 555, boul Roland-Therrien, Longueuil QC J4H 4E7
Tel: 450-679-0540; *Fax:* 450-463-5291
qfa@upa.qc.ca
www.quebecfarmers.org
www.facebook.com/groups/306871089363565
twitter.com/quebecfarmers
To defend the rights of the English-speaking agricultural community within the province of Québec.
Dougal Rattray, Executive Director
Andrew McClelland, Director, Communications

Saskatchewan Agricultural Graduates' Association Inc. (SAGA)
College of Agriculture, University of Saskatchewan, #2D27, 51 Campus Dr., Saskatoon SK S7N 5A8
thesaga@sasktel.net
www.saskaggrads.com
www.facebook.com/saskaggrads
twitter.com/saskaggrads
To promote the social well-being of graduates of the School & College of Agriculture; to ensure close relationships among graduates & between the College & School, including faculty & students; to keep graduates informed of some of the most recent developments in various fields of agriculture; to cooperate with University of Saskatchewan Alumni Association in promoting interests of the University as a whole
Jason Fradette, President

Saskatchewan Agricultural Hall of Fame (SAHF)
2610 Lorne Ave. South, Saskatoon SK S7J 0S6
Tel: 306-536-7892
www.sahf.ca
To honour Saskatchewan people who have contributed to the field of agriculture
Reed Andrew, Chair

Saskatchewan Association of Agricultural Societies & Exhibitions (SAASE)
PO Box 31025, Regina SK S4R 8R6
Tel: 306-565-2121; *Fax:* 306-565-2079
www.saase.ca
To provide the forum for exchange of ideas among association members; To provide educational opportunities for members; To address relevant issues affecting members; To provide for district, board & provincial meetings of members; To promote a fair agricultural industry; To help promote & form new societies; To provide a liaison with the extension program of University of Saskatchewan; To assist governments & universities to reach their agricultural & educational objectives
Glen Duck, Executive Director

Saskatchewan Beekeepers Association (SBA)
PO Box 55, RR#3, Yorkton SK S3N 2X5
Tel: 306-743-5469; *Fax:* 306-743-5528
whowland@accesscomm.ca
www.saskbeekeepers.com
To support Saskatchewan's beekeeping industry; To represent the province's beekeeping industry at both the provincial & national levels
Nathan Wendell, President
Danny Wasylenchuk, Vice-President
Wink Howland, Secretary-Treasurer

Saskatchewan Canola Development Commission
#212, 111 Research Dr., Saskatoon SK S7N 3R2
Tel: 306-975-0262; *Fax:* 306-975-0136
Toll-Free: 877-241-7044
info@saskcanola.com
www.saskcanola.com
SaskCanola enhances canola producers' competitiveness and profitability through research, market development, extension, and policy development.
Catherine Folkersen, Executive Director
Franck Groeneweg, Chair
Ellen Grueter, Manager

SeCan Association / Association SeCan
#400, 300 Terry Fox Dr., Kanata ON K2K 0E3
Tel: 613-592-8600; *Fax:* 613-592-9497
Toll-Free: 800-764-5487
seed@secan.com
www.secan.com
To promote profitability in Canadian agriculture
Jeff Reid, General Manager

SHARE Agriculture Foundation
14110 Kennedy Rd., Caledon ON L7C 2G3
Tel: 905-838-0897; *Fax:* 905-838-0794
Toll-Free: 888-337-4273
info@shareagfoundation.org
www.shareagfoundation.org
www.facebook.com/119869878092172
twitter.com/shareagfoundatn
To help improve the quality of life for agriculturally impoverished communities worldwide
Murray Brownridge, Chair
Les Frayne, Project Manager, Central America
Bob Thomas, Project Manager, South America

Society of Ontario Nut Growers (SONG)
979 Lakeshore Rd., RR#3, Niagara-on-the-Lake ON L0S 1J0
Tel: 519-740-6220
www.songonline.ca
To promote the interests of nut growers; To encourage scientific research in the breeding & culture of nut-bearing plants suited to Ontario conditions; To disseminate information on propagation techniques & cultural practices
Bernice Grimo, Treasurer

Sollio Groupe Coopératif / Sollio Cooperative Group
#200, 9001, boul de l'Acadie, Montréal QC H4N 3H7
Tél: 514-384-6450; *Téléc:* 514-384-7176
info@sollio.coop
sollio.coop
www.youtube.com/user/LaCoopfederee
www.linkedin.com/company/sollio
www.facebook.com/SollioCoop
twitter.com/SollioCoop
Fournit aux agriculteurs, directement ou par l'entremise de ses coopératives sociétaires, une vaste gamme de biens et de services nécessaires à l'exploitation de leur entreprise, y compris des produits pétroliers; de plus, elle transforme et commercialise sur les marchés locaux et internationaux divers produits agricoles: viande porcine, volaille, etc.
Gaétan Desroches, Chef de la direction

Table de développement de la production biologique
#100, 555, boul Roland-Therrien, Longueuil QC J4H 3Y9
Tél: 450-679-0530; *Téléc:* 450-670-4867
biologique@upa.qc.ca
Gérard Bouchard, Président

Union des producteurs agricoles (UPA)
#100, 555, boul Roland-Therrien, Longueuil QC J4H 3Y9
Tél: 450-679-0530
www.upa.qc.ca
www.youtube.com/user/upa1972
www.facebook.com/pageUPA
twitter.com/upaqc
Promouvoir, défendre et développer les intérêts professionnels, économiques, sociaux et moraux des producteurs agricoles et forestiers, sans distinction de race, de nationalité, de sexe, de langue et de croyance
Marcel Groleau, Président général

Vegetable Growers' Association of Manitoba (VGAM)
PO Box 894, Portage la Prairie MB R1N 3C4
Tel: 204-857-4581; *Fax:* 204-239-0260
vgamveggies@hotmail.com
www.vgam.ca
To support Manitoba's vegetable growers
Roland Jeffries, President
Frank Elias, Vice-President
Scott Moorhouse, Director
Todd Giffin, Director
Garry Wiebe, Director

Western Barley Growers Association (WBGA)
Agriculture Centre, 97 East Lake Ramp NE, Airdrie AB T4A 0C3
Tel: 403-912-3998; *Fax:* 403-948-2069
wbga@wbga.org
www.wbga.org
To provide farmers with an informed & effective voice in the agriculture industry of Western Canada
Doug Robertson, President
Douglas McBain, Treasurer
Tom Hewson, Saskatchewan Vice-President

Western Canadian Shippers' Coalition (WCSC)
31 Centennial Pkwy., Delta BC V4L 2C3
Tel: 604-943-8984; *Fax:* 604-943-8936
contact@westshippers.com
www.westshippers.com
www.youtube.com/user/Rhobot
twitter.com/Westshippers

Ian May, Chair

Western Canadian Wheat Growers Association
74 - 3553 31 St. NW, Calgary AB T2L 2K7

Tel: 306-955-0356
info@wheatgrowers.ca
www.wheatgrowers.ca

To promote changes that improve the wheat industry for its members
Dave Quist, Executive Director

Western Grains Research Foundation (WGRF)
#306, 111 Research Dr., Saskatoon SK S7N 3R2

Tel: 306-975-0060; Fax: 306-975-0316
info@westerngrains.com
www.westerngrains.com

To fund & invest in agricultural research that benefits western Canadian crop producers; To give producers a voice in funding decisions; To encourage the long-term sustainability of crop research in western Canada
Garth Patterson, Executive Director

Yukon Agricultural Association
#203, 302 Steele St., Whitehorse YT Y1A 2E5

Tel: 867-668-6864; Fax: 867-393-3566
admin@yukonag.ca
www.yukonag.ca

To provide resources & opportunities to agricultural producers in Yukon
Mike Blumenschein, President
Bev Buckway, Executive Director

AIDS

African & Caribbean Council on HIV/AIDS in Ontario (ACCHO)
20 Victoria St., 4th Fl., Toronto ON M5C 2N8

Tel: 416-977-9955; Fax: 416-977-7664
info@accho.ca
www.accho.ca
www.youtube.com/ACCHOntario
www.facebook.com/ACCHOntario
twitter.com/ACCHOntario

To provide support & resources to members of the African, Caribbean & Black communities in Ontario who are affected by HIV/AIDS
Ky'okusinga Kirunga, Director

AIDS Committee of Durham Region (ACDR)
115 Simcoe St. South, Oshawa ON L1H 4G7

Tel: 905-576-1445; Fax: 905-576-4610
Toll-Free: 877-361-8750
info@aidsdurham.com
www.aidsdurham.com
www.facebook.com/AIDSDurham
twitter.com/AIDSDurham

To provide HIV/AIDS related services to the infected, affected & general community in the Region of Durham
Doug Willoughby, President
Adrian Betts, Executive Director

AIDS Committee of North Bay & Area (ACNBA) / Comité du sida de North Bay et de la région
#201, 269 Main St. West, North Bay ON P1B 2T8

Tel: 705-497-3560; Fax: 705-497-7850
Toll-Free: 800-387-3701
oaacnba@gmail.com
www.aidsnorthbay.com
www.facebook.com/aidscommitteenorthbay
twitter.com/ACNBA

To assist & support all those affected & infected by HIV/AIDS; To limit the spread of the virus through education & awareness strategies
Stacey L. Mayhill, Executive Director

Black Coalition for AIDS Prevention
20 Victoria St., 4th Fl., Toronto ON M5C 2N8

Tel: 416-977-9955; Fax: 416-977-7664
info@black-cap.com
www.black-cap.com
www.facebook.com/blackcapto

To reduce the spread of HIV infection in Black communities; To enhance the quality of life for Black people living with or affected by HIV/AIDS
Shannon Thomas Ryan, Executive Director

Blood Ties Four Directions Centre
405 Ogilvie St., Whitehorse YT Y1A 2S5

Tel: 867-633-2437; Fax: 867-633-2447
admin@bloodties.ca
www.bloodties.ca

To acts as an information & support centre; To promote public awareness of AIDS/AIDS & hepatitis C & aid in their prevention; To assist people living with HIV/AIDS & hep C
Bronte Renwick-Sheilds, Executive Director

Canadian AIDS Society (CAS) / Société canadienne du sida (SCS)
#602, 170 Laurier Ave. West, Ottawa ON K1P 5V5

Tel: 613-230-3580; Fax: 613-563-4998
Toll-Free: 800-499-1986
casinfo@cdnaids.ca
www.cdnaids.ca
www.instagram.com/cdnaids
www.facebook.com/cdnaids
twitter.com/CDNAIDS

To strengthen the response to HIV/AIDS across Canada; To enrich the lives of people living with HIV/AIDS
Gary Lacasse, Executive Director
Kelly Puddister, Manager, Fundraising & National Programs
Patrick Wright, Manager, National Harm Reduction

Canadian AIDS Treatment Information Exchange (CATIE) / Réseau canadien d'info-traitements sida
PO Box 1104, #505, 555 Richmond St. West, Toronto ON M5V 3B1

Tel: 416-203-7122; Fax: 416-203-8284
Toll-Free: 800-263-1638
info@catie.ca
www.catie.ca
www.youtube.com/user/catieinfo
www.linkedin.com/company/canadian-aids-treatment-information-exchange
www.facebook.com/CATIEInfo
twitter.com/CATIEInfo

To improve the health & quality of life of all people living with HIV/AIDS (PHAs) in Canada; To provide HIV/AIDS treatment information to PHAs, caregivers & AIDS service organizations who are encouraged to be active partners in achieving informed decision-making & optimal health care; To promote collaboration among affected populations
Susanne Nicolay, Chair
Laurie Edmiston, Executive Director

Canadian Foundation for AIDS Research (CANFAR) / Fondation canadienne de recherche sur le SIDA
#1600, 2200 Yonge St., Toronto ON M4S 2C6

Tel: 416-361-6281; Fax: 416-361-5736
Toll-Free: 800-563-2873
admin@canfar.com
www.canfar.com
www.youtube.com/user/CANFAR
www.linkedin.com/company/canadian-foundation-for-aids-research
www.facebook.com/canfar
twitter.com/canfar

To raise awareness in order to fund research into all aspects of HIV infection & AIDS
Alex Filiatrault, Chief Executive Officer

Canadian HIV Trials Network (CTN) / Réseau canadien pour les essais VIH
#588, 1081 Burrard St., Vancouver BC V6Z 1Y6

Tel: 604-806-8327; Fax: 604-806-8005
Toll-Free: 800-661-4664
ctninfo@hivnet.ubc.ca
www.hivnet.ubc.ca
www.youtube.com/user/CIHRCTN
www.linkedin.com/company/cihr-canadian-hiv-trials-network
www.facebook.com/CIHR.CTN
twitter.com/CIHR_CTN

To develop treatments, vaccines & a cure for HIV disease & AIDS through the conduct of scientifically sound & ethical clinical trials
Aslam Anis, National Director
Marina Klein, National Co-Director
Sharon Walmsley, National Co-Director

Canadian HIV/AIDS Legal Network / Réseau juridique canadien VIH/sida
#600, 1240 Bay St., Toronto ON M5R 2A7

Tel: 416-595-1666; Fax: 416-595-0094
info@aidslaw.ca
www.aidslaw.ca
www.youtube.com/aidslaw
www.facebook.com/CanadianHIVAIDSLegalNetwork
twitter.com/aidslaw

To promote the human rights of people living with & vulnerable to HIV/AIDS, in Canada & internationally; through research, legal & policy analysis, education, advocacy & community mobilization
Richard Elliot, Executive Director
Janet Butler-McPhee, Director of Communications

Coalition des organismes communautaires québécois de lutte contre le sida (COCQ-SIDA)
1, rue Sherbrooke est, Montréal QC H2X 3V8

Tél: 514-844-2477; Téléc: 514-844-2498
Ligne sans frais: 866-535-0481
info@cocqsida.com
www.cocqsida.com
www.facebook.com/COCQSIDA
twitter.com/COCQSIDA

Représenter les membres afin de favoriser l'émergence et le soutien d'une action concertée dans les dossiers d'intérêt commun; faire reconnaître l'expertise et l'apport des organismes communautaires et non-gouvernementaux dans la lutte contre le sida
Ken Monteith, Directeur général

Maison Plein Coeur
1611, rue Dorion, Montréal QC H2K 4A5

Tél: 514-597-0554; Téléc: 514-597-2788
infompc@maisonpleincoeur.org
www.maisonpleincoeur.org
twitter.com/mpleincoeur

Contribuer à prévenir le VIH-SIDA, et à promouvoir la santé chez les personnes vivant avec la maladie; offrir des services sans aucune discrimination; favoriser des services communautaires visant à stabiliser la situation des personnes présentant des troubles de santé et d'organisation; améliorer la qualité de vie de la personne en offrant un lieu de partage et d'informations
Elaine Mayrand, Présidente
Chris Lau, Directeur général

Positive Living BC
1101 Seymour St., Vancouver BC V6B 0R1

Tel: 604-893-2200; Fax: 604-893-2251
Toll-Free: 800-994-2437
info@positivelivingbc.org
www.positivelivingbc.org
www.facebook.com/positivelivingbc
twitter.com/pozlivingbc

To empower persons in British Columbia who live with HIV/AIDS
Tom McAulay, Chair
Mike Hedges, Director, Operations

RÉZO
CP 246, Succ. C, Montréal QC H2L 4K1

Tél: 514-521-7778; Téléc: 514-521-7665
www.rezosante.org
www.youtube.com/REZOsante
www.facebook.com/REZOsante
twitter.com/rezosante

Développer et coordonner des activités d'éducation et de prévention du VIH-sida et des autres ITSS dans un contexte de promotion de la santé sexuelle auprès des hommes gais, bisexuels et hommes ayant des relations sexuelles avec d'autres hommes de Montréal
Robert Rousseau, Directeur général

Animal Breeding

Alberta Angus Association
PO Box 3725, Olds AB T4H 1P5

Tel: 403-556-9057; Toll-Free: 888-556-9057
office@albertaangus.ca
www.albertaangus.ca

To protect the interests of Angus cattle in Alberta; To promote cooperation between breeders & others interested in Angus cattle
Tiffany Richmond, Vice-President

Alberta Salers Association
5160 Skyline Way NE, Calgary AB T2E 6V1

Tel: 403-264-5850; Fax: 403-264-5895
info@salerscanada.com
www.salerscanada.com

To promote salers cattle in Alberta
Heidi Voegeli-Bleiker, Office Manager

Alberta Sheep Breeders Association (ASBA)
PO Box 7, St Albert AB T8N 1N2

Fax: 403-443-7221
Toll-Free: 866-967-4337
office@albertasheepbreeders.ca
www.albertasheepbreeders.ca

To promote the purebred sheep industry within Alberta
Linda Brandes, Contact, Office

Alberta Shorthorn Association
c/o Albert and Susan Oram, PO Box 939, Castor AB T0C 0X0
Fax: 800-387-6909
Toll-Free: 800-387-6909
albertashorthorn@gmail.com
www.albertashorthorn.com
www.facebook.com/abshorthornassoc
To produce & promote the Shorthorn breed of cattle
Dennis Wishnowski, Executive Director

Appaloosa Horse Club of Canada (ApHCC)
AB
registry@appaloosa.ca
www.appaloosa.ca
To collect records & historical data relating to origin of the
Appaloosa; To file records & issue certificates of registration; To
preserve, improve & standardize the breed

Association des éleveurs de chevaux Belge du Québec / Breeders of Belgian Horses Association of Québec
611, ch Léon-Gérin, Compton QC J0B 1L0
Tél: 819-570-5626
www.belgequebec.com
www.facebook.com/201986326506407
Promouvoir l'élevage de chevaux de race pure de grande qualité
et aider les éleveurs à améliorer leur cheptel chevalin à travers
la province au moyen de concours et d'expositions
Johanne Fréchette, Secrétaire

Association Hereford du Québec
162, rue des Érables, Ste-Catherine-de-la-Jacques-Cartier QC G3N 1A7
Tél: 418-875-2343
CCRBQ@hotmail.com
www.herefordquebec.ca
André Beaumont, Secrétaire

Ayrshire Breeders Association of Canada (ABAC) / Associaton des éleveurs Ayrshire du Canada
4855, boul Laurier ouest, Saint-Hyacinthe QC J2S 3V4
Tel: 450-778-3535; *Fax:* 450-778-3531
info@ayrshire-canada.com
ayrshire-canada.com
www.instagram.com/ayrshirecanadaofficial
www.facebook.com/ayrshire.canada
To bring Ayrshire breeders together for the purpose of
cooperating in their efforts to further the interests of the breed;
To promote breeding of purebred Ayrshire cattle in Canada; To
establish breeding standards; To cooperate with industry
partners to enhance programs
Michel Boudreault, General Manager

British Columbia Hereford Association (BCHA)
c/o Vic Redekop, 25440 - 16th Ave., Aldergrove BC V4W 2R7
Tel: 250-557-4348; *Fax:* 250-557-4468
www.bchereford.ca
To produce Hereford seedstock to meet the demands of British
Columbia's commercial cattle industry
Daryl Kirton, Director

Canadian Angus Association (CAA) / L'Association canadienne Angus
292140 Wagon Wheel Blvd., Rocky View County AB T4A 0E2
Tel: 403-571-3580; *Fax:* 403-571-3599
Toll-Free: 888-571-3580
cdnangus@cdnangus.ca
cdnangus.ca
www.youtube.com/user/CanadianAngusAssoc
www.linkedin.com/company/canadian-angus-association
www.facebook.com/CanadianAngusAssociation
twitter.com/cdnangus
To offer services to enhance the growth & position of the Angus
breed; To maintain breed purity
Shawn Birmingham, President
Myles Immerkar, Chief Executive Officer

Canadian Beef Breeds Council (CBBC)
#165, 6715 - 8th St. NE, Calgary AB T2E 7H7
Tel: 403-730-0350
info@canadianbeefbreeds.com
www.canadianbeefbreeds.com
www.facebook.com/BeefGenetics
twitter.com/CanBeefBreeds
To represent & promote the purebred cattle sector both
domestically & internationally
Michael Latimer, Executive Director

Canadian Belgian Horse Association
17150 Concession 10, Schomberg ON L0G 1T0
Tel: 905-939-1186; *Fax:* 905-939-7547
cbha@csolve.net
www.canadianbelgianhorse.com

To promote the Belgian breed of horse
Terry Morrow, President

Canadian Bison Association (CBA) / Association canadienne du bison
PO Box 3116, #200, 1660 Pasqua St., Regina SK S4P 3G7
Tel: 306-522-4766; *Fax:* 306-522-4768
cba1@sasktel.net
www.canadianbison.ca
www.facebook.com/CanadianBisonAssociation
twitter.com/CanadianBisonAs
To develop the bison industry; To maintain the production of
bison in a natural state; To be the voice for commercial
breeders; To assist in the formation of regulations & guidelines
in commercial production & management of Canadian Plains
Bison; To promote the product & awareness of the bison
industry
Terry Kremeniuk, Executive Director

Canadian Blonde d'Aquitaine Association
c/o Canadian Livestock Records Corporation, 2417 Holly Ln., Ottawa ON K1V 0M7
Tel: 613-731-7110; *Fax:* 613-731-0704
cbda@clrc.ca
www.canadianblondeassociation.ca
www.facebook.com/canadianblondedaquitaine
To improve the practice of breeding Blonde d'Aquitaine cows
Paul Ferguson, President

Canadian Border Collie Association
c/o Tara Dier, PO Box 817, Stirling ON K0K 3E0
Tel: 705-632-9786
registrar@canadianbordercollies.org
www.canadianbordercollies.org
www.facebook.com/canadianbordercollies
To establish a standard of breeding; To maintain a registry of
purebred border collies; To promote & foster the breeding,
training & distribution of reliable border collies; To promote &
foster health improvements in border collies
Tara Dier, Registrar

Canadian Brown Swiss & Braunvieh Association / L'association canadienne de la Suisse Brune et de la Braunvieh
RR#5 5653 Hwy. 6 North, Guelph ON N1H 6J2
Tel: 519-821-2811; *Fax:* 519-763-6582
brownswiss@holstein.ca
browncow.ca
www.facebook.com/117089315003708
To encourage, develop & regulate breeding of Brown Swiss &
Braunvieh dairy cattle
Dave Rousseau, President
Donald Caron, Secretary Manager

Canadian Cattlemen's Association (CCA)
#180, 6815 - 8th St. NE, Calgary AB T2E 7H7
Tel: 403-275-8558; *Fax:* 403-274-5686
feedback@cattle.ca
www.cattle.ca
www.facebook.com/CdnCattlemen
twitter.com/CdnCattlemen
To act as the national voice of beef producers across Canada;
To produce high-quality beef products; To maintain a profitable
Canadian beef industry; To use management practices that
protect the health of the animal & protect the environment
David Moss, General Manager

Canadian Charolais Association (CCA)
2320 - 41st Ave. NE, Calgary AB T2E 6W8
Tel: 403-250-9242; *Fax:* 403-291-9324
cca@charolais.com
charolais.com
www.facebook.com/cdncharolais
twitter.com/canCharolais
To be leaders in predictable beef genetics; To register, record,
transfer & promote Canadian Charolais; To provide services for
membership
Craig Scott, General Manager

Canadian Co-operative Wool Growers Ltd. (CCWG)
PO Box 130, 142 Franktown Rd., Carleton Place ON K7C 3P3
Tel: 613-257-2714; *Fax:* 613-257-8896
ccwghq@wool.ca
wool.ca
To operate as a producer-owned wool marketing cooperative; To
collect, grade & market the majority of the Canadian wool clip to
the global market; To retail farm supplies & animal health &
identification products
Eric Bjergso, General Manager

Canadian Cutting Horse Association (CCHA)
CCHA c/o Robin Powell, 6025 - 60A Ave. Cres., Innisfail AB T4G 1V9
Tel: 403-227-4444; *Fax:* 403-227-3030
CCHAcutting@gmail.com
www.ccha.ca
www.facebook.com/1145068682191323
To promote the cutting horse, a specially trained horse to isolate
or cut an individual animal from large cattle herds
Les Jack, President
Connie Down-Cicoria, Vice-President
Kim Moore, Secretary-Treasurer

Canadian Dexter Cattle Association (CDCA) / Société canadienne des bovins Dexter
2417 Holly Lane, Ottawa ON K1V 0M7
Tel: 613-731-7110; *Fax:* 613-731-0704
www.dextercattle.ca
To preserve & promote the breeding of good quality Dexter
cattle in Canada
Ron Black, Contact

Canadian Donkey & Mule Association (CDMA)
c/o Canadian Livestock Records Corporation, 2417 Holly Lane, Ottawa ON K1V 0M7
Tel: 613-731-7110
www.donkeyandmule.com
To operate registry for donkeys & recordation for mules; To
promote use, well-being & protection of donkeys & mules; To
assist in training & placing donkeys for disabled riding

Canadian Fjord Horse Association
c/o Canadian Livestock Records Corp., 2417 Holly Lane, Ottawa ON K1V 0M7
Tel: 613-731-7110; *Fax:* 613-731-0704
info@cfha.org
cfha.org
www.instagram.com/canadian_fjord_horse_assoc
www.facebook.com/canadianfjord
twitter.com/canadianfjord
To operate under the Animal Pedigree Act; To assure the
success of the purebred registered Norwegian Fjord Horse in
Canada
Gordon Fulton, President
Julie Seibel, CLRC Contact

Canadian Galloway Association (CGA) / Société canadienne Galloway
c/o Canadian Livestock Records Corporation, 2417 Holly Lane, Ottawa ON K1V 0M7
Tel: 613-731-7110; *Fax:* 613-731-0704
galloway@clrc.ca
www.galloway.ca
To promote & regulate the breeding of Galloways, Belted
Galloways & White Galloways in Canada
Vanessa Beach, President
Ron Black, Secretary-Treasurer

Canadian Gelbvieh Association (CGA)
5160 Skyline Way NE, Calgary AB T2E 6V1
Tel: 403-250-8640; *Fax:* 403-291-5624
gelbvieh@gelbvieh.ca
gelbvieh.ca
To promote Gelbvieh cattle in Canada & their registration
Lee Wirgau, President

Canadian Goat Society (CGS) / La Société canadienne des éleveurs de chèvres
PO Box 31084, Stn. Willow West, Guelph ON N1H 8K1
Tel: 226-486-3251
info@goats.ca
goats.ca
www.facebook.com/CanadianGoatSociety
To maintain the integrity of herdbooks, providing accurate
evaluation programs for performance & type & promoting the
responsible & humane treatment of goats
Sandy Howell, President

Canadian Guernsey Association
7660 Mill Rd., Guelph ON N1H 6J1
Tel: 519-836-2141
info@guernseycanada.ca
www.guernseycanada.ca
To provide services to breeders of Guernsey dairy cattle
including records, awards, promotion, sales & shows
Jesse Weir, Administrator

Canadian Hereford Association (CHA) / Association canadienne Hereford
5160 Skyline Way NE, Calgary AB T2E 6V1
Tel: 403-275-2662; *Fax:* 403-295-1333
Toll-Free: 888-836-7242
herefords@hereford.ca
www.hereford.ca
twitter.com/CAN_Hereford
To promote the consistent & economical production of beef; To strive to meet & exceed consumer expectations for tender, juicy & flavourful beef products, through performance measurement, genetic selection, appropriate handling, feeding & processing
Stephen Scott, Executive Director

Canadian Highland Cattle Society (CHCS) / Société canadienne des éleveurs de bovins Highland
Tel: 418-313-1469
highland@chcs.ca
chcs.ca
To regulate & promote breeding of Highland cattle in Canada
Sylvie Rajotte, Secretary

Canadian Icelandic Horse Federation (CIHF)
c/o Canadian Livestock Records Corporation, 2417 Holly Lane, Ottawa ON K1V 0M7
Tel: 613-731-7110; *Fax:* 613-731-0704
Toll-Free: 877-731-7110
www.cihf.ca
To promote & maintain the purity of the Icelandic horse; To keep record of breeding & registration of Icelandic horse under the Canadian National Livestock Record System; To promote the awareness & secure the integrity of purebred Icelandic horses
Victoria Stoncius, President

Canadian Limousin Association (CLA)
#13, 4101 - 19th St. NE, Calgary AB T2E 7C4
Tel: 403-253-7309; *Fax:* 403-253-1704
Toll-Free: 866-886-1605
limousin@limousin.com
www.limousin.com
www.facebook.com/CanadianLimousin
twitter.com/cdnlimousin
To provide collective service for Limousin breeders in Canada; To record registration & produce Records of Performance on all registered animals; To promote & inform producers about Limousin cattle; To develop & implement educational agricultural programs
Laura Ecklund, General Manager

Canadian Livestock Records Corporation (CLRC) / Société canadienne d'enregistrement des animaux
2417 Holly Lane, Ottawa ON K1V 0M7
Tel: 613-731-7110; *Fax:* 613-731-0704
Toll-Free: 877-833-7110
clrc@clrc.ca
www.clrc.ca
To serve the Canadian seed stock industry; To be responsible to the member breed associations & Agriculture Canada for the maintenance of records, issuance of certificates, endorsement of changes of ownership, enrolment of members, registration of individuals, identification letters, collection of fees & the deposit of same into the appropriate breed association account
Jim Washer, General Manager

Canadian Maine-Anjou Association (CMAA)
5160 Skyline Way NE, Calgary AB T2E 6V1
Tel: 403-291-7077; *Fax:* 403-291-0274
cmaa@maine-anjou.ca
maine-anjou.ca
www.facebook.com/848369091908255
To encourage, develop & regulate the breeding of Main-Anjou cattle in Canada
Stuart Byman, President
Josie Pashulka, Secretary
Brian Brown, Treasurer

Canadian Meat Goat Association (CMGA) / Canadienne de la Chèvre de Boucherie
#12, 449 Laird Rd., Guelph ON N1G 4W1
Tel: 519-824-2942; *Fax:* 519-824-2534
info@canadianmeatgoat.com
www.canadianmeatgoat.com
To support the development of a profitable meat goat breeding stock & meat industry in Canada; To provide animal registration; To establish breeding standards; To promote the industry & raise consumer demand for chevon
Stuart Chutter, President

Canadian Milking Shorthorn Society (CMSS)
6A Barrett St., Kensington PE C0B 1M0
Tel: 902-439-9386
milking.shorthorn@gmail.com
www.facebook.com/milkingshorthorn
twitter.com/CanMShorthorn
To promote & encourage the development of milking shorthorn cattle
Ryan Barrett, Secretary-Manager

Canadian Morgan Horse Association (CMHA) / Association des chevaux Morgan canadien inc.
2685 Concession 4, Loretto ON L0G 1L0
Tel: 905-982-0060; *Fax:* 905-729-0972
info@morganhorse.ca
www.morganhorse.ca

Canadian Murray Grey Association (CMGA)
PO Box 157, Bragg Creek AB T0L 0K0
Tel: 403-949-2199
cmgareg@telus.net
www.cdnmurraygrey.ca
To promote the genetics of Murray Grey Beef Cattle

Canadian Palomino Horse Association (CPHA)
c/o Lorraine Holdaway, 631 Hendershott Rd., RR#1, Hannon ON L0R 1P0
Tel: 905-692-4328
canadianpalomino@gmail.com
www.clrc.ca/associations/palomino
To develop & promote the breeding of Palomino horses in Canada; To establish standards of breeding
Lorraine Holdaway, Secretary
Laura Lee Mills, Registrar

Canadian Percheron Association / Association canadienne du cheval Percheron
Dawson Creek BC
Tel: 250-759-4981; *Fax:* 888-423-0049
canadapercheron@uniserve.com
www.canadianpercherons.com
To develop & encourage the breeding of purebred Percheron horses in Canada; To establish standards of breeding; To regulate the breeding of purebred Percheron horses
Kathy Ackles, Secretary/Treasurer

Canadian Pork Council (CPC) / Conseil canadien du porc (CCP)
#900, 220 Laurier Ave. West, Ottawa ON K1P 5Z9
Tel: 613-236-9239
info@cpc-ccp.com
www.cpc-ccp.com
To provide a leadership role in a concerted effort involving all levels of industry & government toward a common understanding & action plan for achieving a dynamic & prosperous pork industry in Canada
John Ross, Executive Director

Canadian Quarter Horse Association (CQHA)
c/o Sherry Clemens, Secretary, PO Box 2132, Moose Jaw SK S6H 7T2
Tel: 306-692-8393
admin@huntseathorses.com
www.cqha.ca
www.facebook.com/192652444096322
To address issues of concern to Canadian owners of American Quarter Horses; to be a communications vehicle for and with Canadian owners of American Quarter Horses; and to promote and market - both globally and within Canada - Canadian-bred and/or Canadian-owned American Quarter Horses.
Haidee Landry, President

Canadian Red Angus Promotion Society
RR#2, New Norway AB T0B 3L0
Tel: 780-678-9069; *Fax:* 780-855-2581
www.redangus.ca
www.facebook.com/CanadianRedAngus
twitter.com/CdnRedAngus
To promote & advertise Canadian Red Angus cattle
Brent Troyer, President

Canadian Red Poll Cattle Association / Société Canadienne des Bovins Red Poll
c/o Canadian Livestock Records Corporation, 2417 Holly Lane, Ottawa ON K1V 0M7
Tel: 613-731-7110; *Fax:* 613-731-0704
Toll-Free: 877-731-7110
redpoll@clrc.ca
www.clrc.ca/associations/redpoll
To encourage development & regulation of breeding of purebred Red Poll cattle in Canada for improvement of Canadian beef cattle industry

Ron Black, Secretary-Treasurer

Canadian Sheep Breeders' Association (CSBA) / La société canadienne des éleveurs de moutons
4350, av de l'Hotel-de-ville, Montréal AB T0C 0M0
Fax: 877-207-2541
Toll-Free: 866-956-1116
office@sheepbreeders.ca
www.sheepbreeders.ca
www.facebook.com/canadiansheepbreeders
To represent & promote sheep breeders
Bruce Sinclair, President
Keith Todd, Vice-President
Jane Underhill, General Manager

Canadian Sheep Federation / Fédération canadienne du mouton
PO Box 10, Williamsburg ON K0C 2H0
Tel: 613-652-1824; *Fax:* 613-652-1599
Toll-Free: 888-684-7739
info@cansheep.ca
www.cansheep.ca
To set national policy for the sheep industry; To endeavour to further the viability, expansion & prosperity of the Canadian sheep & wool industry
Allan Ribbink, Chair
Corlena Patterson, Executive Director

Canadian Shorthorn Association
PO Box 3771, Stn. Evraz Place, Regina SK S4P 3N8
Tel: 306-757-2212; *Fax:* 306-525-5852
office@canadianshorthorn.com
www.canadianshorthorn.com
Dale Asser, President
Belinda Wagner, Secretary-Treasurer

Canadian Simmental Association
#13, 4101 - 19th St. NE, Calgary AB T2E 7C4
Tel: 403-250-7979; *Fax:* 403-250-5121
Toll-Free: 866-860-6051
cansim@simmental.com
www.simmental.com
www.facebook.com/cdnsimmental
twitter.com/CdnSimmental
To encourage, develop & regulate the breeding of Simmental cattle in Canada
Marlin LeBlanc, President
Roger Deeg, First Vice-President
Shane Williams, Second Vice-President
Bruce Holmquist, General Manager

Canadian Swine Breeders' Association (CSBA) / L'Association canadienne des éleveurs de porcs
#2, 408 Dundas St., Woodstock ON N4S 1B9
Tel: 519-421-2354; *Fax:* 519-421-0887
info@canswine.ca
www.canswine.ca
To improve & promote Canadian purebred swine; To lobby on behalf of purebred swine breeders in Canada; To direct & regulate purebred swine industry; To be involved in registration & transfer of following breeds: Berkshire, British Saddleback, Chester White, Duroc, Hampshire, Large Black, Pietrain, Poland China, Spotted, Tamworth, Welsh, Yorkshire, Landrace, Lacombe, Red Wattle (registration forms can be obtained from Canadian Livestock Records Corporation)

Canadian Tarentaise Association (CTA)
c/p Rosalyn Harris, PO Box 1156, Shellbrook SK S0J 2E0
Toll-Free: 800-450-4181
info@tarentaise.ca
www.tarentaise.ca
To develop, register & promote Tarentaise cattle in Canada
Rosalyn Harris, Secretary-Treasurer

Canadian Thoroughbred Horse Society (CTHS) / Société canadienne du cheval Thoroughbred
PO Box 172, Toronto ON M9W 5L1
Tel: 416-675-1370; *Fax:* 416-675-9405
info@cthsnational.com
www.cthsnational.com
To assist & afford a means for promotion of interests of those engaged in breeding of thoroughbreds; To protect members against unbusinesslike methods; To diffuse information among members & others; To secure uniformity in usage & business conditions; To determine requirements of horses as thoroughbreds by the Society; To promote, encourage & assist in livestock & agricultural exhibitions, fairs & racing; To sponsor, assist & conduct sales of thoroughbred stock; To compile statistics of the industry; To maintain efficient supervision of breeders of thoroughbred horses; To prevent, detect & punish fraud (i.e. in registration of throughbreds)
Adrian Munro, President

Canadian Trakehner Horse Society (CTHS)
PO Box 6009, New Hamburg ON N3A 2K6

Tel: 519-662-3209
lkdlive.ca
www.cantrak.on.ca
www.facebook.com/203491652994222

To maintain a public registry of Trakehner horses under the Canadian Livestock Records Corporation; To promote & preserve Trakehner horses in Canada

EastGen
7660 Mill Rd., Guelph ON N1H 6J1

Tel: 519-821-2150; Fax: 519-763-6582
Toll-Free: 888-821-2150
info@eastgen.ca
www.eastgen.ca
www.facebook.com/EastGen
twitter.com/EastGenGenetics

To act as a farmer-directed AI cooperative & offer services to members in Ontario, New Brunswick, PEI, & Newfoundland & Labrador
Robert Wright, President

Farm & Food Care Ontario
#202, 100 Stone Rd. West, Guelph ON N1G 5L3

Tel: 519-837-1326; Fax: 519-837-3209
info@farmfoodcare.org
www.farmfoodcare.org
www.instagram.com/farmfoodcare
www.youtube.com/FarmFoodCare
twitter.com/FarmFoodCareON

To support & promote the responsible production & marketing of livestock & poultry by Ontario farmers & through a variety of initiatives, to better inform the public of the excellence of animal agriculture
Kelly Daynard, Executive Director

Holstein Canada
PO Box 610, Brantford ON N3T 5R4

Tel: 519-756-8300; Fax: 519-756-3502
Toll-Free: 855-756-8300
www.holstein.ca
www.youtube.com/user/HolsteinCanadaVideo
www.facebook.com/HolsteinCanada
twitter.com/HolsteinCanada

To improve the Holstein breed by ascertaining the most desirable characteristics of the breed for current & prospective conditions in Canada; To prepare, maintain & make available a genealogical record of the breed; To promote the best interests of breeders & owners of Holstein cattle
Vincent Landry, Chief Executive Officer
Lynne Berwick, Contact, Human Resources
Linda Ness, Contact, Strategic Communications

Jersey Canada (JC)
#9, 350 Speedvale Ave. West, Guelph ON N1H 7M7

Tel: 519-821-1020; Fax: 519-821-2723
info@jerseycanada.com
jerseycanada.com
www.instagram.com/jerseycanada
www.linkedin.com/company/jersey-canada
www.facebook.com/jerseycanada
twitter.com/jerseycanada

To represent & promote the Jersey breed & encourage market development domestically & internationally; To provide & maintain a registration system, catalogues & pedigree information; To update classification & milk production records
Tim Sargent, President
David Morey, First Vice-President
Patrick MacDougall, Second Vice-President
Kathryn Roxburgh, General Manager

Nova Scotia Mink Breeders' Association
c/o Dan Mullen, 2124 Black Rock Rd., Waterville NS B0P 1V0

Tel: 902-680-5360; Fax: 902-538-7799

To foster better mink breeding among the members; to help secure market advantage.
Dan Mullen, President

Ontario Goat Breeders Association (OGBA)
#12, 449 Laird Rd., Guelph ON N1G 4W1

Tel: 519-824-2942; Fax: 519-824-2534
info@livestockalliance.ca
www.ontariogoat.ca
twitter.com/ontariogoat

To provide & circulate sound information about goats in Ontario; To improve & develop the goat breeds in Ontario; To encourage & promote the expansion of the goat industry in Ontario; To assist the development of chevon, fibre & dairy industries

Ontario Shorthorn Association (OSA)
c/o Doug Brown, 212 Bassett Blvd., Whitby ON L1R 1G6

Tel: 905-431-8496
www.ontarioshorthorns.com
www.facebook.com/ontarioshorthorns

To preserve & promote the Shorthorn breed of cattle in Ontario
Jamie Blenkiron, Vice-President

Prince Edward Island Sheep Breeders Association
PE

peisheepbreeders.weebly.com

Trent Coles, Treasurer

Prince Edward Island Shorthorn Association
PE

Purebred Sheep Breeders Association of Nova Scotia
PO Box 550, Truro NS B2N 5E3

www.sheepnovascotia.ns.ca

To improve the quality of purebred sheep in Nova Scotia; To advance breeders' interests & speak on their behalf when necessary
Andrew Hebda, President

Québec Shorthorn Association / Club Shorthorn du Québec
QC

Ray Dempsey, Contact

Québec Simmental Association (QSA) / Association Simmental du Québec (ASQ)
530, rte 239, Saint-Germain QC J0C 1K0

Tel: 819-395-4453; Fax: 819-395-4453
info@simmentalquebec.ca
www.simmentalquebec.ca

To promote the Québec Simmental breeding programs to the market, purebred as well as commercial, within the province of Québec & abroad
Sylvain Lambert, President

Salers Association of Canada (SAC) / Association salers du Canada
c/o Heidi Voegeli-Bleiker, 5160 Skyline Way NE, Calgary AB T2E 6V1

Tel: 403-264-5850; Fax: 403-264-5895
info@salerscanada.com
salerscanada.com

To develop & register Salers cattle
Heidi Voegeli-Bleiker, Registrar & Office Manager

Sask Pork
#2, 502 - 45th St. West, Saskatoon SK S7L 6H2

Tel: 306-244-7752; Fax: 306-244-1712
info@saskpork.com
www.saskpork.com

To position the Saskatchewan pork industry as a preferred supplier of high quality, competitively priced pork products for the global market.
Neil Ketilson, General Manager

Saskatchewan Stock Growers Association (SSGA)
Main Floor, Canada Centre Building, Evraz Place, PO Box 4752, Regina SK S4P 3Y4

Tel: 306-757-8523; Fax: 306-569-8799
skstockgrowers.com

To serve, protect, & advance the interests of the beef industry in Saskatchewan; To represent the cattle industry in Saskatchewan on the legislative front
Chad MacPherson, General Manager

Standardbred Canada (SC)
2150 Meadowvale Blvd., Mississauga ON L5N 6R6

Tel: 905-858-3060; Fax: 905-858-3111
standardbredcanada.ca
www.youtube.com/user/jporchak
www.facebook.com/standardbred.canada
twitter.com/TrotInsider

To encourage & develop the breeding of Standardbred Horses
Dan Gall, President & CEO
Linda Bedard, Manager & Registrar

Western Ayrshire Club
Cobble Hill BC

Tel: 250-743-6192; Fax: 250-743-6190

To promote the breeding of Ayrshire cattle in British Columbia; to promote the dairy farming industry & the Ayrshire dairy cow as the most economical, productive, profitable & efficient dairy cow to the farmer
Olivier Balme, Director

The Western Stock Growers' Association (WSGA)
PO Box 179, #14, 900 Village Lane, Okotoks AB T1S 1Z6

Tel: 403-250-9121
office@wsga.ca
www.wsga.ca
www.facebook.com/WesternStockGrowers

To support & protect livestock growers by lobbying the government on existing legislation & proposed new legislation; To promote environmentally sound range management practices
Phil Rowland, President

Westgen
PO Box 40, 6681 Glover Rd., Milner BC V0X 1T0

Tel: 604-530-1141; Fax: 604-534-3036
Toll-Free: 800-563-5603
www.westgen.com

To provide Semex Alliance Genetics & other value-added products & services which enhance herd improvement to livestock producers in western Canada
Brent Belluk, General Manager
Darcie Kaye, Marketing Manager

Animals & Animal Science

Alberta Society for the Prevention of Cruelty to Animals
17904 - 118 Ave. NW, Edmonton AB T5S 2W3

Tel: 780-447-3600; Fax: 780-447-4748
info@albertaspca.org
www.albertaspca.org
www.youtube.com/user/AlbertaSPCA
www.linkedin.com/company/alberta-spca
www.facebook.com/AlbertaSPCA
twitter.com/AlbertaSPCA

To promote education of public about welfare of domestic animals & livestock; To deal with wildlife issues; To work on improving legislation; To concentrate on enforcement & education; To have every animal in Alberta humanely treated
Terra Johnston, Executive Director

Alberta Veterinary Medical Association (AVMA)
Bldg. 3, Elm Business Park, #104, 9452 - 51 Ave., Edmonton AB T6E 5A6

Tel: 780-489-5007; Fax: 780-484-8311
Toll-Free: 800-404-2862
www.abvma.ca
www.youtube.com/abvma
www.linkedin.com/company/alberta-veterinary-medical-association
www.facebook.com/ABVMA
twitter.com/abvma

To represent Alberta veterinarians in small animal, large animal & mixed practice as well as those employed in government, industry or other institutions
Darrell Dalton, Registrar

Alberta Veterinary Technologist Association (ABVTA)
#104, 9452 51 Ave. NW, Edmonton AB T6E 5A6

Tel: 587-525-6566
admin.aaaht@abvma.ca
www.abvta.com
www.instagram.com/abvta.official
www.facebook.com/ABVTA.official

To promote professional & educational advancement of the Animal Health Technologist; To enhance the knowledge & skills of the Animal Health Technologist through continuing education programs; To promote positive legislation & to speak for the Animal Health Technologist in regard to legislative action; To develop & maintain a code of ethics & high professional standards of the Animal Health Technologist; To develop & maintain communication & cooperation among Animal Health Technologists, the veterinary medical profession, government & industry; To promote progressive & humane medical care for all animals
Vanessa George, Executive Director

Animal Alliance of Canada (AAC) / Alliance animale du Canada
#101, 221 Broadview Ave., Toronto ON M4M 2G3

Tel: 416-462-9541; Fax: 416-462-9647
contact@animalalliance.ca
www.animalalliance.ca
www.youtube.com/user/AACoffice
www.facebook.com/AnimalAllianceofCanada
twitter.com/Animal_Alliance

To preserve & protect all animals; To promote harmonious relationship between people, animals & the environment; To address issues including pound seizure, cosmetic & product

testing, puppy mills, pet overpopulation, exotic pet trade, the fur trade, sport hunting, factory farming, animals as "entertainment"
Liz White, Coordinator, Fundraising
Lia Laskaris, Coordinator, Donor Relations

Animal Justice
#5700, 100 King St. West, Toronto ON M5X 1C7
info@animaljustice.ca
www.animaljustice.ca
www.instagram.com/animaljustice_
www.facebook.com/animaljusticecanada
twitter.com/AnimalJustice
To advocate for animal protection in Canada; To pass progressive animal protection legislation; To enforce existing animal laws; To ensure the prosecution of animal abusers; To fight on behalf of animals in court
Camille Labchuk, Executive Director

Animal Welfare Foundation of Canada (AWF) / Fondation du bien-être animal du Canada
#643, 1231 Pacific Blvd., Vancouver BC V6Z 0E2
info@awfc.ca
awfc.ca
www.facebook.com/animalwelfarecanada
To improve the quality of life for animals in Canada
Leanne McConnachie, President
Courtney Graham, Secretary

Atlantic Canadian Anti-Sealing Coalition
contact@antisealingcoalition.ca
www.antisealingcoalition.ca
www.facebook.com/260618610812
twitter.com/GreySealHugger
The Atlantic Canadian Anti-Sealing Coalition is a collection of individuals and groups from across the Atlantic Region working to end the commercial seal hunt by peaceful and legal means.

Bird Studies Canada (BSC) / Etudes d'oiseaux Canada (EOC)
PO Box 160, 115 Front St., Port Rowan ON N0E 1M0
Tel: 519-586-3531; Fax: 519-586-3532
Toll-Free: 888-448-2473
hello@birdscanada.org
www.birdscanada.org
www.instagram.com/birds.canada
www.facebook.com/birdscanada
twitter.com/BirdStudiesCan
To advance the understanding, appreciation & conservation of wild birds & their habitats, in Canada & elsewhere, through studies that engage the skills, enthusiasm & support of its members volunteers, staff & the interested public
Steven Price, President
Sean Lindsay, CFO & Vice-President, Finance & Administration
Ruth Friendship-Keller, Director, Communications

Brandon Humane Society
2200 - 17 St. East, Brandon MB R7A 7M6
www.brandonhumanesociety.ca
www.facebook.com/307039086058890
To provide care for & homes for abused companion animals; To educate the public about the value of humane treatment of animals
Tracy Munn, Shelter Manager

British Columbia Society for the Prevention of Cruelty to Animals
1245 East 7th Ave., Vancouver BC V5T 1R1
Tel: 604-681-7271; Toll-Free: 800-665-1868
info@spca.bc.ca
www.spca.bc.ca
www.youtube.com/user/bcspcabc
www.facebook.com/bcspca
twitter.com/BC_SPCA
To protect & enhance the quality of life for domestic, farm, & wild animals in British Columbia
Marylee Davies, President

Calgary Humane Society
4455 - 110 Ave. SE, Calgary AB T2C 2T7
Tel: 403-205-4455; Fax: 403-723-6050
www.calgaryhumane.ca
www.youtube.com/user/CalgaryHumaneSociety
www.facebook.com/CalgaryHumaneSociety
twitter.com/CalgaryHumane
To foster humane treatment of animals & to promote values which demonstrate respect for animals
Carrie Fritz, Executive Director

Canada's Accredited Zoos & Aquariums (CAZA) / Aquariums et zoos accrédités du Canada (AZAC)
#400, 280 Metcalfe St., Ottawa ON K2P 1R7
Tel: 613-567-0099; Fax: 613-233-5438
Toll-Free: 888-822-2907
info@caza.ca
www.caza.ca
www.facebook.com/CAZA.AZAC
To promote the welfare of animals; To provide input into legislative matters & government policy affecting the zoo & aquarium industry
Massimo Bergamini, Executive Director

Canadian Animal Health Institute (CAHI) / Institut canadien de la santé animale (ICSA)
#102, 160 Research Lane, Guelph ON N1G 5B2
Tel: 519-763-7777; Fax: 519-763-7407
cahi@cahi-icsa.ca
www.cahi-icsa.ca
To work closely with allied industry groups for the betterment of Canadian agriculture; To foster & maintain a regulatory & legislative climate which will encourage member companies to develop & market useful animal health products & services; To promote the proper use of animal health & nutrition products by livestock & poultry farmers through user education information programs; To develop a public information program which enhances appreciation of the contributions the animal health & nutrition industry makes to the economy & society
Jean Szkotnicki, President
Colleen McElwain, Director, Programs

Canadian Association for Laboratory Animal Science (CALAS) / Association canadienne pour la science des animaux de laboratoire (ACSAL)
PO Box 20507, 2901 Sheppard Ave. East, Toronto ON M1T 3V5
Tel: 416-593-0268; Fax: 416-979-1819
office@calas-acsal.org
calas-acsal.org
www.facebook.com/CalasAcsal
twitter.com/calasacsal
To elevate standards of laboratory animal science; To promote excellence in research; To eliminate inhumane & unnecessary use of animals in research; To enhance animal welfare
Jason Allen, President
Christina Barnes, Vice-President & Secretary
Karen Gourlay, Chair, Symposium
Stephane Matte, Chair, Membership & Volunteer

Canadian Association of Professional Pet Dog Trainers (CAPPDT)
3226 Cambourne Cres., Mississauga ON L5N 5G2
Toll-Free: 877-748-7829
generalinfo@cappdt.ca
www.cappdt.ca
To further the concept of dog-friendly & humane training techniques; To provide a single source of access to educational opportunities, peer networking & event advertising
Pat Renshaw, Chair

Canadian Association of Veterinary Cannabinoid Medicine (CAVCM)
#357, 2-157 Harwood Ave. North, Ajax ON L1Z 0B6
info.cavcm@gmail.com
www.cavcm.ca
www.facebook.com/CAVCM
To advocate for veterinary access to cannabis; To advance education about the endocannabinoid system & cannabis-based therapies for animals
Sarah Silcox, President

Canadian Coalition for Farm Animals (CCFA) / Coalition Canadienne pour la Protection des Animaux de Ferme
#200/140, 131 Bloor St. West, Toronto ON M5S 1R8
info@humanefood.ca
www.humanefood.ca
www.facebook.com/canadiancoalitionforfarmanimals
To promote the welfare of animals raised for food in Canada through public education, legislative change & consumer choice
Stephanie Brown, Director

Canadian Council on Animal Care (CCAC) / Conseil canadien de protection des animaux (CCPA)
#800, 190 O'Connor St., Ottawa ON K2P 2R3
Tel: 613-238-4031; Fax: 613-238-2837
ccac@ccac.ca
www.ccac.ca
To act on behalf of the people of Canada to ensure, through programs of education, assessment & persuasion, that the use of animals in Canada, where necessary for research, teaching & testing, employs physical & psychological care according to

acceptable scientific standards; To promote an increased level of knowledge, awareness & sensitivity to the relevant ethical principles
Pierre Verreault, Executive Director

Canadian Federation of Humane Societies (CFHS) / Fédération des sociétés canadiennes d'assistance aux animaux
#102, 30 Concourse Gate, Ottawa ON K2E 7V7
Tel: 613-224-8072; Fax: 613-723-0252
Toll-Free: 888-678-2347
info@humanecanada.ca
humanecanada.ca
www.instagram.com/humanecanada
www.linkedin.com/company/humane-canada
www.facebook.com/HumaneCanada
twitter.com/HumaneCanada
To support its member animal welfare organizations across Canada in promoting respect & humane treatment toward all animals
Barbara Cartwright, Chief Executive Officer
Darcy Boucher, Manager, Marketing & Communications

Canadian Horse Defence Coalition (CHDC) / Coalition Canadienne pour la Défense des Chevaux (CCDC)
PO Box 21079, 150 First St., Orangeville ON L9W 4S7
info@defendhorsescanada.org
canadianhorsedefencecoalition.org
www.instagram.com/cdnhorsedefence
www.facebook.com/CanadianHorseDefenceCoalition
twitter.com/defendhorsescan
To ban the slaughter of horses for human consumption; To ban inhumane transport & export of live horses

Canadian Kennel Club (CKC) / Club canin canadien
#400, 200 Ronson Dr., Toronto ON M9W 5Z9
Tel: 416-675-5511; Fax: 416-675-6506
Toll-Free: 855-364-7252
information@ckc.ca
www.ckc.ca
www.instagram.com/ckc4thedogs
www.facebook.com/CKC4thedogs
twitter.com/CKC4thedogs
To provide registry services for all breeds of purebred dogs; To provide governance for all CKC approved events; To encourage, guide & advance the interests of purebred dogs & their owners & breeders in Canada
Lance Novak, Executive Director
Sherry Weiss, General Manager
Jacqueline Boychuk, Manager, Marketing & Communications
Sarah McDowell, Manager, Government & External Relations

Canadian National Goat Federation (CNGF) / Fédération canadienne nationale de la chèvre (FCNC)
7848 Nichol Peel Townline, Fergus ON N1M 2W4
info@cangoats.com
cangoats.com
www.facebook.com/CanadianNationalGoatFederation
To represent all goat producers in Canada, regardless if the goats are raised for meat, dairy, fibre or as pets
Kimberly Sheppard, Executive Director

Canadian Society of Animal Science (CSAS) / Société canadienne de science animale
c/o American Society of Animal Science, PO Box 7410, Champaign IL 61826-7410 USA
Tel: 217-356-9050; Fax: 217-568-6070
www.asas.org/CSAS
To provide opportunities to discuss the problems of the Canadian animal & poultry industries, with the objective of furthering advancements in these industries; To assist in the coordination of research, teaching & technology transfer related to the animal & poultry industries; To encourage publication of scientific information; To provide an annual forum for professionals in the agricultural industry to meet & discuss the most recent technological advancements in the field of animal & poultry science
Flavio Schramm Schenkel, President
Melissa Burnett, Manager, Membership

Canadian Society of Zoologists (CSZ) / Société canadienne de zoologie (SCZ)
c/o Département de biologie, Université Laval, Québec QC G1V 0A6
Tel: 902-820-2979
csz-scz.ca
To promote advancement & public awareness of zoology; To facilitate sharing of knowledge & ideas among all persons interested in science & practice of zoology; To organize discussions & debates of general interest

Helga Guderley, Secretary

Canadian Veterinary Medical Association (CVMA) / Association canadienne des médecins vétérinaires (ACMV)
339 Booth St., Ottawa ON K1R 7K1
Tel: 613-236-1162; *Fax:* 613-236-9681
Toll-Free: 800-567-2862
admin@cvma-acmv.org
www.canadianveterinarians.net
www.youtube.com/user/CVMAACMV
www.facebook.com/CanadianVeterinaryMedicalAssociation
twitter.com/CanVetMedAssoc
To represent the interests of the veterinary profession in Canada; To commit to excellence within the profession & to the well-being of animals; To promote public awareness of the contribution of animals & veterinarians to society
Jost Am Rhyn, Chief Executive Officer
Lori Tarbet, Manager, Communications & Public Relations
Natalie Cummins, Comptroller & Manager, Human Resources

Canadians for Ethical Treatment of Food Animals (CETFA)
PO Box 18024, 2225 - 41st Ave. West, Vancouver BC V6M 4L3
care@cetfa.com
www.cetfa.com
www.facebook.com/cetfa.news
CETFA is an investigation-based, farm animal advocacy organization that promotes the humane treatment of animals raised for food. It works to educate the public about Canada's food industry by providing information on factory farming practices.
Patricia Oswald, President
Twyla Francois, Head, Investigation

College of Veterinarians of Ontario (CVO)
2106 Gordon St., Guelph ON N1L 1G6
Tel: 519-824-5600; *Fax:* 519-824-6497
Toll-Free: 800-424-2856
inquiries@cvo.org
www.cvo.org
linkedin.com/company/the-college-of-veterinarians-of-ontario
twitter.com/cvo_org
To protect the public by regulating & enhancing the veterinary profession in Ontario
Marc Marin, President
Jan Robinson, Registrar & Chief Executive Officer

East Coast Aquarium Society (ECAS)
c/o 91 Deerbrooke Dr., Dartmouth NS B2V 1X2
ECAS.ca
www.facebook.com/eastcoastaquariumsociety
To further the aquarium hobby and promote the practice of keeping tropical fish.
Kathryn Purdy, President
Kelly Lively Jones, Director, Membership

Fort McMurray Society for the Prevention of Cruelty to Animals
155 MacAlpine Cres., Fort McMurray AB T9H 4A5
Tel: 780-743-8997
info@fortmcmurrayspca.ca
www.fortmcmurrayspca.ca
www.facebook.com/307296965992025
To ensure the humane treatment of all animals

Humane Society Yukon
126 Tlingit Rd., Whitehorse YT Y1A 6J2
Tel: 867-633-6019; *Fax:* 867-633-2210
info@humanesocietyyukon.ca
www.humanesocietyyukon.ca
www.facebook.com/153522391419947
To foster a caring, compassionate atmosphere; To promote a humane ethic & responsible pet ownership; To prevent cruelty to animals
Brent Slobodin, President

Manitoba Veterinary Medical Association (MVMA)
1590 Inkster Blvd., Winnipeg MB R2X 2W4
Tel: 204-832-1276; *Fax:* 204-832-1382
Toll-Free: 866-338-6862
www.mvma.ca
To enhance professional excellence for the health & welfare of animals & Manitobans
Andrea Lear, Executive Director

Montréal SPCA
5215, rue Jean-Talon ouest, Montréal QC H4P 1X4
Tél: 514-735-2711; *Téléc:* 514-735-7448
admin@spcamontreal.com
www.spcamontreal.com
www.facebook.com/SPCAMontreal
twitter.com/SPCAMontreal
Recueillir, héberger et soigner les animaux errants ou abandonnés; Rendre les animaux perdus à leurs propriétaires; mettre en adoption les animaux en santé; Inspecter et enquêter sur les plaintes de cruauté
Nicholas Gilman, Directeur général

National Retriever Club of Canada
c/o Laura Danforth, PO Box 601, Irricana AB T0M 1B0
secretary@nrcc-canada.com
www.nrcc-canada.com
www.facebook.com/nrccanada
Jim Andrew, President
Lauara Danforth, Secretary/Treasurer

New Brunswick Society for the Prevention of Cruelty to Animals / Société protectrice des animaux du Nouveau-Brunswick
PO Box 1412, Stn. A, Fredericton NB E3B 5E3
Tel: 506-458-8208; *Fax:* 506-458-8209
www.spca-nb.ca
To prevent cruelty to & encourage consideration for all animals; To pursue program of humane education
Hilary Howes, Executive Director

New Brunswick Veterinary Medical Association (NBVMA) / Association des médecins vétérinaires du Nouveau-Brunswick (AMVNB)
c/o Dr. George Whittle, 1700 Manawagonish Rd., Saint John NB E2M 3Y5
Tel: 506-693-9994
registrar@nbvma-amvnb.ca
www.nbvma-amvnb.ca
To act as the regulatory body for the practice of veterinary medicine in New Brunswick; To establish standards of practice in the profession; To promote animal health & welfare; To prevent public health problems related to animal disease
George Whittle, Registrar

Newfoundland & Labrador Society for the Prevention of Cruelty to Animals
PO Box 29053, St. John's NL A1A 5B5
Tel: 709-726-0301; *Fax:* 709-579-8089
shelter@spcastjohns.com
www.spcastjohns.org
www.instagram.com/spcastjohns
www.facebook.com/SPCAStJohns
twitter.com/spcastjohns
To act as the voice for animal welfare in Newfoundland & Labrador; To promote humane treatment toward all animals
Carolyn Hickey, Secretary

Newfoundland & Labrador Veterinary Medical Association (NALVMA)
PO Box 818, Mount Pearl NL A1N 3C8
nalvmacouncil@gmail.com
www.nalvma.ca
To promote better animal health care; To educate the general public & strive towards continued excellence in veterinary medicine
Tracy Matthews, President
Hilary McKeown, Treasurer-Secretary

Northwest Territories Society for the Prevention of Cruelty to Animals (NWTSPCA)
PO Box 2278, Yellowknife NT X1A 2P7
Tel: 867-920-7722; *Fax:* 867-920-7723
nwtspcayk@gmail.com
www.nwtspca.com
www.facebook.com/nwtspca
To provide animal rescue services in the north; to educate the public about the proper ways to protect & take care of animals
Nicole Spencer, President

Nova Scotia Society for the Prevention of Cruelty to Animals (NS SPCA)
PO Box 38073, Stn. Burnside, 11 Akerley Blvd., Dartmouth NS B3B 1X2
Tel: 902-835-4798; *Fax:* 902-835-7885
Toll-Free: 844-835-4798
info@spcans.ca
www.spcans.ca
www.instagram.com/nsspca
www.facebook.com/nsspca
twitter.com/nsspca
To prevent abuse & neglect of all animals in Nova Scotia; To provide leadership in humane education through outreach

activities & adoption services; To enforce laws on animal cruelty by issuing orders, warrants & laying charges
Elizabeth Murphy, Chief Executive Officer

Nova Scotia Veterinary Medical Association
15 Cobequid Rd., Lower Sackville NS B4C 2M9
Tel: 902-865-1876; *Fax:* 902-865-2001
info@nsvma.ca
www.nsvma.ca
To license Nova Scotia veterinarians in small animal, large animal & mixed practice as well as those employed in government, industry or other institutions
Anthony Snyder, President
Jennifer McKay, Vice-President
Angie Runnalls, Treasurer

Oakville & Milton Humane Society
445 Cornwall Rd., Oakville ON L6J 7S8
Tel: 905-845-1551; *Fax:* 905-845-1973
shelter@omhs.ca
www.omhs.ca
www.youtube.com/user/oakvillehumane
www.facebook.com/OakvilleMiltonHumaneSociety
twitter.com/OakvilleHumane
To promote the human/animal bond & relationship; To assist animals which are sick, have been injured, abused, sick, or abandoned, or are in need of rescue; To legally investigate & prosecute on the animals' behalf; To assist in finding suitable homes for unclaimed stray animals & to assist owners in finding their animals which have strayed or become lost; To construct, equip & maintain places for the reception & care of sick, injured or straying animals & for the humane destruction of unwanted animals.
Kim Millan, Executive Director

Ontario Society for the Prevention of Cruelty to Animals (OSPCA)
16586 Woodbine Ave., Stouffville ON L4A 2W3
Tel: 905-898-7122; *Fax:* 905-853-8643
Toll-Free: 888-668-7722
info@ospca.on.ca
www.ontariospca.ca
www.youtube.com/user/OntarioSPCA
www.linkedin.com/company/ontario-spca
www.facebook.com/OntarioSPCA
twitter.com/ontariospca
To provide care & shelter for animals, especially pets; To enforce animal cruelty laws in the province; To investigate cruelty complaints; To carry out rescues & bring perpetrators to court; To advocate for humane laws; To promote humane education & public awareness of the humane treatment of animals; To operate a Wildlife Rehabilitation Centre in Midland, ON
Kate MacDonald, Chief Executive Officer
Connie Mallory, Chief Inspector

Ontario Veterinary Medical Association (OVMA)
#205, 420 Bronte St. South, Milton ON L9T 0H9
Tel: 905-875-0756; *Fax:* 905-875-0958
Toll-Free: 800-670-1702
info@ovma.org
www.ovma.org
www.youtube.com/user/TheOVMA
www.facebook.com/onvetmedassoc
twitter.com/OnVetMedAssoc
To represent Ontario veterinarians in small animal, large animal & mixed practice as well as those employed in government, industry or other institutions; programs include government & public relations, humane veterinary practice, continuing education in veterinary science & practice management & direct services to members.
Doug Raven, CEO
Melissa Carlaw, Manager, Communications & Public Relations

Ordre des médecins vétérinaires du Québec (OMVQ)
#200, 800, av Ste-Anne, Saint-Hyacinthe QC J2S 5G7
Tél: 450-774-1427; *Téléc:* 450-774-7635
Ligne sans frais: 800-267-1427
www.omvq.qc.ca
Protection du public; contribuer à l'amélioration de la santé et du bien-être des animaux; formation des membres; maintien de la qualité des services vétérinaires
Joël Bergeron, Président
Suzie Prince, Directrice générale/Secrétaire

Pet Industry Joint Advisory Council (PIJAC)
#14, 1010 Polytek St., Ottawa ON K1J 9H9
Tel: 613-730-8111; *Fax:* 613-730-9111
Toll-Free: 800-667-7452
information@pijaccanada.com
www.pijaccanada.com
www.instagram.com/pijaccanada
www.linkedin.com/company/pijac-canada
www.facebook.com/PIJACCanada
twitter.com/pijaccanada
To promote the highest level of pet care for all sectors of the Canadian pet industry; To support research into the best attainable pet care; To engage in legislation & regulation affecting the Canadian pet industry at all levels of government; To promote the humane treatment of animals
Christine Carrière, President & CEO

PIJAC Canada / Conseil consultatif mixte de l'industrie des animaux de compagnie
#14, 1010 Polytek, Ottawa ON K1J 9H9
Tel: 613-730-8111; *Fax:* 613-730-9111
Toll-Free: 800-667-7452
information@pijaccanada.com
pijaccanada.com
www.linkedin.com/company/pijac-canada
To ensure the highest level of pet care attainable & a guarantee of a fair & equitable representation for all facets of the Canadian pet industry
Christine Carrière, President & CEO
Susan Dankert, Director, Communications
Stéphanie Renaud, Manager, Member Services

Prince Edward Island Humane Society (PEIHS)
PO Box 20022, 309 Sherwood Rd., Charlottetown PE C1A 9E3
Tel: 902-892-1190; *Fax:* 902-892-3617
info@peihumanesociety.com
www.peihumanesociety.com
www.facebook.com/peihumanesociety
twitter.com/peihs
To promote & provide the humane treatment of animals recognizing that each is deserving of moral concern
Marla Somersall, Executive Director
Beckie MacLean, Manager, Shelter

Prince Edward Island Veterinary Medical Association (PEIVMA)
PO Box 21097, 465 University Ave., Charlottetown PE C1A 9h6
Tel: 902-367-3757; *Fax:* 902-367-3176
admin.peivma@gmail.com
www.peivma.com
To represent PEI veterinarians in small animal, large animal & mixed practice as well as those employed in government, industry or other institutions; To licence & regulate veterinarians in PEI
Wade Sweet, President
Jenn Reid, Vice-President

Red Deer & District SPCA
4505 - 77th St., Red Deer AB T4P 2J1
Tel: 403-342-7722; *Fax:* 403-341-3147
office@reddeerspca.com
www.reddeerspca.com
www.instagram.com/reddeerspca
www.facebook.com/233609360018185
twitter.com/RedDeerSPCA
To care for & protect companion animals & promote humane treatment of animals & responsible pet ownership
Tara Hellewell, Executive Director

Regina Humane Society Inc.
PO Box 3143, Regina SK S4P 3G7
Tel: 306-543-6363; *Fax:* 306-545-7661
Crisis Hot-Line: 306-543-6363
info@reginahumane.ca
www.reginahumanesociety.ca
www.instagram.com/reginahumanesociety
www.facebook.com/reginahumane
twitter.com/reginahumane
To provide care & shelter for animals; To encourage the humane treatment of animals
Louise Yates, President

Registered Veterinary Technologists & Technicians of Canada (RVTTC)
PO Box 961, Kemptville ON K0G 1J0
Tel: 613-215-0619; *Toll-Free:* 844-626-0796
rvttcanada.ca
www.facebook.com/RVTTC
To provide coordination & resources to support members in the delivery of animal health care services
Shannon Brownrigg, Executive Director

Responsible Dog Owners of Canada (RDOC)
9 Liette Crt., RR1, Kemptville ON K0G 1J0
Tel: 613-206-6885
inquiries@responsibledogowners.ca
www.responsibledogowners.ca
To promote responsible dog ownership and public safety through education and support, cultivate respect for the rights and privileges of all members of society, both dog-owning and non-dog owning, encourage and foster recognition of the contribution that canines make in society through companionship, service/assistance and therapy and assemble a strong network of responsible dog owners to ensure the restoration and preservation of a dog-friendly society.
Candice O'Connell, Chair

Saskatchewan Society for the Prevention of Cruelty to Animals
519 - 45th St. West, Saskatoon SK S7L 5Z9
Tel: 306-382-7722; *Fax:* 306-384-3425
Toll-Free: 877-382-7722
info@sspca.ca
www.sspca.ca
www.facebook.com/SaskSPCA
twitter.com/SaskSPCA
To promote humane treatment of animals
Frances Wach, Executive Director

Société québécoise pour la défense des animaux (SQDA) / Québec Society for the Defense of Animals (QSDA)
#102, 847, rue Cherrier, Montréal QC H2L 1H6
Tél: 514-524-1976
sqda1976@gmail.org
www.sqda.org
Faire connaître et respecter le monde animal par tous les moyens possibles; obtenir une législation modifiée pour la protection de toute espèce; Combattre la destruction de notre faune; exposer l'aberration de l'élevage intensif; Contrôler l'expérimentation animale

World Animal Protection / Protection mondiale des animaux
#960, 90 Eglinton Ave. East, Toronto ON M4P 2Y3
Tel: 416-369-0044; *Fax:* 416-369-0147
Toll-Free: 800-363-9772
info@worldanimalprotection.ca
www.worldanimalprotection.ca
www.instagram.com/worldanimalprotectioncanada
www.facebook.com/WorldAnimalProtectionCanada
twitter.com/movetheworldca
To promote effective means for the prevention of cruelty to, & relief of suffering of animals in any part of the world
Dominique Bellemare, President
Colin Saravanamuttoo, Executive Director

World Small Animal Veterinary Association (WSAVA)
72 Melville St., Dundas ON L9H 2A1
Tel: 905-627-8540
wsavasecretariat@gmail.com
wsava.org
www.youtube.com/WSAVAVet
www.linkedin.com/company/world-small-animal-veterinary-association
www.facebook.com/WSAVA
twitter.com/vetswsava
To advance the health & welfare of small companion animals worldwide through a collaborative global community of veterinary peers; To unite veterinary associations that share common goals; To create a unified standard of care for the benefit of animals & humankind
Shane Ryan, President
Arpita Bhose, Chief Executive Officer

Yukon Schutzhund Association
Whitehorse YT
yukon.schutzhund@gmail.com
www.facebook.com/yukonysa
To promote dog training for the sport of Schutzhund in the Yukon Territory.

ZOOCHECK Canada Inc.
788 1/2 O'Connor Dr., Toronto ON M4B 2S6
Tel: 416-285-1744
zoocheck@zoocheck.com
www.zoocheck.com
www.facebook.com/canadazoocheck
twitter.com/zoocheckcanada
To improve wildlife protection in Canada and to end the abuse, neglect and exploitation of individual wild animals through: investigation & research; public education & awareness campaigns; capacity building initiatives; legal programs; legislative actions.

Antiques

Antiquarian Booksellers' Association of Canada (ABAC) / Association de la librairie ancienne du Canada (ALAC)
c/o Michael Park, Greenfield Books, 217 Academy Rd., Winnipeg MB R3M 0E3
Tel: 204-488-2023
info@abac.org
abac.org
www.facebook.com/210124119032896
To maintain high standards in the antiquarian book trade; To promote interest in rare books & manuscripts
Michael Park, President

Historic Vehicle Society of Ontario (HVSO)
c/o Canadian Transportation Museum & Heritage Village, 6155 Arner Town Line, RR#2, Kingsville ON N9Y 2E5
Tel: 519-776-6909; *Fax:* 519-776-8321
Toll-Free: 886-776-6909
info@ctmhv.com
www.ctmhv.com
To collect, restore & display vehicles, buildings & artifacts that serve to demonstrate the founding settlement of Essex County; to preserve the past to enhance the future.
Kim Brimner, Contact

Manitoba Antique Association (MAA)
PO Box 2881, Winnipeg MB R3C 4B4
mbantiqueassociation@gmail.com
mbantiqueassociation.com
www.facebook.com/MBAntiqueAssociation
To preserve & restore antiques; to promote the admiration of all antiques
Laurie Paradis, President
Audrey German, Contact, Membership

Archaeology

Archaeological Society of Alberta (ASA)
c/o Colleen Haukaas, 190 Tudor Lane, Edmonton AB T6J 3T5
Tel: 780-862-5220
arkysocietyalberta@gmail.com
www.arkyalberta.com
To promote the regulations of the Alberta Historical Act & to disseminate archaeological information by means of publications & seminars
Colleen Haukaas, Executive Secretary-Treasurer
Robyn Crook, Provincial Coordinator

Archaeological Society of British Columbia (ASBC)
c/o Archaeology Unit/G.Hill, Royal BC Museum, 675 Belleville St., Victoria BC V8W 9W2
asbcvictoria@gmail.com
www.asbc.bc.ca
To protect the archaeological heritage of British Columbia; To promote public understanding of the scientific approach to archaeology; To encourage government to preserve archaeological & pre-historic sites
Jacob Earnshaw, President

Association des archéologues du Québec (AAQ)
CP 322, Succ. Haute-Ville, Québec QC G1R 4P8
info@archeologie.qc.ca
www.archeologie.qc.ca
Définir les standards de la profession; veiller à la saine gestion et la mise en valeur du patrimoine archéologique à cause d'une éthique exemplaire et de la qualité de ses membres; agir comme interlocuteur privilégié pour tout ce qui regarde la question archéologique auprès des gouvernements et des organismes, privés ou publics, qui ont à cœur la préservation de notre patrimoine collectif

Association of Professional Archaeologists (APAA)
#600, 3250 Bloor St. West, Toronto ON M8X 2X9
Tel: 647-775-1674
info@apaontario.ca
www.facebook.com/APAOntario
To integrate the concerns of archaeologists in Ontario for all avenues of employment; To maintain commonly recognized standards for dealing with issues affecting archaeological resources
Margie Kenedy, President

Canadian Archaeological Association (CAA) / Association canadienne d'archéologie
www.canadianarchaeology.com
To publish & disseminate archaeological knowledge in Canada; To encourage archaeological research & conservation efforts;

To promote cooperation among archaeological societies & agencies
Gary Warrick, President
Jennifer Campbell, Vice President
Joanne Braaten, Secretary-Treasurer

Nova Scotia Archaeology Society (NSAS)
PO Box 36090, Halifax NS B3J 3S9
nsarchaeology@gmail.com
www.nsarchaeology.com
www.facebook.com/nsarchaeology
twitter.com/NSArchSociety
To promote the preservation of Nova Scotia's archaeological sites & resources
Sarah Ingram, President

The Ontario Archaeological Society
PO Box 62066, Stn. Victoria Terrace, #102, 1444 Queen St. E, Toronto ON M4A 2W1
Tel: 416-406-5959; *Fax:* 416-406-5959
info@ontarioarchaeology.org
www.ontarioarchaeology.org
www.youtube.com/user/OntarioArchaeology
twitter.com/ontarchsoc
To preserve, promote, investigate, record & publish an archaeological record of the province of Ontario
Lorie Harris, Executive Director
Chris Dalton, Director, Chapter Services
Dana Millson, Director, Membership

Saskatchewan Archaeological Society (SAS)
#1, 1730 Quebec Ave., Saskatoon SK S7K 1V9
Tel: 306-664-4124; *Fax:* 306-665-1928
general@thesas.ca
thesas.ca
www.facebook.com/saskarchsoc
twitter.com/saskarchsoc
To promote & conserve archaeology
Tomasin Playford, Executive Director
Belinda Riehl-Fitzsimmons, Business Administrator

Save Ontario Shipwrecks (SOS)
PO Box 2389, Blenheim ON N0P 1A0
Tel: 519-676-4110; *Fax:* 519-676-7058
www.saveontarioshipwrecks.on.ca
To promote & preserve Ontario's marine heritage
Chris Phinney, President
Nicole AuCoin, Secretary

Underwater Archaeological Society of British Columbia (UASBC)
c/o Vancouver Maritime Museum, 1905 Ogden Ave., Vancouver BC V6J 1A3
www.uasbc.com
vimeo.com/uasbc
To promote the science of underwater archaeology; to conserve, preserve & protect the maritime heritage lying beneath our coastal & inland waters

Architecture

Alberta Association of Architects (AAA)
Duggan House, 10515 Saskatchewan Dr. NW, Edmonton AB T6E 4S1
Tel: 780-432-0224; *Fax:* 780-439-1431
info@aaa.ab.ca
www.aaa.ab.ca
www.instagram.com/theabarchitects
www.linkedin.com/company/the-alberta-association-of-architects
www.facebook.com/AlbertaAssociationOfArchitects
twitter.com/theABarchitects
To regulate the practice of architecture & interior design in Alberta for the protection of the public & the administration of the profession; To bring together architects & support commitment to superior architecture
Barbara Bruce, Executive Director

Amis et propriétaires de maisons anciennes du Québec (APMAQ)
2050, rue Amherst, Montréal QC H2L 3L8
Tél: 514-528-8444; *Téléc:* 514-528-8686
apmaq@globetrotter.net
www.maisons-anciennes.qc.ca

Architects Association of Prince Edward Island (AAPEI)
PO Box 1766, 92 Queen St., Charlottetown PE C1A 7N4
Tel: 902-566-3699
www.aapei.com
www.facebook.com/architectsassociationpei
To increase awareness & understanding of architecture & its professional services.

Scott Stewart, Executive Director
David Lopes, Registrar

Architects' Association of New Brunswick (AANB) / Association des architectes du Nouveau-Brunswick
PO Box 5093, 36 Maple Ave., Sussex NB E4E 2N5
Tel: 506-433-5811; *Fax:* 506-432-1122
info@aanb.org
www.aanb.org
To govern & regulate persons in New Brunswick who offer architectural services; To advance & maintain the standards of architecture in New Brunswick
Sylvain Lagace, President
Donald C. Sterritt, Treasurer
Malcolm R. Boyd, Registrar

The Architectural Conservancy of Ontario (ACO)
#206, 401 Richmond St. West, Toronto ON M5V 3A8
Tel: 416-367-8075; *Fax:* 416-367-8630
Toll-Free: 866-221-1420
info@arconserv.ca
acontario.ca
www.instagram.com/arconserv
www.facebook.com/arconserve
twitter.com/arconserve
To preserve buildings & structures of architectural merit & places of natural beauty or interest
F. Leslie Thompson, President
William Coukell, Chief Operating Officer

Architectural Institute of British Columbia (AIBC)
#100, 440 Cambie St., Vancouver BC V6B 2N5
Tel: 604-683-8588; *Fax:* 604-683-8568
Toll-Free: 800-667-0753
info@aibc.ca
www.aibc.ca
twitter.com/AIBConnected
To regulate the profession of architecture in accordance with the Architects Act; to promote & increase the knowledge, skill & proficiency of its members in all things relating to the practice of architecture; to advance & maintain high standards of qualification & professional ethics; to promote public appreciation of architecture, allied arts, sciences & the professions
Mark Vernon, Chief Executive Officer
Grace Battiston, Director, Communications
Paul Becker, Director, Professional Services

Association des Architectes en pratique privée du Québec (AAPPQ) / Association of Architects in Private Practice of Québec
#302, 420, rue McGill, Montréal QC H2Y 2G1
Tél: 514-937-4140; *Téléc:* 514-937-2329
aappq@aappq.qc.ca
www.aappq.qc.ca
Représente et défend les intérêts de firmes d'architecture
Sylvie Perrault, Présidente

Association of Architectural Technologists of Ontario (AATO)
#13, 7611 Pine Valley Dr., Vaughan ON L4L 0A2
Tel: 905-405-0840; *Fax:* 905-405-9882
Toll-Free: 866-805-2286
aato@bellnet.ca
www.aato.ca
To maintain the standard of professional conduct of its members; To advocate to all levels of government on behalf of them & the industry
Italo Marti, Registrar

Canadian Architectural Certification Board (CACB) / Conseil canadien de certification en architecture (CCCA)
#710, 1 Nicholas St., Ottawa ON K1N 7B7
Tel: 613-241-8399; *Fax:* 613-241-7991
info@cacb.ca
www.cacb.ca
The Canadian Architectural Certification Board fulfills two seperate but related mandates: 1- Administer a program of accreditation of the Canadaian schools of architecture in accordance with "Conditions and Procedures for Accreditation" approved by the CCAC and the CCUSA and 2- Administer a program of certification of the educational qualifications of indivdual applicants in accordance withe criteria contained within the "Education Standard" approved by the CCAC.
Branko Kolarevic, President
Myriam Blais, Vice-President

Canadian Centre for Architecture (CCA) / Centre Canadien d'Architecture
1920, rue Baile, Montréal QC H3H 2S6
Tel: 514-939-7026
info@cca.qc.ca
www.cca.qc.ca
www.youtube.com/CCAChannel
www.facebook.com/cca.conversation
twitter.com/ccawire
To advance knowledge, promote public understanding, widen thought & debate on the art of architecture, its history, theory, practice & role in society
Phyllis Lambert, Founding Director Emeritus
Bruce Kuwabara, Chair, Board of Trustees
Giovanna Borasi, Director

Conseil de l'enveloppe du bâtiment du Québec (CEBQ) / Québec Building Envelope Council (QBEC)
12465, 94e av, Montréal QC H1C 1H6
www.cebq.org
Organiser des forums afin de faciliter la discussion et le transfert de technologies auprès de l'industrie de la construction
Mario D. Gonçalves, Président
Nathalie Martin, CPA, CGA, Directrice

Manitoba Association of Architects (MAA)
137 Bannatyne Ave., 2nd Fl., Winnipeg MB R3B 0R3
Tel: 204-925-4620; *Fax:* 204-925-4624
info@mbarchitects.org
www.mbarchitects.org
To protect the public interest & advance the profession of architecture
Judy Pestrak, Executive Director

Newfoundland Association of Architects (NLAA)
PO Box 5204, 7 Downing St., St. John's NL A1C 5V5
Tel: 709-726-8550; *Fax:* 709-726-1549
nlaa@newfoundlandarchitects.com
www.newfoundlandarchitects.com
To support architecture & architects in Newfoundland & Labrador
Jeremy Bryant, President
Grant Genova, Vice-President/Secretary
Lynda Hayward-Kirkland, Executive Director

Northwest Territories Association of Architects (NWTAA)
Administrative Office, Northern Frontier Visitors Centre, PO Box 1394, Yellowknife NT X1A 2P1
Tel: 867-766-4216; *Fax:* 867-973-3654
nwtaa@yk.com
www.nwtaa.ca
To maintain the Register of Architects, in accordance with the NWT Architects Act
Ben Russo, Executive Director
Rod Kirkwood, President

Nova Scotia Association of Architects (NSAA)
1361 Barrington St., Halifax NS B3J 1Y9
Tel: 902-423-7607; *Fax:* 902-425-7024
info@nsaa.ns.ca
www.nsaa.ns.ca
To administer the practice of architecture in Nova Scotia
Margo Dauphinee, Executive Director
Jeremy Martell, Coordinator, Membership

Ontario Association of Architects (OAA)
1 Duncan Mill Rd., Toronto ON M3B 1Z2
Tel: 416-449-6898; *Fax:* 416-449-5756
Toll-Free: 800-565-2724
oaamail@oaa.on.ca
www.oaa.on.ca
To operate in accordance with the Government of Ontario's Architects Act; To serve & protect the public interest by promoting & increasing the knowledge, skill, & proficiency of members
Kristi Doyle, Executive Director
Nedra Brown, Registrar
Christie Mills, Deputy Registrar
Marilyn McInnes, Manager, Finance & Administration
Erik Missio, Manager, Communications
Ellen Savitsky, Manager, Education & Development
Adam Tracey, Manager, Policy & Government Relations

Ordre des architectes du Québec (OAQ)
#200, 420, rue McGill, Montréal QC H2Y 2G1
Tél: 514-937-6168; *Téléc:* 514-933-0242
Ligne sans frais: 800-599-6168
info@oaq.com
www.oaq.com
www.linkedin.com/company/ordre-architectes-qc
www.facebook.com/Ordre.architectes.Qc
twitter.com/OrdreArchiQc

D'assurer la protection du public en régissant l'exercice de la profession d'architecte au Québec
Nathalie Dion, Présidente
Jean-Pierre Dumont, Directeur général

Royal Architectural Institute of Canada (RAIC) / Institut royal d'architecture du Canada
#330, 55 Murray St., Ottawa ON K1N 5M3
Tel: 613-241-3600; *Fax:* 613-241-5750
Toll-Free: 844-856-7242
info@raic.org
www.raic.org
www.instagram.com/raic_irac
www.linkedin.com/in/raicirac
www.facebook.com/theraic.irac
twitter.com/RAIC_IRAC
To represent Canadian architects nationally & internationally; To foster public awareness & appreciation of architecture; To engage in architectural research & education; To lobby government on architectural issues
Mike Brennan, Chief Executive Officer
Tanner Morton, Coordinator, Communications

Saskatchewan Association of Architects (SAA)
#200, 642 Broadway Ave., Saskatoon SK S7N 1A9
Tel: 306-242-0733; *Fax:* 306-664-2598
www.saskarchitects.com
To regulate the profession of architecture in Saskatchewan, in order to ensure the protection of the public interest; To advance the profession of architecture in the province; To ensure that high standards for practice & conduct are followed
Janelle Unrau, Executive Director

Society for the Study of Architecture in Canada (SSAC) / Société pour l'étude de l'architecture au Canada (SEAC)
429 Rossland Rd. East, Ajax ON L1Z 0M7
canada-architecture.org
To promote the study of Canadian architecture including an examination of both historical & cultural issues relating to buildings, districts, cities & the cultural landscapes; To encourage the collection & preservation of Canada's architectural records; To encourage preservation of the built environment
Candace Iron, President

Armed Forces

Together We Stand Foundation
#601, 5775 Yonge St., Toronto ON M2M 4J1
Tel: 416-324-9739
info@twsfoundation.ca
twsfoundation.ca
www.instagram.com/twsfoundationca
www.linkedin.com/company/together-we-stand-military-families-foundation
www.facebook.com/TWSFoundationCA
twitter.com/TWSFoundationCA
To recognize & thank families of Canadian Armed Forces members away during the holidays
Rick Seymour, Chief Executive Officer

Arts

Alberta Foundation for the Arts (AFA)
10708 - 105th Ave., Edmonton AB T5H 0A1
Tel: 780-427-9968; *Toll-Free:* -310-0000
afacontact@gov.ab.ca
affta.ab.ca
www.instagram.com/afa.1991
www.facebook.com/AlbertaFoundationfortheArts
twitter.com/AFA1991
To create the best possible climate for the arts in Alberta
Jeff Brinton, Executive Director

Arts Council of the North Okanagan (ACNO)
2704A Hwy. 6, Vernon BC V1T 5G5
Tel: 250-542-6243
vcacinfo@shaw.ca
www.acno.ca
twitter.com/artscouncilno
To stimulate, encourage, & develop arts & culture in the Greater Vernon Area of BC; To foster an awareness & appreciation of the value of the arts in the community at large
Mary Jo O'Keefe, President
David Woodhouse, Treasurer

Assembly of BC Arts Councils
#301, 1321 Blanshard St., Victoria BC V8W 0B6
Tel: 778-410-5104
info@artsbc.org
www.artsbc.org
www.instagram.com/artsbc
www.facebook.com/ArtsBC
twitter.com/artsbc
To promote & advance the role of arts & culture in building community; To work with community based organizations in furthering the impact & contribution of the arts locally, regionally, & province-wide
Patricia Huntsman, Interim Managing Director

BC Alliance for Arts & Culture
#100, 938 Howe St., Vancouver BC V6Z 1N9
Tel: 604-681-3535; *Fax:* 604-681-7848
info@allianceforarts.com
www.allianceforarts.com
www.youtube.com/user/AllianceArtsCulture
www.facebook.com/AllianceforArtsandCulture
twitter.com/AllianceArts
To project a strong voice for the local arts community; To promote the activities of the arts through a variety of programs, services & marketing strategies; To increase public awareness of & accessibility to the arts & culture
Brenda Leadley, Executive Director
Nancy Lanthier, Director, Communications
Beverly Edgecomb, Manager, Member Relations

Business for the Arts / Affairs pour les arts
#202, 133 Richmond St. West, Toronto ON M5H 2L3
Tel: 416-869-3016; *Fax:* 416-869-0435
www.businessandarts.org
www.instagram.com/businessftarts
www.facebook.com/BusinessftArts
twitter.com/businessftarts
To make the partnership between business & the arts more effective in supporting the nation's creative minds.
Nichole Anderson, President & CEO

Canadian Artists Representation (CARFAC) / Le Front des artistes canadiens
#250, 2 Daly Ave., Ottawa ON K1N 6E2
Tel: 613-233-6161; *Fax:* 613-233-6162
Toll-Free: 866-344-6161
communications@carfac.ca
www.carfac.ca
www.facebook.com/CARFACNational
twitter.com/carfacnational
To act as a national voice for Canada's professional visual artists; To promote a socio-economic climate that is conducive to the production of visual arts
Paddy Lamb, President & Spokesperson
Theresie Tungilik, Vice-President
Daniel Rumbolt, Secretary
David Yazbeck, Treasurer

Canadian Arts Presenting Association (CAPACOA) / Association canadienne des organismes artistiques
#200, 17 York St., Ottawa ON K1N 5S7
Tel: 613-562-3515; *Fax:* 613-562-4005
mail@capacoa.ca
capacoa.ca
www.linkedin.com/company/capacoa
www.facebook.com/CAPACOA
twitter.com/capacoa
To promote the development of the presentation of the arts in Canada; To promote & encourage greater knowledge & appreciation of the presentation of the performing arts; To encourage touring of artists & attractions throughout Canada; To provide information on artists & attractions touring regionally & nationally; To assist presenters of the arts with coordination of bookings; To provide opportunities for professional development of presenters; To promote communication & understanding between presenters of the arts; To provide forum for exchange of views concerning presentation of the performing arts generally; To provide information on regional & federal policies which relate to presentation of the arts; To provide the opportunity to make contacts nationwide
Sue Urquhart, Executive Director
Mélanie Bureau, Manager, Operations

Canadian Celtic Arts Association
c/o Jean Talman, 81 St. Mary St., Toronto ON M5S 1J4
info@canadiancelticarts.ca
www.canadiancelticarts.ca
To promote Celtic culture; To serve as a link between the diverse Celtic communities in Canada
Janice Chan, President
Donald Gillies, Treasurer
Jean Talman, Membership Secretary & Coordinator, Programmes

The Canadian Society for Mesopotamian Studies (CSMS) / La Société canadienne des études mésopotamiennes
c/o RIM Project, University of Toronto, 4 Bancroft Ave., 4th Fl., Toronto ON M5S 1C1
Tel: 416-978-4531; *Fax:* 416-978-3305
csms@chass.utoronto.ca
projects.chass.utoronto.ca/csms
To stimulate interest among the general public in the culture, history & archaeology of Mesopotamia, in particular the civilizations of Sumer, Babylon & Assyria, as well as neighbouring ancient civilizations

Conseil des arts et des lettres du Québec (CALQ)
79, boul René Lévesque est, 3e étage, Québec QC G1R 5N5
Tél: 418-643-1707; *Téléc:* 418-643-4558
Ligne sans frais: 800-897-1707
info@calq.gouv.qc.ca
www.calq.gouv.qc.ca
www.youtube.com/user/LeCALQ
www.facebook.com/LeCALQ
twitter.com/LeCALQ
Soutenir dans toutes les régions du Québec la création, l'expérimentation, la production et la diffusion dans les domaines des arts de la scène (théâtre, danse, musique, chanson, arts du cirque), des arts médiatiques (arts numériques, cinéma et vidéo), des arts multidisciplinaires, des arts visuels, de la littérature et du conte, des métiers d'art et de la recherche architecturale et d'en favoriser la reconnaissance et le rayonnement au Québec, au Canada et à l'étranger
Marie DuPont, Président du conseil d'administration
Stéphan La Roche, Président & Directeur général

Conseil québécois des arts médiatiques (CQAM)
3995, rue Berri, Montréal QC H2L 4H2
Tél: 514-527-5116; *Ligne sans frais:* 888-527-5116
www.cqam.org
Robin Dupuis, Président
Isabelle L'Italien, Directrice générale

Federation of Canadian Artists (FCA)
1241 Cartwright St., Vancouver BC V6H 4B7
Tel: 604-681-2744; *Fax:* 604-681-2740
fcaadmin@artists.ca
artists.ca
To share & promote the visual arts
Dene Croft, President
Jennifer Heine, Vice-President
Patrick E. Meyer, Executive Director
Helen Duckworth, Coordinator, Volunteer & Gallery
Tessa McIntosh, Coordinator, Membership & Studio
Katrin Sarstedt, Coordinator, Education

Governor General's Performing Arts Awards Foundation (GGPAAF) / Les Prix du Gouverneur Général pour les arts du spectacle
#400, 280 Metcalfe St., Ottawa ON K2P 1R7
Tel: 613-241-5297
awards@ggpaa.ca
ggpaa.ca
www.facebook.com/ggawards.prixgg
twitter.com/govgpaa
To honour & celebrate the lifetime artistic achievement of Canada's outstanding performing artists; To foster cross-cultural awareness of Anglophone artists in French Canada & of Francophone artists in English Canada; To foster awareness of Canada's diverse linguistic & cultural groups; To foster awareness of indigenous performing artists; To raise profile among Canadians of the achievements & contributions of Canadian performing artists at home & abroad; To inspire future performing artists
Whitney Taylor, Executive Director

International Association of Art Critics - Canada (IAAC) / Association internationale des Critiques d'art - Canada (AICA)
c/o Ninon Gauthier, President, #301, 150, rue Berlioz, Montréal QC H3E 1K3
Tel: 514-658-2538
aica-canada.org
To contribute to the promotion of contemporary art & freedom of expression in the visual arts; To develop national & international cooperation in art criticism
Ninon Gauthier, President
Earl Miller, Treasurer & Secretary

International Music Software Trade Association (IMSTA)
1160 Ellesmere Rd., Toronto ON M1P 2X4
Tel: 416-789-6850; *Fax:* 416- 78-9166
info@imsta.org
imsta.org
www.instagram.com/imstafesta
twitter.com/IMSTA_FESTA
To promote the message 'Buy the Software You Use'; To end the piracy of music software

Manitoba Arts Council (MAC) / Conseil des arts du Manitoba (CAM)
#525, 93 Lombard Ave., Winnipeg MB R3B 3B1
Tel: 204-945-2237; *Fax:* 204-945-5925
Toll-Free: 866-994-2787
info@artscouncil.mb.ca
artscouncil.mb.ca
www.facebook.com/mbartscouncil
An arms-length agency of the provincial government dedicated to artistic excellence; offers a broad based grant program for professional artists & arts organizations; promotes, preserves, supports & advocates for the arts as essential to the quality of life of all people of Manitoba.
Akoulina Connell, Chief Executive Officer
Charlene Brown, Executive Coordinator
Elly Wittens, Office Manager

Mass Culture Canada
Toronto ON
info@massculture.ca
massculture.ca
www.instagram.com/massculture_
www.linkedin.com/company/mass-culture
www.facebook.com/massculture19
twitter.com/massculture_
To conduct arts & culture research; To see that all communities can mobilize & benefit from arts & culture research
Robin Sokoloski, Director, Organizational Development
Kathryn Geertsema, Office Manager

National Arts Centre Foundation
PO Box 1534, Stn. B, Ottawa ON K1P 5W1
Tel: 613-947-7000
donorscircle@nac-cna.ca
nacfoundation.ca
To raise money on behalf on behalf of the National Arts Centre which funds performing arts projects across Canada
Jayne Watson, CEO

New Brunswick Arts Board
649 Queen St., 2nd Fl., Fredericton NB E3B 1C3
Tel: 506-444-4444; *Fax:* 506-444-5543
Toll-Free: 866-460-2787
artsnb.ca
www.facebook.com/artsnb
twitter.com/artsnb
To achieve the vision of New Brunswick as a place where all residents attend a diversity of quality, live performances in their own community; all students attend performances in their own school by performing artists; artists residing in New Brunswick find a supportive arts community & the resources necessary to establish a career in the performing arts in New Brunswick & beyond; maintain a resource centre; assume an advocacy for the performing arts in the community
Akoulina Connell, Executive Director
Pierre McGraw, Chair

Newfoundland & Labrador Arts Council (NLAC)
The Newman Building, PO Box 98, 1 Springdale St., St. John's NL A1C 5H5
Tel: 709-726-2212; *Fax:* 709-726-0619
Toll-Free: 866-726-2212
nlacmail@nlac.ca
www.nlac.ca
www.facebook.com/NLArtsCouncil
twitter.com/NLArtsCouncil
To foster & promote the creation & enjoyment of the arts for the people of the province
Reg Winsor, Executive Director

Northwest Territories Arts Council / Conseil des arts des TNO
c/o GNWT Education, Culture & Employment, PO Box 1320, Yellowknife NT X1A 2L9
Tel: 867-767-9347; *Fax:* 867-873-0205
Toll-Free: 877-445-2787
www.nwtartscouncil.ca
To promote & encourage the arts in the Northwest Territories
Boris Atamanenko, Manager, Community Cultural Development

Ontario Arts Council (OAC) / Conseil des arts de l'Ontario
121 Bloor St. East, 7th Fl., Toronto ON M4W 3M5
Tel: 416-961-1660; *Toll-Free:* 800-387-0058
info@arts.on.ca
www.arts.on.ca
www.youtube.com/user/OntarioArts
www.facebook.com/OntarioArts
twitter.com/ONArtsCouncil
To serve as Ontario's primary funding body for professional arts activity; To promote & assist in the development of the arts & artists
Carolyn Vesely, Chief Executive Officer
Kirsten Gunter, Director, Communications
Kelly Langgard, Director, Granting

Organization of Saskatchewan Arts Councils (OSAC)
1102 - 8th Ave., Regina SK S4R 1C9
Tel: 306-586-1250; *Fax:* 306-586-1550
info@osac.ca
www.osac.ca
www.instagram.com/osacsask
www.facebook.com/OSACsask
twitter.com/OSACsask
To assist the membership in their endeavors to develop, promote & present the visual arts &/or performing arts
Kevin Korchinski, Executive Director

SaskCulture Inc.
#404, 2125 - 11th Ave., Regina SK S4P 3X3
Tel: 306-780-9284; *Fax:* 306-780-9252
Toll-Free: 855-277-9469
saskculture.info@saskculture.ca
www.saskculture.ca
www.facebook.com/SaskCulture
twitter.com/SaskCulture
To represent the cultural community as a whole & assist the cultural community in its endeavors to develop & promote the cultural life of the province
Rose Gilks, CEO
Dean Kush, Associate CEO
Diane Ell, Manager, Communications
Gloria Walsh, Manager, Administration

Société de Promotion et de Diffusion des Arts et de la Culture (SPDAC)
Festival International Montréal en Arts, #211, 576, rue Sainte-Catherine est, Montréal QC H2L 2E1
Tél: 514-370-2269; *Ligne sans frais:* 877-522-4646
info@mtlenarts.com
mtlenarts.com
www.facebook.com/MtlenArts
twitter.com/mtlenarts
Organisme à but non lucratif qui favorise un rapprochement entre les communautés locales et les artistes; Le Festival International Montréal en Arts accueille plus de 250 artistes en arts visuels et métiers d'arts
Stéphane Mabilais, Directeur général

Union des artistes (UDA) / Artists' Union
#1005, 5445, ave De Gaspé, Montréal QC H2T 3B2
Tél: 514-288-6682; *Téléc:* 514-285-6789
info@uda.ca
uda.ca
www.youtube.com/user/Uniondesartistes
www.facebook.com/UnionDesArtistes
twitter.com/udaquebec
Identification, étude, défense et développement des intérêts économiques, sociaux et moraux de ses membres
Sophie Prègent, Président
Alexandre Curzi, Directeur général

Automotive

Alberta Motor Association (AMA)
#10310, 39A G.A. MacDonald Ave., Edmonton AB T6J 6R7
Tel: 780-430-5555; *Fax:* 780-430-5751
Toll-Free: 800-642-3810
ama.ab.ca
To provide roadside assistance to members
Don Smitten, President

Alfa Romeo Club of Canada (ARCC)
PO Box 62, Stn. Q, Toronto ON M4T 2L7
admin@alfaclub.ca
www.alfaclub.ca
www.facebook.com/alfaclub
To share common interest in use, preservation & appreciation of Alfa Romeo automobiles
Alex Csank, President

Christine Pickering, Secretary

Association des concessionnaires Ford du Québec
16, rue Marguerite-Bourgeoys, Boucherville QC J4B 2H3
Tél: 450-655-2090

Association des spécialistes du pneus et Mécanique du Québec (ASPMQ)
CP 51017, Laval QC H7T 2Z3
Ligne sans frais: 866-454-0477
info@aspmq.ca
www.aspmq.ca
www.linkedin.com/company/aspmq—-association-des-spécialistes-pneu-et-mécanique-du-québec
Cynthia Fredette, Présidente

Automobile Journalists Association of Canada (AJAC) / Association des journalistes automobile du Canada
PO Box 64591, Unionville ON L3R 1M0
office@ajac.ca
www.ajac.ca
www.facebook.com/AJACanada
twitter.com/AJACanada
To report on new vehicles & new industry trends in various print and broadcast media.

Automobile Protection Association (APA) / Association pour la protection automobile
292, boul St-Joseph ouest, Montréal QC H2V 2N7
Tel: 514-272-5555; *Fax:* 514-273-0797
apamontreal@apa.ca
apa.ca
www.facebook.com/AutomobileProtectionAssociation
twitter.com/APA_LEMONAID
To inform & represent the public on major automobile-related issues

Automotive Aftermarket Retailers of Ontario
#10, 5100 South Service Rd., Burlington ON L7L 6A5
Tel: 905-634-4040; *Toll-Free:* 800-268-5400
aaro@aaro.ca
www.aaro.ca
To advance the interests of the independent sector of the Automotive Service Industry
Diane Freeman, Executive Director

Automotive Industries Association of Canada (AIAC) / Association des industries de l'automobile du Canada
#1400, 180 Elgin St., Ottawa ON K2P 2K3
Tel: 613-728-5821; *Fax:* 613-728-6021
Toll-Free: 800-808-2920
info@aiacanada.com
www.aiacanada.com
www.linkedin.com/company/aia-canada
www.facebook.com/AIAofCanada
twitter.com/AIAOFCANADA
To represent the automotive aftermarket industry in Canada; To promote, educate, & represent members
Jean-François Champagne, President
Ibtihal Ridha, Senior Director, Finance & Operations
Courtney DeLaura, Manager, Marketing & Communications
Didina Kyenge, Executive Assisstant & HR Administrator

Automotive Parts Manufacturers' Association (APMA)
#801, 10 Four Seasons Pl., Toronto ON M9B 6H7
Tel: 416-620-4220; *Fax:* 416-620-9730
info@apma.ca
www.apma.ca
www.linkedin.com/company/apmacanada
twitter.com/APMACanada
To promote the manufacture in Canada of automotive parts, systems, components, materials, tools, equipment & supplies, & also the provision of services used in the automotive industry & in particular for the original equipment market; To engage in activities in support of the welfare of the members of the Association
Flavio Volpe, President

Automotive Recyclers of Canada (ARC)
134 Langarth St. East, London ON N6C 1Z5
Tel: 519-858-8761; *Fax:* 905-383-1904
info@autorecyclers.ca
autorecyclers.ca
twitter.com/autorecyclersCA
To act as the national voice for provincial member automotive recycling associations
Steve Fletcher, Managing Director

Automotive Retailers Association of British Columbia
#1, 8980 Fraserwood Ct., Burnaby BC V5J 5H7
Tel: 604-432-7987; *Fax:* 604-432-1756
reception@ara.bc.ca
www.ara.bc.ca
www.facebook.com/autoretailers
twitter.com/autoretailers
To enhance the image & competitive status of association members throughout BC & ensure high quality service to protect the road safety of the motoring public
Ken McCormack, President

BMW Clubs Canada (BMWCC) / Le Club BMW du Canada
info@bmwclub.ca
bmwclub.ca
www.facebook.com/BMW.Canada
To promote the enjoyment & sharing of good will & fellowship derived from owning a BMW automobile or motorcycle
Chris Pawlowicz, President

CAA British Columbia (BCAA)
4567 Canada Way, Burnaby BC V5G 4T1
Tel: 604-268-5500; *Toll-Free:* 877-325-8888
info@bcaa.com
www.bcaa.com
To provide motoring, travel & insurance services to members in British Columbia & the Yukon
Eric Hopkins, President & CEO
Navida Suleman, Chief Financial Officer
Salman Manki, Chief Legal Officer
Grant Stockwell, Chief Mobility Officer

CAA Manitoba
PO Box 1400, 870 Empress St., Winnipeg MB R3G 3H3
Tel: 204-262-6161; *Toll-Free:* 800-222-4357
contact@caamanitoba.com
www.caamanitoba.com
www.instagram.com/caamanitoba
www.facebook.com/caamanitoba
twitter.com/caamanitoba
To provide safety products & services to Manitobans
Michael R. Mager, President & Chief Executive Officer

CAA Québec
444, rue Bouvier, Québec QC G2J 1E3
Tél: 418-624-2424; *Ligne sans frais:* 800-686-9243
info@caaquebec.com
www.caaquebec.com
www.instagram.com/caaquebec
www.linkedin.com/company/caa-quebec
www.facebook.com/caaQc
twitter.com/CAA_Quebec
Veut assurer la sécurité et paix d'esprit à chacun de ses membres ainsi qu'à ses clients en leur offrant des services et des produits de très haute qualité dans les domaines de l'automobile, du voyage, de l'habitation et des services financiers

Canadian Automobile Association Atlantic
Corporate Office & Saint John Member Service Centre, 378 Westmorland Rd., Saint John NB E2J 2G4
Tel: 506-634-1400; *Fax:* 506-653-9500
Toll-Free: 800-561-8807
www.atlantic.caa.ca
www.facebook.com/CAA.Atlantic
twitter.com/CAA_Atlantic
To serve New Brunswick, Newfoundland & Labrador, Nova Scotia, & Prince Edward Island

Canadian Automobile Association Niagara
3271 Schmon Pkwy., Thorold ON L2V 4Y6
Tel: 905-984-8585; *Fax:* 905-688-0289
Toll-Free: 800-263-3616
caaniagara.ca
www.youtube.com/user/CAANiagara1
www.facebook.com/CAANiagara
twitter.com/CAANiagara

Canadian Automobile Association North & East Ontario
2151 Thurston Dr., Ottawa ON K1G 6C9
Tel: 613-820-1890; *Fax:* 613-820-4646
Toll-Free: 800-267-8713
contactcaa@caaneo.on.ca
www.caaneo.ca
www.youtube.com/user/TheCAANEOChannel
www.facebook.com/CAANEO
twitter.com/CAANEO
To deliver automotive, travel, insurance & related services to members & advocate on their behalf
Christina Hlusko, Chief Executive Officer
Mandy Chepeka, Contact, Communications

Canadian Automobile Association Saskatchewan
200 Albert St. North, Regina SK S4R 5E2
Tel: 306-791-4314; *Fax:* 306-949-4461
Toll-Free: 800-564-6222
caa.admin@caasask.sk.ca
caask.ca
www.youtube.com/caasask
www.linkedin.com/company/521051
twitter.com/caasaskatchewan
To guarantee excellent emergency road assistance, travel, & insurance services; To provide services, products, programs, & representations to government in order to meet the needs of members, clients, & employees
Fred Titanich, President

Canadian Automobile Association South Central Ontario
60 Commerce Valley Dr. East, Thornhill ON L3T 7P9
Tel: 416-221-4300; *Fax:* 905-771-3101
Toll-Free: 800-268-3750
membership@caasco.ca
www.caasco.ca
www.youtube.com/caasouthcentralON
www.facebook.com/106112779480473
twitter.com/caasco
To enrich the driving experience of members by providing travel, insurance & automotive services & information
Bill Carter, Chair
Jay Woo, President & CEO
Jeff LeMoine, Consultant, Communications

Canadian Automobile Dealers' Association (CADA) / Corporation des associations de détaillants d'automobiles (CADA)
#303, 123 Commerce Valley Dr. East, Thornhill ON L3T 7W8
Tel: 905-940-4959; *Toll-Free:* 800-463-5289
www.cada.ca
twitter.com/cdnautocada
To deal with issues of a national nature which affect the well-being of franchised automobile & truck dealers in Canada
Tim Reuss, President & CEO

Canadian Automobile Sport Clubs - Ontario Region Inc. (CASC-OR)
#222, 1100 Finch Ave. West, Toronto ON M3J 2T2
Tel: 416-667-9500; *Fax:* 416-667-9555
Toll-Free: 877-667-9505
office@casc.on.ca
www.casc.on.ca
To provide leadership, management, advocacy, & the administrative services, facilities, & equipment necessary to enable members to maximize their enjoyment & participation in motorsport; To maintain controls & standards necessary for safe competition
Gunter Schmidt, President

Canadian Vehicle Manufacturers' Association (CVMA) / Association canadienne des constructeurs de véhicules
#400, 170 Attwell Dr., Toronto ON M9W 5Z5
Tel: 416-364-9333; *Fax:* 416-367-3221
Toll-Free: 800-758-7122
info@cvma.ca
www.cvma.ca
To create a framework within which member companies work together to achieve shared industry objectives on a range of important issues such as consumer protection, the environment, & vehicle safety
Mark A. Nantais, President

Corporation des concessionnaires d'automobiles du Québec inc. (CCAQ)
#750, 140, Grande-Allée est, Québec QC G1R 5M8
Tél: 418-523-2991; *Téléc:* 418-523-3725
Ligne sans frais: 800-463-5189
info@ccaq.com
www.ccaq.com
www.facebook.com/LaCCAQ
twitter.com/CCAQ
Offre une multitude de services aux membres; représenter ses membres
Robert Poëti, Président-directeur général

Halifax-Dartmouth Automobile Dealers' Association (HDADA)
PO Box 142, #502, 5657 Spring Garden Rd., Halifax NS B3J 3R4
Tel: 902-425-2445; *Fax:* 902-425-2441
info@hdada.ca
www.hdada.ca

Japan Automobile Manufacturers Association of Canada
#840, 151 Bloor St. West, Toronto ON M5S 1S4
Tel: 416-968-0150
jama@jama.ca
www.jama.ca
To promote increased understanding of economic & trade matters pertaining to the motor vehicle industry; To encourage closer cooperation between Canada & Japan; To represent the interests of members
Larry Hutchinson, Chair

Manitoba Motor Dealers Association (MMDA)
#112, 1790 Wellington Ave., Winnipeg MB R3H 1B2
Tel: 204-985-4200; *Fax:* 204-775-9125
Toll-Free: 800-949-6632
info@mmda.mb.ca
www.mmda.mb.ca
www.facebook.com/MBMotorDealers
twitter.com/MBMotorDealers
To represent franchised automobile & truck dealers in Manitoba by dealing with provincial issues that affect this membership; To advance the automotive industry in Manitoba; To uphold the code of ethics
Geoff Sine, Executive Director

Motor Dealers' Association of Alberta (MDA)
6248 - 50 St., Edmonton AB T6B 2N7
Tel: 780-465-8854; *Fax:* 780-465-6201
info@mdaalberta.com
www.mdaalberta.com
www.facebook.com/266699400099567
To serve the collective interest of all its members & promote positive relationships with government, industry, suppliers, consumers, & media, by offering needed & effective programs & services.
Denis Ducharme, President

New Car Dealers Association of BC
#70, 10551 Shellbridge Way, Richmond BC V6X 2W9
Tel: 604-214-9964
info@newcardealers.ca
www.newcardealers.ca
To promote benefits & heighten awareness of issues of interest to members
Blair Qualey, President & CEO
Shakira Maqbool, Office Manager

Nova Scotia Automobile Dealers' Association (NSADA)
Park Lane Terraces, PO Box 142, #502, 5657 Spring Garden Rd., Halifax NS B3J 3R4
Tel: 902-425-2445
info@nsada.ca
www.nsada.ca
To assist & protect association members; To act as the voice of new vehicle franchised dealers in Nova Scotia
John Sutherland, Executive Vice-President

Ontario Limousine Owners Association (OLOA)
10 Sunbeam Ave., Toronto ON M3H 1W7
Tel: 416-233-3029; *Fax:* 416-638-1699
Toll-Free: 866-700-6562
info@oloa.ca
www.oloa.ca
To represent limousine operators in Ontario; To provide members with a unified voice to approach regulatory agencies, politicians, & lawmakers with information regarding issues affecting the limousine industry
John Dahdaly, President

Ontario Tire Dealers Association
PO Box 516, 22 John St., Drayton ON N0G 1P0
Tel: 888-207-9059; *Fax:* 866-375-6832
www.otda.com
www.facebook.com/168955833458608
To represent members; To educate members in all areas that impact the continued growth of the tire industry
Robert Bignell, Executive Director

Prince Edward Island Automobile Dealers Association
5 Delta Cres., Charlottetown PE C1E 1Z9
Tel: 902-566-3639; *Fax:* 902-368-7116
peiada@eastlink.ca
www.peiada.com
Lisa Doyle-MacBain, Manager

Recreation Vehicle Dealers Association of Canada (RVDA) / Association des commerçants de véhicules recréatifs du Canada
#145, 11331 Coppersmith Way, Richmond BC V7A 5J9
Tel: 604-718-6325; *Fax:* 604-204-0154
info@rvda.ca
www.rvda.ca
www.youtube.com/user/RVDAofCanada
www.facebook.com/RVDAofCanada
twitter.com/RVDAofCanada
To promote professionalism in the RV industry through educational programs & events; To present the views of the industry to government & the general public
Eleonore Hamm, President

Saskatchewan Automobile Dealers Association (SADA)
610 Broad St., Regina SK S4R 8H8
Tel: 306-721-2208; *Fax:* 306-721-1009
info@saskautodealers.com
www.saskautodealers.com
To address issues faced by automobile & truck dealers; To advance the interests of members
Susan Buckle, Executive Director

Trillium Automobile Dealers' Association (TADA)
85 Renfrew Dr., Markham ON L3R 0N9
Tel: 905-940-6232; *Fax:* 905-940-6235
Toll-Free: 800-668-6510
info@tada.ca
www.tada.ca
www.facebook.com/149581915142339
twitter.com/tada_gr
Brenda Sachdev, Contact

Aviation & Aerospace

Canada's Aviation Hall of Fame (CAHF)
PO Box 6090, Wetaskiwin AB T9A 2E8
Tel: 780-312-2084; *Toll-Free:* 800-661-4726
info@cahf.ca
www.cahf.ca
www.youtube.com/user/cahf1973
www.facebook.com/CanadasAviationHallofFame1
To preserve & publicize the names & deeds of those who have made a significant contribution to Canadian aviation; To house an extensive collection of personal items & memorabilia, as well as a library of about 2,500 books & over 12,000 periodicals
Rod Sheridan, Chair

Helicopter Association of Canada (HAC)
#500, 130 Albert St., Ottawa ON K1P 5G4
Tel: 613-231-1110; *Fax:* 613-369-5097
www.h-a-c.ca
To ensure the financial viability of the Canadian civil helicopter industry; To promote flight safety; To expand utilization of helicopter transport
Teri Northcott, Chair
Fred L. Jones, BA LLB, President & Chief Executive Officer
Sylvain Seguin, Vice-President & Director, Marketing
Gary McDermid, Secretary
Maureen Crockett, Treasurer

International Civil Aviation Organization: Legal Affairs & External Relations Bureau
999, boul Robert-Bourassa, Montréal QC H3C 5H7
Tel: 514-954-8219; *Fax:* 514-954-6077
icaohq@icao.int
www.icao.int
www.youtube.com/icaovideo
twitter.com/icao
To promote the safe & orderly development of civil aviation in the world; To set international standards & regulations necessary for the safety, security, efficiency & regularity of air transport; To serve as the medium for cooperation in all fields of civil aviation
Fang Liu, Secretary General

International Federation of Air Line Pilots' Associations (IFALPA)
#700, 485, rue McGill, Montréal QC H2Y 2H4
Tel: 514-419-1191
communications@ifalpa.org
www.ifalpa.org
www.linkedin.com/company/ifalpa
www.facebook.com/ifalpa
twitter.com/IFALPA
To promote aviation safety worldwide; To be the global advocate of the piloting profession
Christoph Schewe, Managing Director
Ana Zachovay, Head, Administration

Ontario Aerospace Council (OAC)
1701 Aberfoyle Ct., Pickering ON L1V 4W4
Tel: 905-492-2296
www.theoac.ca
www.linkedin.com/company/ontario-aerospace-council
To enhance Ontario's aerospace industry in the global market; to ensure growth & prosperity
Moira Harvey, Executive Director

Better Business Bureaux

Better Business Bureau of Central & Northern Alberta
16102 - 100 Ave., Edmonton AB T5P 0L3
Fax: 780-482-1150
Toll-Free: 800-232-7298
edmonton.bbb.org
To handle inquiries & complaints; To provide an ad review program; To educate the public
Seanna Lawrence, President & CEO

Better Business Bureau of Eastern & Northern Ontario & Quebec / Bureau d'éthique commerciale de l'Est et Nord de l'Ontario et Québec
#505, 700 Industrial Ave., Ottawa ON K1G 0Y9
Tel: 613-237-4856; *Fax:* 613-237-4878
Toll-Free: 877-859-8566
info@ottawa.bbb.org
www.bbb.org
www.instagram.com/bbb_ottawa
www.facebook.com/BBBottawa
twitter.com/BBBOttawa
To promote & foster the highest ethical relationship between business & the public through voluntary self-regulation, consumer & business education & service excellence

Better Business Bureau of Mainland BC
#404, 788 Beatty St., Vancouver BC V6B 2M1
Tel: 604-682-2711; *Fax:* 604-681-1544
Toll-Free: 888-803-1222
contactus@mbc.bbb.org
www.bbb.org/local-bbb/bbb-of-mainland-bc
www.instagram.com/bbb_mbc
www.linkedin.com/company/bbbmbc
www.facebook.com/BBBmainlandBC
twitter.com/BBB_BC
To promote, develop & encourage an ethical marketplace

Better Business Bureau of Manitoba & Northwest Ontario
1030B Empress St., Winnipeg MB R3G 3H4
Tel: 204-989-9010; *Fax:* 204-989-9016
www.bbb.org/local-bbb/bbb-serving-manitoba-and-nw-ontario
www.linkedin.com/company/bbb-manitoba-and-nw-ontario
www.facebook.com/BBBmanitoba
twitter.com/BBBManitoba
To encourage ethical business practices through self-regulation in Manitoba & Northwestern Ontario

Better Business Bureau of Saskatchewan, Inc. (BBB of SK)
980 Albert St., Regina SK S4R 2P7
Tel: 306-352-7601; *Fax:* 306-565-6236
Toll-Free: 888-352-7601
info@sask.bbb.org
www.bbb.org/local-bbb/bbb-of-saskatchewan
www.linkedin.com/company/better-business-bureau-of-saskatchewan-inc-
www.facebook.com/BBBSask
twitter.com/BBBSask
To promote & foster high ethical relationships between business & the public through voluntary self-regulation, consumer & business education & service excellence; To serve as a marketplace where buyers & sellers trust one another

Better Business Bureau Serving Central Ontario
#903, 30 Duke St. West, Kitchener ON N2H 3W5
Tel: 519-579-3080; *Fax:* 519-570-0072
Toll-Free: 800-459-8875
info@mwco.bbb.org
www.bbb.org/local-bbb/bbb-serving-central-ontario
www.instagram.com/bbbcentralon
www.linkedin.com/company/bbb-central-ontario
www.facebook.com/BBBCentralON
twitter.com/BBBCentralON
To encourage ethical business practices through self-regulation in Central Ontario

Better Business Bureau Serving Southern Alberta & East Kootenay
#5, 1709 8 Ave. NE, Calgary AB T2E 0S9
Tel: 403-531-8784; *Fax:* 403-640-2514
www.bbb.org
www.facebook.com/CalgaryBBB
twitter.com/calgarybbb
To promote & encourage ethical practices in retail market for goods & services through provision of a wide range of consultative, informative & conciliatory arbitration services for businesses & consumers

Better Business Bureau Serving the Atlantic Provinces
#279, 7071 Bayers Rd., Halifax NS B3L 2C2
Tel: 902-422-6581; *Fax:* 902-429-6457
Toll-Free: 877-663-2363
info@ap.bbb.org
www.bbb.org
www.instagram.com/bbbatlantic
www.linkedin.com/company/bbb-better-business-bureau-serving-the-atlantic-provinces
www.facebook.com/BBBAtlantic
twitter.com/BBBAtlantic
To provide mutually beneficial relationships between buyer & seller based on responsible business practices
Peter Moorhouse, President & CEO

Better Business Bureau Serving Vancouver Island
#220, 1175 Cook St., Victoria BC V8V 4A1
Tel: 250-386-6348; *Fax:* 250-386-2367
info@vi.bbb.org
www.bbb.org/local-bbb/bbb-serving-vancouver-island
www.youtube.com/user/BBBVancouverIsland
www.linkedin.com/company/better-business-bureau-of-vancouver-island
www.facebook.com/BBBVancouverIsland
twitter.com/VIBBB
Committed to the principle that fair dealing is good business for both buyer & seller & the majority of buyers & sellers are honest & responsible

Better Business Bureau Serving Western Ontario
#206, 190 Wortley Rd., London ON N6C 4Y7
Tel: 519-673-3222; *Fax:* 519-673-5966
info@westernontario.bbb.org
www.bbb.org/local-bbb/bbb-serving-western-ontario
www.instagram.com/bbbwesternont
www.linkedin.com/company/better-business-bureau-serving-western-ontario
www.facebook.com/BBBWesternOnt
twitter.com/BBBWesternOnt
To promote the vitality of the free enterprise system & ethical business practices; To serve the concerns of business & the consuming public

International Association of Better Business Bureaus, Inc. (IABBB)
#600, 4250 North Fairfax Dr., Arlington VA 22203 USA
Tel: 703-276-0100
www.bbb.org
www.linkedin.com/company/international-association-of-better-business-bureaus
www.facebook.com/BetterBusinessBureau
twitter.com/bbb_us
To protect consumers & the free enterprise system; To foster high standards in business practice by advocating truth in advertising, by assuring integrity in performance of business services & by voluntary regulation & monitoring activities designed to enhance public trust & confidence in business
Jim Hegarty, Chair
Colleen Rudio, Interim Executive Director

Broadcasting

Alliance des radios communautaires du Canada
#1206, 1, rue Nicholas, Ottawa ON K1N 7B7
Tél: 613-562-0000; *Téléc:* 613-562-2182
radiorfa.com
www.youtube.com/arcducanada
www.facebook.com/arcducanada
twitter.com/arcducanada
François Côté, Secrétaire général

Audio Engineering Society (AES)
AES Toronto Section, PO Box 292, #32E, 223 Pioneer Dr., Kitchener ON N2P 1L9
Tel: 519-894-5308
torontoaes@torontoaes.org
www.torontoaes.org
www.linkedin.com/groups/2023730

Dedicated to audio technology
Blair Francey, Chair
Karl Machat, Secretary
Frank Lockwood, Vice Chair

British Columbia Association of Broadcasters (BCAB)
BC

www.bcab.ca
www.facebook.com/BCBroadcasters
twitter.com/bcabinfo
To unify the broadcasting community in British Columbia
James Stewart, President

Broadcast Research Council of Canada (BRC)
c/o NABS, #130, 55 St. Clair Ave. West, Toronto ON M4V 2Y7
thebrccanada@gmail.com
www.brc.ca
www.facebook.com/117260268358077
twitter.com/BroadcastBRC
To provide a forum for presentations relating to the broadcast advertising business; To provide awards to the most promising students at colleges that train people to enter the advertising business
Boris Cho, President

Canadian Association of Broadcasters (CAB) / Association canadienne des radiodiffuseurs (ACR)
#770, 45 O'Connor St., Ottawa ON K1P 1A4
Tel: 613-233-4035; Fax: 613-233-6961
www.cab-acr.ca
To act as the national voice of Canada's private broadcasters
Sylvie Bissonnette, Vice-President, Finance & Administration

Canadian Communications Foundation (CCF)
Toronto ON
www.broadcasting-history.ca
To document the history of Canadian broadcasting on the foundation's online electronic database.
Pip Wedge, President
Fil Fraser, Vice-President

Canadian Media Educators (CME) / Educateurs de Media Canadienne (EMC)
cme@canadianmediaeducators.ca
www.canadianmediaeducators.ca
www.instagram.com/canadianmediaeducators
www.facebook.com/canadianmediaeducators
twitter.com/canadianmediaed
To provide a forum to reflect on & respond collectively to issues & directions relevant to individual, institutonal & industry needs
Alana Gieck, President

Central Canada Broadcast Engineers (CCBE)
3 Jasmine Dr., Paris ON N3L 3P7
Fax: 519-442-1912
Toll-Free: 800-481-4649
information@ccbe.ca
www.ccbe.ca
To provide up-to-date technical information regarding the broadcast industry, including the following areas: television, radio, post production, towers & safety issues.
Peter Warth, President

Friends of Canadian Broadcasting (FCB)
#200-238, 131 Bloor St. West, Toronto ON M5S 1R8
Tel: 416-968-7496; Fax: 416-968-7406
friends@friends.ca
friends.ca
www.youtube.com/user/FriendsCB
www.facebook.com/friendscb
twitter.com/friendscb
To defend & enhance the quality & quantity of Canadian programming in the Canadian audio-visual system
Daniel Bernhard, Executive Director & Spokesperson

Interactive Ontario (IO)
#600, 431 King St. West, Toronto ON M5V 1K4
Tel: 416-516-0077
info@interactiveontario.com
www.interactiveontario.com
www.flickr.com/photos/32406922@N04
www.linkedin.com/groups/2096721
www.facebook.com/28971906704
twitter.com/ionews
To advance the digital media industry in Ontario, including e-Learning, video & online games, mobile, television & social media.
Peter Miller, Chair
Lucie Lalumière, Vice-Chair
Spence McDonnell, Treasurer
David Dembroski, Secretary
Christa Dickenson, Executive Director

National Campus & Community Radio Association (NCRA) / Association nationale des radio étudiantes et communautaires (ANREC)
#601, 331 Cooper St., Ottawa ON K2P 0G5
Tel: 613-321-1440; Toll-Free: 866-859-8086
info@ncra.ca
www.ncra.ca
www.linkedin.com/company/national-campus-and-community-radio-association
www.facebook.com/ncracanada
twitter.com/NCRACanada
To encourage development of community & student radio in Canada by providing core services to community-oriented radios & representing them to government, industry, agencies & the public; To promote community radio in Canada
Barry Rooke, Executive Director
Luke Smith, Officer, Learning & Development

North American Broadcasters Association (NABA)
PO Box 500, Stn. A, #6C300, 25 John St., Toronto ON M5V 3G7
Tel: 416-205-3363
contact@nabanet.com
nabanet.com
www.linkedin.com/company/north-american-broadcasters-association
www.facebook.com/2705058279524102
twitter.com/NABA_ORG
To advance the interests of broadcasters in Canada, the United States, & Mexico; To identify & respond to technical, operational & regulatory issues affecting the broadcasting industry in North America
Michael McEwen, Director General
Anh Ngo, Director, Administration

Numeris
1500 Don Mills Rd., 3rd Fl., Toronto ON M3B 3L7
Tel: 416-445-9800; Fax: 416-445-8644
en.numeris.ca
www.linkedin.com/company/numeris-canada
To provide broadcast measurement & consumer behaviour data to broadcasters, advertisers & agencies
Neil McEneaney, President & CEO
Catherine Malo, Senior Vice-President, Cross-media, Business Development & Communication
Laura Da Re, Vice-President, Finance
Vita DiSerio, Vice-President, People & Culture
Jacques Gaboury, Vice-President, Legal
Ricardo Gomez-Insausti, Vice-President, Research
Derek Matisz, Vice-President, Operations
Shawn Sheridan, Vice-President, Information Technology

Ontario Association of Broadcasters (OAB)
PO Box 54040, 5762 Hwy. 7 East, Markham ON L3P 7Y4
Tel: 905-554-2730; Fax: 905-554-2731
www.oab.ca
Doug Bingley, President
Chris Byrnes, Treasurer
Paul Evanov, Vice-President

Ontario Campus Radio Organization
c/o CFRU-FM, Radio Gryphon, University of Guelph, Level 2 UC, Guelph ON N1G 2W1
Tel: 519-824-4120

Radio Advisory Board of Canada (RABC) / Conseil consultatif canadien de la radio
2583 Carling Ave., #M038, Ottawa ON K2B 7H7
www.rabc-cccr.ca
twitter.com/RABC_CCCR
To consult & advise Industry Canada on behalf of industry on the development, management & regulation of radio services in Canada
David Farnes, General Manager

Radio Amateurs of Canada Inc. (RAC) / Radio Amateurs du Canada inc.
#217, 720 Belfast Rd., Ottawa ON K1G 0Z5
Tel: 613-244-4367; Toll-Free: 877-273-8304
www.rac.ca
www.facebook.com/radioamateurscdn
twitter.com/ractweets
To act as coordinating body of amateur radio organizations in Canada, liaison agency between members & other amateur organizations in Canada & other countries, coordinating & advisory agency between members & industry Canada; To promote interests of amateur radio operators through program of technical & general education in amateur matters
Glenn MacDonell, President
Al Masse, Corporate Secretary

Radio Television Digital News Association (Canada) (RTDNA Canada) / Association canadienne des directeurs de l'information en radio-télévision
#300, 1201 West Pender St., Vancouver BC V6E 2V2
Tel: 604-681-2153
admin@rtdnacanada.com
www.rtdnacanada.com
www.linkedin.com/groups/1800955
www.facebook.com/RTDNA.CAN
twitter.com/RTDNA_Canada
To represent electronic & digital journalists & news managers in Canada; To act as a progressive voice in the Canadian broadcast news industry; To foster education, professional development & recognition while encouraging active dialogue within its membership
Fiona Conway, President
Leya Duigu, Manager

Thinktv Inc.
tvb@tvb.ca
thinktv.ca
www.linkedin.com/company/thinktv-canada
twitter.com/thinktvca
To promote sales, marketing & research of commercial television industry in Canada
Alan Dark, Chair
Cahterine MacLeod, President & CEO
Laura Baehr, Vice-President, Marketing
Kathy Gardner, Vice-President, Media Insights
Rhonda Bagnall, Director, Thinktv Clearance

VISION TV
64 Jefferson Ave., Toronto ON M6K 1Y4
Tel: 416-368-3194; Fax: 416-368-9774
Toll-Free: 888-321-2567
TTY: 416-216-6311
www.visiontv.ca
www.facebook.com/visiontelevision
twitter.com/visiontv
To air multi-faith, multicultural & family-oriented entertainment
Znaimer Moses, Executive Producer

Western Association of Broadcast Engineers (WABE)
#319, 300, 8120 Beddington Blvd. NW, Calgary AB T3K 2A8
Tel: 403-630-4907; Fax: 403-295-3135
info@wabe.ca
www.wabe.ca
www.linkedin.com/company/651175
www.facebook.com/wabe.convention
twitter.com/WABE_Convention
Kathy Watson, Office Manager

Western Association of Broadcasters (WAB)
#507, 918 - 16th Ave. NW, Calgary AB T2M 0K3
Toll-Free: 877-814-2719
info@wab.ca
www.wab.ca
To represent private television & radio stations in Alberta, Saskatchewan & Manitoba.
John Vos, President
Vanessa Ong, Manager

Women in Film & Television - Toronto
#601, 110 Eglinton Ave. East, Toronto ON M4P 2Y1
Tel: 416-322-3430; Fax: 416-322-3703
wift@wift.com
www.wift.com
vimeo.com/wift
www.linkedin.com/groups/2908431
www.facebook.com/WIFT.Toronto
twitter.com/WIFT
To provide year-round training programs, industry events, & professional awards for women & men in Canadian screen based media
Prentiss Fraser, Chair
Heather Webb, Executive Director

Women in Film & Television Alberta (WIFTA)
c/o Luanne Morrow, Borden Ladner Gervais, Canterra Tower, #1000, 400 - 3rd Ave. SW, Calgary AB T2P 4H2
admin@wifta.ca
www.wifta.ca
www.linkedin.com/groups/4165901
www.facebook.com/WIFTAlberta
twitter.com/WIFTAlberta
To promote & assist the professional development, equitable treatment, recognition of achievements & the creation of new opportunities for professional women in the film, video, multimedia & television industries
Susan Feddena-Leonard, President

Women in Film & Television Vancouver (WIFTV)
Dominion Building, #306, 207 West Hastings St., Vancouver BC V6B 1H7

Tel: 604-685-1152; *Fax:* 604-685-1124
info@womeninfilm.ca
www.womeninfilm.ca
www.youtube.com/user/wiftv
www.facebook.com/Womeninfilm
twitter.com/WIFTV

To support, advance, promote & celebrate the professional development & achievements of women working in British Columbia's film, television, video & multimedia industries
Rachelle Chartrand, President
Michelle Billy Povill, Vice-President
Christine Larsen, Secretary

Youth Media Alliance (AMJ) / Alliance Médias Jeunesse (AET)
#407, 5165, rue Sherbrooke ouest, Montréal QC H4A 1T6

Tel: 514-597-5417
alliance@ymamj.org
www.ymamj.org
www.facebook.com/ymamj
twitter.com/YMAMJ

To promote the production & carriage of quality Canadian television programming for children; To ensure the development of critical viewing skills so that families are able to use media more effectively in the home; To promote awareness of the need to help young people make the most of their experience of television & other screen-based media
Chantal Bowen, Executive Director

Building & Construction

Alberta Construction Association (ACA)
18004 - 107 Ave., Edmonton AB T5S 2J5

Tel: 780-455-1122; *Fax:* 780-451-2152
info@albertaconstruction.net
www.albertaconstruction.net
www.facebook.com/albertaconstruction
twitter.com/aca_social

To represent & promote Alberta's construction industry
Ken Gibson, Executive Director
Shelley Andrea, Director, Administration

Alberta Ready Mixed Concrete Association (ARMCA)
4944 Roped Rd. NW, Edmonton AB T6B 3T7

Tel: 780-436-5645; *Fax:* 780-436-6503
info@concretealberta.ca
www.concretealberta.ca
www.facebook.com/concretealberta
twitter.com/concretealberta

To provide industry representation for the advancement of quality concrete in Alberta
Dan Hansen, Executive Director
Paul Masson, Director, Technical Services & Training

Alberta Roadbuilders & Heavy Construction Association (ARHCA)
#201, 9333 - 45 Ave., Edmonton AB T6E 5Z7

Tel: 780-436-9860; *Fax:* 780-436-4910
Toll-Free: 866-436-9860
administration@arhca.ab.ca
www.arhca.ab.ca
twitter.com/AB_Roadbuilders

To represent contractors, suppliers & consulting engineers who work in the heavy construction industry; To support long-term investment in transportation infrastructure
Ron Glen, Chief Executive Officer
Vacant, Director, Government & External Relations
Paul Cashman, Manager, Communications & Media Relations
Jenna Klynstra, Manager, Environment, Safety & Education

Alberta Roofing Contractors Association (ARCA)
2380 Pegasus Rd. NE, Calgary AB T2E 8G8

Tel: 403-250-7055; *Fax:* 403-250-1702
Toll-Free: 800-382-8515
info@arcaonline.ca
www.arcaonline.ca

To provide continuing education for roofing contractors, their personnel & interested others; to represent the roofing contracting industry in its relationships with legislative & regulating bodies; to work closely with affiliate organizations & liaison groups in advancing professionalism of roofing contracting; to provide a forum for interaction of members; to encourage high standards of professional conduct among roofing contractors; to develop a comprehensive body of knowledge about roofing management & technology, & disseminate ideas & knowledge to members & others; to monitor new products & systems; to work for cooperation & greater

understanding between contracting, inspection, manufacturing & supply segments of the roofing industry

Architectural Glass & Metal Contractors Association (AGMCA)
619 Liverpool Rd., Pickering ON L1W 1R1

Tel: 905-420-7272; *Fax:* 905-420-7288
info@agmca.ca
www.agmca.ca

Kline Holland, Director, Labour Relations

Architectural Woodwork Manufacturers Association of British Columbia (AWMA-BC)
#101, 4238 Lozells Ave., Burnaby BC V5A 0C4

Tel: 604-298-3555; *Fax:* 604-298-3558
info.bc@awmac.com
bc.awmac.com

To advance the highest standards of education, quality workmanship, warranties & business practices in architectural woodwork manufacturing in British Columbia
Martin Berryman, President

Architectural Woodwork Manufacturers Association of Canada (AWMAC) / Association des manufacturiers de menuiserie architecturale du Canada
PO Box 36525, Stn. MacTaggart, Edmonton AB T6R 0T4

Tel: 403-981-7300
info@awmac.com
www.awmac.com

To develop & promote the use of AWMAC's quality standards for the manufacturing & installation of architectural woodwork; To promote assurance of adherence to those quality standards & sustainable practices in the woodworking industry
Michelle Morrell, National Executive Director

Architectural Woodwork Manufacturers Association of Canada - Atlantic
PO Box 38136, Dartmouth NS B3B 1X2

Tel: 902-483-4213
atlantic@awmac.com
atl.awmac.com

To promote the interests of individuals & organizations in the architectural wood manufacturing, supply & installation industry
Tim Pedersen, President

Architectural Woodwork Manufacturers Association of Canada - Manitoba
1447 Waverly St., Winnipeg MB R3T 0P7

Tel: 204-333-6137
manitoba@awmac.com
mb.awmac.com

To foster & advance the interests of those who are engaged in or who are directly or indirectly connected with or affected by the production & installation of architectural woodwork; To endeavor to achieve a closer relationship & a better understanding among the various branches of the industry
Dave Hudon, President

Architectural Woodwork Manufacturers Association of Canada - Northern Alberta
c/o Margo Love, 12816 - 89 St. NW, Edmonton AB T5E 3J9

Tel: 780-937-8572
northernalberta@awmac.com
nab.awmac.com

To promote the architectural woodwork field in Northern Alberta
Kevin Balicki, President

Architectural Woodwork Manufacturers Association of Canada - Québec
89, av Godfrey, Saint-Sauveur QC J0R 1R5

Tel: 450-227-4048
info@awmacquebec.com
qc.awmac.com

To promote the interests of the architectural woodwork industry in Québec
Gaëtan Lauzon, Executive Director

Architectural Woodwork Manufacturers Association of Canada - Saskatchewan
PO Box 26032, Stn. Lawson Heights, Saskatoon SK S7K 8C1

Tel: 306-652-2704; *Fax:* 306-664-2552
saskatchewan@awmac.com
sk.awmac.com

To foster & advance the interests of those who are engaged in or who are directly or indirectly connected with or affected by the production & installation of architectural woodwork
Kasia Robinson, President

Architectural Woodwork Manufacturers Association of Canada - Southern Alberta
210 - 3700 78 Ave. SE, Calgary AB T2C 2L8

Tel: 403-264-5979
southernalberta@awmac.com
sab.awmac.com

To advance the interests of those related to the production & installation of architectural woodwork; To foster a closer relationship among the various branches of the industry

Associated Research Centres for the Urban Underground Space (ACUUS) / Association des Centres de recherche sur l'utilisation urbaine du sous-sol
34, rue de Séville, Montréal QC H9B 2S5

Tel: 514-982-6606; *Fax:* 514-982-6122
info@acuus.org
www.acuus.org
www.linkedin.com/groups/4204639

To promote partnerships amongst all actors in the field of planning, management, research & uses of urban underground space; To members into a cohesive network of mutual cooperation for the benefit of all
Dimitris Kaliampakos, President
Jacques Besner, General Manager

Association Béton Québec (ABQ)
#2200, 520, rue D'Avaugour, Boucherville QC J4B 0G6

Tel: 450-650-0930; *Fax:* 450-650-0935
Toll-Free: 855-650-0930
info@betonabq.org
betonabq.org
www.youtube.com/user/BetonABQ
www.linkedin.com/company/association-b-ton-qu-bec
www.facebook.com/betonquebec
twitter.com/BetonQc

Promouvoir l'utilisation du béton prêt à l'emploi dans le respect des bonnes pratiques de l'industrie, mobiliser nos membres et partenaires envers l'amélioration continue des connaissances et des pratiques
Luc Bédard, Directeur général

Association de la construction du Québec (ACQ) / Construction Association of Québec
9200, boul Métropolitain est, Anjou QC H1K 4L2

Tél: 514-354-0609; *Téléc:* 514-354-8292
Ligne sans frais: 888-868-3424
info@prov.acq.org
www.acq.org
www.youtube.com/user/ACQprovinciale
www.linkedin.com/company/association-de-la-construction-du-q
u-bec
www.facebook.com/ACQprovinciale
twitter.com/ACQprovinciale

Promotion et défense des intérêts des entreprises de construction, de gestionnaire de plans de garantie des bâtiments résidentiels neufs (Qualité Habitation) et d'agent patronal négociateur pour tous les employeurs des secteurs institutionnel/commercial et industriel (IC/I)

Association des constructeurs de routes et grands travaux du Québec (ACRGTQ) / Québec Road Builders & Heavy Construction Association
435, av Grande-Allée est, Québec QC G1R 2J5

Tél: 418-529-2949; *Téléc:* 418-529-5139
Ligne sans frais: 800-463-4672
acrgtq@acrgtq.qc.ca
www.acrgtq.qc.ca
www.linkedin.com/company/association-des-constructeurs-de-ro
utes-et-grands-travaux-du-québec-acrgtq-
www.facebook.com/ACRGTQ
twitter.com/acrgtq

Défendre les intérêts des entrepreneurs en génie civil et voirie du Québec
Sébastien Marcoux, Président
Gisèle Bourque, Directrice générale

Association des entrepreneurs en construction du Québec (AECQ) / Association of Building Contractors of Québec (ABCQ)
#101, 7905, boul Louis-H. Lafontaine, Anjou QC H1K 4E4

Tél: 514-353-5151; *Téléc:* 514-353-6689
Ligne sans frais: 800-361-4304
info@aecq.org
www.aecq.org

Étudier, promouvoir, protéger et défendre les intérêts des employeurs en matière de relations de travail; négocier les clauses du tronc commun à chacune des quatre conventions collectives sectorielles
Dominic Robert, Directeur général

Association des maîtres couvreurs du Québec (AMCQ) / Québec Master Roofers Association
3001, boul Tessier, Laval QC H7S 2M1
Tél: 450-973-2322; Téléc: 450-973-2321
Ligne sans frais: 888-973-2322
amcq@amcq.qc.ca
www.amcq.qc.ca
Promouvoir les intérêts généraux des entreprises de couvertures et ceux de diverses entreprises des secteurs connexes dans la province de Québec; promouvoir la hausse de la qualité des travaux de couvertures
Marc Savard, Directeur général

Association of Commercial & Industrial Contractors of PEI
PO Box 1685, Charlottetown PE C1A 7N4
Tel: 902-566-3456; Fax: 902-368-2754
wmm@wmm93.pe.ca
Mary MacDonald, Contact

Association québécoise de la quincaillerie et des matériaux de construction (AQMAT) / The Building Materials Retailers Association of Québec
#3, 400, rue Sainte-Hélène, Longueuil QC J4K 3R2
Tél: 450-646-5842
information@aqmat.org
www.aqmat.org
www.facebook.com/408490452586398
twitter.com/aqmat_impact
Promouvoir l'intérêt général de ses membres-clients engagés dans la vente au détail de matériaux de construction et de quincaillerie, en leur offrant une panoplie de produits et services visant à faciliter la gestion de leurs commerces, des Québécois et la rénovation
Richard Darveau, Président-chef de la direction

Atlantic Building Supply Dealers Association (ABSDA)
70 Englehart St., Dieppe NB E1A 8H3
Tel: 506-858-0700; Fax: 506-859-0064
absda@nb.aibn.com
www.absda.ca
twitter.com/absdadealers
To keep membership informed of new trends & developments in the industry; To provide a forum to discuss mutual problems & ideas; To provide continuing education programs for members
Denis Melanson, President
John Logan, Manager

Atlantic Concrete Association (ACA) / Association béton Atlantique (ABA)
#301, 3845 Joseph Howe Dr., Halifax NS B3L 4H9
Tel: 902-443-4456; Fax: 902-404-8074
info@atlanticconcrete.ca
www.atlanticconcrete.ca
www.facebook.com/atlanticconcrete
twitter.com/atlanticconc
To promote the use of ready-mixed concrete while providing leadership to the industry through the exchange of ideas & information
Pam Woodman, Executive Director

British Columbia Construction Association (BCCA)
#401, 655 Tyee Rd., Victoria BC V9A 6X5
Tel: 250-475-1077; Fax: 250-475-1078
info@bccassn.com
www.bccassn.com
www.youtube.com/user/BCCASSN
www.linkedin.com/company/british-columbia-construction-associ
ation-bcca
www.facebook.com/ThisisBCCA
To provide excellence in the representation of & service to British Columbia's construction industry
Chris Atchison, President
Jackie Knutson, Director, Finance
Warren Perks, Vice-President, Industry Standard Practices

British Columbia Road Builders & Heavy Construction Association (BCRB&HCA)
#307, 8678 Greenall Ave., Burnaby BC V5J 3M6
Tel: 604-436-0220; Fax: 604-436-2627
info@roadbuilders.bc.ca
www.roadbuilders.bc.ca
twitter.com/BCRoadBuilders
To represent the interests of member companies to government, media, other organizations & the public
Kelly Scott, President
Tanjeet Kalsi, Manager, Operations
Parveen Parhar, Manager, Communications & Membership

Building Supply Industry Association of British Columbia (BSIA of BC)
#2, 19299 - 94th Ave., Surrey BC V4N 4E6
Tel: 604-513-2205; Fax: 604-513-2206
Toll-Free: 888-711-5656
www.bsiabc.ca
www.linkedin.com/company/building-supply-industry-association
-of-bc
www.facebook.com/BSIABC
twitter.com/BSIAofBC
To act as the official voice of the building supply industry in British Columbia; To provide services to members
Thomas Foreman, President

Canada Backyard Housing Association
11824 - 52 St. NW, Edmonton AB T5W 3J4
Tel: 780-722-5699
www.canadabackyardhousing.com
www.instagram.com/yegardensuites
www.facebook.com/YEGardenSuites
twitter.com/YEGardenSuites
To support the development of backyard housing in urban centres across Canada
Travis Fong, Director
Ashley Salvador, Director

Canadian Concrete Masonry Producers Association (CCMPA)
c/o Andrea McChesney, PO Box 1492, Waterdown ON L0R 2H0
information@ccmpa.ca
ccmpa.ca
www.linkedin.com/company/canadian-concrete-masonry-produc
ers-association
www.facebook.com/CanadianConcreteMasonryProducers
twitter.com/CCMasonryPA
To work on behalf of concrete masonry producers
Paul Hargest, President
Andrea McChesney, Executive Director

Canadian Concrete Pipe Association (CCPA) / Association canadienne des fabricants de tuyaux de béton (ACTB)
205 Miller Dr., Halton Hills ON L7G 6G4
Tel: 905-877-5369; Fax: 905-877-5369
info@ccpa.com
www.ccpa.com
www.youtube.com/user/CanadianConcretePipe
www.linkedin.com/groups/1920373
To coordinate research & development, promotion, education & federal government relations programs pertaining to the marketing of high quality precast concrete waste water & storm drainage products in Canada.
John Greer, Chair

Canadian Construction Association (CCA) / Association canadienne de la construction (ACC)
#1900, 275 Slater St., Ottawa ON K1P 5H9
Tel: 613-236-9455; Fax: 613-236-9526
cca@cca-acc.com
www.cca-acc.com
www.youtube.com/user/ConstructionCAN
www.linkedin.com/company/canadian-construction-association—
-association-canadienne-de-la-construction
twitter.com/ConstructionCAN
To act as the national voice of the construction industry; To serve, promote & enhance the construction industry by acting on behalf of its members in matters of national concern
Mary Van Buren, President
Mark Belton, Director, Finance

Canadian Hoisting & Rigging Safety Council / Conseil Canadien de la sécurité du levage et du gréage
PO Box 282, Stn. B, Ottawa ON K1P 6C4
Tel: 604-336-4699; Fax: 604-336-4510
input@chrsc.ca
chrsc.ca
To create standardized regulations throughout the nation with regards to cranes, hoisting & rigging
Tim Bennett, Chair
Fraser Cocks, Executive Director

Canadian Masonry Contractors' Association (CMCA)
Canada Masonry Centre, 360 Superior Blvd., Mississauga ON L5T 2N7
Tel: 905-564-6622; Fax: 905-564-5744
canadianmasonrycontractors.com
To advance masonry technology, skills development & the use of masonry products in construction across Canada

Canadian Paint & Coatings Association (CPCA) / Association canadienne de l'industrie de la peinture et du revêtement
#900, 170 Laurier Ave. West, Ottawa ON K1P 5V5
Tel: 613-231-3604; Fax: 613-231-4908
cpca@canpaint.com
www.canpaint.com
www.linkedin.com/company/canadian-paint-and-coatings-associ
ation
www.facebook.com/CanadianPaint
twitter.com/Can_Paint
To represent the paint industry among the provincial, federal & municipal governments
Gary LeRoux, President & CEO

Canadian Precast / Prestressed Concrete Institute (CPCI) / Institut canadien du béton préfabriqué et précontraint
PO Box 24058, Stn. Hazeldean, Ottawa ON K2M 2C3
Tel: 613-232-2619; Fax: 613-232-5139
Toll-Free: 877-937-2724
helpdesk@cpci.ca
www.cpci.ca
www.facebook.com/CPCIPrecast
To promote & advance the interests & general welfare of the structural precast / prestressed concrete industry, the architectural precast concrete industry & the post-tensioned concrete industry in Canada
Rob Burak, President
Brian Hall, Managing Director

Canadian Roofing Contractors' Association (CRCA) / Association canadienne des entrepreneurs en couverture (ACEC)
#100, 2430 Don Reid Dr., Ottawa ON K1H 1E1
Tel: 613-232-6724; Fax: 613-232-2893
Toll-Free: 800-461-2722
crca@roofingcanada.com
www.roofingcanada.com
www.facebook.com/113028683592871
To provide leadership & guidance to members of the Canadian roofing industry
Bob Brunet, Executive Director

Canadian Welding Bureau (CWB)
8260 Parkhill Dr., Milton ON L9T 5V7
Fax: 905-542-1318
Toll-Free: 800-844-6790
info@cwbgroup.org
www.cwbgroup.org
www.youtube.com/user/cwbgroup
www.facebook.com/cwbgroupwelding
To administrator certification programs for CSA Standards W47.1, W47.2, W186, W178.1 & W48 series; To provide support for welding-based programs in schools, education institutions, welding professionals & companies employing welding technology
Dan Tadic, Executive Director

Cement Association of Canada (CAC) / Association canadienne du ciment
#1105, 350 Sparks St., Ottawa ON K1R 7S8
Tel: 613-236-9471; Fax: 613-563-4498
www.cement.ca
twitter.com/rediscoverconc
To represent all of Canada's cement producers; To improve & extend the uses of cement & concrete through market development, engineering, research, education & public affairs work
Michael McSweeney, President & CEO

Concrete BC (BCRMCA)
26162 - 30A Ave., Langley BC V4W 2W5
Tel: 604-626-4141; Fax: 604-626-4143
concrete@concretebc.ca
www.concretebc.ca
To work cooperatively with all levels of government to ensure the ready-mix concrete industry operates with a focus on B.C.'s communities & the environment
Charles Kelly, President
Carolyn Campbell, Vice-President, Operations & Membership

Concrete Canada
#102B, 1 Prologis Blvd., Mississauga ON L5W 0G2
Tel: 905-564-2726; Fax: 905-564-5680
www.crmca.ca
To represent federally legislated issues impacting the members of the ready mixed concrete industry

Concrete Manitoba (MRMCA)
PO Box 1787, Stn. Main, Winnipeg MB R3C 2Z9
Tel: 204-667-8539; *Fax:* 204-661-8489
info@concretemanitoba.ca
www.concretemanitoba.ca
twitter.com/concretemb
To market & promote concrete, while advocating for its use in the development of Manitoba's infrastructure
Fred Kennell, Chair
Hubert Boulet, Vice-Chair

Concrete Ontario (RMCAO)
#102B, 1 Prologis Blvd., Mississauga ON L5W 0G2
Tel: 905-564-2726; *Fax:* 905-564-5680
www.rmcao.org
www.youtube.com/concreteontario
www.facebook.com/ConcreteOntario
twitter.com/ConcreteOntario
To promote & further the business, technology & use of quality concrete through partnership between producers & the construction & specifying industriesin Ontario
Bart Kanters, Vice President
Sylvia Benevides, Director, Meetings & Industry Event Planner
Alen Keri, Engineer, Technical Services

Concrete Sask (SRMCA)
#101, 1102 - 8th Ave., Regina SK S4R 1C9
Tel: 306-757-2788; *Fax:* 306-546-3477
acampbell@concretesask.org
www.concretesask.org
www.facebook.com/ConcreteSask
twitter.com/srmcaconcrete
To promote the highest quality of concrete produced by its members; To improve the industry in all aspects & represent its members in relation to governments, environmental agencies & other industry-related associations
Rod Smith, President
Garth Sanders, Executive Director, Finance

Construction Association of New Brunswick (CANB) / Association de la construction du nouveau-brunswick
59 Avonlea Ct., Fredericton NB E3C 1N8
Tel: 506-459-5770; *Fax:* 506-457-1913
canb4@nbnet.nb.ca
www.constructnb.ca
To co-ordinate a consensus to effectively present the Industry's collective views to various client groups, particularly to relevant departments & agencies of the provincial government
Rob Carvell, President
John Landry, Executive Director

Construction Association of Nova Scotia
#103, 134 Eileen Stubbs Ave., Dartmouth NS B3B 0A9
Tel: 902-468-2267; *Fax:* 902-468-2470
cans@cans.ns.ca
www.cans.ns.ca
To represent the interests of its members
Duncan Williams, President

Construction Association of Prince Edward Island (CAPEI)
PO Box 728, #223, 40 Enman Cres., Charlottetown PE C1A 7L3
Tel: 902-368-3303; *Fax:* 902-894-9757
admin@capei.ca
www.capei.ca
To foster, promote & advance the interests & efficiency of Prince Edward Island's construction industry
Stanley (Sam) Sanderson, General Manager
Grant MacPherson, President

Construction Specifications Canada (CSC) / Devis de construction Canada
#312, 120 Carlton St., Toronto ON M5A 4K2
Tel: 416-777-2198; *Fax:* 416-777-2197
info@csc-dcc.ca
www.csc-dcc.ca
www.instagram.com/csc_dcc
www.linkedin.com/company/construction-specifications-canada
www.facebook.com/CSCDCC
twitter.com/csc_dcc
To improve communication, contract documentation & technical information in the construction industry
Wyatt Eckert, President
Nick Franjic, Executive Director

Council of Ontario Construction Associations (COCA)
#2001, 180 Dundas St. West, Toronto ON M5G 1Z8
Tel: 416-968-7200; *Fax:* 416-968-0362
info@coca.on.ca
www.coca.on.ca
www.linkedin.com/company/2397076
www.facebook.com/MyICIConstruction
twitter.com/ICIconstruction
To contribute to the long-term growth & profitability of the construction industry in Ontario; To speak with a unified voice to government, the industry & the public
Ian Cunningham, President
Martin Benson, Manager, Operations & Member Services

Glass & Architectural Metals Association (GAMA)
619 Liverpool Rd., Pickering ON L1W 1R1
Tel: 905-420-7272
www.pgaa.ca/gama
To advance the glass & architectural metals industry
Noel Marsella, Executive Director
Kline Holland, Director, Labour Relations

Heavy Civil Association of Newfoundland & Labrador, Inc. (HCANL)
PO Box 23038, 25 Kenmount Rd., St. John's NL A1B 4J9
Tel: 709-364-8811; *Fax:* 709-364-8812
heavycivilnl.ca
To act as the voice of the heavy construction industries in Newfoundland & Labrador; To develop standard tendering & contractual practices & procedures
Jim Organ, Executive Director
Lorraine Richards, Manager, Operations

Infrastructure Health & Safety Association (IHSA)
Centre for Health & Safety Innovation, #400, 5110 Creekbank Rd., Mississauga ON L4W 0A1
Tel: 905-625-0100; *Fax:* 905-625-8998
Toll-Free: 800-263-5024
info@ihsa.ca
www.ihsa.ca
twitter.com/IHSAnews
To serve the utilities, electrical, natural gas, aggregates, ready-mix, construction & transportation industries in Ontario; To develop prevention solutions for work environments
Michael Frolick, Chief Executive Officer & President

Lumber & Building Materials Association of Ontario (LBMAO)
391 Matheson Blvd. East, #A, Mississauga ON L4Z 2H2
Tel: 905-625-1084; *Fax:* 905-625-3006
Toll-Free: 888-365-2626
www.lbmao.on.ca
To promote the welfare of members so that they are able to build a competitive advantage & remain at the leading edge of the lumber & building materials industry
Ken Forbes, Chair

Manitoba Heavy Construction Association (MHCA)
#3, 1680 Ellice Ave., Winnipeg MB R3G 0Z2
Tel: 204-947-1379; *Fax:* 204-943-2279
info@mhca.mb.ca
www.mhca.mb.ca
twitter.com/ManitobaHeavy
To promote a safe workplace for employees in Manitoba's heavy construction industry; To represent the heavy construction industry in Manitoba
Christopher Lorenc, President
Wendy Greund Summerfield, Manager, Finance & Human Resources
Don Hurst, Director, WORKSAFELY, Education & Training
Christine Miller, Manager, Operations
Catherine Mitchell, Manager, Policy & Communications

Master Insulators' Association of Ontario Inc.
Building 1, #101, 2600 Skymark Ave., Mississauga ON L4W 5B2
Tel: 905-279-6426; *Fax:* 905-279-6422
miapublic1@miaontario.org
www.miaontario.org
To promote & advance the insulation industry
Caroline O'Keeffe, Office Manager

Master Painters & Decorators Association (MPDA)
2800 Ingleton Ave., Burnaby BC V5C 6G7
Tel: 604-298-7578; *Fax:* 604-298-7571
Toll-Free: 888-674-8708
info@paintinfo.com
www.paintinfo.com/assoc/mpda
To set & raise standards of industrial organizations
Greg Boshard, President
Joe Racanelli, Vice-President
Doreen Tan, Secretary-Treasurer

Mechanical Contractors Association of Alberta (MCA AB)
#204, 2725 - 12 St. NE, Calgary AB T2E 7J2
Tel: 403-250-7237; *Fax:* 403-291-0551
Toll-Free: 800-251-0620
info@mca-ab.ca
www.mca-ab.com
To promote plumbing & mechanical contractors; To provide educational programs to foster improved management & productivity in mechanical contracting; To represent mechanical contractors with their various publics - governments, design authorities, labour; To foster professional advancement & profitability of the plumbing, heating & mechanical contracting industry through its member services; To advocate on behalf of members
Russ Evans, Executive Director

Mechanical Contractors Association of British Columbia (MCABC)
#223, 3989 Henning Dr., Burnaby BC V5C 6N5
Tel: 604-205-5058; *Fax:* 604-205-5075
Toll-Free: 800-663-8473
www.mcabc.org
www.flickr.com/photos/mcabc
www.linkedin.com/company/mechanical-contractors-association-of-bc
twitter.com/mcabc
To encourage, support & promote the advancement of the mechanical contracting industry; to provide leadership, assistance & training to members.
Dana Taylor, Executive Vice President

Mechanical Contractors Association of Canada (MCAC) / Association des entrepreneurs en mécanique du Canada
#701, 280 Albert St., Ottawa ON K1P 5G8
Tel: 613-232-0492; *Fax:* 613-235-2793
mcac@mcac.ca
www.mcac.ca
www.linkedin.com/company/mcacanada
twitter.com/MecConCA
To promote plumbing & mechanical contractors; to provide educational programs to foster improved management & productivity in mechanical contracting; to represent mechanical contractors to their various publics - governments, design authorities, labour.
Dave Holek, President
Tania Johnston, Chief Executive Officer

Mechanical Contractors Association of Manitoba (MCAM)
#320, 830 King Edward St., Winnipeg MB R3H 0P4
Tel: 204-774-2404; *Fax:* 204-772-0233
mcam@mts.net
www.mca-mb.com
To continually improve mechanical industry standards while providing a high level of value performance & customer service for our members
Betty McInerney, Executive Director

Mechanical Contractors Association of New Brunswick (MNECA)
c/o Moncton Northeast Construction Association, 297 Collishaw St., Moncton NB E1C 9R2
Tel: 506-857-4038; *Fax:* 506-857-8861
info@mneca.ca
www.mneca.ca
To provide leadership & service to members; To act on behalf of members in labour relations matters, including collective bargaining; To advance & develop the industry, primarily in New Brunswick; To endeavour to improve legislation affecting the industry; To promote sound labour relations
Nadine Fullarton, President

Mechanical Contractors Association of Newfoundland & Labrador
PO Box 1674, 240 Waterford Bridge Rd., St. John's NL A1C 5P5
Tel: 709-745-0225; *Fax:* 709-368-3502
ddawe@cahill.ca
David Dawe, Executive Director

Mechanical Contractors Association of Nova Scotia (CANS)
#103, 134 Eileen Shabbs Ave., Dartmouth NS B3B 0A9
Tel: 902-468-2267; *Fax:* 902-468-2470
dwilliams@cans.ns.ca
www.cans.ns.ca
To be the leading voice of the construction industry in Nova Scotia
Duncan Williams, President

Mechanical Contractors Association of Ontario (MCAO)
#103, 10 Director Ct., Woodbridge ON L4L 7E8
Tel: 905-856-0342; *Fax:* 905-856-0385
mcao@mcao.org
www.mcao.org
To provide leadership & assistance to members of the mechanical contracting industry in Ontario
Steve Coleman, Executive Vice-President

Mechanical Contractors Association of Saskatchewan Inc. (MCAS)
Heritage Business Park, #105, 2750 Faithfull Ave., Saskatoon SK S7K 6M6
Tel: 306-664-2154; *Fax:* 306-653-7233
admin@mca-sask.com
www.mca-sask.com
To represent plumbing & heating contractors in relation to the construction industry, legislative departments of municipal & provincial government & other industry-related bodies.
Ryan Tynning, President
Carolyn Bagnell, Executive Director

Mechanical Service Contractors of Canada (MSCC)
#701, 280 Albert St., Ottawa ON K1P 5G8
Tel: 613-232-0017; *Fax:* 613-235-2793
Toll-Free: 877-622-2668
www.servicecontractor.ca
To be dedicated to mechanical service, repair & retrofit contractors
Daryl Sharkey, Executive Director

National Elevator & Escalator Association (NEEA)
#708, 6299 Airport Rd., Mississauga ON L4V 1N3
Andrew Reistetter, Executive Director

National Home Inspector Certification Council (NHICC)
PO Box 22028, Windsor ON N8N 5G6
nhicc1@gmail.com
nationalhomeinspector.org
To run an independent national certification program for home & property inspectors in Canada
Claude Lawrenson, President

National Trade Contractors Council of Canada (NTCCC)
#701, 280 Albert St., Ottawa ON K1P 5G8
Tel: 613-232-0492
ntccc@ntccc.ca
www.ntccc.ca
www.linkedin.com/company/national-trade-contractors-council-of-canada
To identify issues of common interest among like-minded national trade associations
Pierre Boucher, Contact

New Brunswick Road Builders & Heavy Construction Association
#5, 59 Avonlea Ct., Fredericton NB E3C 1N8
Tel: 506-454-5079; *Fax:* 506-452-7646
rbanb@nb.aibn.com
www.rbanb.ca
To foster & enhance relations between members, & between the members of other associations in construction; To acquire & disseminate information of value to the industry & to its membership; To improve & extend standards, conditions, methods & practices within the industry
Jamie Weatherbee, President
Tom McGinn, Executive Director

New Brunswick Roofing Contractors Association, Inc. (NBRCA) / Association des entrepreneurs en couverture du Nouveau-Brunswick
1010 Fairville Blvd., Saint John NB E2M 5T5
Tel: 506-652-7003; *Fax:* 506-696-0380
Toll-Free: 888-652-7003
info@nbrca.ca
www.nbrca.ca
To protect the public's interest in relation to roofing; To act as the voice of New Brunswick's roofing industry; To facilitate a competent & profitable roofing & sealed membrane system industry in the province; To foster excellence in roofing related activities; to ensure that members uphold the code of ethics
Andrew Lunn, President
Ron Hutton, Executive Director

Newfoundland & Labrador Construction Association (NLCA)
#202, 397 Stavanger Dr., St. John's NL A1A 0A1
Tel: 709-753-8920; *Fax:* 709-754-3968
info@nfld.com
www.nlca.ca
www.facebook.com/NLCA1
twitter.com/NLCA1
To act as the voice of the construction industry in Newfoundland & Labrador; To enhance the professionalism & productivity of members through the development of policies
Rhonda Collings, Chair
Rhonda Neary, President & Chief Operating Officer

Northwest Territories & Nunavut Construction Association (NNCA)
PO Box 2277, 4921 - 49th St., 3rd Fl., Yellowknife NT X1A 2P7
Tel: 867-873-3949; *Fax:* 867-873-8366
bulletin@nnca.ca
nnca.ca
To act as a voice for construction-related business in the Northwest Territories & Nunavut
Louise Elder, Executive Director

Nova Scotia Construction Labour Relations Association Limited (NSCLRA)
#1, 260 Brownlow Ave., Dartmouth NS B3B 1V9
Tel: 902-468-2283; *Fax:* 902-468-3705
admin@nsclra.ca
www.nsclra.ca
www.youtube.com/user/ReseauFADOQ
www.facebook.com/reseaufadoq
To represent construction industry employers in collective bargaining with trade unions in the industrial & commercial sectors
Allan Stapleton, President
Nancy Canales, Administrator

Nova Scotia Road Builders Association
#217, 11 Thornhill Dr., Dartmouth NS B3B 1R9
www.nsrba.ca
To speak for the heavy construction industry in Nova Scotia; To liaise with provincial Department of Transportation
Grant Feltmate, Executive Director
Carol Ingraham, Office Manager

Ontario Concrete Pipe Association (OCPA)
447 Frederick St., 2nd Fl, Kitchener ON N2H 2P4
Tel: 519-489-4488; *Fax:* 519-578-6060
admin@ocpa.com
www.ocpa.com
www.linkedin.com/company/2126103
www.facebook.com/ocpa.fb
To represent the concrete pipe & maintenance hole industry throughout Ontario; To promote engineered concrete products of permanence
Gerrard F. Mulhern, Executive Director

Ontario Formwork Association (OFA)
#25, 111 Zenway Blvd., Woodbridge ON L4H 3H9
Tel: 905-856-4747; *Fax:* 905-856-4474
ontariofoamwork@bellaliant.ca
www.ontarioformworkassociation.com
To discuss issues related to the formwork sector of the construction industry in Ontario

Ontario General Contractors Association (OGCA)
#280, 180 Attwell Dr., Toronto ON M9W 6A9
Tel: 905-671-3969; *Fax:* 905-671-8212
info@ogca.ca
ogca.ca
www.linkedin.com/company/ontario-general-contractors-association
twitter.com/OGCAinfo
To offer experience & expertise dealing with contractors, architects, engineers & owners
Giovanni Cautillo, President

Ontario Industrial Roofing Contractors' Association (OIRCA)
#301, 940 The East Mall, Toronto ON M9B 6J7
Tel: 416-695-4114; *Fax:* 416-695-9920
Toll-Free: 888-336-4722
oirca@ontarioroofing.com
www.ontarioroofing.com
www.linkedin.com/company/3499282
To act as the voice of the industrial-commercial roofing industry in Ontario; To promote excellence in roofing construction
Wesley Lamb, President
Peter Serino, Treasurer

Ontario Painting Contractors Association (OPCA)
#10, 7611 Pine Valley Dr., Woodbridge ON L4L 0A2
Tel: 416-498-1897; *Fax:* 416-498-6757
Toll-Free: 800-461-3630
info@opca.org
www.ontpca.org
To foster, develop & maintain unity & stability among members by acting as a bargaining agent; providing services & educational opportunities; acting as a liaison between industry groups; upholding & improving the standards of the industry; promoting the use of modern specifications; advancing an attitude of ethical responsibility & pride
Thomas Corbett, President
Andrew Sefton, Executive Director

Ontario Pipe Trades Council
#206, 400 Dundas St. East, Whitby ON L1N 3X2
Tel: 905-665-3500; *Fax:* 905-665-3400
info@optc.org
www.optc.org
www.facebook.com/pipetradescouncil
twitter.com/Pipe_Trades
To promote the many technical, commercial & environmental benefits of the Pipe Trades & maximize their use in the construction industry; to promote the interest of the plumbing, pipe fitting, sprinkler fitting & HVAC industry in the province of Ontario
Neil McCormack, Business Manager

Ontario Road Builders' Association (ORBA)
#1, 365 Brunel Rd., Mississauga ON L4Z 1Z5
Tel: 905-507-1107; *Fax:* 905-890-8122
info@orba.org
www.orba.org
www.facebook.com/OntarioRoadBuildersAssociation
twitter.com/onroadbuilders
To act as the voice of the Ontario road building industry; To maintain high standards in the road building industry & promote worker health & safety
Geoffrey Stephens, President
Vince Aurilio, Executive Director, Ontario Asphalt Pavement Council
David Caplan, Chief Operating Officer
Andrew Hurd, Director, Policy & Stakeholder Relations

Ontario Stone, Sand & Gravel Association (OSSGA)
#103, 5720 Timberlea Blvd., Mississauga ON L4W 4W2
Tel: 905-507-0711; *Fax:* 905-507-0717
www.ossga.com
www.instagram.com/_ossga
www.facebook.com/OntarioStoneSandGravel
twitter.com/_OSSGA
Norm Cheesman, Executive Director

Ottawa Construction Association (OCA) / L'Association de la construction d'Ottawa
196 Bronson Ave., Ottawa ON K1R 6H4
Tel: 613-236-0488; *Fax:* 613-238-6124
oca@oca.ca
www.oca.ca
www.facebook.com/OttawaConstructionAssociation
twitter.com/ConstructionOtt
To act as the voice of the non-residential construction industry in Ottawa; To promote & maintain industry best practices & high ethical standards
John DeVries, President & General Manager

Pipe Line Contractors Association of Canada (PLCAC)
#201, 1075 North Service Rd. West, Oakville ON L6M 2G2
Tel: 905-847-9383; *Fax:* 905-847-7824
plcac@pipeline.ca
www.pipeline.ca
www.linkedin.com/company/pipe-line-contractors-association-of-canada
To represent contractors in labour relations matters & to establish training courses for the development of Canadian workers in special pipeline consturction skills
Neil G. Lane, Executive Director
Ella Matteucci, Contact, Communications & Memeber Services

Prince Edward Island Road Builders & Heavy Construction Association
PO Box 1901, #223, 40 Enman Cres., Charlottetown PE C1A 7N5
Tel: 902-894-9514; *Fax:* 902-894-9512
info@peirb.ca
www.peirb.ca
To be a strong, effective voice in the heavy construction industry
Steve Campbell, President

Provincial Building & Construction Trades Council of Ontario
#401, 75 International Blvd., Toronto ON M9W 6L9
Tel: 416-679-8887; *Fax:* 416-679-8882
info@ontariobuildingtrades.com
www.ontariobuildingtrades.com
To give construction workers a collective voice in the workplace; To ensure that workers are well-trained to meet industry needs; To promote healthy & safe working conditions with decent wages, pensions & benefits
Patrick J. Dillon, Business Manager

Resilient Flooring Contractors Association of Ontario (RFCAO)
70 Leek Cres., Richmond Hill ON L4B 1H1
Tel: 416-499-4000; *Fax:* 416-499-8752
info@resilientflooring.ca
www.resilientflooring.ca
To advance the interests of members; To promote & implement trade practices & regulations; To negotiate among & between members of the corporation
Eric Babiak, President

Roofing Contractors Association of British Columbia (RCABC)
9734 - 201st St., Langley BC V1M 3E8
Tel: 604-882-9734
roofing@rcabc.org
www.rcabc.org
To provide continuing education for roofing contractors, their workers & interested others; to represent the roofing contracting industry in its relationships with legislative & regulating bodies; to work closely with affiliate organizations & liaison groups in advancing the professionalism of roofing contracting; to provide a forum for the interaction of members; to encourage high standards of professional conduct among roofing contractors; to develop a comprehensive body of knowledge about roofing management & technology; to disseminate ideas & knowledge to members & others; to monitor new products & systems; to work for cooperation & greater understanding between contracting, inspection, manufacturing & supply segments of the roofing industry
Bryan L. Wallner, Chief Executive Officer

Roofing Contractors Association of Manitoba Inc. (RCAM)
1447 Waverley St., Winnipeg MB R3T 0P7
Tel: 204-783-6365; *Fax:* 204-783-6446
office@rcam.ca
www.rcam.ca
Marian Davidson Boles, Executive Director

Roofing Contractors Association of Nova Scotia (RCANS)
7 Frederick Ave., Mount Uniacke NS B0N 1Z0
Tel: 902-866-0505; *Fax:* 902-866-0506
Toll-Free: 888-278-0133
contact@rcans.ca
www.rcans.ca
To promote quality workmanship in the commerical, industrial & institutional roofing industry; to encourage training for roofers
Paula Webber, President

Saskatchewan Construction Association (SCA)
320 Gardiner Park Court, Regina SK S4V 1R9
Tel: 306-525-0171
sca@scaonline.ca
www.scaonline.ca
www.facebook.com/SaskConstAssociation
twitter.com/webuildsk
To provide industry leadership, encourage investment in Saskatchewan, grow opportunities for its members & maintain a stable oranization
Mark Cooper, President
Amanda Thick, Director, Operations

Saskatchewan Heavy Construction Association (SHCA)
1939 Elphinstone St., Regina SK S4T 3N3
Tel: 306-586-1805; *Fax:* 306-585-3750
www.saskheavy.ca
www.youtube.com/user/saskheavy
www.facebook.com/SaskHeavy
twitter.com/saskheavy
To commit to the heavy construction industry by actively promoting quality, cost-effective & socially responsible services for the public & its members
Carmen Duncan, Chairman

Sealant & Waterproofing Association (SWA)
70 Leek Cres., Richmond Hill ON L4B 1H1
Tel: 416-499-4000; *Fax:* 416-499-8752
info@swao.com
www.swao.com
www.linkedin.com/company/sealant-and-waterproofing-associati
on-of-ontario
To promote the exchange of ideas for the development of the highest standards & operating efficiency within the sealant & waterproofing industry
Bill MacKay, President
Jeremy Horst, Vice-President

Terrazzo Tile & Marble Association of Canada (TTMAC) / Association canadienne de terrazzo, tuile et marbre
#8, 163 Buttermill Ave., Concord ON L4K 3X8
Tel: 905-660-9640; *Fax:* 905-660-0513
Toll-Free: 800-201-8599
association@ttmac.com
www.ttmac.com
www.youtube.com/user/TTMACCanada
www.linkedin.com/company/terrazzo-tile-&-marble-association-of
-canada
www.facebook.com/TerrazzoTileMarbleAssociationofCanada
twitter.com/TTMACCanada
To standardize terrazzo, tile, marble & stone installation techniques, so that the industry will grow & proper; To support the hardsurface industry & its members
Violeta Ivanescu, General Manager

Thermal Insulation Association of Canada (TIAC) / Association Canadienne de l'Isolation Thermique (ACIT)
1485 Laperriere Ave., Ottawa ON K1Z 7S8
Tel: 613-724-4834; *Fax:* 613-729-6206
info@tiac.ca
www.tiac.ca
Bob Fellows, President

Western Canada Roadbuilders & Heavy Construction Association
c/o Manitoba Heavy Construction Association, #3, 1680 Ellice Ave., Winnipeg MB R3H 0Z2
Tel: 204-947-1379; *Fax:* 204-943-2279
www.wcrhca.org
To represent four western provincial roadbuilders & heavy construction associations at the provincial & federal level

Western Retail Lumber Association (WRLA)
Western Retail Lumber Association Inc., #1004, 213 Notre Dame Ave., Winnipeg MB R3B 1N3
Toll-Free: 800-661-0253
wrla@wrla.org
www.wrla.org
Membership: membership@wrla.org
To serve & promote needs & common interests of lumber, building materials & hard goods industry on the Prairies
Liz Kovach, President

Winnipeg Construction Association
1447 Waverly St., Winnipeg MB R3T 0P7
Tel: 204-775-8664; *Fax:* 204-783-6446
wca@winnipegconstruction.ca
www.winnipegconstruction.ca
twitter.com/wcanews
To encourage a high level of standards among the construction industry in Manitoba & to promote the industry as a whole
Ronald Hambley, President

Business

Alberta Chambers of Commerce (ACC)
#1808, 10025 - 102A Ave., Edmonton AB T5J 2Z2
Tel: 780-425-4180; *Fax:* 780-429-1061
Toll-Free: 800-272-8854
tacorn@abchamber.ca
www.abchamber.ca
www.linkedin.com/company/albertachambers
www.facebook.com/ABChambersofCommerce
twitter.com/albertachambers
To enhance private enterprise in Alberta
Shawna Miller, Chair
Ken Kobly, President & CEO

Alliston & District Chamber of Commerce
PO Box 32, 60B Victoria St. West, Alliston ON L9R 1T9
Tel: 705-435-7921; *Fax:* 705-435-0289
www.adcc.ca
www.youtube.com/user/AllistonChamber
www.facebook.com/allistonchamber
twitter.com/allistonchamber

Crystal Kellard, Executive Director

Assiniboia Chamber of Commerce (MB) (ACC)
PO Box 42122, Stn. Ferry Road, 1867 Portage Ave., Winnipeg MB R3J 3X7
Tel: 204-774-4154; *Fax:* 204-774-4201
info@assiniboiacc.mb.ca
www.assiniboiacc.mb.ca
twitter.com/assiniboiacc
To promote entrepreneurship & competitive enterprise in West Winnipeg
Ernie Nairn, Executive Director

Association for Corporate Growth, Toronto Chapter (ACG)
#200, 411 Richmond St. East, Toronto ON M5A 3S5
Tel: 416-868-1881; *Fax:* 416-929-5256
toronto@acg.org
www.acg.org/toronto
To foster sound corporate growth by providing its members with an opportunity to gain new ideas from speakers, seminars & discussions with people working in the field of corporate growth; To develop additional skills & techniques which will contribute to the growth of their respective organizations; To meet other corporate growth professionals who can provide counsel & valuable contacts
Mike Fenton, Executive Director

Association of International Customs & Border Agencies (AICBA) / Association Des Courtiers et Intervenants Frontaliers (ACIFI)
PO Box 60022, Ottawa ON K1T 0K9
Tel: 613-822-6969
aicba.org
To secure public support; To represent its members to government; To coordinate activities with other organizations
Sandi Villeneuve, President
Denise Dydynsky, General Manager

Association of Professional Economists of British Columbia (APEBC)
#102, 211 Columbia St., Vancouver BC V6A 2R5
Tel: 604-689-1455; *Fax:* 604-681-4545
info@apebc.ca
www.apebc.ca
Jacob Helliwell, President

Atlantic Association of Applied Economists (AAAE)
1701 Hollis St., 13th Fl., Halifax NS B3J 3M8
Tel: 902-420-4601
www.cabe.ca/aaae
To provide opportunities for professional development & networking with other economists & analysts
Sarah Miller, President
Tara Ainsworth, Treasurer

The Brampton Board of Trade (BBOT)
#101, 36 Queen St. East, Brampton ON L6V 1A2
Tel: 905-451-1122
admin@bramptonbot.com
www.bramptonbot.com
www.youtube.com/user/BramptonBoT
www.linkedin.com/company/2087561
www.facebook.com/BramptonBOT
twitter.com/BramptonBOT
To represent & actively promote the interests of Brampton business, members & the private enterprise system
Todd Letts, Chief Executive Officer
Lorraine De Nardis-Assenza, Office Manager

British Columbia Chamber of Commerce
#705, 750 West Pender St., Vancouver BC V6C 2T8
Tel: 604-683-0700; *Fax:* 604-683-0416
bccc@bcchamber.org
bcchamber.org
www.youtube.com/user/bcchamberofcom
www.linkedin.com/company/bc-chamber-of-commerce
www.facebook.com/bcchamber
twitter.com/bcchamberofcom
To make British Columbia a great place to do business; To be the leadership voice of BC business; To build a strong Chamber of Commerce network
Dan Baxter, Interim Chief Executive Officer
Rosaline Chan, Director, Finance & Administration

Burlington Chamber of Commerce
#201, 414 Locust St., Burlington ON L7S 1T7
Tel: 905-639-0174; *Fax:* 905-333-3956
info@burlingtonchamber.com
www.burlingtonchamber.com
www.youtube.com/user/BurlingtonChamber
www.facebook.com/burlington.chamber
twitter.com/burlingtoncofc

To be the focus for business in Burlington; to encourage & promote a strong Burlington business community through sound practices that support social & economic development
Bruce Nicholson, Chair
Keith Hoey, President

Business Council of Canada / Conseil canadien des affaires
#1001, 99 Bank St., Ottawa ON K1P 6B9
Tel: 613-238-3727; *Fax:* 613-238-3247
info@thebusinesscouncil.ca
www.thebusinesscouncil.ca
www.youtube.com/c/BusinessCouncilofCanada
www.linkedin.com/company/business-council-of-canda
twitter.com/BizCouncilofCan
To engage in policy work in Canada, North America & the world
Goldy Hyder, President & CEO
Susan Scotti, Executive Vice-President
John R. Dillon, Corporate Counsel & Senior Vice-President, Policy
Ross H. Laver, Senior Vice-President, Strategy
Nancy Wallace, Vice-President, Corporate Services

Calgary Chamber of Commerce
#600, 237 - 8th Ave. SE, Calgary AB T2G 5C3
Tel: 403-750-0400
info@calgarychamber.com
www.calgarychamber.com
www.linkedin.com/company/calgary-chamber-of-commerce
www.facebook.com/CalgaryChamber
twitter.com/calgarychamber
To lead & serve the Calgary business community valuing its diversity
Rob Hawley, Chair
Adam Legge, President & CEO
Rebecca Wood, Director, Member Services

Cambridge Chamber of Commerce
750 Hespler Rd., Cambridge ON N3H 5L8
Tel: 519-622-2221; *Fax:* 519-622-0177
Toll-Free: 800-749-7560
cchamber@cambridgechamber.com
www.cambridgechamber.com
www.youtube.com/thecambridgechamber
www.linkedin.com/in/cambridgechamber
twitter.com/My_Chamber
Greg Durocher, President & CEO

Campbell River & District Chamber of Commerce
900 Alder St., Campbell River BC V9W 2P6
Tel: 250-287-4636; *Fax:* 250-286-6490
admin@campbellriverchamber.ca
www.campbellriverchamber.ca
www.youtube.com/user/CampbellRiverChamber
www.facebook.com/CampbellRiverChamber
twitter.com/ChamberCR
Colleen Evans, President & CEO

Canada-Finland Chamber of Commerce
c/o Finnish Credit Union, 191 Eglinton Ave. East, Toronto ON M4P 1K1
Tel: 416-486-1533; *Fax:* 416-486-1592
info@canadafinlandcc.com
www.canadafinlandcc.com
www.linkedin.com/company/canada-finland-chamber-of-commerce
www.facebook.com/CanadaFinlandChamber
To promote investment, trade & business relations between Finland & Canada
Lauri Asikainen, President

Canadian Association for Business Economics (CABE) / Association canadienne de science économique des affaires
PO Box 186, 31 Adelaide St. East, Toronto ON M5C 2J1
Toll-Free: 855-222-3321
secretariat@cabe.ca
www.cabe.ca
www.facebook.com/CABEconomics
twitter.com/CABE_Economics
To represent the interests of business economists in Canada; To enhance the professionalism of business economists

Canadian Australian Chamber of Commerce
19-29 Martin Pl., Sydney NSW 2000 Australia
admin@cacc.com.au
www.cacc.com.au
www.linkedin.com/company/canadian-australian-chamber-of-commerce
twitter.com/CACC_AUS
To enhance the trade & business relationship between Canada & Australia
John Secker, Executive Director

Canadian Black Chamber of Commerce (CBCC) / Chambre de commerce noire du Canada (CCNC)
#1901, 5000 Yonge St., Toronto ON M2N 7E9
Tel: 416-613-6206; *Toll-Free:* 855-687-6222
info@blackchamber.ca
www.blackchamber.ca
www.instagram.com/canadianblackchamber
www.linkedin.com/company/canadian-black-chamberofcommerce
www.facebook.com/CanadianBlackChamber
twitter.com/cdnblackchamber
To be the hub of Canadian Black businesses by creating value & collaborating opportunities between all the players in the ecosystem

The Canadian Chamber of Commerce / La Chambre de commerce du Canada
#1700, 275 Slater St., Ottawa ON K1P 5H9
Tel: 613-238-4000; *Fax:* 613-238-7643
info@chamber.ca
www.chamber.ca
www.youtube.com/user/CdnChamberofCommerce
www.linkedin.com/company/the-canadian-chamber-of-commerce-canada-
www.facebook.com/CanadianChamberofCommerce
twitter.com/CdnChamberofCom
To create a climate for competitiveness, profitability & job creation for enterprises of all sizes in all sectors across Canada
Perrin Beatty, President & CEO
Jackie King, Chief Operating Officer
Manuela Lacroix, Vice-President, Finance
Catherine Long, Manager, Payroll & Human Resources

The Canadian Council for Public-Private Partnerships (CCPPP) / Le Conseil canadien pour les partenariats public-privé
#608, 55 University Ave., Toronto ON M5J 2H7
Tel: 416-861-0500
partners@pppcouncil.ca
www.pppcouncil.ca
www.youtube.com/user/CCPPPVideo
twitter.com/pppcouncil
To act as a proponent for improvements in the quality & cost of public services provided to Canadians through innovative partnerships between the public & private sectors
Mark Romoff, President & CEO
Dave Trafford, Director, Communications & Media Relations

Canadian Council for Small Business & Entrepreneurship (CCSBE) / Conseil canadien des PME et de l'entrepreneuriat (CCPME)
6382 Young St., Halifax NS B3L 2A1
Tel: 902-478-8634
ccsbeinfo@gmail.com
www.ccsbe.org
www.linkedin.com/groups/2431087
www.facebook.com/ccsbe
twitter.com/ccsbe
To promote & advance the developmet of small business & entreprenurship through research, education & training, networking, & dissemination of scholarly & policy-oriented information.
Mike Henry, President
Mary Kilfoil, Executive Director

Canadian Federation of Independent Business (CFIB) / Fédération canadienne de l'entreprise indépendante
#401, 4141 Yonge St., Toronto ON M2P 2A6
Tel: 416-222-8022; *Fax:* 416-222-4337
Toll-Free: 844-242-4400
cfib@cfib.ca
www.cfib-fcei.ca
www.youtube.com/user/cfibdotca
www.linkedin.com/company/62788
www.facebook.com/CFIB
twitter.com/CFIBbuzz
To act as the voice for small businesses in Canada
Dan Kelly, Chief Executive Officer
Laura Jones, Executive Vice-President

Canadian Franchise Association (CFA) / Association canadienne de la franchise
#116, 5399 Eglinton Ave. West, Toronto ON M9C 5K6
Tel: 416-695-2896; *Fax:* 416-695-1950
Toll-Free: 800-665-4232
info@cfa.ca
www.cfa.ca
www.linkedin.com/company/canadian-franchise-association
www.facebook.com/canadianfranchiseassociation
twitter.com/CFAfranchise

To promote & represent franchise excellence through a national association of businesses united by a common interest in ethical franchising
Sherry McNeil, President & CEO
Kenny Chan, Vice-President, Content & Marketing
David Black, Director, Government Relations & Public Policy
Lou Gervasi, Senior Manager, Development & Member Relationships

Canadian Gaming Association (CGA)
#503, 131 Bloor St. West, Toronto ON M5S 1P7
Tel: 416-304-7800; *Fax:* 416-304-7805
info@canadiangaming.ca
www.canadiangaming.ca
To act as the voice of companies & organizations involved in the gaming & entertainment industry throughout Canada; To foster a greater understanding of the gaming industry
Paul Burns, President & CEO

Canadian German Chamber of Industry & Commerce Inc. (CGCIC) / Deutsch-Kanadische Industrie- und Handelskammer
#1500, 480 University Ave., Toronto ON M5G 1V2
Tel: 416-598-3355; *Fax:* 416-598-1840
info@germanchamber.ca
kanada.ahk.de
To promote trade & investment between Germany & Canada; offices in Toronto & Montreal
Goetz Milcke, Vice-President, Finance & Administration

Canadian Institute of Chartered Business Valuators (CICBV) / L'Institut canadien des experts en évaluation d'entreprises
#808, 277 Wellington St. West, Toronto ON M5V 3E4
Tel: 416-977-1117; *Fax:* 416-977-7066
Toll-Free: 866-770-7315
info@cbvinstitute.com
cbvinstitute.com
To develop high professional standards for Canadian Chartered Business Valuators; To manage the Chartered Business Valuator (CBV) designation; To govern members of the Institute with a strict Code of Ethics & Practice Standards
Christine Sawchuk, President & CEO
Bob Boulton, Executive Vice-President & COO
Deborah Hanlon, Manager, Administration & Events
Kevin Floether, Coordinator, Communications

Canadian International Institute of Applied Negotiation (CIIAN) / L'Institut international canadien de la négociation pratique
BC V9C 2V1
ciian@ciian.org
ciian.org
www.linkedin.com/company/the-canadian-international-institute-of-applied-negotiation
www.facebook.com/CIIANCanada
twitter.com/CIIAN
To build sustainable peace at local, national & international levels

Canadian Professional Sales Association (CPSA) / Association canadienne des professionnels de la vente
PO Box 116, 2 Bloor St. East, Toronto ON M4W 1A8
Tel: 416-408-2685; *Fax:* 416-408-2684
Toll-Free: 888-267-2772
customerservice@cpsa.com
www.cpsa.com
www.linkedin.com/groups/1589497
www.facebook.com/CanadianProfessionalSalesAssociation
twitter.com/cpsa
To develop & serve sales professionals
Joy Sayers, President & CEO
Nicholas Crowe, Vice-President, Learning Solutions
Marie Meagher, Director, Sales
Mandy Unger, Manager, Membership & Association Services

Canadian Society of Customs Brokers (CSCB) / Société canadienne des courtiers en douane
#320, 55 Murray St., Ottawa ON K1N 5M3
Tel: 613-562-3543; *Fax:* 613-562-3548
cscb@cscb.ca
www.cscb.ca
www.linkedin.com/groups/3997661
twitter.com/CSCB_CA
To act as voice of the industry to all levels of government; To provide information to members on all matters affecting customs brokerage
David Bosse, Chair

Canadian Society of Technical Analysts (CSTA)
#436, 157 Adelaide St. West, Toronto ON M5H 4E7
Tel: 519-807-9178
toronto@csta.org
www.csta.org
To provide a forum for those interested in & working in technical analysis; To promote technical analysis within the financial community
Reagan Yuke, Business Manager

Canadian Tamils' Chamber of Commerce
#209, 5200 Finch Ave. East, Toronto ON M1S 4Z4
Tel: 416-335-9791
info@ctcc.ca
www.ctcc.ca
www.instagram.com/cantamilchamber
www.facebook.com/CTCC25
twitter.com/CANTAMILChamber
To enhance entrepreneurship & socioeconomic development within the Tamil-Canadian community
Dilani Gunarajah, President

Canadian-Croatian Chamber of Commerce
630 The East Mall, Toronto ON M9B 4B1
Tel: 416-641-2829; Fax: 416-641-2700
contactus@croat.ca
www.croat.ca
www.linkedin.com/company/the-canadian-croatian-chamber-of-commerce
www.facebook.com/CanadianCroatianChamberofCommerce
twitter.com/CroatChamber
To represent Croatian-Canadian business in Canada
Wanita Kelava, Manager

Castlegar & District Chamber of Commerce (CDCoC)
1995 - 6th Ave., Castlegar BC V1N 4B7
Tel: 250-365-6313; Fax: 250-365-5778
info@castlegar.com
www.castlegar.com
To encourage a business climate which enables our membership & community to prosper
Jane Charest, President

Centre for Entrepreneurship Education & Development Inc. (CEED)
Bayers Road Centre, #225, 7071 Bayers Rd., Halifax NS B3L 2C2
Tel: 902-421-2333; Fax: 902-482-0291
Toll-Free: 800-590-8481
info@ceed.ca
www.ceed.ca
www.youtube.com/ceedhalifax
www.linkedin.com/company/314065
www.facebook.com/ceed.ca
twitter.com/ceed_halifax
To build entrepreneurial awareness & capacity throughout Atlantic Canada
Craig MacMullin, President & CEO

Chamber of Digital Commerce Canada
Ottawa ON
canada@digitalchamber.org
digitalchamber.org/canada
twitter.com/DigiChamberCDN
To support employment growth & career opportunities in blockchain technology; To promote & sustain community development initiatives across Canada; To enhance consumer safety & industry competitiveness
Tanya Woods, Managing Director

Chambre de commerce au Coeur de la Montérégie (CCCM)
319, ch de Chambly, Marieville QC J3M 1N9
Tél: 450-460-4019; Téléc: 450-460-2362
info@coeurmonteregie.com
www.coeurmonteregie.com
Regroupement volontaire de personnes du milieu dans un but de développement économique, civique et social des membres
Véronique Côté, Directrice générale

Chambre de commerce Canado-Suisse (Québec) Inc. (SCCCQ) / Swiss Canadian Chamber of Commerce (Québec) Inc.
#152, 3450, rue Drummond, Montréal QC H3G 1Y4
Tél: 514-937-5822
www.cccsqc.ca
D'assumer un rôle de premier plan dans la promotion des relations commerciales, industrielles et financières entre la Suisse et le Canada, tout en se concentrant sur l'est du Canada
Marie Habre, Présidente

Chambre de commerce Canado-Tunisienne (CCCT) / Tunisian Canadian Chamber of Commerce
#810, 276, rue Saint-Jacques, Montréal QC H2Y 1N3
Tél: 514-847-1281
info@cccantun.ca
www.cccantun.ca
www.facebook.com/cccantun
Le fer de lance du partenariat canado-tunisien; fournir des informations privilégiées sur les spécificités du marché tunisien; soutenir dans votre recherche de partenaires d'affaires tunisiens; appuyer dans la démarche de mise en marché de vos produits et services en Tunisie
Abdeljelil Ouanès, Président

Chambre de commerce de Charlevoix
#209, 11, rue Saint-Jean-Baptiste, Baie-Saint-Paul QC G3Z 1M1
Tél: 418-760-8648
info@creezdesliens.com
www.creezdesliens.com
De promouvoir les intérêts de ses membres afin de les aider à prospérer
Johanne Côté, Directrice générale

Chambre de commerce de Forestville
40, rte 138 ouest, Forestville QC G0T 1E0
Tél: 418-587-1585
chcommforestville@cgocable.ca
www.facebook.com/501570453233107

Chambre de commerce de l'Ouest-de-l'Île de Montréal / West Island Chamber of Commerce
#106, 1870, boul des Sources, Pointe-Claire QC H9R 5N4
Tél: 514-697-4228; Téléc: 514-697-2562
info@ccoim.ca
www.ccoim.ca
www.facebook.com/CCOIM.WIMCC
twitter.com/chambrewest
D'assurer le bien-être économique de ses membres et de sa communauté d'affaires
Joseph Huza, Directeur exécutif

Chambre de commerce de la Haute-Matawinie
521, rue Brassard, Saint-Michel-des-Saints QC J0K 3B0
Tél: 450-833-1334; Téléc: 450-833-1334
infocchm@satelcom.qc.ca
www.haute-matawinie.com
Regrouper les leaders de tout son territoire intéressés à travailler au bien-être économique, civique et social du milieu et au développement de ses ressources
France Chapdelaine, Directrice générale

Chambre de commerce de la région d'Acton
Édifice de la Gare, 980, rue Boulay, Acton Vale QC J0H 1A0
Tél: 450-546-0123; Téléc: 450-546-2709
ccracton@cooptel.qc.ca
www.chambredecommerce.info
Promouvoir l'action commerciale, sociale et communautaire
Alain Giguère, Président

Chambre de commerce de la region de Cap-Pelé
CP 1219, Cap-Pelé NB E4N 3B1
Tél: 506-332-0118
chambre_de_commerce@rogers.com
www.cap-pele.com
Albert E. LeBlanc, Président
Gilles Haché, Secrétaire

Chambre de commerce de la région de Weedon
280, 9e av, Weedon QC J0B 3J0
Tél: 819-560-8555
Favoriser le développement économique par le réseautage et la concertation

Chambre de commerce de Lac-Brome
CP 3654, #316, 1, rue Knowlton, Lac-Brome QC J0E 1V0
Tél: 450-242-2870
info@cclacbrome.com
www.cclacbrome.com
Pour promouvoir le commerce dans la ville et d'offrir à ses membres des services pour aider à développer leur entreprise
Suzanne Gregory, Directrice générale

Chambre de commerce de Saint-Côme
1661A, rue Principale, Saint-Côme QC J0K 2B0
Tél: 450-883-2730
tourisme@stcomelanaudiere.ca
www.stcomelanaudiere.com
Promouvoir les ressources axées sur le développement économique local en stimulant le commerce, l'industrie et le tourisme
Marie-Marthe Venne, Présidente par intérim

Chambre de commerce de Sainte-Adèle
1370, boul de Sainte-Adèle, Sainte-Adèle QC J8B 2N5
Tél: 450-229-2644; Téléc: 450-229-1436
chambredecommerce@sainte-adele.net
www.sainte-adele.net
www.facebook.com/sainteadele
twitter.com/sainteadele
Pour promouvoir le commerce et à aider leurs membres à prospérer
Guy Goyer, Directeur général

Chambre de commerce de Ste-Justine
167, rte 204, Sainte-Justine QC G0R 1Y0
Tél: 418-383-3207; Téléc: 418-383-3223
chambredecommercestejustine@sogetel.net
www.ccstejustine.ca
Pour maintenir une économie saine à Saint-Justine
Bruno Turcotte, Président

Chambre de commerce de Saint-Quentin Inc.
144D, rue Canada, Saint-Quentin NB E8A 1G7
Tél: 506-235-3666; Téléc: 506-235-1804
www.saintquentinnb.com
www.facebook.com/ChambreDeCommerceDeStQuentin
Réunir ceux et celles qui veulent promouvoir et protéger les intérêts de la ville de Saint-Quentin et de sa région immédiate; encourager tous les citoyens à participer à la prospérité et croissance de la communauté; favoriser et améliorer l'industrie, le commerce et le bien-être économique, civique et social de la communauté
Pascale Bellavance, Présidente
Sandra Aubut, Secrétaire

Chambre de commerce de Sherbrooke
#202, 9, rue Wellington sud, Sherbrooke QC J1H 5C8
Tél: 819-822-6151; Téléc: 819-822-6156
info@ccsherbrooke.ca
www.ccsherbrooke.ca
www.facebook.com/ccsherbrooke
De favoriser et promouvoir le développement socio-économique de l'entreprise privée, défendre les intérêts de ses membres grâce à l'exercice de son leadership et assurer le maintien de conditions propices à la croissance des affaires de sa communauté
Louise Bourgault, Directrice générale

Chambre de commerce de St-Léonard
8370, boul Lacordaire, Saint-Léonard QC H1R 3Y6
Tél: 514-325-4232; Téléc: 514-955-8544
info@saintleonardenaffaires.com
saintleonardenaffaires.com
www.facebook.com/207992709237477
twitter.com/chambrestleo
Défendre des intérêts de ses membres et de la communauté d'affaires de son territoire
Salvatore Andricciola, Président

Chambre de commerce de Valcourt et Région
980, rue St-Joseph, Valcourt QC J0E 2L0
Tél: 450-532-3263; Téléc: 450-532-5855
info@valcourtregion.com
www.valcourtregion.com
www.facebook.com/ccirv
twitter.com/valcourtregion
D'améliorer les activités économiques, sociales et civiques de la région de vacourt
Pierre Bonneau, Président

Chambre de commerce du grand de Châteauguay
#100, 15, boul Maple, Châteauguay QC J6J 3P7
Tél: 450-698-0027; Téléc: 450-698-0088
info@ccgchateauguay.ca
www.ccgchateauguay.ca
www.facebook.com/ChambreDeCommerceChateauguay
Agit comme un catalyseur à la promotion des forces économiques présentes sur son territoire
Isabelle Poirier, Directrice générale

Chambre de commerce du Grand Tracadie-Sheila
#4104, rue Principale, Tracadie-Sheila NB E1X 1B8
Tél: 506-394-4028
www.ccgts.ca
www.facebook.com/111012852315372
twitter.com/CCG_TracadieS
De promouvoir et de développer le commerce dans la région
Rebecca Preston, Directrice générale

Chambre de commerce du Haut-Richelieu
Centre Ernest-Thuot, 75, 5e av, Saint-Jean-sur-Richelieu QC J2X 1T1
Tél: 450-346-2544; Téléc: 450-346-3812
info@ccihr.ca
www.ccihr.ca
www.linkedin.com/company/chambre-de-commerce-du-haut-rich elieu
Pour aider à développer l'économie de la région et aider à développer le commerce
Stéphane Legrand, Directeur général

Chambre de commerce et d'entrepreneuriat des Sources (CCES)
CP 599, Danville QC J0A 1A0
Tél: 819-839-2742; Téléc: 819-839-2347
www.facebook.com/ChambreCommerceEntrepreneuriatSources
Favoriser le développement des affaires dans sa collectivité
Isabelle Lodge, Présidente
Kathy Breton, Secrétaire

Chambre de commerce et d'industrie Beauharnois-Valleyfield-Haut Saint-Laurent
#400, 100, rue Sainte-Cécile, Salaberry-de-Valleyfield QC J6T 1M1
Tél: 450-373-8789; Téléc: 450-373-8642
info@ccibvhsl.ca
www.ccibv.ca
www.facebook.com/ccibv
De mettre sur pied d'activités et de services propres à aider les gens d'affaires; de promouvoir des intérêts économiques régionaux face aux décideurs politiques et cela sous forme d'études, de consultations, d'expertises, de propositions et de représentations et enfin promotion du commerce local et régional
Sylvie Villemure, Directrice générale

Chambre de commerce et d'industrie de la région de Richmond
CP 3119, Richmond QC J0B 2H0
Tél: 819-826-5854
info@ccrichmond.com
www.ccrichmond.com
De travailler au bien être économique, civique, et social de la région de Richmond, et au développement de ses ressources en stimulant le commerce, l'industrie et le tourisme
Hélène Tousignant, Présidente
Ginette Coutu-Poirier, Trésorière

Chambre de commerce et d'industrie de la Rive-Sud
#101, 85, rue Saint-Charles ouest, Longueuil QC J4H 1C5
Tél: 450-463-2121; Téléc: 450-463-1858
info@ccirs.qc.ca
www.ccirs.qc.ca
www.linkedin.com/groups/1621977
www.facebook.com/ccirsrivesud
twitter.com/CCIRS2010
De représenter les entreprises agissant sur son territoire; De prendre position sur les grands enjeux; D'offrir des services en lien avec leurs objectifs de réussite; en développant des partenariats et des occasions de maillage
Hélène Bergeron, Codirectrice générale
Stéphanie Brodeur, Codirectrice générale

Chambre de commerce et d'industrie de la Vallée-du-Richelieu
#203, 230, rue Brébeuf, Beloeil QC J3G 5P3
Tél: 450-464-3733; Téléc: 450-446-4163
www.ccivr.com
www.linkedin.com/groups/4077118
www.facebook.com/CCIVR
twitter.com/CCIVR
De développer continuellement de nouveaux services pour ses membres, des services et des activités qui peuvent contribuer à faire connaître leur entreprise
Julie La Rochelle, Directrice générale

Chambre de commerce et d'industrie de Québec
#600, 900, boul René-Lévesque est, Québec QC G1R 2B5
Tél: 418-692-3853; Téléc: 418-694-2286
info@cciquebec.ca
www.cciquebec.ca
www.youtube.com/channel/UC6knYpzSAWYkHtfTqnlV6SA
www.linkedin.com/company/chambre-de-commerce-et-d%27ind ustrie-de-qu-bec
www.facebook.com/cciquebec
twitter.com/cciquebec
Pour représenter les entreprises au Québec
Alain Aubut, Président et chef de la direction

Chambre de commerce et d'industrie de Sorel-Tracy
67, rue George, Sorel-Tracy QC J3P 1C2
Tél: 450-742-0018; Téléc: 450-742-7442
www.ccstm.qc.ca
www.youtube.com/channel/UC2_SG-MoqKsusKJulFD6m5w
www.linkedin.com/groups/4147723
Promouvoir la liberté d'entreprendre; favorisant ainsi un environnement d'affaires innovant et concurrentiel
Sylvain Dupuis, Directeur général

Chambre de commerce et d'industrie de St-Laurent-Mont-Royal
#101, 5255, boul Henri-Bourassa, Montréal QC H4R 2M6
Tél: 514-333-5222; Téléc: 514-333-0937
info@ccsl-mr.com
www.ccsl-mr.com
De rassembler, informer et défendre les intérêts de ses membres
Sylvie Séguin, Directrice générale

Chambre de commerce et d'industrie de Varennes (CCIV)
2102, Marie-Victorin, #B, Varennes QC J3X 1R4
Tél: 450-652-4209; Téléc: 450-652-4244
info@cciv.ca
www.cciv.ca
De défendre les intérêts de ses membres afin de faire prospérer leur entreprise
Marie-Claude Lévesque, Directrice générale

Chambre de commerce et d'industrie française au canada (CCIFC) / French Chamber of Commerce
#2B, 1455, rue Drummond, Montréal QC H3G 1W3
Tél: 514-281-1246; Téléc: 514-289-9594
info@ccifcmtl.ca
www.ccifcmtl.ca
www.linkedin.com/company/chambre-de-commerce-et-d'industri e-française-au-canada
www.facebook.com/ccifcmtl
twitter.com/CCIFCcanada
Favoriser les échanges entre la France et le Canada; aider à trouver des partenaires
Sandrine Perreault, Directrice générale

Chambre de commerce et d'industrie MRC de Deux-Montagne (CCI2M)
67A, boul Industriel, Saint-Eustache QC J7R 5B9
Tél: 450-491-1991; Téléc: 450-491-1648
info@chambrecommerce.com
www.chambrecommerce.com
www.linkedin.com/groups/3250810
twitter.com/CCI2M
Mélanie Laroche, Directrice générale

Chambre de commerce et d'industrie Thérèse-De Blainville (CCITB)
#202, 141, rue St-Charles, Sainte-Thérèse QC J7E 2A9
Tél: 450-435-8228; Téléc: 450-435-0820
info@ccitb.ca
www.ccitb.ca
www.youtube.com/user/CCITB85
www.linkedin.com/company/chambre-de-commerce-et-d'industri e-th-r-se-de-blainville
www.facebook.com/CCITB
twitter.com/laccitb
Cynthia Kabis, Directrice générale

Chambre de commerce et d'industries de Trois-Rivières
CP 1045, #200, 225, rue des Forges, Trois-Rivières QC G9A 5K4
Tél: 819-375-9628; Téléc: 819-375-9083
info@ccitr.net
www.ccitr.net
www.facebook.com/158875090821998
Défendre les entreprises privées et d'améliorer la communauté
Marie-Pier Matteau, Directrice générale

Chambre de commerce francophone de Vancouver (CCFC)
1555, 7e av ouest, Vancouver BC V6J 1S1
Tél: 604-601-2124
info@ccfvancouver.com
ccfvancouver.com
www.linkedin.com/company/chambre-de-commerce-francophon e-de-vancouver
www.facebook.com/ccfvancouver
twitter.com/ccfvancouver
Organisme à but non-lucratif dont le mandat est de développer et d'améliorer les rapports commerciaux entre gens d'affaires d'expression française en Colombie-Britannique
Daniel Wang, Président

Chambre de commerce LGBT du Québec (CCLGBTQ) / The Québec LGBT Chamber of Commerce
#303.3, 372, rue Sainte-Catherine ouest, Montréal QC H3B 1A2
Tél: 514-522-1885
info@cclgbtq.org
www.cclgbtq.org
Défendre et promouvoir les intérêts de la communauté lesbienne et gaie d'affaires du Québec et favoriser le rayonnement de ses membres
Steve Foster, Président

Chambre de commerce régionale de St-Raymond (CCRSR)
#100, 1, av St-Jacques, Saint-Raymond QC G3L 3Y1
Tél: 418-337-4049; Téléc: 418-337-8017
ccrsr@cite.net
www.ccrsr.qc.ca
De soutenir et appuyer ses membres commerçants, entrepreneurs, gens d'affaires et individus évoluant dans le milieu des affaires de Saint-Raymond, Saint-Léonard et de Rivière-à-Pierre
Jean-François Drolet, Président

Chambre de commerce régionale de Windsor
CP 115, Windsor QC J1S 2L7
Tél: 819-434-5936
info@ccrwindsor.com
www.ccrwindsor.com
Pour aider à développer le commerce dans la région de Windsor afin que leurs membres sont en mesure de prospérer
Serge Ranger, Président

Chambre de commerce Ste-Émélie-de-l'Énergie
400, rue St-Michel, Sainte-Émélie-de-l'Énergie QC J0K 2K0
Tél: 450-886-1658

Chambre de commerce St-Félix de Valois
5306, rue Principale, Saint-Félix-de-Valois QC J0K 2M0
Tél: 450-889-8161; Téléc: 450-889-1590
ccst-flx@stfelixdevalois.qc.ca
www.stfelixdevalois.qc.ca
Travailler au bien-être économique, civique et social de Saint-Félix-de-Valois
Johanne Dufresne, Directrice générale

Chambre de commerce St-Jean-de-Matha
185, rue Laurent, Saint-Jean-de-Matha QC J0K 2S0
Tél: 450-886-0599; Téléc: 450-886-3123
info@chambrematha.com
www.chambrematha.com
Travailler à la promotion de ses membres, ainsi qu'au développement commercial, culturel et social de son village
Steve Adam, Président par intérim
Mélanie Paquin, Directrice

Chambre de commerce St-Martin de Beauce
CP 2022, 131, 1e av est, Saint-Martin QC G0M 1B0
Tél: 418-382-5549
chambre@st-martin.qc.ca
www.st-martin.qc.ca
Travailler au développement économique civique et social de la localité de St-Martin-De-Beauce
Pascal Bergeron, Président

Chambre de commerce Vallée de la Missisquoi
Rte 245, Bolton Centre QC J0E 1G0
Tél: 450-292-4217; Téléc: 450-292-4224
Promouvoir la région et ses commerces; encourager la venue de nouveaux commerces; encourager et accueillir les jeunes entrepreneurs

Chambre de commerce Vallée de la Petite-Nation
185, rue Henri-Bourassa, Papineauville QC J0V 1R0
Tél: 819-427-8450
direction.ccvpn@videotron.ca
www.ccvpn.org
Pour stimuler l'économie et la croissance des entreprises locales à travers des projets d'intérêt commun
Jean Careau, Directeur général

Chatham-Kent Chamber of Commerce
54 - 4th St., Chatham ON N7M 2G2
Tel: 519-352-7540
www.chatham-kentchamber.ca
linkedin.com/company/chatham-kent-chamber-of-commerce
www.facebook.com/ChathamKentChamberofCommerce
twitter.com/CKChamber
G.A. (Gail) Antaya, President & CEO

Comox Valley Chamber of Commerce (CVCC)
2040 Cliffe Ave., Courtenay BC V9N 2L3
Tel: 250-334-3234; Fax: 250-334-4908
Toll-Free: 888-357-4471
events@comoxvalleychamber.com
www.comoxvalleychamber.com
www.facebook.com/ComoxValleyChamber
twitter.com/cxValleyChamber
To support, promote & represent the interests of members in municipal, provincial & national issues
Kevin East, Chair
Dianne Hawkins, CEO

Conseil du patronat du Québec (CPQ) / Québec Employers Council
#510, 1010, rue Sherbrooke ouest, Montréal QC H3A 2R7
Tél: 514-288-5161; Téléc: 514-288-5165
Ligne sans frais: 877-288-5161
www.cpq.qc.ca
www.youtube.com/user/CPQ2010
www.linkedin.com/groups/Conseil-patronat-Québec-2908454
www.facebook.com/conseilpatronat
twitter.com/conseilpatronat
Le Conseil du patronat du Québec a pour mission de s'assurer que les entreprises puissent disposer au Québec des meilleures conditions possibles- notamment en metière de capital humain- afin de prosperear de fason durable dans un contexte de concurrence mondiale.
Yves-Thomas Dorval, Président
Camilla Sironi, Conseillère principale, Communications

Cranbrook & District Chamber of Commerce
Cranbrook & District Chamber of Commerce, PO Box 84, Cranbrook BC V1C 4H6
Tel: 250-426-5914; Fax: 250-426-3873
Toll-Free: 800-222-6174
info@cranbrookchamber.com
www.cranbrookchamber.com
www.facebook.com/cranbrookchamber
twitter.com/cranbrookchambr
To promote the community & its businessess; To protect the interests of businesses; To attract new businesses to the area
David Struthers, President
David Hull, Executive Director

Crowsnest Pass Chamber of Commerce
PO Box 706, 12707 - 20th Ave., Blairmore AB T0K 0E0
Tel: 403-562-7108; Fax: 403-562-7493
Toll-Free: 888-562-7108
office@crowsnestpasschamber.ca
www.crowsnestpasschamber.ca
www.linkedin.com/in/crowsnest-pass-chamber-of-commerce-45a
b946a
www.facebook.com/CrowsnestPassChamber
To act as a link for business, marketing, & tourism for the Crowsnest Pass area of Alberta
Sacha Anderson, President
Tim May, Treasurer
Claire Rogers, Secretary

Duncan-Cowichan Chamber of Commerce (DCCC)
381 Trans-Canada Hwy., Duncan BC V9L 3R5
Tel: 250-748-1111; Fax: 250-746-8222
chamber@duncancc.bc.ca
www.duncancc.bc.ca
www.facebook.com/DuncanCowichanChamber
twitter.com/DuncanCowichan
To advocacy, service, education, support, & opportunity to engage the business community
Sonja Nagel, Executive Director

Edmonton Chamber of Commerce
World Trade Centre, Sun Life Place, #600, 9990 Jasper Ave., Edmonton AB T5J 1P7
Tel: 780-426-4620; Fax: 780-424-7946
info@edmontonchamber.com
www.edmontonchamber.com
www.linkedin.com/company/edmonton-chamber-of-commerce
www.facebook.com/EdmontonChamber
twitter.com/edmontonchamber
To facilitate economic growth by providing information, business opportunities, educational programs & services to members; To positively influence Edmonton's business environment
Janet M. Riopel, President & CEO

European Union Chamber of Commerce in Canada (EUCCAN)
#201F, 622 College St., Toronto ON M6G 1B6
Tel: 416-598-7087
info@euccan.com
euccan.com
www.linkedin.com/groups/2924006
www.facebook.com/EUCCAN
twitter.com/EUCCAN_
To strengthen economic ties between Canada & Europe; To act as the business voice of & the point of contact for European business interests in Canada
Stephen Klus, President

Excellence Canada
#402, 154 University Ave., Toronto ON M5H 3Y9
Tel: 416-251-7600; Fax: 416-251-9131
Toll-Free: 800-263-9648
info@excellence.ca
www.excellence.ca
www.linkedin.com/company/excellence-canada
www.facebook.com/82765064279
twitter.com/excellencecan
To inspire & foster excellence in Canadian organizations; to enhance Canada's national well-being & global leadership through the incorporation of quality principles in business, government, education & health care; to promote, encourage & support the understanding & adoption of total quality principles & practices in all sectors of the economy across Canada; & to recognize outstanding achievement through the Canada Awards for Excellence
Allan Ebedes, President & CEO

Family Enterprise Xchange (FEX)
#135, 690 Dorval Dr., Oakville ON L6K 3W7
Tel: 905-337-8375; Fax: 905-337-0572
Toll-Free: 866-849-0099
info@family-enterprise-xchange.com
family-enterprise-xchange.com
www.youtube.com/user/CAFECanada1
www.linkedin.com/company/family-enterprise-xchange
www.facebook.com/FamilyEnterpriseXchange
twitter.com/FEXcanada
To help business families across Canada succeed
Bill Brushett, President & CEO
Lorraine Bauer, National Director, Membership & Community Engagement
Russel Baskin, Director, Education & Programs

Flin Flon & District Chamber of Commerce
#235, 35 Main St., Flin Flon MB R8A 1J7
Tel: 204-687-4518
flinflonchamber@mymts.net
www.flinflondistrictchamber.com
www.facebook.com/flinflondistrictchamber
twitter.com/FlinFlonChamber
To promote & improve trade & commerce & the economic, civic & social welfare of the district; the Chamber represents the communities of Flin Flon, Creighton, Denare Beach, & Cranberry Portage.
Dianne Russell, President
Karen MacKinnon, President Elect

Fredericton Chamber of Commerce / La Chambre de Commerce de Fredericton
PO Box 275, #200, 364 York St., Fredericton NB E3B 4Y9
Tel: 506-458-8006; Fax: 506-451-1119
fchamber@frederictonchamber.ca
www.frederictonchamber.ca
www.facebook.com/frederictonchamber
twitter.com/Fton_Chamber
To contribute to the economic development of the community by being the advocate of business in the Greater Fredericton area
Stephen Hill, President
Krista Ross, Chief Executive Officer

Futurpreneur Canada
#700, 133 Richmond St. West, Toronto ON M5H 2L3
Fax: 877-408-3234
Toll-Free: 866-646-2922
info@futurpreneur.ca
www.futurpreneur.ca
www.youtube.com/user/CYBF
www.linkedin.com/company/futurpreneur-canada
www.facebook.com/futurpreneur
twitter.com/Futurpreneur
To provide financing, mentoring, & support tools to aspiring business owners aged 18-39
Julia Deans, CEO
Rebecca Dew, CFO
Terry Campbell, COO
Mitchell Krakower, Senior Vice-President, Programs & Business Development

Dan Ouimet, Senior Vice-President, External Engagement

Glendon & District Business Alliance (GDBA)
c/o Bonnyville & District Chamber of Commerce, PO Box 6054, Hwy. 28 West, Bonnyville AB T9N 2G7
Tel: 780-826-3252
www.bonnyvillechamber.com
To drive local economic development; To represent, support & promote businesses in the area
Julie Kissel, Chair

Greater Bathurst Chamber of Commerce / Chambre de commerce du Grand Bathurst
Keystone Bldg., #101, 270 Douglas Ave., Bathurst NB E2A 1M9
Tel: 506-546-8100; Fax: 506-548-2200
info@bathurstchamber.ca
www.bathurstchamber.ca
www.facebook.com/335718759975
twitter.com/bathurstchamber
To facilitate economic growth in the Chaleur area; To advocate for the business community of Greater Bathurst
Mitch Poirier, General Manager
Bernard Cormier, President
Linda Rogers, Treasurer

Greater Charlottetown & Area Chamber of Commerce
PO Box 67, #230, 134 Kent St., Charlottetown PE C1A 7K2
Tel: 902-628-2000; Fax: 902-368-3570
www.charlottetownchamber.com
www.linkedin.com/company/the-greater-charlottetown-area-cha
mber-of-commerce
www.facebook.com/CharlottetownChamber
twitter.com/GCACCbuzz
To be the voice of business on economic issues; to provide services & opportunities for members to enhance their ability to do business
Pam Williams, President
Penny Walsh McGuire, Executive Director
Angela Smith, Office Manager

Greater Kingston Chamber of Commerce (GKCC)
945 Princess St., Kingston ON K7L 3N6
Tel: 613-548-4453; Fax: 613-548-4743
info@kingstonchamber.on.ca
www.kingstonchamber.on.ca
www.youtube.com/channel/UC1Pmf1i3uKXFF7PM_3_5cAA
www.linkedin.com/company/greater-kingston-chamber-of-comm
erce
www.facebook.com/greaterkingstonchamber
twitter.com/kingstonchamber
To advance economic progress, free enterprise, & the quality of life
Martin Sherris, CEO

Greater Kitchener & Waterloo Chamber of Commerce
PO Box 2367, 80 Queen St. North, Kitchener ON N2H 6L4
Tel: 519-576-5000; Fax: 519-742-4760
admin@greaterkwchamber.com
www.greaterkwchamber.com
www.youtube.com/user/GreaterKWChamber
www.linkedin.com/groups/2056325
www.facebook.com/GKWCC
twitter.com/gkwcc
To serve business in the Greater Kitchener Waterloo area & be its voice in the betterment of the community
Ian McLean, President & CEO

Greater Moncton Chamber of Commerce (GMCC) / Chambre de commerce du Grand Moncton
#200, 1273 Main St., Moncton NB E1C 0P4
Tel: 506-857-2883
info@gmcc.nb.ca
www.gmcc.nb.ca
www.youtube.com/user/GreaterMonctonCham
www.linkedin.com/company/greater-moncton-chamber-of-comm
erce
www.facebook.com/GreaterMonctonChamberOfCommerce
twitter.com/MonctonChamber
To strengthen business & community in the Greater Moncton area through leadership, member services, & advocacy on business issues at the municipal, provincial, & national levels
Carol O'Reilly, CEO
Scott Lewis, Chair

Greater Nanaimo Chamber of Commerce
2133 Bowen Rd., Nanaimo BC V9S 1H8
Tel: 250-756-1191; Fax: 250-756-1584
info@nanaimochamber.bc.ca
www.nanaimochamber.bc.ca

To act as the voice of business in Greater Nanaimo; To ensure a healthy economic base & socio-economic structure to benefit the central Vancouver Island area
Kim Smythe, CEO
David Littlejohn, Chair
Justin Schley, Treasurer

Greater Niagara Chamber of Commerce (GNCC)
#103, 1 St. Paul St., St Catharines ON L2R 7L2
Tel: 905-684-2361; *Fax:* 905-684-2100
info@gncc.ca
www.gncc.ca
www.linkedin.com/groups/4151488
www.facebook.com/NiagaraChamber
twitter.com/The_GNCC
To support business growth & prosperity in the Niagara region
Mishka Balsom, President & CEO

Greater Peterborough Chamber of Commerce (GPCC)
175 George St. North, Peterborough ON K9J 3G6
Tel: 705-748-9771; *Fax:* 705-743-2331
Toll-Free: 887-640-4037
info@peterboroughchamber.ca
www.peterboroughchamber.ca
www.youtube.com/user/PeterboroughChamber
www.linkedin.com/groups/2934106
www.facebook.com/peterboroughchamber
twitter.com/ptbochamber
To create a prosperous community by promoting the free enterprise system, a healthy business environment, & acting as the voice of business
Stuart Harrison, President & CEO

Greater Summerside Chamber of Commerce (GSCC)
#10, 263 Heather Moyse Dr., Summerside PE C1N 5P1
Tel: 902-436-9651; *Fax:* 902-436-8320
info@summersidechamber.com
www.summersidechamber.com
www.instagram.com/summersidechamber
www.linkedin.com/groups/8208866
www.facebook.com/120850442004
twitter.com/GSSideCC
To provide a voice on behalf of business in the City of Summerside & area; To work towards the prosperity & betterment of Greater Summerside
Jan Sharpe, Executive Director

Greater Victoria Chamber of Commerce (GVCC)
#100, 852 Fort St., Victoria BC V8W 1H8
Tel: 250-383-7191; *Fax:* 250-385-3552
chamber@victoriachamber.ca
www.victoriachamber.ca
www.youtube.com/user/victoriachamber
www.linkedin.com/groups/1795424
www.facebook.com/VictoriaChamber
twitter.com/ChamberVictoria
To act as the voice of business for the Greater Victoria region; To ensure that the area maintains & enhances its prosperous & vibrant business climate
Bruce Carter, CEO
Frank Bourree, Chair
Sang-Kiet Ly, Treasurer

Greenwood Board of Trade
c/o City of Greenwood, PO Box 129, 202 South Government Ave., Greenwood BC V0H 1J0
Tel: 250-445-6644; *Fax:* 250-445-6441
greenwoodbot@gmail.com
www.greenwoodbot.com
To promote & improve trade, commerce & the economic, civic & social welfare of the district
Dave Evans, President

Grimsby & District Chamber of Commerce
33 Main St. West, Grimsby ON L3M 3H1
Tel: 905-945-8319; *Fax:* 905-945-1615
www.grimsbychamber.ca
www.youtube.com/channel/UCN036EfnmnpKPG2rWqElCqA
www.facebook.com/grimsbychamberofcommerce
twitter.com/grimsbychamber
To promote commerce in the community
Marion Thorp, President

Guelph Chamber of Commerce (GCC)
PO Box 1268, 111 Farquhar St., Guelph ON N1H 3N4
Tel: 519-822-8081; *Fax:* 519-822-8451
chamber@guelphchamber.com
www.guelphchamber.com
www.youtube.com/user/GuelphChamberComerc1
www.linkedin.com/groups/2053342
www.facebook.com/guelphchamber

To serve as the voice of the business community in Guelph; To help strengthen the economy of Guelph & adjacent townships; To provide a forum for the development of discussion & programs that will contribute to the social, economic & physical quality of life in Guelph; To promote Guelph as a good place to live, work & visit
Kithio Mwanzia, President & CEO

Halifax Chamber of Commerce
#100, 32 Akerley Blvd., Dartmouth NS B3B 1N1
Tel: 902-468-7111; *Fax:* 902-468-7333
info@halifaxchamber.com
www.halifaxchamber.com
www.linkedin.com/company/halifax-chamber-of-commerce
www.facebook.com/halifaxchamberofcommerce
twitter.com/halifaxchamber
To build & strengthen the business culture in Metro Halifax through advocacy, networking & leadership
Cynthia Dorrington, Chair

Hamilton Chamber of Commerce (HCC)
Plaza Level, 120 King St. West, Hamilton ON L8P 4V2
Tel: 905-522-1151; *Fax:* 905-522-1154
hcc@hamiltonchamber.ca
www.hamiltonchamber.ca
www.linkedin.com/company/hamilton-chamber-of-commerce
www.facebook.com/140038556040986
twitter.com/hamiltonchamber
To make greater Hamilton a great place to live, work, play, visit & invest; To recognize the importance of the individual as the most significant contributor to achieving community objectives
Keanin Loomis, President & CEO

Hellenic Canadian Board of Trade (HCBT)
PO Box 801, 31 Adelaide St. East, Toronto ON M4C 2K1
Tel: 416-410-4228
membership@hcbt.com
www.hcbt.com
www.instagram.com/helleniccanadianboardoftrade
www.facebook.com/helleniccanadianboardoftrade
twitter.com/HCBT_Toronto
Michael Gekas, President

Hong Kong-Canada Business Association (HKCBA) / L'Association commerciale Hong Kong-Canada
PO Box 18463, Stn. West Georgia, Vancouver BC V6Z 0B3
Tel: 778-990-4756
nationaled@hkcba.com
www.hkcba.com
To encourage & promote trade & commercial activities across a broad range of industries between Canada & Hong Kong, & through Hong Kong to China & the Asia Pacific Region
Craig Lindsay, National Chair
Vanessa Wright, Executive Director

IntegrityLink
#302, 880 Ouellette Ave., Windsor ON N9A 1C7
Tel: 519-258-7222; *Fax:* 519-258-1198
info@integritylink.ca
www.integritylink.ca
To promote & foster the highest ethical relationship between businesses & the public through voluntary self-regulation, consumer & business education & service education
Joe Amort, President & CEO

International Coaching Federation (ICF)
#A325, 2365 Harrodsburg Rd., Lexington KY 40504 USA
Tel: 859-219-3580; *Fax:* 859-226-4411
Toll-Free: 888-423-3131
icfheadquarters@coachingfederation.org
coachfederation.org
www.youtube.com/user/ICFHeadquarters
www.linkedin.com/groups/87212
www.facebook.com/icfhq
twitter.com/icfhq
To be a support network for professional coaches of any kind
Rajat Garg, Chair
Magdalena Nowicka Mook, Chief Executive Officer

Italian Chamber of Commerce of Ontario (ICCO)
#201F, 622 College St., Toronto ON M6G 1B6
Tel: 416-789-7169; *Fax:* 416-789-7160
trade@italchambers.ca
www.italchambers.ca
www.instagram.com/italchambers
www.linkedin.com/company/icco-italian-chamber-of-commerce-of-ontario
www.facebook.com/IccoItalianChamberOfCommerceOfOntario
twitter.com/italchambers
To enhance & promote business, trade & cultural relations between Canada & Italy
Tony Altomare, Co-President
Patrick Pelliccione, Co-President

Corrado Paina, Executive Director

Kapuskasing & District Chamber of Commerce
25 Millview Rd., Kapuskasing ON P5N 2X6
Tel: 705-335-2332; *Fax:* 705-335-2359
info@kapchamber.ca
www.kapchamber.ca
www.facebook.com/KDCofC
twitter.com/KDCC2
To help businesses & the community thrive & grow
Martin Proulx, President

Kelowna Chamber of Commerce
544 Harvey Ave., Kelowna BC V1Y 6C9
Tel: 250-861-3627; *Fax:* 250-861-3624
info@kelownachamber.org
www.kelownachamber.org
www.linkedin.com/groups/3972388
www.facebook.com/KelownaChamberofCommerce
twitter.com/KelownaChamber
To improve trade & commerce & the economic, civic & social welfare of the city of Kelowna
Tom Dyas, President
Caroline Grover, Chief Executive Officer

Lethbridge Chamber of Commerce
#200, 529 - 6 St. South, Lethbridge AB T1J 2E1
Tel: 403-327-1586; *Fax:* 403-327-1001
office@lethbridgechamber.com
www.lethbridgechamber.com
www.youtube.com/lethchamber
www.facebook.com/LethbridgeChamber
twitter.com/lethchamber
To serve and represent the interests of its members by promoting and enhancing free enterprise, for the benefit of the social and economic environment of the City of Lethbridge
Karla Pyrch, Executive Director

Lindsay & District Chamber of Commerce
180 Kent St. West, Lindsay ON K9V 2Y6
Tel: 705-324-2393; *Fax:* 705-324-2473
info@lindsaychamber.com
www.lindsaychamber.com
www.linkedin.com/company/lindsay-&-district-chamber-of-commerce
twitter.com/LDChamber
To protect the interests of the business community of Lindsay & district
Marlene Morrison Nicholls, President
Colleen Collins, Administrative Officer

Lloydminster Chamber of Commerce
4419 - 52 Ave., Lloydminster AB T9V 0Y8
Tel: 780-875-9013; *Fax:* 780-875-0755
info@lloydminsterchamber.com
www.lloydminsterchamber.com
www.youtube.com/user/LloydminsterChamber
www.facebook.com/LloydChamber
twitter.com/LloydChamber
To enhance private enterprise in Lloydminster & surrounding area
Serena Sjodin, Executive Director

Lunenburg Board of Trade
Visitor's Information Centre, PO Box 1300, 11 Blockhouse Hill Rd., Lunenburg NS B0J 2C0
Tel: 902-634-3170; *Fax:* 902-634-3194
Toll-Free: 888-615-8305
ed@lunenburgns.com
www.lunenburgns.com/lunenburg-board-of-trade
To advance commercial, industrial & civic interests of Lunenburg and its area
Mike Smith, President

Manitoba Association for Business Economics (MABE)
MB
www.cabe.ca/mabe
To bring together individuals in Manitoba interested in the field of economics; To provide regular meetings for discussion & the exchange of ideas on current economic problems, issues & achievements; To foster further education in the field of economics
John Harper, President

Manitoba Quality Network
#660, 175 Hargrave St., Winnipeg MB R3C 3R8
Tel: 204-949-4999; *Fax:* 204-949-4990
www.qnet.ca
To help organizations pursue continuous excellence & improvement
Trish Wainikka, Executive Director

Maple Ridge Pitt Meadows Chamber of Commerce
12492 Harris Rd., Pitt Meadows BC V3Y 2J4
Tel: 604-457-4599; *Fax:* 604-457-4598
info@ridgemeadowschamber.com
www.ridgemeadowschamber.com
www.instagram.com/pmmrchamber
www.facebook.com/RidgeMeadowsChamber
twitter.com/PMMRChamber
Andrea Madden, Executive Director

Markham Board of Trade (MBT)
#105, 3600 Steeles Ave., C1, Markham ON L3R 9Z7
Tel: 905-474-0730; *Fax:* 905-474-0685
info@markhamboard.com
www.markhamboard.com
www.linkedin.com/company/markham-board-of-trade
www.facebook.com/MarkhamBoard
twitter.com/MarkhamBoard
To enhance the success of members & the Markham business
community
Richard Cunningham, President & CEO
Mary Ann Quagliara, Director, Member Services

Medicine Hat & District Chamber of Commerce
413 - 6th Ave. SE, Medicine Hat AB T1A 2S7
Tel: 403-527-5214; *Fax:* 403-527-5182
info@medicinehatchamber.com
www.medicinehatchamber.com
www.linkedin.com/company/medicine-hat-and-district-chamber-o
f-commerce
www.facebook.com/MHChamber
twitter.com/mhdchamber
To promote a healthy business environment
Khrista Vogt, President
Lisa Kowalchuk, Executive Director

Mission Regional Chamber of Commerce
34033 Lougheed Hwy., Mission BC V2V 5X8
Tel: 604-826-6914; *Fax:* 604-826-5916
info@missionchamber.bc.ca
www.missionchamber.bc.ca
www.youtube.com/TheMissionChamber
www.facebook.com/Mission.Business.Network
twitter.com/MissionCommerce
To foster a network for entrepreneurial leaders to partner in
education, communication & representation
Kristin Parsons, Executive Director

Mouvement québécois de la qualité (MQQ)
#1710, 360, rue Saint-Jacques ouest, Montréal QC H2Y 1P5
Tél: 514-874-9933; *Téléc:* 514-866-4600
Ligne sans frais: 888-874-9933
mqq@qualite.qc.ca
www.qualite.qc.ca
www.facebook.com/MouvementQuebecoisQualite
Promouvoir et rendre accessibles aux organisations les
meilleures pratiques d'affaire pour accroître leur performance et
leur compétitivité
Roch Dubé, Président

New Brunswick Chamber of Commerce (NBCC)
1, ch Canada, Edmundston NB E3V 1T6
Tel: 506-737-1868; *Fax:* 506-737-1862

Next Canada
North Bldg., #200, 175 Bloor St. East, Toronto ON M4W 3R8
Tel: 647-259-8943
info@nextcanada.com
www.nextcanada.com
www.instagram.com/next_canada
www.linkedin.com/company/next-canada
www.facebook.com/nextcanadaorg
twitter.com/next_canada
To offer education, mentorship, funding, & network access to
entrepreneurs
Joe Canavan, Chief Executive Officer
Kyle J. Winters, Chief Development Officer
Jon French, Senior Director, Global Recruitment, Community &
Alumni

North Grenville Chamber of Commerce
PO Box 1047, 509 Kernahan St., Kemptville ON K0G 1J0
Tel: 613-258-4838
www.northgrenvillechamber.com
To promote business community & quality of life
Mark Thornton, Chair

North Queens Board of Trade
North Queens Community School, 40 Caledonia Rd. West,
Caledonia NS B0T 1B0
Tel: 902-682-3116
To support & promote commerce and trade in the North Queens
area

Peter van Dyk, President

North Vancouver Chamber of Commerce (NVCC)
1250 Lonsdale Ave., Vancouver BC V7M 2H6
Tel: 604-987-4488; *Fax:* 604-987-8272
www.nvchamber.ca
www.instagram.com/nvchamber
www.linkedin.com/company/north-vancouver-chamber-of-comm
erce
www.facebook.com/nvchamber
To ensure a healthy socio-economic base for the benefit of the
North Shore region by supporting business prosperity, economic
growth, & diversification
Louise Ranger, Chief Executive Officer
Misha Wilson, Manager, Membership

Northwest Territories Chamber of Commerce
NWT Commerce Place, #13, 4802 - 50th Ave., Yellowknife NT
X1A 1C4
Tel: 867-920-9505; *Fax:* 867-873-4174
admin@nwtchamber.com
www.nwtchamber.com
To act as the voice for northern business; To create a business
climate of profitability & competitiveness in the Northwest
Territories; To foster business development; To promote
business in the Northwest Territories; To involve & assist First
Nations organizations; To conduct operations in an
environmentally responsible manner
Trevor Wever, President

**L'Office de Certification Commerciale du Québec
Inc. (OCCQ) / Québec Commercial Certification
Office Inc. (QCCO)**
#206, 1565, boul de l'Avenir, Laval QC H7S 2N5
Tél: 514-905-3893; *Téléc:* 450-663-6316
info@occq-qcco.com
www.occq-qcco.com

Ontario Chamber of Commerce (OCC)
#2105, 180 Dundas St. West, Toronto ON M5G 1Z8
Tel: 416-482-5222; *Fax:* 416-482-5879
info@occ.on.ca
occ.ca
www.youtube.com/user/OntarioChamber
www.linkedin.com/company/ontario-chamber-of-commerce
www.facebook.com/ontchamberofcommerce
twitter.com/OntarioCofC
To support economic growth in Ontario by representing business
priorities to the provincial government
Rocco Rossi, President & CEO
Victor Korchenko, Vice-President, Finance

Ontario Gay & Lesbian Chamber of Commerce
#118, 2 College St., Toronto ON M5G 1K3
Tel: 416-646-1600
info@oglcc.com
www.oglcc.com
www.linkedin.com/groups/2487217
www.facebook.com/OGLCC
twitter.com/OGLCC
To create an environment in which the Ontario gay & lesbian
business & professional communities can thrive through the
sharing of knowledge, resources, & communications
Sadhisha Ambagahawita, President

Ontario Public Buyers Association (OPBA)
OPBA Central Office, #361, 111 Fourth Ave., St Catharines
ON L2S 3P5
Tel: 905-682-2644
info@opba.ca
www.opba.ca
To promote the ethical & effective expenditure of public funds
through the principles of professional procurement
Michelle Palmer, President
Tina Iacoe, Vice President
David Allan, Secretary
Michelle Rasiulis, Treasurer

**Organisme de développement d'affaires
commerciales et économiques (ODACE)**
924, rue King est, Sherbrooke QC J1G 1E2
Tél: 819-565-7991; *Téléc:* 819-565-3160
info@odace.quebec
www.odace.quebec
www.facebook.com/OdaceQuebec
Assurer un développement économique prospère dans le grand
Sherbrooke et générer des retombées sur l'ensemble du
territoire de la ville de Sherbrooke
Louis Longchamps, Directeur général

Ottawa Chamber of Commerce (OCC)
328 Somerset St. West, Ottawa ON K2P 0J9
Tel: 613-236-3631; *Fax:* 613-236-7498
www.ottawachamber.ca
www.facebook.com/ottawachamberofcommerce
twitter.com/ottawachamber
To provide leadership in the community to enhance economic
prosperity & quality of life
Ian Faris, President & CEO
Alexandra Walsh, Director, Membership Services
Kenny Leon, Director, Communications

Ottawa Economics Association (OEA)
PO Box 264, Stn. B, Ottawa ON K1P 6C4
Tel: 613-837-9415
www.cabe.ca/oea
twitter.com/OEAEconomics
To organize programs of interest to members
Brian Kingston, President
Jasmin Thomas, Treasurer

Pacific Corridor Enterprise Council (PACE)
PO Box 3032, Vancouver BC V6B 3X5
Tel: 604-682-8278; *Fax:* 888-402-0708
pace@pacebordertrade.org
www.pacebordertrade.org
To build relationships through the production & dissemination of
new information, the communication of information relevant to
cross border business; To promote public policy that removes
barriers to the free flow of capital, people goods & services
across borders, & the facilitation of networking among members
& the public/private sector
K. David Andersson, Chair
Greg Boos, President

Parksville & District Chamber of Commerce
PO Box 99, Parksville BC V9P 2G3
Tel: 250-248-3613; *Fax:* 250-248-5210
info@parksvillechamber.com
www.parksvillechamber.com
www.youtube.com/user/ParksvilleChamber1
www.facebook.com/parksvillechamber
twitter.com/parksvillechmbr
Kim Burden, Executive Director
Linda Tchorz, Manager, Member Services
Lynda Schneider, Bookkeeper
Patti Lee, Manager, Visitor Centre

Penticton & Wine Country Chamber of Commerce
553 Vees Dr., Penticton BC V2A 8S3
Tel: 250-492-4103
admin@penticton.org
www.penticton.org
www.facebook.com/200338503334345
twitter.com/PentChamber
Brandy Maslowski, Executive Director
Jason Cox, President

Pictou County Chamber of Commerce
#3C, 115 MacLean St., New Glasgow NS B2H 4M5
Tel: 902-755-3463
info@pictouchamber.com
www.pictouchamber.com
www.linkedin.com/company/pictou-county-chamber-of-commerc
e
www.facebook.com/173337132712998
twitter.com/PCChamberCommer
To distinguish itself as the pre-eminent voice of business in our
region
Jack Kyte, Executive Director

Portage la Prairie & District Chamber of Commerce
56 Royal Rd. North, Portage la Prairie MB R1N 1V1
Tel: 204-857-7778; *Fax:* 204-856-5001
info@portagechamber.com
www.portagechamber.com
www.facebook.com/PortageLaPrairieDistrictChamberOfCommer
ce
To foster an environment which will enhance the commercial
development of the district
Dave Omichinski, President
Cindy McDonald, Executive Director

Powell River Chamber of Commerce
6807 Wharf St., Powell River BC V8A 2T9
Tel: 604-485-4051
office@powellriverchamber.com
www.powellriverchamber.com
www.facebook.com/188501364559861
Jack Barr, President
Kim Miller, General Manager

Prince George Chamber of Commerce (PGCOC)
890 Vancouver St., Prince George BC V2L 2P5
Tel: 250-562-2454; *Fax:* 250-562-6510
chamber@pgchamber.bc.ca
www.pgchamber.bc.ca
www.youtube.com/channel/UCzQhi2Ttff84-lkN_Vb6NkQ
www.linkedin.com/company/prince-george-chamber-of-commerc
e
www.facebook.com/PrinceGeorgeChamber
twitter.com/PGChamber1
To enhance the quality of life in the community by fostering an
environment that enables local businesses to thrive
Christie Ray, CEO

Red Deer Chamber of Commerce
3017 Gaetz Ave., Red Deer AB T4N 5Y6
Tel: 403-347-4491; *Fax:* 403-343-6188
rdchamber@reddeerchamber.com
www.reddeerchamber.com
www.linkedin.com/groups/2518693
www.facebook.com/109831038638
twitter.com/RedDeerChamber
To promote a thriving environment by advocating for Red Deer &
area members on issues affecting business in the community
Bradley Williams, President
Tim Creedon, Executive Director

Richmond Chamber of Commerce
North Tower, #202, 5811 Cooney Rd., Richmond BC V6X
3M1
Tel: 604-278-2822; *Fax:* 604-278-2972
rcc@richmondchamber.ca
www.richmondchamber.ca
www.youtube.com/user/RichmondchamberBC
www.linkedin.com/company/1026185
www.facebook.com/RichmondChamberCommerce
twitter.com/richmondchamber
To support & represent the interests of business in the city on
behalf of its membership; to promote, enhance & improve trade
& commerce, & the economic, civic & social well-being of
Richmond; to support & communicate to all levels of government
the informed opinion & positions of policy of its members on key
local, provincial & national issues
Matt Pitcairn, President & CEO

Richmond Hill Chamber of Commerce (RHCOC)
376 Church St. South, Richmond Hill ON L4C 9V8
Tel: 905-884-1961; *Fax:* 905-884-1962
info@rhcoc.com
www.rhcoc.com
www.youtube.com/user/richmondhillchamber
www.linkedin.com/groups/1443337
www.facebook.com/RHCOC
twitter.com/RHChamber
To foster a business enviornment that enhances the success of
our members & improves the quality of life in Richmond Hill
Bryon Wilfert, Chair
Elio Fulan, Executive Director

St Thomas & District Chamber of Commerce
#115, 300 South Edgeware Rd., St Thomas ON N5P 4L1
Tel: 519-631-1981; *Fax:* 519-631-0466
mail@stthomaschamber.on.ca
www.stthomaschamber.on.ca
To serve as the voice of the business community & to work to
ensure economic success in central Elgin county
Bob Hammersley, President & CEO

Saskatchewan Chamber of Commerce
#200, 2221 Cornwall St., Regina SK S4P 2L1
Tel: 306-352-2671; *Fax:* 306-781-7084
info@saskchamber.com
www.saskchamber.com
www.youtube.com/user/SaskChamber
www.linkedin.com/company/saskatchewan-chamber-of-commer
ce
www.facebook.com/saskchamber
twitter.com/SaskChamber
To act as the voice of business in Saskatchewan; To make
Saskatchewan a better place for living, working, & investing; To
promote commercial & industrial progress in Saskatchewan; To
improve the competitiveness of Saskatchewan's economy
Steve McLellan, Chief Executive Officer

Saskatchewan Economics Association (SEA)
c/o Rahatjan Judge, Treasurer, 826 Ave. K south, Saskatoon
SK S7M 2E8
sea@cabe.ca
www.cabe.ca/jmv3/index.php/cabe-chapters/oskaer
Aaron Murray, President
Rahatjan Judge, Treasurer

Sechelt & District Chamber of Commerce
PO Box 360, #102, 5700 Cowrie St., Sechelt BC V0N 3A0
Tel: 604-885-0662; *Fax:* 604-885-0691
sdcoc9@telus.net
www.secheltchamber.bc.ca
www.facebook.com/SecheltChamberofCommerce
twitter.com/SecheltChamber
To provide resources & services to members, including business
information, community profiles, discounts & benefits plans,
payroll services & networking opportunities
Kim Darwin, President
Colleen Clark, Executive Director

Stratford & District Chamber of Commerce
55 Lorne Ave. East, Stratford ON N5A 6S4
Tel: 519-273-5250; *Fax:* 519-273-2229
info@stratfordchamber.com
www.stratfordchamber.com
www.facebook.com/stratforddistrict.chamberofcommerce
twitter.com/stratfordchambr
To maintain & improve trade & commerce, conservation & good
management of community resources; To promote the
economic, commercial, industrial, tourist & convention, civic,
agricultural & environmental welfare of the City of Stratford & the
surrounding district
Brad Beatty, General Manager

**Swiss Canadian Chamber of Commerce (Ontario)
Inc. (SCCC)**
756 Royal York Rd., Toronto ON M8Y 2T6
Tel: 416-236-0039; *Fax:* 416-551-1011
sccc@swissbiz.ca
www.swissbiz.ca
www.linkedin.com/groups/8282978
www.facebook.com/swiss.chamber
To assume a prominent role in promoting commercial, industrial
& financial relations between Switzerland & Canada, with
primary focus on membership in Ontario
Alexandra Soriano, President

Thunder Bay Chamber of Commerce (TBCC)
#102, 200 Syndicate Ave. South, Thunder Bay ON P7E 1C9
Tel: 807-624-2626; *Fax:* 807-622-7752
chamber@tbchamber.ca
www.tbchamber.ca
www.linkedin.com/company/thunder-bay-chamber-of-commerce
www.facebook.com/tbchamber
twitter.com/tbchamber
To serve the membership by providing leadership & influencing
effective change for a healthy business environment
Charla Robinson, President

**Toronto Association for Business Economics Inc.
(TABE)**
PO Box 955, 31 Adelaide St. East, Toronto ON M5C 2K3
Tel: 647-693-7418
tabe@cabe.ca
www.cabe.ca/tabe
twitter.com/TABE_Economics
To promote a better understanding of economic issues; To
contribute to the professional development of members; To
encourage the availability of economic information & to broaden
awareness of business economics; To recognize achievement of
business economists
Bonnie Lemcke, President

Truro & Colchester Chamber of Commerce
605 Prince St., Truro NS B2N 1G2
Tel: 902-895-6328; *Fax:* 902-897-6641
oa@tcchamber.ca
www.trurocolchesterchamber.com
www.facebook.com/tdcoc
twitter.com/TruColCoC
To be the principal advocate for business in Truro &
Colchester Region in matters of economic, social & political
importance
Sherry Martell, Executive Director
Trish Petrie, Office Administrator

Vaughan Chamber of Commerce (VCC)
#2, 25 Edilcan Dr., Vaughan ON L4K 3S4
Tel: 905-761-1366; *Fax:* 905-761-1918
info@vaughanchamber.ca
www.vaughanchamber.ca
www.facebook.com/vaughanchamberofcommerce
To be the voice of business; To promote & improve business in
the City of Vaughan
Brian Shifman, President & CEO
Lori Suffern, Office Manager

WABC Coaches Inc. (WABC)
wabccoaches.com

To develop, advance & promote the emerging profession of
business coaching, worldwide
Wendy Johnson, President & CEO

Wellesley & District Board of Trade
c/o Wendy Sauder, Wellesley Service Centre, 1220 Queens
Bush Rd., Wellesley ON N0B 2T0
Tel: 519-656-3494
wellesleyboardoftrade@gmail.com
wellesleyboardoftrade.com
To improve the economic & social welfare of the community; To
strengthen the business climate in Wellesley & area
Kim Heinmiller, President

West Vancouver Chamber of Commerce
2235 Marine Dr., West Vancouver BC V7V 1K5
Tel: 604-926-6614; *Fax:* 604-926-6647
info@westvanchamber.com
www.westvanchamber.com
www.linkedin.com/company/west-vancouver-chamber-of-comme
rce
www.facebook.com/WestVanChamber
twitter.com/westvanchamber
To promote, enhance, & facilitate business in the community
Leagh Gabriel, Executive Director

Whitby Chamber of Commerce (WCC)
209 Dundas St. East, Whitby ON L1N 7H8
Tel: 905-668-4506; *Fax:* 905-668-1894
info@whitbychamber.org
www.whitbychamber.org
www.linkedin.com/company/whitby-chamber-of-commerce
www.facebook.com/WhitbyChamber
twitter.com/whitbychamber
To empower, connect, & advocate for business across the
Durham Region
Brenda Bemis, Office Manager
Natalie Prychitko, Chief Executive Officer
Heather Bulman, Manager, Marketing & Communications

Whitecourt & District Chamber of Commerce
Synergy Business Centre, PO Box 1011, 4907 - 52 Ave.,
Whitecourt AB T7S 1N9
Tel: 780-778-5363; *Fax:* 780-778-2351
manager@whitecourtchamber.com
www.whitecourtchamber.com
www.facebook.com/whitecourtchamber
To promote trade & commerce & the economic, civic & social
welfare of the district
Rand Richards, President

Whitehorse Chamber of Commerce (WCC)
#101, 302 Steele St., Whitehorse YT Y1A 2C5
Tel: 867-667-7545; *Fax:* 867-667-4507
business@whitehorsechamber.ca
www.whitehorsechamber.ca
To promote & improve trade & commerce; to contribute to the
economic, civic & social well-being of Whitehorse
Rick Karp, President

Windsor-Essex Regional Chamber of Commerce
2575 Ouellette Place, Windsor ON N8X 1L9
Tel: 519-966-3696; *Fax:* 519-966-0603
www.windsorchamber.org
www.linkedin.com/groups/2762020
www.facebook.com/125412597496221
twitter.com/WERCofC
To serve the business community of Windsor & district by
providing networking opportunities, & by communicating
positions & opinions on government policy & other issues on
behalf of its membership
Jeffrey MacKinnon, Chair
Matt Marchand, President & CEO

**Winnipeg Chamber of Commerce (WCC) / Chambre
de commerce de Winnipeg**
#100, 259 Portage Ave., Winnipeg MB R3B 2A9
Tel: 204-944-8484; *Fax:* 204-944-8492
info@winnipeg-chamber.com
www.winnipeg-chamber.com
www.youtube.com/wpgchamber
www.linkedin.com/company/the-winnipeg-chamber-of-commerce
www.facebook.com/WpgChamber
twitter.com/TheWpgChamber
To act as the voice of business in Winnipeg; To foster an
environment in which Winnipeg businesses can proper
Dave Angus, President & Chief Executive Officer
Maxine Kashton, Vice-President, Finance & Operations
Karen Weiss, Vice-President, Membership & Marketing

Yarmouth & Area Chamber of Commerce (YCC)
PO Box 532, Yarmouth NS B5A 4B4
Tel: 902-742-3074; *Fax:* 902-749-1383
info@yarmouthchamberofcommerce.com
www.yarmouthchamberofcommerce.com
www.linkedin.com/groups/2910385
www.facebook.com/YarmouthNSChamber
To promote a positive economic & business climate in Yarmouth county
Chris Atwood, President
Neil Rogers, 1st Vice-President
Angie Greene, 2nd Vice-President

Yellowknife Chamber of Commerce
#21, 4802 - 50th Ave., Yellowknife NT X1A 1C4
Tel: 867-920-4944; *Fax:* 867-920-4640
admin@ykchamber.com
www.ykchamber.com
www.facebook.com/ykchamber
twitter.com/YKChamber
Daneen Everett, Executive Director

Yukon Chamber of Commerce (YCC)
#205, 2237 - 2 Ave., Whitehorse YT Y1A 0K7
Tel: 867-667-2000; *Fax:* 867-667-2001
office@yukonchamber.com
www.yukonchamber.com
www.facebook.com/YukonChamberOfCommerceYukonCanada
To create a climate conducive to a strong private sector economy by providing leadership & representation
Peter Turner, President

Chemical Industry

Alberta Sulphur Research Ltd. (ASRL)
University Research Centre, #6, 3535 Research Rd. NW, Calgary AB T2L 2K8
Tel: 403-220-5346; *Fax:* 403-284-2054
asrinfo@ucalgary.ca
albertasulphurresearch.ca
To offer technological support for producers & users of sulfur, as well as research & technology training through seminars & courses; To provide contact between industry & academia for applied catalysis & industrial sulfur chemistry; To examine the chemistry & technology of sulfur & its compunds; To focus on research relevant to sour gas, sulfur & refining industries
Paul Davis, General Manager

Canadian Association of Agri-Retailers (CAAR)
#205, 1 Wesley Ave., Winnipeg MB R3C 4C6
Tel: 204-989-9300; *Fax:* 204-989-9306
Toll-Free: 800-463-9323
info@caar.org
www.caar.org
twitter.com/CdnAgRetail
To represent & protect the interests of Canadian agricultural retailers
Mitch Rezansoff, Executive Director
Lisa Defoort, Manager, Communications & Events

Canadian Consumer Specialty Products Association (CCSPA) / Association canadienne de produits de consommation spécialisés (ACPCS)
#800, 130 Albert St., Ottawa ON K1P 5G4
Tel: 613-232-6616; *Fax:* 613-233-6350
assoc@ccspa.org
www.ccspa.org
twitter.com/CCSPA_ACPCS
To represent the specialty chemical & formulated products industry; To promote the interests of member companies by providing a national voice, encouraging ethical practices, negotiating with government & fostering industry cooperation
Shannon Coombs, President
Nancy Hitchins, Director, Administration & Member Services

Chemical Institute of Canada (CIC) / Institut de chimie du Canada
#1009, 222 Queen St., Ottawa ON K1P 5V9
Tel: 613-232-6252; *Fax:* 613-232-5862
Toll-Free: 888-542-2242
info@cheminst.ca
www.cheminst.ca
www.instagram.com/cic_cheminst
www.linkedin.com/company/chemical-institute-of-canada
twitter.com/CIC_ChemInst
To maintain all branches of the professions of chemical sciences & chemical engineering in their proper status among other learned & scientific professions; To encourage original research & develop & maintain high standards in profession; To enhance usefulness of profession to the public
Paul Smith, Interim Executive Director

Fertilizer Canada
#907, 350 Sparks St., Ottawa ON K1R 7S8
Tel: 613-230-2600; *Fax:* 613-230-5142
info@fertilizercanada.ca
fertilizercanada.ca
www.youtube.com/user/CanadianFertilizer
www.facebook.com/fertilizercanada
twitter.com/FertilizerCA
To represent manufacturers, wholesale & retail distributors of nitrogen, phosphate & potash fertilizers
Garth Whyte, President & CEO
Clyde Graham, Executive Vice-President
Cassandra Cotton, Vice-President, Policy & Programs
Catherine King, Vice-President, Public Affairs
Rabya Khanan, Manager, Communications

Ordre des chimistes du Québec (OCQ)
Place du Parc, #2199, 300, rue Léo-Pariseau, Montréal QC H2X 4B3
Tél: 514-844-3644; *Téléc:* 514-844-9601
information@ocq.qc.ca
www.ocq.qc.ca
www.facebook.com/1285160824849865
L'Ordre est une corporation professionnelle dont la raison d'être est la protection du public
Guy Collin, Président du Conseil d'administration

Responsible Distribution Canada (RDC)
#1, 1160 Blair Rd., Burlington ON L7M 1K9
Tel: 905-332-8777; *Toll-Free:* 844-237-4039
www.rdcanada.ca
www.linkedin.com/company/canadian-association-of-chemical-distributors
twitter.com/RDCDRC
Cathy Campbell, President
Catherine Wieckowska, Vice-President

Child & Family Services

Affected Families of Police Homicide (AFPH)
Tel: 289-880-9950
grief2action@gmail.com
www.facebook.com/groups/BFRJC
To promote change in the methods that police officers utilize to deal with mental illness & use of force in Ontario
Karyn Greenwood-Graham, Contact

CARE Jeunesse
Montréal QC
carejeunesse@gmail.com
carejeunesse.ca
www.facebook.com/carejeunesse
twitter.com/care_jeunesse
Fournir des supports pour les jeunes placés et ancien(ne)s placés au Québec, y compris, mais sans s'y limiter: les foyers d'accueil, les foyers de groupe et une variété de centres résidentiels
Amanda Keller, Présidente et fondatrice
Jennifer Dupuis, Vice-Présidente

Centre Sportif de la Petite Bourgogne / Little Burgundy Sports Centre
1825, rue Notre-Dame ouest, Montréal QC H3J 1M5
Tél: 514-932-0800
centresportifdelapetitebourgogne.com
Dickens Mathurin, Director General

Elizabeth House / Maison Elizabeth
2131, av Marlowe, Montréal QC H4A 3L4
Tel: 514-482-2488; *Fax:* 514-482-9467
questions@maisonelizabethhouse.com
www.maisonelizabethhouse.com
To provide a continuum of specialized services to pregnant adolescents & women, mothers & babies, fathers & families experiencing significant difficulty in adjusting to pregnancy & to their new roles as parents & caregivers; To support clients as they make choices & are directed to appropriate resources either in-house or in the community; To serve the anglophone community throughout the province of Quebec
Linda Schachtler, Executive Director

Federation of BC Youth in Care Networks (FBCYICN)
#500, 625 Agnes St., New Westminster BC V3M 5Y4
Tel: 604-527-7762; *Fax:* 604-527-7764
Toll-Free: 800-565-8055
Crisis Hot-Line: 866-872-0113
info@fbcyicn.ca
www.fbcyicn.ca
www.facebook.com/YouthInCareBC
twitter.com/fbcyicn
To improve the lives of young people in & from government care in BC

Jules Wilson, Executive Director
Brittaney Andreychuk, Manager, Operations

Missing Children Society of Canada (MCSC)
#219, 3501 - 23 St. NE, Calgary AB T2E 6V8
Tel: 403-291-0705; *Fax:* 403-291-9728
Toll-Free: 800-661-6160
info@mcsc.ca
www.mcsc.ca
www.youtube.com/user/MissingChildCanada
www.facebook.com/MissingChildrenSocietyofCanada
twitter.com/MCSCanada
To return missing children to a safe haven through professional investigations, emergency response, public awareness, & family support programs; To eliminate child abduction in Canada
Amanda Pick, Chief Executive Officer
Craig Peterson, Director, Business Development & Technology

National Youth in Care Network (YICC) / Reseau National des Jeunes Pris en Charge
PO Box 96, 223 Main St., Ottawa ON K1S 1C4
Tel: 613-327-4317; *Toll-Free:* 800-790-7074
info@youthincare.ca
www.youthincare.ca
www.facebook.com/youthincarecanada
twitter.com/youthincare
To increase the awareness of the needs of youth in & from government care by researching the issues & presenting the results to youth, professionals & the general public through publications & speaking engagements; To provide emotional support to youth in or from government care & to guide the development of youth in care groups
Connor Lowes, President

New Brunswick Youth in Care Network
535 Beaverbrook Ct., #B-10, Fredericton NB E3B 1X6
Tel: 506-462-0323; *Fax:* 506-462-0328
www.partnersforyouth.ca
www.facebook.com/NBYICN
twitter.com/VoicesMYICN
To advocate for & support youth in or from government care in New Brunswick
Zoe Bourgeois, Project Coordinator

Saskatchewan Youth in Care & Custody Network (SYICCN)
Cornwall Professional Building, #510, 2125 - 11th Ave., Regina SK S4P 3X3
Tel: 306-522-1533; *Fax:* 306-522-1507
info@syiccn.ca
www.syiccn.ca
www.facebook.com/SYICCN
twitter.com/syiccninc
To advocate for & support youth in or from government care or young offender systems in Saskatchewan; To ensure that youth in care or custody have a voice in their lives & communities
Stephanie Bustamante, Executive Director
Sarah Caldwell, Coordinator, Provincial Outreach
Darlene Domshy, Coordinator, Research

Voices: Manitoba's Youth in Care Network
61 Juno St., 3rd Fl., Winnipeg MB R3A 1T1
Tel: 204-982-4956; *Fax:* 204-982-4950
Toll-Free: 866-982-4956
info@voices.mb.ca
www.voices.mb.ca
www.facebook.com/VoicesMB
twitter.com/VoicesMYICN
To advocate for & support youth in or from government care in Manitoba
Marie Christian, Program Director

Youth in Care in Ontario
ON
youthcan@oacas.org
ontarioyouthcan.org
To be the unifying voice for youth in care of Children's Aid Societies in the province of Ontario; To improve the quality of care for youth in Ontario's Child Welfare System
Patricia McMahon, Sec.-Treas.
Joyce Kehler, President

Yukon Child Care Association (YCCA)
PO Box 31103, Whitehorse YT Y1A 5P7
Tel: 867-668-5130
ycca1974@gmail.com
www.yukonchildcareassociation.org
www.facebook.com/YukonCCA
twitter.com/YukonChildCare
To develop a high quality, universally accessible & affordable child care system in the Yukon; To represent caregivers & families
Cyndi Desharnais, President

Childbirth

Alberta Association of Midwives (AAM)
8210, 11500 - 35th St. SE, Calgary AB T2Z 3W4
Tel: 888-316-5457; *Fax:* 888-859-5228
info@alberta-midwives.com
www.alberta-midwives.com
www.instagram.com/albertamidwives
twitter.com/albertamidwives
To promote awareness of the profession of midwifery, supports midwifery-centered research, participates in a provincial education program
Chelsea Miklos, President
Marita Obst, Vice-President
Erin Braaten, Treasurer

Association of Ontario Midwives (AOM) / Association des sages-femmes de l'Ontario
#800, 365 Bloor St. East, Toronto ON M3W 3L4
Tel: 416-425-9974; *Toll-Free:* 866-418-3773
reception@aom.on.ca
www.ontariomidwives.ca
www.instagram.com/ontariomidwives
www.facebook.com/OntarioMidwives
twitter.com/ontariomidwives
To represent midwives & the practice of midwifery in Ontario
Juana Berinstein, Interim Executive Director

College of Midwives of British Columbia (CMBC)
#603, 601 West Broadway, Vancouver BC V5Z 4C2
Tel: 604-742-2230; *Fax:* 604-730-8908
information@cmbc.bc.ca
www.cmbc.bc.ca
To serve & protect the public interest by registering competent midwives who will practise safely & ethically in British Columbia
Louise Aerts, Registrar & Executive Director

Infant Feeding Action Coalition
533 Colborne St., London ON N6B 2T5
Tel: 416-595-9819
info@infactcanada.ca
www.infactcanada.ca
To protect, promote & support breastfeeding in Canada & globally; to promote better infant & maternal health; to foster appropriate mother & infant nutrition
Elisabeth Sterken, National Director

La Leche League Canada (LLLC) / Ligue La Leche Canada
PO Box 147, Pickering ON L1V 2R2
Tel: 289-660-5900
office@lllc.ca
www.lllc.ca
To act as a support network for breastfeeding/chestfeeding mothers; To promote the importance of breastfeeding/chestfeeding in Canada; To disseminate information on how to help mothers succeed in breastfeeding/chestfeeding
Nikki Bell, Office Manager

Multiple Births Canada (MBC) / Naissances multiples Canada
#246, 13 - 280 West Beaver Creek Rd., Richmond Hill ON L4B 3Z1
Toll-Free: 866-228-8824
office@multiplebirthscanada.org
www.multiplebirthscanada.org
www.facebook.com/MultipleBirthsCanada
twitter.com/Multiple_Births
To improve the quality of life for multiple birth individuals & their families through research, education, service & advocacy
Frances Keech, Office Manager

Ordre des sages-femmes du Québec
#450, 1200, av Papineau, Montréal QC H2K 4R5
Tél: 514-286-1313; *Ligne sans frais:* 877-711-1313
info@osfq.org
www.osfq.org
L'Ordre professionnel des sages-femmes du Québec veille à la qualité d'exercice de la profession sage-femme au bénéfice de la population
Johanne Côté, Directrice générale

Serena Canada
151 Holland Ave., Ottawa ON K1Y 0Y2
Tel: 613-728-6536; *Toll-Free:* 888-373-7362
sc@serena.ca
serena.ca
To promote natural family planning methods based on information from a woman's body

Children & Youth

Adoption Council of Ontario (ACO)
#503, 36 Eglinton Ave. West, Toronto ON M4R 1A1
Tel: 416-482-0021; *Fax:* 416-482-1586
Toll-Free: 877-236-7820
info@adoption.on.ca
www.adoption.on.ca
www.facebook.com/adoptioncouncilontario
twitter.com/ontarioadopts
To education, support & advocate on behalf of those touched by adoption in Ontario

Alberta Associations for Bright Children (AABC)
c/o Edmonton Association for Bright Children, 1644 Tompkins Place, Edmonton AB T6R 2Y6
www.edmontonabc.org/aabc
To inform & support professionals & parents who are facing the challenge of dealing with bright, gifted, talented children; to advocate at the school board & government levels to ensure that resources & expertise are allocated in a manner that serves the children best

Alberta Family Child Care Association (AFCCA)
c/o Child Development Dayhomes, #202, 222 - 16 Ave. NE, Calgary AB T2E 1J8
Tel: 403-230-2233; *Fax:* 403-230-2220
www.afcca.ca
To promote a high standard of well being for children & the child care industry
Michelle Tamashiro, Contact

ARC Foundation
#215, 312 Main St., Vancouver BC V6A 2T2
Tel: 778-819-2135
info@arcfoundation.ca
www.arcfoundation.ca
To help children & youth live full lives no matter their sexual orientation or gender identity
Brad Beattie, Executive Director
Heather Vause, Director, Community Engagement

Association for Bright Children (Ontario) (ABC Ontario) / Société pour enfants doués et surdoués (Ontario)
c/o 135 Brant St., Oakville ON L6K 2Z8
Tel: 416-925-6136
abcinfo@abcontario.ca
www.abcontario.ca
To provide information & support to parents of bright & gifted children; To increase the understanding & acceptance of bright & gifted children/youth at home, at school & in the community
Kathleen Keane, President

Association francophone à l'éducation des services à l'enfance de l'Ontario (AFÉSEO)
#206, 435, rue Donald, Ottawa ON K1K 4X5
Tél: 613-741-5107; *Téléc:* 613-746-6140
communications@afeseo.ca
afeseo.ca
Pour aider les personnes en Ontario qui ont un intérêt dans l'éducation de la petite enfance
Martine St-Onge, Directrice générale
Manon Bélanger, Administration
Sophie Lavoie, Coordinatrice, Coordonnatrice aux services des membres et des partenaires

Association of Day Care Operators of Ontario (ADCO)
#1, 188 Bunting Rd., St Catharines ON L2M 3Y1
Fax: 877-685-4288
Toll-Free: 800-567-7075
www.adco-o.on.ca
To promote the growth of private & independent (non-profit) licensed child care programs & safeguard the interests of the providers of this service in Ontario through public education, advocacy, professional (management) development & advisory activities locally & provincially

Association of Early Childhood Educators of Alberta (AECEA)
#54, 9912 - 106 St., Edmonton AB T5K 1C5
Tel: 780-421-7544; *Toll-Free:* 877-421-9937
info@aecea.ca
www.aecea.ca
twitter.com/AECEA_
To transform Alberta's early learning & child care workforce into a recognized profession
Manna Middleton, Chair

Association of Early Childhood Educators of Nova Scotia (AECENS)
#102, 3845 Joseph Howe Dr., Halifax NS B3L 4H9
Tel: 902-423-8199
info@aecens.ca
aecens.ca
To promote high standards in service in the child care industry; To be a voice for its members

Association of Early Childhood Educators of Quebec (AECEQ)
1001, rue Lenoir, #A2-10, Montréal QC H4C 2Z6
membership@aeceq.ca
www.aeceq.ca
To improve the quality of early childhood education in Quebec
Julie Butler, Contact

L'Association québécoise des centres de la petite enfance (AQCPE)
#401, 7245, rue Clark, Montréal QC H2R 2Y4
Tél: 514-326-8008; *Téléc:* 514-326-3322
Ligne sans frais: 888-326-8008
info@aqcpe.com
www.aqcpe.com
www.youtube.com/user/aqcpe1
www.facebook.com/aqcpe
twitter.com/aqcpe
A pour mandat la concertation des acteurs du réseau, la représentation politique de ses membres et la promotion des centres de la petite enfance, et services de soutien; représente les employeurs du secteur des CPE à l'occasion de négociations, en matière de relations du travail et de main-d'oeuvre; l'AQCPE est reconnue par le Min. de la Famille et des Aînés pour la tenue des négociations provinciales
Claude Deraîche, Directeur, Communications

B'nai Brith Youth Organization (BBYO)
Lake Ontario Region, #1-22, 4700 Bathurst St., Toronto ON M2R 1W8
Tel: 416-398-2004; *Fax:* 416-398-5780
info@bbyo.ca
www.bbyo.ca
www.facebook.com/lorbbyo
twitter.com/lorbbyo
To educate young people about the richness of Jewish culture & heritage
Kevin Goodman, Executive Director

Boys & Girls Clubs of Canada (BGCC) / Clubs garçons & filles du Canada
#400, 2005 Sheppard Ave. East, Toronto ON M2J 5B4
Tel: 905-477-7272; *Fax:* 416-640-5331
info@bgccan.com
www.bgccan.com
www.youtube.com/user/bgccan
www.linkedin.com/company/boys-and-girls-clubs-of-canada
www.facebook.com/BGCCAN
twitter.com/BGCCAN
To provide a safe, supportive place where children & youth can experience new opportunities, overcome barriers, build positive relationships & develop confidence & skills for life
Owen Charters, President & CEO

Boys & Girls Clubs of Canada Foundation / Fondation des Clubs Garçons et Filles du Canada
Boys & Girls Clubs of Canada, #400, 2005 Sheppard Ave. East, Toronto ON M2J 5B4
Tel: 905-477-7272; *Fax:* 416-640-5331
www.bgccan.com
www.instagram.com/bgccan
www.facebook.com/BGCCAN
twitter.com/BGCCAN
To support the Boys & Girls Clubs of Canada
David Mather, Chair

British Columbia Family Child Care Association (BCFCCA)
#100, 6878 King George Blvd., Surrey BC V3W 4Z9
Tel: 604-590-1497; *Fax:* 604-590-1427
Toll-Free: 800-686-6685
office@bcfcca.ca
www.bcfcca.ca
www.facebook.com/1433767050225700
twitter.com/BCFCCA
To act as a voice for family child care providers in British Columbia; To promote awareness of professionalism in family child care
Janeen Fowler, Administrator

Canadian Association for Young Children (CAYC) / Association canadienne pour les jeunes enfants (ACJE)
www.cayc.ca

To influence policies & programs affecting critical issues related to the education & welfare of Canadian young children from birth through age nine
Randa Khattar, President
Christine McLean, Contact, Membership Service

Canadian Child Care Federation (CCCF) / Fédération canadienne des services de garde à l'enfance (FCSGE)
#600, 700 Industrial Ave., Ottawa ON K1G 0Y9
Tel: 613-729-5289; *Fax:* 613-729-3159
Toll-Free: 800-858-1412
info@cccf-fcsge.ca
www.cccf-fcsge.ca
www.youtube.com/user/Qualitychildcare
www.facebook.com/groups/5657406573
To promote excellence in child care & early learning
Don Giesbrecht, Chief Executive Officer
Claire McLaughlin, Manager, Publications & Marketing

Canadian Young Judaea
788 Marlee Ave., Toronto ON M6J 0B8
Tel: 416-781-5156
admin@youngjudaea.ca
www.youngjudaea.ca
www.facebook.com/youngjudaea
twitter.com/CdnYoungJudaea
To empower its members through their Jewish identity
Risa Epstein, National Executive Director

Child Find British Columbia
#208, 2722 Fifth St., Victoria BC V8T 4B2
Tel: 250-382-7311; *Fax:* 250-382-0227
Toll-Free: 888-689-3463
childvicbc@shaw.ca
childfindbc.com
To assist in the search & location of missing children, providing support to law enforcement & families; To educate & prevent the abduction & exploitation of children & provide awareness
Steve Orcherton, Executive Director

Child Find Canada Inc. (CFC)
PO Box 237, Oakville MB R0H 0Y0
Tel: 204-870-1298
childcan@aol.com
www.childfind.ca
Supports provincial Child Find organizations in the location of & education in the prevention of missing children; increases national awareness of issues relating to missing children; advocates for the protection & rights of children.

Child Find Newfoundland & Labrador
PO Box 13232, St. John's NL A1B 4A5
Tel: 709-738-4400
childfindnl@bellaliant.com
www.childfind.ca
To prevent missing children; To support the search for missing children

Child Find Ontario
#303B, 75 Front St. East, Toronto ON M5E 1V9
Tel: 416-987-9684; *Toll-Free:* 866-543-8477
mail@childfindontario.ca
www.childfindontario.ca
To assist in the search & recovery process of missing children

Child Find PEI Inc.
39 Riverbank Dr., Johnston's River PE C1B 3E7
Tel: 902-566-5935; *Fax:* 902-368-1389
Toll-Free: 800-387-7962
childfindpei@gmail.com
www.childfindpei.com
www.facebook.com/459667334088816
To assist in the location of missing children; to increase awareness of the problem of missing children; to teach ways to prevent abduction; to provide assistance & support to families of a missing child.
Megan DeCoste, President

Child Find Saskatchewan Inc.
#202, 3502 Taylor St. East, Saskatoon SK S7H 5H9
Tel: 306-955-0070; *Fax:* 306-373-1311
Toll-Free: 800-513-3463
childfind@childfind.sk.ca
www.childfind.sk.ca
To locate missing & abducted children & reunite them with their lawful parent or guardian; To increase public awareness of the need to protect children; To educate both parents & child on street proofing technology & to support families of missing children
Phyllis Hallatt, President

Children's Miracle Network
#200, 8001 Weston Rd., Vaughan ON L4L 9C8
Tel: 905-265-9750; *Fax:* 905-265-9749
info@childrenshospitals.ca
childrensmiraclenetwork.ca
www.youtube.com/cmnhospitals
www.facebook.com/cmnhospitals
twitter.com/cmncanada
To raise funds for children's hospitals
Teri Nestel, Chief Executive Officer
Maureen Carlson, Chief Program Officer
Clark Sweat, Exectuve Vice-President & COO
Barbara Walczyk, Secretary

Children's Wish Foundation of Canada / Fondation canadienne rêves d'enfants
#350, 1101 Kingston Rd., Pickering ON L1V 1B5
Tel: 905-839-8882; *Fax:* 905-839-3745
Toll-Free: 800-700-4437
grantawish@childrenswish.ca
www.childrenswish.ca
www.instagram.com/childrenswishfoundation
www.linkedin.com/company/children's-wish-foundation-of-canada
www.facebook.com/ChildrensWish
twitter.com/Childrens_wish
To grant wishes to children suffering from high risk, life-threatening illnesses
Jennifer Klotz-Ritter, CEO
Chris Kotsopoulos, CEO
Dimple Joshi, National Director, Human Resources & Volunteer Services
Lyanne Goulin, National Director, Wish Granting

CIVIX
#504, 639 Queen St. West, Toronto ON M5V 2B7
Toll-Free: 866-488-8775
hello@civix.ca
civix.ca
www.facebook.com/CIVIXcanada
twitter.com/CIVIX_Canada
To prepare young Canadians to actively take part in democracy
Taylor Gunn, President & Chief Election Officer
Lindsay Mazzucco, Chief Operating Officer

Concerned Children's Advertisers
#200, 10 Alcorn Ave., Toronto ON M4V 3A9
Tel: 416-484-0871; *Fax:* 416-484-6564
info@cca-arpe.ca
cca-arpe.ca
To produce campaigns such as public service announcements, curricula & advice for families, in order to responsibly handle issues such as drug abuse, child abuse, child safety, self-esteem, bullying, media literacy & healthy lifestyles.
Craig Hutchison, Chair
Sherry MacLauchlan, Vice-Chair
Russ Ward, Treasurer

Enfant-Retour Québec / Missing Children Quebec
#420, 6830, av du Parc, Montréal QC H3N 1W7
Tél: 514-843-4333; *Téléc:* 514-843-8211
Ligne sans frais: 888-692-4673
info@enfant-retourquebec.ca
www.enfant-retourquebec.ca
www.facebook.com/182144014082
twitter.com/enfantretourqc
Assister les parents à la recherche de leurs enfants portés disparus; aider également les professionnels, avocats, policiers, travailleurs sociaux impliqués dans une situation de disparition d'enfant ou de prévention contre une disparition; réseau international de communication et d'aide qui oeuvre également à sensibiliser la population au problème des enfants disparus et exploités par des affiches, émissions, documents
Yves J. Beauchesne, Président
Pina Arcamone, Directrice générale
Nancy Duncan, Directrice, Progreammes d'assistance aux familles

Future Possibilities for Kids
120 Eglinton Ave. East, Toronto ON M4P 1E2
Tel: 416-923-0777; *Fax:* 866-619-6599
info@fpcanada.or
www.fpcanada.org
www.instagram.com/fpk.canada
www.linkedin.com/company/future-possibilities-for-kids
www.facebook.com/FuturePossibilitiesforKids
twitter.com/FPKCanada
To aid children from under-served communities in reaching their full potential
Rickesh Lakhani, Executive Director
Nicole Thibideau, Director, Program & Operations

Girl Guides of Canada (GGC) / Guides du Canada
50 Merton St., Toronto ON M4S 1A3
Tel: 416-487-5281; *Toll-Free:* 800-565-8111
www.girlguides.ca
www.youtube.com/user/ggcanada
www.linkedin.com/company/girl-guides-of-canada
www.facebook.com/GirlGuidesofCanada.GuidesduCanada
twitter.com/girlguidesofcan
To prepare girls to meet the challenges of life, in a safe environment, by teaching them such skills as bandaging wounds & coping with bullies; To encourage girls to foster friendships & develop a sense of leadership
Robyn McDonald, Chair, Board of Directors
Jill Zelmanovits, CEO

Infant & Toddler Safety Association (ITSA) / Association pour la sécurité des bébés et des tout petits
#154, 23 - 500 Fairway Rd. South, Kitchener ON N2C 1X3
Tel: 519-570-0181; *Fax:* 519-570-1078
Toll-Free: 888-570-0181
www.infantandtoddlersafety.ca
To offer information & resources to promote & increase the safety of young children & prevent paediatric injury & death

Jeunesse Acadienne et Francophone de l'Ile-du-prince-Édouard (JAFLIPE)
Centre Belle-Alliance, 5, av Maris Stella, Summerside PE C1N 6M9
Tél: 902-888-3346; *Téléc:* 902-436-6936
coord1@ssta.org
www.jeunesseacadienne.ca
www.facebook.com/JeunesseAcadienne
twitter.com/JeunesseAcadie
Permettre aux jeunes acadiens et francophones de la province à vivre et s'épanouir en français
Myranda Kelly, Présidente
Katelyn Gill, Vice-Président
Kelly McGrath, Secrétaire-trésoriaire

Junior Achievement Canada / Jeunes Entreprises du Canada
161 Bay St., 27th Fl., Toronto ON M5J 2S1
Tel: 416-622-4602; *Fax:* 416-622-6861
Toll-Free: 800-265-0699
www.jacan.org
www.youtube.com/user/juniorachievementcan
www.linkedin.com/company/junior-achievement-of-canada
www.facebook.com/JAchievement
twitter.com/ja_canada
To provide practical business & economic education programs & experience for young people, through partnerships with business & education communities
Scott Hillier, President & CEO
Karen Gallant, Vice-President, Programs & Charter Services
Andre Gallant, Director, Program Development & Services
Vanessa Underwood, Director, Finance

Junior Chamber International Canada / Jeune chambre internationale du Canada
c/o JCI, World Headquarters, 15645 Olive Blvd., Chesterfield MO 63017 USA
Toll-Free: 844-746-3544
info@jcicanada.com
jci.cc
www.facebook.com/jcicanada
To contribute to the advancement of the global community by providing the opportunity for young people to develop the leadership skills, social responsibility & fellowship necessary to create positive change

Justice for Children & Youth (JFCY)
55 University Ave., 15th Fl., Toronto ON M5J 2H7
Tel: 416-920-1633; *Fax:* 416-920-5855
Toll-Free: 866-999-5329
info@jfcy.org
www.jfcy.org
To assist & empower children & youth in obtaining fair & equal access to legal, educational, medical & social resources; To provide direct legal assistance in all areas of children's law to eligible children & youth of Metro Toronto & vicinity; To provide summary legal advice, information & assistance to young people, parents, professionals & community groups on a province-wide basis; To advocate for law & policy reform; To monitor & respond to developments & changes to the laws which affect children
Emily Chan, Acting Executive Director
Karien Gibson, Office Manager

Make-A-Wish Canada / Fais-Un-Voeu Canada
#520, 4211 Yonge St., Toronto ON M2P 2A9
Tel: 416-224-9474; *Fax:* 416-224-8795
Toll-Free: 888-822-9474
nationaloffice@makeawish.ca
makeawish.ca
www.youtube.com/user/makeawishcanada
www.linkedin.com/company/make-a-wish-canada
www.facebook.com/makeawish.ca
twitter.com/MakeAWishCA
To create life-changing wishes for children with critical illnesses
Jennifer Klotz-Ritter, President & CEO

Manitoba Child Care Association (MCCA)
2350 McPhillips St., 2nd Fl., Winnipeg MB R2V 4J6
Tel: 204-586-8587; *Fax:* 204-589-5613
Toll-Free: 888-323-4676
info@mccahouse.org
www.mccahouse.org
www.instagram.com/manitobachildcare
www.facebook.com/manitobachildcare
twitter.com/MCCAHOUSE
To act as the voice of child care in Manitoba; To advocate for a quality system of child care; To advance early childhood education as a profession
Jodie Kehl, Executive Director

National Alliance for Children & Youth (NACY) / Alliance nationale pour l'enfance et la jeunesse (ANEJ)
#707, 331 Cooper St., Ottawa ON K2P 0G5
Tel: 613-292-0569
info@nacy.ca
www.nacy.ca
www.facebook.com/189588222849
twitter.com/NACY_ANEJ
To promote the health & well being of children in Canada.
Gordon Floyd, Chair

Parachute
#300, 150 Eglinton Ave. East, Toronto ON M4P 1E8
Tel: 647-776-5100; *Toll-Free:* 888-537-7777
info@parachutecanada.org
www.parachutecanada.org
www.linkedin.com/company/parachute—leaders-in-injury-prevention
www.facebook.com/parachutecanada
twitter.com/parachutecanada
To promote effective strategies to prevent unintentional injuries; To build partnerships & uses a comprehensive approach to advance safety & reduce the burden of injuries to Canada's children & youth
Louise Logan, President & CEO

Ranch Ehrlo Society
1951 Francis St., Regina SK S4V 6V1
Tel: 306-781-1800; *Fax:* 306-757-0599
inquiries@ranchehrlo.ca
www.ehrlo.ca
www.youtube.com/user/ranchehrlo1
www.facebook.com/RanchEhrlo
twitter.com/RanchEhrlo
To provide a range of quality assessment, treatment, education & support services that improve the social & emotional functioning of children & youth
Andrea Brittin, President & CEO

Roots of Empathy
#1501, 250 Ferrand Dr., Toronto ON M3C 3G8
Tel: 416-944-3001; *Fax:* 416-944-9295
Toll-Free: 866-766-8763
mail@rootsofempathy.org
rootsofempathy.org
www.youtube.com/user/rootsofempathy
www.facebook.com/RootsofEmpathy
twitter.com/rootsofempathy
To develop empathy in children & adults in order to build caring, peaceful, & civil societies
Mary Gordon, Founder & President
Leah Starrett, Canada President
Catherine Talbot, National Contact

Scouts Canada / Scouts du Canada
1345 Baseline Rd., Ottawa ON K2C 0A7
Tel: 613-224-5134; *Toll-Free:* 888-855-3336
helpcentre@scouts.ca
www.scouts.ca
www.youtube.com/scoutscanada
www.linkedin.com/company/scouts-canada
www.facebook.com/scoutscanada
twitter.com/scoutscanada
To contribute to the education of young people through a value system based on the Scout Promise & Law; To emphasize

learning by doing, particularly in small groups, with outdoor activities as a learning resource
Tim Welch, National Commissioner
Annabelle Loder, National Youth Commissioner
Andrew Price, Executive Commissioner & CEO
Valarie Dillon, Executive Director, Human Resources & Volunteer Services
Ian Mitchell, Executive Director, Field Services
John Petitti, Executive Director, Marketing & Communications
Peter Valters, Executive Director, Business Services

Youth Coalition for Sexual & Reproductive Rights (YCSRR)
123 Slater St., 6th Fl., Ottawa ON K1P 5H2
admin@youthcoalition.org
www.youthcoalition.org
www.facebook.com/YouthCoalition
twitter.com/youth_coalition
To promote adolescent & youth sexual & reproductive rights regionally, nationally, & internationally
Aramide Odutayo, Chair
Aminata Bintu Wurie, Executive Coordinator

Citizenship & Immigration

Association for New Canadians (ANC) / L'association des nouveaux Canadiens (ANC)
Head Office & Settlement Services, PO Box 2031, Stn. C, 144 Military Rd., St. John's NL A1C 5R6
Tel: 709-722-9680; *Fax:* 709-754-4407
settlement@nfld.net
www.ancnl.ca
To provide full service immigrant settlement programs & services to the newcomer community in Newfoundland & Labrador; To support integration, & cross cultural understanding

Canadian Association of Professional Immigration Consultants (CAPIC) / Association Canadienne des Conseillers Professionnels en Immigration (ACCPI)
#602, 245 Fairview Mall Dr., Toronto ON M2J 4T1
Tel: 416-483-7044; *Fax:* 416-309-1985
info@capic.ca
www.capic.ca
www.facebook.com/684073984953919
twitter.com/capicaccpi
To represent Certified Canadian Immigration Consultants (CCIC), or full members of the Canadian Society of Immigration Consultants (CSIC)
Katarina Onuschak, Executive Director
Monica Poon, National Coordinator
Christopher Daw, Director, Lobbying
Lynn Gaudet, Director, Communications
Deepak Kohli, Director, Membership
Tanveer Sharief, Director, Education & Training

Canadian Ukrainian Immigrant Aid Society (CUIAS)
2383 Bloor St. West, 2nd Fl., Toronto ON M6S 1P9
Tel: 416-767-4595; *Fax:* 416-767-2658
cuias@cuias.org
cuias.org
To sponsor & aid in settlement of Ukrainian refugees
Ludmila Kolesnichenko, Executive Director

Centre for Immigrant & Community Services (CICS)
c/o Immigrant Resource Centre, 2330 Midland Ave., Toronto ON M1S 5G5
Tel: 416-292-7510; *Fax:* 416-292-7579
info@cicscanada.com
www.cicscanada.com
www.facebook.com/cicscanada
twitter.com/cicscanada
To provide a wide range of cost-effective, culturally-sensitive & professional services; To empower newcomers to settle & integrate into Canadian society; To promote active citizenship in the community
Moy Wong-Tam, Executive Director

Collectif des femmes immigrantes du Québec (CFIQ)
7124, rue Boyer, Montréal QC H2S 2J8
Tél: 514-279-4246; *Téléc:* 514-279-8536
info@cfiq.ca
www.cfiq.ca
Préparation à l'emploi des immigrants, formation, placement à Montréal et en région
Aoura Bizzarri, Directrice générale

Immigrant Centre Manitoba Inc.
100 Adelaide St., Winnipeg MB R3A 0W2
Tel: 204-943-9158; *Fax:* 204-949-0734
info@icmanitoba.com
icmanitoba.com

To encourage pride in Canada & appreciation of Canadian citizenship; To encourage intercultural understanding in multicultural Canada; To support immigration & provide caring services to newcomers
Robert Vineberg, Chair

Korean Canadian Women's Association (KCWA)
27 Madison Ave., Toronto ON M5R 2S2
Tel: 416-340-1234; *Fax:* 416-340-7755
kcwa@kcwa.net
www.kcwa.net
www.facebook.com/kcwaservice
To empower Korean Canadian families and other vulnerable members of the community-at-large to live free from violence, poverty and inequity through the provision of culturally sensitive and linguistically appropriate services for the purpose of enhancing the well-being of immigrant families and promoting their successful integration into Canadian society
Shine Chung, Executive Director
Eunyoung Baek, Operations Manager

Ontario Council of Agencies Serving Immigrants (OCASI)
#200, 110 Eglinton Ave. West, Toronto ON M4R 1A3
Tel: 416-322-4950; *Fax:* 416-322-8084
TTY: 416-322-1498
generalmail@ocasi.org
ocasi.org
twitter.com/OCASI_Policy
To act as a collective voice for immigrant services; to provide access for immigrants & refugees to settlement services; to provide social organizational development with community groups, policy analysis & government relations, professional development of member agency staff & research into issues facing immigrant service agencies
Carl Nicholson, President
Debbie Douglas, Executive Director

Ottawa Community Immigrant Services Organization (OCISO) / Organisme communautaire des services aux immigrants d'Ottawa
959 Wellington St. West, Ottawa ON K1Y 2X5
Tel: 613-725-0202; *Fax:* 613-725-9054
info@ociso.org
www.ociso.org
www.youtube.com/user/OCISOTV
twitter.com/OttawaOCISO
To enable newcomers & their families to fully participate in an open & welcoming Ottawa, through innovative services, community building & public engagement
Leslie Emory, Executive Director

Tamil Eelam Society of Canada (TEOSC)
#1A, 1160 Birchmount Rd., Toronto ON M1P 2B8
Tel: 416-757-6043; *Fax:* 416-757-6851
ed@tesoc.org
www.tesoc.org
To provide opportunities & services to newcomers & immigrants from the Tamil community & other ethno cultures; To promote a smooth integration into Canada by enhancing the lives of newcomers through programs designed for settlement, employment & personal growth

Civil Liberties

Committee of Progressive Pakistani-Canadians (CPPC)
info@pakistanicanadians.ca
pakistanicanadians.ca
www.facebook.com/pakistanicanadians
To reach the ideal of Canada & Pakistan as pluralistic, socialist democracies with strong structural & institutional guarantees for protection of all persons

Computers

Compute Canada / Calcul Canada
#302, 155 University Ave., Toronto ON M5H 3B7
Tel: 416-228-1234; *Fax:* 800-716-9417
info@computecanada.ca
www.computecanada.ca
www.youtube.com/c/ComputeCanadaetCalculCanada
www.linkedin.com/company/compute-canada-calcul-canada
twitter.com/computecanada
To enable excellence in research & innovation in Canada through effective, efficient & sustainable deployment of a research computing network; To use the network to support a growing base of researchers; To serve researchers as a national voice for advanced research computing
Christopher Loomis, PhD, FCAHS, Chair

Construction

Association des professionnels à l'outillage municipal (APOM)
11, av du Ruisseau, Montréal QC H4K 2C8
Téléc: 866-334-1264
Ligne sans frais: 866-337-5136
info@apom-quebec.ca
www.apom-quebec.ca
www.facebook.com/apomquebec
Répondre aux besoins créés par l'achat, l'entretien et la réparation de l'outillage utilisé dans l'exécution des travaux publics municipaux; Encourager la coopération entre ses organisations membres
Eric Landry, President

Construction Owners Association of Alberta (COAA)
Sun Life Place, #800, 10123 - 99th St. NW, Edmonton AB T5J 3H1
Tel: 780-420-1145; *Fax:* 780-425-4623
coaa.admin@coaa.ab.ca
www.coaa.ab.ca
To provide leadership enabling the Alberta heavy industrial construction & industrial maintenance industries to be successful in a drive for safe, effective, timely & productive project execution
Neil Shelly, P.Eng., Executive Director
Amanda Rose, Comminications Officer

Consumers

Consumers Council of Canada (CCC)
Commercial Bldg., #201, 1920 Yonge St., Toronto ON M4S 3E2
Tel: 416-483-2696
www.consumerscouncil.com
To enhance the marketplace in Canada
Don Mercer, President
Ken Whitehurst, Executive Director

Consumers' Association of Canada (CAC) / Association des consommateurs du Canada (ACC)
Ottawa ON
Tel: 604-418-8359
consumer@rogers.com
www.consumer.ca
www.facebook.com/consumercanada
twitter.com/ConsumerCanada
To represent & articulate the best interests of Canadian consumers to all levels of government & to all sectors of society by continually earning recognition as the trusted voice of the consumer on a national basis; To inform & educate consumers on marketplace issues; To work with government & industry to solve marketplace problems; To focus its work in the areas of food, health, trade, standards, financial services, communications industries & other marketplace issues as they emerge
Bruce Cran, President & Director

Tobacco Harm Reduction Association of Canada (THRA)
thra.ca
To increase public awareness about tobacco harm reduction products, & to promote the availability of those products

Culture

Association des francophones de Fort Smith (AFFS)
212, ch McDougal, Fort Smith NT X0E OPO
Tél: 867-872-2338; *Téléc:* 867-872-5710
affs@northwestel.net
www.associationfrancophonesfortsmith.ca
Afin de préserver et de développer la communauté francophone de Fort Smith
Marie-Christine Aubrey, Présidente

Association des francophones du delta du Mackenzie (AFDM)
CP 2845, Inuvik NT X0E OTO
Tél: 867-678-2661; *Téléc:* 867-777-2799
afdm@hotmail.ca
www.afdm.ca
Pour représenter les intérêts et les droits de la communauté francophone de delta du Mackenzie
André Church, Président

Association des parents ayants droit de Yellowknife (APADY)
CP 2103, Yellowknife NT X1A 2P5
Tél: 867-446-6821
apady@franco-nord.com
apady.ca
Les parents ayants droit de Yellowknife interviennent pour mettre en place toutes les conditions indispensables à la prestation de services d'éducation de qualité en français favorisant l'épanouissement de leurs enfants et la transmission de l'identité canadienne-française
Jacques Lamarche, Président

Association franco-culturelle de Hay River
CP 4482, 77A, rue Woodland, Hay River NT XOE 1G2
Tél: 867-674-3171
afchr.ca
www.facebook.com/AssociationFrancoCulturelleDeHayRiver
Pour représenter la communauté francophone de Hay River et de défendre leurs droits
Christian Girard, Président

Association franco-culturelle de Yellowknife (AFCY)
CP 1586, Succ. Principale, 5016, 48 rue, Yellowknife NT X1A 2P2
Tél: 867-873-3292; *Téléc:* 867-873-2158
dgafcy@franco-nord.com
afcy.info
www.facebook.com/afcy.yellowknife
twitter.com/AFCYTNO
Pascaline Gréau, Direction générale

Calgary Exhibition & Stampede
PO Box 1060, Stn. M, 1410 Olympic Way SE, Calgary AB T2P 2K8
Tel: 403-261-0101; *Toll-Free:* 800-661-1767
info@calgarystampede.com
www.calgarystampede.com
www.youtube.com/calgarystampede
www.facebook.com/calgarystampede
twitter.com/calgarystampede
To preserve & promote Western heritage & values
Warren Connell, CEO
Paul Rosenberg, Chief Operating Officer
Shelly Flint, Chief Financial Officer

Canada-Israel Cultural Foundation (CICF) / Fondation culturelle Canada-Israël
4700 Bathurst St., 2nd Fl., Toronto ON M2R 1W8
Tel: 416-932-2260; *Fax:* 416-633-1956
cicf@bellnet.ca
www.cicfweb.ca
To act as a cultural bridge between Canada and Israel, promoting and supporting intercultural exchange with a special focus on young artists, and developing artistic life by awarding scholarships and grants
Janet Klugsberg, Executive Director

Canadian Alliance of Chinese Associations
#3025, 888 Odlin Cres., Richmond BC V6X 3Z8
info@ca-ca.ca
www.ca-ca.ca
To help Chinese people integrate into Canadian life & to promote solidarity & cooperations; To unite the Chinese community to respond to emergencies; To protect the rights of Chinese-Canadians & member organizations & liaise with government

Canadian Italian Heritage Foundation (CIHF)
11 Director Ct., Woodbridge ON L4L 4S5
Tel: 905-850-4500; *Fax:* 905-850-4516
To work with the Italian Canadian community to undertake projects in collaboration with other existing organizations that support & promote Italian heritage & culture through activities within Canada
Michael Tibollo, President

Canadian-Scandinavian Foundation (CSF) / Fondation Canada-Scandinavie
1438, rue Fullum, Montréal QC H2K 3M1
www.thecsfoundation.com
To raise funds to distribute to Canadian students who wish to travel to Denmark, Finland, Iceland, Norway or Sweden, to undertake studies at a Scandinavian institution; To promote study / research projects by offering travel busaries
Noami Kramer, President

Centre francophone de Toronto (CFT)
#303, 555, rue Richmond ouest, Toronto ON M5V 3B1
Tél: 416-922-2672; *Téléc:* 416-203-1165
infos@centrefranco.org
www.centrefranco.org
www.youtube.com/channel/UCK-ySdR14i29fBcm-xBVFYw
www.facebook.com/Centre.francophone.de.Toronto
twitter.com/CentrefrancoT
Permettre à la population francophone du grand Toronto d'avoir accès à des services d'information, d'orientation et d'encadrement susceptibles de promouvoir la dimension humaine, culturelle et communautaire des multiples visages de la francophonie
Lise Marie Baudry, Directrice générale

Chinese Canadian Association of Prince Edward Island (CCAPEI)
36 Massey Dr., Charlottetown PE C1E 1R6

Commission nationale des parents francophones (CNPF)
#300, 450 rue Rideau, Ottawa ON K1N 574
Tél: 613-288-0958; *Téléc:* 613-688-1367
Ligne sans frais: 800-665-5148
info@cnpf.ca
cnpf.ca
www.vimeo.com/cnpf
www.facebook.com/LaCNPF
twitter.com/LaCNPF
Pour soutenir les branches provinciales de l'organisation et les aider à fournir de l'aide aux parents
Véronique Legault, Présidente

The Council of Canadians (COC) / Le Conseil des Canadiens
#200, 240 Bank St., Ottawa ON K2P 1X4
Tel: 613-233-2773; *Fax:* 613-233-6776
Toll-Free: 800-387-7177
inquiries@canadians.org
www.canadians.org
www.youtube.com/councilofcanadians
www.facebook.com/CouncilofCDNS
twitter.com/councilofcdns
To protect Canadian independence in areas such as energy & environment, health care & fair trade; To provide a national on the following issues: social programs, economic justice, democracy, sovereignty, alternatives to corporate-style free trade & preserving the environment
Molly Kane, Executive Director

Fédération culturelle canadienne-française (FCCF)
Place de la Francophonie, #405, 450, rue Rideau, Ottawa ON K1N 5Z4
Tél: 613-241-8770; *Téléc:* 613-241-6064
Ligne sans frais: 800-267-2005
info@fccf.ca
www.fccf.ca
www.facebook.com/infofccf
twitter.com/infofccf
Défendre et promouvoir les arts et la culture de la francophonie canadienne hors-Québec.
Maggy Razafimbahiny, Directrice générale

Federation for Scottish Culture in Nova Scotia (FSCNS)
PO Box 811, Lower Sackville NS B4C 3V3
info@scotsns.ca
www.scotsns.ca
To act as the voice for Nova Scotia's clans, Scottish-cultural communities & cultural associations; To create appreciation for Scottish culture, traditions & heritage
Thomas (Tom) E.S. Wallace, President
Daniel G. Campbell, 1st Vice-President
Audrey Manzer, Secretary
Al Matheson, Treasurer

Fondation franco-ontarienne (FFO)
CP 7340, Ottawa ON K1L 8E4
Tél: 613-565-4720; *Téléc:* 613-565-8539
info@fondationfranco-ontarienne.ca
www.fondationfranco-ontarienne.ca
www.facebook.com/Fondationfranco
twitter.com/fondationfranco
La Fondation franco-ontarienne appuie financièrement la réalisation d'initiatives qui assurent la vitalité de la communauté franco-ontarienne
Martin Arseneau, Directeur général par intérim

L'Institut canadien de Québec (ICQ)
1445, av Maguire, Québec QC G1T 2W9
Tél: 418-641-6788; Téléc: 418-641-6787
courriel@institutcanadien.qc.ca
institutcanadien.qc.ca
www.linkedin.com/company/l'institut-canadien-de-qu-bec
www.facebook.com/LICQuebec
twitter.com/LICQuebec
Démocratiser l'accès au savoir et aux oeuvres d'imagination par
un service de bibliothèque universellement accessible;
Sensibiliser le public aux arts et à la culture; Gestion de
bibliothèques publiques de la Ville de Québec
Frédéric Fortin, Directeur général

**The Japan Foundation, Toronto / Kokosai Koryu
Kikin Toronto Nihon Bunka Centre**
#300, 2 Bloor St. East, Toronto ON M4W 1A8
Tél: 416-966-1600
info@jftor.org
jftor.org
www.youtube.com/c/JFToronto
www.facebook.com/JFToronto
twitter.com/JFToronto
To promote Japanese culture abroad; To offer a broad range of
programs designed to further cultural exchange with Japan, with
an emphasis on Japanese studies at the post-secondary level &
Japanese language study
Yuko Shimizu, Executive Director
Masahiro Saito, Director

**The Royal Commonwealth Society of Canada (RCS)
/ La Société royale du Commonwealth du Canada**
c/o RCS Ottawa, PO Box 8023, Stn. T, Ottawa ON K1G 3H6
www.rcs.ca
www.facebook.com/RCSCanada
twitter.com
A charitable, non-partisan organization which promotes
knowledge of the Commonwealth & its member countries;
fosters unity in diversity in matters of common concern;
promotes international understanding, cooperation & peace;
upholds the best traditions of the Commonwealth
Norman Macfie, Chair

Saskatchewan Cultural Exchange Society (SCES)
2431 - 8th Ave., Regina SK S4R 5J7
Tél: 306-780-9494; Fax: 306-780-9487
james@culturalexchnage.ca
culturalexchange.ca
twitter.com/TheExchangeClub
To encourage interactive & diverse artistic experienes through
creative programming in Saskatchewan
John Kennedy, Executive Director

**Société de développement des entreprises
culturelles (SODEC)**
905, av de Lorimier, Montréal QC H2K 3V9
Tél: 514-841-2200; Ligne sans frais: 800-363-0401
info@sodec.gouv.qc.ca
www.sodec.gouv.qc.ca
www.instagram.com/la.sodec
www.linkedin.com/company/sodec
www.facebook.com/SODEC.gouv.qc.ca
twitter.com/la_sodec
Soutient la production et la diffusion de la culture québécoise
dans le champ des industries culturelles
Suzanne Guèvremont, Président par interim du conseil
Louise Lantagne, Présidente et chef de la direction

Société nationale de l'Acadie (SNA)
#403, 236, rue St-George, Moncton NB E1C 1W1
Tél: 506-853-0404; Téléc: 506-853-0400
info@snacadie.org
www.snacadie.org
Mène différentes activités sur les scènes interprovinciales et
internationales afin de promouvoir et de défendre les droits et
intérêts du peuple acadien
Martin Arseneau, Directeur, Comunications

Société Saint-Jean-Baptiste de Montréal (SSJBM)
82, rue Sherbrooke ouest, Montréal QC H2X 1X3
Tél: 514-843-8851; Téléc: 514-844-6369
info@ssjb.ca
www.ssjb.ca
www.youtube.com/user/ssjbmofficiel
www.facebook.com/SSJBM
twitter.com/ssjbm
Une société nationale qui participe de façon non partisane à
l'évolution politique, sociale, économique et culturelle du Québec
par ses actions, ses études, ses interventions et ses campagnes
d'opinion
Guy Raynault, Directeur général

**Townshippers' Association (TA) / Association des
Townshippers**
#100, 257, rue Queen, Sherbrooke QC J1M 1K7
Tel: 819-566-5717; Toll-Free: 866-566-5717
ta@townshippers.org
www.townshippers.org
twitter.com/townshippersTA
To promote the interests of the English-speaking community in
the historical Eastern Townships; To strengthen the cultural
identity of this community; To encourage the full participation of
the English-speaking population in the community at large
Gerald Cutting, President
Rachel Hunting, Executive Director

L'Union culturelle des Franco-Ontariennes (UCFO)
#302, 450, rue Rideau, Ottawa ON K1N 5Z4
Tél: 613-741-1334; Téléc: 613-741-8577
Ligne sans frais: 877-520-8226
ucfo@on.aibn.com
www.unionculturelle.ca
Améliorer les conditions et les réalités sociales des femmes
francophones de l'Ontario; faciliter l'épanouissement de la
femme tout en favorisant son autonomie
Madeleine Chabot, Présidente provinciale

Dental

Alberta Dental Association & College (ADAC)
#402, 7609 - 109 St. NW, Edmonton AB T6G 1C3
Tel: 780-432-1012; Fax: 780-433-4864
Toll-Free: 800-843-3848
reception@adaandc.com
www.dentalhealthalberta.ca
www.facebook.com/DentalHealthAB
twitter.com/DentalHealthAB
To provide guidence & leadership to dentists in Alberta; To
maintain patient care standards set by the association

**Association des assistant(e)s-dentaires du Québec
(CDAA/AADQ)**
#403, 2030, boul Pie-IX, Montréal QC H1V 2C8
Tél: 514-722-9900; Téléc: 514-355-4159
aadq@spg.qc.ca
www.aadq.ca
www.facebook.com/199089516940427
Aider ses membres à parfaire leurs connaissances par des
cours pratiques et théoriques; moderniser le domaine dentaire;
règlementer les assistants-dentaires
Denise Longpré, Présidente

Association des denturologistes du Québec (ADQ)
#230, 8150, boul Métropolitain est, Anjou QC H1K 1A1
Tél: 514-252-0270; Téléc: 514-252-0392
Ligne sans frais: 800-563-6273
denturo@adq-qc.com
www.adq-qc.com
www.facebook.com/denturo
Protéger et développer les intérêts professionnels, moraux,
sociaux et économiques de ses membres
Marie-France Brisson, Directrice générale

British Columbia Dental Association
#400, 1765 - 8th Ave. West, Vancouver BC V6J 5C6
Tel: 604-736-7202; Fax: 604-736-7588
Toll-Free: 888-396-9888
info@bcdental.org
www.bcdental.org
www.facebook.com/yourdentalhealth
To act as the voice of dentistry in British Columbia; To prevent
oral disease
Ann Heald, Director, Operations

**Canadian Academy of Endodontics / L'Académie
canadienne d'endodontie**
#301, 400 St. Mary Ave., Winnipeg MB R3C 4K5
Tel: 204-942-2511; Fax: 204-956-4147
info@caendo.ca
www.caendo.ca
To advance endodontics by providing lectures, information,
forums for interaction & resources; To enhance the health of the
public
Shane Lipyon, President
Ian Watson, Executive Director

**Canadian Association for Dental Research (CADR) /
Association canadienne de recherches dentaires
(ACRD)**
c/o Western University, 1151 Richmond St., London ON N6A
5B8
Tel: 519-661-2111
www.iadr.org/CADR

To advance research & increase knowledge in order to improve
oral health in Canada; To support & represent Canadian oral
health researchers
Walter Siqueira, President
Belinda Nicolau, Vice-President
Amir Azarpazhooh, Secretary-Treasurer

**Canadian Association of Orthodontists (CAO) /
Association canadienne des orthodontists (aco)**
#210, 2800 - 14th Ave., Markham ON L3R 0E4
Tel: 416-491-3186; Fax: 416-491-1670
Toll-Free: 877-226-8800
cao@associationconcepts.ca
www.cao-aco.org
www.linkedin.com/in/caosmiles
www.facebook.com/CAOSmiles
To advance the science & art of orthodontics; To promote the
highest quality of orthodontic care in Canada; To act as the
official voice of Canadian orthodontic specialists
Mike Wagner, President
Brian Phee, Vice-President
Donald Johnston, Secretary-Treasurer

**Canadian Dental Assistants Association (CDAA) /
Association canadienne des assistants(es)
dentaires (ACAD)**
#200, 440 Laurier Ave. West, Ottawa ON K1R 7X6
Tel: 613-521-5495; Toll-Free: 800-345-5137
info@cdaa.ca
www.cdaa.ca
twitter.com/CDAA_ACAD
To foster opportunities for growth; To be the voice for Canadian
dental assistants; To represent the interests of provincial &
military dental associations
Sina Allegro-Sacco, President
Stephanie Mullen-Kavanagh, Executive Director,
skavanagh@cdaa.ca

**Canadian Dental Association (CDA) / L'Association
dentaire canadienne (ADC)**
1815 Alta Vista Dr., Ottawa ON K1G 3Y6
Tel: 613-523-1770
reception@cda-adc.ca
www.cda-adc.ca
www.facebook.com/CanadianDentalAssociation
twitter.com/CdnDentalAssoc
To represent & advance dentistry nationally & internationally; To
promote oral health
Alexander Mutchmor, President

**Canadian Dental Hygienists Association (CDHA) /
Association canadienne des hygiènistes dentaires**
1122 Wellington St. West, Ottawa ON K1Y 2Y7
Tel: 613-224-5515; Fax: 613-224-7283
Toll-Free: 800-267-5235
info@cdha.ca
www.cdha.ca
www.youtube.com/thecdha
twitter.com/theCDHA
To act as the collective voice of dental hygiene in Canada; To
advance the profession in support of members; To contribute to
the health & well-being of the public
Ondina Love, Chief Executive Officer
Michelle Charest, Director, Finance & Operations
Angie D'Aoust, Director, Marketing & Communications
Melanie Martin, Director, Dental Hygiene Practice
Brigitte Gauthier, Manager, Membership Services

Certified Dental Assistants of BC (CDABC)
#102, 211 Columbia St., Vancouver BC V6A 2R5
Tel: 604-714-1766; Fax: 604-714-1767
Toll-Free: 800-579-4440
info@cdabc.org
www.cdabc.org
www.linkedin.com/company/certified-dental-assistants-of-bc-cda
bc-
www.facebook.com/76934117515
twitter.com/CDABC
To promote the dental assisting profession in British Columbia;
To protect the interests of members
Chelsie Trask-Soltesz, President

**College of Dental Hygienists of Nova Scotia
(CDHNS)**
Armdale Professional Centre, #11, 2625 Joseph Howe Dr.,
Halifax NS B3L 4G4
Tel: 902-444-7241; Fax: 902-444-7242
info@cdhns.ca
www.cdhns.ca
To advance the profession & contribute to the health of the
public
Stacy Bryan, Registrar

College of Dental Surgeons of British Columbia (CDSBC)
#110, 1765 West 8th Ave., Vancouver BC V6J 5C6
Tel: 604-736-3621; *Fax:* 604-734-9448
Toll-Free: 800-663-9169
info@cdsbc.org
www.cdsbc.org
www.youtube.com/user/TheCDSBC
twitter.com/cdsbc
To register, license & regulate dentists & certified dental assistants; To assure British Columbians of professional standards of health care, ethics & competence by regulating dentistry in a fair & reasonable manner; To administer the Dentists Act
Chris Hacker, Registrar & CEO
Róisín O'Neill, Director, Registration & Human Resources
Anita Wilks, Director, Communications
Dan Zeng, Director, Finance & Administration

College of Dental Surgeons of Saskatchewan
Tower at Midtown, #1202, 201 - 1 Ave. South, Saskatoon SK S7K 1J5
Tel: 306-244-5072; *Fax:* 306-244-2476
cdss@saskdentists.com
www.saskdentists.com
To operate as a provincial licensing body

College of Dental Technologists of Ontario
#904, 305 Milner Ave., Toronto ON M1B 3V4
Tel: 416-438-5003; *Fax:* 416-438-5004
Toll-Free: 877-391-2386
info@cdto.ca
www.cdto.ca
To serve & protect the public interest by regulating & guiding the dental technology profession
Judy Rigby, Registrar

Dental Association of Prince Edward Island (DAPEI)
184 Belvedere Ave., Charlottetown PE C1A 2Z1
Tel: 902-892-4470; *Fax:* 902-892-0234
dapei@eastlink.ca
www.dapei.ca
To stimulate professional growth in dentistry; To regulate dentistry in Prince Edward Island
Michael J. Connolly, President
Brian Barrett, Executive Director

Dental Council of Prince Edward Island
184 Belvedere Ave., Charlottetown PE C1A 2Z1
Tel: 902-628-8156; *Fax:* 902-892-0234
info@dcpei.ca
www.dcpei.ca
Maurice Coady, Registrar

Denturist Association of British Columbia
PO Box 23069, Prince George BC V2N 6Z2
Tel: 604-886-1705
info@denturist.bc.ca
www.denturist.bc.ca
Gary Sallaway, President

Denturist Association of Canada (DAC) / Association des denturologistes du Canada (ADC)
66 Dundas St. East, Belleville ON K8N 1C1
Tel: 613-968-9467; *Toll-Free:* 877-538-3123
dacdenturist@bellnet.ca
www.denturist.org
To promote oral health in Canada through the profession of denturism
Steve Sailer, Vice-President, Administration

Denturist Association of Manitoba
PO Box 69012, Stn. Tuxedo Park, Winnipeg MB R3P 2G9
Tel: 204-897-1087; *Fax:* 204-488-2872
administrator@denturistmb.org
www.denturistmb.org
To represent Manitoba denturists & ensure high quality, low cost delivery of dentures direct to the public
Jamshid Zehtab-Jadid, President
Jennifer Peters, Executive Director

Denturist Association of Newfoundland & Labrador
323 Freshwater Rd., St. John's NL A1B 1C3
Tel: 709-364-4813
info@denturistassociationnl.ca
www.denturistassociationnl.ca
To promote denturism as a profession & provide services for its members
Steve Browne, President

Denturist Association of Ontario (DAO)
#9, 2285 Dunwin Dr., Mississauga ON L5L 3S3
Tel: 905-238-6090; *Fax:* 905-238-7090
Toll-Free: 800-284-7311
info@denturistassociation.ca
denturistassociation.ca
To develop services & tools that help denturists in their practices as well as address denturist needs & concerns
Frank Odorico, President

Denturist Society of Nova Scotia
c/o Della Sangster, 134 Arthur St., Truro NS B2N 1Y1
Tel: 902-893-8010
info@nsdenturistsociety.ca
www.nsdenturistsociety.ca
To promote denturists in Nova Scotia
Della Sangster, President

Denturist Society of Prince Edward Island
222 University Ave., Charlottetown PE C1A 4C7
Tel: 902-892-3253
dspei@live.ca
www.denturist.org
Pat Rhyno, Registrar

Manitoba Dental Assistants Association
#142, 99 Scurfield Blvd., Winnipeg MB R3Y 1Y1
Tel: 204-586-7378; *Fax:* 204-489-8033
Toll-Free: 877-475-6322
mdaa@mdaa.ca
www.mdaa.ca
www.facebook.com/manitobaRDA
twitter.com/MDAA_RDA
To promote & advance the profession of dental assisting
Kathleen Cook, Executive Director

Manitoba Dental Association (MDA)
#202, 1735 Corydon Ave., Winnipeg MB R3N 0K4
Tel: 204-988-5300; *Fax:* 204-988-5310
Toll-Free: 888-592-7727
office@manitobadentist.ca
www.manitobadentist.ca
To act as the governing body for dentists & dental assistants in Manitoba; To ensure that the oral health of Manitobans is met
Marc Mollot, President
Christopher Cottick, Vice-President
Rafi Mohammed, Executive Director & Secretary-Treasurer

National Dental Examining Board of Canada / Le bureau national d'examen dentaire du Canada
80 Elgin St., 2nd Fl., Ottawa ON K1P 6R2
Tel: 613-236-5912; *Fax:* 613-236-8386
info@ndeb-bned.ca
www.ndeb-bned.ca
To establish qualifying conditions for a national standard of dental competence for general practitioners; To establish & maintain an examination facility to test for this national standard of dental competence; To issue certificates to dentists who successfully meet this national standard
Marie Dagenais, Executive Director & Registrar

New Brunswick Dental Assistants Association (NBDAA) / Association des Assistantes Dentaires du Nouveau-Brunswick (AADNB)
PO Box 2095, Richibucto NB E4W 5P2
Tel: 506-876-4662; *Fax:* 506-532-3635
Toll-Free: 866-530-9189
.nbdaa.ca
www.facebook.com/309506835839025
To provide opportunities Dental Assistants in New Brunswick
Angela Cselenyi, President

New Brunswick Dental Society / Société dentaire du Nouveau-Brunswick
HSBC Place, PO Box 488, Stn. A, #820, 520 King St., Fredericton NB E3B 4Z9
Tel: 506-452-8575; *Fax:* 506-452-1872
nbds@nb.aibn.com
www.nbdental.com
www.facebook.com/NBDentalSociety
twitter.com/NBDentalNB
To regulate & promote the dentistry profession in New Brunswick; To support professional growth & ensure the provision of high standards & quality care
Lia A. Daborn, Executive Director

New Brunswick Denturists Society / Société des denturologistes du Nouveau-Brunswick
PO Box 5566, 288 West Blvd. St. Pierre, Caraquet NB E1W 1B7
Tel: 506-727-7411; *Fax:* 506-727-6728
www.nbdenturistsociety.ca
To promote & support denturists in New Brunswick

Ashley Richard, President
Claudette Boudreau, Administrative Assistnat

Newfoundland & Labrador Dental Association
#102, 1 Centennial St., Mount Pearl NL A1N 0C9
Tel: 709-579-2362; *Fax:* 709-579-1250
nfdental@nfld.net
www.nlda.net
www.facebook.com/NLDentalAssociation
twitter.com/nldental
To promote & advance dentistry or dental surgery & related arts & sciences in all their branches; To increase the knowledge, skill, standard & proficiency of its members in the practice of dentistry or dental surgery; To maintain the honour & integrity of the dental profession; To aid in the furtherance of measures designed to improve dental health & prevent disease & disability; To cooperate with & to assist public & private dental associations, agencies & commissions in the task of providing or financing dental care; To promote measures designed to improve standards of dental care & the practice of dentistry or dental surgery; To improve the welfare & social standards of its members & encourage the cooperation of its members in the protection of their rights
Anthony Patey, Executive Director

Newfoundland & Labrador Dental Board
#204, 49-55 Elizabeth Ave., St. John's NL A1A 1W9
Tel: 709-579-2391; *Fax:* 709-579-2392
nldb@nf.aibn.com
www.nldb.ca
To establish standards of qualification, practice, knowledge & ethics for the dentistry, dental assisting & dental technician professions
Paul O'Brien, Secretary-Registrar

Newfoundland Dental Assistants Association (NLDAA)
PO Box 28023, Stn. Avalon Mall, St. John's NL A1B 4J8
Tel: 709-579-2391
nldentalassistants@gmail.com
www.nldaa.ca
To advance the career of dental assisting in Newfoundland
Laura Candow, President

Northwest Territories & Nunavut Dental Association
PO Box 46817, Vancouver BC V6J 5M4
Tel: 867-988-0151; *Fax:* 877-389-6876
www.nwtnudentalassociation.ca
To act as the voice of dentists in the Northwest Territories & Nunavut
Elisabeth Specht, President

Nova Scotia Dental Assistants' Association (NSDAA)
PO Box 9142, Stn. A, Halifax NS B3K 5M8
Tel: 902-405-1122; *Fax:* 902-405-1133
nsdaa@eastlink.ca
www.nsdaa.ca
To affiliate at local, provincial & national levels for the betterment of the dental assistant profession & patient care
Natalie Marsh, President
Lynda Foran, Executive Director

Nova Scotia Dental Association (NSDA)
#101, 210 Waterfront Dr., Bedford NS B4A 0H3
Tel: 902-420-0088; *Fax:* 902-423-6537
Toll-Free: 888-238-1726
nsda@eastlink.ca
www.nsdental.org
www.instagram.com/nsdentalassociation
www.facebook.com/NovaScotiaDentalAssociation
twitter.com/theNSDA
To help dentists in Nova Scotia better serve their patients
Steve Jennex, Executive Director
Patricia Pellerine, Manager, Operations
Penny Miller, Manager, Communications
Kyla Romard, Manager, Clinical Affairs

Ontario Dental Assistants Association (ODAA)
869 Dundas St., London ON N5W 2Z8
Tel: 519-679-2566; *Fax:* 519-679-8494
Toll-Free: 800-461-4348
info@odaa.org
www.odaa.org
www.facebook.com/yourODAA
To act as the certifying body for dental assistants in Ontario
Billy Jo Santoro, President
Kathryn Bureau, Vice-President
Carolyn Hibbs, Executive Director

Ontario Dental Association (ODA)
4 New St., Toronto ON M5R 1P6
Tel: 416-922-3900; *Fax:* 416-922-9005
Toll-Free: 800-387-1393
info@oda.ca
www.oda.ca
www.youtube.com/user/OntarioDentalAssoc
www.linkedin.com/company/ontario-dental-association
www.facebook.com/OntarioDentalAssociation
twitter.com/ONDentalAssn
To represent the dentists of Ontario; To provide exemplary oral health care & promote the attainment of optimal health for the people of Ontario
Kim Hansen, President
Frank Hansen, Chief Executive Officer
Ian Farmer, Director, Finance & Administration
David Gentili, Director, Professional & Government Affairs
Alex Glazduri, Director, Membership Services & IT Services
Marcus Staviss, Director, Communications, Public Affairs & Events

Ordre des dentistes du Québec (ODQ)
#1640, 800, boul René-Lévesque ouest, Montréal QC H3B 1X9
Tél: 514-875-8511; *Téléc:* 514-393-9248
Ligne sans frais: 800-361-4887
info@odq.qc.ca
www.odq.qc.ca
www.youtube.com/webmestreodq
www.facebook.com/maboucheensante
twitter.com/ordredentistes
Assurer la qualité des services en médecine dentaire par le respect de normes élevées de pratique et d'éthique et de promouvoir la santé bucco-dentaire auprès de la population du Québec
Caroline Daoust, Directrice générale et secrétaire
André Lavoie, Directeur, Affaires publiques et communications

Ordre des denturologistes du Québec (ODQ)
395, rue du Parc-Industriel, Longueuil QC J4H 3V7
Tél: 450-646-7922; *Téléc:* 450-646-2509
Ligne sans frais: 800-567-2251
info@odq.com
www.odq.com
www.facebook.com/ordredesdenturologistesduquebec
Robert Cabana, Président
Monique Bouchard, Directrice générale et secrétaire

Provincial Dental Board of Nova Scotia
#103, 210 Waterfront Dr., Halifax NS B4A 0H3
Tel: 902-420-0083; *Fax:* 902-492-0301
Toll-Free: 866-326-1046
info@pdbns.ca
www.pdbns.ca
To protect the public in the delivery of dental care through licensure & regulation
Martin Gillis, Registrar

Royal College of Dental Surgeons of Ontario
6 Crescent Rd., Toronto ON M4W 1T1
Tel: 416-961-6555; *Fax:* 416-961-5814
Toll-Free: 800-565-4591
info@rcdso.org
www.rcdso.org
To operate as the governing body for dentists in Ontario; To protect the public's right to quality dental services by providing leadership to the dental profession in self-regulation
Flavio Turchet, President
Irwin W. Fefergrad, Registrar

Royal College of Dentists of Canada (RCDC) / Collège Royal des Chirurgiens Dentistes du Canada
#1501, 110 Yonge St., Toronto ON M5C 1T4
Tel: 416-512-6571; *Fax:* 416-512-6468
office@rcdc.ca
www.rcdc.ca
To provide examinations for dental sciences & for nationally recognized dental specialties in Canada
Hugh Lamont, President
Leland McFadden, Registrar
James Posluns, Treasurer
Christine Corbeil, Examiner-in-Chief

Saskatchewan Dental Assistants' Association (SDAA)
PO Box 294, 603 - 3rd St., Kenaston SK S0G 2N0
Tel: 306-252-2769; *Fax:* 306-252-2089
sdaa@sasktel.net
www.sdaa.sk.ca
www.facebook.com/111269682301325
To promote excellence in dental health care; To advance public protection through enforcement of regulations, education, ethical practice, & standardization

Gillian Nault, President
Susan Anholt, Executive Director
Tracey Taylor, Coordinator, Professional Development

Yukon Professional Licensing (Dental)
PO Box 2703, C-5, Whitehorse YT Y1A 2C6
Tel: 867-667-5111; *Fax:* 867-667-3609
plra@gov.yk.ca
www.community.gov.yk.ca/dental

Developing Countries

Canadian Christian Relief & Development Association (CCRDA)
CCRDA c/o Joella Reitsma, 16 Soper Creek Dr., Bowmanville ON L1C 4G1
Tel: 289-385-7307; *Fax:* 519-885-5225
joellareitsma@ccrda.ca
www.ccrda.ca
www.facebook.com/CCRDACanada
twitter.com/CCRDACanada
Building partnerships to effectively provide emergency relief, facilitate sustainable development, promote justice, and speak with one voice on behalf of the world's poor and disadvantaged peoples.

Crossroads International / Carrefour International
#201, 49 Bathurst St., Toronto ON M5V 2P2
Tel: 416-967-1611; *Fax:* 416-967-9078
Toll-Free: 877-967-1611
info@cintl.org
cintl.org
www.youtube.com/user/CanadianCrossroads
www.linkedin.com/company/crossroads-international
www.facebook.com/CanadianCrossroads
twitter.com/CrossroadsIntl
To reduce poverty & increase women's rights around the world; To work with local organizations in West Africa, Southern Africa & South America; To uphold ethical relationships with stakeholders; To help develop programs & meet development goals of developing countries; To support the exchange of skilled volunteers
Simone Philogène, Chair
Heather Shapter, Executive Director

Dignitas International
c/o ICES, Attn: Dr. Michael Schull, 2075 Bayview Ave., #G106, Toronto ON M4N 3M5
Tel: 416-260-3100; *Toll-Free:* 866-576-3100
info@dignitasinternational.org
dignitasinternational.org
www.instagram.com/dignitasintl
www.linkedin.com/company/dignitas-international
www.facebook.com/DignitasInternational
twitter.com/dignitasintl
To improve access to quality health care for people facing a high burden of disease & unequal access to services; To educate health care workers in remote areas on ways to treat HIV, TB & malaria; To work towards the eradication of the AIDS epidemic in Malawi
Jennifer Keenan, Chair
Catherine Collins, Senior Officer, Special Projects
Chavenet Telfort, Director, Finance & Operations
Maria Pata, Administrator, Finance & HR

Micro-Recyc-Coopération
#310, 7000, av du Parc, Montréal QC H3N 1X1
Tél: 514-227-5776
info@microrecyccoop.org
www.microrecyccoop.org
www.facebook.com/MicroRecycCoop
Informatiser les établissements d'enseignements au Sud; Sensibiliser le public aux edéchets au Nord
Philippe Nguene, Président

Partenariat pour le développement des communautés (PARDEC)
6450, av Christophe-Colomb, Montréal QC H2S 2G7
Tél: 514-690-5222; *Téléc:* 514-843-3061
info@pardec.org
www.pardec.org
www.instagram.com/pardec_organisme
www.facebook.com/pardecqc
Marguerite Kephart, Présidente
Baudouin Kutuka Makasi, Cofondateur et Directeur général

Projet Accompagnement Québec-Guatemala (PAQG)
#2.115, 660, rue Villeray, Montréal QC H2R 1J1
Tél: 514-495-3131
paqg@paqg.org
www.paqg.org
www.facebook.com/PAQcG
Soutien à l'attention des défenseur.e.s guatémaltèques des droits civils, politiques, sociaux, culturels et économiques
Oscar Benavides Calvachi, Coordination générale

Teamwork Children's Services International
5983 Ladyburn Cres., Mississauga ON L5M 4V9
Tel: 905-542-1047
www.teamworkchildrenservices.com
To provide a safe environment for disadvantaged children in rural areas of Africa; To help children become productive citizens through the provision of physical & mental care, education & vocational training
Joel Chacha, Executive Director

Disabled Persons

AboutFace
51 Wolseley St., Toronto ON M5T 1A4
Tel: 416-597-2229; *Fax:* 416-597-8494
Toll-Free: 800-665-3223
info@aboutface.ca
www.aboutface.ca
www.youtube.com/user/AboutFaceEvents
www.linkedin.com/company/aboutface
twitter.com/AboutFace
To provide emotional support & information to, & on behalf of, individuals who have a facial difference & their families
Danielle Griffin, Executive Director
Christina Vasilopoulos, Program Manager

Alberta Association of Rehabilitation Centres (AARC)
#160, 3015 - 12th St. NE, Calgary AB T2E 7J2
Tel: 403-250-9495; *Fax:* 403-291-9864
acds@acds.ca
www.acds.ca
www.youtube.com/user/acdsonline
www.linkedin.com/company/acdsonline
www.facebook.com/acds.ca
twitter.com/ACDS_online
To support organizations that provide services & supports to people with disabilities; To act as a voice for the field of community rehabilitation to the political & administrative arms of government; To focus on human resource initiatives for the services sector; To provide in-service training opportunities for people employed in the field; To accredit & certify service in Alberta
Andrea Hesse, Chief Executive Officer

Alberta Easter Seals Society
#103, 811 Manning Rd. NE, Calgary AB T2E 7L4
Tel: 403-235-5662; *Fax:* 403-248-1716
Toll-Free: 877-732-7837
calgary@easterseals.ab.ca
www.easterseals.ab.ca
www.pinterest.ca/eastersealssab
www.facebook.com/EasterSealsAlberta
twitter.com/eastersealsAB
To represent interests of all people with disabilities in Alberta; to promote change at all policy-making levels through public awareness campaigns, projects, seminars; to provide mobility equipment; to conduct public awareness programs; to provide recreational activities through summer camp - Camp Horizon; to provide a residential home program - Easter Seals McQueen Residence
Larry Mathieson, Chief Executive Officer

ARCH Disability Law Centre
55 University Ave., 15th Fl., Toronto ON M5J 2H7
Tel: 416-482-8255; *Fax:* 416-482-2981
Toll-Free: 866-482-2724
TTY: 416-482-1254
archgen@lao.on.ca
www.archdisabilitylaw.ca
www.facebook.com/ARCHDisabilityLawCentre
twitter.com/ARCHDisability
To defend & advance the equality rights of persons with disabilities; assisting individuals with disabilities to understand their rights & how to enforce them; working with groups representing people with disabilities throughout Ontario; representing in precedent setting cases where client cannot be represented appropriately by other legal services; summary advice & referral - lawyers who specialize in areas of law as they

relate to disability provide free, confidential, basic legal advice & referral to other sources of assistance
Roberto Lattanzio, Executive Director

Association du Québec pour enfants avec problèmes auditifs (AQEPA)
3700, rue Berri, #A-446, Montréal QC H2L 4G9
Tél: 514-842-8706; *Téléc:* 514-842-4006
Ligne sans frais: 877-842-4006
info@aqepa.org
www.aqepa.org
www.instagram.com/aqepa_provinciale
www.linkedin.com/company/aqepa-provinciale
www.facebook.com/AQEPA
twitter.com/AQEPA
Regrouper les parents d'enfants sourds et malentendants; informer et sensibiliser les parents et le public
Pier-Alain Roy, Président
Claire Moussel, Directrice Générale

Association québécoise pour le loisir des personnes handicapées (AQLPH)
858, rue Laviolette, Trois-Rivières QC G9A 5J1
Tél: 819-693-3339
info@aqlph.qc.ca
www.aqlph.qc.ca
Promouvoir le droit à un loisir de qualité (éducatif, sécuritaire, valorisant et de détente); promouvoir la participation et la libre expression de la personne face à son loisir; promouvoir l'accès à tous les champs d'application du loisir (tourisme, plein air, sport et activité physique, loisir scientifique, socio-éducatif et socioculturel) pour toutes les personnes handicapées du Québec sans restriction d'âge, de sexe, ni de type d'handicap
Marc St-Onge, Directeur

Autistics United Canada (AU)
Vancouver BC
info@autisticsunitedca.org
www.autisticsunitedca.org
autisticsunitedca.tumblr.com
www.facebook.com/AutisticsUnitedCA
twitter.com/AutisticsUnited
To improve the lives of Autistic people in Canada
Vivian Ly, Chapter Leader, Vancouver
Sam McCulligh, Chapter Leader, Vancouver

BALANCE for Blind Adults
#302, 4920 Dundas St. West, Toronto ON M9A 1B7
Tel: 416-236-1796; *Fax:* 416-236-4280
info@balancefba.org
www.balancefba.org
www.facebook.com/balanceforblindadults
twitter.com/balancefba
To provide instruction & support to individuals with visual impairment to enable them to live independently & confidently in their community; To promote independence, decision making, & self-fulfillment
Susan Archibald, Executive Director

BC People First Society
BC
www.selfadvocatenet.com
www.facebook.com/bcpeoplefirst
To change attitudes towards individuals with disabilities; To encourage self-advocacy among individuals with disabilities; To provide information & mentoring services; To raise public awareness about disabilities in the community
Bryce Schaufelberger, Contact

Bob Rumball Canadian Centre of Excellence for the Deaf (BRCED)
2395 Bayview Ave., Toronto ON M2L 1A2
Tel: 416-449-9651; *Fax:* 416-449-8881
TTY: 416-449-2728
info@bobrumball.org
www.bobrumball.org
www.facebook.com/bobrumballfoundation
twitter.com/BobRumball
To provide opportunities for a higher quality of life for deaf people while preserving & promoting their language & culture; To foster & develop good relations with the community at large & actively promote the Centre; To work closely with the various ministries of the provincial government & related agencies
Jane Hooey, Chair

Canadian Abilities Foundation
#803, 255 Duncan Mill Rd., Toronto ON M3B 3H9
Tel: 416-421-7944; *Fax:* 416-421-8418
abilities@bcsgroup.com
www.abilities.ca
twitter.com/abilitiescanada
To provide information, inspiration & opportunity to Canadians with disabilities

---

Caroline Tapp-McDougall, Executive Director & Managing Editor

Canadian Association for Community Living (CACL) / Association canadienne pour l'intégration communautaire
20-850 King St. West, Oshawa ON L1J 8N5
Tel: 416-661-9611; *Fax:* 905-436-3587
Toll-Free: 855-661-9611
inform@cacl.ca
www.cacl.ca
www.youtube.com/canadianacl
www.facebook.com/canadianacl
twitter.com/cacl_acic
To ensure the following for people with intellectual disabilities: the same rights, & access to choice, services, & supports as others; the same opportunities to live in freedom & dignity with the necessary supports to do so; & the ability to articulate & realize their rights & aspirations
Robin Acton, President
Krista Carr, Executive Vice-President
Sue Talmey, National Director, Finance & Administration
Tara Levandier, National Director, Policy & Program Operations
Gordon Porter, National Director, Inclusive Education Initiatives

Canadian Association of the Deaf (CAD) / Association des sourds du Canada (ASC)
#606, 251 Bank St., Ottawa ON K2P 1X3
Tel: 613-565-2882; *Fax:* 613-565-1207
TTY: 613-565-8882
info@cad.ca
www.cad.ca
www.facebook.com/1940CADASC
twitter.com/CADASC
To protect & promote the rights, needs & concerns of deaf Canadians
Frank Folino, President
James Roots, Executive Director
Pavel Chernousov, Project Coordinator

The Canadian Council of the Blind (CCB) / Le Conseil canadien des aveugles
#100, 20 James St., Ottawa ON K2P 0T6
Tel: 613-567-0311; *Fax:* 613-567-2728
Toll-Free: 877-304-0968
ccb@ccbnational.net
www.ccbnational.net
www.facebook.com/ccbnational
twitter.com/ccbnational
To promote the well-being of individuals who are blind or vision-impaired through higher education, profitable employment, & social association; To create a closer relationship between blind & sighted friends; To organize a nation-wide organization of people who are blind & vision-impaired & groups of blind persons throughout Canada; To promote measures for the conservation of sight & the prevention of blindness
Louise Gillis, National President

Canadian Council on Rehabilitation & Work (CCRW) / Le Conseil canadien de la réadaptation et du travail (CCRT)
#105, 477 Mount Pleasant Rd., Toronto ON M4S 2L9
Tel: 416-260-3060; *Fax:* 416-260-3093
Toll-Free: 800-664-0925
TTY: 416-260-9223
info@ccrw.org
www.ccrw.org
www.linkedin.com/company/2458107
www.facebook.com/CCRW.org
twitter.com/ccrw
To improve employment opportunities for persons with disabilities in Canada; To promote the equitable & meaningful employment of persons with disabilities
Maureen Haan, President & CEO

Canadian Cultural Society of The Deaf, Inc. (CCSD)
15 Mill Lane, Toronto ON M5A 3R6
info@deafculturecentre.ca
www.deafculturecentre.ca
www.facebook.com/deafculturecentre
twitter.com/DeafCulture
To ensure that the cultural needs of deaf & hard-of-hearing people are being met; To concentrate efforts in the areas of the performing arts, sign language, deaf literature, the visual arts & heritage resources
Joanne Cripps, Executive Director

Canadian Deafblind Association (National) (CDBA) / Association canadienne de la surdicécité (Bureau National)
#14, 1860 Appleby Line, Burlington ON L7L 7H7
Fax: 905-331-2043
Toll-Free: 866-229-5832
info@cdbanational.com
www.cdbanational.com
www.facebook.com/cdbanational
twitter.com/CDBANational
To promote & enhance the well-being of people who are deafblind through awareness, education, & provision of support for chapters, members, & community partners
Carolyn Monaco, President
Tom McFadden, National Executive Director
Paul Nobes, IT Officer

Canadian Foundation for Physically Disabled Persons (CFPDP)
#265, 6 Garamond Ct., Toronto ON M3C 1Z5
Tel: 416-760-7351; *Fax:* 416-760-9405
info@cfpdp.com
www.cfpdp.com
www.facebook.com/cffpdp
twitter.com/cffpdp
To provide financial assistance to organizations sharing concern for physically disabled adults; To help create awareness in the public & business communities, & in government of the needs of physically disabled adults in the areas of housing, employment, education, accessibility, sports & recreation, & research
Vim Kochhar, Chair
Deborah Lewis, Executive Director

Canadian Guide Dogs for the Blind (CGDB)
National Office & Training Centre, PO Box 280, 4120 Rideau Valley Dr. North, Manotick ON K4M 1A3
Tel: 613-692-7777; *Fax:* 613-692-0650
info@guidedogs.ca
www.guidedogs.ca
To assist visually-impaired Canadians with their mobility by providing & training them in the use of professionally trained guide dogs
Jane Thornton, Co-Founder & Chief Operating Officer

Canadian Hard of Hearing Association (CHHA) / Association des malentendants canadiens (AMEC)
#905, 75 Albert St., Ottawa ON K1P 5E7
Tel: 613-526-1584; *Fax:* 613-526-4718
Toll-Free: 800-263-8068
TTY: 613-526-2692
info@chha.ca
www.chha.ca
www.facebook.com/CHHANational
twitter.com/CHHA_AMEC
To act as the voice of all hard of hearing Canadians; To promote the integration of hard of hearing people into society
Marilyn J. Kingdon, President
Lee Pigeau, National Executive Director

Canadian Hearing Society (CHS) / Société canadienne de l'ouïe
271 Spadina Rd., Toronto ON M5R 2V3
Toll-Free: 866-518-0000
TTY: 877-215-9530
info@chs.ca
www.chs.ca
www.youtube.com/user/CHSCanadaTV
www.facebook.com/chssco
twitter.com/CHSCanada
To provide services that enhance the independence of deaf, deafened & hard of hearing people, & that encourage prevention of hearing loss
Julia Dumanian, President & CEO
Chantal Graveline, Vice-President, Clinical & Community Services
Raymond D. King, Vice-President, Business Development

Canadian National Institute for the Blind (CNIB) / INCA (INCA)
1929 Bayview Ave., Toronto ON M4G 3E8
Toll-Free: 800-563-2642
info@cnib.ca
www.cnib.ca
www.youtube.com/cnibnatcomm
www.facebook.com/myCNIB
twitter.com/CNIB
To ameliorate the condition of persons with vision loss in Canada; To prevent blindness; To promote sight enhancement services; To direct services to more than 100,000 Canadians with vision loss, provided through a network of more than 50 offices across the country; To provide library services, research, advocacy, public education, & accessible design consulting; To

---

produce materials in alternative formats, including Braille & DAISY talking books; To supply assistive technologies for persons with vision loss
John M. Rafferty, President & CEO
Kathy Rabideau, Chief Financial Officer
Maria Ash, Senior Vice-President, Business Support Services
Diane Bergeron, Vice-President, Engagement & International Affairs
Garry Nenson, Vice-President, Philanthropy
Shane Silver, Vice-President, Social Enterprise & Innovation

Centre de réadaptation Constance-Lethbridge (CRCL) / Constance Lethbridge Rehabilitation Centre
7005, boul de Maisonneuve ouest, Montréal QC H4B 1T3
Tél: 514-487-1770; Ligne sans frais: 866-487-1891
www.constance-lethbridge.qc.ca
www.linkedin.com/company/centre-de-readaptation-constance-le thbridge-rehabilitation-centre
www.facebook.com/ConstanceLethbridge
Offrir des services spécialisés et ultraspécialisés à des adultes ayant une déficience motrice, en externe ou à domicile, de réadaptation, d'adaptation, de préparation et de support à l'intégration sociale ou professionnelle aux clientèles ayant des problèmes orthopédiques, neurologiques et rhumatologiques; offrir aussi une expertise d'évaluation de la conduite automobile, d'évaluation et d'orientation des capacités de travail de la personne handicapée

Community Living Manitoba
#6, 120 Maryland St., Winnipeg MB R3G 1L1
Tel: 204-786-1607; Fax: 204-789-9850
aclmb@aclmb.ca
www.aclmb.ca
www.facebook.com/370890112967949
twitter.com/aclmanitoba
To promote the welfare of people with handicaps & their families; To speak on behalf of people with developmental disabilities in Manitoba; To ensure that every person in Manitoba has access to supports necessary to live with dignity & to participate fully in the community of their choice
Aileen Najduch, President
Sheryl Giesbrecht, Vice-President
Brian Goodman, Secretary

Community Living Ontario (CLO) / Intégration communautaire Ontario
1 Valleybrook Dr., Toronto ON M3B 2S7
Tel: 416-447-4348; Fax: 416-447-8974
Toll-Free: 800-278-8025
info@communitylivingontario.ca
www.communitylivingontario.ca
www.youtube.com/user/comlivon
www.facebook.com/communitylivingontario
twitter.com/CLOntario
To lobby on behalf of people with intellectual disabilities in Ontario; To ensure that every person in Ontario has access to supports to live with dignity & to participate in the community of their choice
Chris Beesley, Chief Executive Officer
Marcy Galipeau, Director, Communications, Marketing & Fund Development
Megan Mitchell, Director, Membership Services
Shawn Pegg, Director, Policy Analysis, Planning & Accountability

Council of Canadians with Disabilities (CCD) / Conseil des Canadiens avec déficiences
#909, 294 Portage Ave., Winnipeg MB R3C 0B9
Tel: 204-947-0303; Fax: 204-942-4625
TTY: 204-943-4757
ccd@ccdonline.ca
www.ccdonline.ca
www.youtube.com/ccdonline
www.facebook.com/ccdonline
twitter.com/ccdonline
To improve the status of disabled citizens in Canadian society; To promote self-help for persons with disabilities; To provide a democratic structure for disabled citizens to voice concerns; To monitor federal legislation; To share information & cooperate with disabled persons' organizations in Canada & in other countries; To establish a positive image of disabled Canadians
Jewelles Smith, Chair
Roxana Jahani Aval, Secretary

DIRECTIONS Council for Vocational Services Society
#920, 99 Wyse Rd., Dartmouth NS B3A 4S5
Tel: 902-466-2220; Fax: 902-461-2220
www.directionscouncil.org
To promote the abilities & inclusion of persons with disabilities in the every day activities of their community

Bob Bennett, President

Disability Alliance British Columbia (DABC)
#204, 456 West Broadway, Vancouver BC V5Y 1R3
Tel: 604-875-0188; Fax: 604-875-9227
Toll-Free: 800-663-1278
TTY: 604-875-8835
feedback@disabilityalliancebc.org
www.disabilityalliancebc.org
www.youtube.com/user/TheBCCPD
www.linkedin.com/company/4863769
www.facebook.com/DisabilityAllianceBC
twitter.com/DisabAllianceBC
To raise public & political awareness of issues concerning people with disabilities; To facilitate full participation of disabled people in society by promoting independence & the self-help model; To lobby government on policies & attitudes which affect people with disabilities
Jane Dyson, Executive Director
Sam Turcott, Director, Advocacy Access Program
Justina Loh, Administrative Director

DisAbled Women's Network of Canada / Réseau d'Action des Femmes Handicapées du Canada
#215, rue 469 Jean Talon ouest, Montréal QC H3N 1R4
Tel: 514-396-0009; Fax: 514-396-6585
Toll-Free: 866-396-0074
www.dawncanada.net
www.youtube.com/user/DAWNRAFHCanada
www.linkedin.com/company/dawncanada
www.facebook.com/dawnrafhcanada
twitter.com/DAWNRAFHCanada
To end the poverty, isolation, discrimination & violence experienced by women with disabilities; To ensure the accessibility of services to women with disabilities; To address key issues concerning women with disabilities
Bonnie Brayton, National Executive Director
Hanane Khales, Coordinator, Communications

Easter Seals Canada / Timbres de Pâques Canada
#401, 40 Holly St., Toronto ON M4S 3C3
Tel: 416-932-8382; Fax: 416-932-9844
Toll-Free: 877-376-6362
info@easterseals.ca
www.easterseals.ca
www.instagram.com/eastersealscanada
www.facebook.com/eastersealscanada
twitter.com/easterseals
To enhance the quality of life, self-esteem, & self-determination of Canadians with physical disabilities; To support the social & economic integration of people with disabilities
Dave Starrett, Chief Executive Officer
Ana Maria Faria, Vice-President, National Development
Frank Williamson, Director, Finance

Easter Seals New Brunswick (ESNB) / Les Timbres de Pâques N.-B.
65 Brunswick St., Fredericton NB E3B 1G5
Tel: 506-458-8739; Fax: 506-457-2863
Toll-Free: 888-280-8155
info@easterseals.nb.ca
www.easterseals.nb.ca
twitter.com/EasterSealsNB
To provide rehabilitation services & programs to persons with disabilities in New Brunswick; To improve public attitudes towards disabled persons; To provide disabled persons with new opportunities; To provide orthopedic appliances, rehabilitative equipment, technical aids & computers; To advocate on behalf of disabled persons; To serve as information resource centre for disabled persons, students, the public & health professionals; To hold the franchise for the Easter Seals campaign; To provide interprovincial transportation assistance to treatment & diagnostic centres
Julia Latham, Executive Director

Easter Seals Newfoundland & Labrador
Husky Energy Easter Seals House, 206 Mount Scio Rd., St. John's NL A1B 4L5
Tel: 709-754-1399; Fax: 709-754-1398
info@easterseals.nf.ca
www.easterseals.nf.ca
www.linkedin.com/company/easter-seals-newfoundland-and-labr ador
www.facebook.com/EasterSealsNL
twitter.com/easterssealsnl
To maximize the abilities & enhancing the lives of children & youth with physical disabilities through recreational, social & other therapeutic programs, direct assistance, education & advocacy
Mark Bradbury, Chief Executive Officer

Easter Seals Nova Scotia (AFNS)
22 Fielding Ave., Dartmouth NS B3B 1E2
Tel: 902-453-6000
mailing@easterseals.ns.ca
www.easterseals.ns.ca
www.youtube.com/user/easterssealsns
www.facebook.com/ESnovascotia
twitter.com/Easterssealsns
To enable Nova Scotians with physical disabilities to enhance their quality of life by realizing their individual potential
Joanne Bernard, President & CEO

Easter Seals Ontario (TESS) / Société du timbre de Pâques de l'Ontario
#700, 1 Concorde Gate, Toronto ON M3C 3N6
Tel: 416-421-8377; Fax: 416-696-1035
Toll-Free: 800-668-6252
info@easterseals.org
www.easterseals.org
www.youtube.com/user/Easterssealsont
www.linkedin.com/company/easter-seals-ontario
www.facebook.com/EasterSealsON
twitter.com/easterssealson
To help children with physical disabilities achieve their full individual potential & future independence
John M. Herhalt, Chair
Kevin J. Collins, President & CEO

La fédération des mouvements personne d'abord du Québec
3958, rue Dandurand, #S-4, Montréal QC
Tel: 514-723-7507; Téléc: 514-723-2517
Ligne sans frais: 877-475-1617
fmpdaq@bellnet.ca
www.fmpdaq.org
Défendre les droits et intérêts des personnes ayant une déficience intellectuelle; Promouvoir l'auto-défense
Françoise Charbonneau, Coordinatrice

Fondation Papillon / Butterfly Foundation
2300, boul René-Lévesque ouest, Montréal QC H3H 2R5
Tél: 514-937-6171; Téléc: 514-937-0082
Ligne sans frais: 877-937-6171
www.fondationpapillon.ca
www.youtube.com/channel/UCfFKb66-XlfUSN1xZ6lIS_Q
www.facebook.com/fondationpapillon.ca
twitter.com/SEHQ
Voué au bien-être des enfants handicapés et de leur famille; grâce aux contributions publiques qui lui sont versées et aux efforts conjugués de bénévoles et de permanents, la société offre des services directs et professionnels qui favorisent le développement personnel des enfants et leur intégration dans la communauté
Jean Duchesneau, Directeur général

Humanity & Inclusion Canada
#400, 50, rue Sainte-Catherine ouest, Montréal QC H2X 3V4
Tel: 514-908-2813; Fax: 514-937-6685
Toll-Free: 877-908-2813
hi-canada.org
www.instagram.com/hi_canada
www.linkedin.com/company/humanite-inclusion-canada
www.facebook.com/Humanite.Inclusion.Canada
twitter.com/HI_Canada
To provide assistance through work in various fields for people in developing countries with disabilities; To prevent disabilities through the clearing of anti-personnel mines & cluster munitions; To provide support for disabled persons in the aftermath of natural disasters & other humanitarian crises
Jérôme Bobin, Executive Director
Elena Pukhaeva, Manager, Administration & Finance
Gabriel Perriau, Communications Officer

Inclusion Alberta (AACL)
11724 Kingsway Ave., Edmonton AB T5G 0X5
Tel: 780-451-3055; Fax: 780-453-5779
Toll-Free: 800-252-7556
mail@inclusionalberta.org
inclusionalberta.org
www.linkedin.com/company/inclusionalberta
www.facebook.com/InclusionAlberta
twitter.com/inclusionAB
To advocate for fully inclusive community lives for children & adults with developmental disabilities
Trish Bowman, Chief Executive Officer
Wendy McDonald, Chief Operating Officer

Inclusion BC
227 - 6th St., New Westminster BC V3L 3A5
Tel: 604-777-9100; *Fax:* 604-777-9394
Toll-Free: 800-618-1119
info@inclusionbc.org
www.inclusionbc.org
www.youtube.com/user/BCACL
www.linkedin.com/company/inclusion-bc
www.facebook.com/InclusionBC
twitter.com/InclusionBC
To enhance the lives of persons with developmental disabilities & their families; To promote the participation of people with developmental disabilities in all aspects of community life; To support activities dedicated to building inclusive communities that value the diverse abilities of all people
Fiona Whittington-Walsh, President
Karla Verschoor, Executive Director
Frank Peng, Director, Finance & Administration

Inclusion NWT (YKACL)
Abe Miller Bldg., PO Box 981, 4912 - 53 St., Yellowknife NT X1A 2N7
Tel: 867-920-2644; *Fax:* 867-920-2348
inclusionnwt.org
www.facebook.com/InclusionNWT
To promote the welfare of people with handicaps & their families; To lobby on behalf of people with developmental disabilities in the Northwest Territories; To ensure that every person in Northwest Territories has access to supports to live with dignity & to participate in the community of their choice
Lynn Elkin, Executive Director

Inclusion Saskatchewan
3031 Louise St., Saskatoon SK S7J 3L1
Tel: 306-955-3344; *Fax:* 306-373-3070
info@inclusionsk.com
www.inclusionsk.com
www.facebook.com/InclusionSK
twitter.com/InclusionSK
To enhance the lives of individuals with intellectual disabilities throughout Saskatchewan; To develop programs & services to meet the needs of people with intellectual disabilities
Kevin McTavish, Executive Director
Christina Martens-Funk, Director, Finance
Connie Andersen, Director, Community Development
Travis Neufeld, Manager, Communications & Marketing
Nicole Graham, Coordinator, Youth Program & Family Network

Inclusion Yukon
#7, 4230 - 4 Ave., Whitehorse YT Y1A 1K1
Tel: 867-667-4606; *Fax:* 867-667-4606
yaclwhse@northwestel.net
www.inclusionyukon.org
www.facebook.com/InclusionYukon
To promote the welfare of people with intellectual disabilities & their families; To ensure that every person in the Yukon has access to supports necessary to live with dignity & to participate fully in the community of their choice
Shonagh McCrindle, Executive Director

Independent Living Canada (ILC) / Vie autonome Canada (VAC)
c/o House of Sport, RA Centre, 2451 Riverside Dr., Ottawa ON K1H 7X7
Tel: 613-563-2581; *Fax:* 613-563-3861
Toll-Free: 877-713-3373
info@ilcanada.ca
www.ilc-vac.ca
www.facebook.com/MyIndependentLivingCanada
twitter.com/IL_Canada
To represent & coordinate the network of independent living centres; To guide & support independent living centres in the delivery of programs & services
Carole J. Barron, National Chair
Kathleen Odell, Secretary

Kinsmen Foundation of British Columbia & Yukon (KRF)
PO Box 64789, Stn. Sunwood Square, Coquitlam BC V3B 0H1
Tel: 604-852-4501; *Fax:* 604-852-4501
kinsmenfoundationofbc@shaw.ca
www.kinsmenfoundationofbc.ca
Committed to providing funding for services & technologies empowering British Columbians with physical disabilities to live more independently
Phillip Jewel, Chief Operating Officer

LakeCity Employment Services Association
386 Windmill Rd., Dartmouth NS B3A 1J5
Tel: 902-465-5000; *Fax:* 902-465-5009
lesa@lakecityemployment.com
www.lakecityemployment.com

To assist mental health consumers in improving their quality of life by helping them to assume responsibility & independence through work
Andre McConnell, Chair
Chris Fyles, Executive Director

Manitoba Possible (SMD)
825 Sherbrook St., Winnipeg MB R3A 1M5
Tel: 204-975-3010; *Fax:* 204-975-3073
Toll-Free: 866-282-8041
TTY: 204-975-3083
info@manitobapossible.ca
www.manitobapossible.ca
www.youtube.com/user/TheSmdfoundation
www.linkedin.com/company/manitobapossible
www.facebook.com/manitoba.possible
twitter.com/manitobapossibl
To promote the full participation & equality of people with disabilities: To provide a full range of rehabilitation services; To facilitate the development of a receptive & supportive environment

Nanaimo Association for Community Living (NACL)
#201, 96 Cavan St., Nanaimo BC V9L 2V1
Tel: 250-741-0224; *Fax:* 250-741-0227
info@nanaimoacl.com
www.nanaimoacl.com
www.facebook.com/nanaimoacl
To support all people with disabilities to achieve the highest quality of life through participation, independence, inclusion & education
Marlena Stewart, Executive Assistant

National Institute of Disability Management & Research (NIDMAR) / Institut national de recherche et de gestion de l'incapacité au travail
c/o Pacific Coast University for Workplace Health Sciences, 4755 Cherry Creek Rd., Port Alberni BC V9Y 0A7
Tel: 778-421-0821; *Fax:* 778-421-0823
nidmar@nidmar.ca
www.nidmar.ca
Committed to reducing the human, social, & economic cost of disability to workers, employers, & society by providing education, research, policy development, & implementation resources to promote workplace-based integration programs
Wolfgang Zimmermann, Executive Director

New Brunswick Association for Community Living (NBACL) / Association du Nouveau-Brunswick pour l'intégration communautaire
800 Hanwell Rd., Fredericton NB E3B 2R7
Tel: 506-453-4400; *Fax:* 506-453-4422
Toll-Free: 866-622-2548
nbacl@nbnet.nb.ca
www.nbacl.nb.ca
www.youtube.com/communitylivingnb
www.facebook.com/nbacl
twitter.com/nbacl
To promote the welfare of people with handicaps & their families; To lobby for developmentally disabled people in New Brunswick; To ensure that every person in New Brunswick has access to supports to live with dignity & participate in the community of their choice
Sarah Wagner, Executive Director
Lindsey Gillies, Director, Finance & Office Administration

Newfoundland & Labrador Association for Community Living (NLACL)
PO Box 8414, 74 O'Leary Ave., St. John's NL A1B 3N7
Tel: 709-722-0790; *Fax:* 709-722-1325
Toll-Free: 800-701-8511
nlacl@nlacl.ca
www.nlacl.ca
www.facebook.com/nlacl
twitter.com/nlacl1
To develop communities in Newfoundland & Labrador that welcome individuals with developmental disabilities
Dennis Gill, President
Lori Moulton, Vice-President
Una Tucker, Secretary
Marg Pike, Acting Treasurer
Hope Colbourne, Executive Director

Nova Scotia Association for Community Living (NSACL)
#101, 3845 Joseph Howe Dr., Halifax NS B3L 4H9
Tel: 902-469-1174; *Toll-Free:* 844-469-1174
inform@nsacl.ca
www.nsacl.ca
www.facebook.com/nsacl
twitter.com/NSACL
To work for the benefit of persons of all ages who have an intellectual disability in Nova Scotia; To ensure those with an

intellectual disability have the same rights & access as all other persons
Ruth Strubank, Executive Director

Nova Scotia Hearing & Speech Centres
Park Lane Terraces, PO Box 120, #401, 5657 Spring Garden Rd., Halifax NS B3S 3R4
Tel: 902-492-8289; *Fax:* 902-423-0532
Toll-Free: 888-780-3330
info@nshsc.nshealth.ca
www.nshsc.nshealth.ca
To provide hearing services to all Nova Scotians & speech-language services to preschool children & adults; To work with community volunteer leaders, the families & friends of those who are hearing or speech impaired, our partners in government & the medical & academic communities; To raise funds to support critical Centres' needs
Bert Lewis, Chair
Anne Mason-Browne, Chief Executive Officer

Nunavummi Disabilities Makinnasuaqtiit Society (NDMS) / Société Nunavummi Disabilities Makinnasuaqtiit
PO Box 4212, #105, 8 Storey Bldg., Iqaluit NU X0A 1H0
Tel: 867-979-2228; *Toll-Free:* 877-354-0916
connect@nuability.ca
www.nuability.ca
To improve the quality of life for people with disabilities in Nunavut through encouragement, advocacy & promotion of opportunities

Ontario Federation for Cerebral Palsy (OFCP)
#104, 1630 Lawrence Ave. West, Toronto ON M6L 1C5
Tel: 416-244-9686; *Fax:* 416-244-6543
Toll-Free: 877-244-9686
info@ofcp.ca
www.ofcp.ca
www.facebook.com/OntarioFederationforCerebralPalsy
twitter.com/OntarioFCP
To address the changing needs of people in Ontario with cerebral palsy; To improve the quality of life of persons with cerebral palsy through a broad range of programs, education, support of research & the delivery of needed services to people with cerebral palsy & other physical disabilities & their families
Gordana Skrba, Interim Executive Director

Pamiqsaiji Association for Community Living
PO Box 708, Rankin Inlet NU X0C 0G0
Tel: 867-645-2542; *Fax:* 867-645-2543
pamiqad@qiniq.com
To provide support for adults with intellectual disabilities

PEI People First
81 Prince St., Charlottetown PE C1A 4R3
Tel: 902-892-8989
www.facebook.com/312960685412957
To encourage self-advocacy among individuals labelled with an intellectual disability

People First of Canada (PFC) / Personnes d'abord du Canada
#20, 226 Osborne St. North, Winnipeg MB R3C 1V4
Tel: 204-784-7362; *Fax:* 204-784-7364
info@peoplefirstofcanada.ca
www.peoplefirstofcanada.ca
www.youtube.com/user/PeopleFirstofCanada
www.facebook.com/PeopleFirstofCanada
twitter.com/PeopleFirstCA
To educate the public on issues faced by persons with intellectual disabilities; To promote equality; To work toward the deinstitutionalization of persons with intellectual disabilities
Shelley Fletcher, Executive Director

People First of Manitoba
AB
To promote & educate the community about the values of inclusion; To assist individuals labelled with a disability in living a full & inclusive life

People First of Newfoundland & Labrador
#5A, Limerick Pl., St. John's NL A1B 2H2
peoplefirst@nl.rogers.com
www.peoplefirstnl.ca
To educate the public about issues that affect individuals labelled with a disability; To encourage self-advocacy among labelled individuals

People First Society of Yukon
PO Box 31478, Whitehorse YT Y1A 6K8
Tel: 867-667-4606; *Fax:* 867-668-8169
peoplefirstyukon@hotmail.com
www.facebook.com/PeopleFirstSocietyOfYukon
To encourage self-advocacy among individuals labelled with an intellectual disability

Prince Edward Island Association for Community Living (PEIACL)
Royalty Centre, #234, 40 Enman Cres., Stratford PE C1E 1E6
Tel: 902-439-4607
familysupport@peiacl.org
www.peiacl.org
www.youtube.com/channel/UCR951HZ9Ah9xD6VjYTsb8mQ
www.facebook.com/PEIACL
twitter.com/PEIACL
To work on behalf of individuals with an intellectual disability & their families; To empower families to increase options available to Islanders with an intellectual disability
Julie Smith, Executive Director

Prince Edward Island Council of People with Disabilities (PEICOD)
Landmark Plaza, #2, 5 Lower Malpeque Rd., Charlottetown PE C1E 1R4
Tel: 902-892-9149; *Fax:* 902-566-1919
Toll-Free: 888-473-4263
peicod@peicod.pe.ca
www.peicod.pe.ca
www.facebook.com/PEICOD
To improve the quality of life of people with disabilities on PEI
Marcia Carroll, Executive Director

Saskatchewan Abilities Council
2310 Louise Ave., Saskatoon SK S7J 2C7
Tel: 306-374-4448; *Fax:* 306-373-2665
provincialservices@saskabilities.ca
www.saskabilities.ca
www.linkedin.com/company/saskatchewan-abilities-council
To enhance the independence & community participation of people of varying abilities in Saskatchewan
Ian Wilkinson, Executive Director

Silent Voice Canada Inc.
#400, 60 St. Clair Ave. East, Toronto ON M4T 1N5
Tel: 416-463-1104; *Fax:* 416-778-1876
TTY: 416-463-3928
silent.voice@silentvoice.ca
www.silentvoice.ca
www.instagram.com/silentvoicecanada
www.facebook.com/SilentVoiceCan
twitter.com/silentvoiceca
To serve deaf children, deaf youth & adults & their families in the GTA; To improve communication & relationships between the deaf & hearing in families & in our community; To provide services in a sign language environment
Kelly MacKenzie, Executive Director
Mike Cyr, Director, Community Programs

Société québécoise pour la déficience intellectuelle / Québec Intellectual Disability Society
3958, rue Dandurand, Montréal QC H1X 1P7
Tél: 514-725-7245; *Téléc:* 514-725-7245
info@sqdi.ca
www.sqdi.ca
www.facebook.com/sqdi.ca
Défendre les droits et promouvoir les intérêts des personnes ayant une déficience intellectuelle
Roger Duchesneau, Président

Special Needs Planning Group
70 Ivy Cres., Stouffville ON L4A 5A9
Tel: 905-640-8285; *Fax:* 905-640-8285
www.specialneedsplanning.ca
To provide planning services for disabled persons & their families
Graeme S. Treeby, Contact

The Speech & Stuttering Institute
#308, 95 Barber Greene Rd., Toronto ON M3C 3E9
Tel: 416-491-7771; *Fax:* 416-491-7215
info@speechandstuttering.com
www.speechandstuttering.com
www.youtube.com/channel/UC_a2M5vTFVYLr0VeDXTWayw
www.linkedin.com/company/the-speech-and-stuttering-institute
www.facebook.com/speechandstuttering
twitter.com/SpchStutterInst
To provide treatment of & foster the development of innovative speech/language therapy programs; To support education & research in communication disorders
Frank Ientile, Executive Director

Vecova Centre for Disability Services & Research
3304 - 33 St. NW, Calgary AB T2L 2A6
Tel: 403-284-1121; *Fax:* 403-284-1146
info@vecova.ca
www.vecova.ca
www.youtube.com/user/Vecovadisability
www.linkedin.com/company/vecova
www.facebook.com/Vecova
twitter.com/Vecova
To meet the changing needs of individuals with disabilities & the community-at-large through services, research, & enterprises
Joan Lee, Chief Executive Officer
Kaitlyn Pecson, Manager, Communications

Vision Institute of Canada (VIC)
#205, 4025 Yonge St., Toronto ON M2P 2E3
Tel: 416-224-2273; *Fax:* 416-224-9234
visioninstitute@rogers.com
www.visioninstitutecanada.com
To improve the quality of vision care in the community; To provide eye & vision care to persons with special needs
Frances J. MacCusworth, Executive Director

Voice of Albertans with Disabilities (VAD)
PO Box 406, Stn. Hys Centre, 11010 - 101 St., Edmonton AB T5H 4B9
Tel: 780-488-9088
vad@vadsociety.ca
vadsociety.ca
www.facebook.com/accdisabilities
twitter.com/accdisabilities
To promote full participation in society for Albertans with disabilities
Margot Brunner, Executive Director

Disarmament

Mines Action Canada (MAC)
PO Box 4668, Stn. E, Ottawa ON K1S 5H8
Tel: 613-241-3777
info@minesactioncanada.org
www.minesactioncanada.org
www.instagram.com/MinesActionCan
www.facebook.com/minesactioncanada
twitter.com/MinesActionCan
To alleviate the impact that indiscriminate weapons have on the rights, dignity & well being of civilian populations
Paul Hannon, Executive Director

Drilling

Alberta Water Well Drilling Association (AWWDA)
PO Box 130, Lougheed AB T0B 2V0
Tel: 780-386-2335; *Fax:* 780-386-2344
awwda@xplornet.com
www.awwda.com
To assist, promote, encourage, & support the interest and welfare of the water well industry in all of its phases; To foster aid and promote scientific education, standard research, and technique in order to improve methods of well construction: To advance the science of groundwater in Alberta
Michael Schmidt, Secretary Manager

Association des entreprises spécialisées en eau du Québec
5325, Jean-Talon est, Montréal QC H1S 1L5
Tél: 438-340-1364
info@aeseq.com
www.aeseq.com
Regrouper les entrepreneurs de construction oeuvrant dans tous les secteurs du cycle de l'eau décentralisé au Québec
Daniel Schanck, Directeur général

British Columbia Ground Water Association (BCGWA)
1708 - 197A St., Langley BC V2Z 1K2
Tel: 604-530-8934; *Fax:* 604-530-8934
secretary@bcgwa.org
www.bcgwa.org
Joan Perry, Secretary

Canadian Association of Oilwell Drilling Contractors (CAODC)
#2050, 717 - 7th Ave. SW, Calgary AB T2P 0Z3
Tel: 403-264-4311; *Fax:* 403-263-3796
info@caodc.ca
www.caodc.ca
www.youtube.com/user/TheCAODC
www.linkedin.com/company/5607531
www.facebook.com/thecaodc
twitter.com/thecaodc
To represent drilling rig contractors; To provide ongoing means of communication between drilling & well servicing contractors, governments, other industry sector participants, & the general public; To improve standards for safety & training, equipment & technical procedures; To coordinate programs between government bodies & contractors; To oversee the Rig Technician Trade & Apprenticeship Program in Alberta, British Columbia, & Saskatchewan
Mark A. Scholz, President & CEO
John Bayko, Vice-President, Communications
Russell Nibogie, Vice-President, Operations

Canadian Diamond Drilling Association (CDDA)
City Centre Building, #337, 101 Worthington St. East, North Bay ON P1B 1G5
Tel: 705-476-6992; *Fax:* 705-476-9494
office@cdda.ca
www.cdda.ca
To foster the commercial interests of members; To promote the simplifications, standardization & interchangeability of diamond drilling equipment; To recognize the safety & health of employees; To foster the protection of the natural environment; To secure the elimination of unfair or uneconomic practices within the industry & freedom from unjust or unlawful exactions; To establish & maintain uniformity & equity in the customs & commercial usages of the diamond drilling business; To acquire & disseminate valuable business information; To promote communication among those engaged in the industry
Ryan Samis, President

Manitoba Water Well Association (MWWA)
1082 Main St., Winnipeg MB R2W 5J3
Tel: 204-589-6166
mwwa@mwwa.ca
www.mwwa.ca
To promote & support the water well industry in Manitoba
Inez Miller, Executive Director

New Brunswick Ground Water Association
1278 Route 260, St-Martin de Restigouche NB E8A 2M8
Tel: 506-235-5002
nbgwa@nb.sympatico.ca
www.nbgwa.ca
To preserve & protect New Brunswick's water; To promote education of members & the public; To encourage the development of ground water guidelines & strategies
Danny Constantine, President
Terry Burpee, Sec.-Treas.

Newfoundland & Labrador Ground Water Association
PO Box 160, Doyles NL A0N 1J0
Tel: 709-955-2561; *Fax:* 709-955-3402
gwater@nf.sympatico.ca
To promote the protection & management of ground water in Newfoundland & Labrador
Francis Gale, Contact

Nova Scotia Ground Water Association (NSGWA)
119 Baker's Point Rd., East Jeddore NS B0J 1W0
Tel: 902-845-1084; *Fax:* 902-435-0089
Toll-Free: 888-242-4440
nsgwa@ns.aliantzinc.ca
www.nsgwa.ca
To act as the voice of the industry to all levels of government; To encourage the management & protection of ground water
Noreene McGuire, Secretary-Treasurer

Ontario Ground Water Association (OGWA)
232 Central Ave., London ON N6A 1M8
Tel: 519-245-7194; *Fax:* 519-245-7196
www.ogwa.ca
To protect & promote Ontario's ground water; To provide guidance to members, government representatives, & the public
Craig Stainton, Executive Director

Prince Edward Island Ground Water Association
PO Box 530, 105 Donly Dr. South, Simcoe ON N3Y 4N5
Tel: 902-675-2360; *Fax:* 902-675-2360
To promote the protection of ground water in Prince Edward Island
Watson MacDonald, Contact

Saskatchewan Ground Water Association (SGWA)
PO Box 9434, Saskatoon SK S7K 7E9
Tel: 306-244-7551; *Fax:* 306-343-0001
teksmarts.com/skgwa
To act as the voice of the ground water indusity throughout
Saskatchewan; To promote the management of ground water
throughout the province
Kathleen Watson, Contact

Economics

Association des économistes québécois (ASDÉQ)
#7118, 385, rue Sherbrooke est, Montréal QC H2X 1E3
Tél: 514-342-7537; *Téléc:* 514-342-3967
Ligne sans frais: 866-342-7537
info@economistesquebecois.com
www.economistesquebecois.com
www.linkedin.com/groups/3809359
www.facebook.com/127117010671812
twitter.com/EconomistesQc
Assurer la promotion professionnelle des économistes
Bernard Barrucco, Directeur général

**Association des professionnels en développement
économique du Québec (APDEQ) / Economic
Development Professionals Association of Québec**
CP 297, 455, rue McDonald, Magog QC J1X 3W8
Tél: 819-868-9778; *Téléc:* 819-868-9907
Ligne sans frais: 800-361-8470
info@apdeq.qc.ca
www.apdeq.qc.ca
twitter.com/apdeq
Pour aider les artisans du Développement économique à
acquérir des compétences et de la formation afin de les aider à
réussir
Patrice Gagnon, Directeur général

**Atlantic Provinces Economic Council (APEC) /
Conseil économique des provinces de l'Atlantique**
#500, 5121 Sackville St., Halifax NS B3J 1K1
Tel: 902-422-6516; *Fax:* 902-429-6803
info@apec-econ.ca
www.apec-econ.ca
www.linkedin.com/company/atlantic-provinces-economic-council
twitter.com/APECatlantic
To be the leading advocate for the economic development of the
Atlantic region; To monitor & analyze current & emerging
economic trends & policies; To communicate the results of this
analysis to its members on a regular basis; To consult with a
wide audience; To disseminate its research & policy analysis to
business, government, & the community at large; To advocate
the appropriate public & private sector policy responses
Finn Poschmann, President & CEO

Canada West Foundation (CWF)
#110, 134 - 11th Ave. SE, Calgary AB T2G 0X5
Tel: 403-264-9535; *Toll-Free:* 888-825-5293
cwf@cwf.ca
www.cwf.ca
www.linkedin.com/company/2262878
twitter.com/CanadaWestFdn
A leading source of strategic insight, conducting and
communicating non-partisan economic and public policy
research of importance to the four western provinces and all
Canadians.
Martha Hall Findlay, President & Chief Executive Officer
Colleen Collins, Vice-President, Research
Hector Humphrey, Director, Finance & Administration
Jamie Gradon, Manager, Communications

**Canadian Agricultural Economics Society (CAES) /
Société canadienne d'agroéconomie (SCAE)**
CAES Accounting, PO Box 87030, 331 Bank St., Ottawa ON
K2P 1X0
contact@caes-scae.ca
caes-scae.ca
twitter.com/CAES_AgEcon
To address problems related to the economics of food
production & marketing & the quality of rural life through
extension, research, teaching & policy making in government &
private industry
Emmanuel Yiridoe, President

Canadian CED Network / Réseau canadien de DÉC
PO Box 119E, 59, rue Monfette, Victoriaville QC G6P 1J8
Tel: 819-795-3056; *Fax:* 819-758-2906
Toll-Free: 877-202-2268
info@ccednet-rcdec.ca
ccednet-rcdec.ca
www.youtube.com/user/ccednet
www.linkedin.com/company/canadian-community-economic-dev
elopment-network
www.facebook.com/CCEDNet
twitter.com/CCEDNet_RCDEC
To strengthen communities in Canada by creating economic
opportunities that improve local social & environmental
conditions
Michael Toye, Executive Director
Guylaine Simard, Director, Finance
Melissa Lessard, Coordinator, Administration

**Canadian Economics Association (CEA) /
Association canadienne d'économique**
2053 Main Mall, Vancouver BC V6T 1Z2
Tel: 613-454-5275
office@economics.ca
www.economics.ca
To represent academic economists; To advance economic
knowledge
Nicole Fortin, President
Sonya K. Marion, Executive Director

Canadian Law & Economics Association (CLEA)
Faculty of Law, University of Toronto, 84 Queen's Park
Cres., Toronto ON M5S 2C5
Tel: 416-978-0210; *Fax:* 416-978-7899
www.canlecon.org
To organize & present the CLEA Conference
Nadia Gulezko, Contact

C.D. Howe Institute / Institut C.D. Howe
#300, 67 Yonge St., Toronto ON M5E 1J8
Tel: 416-865-1904; *Fax:* 416-865-1866
cdhowe@cdhowe.org
www.cdhowe.org
www.linkedin.com/company/c.d.-howe-institute
www.facebook.com/cdhoweinstitute
twitter.com/cdhoweinstitute
To identify current & emerging economic & social policy issues
facing Canadians; to recommend particular policy options; to
communicate conclusions of research to domestic &
international audiences.
William B.P. Robson, President & CEO
Daniel Schwanen, Vice-President, Research

**Centre interuniversitaire de recherche en économie
quantitative (CIREQ)**
Pavillon Lionel-Groulx, Université de Montréal, CP 6128,
Succ. Centre-Ville, 3150, rue Jean-Brillant, #C-6088,
Montréal QC H3C 3J7
Tél: 514-343-6557; *Téléc:* 514-343-5831
www.cireqmontreal.com
Recherches dans les domaines de l'économétrie théorique et
appliquée, de l'économie financière et de la théorie économique
Benoît Perron, Directeur

**The Conference Board of Canada / Le Conference
Board du Canada**
Tel: 613-526-3280; *Fax:* 613-526-4857
Toll-Free: 866-711-2262
contactcboc@conferenceboard.ca
www.conferenceboard.ca
www.youtube.com/user/CBoCanada
www.linkedin.com/company/the-conference-board-of-canada
www.facebook.com/ConferenceBoardofCanada
twitter.com/ConfBoardofCda
To be dedicated to applied research, notably in public policy,
economic trends & organizational performance
Susan Black, Chief Executive Officer

**Economic Developers Association of Canada
(EDAC) / Association canadienne de développement
économique (ACDE)**
#205, 1100 South Service Rd., Stoney Creek ON L8E 0C5
Tel: 289-649-1771
info@edac.ca
edac.ca
www.facebook.com/edacacde
twitter.com/E_D_A_C
To contribute to Canada's economic, social & environmental
well-being by advancing economic development; To enhance
professional competence & ethical service
Aileen Murray, President
Penny A. Gardiner, Chief Executive Officer

**Economic Developers Council of Ontario Inc.
(EDCO)**
6506 Marlene Ave., Cornwall ON K6H 7H9
Tel: 613-931-9827; *Fax:* 613-931-9828
edco@edco.on.ca
www.edco.on.ca
www.linkedin.com/company/economic-developers-council-of-ont
ario
www.facebook.com/EDCO1EDCO
twitter.com/edco1edco
To provide a forum for economic development related
educational activities; To increase the profile of EDCO & the
profession; To encourage & create an awareness of economic
development issues with relevant government agencies; To
promote & develop Ontario as a premier location for economic
activity by increasing employment & prosperity, & enhancing the
quality of life within the Ontario municipalities
Heather Lalonde, Executive Director

The Fraser Institute
1770 Burrard St., 4th Fl., Vancouver BC V6J 3G7
Tel: 604-688-0221; *Fax:* 604-688-8539
info@fraserinstitute.org
www.fraserinstitute.org
www.youtube.com/FraserInstitute
www.linkedin.com/company/the-fraser-institute
www.facebook.com/fraserinstitute
twitter.com/FraserInstitute
To redirect public attention to the role competitive markets play
in the economic well-being of all Canadians
Niels Veldhuis, President
Jason Clemens, Executive Vice-President
Manpreet Brar, Director, Human Resources

The North-South Institute (NSI) / L'Institut Nord-Sud
River Building, 1124 Colonel By Dr., 5th Floor, Ottawa ON
K1S 5B6
Tel: 613-520-6655; *Fax:* 613-520-2889
nsi@nsi-ins.ca
www.nsi-ins.ca
www.facebook.com/NSIINS
twitter.com/NSI_INS
To analyze, for Canadians & others, the economic, social &
political implications of global change & to propose policy
alternatives to promote global development & justice

Rotman Institute for International Business (RIIB)
University of Toronto, 105 St. George St., Toronto ON M5S
3E6
Tel: 416-978-5781
riib@rotman.utoronto.ca
www.rotman.utoronto.ca
RIIB merges the former Institute for Policy Analysis & the
Institute for International Business, & focusses on research on
the global business environment, enterprise decision making in
the global economy, & the urban service economy.
Wendy Dobson, Co-Director
Ig Horstman, Co-Director

**Saskatchewan Economic Development Alliance
(SEDA)**
PO Box 113, 131 Wall St., Saskatoon SK S7K 3K1
Tel: 306-384-5817; *Fax:* 306-384-5818
Toll-Free: 877-551-7332
seda@seda.sk.ca
www.seda.sk.ca
www.linkedin.com/company/saskatchewan-economic-developm
ent-association
www.facebook.com/SEDASaskatchewan
twitter.com/saskecdevassoc
To secure the economic future of Saskatchewan by helping
communities to grow
Verona Thibault, Chief Executive Officer

Education

Agence universitaire de la Francophonie (AUF)
CP 49714, Succ. Musée, Montréal QC H3T 2A5
Tél: 514-343-6630; *Téléc:* 514-343-5783
rectorat@auf.org
www.auf.org
www.youtube.com/planeteauf
www.linkedin.com/company/auf
www.facebook.com/aufinternational
twitter.com/auf_org
Le développement, au sein de l'espace francophone, d'une
coopération internationale pour assurer à la fois le dialogue
permanent des cultures et la circulation des personnes, des
idées, des expériences entre institutions universitaires, dans
l'intérêt de l'éducation et du progrès de la science
Slim Khalbous, Recteur

Alberta Assessment Consortium (AAC)
#700, 11010 - 142nd St., Edmonton AB T5N 2R1
Tel: 780-761-0530; *Fax:* 780-761-0533
info@aac.ab.ca
www.aac.ab.ca
twitter.com/AACinfo
Develops a broad range of classroom assessment materials, directly aligned to Alberta curriculum, that address both formative and summative processes.
Sherry Bennett, Executive Director

Alberta Association of Family School Liaison Workers (AAFSLW)
c/o Tonia Koversky, St. Albert Family & Community Support Services, #10, 50 Bellerose Dr., St Albert AB T8N 3L5
Tel: 780-459-1749; *Fax:* 780-458-1260
www.aafslw.ca
www.linkedin.com/groups/6609871
www.facebook.com/AAFSLW
AAFSLW provides an opportunity for networking among professionals through conferences, regional meetings, newsletters, resource sharing, and case conferencing.
Christine Payne, President

Alberta College of Combined Laboratory & X-Ray Technologists (ACCLXT)
206 Pembina Rd., Sherwood Park AB T8H 0L8
Tel: 780-438-3323; *Fax:* 855-299-0829
info@acclxt.ca
www.acclxt.ca
To be responsible for the registration, discipline & competency of all registered Combined Laboratory & X-Ray Technicians / Technologists currently practicing in the province of Alberta; To strive to provide excellence in the combined fields of laboratory, radiography & electrocardiography medicine
Nichol Roy, President
Nicole Stewart, Vice-President
Lyndsay Arndt, Executive Director & Registrar
Sandi Toepfer, Director, Competency & Evaluation

Alberta Educational Facilities Administrators Association (AEFAA)
7 White Pelican Way, Lake Newell Resort AB T1R 0X5
Tel: 403-376-0461
www.aefaa.ca
twitter.com/AlanKloepper
Alan Kloepper, Executive Director

Alberta Home Education Association (AHEA)
AB
www.aheaonline.com
To serve home schooling parents; To support local groups of parents & individuals; To interact with various levels of government to protect the responsibilities of parents
Paul van den Bosch, President

Alberta School Boards Association (ASBA)
#1200, 9925 - 109th St., Edmonton AB T5K 2J8
Tel: 780-482-7311
reception@asba.ab.ca
www.asba.ab.ca
twitter.com/ABSchoolBoards
To promote the availability of high quality schooling for all; To assist member boards in fulfilling their mission of achieving excellence in education
Scott McCormack, Executive Director
Heather Massel, Director, Communications
Heather Rogers, Director, Finance & Corporate Services

Alberta School Councils' Association (ASCA)
#1200, 9925 - 109th St., Edmonton AB T5K 2J8
Tel: 780-454-9867; *Fax:* 780-455-0167
Toll-Free: 800-661-3470
www.albertaschoolcouncils.ca
www.linkedin.com/company/3862745
www.facebook.com/ABschoolcouncil
twitter.com/ABschoolcouncil
To be the voice of parents / families committed to the best possible education for Alberta children, so that they may reach their potential to participate in society in a meaningful & responsible way
Allison Pike, President
Wendy Keiver, Acting Executive Director
Jolaine Kochisarli, Manager, Communications

Alberta Teachers' Association (ATA)
Barnett House, 11010 - 142nd St. NW, Edmonton AB T5N 2R1
Tel: 780-447-9400; *Fax:* 780-455-6481
Toll-Free: 800-232-7208
postmaster@ata.ab.ca
www.teachers.ab.ca
www.youtube.com/user/albertateachers
www.facebook.com/ABteachers
twitter.com/albertateachers
To advance the cause of education in Alberta; To improve the teaching profession; To increase public interest in & support for education; To cooperate with other bodies having similar objectives
Jason C. Schilling, President

Alliance des professeures et professeurs de Montréal (APPM)
8225, boul Saint-Laurent, Montréal QC H2P 2M1
Tél: 514-383-4880; *Téléc:* 514-384-5756
presidence@alliancedesprofs.qc.ca
www.alliancedesprofs.qc.ca
Alain Marois, Président

Association canadienne d'éducation de langue française (ACELF)
#303, 265, rue de la Couronne, Québec QC G1K 6E1
Tél: 418-681-4661; *Téléc:* 418-681-3389
info@acelf.ca
www.acelf.ca
www.youtube.com/acelfcanada
www.facebook.com/acelf.ca
twitter.com/_ACELF
Inspire et soutient le développement et l'action des institutions éducatives francophones du Canada; renforcer la vitalité des communautés francophones
Anne Vinet-Roy, Présidente
Richard Lacombe, Directeur général

Association canadienne des professeurs d'immersion (ACPI) / Canadian Association of Immersion Teachers (CAIT)
#1104, 170, rue Gloucester, Ottawa ON K15 5V5
Tél: 613-230-9111; *Ligne sans frais:* 866-230-9114
bureau@acpi.ca
www.acpi.ca
www.facebook.com/acpimmersion
twitter.com/acpi_
Chantal Bourbonnais, Directrice générale

Association des cadres des centres de la petite enfance (ACCPE) / Association of Managers of Childcare Centers (AMCC)
CP 4042, Succ. D, Montréal QC
Tél: 514-933-3954
info@associationdescadres.ca
www.associationdescadres.ca
Réunir les cadres de centres de la petite enfance; Travailler en collaboration avec le Ministère de la Famille
Isabelle Palardy, Directrice générale

Association des collèges privés du Québec (ACPQ)
1940, boul Henri-Bourassa est, Montréal QC H2B 1S2
Tél: 514-381-8891; *Téléc:* 514-381-4086
Ligne sans frais: 888-381-8891
acpq@acpq.net
www.acpq.net
www.facebook.com/campleadershipacpq
twitter.com/acpq_net
Défendre les intérêts de ses collèges membres et contribuer au développement de l'enseignement collégial privé au Québec
Pierre L'Heureux, Directeur général
Marili B. Desrochers, Chargée de projets

Association des directeurs généraux des commissions scolaires du Québec (ADIGECS)
a/s Directeur exécutif, #212, 195, ch de Chambly, Longueuil QC J4H 3L3
Tél: 450-674-6700; *Téléc:* 450-674-7337
adigecs.qc.ca
Contribuer à l'avancement de l'éducation au Québec; protéger les intérêts de ses membres notamment au chapitre des conditions de travail
Raynald Thibeault, Président
Serge Lefebvre, Directeur exécutif

Association des enseignantes et des enseignants franco-ontariens (AEFO) / Franco-Ontarian Teachers' Association
290 Dupuis St., 4th Fl., Ottawa ON K1L 1B5
Tél: 613-244-2336; *Téléc:* 613-563-7718
Ligne sans frais: 800-267-4217
aefo@aefo.on.ca
www.aefo.on.ca
www.linkedin.com/company/aefo
www.facebook.com/aefo.on.ca
twitter.com/AEFO_ON_CA
De regrouper les travailleuses et les travailleurs au service des établissements publics et privés francophones en Ontario
Pierre Léonard, Directeur général

Association des enseignantes et des enseignants francophones du Nouveau-Brunswick (AEFNB)
CP 712, 650, rue Montgomery, Fredericton NB E3B 5B4
Tél: 506-452-8921; *Téléc:* 506-452-1838
www.aefnb.ca
www.youtube.com/channel/UCjZukUoeNt4styGTFsrxF0A
www.facebook.com/aefnb/
twitter.com/aefnb
Représenter les intérêts des enseignantes et des enseignants francophones de la province; favoriser et maintenir au Nouveau-Brunswick des services éducatifs de langue française de première qualité
Marc Arseneau, Président

Association francophone pour le savoir (ACFAS)
425, rue de la Gauchetière, Montréal QC H2L 2M7
Tél: 514-849-0045; *Téléc:* 514-849-5558
www.acfas.ca
www.youtube.com/user/AcfasTV
linkedin.com/company/acfas----association-francophone-pour-le-savoir
www.facebook.com/acfas
twitter.com/_Acfas
Promouvoir et soutenir la science et la technologie pour encourager le développement culturel et économique de la société
Sophie Montreuil, Directrice générale
Isabelle Gandilhon, Directrice, Opérations

Association of Atlantic Universities (AAU) / Association des universités de l'Atlantique
#403, 5657 Spring Garden Rd., Halifax NS B3J 3R4
Tel: 902-425-4230; *Fax:* 902-425-4233
info@atlanticuniversities.ca
www.atlanticuniversities.ca
www.facebook.com/AssociationOfAtlanticUniversities
twitter.com/aau_aua
To assist in assuring the quality & coordination of higher education in Atlantic Provinces; to provide a forum for university administrators to discuss & coordinate their views, interests & concerns in support of higher education in the Atlantic provinces
Peter Halpin, Executive Director

Association of British Columbia Teachers of English as an Additional Language (BC TEAL)
#206, 640 West Broadway, Vancouver BC V5Z 1G4
Tel: 604-736-6330; *Fax:* 604-736-6306
admin@bcteal.org
www.bcteal.org
To foster & promote effective instruction in English as a second language in BC; To raise the professional status of BC ESL teachers; To promote communication among BC ESL professionals
Jaimie Evoy, Administrative Manager

Association of Canadian Deans of Education (ACDE) / Association Canadienne des Doyens et Doyennes d'Éducation
c/o ACDE Secretariat, 1144 Skana Dr., Delta BC V4M 2L4
Tel: 604-943-6374
acde@telus.net
csse-scee.ca/associations/acde
To advance knowledge & inform practice in educational settings
Sal Badali, President
Katy Ellsworth, Executive Director

Association of Canadian Faculties of Dentistry (ACFD) / Association des facultés dentaires du Canada (AFDC)
University of Manitoba, Dental Bldg., 780 Bannatyne, #D113, Winnipeg MB R3E 0W2
admin@acfd.ca
www.acfd.ca
To assure the quality of dental education & research in Canada; To keep members informed of issues regarding University-based dental education & promote communication between its members

Andrea Esteves, President
Paul Major, Vice-President & Treasurer

Association of Canadian Universities for Northern Studies (ACUNS) / Association universitaire canadienne d'études nordiques
#200, 32 Colonnade Rd., Ottawa ON K2E 7J6
Tel: 613-820-8300
office@acuns.ca
www.acuns.ca
www.instagram.com/acunsaucen
www.facebook.com/acunsaucen
twitter.com/acunsaucen
To encourage the government & private sector to support polar scholarship, which fosters programs to increase public awareness of polar sciences & research; to represent its member universities & colleges, encouraging the establishment of funds & resources to ensure a network of trained researchers, regional managers & educators.
Gary Wilson, President
Jeanette Doucet, Executive Director

Association of Early Childhood Educators Ontario (AECEO)
#206, 489 College St., Toronto ON M6G 1A5
Tel: 416-487-3157; *Fax:* 416-487-3758
Toll-Free: 866-932-3236
info@aeceo.ca
www.aeceo.ca
www.facebook.com/AECEOntario
twitter.com/AECEO
To support early childhood educators throughout Ontario
Rachel Lafferty, Executive Coordinator
Sonia Tavares, Coordinator, Community Organizing & Communications
Sue Parker, Office Manager

Association of Educational Researchers of Ontario (AERO) / Association ontarienne des chercheurs et chercheuse en éducation
c/o Research & Information Services, Toronto District School Board, 1 Civic Centre Court, Lower Level, Toronto ON M9C 2B3
Tel: 416-394-4929; *Fax:* 416-394-4946
info@aero-aoce.org
www.aero-aoce.org
To promote & improve research, education, planning & development pertaining to education in the Ontario school system
Terry Spencer, President

Association of Faculties of Medicine of Canada (AFMC) / L'Association des facultés de médecine du Canada (AFMC)
#100, 2733 Lancaster Rd., Ottawa ON K1B 0A9
Tel: 613-730-0687; *Fax:* 613-730-1196
info@afmc.ca
www.afmc.ca
www.youtube.com/user/afmcottawa
linkedin.com/company/the-association-of-faculties-of-medicine-of-canada
twitter.com/afmc_e
To represent the interests of members in medical research policy formulation; To promote & advance academic medicine through the review & development of standards for medical education, through the development of national policies appropriate to the aims & purposes of Canadian faculties of medicine, through the fostering of research & through representation of Canadian faculties of medicine to professional associations & governments
Genevieve Moineau, President & CEO

Association of Independent Schools & Colleges in Alberta (AISCA)
#201, 11830 - 111 Ave., Edmonton AB T5G 0E1
Tel: 780-469-9868; *Fax:* 780-469-9880
office@aisca.ab.ca
www.aisca.ab.ca
To defend & promote the right of parents to determine the context for their children's education; To create a positive social, fiscal & political environment in which independent schools are free to maintain their identity as they serve the public interest; To support & encourage independent schools in providing significant educational choices for parents & their children; To foster public understanding & appreciation of independent schools & their services
John Jagersma, Executive Director

Association of Registrars of the Universities & Colleges of Canada (ARUCC) / Association des registraires des universités et collèges du Canada
c/o Greg McPherson, PO Box 71157, Stn. Silver Springs, Calgary AB T3B 5K2
Tel: 403-541-0911
info@arucc.ca
www.arucc.ca
To address the professional needs of student administrative services personnel in universities
Romesh Vadivel, President

Association of University Forestry Schools of Canada (AUFSC) / Association des écoles forestières universitaires du Canada
c/o University of New Brunswick, Fredericton NB E3B 5A3
Tel: 506-458-7775
www.aefuc-aufsc.ca
Van Lantz, Chair

Association pour une solidarité syndicale étudiante (ASSE)
CP 383, 2065, rue Parthenais, Montréal QC H2K 3T1
Tél: 514-390-0110
executif@asse-solidarite.qc.ca
www.asse-solidarite.qc.ca
Voué à la défense des intérêts des étudiants et étudiantes du Québec
Mireille Allard, Secrétaire aux finances

Association provinciale des enseignantes et enseignants du Québec (APEQ) / Québec Provincial Association of Teachers (QPAT)
#1, 17035, boul Brunswick, Kirkland QC H9H 5G6
Tél: 514-694-9777; *Téléc:* 514-694-0189
Ligne sans frais: 800-361-9870
www.qpat-apeq.qc.ca
www.facebook.com/qpatapeq
Alan Lombard, Executive Director

Association québécoise des cadres scolaires (AQCS)
#170, 1195, av Lavigerie, Québec QC G1V 4N3
Tél: 418-654-0014; *Téléc:* 418-654-1719
info@aqcs.ca
www.aqcs.ca
www.youtube.com/user/ACSQ72
www.facebook.com/230806163669399
twitter.com/ACSQ_LT
L'AQCS rassemble, forme et soutient ses membres. Elle les représente et prend position dans tous les aspects qui affectent leur vie professionnelle. Elle contribue également au développement du réseau de l'éducation.
Rémi Asselin, Président
Jean-François Parent, Directeur général

Association québécoise des professeurs de français (AQPF)
75, rue Jérémie, St-Boniface QC G0X 2L0
Tél: 450-923-9422
info@aqpf.qc.ca
www.aqpf.qc.ca
www.facebook.com/aqpfqc
Les principaux champs d'intervention sont - la didactique et l'enseignement du français langue maternelle du préscolaire à l'université; l'enseignement du français aux adultes; l'alphabétisation; l'enseignement du français langue seconde; promotion de la langue française, de la culture québécoise et de la francophonie
Katya Pelletier, Présidente
Anne Robitaille, Vice-présidente, Administration

Association québécoise du personnel de direction des écoles (AQPDE)
#235, 3291, ch Ste-Foy, Québec QC G1X 3V2
Tél: 418-781-0700; *Téléc:* 418-781-0276
info@aqpde.ca
www.aqpde.ca
Défendre et promouvoir les intérêts professionnels, sociaux et économiques des membres, favoriser leur participation et établir une concertation avec les autres organismes du réseau de l'éducation pour assurer les meilleures conditions de ses membres
Danielle Boucher, Présidente

Atlantic Conference of Independent Schools (ACIS)
708 Main St., Wolfville NS B4P 1G4
Tel: 902-542-2237
gmitchell@landmarkeast.org
To promote the role of independent school education in the Maritime provinces; To coordinate educational, sporting & other activities of mutual interest to member schools

Black Educators Association of Nova Scotia (BEA)
2136 Gottingen St., Halifax NS B3K 3B3
Tel: 902-424-7036; *Fax:* 902-424-0636
Toll-Free: 800-565-3398
info@theblackeducators.ca
www.theblackeducators.ca
To monitor & ensure the development of an equitable education system, so that African Nova Scotians are able to achieve their maximum potential
Ken Fells, President
Robert Upshaw, Executive Director

Black Studies Centre (BSC)
1968, boul de Maisonneuve ouest, Montréal QC H3H 1K5
Tel: 514-933-0798
To provide a wide range of services to the Montreal community & to its various institutions; To be committed to the continued educational development of Montreal's Black community & to the recognition of the contributions they have made in helping Montreal to grow as a city
Clarence S. Bayne, President

British Columbia Career College Association (BCCCA)
10040 King George Ave., Surrey BC V37 2W4
Tel: 778-869-2605
membership@bccca.com
www.bccca.com
twitter.com/thebccca
To promote & support post secondary schools, stakeholders, students & all other interested parties involved in private post-secondary education & training in BC
Vacant, Chief Executive Officer
Lois McNestry, President

British Columbia Confederation of Parent Advisory Councils (BCCPAC)
#2288 Elgin Ave., #C, Port Coquitlam BC V3C 2B2
Tel: 604-474-0524; *Toll-Free:* 866-529-4397
info@bccpac.bc.ca
www.bccpac.bc.ca
www.facebook.com/YOURBCCPAC
twitter.com/bccpac
To advance the public school education & well-being of children in British Columbia
John Gaiptman, Chief Executive Officer

British Columbia Principals & Vice-Principals Association (BCPVPA)
#200, 525 - 10 Ave. West, Vancouver BC V5Z 1K9
Tel: 604-689-3399; *Fax:* 604-877-5380
Toll-Free: 800-663-0432
www.bcpvpa.bc.ca
www.instagram.com/bcpvpa
twitter.com/bcpvpa
To provide legal & contractual services advice, organize student leadership activities, & provide professional development programs
Kevin Reimer, Executive Director

British Columbia School Trustees Association (BCSTA) / Association des commissaires d'écoles de Colombie-Britannique
1580 West Broadway, 4th Fl., Vancouver BC V6J 5K9
Tel: 604-734-2721; *Fax:* 604-732-4559
bcsta@bcsta.org
www.bcsta.org
www.linkedin.com/company/bc-school-trustees-association
twitter.com/bc_sta
To promote effective boards of public school trustees working together for BC students; To improve student achievement through community engagement
Mike Roberts, Chief Executive Officer
Jodi Olstead, Director, Finance & Human Resources
Mike P. Gagel, Director, Information & Education Technology

British Columbia Science Teachers' Association (BCScTA)
BC
bcscta@gmail.com
bcscta.ca
www.youtube.com/user/bcscta
www.facebook.com/bcscta
twitter.com/bcscta
John Munro, President
Favian Yee, Secretary

British Columbia Teachers of English Language Arts
BC
psac46@bctf.ca
bctela.ca
www.instagram.com/bctela
www.facebook.com/groups/15625655071
twitter.com/BCTELA
Kyle McKillop, President

British Columbia Teachers' Federation (BCTF) / Fédération des enseignants de la Colombie-Britannique
#100, 550 West 6th Ave., Vancouver BC V5Z 4P2
Tel: 604-871-2283; Toll-Free: 800-663-9163
webinfo@bctf.ca
bctf.ca
www.youtube.com/user/BCTFvids
www.facebook.com/BCTeachersFederation
twitter.com/bctf
To represent public school teachers in the province of British Columbia; To support provincial specialist associations, such as the British Columbia Teacher-Librarians' Association & the British Columbia Music Educators' Association; To advocate for the professional, economic & social goals of teachers
Teri Mooring, President
Amber Mitchell, Executive Director

Bureau de coopération interuniversitaire (BCI)
#200, 500, rue Sherbrooke ouest, Montréal QC H3A 3C6
Tél: 514-288-8524; Téléc: 514-288-0554
info@bci-qc.ca
www.bci-qc.ca
Est un organisme privé qui regroupe, sur une base volontaire, tous les établissements universitaires québécois; sert de forum permanent d'échanges et de concertation qui permet aux gestionnaires de partager leurs expériences en vue d'améliorer l'efficacité générale du système universitaire québécois.
Claude Bédard, Directeur général

Canadian Accredited Independent Schools (CAIS)
PO Box 56, Jordan ON L0R 1S0
Tel: 905-683-5658
www.cais.ca
www.linkedin.com/company/canadian-accredited-independent-schools-cais-
twitter.com/CAIS_Schools
Patti MacDonald, Executive Director
Tracey Nolan, Executive Assistant

Canadian Alliance of Student Associations (CASA) / Alliance canadienne des associations étudiantes (ACAE)
410 Slater St., Ottawa ON K1P 6E2
Tel: 613-236-3457; Fax: 613-236-2386
www.casa-acae.com
www.youtube.com/user/CASAACAE
www.facebook.com/casa.acae
twitter.com/casadaily
To be a national voice for Canada's post-secondary students
Shifrah Gadansetti, Chair
Michael McDonald, Executive Director
MacAndrew Clarke, Officer, Government & Stakeholder Relations
Lindsay Boyd, Officer
Rosanne Waters, Policy & Research Analyst

Canadian Association for American Studies (CAAS) / Association d'études américaines au Canada (AEAC)
webmaster@american-studies.ca
american-studies.ca
www.facebook.com/groups/75085833950
twitter.com/CAASCanada
To encourage study & research concerning the United States; To examine the implications of American studies for Canada & the world
Ross Bullen, President

Canadian Association for Curriculum Studies (CACS)
c/o Canadian Society for the Study of Education, #204, 260 Dalhousie St., Ottawa ON K1N 7E4
Tel: 613-241-0018; Fax: 613-241-0019
csse-scee@csse.ca
csse-scee.ca/associations/cacs-acec
twitter.com/cacs_acec
To support inquiries into & discussions of curricula that are of interest to Canadian educators
Sean Wiebe, Co-President
Paul Zanazanian, Co-President

Canadian Association for Educational Psychology (CAEP) / L'association Canadienne en psychopedagogie (ACP)
c/o Canadian Society for the Study of Education, #204, 260 Dalhousie St., Ottawa ON K1N 7E4
Tel: 613-241-0018; Fax: 613-241-0019
caepacp.wordpress.com
www.facebook.com/CAEP.ACP
To research, discuss & encourage the study of educational psychology
Jeffrey MacCormack, President

Canadian Association for Graduate Studies (CAGS) / Association canadienne pour les études supérieures (ACES)
#301, 260 St. Patrick St., Ottawa ON K1N 5K5
Tel: 613-562-0949; Fax: 613-562-9009
info@cags.ca
www.cags.ca
To promote excellence in graduate education; To foster research, scholarship, & creative activity; To provide a nationwide link for the exchange of information between graduate schools & granting councils, research, business, & industrial sectors, & all levels of government; To hold meetings & conferences; To publish materials to advance graduate education; To develop & maintain national standards for graduate degree programs; To support the regular external evaluation of these standards; To deal with other matters of concern to Deans & Associate Deans of graduate studies
Sally Rutherford, Executive Director
Brigitte Lawson, Administrator

Canadian Association for Social Work Education (CASWE) / Association canadienne pour la formation en travail social (ACFTS)
#410, 383 Parkdale Ave., Ottawa ON K1Y 4R4
Tel: 613-792-1953; Toll-Free: 888-342-6522
admin@caswe-acfts.ca
caswe-acfts.ca
To advance university education for the profession of social work; To accredit professional social work educational programs, based on high educational standards; To increase understanding of the nature & role of social work practice & social welfare
Stéphane Grenier, President, -
Alexandra Wright, PhD, Executive Director

Canadian Association for Teacher Education (CATE) / Association canadienne pour la formation des enseignants (ACFE)
c/o Canadian Society for the Study of Education, #204, 260 Dalhousie St., Ottawa ON K1N 7E4
Tel: 613-241-0018; Fax: 613-241-0019
cate-acfe.ca
twitter.com/AcfeCate
To encourage scholarly study & research in education, with special emphasis on teacher education; to provide for the membership a national forum for the presentation & discussion of significant studies in education, with special emphasis on teacher education
Cathryn Smith, President

Canadian Association for the Advancement of Netherlandic Studies (CAANS) / Association canadienne pour l'avancement des études néerlandaises (ACAEN)
c/o Peter Tijssen, 76 Winston Circle, Montréal QC H9S 4X6
caans-acaen.ca
To stimulate awareness & interest in & to promote the study of Netherlandic languages (Dutch, Flemish, Afrikaans), as well as Netherlandic literature, history & culture; To provide a forum for discussion in these areas, hold an annual conference, publish research & sponsor relevant cultural & scholarly activities such as meetings, presentations, lectures & discussions
Tanja Collet, President
Peter Tijssen, Secretary-Treasurer

Canadian Association for the Study of Discourse & Writing (CASDW) / Association canadienne de rédactologie (ACR)
c/o W. Brock MacDonald, Woodsworth College, University of Toronto, 119 St. George St., Toronto ON M5S 1A9
casdwacr.wordpress.com
To advance the study & teaching of discourse, writing & communication in both academic & nonacademic settings
W. Brock MacDonald, Treasurer, Membership

Canadian Association for the Study of Educational Administration (CASEA) / Association canadienne pour l'étude de l'administration scolaire (ACÉAS)
c/o Canadian Society for the Study of Education, #204, 260 Dalhousie St., Ottawa ON K1N 7E4
Tel: 613-241-0018; Fax: 613-241-0019
csse-scee.ca/associations/casea-aceas
To promote the study of educational administration among scholars & practitioners
Jacqueline Kirk, President

Canadian Association for the Study of Women & Education (CASWE) / Association canadienne pour l'étude sur les femmes et l'éducation (ACÉFÉ)
c/o Canadian Society for the Study of Education, #204, 260 Dalhousie St., Ottawa ON K1N 7E4
Tel: 613-241-0018; Fax: 613-241-0019
canadianwomenineducation.net
twitter.com/CASWE1
Kathy Sanford, President

Canadian Association for University Continuing Education (CAUCE) / Association pour l'éducation permanente dans les universités du Canada (AEPUC)
c/o CAUCE Secretariat, Univ. of Saskatchewan, 221 Cumberland Ave. North, Saskatoon SK S7N 1M3
Tel: 306-966-5604; Fax: 306-966-5590
www.cauce-aepuc.ca
www.linkedin.com/groups/13527992
twitter.com/CAUCE_AEPUC
To enlarge the quality & scope of educational opportunities for adults at the university level
Carolyn Young, President

Canadian Association of College & University Student Services (CACUSS) / Association des services aux étudiants des universités et collèges du Canada (ASEUCC)
#402, 150 Eglinton Ave. East, Toronto ON M4P 1E8
Tel: 647-345-1116
contact@cacuss.ca
www.cacuss.ca
www.facebook.com/cacuss
twitter.com/cacusstweets
To represent & serve persons who work in Canadian post-secondary institutions in student affairs & services; To offer advocacy & assistance on issues that affect the quality of student life on Canadian university & college campuses
Mark Solomon, President
Jennifer Hamilton, Executive Director
Jonathan Elias, Coordinator, Digital Communications & Technology

Canadian Association of Foundations of Education (CAFE) / Association canadienne des fondements de l'éducation (ACFE)
c/o Canadian Society for the Study of Education, #204, 260 Dalhousie St., Ottawa ON K1N 7E4
Tel: 613-241-0018; Fax: 613-241-0019
cafe.acefe@gmail.com
www.cafe-acefe.com
To provide a forum for discussing the contribution of the social sciences & humanities (eg. history of education, philosophy of education, sociology of education) to educational theory, research & practice
Lynn Lemisko, President

Canadian Association of Geographers (CAG) / Association canadienne des géographes
60 University Private, Ottawa ON K1N 6N5
Tel: 613-562-5208
info@cag-acg.ca
www.cag-acg.ca
To promote the discipline of geography in Canada & internationally
Sanjay Nepal, President
Joseph Leydon, Secretary-Treasurer

Canadian Association of Montessori Teachers (CAMT)
312 Oakwood Crt., Newmarket ON L3Y 3C8
Tel: 416-755-7184; Fax: 866-328-7974
info@camt100.ca
www.camt100.ca
www.facebook.com/montessoriCAMT
To advance the standards of Montessori teaching & to improve the quality of Montessori education throughout Canada
Claudia Langlois, President

Canadian Association of Principals (CAP) / Association canadienne des directeurs d'école
#220, 300 Earl Grey Dr., Ottawa ON K2T 1C1

Tel: 613-839-0768
cdnprincipals.com
www.facebook.com/599842980034960
twitter.com/CdnPrincipals

To represent the professional perspectives of principals & vice-principals at the national level & to provide the leadership necessary to ensure quality educational opportunities for Canadian students
Jill Sooley-Perley, Executive Assistant

Canadian Association of Research Administrators (CARA) / Association canadienne des administratrices et des administrateurs de recherche (ACAAR)
#1710, 350 Albert St., Ottawa ON K1R 1B1

Tel: 289-244-3744
webinars@cara-acaar.ca
cara-acaar.ca
twitter.com/cara_acaar

To advance the research administrator profession; To improve the efficiency & effectiveness of research administration at post-secondary institutions; To advocate for its membership through representation & unity; To foster & encourage collaboration with organizations in related disciplines
Sarah Lampson, Executive Director
Kaleb Antonides, Coordinator, Professional Development & Membership Services

Canadian Association of Schools of Nursing (CASN) / Association canadienne des écoles de sciences infirmières (ACESI)
#450, 1145 Hunt Club Rd., Ottawa ON K1V 0Y3

Tel: 613-235-3150; *Fax:* 613-235-4476
inquire@casn.ca
www.casn.ca
www.linkedin.com/company/canadian-association-of-schools-of-nursing-association-canadienne-des-ecole-de-sciences-infirmier
es
www.facebook.com/574645555928679
twitter.com/CASN43

To represent Canadian nursing programs; To act as the national voice for nursing education & nursing research
Cynthia Baker, Executive Director

Canadian Association of Second Language Teachers (CASLT) / Association canadienne des professeurs de langues secondes (ACPLS)
2490 Don Reid Dr., Ottawa ON K1H 1E1

Tel: 613-727-0994; *Toll-Free:* 877-727-0994
admin@caslt.org
www.caslt.org
www.youtube.com/channel/UCcSs2AnBpazKmo4N1H5YVVw
www.facebook.com/CASLT.ACPLS
twitter.com/CASLT_ACPLS

To promote & advance nationally learning of second languages; To encourage activities & research in field of second language; To create opportunities for professional development; To promote research & information exchange among second language educators
Francis Potié, Executive Director

Canadian Association of Slavists (CAS) / Association canadienne des slavistes
Dept. of History & Classics, University of Alberta, #2, 28 Tory Bldg., Edmonton AB T6G 2H4

Tel: 780-492-2566; *Fax:* 780-492-9125
csp@ualberta.ca
www.ualberta.ca/~csp/cas/contact.html

To operate a learned society comprising scholars & professionals with interests in the social, economic, & political life of Slavic people, in addition to their languages, cultures, & histories; To promote understanding of Slavic societies & dialogue; To disseminate information about the past & present of the Slavic world
Alison Rowley, President

Canadian Association of University Business Officers (CAUBO) / Association canadienne du personnel administratif universitaire (ACPAU)
#315, 350 Albert St., Ottawa ON K1R 1B1

Tel: 613-230-6760; *Fax:* 613-563-7739
caubo-acpau@caubo.ca
www.caubo.ca

To promote the professional & effective management of the administrative, financial & business affairs of higher education; To have the professional standards of its members & to strengthen the contribution of higher education to the well being of Canada
Nathalie Laporte, Executive Director

James Butler, Director, Faculty Bargaining Services
Tamara Nemchin, Associate Director

Canadian Association of University Teachers (CAUT) / Association canadienne des professeures et professeurs d'université (ACPPU)
2705 Queensview Dr., Ottawa ON K2B 8K2

Tel: 613-820-2270
acppu@caut.ca
www.caut.ca
www.linkedin.com/company/canadian-association-of-university-t
eachers
www.facebook.com/CAUT.ACPPU
twitter.com/CAUT_ACPPU

To act as the national voice for academic staff; To promote academic freedom; To improve the quality & accessibility of post-secondary education in Canada
David Robinson, Executive Director

Canadian Association of University Teachers of German (CAUTG) / L'Association des professeurs d'allemand des universités canadiennes (APAUC)
c/o Michel Mallet, Université de Moncton, 18, av Antonine-Maillet, Moncton NB E1A 3E9

www.cautg.org

To promote studies & research in Germanic Studies at the post-secondary level
Michel Mallet, Secretary
James M. Skidmore, Treasurer

Canadian Bureau for International Education (CBIE) / Bureau canadien de l'éducation internationale (BCEI)
#1550, 220 Laurier Ave. West, Ottawa ON K1P 5Z9

Tel: 613-237-4820; *Fax:* 613-237-1073
communications@cbie.ca
www.cbie-bcei.ca
www.youtube.com/user/cbiebcei
www.linkedin.com/company/the-canadian-bureau-for-internation
al-education.com
www.facebook.com/cbie.ca
twitter.com/cbie_bcei

To be the national voice advancing Canadian international education by creating & mobilizing expertise, knowledge, opportunity & leadership
Larissa Beoz, President & CEO
Karen Dalkie, Vice-President, Development & Partnerships

Canadian Committee of Graduate Students in Education (CCGSE) / Comité canadien des étudiants et étudiantes aux cycles supérieurs en éducation (CCÉÉCSÉ)
c/o Canadian Society for the Study of Education, #204, 260 Dalhousie St., Ottawa ON K1N 7E4

Tel: 613-241-0018; *Fax:* 613-241-0019
csse-scee.ca/associations/ccgse-ccee

To be the graduate student caucus within the Canadian Society for the Study of Education
Josianne Robert, President

Canadian Council for the Advancement of Education (CCAE) / Le Conseil canadien pour l'avancement de l'éducation
#310, 4 Cataraqui St., Kingston ON K7K 1Z7

Tel: 613-531-9213; *Fax:* 613-531-0626
admin@ccaecanada.org
www.ccaecanada.org
twitter.com/CCAECanada

To promote excellence in educational advancement through networking opportunities, professional development, & mutual support
Mark Hazlett, Executive Director

Canadian Education Association (CEA) / Association canadienne d'éducation (ACE)
#703, 60 St. Clair Ave. East, Toronto ON M4T 1N5

Tel: 416-591-6300; *Fax:* 416-591-5345
Toll-Free: 866-803-9549
info@edcan.ca
www.edcan.ca
www.youtube.com/user/CdnEducAssn
www.linkedin.com/company/canadian-education-association-cea
-association-canadienne-d-ducation-ace
www.facebook.com/cea.ace
twitter.com/EdCanNet

To promote educational change in Canada
Max Cooke, Chief Executive Officer
Mia San Jose, Manager, Operations

Canadian Educational Researchers' Association (CERA)
c/o Canadian Society for the Study of Education, #204, 260 Dalhousie St., Ottawa ON K1N 7E4

Tel: 613-241-0018; *Fax:* 613-241-0019
www.ceraacce.ca

To improve the quality & quantity of educational research; To act as the voice for the educational research community throughout Canada
Christopher DeLuca, President
Laurie Hellsten-Bzovey, Executive Officer

Canadian Faculties of Agriculture & Veterinary Medicine (CFAVM) / Facultés d'agriculture et de médecine vétérinaire du Canada
#204, 532 Montreal Rd., Ottawa ON K1K1 4R4

Tel: 613-822-4442
info@acfavm.ca
www.cfavm.ca

To work collaboratively to strengthen Canadian academic research & teaching; to be the representative for faculties of agriculture & veterinary medicine; to form ties with faculties of agriculture & veterinary medicine around the world
Roger Larson, P.Ag., Executive Director

Canadian Federation of Business School Deans (CFBSD) / Fédération canadienne des doyens des écoles d'administration (FCDEA)
3000, ch de la Côte-Sainte-Catherine, Montréal QC H3T 2A7

Tel: 514-340-7116; *Fax:* 514-340-7275
info@cfbsd.ca
cfbsd.ca

To encourage the professional development of business school administrators; To promote excellence in management education; To represent management education to the government, the business community, & the media
Timothy Daus, Executive Director
Bahram Dadgostar, Chair
Jerry Tomberlin, Vice-Chair
Robert Mantha, Secretary-Treasurer

Canadian Federation of Students (CFS) / Fédération canadienne des étudiantes et étudiants (FCEE)
#200, 2725 Queensview Dr., Ottawa ON K2B 0A1

Tel: 613-232-7394
info@cfs-fcee.ca
www.cfs-fcee.ca
www.facebook.com/cfsfcee
twitter.com/CFSFCEE

To represent the collective interests of college & university students across Canada; To act as a unified voice for Canadian university & college students
Kien Saningong Azinwi, Chair
Nicole Brayiannis, Deputy Chair
Alannah Mckay, Treasurer

Canadian Federation of University Women (CFUW) / Fédération canadienne des femmes diplômées des universités (FCFDU)
#502, 331 Cooper St., Ottawa ON K2P 0G5

Tel: 613-234-8252; *Fax:* 613-234-8221
Toll-Free: 888-220-9606
cfuwgen@rogers.com
www.cfuw.org
www.facebook.com/cfuw.fcfdu
twitter.com/cfuwfcfdu

To pursue knowledge, promote education & improve the status of women & human rights; To participate actively in public affairs in a spirit of cooperation & friendship
Robin Jackson, Executive Director
Betty Dunlop, Manager, Fellowship Program
Yasmin Strautins, Coordinator, Advocacy

Canadian Foundation for Economic Education (CFEE) / Fondation d'éducation économique
#201, 110 Eglinton Ave. West, Toronto ON M4R 1A3

Tel: 416-968-2236; *Fax:* 416-968-0488
Toll-Free: 888-570-7610
mail@cfee.org
www.cfee.org
www.instagram.com/cfee_
www.facebook.com/886569074767378
twitter.com/cfee1

To enhance the economic capabilities of Canadians
Gary Rabbior, President
Joe Clark, Director, Communications

Canadian History of Education Association (CHEA) / L'Association canadienne d'histoire de l'éducation (ACHE)
University of Saskatchewan, College of Education, 28 Campus Dr., Saskatoon SK S7N 0X1
www.ache-chea.ca
www.facebook.com/achechea
twitter.com/CHEA_ACHE
Kristina Llewellyn, President

Canadian Home & School Federation (CHSF) / Fédération canadienne des associations foyer-école (FCAFE)
618 Bronson Settlement Rd., Red Bank Queens County NB E4A 2K9
www.canadianhomeandschoolfederation.ca
To improve the quality of Canadian public education available to children & youth; To act as the national voice of parents with children in public schools
Arlene Morell, President

Canadian Network for Innovation in Education (CNIE) / Réseau canadien pour l'innovation en éducation (RCIÉ)
#204, 260 Dalhousie St., Ottawa ON K1N 7E4
Tel: 613-241-0018; Fax: 613-241-0019
cnie-rcie@cnie-rcie.ca
www.cnie-rcie.ca
www.facebook.com/CNIE.RCIE
twitter.com/CNIE_RCIE
To develop & promote the use of technologies, practices & policies that foster access to learning for students
Michael Dabrowski, President
Tim Howard, Director, Administration

Canadian School Boards Association (CSBA) / L'Association canadienne des commissions/conseils scolaires (ACCCS)
91 Sherwood Dr., Wolfville NS B4P 2K5
Tel: 902-456-5574
info@cdnsba.org
www.cdnsba.org
www.facebook.com/cdnsba
twitter.com/cdnsba
To support jurisdictional school board associations in their mandates; To advocate on national, collective interests of Canadian children; To promote the role democratically elected school boards play in ensuring quality & equitable education in Canada
Laurie French, President
Carolyn Broady, Vice-President

Canadian Society for Education through Art (CSEA) / Société canadienne d'éducation par l'art (SCEA)
PO Box 1700, Stn. CSC, University of Victoria, Victoria BC V8W 2Y2
Tel: 250-721-7896; Fax: 250-721-7598
office.csea@gmail.com
www.instagram.com/csea_scea
www.facebook.com/ArtEducationCanada
twitter.com/CSEA_SCEA
To unite art educators, gallery educators, & others wtih similar interests & concerns
Peter Vietgen, President
Mary-Jane Emme, Secretary General

Canadian Society for the Study of Education (CSSE) / Société canadienne pour l'étude de l'éducation (SCÉÉ)
#204, 260 Dalhousie St., Ottawa ON K1N 7E4
Tel: 613-241-0018; Fax: 613-241-0019
csse-scee@csse.ca
csse-scee.ca
twitter.com/CSSESCEE
To advance knowledge & inform practice in educational settings; To promote the advancement of Canadian research & scholarship in education; To provide for the discussion of studies, issues & trends in education & for the dissemination of research findings; To promote exchange among members & other educational researchers in Canada & internationally; To foster partnerships &, through educational research, influence public policy & help determine the nature, structure & funding of the research agenda
Tim Howard, Director, Administration

Canadian Society for the Study of Higher Education (CSSHE) / La Société canadienne pour l'étude de l'enseignement supérieur (SCEES)
#204, 260 Dalhousie St., Ottawa ON K1N 7E4
Tel: 613-241-0018; Fax: 613-241-0019
csshe-scees@csse.ca
www.csshe-scees.ca
twitter.com/csshescees
To advance the knowledge of post-secondary education through the promotion of research & its dissemination through publications & learned meetings
Kathleen Matheos, President
Tim Howard, Director, Administration

Canadian Teachers' Federation (CTF) / Fédération canadienne des enseignantes et des enseignants (FCE)
2490 Don Reid Dr., Ottawa ON K1H 1E1
Tel: 613-232-1505; Fax: 613-232-1886
Toll-Free: 866-283-1505
info@ctf-fce.ca
www.ctf-fce.ca
www.youtube.com/user/canadianteachers
www.facebook.com/CTF.FCE
twitter.com/CanTeachersFed
To promote a strong publicly funded education system for Canada, one that enhances the country's competitiveness in a knowledge based global economy & gives children the opportunity to become active, engaged citizens
Shelley L. Morse, President
Cassandra Hallett, Secretary General

Canadian Test Centre Inc. (CTC) / Services d'évaluation pédagogique
#10, 80 Citizen Ct., Markham ON L6G 1A7
Tel: 905-513-6636; Fax: 905-513-6639
Toll-Free: 800-668-1006
info@canadiantestcentre.com
www.canadiantestcentre.com
www.youtube.com/user/CanadianTestCentre
To publish & distribute test products; To support teachers to make their testing programs work; To invest in research & development projects which aim to improve the measurement & evaluation of student ability & achievement
Ernest W. Cheng, Managing Director

Canadian University & College Conference Organizers Association (CUCCOA) / Association des coordonnateurs de congrès des universités et des collèges du Canada (ACCUCC)
312 Oakwood Ct., Newmarket ON L3Y 3C8
Tel: 905-954-0102; Fax: 905-895-1630
inquiries@cuccoa.org
www.cuccoa.org
Exists for the purpose of information sharing, professional development & group marketing
Carol Ford, Manager

Career Colleges Ontario (CCO)
#2, 155 Lynden Rd., Brantford ON N3R 8A7
Tel: 519-752-2124; Fax: 519-752-3649
www.careercollegesontario.ca
www.linkedin.com/company/ontario-association-of-career-colleges
www.facebook.com/careercollegesontario
twitter.com/c_c_ontario
To act as the voice for the private career college sector in Ontario
Paul Kitchin, Executive Director
Lorna Mills, Manager, Office & Financial Aid

Centre d'animation de développement et de recherche en éducation (CADRÉ)
1940, boul Henri-Bourassa est, Montréal QC H2B 1S2
Tél: 514-381-8891; Ligne sans frais: 888-381-8891
www.cadre21.org
twitter.com/LeCADRE21
Accompagner les intervenants francophones du monde de l'éducation dans leur réflexion, leur développement professionnel et leur veille sur les grands enjeux de l'éducation
Jacques Cool, Directeur

Centre franco-ontarien de ressources pédagogiques (CFORP)
435, rue Donald, Ottawa ON K1K 4X5
Tél: 613-747-8000; Téléc: 613-747-2808
Ligne sans frais: 877-742-3677
cforp@cforp.ca
www.cforp.ca
www.instagram.com/cforp
www.linkedin.com/company/cforp
www.facebook.com/cforp
twitter.com/CFORP
Produit et diffuse des ressources pédagogiques et offrir des services destinés à soutenir l'éducation en langue française
Claude Deschamps, Directeur général
Penny Bell, Directrice exécutive, Administration, Finances et Ressources humaines

Colleges and Institutes Canada (CICan) / Collèges et instituts Canada
#701, 1 Rideau St., Ottawa ON K1N 8S7
Tel: 613-746-2222; Fax: 613-746-6721
info@collegesinstitutes.ca
www.collegesinstitutes.ca
www.instagram.com/College_can
www.linkedin.com/company/collegesinstitutes
www.facebook.com/collegesinstitutes
twitter.com/CollegeCan
To represent publicly supported colleges, institutes, cégeps, & polytechnics in Canada & internationally
Denise Amyot, President & CEO
Leah Jurkovic, Director, Communications & Stakeholder Engagement
Pat Serediuk, Manager, Human Resources

Colleges Ontario
PO Box 88, #1600, 20 Bay St., Toronto ON M5J 2N8
Tel: 647-258-7670; Fax: 647-258-7699
www.collegesontario.org
www.youtube.com/user/CollegesOntario1
www.linkedin.com/company/network-for-innovation-and-entrepreneurship
www.facebook.com/CollegesOntario
twitter.com/CollegesOntario
To represent Ontario colleges; To advocate on provincial & national issues on behalf of its membership
Linda Franklin, President & CEO
Rob Savage, Director, Communications
Caroline Donkin, Director, Member Services & Special Projects
Bill Summers, Vice-President, Research & Policy

The Commonwealth of Learning (COL)
#2500, 4710 Kingsway, Burnaby BC V5H 4M2
Tel: 604-775-8200; Fax: 604-775-8210
info@col.org
www.col.org
www.youtube.com/user/comlearn
www.linkedin.com/company/commonwealth-of-learning
www.facebook.com/COL4D
twitter.com/COL4D
To create & widen access to education & to improve its quality, utilising distance education techniques & associated communications technologies to meet the particular requirements of member countries
Asha S. Kanwar, President & CEO
Doris McEachern, Director, Finance, Administration & Human Resources

The Comparative & International Education Society of Canada (CIESC) / La Société canadienne d'éducation comparée et internationale (SCECI)
c/o Canadian Society for the Study of Education, #204, 260 Dalhousie St., Ottawa ON K1N 7E4
Tel: 613-241-0018; Fax: 613-241-0019
ciescanada.ca
www.facebook.com/ciescsceci
To promote international knowledge & understanding in education; To examine educational systems in international & comparative framework
Kumari Beck, President

Confederation of Alberta Faculty Associations (CAFA)
8909S - 112 St., Edmonton AB T6G 2C5
Tel: 780-492-5630
cafa-ab.ca
twitter.com/cafaab
To promote the quality of education in the province & to promote the well-being of Alberta Universities & their academic staff. Comprised of four associations: The Association of Academic Staff University of Alberta, Athabasca University Faculty Association, The Faculty Association of the University of Calgary, & The University of Lethbridge Faculty Association.

Lori Morinville, Administrative Officer

Confederation of University Faculty Associations of British Columbia (CUFA BC)
#315, 207 West Hastings St., Vancouver BC V6B 1H7
Tel: 604-646-4677; *Fax:* 604-646-4676
www.cufa.bc.ca

Jim Johnson, President
Michael Conlon, Executive Director
Haida Antolick, Resource Coordinator

Conference of Independent Schools (Ontario) (CIS)
PO Box 442, Oakville ON L6K 0A6
Tel: 905-665-8622
communications@cisontario.ca
www.cisontario.ca
twitter.com/CISOntario
To provide a collegial forum to promote excellence in education among its member schools
Sarah Craig, Executive Director
Sheri Little, Executive Assistant & Event Manager

Co-operative Education & Work-Integrated Learning Canada (CEWIL)
#705, 1 Eglinton Ave. East, Toronto ON M4P 3A1
Tel: 416-483-3311
cewil@cewilcanada.ca
www.cewilcanada.ca
www.linkedin.com/groups/4257621
twitter.com/CEWILCanada
To act as the voice for post-secondary co-operative education in Canada; To advance post-secondary co-operative education throughout the country; To establish national standards
Cara Krezek, President

Council of Atlantic Ministers of Education & Training (CAMET) / Conseil atlantique des ministres de l'Éducation et de la Formation (CAMEF)
PO Box 2044, Halifax NS B3J 2Z1
Tel: 902-424-3295; *Fax:* 902-424-8976
camet-camef@cap-cpma.ca
www.camet-camef.ca
To allow the ministers responsible for education & training in the Atlantic provinces to collaborate & respond to needs identified in public & post-secondary education; To enhance cooperation in public & post-secondary education to improve learning for Atlantic Canadians
Rhéal Poirier, Secretary
Sylvie Martin, Regional Coordinator

Council of Canadian Law Deans (CCLD) / Conseil des doyens et des doyennes des facultés de droit du Canada (CDFDC)
c/o Brigitte Pilon, Executive Director, PO Box 58051, Stn. Orléans Garden, Ottawa ON K1C 7H4
Tel: 613-824-9233; *Fax:* 613-824-9233
www.ccld-cdfdc.ca
To consult on matters of mutual concern, including legal education in Canada, legal research, cooperation among law schools & relations with law teachers, accreditation bodies, the legal profession & others
Brigitte Pilon, Executive Director

Council of Ontario Universities (COU) / Conseil des universités de l'Ontario
#1800, 180 Dundas St. West, Toronto ON M5G 1Z8
Tel: 416-979-2165; *Fax:* 416-979-8635
cou@cou.on.ca
www.cou.on.ca
www.linkedin.com/company/council-of-ontario-universities
www.facebook.com/CouncilofOntarioUniversities
twitter.com/OntUniv
To work with & on behalf of members to meet public policy expectations related to accountability, diversity of educational opportunity, financial self-reliance, & responsiveness to educational & marketplace needs
Patrick Deane, Chair
David Lindsay, President & CEO
Marina Piao, Executive Director, Corporate Services
Brian Timney, Executive Director, Quality Assurance
Barbara Hauser, Secretary to Council

Dufferin Peel Educational Resource Workers' Association (DPERWA)
#106, 5805 Whittle Rd., Mississauga ON L4Z 2J1
Tel: 905-501-1622; *Fax:* 905-501-1623
www.dperwa.com
DPERWA is the official, certified bargaining body for all Educational Assistants, Designated Early Childhood Educators & Supply ERWs employed with the Dufferin Peel Catholic District School Board.
Diane Kossel, President

EduNova
#300, 1533 Barrington St., Halifax NS B3J 1Z4
Tel: 902-424-8274; *Fax:* 902-424-8134
info@edunova.ca
studynovascotia.ca
www.youtube.com/edun0va
www.facebook.com/212866282085259
twitter.com/edunova_news
To raise the profile of education & training expertise in Nova Scotia
Wendy Luther, President & CEO
Michael Hennigar, Director, Recruitment & Marketing
Natasha McNeil, Manager, Operations & Accounts

Elementary Teachers' Federation of Ontario (ETFO) / Fédération des enseignantes et des enseignants de l'élémentaire de l'Ontario (FEEO)
136 Isabella St., Toronto ON M4Y 0B5
Tel: 416-962-3836; *Fax:* 416-642-2424
Toll-Free: 888-838-3836
info@etfo.org
www.etfo.ca
www.youtube.com/user/ETFOprovincial
www.facebook.com/ETFOprovincialoffice
twitter.com/ETFOeducators
To regulate relations between employees & employer; To advance the cause of education & the status of teachers & educational workers; To promote a high standard of professional ethics & a high standard of professional competence; To foster a climate of social justice in Ontario & continue a leadership role in such areas as anti-poverty, non-violence & equity; To promote & protect the interests of all members of the Federation & the students in their care; To cooperate with other organizations in Ontario, Canada & elsewhere
Sam Hammond, President
Karen Campbell, Vice-President
Susan Swackhammer, Vice-President
Nancy Lawler, Vice-President

Experiences Canada
#202, 2148 Carling Ave., Ottawa ON K2A 1H1
Tel: 613-727-3832; *Fax:* 613-727-3831
Toll-Free: 800-387-3832
info@experiencescanada.ca
www.experiencescanada.ca
www.instagram.com/experiencescanada
www.linkedin.com/company/experiences-canada
www.facebook.com/experiences.canada
twitter.com/experiencescan
To create, facilitate & promote enriching educational opportunities within Canada for the development of mutual respect & understanding through programs of exploration in language & culture
Deborah Morrison, President & CEO
Ellen Glouchkow, Director, Finance & Administration
Jamie McCullough, Director, Programs

Fédération des cégeps
500, boul Crémazie est, Montréal QC H2P 1E7
Tél: 514-381-8631; *Téléc:* 514-381-2263
comm@fedecegeps.qc.ca
www.fedecegeps.qc.ca
www.facebook.com/monretouraucegep
De promouvoir le développement de l'enseignement collégial; au nom de ses membres, la Fédération établit des contacts et étudie des dossiers communs avec différents partenaires gouvernementaux et privés, notamment en ce qui concerne les affaires pédagogiques, étudiantes, matérielles et financières, et les ressources humaines du réseau
Marie-France Bélanger, Présidente
Bernard Tremblay, Président-directeur général

Fédération des comités de parents du Québec inc. (FCPQ)
2263, boul Louis-XIV, Québec QC G1C 1A4
Tél: 418-667-2432; *Téléc:* 418-667-6713
Ligne sans frais: 800-463-7268
courrier@fcpq.qc.ca
www.fcpq.qc.ca
www.facebook.com/fcpq.parents
twitter.com/fcpq
De défendre et de promouvoir les droits et les intérêts des parents des élèves des écoles publiques primaires et secondaires de façon à assurer la qualité de l'éducation offerte aux enfants
Gaston Rioux, Président
Marc Charland, Directeur général
Jonatan Bérubé, Conseiller aux communications

La Fédération des commissions scolaires du Québec (FCSQ)
1001, av Bégon, Québec QC G1X 3M4
Tél: 418-651-3220; *Téléc:* 418-651-2574
Ligne sans frais: 800-463-3311
info@fcsq.qc.ca
www.fcsq.qc.ca
www.youtube.com/user/fcsq2011
www.linkedin.com/company/736250
www.facebook.com/LaFCSQ
twitter.com/fcsq
Tout en conservant ses tâches premières de coordination et d'unification, la mission de la Fédération s'est élargie, au fil des ans, pour rencontrer deux objectifs principaux : contribuer à promouvoir l'éducation ainsi que représenter et défendre avec détermination les intérêts des commissions scolaires.
Josée Bouchard, Présidente
Pâquerette Gagnon, Directrice générale

Fédération des établissements d'enseignement privés (FEEP)
1940, boul Henri-Bourassa est, Montréal QC H2B 1S2
Tél: 514-381-8891; *Téléc:* 514-381-4086
Ligne sans frais: 888-381-8891
info@feep.qc.ca
www.feep.qc.ca
www.instagram.com/lafeep1940
www.facebook.com/Federationdesetablissementsdenseignemen
tprives
twitter.com/lafeep
Soutien des établissements membres sur les plans administratifs, pédagogiques et de la vie scolaire; représentation auprès du gouvernement
Nancy Brosseau, Directrice générale

Fédération des parents du Manitoba (FPCP)
MB
www.lapfm.com
Appuyer les membres dans le développement des milieux, familial, éducatif (préscolaire et scolaire) et communautaire, propices à l'épanouissement des familles francophones

Fédération du personnel professionnel des collèges (FPPC)
9405, rue Sherbrooke est, Montréal QC H1L 6P3
Tél: 514-356-8888; *Téléc:* 514-356-3377
fppc@csq.qc.net
fppc.qc.ca
www.facebook.com/fppc.csq
twitter.com/fppc_csq
Défendre et promouvoir la fonction professionnelle dans les collèges
Bernard Bérubé, Président

Fédération nationale des enseignants et des enseignantes du Québec (FNEEQ) / National Federation of Québec Teachers
1601, av de Lorimier, Montréal QC H2K 4M5
Tél: 514-598-2241; *Téléc:* 514-598-2190
Ligne sans frais: 877-312-2241
fneeq.reception@csn.qc.ca
www.fneeq.ca
www.facebook.com/FneeqCSN
twitter.com/FneeqCSN
La Fédération nationale des enseignantes et des enseignants du Québec (FNEEQ) est une fédération de la CSN qui regroupe les syndicats de l'enseignement. La mission première de la FNEEQ est l'amélioration des conditions de travail par l'entremise de la négociation et de l'application d'une convention collective entre un employeur et le personnel enseignant et salarié
Caroline Senneville, Présidente
Jean Murdock, Secrétaire général et trésorier

Federation of Independent School Associations of BC (FISA)
4885 Saint John Paul II Way, Vancouver BC V5Z 0G3
Tel: 604-684-6023; *Fax:* 604-684-3163
info@fisabc.ca
www.fisabc.ca
To assist independent schools in maintaining their independence while seeking fair treatment for them in legislative & financial terms
Shawn Chisholm, Executive Director

Federation of New Brunswick Faculty Associations (FNBFA) / Fédération des associations de professeurs et professeurs d'université du Nouveau-Brunswick (FAPPUNB)
#204, 361 Victoria St., Fredericton NB E3B 1W5
Tel: 506-458-8977; *Fax:* 506-458-5620
www.fnbfa.ca

To promote interests of teachers, librarians & researchers in universities & colleges of New Brunswick; To advance standards of professions & to seek to improve quality of higher education in the Province
Jean Sauvageau, President
Elisabeth Hans, Executive Director

Fédération québécoise des directions d'établissements d'enseignement (FQDE)
#100, 7855, boul Louis-H-Lafontaine, Anjou QC H1K 4E4
Tél: 514-353-7511; *Téléc:* 514-353-2064
www.fqde.qc.ca
www.facebook.com/FQDE1
twitter.com/fqde
Défendre les droits des directeurs, directrices, directeurs adjoints, directrices adjointes d'établissements d'enseignement, sans oublier de promouvoir l'excellence dans la direction des établissements d'enseignement au Québec: en supportant des associations de directions d'établissement d'enseignement; en faisant en sorte que les directions d'établissement d'enseignement aient un environnement de travail favorisant la réalisation du projet éducatif; en s'assurant que les directions d'établissement d'enseignement maintiennent une compétence de gestionnaire de haute qualité
Lorraine Normand-Charbonneau, Présidente
Marie Boucher, Coordonnatrice, Affaires professionnelles

Fédération québécoise des professeures et professeurs d'université (FQPPU) / Québec Federation of University Professors
#300, 666, rue Sherbrooke, Montréal QC H3A 1E7
Tél: 514-843-5953; *Téléc:* 514-843-6928
Ligne sans frais: 888-843-5953
federation@fqppu.org
www.fqppu.org
twitter.com/fqppu
Ouvrer au maintien, à la défense, à la promotion et au développement de l'université comme service public; défendre une université accessible et de qualité
Jean-Marie Lafortune, Président

First Nations SchoolNet (FNS)
Indian & Northern Affairs Canada, Education Program Directorate, 10, rue Wellington, Tour nord, Gatineau QC K1A 0H4
Toll-Free: 800-567-9604
TTY: 866-553-0554
pnr-fns@ainc-inac.gc.ca
www.ainc-inac.gc.ca/edu/ep/index1-eng.asp
Established by the federal government, FNS provides internet access, computer equipment & technical support to First Nations schools on reserves across the country. Students can connect with each other, develop new skills, & participate in national & international events. Six non-profit, regional management organizations deliver the program in their respective region, working with Indian & Northern Affairs Canada.

Foundation for Educational Exchange Between Canada & the United States of America
#2015, 350 Albert St., Ottawa ON K1R 1A4
Tel: 613-688-5540; *Fax:* 613-237-2029
info@fulbright.ca
www.fulbright.ca
www.youtube.com/user/FulbrightCanada
www.facebook.com/fulbright.canada
twitter.com/FulbrightPrgrm
To support outstanding graduate students, faculty, professionals & independent researchers in order to enhance understanding between the people of Canada & the United States
Michael K. Hawes, Executive Director

IAESTE Canada (International Association for the Exchange of Students for Technical Experience) (IAESTE)
194 Boteler St., Ottawa ON K1N 5A7
canada@iaeste.org
iaestecanada.org
To provide technical students with international work experience related to their studies
David Fraser, National Secretary

Independent School Advancement Professionals Canada (ISAPC)
isapcanada@gmail.com
www.isapc.ca
www.linkedin.com/groups/2071818
www.facebook.com/ISAPCanada
twitter.com/isap_canada
The Independent School Advancement Professionals Canada is an association of development and advancement directors and officers.

Institut de coopération pour l'éducation des adultes (ICEA)
#304, 5000, rue d'Iberville, Montréal QC H2H 2S6
Tél: 514-948-2044
icea@icea.qc.ca
icea.qc.ca
www.facebook.com/icea.reseau
twitter.com/icea_
Promouvoir l'exercice du droit des adultes à l'éducation tout au long de la vie
Daniel Baril, Directeur général

International Association for Educational & Vocational Guidance (IAEVG) / Association internationale d'orientation scolaire et professionnelle (AIOSP)
ON
membership@iaevg.com
iaevg.com
www.facebook.com/IAEVG
twitter.com/iaevg
To ensure access to vocational guidance to all who want it; To guarantee a standard of service offered by practitioners; To encourage the permanent development of ideas, practice & research in this field on national & international levels; To address isues of social justice in education and work
Gert van Brussel, President
Laurent Matte, Secretary General

Learning Assistance Teachers' Association of British Columbia (LATA)
BC
psac53@bctf.ca
www.latabc.ca
www.facebook.com/LATABC
twitter.com/latabc
To provide equal access to the educational system, a position that supports the opportunity for students to pursue their goals in all aspects of education; To work together with parents & the community to give all students the best opportunities for success
Dennis Mousseau, President
Danielle Neer, Vice-President

Learning Disabilities Association of Alberta (LDAA) / Troubles d'apprentissage - Association de l'Alberta
PO Box 29011, Stn. Pleasantview, Edmonton AB T6H 5Z6
Tel: 780-448-0360
www.ldalberta.ca
www.facebook.com/ldalberta
To foster public understanding & build support networks to maximize the potential of individuals with learning disabilities; To support children, families & adults affected by learning disabilities & ADHD
Toby Rabinovitz, Executive Director

Learning Disabilities Association of British Columbia (LDAV) / Troubles d'apprentissage - Association de la Colombie-Britannique
#5, 774 Bay St., Victoria BC V8T 5E4
Tel: 250-370-9513
info@ldabc.ca
www.ldabc.ca
www.facebook.com/LDABC
twitter.com/LDABC
To advance the education, employment, social development, legal rights & general well-being of people with learning disabilities; To operate as a coordinating body, information centre & provincial representative for chapters within BC
Lynne Kent, Chair

Learning Disabilities Association of Canada (LDAC) / L'association Canadienne des troubles d'apprentissage (ACTA)
#20, 2420 Bank St., Ottawa ON K1V 8S1
Tel: 613-238-5721
info@ldac-acta.ca
www.ldac-acta.ca
www.youtube.com/ldacacta
www.facebook.com/ldacacta
twitter.com/ldacacta
To advance the education, employment, social development, legal rights & general well-being of people with learning disabilities; To create a greater public awareness & understanding of learning disabilities; To promote & develop early recognition, diagnosis, treatment & appropriate educational, social, recreational & career-oriented programs for people with learning disabilities; To promote legislation, research & training of personnel in the field of learning disabilities
Thealzel Lee, Chair
Claudette Larocque, Executive Director

Learning Disabilities Association of Manitoba (LDAM) / Troubles d'apprentissage - Association de Manitoba
617 Erin St., Winnipeg MB R3G 2W1
Tel: 204-774-1821; *Fax:* 204-788-4090
info@ldamanitoba.org
www.ldamanitoba.org
www.instagram.com/ldamanitoba
www.linkedin.com/in/lda-manitoba-98261b198
www.facebook.com/ldamb
twitter.com/ldamcentre
To provide support to all those who are concerned with learning disabilities; To represent individuals & families with learning disabilities
Karen Velthuys, Executive Director

Learning Disabilities Association of New Brunswick (LDANB) / Troubles d'apprentissage - Association du Nouveau-Brunswick (TA-ANB)
#203, 403 Regent St., Fredericton NB E3B 3X6
Tel: 506-459-7852; *Fax:* 506-455-9300
admin@ldanb-taanb.ca
www.ldanb-taanb.ca
vimeo.com/user19549796
www.facebook.com/LDANBTAANB
twitter.com/LDANB
Promotes the understanding & acceptance of the ability of persons with learning disabilities to lead meaningful & successful lives. Satellite office in Saint John.
Ainsley Congdon, Acting Executive Director

Learning Disabilities Association of Newfoundland & Labrador Inc. (LDANL)
The Board of Trade Bldg., #301, 66 Kenmount Rd., St. John's NL A1B 3V7
Tel: 709-753-1445; *Fax:* 709-753-4747
info@ldanl.ca
www.ldanl.ca
www.facebook.com/LearningDisabilitiesNL
twitter.com/LDANL
To work towards the advancement of legal rights, social development, education, employment & the general well-being of people with learning disabilities
Edie Dunphy, Executive Director
Karen Nelson, Office Manager

Learning Disabilities Association of Ontario (LDAO) / Troubles d'apprentissage - Association de l'Ontario
#202, 365 Evans Ave., Toronto ON M8Z 1K2
Tel: 416-929-4311; *Fax:* 416-929-3905
info@ldao.ca
www.ldao.ca
www.facebook.com/LDAOntario
twitter.com/ldatschool
To provide leadership in learning disabilities advocacy, research, education & services; To advance the full participation of children, youth & adults with learning disabilities in today's society
Lawrence Barns, President & CEO
Felicity Barns, Office Administrator

Learning Disabilities Association of Prince Edward Island (LADPEI)
#236, 40 Enman Cres., Charlottetown PE C1E 1E6
Tel: 902-894-5032
ldapei@eastlink.ca
www.ldapei.ca
www.facebook.com/ldapei
twitter.com/LDAPEI
To advance the interests of people with learning disabilities; To act as a voice for learning disabled people of Prince Edward Island
Martin Dutton, Executive Director

Learning Disabilities Association of Saskatchewan (LDAS) / Troubles d'apprentissage - Association de la Saskatchewan
221 Hanselman Ct., Saskatoon SK S7L 6A8
Tel: 306-652-4114; *Fax:* 306-652-3220
reception@ldas.org
www.ldas.org
To advance the education, employment, social development, legal rights & general well-being of people with learning disabilities
Wayne Stadnyk, Executive Director

Learning Disabilities Association of The Northwest Territories (LDA-NWT)
PO Box 242, Yellowknife NT X1A 2N2
Tel: 867-873-6378; *Fax:* 867-873-6378
lda-nwt@arcticdata.ca

To help people with learning disabilities achieve their potential in school, the workplace & in society

Learning Disabilities Association of Yukon Territory (LDAY)
128A Copper Rd., Whitehorse YT Y1A 2Z6
Tel: 867-668-5167; *Fax:* 867-668-6504
office@ldayukon.com
www.ldayukon.com
www.facebook.com/LDAYukon
To provide services & programs for Yukoners with learning disabilities so that they reach their potential & become productive members of society
Stephanie Hammond, Executive Director
Mark Browning, President

Learning Enrichment Foundation (LEF)
116 Industry St., Toronto ON M6M 4L8
Tel: 416-769-0830; *Fax:* 416-769-9912
info@lefca.org
www.lefca.org
To provide programs & services to help individuals become contributors to their community's social & economic development
James McLeod, President
Fotios Saratsiotis, Vice-President
Alex Kroon, Vice-President
Arthur Kennedy, Secretary-Treasurer

Manitoba Association of Parent Councils (MAPC)
#1005, 401 York Ave., Winnipeg MB R3C 0P8
Tel: 204-956-1770; *Fax:* 204-948-2855
Toll-Free: 877-290-4702
info@mapc.mb.ca
www.mapc.mb.ca
www.youtube.com/MBParentCouncils
www.facebook.com/mapcmb
twitter.com/mapcmb
Naomi Kruse, Executive Director

Manitoba Association of School Business Officials (MASBO)
MB
masbo@mymts.net
www.masbo.ca
To provide leadership in the areas of finance, maintenance & transportation
Paul Ilchena, Executive Director

Manitoba Association of School Superintendents (MASS)
375 Jefferson Ave., Winnipeg MB R2V 0N3
Tel: 204-487-7972; *Fax:* 204-487-7974
www.mass.mb.ca
To provide leadership for public education by advocating in the best interest of learners, & supports its members through professional services.
Ken Klassen, Executive Director

Manitoba Federation of Independent Schools Inc. (MFIS)
630 Westminster Ave., Winnipeg MB R3C 3S1
Tel: 204-783-4481
director@mfis.ca
www.mfis.ca
To support & encourage high educational standards & values unique to members' various school communities; Tto represent interests & concerns of member independent schools in Manitoba
Bruce Neal, Executive Director

Manitoba School Boards Association
191 Provencher Blvd., Winnipeg MB R2H 0G4
Tel: 204-233-1595; *Fax:* 204-231-1356
Toll-Free: 800-262-8836
webmaster@mbschoolboards.ca
www.mbschoolboards.ca
twitter.com/mbschoolboards
To provide services to school boards in Manitoba; To advocate for public education
Josh Watt, Executive Director
Heather Demetrioff, Director, Education & Communication Services
George Coupland, Director, Labour Relations & Human Resource Services

Manitoba School Counsellors' Association (MSCA) / Association manitobaine des conseillers d'Orientation
c/o Manitoba Teachers' Society, 191 Harcouty St., Winnipeg MB R3J 3H2
Tel: 204-888-7961; *Fax:* 204-831-0877
Toll-Free: 800-262-8803
www.msca.mb.ca
To promote & develop guidance & counselling services for children & youth; To provide a forum & a voice for those interested in promoting the personal, social, educational & career development of young Manitobans
Jennifer Stewart, President
Joëlle Émond, President-Elect
Shamain Hartman, Coordinator, Media

Manitoba Teachers' Society (MTS)
McMaster House, 191 Harcourt St., Winnipeg MB R3J 3H2
Tel: 204-888-7961; *Fax:* 204-831-0877
Toll-Free: 800-262-8803
info@mbteach.org
www.mbteach.org
www.instagram.com/mbteachers
www.facebook.com/manitobateachers
twitter.com/mbteachers
To work towards a public education system that provides equal accessibility & equal opportunity for all children, that optimizes the potential of all students as individuals & citizens, that fosters lifelong learning & that ensures a safe learning environment respectful of diversity & human dignity
Danielle Fullan Kolton, General Secretary
Kim Kummen, Chief Financial Officer
Debbie Guillas, Administrator, Human Resources

McMaster University Retirees Association (MURA)
c/o McMaster University, Gilmour Hall, #B108, 1280 Main St. West, Hamilton ON L8S 4L8
Tel: 905-525-9140
mura@mcmaster.ca
www.mcmaster-retirees.ca
To contribute in as many ways as possible to the welfare, prestige & excellence of the University; To encourage & promote a spirit of fraternity & unity among the members of the Association; To provide means for continuing the associations which retirees enjoyed as employees of the University

Mensa Canada Society / La Société Mensa Canada
#705, 1 Eglinton Ave. East, Toronto ON M4P 3A1
Toll-Free: 844-202-6761
info@mensacanada.org
www.mensacanada.org
www.linkedin.com/groups/40194
www.facebook.com/MensaCanada
twitter.com/MensaCanada
To identify & foster human intelligence for the benefit of humanity; To encourage research; To provide an intellectual & social environment for members
Marjorie Bentley, President
Raj Krishnan, Vice-President, Communications

National Educational Association of Disabled Students (NEADS) / Association nationale des étudiant(e)s handicapé(e)s au niveau postsecondaire
Carleton University, Unicentre, #514, 1125 Colonel By Dr., Ottawa ON K1S 5B6
Tel: 613-380-8065; *Fax:* 613-369-4391
Toll-Free: 877-670-1256
info@neads.ca
www.neads.ca
www.facebook.com/myNEADS
twitter.com/myneads
To encourage the self-empowerment of post-secondary students with disabilities; To advocate for increased accessibility at all levels so that disabled students may gain equal access to a college or university education; To provide an information resource base on services for disabled students nationwide according to a file of material from post-secondary institutions
Frank Smith, National Coordinator

National Reading Campaign, Inc.
#300, 2 Toronto St., Toronto ON M5C 2B6
Tel: 416-847-0309
info@nationalreadingcampaign.ca
www.nationalreadingcampaign.ca
www.youtube.com/user/NationalReadCampaign
www.facebook.com/NationalReadingCampaign
twitter.com/readingcampaign
To help make Canada a nation of readers
Sandy Crawley, Executive Director

New Brunswick Federation of Home & School Associations, Inc. (NBFHSA)
#202A, 212 Queen St., Fredericton NB E3B 1A8
Tel: 506-451-6247
www.nbfhsa.org
To ensure a quality education, enhanced by parental involvement, & a safe environment for all children
Leola Langille, President

New Brunswick Teachers' Association (NBTA) / Fédération des enseignants du Nouveau-Brunswick (FENB)
PO Box 752, 650 Montgomery St., Fredericton NB E3B 5G2
Tel: 506-452-8921; *Fax:* 506-453-9795
www.nbta.ca
www.facebook.com/219814221400600
Guy Arseneault, President
Larry Jamieson, Executive Director

New College Alumni Association (NCAA)
#118, 300 Huron St., Toronto ON M5S 3J6
Tel: 416-978-8273; *Fax:* 416-978-0554
alumni.newcollege@utoronto.ca
www.utoronto.ca/ncaa
To develop a visible & mutually supportive communication network that connects New College Alumni with the other stake holders of New College & the University of Toronto
Lesley Reidstra, President

Newfoundland & Labrador School Boards Association (NLSBA)
40 Strawberry Marsh Rd., St. John's NL A1B 2V5
Tel: 709-722-7171; *Fax:* 709-722-8214
www.schoolboardsnl.ca
To promote the interests of education in Newfoundland & Labrador
Brian Shortall, Executive Director

Newfoundland & Labrador Teachers' Association (NLTA) / Association des enseignants de Terre-Neuve
3 Kenmount Rd., St. John's NL A1B 1W1
Tel: 709-726-3223; *Fax:* 709-726-4302
Toll-Free: 800-563-3599
mail@nlta.nl.ca
www.nlta.nl.ca
www.facebook.com/nlta.nl.ca
twitter.com/NLTeachersAssoc
To strive towards the professional excellence & personal well-being of teachers
Don Ash, Executive Director

Northwest Territories Teachers' Association (NWTTA)
PO Box 2340, 5018 - 48th St., Yellowknife NT X1A 2P7
Tel: 867-873-8501; *Fax:* 867-873-2366
nwtta@nwtta.nt.ca
nwtta.nt.ca
www.facebook.com/nwtta
twitter.com/nwtta
To be the professional voice of educators in providing education to Northwest Territories students; To represent all regions equally, advocates for public education & promotes the teaching profession
Matthew Miller, President
Sara McCrea, Assistant Executive Director

Nova Scotia Federation of Home & School Associations (NSFHSA)
PO Box 28123, Stn. Tacoma Dr., Dartmouth NS B2W 6E2
Tel: 902-266-9507; *Toll-Free:* 800-214-9507
nsfhsapresident@gmail.com
www.nsfhsa.org
To provide a forum for discussion between the home & school beyond the parent-teacher interview; To promote & secure legislation for the care & protection of & equality of educational opportunities for children; To give parents an understanding of the school & its work, assisting in interpreting the school to the public; To confer & cooperate with organizations other than the schools which concern themselves with the training & development of children & youth
Charla Dorrington, President

Nova Scotia School Boards Association (NSSBA) / Association des conseils scolaires de la Nouvelle-Écosse
#395, 3 Spectacle Lake Dr., Dartmouth NS B3B 1W8
Tel: 902-491-2888
info@nssba.ca
www.nssba.ca
www.youtube.com/user/NSSBA2012
www.linkedin.com/company/nova-scotia-school-boards-associati
on
www.facebook.com/NovaScotiaSchoolBoardsAssociation
twitter.com/NSSchoolBoards
To act as the voice for school boards in Nova Scotia; To strive towards excellence in public education for students in the province
Nancy Pynch-Worthylake, Executive Director

Nova Scotia School Counsellor Association (NSSCA)
c/o Nova Scotia Teachers Union, 3106 Joseph Howe Dr., Halifax NS B3L 4L7
nssca.nstu.ca

Martia MacLean, President

Nova Scotia Teachers Union (NSTU) / Syndicat des enseignants de la Nouvelle-Écosse
Dr. Tom Parker Bldg., 3106 Joseph Howe Dr., Halifax NS B3L 4L7
Tel: 902-477-5621; *Fax:* 902-477-3517
Toll-Free: 800-565-6788
centraloffice@nstu.ca
www.nstu.ca
www.youtube.com/nstuwebcast
www.facebook.com/nsteachersunion
twitter.com/NSTeachersUnion
To unify the teaching profession in Nova Scotia; To improve the quality of education
Joan Ling, Executive Director

Nunavut Teachers' Association (NTA)
PO Box 2458, Iqaluit NU X0A 0H0
Tel: 867-979-0750; *Fax:* 867-979-0780
www.ntanu.ca
To represent & negotiate for teachers, vice-principals, & principals, as well as RSO & TLC coordinators in Nunavut; To ensure that members' rights & benefits are advocated & protected
John Fanjoy, President
Emile Hatch, Executive Director
Jeff Avery, Coordinator, Professional Improvement

Ontario Association of Deans of Education (OADE)
c/o Council of Ontario Universities, #1100, 180 Dundas St. West, Toronto ON M5G 1Z8
Tel: 416-979-2165; *Fax:* 416-979-8635
cou.on.ca
Peter Gooch, Contact

Ontario Association of School Business Officials (OASBO)
#207, 144 Main St. North, Markham ON L3P 5T3
Tel: 905-209-9704
office@oasbo.org
www.oasbo.org
To support quality education for all students; To improve the quality of school business management & the status, competency, leadership qualities & ethical standards of school business officials at all levels
Gerry Cullen, Executive Director

Ontario Catholic School Trustees' Association (OCSTA)
PO Box 2064, #1804, 20 Eglinton Ave. West, Toronto ON M4R 1K8
Tel: 416-932-9460; *Fax:* 416-932-9459
ocsta@ocsta.on.ca
www.ocsta.on.ca
www.youtube.com/user/OCSTAVideo1
www.facebook.com/CatholicEducationInOntario
twitter.com/catholicedu
To protect & support the interests of Catholic education in Ontario
Patrick J. Daly, President
Nick Milanetti, Executive Director

Ontario Confederation of University Faculty Associations (OCUFA) / Union des associations des professeurs des universités de l'Ontario
17 Isabella St., Toronto ON M4Y 1M7
Tel: 416-979-2117; *Fax:* 416-593-5607
ocufa@ocufa.on.ca
www.ocufa.on.ca
www.facebook.com/OCUFA
twitter.com/ocufa
To act as the voice of Ontario's approximately 15,000 university faculty & academic librarians; To advance the professional & economic interests of university faculty & academic librarians; To enhance the quality of Ontario's higher education system
Kate Lawson, President
Judy Bates, Vice-President
Mark Rosenfeld, Executive Director
Mark Rosenfeld, Associate Executive Director, Research & Communications
Glen Copplestone, Treasurer

Ontario Council for University Lifelong Learning (OCULL)
c/o Centre for Academic Excellence, Laurentian University, 935 Ramsey Lake Rd., Sudbury ON P3E 2C6
ocull@yahoo.ca
www.ocull.ca
www.linkedin.com/grps/OCULL-Ontario-Council-University-Lifelo
ng-7423612
twitter.com/OCULL_CUEP
To advocate for adult learners at Ontario universities, a collegial network, and a vehicle for professional development for its members.
Bettina Brockerhoff-Macdonald, President

Ontario Council on Graduate Studies (OCGS) / Conseil ontarien des études supérieures
#1100, 180 Dundas St. West, Toronto ON M5G 1Z8
Tel: 416-979-2165; *Fax:* 416-979-8635
cou.on.ca/ocgs-1
To ensure quality graduate education & research across Ontario
Peter Gooch, Secretariat, COU
Clarke Anthony, Chair

Ontario Federation of Home & School Associations Inc. (OFHSA)
51 Stuart St., Hamilton ON L8L 1B5
Tel: 905-308-9563
info@ofhsa.on.ca
www.ofhsa.on.ca
www.instagram.com/ofhsa1916
www.facebook.com/OFHSA1916
twitter.com/OFHSA1916
To provide facilities for the bringing together of members of Home & School Associations for discussion of matters of general interest & to stimulate cooperative effort; To assist in forming public opinion favorable to reform & advancement of the education of the child; To develop between educators & the general public such united effort as shall secure for every child the highest advantage in physical, mental, moral & spiritual education; To raise the standard of home & national life; To maintain a non-partisan, non-commercial, non-racial & non-sectarian organization
Arlene Morell, President

Ontario Federation of Independent Schools (OFIS)
PO Box 29011, 101 Holiday Inn Dr., Cambridge ON N3C 0E6
Tel: 519-249-1665
info@ofis.ca
www.ofis.ca
www.facebook.com/OFISOntario
twitter.com/OFIS_Ontario
To secure guarantees from Ontario government for independent schools' right to exist, curricular freedom, self-governance & acceptance by government of its responsibility to let education grants follow a child to any bona fide school that meets acceptable social & educational criteria
Barbara Bierman, Executive Director

Ontario Modern Language Teachers Association (OMLTA) / Association ontarienne des professeurs de langues vivantes (AOPLV)
PO Box 268, 71 George St., Lanark ON K0G 1K0
omlta@omlta.org
www.omlta.org
www.facebook.com/omlta
twitter.com/omlta
To represent French & international languages teachers in the province of Ontario; To advocate on behalf of language educators; To promote the benefits of learning languages
Jennifer Rochon, President

Ontario Principals' Council (OPC)
#2700, 20 Queen St. West, Toronto ON M5H 3R3
Tel: 416-322-6600; *Fax:* 416-322-6618
Toll-Free: 800-701-2362
admin@principals.ca
www.principals.ca
www.facebook.com/Ontario-Principals-Council
twitter.com/OPCouncil
To support the work of Ontario's principals & vice-principals to provide excellent leadership in the public education system
Allyson Otten, Executive Director

Ontario Public School Boards Association (OPSBA)
#1850, 439 University Ave., Toronto ON M5G 1Y8
Tel: 416-340-2540; *Fax:* 416-340-7571
webmaster@opsba.org
www.opsba.org
www.linkedin.com/company/ontario-public-school-boards-associ
ation
twitter.com/OPSBA
To represent Ontario's public school authorities & public district school boards; To advocate on behalf of the public school system in Ontario; To promote & enhance public education
Michael Barrett, President
Gail Anderson, Executive Director
Florenda Tingle, Executive Coordinator

Ontario Secondary School Teachers' Federation (OSSTF) / Fédération des enseignants des écoles secondaires de l'Ontario (FEESO)
49 Mobile Dr., Toronto ON M4A 1H5
Tel: 416-751-8300; *Fax:* 416-751-3394
Toll-Free: 800-267-7867
www.osstf.on.ca
www.youtube.com/user/OSSTF
www.facebook.com/osstfnews
twitter.com/osstf
To protect & enhance Ontario's public education system; To establish working conditions for members
Harvey Bischof, President & CEO
Pierre Côté, General Secretary

Ontario Teachers' Federation (OTF) / Fédération des enseignantes et des enseignants de l'Ontario (FEO)
#100, 10 Alcorn Ave., Toronto ON M4V 3A9
Tel: 416-966-3424; *Fax:* 416-966-5450
Toll-Free: 800-268-7061
www.otffeo.on.ca
www.youtube.com/c/OntarioTeachersFederationOTF
www.facebook.com/otffeo
twitter.com/otffeo
To represent the interests of all registered teachers in Ontario's publicly funded schools
Parker Robinson, President
Scott Perkin, Secretary-Treasurer
Lindy Amato, Director, Professional Affairs
Debbie Farrow, Manager, Human Resources & Office

Ontario University Registrars' Association (OUSA)
900 McGill Rd., Kamloops BC V2C 0C8
Tel: 250-828-5019
www.oura.ca

Lucy Bellissimo, President

ORT Canada
c/o ORT Toronto, 272 Codsell Ave., Toronto ON M3H 3X2
Tel: 416-787-0339; *Fax:* 416-787-9420
Toll-Free: 866-991-3045
info@ort-toronto.org
www.ort.org/whereweare/canada
www.facebook.com/299243785455
To fundraise in support of the worldwide vocational-training-school network of ORT
Rick Wellen, Director, Development
Lindy Meshwork, Executive Director

Parent Cooperative Preschools International (PCPI)
8725 Westport Dr., Niagara Falls ON L2H 0A2
Tel: 905-374-6605
enquiries@preschools.coop
www.preschools.coop
www.facebook.com/parentcooperatives
To promote the family & community; to strengthen & expand the parent cooperative movement & community appreciation of parent education for adults & preschool education for children; to promote desirable standards for program, practices & conditions in parent cooperative preschools & encourage continuing education for parents, teachers & directors; to promote interchange of information among parent cooperative nursery schools, kindergartens & other parent-sponsored preschool programs; to cooperate with family living, adult education & early childhood educational organizations in the interest of more effective service relationships with parents of young children; to

study & promote legislation designed to further the health & well-being of children & families
Mariah Battiston, Co-President
Lesley Romanoff, Co-President

Parents as First Educators (PAFE)
PO Box 84556, Toronto ON M6S 4Z7
Tel: 416-763-7233
pafe4you@gmail.com
www.p-first.com
www.facebook.com/pafe4
twitter.com/PAFE4
To ensure Ontario Catholic school board trustees are promoting Catholic teachings & to make parents aware of the work trustees are doing

Parents partenaires en éducation (PPE)
#204, 435, rue Donald, Ottawa ON K1K 4X5
Tél: 613-741-8846; *Téléc:* 613-741-7322
Ligne sans frais: 800-342-0663
info@ppeontario.ca
ppeontario.ca
www.youtube.com/reseauppe
www.facebook.com/ppeontario
twitter.com/ppeontario
Travailler en étroite collaboration avec ses partenaires en éducation, outiller les parents dans leur rôle de partenaires en éducation et agir comme porte-parole provincial des parents; promouvoir l'excellence de l'éducation de langue française et l'épanouissement global des enfants francophones
Badrieh Kojok, Présidente
Julie Béchard, Directrice générale

Pathways to Education Canada
439 University Ave., 16th Fl., Toronto ON M5G 1Y8
Tel: 416-646-0123; *Fax:* 416-646-0122
Toll-Free: 877-516-0123
info@pathwayscanada.ca
www.pathwaystoeducation.ca
www.instagram.com/pathwayscanada
www.linkedin.com/company/pathways-to-education-canada
www.facebook.com/pathwaystoeducationcanada
twitter.com/PathwaysCanada
To assist youth in low-income communities graduate high school & transition into post-secondary education opportunities
Sue Gillespie, President & CEO

People for Education (P4E)
641 Bloor St. West, Toronto ON M6G 1L1
Tel: 416-534-0100; *Fax:* 416-536-0100
info@peopleforeducation.ca
www.peopleforeducation.ca
www.facebook.com/peopleforeducation
www.twitter.com/Anniekidder
People for Education is an independent organization working to support public education in Ontario's English, Catholic and French schools.
Annie Kidder, Executive Director

Prince Edward Island Home & School Federation Inc. (PEIHSF)
PO Box 1012, 40 Enman Cres., Charlottetown PE C1A 7M4
Tel: 902-620-3186; *Fax:* 902-620-3187
Toll-Free: 800-916-0664
peihsf@edu.pe.ca
peihsf.ca
www.facebook.com/peihsf
twitter.com/peihsf
To improve standards of education in the province
Lisa MacDougall, President
Shirley Smedley Jay, Executive Director

Prince Edward Island Teachers' Federation (PEITF) / Fédération des enseignants de l'Ile-du-Prince-Édouard
PO Box 6000, Charlottetown PE C1A 8B4
Tel: 902-569-4157; *Fax:* 902-569-3682
Toll-Free: 800-903-4157
www.peitf.com
www.facebook.com/PEITF
twitter.com/PEITF
To promote & support education as well as the professional & economic well-being of PEI teachers
McLeod Bethany, President
Shaun MacCormac, General Secretary

Québec Association of Independent Schools (QAIS) / Association des écoles privées du Québec
3635, av Atwater, Montréal QC H3H 1Y4
Tel: 514-483-6111; *Fax:* 514-483-0865
Toll-Free: 866-909-6111
www.qais.qc.ca

To promote collaboration, provide services that further educational leadership & advocate for independent English language education in Quebec on behalf of its member schools
Holly Hampson, Executive Director

Québec Board of Black Educators (QBBE)
#310, 3333 boul Cavendish, Montréal QC H4B 2M5
Tel: 514-481-9400; *Fax:* 514-481-0611
qbbe@videotron.ca
www.qbbe.org
www.facebook.com/qbbe.ca
To promote the development of educational services for Black Youth & other youth between the ages of 5 to 25 who reside in the Greater Montreal area
Phylicia Burke, Contact
Clarence Bayne, President

Québec English School Boards Association (QESBA) / Association des commissions scolaires anglophones du Québec (ACSAQ)
#515, 1410, rue Stanley, Montréal QC H3A 1P8
Tel: 514-849-5900; *Fax:* 514-849-9228
Toll-Free: 877-512-7522
qesba@qesba.qc.ca
www.qesba.qc.ca
twitter.com/qesba
To represent English school boards in Québec
Marcus Tabachnick, Executive Director

Québec Federation of Home & School Associations Inc. (QFHSA) / Fédération des associations foyer-école du Québec Inc.
#560, 3285, boul Cavendish, Montréal QC H4B 2L9
Tel: 514-481-5619; *Fax:* 514-481-5610
Toll-Free: 888-808-5619
info@qfhsa.org
www.qfhsa.org
www.facebook.com/QFHSA
To provide facilities for the bringing together of members of home & school associations for discussion & to stimulate cooperative effort; To assist in forming public opinion favorable to reform & advancement of the education of the child; To develop between educators & the general public such a united effort as shall secure for every child the highest advantage in physical, mental, moral & spiritual education; To raise the standard of home & national life; To maintain non-partisan, non-commercial, non-racial & non-sectarian organization
Brian Rock, President

Le Réseau d'enseignement francophone à distance du Canada (REFAD)
CP 47542, Succ. Plateau Mont-Royal, Montréal QC H2H 2S8
Tél: 514-284-9109
refad@sympatico.ca
www.refad.ca
twitter.com/_refad
Favoriser la collaboration entre les personnes et les organisations intéressées par l'enseignement à distance en français; rassembler en réseau les établissements qui ont recours à la formation à distance en français; appuyer et compléter d'autres réseaux d'enseignement à distance existant déjà à travers le Canada; promouvoir et accroître la qualité et la quantité des programmes et des cours offerts dans la francophonie canadienne.
Alain Langlois, Directeur général

The Retired Teachers of Ontario (RTO) / Les Enseignants et enseignantes retraités de l'Ontario (ERO)
#300, 18 Spadina Rd., Toronto ON M5R 2S7
Tel: 416-962-9463; *Fax:* 416-962-1061
Toll-Free: 800-361-9888
info@rto-ero.org
www.rto-ero.org
www.facebook.com/rto.ero
twitter.com/rto_ero
To promote the interests of persons in receipt of a pension under the Ontario Teachers' Pension Act
Jim Grieve, Executive Director

Saskatchewan Association for Multicultural Education (SAME)
2454 Atkinson St., Regina SK S4N 3X5
Tel: 306-780-9428
same@sk.sympatico.ca
To promote multicultual & anti-racist education throughout Saskatchewan; To raise awareness & acceptance of cultural diversity in the province; To respond to changes in multicultural policies & demographics; To address social justice issues

Saskatchewan Association of School Councils (SASC)
#301, 221 Cumberland Ave. North, Saskatoon SK S7N 1M3
Tel: 306-955-5723; *Fax:* 306-445-7707
sasc@sasktel.net
To enhance the education & general well-being of children & youth; To promote the involvement of parents, students, educators & the community at large in the advancement of learning & to act as a voice for parents; To promote effective communication between the home & the school; To encourage parents to participate in educational activities & decision making

Saskatchewan School Boards Association (SSBA)
#400, 2222 - 13th Ave., Regina SK S4P 3M7
Tel: 306-569-0750; *Fax:* 306-352-9633
admin@saskschoolboards.ca
www.saskschoolboards.ca
www.facebook.com/saskschoolboards
twitter.com/saskschoolboard
To represent boards of education, including division boards, conseils scolaires & local or district boards; To ensure advocacy, leadership & support for member boards by speaking as the voice for quality public education for all children; To offer opportunities for trustee development
Darren McKee, Executive Director
Catherine Vu, Director, Corporate Services
Jill Welke, Director, Communications Services

Saskatchewan Teachers' Federation (STF) / Fédération des enseignants et des enseignantes de la Saskatchewan
2317 Arlington Ave., Saskatoon SK S7J 2H8
Tel: 306-373-1660; *Fax:* 306-374-1122
Toll-Free: 800-667-7762
stf@stf.sk.ca
www.stf.sk.ca
www.youtube.com/channel/UCIw3RFPZPxTzbldiTocbknA
twitter.com/SaskTeachersFed
To help provide the best possible education to children
Patrick Maze, President
Gwen Dueck, Executive Director

Skills/Compétences Canada
#201, 294 Albert St., Ottawa ON K1P 6E6
Fax: 613-691-1404
Toll-Free: 877-754-5226
www.skillscompetencescanada.com
www.youtube.com/user/SkillsCanadaOfficial
www.linkedin.com/company/skills-competences-canada
www.facebook.com/skillscanada
twitter.com/Skills_Canada
To encourage & support a coordinated approach in promoting skilled trades & technologies to Canadian youth
Shaun Thorson, Chief Executive Officer
Karine R. Dupuis, Director, Competitions
Gail Vent, Director, Business Development & Marketing

Society for Quality Education (SQE)
57 Twyford Rd., Toronto ON M9A 1W5
Tel: 416-231-7247; *Fax:* 416-237-0108
Toll-Free: 888-856-5535
info@societyforqualityeducation.org
www.societyforqualityeducation.org
www.facebook.com/SQEducation
twitter.com/SQESocQualEd
To advance public & private education in Canada by disseminating authoritative information on educational governance & methodology.
Doretta Wilson, Executive Director
Malkin Dare, President

Society for the Promotion of the Teaching of English as a Second Language in Quebec (SPEAQ) / Société pour le perfectionnement de l'enseignement de l'anglais, langue seconde, au Québec
6662, rue Saint-Denis, #C, Montréal QC H2S 2R9
Tel: 514-271-3700; *Fax:* 514-271-4587
speaq@speaq.qc.ca
www.speaq.qc.ca
To unite individuals engaged or interested in the teaching of English as a second language in Quebec; To promote & develop the professional & economic interests of members; To ensure favourable conditions for the development of teaching English as a second language in Quebec//Promouvoir l'enseignement de l'anglais, langue seconde au Québec
Gwenn Gauthier, President
Monique Mainella, Vice President

Renewable Industries Canada
#450, 54 Murray St., Ottawa ON K1N 5M3
info@ricanada.org
www.ricanada.org
www.linkedin.com/company/renewable-industries-canada
twitter.com/RenewCan
To promote renewable fuel development & usage

Wood Energy Technology Transfer Inc. (WETT)
1 - 189 Queen St. East, Toronto ON M5A 1S2
Tel: 416-968-7718; *Fax:* 416-968-6818
Toll-Free: 888-358-9388
info@wettinc.ca
www.wettinc.ca
To develop, maintain, promote, & deliver professional training courses within the framework of the WETT Program for practitioners of trades related to the sale, installation, maintenance, & inspection of systems using wood & other biomass fuels; To maintain a registry containing the names of holders of valid WETT certificates & those who are students under the program; To foster & promote among certificate holders the highest level of professional conduct in the delivery of services to the public; To encourage & promote the safe & efficient use of wood energy through the distribution of public information materials & through collaboration with government agencies & related industries; To foster & promote research & education in the utilization of wood as a source of energy; To promote the interests & activities of the members of the organization in a reasonable & legal manner; To provide a forum for the discussion of issues of importance or interest to the members & to share information & opinions for the mutual benefit of the member
Anthony Laycock, Executive Director

Engineering & Technology

Applied Science Technologists & Technicians of British Columbia (ASTTBC)
10767 - 148th St., Surrey BC V3R 0S4
Tel: 604-585-2788
techinfo@asttbc.org
asttbc.org
www.youtube.com/user/ASTTBC
www.linkedin.com/company/asttbc
twitter.com/asttbc
To advance the profession of applied science technology & the professional recognition of applied science technologists, certified technician & other members in a manner that serves & protects the public interest
Theresa McCurry, BSc, PMP, Chief Executive Officer
Karen Taylor, Director, Operations
Cara Christopherson, Manager, Marketing Communications
Jason Jung, Manager, Professional Practice & Development
Evan Triste, Manager, Finance

Association des firmes de génie-conseil - Québec (AFG) / Association of Consulting Engineering Companies - Quebec
#930, 1440, rue Sainte-Catherine ouest, Montréal QC H3G 1R8
Tél: 514-871-2229; *Téléc:* 514-871-9903
info@afg.quebec
afg.quebec
www.youtube.com/aicqtv
Promouvoir et développer l'industrie du génie-conseil en regroupant des membres qui offrent des services de qualité
Beaudoin Bergeron, Président du Conseil
André Rainville, Président-directeur général
Pierre Nadeau, Directeur, Communications

Association des ingénieurs municipaux du Québec (AIMQ) / Association of Québec Municipal Engineers
CP 792, Succ. B, Montréal QC H3B 3K5
Tél: 514-845-5303
www.aimq.net
Améliorer les connaissances et le statut de l'ingénieur municipal par l'échange d'information, la coopération entre ingénieurs municipaux et avec d'autres associations professionnelles et la promotion des intérêts communs des membres de l'Association
Robert Millette, Directeur général

Association of Consulting Engineering Companies - British Columbia (ACEC-BC)
#1258, 409 Granville St., Vancouver BC V6C 1T2
Tel: 604-687-2811; *Fax:* 604-688-7110
info@acec-bc.ca
www.acec-bc.ca
To improve the commercial environment for consulting engineering firms
Catherine Fritter, Chair
Keith Sashaw, President & CEO

Alla Samusevich, Coordinator, Accounting & Events

Association of Consulting Engineering Companies - Canada (ACEC) / L'Association des firmes d'ingénieurs-conseils - Canada (AFIC)
#420, 130 Albert St., Ottawa ON K1P 5G4
Tel: 613-236-0569; *Fax:* 613-236-6193
Toll-Free: 800-565-0569
info@acec.ca
www.acec.ca
www.youtube.com/ACECAFIC
www.linkedin.com/groups/7450101
twitter.com/ACECCanada
To assist in promoting satisfactory business relations between its Member Firms & their clients; To promote cordial relations among the various consulting engineering firms in Canada & to foster the interchange of professional, management & business experience & information among them; To safeguard the interest of the consulting engineer; To further the maintenance of high professional standards in the consulting engineering profession
John D. Gamble, CET, P.Eng., President
Martine Proulx, Vice-President
Michael Courtright, CPA, CGA, Director, Finance & Administration
Christina Locmelis, Manager, Communications

Association of Consulting Engineering Companies - Manitoba (ACEC-MB)
PO Box 1547, Stn. Main, Winnipeg MB R3C 2Z4
Tel: 204-774-5258; *Fax:* 204-779-0788
acec-mb.ca
twitter.com/acec_manitoba
To promote & enhance the business interests of the consulting engineers of Manitoba; to lead in the application of technology for the benefit of society
Cameron Dyck, P.Eng., P.E., President
Shirley E. Tillett, Executive Director

Association of Consulting Engineering Companies - New Brunswick (ACEC-NB) / Association des firmes d'ingénieurs-conseils - Nouveau-Brunswick
PO Box 415, Moncton NB E1C 8L4
Tel: 506-380-5776
info@acec-nb.ca
www.acec-nb.ca
To develop & support member firms; To improve the business environment for member firms & their clients; To further the professional standards of the consulting engineering profession
Nadine Boudreau, Executive Director

Association of Consulting Engineering Companies - Prince Edward Island (ACEC-PEI)
c/o James C Johnson Associates Inc., #2, Pickard Bldg., Harbourside II, Charlottetown PE C1A 8R4
Tel: 902-629-5895; *Fax:* 902-368-2196
Hal Brothers, Acting Executive Director

Association of Consulting Engineering Companies - Saskatchewan (ACEC-SK)
#12, 2010 - 7 Ave., Regina SK S4R 1C2
Tel: 306-359-3338; *Fax:* 306-522-5325
info@acec-sk.ca
www.acec-sk.ca
To further the maintenance of high professional standards in consulting engineering profession; To promote cordial relations among various consulting firms in Saskatchewan; To foster interchange of professional management & business experience & information among consulting engineers; To develop regional representation & participation in affairs of the association
Jason Gasmo, P.Eng, Chair
Beverly MacLeod, Executive Director

Association of Engineering Technicians & Technologists of Newfoundland & Labrador (AETTNL)
#301, 2197 Riverside Dr., Ottawa ON K1H 7X3
Tel: 613-238-8123; *Fax:* 613-238-8822
Toll-Free: 888-238-8600
cctt@cctt.ca
www.aettnl.ca
To advance the profession of Applied Science / Engineering Technology & the professional recognition of Certified Technicians & Technologists
Rick Tachuk, President & CEO
Darlene Pilon, Finance Manager
Valery Vidershpan, Project Manager

Association of Professional Engineers & Geoscientists of Alberta (APEGA)
Scotia One, #1500, 10060 Jasper Ave. NW, Edmonton AB T5J 4A2
Tel: 780-426-3990; *Fax:* 780-426-1877
Toll-Free: 800-661-7020
email@apega.ca
www.apega.ca
www.youtube.com/c/APEGAabca
www.linkedin.com/company/apega-ab
twitter.com/APEGA_AB
To register & set practice standards & codes of professional conduct & ethics for professional engineers, geologists, & geophysicists in Alberta, according to The Engineering, Geological & Geophysical Professions Act
Jay Nagendran, P.Eng., FEC, QE, Registrar & Chief Executive Officer
Matthew Oliver, CD, P.Eng., Deputy Registrar & Chief Regulatory Officer
Sharilee Fossum, MBA, CPA, CMA, Chief Financial & Corporate Officer

Association of Professional Engineers & Geoscientists of New Brunswick (APEGNB) / Association des ingénieurs et géoscientifiques du Nouveau-Brunswick (AINB)
183 Hanwell Rd., Fredericton NB E3B 2R2
Tel: 506-458-8083; *Fax:* 506-451-9629
Toll-Free: 888-458-8083
info@apegnb.com
www.apegnb.com
www.instagram.com/apegnb_aignb
www.linkedin.com/company/apegnb
www.facebook.com/apegnb
twitter.com/APEGNB_AIGNB
To establish, maintain & develop standards of knowledge & skill, qualification & practice, & professional ethics; To promote public awareness of the role of the association
Marlo Rose, P.Eng., President
Maggie Stothart, P.Eng., Vice-President
Lia Daborn, Chief Executive Officer

Association of Professional Engineers & Geoscientists of Saskatchewan (APEGS)
#300, 4581 Parliament Ave., Regina SK S4W 0G3
Tel: 306-525-9547; *Fax:* 306-525-0851
Toll-Free: 800-500-9547
apegs@apegs.ca
www.apegs.ca
To achieve a safe & prosperous future through engineering & geoscience in Saskatchewan; To regulate the practice of engineering & geoscience at a business level
Bob McDonald, P.Eng., MBA, LL, Executive Director & Registrar
Shawna Argue, P.Eng., FEC, FC, Director, Registration
Ferguson Earnshaw, P.Eng., Director, Corporate Practice & Compliance
Kate MacLachlan, Ph.D., P.Geo., Director, Academic Review
Tina Maki, P.Eng., FEC, FG, Director, Special Projects
Chris Wimmer, P.Eng., FEC, Director, Professional Standards

Association of Professional Engineers & Geoscientists of the Province of British Columbia (EGBC)
#200, 4010 Regent St., Burnaby BC V5C 6N2
Tel: 604-430-8035; *Fax:* 604-430-8085
Toll-Free: 888-430-8035
info@egbc.ca
www.egbc.ca
www.linkedin.com/company/engineersandgeoscientistsbc
twitter.com/EngGeoBC
To protect the public interest in matters related to geoscience & engineering; To regulate & govern the professions of professional engineers & geoscientists in British Columbia, according to the Engineers & Geoscientists Act; To strive for professional excellence, by establishing academic, experience & professional practice standards
Ann English, P.Eng., Chief Executive Officer & Registrar
Tony Chong, P.Eng., Chief Regulatory Officer & Deputy Registrar
Jennifer Cho, Chief Financial & Administration Officer

The Association of Professional Engineers & Geoscientists of the Province of Manitoba (APEGM)
870 Pembina Hwy., Winnipeg MB R3M 2M7
Tel: 204-474-2736; *Fax:* 204-474-5960
Toll-Free: 866-227-9600
info@enggeomb.ca
www.enggeomb.ca
www.facebook.com/EngGeoMB
twitter.com/enggeomb

To serve & protect public interest by governing & advancing the practice of engineering in accordance with the Engineering Profession Act of Manitoba
Grant Koropatnick, P.Eng., FEC, Chief Executive Officer & Registrar
Michael Gregoire, P.Eng., FEC, Director, Professional Standards
Sharon E. Sankar, P.Eng., FEC, Director, Admissions
C. Scott Sarna, Director, Government Relations

Association of Professional Engineers of Prince Edward Island (APEPEI)
135 Water St., Charlottetown PE C1A 1A8
Tel: 902-566-1268; *Fax:* 902-566-5551
info@engineerspei.com
www.engineerspei.com
www.facebook.com/259153067491096
twitter.com/EngineersPEI
To regulate the practice of professional engineering in P.E.I., with authority over members, licensees, engineers-in-training, & holders of certificates of authorization
Jason Lindsay, P.Eng., President
Jim Landrigan, P.Eng., Executive Director, Registrar & Treasurer

Association of Professional Engineers of Yukon (APEY)
312B Hanson St., Whitehorse YT Y1A 1Y6
Tel: 867-667-6727; *Fax:* 867-668-2142
staff@apey.yk.ca
www.apey.yk.ca
To establish, maintain & develop standards of knowledge & skill; qualification & practice; & professional ethics; To promote public awareness of the role of the association

Association of Science & Engineering Technology Professionals of Alberta (ASET)
#1600, 9888 Jasper Ave., Edmonton AB T5J 5C6
Tel: 780-425-0626; *Fax:* 780-424-5053
Toll-Free: 800-272-5619
asetadmin@aset.ab.ca
www.aset.ab.ca
www.linkedin.com/company/asetmembers
www.facebook.com/ASETmembers
twitter.com/asetmembers
To benefit the public & the profession by regulating & promoting safe, high quality, professional technology practice; To focus on the engineering technology, applied science, & information technology fields; To issue credentials to qualified individuals; To accredit training programs. There are 9 chapters across the province
Barry Cavanaugh, CEO & General Counsel
Nicole Miller, Privacy Officer & Director, Finance & Administration
Melanie Leaf, Interim Director, Registration & Practice

Blockchain Technology Coalition of Canada (BTCC)
1 Yonge St., Toronto ON M5E 1W7
support@thememom.com
joinbtcc.org
www.linkedin.com/company/joinbtcc
www.facebook.com/joinbtcc
twitter.com/joinbtcc
To create standards & shape public policy in order to protect consumers, support innovation, & stimulate growth in Canadian blockchain jobs
Bill Rayburn, Executive Board Member

Canada BIM Council Inc.
PO Box 17017, Stn. Yonge-King, Toronto ON M5E 1Y2
Toll-Free: 877-778-5194
www.canbim.com
www.facebook.com/125791377505468
twitter.com/CanBIM
To serve & benefit members who work with Building Information Modeling (BIM) technologies in the fields of architecture, engineering, construction, building ownership & facility management, construction law & education
Allan Partridge, President
Gerry Lattmann, Executive Director

Canadian Acoustical Association (CAA) / Association canadienne d'acoustique (ACA)
c/o JASCO Applied Sciences, #2305, 4464 Markham St., Victoria BC V8Z 7X8
secretary@caa-aca.ca
www.caa-aca.ca
www.linkedin.com/groups/3526930
twitter.com/canacoustical
To foster communication among people working in all areas of acoustics in Canada; To promote the growth & practical application of knowledge in acoustics; To encourage education, research & employment in acoustics
Jérémie Voix, President
Dalila Giusti, Treasurer

Roberto Racca, Executive Secretary

Canadian Advanced Technology Alliance (CATA Alliance) / Association canadienne de technologie de pointe
#416, 207 Bank St., Ottawa ON K2P 2N2
Tel: 613-236-6550
info@cata.ca
www.cata.ca
www.linkedin.com/groups/37239
www.facebook.com/CATAAlliance
twitter.com/CATAAlliance
To provide members with a network to establish partnerships, to match up with global business opportunities; To offer communication & advocacy services, notably in dealing with the government; To work to ensure that policies are favourable to Canadian technology companies; To maintain a research repository where members can access information to advance their agendas
Suzanne Grant, Chief Executive Officer

Canadian Air Cushion Technology Society (CACTS)
c/o Canadian Aeronautics & Space Institute, #104, 350 Terry Fox Dr., Kanata ON K2K 2W5
Tel: 613-591-8787; *Fax:* 613-591-7291
www.casi.ca/canadian-air-cushion-tech-soc
To serve the air cushion technology (hovercraft) community throughout Canada; To advance the science, technologies, & applications of air cushion technology
Jacques Laframboise, Society Chair

Canadian Association for Composite Structures & Materials (CACSMA) / Association canadienne pour les structures et matériaux composites (ACSMAC)
c/o Peter Richter, WPR Consulting, Lansdowne Rd. North, Cambridge ON
www.cacsma.ca
To support composites companies in Canada; To promote Canadian composites capabilities; To encourage the application of composites in all sectors
Pierre Mertiny, President
Peter Richter, Secretary
Pascal Hubert, Treasurer

Canadian Council of Technicians & Technologists (CCTT) / Conseil canadien des techniciens et technologues
#405, 2197 Riverside Dr., Ottawa ON K1H 7X3
Tel: 613-238-8123; *Fax:* 613-238-8822
cctt@cctt.ca
www.cctt.ca
www.linkedin.com/company/canadian-council-of-technicians-&-technologists
twitter.com/CCTTCanada
To advocate on behalf of Canada's certified technicians & technologists; To establish & maintain national competency standards
Rick Tachuk, President & CEO
Darlene Pilon, Manager, Finance
Valery Vidershpan, Manager, Projects

Canadian Explosive Technicians' Association (CETA) / Association canadienne des techniciens en explosif
Explosive Disposal Unit, Halton Regional Police Service, 1151 Bronte Rd., Oakville ON L6M 3L1
www.cetatechs.com
To enhance public safety by supporting & advocating for explosive technicians

Canadian Hydrogen & Fuel Cell Association (CHFCA)
#900, 1188 West Georgia St., Vancouver BC V6E 4A2
Tel: 604-283-1040; *Fax:* 604-283-1043
info@chfca.ca
www.chfca.ca
www.youtube.com/chfca
www.facebook.com/poweringnow
twitter.com/poweringnow
To act as the collective voice of the hydrogen & fuel cell technologies & products sector; To support Canadian corporations, educational institutions, & governments which develop & deploy hydrogen & fuel cell products & services in Canada
Eric Denhoff, President & Chief Executive Officer

Canadian Remote Sensing Society (CRSS) / Société canadienne de télédétection
c/o Canadian Aeronautics & Space Institute, #104, 350 Terry Fox Dr., Kanata ON K2K 2W5
Tel: 613-591-8787; *Fax:* 613-591-7291
casi@casi.ca
www.crss-sct.ca

To advance the art, science, engineering, & application of remote sensing in Canada; To uphold the Society's Code of Ethics
Monique Bernier, Chair
Anne Smith, Vice-Chair
Richard Fournier, Secretary-Treasurer

Canadian Society for Civil Engineering (CSCE) / Société canadienne de génie civil
#521, 300, rue St-Sacrement, Montréal QC H2Y 1X4
Tel: 514-933-2634; *Fax:* 514-933-3504
info@csce.ca
www.csce.ca
www.linkedin.com/groups/1812786
www.facebook.com/Canadiansocietyforcivilengineering
twitter.com/csce2
To develop & maintain high standard of civil engineering practice in Canada; To enhance the public image of the civil engineering profession
Catherine Mulligan, President
Lois Arkwright, Director, Administration & Events
Lyanne St-Jacques, Director, Marketing & Communications

Canadian Society for Engineering Management (CSEM) / Société canadienne de gestion en ingénierie
PO Box 40140, Stn. Bank / Hunt Club, Ottawa ON K1V 0W8
Tel: 613-400-1786
admin.officer@eic-ici.ca
www.csem-scgi.org
www.linkedin.com/groups/4818149
To represent the interests & enhance the capabilities of engineers in management in order to promote & advance efficient management of commerce, industry & public affairs
Aidan Gordon, President

Canadian Society for Mechanical Engineering (CSME) / Société canadienne de génie mécanique (SCGM)
PO Box 40140, Ottawa ON K1V 0W8
admin.officer@csme-scgm.ca
www.csme-scgm.ca
www.facebook.com/CSMESCGM
twitter.com/CSME_SCGM
To benefit Canada & the world by fostering excellence in the practice of mechanical engineering; To support members
Guy Gosselin, Executive Director

Canadian Society of Iranian Engineers & Architects
PO Box 217, 6021 Yonge St., Toronto ON M2N 3W2
Tel: 905-771-7147
kanoon@mohandes.com
mohandes.com
www.linkedin.com/company/kanoon-mohandes
www.facebook.com/KanoonMohandes
twitter.com/KanoonMohandes
To represent Iranian engineers & architects in Canada; To promote their contributions to the Canadian economy; To establish relationships with other technical & professional organizations; To provide services for members
Mehran Mohaghegh, Chair

Canadian Technical Asphalt Association (CTAA) / Association technique canadienne du bitume
#174, 2417 Main St., Kelowna BC V4T 2H8
Tel: 250-361-9187; *Fax:* 250-361-9187
admin@ctaa.ca
www.ctaa.ca
www.linkedin.com/groups/3266673
www.facebook.com/CanadianTechnicalAsphalt
To organize efforts of membership on a non-profit, public service basis; To assemble, correlate & disseminate technical information on characteristics & uses of bituminous materials; To encourage research on uses of asphaltic materials; To encourage colleges to teach students to study asphalt technology
Chuck McMillan, Secretary-Treasurer

Certified Technicians & Technologists Association of Manitoba (CTTAM)
#602, 1661 Portage Ave., Winnipeg MB R3J 3T7
Tel: 204-784-1088; *Fax:* 204-784-1084
admin@cttam.com
www.cttam.com
To advance the professional recognition & development of certified applied science technicians & technologists in a manner that serves the public interest
Neil Klassen, CET, President
Terry Gifford, CAE, Executive Director
Robert D. Okabe, CET; IntET, Registrar

Consulting Engineers of Alberta (CEA)
**Phipps-McKinnon Building, #870, 10020 - 101A Ave.,
Edmonton AB T5J 3G2**
Tel: 780-421-1852; *Fax:* 780-424-5225
info@cea.ca
www.cea.ca
www.linkedin.com/company/consulting-engineers-of-alberta
www.facebook.com/749479441765790
twitter.com/ConsultingEngAB
To provide leadership to foster a positive business environment
for the consulting engineering firms in Alberta; To promote the
engineering industry; To enhance interests & opportunities of
CEA members; To provide society with high standards of
engineering design & safety
Matt Brassard, President
Ken Pilip, CEO & Registrar
Lisa Krewda, Director, Operations
Chantal Sargent, Manager, Events

Consulting Engineers of Newfoundland & Labrador (CENL)
PO Box 1236, St. John's NL A1C 5M9
Tel: 709-726-3468
www.consultingengineersofnl.ca
To unite the local industry; to promote & advocate common
business interests; to support the development & successs of
member firms.
Mike Brady, P.Eng., PMP, President

Consulting Engineers of Nova Scotia (CENS)
PO Box 613, Stn. M, Halifax NS B3J 2R7
Tel: 902-461-1325; *Fax:* 902-461-1321
cens@eastlink.ca
www.cens.org
To enable the consulting engineering industry in Nova Scotia to
capitalize on opportunities to grow; To promote employment of
member firms
Scott Kyle, President
Skit Ferguson, Executive Director

Consulting Engineers of Ontario (CEO)
#405, 10 Four Seasons Pl., Toronto ON M9B 6H7
Tel: 416-620-1400; *Fax:* 416-620-5803
www.ceo.on.ca
www.youtube.com/user/CEOYT
www.linkedin.com/company/consulting-engineers-of-ontario
www.facebook.com/ConsultingEngON
twitter.com/ConsultingEngON
To further the maintenance of high professional standards in
consulting engineering profession; to promote cordial relations
among various consulting firms in Ontario; to foster interchange
of professional management & business experience &
information among consulting engineers; to develop regional
representation & participation in affairs of the association
Bruce Potter, Chair
Barry Steinburg, Chief Executive Officer
Jennifer Parent, Manager, Events & Member Services
Diane Lee, Coordinator, Communications

Consulting Engineers of the Northwest Territories (CENT)
**c/o NAPEG, Bowling Green Bldg., #201, 4817 - 49th St.,
Yellowknife NT X1A 3S7**
info@cent-nt.ca
www.cent-nt.ca
To promote positive business relationships between member
firms & clients; to promote members' business interests.
Carlos Philipovsky, President

Consulting Engineers of Yukon (CEY)
**c/o EBA Engineering Consultants Ltd., #6, 151 Industrial
Rd., Whitehorse YT Y1A 2V3**
Tel: 867-668-3068; *Fax:* 867-668-4349
cey@eba.ca
www.cey.ca
To maintain high professional standards in the consulting
engineering profession; To promote cordial relations among
various consulting firms in the Yukon; to foster interchange of
professional management & business experience & information
among consulting engineers; To develop regional representation
& participation in affairs of the association

Continental Automated Buildings Association (CABA) / Association continentale pour l'automatisation des bâtiments
#210, 1173 Cyrville Rd., Ottawa ON K1J 7S6
Tel: 613-686-1814; *Fax:* 613-744-7833
Toll-Free: 888-798-2222
caba@caba.org
www.caba.org
www.youtube.com/user/cabaconf
www.linkedin.com/company/continental-automated-buildings-ass
ociation-caba-
twitter.com/caba_news
To promote advanced technologies for the automation of homes
& buildings in North America; To create opportunities for
members
Ronald J. Zimmer, President & CEO
Aruna Gamage, Financial Administrator
Greg Walker, Director, Research
Conrad McCallum, Director, Communications

The Engineering Institute of Canada (EIC) / L'Institut canadien des ingénieurs (ICI)
PO Box 40140, Ottawa ON K1V 0W8
www.eic-ici.ca
www.linkedin.com/company/the-engineering-institute-of-canada
To further the development of engineering in Canada; To
stimulate the advancement of the quality & scope of Canadian
engineering; To meet regularly with other engineering
organizations & industries to promote understanding &
improvement of the profession, the diffusion of engineering
information & to provide Canadian representation in specialized
engineering fields; To interact with government agencies &
departments for the purpose of influencing decision making on
matters relating to engineering & technology; To cooperate with
the provincial engineering licensing bodies, The Canadian
Council of Professional Engineering, The Association of
Consulting Engineers of Canada, The Canadian Academy of
Engineering & other engineering organizations in matters of
common interest; To promote interaction with specific interest
groups; To collaborate with universities & educational institutions
Guy Gosselin, Executive Director
Mohammud Emamally, Administrative Officer

Engineers Canada / Ingénieurs Canada
#300, 55 Metcalfe St., Ottawa ON K1P 6L5
Tel: 613-232-2474; *Fax:* 613-230-5759
Toll-Free: 877-408-9273
info@engineerscanada.ca
www.engineerscanada.ca
www.youtube.com/user/EngineersCanada
www.linkedin.com/company/engineers-canada
www.facebook.com/EngineersCanada
twitter.com/engineerscanada
To establish & maintain a common bond between constituent
associations; To assist constituent associations to meet their
common needs & those of their members by coordinating
standards, procedures, & programs across Canada; To
represent the engineering profession with respect to national &
international affairs; To increase the profile & prestige of the
engineering profession
Gerard McDonald, Chief Executive Officer
Stephanie Price, Executive Vice-President, Regulatory Affairs
Jeanette M. Southwood, Vice-President, Corporate Affairs &
Strategic Partnerships
Sylvie Francoeur, Director, Human Resources

Engineers Nova Scotia
1355 Barrington St., Halifax NS B3J 1Y9
Tel: 902-429-2250; *Fax:* 902-423-9769
Toll-Free: 888-802-7367
info@engineersnovascotia.ca
www.engineersnovascotia.ca
To establish, maintain & develop standards of knowledge & skill;
qualification & practice; & professional ethics; To promote pthe
value & proficiency of the Engineering profession
Len White, P.Eng., Chief Executive Officer & Registrar
Katherine MacLeod, P.Eng., President

Ingénieurs Sans Frontières Québec (ISFQ) / Engineers Without Borders Quebec
#204, 8440, boul St-Laurent, Montréal QC H2P 2M5
Tél: 438-320-4737
isfq@isfq.ca
isfq.ca
www.instagram.com/isf_qc
www.linkedin.com/company/ing-nieurs-sans-fronti-res-qu-bec-isf
q-
www.facebook.com/ingenieurssansfrontieresquebec
Améliorer la qualité de vie dans les pays en développement à
travers le développement durable; Fournir des services
d'ingénierie dans les pays en développement; Informer le public
sur l'importance de la coopération internationale

Pierre-Luc Huot, Directrice générale

Innovate Calgary
**Alastair Ross Technology Centre, 3553 - 31 St. NW, Calgary
AB T2L 2K7**
Tel: 403-284-6400; *Fax:* 403-267-5699
info@innovatecalgary.com
www.innovatecalgary.com
www.linkedin.com/company/innovate-calgary
www.facebook.com/innovatecalgary
twitter.com/innovatecalgary
To aid in acceleration & innovation of business in the technology
sector
Peter Garrett, President
Susan Delesalle, Chief Financial Officer

Institut national d'optique (INO) / National Optics Institute
2740, rue Einstein, Québec QC G1P 4S4
Tel: 418-657-7006; *Toll-Free:* 866-657-7406
info@ino.ca
www.ino.ca
www.youtube.com/user/INOphotonique
www.linkedin.com/company/ino
www.facebook.com/INOCanada
twitter.com/inocanada
To be an international leader in optics & photonics R&D,
promoting economic expansion in the country by providing
assistance to companies seeking to be more competitive
Alain Chandonnet, President & CEO
Michel Arnault, Chief Operations Officer

Island Technology Professionals (ITP)
PO Box 1436, 92 Queen St., Charlottetown PE C1A 7N1
Tel: 902-892-8324
registrar@techpei.ca
www.techpei.ca
www.facebook.com/IslandTechnologyProfessionals
twitter.com/Tech_PEI
To benefit society by advancing the professions of applied
science & engineering technology in Prince Edward Island
Bryan Burt, CET, President
Marea O'Halloran, CET, Vice-President
Laurie Eveleigh, CET, Treasurer
Troy Livingstone, CET, Registrar

NACE International (NACE)
15835 Park Ten Pl., Houston TX 77084 USA
Tel: 281-228-6200; *Fax:* 281-228-6300
firstservice@nace.org
www.nace.org
www.linkedin.com/company/nace-international
www.facebook.com/NACEinternational
twitter.com/NACEtweet
To protect people, assets & the environment from the effects of
corrosion; Northern Area sections include: Atlantic Canada, BC,
Calgary, Canadian National Capital Section, Edmonton,
Montreal, Saskatchewan & Toronto
Bob Chalker, Executive Director

Natural Sciences & Engineering Research Council of Canada (NSERC) / Conseil de recherches en sciences naturelles et en génie du Canada (CRSNG)
350 Albert St., 16th Fl., Ottawa ON K1A 1H5
Tel: 613-995-4273; *Fax:* 613-992-5337
Toll-Free: 855-275-2861
comm@nserc-crsng.gc.ca
www.nserc-crsng.gc.ca
www.youtube.com/user/NSERCTube
www.linkedin.com/company/nserc-crsng
www.facebook.com/nserccanada
twitter.com/nserc_crsng
To support university students in advanced studies; To promote
discovery research; To foster innovation through Canadian
investment in postsecondary research projects
Alejandro Adem, President

New Brunswick Society of Certified Engineering Technicians & Technologists (NBSCETT) / Société des techniciens et des technologues agréés du génie du Nouveau-Brunswick (STTAGN-B)
#12B, 102 Main St., Fredericton NB E3A 9N6
Tel: 506-454-6124; *Fax:* 506-452-7076
Toll-Free: 800-665-8324
nbscett@nbscett.nb.ca
www.nbscett.nb.ca
www.facebook.com/nbscett
To grant certification to applied science & engineering
technology technicians & technologists; To protect titles &
powers of discipline for its members
Edward F. Leslie, Executive Director & CEO
Kenneth C. Brown, Registrar

Northwest Territories & Nunavut Association of Professional Engineers & Geoscientists (NAPEG)
#201, 4817 - 49th St., Yellowknife NT X1A 3S7
Tel: 867-920-4055; *Fax:* 867-873-4058
www.napeg.nt.ca
www.facebook.com/208781715979685
twitter.com/napeg_north
To license professional engineers & professional geoscientists in the Northwest Territories & Nunavut; To regulate the practices of professional engineering & professional geoscience; To establish & maintain standards of knowledge, skill, care, & professional ethics among registrants
Sudhir Jha, P.Eng., President
Linda Golding, FEC (Hon), FGC, Executive Director & Registrar

Ontario Association of Certified Engineering Technicians & Technologists (OACETT)
#404, 10 Four Seasons Pl., Toronto ON M9B 6H7
Tel: 416-621-9621; *Fax:* 416-621-8694
info@oacett.org
www.oacett.org
www.instagram.com/oacett
www.linkedin.com/company/oacett
www.facebook.com/OACETT
twitter.com/OACETT
To advance the profession of applied science & engineering technology through standards for society's benefit
David J. Thomson, Chief Executive Officer
Stephen Morley, President

Ordre des ingénieurs du Québec (OIQ)
#350, 1100, av des Canadiens-de-Montréal, Montréal QC H3B 2S2
Tél: 514-845-6141; *Téléc:* 514-845-1833
Ligne sans frais: 800-461-6141
sac@oiq.qc.ca
oiq.qc.ca
www.youtube.com/user/ordredesingenieurs
www.linkedin.com/company/ordreingenieursqc
www.facebook.com/oiq.qc.ca
twitter.com/OIQ
Faire de la promotion et s'assurer de la qualité des services rendus à la société par les ingénieurs, individuellement et collectivement, en tant que membres d'un corps professionnel; Favoriser leur épanouissement professionnel et personnel; Contribuer au développement socio-économique de la société
Kathy Baig, Présidente
Louis Beauchemin, Directeur générale

Ordre des technologues professionnels du Québec (OTPQ)
#505, 606, rue Cathcart, Montréal QC H3B 1K9
Tél: 514-845-3247; *Téléc:* 514-845-3643
Ligne sans frais: 800-561-3459
info@otpq.qc.ca
www.otpq.qc.ca
www.youtube.com/user/TechnologuePro1
www.linkedin.com/groups/4134994
www.facebook.com/TechnologuesProfessionnels
twitter.com/otpq
Promouvoir et assurer la compétence des technologues professionnels dans l'intérêt public
Denis Beauchamp, Directeur général et secrétaire

PEMAC Asset Management Association of Canada
#750, 2 Robert Speck Pkwy., Mississauga ON L4Z 1H8
Tel: 905-823-7255; *Fax:* 905-823-8001
Toll-Free: 877-523-7255
admin@pemac.org
www.pemac.org
www.linkedin.com/company/pemac-asset-management-associati
on-of-canada
www.facebook.com/163677003698891
twitter.com/PEMACexec
To be recognized as a nationwide centre of excellence in plant engineering & maintenance; To form positive & constructive links with industry & service sectors, in support of local & nationwide developments & productivity; To deliver strongly identifiable services & commitments across the range of disciplines embraced by the association; To educate & introduce new concepts; To provide representation at all government levels; To provide career enhancement & networking opportunities; To promote research in the field of plant engineering & maintenance
Cindy Snedden, Executive Director

Professional Engineers & Geoscientists Newfoundland & Labrador (PEGNL)
Baine Johnston Centre, PO Box 21207, #203, 10 Fort William Pl., St. John's NL A1A 5B2
Tel: 709-753-7714; *Fax:* 709-753-6131
main@pegnl.ca
www.pegnl.ca

To provide competent & ethical practice of engineering & geoscience in Newfoundland & Labrador; To ensure public confidence, sustainability, & stewardship of the professions; To provide leadership to enhance quality of life through the application & management of engineering & geoscience
Geoff Emberley, P.Eng., FEC, Chief Executive Offiver & Registrar
Mark Fewer, Chief Operating Officer & Deputy Registrar
Janet Bradshaw, P.Eng., FEC, Director, Professional Standards

Professional Engineers Ontario (PEO)
#101, 40 Sheppard Ave. West, Toronto ON M2N 6K9
Tel: 416-224-1100; *Fax:* 416-224-8168
Toll-Free: 800-339-3716
www.peo.on.ca
www.youtube.com/c/PeoOnCa
www.linkedin.com/company/peo—-professional-engineers-ontari
o
www.facebook.com/ProfessionalEngineersOntario
twitter.com/PEO_HQ
To meet the needs of Ontario society by licensing & regulating the entire practice of professional engineering in an open, transparent, inclusive manner
Marisa Sterling, P.Eng., FEC, President
Johnny Zuccon, P.Eng., FEC, CEO/Registrar
Linda Latham, P.Eng., Deputy Registrar, Regulatory Compliance
David Smith, Director, Communications
Mehta Chetan, Director, Finance & PEO Controller

Saskatchewan Applied Science Technologists & Technicians (SASTT)
363 Park St., Regina SK S4N 5B2
Tel: 306-721-6633; *Fax:* 306-721-0112
info@tpsk.ca
www.tpsk.ca
To regulate the professional conduct of applied science technologists & certified technicians in Saskatchewan, in order to protect the public

Shad Canada
419-A Phillip St., Waterloo ON N2L 3X2
Tel: 519-884-8844; *Fax:* 519-884-0665
info@shad.ca
www.shad.ca
www.youtube.com/user/SHADVideoChannel
www.linkedin.com/company/shadcanada
www.facebook.com/ShadProgram
twitter.com/shadnetwork
To advance the scientific & technological capabilities of youth, integrated with the development of their entrepreneurial spirit; To collaborate with education, business & other communities, both domestic & international, to provide exceptional development opportunities
Tim Jackson, President & CEO

Society of Motion Picture & Television Engineers (SMPTE)
#601, 445 Hamilton Ave., White Plains NY 10601-1827 USA
Tel: 914-761-1100; *Fax:* 914-206-4216
membership@smpte.org
www.smpte.org
www.youtube.com/user/smpteconnect
www.linkedin.com/groups/71716
www.facebook.com/smpteconnect
twitter.com/smpteconnect
Barbara H. Lange, Executive Director

Society of Tribologists & Lubrication Engineers / Société des tribologistes et ingénieurs en lubrification
840 Busse Hwy., Park Ridge IL 60068-2302 USA
Tel: 847-825-5536; *Fax:* 847-825-1456
information@stle.org
www.stle.org
www.youtube.com/user/STLEMedia
www.facebook.com/stle.org
twitter.com/stle_tribology
To promote study of tribology, friction, wear & lubrication; To function as resource for distribution of new information & techniques
Edward Salek, Executive Director
Myrna Scott-Perez, Director, Operations & Technology
Stefan Carrera, Manager, Education
Bruce Margueitio, Manager, Digital Marketing
Tracy Vanee, Manager, National Sales

Structural Innovation & Monitoring Technologies Resources Centre
Agricultural & Civil Engineering Building, University of Manitoba, #A250, 96 Dafoe Rd., Winnipeg MB R3T 2N2
Tel: 204-474-8506
info@simtrec.ca
simtrec.ca

To advance civil engineering in Canada to a world leadership position through the development & application of fibre-reinforced polymers & integrated intelligent fibre optic sensing technologies
Donald Whitmore, Chair
Aftab Mufti, Director

TechNova
#310, 202 Brownlow Ave., Dartmouth NS B3B 1T5
Tel: 902-463-3236; *Fax:* 902-465-7567
Toll-Free: 866-723-8867
info@technova.ca
www.technova.ca
twitter.com/NSTechNova
To certify engineering & applied science technicians & technologists for the betterment of the public & the welfare of the environment
Mike Maclean, President
Joe Simms, Registrar

Tunnelling Association of Canada (TAC) / Association canadienne des tunnels
8828 Pigott Rd., Richmond BC V7A 2C4
Tel: 604-241-1297; *Fax:* 604-241-1399
admin@tunnelcanada.ca
www.tunnelcanada.ca
To promote Canadian tunnelling & underground excavation technologies; To represent the tunnelling community in matters of public & technical concern
Derek Zoldy, Secretary-Treasurer
Rick Staples, President

Environmental

Alberta Ecotrust Foundation
#1020, 105 - 12th Ave. SE, Calgary AB TSG 1A1
Tel: 403-209-2245; *Toll-Free:* 800-465-2147
info@albertaecotrust.com
albertaecotrust.com
twitter.com/AlbertaEcotrust
To provide grants to environmental groups that work towards improving Alberta's eco health
Pat Letizia, Executive Director

Alberta Environmental Network (AEN)
PO Box 4541, Edmonton AB T6E 5G4
Tel: 780-757-4872
admin@aenweb.ca
www.aenweb.ca
twitter.com/ABEnvNet
To facilitate communication & cooperation among environmental groups in Alberta in order to contribute to the enhancement & protection of the environment
Melissa Gorrie, Co-Chair
Nikki Way, Co-Chair

Alberta Fish & Game Association (AFGA)
6924 - 104 St., Edmonton AB T6H 2L7
Tel: 780-437-2342; *Fax:* 780-438-6872
office@afga.org
www.afga.org
www.facebook.com/120693761350755
twitter.com/AlbertaFishGame
To ensure fish & wildlife habitat & resources in Alberta
Martin Sharren, Executive Vice-President

Alberta Water Council
Petroleum Plaza, South Tower, #1400, 9915 - 108 St., Edmonton AB T5K 2G8
Tel: 780-644-7380
info@awchome.ca
www.awchome.ca
The Alberta Water Council is a stakeholder partnership that provides leadership, expertise and advocacy, to engage and empower individuals, organizations, business and governments to achieve the outcomes of the Water for Life strategy.
Gord Edwards, Executive Director

Alberta Wilderness Association (AWA)
455 - 12th St. NW, Calgary AB T2N 1Y9
Tel: 403-283-2025; *Fax:* 403-270-2743
awa@abwild.ca
albertawilderness.ca
www.youtube.com/user/AlbertaWilderness
www.facebook.com/AlbertaWilderness
twitter.com/ABWilderness
To promote the protection of Alberta's rivers & wildlands areas; To restore the natural ecosystems of Alberta; To educate Albertans on wilderness conservation & sustainable use of natural lands & waters
Jim Campbell, President
Christyann Olson, Executive Director

Arctic Institute of North America (AINA)
Earth Sciences Bldg., University of Calgary, 2500 University Dr. NW, #ES-1040, Calgary AB T2N 1N4
Tel: 403-220-7515; *Fax:* 403-282-4609
arctic@ucalgary.ca
www.arctic.ucalgary.ca
www.instagram.com/aina_arcticsynthesis
www.facebook.com/ArcticInstituteofNorthAmerica
twitter.com/ArcticSynthesis
To encourage & support scientific research pertaining to the polar regions
Maribeth Murray, Executive Director

Association for Literature, Environment, & Culture in Canada (ALECC) / Association pour la littérature, l'environnement et la culture au Canada
c/o Department of English, University of Calgary, 2500 University Dr. NW, 11th Fl., Calgary AB T2N 1N4
contactus@alecc.ca
www.alecc.ca
To promote & support artistic, critical & cultural studies work on a wide range of environmental issues
Robert Boschman, President

Big Rideau Lake Association (BRLA)
PO Box 93, Portland ON K0G 1V0
Tel: 613-272-3629
brla@brla.on.ca
www.brla.on.ca
To protect & conserve Big Rideau Lake and share its resources.
Doug Good, President

BIOQuébec / Québec Bio-Industries Business Network
#205, 1460, boul de l'Innovation, Bromont QC J2L 0J8
Tél: 514-360-4565; *Téléc:* 450-919-0827
direction@bioquebec.com
www.bioquebec.com
www.youtube.com/channel/UChbVHD9WA91i8iZ_la7TFHw
www.linkedin.com/company/bioquébec
www.facebook.com/BIOQuebec
twitter.com/BIO_Qc
Ôtre le porte-parole des entreprises biotechnologiques du Québec; favoriser le développement et la mise en valeur des biotechnologies et des bioindustries québécoises, et ce au bénéficie de ses membres; To promote the development & the upgrading of biotechnologies; to supply strategic information of technical & economical content as well as carry out projects, events & activities; to stimulate collaboration between private industry, governments & universities; to stimulate the growth of structuring economical activities in this field; to act as a spokesman for the bio-industry in Québec
Anie Perrault, Directrice générale

British Columbia Environment Industry Association (BCEIA)
#400, 602 West Hastings St., Vancouver BC V6B 1P2
Tel: 604-683-2751; *Fax:* 604-677-5960
info@bceia.com
www.bceia.com
twitter.com/BCEIA_
To foster the growth of the environmental industry & to promote technology development and innovation in the sector
Brian S. White, President
Chris McCue, 1st Vice President
Kate Branch, 2nd Vice President

British Columbia Environmental Network (BCEN)
PO Box 1209, 150 Mile House BC V0K 2G0
Tel: 604-984-7030
www.bcen.info
To facilitate communication among environmental groups & individuals so that ecological sustainability & economic stability prevail, & biological diversity & human health remain viable
Rod Marining, Contact

BurlingtonGreen Environmental Association
3281 Myers Lane, Burlington ON L7N 1K6
Tel: 905-466-2171
www.burlingtongreen.org
www.facebook.com/burlington.green.environment
twitter.com/burlingtongreen
To advocate for local environmental issues
Amy Schnurr, Executive Director

Campaign for Nuclear Phaseout (CNP)
#412, 1 Nicholas St., Ottawa ON K1N 7B7
www.cnp.ca
The Campaign for Nuclear Phaseout (CNP) represents a coalition of Canadian public interest organizations concerned with the environmental consequences of nuclear power generation.

Canadian Arctic Resources Committee
488 Gladstone Ave., Ottawa ON K1N 8V4
Tel: 613-759-4284; *Fax:* 613-237-3845
Toll-Free: 866-949-9006
davidg@carc.org
www.carc.org
www.facebook.com/168782596508551
The Canadian Arctic Resources Committee (CARC) is a citizens' organization dedicated to the long-term environmental and social well being of northern Canada and its peoples.
Ben McDonald, Acting Chair

Canadian Association for Laboratory Accreditation Inc. (CALA)
#102, 2934 Baseline Rd., Ottawa ON K2H 1B2
Tel: 613-233-5300; *Fax:* 613-233-5501
info@cala.ca
www.cala.ca
www.linkedin.com/company/canadian-association-for-laboratory-accreditation-cala-
www.facebook.com/161209647296775
To provide internationally-recognized accreditation services; To assist laboratories in the achievement of high levels of scientific & management excellence; To improve environmental quality & public health & safety
Andrew Adams, President & CEO
Stephen Williamson, Chief Financial Officer
Ken Middlebrook, Manager, Proficiency Testing
Andrew Morris, Manager, Data & Information

Canadian Association of Recycling Industries (CARI) / Association canadienne des industries du recyclage (ACIR)
PO Box 67094, Stn. Westboro, Ottawa ON K2A 4E4
Tel: 613-728-6946
info@cari-acir.org
www.cari-acir.org
www.linkedin.com/company/cariacir
www.facebook.com/CARIACIRScrap
twitter.com/CARI_Recycling
To address issues facing the recycling industry in Canada & internationally; To promote commercial recycling activities
Tracy Shaw, President & CEO
Donna Turner, Director, Events
Marie Binette, Manager, Communications

Canadian Council on Invasive Species (CCIS)
72 - 7th Ave. South, Williams Lake BC V2G 4N5
Tel: 249-353-2247
infocanadainvasives
canadainvasives.ca
www.youtube.com/channel/UCkxytu3iSXvbeB51isN1kNw
www.facebook.com/canadainvasives
To be a national voice & hub of conversation for the impacts of invasive species on Canada's environment
Barry Gibbons, Executive Director

Canadian Environmental Certification Approvals Board (CECAB) / Bureau canadien de reconnaissance professionnelle des spécialistes de l'environnement
#200, 308 - 11th Ave. SE, Calgary AB T2G 0Y2
Tel: 403-233-7484; *Fax:* 403-264-6240
certification@eco.ca
www.cecab.org
CECAB is a professional autonomous body providing national certification for Canadian environmental practitioners.
Victor Nowicki, Chair

Canadian Environmental Law Association (CELA) / Association canadienne du droit de l'environnement
#1500, 55 University Ave., Toronto ON M5J 2H7
Tel: 416-960-2284; *Fax:* 416-960-9392
Toll-Free: 844-755-1420
articling@cela.ca
www.cela.ca
www.instagram.com/canadianenvironmentallawassoc
www.linkedin.com/company/canadian-environmental-law-association-cela
www.facebook.com/CanadianEnvironmentalLawAssociation
twitter.com/CanEnvLawAssn
To advocate for environmental law reform; To act in court or during hearings on behalf of citizens' groups & individuals who would otherwise be unable to afford legal assistance
Theresa McClenaghan, Executive Director & Counsel
Tracy Tucker, Office Manager/Executive Assistant

Canadian Environmental Network (RCEN) / Réseau canadien de l'environnement
214 Manchester Ave., Ottawa ON K1Y 1Y9
Tel: 613-728-9810; *Fax:* 613-728-2963
secretary@rcen.ca
rcen.ca
www.youtube.com/user/RCEN1
www.facebook.com/CanadianEnvironmentalNetwork
twitter.com/RCEN
To promote ecologically sound ways of life; To enhance members' work to restore, protect, & promote a clean & sustainable environment
Ian Peace, Acting Chair

Canadian Environmental Technology Advancement Corporation - West (CETAC)
3608 - 33rd St. NW, Calgary AB T2L 2A6
Tel: 403-777-9595; *Fax:* 403-777-9599
cetac@cetacwest.com
cetacwest.com
www.linkedin.com/company/2128202
www.facebook.com/431936763529236
To be committed to helping small & medium-sized enterprises that are engaged in the development & commercialization of new environmental technologies

Canadian Institute of Resources Law (CIRL) / Institut canadien du droit des ressources
Murray Fraser Hall, University of Calgary, #3353, 2500 University Dr. NW, Calgary AB T2N 1N4
Tel: 403-220-3200; *Fax:* 403-282-6182
cirl@ucalgary.ca
cirl.ca
www.facebook.com/theCIRL
To undertake & promote research, education & publication on the law relating to Canada's renewable & non-renewable natural resources
Allan Ingelson, LLM, JD, BSc, B, Executive Director

Canadian Land Reclamation Association (CLRA) / Association canadienne de réhabilitation des sites dégradés (ACRSD)
#202, 5405 - 99th St. NW, Edmonton AB T6E 3N8
Tel: 780-437-0044; *Fax:* 780-413-0076
info@clra.ca
www.clra.ca
www.linkedin.com/company/canadianlandreclamationassociation national
www.facebook.com/CanadianLandReclamationAssociation
twitter.com/CLRA_National
To encourage involvement in reclamation projects of disturbed land
Andrea McEachern, President
Shauna Prokopchuk, Coordinator

Canadian Network for Environmental Education & Communication (EECOM) / Réseau canadien d'éducation et de communication relatives à l'environnement
c/o 336 Rosedale Ave., Winnipeg MB R3L 1L8
nswayze@eecom.org
www.eecom.org
www.facebook.com/EECOM.Canada
To advance environmental learning in Canada; To promote environmental literacy & environmental stewardship; To contribute to a sustainable future
Natalie Swayzer, Executive Director
Grant Gardner, Chair
Rick Wishart, Treasurer

Canadian Peregrine Foundation (CPF)
#20, 25 Crouse Rd., Toronto ON M1R 5P8
Tel: 416-481-1233; *Toll-Free:* 888-709-3944
info@peregrine-foundation.ca
www.peregrine-foundation.ca
The Canadian Peregrine Foundation is a registered charity dedicated to assisting the recovery of the peregrine falcon and other raptors at risk.

Canadian Society of Environmental Biologists (CSEB) / Société canadienne des biologistes de l'environnement
PO Box 962, Stn. F, Toronto ON M4Y 2N9
cseb-scbe.org
To further the conservation of natural resources of Canada & to promote the prudent management of these resources so as to minimize adverse environmental effects; To ensure high professional standards in education, research & management related to resources & environment; To advance the education of the public & to protect public interest on matters pertaining to the use of natural resources & the protection & management of the environment; To undertake environmental research &

education programs; To assess & evaluate administrative & legislative policies having ecological significance in terms of conservation of resources & quality of the environment; To develop & promote policies that seek to achieve balance among resource management & utilization, protection of the environment & quality of life; To foster liaison among environmental biologists working within governmental, industrial & educational frameworks across Canada
Curt Schroeder, President

Canadian Wildlife Federation (CWF) / Fédération canadienne de la faune (FCF)
350 Michael Cowpland Dr., Ottawa ON K2M 2W1
Tel: 613-599-9594; *Fax:* 613-599-4428
Toll-Free: 800-563-9453
info@cwf-fcf.org
cwf-fcf.org
www.youtube.com/user/CanadianWildlifeFed
www.linkedin.com/company/canadian-wildlife-federation
www.facebook.com/CanadianWildlifeFederation
twitter.com/CWF_FCF
To promote the conservation of fish & wildlife, wildlife habitat & quality aquatic environments; To foster an understanding of natural processes; To ensure adequate stocks of wildlife for the use & enjoyment of all Canadians; To sponsor research; To cooperate with legislators, government & non-government agencies in achieving conservation objectives
Rick Bates, Executive Vice-President & CEO
Pamela Logan, Director, Communications
Maria Vallee, Director, Finance

Canadians for Clean Prosperity
#503, 460 Richmond St. West, Toronto ON M5V 1Y1
Tel: 416-777-2327; *Fax:* 416-777-2524
info@cleanprosperity.ca
www.cleanprosperity.ca
www.facebook.com/cleanprosperity
twitter.com/CleanProsperity
To build a strong economy using pollution fees to cut taxes
Mark Cameron, Executive Director
Tom Chervinsky, Acting Executive Director & Vice-President, Campaigns
Mollie Anderson, Coordinator, Engagement

Carolinian Canada Coalition
Grosvenor Lodge, 1017 Western Rd., London ON N6G 1G5
Tel: 519-433-7077; *Fax:* 519-645-0981
info@carolinian.org
www.carolinian.org
www.youtube.com/user/CarolinianCanada
www.facebook.com/caroliniancanada
twitter.com/caroliniancan
To promote the protection and conservation of the Carolinian Life Zone of Southwestern Ontario.
Michelle Kanter, Executive Director

Citizens for a Safe Environment (CSE)
Tel: 416-461-1092
info@csetoronto.org
www.csetoronto.org
To promote waste management practices that protect the health of Toronto citizens, their communities and the environment.

Citizens Opposed to Paving the Escarpment (COPE)
PO Box 20014, 2211 Brant St., Burlington ON L7P 0A4
mail@cope-nomph.org
www.cope-nomph.org
To preserve the Niagara Escarpment, by ensuring that no new highway corridors are paved across the Niagara Escarpment & that all viable alternatives to the proposed Mid-Peninsula Highway are fully considered

Citizens' Environment Watch (CEW)
#380, 401 Richmond St. West, Toronto ON M5V 3A8
Tel: 647-258-3280; *Fax:* 416-979-3155
info@citizensenvironmentwatch.org
www.citizensenvironmentwatch.org
To provide communities the tools for education, monitoring and influencing positive change and to encourage people to take an active role in restoring and sustaining nature.
Meredith Cochrane, Executive Director

Clean Nova Scotia Foundation (CNS)
126 Portland St., Dartmouth NS B2Y 1H8
Tel: 902-420-3474; *Fax:* 902-982-6768
Toll-Free: 855-736-3474
info@clean.ns.ca
www.clean.ns.ca
www.youtube.com/CleanFoundation
www.facebook.com/CleanFoundation
twitter.com/CleanFoundation

To inspire positive environmental change in Nova Scotia; To support clean leaders; To work towards achieving a clean environment & clean water
Scott Skinner, Executive Director
Gina Patterson, Director, Policy & Strategic Relations
Geoff McCain, Senior Manager, Finance & Administration
Erin Burbridge, Director, Programs & Regulatory Affairs
Charlynne Robertson, Coordinator, Waste Programs
Camilla Melrose, Coordinator, Water Programs

Compost Council of Canada / Conseil canadien du compost
16 Northumberland St., Toronto ON M6H 1P7
Tel: 416-535-0240; *Fax:* 416-536-9892
Toll-Free: 877-571-4769
info@compost.org
www.compost.org
www.facebook.com/compost.council
To advance organics residuals recycling & compost use; To contribute to environmental sustainability
Susan Antler, Executive Director

Conservation Council of New Brunswick (CCNB) / Conseil de la conservation du Nouveau-Brunswick
180 St. John St., Fredericton NB E3B 4A9
Tel: 506-458-8747; *Fax:* 506-458-1047
info@conservationcouncil.ca
www.conservationcouncil.ca
www.facebook.com/conservationcouncil
twitter.com/cc_nb
To generate awareness of the ecological foundations of quality of life; To promote public policies with respect to the integrity of natural systems & to contribute to a sustainable society; To advocate appropriate remedies to pressing environmental problems such as ground water contamination & hazardous wastes
Lois Corbett, Executive Director

Conservation Council of Ontario (CCO) / Conseil de conservation de l'Ontario
c/o Hardy Stevenson & Associates, 364 Davenport Rd., Toronto ON M5R 1K6
Tel: 416-533-1635; *Fax:* 416-979-3936
conserveontario.ca
www.instagram.com/weconserve
www.linkedin.com/company/2458603
www.facebook.com/ontarioconserves
twitter.com/ccoweconserve
To build a strong conservation movement across Ontario

Conservation Ontario
PO Box 11, 120 Bayview Pkwy., Newmarket ON L3R 4W3
Tel: 905-895-0716; *Fax:* 905-895-0751
info@conservationontario.ca
www.conservation-ontario.on.ca
www.instagram.com/con_ont
www.facebook.com/1268611190733330
twitter.com/conont
To represent & support a network of community-based environmental organizations; To ensure conservation, restoration, & responsible management of Ontario's wetlands, woodlands, & natural habitat
Dick Hibma, Chair
Kim Gavine, General Manager
Bonnie Fox, Manager, Policy & Planning
Jane Lewington, Specialist, Marketing & Communications

Construction Resource Initiatives Council (CRI) / Conseil d'initiatives des ressources de construction
#609 Donald B. Munro Dr., Carp ON K0A 1L0
Tel: 613-795-4632; *Fax:* 613-839-0704
info@cricouncil.com
www.cricouncil.com
www.linkedin.com/groups/3819158
www.facebook.com/330962370266752
twitter.com/CRICouncil
To develop strategies that help the building industry achieve the goal of zero waste production.
Renée L. Gratton, President & CEO

Cumulative Environmental Management Association (CEMA)
Morrison Center, #214, 9914 Morrison St., Fort McMurray AB T9H 4A4
Tel: 780-799-3947; *Fax:* 780-714-3081
info@cemaonline.ca
www.cemaonline.ca
www.facebook.com/111309945551863
twitter.com/cemacomms
To study the cumulative environmental effects of industrial development in the region and produce guidelines and management frameworks.
Glen Semenchuk, Executive Director

Ducks Unlimited Canada (DUC) / Canards Illimités Canada (CIC)
PO Box 1160, Stonewall MB R0C 2Z0
Tel: 204-729-3500; *Fax:* 204-467-9028
Toll-Free: 800-665-3825
communications@ducks.ca
www.ducks.ca
www.youtube.com/channel/UCR5V5lumfBOHkGOYxKbghsg
www.linkedin.com/company/ducks-unlimited-canada
www.facebook.com/ducksunlimitedcanada
twitter.com/ducanada
To conserve, restore & manage wetlands & associated habitats for waterfowl, as well as for the benefit of other wildlife & people
David Blom, Chair
Kevin Harris, President
Karla Guyn, Chief Executive Officer

Earth Day Canada (EDC) / Jour de la terre Canada
276 Roncesvalles Ave., Toronto ON M6R 2M2
Tel: 416-599-1991; *Fax:* 416-599-3100
Toll-Free: 888-283-2784
info@earthday.ca
www.earthday.ca
www.youtube.com/user/EarthDayCanada
www.facebook.com/EarthDayCanada
twitter.com/earthdaycanada
To inspire & support Canadians to connect with nature & build resilient communities
Deb Doncaster, President

Ecojustice Canada Society
#390, 425 Carrall St., Vancouver BC V6B 6E3
Tel: 604-685-5618; *Fax:* 604-685-7813
Toll-Free: 800-926-7744
info@ecojustice.ca
www.ecojustice.ca
www.facebook.com/ecojustice
twitter.com/ecojustice_ca
To provide legal representation to environmental groups that cannot afford to go to court against large institutions when important wilderness values are at stake; to bring selected cases with the ultimate goal of establishing an aggregate of strong legal precedents that recognize environmental values; to provide professional advice on the development of environmental legislation
Devon Page, Executive Director
Marion Greene, Chief Financial Officer
Andrea Gutierrez, Director, Operations
Huda Al-Saedy, Director, Philanthropy
Kimberly Shearon, Director, Strategic Communications

Ecology Action Centre (EAC)
2705 Fern Lane, Halifax NS B3K 4L3
Tel: 902-429-2202; *Fax:* 902-405-3716
info@ecologyaction.ca
www.ecologyaction.ca
www.facebook.com/EcologyActionCentre
twitter.com/ecologyaction
To act as a voice for Nova Scotia's environment; To build a healthier, more sustainable Nova Scotia
Marla MacLeod, Managing Director
Mark Butler, Policy Director
Carla Vandenberg, Financial Director

Ecotrust Canada
#90, 425 Carrall St., Vancouver BC V6B 6E3
Tel: 604-682-4141; *Fax:* 604-862-1944
info@ecotrust.ca
ecotrust.ca
www.youtube.com/user/EcotrustCanada
www.facebook.com/ecotrustcanada
twitter.com/ecotrustcanada
To improve environmental sustainability in British Columbia
Brenda Reid-Kuecks, President

Elsa Wild Animal Appeal of Canada
To help save endangered wildlife species in Canada

Enviro-Accès Inc.
#150, 85, rue Belvédère nord, Sherbrooke QC J1H 4A7
Tél: 819-823-2230; *Téléc:* 819-823-6632
enviro@enviroaccess.ca
www.enviroaccess.ca
Supporter les petites et moyennes entreprises qui oeuvrent dans le domaine de l'environnement en leur offrant les services professionnels nécessaires au développement de leurs projets et de leurs affaires.
Manon Laporte, Présidente-directrice générale

Environmental Careers Organization of Canada / L'Organisation pour les carrières en environnement du Canada
#400, 105 - 12th Ave. SE, Calgary AB T2G 1A1
Tel: 403-233-0748; *Fax:* 403-269-9544
Toll-Free: 800-890-1924
info@eco.ca
www.eco.ca
www.facebook.com/ecocanada
twitter.com/ecocanada
To provide services to all participants in the environmental sector, including educators, students, practitioners & employers
Faramarz Bogzaran, Chair
John Wiebe, Secretary-Treasurer
Kevin Nilson, President & CEO

Environmental Education Association of the Yukon (EEAY)
Whitehorse YT
eeyukon@gmail.com
taiga.net/YukonEE
To promote environmental education in the Yukon; To foster communication between individuals & groups with an interest in environmental education

Environmental Health Association of British Columbia (EHABC)
PO Box 30033, RPO Reyolds, Victoria BC V8X 5E1
Tel: 250-658-2027
info@ehabc.org
www.ehabc.org
www.facebook.com/353025931439290
To raise awareness within the medical community, educational institutions, & the general public to prevent further cases of environmental sensitivity from occurring

The Environmental Law Centre (Alberta) Society (ELC)
#410, 10115 - 100A St., Edmonton AB T5J 2W2
Tel: 780-424-5099; *Fax:* 780-424-5133
Toll-Free: 800-661-4238
elc@elc.ab.ca
www.elc.ab.ca
www.youtube.com/ELCAlberta
www.facebook.com/environmentallawcentre
twitter.com/ELC_Alberta
To conduct research in environmental & natural resources law, policy & procedure; To educate the public on environmental law; To operate an environmental law information & referral service for the benefit of the public; To monitor relevant municipal, provincial & federal environmental laws, policies & procedures, & make recommendations for reform
Jason Unger, Acting Executive Director

Environmental Managers Association of British Columbia (EMABC)
PO Box 3741, Vancouver BC V6B 3Z8
Tel: 604-998-2226; *Fax:* 604-998-2226
info@emaofbc.com
www.emaofbc.com
www.linkedin.com/groups/1856767
twitter.com/emaofbc
To encourage education, share knowledge among members and create a forum for environmental management issues in the industrial, commercial and institutional sectors, serve as a key resource of environmental information for members and explore existing and emerging environmental issues.
Leanne Harris, B.Sc., President
Don Bryant, MBA, P.Eng, P.E, Executive Director

Environmental Services Association of Alberta (ESAA)
#102, 2528 Ellwood Dr. SW, Edmonton AB T6X 0A9
Tel: 780-429-6363; *Fax:* 780-429-4249
Toll-Free: 800-661-9278
info@esaa.org
www.esaa.org
To act as the voice of Alberta's environment industry
Joe Chowaniec, Director, Program & Event Development

Environmental Services Association of Nova Scotia (ESANS)
Woodside Industrial Park, #211-2, 1 Research Dr., Dartmouth NS B2Y 4M9
Tel: 902-463-3538; *Fax:* 902-466-6889
contact@esans.ca
www.esans.ca
To the promote environmental products, services & organizations within the environmental industry
Norval Collins, President
Sandra Lynch, Operations Manager

Environnement jeunesse
Maison du développement durable, #400, 50, rue Sainte-Catherine ouest, Montréal QC H2X 3V4
Tél: 514-252-3016; *Téléc:* 514-254-5873
Ligne sans frais: 866-377-3016
infoenjeu@enjeu.qc.ca
enjeu.qc.ca
vimeo.com/channels/enjeu
www.facebook.com/environnement.jeunesse
twitter.com/ENJEUquebec
Promouvoir la conservation et l'amélioration de la qualité de l'environnement; développer chez les jeunes les qualités favorisant leur implication sociale
Jérôme Normand, Directeur général

Evergreen
Evergreen Brick Works, #300, 550 Bayview Ave, Toronto ON M4W 3X8
Tel: 416-596-1495; *Fax:* 416-596-1443
Toll-Free: 888-426-3138
info@evergreen.ca
www.evergreen.ca
www.instagram.com/EvergreenCanada
www.facebook.com/EvergreenCanada
twitter.com/EvergreenCanada
To bring communities & nature together for the benefit of both; To create sustaining, healthy, dynamic outdoor spaces by engaging people & encouraging local stewardship
Geoff Cape, Executive Director
Seana Irvine, Chief Strategy officer

FaunENord
CP 422, 512, rte 167 sud, Chibougamau QC G8P 2X8
Tél: 418-748-4441; *Téléc:* 418-748-1110
faunenord@lino.com
www.faunenord.org
www.facebook.com/FaunENord
Une entreprise vouée à la promotion & à l'aménagement durable des ressources fauniques & des écosystèmes
Isabelle Milord, Présidente

Fédération québécoise des chasseurs et pêcheurs
162, rue du Brome, Québec QC G3A 2P5
Tél: 418-878-8901; *Téléc:* 418-878-8980
Ligne sans frais: 888-523-2863
info@fedecp.qc.ca
www.fedecp.qc.ca
www.facebook.com/116805682100
www.facebook.com/FederationCP
Contribuer, dans le respect de la faune et de ses habitats, à la gestion du développement et à la perpétuation de la chasse et de la pêche comme activités traditionnelles et sportives
Pierre Latraverse, Président

First Nations Environmental Network
PO Box 394, Tofino BC V0R 2Z0
Tel: 250-726-5265; *Fax:* 250-725-2357
councilfire@hotmail.com
www.fnen.org
The First Nations Environmental Network is a circle of First Nations people committed to protecting, defending, and restoring the balance of all life by honouring traditional Indigenous values and the path of our ancestors.

Fondation de la faune du Québec (FFQ)
#420, 1175, av Lavigerie, Québec QC G1V 4P1
Tél: 418-644-7926; *Téléc:* 418-643-7655
Ligne sans frais: 877-639-0742
ffq@fondationdelafaune.qc.ca
www.fondationdelafaune.qc.ca
www.facebook.com/fondationdelafauneduquebec
Promouvoir la conservation et la mise en valeur de la faune et de son habitat
André Martin, Président-directeur général

FortWhyte Alive
1961 McCreary Rd., Winnipeg MB R3P 2K9
Tel: 204-989-8355; *Fax:* 204-895-4700
info@fortwhyte.org
www.fortwhyte.org
www.facebook.com/FortWhyteAlive
twitter.com/fortwhytealive
FortWhyte Alive is dedicated to providing programming, natural settings and facilities for environmental education and outdoor recreation. In so doing, FortWhyte promotes awareness and understanding of the natural world and actions leading to sustainable living.
Bill Elliott, President/CEO

Fraser Basin Council (FBC)
Main Office, 470 Granville St., 1st Fl., Vancouver BC V6C 1V5
Tel: 604-488-5350; *Fax:* 604-488-5351
info@fraserbasin.bc.ca
www.fraserbasin.bc.ca
To advance sustainability in the Fraser River Basin & across British Columbia
David Marshall, Executive Director
Charlotte Argue, Program Manager, Climate Change & Air Quality Program

Fresh Outlook Foundation (FOF)
12510 Ponderosa Rd., Lake Country BC V4V 2G9
Tel: 250-766-1777; *Fax:* 250-766-1767
www.freshoutlookfoundation.org
www.facebook.com/FreshOutlookFoundation
twitter.com/FreshOutlook
The Fresh Outlook Foundation (FOF) builds sustainable communities through a focus on the social, cultural, environmental, and economic aspects of community sustainability.
Joanne de Vries, CEO

Friends of Red Hill Valley
PO Box 61536, Hamilton ON L8T 5A1
Tel: 905-664-8796
redhill@hwcn.org
To protect & enhance the Red Hill Valley in Hamilton, Ontario
Don McLean, Chair

Friends of the Earth Canada (FoE) / Les Ami(e)s de la Terre Canada
#150, 18 Louisa St., Ottawa ON K2P 1X3
Tel: 613-241-0085; *Fax:* 613-566-3449
Toll-Free: 888-385-4444
foe@foecanada.org
foecanada.org
www.instagram.com/foe_canada
www.facebook.com/foe_canada
twitter.com/FoE_Canada
To serve as a national voice for the environment, working with others to inspire the renewal of our communities & the earth, through research, education, advocacy & cooperation
Arlye Waring, President
Beatrice Olivastri, Chief Executive Officer

Fuse Collective
University of Calgary, 2500 University Dr. NW, Calgary AB T2N 1N4
info@fusecollective.org
fusecollective.org
www.instagram.com/fuseyyc
www.linkedin.com/company/institute-for-sustainable-energy-environment-and-economy-students'-association-iseeesa-
www.facebook.com/FUSEYYC
twitter.com/fusecollective
To promote & create initiatives that reflect the growing movement to obtain a cleaner energy supply, healthy environment & efficient economy

Green Action Centre (RCM)
303 Portage Ave., 3rd Fl., Winnipeg MB R3B 2B4
Tel: 204-925-3777; *Fax:* 204-942-4207
Toll-Free: 866-394-8880
info@greenactioncentre.ca
greenactioncentre.ca
www.pinterest.com/gacentre
www.facebook.com/GreenActionCentre
twitter.com/greenactionctr
To promote ecological sustainability by developing alternatives to currently unsustainable practices; their principal activity is environmental education; our partners & clients include businesses, schools, non-profit groups, governments, recyclers, home gardeners & general public
Tracy Hucul, Executive Director

Greenbelt Foundation
#500, 661 Yonge St., Toronto ON M4Y 1Z9
Tel: 416-960-0001; *Fax:* 416-960-0030
info@greenbelt.ca
www.greenbelt.ca
www.instagram.com/ongreenbelt
www.linkedin.com/company/friends-of-the-greenbelt-foundation
www.facebook.com/ontariogreenbelt
twitter.com/greenbeltca
To help foster the Greenbelt's living countryside by nurturing & supporting activities that preserve its environmental & agricultural integrity
Edward McDonnell, Chief Executive Officer

Greenpeace Canada
33 Cecil St., Toronto ON M5T 1N1
Tel: 416-597-8408; *Fax:* 416-597-8422
supporter.ca@greenpeace.org
www.greenpeace.org/canada
www.youtube.com/user/GreenpeaceCanada
www.facebook.com/greenpeace.canada
twitter.com/greenpeaceCA
To raise awareness on issues such as biodiversity, pollution of the Earth, nuclear threats & disarmament; To bring public opinion to bear on decisions makers; To conduct scientific, economic & political research, publicize environmental problems, recommend environmentally sound solutions & lobby for change
Christy Ferguson, Executive Director

Greenspace Alliance of Canada's Capital
PO Box 55085, 240 Sparks St., Ottawa ON K1P 1A1
greenspace@greenspace-alliance.ca
www.greenspace-alliance.ca
To preserve green spaces in the National Capital area.
Amy Kempster, Chair

Hamilton Industrial Environmental Association (HIEA)
PO Box 35545, Hamilton ON L8H 7S6
Tel: 905-561-4432
info@hiea.org
www.hiea.org
To improve the local environment - air, land and water - through joint and individual activities, and by partnering with the community to enhance future understanding of environmental issues and help establish priorities for action.
Jim Stirling, Chair

Harmony Foundation of Canada / Fondation Harmonie du Canada
PO Box 50022, #15, 1594 Fairfield Rd., Victoria BC V8S 1G1
Tel: 250-380-3001; *Fax:* 250-380-0887
harmony@islandnet.com
www.harmonyfdn.ca
www.youtube.com/user/harmonyfdn
www.facebook.com/HarmonyFoundationCanada
twitter.com/HarmonyFDN
To encourage development which is socially & environmentally sustainable; To strive towards ecological stability, long-term prosperity, & social harmony
Robert Bateman, Honorary Chair
Jean-Pierre Soublière, President
Michael Bloomfield, Founder & Executive Director

Hope for Wildlife Society
5909 Hwy. 207, Seaforth NS B0J 1N0
Tel: 902-452-3339
Crisis Hot-Line: 902-407-9453
info@hopeforwildlife.net
www.hopeforwildlife.net
www.facebook.com/hopeforwildlife
twitter.com/hopeforwildlife
Specializing in the care, treatment and rehabilitation of injured or orphaned native fur bearing mammals, sea birds and songbirds both indigenous to the Nova Scotia area as well as non-indigenous species and pets.
Hope Swinimer, Founder & Director

Institut de recherche en biologie végétale (IRBV) / Plant Biology Research Institute (PBRI)
4101, rue Sherbrooke est, Montréal QC H1X 2B2
Tél: 514-343-2121; *Téléc:* 514-343-2288
irbv@irbv.umontreal.ca
www.irbv.umontreal.ca
To develop a centre of excellence in plant biology, both in fundamental research & its applicaitons; To train students in plant biology at the master, doctoral & post-doctoral levels; To further training and knowledge of its researchers & technical personnel; To promote the technological transfer of its scientific research results to users; To provide complementary services to the community in fields relevant to plant biology, where expertise in the field is lacking
Anne Bruneau, Directrice

International Institute for Sustainable Development (IISD) / Institut international du développement durable (IIDD)
#325, 111 Lombard Ave., Winnipeg MB R3B 0T4
Tel: 204-958-7700
info@iisd.org
www.iisd.org
www.youtube.com/user/iisdvideo
www.facebook.com/IISDnews
twitter.com/IISD_news
To promote sustainable development in decision-making in Canada & abroad by undertaking sustainable development research, advising government, business & organizations,

analyzing & reporting on issues & events & publishing & disseminating sustainable development information
Richard Florizone, President & CEO
Grace Mota, Treasurer & Chief Financial Officer
Zahra Sethna, Director, Communications

Jasper Environmental Association (JEA)
PO Box 2198, Jasper AB T0E 1E0
Tel: 780-852-4152
jea2@telus.net
www.jasperenvironmental.org
To support Parks Canada in administering Jasper National Park in accordance with Canadian legislation, Parks Canada principles and policies and the wishes of the Canadian public.

Manitoba Association of Watersheds (MAW)
#200, 1765 Sargent Ave., Winnipeg MB R3H 0C6
office@manitobawatersheds.org
manitobawatersheds.org
www.facebook.com/mbconsdistassoc
twitter.com/MBConsDistAssoc
To represent the 14 Watershed Districts within Manitoba
Lynda Nicols, Executive Director

Manitoba Eco-Network Inc. (MEN) / Réseau écologique du Manitoba inc.
#3, 303 Portage Ave., Winnipeg MB R3B 2B4
Tel: 204-947-6511; *Fax:* 866-237-3130
info@mbeconetwork.org
www.mbeconetwork.org
www.youtube.com/user/ManitobaEcoNetwork
www.facebook.com/Manitoba.Eco.Network
twitter.com/MB_EcoNetwork
To educate the public on environmental issues; To conduct research on environmental issues; To facilitate communications between environmental groups & the general public
Peters Karen, Executive Director

Manitoba Environment Officers Association Inc. (MEOA)
147 Norcross Cres., Winnipeg MB R3X 1J2
meoa@mts.net
www.meoa.ca
To enhance the public health and safety of Manitobans and to protect, maintain and rehabilitate Manitoba's environment ecosystems through the diligent duties of educated Environment Officers and to obtain for Environment Officers continued education and recognition of their efforts.
Bill Barr, President

Manitoba Environmental Industries Association Inc. (MEIA)
#100, 62 Albert St., Winnipeg MB R3B 1E9
Tel: 204-783-7090; *Fax:* 204-783-6501
admin@meia.mb.ca
www.meia.mb.ca
To assist members in the business of the environment; To connect business, government, & stakeholders with environmental issues
John Fjeldsted, Executive Director
Vaughn Bullough, President
Rosemary Deans, Coordinator, Education & Training
Deb Tardiff, Coordinator, Education & Training
Sheldon McLeod, Secretary
John Pikel, Treasurer

Manitoba Wildlife Federation (MWF)
70 Stevenson Rd., Winnipeg MB R3H 0W7
Tel: 204-633-5967; *Toll-Free:* 877-633-4868
info@mwf.mb.ca
www.mwf.mb.ca
To devote members to the causes of conservation & the participation in the wise use of natural resources; To encourage the propagation of game & fish; To promote the enforcement of game laws; To cooperate with government departments
Rob Olson, Managing Director

Municipal Waste Association (MWA)
PO Box 1894, Guelph ON N1H 7A1
Tel: 519-823-1990; *Fax:* 519-823-0084
www.municipalwaste.ca
To expedite the flow of information regarding 3R programs to municipalities & other community & government groups; To act as an information forum for municipal recycling coordinators; To allow member municipalities to act as a unified voice in promoting progressive waste reduction & recycling alternatives
Ben Bennett, Executive Director
Melissa Campbell, Coordinator, Membership

The Nature Conservancy of Canada (NCC) / La Société canadienne pour la conservation la nature
#410, 245 Eglinton Ave. East, Toronto ON M4P 3J1
Toll-Free: 877-231-3552
nature@natureconservancy.ca
www.natureconservancy.ca
www.instagram.ca/ncc_cnc
www.linkedin.com/company/the-nature-conservancy-of-canada
www.facebook.com/natureconservancy.ca
twitter.com/NCC_CNC
To protect Canada's biodiversity through long-term stewardship & property securement
Catherine Grenier, President & CEO
Jane Gilbert, Vice-President, Public Affairs & Communications

New Brunswick Environmental Network (NBEN) / Réseau environnemental du Nouveau-Brunswick (RENB)
#103, 30 Gordon St., Moncton NB E1C 1L8
Tel: 506-855-4144
nben@nben.ca
www.nben.ca
www.facebook.com/renb.nben
To strengthen the environmental movement throughout New Brunswick; To promote ecologically sound ways of life
Raissa Marks, Executive Director

New Brunswick Wildlife Federation (NBWF) / Fédération de la faune du Nouveau-Brunswick
PO Box 549, Moncton NB E1C 8L9
nbwildlifefederation.org
To foster sound management & wise use of the renewable & non-renewable natural resources of New Brunswick; To assist & encourage the enforcement of those game laws which are in keeping with the objectives of the Federation & to strive for better management & game laws where & when necessary; To educate membership & the public, with particular emphasis upon conservation & safety; To represent the interests & concerns of New Brunswick sportsmen; to cooperate with government departments & all related groups, where interests are mutual
Charlie Leblanc, President

Newfoundland & Labrador Environmental Industry Association (NEIA)
#207, 90 O'Leary Ave., St. John's NL A1B 2C7
Tel: 709-237-8090
info@neia.org
neia.org
www.linkedin.com/company/3194901
www.facebook.com/NEIAssoc
twitter.com/NEIAssoc
To promote the growth & development of the environmental industry of Newfoundland & Labrador; To promote ethical behavior & high standards for environmental products & services; To provide a strong, unified voice toward all private sector, government & non-profit entities involved in the Newfoundland environmental industry
Ted Lomond, Executive Director
Frank Ricketts, Chair

Newfoundland & Labrador Wildlife Federation (NWLF)
15 Conran St., St. John's NL A1E 5L8
Tel: 709-364-8415
www.nlwf.ca
To foster awareness & enjoyment of the natural world; To promote the sustainable use of natural resources; To protect wildlife & its habitat through conservation & effective wildlife management
Rick Bouzan, President

North American Recycled Rubber Association (NARRA)
#24, 1621 McEwen Dr., Whitby ON L1N 9A5
Tel: 905-433-7769; *Fax:* 905-433-0905
narra@oix.com
www.recycle.net/recycle/assn/narra
The Association provides a unified voice, as well as a communication network & research facility, for issues of concern to those involved in rubber recycling across North America.
Diane Sarracini, Office Manager

Nova Scotia Federation of Anglers & Hunters (NSFAH)
PO Box 654, Halifax NS B3J 2T3
Tel: 902-477-8898; *Fax:* 902-444-3883
www.nsfah.ca
To be dedicated to the conservation & propagation of wildlife in the province for those who hunt, fish, trap or otherwise enjoy the wildlife resources of Nova Scotia, through education, cooperation & exchange of information

Nova Scotia Nature Trust (NSNT)
PO Box 2202, 2085 Maitland St., Halifax NS B3J 3C4
Tel: 902-425-5263; *Fax:* 902-429-5263
Toll-Free: 877-434-5263
nature@nsnt.ca
www.nsnt.ca
www.youtube.com/user/naturetrust
www.facebook.com/novascotianaturetrust
twitter.com/nsnaturetrust
To protect Nova Scotia's outstanding natural legacy through land conservation.
Corey Miller, President
Bonnie Sutherland, Executive Director

Oak Ridges Moraine Foundation (ORMF)
120 Bayview Pkwy., Newmarket ON L3Y 4X1
Tel: 289-279-5733
support@ormf.com
www.ormf.com
twitter.com/ormoraine
To provide support and encouragement for activities that preserve, protect, and restore the environmental integrity of the Oak Ridges Moraine and support a trail along it.
Michele Donnelly, Senior Administrative Assistant

Ontario Environment Industry Association (ONEIA)
#306, 192 Spadina Ave., Toronto ON M5T 2C2
Tel: 416-531-7884
info@oneia.ca
www.oneia.ca
www.instagram.com/onenvironmentbiz
www.linkedin.com/company/oneia
twitter.com/ONEIAnetwork
To promote the growth of environment business in Ontario
Alex Gill, Executive Director
Janelle Yanishewski, Manager, Operations

Ontario Environmental Network (OEN)
#11, 2675 Bloor St, West, Toronto ON M8X 1A4
oen@oen.ca
www.oen.ca
www.youtube.com/ontarioenvironment
www.facebook.com/OntarioEnvironmentNetwork
twitter.com/ONTenvironment
To encourage discussions of ways to protect the environment; To increase environmental awareness throughout Ontario; To serve the environmental non-profit, non-governmental community in Ontario
Phillip Penna, Coordinator

Ontario Federation of Anglers & Hunters (OFAH)
PO Box 2800, 4601 Guthrie Dr., Peterborough ON K9J 8L5
Tel: 705-748-6324; *Fax:* 705-748-9577
ofah@ofah.org
www.ofah.org
www.youtube.com/ofahcommunications
www.facebook.de/theOFAH
twitter.com/ofah
To save & defend from waste the natural resources of Ontario, its soils, minerals, air, water, forests & wildlife
Angelo Lombardo, Executive Director

Ontario Pollution Control Equipment Association (OPCEA)
6514 Mississauga Rd., #C, Mississauga ON L5N 1A6
Tel: 416-307-2185
opcea@opcea.com
www.opcea.com
To assist members in the promotion of their services & equipment in Ontario
Max Rao, President
Robert Lee, Vice President
Greg Jackson, Treasurer

Ontario Steelheaders
PO Box 604, Brantford ON N3T 5T3
president@ontariosteelheaders.ca
www.ontariosteelheaders.ca
www.facebook.com/OntarioSteelheaders
twitter.com/ONSteelheaders
To improve access and habitat for migratory rainbow trout, provide young rainbow trout with suitable nursery habitat, provide relevent and appropriate input to government, agencies and other organizations, and to educate members and the public on relevent issues, conservation practices and proper angling techniques.
Karl Redin, President

Ontario Streams
50 Bloomington Rd. West, Aurora ON L4G 3G8
Tel: 905-713-7399; *Fax:* 905-713-7361
www.ontariostreams.on.ca

To promote the conservation & rehabilitation of streams & wetlands, through education & community involvement
Doug Forder, General Manager

Ontario Waste Management Association (OWMA) / Société ontarienne de gestion des déchets
#3, 2005 Clark Blvd., Brampton ON L6T 5P8
Tel: 905-791-9500; *Fax:* 905-791-9514
info@owma.org
www.owma.org
www.linkedin.com/company/ontario-waste-management-association
twitter.com/OWMA1
To act as the voice of the private sector waste industry in Ontario; To protect the enviroment by properly managing waste & recyclable materials

Ottawa Riverkeeper / Sentinelle Outaouais
#301, 1960 Scott St., Ottawa ON K1Z 8L8
Tel: 613-321-1120; *Fax:* 613-822-5258
Toll-Free: 888-953-3737
info@ottawariverkeeper.ca
www.ottawariverkeeper.ca
www.instagram.com/ottawariverkeeper
www.facebook.com/ottawa.riverkeeper
twitter.com/ottriverkeeper
To protect and promote the ecological health and diversity of the Ottawa River and its tributaries; To ensure swimmable, fishable, drinkable waterways
Patrick Nadeau, Executive Director

Ottawa Valley Wild Bird Care Centre (WBCC)
PO Box 11159, Stn. H, Nepean ON K2H 7T9
Tel: 613-828-2849
mojo@wildbirdcarecentre.org
www.wildbirdcarecentre.org
To assess, treat, & rehabilitate ill, injured, & orphaned wild birds in order to release them back into the wild
Mireille Goguen, Executive Director

The Pembina Institute
219 - 19th St. NW, Calgary AB T2N 2H9
Tel: 403-269-3344; *Fax:* 403-269-3377
www.pembina.org
www.instagram.com/pembinainstitute
www.linkedin.com/company/pembina-institute
www.facebook.com/pembina.institute
twitter.com/pembina
To develop & promote public policy & educational programs which protect the environment & encourage environmentally sound resource management strategies; to implement a conserver society
Glen R. Murray, Executive Director
Andrew Aziz, Director, Communications

Pitch-In Canada (PIC) / Passons à l'action Canada
#1, 964 Shoppers Row, Campbell River BC V9w 2c5
Tel: 250-914-3202
pitch-in@pitch-in.ca
pitch-in.ca
www.facebook.com/pitchincanada
twitter.com/pitch_in_canada
To improve communities & the envionment by providing programs to reduce, re-use, recycle & properly manage & dispose waste
Misha Cook, Executive Director
Chantelle Slaneff, Office Administrator

The Pollution Probe Foundation (PPF)
#208, 150 Ferrand Dr., Toronto ON M3C 3E5
Tel: 416-926-1907; *Toll-Free:* 877-926-1907
pprobe@pollutionprobe.org
www.pollutionprobe.org
www.linkedin.com/company/pollution-probe
www.facebook.com/PollutionProbe
twitter.com/PollutionProbe
To define environmental problems through research; To promote understanding through education & to press for practical solutions through advocacy; To work collaboratively with government agencies, other non-profit organizations & private business to engage key issues & find solutions
Christopher Hilkene, Chief Executive Officer
Steve McCauley, Senior Director
Richard Carlson, Director, Energy Exchange & Energy Policy

Prince Edward Island Eco-Net (PEIEN)
#216, 40 Enman Cres., Charlottetown PE C1E 1E6
Tel: 902-566-4170; *Fax:* 902-566-4037
network@eastlink.ca
www.facebook.com/peieconet
To promote communication & cooperation among ENGO's (Environmental NGO's) & between ENGO's & governments; to provide referral services; to coordinate workshops &

conferences; to provide consultations; to publish & distribute information
Matthew McCarville, Executive Director

Prince Edward Island Wildlife Federation
#103B, 420 University Ave., Charlottetown PE C1A 7Z5
Tel: 902-626-9699
www.facebook.com/145488672186392
To foster sound management & wise use of the renewable resources of PEI; to assist & encourage the enforcement of those game laws which are in keeping with the objectives of the Federation & to strive for better management & game laws where & when necessary; to cooperate with government departments & related groups where interests are mutual; to educate membership & the public, with particular emphasis upon conservation & safety; to represent the interests & concerns of PEI sportsmen
Duncan Crawford, Contact

Quetico Foundation
#216, 642 King St. West, Toronto ON M5V 1M7
Tel: 416-941-9388; *Fax:* 416-941-9236
office@queticofoundation.org
www.queticofoundation.org
www.facebook.com/QueticoFoundation
To preserve wilderness areas of Ontario, particularly Quetico Provincial Park, for recreation & scientific use
Glenda McLachlan, Executive Director

Recycling Council of Alberta (RCA)
PO Box 23, Bluffton AB T0C 0M0
Tel: 403-843-6563; *Fax:* 403-843-4156
info@recycle.ab.ca
www.recycle.ab.ca
www.facebook.com/RecyclingCouncilOfAlberta
twitter.com/3RsAB
To promote & facilitate waste reduction, recycling, & resource conservation in Alberta
Christina Seidel, Executive Director

Recycling Council of British Columbia (RCBC)
#10, 119 West Pender St., Vancouver BC V6B 1S5
Tel: 604-683-6009; *Fax:* 604-683-7255
Toll-Free: 800-667-4321
rcbc@rcbc.ca
www.rcbc.ca
www.facebook.com/RecyclingBC
twitter.com/RecyclingBC
To promote the principles of zero waste; To decrease British Columbia's environmental footprint
Brock Macdonald, Chief Executive Officer
Anna Rochelle, Director, Finance
Harvinder Aujala, Manager, Information Services
Ben Ramos, Manager, Member Services

Recycling Council of Ontario (RCO) / Conseil du recyclage de l'Ontario
PO Box 83, Orangeville ON L9W 2Z5
Tel: 416-657-2797; *Toll-Free:* 888-501-9637
rco@rco.on.ca
www.rco.on.ca
www.facebook.com/RecyclingCouncilofOntario
twitter.com/RCOntario
To inform & educate society about the generation & avoidance of waste; To encourage recycling & the efficient use of resources
Jo-Anne St. Godard, Executive Director

Réseau environnement
#750, 255, bould Crémazie est, Montréal QC H2M 1L5
Tél: 514-270-7110; *Téléc:* 514-270-7154
Ligne sans frais: 877-440-7110
info@reseau-environnement.com
www.reseau-environnement.com
www.linkedin.com/company/2382510
www.facebook.com/reseauenvironnement
twitter.com/Reseau_Envt
Regrouper des entreprises spécialisées dans la gestion des déchets commerciaux, industriels et des services municipaux reliés à l'environnement; Assurer l'avancement des technologies et de la science, la promotion des expertises et le soutien des activités en environnement
Stéphanie Myre, Présidente-directrice générale
Mario Laplante, Directeur général adjoint
Josianne Lafantaisie, Coordonnatrice principale, Communications et relations publiques
Romy Regis, Coordonnatrice, Événements
Lyne Dubois, Merlicom
Mihaela Sandor, Comptable

Réseau québécois des groupes écologistes (RQGE)
454, av Laurier est, Montréal QC H2J 1E7
Tél: 514-587-8194
info@rqge.qc.ca
www.rqge.qc.ca
www.youtube.com/user/RQgroupesecologistes
www.facebook.com/Reseau.quebecois.des.groupes.ecologistes
twitter.com/InfoRQGE
Pour recueillir de services et d'information pour les groupes écologiques du Québec; aider les groupes à communiquer entre eux
Stéphane Gingras, Président
Bruno Massé, Coordonnateur général

Resource Efficient Agricultural Production (REAP Canada)
#21, 111, rue Lakeshore, Sainte-Anne-de-Bellevue QC H9X 3V9
Tel: 514-398-7743; *Fax:* 514-398-7972
info@reap-canada.com
www.reap-canada.com
To improve farm profits & productivity while minimizing adverse health & environmental effects
Roger Samson, Executive Director

Rideau Environmental Action League (REAL)
PO Box 1061, Smiths Falls ON K7A 5A5
Tel: 613-283-9500
info@realaction.ca
www.realaction.ca
twitter.com/RideauEnvActL
To conduct community-wide environmental projects and promote environmental improvements within the Town of Smiths Falls and Lanark, Leeds and Grenville Counties.
Larry Manson, President

Rideau Valley Conservation Authority (RVCA)
PO Box 599, 3889 Rideau Valley Dr., Manotick ON K4M 1A5
Tel: 613-692-3571; *Fax:* 613-692-0831
Toll-Free: 800-267-3504
info@rvca.ca
www.rvca.ca
www.facebook.com/RideauValleyConservationAuthority
twitter.com/RideauValleyCA
To advocate for clean water, natural shorelines & sustainable land use throughout the Rideau Valley watershed
Sommer Casgrain-Robertson, General Manager
Diane Downey, Manager, Communications

Sackville Rivers Association (SRA)
PO Box 45071, Sackville NS B4E 2Z6
Tel: 902-865-9238; *Fax:* 902-864-3564
sackvillerivers@ns.sympatico.ca
www.sackvillerivers.ns.ca
To promote the preservation, restoration and enhancement of the Sackville River Watershed.
Damon Conrad, Contact

Saskatchewan Eco-Network (SEN)
535 - 8th St. East, Saskatoon SK S7K 0P9
Tel: 306-652-1275
info@econet.ca
www.econet.sk.ca
To provide educational activities to develop an awareness of conservation & enhancement of the environment
Rick Morrell, Executive Director

Saskatchewan Environmental Industry & Managers' Association (SEIMA)
2341 McIntyre St., Regina SK S4P 2S3
Tel: 306-543-1567; *Fax:* 306-543-1568
info@seima.sk.ca
www.seima.sk.ca
To act as the voice of practitioners in Saskatchewan's environmental industry on environmental matters; To promote responsible environmental management in the province; To develop the environmental industry in Saskatchewan
Kathleen Livingston, Executive Director & COO
Al Shpyth, President
Lenore Swystun, Vice-President
Lois Miller, Treasurer
Cheryl Hender, Secretary

Saskatchewan Environmental Society (SES)
PO Box 1372, Saskatoon SK S7K 3N9
Tel: 306-665-1915
info@environmentalsociety.ca
www.environmentalsociety.ca
www.youtube.com/user/EnvironmentalSociety
www.linkedin.com/company/saskatchewan-environmental-societ
y
www.facebook.com/environmentalsociety
twitter.com/skenvsociety

To maintain the integrity of Saskatchewan's forests, farmlands & natural prairie landscapes; To promote conservation & the development of renewable energy resources; To build sustainable communities, enhanced waste management, & enhanced water quality in the province's lakes & rivers
Allyson Brady, Executive Director
Peter Prebble, Director, Environmental Policy
Angie Bugg, Coordinator, Energy Conservation
Lynette Suchar, Coordinator, Communications

Saskatchewan Soil Conservation Association (SSCA)
PO Box 1360, Indian Head SK S0G 2K0
Tel: 306-695-4233; *Fax:* 306-695-4236
Toll-Free: 800-213-4287
info@ssca.ca
www.ssca.ca
To improve the land & environment; To increase public awareness of soil conservation; To promote conservation production systems to Saskatchewan producers
Tim Nerbas, President
Marilyn Martens, Office Manager

Saskatchewan Waste Reduction Council (SWRC)
#208, 220 - 20th St. West, Saskatoon SK S7M 0W9
Tel: 306-931-3242; *Fax:* 306-955-5852
info@saskwastereduction.ca
www.saskwastereduction.ca
www.instagram.com/skwastereduction
www.facebook.com/saskwastereduction
To lead in addressing the underlying causes of waste by identifying opportunities, creating connections & promoting solutions.
Joanne Fedyk, Executive Director

Saskatchewan Wildlife Federation (SWF)
9 Lancaster Rd., Moose Jaw SK S6J 1M8
Tel: 306-692-8812; *Fax:* 306-692-4370
Toll-Free: 877-793-9453
sask.wildlife@sasktel.net
www.swf.sk.ca
www.facebook.com/SaskatchewanWildlifeFederation
twitter.com/saskwildlife
To promote the wise use & management of natural resources in Saskatchewan
Darrell Crabbe, Executive Director
Darren Newberry, Coordinator, Habitat Land Trust
Laurel Waldner, Coordinator, Education Program
Adam Matichuk, Coordinator, Fisheries Project
Darby Briggs, Coordinator, Communications

Sea Shepherd Conservation Society (SSCS)
PO Box 48446, Vancouver BC V7X 1A2
Tel: 604-688-7325
canada@seashepherd.org
www.seashepherd.org
To investigate & document violations of international laws, regulations & treaties protecting marine wildlife species

SEEDS Connections
#309, 223 - 12th Ave. SW, Calgary AB T2R 0G9
Tel: 403-264-5959; *Fax:* 403-234-9532
Toll-Free: 800-661-8751
seedsconnections.org
To provide educational support materials & professional assistance to teachers in the area of energy, environment & sustainable development; To work toward the development of a society which understands & is committed to actions leading to wise stewardship of resources, resource use & the environment
MacDonald Alexandra, President

Sierra Club of Canada (SCC) / Sierre club du Canada
#412, 1 Nicholas St., Ottawa ON K1N 7B7
Tel: 613-241-4611; *Fax:* 613-241-2292
Toll-Free: 888-810-4204
info@sierraclub.ca
www.sierraclub.ca
www.youtube.com/sierraclubcanada
www.facebook.com/sierraclubcanada
twitter.com/SierraClubCan
To develop a diverse, well-trained grassroots network, working to protect the integrity of our global ecosystems; To focus on five overriding threats: loss of animal & plant species, deterioration of the planet's oceans & atmosphere, the ever-growing presence of toxic chemicals in all living things, destruction of our remaining wilderness, spiralling population growth & overconsumption
John Bennett, Executive Director
Anowara Baqi, CFO
Tania Beriau, Development Director
Daniel Spence, Director, Communications

Small Water Users Association of BC
PO Box 187, Balfour BC V0G 1C0
Tel: 250-229-5704
smallwaterusers@shaw.ca
www.smallwaterusers.com
To foster cooperation & information sharing amongst small water systems throughout BC in order to improve system operations & reduce costs; To represent the interests & concerns of small water systems
Denny Ross-Smith, Executive Director

Smart Prosperity Institute
1 Stewart St., 3rd Fl., Ottawa ON K1N 6N5
info@smartprosperity.ca
institute.smartprosperity.ca
www.linkedin.com/company/1463541
www.facebook.com/SmartProsperityInstitute
twitter.com/SP_Inst
To advance practical policies & market solutions for a stronger, cleaner economy through research & work with public & private partners
Stewart Elgie, Executive Chair
Mike Wilson, Executive Director
Stephanie Cairns, Director, Cities & Communities
Eric Campbell, Director, Communications & Outreach
Geoff McCarney, Director, Research

Society Promoting Environmental Conservation (SPEC)
2305 West 7th Ave., Vancouver BC V6K 1Y4
Tel: 604-736-7732
admin@spec.bc.ca
www.spec.bc.ca
www.youtube.com/user/SPECbc
www.facebook.com/137945192900176
To provide our community with practical solutions for urban sustainability
Rob Baxter, President
Oliver Lane, Coordinator

Southeast Environmental Association (SEA)
41 Woods Islands Hill, Montague PE C0A 1R0
Tel: 902-838-3351; *Fax:* 902-838-0610
seapei.org
To protect, maintain, and enhance the ecology of south eastern Prince Edward Island for the environmental, social, and economic well being of area residents.
Jackie Bourgeois, Executive Director
Lawrence Millar, Chair

Spruce City Wildlife Association (SCWA)
1384 River Rd., Prince George BC V2L 5S8
Tel: 250-563-5437; *Fax:* 250-563-5438
info@scwa.bc.ca
www.scwa.bc.ca
To perform environmental acts that improve the BC wilderness
Jim Glaicar, President

Sustainable Urban Development Association (SUDA)
2637 Council Ring Rd., Mississauga ON L5L 1S6
Tel: 416-400-0553
mail@suda.ca
www.suda.ca
To foster a healthy natural environment by providing information about ways in which cities can become more efficient in the land, material, water and energy resources, and highly supportive of sustainable transportation.
John Banka, President

TD Friends of the Environment Foundation / Fondation des amis de l'environnement TD
TD Bank Tower, PO Box 1, 66 Wellington St., Toronto ON M5K 1A2
Toll-Free: 800-361-5333
tdfef@td.com
www.fef.td.com
To protect & preserve the Canadian environment
Natasha Alleyne-Martin, Manager, National Programs
Sarah Lawless-Ajibade, Regional Manager, Ontario North & East, Quebec and Atlantic Provinces
Mandip Kharod, Regional Manager, BC, Alberta, Yukon & Northwest Territories, Saskatchewan & Manito
Carolyn Scotchmer, Regional Manager, Greater Toronto Region & Western Ontario

USC Canada
#600, 56 Sparks St., Ottawa ON K1P 5B1
Tel: 613-234-6827; Fax: 613-234-6842
Toll-Free: 800-565-6872
info@usc-canada.org
www.usc-canada.org
www.youtube.com/user/USCCanada
www.facebook.com/78368904729
twitter.com/usccanada
Committed to enhancing human development through an
international partnership of people linked in the challenge to
reduce poverty
Martin Settle, Co-Executive Director
Jane Rabinowicz, Co-Executive Director
Sheila Petzold, Director, Communications
Jeff de Jong, Director, International Programs
Faris Ahmed, Director, Policy & Campaigns
Brian McFarlane, Director, Fundraising

Water Environment Association of Ontario (WEAO)
PO Box 176, Milton ON L9T 4N9
Tel: 416-410-6933; Fax: 416-410-1626
weao@weao.org
www.weao.org
twitter.com/WEAOYP
To advance the water environment industry; To promote sound
public policy
Julie Vincent, Executive Administrator

Western Canada Water (WCW)
PO Box 1708, Cochrane AB T4C 1B6
Tel: 403-709-0064; Fax: 403-709-0068
Toll-Free: 877-283-2003
info@wcwwa.ca
www.wcwwa.ca
To advance support for water professionals throughout western
Canada
Audrey Arisman, Executive Director

Western Canada Wilderness Committee (WCWC)
46 East 6th Ave., Vancouver BC V5T 1J4
Tel: 604-683-8220; Fax: 604-683-8229
Toll-Free: 800-661-9453
info@wildernesscommittee.org
www.wildernesscommittee.org
www.instagram.com/wildernews
www.facebook.com/wildernesscommittee
twitter.com/wildernews
To work for the protection of Canadian & the Earth's wilderness
through research & education; To promote the principles which
achieve ecologically sustainable communities
Beth Clarke, Executive Director
Torrance Coste, Direactor, National Campaign
Michael Lawrence, Director, Administration

Wildlife Habitat Canada (WHC) / Habitat faunique Canada (HFC)
#247, 2039 Robertson Rd., Ottawa ON K2H 8R2
Tel: 613-722-2090; Fax: 613-722-3318
Toll-Free: 800-669-7919
admin@whc.org
www.whc.org
www.linkedin.com/company/wildlife-habitat-canada
www.facebook.com/WildlifeHCanada
twitter.com/WildlifeHCanada
To support conservation initiatives for wildlife & their habitats; To
provide funds that support habitat restoration, enhancement, &
protection all over Canada through the grant program; To impact
the decisions that directly affect biodiversity in wildlife & habitats
as part of the solutions to climate change
Cameron Mack, Executive Director

Wildlife Preservation Canada (WPC) / Conservation de la faune au Canada
RR#5, 5420 Hwy. 6 North, Guelph ON N1H 6J2
Tel: 519-836-9314; Toll-Free: 800-956-6608
admin@wildlifepreservation.ca
www.wildlifepreservation.ca
www.facebook.com/WildlifePreservationCanada
twitter.com/WPCWild911
To save endangered animal species from extinction in Canada &
internationally
Elaine Williams, Executive Director
Ian Glen, President
Jessica Steiner, Recovery Biologist

World Wildlife Fund - Canada (WWF-Canada) / Fonds mondial pour la nature
#400, 410 Adelaide St. West, Toronto ON M5V 1S8
Tel: 416-489-8800; Toll-Free: 800-267-2632
ca-panda@wwfcanada.org
wwf.ca
www.youtube.com/wwfcanada
www.linkedin.com/company/wwf-canada
www.facebook.com/WWFCanada
twitter.com/wwfcanada
To conserve wild animals, plants & habitats for their own sake &
the long-term benefit of people; To protect the diversity of life on
earth; To stop, & eventually reverse, the accelerating
degradation of our planet's natural environment; To help build a
future in which humans live in harmony with nature
Megan Leslie, President & CEO
Mary MacDonald, Chief Conservation Officer & Senior VP
Kathrin Majic, Senior Vice-President, Development

Yukon Conservation Society (YCS)
302 Hawkins St., Whitehorse YT Y1A 1X6
Tel: 867-668-5678; Fax: 867-668-6637
ycs@ycs.yk.ca
www.yukonconservation.org
To pursue ecosystem well-being throughout the Yukon & beyond
Karen Baltgailis, Executive Director
Georgia Greetham, Coordinator, Office
Sue Kemmett, Coordinator, Forestry
Anne Middler, Coordinator, Energy
Lewis Rifkind, Coordinator, Mining

Yukon Fish & Game Association (YFGA)
509 Strickland St., Whitehorse YT Y1A 2K5
Tel: 867-667-4263
yfga@klondiker.com
www.yukonfga.ca
www.facebook.com/yukonfga
To ensure the long-term management of fish, wildlife, & outdoor
recreational resources in the Yukon; To improve wildlife habitat
Gord Zealand, Executive Director

Yukon Territory Environmental Network
302 Hawkins St., Whitehorse YT Y1A 1X6
Tel: 867-668-5678; Fax: 867-668-6637
yukonenvironet@gmail.com
Susan Davis, Coordinator

Equipment & Machinery

Agricultural Manufacturers of Canada (AMC)
#5, 725 Corydon Ave., Winnipeg MB R3M 0W4
Tel: 204-666-3518
admin@a-m-c.ca
www.a-m-c.ca
To foster & promote the growth & development of the agricultural
equipment manufacturing industry in Canada; To encourage
governments to enact legislation & offer programs that enhance
the growth potential of the industry; To provide a forum for
members to exchange ideas & discuss their industry as it relates
to the national & international economy
Donna Boyd, President
Cherrille Price, Member Services and Administration
April Jackman, Manager, Marketing & Communications

Association des marchands de machines aratoires de la province de Québec (AMMAQ)
7, rue Bernier, Bedford QC J0J 1A0
Tél: 450-248-7946; Téléc: 450-248-3264
info@ammaq.ca
www.ammaq.ca
Aider et regrouper tous les concessionnaires de machineries
agricoles de toute la province; compiler des statistiques et des
renseignements sur la vente de machines aratoires dans la
province du Québec; obtenir une plus grande coopération entre
les marchands de machines aratoires des diverses régions de la
province; promouvoir la vente et l'utilisation des machines
aratoires
Peter Maurice, Directeur général

Association des propriétaires de machinerie lourde du Québec inc. (APMLQ)
Plaza Laval, #259, 2750, ch Ste-Foy, Québec QC G1V 1V6
Tél: 418-650-1877; Téléc: 418-650-3361
Ligne sans frais: 800-268-7318
info@apmlq.com
www.apmlq.com
Informer et instruire ses membres au moyen de publications;
maintenir un secrétariat permanent dans un but de liaison entre
les membres et de contact avec différentes autorités; négocier
avec les autorités publiques toutes ententes susceptibles de
promouvoir les buts de l'Association et ceux de ses membres

Yvan Grenier, Directeur général

Association of Equipment Manufacturers - Canada (AEM-Canada)
#700, 123 Slater St., Ottawa ON K1P 5H2
Tel: 613-566-4568
www.aem.org
To act as a voice for its members to the public & on a
governmental level; To regulate safety standards & offer
educational programs & seminars
Dennis Slater, President

Canada East Equipment Dealers' Association (CEEDA)
#623, 92 Caplan Ave., Barrie ON L4N 9J2
Tel: 705-726-2100; Fax: 705-719-7055
office@ceeda.ca
www.ceeda.ca
www.linkedin.com/groups/3210864
www.facebook.com/CEEDACanadaEast
twitter.com/ceedaCanadaEast
To promote the welfare of equipment trade retailers in the
Maritimes & Ontario; To represent dealer interests in
government legislation & regulation; To foster cooperation
among manufacturers & distributors; To promote high standards
for the retail equipment industry
Beverly J. Leavitt, President & CEO

Canadian Association of Defence & Security Industries (CADSI) / Association des industries canadiennes de défense et de sécurité (AICDS)
#300, 251 Laurier Ave. West, Ottawa ON K1P 5J6
Tel: 613-235-5337; Fax: 613-235-0784
cadsi@defenceandsecurity.ca
www.defenceandsecurity.ca
www.linkedin.com/company/canadian-association-of-defence-an
d-security-industries
twitter.com/cadsicanada
To represent Canadian defence & security industries
domestically & internationally
Christyn Cianfarani, President
Paul Keogh, Vice-President, Operations
Steven Hillier, Vice-President, Government Relations &
Communications
Bal Mahal, Comptroller & Director, Human Resources & Office
Environment

Canadian Process Control Association (CPCA)
146 Delarmbro Dr., Erin ON N0B 1T0
Tel: 519-833-7414
cpca@cpca-assoc.com
cpca-assoc.com
www.linkedin.com/company/canadian-process-control-associatio
n
twitter.com/cpca_assoc
To promote the industry & its members to customers, academia
& public bodies; To provide a forum for the exchange of
technical, industry & regulatory information; To develop industry
statistics; To encourage professional & ethical behaviour &
quality standards among members
Paul Bastel, President

Events & Festivals

Alberta Music Festival Association
AB
info@albertamusicfestival.org
www.albertamusicfestival.org
www.facebook.com/AlbertaMusicFestivalOrganization
To coordinate, regulate & assist activities of local Alberta
festivals of music & speech arts; To encourage formation of
additional local festivals
Wendy Durieux, Provincial Administrator

Associated Manitoba Arts Festivals, Inc. (AMAF)
#2, 88 St. Anne's Rd., Winnipeg MB R2M 2Y7
Tel: 204-231-4507; Fax: 204-231-4510
www.amaf.mb.ca
To promote & encourage participation in growth & development
of & appreciation for creative & performing arts in partnership
with local festivals
William Gordon, President
Judith Oatway, Secretary
Tannie Lam, Treasurer

Association des professionnels en exposition du Québec (APEQ)
Succ. 89022, L'Ile-Bizard QC H9C 2Z3
Tél: 514-315-1794; Ligne sans frais: 888-276-1633
info@apeq.org
www.apeq.org

Faire reconnaître le rôle vital de l'industrie des expositions dans la vie économique, industrielle, culturelle et sociale au Québec; Promouvoir, auprès du monde des affaires, l'efficacité des expositions comme moyen de promotion, de commercialisation et de communication; Favoriser l'éducation de ses membres
Jacques Perreault, Directeur général

Canadian Association of Exposition Management (CAEM) / Association canadienne des directeurs d'expositions
#705, 1 Eglinton Ave. East, Toronto ON M4P 3A1
Tel: 416-787-9377; Toll-Free: 866-441-9377
info@caem.ca
caem.ca
www.instagram.com/caemevents
www.facebook.com/CAEM.ACGE
twitter.com/caemevents
To represent & improve the exposition & trade show industry in Canada

Canadian Association of Fairs & Exhibitions (CAFE) / Association canadienne des foires et expositions
PO Box 21053, Stn. WEPO, Brandon MB R7B 3W8
Toll-Free: 800-663-1714
info@canadian-fairs.ca
www.canadian-fairs.ca
www.instagram.com/canadianfairs
www.facebook.com/canadianfairs
twitter.com/CdnAssocofFairs
To provide leadership in the development of the Canadian fair industry; To represent the Canadian fairs & exhibitions sector at the national level
Amanda Frigon, President
Christina Franc, Executive Director

Canadian Music Week Inc. (CMW)
5355 Vail Ct., Mississauga ON L5M 6G9
Tel: 905-858-4747; Fax: 905-858-4848
cmw.net
www.facebook.com/canadianmusicweek
twitter.com/CMW_Week
To organize the annual Canadian Music Week festival, convention & trade show
Neill Dixon, President
Verle Mobbs, General Manager
Cameron Wright, Director, Festival

Carnaval de Québec / Québec Winter Carnival
205, boul des Cèdres, Québec QC G1L 1N8
Tél: 418-626-3716; Ligne sans frais: 866-422-7628
bonhomme@carnaval.qc.ca
carnaval.qc.ca
www.instagram.com/carnavaldequebec
www.linkedin.com/company/carnaval-de-qu-bec
www.facebook.com/CarnavaldeQuebec
twitter.com/CarnavalQc
Organiser annuellement une fête populaire hivernale dans le but de faire bénéficier à Québec une activité économique, touristique et sociale de première qualité dont les gens de la région seront fiers
Serge Ferland, Président
Mélanie Raymond, Directrice générale

Edmonton Kiwanis Music Festival
14205 109 Ave., Edmonton AB T5N 1H5
Tel: 780-488-3498; Fax: 780-488-6925
musicfest@edmontonkiwanis.com
www.edmontonkiwanis.com
www.facebook.com/EdmontonKiwanisMusicFestival
To create opportunities for music students, musicians, actors, & music lovers
Heather Bedford-Clooney, Executive Director

Exhibitions Association of Nova Scotia (EANS)
40 Gateway Rd., Halifax NS B3M 1M9
Tel: 902-443-2039
www.eans.ca
To promote such events as fairs & exhibitions across the province
Glen E. Jefferson, Executive Director

Federation of Canadian Music Festivals (FCMF) / La Fédération canadienne des festivals de musique
c/o Barbara Long, Executive Director, 11119 rte 130, Somerville NB E7P 2S4
Tel: 506-375-6752; Toll-Free: 866-245-1680
info@fcmf.org
www.fcmf.org
www.facebook.com/nationalmusicfestival
To act as an umbrella organization for 230+ local & provincial festivals; To develop & encourage Canadian talent in the performance & knowledge of classical music; To encourage the study & practice of the art of music alone or in conjunction with

related arts; To organize the National Music Festival in which winners from each province participate
Judy Urbonas, Chair
Barbara Long, Executive Director

Federation of Music Festivals of Nova Scotia
PO Box 31, Lunenburg NS B0J 2C0
Tel: 902-640-2448
www.musicfestivalsnovascotia.ca
Pamela Rogers, Secretary

Festivals & Events Ontario (FEO)
#301, 5 Graham St., Woodstock ON N4S 6J5
Tel: 519-537-2226; Fax: 519-537-2226
info@festivalsandeventsontario.ca
www.festivalsandeventsontario.ca
www.facebook.com/FestivalsandEventsOntario
twitter.com/FEOntario
Festivals & Events Ontario (FEO) is an association devoted to the growth and stability of the festival and event industry in Ontario. FEO provides festival and event organizers across the province with a networking forum offering professional development opportunities and resources aimed to encourage professionalism and excellence in the delivery of festivals and special events.
Debbie Mann, Interim Executive Director
Martha Cookson, Administrative Coordinator

Festivals et Événements Québec (FEQ)
4545, av Pierre-de Coubertin, Montréal QC H1V 0B2
Tél: 514-252-3037; Téléc: 514-254-1617
Ligne sans frais: 800-361-7688
info@satqfeq.com
www.attractionsevenements.com
twitter.com/SATQFEQ
Regrouper les fêtes, festivals et événements, de les promouvoir et de leur offrir des services qui favorisent leur développement
Pierre-Paul Leduc, Directeur général
Luc Martineau, Directeur, Marketing
Sylvain Martineau, Directeur-adjoint, Marketing et des ventes
Sylvie Théberge, Directrice générale adjointe
Mélanie Sigouin, Agente aux communications

International Live Events Association Canada (ILEA)
312 Oakwood Ct., Newmarket ON L3Y 3C8
Tel: 905-898-7434; Fax: 905-895-1630
Toll-Free: 866-729-4737
info@ileacanada.com
ileacanada.com
To provide a forum for creative events professionals in all disciplines across the country to foster creativity, find inspiration, promote teamwork & communication, & learn & share best practices
Dustin Westling, Chair

Jazz Festivals Canada
295 West 7th Ave., 2nd Fl., Vancouver BC V5Y 1L9
Tel: 902-489-5885
info@jazzfestivalscanada.ca
www.jazzfestivalscanada.ca
twitter.com/JazzFestsCanada
To advocate for the advancement & development of Canadian jazz festivals & jazz presenters; To represent the interests of members
Petr Cancura, President

New Brunswick Federation of Music Festivals Inc. (NBFMF) / La Fédération des festivals de musique du Nouveau-Brunswick inc. (FFMNB)
NB
info@nbfmf.org
nbfmf.org
Barbara Long, Executive Director/President

Newfoundland Federation of Music Festivals
1 Marigold Place, St. John's NL A1A 3T1
Tel: 709-722-9376
To coordinate activities of local music festivals & conduct a provincial music festival annually; to participate in the CIBC National Music Festival.
Joan Woodrow, Provincial Administrator

Ontario Music Festivals Association (OMFA)
17 Pinemore Cres., Toronto ON M3A 1W5
Toll-Free: 888-307-6632
mail@omfa.ca
www.omfa.ca
www.facebook.com/ONTMUSFEST
To promote the performance of classical music by Ontario's youth; To encourage knowledge of classical music
Martha Gregory, President
Pam Allen, Festival Administrator

Performing Arts BC
PO Box 1484, Stn. A, Comox BC V9M 8A2
Tel: 250-493-7279
festival@bcprovincials.com
www.bcprovincials.com

Prince Edward Island Kiwanis Music Festival Association
c/o Diane Campbell, Administrator, 227 Keppoch Rd., Stratford PE C1B 2J5
Tel: 902-569-2885
www.peikiwanismusicfestival.ca
To make possible performances of young & older musicians in a semi-professional atmosphere; To adjudicate using professionals; & to encourage performance & study in music
Diane Campbell, Provincial Administrator

Provincial Exhibition of Manitoba
115 - 10th St., Brandon MB R7A 4E7
Tel: 204-726-3590; Fax: 204-725-0202
Toll-Free: 877-729-0001
info@provincialexhibition.com
www.provincialexhibition.com
www.facebook.com/provincial.exhibition
twitter.com/ProvincialEx
To showcase agriculture; To link urban & rural regions through education & awareness while providing entertainment, community pride & economic enhancement to the region
Ron Kristjansson, General Manager

Québec Competitive Festival of Music / Festival de concours du Québec
136, av Duke-of-Kent, Pointe-Claire QC H9R 1X9
Tel: 514-398-4535; Fax: 514-398-8061
Tom Davidson, Provincial Administrator

Royal Agricultural Winter Fair Association (RAWF) / Foire agricole royale d'hiver
100 Prince's Blvd., Toronto ON M6K 3C3
Tel: 416-263-3400
info@royalfair.org
www.royalfair.org
www.youtube.com/user/royalhorseshow
www.facebook.com/royalfair
twitter.com/THERAWF
To promote excellence in agricultural & equestrian activities through world class competition, exhibitions & education
Charlie Johnstone, Chief Executive Officer

Saskatchewan Music Festival Association Inc.
PO Box 37005, Regina SK S4S 7K3
Tel: 306-757-1722; Fax: 306-347-7789
Toll-Free: 888-892-9929
sask.music.festival@sasktel.net
www.smfa.ca
twitter.com/SKMusicFestival
To provide a classical competitive music festival system of the highest standard at the local, provincial & national levels
Carol Donhauser, Executive Director

Vancouver International Children's Festival
#301, 601 Cambie St., Vancouver BC V6B 2P1
Tel: 604-708-5655
info@childrensfestival.ca
www.childrensfestival.ca
www.youtube.com/user/VanKidsFest
www.facebook.com/KidsFest
twitter.com/VICF
To provide performing arts programs to young people in a festival environment; to encourage critical thinking & a lifelong interest in learning, the arts & cultural development
Nicole Yeasting, Chair
Katharine Carol, Artistic & Executive Director

Farming

Association des producteurs maraîchers du Québec (APMQ) / Québec Produce Growers Association (QPGA)
905, rue du Marché-Central, Montréal QC H4N 1K2
Tél: 514-387-8319
apmq@apmquebec.com
www.apmquebec.com
Favorise le développement du secteur horticole québécois et veille à la promotion des fruits et légumes cultivés au Québec, sur le marché local et sur les marchés extérieurs

Canadian Agricultural Safety Association (CASA) / Association canadienne de sécurité agricole (ACSA)
3325-C Pembina Hwy., Winnipeg MB R3V 0A2
Tel: 204-452-2272; Fax: 204-261-5004
Toll-Free: 877-452-2272
info@casa-acsa.ca
www.casa-acsa.ca
www.youtube.com/planfarmsafety
www.linkedin.com/company/canadian-agricultural-safety-association
www.facebook.com/planfarmsafety
twitter.com/planfarmsafety
To address problems of illness, injuries & accidental death in farmers, their families & agricultural workers; To improve health & safety conditions of those that live or work on Canadian farms
Marcel L. Hacault, Executive Director

Ontario Ginseng Growers Association
PO Box 587, 1283 Blueline Rd., Simcoe ON N3Y 4N5
Tel: 519-426-7046; Fax: 519-426-9087
info@ginsengontario.com
www.ginsengontario.com
www.facebook.com/GinsengOntario
To conduct research on how to improve ginseng growing, as well as new varieties of ginseng; To help market North American ginseng
Rebecca Coates, Executive Director

Ontario Greenhouse Vegetable Growers (OGVG)
32 Seneca Rd., Leamington ON N8H 5H7
Tel: 519-326-2604; Fax: 519-326-7842
Toll-Free: 800-265-6926
admin@ogvg.com
www.ogvg.com
www.instagram.com/ongreenhouseveg
www.linkedin.com/company/ontario-greenhouse-vegetable-growers
www.facebook.com/ONgreenhouseVeg
twitter.com/ONgreenhouseVeg
To represent growers' interests & ensure that they have the necessary resources to continue to prosper
Joe Sbrocchi, General Manager

Potatoes New Brunswick / Pommes de terre Nouveau-Brunswick
PO Box 7878, Grand Falls NB E3Z 3E8
Tel: 506-473-3036; Fax: 506-473-4647
gfpotato@potatoesnb.com
www.potatoesnb.com
www.facebook.com/newbrunswickpotatoes
To work in close collaboration with industry partners in advocating, coordinating, promoting, negotiating, & leading growth & development of New Brunswick potato producers
Joe Brennan, Chair
Matt Hemphill, Executive Director
Robert Corriveau, Director, Finance
Gisele Beardsley, Bookkeeper & Translator

Prince Edward Island Certified Organic Producers Co-op
PO Box 1776, #110, 420 University Ave., Charlottetown PE C1A 7Z5
Tel: 902-894-9999; Toll-Free: 866-850-9799
www.organicpei.com
www.facebook.com/organicpei
To increase organic production, research and market development; invite growers into the organic industry and promote and educate Islanders about organic food.
Fred Dollar, President

Union des cultivateurs franco-ontariens (UCFO)
2474 rue Champlain, Clarence Creek ON K0A 1N0
Tél: 613-488-2929; Télec: 613-488-2541
Ligne sans frais: 877-425-8366
info@ucfo.ca
www.ucfo.ca
www.facebook.com/UCFO.ca
Regrouper les franco-ontariens et les franco-ontariennes qui oeuvrent dans le secteur agricole; concerter pour la protection de nos droits; promouvoir nos intérêts; informer notre communauté; appuyer les institutions et groupements qui favorisent notre développement; développer notre sentiment et fierté; stimuler le développement social et économique des régions agricoles et rurales
Marc Laflèche, Président
Simon Durand, Directeur exécutif
Marc-André Tessier, Agent, Communication et développement du leadership

Fashion & Textiles

Alberta Men's Wear Agents Association
PO Box 23022, Stn. Citadel, St Albert AB T8N 6Z9
Tel: 780-920-8932
info@trendsapparel.com
www.trendsapparel.com
Ken Melnychuk, President

Allied Beauty Association
PO Box 30068, Stn. Cityside, Mississauga ON
Toll-Free: 800-268-6644
communication@abacanada.com
abacanada.com
www.instagram.com/ABACanada
www.linkedin.com/company/allied-beauty-association
www.facebook.com/ABACanada
twitter.com/abacanada
To encourage & create a greater understanding & knowledge of the professional beauty industry to the salons, the public, the federal & provincial governments & to members
Marc Speir, Executive Director

BeautyCouncil (BC)
899 West 8th Ave., Vancouver BC V5Z 1E3
Tel: 604-871-0222; Fax: 604-871-0299
Toll-Free: 800-663-9283
info@beautycouncil.ca
beautycouncil.ca
www.pinterest.com/beautycouncil
www.facebook.com/beautycouncilwesterncanada
twitter.com/beautycouncil
To strive for the highest standards of excellence in professional cosmetology services through its member enhancement programs & to service the public through education & knowledge.
Bill Moreland, Chair
Debbie Nickel, Executive Director

Canadian Apparel Federation (CAF) / Fédération canadienne du vêtement
#404, 116 Albert St., Ottawa ON K1P 5G3
Tel: 613-231-3220; Fax: 613-231-2305
info@apparel.ca
www.apparel.ca
www.linkedin.com/company/canadian-apparel-federation
www.facebook.com/CanadianApparelFed
twitter.com/caf_apparel
To provide a forum for provincial apparel associations representing the vast majority of the country's manufacturers; To exercise leadership in relations with government, suppliers & the general public
Bob Kirke, Executive Director

Canadian Association of Wholesale Sales Representatives (CAWS) / Association canadienne des représentants de ventes en gros
PO Box 1342, 2708 Yonge St., Toronto ON M4P 3J4
Tel: 416-782-8961; Fax: 416-782-5876
info@caws.ca
caws.ca
To represent comission sales agents on a national level; To serve as an umbrella organization for affiliate markets across Canada
Kim Crawford, President

Canadian Textile Industry Association (CTIA)
#708, 151 Slater St., Ottawa ON K1P 5M9
www.canadiantextiles.ca
To protect the interests of the textile industry in Canada
Alexander Artus, Chair

Cosmetology Association of Nova Scotia (CANS)
126 Chain Link Dr., Halifax NS B3S 1A2
Tel: 902-468-6477; Fax: 902-468-7147
Toll-Free: 800-765-8757
info@nscosmetology.ca
www.nscosmetology.ca
www.facebook.com/cosmetologyns
To apply standards ensuring the safety of the public & practitioners
Dana Sharkey, Executive Director

Groupe CTT Group
3000, rue Boullé, Saint-Hyacinthe QC J2S 1H9
Tél: 450-778-1870; Télec: 450-778-3901
Ligne sans frais: 877-288-8378
info@gcttg.com
www.gcttg.com
www.linkedin.com/company/groupe-ctt
www.facebook.com/GroupeCTT
twitter.com/GroupeCTTGroup
Favoriser le développement des matériaux textiles et de stimuler l'avancement technologique de l'industrie textile et géosynthétique par des activités telles que la recherche et le développement, l'assistance technique, la formation sur mesure, l'information spécialisé et l'animation du milieu
Jacek Mlynarek, Ph.D., Président-directeur-général

Luggage, Leathergoods, Handbags & Accessories Association of Canada (LLHA)
96 Karma Rd., Markham ON L3R 4Y3
Tel: 519-624-9085; Fax: 416-296-0994
Toll-Free: 866-872-2420
info@llha.ca
www.llha.ca
www.instagram.com/llhatradeshow
www.linkedin.com/in/llhatradeshow
www.facebook.com/LLHAShow
twitter.com/llhatradeshow
To promote the growth of the industry in Canada; To foster the interchange of ideas
Tammy Mang, Executive Administrator

METROSHOW Vancouver
#103, 1951 Glen Dr., Vancouver BC V6A 4J6
Tel: 604-929-8995; Fax: 604-357-1995
info@metroshow.ca
www.metroshow.ca
www.facebook.com/MetroShowVan
twitter.com/MetroShowVan
To produce the METROSHOW, an event held four times a year in Vancouver which houses vendors selling apparel, footwear & giftware
Karen James, President

Prairie Apparel Market
PO Box 55065, Stn. Dakota Crossing, Winnipeg MB R2N 0A8
Tel: 204-973-3256; Fax: 204-947-0561
To sell women's & children's apparel
Dan Kelsch, President

Shoe Manufacturers' Association of Canada (SMAC) / Association des manufacturiers de chaussures du Canada
To represent & serve Canadian footwear manufacturers; To protect the Canadian domestic shoe industry

Western Canada Children's Wear Markets (WCCWM)
#245, 1868 Glen Dr., Vancouver BC V6A 4K4
Tel: 604-634-0909; Fax: 888-595-9360
www.wccwm.com
To provide showcases for children's & maternity goods
Doug Fulton, President

Film & Video

Academy of Canadian Cinema & Television (ACCT) / Académie canadienne du cinéma et de la télévision
#9, 411 Richmond St. East, Toronto ON M5A 3S5
Tel: 416-366-2227; Fax: 416-366-8454
Toll-Free: 800-644-5194
communications@academy.ca
www.academy.ca
www.instagram.com/thecdnacademy
www.linkedin.com/company/academy-of-canadian-cinema-&-television
www.facebook.com/TheCdnAcademy
twitter.com/TheCdnAcademy
To promote & celebrate exceptional creative achievement in the Canadian film & television industries; To heighten public awareness & increase audience appreciation of Canadian film & television productions through its national Award program
Beth Janson, Chief Executive Officer

Alberta Media Production Industries Association (AMPIA)
#200, 7316 - 101 Ave., Edmonton AB T6A 0J2
Tel: 780-944-0707
action@ampia.org
www.ampia.org
www.instagram.com/yourampia
www.facebook.com/yourAMPIA
twitter.com/yourampia
To develop & sustain the motion picture industry indigenous to Alberta
Bill Evans, Executive Director
Colette Switzer, Program Director
Joe Hartfeil, Coordinator, Communications & Membership

Association des réalisateurs et réalisatrices du Québec (ARRQ)
5154, rue St-Hubert, Montréal QC H2J 2Y3
Tél: 514-842-7373; *Téléc:* 514-842-6789
realiser@arrq.qc.ca
www.arrq.qc.ca
Défendre les intérêts et les droits professionnels, économiques, culturels, sociaux et moraux des réalisateurs pigistes membres, travaillant principalement dans les domaines du cinéma et de la télévision
Caroline Fortier, Directrice générale

Association of Canadian Film Craftspeople
Local 2020 Communications, Energy & Paperworkers Union of Canada, #108, 3993 Henning Dr., Burnaby BC V5C 6P7
Tel: 604-299-2232; *Fax:* 604-299-2243
info@acfcwest.com
www.acfcwest.com
To create the best working conditions for members of the technical film industry in British Columbia
Perm Marimuthu, President
Ken Frost, Ssecretary/Treasurer
Greg Chambers, Business Manager

Association québécoise de la production médiatique (AQPM)
#950, 1470, rue Peel, Montréal QC H3A 1T1
Tél: 514-397-8600; *Téléc:* 514-392-0232
www.aqpm.ca
Représente les entreprises de production indépendante en cinéma, en télévision et en web au Quebec
Hélène Messier, Présidente

Atlantic Filmmakers Cooperative (AFCOOP)
1531 Grafton St., Halifax NS B3J 2B9
Tel: 902-405-4474; *Fax:* 902-405-4485
membership@afcoop.ca
afcoop.ca
www.youtube.com/afcoophalifax
www.facebook.com/117025119810
twitter.com/afcoop
To provide a space where media artists can meet & produce films; To give members access to production equipment & facilities
Martha Cooley, Executive Director
Josh Fifield, Coordinator, Technical
Iain MacLeod, Coordinator, Program & Outreach

Canadian Association of Film Distributors & Exporters (CAFDE) / Association canadienne des distributeurs et exportateurs de films (ACDEF)
#1605, 85 Albert St., Ottawa ON K1P 6A4
Tel: 613-238-3557
info@CAFDE.ca
cafde.ca
To foster & promote the health of the Canadian motion picture industry by strengthening the Canadian owned & controlled distribution / export sector
Emily Harris, President

Canadian Film Centre (CFC) / Centre canadien du film
2489 Bayview Ave., Toronto ON M2L 1A8
Tel: 416-445-1446; *Fax:* 416-445-9481
info@cfccreates.com
www.cfccreates.com
www.instagram.com/cfccreates
www.facebook.com/cfccreates
twitter.com/cfccreates
To operate as Canada's foremost film, television & new media institution; To advance Canadian creative talent, content & values worldwide, through training, production, promotion & investment
Slawko Klymkiw, Chief Executive Officer

Canadian Film Institute (CFI) / Institut canadien du film (ICF)
#120, 2 Daly Ave., Ottawa ON K1N 6E2
Tel: 613-232-6727; *Fax:* 613-232-6315
info@cfi-icf.ca
www.cfi-icf.ca
www.instagram.com/canadianfilminstitute
www.facebook.com/CanadianFilmInstitute
twitter.com/Canadian_Film
To promote Canadian cinema; To assist in locating sources for rental or purchase of individual films & videos; To give subject & content information on theatrical & non-theatrical films & videos from both private & public sources; To give general information on Canadian & international film, video & television production, distribution, exhibition & related subjects
Jim McKeen, Chair
Tom McSorley, Executive Director

Canadian Filmmakers Distribution Centre (CFMDC)
PO Box 127, Stn. C, 32 Lisgar St., Toronto ON M6J 3M9
Tel: 416-588-0725
info@cfmdc.org
www.cfmdc.org
To promote & distribute the work of independent Canadian filmmakers
Lauren Howes, Executive Director

Canadian Media Producers Association (CMPA)
251 Laurier Ave. West, 11th Fl., Ottawa ON K1P 5J6
Tel: 613-233-1444; *Toll-Free:* 800-656-7440
ottawa@cmpa.ca
www.cmpa.ca
www.youtube.com/CMPAOnline
www.linkedin.com/company/canadian-media-producers-association-cmpa
www.facebook.com/theCMPA
twitter.com/the_cmpa
To represent the interests of media companies engaged in the production & distribution of English language television programs, feature films & new media content throughout Canada
Reynolds Mastin, President & CEO
Liz Shorten, Chief Operating Officer

Canadian Picture Pioneers (CPP)
#1762, 225 The East Mall, Toronto ON M9B 0A9
Tel: 416-368-1139; *Fax:* 416-368-1139
canadianpicturepioneers.ca
To provide assistance for the welfare of those in the motion picture industry in Canada
Jason Fulson, President
John Freeborn, Executive Director

Canadian Society of Cinematographers (CSC)
#131, 3085 Kingston Rd., Toronto ON M1M 1P1
Tel: 416-266-0591; *Fax:* 416-266-3996
admin@csc.ca
www.csc.ca
www.instagram.com/canadiancinematographer
www.facebook.com/groups/canadiansocietyofcinematographers
twitter.com/csc_CDN
To promote the art & craft of cinematography
George Willis, President
Susan Saranchuk, Executive Officer

La cinémathèque québécoise
335, boul de Maisonneuve est, Montréal QC H2X 1K1
Tél: 514-842-9763; *Téléc:* 514-842-1816
info@cinematheque.qc.ca
www.cinematheque.qc.ca
www.instagram.com/cinemathequeqc
www.facebook.com/cinematheque.quebecoise
twitter.com/cinemathequeqc
Conservation et mise en valeur du patrimoine cinématographique et télévisuel; promouvoir la culture cinématographique; créer des archives de cinéma; acquérir et conserver des films ainsi que toute la documentation qui s'y rattache; projeter ces films et exposer ces documents de façon non commerciale à des fins historique, pédagogique et artistique.
Louis-Philippe Rochon, Président
Dominique Dugas, Vice Président
Christian Pitchen, Vice Président
Frédérick Pelletier, Secrétaire
Normand Grégoire, Trésorier

Directors Guild of Canada (DGC) / La Guilde canadienne des réalisateurs
#600, 111 Peter St., Toronto ON M5V 2H1
Tel: 416-925-8200; *Fax:* 416-925-8400
Toll-Free: 888-972-0098
mail@dgc.ca
www.dgc.ca
vimeo.com/dgcnational
twitter.com/DGCTalent
To represent key creative & logistical personnel in the film & television industry; To promote & advance the quality & vitality of Canadian feature film
Warren P. Sonoda, President
David Forget, National Executive Director

FilmOntario
625 Church St., 2nd Fl., Toronto ON M4Y 2G1
Tel: 416-642-6704
www.filmontario.ca
twitter.com/film_ontario
To market Ontario as a creator of film content & a location for film & television production
Cynthia Lynch, Managing Director & Counsel

Harold Greenberg Fund / Le Fonds Harold Greenberg
299 Queen St. West, Toronto ON M5V 2Z5
Tel: 416-384-3446
hgfund@bellmedia.ca
www.bellmedia.ca/harold-greenberg-fund
To foster the development & production of feature-length movies written by Canadians & the production of family television series
John Galway, President

Independent Media Arts Alliance (IMAA) / Alliance des arts médiatiques indépendants (AAMI)
#200-A, 4067, boul Saint-Laurent, Montréal QC H2W 1Y7
Tel: 514-522-8240; *Fax:* 514-987-1862
info@imaa.ca
www.imaa.ca
www.youtube.com/user/IMAAMIvideo
twitter.com/IMAA_AAMI
To promote discussion among media art centres; To coordinate independent film & video centres
Emmanuel Madan, National Director
Mercedes Pacho, Director, Communications & Development

Motion Picture Association - Canada / Association Cinématographique - Canada
#210, 55 St Clair Ave. West, Toronto ON M4V 2Y7
Tel: 416-961-1888; *Fax:* 416-968-1016
mpa-canada@motionpictures.org
mpa-canada.org
twitter.com/mpacanada
To act as the voice of U.S.A. studios who market feature films, prime time entertainment programming for television & pay TV & pre-recorded videos & DVDs in Canada; To coordinate recommendations on matters affecting national distributors of feature films, pre-recorded videocassettes & television programs; To protect the rights of copyright owners
Sydney Grieve, Director of Public Affairs & Communications, Public Affairs

NABET 700 CEP
#203, 100 Lombard St., Toronto ON M5C 1M3
Tel: 416-536-4827; *Fax:* 416-536-0859
info@nabet700.com
www.nabet700.com
To be a union serving television & film technicians in Toronto; in 1994 NABET 700 merged with the Communications, Energy & Paperworkers Union of Canada (CEP).
Jonathan Ahee, President
Craig Steele, Senior Vice-President
Frank Iacobucci, Secretary-Treasurer

National Screen Institute - Canada (NSI) / L'Institut national des arts de l'écran - Canada
#400, 141 Bannatyne Ave., Winnipeg MB R3B 0R3
Tel: 204-956-7800; *Fax:* 204-956-5811
Toll-Free: 800-952-9307
info@nsi-canada.ca
nsi-canada.ca
www.facebook.com/nsicanada
twitter.com/nsicanada
To supply innovative, focused, applied professional training to lead participants in successful careers as writers, directors & producers in Canada's film & television industry
Joy Loewen, Chief Executive Officer

North of Superior Film Association (NOSFA)
#352, 1100 Memorial Ave., Thunder Bay ON P7B 4A3
Tel: 807-625-5450
info@nosfa.ca
www.nosfa.ca
To promote film and appreciation of film in the Thunder Bay area.
Marty Mascarin, President
Catherine Powell, Festival Coordinator

Northern Film & Video Industry Association (NFVIA)
PO Box 31340, Whitehorse YT Y1A 5P7
Tel: 867-456-2978
info@nfvia.com
www.nfvia.com
To support the film & video sector in Yukon by focussing on areas such as human resource development in the industry, development of infrastructure & production support, marketing, strategic alliances & partnerships & membership services

On Screen Manitoba
#003, 100 Albert St., Winnipeg MB R3B 1H3
Tel: 204-927-5898; *Fax:* 204-272-8792
info@onscreenmanitoba.com
www.onscreenmanitoba.com
www.youtube.com/user/OnScreenManitoba
www.facebook.com/onscreenmanitoba
twitter.com/OnScreenMB

To build & represent the motion picture industry in Manitoba; To foster excellence & innovation in the industry
Nicole Matiation, Executive Director
Trevor Suffield, Coordinator, Communications

Saskatchewan Motion Picture Industry Association (SMPIA)
Canada Saskatchewan Production Studios, #312, 1831 College Ave., Regina SK S4P 4V5
Tel: 306-780-9840
office@smpia.sk.ca
www.smpia.sk.ca
twitter.com/smpiaoffice
Committed to the intrinsic cultural & economic value of motion pictures;to work toward the creation & advancement of opportunities for the production, promotion & appreciation of motion pictures in Saskatchewan
Lioz Bouganin, President
Max Berdowski, Executive Director

Writers Guild of Canada (WGC)
#401, 366 Adelaide St. West, Toronto ON M5V 1R9
Tel: 416-979-7907; *Fax:* 416-979-9273
Toll-Free: 800-567-9974
info@wgc.ca
www.wgc.ca
www.facebook.com/writers.guild.12
twitter.com/WGCtweet
To be the voice of professional Canadian screenwriters; To lobby on their behalf, protect their interests & raise the profile of screenwriters & screenwriting
Jill Golick, President
Maureen Parker, Executive Director

Yukon Film Society (YFS)
212 Lambert St., Whitehorse YT Y1A 1Z4
Tel: 867-393-3456; *Fax:* 867-393-3456
yfs@yukonfilmsociety.com
www.yukonfilmsociety.com
To present independent & alternative media art works to Yukon audiences & to support the production & distribution of works by Yukon media artists
Noel Sinclair, President
Zoë Toupin, General Manager

Film Festivals

The Atlantic Film Festival Association (AFFA)
PO Box 36139, Halifax NS B3J 3S9
Tel: 902-422-3456
festival@atlanticfilm.com
www.atlanticfilm.com
www.facebook.com/atlanticinternationalfilmfestival
twitter.com/thefilmfest
To promote & to build a strong film industry in Atlantic Canada
Wayne Carter, Executive Director

Canadian Labour International Film Festival (CLiFF)
Toronto ON
Tel: 416-579-0481
info@labourfilms.ca
labourfilms.ca
To produce a labour-oriented film festival in Canada, featuring films about workers & their conditions from Canada & around the world; To provide a venue where working people can tell their own stories in their own words & images; To encourage the production of films about working people
Frank Saptel, Festival Founder & Director

Edmonton International Film Festival Society (EIFFS)
#201, 10816A - 82nd Ave., Edmonton AB T6E 2B3
Tel: 780-423-0844
info@edmontonfilmfest.com
edmontonfilmfest.com
www.youtube.com/user/Edmontonfilmfest
www.facebook.com/Edmontonfilmfest
twitter.com/edmfilmfest
To produce a film festival for 9 days each autumn showing international, independent films in categories that include contemporary, world cinema, Canadian, documentary, alternative, shorts

Greater Vancouver International Film Festival Society (VIFF)
1181 Seymour St., Vancouver BC V6B 3M7
Tel: 604-685-0260; *Fax:* 604-688-8221
info@viff.org
viff.org
www.youtube.com/user/VIFFest
www.facebook.com/VIFFest
twitter.com/VIFForum

To operate the Annual Vancouver International Film Festival & year-round programming of the Vancity Theatre at the Vancouver International Film Centre
Dave Hewitt, Chair
Jacqueline Dupuis, Executive Director

ReelWorld Film Festival
#300, 438 Parliament St., Toronto ON M5A 3A2
Tel: 416-598-7933
www.reelworld.ca
www.youtube.com/user/ReelWorldFestival
www.facebook.com/ReelWorld.Film.Festival.Toronto
twitter.com/ReelWorldFilm
To present a culturally & racially diverse film festival showcasing films & music videos, & to connect filmmakers with producers, acquisitions personnel & distributors through The RealWorld Foundation.
Moe Jiwan, Chair & Treasurer
Tonya Lee Williams, Founder, Executive Director & Head, Programming

St. John's International Women's Film Festival (SJIWFF)
PO Box 984, Stn. C, St. John's NL A1C 5M3
Tel: 709-754-3141; *Fax:* 709-754-0049
info@womensfilmfestival.com
www.womensfilmfestival.com
www.youtube.com/user/womensfilmfest
www.linkedin.com/company/st-john%27s-international-women%27s-film-festival
www.facebook.com/womensfilmfestival
twitter.com/sjiwff
To promote international women filmmakers through the annual film festival
Noreen Golfman, Chair
Kelly Davis, Executive Director

Toronto International Film Festival Inc. (TIFF)
TIFF Bell Lightbox, 250 King St. West, Toronto ON M5V 3K5
Tel: 416-599-8433; *Toll-Free:* 888-599-8433
customerrelations@tiff.net
tiff.net
www.youtube.com/user/tiff
www.facebook.com/TIFF
twitter.com/TIFF_net
To lead in creative & cultural discovery through the moving image
Jennifer Troye, Chair

Finance

Association de planification fiscale et financière (APFF) / Fiscal & Financial Planning Association
#660, 1100, boul René-Lévesque ouest, Montréal QC H3B 4N4
Tél: 514-866-2733; *Téléc:* 514-866-0113
Ligne sans frais: 877-866-0113
apff@apff.org
www.apff.org
www.linkedin.com/groups/3958598
Regrouper les personnes intéressées à la planification fiscale successorale et financière; publier et diffuser l'information dans ces domaines; favoriser la recherche
Maurice Mongrain, Président et directeur général

Association des cadres municipaux de Montréal (ACMM)
#305, 7245, rue Clark, Montréal QC H2R 2Y4
Tél: 514-499-1130; *Téléc:* 514-499-1737
acmm@acmm.qc.ca
www.acmm.qc.ca
A pour objet l'établissement de relations ordonnées entre l'employeur et les membres ainsi que l'étude, la défense et le développement des intérêts économiques sociaux, moraux et professionnels de ces derniers
Pascale Tremblay, Présidente

Association of Canadian Pension Management (ACPM) / Association canadienne des administrateurs de régimes de retraite
#304, 1255 Bay St., Toronto ON M5R 2A9
Tel: 416-964-1260; *Fax:* 416-964-0567
info@acpm.com
www.acpm.com
www.linkedin.com/company/the-association-of-canadian-pension-management
twitter.com/ACPM_ACARR
To act as the voice of Canada's pension industry; To foster the growth of the the national retirement income system
Ric Marrero, Chief Executive Officer
Judy Lei, Manager

ATM Industry Association Canada Region (ATMIA)
c/o Curt Binns, Executive Director, #218, 10520 Yonge St., Unit 35B, Richmond Hill ON L4C 3C7
Tel: 416-970-7954; *Fax:* 905-770-6230
www.atmia.com/regions/canada
www.youtube.com/user/TheATMIA
www.linkedin.com/company/atm-industry-association
twitter.com/ATM_Industry
To promote ATM convenience, growth, & usage worldwide; To protect the ATM industry's assets, interests, & reputation; To provide education, networking opportunities, & best practices
Curt Binns, Executive Director, Canada

Caisse Groupe Financier / Caisse Financial Group
#400, 205 Provencher Blvd., Winnipeg MB R2H 0G4
Tél: 204-237-8988; *Téléc:* 204-233-6405
Ligne sans frais: 866-926-0706
info@caisse.biz
www.caisse.biz
www.linkedin.com/company/caisse
www.facebook.com/caissefinancialgroup
Contribuer à l'essor économique et socio-culturel des manitobains en poursuivant le développement des services et du réseau financiers dont les avoirs sont gérés, administrés et contrôlés par des francophones
Joël Rondeau, Directeur général

Canadian Association of Insolvency & Restructuring Professionals (CAIRP) / Association canadienne des professionnels de l'insolvabilité et de la réorganisation (ACPIR)
277 Wellington St. West, Toronto ON M5V 3H2
Tel: 647-695-3090; *Fax:* 647-695-3149
info@cairp.ca
www.cairp.ca
www.linkedin.com/company/3239103
www.facebook.com/CAIRP.ca
twitter.com/CAIRP_ACPIR
To develop, educate, support & give value to members; To foster the provision of insolvency, business recovery service with integrity, objectivity & competence, in a manner that instils the highest degree of public trust; To advocate for a fair, transparent & effective system of insolvency / business recovery administration throughout Canada
Anne Wettlaufer, President & CEO
Steve D'Alessandro, Chief Operating Officer
Natalie Alfano, Director, Professional Development
Gina Létourneau, Director, Education Programs

Canadian Association of Pension Supervisory Authorities (CAPSA) / Association canadienne des organismes de contrôle des régimes de retraite (ACOR)
c/o CAPSA Secretariat, 5160 Yonge St., 16th Fl., Toronto ON M2N 6L9
Tel: 416-590-7579; *Fax:* 416-590-7070
Toll-Free: 800-668-0128
capsa-acor@fsrao.ca
www.capsa-acor.org
To facilitate an efficient & effective pension regulatory system in Canada
Raseema Alam, Manager, Policy

Canadian Association of Student Financial Aid Administrators (CASFAA)
c/o Treasurer, Lakehead University, 955 Oliver Rd., Thunder Bay ON P7B 5E1
Tel: 807-343-8150
info@casfaa.ca
www.casfaa.ca
To represent financial aid administrators & awards officers in universities & colleges across Canada
Stephanie Williams, President
Josh Levac, Treasurer

Canadian Association of Urban Financial Professionals (CAUFP)
Toronto ON
info@caufp.ca
caufp.ca
www.instagram.com/caufp
www.linkedin.com/company/caufp
www.facebook.com/caufp
twitter.com/caufp
To develop & advance Black professionals
Meryl Afrika, President

Canadian Bankers Association (CBA) / Association des banquiers canadiens
PO Box 348, Stn. Commerce Court West, 199 Bay St., 30th Fl., Toronto ON M5L 1G2
Tel: 416-362-6092; *Fax:* 416-362-7705
Toll-Free: 800-263-0231
inform@cba.ca
www.cba.ca
www.youtube.com/user/cdnbankers
www.linkedin.com/company/canadian-bankers-association
www.facebook.com/YourMoneySeniors
twitter.com/CdnBankers
To advocate for policies that contribute to a beneficial banking system
Neil Parmenter, President & CEO

Canadian Community Reinvestment Coalition (CCRC)
PO Box 821, Stn. B, Ottawa ON K1P 241
Tel: 613-789-5753; *Fax:* 613-241-4758
info@cancrc.org
www.cancrc.org
To increase the accountability of Canada's financial institutions, increase their reinvestment in the Canadian ecomony, strengthen Canada's economy, strengthen community economic development efforts across Canada, & develop leadership in the Canadian financial sevices consumer movement.

Canadian Credit Union Association (CCUA) / Association canadienne des coopératives financières (ACCF)
Corporate Office, #1000, 151 Yonge St., Toronto ON M5C 2W7
Tel: 416-232-1262; *Toll-Free:* 800-649-0222
inquiries@ccua.com
www.ccua.com
www.linkedin.com/company/canadian-credit-union-association
www.facebook.com/CCUA.ACCF
twitter.com/CCUA_ACCF
To act as the national voice for the Canadian credit union system; To facilitate the national cooperative movement; To provide services to ensure best practices are met at all credit unions; To develop opportunities for cooperative growth
Martha Durdin, President & CEO
Korinne Collins, Vice-President, Professional Development & Education
Jeff Erickson, Chief Financial Officer & Vice-President, Corporate Services
Martin Reed, Vice-President, Marketing & Research
Brenda O'Connor, Vice-President, Governance & Strategy
Athana Mentzelopoulos, Vice-President, Government Relations

Canadian ETF Association (CETFA)
Toronto ON
www.cetfa.ca
www.youtube.com/cetfassn
twitter.com/cetfassn
To promote awareness of the Canadian exchange trade fund (ETF) industry
Kevin Gopaul, Chair

Canadian Finance & Leasing Association (CFLA) / Association canadienne de financement et de location (ACFL)
#301, 15 Toronto St., Toronto ON M5C 2E3
Tel: 416-860-1133; *Fax:* 416-860-1140
Toll-Free: 877-213-7373
info@cfla-acfl.ca
www.cfla-acfl.ca
www.linkedin.com/company/1360377
To ensure an environment in Canada where asset-based financing, equipment & vehicle-leasing industry can be profitable
Michael Rothe, President & CEO
Charlene Forde, Director, Events & Member Services
Lalita Sirnaik, Director, Finance & Administration
Marcel Buerkler, Manager, Policy

Canadian Institute of Financial Planners (CIFPs)
#600, 3660 Hurontario St., Mississauga ON L5B 3C4
Tel: 647-723-6445; *Fax:* 647-723-6457
Toll-Free: 866-933-0233
cifps@cifps.ca
www.cifps.ca
To train & qualify advisors to become Certified Financial Planners; To represent members on matters of common interest
Keith Costello, President & Chief Executive Officer
Anthony Williams, Vice-President, Academic Affairs
Andrew Cunningham, Director, Operations, Information & Education Services
Justin Warren, Director, Member Services & Business Development
Odele Burton, Office Manager

Canadian Investor Relations Institute (CIRI) / Institut canadien de relations avec les investisseurs
#601, 67 Yonge St., Toronto ON M5E 1J8
Tel: 416-364-8200; *Fax:* 416-364-2805
enquiries@ciri.org
www.ciri.org
To advance the practice of investor relations; To raise the stature of the profession in Canada; To act as the voice of investor relations professionals throughout Canada
Yvette Lokker, President & Chief Executive Officer
Salisha Hosein Ilyas, Director, Professional Development & Sponsorship
Patricia MacPherson, Manager, Membership

Canadian Lenders Association (CLA) / Association des Prêteurs Canadiens (APC)
120 Albany Ave., Toronto ON M5R 3C4
www.canadianlenders.org
www.linkedin.com/company/canadianlenders
twitter.com/canadianlenders
To foster safe & ethical lending practices by providing members with the means to be innovative & grow their businesses
Neil Wechsler, Chair
Gary Schwartz, President

Canadian Payroll Association (CPA) / L'Association canadienne de la paie (ACP)
#1600, 250 Bloor St. East, Toronto ON M4W 1E6
Tel: 416-487-3380; *Fax:* 416-487-3384
Toll-Free: 800-387-4693
infoline@payroll.ca
www.payroll.ca
www.youtube.com/user/CanadianPayrollAssoc
www.linkedin.com/company/the-canadian-payroll-association
www.facebook.com/canadianpayroll
twitter.com/cdnpayroll
To provide payroll leadership, through advocacy & education
Peter Tzanetakis, President

Canadian Pension & Benefits Institute (CPBI) / Institut canadien de la retraite et des avantages sociaux (ICRA)
#1210, 505, boul René-Lévesque ouest, Montréal QC H2Z 1Y7
Tel: 514-288-1222; *Fax:* 514-288-1225
info@cpbi-icra.ca
www.cpbi-icra.ca
linkedin.com/company/canadian-pension-&-benefits-institute
twitter.com/cpbi_icra
Caroline Tison, Executive Director

Canadian Securities Administrators (CSA) / Autorités canadiennes en valeurs mobilières (ACVM)
CSA Secretariat, Tour de la Bourse, #2510, 800, rue du Victoria-Square, Montréal QC H4Z 1J2
Tel: 514-864-9510; *Fax:* 514-864-9512
csa-acvm-secretariat@acvm-csa.ca
www.securities-administrators.ca
twitter.com/CSA_News
To give Canada a securities regulatory system that protects investors from unfair, improper or fraudulent practices & fosters fair, efficient & vibrant capital markets, by developing a national system of harmonized securities regulation, policy & practice.
Louis Morisset, Chair
Laura Belloni, Secretary General

Canadian Securities Institute (CSI) / L'Institut canadien des valeurs mobilières
200 Wellington St. West, 15th Fl., Toronto ON M5V 3C7
Tel: 416-364-9130; *Fax:* 416-359-0486
Toll-Free: 866-866-2601
customer_support@csi.ca
www.csi.ca
www.youtube.com/user/CSIGlobalEd
www.linkedin.com/groups/3720042
www.facebook.com/csiglobal
twitter.com/CSIGlobalEd
To enhance the knowledge of securities & financial industry professionals & promote knowledge & understanding of investing among the public
Marie Muldowney, Managing Director

Canadian Security Traders Association, Inc. (CSTA)
PO Box 3, 31 Adelaide St. East, Toronto ON M5C 2H8
www.canadiansta.org
www.linkedin.com/groups/3922676
twitter.com/canadiansta
Stéphane Ouellette, Chair

Canadian Venture Capital & Private Equity Association (CVCA) / Association canadienne du capital de risque et d'investissement (ACCR)
#1201, 372 Bay St., Toronto ON M5H 2W9
Tel: 416-487-0519
reception@cvca.ca
www.cvca.ca
www.linkedin.com/company/cvca
twitter.com/cvcacanada
To help its members fuel the economy of the future by growing the businesses of today; to support and connect the private capital industry with advocacy, research, and education.
Kim Furlong, Chief Executive Officer
Darrell Pinto, Vice-President, Research & Industry Advancement
Matt Ivis, Director, Government Relations & Policy
Elaine Bedell, Head, Talent & Operations
Jon Jackson, Head, Communications
Fil Varino, Head, Development & Member Engagement
Karen Hung, International Trade Liaison Officer
David Kornacki, Associate
Igli Panariti, Membership Coordinator

Chambre de commerce Canada-Pologne
5570, rue Waverly, Montréal QC H2T 2Y1
Tél: 514-278-7617

Co-operatives & Mutuals Canada (CMC) / Coopératives et mutuelles Canada
#400, 275 Bank St., Ottawa ON K2P 2L6
Tel: 613-238-6712; *Fax:* 613-567-0658
info@canada.coop
www.canada.coop
www.facebook.com/coopscanada
twitter.com/CoopsCanada
To unite co-operatives & mutuals from various industry sectors & regions of Canada
Doug Potentier, President
André Beaudry, Executive Director
Madeleine Brillant, Director, Corporate Affairs
Daniel Brunette, Director, Advocacy & Partnerships
René Bernatchez, Manager, Finance
Grace Busanga, Coordinator, Communications

Council of Ukrainian Credit Unions of Canada
145 Evans Ave., Toronto ON M8Z 5X8
Tel: 416-323-3495; *Fax:* 416-923-7904
info@cucuc.ca
www.cucuc.ca
To unite & promote Ukrainian member credit unions in Canada; To assist with the development of credit unions in Ukraine
Olya Sheweli, President

Credit Counselling Canada (CCC) / Conseil en crédit du Canada
#1600, 401 Bay St., Toronto ON M5H 2Y4
Toll-Free: 866-398-5999
contact@creditcounsellingcanada.ca
www.creditcounsellingcanada.ca
www.youtube.com/channel/UCj1dgARyEE1aya5RtJxvuUw
twitter.com/Creditcc
To ensure all Canadians have access to not-for-profit credit counselling; to ensure a quality of service is provided to Canadians by member agencies; to advocate on issues relevant to money management & the wise use of credit along with public policy & legislative issues around these; to promote awareness of the existence & availability of non-profit credit counselling; to cultivate positive working relationships with stakeholders

Credit Institute of Canada (CIC) / L'Institut canadien du crédit
#211, 3 Concorde Gate, Toronto ON M3C 3N7
Tel: 416-572-2615; *Fax:* 416-572-2619
Toll-Free: 888-447-3324
geninfo@creditedu.org
www.creditedu.org
www.youtube.com/user/creditinstitute
www.linkedin.com/groups/2370374
www.facebook.com/creditedu
twitter.com/creditinstitute
To provide credit education for credit & financial professionals in Canada
Nawshad Khadaroo, General Manager

Financial Executives International Canada (FEIC)
#300, 116 Simcoe St., Toronto ON M5H 4E2
Tel: 416-366-3007; *Toll-Free:* 866-677-3007
membership@feicanada.org
www.feicanada.org
www.instagram.com/fei_canada
www.linkedin.com/company/fei-canada
www.facebook.com/financialexecs
twitter.com/FEICanada

To promote ethical conduct in the practice of financial management; To contribute to the legal & policy making process in Canada; To provide advocacy, leadership & professional development services to members
Catherine Fels-Smith, Interim President

FP Canada
#902, 375 University Ave., Toronto ON M5G 2J5
Tel: 416-593-8587; *Fax:* 416-583-6903
Toll-Free: 800-305-9888
info@fpcanada.ca
www.fpcanada.ca
www.instagram.com/OfficialFPCanada
www.linkedin.com/company/fpcanada
www.facebook.com/OfficialFPCanada
twitter.com/OfficialFPCan
To develop, enforce, & promote competency & ethical standards in financial planning by those who have earned the designation of Certified Financial Planner (CFP) & Qualified Associate Financial Planner (QAFP)
Tashia Batstone, President & CEO
Joanna Tukums, Chief Operating Officer
Ralph Vizi, Chief Strategy Officer
Stephen Rotstein, Vice-President, Policy & Regulatory Affairs
Joan Yudelson, Vice-President, Professional Practice
Damienne Lebrun-Reid, Executive Director, Standards Council

The Institute of Internal Auditors (IIA) / L'Institut des vérificateurs internes
#401, 1035 Greenwood Blvd., Lake Mary FL 32746 USA
Tel: 407-937-1111; *Fax:* 407-937-1101
customerrelations@theiia.org
www.theiia.org
www.linkedin.com/company/the-institute-of-internal-auditors-inc
www.facebook.com/TheInstituteofInternalAuditors
twitter.com/theiia
To provide leadership for the global profession of internal auditing; To advocate for the profession's value
Richard F. Chambers, CIA, QIAL, CGAP, President & CEO

Interac Association / L'Association Interac
Royal Bank Plaza, North Tower, PO Box 45, #2400, 200 Bay St., Toronto ON M5J 2J1
Tel: 416-362-8550; *Toll-Free:* 855-789-2979
info@interac.ca
www.interac.ca
www.youtube.com/user/InteracBrand
www.linkedin.com/company/interac-corp
www.facebook.com/interac
twitter.com/interac
To provide debit card services in Canada
Mark O'Connell, President & CEO

International Organization of Securities Commissions (IOSCO) / Organisation internationale des commissions de valeurs (OICV)
General Secretariat, C/ Oquendo 12, Madrid 28006 Spain
info@iosco.org
www.iosco.org
www.linkedin.com/groups/4849117
twitter.com/IOSCOPress
To cooperate together to ensure a better regulation of the markets, on both the domestic & international level, in order to maintain just & efficient securities markets; To exchange information in order to promote development of domestic markets; To unite efforts to establish standards & effective surveillance of international securities transactions; To provide mutual assistance to ensure the integrity of the markets by rigorous application of standards & by effective enforcement against offences
Paul P. Andrews, Secretary General
Tajinder Singh, Deputy Secretary General

Investment Funds Institute of Canada (IFIC) / L'Institut des fonds d'investissement du Canada
11 King St. West, 4th Fl., Toronto ON M5H 4C7
Tel: 416-363-2150; *Toll-Free:* 866-347-1961
member-services@ific.ca
www.ific.ca
www.linkedin.com/company/266541
www.facebook.com/ific.ca
twitter.com/ific
To act as the voice of the investment funds industry in Canada; To enhance the integrity & growth of the Canadian mutual fund industry
Paul C. Bourque, President & CEO
Parker John, CFO & Vice-President, Finance

Investment Industry Regulatory Organization of Canada (IIROC) / Organisme canadien de réglementation du commerce des valeurs mobilières (OCRCVM)
#2000, 121 King St. West, Toronto ON M5H 3T9
Tel: 416-364-6133; *Fax:* 416-364-0753
Toll-Free: 877-442-4322
publicaffairs@iiroc.ca
www.iiroc.ca
To oversee investment dealers & trading activity on debt & equity marketplaces in Canada; To focus on regulatory & investment industry standards, protecting investors & strengthening market integrity
Andrew J. Kriegler, President & CEO
Ian Campbell, Chief Information Officer
Lucy Becker, Vice-President, Public Affairs & Member Education Services

Municipal Finance Officers' Association of Ontario (MFOA)
2169 Queen St. East, 2nd Fl., Toronto ON M4L 1J1
Tel: 416-362-9001; *Fax:* 416-362-9226
office@mfoa.on.ca
www.mfoa.on.ca
To represent the interests of municipal finance officers throughout Ontario; To promote the interests of members
Dan Cowin, Executive Director
Shelley Stedall, President
Nancy Taylor, Vice-President

Mutual Fund Dealers Association of Canada (MFDA) / Association canadienne des courtiers de fonds mutuels
#1000, 121 King St. West, Toronto ON M5H 3T9
Tel: 416-361-6332; *Toll-Free:* 888-466-6332
mfda@mfda.ca
www.mfda.ca
www.linkedin.com/company/mfda
twitter.com/MFDA_News
To be the national self-regulatory organization (SRO) for the distribution side of the Canadian mutual fund industry
Christopher Nicholls, BA, LL.B., LL.M, Chair
Mark T. Gordon, LL.B., President & CEO
Shaun Devlin, Senior Vice-President, Member Regulation - Enforcement
Karen L. McGuinness, Senior Vice-President, Member Regulation - Compliance
Paige L. Ward, General Counsel, Corporate Secretary & VP, Policy

Ontario Association of Credit Counselling Services (OACCS)
ON
info@oaccs.ca
www.oaccs.com
To represent member agencies & provide them with a forum for the pursuit of common interests in order to support, strengthen & enhance not-for-profit credit counselling services; To enhance the quality & availability of not-for-profit credit counselling

Payments Canada / Paiements Canada
Tower II, Constitution Sq., #800, 350 Albert St., Ottawa ON K1R 1A4
Tel: 613-238-4173
info@payments.ca
www.payments.ca
www.linkedin.com/company/payments-canada
www.facebook.com/paymentscanada
twitter.com/paymentscanada
To be responsible for the clearing & settlement infrastructure, processes & rules essential to transactions in the Canadian economy
Tracey Black, President & CEO
Tricia Weagant, Contact, Marketing & Communications

Pension Investment Association of Canada (PIAC) / Association canadienne des gestionnaires de fonds de retraite
#123, 20 Carlton St., Toronto ON M5B 2H5
Tel: 416-640-0264
www.piacweb.org
www.linkedin.com/company/pension-investment-association-of-canada
To promote the financial security of pension fund beneficiaries through sound investment policy & practices
Peter Waite, Executive Director

Portfolio Management Association of Canada (PMAC)
#1210, 155 University Ave., Toronto ON M5H 3B7
Tel: 416-504-1118; *Fax:* 416-504-1117
info@portfoliomanagement.org
www.portfoliomanagement.org
www.linkedin.com/company/portfolio-management-association-of-canada
twitter.com/PMACnews
To represent the Investment Counsel & portfolio managers in Canada; To advocate high standards of unbiased portfolio management in the interest of investors
Katie Walmsley, President
Alex Stephen, Manager, Member Services

Registered Deposit Brokers Association (RDBA)
#614, 55 Cedar Pointe Dr., Barrie ON L4N 5R7
Tel: 705-730-7599; *Fax:* 705-730-0477
Toll-Free: 866-261-6263
headoffice@rdba.ca
www.rdba.ca
To represent interests of deposit clients & independent deposit brokers

Responsible Investment Association (RIA)
#300, 215 Spadina Ave., Toronto ON M5T 2C7
Tel: 416-461-6042
staff@riacanada.ca
www.riacanada.ca
www.linkedin.com/company/responsible-investment-association
www.facebook.com/ResponsibleInvestmentAssociation
twitter.com/riacanada
To take a leadership role in coordinating the responsible investing (RI) agenda in Canada; To raise public awareness of RI in Canada; To reach out to other groups interested in RI; To provide information on RI to members & the public
Dustyn Lanz, Chief Executive Officer
Wendy Mitchell, Chief Financial Officer

Society of Actuaries (SOA)
#600, 475 North Martingale Rd., Schaumburg IL 60173 USA
Tel: 847-706-3500; *Fax:* 847-706-3599
customerservice@soa.org
www.soa.org
twitter.com/soasupport
To advance actuarial knowledge & improve decision making to benefit society
Gregory Heidrich, Executive Director
Stacy D.R. Lin, Chief Financial Officer

Startup Canada
#300, 56 Sparks St., Ottawa ON K1P 5A9
Tel: 613-627-0787
hello@startupcan.ca
www.startupcan.ca
www.youtube.com/user/StartupCanada
www.facebook.com/startupcanada
twitter.com/Startup_Canada
To be a national, grassroots, non-profit organization dedicated to strengthening & enhancing Canada's entrepreneurial culture
Brenda Halloran, Chair
Victoria Lennox, President
Cyprian Szalankiewicz, Director, Production
Tomasz Popiel, Director, Finance

UNI Coopération financière / UNI Financial Cooperation
Édifice Martin-J.-Légère, CP 5554, 295, boul St-Pierre ouest, Caraquet NB E1W 1B7
Tél: 506-726-4000; *Téléc:* 506-726-4001
www.uni.ca
www.linkedin.com/company/uni-cooperation-financiere
www.facebook.com/unicooperation
twitter.com/UNIcooperation
Améliorer la qualité de vie de ceux et celles qui y adhèrent tout en contribuant à l'autosuffisance socio-économique de la collectivité acadienne du Nouveau-Brunswick, dans le respect de son identité linguistique et ses valeurs coopératives
Robert Moreau, Chef de la direction

Women in Capital Markets (WCM) / Les femmes sur les marchés financiers
#300, 37 Front St. East, Toronto ON M5E 1B3
Tel: 416-502-3614
info@wcm.ca
www.wcm.ca
www.linkedin.com/groups/1681457
www.facebook.com/WomenInCapitalMarkets
twitter.com/WCMCanada
To enable capital markets professionals to reach their greatest potential for success; to advance women within Canadian financial services
Mari Jenson, Chair

Camilla Sutton, President & CEO

World Council of Credit Unions, Inc. (WOCCU)
PO Box 2982, 5710 Mineral Point Rd., Madison WI
53705-4493 USA

Tel: 608-395-2000; *Fax:* 608-395-2001
mail@woccu.org
www.woccu.org
www.youtube.com/user/WOCCU
www.linkedin.com/company/world-council-of-credit-unions
www.facebook.com/woccu
twitter.com/woccu

To promote the sustainable growth & expansion of credit unions
& financial cooperatives worldwide; To provide technical
assistance & trade association services to members
Brian Branch, President & CEO
Steven Funk, Chief Financial Officer
Paul Treinen, Chief Operating Officer
Jack Van Kauwenbergh, Chief Information Officer
JoAnna Vanderpoel, Vice-President, Human Resources

Fisheries & Fishing Industry

Association québécoise de l'industrie de la pêche (AQIP) / Québec Fish Processors Association
Place de la Cité, Tour Cominar, #0150, 2640, boul Laurier,
Québec QC G1V 5C2

Tél: 418-654-1831; *Téléc:* 418-654-1376
info@aqip.com
aqip.com
www.instagram.com/aqipqc
www.facebook.com/AQIPQC

Défendre les intérêts professionnels des industries québécoises
de la transformation des produits marins; travailler au
développement des services; aider à l'amélioration de la
productivité en usines

Atlantic Canada Fish Farmers Association (ACFFA)
226 Limekiln Rd., Letang NB E5C 2A8

Tel: 506-755-3526; *Fax:* 506-755-6237
info@atlanticfishfarmers.com
atlanticfishfarmers.com
www.youtube.com/user/acffavideos
www.facebook.com/150506105026651
twitter.com/AtlFishFarmers

To act as the voice of Atlantic Canada's salmon farming
industry; To implement fish health initiatives to produce
high-quality finfish
Pamela Parker, Executive Director
Tobi Taylor, Manager, Operations
Betty House, Coordinator, Research & Development
Jim Hanley, Manager, Wharf

Atlantic Salmon Federation (ASF) / Fédération du saumon atlantique
15 Rankine Mill Rd., St Andrews NB E5B 3A9

Tel: 506-529-4581; *Toll-Free:* 800-565-5666
savesalmon@asf.ca
www.asf.ca
www.facebook.com/AtlanticSalmonFederation
twitter.com/SalmonNews

To protect, conserve & restore wild Atlantic salmon & their
ecosystems
Bill Taylor, President & CEO
Robert Otto, Chief Operating Officer
Jamie LeBlanc, Chief Financial Officer
Jonathan Carr, Vice-President, Research & Environment
Kirsten Rouse, Vice-President, Development

British Columbia Salmon Farmers Association (BCSFA)
#201, 911 Island Hwy., Campbell River BC V9W 2C2

Tel: 250-286-1636; *Fax:* 800-849-9430
Toll-Free: 800-661-7256
info@bcsalmonfarmers.ca
www.bcsalmonfarmers.ca
www.facebook.com/BCSalmonFarmers
twitter.com/BCSalmonFarmers

To act as the voice of British Columbia's farmed salmon
industry; To advance the competitiveness & sustainable growth
of the salmon farming industry; To increase fish farming
opportunities in British Columbia
Jeremy Dunn, Executive Director
Sabrina Santoro, Manager

British Columbia Seafood Alliance (BCSA)
#1100, 1200 West 73rd Ave., Vancouver BC V6P 6G5

Tel: 604-377-9213; *Fax:* 604-683-4510
www.bcseafoodalliance.com

To represent the interests & values of a majority of BC's seafood
industries to the federal & provincial governments & to the
general public; to promote the conservation & environmentally

sustainable use & production of seafood resources in BC; to
foster an economically viable & internationally competitive
seafood industry
Christina Burridge, Executive Director

British Columbia Shellfish Growers Association (BCSGA)
2002 Comox Ave., #F, Comox BC V9M 3M6

Tel: 250-890-7561
admin@bcsga.ca
www.bcsga.ca

To advance the sustainable growth & prosperity of the BC
shellfish industry in a global economy by providing leadership &
advocacy to members & stakeholders while maintaining the
integrity of the marine environment
Steve Pocock, President
Darlene Winterburn, Executive Director

Canadian Aquaculture Industry Alliance (CAIA) / Alliance de l'industrie canadienne de l'aquiculture
#650, 220 Laurier Ave. West, Ottawa ON K1P 5Z9

Tel: 613-239-0612; *Fax:* 613-239-0619
info@aquaculture.ca
aquaculture.ca
www.facebook.com/155794491097836
twitter.com/CDNaquaculture

To represent the interests of aquaculture operators, feed
companies, suppliers, & provincial finfish & shellfish aquaculture
associations on both the national & international scenes; To
ensure the international competitiveness of the Canadian
aquaculture industry
Timothy J. Kennedy, President, CEO & Executive Dir.

Canadian Association of Prawn Producers (CAPP)
1362 Revell Dr., Manotick ON K4M 1K8

Tel: 613-692-8249; *Fax:* 613-692-8250
office@shrimp-canada.com
www.shrimp-canada.com

To represent the interests of Canadian at-sea producers of
coldwater shrimp; To advocate for sustainable & responsible
resource management; To provide a platform through which
Canadian prawn producers can communicate their issues to
government & the general public
Bruce Chapman, Executive Director

Canadian Centre for Fisheries Innovation (CCFI) / Centre canadien d'innovations des pêches
PO Box 4920, St. John's NL A1C 5R3

Tel: 709-778-0517; *Fax:* 709-778-0516
ccfi@mi.mun.ca

To work with the fishing industry to improve productivity &
profitability of fishery through science & technology
Robert Verge, Managing Director

Canadian Council of Professional Fish Harvesters (CCPFH) / Conseil canadien des pêcheurs professionnels (CCPP)
33, rue Laval, Gatineau QC J8X 3G8

Tel: 819-777-3474; *Fax:* 613-231-4313
www.fishharvesterspecheurs.ca
www.linkedin.com/groups/3881175
www.facebook.com/CCPFHCCPP
twitter.com/CCPFH_CCPP

To represent the interests of professional fish harvesters across
Canada in their dealings with the federal, provincial & territorial
governments on national issues of common concern; To act as a
national industry sector council to plan & implement training &
adjustment & human resources programs for the fish harvesting
industry in Canada
Jonattan Wettel, Office Administrator
Martin Picard, Project Manager

Environment Resources Managment Association
PO Box 857, Grand Falls-Windsor NL A2A 2P7

Tel: 709-489-7350
info@exploitsriver.ca
www.exploitsriver.ca/association.php

To promote the development of the Exploits River as a major
Atlantic Salmon producing river.

Fédération québécoise pour le saumon atlantique (FQSA)
3137, rue Laberge, Québec QC G1X 4B5

Tél: 418-847-9191; *Ligne sans frais:* 888-847-9191
info@fqsa.ca
www.saumonquebec.com
www.instagram.com/saumonquebec
www.facebook.com/SaumonQuebec

Organisme à but non lucratif dont la raison d'être est d'unir et de
représenter les intérêts de l'ensemble des saumoniers du
Québec
Myriam Bergeron, Directrice général

Fisheries Council of Canada (FCC) / Conseil Canadien des Pêches
#610, 170 Laurier Ave. West, Ottawa ON K1P 5V5

Tel: 613-727-7450; *Fax:* 613-727-7453
info@fisheriescouncil.org
fisheriescouncil.com

To represent Canada's fish & seafood industry
Paul Lansbergen, President

Fishermen & Scientists Research Society (FSRS)
PO Box 25125, Halifax NS B3M 4H4

Tel: 902-876-1160; *Fax:* 902-876-1320
www.fsrs.ns.ca

To establish and maintain a network of fishermen and scientific
personnel that are concerned with the long-term sustainability of
the marine fishing industry in the Atlantic Region.
Patricia King, General Manager

International Association of Fish Inspectors (IAFI)
PO Box 225, 1568 Merivale Rd., Nepean ON K2G 5Y7

Tel: 613-721-6968; *Fax:* 613-726-7778
info@iafi.net
www.iafi.net
www.linkedin.com/groups/4121747
twitter.com/IAFInet

To bring together fish inspectors & others interested in the field,
from backgrounds such as government, fish & seafood
harvesting, processing & marketing industries, academia, public
& private organizations, & others
John Emberley, Executive Director

International Commission for the Conservation of Atlantic Tunas (ICCAT)
Calle Corazón de María, 8, 6th Fl., Madrid 28002 Spain

info@iccat.int
www.iccat.int

Driss Meski, Executive Secretary
Juan Antonio Moreno, Department Head, Administration &
Finance

North Atlantic Salmon Conservation Organization (NASCO)
11 Rutland Sq., Edinburgh EH1 2AS United Kingdom

hq@nasco.int
nasco.int

To promote the conservation, restoration, enhancement &
rational management of salmon stocks in North Atlantic
S. Doucet, President
Emma Hatfield, Secretary

North Pacific Anadromous Fish Commission (NPAFC)
#502, 889 West Pender St., Vancouver BC V6C 3B2

Tel: 604-775-5550; *Fax:* 604-775-5577
secretariat@npafc.org
www.npafc.org

To promote the conservation of anadromous stocks in the North
Pacific Ocean
Vladimir Radchenko, Executive Director
Nancy Davis, Deputy Director

Northwest Atlantic Fisheries Organization (NAFO)
PO Box 638, Dartmouth NS B2Y 3Y9

Tel: 902-468-5590; *Fax:* 902-468-5538
info@nafo.int
www.nafo.int
www.linkedin.com/company/nafo1979
www.facebook.com/NAFO.Info
twitter.com/NAFO1979

To contribute through consultation & cooperation to the optimum
utilization, rational management & conservation of the fishery
resources of the Northwest Atlantic
Fred Kingston, Executive Secretary

Nova Scotia Salmon Association (NSSA)
PO Box 396, Chester NS B0J 1J0

nssasalmon@gmail.com
www.nssalmon.ca

To further the conservation & wise management of wild Atlantic
salmon & trout
Rene Aucoin, President

Prince Edward Island Aquaculture Alliance (PEIAA)
101 Longworth Ave., 1st Fl., Charlottetown PE C1A 5A9

Tel: 902-368-2757; *Fax:* 902-626-3954
peiaqua@aquaculturepei.com
www.aquaculturepei.com

To provide focus for the Prince Edward Island aquaculture
industry; To enhance industry prosperity through its
development as an effective world competitor
Peter Warris, Coordinator, Research & Development
Sharon Gilbank, Manager, Accounts & Officer

Prince Edward Island Fishermen's Association Ltd. (PEIFA)
#102, 420 University Ave., Charlottetown PE C1A 7Z5
Tel: 902-566-4050; *Fax:* 902-368-3748
adminpeifa@pei.eastlink.ca
www.peifa.org
To represent fishermen across Prince Edward Island; To act as a single, united voice on behalf of Island fishers on industry issues
Craig Avery, President
Ian MacPherson, Manager

Seafood Producers Association of Nova Scotia
45 Alderney Dr., Dartmouth NS B2Y 2N6
Tel: 902-463-7790
spans@ns.sympatico.ca

Food & Beverage Industry

Association des brasseurs du Québec (ABQ) / Québec Brewers Association
#888, 2000, rue Peel, Montréal QC H3A 2W5
Tél: 514-284-9199
brasseurs.qc.ca
De représenter les intérêts de ses membres à des organismes et des intervenants govenment
Patrice Léger Bourgoin, Directeur général

Association of Canadian Distillers (ACD) / Association des distillateurs canadiens
#2-B, 219 Dufferin St., Toronto ON M6K 1Y9
Tel: 416-626-0100
info@spiritscanada.ca
www.spiritscanada.ca
www.instagram.com/spiritscanada
www.facebook.com/spiritscanada
twitter.com/SpiritsCanada
To protect & advance the interests of its members; To promote & protect, both nationally & internationally, the well-being & viability of the Canadian distilling industry; To foster responsible attitudes toward the consumption of distilled spirits (gin, vodka, rum, Canadian Whisky) in Canada; To enhance the recognition of the name & reputation of Canadian Whisky as Canada's unique appellation distilled spirits product; To preserve & protect the integrity & standards of all distilled products
Jan Westcott, President & CEO

Breakfast Cereals Canada (BCC)
#600, 100 Sheppard Ave. East, Toronto ON M2N 6N5
Tel: 416-510-8024; *Fax:* 416-510-8043
breakfastcereals.ca
To provide a forum for members to review issues of significance to the breakfast industry; to represent industry with government
Kathryn Fitzwilliam, Contact

Brewers Association of Canada / L'association des brasseurs du Canada
#650, 45 O'Connor St., Ottawa ON K1P 1A4
cheers@beercanada.com
www.beercanada.com
www.instagram.com/beercanadacheers
www.linkedin.com/company/beer-canada
www.facebook.com/BeerCanadaCheers
twitter.com/beercanada
To represent brewing companies operating in Canada; To collect information & statistics about the brewing industry; To provide information about the industry to the public
Luke Chapman, Interim President
Dana Miller, Director, Communications & Engagement
Ed Gregory, Senior Research Advisor
Tanya Bernier, Senior Manager, Operations & Member Services

Brewing & Malting Barley Research Institute (BMBRI) / Institut de recherche - brassage et orge de maltage
PO Box 39120, Stn. Lakewood, Saskatoon SK S7V 0A9
Tel: 306-370-1787
www.bmbri.ca
To support the development & evaluation of new malting barley varieties in Canada
Gina Feist, Executive Director

CanadaGAP
#312, 245 Menten Pl., Ottawa ON K2H 9E8
Tel: 613-829-4711; *Fax:* 613-829-9379
info@canadagap.ca
www.canadagap.ca
To operate a food safety program for companies that produce & handle fruits & vegetables; To develop & disseminate manuals for Greenhouse & fruit & vegetable operations; To encourage

Good Agricultural Practices (GAPs); To encourage best practices for food supply management
Heather Gale, Executive Director

Canadian Beverage Association / Association canadienne des boissons
WaterPark Place, 20 Bay St., 11th Fl., Toronto ON M5J 2N8
Tel: 416-362-2424; *Fax:* 416-362-3229
info@canadianbeverage.ca
www.canadianbeverage.ca
www.linkedin.com/company/canadian-beverage-association
www.facebook.com/CanadianBeverageAssociation
twitter.com/CanadaBev
To represent beverage bottlers, distributors, franchise houses & industry suppliers on a variety of issues
Jim Goetz, President
Carolyn Fell, Vice-President
Gabrielle Gallant, Senior Director, Government Affairs

Canadian Bottled Water Association (CBWA) / Association canadienne des embouteilleurs d'eau
#617, 7357 Woodbine Ave., Markham ON L3R 6R3
Tel: 416-618-1763; *Fax:* 877-354-2788
www.cbwa.ca
To represent the Canadian bottled water industry; To ensure a high standard of quality for bottled water
Elizabeth Griswold, Executive Director

Canadian College & University Food Service Association (CCUFSA)
c/o Drew Hall, University of Guelph, Gordon St., Guelph ON N1G 2W1
Tel: 519-824-4120; *Fax:* 519-837-9302
mcollins@hrs.uoguelph.ca
www.ccufsa.on.ca
To enhance the quality of campus life through the growth & development of food service operations in colleges & universities
Chris Roberts, President
Ed Townsley, Executive Director

Canadian Craft Brewers Association (CCBA) / Association des microbrasseries canadiennes (AMBC)
#1400, 340 Albert St., Ottawa ON K1R 7Y6
info@ccba-ambc.org
ccba-ambc.org
www.linkedin.com/company/ccba-ambc
www.facebook.com/craftbeercanada.org
twitter.com/CdnCraftBrewers
To promote & protect members' interests

Canadian Federation of Independent Grocers (CFIG) / Fédération canadienne des épiciers indépendants
#401, 105 Gordon Baker Rd., Toronto ON M2H 3P8
Tel: 416-492-2311; *Fax:* 416-492-2347
Toll-Free: 800-661-2344
info@cfig.ca
www.cfig.ca
www.linkedin.com/company/canadian-federation-of-independent-grocers
www.facebook.com/CFIGFCEI
twitter.com/cfigfcei
To equip & enable independent, franchised, & specialty grocers for sustainable success; To act as a united voice for independent grocers across Canada
Tom Shurrie, President & CEO
Nancy Kwon, Vice-President, Communications & Marketing

Canadian Health Food Association (CHFA) / Association canadienne des aliments de santé
#201, 235 Yorkland Blvd., Toronto ON M2J 4Y8
Tel: 416-497-6939; *Fax:* 416-497-3214
Toll-Free: 800-661-4510
info@chfa.ca
www.chfa.ca
www.instagram.com/canadianhealthfoodassociation
www.facebook.com/CanadianHealthFoodAssociation
twitter.com/cdnhealthfood
To create opportunities for members to thrive by cultivating an innovative industry through advocacy, education, & experience
Mike Fata, Chair

Canadian Meat Council (CMC) / Conseil des viandes du Canada
#930, 220 Laurier Ave. West, Ottawa ON K1P 5Z9
Tel: 613-729-3911; *Fax:* 613-729-4997
info@cmc-cvc.com
cmc-cvc.com
twitter.com/CMCCVC
To express the views of the membership with government, all elements of the food industry, consumer organizations, the research & academic community & the media; To foster high

standards of industry integrity & a vast range of wholesome, nutritional meat products
Chris White, President & CEO
Jorge Correa, Vice-President, Market Access & Technical Affairs

Canadian Meat Science Association (CMSA) / Association scientifique canadienne de la viande (ASCB)
Dept. of Agricultural, Food & Nutritional Science, Univ. of Alberta, #4-10, Agriculture / Forestry Centre, Edmonton AB T6G 2P5
admin@cmsa-ascv.ca
www.cmsa-ascv.ca
To promote the application of science & technology to the production, processing, packaging, distribution, preparation, evaluation & utilization of all meat & meat products; To develop & promote useful, coordinated research, educational techniques & service activities
Eric Pouliot, President
Bethany Uttaro, Sec.-Treas.

Canadian National Millers Association (CNMA)
#303, 236 Metcalfe St., Ottawa ON K2P 1R3
Tel: 613-238-2293; *Fax:* 613-271-1112
www.canadianmillers.ca
To serve as a vehicle for consultation between the milling industry, government departments & agencies; To promote regulatory & public policy environment that enhances international competitiveness; To provide international trade development to the industry; To disseminate information about the industry & Canadian wheat flour quality; To work directly & in cooperation with the trade offices abroad
Gordon Harrison, President

Canadian Snack Food Association (CSFA) / Association canadienne des fabricants des grignotines
c/o Ileana Lima, PO Box 42252, 128 Queen St. South, Mississauga ON L5M 4Z0
Tel: 289-997-1379
canadiansnack.com
To provide the leadership required for sustained growth & competitiveness of the industry; To influence policy formulation, legislation & regulations at all levels of government in the best interests of the industry; To encourage high standards for the protection of public health
Kent Hawkins, President
Ileana Lima, Executive Vice-President

Canadian Spice Association (CSA) / Association canadienne des épices
PO Box 88059, 7235 Bellshire Gate, Mississauga ON L5N 8A0
contact@canadianspiceassociation.com
www.canadianspiceassociation.com
To foster & promote fellowship & goodwill among members; To advance the welfare of the Spice Trade & its commonly associated lines in Canada
Beverley Tschirhart, Executive Director

Canadian Sugar Institute (CSI) / Institut canadien du sucre
#801, 277 Wellington St. West, Toronto ON M5V 3E4
Tel: 416-368-8091; *Fax:* 416-368-6426
info@sugar.ca
sugar.ca
www.linkedin.com/company/canadian-sugar-institute
twitter.com/CdnSugarTrade
To collect, analyze & provide nutrition information on sugars, carbohydrates & health
Sandra Marsden, President
Flora Wang, Manager, Nutrition & Scientific Affairs

Canadian Vintners Association (CVA) / L'Association des vignerons du Canada
#200, 440 Laurier Ave. West, Ottawa ON K1R 7X6
Tel: 613-782-2283
info@canadianvintners.com
www.canadianvintners.com
www.facebook.com/CVAwine
twitter.com/cvawine
To formulate & promote policies that will advance the interests & goals of the Canadian wine sector
Dan Paszkowski, President & CEO

Coffee Association of Canada (CAC) / Association du café du Canada
#207, 133 Richmond St. West, Toronto ON M5H 2L3
Tel: 416-510-8032
info@coffeeassoc.com
www.coffeeassoc.com

To address industry-wide issues on behalf of members, keeping them fully informed, & allowing them to focus on the proprietary concerns of building their businesses

Conseil de la transformation agroalimentaire et des produits de consommation (CTAC) / Council of Food Processing & Consumer Products
216, rue Denison est, Granby QC J2H 2R6
Tél: 450-349-1521; *Téléc:* 450-349-6923
info@conseiltac.com
www.conseiltac.com
www.linkedin.com/company/1237456
Le porte-parole officiel des manufacturiers de produits alimentaires du Québec qui s'y regroupent à titre de membres fabricants; canalise les représentations des manufacturiers, en particulier auprès des gouvernements; coordonne l'action des membres en vue de promouvoir leurs intérêts économiques, sociaux et professionnels; suscite l'éducation des consommateurs sur les valeurs d'une bonne alimentation; favorise la promotion des produits fabriqués par les membres; établit des liaisons entre les manufacturiers, les producteurs, les fournisseurs, les distributeurs, les consommateurs et les autres maillons de la chaîne alimentaire; encourage la recherche dans les domaines de l'agriculture, de l'alimentation et du marketing
Sylvie Cloutier, Présidente-directrice générale

Flavour Manufacturers Association of Canada (FMAC) / Association canadienne de fabricants des arômes
#602E, 2700 Matheson Blvd. East, Mississauga ON L4W 4V9
Tel: 416-510-8036; *Fax:* 416-510-8043
info@flavourcanada.ca
www.flavorcanada.com
To serve the needs of the Canadian flavour industry by providing a forum for the examination of industry problems, assisting in the implementation of solutions, & fostering a global perspective for creativity, innovation & competition

Food & Beverage Atlantic (FBA)
36 Albert St., Moncton NB E1C 1A9
Tel: 506-857-4255
admin@atlanticfood.ca
www.atlanticfood.ca
www.linkedin.com/company/food-beverage-atlantic
www.facebook.com/foodandbeverageatlantic
To help grow food & beverage companies in Atlantic Canada
Tammy Brideau, Executive Director

Food Processors of Canada (FPC) / Fabricants de produits alimentaires du Canada
#900, 350 Sparks St., Ottawa ON K1R 7S8
Tel: 613-722-1000; *Fax:* 613-722-1404
info@foodprocessorsofcanada.ca
foodprocessorsofcanada.ca
To provide professional services & advice to members on matters such as manufacturing, trade, & commerce
Denise Allen, President & CEO

Food, Health & Consumer Products of Canada (FHCPC) / Produits alimentaires, de santé et de consommation du Canada (PASCC)
#602E, 2700 Matheson Blvd. East, Mississauga ON L4W 4V9
Tel: 416-510-8024; *Fax:* 416-510-8043
info@fhcp.ca
www.fhcp.ca
www.youtube.com/channel/UCiPucOT4GdBEv5XaN-SpGAQ
www.linkedin.com/company/fhcp-canada
www.facebook.com/fhcpcanada
twitter.com/FHCP_CA
To represent the food & consumer products industry, from small independently-owned companies to large multinationals
Michael Graydon, Chief Executive Officer

Islamic Food & Nutrition Council of Canada (IFANCC)
#206, 130 Dundas St. East, Mississauga ON L5A 3V8
Tel: 905-275-0477
halal@ifancc.org
ifancc.org
www.facebook.com/ifancc
twitter.com/ifancc
To provide Halal certification services; To help companies develop Halal standards
Haider Khattak, Administrator

Master Brewers Association of The Americas (MBAA)
3340 Pilot Knob Rd., St Paul MN 55121-2097 USA
Tel: 651-454-7250; *Fax:* 651-454-0766
mbaa@mbaa.com
www.mbaa.com
www.facebook.com/MasterBrewers
twitter.com/masterbrewers

To advance brewing, fermentation & allied industries
Amy Hope, Executive Vice-President

New Brunswick Maple Syrup Association (NBMSA)
250 Sheriff St., Grand Falls NB E3Z 3A2
Tel: 506-473-2271
maple.infor.ca
To represent the interests of its members, & facilitate the industry through advertisement & the constant improvement of quality & standards of the maple industry
Louise Poitras, Executive Director

Ontario Food Protection Association (OFPA)
PO Box 53128, Stn. Royal Orchard, Thornhill ON L3T 7R9
Tel: 647-573-4940
info@ofpa.on.ca
ofpa.on.ca
www.instagram.com/ofpa_food
www.linkedin.com/company/ontario-food-protection-association
www.facebook.com/OntarioFoodProtectionAssociation
twitter.com/ofpamedia
To provide a common forum for those associated with food safety in the food industry & enables them to exchange ideas, experiences & information
Joe Myatt, President

Ontario Independent Meat Processors (OIMP)
52 Royal Rd., #B-1, Guelph ON N1H 1G3
Tel: 519-763-4558; *Fax:* 519-763-4164
info@oimp.ca
www.oimp.ca
www.instagram.com/ontariomeatpoultry
www.linkedin.com/company/1368588
www.facebook.com/ONTARIOINDEPENDENTMEATPROCESSORS
twitter.com/OIMPa
To provide leadership for Ontario's meat & poultry industry by fostering innovation, promoting food safety & recognizing excellence
Laurie Nicol, Executive Director

Pet Food Association of Canada (PFAC) / Association des fabricants d'aliments pour animaux familiers du Canada
PO Box 238, Carleton Place ON K7C 3P4
Tel: 416-447-9970
pfac.com
To provide association members with a unified voice on issues that affect the pet food industry in Canada

Soy Canada
#703, 350 Sparks St., Ottawa ON K1R 7S8
Tel: 613-233-0500
info@soycanada.ca
soycanada.ca
twitter.com/soy_canada
To unite the Canadian soybean industry
Ron Davidson, Executive Director

Tea & Herbal Association of Canada (THAC) / Association du thé et des tisanes du Canada
#207, 133 Richmond St. West, Toronto ON M5H 2L3
Tel: 416-510-8647
info@tea.ca
www.tea.ca
www.instagram.com/canadatea
twitter.com/Canadatea
To represent & advance the interests of Canada's tea industry to all levels of government in an effort to improve the conditions under which the industry operates & to promote better business relations between the industry's players
Shabnam Weber, President

Wine Country Ontario
PO Box 4000, 4890 Victoria Ave. North, Vineland ON L0R 2E0
Tel: 905-684-8070; *Fax:* 905-562-1993
info@winecountryontario.ca
winecountryontario.ca
www.instagram.com/winecountryont
www.facebook.com/WineCountryOntario
twitter.com/winecountryont
A non-profit trade association which plays a leadership role in the marketing, promotion & future direction of the Ontario wine industry
Sylvia Augaitis, Executive Director, Marketing
Magdalena Kaiser, Director, Public Relations - Marketing & Tourism

Forestry & Forest Products

Alberta Forest Products Association (AFPA)
#900, 10707 - 100 Ave., Edmonton AB T5J 3M1
Tel: 780-452-2841; *Fax:* 780-455-0505
info@albertaforestproducts.ca
www.albertaforestproducts.ca
www.facebook.com/albertaforests
twitter.com/albertaforests
To represent companies that manufacture forest products throughout Alberta
Paul Whittaker, President & CEO
Brock Mulligan, Director, Communications
Keith Murray, Director, Industry/Government Relations
Carola von Sass, Director, Health, Safety & Transportation
Dan Wilkinson, Director, Markets
Leslie Loudon, Office Administrator

Association of British Columbia Forest Professionals (ABCFP)
#602 - 1281 West Georgia St., Vancouver BC V6E 3J7
Tel: 604-687-8027; *Fax:* 604-687-3264
info@abcfp.ca
www.abcfp.ca
www.youtube.com/user/TheABCFP
www.facebook.com/ABCFP
twitter.com/abcfp
To protect the public interest in the practice of professional forestry by ensuring the competence, independence & integrity of its members; to ensure that every person practising professional forestry is accountable to the association & to the public
Christine Gelowitz, Chief Executive Officer
Mike Larock, Director, Professional Practice & Forest Stewardship
Dean Pelkey, Director, Communications

Association of Registered Professional Foresters of New Brunswick (ARPFNB) / Association des forestiers agréés du Nouveau-Brunswick (AFANB)
#221, 1350 Regent St., Fredericton NB E3C 2G6
Tel: 506-452-6933; *Fax:* 506-450-3128
info@arpfnb.ca
www.arpfnb.ca
www.facebook.com/arpfnb
To manage the forest resources of New Brunswick for the sustained development of these resources; To assure the proficiency & competency of Registered Professional Foresters in New Brunswick
Edward Czerwinski, Executive Director
Jody Jenkins, President
Jasen Golding, Secretary-Treasurer

BC Council of Forest Industries (COFI)
#1220, 595 Howe St., Vancouver BC V6C 2T5
Tel: 604-684-0211; *Fax:* 604-687-4930
info@cofi.org
www.cofi.org
To be the voice of the British Columbia forest industry
Susan Yurkovich, President & CEO
Michael Armstrong, Vice-President, Policy & Operations
Mina Laudan, Vice-President, Public Affairs

Canadian Hardwood Plywood & Veneer Association (CHPVA) / Association canadienne du Contreplaqué et de Placages de bois dur (ACCPBD)
89, av Godfrey, Saint-Sauveur QC J0R 1R5
Tel: 450-227-4048
www.chpva.com
To protect the interests & conserve the rights of those involved in the manufacture & distribution of hardwood veneer & plywood & their suppliers in Canada
Gaëtan Lauzon, Executive Vice-President
Carole Aussant, Coordinator

Canadian Institute of Forestry (CIF) / Institut forestier du Canada (IFC)
PO Box 99, 6905 Hwy. 17 West, Mattawa ON P0H 1V0
Tel: 705-744-1715; *Fax:* 705-744-1716
admin@cif-ifc.org
www.cif-ifc.org
www.youtube.com/user/CIFtube
www.linkedin.com/company/canadian-institute-of-forestry
www.facebook.com/CIF.IFC
twitter.com/CIF_IFC
To act as the national voice of forest practitioners
Mark Pearson, Executive Director
Kerry Spencer, Manager, Office & Finance

Canadian Lumber Standards Accreditation Board (CLSAB)
#102, 28 Deakin St., Ottawa ON K2E 8B7
Tel: 613-482-2480; *Fax:* 613-482-6044
info@clsab.ca
www.clsab.ca
To monitor the identification & certification of lumber used in or exported from Canada, or manufactured in accordance with Canadian standards; To provide lumber grading agencies with the authority to supervise lumber manufacturers; To review & advise upon grading rules & standards
Chuck Dentelbeck, President & CEO

Canadian Plywood Association
#100, 375 Lynn Ave., North Vancouver BC V7J 2C4
Tel: 604-981-4190; *Fax:* 604-985-0342
info@canply.org
www.canply.org
Canadian plywood organization.
Judy White, Office Manager
Nick Nagy, President

Canadian Well Logging Society (CWLS)
c/o Associations Plus Inc., #600, 900 - 6th Ave. SW, Calgary AB T2P 3K2
Tel: 403-244-4487; *Fax:* 403-244-2340
info@cwls.org
www.cwls.org
www.linkedin.com/groups/4852822
To provide resources & support for those interested in log analysis & petrophysics
Christa Williams, President

Canadian Wood Council (CWC) / Conseil canadien du bois (CCB)
#400, 99 Bank St., Ottawa ON K1P 6B9
Tel: 613-747-5544; *Fax:* 613-747-6264
www.cwc.ca
www.linkedin.com/company/canadian-wood-council
twitter.com/CdnWoodFacts
To represent Canadian manufacturers of wood products; To ensure market access for wood products; To communicate technical information; To organize educational programs for students & construction professionals
Kevin McKinley, President & CEO
Helen Griffin, Vice-President, Codes & Engineering
Étienne Lalonde, Vice-President, Market Development
Natalie Tarini, Director, Communications, Events & Member Services

Canadian Wood Pallet & Container Association (CWPCA) / Association canadienne des manufacturiers de palettes et contenants (ACMPC)
PO Box 280, Carleton Place ON K7C 3P4
Tel: 613-521-6468; *Fax:* 613-521-1835
Toll-Free: 877-224-3555
info@canadianpallets.com
www.canadianpallets.com
twitter.com/canadianpallets
To promote the general welfare of the wooden pallet & container manufacturing industry; To improve services directly or otherwise; To cooperate with officers of government & business in any program considered essential to the national welfare or economy; To engage in any other lawful activities & enjoy powers, rights & privileges granted or conferred upon associations of a similar nature
Scott Geffros, General Manager
Lori Devlin, Office Manager

Christmas Tree Farmers of Ontario (CFTO)
4611 Mohrs Rd., Arnprior ON K7S 3G7
Tel: 613-623-4312; *Fax:* 905-729-0548
Toll-Free: 800-661-3530
www.christmastrees.on.ca
Shirley Brennan, Executive Director

College of Alberta Professional Foresters
#200, 10544 - 106 St., Edmonton AB T5H 2X6
Tel: 780-432-1177; *Fax:* 780-432-7046
office@capf.ca
www.capf.ca
To maintain an accurate register of registered professional foresters in Alberta; To set standards of professional conduct & competence for members; To administer the title, Registered Professional Forester (RPF)
Noel St. Jean, President
Doug Krystofiak, Executive Director & Registrar

Conseil de l'industrie forestière du Québec (CIFQ) / Québec Forestry Industry Council (QFIC)
#200, 1175, av Lavigerie, Québec QC G1V 4P1
Tél: 418-657-7916; *Téléc:* 418-657-7971
info@cifq.qc.ca
www.cifq.qc.ca
www.linkedin.com/company/conseil-de-l-industrie-foresti-re-du-q
u-bec
twitter.com/CIFQ
Représente la très grande majorité des entreprises de sciage résineux, de pâtes, papiers, cartons et panneaux oeuvrant au Québec; Consacre à la défense des intérêts de ces entreprsies, à la promotion de leur contribution au développement socio-économique, à la gestion intégrée et à l'aménagement durable des forêts, de même qu'à l'utilisation optimale des ressources naturelles; Oeuvre auprès des instances gouvernementales, des organismes publics et parapublics, des organisations et de la population; Encourage un comportement responsable de ses membres en regard des dimensions environnementales, économiques et sociales de leurs activités
Jean-François Samray, Président-directeur général
Mario St-Laurent, Directeur, Communications, affaires publiques et ressources humaines
Pierre Vézina, Directeur, Énergie et environnement

Fédération des producteurs forestiers du Québec
#565, 555, boul Roland-Therrien, Longueuil QC J4H 4E7
Tél: 450-679-0530; *Téléc:* 450-679-4300
bois@upa.qc.ca
www.foretprivee.ca
www.facebook.com/federationdesproducteursforestiers
Défendre les intérêts de l'ensemble des propriétaires de boisés du Québec ainsi que l'élaboration et la promotion des politiques souhaitables et nécessaires pour atteindre cet objectif;
Représenter les propriétaires de boisés privés auprès des pouvoirs publics et des autres groupes de la société au niveau provincial et national; Coordonner l'ensemble des activités des Syndicats et Offices de producteurs de bois ainsi que l'établissement, le maintien et le développement entre eux d'une étroite collaboration
Marc-André Côté, Directeur

Fédération québécoise des coopératives forestières (FQCF)
#350, 3375, ch Sainte-Foy, Québec QC G1X 1S7
Tél: 418-651-0388; *Téléc:* 418-651-3860
cathyg@fqcf.coop
www.fqcf.coop
www.linkedin.com/company/2474726
www.facebook.com/laFQCF
twitter.com/LaFQCF
La Fédération québécoise des coopératives forestières (FQCF) regroupe et représente dans des domaines d'intérêts communs l'ensemble des coopératives forestières de travailleurs, les coopératives de travailleurs actionnaires et les coopératives de solidarité actives dans le milieu forestier, et ce dans toutes les régions du Québec
Jocelyn Lessard, Directeur général
Cathy Gagnon, Adjointe administrative

Forest Nova Scotia
PO Box 696, Truro NS B2N 5E5
Tel: 902-895-1179; *Fax:* 902-893-1197
forestns.ca
To act as the voice of the forest industry in Nova Scotia; To cooperate with industry, federal, provincial, & municipal governments, & other stakeholders to ensure adherence to forest management & stewardship policies; To promote sustainable management & viability of the forest industry

Forest Products Association of Canada (FPAC) / Association des produits forestiers du Canada
#410, 99 Bank St., Ottawa ON K1P 6B9
Tel: 613-563-1441; *Fax:* 613-563-4720
ottawa@fpac.ca
www.fpac.ca
www.youtube.com/ForestProdsAssocCan
www.facebook.com/FPAC.APFC
twitter.com/FPAC_APFC
To be the voice of Canada's wood, pulp & paper producers nationally & internationally in the areas of government, trade, & environmental affairs; To advance the Canadian forest products industry's global competitiveness & sustainable stewardship; To operate in a mannner which is economically viable, environmentally responsible, & socially desirable
Derek Nighbor, President & CEO

Forests Ontario
#700, 144 Front St. West, Toronto ON M5J 2L7
Tel: 416-646-1193; *Fax:* 416-493-4608
Toll-Free: 877-646-1193
info@treesontario.ca
www.forestsontario.ca
www.youtube.com/user/ontforest
www.linkedin.com/company/1243400
www.facebook.com/Forests.Ontario
twitter.com/Forests_Ontario
To promote sound land use & full development protection & utilization of Ontario's forest resources for maximum public advantage; To increase public awareness, school education & natural appreciation of forests; To bring about better understanding of forests to people of all ages & backgrounds
Rob Keen, CEO
Al Corlett, Director of Programs
Shelley McKay, Director of Communications & Development

Maritime Lumber Bureau (MLB) / Bureau de bois de sciage des Maritimes
PO Box 459, Amherst NS B4H 4A1
Tel: 902-667-3889; *Fax:* 902-667-0401
Toll-Free: 800-667-9192
info@mlb.ca
www.mlb.ca
An accredited quality control agency for the lumber industry in the region.

National Aboriginal Forestry Association (NAFA)
#302, 359 Kent St., Ottawa ON K2P 0R6
Tel: 613-233-5563; *Fax:* 613-233-4329
www.nafaforestry.org
To promote & support increased Aboriginal involvement in forest management & related commercial opportunities; to assist Aboriginal communities in their quest to achieve a standard of land care which is balanced, sustainable & reflective of the traditional knowledge & forest values of Aboriginal peoples; to facilitate capacity-building in forest management through the development of human resource strategies & models for increased participation in natural resource decision making; to address the need for Aboriginal forest land rehabilitation & increased Aboriginal control over forest resources through the development of appropriate policy & programming
Bradley Young, Executive Director
Janet Pronovost, Office Manager

National Lumber Grades Authority (NLGA) / Commission Nationale de Classification des Sciages
#309, 409 Granville St., Vancouver BC V6C 1T2
Tel: 604-673-9100
info@nlga.org
nlga.org
To be the only recognized rules writing body for lumber grades and standards in Canada

New Brunswick Forest Products Association Inc. (NBFPA) / L'Association des produits forestiers du Nouveau-Brunswick (APFNB)
Hugh John Flemming Forestry Centre, 1350 Regent St., Fredericton NB E3C 2G6
Tel: 506-452-6930; *Fax:* 506-450-3128
info@nbforestry.com
www.nbforestry.com
To represent forest industry members by serving as a common voice in relations with the government and the public, promoting a healthy New Brunswick forest, raise public awareness of sustainable forest management practices & provide a forum for the exchange of information, ideas & concerns.
Jacques Cormier, Chair

Ontario Forest Industries Association (OFIA) / l'Industrie forestière de l'Ontario
#1704, 8 King St. East, Toronto ON M5C 1B5
Tel: 416-368-6188; *Fax:* 416-368-5445
info@ofia.com
www.ofia.com
www.linkedin.com/company/ontario-forest-industries-association
www.facebook.com/OntarioForestIndustriesAssociation
twitter.com/OFIA_info
To act as a unified voice on behalf of member companies to ensure industry positions are considered; To respond to industry issues, such as economic, environmental, & technological developments

Ontario Lumber Manufacturers Agency (OLMA)
244 Viau Rd., Noelville ON P0M 2N0
Tel: 705-898-1036; *Fax:* 705-898-3403
info@olma.ca
olma.ca
www.linkedin.com/pub/olmalumber
twitter.com/olma_lumber

To ensure a sound & renewable forest economy; To oversee lumber grading licenses & quality control at member sawmills in Ontario; To ensure market access within Northern America, Europe, & Japan
André G. Boucher, President/Chief Lumber Grading Inspector
Dianne Boucher, Vice President
Lise Carrière, Executive Assistant

Ontario Professional Foresters Association (OPFA)
#201, 5 Wesleyan St., Georgetown ON L7G 2E2
Tel: 905-877-3679; *Fax:* 905-877-6766
opfa@opfa.ca
www.opfa.ca
www.facebook.com/OntarioProfessionalForestersAssociation
To operate as a regulatory body for the practice of professional forestry in Ontario; To be committed to the development, management, conservation & sustainability of forest & urban forests
Fred Pinto, R.P.F, Executive Director
Susan Jarvis, R.P.F, Registrar

Ontario Urban Forest Council (OUFC)
PO Box 32166, Stn. Harding Post Office, Richmond Hill ON L4C 9SC
Tel: 416-936-6735; *Fax:* 416-291-5709
info@oufc.org
www.oufc.org
www.facebook.com/oufc.org
twitter.com/oufc_canada
To be dedicated to the the health of urban forests in the province of Ontario
Peter Wynnyczuk, Executive Director

Ordre des ingénieurs forestiers du Québec (OIFQ)
#110, 2750, rue Einstein, Québec QC G1P 4R1
Tél: 418-650-2411; *Téléc:* 418-650-2168
oifq@oifq.com
www.oifq.com
www.linkedin.com/company/8337438
www.facebook.com/OIFQc
twitter.com/oifqc
Assurer la protection du public; assurer la qualité des services rendus au public québécois; favoriser l'amélioration continue de l'expertise et de la compétence des ingénieurs forestiers; mettre en place des actions favorisant la durabilité de l'aménagement forestier pour le bénéfice de l'ensemble de la société
Denis Villeneuve, Président

Pulp & Paper Centre
University of British Columbia, 2385 East Mall, Vancouver BC V6T 1Z4
Tel: 604-822-8560
ppc-info@ubc.ca
www.ppc.ubc.ca
To act as a university-industry partnership for innovation & education; To house inter-disciplinary, cross-faculty post-graduate research programs relevant to the pulp & paper industry
Mark Martinez, Director
George Soong, Safety & Operations Officer, Building/Technical Inquiries
Chitra Arcot, Coordinator, Communications

Registered Professional Foresters Association of Nova Scotia (RPFANS)
PO Box 1031, Truro NS B2N 5G9
Tel: 902-893-0099
contact@rpfans.ca
www.rpfans.ca
To improve the holistic management of forest resources in Nova Scotia
Roger Aggas, Registrar
John Ross, President
Mike Brown, Treasurer

Western Forestry Contractors Association (WFCA)
#720, 999 West Broadway, Vancouver BC V5Z 1K5
Tel: 604-736-8660; *Fax:* 604-728-4080
info@wfca.ca
www.wfca.ca
John Betts, Executive Director
Karline Mark-Eng, Administrative Secretary

Wood Preservation Canada (WPC) / Préservation du bois Canada
#141, 2420 Bank St., Ottawa ON K1V 8S1
Tel: 613-737-4337; *Toll-Free:* 800-463-8733
woodpreservation.ca
To provide a quality assurance program for the treated wood industry

Alliance Française (AF)
c/o Alliance française de Toronto, 24 Spadina Rd., Toronto ON M5R 2S7
www.af.ca
Promotion de la langue et de la culture française

Assemblée communautaire fransaskoise (ACF)
#215, 1440, 9 av Nord, Regina SK S4R 8B1
Tél: 306-569-1912; *Téléc:* 306-781-7916
Ligne sans frais: 800-991-1912
acf@fransaskois.sk.ca
www.fransaskois.sk.ca
www.facebook.com/assembleecommunautairefransaskoise.acf
Travaille au développement, à l'épanouissement et au rayonnement de tous ses membres; est l'entité gouvernante de la communauté fransaskoise
Dominique Sarny, Directeur général
Marc Masson, Directeur des communications

Assemblée de la francophonie de l'Ontario (AFO)
1490, ch Star Top, Ottawa ON K1B 3W6
Tél: 613-744-6649; *Téléc:* 416-744-8861
Ligne sans frais: 866-596-4692
ad@monassemblee.ca
www.monassemblee.ca
www.youtube.com/monassemblee
www.facebook.com/monassemblee
twitter.com/MonAssemblee
Pour représenter la voix politique des francophones en Ontario
Peter Hominuk, Directeur général

Assemblée parlementaire de la Francophonie (APF)
Région Amérique, Assemblée nationale, 1050, rue des Parlementaires, 4e étage, Québec QC G1A 1A3
Tél: 418-643-7391; *Téléc:* 418-643-1865
www.regionamerique-apf.org
Promouvoir la langue et la culture française; Promouvoir les droits de l'homme et la démocratie
André Lavoie, Secrétaire administrative régionale

Association canadienne-française de l'Alberta (ACFA)
#303, Pav. II, 8627, rue Marie-Anne-Gaboury, Edmonton AB T6C 3N1
Tél: 780-466-1680; *Téléc:* 780-465-6773
acfa@acfa.ab.ca
www.acfa.ab.ca
www.youtube.com/user/acfaab
www.facebook.com/acfaab
Représenter la population francophone de l'Alberta; promouvoir le bien-être intellectuel, culturel et social des francophones de l'Alberta; encourager, faciliter et développer l'enseignement en français; entretenir des relations amicales avec les groupes de différentes origines ethniques et anglophones dans la province
Isabelle Laurin, Directrice générale

Association canadienne-française de l'Ontario, Mille-îles (ACFOMI)
Barriefield Centre, 760, Hwy. 15, Kingston ON K7L 0C3
Tél: 613-546-7863; *Téléc:* 613-546-7918
Ligne sans frais: 800-561-4695
info@acfomi.org
www.acfomi.org/acfo
Appuyer le développement communautaire; rassembler les forces vives de la communauté franco-ontarienne; faire des représentations politiques
Lucie Mercier, Directrice générale

Association des francophones du Nunavut (AFN)
CP 880, Iqaluit NU X0A 0H0
Tél: 867-979-4606; *Téléc:* 867-979-0800
cuerrier@nunafranc.ca
www.afnunavut.ca
Pour représenter la communauté française et l'aider à développer
Mylène Chartrand, Présidente

Association des parents fransaskois (APF) / Fransaskois Parents Association
910, 5, rue est, Saskatoon SK S7H 2C6
Tél: 306-653-7444; *Téléc:* 306-653-7001
Ligne sans frais: 800-653-7444
apf.info@sasktel.net
www.parentsfransaskois.ca
www.facebook.com/148583571881687
Assurer la mise sur pied et le développement d'un système scolaire complet de qualité, conforme au Projet éducatif de la communauté des familles fransaskoises
Carol-Guillaume Gagné, Directeur général

Centre culturel franco-manitobain (CCFM)
340, boul Provencher, Winnipeg MB R2H 0G7
Tél: 204-233-8972; *Téléc:* 204-233-3324
reception@ccfm.mb.ca
www.ccfm.mb.ca
www.facebook.com/CCFManitobain
twitter.com/CCFManitobain
De maintenir, d'encourager, de favoriser et de patronner, par tous les moyens possibles, toutes les formes d'activités culturelles de langue française, et de rendre la culture canadienne-française accessible à tous les résidents de la province
Ginette Lavack, Directrice générale

Le Collège du Savoir
20, rue Nelson ouest, Brampton ON L6X 2M5
Tél: 905-457-7884
www.lecollegedusavoir.com
www.linkedin.com/in/le-collège-du-savoir-040077b0
Assurer l'éducation et la formation de l'emploi aux francophones de la région de Peel; Préparer les adultes pour obtenir une équivalence d'études secondaires
Anna Veltri, Directrice

Les EssentiElles
Centre de la francophonie, 302, rue Strickland, Whitehorse YT Y1A 2K1
Tél: 867-668-2636; *Téléc:* 867-668-3511
elles@lesessentielles.ca
lesessentielles.ca
www.facebook.com/lesessentiellesyukon
twitter.com/elles_yukon
De représenter les intérêts des femmes francophones du Yukon
Paige Galette, Présidente
Elaine Michaud, Directrice

Fédération acadienne de la Nouvelle-Écosse (FANE)
La Maison acadienne, 54, rue Queen, Dartmouth NS B2Y 1G3
Tél: 902-433-0065; *Téléc:* 902-433-0066
info@federationacadienne.ca
www.acadiene.ca
www.facebook.com/1FANE
twitter.com/faneacadie
Un regroupement d'organismes régionaux, provinciaux et institutionnels d'expression française qui s'engage à promouvoir l'épanouissement et le développement global de la communauté acadienne et francophone de la Nouvelle-Écosse
Marie-Claude Rioux, Directrice générale

Fédération de la jeunesse canadienne-française inc. (FJCF)
#403, 450 Rideau St., Ottawa ON K1N 5Z4
Tél: 613-562-4624; *Téléc:* 613-562-3995
Ligne sans frais: 800-267-5173
admin@fjcf.ca
fjcf.ca
www.facebook.com/FJCF_Canada
twitter.com/FJCF_Canada
Etre le porte-parole national de la jeunesse canadienne-française et acadienne; assurer l'épanouissement de la jeunesse dans les secteurs de l'éducation, des arts et communications, des loisirs et de l'économie; augmenter la visibilité de la FJCF et de ses membres auprès de leurs différentes clientèles; augmenter les occasions pour les jeunes d'utiliser la langue française; renforcer le sentiment d'appartenance des jeunes, pour qu'ils soient des agents de changement dans leur communauté
Sue Duguay, Président

Fédération des communautés francophones et acadienne du Canada (FCFAC)
#300, 450, rue Rideau, Ottawa ON K1N 5Z4
Tél: 613-241-7600; *Téléc:* 613-241-6046
info@fcfa.ca
fcfa.ca
www.facebook.com/FCFACanada
twitter.com/fcfacanada
Défendre et promouvoir les droits et les intérêts des communautés francophones et acadiennes qu'elle représente
Alain Dupuis, Directeur général

Fédération franco-ténoise (FFT)
5016 - 48e rue, Yellowknife NT X1A 2N9
Tél: 867-920-2919; *Téléc:* 867-873-2458
info@franco-nord.com
www.federation-franco-tenoise.com
www.facebook.com/infolafft
twitter.com/La_FFT
Afin de promouvoir et de préserver la communauté francophone des Territoires du Nord-Ouest
Rachelle Francoeur, Président

La Passerelle - Intégration et Développement Économique
2, rue Carlton, Mezzanine ouest, Toronto ON M5B 1J3
Tél: 416-934-0558; *Téléc:* 416-934-0590
info@passerelle-ide.com
www.paserelle-ide.com
www.youtube.com/user/passerelleide
www.facebook.com/lapasserelleide
twitter.com/Passerelle_IDE
Pour répondre aux besoins d'intégration et économiques des francophones dans la Région du Grand Toronto (RGT)
Léonie Tchatat, Directrice générale

Reflet Salvéo
#202B, 1415 Bathurst St., Toronto ON M5R 3H8
Tél: 647-345-5502; *Téléc:* 647-345-5520
TTY: 800-855-0511
info@refletsalveo.ca
www.refletsalveo.ca
www.facebook.com/pagerefletsalveo
twitter.com/refletsalveo
Assurer que les francophones ont un accès égal à des soins de santé de qualité, en français, indépendamment de l'origine, la race, l'orientation, ou le statut
Gilles Marchildon, Directeur général

Société de l'Acadie du Nouveau-Brunswick (SANB)
#204, 702, rue Principale, Petit-Rocher NB E8J 1V1
Ligne sans frais: 888-722-2343
info@sanb.ca
www.sanb.ca
www.facebook.com/sanb.ca
twitter.com/SAcadieNB
La Société vise à unir tous les Acadiens et Acadiennes du Nouveau-Brunswick et les sensibiliser aux problèmes sociaux, économiques, culturels et politiques qu'ils doivent affronter; s'occuper de tout sujet ayant trait à la protection et à la promotion des droits et à l'avancement des intérêts des Acadiens et Acadiennes du Nouveau-Brunswick; entretenir des liens aussi étroits que possible avec les groupements analogues des autres provinces canadiennes et de l'étranger
Ali Chaisson, Directeur général

Société de la francophonie manitobaine (SFM)
#106, 147, boul Provencher, Saint-Boniface MB R2H 0G2
Tél: 204-233-4915; *Téléc:* 204-977-8551
Ligne sans frais: 800-665-4443
sfm@sfm-mb.ca
www.sfm.mb.ca
www.facebook.com/societe.franco.manitobaine
twitter.com/SocieteFM
Veiller à l'épanouissement de cette communauté
Christian Monnin, Président
Daniel Boucher, Directeur général

Société Saint-Thomas-d'Aquin (SSTA)
5, av Maris Stella, Summerside PE C1N 6M9
Tél: 902-436-4881; *Téléc:* 902-436-6936
colette.aesenault@ssta.org
ssta.org
www.facebook.com/SaintThomasdAquin
twitter.com/commSSTA
Travailler pour que tout Acadien, Acadienne ou francophone puissent vivre et s'épanouir (individuellement et collectivement) en français à l'Ile-du-Prince-Édouard; regrouper les Acadiens, Acadiennes et francophones de l'Ile-du-Prince-Édouard au sein d'une même association; représenter ses membres auprès du gouvernement municipal, provincial et national; revendiquer leurs droits; établir et administrer un fonds devant servir d'aide financière aux étudiant(e)s acadiens, acadiennes et francophones de l'Ile-du-Prince-Édouard dans tous les secteurs; développer des relations amicales entre les Acadiens, Acadiennes et francophones de l'Ile-du-Prince-Édouard et les autres francophones du Canada et des pays étrangers
Jeannita Bernard, Directrice Générale par intérim
Crystal Barriault, Contact

Fraternal

Benevolent & Protective Order of Elks of Canada
#100, 2629 - 29 Ave., Regina SK S4S 2N9
Tel: 306-359-9010; *Fax:* 306-565-2860
Toll-Free: 888-843-3557
grandlodge@elksofcanada.ca
www.elksofcanada.ca
www.facebook.com/ElksofCanada
twitter.com/ElksOfCanada
To promote & support community needs, through volunteer efforts of local lodges
Ron Potter, National President

Benevolent Irish Society of Prince Edward Island (BIS)
Benevolent Irish Society Hall, PO Box 34, 582 North River Rd., Charlottetown PE C1A 7K4
Tel: 902-892-2367
www.benevolentirishsocietyofpei.com
www.facebook.com/bishallpei
To enhance & preserve Irish heritage & culture; To assist the poor & indigent of all denominations; To promote friendship & unity among Irish people & their descendants for mutual benefit
Shane O'Neill, Secretary

Les Chevaliers de Colomb du Québec / Knights of Columbus of Québec
670, av Chambly, Saint-Hyacinthe QC J2S 6V4
Tél: 450-768-0616; *Téléc:* 450-768-1660
Ligne sans frais: 866-893-3681
conact@chevaliersdecolomb.com
www.chevaliersdecolomb.com
Un groupe d'entraide et une société fraternelle, qui unit des hommes de foi; l'ordre n'est pas rattaché à la structure juridique de l'Église catholique mais c'est un ordre de laïcs catholiques et exclusivement masculin
Fernand Rochon, Directeur général

Empire Club of Canada
Fairmont Royal York Hotel, 100 Front St. West, Level H, Toronto ON M5J 1E3
Tel: 416-364-2878
info@empireclub.org
www.empireclubofcanada.com
www.flickr.com/photos/empire_club
www.linkedin.com/company/empire-club-of-canada
www.facebook.com/empireclubofcanada
twitter.com/Empire_Club
To present prominent speakers from professions such as businesses, labour, education, government & cultural organizations
Antoinette Tummillo, President
Jehan Karsan, Executive Director
Ashley Gregory, Manager, Event & Communications

Foresters
789 Don Mills Rd., Toronto ON M3C 1T9
Tel: 416-429-3000; *Fax:* 416-467-2518
Toll-Free: 800-828-1540
service@foresters.com
www.foresters.com
www.youtube.com/c/foresters
www.linkedin.com/company/foresters
www.facebook.com/Foresters
twitter.com/weareforesters
A fraternal benefit society that provides life insurance & other financial products to its members
James Boyle, President & CEO

International Association of Rebekah Assemblies
c/o The Sovereign Grand Lodge IOOF, 422 Trade St., Winston-Salem NC 27101 USA
Tel: 336-725-6037; *Fax:* 336-773-1066
Toll-Free: 800-766-1838
iarasec@aol.com
www.ioof.org
The Rebekah lodges are the female auxiliary of the Independent Order of Odd Fellows, but are open to both women and men.

IODE Canada (IODE)
#219, 40 Orchard View Blvd., Toronto ON M4R 1B9
Tel: 416-487-4416; *Fax:* 416-487-4417
Toll-Free: 866-827-7428
iodecanada@bellnet.ca
www.iode.ca
www.facebook.com/IODECanada
twitter.com/IODECanada
To operate as a women's charitable organization; To enhance the quality of life for individuals, through education support, community service, & citizenship programs
Bonnie G. Rees, National President
Carol McCall, 1st Vice-President & National Treasurer

Knights of Columbus / Chevaliers de Colomb
1 Columbus Plaza, New Haven CT 06510 USA
Tel: 203-752-4000
www.kofc.org
www.youtube.com/knightsofcolumbus
www.facebook.com/KnightsofColumbus
twitter.com/kofc
To render financial aid to members & their families; To render mutual aid & assistance to sick, disabled & needy members; To promote social & intellectual intercourse among members; To promote & conduct educational, charitable, religious, social welfare, war relief & welfare & public relief work
Carl A. Anderson, Supreme Knight

Michael J. O'Connor, Supreme Secretary

Knights of Pythias - Domain of British Columbia
BC
knightsofpythiasbritishcolumbia.ca
Roger Murray, Chancellor

Order of Sons of Italy of Canada (OSIC)
To assist the needy, the ill & disabled through financial support, the provision of housing & other support programs; To encourage the active participation of members in the political, social & economic life of their community; to participate in programs combating discrimination, racism & social injustice; To promote & preserve the Italian language, culture & traditions in Canada
Carmine Filice, National President

The Order of United Commercial Travelers of America (UCT)
Canadian Office, #300, 901 Centre St. North, Calgary AB T2E 2P6
Tel: 403-277-0745; *Fax:* 403-277-6662
Toll-Free: 800-267-2371
customerservice@uct.org
www.uct.org
www.youtube.com/UCTinaction
www.facebook.com/UCTinAction
To provide members with affordable insurance & support through fraternal benefit & discount programs
Mary Applegate, President
Kevin Hecker, Chief Executive Officer

Réseau Hommes Québec (RHQ)
4545, av Pierre-De Coubertin, Montréal QC H1V 0B2
Tél: 514-273-6162; *Ligne sans frais:* 877-908-4545
info@hommesquebec.ca
hommesquebec.ca
www.facebook.com/hommesquebec
Organisme sans but lucratif; a pour mission d'entretenir un réseau de groupes autogérés d'écoute, de parole & d'entraide aux hommes
Martin Dufour, Président

Royal Arch Masons of Canada
361 King St. West. 2nd Fl., Hamilton ON L8P 1B4
Tel: 905-522-5775; *Fax:* 905-522-5099
office@royalarchmasons.on.ca
www.royalarchmasons.on.ca
Melvyn J. Duke, Grand Scribe E.

Society of Kabalarians of Canada
1160 West 10th Ave., Vancouver BC V6H 1J1
Tel: 604-263-9551; *Fax:* 604-263-5514
Toll-Free: 866-489-1188
info1@kabalarians.com
kabalarians.com
To promote Kabalarian philosophy, which teaches a constructive way of life through the understanding of the Mathematical Principle, encouraging people to live a more progressive, constructive life.
Lorenda Bardell, President

Funeral Services

Alberta Funeral Service Association (AFSA)
#202, 5405 - 99 St., Edmonton AB T6E 3N8
Tel: 780-412-1310; *Fax:* 780-413-0076
Toll-Free: 800-803-8809
inquiry@afsa.ca
www.afsa.ca
To promote & improve funeral service in Alberta
Stuart Murray, President

British Columbia Funeral Association (BCFA)
#211, 2187 Oak Bay Ave., Victoria BC V8R 1G1
Tel: 250-592-3213; *Fax:* 250-592-4362
Toll-Free: 800-665-3899
info@bcfunerals.com
www.bcfunerals.com
www.facebook.com/bcfunerals
twitter.com/bcfunerals
To promote, through education, communication, & leadership, the highest standards of ethics & service in the funeral profession
Sharla MacKay, President
Lori Cascaden, Executive Director

Corporation des thanatologues du Québec (CTQ)
#115, 4600, boul Henri-Bourassa, Québec QC G1H 3A5
Tél: 418-622-1717; *Téléc:* 418-622-5557
Ligne sans frais: 800-463-4935
info@corpothanato.com
www.domainefuneraire.com
www.facebook.com/corporation.thanatologues.quebec
twitter.com/corpothanato
Représenter le domaine funéraire, supporter son évolution
promouvoir l'excellence et contribuer au développement d'affaire
de ses membres pour le mieux être de la population
René Goyer, Président

Funeral & Cremation Services Council of Saskatchewan (FCSCS)
3847C Albert St., Regina SK S4S 3R4
Tel: 306-584-1575; *Fax:* 306-584-1576
administration@funeralinfo.ca
www.fcscs.ca
To outline standard practices for the funeral industry for the
benefit of the public
Raymond Bailey, Chair
Sandy Mahon, Registrar

Funeral Advisory & Memorial Society (FAMS)
PO Box 65, Stn. F, 55 St. Phillips Rd., Toronto ON M9P 2N8
Tel: 416-241-6274
info@fams.ca
www.fams.ca
To provide consumer advice on funeral planning
Margaret Adamson, Chair
Shirley Zinman, Vice Chair
Albert Tucker, Treasurer

Funeral Service Association of Canada (FSAC) / Association des services funéraires du Canada (ASFC)
#800, 1730 St. Laurent Blvd., Ottawa ON K1G 3Y7
Tel: 613-505-0277; *Toll-Free:* 888-507-3722
info@fsac.ca
www.fsac.ca
www.facebook.com/FuneralAssociation
twitter.com/fsac_asfc
To provide a collective voice for the Canadian funeral
professional; To provide high quality professional services with
dignity & competence; To ensure compliance with all provisions
of the law; To provide information about services
Yves Berthiaume, President

Manitoba Funeral Service Association (MFSA)
#610, 55 Garry St., Winnipeg MB R3C 4H4
Tel: 204-947-0927
info@mfsa.mb.ca
www.mfsa.mb.ca
To serve funeral directors & funeral homes throughout Manitoba;
To advance funeral service; To uphold a code of ethics
Owen McKenzie, President
Thorunn Petursdottir, Executive Director
Matt Nichol, Secretary-Treasurer

Newfoundland & Labrador Funeral Services Association (NLFSA)
PO Box 138, Winterton NL A0G 3M0
Tel: 709-586-2721; *Fax:* 709-586-2888
To offer funeral service support for the province.

Ontario Association of Cemetery & Funeral Professionals (OACFP)
PO Box 24040, RPO Josephine, North Bay ON P1B 0C7
Tel: 905-383-6528; *Toll-Free:* 888-558-3335
info@oacfp.com
oacfp.com
www.facebook.com/OACFP
twitter.com/theOACFP
To promote high standards of service & the professional
operation of cemeteries, funeral homes, crematoria & related
bereavement services
Steve Reynolds, President
Denomme Denomme, Executive Director

Ontario Funeral Service Association (OFSA)
#103, 3228 South Service Rd., Burlington ON L7N 3N1
Tel: 905-637-3371; *Fax:* 905-637-3583
Toll-Free: 800-268-2727
info@ofsa.org
www.ofsa.org
www.facebook.com/OFSA.socialmedia
twitter.com/OFSAsocialmedia
To maintain high standards of services & ethical business
practices among Ontario's funeral homes for the welfare of the
public; To represent & support Ontario's independently owned
funeral establishments
Scott Davidson, President

Kerri Douglas, Executive Director

Prince Edward Island Funeral Directors & Embalmers Association
PO Box 540, Kensington PE C0B 1M0
Tel: 902-836-3313; *Fax:* 902-836-4461
To ensure professional services of the highest standards

Fur Trade

Canadian Association for Humane Trapping (CAHT)
PO Box 36534, Stn. Eastgate, 75 Centennial Pkwy. North, Hamilton ON L8E 2P0
info@caht.ca
www.caht.ca
www.facebook.com/caht.ca
To reduce & eliminate suffering of animals trapped for whatever
reason; To work with governments, trappers, the commercial fur
industry, animal welfare organizations & the public-at-large to
bring about actual trapping improvements
Carl Bandow, Executive Director
Donald Mitton, Project Director

Fur Council of Canada (FCC) / Conseil canadien de la fourrure
#1270, 1435, rue Saint-Alexandre, Montréal QC H3A 2G4
Tel: 514-844-1945; *Fax:* 514-844-8593
info@furcouncil.com
www.furcouncil.com
www.youtube.com/user/EcoFurs
www.facebook.com/FurCouncilofCanada
twitter.com/Councilfur
To promote all aspects of the fur trade

Fur Institute of Canada (FIC) / Institut de la fourrure du Canada (IFC)
#701, 331 Cooper St., Ottawa ON K2P 0G5
Tel: 613-231-7099; *Fax:* 613-231-7940
www.fur.ca
www.facebook.com/FurInstituteOfCanada
twitter.com/furinstitute
To promote the sustainable & wise use of Canadian fur
resources
Dion Dakins, Chair
James Baker, Executive Director

The Fur-Bearers
#701, 718 - 333 Brooksbank Ave., North Vancouver BC V7J 3V8
Tel: 604-435-1850
info@thefurbearers.com
thefurbearers.com
www.youtube.com/furbearerdefenders
www.facebook.com/FurFree
twitter.com/FurBearers
To stop trapping cruelty & protect fur-bearing animals
Lesley Fox, Executive Director

Galleries & Museums

Alberta Museums Association
#404, 10408 - 124 St., Edmonton AB T5N 1R5
Tel: 780-424-2626; *Fax:* 780-425-1679
info@museums.ab.ca
www.museums.ab.ca
www.linkedin.com/company/alberta-museums-association
twitter.com/AlbertaMuseums
To promote understanding, access & excellence within Alberta's
museums for the benefit of society
Meaghan Patterson, Executive Director

Association Heritage New Brunswick (AHNB) / Association du patrimoine Nouveau-Brunswick (APNB)
163 St John St., Fredericton NB E3B 4A8
Tel: 506-454-3561
info@amnb.ca
ahnb-apnb.ca
twitter.com/AHNB_APNB
To preserve New Brunswick's heritage & history by uniting,
promoting, & advancing heritage workers, supporters, &
organizations
Koral LaVorgna, Executive Director
Chantal Brideau, Administrative Officer

Association of Manitoba Museums (AMM)
#1040, 555 Main St., Winnipeg MB R3B 1C3
Tel: 204-947-1782; *Fax:* 204-942-3749
www.museumsmanitoba.com
To strengthen the museum community by promoting excellence
in preserving & presenting Manitoba's heritage; To improve the

AMM's ability to communicate with its members; To continue a
training program
Monique Brandt, Executive Director
Beryth Strong, Coordinator, Training & Communications
Jane Dalley, Conservator, Cultural Stewardship Program

Association of Nova Scotia Museums (ANSM)
1113 Marginal Rd., Halifax NS B3H 4P7
Tel: 902-423-4677; *Fax:* 902-422-0881
admin@ansm.ns.ca
ansm.ns.ca
www.facebook.com/AssociationNSMuseums
To promote museums through education, outreach, networking,
& advocacy
Anita Price, Executive Director

Atlantic Provinces Art Gallery Association (APAGA) / Association des galeries d'art des provinces de l'Atlantique (AGAPA)
c/o Kevin Rice, Confederation Centre of the Arts, 145 Richmond St., Charlottetown PE C1A 1J1
apagaagapa.wordpress.com
To pursue & promote high standards of excellence in care &
presentation of works of art in public art galleries in the Atlantic
region; To encourage the closest possible cooperation between
art galleries, museums & artists; To serve as an advisory body in
matters of professional interest
Kevin Rice, President

British Columbia Museums Association (BCMA)
675 Belleville St., Victoria BC V8W 9W2
Tel: 250-356-5700
bcma@museumsassn.bc.ca
www.museumsassn.bc.ca
www.facebook.com/BCMuseumsAssn
twitter.com/museumsassn
To promote the protection & preservation of the objects,
specimens, records & sites significant to the natural, creative &
human history of British Columbia; To aid in the improvement of
museums & galleries as educational institutions; To assist in the
development of the museum profession; To support & advocate
for the museum community of British Columbia
Erica Mattson, Executive Director
Heather Jeliazkov, Manager, Marketing & Membership Services

Canadian Federation of Friends of Museums (CFFM) / Fédération canadienne des amis de musées (FCAM)
#400, 280 Metcalfe St., Ottawa ON K2P 1R7
Tel: 514-284-0723
info@cffm-fcam.ca
www.cffm-fcam.ca
www.facebook.com/cffmfcam
To serve as source of information & expertise for friends of
museums; To serve as communications network & national
voice for those who are dedicated to the support & promotion of
museums for the benefit of all Canadians
Bruce Bolton, President

Canadian Museums Association (CMA) / Association des musées canadiens (AMC)
#400, 280 Metcalfe St., Ottawa ON K2P 1R7
Tel: 613-567-0099; *Fax:* 613-233-5438
Toll-Free: 888-822-2907
info@museums.ca
www.museums.ca
www.youtube.com/museumsdotca
www.linkedin.com/company/canadian-museums-association
www.facebook.com/musecdn
twitter.com/musecdn
To advance a strong, vital & valued Canadian museum sector
Vanda Vitali, Executive Director & CEO

Community Museums Association of Prince Edward Island
PO Box 22002, Charlottetown PE C1A 9J2
Tel: 902-892-8837; *Fax:* 902-892-1459
info@museumspei.ca
www.museumspei.ca
wwww.facebook.com/116764358400112
To foster & support museums, historical societies & other
non-profit organizations concerned with heritage of PEI.
David Panton, President
Barry King, Executive Director

Design Exchange (DX)
Toronto Dominion Centre, PO Box 18, 234 Bay St., Toronto ON M5K 1B2
Tel: 416-363-6121; *Fax:* 416-368-0684
info@dx.org
www.dx.org
www.instagram.com/designexchange
www.facebook.com/DesignExchange
twitter.com/designexchange
To provide a design museum & centre for design research & education; To raise awareness & understanding of design
Alex James, Chief Financial Officer
Shauna Levy, President & CEO

ICOM Museums Canada / ICOM Musées Canada
#400, 280 Metcalfe St., Ottawa ON K2P 1R7
Tel: 613-567-0099
network.icom.museum/icom-canada
www.facebook.com/ICOMCanada
twitter.com/ICOMCanada
To advance the cause of museums throughout the world & in Canada; To provide liaison with International Council of Museums in Paris; To hold annual meeting in conjunction with Canadian Museums Association

Museum Association of Newfoundland & Labrador (MANL)
PO Box 5785, St. John's NL A1C 5X3
Tel: 709-722-9034; *Fax:* 709-722-9035
www.manl.nf.ca
www.flickr.com/photos/manl
www.facebook.com/museumassociationofnl
twitter.com/manltweets
To protect & preserve the cultural & natural heritage of Newfoundland & Labrador; To unite, support & promote members; To improve & promote museums
Ken Flynn, Executive Director

Museum London
421 Ridout St. North, London ON N6A 5H4
Tel: 519-661-0333
www.museumlondon.ca
To enrich public knowledge & enjoyment of the art & history of the London region & Canada
Brian Meehan, Executive Director

Museums Association of Saskatchewan (MAS)
424 McDonald St., Regina SK S4N 6E1
Tel: 306-780-9279; *Fax:* 306-780-9463
Toll-Free: 866-568-7386
mas@saskmuseums.org
www.saskmuseums.org
www.facebook.com/saskmuseums
twitter.com/saskmuseums
To work for the advancement of strong & vibrant museums in Saskatchewan; To encourage the preservation & understanding of the province's cultural & natural heritage; To serve Saskatchewan museums
Wendy Fitch, Executive Director
Robert Hubick, President

Ontario Association of Art Galleries (OAAG)
#395, 401 Richmond St. West, Toronto ON M5V 3A8
Tel: 416-598-0714; *Fax:* 416-598-4128
oaag@oaag.org
oaag.org
To encourage the highest standards for the exhibition, interpretation, & conservation of the visual arts; To develop tools to assist gallery professionals in achieving institutional goals; To advance positive, responsive relations with government, its agencies & the citizens of Ontario
Zainub Verjee, Executive Director

Ontario Museum Association (OMA) / Association des musées de l'Ontario
George Brown House, 50 Baldwin St., Toronto ON M5T 1L4
Tel: 416-348-8672; *Fax:* 416-348-0438
Toll-Free: 866-662-8672
www.museumsontario.ca
www.facebook.com/museumsontario
twitter.com/museumsontario
To enhance museums as significant cultural resources in the service of Ontario society & its development
Marie Lalonde, Executive Director

Organization of Military Museums of Canada, Inc. (OMMC) / L'Organisation des musées militaires du Canada, inc.
PO Box 36081, Stn. Lakeview, 6449 Crowchild Trail SW, Calgary AB T3E 7C3
Tel: 204-223-0905
ommcinc2@gmail.com
www.ommcinc.ca
www.facebook.com/OMMCInc
To preserve the military heritage of Canada by encouraging the establishment & operation of military museums; To educate museum staff & cooperate with others having the same or similar purposes
Léon Chamois, President
Bradley S. Froggatt, Secretary
Richard Ruggle, Treasurer

Prince Edward Island Museum & Heritage Foundation (PEIMHF) / Le Musée et la fondation du patrimoine de l'Ile-du-Prince-Édouard
2 Kent St., Charlottetown PE C1A 1M6
Tel: 902-368-6600; *Fax:* 902-368-6608
mhpei@gov.pe.ca
www.peimuseum.com
www.facebook.com/124989037532122
twitter.com/PEIMUSEUM
To study, preserve, interpret & protect the human & natural heritage of PEI
David L. Keenlyside, Executive Director
Mary Paquet, Business Administrator
Nora J. Young, Executive Assistant

Société des musées du Québec (SMQ)
CP 8888, Succ. Centre-Ville, Montréal QC H3C 3P8
Tél: 514-987-3264; *Téléc:* 514-987-3379
info@smq.qc.ca
www.musees.qc.ca
www.facebook.com/societedesmuseesduquebec
twitter.com/museesdecouvrir
Au service du développement de la muséologie au Québec
Stéphane Chagnon, Directeur général

Yukon Historical & Museums Association (YHMA)
3126 - 3rd Ave., Whitehorse YT Y1A 1E7
Tel: 867-667-4704; *Fax:* 867-667-4506
info@heritageyukon.ca
heritageyukon.ca
twitter.com/Yukonheritage
To preserve & foster an appreciation of the Yukon's history & culture; to act as forum for other museum & heritage organizations in the region
Nancy Oakley, Executive Director

Gas & Oil

Association de l'énergie du Québec (AEQ) / Quebec Energy Association
1743, rue Holmes, Longueuil QC J4T 1R3
D'encourager le dialogue sur le potentiel d'une nouvelle industrie au Québec
Éric Tetrault, Président

Canadian Heavy Oil Association (CHOA)
c/o RGL Reservoir Management Inc., #610, 700 - 2nd St. SW, Calgary AB T2P 2W1
Tel: 403-269-1755
office@choa.ab.ca
choa.ab.ca
www.linkedin.com/company/canadian-heavy-oil-association
www.facebook.com/canadianheavyoilassociation
twitter.com/CDN_CHOA
To provide a technical, educational, & social forum for people employed in, or associated with, the oil sands & heavy oil industries
Caralyn Bennett, President

Canadian Independent Petroleum Marketers Association (CIPMA)
411 Donald B. Munro Dr., Ottawa ON K0A 1L0
www.cipma.org
twitter.com/CIPMAssoc
To lobby & represent members' interests
Jennifer Stewart, President & CEO

Gems & Jewellery

Canadian Gemmological Association (CGA)
#105, 55 Queen St. East, Toronto ON M5C 1R6
Tel: 647-466-2436; *Fax:* 416-366-6519
info@canadiangemmological.com
canadiangemmological.com
www.instagram.com/canadiangemassoc
www.facebook.com/194830677283253
twitter.com/CanGem3
To set a standard for excellence in the practice of gemmology
Donna Hawrelko, FGA, FCGmA, President
JoAnne Larmond, Office Administrator

Canadian Institute of Gemmology (CIG) / Institut canadien de gemmologie
c/o School of Jewellery Arts, PO Box 57010, Vancouver BC V5K 5G6
Tel: 604-530-8569; *Toll-Free:* 604-530-8569
info@cigem.ca
www.cigem.ca
www.facebook.com/CanadianInstituteOfGemmology
twitter.com/CIGemNews
To serve the jewellery industry & the general public
Wolf Kuehn, Executive Director

Canadian Jewellers Association (CJA)
#600, 27 Queen St. East, Toronto ON M5C 2M6
Tel: 416-368-7616; *Fax:* 416-368-1986
Toll-Free: 800-580-0942
info@canadianjewellers.com
www.canadianjewellers.com
www.instagram.com/canadianjewellersassociation
www.facebook.com/505697319910050
To provide its members with information, services & techonology that allow them to flourish in their profession
Marco Miserendino, Chair

Corporation des bijoutiers du Québec (CBQ) / Québec Jewellers' Corporation
868, rue Brissette, Sainte-Julie QC J3E 2B1
Tél: 514-485-3333; *Téléc:* 450-649-8984
info@cbq.qc.ca
www.cbq.qc.ca
La promotion des membres, la défence de leurs intérêts économiques et sociaux et le développement du professionnalisme chez les membres; garantir au public un meilleur service et l'intégrité des bijoutiers membres; accroître la compétence des gens du métier; favoriser l'exercice du métier selon l'art et la science
André Marchand, Président
Lise Petitpas, Directrice générale

Gem & Mineral Federation of Canada (GMFC) / Fédération canadienne des gemmes et des minéraux
PO Box 42015, RPO North, Winfield BC V4V 1Z8
Tel: 250-766-4353
president@gmfc.ca
www.gmfc.ca
To promote earth sciences; to protect collecting sites; to educate collectors; to foster good will, friendship & rapport among all
Peter Hagar, President

Government & Public Administration

Alberta Municipal Clerks Association (AMCA)
c/o Town of Canmore, 902 7th Ave., Canmore AB T1W 3K1
Tel: 403-678-1500
www.albertamunicipalclerks.com
To provide a forum for exchange of ideas among the municipal clerks of the municipalities of Alberta; To provide a means for presentation of suggested amendments in legislation to senior government; To work in conjunction with any other organization, having as its objective the betterment of administration of local government
Cheryl Hyde, Director
Bonnie Hilford, Director

Alberta Rural Municipal Administrators Association
PO Box 217, LaGlace AB T0H 2J0
Tel: 780-831-4195
www.armaa.ca
To represent administrators in Alberta municipal governments
Irene Cooper, Executive Director

Alberta Urban Municipalities Association (AUMA)
#300, 8616 51 Ave., Edmonton AB T6E 6E6
Tel: 780-433-4431; *Fax:* 780-433-4454
Toll-Free: 877-421-6644
main@auma.ca
www.auma.ca
www.youtube.com/channel/UC_HJ3RFfvOwFpdVDcLifGLw/feed
www.linkedin.com/company/alberta-urban-municipalities-associa
tion
www.facebook.com/theauma
twitter.com/theauma
To provide leadership in advocating local government interests
to the provincial government & other organizations, & to provide
services that address the needs of its membership
Sue Bohaichuk, FCPA (CMA); ICD, Chief Executive Officer

Association des directeurs généraux des municipalités du Québec
#470, 43, rue de Buade, Québec QC G1R 4A2
Tél: 418-660-7591; *Téléc:* 418-660-0848
adgmq@adgmq.qc.ca
adgmq.qc.ca
Permettre l'amélioration des connaissances et du statut de ses
membres et la promotion de la formule de gestion
conseil/directeur général
Jean Matte, Directeur général

Association des directeurs municipaux du Québec (ADMQ)
Hall Est, #535, 400, boul Jean-Lesage, Québec QC G1K 8W1
Tél: 418-647-4518; *Téléc:* 418-647-4115
admq@admq.qc.ca
admq.qc.ca
www.facebook.com/admq.qc.ca
De voir à la promotion et à la défense des membres en plus
d'offrir un soutien professionnel constant au niveau des outils de
formation et de communication
Marc Laflamme, Directeur général

Association francophone des municipalités du Nouveau-Brunswick Inc. (AFMNB)
#322, 702, rue Principale, Petit-Rocher NB E8J 1V1
Tél: 506-542-2622; *Téléc:* 506-542-2618
Ligne sans frais: 888-236-2622
afmnb@afmnb.org
www.afmnb.org
www.facebook.com/afmnb
www.twitter.com/AFMNB
Promouvoir le développement des municipalités francophones
du Nouveau-Brunswick
Frédérick Dion, Directeur général
Roger Doiron, Président

Association internationale des maires francophones - Bureau à Québec (AIMF)
CP 700, Succ. Haute-Ville, #312, 2, rue des Jardins, Québec
QC G1R 4S9
Tél: 418-641-6188; *Téléc:* 418-641-6437
Favoriser les échanges et la coopérations entre les villes
membres
Régis Labeaume

Association of Manitoba Municipalities (AMM)
1910 Saskatchewan Ave. West, Portage la Prairie MB R1N
0P1
Tel: 204-857-8666; *Fax:* 204-856-2370
amm@amm.mb.ca
www.amm.mb.ca
www.facebook.com/AMMMB
twitter.com/AMMManitoba
To provide communications link between municipalities; To lobby
for municipal governments with senior levels of government
Joe Masi, Executive Director
Linda Hargest, Director, Administration & Marketing
Denys Volkov, Director, Advocacy & Communications

Association of Municipal Administrators of New Brunswick (AMANB) / Association des administrateurs municipaux du Nouveau-Brunswick (AAMNB)
20 Courtney St., Douglas NB E3G 8A1
Tel: 506-453-4229; *Fax:* 506-444-5452
amanb@nb.aibn.com
www.amanb-aamnb.ca
To promote & advance status of persons employed in field of
municipal administration; to advance quality of administration of
municipal services; to encourage closer official & personal
relationship among members to facilitate interchange of ideas &
experience; to establish & maintain standards of performance for
members; to assist in provision of formal training & educational
facilities
Melanie MacDonald, President

Danielle Charron, Executive Director

Association of Municipal Administrators, Nova Scotia (AMANS)
CIBC Building, #1106, 1809 Barrington St., Halifax NS B3J
3K8
Tel: 902-423-2215; *Fax:* 902-425-5592
info@amans.ca
www.amans.ca
To improve the quality of local government in Nova Scotia
through the development of educational programs; To provide a
forum for the exchange of ideas; to provide a resource to
municipal officials; To provide service to members to improve
their professional capabilities
Janice Wentzell, Executive Director
Kristy Hardie, Event Coordinator/ Financial Officer

Association of Municipal Managers, Clerks & Treasurers of Ontario (AMCTO) / Association des directeurs généraux, secrétaires et trésoriers municipaux de l'Ontario (ASTMO)
#610, 2680 Skymark Ave., Mississauga ON L4W 5L6
Tel: 905-602-4294; *Fax:* 905-602-4295
amcto@amcto.com
www.amcto.com
To foster administrative excellence in local government; To
identify & meet training & education needs in local government;
To be an influential voice for local government; To provide an
effective communication forum for local government; To promote
public awareness of & confidence in local government; To
facilitate change within AMCTO
Andy Koopmans, Executive Director
Roger Ramkissoon, Manager, Finance & Administration

Association of Municipalities of Ontario (AMO)
#801, 200 University Ave., Toronto ON M5H 3C6
Tel: 416-971-9856; *Fax:* 416-971-6191
Toll-Free: 877-426-6527
amo@amo.on.ca
www.amo.on.ca
twitter.com/AMOPolicy
To support & enhance strong & effective municipal government
in Ontario; To represent almost all of Ontario's 444 municipal
governments
Pat Vanini, Executive Director
Monika Turner, Director, Policy
Afshin Majidi, Director, Finance & Operations

Association of Public Sector Information Professionals (DPI) / Association des professionnels de l'information du secteur public (DPI)
PO Box 424, 2647 Alta Vista Drive, Ottawa ON K1V 7T5
Tel: 613-737-4374
dpi-canada.com
To promote public sector professionals & the application of
Information Management & Technology in the federal
government & other public spheres
Denis Skinner, President
Rachel Porteous, Co-Director, Advisory Council
Paul Wagner, Co-Director, Advisory Council
Rochelle Bryerton, Director, Communications

Association of Yukon Communities (AYC)
#140, 2237 2nd Ave., Whitehorse YT Y1A 0K7
Tel: 867-668-4388; *Fax:* 867-668-7574
www.ayc-yk.ca
To further the establishment of responsible government at the
community level; To provide a united approach to issues
affecting local governments; To advance ambitions & goals of
member communities by developing a shared common vision of
the future; To represent members in matters affecting them &
the welfare of their communities; To provide programs &
services of common interest & benefit to members
Bev Buckway, Executive Director

Association paritaire pour la santé et la sécurité du travail - Secteur Affaires municipales (APSAM)
#710, 715, rue du Square-Victoria, Montréal QC H2Y 2H7
Tél: 514-849-8373; *Téléc:* 514-849-8873
Ligne sans frais: 800-465-1754
info@apsam.com
www.apsam.com
www.facebook.com/apsamsst
twitter.com/APSAM
Denise Soucy, Directrice générale

Association québécoise du loisir municipal (AQLM)
4545, av Pierre-de Coubertin, Montréal QC H1V 0B2
Tél: 514-252-5244; *Téléc:* 514-252-5220
infoaqlm@loisirmunicipal.qc.ca
www.loisirmunicipal.qc.ca

Intégrer le domaine de vie communautaire au mandat de loisir;
Affirmer la maîtrise d'oeuvre de la municipalité en loisir; faire
valoir le service municipal de loisir comme partenaire du réseau
des organisations locales (institutionnelles et associatives);
Promouvoir l'expertise des professionnels du loisir; démontrer
l'utilité et les bénéfices du loisir; Développer des pratiques
professionnelles en loisir
Luc Toupin, Directeur général
Pierre Waters, Directeur, Services aux membres affaires
Joëlle Derulle, Conseillère, Formations et développement

Canada's Public Policy Forum / Forum des politiques publiques du Canada
#1405, 130 Albert St., Ottawa ON K1P 5G4
Tel: 613-238-7160; *Fax:* 613-238-7990
mail@ppforum.ca
www.ppforum.ca
www.youtube.com/user/PublicPolicyForum
www.facebook.com/publicpolicyforum
twitter.com/ppforumca
To promote better public policy & better public management
through dialogue among leaders from the public, private, labour
& voluntary sectors
Larry Murray, Chair
David J. Mitchell, President & CEO
Julie Cafley, Vice-President
Natasha Gauthier, Director, Communications

Canadian Association of Municipal Administrators (CAMA) / Association canadienne des administrateurs municipaux (ACAM)
PO Box 128, Stn. A, Fredericton NB E3B 4Y2
Toll-Free: 866-771-2262
camalink@camacam.ca
www.camacam.ca
www.youtube.com/user/CAMALink
www.linkedin.com/company/camalink
www.facebook.com/CAMALink
twitter.com/camalink
To advance excellence in municipal management throughout
Canada
Jake Rudolph, President
Jennifer Goodine, Executive Director

Canadian Council on Social Development (CCSD) / Conseil canadien de développement social (CCDS)
PO Box 13713, Kanata ON K2K 1X6
Tel: 613-236-8977
info@ccsd.ca
www.ccsd.ca
To develop & promote progressive social policies, on issues
such as child well-being, poverty, housing, employment, cultural
diversity & social inclusion
Peggy Taillon, President & CEO
Katherine Scott, Vice-President, Research & Policy

Cities of New Brunswick Association (CNBA)
PO Box 1421, Stn. A, Fredericton NB E3B 5E3
Tel: 506-452-9292; *Fax:* 506-452-9898
info@8citiesnb.com
www.8citiesnb.com
twitter.com/CNBA_ACNB
To promote the exchange of information among members; To
co-operate & liaise with other agencies & associations having a
municipal interest; To strive for a united front in all matters
pertaining to the realization of municipal goals
Eric Megarity, President
Charline McCoy, Acting Executive Director

Corporation des officiers municipaux agréés du Québec (COMAQ) / Corporation of Chartered Municipal Officers of Québec
Édifice Lomer-Gouin, 575, rue Jacques-Parizeau, #R02,
Québec QC G1R 2G4
Tél: 418-527-1231; *Téléc:* 418-527-4462
Ligne sans frais: 800-305-1031
info@comaq.qc.ca
www.comaq.qc.ca
Regrouper les cadres municipaux des cités et villes du Québec;
promouvoir la formation professionnelle par l'organisation de
cours; protéger les intérêts sociaux-économiques des membres
Julie Faucher, Directrice générale

Council of Atlantic Premiers (CAP)
Council Secretariat, PO Box 2044, #1006, 5161 George St.,
Halifax NS B3J 2Z1
Tel: 902-424-7590; *Fax:* 902-424-8976
info@cap-cpma.ca
www.cap-cpma.ca
The mandate of the Council is to promote Atlantic Canadian
interests on national issues. To accomplish this, the Council
seeks to establish common views & positions to ensure that
Atlantic Canadians & their interests are well represented in

national debates. The work of the Council of Atlantic Premiers builds on the ongoing work of the Council of Maritime Premiers & the Conference of Atlantic Premiers. The premiers are committed to work together on behalf of Atlantic Canadians to strengthen the economic competitiveness of the region, improve the quality of public services to Atlantic Canadians and/or improve the cost-effectiveness of delivering public services to Atlantic Canadians.
Tim Porter, Secretary to Council

Democracy Watch
PO Box 821, Stn. B, #412, 1 Nicholas St., Ottawa ON K1P 5P9
Tel: 613-241-5179; *Fax:* 613-241-4758
info@democracywatch.ca
democracywatch.ca
www.youtube.com/dwatchcda
www.facebook.com/DemocracyWatch
twitter.com/democracywatchr
To advocate for democratic reform, government accountability, and corporate responsibility.
Duff Conacher, Coordinator

Federation of Canadian Municipalities (FCM) / Fédération canadienne des municipalités
24 Clarence St., Ottawa ON K1N 5P3
Tel: 613-241-5221; *Fax:* 613-241-7440
info@fcm.ca
www.fcm.ca
www.youtube.com/user/FCMChannel
linkedin.com/company/federation-of-canadian-municipalities
www.facebook.com/FederationofCanadianMunicipalities
twitter.com/FCM_online
To represent the interests of municipalities on policy & program matters that fall within federal jurisdiction; To improve the quality of life in all communities
Carole Saab, Chief Executive Officer
Sebastien Hamel, Executive Director
Stefano Biscotti, Senior Director, People & Culture

Federation of Northern Ontario Municipalities (FONOM)
615 Hardy St., North Bay ON P1B 8S2
fonom.info@gmail.com
www.fonom.org
To act as the voice for the people of northeastern Ontario communities; To work for the betterment of municipal government by striving for improved legislation respecting local government in northern Ontario
Alison Stanley, Executive Director

Federation of Prince Edward Island Municipalities Inc. (FPEIM)
1 Kirkdale Rd., Charlottetown PE C1E 1R3
Tel: 902-566-1493; *Fax:* 902-566-2880
info@fpeim.ca
fpeim.ca
To represent the interests of the cities, towns & communities within PEI; To secure united action for the protection of individual municipalities & municipal interests as a whole; To act as a clearing house for the collection, exchange & dissemination of information of concern & interest to member municipalities; To provide training, education & development opportunities for elected & appointed municipal officials
John Dewey, Executive Director

Fédération Québécoise des Municipalités (FQM)
#560, 2954, boul Laurier, Sainte-Foy QC G1V 4T2
Tél: 418-651-3343; *Téléc:* 418-651-1127
Ligne sans frais: 866-951-3343
info@fqm.ca
www.fqm.ca
www.facebook.com/FQMenligne
twitter.com/fqmenligne
Etre la porte-parole des régions; défendre les intérêts de ses membres
Bernard Généreux, Président
Ann Bourget, Directrice générale

Institute of Public Administration of Canada (IPAC) / Institut d'administration publique du Canada (IAPC)
#401, 1075 Bay St., Toronto ON M5S 2B1
Tel: 416-924-8787; *Fax:* 416-924-4992
ipac@ipac.ca
www.ipac.ca
www.linkedin.com/groups/1937184
www.facebook.com/IPACIAPC
twitter.com/IPAC_IAPC
To advance public service excellence, by sharing effective practices & policy in public administration; To lead public administration research in Canada; To further professional, non-artisan public service
Suzanne Patterson, Acting Chief Executive Officer

Zachary Spicer, Director, Research & Outreach
Christy Paddick, Managing Editor

Institute On Governance (IOG) / Institut sur la gouvernance
60 George St., Ottawa ON K1N 1J4
Tel: 613-562-0090; *Fax:* 613-562-0087
info@iog.ca
www.iog.ca
www.linkedin.com/groups/4179557
www.facebook.com/IOGca
twitter.com/IOGca
To advance governance in the public interest
Maryantonett Flumian, President
Jennifer Smith, Chief Operating Officer
Laura Edgar, Vice President, Board & Organizational Governance
Sylvain Dubois, Vice President, Public Governance
Toby Fyfe, Vice President, Learning Lab
Barry Christoff, Vice President, Indigenous Governance

Local Government Administrators of the Northwest Territories (LGANT)
PO Box 2083, 5018 - 52nd St., 2nd Fl., Yellowknife NT X1A 2P6
Tel: 867-765-5630; *Fax:* 867-765-5635
information@lgant.com
www.lgant.com
To ensure effectiveness & professionalism in the Northwest Territories' local government administration field
Grant Hood, President

Local Government Management Association of British Columbia (LGMA BC)
710 - 880 Douglas St., Victoria BC V8W 1B7
Tel: 250-383-7032; *Fax:* 250-384-4879
office@lgma.ca
www.lgma.ca
To promote professional management & leadership excellence in local government; To create awareness of local government officers' roles in the community; To support professional networking & connections development; To encourage idea exchanges among members
Nancy Taylor, Executive Director
Ana Fuller, Manager, Programs
Randee Platz, Officer, Finance

Manitoba Municipal Administrators' Association Inc.
5204 Roblin Blvd., Winnipeg MB R3R 0H1
Tel: 204-255-4883
mmaa@mts.net
www.mmaa.mb.ca
To promote the needs of membership & their professional development.
Mel Nott, Executive Director

Municipalities Newfoundland & Labrador (MNL)
460 Torbay Rd., St. John's NL A1A 5J3
Tel: 709-753-6820; *Fax:* 709-738-0071
Toll-Free: 800-440-6536
info@municipalitiesnl.com
www.municipalitiesnl.com
www.instagram.com/municipal_nl
www.linkedin.com/groups/4094976
www.facebook.com/MunicipalitiesNL
twitter.com/MunicipalNL
To assist communities in their endeavour to achieve & sustain strong & effective local government thereby improving the quality of life for all the people of this province.
Craig Pollett, Chief Executive Officer
Gail Woodfine, Contact, Communications & Public Relations

National Association of Federal Retirees (FSNA) / Association nationale des retraités fédéraux (ANRF)
865 Shefford Rd., Ottawa ON K1J 1H9
Tel: 613-745-2559; *Fax:* 613-745-5457
Toll-Free: 855-304-4700
service@federalretirees.ca
www.federalretirees.ca
www.linkedin.com/company/federalretirees
www.facebook.com/FederalRetirees
twitter.com/fedretirees
To protect & enhance the rights & benefits of retired federal employees, & seniors in general, & to cooperate with other seniors'/pensioners' organizations on objectives of mutual interest
Simon Coakeley, Chief Executive Officer
Nikki Dignard, Director, Finance & Administration
Andrew McGillivary, Director, Communications & Marketing

Northwest Territories Association of Communities (NWTAC)
Finn Hansen Bldg., #200, 5105 - 50th St., Yellowknife NT X1A 1S1
Tel: 867-873-8359; *Fax:* 867-873-3042
Toll-Free: 866-973-8359
communications@nwtac.com
www.nwtac.com
www.flickr.com/photos/nwtac
twitter.com/nwtac
To promote the exchange of information amongst the community governments of the Northwest Territories and to provide a united front for the realization of goals.
Sara Brown, CEO

Northwestern Ontario Municipal Association (NOMA)
PO Box 10308, Thunder Bay ON P7B 6T8
Tel: 807-683-6662
admin@noma.on.ca
www.noma.on.ca
To consider matters of interest to municipalities in northwestern Ontario; To procure enactment of legislation which may be advantageous to northwestern Ontario's municipalities
Kristen Oliver, Executive Director

Ontario Municipal Administrators' Association (OMAA)
14 Caledonia Terrace, Goderich ON N7A 2M8
Toll-Free: 855-833-6622
www.omaa.on.ca
To support, promote, & strengthen Ontario's municipal administrators
Gary Dyke, President

Ontario Municipal Human Resources Association (OMHRA)
PO Box 1090, Waterford ON N0E 1Y0
Tel: 519-443-6549
customerservice@omhra.on.ca
www.omhra.on.ca
To provide direction on issues of human resources management; To represent the interests of the association, related to legislation & policies
Kandy Webb, Executive Director

Ontario Municipal Management Institute (OMMI)
618 Balmoral Dr., Oshawa ON L1J 3A7
Tel: 905-434-8885; *Fax:* 905-434-7381
ommi@bellnet.ca
www.ommi.on.ca
To enhance management skills in order to strengthen local government administration
Bill McKim, Executive Director
Sandra Barter, Administrative Coordinator

Ontario Small Urban Municipalities (OSUM)
c/o Town of Goderich, 57 West St., Goderich ON N7A 2K5
Tel: 519-524-8344
amo@amo.on.ca
www.osum.ca
To take matters which affect Ontario's small urban communities to the attention of the provincial & federal governments
Paul Grenier, Chair
Jim Collard, Vice-Chair & Conference Chair
Larry McCabe, Administrative Member, OSUM Executive Committee

Parliamentary Centre / Le Centre parlementaire
#710, 155 Queen St., Ottawa ON K1P 6L1
Tel: 613-947-4999
parlcent@parl.gc.ca
parlcent.org
www.linkedin.com/company/parliamentarycentre
www.facebook.com/parliamentarycentre
twitter.com/parlcent
To strengthen legislatures through continuous learning & innovation in parliamentary development, mutual sharing & practical parliamentary experience & the provision of advisory services
Tom Cormier, President & CEO
Lola Giraldo, Director, Operations
Stéphane Courtemanche, Director, Programs

The Public Affairs Association of Canada (PAAC) / Association des affaires publiques du Canada
c/o Lois Marsh, #1801, 1 Yonge St., Toronto ON M5E 1W7
Tel: 416-214-7837; *Fax:* 416-369-0515
www.publicaffairs.ca
www.linkedin.com/groups/4790500
www.facebook.com/PublicAffairsAssociationCanada
twitter.com/PAAC84

To improve the professionalism of members to enhance the relations of members' organizations with their publics
Lois Marsh, Managing Director

Rural Municipal Administrators' Association of Saskatchewan (RMAA)
PO Box 130, Wilcox SK S0G 5E0
Tel: 306-732-2030; *Fax:* 306-732-4495
rmaa@sasktel.net
www.rmaa.ca
To address the needs of rural administrators in Saskatchewan
Kevin Ritchie, Executive Director
Tim Leurer, President

Rural Municipalities of Alberta (RMA)
2510 Sparrow Dr., Nisku AB T9E 8N5
Tel: 780-955-3639; *Fax:* 780-955-3615
Toll-Free: 855-548-7233
rma@rmalberta.com
rmalberta.com
www.flickr.com/photos/45829734@N03
twitter.com/ruralma
Gerald Rhodes, Executive Director

Rural Ontario Municipal Association (ROMA)
#801, 200 University Ave., Toronto ON M5H 3C6
Tel: 416-971-9856; *Fax:* 416-971-6191
Toll-Free: 877-426-6527
www.roma.on.ca
twitter.com/share
Ron Eddy, Chair

Saskatchewan Association of Rural Municipalities (SARM)
2301 Windsor Park Rd., Regina SK S4V 3A4
Tel: 306-757-3577; *Fax:* 306-565-2141
Toll-Free: 800-667-3604
sarm@sarm.ca
www.sarm.ca
To represent & advocate for rural municipal government in Saskatchewan
Jay Meyer, Executive Director

Saskatchewan Urban Municipalities Association (SUMA)
#200, 2222 - 13th Ave., Regina SK S4P 3M7
Tel: 306-525-3727; *Fax:* 306-525-4373
suma@suma.org
www.suma.org
www.facebook.com/SUMAamplify
twitter.com/suma_amplify
To work to enhance urban life in Saskatchewan, by providing administrative & consultative services to members, a forum for the discussion & resolution of current issues, & a negotiating vehicle for improvements in legislation, financing & programs; To provide information & training for aldermen & mayors, & group benefits for members
Jean-Marc Nadeau, Chief Executive Officer
Lindsay Peel, Director, Operations & Financial Services

Society of Local Government Managers of Alberta
PO Box 308, 4629 - 54 Ave., Bruderheim AB T0B 0S0
Tel: 780-796-3836; *Fax:* 780-796-2081
www.clgm.net
To govern & promote the profession of municipal government managers
Linda M. Davies, Executive Director/Registrar

Union des municipalités du Québec (UMQ)
#210, 2020, boul Robert-Bourassa, Montréal QC H3A 2A5
Tél: 514-282-7700; *Téléc:* 514-282-8893
info@umq.qc.ca
umq.qc.ca
www.linkedin.com/company/union-des-municipalit-s-du-qu-bec
twitter.com/UMQuebec
Au bénéfice des citoyens, représenter les municipalités auprès du gouvernement et contribuer à l'efficience de gestion des municipalités
Jasmin Savard, Directeur général
Jacinthe Olivier, Directrice, Finances et opérations
François Sormany, Directeur, Communications et marketing

Union of British Columbia Municipalities (UBCM)
#60, 10551 Shellbridge Way, Richmond BC V6X 2W9
Tel: 604-270-8226; *Fax:* 604-270-9116
ubcm@ubcm.ca
www.ubcm.ca
twitter.com/UBCM
To provide a common voice for local government
Gary MacIsaac, Executive Director

Union of Municipalities of New Brunswick (UMNB) / Union des municipalités du Nouveau-Brunswick
#145, 9 Main St., Rexton NB E4W 2A6
Tel: 506-523-7991; *Fax:* 506-523-7992
umnb@nb.aibn.com
www.umnb.ca
To unite the municipalities of New Brunswick through their respective councils into a body whose efforts shall be devoted to the achievement of the common good of all
Bev Gaston, President

Union of Nova Scotia Municipalities (UNSM)
#1106, 1809 Barrington St., Halifax NS B3J 3K8
Tel: 902-423-8331; *Fax:* 902-425-5592
info@unsm.ca
www.unsm.ca
To represent the interests of municipalities on policy & program matters that fall within the Nova Scotia provincial jurisdiction
Betty MacDonald, Executive Director
Judy Webber, Event Planner/Financal Officer

Urban Municipal Administrators' Association of Saskatchewan (UMAAS)
PO Box 730, Hudson Bay SK S0E 0Y0
Tel: 306-865-2261; *Fax:* 306-865-2800
umaas@sasktel.net
www.umaas.ca
Richard Dolezsar, Executive Director

West Vancouver Municipal Employees' Association (WVMEA) / Association des employés municipaux de Vancouver-Ouest
#118, 2419 Bellevue Ave., West Vancouver BC V7V 4T4
Tel: 604-925-7447; *Fax:* 604-926-7059
info@wvmea.com
www.wvmea.com
Public Sector Union representing West Vancouver workers in four (4) bargaining units
Conner Payne, President, Facilities, School District 45
Bruce Scott, Business Manager, Union Office

Health & Medical

Abortion Rights Coalition of Canada (ARCC) / Coalition pour le droit à l'avortement au Canada (CDAC)
PO Box 2663, Stn. Main, Vancouver BC V6B 3W3
Crisis Hot-Line: 888-642-2725
info@arcc-cdac.ca
www.arcc-cdac.ca
www.instagram.com/abortionrightscoalitioncan
www.facebook.com/AbortionRights
twitter.com/abortionrights
To ensure that women can access abortion services equitably & without barriers

Acoustic Neuroma Association of Canada (ANAC) / Association pour les neurinomes acoustiques du Canada
PO Box 1005, 7B Pleasant Blvd., Toronto ON M4T 1K2
Tel: 416-546-6426; *Toll-Free:* 800-561-2622
www.anac.ca
www.facebook.com/659626160751984
To provide support & information for those who have experienced acoustic neuromas or other tumors affecting the cranial nerves; To furnish information on patient rehabilitation to physicians & health care personnel; To promote & support research; To educate the public regarding symptoms suggestive of acoustic neuromas, thus promoting early diagnosis & consequent successful treatment
Carole Humphries, Executive Director, director@anac.ca

Active Healthy Kids Canada / Jeunes en forme Canada
401 Smyth Rd., Ottawa ON K1H 8L1
info@activehealthykids.ca
www.activehealthykids.ca
www.youtube.com/user/ActiveHealthyKids
www.facebook.com/ActiveHealthyKidsCanada
twitter.com/ActiveHealthyKi
To advocate the importance of quality, accessible & enjoyable physical activity participation experiences for children & youth; To provide expertise & direction to decision makers at all levels, from policy-makers to parents, in order to increase the attention given to, investment in, & effective implementation of physical activity opportunities for all Canadian children & youth
Mark Tremblay, President

Acupuncture Canada
Tower II, #109, 895 Don Mills Rd., Toronto ON M3C 1W3
Tel: 416-752-3988; *Fax:* 416-752-4398
info@acupuncturecanada.org
www.acupuncturecanada.org
www.linkedin.com/company/acupuncture-canada
www.facebook.com/AcupunctureCan
To define & maintain the highest professional standards for the use of acupuncture; To gain recognition of acupuncture's legitimate place in western medicine as a safe, efficient complement to conventional medical treatment; To design educational training programs for clinicians, physiotherapists, RNs, dentists, chiropractors & naturopaths in the methodology & practice of acupuncture
Catharine Maxwell-Palmer, President
Ronda Kellington, Executive Director

African Medical & Research Foundation Canada (AMREF Canada)
#403, 489 College St., Toronto ON M6G 1A5
Tel: 416-961-6981; *Fax:* 416-961-6984
Toll-Free: 888-318-4442
info@amrefcanada.org
www.amrefcanada.org
www.youtube.com/amrefcanada
www.facebook.com/amrefcanada
twitter.com/amrefcanada
Development agency working to enhance community health in East & Southern Africa; headquartered in Nairobi, Kenya; eleven national offices in both Europe & America; acts as support office in raising private & public funds for overseas health programs & also plays active role in maintaining working relations with Canadian International Development Agency (CIDA)
Onome Ako, Executive Director

Alberta Association of Optometrists (AAD)
#100, 8407 Argyll Rd., Edmonton AB T6C 4B2
Tel: 780-451-6824; *Fax:* 780-452-9918
Toll-Free: 800-272-8843
alberta.association@optometrists.ab.ca
www.optometrists.ab.ca
twitter.com/AAOOptometrists
To promote excellence in the practice of Optometry; To enhance public recognition of Optometry as the primary vision care provider in Alberta; To advance the interests of the profession
Brian Wik, Executive Director

Alberta Children's Hospital Foundation
2888 Shaganappi Trail NW, Calgary AB T3B 6A8
Tel: 403-955-8818; *Fax:* 403-955-8840
Toll-Free: 877-715-5437
kids@achf.com
www.childrenshospital.ab.ca
www.youtube.com/user/ACHF1
www.facebook.com/AlbertaChildrensHospitalFoundation
To raise money on behalf of the Alberta Children's Hospital in order to improve the services provided to patients & to fund research
Saifa Koonar, President & CEO

Alberta College & Association of Chiropractors (ACAC)
Manulife Place, 11203 - 70 St. NW, Edmonton AB T5B 1T1
Tel: 780-420-0932; *Fax:* 780-425-6583
office@albertachiro.com
www.albertachiro.com
www.youtube.com/user/albertachiro
www.facebook.com/AlbertaChiropractors
twitter.com/AlbertaChiro
To ensure quality chiropractic care that enhances the well-being & protects the rights of the people of Alberta; To promote the art, science & philosophy of chiropractic & its value in the health care community
Sheila Steger, Chief Executive Officer

Alberta College of Occupational Therapists (ACOT)
#312, 8925 - 51 Ave., Edmonton AB T6E 5J3
Tel: 780-436-8381; *Fax:* 780-434-0658
Toll-Free: 800-561-5429
info@acot.ca
www.acot.ca
To operate as the regulatory body in Alberta for the profession of occupational therapists; To ensure competent & ethical occupational therapy services for the public of the province; To uphold the Code of Ethics & the Standards of Practice for occupational therapists in Alberta
Elizabeth Taylor, President
Peter Portlock, Interim Registrar

Alberta Hospice Palliative Care Association (AHPCA)
#110, 105 - 12th Ave. SE, Calgary AB T2G 1A1
Tel: 403-206-9938; Fax: 403-206-9958
director@ahpca.ca
ahpca.ca
www.linkedin.com/company/alberta-hospice-palliative-care-association
www.facebook.com/AlbertaHospicePalliativeCare
twitter.com/AHPCA
To engage in actions & strategies that result in comprehensive, equitable & quality end of life care for Albertans
Elaine Klym, Chair
Leslie Penny, Treasurer
Kristi Puchbauer, Executive Director
Theresa Bellows, Road Show Coordinator

Alberta Innovates
#1500, 10104 - 103 Ave., Edmonton AB T5J 4A7
Tel: 780-423-5727; Fax: 780-429-3509
Toll-Free: 877-423-5727
albertainnovates.ca
www.youtube.com/user/AlbertaInnovates
www.linkedin.com/company/alberta-innovates
www.facebook.com/AlbertaInnovates
twitter.com/abinnovates
To support basic biomedical, clinical & health research in Alberta; To contribute funds to scientific community to carry out research
Laura Kilcrease, Chief Executive Officer

Alberta Medical Association (AMA)
12230 - 106 Ave. NW, Edmonton AB T5N 3Z1
Tel: 780-482-2626; Fax: 780-482-5445
Toll-Free: 800-272-9680
amamail@albertadoctors.org
www.albertadoctors.org
www.youtube.com/user/ABMedAssoc
www.linkedin.com/company/alberta-medical-association
www.facebook.com/AlbertaMedicalAssociation
twitter.com/Albertadoctors
To advocate on behalf of its physician members; To provide leadership & support for their role in the provision of quality health care
Alison Clark, President
Michael A. Gormley, Executive Director
Cameron N. Plitt, Chief Financial Officer

Alberta Occupational Health Nurses Association (AOHNA)
PO Box 12104, Sylvan Lake AB T4S 2K9
Fax: 866-877-0228
Toll-Free: 888-566-3343
info@aohna.org
aohna.org
www.linkedin.com/company/alberta-occupational-health-nurses%27-association
twitter.com/AOHNA1
To promote healthy work environments for Occupational Health Nurses in Alberta; To provide growth & develop opportunities for its membership
Kristi Hines, President

Alberta Public Health Association (APHA)
c/o Injury Prevention Centre, University of Alberta, #4075 RTF, 8308 - 114 St., Edmonton AB T6G 2E1
apha.comm@gmail.com
www.apha.ab.ca
To protect public health through advocacy, partnerships, & education
Lindsay McLaren, President

Alliance for Chiropractic (AFC)
#126, 17A - 218 Silvercreek Pkwy. North, Guelph ON N1H 8E8
Tel: 519-822-1879; Fax: 519-822-1239
Toll-Free: 877-997-9927
www.allianceforchiropractic.com
www.instagram.com/all4chiro
www.facebook.com/all4chiro
twitter.com/all4chiro
To promote public awareness of chiropractic life principles by promoting an awareness of the devastating effects of vertebral subluxation complex on the expression of human health potential; To educate the public with the conviction that chiropractic care is an integral aspect of health for people of all ages & to society in general
Craig Hazel, Chair

ALS Society of Canada (ALS) / La Société canadienne de la SLA (SLA)
#1701, 393 University Ave., Toronto ON M5G 1E6
Tel: 416-497-2267; Fax: 416-497-8545
Toll-Free: 800-267-4257
www.als.ca
www.linkedin.com/company/als-society-of-canada
www.facebook.com/ALSCanada
twitter.com/alscanada
To support research towards a cure for ALS; To support ALS partners in their provision of quality care for persons affected by ALS
Tammy Moore, Chief Executive Officer

Alzheimer Manitoba
#10, 120 Donald St., Winnipeg MB R3C 4G2
Tel: 204-943-6622; Fax: 204-942-5408
Toll-Free: 800-378-6699
alzmb@alzheimer.mb.ca
www.alzheimer.mb.ca
www.facebook.com/AlzheimerSocietyManitoba
twitter.com/AlzheimerMB
To alleviate the individual, family & social consequences of Alzheimer type dementia while supporting the search for a cure
Wendy Schettler, Chief Executive Officer

Alzheimer Society of Alberta & Northwest Territories
High Park Corner, #306, 10430 - 61 Ave., Edmonton AB T6H 2J3
Tel: 780-761-0030; Fax: 780-761-0031
Toll-Free: 866-950-5465
reception@alzheimer.ab.ca
www.alzheimer.ca/ab
www.instagram.com/dementiaab_nt
www.facebook.com/Dementiaabnt
twitter.com/DementiaAB_NT
To alleviate the personal & social consequences of Alzheimer's disease through the development, support & coordination of local societies & chapters; To promote the search for a cure through education & research
Michele Mulder, Chief Executive Officer

Alzheimer Society of British Columbia
#300, 828 West 8th Ave., Vancouver BC V5Z 1E2
Tel: 604-681-6530; Fax: 604-669-6907
Toll-Free: 800-667-3742
info@alzheimerbc.org
www.alzheimerbc.org
www.youtube.com/AlzheimerBC
www.linkedin.com/company/alzheimer-society-of-b.c.
www.facebook.com/AlzheimerBC
twitter.com/AlzheimerBC
To alleviate the personal & social consequences of Alzheimer disease & related dementias; To promote public awareness & to search for the causes & the cures
Maria Howard, Chief Executive Officer

Alzheimer Society of Canada (ASC) / Société Alzheimer du Canada
20 Eglinton Ave. West, 16th Fl., Toronto ON M4R 1K8
Tel: 416-488-8772; Fax: 416-322-6656
Toll-Free: 800-616-8816
info@alzheimer.ca
www.alzheimer.ca
www.youtube.com/alzheimercanada
www.facebook.com/AlzheimerCanada
twitter.com/AlzCanada
To identify, develop & facilitate national priorities that enable members to alleviate personal & social consequences of Alzheimer's disease & related disorders; To promote research & lead the search for a cure
Ian Rea, Chair

Alzheimer Society of New Brunswick / Société alzheimer du nouveau brunswick
PO Box 1553, Stn. A, Fredericton NB E3B 5G2
Tel: 506-459-4280; Fax: 506-452-0313
Toll-Free: 800-664-8411
info@alzheimernb.ca
www.alzheimernb.ca
www.facebook.com/AlzheimerSocietyNB
twitter.com/AlzheimerNB
To alleviate the personal & social consequences of Alzheimer disease; To promote the search for a cause & cure
Chandra MacBean, Executive Director

Alzheimer Society of Newfoundland & Labrador
#107, 835 Topsail Rd., Mount Pearl NL A1N 3J6
Tel: 709-576-0608; Fax: 709-576-0798
Toll-Free: 877-776-0608
info@alzheimernl.ca
alzheimer.ca/en/nl
www.facebook.com/ASNL2
twitter.com/asnl2
To support the search for the cause & cure of Alzheimer Disease; To raise public awareness of the personal & social impact of the disease; To promote the provision of support to families & caregivers in Newfoundland
Shirley Lucas, Chief Executive Officer

Alzheimer Society of Nova Scotia
Gladstone Ridge Professional Centre, #112, 2719 Gladstone St., Halifax NS B3K 4W6
Tel: 902-422-7961; Fax: 902-422-7971
Toll-Free: 800-611-6345
alzheimer@asns.ca
www.alzheimer.ca/ns
www.youtube.com/user/alzheimerns
www.facebook.com/alzheimersocietyns
twitter.com/alzheimerns
To enhance the quality of life of people with Alzheimer disease through providing & promoting public education & family support; To engage in advocacy on behalf of people with Alzheimer disease & their families; To promote research at the provincial & national levels
John Britton, Executive Director
Andrew MacIsaac, President

Alzheimer Society of Ontario / Société Alzheimer Ontario
20 Eglinton Ave. West, 16th Fl., Toronto ON M4R 1K8
Tel: 416-967-5900; Fax: 416-967-3826
Toll-Free: 800-879-4226
staff@alzon.ca
alzheimer.ca/en/on
www.youtube.com/alzheimersocietyont
www.facebook.com/AlzheimerSocietyofOntario
twitter.com/alzheimeront
To improve the quality of life for persons with Alzheimer disease & their families; To inform & educate the public & health care professionals about Alzheimer disease; To coordinate a chapter network & liaison in order to present a united voice to the Government of Ontario & other provincial groups on matters relating to legal concerns, health care, research & community needs; To raise funds for research
Keith Gibbons, Chair

Alzheimer Society of PEI
166 Fitzroy St., Charlottetown PE C1A 1S1
Tel: 902-628-2257; Fax: 902-368-2715
Toll-Free: 866-628-2257
society@alzpei.ca
www.alzheimer.ca/pei
www.youtube.com/user/Alzpei
www.facebook.com/AlzheimerPEI
twitter.com/AlzheimerPEI
To support & assist Islanders affected by Alzheimer Disease; To raise the level of awareness & educate the public at large about the disease
Corrine Hendricken-Eldershaw, Chief Executive Officer

Alzheimer Society of Saskatchewan Inc. (ASOS)
#301, 2550 - 12th Ave., Regina SK S4P 3X1
Tel: 306-949-4141; Fax: 306-949-3069
Toll-Free: 800-263-3367
info@alzheimer.sk.ca
alzheimer.ca/en/sk
www.youtube.com/thealzheimersociety
www.facebook.com/AlzheimerSK
twitter.com/AlzheimerSK
To alleviate the personal & social consequences of Alzheimer's disease & related disorders; To promote the search for a cause & a cure
Joanne Bracken, Chief Executive Officer

Aplastic Anemia & Myelodysplasia Association of Canada (AAMAC)
#4, 2201 King Rd., King City ON L7B 1G2
Tel: 905-780-0698; Fax: 905-780-1648
Toll-Free: 888-840-0039
info@aamac.ca
www.aamac.ca
To disseminate information concerning the disease; To form a nation-wide support network for patients, families & medical professionals; To support Canadian Blood Services & their programs; To raise funds for research
Hayden Liang, President
Gwen Barry, Secretary

Arthritis Society / Société de l'arthrite
#1700, 393 University Ave., Toronto ON M5G 1E6
Tel: 416-979-7228; *Fax:* 416-979-8366
Toll-Free: 800-321-1433
info@arthritis.ca
www.arthritis.ca
www.facebook.com/arthritissociety
twitter.com/arthritisoc
To fund & promote arthritis research, programs & patient care.
There are division offices in each province & nearly 1,000
community branches throughout Canada
Trish Barbato, President & CEO
Cheryl McClellan, Chief Operating Officer
Laura Syron, Chief Development Officer

Association canadienne des ataxies familiales (ACAF) / Canadian Association for Familial Ataxias (CAFA)
#5400, 1751, rue Radisson, Montréal QC H3K 1G6
Tél: 514-321-8684; *Ligne sans frais:* 855-321-8684
ataxie@lacaf.org
www.lacaf.org
www.youtube.com/user/LACAF2010
www.facebook.com/ataxie.canada
twitter.com/ataxiecanada
Recueillir des dons du public pour financer les recherches
médicales qui se font sur l'Ataxie familial ainsi que d'améliorer la
condition de vie des personnes ataxiques (personnes qui sont
affligées par la maladie de l'Ataxie de Friedreich)
Jean Luk Pellerin, Présidente
André De Montigny, Vice-Présidente
François-Olivier Théberge, Directeur général

Association d'orthopédie du Québec
Tour de L'Est, CP 216, Succ. Desjardins, 2, Complexe
Desjardins, 30e étage, Montréal QC H5B 1G8
Tél: 514-844-0803; *Téléc:* 514-844-6786
aoq@fmsq.org
www.orthoquebec.ca
Valoriser le statut professionnel de ses membres; promouvoir
leurs intérêts économiques; contribuer au développement de la
chirurgie orthopédique et de la traumatologie par le biais
d'activités de formation médicale continue
Jean-François Joncas, Président

Association d'oto-rhino-laryngologie et de chirurgie cervico-faciale du Québec
CP 216, Succ. Desjardins, #3000, 2, Complexe Desjardins,
Montréal QC H5B 1G8
Tél: 514-350-5125; *Téléc:* 514-350-5165
assorl@fmsq.org
www.orlquebec.org
Valoriser le statut professionnel de ses membres, promouvoir
leurs intérêts scientifiques, économiques et professionnels, et
contribuer au développement de l'oto-rhino-laryngologie
Luc Monette, Président
Jocelyne Fortin, Directrice, Administration

Association de neurochirurgie du Québec (ANCQ)
CP 216, Succ. Desjardins, #3000, 2, Complexe Desjardins,
Montréal QC H5B 1G8
Tél: 514-350-5120; *Téléc:* 514-350-5100
ancq@fmsq.org
www.ancq.net
www.facebook.com/neurochirurgiequebec
Pour représenter les médecins spécialistes et de promouvoir
leurs intérêts
Louis Crevier, Président
Manon Gaudry, Directrice, Administration

L'Association de spina-bifida et d'hydrocéphalie du Québec (ASBHQ)
QC
Tél: 514-340-9019; *Ligne sans frais:* 800-567-1788
www.spina.qc.ca
www.facebook.com/asbhq
twitter.com/ASBHQ
Promouvoir et défendre les droits, les intérêts et le bien-être des
personnes ayant le spina-bifida et l'hydrocéphalie; sensibiliser le
public à la nature du spina-bifida et de l'hydrocéphalie ainsi
qu'aux besoins des personnes ayant ces malformations;
favoriser et soutenir la recherche sur les causes, les nouveaux
traitements et les techniques de prévention du spina-bifida et de
l'hydrocéphalie
Nathalie Boëls, Président

Association des Allergologues et Immunologues du Québec
CP 216, Succ. Desjardins, #3000, 2, Complexe Desjardins,
Montréal QC H5B 1G8
Tél: 514-350-5101
aaiq@fmsq.org
www.allerg.qc.ca

Association des bénévoles du don de sang (ABDS) / Association of Blood Donation Volunteers (ABDV)
4045, boul Côte-Vertu, Montréal QC H4R 2W7
Tél: 514-832-5000; *Téléc:* 514-832-0872
Ligne sans frais: 888-666-4362
abdsdondesang@gmail.com
www.abdsdondesang.com
www.linkedin.com/in/abdsdondesang
www.facebook.com/ABDS-333369506845428
Soutenir le recrutement de nouveaux donneurs en partenariat
avec Héma-Québec; Promouvoir le don de sang
Florentina Costache, Directrice des opérations

Association des cardiologues du Québec (ACQ)
CP 216, Succ. Desjardins, #3000, 2, Complexe Desjardins,
Montréal QC H5B 1G8
Tél: 514-350-5106; *Téléc:* 514-350-5156
acq@fmsq.org
cardioquebec.ca
Arsène Basmadjian, Président
Yasmina Ait El Hadi, Directrice

Association des chiropraticiens du Québec
7960, boul Métropolitain est, Montréal QC H1K 1A1
Tél: 514-355-0557; *Téléc:* 514-355-0070
Ligne sans frais: 866-292-4476
acq@chiropratique.com
www.chiropratique.com
www.youtube.com/user/AssoDesChirosQc
www.facebook.com/AssoDesChirosQc
twitter.com/AssoChiroQc
Défendre les intérêts professionnels, sociaux et économiques de
ses membres
Marie-Hélène Boivin, Présidente
Sylvie Des Ruisseaux, Directrice générale

Association des conseils des médecins, dentistes et pharmaciens du Québec (ACMDP) / Association of Councils of Physicians, Dentists & Pharmacists of Québec
#214, 81, rue Notre-Dame ouest, Thetford Mines QC G6G
1J4
Tél: 514-858-5885; *Téléc:* 514-858-6767
acmdp@acmdp.qc.ca
www.acmdp.qc.ca
Offrir l'information, la motivation, et la formation
médico-administrative nécessaire aux Conseils des médecins,
dentistes, et pharmaciens membres afin qu'ils accomplissent
adéquatement leurs tâches
Martin Arata, Président-Directeur général

Association des gastro-entérologues du Québec (AGEQ)
CP 216, Succ. Desjardins, 2, Complexe Desjardins, Montréal
QC H5B 1G8
Tél: 514-350-5112; *Téléc:* 514-350-5146
www.ageq.net
D'informer et de formations aux médecins de première ligne, aux
patients souffrant de pathologies gastro-intestinales et aux
autres médecins intéressés par la gastro-entérologie; de créer
des liens avec la communauté médicale internationale
Josée Parent, Présidente
Sylvie Bergeron, Directrice, Administration

Association des médecins biochimistes du Québec (AMBQ)
CP 216, Succ. Desjardins, #3000, 2, Complexe Desjardins,
Montréal QC H5B 1G8
Tél: 514-350-5105; *Téléc:* 514-350-5151
ambq@fmsq.org
ambq.org
Promouvoir l'utilisation optimale des tests de laboratoire au
Québec en offrant, au professionnel de la santé et au patient, les
meilleurs services de diagnostic et de dépistage de maladies
grâce à des techniques biochimiques et immunologiques
Yves Giguère, Président

Association des médecins endocrinologues du Québec
CP 216, Succ. Desjardins, #3000, 2, Complexe Desjardins,
Montréal QC H5B 1G8
Tél: 514-350-5135; *Téléc:* 514-350-5049
Ligne sans frais: 800-561-0703
ameq@fmsq.org
www.ameq.qc.ca
L'Association est un porte-parole des endocrinologues; elle
favorise les intérêts scientifiques de ses membres et organise
plusieurs réunions afin de permettre une formation médicale
continue des endocrinologues
Jean Palardy, Président
Marie-Eve Lefebvre, Directrice

Association des médecins généticiens du Québec
#3000, 2, Complexe Desjardins, Montréal QC H5B 1G8
Tél: 514-350-5141; *Téléc:* 514-350-5116
www.medecingeneticien.ca
Bruno Maranda, M.D., Président
Sandrine Guillot, Directrice

Association des médecins gériatres du Québec
CP 216, Succ. Desjardins, #3000, 2, Complexe Desjardins,
Montréal QC H5B 1G8
Tél: 514-350-5145; *Téléc:* 514-350-5151
info@amgq.ca
www.amgq.ca
Serge Brazeau, Président
Lillian Plasse, Directrice, Administration

Association des médecins hématologistes-oncologistes du Québec (AMHOQ)
CP 216, Succ. Desjardins, 2, Complexe Desjardins, Montréal
QC H5B 1G8
Tél: 514-350-5121; *Téléc:* 514-350-5126
info@amhoq.org
amhoq.org
Martin Champagne, Président
Nathalie Latendresse, Directrice administrative

Association des médecins microbiologistes-infectiologues du Québec (AMMIQ)
#3000, 2, Complexe Desjardins, Montréal QC H5B 1G8
Tél: 514-350-5104; *Téléc:* 514-350-5144
info@ammiq.org
www.ammiq.org
Regroupe des médecins (de laboratoire et dans le diagnostic
clinique) spécialisés dans l'épidémiologie, le traitement et la
prévention des maladies infectieuses
Karl Weiss, Président
Charlotte Lavoie, Directrice

Association des médecins ophtalmologistes du Québec (AMOQ)
CP 216, Succ. Desjardins, #3000, 2, Complexe Desjardins,
Montréal QC H5B 1G8
Tél: 514-350-5124; *Téléc:* 514-350-5174
amoq@fmsq.org
www.fmsq.org
Promouvoir les intérêts professionnels et économiques de ses
membres; se préoccuper du maintien de la compétence; susciter
et appuier des activités scientifiques susceptibles de favoriser
l'avancement de l'ophtalmologie; se préoccuper de l'accessibilité
aux soins ophtalmologiques
Salim Lahoud, Président
Sylvie Gariépy, Directrice, Administration

Association des médecins rhumatologues du Québec (AMRQ)
CP 216, Succ. Desjardins, Montréal QC H5B 1G8
Tél: 514-350-5136; *Téléc:* 514-350-5029
Ligne sans frais: 800-561-0703
info@rhumatologie.org
www.rhumatologie.org
La rhumatologie se consacre au diagnostic et au traitement des
pathologies qui touchent les articulations, les os, les muscles et
tendons et parfois tout organe dans le cadre de maladies
systémiques. Ceci regroupe au-delà de 100 conditions pouvant
aller de l'arthrite rhumatoïde au lupus érythémateux disséminé
en passant par l'arthrose, les vasculites et l'ostéoporose
Frédéric Massicotte, Président
Nancy Fortin, Direction générale

Association des médecins spécialistes dermatologues du Québec (AMSDQ)
CP 216, Succ. Desjardins, #3000, 2, Complexe Desjardins,
Montréal QC H5B 1G8
Tél: 514-350-5111; *Téléc:* 514-350-5161
dermato@fmsq.org
www.dermatoqc.org
Syndicat professionnel: assure la défense des intérêts
économiques, professionnels et scientifiques de ses membres
Dominique Hanna, Présidente

Association des médecins spécialistes en médecine nucléaire du Québec (AMSMNQ)
CP 216, Succ. Desjardins, #3000, 2, Complexe Desjardins,
Montréal QC H5B 1G8
Tél: 514-350-5133; *Téléc:* 514-350-5151
Ligne sans frais: 800-561-0703
amsmnq@fmsq.org
www.medecinenucleaire.com
Pour former ses membres et maintenir un haut niveau de
professionnalisme
Norman Laurin, Président
Michelle Laviolette, Directrice administrative

Association des médecins spécialistes en santé communautaire du Québec (AMSSCQ)
CP 216, #3000, 2, Complexe Desjardins, Montréal QC H5B 1G8

Tél: 514-350-5138; *Téléc:* 514-350-5151
asmpq@fmsq.org
www.amscq.org
De promouvoir les intérêts professionnels et économiques de ses membres
Isabelle Samson, Présidente

Association des néphrologues du Québec
CP 216, Succ. Desjardins, #3000, 2, Complexe Desjardins, Montréal QC H5B 1G8

Tél: 514-350-5134; *Téléc:* 514-350-5151
nephrologie@fmsq.org
Robert Charbonneau, Président
Lillian Plasse, Directrice, Administration

Association des neurologues du Québec (ANQ)
CP 216, Succ. Desjardins, #3000, 2, Complexe Desjardins, Montréal QC H5B 1G8

Tél: 514-350-5122; *Téléc:* 514-350-5172
anq@fmsq.org
www.anq.qc.ca
www.facebook.com/109136899239391
twitter.com/assneuroquebec
Représenter des médecins spécialistes qui diagnostique et traite les maladies affectant le système nerveux central ainsi que le système nerveux périphérique
François Evoy, Président
Mari-Claude Hotte, Directrice, Administration

Association des obstétriciens et gynécologues du Québec (AOGQ)
CP 216, Succ. Desjardins, #3000, 2, Complexe Desjardins, Montréal QC H5B 1G8

Tél: 514-849-4969; *Téléc:* 514-849-5011
info@gynecoquebec.com
www.gynecoquebec.com
Promouvoir l'intérêt professionnel scientifique et économique de ses membres
Violaine Marcoux, Présidente
Léa Desjardins, Directrice, Administration

Association des optométristes du Québec (AOQ) / Québec Optometric Association
#217, 1255, boul Robert-Bourassa, Montréal QC H3B 3B2

Tél: 514-288-6272; *Téléc:* 514-288-7071
aoq@aoqnet.qc.ca
www.aoqnet.qc.ca
www.linkedin.com/company/association-des-optom-tristes-du-qu
-bec
www.facebook.com/109631962406806
De développer meilleures conditions de pratique économiques et professionnelles pour les optométristes du Québec
Steven Carrier, Président
Maryse Nolin, Directrice générale

Association des pathologistes du Québec (APQ)
CP 216, Succ. Desjardins, #3000, 2, Complexe Desjardins, Montréal QC H5B 1G8

Tél: 514-350-5102; *Téléc:* 514-350-5152
Ligne sans frais: 800-561-0703
patho@fmsq.org
www.apq.qc.ca
Promouvoir les intérêts professionnels et économiques de ses membres
Badia Issa-Chergui, Président
Danielle Joncas, Directrice, Administration

Association des pédiatres du Québec
CP 216, Succ. Desjardins, #3000, 2, Complexe Desjardins, 32e étage, Montréal QC H5B 1G8

pediatrie@fmsq.org
www.pediatres.ca
Marc Lebel, Président

Association des pharmaciens des établissements de santé du Québec (APES)
#320, 4050, rue Molson, Montréal QC H1Y 3N1

Tél: 514-286-0776; *Téléc:* 514-286-1081
info@apesquebec.org
www.apesquebec.org
www.facebook.com/PharmaciensEtablissements
twitter.com/pharmaciensAPES
Linda Vaillant, Directrice générale
France Boucher, Directrice générale adjointe

Association des physiatres du Québec (APQ)
CP 216, Succ. Desjardins, #3000, 2, Complexe Desjardins, Montréal QC H5B 1G8

Tél: 514-350-5119; *Téléc:* 514-350-5147
apq@fmsq.org
www.fmsq.org
Pour ouvrir à la prévention, au diagnostic et au traitement médical des douleurs et des troubles de l'appareil locomoteur (la colonne vertébrale, les os, les muscles, les tendons, les articulations, les vaisseaux et le cerveau)
Claude Bouthillier, Président
Elsa Fournier, Directrice, Administration

Association des pneumologues de la province de Québec (APPQ)
CP 216, Succ. Desjardins, #3000, 2, Complexe Desjardins, Montréal QC H5B 1G8

Tél: 514-350-5117; *Téléc:* 514-350-5153
appq@fmsq.org
www.fmsq.org
Promouvoir les intérêts professionnels et économiques de ses membres; se préoccuper du maintien de leur compétence; se prononcer sur les problématiques de la pneumologie dans les meilleurs intérêts de la population
Antoine Delage, Président
Elsa Fournier, Directrice, Administration

Association des radiologistes du Québec
CP 216, Succ. Desjardins, #3000, 2, Complexe Desjardins, Montréal QC H5B 1G8

Tél: 514-350-5129; *Téléc:* 514-350-5179
bureau@arq.qc.ca
www.arq.qc.ca
Regrouper les médecins spécialisés en radiologie; défendre leurs intérêts et promouvoir leur spécialité
Vincent Oliva, Président
Djinène Meziane, Directrice, Administration

Association des radio-oncologues du Québec (AROQ)
CP 216, Succ. Desjardins, #3000, 2, Complexe Desjardins, Montréal QC H5B 1G8

Tél: 514-350-5130; *Téléc:* 514-350-5126
aroq@fmsq.org
www.aroq.ca
De fournir un forum où ses membres peuvent échanger des idées afin d'aider à améliorer leurs méthodes de traitement
Michael Yassa, Président
Sylvie Pelletier, Directrice, Administration

Association des sexologues du Québec (ASQ)
CP 22147, Succ. Iberville, Montréal QC H1Y 3K8

Tél: 514-270-9289
info@associationdessexologues.com
www.associationdessexologues.com
www.facebook.com/Associationasq
Susciter auprès du public une meilleure connaissance de la sexologie et du rôle du sexologue, en favorisant et en maintenant les normes scientifiques et professionnelles les plus élevées dans l'exercice de la sexologie et dans la formation des sexologues

Association des spécialistes en chirurgie plastique et esthétique du Québec (ASCPEQ)
CP 216, Succ. Desjardins, 2, Complexe Desjardins, Montréal QC H5B 1G8

Tél: 514-350-5109; *Téléc:* 514-350-5246
ascpeq@fmsq.org
www.ascpeq.org
Se consacrer essentiellement au développement continu de l'art et de la science de la chirurgie plastique et esthétique, entre autres par la diffusion de renseignements pertinents auprès du public, par la promotion d'une relation médecin-patient fondée sur la communication, la compréhension et le respect mutuel, ainsi que par une contribution active aux programmes d'éducation et de formation continue et par une participation critique aux débats relatifs au rôle et à la place des professionnels de la santé au sein de la société québécoise
Éric Bensimon, Président

Association des spécialistes en médecine d'urgence du Québec
Tour de l'Est, #3000, 2, Complexe Desjardins, Montréal QC H5B 1G8

Tél: 514-350-5115; *Téléc:* 514-350-5116
asmuq@fmsq.org
www.asmuq.org
twitter.com/asmuq
Gilbert Boucher, Président

Association des spécialistes en médecine interne du Québec
Tour Est, 2, Complexe Desjardins, 30e étage, Montréal QC H5B 1G8

Tél: 514-350-5118; *Téléc:* 514-350-5168
asmiq.org
Hoang Duong, Président

Association des urologues du Québec (AUQ) / Quebec Urological Association (QUA)
Tour de l'est, 2, Complexe Desjardins, 32e étage, Montréal QC H5B 1G8

Tél: 514-350-5131; *Téléc:* 514-350-5181
auq@fmsq.org
www.auq.org
Steven P. Lapointe, Président
Thierry Lebeau, Secrétaire

Association médicale du Québec (AMQ) / Québec Medical Association (QMA)
#3200, 380, rue Saint-Antoine ouest, Montréal QC H2Y 3X7

Tél: 514-866-0660; *Téléc:* 514-866-0670
Ligne sans frais: 800-363-3932
admin@amq.org
www.amq.ca
www.facebook.com/AMQ.QUEBEC
twitter.com/amquebec
Rassembler et soutenir les médecins du Québec afin de garantir à la population québécoise des conditions et des soins de santé de qualité
Normand Laberge, Directeur général

Association of Local Public Health Agencies (ALPHA)
#1306, 2 Carlton St., Toronto ON M5B 1J3

Tel: 416-595-0006; *Fax:* 416-595-0030
info@alphaweb.org
www.alphaweb.org
To provide leadership in public health management to health units in Ontario; To assist local public health units in the provision of efficient & effective services
Loretta Ryan, Executive Director
Gordon Fleming, Manager, Public Health Issues
Susan Lee, Manager, Administrative & Association Services

Association of Medical Microbiology & Infectious Disease Canada (AMMI Canada) / Association pour la microbiologie médicale et l'infectiologie Canada
192 Bank St., Ottawa ON K2P 1W8

Tel: 613-260-3233; *Fax:* 613-260-3235
communications@ammi.ca
www.ammi.ca
www.facebook.com/AMMICanada
twitter.com/AMMICanada
To represent the broad interests of researchers & physicians who specialize in the fields of infectious diseases & medical microbiology in Canada; To contribute to the health of people at risk of, or affected by, infectious diseases; To promote & facilitate research; To develop policies for the prevention, diagnosis & management of infectious diseases
Riccarda Galioto, Executive Director
Alison Peverley, Coordinator, Meetings & Membership

Association pour la santé publique du Québec (ASPQ) / Québec Public Health Association
#102, 4529, rue Clark, Montréal QC H2T 2T3

Tél: 514-528-5811; *Téléc:* 514-528-5590
info@aspq.org
www.aspq.org
www.facebook.com/AssociationPourLaSantePubliqueDuQuebec
aspq
twitter.com/ASPQuebec
Favoriser un regard critique sur les enjeux de santé publique au Québec en constituant un regroupement volontaire, autonome, multidisciplinaire et multisectoriel de personnes et d'organisations provenant des milieux tant institutionnels et professionnels que communautaires; offre un espace à ses membres pour développer des prises de position communes ou concertées, appuyer des politiques favorables à la santé et au bien-être et développer des coalitions et des projets en collaboration avec d'autres partenaires de santé publique ou du milieu
Lilianne Bertrand, Présidente
Lucie Granger, Directrice générale

Association Québécoise de chirurgie
CP 216, Succ. Desjardins, #3000, 2, Complexe Desjardins, Montréal QC H5B 1G8

Tél: 514-350-5107; *Téléc:* 514-350-5157
info@chirurgiequebec.ca
www.chirurgiequebec.ca

Objectifs sont la protection et défense des intérêts professionnels collectifs des chirurgiens et l'enseignement chirurgical continu
Serge Legault, Président
Chantale Jubinville, Directrice

Association québécoise de l'épilepsie
#204, 1650, boul de Maisonneuve ouest, Montréal QC H3H 2P3
Tél: 514-875-5595; *Téléc:* 514-875-6734
info@associationquebecoiseepilepsie.com
www.associationquebecoiseepilepsie.com
www.facebook.com/associationquebecoiseepilepsie
twitter.com/AssEpilepsieQc
Veiller au mieux-être des personnes épileptiques et à leurs familles; promouvoir les droits des personnes épileptiques; sensibiliser le public à l'épilepsie; promouvoir l'intégration scolaire et au travail

Asthma Canada
#401, 124 Merton St., Toronto ON M4S 2Z2
Tel: 416-787-4050; *Fax:* 416-787-5807
Toll-Free: 866-787-4050
info@asthma.ca
www.asthma.ca
www.instagram.com/asthma_canada
www.linkedin.com/company/asthma-society-of-canada
www.facebook.com/AsthmaCanada
twitter.com/AsthmaCanada
To optimize the health of people with asthma through education & asthma awareness
Vanessa Foran, President & CEO
Jenna Reynolds, Director, Programs & Services
Zhen Liu, Manager, Operations & Administration

Autism Canada / Société canadienne d'autisme
#200, 140 Yonge St., Toronto ON M5C 1X6
Tel: 647-362-5610; *Toll-Free:* 800-983-1795
info@autismcanada.org
www.autismcanada.org
www.linkedin.com/company/autism-canada
www.facebook.com/autismcanada
twitter.com/autismcanada
To provide support on a national basis to people affected by autism & related conditions through the collective efforts of Canadian provincial & territorial autism societies; To provide information & general referrals to the public regarding autism & related conditions; To promote public awareness of autism & related conditions; To encourage research in fields related or relevant to autism & related conditions; To communicate with government, agencies, & other organizations on behalf of persons affected by autism & related conditions; To promote actions to ensure people with autism & related conditions live in an environment that supports their well-being & enables them to reach their full potential; To promote & encourage the convening of conferences focused on autism & related conditions
Dermot Cleary, Chair
Michelle Colero, Executive Director

Autism Nova Scotia (ANS)
5945 Spring Garden Rd., Halifax NS B3H 1Y4
Tel: 902-446-4995; *Fax:* 902-446-4997
Toll-Free: 877-544-4495
info@autismns.ca
www.autismnovascotia.ca
www.facebook.com/AutismNovaScotia
twitter.com/autismns
A community-based organization that fosters understanding, acceptance, & inclusion for those living with autism spectrum disorder (ASD) throughout Nova Scotia. Chapters are located in each region of the province.
Victoria Ettinger, Family Support, Family, Respite, & Community Support
Holly MacLellan, Autism Employment & Outreach Coordinator, Employment Support
Vicki Harvey, Chapter Coordinator
Chrissy Pace, Program Coordinator, Social & Community Inclusion Programming

Autism Ontario
#004, 1179 King St. West, Toronto ON M6K 3C5
Tel: 416-246-9592; *Fax:* 416-246-9417
Toll-Free: 800-472-7789
www.autismontario.com
www.instagram.com/autismontario
www.linkedin.com/company/autism-ontario
www.facebook.com/autismontarioprovincial
twitter.com/AutismONT
To ensure that individuals with autism spectrum disorders are provided the means to achieve quality of life as respected members of society
Marg Spoelstra, Executive Director

Autism Society Alberta (ASA)
3639 26 St. NE, Calgary AB T1Y 5E1
Toll-Free: 877-777-7192
info@autismalberta.ca
www.facebook.com/autismalberta
twitter.com/AutismSocietyAB
To improve the understanding of autism throughout Alberta by the dissemination of information to parents, health care workers, educators, government, private agencies & the public
Jason Scheyen, President
Brooke Pinsky, Secretary

Autism Society Manitoba
825 Sherbrook St., Winnipeg MB R3A 1M5
Tel: 204-783-9563; *Fax:* 204-975-3027
info@autismmanitoba.com
www.autismmanitoba.com
www.facebook.com/AutismSocietyOfManitoba
twitter.com/manitobaautism
To enhance the quality of life of people with Autism Spectrum Disorder & their families; To promote full inclusion, dignity & development of personal skills & abilities for our members

Autism Society Newfoundland & Labrador (ASNL)
PO Box 14078, St. John's NL A1B 4G8
Tel: 709-722-2803; *Fax:* 709-722-4926
info@autism.nf.net
www.autism.nf.net
twitter.com/AutismSocietyNL
To promote the diagnosis, treatment, education & integration into the community of all autistic persons; To provide information about autism; To promote research; To promote integrated care for autistic persons; To encourage the formation of parent support groups around the province
Scott Crocker, Executive Director

Autism Society Northwest Territories
5204 - 54th St., Yellowknife NT X1A 1W8
Tel: 867-446-0985; *Fax:* 867-873-4124
www.nwtautismsociety.org
www.facebook.com/nwtautismsociety
To ensure that autistic individuals & their families have access to resources
Denise McKee, President

Autism Society of British Columbia
3688 Cessna Dr., Richmond BC V7B 1C7
Tel: 604-434-0880; *Toll-Free:* 888-437-0880
hello@autismbc.ca
www.autismbc.ca
www.facebook.com/autismbc
twitter.com/autismbc
To enhance & improve the lives of those affected by autism in BC; To work towards an inclusive society where people on the autism spectrum reach their full potential
Julia Boyle, Director, Operations

Autism Society of PEI
PO Box 3243, Charlottetown PE C1A 8W5
Tel: 902-566-4844; *Toll-Free:* 888-360-8681
www.autismsociety.pe.ca
www.facebook.com/autismsocietypei
To provide austim resources to families in PEI
Nathalie Walsh, Executive Director

Autism Yukon
108 Copper Rd., Whitehorse YT Y1A 2Z6
Tel: 867-667-6406
info@autismyukon.org
www.autismyukon.org
www.facebook.com/162869033819118
twitter.com/yukon_autism
To provide support for individuals & families affected by autism
Leslie Peters, Executive Director

Baby's Breath
PO Box 5005, St Catharines ON L2R 7T4
Tel: 905-688-8884; *Fax:* 905-688-3300
Toll-Free: 800-363-7437
info@babysbreathcanada.ca
www.babysbreathcanada.ca
www.facebook.com/babysbreathca
twitter.com/babysbreathca
To support & represent families in Canada who are coping with the loss of an infant; To promote research on the health or medical conditions associated with infant deaths & stillbirths
Wendy Potter, Chair
Mary Margaret Murphy, Executive Director, marymargaretmurphy@babysbreathcanada.ca

Barth Syndrome Foundation of Canada
#115, 162 Guelph St., Georgetown ON L7G 5X7
Tel: 905-873-2391; *Toll-Free:* 888-732-9458
www.barthsyndrome.ca
www.facebook.com/barthsyndromecanada
To find research grants into the cause, treatments & cure for Barth Syndrome; To assist Canadian families & physicians dealing with the disease
Susan Hone, President

Bladder Cancer Canada (BCC) / Cancer de la vessie Canada
#1000, 4936 Yonge St., Toronto ON M2N 6S3
Toll-Free: 866-674-8889
info@bladdercancercanada.org
www.bladdercancercanada.org
www.youtube.com/user/BladderCancerCA
www.linkedin.com/company/2599127
www.facebook.com/BladderCancerCanada
twitter.com/BladderCancerCA
To improve patient support by having a patient to patient support system in place; To offer information about available treatment options; To create greater awareness of bladder cancer
Ferg Devin, Chair
Tammy Northam, Executive Director

Brain Tumour Foundation of Canada (BTFC) / La Fondation canadienne sur les tumeurs cérébrales
#203, 205 Horton St. East, London ON N6B 1K7
Tel: 519-642-7755; *Fax:* 519-642-7192
Toll-Free: 800-265-5106
www.braintumour.ca
www.youtube.com/BrainTumourFdn
www.linkedin.com/company/braintumourfdn
www.facebook.com/BrainTumourFdn
twitter.com/BrainTumourFdn
To find a cure for brain tumors & to improve the quality of life for those affected; To fund brain tumor research; To provide patient & family support services; To educate the public
Susan Marshall, Chief Executive Officer

Breast Cancer Society of Canada (BCSC) / Société du cancer du sein du Canada
#101, 415 Exmouth St., Sarnia ON N7T 8A4
Tel: 519-336-0746; *Fax:* 519-336-5725
Toll-Free: 800-567-8767
bcsc@bcsc.ca
www.bcsc.ca
www.youtube.com/user/BreastCancerSociety
www.linkedin.com/company/breast-cancer-society-of-canada
www.facebook.com/breastcancersocietyofcanada
twitter.com/bcsc
To support research into the prevention, detection & treatment of breast cancer
Kimberly Carson, Chief Executive Officer

British Columbia Cancer Foundation (BCCF)
#150, 686 West Broadway, Vancouver BC V5Z 1G1
Tel: 604-877-6040; *Fax:* 604-877-6161
Toll-Free: 888-906-2873
bccfinfo@bccancer.bc.ca
www.bccancerfoundation.com
www.youtube.com/user/BCCancerFoundation
www.facebook.com/BCCancerFoundation
twitter.com/bccancerfdn
To reduce the incidence of cancer, reduce the mortality rate from cancer & improve the quality of life for those living with cancer, through the acquisition, development & stewardship of resources
Sara Roth, President & CEO
Luigi (Lou) Del Gobbo, Chief Financial Officer & Vice-President
Allison Colina, Senior Director, Marketing & Communications

British Columbia Centre for Ability Association (BCCFA)
2805 Kingsway, Vancouver BC V5R 5H9
Tel: 604-451-5511; *Fax:* 604-451-5651
www.bc-cfa.org
www.youtube.com/channel/UCIjOVwg7zWgpD5WLT6RNzzA
www.linkedin.com/company/bc-centre-for-ability
twitter.com/bccfa
To provide community-based services that promote inclusion & improve the quality of life for children, youth & adults with disabilities & their families
Jennifer Baumbusch, President

British Columbia Chiropractic Association (BCCA)
#125, 3751 Shell Rd., Richmond BC V6X 2W2
Tel: 604-270-1332; *Fax:* 604-278-0093
Toll-Free: 866-256-1474
info@bcchiro.com
www.bcchiro.com
www.youtube.com/bcchiropractic
www.linkedin.com/company/british-columbia-chiropractic-associ
ation
www.facebook.com/bcchiro
twitter.com/bcchiro
To represent BC chiropractors in matters relating to health
policy, public relations & health authorities
Clark Konczak, President
Angie Knott, Executive Director

British Columbia Doctors of Optometry (BCDO)
121 - 10551 Shellbridge Way, Richmond BC V6X 2W8
Tel: 604-737-9907; *Fax:* 604-737-9967
Toll-Free: 888-393-2226
info@optometrists.bc.ca
bc.doctorsofoptometry.ca
To maintain standards; To represent membership to government
& other health care professions; To raise public levels of
awareness about optometry, good vision & eye care
Pria Sandhu, Chief Executive Officer

British Columbia Lung Association (BCLA)
2675 Oak St., Vancouver BC V6H 2K2
Tel: 604-731-5864; *Fax:* 604-731-5810
Toll-Free: 800-665-5864
info@bc.lung.ca
www.bc.lung.ca
www.facebook.com/BCLungAssociation
twitter.com/BCLungAssoc
To support lung health research, education, prevention &
advocacy; To help people manage respiratory diseases,
including asthma, COPD (chronic bronchitis & emphysema),
lung cancer, sleep apnea & tuberculosis
Christopher Lam, President & CEO
Kelly Ablog-Morrant, Vice-President, Advocacy & Partnerships
Menn Biagtan, Vice-President, Health Programs & Initiatives

British Columbia Lupus Society (BCLS)
#210, 888 West 8th Ave., Vancouver BC V5Z 3Y1
Tel: 604-714-5564; *Toll-Free:* 866-585-8787
info@bclupus.org
www.bclupus.org
To provide education & support to Lupus patients & their friends
& families; To increase public awareness of lupus
Josie Bradley, President

British Columbia Naturopathic Association (BCNA)
2238 Pine St., Vancouver BC V6J 5G4
Tel: 604-736-6646; *Fax:* 604-736-6048
Toll-Free: 800-277-1128
www.bcna.ca
www.youtube.com/user/BCNaturopathicAssoc
www.facebook.com/BCNaturopathicAssociation
twitter.com/BCnaturopath
To act on behalf of the naturopathic profession in British
Columbia; To advance the welfare of members of the profession
Janine Fraser, President
Glenn Cassie, Executive Director

British Columbia Provincial Renal Agency (BCPRA)
#260, 1770 West 7th St., Vancouver BC V6J 4Y6
Tel: 604-875-7340
bcpra@bcpra.ca
www.bcrenalagency.ca
To make BC a leader in kidney care delivery in Canada, through
enhancing the network of kidney care, providing a coordinated
patient-focused information system & monitoring & maintaining
quality & standards of care

British Columbia Transplant Society (BCTS)
#260, 1770 West 7th Ave., Vancouver BC V6J 4Y6
Tel: 604-877-2240; *Fax:* 604-877-2111
Toll-Free: 800-663-6189
info@bct.phsa.ca
www.transplant.bc.ca
www.facebook.com/BCTransplant
twitter.com/bc_transplant
To lead & coordinate all activities related to organ transplantation
& donation, ensuring high standards of quality & efficient
management
Ed Ferre, Executive Director
Tina Robinson, Manager, Communications & Community
Relations

Calgary Health Trust
#800, 11012 Macleod Trail SE, Calgary AB T2J 6A5
Tel: 403-943-0615; *Fax:* 403-943-0628
fundraising@calgaryhealthtrust.ca
www.calgaryhealthtrust.ca
www.youtube.com/user/YYCHealthTrust
www.linkedin.com/company/calgary-health-trust
www.facebook.com/YYCHealthTrust
twitter.com/YYCHealthTrust
To receive & distribute philanthropic health care gifts & funds
across Calgary; To work closely with Alberta Health Services to
identify key priorities for allocation of philanthropic support; To
enhance the development of health care, patient care,
technology, & services at medical centres across Calgary
Jill Olynyk, Chief Executive Officer
Susan Cuerrier, Chief Financial Officer

Canada Health Infoway / Inforoute Santé du Canada
#1200, 1000, rue Sherbrooke ouest, Montréal QC H3A 3G4
Tel: 514-868-0550; *Fax:* 514-868-1120
Toll-Free: 866-868-0550
www.infoway-inforoute.ca
www.youtube.com/user/InfowayInforoute
www.linkedin.com/company/canada-health-infoway
www.facebook.com/CanadaHealthInfoway
twitter.com/infoway
To accelerate the development of compatible electronic health
information systems, which provide healthcare professionals with
rapid access to complete & accurate patient information,
enabling better decisions about diagnosis & treatment
Michael Green, President & CEO

**Canadian Agency for Drugs & Technologies in
Health (CADTH) / Agence canadienne des
médicaments et des technologies de la santé
(ACMTS)**
#300, 154 University Ave., Ottawa ON M5H 3Y9
Tel: 613-226-2553; *Fax:* 866-662-1778
Toll-Free: 866-988-1444
requests@cadth.ca
www.cadth.ca
www.youtube.com/user/CADTHACMTS
www.linkedin.com/company/cadth
www.facebook.com/CADTH.ACMTS
twitter.com/CADTH_ACMTS
To offer evidence-based information & impartial advice to health
care decision makers about the effectiveness of drugs & other
health technologies
Brian O'Rourke, President & CEO

**Canadian Alliance of Physiotherapy Regulators
(CARP) / Alliance canadienne des organismes de
réglementation de la physiothérapie (ACORP)**
#501, 1243 Islington Ave., Toronto ON M8X 1Y9
Tel: 416-234-8800; *Fax:* 416-234-8820
email@alliancept.org
www.alliancept.org
www.facebook.com/1809229349290551
To facilitate the sharing of information & build consensus on
national regulatory issues in order to assist member regulators in
fulfilling their mandate of protecting the public interest
Katya Masnyk, Chief Executive Officer
Diana Sinnige, Director, Policy & Communications

**Canadian Anesthesiologists' Society (CAS) / Société
canadienne des anesthésiologistes (SCA)**
#208, 1 Eglinton Ave. East, Toronto ON M4P 3A1
Tel: 416-480-0602; *Fax:* 416-480-0320
anesthesia@cas.ca
www.cas.ca
www.facebook.com/CanadianAnesthesiologistsSociety
twitter.com/CASUpdate
To advance the medical practice of anesthesia throughout
Canada
Debra M. Thomson, Executive Director
Amanda Cormier, Director, Communications, Marketing &
Events
Iris Li, Director, Finance, HR & IT

**Canadian Association for Clinical Microbiology &
Infectious Diseases (CACMID) / Association
canadienne de microbiologie clinique et des
maladies contagieuses**
c/o National Microbiology Laboratory, 1015 Arlington St.,
Winnipeg MB R3E 3R2
Fax: 204-789-2097
www.cacmid.ca
www.facebook.com/CACMID
To enhance the cooperation of professionals specializing in
clinical microbiology & infectious disease; To act as the voice for
clinical microbiology & infectious disease professionals; To
develop standards in the field of clinical microbiology

**Canadian Association for Health Services & Policy
Research (CAHSPR) / Association canadienne pour
la recherche sur les services et les politiques de la
santé (ACRSPS)**
c/o Face 2 Face Events Management, #105, 555 Legget Dr.,
Ottawa ON K2K 2X3
Tel: 613-288-9239; *Fax:* 613-599-7805
info@cahspr.ca
www.cahspr.ca
www.youtube.com/CAHSPR
twitter.com/CAHSPR
To provide a multidisciplinary association fostering & supporting
linkages between researchers & decision makers; knowledge
translation & exchange; education & training; advocacy for
research & its more effective use in planning, practice &
policy-making
Roxane Borges Da Silva, President
Maggie Keresteci, Executive Director

**Canadian Association for HIV Research (CAHR) /
L'Association Canadienne de recherche sur le HIV
(ACRV)**
#200, 440 Laurier Ave. West, Ottawa ON K1R 7X6
Toll-Free: 888-374-2247
info@cahr-acrv.ca
www.cahr-acrv.ca
www.youtube.com/user/CAHRACRV
www.facebook.com/CanadianAssociationforHIVResearch
twitter.com/CAHR_ACRV
Carol Strike, President
Shariq Haider, Secretary
Marissa Becker, Treasurer
Andrew Matejcic, Executive Director

Canadian Association for Neuroscience (CAN)
2661 Queenswood Dr., Victoria BC V8N 1X6
Tel: 250-472-7644
info@can-acn.org
can-acn.org
www.instagram.com/canneuro
www.facebook.com/can.acn
twitter.com/CAN_ACN
To promote communication among Canadian neuroscientists &
encourage research related to the nervous system; To educate
about current neuroscience research
Julie Poupart, Chief Operating & Advocacy Officer

**Canadian Association for Porphyria, Inc. (CAP) /
Association Canadienne de Porphyrie (ACP)**
canadianassociationforporphyria.ca
To improve the quality of life for Canadians affected by the
porphyrias through programs of awareness, education, service,
advocacy & research; To promoting public & medical
professional awareness; To provide up-to-date educational
information to physicians, health care personnel, diagnosed
patients & others affected by porphyria; To offer support
programs to affected individuals & their families; To promote the
family social welfare of affected individuals; To promote &
provide financial assistance for research
Wendy Sauvé, President

**Canadian Association of Cardio-Pulmonary
Technologists (CACPT)**
PO Box 848, Stn. A, Toronto ON M5W 1G3
contactus@cacpt.ca
www.cacpt.ca
To establish maintain high standards for Registered
Cardio-Pulmonary Technologists
Laura Seed, President

**Canadian Association of Child Neurology (CACN) /
L'Association canadienne de neurologie pédiatrique
(ACNP)**
#709, 7015 Macleod Trail SW, Calgary AB T2H 2K6
Tel: 403-229-9544; *Fax:* 403-229-1661
www.cnsfederation.org
To advance knowledge about the development of the nervous
system from conception, as well as the diseases of the nervous
system in children; To improve treatment of young people with
neurological handicaps
Simon Levin, President

**Canadian Association of Critical Care Nurses
(CACCN) / Association canadienne des infirmières
et infirmiers en soins intensifs (ACIISI)**
PO Box 25322, London ON N6B 6B1
Fax: 519-649-1458
Toll-Free: 866-477-9077
caccn@caccn.ca
www.caccn.ca
www.facebook.com/CanACCN

To engage & inform Canadian critical care nurses through education & networking & provide a strong unified national identity; To develop standards of critical care nursing practice
Christine Halfkenny-Zellas, Chief Operating Officer

Canadian Association of Gastroenterology / Association canadienne de gastroentérologie
#224, 1540 Cornwall Rd., Oakville ON L6J 7W5
Tel: 905-829-2504; *Fax:* 905-829-0242
Toll-Free: 888-780-0007
general@cag-acg.org
www.cag-acg.org
www.linkedin.com/company/canadian-association-of-gastroenterology
www.facebook.com/canadianassociationofgastroenterology
twitter.com/CanGastroAssn
To support & engage in the study of gastroenterology; To promote patient care, research, teaching & professional development in the field; To promote & maintain the highest ethical standards of practice
Paul Sinclair, Executive Director

Canadian Association of General Surgeons (CAGS) / Association canadienne des chirurgiens généraux (ACCG)
#300, 233 Argyle Ave., Ottawa ON K2P 1B8
Tel: 613-882-6510
cags@cags-accg.ca
www.cags-accg.ca
www.facebook.com/220880261312881
twitter.com/CAGS_ACCG
To assist all general surgeons with continuing education; To facilitate & promote surgical research; To develop policies & new ideas in the areas of clinical care, education & research
Dawn Wilson, Executive Director

Canadian Association of Medical Biochemists (CAMB) / Association des médecins biochimistes du Canada (AMBC)
2083 Black Friars Rd., Ottawa ON K2A 3K6
Tel: 613-680-8526; *Fax:* 613-249-3557
camb.ambc@gmail.com
www.camb-ambc.ca
Pierre Douville, President

Canadian Association of Medical Device Reprocessing (CAMDR)
#310, 4 Cataraqui St., Kingston ON K7K 1Z7
info@camdr.ca
www.camdr.ca
www.facebook.com/CAMDRCanada
twitter.com/CAMDR_Canada
To address issues including patient safety, infection prevention & control, technology assessments, vendor relations, organizational management & education
Albert Csapó, President

Canadian Association of Medical Oncologists (CAMO) / Association canadienne des oncologues médicaux (ACOM)
PO Box 35164, Stn. Westgate, 1309 Carling Ave., Ottawa ON K1Z 1A2
Tel: 613-415-6033; *Fax:* 866-839-7501
info@camo-acom.ca
camo-acom.ca
Bruce Colwell, President, bruce.colwell@nshealth.ca
Alexi Campbell, Executive Director
Sharlene Gill, Secretary-Treasurer

Canadian Association of Medical Radiation Technologists (CAMRT) / Association canadienne des technologues en radiation médicale (ACTRM)
#1300, 180 Elgin St., Ottawa ON K2P 2K3
Tel: 613-234-0012; *Fax:* 613-234-1097
Toll-Free: 800-463-9729
info@camrt.ca
www.camrt.ca
www.linkedin.com/company/canadian-association-of-medical-radiation-technologists
www.facebook.com/CAMRTactrm
twitter.com/CAMRT_ACTRM
To act as the certifying body for medical radiation technologists & therapists throughout Canada
Irving Gold, Chief Executive Officer

The Canadian Association of Naturopathic Doctors (CAND) / Association canadienne des docteurs en naturopathie
#200, 20 Holly St., Toronto ON M2S 3B1
Tel: 416-496-8633; *Fax:* 416-496-8634
Toll-Free: 800-551-4381
www.cand.ca
www.facebook.com/NaturopathicDrs
twitter.com/naturopathicdrs
To promote naturopathic medicine to the public, insurance companies & corporations; To encourage professional, educational & networking activities among its members, & standardization of educational requirements for practitioners
Shawn O'Reilly, Executive Director

Canadian Association of Neuropathologists (CANP) / Association canadienne de neuropathologistes
c/o Service d'Anatomo-pathologie, CHA Hopital de l'Enfant-Jesus, 1401, 18e rue, Québec QC G1J 1Z4
Tel: 418-649-5725; *Fax:* 418-649-5856
www.canp.ca
To promote the professional & educational objectives of neuropathologists; To ensure high standards in the neuropathology field
Peter Gould, President
Peter Schutz, Secretary-Treasurer

Canadian Association of Nuclear Medicine (CANM) / Association canadienne de médecine nucléaire (ACMN)
PO Box 4383, Stn. E, Ottawa ON K1S 2L0
Tel: 613-882-5097
canm@canm-acmn.ca
www.canm-acmn.ca
To strive for excellence in the practice of diagnostic & therapeutic nuclear medicine; To promote the continued professional competence of nuclear medicine specialists; To establish guidelines of clinical practice; To encourage biomedical research
Francois Lamoureux, President
Denise Chan, Vice-President
Salem Yuoness, Secretary-Treasurer

Canadian Association of Occupational Therapists (CAOT) / Association canadienne des ergothérapeutes (ACE)
#100, 34 Colonnade Rd., Ottawa ON K2E 7J6
Tel: 613-523-2268; *Fax:* 613-523-2552
Toll-Free: 800-434-2268
membership@caot.ca
www.caot.ca
www.instagram.com/caotace
www.linkedin.com/company/the-canadian-association-of-occupational-therapists-caot
www.facebook.com/CAOT.ca
twitter.com/CAOT_ACE
To develop & promote the profession of occupational therapy in Canada & abroad; To assist occupational therapists achieve excellence in their professional practice by offering services, products, events & networking opportunities
Hélène Sabourin, Interim Executive Director
Havelin Anand, Director, Government Affairs & Policy
Pat Underwood, Director, Communications
Karen Tittonel, Director, Finance
Randy St. Louis, Manager, Business Development & Marketing

Canadian Association of Occupational Therapists - British Columbia (CAOT-BC)
c/o National Office, #100, 34 Colonnade Rd., Ottawa ON K2E 7J6
Tel: 613-523-2268; *Fax:* 613-523-2552
Toll-Free: 800-434-2268
www.caot.ca/default.asp?pageid=4125
www.facebook.com/caotbc
twitter.com/Caot_bc
To promote the profession of occupational therapy throughout the province & represent its members to regional health boards & government, health professional groups & the public; To foster the growth & development of the profession in BC; To provide a variety of services to its members including continuing education, reentry & participation in professional issues
Tanya Fawkes, Managing Director

Canadian Association of Optometrists (CAO) / Association canadienne des optométristes (ACO)
234 Argyle Ave., Ottawa ON K2P 1B9
Tel: 613-235-7924; *Fax:* 613-235-2098
Toll-Free: 888-263-4676
info@opto.ca
www.opto.ca
www.facebook.com/CanadianOpto
twitter.com/CanadianOpto

To represent & assist the profession of optometry in Canada; To improve the quality, availability & accessibility of vision & eye care
Francois Couillard, Chief Executive Officer
Ibrahim Daibes, Director, Policy, Research & Advocacy
Jeanne Franche, Director, Finance & Operations
Rhona Lahey, Director, Communications & Marketing

Canadian Association of Oral & Maxillofacial Surgeons (CAOMS) / Association canadienne de spécialistes en chirurgie buccale et maxillo-faciale (ACSCBMF)
#100, 32 Colonnade Rd., Ottawa ON K2E 7J6
Tel: 613-721-1816; *Fax:* 613-721-3581
Toll-Free: 888-369-5641
caoms@caoms.com
www.caoms.com
To support & meet the needs of oral & maxillofacial surgeons in Canada
Kevin McCann, President
Pierre-Éric Landry, Executive Director

Canadian Association of Paediatric Surgeons (CAPS) / Association de la chirurgie infantile canadienne
c/o Children's Hospital of Western Ontario, 800 Commissioners Rd. East, London ON N6G 2S1
Tel: 519-685-8401; *Fax:* 519-685-8421
admin@caps.ca
www.caps.ca
www.facebook.com/CAPSsurgeons
twitter.com/CAPSsurgeons
To improve the surgical care of infants & children in Canada
Sarah Jones, Secretary-Treasurer

Canadian Association of Pathologists (CAP) / Association canadienne des pathologistes (ACP)
#310, 4 Cataraqui St., Kingston ON K7K 1Z7
Tel: 613-507-8528; *Fax:* 866-531-0626
info@cap-acp.org
cap-acp.org
www.linkedin.com/in/capacp
www.facebook.com/canadian.association.pathologists
twitter.com/CAPACP
To maintain high standards for patient practices & care for pathologists & laboratory medicine
Catherine Ross, President
Heather Dow, Executive Director

Canadian Association of Radiologists (CAR) / L'Association canadienne des radiologistes
#600, 294 Albert St., Ottawa ON K1P 6E6
Tel: 613-860-3111; *Fax:* 613-860-3112
info@car.ca
www.car.ca
www.linkedin.com/company/canadian-association-of-radiologists
www.facebook.com/CARadiologists
twitter.com/CARadiologists
To represent the goals & the interests of imaging specialists; To promote the clinical, educational, research & political goals of Canadian radiology to members, organized radiology, medical associations, government & the public
Nick Neuheimer, Chief Executive Officer

Canadian Association of Thoracic Surgeons (CATS) / Association canadienne des chirurgiens thoraciques
PO Box 175, 501 Smyth Rd., Ottawa ON K1H 8L6
cats@canadianthoracicsurgeons.ca
www.canadianthoracicsurgeons.ca
www.linkedin.com/company/canadian-association-of-thoracic-surgeons
twitter.com/ThoracicsCanada
To enable thoracic surgeons in Canada to provide the highest level of care to patients; To promote excellence in patient centered care & enhance quality through education, research & advocacy
Andrew Seely, President
Gail Darling, Vice-President
John Dickie, Secretary-Treasurer

Canadian Association of Transplantation
114 Cheyenne Way, Ottawa ON K2J 0E9
Toll-Free: 877-968-9449
admin@cst-transplant.ca
www.cst-transplant.ca
twitter.com/cst_transplant
To facilitate & enhance physicians in the transplant process
S. Joseph Kim, President
Jeffrey Schiff, Vice-President
Aviva Goldberg, Secretary
Jagbir Gill, Treasurer

Canadian Blood Services (CBS) / Société canadienne du sang
1800 Alta Vista Dr., Ottawa ON K1G 4J5
Tel: 613-739-2300; Fax: 613-731-1411
Toll-Free: 888-236-6283
feedback@blood.ca
www.blood.ca
www.youtube.com/18882DONATE
www.linkedin.com/company/canadian-blood-services
www.facebook.com/CanadasLifeline
twitter.com/CanadasLifeline
To manage the blood supply for Canadians; To ensure blood safety
Mel Cappe, Chair
Graham D. Sher, Chief Executive Officer

Canadian Brain Tumour Tissue Bank
London Health Sciences Centre, University of Western Ontario, 339 Windermere Rd., #C7108, London ON N6A 5A5
Tel: 519-663-3427; Fax: 519-663-2930
www.braintumor.ca
To supply optimally collected brain tumour tissue to researchers all over the country, internationally & locally in the hopes that some day the cause of & the cure for brain tumours will be found
Marcela White, Coordinator

Canadian Cancer Research Alliance (CCRA) / Alliance canadienne pour la recherche sur le cancer (ACRC)
#900, 145 King St. West, Toronto ON M5H 1J8
info@ccra-acrc.ca
www.ccra-acrc.ca
www.linkedin.com/company/canadian-cancer-research-alliance
twitter.com/ccralliance
To foster partnerships & promote the development of national research priorities; To coordinate funding
Cindy L. Bell, Chair
Sara Urowitz, MSW, PhD, Executive Director

Canadian Cancer Society (CCS) / Société canadienne du cancer
National Office, #500, 55 St. Clair Ave. West, Toronto ON M4V 2Y7
Tel: 416-961-7223; Fax: 416-961-4189
Toll-Free: 888-939-3333
ccs@cancer.ca
www.cancer.ca
www.youtube.com/user/CDNCancerSociety
www.facebook.com/canadiancancersociety
twitter.com/cancersociety
To collect donations to fund cancer research in Canada; To disseminate information on cancer prevention & treatments, advocating for healthy environment & lifestyle to reduce the incidence of cancer; To offer individual & group support programs for caregivers, family & friends of cancer patients
Robert Lawrie, Chair
Andrea Seale, Chief Executive Officer
Sara Oates, Executive Vice-President, Finance & Operations
Paula Roberts, Executive Vice-President, Marketing & Communications

Canadian Cancer Society Research Institute
#300, 55 St. Clair Ave. West, Toronto ON M4V 2Y7
Tel: 416-961-7223; Fax: 416-961-4189
research@cancer.ca
www.cancer.ca/research
To act as a strong voice in the cancer research community; To support a broad range of projects that involve Canadian investigators across the spectrum of cancer research
Judy Bray, Vice-President, Research
Lori Moser, Manager, Research Programs

Canadian Cancer Survivor Network (CCSN)
#210, 1750 Courtwood Cres., Ottawa ON K2C 2B5
Tel: 613-898-1871
info@survivornet.ca
survivornet.ca
www.facebook.com/CanadianSurvivorNet
twitter.com/survivornetca
To help cancer patients & their families cope with their situation; To educate the public about the costs of cancer
Jackie Manthorne, President & CEO
Mona Forrest, Manager, Operations

Canadian Cannabis Nurses Association (CCNA) / Association canadienne des infirmières et infirmiers pour le cannabis
Victoria BC
cannabisnurses@gmail.com
www.canadiancannabisnursesassociation.com
www.facebook.com/CanadianCannaNursesAssociation
twitter.com/CCNACanad

To help nurses to support patients by providing education on endocannabinoid medicine
Kelly Insley, Founder & President

Canadian Cardiovascular Society (CCS) / Société canadienne de cardiologie
#1100, 222 Queen St., Ottawa ON K1P 5V9
Tel: 613-569-3407; Fax: 613-569-6574
Toll-Free: 877-569-3407
info@ccs.ca
www.ccs.ca
www.facebook.com/SCC.CCS.ca
twitter.com/SCC_CCS
To promote cardiovascular health & care through knowledge translation, dissemination of research & encouragement of best practices, professional development & leadership in health policy
Andrew D. Krahn, President
Carolyn Pullen, Chief Executive Officer

Canadian Celiac Association (CCA) / L'Association canadienne de la maladie coeliaque
#503, 1450 Meyerside Dr., Mississauga ON L5T 2N5
Tel: 905-507-6208; Fax: 905-507-4673
Toll-Free: 800-363-7296
info@celiac.ca
www.celiac.ca
www.pinterest.ca/canadianceliac
www.facebook.com/CCAceliac
twitter.com/ccaceliac
To increase awareness of celiac & dermatitis herpetiformis among government institutions, health care professionals & the public; To provide information about the disease & a gluten-free diet; To encourge research through the establishment of the J.A. Campbell Research Fund
Treena Duncan, President

Canadian Chiropractic Association (CCA) / Association chiropratique canadienne (ACC)
#6, 186 Spadina Ave., Toronto ON M5T 3B2
Tel: 416-585-7902; Fax: 416-585-2970
Toll-Free: 877-222-9303
info@chiropractic.ca
www.chiropractic.ca
www.youtube.com/CanChiroAssoc
www.linkedin.com/company/canadian-chiropractic-association
www.facebook.com/canadianchiropracticassociation
twitter.com/CanChiroAssoc
To see every Canadian have full & equitable access to chiropractic care; To promote the integration of chiropractic care into the Canadian health care system
Alison Dantas, Chief Executive Officer
Tari Stork, Director, Public Affairs

Canadian Coalition for Genetic Fairness (CCGF) / Coalition Canadienne pour L'Équité Génétique (CCEG)
#801, 20 Erb St. West, Waterloo ON N2L 1T2
Fax: 519-749-8965
Toll-Free: 800-998-7398
info@ccgf-cceg.ca
www.ccgf-cceg.ca
www.facebook.com/FightingGeneticDiscrimination
twitter.com/GeneticFairness
To prevent genetic discrimination for Canadians

Canadian College of Health Leaders (CCHL) / Collège canadien des leaders en santé (CCLS)
#1102, 150 Isabella St., Ottawa ON K1S 1V7
Tel: 613-235-7218; Fax: 613-235-5451
Toll-Free: 800-363-9056
info@cchl-ccls.ca
www.cchl-ccls.ca
www.youtube.com/HealthLeadersCanada
www.linkedin.com/company/canadian-college-of-health-leaders
www.facebook.com/CCHL.National
twitter.com/CCHL_CCLS
To advance excellence in health leadership; To act as a collective voice for the profession
Alain Doucet, President & CEO
Jaime Cleroux, Vice-President, Corporate Partnership Excellence
Tatjana Solowjew, Director, Finance
Christian Coulombe, Director, Marketing & Communications
Kathy Ivey, Manager, Marketing & Communications

Canadian College of Medical Geneticists (CCMG) / Collège canadien de généticiens médicaux
#310, 4 Cataraqui St., Kingston ON K7K 1Z7
Tel: 613-507-8345; Fax: 866-303-0626
info@ccmg-ccgm.org
www.ccmg-ccgm.org
To establish & maintain professional & ethical standards for medical genetics services in Canada; To certify individuals who

provide medical genetics services; To encourage research activities
Tracy Stockley, President
Marjan Nezarati, Treasurer

Canadian Critical Care Society (CCCS) / Société canadienne de soins intensifs (SCSI)
#6, 20 Crown Steel Dr., Toronto ON L3R 9X9
Tel: 905-604-0166; Fax: 905-415-0071
Toll-Free: 855-415-3917
cccs@secretariatcentral.com
www.canadiancriticalcare.org
www.facebook.com/CritCareSociety
twitter.com/CritCareSociety
To promote & develop critical care medicine in Canada
Bojan Paunovic, President

Canadian Dermatology Association (CDA) / Association canadienne de dermatologie (ACD)
#425, 1385 Bank St., Ottawa ON K1H 8N4
Tel: 613-738-1748; Fax: 613-738-4695
Toll-Free: 800-267-3376
info@dermatology.ca
www.dermatology.ca
www.youtube.com/user/canadiandermatology
www.linkedin.com/company/canadian-dermatology-association
www.facebook.com/CdnDermatology
twitter.com/cdndermatology
To advance the science of medicine & surgery related to the health of the skin; To support & advance patient care; To represent dermatologists in Canada
Kerri Purdy, President
Linda M. Jones, Interim Chief Executive Officer

Canadian Down Syndrome Society (CDSS) / Société canadienne du syndrome de Down
#103, 2003 - 14 St. NW, Calgary AB T2M 3N4
Tel: 403-270-8500; Fax: 403-270-8291
Toll-Free: 800-883-5608
www.cdss.ca
www.youtube.com/user/CdnDownSyndrome
www.facebook.com/cdndownsyndrome
twitter.com/CdnDownSyndrome
To ensure equitable opportunities for all Canadians with Down Syndrome
Ed Casagrande, Chair
Kirk Crowther, Executive Director

Canadian Dyslexia Association (CDA) / Association canadienne de la dyslexie
207 Bayswater Ave., Ottawa ON K1Y 2G5
Tel: 613-853-6539; Fax: 819-684-0672
info@dyslexiaassociation.ca
www.dyslexiaassociation.ca

Canadian Epilepsy Alliance (CAE) / L'Alliance canadienne de l'épilepsie (ACE)
Toll-Free: 866-374-5377
www.canadianepilepsyalliance.org
www.instagram.com/ceaofficialnews
www.linkedin.com/company/canadian-epilepsy-alliance
www.facebook.com/ceaofficialnews
twitter.com/ceaofficialnews
To promote independence & quality of life for people with epilepsy & their families, through support services, information, advocacy & public awareness
Deidre Floyd, President

Canadian Fabry Association / L'association canadienne de fabry
748 Kelly St., Thunder Bay ON P7E 2A1
www.fabrycanada.com
www.instagram.com/canadianfabryassociation
www.facebook.com/canadianfabryassociation
twitter.com/CdnFabry
To educate the public & offer information on treatments; To encourage & support research; To increase facilities for those suffering from the disease
Julia Alton, Executive Director

Canadian Federation of Aromatherapists / La fédération canadienne d'aromathérapistes
PO Box 10059, Stn. Alcona Beach, Innisfil ON L9S 4Y7
Tel: 613-330-6395; Fax: 519-746-9493
cfamanager@cfacanada.com
www.cfacanada.com
www.facebook.com/CanadianAromatherapy
To maintain a register of aromatherapy practitioners, schools & instructors who meet established minimum standards; To act as a unified voice of the profession; To maintain the highest ethical standards of the profession
Krista Grear, President

Canadian Foundation for Dietetic Research (CFDF)
c/o Dietitians of Canada, 99 Yorkville Ave., 2nd Fl., Toronto ON M5R 1C1

Tel: 416-642-9309; *Fax:* 416-596-0603
info@cfdr.ca
www.cfdr.ca

To provide grants for research in dietetics & nutrition
Pierrette Buklis, Chair
Janis Randall Simpson, Executive Director

Canadian Health Coalition (CHC) / Coalition canadienne de la santé
#300, 116 Albert St., Ottawa ON K1P 5G3

Tel: 613-699-9898
hello@healthcoalition.ca
www.healthcoalition.ca
www.youtube.com/user/HealthCoalition
www.facebook.com/CanadianHealthCoalition
twitter.com/healthcoalition

To create good health; To preserve & strengthen the Canada Health Act, the foundation of Medicare; To make the health care system democratic, accountable & representative; To provide a continuum of care from large institutions to the home; To protect our investment in the skills & abilities of our health care workers; To ensure fair wages for all health care providers; To eliminate profit-making from illness; To reduce over-prescribing & make drugs affordable; To stop fee-for-service payments; To expand methods of health care & the role of non-physician health providers
Amélie Baillargeon, National Director, Operations & Projects
Melanie Benard, National Director, Policy & Advocacy

Canadian Hematology Society (CHS) / Société canadienne d'hématologie
#199, 435 St. Laurent Blvd., Ottawa ON K1K 2Z8

Tel: 613-748-9613; *Fax:* 613-748-6392
office@canadianhematologysociety.org
www.canadianhematologysociety.org

To represent members of the Society & provide information about hematology
Nicole Laferriere, President

Canadian Hemochromatosis Society (CHS) / Société canadienne de l'hémochromatose
#285, 7000 Minoru Blvd., Richmond BC V6Y 3Z5

Tel: 604-279-7135; *Fax:* 604-279-7138
Toll-Free: 877-223-4766
office@toomuchiron.ca
www.toomuchiron.ca
www.youtube.com/user/toomuchiron
www.facebook.com/TooMuchIron
twitter.com/IronOutCanada

To increase awareness among the public & medical community with regards to the importance of family screening, early diagnosis & treatment of Hemochromatosis
Paul Johnston, President & Chair

Canadian Hemophilia Society (CHS) / Société canadienne de l'hémophilie (SCH)
#301, 666, rue Sherbrooke ouest, Montréal QC H3A 1E7

Tel: 514-848-0503; *Fax:* 514-848-9661
Toll-Free: 800-668-2686
chs@hemophilia.ca
www.hemophilia.ca
www.youtube.com/user/CanadianHemophilia
www.facebook.com/CanadianHemophiliaSociety
twitter.com/CHShemophilia

To improve the health & quality of life of all people in Canada with inherited bleeding disorders; To find cures for inherited bleeding disorders; To achieve a world free from the pain & suffering of inherited bleeding disorders
Hélène Bourgaize, National Co-Executive Director

Canadian Hospice Palliative Care Association (CHPCA) / Association canadienne de soins palliatifs (ACSP)
Annex D, Saint-Vincent Hospital, 60 Cambridge St. North, Ottawa ON K1R 7A5

Tel: 613-241-3663; *Fax:* 613-241-3986
Toll-Free: 800-668-2785
info@chpca.net
www.chpca.net
www.facebook.com/CanadianHospicePalliativeCare
twitter.com/CanadianHPCAssn

To be the national leader in the pursuit of quality hospice palliative care in Canada through: public policy, education, knowledge translation, awareness, & collaboration; To ensure that all Canadians have access to quality hospice palliative care
Sharon Baxter, Executive Director

Canadian Hypnosis Association (CHA)
www.canadianhypnosisassociation.ca

To determine standards for hypnotherapy in Canada; To promote the therapeutic value of hypnosis
Detlef Joe Friede, President

Canadian Institute of Public Health Inspectors (CIPHI) / Institut Canadien des inspecteurs en santé publique (ICISP)
#720, 999 West Broadway Ave., Vancouver BC V5Z 1K5

Tel: 604-739-8180; *Fax:* 604-738-4080
Toll-Free: 888-245-8180
office@ciphi.ca
www.ciphi.ca
www.facebook.com/CIPHI.ICISP
twitter.com/ciphi_national

To protect the health of all Canadians; To advance the environmental & health sciences; To enhance the field of public health inspection through certification, information & advocacy
Kari Engele-Carter, National President

Canadian League Against Epilepsy (CLAE)
c/o Secretariat Central, #6, 20 Crown Steel Dr., Markham ON L3R 9X9

Tel: 905-415-3917
clae@secretariatcentral.com
www.claegroup.org
www.facebook.com/CLAE.Epilepsy
twitter.com/CLAE_LCCE

To help Canadians affected by epilepsy; To develop therapeutic & preventative strategies to prevent the effects of epilepsy
Dang Nguyen, President
Esther Bui, Secretary
Paula Brna, Treasurer

Canadian Liver Foundation (CLF) / Fondation canadienne du foie (FCF)
#801, 3100 Steeles Ave. East, Toronto ON L3R 8T3

Tel: 416-491-3353; *Fax:* 905-752-1540
Toll-Free: 800-563-5483
clf@liver.ca
www.liver.ca
www.youtube.com/user/clfwebmaster
www.facebook.com/CanadianLiverFoundation
twitter.com/CdnLiverFdtn

To reduce the incidence & impact of all liver disease by funding liver research & education; To promote liver health through programs & publications
Jennifer Nebesky, President & CEO
Veronica Herfindahl, National Director, Marketing & Communications
Nem Maksimovic, National Director, Health Promotion & Education
Karen Seto, National Director, Research & Education

Canadian Lung Association (CLA) / Association pulmonaire du Canada
National Office, #502, 885 Meadowlands Dr., Ottawa ON K2C 3N2

Tel: 613-569-6411; *Toll-Free:* 888-566-5864
info@lung.ca
www.lung.ca
www.youtube.com/user/TheLungAssociation
www.facebook.com/canadianlungassociation
twitter.com/canlung

To improve & promote lung health across Canada
Terry Dean, President & Chief Executive Officer
Monte Weber, Chief Financial Officer
Marketa Stastna, Manager, Communications & Marketing

Canadian Lyme Disease Foundation / Fondation canadienne de la maladie de lyme
www.canlyme.org
www.facebook.com/CanLyme
twitter.com/canlyme

To advance research about Lyme Disease in Canada
Jim Wilson, President & Founder

Canadian Massage Therapist Alliance (CMTA) / Alliance Canadienne de Massothérapeutes
#22, 1738 Quebec Ave., Saskatoon SK S7K 1V9

Tel: 306-384-7077
info@crmta.ca
www.crmta.ca
www.facebook.com/CRMTA

To foster & advance the art, science & philosophy of massage therapy through nationwide cooperation in a professional, ethical & practical manner for the betterment of health care in Canada

Canadian Medical Association (CMA) / Association médicale canadienne (AMC)
1410 Blair Towers Pl., Ottawa ON K1J 9B9

Tel: 613-731-8610
cmamsc@cma.ca
www.cma.ca
www.youtube.com/user/CanadianMedicalAssoc
www.linkedin.com/company/canadian-medical-association
www.facebook.com/CanadianMedicalAssociation
twitter.com/CMA_Docs

To act as the national voice of physicians in Canada; To serve the Canadian medical community; To promote the highest standards of health & health care
Suzanne Strasberg, Chair
Katharine Smart, President
Tim Smith, CEO
Jimmy Mui, COO & CFO
Owen Adams, Senior Advisor to the CEO
Jeff Blackmer, Executive Vice-President, International Health
John Feeley, Executive Vice-President, Engagement & Partners
Luce Lavoie, Executive Vice-President, Enterprise Marketing & Communications
Joseph Mayer, Executive Vice-President, Access to Care
Jean Nelson, Exec. Vice-President & Chief Privacy Officer, Legal & Governance
Deborah Scott-Douglas, Executive Vice-President, Innovation

Canadian Medical Foundation (CMF) / La Fondation médicale canadienne
720 Bathurst St., Ottawa ON M5S 2R4

Tel: 613-518-6010
info@cmf.ca
www.medicalfoundation.ca
www.youtube.com/CdnMedicalFoundation
www.linkedin.com/company/canadian-medical-foundation
www.facebook.com/Canadianmedicalfoundation1
twitter.com/CdnMedicalFound

To improve health outcomes in Canada by providing programs for vulnerables communities, offering assistance to physicians-in-training & other organizations & engaging in philanthropic activity
Lee Gould, President & CEO

The Canadian Medical Protective Association (CMPA) / Association canadienne de protection médicale
PO Box 8225, Stn. T, Ottawa ON K1G 3H7

Tel: 613-725-2000; *Fax:* 613-725-1300
Toll-Free: 800-267-6522
inquiries@cmpa.org
www.cmpa-acpm.ca
www.youtube.com/user/cmpamembers
www.linkedin.com/company/canadian-medical-protective-association
twitter.com/CMPAmembers

To offer advice, assistance, & resources to members facing medical-legal issues; To provide compensation to patients proven to have been hurt by negligent care
Hartley Stern, MD, FRCSC, FACS, Executive Director & CEO
Stephen M. Bryan, OMM, CPA, CMA, Chief Financial Officer & Managing Director, Enterprise Management
W. Todd Watkins, BSc(Hon), MD, C, Managing Director, Physician Services
Pascale Belleau, M.A., M.Sc., Director, Communications
Leah Keith, Acting Director, Human Resources

Canadian MedicAlert Foundation / Fondation canadienne MedicAlert
Morneau Shepell Centre II, #600, 895 Don Mills Rd., Toronto ON M3C 1W3

Tel: 416-696-0267; *Fax:* 800-392-8422
Toll-Free: 800-668-1507
customerservice@medicalert.ca
www.medicalert.ca
www.youtube.com/medicalertCA
www.facebook.com/medicalertcanada
twitter.com/medicalertCA

To provide lifelong access to personal & medical information in order to protect & save the lives of its members; To provide Canadians with medical protection in an emergency situation
Françoise Fortin-Faverjon, President & CEO

Canadian Memorial Chiropractic College (CMCC)
6100 Leslie St., Toronto ON M2H 3J1

Tel: 416-482-2340; *Fax:* 416-646-1114
Toll-Free: 800-463-2923
communications@cmcc.ca
www.cmcc.ca

To deliver world class chiropractic education, research, & patient care
David Wickes, President

Mara Bartolucci, AVP, Institutional Advancement & Communications

Canadian Natural Health Association (CNHA)
#105, 5 Wakunda Pl., Toronto ON M4A 1A2
Tel: 416-686-7056
To establish leadership in healthy, natural lifestyle education & support services; to assist by providing resources to help make people healthier

Canadian Network of Palliative Care for Children (CNPCC) / Reseau canadien de soins palliatifs pour les enfants
c/o Canadian Hospice Palliative Care Assn., Saint-Vincent Hospital, 60 Cambridge St. North, Ottawa ON K1R 7A5
Tel: 613-241-3663; Fax: 613-241-3986
Toll-Free: 800-668-2785
www.chpca.net
www.facebook.com/CanadianHospicePalliativeCare
twitter.com/CanadianHPCAssn
To improve palliative care for infants, children, & youth

Canadian Neurological Sciences Federation (CNSF) / Fédération des sciences neurologiques du Canada
#143N, 8500 Macleod Trail SE, Calgary AB T2H 2N1
Tel: 403-229-9544; Fax: 403-229-1661
www.cnsfederation.org
www.facebook.com/CNSFNeuroLinks
twitter.com/CNSFNeuroLinks
To support the neuroscience professions in Canada, particularly those members of the CNSF Societies, through education, advocacy, membership services & research promotion
Dan Morin, Chief Executive Officer
Marika Fitzgerald, Manager, Finance & Administration
Donna Irvin, Administrator, Membership Services

Canadian Neurological Society (CNS) / Société canadienne de neurologie
#709, 7015 Macleod Trail SW, Calgary AB T2H 2K1
Tel: 403-229-9544; Fax: 403-229-1661
www.cnsfederation.org
To promote & encourage all aspects of neurology, including research, education, assessment & accreditation; provide for annual scientific sessions to promote the knowledge & practice of neurology
Dan Morin, CNSF CEO

Canadian Occupational Therapy Foundation (COTF) / La Fondation canadienne d'ergothérapie (FCE)
#64, 2420 Bank St., Ottawa ON K1V 8S1
Tel: 613-319-6890
www.cotfcanada.org
To fund & promote research & scholarship in occupational therapy in Canada
Sangita Kamblé, Executive Director
Anne McDonald, Executive Assistant

Canadian Ophthalmological Society (COS) / Société canadienne d'opthalmologie (SCO)
#110, 2733 Lancaster Rd., Ottawa ON K1B 0A9
Tel: 613-729-6779; Fax: 613-729-7209
cos@cos-sco.ca
www.cos-sco.ca
To assure the provision of optimal eye care to all Canadians by promoting excellence in ophthalmology & providing services to support its members in practice
Elisabeth Fowler, Chief Executive Officer
Eric Johnson, Manager, Communications & Public Affairs

Canadian Organization for Rare Disorders (CORD)
#600, 151 Bloor St. West, Toronto ON M5S 1S4
Tel: 416-969-7464; Fax: 416-969-7420
Toll-Free: 877-302-7273
info@raredisorders.ca
raredisorders.ca
www.youtube.com/user/CORDRareDisorders
www.facebook.com/RareDisorders
twitter.com/raredisorders
To advocate for health policy that works for people with rare disorders; to promote research & services for all rare disorders in Canada; To increase access to genetic screening & genetic counselling for rare disorders
Durhane Wong-Rieger, President & CEO

Canadian Orthopaedic Association (COA) / Association canadienne d'orthopédie
#620, 4060, rue Sainte-Catherine ouest, Westmount QC H3Z 2Z3
Tel: 514-874-9003; Fax: 514-874-0464
info@canorth.org
www.coa-aco.org
www.instagram.com/coa.aco
www.linkedin.com/in/coaaco
twitter.com/CdnOrthoAssoc
To provide continuing medical education & training for orthopaedic surgeons
Cynthia Vezina, Chief Executive Officer

Canadian Orthopaedic Foundation (COF) / Fondation orthopédique du Canada (FOC)
PO Box 1036, Toronto ON M5K 1P2
Tel: 416-410-2341; Fax: 416-352-5078
Toll-Free: 800-461-3639
mailbox@canorth.org
whenithurtstomove.org
www.facebook.com/OrthopaedicFoundation
twitter.com/canorthofound
To foster excellence in the provision of health care to patients with musculoskeletal disease or injury, in a cost effective manner, based on significant outcome studies, by supporting research, educating its members & securing funding from government & other health care funding agencies
Pierre Guy, Chair & President
Isla Horvath, Executive Director & CEO

Canadian Orthoptic Council / Conseil canadien d'orthoptique
CHUL, 2705, boul Laurier, Sainte-Foy QC G1V 4G2
Fax: 418-654-2188
info@orthopticscanada.org
www.orthopticscanada.org
To establish standards in the training of orthoptic students; To establish standards for orthoptic training centres; To provide examinations of orthoptic students in order to determine their proficiency in orthopotics & to award a certificate of competency to qualified students who pass the examinations; To require evidence of continuing education of certified orthoptists; To establish standards for the professional ethical conduct of certified orthoptists
Louis-Etienne Marcoux, Secretary-Treasurer
Ann Haver, Administrative Coordinator

Canadian Paediatric Society (CPS) / Société canadienne de pédiatrie
#100, 2305 St. Laurent Blvd., Ottawa ON K1G 4J8
Tel: 613-526-9397; Fax: 613-526-3332
www.cps.ca
www.youtube.com/canpaedsociety
www.linkedin.com/company/canadian-paediatric-society
www.facebook.com/CanPaedSociety
twitter.com/canpaedsociety
To advocate for the health needs of children & youth; To provide continuing education to paediatricians; To establish national guidelines for paediatric care & practice
Ellen P. Wood, President
Marie Adèle Davis, Executive Director
Elizabeth Moreau, Director, Communications & Knowledge Translation

Canadian Pain Society / Société canadienne pour le traitement de la douleur
#301, 250 Consumers Rd., Toronto ON M2J 4V6
Tel: 416-642-6379; Fax: 416-495-8723
office@canadianpainsociety.ca
www.canadianpainsociety.ca
www.facebook.com/CanadianPain
twitter.com/canadianpain
To foster research on pain; To improve the management of patients with acute & chronic pain
Fiona Campbell, President
Eloise Carr, Secretary
Mojgan Hodaie, Treasurer

Canadian Partnership Against Cancer
#900, 145 King St. West, Toronto ON M5H 1J8
Tel: 416-915-9222; Fax: 416-915-9224
Toll-Free: 877-360-1665
info@partnershipagainstcancer.ca
www.partnershipagainstcancer.ca
www.youtube.com/CanadianPartnershipAgainstCancer
linkedin.com/company/canadian-partnership-against-cancer
www.facebook.com/CanadianPartnershipAgainstCancer
twitter.com/CancerStratCA
To advance cancer control in Canada; To reduce instances of cancer & deaths caused by cancer; To influence policy & practice throughout Canada in order to improve the lives of

individuals with cancer; To assist provinces & territories in developing cancer management strategies
Cynthia Morton, Chief Executive Officer
Nicole Beben, Vice-President, Strategy
Craig Earle, Vice-President, Cancer Control
David Lynch, Vice-President, Finance & Corporate Services

Canadian Pediatric Foundation (CPF) / La fondation canadienne de pédiatrie
#100, 2305 St. Laurent Blvd., Ottawa ON K1G 4J8
Tel: 613-526-9397; Fax: 613-526-3332
www.cps.ca
www.youtube.com/canpaedsociety
www.linkedin.com/company/canadian-paediatric-society
www.facebook.com/CanPaedSociety
twitter.com/canpaedsociety
To promote improved health care & social well-being for the children of Canada, particularly for disadvantaged groups; To promote better standards of health care for children throughout the world, particularly where Canadian aid is active
Marie Adèle Davis, Executive Director
Elizabeth Moreau, Director, Communications & Knowledge Translation
Jackie Millette, Director, Education, Committees & Sections
Bonnie Sowiak, Director, Finance & Administration

Canadian Physiotherapy Association (CPA) / L'Association canadienne de physiothérapie
#270, 955 Green Valley Cres., Ottawa ON K2C 3V4
Tel: 613-564-5454; Fax: 613-564-1577
Toll-Free: 800-387-8679
information@physiotherapy.ca
www.physiotherapy.ca
www.linkedin.com/company/canadian-physiotherapy-association
www.facebook.com/CPA.ACP
twitter.com/physiocan
To provide leadership & direction to the profession; To foster excellence in practice, education & research; To promote high standards of health in Canada
John-Paul Cody-Cox, Chief Executive Officer

Canadian PKU and Allied Disorders Inc. (CANPKU)
#180, 260 Adelaide St. East, Toronto ON M5A 1N1
Fax: 877-789-2462
Toll-Free: 877-226-7581
info@canpku.org
www.canpku.org
twitter.com/canpku
To provide news, information & support to families & professionals dealing with phenylketonuria and similar, rare, inherited metabolic disorders
John Adams, President & CEO

Canadian Podiatric Medical Association (CPMA) / Association médicale podiatrique canadienne
#305, 120 Carlton St., Toronto ON M5A 4K2
Tel: 780-720-8771; Toll-Free: 888-220-3338
askus@podiatrycanada.org
www.podiatrycanada.org
www.facebook.com/PodiatryCanada
twitter.com/PodiatryCanada
To effectively serve & provide guidance to its members & the podiatry profession in Canada; To serve the public; to provide the authoritative national voice for podiatrists in Canada; To recognize a particular responsibility to contribute to the development of national positions & standards related to the podiatric medical profession through education, research, materials & personnel
Joel Alleyne, Executive Director

Canadian Point of Care Ultrasound Society (CPoCUS) / Société canadienne d'échographie au département d'urgence (SCÉC)
www.cpocus.ca
twitter.com/ceus_scedu
To promote & certify high standards for Point of Care Ultrasound use

Canadian Post-MD Education Registry (CAPER) / Système informatisé sur les stagiaires post-MD en formation clinique
#100, 2733 Lancaster Rd., Ottawa ON K1B 0A9
Tel: 613-730-1204; Fax: 613-730-1196
caper@afmc.ca
www.caper.ca
twitter.com/CAPERCanada
To provide accurate & timely data pertaining to Post-MD training & physician resources in Canada to assist medical schools, governments & other work longitudinal research pertaining to physicians training & supply
Geoffrey Barnum, Manager

Canadian Public Health Association (CPHA) / Association canadienne de santé publique (ACSP)
#404, 1525 Carling Ave., Ottawa ON K1Z 8R9
Tel: 613-725-3769; *Fax:* 613-725-9826
info@cpha.ca
www.cpha.ca
www.linkedin.com/company/cpha-acsp
www.facebook.com/cpha.acsp
twitter.com/CPHA_ACSP
To represent public health in Canada; To support universal & equitable access to the necessary conditions to achieve health for all Canadians; To provide links to the international public health community
Ian Culbert, Executive Director

Canadian Public Health Association - NB/PEI Branch
NB
nbpei.pha@gmail.com
To maintain & improve the level of personal & community health
Tracey Rickards, President
Anne Lebans, Secretary-Treasurer

Canadian Public Health Association - NWT/Nunavut Branch (NTNUPHA)
PO Box 1709, Yellowknife NT X1A 2P3
To represent public health professionals
Cheryl Case, President

Canadian Retina Society / Société canadienne de la rétine
c/o Canadian Ophthalmological Society, #110, 2733 Lancaster Rd., Ottawa ON K1B 0A9
Toll-Free: 800-267-5763
admin@crssrc.ca
www.crssrc.ca
To promote & support retina specialists in Canada
Amin Kherani, President

Canadian Rheumatology Association (CRA) / Société canadienne de rhumatologie
#108, 9-6975 Meadowvale Town Centre Circle, Mississauga ON L5N 2V7
Tel: 905-952-0698; *Fax:* 905-952-0708
info@rheum.ca
rheum.ca
www.linkedin.com/company/canadian-rheumatology-association
twitter.com/CRASCRRheum
To represent Canadian rheumatologists & promote their pursuit of excellence in arthritis care & research in Canada through leadership, education & communication
Evelyn Sutton, President
John Wade, Secretary-Treasurer

Canadian Society for Clinical Investigation (CSCI) / Société canadienne de recherches cliniques (SCRC)
114 Cheyenne Way, Ottawa ON K2J 0E9
Fax: 613-491-0073
Toll-Free: 877-968-9449
office@csci-scrc.ca
www.csci-scrc.ca
To promote research in the field of human health throughout Canada; to lobby for research funding; To support Canadian researchers in their endeavours & at all stages of their careers by supporting knowledge translation & fostering communities of health science researchers
Jason Berman, President

Canadian Society for International Health (CSIH) / Société canadienne de la santé internationale
#1003, 75 Albert St., Ottawa ON K1P 1E3
Tel: 613-241-5785
csih@csih.org
www.csih.org
www.facebook.com/CSIH.org
twitter.com/CSIH_
To promote international health & development through mobilization of Canadian resources; To advocate & facilitate research, education, & service activities in international health; To further Canadian strengths of progressive health policy & programming in all fields where global & domestic health concerns meet; To contribute to the evolving global understanding of health & development
Geneviève Dubois-Flynn, Co-Chair
Shawna O'Hearn, Co-Chair
Eva Slawecki, Executive Director

Canadian Society for Medical Laboratory Science (CSMLS) / Société canadienne de science de laboratoire médical (SCSLM)
33 Wellington St. North, Hamilton ON L8R 1M7
Tel: 905-528-8642; *Fax:* 905-528-4968
Toll-Free: 800-263-8277
info@csmls.org
www.csmls.org
www.youtube.com/user/csmls
www.facebook.com/csmls
twitter.com/csmls
To promote & maintain a nationally accepted standard of medical laboratory technology; To promote, maintain & protect professional identity & interests of medical laboratory technologists
Christine Nielsen, Chief Executive Officer
Joe Davies, Chief Financial Officer
Michael Grant, Director, Marketing & Communications

Canadian Society for Pharmaceutical Sciences (CSPS) / Société canadienne des sciences pharmaceutiques (SCSP)
275 Bay St., Ottawa ON K1R 5Z5
Tel: 613-238-4870; *Fax:* 613-236-2727
csps@intertaskconferences.com
www.cspscanada.org
www.linkedin.com/company/canadian-society-for-pharmaceutical-sciences
www.facebook.com/CanadaCSPS
twitter.com/canadacsps
To advance pharmaceutical R&D & education; To provide a forum for researchers, industry & government to advance pharmaceutical sciences & increase drug discovery & development in Canada
Christine Allen, President

Canadian Society for Surgical Oncology (CSSO) / Société canadienne d'oncologie chirurgicale
c/o Jane Hanes, Princess Margaret Hospital, #3-130, 610 University Ave., Toronto ON M5G 2M9
Tel: 416-946-6583; *Fax:* 416-946-6590
www.csso.surgery
To encourage optimum cancer patient care through a multi-disciplinary treatment approach; To promote surgical oncology training programs in Canadian universities
Andrew McKay, President
Rebecca Auer, Secretary

Canadian Society for the History of Medicine (CSHM) / Société canadienne d'histoire de la médecine (SCHM)
c/o University of Ottawa, #14022, 120 University, Ottawa ON K1N 6N5
Tel: 613-562-5700
info@cshm-schm.ca
www.cshm-schm.ca
To promote the study & communication of the history of health & medicine
Catherine Carstairs, President
Esyllt Jones, Vice-President
Jenna Healey, Secretary-Treasurer & Coordinator, Membership

Canadian Society for Transfusion Medicine (CSTM) / Société canadienne de médecine transfusionnelle
#6, 20 Crown Steel Dr., Markham ON L3R 9X9
Tel: 905-415-3917; *Fax:* 905-415-0071
Toll-Free: 855-415-3917
office@transfusion.ca
www.transfusion.ca
www.instagram.com/cstm_transfusion
www.facebook.com/290163767690083
twitter.com/CanSocTransMed
To promulgate throughout Canada a high level of ethics & professional standards; To create national & regional opportunities for the presentation & discussion of research & developments in these & allied fields; To initiate & maintain a program of continuing education; To promote good laboratory & good manufacturing practices; To establish mutually beneficial working relationships with relevant national & international societies & organizations; To be the primary voice for transfusion medicine in Canada
Ann Wilson, President

Canadian Society for Vascular Surgery (CSVS) / Société canadienne de chirurgie vasculaire
PO Box 58062, Ottawa ON K1C 7H4
Tel: 613-286-7583
csvs@vascular.ca
canadianvascular.ca
To promote vascular health for Canadians
Keith Baxter, President
John Harlock, Secretary

Joshua Koulack, Treasurer

Canadian Society of Allergy & Clinical Immunology (CSACI) / Société canadienne d'allergie et d'immunologie clinique
PO Box 51045, Orléans ON K1E 3W4
Tel: 613-986-5869; *Fax:* 866-839-7501
info@csaci.ca
www.csaci.ca
www.linkedin.com/company/csaciscaic
www.facebook.com/csaciscaic
twitter.com/CSACI_ca
To ensure optimal patient care by advancing the knowledge & practice of allergy, clinical immunology & asthma
Harold Kim, President
Tim Vander Leek, Vice-President
Anne Ellis, Secretary-Treasurer

Canadian Society of Cardiac Surgeons (CSCS) / Société des chirurgiens cardiaques
#1100, 222 Queen St., Ottawa ON K1P 5V9
Tel: 613-569-3407; *Fax:* 613-569-6574
Toll-Free: 877-569-3407
cscs@ccs.ca
www.ccs.ca/en/affiliate-societies/cscs-home
www.facebook.com/SCC.CCS.ca
twitter.com/SCC_CCS
To represent cardiovascular clinicians & scientists in Canada
Jean-François Légaré, President
Ansar Hassan, Secretary-Treasurer

Canadian Society of Celebrants (CSOC)
4673 Jane St., Toronto ON M3N 2L1
Tel: 416-920-5464
canadiansocietyofcelebrantss@gmail.com
www.facebook.com/CanadianSocietyOfCelebrants
twitter.com/CSOC87854277
To provide a curriculum through self study books & online presence to assist in certifiable courses as well as mentoring from other members in practical Celebrant Training

Canadian Society of Clinical Neurophysiologists (CSCN) / Société canadienne de neurophysiologistes cliniques
#709, 7015 Macleod Trail SW, Calgary AB T2H 2K6
Tel: 403-229-9544; *Fax:* 403-229-1661
www.cnsfederation.org
To promote & encourage all aspects of neurophysiology, including research & education, in addition to assessment & accreditation in the field
Fraser Moore, President

Canadian Society of Cytopathology (CSC)
c/o Canadian Association of Pathologists, #310, 4 Cataraqui St., Kingston ON K7K 1Z7
Tel: 613-507-8528; *Fax:* 866-531-0626
cytopathology.ca
To promote & support education in cytology; To maintain a high standard of practice within the discipline of cytopathology; To foster the development of cytopathology in Canada
Fadi Brimo, Chair

Canadian Society of Endocrinology & Metabolism (CSEM) / Société canadienne d'endocrinologie et métabolisme (SCEM)
192 Bank St., Ottawa ON K2P 1W8
Tel: 613-594-0005; *Fax:* 613-260-3235
info@endo-metab.ca
www.endo-metab.ca
twitter.com/CSEM_SCEM
To advance the endocrinology & metabolism field in Canada
Heather Lochnan, President
Breay Paty, Secretary-Treasurer
Inika Anderson, Executive Director

Canadian Society of Gastroenterology Nurses & Associates (CSGNA)
#310, 4 Cataraqui St., Kingston ON K7K 1Z7
Tel: 613-507-6130
csgnaexecutiveassistant@csgna.com
www.csgna.com
www.instagram.com/multimediadirector
twitter.com/CSGNA
To enhance the educational & professional growth of the membership within the resources available
Cathy Arnold Cormier, President
Katherine Mansfield, Treasurer

Canadian Society of Hand Therapists (CSHT) / Societe canadienne des therapeutes de la main (SCTM)
#101, 10277 154 St., Surrey BC V3R 4J7
secretary@csht.org
www.csht.org
www.facebook.com/324550384259629
To provide education, information, & enhanced care for the improvement of upper extremity rehabilitation
Marie Eason Klatt, President

Canadian Society of Internal Medicine (CSIM) / Société canadienne de médecine interne (SCMI)
#200, 421 Gilmour St., Ottawa ON K2P 0R5
Tel: 613-422-5977; Fax: 613-249-3326
Toll-Free: 855-893-2746
info@csim.ca
csim.ca
www.facebook.com/canadiansocietyofinternalmedicine
twitter.com/CSIMSCMI
To promote healthy living among Canadians; To provide leadership for physicians; To conduct research & education
Nadine Lahoud, President

Canadian Society of Nephrology (CSN) / Société canadienne de néphrologie (SCN)
PO Box 25255, Stn. RDP, Montréal QC H1E 7P9
Tel: 514-643-4985
info@csnscn.ca
www.csnscn.ca
www.facebook.com/1498868453774190
twitter.com/CSNSCN
To advance the care of Canadians with, or at risk of, kidney disease; To create opportunities to share challenges, solutions, experiences, knowledge, & best practices for individuals working in the kidney health & disease field; To set standards for kidney care & promote research; To support Canadian Nephrologists by promoting & providing continuing education & professional development
Filomena Picciano, Director, Operations

Canadian Society of Nutrition Management / Société canadienne de gestion de la nutrition
#300, 1370 Don Mills Rd., Toronto ON M3B 3N7
Fax: 416-441-0591
Toll-Free: 866-355-2766
csnm@csnm.ca
www.csnm.ca
www.linkedin.com/in/thecsnm
twitter.com/TheCSNM
To foster an environment in which members can achieve success in their chosen field
David Lebert, President
Heather Shannon, Secretary-Treasurer

Canadian Society of Otolaryngology - Head & Neck Surgery (CSO-HNS) / Société canadienne d'otolaryngologie et de chirurgie cervico-faciale
Administrative Office, 68 Gilkison Rd., Elora ON N0B 1S0
Tel: 519-846-0630; Fax: 519-846-9529
Toll-Free: 800-655-9533
cso.hns@sympatico.ca
www.entcanada.org
twitter.com/ent_canada
To improve patient care in otolaryngology - head & neck surgery; To maintain high professional & ethical standards
Ian Witterick, President
Jodi Jones, Secretary
John Yoo, Treasurer
Donna Humphrey, General Manager

Canadian Society of Palliative Care Physicians (CSPCP) / Société canadienne des médecins de soins palliatifs (SCMSP)
#584, 1A-12830-96 Ave., Surrey BC V3V 0C2
Tel: 604-341-3174; Fax: 604-583-0645
office@cspcp.ca
www.cspcp.ca
www.facebook.com/CSPCPSCMSP
twitter.com/CSPCP_SCMSP
Leonie Herx, President
Kim Taylor, Executive Director

Canadian Society of Plastic Surgeons (CSPS) / Société canadienne des chirurgiens plasticiens
PO Box 60192, Stn. Saint-Denis, Montréal QC H2J 4E1
Tel: 514-843-5415; Fax: 514-843-7005
Toll-Free: 800-665-5415
csps_sccp@bellnet.ca
www.plasticsurgery.ca
To represent, promote & provide leadership for the descipline of plastic surgery across Canada

Bing Siang Gan, President
Carolyn Levis, Vice-President
Earl Campbell, Secretary-Treasurer
Karyn Wagner, Executive Director

Canadian Society of Respiratory Therapists (CSRT) / La Société canadienne des thérapeutes respiratoires (SCTR)
#201, 2460 Lancaster Rd., Ottawa ON K1B 4S5
Tel: 613-731-3164; Fax: 613-521-4314
Toll-Free: 800-267-3422
www.csrt.com
www.instagram.com/csrt_sctr
www.linkedin.com/company/csrt
www.facebook.com/csrt.sctr
twitter.com/CSRT_tweets
To provide leadership toward the advancement of cardiorespiratory care; To achieve excellence through the definition of roles, standards & scope of clinical practice
Adam Buettner, President
Paul Williams, Treasurer
Andrew West, Chief Executive Officer

Canadian Society of Transplantation (CST) / Société canadienne de transplantation
114 Cheyenne Way, Ottawa ON K2J 0E9
Toll-Free: 877-968-9449
admin@cst-transplant.ca
www.cst-transplant.ca
To provide leadership for the advancement of educational, scientific, & clinical aspects of transplantation in Canada
Michael Mengel, President
Joseph Kim, Secretary-Treasurer

Canadian Spinal Research Organization (CSRO)
#601, 90 Eglinton Ave. East, Toronto ON M4P 2Y3
Tel: 905-508-4000; Fax: 905-508-4002
Toll-Free: 800-361-4004
info@csro.com
www.csro.com
www.youtube.com/user/CSROVideos
www.facebook.com/CSROASRO
twitter.com/canadian_spinal
To improve the physical quality of life for people with spinal injuries; To reduce the incidence of spinal cord injuries through awareness programs for the public & prevention programs with targeted groups
Barry Munro, President

Canadian Thoracic Society (CTS) / Société canadienne de thoracologie (SCT)
#27, 30 Concourse Gate, Ottawa ON K2E 7V7
Tel: 613-235-6650
info@cts-sct.ca
cts-sct.ca
www.linkedin.com/in/canadian-thoracic-society-cts-65b84115b
www.facebook.com/334691136607567
twitter.com/CTS_SCT
To enhance the prevention & treatment of respiratory diseases
Janet Sutherland, Executive Director
Anne Van Dam, Director, Knowledge Mobilization
Banu Pamukcu, Manager, Education & Continuing Professional Development

Canadian Transplant Association (CTA) / Association canadienne des greffes
PO Box 71530, Stn. Hillcrest, 1463 Johnston Rd., White Rock BC V4B 3Z0
Toll-Free: 877-779-5991
cta@txworks.ca
www.canadiantransplant.com
www.linkedin.com/company/canadian-transplant-association
www.facebook.com/CanadianTransplantAssociationandGames
twitter.com/CTACanada
To promote a healthy lifestyle for transplant recipients
Brenda Brown, President
Heather Lannon, Secretary
Earl Howell, Treasurer
Kennedie Maidment, Director, Membership Development

Canadian Urological Association (CUA) / Association des urologues du Canada
#401, 185, av Dorval, Dorval QC H9S 5J9
Tel: 514-395-0376; Fax: 514-395-1664
corporate.office@cua.org
www.cua.org
www.instagram.com/cualauc
www.linkedin.com/company/canadian-urological-association-jour-nal-cuaj-
www.facebook.com/CanadianUrologyAssociation
twitter.com/CanUrolAssoc
To advance the urology field; To promote high standards of urologic care in Canada

Tiffany Pizioli, Chief Executive Officer
Nadia Pace, Director, Communications
Denise Toner, Manager, Advertising & Membership

Canadian Virtual Hospice
1 Morley Ave., #PE469, Winnipeg MB R3L 2P4
info@virtualhospice.ca
www.virtualhospice.ca
www.youtube.com/user/cvhvcvcsp
www.linkedin.com/company/canadian-virtual-hospice
www.facebook.com/CanadianVirtualHospice
twitter.com/VirtualHospice
To provide support & personalized information on palliative & end-of-life care to patients, families, health care providers, researchers, & educators
Harvey Max Chochinov, OM, MD, PhD, FR, Founder
Shelly Cory, MA, Executive Director

Cancer Education Research Foundation (CERF)
#101, 7800 Kennedy Rd., Markham ON L3R 2C7
Tel: 905-470-8111; Fax: 905-470-8121
info@cerfcanada.com
cerfcanada.com
To raise funds for the purchase of cancer treatment equipment & the construction and expansion of Shaukat Khanum Hospital in Lahore, Peshawar & Karachi, Pakistan
Khalid Usman, President

CancerCare Manitoba (CCMB)
MacCharles Unit, 675 McDermot Ave., Winnipeg MB R3E 0V9
Tel: 204-787-2197; Toll-Free: 866-561-1026
donate@cancercare.mb.ca
www.cancercare.mb.ca
www.youtube.com/user/CancerCareMB
twitter.com/cancercaremb
To provide exceptional care for patients & their families
Sri Navaratnam, President & CEO
Piotr Czaykowski, Chief Medical Officer
Paul Penner, Chief Operating Officer

Cape Breton Regional Hospital Foundation
#209, 45 Weatherbee Rd., Sydney NS B1M 0A1
Tel: 902-567-7752
foundation@cbdha.nshealth.ca
www.becauseyoucare.ca
www.instagram.com/becauseucare
www.facebook.com/CapeBretonCares
twitter.com/BecauseUCare
To raise money on behalf of the Cape Breton Regional Hospital in order to improve the services provided to patients & to fund research
Brad Jacobs, CEO

Carcinoid NeuroEndocrine Tumour Society Canada
1608 Blakely Dr., Cornwall ON K6J 5P4
Toll-Free: 844-628-6788
info@cnetscanada.org
www.cnetscanada.org
www.youtube.com/user/cnetscanada
www.facebook.com/cnetscanada
twitter.com/CNETSCanada
To raise awareness about neuroendocrine tumours; To provide help & support to those suffering from this type of cancer; To fund research that treats neuroendocrine tumours
Enrico Mandarino, Executive Manager

Carers Canada / Proches aidants au Canada
c/o Canadian Home Care Association, #302, 2000 Argentia Rd., Plaza 3, Mississauga ON L5N 1W1
Tel: 905-567-7373
www.carerscanada.ca
To provide partnerships & advocacy to carers across Canada in order to enhance their quality of life
Catherine Suridjan, Lead, Policy and Stakeholder Engagement

Cell Therapy Transplant Canada (CTTC) / Transplantation et Therapie Cellulaire Canada
#301, 750 West Pender St., Vancouver BC V6C 2T7
Tel: 604-874-4944; Fax: 604-874-4378
info@cttcanada.org
cttcanada.org
twitter.com/CTTC_ORG
To provide leadership in the field of blood & marrow transplantation (BMT); To recognize & promote advances in clinical care; To promote basic, translational & clinical research & education; To represent BMT issues to government agencies, health care organizations & the public; To collaborate with fellow organizations
Donna Wall, President

Cerebral Palsy Association of British Columbia (CPABC)
#330, 409 Granville St., Vancouver BC V6C 1T2
Tel: 604-408-9484; *Fax:* 604-408-9489
Toll-Free: 800-663-0004
info@bccerebralpalsy.com
www.bccerebralpalsy.com
www.facebook.com/cerebral.palsy.39
To raise awareness of cerebral palsy in the community; To assist those living with cerebral palsy to reach to maximum; To work to see those living with cerebral palsy realize their place as equals within a diverse society; To provide support & services that facilitate these needs; To make a Life Without Limits for people with disabilities
Feri Dehdar, Executive Director

Certified Celebrants Association of Canada (CCAOC)
ccaoc.ca
To connect & certify funeral celebrants

Childhood Cancer Canada Foundation
#702, 20 Queen St. West, Toronto ON M5H 3R3
Tel: 416-489-6440; *Fax:* 416-489-9812
Toll-Free: 800-363-1062
info@childhoodcancer.ca
www.childhoodcancer.ca
www.instagram.com/childhoodcancercanada
www.facebook.com/ChildhoodCancerCanada
twitter.com/chldhdcancercan
To help improve the lives of children suffering from cancer through family support programs; To fund cancer research
Jaime Wilson, President & CEO

Children's Hospital Foundation of Manitoba
840 Sherbrook St., #CE501, Winnipeg MB R3A 1S1
Tel: 204-787-4000; *Fax:* 204-787-4114
Toll-Free: 866-953-5437
info@goodbear.ca
goodbear.ca
www.youtube.com/user/DRGoodbear1
www.linkedin.com/company/chfmanitoba
www.facebook.com/chfmanitoba
twitter.com/chfmanitoba
To help raise funds in order to fund research & to provide young patients from Manitoba, Northwestern Ontario & Nunavut with improved health care services
Stefano Grande, President & CEO

Children's Hospital Foundation of Saskatchewan
#1, 345 - 3 Ave. South, Saskatoon SK S7K 1M6
Tel: 306-931-4887; *Toll-Free:* 888-808-5437
info@chfsask.ca
www.childrenshospitalsask.ca
www.youtube.com/user/ChildHospitalSK
www.facebook.com/CHFSask
twitter.com/childhospitalsk
To help raise funds for the Children's Hospital of Saskatchewan in order to provide patients with improved health care services & to fund research
Brynn Boback-Lane, President & CEO

Children's Hospital of Eastern Ontario Foundation
415 Smyth Rd., Ottawa ON K1H 8M8
Tel: 613-737-2780; *Fax:* 613-738-4818
Toll-Free: 800-561-5638
www.cheofoundation.com
www.youtube.com/user/CHEOvideos
www.facebook.com/CHEOkids
twitter.com/cheohospital
To advance the physical, mental, & social well-being of children & their families in Eastern Ontario & Western Quebec by raising, managing, & disbursing funds; To support the Children's Hospital of Eastern Ontario
Mahesh Mani, Chair
Len Hanes, Director, Communications

Chronic Pain Association of Canada (CPAC)
PO Box 66017, Stn. Heritage, Edmonton AB T6J 6T4
Tel: 780-482-6727; *Fax:* 780-433-3128
cpac@chronicpaincanada.com
www.chronicpaincanada.com
www.facebook.com/chronicpainca
twitter.com/canada_pain
To advance the treatment & management of chronic intractable pain; To develop research projects to promote the discovery of a cure for this disease; To educate both the health care community & the public
Terry Bremner, President
Barry Ulmer, Executive Director

Collège des médecins du Québec (CMQ)
#3500, 1250, boul René-Lévesque ouest, Montréal QC H3B 0G2
Tél: 514-933-4441; *Téléc:* 514-933-3112
Ligne sans frais: 888-633-3246
info@cmq.org
www.cmq.org
www.facebook.com/CollegeMedecinsQuebec
twitter.com/CMQ_org
Promouvoir une médecine de qualité pour protéger le public et contribuer à l'amélioration de la santé des Québécois
Mauril Gaudreault, Président
Yves Robert, Secrétaire

College of Dietitians of Alberta
#1320, 10123 - 99 St., Edmonton AB T5J 3H1
Tel: 780-448-0059; *Fax:* 780-489-7759
Toll-Free: 866-493-4348
office@collegeofdietitians.ab.ca
www.collegeofdietitians.ab.ca
The College is the regulatory body of registered dietitians/nutritionists in Alberta, setting entry requirements, standards of practice. It is accountable to both the government & the public.
Doug Cook, Executive Director & Registrar

College of Dietitians of British Columbia (CDBC)
#900, 200 Granville St., Vancouver BC V6C 1S4
Tel: 604-742-6395; *Fax:* 604-357-1873
Toll-Free: 888-742-6395
info@collegeofdietitiansbc.org
www.collegeofdietitiansofbc.org
To serve & protect the nutritional health of the public through quality dietetic practice
Joanie Bouchard, Registrar
Mélanie Journoud, Deputy Registrar, Quality Assurance

College of Dietitians of Manitoba
#36, 1313 Border St., Winnipeg MB R3H 0X4
Tel: 204-694-0532; *Fax:* 204-889-1755
Toll-Free: 866-283-2823
office@collegeofdietitiansmb.ca
www.collegeofdietitiansmb.ca
To act as the regulating body within the province for dietitians & the profession of dietetics; To set education standards; To ensure competency of members
Shaunda Durance-Tod, Registrar

College of Dietitians of Ontario (CDO) / L'Ordre des diététistes de l'Ontario
PO Box 30, #1810, 5775 Yonge St., Toronto ON M2M 4J1
Tel: 416-598-1725; *Fax:* 416-598-0274
Toll-Free: 800-668-4990
information@collegeofdietitians.org
www.collegeofdietitians.org
www.youtube.com/user/CollegeofDietitians
www.facebook.com/CollegeDietitiansOntario
twitter.com/CDOntario
To promote awareness of & access to competent, high quality nutritional care for Ontarians
Melisse L. Willems, Registrar & Executive Director

College of Family Physicians of Canada (CFPC) / Collège des médecins de famille du Canada
2630 Skymark Ave., Mississauga ON L4W 5A4
Tel: 905-629-0900; *Fax:* 888-843-2372
Toll-Free: 800-387-6197
info@cfpc.ca
www.cfpc.ca
www.youtube.com/user/CFPCMedia
www.facebook.com/CFPC.CMFC
twitter.com/FamPhysCan
To lead family medicine and to improve the health of all people in Canada, by setting standards for education, certifying & supporting family physicians, championing advocacy & research, & honouring the patient-physician relationship as being core to the profession
Francine Lemire, MD CM, CCFP, FC, Executive Director & CEO

College of Naturopathic Doctors of Alberta (CNDA)
#216, 20 Sunpark Plaza SE, Calgary AB T2X 3T2
Tel: 403-266-2446; *Fax:* 403-226-2433
info@cnda.net
www.cnda.net
twitter.com/CollegeNDAB
To maintain a high standard of practice among naturopathic doctors
Beverly Huang, President
Cherie Baruss, Registrar

College of Occupational Therapists of British Columbia (COTBC)
#402, 3795 Carey Rd., Victoria BC V8Z 6T8
Tel: 250-386-6822; *Fax:* 250-386-6824
Toll-Free: 866-386-6822
info@cotbc.org
www.cotbc.org
www.linkedin.com/company/college-of-occupational-therapists-of-british-columbia
www.facebook.com/OTCollegeBC
twitter.com/OTCollegeBC
To establish standards of practice & conduct; To enhance quality assurance; To monitor quality of practice & continuing competence; To improve competence of occupational therapists; To investigate complaints; To enforce standards
Kathy Corbett, Registrar
Andrea Bowden, Deputy Registrar

College of Physicians & Surgeons of Alberta (CPSA)
#2700, 10020 - 100 St. NW, Edmonton AB T5J 0N3
Tel: 780-423-4764; *Fax:* 780-420-0651
Toll-Free: 800-561-3899
publicinquiries@cpsa.ab.ca
www.cpsa.ca
To serve the public & guide the medical profession; To identify factors affecting competent medical practice; To promote quality improvement in medical practice; To ensure practitioners meet our registration standards; To resolve complaints involving practitioners fairly & effectively
Kate Wood, President

College of Physicians & Surgeons of British Columbia (CPSBC)
#300, 699 Howe St., Vancouver BC V6C 0B4
Tel: 604-733-7758; *Fax:* 604-733-3503
Toll-Free: 800-461-3008
www.linkedin.com/company/2905395
www.facebook.com/cpsbc.ca
twitter.com/cpsbc_ca
To protect British Columbia's patients by regulating the practice of medicine; To ensure physicians adhere to standards of practice & conduct
Heidi Oetter, CEO & Registrar
Corinne du Bruin, Executive Director

College of Physicians & Surgeons of Manitoba (CPSM)
#1000, 1661 Portage Ave., Winnipeg MB R3J 3T7
Tel: 204-774-4344; *Fax:* 204-774-0750
Toll-Free: 877-774-4344
cpsm@cpsm.mb.ca
cpsm.mb.ca
Eric Sigurdson, President
Anna Ziomek, Registrar

College of Physicians & Surgeons of New Brunswick / Collège des médecins et chirurgiens du Nouveau-Brunswick
#300, 1 Hampton Rd., Rothesay NB E2E 5K8
Tel: 506-849-5050; *Fax:* 506-849-5069
Toll-Free: 800-667-4641
info@cpsnb.org
www.cpsnb.org
Stéphane E. Paulin, President
Ed Schollenberg, Registrar

College of Physicians & Surgeons of Newfoundland & Labrador
120 Torbay Rd., #W100, St. John's NL A1A 2G8
Tel: 709-726-8546; *Fax:* 709-726-4725
cpsnl@cpsnl.ca
www.cpsnl.ca
To regulate the practice of medicine & medical practitioners; To promote high standards of practice, as well as continuing competence & quality improvement through continuing medical education; To administer a quality assurance program; To enforce standards of conduct
Linda Inkpen, Registrar
Oscar Howell, Deputy Registrar
Jamie Osmond, Associate Registrar, Licensing & Quality
Elyse Bruce, Legal Counsel

College of Physicians & Surgeons of Nova Scotia (CPSNS)
#5005, 7071 Bayers Rd., Halifax NS B3L 2C2
Tel: 902-422-5823; *Fax:* 902-422-7476
Toll-Free: 877-282-7767
info@cpsns.ns.ca
www.cpsns.ns.ca
www.linkedin.com/company/2497006
To govern the practice of medicine in the public interest

Mary Oxner, President

College of Physicians & Surgeons of Ontario (CPSO)
80 College St., Toronto ON M5G 2E2
Tel: 416-967-2603; *Fax:* 416-961-3330
Toll-Free: 800-268-7096
feedback@cpso.on.ca
www.cpso.on.ca
www.youtube.com/user/theCpso
www.linkedin.com/groups/4760466
www.facebook.com/thecpso
twitter.com/cpso_ca
To ensure the best quality care for the people of Ontario by the doctors of Ontario
Brenda Copps, President
Nancy Whitmore, Registrar

College of Physicians & Surgeons of Prince Edward Island
14 Paramount Dr., Charlottetown PE C1E 0C7
Tel: 902-566-3861; *Fax:* 902-566-3986
cpspei.ca
To act as the regulatory body for physicians in the province, responsible for licensing all medical doctors, maintaining medical standards, handling complaints from the public & delivering disciplinary action
Cyril Moyse, Registrar
Melissa MacDonald, Office Manager

College of Physicians & Surgeons of Saskatchewan (CPSS) / Collège des médecins et chirurgiens de la Saskatchewan
#101, 2174 Airport Dr., Saskatoon SK S7L 6M6
Tel: 306-244-7355; *Fax:* 306-244-0090
Toll-Free: 800-667-1668
cpssinfo@cps.sk.ca
www.cps.sk.ca
To serve the public by regulating the practice of medicine & guiding the profession to achieve the highest standards of care
Karen Shaw, Registar & Chief Executive Officer

Conseil québécois sur le tabac et la santé / Québec Council on Tobacco & Health
#302, 4126, rue Saint-Denis, Montréal QC H2W 2M5
Tél: 514-948-5317; *Téléc:* 514-948-4582
info@cqts.qc.ca
www.cqts.qc.ca
www.facebook.com/quebecsanstabac
twitter.com/cqts
Promouvoir la santé du fumeur et du non-fumeur; faire le lien entre les associations, groupes bénévoles et autres intéressés à la santé publique; trouver des approches et des moyens pour améliorer l'éducation face à l'usage du tabac
Annie Papageorgiou, Directrice général
Isabelle Mailhiot, Directrice, Communications

Consumer Health Organization of Canada (CHOC)
#1901, 355 St Clair Ave. West, Toronto ON M5P 1N5
Tel: 416-924-9800; *Fax:* 416-924-6404
info@consumerhealth.org
www.consumerhealth.org
To encourage the prevention of all kinds of illness through knowledge; To help the individual, the family & the community to enjoy the benefits of a more wholesome lifestyle; To promote harmony & cooperation between like-minded groups
Libby Gardon, President

Crohn's & Colitis Canada / Crohn's et Colitis Canada
#600, 60 St. Clair Ave. East, Toronto ON M4T 1N5
Tel: 416-920-5035; *Fax:* 416-929-0364
Toll-Free: 800-387-1479
support@crohnsandcolitis.ca
www.crohnsandcolitis.ca
www.youtube.com/user/getgutsy
www.linkedin.com/company/crohn's-and-colitis-foundation-of-canada
www.facebook.com/crohnsandcolitis.ca
twitter.com/getgutsyCanada
To find a cure for Crohn's disease & ulcerative colitis; To raise funds for medical research; To educate individuals with inflammatory bowel disease, their families, health professionals & the public
Mina Mawani, President & CEO
Zoe Charalambous, Vice-President, Finance & Administration
Angie Specic, Vice-President, Marketing & Communications

Cystic Fibrosis Canada / Fibrose Kystique Canada
National Office, #800, 2323 Yonge St., Toronto ON M4P 2C9
Tel: 416-485-9149; *Fax:* 416-485-0960
Toll-Free: 800-378-2233
info@cysticfibrosis.ca
www.cysticfibrosis.ca
www.youtube.com/CysticFibrosisCanada
www.facebook.com/CysticFibrosisCanada
twitter.com/CFCanada
To help people with Cystic Fibrosis through funding research towards a cure or control; To support high quality care; To promote public awareness; To raise & allocate funds
Kelly Grover, Chief Executive Officer & President
John Wallenberg, Chief Scientific Officer

Diabète Québec (ADQ) / Diabetes Quebec
#500, 3750, boul Crémazie est, Montréal QC H2A 1B6
Tél: 514-259-3422; *Téléc:* 514-259-9286
Ligne sans frais: 800-361-3504
infodiabete@diabete.qc.ca
www.diabete.qc.ca
www.facebook.com/diabetequebec
twitter.com/DiabeteQuebec
Regrouper les diabétiques et favoriser l'entraide; les renseigner sur les façons de faire face à la maladie; informer le grand public et le sensibiliser à la condition de personnes souffrant du diabète; ouvrir de nouvelles voies dans le domaine de la recherche pour en venir à triompher du diabète
Marcel Breton, Présidente

Diabetes Canada (CDA) / Association canadienne du diabète
#1300, 522 University Ave., Toronto ON M5G 2R5
Tel: 416-363-3373; *Fax:* 416-363-7465
Toll-Free: 800-226-8464
info@diabetes.ca
www.diabetes.ca
www.instagram.com/DiabetesCanada
www.linkedin.com/company/diabetescanada
www.facebook.com/DiabetesCanada
twitter.com/DiabetesCanada
To advance the welfare of Canadians with diabetes; To support research into the causes, complications, treatment & cure of diabetes; To promote & strengthen services for people affected by diabetes & their families; To work with health professionals to improve standards in care the & treatment of diabetes; To develop guidelines for diabetes education in Canada; To promote the rights of Canadians affected by diabetes in an effort to bring about positive change in the areas of public awareness, government policy, health policy issues & employment
Russel Williams, Acting President & Senior Vice-President
Mary Ann Azzarello, Vice-President, Fund Development
Halinka Dybka, Vice-President, Marketing & Knowledge Innovation
Seema Nagpal, Vice-President, Science & Policy
Shannon Shannon, President & CEO, National Diabetes Trust

Dietitians of Canada (DC) / Les diététistes du Canada
#604, 480 University Ave., Toronto ON M5G 1V2
Tel: 416-596-0857; *Fax:* 416-596-0603
contactus@dietitians.ca
www.dietitians.ca
To advance health, through food & nutrition; To act as the voice of the dietitian profession in Canada
Nathalie Savoie, Chief Executive Officer

Doctors Manitoba
20 Desjardins Dr., Winnipeg MB R3X 0E8
Tel: 204-985-5888; *Fax:* 204-985-5844
Toll-Free: 888-322-4242
general@doctorsmanitoba.ca
doctorsmanitoba.ca
To unite & advocate for Manitoba physicians; To encourage the highest standards of health care for the people of Manitoba
Theresa Oswald, Chief Executive Officer
Rick Sawyer, Chief Administrative Officer
Alana Brooker, Director, Marketing & Communications

Doctors Nova Scotia
25 Spectacle Lake Dr., Dartmouth NS B3B 1X7
Tel: 902-468-1866; *Fax:* 902-468-6578
Toll-Free: 800-563-3427
info@doctorsns.com
www.doctorsns.com
www.facebook.com/DoctorsNovaScotia
twitter.com/Doctors_NS
To maintain the integrity of the medical profession; To represent members; To promote high quality health care & disease prevention in Nova Scotia
Nancy MacCready-Williams, Chief Executive Officer

Doctors of BC
#115, 1665 West Broadway, Vancouver BC V6J 5A4
Tel: 604-736-5551; *Fax:* 604-638-2917
Toll-Free: 800-665-2262
communications@doctorsofbc.ca
www.doctorsofbc.ca
www.linkedin.com/company/bc-medical-association
www.facebook.com/bcsdoctors
twitter.com/doctorsofbc
To promote a social, economic, & political climate in which members can provide the citizens of British Columbia with the highest standard of health care while achieving maximum professional satisfaction & fair economic reward
Allan Seckel, Chief Executive Officer

Dystonia Medical Research Foundation Canada / Fondation de recherches médicales sur la dystonie
#209, 550 St. Clair Ave. West, Toronto ON M6C 1A5
Tel: 416-488-6974; *Fax:* 416-488-5878
Toll-Free: 800-361-8061
info@dystoniacanada.org
www.dystoniacanada.org
www.facebook.com/DMRFC
To advance & support research relating to dystonia; To build awareness about the illness in order to educate both medical & lay communities; To sponsor patient & family support groups & programs
Stefanie Ince, Executive Director

Eating Disorder Association of Canada (EDAC) / Association des Troubles Alimentaires du Canada (ATAC)
edacatac@gmail.com
www.edac-atac.ca
twitter.com/EDACATAC
EDAC-ATAC aims to serve the needs of those whose lives are impacted by eating disorders.
Nicole Obeid, President

Edmonton (Alberta) Nerve Pain Association (EANPA)
14016 - 91 A Ave., Edmonton AB T5R 5A7
Tel: 780-217-9306
neuropathy_nervepain@hotmail.com
www.edmontonnervepain.ca
To support people suffering from neuropathic pain
Claude M. Roberto, President

effect:hope
#200, 90 Allstate Pkwy., Markham ON L3R 6H3
Tel: 905-886-2885; *Fax:* 905-886-2887
Toll-Free: 888-537-7679
info@effecthope.org
effecthope.org
www.youtube.com/user/effecthope
www.linkedin.com/company/3068053
www.facebook.com/effecthope
twitter.com/effecthope
To provide care & support to leprosy patients in many parts of the world including India, Bangladesh & Nigeria
Kim Evans, Chief Executive Officer

Epilepsy & Seizure Association of Manitoba
#4, 1805 Main St., Winnipeg MB R2V 2A2
Tel: 204-783-0466; *Fax:* 204-784-9689
esam@manitobaepilepsy.org
www.manitobaepilepsy.org
To improve the quality of life of persons with epilepsy by providing programs & education, & supporting research & services
Chris Kullman, President
Kim Boulet, Vice-President
Diane Wall, Treasurer
Dennis Weedon, Secretary

Epilepsy Canada (EC) / Épilepsie Canada
#600, 3250 Bloor St. West, East Tower, Toronto ON M8X 2X9
Tel: 647-775-1611; *Fax:* 905-764-1231
Toll-Free: 877-734-0873
epilepsy@epilepsy.ca
www.epilepsy.ca
www.instagram.com/epilepsycanada
www.facebook.com/EpilepsyCanada
twitter.com/epilepsycanada
To enhance the quality of life for persons affected by epilepsy; To promote & support research into all aspects of epilepsy; To facilitate educational initiatives; To increase public & professional awareness of epilepsy; To fund research; To encourage governments to address the needs of people with epilepsy
Gary N. Collins, National President

Epilepsy Ontario / Épilepsie Ontario
#15, 470 North Rivermede Rd., Concord ON L4K 3R8
Tel: 905-738-9431
info@epilepsyontario.org
www.epilepsyontario.org
www.instagram.com/epilepsyontario
www.facebook.com/epilepsy.ontario
twitter.com/EpilepsyOntario
To promote optimal quality of life for people living with seizure disorders; To advocate for awareness, support services & research into these disorders & maintains a network of local agencies, contacts & associates to provide services, counselling & referrals
Paul Raymond, Executive Director

Ethiopiaid
484 Gladstone Ave., Ottawa ON K1R 5N8
Tel: 613-238-4481
info@ethiopiaid.ca
www.ethiopiaid.ca
www.facebook.com/EthiopiaidCanada
twitter.com/EthiopiaidCAN
To create lasting & positive change in Ethiopia by tackling the problems of poverty, ill health & poor education; To donate to local community projects in Ethiopia
Kristin Douglas, Executive Director

Evangelical Medical Aid Society Canada (EMAS)
Crossroads Building, 1295 North Service Rd., Burlington ON L7R 4M2
Tel: 905-319-3415; Toll-Free: 866-648-0664
info@emascanada.org
www.emascanada.org
www.facebook.com/EMASCANADA
twitter.com/emascanada
To provide medical care for those in need in a Christlike manner
Peter Agwa, Executive Director

Eye Bank of BC (EBBC)
Jim Pattison Pavilion North - B205, 855 West 12th Ave, Vancouver BC V5Z 1M9
Tel: 604-875-4567; Fax: 604-875-5316
Toll-Free: 800-667-2060
eyebankofbc@vch.ca
www.eyebankofbc.ca
www.facebook.com/EyeBankBC
twitter.com/VCHEyeBankBC
To acquire human donor eye tissue for the purposes of corneal transplant, scelra grafts & medical research
Marlene Matsuba, Manager
Sonia Yeung, Medical Director

Eye Bank of Canada - Ontario Division
340 College St., #B100, Toronto ON M5T 3A9
Tel: 416-978-7355
www.kensingtonhealth.org/eye-bank
To provide donated eye tissue for surgical use in those whose vision can be restored or improved through corneal transplantation or other eye surgery
John Yip, President & CEO

Fédération des médecins omnipraticiens du Québec (FMOQ) / Québec Federation of General Practitioners
Place Alexis Nihon, #2, 3500, boul de Maisonneuve ouest, 20e étage, Westmount QC H3Z 3C1
Tél: 514-878-1911; Ligne sans frais: 800-361-8499
info@fmoq.org
www.fmoq.org
twitter.com/FMOQ
Étude et défense des intérêts économiques, sociaux, moraux et scientifiques des associations et de leurs membres; promouvoir et développer le rôle de l'omnipraticien dans les sphères de la vie économique, sociale, scientifique et culturelle en définissant d'une façon objective le statut propre à l'omnipraticien
Louis Godin, Président-directeur général

Fédération des médecins spécialistes du Québec (FMSQ)
CP 216, Succ. Desjardins, #3000, 2, Complexe Desjardins, Montréal QC H5B 1G8
Tél: 514-350-5000; Téléc: 514-350-5100
Ligne sans frais: 800-561-0703
www.fmsq.org
www.facebook.com/laFMSQ
twitter.com/FMSQ
Défendre et promouvoir les intérêts économiques, professionnels et scientifiques des médecins spécialistes
Diane Francoeur, Présidente

Federation of Medical Regulatory Authorities of Canada (FMRAC) / Fédération des ordres des médecins du Canada
#103, 2283 St. Laurent Blvd., Ottawa ON K1G 5A2
Tel: 613-738-0372; Fax: 613-738-9169
info@fmrac.ca
www.fmrac.ca
To provide a national structure for the provincial & territorial medical regulatory authorities; To present & pursue issues of common concern & interest; To share, consider & develop positions on such matters
Fleur-Ange Lefebvre, Executive Director & CEO

Fédération québécoise de l'autisme (FQA) / Québec Federation for Autism
3396, rue Jean-Talon est, Montréal QC H2A 1W8
Tél: 514-270-7386; Téléc: 514-270-9261
Ligne sans frais: 888-830-2833
info@autisme.qc.ca
www.autisme.qc.ca
www.facebook.com/autisme.qc.ca
Promouvoir et défendre les droits et les intérêts de la personne autiste ou ayant un trouble envahissant du développement afin qu'elle accède à une vie digne et à une meilleure autonomie sociale possible; mobiliser tous les acteurs concernés afin de promouvoir le bien-être des personnes, sensibiliser et informer la population sur le trouble du spectre de l'autisme ainsi que sur la situation des familles, et contribuer au développement des connaissances et à leur diffusion
Luc Chulak, Directrice générale

Fédération québécoise des massothérapeutes (FQM)
#400, 4428, boul St-Laurent, Montréal QC H2W 1Z5
Tél: 514-597-0505; Téléc: 514-597-0141
Ligne sans frais: 800-363-9609
administration@fqm.qc.ca
www.fqm.qc.ca
www.youtube.com/user/FQMmassotherapie
www.facebook.com/massotherapie.FQM
twitter.com/FederationFQM
Regrouper les massothérapeutes afin de promouvoir la massothérapie sous l'intérêt public et de valoriser la profession de la massothérapie
Sylvie Bédard, Présidente

Fédération québécoise des sociétés Alzheimer (FQSA) / Federation of Québec Alzheimer Societies
#200, 5165, rue Sherbrooke ouest, Montréal QC H4A 1T6
Tél: 514-369-7891; Téléc: 514-369-7900
Ligne sans frais: 888-636-6473
www.alzheimerquebec.ca
www.youtube.com/user/FQSA1
www.facebook.com/LaFederationQuebecoiseDesSocietesAlzheimer
twitter.com/FqsaAlzh
Alléger les conséquences personnelles et sociales de la maladie d'Alzheimer; diffuser l'information auprès du public sur la maladie d'Alzheimer et sur les services offerts par notre réseau; soutenir les sociétés qui offrent aide et formation; promouvoir et encourager la recherche sur la maladie d'Alzheimer entre autres par la gestion d'un fonds provincial de la recherche; établir des relations et faire des représentations auprès des autorités concernées
Sylvie Grenier, Directrice générale

Fibrose kystique Québec (FKQ) / Cystic Fibrosis Québec (CFQ)
#505, 625, av du Président-Kennedy, Montréal QC H3A 1K2
Tél: 514-877-6161; Téléc: 514-877-6116
Ligne sans frais: 800-363-7711
www.fibrosekystique.ca/quebec
www.facebook.com/FKQuebec
twitter.com/FKQuebec
Sensibiliser la population sur la fibrose kystique; amasser des fonds pour la recherche médicale; améliorer la qualité de vie des personnes atteintes de FK; découvrir un remède ou un moyen de contrôler la fibrose kystique
Olivier Jérôme, Directeur général

Fondation des étoiles / Foundation of Stars
#205, 370, rue Guy, Montréal QC H3J 1S6
Tél: 514-595-5730; Téléc: 514-595-5745
Ligne sans frais: 800-665-2358
info@fondationdesetoiles.ca
www.fondationdesetoiles.ca
www.instagram.com/fondationdesetoiles
www.linkedin.com/company/foundation-of-stars
www.facebook.com/FondationDesEtoiles
twitter.com/Fondationetoile
Amasser des fonds pour la recherche sur les maladies infantiles au Québec; ces fonds sont distribués aux quatre centres de recherche suivants: Centre de recherche de l'Hôpital Ste-Justine, Institut de recherche de l'Hôpital de Montréal pour enfants, Centre Hospitalier Universitaire de Québec et Centre Hospitalier Universitaire de Sherbrooke
Josée Saint-Pierre, Présidente-directrice générale
Sylviane Chatel, Directeur, Développement

Fondation des maladies du coeur du Québec (FMCQ) / Heart & Stroke Foundation of Québec
#500, 1434, rue Sainte-Catherine ouest, Montréal QC H3G 1R4
Tél: 514-871-1551; Téléc: 514-871-9385
Ligne sans frais: 800-567-8563
www.coeuretavc.ca
Forte de l'engagement de ses donateurs, de ses bénévoles et de ses employés, a pour mission de contribuer à l'avancement de la recherche et de promouvoir la santé du coeur, afin de réduire les invalidités et les décès dus aux maladies cardiovasculaires et aux accidents vasculaires cérébraux
Dana Ades-Landy, Vice-présidente principale

Fondation québécoise du cancer
2075, rue de Champlain, Montréal QC H2L 2T1
Tél: 514-527-2194; Téléc: 514-527-1943
Ligne sans frais: 877-336-4443
cancerquebec.mtl@fqc.qc.ca
www.fqc.qc.ca
www.youtube.com/user/fqcancer
www.facebook.com/fqcancer
twitter.com/fqcancer
Vouée à l'amélioration de la condition de la personne atteinte de cancer et de ses proches; offrir des services d'hôtellerie, d'écoute et d'information pour gens atteints du cancer; améliorer la qualité de vie des patients et celle de leurs proches
Marco Décelles, Directeur général

Foundation Fighting Blindness (FFB)
890 Yonge St., 12th Fl., Toronto ON M4W 3P4
Tel: 416-360-4200; Fax: 416-360-0060
Toll-Free: 800-461-3331
info@fightingblindness.org
www.fightingblindness.org
www.youtube.com/user/FndFightingBlindness
www.facebook.com/FoundationFightingBlindness
twitter.com/fightblindness
To support & promote research directed to finding the causes, treatments & ultimately the cures for retinitis pigmentosa, macular degeneration & related retinal diseases
Benjamin R. Yerxa, Chief Executive Officer
Jason Menzo, Chief Operating Officer
Patricia A. Dudley, Chief Human Resources Officer

Foundation for Advancing Family Medicine of the College of Family Physicians of Canada (FAFM)
2630 Skymark Ave., Mississauga ON L4W 5A4
Tel: 905-629-0900; Toll-Free: 800-387-6197
fafm.cfpc.ca
www.flickr.com/photos/cfpc
www.linkedin.com/company/991629
www.facebook.com/foundationforadvancingfamilymedicine
twitter.com/fafm_cfpc
To advance the discipline of family medicine through research & education initiatives
Sarah Delaney, Director, Awards & Development
Sandeep Kumar, Director, Finance & Asset Management
Siobhan Juniku, Marketing Lead & Coordinator, Programs
Nikita Mistry, Adminsitrative Coordinator

Garrod Association
11797 rue Poincaré, Montréal QC H3L 3L6
garrodassociation@outlook.com
www.garrod.ca
To coordinate the management of inherited metabolic disorders; To provide a forum for the exchange of information & develop guidelines for the investigation & treatment of the diseases
Pranesh Chakraborty, President
Japdeep Walia, Secretary-Treasurer

Genetic Aortic Disorders Association Canada (GADA) / Association Canadienne des Maladies Génétiques de l'Aorte
PO Box 42257, Stn. Centre Plaza, 128 Queen St. South, Mississauga ON L5M 4Z0
Tel: 905-826-3223; Fax: 905-826-2125
Toll-Free: 866-722-1722
info@gadacanada.ca
www.gadacanada.ca
www.youtube.com/user/CdnMarfanAssociation
www.facebook.com/GeneticAorticDisordersAssociationCanada
twitter.com/AorticDisorders
To support individuals diagnosed with genetic aortic disorders; To raise awareness of genetic aortic disorders
Chrisanne Campos, Executive Director

Geneva Centre for Autism (GCA)
112 Merton St., Toronto ON M4S 2Z8
Tel: 416-322-7877; *Fax:* 416-322-5894
Toll-Free: 866-436-3829
info@autism.net
www.autism.net
www.linkedin.com/company/geneva-centre-for-autism
www.facebook.com/genevacentre
twitter.com/geneva_centre
To provide people with autism & other related disorders with
opportunities & resources to fully participate in their communities
Abe Evreniadis, Chief Executive Officer
Kathy Shaw, Chief Financial Officer
Renita Paranjape, Senior Director, Programs & Services
Kim Takata, Director, Human Resources

GI (Gastrointestinal) Society
#231, 3665 Kingsway, Vancouver BC V5R 5W2
Tel: 604-873-4876; *Fax:* 604-875-4429
Toll-Free: 866-600-4875
www.badgut.org
www.youtube.com/user/badgutcanada
www.facebook.com/GISociety
twitter.com/GISociety
To improve the lives of people with GI and liver conditions,
support research, advocate for appropriate patient access to
healthcare & promote gastrointestinal & liver health
Ron Goetz, Chair
Gail Attara, Co-Founder & CEO

**Glaucoma Research Society of Canada / Société
canadienne de recherche sur le glaucome**
#215E, 1929 Bayview Ave., Toronto ON M4G 3E8
Tel: 416-483-0200; *Fax:* 416-483-6673
Toll-Free: 877-483-0204
info@glaucomaresearch.ca
www.glaucomaresearch.ca
To fund research into the causes, diagnosis, prevention &
treatment of glaucoma
James M. Park, President
Mary Ghazalian, Administrator

Health Action Network Society (HANS)
#212, 312 Main St., vancouver BC V6A 2T2
Tel: 604-435-0512; *Fax:* 604-435-1561
Toll-Free: 855-787-1891
info@hans.org
www.hans.org
www.facebook.com/HANSHealthAction
twitter.com/JoinHANS
To support complementary & alternative health care; To provide
resources about preventive medicine & natural therapeutics; To
facilitate delivery of integrated health care; To act as a voice for
natural health consumers in Canada
Lorna Hancock, Director

Health Association of African Canadians (HAAC)
c/o Black Cultural Centre for Nova Scotia, 10 Cherry Brook
Rd., Cherry Brook NS B2Z 1A8
Tel: 902-405-4222
info@haac.ca
www.haac.ca
To promote & improve the health of African Canadians in Nova
Scotia through community engagement, education, policy
recommendations, partnerships, & research participation
Donna Smith-Darrell, Co-Chair
Sharon Davis-Murdoch, Co-Chair

**Health Sciences Association of British Columbia
(HSABC)**
180 East Columbia St., New Westminster BC V3L 0G7
Tel: 604-517-0994; *Fax:* 604-515-8889
Toll-Free: 800-663-2017
webmaster@hsabc.org
www.hsabc.org
www.facebook.com/HSABC
twitter.com/hsabc
To negotiate collective agreements for members; To preserve &
promote public health care in Canada
Val Avery, President

Health Sciences Centre Foundation (HSCF)
700 William Ave., #PW112, Winnipeg MB R3E 0Z3
Tel: 204-515-5612; *Fax:* 204-813-0131
Toll-Free: 800-679-8493
info@hscfoundation.mb.ca
www.hscfoundation.mb.ca
www.instagram.com/hsc.foundation
www.facebook.com/hscfdn
twitter.com/hscfoundation
To support the people who provide health care at Health
Sciences Centre Winnipeg by funding research, education,
advanced technology & infrastructure enhancements

Jonathon Lyon, President & CEO
Susan Robinson, Vice-President, Operations

Heart & Stroke Foundation of Alberta & NWT (HSFA)
#100, 119 - 14 St. NW, Calgary AB T2N 1Z6
Tel: 403-264-5549; *Fax:* 403-237-0803
Toll-Free: 888-473-4636
www.heartandstroke.ca
To disseminate information about heart disease & stroke; To
promote research into new drugs, therapies, treatments in
disorders leading to heart disease & stroke; To conduct several
events to campaign for funds
Donna Hastings, Chief Executive Officer

**Heart & Stroke Foundation of British Columbia &
Yukon (HSFBCY)**
#200, 1212 West Broadway, Vancouver BC V6H 3V2
Tel: 778-372-8000; *Fax:* 604-736-8732
Toll-Free: 888-473-4636
www.heartandstroke.ca
To further the study, prevention & relief of cardiovascular
disease
Diego Marchese, Executive Vice-President, Western Canada

**Heart & Stroke Foundation of Canada (HSFC) /
Fondation des maladies du coeur du Canada**
#110, 1525 Carling Ave., Ottawa ON K1Z 8R9
Toll-Free: 888-473-4636
www.heartandstroke.ca
www.youtube.com/c/HeartandStrokeCAN
www.facebook.com/heartandstroke
twitter.com/heartandstroke
To further the study, prevention & reduction of disability & death
from heart disease & stroke through research, education & the
promotion of healthy lifestyles
Doug Roth, Chief Executive Officer

Heart & Stroke Foundation of Manitoba (HSFM)
1379 Kenaston Blvd., Winnipeg MB R3P 2T5
Tel: 204-949-2000; *Fax:* 204-957-1365
Toll-Free: 888-473-4636
www.heartandstroke.ca
To eliminate heart disease & stroke through education,
advocacy, & research
Allison Kesler, Chief Executive Officer
Dale Oughton, Director, Development

**Heart & Stroke Foundation of New Brunswick /
Fondation des maladies du coeur du
Nouveau-Brunswick**
580 Main St., #B210, Saint John NB E2K 1J5
Tel: 506-634-1620; *Fax:* 506-648-0098
Toll-Free: 800-663-3600
www.heartandstroke.ca
To improve the health of residents of New Brunswick by
preventing & reducing disability & death from heart disease &
stroke, through research, health promotion & advocacy
Kurtis Sisk, Chief Executive Officer

**Heart & Stroke Foundation of Newfoundland &
Labrador**
1037 Topsail Rd., Mount Pearl NL A1N 5E9
Tel: 709-753-8521; *Fax:* 709-753-3117
Toll-Free: 888-473-4636
www.heartandstroke.ca
To work in Newfoundland & Labrador to advance research,
advocate, & promote healthy lifestyles so that heart disease &
stroke will be eliminated & their impact reduced
Mary Ann Butt, Chief Executive Officer

Heart & Stroke Foundation of Nova Scotia (HSFNS)
Park Lane - Mall Level 3, PO Box 245, 5657 Spring Garden
Rd., Halifax NS B3J 3R4
Tel: 902-423-7530; *Fax:* 902-492-1464
Toll-Free: 800-423-4432
www.heartandstroke.ca
To eliminate heart disease & stroke; To advance research; To
promote healthy living; To engage in advocacy activities
Christine Baker, Vice-President, Philanthropy
Sharon Hollingsworth, Manager, Communications

Heart & Stroke Foundation of Ontario (HSFO)
PO Box 2414, #1300, 2300 Yonge St., Toronto ON M4P 1E4
Tel: 416-489-7111; *Fax:* 416-489-6885
Toll-Free: 888-473-4636
www.heartandstroke.ca
To eliminate heart disease & stroke by advancing research &
promoting healthy living; To advocate in areas such as a
smoke-free world, equal access to quality stroke care, obesity
targeting, elimination of trans-fat, & resuscitation/CPR
Aleksandar Zakonovic, Vice-President, Development
Teresa Roncon, Senior Manager, Communications

**Heart & Stroke Foundation of Prince Edward Island
Inc.**
PO Box 279, 180 Kent St., Charlottetown PE C1A 7K4
Tel: 902-892-7441; *Fax:* 902-368-7068
Toll-Free: 888-473-4636
www.heartandstroke.ca
To improve the health of Islanders through the funding of heart
disease & stroke research & the provision of heart & stroke
education & programs
Charlotte Comrie, Chief Executive Officer

**Heart & Stroke Foundation of Saskatchewan (HSFS)
/ Fondation des maladies du coeur de la
Saskatchewan**
#26, 1738 Quebec Ave., Saskatoon SK S7K 1V9
Tel: 306-244-2124; *Fax:* 306-664-4016
Toll-Free: 888-473-4636
www.youtube.com/saskheart
www.linkedin.com/company/heart-and-stroke-foundation-saskatc
hewan
To eliminate & reduce the impact of heart disease & stroke; To
advance research, promote healthy living, & advocates a healthy
public policy
Allison Kesler, Chief Executive Officer
Dale Oughton, Director, Development

Hepatitis Outreach Society of Nova Scotia (HepNS)
PO Box 29120, RPO Halifax Shopping Centre, Dartmouth NS
B2Y 1C3
Tel: 902-420-1767; *Fax:* 902-463-6725
Toll-Free: 800-521-0572
info@hepns.ca
www.hepns.ca
www.youtube.com/user/HepNSca
www.facebook.com/114379611934070
twitter.com/HepNSca
To educate Nova Scotians about Hepatitis & its prevention; To
reduce social stigmatization & isolation; To prevent the spread of
Hepatitis
Carla Densmore, Executive Director

Hospital for Sick Children Foundation (HSCF)
#835, 525 University Ave., Toronto ON M5G 2L3
Tel: 416-813-6166; *Fax:* 416-813-5024
Toll-Free: 800-661-1083
www.sickkidsfoundation.com
www.youtube.com/sickkidsfoundation
www.linkedin.com/company/sickkids-foundation
www.facebook.com/sickkidsfoundation
twitter.com/sickkids
To invest contributions in paediatric care, research & education
to help children at The Hospital for Sick Children, throughout
Canada & around the world
Kevin Goldthorp, President & Chief Development Officer
Ted Garrard, Chief Executive Officer
Emily Pang, Chief Operating Officer
Heather Clark, Vice-President, Direct & Digital Marketing
Lori Davison, Vice-President, Brand Strategy & Communications
Seanna Millar, Vice-President, Corporate Partnerships

**Huntington Society of Canada (HSC) / Société
Huntington du Canada**
#801, 20 Erb St. West, Waterloo ON N2L 1T2
Tel: 519-749-7063; *Fax:* 519-749-8965
Toll-Free: 800-998-7398
info@huntingtonsociety.ca
www.huntingtonsociety.ca
www.youtube.com/user/HuntSocCanada
www.linkedin.com/company/huntington-society-of-canada
www.facebook.com/HuntingtonSC
twitter.com/HuntingtonSC
To aspire for a world free of Huntington disease; To maximize
the quality of life of people living with HD
Bev Heim-Myers, Chief Executive Officer

Hypertension Canada
#211, 3780 - 14th Ave., Markham ON L3R 9Y5
Tel: 905-943-9400; *Fax:* 905-943-9401
www.hypertension.ca
www.youtube.com/user/hypertensioncanada
www.facebook.com/HypertensionCanada
twitter.com/HTNCANADA
To advance health by preventing & controlling high blood
presseure
Nadia Khan, President
Angelique Berg, Chief Executive Officer
Ross Tsuyuki, Vice-President
Trevor Hudson, Treasurer

Immunize Canada / Immunisation Canada
c/o Canadian Public Health Association, #404, 1525 Carling Ave., Ottawa ON K1Z 8R9
Tel: 613-725-3769; *Fax:* 613-725-9826
www.immunize.ca
www.youtube.com/user/ImmunizeCanada
www.facebook.com/ImmunizeCanada
twitter.com/immunizedotca
To contribute to the control, elimination, & eradication of vaccine preventable diseases in Canada; To increase awareness of the benefits & risks of immunization for all ages
Anne Pham-Huy, Chair
Angel Chu, Vice-Chair

Infection & Prevention Control Canada
PO Box 46125, Stn. Westdale, Winnipeg MB R3R 3S3
Tel: 204-897-5990; *Fax:* 204-895-9595
Toll-Free: 866-999-7111
info@ipac-canada.org
www.ipac-canada.org
www.youtube.com/c/IPACCanadaVideos
www.linkedin.com/company/ipac-canada
www.facebook.com/IPACCanada
twitter.com/IPACCanada
To promote excellence in the practice of infection prevention & control; To employ evidence based practice & application of epidemiological principles to improve the health of Canadians
Gerry Hansen, Execurive Director

Institut national d'excellence en santé et en services sociaux (INESSS)
2535, boul Laurier, 5e étage, Québec QC G1V 4M3
Tél: 418-643-1339; *Téléc:* 418-646-8349
inesss@inesss.qc.ca
www.inesss.qc.ca
www.linkedin.com/company/institut-national-d'excellence-en-san t-et-en-services-sociaux-inesss-
www.facebook.com/INESSSQUEBEC
twitter.com/INESSS_Qc
La promotion de l'excellence clinique et de l'utilisation efficace des ressources dans le secteur de la santé et des services sociaux
Roger Paquet, Président

International Association for Medical Assistance to Travellers (IAMAT)
#036, 67 Mowat Ave., Toronto ON M6K 3E3
Tel: 416-652-0137; *Fax:* 416-652-1983
www.iamat.org
www.flickr.com/photos/iamat_photo_contest/
www.facebook.com/IAMATHealth
twitter.com/IAMAT_Travel
To make competent care available to the traveller around the world; to make direct grants to medical institutions
Assunta Uffer-Marcolongo, President
Tullia Marcolongo, Executive Director
Nadia Sallete, Membership Officer

International Dyslexia Association (IDA)
40 York Rd., 4th Fl., Baltimore MD 21204 USA
Tel: 410-296-0232; *Fax:* 410-321-5069
info@dyslexiaida.org
dyslexiaida.org
www.youtube.com/user/idachannel
www.linkedin.com/company/international-dyslexia-association
www.facebook.com/DyslexiaIDA
twitter.com/DyslexiaIDA
To promote effective teaching approaches & related clinical educational intervention strategies for people with dyslexia
Sonja Banks, Chief Executive Officer

IRIS Mundial
#1200, 3030, boul Le Carrefour, Laval QC H7T 2P5
Tel: 450-688-9060
irismundial-info@iris.ca
irismundial.ca
www.facebook.com/irismundial
To improve the ocular health of underserved people in developing countries through access to preventive & curative eye care services
Catherine Rioux, General Manager

Juvenile Diabetes Research Foundation Canada (JDRF)
#600, 235 Yorkland Blvd., Toronto ON M2J 4Y8
Tel: 647-789-2000; *Fax:* 416-491-2111
Toll-Free: 877-287-3533
general@jdrf.ca
www.jdrf.ca
www.youtube.com/JDRFCanada
www.facebook.com/JDRFCanada
twitter.com/JDRF_Canada

To support research to find a cure for diabetes & its complications; To increase awareness of diabetes, particularly Juvenile (Type 1) diabetes
Lorne Shiff, Chair
Dave Prowten, President & CEO

Kidney Cancer Canada Association
#226, 4936 Yonge St., Toronto ON M2N 6S3
Tel: 416-603-0277; *Fax:* 416-603-0277
Toll-Free: 866-598-7166
info@kidneycancercanada.ca
www.kidneycancercanada.ca
www.youtube.com/KidneyCancerCanada
www.linkedin.com/company/kidney-cancer-canada
www.facebook.com/KidneyCancerCanada
twitter.com/KidneyCancer_Ca
To support & improve the lives of patients & families living with kidney cancer; To raise awareness of kidney cancer treatment options; To promote quality care across Canada; To increase funding for kidney cancer research
Andrew Weller, Chair
Stephen Andrew, Executive Director
Gerry Backs, Director, Development & Donor Relations

Kidney Foundation of Canada (KFOC) / Fondation canadienne du rein
#310, 5160, boul Decarie, Montréal QC H3X 2H9
Tel: 514-369-4806; *Fax:* 514-369-2472
Toll-Free: 800-361-7494
info@kidney.ca
www.kidney.ca
www.youtube.com/kidneycanada
www.linkedin.com/company/the-kidney-foundation-of-canada
www.facebook.com/kidneyfoundation
twitter.com/kidneycanada
To improve the health & quality of life of people living with kidney disease; To fund research & related clinical education; To provide services for the special needs of individuals living with kidney disease; To advocate for access to high quality health care; To actively promote awareness of & commitment to organ donation
Greg Robbins, National President
Elizabeth Myles, National Executive Director
Teresa Havill, National Director, Human Resources
Carole Larouche, National Director, Finance
Stéphanie Lord-Fontaine, National Director, Research
Wendy Kudeba, National Director, Communications & Marketing

Leucan - Association pour les enfants atteints de cancer / Leucan - Association for Children with Cancer
#300, 550, av Beaumont, Montréal QC H3N 1V1
Tél: 514-731-3696; *Téléc:* 514-731-2667
Ligne sans frais: 800-361-9643
www.leucan.qc.ca
www.instagram.com/leucan
www.linkedin.com/company/leucan
www.facebook.com/leucanpageprovinciale
twitter.com/leucan
Accroître la confiance en l'avenir des enfants atteints de cancer et de leurs familles
Pascale Bouchard, Directrice générale

The Leukemia & Lymphoma Society of Canada (LLSC) / Société de leucémie et lymphome du Canada
#804, 2 Lansing Square, Toronto ON M2J 4P8
Tel: 416-661-9541; *Fax:* 416-661-7799
Toll-Free: 877-668-8326
AdminCanada@lls.org
www.llscanada.org
www.youtube.com/llscanada
www.linkedin.com/company/5127044
www.facebook.com/LeukemiaandLymphomaSocietyofCanada
twitter.com/llscanada
To cure leukemia, lymphoma, Hodgkin's disease & myeloma & to improve the quality of life of patients & their families
Alicia Talarico, President
Ted Moroz, Chair

Lieutenant Governor's Circle on Mental Health & Addiction
c/o Duncan Craig LLP, 2800 Scotia Place, 10060 Jasper Ave., Edmonton AB T5J 3V9
Tel: 780-850-0533
execdir@lgcirclealberta.ca
www.lgcircle.ca
www.facebook.com/LGCircle
twitter.com/LGCircle
To increase public knowledge of mental illness & addiction
Sol Rolingher, Chair

The Lung Association AB & NWT
PO Box 4500, Stn. South, #208, 17420 Stony Plain Rd., Edmonton AB T6E 6K2
Tel: 780-488-6819; *Fax:* 780-488-7195
Toll-Free: 888-566-5864
info@ab.lung.ca
www.ab.lung.ca
www.facebook.com/lungassociationabnwt
twitter.com/lungabnwt
To raise funds for research, prevention of lung disease, & patient supports
Evangeline Berube, Chair
Nina Snyder, COO

The Lung Association of Nova Scotia (LANS)
#200, 6331 Lady Hammond Rd., Halifax NS B3K 2S2
Tel: 902-443-8141; *Fax:* 902-445-2573
Toll-Free: 888-566-5864
info@ns.lung.ca
www.ns.lung.ca
www.instagram.com/ns_lung
www.facebook.com/LungNS
twitter.com/NSLung
To control & prevent lung disease in Nova Scotia; To help people who live with lung disease
Robert MacDonald, President & CEO
Mohammed Al-Hamdani, Director, Health Initiatives
Maria Caines, Senior Manager, Finance
Michelle Donaldson, Manager, Communications & Special Projects
Lynette Hollett, Manager, Donor Relations

Lung Health Foundation
#401, 18 Wynford Dr., Toronto ON M3C 0K8
Tel: 416-864-9911
info@lunghealth.ca
lunghealth.ca
www.youtube.com/user/ONLungAssociation
www.linkedin.com/company/lunghealthfoundation
www.facebook.com/lunghealthfoundation
twitter.com/LungHealthFdn
To promote respiratory health through medical research & education
George Habib, President & CEO

Lupus Canada
#306, 615 Davis Dr., Newmarket ON L3Y 2R2
Tel: 905-235-1714; *Toll-Free:* 800-661-1468
info@lupuscanada.org
www.lupuscanada.org
www.facebook.com/LupusCanada
twitter.com/lupuscanada
To improve the lives of people living with lupus; To encourage cooperation among the lupus organizations in Canada
Tanya Carlton, President
Shane Dungey, Vice-President
Malcolm Gilroy, Treasurer
Leanne Mielczarek, Executive Director

Lupus Foundation of Ontario (LFO)
PO Box 687, 294 Ridge Rd. North, Ridgeway ON L0S 1N0
Tel: 905-894-4611; *Fax:* 905-894-4616
Toll-Free: 800-368-8377
lupusont@vaxxine.com
www.vaxxine.com/lupus
To serve the lupus patient community as a charitable organization
Laurie Kroeker, President

Lupus New Brunswick
#17, 55 Grant St., Moncton NB E1A 3R3
Tel: 506-384-6227; *Toll-Free:* 877-303-8080
lupins@rogers.com
To promote eduction & public awareness of lupus; To bring together lupus patients, friends, family & other interested persons for a network of support

Lupus Newfoundland & Labrador
PO Box 8121, Stn. A, St. John's NL A1B 3M9
Tel: 709-368-8130
lupus.nl.ca@gmail.com
www.envision.ca/webs/lupusnfldlab
To support individuals with lupus; to promote education & awareness of lupus; To support research & treatment of the disease

Lupus Ontario
#10, 25 Valleywood Dr., Toronto ON L3R 5L9
Tel: 905-415-1099; *Fax:* 905-415-9874
Toll-Free: 877-240-1099
admin@lupusontario.org
www.lupusontario.org
twitter.com/LupusON

To serve the needs of Lupus sufferers in Ontario
Cathy Ferren, President
Karen Furlotte, Office Manager & Coordinator

Lupus SK Society
c/o Royal University Hospital, PO Box 88, 103 Hospital Dr.,
Saskatoon SK S7N 0W8
Toll-Free: 877-566-6123
lupus@lupussk.com
www.lupussk.com
www.facebook.com/lupus.sask
twitter.com/Lupus_SK
To assist individuals affected by lupus by providing education,
raising awareness, & supporting research
Irene Driedger, Treasurer

Lupus Society of Alberta (LESA)
#900, 105 - 12 Ave. SE, Calgary AB T2G 1A1
Tel: 403-228-7956; Fax: 403-228-7853
Toll-Free: 888-242-9182
lupuslsa@shaw.ca
www.lupus.ab.ca
www.instagram.com/challengelupus
www.facebook.com/lupussocietyofalberta
twitter.com/lupussocietyab
To provide education & support on lupus issues & enable
research to find a cure
Donna Campeau, Executive Director

Lupus Society of Manitoba
#105, 105 Fort Whyte Way, Oak Bluff MB R4G 0B1
Tel: 204-942-6825; Fax: 204-832-6912
lupus@mymts.net
www.lupusmanitoba.com
www.facebook.com/lupus.manitoba
To provide support, encouragement & education to lupus
patients & their families
Debbie Dohan, President

Manitoba Association of Optometrists (MAO)
#217, 530 Century St., Winnipeg MB R3H 0Y4
Tel: 204-943-9811; Fax: 204-943-1208
mao@mb-opto.ca
www.mb-opto.ca
To regulate the practice of optometry in Manitoba, in accordance
with The Optometry Act & Regulation; To represent optometrists
in Manitoba; To protect & promote the vision care needs & eye
health of Manitobans
Laureen Goodridge, Executive Director

Manitoba Chiropractors' Association (MCA)
#610, 1445 Portage Ave., Winnipeg MB R3G 3P4
Tel: 204-942-3000; Fax: 204-942-3010
Toll-Free: 855-430-0383
info@mbchiro.org
manitobachiropractors.ca
To act as both a regulatory body & a professional association to
serve the public & the chiropractors of Manitoba; To foster high
standards of chiropractic health care for Manitobans; To ensure
that safe, ethical & competent services are provided by Manitoba
chiropractors
Karen Woloschuk, Executive Director
E. Audrey Toth, Registrar

Manitoba Lung Association
#204, 825 Sherbrook St., Winnipeg MB R3A 1M5
Tel: 204-774-5501
info@mb.lung.ca
www.mb.lung.ca
www.youtube.com/channel/UC3OyzjhurY-5KBPZvsG1G4Q
www.facebook.com/manitobalungassociation
twitter.com/ManitobaLung
To improve lung health
Brenda Dyck, Chair
Neil Johnston, President & CEO

Manitoba Medical Service Foundation Inc. (MMSF)
PO Box 1046, Stn. Main, Winnipeg MB R3G 3P3
Tel: 204-788-6801; Fax: 204-774-1761
info@mmsf.ca
www.mmsf.ca
To consider the provision of funds for the advancement of
scientific, educational & other activities to maintain & improve
the health & welfare of the citizens of Manitoba
Greg Hammond, Executive Director
Lindsay Du Val, Chair

Manitoba Naturopathic Association (MNA)
PO Box 434, 971 Corydon Ave., Winnipeg MB R3M 0Y0
Tel: 204-947-0381
directormna@gmail.com
www.mbnd.ca

To act as a regulatory body for the profession of naturopathy, in
accordance with The Naturopathic Act of Manitoba
Lesley Phimister, Registrar

Manitoba Paraplegia Foundation Inc.
825 Sherbrook St., Winnipeg MB R3A 1M5
Tel: 204-786-4753; Fax: 204-786-1140
winnipeg@canparaplegic.org
www.cpamanitoba.ca/mpf
To provide support for research & prevention activities; To
provide direct aid to paraplegics & quadriplegics for home
modifications, vocational aid & other items to assist spinal cord
injured Manitobans to lead independent lives within the
community; To provide support for special projects undertaken
on behalf of spinal cord injured persons in Manitoba
Doug Finkbeiner, President

Manitoba Public Health Association (MPHA)
MB
admin@manitobapha.ca
www.manitobapha.ca
To influence health, social, environmental, & economic policy
decisions, in order to improve the well-being of people in
Manitoba; To ensure that health promotion, health protection &
disease protection are part of services
Stephanie van Haute, President

Manitoba Society of Occupational Therapists (MSOT)
#7, 120 Maryland St., Winnipeg MB R3G 1L1
Tel: 204-957-1214; Fax: 204-775-2340
msot@msot.mb.ca
www.msot.mb.ca
www.facebook.com/TheMSOT
To build & strengthen occupational therapy in Manitoba
Heidi Garcia, Executive Officer

Médecins francophones du Canada
8355, boul Saint-Laurent, Montréal QC H2P 2Z6
Tél: 514-388-2228; Téléc: 514-388-5335
Ligne sans frais: 800-387-2228
info@medecinsfrancophones.ca
www.medecinsfrancophones.ca
www.linkedin.com/company/medecins-francophones-du-canada
www.facebook.com/MdFCanada
twitter.com/MdFCanada
Diane Poirier, Présidente
Nicole Parent, Directrice générale

Medical Council of Canada (MCC) / Le Conseil médical du Canada (CMC)
1021 Thomas Spratt Pl., Ottawa ON K1G 5L5
Tel: 613-520-2240; Fax: 613-248-5234
service@mcc.ca
www.mcc.ca
www.youtube.com/user/medicalcouncilcanada
www.linkedin.com/company/medical-council-of-canada
www.facebook.com/MedicalCouncilOfCanada
twitter.com/MedCouncilCan
To establish & promote a qualification in medicine, known as the
Licentiate of the Medical Council of Canada, such that the
holders thereof are acceptable to medical licensing authorities
for the issuance of a licence to practise medicine
Maureen Topps, Executive Director & CEO

Medical Society of Prince Edward Island (MSPEI)
2 Myrtle St., Stratford PE C1B 2W2
Tel: 902-368-7303; Fax: 902-566-3934
www.mspei.org
twitter.com/MSPEI_Docs
To promote health & improvement of medical services; To
prevent disease; To represent members at national bodies &
government; To consider all matters concerning the professional
welfare of members
Lea Bryden, Chief Executive Officer
Doug Carr, Finance Manager
Heather Mullen, Membership Coordinator

The Michener Institute for Applied Health Sciences
222 St. Patrick St., Toronto ON M5T 1V4
Tel: 416-596-3101; Toll-Free: 800-387-9066
info@michener.ca
www.michener.ca
www.youtube.com/user/TheMichenerInstitute
www.facebook.com/TheMichenerInstitute
twitter.com/michenerinst
To design, develop & deliver the best educational programs,
products & services in applied health sciences
Cornell Wright, Chair
Kevin Smith, Chief Executive Officer

Multiple Sclerosis Society of Canada (MS) / Société canadienne de la sclérose en plaques
North Tower, #500, 250 Dundas St. West, Toronto ON M5T 2Z5
Tel: 416-922-6065; Fax: 416-922-7538
Toll-Free: 800-268-7582
info@mssociety.ca
mssociety.ca
www.youtube.com/MSSocietyCanada
www.linkedin.com/company/ms-society-of-canada
www.facebook.com/MSSocietyCanada
twitter.com/mssocietycanada
To be a leader in finding a cure for multiple sclerosis & enabling
people affected by MS to enhance their quality of life
Pamela Valentine, President & CEO

Muscular Dystrophy Canada (MDC) / Dystrophie musculaire Canada (DMC)
#500, 40 Eglinton Ave. East, Toronto ON M4P 3A2
Toll-Free: 800-567-2873
info@muscle.ca
www.muscle.ca
www.youtube.com/user/musculardystrophycan
www.linkedin.com/company/muscular-dystrophy-canada
www.facebook.com/MuscularDystrophyCA
twitter.com/md_canada
To work towards finding a cure & providing support for those
living with neuromuscular disorders, their family members &
caregivers, health professionals & researchers; To enhance the
lives of those with neuromuscular disorders by providing ongoing
support & resources while searching for a cure through
well-funded research
Barbara Stead-Coyle, CEO

Myasthenia Gravis Association of British Columbia (MGABC)
2805 Kingsway, Vancouver BC V5R 5H9
Tel: 604-451-5511; Fax: 604-451-5651
myasthenia.gravis@bc-cfa.org
www.myastheniagravis.ca
To provide information & support to British Columbians who
suffer from Myasthenia Gravis (Grave Muscular Disease) & to
their caregivers; to increase public awareness of the disease; to
gather & disseminate specific information on Myasthenia Gravis
to healthcare providers in British Columbia; to foster & support
research into the causes & treatment of Myasthenia Gravis
Brenda Kelsey, President

National Eating Disorder Information Centre (NEDIC)
200 Elizabeth St., #ES7-421, Toronto ON M5G 2C4
Tel: 416-340-4156; Fax: 416-340-4736
Toll-Free: 866-633-4220
nedic@uhn.ca
www.nedic.ca
www.instagram.com/the_nedic
www.facebook.com/thenedic
twitter.com/theNEDIC
To provide information & resources on eating disorders, food &
weight preoccupation; To raise public awareness about eating
disorders & related issues
Suzanne Phillips, Manager, Program
Ary Maharaj, Coordinator, Education & Outreach

National ME/FM Action Network / Réseau national d'action EM/FM encéphalomyélite myalgique/fibromyalgie
#512, 33 Banner Rd., Nepean ON K2H 8V7
Tel: 613-829-6667; Fax: 613-829-8518
mefminfo@mefmaction.com
www.mefmaction.com
www.facebook.com/MEFMActionNetwork
twitter.com/mefmaction
To offer support, advocacy, education & research into the many,
varied, anomalies connected with Myalgic Encephalomyelitis /
Chronic Fatigue Syndrome & Fibromyalgia (ME/FM)
Lydia E. Neilson, M.S.M., Founder & CEO

Neurological Health Charities Canada (NHCC)
c/o Parkinson Canada, #316, 4211 Yonge St., Toronto ON M2P 2A9
Tel: 416-227-9700; Fax: 416-227-9600
Toll-Free: 800-565-3000
info@mybrainmatters.ca
www.mybrainmatters.ca
www.youtube.com/MyBrainMatters
www.facebook.com/MyBrainMatters
twitter.com/MyBrainMatters
To improve quality of life for persons with chronic brain
conditions & their caregivers; To increase awareness in the
government about neurological issues; To support research
Joyce Gordon, Chair

New Brunswick Association of Dietitians (NBAD) / Association des diététistes du Nouveau-Brunswick (ADNB)
PO Box 7022, Riverview NB E1B 4T8

Tel: 506-386-5903; *Fax:* 506-450-9375
registrar@adnb-nbad.com
www.adnb-nbad.com

To regulate & maintain excellence in dietetic practice in New Brunswick
Nicole Arsenault Bishop, Executive Director & Registrar
Véronique Ferguson, President

New Brunswick Association of Naturopathic Doctors (NBAND)
c/o Crystal Charest, 2278 King George Hwy., Miramichi NB E1V 6N6

Tel: 506-773-3700; *Fax:* 506-773-3704
www.nband.ca
twitter.com/NewBrunswickNDs

To educate the public on the philosophies & values of Naturopathic Medicine; To promote the profession within the province
Crystal Charest, Contact

New Brunswick Association of Optometrists (NBAO) / Association des optométristes du Nouveau-Brunswick
#1, 490 Gibson St., Fredericton NB E3A 4E9

Tel: 506-458-8759; *Fax:* 506-450-1271
nbao@nbao.ca
www.nbao.ca

To represent Doctors of Optometry in New Brunswick
Krista McDevitt, President

New Brunswick Chiropractors' Association (NBCA) / Association des chiropraticiens du Nouveau-Brunswick
#202, 327 St. George St., Moncton NB E1C 1W8

Tel: 506-455-6800; *Fax:* 506-455-4430
comments@nbchiropractic.ca
www.nbchiropractic.ca

To regulate the practice of chiropractic medicine & govern its members in accordance with the Act & the by-laws, in order to serve & protect the public interests; To establish, maintain, develop & enforce standards of qualification for the practice of chiropractic, including the required knowledge, skill & efficiency; To establish, maintain, develop & enforce standards of professional ethics; To promote public awareness of the role of the Association & the work of chiropractic; To communicate & cooperate with other professional organizations for the advancement of the best interests of the Association, including the publication of books, papers & journals; To encourage studies in chiropractic & provide assistance & facilities for special studies & research
Frances LeBlanc, Chief Executive Officer

New Brunswick Lung Association / Association pulmonaire du Nouveau-Brunswick
65 Brunswick St., Fredericton NB E3B 1G5

Tel: 506-455-8961; *Fax:* 506-462-0939
Toll-Free: 888-566-5864
info@nb.lung.ca
www.nb.lung.ca
www.youtube.com/user/TheNBLungAssociation
www.facebook.com/nblung
twitter.com/NBlung

To promote wellness throughout New Brunswick & prevent lung disease
Barbara MacKinnon, President & CEO
Ted Allingham, Director, Finance & Administration
Monica Brewer, Director, Fundraising & Donor Relations
Liz Smith, Director, Public Education
Barbara Walls, Director, Health Promotion

New Brunswick Medical Society (NBMS) / Société médicale du Nouveau-Brunswick
21 Alison Blvd., Fredericton NB E3C 2N5

Tel: 506-458-8860; *Fax:* 506-458-9853
Toll-Free: 800-661-2001
info@nbms.nb.ca
www.facebook.com/NBDocs
twitter.com/nb_docs

To advance medical science in all its branches; To promote improvement of medical services; To prevent disease in cooperation with health officers & all others engaged in such work; To maintain high scientific & professional status for its members; To promote medical science & related arts & sciences
Anthony Knight, Chief Executive Officer
Lisa LePage, Chief Operating Officer
Marcelle Saulnier, Policy & Communications Officer

Newfoundland & Labrador Association of Optometrists (NLAO)
PO Box 8042, St. John's NL A1B 3M7

Tel: 709-765-1096; *Fax:* 709-739-8378
nlao@bellaliant.net
www.nlao.org

To provide an online resource for Doctors of Optometry & other health care providers in Newfoundland & Labrador
Ed Breen, Executive Director

Newfoundland & Labrador Chiropractic Association
#285W, 120 Torbay Rd., St. John's NL A1A 2G8

Tel: 709-739-7762; *Fax:* 709-739-7703
www.nlchiropractic.ca

Newfoundland & Labrador College of Dietitians (NLCD)
PO Box 1756, Stn. C, St. John's NL A1C 5P5

Tel: 709-753-4040; *Fax:* 709-781-1044
Toll-Free: 877-753-4040
registrar@nlcd.ca
www.nlcd.ca

To regulate Registered Dietitians & to ensure competency in the dietetic profession, in the interest of the people in Newfoundland
Cynthia Whalen, Registrar

Newfoundland & Labrador Lung Association (NLLA)
PO Box 13457, Stn. A, St. John's NL A1B 4B8

Tel: 709-726-4664; *Fax:* 709-726-2550
Toll-Free: 888-566-5864
info@nf.lung.ca
www.nf.lung.ca
www.facebook.com/NLLung
twitter.com/nllung

To achieve healthy breathing for the people of Newfoundland & Labrador
Greg Noel, President & CEO

Newfoundland & Labrador Medical Association (NLMA)
164 MacDonald Dr., St. John's NL A1A 4B3

Tel: 709-726-7424; *Fax:* 709-726-7525
Toll-Free: 800-563-2003
nlma@nlma.nl.ca
www.nlma.nl.ca
www.youtube.com/user/nlmavideo
www.facebook.com/nlma.nl.ca
twitter.com/_nlma

To represent & support physicians in Newfoundland & Labrador; To provide leadership in the promotion of good health & the provision of quality health care to the people of the province
Robert Thompson, Executive Director
J. David Mitchell, Director, Administration & Membership
Jonathan Carpenter, Director, Communications & Public Affairs

Newfoundland & Labrador Public Health Association (NLPHA)
PO Box 8172, St. John's NL A1B 3M9

Tel: 709-364-1589
info@nlpha.ca
www.nlpha.ca
twitter.com/NLPHA_PubHealth

To advocate for the physical, emotional, social & environmental well-being of Newfoundland & Labrador's people & communities
Holly LeDrew, President
Hayley Cooze, Secretary
Pat Murray, Treasurer

Northwest Territories Medical Association (NWTMA)
PO Box 1732, Yellowknife NT X1A 2P3

Tel: 867-920-4575; *Fax:* 867-920-4578
nwtmda@gmail.com
www.nwtma.ca

To advocate on behalf of its members & citizens for access to quality health care; To provide leadership & guidance to its members
Katherine Breen, President

Nova Scotia Association of Naturopathic Doctors (NSAND)
PO Box 245, Lower Sackville NS B4C 2S9

Tel: 902-431-8001
info@nsand.ca
www.nsand.ca
www.facebook.com/novascotiaassociationofNDs
twitter.com/NSAND_

To be a resource for its members & to inform the public about naturopathic medicine
Bryan Rade, President
Florence Woolaver, Administrator

Nova Scotia Association of Optometrists (NSAO)
PO Box 142, #502, 5657 Spring Garden Rd., Halifax NS B3J 3R4

Tel: 902-435-2845; *Fax:* 902-425-2441
nsao@accesswave.ca
www.nsoptometrists.ca

To foster excellence in the delivery of vision & eye health services in Nova Scotia; To act as the voice of optometry in Nova Scotia

Nova Scotia College of Chiropractors (NSCC)
Park Lane Terraces, PO Box 142, #502, 5657 Spring Garden Rd., Halifax NS B3J 3R4

Tel: 902-407-4255; *Fax:* 902-425-2441
inquiries@chiropractors.ns.ca
www.chiropractors.ns.ca

To promote & improve the proficiency of chiropractors in all matters relating to the practice of chiropractic; To protect the public from untrained & unqualified persons acting as chiropractors; To advance the chiropractic profession
John K. Sutherland, Executive Director

Nova Scotia Dietetic Association (NSDA)
#301, 380 Bedford Hwy., Halifax NS B3M 2L4

Tel: 902-493-3034
info@nsdassoc.ca
www.nsdassoc.ca

To regulate dietitians & nutritionists in the province, & register & discipline (when necessary) practitioners to ensure safe, ethical & competent dietetic practice
Melissa Campbell, President
Jennifer Garus, Executive Manager

Occupational & Environmental Medical Association of Canada (OEMAC) / Association canadienne de la médecine du travail et de l'environnement (ACMTE)
#503, 386 Broadway, Winnipeg MB R3C 3R6

Fax: 877-947-9767
Toll-Free: 888-223-3808
info@oemac.org
oemac.org

To act as the voice of the Canadian occupational & environmental medicine sector
Olufemi Adekeye, President
Coralee Dolyniuk, Executive Director

Ontario Association of Naturopathic Doctors (OAND)
#603, 789 Don Mills Rd., Toronto ON M3C 1T5

Tel: 416-233-2001; *Fax:* 416-233-2924
Toll-Free: 877-628-7284
info@oand.org
www.oand.org
www.facebook.com/ndontario
twitter.com/OANDorg

To act as a voice for naturopathic doctors in Ontario
John Wellner, Chief Executive Officer

Ontario Association of Optometrists (OAO)
PO Box 16, #801, 20 Adelaide St. East, Toronto ON M5C 2T6

Tel: 905-826-3522; *Fax:* 905-826-0625
Toll-Free: 800-540-3837
info@optom.on.ca
www.optom.on.ca
www.youtube.com/user/OntarioOptometrists
www.linkedin.com/company/onoptometrists
www.facebook.com/OntarioOptometrists
twitter.com/ONOptometrists

To advance the profession of optometry at the government, regulatory & public levels
Justin Brown, Chief Executive Officer
Bethany Carey, Director, Member Services & Professional Affairs

Ontario Chiropractic Association (OCA) / Association chiropratique de l'Ontario
#201, 70 University Ave., Toronto ON M5J 2M4

Tel: 416-860-0070; *Fax:* 416-860-0857
Toll-Free: 877-327-2273
oca@chiropractic.on.ca
www.chiropractic.on.ca
www.youtube.com/user/OntarioChiropractic
www.linkedin.com/company/ontario-chiropractic-association
www.facebook.com/ontariochiropracticassociation
twitter.com/ONChiroAssoc

To serve its members by promoting the philosophy, art, & science of chiropractic & thereby enhance the health & well-being of the citizens of Ontario
Ken Brough, President
Caroline Brereton, Chief Executive Officer

Ontario Medical Association (OMA)
#900, 150 Bloor St. West, Toronto ON M5S 3C1
Tel: 416-599-2580; *Fax:* 416-599-9309
Toll-Free: 800-268-7215
info@oma.org
www.oma.org
www.youtube.com/user/OntMedAssociation
www.linkedin.com/company/ontario-medical-association
www.facebook.com/Ontariosdoctors
twitter.com/OntariosDoctors
To represent the clinical, political & economic interests of
Ontario physicians; To promote an accessible, quality
health-care system
Allan O'Dette, Chief Executive Officer
Terry Caputo, Chief Financial Officer

Ontario Occupational Health Nurses Association (OOHNA)
#504, 701 Evans Ave., Toronto ON M9C 1A3
Tel: 416-239-6462; *Toll-Free:* 866-664-6276
administration@oohna.on.ca
www.oohna.on.ca
www.linkedin.com/in/oohna
twitter.com/OOHNA1
To foster a climate of excellence, innovation & partnership
enabling Ontario Occupational Health Nurses to achieve positive
workplace health & safety objectives
Drew Sousa, Executive Director

Ontario Public Health Association (OPHA) / Association pour la santé publique de l'Ontario
#200, 154 Pearl St., Toronto ON M5H 1L3
Tel: 416-367-3313; *Fax:* 416-367-2844
admin@opha.on.ca
www.opha.on.ca
www.linkedin.com/company/ontario-public-health-association
www.facebook.com/opha1949
twitter.com/OPHA_Ontario
To provide leadership on issues affecting public health in
Ontario, such as preserving the environment, promoting disease
prevention, narrowing health disparities & reducing poverty; To
strengthen the influence of persons involved in public &
community health across Ontario
Karen Ellis-Scharfenberg, President
Pegeen Walsh, Executive Director

Ontario Rheumatology Association (ORA)
#262, 6 - 14845 Yonge St., Aurora ON L4G 6H8
Tel: 905-952-0698; *Fax:* 905-952-0708
admin@ontariorheum.ca
ontariorheum.ca
To represent Ontario Rheumatologists & promote their pursuit of
excellence in Arthritis care in Ontario
Jane Purvis, President
Denis Morrice, Executive Director

Ontario Society of Occupational Therapists (OSOT)
#210, 55 Eglinton Ave. East, Toronto ON M4P 1G8
Tel: 416-322-3011; *Fax:* 416-322-6705
Toll-Free: 877-676-6768
osot@osot.on.ca
www.osot.on.ca
www.linkedin.com/company/ontario-society-of-occupational-therapists
www.facebook.com/OntarioOTs
twitter.com/osotvoice
To promote & represent the profession of occupational therapy
in the areas of government affairs, education, professional
issues & public relations in Ontario
Christie Benchley, Executive Director

Opticians Association of Canada (OAC)
#2706, 83 Garry St., Winnipeg MB R3C 4J9
Tel: 204-982-6060; *Fax:* 204-947-2519
Toll-Free: 800-842-3155
canada@opticians.ca
www.opticians.ca
www.youtube.com/user/opticianstv
www.linkedin.com/company/opticians-association-of-canada
www.facebook.com/OpticiansAssociationofCanada
twitter.com/OACexecutiveDr
Robert Dalton, Executive Director

Ordre des ergothérapeutes du Québec (OEQ)
#920, 2021, av Union, Montréal QC H3A 2S9
Tél: 514-844-5778; *Téléc:* 514-844-0478
Ligne sans frais: 800-265-5778
ergo@oeq.org
www.oeq.org
Protéger le public; assurer la qualité d'ergothérapie; promouvoir
l'accessibilité aux services d'ergothérapie; soutenir la pratique
professionnelle et son évolution; favoriser le rayonnement de la
profession

Alain Bibeau, Président-directeur général
Louise Tremblay, Secrétaire générale

Ordre des orthophonistes et audiologistes du Québec (OOAQ)
#800, 630, rue Sherbrooke ouest, Montréal QC H3A 1E4
Tél: 514-282-9123; *Téléc:* 514-282-9541
Ligne sans frais: 888-232-9123
info@ooaq.qc.ca
www.ooaq.qc.ca
www.youtube.com/channel/UCOMI_RSI03Dzg5zTRX1izcA
www.linkedin.com/company/ooaq
www.facebook.com/286966305093140
D'assurer la protection du public en regard du domaine
d'exercice de ses membres, soit les troubles de la
communication humaine; surveiller l'exercice professionnel des
orthophonistes et des audiologistes et voir à favoriser
l'accessibilité du public à des services de qualité; contribuer à
l'intégration sociale des individus et à l'amélioration de la qualité
de vie de la population québécoise
Maya Raic, Directrice générale

Ordre des techniciens et techniciennes dentaires du Québec (OTTDQ)
#900, 500, rue Sherbrooke ouest, Montréal QC H3A 3C6
Tél: 514-282-3837; *Téléc:* 514-844-7556
secretariat@ottdq.org
www.ottdq.org
www.facebook.com/OTTDQ
De réglementer la profession des techniciens dentaires afin de
protéger le public et d'assurer la meilleure qualité de service
possible est fournie
Stéphan Provencher, Président
Emmanuelle Duquette, Directrice générale et secrétaire

Ordre professionnel de la physiothérapie du Québec (OPPQ)
#1000, 7151, rue Jean-Talon est, Anjou QC H1M 3N8
Tél: 514-351-2770; *Téléc:* 514-351-2658
Ligne sans frais: 800-361-2001
physio@oppq.qc.ca
www.oppq.qc.ca
Assurer la protection du public en surveillant l'exercice de la
physiothérapie par ses membres et en contribuant à leur
développement professionnel
Denis Pelletier, Président
Claude Laurent, Directeur général et secrétaire

Ordre professionnel des diététistes Québec / Québec Professional Union of Dieticians
Tour Ouest, 550, rue Sherbrooke ouest, Montréal QC H3A 1B9
Tél: 514-393-3733; *Téléc:* 514-393-3582
Ligne sans frais: 888-393-8528
Claudette Péloquin-Antoun, Présidente

Ordre professionnel des sexologues du Québec (OPSQ)
1200, rue Papineau, Montréal QC H2K 4R5
Tél: 438-386-6777; *Ligne sans frais:* 855-386-6777
info@opsq.org
opsq.org
De réglementer la profession des sexologues afin de protéger le
public et d'assurer la meilleure qualité de service possible est
fournie
Isabelle Beaulieu, Directrice générale et secrétaire de l'Ordre

Orthotics Prosthetics Canada (OPC) / Orthèse Prothèse Canada
#705, 1 Eglinton Ave. East, Toronto ON M4P 3A1
Tel: 613-623-6687
info@opcanada.ca
www.opcanada.ca
www.linkedin.com/company/orthotics-prosthetics-canada----orthèse-prothèse-canada
www.facebook.com/OPCanada
twitter.com/CanadaOPC
To promote high standards of patient care & professionalism in
the prosthetic & orthotic profession throughout Canada; To
represent members with government, related organizations &
the general public
Jesse Cornell, President
Séamus Gearin, Executive Director

Osteoporosis Canada / Ostéoporose Canada
#201, 250 Ferrand Dr., Toronto ON M3C 3G8
Tel: 416-696-2663; *Fax:* 416-696-2673
Toll-Free: 800-463-6842
www.osteoporosis.ca
www.youtube.com/user/osteoporosisca
www.linkedin.com/company/osteoporosis-canada
www.facebook.com/osteoporosiscanada
twitter.com/OsteoporosisCA

To encourage research into the prevention, diagnosis &
treatment of osteoporosis; To improve access to osteoporosis
care & support
Famida Jiwa, President & CEO

Ostomy Canada Society
#210, 5800 Ambler Dr., Mississauga ON L4W 4J4
Tel: 905-212-7111; *Fax:* 905-212-9002
Toll-Free: 888-969-9698
info1@ostomycanada.ca
www.ostomycanada.ca
www.youtube.com/user/ostomycanada
www.linkedin.com/company/ostomy-canada-society
www.facebook.com/OstomyCanada
twitter.com/OstomyCanada
To assist all persons with gastrointestinal or urinary diversions,
as well as their families & caregivers, by providing emotional &
practical support & help, information & instruction
Ann Ivol, President

Ovarian Cancer Canada (OCC) / Cancer de l'ovaire Canada (COC)
#205, 145 Front St. East, Toronto ON M5A 1E3
Tel: 416-962-2700; *Fax:* 416-962-2701
Toll-Free: 877-413-7970
info@ovariancanada.org
www.ovariancanada.org
www.youtube.com/OvarianCancerCanada
www.linkedin.com/company/ovarian-cancer-canada
www.facebook.com/OvarianCancerCanada
twitter.com/OvarianCanada
To support women & their families living with the disease; To
raise awareness in the general public & with health care
professionals; To fund research to develop reliable early
detection techniques, improved treatments & a cure
Elisabeth Baugh, Chief Executive Officer
Mapy Villaudy, Vice-President, Marketing, Communications &
Development
Bo Wang-Frape, Vice-President, Finance & Administration

Pain Society of Alberta (PSA)
132 Warwick Rd., Edmonton AB T5X 4P8
Tel: 780-457-5225; *Fax:* 780-475-7968
team@painab.ca
painab.ca
To provide support for patients & health care professionals in
Alberta who are concerned with pain management & treatment
Dawn Petit, President
Glyn Smith, Administrator

Pallium Canada
Ottawa ON
Toll-Free: 833-888-5327
info@pallium.ca
www.pallium.ca
www.youtube.com/user/palliumcanada
www.linkedin.com/company/palliumcanada
www.facebook.com/PalliumCanada
twitter.com/palliumcanada
To improve the quality & accessibility of palliative care in Canada
Jeffrey B. Moat, Chief Executive Officer
José Pereira, Scientific Officer
Jonathan Faulkner, Vice-President, Operations

Parkinson Association of Alberta (PAA)
#120, 6835 Railway St. SE, Calgary AB T2H 2V6
Tel: 403-243-9901; *Fax:* 403-243-8283
Toll-Free: 800-561-1911
info@parkinsonassociation.ca
parkinsonassociation.ca
www.youtube.com/user/ParkinsonAlberta
www.facebook.com/ParkinsonAssociationofAlberta
twitter.com/PDAssocAB
To help people & families of Southern Alberta who live with
Parkinson's & related disorders
Lana Tordoff, Acting Chief Executive Officer

Parkinson Canada
#316, 4211 Yonge St., Toronto ON M2P 2A9
Tel: 416-227-9700; *Fax:* 844-440-8963
Toll-Free: 800-565-3000
info@parkinson.ca
www.parkinson.ca
www.facebook.com/parkinsoncanada
twitter.com/parkinsoncanada
To raise funds for research into the causes & treatment of
Parkinsons; to provide services which support Parkinsonians &
their families; to disseminate information about the condition to
individuals & organizations across Canada
Joyce Gordon, President & CEO
Marina Joseph, Director, Marketing & Communication

Parkinson Society Atlantic Canada / Société Parkinson - Atlantique
#150, 7071 Bayers Rd., Halifax NS B3L 2C2
Tel: 902-422-3656; *Fax:* 902-422-3797
Toll-Free: 800-663-2468
info@parkinson.ca
www.parkinson.ca
twitter.com/psmr
To give information to people with Parkinson & their family, children & caregivers
Ryan Underhill, Managing Director, Atlantic

Parkinson Society British Columbia (PSBC)
#600, 890 West Pender St., Vancouver BC V6C 1J9
Tel: 604-662-3240; *Fax:* 604-687-1327
Toll-Free: 800-668-3330
info@parkinson.bc.ca
www.parkinson.bc.ca
www.youtube.com/user/ParkinsonSocietyBC
www.facebook.com/ParkinsonSocietyBritishColumbia
twitter.com/ParkinsonsBC
Jean Blake, Chief Executive Officer

Parkinson Society Central & Northern Ontario
#321, 4211 Yonge St., Toronto ON M2P 2A9
Tel: 416-227-1200; *Fax:* 416-227-1520
Toll-Free: 800-565-3000
info.cno@parkinson.ca
www.cno.parkinson.ca
www.facebook.com/101248525517
twitter.com/ParkinsonCNO
Debbie Davis, CEO

Parkinson Society Newfoundland & Labrador
The Viking Bldg., #305, 136 Crosbie Rd., St. John's NL A1B 3K3
Tel: 709-574-4428; *Fax:* 709-754-5868
Toll-Free: 800-567-7020
parkinson@nf.aibn.com
nlparkinson.ca
www.facebook.com/ParkinsonSocietyNewfoundlandAndLabrador
twitter.com/Parkinsons_NL
Derek Staubitzer, Executive Director

Parkinson Society of Eastern Ontario / Société Parkinson de l'est de l'Ontario
#1, 200 Colonnade Rd., Ottawa ON K2E 7M1
Tel: 613-722-9238; *Fax:* 613-722-3241
psoc@toh.on.ca
www.parkinsons.ca
twitter.com/ParkinsonEastOn
To improve the lives of individuals & families affected by Parkinson's disease
Alan Muir, Manager, Resource Development
Ginette Trottier, Coordinator, Community Development

Partenariat communauté en santé (PCS)
#328, 302, rue Strickland, Whitehorse YT Y1A 2K1
Tél: 867-668-2663; *Téléc:* 867-668-3511
pcsyukon@francosante.ca
www.francosante.org
Favorise l'offre de services de santé en français
Sandra St-Laurent, Directrice

Partners In Health Canada (PIH)
#603, 890 Yonge St., Toronto ON M4W 3P4
Tel: 416-646-0666
pihcanada@pih.org
pihcanada.org
www.instagram.com/pihcanada
www.facebook.com/PIHCanada
twitter.com/pihcanada
To provide modern medical science to those most in need around the world
Mark Brender, National Director
Emily Antze, Senior Manager, Programs & Development

Patients Canada
PO Box 68, #2010, 65 Queen St. West, Toronto ON M5H 2M5
Tel: 416-900-2975
communications@patientscanada.ca
www.patientscanada.ca
twitter.com/patientscanada
To bring changes & improvements to health care policy & delivery in Canada; To represent patients in health care decision-making
Francesca Grosso, Chair

Post-Polio Awareness & Support Society of BC (PPASS/BC)
#222, 2453 Beacon Ave., Sidney BC V8L 1X7
Tel: 250-655-8849; *Fax:* 250-655-8859
ppass@ppassbc.com
www.ppassbc.com
To develop awareness, communication & education between society & community; To disseminate information concerning research & treatment about Post-Polio Syndrome; To support polio survivors other than through direct financial aid
Joan Toone, President

Post-Polio Network Manitoba Inc. (PPN-MB)
c/o SMD Self-Help Clearinghouse, 825 Sherbrook St., Winnipeg MB R3A 1M5
Tel: 204-975-3037; *Fax:* 204-975-3027
postpolionetwork@gmail.com
www.postpolionetwork.ca
To serve as a support group & information centre for polio survivors throughout Manitoba, especially those suffering from post-polio syndrome; To acquaint the medical community & those responsible for government services as to the nature & extent of the problems associated with the late effects of polio
Cheryl Currie, President
Donna Remillard, Treasurer
Clare Simpson, Secretary

Prince County Hospital Foundation (PCHF)
PO Box 3000, 65 Roy Boates Ave., Summerside PE C1N 2A9
Tel: 902-432-2547; *Fax:* 902-432-2551
info@pchcare.com
www.pchcare.com
www.facebook.com/PCHFoundation
twitter.com/PCHFoundation
To raise money for Prince County Hospital in order to keep up with medical equipment needs
Heather Matheson, Managing Director
Bevan Woodacre, Officer, Communications
Lisa Schurman-Smith, Manager, Finance & Administration
Kelly Arsenault, Administrator, Database

Prince Edward Island Association of Optometrists (PEIAO)
PO Box 1812, Charlottetown PE C1A 7N5
Tel: 902-566-4418; *Fax:* 902-566-4694
peiregistrar@peisympatico.ca
www.peioptometrists.ca
www.facebook.com/CanadianOpto
twitter.com/CanadianOpto
To promote the professional interests of optometrists in Prince Edward Island Association; To improve optometrists' proficiency
Carolyn Acorn, President
Jayne Toombs, Vice-President
Bonnie Gallant, Secretary
Joe E. Hickey, Treasurer

Prince Edward Island Chiropractic Association (PEICA)
1A Harbourside Access Rd., Charlottetown PE C1A 8R4
Tel: 902-894-4400; *Fax:* 902-894-3762
www.peichiropractic.ca
To represent the chiropractic profession in Prince Edward Island; To advance the chiropractic profession in the province; To encourage high standards of service; To protect the residents of Prince Edward Island from unqualified individuals acting as chiropractors
Christopher McCarthy, Registrar

Prince Edward Island Dietetic Association (PEIDA)
c/o Prince Edward Island Dietitians Registration Board, PO Box 362, Charlottetown PE C1A 7K7
peidietitians@gmail.com
www.peidietitians.ca
www.facebook.com/peidieteticassociation
To promote, encourage & improve the status of dietitians & nutritionists in the province of PEI; To promote & increase the knowledge & proficiency of its members in all matters relating to nutrition & dietetics; To promote public awareness
Doreen Pippy, President

Prince Edward Island Lung Association
81 Prince St., Charlottetown PE C1A 4R3
Tel: 902-892-5957; *Toll-Free:* 888-566-5864
peilungassociation@gmail.com
www.pei.lung.ca
www.facebook.com/196098560534899
twitter.com/PEI_Lung
To improve the respiratory health of Islanders through education, advocacy & research; To raise funds to support medical research
Robert MacDonald, Executive Director

Prince Edward Island Society for Medical Laboratory Science (PEISMLS)
PO Box 20061, Stn. Sherwood, 161 St. Peters Rd., Charlottetown PE C1A 9E3
peismls@gmail.com
peismls.com
www.facebook.com/320495861437823
twitter.com/peismls
To promote, maintain & protect the professional identity & interests of medical laboratory technologists & of the profession; To promote the development of continuing education; To provide information on current developments in medical laboratory technology
Rosalie Richard, President

Psoriasis Society of Canada / Société psoriasis du Canada
National Office, PO Box 25015, Halifax NS B3M 4H4
Fax: 902-443-2073
Toll-Free: 800-656-4494
www.psoriasissociety.org
To provide programs & services to people who suffer from psoriasis in Canada; To encourage formation of support groups where individual sufferers may share experiences & exchange information; To provide facts about psoriasis to medical community, general public & teaching profession; To promote & encourage research directed towards treatment & cure for psoriasis
Judy Misner, President

Public Health Association of British Columbia (PHABC)
#210, 1027 Pandora Ave., Victoria BC V8V 3P6
Tel: 250-595-8422; *Fax:* 250-595-8622
staff@phabc.org
www.phabc.org
To constitute a special resource in BC for the betterment & maintenance of the population's health at the community & personal level

Public Health Association of Nova Scotia (PHANS)
PO Box 33074, Halifax NS B3L 4T6
info@phans.ca
www.phans.ca
www.facebook.com/PHANovaScotia
To build public health capacity & to make progress on the determinants of health in Nova Scotia
Brian Condran, President
Cheryl MacNeil, Vice-President

Quality End-of-Life Care Coalition of Canada (QELCCC)
c/o Canadian Hospice Palliative Care Assn., Saint-Vincent Hospital, 60 Cambridge St. North, Ottawa ON K1R 7A5
Tel: 613-241-3663; *Toll-Free:* 800-668-2785
info@chpca.net
www.qelccc.ca
www.facebook.com/CanadianHospicePalliativeCare
twitter.com/canadianhpcassn
To create & fund a national strategy for hospice palliative & end-of-life care

Québec Black Medical Association
PO Box 49052, Stn. Place Versailles, Montréal QC H1N 3T6
www.qbma.ca
To enable young people from the Black community to pursue careers as health professionals & to advance medical practice & research in Quebec
Edouard Kouassi, President

Québec Lung Association (QLA) / Association pulmonaire du Québec (APQ)
#104, 6070, rue Sherbrooke est, Montréal QC H1N 1C1
Tel: 514-287-7400; *Fax:* 514-287-1978
Toll-Free: 888-768-6669
info@pq.poumon.ca
www.pq.poumon.ca
www.youtube.com/user/PoumonAPQ
www.facebook.com/poumon.qc
twitter.com/AssoPulmonaireQ
To provide resources in Québec about lung cancer, chronic obstructive pulmonary disease, sarcoidosis, tuberculosis, asthma, chronic bronchitis, sleep apnea, pneumonia & emphysema
Dominique Massie, Executive Director

Regroupement québécois des maladies orphelines (RQMO) / Québec Coalition for Orphan Diseases
l'Institut de recherches cliniques de Montréal (IRCM), 110, av des Pins ouest, Montréal QC H2W 1R7

Tél: 514-987-5659
administration@rqmo.org
www.rqmo.org
www.youtube.com/user/RQMOMalOrph
www.facebook.com/139256366104757
twitter.com/maladorphelines
Améliorer la recherche, le financement, et la sensibilisation concernant les maladies rares au Québec
Gail Ouellette, Directrice générale

Réseau de Santé en Français au Nunavut
CP 1516, Iqaluit NU X0A 0H0

Tél: 867-222-2107
info@resefan.ca
www.resefan.ca
www.facebook.com/resefan
twitter.com/ResefanNunavut
Contribuer à l'amélioration de la santé des francophones du Nunavut
Jérémie Roberge, Directeur générale

Réseau des services de santé en français de l'Est de l'Ontario
#300, 1173, ch Cyrville, Ottawa ON K1J 7S6

Tél: 613-747-7431; *Téléc:* 613-747-2907
Ligne sans frais: 877-528-7565
reseau@rssfe.on.ca
www.rssfe.on.ca
Améliorer l'offre active et l'accès à un continuum de services de santé de qualité en français
Jacinthe Desaulniers, Directrice générale

Réseau du mieux-être francophone du Nord de l'Ontario
#270, 469, rue Bouchard, Sudbury ON P3E 2K8

Tél: 705-674-9381; *Ligne sans frais:* 866-489-7484
www.reseaudumieuxetre.ca
www.facebook.com/rmefno
twitter.com/rmefno
Favorisant l'offre de services de santé en français
Diane Quintas, Directrice générale

Réseau franco-santé du Sud de l'Ontario (RFSSO)
CP 90057, 1000, rue Golf Links, Ancaster ON L9K 0B4

Tél: 416-413-1717; *Ligne sans frais:* 888-549-5775
www.francosantesud.ca
www.facebook.com/RFSSO
twitter.com/RFSSO
Contribue au développement des services de santé en français
Julie Lantaigne, Directrice générale

Réseau québécois de l'asthme et de la MPOC (RQAM)
Institut universitaire de cardiologie et de pneumologie de Québec, 2725, ch Sainte-Foy, #U-2765, Québec QC G1V 4G5

Tél: 418-650-9500; *Téléc:* 418-650-9391
Ligne sans frais: 877-441-5072
info@rqam.ca
qww.rqam.ca
De fournir un soutien aux professionnels travaillant dans l'asthme dans le secteur de la santé et de leurs patients
Véronique Paradis, Président
Sara-Edith Penney, Directrice générale

Réseau Santé - Nouvelle-Écosse
#204, 25 Wentworth St., Dartmouth NS B4B 1G7

Tél: 902-222-5871
reseau@reseausantene.ca
www.reseausantene.ca
www.facebook.com/reseausantenouvelleecosse
twitter.com/ReseauSanteNE
Promouvoir et d'améliorer l'accessibilité en français aux services de santé et de mieux-être de qualité
Pierre Roisné, Directrice générale

Réseau santé albertain
#230, 6940, rte Fisher SE, Calgary AB T2H 0W3

Tél: 780-466-9816
info@rsa-ab.ca
www.reseausantealbertain.ca
www.facebook.com/rsaAlberta
Paul Denis, Directeur générale

Réseau Santé en français de la Saskatchewan (RSFS)
#220, 308 4e av Nord, Saskatoon SK S7K 2L7

Tél: 306-653-7445; *Téléc:* 306-664-6447
www.rsfs.ca
www.facebook.com/rsfsaskatchewan

D'assurer un meilleur accès à des programmes et services sociaux et de santé en français
Frédérique Baudemont, Directrice générale

Réseau Santé en français I.-P.-É
CP 58, 48, ch Mill, Wellington PE C0B 2E0

Tél: 902-854-7444; *Téléc:* 902-854-7255
info@santeipe.ca
www.santeipe.ca
www.facebook.com/RSFIPE
Améliorer l'accès à des programmes et services de santé de qualité en français
Élise Arsenault, Directrice

Réseau santé en français Terre-Neuve-et-Labrador (RSFTNL)
Centre scolaire et communautaire des Grads-Vants, #233, 65 ch Ridge, St. John's NL A1B 4P5

Tél: 709-575-2862; *Téléc:* 709-722-9904
sante@fftnl.ca
www.francotnl.ca/en/organizations/fftnl/reseau-sante-en-francais
Améliorer l'offre de services de santé en français
Lise Richard, Directrice

Réseau TNO Santé en français
CP 1325, 5016, 48 rue, Yellowknife NT X1A 2N9

Tél: 867-920-2919; *Téléc:* 867-873-2158
santetno@franco-nord.com
www.reseautnosante.ca
www.facebook.com/tnosante
twitter.com/SanteTno
Contribuer à l'amélioration de l'accès à des services de santé de qualité en français
Audrey Fournier, Coordonnatrice

RésoSanté Colombie-Britannique (RSCB)
#102, 1575, West 7th Av, Vancouver BC V6J 1S1

Tél: 604-629-1000
info@resosante.ca
www.resosante.ca
www.linkedin.com/company/résosanté-colombie-britannica
www.facebook.com/resosante
twitter.com/resosante
Promouvoir des services de la santé et du bien-être en français en Colombie-Britannique
Benjamin Stoll, Directeur général

Ronald McDonald House Toronto
240 McCaul St., Toronto ON M5T 1W5

Tél: 416-977-0458; *Fax:* 416-977-8807
info@rmhtoronto.ca
www.rmhtoronto.ca
www.linkedin.com/company/ronald-mcdonald-house-toronto
www.facebook.com/RMHCToronto
twitter.com/RMHToronto
To provide a home & support services for out-of-town families whose children are receiving treatment in Toronto hospitals for serious illness
Sally Ginter, Chief Executive Officer
Anita Price, Office Manager

The Royal College of Physicians & Surgeons of Canada (RCPSC) / Le Collège royal des médecins et chirurgiens du Canada (CRMCC)
774 Echo Dr., Ottawa ON K1S 5N8

Tél: 613-730-8177; *Fax:* 613-730-8830
Toll-Free: 800-668-3740
feedback@royalcollege.ca
www.royalcollege.ca
www.linkedin.com/company/royal-college-of-physicians-and-surgeons-of-canada
www.facebook.com/TheRoyalCollege
twitter.com/Royal_College
To serve patients, diverse populations, & Fellows by setting the standards in specialty medical education & lifelong learning & by advancing professional practice & health care
Andrew Padmos, CEO

Saint Elizabeth Health Care (SEHC) / Les soins de santé Sainte-Elizabeth
#300, 90 Allstate Pkwy., Markham ON L3R 6H3

Tél: 905-940-9655; *Fax:* 905-940-9934
Toll-Free: 800-463-1763
TTY: 800-855-0511
communications@saintelizabeth.com
www.saintelizabeth.com
www.youtube.com/user/SaintElizabethSEHC
www.linkedin.com/company/saint-elizabeth-health-care
www.facebook.com/SaintElizabethSEHC
twitter.com/stelizabethSEHC
To serve the physical, emotional, & spiritual needs of people in their homes & communities
Noreen Taylor, Chair

Shirlee Sharkey, President & CEO
Heather McClure, Treasurer
Don McCutchan, Secretary

Santé en français
#400, 400, av Taché, Saint-Boniface MB R2H 3C3

Tél: 204-235-3293; *Téléc:* 204-237-0984
santeenfrancais@santeenfrancais.com
www.santeenfrancais.com
www.facebook.com/santeenfrancais
twitter.com/Santeenfrancais
Promouvoir l'accès à des services de qualité en français
Annie Bédard, Directrice générale

Saskatchewan Association of Naturopathic Practitioners (SANP)
#206, 3775 Pasqua St., Regina SK S4S 6W8

Tél: 306-543-4325; *Fax:* 306-543-4330
info@sanp.ca
www.sanp.ca
www.facebook.com/SaskNDs
To act as the governing body for naturopathic doctors in Saskatchewan; To license & regulate naturopathic physicians in the province; To ensure members are educated & trained according to strict standards
Laura Stark, President
Stephanie Liebrecht, Vice-President
Wendy Davis, Secretary
Cristina Harabor, Treasurer
Vanessa DiCicco, Registrar
Ken Alexce, Executive Director

Saskatchewan Association of Optometrists (SAO)
#102, 202 Wellman Cres., Saskatoon SK S7T 0J1

Tel: 306-652-2069; *Fax:* 306-652-2642
Toll-Free: 877-660-3937
admin@saosk.ca
optometrists.sk.ca
twitter.com/SaskEyecare
To license the delivery of optometric care in Saskatchewan; To regulate doctors of optometry throughout the province; To ensure excellence in the delivery of vision & eye health services across Saskatchewan; To enforce high standards of optometric eye care, in order to protect the public; To act as the voice of optometry in Saskatchewan
Sheila Spence, Executive Director

Saskatchewan Cerebral Palsy Association (SCPA)
2310 Louise Ave., Saskatoon SK S7J 2C7

Tel: 306-955-7272; *Fax:* 306-373-2665
saskcpa@shaw.ca
cpsk.ca
www.facebook.com/Saskcp
twitter.com/SaskCp
To improve the quality of life of persons with cerebral palsy through a broad range of programs, education, support of research & the delivery of needed services to people with cerebral palsy & their families
Jaime Winkler, President

Saskatchewan Dietitians Association (SDA)
#17, 2010 - 7th Ave., Regina SK S4R 1C2

Tel: 306-359-3040; *Fax:* 306-359-3046
registrar@saskdietitians.org
www.saskdietitians.org
To protect the public by registering competent dietitians; To set standards of practice; To uphold codes of conduct; To provide a framework for continuing competence, consisting of a self-assessment tool, a learning plan & a quality assurance audit
Bronwyn Bone, President
Lana Moore, Registrar

Saskatchewan Lung Association
Saskatoon Office, 1231 - 8 St. East, Saskatoon SK S7H 0S5

Tel: 306-343-9511; *Fax:* 306-343-7007
Toll-Free: 888-566-5864
info@sk.lung.ca
www.lungsask.ca
www.youtube.com/user/LungAssociation1
www.linkedin.com/company/lung-association-of-saskatchewan
www.facebook.com/LungSask
twitter.com/lungsk
To improve respiratory health & overall quality of life; To advocate for support of education & research
Erin Kuan, President & CEO
Trent Litzenberger, Vice-President, Community Care
Jennifer May, Vice-President, Community Engagement
Rod Ollerhead, Vice-President, Enterprise Technology

Saskatchewan Medical Association (SMA)
#201, 2174 Airport Dr., Saskatoon SK S7L 6M6
Tel: 306-244-2196; *Fax:* 306-653-1631
Toll-Free: 800-667-3781
sma@sma.sk.ca
www.sma.sk.ca
www.facebook.com/SMAdocs
twitter.com/SMA_docs
To represent physicians in Saskatchewan; To advance the professional, educational & economic welfare of physicians in the province
Bonnie Brossart, Chief Executive Officer

Saskatchewan Public Health Association Inc.
PO Box 845, Regina SK S4P 3B1
mail@saskpha.ca
www.saskpha.ca
twitter.com/saskpha
To constitute a resource in Saskatchewan for the improvement & maintenance of health
Wanda Martin, President

Screen Colons Canada (SCC)
#215, 1920 Yonge St., Toronto ON M4S 3E2
Tel: 416-365-0806
info@screencolons.ca
www.screencolons.ca
To promote screening for colon cancer; To raise awareness about the prevalence & preventability of the disease
Mariellen Black, Founder
Scott Clarke, Chair

SE Health
#300, 90 Allstate Pkwy., Markham ON L3R 6H3
Tel: 905-940-9655; *Toll-Free:* 800-463-1763
CommunicationsSEHC@sehc.com
sehc.com
www.youtube.com/user/SaintElizabethSEHC
www.linkedin.com/company/saint-elizabeth-health-care
www.facebook.com/sehealth.sehc
twitter.com/sehealth_sehc
To provide quality, trusted home care; To enhance seniors' lifestyles; To provide family caregiving
Shirlee M. Sharkey, CHE, MHSc, BScN, President & CEO

Sivananda Ashram Yoga Camp
673 8e av, Val Morin QC J0T 2R0
Tel: 819-322-3226; *Toll-Free:* 800-263-9642
hq@sivananda.org
www.sivananda.org
www.youtube.com/user/SivanandaYogaCampHq
www.facebook.com/SivanandaYogaCamp
twitter.com/sivanandacamp
To practice classical Indian yoga

Société canadienne de la sclérose en plaques (Division du Québec) (SCSP) / Multiple Sclerosis Society of Canada (Québec Division)
Tour Est, #1010, 550, rue Sherbrooke ouest, Montréal QC H3A 1B9
Tél: 514-849-7591; *Téléc:* 514-849-8914
Ligne sans frais: 800-268-7582
info.qc@mssociety.ca
scleroseenplaques.ca/division/division-du-quebec
www.youtube.com/SocieteSPCanada
www.facebook.com/SocieteSPCanada
twitter.com/SocCanDeLaSP
Soutenir la recherche sur la SP; offrir des services aux personnes atteintes de la maladie et à leurs familles; sensibiliser le public à la sclérose en plaques et maintenir les relations avec les gouvernements
Louis Adam, Directeur général

Société Huntington du Québec (SHQ) / Huntington Society of Québec (HSQ)
2300, boul René-Lévesque ouest, Montréal QC H3R 3R5
Tél: 514-282-4272; *Ligne sans frais:* 800-220-0226
shq@huntingtonqc.org
www.huntingtonqc.org
www.facebook.com/societehuntingtonduquebec
Pour aider les personnes atteintes de la maladie de Huntington à faire face
Francine Lacroix, Directrice générale

Société Parkinson du Québec / Parkinson Society Québec
560, rue Ontario est, Montréal QC H2L 0B6
Tél: 514-861-4422; *Ligne sans frais:* 800-720-1307
www.parkinsonquebec.ca
www.facebook.com/parkinsonquebec
twitter.com/parkinsonquebec
Nicole Charpentier, Directrice générale

Société Santé en français (SSF)
223, rue Main, Ottawa ON K1S 1C4
Tél: 613-244-1889; *Téléc:* 613-244-0283
Ligne sans frais: 888-684-4253
info@santefrancais.ca
www.santefrancais.ca
www.facebook.com/santefrancais
twitter.com/santefrancais
Pour améliorer l'accès et la qualité des services de soins de santé en français au Canada
Anne Leis, Président

Société Santé et Mieux-être en français du Nouveau-Brunswick (SSMEFFNB)
CP 1764, Moncton NB E1C 9X6
Tél: 506-389-3351; *Téléc:* 506-389-3366
ssmefnb@nb.aibn.com
www.ssmefnb.ca
www.facebook.com/SSMEFNB
twitter.com/SSMEFNB
Gilles Vienneau, Directeur général

Society for Treatment of Autism / Association canadienne pour l'obtention des services aux personnes autistiques
404 - 94 Ave. SE, Calgary AB T2J 0E8
Tel: 403-253-2291; *Fax:* 403-253-6974
Toll-Free: 888-301-2872
intake@sta-ab.com
www.sta-ab.com
www.linkedin.com/company/society-for-treatment-of-autism
www.facebook.com/SocietyForTreatmentOfAutism
twitter.com/Autism_STA
To ensure that a comprehensive range of services exists across Canada to meet the needs of individuals with autism & their families, & that autistic people are given the opportunity to achieve maximum independence & productivity within the community
Peter Johnson, Chair
Kimberley Ward, Executive Director

Society of Obstetricians & Gynaecologists of Canada (SOGC) / Société des obstétriciens et gynécologues du Canada
#200, 2781 Lancaster Rd., Ottawa ON K1B 1A7
Tel: 613-730-4192; *Fax:* 613-730-4314
Toll-Free: 800-561-2416
info@sogc.com
www.sogc.org
www.instagram.com/sogcorg
www.linkedin.com/company/the-society-of-obstetricians-and-gyn aecologists-of-canada
www.facebook.com/sogc.org
twitter.com/SOGCorg
To promote excellence in the practice of obstetrics & gynaecology; To produce national clinical guidelines for medical education on women's health issues; To promote optimal, comprehensive women's health care
B. Anthony Armson, President
Jennifer Blake, Chief Executive Officer

Society of Rural Physicians of Canada (SRPC) / Société de la médecine rurale du Canada
PO Box 893, #383, Route 148, Shawville QC J0X 2Y0
Tel: 819-647-7054; *Fax:* 819-647-2485
Toll-Free: 877-276-1949
info@srpc.ca
www.srpc.ca
vimeo.com/srpc
www.facebook.com/theSRPC
twitter.com/srpcanada
To provide equitable medical care for rural communities; to provide sustainable working conditions for rural physicians
Margaret Tromp, President
Jennifer Barr, Office Manager

Speech-Language & Audiology Canada (SAC) / Orthophonie et Audiologie Canada (OAC)
#1000, 1 Nicholas St., Ottawa ON K1N 7B7
Tel: 613-567-9968; *Fax:* 613-567-2859
Toll-Free: 800-259-8519
info@sac-oac.ca
www.sac-oac.ca
www.linkedin.com/groups/4226965
www.facebook.com/sac.oac
twitter.com/sac_oac
To support & represent the professional needs & development of speech-language pathologists & audiologists; To champion the needs of people with communication disorders
Joanne Charlebois, Chief Executive Officer
Jessica Bedford, Chief Operating Officer
Phil Bolger, Chief Financial Officer

Spina Bifida & Hydrocephalus Association of Canada (SBHAC) / Association de spina-bifida et d'hydrocephalie du Canada
#472, 167 Lombard Ave., Winnipeg MB R3B 0T6
Tel: 204-925-3650; *Fax:* 204-925-3654
Toll-Free: 800-565-9488
info@sbhac.ca
www.sbhac.ca
www.facebook.com/167743789940812
To improve the quality of life of all individuals with spina bifida &/or hydrocephalus & their families through awareness, education, advocacy & research; To reduce the incidence of neural tube defects
Bonnie Hidlebaugh, Executive Director

Spinal Cord Injury Canada / Lésions Médullaires Canada
#105, 477 Mt. Pleasant Rd., Ottawa ON M4S 2L9
Tel: 416-200-5814
info@sci-can.ca
www.sci-can.ca
To assist persons with spinal cord injuries & other physical disabilitieto to cope with the changes caused by their injury, to become independent & self-reliant & to lead productive lives
Bill Adair, Executive Director

The Terry Fox Foundation / La Fondation Terry Fox
#150, 8960 University High St., Burnaby BC V5A 4Y6
Tel: 604-200-0541; *Fax:* 604-701-0247
Toll-Free: 877-363-2467
national@terryfoxrun.org
www.terryfoxrun.org
www.youtube.com/terryfoxcanada
www.facebook.com/TheTerryFoxFoundation
twitter.com/TerryFoxCanada
To maintain the vision & principles of Terry Fox while raising money for cancer research through the annual Terry Fox Run, memoriam donations & planned gifts
Ara Sahakian, Interim Executive Director
Katherine Koyko, Director, Marketing & Communications
Heather Scott, Director, Development
Rhonda Risebrough, International Director

Thalidomide Victims Association of Canada (TVAC) / Association canadienne des victimes de la thalidomide (ACVT)
#102, 7744, rue Sherbrooke est, Montréal QC H1L 1A1
Tel: 514-355-0811; *Fax:* 514-355-0860
Toll-Free: 877-355-0811
tvac.acvt@sympatico.ca
www.thalidomide.ca
To monitor the drug thalidomide & to meet the needs of thalidomide survivors; To empower & enhance the quality of life of Canadians living with the effects of thalidomide
Mercedes Benegbi, Executive Director

Thrombosis Canada (TC) / Thrombose Canada
128 Halls Rd., Whitby ON L1P 1Y8
Tel: 647-528-8586
info@thrombosiscanada.ca
thrombosiscanada.ca
www.youtube.com/user/ThrombosisCanada
www.facebook.com/ThrombosisCan
twitter.com/thrombosiscan
To promote patient care & improved outcomes for patients with thrombosis
James Douketis, President
David Airdrie, Executive Director

Thyroid Cancer Canada (TCC) / Cancer de la thyroïde Canada (CTC)
308 Main St., 1st Fl., Toronto ON M4C 4X7
Tel: 416-487-8267; *Fax:* 416-487-0601
info@thyroidcancercanada.org
www.thyroidcancercanada.org
www.facebook.com/344492466005996
twitter.com/ThyroidCancerCa
To provide emotional support & information to individuals affected by thyroid cancer

Thyroid Foundation of Canada / La Fondation canadienne de la Thyroïde
PO Box 298, Bath ON K0H 1G0
Toll-Free: 800-267-8822
www.thyroid.ca
www.facebook.com/138316539676468
To provide leadership to the fight against thyroid disease
Laz Bouros, President
Parisa Zareapour, Treasurer

Tourette Canada
#245, 5955 Airport Rd., Mississauga ON L4V 1R9
Tel: 905-673-2255; *Fax:* 905-673-2638
Toll-Free: 800-361-3120
admin@tourette.ca
www.tourette.ca
www.youtube.com/TSFCanada
www.linkedin.com/company/tourette-syndrome-foundation-of-canada
www.facebook.com/TouretteCanada
twitter.com/TouretteCanada
To educate & increase public awareness about Tourette
Syndrome
Janet Rumsey, President

Trillium Gift of Life Network
#900, 522 University Ave., Toronto ON M5G 1W7
Tel: 416-363-4001; *Fax:* 416-363-4002
Toll-Free: 800-263-2833
www.giftoflife.on.ca
www.linkedin.com/company/1426658
www.facebook.com/TrilliumGiftofLife
twitter.com/TrilliumGift
To enable every Ontario resident to make an informed decision
to donate organs & tissue; To support healthcare professionals
in implementing their wishes; To maximize organ & tissue
donation in Ontario in a respectful & equitable manner through
education, research, services & support
Ronnie Gavsie, President & CEO

**Turner Syndrome Society of Canada (TSS) / Société
du syndrome de Turner du Canada**
#7A, 2100 Thurston Dr., Ottawa ON K1G 4K8
Tel: 613-321-2267; *Fax:* 613-321-2268
Toll-Free: 800-465-6744
info@turnersyndrome.ca
www.turnersyndrome.ca
www.facebook.com/TurnerSyndromeSocietyOfCanada
To improve the quality of life for individuals & families affected by
Turner's Syndrome; To strive to accomplish this through
providing public & professional awareness about the needs &
concerns of individuals with Turner's Syndrome & their families
through the development of communication networks to provide
mutual support
Krista Kamstra-Cooper, President

**Vocational Rehabilitation Association of Canada
(VRA Canada)**
#2, 555 Hall Ave. East, Renfrew ON K7V 4M7
Fax: 613-432-6840
Toll-Free: 888-876-9992
www.vracanada.com
www.linkedin.com/company/vracanada
www.facebook.com/VRACanada
twitter.com/VRACanada
To support members in promoting & providing vocational &
pre-vocational rehabilitation services
Tricia Gueulette, President

VOICE for Children Who Are Deaf & Hard of Hearing
PO Box 30045, 478 Dundas St. West, Oakville ON L6H 6Y3
Tel: 416-487-7719
TTY: 416-487-7719
admin@voicefordeafkids.com
www.voicefordeafkids.com
www.facebook.com/VOICEfordeafandhardofhearingchildren
To ensure that all children who are deaf &/or hard of hearing
have the right to develop their ability to listen & speak & have
access to services which will enable them to listen & speak
Mary Kay McCoy, Chair

**World Federation of Occupational Therapists
(WFOT)**
PO Box 53187, London E18 9DF United Kingdom
admin@wfot.org
www.wfot.org
To promote health occupation & participation within a worldwide
perspective; To increase & maintain the awareness,
understanding, & use of the services of occupational therapists
by government, employers, & the wider community through
collaborative action; To develop & promote a standard of
excellence in occupational therapy practice; To ensure the
ongoing development & accessibility of quality education &
research for occupational therapists worldwide; To develop &
maintain WFOT as an efficient & effective organization
Ritchard Ledgerd, Executive Director

Yukon Medical Association
5 Hospital Rd., Whitehorse YT Y1A 3H7
Tel: 867-393-8749
office@yukondoctors.ca
www.yukondoctors.ca

To advocate on behalf of members; To promote professionalism
in medical practice & accessibility to quality health care for
Yukoners
Alex Poole, President

Heating, Air Conditioning, Plumbing

**Canadian Institute of Plumbing & Heating (CIPH) /
Institut canadien de plomberie et de chauffage**
#504, 295 The West Mall, Toronto ON M9C 4Z4
Tel: 416-695-0447; *Toll-Free:* 800-639-2474
info@ciph.com
www.ciph.com
www.youtube.com/user/CIPHvideos
twitter.com/ciphnews
To act as a unified voice for plumbing, heating, hydronic, PVF &
waterworks across Canada
Ralph Suppa, CAE, President & General Manager
Elizabeth McCullough, CDE, General Manager, Trade Shows
Therese Kasongo, Manager, Program
Geeta Persaud, Manager, Program

**Heating, Refrigeration & Air Conditioning Institute of
Canada (HRAI) / Institut canadien du chauffage, de
la climatisation et de la réfrigération (ICCCR)**
#101, 2350 Matheson Blvd. East, Mississauga ON L4W 5G9
Tel: 905-602-4700; *Fax:* 905-602-1197
Toll-Free: 800-267-2231
hraimail@hrai.ca
www.hrai.ca
www.youtube.com/hraichannel
www.facebook.com/HRAI.ca
twitter.com/HRAI_Canada
To serve the HRAI membership & HVACR industry in Canada by
facilitating industry solutions, coordinating a strong national
membership, representing the industry to their publics,
conducting accountable association activities, providing quality
member / customer services, & educating & training industry
members
Sandy MacLeod, President & CEO
Martin Luymes, Vice-President, Government & Stakeholder
Relations
Frank Diecidue, Director, Operations & Services

Ontario Geothermal Association (OGA)
ON
Tel: 905-602-4700; *Toll-Free:* 800-267-2231
office@ontariogeothermal.ca
www.ontariogeothermal.ca
www.linkedin.com/company/ontario-geothermal-association
www.facebook.com/OGACanada
twitter.com/OGACanada
Stan Reitsma, President

Ontario Plumbing Inspectors Association (OPIA)
c/o Ursula Wengler, 22 Dalegrove Cres., Toronto ON M9B
6A7
www.opia.info
To promote uniform enforcement of plumbing regulations; To
close liaison & interchange of ideas & knowledge between
members of the OPIA & members of other associations; To
provide education & training to members & the industry
Jerry Monaco, President
Bryan Heyl, Vice-President
Ursula Wengler, Treasurer

**Ontario Refrigeration & Air Conditioning
Contractors Association (ORAC)**
#104, 133 Milani Blvd., Vaughan ON L4H 4M4
Tel: 905-670-0010; *Fax:* 905-670-0474
www.orac.ca
To represent Ontario's contractor practitioners in the
refrigeration & air conditioning trade; To enhance quality &
efficiency in the industry to benefit customers
Mike Verge, Managing Director

**Plumbing Officials' Association of British Columbia
(POABC)**
2328 Hollyhill Pl., Victoria BC V8N 1T9
Tel: 250-361-0342; *Fax:* 250-385-1128
bhusband@victoria.ca
www.bcplumbingofficials.com
Brian Husband, President

**Refrigeration Service Engineers Society (Canada)
(RSES Canada)**
www.rsescanada.com
To lead all segments of the HVAC industry by providing superior
educational & training programs; To create an environment that
encourages maximum member participation in the development
& decision process of the Society

Thermal Environmental Comfort Association (TECA)
PO Box 73105, Stn. Evergreen RO, Surrey BC V3R 0J2
Tel: 604-594-5956; *Toll-Free:* 888-577-3818
office@teca.ca
www.teca.ca
To offer the residential heating, cooling & ventilation industry
up-to-date training courses & a collective voice in local &
provincial issues
Gary Milligan, President

History, Heritage, Genealogy

Action Patrimoine
82, Grande-Allée ouest, Québec QC G1R 2G6
Tél: 418-647-4347; *Téléc:* 418-647-6483
Ligne sans frais: 800-494-4347
info@actionpatrimoine.ca
actionpatrimoine.ca
www.facebook.com/Actionpatrimoine
Afin de préserver et de promouvoir repères culturels au Québec
Émilie Vézina-Doré, Directrice générale

Alberta Family History Society (AFHS)
712 - 16 Ave. NW, Calgary AB T2M 0J8
Tel: 403-214-1447
www.afhs.ab.ca
www.facebook.com/AlbertaFHS
To encourage accuracy & thoroughness in family histories &
genealogical research
Irene Oickle, Membership Chair
Lorna Loughton, President

Alberta Historical Resources Foundation (AHRF)
Old St. Stephen's College, 8820 - 112 St., Edmonton AB T6G
2P8
Tel: 780-431-2300; *Fax:* 780-427-5598
To assist in the preservation of Alberta's historic sites, buildings
& objects; To encourage & promote public awareness of the
province's past
Laurel Halladay, Chair
Aimee Benoit, Vice Chair

Antique Motorcycle Club of Manitoba Inc. (AMCM)
1377 Niakwa Rd. East, Winnipeg MB R2J 3T3
www.amcm.ca
www.facebook.com/groups/862177597223304
Rick Poirier, President
Dan Catte, Librarian

**Architectural Heritage Society of Saskatchewan
(AHSS)**
#202, 1275 Broad St., Regina SK S4R 1Y2
Tel: 306-359-0933; *Fax:* 306-359-3899
sahs@sasktel.net
www.ahsk.ca
To promote, support & facilitate the preservation, conservation,
restoration & reuse of distinct architectural & historical heritage
properties (designated or potential) throughout the province,
ensuring that our built heritage is maintained for present & future
citizens to appreciate the contributions & craftsmanship of past
generations; to enhance the current social, economic &
environmental quality of life

**Association québécoise des interprètes du
patrimoine (AQIP)**
CP 11003, Succ. Le Plateau, Gatineau QC J9A 0B6
Tél: 819-595-2190
aqip@aqip.ca
www.aqip.ca
www.facebook.com/AssoQuebecoiseInterpretePatrimoine
Stimuler la communication entre les individus et les organismes
intéressés à l'interprétation du patrimoine naturel, culturel,
historique et industriel; promouvoir l'interprétation du patrimoine
québécois auprès des gouvernements, des organismes, des
médias et du public en général; stimuler l'acquisition de
connaissances et la recherche liée à l'interprétation du
patrimoine
Gabrielle Normand, Présidente
Christian Arcand, Vice Présidente
Éliane Bélec, Secrétaire

British Columbia Genealogical Society (BCGS)
PO Box 88054, Stn. Lansdowne Mall, Richmond BC V6X 3T6
Tel: 604-502-9119; *Fax:* 604-502-9119
bcgs@bcgs.ca
www.bcgs.ca
To perpetuate the heritage of BC; To collect, preserve & publish
material relevant to promotion of ethical principles, scientific
methods & effective techniques in genealogical & historical
research
Eunice Robinson, President

British Columbia Historical Federation (BCHF)
PO Box 5254, Stn. B, Victoria BC V8R 6N4
info@bchistory.ca
www.bchistory.ca
www.facebook.com/bchistoricalfederation
To encourage interest in the history of British Columbia through financial support, research, & presentation
Gary Mitchell, President
Sandra Martins, Secretary

Bus History Association, Inc. (BHA)
c/o Bernie Drouillard, 965 McEwan Ave., Windsor ON N9B 2G1
www.bus-history.org
To preserve & record data, information & other related materials of the bus industry, both within North America & worldwide
David Vincent, Chair
Bernard Drouillard, Secretary-Treasurer

Canada's History / Histoire Canada
PO Box 699, Alliston ON L9R 1V9
Tel: 204-988-9300; *Toll-Free:* 888-816-0997
memberservices@canadashistory.ca
www.canadashistory.ca
www.youtube.com/canadashistory
www.facebook.com/CanadasHistory
twitter.com/canadashistory
To promote greater popular interest in Canadian history
Janet Walker, President & CEO
Danielle Chartier, Manager, Marketing & Circulation
Joanna Dawson, Director, Programs

Canadian Association for Conservation of Cultural Property (CAC) / Association canadienne pour la conservation et la restauration des biens culturels (ACCR)
#268, 1554 Carling Ave., Ottawa ON K1Z 7M4
Tel: 613-231-3977
administrator@cac-accr.ca
www.cac-accr.ca
www.facebook.com/cac.accr.ca
To promote conservation of Canadian cultural property
Alison Freake, President
Gyllian Porteous, Vice-President
Lauara Hashimoto, Secretary
Rebecca Latourel, Treasurer

Canadian Association of Heritage Professionals (CAPHC) / Association canadienne d'experts-conseils en patrimoine (ACECP)
190 Bronson Ave., Ottawa ON K1R 6H4
Tel: 613-569-7455
admin@cahp-acecp.ca
www.caphc.ca
www.facebook.com/cahpacecp
twitter.com/cahpacecp
To represent & further the professional interests of heritage consultants active in both the private & public sectors; To establish & maintain principles & standards of practice for heritage consultants; To enhance awareness & appreciation of heritage resources, & the contribution of heritage consultants; To foster communication among private practitioners, public agencies & the public at large in matters related to heritage conservation
Dima Cook, President

Canadian Heritage Information Network (CHIN) / Réseau canadien d'information sur le patrimoine (RCIP)
1030 Innes Rd., Ottawa ON K1B 4S7
Tel: 613-998-3721; *Fax:* 613-998-4721
Toll-Free: 800-520-2446
TTY: 888-997-3123
pch.rcip-chin.pch@canada.ca
www.canada.ca/en/heritage-information-network
To engage national & international audiences in Canadian heritage, through leadership & innovation in digital content, partnerships & lifelong learning opportunities
Bruno Lemay, Director, Heritage Information
Paul Lima, Manager, Business Innovation

Canadian Historical Association (CHA) / Société historique du Canada (SHC)
#1912, 130 Albert St., Ottawa ON K1P 5G4
Tel: 613-233-7885; *Fax:* 613-565-5445
cha-shc@cha-shc.ca
cha-shc.ca
www.facebook.com/215430858536628
twitter.com/CndHistAssoc
To encourage historical research; To stimulate public interest in history; To promote the preservation of Canadian heritage
Michel Duquet, Executive Director

Canadian Oral History Association (COHA) / Société canadienne d'histoire orale (SCHO)
MB
www.canoha.ca
To encourage & support the creation & preservation of sound recordings which document the history & culture of Canada; To develop standards of excellence & increase competence in the field of oral history through study, education & research

Canadian Society for the Study of Names (CSSN) / Société canadienne d'onomastique (SCO)
PO Box 2164, Stn. Hull, Gatineau QC J8X 3Z4
www.csj.ualberta.ca/sco
To promote the study of all aspects of names & naming in Canada & elsewhere
Carol J. Léonard, Chair
Léo La Brie, Secretary-Treasurer

Canadian Society of Mayflower Descendants
info@csmd.org
csmd.org
www.facebook.com/canadiansocietyofmayflowerdescendants
To promote the memory of the Mayflower pilgrims & to inform the public of this era of Canadian history
Bill Curry, Governor

Canadian Society of Presbyterian History
c/o Burns Presbyterian Church, 765 Myrtle Rd. West, Ashburn ON L0B 1A0
Tel: 905-655-8509
www.csph.ca
To study Presbyterian & Reformed history
A. Donald MacLeod, President

Canadian Vintage Motorcycle Group (CVMG)
c/o Dale Prisley, Membership Secretary, 467 Thorn Ridge Cres., Amherstburg ON N9V 3X4
www.cvmg.ca
To promote the use, restoration & interest in older motorcycles & those of historic interest
Jim Briggs, President
Bill Hoar, Correspondence Secretary
Dale Prisley, Membership Secretary

Canadiana
c/o Canadian Research Knowledge Network, #411, 11 Holland Ave., Ottawa ON K1Y 4S1
Tel: 613-907-7035
info@crkn.ca
www.canadiana.ca
twitter.com/CRKN_RCDR
To specialize in the digitization of, preservation of & access to Canada's documentary heritage
Clare Appavoo, Executive Director, CRKN

The Champlain Society
University of Toronto Press, 5201 Dufferin St., Toronto ON M3H 5T8
Tel: 416-667-7777; *Fax:* 416-667-7881
info@champlainsociety.ca
www.champlainsociety.ca
www.facebook.com/ChamplainSoc
twitter.com/ChamplainSoc
To preserve & promote the eye-witness accounts of Canada's past, including journals, diaries, books, letters & documents
Lauren Naus, Contact

Family History Society of Newfoundland & Labrador
PO Box 8008, #101A, 66 Kenmount Rd., St. John's NL A1B 3V7
Tel: 709-754-9525; *Fax:* 709-754-6430
fhs@fhsnl.ca
www.fhsnl.ca
www.facebook.com/144749998869923
twitter.com/fhsnl
To encourage & promote the study of family history in Newfoundland & Labrador; To collect & preserve local genealogical & historical records & materials; to foster education in genealogical research
Smith Frederick, President
Dunne Paul, Secretary

Fédération des sociétés d'histoire du Québec
4545, av Pierre-de Coubertin, Montréal QC H1V 0B2
Tél: 514-252-3031; *Téléc:* 514-251-8038
Ligne sans frais: 866-691-7207
fshq@histoirequebec.qc.ca
www.histoirequebec.qc.ca
twitter.com/FederationHQ
Regrouper les organisations historiques du Québec.
Richard M. Bégin, Président

Fédération québécoise des sociétés de généalogie (FQSG)
CP 9454, Succ. Sainte-Foy, 1055, av du Séminaire, Québec QC G1V 4B8
Tél: 418-653-3940; *Téléc:* 418-653-3940
www.federationgenealogie.qc.ca
Représenter les sociétés de généalogie locales et régionales; la promotion et l'épanouissement de la généalogie au Québec et son rayonnement à l'étranger sont les buts visés
Pierre Soucy, Directeur général

Genealogical Association of Nova Scotia (GANS) / Association généalogique de la Nouvelle-Écosse
PO Box 333, 3045 Robie St., Halifax NS B3K 4P6
Tel: 902-454-0322
info@novascotiaancestors.ca
www.novascotiaancestors.ca
www.facebook.com/NovaScotiaAncestors
twitter.com/NSAncestors
To encourage interest in & to raise standards of research in genealogy through workshops & publications; to acquaint members with research materials & methods to serve as medium of exchange for genealogical information; to support the collection & preservation of documents & other genealogical materials; to foster recognition of the value of genealogy to a proper study of the social sciences.
Allan Marble, President

Genealogical Institute of The Maritimes (GIM) / Institut généalogique des Provinces Maritimes
c/o Nathaniel Smith, Registrar, 9501 Donnell Rd. NW, Edmonton AB T6C 4C2
nsgna.ednet.ns.ca/gim
To pursue geneaology; To upgrade the quality of professional family history research in the Maritimes
Nathaniel Smith, Registrar

L'Héritage canadien du Québec (HCQ) / The Canadian Heritage of Québec (CHQ)
#1201, 1350 rue Sherbrooke ouest, Montréal QC H3G 1J1
Tél: 514-393-1417; *Téléc:* 514-393-9444
mail@hcq-chq.org
www.hcq-chq.org
www.facebook.com/1723406467941985
Organisme qui se consacre à la préservation des terrains & des constructions revêtant une valeur historique/architecturale dans la province du Québec
Jacques Archambault, General Manager

Heritage Foundation of Newfoundland & Labrador (HFNL)
The Newman Building, PO Box 5171, 1 Springdale St., St. John's NL A1C 5V5
Tel: 709-739-1892; *Fax:* 709-739-5413
Toll-Free: 888-739-1892
info@heritagefoundation.ca
www.heritagefoundation.ca
To stimulate an understanding of & appreciation for the architectural heritage of Newfoundland & Labrador; To support & contribute to the preservation, maintenance & restoration of buildings of architectural or historical significance; To designate buildings & structures as Registered Heritage Structures; may make grants for purpose of preservation, maintenance, or restoration (Deadline for submitting grant application is Mar. 1 & Sept. 1 of each year)
George Chalker, Executive Director
Frank Crews, Chairperson

Heritage Society of British Columbia
1459 Barclay St., Victoria BC V6G 1J6
Tel: 604-417-7243
hsbc@islandnet.com
www.heritagebc.ca
www.facebook.com/heritagebccanada
twitter.com/HeritageBCanada
To support heritage conservation across British Columbia
Laura Saretsky, Heritage Program Manager
Nathan Macdonald, Coordinator, Operations & Events

Historic Sites Association of Newfoundland & Labrador (HSANL)
Chelsea Building, #204, 10 Forbes St., St. John's NL A1E 3L5
Tel: 709-753-5515; *Fax:* 709-753-0879
Toll-Free: 877-753-9262
marketing@historicsites.ca
www.historicsites.ca
www.facebook.com//131036186980761
twitter.com/historicsitesnl
To preserve, promote & present the history & heritage of Newfoundland & Labrador
Andrea MacDonald, Executive Director
Mandy White, Financial Officer

Historica Canada
East Mezzanine, 2 Carlton St., Toronto ON M5B 1J3
Tel: 416-506-1867; Fax: 416-506-0300
Toll-Free: 866-701-1867
info@historicacanada.ca
www.historicacanada.ca
www.youtube.com/c/HistoricaCanada
www.facebook.com/Historica.Canada
twitter.com/HistoricaCanada
To conduct original research into Canadians' knowledge of the
country's past & to build innovative programs that broaden
appreciation of the richness & complexity of Canadian history
Anthony Wilson-Smith, President & CEO
Brigitte d'Auzac de Lamartinie, Director, Programs &
Development

Historical Society of Alberta (HSA)
PO Box 4035, Stn. C, Calgary AB T2T 5M9
Tel: 403-261-3662; Fax: 403-269-6029
info@albertahistory.org
www.albertahistory.org
To preserve & promote the history of Alberta; To encourage the
study & preservation of Canadian & Albertan history; To rescue
from oblivion the memories, experiences & knowledge of early
inhabitants
Timothy Marriott, President

ICOMOS Canada
PO Box 737, Stn. B, Ottawa ON K1P 5P8
Tel: 613-749-0971; Fax: 613-749-0971
secretariat@canada.icomos.org
canada.icomos.org
To further the conservation, protection, rehabilitation, &
enhancement of monuments, groups of buildings & sites; To
encourage primary research in many important fields
Christophe Rivet, President
Robert Buckle, Vice-President, Strategic Planning
Michael McClelland, Vice-President, Memberships & Funding

J. Douglas Ferguson Historical Research Foundation
PO Box 78085, 1460 Merivale Rd., Ottawa ON K2E 1B1
Tel: 506-532-6025
www.jdfergusonfoundation.ca
To give financial support to a broad range of activities aimed at
preserving the heritage of early historical currency, banks &
other issuers of money, coins, tokens & paper money issued
throughout Canada since the 18th century.
Christopher Faulkner, Chair

Jewish Genealogical Society of Toronto (JGST)
2901 Bayview Ave., Toronto ON M2K 2S3
Tel: 647-247-6414
info@jgstoronto.ca
www.jgstoronto.ca
www.jgstoronto.blogspot.com
www.facebook.com/jgstoronto
twitter.com/jgsoftoronto
To foster interest in Jewish genealogical research; To facilitate
the pursuit of Jewish genealogical research domestically &
internationally; To provide a forum for the exchange of
knowledge & information among people interested in Jewish
genealogy
Marla Waltman, President
Les Kelman, Past President
Neil Richler, Coordinator, Membership

Literary & Historical Society of Québec (LHSQ) / Société littéraire et historique de Québec
44, Chaussée des Écossais, Québec QC G1R 4H3
Tel: 418-694-9147; Fax: 418-694-0754
info@morrin.org
www.morrin.org
To preserve, develop & share the diverse cultural life of the
Québec City region's English-speaking community through
innovative, responsive & effective services
Barry McCullough, Executive Director

Manitoba Genealogical Society Inc. (MGS)
1045 St James St., #E, Winnipeg MB R3H 1B1
Tel: 204-783-9139; Fax: 204-783-0190
contact@mbgenealogy.com
www.mbgenealogy.com
www.facebook.com/7054423205
twitter.com/MbGenealogy
To collect & preserve local genealogical & historical records &
materials; To foster education in genealogical research through
society workshops & seminars; To encourage production of
genealogical publications relating especially to Manitoba
Kathy Stokes, President
Mary Bole, Library Chair

Manitoba Historical Society (MHS)
#710A, 1 Lombard Place, Winnipeg MB R3B 0X3
Tel: 204-947-0559
info@mhs.mb.ca
www.mhs.mb.ca
To promote public interest in, & preservation of Manitoba's
historical resources; To encourage research relating to the
history of Manitoba
Gary McEwen, President
Gordon Clarke, Chief Administrative Officer
Victor Sawelo, Manager, Ross House

Monarchist League of Canada (MLC) / Ligue Monarchiste du Canada
PO Box 1057, Stn. Lakeshore West, Oakville ON L6K 0B2
Tel: 905-912-0916; Toll-Free: 800-465-6925
domsec@monarchist.ca
www.monarchist.ca
www.youtube.com/LigueMonarchLeague
www.facebook.com/canadamonarchist
twitter.com/monarchist
To promote loyalty to the Sovereign & a broader understanding
of constitutional monarchy as part of Canada's parliament,
history, social fabric, culture & traditions
Robert Finch, Dominion Chairman

National Trust for Canada / Fiducie Nationale du Canada
190 Bronson Ave., Ottawa ON K1R 6H4
Tel: 613-237-1066; Fax: 613-237-5987
Toll-Free: 866-964-1066
nationaltrust@nationaltrustcanada.ca
www.nationaltrustcanada.ca
www.instagram.com/nationaltrust
www.facebook.com/NationalTrustCanada
twitter.com/nationaltrustca
To be a resource for people who care about historic places by
offering services, tools, inspiration, & funding
Natalie Bull, Executive Director
Alison Faulknor, Director, New Initiatives

New Brunswick Genealogical Society Inc. (NBGS, Inc.) / Société Généalogique du Nouveau-Brunswick Inc.
PO Box 3235, Stn. B, Fredericton NB E3A 5G9
webmanager@nbgs.ca
www.nbgs.ca
To promote & facilitate family historical research in New
Brunswick
Stephanie Heenan-Orr, President
Ron Green, Treasurer
Shirley Graves, Secretary

New Brunswick Historical Society
Loyalist House, 120 Union St., Saint John NB E2L 1A3
Tel: 506-652-3590
info@LoyalistHouse.com
www.loyalisthouse.com
To promote the study, research & discussion of New Brunswick
history; to collect & preserve New Brunswick history; to publish &
educate. The Society owns & operates Loyalist House.

Newfoundland Historical Society (NHS)
PO Box 23154, Stn. Churchill Square, St. John's NL A1B 4J9
Tel: 709-722-3191; Fax: 709-722-9035
nhs@nf.aibn.com
www.nlhistory.ca
To promote study, research & public discussion of
Newfoundland & Labrador's history; to record the history of the
province; to promote preservation of historic sites
Fred Smith, President

Ontario Black History Society (OBHS) / Société historique des Noirs de l'Ontario
#402, 10 Adelaide St. East, Toronto ON M5C 1J3
Tel: 416-867-9420; Fax: 416-867-8691
admin@blackhistorysociety.ca
www.blackhistorysociety.ca
www.youtube.com/user/OntarioBlackHistory
www.facebook.com/109773629168
twitter.com/tweetOBHS
To study Black history in Canada; to recognize, preserve &
promote the contribution of Black peoples & their collective
histories through education, research & cooperation; to promote
the inclusion of material on Black history in school curricula; to
sponsor & support educational conferences & exhibits in this
field.

Ontario Electric Railway Historical Association
PO Box 578, Milton ON L9T 5A2
Tel: 519-856-9802; Fax: 519-856-1399
streetcar@hcry.org
www.hcry.org
twitter.com/streetcarmuseum
To collect & return to operating capacity, electric railway
equipment representing North American city & interurban
systems

Ontario Genealogical Society (OGS)
#202, 2100 Steeles Ave. West, Concord ON L4K 2V1
Tel: 416-489-0734; Fax: 855-695-8080
Toll-Free: 855-697-6687
info@ogs.on.ca
www.ogs.on.ca
www.linkedin.com/company/the-ontario-genealogical-society
www.facebook.com/OntarioGenealogicalSociety
twitter.com/OntGenSociety
To support, unite & help all those interested in pursuing family
history; To promote the study of genealogy & genealogical
research in Ontario
Peter D. Taylor, Executive Director
Coral Harkies, Administrative Coordinator

Ontario Heritage Trust (OHT) / Fiducie du patrimoine ontarien
10 Adelaide St. East, Toronto ON M5C 1J3
Tel: 416-325-5000; Fax: 416-325-5071
marketing@heritagefdn.on.ca
www.heritagetrust.on.ca
www.facebook.com/OntarioHeritageTrust
twitter.com/ONheritage
To be dedicated to the preservation, protection & promotion of
Ontario's built, natural & cultural heritage for public enjoyment
Nimet Manji, Executive Assistant

Ontario Historical Society (OHS) / La Société historique de l'Ontario
34 Parkview Ave., Willowdale ON M2N 3Y2
Tel: 416-226-9011; Fax: 416-226-2740
Toll-Free: 866-955-2755
ohs@ontariohistoricalsociety.ca
www.ontariohistoricalsociety.ca
www.facebook.com/OntarioHistoricalSociety
twitter.com/OntarioHistory
To bring people who are interested in preserving some aspect of
Ontario's history together; To encourage & assist museums,
historical societies & other heritage groups to research, preserve
& interpret artifacts, architecture, archaeological sites & archival
resources of local communities; To provide a forum to exchange
ideas, research & experiences related to the history of Ontario;
To sponsor programs & projects with a wide general appeal that
help illustrate Ontario's history
Robert Leverty, Executive Director

Pier 21 Society
1055 Marginal Rd., Halifax NS B3H 4P6
Tel: 902-425-7770; Fax: 902-423-4045
Toll-Free: 855-526-4721
info@pier21.ca
www.pier21.ca
www.youtube.com/Pier21Museum
www.facebook.com/CanadianMuseumofImmigration
twitter.com/pier21
To preserve & share information about the Canadian immigration
experience through history
Tung Chan, Chair
Marie Chapman, Chief Executive Officer
Monica MacDonald, Manager, Research
Cailin MacDonald, Manager, Communication

Postal History Society of Canada (PHSC)
10 Summerhill Ave., Toronto ON M4T 1A8
phscdb@postalhistorycanada.net
www.postalhistorycanada.net
To promote the study of postal history of Canada
Chris Green, Contact

Prince Edward Island Genealogical Society Inc. (PEIGS)
PO Box 2744, Charlottetown PE C1A 8C4
peigs_queries@yahoo.ca
www.peigs.ca
To encourage & promote the study of family history in PEI; to
collect & preserve local genealogical & historical records &
materials; to foster education in genealogical research

Québec Family History Society (QFHS) / Société de l'histoire des familles du Québec
PO Box 7156, Stn. Pointe Claire-Dorval, 15, av Donegani, Pointe-Claire QC H9R 4S8
Tel: 514-695-1502; *Fax:* 514-695-3508
qfhs@bellnet.ca
www.qfhs.ca
To promote genealogy & genealogical research in Québec (particularly English & Protestant records); To collect & preserve books, manuscripts & other related material
Gary Schroder, President
Jackie Billingham, Executive Secretary

Réseau du patrimoine franco-ontarien (RPFO)
267, rue Dalhousie, Ottawa ON K1N 7E3
Tél: 613-729-5769; *Téléc:* 613-729-2209
Ligne sans frais: 866-307-9995
www.rpfo.ca
www.facebook.com/RPFO.projets
twitter.com/RPFO_projets
Permettre à ses membres de découvrir le patrimoine franco-ontarien par l'entremise de l'histoire et de la généalogie
Soukaïna Boutiyeb, Directrice générale

Richard III Society of Canada
c/o 156 Drayton Ave., Toronto ON M4C 3M2
info@richardiii.ca
richardiii.ca
twitter.com/RichardIIICA
To promote research into the life & times of Richard III to secure a re-assessment of the material relating to this period & this monarch's role in English history.

Royal Heraldry Society of Canada / Société royale héraldique du Canada
PO Box 8128, Stn. T, Ottawa ON K1G 3H9
secretary@heraldry.ca
www.heraldry.ca
To maintain, foster & develop the heraldic traditions of Canadians by: increasing public awareness of heraldry & the society; advocating with governments for the protection & proper use of heraldry in Canada; advising the Canadian Heraldic Authority on matters of mutual concern
Vicken Koundakjian, President
Jason Burgoin, 1st Vice-President
Ian C. Steingaszner, 2nd Vice-President

Saskatchewan Genealogical Society (SGS)
#110, 1514 - 11th Ave., Regina SK S4P 0H2
Tel: 306-780-9207
www.saskgenealogy.com
www.facebook.com/216892188363312
To provide assistance in researching family history throughout the world; To preserve heritage documents; To collect materials for study
Linda Dunsmore-Porter, Executive Director

Société de généalogie de Québec (SGQ)
CP 9066, Succ. Sainte-Foy, #3112, 1055, av du Séminaire, Québec QC G1V 4A8
Tél: 418-651-9127; *Téléc:* 418-651-2643
sgq@uniserve.com
www.sgq.qc.ca
www.facebook.com/553614701384842
Regrouper les personnes intéressées à promouvoir les recherches sur les histoires de familles des ancêtres et à répandre les connaissances généalogiques; favoriser la conservation des documents relatifs à la généalogie; être un lieu de conservation du patrimoine familial
Solange Talbot, Registraire

Société généalogique canadienne-française (SGCF)
3440, rue Davidson, Montréal QC H1W 2Z5
Tél: 514-527-1010; *Téléc:* 514-527-0265
info@sgcf.com
www.sgcf.com
Regrouper toutes les personnes désireuses de partager des connaissances généalogiques et leur histoire de famille par les conférences et la publication de travaux de recherche
Richard Masson, Présidente
Lisa Bertrand, Vice Présidente
Suzanne Houle, Secrétaire
Bissonnette Yves, Trésorier

Société historique de Québec
#158, 6, rue de la Vieille-Université, Québec QC G1R 5X8
Tél: 418-694-1020
shq1@bellnet.ca
www.societehistoriquedequebec.qc.ca
www.facebook.com/157594394301478
Étudier et diffuser l'histoire de la ville de Québec et de sa région; relever et mettre en valeur le patrimoine de la même région
Jean Dorval, Président

Jean-François Caron, Trésorier
Doris Drolet, Secrétaire

United Empire Loyalists' Association of Canada (UELAC)
Dominion Office, The George Brown House, #202, 50 Baldwin St., Toronto ON M5T 1L4
Tel: 416-591-1783
uelac@uelac.org
uelac.ca
www.facebook.com/UELAC
twitter.com/uelac
To unite together descendants of those families who, as a result of the American revolutionary war, sacrificed their homes in retaining their loyalty to the British Crown; To keep alive the knowledge of the early contributions of hundreds of thousands of Loyalists of many cultures, creeds & colours
Sue Hines, President

The Vimy Foundation / La Fondation Vimy
#726, 1470, rue Peel, Montréal QC H3A 1T1
Tel: 514-904-1007
info@vimyfoundation.ca
www.vimyfoundation.ca
twitter.com/vimyfoundation
To preserve & promote Canada's First World War legacy as symbolized with the 1917 victory at Vimy Ridge
Rick Hillier, Honorary Chair
Christopher Sweeney, Chair

Yukon Heritage Resources Board (YHRB)
PO Box 31115, 509A Strickland St., Whitehorse YT Y1A 5P7
Tel: 867-668-7150
www.yhrb.ca
To advise on heritage-related issues; To make recommendations to Governments regarding management of heritage resources & sites; To determine ownership of heritage resources
Morgen Smith, Executive Director

Horticulture & Gardening

Les Amis du Jardin botanique de Montréal / Friends of the Montréal Botanical Garden
#206A, 4101, rue Sherbrooke est, Montréal QC H1X 2B2
Tél: 514-872-1493; *Téléc:* 514-872-3765
amisjardin@ville.montreal.qc.ca
www.amisjardin.qc.ca
www.facebook.com/LesAmisduJardinbotaniquedeMontreal
Maud Fillion, Contact
Paule Lamontagne, Présidente

British Columbia Landscape & Nursery Association (BCLNA)
#102, 19289 Langley Bypass, Surrey BC V3S 6K1
Tel: 604-575-3500; *Fax:* 604-574-7773
Toll-Free: 800-421-7963
www.bclna.com
www.linkedin.com/groups/2387526
www.facebook.com/bclna
twitter.com/bclna
To work together to improve quality & standards of the landscape horticulture industry
Hedy Dyck, Chief Operating Officer

Canadian Horticultural Council (CHC) / Conseil canadien de l'horticulture
#102, 2200 Prince of Wales Dr., Ottawa ON K2E 6Z9
Tel: 613-226-4880; *Fax:* 613-226-4497
admin@hortcouncil.ca
www.hortcouncil.ca
www.linkedin.com/company/canadian-horticultural-council
twitter.com/chc_cch
To improve horticultural & allied industries including production, grading, packing, transportation, storage & marketing
Brian Gilroy, President
Rebecca Lee, Executive Director

Canadian Iris Society (CIS)
c/o Ed Jowett, 1960 Sideroad 15, RR#2, Tottenham ON L0G 1W0
Tel: 905-936-9941
cdniris@gmail.com
www.cdn-iris.ca
To encourage, improve & extend the cultivation of the Iris & to collaborate with other societies for this purpose, as well as to regulate the nomenclature & colour classification of this flower.
Ed Jowett, President
Nancy Kennedy, Secretary

Canadian Nursery Landscape Association (CNLA)
7856 - 5th Line South, Milton ON L9T 2X8
Tel: 905-875-1399; *Fax:* 905-875-1840
Toll-Free: 888-446-3499
info@cnla-acpp.ca
cnla.ca
www.linkedin.com/groups/985377
www.facebook.com/canadanursery
twitter.com/CNLA_ACPP
To coordinate provincial member groups in the Canadian horticultural industry; To set national standards; To work with government; To develop national priorities
Victor Santacruz, Executive Director

Canadian Ornamental Horticulture Alliance (COHA) / Alliance Canadienne de l'Horticulture Ornamentale (ACHO)
PO Box 30025, Stn. East Main, Grimsby ON L3M 0A3
Tel: 905-945-6791
coha-acho.ca
To represent Canada's ornamental horticulture value chain at the national level
James Farrar, Alliance Director

Canadian Ornamental Plant Foundation (COPF) / Fondation canadienne des plantes ornementales
7856 - 5th Line South, Milton ON L9T 2X8
Tel: 519-341-6761; *Toll-Free:* 888-446-3499
info@copf.org
www.copf.org
To encourage new plant development by strengthening relations between growers & breeders for the benefit of the horticulture industry
Teagan Giddings, Contact
Megan Farias, Contact

Canadian Rose Society (CRS)
c/o Richard Clayton, 233 Covewood Circle NE, Calgary AB T3K 5S7
canrosesociety@aol.com
canadianrosesociety.org
www.facebook.com/canadianrosesociety
To provide information about rose growing, speakers, judges, nurseries & suppliers & rose shows; To correspond with people with similar interests throughout Canada & around the world

Canadian Society for Horticultural Science (CSHS) / Société canadienne de science horticole (SCSH)
www.cshs.ca
www.instagram.com/canadian_horticultural_science
www.facebook.com/CSHSwebcommittee
twitter.com/CanadianHortSci
To advance research, teaching, information & technology related to all horticultural crops
Valérie Gravel, President

City Farmer - Canada's Office of Urban Agriculture
PO Box 74567, Stn. Kitsilano, Vancouver BC V6K 4P4
Tel: 778-990-9326
cityfarmer@gmail.com
www.cityfarmer.info
To encourage gardening in an urban environment
Michael Levenston, Executive Director

Fédération des sociétés d'horticulture et d'écologie du Québec (FSHÉQ)
4545, av Pierre-de-Coubertin, Montréal QC H1V 3R2
Tél: 514-252-3010; *Téléc:* 514-251-8038
fsheq@fsheq.com
www.fsheq.com
www.facebook.com/fsheq
Regrouper tous les organismes voués à l'horticulture; faire la promotion de l'horticulture
Pierre Blain, Directrice générale

Fédération interdisciplinaire de l'horticulture ornementale du Québec (FIHOQ)
3230, rue Sicotte ouest, #E-300, Saint-Hyacinthe QC J2S 2M2
Tél: 450-774-2228; *Téléc:* 450-774-3556
renseignement@quebecvert.com
quebecvert.com
www.facebook.com/fihoq
Grouper en fédération les associations professionnelles qui s'occupent d'horticulture ornementale au Québec; étudier, promouvoir, protéger et développer de toutes manières les intérêts économiques, sociaux et professionnels de ses membres; imprimer, éditer des revues, journaux, périodiques et plus généralement, toutes publications du domaine de l'horticulture ornementale aux fins d'information, de culture professionnelle et de propagande; organiser et tenir des cours, conférences, congrès, assemblées, expositions et autres réunions pour la promotion, le développement et la vulgarisation

de l'horticulture ornementale; promouvoir la protection du consommateur dans le domaine de l'horticulture ornementale; assurer une répresentation tant sur le plan local et national, que sur le plan international des personnes oeuvrant dans le domaine de l'horticulture ornementale au Québec
Luce Daigneault, Directrice générale

Flowers Canada (FC) / Fleurs Canada
Retail & Distribution Sector, #406, 150 Bank St., Ottawa ON K1H 1B8

Fax: 866-671-8091
Toll-Free: 800-447-5147
flowers@flowerscanada.org
www.flowerscanada.org
To act as the voice of & help to improve the Canadian floriculture industry
Susan Clarke, Senator
James Fuller, Chairman
Jeff Walters, President

Flowers Canada Growers
#7, 45 Speedvale Ave. East, Guelph ON N1H 1J2
Tel: 519-836-5495; *Fax:* 519-836-7529
Toll-Free: 800-698-0113
flowers@fco.on.ca
www.flowerscanadagrowers.com
To help members increase their exposure & sales by addressing issues pertaining to the industry
Andrew Morse, Executive Director

International Commission for Plant-Pollinator Relationships (ICPPR)
School of Environmental Sciences - Bovey, University of Guelph, Guelph ON N1G 2W1
www.icppr.com
To conduct research on the relationships between plants and all types of bees
Peter Kevan, Chair

Landscape Alberta Nursery Trades Association
#200, 10331 - 178 St. NW, Edmonton AB T5S 1R5
Tel: 780-489-1991; *Fax:* 780-444-2152
Toll-Free: 800-378-3198
admin@landscape-alberta.com
www.landscape-alberta.com
www.linkedin.com/company/landscape-alberta-nursery-trade-ass ociation
twitter.com/LandscapeAB
To advance the Alberta ornamental horticulture industry through unity, education & professionalism
Joel Beatson, Executive Director

Landscape New Brunswick Horticultural Trades Association (LNBHTA)
PO Box 742, Saint John NB E2L 4B3

Fax: 866-595-5467
Toll-Free: 866-752-6862
lnb@nbnet.nb.ca
www.landscapenbmember.com
www.facebook.com/Landscapenewbrunswick
To further the development of the ornamental horticulture industry by focusing on the environment, education, promotion & professionalism; To represent members & to help them achieve their goals
Joe Wynberg, President

Landscape NL Horticultural Association (LNLHA)
PO Box 8062, St. John's NL A1B 3M9
Tel: 709-700-2165; *Fax:* 709-700-2165
lnl@landscapenl.ca
www.landscapenl.ca
www.pinterest.com/landscapenl
www.facebook.com/landscapenlevents
To promote professionalism at all levels of the Industry & achieve the highest standards of excellence in delivery of services & products across all sectors of our industry
David Kiell, Executive Director

Landscape Nova Scotia
Executive Plus Business Centre, Burnside Industrial Park, #44, 201 Brownlow Ave., Dartmouth NS B3B 1W2
Tel: 902-463-0519; *Fax:* 902-446-8104
Toll-Free: 877-567-4769
info@landscapenovascotia.ca
www.landscapenovascotia.ca
www.facebook.com/1991351368222813
To promote high standards in product quality, professional service and conduct in the landscape and horticulture industry
Pam Woodman, Executive Director

Landscape Ontario Horticultural Trades Association (LOHTA)
7856 - 5th Line South, RR#4, Milton ON L9T 2X8
Tel: 905-875-1805; *Toll-Free:* 800-265-5656
www.horttrades.com
www.linkedin.com/company/landscape-ontario
www.facebook.com/landscapeontario
To be a leader in representing, promoting & fostering a favourable environment for the advancement of the horticultural industry in Ontario
Tony DiGiovanni, Executive Director

North American Native Plant Society (NANPS)
PO Box 69070, Stn. St. Clair, Toronto ON M4T 3A1
nanps@nanps.org
www.nanps.org
www.instagram.com/nativeplant_society
www.facebook.com/nativeplant
twitter.com/tnanps
Dedicated to the study, conservation & cultivation of North America's wild flora.

Ontario Horticultural Association (OHA)
448 Paterson Ave., London ON N5W 5C7
secretary@gardenontario.org
www.gardenontario.org
twitter.com/gardenontario
To promote civic beautification, preservation of the environment, youth work & education of many aspects of horticulture
Kathy Smyth, President

Royal Botanical Gardens (RBG) / Les jardins botaniques royaux
680 Plains Rd. West, Hamilton ON L7T 4H4
Tel: 905-527-1158; *Fax:* 905-577-0375
Toll-Free: 800-694-4769
www.rbg.ca
www.youtube.com/user/royalbotanicalgarden
www.facebook.com/140038459379746
twitter.com/RBGCanada
To be recognized in Canada & throughout the world for its unique contribution to the collection, research, exhibition, & interpretation of the plant world & for the development of public understanding & appreciation of the relationship between the plant world, humanity, & the rest of nature
Mark C. Runciman, CEO

Saskatchewan Nursery Landscape Association (SNLA)
c/o Landscape Alberta Nursery Trades Association, 18051 107 Ave. NW, Edmonton AB T5S 1K3
Toll-Free: 800-378-3198
admin@landscape-alberta.com
www.snla.ca
To encourage people in the landscaping industry to network in order to spread their wealth of knowledge among each other
Leslie Cornell, President

Seeds of Diversity Canada (SoDC) / Semences du patrimoine Canada
#1, 12 Dupont St. West, Waterloo ON N2L 2X6
Tel: 226-600-7782
mail@seeds.ca
www.seeds.ca
To search out, preserve, perpetuate, study & encourage the cultivation of heirloom & endangered varieties of food crops
Bob Wildfong, Executive Director

Hospitals

Accreditation Canada / Agrément Canada
1150 Cyrville Rd., Ottawa ON K1J 7S9
Tel: 613-738-3800; *Fax:* 613-738-7755
Toll-Free: 800-814-7769
www.accreditation.ca
www.linkedin.com/company/accreditation-canada
twitter.com/AccredCanada
To improve quality in health services through accreditation; To provide health care organizations with a voluntary, external peer review to assess the quality of their services
Leslee Thompson, Chief Executive Officer
Asmita Gillani, Executive Director, Canadian Accreditation
Katerina Tarasova, Executive Director, International Accreditation

Alliance for Healthier Communities
#500, 970 Lawrence Ave. West, Toronto ON M6A 3B6
Tel: 416-236-2539; *Fax:* 416-236-0431
mail@allianceon.org
allianceon.org
To promote community based primary care, health promotion & illness prevention services, focusing on the broader

determinants of health such as education, employment, poverty, isolation & housing
Claudia den Boer, Chair

Association des établissements privés conventionnés - santé services sociaux (AEPC)
#200, 1076, rue de Bleury, Montréal QC H2Z 1N2
Tél: 514-499-3630; *Téléc:* 514-873-7063
info@aepc.qc.ca
www.aepc.qc.ca
www.facebook.com/AEPC.SSS
twitter.com/AEPC_SSS
Promouvoir l'amélioration continue de la qualité des soins et des services donnés au sein des entreprises membres; protéger et promouvoir l'entreprise privée dans le domaine de la santé et du bien-être
Ann Lavoie, Directrice générale

Canadian Home Care Association (CHCA) / Association canadienne de soins et services à domicile
#302, 2000 Argentia Rd., Mississauga ON L5N 1W1
Tel: 905-567-7373
chca@cdnhomecare.ca
www.cdnhomecare.ca
www.youtube.com/user/cdnhomecare
twitter.com/CdnHomeCare
To promote the development, integration, delivery, public awareness & evaluation of quality home care services in Canada; To provide national leadership to strengthen & unify the home care sector; To collect & disseminate information about home care; To encourage or commission research; To influence policy & legislation; To establish a code of ethics
Alice Kennedy, President
Nadine Henningsen, Executive Director

Children's Healthcare Canada (CHC) / Santé des enfants Canada
#102, 495 Richmond Rd., Ottawa ON K2A 4H6
Tel: 613-738-4164; *Fax:* 613-738-3247
info@childrenshealthcarecanada.ca
www.childrenshealthcarecanada.ca
www.linkedin.com/company/childrenshealthcarecanada
www.facebook.com/ChildHealthCAN
twitter.com/ChildHealthCan
To improve the health of children within Canada through research activities & through advocacy with governments & health care organizations; To provide information exchange amongst members
Emily Gruenwoldt, President & CEO
Doug Maynard, Associate Director, Business Development

Continuing Care Association of Nova Scotia (CCANS)
NS
continuingcareassociationns.com
www.facebook.com/continuingcarens
To represent continuing care facilities throughout Nova Scotia
Sheila Peck, President

Health Association Nova Scotia
2 Dartmouth Rd., Halifax NS B4A 2K7
Tel: 902-832-8500; *Fax:* 902-832-8505
contactus@healthassociation.ns.ca
www.healthassociation.ns.ca
www.linkedin.com/company/health-association-nova-scotia
twitter.com/HealthAssnNS
To promote an effective, efficient & integrated quality health system for all Nova Scotians through leadership in influencing the development of public policy, representing & advocating members' interests & providing services to assist its members meet the health care needs of their communities
Joyce d'Entremont, Chair
Mary Lee, President & CEO

Health Employers Association of British Columbia (HEABC)
#300, 2889 East 12th Ave., Vancouver BC V5M 4T5
Tel: 604-736-5909; *Fax:* 604-736-2715
contact@heabc.bc.ca
www.heabc.bc.ca
www.youtube.com/user/BCHealthCareAwards
www.linkedin.com/company/heabc
www.facebook.com/BCHealthCareAwards
twitter.com/heabcnews
To serve a diverse group of over 218 publicly funded healthcare employers; To deliver high quality labour relations services; To advance the efficiency & productivity of human resources system-wide
Michael McMillan, President & CEO
Lyn Kocher, CFO & Executive Director, Corporate Services

HealthCareCAN / SoinsSantéCAN
#100, 17 York St., Ottawa ON K1N 5S7
Tel: 613-241-8005; Fax: 613-241-5055
Toll-Free: 855-236-0213
info@healthcarecan.ca
www.healthcarecan.ca
www.linkedin.com/company/healthcarecan
www.facebook.com/healthcarecan.soinssantecan
twitter.com/healthcarecan
To improve the delivery of health services in Canada through policy development, advocacy & leadership
Paul-Émile Cloutier, President & CEO
Catherine Barton, Chief Operating Officer
Steve Wharry, Director, Communications & Member Services
Chantal Easy, Office Manager

Ontario Association of Medical Laboratories (OAML)
#1802, 5000 Yonge St., Toronto ON M2N 7E9
Tel: 416-250-8555; Fax: 416-250-8464
oaml@oaml.com
www.oaml.com
www.facebook.com/234214510271204
twitter.com/TheOAML
To act as the voice of Ontario's community laboratory sector; To promote professionalism, technical excellence & accountability in the delivery of laboratory services throughout Ontario

Ontario Hospital Association (OHA)
#2800, 200 Front St. West, Toronto ON M5V 3L1
Tel: 416-205-1300; Fax: 416-205-1301
Toll-Free: 800-598-8002
info@oha.com
www.oha.com
www.youtube.com/onthospitalassn
www.linkedin.com/company/ontario-hospital-association
www.facebook.com/onthospitalassn
twitter.com/OnthHospitalAssn
To build a strong, innovative & sustainable health care system that meets patient care needs throughout Ontario; To promote an efficent & effective health care system
Altaf Stationwala, Chair
Anthony Dale, President & CEO

Ontario Long Term Care Association (OLTCA)
#500, 425 University Ave., Toronto ON M5G 1T6
Tel: 647-256-3490; Fax: 416-642-0635
info@oltca.com
www.oltca.com
www.youtube.com/user/OLTCA345
twitter.com/oltcanews
To provide professional leadership to the long-term care sector; To empower long-term care facilities to provide high quality & cost-effective health care & accommodation services
Candace Chartier, Chief Executive Officer
Judy Irwin, Senior Manager, Communications

Saskatchewan Association of Health Organizations (SAHO)
#500, 2002 Victoria Ave., Regina SK S4P 0R7
Tel: 306-347-1740; Fax: 306-347-1043
info@saho.ca
www.saho.ca
To serve members through services, support & programs

Housing

Alberta Public Housing Administrators' Association (APHAA)
14220 - 109th Ave. NW, Edmonton AB T5N 4B3
Tel: 780-498-1971; Fax: 780-464-7039
www.aphaa.org
twitter.com/AphaaInfo
Works with the Province of Alberta in the publicly-funded housing industry to promote excellence in publicly funded housing administration through education, information and networking
Raymond Swonek, President

Association of Condominium Managers of Ontario (ACMO)
#100, 2233 Argentia Rd., Mississauga ON L5N 2X7
Tel: 905-826-6890; Fax: 905-826-4873
Toll-Free: 800-265-3263
www.acmo.ca
www.instagram.com/acmo_org
www.linkedin.com/company/acmo
www.facebook.com/ACMO.org1977
twitter.com/ACMO_org
To enhance the quality performance of condominium property managers & management companies in Ontario
Audrey McGuire, President

Association provinciale des constructeurs d'habitations du Québec inc. (APCHQ) / Provincial Association of Home Builders of Québec
5930, boul Louis-H.-Lafontaine, Anjou QC H1M 1S7
Tél: 514-353-9960; Téléc: 514-353-4825
Ligne sans frais: 800-468-8160
www.apchq.com
www.youtube.com/APCHQinc/
www.linkedin.com/company/apchq/
www.facebook.com/apchq
twitter.com/APCHQ
Depuis 1997, l'APCHQ est la plus importante gestionnaire de mutuelles de prévention du domaine de la construction. Étant le seul agent négociateur patronal des relations de travail dans le secteur résidentiel, elle défend les intérêts de quelque 12 000 employeurs et 25 000 travailleurs
Mario Dargis, Président
Luc Bélanger, Directeur général

Canadian Association of Home & Property Inspectors (CAHPI) / Association canadienne des inspecteurs de biens immobiliers
PO Box 76065, Stn. Morgan's Grant, 832 March Rd., Ottawa ON K2W 0E1
Toll-Free: 888-748-2244
info@cahpi.ca
www.facebook.com/cahpi.ca
To promote & enhance the professionalism & competency of professional home & property inspectors
Peter Weeks, President
Sharry Featherston, Executive Director

Canadian Condominium Institute (CCI) / Institut canadien des condominiums
#210, 2800 - 14th Ave., Markham ON L3R 0E4
Tel: 416-491-6216; Fax: 416-491-1670
Toll-Free: 866-491-6216
info@cci.ca
cci.ca
To provide education, information, awareness & access to expertise by, but also for, its members; To serve as a central clearinghouse & research centre on condominium issues & activities across the country; To provide objective research for practitioners & government agencies regarding all aspects of condominium operations; To offer professional assistance; To improve legislation & represent condominiums
Sherry Denesha, Executive Director

Canadian Federation of Apartment Associations (CFAA) / Fédération canadienne des Associations de propriétaires immobiliers
#640, 1600 Carling Ave., Ottawa ON K1Z 1G3
Tel: 613-235-0101; Fax: 613-238-0101
admin@cfaa-fcapi.org
cfaa-fcapi.org
To represent members on political & economic issues at the national level & to facilitate the exchange of information & materials amongst members while maintaining the highest professional & ethical standards in all activities
John Dickie, President
David Benes, Administrator

Canadian Home Builders' Association (CHBA) / Association canadienne des constructeurs d'habitations
#500, 150 Laurier Ave. West, Ottawa ON K1P 5J4
Tel: 613-230-3060; Fax: 613-232-8214
chba@chba.ca
www.chba.ca
www.instagram.com/chbanational
www.linkedin.com/company/canadian-home-builders
www.facebook.com/chbanational
twitter.com/chbanational
To assist its members in serving the needs & meeting the aspirations of Canadians for housing; To be the voice of the residential construction industry in Canada; To achieve an environment in which members can operate profitably; To promote affordability & choice in housing for all Canadians; To support the professionalism of members
Kevin Lee, Chief Executive Officer

Canadian Housing & Renewal Association (CHRA) / Association canadienne d'habitation et de rénovation urbaine (ACHRU)
#902, 75 Albert St., Ottawa ON K1P 5E7
Tel: 613-594-3007
info@chra-achru.ca
www.chra-achru.ca
www.facebook.com/CHRA.ACHRU.ca
twitter.com/CHRA_ACHRU
To provide access to adequate & affordable housing

Jeff Morrison, Executive Director

Canadian Manufactured Housing Institute (CMHI)
#500, 150 Laurier Ave. West, Ottawa ON K1P 5J4
Tel: 613-563-3520
cmhi@cmhi.ca
www.cmhi.ca
www.linkedin.com/company/canadian-manufactured-housing-institute
To be the voice of the manufactured housing industry in Canada; To seek, identify & solidify the development of new, profitable market opportunities for manufactured housing, both domestically & internationally; To promote housing affordability for all Canadians

Cooperative Housing Federation of British Columbia (CHFBC)
#220, 1651 Commercial Dr., Vancouver BC V5L 3Y3
Tel: 604-879-5111; Fax: 604-879-4611
Toll-Free: 866-879-5111
info@chf.bc.ca
www.chf.bc.ca
www.youtube.com/user/coopsbc
www.facebook.com/coophousingbc
twitter.com/chfbc
To unit, represent & serve members in a thriving cooperative housing movement
Thom Armstrong, Executive Director

Cooperative Housing Federation of Canada (CHF Canada) / Fédération de l'habitation coopérative du Canada (FHCC)
#311, 225 Metcalfe St., Ottawa ON K2P 1P9
Tel: 613-230-2201; Fax: 613-230-2231
Toll-Free: 800-465-2752
info@chfcanada.coop
chfcanada.coop
www.youtube.com/user/coophousing
www.facebook.com/chfcanada
twitter.com/CHFCanada
To unite, represent & serve the co-op housing community across Canada
Tim Ross, Executive Director

Federation of Metro Tenants' Associations (FMTA)
PO Box 73102, Stn. Wood St., Toronto ON M4Y 2W5
Tel: 416-646-1772
Crisis Hot-Line: 416-921-9494
fmta@torontotenants.org
www.torontotenants.org
To inform & educate tenants; to encourage the organization of tenants; to lobby for tenant protection laws; to promote affordable housing

Front d'action populaire en réaménagement urbain (FRAPRU)
#201, 1431, rue Fullum, Montréal QC H2K 0B5
Tél: 514-522-1010; Téléc: 514-527-3403
frapru@frapru.qc.ca
www.frapru.qc.ca
www.youtube.com/user/TheFRAPRU
www.facebook.com/FRAPRU.logement
twitter.com/frapru
Marie-José Corriveau, Coordonnatrice

Modular Housing Association Prairie Provinces (MMHA)
PO Box 3538, Stn. Main, Sherwood Park AB T8H 2T4
Tel: 780-429-1798; Fax: 780-429-1871
Toll-Free: 866-866-8106
www.mhaprairies.ca
www.linkedin.com/company/modular-housing-association-prairie-provinces
www.facebook.com/ModularHousingAssociationPrarieProvinces
To promote the interests of the manufactured housing industry in Alberta, Manitoba, & Saskatchewan
Sandra Nigro, Executive Director

Ontario Association of Property Standards Officers Inc.
PO Box 43209, 3980 Grand Park Dr., Mississauga ON L5B 4A7
www.oapso.ca
www.facebook.com/OAPSO.ca
To provide training for professionals involved in the governing of property & the environment
Italo Joe Luzi, President

Ontario Non-Profit Housing Association (ONPHA)
#400, 489 College St., Toronto ON M6G 1A5
Tel: 416-927-9144; *Fax:* 416-927-8401
Toll-Free: 800-297-6660
mail@onpha.org
www.onpha.on.ca
www.linkedin.com/company/ontario-non-profit-housing-associati
on
www.facebook.com/ONPHA
To build a strong non-profit housing sector in Ontario; To strive for excellence in non-profit housing management; To represent non-profit housing
Marlene Coffey, Executive Director
Michelle Coombs, Manager, Member Services
Sarah Fisch, Coordinator, Communications
Helen Harris, Coordinator, Policy & Research

Réseau québécois des OSBL d'habitation (RQOH)
#102, rue Fullum, Montréal QC H2K 0B5
Tél: 514-846-0163; *Téléc:* 514-846-3402
Ligne sans frais: 866-846-0163
info@rqoh.com
www.rqoh.com
www.facebook.com/ReseauQuebecoisOsblHabitation
twitter.com/RQOH_
Pour représenter les organismes de logement à but non lucratif; Pour répondre aux besoins de logement des personnes vulnérables et exclus de la province
Isabelle Leduc, Présidente
Stéphan Corriveau, Directeur général

ShareOwner Education Inc.
#201, 862 Richmond St. West, Toronto ON M6J 1C9
Tel: 416-595-9600; *Fax:* 416-595-0400
Toll-Free: 800-268-6881
customercare@shareowner.com
www.shareowner.com
To offer practical education & portfolio training to individual investors & investment clubs, so that they may invest successfully in quality growth stocks; To increase stock market literacy

Human Rights & Civil Liberties

Alberta Civil Liberties Research Centre (ACLRC)
c/o Murray Fraser Hall, Faculty of Law, University of Calgary, 2500 University Dr. NW, Calgary AB T2N 1N4
Tel: 403-220-2505; *Fax:* 403-284-0945
aclrc@ucalgary.ca
www.aclrc.com
To promote awareness among Albertans about civil liberties & human rights through research & education
Doreen Barrie, Chair
Michael I. Wylie, Treasurer

Amnesty International - Canadian Section (English Speaking)
312 Laurier Ave. East, Ottawa ON K1N 1H9
Tel: 613-744-7667; *Fax:* 613-746-2411
Toll-Free: 800-266-3789
info@amnesty.ca
www.amnesty.ca
www.facebook.com/amnestycanada
twitter.com/AmnestyNow
To bring public attention to abuses of human rights standards; To prevent & end human rights violations; To abolish the death penalty, torture, & other cruel treatment of prisoners, & to end political killings
Lana Verran, President
Jayne Stoyles, Executive Director

Amnistie internationale, Section canadienne (Francophone) / Amnesty International, Canadian Section (Francophone)
#500, 50, rue Sainte-Catherine ouest, Montréal QC H2X 3V4
Tél: 514-766-9766; *Téléc:* 514-766-2088
Ligne sans frais: 800-565-9766
accueil@amnistie.ca
www.amnistie.ca
www.facebook.com/Amnistie.internationale.Canada.francophone
twitter.com/AmnistieCa
Mouvement d'intervention directe formé de bénévoles qui visent à la libération des prisonniers d'opinion, la tenue de procès équitables pour les prisonniers politiques, l'abolition de la torture et la cessation des "disparitions" et assassinats politiques
Béatrice Vaugrante, Directrice générale

Black Coalition of Québec / La Ligue des Noirs du Québec
5201, boul Decarie, Montréal QC H3W 3C2
Tel: 514-489-3830
info@liguedesnoirs.org
www.liguedesnoirs.org
To speak for the Black community in the defence of individual human rights & against all forms of discrimination
Peterson Frederick, President

Black Lives Matter - Canada
76 Geary Ave., Toronto ON M6H 2B5
info@blacklivesmatter.ca
blacklivesmatter.ca
www.facebook.com/blacklivesmatterTO
twitter.com/blm_to
To dismantle all forms of anti-Black racism; To support Black healing; To create & build community spaces; To support Indigenous liberation & decolonization of Turtle Island & Nunavut Nunangat

British Columbia Civil Liberties Association (BCCLA)
900 Helmcken St., 2nd Fl., Vancouver BC V6Z 1B3
Tel: 604-687-2919; *Fax:* 604-687-3045
Toll-Free: 866-731-7507
www.bccla.org
www.youtube.com/user/BCCivilLiberties
www.facebook.com/BCCivLib
twitter.com/bccla
To protect & enhance civil liberties & human rights in British Columbia
Josh Paterson, Executive Director
Micheal Vonn, Policy Director

Canada Tibet Committee (CTC)
1425, boul René-Lévesque ouest, 3e étage, Montréal QC H3G 1T7
Tel: 514-487-0665
ctcoffice@tibet.ca
tibet.ca
www.youtube.com/tibetchannel
www.facebook.com/CanadaTibet
twitter.com/canadatibet
To defend & promote human rights & democratic freedoms of Tibetan people; To encourage support for Tibet from the government of Canada
Sherap Therchin, Executive Director

Canadian Anti-Hate Network
info@antihate.ca
www.antihate.ca
www.facebook.com/antihateca
twitter.com/antihateca
To monitor, research & counter hate groups; To educate & inform the public, media, researchers, courts, law enforcement & community groups
Evan Balgord, Executive Director

Canadian Association of Statutory Human Rights Agencies (CASHRA) / Association canadienne des commissions et conseil des droits de la personne (ACCCDP)
#170, 99 - 5th Ave., Ottawa ON K1P 5P5
www.cashra.ca
An umbrella organization for the federal, provincial and territorial human rights commissions.

Canadian Civil Liberties Association (CCLA) / Association canadienne des libertés civiles
#900, 90 Eglinton Ave. East, Toronto ON M4P 2Y3
Tel: 416-363-0321; *Fax:* 416-861-1291
mail@ccla.org
ccla.org
www.youtube.com/cancivlib
www.facebook.com/cancivlib
twitter.com/cancivlib
To protect the civil liberties, human rights & democratic freedoms of all Canadians
Michael Bryant, Executive Director & General Counsel

Canadian Tribute to Human Rights (CTHR) / Monument canadien pour les droits de la personne (MCDP)
#170, 99 - 5th Ave., Ottawa ON K1P 5P5
contact@cthr-mcdp.com
www.cthr-mcdp.com
To ensure public awareness of the presence in Ottawa of the Tribute monument as a symbol of Canadians' committment to preserving & fostering human rights; To promote use of the site as a focal point for all groups working for human rights in Canada & internationally; To spread the concept of public places

dedicated to human rights in other capital cities of countries that have affirmed the UN Universal Declaration of Human Rights.

CPJ Corp. (CPJ)
#501, 309 Cooper St., Ottawa ON K2P 0G5
Tel: 613-232-0275; *Fax:* 613-232-1275
Toll-Free: 800-667-8046
cpj@cpj.ca
www.cpj.ca
www.youtube.com/user/c4pj
www.facebook.com/citizensforpublicjustice
twitter.com/publicjustice
To promote public justice in Canada by shaping key public policy debates through research & analysis, publishing & public dialogue; To encourage citizens, leaders in society & governments to support policies & practices which reflect God's call for love, justice & stewardship
Joe Gunn, Executive Director

Equitas - International Centre for Human Rights Education / Equitas - Centre international d'éducation aux droits humains
#1100, 666, rue Sherbrooke ouest, Montréal QC H3A 1E7
Tel: 514-954-0382; *Fax:* 514-954-0659
info@equitas.org
equitas.org
www.youtube.com/user/EquitasHRE
www.linkedin.com/groups/1828397
www.facebook.com/equitas
twitter.com/equitasintl
To provide human rights education in Canada & abroad, based on the principles elaborated in the Universal Declaration of Human Rights
Ian Hamilton, Executive Director
Catalina Lomanto, Office Manager

International Bureau for Children's Rights (IBCR) / Bureau international des droits des enfants
805, rue Villeray, Montréal QC H2R 1J4
Tel: 514-932-7656
info@ibcr.org
www.ibcr.org
www.instagram.com/bureau_ibcr
www.linkedin.com/company/international-bureau-for-childrens'%
E2%80%8B-rights
www.facebook.com/BureauBCR
twitter.com/BureauIBCR
To ensure children's rights around the world
Guillaume Landry, General Manager

Joy Smith Foundation Inc.
2141 Henderson Hwy., #D, Winnipeg MB R2G 1P8
Tel: 204-691-2455; *Fax:* 204-421-2435
Toll-Free: 855-614-2532
info@joysmithfoundation.com
www.joysmithfoundation.com
www.instagram.com/joy.smith.foundation
www.facebook.com/TheJoySmithFoundation
twitter.com/JoySmithFdn
To ensure that every Canadian person is safe from manipulation, force, or abuse of power designed to lure & exploit them into the sex trade or forced labour
Joy Smith, Founder & President

League for Human Rights of B'nai Brith Canada / Ligue des droits de la personne de B'nai Brith Canada
15 Hove St., Toronto ON M3H 4Y8
Tel: 416-633-6224; *Fax:* 416-630-2159
Toll-Free: 800-892-2624
Crisis Hot-Line: 800-892-2624
league@bnaibrith.ca
www.bnaibrith.ca/league
To strive for human rights for all Canadians; to improve inter-community relations; to combat racism & racial discrimination; to prevent bigotry & anti-Semitism.
Frank Dimant, CEO

Macedonian Human Rights Movement International (MHRMI) / Mouvement canadien de défense des droits de la personne dans la communauté macédonienne
#434, 157 Adelaide St., Toronto ON M5H 4E7
Tel: 416-850-7125; *Fax:* 416-850-7127
info@mhrmi.org
www.mhrmi.org
www.facebook.com/MHRMI
twitter.com/mhrmi
To secure & maintain the human rights of all Macedonians wherever they live through advocacy & education
Bill Nicholov, President
Luby Vidinovski, Vice-President

Mark Opashinov, Secretary
Andy Plukov, Treasurer

PEN Canada, The Canadian Centre of PEN International (PEN)
#258, 401 Richmond St. West, Toronto ON M5V 3A8
Tel: 416-703-8448
queries@pencanada.ca
www.pencanada.ca
www.youtube.com/canadapen
www.facebook.com/PENCanadaCentre
twitter.com/PENCanada
To foster understanding among writers of all nations; To fight for freedom of expression wherever it is endangered; To work for preservation of world's literature
Brendan de Caires, Executive Director
Vera DeWaard, Office Manager

Philanthropic Foundations Canada (PFC) / Fondations philanthropiques Canada (FPC)
#1220, 615, boul René-Lévesque ouest, Montréal QC H3B 1P5
Tel: 514-866-5446; *Fax:* 514-866-5846
info@pfc.ca
pfc.ca
To encourage public policies that promote philanthropy; to increase awareness of philanthropy & provide opportunities for foundations to learn from one another
Hilary Pearson, President & CEO
Liza Goulet, Director, Research & Member Services

Pivot Legal Society
121 Heatley Ave., Vancouver BC V6A 3E9
Tel: 604-255-9700; *Fax:* 604-255-1552
www.pivotlegal.org
www.facebook.com/PivotLegalSociety
twitter.com/pivotlegal
To use the law to address the root causes of social exclusion & poverty; To pressure authorities in order to shift society's values toward equality & inclusivity
Katrina Pacey, Executive Director

Immigration

Iranian-Canadian Association of Immigration Consultants (ICAIC)
#316, 10271 Yonge St., Richmond Hill ON L4C 3B5
Tel: 647-362-5687
info@icaic.ca
icaic.ca
www.linkedin.com/company/kanoon-mohandes
www.facebook.com/KanoonMohandes
twitter.com/KanoonMohandes
To protect the interests of Iranian-Canadian immigration consultants
Nazgol Momeni, President

Industry

Arts Consultants Canada (ACC) / Consultants canadiens en arts (CCA)
#214, 2055 Danforth Ave., Toronto ON M4C 1J8
info@artsconsultants
artsconsultants.ca
www.linkedin.com/company/arts-consultants-canada-consultants-canadiens-en-arts
www.facebook.com/ArtsConsultantsCanada
twitter.com/consult_arts
To support art consultants & promote the profession to the public
Victoria Steele, President

Electronic Cigarette Trade Association (ECTA)
#6, 1295 Mosley St., Wasaga Beach ON L9Z 2Y7
info@ectaofcanada.com
ectaofcanada.com
www.facebook.com/groups/107871806005243
twitter.com/ECTAofCanada
To establish an Industry Standard of Excellence & ensure that member companies adhere to it

Vaping Advocacy & Education Project Inc. (VAEP)
Westlock AB
info@vaepworld.com
vaepworld.com
www.instagram.com/vaepworld
www.facebook.com/groups/147582955637632
twitter.com/VAEPworld
To spread accurate & comprehensive information about vaping to the general public, through advocacy & education

Vaping Industry Trade Association (VITA) / Association des Représentants de l'Industrie du Vapotage (ARIV)
Ottawa ON
vitaofcanada.com
To represent vaping industry manufacturers, importers, distributors & retailers; To work with government & stakeholders to set & maintain regulations
Daniel David, President & CEO

Information Technology

ASM International
9639 Kinsman Rd., Materials Park OH 44073-0002 USA
Tel: 440-338-5151; *Fax:* 440-338-4634
Toll-Free: 800-336-5152
memberservicecenter@asminternational.org
www.asminternational.org
www.linkedin.com/company/asm-international
www.facebook.com/asminternational
twitter.com/asminternationa
To gather, process & disseminate technical information; to foster understanding & application of engineered materials; to provide career support & education for business & information systems professionals
Jon D. Tirpak, President

Association for Image & Information Management International - 1st Canadian Chapter (AIIM Canada)
Toronto ON
www.aiim.org
To connect users & suppliers of e-business technologies & services

Association of Professional Canadian Consultants (APCC)
#703, 157 Adelaide St. West, Toronto ON M5H 4E7
Tel: 416-545-5213; *Toll-Free:* 800-483-0766
www.apcconline.com
To promote the interests of independent contractors in Canada; To provide education to the independent contractor community; To provide members with a forum for interaction & exchange
Frank McCrea, President

Association québécoise des informaticiennes et informaticiens indépendants (AQIII) / Québec Association for ICT Freelancers
#101, 405, av Ogilvy, Montréal QC H3N 1M3
Tél: 514-388-6147
aqiii@aqiii.org
www.aqiii.org
www.linkedin.com/company/aqiii
www.facebook.com/AQIII.org
twitter.com/aqiii
Offrir une communauté de partage aux consultants indépendants en TIC afin qu'ils bénéficient des forces d'un réseau pour favoriser leur réussite et préserver leur liberté d'entrepreneuriat indépendant
Lamy Hugues, Président
François Marchal, Directeur général

Canada's Advanced Internet Development Organization (CANARIE)
#500, 45 O'Connor St., Ottawa ON K1P 1A4
Tel: 613-943-5454; *Fax:* 613-943-5443
info@canarie.ca
www.canarie.ca
www.linkedin.com/groups/3712846
www.facebook.com/CanarieInc
twitter.com/CANARIE_Inc
Canada's advanced internet development organization; to facilitate & promote the development of Canada's communications infrastructure; to stimulate next-generation products, applications & services; to communicate the benefits of an information-based society. CANARIE also intends to act as a catalyst and partner with governments, industry and the research community to increase overall IT awareness, ensure continuing promotion of Canadian technological excellence and ultimately, foster long-term productivity and improvement of living standards.
Jim Ghadbane, President & CEO
Nancy E. Carter, Chief Financial Officer

Canadian Association of Wireless Internet Service Providers / Association des fournisseurs de service internet sans fil
#300, 162 Metcalfe St., Ottawa ON K2P 1P2
Toll-Free: 844-370-0404
info@canwisp.ca
www.canwisp.ca

To foster the growth of a healthy & competitive Internet service industry in Canada through collective & cooperative action on issues of mutual interest
Eric Lay, Executive Director
Cathi Malette, Manager, Member Services

Canadian Image Processing & Pattern Recognition Society (CIPPRS) / Association canadienne de traitement d'images et de reconnaissance des formes (ACTIRF)
Lassonde School of Engineering, York Univ., 4700 Keele St., Toronto ON M3J 1P3
www.cipprs.org
To promote research & development activities in image & signal processing for solving pattern recognition problems
Michael Jenkin, President
Steven Waslander, Treasurer
Jim Little, Secretary

Canadian Information Processing Society (CIPS) / L'Association canadienne de l'informatique (ACI)
#802, 1375 Southdown Rd., Unit 16, Mississauga ON L5J 2Z1
Tel: 905-602-1370; *Fax:* 905-602-7884
Toll-Free: 877-275-2477
info@cips.ca
www.cips.ca
www.linkedin.com/company/canadian-information-processing-society
www.facebook.com/CIPS.ca
twitter.com/cips
To define & foster the IT profession; To encourage & support the IT practitioner; To advance the theory & practice of IT, while safeguarding the public interest
Derek Burt, Chair

Digital Health Canada
#1100, 151 Yonge St., Toronto ON M5C 2W7
Tel: 647-775-8555
info@digitalhealthcanada.com
digitalhealthcanada.com
www.linkedin.com/company/415342
www.facebook.com/digitalhealthcdn
twitter.com/DigiHealthCA
To improve the health of Canadians & enhance the management of Canada's health system by advancing the practice of health information management & effective utilization of associated technologies
Mark Casselman, Chief Executive Officer
Shannon Bott, Executive Director, Operations

Digital Nova Scotia (ITANS)
Technology Innovation Centre, 1 Research Dr., Dartmouth NS B2Y 4M9
Tel: 902-423-5332; *Fax:* 877-282-9506
info@digitalnovascotia.com
www.digitalnovascotia.com
www.youtube.com/user/digitalnovascotia
www.linkedin.com/groups/1801099
twitter.com/digitalns
To be dedicated to the development & growth of the digital technologies industry in Nova Scotia
Ulrike Bahr-Gedalia, President & CEO
Bruce MacDougall, Chair
Emily Boucher, Director, Marketing & Research

Electronic Frontier Canada Inc. (EFC) / Frontière électronique du Canada
20 Richmond Ave., Kitchener ON N2G 1Y9
Tel: 905-525-9140; *Fax:* 905-546-9995
www.efc.ca
To ensure that the principals embodied in the Canadian Charter of Rights & Freedoms are protected as new computing, communications & information technologies emerge.
David Jones, President
Jeffrey Shallit, Vice-President/Treasurer
Richard Rosenberg, Vice-President

GS1 Canada
#800, 1500 Don Mills Rd., Toronto ON M3B 3K4
Tel: 416-510-8039; *Fax:* 416-510-1916
Toll-Free: 800-567-7084
info@gs1ca.org
www.gs1ca.org
To act as a facilitator for the use of electronic information transactions in support of Canadian users
N. Arthur Smith, Chief Executive Officer

Information & Communications Technology Council of Canada (ICTC) / Conseil des technologies de l'information et des communications du Canada (CTIC)
#300, 116 Lisgar St., Ottawa ON K2P 0C2
Tel: 613-237-8551; Fax: 613-230-3490
info@ictc-ctic.ca
www.ictc-ctic.ca
www.youtube.com/user/DigitalEconomyPulse
www.linkedin.com/company/information-and-communications-technology-council
www.facebook.com/196829353752455
twitter.com/ictc_ctic

To serve the software development profession by developing joint ventures in courseware design & delivery, by integrating training & education processes, by helping to ensure sufficient supply & quality of new entrants to the profession & by promoting an attractive image & definition of software workers
Namir Anani, President & CEO

Information Resource Management Association of Canada (IRMAC)
#4800 - 46, 1 King St. West, Toronto ON M5H 1A1
Tel: 416-887-2837
www.irmac.ca

To provide a forum for members to exchange information about data administration & information resource management

Information Technology Association of Canada (ITAC) / Association canadienne de la technologie de l'information
#801, 5090 Explorer Dr., Mississauga ON L4W 4T9
Tel: 905-602-8345; Fax: 905-602-8346
info@itac.ca
www.itac.ca
www.youtube.com/user/itacacti

To represent companies in the computing & telecommunications hardware, software, services & electronic content sectors; To identifys & lead resolution on issues that affect the industry; To advocate for initiatives that enable continued growth & development in the industry
Angela Mondou, President & CEO
Andrew Leduc, Senior Vice-President, GR & Policy
Jan Hall, Director, Human Resources
Owais Khalid, Director, Finance

IntelliFLEX Innovation Alliance
170 Cheyenne Way, Ottawa ON K2J 5S6
Tel: 613-795-8181
intelliflex.org
www.linkedin.com/company/intelliflexorg
twitter.com/intelliflex_org

To connect key Canadian & international players in industry, academia & government to build a strong Canadian PE sector
Mark Majewski, President & CEO
Naudia Banton, Director, Operations

National Capital FreeNet (NCF) / Libertel de la Capitale Nationale
Richmond Square, #206, 1305 Richmond Rd., Ottawa ON K2B 7Y4
Tel: 613-721-1773
ncf@ncf.ca
www.ncf.ca

Newfoundland & Labrador Association of Technology Industries (NATI)
#5, 391 Empire Ave., St. John's NL A1E 1W6
Tel: 709-772-8324; Fax: 709-757-6284
info@nati.net
www.nati.net
www.linkedin.com/company/nati
twitter.com/NATI_NL

To act collectively for technical organizations in Newfoundland industry in cooperation with educational & public sectors to promote the growth of innovative technical industries in Newfoundland & Labrador & the rest of Canada
Ron Taylor, Chief Executive Officer

reBOOT Canada
#1, 2450 Lawrence Ave. East, Toronto ON M1P 2R7
Tel: 416-534-6017; Fax: 416-534-6083
rose@rebootcanada.ca
www.rebootcanada.ca

Refurbishes old computers received from individual & corporate donors & distributes them, free of charge, to other charitable organizations
Nicholas Brinckman, Executive Director

Insurance Industry

Advocis
#600, 10 Lower Spadina Ave., Toronto ON M5V 2Z2
Tel: 416-444-5251; Toll-Free: 877-773-6765
info@advocis.ca
www.advocis.ca
www.youtube.com/user/AdvocisTFAAC
www.linkedin.com/company/advocis
www.facebook.com/advocis
twitter.com/Advocis

To represent Advice & Advocacy; To carry on the tradition of effectively representing members' interests with all levels of government, regulators & industry, always with the intention of putting the interests of consumers first
Greg Pollock, President & CEO

Canadian Association of Blue Cross Plans (CABCP) / Association Canadienne des Croix Bleue (ACCB)
PO Box 2005, #610, 185 The West Mall, Toronto ON M9C 5P1
Toll-Free: 866-732-2583
www.bluecross.ca

To maintain & monitor standards of performance by association members; To ensure members manage effectively supplementary health, dental, life insurance & disability income products on an individual and group basis

Canadian Association of Independent Life Brokerage Agencies (CAILBA)
#213, 13-4 Alliance Blvd., Barrie ON L4M 7G3
Tel: 416-931-2166
info@cailba.com
www.cailba.com
www.linkedin.com/company/10963663

To lobby provincial & federal governments on legislative issues affecting the life & health insurance brokerage industry; To provide a forum for networking & relationship building among members, insurance companies & industry vendors
Michael Williams, President
Clementine Peacock, Executive Director
Andrew Harris, Administrator

Canadian Association of Mutual Insurance Companies (CAMIC) / Association canadienne des compagnies d'assurance mutuelles (ACCAM)
#516, 250 City Centre Ave., Ottawa ON K1R 6K7
Tel: 613-789-6851; Toll-Free: 888-366-7807
www.camic.ca

To provide information, research, advocacy to its members in areas of general concerns & to negotiate supply agreements for goods & services of common needs; To promote a strong, health & competitive insurance market; To support regulatory efficiency & legislative change; To inform member companies on matters affecting the industry & to build consensus on action plans; To promote self-regulation for the property & casualty insurance industry
Sangita Kamblé, President & CEO

Canadian Board of Marine Underwriters (CBMU)
#304, 2233 Argentia Rd., Mississauga ON L5N 2X7
Tel: 905-826-4768; Fax: 905-826-4873
cbmu@cbmu.com
www.cbmu.com
www.linkedin.com/groups/4581774
twitter.com/TheCBMU

To procure & disseminate information of interest to marine underwriters & others; To facilitate the exchange of views & ideas which work to improve the marine underwriting industry & marine insurance; To promote & protect the interest of the underwriting community
Matthew Lewis, President
Halyna Troian, Secretary-Treasurer

Canadian Independent Adjusters' Association (CIAA) / Association canadienne des experts indépendants (ACEI)
#308, 132 Commerce Park Dr., #K, Barrie ON L4N 0Z7
Tel: 416-621-6222; Toll-Free: 877-255-5589
info@ciaa-adjusters.ca
www.ciaa-adjusters.ca
www.linkedin.com/company/canadian-independent-adjusters-association
twitter.com/CIAAOfficial1

To provide leadership for independent adjusters in Canada; To develop & maintain high standards of professionalism; To represent the interests of independent adjusters at the regional, provincial & national levels
Christopher Bartlett, President
Patricia M. Battle, Executive Director

Canadian Institute of Actuaries (CIA) / Institut canadien des actuaires (ICA)
Secretariat, #1740, 360 Albert St., Ottawa ON K1R 7X7
Tel: 613-236-8196; Fax: 613-233-4552
head.office@cia-ica.ca
www.cia-ica.ca
www.linkedin.com/company/canadian-institute-of-actuaries
www.facebook.com/CanadianInstituteofActuaries
twitter.com/CIA_Actuaries

To set & ensure educational & professional standards for members; To operate a review & disciplinary system; To maintain liaison with government authorities & other professions & organizations; To promote research
Michel C. Simard, Executive Director
Lynn Blackburn, Director, Professional Practice & Governance
Les Dandridge, Director, Communications & Public Affairs
Jacques Leduc, Director, Membership & Operations
Alicia Rollo, Director, Education & International Affairs

Canadian Life & Health Insurance Association Inc. (CLHIA) / Association des compagnies d'assurances de personnes inc. (ACCAP)
PO Box 99, #2300, 79 Wellington St. West, Toronto ON M5K 1G8
Tel: 416-777-2221; Fax: 416-777-1895
Toll-Free: 888-295-8112
info@clhia.ca
www.clhia.ca
www.linkedin.com/company/clhia
www.facebook.com/clhia
twitter.com/clhia

To represent the interests of member life & health insurance companies
Stephen Frank, President & CEO

Centre for Study of Insurance Operations (CSIO) / Centre d'étude de la pratique d'assurance
#500, 110 Yonge St., Toronto ON M5C 1T4
Tel: 416-360-1773; Toll-Free: 800-463-2746
helpdesk@csio.com
www.csio.com
www.linkedin.com/company/csio
www.facebook.com/CSIOCANADA
twitter.com/csio

To act as the national standards association for property & casualty insurance by representing property & casualty industry initiatives; To provide a competitive advantage for the independent broker distribution channel
Steve Whitelaw, Chair
Catherine Smola, President & CEO

Chambre de l'assurance de dommages (CHAD)
#1200, 999, boul de Maisonneuve ouest, Montréal QC H3A 3L4
Tél: 514-842-2591; Téléc: 514-842-3138
Ligne sans frais: 800-361-7288
info@chad.qc.ca
www.chad.ca
www.linkedin.com/company/chambre-de-l'assurance-de-dommages

Assurer la protection du public en matière d'assurance de dommages et d'expertise en règlement de sinistres; encadrer de façon préventive et disciplinaire la pratique professionnelle des individus et des organisations oeuvrant dans ces domaines
Diane Beaudry, CPA, CA, ICD.D., Présidente
Anne-Marie Poitras, Directrice générale

Chambre de la sécurité financière (CSF)
2000, av McGill College, Montréal QC H3A 3H3
Tél: 514-282-5777; Téléc: 514-282-2225
Ligne sans frais: 800-361-9989
renseignements@chambresf.com
www.chambresf.com
www.youtube.com/chambresf
www.linkedin.com/company/1004475
www.facebook.com/ChambreSF
twitter.com/ChambreSF

Assurer la protection du public en maintenant la discipline et en veillant à la formation et à la déontologie de ses membres
Marie Elaine Farley, Présidente et chef de la direction
Lyne Boisvert, Directrice principale, Performance et opérations
Nancy De Bruyn, Directrice principale, Ressources humaines et affaires corporatives
Julie Chevrette, Directrice, Communications
Nathalie Lajeunesse, Directrice, Information et des services aux membres
Valérie Sauvé, Directrice, Finances et amélioration continue

Facility Association
PO Box 121, #2400, 777 Bay St., Toronto ON M5G 2C8
Tel: 416-863-1750; *Fax:* 416-868-0894
Toll-Free: 800-268-9572
mail@facilityassociation.com
www.facilityassociation.com
To ensure the availability of automobile insurance for owners & licensed drivers of motor vehicles who may otherwise have difficulty obtaining such insurance
Saskia Matheson, President & CEO

Financial Services Commission of Ontario (FSCO) / Commission des services financiers de l'Ontario (CSFO)
5160 Yonge St., 16th Fl., Toronto ON M2N 6L9
Tel: 416-250-7250; *Fax:* 416-590-7070
Toll-Free: 800-668-0128
TTY: 800-387-0584
contactcentre@fsco.gov.on.ca
www.fsco.gov.on.ca
To regulate the following sectors in Ontario: insurance; pension plans; loan & trust companies; credit unions & caisses populaires; mortgage brokering; co-operative corporations in Ontario; & service providers who invoice auto insurers for statutory accident benefits claims.
Brian Mills, Chief Executive Officer

GAMA International Canada / GAMA International du Canada
#600, 10 Lower Spadina Ave., Toronto ON M5V 2Z2
Tel: 416-444-5251; *Fax:* 416-444-8031
Toll-Free: 800-563-5822
info@gamacanada.com
www.gamacanada.com
www.youtube.com/user/AdvocisTFAAC
www.linkedin.com/groups/1952201
www.facebook.com/gama.canada
To focus on professional development for leaders involved in the distribution of financial services

Groupement des assureurs automobiles (GAA)
#620, 1981 av McGill College, Montréal QC H3A 2Y1
Tél: 514-288-4321; *Ligne sans frais:* 877-288-4321
cinfo@gaa.qc.ca
www.gaa.qc.ca
Administrer, de façon efficace et selon les décisions du conseil d'administration, tous les mandats certifiés au Groupement des assureurs automobiles par la Loi sur l'assurance automobile du Québec
Johanne Lamanque, Directrice générale

L'Institut d'assurance de dommages du Québec (IADQ)
#575, 2055, rue Peel, Montréal QC H3A 1T6
Tél: 514-393-8156; *Téléc:* 514-393-9222
iadq@institutdassurance.ca
insuranceinstitute.ca/fr/institutes-and-chapters/Quebec.aspx
Organiser des cours, des séminaires et des conférences; promouvoir le rayonnement des titres professionnels PAA et FPAA d'assurance du Canada (AIAC & FIAC). Organisme sans but lucratif, qui a été mis sur pied par l'industrie de l'assurance de dommages pour donner la formation professionnelle à tous ceux qui oeuvrent dans ce secteur au Québec
Julie Saucier, Directrice générale

Insurance Bureau of Canada (IBC) / Bureau d'assurance du Canada
Head Office / Ontario Office, PO Box 121, #2400, 777 Bay St., Toronto ON M5G 2C8
Tel: 416-362-2031; *Fax:* 416-361-5952
Toll-Free: 844-227-5422
www.ibc.ca
www.youtube.com/insurancebureau
www.linkedin.com/company/insurance-bureau-of-canada
www.facebook.com/insurancebureau
twitter.com/InsuranceBureau
To foster a healthy property & casualty insurance marketplace & strenghten the ability of our members to serve the needs of Canada's insurance consumers; To advocate public policies that foster a healthy insurance marketplace; To facilitate communication, seek consensus & when in a unique position to do so, undertake industry solutions to common insurance industry concerns
Don Forgeron, President & CEO

Insurance Council of British Columbia
PO Box 7, #300, 1040 West Georgia St., Vancouver BC V6E 4H1
Tel: 604-688-0321; *Fax:* 604-662-7767
Toll-Free: 877-688-0321
info@insurancecouncilofbc.com
www.insurancecouncilofbc.com

Has the authority to license insurance agents, salespersons, & adjusters, & to investigate & discipline licensees. The Council is accountable to the provincial government & reports to the Minister of Finance.
Gerald Matier, Executive Director

Insurance Institute of British Columbia (IIBC)
#1110, 800 West Pender St., Vancouver BC V6C 2V6
Tel: 604-681-5491; *Fax:* 604-681-5479
Toll-Free: 888-681-5491
IIBCmail@insuranceinstitute.ca
www.insuranceinstitute.ca
Danielle Bolduc, Manager

Insurance Institute of Canada (IIC) / Institut d'assurance du Canada (IAC)
18 King St. East, 6th Fl., Toronto ON M5C 1C4
Tel: 416-362-8586; *Fax:* 416-362-1126
Toll-Free: 866-362-8585
IICmail@insuranceinstitute.ca
www.insuranceinstitute.ca
To design, develop, & deliver insurance educational programs & texts; To prepare examinations & awards; To provide a graduate society; To develop career information on behalf of the property/casualty insurance industry
Peter Hohman, MBA, FCIP, ICD., President & CEO
Mike Divjak, BComm, FCIP, CR, Vice-President, Operations
Linda Love, MHRM, BA, CHRP, Senior Director, Human Resources
Fahed Malik, MBA, BComm, Director, Marketing & Communications
Harry Vizi, CPA, CA, Director, Finance

Insurance Institute of Manitoba (IIM)
#303, 175 Hargrave St., Winnipeg MB R3C 3R8
Tel: 204-956-1702; *Fax:* 204-956-0758
IIMmail@insuranceinstitute.ca
www.insuranceinstitute.ca
To provide educational services in the general insurance industry in both English and French, such as the Chartered Insurance Professional (CIP), & Fellow Chartered Insurance Professional (FCIP) programs
Jessica Hutchings, Manager

Insurance Institute of New Brunswick (IINB)
#101, 1010 St-George Blvd., Moncton NB E1E 4R5
Tel: 506-386-5896; *Fax:* 506-386-1130
IINBmail@insuranceinstitute.ca
www.insuranceinstitute.ca
Monique LeBlanc, Manager

Insurance Institute of Newfoundland & Labrador Inc. (IINL)
Chimo Bldg., 151 Crosbie Rd., St. John's NL A1B 4B4
Tel: 709-754-4398; *Fax:* 709-754-4399
IINLmail@insuranceinstitute.ca
www.insuranceinstitute.ca
Leona Rowsell, Manager

Insurance Institute of Northern Alberta (IINA)
#204, 10109 - 106 St., Edmonton AB T5J 3L7
Tel: 780-424-1268; *Fax:* 780-420-1940
IINAmail@insuranceinstitute.ca
www.insuranceinstitute.ca
The Insurance Institute of Northern Alberta provides products and sevices to the general insurance industry, and ensures the maintenance of a uniform standard of education for the general Insurance Business throughout Canada
Dawn Horne, Manager

Insurance Institute of Nova Scotia (IINS)
#220, 250 Baker Dr., Dartmouth NS B2W 6L4
Tel: 902-433-0070; *Fax:* 902-433-0072
IINSmail@insuranceinstitute.ca
www.insuranceinstitute.ca
twitter.com/insuranceinsns
To provide educational products & services to the general insurance industry, such as the Chartered Insurance Professional (CIP) & the Fellow Chartered Insurance Professional (FCIP) designation programs
Jenny Renyo, Manager

Insurance Institute of Ontario (IIO)
18 King St. East, 16th Fl., Toronto ON M5C 1C4
Tel: 416-362-8586; *Fax:* 416-362-8081
iiomail@insuranceinstitute.ca
insuranceinstitute.ca/en/institutes-and-chapters/Ontario.aspx
To deliver general insurance educational services in English & French, which are consistent with the standardized curriculum offered throughout Canada, such as the Fellow Chartered Insurance Professional (FCIP) & the Fellow Chartered Insurance Professional (FCIP) designation programs
Margaret Wasserman, Senior Director

Insurance Institute of Prince Edward Island (IIPEI)
c/o The Insurance Institute of Canada, 18 King St. East, 6th Fl., Toronto ON M5C 1C4
Tel: 902-892-1692; *Fax:* 902-368-7305
IIPEImail@insuranceinstitute.ca
www.insuranceinstitute.ca
twitter.com/insuranceinspei
Kent Hudson, Marketing Coordinator

Insurance Institute of Saskatchewan (IIS)
#310, 2631 - 28 Ave., Regina SK S4S 6X3
Tel: 306-525-9799; *Fax:* 306-525-8169
IISmail@insuranceinstitute.ca
www.insuranceinstitute.ca
To offer educational products & services to the general insurance industry in both English & French, such as the Fellow Chartered Insurance Professional (FCIP) & the Chartered Insurance Professional (CIP) designation programs
Shannon Karok, Manager

Insurance Institute of Southern Alberta (IISA)
#1110, 833 - 4 Ave. SW, Calgary AB T2P 3T5
Tel: 403-266-3427; *Fax:* 403-269-3199
IISAmail@insuranceinstitute.ca
www.insuranceinstitute.ca
To advance the efficiency, expertise & ability of people employed in the insurance & financial services industry
Seti Mazaheri, Manager

LOMA Canada
East Tower, 675 Cochrane Dr., 6th Floor, Markham ON L3R 0B8
Tel: 905-530-2309; *Fax:* 905-530-2001
lomacanada@loma.org
www.loma.org/canada
To serve its member companies by encouraging & assisting individuals to acquire knowledge & understanding of business of life & health insurance & related financial services

Marine Insurance Association of British Columbia (MIABC)
c/o Tina Antonio, Aon Risk Solutions, PO Box 3228, #1200, 401 West Georgia St., Vancouver BC V6B 3X8
Tel: 604-844-7654; *Fax:* 604-682-4026
marineinsuranceassociationbc.ca
To represent the goals & interests of the marine insurance industry in British Columbia
Tina Antonio, President

Nuclear Insurance Association of Canada (NIAC) / Association canadienne d'assurance nucléaire
#1600, 401 Bay St., Toronto ON M5H 2Y4
Tel: 416-646-6232
www.niac.biz
www.youtube.com/channel/UCpwR0r-ONaYt6TDZXwf64hA
www.linkedin.com/company/nuclear-insurance-association-of-canada
www.facebook.com/NIAC.biz
twitter.com/NIACanada
Colleen P. DeMerchant, Manager

Ontario Insurance Adjusters Association (OIAA)
29 De Jong Dr., Mississauga ON L5M 1B9
Tel: 905-542-0576; *Fax:* 905-542-1301
Toll-Free: 888-259-1555
www.oiaa.com
www.facebook.com/OntarioInsuranceAdjustersAssociation
twitter.com/OIAAOfficial
To promote & maintain a high standard of ethics in the business of insurance claims adjusting
Jennifer Graham, President

Ontario Mutual Insurance Association (OMIA)
350 Pinebush Rd., Cambridge ON N1T 1Z6
Tel: 519-622-9220; *Fax:* 519-622-9227
www.omia.com
To assist mutual insurance companies to achieve excellence in service provision

Reinsurance Research Council (RRC) / Conseil de recherche en réassurance (CRR)
#1, 189 Queen St. East, Toronto ON M5A 1S2
Tel: 416-968-0183; *Fax:* 416-968-6818
manager@rrccanada.org
rrccanada.org
To represent professional reinsurers registered in Canada; To conduct research into all lines of property / casualty reinsurance; To present the views of its members & provides liaison with governments, the primary insurance market & other interested parties; To promote high standards of service & ethical business practices; To develop & maintain cordial relations among members & with kindred associations & the public
John Chagnon, General Manager

Risk & Insurance Management Society Inc. (RIMS)
RIMS Canada Council, #202, 10 Morrow Ave., Toronto ON M6R 2J1

Tel: 416-538-1212
www.rimscanada.ca
www.linkedin.com/groups/4701774
twitter.com/RIMSCanada
To advance the practice of risk management in Canada
Ren Lips, Chair

Saskatchewan Municipal Hail Insurance Association (SMHI)
2100 Cornwall St., Regina SK S4P 2K7

Tel: 306-569-1852; *Fax:* 306-522-3717
Toll-Free: 877-414-7644
smhi@municipalhail.ca
www.smhi.ca
twitter.com/MunicipalHail
To provide spot-loss hail insurance coverage to Saskatchewan grain farmers at cost
Rodney Schoettler, Chief Executive Officer
Mark Holfeld, Chief Operating Officer

Society of Public Insurance Administrators of Ontario (SPIAO)
c/o The Municipality Of Clarington, 40 Temperance St., Bowmanville ON L1C 3A6

info@spiao.ca
www.spiao.ca
To exchange knowledge & pursue matters dealing with risk & insurance management; to promote cooperation among all local government bodies which have interests in the field of risk & insurance management; to encourage development of educational training programs; to collect & disperse information
Marie Endicott, President
Catherine Carr, Treasurer

Underwriters' Laboratories of Canada (ULC) / Laboratoires des assureurs du Canada
7 Underwriters Rd., Toronto ON M1R 3A9

Tel: 416-757-3611; *Fax:* 416-757-8727
Toll-Free: 866-937-3852
cec@ul.com
canada.ul.com
To support domestic governmental product safety regulations; To work with international safety systems to help further trade with adherence to local safety requirements
Jennifer Scanlon, President & CEO

Interior Design

Association des designers industriels du Québec (ADIQ)
#406, 420, rue McGill, Montréal QC H2Y 2G1

Tél: 514-287-6531; *Téléc:* 514-278-3049
info@adiq.ca
www.adiq.ca
www.facebook.com/adiquebec
De soutenir, de représenter et de promourvoir les membres professionels et de mettre en valeur la profession.
Mario Gagnon, Président

Association of Canadian Industrial Designers (ACID) / Association des designers industriels du Canada
#251, 157 Adelaide St. West, Toronto ON M5H 4E7

info@designcanada.org
www.designcanada.org
To represent Canadian industrial designers throughout world; To represent the collective interests of designers; To increase the knowledge, skill, & proficiency of its members through networking, discussion forums, seminars, & trade events

Association of Interior Designers of Nova Scotia (IDNS)
PO Box 2042, Halifax NS B3J 3B4

Tel: 902-425-4367
idns.ca
To promote the profession; to serve both the interests of public and the interior design industry.
Fran Underwood, President

Association of Registered Interior Designers of New Brunswick (ARIDNB) / Association des designers d'intérieur immatriculés du Nouveau-Brunswick (ADIINB)
PO Box 1541, Fredericton NB E3B 5G2

Tel: 506-459-3014
info@aridnb.ca
www.aridnb.ca
To establish & maintain standards of knowledge, skill, & professional ethics among association members; To serve the public interest by governing the practice of interior design in New Brunswick
Rachel Mitton, President
Lyn Van Tassel, Vice-President
Chrystalla Wilde, Treasurer & Registrar
Ginette Fougère, Secretary

Association of Registered Interior Designers of Ontario (ARIDO)
43 Hanna Ave., #C536, Toronto ON M6K 1X1

Tel: 416-921-2127; *Toll-Free:* 800-334-1180
info@arido.ca
www.arido.ca
To govern the conduct & professional standards of members; To increase awareness of the profession & ensure rights of interior designers & the public they serve
Sharon Portelli, Executive Director & Registrar

Association professionnelle des designers d'intérieur du Québec (APDIQ)
Maison de l'Architecture, du Design et de l'Urbanisme (MADU), #406, 420, rue McGill, Montréal QC H2Y 2G1

Tél: 514-284-6263
info@apdiq.com
www.apdiq.com
Promouvoir la reconnaissance des designers d'intérieur comme ordre professionnel; assurer la qualité de leurs services; les regrouper pour faire évoluer leur profession; veiller aux intérêts du public; édicter et assurer le respect des règles d'éthique professionnelle
Marie-Claude Parenteau-Lebeuf, Directrice générale

British Columbia Industrial Designer Association (BCID)
PO Box 33943, Vancouver BC V6J 4L7

Tel: 604-608-3204; *Fax:* 604-608-3204
email@bcid.com
www.bcid.com
To act as the public voice for its members; to represent their interests nationally; to maintain a set of standards to preserve the integrity of the profession; to keep a register of professional industrial designers in the province.

Decorators & Designers Association of Canada (DDAC)
#705, 1 Eglinton Ave. East, Toronto ON M4P 3A1

Tel: 416-231-6202; *Toll-Free:* 866-878-2155
office@ddacanada.com
ddacanada.com
www.instagram.com/ddacanada
www.linkedin.com/company/ddacanada
www.facebook.com/DecorDesignCanada
twitter.com/DDACanada
To represent interior decorators & interior designers in Canada
Andria Cowan-Molyneaux, Acting National Chair

Interior Designers Association of Saskatchewan (IDAS)
PO Box 32005, Stn. Erindale, Saskatoon SK S7S 1N8

Tel: 306-343-3311
idasadmin@idas.ca
www.idas.ca
To promote an understanding of the profession to the public & to support members in their profession through continuing education & networking
Lucienne Van Langen, President
Catherine Folkersen, Contact

Interior Designers Institute of British Columbia (IDIBC)
#400, 601 West Broadway, Vancouver BC V5Z 4C2

Tel: 604-298-5211; *Fax:* 604-421-5211
info@idibc.org
www.idibc.org
www.linkedin.com/company/idibc---the-interior-designers-institute-of-bc
www.facebook.com/IDIBC
twitter.com/idibc
To act as the single representative voice of the Interior Design profession in British Columbia; To advance the profession through public recognition & provide leadership & services to members through programs, communication & education; To benefit public health, safety & welfare, contribute to the enhancement of the environment & increase the perception, appreciation & value of design in the community
Erica Wickes, President

Interior Designers of Alberta (IDA)
c/o ManageWise Inc., PO Box 21171, #202, 5405 - 99 St., Edmonton AB T6R 2V4

Tel: 780-413-0013; *Fax:* 780-413-0076
info@idalberta.ca
www.idalberta.ca
To develop & maintain standards of practice of interior design; to encourage excellence in interior design; to develop standards of & encourage continuing education of practicing designers; & to provide a liaison between the profession & the general public.
Kelly Vander Hooft, President
Adele Bonetti, Registrar

Interior Designers of Canada (IDC) / Designers d'intérieur du Canada
#400, 901 King St. West, Toronto ON M5V 3H5

Tel: 416-649-4425; *Toll-Free:* 877-443-4425
info@idcanada.org
www.idcanada.org
www.instagram.com/interiordesignersofcanada
www.linkedin.com/company/interior-designers-of-canada
www.facebook.com/InteriorDesignersOfCanada
twitter.com/IDCanadaTweets
To advance the interior design industry in Canada through high standards of education for the profession, professional responsibility, professional development & communication
Trevor Kruse, Chief Executive Officer
Vesna Plazacic, Director, Communications & Marketing

Interior Designers of Newfoundland & Labrador (IDNL)
NL

idnl.ca

Professional Interior Designers Institute of Manitoba
137 Bannatyne Ave. East, 2nd Fl., Winnipeg MB R3B 0R3

Tel: 204-925-4625
pidim@shaw.ca
www.pidim.ca
To practice interior design in order to improve the lives of the public

International Cooperation/International Relations

AFS Interculture Canada (AFSIC)
#805, 1001 rue Sherbrooke est, Montréal QC H2L 1L3

Tel: 514-288-3282; *Toll-Free:* 800-361-7248
info-canada@afs.org
www.afscanada.org
www.instagram.com/afscanada
www.facebook.com/afsinterculturecanada
To promote global education & international development through intercultural exchange programs for both young people & adults; To offer international internships; To work as part of the largest network of international exchange programs in the world
Anisara Creary, National Director

Aga Khan Foundation Canada (AKFC)
The Delegation of the Ismaili Imamat, 199 Sussex Dr., Ottawa ON K1N 1K6

Tel: 613-237-2532; *Fax:* 613-567-2532
Toll-Free: 800-267-2532
www.akfc.ca
www.youtube.com/user/akfcadmin
www.facebook.com/akfcanada
twitter.com/AKFCanada
To support cost-effective development projects in Asia & Africa in the fields of primary health care, education & rural development, with special attention paid to the needs of women; Major initiatives include: The Pakistan-Canada Social Institutions Development Program; the Tajikistan Institutional Support Program and the Non-Formal Education Program of the Bangladesh Rural Advancement Committee
Khalil Z. Shariff, Chief Executive Officer

Canada World Youth (CWY) / Jeunesse Canada Monde (JCM)
#300, 2330, rue Notre-Dame ouest, Montréal QC H3J 1N4

Tel: 514-931-3526; *Fax:* 514-360-3881
Toll-Free: 800-605-3526
info@cwy-jcm.org
canadaworldyouth.org
www.instagram.com/cwyjcm
www.linkedin.com/company/canada-world-youth-official-website-jeunesse-canada-monde-site-officiel-
www.facebook.com/CanadaWorldYouth.JeunesseCanadaMonde
twitter.com/cwyjcm
To increase people's ability to participate actively in the development of just, harmonious & sustainable societies; To create exceptional learning opportunities for communities, groups & individuals wishing to acquire skills & explore new ideas
Susan Handrigan, President & CEO
Mike Power, Vice-President, Programming & Operations

Canada-UK Foundation
Canada House, Trafalgar Sq., London SW1Y 5BJ United Kingdom

admin@canadaukfoundation.org
www.canadaukfoundation.org
www.linkedin.com/company/canada-uk-foundation1
www.facebook.com/CanUKFoundation
twitter.com/CanUKFoundation

To foster understanding of Canada & Canadians in the UK; To create partnerships between the academic & non-academic world to foster understanding of Canadian contributions in various subjects
Wanda Hamilton, Chief Executive Officer

Canadian Association for Latin American & Caribbean Studies (CALACS) / Association canadienne des études latino-américaines et caraïbes (ACELAC)
c/o Juan Pablo Crespo Vasquez, York Research Tower, York University, #8-17, 4700 Keele St., Toronto ON M3J 1P3

Tel: 416-736-2100; Fax: 519-971-3610
calacs@yorku.ca
www.can-latam.org

To facilitate networking & the exchange of information among those engaged in teaching & research on Latin America & the Caribbean in Canada & abroad; To foster throughout Canada, especially within the universities, colleges, & other centres of higher education, the expansion of information on & interest in Latin America & the Caribbean; To represent the academic & professional interest of Canadian Latin Americanists
Pablo Crespo Vasquez Juan, Contact, Administration
Steven Palmer, Secretary-Treasurer

Canadian Association for the Study of International Development (CASID) / L'Association canadienne d'études du développement international (ACEDI)
c/o The Canadian Federation for the Humanities & Social Sciences, #300, 275 Bank St., Ottawa ON K2P 2L6

Tel: 613-238-6112; Fax: 613-238-6114
www.casid-acedi.ca

To be a national, bilingual, interdisciplinary & pluralistic association devoted to the study of international development
Ann Miller, Contact

Canadian Commission for UNESCO (CCUNESCO) / Commission canadienne pour l'UNESCO
PO Box 1047, 150 Elgin St., Ottawa ON K1P 5V8

Tel: 613-566-4414; Fax: 613-566-4405
Toll-Free: 800-263-5588
ccunesco@unesco.ca
www.unesco.ca

To promote Canadian participation in the programmes & activities of UNESCO; To advise the government of Canada on its policies toward UNESCO; To act as a forum for Canadian civil society & government to discuss matters relating to UNESCO
Sébastien Goupil, Secretary-General

Canadian Council for International Co-operation (CCIC) / Conseil canadien pour la coopération internationale
39 McArthur Ave., Ottawa ON K1L 8L7

Tel: 613-241-7007; Fax: 613-241-5302
info@ccic.ca
www.ccic.ca
www.youtube.com/user/CCICable
www.facebook.com/ccciccic
twitter.com/CCCICCIC

To work globally to achieve sustainable human development; To seek to end global poverty; To promote social justice & human dignity for all
Nicolas Moyer, President & CEO
Monika Latta, Manager, Finance & Administration

Canadian Expat Association
#117, 724 Sea Terrace, Victoria BC V9A 3R6

Tel: 250-415-0051
info@thecanadianexpat.com
www.thecanadianexpat.com
www.instagram.com/thecanadianexpat
www.facebook.com/CanadianExpat

To connect all Canadians living abroad under one platform
Ivan Ross Vrána, Executive Director

Canadian Friends of Burma (CFOB) / Les amis canadiens de la Birmanie
#206, 145 Spruce St., Ottawa ON K1R 6P1

Tel: 613-237-8056; Fax: 613-563-0017
cfob@cfob.org
www.cfob.org

To promote democracy & human rights in Burma by working within the global movement, & educating & activating Canadian involvement in the struggle for peace in Burma
Tin Maung Htoo, Executive Director

Canadian Institute for Conflict Resolution (CICR) / Institut canadien pour la résolution des conflits (ICRC)
c/o St. Paul University, PO Box 79, 223 Main St., Ottawa ON K1S 1C4

Tel: 613-235-5800; Fax: 613-235-5801
info@cicr-icrc.ca
www.cicr-icrc.ca

To empower & build capacity in individuals, communities, & organizations to resolve conflicts peacefully
Daniel Markus, Executive Director
Miranda Merry, Office Manager

Canadian Institute of Cultural Affairs / Institut canadien des affaires culturelles
#405, 401 Richmond St. West, Toronto ON M5V 3A8

Tel: 416-691-2316
ica@icacan.org
www.icacan.org
www.instagram.com/ica_canada
www.linkedin.com/company/institute-of-cultural-affairs-canada
www.facebook.com/positivesocialchange
twitter.com/ICA_Canada

To empower people to develop leadership capacity; To contribute to positive social change
Ekta Bromley, Chair

Canadian International Council (CIC) / Conseil international du Canada
6 Hoskin Ave., Toronto ON M5S 1H8

Tel: 416-946-7209
info@thecic.org
thecic.org
www.youtube.com/user/onlinecicvideos
www.facebook.com/CanadianInternationalCouncil
twitter.com/TheCIC

To strengthen Canada's role in international affairs; To advance research & dialogue on international affairs
Ben Rowswell, President & Director, Research

Canadian Peace Alliance (CPA) / Alliance canadienne pour la paix
1 Front St., Toronto ON

Tel: 647-984-9482
info@acp-cpa.ca
www.acp-cpa.ca
www.facebook.com/CanadianPeaceAlliance
twitter.com/CanadianPeace

To involve Canadians in the worldwide movement to stop the arms race, ensure the non-violent settlement of disputes & guarantee the security & well-being of all peoples

Canadian Physicians for Aid & Relief (CPAR)
#401, 240 Bank St., Ottawa ON K2P 1X4

Tel: 416-369-0865; Fax: 416-369-0294
Toll-Free: 800-263-2727
info@cpar.ca
www.cpar.ca
linkedin.com/company/canadian-physicians-for-aid-and-relief
www.facebook.com/cparcan
twitter.com/cpar

To help impoverished communities in developing nations become prosperous, while maintaining harmony with the environment; To tackle all aspects of poverty; To emphasize healthy community empowerment & integrated community based development; To advance a world in which the basic needs of all individuals & communities are met
Kathrina Loeffler, Executive Director

CARE Canada
#200, 9 Gurdwara Rd., Ottawa ON K2E 7X6

Tel: 613-228-5600; Fax: 613-226-5777
Toll-Free: 800-267-5232
info@care.ca
care.ca
www.instagram.com/carecanada
www.linkedin.com/company/care-canada
www.facebook.com/carecanada
twitter.com/carecanada

To serve individuals & families in developing communities; To provide economic opportunity & emergency relief to those in need
Barbara Grantham, President & CEO

Carrefour de solidarité internationale de Sherbrooke inc.
165, rue Moore, Sherbrooke QC J1H 1B8

Tél: 819-566-8595; Téléc: 819-566-8076
info@csisher.com
www.csisher.com
www.facebook.com/carrefour.solidarite.internationale

Susciter la solidarité de la population de l'Estrie pour la justice sociale au plan international
Pier-Olivier St-Arnaud, Président
Étienne Doyon, Directeur général

Centre canadien d'étude et de coopération internationale (CECI) / Canadian Centre for International Studies & Cooperation
3000, rue Omer-Lavallée, Montréal QC H1Y 3R8

Tél: 514-875-9911; Téléc: 514-875-6469
info@ceci.ca
www.ceci.ca
www.youtube.com/commceci
www.linkedin.com/company/ceci
www.facebook.com/cecicooperation
twitter.com/CECI_Canada

Le CECI combat la pauvreté et l'exclusion; renforce les capacités de développment des communautés défavorisées; appuie des initiatives de paix, de droits humains et d'équité; mobilise des ressources et favorise l'échange de savoir-faire
Claudia Black, Directrice générale

Centre international de transfert d'innovations et de connaissances en économie sociale et solidaire (CITIES) / International Center for Innovation & Knowledge Transfer on the Social & Solidarity Economy
#205, 1431, rue Fullum, Montréal QC H2K 0B5

info@cities-ess.org
cities-ess.org
www.linkedin.com/company/cities-ess
www.facebook.com/cities.ess
twitter.com/CitiesEss

To support international gathering, sharing & transfer of knowledge & best practices in the social economy, focusing on collaboration between local government & civil society to enable territorial development

Children's International Summer Villages (Canada) Inc. (CISV) / Villages internationaux d'enfants
1 Gregory St., Brampton ON L6Y 1E9

Tel: 416-417-2591
canada@cisv.org
cisvcanada.org
www.facebook.com/CISV.Canada.Official

To promote cross-cultural friendship, through educational programs for youth & adults in 60 countries; To prepare indivduals to become active & contributing members of a peaceful society; To stimulate the life-long development of amicable relationships & effective & appropriate leadership towards a fair & just world
Rizwan Kassam, National President

Coady International Institute (CII)
St. Francis Xavier University, PO Box 5000, 4780 Tompkins Lane, Antigonish NS B2G 2W5

Tel: 902-867-3960; Fax: 902-867-3907
Toll-Free: 866-820-7835
coadycom@stfx.ca
coady.stfx.ca
www.youtube.com/user/CoadyInstitute
twitter.com/coadystfx

To promote learning in individuals & organizations engaged in community-driven action to achieve wellbeing, global justice, peace & participating democracy
Gord Cunningham, Executive Director

CODE
321 Chapel St., Ottawa ON K1N 7Z2

Tel: 613-232-3569; Fax: 613-232-7435
Toll-Free: 800-661-2633
info@code.ngo
code.ngo
www.youtube.com/channel/UC5ctRHh2_b-RYuTsm_Hta_Q
www.facebook.com/codecan.org
twitter.com/codengo

To enable people to learn by developing partnerships that provide resources for learning, to promote awareness & understanding & to encourage self-reliance; To support training for teachers & librarians; To coordinate book donations from North American publishers to schools & libraries in the developing world
Scott Walter, Executive Director
Andrea Helfer, Director, Fund Development & Marketing
Marc Molnar, Director, Finance & Administration

Hila Olyan, Director, Program Development & Innovation

CoDevelopment Canada (CODEV)
#260, 2747 East Hastings St., Vancouver BC V5K 1Z8
Tel: 604-708-1495; *Fax:* 604-708-1497
codev@codev.org
www.codev.org
www.facebook.com/CoDevCanada
twitter.com/CoDevCanada
To initiate social change in Latin American, facilitating
relationships between Northern & Southern organizations that
share a commitment to workers' rights, community development
& women's rights
Nancy Hawkins, President
Carol Wood, Vice-President
Frank Lee, Treasurer

Compassion Canada
PO Box 5591, London ON N6A 5G8
Tel: 519-668-0224; *Fax:* 866-685-1107
Toll-Free: 800-563-5437
info@compassion.ca
www.compassion.ca
www.youtube.com/user/CompassionCAD
www.facebook.com/CompassionCA
twitter.com/compassionCA
To provide sponsors for children in Third World countries; To aid
community development projects in cooperation with Canadian
International Development Agency; To be an advocate for
children, to release them from their spiritual, economic, social &
physical poverty & to enable them to become responsible &
fulfilled Christian adults
Allison Alley, President & CEO

Conseil canadien de la coopération et de la mutualité (CCCM)
#400, 275, rue Bank, Ottawa ON K2P 2L6
Tél: 613-238-6712; *Téléc:* 613-567-0658
info@coopscanada.coop
canada.coop
www.facebook.com/792260167456516
twitter.com/CoopFrancoCan
Le Conseil vise à promouvoir la coopération en vue du
développement socio-économique des communautés
francophones du Canada.
Denyse Guy, Directrice générale

Conseil de la coopération de l'Ontario (CCO)
#212, 192 Spadina Ave., Toronto ON M5T 2C2
Tel: 416-364-4545
info@cco.coop
www.cco.coop
www.youtube.com/user/conseilcoopontario
www.linkedin.com/company/conseil-de-la-coop-ration-de-l%27on
tario
www.facebook.com/coop.ontariofr
twitter.com/coop_ontariofr
Favoriser la prise en charge socio-économique de la
communauté francophone de l'Ontario par le biais de la
coopération
Julien Geremie, Directeur général

Conseil québécois de la coopération et de la mutualité (CCQ)
#204, 5955, rue Saint-Laurent, Lévis QC G6V 3P5
Tel: 418-835-3710; *Téléc:* 418-835-6322
info@cqcm.coop
www.cqcm.coop
www.facebook.com/quebec.coop
twitter.com/CQCMCOOP
Pour unir des organisations coopératives du Québec pour
favoriser l'action concertée de ses membres, promouvoir
l'authenticité coopérative, défendre les intérêts de ses membres
Gaston Bédard, Président-directeur général

Cuso International
#200, 44 Eccles St., Ottawa ON K1R 6S4
Tel: 613-829-7445; *Toll-Free:* 888-434-2876
questions@cusointernational.org
cusointernational.org
www.youtube.com/cusointernational
www.linkedin.com/company/cuso-international
www.facebook.com/CusoInternational
twitter.com/CusoIntl
To eradicate poverty & inequality through volunteers,
collaborative partnerships & donors
Glenn Mifflin, CEO

The Duke of Edinburgh's International Award - Canada
#100, 215 Niagara St., Toronto ON M6J 2L2
Tel: 416-203-0674; *Toll-Free:* 800-872-3853
info@dukeofed.org
www.dukeofed.org
www.instagram.com/dukeofedcanada
www.linkedin.com/company/dukeofedcanada
www.facebook.com/dukeofedcanada
twitter.com/dukeofedcanada
To give out an award that empowers young people (ages 14 to
24) to take action
Melissa MacAdam, National President
Stephen De-Wint, National Executive Director

Forum for International Trade Training (FITT) / Forum pour la formation en commerce international
#100, 116 Lisgar St., Ottawa ON K2P OC2
Tel: 613-230-3553; *Toll-Free:* 800-561-3488
info@fitt.ca
fittfortrade.com
www.linkedin.com/company/fitt-forum-for-international-trade-train
ing-
www.facebook.com/FITTNews
twitter.com/FITTNews
To provide quality programs' training & certification in
international trade designed to prepare businesses & individuals
to compete successfully in world markets
Caroline Tompkins, President & CEO

Group of 78 / Groupe des 78
#608, 63 Sparks St., Ottawa ON K1P 5A6
Tel: 613-565-9449
group78@group78.org
group78.org
www.facebook.com/groupof78
To advocate for peace, disarmament, sustainable development
& strengthening of the United Nations.
Roy Culpeper, Chair

HOPE International Development Agency
#410, 713 Columbia St., New Westminster BC V3M 1B2
Tel: 604-525-5481; *Fax:* 604-525-3471
Toll-Free: 866-525-4673
hope@hope-international.com
hope-international.com
twitter.com/HOPEInt
To help people in the poverty-stricken section of the developing
world to attain the basic necessities of life; To inform Canadians
regarding issues related to the developing world & HOPE's
activities; To provide alternative technological & educational
support to people in developing countries where environmental,
economic or social circumstances have interfered with the ability
of local communities to sustain themselves by using traditional
methods
Kim Savage, Executive Director

Horizons of Friendship (HOF)
PO Box 402, 50 Covert St., Cobourg ON K9A 4L1
Tel: 905-372-5483; *Fax:* 905-372-7095
Toll-Free: 888-729-9928
info@horizons.ca
www.horizons.ca
www.youtube.com/user/HorizonsofFriendship
www.facebook.com/HorizonsFriends
twitter.com/HorizonsFriends
To address the root causes of poverty & injustice through the
cooperation of people from the south & north; To support Central
American & Mexican partner organizations which undertake local
initiatives; To raise awareness in Canada of global issues; To
work with Canadian organizations at the local & national levels
Patricia Rebolledo-Kloques, Executive Director

Inter Pares / Among Equals
221 Laurier Ave. East, Ottawa ON K1N 6P1
Tel: 613-563-4801; *Fax:* 613-594-4704
Toll-Free: 866-563-4801
info@interpares.ca
interpares.ca
www.youtube.com/InterParesCanada
www.linkedin.com/company/inter-pares
www.facebook.com/InterParesCanada
twitter.com/Inter_Pares
To build equality of people, North & South, by collaborating with
& supporting justice for people around the world; To advance
peace & justice through the provision of programs that address
global issues, including food sovereignty, women's equality,
democracy, economic justice, health & migration
Charlotte Kiddell, Co-Executive Director
Samantha McGavin, Co-Executive Director

Mahatma Gandhi Canadian Foundation for World Peace
PO Box 60002, RPO University of Alberta, Edmonton AB T6G 2S4
Tel: 780-492-5504; *Fax:* 780-492-0113
gandhifoundationcanada@gmail.com
www.gandhi.ca
To conduct programs & activities that promote the teachings &
philosophy of Mahatma Gandhi in order to advance peace &
understanding amongst peoples of the world
Jaime Beck, Educational Coordinator

Manitoba Council for International Cooperation (MCIC) / Conseil du Manitoba pour la coopération internationale
#302, 280 Smith St., Winnipeg MB R3C 1K2
Tel: 204-987-6420; *Fax:* 204-956-0031
info@mcic.ca
mcic.ca
www.facebook.com/mcic.ca
twitter.com/MCIC_CA
To promote international development that protects the
environment; To coordinate the development work of member
agencies
Janice Hamilton, Executive Director

The Marquis Project, Inc.
PO Box 50045, Brandon MB R7A 7E4
Tel: 204-727-5675
marquis@marquisproject.com
www.marquisproject.com
To inform rural Manitobans of global issues; To link concerns to
those of Third World peoples; To encourage concrete positive
action in response to global concerns
Zack Gross, President

NATO Association of Canada / Association canadienne pour l'OTAN
60 Harbour St., 4th Fl., Toronto ON M5J 1B7
Tel: 416-979-1875
info@natoassociation.ca
natoassociation.ca
www.linkedin.com/company/atlantic-council-of-canada
www.facebook.com/NATOAssociationofCanada
twitter.com/NATOCanada
To promote peace, prosperity, & security by informing
Canadians about NATO
Robert Baines, President

Ontario Council for International Cooperation (OCIC) / Conseil de l'Ontario pour la coopération internationale
#424, 192 Spadina Ave., Toronto ON M5T 2C2
Tel: 416-972-6303
info@ocic.on.ca
www.ocic.on.ca
www.linkedin.com/company/ontario-council-for-international-coo
peration
www.facebook.com/LikeOCIC
twitter.com/ocictweets
Kimberly Gibbons, Executive Director

Operation Eyesight Universal
#200, 4 Parkdale Cres. NW, Calgary AB T2N 3T8
Tel: 403-283-6323; *Fax:* 403-270-1899
Toll-Free: 800-585-8265
www.operationeyesight.com
www.youtube.com/user/OpEyesightUniversal
www.linkedin.com/company/operation-eyesight
www.facebook.com/OperationEyesightUniversal
twitter.com/OpEyesight
To eliminate avoidable blindness through the development &
support of permanent, self-sustaining, quality blindness
prevention & sight restoration programs for those people in
greatest need
Aly Bandali, President & CEO
Lisa Dent, Chief Financial Officer

Oxfam Canada
39 McArthur Ave., Ottawa ON K1L 8L7
Tel: 613-237-5236; *Fax:* 613-237-0524
Toll-Free: 800-466-9326
info@oxfam.ca
www.oxfam.ca
www.youtube.com/user/OxfamCanada
www.facebook.com/OxfamCanada
twitter.com/oxfamcanada
To build lasting solutions to the injustice of poverty & inequality
Ricardo Acuna, Chair
Julie Delahanty, Executive Director, Ottawa

Partners International
#56, 8500 Torbram Rd., Brampton ON L6T 5C6
Tel: 905-458-1202; *Fax:* 905-458-4339
Toll-Free: 800-883-7697
info@partnersinternational.ca
www.partnersinternational.ca
www.youtube.com/user/partnerscanada
twitter.com/Partnersintlcan
To partner Canadians with indigenous Christian ministries to spread the Word of God
Kevin McKay, President

Peace Brigades International (Canada) (PBI)
#220, 211 Bronson Ave., Ottawa ON K1R 6H5
Tel: 613-237-6968
direction@pbicanada.org
pbicanada.org
www.facebook.com/pbicanada
twitter.com/pbicanada
To explore & implement non-violent approaches to peacekeeping & support for basic human rights; To provide protective accompaniment & peace education training in Colombia, Indonesia & Mexico
Brent Patterson, Executive Director

Physicians for Global Survival (Canada) (PGS) / Médecins pour la survie mondiale (Canada)
30 Cleary Ave., Ottawa ON K2A 4A1
Tel: 613-233-1982
pgsadmin@web.ca
www.pgs.ca
www.youtube.com/user/pgsottawa
www.facebook.com/PhysiciansforGlobalSurvival
Committed to the abolition of nuclear weapons, the prevention of war, the promotion of non-violent means of conflict resolution & social justice in a sustainable world
Vinay Jindal, President

Project Ploughshares
140 Westmont Rd. North, Waterloo ON N2L 3G6
Tel: 519-888-6541; *Fax:* 519-888-0018
Toll-Free: 888-907-3223
plough@ploughshares.ca
ploughshares.ca
www.facebook.com/206928856016444
twitter.com/ploughshares_ca
Ecumenical peace agency of the Canadian Council of Churches that identifies, develops & advances approaches that build peace & prevent war
Cesar Jaramillo, Executive Director

Saskatchewan Council for International Co-operation (SCIC) / Conseil de la Saskatchewan pour la co-opération internationale
2138 McIntyre St., Regina SK S4P 2R7
Tel: 306-757-4669; *Fax:* 306-757-3226
info@saskcic.org
www.saskcic.org
www.youtube.com/user/SCICYouth
www.facebook.com/SaskCIC
www.twitter.com/saskCIC
To act as the umbrella organization for international development agencies in Saskatchewan; To distribute international development funds provided by the Government of Saskatchewan; To facilitate communications among member agencies in Saskatchewan and across Canada; To support cooperative government relations, public education & fundraising
Jessica Wood, Executive Director

Save a Family Plan (SAFP)
c/o St. Peter's Seminary, 1040 Waterloo St., London ON N6A 3Y1
Tel: 519-672-1115; *Fax:* 519-672-6379
safpinfo@safp.org
www.safp.org
www.facebook.com/saveafamilyplan
twitter.com/SaveaFamilyPlan
To implement sustainable family & community development programs in 5 states in India
Lois Côté, President
Marisa Thorburn, Executive Director

Save the Children Canada (SCC) / Aide à l'enfance Canada
#300, 4141 Yonge St., Toronto ON M2P 2A8
Tel: 416-221-5501; *Toll-Free:* 800-668-5036
info@savethechildren.ca
www.savethechildren.ca
www.youtube.com/savethechildrenCA
www.linkedin.com/company/save-the-children-canada
www.facebook.com/SaveChildrenCanada
twitter.com/SaveChildrenCan

To fight for children's rights; To deliver immediate & lasting improvements to children's lives worldwide in Canada, Africa, Asia, Latin America & the Caribbean & the Middle East
Bill Chambers, President & CEO

Science for Peace (SfP) / Science et paix
c/o University College, #355, 15 King's College Circle, Toronto ON M5S 3H7
Tel: 416-978-3606
sfp@physics.utoronto.ca
scienceforpeace.ca
www.youtube.com/user/Science4Peace
www.facebook.com/science4peace
twitter.com/ScienceforPeace
To understand & act against forces of militarism, social injustice & environmental destruction
Richard Sandbrook, President
Ellie Kirzner, Secretary
Rob Acheson, Treasurer
Melisa Kuc, Executive Secretary & Office Coordinator

United Nations Association in Canada (UNAC) / Association canadienne pour les Nations Unies (ACNU)
#300, 309 Cooper St., Ottawa ON K2P 0G5
Tel: 613-232-5751; *Fax:* 613-563-2455
info@unac.org
www.unac.org
www.linkedin.com/company/1177974
www.facebook.com/canimunconference
twitter.com/UNACanada
To study international problems & Canada's relationship to them as a member of the UN & its related agencies; To foster mutual understanding, goodwill & cooperation between the people of Canada & those of other countries, with the object of promoting peace & justice; To study possible courses of action in the field of international affairs; To work for support by the government & the people of Canada for desirable policies; To provide information on & stimulate public interest in the UN & its various agencies which have been established for direct or indirect promotion of international order, justice & security; To foster national commitment to principles of multilateralism & international cooperation
Kathryn White, President & CEO

Vides Canada
17 Porterfield Rd., Toronto ON M9W 3J2
Tel: 416-803-3558
videscanada.ca
www.facebook.com/videscanada
To improve the lives of underpriviledged children; To train volunteers & send them to developing countries in order to help the children who live there
Jeannine Landry, Director

World Federalist Movement - Canada (WFMC)
#110, 323 Chapel St., Ottawa ON K1N 7Z2
Tel: 613-232-0647
www.wfmcanada.org
www.facebook.com/WorldFederalistMovementCanada
twitter.com/WFMCanada
Education, research, political support for strengthening the United Nations & rule of law in world affairs
Walter Dorn, National President
Fergus Watt, Executive Director
Monique Cuillerier, Director, Membership & Communications

World University Service of Canada (WUSC) / Entraide universitaire mondiale du Canada (EUMC)
1404 Scott St., Ottawa ON K1Y 4M8
Tel: 613-798-7477; *Fax:* 613-798-0990
Toll-Free: 800-267-8699
wusc@wusc.ca
wusc.ca
www.youtube.com/wusceumc
www.linkedin.com/company/world-university-service-of-canada-wusc-—-eumc
www.facebook.com/wusc.ca
twitter.com/worlduniservice
To foster human development & global understanding through education & training
Chris Eaton, Executive Director
Stefan Hollmann, Chief Financial Officer
Sylvie Villemure, Chief Human Resources Officer
Stephanie Leclair, Senior Manager, Communications & Philanthropy

World Vision Canada (WVC) / Vision Mondiale
1 World Dr., Mississauga ON L5T 2Y4
Fax: 866-219-8620
Toll-Free: 866-595-5550
www.worldvision.ca
www.youtube.com/WorldVisionCanada
www.facebook.com/WorldVisionCan
twitter.com/worldvisioncan
To act as an international partnership of Christians that provides relief to children, families & communities; To work towards overcoming poverty & injustice; To aid people regardless of religion, race, ethnicity or gender
Michael Messenger, President & CEO

Labour Relations

ADR Institute of Canada (ADRIC) / Institut d'arbitrage et de médiation du Canada
#407, 234 Eglinton Ave. East, Toronto ON M4P 1K5
Tel: 416-487-4733; *Fax:* 416-901-4736
Toll-Free: 877-475-4353
admin@adric.ca
adric.ca
www.linkedin.com/company/adr-institute-of-canada
www.facebook.com/ADRIC.IAMC
twitter.com/adrcanada
To promote the use of arbitration & mediation (ADR - alternative dispute resolution) to settle disputes; To provide information & education on ADR to practitioners, parties, the public & the business, professional & government communities; To assist those wishing to use ADR through the provision of Arbitration & Mediation Rules, administrative services & information about the process & member arbitrators & mediators
Janet McKay, Executive Director

Association canadienne des relations industrielles (ACRI) / Canadian Industrial Relations Association (CIRA)
École de relations industrielles, Université de Montréal, 150, rue Jean-Brillant, Montréal QC H3T 1N8
communications.cira@gmail.com
www.cira-acri.ca
www.linkedin.com/company/ciraacri
www.facebook.com/CIRAACRI
twitter.com/cira_acri
Promouvoir la discussion, la recherche, et la formation dans le domaine des relations industrielles
Patrice Jalette, Président

Association of Workers' Compensation Boards of Canada (AWCBC) / Association des commissions des accidents du travail du Canada (ACATC)
#1007, 40 University Ave., Toronto ON M5J 1T1
Tel: 416-581-8875; *Toll-Free:* 855-282-9222
contact@awcbc.org
www.awcbc.org
twitter.com/awcbc_acatc
To provide safe & healthy workplaces & a fair, affordable workers' compensation insurance system; To achieve excellence through data analysis, shared knowledge, education, & networking
Cheryl Tucker, Chief Executive Officer

Canadian Association of Administrators of Labour Legislation (CAALL) / Association canadienne des administrateurs de la législation ouvrière (ACALO)
CAALL Secretariat, Phase II, Place du Portage, 165, rue Hôtel-de-Ville, 8e étage, Gatineau QC K1A 0J2
Tel: 819-654-4123; *Fax:* 819-654-4125
caall-secretariat@hrsdc-rhdsc.gc.ca
www.caall-acalo.org
To provide a forum for federal, provincial, & territorial senior officials; To develop agenda, background papers & logistics for meetings of Ministers responsible for Labour; To follow-up on issues as directed by Ministers

Canadian Association of Labour Media (CALM) / Association canadienne de la presse syndicale (ACPS)
196, Rene-Levesque ouest, Québec QC G1R 2A5
Tel: 647-428-8028
editor@calm.ca
www.calm.ca
www.facebook.com/canadian.association.of.labour.media
twitter.com/CanLabourMedia
To provide training, labour-friendly news, & graphics for labour communicators
Catherine Louli, President
Nora Loreto, Editor
Virginia Ridley, Coordinator

Canadian Committee on Labour History (CCLH) / Comité canadien sur l'histoire du travail
c/o Canadian Committee on Labour History, Athabasca University, #1200, 10011 - 109 St. NW, Edmonton AB T5J 3S8
Tel: 780-497-3412; *Fax:* 780-421-3298
cclh@athabascau.ca
www.cclh.ca
twitter.com/CCLHTweets
To promote & publish scholarly research in the area of Canadian labour history & related topics
G.S. Kealey, Treasurer

Canadian Injured Workers Alliance (CIWA) / L'Alliance canadienne des victimes d'accidents et de maladies du travail (ACVAMT)
1201 Jasper Dr., Thunder Bay ON P7B 6R2
Tel: 807-345-3429; *Fax:* 807-344-8683
Toll-Free: 877-787-7010
ciwa@tbaytel.net
www.ciwa.ca
To support & strengthen the work of local & provincial groups by providing a forum for exchanging information & experiences
Bill Chedore, National Coordinator

Cape Breton Injured Workers' Association (CBIWA)
714 Alexandra St., Sydney NS B1S 2H4
Tel: 902-539-4650; *Fax:* 902-539-4171
cbiwa@ns.aliantzinc.ca
The Cape Breton Injured Workers Association is a volunteer group, located in Sydney, Nova Scotia working on behalf of injured workers by providing information, assisting with claims and appeals, and continuing a dialogue with the Workers' Compensation Board of Nova Scotia.

Centre canadien d'arbitrage commercial (CCAC) / Canadian Commercial Arbitration Centre (CCAC)
Place du Canada, #905, 1010, rue de la Gauchetière ouest, Montréal QC H3B 2N2
Tél: 514-448-5980; *Téléc:* 514-448-5948
www.ccac-adr.org
www.linkedin.com/company/centre-canadien-d-arbitrage-commercial
Fournir des services de conciliation, de médiation et d'arbitrage pour les activités commerciales et de consommation; offrir des activités de formation aux arbitres et médiateurs; analyse de dossiers litigieux et études pour des organismes privés et publics
Julie Houle, Coordonnatrice

Construction Labour Relations - An Alberta Association (CLRA)
Calgary Office, #207, 2725 - 12th St. NE, Calgary AB T2E 7J2
Tel: 403-250-7390; *Fax:* 403-250-5516
Toll-Free: 800-450-7204
www.clra.org
To represent construction employers in collective bargaining, collective agreement administration, administrative labour law, lobbying.

Construction Labour Relations Association of British Columbia
97 - 6 St., New Westminster BC V3L 5H8
Tel: 604-524-4911; *Fax:* 604-524-3925
www.clra-bc.com
To represent members & building trades-signatory contractors in matters of labour relations & human resources
Clyde Scollan, President
Dave Earle, Vice-President, Government Relations & HR Services
Gregg Sewell, Vice-President, Labour Relations

Construction Labour Relations Association of Newfoundland & Labrador (CLRA)
69 Mews Pl., St. John's NL A1B 4N2
Tel: 709-753-5770; *Fax:* 709-753-5771
lrideout@clranl.com
www.clranl.com
To be the sole & exclusive bargaining agent for all unionized employers employing unionized trades persons in the commercial & industrial sectors of Newfoundland & Labrador's construction industry
Neil Chaplin, President

Institut de médiation et d'arbitrage du Québec (IMAQ)
#1501, 1445, rue Stanley, Montréal QC H3A 3T1
Tél: 514-282-2327; *Téléc:* 514-282-2214
Ligne sans frais: 855-482-3327
info@imaq.org
www.imaq.org
www.youtube.com/user/IMAQuebec
www.linkedin.com/company/institut-de-m-diation-et-d%27arbitrage-du-qu-bec

Promouvoir les méthodes alternatives de résolution de conflits (médiation, arbitrage); donner accès par internet à la population et aux entreprises à une banque de médiateurs et d'arbitres accrédités selon leur: spécialité (médiateur ou arbitre), région, langue de communication, catégorie de membre, profession, domaine d'expertise
Pierre Grenier, Président
Ginette Gamache, Directrice, Opérations

Pulp & Paper Employee Relations Forum
c/o Westcott Consulting, 6627 Westcott Rd., Duncan BC V9L 6A4
Tel: 250-748-9445
westcot@telus.net
paperforum.com
To act primarily as a research & information service for the industry; To service the pulp & paper industry in job evaluation, benefit & pension plan administration & trusteeship, contract interpretation & any other matters relating to labour relations
Fred Oud, Executive Director

Union of Injured Workers of Ontario
2888 Dufferin St., Toronto ON M6B 3S6
Tel: 416-785-8787; *Fax:* 416-785-6390
To serve injured workers & their families in Ontario
Philip Biggin, Executive Director

Western Employers Labour Relations Association
#203, 27126 Fraser Hwy., Langley BC V4W 3P6
Tel: 604-857-5540; *Fax:* 604-857-5547
To provide employee relations services for both union & non-union employers

World at Work
14041 Northside Blvd. North, Scottsdale AZ 85260 USA
Toll-Free: 877-951-9191
customerrelations@worldatwork.com
www.worldatwork.org
www.youtube.com/worldatworktv
www.linkedin.com/groups/84761
www.facebook.com/WorldatWorkAssociation
twitter.com/worldatwork
To promote the education for, compensation of & benefits to professionals
Anne Ruddy, President
Marcia Rhodes, Contact, Media Relations

Labour Unions

Agriculture Union / Syndicat Agriculture
#1000, 233 Gilmour St., Ottawa ON K2P 0P2
Tel: 613-560-4306; *Fax:* 613-235-0517
agrunion@psac-afpc.com
www.agrunion.com
To advance the workplace interests of its membership; To fight for a society that recognizes the value of the important public services provided by Agriculture Union members
Fabian Murphy, National President

Alberta Federation of Labour (AFL) / Fédération du travail de l'Alberta
#300, 10408 - 124th St., Edmonton AB T5N 1R5
Tel: 780-483-3021; *Fax:* 780-484-5928
Toll-Free: 800-661-3995
afl@afl.org
www.afl.org
twitter.com/abfedlabour
To act as a central labour body, representing Alberta's organized workers & their families; To improve conditions for Alberta's workers, their families & communities
Gil McGowan, President

Alberta Union of Provincial Employees / Syndicat de la fonction publique de l'Alberta
10451 - 170 St., Edmonton AB T5P 4S7
Tel: 780-930-3300; *Fax:* 780-930-3392
Toll-Free: 800-232-7284
www.aupe.org
www.youtube.com/user/AlbertaUnion
www.facebook.com/yourAUPE
twitter.com/_AUPE_
Carl Soderstrom, Executive Director
Tim Gough, Director, Labour Relations
Jim Petrie, Director, Labour Relations

Alliance du personnel professionnel et technique de la santé et des services sociaux (APTS)
#1050, 1111, rue Saint-Charles ouest, Longueuil QC J4K 5G4
Tél: 450-670-2411; *Téléc:* 450-679-0107
Ligne sans frais: 866-521-2411
info@aptsq.com
www.aptsq.com
www.facebook.com/SyndicatAPTS
twitter.com/APTSQ
Regrouper les organisations syndicales représentant toutes les catégories des personnes salariées professionnelles ou paramédicales travaillant dans le domaine de la santé; défendre, promouvoir et sauvegarder les intérêts collectifs des membres
Carolle Dubé, Présidente

Alliance of Canadian Cinema, Television & Radio Artists (ACTRA) / Alliance des artistes canadiens du cinéma, de la télévision et de la radio
625 Church St., 3rd Fl., Toronto ON M4Y 2G1
Tel: 416-489-1311; *Fax:* 416-489-8076
Toll-Free: 800-387-3516
actra@actra.ca
www.actra.ca
www.youtube.com/user/ACTRANational
www.facebook.com/ACTRANational
twitter.com/ACTRAnat
To represent performers in recorded media; To negotiate & administer collective agreements which set minimum rates & basic conditions governing work; To advocate public policies designed to create strong Canadian broadcasting & film industries in order to provide work opportunities for members in their own country
Marie Kelly, National Executive Director
Daintry Dalton, Regional Executive Director
Anna Bucci, Senior Director, Finance & Administration
Christine Basdeo, Director, People, LR & Operations
Lisa Blanchette, Director, Public Policy & Communications

American Federation of Labor & Congress of Industrial Organizations (AFL-CIO) / Fédération Américaine du travail et congrès des organisations industrielles (FAT-COI)
815 - 16th St. NW, Washington DC 20006 USA
Tel: 202-637-5000; *Fax:* 202-637-5058
aflcio.org
www.youtube.com/c/AFLCIO
www.linkedin.com/company/afl-cio
www.facebook.com/aflcio
twitter.com/AFLCIO
Richard Trumka, President
Elizabeth Shuler, Secretary-Treasurer
Tefere Gebre, Executive Vice-President

Association canadienne des métiers de la truelle, section locale 100 (CTC) / Trowel Trades Canadian Association, Local 100 (CLC)
#2000, 565, rue Crémazie est, Montréal QC H2M 2V6
Tél: 514-326-3691; *Téléc:* 514-326-5562
Ligne sans frais: 888-326-3691
acmt@qc.aira.com
truellelocal100.org
www.facebook.com/ACMTLOCAL100
La FTQ-Construction a, bien entendu, de manière très précise le mandat de négocier les conventions collectives applicables dans les sous secteurs d'activités (industriel, commercial et institutionnel, génie civil et voirie, résidentiel) et de voir à leur application. Mais bien au-delà de ce mandat traditionnel, la FTQ-Construction veut s'assurer d'être présent dans l'ensemble des débats représentant un intérêt pour les travailleurs et les travailleuses qu'il représente.
Roger Poirier, Directeur-général

Association nationale des peintres - locale 99 / National Association of Painters - Local 99
#202, 8300, boul Métropolitain est, Anjou QC H1K 1A2
Tél: 438-382-9990; *Téléc:* 438-383-9991
Ligne sans frais: 855-382-9990
www.local99.ca
www.facebook.com/ftqlocal99
twitter.com/ftqlocal99
Aider nos membres dans leur métier; faire respecter les conventions collectives sur les chantiers

Association of Allied Health Professionals: Newfoundland & Labrador (Ind.) (AAHP) / Association des professionnels unis de la santé: Terre-Neuve et Labrador (ind.)
6 Mount Carson Ave., Mount Pearl NL A1N 3K4
Tel: 709-631-4862; *Fax:* 709-722-0987
Toll-Free: 800-728-2247
info@aahp.ca
aahp.ca
www.youtube.com/channel/UCaOAL5CSpeHC3XieNndBhhw
www.facebook.com/aahp.ca
twitter.com/AAHP_NL

Association of Canadian Financial Officers (ACFO) / Association canadienne des agents financiers (ACAF)
#400, 2725 Queensview Dr., Ottawa ON K2B 0A1
Tel: 613-728-0695; *Fax:* 613-761-9568
Toll-Free: 877-728-0695
information@acfo-acaf.com
acfo-acaf.com
www.linkedin.com/company/401947
twitter.com/acfoacaf

To unite in a democratic organization all public service financial administrators for which the association becomes or applies to become a bargaining agent; to serve the welfare of its members through effective collective bargaining with their employers; to obtain for members the best levels of compensation for services rendered to their employers & the best terms & conditions of employment; to protect the rights & interests of all members in all matters upon their employment or upon their relationship with their employers; to seek to maintain high professional standards & promote their professional development; to affiliate as appropriate with other associations, unions or labour organizations for the purpose of enhancing the interests of members in the attainment of their professional & bargaining goals
Milt Isaacs, President

Association of New Brunswick Professional Educators (ANBPE) / Association des éducateurs professionnels du Nouveau-Brunswick
To operate as a bargaining unit of the New Brunswick Union of Public & Private Employees (NBUPPE / NUPGE)

Association professionnelle des ingénieurs du gouvernement du Québec (ind.) (APIGQ) / Association of Professional Engineers of the Government of Québec (Ind.)
Complexe Iberville Trois, #218, 2960, boul Laurier, Québec QC G1V 4S1
Tél: 418-683-3633; *Téléc:* 418-683-6878
info@apigq.qc.ca
www.apigq.qc.ca
Pour représenter les intérêts de leurs membres
Michel Gagnon, Président

Atlantic Federation of Musicians, Local 571 (AFM, Local 571)
16 Balcomes Dr., Halifax NS B3N 1H9
Tel: 902-479-3200; *Fax:* 902-479-1312
Toll-Free: 866-240-4809
admin@cfm571.ca
www.atlanticmusicians.org
Tom Roach, President
Varun Vyas, Secretary-Treasurer

Bakery, Confectionery, Tobacco Workers & Grain Millers International Union (AFL-CIO/CLC)
US
bctgmwebmaster@gmail.com
www.bctgm.org
www.instagram.com/bctgm
www.facebook.com/BCTGM
twitter.com/BCTGM
To represent members & bring justice in the workplace in all jurisdictions
Anthony Shelton, International President
David Woods, International Secretary-Treasurer
Ron Piercey, International Vice-President, Canadian Region

Bricklayers, Masons Independent Union of Canada (CLC) / Syndicat indépendant des briqueteurs et des maçons du Canada (CTC)
PO Box 105, #307, 1263 Wilson Ave., Toronto ON M3M 3G3
Tel: 416-247-9841; *Fax:* 416-241-9636
local1.ca
Tony Rizzuto, President
John Meiorin, Secretary-Treasurer

British Columbia Federation of Labour (BCFL) / Fédération du travail de la Colombie-Britannique
#200, 5118 Joyce St., Vancouver BC V5R 4H1
Tel: 604-430-1421; *Fax:* 604-430-5917
bcfed@bcfed.ca
bcfed.com
www.facebook.com/bcfed
www.facebook.com/bcfed
To promote the interests of affiliated unions & their members; To advance the economic & social welfare of the workers of British Columbia; To act as the single voice for workers' rights in British Columbia
Nina Hansen, Executive Director
Rob Cottingham, Director, Communications

British Columbia Government & Service Employees' Union (BCGEU) / Syndicat des fonctionnaires provinciaux et de service de la Colombie-Britannique
4911 Canada Way, Burnaby BC V5G 3W3
Tel: 604-291-9611; *Fax:* 604-291-6030
Toll-Free: 800-663-1674
www.bcgeu.ca
Judi Filion, Treasurer
Darryl Walker, President

British Columbia Teacher Regulation Branch (BCCT)
#400, 2025 West Broadway, Vancouver BC V6J 1Z6
Tel: 604-660-6060; *Fax:* 604-775-4859
Toll-Free: 800-555-3684
www.bcteacherregulation.ca
To establish standards for the education, professional responsibility & competence of its members; To certify educators
Sarvi Brent, Director, Operations
Sally Mercer, Manager, Communications

Canada Employment & Immigration Union (CEIU) / Syndicat de l'emploi et de l'immigration du Canada (SEIC)
#1204, 275 Slater St., Ottawa ON K1P 5H9
Tel: 613-236-9634; *Fax:* 613-236-7871
Toll-Free: 855-271-3848
www.ceiu-seic.ca
www.instagram.com/ceiuseic
www.facebook.com/CEIUSEIC
twitter.com/ceiuseic
To unite all the union members at Service Canada, Human Resources & Social Development, Citizenship & Immigration Canada, the Immigration & Refugee Board & others who wish to join in a single union acting on their behalf by processing appeals & grievances; To unite all members by fostering an understanding of the fundamental differences between the interests of the members & those of the employer; To assure a union presence at the workplace through collective strength of membership
Eddy Bourque, National President
Crystal Warner, National Executive Vice-President
Alain Normand, Director, Finance & Administration

Canadian Actors' Equity Association (CLC) (CAEA)
44 Victoria St., 12th Fl., Toronto ON M5C 3C4
Tel: 416-867-9165; *Fax:* 416-867-9246
info@caea.com
www.caea.com
To negotiate & administer collective agreements, provides benefit plans, information & support; to act as an advocate for its membership.
Allan Teichman, President
Arden R. Ryshpan, Executive Director
Lynn McQueen, Director, Communications

Canadian Association of Professional Employees (CAPE) / Association canadienne des employés professionnels (ACEP)
World Exchange Plaza, 100 Queen St., 4th Fl., Ottawa ON K1P 1J9
Tel: 613-236-9181; *Fax:* 613-236-6017
Toll-Free: 800-265-9181
general@acep-cape.ca
www.acep-cape.ca
www.facebook.com/acepcape
twitter.com/cape_acep
To negotiate & monitor collective agreement for all federal government economists, sociologists & statisticians
Greg Phillips, President

Canadian Federal Pilots Association (CFPA) / Association des pilotes fédéraux du Canada (APFC)
#107, 18 Deakin St., Ottawa ON K2E 8B7
Tel: 613-230-5476; *Fax:* 613-230-2668
cfpa@cfpa-apfc.ca
www.cfpa-apfc.ca

Greg McConnell, Chair
Denis Brunelle, Vice-Chair
Ron Graham, Secretary-Treasurer
Greg Holbrook, Director, Operations

Canadian Federation of Nurses Unions (CFNU) / La Fédération canadienne des syndicats d'infirmières/infirmiers
2841 Riverside Dr., Ottawa ON K1V 8X7
Tel: 613-526-4661; *Fax:* 613-526-1023
Toll-Free: 800-321-9821
www.nursesunions.ca
www.facebook.com/NursesUnions
twitter.com/CFNU
To advance the social, economic & general welfare of its members; To act on national matters of significant concern to the Federation; To promote unity among nurses' unions & other allied health care workers who share the objectives of the CFNU; To provide a national forum to promote desirable legislation on matters of national significance; To preserve free democratic unionism & collective bargaining in Canada; To support other organizations sharing the Union's objectives
Linda Silas, President

Canadian Independent Fish Harvesters Federation / Fédération des pêcheurs indépendants du Canada
408 Main St., Shediac NB E4P 2G1
Tel: 506-532-2485; *Fax:* 506-532-2487
info@fed-fede.ca
fed-fede.ca
To be a national advocacy voice for people who fish
Melanie Sonnenberg, President

Canadian Labour Congress (CLC) / Congrès du travail du Canada (CTC)
2841 Riverside Dr., Ottawa ON K1V 8X7
Tel: 613-521-3400; *Fax:* 613-521-4655
canadianlabour.ca
www.youtube.com/canadianlabour
www.facebook.com/clc.ctc
twitter.com/canadianlabour
To represent the interests of affiliated workers across Canada; To act as an umbrella organization for affiliated regional labour councils, provincial federations, Canadian unions & international unions
Hassan Yussuff, President

Canadian Media Guild (CMG) / La Guilde canadienne des médias
#101, 311 Adelaide St. East, Toronto ON M5A 1N2
Tel: 416-591-5333; *Fax:* 416-591-5333
Toll-Free: 800-465-4149
info@cmg.ca
www.cmg.ca
twitter.com/CMGLaGuilde
To advance the interests of Guild members through collective bargaining
Sue Beres, Office Coordinator

Canadian Merchant Service Guild (CMSG) / Guilde de la marine marchande du Canada (GMMC)
#234, 9 Antares Dr., Ottawa ON K2E 7V5
Tel: 613-727-6079; *Fax:* 613-727-6079
cmsgott@on.aibn.com
www.cmsg-gmmc.ca
To promote the social, economic, cultural, educational & material interests of ships' masters, chief engineers, officers, pilots & of other persons whose employment is directly related to maritime operations
Mark Boucher, National President

Canadian National Federation of Independent Unions (CNFIU) / Fédération canadienne nationale des syndicats indépendants (FCNSI)
PO Box 416, 36 Main St. North, Campbellville ON L0P 1B0
Toll-Free: 800-638-9438
canadiannationalfederationofin.canic.ws
To encourage & promote the formation of independent unions

Canadian Office & Professional Employees Union (COPEU) / Le Syndicat canadien des employées et employés professionnels et de bureau (SEPB)
c/o Kateri Lefebvre, #11100, 565 boul Crémazie est, Montréal QC H2M 2W2
copesepb.ca
A national labour union organization made up of 3 regional Councils and 47 Local unions comprising tens of thousands of members in several provinces across Canada.
David Black, National President
Kateri Lefebvre, National Secretery-Treasurer

Canadian Postmasters & Assistants Association (CPAA) / Association canadienne des maîtres de poste et adjoints (ACMPA)
281 Queen Mary St., Ottawa ON K1K 1X1
Tel: 613-745-2095; *Fax:* 613-745-5559
mail@cpaa-acmpa.ca
cpaa-acmpa.ca

Brenda McAuley, National President
Sylvie Duguay, Office Manager

Canadian Union of Postal Workers (CUPW) / Syndicat des travailleurs et travailleuses des postes (STTP)
377 Bank St., Ottawa ON K2P 1Y3
Tel: 613-236-7238; *Fax:* 613-563-7861
TTY: 613-236-9753
feedback@cupw-sttp.org
www.cupw-sttp.org
www.youtube.com/user/cupwsttp
www.linkedin.com/company/canadian-union-of-postal-workers
www.facebook.com/cupwsttp
twitter.com/cupw
To be involved with various campaigns & activities which help support their members
Jan Simpson, National President

Canadian Union of Public Employees (CUPE) / Syndicat canadien de la fonction publique (SCFP)
1375 St. Laurent Blvd., Ottawa ON K1G 0Z7
Tel: 613-237-1590; *Fax:* 613-237-5508
Toll-Free: 844-237-1590
www.cupe.ca
www.linkedin.com/company/canadian-union-of-public-employees
www.facebook.com/cupescfp
twitter.com/cupenat
To advance the social, economic & general welfare of both active & retired employees; To promote required legislation
Mark Hancock, National President
Charles Fleury, National Secretary-Treasurer

Centrale des syndicats démocratiques (CSD)
#600, 990, av de Bourgogne, Québec QC G1W 0E8
Tél: 418-529-2956; *Fax:* 418-529-6323
Ligne sans frais: 866-651-0050
info@csd.qc.ca
www.csd.qc.ca
www.youtube.com/c/CsdQcCa1972
www.facebook.com/CSDCentrale
twitter.com/CSDCentrale

Luc Vachon, Président

Centrale des syndicats du Québec (CSQ)
9405, rue Sherbrooke est, Montréal QC H1L 6P3
Tél: 514-356-8888; *Téléc:* 514-356-9999
Ligne sans frais: 800-465-0897
www.lacsq.org
www.youtube.com/user/csqvideos
www.facebook.com/lacsq
twitter.com/csq_centrale
De regrouper dans un même mouvement des personnels salariés ayant des aspirations et des intérêts communs et de promouvoir leurs intérêts professionnels, sociaux, et économiques; dans cette perspective, elle travaille à établir un environnement syndical et professionnel exempt de harcèlement sexuel et favorise la vie syndicale par le partage des ressources; elle intervient au soutien direct de ses affiliés et assure différents services liés aux relations de travail et à la vie professionnelle (recherche dans le domaine de l'éducation, etc.)
Sonia Ethier, Présidente

Comité Syndical Francophone de l'Éducation et de la Formation (CSFEF)
9405, rue Sherbrooke est, Montréal QC H1L 6P3
Tél: 514-356-8888; *Téléc:* 514-356-9999
www.csfef.org
www.facebook.com/francophonie.syndicale
Jean-Hervé Cohen, Président

Compensation Employees' Union (Ind.) (CEU) / Syndicat des employés d'indemnisation (ind.)
#120, 13775 Commerce Pkwy., Richmond BC V6V 2V4
Tel: 604-278-4050; *Fax:* 604-278-5002
www.ceu.bc.ca
www.facebook.com/313873122023339
twitter.com/CEUOurUnion
To represent all workers at the Workers' Compensation Board that are not excluded by law
Sandra Wright, President
Candace Philpitt, Secretary

Confédération des syndicats nationaux (CSN) / Confederation of National Trade Unions
1601, av De Lorimier, Montréal QC H2K 4M5
Tél: 514-598-2271; *Téléc:* 514-598-2052
sesyndiquer@csn.qc.ca
www.csn.qc.ca
www.instagram.com/mouvementcsn
www.facebook.com/LaCSN
twitter.com/laCSN
La Confédération limite ses activités principalement au Québec, quoique certains locaux soient établis hors de la province
Jacques Létourneau, Président
Jean Lortie, Secrétaire général
Pierre Patry, Trésorier

Congress of Union Retirees Canada (CURC) / Association des syndicalistes retraités du Canada (ASRC)
2841 Riverside Dr., Ottawa ON K1V 8X7
Tel: 613-526-7422; *Fax:* 613-521-4655
unionretiree.ca
www.facebook.com/315702295180775
twitter.com/UnionRetirees
To ensure that the concerns of senior citizens & union retirees are heard across Canada
Bill Chedore, President
Louisette Hinton, First Vice-President
Janice Berner, Second Vice-President
Janice Gairey, Secretary
Lucienne Bahuaud, Treasurer

Customs & Immigration Union (CIU) / Syndicat des douanes et de l'immigration (SDI)
1741 Woodward Dr., Ottawa ON K2C 0P9
Tel: 613-723-8008; *Fax:* 613-723-7895
web@ciu-sdi.ca
www.ciu-sdi.ca
www.facebook.com/ciu-sdi
twitter.com/ciu_sdi
To address CIU-SDI members' concerns on a timely basis
Jean-Pierre Fortin, National President
Mark Weber, First National Vice-President

Employees' Union of St. Mary's of the Lake Hospital - CNFIU Local 3001 / Association des employés, l'Hôpital Saint Mary's of the Lake (FCNSI)
340 Union St., Kingston ON K7L 5A2
Tel: 613-544-5220; *Fax:* 613-544-8527

Fédération autonome du collégial (ind.) (FAC) / Autonomous Federation of Collegial Staff (Ind.)
#400, 1259, rue Berri, Montréal QC H2L 4C7
Tél: 514-848-9977; *Téléc:* 514-848-0166
Défendre et développer les intérêts économiques, sociaux, pédagogiques et professionnels du personnel enseignant des cégeps; défendre le droit d'association, la libre négociation et la liberté d'action syndicale; négocier et s'assurer de l'application des conventions collectives; de représenter ses syndicats affiliés partout où leurs intérêts sont débattus

Fédération CSN - Construction (CSN) / CNTU Federation - Construction (CNTU)
2100, boul de Maisonneuve est, 4e étage, Montréal QC H2K 4S1
Tél: 514-598-2044; *Téléc:* 514-598-2040
www.csnconstruction.qc.ca
www.facebook.com/csnconstruction
Pour défendre les droits de leurs membres et de leur assurer de bonnes conditions de travail
Pierre Brassard, Président
Karyne Prégent, Secrétaire général

Fédération de l'industrie manufacturière (FIM-CSN)
#3500, 1601, boul de Lorimier, Montréal QC H2K 4M5
Tél: 514-529-4937; *Téléc:* 514-529-4935
Ligne sans frais: 877-529-4977
fim@csn.qc.ca
www.fim.csn.qc.ca
www.facebook.com/FIMCSN
Améliorer les conditions de travail et de vie de ses membres et pour développer des emplois de qualité
Louis Bégin, Président

Fédération de la santé et des services sociaux (FSSS)
1601, av de Lorimier, Montréal QC H2K 4M5
Tél: 514-598-2210
www.fsss.qc.ca
www.youtube.com/user/f3sscsn
www.facebook.com/FSSSCSN
twitter.com/FSSSCSN
De promouvoir et sauvegarder la santé, la sécurité et les intérêts des personnes employées des établissements affiliés ou en voie

d'affiliation; de représenter ses membres auprès de la Confédération des syndicats nationaux en lui soumettant toutes questions d'intérêt général; de représenter ses membres, de concert avec la CSN, partout où les intérêts généraux des travailleuses et travailleurs le justifient; d'aider à conclure, en faveur des syndicats affiliés, des conventions collectives de travail et en favoriser l'application; de collaborer à l'éducation des travailleuses et travailleurs et à la formation de responsables et militantes et militants syndicaux; d'assurer les services à ses syndicats affiliés; de favoriser et d'établir des liens inter-syndicaux avec les autres travailleuses et travailleurs dans le secteur public et para-public et dans le secteur privé du Québec et du Canada
Jeff Begley, Président
Nadine Lambert, Secrétaire générale-trésorière

Fédération des employées et employés de services publics inc. (CSN) (FEESP) / Federation of Public Service Employees Inc. (CNTU)
1601, av de Lorimier, Montréal QC H2K 4M5
Tél: 514-598-2231; *Téléc:* 514-598-2398
feesp.courrier@csn.qc.ca
www.feesp.csn.qc.ca
www.facebook.com/feespcsn
Il est composé de quatre personnes élues, du coordonnateur ou coordonnatrice des services et de la personne déléguée syndicale
Nathalie Arguin, Secréaire-générale

Fédération des enseignantes et enseignants de cégeps
9405, rue Sherbrooke est, Montréal QC H1L 6P3
Tél: 514-356-8888; *Téléc:* 514-354-8535
Ligne sans frais: 800-465-0897
fec@lacsq.org
fec.lacsq.org
www.facebook.com/feccsq
twitter.com/feccsq
De protéger les intérêts de ses membres
Lucie Piché, Présidente

Fédération des intervenantes en petite enfance du Québec (FIPEQ)
9405, rue Sherbrooke est, Montréal QC H1L 6P3
Tél: 514-356-8888; *Téléc:* 514-356-9999
Ligne sans frais: 800-465-0897
fipeq@csq.qc.net
La Fédération des intervenantes en petite enfance du Québec (FIPEQ) est vouée à la promotion de la profession, à la défense des droits et des intérêts ainsi qu'à l'amélioration des conditions de vie de toutes les intervenantes, tant travailleuses autonomes que salariées, oeuvrant au service des centres de la petite enfance
Kathleen Courville, Présidente

Fédération des médecins résidents du Québec inc. (ind.) (FMRQ) / Québec Federation of Residents (Ind.)
#510, 630, rue Sherbrooke ouest, Montréal QC H3A 1E4
Tél: 514-282-0256; *Téléc:* 514-282-0471
Ligne sans frais: 800-465-0215
info@fmrq.qc.ca
fmrq.qc.ca
www.facebook.com/fmrqc
D'étudier, de défendre et de développer des intérêts économiques, sociaux, moraux et scientifiques des syndicats et des leurs membres
Patrice Savignac Dufour, Executive Director

Fédération des policiers et policières municipaux du Québec (ind.) (FPMQ) / Québec Federation of Policemen (Ind.)
7955, boul Louis-Hippolyte-La Fontaine, Anjou QC H1K 4E4
Tél: 514-356-3321; *Téléc:* 514-356-1158
Ligne sans frais: 800-361-0321
info@fpmq.org
www.fpmq.org
www.facebook.com/policiersMun
twitter.com/policiersmun
L'étude et la défense des intérêts économiques, professionnels, sociaux et moraux de ses associations-membres et de tous les policiers que celles-ci regroupent.
Denis Côté, Président
Luc Lalonde, Directeur exécutif

Fédération des professionnèles (FPCSN) / Quebec Federation of Managers & Professional Salaried Workers (CNTU)
#2400, 1601, av de Lorimier, Montréal QC H2K 4M5
Tél: 514-598-2143; *Téléc:* 514-598-2491
Ligne sans frais: 888-633-2143
www.fpcsn.qc.ca

Regroupe plus de 7000 professionnèles oeuvrant dans différents secteurs d'activités: santé et services sociaux, organismes gouvernementaux, éducation, secteur municipal, médecines alternatives, secteur juridique, intégration à l'emploi, professionnèles autonomes, organismes communautaires, etc
Ginette Langlois, Présidente
Catherine Gauvreau, Secrétaire générale

Fédération des professionnelles et professionnels de l'éducation du Québec (FPPE) / Québec Federation of Professional Employees in Education
9405, rue Sherbrooke est, Montréal QC H1L 6P3
Tél: 514-356-0505; *Téléc:* 514-356-1324
infos@fppe.qc.ca
www.fppe.qc.ca
www.youtube.com/user/FPPECSQ
www.facebook.com/FPPECSQ
twitter.com/FPPECSQ
De promouvoir et de développer les intérêts professionnels, sociaux et économiques des professionnelles et professionnels de l'éducation du Québec que de défendre les droits fondamentaux compris à l'intérieur des chartes, le droit d'association, le droit à la libre négociation et le droit à la liberté d'action syndicale; de représenter ses syndicats affiliés à un niveau national; d'orienter et de coordonner la représentation de ses syndicats affiliés auprès des instances de la Centrale; de diriger et de coordonner la négociation des conventions collectives; de concilier les conflits qui peuvent naître entre les syndicats affiliés; de mettre à la disposition des syndicats affiliés et de leurs membres des services de qualité en matière de négociation et d'application des conditions de travail et des droits sociaux, d'information et de formation syndicale
Jacques Landry, Président
Sophie Massé, Vice-présidente

Fédération des syndicats de l'action collective (FSAC)
9405, rue Sherbrooke est, Montréal QC H1L 6P3
Tél: 514-606-8263
www.fsac-csq.org
Regroupe les syndicats qui représentent le personnel oeuvrant dans les secteurs du loisir, du sport, de la culture du tourisme, du communautaire, l'économie sociale, le tourisme social, les bibliothèques et les services d'intégration
Jacques Legault, Président
Richard Vennes, Secrétaire général

Fédération des Syndicats de l'Enseignement (FSE)
CP 100, 320, rue Saint-Joseph est, Québec QC G1K 9E7
Tél: 418-649-8888; *Téléc:* 418-649-1914
Ligne sans frais: 877-850-0897
fse@fse.lacsq.org
www.lafse.org
www.youtube.com/c/FédérationdessyndicatsdelenseignementFS
ECSQ
www.facebook.com/FSECSQ
twitter.com/FSECSQ
Promouvoir les intérêts professionnels, sociaux et économiques du personnel enseignant des commissions scolaires; orienter et coordonner la représentation des syndicats affiliés auprès des instances de la Centrale et de représenter les syndicats affiliés là où leurs intérêts et leurs droits sont débattus; assumer prioritairement la responsabilité des négociations, les aspects sectoriels des relations du travail et de l'action juridique ainsi que les questions professionnelles à caractère sectoriel; favoriser la concertation entre les syndicats affiliés et concilier les divergences qui pourraient naître entre eux
Denis St-Hilaire, Directeur général

Fédération des travailleurs et travailleises du Québec (FTQ) / Québec Federation of Labour
#12100, 565, boul Crémazie est, Montréal QC H2M 2W3
Tél: 514-383-8000; *Téléc:* 514-383-8004
Ligne sans frais: 877-897-0057
www.ftq.qc.ca
www.facebook.com/laFTQ
twitter.com/FTQnouvelles
Michel Arsenault, Président

Fédération des travailleurs et travailleuses du Québec - Construction
#201, 9671 boul Métropolitain est, Montréal QC H1J 3C1
Tél: 514-381-7300; *Téléc:* 514-381-5173
Ligne sans frais: 877-666-4060
info@ftqconstruction.org
ftqconstruction.org
www.facebook.com/ConstructionFTQ
twitter.com/FTQConstruction
De négocier les conventions collectives applicables dans les sous secteurs d'activités (industriel, commercial et institutionnel, génie civil et voirie, résidentiel) et de voir à leur application

Fédération du commerce (CSN)
1601, av De Lorimier, Montréal QC H2K 4M5
Tél: 514-598-2421; *Téléc:* 514-598-2304
infofc@csn.qc.ca
www.fc-csn.ca
Serge Fournier, Président

Fédération du personnel de l'enseignement privé (FPEP)
9405, rue Sherbrooke est, Montréal QC H1L 6P3
Tél: 514-356-8888; *Téléc:* 514-356-1866
fpep@lacsq.org
www.fpep.lacsq.org
Stéphane Lapointe, Président

Fédération du personnel de soutien scolaire (CSQ) (FPSS) / Federation of Support Staff
9405, rue Sherbrooke est, Montréal QC H1L 6P3
Tél: 514-356-8888; *Téléc:* 514-493-3697
Ligne sans frais: 800-465-0897
fpss@csq.qc.net
www.fpss.lacsq.org
www.facebook.com/fpss.csq
twitter.com/FPSSCSQ
Le seul regroupement au Québec représentant du personnel de soutien scolaire des écoles et des centres
Éric Pronovost, Présidente

Fédération du personnel professionnel des universités et de la recherche (FPPU)
2277, rue Sheppard, Montréal QC H2K 3L1
Tél: 819-840-4544; *Téléc:* 514-522-6445
info@fppu.ca
www.fppu.ca
www.facebook.com/LaFPPU
twitter.com/LaFPPU
La FPPU est la seule organisation syndicale regroupant exclusivement le personnel professionnel des universités et de la recherche
Bernard Gaucher, Président

Fédération indépendante des syndicats autonomes (FISA) / Independent Federation of Autonomous Unions
#201, 1778, boul Wilfrid-Hamel, Québec QC G1N 3Y8
Tél: 418-529-4571; *Téléc:* 418-529-4695
Ligne sans frais: 800-407-3472
info@fisa.ca
www.fisa.ca
Fournir des services d'organisation, de conseils, de représentation et d'aide financière aux associations membres.
Jean Gagnon, Président

Fédération nationale des communications (CSN) (FNC) / National Federation of Communication Workers (CNTU)
1601, av de Lorimier, Montréal QC H2K 4M5
Tél: 514-598-2132
fnc@fncom.org
www.fncom.org
La défense des intérêts économiques, sociaux, politiques et professionnels des membres
Pascale St-Onge, Présidente
Patricia Lévesque, Coordonnatrice

Fraternité interprovinciale des ouvriers en électricité (CTC) (FIPOE) / Interprovincial Brotherhood of Electrical Workers (CLC)
10200, boul du Golf, Montréal QC H1J 2Y7
Tél: 514-385-3476; *Téléc:* 514-385-9298
Ligne sans frais: 855-453-4763
info@fipoe.org
www.fipoe.org
www.facebook.com/FIPOE
twitter.com/fipoeorg
Regrouper des électriciens de construction, des installateurs de systèmes d'alarmes et des monteurs de ligne
Arnold Guérin, Directeur général

Fraternité nationale des forestiers et travailleurs d'usine (CTC) / National Brotherhood of Foresters & Industrial Workers (CLC)
Locale 9, #8, rue Père Divet, Sept-Iles QC G4R 3N2
Tél: 418-968-3008
L'étude, la sauvegarde et le développement des intérêts économiques, et l'application de conventions collectives
Yves Guérette, Président

Government Services Union (GSU) / Syndicat des services gouvernementaux
#705, 233 Gilmour St., Ottawa ON K2P 0P2
Tel: 613-560-4395; *Fax:* 613-230-6774
Toll-Free: 888-220-2414
info@gsu-ssg.com
www.gsu-ssg.ca
twitter.com/GSUPSAC
To assist & represent members on grievances, staffing issues, disability & workers' compensation claims & union / management consultation
Randy Howard, National President

Grain Services Union (CLC) (GSU) / Syndicat des services du grain (CTC)
2334 McIntyre St., Regina SK S4P 2S2
Tel: 306-522-6686; *Fax:* 306-565-3430
Toll-Free: 866-522-6686
gsu.regina@sasktel.net
www.gsu.ca
They represent Saskatchewan Wheat Pool Workers and represent members working for a variety of companies within Canada.
Jim Brown, President
Hugh J. Wagner, General Secretary

Health Sciences Association of Alberta (HSAA) / Association des sciences de la santé de l'Alberta (ind.)
18410 - 100 Ave. NW, Edmonton AB T5S 0K6
Tel: 780-488-0534; *Toll-Free:* 844-280-4722
mrc@hsaa.ca
www.hsaa.ca
www.facebook.com/HSAAlberta
twitter.com/HSAAlberta
To conduct activities as a labour union to enhance the quality of life for HSAA members & society
Michael Parker, President
Mike Boyle, Executive Director

Health Sciences Association of Saskatchewan (HSAS) / Association des sciences de la santé de la Saskatchewan (ind.)
#42, 1736 Quebec Ave., Saskatoon SK S7K 1V9
Tel: 306-955-3399; *Fax:* 306-955-3396
Toll-Free: 888-565-3399
www.hsas.ca
www.youtube.com/user/HealthScienceSask
www.facebook.com/HealthSciencesSK
To conduct activities as an independent union representing its members who are health sciences professionals in Saskatchewan
Dean Job, Executive Director
Karen Wasylenko, President
Maureen Kraemer, Vice-President
Angela Barsalou, Secretary

Hospital Employees' Union (HEU) / Syndicat des employés d'hôpitaux
5000 North Fraser Way, Burnaby BC V5J 5M3
Tel: 604-438-5000; *Fax:* 604-739-1510
Toll-Free: 800-663-5813
info@heu.org
www.heu.org
www.youtube.com/user/MyHEUTube
www.facebook.com/hospitalemployeesunion
twitter.com/HospEmpUnion
To unite & associate together all employees employed in hospital, medical or related work for the purpose of securing concerted action in whatever may be regarded as conducive to their best interests; To embrace the concept of equality of treatment for all in hospital, medical or related employment, with respect to wages & job opportunities, recognizing their obligation to provide high-quality care; To defend & preserve the right of all persons to high standards of medical & hospital treatment
Barb Nederpel, President
Jennifer Whiteside, Secretary & Business Manager

International Alliance of Theatrical Stage Employees, Moving Picture Technicians, Artists & Allied Crafts of the US, Its Territories & Canada (IATSE)
207 West 25th St., 4th Fl., New York NY 10001 USA
Tel: 212-730-1770; *Fax:* 212-730-7809
www.iatse.net
www.instagram.com/iatse
www.facebook.com/iatse
twitter.com/iatse
To represent workers in the entertainment industry
Matthew D. Loeb, International President
James B. Wood, General Secretary-Treasurer
John M. Lewis, Director, Canadian Affairs

International Brotherhood of Boilermakers, Iron Ship Builders, Blacksmiths, Forgers & Helpers (AFL-CIO) (IBB) / Fraternité internationale des chaudronniers, constructeurs de navires en fer, forgerons, forgeurs et aides (FAT-COI)
#750, 753 State Ave., Kansas City KS 66101 USA
Tel: 913-371-2640; *Fax:* 913-281-8101
boilermakers.org
www.youtube.com/user/ibbwebguy
www.facebook.com/Boilermakers.Union
twitter.com/boilermakernews
To represent workers employed in shipbuilding, manufacturing, railroads, cement, mining & related industries
Newton B. Jones, International President

International Brotherhood of Teamsters (AFL-CIO/CLC) / Fraternité internationale des teamsters (FAT-COI/CTC)
25 Louisiana Ave. NW, Washington DC 20001 USA
Tel: 202-624-6800
teamster.org
www.youtube.com/TeamsterPower
www.facebook.com/teamsters
twitter.com/teamsters
To act as North America's strongest & most diverse labour union
James P. Hoffa, General President
Ken Hall, General Secretary-Treasurer

International Federation of Employees in Public Service (INFEDOP) / Fédération internationale du personnel des services publics
Montoyerstraat 39 bus 20, Rue Montoyer 39 boîte 20, Brussels 1000 Belgium
infedop@infedop.org
www.infedop.org
Bert Van Caelenberg, Secretary General

International Federation of Professional & Technical Engineers (AFL-CIO/CLC) (IFPTE) / Fédération internationale des ingénieurs et techniciens (FAT-COI/CTC)
#701, 501 - 3rd St. NW, Washington DC 20001 USA
Tel: 202-239-4880; *Fax:* 202-239-4881
generalinfo@ifpte.org
www.ifpte.org
www.facebook.com/IFPTE
twitter.com/IFPTE
To represent employees in a wide variety of occupations in the technical, administrative & professional fields
Paul Shearon, International President
Matthew Biggs, Secretary-Treasurer

International Longshore & Warehouse Union (CLC) / Syndicat international des débardeurs et magasiniers (CTC)
1188 Franklin St., 4th Fl., San Francisco CA 94109 USA
Tel: 415-775-0533; *Fax:* 415-775-1302
www.ilwu.org
To represent the rights of their members, who work in the warehouse industry
William E. Adams, President

International Union of Bricklayers & Allied Craftworkers (AFL-CIO/CFL) (BAC) / Union internationale des briqueteurs et métiers connexes (FAT-COI/FCT)
620 F St. NW, Washington DC 20004 USA
Tel: 202-783-3788; *Toll-Free:* 888-880-8222
askbac@bacweb.org
bacweb.org
www.youtube.com/user/BACInternational
www.facebook.com/IUBAC
twitter.com/IUBAC
To improve the quality of life of their members
Timothy J. Driscoll, President

International Union, United Automobile, Aerospace & Agricultural Implement Workers of America (UAW) / Syndicat international des travailleurs unis de l'automobile, de l'aérospatiale et de l'outillage agricole d'Amérique
8000 East Jefferson Ave., Detroit MI 48214 USA
Tel: 313-926-5000
feedback@uaw.org
www.uaw.org
www.youtube.com/uaw
www.facebook.com/uaw.union
twitter.com/uaw
To act as the collective bargaining body for its members, negotiating for wages & benefits
Rory Gamble, President

Laborers' International Union of North America (AFL-CIO/CLC) (LiUNA) / Union internationale des journaliers d'Amérique (FAT-COI/CTC)
905 - 16th St. NW, Washington DC 20006 USA
Tel: 202-737-8320
communications@liuna.org
www.liuna.org
www.youtube.com/user/liunavideo
www.linkedin.com/company/liuna
www.facebook.com/LaborersInternationalUnionofNorthAmerica
twitter.com/LIUNA
To represent construction workers & other public service employees
Terry O'Sullivan, President
Erin Hutson, Director, Corporate Affairs
Brendan O'Sullivan, Director, Construction
John R. Billi, Inspector General

Manitoba Association of Health Care Professionals (MAHCP) / Association des professionnels de la santé du Manitoba
#101, 1500 Notre Dame Ave., Winnipeg MB R3E 0P9
Tel: 204-772-0425; *Fax:* 204-775-6829
Toll-Free: 800-315-3331
info@mahcp.ca
mahcp.com
www.facebook.com/manitobaahcp
twitter.com/MAHCP_MB
To protect, advocate for & advance the rights of its members through labour relations activities
Bob Moroz, President
Lee Manning, Executive Director

Manitoba Federation of Labour / Fédération du travail du Manitoba
#303, 275 Broadway Ave., Winnipeg MB R3C 4M6
Tel: 204-947-1400; *Fax:* 204-943-4276
admin@mfl.mb.ca
www.mfl.mb.ca
www.youtube.com/user/MFLabour
www.facebook.com/ManitobaLabour
twitter.com/MFLabour
To advance economic & social welfare of working people in Manitoba; To encourage workers to vote & exercise full rights & responsibilities
Kevin Rebeck, President
Anna Rothney, Executive Director

Manitoba Government & General Employees' Union (MGEU)
#601, 275 Broadway, Winnipeg MB R3C 4M6
Tel: 204-982-6438; *Fax:* 204-942-2146
Toll-Free: 866-982-6438
TTY: 204-982-6599
resourcecentre@mgeu.ca
www.mgeu.ca
www.youtube.com/user/mgeulogin
www.facebook.com/MGEUnion
twitter.com/MGEUnion
Michelle Gawronsky, President
Debbie O'Hare, Executive Assistant

Maritime Fishermen's Union (CLC) (MFU) / Union des pêcheurs des Maritimes (CTC) (UPM)
408 Main St., Shediac NB E4P 2G1
Tel: 506-532-2485; *Fax:* 506-532-2487
shediac@mfu-upm.com
www.mfu-upm.com
twitter.com/upmmfu
To maintain a sustainable inshore fishery & defend the principal of the fishermen/owner-operator.
Gaetan Robichaud, President

Mount Royal Staff Association (MRSA)
#W301, 4825 Mount Royal Gate SW, Calgary AB T3E 6K6
Tel: 403-440-5993; *Fax:* 403-440-6763
mrsa@mtroyal.ca
www.mrssa.ca
To ensure Mount Royal University staff work in a fair environment
Baset Zarrugr, President

National Union of Public & General Employees (NUPGE)
15 Auriga Dr., Nepean ON K2E 1B7
Tel: 613-228-9800; *Fax:* 613-228-9801
national@nupge.ca
nupge.ca
To deliver public services of every kind to the citizens of their home provinces
Larry Brown, National President

Native Brotherhood of British Columbia (NBBC) / Fraternité des Indiens de la Colombie-Britannique
#110, 100 Park Royal South, West Vancouver BC V7T 1A2
Tel: 604-913-2997; *Fax:* 604-913-2995
nativebrotherhood.ca
To improve the social, spiritual, economic & physical conditions of its members, including education, health & living; To cooperate with other organizations which are involved with the advancement of Indian welfare; To focus on capacity building, particularly resources with economic potential

New Brunswick Federation of Labour (NBFL) / Fédération des travailleurs et travailleuses du Nouveau-Brunswick
#314, 96 Norwood Ave., Moncton NB E1C 6L9
Tel: 506-857-2125; *Fax:* 506-383-1597
info@fednb.ca
www.nbfl-fttnb.ca
www.facebook.com/NewBrunswickFederationOfLabour
twitter.com/NBFL_FTTNB
To act as the central voice of labour in New Brunswick; To build solidarity & support between unions; To advance the economic & social welfare of New Brunswick's workers
Patrick Colford, President
John Gagnon, First Vice-President

Newfoundland & Labrador Association of Public & Private Employees (NAPE)
PO Box 8100, 330 Portugal Cove Pl., St. John's NL A1B 3M9
Tel: 709-754-0700; *Fax:* 709-754-0726
Toll-Free: 800-563-4442
www.nape.ca
The largest union in Newfoundland & Labrador
Jerry Earle, President
Bert Blundon, Secretary-Treasurer
Arlene Sedlickas, General Vice-President

Newfoundland & Labrador Federation of Labour (NLFL) / Fédération du travail de Terre-Neuve et du Labrador
NAPE Bldg., PO Box 8597, Stn. A, 330 Portugal Cove Pl., 2nd Fl., St. John's NL A1B 3P2
Tel: 709-754-1660; *Fax:* 709-754-1220
fed@nlfl.nf.ca
www.nlfl.nf.ca
www.youtube.com/user/NLLABOUR
www.facebook.com/189773034381902
twitter.com/NLFL_labour
To represent the interests of its members
Mary Shortall, President
Linda Rideout, Executive Secretary

Northern Territories Federation of Labour / Fédération du travail des Territoires du Nord
PO Box 2787, Yellowknife NT X1A 2R1
Tel: 867-873-3695; *Fax:* 867-873-6979
Toll-Free: 888-873-1956
ntfl@yk.com
www.ntfl.ca
www.facebook.com/NTFed
To promote the interests of its members
Gayla Thunstrom, Acting President

Nova Scotia Federation of Labour / Fédération du travail de la Nouvelle-Écosse
#225, 3700 Kempt Rd., Halifax NS B3K 4X8
Tel: 902-454-6735; *Fax:* 902-454-7671
nsfl@ns.aliantzinc.ca
www.nsfl.ns.ca
To speak on behalf of & represent the interests of organized & unorganized workers; to promote decent wages & working conditions, improved health & safety laws & lobbies for fair taxes & strong social programs; to work for social equality & to end racism & discrimination.
Rick Clarke, President
Kyle Buott, Secretary-Treasurer

Nova Scotia Government & General Employees Union (NSGEU) / Syndicat de la fonction publique de la Nouvelle-Écosse
255 John Savage Ave., Dartmouth NS B3B 0J3
Tel: 902-424-4063; *Fax:* 902-424-2111
Toll-Free: 877-556-7438
www.nsgeu.ns.ca
Joan Jessome, President
Keiren Tompkins, Executive Director

Nova Scotia Union of Public & Private Employees (CCU) (NSUPE) / Syndicat des employés du secteur public de la Nouvelle-Écosse (CCU)
#402A, 7020 Mumford Rd., Halifax NS B3L 4S9
Tel: 902-422-9495; *Fax:* 902-429-7655
www.nsupe.ca
To better & protect the livelihood and the social and economic well-being of its members, their families and fellow citizens.
Joe Kaiser, President
Claudia MacFarlane, Vice-President

Nunavut Employees Union (NEU)
Bldg. #165, PO Box 869, Nipisa St., Iqaluit NU X0A 0H0
Tel: 867-979-4209; *Fax:* 867-979-4522
Toll-Free: 877-243-4424
reception@neu.ca
www.neu.ca
www.facebook.com/232407933602621
To represent the interests of the employees of the Government of Nunavut, the Northwest Territories Power Corporation, Workers Compensation Board in Nunavut, Nunavut Housing Corporation, & the unionized employees of Nunavut municipalities & Housing Associations
Bill Fennell, President
Brian Boutilier, Executive Director

Office & Professional Employees International Union (AFL-CIO/CLC) / Union internationale des employés professionnels et de bureau (FAT-COI/CTC)
80 - 8th Ave., 20th Fl., New York NY 10011 USA
Tel: 800-346-7348
frontdesk@opeiu.org
www.opeiu.org
www.facebook.com/opeiu
twitter.com/opeiu

Richard Lanigan, President

Ontario Federation of Labour (OFL) / Fédération du travail de l'Ontario
#202, 15 Gervais Dr., Toronto ON M3C 1Y8
Tel: 416-441-2731; *Fax:* 416-441-0722
Toll-Free: 800-668-9138
TTY: 416-443-6305
info@ofl.ca
ofl.ca
www.linkedin.com/company/ontario-federation-of-labour
www.facebook.com/OFLabour
twitter.com/OFLabour
To represent the interests of organized workers in Ontario; To provide support services to its affiliated local unions & labour councils
Patty Coates, President
Ahmad Gaied, Secretary-Treasurer

Ontario Professional Fire Fighters Association (OPFFA) / Association des pompiers professionnels de l'Ontario (ind.)
637 King St. West, #A, Toronto ON M5V 1M5
Tel: 905-681-7111; *Fax:* 905-681-1489
Toll-Free: 800-387-4418
www.opffa.org

Rob Hyndman, President

Ontario Public Service Employees Union (OPSEU) / Syndicat des employées et employés de la fonction publique de l'Ontario
100 Lesmill Rd., Toronto ON M3B 3P8
Tel: 416-443-8888; *Fax:* 416-443-9670
Toll-Free: 800-268-7376
opseu@opseu.org
www.opseu.org
www.youtube.com/user/OPSEUSEFPO
www.facebook.com/OPSEU
twitter.com/OPSEU
To negotiate collective agreements; To conduct membership education; To lobby governments to maintain & improve public services; To defend the principle of social unionism by speaking out on public policy issues such as taxes, free trade, privatization, health care, social services, occupational health & safety & employment equity
Warren (Smokey) Thomas, President

Operative Plasterers' & Cement Masons' International Association of the US & Canada (AFL-CIO/CFL) - Canadian Office
Varette Bldg., #1902, 130 Albert St., Ottawa ON K1P 5G4
Tel: 613-236-0653; *Fax:* 613-230-5138
www.buildingtrades.ca
www.youtube.com/user/Buildingtrades12
twitter.com/CDNTrades

To represent the interests of those employed in the building, construction, fabrication & maintenance industry in Canada ensuring safe working conditions
Robert Blakely, Canadian Operating Officer

Prince Edward Island Federation of Labour / Fédération du travail de l'Île-du-Prince-Édouard
326 Patterson Dr., Charlottetown PE C1A 8K4
Tel: 902-368-3068
peifed@pei.aibn.com
www.peifl.ca

Carl Pursey, President

Prince Edward Island Union of Public Sector Employees / Syndicat de la fonction publique de l'Île-du-Prince-Édouard
4 Enman Cres., Charlottetown PE C1E 1E6
Tel: 902-892-5335; *Fax:* 902-569-8186
Toll-Free: 800-897-8773
peiupse@peiupse.ca
www.peiupse.ca
To represent & advocate on behalf of its members in order to ensure safe & fair working conditions
Debbie Bovyer, President

Professional Association of Foreign Service Officers (PAFSO) / L'Association professionnelle des agents du service extérieur (APASE)
#412, 47 Clarence St., Ottawa ON K1N 9K1
Tel: 613-241-1391; *Fax:* 613-241-5911
info@pafso-apase.com
www.pafso.com
www.linkedin.com/company/pafso-apase
www.facebook.com/pafso.apase
twitter.com/PafsoApase
To be the bargaining agent & the professional association for Canadian Foreign Service Officers
Ron Cochrane, Executive Director

Professional Association of Residents & Interns of Manitoba (PARIM) / Association professionnelle des résidents et internes du Manitoba
Health Sciences Centre, 820 Sherbrook St., #GF132, Winnipeg MB R3A 1R9
Tel: 204-787-3673; *Fax:* 204-787-2692
www.parim.org
www.instagram.com/parim_docs
www.facebook.com/PARIMresidents
twitter.com/parimresidents
To represent the concerns of all residents & interns in Manitoba; To advocate for the well-being of residents & interns; To promote quality medical education & excellent patient care
Jessica Burleson, Executive Director

Professional Association of Residents in the Maritime Provinces (PARI-MP) / Association professionnelle des résidents des provinces maritimes
Halifax Professional Centre, #460, 5991 Spring Garden Rd., Halifax NS B3H 1Y6
Tel: 902-404-3597; *Toll-Free:* 877-972-7467
www.parimp.ca
To represent the interests of resident physicians who train at Dalhousie University; To improve the well-being & working conditions of residents in the Maritimes; To advocate on the behalf of residents
Philip Davis, President
Sandi Carew Flemming, Executive Director

Professional Association of Residents of Alberta (PARA) / Association professionnelle des résidents de l'Alberta
Garneau Professional Center, #340, 11044 - 82 Ave., Edmonton AB T6G 0T2
Tel: 780-432-1749; *Fax:* 780-432-1778
Toll-Free: 877-375-7272
para@para-ab.ca
www.para-ab.ca
www.facebook.com/ProfessionalAssociationofResidentPhysiciansofAB
twitter.com/para_ab
To represent physicians completing further training in residency programs; To promote excellence in education & patient care; To advocate for health care issues & for improvement in working conditions, salary, & benefits for resident physicians of Alberta
Catherine Cheng, President
Rob Key, Chief Executive Officer
Kiersten Doblanko, Specialist, Communications

Professional Association of Residents of Newfoundland & Labrador (PARNL)
NL
info@parnl.ca
parnl.ca
To collaborate with local & national health care organizations to advocate on behalf of internes, resident physicians & fellows of Newfoundland & Labrador; To advocate for the acknowledgement of the resident's role in medical education
Samantha Mullett, President
Laura Chu, Vice-President
Patricia Penton, Executive Director

Professional Employees Association (Ind.) (PEA) / Association des employés professionnels (ind.)
#505, 1207 Douglas St., Victoria BC V8W 2E7
Tel: 250-385-8791; *Fax:* 250-385-6629
Toll-Free: 800-779-7736
www.pea.org
www.instagram.com/peainbc
www.facebook.com/peainbc
To provide collective bargaining representation to professionals employed in the provincial public service & elsewhere in the BC public sector
Scott McCannell, Executive Director

Professional Engineers Government of Ontario
4711 Yonge St., 10th Fl., Toronto ON M2N 6K8
Tel: 416-784-1284; *Fax:* 416-784-1366
pego@pego.on.ca
www.pego.on.ca
The Professional Engineers Government of Ontario (PEGO) is a certified bargaining association representing Professional Engineers and Ontario Land Surveyors working directly for the Government of the Province of Ontario.

The Professional Institute of the Public Service of Canada (PIPSC) / Institut professionnel de la fonction publique du Canada
250 Tremblay Rd., Ottawa ON K1G 3J8
Tel: 613-228-6310; *Fax:* 613-228-9048
Toll-Free: 800-267-0446
www.pipsc.ca
www.youtube.com/user/PIPSCOMM
www.facebook.com/PIPSC.IPFPC
twitter.com/PIPSC_IPFPC
To serve members by serving as their collective bargaining agent & by providing representational services
Debi Daviau, President
Edward Gillis, COO & Executive Secretary

Public & Private Workers of Canada (PPWC)
#201, 1184 - West 6th Ave., Vancouver BC V6H 1A4
Tel: 604-731-1909; *Fax:* 604-731-6448
Toll-Free: 888-992-7792
admin@ppwc.ca
www.ppwc.ca
www.youtube.com/user/PPWCUnion
www.facebook.com/PublicandPrivateWorkersofCanada
twitter.com/PPWCUnion
To ensure fair working conditions for its members
Gary Fiege, President

Public Service Alliance of Canada (PSAC) / Alliance de la Fonction publique du Canada (AFPC)
233 Gilmour St., Ottawa ON K2P 0P1
Tel: 613-560-4200; *Toll-Free:* 888-604-7722
info@psac-afpc.com
www.psacunion.ca
www.youtube.com/user/PSACwebmaster
www.facebook.com/psac.national
twitter.com/psac_afpc
To unite all workers in a single democratic organization; To obtain for all public service employees the best standards of compensation & other conditions of employment & to protect the rights & interests of all public service employees; To maintain & defend the right to strike
Chris Aylward, National President
Magali Picard, National Executive Vice-President

Public Services International (PSI) / Internationale des services publics
Centre d'Aumard, PO Box 9, 45, av Voltaire, Ferney-Voltaire Cedex F-01211 France
psi@world-psi.org
publicservices.international
www.youtube.com/user/PSIglobalunion
www.facebook.com/PSIglobalunion
twitter.com/PSIglobalunion
To represent public sector trade unions in countries around the world; has consultative status with ECOSOC & observer status with other UN bodies such as UNCTAD & UNESCO
Rosa Pavanelli, General Secretary

Research Council Employees' Association (Ind.) (RCEA) / Association des employés du conseil de recherches (ind.) (AECR)
PO Box 8256, Stn. Alta Vista Terminal, Ottawa ON K1G 3H7
Tel: 613-746-9341; *Fax:* 613-745-7868
office@rcea.ca
www.rcea.ca
To act as the certified bargaining agent for six groups and categories and represents the majority of NRC employees, which are: AD (Administrative Support) Group, AS (Administrative Services) Group, CS (Computer Systems Administration) Group, OP (Operational) Category, PG (Purchasing and Supply) Group, and TO(Technical) Category.
Cathie Fraser, President

Resident Doctors of British Columbia (RDBC)
#350, 1665 West Broadway, Vancouver BC V4C 7J7
Tel: 604-876-7636; *Toll-Free:* 888-877-2722
info@residentdoctorsbc.ca
www.residentdoctorsbc.ca
www.facebook.com/ResidentDoctorsBC
twitter.com/ResidentDocsBC
To bargain collectively on behalf of residents in British Columbia; To foster the personal well-being of members
Nicholas Monfries, President
Harry Gray, Executive Director

Retail, Wholesale & Department Store Union (AFL-CIO/CLC) (RWDSU) / Union des employés de gros, de détail et de magasins à rayons (FAT-COI/CTC)
#501, 370 - 7th Ave., New York NY 10001 USA
Tel: 212-684-5300
admin@rwdsu.org
www.rwdsu.org
www.youtube.com/RetailUnion
www.facebook.com/RWDSU.UFCW
twitter.com/RWDSU
To represent workers throughout much of the United States & Canada
Stuart Appelbaum, President
Jack Wurm, Secretary-Treasurer

Royal Newfoundland Constabulary Association (RNCA) / Association de la gendarmerie royale de Terre-Neuve
125 East White Hills Rd., St. John's NL A1A 5R7
Tel: 709-739-5946; *Fax:* 709-739-6276
office@rnca.ca
www.rnca.ca
To improve benefits & working conditions for police officers; to improve public safety & strive to create a positive relationship between the police & the community they protect
Tim Buckle, President
Warren Sullivan, 1st Vice-President
Albert Gibbons, 2nd Vice-President

Saskatchewan Government & General Employees' Union (SGEU) / Syndicat de la fonction publique de la Saskatchewan
1440 Broadway Ave., Regina SK S4P 1E2
Tel: 306-522-8571; *Fax:* 306-352-1969
Toll-Free: 800-667-5221
general@sgeu.org
www.sgeu.org
www.youtube.com/user/SGEUtube
www.facebook.com/SGEU.SK
twitter.com/sgeu
To represent & protect the interests of its members who work in the public sector in Saskatchewan
Bob Bymoen, President

Saskatchewan Joint Board Retail, Wholesale & Department Store Union (SJBRWDSU)
1233 Winnipeg St., Regina SK S4R 1K1
Tel: 306-569-9311; *Fax:* 306-569-9521
Toll-Free: 877-747-9378
rwdsu.regina@sasktel.net
www.rwdsu.sk.ca
Garry Burkart, Secretary-Treasurer

Seafarers' International Union of Canada / Syndicat international des marins canadiens
#200, 1333, rue Saint-Jacques, Montréal QC H3C 4K2
Tel: 514-931-7859; *Fax:* 514-931-3667
siuofcanada@seafarers.ca
www.seafarers.ca
www.facebook.com/SIUofCanada
twitter.com/SIUCanada
To ensure its members safe & fair working conditions
James Given, President
Patrice Caron, Executive Vice-President

Service Employees International Union (AFL-CIO/CLC) / Union internationale des employés des services (FAT-COI/CTC)
1800 Massachusetts Ave. NW, Washington DC 20036 USA
Tel: 202-730-7000; *Toll-Free:* 800-424-8592
TTY: 202-730-7481
www.seiu.org
www.youtube.com/user/SEIU
www.facebook.com/SEIU
twitter.com/SEIU
To unite workers in 3 sectors: healthcare, property services & public services; To improve the lives of its members, their families & the services they provide
Mary Kay Henry, President

Société des Auteurs de Radio, Télévision et Cinéma (SARTEC) / Society of Writers in Radio, Television & Cinema
1229, rue Panet, Montréal QC H2L 2Y6
Tél: 514-526-9196; *Téléc:* 514-526-4124
information@sartec.qc.ca
www.sartec.qc.ca
vimeo.com/user8816585
twitter.com/SARTEC_auteur
Regroupe les auteurs de langue française oeuvrant au Canada dans les domaines de la radio, de la télévision, du cinéma ou de l'audiovisuel; a pour objet l'étude, la défense et le développement des intérêts économiques, sociaux et moraux de ses membres
Stéphanie Hénault, Directrice générale

Society of Professional Engineers & Associates (SPEA) / Société des ingénieurs professionnels et associés
#2, 2275 Speakman Dr., Mississauga ON L5K 1B1
Tel: 905-823-3606; *Fax:* 905-823-9602
www.spea.ca
To represent scientists, engineers, technologists, & tradespeople who work for Atomic Energy of Canada Limited (AECL) in Mississauga, Ontario & abroad
Michael Ivanco, President
Brian Girard, Chair, Membership
Vincent Tume, Secretary
Val Aleyaseen, Treasurer

Syndicat de la fonction publique et parapublique du Québec inc. (ind.) (SFPQ) / Québec Government Employees' Union (Ind.)
5100, boul des Gradins, Québec QC G2J 1N4
Tél: 418-623-2424; *Téléc:* 418-623-6109
Ligne sans frais: 855-623-2424
communication@sfpq.qc.ca
www.sfpq.qc.ca
www.youtube.com/user/SFPQ
www.linkedin.com/company/syndicat-de-la-fonction-publique-du-qu-bec
www.facebook.com/SFPQ.Syndicat
twitter.com/SFPQ_Syndicat
Assurer la défense des intérêts économiques, politiques et sociaux des membres et le développement de leurs conditions de vie; faire la promotion des services publics comme moyen démocratique de répondre aux besoins de la population
Christian Daigle, Président général

Syndicat de professionnelles et professionnels du gouvernement du Québec (SPGQ) / Union of Professional Employees of the Québec Government
7, rue Vallière, Québec QC G1K 6S9
Tél: 418-692-0022; *Téléc:* 418-692-1338
Ligne sans frais: 800-463-5079
info@spgq.qc.ca
spgq.qc.ca
www.youtube.com/spgqinformation
www.linkedin.com/company/spgq
www.facebook.com/lespgq
twitter.com/spgq

Syndicat des Agents Correctionnels du Canada (CSN) (SACC-CSN) / Union of Canadian Correctional Officers (UCCO-CSN)
1601, av De Lorimier, Montréal QC H2K 4M5
Tel: 514-598-2263; *Fax:* 514-598-2943
Toll-Free: 866-229-5566
ucco-sacc@csn.qc.ca
www.ucco-sacc.csn.qc.ca
www.facebook.com/216852691687729
Kevin Grabosky, Président

Syndicat des agents de la paix en services correctionnels du Québec (SAPSCQ) / Union of Prison Guards of Québec
4906, boul Gouin est, Montréal QC H1G 1A4
Tél: 514-328-7774; *Téléc:* 514-328-0889
Ligne sans frais: 800-361-3559
support@sapscq.com
www.sapscq.com
Service syndical pour les agents de la paix en services correctionnels du Québec
Mathieu Lavoie, Président national
Michel Désourdie, Vice Président
Jean-Pascal Bélisle, Secrétaire général

Syndicat des agents de maîtrise de TELUS (ind.) (SAMT) / TELUS Professional Employees Union (Ind.) (TPEU)
#605, 2, St-Germain est, Rimouski QC G5L 8T7
Tél: 418-722-6144; *Téléc:* 418-724-0765
info@samt.qc.ca
www.samt.qc.ca/apropos.php
La sauvegarde et la promotion des intérêts professionnels, scientifiques, économiques, sociaux, culturels et politiques de ses membres; faire bénéficier les membres et les travailleurs en général des avantages de l'entraide et des négociations collectives; obtenir pour ses membres un meilleur niveau de vie et de meilleures conditions de travail; représenter les membres auprès de l'employeur
Harold Morrissey, Président
Lynda Fortin, Secrétaire

Syndicat des employé(e)s de magasins et de bureau de la Société des alcools du Québec (ind.) (SEMB SAQ) / Québec Liquor Board Store & Office Employees Union (Ind.)
1065, rue Saint-Denis, Montréal QC H2X 3J3
Tél: 514-849-7754; *Téléc:* 514-849-7914
Ligne sans frais: 800-361-8427
info@semb-saq.com
www.semb-saq.com
www.facebook.com/semb.saq
Katia Lelièvre, Présidente

Syndicat des employés en radio-télédiffusion de Télé-Québec (CSQ) / Télé-Québec Television Broadcast Employees' Union
c/o Télé-Québec, 1000, rue Fullum, Montréal QC H2K 3L7
Tél: 514-529-2805
sert@colba.net
Sylvain Leboeuf, Président

Syndicat des pompiers et pompières du Québec (CTC) (SPQ) / Québec Union of Firefighters (CLC)
#3900, 565, boul Crémazie est, Montréal QC H2M 2V6
Tél: 514-383-4698; *Téléc:* 514-383-6782
Ligne sans frais: 800-461-4698
www.spq-ftq.com
Daniel Pépin, Président

Syndicat des professeures et professeurs de l'Université du Québec à Chicoutimi (SPPUQAC)
555, boul de l'Université, #P2-1000, Chicoutimi QC G7H 2B1
Tél: 418-545-5378; *Téléc:* 418-545-6659
sppuqac@uqac.ca
www.uqac.ca/sppuqac
Lison Bergeron, Secrétaire

Syndicat des professeurs de l'État du Québec (ind.) (SPEQ) / Union of Professors for the Government of Québec (Ind.)
#1003, 2120, rue Sherbrooke est, Montréal QC H2K 1C3
Tél: 514-525-7979; *Téléc:* 514-525-4655
Ligne sans frais: 877-525-7979
info@speq.org
www.speq.org
Pour représenter les fonctionnaires enseignants salariés.
Claude Tanguay, Président

Syndicat des technicien(ne)s et artisan(e)s du réseau français de Radio-Canada (ind.) (STARF) / CBC French Network Technicians' Union (Ind.)
1250, rue de la Visitation, Montréal QC H2L 3B4
Tél: 514-524-1100; *Téléc:* 514-524-6023
Ligne sans frais: 888-838-1100
secretariat@starf.qc.ca
www.starf.qc.ca
Benoît Celestino, Président
Marie-Lou Faille, Secrétaire-trésorier

Syndicat des technologues en radiologie du Québec (STRQ) / Union of Radiology Technicians of Québec
#850, 1001, rue Sherbrooke est, Montréal QC H2L 1L3
Tél: 514-521-4469; *Téléc:* 514-521-0086
Étude, développement et la défense des intérêts professionnels, économiques, sociaux et éducatifs de ses membres et particulièrement la négociation et l'application de conventions collectives.

Syndicat des travailleurs de la construction du Québec (CSD)
#300, 801, 4e rue, Québec QC G1J 2T7
Tél: 418-522-3918; *Téléc:* 418-529-6323
info@csdconstruction.qc.ca
www.csdconstruction.qc.ca
www.youtube.com/user/LaCSDConstruction
www.facebook.com/csdconstruction
twitter.com/csdconstruction
Défendre et promouvoir les intérêts sociaux et économiques de ses membres
Daniel Laterreur, Président
Guy Terrault, Vice-président
Gilles C. Coulombe, Secrétaire

Syndicat du personnel technique et professionnel de la Société des alcools du Québec (ind.) (SPTP-SAQ) / Québec Liquor Board's Union of Technical & Professional Employees (Ind.)
905, rue de Lorimier, Montréal QC H2K 3V9
Tél: 514-873-5878; *Téléc:* 514-873-5896
intra.sptp-saq.ca

Steve d'Agostino, Président
Patrick Bray, Vice-Président
Hélène Daneault, Directrice
Johanne Morrisseau, Directrice
Lisanne Racine, Directrice

Syndicat interprovincial des ferblantiers et couvreurs, la section locale 2016 à la FTQ-Construction
#200, 8300, boul Métropolitain est, Anjou QC H1K 1A2
Tél: 514-374-1515; *Téléc:* 514-448-2265
Ligne sans frais: 866-374-1515
info@ftq2016.org
www.ftq2016.org
Voir à la promotion et à la défense des intérêts économiques et sociaux des membres; assurer l'intégrité du métier de ferblantier et couvreur en défendant sa juridiction professionnelle et en assurant sa sécurité d'emploi; représenter les travailleurs, que leur travail soit effectué à l'intérieur du chantier de construction ou non; cultiver des sentiments de solidarité parmis les travailleurs; obtenir des améliorations dans les conditions de travail de ses membres
Dorima Aubut, Directeur provincial

Syndicat québécois de la construction (SQC) / North Shore Construction Inc. (Ind.)
2121, av Sainte-Anne, Saint-Hyacinthe QC J2S 5H5
Tél: 450-773-8833; *Téléc:* 450-773-2232
Ligne sans frais: 888-773-8834
info@sqc.ca
www.sqc.ca
www.facebook.com/SyndicatQuebecoisConstruction
Sylvain Gendron, Président

Teaching Support Staff Union (TSSU)
Academic Quadrangle, Simon Fraser University, #5129/5130, 8888 University Dr., Burnaby BC V5A 1S6
Tel: 778-782-4735
tssu@tssu.ca
www.tssu.ca
www.facebook.com/TSSU.ca
twitter.com/TSSU
A feminist, non-hierarchical, independent labour union representing all teaching support staff during collective bargaining agreements & in employee-employer conflicts.
Alicia Massie, Coordinator
Zachary Williams, Organizer
Scott Yano, Chief Steward I
Lillian Deeb, Chief Steward II

Toronto Musicians' Association (TMA)
#500, 15 Gervais Dr., Toronto ON M3C 1Y8
Tel: 416-421-1020; *Fax:* 416-421-7011
Toll-Free: 800-762-3444
info@tma149.ca
www.torontomusicians.org
www.facebook.com/torontomusicians
twitter.com/TMA149
To represent professional musicians in all facets of music in the greater Toronto area; To offer legal protection, assistance & advice; To help musicians have a successful professional career

Michael Adam Murray, Executive Director

UNIFOR
205 Placer Ct., Toronto ON M2H 3H9
Tel: 416-497-4110; *Toll-Free:* 800-268-5763
communications@unifor.org
www.unifor.org
www.youtube.com/user/UniforCanada
www.facebook.com/UniforCanada
twitter.com/UniforTheUnion
To improve the working conditions & general economic & social conditions of Canadian workers in the industries of: aerospace, mining, fishing, auto & specialty vehicle assembly, auto parts, hotels, airlines, rail, education, hospitality, retail, road transportation, health care, manufacturing, shipbuilding & others
Jerry Dias, National President
Lana Payne, Secretary-Treasurer

UniforACL
c/o Unifor Local 2289, #100, 6300 Lady Hammond Rd., Halifax NS B3K 2R6
Tel: 902-425-2440; *Fax:* 902-422-4647
Toll-Free: 800-565-2289
unifor-acl.ca

Penny Fawcett, Chair

Union des Artistes (FIA) - Bureau de Québec (UDA)
#520, rue De Saint-Vallier est, Québec QC G1K 9G4
Tél: 418-523-4241; *Téléc:* 418-523-0168
Ligne sans frais: 877-523-4299
pcauffope@uda.ca

Union of Calgary Co-op Employees (UCCE)
420 - 35th Ave. NE, Calgary AB T1Y 5R8
Tel: 403-299-6700; *Fax:* 403-299-6710
reception@ucce.info
www.ucce.info
To represent members employed in occupations including trades, janitorial, clerical & technical positions in the field of retail grocery
Pat Rose, President
Shelley Winters, Vice President
Kim Revenco, Treasurer

Union of Health & Environment Workers (UHEW) / Syndicat des travailleurs de la santé et de l'environnement (STSE)
#400, 2781 Lancaster Rd., Ottawa ON K1B 1A7
Tel: 613-731-5533; *Fax:* 613-526-5537
Toll-Free: 833-731-5533
info@uhew-stse.ca
www.uew-ste.ca
twitter.com/UHEW5
To protect members by ensuring safe working conditions & fair wage rights & benefits
Shimen Fayad, National President

Union of National Defence Employees (UNDE) / Union des employés de la Défense nationale (UEDN)
#700, 116 Albert St., Ottawa ON K1P 5G3
Tel: 613-594-4505; *Fax:* 613-594-8233
Toll-Free: 866-594-4505
www.unde-uedn.com
To represent the interests of their members & ensure safe working conditions for them
June Winger, National President

Union of National Employees (UNE) / Syndicat des employées et employés nationaux (SEN)
#900, 150 Isabella St., Ottawa ON K1S 1V7
Tel: 613-560-4364; *Fax:* 613-560-4208
Toll-Free: 800-663-6685
info@une-sen.org
une-sen.org
www.youtube.com/user/UnionNESyndicatEN
www.facebook.com/Union.NE.Syndicat.EN
twitter.com/UNE_SEN
To protect members by ensuring safe working conditions & fair wage rights & benefits
Kevin King, National President
Georges St-Jean, Director, Finance & Administration

Union of Northern Workers / Syndicat des travailleurs du Nord
#400, 4910 - 53rd St., Yellowknife NT X1A 1V2
Tel: 867-873-5668; *Fax:* 867-920-4448
Toll-Free: 877-906-4447
hq@unw.ca
www.unw.ca
twitter.com/UNW_NWT
To represent the interests of its members in contract negotiatons & grievances
Todd Parsons, President

Kim Bailey, Director, Finance & Administration

Union of Postal Communications Employees (UPCE) / Syndicat des employés des postes et des communications (SEPC)
#701, 233 Gilmour St., Ottawa ON K2P 0P1
Tel: 613-560-4342; *Fax:* 613-594-3849
Toll-Free: 877-841-9998
www.upce-sepc.ca
To represent Canada Post members employed in administrative, clerical, technical & professional capacities
François Paradis, National President

Union of Safety & Justice Employees / Syndicat des employés de la Sécurité de la Justice
#1004, 233 Gilmour St., Ottawa ON K2P 0P2
Tel: 613-560-5554; *Fax:* 613-232-3311
usjemembers_membressesj@psac-afpc.com
www.usje-sesj.com
www.facebook.com/USJESESJ
To unite & represent public service workers across the federal justice system
Stan Stapleton, National President

Union of Taxation Employees (UTE) / Syndicat des employé(e)s de l'impôt (SEI)
#800, 233 Gilmour St., Ottawa ON K2P 0P2
Tel: 613-235-6704; *Fax:* 613-234-7290
communications@ute-sei.org
www.ute-sei.org
www.youtube.com/user/utesei
www.facebook.com/UnionofTaxationEmployees
twitter.com/utesei
To represent employees of Canada Revenue Agency
Marc Brière, National President

Union of Veterans' Affairs Employees (UVAE) / Syndicat des employé(e)s des affaires des anciens combattants (SEAC)
#703, 233 Gilmour St., Ottawa ON K2P 0P2
Tel: 613-560-5460; *Fax:* 613-237-8282
www.uvae-seac.ca
To represent the interests of employees of Veterans' Affairs Canada
Virginia Vaillancourt, National President

UNITE HERE
275 - 7th Ave., New York NY 10001-6708 USA
Tel: 212-265-7000
unitehere.org
www.instagram.com/unitehere
www.facebook.com/UniteHere
twitter.com/unitehere
To represent workers in the following major sectors: apparel & textile manufacturing, apparel distribution centers, apparel retail, industrial laundries, hotels, casinos, foodservice, airport concessions & restaurants
D. Taylor, President
Nia Winston, General Vice-President
Gwen Mills, Scretary-Treasurer

UNITE HERE Canada
12836 - 146th St. NW, Edmonton AB T5L 2H7
Tel: 780-453-2607; *Fax:* 780-426-5098
info@uniterehecanada.ca
unitehere.org/affiliates/unite-here-canada-headquarters
To organize & represent individuals who work in the hospitality, gaming, food service, manufacturing, textile, laundry & airport industries
Ian Robb, Canadian Director

United Brotherhood of Carpenters & Joiners of America (AFL-CIO/CLC) / Fraternité unie des charpentiers et menuisiers d'Amérique (FAT-COI/CTC)
101 Constitution Ave. NW, Washington DC 20001 USA
Tel: 202-546-6206; *Fax:* 202-543-5724
www.carpenters.org
www.instagram.com/ubcja
www.facebook.com/CarpentersUnited
twitter.com/UBCJA_Official
Douglas J. McCarron, General President

United Food & Commercial Workers Canada (UFCW CANADA)
#300, 61 International Blvd., Toronto ON M9W 6K4
Tel: 416-675-1104; *Fax:* 416-675-6919
ufcw@ufcw.ca
www.ufcw.ca
www.youtube.com/user/UFCWCanada
www.facebook.com/ufcwcanada
twitter.com/ufcwcanada
One of Canada's largest private sector unions

Paul Meinema, National President

United Food & Commercial Workers' International Union (UFCW) / Union internationale des travailleurs et travailleuses unis de l'alimentation et du commerce
1775 K St. NW, Washington DC 20006 USA
Tel: 202-223-3111; Fax: 202-466-1562
ufcw@ufcw.ca
www.ufcw.org
www.youtube.com/UFCWInternational
www.facebook.com/ufcwinternational
twitter.com/UFCW
To empower workers to unite & find their voice
Marc Perrone, International President
Shaun Barclay, International Secretary-Treasurer

United Mine Workers of America (CLC) / Mineurs unis d'Amérique (CTC)
#200, 18354 Quantico Gateway Dr., Triangle VA 22172-1179 USA
Tel: 703-291-2400
info@umwa.org
umwa.org
www.youtube.com/user/UMWAunion
www.facebook.com/UMWAunion
twitter.com/mineworkers
Cecil Roberts, President

United Steelworkers of America (AFL-CIO/CLC) / Métallurgistes unis d'Amérique (FAT-COI/CTC)
60 Blvd. of the Allies, Pittsburgh PA 15222 USA
Tel: 412-562-2400
webmaster@uswa.org
www.usw.org
www.youtube.com/steelworkers
www.facebook.com/steelworkers
twitter.com/steelworkers
To represent workmen & working women in various industries
Thomas Conway, President
John Shinn, Secretary-Treasurer

Winnipeg Association of Non-Teaching Employees (WANTE) / Association des employés non enseignants de Winnipeg
#111, 1555 St. James St., Winnipeg MB R3H 1B5
Tel: 204-953-0250; Fax: 204-953-0259
wante@wante.org
www.wante.org
To act as a bargaining agent for members to help regulate relations between members & their employers
Gale Hladik, President

Yukon Employees Union (YEU) / Syndicat des employés du Yukon
#201, 2285 - 2nd Ave., Whitehorse YT Y1A 1C9
Tel: 867-667-2331; Fax: 867-667-6521
Toll-Free: 888-938-2331
contact@yeu.ca
www.yeu.ca
www.youtube.com/user/YukonEmployeesUnion
www.facebook.com/YukonEmployeesUnion
twitter.com/YEUPSAC
To obtain for all members the best possible standards of wages, salaries & other conditions of employment; To protect the interests, rights & privileges of all such employees
Steve Geick, President

Yukon Federation of Labour (YFL) / Fédération du travail du Yukon
#102, 106 Strickland St., Whitehorse YT Y1A 2J5
Tel: 867-456-8250; Fax: 867-668-3426
yfl@yukonfed.com
www.yukonfed.com
www.facebook.com/yukonworkers
twitter.com/yukonworkers
To advocate on behalf of its memebers
Vikki Quocksister, President

Landscape Architecture

Alberta Association of Landscape Architects (AALA)
#248, 17008 90 Ave. NW, Edmonton AB T5T 1L6
Tel: 780-435-9902; Fax: 780-435-9902
aala@aala.ab.ca
www.aala.ab.ca
To advance the quality of the professional practice of landscape architecture in Alberta
Todd Reade, Executive Director
Mark Nolan, Registrar

Association des architectes paysagistes du Québec (AAPQ)
#406, 420, rue McGill, Montréal QC H2Y 2G1
Tél: 514-526-6385; Téléc: 514-526-6385
info@aapq.org
www.aapq.org
www.facebook.com/pageaapq
twitter.com/AAPQ_paysages
Promouvoir la création et la valorisation du paysage en milieu naturel et construit dans le but de constituer un cadre de vie sain, fonctionnel, esthétique, axé sur les besoins de la population et répondant aux exigences écologiques
Édith Normandeau, Directrice générale par intérim

Atlantic Provinces Association of Landscape Architects (APALA)
PO Box 38051, Stn. Burnside, Dartmouth NS B3B 1X2
info@apala.ca
www.apala.ca
To promote, improve & advance the profession; To maintain standards of professional practice & conduct consistent with the need to serve & to protect the public interest; To support improvement &/or conservation of the natural, cultural, social & built environment
Matthew Mills, President
Angela Morin, Secretary-Treasurer

British Columbia Society of Landscape Architects (BCSLA)
#450, 355 Burrard St., Vancouver BC V6C 2G8
Tel: 604-682-5610; Toll-Free: 855-682-5610
admin@bcsla.org
www.bcsla.org
www.facebook.com/BCSocietyofLandscapeArchitects
twitter.com/BCSLA
To promote, improve & advance the profession; To maintain standards of professional practice & conduct consistent with the need to serve & protect the public interest; To support the improvement &/or conservation of the natural, cultural, social & built environment
Tara Culham, Executive Director

Canadian Society of Landscape Architects (CSLA) / Association des architectes paysagistes du Canada (AAPC)
12 Forillon Cres., Ottawa ON K2M 2S5
Tel: 866-781-9799; Fax: 866-871-1419
info@csla.ca
www.csla.ca
www.instagram.com/csla_aapc
www.linkedin.com/company/canadian-society-of-landscape-archi tects
www.facebook.com/CSLA.AAPC
To support the improvement &/or conservation of the natural, cultural, social & built environment; to promote visibility, recognition, acceptance & understanding of the profession by communicating its value in relation to that of the public good
Michelle Legault, Executive Director

Manitoba Association of Landscape Architects (MALA)
131 Callum Cres., Winnipeg MB R2G 2C7
Tel: 204-663-4863; Fax: 204-668-5662
www.mala.net
To promote, improve & advance the profession; to maintain standards of professional practice & conduct consistent with the need to serve & protect public interest; to support improvement &/or conservation of the natural, cultural, social & built environment
Monica Giesbrecht, President

Northwest Territories Association of Landscape Architects (NWTALA)
PO Box 1394, Yellowknife NT X1A 2P1
Tel: 867-920-2986; Fax: 867-920-2986
atborow@internorth.com
www.csla-aapc.ca/society/nwtala
To represent landscape architects in the Northwest Territories

Nunavut Association of Landscape Architects (NuALA)
PO Box 58, Iqaluit NU X0A 0H0
nualainfo@gmail.com
Jim Floyd, President

Ontario Association of Landscape Architects (OALA)
#506, 3 Church St., Toronto ON M5E 1M2
Tel: 416-231-4181; Fax: 416-231-2679
oala@oala.ca
www.oala.ca
www.facebook.com/109687249113317
twitter.com/OALA_ON

To promote, improve & advance the landscape architecture profession; To maintain standards of professional practice & conduct consistent with the need to serve & to protect the public interest; To support improvement &/or conservation of the natural, cultural, social & built environment
Doris Chee, President
Aina Budrevics, Executive Director
Ingrid Little, Registrar
Sarah Manteuffel, Coordinator

Saskatchewan Association of Landscape Architects (SALA)
PO Box 20015, Regina SK S4P 4J7
www.sala.sk.ca
To promote, improve, & advance the profession of landscape architecture; To maintain standards of professional practice & conduct
Laureen Snook, President

Language, Linguistics, Literature

ABC Life Literacy Canada
#604, 110 Eglinton Ave. East, Toronto ON M4P 2Y1
Tel: 416-218-0010; Fax: 416-218-0457
Toll-Free: 800-303-1004
info@abclifeliteracy.ca
abclifeliteracy.ca
www.facebook.com/abclifeliteracy
twitter.com/abclifeliteracy
To inspire Canadians to increase their literacy skills
Mack Rogers, Executive Director

L'arc-en-ciel littéraire
CP 180, Succ. C, Montréal QC H2L 4K1
arcenciellitteraire@yahoo.ca
arcenciellitteraire.site.voila.fr
Promouvoit la littérature gaie et des auteurs gais
Réjean Roy, Président fondateur

Association canadienne de traductologie (ACT) / Canadian Association for Translation Studies (CATS)
info@act-cats.ca
www.act-cats.ca
Société savante qui regroupe des chercheurs, des professeurs et des praticiens qui se consacrent ou s'intéressent à l'étude ou à l'enseignement de la traduction et des disciplines apparentées
Christine York, Président
Julie McDonough Dolmaya, Secrétaire

Association of Canadian Corporations in Translation & Interpretation (ACCTI) / Association canadienne de compagnies de traductions et d'interpretation
#306, 421 Bloor St. East, Toronto ON M4W 3T1
Tel: 416-975-5000; Fax: 416-975-0505
english_info@accti.org
www.accti.org
To unite the Canadian translation industry, providing a quality standard to protect the public & service providers alike; to arrange for arbitration in the event of a dispute; to operate in the best interest of members
Paul Penzo, President
Maryse M. Benhoff, Vice-President

Association of Translators & Interpreters of Alberta (ATIA) / Association des traducteurs et interprètes de l'Alberta
PO Box 546, Stn. Main, Edmonton AB T5J 2K8
Tel: 780-434-8384
www.atia.ab.ca
To protect the interests of its members
Hellen Martinez, President

Association of Translators & Interpreters of Nova Scotia (ATINS) / Association des traducteurs et interprètes de la nouvelle-écosse
PO Box 372, Halifax NS B3J 2P8
info@atins.org
www.atins.org
To ensure that clients have access to a body of qualified professionals; to promote the profession & the development of its members
Bassima Jurdak O'Brien, President

Association of Translators & Interpreters of Ontario (ATIO) / Association des traducteurs et interprètes de l'Ontario
#1202, 1 Nicholas St., Ottawa ON K1N 7B7
Tel: 613-241-2846; *Fax:* 613-241-4098
Toll-Free: 800-234-5030
info@atio.on.ca
www.atio.on.ca
To promote a high degree of professionalism & to protect the interest of those who use the language services provided by its members; To organize professional development activities & to encourage exchanges among its members
Philippe Ramsay, Executive Director

Association of Translators & Interpreters of Saskatchewan (ATIS) / Association des traducteurs et interprètes de la Saskatchewan
SK
atisask.ca
To provide a collective voice for members; To ensure that members exercise the profession in accordance with their code of ethics; To administer admission procedures of national certification examination; To provide a list of current certified members
Estelle Bonetto, President

Association of Translators, Terminologists & Interpreters of Manitoba (ATIM) / Association des traducteurs, terminologues et des interprètes du Manitoba
PO Box 83, 200 Cathédrale Ave., Winnipeg MB R2H 0H7
Tel: 204-797-3247
info@atim.mb.ca
www.atim.mb.ca
To provide a collective voice for its members, ensure that members exercise their profession in accordance with its Code of Ethics, & protect the public interest by ensuring the quality of the services rendered by its members
Vacant, President
Vacant, Vice-President
Karine Doiron, Secretary
Carole Meneghel, Treasurer

Association of Visual Language Interpreters of Canada (CASLI) / Association des interprètes en langage visuel du Canada
#562, 125A - 1030 Denman St., Vancouver BC V6G 2M6
Tel: 778-874-3165
avlic@avlic.ca
www.avlic.ca
www.youtube.com/user/TheAVLIC
www.facebook.com/candacasli
twitter.com/AVLIC_Canada
To represent interpreters whose working languages are English & American Sign Language (ASL); To promote high standards & uniformity within the profession of interpreting
Wayne Nicholson, President
Becky Stuckless, Vice-President
Anne Websdale, Treasurer

Association québécoise des enseignants de français langue seconde (AQEFLS) / Québec Association of Teachers of French as a Second Language
#350, 5165, ch Queen-Mary, Montréal QC H3W 1X7
Tél: 438-764-6470
info@aqefls.org
www.aqefls.org
www.facebook.com/groups/362001934314
twitter.com/aqefls
Promouvoir l'enseignement du français langue seconde et les aspects qui s'y rattachent; coordonner et encourager les recherches d'ordre pratique dans le domaine de la pédagogie et dans tout autre domaine touchant l'enseignement du français langue seconde; permettre la diffusion des derniers développements de la recherche et les techniques dans le domaine de l'enseignement du français langue seconde
Louise Outland, Présidente
Neli Guedova, Secrétaire générale

Bronte Historical Society (BHS)
7 West Rivers St., Oakville ON L6L 6N9
Tel: 905-825-5552
info@brontehistoricalsociety.ca
www.brontehistoricalsociety.ca
www.facebook.com/478210789179044
To bring closer together all who honour the Brontë sisters; To act as the guardian of such letters, writings & personal belongings as could be acquired for the Museum; To dispel legend & false sentiments regarding the Brontë story

Canadian Association for Commonwealth Literature & Language Studies (CACLALS) / Association canadienne pour l'étude des langues et de la littérature du Commonwealth
info@caclals.ca
caclals.ca
twitter.com/caclals_ca
To promote the study of Commonwealth literature in Canada; To encourage the reading of Canadian literature abroad
Asma Sayed, President
Jesse Arsenault, Secretary-Treasurer

Canadian Comparative Literature Association (CCLA) / Association canadienne de littérature comparée (ACLC)
c/o Markus Reisenleitner, Department of Humanities, York University, 217 Vanier College, Toronto ON M3H 1P3
complit.ca
Karin Beeler, President
Susan Ingram, Vice-President
Pascal Gin, Secretary
Markus Reisenleitner, Treasurer

Canadian Linguistic Association (CLA) / Association canadienne de linguistique (ACL)
c/o Craigie Hall, University of Calgary, 2500 University Dr. NW, #D310, Calgary AB T2N 1N4
www.cla-acl.ca
To advance scientific study of linguistics & language in Canada
Dennis Ryan Storoshenko, Secretary
Arsalan Kahnemuyipour, Treasurer

Canadian Parents for French (CPF)
#1104, 170 Laurier Ave. West, Ottawa ON K1P 5V5
Tel: 613-235-1481; *Fax:* 613-230-5940
cpf@cpf.ca
cpf.ca
www.youtube.com/user/CPFNational1977
www.facebook.com/CanadianParentsForFrench
twitter.com/CPFNational
To provide educational opportunities for young Canadians to learn & use the French language; To recognize & support English & French as Canada's two official languages; To create & promote opportunities for young Canadians to learn & use French as a second language
Nicole Thibault, National Executive Director
Cathy Stone, Director, Operations & Human Resources

Canadian Translators, Terminologists & Interpreters Council (CTTIC) / Conseil des traducteurs, terminologues et interprètes du Canada (CTTIC)
#1202, 1 Nicholas St., Ottawa ON K1N 7B7
Tel: 613-562-0379; *Fax:* 613-562-0379
info@cttic.org
cttic.org
To ensure uniform standards for the practice of the profession; To make available to the public a body of reliable professionals in translation, terminology & interpretation
Alexandre Coutu, President
Natalia Terekhova, Secretary

Canadian Writers' Foundation Inc. (CWF) / La Fondation des écrivains canadiens inc.
PO Box 13281, Stn. Kanata, Ottawa ON K2K 1X4
Tel: 613-257-3831; *Fax:* 613-257-8348
info@canadianwritersfoundation.org
www.canadianwritersfoundation.org
Strives to continue building the capital fund through donations
Marianne Scott, President
Suzanne Williams, Executive Secretary

Centre interdisciplinaire de recherches sur les activités langagières (CIRAL)
Pavillon Charles-de-Koninck, Université Laval, #2260-A, Faculté des lettres, Québec QC G1V 0A6
Tél: 418-656-2131; *Téléc:* 418-656-2622
www.lli.ulaval.ca/recherche/groupes-et-laboratoires
Le Centre interdisciplinaire de recherches sur les activités langagières (CIRAL) regroupe cinq équipes régulières, une vingtaine de chercheurs et quelque soixante-dix étudiants de deuxième et troisième cycles. Tous partagent la même conception des questions linguistiques : la langue est indissociable de l'histoire et de la culture des groupes qui la parlent, et elle évolue en fonction des contacts interethniques et des pressions socioculturelles qui s'exercent sur elle
Aline Francoeur, Directrice

Copian
Sterling House, 767 Brunswick St., Fredericton NB E3B 1H8
Tel: 506-457-6900; *Fax:* 506-457-6910
Toll-Free: 800-720-6253
contact@copian.ca
www.copian.ca
twitter.com/Copian_E
To provide an information network, in both official languages; to support the Canadian literacy community: adult learners, practitioners, organizations & governments
Bill Stirling, CEO

Corporation des traducteurs, traductrices, terminologues et interprètes du Nouveau-Brunswick (CTINB) / Corporation of Translators, Terminologists & Interpreters of New Brunswick
CP 427, Fredericton NB E3B 4Z9
Tél: 506-458-1519
ctinb@nbnet.nb.ca
www.ctinb.nb.ca
Donner à ses membres une voix collective; promouvoir le perfectionnement professionnel de ses membres; veiller à ce que ses membres respectent son Code de déontologie; faire connaître le rôle professionnel de ses membres dans la société; protéger l'intérêt public en faisant subir des examens d'admission à la CTINB et d'agrément des membres ainsi qu'en examinant les plaintes reçues à l'égard des membres; entretenir des liens avec les organismes semblables et avec les établissements de formation universitaire dans les domaines de la traduction, de la terminologie et de l'interprétation

Esperanto Association of Canada (KEA) / Association canadienne d'esperanto
#414, 110 Grand Ave., London ON N6C 1L8
esperanto.ca
To promote & teach the neutral international language of Esperanto
Paul Hopkins, President

Fédération québécoise du loisir littéraire (FQLL)
4545, av Pierre-de Coubertin, Montréal QC H1V 0B2
Tél: 514-252-3033; *Ligne sans frais:* 866-533-3755
fqll.ca
Offre au grand public l'accès à toutes les formes de l'expression littéraire et artistique dans un contexte de loisir, d'éducation et de perfectionnement
Diane Robert, Présidente
Serge Larochelle, Vice Présidente
Lisa D'amico, Secrétaire-Trésorière

International Literacy Association (ILA)
PO Box 8139, Newark DE 19714-8139 USA
Tel: 302-731-1600; *Fax:* 302-731-1057
Toll-Free: 800-336-7323
customerservice@reading.org
www.literacyworldwide.org
www.instagram.com/ilatoday
www.linkedin.com/company/international-literacy-association
www.facebook.com/InternationalLiteracyAssociation
twitter.com/ILAToday
To promote high levels of literacy for all; To improve the quality of reading instruction through study; To encourage a lifetime reading habit; To advocate for policy, curriculum & education reform that supports both teachers & learners; To foster & encourage collaboration among professionals on an international scale
Marcie Craig Post, Executive Director

Jane Austen Society of North America (JASNA)
Toronto ON
Tel: 206-739-6225
info@jasna.org
www.jasna.org
www.facebook.com/JaneAustenSocietyofNorthAmerica
To promote an appreciation of Jane Austen & her writings
Phyllis Ferguson, Canadian Membership Secretary

Languages Canada / Langues Canada
c/o Member Services, 27282 - 12B Ave., Aldergrove BC V4W 2P6
Tel: 604-625-1532
info@languagescanada.ca
www.languagescanada.ca
www.instagram.com/langcanada
www.linkedin.com/company/languages-canada
www.facebook.com/languagescanada
twitter.com/LangCanada
To promote quality, accredited English & French language training in Canada, & to represent Canada as a destination for excellent English & French language training
Gonzalo Peralta, Executive Director

Literary Translators' Association of Canada (LTAC) / Association des traducteurs et traductrices littéraires du Canada (ATTLC)
Concordia University, 1455, boul Maisonneuve ouest, #LB631.03, Montréal QC H3G 1M8

Tel: 514-848-2424
info@attlc-ltac.org
www.attlc-ltac.org
www.facebook.com/ATTLC.LTAC
twitter.com/attlc_ltac
To promote literary translation & interests of literary translators
Bilal Hashmi, President

L.M. Montgomery Institute (LMMI)
University of Prince Edward Island, 550 University Ave., Charlottetown PE C1A 4P3

Tel: 902-628-4346; *Fax:* 902-628-4305
lmmi@upei.ca
www.lmmontgomery.ca
www.facebook.com/LMMInstitute
twitter.com/LMMI_PEI
To focus on scholarship & teaching, while providing resources & educational opportunities to students & scholars researching the life, works & influence of L.M. Montgomery
Mark Leggott, Chair

Ordre des traducteurs, terminologues et interprètes agréés du Québec (OTTIAQ)
#1108, 2021, rue Union, Montréal QC H3A 2S9

Tél: 514-845-4411; *Fax:* 514-845-9903
Ligne sans frais: 800-265-4815
info@ottiaq.org
www.ottiaq.org
L'OTTIAQ assure la protection du public en octroyant les titres de traducteur agréé, de terminologue agréé et d'interprète agréé, en veillant au respect de son code de déontologie et des normes professionnelles et en mettant en ouvre les mécanismes prévus au Code des professions.
Johanne Boucher, Directrice générale

Quebec English Literacy Alliance (QELA)
PO Box 3542, #236, 410, rue St-Nicholas, Montréal QC H2Y 2P5

Tel: 450-242-2360; *Fax:* 450-242-2543
Toll-Free: 866-942-7352
info@qela.qc.ca
qela.qc.ca
To be the unified voice of Quebec English literacy providers nationally & provincially
Louise Quinn, Executive Director

Réseau pour le développement de l'alphabétisme et des compétences (RESDAC)
#205, 235 ch Montréal, Ottawa ON K1L 6C7

Tél: 613-749-5333; *Téléc:* 613-749-2252
Ligne sans frais: 888-906-5666
info@resdac.net
www.resdac.net
www.facebook.com/128384640568102
Promouvoir l'alphabétisation en français au Canada; assurer une concertation des intervenantes en alphabétisation en français au Canada.
Normand Lévesque, Directeur général
Isabelle Salesse, Présidente
Donald Desroches, Vice-président

Saskatchewan Elocution & Debate Association (SEDA) / Association d'élocution et des débats de la Saskatchewan
1860 Lorne St., Regina SK S4P 2L7

Tel: 306-780-9243; *Fax:* 306-781-6021
info@saskdebate.com
www.saskdebate.com
www.facebook.com/sask.debate
twitter.com/SaskDebate
To foster debate & public speaking
Lorelie DeRoose, Executive Director

Saskatchewan Organization for Heritage Languages Inc. (SOHL)
2144 Cornwall St., Regina SK S4P 2K7

Tel: 306-780-9275; *Fax:* 306-780-9407
sohl@sasktel.net
www.heritagelanguages.sk.ca
www.linkedin.com/in/sohl-sk-aa554151
www.facebook.com/sohl.sask
twitter.com/sohl_sk
To promote & develop teaching of heritage languages in Saskatchewan; to act in advocacy capacity to make representation to government, institutions & boards regarding matters pertaining to heritage languages; to promote cooperation with & mutual support of provincial organizations with similar

aims & objectives; to encourage inter-provincial & national liaison
Tamara Ruzic, Executive Director

Société québécoise d'espéranto (SQE) / Québec Esperanto Society (QES)
6358A, rue de Bordeaux, Montréal QC H2G 2R8

www.esperanto.qc.ca
Faire connaître et aider à l'apprentissage de l'espéranto; organiser des rencontres et favoriser l'utilisation de la langue; présenter les avantages de la langue et le mouvement mondial
Normand Fleury, Président
Sylvano Auclair, Secrétaire-trésorier

Society of Translators & Interpreters of British Columbia (STIBC)
#400, 1501 West Broadway, Vancouver BC V6J 4Z6

Tel: 604-684-2940
www.stibc.org
www.linkedin.com/groups/135809
www.facebook.com/200542026628804
twitter.com/STIBC2012
To promote the interests of translators & interpreters in BC; To serve the public by applying a Code of Ethics members must comply with, by setting & maintaining high professional standards through education & certification
Michael Radano, Chief Executive Officer

Stephen Leacock Associates
PO Box 854, Orillia ON L3V 6K8

Tel: 705-835-3218; *Fax:* 705-835-5171
www.leacock.ca
www.facebook.com/1480603219155484
twitter.com/leacockmedal
To honour & promote Stephen Leacock & his body of writing
Michael Hill, President

Law

The Advocates' Society
#2700, 250 Yonge St., Toronto ON M5B 2L7

Tel: 416-597-0243; *Fax:* 416-597-1588
Toll-Free: 888-597-0243
mail@advocates.ca
www.advocates.ca
www.linkedin.com/company/1311912
www.facebook.com/TheAdvocatesSociety
twitter.com/Advocates_Soc
To teach the skills & ethics of advocacy through information sharing, educational programs, seminars, conferences & workshops; To speak out on behalf of advocates; To protect the right to representation by an independent bar; To initiate appropriate reforms to the legal system
Vicki White, Executive Director

Alberta Association of Police Governance (AAPG)
PO Box 36098, Stn. Lakeview Post Office, Calgary AB T3E 7C6

Tel: 587-892-7874
admin@aapg.ca
www.aapg.ca
To support excellence in civilian governance & oversight of policing services in Alberta

Alberta Civil Trial Lawyers' Association (ACTLA)
#550, 10055 - 106 St., Edmonton AB T5J 2Y2

Tel: 780-429-1133; *Fax:* 780-429-1199
Toll-Free: 800-665-7248
admin@actla.com
www.actla.com
To advocate for a strong civil justice system that protects the rights of all Albertans
Sandy Leske, Executive Director
Maureen McCartney-Cameron, President

Alberta Federation of Police Associations (AFPA)
10150 - 97 Ave. NW, Edmonton AB T5K 2T5

Tel: 780-496-8600; *Fax:* 780-428-0374
www.albertapolice.ca
To represent the interests of members; To address the issues affecting local, provincial & national police associations
Michael Elliot, President

Alberta Law Foundation (ALF)
#980, 105 - 12 Ave. SE, Calgary AB T2G 1A1

Tel: 403-264-4701; *Fax:* 403-294-9238
info@albertalawfoundation.org
www.albertalawfoundation.org
To conduct research into & recommend reform of law & administration of justice in Alberta; To establish, maintain & operate law libraries; To contribute to legal education &

knowledge of people of Alberta; To provide assistance to Native people's legal & student programs
Deborah Duncan, Executive Director
Diana M. Porter, Administrative Assistant

Alberta Restorative Justice Association (ARJA)
PO Box 1053, Stn. Main, Edmonton AB T5J 2M1

Tel: 780-628-6801; *Toll-Free:* 800-601-7310
info@arja.ca
www.arja.ca
www.facebook.com/RJAlberta
twitter.com/RJAlberta
To be a collective voice to strengthen Restorative Justice in Alberta communities by establishing and providing information, education, and awareness towards best practices in Restorative Justice.
Barb Barclay, Chair

Association canadienne des juristes-traducteurs (ACJT) / Canadian Association of Legal Translators (CALT)
a/s OOTTIAQ, #1108, 2021, av Union, Montréal QC H3A 2S9

info@acjt.ca
acjt.ca
Pour promouvoir le double qualification comme avocat (ou juriste) et comme traducteur pour la traduction de documents juridiques
Louis Fortier, President

Association des juristes d'expression française de l'Ontario (AJEFO)
#1400, 85, rue Albert, Ottawa ON K1P 6A4

Tél: 613-842-7462; *Téléc:* 613-842-8389
bureau@ajefo.ca
www.ajefo.ca
www.youtube.com/c/CliquezJustice
www.linkedin.com/in/ajefo
www.facebook.com/ajefo
twitter.com/ajefo_justice
Représenter les intérêts des avocates, des avocats, des juges, des fonctionnaires de la justice, des professeures, des professeurs, des étudiantes et des étudiants en droit, et des autres participants et participantes du monde juridique, qui travaillent à la promotion des services juridiques en français sur le territoire de l'Ontario; viser à assurer un accès égal à la justice, sans pénalité, délai, obstacle ou hésitation à l'utilisation du français par l'appareil judiciaire, les membres du Barreau ou la population francophone de notre province
Marc Sauvé, Président
Andrée-Anne Martel, Directrice générale

Association des juristes d'expression française de la Saskatchewan (AJEFS) / French Jurists Association of Saskatchewan
#219, 1440, 9e av nord, Regina SK S4R 8B1

Tél: 306-924-8543; *Téléc:* 306-781-7916
Ligne sans frais: 855-924-8543
centre@saskinfojustice.ca
www.saskinfojustice.ca
www.instagram.com/ajefsjustice
www.facebook.com/saskinfojustice.ca
twitter.com/AJEFS1
Développer et promouvoir les droits et services en français auprès des instances juridiques et gouvernementales; informer et sensibiliser la population fransaskoise sur la vulgarisation des lois et l'utilisation des services juridiques en français
Romain Baudemont, Président

Association des policières et policiers provinciaux du Québec (APPQ) / Québec Provincial Police Association
1981, rue Léonard-De Vinci, Sainte-Julie QC J3E 1Y9

Tél: 450-922-5414; *Téléc:* 450-922-5417
info@appq-sq.qc.ca
www.appq-sq.qc.ca
Promouvoir le bien-être de ses membres et voir à leurs intérêts sociaux, moraux et culturels
Pierre Veilleux, Président
Jocelyn Boucher, Vice-président, Ressources humaines
Luc Fournier, Vice-président, Finances
Jacques Painchaud, Vice-président, Discipline et déontologie
Pierre Lemay, Vice-président, Griefs et formation
Daniel Rolland, Vice-président, Ress. matérielles et santé et sécurité du travail

Association of Legal Court Interpreters & Translators (ALCIT) / Association des traducteurs et interprètes judiciaires (ATIJ)
438, rue St-Antoine est, Montréal QC H2Y 1A5

Tel: 514-845-3113; *Fax:* 514-845-3006
admin@atij.ca
www.atij.ca

To provide translation & interpretation services, mainly for the Municipal Court of Montréal and the City of Montréal Police Department

Avocats sans frontières Canada (ASFC) / Lawyers Without Borders Canada (LWBC)
#230, 825, rue St-Joseph est, Québec QC G1K 3C8
Tél: 418-907-2607; Téléc: 418-948-2241
info@asfcanada.ca
www.asfcanada.ca
www.linkedin.com/company/avocats-sans-frontières-canada
www.facebook.com/asfcanada.ca
twitter.com/ASFCanada
Pour aider à défendre les droits humains dans les endroits où ils sont le plus négligés
Me Délia Cristea, Présidente, Conseil d'administration

Barreau de Montréal / Bar of Montréal
460, rue Saint-Gabriel, 2e étage, Montréal QC H2Y 2Z9
Tél: 514-866-9392; Téléc: 514-866-1488
info@barreaudemontreal.qc.ca
www.barreaudemontreal.qc.ca
Administrer une corporation professionnelle
Doris Larrivée, Directrice générale
Gislaine Dufault, Directrice des communications

Black Female Lawyers Network (BFLN)
PO Box 20010, 333 Bay St. West, Toronto ON M5H 2R0
info@bfln.ca
bfln.ca
www.instagram.com/black_female_lawyers_network
www.linkedin.com/groups/6501715
www.facebook.com/sistahs.inlaw
To advocate for diversity & inclusion in law; To support promotion, advancement & retention of black female lawyers; To empower marginalized youth; To celebrate & showcase the achievements of black female law professionals; To provide a safe forum for dialogue
Denise Dwyer, Founder & President

Black Law Students' Association of Canada (BLSA) / L'Association des etudiants noirs en droit du Canada
admin@blsacanada.com
blsacanada.com
www.facebook.com/blsacanada
To support & enhance academic & professional opportunities for black law students in both official languages
Tiana Knight, President

British Columbia Law Institute (BCLI)
University of British Columbia, 1822 East Mall, Vancouver BC V6T 1Z1
Tel: 604-822-0142; Fax: 604-822-0144
Toll-Free: 800-565-5297
bcli@bcli.org
www.bcli.org
www.linkedin.com/company/2281377
www.facebook.com/BCLawInstitute
twitter.com/BCLawInstitute
To perform research & studies to change & modernize law in British Columbia
Kathleen Cunningham, Executive Director
Krista James, National Director

British Columbia Police Association
c/o 1819 Victoria Diversion, Vancouver BC V5N 2K2
Tel: 604-685-6486
contact@bc-pa.ca
www.bc-pa.ca
To represent the interests of its members
Tom Stamatakis, President

British Columbia Public Interest Advocacy Centre (BCPIAC)
#208, 1090 West Pender St., Vancouver BC V6E 2N7
Tel: 604-687-3063; Fax: 604-682-7896
support@bcpiac.com
www.bcpiac.com
www.facebook.com/443550842340768
twitter.com/BCPIAC
To advance the interests of groups that are generally unrepresented or underrepresented in issues of major public concern, such as welfare, disability, human, farmworkers & consumers rights
Tannis Braithwaite, Executive Director
Grace Matsutani, Administrator

Canadian Association of Black Lawyers (CABL) / L'Association des Avocats Noirs du Canada
#300, 20 Toronto St., Toronto ON M5C 2B8
info@cabl.ca
www.cabl.ca
www.linkedin.com/groups/3951435
www.facebook.com/150574661678680
twitter.com/cablnational
To bring together law professionals & other interested Canadians to cultivate & maintain the Association of Black Professionals in Canada
Shawn Richard, President
Rosemarie Mercury, Vice President
Esi Codjoe, Secretary
Charlene Theodore, Treasurer

Canadian Association of Chiefs of Police (CACP) / Association canadienne des chefs de police (ACCP)
#100, 300 Terry Fox Dr., Ottawa ON K2K 0E3
Tel: 613-595-1101; Fax: 613-383-0372
cacp@cacp.ca
www.cacp.ca
To encourage & develop cooperation among all Canadian police organizations & members in pursuit & attainment of common objects to create & develop the highest standards of efficiency in law enforcement through the fostering & encouragement of police training, education & research; To promote & maintain a high standard of ethics, integrity, honour & conduct in profession of law enforcement; To encourage & advance the study of modern & progressive practices in prevention & detection of crime; To foster uniformity of police practices & cooperation for the protection & security of the people of Canada
William Moore, Executive Director

Canadian Association of Counsel to Employers (CACE) / Association canadienne des avocats d'employeurs (ACAE)
c/o Tracy Scanks, Pro Conference Advantage, 19750 - 50th Ave., Langley BC V3A 4J2
Tel: 604-427-1491
www.counseltoemployers.ca
www.linkedin.com/groups/2681581
twitter.com/CACE_Assoc
To promote excellence in labour & employment law; To engage in legislation & law reform lobbying at the provincial & federal level
Tracy Scanks, Executive Director

Canadian Association of Crown Counsel (CACC) / Association canadienne des juristes de l'État (ACJE)
#700, 1625 Grafton St., Halifax NS B3J 0E8
Tel: 902-424-8734
info@cacc-acje.ca
www.cacc-acje.ca
To represent the collective interests of its members on a national level
Rick Woodburn, President

Canadian Association of Provincial Court Judges (CAPCJ) / L'Association canadienne des juges de cours provinciales
c/o Executive Secretary, Provincial Court of Newfoundland & Labrador, PO Box 1060, Whiteway Dr., Wabush NL A0R 1B0
Tel: 709-282-6617; Fax: 709-282-6905
www.judges-juges.ca
To ensure the soundness of provincial & territorial courts across Canada; To promote judicial independence & the rule of law
Joseph De Filippis, Treasurer
Wynne Anne Trahey, Executive Secretary

Canadian Association of Refugee Lawyers
281 Eglinton Ave. East, Toronto ON M4P 1L3
info@carl-acaadr.ca
www.carl-acaadr.ca
www.facebook.com/CARLadvocates
twitter.com/CARLadvocates
To advocate for the rights of refugees & forced migrants; To research issues related to refugees; To promote equitable practices in the treatment of refugees in Canada
Mitchell Goldberg, President

Canadian Bar Association (CBA) / Association du barreau canadien (ABC)
#1200, 66 Slater St., Ottawa ON K1P 5H1
Tel: 613-237-2925; Fax: 613-237-0185
Toll-Free: 800-267-8860
info@cba.org
www.cba.org
www.youtube.com/user/cbaspin
www.linkedin.com/company/canadian-bar-association
www.facebook.com/CanadianBarAssociation
twitter.com/CBA_News
To promote improvements in the law; To promote improvements in the administration of justice; To promote individual lawyer training; To advocate in the public interest; To represent the profession on a national & international level; To promote the interests of the CBA; To promote equality in the profession
Cheryl Farrow, Chief Executive Officer
Susan Landry, Director, Human Resources & Office Administration

Canadian Corporate Counsel Association (CCCA) / Association canadienne des conseillers juridiques d'entreprises
#1210, 20 Toronto St., Toronto ON M5C 2B8
Tel: 416-869-0522; Fax: 416-869-0946
ccca@ccca-cba.org
www.ccca-accje.org
twitter.com/CCCA_News
To provide quality education, information & other services & resources of specific interest to corporate counsel in Canada, & to facilitate communication & networking among such counsel
Christine Staley, Executive Director

Canadian Council on International Law (CCIL) / Conseil canadien de droit international (CCDI)
275 Bay St., Ottawa ON K1R 5Z5
Tel: 613-235-0442; Fax: 613-232-8228
ccil-ccdi@intertaskconferences.com
www.ccil-ccdi.ca
www.linkedin.com/company/canadian-council-on-international-law
www.twitter.com/ccil_ccdi
To bring together scholars of international law & organizations engaged in teaching & research at Canadian universities; To encourage & conduct studies in international law with a view to its progressive development & codification; To foster the study of legal aspects of Canada's international problems & to advocate their solution in accordance with existing or developing principles of international law
Céline Lévesque, President

Canadian Criminal Justice Association (CCJA) / Association canadienne de justice pénale (ACJP)
#101, 320 Parkdale Ave., Ottawa ON K1Y 4X9
Tel: 613-725-3715; Fax: 613-725-3720
ccja-acjp@ccja-acjp.ca
www.ccja-acjp.ca
www.facebook.com/ccjacjp
twitter.com/AcjpCcja
To promote a humane, equitable & effective criminal justice system in Canada
Angela Falk, President
Irving Kulik, Executive Director

Canadian Institute for the Administration of Justice (CIAJ) / Institut canadien d'administration de la justice (ICAJ)
Faculté de droit, Univ. de Montréal, PO Box 6128, Stn. Centre-Ville, 3101, chemin de la Tour, #A-3421, Montréal QC H3C 3J7
Tel: 514-343-6157
ciaj@ciaj-icaj.ca
www.ciaj-icaj.ca
www.linkedin.com/company/ciaj-icaj
www.facebook.com/ciaj_icaj
twitter.com/ciaj_icaj
To improve the quality of justice for all Canadians
Christine O'Doherty, Executive Director
Isabelle Ligot, Manager, Communications

Canadian Law & Society Association (CLSA) / Association canadienne droit et société (ACDS)
www.acds-clsa.com
To encourage socio-legal inquiry both domestically & internationally
Nicole O'Byrne, President

The Canadian Maritime Law Association / L'Association canadienne de droit maritime
#900, 1000, rue de la Gauchetière ouest, Montréal QC H3B 5H4

Tel: 514-954-3184; *Fax:* 514-954-1905
cmla@cmla.org
www.cmla.org

To promote the study & advancement of maritime law in Canada; To promote the harmonization of maritime law internationally
Shelley Chapelski, President
Paul M. Harquail, National Vice-President
Robert C. Wilkins, Secretary-Treasurer

Chambre des notaires du Québec
#600, 1801, av McGill College, Montréal QC H3A 0A7

Tél: 514-879-1793; *Téléc:* 514-879-1923
Ligne sans frais: 800-263-1793
www.cnq.org
www.youtube.com/user/ChambreDesNotaires

D'assurer principalement la protection du public utilisateur des services professionnels de notaire.
Christian Tremblay, Directeur général

Community Legal Education Association (Manitoba) Inc. (CLEA) / Association d'éducation juridique communautaire (Manitoba) inc.
#205, 414 Graham Ave., Winnipeg MB R3C 0L8

Tel: 204-943-2382; *Fax:* 204-943-3600
mctroszko@communitylegal.mb.ca
www.communitylegal.mb.ca
www.facebook.com/339159352882635

To provide legal education & information programs to Manitobans
Mary Troszko, Executive Director
Geof Langen, President

Community Legal Education Ontario (CLEO)
#506, 180 Dundas St. West, Toronto ON M5G 1Z8

Tel: 416-408-4420; *Fax:* 416-408-4424
info@cleo.on.ca
www.cleo.on.ca

To provide public legal education services & programs that benefit the low income community, disadvantaged persons, such as immigrants & refugees, seniors, women, & injured workers in Ontario
Julie Mathews, Executive Director
Jane Withey, Director, Clinic Operations

Community Legal Information Association of Prince Edward Island (CLIA PEI)
Royalty Centre, #11, 40 Enman Cres., Charlottetown PE C1A 7K4

Tel: 902-892-0853; *Toll-Free:* 800-240-9798
clia@cliapei.ca
www.cliapei.ca
www.youtube.com/CLIAPEI
www.facebook.com/CLIAPEI
twitter.com/cliapei

To provide Islanders with understandable, useful information about the Canadian laws & the justice system
Warren Banks, President
David Daughton, Executive Director

Community Planning Association of Alberta (CPAA)
#205, 10940 - 166A St., Edmonton AB T5P 3V5

Tel: 780-432-6387; *Fax:* 780-452-7718
cpaa@cpaa.biz
www.cpaa.biz

The Community Planning Association of Alberta is an organization dedicated to the promotion of community planning in the Province of Alberta.
Gloria Wilkinson, Chair

Congress of Black Lawyers & Jurists of Québec
445, boul St-Laurent, 5e étage, Montréal QC H3S 2B8

Tel: 514-954-3471

Please call prior to visit

Continuing Legal Education Society of BC
#500, 1155 West Pender St., Vancouver BC V6E 2P4

Tel: 604-669-3544; *Fax:* 604-669-9260
Toll-Free: 800-663-0437
custserv@cle.bc.ca
www.cle.bc.ca
www.youtube.com/user/TheCLEBC
www.linkedin.com/company/continuing-legal-education-society-of-bc
www.facebook.com/clebc
www.twitter.com/clebc

To meet the present & future educational needs of the legal profession in British Columbia
Gwendoline C. Allison, Chair

Ronald G. Friesen, Chief Executive Officer

Criminal Lawyers' Association (CLA)
#1, 189 Queen St. East, Toronto ON M5A 1S2

Tel: 416-214-9875; *Fax:* 416-968-6818
admin@criminallawyers.ca
www.criminallawyers.ca

To be the voice for criminal justice & civil liberties in Canada
John Struthers, President
Anthony Laycock, Executive Director

Fédération des associations de juristes d'expression française de common law (FAJEF)
#1, 242, rue Goulet, Winnipeg MB R2H 0S2

Tél: 204-415-7551; *Téléc:* 204-415-4482
bureau@ajefa.ca
fajef.ca

Pour fournir un soutien et de représenter ses membres
Rénald Rémillard, Directeur général

Federation of Asian Canadian Lawyers (FACL)
#300, 20 Toronto St, Toronto ON M5C 2B8

communications@facl.ca
on.facl.ca

To promote equity, justice & opportunity for Asian Canadian legal professionals & the community

Federation of Law Reform Agencies of Canada (FOLRAC)
c/o Manitoba Law Reform Commission, 405 Broadway, 12th Fl., Winnipeg MB R3C 3L6

Tel: 604-822-0142; *Fax:* 604-822-0144
folracanada@gmail.com
www.folrac.com

Collection of 8 law reform agencies, from various provinces, who meet yearly to exchange information.
Greg Steele, President

Federation of Law Societies of Canada (FLSC) / Fédération des ordres professionnels de juristes du Canada
World Exchange Plaza, #1810, 45 O'Connor St., Ottawa ON K1P 1A4

Tel: 613-236-7272; *Fax:* 613-236-7233
info@flsc.ca
www.flsc.ca

To coordinate the law societies of Canada; To act as a voice for Canadian law societies
Jonathan G. Herman, Chief Executive Officer
Bob Linney, Director, Communications

Fondation du barreau du Québec
Maison du Barreau, 445, boul Saint-Laurent, Montréal QC H2Y 3T8

Tél: 514-954-3400; *Ligne sans frais:* 800-361-8495
information@barreau.qc.ca
www.barreau.qc.ca
www.linkedin.com/groups/2206718
www.facebook.com/barreauduquebec
twitter.com/BarreauduQuebec

Subventionner, primer et supporter des travaux axés vers l'intérêt public et utiles à la pratique du droit.
Bernard Synnott, Président

Foundation for Legal Research (FLR) / La foundation pour la recherche juridique
c/o Stephanie Elyea, Administrator, #500, 865 Carling Ave., Ottawa ON K1S 5S8

Toll-Free: 800-267-8860
foundationforlegalresearch.org

To support & maintain scholarships, bursaries & prizes in the field of legal research
Nicholas Kasirer, Chair
Francois Letourneaux, Secretary
Stephen Bresolin, Treasurer

Hamilton Police Association (HPA) / Association de la police de Hamilton
555 Upper Wellington St., Hamilton ON L9A 3P8

Tel: 905-574-6044; *Fax:* 905-574-3223
hpa@hpa.on.ca
www.hpa.on.ca

To promote high quality professional policing through labour relations & political activity
Brad Boyce, Administrator
Mike Cruse, Executive Officer

Institute of Law Clerks of Ontario (ILCO)
PO Box 44, #502, 20 Adelaide St. East, Toronto ON M5C 2T6

Tel: 416-214-6252; *Fax:* 416-214-6255
reception@ilco.on.ca
www.ilco.on.ca
www.linkedin.com/company/institute-of-law-clerks-of-ontario
www.facebook.com/InstituteLCO
twitter.com/InstituteLCO

To provide an organized network for promoting unity, cooperation & mutual assistance among law clerks in Ontario; to advance & protect their status & interests; to promote their education for the purpose of increasing their knowledge, efficiency & professional ability
Lisa Matchim, President
Karen Daly, Office Administrator

International Centre for Criminal Law Reform & Criminal Justice Policy (ICCLR)
1822 East Mall, Vancouver BC V6T 1Z1

Tel: 604-822-9875; *Fax:* 604-822-9317
icclr@allard.ubc.ca
www.icclr.law.ubc.ca
twitter.com/theicclr

To improve the quality of justice through reform of criminal law, policy & practice; To provide advice, information, research & proposals for policy development & legislation
Peter German, President & Executive Director

International Commission of Jurists (Canadian Section) (ICJ) / La Commission internationale de juristes (section canadienne) (CIJ)
#554, 57 Louis Pasteur Pvt., Ottawa ON K1S 5S8

Tel: 613-237-2925; *Fax:* 613-237-0185
info@icjcanada.org
www.icjcanada.org

To works internationally with the parent organization to monitor & promote the rule of law & the impartiality & independence of the judiciary in countries where these are threatened or non-existent; To act nationally & locally to promote awareness of these issues & human rights generally
Errol P. Mnedes, President
Stéphanie Plante, Executive Director

Iranian Canadian Legal Professionals (ICLP)
#200, 5700 Yonge St., Toronto ON M2M 4K2

Tel: 416-226-7260
contact@iclp.ca
www.iclp.ca
www.linkedin.com/company/iranian-canadian-legal-professionals
www.facebook.com/iclp.ca

To build & maintain a network of Iranian legal professionals in Canada; To establish mentorship programs & provide guidance; To promote & advocate for Iranian Canadian legal professionals

Law Foundation of British Columbia
#1340, 605 Robson St., Vancouver BC V6B 5J3

Tel: 604-688-2337; *Fax:* 604-688-4586
info@lawfoundationbc.org
www.lawfoundationbc.org

To allocate funds to programs that will benefit the general public of British Columbia; To act in accordance with The Legal Profession Act & distribute income in areas such as legal aid, law libraries, legal education, legal research & law reform; To conduct operations with recognition of the diverse population of British Columbia
Wayne Robertson, Executive Director
Jo-Anne Kaulius, Director, Finance

Law Foundation of Newfoundland & Labrador
PO Box 5907, #49, 55 Elizabeth Ave., St. John's NL A1C 5X4

Tel: 709-754-4424; *Fax:* 709-754-4320
lfnl@lawfoundationanl.com
www.lawfoundationnl.com

To provide grants that advance public understanding of the law & access to legal services, in the areas of: law libraries; legal research; legal education; scholarships for studies relevant to law; law reform; legal aid; & legal referral services
Lawrence E. Collins, Executive Director
Janet Kiely, Office Secretary

Law Foundation of Nova Scotia
Cogswell Tower, #1305, 2000 Barrington St., Halifax NS B3J 3K1

Tel: 902-422-8335; *Fax:* 902-492-0424
nslawfd@nslawfd.ca
www.nslawfd.ca

To establish & maintain a fund to be used for the examination, research, revision & reform of & public access to the law, legal education, the administration of justice in the province & any other purposes incidental or conducive to or consequential upon the attainment of any such objects
Kerry L. Oliver, Executive Director

Law Foundation of Ontario (LFO) / La fondation du droit de l'Ontario
PO Box 19, #3002, 20 Queen St. West, Toronto ON M5H 3R3
Tel: 416-598-1550; *Fax:* 416-598-1526
general@lawfoundation.on.ca
www.lawfoundation.on.ca
www.facebook.com/LawFoundationOn
twitter.com/LawFoundationOn
An organization that provides funding to a wide range of organizations to foster excellence in the work of lawyers, paralegals and other legal professionals.
Mark J. Sandler, Chair
Elizabeth Goldberg, Chief Executive Officer

Law Foundation of Prince Edward Island
49 Water St., Charlottetown PE C1A 7K2
Tel: 902-620-1763
info@lawfoundationpei.ca
www.lawfoundationpei.ca
To establish & maintain a fund & use the proceeds for the purposes of: legal education & research on law reform; the editing & printing of decisions of the Supreme Court & the Provincial Court of PEI; the promotion of legal aid; aid in the establishment, operation & maintenance of law libraries in PEI
Sheila Lund MacDonald, Executive Director

Law Foundation of Saskatchewan
#200, 2208 Scarth St., Regina SK S4P 2J6
Tel: 306-352-1121; *Fax:* 306-522-6222
www.lawfoundation.sk.ca
To maintain a fund to support legal aid, law reform, law libraries, legal education & legal research in Saskatchewan
Bob Watt, Executive Director
Eileen Libby, Chair

Law Society of Alberta (LSA)
#700, 333 - 11th Ave. SW, Calgary AB T2R 1P3
Tel: 403-229-4700; *Toll-Free:* 800-661-9003
www.lawsociety.ab.ca
www.linkedin.com/company/the-law-society-of-alberta
twitter.com/LawSocietyofAB
To serve the public by promoting a high standard of legal services & professional conduct through the governance & regulation of an independent legal profession; To govern all lawyers who practise law in Alberta; To admit lawyers to the Bar; To supervise professional conduct & disciplinary actions as required
Elizabeth Osler, Chief Executive Officer & Executive Director
Cori Ghitter, Deputy Executive Director & Director, Policy & Education
Nadine Meade, Chief Financial Officer
David Weyant, Chief Operating Officer
Brita Wahl, Director, Human Resources

Law Society of British Columbia
845 Cambie St., Vancouver BC V6B 4Z9
Tel: 604-669-2533; *Fax:* 604-669-5232
Toll-Free: 800-903-5300
TTY: 604-443-5700
communications@lsbc.org
www.lawsociety.bc.ca
www.youtube.com/user/lawsocietyofbc
www.linkedin.com/company/law-society-of-british-columbia
twitter.com/LawSocietyofBC
To ensure that the public is well served by a competent, honourable & independent legal profession
Don Avison, QC, CEO & Executive Director

Law Society of Manitoba (LSM) / La Société du Barreau du Manitoba
219 Kennedy St., Winnipeg MB R3C 1S8
Tel: 204-942-5571; *Fax:* 204-956-0624
admin@lawsociety.mb.ca
www.lawsociety.mb.ca
twitter.com/lawsocietymb
To ensure the public in Manitoba is well served by the legal profession
Kristin Dangerfield, CEO
Richard Porcher, Director, Admissions & Membership

Law Society of New Brunswick / Barreau du Nouveau-Brunswick
68 Avonlea Court, Fredericton NB E3C 1N8
Tel: 506-458-8540; *Fax:* 506-451-1421
general@lawsociety-barreau.nb.ca
www.lawsociety-barreau.nb.ca
The Law Society was officially created in 1846. The Provincial Legislative Assembly adopted Chapter 48 of the Provincial Statutes which in effect incorporated what was then called the "Barristers' Society" for the "purpose of securing in the Province a learned and honourable legal profession, for establishing order and good conduct among its members and for promoting knowledgeable development and reform of the law".

Hélène L. Beaulieu, President
Marc L. Richard, Executive Director

Law Society of Newfoundland & Labrador
PO Box 1028, 196-198 Water St., St. John's NL A1C 5M3
Tel: 709-722-4740; *Fax:* 709-722-8902
thelawsociety@lawsociety.nf.ca
www.lawsociety.nf.ca
To ensure that law students are appropriately educated and trained through articling and Bar Admission programs and exams, and provides continuing legal education to practititoners.
Brenda B. Grimes, Executive Director

Law Society of Nunavut (LSNU)
PO Box 149, Iqaluit NU X0A 0H0
Tel: 867-979-2330; *Fax:* 867-979-2333
administrator@lawsociety.nu.ca
lawsociety.nu.ca
To govern its membership & protect the public
Nalini Vaddapalli, CEO

Law Society of Ontario / Barreau de l'Ontario
Osgoode Hall, 130 Queen St. West, Toronto ON M5H 2N6
Tel: 416-947-3300; *Toll-Free:* 800-668-7380
TTY: 416-644-4886
lawsociety@lso.ca
www.lso.ca
www.youtube.com/c/LawSocietyofOntario
www.linkedin.com/company/law-society-of-ontario
www.facebook.com/LawSocietyLSO
twitter.com/LawsocietyLSO
To govern Ontario's lawyers & paralegals in the public interest by ensuring that the people of Ontario are served by lawyers & paralegals who meet high standards of learning, competence, & professional conduct
Diana Miles, Chief Executive Officer

Law Society of Prince Edward Island
PO Box 128, 49 Water St., Charlottetown PE C1A 7K2
Tel: 902-566-1666; *Fax:* 902-368-7557
lawsociety@lspei.pe.ca
www.lspei.pe.ca
To uphold & protect the public interest in the administration of justice; to establish standards for the education, professional responsibility & competence of members & applicants for membership; to ensure the independence, integrity & honour of the society & its members; to regulate the practice of law; to uphold & protect the interests of members.
Susan M. Robinson, Executive Director & Sec.-Treas.

Law Society of Saskatchewan
#1100, 2002 Victoria Ave., Regina SK S4P 0R7
Tel: 306-569-8242; *Fax:* 306-352-2989
reception@lawsociety.sk.ca
www.lawsociety.sk.ca
To govern the legal profession by upholding high standards of competence & integrity; ensuring the independence of the profession; advancing the administration of justice, the profession & the rule of law, all in the public interest
Donna Sigmeth, Deputy Director
Tim Huber, Counsel
Ruth Armstrong, Office Administrator

Law Society of the Northwest Territories / Le Barreau des Territoires du Nord-Ouest
Diamond Plaza, PO Box 1298, Stn. Main, 5204 - 50th Ave., 4th Fl., Yellowknife NT X1A 2N9
Tel: 867-873-3828; *Fax:* 867-873-6344
info@lawsociety.nt.ca
www.lawsociety.nt.ca
twitter.com/LawSocietyNWT
To serve the public by an independent, responsible & responsive legal profession
Pamela Naylor, Executive Director

Law Society of Yukon (LSY)
#202, 302 Steele St., Whitehorse YT Y1A 2C5
Tel: 867-668-4231; *Fax:* 867-667-7556
info@lawsocietyyukon.com
www.lawsocietyyukon.com
To govern legal profession in the Yukon.
Lynn Daffe, Executive Director

Legal Education Society of Alberta (LESA)
#2610, 10104 - 103 Ave., Edmonton AB T5J 0H8
Tel: 780-420-1987; *Fax:* 780-425-0885
Toll-Free: 800-282-3900
lesa@lesa.org
www.lesa.org
www.linkedin.com/company/legal-education-society-of-alberta
www.facebook.com/lesaonline
twitter.com/lesaonline

To educate providers of legal services in Alberta; To increase awareness of issues affecting the legal profession; To maintain & increase professional responsibility & competence; To develop & provide education in law, skills, & ethics
Christine Sanderman, Interim Executive Director

Legal Information Society of Nova Scotia (LISNS)
5523B Young St., Halifax NS B3K 1Z7
Tel: 902-454-2198; *Fax:* 902-455-3105
Toll-Free: 800-665-9779
lisns@legalinfo.org
www.legalinfo.org
www.facebook.com/LegalSeagull
twitter.com/LegalInfoNS
To provide Nova Scotians easy access to information & resources about the law
Kevin A. MacDonald, President

The Manitoba Law Foundation / La Fondation manitobaine du droit
#300, 207 Donald St., Winnipeg MB R3C 1M5
Tel: 204-947-3142; *Fax:* 204-942-3221
mblawfoundation@gatewest.net
manitobalawfoundation.org
To provide funds for legal education, legal research, legal aid, law reform & the establishment, operation & maintenance of law libraries
Barbara Palace Churchill, Executive Director

Migrant Workers Centre
#302, 119 West Pender St., Vancouver BC V6B 1S5
Tel: 604-669-4482; *Fax:* 604-669-6456
Toll-Free: 888-669-4482
info@mwcbc.ca
www.mwcbc.ca
To promote & advance access to justice for migrant workers by providing legal services, advocacy, research, & public education & engaging in law & policy reform initiatives
Natalie Drolet, Lawyer & Executive Director

Municipal Law Enforcement Officers' Association (MLEOA)
1 Carden St., Guelph ON N1H 3A1
Tel: 519-822-1260
mleo@mleoa.ca
www.mleoa.ca
www.facebook.com/mleoaOntario
To help bring members into association with each other to maintain professional standards; To encourage & assist in the education & training programs for Municipal Law Enforcement Officers
Doug Godfrey, President
Yves Roy, Vice President

National Judicial Institute (NJI) / Institut national de la magistrature (INM)
#400, 250 Albert St., Ottawa ON K1P 6M1
Tel: 613-237-1118; *Fax:* 613-237-6155
nji@nji-inm.ca
www.nji.ca
Based in Ottawa, the National Judicial Institute (NJI) is an independent, not-for-profit institution committed to building better justice through leadership in the education of judges in Canada and internationally. Since its inception in 1988, the NJI has continued to develop and deliver stimulating programs and a variety of electronic resources that foster judicial excellence. Alone or in partnership with courts and other organizations, the NJI is involved in the delivery of the majority of education taken by judges in Canada.
C. Adèle Kent, Executive Director
Lynn O'Shaughnessy, Library/Information Technician, Operations

New Brunswick Law Foundation / La Fondation pour l'avancement du droit au Nouveau-Brunswick
68 Avonlea Court, Fredericton NB E3C 1N8
Tel: 506-458-8540; *Fax:* 506-451-1421
general@lawsociety-barreau.nb.ca
lawsociety-barreau.nb.ca/en/public/new-brunswick-law-found
To fund law-related activities related to the areas of legal reform, legal aid & legal education
Marc L. Richard, Executive Director
R. Bruce Eddy, Chair

Northwest Territories Association of Provincial Court Judges
c/o Judge Garth Malakoe, Territorial Court of Northwest Territories, PO Box 550, 4093 - 49th St., Yellowknife NT X1A 2N4
Tel: 867-873-7602; *Fax:* 867-873-0291
Toll-Free: 866-822-5864
Garth Malakoe, Northwest Territories Director, Canadian Association of Provincial Court Judges

Nova Scotia Barristers' Society (NSBS)
800 - 2000 Barrington St., Halifax NS B3J 3K1
Tel: 902-422-1491; *Fax:* 902-429-4869
www.nsbs.org
https://www.linkedin.com/company/ns-barristers'-society
www.facebook.com/NSBarristers
twitter.com/nsbs
To set & enforce standards of professional responsibility & ethics for lawyers; To license & discipline members of the profession, in accordance with the Legal Profession Act
Darrel Pink, Executive Director

Ontario Association of Police Services Boards (OAPSB)
Suite A, 10 Peel Centre Dr., Brampton ON L6T 4B9
Tel: 905-458-1488; *Fax:* 905-458-2260
Toll-Free: 800-831-7727
admin@oapsb.ca
www.oapsb.ca
To act as the voice of police services boards to government; To provide services to assist police services boards in Ontario
Fred Kaustinen, Executive Director

Ontario Criminal Justice Association (CJAO)
PO Box 949, Stn. K, Toronto ON M4P 2V3
cjao.info
To encourage co-operation among individuals, groups & governmental organizations interested & active in the field of criminal justice; to further the study of criminal justice issues.

Ontario Crown Attorneys Association (OCAA) / Association des procureurs de la couronne de l'Ontario (APCO)
PO Box 30, #2100, 180 Dundas St. West, Toronto ON M5G 1Z8
Tel: 416-977-4517; *Fax:* 416-977-1460
reception@ocaa.ca
www.ocaa.ca
To promote & protect the professional interests of crown counsels, assistant crown attorneys, & articling students
Laurie Gonet, President

People's Law School
#150, 900 Howe St., Vancouver BC V6Z 2M4
Tel: 604-331-5400; *Fax:* 604-331-5401
info@peopleslawschool.ca
www.peopleslawschool.ca
www.youtube.com/user/plsbc
www.linkedin.com/company/people's-law-school
www.facebook.com/peopleslawschool
twitter.com/PLSBC
To make law & the legal system understandable & accessible to residents of British Columbia
Patricia Byrne, Executive Director

Police Association of Nova Scotia (PANS) / Association des policiers de la Nouvelle-Écosse
#2, 1000 Windmill Rd., Dartmouth NS B3B 1L7
Tel: 902-468-7555; *Fax:* 902-468-2202
Toll-Free: 888-468-2798
www.pansguide.com
David W. Fisher, CEO

Police Association of Ontario (PAO) / Association des policiers de l'Ontario
#901, 2 Carlton St., Toronto ON M5B 1J3
Tel: 416-487-9367; *Fax:* 416-487-3170
pao@pao.ca
pao.ca
www.facebook.com/PoliceAssociationofOntario
twitter.com/PoliceAssocON
To act as the official voice & representative body for Ontario's front line police personnel; To represent & support Ontario police associations
Stephen Reid, Executive Director

Police Sector Council (PSC) / Conseil sectoriel de la police (CSP)
#303, 1545 Carling Ave., Ottawa ON K1Z 8P9
Tel: 613-729-2789
info@policecouncil.ca
www.policecouncil.ca
twitter.com/PoliceCouncil
Improving the ways in which human resource planning & management support police operations & enhance police service in communities across Canada
Geoff Gruson, Executive Director

Probation Officers Association of Ontario (POAO)
#6245, 2100 Bloor St. West, Toronto ON M6S 5A5
www.poao.org
www.facebook.com/POAOntario
twitter.com/POAOntario

To represent the professional interests of the probation & parole Officers across the province; to provide representation on legislative issues to policy makers; to act as a forum for exchange of experience & information.
Elana Lamese, President

The Public Interest Advocacy Centre (PIAC) / Centre pour la défense de l'intérêt public
#200, 285 McLeod St., Ottawa ON K1N 7B7
Tel: 613-562-4002
piac@piac.ca
www.piac.ca
www.facebook.com/CanadaPIAC
twitter.com/CanadaPIAC
To provide legal services to groups & individuals addressing public interest issues of broad concern who would not otherwise have access to such services; The centre's special interests are telecommunications, energy, transportation, broadcasting, privacy, technical services & consumer protection
John Lawford, Executive Director & General Counsel

Public Legal Education Association of Saskatchewan, Inc. (PLEA Sask.)
#500, 333 - 25th St. East, Saskatoon SK S7K 0L4
Tel: 306-653-1868; *Fax:* 306-653-1869
www.plea.org
To provide the public with information regarding the law
Joel Janow, Executive Director

Public Legal Information Association of Newfoundland (PLIAN)
Tara Place, #227, 31 Peet St., St. John's NL A1B 3W8
Tel: 709-722-2643; *Fax:* 709-722-0054
Toll-Free: 888-660-7788
info@publiclegalinfo.com
www.publiclegalinfo.com
twitter.com/PLIAN_NL
To provide plain language legal information to the general public of Newfoundland, in both official languages, through a telephone enquiry line, public speaking engagements, publications, & a lawyer referral service
Kevin O'Shea, Executive Director

Saskatchewan Federation of Police Officers (SFPO)
SK
Tel: 306-539-0960
www.saskpolice.com
To advance police work as a profession; To support members in their police careers
Bernie Eiswirth, Executive Officer
Evan Bray, President
Jason Stonechild, Executive Vice-President

Société de criminologie du Québec (SCQ)
#38, 2000, boul Saint-Joseph est, Montréal QC H2H 1E4
Tel: 514-529-4391; *Téléc:* 514-529-6936
crimino@societecrimino.qc.ca
www.societecrimino.qc.ca
www.facebook.com/SocieteCrimino
twitter.com/societecrimino
De contribuer à l'évolution du système de justice pénale, de favoriser les échanges & les débats entre tous les intéressés à l'avancement de la justice pénale, & de favoriser & encourager la recherche
Caroline Savard, Directrice générale

The Society of Notaries Public of British Columbia
PO Box 44, #700, 625 Howe St., Vancouver BC V6C 2T6
Tel: 604-681-4516; *Fax:* 604-681-7258
Toll-Free: 800-663-0343
www.notaries.bc.ca
www.linkedin.com/company/2169593
www.facebook.com/BCNotaries
To ensure that its members provide high quality services to their clients
Jacqui Mendes, Chief Executive Officer

Yukon Law Foundation
PO Box 31789, Whitehorse YT Y1A 6L3
Tel: 867-667-7500; *Fax:* 867-393-3904
info@yukonlawfoundation.com
www.yukonlawfoundation.com
To maintain & manage a fund accumulated primarily from the interest on lawyers' trust accounts
Deana Lemke, Executive Director

Yukon Public Legal Education Association (YPLEA)
Tutshi Building, #102, 2131 Second Ave., Whitehorse YT Y1A 1C3
Tel: 867-668-5297; *Toll-Free:* 866-667-4305
www.yplea.com
To provide free legal information to the public & promote greater accessibility to the legal system

Carmen Gustafson, Executive Director

LGBTQ

Alliance des gais et lesbiennes Laval-Laurentides (AGLLL Inc.)
CP 98030, 95, boul Labelle, Sainte-Thérèse QC J7E 5R4
aglll@hotmail.com
www.algi.qc.ca/asso/aglll
Groupe de discussion; activités

AlterHéros
CP 56073, Succ. Alexis-Nihon, Montréal QC H3Z 1X5
Tel: 514-360-1320
info@alterheros.com
www.alterheros.com
www.facebook.com/alterheros
twitter.com/alterheros
Favorise l'insertion sociale des personnes d'orientation homosexuelle, bisexuelle et d'identité transsexuelle
Véronique Daneau, Directrice générale

Amazones des grands espaces
Montréal QC
Tél: 514-525-3663
info@plein-air-amazones.org
www.plein-air-amazones.org
Club de plein air pour lesbiennes

ARC - Aînés et retraités de la communauté
#110, 2075, rue Plessis, Montréal QC H2L 2Y4
Tél: 514-730-8870
info@arcmontreal.org
www.arcmontreal.org
www.facebook.com/arc.montreal
Regroupement d'hommes gais aînés retraités ou préretraités, visant à briser l'isolement et à demeurer actifs dans la communauté
Richard Desjardins, Président

Association des Gais et Lesbiennes Sourds (AGLS)
Montréal QC
agls@live.ca
www.agls.ca
www.facebook.com/214130285283518
L'Association des Gais et Lesbiennes Sourds est un organisme provincial à but non lucratif qui offre des activités sociales et des ateliers sur l'homophobie auprès de la communauté sourde et malentendante du Québec et du Grand Montréal.

Association des lesbiennes et des gais sur Internet (ALGI)
CP 476, Succ. C, Montréal QC H2L 4K4
Tél: 514-528-8424
info@algi.qc.ca
www.algi.qc.ca
www.facebook.com/algi.qc.ca
Favoriser l'expression des lesbiennes et des gais au moyen de l'Internet; favoriser l'échange entre les individus et les organismes de la communauté gaie et lesbienne dans un esprit d'entraide

Association des pères gais de Montréal inc. (APGM) / Gay Fathers of Montréal Inc.
Montréal QC H2L 4K4
Tél: 855-237-2746
peresgais@gmail.com
apgmqc.wordpress.com
www.facebook.com/equipe.APGM
Regrouper les hommes qui sont à la fois pères et gais; offrir support et aide aux hommes gais soucieux d'éduquer leurs enfants; permettre au père gai de se situer face à la condition de vie au moyen d'échanges, de discussion et d'information; promouvoir la condition des pères gais et la défense de leurs intérêts communs

BC Rainbow Alliance of the Deaf
BC
info@bcrad.com
www.bcrad.com
www.facebook.com/BCRAD.YVR
The British Columbia Rainbow Alliance of the Deaf (BCRAD) is an educational and social recreation organization for all people on the Deaf and queer spectrums.
Zoée Montpetit, President

Bi Unité Montréal (BUM)
CP 476, Succ. C, Montréal QC H2L 4K4
info@biunitemontreal.org
www.algi.qc.ca/asso/bum

Connaître la bisexualité et de rassembler les bisexuel(le)s dans un lieu commun pour qu'ils / qu'elles puissent s'informer, se divertir, et se supporter

Les Bolides
3350, rue Ontario est, Montréal QC H1W 1P7

Tél: 514-522-7773
info@lesbolides.org
www.lesbolides.org

Ligue de quilles

Canadian Centre for Gender & Sexual Diversity (CCGSD) / Centre canadien pour la diversité des genres et de la sexualité (CCDGS)
Albert Street Educational Centre, 440 Albert st., #C304, Ottawa ON K1R 5B5

Tel: 613-400-1875
info@ccgsd-ccdgs.org
ccgsd-ccdgs.org
www.instagram.com/ccgsd_ccdgs
www.linkedin.com/company/canadian-centre-for-gender-sexual-diversity
www.facebook.com/ccgsd.ccdgs
twitter.com/ccgsd_ccdgs
To advocate for a discrimination-free gender & sexually diverse world; To serve Canadian & indigenous communities across the country
Cameron Aitken, Acting Executive Director
Adri Bravo, Interim Office Manager

Canadian Lesbian & Gay Archives (CLGA)
PO Box 699, Stn. F, 34 Isabella St., Toronto ON M4Y 1N1

Tél: 416-777-2755
queeries@clga.ca
www.clga.ca
www.facebook.com/116735553447
twitter.com/clgarchives
To acquire, preserve & make available to the public information in any medium about lesbians & gays, with an emphasis on Canada.
Robert Windrum, President

Canadian Professional Association for Transgender Health (CPATH)
#201, 1770 Fort St., Ottawa ON V8R 1J5

Tel: 250-592-6183; *Fax:* 250-592-6123
info@cpath.ca
www.cpath.ca
To support the health, wellbeing & dignity of trans & gender diverse people with an interdisciplinary approach
Jack Woodman, President

Centre communautaire LGBTQ+ de Montréal
#110, 2075, rue Plessis, Montréal QC H2L 2Y4

Tél: 514-528-8424; *Téléc:* 514-528-9708
info@ccglm.org
cclgbtqplus.org
www.facebook.com/cclgbtqplus
Organisme sans but lucratif qui agit pour améliorer la condition des membres de nos communautés - lesbiennes, gais, bisexuels(les), transexuel(les), transgenres, et allosexuel(les); bibliothèque
Christian Tanguay, Directeur général

Centre d'orientation sexuelle de l'université McGill (COSUM) / McGill University Sexual Identity Centre (MUSIC)
Dép. de psychiatrie, Hôpital général de Montréal, 1650, av Cedar, #A2-160, Montréal QC H3G 1A4

Tél: 514-934-1934; *Téléc:* 514-934-8471
music-cosum@mcgill.ca
www.mcgill.ca/cosum
Offre des psychothérapies individuelles à court terme, psychothérapies de groupe & de couple ou familiales
Karine J. Igartua, Psychiatre

Centre de solidarité lesbienne (CSL)
#301, 4126, rue Saint-Denis, Montréal QC H2W 2M5

Tél: 514-526-2452; *Téléc:* 514-526-3570
info@solidaritelesbienne.org
www.solidaritelesbienne.qc.ca
www.facebook.com/centredesolidarite
D'améliorer les conditions de vie des lesbiennes en leur offrant des services et des interventions adaptés à leur réalité et ce, dans les domaines de la violence conjugales, du bien-être et de la santé
Audrey Mantha, Coordonnatrice générale

Coalition des familles LGBT / LGBT Family Coalition
3155, rue Hochelaga, Montréal QC H1W 1G4

Tél: 514-846-7600
info@familleslgbt.org
www.familleslgbt.org
www.instagram.com/CoalitiondesfamillesLGBT
www.facebook.com/coalitionfamilleslgbt
twitter.com/familleslgbt
Milite pour la reconnaissance légale et sociale des familles homoparentales; groupe bilingue de parents lesbiens, gais, bisexuels et transgenres
Mona Greenbaum, Directrice générale

Community One Foundation
PO Box 760, Stn. F, Toronto ON M4Y 2N6

Tel: 416-920-5422
info@communityone.ca
www.communityone.ca
www.instagram.com/c1foundation
www.facebook.com/CommunityOneFoundation
twitter.com/C1Foundation
To raise & disburse funds for the advancement of lesbian, gay, bisexual & transgender projects, artists & organizations; To fund projects in the areas of health & social services, arts & culture, research & education, political & legal
Terrance Greene, Co-Chair
Kevin Ormsby, Co-Chair

Conseil central du Montréal métropolitain (CCMM-CSN)
1601, av De Lorimier, Montréal QC H2K 4M5

Tél: 514-598-2021; *Téléc:* 514-598-2020
receptionccmm@csn.qc.ca
www.ccmm-csn.qc.ca
www.facebook.com/Conseil.Central.Montreal.Metropolitain.CSN
Mireille Bénard, Coordonnatrice

Conseil québécois des gais et lesbiennes du Québec (CQGL)
CP 182, Succ. C, Montréal QC H2L 4K1

Tél: 514-759-6844
info@conseil-lgbt.ca
www.cqgl.ca
www.facebook.com/CQLGBT
twitter.com/cqlgbt
Concrétiser notre leitmotive s'engager pour l'égalité sociale
Steve Foster, Directeur général

Egale Canada
#217, 120 Carlton St., Toronto ON M5A 4K2

Tél: 416-964-7887; *Fax:* 416-963-5665
Toll-Free: 888-204-7777
egale.canada@egale.ca
egale.ca
www.instagram.com/egalecanada
www.linkedin.com/company/egale-canada
www.facebook.com/EgaleCanada
twitter.com/egalecanada
To advance equality & justice for lesbian, gay, bisexual & transgender persons & their families in Canada
Helen Kennedy, Executive Director

Fondation Mario-Racine / Mario Racine Foundation
#110, 2075, rue Plessis, Montréal QC H2L 2Y4

Tél: 514-528-5940
fondationmarioracine99@gmail.com
www.algi.qc.ca/asso/fmr
Favoriser le développement communautaire et culturel des gais et lesbiennes à Montréal; est engagée dans la réalisation du Centre communautaire des gais et lesbiennes de Montréal
Michel Durocher, Président

Gay Fathers of Toronto
c/o The 519 Church St. Community Centre, 519 Church St., Toronto ON M4Y 2C9

info@gayfathers-toronto.com
www.gayfathers-toronto.com
To offer a supportive environment to fathers who are gay-oriented by providing assistance in building a positive self-image & by encouraging them to be loving & responsible

GRIS-Mauricie/Centre-du-Québec
#232, 255 rue Brock, Drummondville QC J2C 1M5

Tél: 819-445-0007; *Ligne sans frais:* 877-745-0007
info@grismcdq.org
www.grismcdq.org
De promouvoir la diversité de l'acceptation
Nathalie Niquette, Directrice générale

Groupe de recherche et d'intervention sociale (GRIS-Montréal)
CP 476, Succ. C, Montréal QC H2L 4K4

Tél: 514-590-0016; *Téléc:* 514-590-0764
info@gris.ca
www.gris.ca
www.facebook.com/grismontreal
twitter.com/GRISmontreal
Favoriser un meilleure connaissance des réalités homosexuelles et de faciliter l'intégration des gais, lesbiennes et bisexuel(les) dans la société
David Platts, Président

Groupe gai de l'Outaouais
#003, 109, rue Wright, Gatineau QC J8X 2G7

Tél: 819-776-2727; *Téléc:* 819-776-2001
Ligne sans frais: 877-376-2727
info@lebras.qc.ca
www.algi.qc.ca/asso/gdhgfo

Groupe gai de l'Université Laval (GGUL)
Pavillon Mauice-Pollack, #2223, 2305, rue de l'Université, Québec QC G1V 0A6

Tél: 418-656-2131
ggul@public.ulaval.ca
www.ggul.org
www.youtube.com/user/GGULULAVAL
twitter.com/ggul_ulaval

Groupe régional d'intervention social - Québec (GRIS-Québec)
#202, 363, rue de la Couronne, Québec QC G1K 6E9

Tél: 418-523-5572
info@grisquebec.org
www.grisquebec.org
www.facebook.com/GrisQuebec
André Tardiff, Directeur général

Hors sentiers
#925, 400, de l'Inspecteur, Montréal QC H3C 4A8

Tél: 450-433-7508
sentiers@horssentiers.ca
www.horssentiers.ca
Groupe de plein air

Jeunesse Lambda
CP 321125, Succ. Saint-André, Montréal QC H2L 4Y5

Tél: 514-528-7535
info@jeunesselambda.org
www.algi.qc.ca/asso/jlambda
www.facebook.com/JLAMBDA.MTL
Groupe d'accueil francophone de discussion et d'activités par et pour les jeunes gais, lesbiennes, bisexuel(les)

Ontario Rainbow Alliance of the Deaf (ORAD)
c/o The 519 Community Centre, 519 Church St., Toronto ON M4Y 2C9

info@orad.ca
new2.orad.ca
www.youtube.com/ontariorad
www.facebook.com/176398609081793
www.twitter.com/OntarioRAD
Ontario Rainbow Alliance for the Deaf (ORAD) is a not for profit organization serving Deaf, deaf, deafened, hard of hearing and hearing people who are LGBTTIQQ2S* communities in the Province of Ontario.
Nicka Noble, Acting President/Vice-President

Projet 10 (P10) / Project 10
1575, rue Amherst, Montréal QC H2L 3L4

Tel: 514-989-0001
questions@p10.qc.ca
www.p10.qc.ca
www.instagram.com/p10_mtl
www.facebook.com/P10montreal
twitter.com/p10_mtl
To provide advocacy, education, & services to support the personal, social, sexual, & mental well-being of lesbian, gay, bisexual, transgender, transsexual, two-spirit, intersexed, & questioning youth; To empower youth at individual, community, & institutional levels; To support oppressed groups & individuals
Otto Vicé, Co-Coordinator
Sarah Butler, Co-Coordinator

Queer Ontario
Community Centre, 519 Church St., Toronto ON M4Y 2C9

info@queerontario.org
queerontario.org
twitter.com/queerontario
To question, challenge & reform the laws, institutional practices & social norms that regulate queer people; to fight for accessibility, recognition & pluralism; to use social media & other

tactics to engage in political action, public education & coalition-building
Richard Hudler, Chair

Réseau des lesbiennes du Québec (RLQ) / Québec Lesbian Network
CP 6, Succ. C, Montréal QC H2L 4J7
Tél: 438-929-6928
dg@rlq-qln.ca
rlq-qln.algi.qc.ca
www.instagram.com/RLQ_QLN
www.facebook.com/RLQQLN
twitter.com/rlq_qln

Julie Antoine, Directrice générale

La Trame
CP 845, Succ. Desjardins, Montréal QC H5B 1B9
Tél: 514-374-0227
la.trame@hotmail.com
la-trame.ca
Regroupement pour lesbiennes dans le domaine des arts, de la culture et du loisir
Mireille Robillard, Contact

TransParent Canada
NS
Tel: 902-431-8500
transparentcanada17@gmail.com
www.transparentcanada.ca
To support & provide resources for parents of trans children

Welcome Friend Association (WFA)
PO Box 242, 76 Dawson St., Thessalon ON P0R 1L0
Fax: 705-998-2612
Toll-Free: 888-909-2234
info@welcomefriend.ca
www.welcomefriend.ca
www.facebook.com/welcomefriendassociation
twitter.com/WelcomeFriend
To educate & promote awareness in society regarding gender, sexual identities, & expressions; To support individuals facing gender & sexual issues; To increase understanding of the queer community; To work towards a society that includes & respects all persons regardless of gender or sexual orientation
Harry Stewart, Chair

Libraries & Archives

Alberta Association of Academic Libraries (AAAL)
AB
aaal.executive@gmail.com
aaal.ca
www.facebook.com/AlbertaAssociationofAcademicLIbraries
twitter.com/AlbertaAAL
To facilitate planning, cooperation, & communication among Alberta's academic libraries; To promote continuing education
Madelaine Vanderwerff, Chair
Marc D'Avernas, Treasurer

Alberta Association of Library Technicians (AALT)
PO Box 700, Edmonton AB T5J 2L4
Toll-Free: 866-350-2258
www.aalt.org
www.linkedin.com/in/librarytechnicians
twitter.com/AALTLibraryTech
To foster & enhance the professional image of library technicians in Alberta; To support library technicians throughout the province
Brenna Burwash, President
Tracy Belsher, Director, Communication Services
Christy Nichols, Director, Online Services
Lynda Shurko, Director, Administrative Services

Alberta Library Trustees Association (ALTA)
4024 - 37A Ave., Edmonton AB T6L 7A1
Tel: 780-761-2582; *Fax:* 866-419-1451
librarytrustees.ab.ca
www.linkedin.com/company/alberta-library-trustees-association
www.facebook.com/librarytrustees
twitter.com/librarytrustees
To act as the collective voice for library trustees in Alberta; To develop effective trustees
Heather Coulson, Executive Director

Alberta School Learning Commons Council (ASLC)
AB
aslc.ca
www.facebook.com/ASLCLearn
twitter.com/ASLC_Learn
To advance teaching & learning excellence through effective school library practices; To cultivate & enhance effective school

library operation through leadership, information & professional development
Lisa Hauk-Meeker, President

Archives Association of British Columbia (AABC)
#249, 34A-2755 Lougheed Hwy., Port Coquitlam BC V3B 5Y9
info@aabc.ca
www.aabc.ca
www.facebook.com/ArchivesAssociationBC
To act as the voice of archivists & archival institutions in British Columbia; To undertake projects that strengthen the archival network in the province; To preserve & promote access to British Columbia's documentary heritage
Alysa Routtenberg, President
Victoria McAuley, Secretary
Stacey Gilkinson, Treasurer

Archives Association of Ontario (AAO) / L'Association des archives de l'Ontario
#200, 411 Richmond St. East, Toronto ON M5A 3S5
Tel: 647-343-3334
aao@aao-archivists.ca
aao-archivists.ca
www.instagram.com/archives.assoc.ontario
www.linkedin.com/company/archives-association-of-ontario
www.facebook.com/ArchivesAssociationOfOntario
twitter.com/AAO_tweet
To encourage, through the establishment of networks, the public knowledge & appreciation of archives & their function; To promote the advancement of general education in the preservation of the cultural heritage & identity of the various regions of the province; To represent the interests of the archival community before the government of Ontario, local government & other provincial institutions of a public or private nature; To provide professional guidance & leadership through communication & cooperation with all persons, groups & associations interested in the preservation & use of records of the human experience in Ontario
Jennifer Grant, President
Jessica Barr, Secretary & Treasurer

Archives Council of Prince Edward Island
PO Box 1000, Charlottetown PE C1A 7M4
acpei@gov.pe.ca
www.archives.pe.ca
To facilitate the development of the archival system in PEI; To make recommendations about the system's operation & financing; To develop & facilitate the implementation & management of programs to assist the archival community; To communicate archival needs & concerns to decision-makers, researchers & the general public
Simon Lloyd, President

Archives Society of Alberta (ASA)
#114C, 10440 - 108th Ave. NW, Edmonton AB T5H 3Z9
Tel: 780-424-2697
info@archivesalberta.org
www.archivesalberta.org
www.facebook.com/groups/archivesalberta
twitter.com/ArchivesAlberta
To provide professional leadership & development among persons engaged in practice of archival science; To promote development of archives & archivists in Alberta; To encourage cooperation of archivists & archives with all those interested in preservation & use of documents of human experience
Rene Georgopalis, Executive Director

Association des archivistes du Québec (AAQ)
#3240D, 1055, av du Séminaire, Québec QC G1V 5C8
Tél: 418-652-2357
infoaaq@archivistes.qc.ca
archivistes.qc.ca
www.youtube.com/user/ArchivistesQc
www.linkedin.com/company/association-des-archivistes-du-québ
ec
www.facebook.com/ArchivistesQc
twitter.com/archivistesQc
Regrouper les personnes qui offrent aux organisations et à leurs clientèles des services liés à la gestion de leur information organique et consignée; offrir à ses membres des services en français et propres à assurer le développement, l'enrichissement et la promotion de leur profession et de leur discipline; assurer aux membres les services susceptibles de favoriser et d'accroître les échanges et la communication internes et externes des idées et des connaissances; promouvoir le développement professionnel des membres en s'impliquant activement au plan de la formation et du perfectionnement, en favorisant la recherche et le développement et en assurant une représentation adéquate de la profession au sein de la société et auprès des corps politiques
Frédéric Giuliano, Président
Louis Germain, Directeur général

Association des bibliothèques de droit de Montréal (ABDM) / Montréal Association of Law Libraries (MALL)
CP 482, 800, carré Victoria, Montréal QC H4Z 1J7
info@abdm-mall.org
abdm-mall.org
Vise à permettre aux gens qui travaillent dans les bibliothèques de droit et qui exercent des fonctions connexes de communiquer et d'échanger des idées; d'encourager l'avancement de la profession; de maintenir et d'accroître l'utilité des bibliothèques de droit; promouvoir la coopération
Ruth Veilleux, Présidente

Association des bibliothèques publiques de l'Estrie (ABIPE)
1002, av J.-A.-Bombardier, Valcourt QC J0E 2L0
Tél: 450-532-2250
www.bpq-estrie.qc.ca
Regrouper les bibliothèques publiques d'Estrie pour en favoriser le développement; informer les membres et échanger sur toute question pertinente au dossier des bibliothèques; représenter les intérêts des bibliothèques membres de la région 05 en étant leur porte-parole officiel auprès des instances gouvernementales et autres; organiser et réaliser des activités d'animation culturelle; sensibiliser le milieu au rôle et à l'importance de la bibliothèque publique dans la communauté
Karine Corbeil, Présidente

Association des bibliothèques publiques du Québec (ABPQ) / Québec Public Library Association
#215, 1453, rue Beaubien est, Montréal QC H2G 3C6
Tél: 514-279-0550; *Téléc:* 514-845-1618
info@abpq.ca
abpq.ca
www.facebook.com/ABPQc
Agit à titre de représentant officiel des bibliothèques publiques du Québec
Eve Lagacé, Directrice générale
Fannie Labonté, Coordonnatrice, Services aux membres et événements

Association for Manitoba Archives (AMA)
#606, 100 Arthur St., Winnipeg MB R3B 1H3
Tel: 204-942-3491
ama1@mts.net
mbarchives.ca
To promote understanding & awareness of the role & use of archives; To promote standards, procedures, & practices in the management of archives; To provide assistance & education to persons seeking to improve their skills in the development, management or operation of archives
David Cuthbert, Chair

Association of Canadian Archivists (ACA) / Association canadienne des archivistes
#1912, 130 Albert St., Ottawa ON K1P 5G4
Tel: 613-234-6977; *Fax:* 613-234-8500
aca@archivists.ca
archivists.ca
www.youtube.com/user/archivistsdotca
www.linkedin.com/company/association-of-canadian-archivists
www.facebook.com/AssociationofCanadianArchivists
twitter.com/archivistsdotca
To ensure the preservation & accessibility of Canada's documentary heritage; To provide professional leadership among persons engaged in the discipline & practice of archival science; To promote the development of archives & archivists in Canada; To encourage cooperation of archivists with all those interested in the preservation & use of documents of human experience
J.M. McCutcheon, Executive Director
Maureen Tracey, Coordiantor, Membership Services

Association of Canadian Map Libraries & Archives (ACMLA) / Association des cartothèques et archives cartographiques du Canada (ACACC)
acmla-acacc.ca
To represent Canadian map librarians & cartographic archivists, as well as others who are interested in geographic information; To develop professional standards & international cataloguing rules for the management & access to geographic information; To promote the contributions of map libraries & cartographic archives
Martin Chandler, President
Rosa Orlandini, Vice-President, Communications & Outreach
Francine Berish, Secretary
Dan Jakubek, Treasurer

Association of Newfoundland & Labrador Archives (ANLA)
PO Box 23155, St. John's NL A1B 4J9
Tel: 709-726-2867; *Fax:* 709-722-9035
anla@nf.aibn.ca
anla.nf.ca
www.facebook.com/ANLArchives
To provide professional leadership among persons engaged in practice of archival science; To promote development of archives & archivists in Newfoundland & Labrador; To encourage cooperation of archivists with all those interested in preservation & use of documents of human experience
Nicole Penney, Treasurer
Mary Ellen Wright, Officer, Professional Development & Outreach

Association of Parliamentary Libraries in Canada (APLIC) / Association des bibliothèques parlementaires au Canada (ABPAC)
AB
president@aplic-abpac.org
aplic-abpac.ca
To improve parliamentary library service in Canada; To encourage cooperation with related officials & organizations

Association of Prince Edward Island Libraries (APEIL)
c/o Trina O'Brien Leggott, 187 North River Rd., Charlottetown PE C1A 3L4
apeilibraries@gmail.com
www.apeilibraries.wordpress.com
www.facebook.com/peilibraries
To represent the interests of individuals working or interested in library services; To promote library & information services in Prince Edward Island
Trina O'Brien Leggott, President
Jennie Thompson, Vice-President
Ray MacLeod, Secretary & Treasurer

Association of Professional Librarians of New Brunswick (APLNB) / Association des bibliothécaires professionnel(le)s de Nouveau-Brunswick (ABPNB)
c/o Tyler Griffin, Fredericton Public Library, 12 Carleton St., Fredericton NB E3B 5P4
www.aplnb-abpnb.ca
twitter.com/APLNB
To promote librarians & libraries in New Brunswick
Tyler Griffin, President

Association pour la promotion des services documentaires scolaires (APSDS)
#5, 7870, rue Madeleine-Huguenin, Montréal QC H1L 6M7
Tél: 514-588-9400
apsds@apsds.org
apsds.org
www.facebook.com/APSDS.QC
twitter.com/apsds_
Contribue au développement des services documentaires dans les commissions scolaires du Québec, dans les écoles primaires et secondaires, publiques et privées, et qui en assure la promotion
Ariane Régnier, Présidente

Atlantic Provinces Library Association (APLA)
c/o Kenneth C. Rowe Management Bldg., Dalhousie University, Stn. 15000, #4010, 6100 University Ave., Halifax NS B3H 4R2
www.apla.ca
twitter.com/APLAcontact
To promote library & information service & workers throughout the Atlantic region; To represent & support the interests of persons who work in libraries in the Atlantic provinces; To cooperate with other library associations & similar organizations; To develop & offer effective continuing education programs
Ann Smith, President
Erin Alcock, Vice-President, Membership
Amy Lorencz, Secretary

Les bibliothèques publiques des régions de la Capitale-Nationale et Chaudière-Appalaches
a/s Réseau BIBLIO de la Capitale-Nationale, 3189, rue Albert-Demers, Lévis QC G6X 3A1
Tél: 418-832-6166; *Téléc:* 418-832-6168
abpq.ca/regions_capitale-nationale.php
Regrouper les responsables des bibliothèques publiques des régions; promouvoir et défendre les intérêts de ces bibliothèques; représenter le secteur des bibliothèques publiques des ces régions au sein des organismes à caractère culturel et social
Philippe Cadieux, Présidente
Michaël Lessard-Quintal, Trésorière

Johanne Labbé, Administrateur

British Columbia Courthouse Library Society
800 Smithe St., Vancouver BC V6Z 2E1
Tel: 604-660-2841; *Fax:* 604-660-2821
Toll-Free: 800-665-2570
librarian@courthouselibrary.ca
www.courthouselibrary.ca
www.linkedin.com/company/theclbc
www.facebook.com/theCLBC
twitter.com/theclbc
To offer legal information services to librarians, legal professionals & the public
Caroline Nevin, Chief Executive Officer
Paul Hargreaves, Chief Financial Officer
Brenda Rose, Director, Community Engagement

British Columbia Library Association (BCLA)
PO Box 19008, Stn. Rocky Point, Port Moody BC V3H 0J1
Tel: 604-683-5354
bclaoffice@bcla.bc.ca
bclaconnect.ca
twitter.com/bclaconnect
To encourage library development throughout British Columbia; To coordinate library services to various parts of the province; To promote cooperation between libraries; To advance the mutual interests of libraries & library personnel
Annette DeFaveri, Executive Director
Angie Ayupova, Office Manager

British Columbia Library Trustees' Association (BCLTA)
#108, 9865 - 140th St., Surrey BC V3T 4M4
Tel: 604-913-1424; *Toll-Free:* 888-206-1245
www.bclta.ca
www.linkedin.com/in/bclta-bc-library-trustees-association-31a14
4150
twitter.com/BCLTA
To develop & support library trustees who govern local public libraries in British Columbia; To advance public library service in the province
Jerrilyn Kirk, Executive Director

Canadian Association for Information Science (CAIS) / Association canadienne des sciences de l'information (ACSI)
info@cais-acsi.ca
cais-acsi.ca
twitter.com/cais_acsi
To advance information science in Canada by encouraging & facilitating the exchange of information on the use, access, retrieval, organization, management & dissemination of information
Philippe Mongeon, President
Michael Ridley, Treasurer
Fei Shu, Secretary

Canadian Association of Law Libraries (CALL) / Association canadienne des bibliothèques de droit (ACBD)
#705, 1 Eglinton Ave. East, Toronto ON M4P 3A1
Tel: 647-346-8723
office@callacbd.ca
www.callacbd.ca
www.linkedin.com/groups/2006070
www.facebook.com/callacbd
twitter.com/callacbd
To promote law librarianship; To develop Canadian law libraries; To promote access to legal information
Shaunna Mireau, President

Canadian Association of Music Libraries, Archives & Documentation Centres (CAML) / Association canadienne des bibliothèques, archives et centres de documentation musicaux inc. (ACBM)
Edward Johnson Bldg., University of Toronto, 80 Queen's Park Cres., Toronto ON M5S 2C5
contact@caml-acbm.org
caml-acbm.org
To represent librarians, researchers & archivists in the field of music
Houman Behzadi, President
Becky Smith, Membership Secretary
Marc Stoeckle, Officer, Communications

Canadian Association of Professional Academic Librarians (CAPAL)
PO Box 19606, Stn. Manulife, Toronto ON M4W 3T9
capalibrarians@gmail.com
capalibrarians.org
To represent the interests of professional academic librarians in the areas of education, standards, professional practice, ethics & core principles to local, provincial & national organizations

---

Canadian Association of Research Libraries (CARL) / Association des bibliothèques de recherche du Canada (ABRC)
#203, 309 Cooper St., Ottawa ON K2P 0G5
Tel: 613-482-9344
info@carl-abrc.ca
www.carl-abrc.ca
www.youtube.com/channel/UCK59-sdDLfQgUUoAuiOVQeQ
www.linkedin.com/company/canadian-association-of-research-lib raries—-association-des-biblioth-ques-de-recherche-du-canada
www.facebook.com/1814343425522910
twitter.com/carlabrc
To provide leadership to the Canadian research library community; To address issues affecting research libraries, such as federal research policy, copyright, open access publication & preservation; To encourage broad access to scholarly information; To seek public policy encouraging of research
Susan Haigh, Executive Director
Katherine McColgan, Manager, Administration & Programs

Canadian Committee on Cataloguing / Comité canadien de catalogage
Library & Archives Canada, 550, boul de la Cité, Gatineau QC K1A 0N4
bac.normesdecatalogage-cataloguingstandards.lac@canada.ca
www.bac-lac.gc.ca
To formulate policy on questions concerning cataloguing & bibliographic control, including subject analysis, referred to it by any of the organizations represented on the Committee; To provide representative Canadian opinion for presentation at international meetings, committees & working groups; To be involved with the revision of the Anglo-American Cataloguing Rules

Canadian Committee on MARC / Comité canadien du MARC
Description Div., Published Heritage Branch, Library & Archives Canada, 395 Wellington St., Ottawa ON K1A 0N4
Fax: 819-934-4388
bac.marc21.lac@bac-lac.gc.ca
www.marc21.ca/040010-203-e.html
To act as a Canadian MARC Advisory Committee to the National Library by examining the MARC 21 communication formats & making recommendations on the formats; To examine MARC 21 communication formats as a medium for the exchange of machine-readable bibliographic information in Canada; To establish procedures for receiving, evaluating & making recommendations on proposed national & international standards for the representation in machine-readable form of bibliographic information & other related standards; To maintain liaison with its constituent organizations & relevant outside agencies
Pat Riva, Chair
Bill Leonard, Contact

Canadian Council of Archives (CCA) / Conseil canadien des archives
#1912, 130 Albert St., Ottawa ON K1P 5G4
Tel: 613-565-1222; *Fax:* 613-565-5445
Toll-Free: 866-254-1403
cca@archivescanada.ca
archivescanada.ca/AboutCCA
To preserve & provide access to Canadian documentary heritage; To facilitate development of Canadian archival system & its operation; To develop & facilitate implementation & management of programs to assist archival community; To communicate archival needs & concerns to decision-makers, researchers & the general public
Joanna Aiton-Kerr, Chair
Christina Nichols, Executive Director

Canadian Federation of Library Associations (CFLA) / Fédération canadienne des associations de bibliothèques (FCAB)
c/o Canadian Association of Research Libraries, #203, 309 Cooper St., Ottawa ON K2P 0G5
Tel: 613-867-7789
info@cfla-fcab.ca
cfla-fcab.ca
www.linkedin.com/company/canadian-federation-of-library-assoc iations-fédération-canadienne-des-associations-de-bibliothèques
www.facebook.com/cflafcab
twitter.com/cflafcab
To represent Canada's library community; To promote library values & the value of libraries; To influence public policy affecting libraries; To advance libraries in Canada; To strengthen the library community; To help preserve Canada's heritage
Todd Kyle, Chair
Mary Chevreau, Treasurer
Rebecca Raven, Executive Director

Canadian Health Information Management Association (CHIMA)
201 King St., London ON N6A 1C9
Tel: 519-438-6700; *Fax:* 519-438-7001
Toll-Free: 877-332-4462
www.echima.ca
www.linkedin.com/groups/4445368
www.facebook.com/OfficialCHIMA
twitter.com/E_CHIMA

To contribute to the promotion of wellness & the provision of quality healthcare through excellence in health information management; To assure competency of practice through credentialing, standards, & continuing education; To promote value of health information management professionals
Jeff Nesbitt, CEO & Registrar

Canadian Health Libraries Association (CHLA) / Association des bibliothèques de la santé du Canada (ABSC)
Toronto ON
info@chla-absc.ca
www.chla-absc.ca
www.instagram.com/chla_absc
www.facebook.com/CHLA.ABSC
twitter.com/chlaabsc

To lead health librarians towards excellence
Francesca Frati, President
Sarah Visintini, Secretary
Alison Manley, Director, Public Relations
Perry Ruehlen, Executive Director

Canadian School Libraries (CSL)
299 Canterbury Dr., Waterloo ON N2K 3C1
info@canadianschoollibraries.ca
www.canadianschoollibraries.ca
www.facebook.com/CanadianSchoolLibraries
twitter.com/CdnSchoolLibrar

To contribute to professional research & development in the school library learning commons field in Canada; To help students across Canada improve their learning skills; To unite library practitioners & educators in Canada; To collaborate with other school library organizations, programs & communities
Anita Brooks Kirkland, Chair & Treasurer

Canadian Urban Libraries Council (CULC) / Conseil des Bibliothèques Urbaines du Canada (CBUC)
349 Main St., Bloomfield ON K0K 1G0
Tel: 416-699-1938; *Fax:* 866-211-2999
culc.ca
twitter.com/culc_cbuc

To identify the issues & choices available in developing urban public library services; To explore the philosophy & principles that govern public library service in urban areas; To comment on the state of public library service in Canada; To facilitate the exchange of ideas & information between member libraries; To influence legislation & financing of urban public libraries; To promote & work in conjunction with other library organizations in Canada to achieve an urban public library service which is comprehensive, economic & efficient; To provide the means for communication & information sharing between members of the public library community; To promote formal & informal cooperation with organizations & institutions in Canada & outside Canada whose goals & objectives are relevant to large urban public library service
Mary Chevreau, Chair
Jefferson Gilbert, Executive Director

Colchester-East Hants Public Library Foundation
754 Prince St., Truro NS B2N 1G9
Tel: 902-895-4183; *Fax:* 902-895-7149
Toll-Free: 888-632-9088
gift@lovemylibrary.ca
lovemylibrary.ca/foundation
www.facebook.com/GiftMyLibrary

To maintain & enhance the library system
Mary Brown, Chair

Corporation des bibliothécaires professionnels du Québec (CBPQ) / Corporation of Professional Librarians of Québec
#387, 2065, rue Parthenais, Montréal QC H2K 3T1
Tél: 514-845-3327
info@cbpq.qc.ca
www.cbpq.qc.ca
www.facebook.com/cbpq.qc.ca

Développer les services de bibliothèques; établir des normes de compétence; encourager et stimuler la recherche en bibliothéconomie; promouvoir et développer les intérêts professionnels de ses membres
Paolo Miriello, Directeur général
Angelica Bru, Secrétariat

Council of Archives New Brunswick (CANB) / Conseil des archives du Nouveau-Brunswick
PO Box 1204, Stn. A, Fredericton NB E3B 5C8
Tel: 506-453-4327; *Fax:* 506-453-3288
archives.advisor@gnb.ca
www.canbarchives.ca
www.facebook.com/CANBarchives
twitter.com/CANBarchives

To address the needs of the archival institutions in New Brunswick; To provide training & information on developments in the profession; To encourage information sharing & cooperation in educational opportunities with Maritime sister provinces & national associations
David Mawhinney, President

Council of Nova Scotia Archives (CNSA)
6016 University Ave., Halifax NS B3H 1W4
Tel: 902-424-7093
advisor@councilofnsarchives.ca
www.councilofnsarchives.ca
www.facebook.com/CouncilofNSArchives
twitter.com/ArchivesInNS

To foster education of archival standards & practices to preserve Nova Scotia's documentary heritage; To promote archival standards, procedures & practices

Council of Prairie & Pacific University Libraries (COPPUL)
High Density Library, University of Calgary, #150B, 11711 - 85th St. NW, Calgary AB T3R 1J3
Tel: 403-220-2414
www.coppul.ca
twitter.com/coppul

To work together to leverage members' collective expertise, resources & influence; To increase capacity & infrastructure; To enhance learning, teaching, student experiences & research at member institutions
Vivian Stieda, Executive Director

Families Canada / Familles Canada
#149, 150 Isabella St., Ottawa ON K1S 1V7
Tel: 613-237-7667; *Fax:* 613-237-8515
Toll-Free: 866-637-7226
info@familiescanada.ca
familiescanada.ca
www.linkedin.com/company/families-canada
www.facebook.com/FamiliesCanada
twitter.com/familiescanada

To promote the well-being of families, through provision of leadership, consultation & resources to organizations which care for children & support families; To act as the national voice for family resource programs; To advance social policy, research, resource development & training for those who support the capacity of families to raise their children
Kelly Stone, President & CEO
Zindu Salih, Director, Operations

Fédération des milieux documentaires (FMD)
#387, 2065, rue Parthenais, Montréal QC H2K 3T1
Tél: 514-281-5012; *Téléc:* 514-281-8219
info@fmdoc.org
fmdoc.org

Pour promouvoir les intérêts de ses membres
Réjean Savard, Président
Tristan Muller, Vice-président
Guy Gosselin, Trésorière
Mireille Laforce, Secrétaire
Lionel Villalonga, Directeur général

Federation of Ontario Public Libraries (FOPL)
Lower level, Toronto Reference Library, 789 Yonge St., Toronto ON M4W 2G8
Tel: 416-395-0746; *Fax:* 416-395-0743
admin@fopl.ca
www.fopl.ca
www.facebook.com/1601735406759944
twitter.com/foplnews

To represent Ontario's public library systems; To advocate for support, programs & resources that will contribute to the success of Ontario public libraries
Stephen Abram, Executive Director

The Friends of Library & Archives Canada / Les Amis de Bibliothèque et archives Canada
395 Wellington St., Ottawa ON K1A 0N4
Tel: 613-943-1544; *Fax:* 613-943-2343
friends.amis@bac-lac.gc.ca
www.friendsoflibraryandarchivescanada.ca

To promote & encourage public interest in & support for the work of Library & Archives Canada in fulfilling its role as a preserver of the national published & unpublished heritage; To provide interested persons & organizations with the opportunity to share in the activities of Library & Archives Canada; To attract collections of Canadiana as gifts to Library & Archives Canada; To organize fundraising events in support of a variety of its endeavours, including special acquisitions
Marianne Scott, President
Kathleen Shaw, Vice-President
Michael Gnarowski, Treasurer

Halifax Library Association
NS
halifaxlibraryassociation@gmail.com
halifaxla.wordpress.com
www.facebook.com/HalifaxLibraryAssociation

To promote libraries & library services; To promote cooperation among libraries in the Halifax Regional Municipality; To serve the interests of library workers
Siobhan Wiggans, President

Health Libraries Association of British Columbia (HLABC)
c/o Shannon Cheng, BC Cancer Agency Library, 675 West 10th Ave., Vancouver BC V5Z 1L3
hlabcexec@gmail.com
hlabc.chla-absc.ca

To promote effectiveness in health libraries in British Columbia; To foster communication & cooperation between health libraries & health library staff; To advance education in the health library field
Pamela Harrison, President
Eleri Staiger, Secretary
Shannon Cheng, Treasurer & Contact, Membership

Indexing Society of Canada (ISC) / Société canadienne d'indexation (SCI)
133 Major St., Toronto ON M5S 2K9
indexers.ca
www.linkedin.com/company/indexing-society-of-canada-isc-sci
www.facebook.com/indexingsocietyofcanada
twitter.com/indexerscanada

To encourage the production & use of indexes & abstracts; To promote the recognition of indexers & abstractors; To improve indexing & abstracting techniques; To improve communication among individual indexers & abstractors
Alexandra Pearce, President
Julia White, Membership Secretary
Judith Clark, Director, Communications

Library Association of Alberta (LAA)
c/o The Alberta Library, #623, 7 Sir Winston Churchill Sq. NW, Edmonton AB T5J 2V5
info@laa.ca
www.laa.ca
www.facebook.com/LibraryAssociationOfAlberta
twitter.com/Lib_Assn_AB

To facilitate the improvement of library services in Alberta; To promote library service throughout Alberta; To encourage cooperation among libraries & information centres across the province; To promote intellectual freedom in Alberta
Kirk MacLeod, President

Library Boards Association of Nova Scotia (LBANS)
135 North Park St., Bridgewater NS B4V 9B3
Tel: 902-543-2548

To preserve & support quality public library service throughout Nova Scotia

Manitoba Association of Health Information Providers (MAHIP)
c/o Neil John Maclean Health Sciences Library, University of Manitoba, 727 McDermott Ave., Winnipeg MB R3E 3P5
Fax: 204-789-3922
contact.mahip@gmail.com
mahip.chla-absc.ca
twitter.com/MAHIP_CHLAABSC

To promote the provision of quality library service to the health community in Manitoba by communication & mutual assistance
Carol Cooke, President
Nicole Askin, Secretary

Manitoba Library Association (MLA)
#606, 100 Arthur St., Winnipeg MB R3B 1H3
secretary@mla.mb.ca
www.mla.mb.ca
www.instagram.com/mb_library_assoc
www.linkedin.com/in/manitoba-library-association-2a24325b
www.facebook.com/MBLibAssn
twitter.com/MB_Lib_Assn

To develop, support & promote library & information services in Manitoba for the benefit of the library community & Manitoba residents
Melanie Sucha, President
Caralie Heinrichs, Secretary
Victoria Ho, Director, Membership
Shawn Simpson, Director, Communications

**Manitoba Library Consortium Inc. (MLCI) /
Consortium de bibliothèques du Manitoba**
c/o Library Administration, University of Winnipeg, 515
Portage Ave., Winnipeg MB R3B 2E9
Fax: 204-783-8910
manitobalibraryconsortium@gmail.com
www.mlcinc.mb.ca
To facilitate resource sharing among the libraries in Manitoba;
To build a public information network to contribute to a
community's economic goals; To strengthen library services for
the residents of Manitoba; To promote the exchange of
information related to preservation
Heather Brydon, Chair
Colleen Slight, Secretary
Meagan Morash, Treasurer

Manitoba School Library Association (MSLA)
307 Shaftesbury Blvd., Winnipeg MB R3P 0L9
www.manitobaschoollibraries.ca
www.facebook.com/246439115416779
twitter.com/_MSLA_
To support school library personnel in Manitoba; To promote
high quality education programs & equity of service in school
libraries across Manitoba
Brandi Bartok, President
Erin Thomas, Treasurer
Alison Bodner, Director, Membership

**Maritimes Health Libraries Association (MHLA) /
Association des bibliothèques de la santé des
Maritimes (ABSM)**
c/o Lara Killian, Hugh Bell Library, #200, 302 Pleasant St.,
Dartmouth NS B2Y 3S1
mhla.absm@gmail.com
library.nshealth.ca/MHLA
To support members in the provision of quality information
services for the health care community in the Maritime provinces
Katie McLean, President
Lara Killian, Treasurer

**New Brunswick Library Trustees' Association
(NBLTA) / Association des commissaires de
bibliothèque du Nouveau-Brunswick, inc.**
PO Box 34, St Antoine NB E0A 2X0
To train effective library trustees in New Brunswick; To promote
public library services in New Brunswick

**Newfoundland & Labrador Health Libraries
Association (NLHLA)**
c/o Health Sciences Library, Memorial University of
Newfoundland, St. John's NL A1B 3V6
nlhla@chla-absc.ca
nlhla.chla-absc.ca
To promote the provision of a high quality library service to the
health community in Newfoundland & Labrador through mutual
assistance & communication; To provide professional support to
the membership by offering continuing education opportunities
Lindsay Alcock, President
Jordan Pike, Secretary & Treasurer

**Newfoundland & Labrador Library Association
(NLLA)**
PO Box 23192, Stn. Churchill Square, St. John's NL A1B 4J9
nlla.executive@gmail.com
nlla.ca
www.facebook.com/newfoundlandandlabradorlibraryassociation
twitter.com/NLLA_NL
To ensure the excellence of Newfoundland & Labrador's public,
special, academic & school libraries; To foster interest in
libraries
Katie Lawton, President
Janet Goosney, Secretary

Northern Alberta Health Libraries Association
c/o J.W. Scott Health Sciences Library, University of
Alberta, 2K3.28 Walter MacKenzie Centre, Edmonton AB
T6G 2R7
contact.nahla@gmail.com
nahla.chla-absc.ca
To provide a forum for networking, education & advocacy among
librarians, library technicians & others interested in health
libraries & health information; To encourage health information
specialists to support health care services & research
Jody Nelson, President
Nicole Loroff, Treasurer

Northwest Territories Archives Council (NWTAC)
PO Box 1320, Yellowknife NT X1A 2L9
nwtarchivescouncil@gmail.com
nwtarchivescouncil.wordpress.com
www.facebook.com/nwtarchivescouncil
To facilitate development of the archival system in the Northwest
Territories; To make recommendations about the system's

operation & financing; To develop & facilitate implementation &
management of programs to assist the archival community; To
communicate archival needs & concerns to decision-makers,
researchers & the general public
Rebecca Mahler, President

Northwest Territories Library Association (NWTLA)
c/o Yellowknife Public Library, PO Box 694, Yellowknife NT
X1A 2N5
nwtlibraryassociation@gmail.com
nwtlibraryassociation.wordpress.com
To facilitate the exchange of ideas among persons involved in
library services in the Northwest Territories; To recommend
policies for the provision of library services; To promote
intellectual freedom
Alessandra Waddell, President

Nova Scotia Library Association (NSLA)
c/o Nova Scotia Provincial Library, 6016 University Ave., 5th
Fl., Halifax NS B3H 1W4
www.nsla.ns.ca
www.facebook.com/NSLibraryAssociation
twitter.com/NSLAssn
To promote the value of libraries; To facilitate the exchange of
ideas & information among library workers in Nova Scotia
Denise Corey, President
Yvette Frost, Secretary
Tim Jackson, Interim Treasurer
Dale MacMillan, Convener, Membership

Nunavut Library Association (NLA)
c/o Nunavut Legislative Library, PO Box 1200, Iqaluit NU
X0A 0H0
nunavutlibraryassociation@gmail.com
nunavutlibraryassociation.ca
To support persons who work in Nunavut libraries; To advocate
for excellent library services for Nunavut; To promote library
services & literacy; To provide professional development for
members

**Ontario Association of Library Technicians (OALT) /
Association des bibliotechniciens de l'Ontario
(ABO)**
Abbey Market, PO Box 76010, 1500 Upper Middle Rd. West,
Oakville ON L6M 3H5
info@oaltabo.on.ca
oaltabo.on.ca
www.instagram.com/oaltabo
www.linkedin.com/company/oalt-abo
www.facebook.com/OALTABO
twitter.com/OALTABO
To promote the interests of library & information technician
graduates & students throughout Ontario; To advance library &
information technician graduates & students
Vincent Elit, President
Lori O'Connor, Treasurer
Kate Terech, Coordinator, External Communications

**Ontario College & University Library Association
(OCULA)**
c/o Ontario Library Association, 2 Toronto St., 3rd Fl.,
Toronto ON M5C 2B6
Tel: 416-363-3388; *Fax:* 416-941-9581
Toll-Free: 866-873-9867
info@accessola.com
accessola.com/divisions/about-ocula
To support librarians & to improve Library Science in Ontario's
college & university libraries
Angela Henshilwood, President

Ontario Council of University Libraries (OCUL)
Robarts Library, 130 St George St., 7th Fl., Toronto ON M5S
1A5
ocul@ocul.on.ca
ocul.on.ca
twitter.com/ocul_libraries
To collaborate in the delivery & development of effective
information resources for Ontario's universities
Anika Ervin-Ward, Coordinator, Administration &
Communications
Nur Artok, Business Officer

Ontario Health Libraries Association (OHLA)
c/o Orien Duda, Health Sciences Library, 1030 Ouellette
Ave., Windsor ON N9A 1E1
Tel: 519-254-5577
ohla.inquiries@gmail.com
ohla.on.ca
www.linkedin.com/groups/2670522
To represent views of members; To advocate for the value of
health libraries & specialists; To provide a forum for leadership,
education & communications; To build & strengthen relationships
with members & other organizations

Sarah Bonato, President
Orien Duda, Treasurer

**Ontario Library & Information Technology
Association (OLITA)**
c/o Ontario Library Association, 2 Toronto St., 3rd Fl.,
Toronto ON M5C 2B6
Tel: 416-363-3388; *Fax:* 416-941-9581
Toll-Free: 866-873-9867
accessola.com/divisions/about-olita
twitter.com/olitassoc
To engage in the planning, development, design, application &
integration of technology in the library & information environment
with the impact of emerging technologies on library service, &
with the effect of automated technologies on people
Sarah Macintyre, President

Ontario Library Association (OLA)
2 Toronto St., 3rd Fl., Toronto ON M5C 2B6
Tel: 416-363-3388; *Fax:* 416-941-9581
Toll-Free: 866-873-9867
info@accessola.com
accessola.org
www.youtube.com/ONLibraryAssoc
www.linkedin.com/company/ontario-library-association
www.facebook.com/accessola
twitter.com/onlibraryassoc
To provide opportunities for people in the library & information
field to share experience & expertise & to create inclusive
communities
Shelagh Paterson, Executive Director
Stephanie Pimentel, Director, Operations
Meredith Tutching, Director, Forest of Reading
Melissa Macks, Officer, Member Engagement
Lauren Hummel, Manager, Marketing & Communications
Destiny Laldeo, Specialist, Education & Training

Ontario Library Boards' Association (OLBA)
c/o Ontario Library Association, 2 Toronto St., 3rd Fl.,
Toronto ON M5C 2B6
Tel: 416-363-3388; *Fax:* 416-941-9581
Toll-Free: 866-873-9867
info@accessola.com
accessola.com/divisions/about-olba
To represent Ontario public library board members on issues
that affect library board leadership; To advance public library
board development & improve the management & services of
libraries throughout Ontario; To enhance the visibility of library
boards
Caroline Goulding, President

Ontario Public Library Association (OPLA)
c/o Ontario Library Association, 2 Toronto St., 3rd Fl.,
Toronto ON M5C 2B6
Tel: 416-363-3388; *Fax:* 416-941-9581
Toll-Free: 866-873-9867
info@accessola.com
accessola.com/divisions/about-opla
To foster the expansion & improvement of public library service
in Ontario; To support public librarians throughout Ontario; To
encourage standards & certification for public library workers
Erika Heesen, President

Ontario School Library Association (OSLA)
c/o Ontario Library Association, 2 Toronto St., 3rd Fl.,
Toronto ON M5C 2B6
Tel: 416-363-3388; *Fax:* 416-941-9581
Toll-Free: 866-873-9867
info@accessola.com
accessola.com/divisions/about-osla
twitter.com/oslacouncil
To act as the voice of elementary & secondary school
teacher-librarians in Ontario; To promote teacher-librarians as
curriculum leaders; To support student success
Maureen McGrath, President

**Ottawa Valley Health Libraries Association (OVHLA)
/ Association des bibliothèques de santé de la
Vallée d'Outaouais**
c/o Alexandra Hickey, OVHLA Treasurer, Joule Inc., 1031
Bank St., Ottawa ON K1S 3W7
ovhla.executive@gmail.com
ovhla.chla-absc.ca
To support the provision of health library services throughout the
Ottawa Valley & the Outaouais
Kelly Farrah, President
Sarah Visintini, Treasurer

PEI Teacher-Librarians' Association (PEITLA)
c/o Carrie St. Jean, PO Box 6500, Glen Stewart Primary
School, Charlottetown PE C1I 8B5
To represent Teacher-Librarians in PEI
Carrie St. Jean, President

Provincial & Territorial Public Library Council (PTPLC) / Conseil provincial et territorial des bibliotheques (CPTBP)

ptplc-cptbp.ca

To act as a forum in which provincial & territorial public libraries can share experience, information & resources; To serve as a point of contact between national library organizations & the federal government
Mari Martin, Chair

Québec Library Association (QLA) / Association des bibliothécaires du Québec (ABQLA)
PO Box 26717, Stn. Beaconsfield, 50, boul St-Charles, Montréal QC H9W 6G7

Tel: 514-697-0146; *Fax:* 514-697-0146
abqla@abqla.qc.ca
abqla.qc.ca
www.linkedin.com/groups/5071380
www.facebook.com/124766477552846
twitter.com/ABQLA

To promote the role of library & information specialists in the greater Québec community; To foster & encourage the exchange of information on library-related issues; To strengthen relationships with national, provincial & local library associations
Sandy Hervieux, President

Reseau Biblio de l'Abitibi-Témiscamingue Nord-du-Québec
20, av Québec, Rouyn-Noranda QC J9X 2E6

Tél: 819-762-4305; *Téléc:* 819-762-5309
info@reseaubiblioatnq.qc.ca
mabiblio.quebec
www.youtube.com/user/Mouvi1
www.facebook.com/reseaubiblioatnq

Promotion du livre et de la lecture en Abitibi-Témiscamingue; promotion des bibliothèques
Cloé Gingras, Directrice générale

Réseau BIBLIO de la Côte-Nord
59, rue Napoléon, Sept-Iles QC G4R 5C5

Tél: 418-962-1020
biblio@reseaubibliocn.qc.ca
www.reseaubibliocn.qc.ca
www.facebook.com/reseaubibliocn

Promouvoir les bibliothèques publiques; concertation dans des dossiers concernant les bibliothèques publiques; faire connaître nos services
Marie-Soleil Vigneault, Directrice générale

Réseau BIBLIO du Québec
29, rue Brissette, Sainte-Agathe-des-Monts QC J8C 3L1

www.reseaubiblioduquebec.qc.ca

Le Réseau BIBLIO du Québec est un regroupement national qui vise à unir les ressources des Réseaux BIBLIO régionaux pour maintenir et développer leur réseau de bibliothèques et de les représenter auprès des diverses instances sur des dossiers d'intérêts communs.
JoAnne Turnbull, Présidente
Julie Blais, Trésorière
Jacqueline Labelle, Secrétaire générale

Réseau BIBLIO du Saguenay-Lac-Saint-Jean (RBSLSJ)
100, rue Price ouest, Alma QC G8B 4S1

Tél: 418-662-6425; *Ligne sans frais:* 800-563-6425
info@reseaubibliolsj.qc.ca
www.reseaubibliolsj.qc.ca
www.facebook.com/reseaubiblioSLSJ

Promouvoir les bibliothèques publiques; concertation dans des dossiers concernant les bibliothèques publiques; faire connaître nos services
Sophie Bolduc, Directrice générale

Réseau des services d'archives du Québec (RAQ)
a/s Archives nationales du Québec à Montréal, #5.27.1, 535, av Viger est, Montréal QC H2L 2P3

Tél: 514-864-9213
archiviste.conseil.raq@gmail.com
archivisteraq.com
www.facebook.com/293550674109606
twitter.com/reseauraq

Promouvoir le développement et la mise en valeur des archives historiques; favoriser l'échange et la mise en commun d'information, d'expérience et de ressources; devenir un instrument de consultation et un groupe de pression reconnu des divers intervenants des milieux archivistiques
Karine Foisy, Présidente

Saskatchewan Association of Library Technicians, Inc. (SALT)
349 Carleton Dr., Saskatoon SK S7H 3P2

sasksalt@gmail.com
www.sasksalt.ca
www.facebook.com/sasksalt

To support library technicians throughout Saskatchewan; To encourage & provide continuing education for library technicians; To foster the sharing of ideas & information between library technicians
Carole-Anne Wilson, President
Elisabeth Eilinger, Treasurer
Desirae Munro, Membership Secretary

Saskatchewan Council for Archives & Archivists (SCAA)
PO Box 31122, RPO Normanview, Regina SK S4R 8R6

Tel: 306-780-9414; *Fax:* 306-585-1765
scaa@sasktel.net
www.scaa.sk.ca
www.facebook.com/SCAArchivists

To facilitate the development of the archival system in Saskatchewan; To develop standard archival policies & practices; To promote public awareness of the use of archives
Mark Vajcner, President

Saskatchewan Health Libraries Association (SHLA)
SK

shlasask@gmail.com
shla.chla-absc.ca

To promote access to health library service to the Saskatchewan health community; To provide professional support & development to members
Lance Fox, President
Erin Langman, Secretary & Treasurer

Saskatchewan Library Association (SLA)
#10, 2010 - 7th Ave., Regina SK S4R 1C2

Fax: 306-780-3633
www.saskla.ca
www.facebook.com/sasklibraryassociation
twitter.com/sklibrary

To further the development of library services in Saskatchewan
Dorothea Warren, Executive Director
Anne Pennylegion, Program Coordinator

Saskatchewan Library Trustees' Association (SLTA)
c/o Nancy Kennedy, 79 Mayfair Cres., Regina SK S4S 5T9

Tel: 306-584-2495; *Fax:* 306-585-1473
slta.ca
www.facebook.com/sasklibrarytrusteesassoc

To foster the development of libraries & library services throughout Saskatchewan
Nancy Kennedy, Executive Director

Southern Alberta Health Libraries Association (SAHLA)
AB

sahla@chla-absc.ca
sahla.chla-absc.ca

To promote good health information service in southern Alberta; To encourage cooperation & communication among members; To promote educational development
Kathryn Tippell-Smith, President
Nicole Dunnewold, Secretary
Ashley Jane Leonard, Treasurer

Toronto Health Libraries Association (THLA)
ON

secretary@thla.ca
thla.chla-absc.ca
twitter.com/THLA_1

To promote the provision of quality library service to the health community; To encourage communication & cooperation among members & to foster their professional development; To consult & collaborate with other professional, technical & scientific organizations in matters of mutual interest
Naz Torabi, President
Mellisha McKenzie, Secretary
Caleb Nault, Secretary

Wellington Waterloo Dufferin Health Library Network (WWDHLN)
ON

wwdhln-l@mailman.uwaterloo.ca
wwdhln.chla-absc.ca

To support & enhance the ability of its members to provide high quality knowledge information services to member organizations; To promote communication among members; To co-operate with other health library networks to promote the efficient delivery of service; To support health library development
Tanya Harron, President

Yukon Council of Archives (YCA)
PO Box 31089, Whitehorse YT Y1A 5P7

Tel: 867-333-1700
yukoncnclarch@gmail.com
www.yukoncouncilofarchives.ca
www.instagram.com/yukon.yca.archives
www.facebook.com/Yukon.YCA

To facilitate the development of the archival system in the Yukon; To make recommendations about the system's operation & financing; To develop & facilitate implementation & management of programs to assist the archival community; To communicate archival needs & concerns to decision-makers, researchers & the general public
Karly Leonard, President

Management & Administration

Administrative Sciences Association of Canada (ASAC) / Association des sciences administratives du Canada

info@asac.ca
asac.ca

To develop teaching & research in management studies at Canadian universities
Trish McLaren, President
Amy Thurlow, Secretary

ARMA Canada
6, rue Viateur Gauvreau, Chambly QC J3L 6V3

armacanada.org
www.linkedin.com/groups/6629965
twitter.com/armacanada

To work to advance records & information management as a discipline & a profession; To organize programs of research, education, training & networking
Christy Walters, Region Director
Dawn Bassett, Secretary & Treasurer

Association des MBA du Québec (AMBAQ)
1370, rue Notre-Dame ouest, Montréal QC H3C 1K8

Tél: 514-323-8480; *Téléc:* 514-282-4292
Ligne sans frais: 888-321-3777
www.ambaq.com
www.facebook.com/ambaq
twitter.com/AMBAQ

Ôtre le porte-parole des MBA du Québec; constituer un réseau actif de diplômés et étudiants MBA; favoriser le développement personnel et professionnel des membres; valoriser et promouvoir le diplôme MBA
Charles Beaudoin, Directeur général

Association of Administrative Professionals (AAP) / Association des professionnels de l'administration
PO Box 114, 5589 Rd. 38, Hartington ON K0H 1W0

Tel: 905-580-7855
contact@canadianadmin.ca
canadianadmin.ca
www.instagram.com/administrative.professionals
www.linkedin.com/groups/13559707
www.facebook.com/association.administrative.professionals
twitter.com/canada_aaa

To promote the professional growth & advancement of members; To assist members in the continuing development of administrative skills

Association of Fundraising Professionals (AFP)
#300, 4300 Wilson Blvd., Arlington VA 22203 USA

Tel: 703-684-0410; *Fax:* 703-684-1950
Toll-Free: 800-666-3863
afp@afpnet.org
www.afpnet.org
www.linkedin.com/company/878282
www.facebook.com/AFPFan
twitter.com/afpihq

To promote stewardship, donor trust & effective & ethical fundraising
Martha Schumacher, CFRE, ACFRE, MI, Chair
Mike Geiger, President & CEO
Lisa Davey, Vice-President, AFP Canada
David Sigman, Vice-President, Finance & Administration
Michael Nilsen, Vice-President, Communications & Public Policy

Association of MBAs in Canada (AMBA)

admin@ambac.ca
ambac.ca
www.linkedin.com/company/the-association-of-mbas-in-canada

The prominent body in Canada representing and supporting those who have invested in an MBA.
Muradali Amir, President

Association of Professional Executives of the Public Service of Canada (APEX) / L'Association professionnelle des cadres de la fonction publique du Canada
#400, 75 Albert St., Ottawa ON K1P 5E7
Tel: 613-995-6252; *Fax:* 613-943-8919
info@apex.gc.ca
www.apex.gc.ca
www.linkedin.com/company/apex-goc
twitter.com/apex_gc
To represent the interests of the executive community
Jacqueline Rigg, Chief Executive Officer
Ilona Rehberg, Chief Operating Officer

Canadian Association of Management Consultants (CMC-Canada) / Association canadienne des conseillers en management
2 St. Clair Ave. West, 18th Fl., Toronto ON M4V 1L5
Tel: 416-860-1515; *Fax:* 416-860-1535
Toll-Free: 800-268-1148
consulting@cmc-canada.ca
www.cmc-canada.ca
www.youtube.com/user/CMCCanada1
www.linkedin.com/company/canadian-association-of-management-consultants
www.facebook.com/CMCCanada1
twitter.com/CMCCanada1
To foster excellence & integrity in the management consulting profession; To administer the Certified Management Consultant (CMC) designation in Canada; To advance the practice & profile of the profession of management consulting in Canada; To promote ethical standards
Donna Ringrose, Interim Executive Director
Jason Blow, Director, Business Development & Membership
Jordan Sandler, Director, Marketing & Communications

Canadian Association of School System Administrators (CASSA) / Association canadienne des administrateurs et des administratrices scolaires (ACGCS)
1123 Glenashton Dr., Oakville ON L6H 5M1
Tel: 905-845-2345; *Fax:* 905-845-2044
www.cassa-acgcs.ca
twitter.com/CASSAACGCS
To promote & enhance effective administration & leadership in provision of quality education in Canada; to provide a national voice on educational matters; to promote & provide opportunity for professional development to the membership; to promote communication & liaison with national & international organizations having an interest in education; to provide a variety of services to the membership; to recognize outstanding contributions to education in Canada
Ken Bain, Executive Director

Canadian Council of Professional Certification (CCPC)
20 Bergen Rd., Toronto ON M1P 1R9
Tel: 416-724-5339; *Fax:* 877-727-9218
Toll-Free: 877-727-9217
info@ccpcglobal.com
www.ccpcglobal.com
www.linkedin.com/company/ccpc-global
www.facebook.com/ccpcglobal
To grant certification & professional designation to qualified applicants

Canadian Executive Service Organization (CESO) / Service d'assistance canadienne aux organismes (SACO)
#800, 700 Bay St., Toronto ON M5G 1Z6
Tel: 416-961-2376; *Fax:* 416-961-1096
Toll-Free: 800-268-9052
info@ceso-saco.com
www.ceso-saco.com
www.youtube.com/CESOSACO
www.facebook.com/cesosaco
twitter.com/cesosaco
To enhance the socio-economic well-being of the peoples & the communities of Canada, developing nations & emerging market economies
Wendy Harris, President & CEO
Geoffrey Bonner, Director, Finance
Gale Lee, Director, International Services (Asia, Americas & the Caribbean)
Apollinaire Ihaza, Director, International Services (Africa & Haiti)

Canadian Institute of Management (CIM) / Institut canadien de gestion
#311, 80 Bradford St., Barrie ON L4N 6S7
Tel: 705-725-8926; *Fax:* 705-725-8196
Toll-Free: 800-387-5774
office@cim.ca
www.cim.ca
www.instagram.com/cim_charteredmanager
www.linkedin.com/company/canadian-institute-of-management
www.facebook.com/CanadianInstituteofManagement
twitter.com/CIM_National
To promote the senior management profession by offering a series of educational programs from single courses to professional certification
Matthew Jelavic, C.Mgr., National President & CEO

Canadian Management Centre (CMC)
#320, 33 Yonge St., Toronto ON M5E 1G4
Tel: 416-214-6047; *Toll-Free:* 877-262-2519
cmcinfo@cmcoutperform.com
www.cmcoutperform.com
www.youtube.com/user/CdnMgmtCtr
www.linkedin.com/company/35861
www.facebook.com/CanadianMgmt
twitter.com/canadianmgmt
To play a key role in strengthening the ability of Canada's business leaders, managers, & organizations to compete & succeed in today's challenging & changing business environment; To provide a full range of professional development & management education services to companies, government agencies & individuals
John Wright, President & Managing Director
Bernadette Smith, Vice-President, Talent Solutions

Canadian Public Relations Society Inc. (CPRS) / La Société canadienne des relations publiques
#200, 411 Richmond St. East, Toronto ON M5A 3S5
Tel: 416-239-7034; *Fax:* 416-929-5256
admin@cprs.ca
www.cprs.ca
www.instagram.com/CPRSNational
www.linkedin.com/company/canadian-public-relations-society-inc.
www.facebook.com/CPRSNational
twitter.com/CPRSNational
To oversee the practice of public relations practitioners in Canada, to ensure the protection of the public interest; To advance the professional stature of public relations practitioners; To promote the ethical practice of public relations & communications management
Kiki Cloutier, Interim Executive Director
Aisling Bermingham, Coordinator, Certification
Laura Mills, Coordinator, Awards, Membership & Chapter Relations

Canadian Society of Association Executives (CSAE) / Société canadienne des directeurs d'association (SCDA)
#1100, 10 King St. East, Toronto ON M5C 1C3
Tel: 416-363-3555; *Fax:* 416-363-3630
Toll-Free: 800-461-3608
www.csae.com
www.linkedin.com/company/csae-canadian-society-of-association-executives
www.facebook.com/AssociationExecutives
twitter.com/csaeconnect
To provide members with the environment, knowledge, & resources to develop excellence in not-for-profit leadership through networking, education, advocacy, information, & research
Tracy Folkes Hanson, President & CEO
Danielle Lamothe, Vice-President, Learning & Innovation
Edward Byers, Director, Membership & Business Development
Rhonda McIntyre, Director, Finance & Corporate Services
Penny Tantakis, Director, Marketing & Communications
Yowali Kabamba, Network Administrator, Alberta, Atlantic, British Columbia, Manitoba & Quebec
Casey Pope, Network Administrator, Ottawa-Gatineau, Trillium

Canadian Society of Physician Leaders (CSPL) / Société canadienne des leaders médicaux
#223, 875 Carling Ave., Ottawa ON K1S 5P1
Tel: 613-369-8322
physicianleaders.ca
www.linkedin.com/company/canadian-society-of-physician-leaders
twitter.com/CSPLeaders
To develop physician leaders to be successful in health care leadership & management roles
Carol Rochefort, Executive Director

Canadian Student Leadership Association (CSLA)
2460 Tanner Rd., Victoria BC V8Z 5R1
studentleadership.ca
www.facebook.com/CanadianStudentLeadershipAssociation
twitter.com/CSLA_Leaders
Don Homan, Chair
Bill Conconi, Executive Director

The Chartered Governance Institute of Canada (CGIC)
#739, 1568 Merivale Rd., Ottawa ON K2G 5Y7
Tel: 613-595-1151; *Toll-Free:* 800-501-3440
info@charteredgovernanceinstitute.ca
www.cgiofcanada.ca
www.linkedin.com/company/cgiofcanada
www.facebook.com/297017093984978
twitter.com/CGIofCanada
To represent & serve chartered secretaries & administrators, professionals who are hired by organizations to administer key areas such as corporate governance, director / officer / shareholder matters, compliance & regulatory matters & financial matters
Patricia Thacker, CAE, Executive Director
David Miriguay, CAE, Director, Education

CIO Association of Canada (CIOCAN)
National Office, #305, 7270 Woodbine Ave., Markham ON L3R 4B9
Tel: 905-752-1899; *Fax:* 905-513-1248
Toll-Free: 877-865-9009
www.ciocan.ca
www.linkedin.com/company/cio-association-of-canada
twitter.com/CIO_CAN
To facilitate networking, sharing of best practices & executive development, & to drive advocacy on issues facing IT Executives/CIOs. Chapters: Calgary, Edmonton, Manitoba, Montreal, Ottawa, Toronto & Vancouver
Tracy Blyth, Executive Director
Alison Toscano, Director, Operations

Corporation des approvisionneurs du Québec (CAQ)
Complexe Tassé, #302, 895, boul Séminaire nord, Saint-Jean-sur-Richelieu QC J3A 1J2
Tél: 450-357-0033; *Téléc:* 450-357-0044
Ligne sans frais: 800-977-1877
info@caq.qc.ca
www.caq.qc.ca
www.facebook.com/CorpoAppQc
La Corporation des approvisionneurs du Québec assure le développement professionnel de ses membres et veille à promouvoir et favoriser l'implantation des meilleures pratiques en matière de gestion de la chaîne d'approvisionnement au sein des entreprises québécoises afin que la valeur stratégique de l'approvisionnement puisse contribuer pleinement à l'essor des entreprises et à la société québécoise.
Pierre St-Jean, Président

Couchiching Institute on Public Affairs (CIPA)
#240, 65 Overlea Blvd., Toronto ON M4H 1P1
Toll-Free: 866-647-6374
couch@couchichinginstitute.ca
www.facebook.com/couchichinginstitute
twitter.com/couchiching
To bring together interested Canadians to discuss important public policy issues with experts & other members of the general public

Fédération des secrétaires professionnelles du Québec (FSPQ)
#390-1, 1173, boul Charest ouest, Québec QC G1N 2C9
Tél: 418-527-5041; *Téléc:* 418-527-2160
Ligne sans frais: 866-527-5041
info@fspq.qc.ca
www.fspq.qc.ca
www.linkedin.com/groups/2340718
twitter.com/FSPQ
Travail à la valorisation de la profession
Anick Blouin, Présidente

Global Network of Director Institutes (GNDI)
c/o Institute of Directors in Southern Africa, 144 Katherine St., Sandton 2196 South Africa
www.gndi.org
To help members stay abreast of leading practices as well as current & emerging governance issues; To foster closer cooperation between members
Angela Cherrington, Chair

Governance Professionals of Canada (GPC)
#802, 21 St. Clair Ave. East, Toronto ON M4T 1L9
Tel: 416-921-5449; *Fax:* 416-967-6320
Toll-Free: 800-774-2850
info@gpcanada.org
gpcanada.org
www.linkedin.com/company/governance-professionals-of-canad
a
To promote & advance governance practices in private, public, & not-for-profit organizations
Lynn Beauregard, President
Albert Orellana, Manager, Events & Special Projects
Crystal Singh, Coordinator, Membership & Events

Institute of Certified Management Consultants of Alberta (CMC-Alberta)
c/o CMC-Canada National Office, PO Box 20, #2004, 410 Bay St., Toronto ON M5H 2Y4
Tel: 416-860-1515; *Fax:* 416-860-1535
Toll-Free: 800-268-1148
consulting@cmc-canada.ca
www.cmc-canada.ca/provincial_institutes.cfm?Portal_ID=1
To act under the regulations of the Professional & Occupational Associations Registration Act; To work as the regulatory authority for provisional registrants, certified management consultants, & fellow certified management consultants in Alberta; To ensure that members abide by professional & ethical standards
Greg McIntyre, Vice-President
Jeff Griffiths, Registrar

Institute of Certified Management Consultants of Atlantic Canada
c/o CMC-Canada National Office, 2 St Clair Ave. West, 18th Fl., Toronto ON M4V 1L5
Tel: 416-860-1515; *Fax:* 416-860-1535
Toll-Free: 800-268-1148
consulting@cmc-canada.ca
www.cmc-canada.ca/instituteschapters
To foster excellence & integrity in the management consulting profession.
Jerrold White, President
Blaine Atkinson, Registrar

Institute of Certified Management Consultants of British Columbia (CMC-BC)
c/o CMC-Canada National Office, PO Box 20, #2004, 401 Bay St., Toronto ON M5H 2Y4
Tel: 416-860-1515; *Fax:* 416-860-1535
Toll-Free: 800-268-1148
consulting@camc.com
www.cmc-canada.ca/provincial_institutes.cfm?Portal_ID=3
To protect the general public & clients by ensuring that the Institute's Code of Professional Conduct is followed by the certified management consultant profession; To ensure that certified members comply with all applicable legislation & laws
Stephen Spooner, President
Lyn Blanchard, Vice-President
Shayda Kassam, Treasurer

Institute of Certified Management Consultants of Manitoba (CMC-Manitoba) / Institut manitobain des conseillers en administration agréés
c/o CMC-Canada National Office, 2 St Clair Ave. West, 18th Fl., Toronto ON M4V 1L5
Tel: 416-860-1515; *Fax:* 416-860-1535
Toll-Free: 800-268-1148
consulting@cmc-canada.ca
www.cmc-canada.ca/instituteschapters
To foster & promote the development & acceptance of the profession of management consulting; to promote excellence in the practice of the profession for the benefit of members, clients & the community at large.
Timothy Wildman, President
Warren Thompson, Registrar

Institute of Certified Management Consultants of Saskatchewan
c/o CMC-Canada National Office, PO Box 20, #2004, 401 Bay St., Toronto ON M5H 2Y4
Tel: 416-860-1515; *Fax:* 416-860-1535
Toll-Free: 800-662-2972
consulting@cmc-canada.ca
www.cmc-canada.ca/provincial_institutes.cfm?Portal_ID=7
www.facebook.com/CMC.Saskatchewan
Richmond Graham, President
Jeremy Hall, Registrar

Institute of Corporate Directors (ICD) / Institut des administrateurs de sociétés
#2701, 250 Yonge St., Toronto ON M5B 2L7
Tel: 416-593-7741; *Toll-Free:* 877-593-7741
info@icd.ca
www.icd.ca
www.linkedin.com/school/icdcanada
twitter.com/ICDCanada
To enhance the quality of corporate governance in Canada
Rahul Bhardwaj, LLB, ICDD, President & CEO

Institute of Professional Management (IPM)
#2210, 1081 Ambleside Dr., Ottawa ON K2B 8C8
Tel: 613-721-5957; *Fax:* 613-721-5850
info@workplace.ca
www.workplace.ca
www.facebook.com/InstituteofProfessionalManagement

International Personnel Management Association - Canada (IPMA-Canada)
PO Box 4011, Mount Pearl NL A1N 0A1
Toll-Free: 888-226-5002
ipmacanada@ipma-aigp.com
ipma-aigp.com
www.linkedin.com/in/ipmaaigpcanada
twitter.com/IPMACanada
To promote excellence in the practice of human resource management; to promote & enhance the HR profession in Canada & globally; To provide professional development & training for the HR community; to maintain a code of ethics & standards of practice; To recognize excellence through national & local awards programs

Ontario Association of Emergency Managers (OAEM)
c/o McCauley Nichols, 14 Caledonia Terrace, Goderich ON N7A 2M8
Tel: 519-524-5992; *Fax:* 519-612-1992
secretary@oaem.ca
www.oaem.ca
To unite emergency management professionals in Ontario; To promote, support, & improve the profession of emergency management in Ontario
Amber Rushton, Coordinator, Membership

Ordre des administrateurs agréés du Québec (OAAQ)
#360, 1050, côte du Beaver Hall, Montréal QC H2Z 0A5
Tél: 514-499-0880; *Téléc:* 514-499-0892
Ligne sans frais: 800-465-0880
info@adma.qc.ca
www.adma.qc.ca
www.instagram.com/ordreadma
www.linkedin.com/company/ordreadma
www.facebook.com/OrdreAdmA
twitter.com/OrdreAdmA
Favorise auprès des professionnels de l'administration, l'innovation et l'atteinte d'un niveau de compétence supérieur pour qu'ils contribuent de façon proactive et dynamique au développement des entreprises et des organisations; Assure la protection du public en garantissant le respect des normes et standards professionnels en administration, en conformité avec le code de déontologie et par le biais des mécanismes prévus au code des professions; Contribue à l'avancement de l'administration, discipline essentielle au développement social et économique du Québec
Francine Sabourin, Directrice générale

Supply Chain Management Association (SCMA) / Association de la gestion de la chaîne d'approvisionnement (AGCA)
PO Box 64, #2704, 1 Dundas St. West, Toronto ON M5G 1Z3
Tel: 416-977-7111; *Fax:* 416-977-8886
Toll-Free: 888-799-0877
info@scmanational.ca
scma.com
www.linkedin.com/groups/2888933
www.facebook.com/scmanational
twitter.com/scmanational
To advance strategic supply chain management by providing training, education, & professional development for supply chain management professionals in Canada
Christian Buhagiar, President & CEO
Lynne Coles, Chief Marketing Officer

Supply Chain Management Association - Alberta (SCMAAB)
Sterling Business Centre, #115, 17420 Stony Plain Rd., Edmonton AB T5S 1K6
Tel: 780-944-0355; *Fax:* 780-944-0356
Toll-Free: 866-610-4089
info@scmaab.ca
www.scmaab.ca
www.linkedin.com/groups/4259963
www.facebook.com/332429763455410
twitter.com/SCMA_alberta
To develop the profession by ensuring that professional status is accessible to all purchasing practitioners in the province; high standards of eligibility & professional conduct will be developed, maintained & enforced to enhance the profession & protect public interest in the province of Alberta
Allan To, President

Supply Chain Management Association - British Columbia (SCMABC)
#300, 435 Columbia St., New Westminster BC V3L 5N8
Tel: 604-540-4494; *Fax:* 604-540-4023
Toll-Free: 800-411-7622
info@scmabc.ca
www.scmabc.ca
www.facebook.com/scmanational
twitter.com/scmabc
BC Institute PMAC is an incorporated, not-for-profit association that maintains a code of ethics for the profession to regulate quality & integrity.
Barrie Lynch, Executive Director
Ron Wiebe, President

Supply Chain Management Association - Manitoba (SCMAMB)
#200, 5 Donald St., Winnipeg MB R3L 2T4
Tel: 204-231-0965; *Fax:* 204-233-1250
Toll-Free: 877-231-0965
info@scmamb.ca
www.scmamb.ca
www.linkedin.com/groups/4546716
www.facebook.com/supplychaincanada
twitter.com/scmanational
SCMAMB is committed to offering a professional development program coupled with networking opportunities to advance supply chain management.
Jay Anderson, President
Rick Reid, Executive Director

Supply Chain Management Association - New Brunswick (SCMANB)
#402, 527 Dundonald St., Fredericton NB E3B 1X5
Tel: 506-458-9414
info@scmanb.ca
www.scmanb.ca
www.linkedin.com/groups/2888933
www.facebook.com/NBPMI
twitter.com/scmanational
NBPMI is dedicated to being the leading source of education, training, & development in the field of purchasing & supply chain management. It provides members with networking opportunities & offers them training for a Supply Chain Management Professional (SCMP) designation.
Ryan McPherson, President
Wendy Piercy, Administrator

Supply Chain Management Association - Newfoundland & Labrador (SCMANL)
PO Box 29011, Stn. Torbay Road, St. John's NL A1A 5B5
Tel: 709-778-4033; *Fax:* 709-724-5625
info@scmanl.ca
www.scmanl.ca
www.linkedin.com/groups/2888933
www.facebook.com/scmanational
twitter.com/scmanational
To deliver education, training, & professional development programs in the province, so members may earn a Supply Chain Management Professional (SCMP) designation
Shauna Clark, President

Supply Chain Management Association - Northwest Territories (SCMANWT)
PO Box 2736, Yellowknife NT X1A 2R1
Tel: 867-873-9324
info@scmanwt.ca
www.scmanwt.ca
A non profit organization registered with the Societies Act in the Northwest Territories. They provide information and Education leading to a professional designation as a C.P.P. (Certified Professional Purchaser) the only accredited and legally recognized designation in the fields of Purchasing and Supply Management in Canada.

John Vandenberg, President

Supply Chain Management Association - Nova Scotia (SCMANS)
PO Box 21, Stn. CRO, Halifax NS B3J 2L4
Tel: 902-425-4029; *Fax:* 902-431-7220
info@scmans.ca
www.scmans.ca
www.linkedin.com/groups/2888933
www.facebook.com/supplychaincanada
twitter.com/scmanational
NSIPMAC delivers education, training & professional development programs in the province, so members may earn a Supply Chain Management Professional (SCMP) designation.
Joe McKenna, President

Supply Chain Management Association - Ontario (SCMAO)
PO Box 64, #2704, 1 Dundas St. West, Toronto ON M5G 1Z3
Tel: 416-977-7566; *Fax:* 416-977-4135
Toll-Free: 877-726-6968
info@scmao.ca
www.scmao.ca
www.youtube.com/user/OIPMAC
twitter.com/SCMAOnt
The preeminent supply chain managemen organisation in Ontario, supporting a growing global SCM community of over 20,00 active members and program participants in meeting their professional and lifelong learning goals. Their programs taught by leading North American academics and professional trainers, are designed to build/enhance the professional competence and strategic perspective of practitioners at all levels of career progression, from entry-, to mid-, to senior/executive levels of functional responsibility.
Kelly Duffin, Executive Director

Supply Chain Management Association - Saskatchewan (SCMASK)
#221A, 3521 - 8th St. East, Saskatoon SK S7H 0W5
Tel: 306-653-8899; *Fax:* 306-653-8870
Toll-Free: 866-665-6167
info@scmask.ca
www.scmask.ca
www.linkedin.com/company/3549789
www.facebook.com/SCMASK
twitter.com/SCMASK
To promote & improve supply management practices in the profession through education & raising the awareness of the supply management profession within Saskatchewan
Nicole Burgess, Executive Director

Manufacturing & Industry

Alberta Floor Covering Association (AFCA)
60 Martindale Close NE, Calgary AB T3J 2V1
Tel: 403-280-6006; *Fax:* 403-280-6056
Toll-Free: 800-292-9712
afca@shaw.ca
www.albertafloors.com
To ensure professionalism in Alberta's floor covering industry; To promote high standards within the industry, by upholding the Code of Ethics & the Code of Trade & Practice; To represent members on issues related to the construction industry
Peggy Alkenbrack, Executive Director

Association de la recherche industrielle du Québec (ADRIQ)
#1120, 555, boul René-Lévesque ouest, Montréal QC H2Z 1B1
Tél: 514-337-3001; *Téléc:* 514-337-2229
adriq@adriq.com
www.adriq.com
www.linkedin.com/groups/2999463
twitter.com/ADRIQ_RCTi
De promouvoir les nouvelles technologies afin d'accroître le commerce concurrentiel au Québec et à l'étranger
Pascal Monette, Président-directeur général

Association for Operations Management (APICS)
#300, 1370 Don Mills Rd., Toronto ON M3B 3N7
Tel: 416-366-5388; *Fax:* 416-381-4054
info@apics.ca
www.apics.ca
To offer programs & materials on business management techniques; To promote education in resource management
Mauro Girardo, President

Association of Home Appliance Manufacturers Canada Council (AHAM)
#1200, 130 Albert St., Ottawa ON K1P 5G4
Tel: 613-236-8428
info@aham.org
www.aham.org/AHAM/AuxAHAMCanada
twitter.com/AHAM_Voice
To represent member interests in the establishment of product standards & in environmental legislation; To advocate the safe removal of mercury & other ozone depleting substances from older appliances; To support the development of energy efficient products
Kevin Girdharry, Manager, Policy & Data Analysis
Meagan Hatch, Director, Government Relations

Association of Independent Corrugated Converters
PO Box 35, 43 King St. West, Toronto ON L7E 5T1
Fax: 833-200-8333
Toll-Free: 833-200-8333
info@aiccbox.com
www.aiccbox.ca
www.facebook.com/canadaaicc
twitter.com/CanadaAicc
To provide a forum for independent corrugated converters on legitimate matters of mutual interest; To enhance the level of professionalism of the independent converter in the operation of their business; To implement democratically determined goals on matters civil & governmental that have a positive effect on all independent corrugated converters

British Columbia Paint Manufacturers' Association (BCPMA)
c/o Cloverdale Paint Inc., #400, 2630 Croydon Dr., Surrey BC V3Z 6T3
Tel: 604-596-6261
helpdesk@cloverdalepaint.com
www.cloverdalepaint.com
To act as the voice of paint manufacturers in British Columbia; To promote the welfare of association members

Business & Institutional Furniture Manufacturer's Association (BIFMA)
#150, 678 Front Ave. NW, Grand Rapids MI 49504-5368 USA
Tel: 616-285-3963; *Fax:* 616-285-3765
email@bifma.org
www.bifma.org
www.linkedin.com/company/BIFMA
twitter.com/BIFMA
To promote the interests of the commercial furniture industry
Tom Reardon, Executive Director

Canadian Association of Moldmakers (CAMM)
c/o St. Clair College (FCEM), PO Box 16, 2000 Talbot Rd. West, Windsor ON N9A 6S4
Tel: 519-255-7863; *Fax:* 519-255-9446
info@camm.ca
www.camm.ca
To represent companies in Mold, Tool, Die, & Automation; To promote & develop a global exposure for the mold making industry
Jonathon Azzopardi, Chair
Diane Deslippe, Executive Director

Canadian Explosives Industry Association (CEAEC) / Association Canadienne de L'industrie des Explosifs
164, Ruskin, Beaconsfield QC H9W 2Y2
www.ceaec.ca
To promote & represent the general interests of distributors, manufacturers & users of explosives; To promote & maintain high standards concerning the use, handling & transport of explosives; To co-operate with government authorities in the promotion of safety standards; To encourage the adoption & adherence to uniform legislation concerning the Canadian explosives industry
Nicholas Ebsworth, Executive Director

Canadian Fire Alarm Association (CFAA)
#3-4, 85 Citizen Ct., Markham ON L6G 1A8
Tel: 905-944-0030; *Fax:* 905-479-3639
Toll-Free: 800-529-0552
admin@cfaa.ca
www.cfaa.ca
To maximize the effectiveness and use of fire alarm systems in the protection of life and property in Canada.
Suzanne Alfano, Executive Director
Ruth Kavanagh, Manager, Membership & Finance

Canadian Hardware & Housewares Manufacturers' Association (CHHMA) / Association canadienne des fabricants de produits de quincaillerie et d'articles ménagers
#101, 1335 Morningside Ave., Toronto ON M1B 5M4
Tel: 416-282-0022
www.chhma.ca
www.linkedin.com/company/chhma
twitter.com/theCHHMA
To assist members to sell more & do it more profitably
Sam Moncada, President
Nicole Gamble, Manager, Operations & Events Manager
Michael Jorgenson, Manager, Marketing & Communications
Pam Winter, Coordinator, Events

Canadian Innovation Centre (CIC)
c/o Waterloo Research & Technology Park, #15, 295 Hagey Blvd., Waterloo ON N2L 6R5
Tel: 519-885-5870; *Fax:* 519-513-2421
Toll-Free: 800-265-4559
info@innovationcentre.ca
www.innovationcentre.ca
www.linkedin.com/company/canadian-innovation-centre
twitter.com/innovationctre
To advance innovation by helping our clients make better business decisions through information, education & commercialization.
Ted Cross, Chair
Josie Graham, CEO & Director, Projects and Studies

Canadian Kitchen Cabinet Association (CKCA) / Association canadienne de fabricants d'armoires de cuisine (ACAC)
PO Box 34018, 3781 Strandherd Dr., Ottawa ON K2J 5B1
Tel: 613-493-5858
info@ckca.ca
www.ckca.ca
To promote the interests & conserve the rights of those engaged in the manufacture of kitchen cabinets, bathroom vanities & related millwork as well as their suppliers & dealers
Mike Slobodian, President
Sandra Wood, Executive Director

Canadian Laboratory Suppliers Association (CLSA) / Association canadienne de fournisseurs de laboratoire
#220, 245 King George Rd., Brantford ON N3R 7N7
Tel: 519-758-9984; *Fax:* 519-758-9736
www.clsassoc.com
To promote & serve the Canadian laboratory marketplace; To provide a non-competitive environment for executives of Canada's leading scientific suppliers to share ideas & concepts; To provide market analysis on the scientific industry; To understand & discuss issues that influence the Canadian laboratory scientific market
Richard Blais, President & Chair

Canadian Manufacturers & Exporters (CME) / Manufacturiers et Exportateurs Canada
#402, 270 Albert St., Ottawa ON K1P 5G8
www.cme-mec.ca
www.youtube.com/user/manufacturingTV
www.linkedin.com/company/canadian-manufacturers-&-exporters
twitter.com/cme_mec
To continuously improve the competitiveness of Canadian industry & to expand export business by: aggressive, effective advocacy to government at all levels; delivering timely, relevant information, programs & support of superior quality & value; providing opportunities for education, learning & professional growth; & promoting the development & implementation of advanced technology
Dennis Darby, President & CEO
Mathew Wilson, Senior Vice-President, Policy & Government Relations

Canadian Office Products Association (COPA)
#101, 1335 Morningside Ave., Toronto ON M1B 5M4
Tel: 905-624-9462; *Fax:* 905-624-0830
info@copa.ca
www.copa.ca
www.linkedin.com/company/2675440
www.facebook.com/CanadianOfficeProductsAssociation
twitter.com/COPA_network
To help their memebers by providing them with business solutions that allow them to grow
Jordan Hoxie, Chair

Canadian Tooling & Machining Association (CTMA)
#3, 140 McGovern Dr., Cambridge ON N3H 4R7
Tel: 519-653-7265; *Fax:* 519-653-6764
info@ctma.com
www.ctma.com
www.linkedin.com/company/canadian-tooling-machining-associa
tion
www.facebook.com/111451842271079
twitter.com/CTMA_Voice
To be an effective, broad-based, respected organization, representing the Canadian tooling & machining industry, nationally & internationally
Robert Cattle, Executive Director
Julie McFarlane, Office Manager

Canadian Toy Association / Canadian Toy & Hobby Fair (CTA) / L'Association canadienne du Jouet
PO Box 218, #2219, 160 Tycos Dr., Toronto ON M6B 1W8
Tel: 416-596-0671; *Fax:* 416-596-1808
info@canadiantoyassociation.ca
www.canadiantoyassociation.ca
www.linkedin.com/company/canadian-toy-association
twitter.com/CdnToy
To represent the toy industry in Canada
Serge Micheli, Executive Director

Cosmetics Alliance Canada / L'Alliance de l'industrie cosmétique du Canada
#102, 420 Britannia Rd. East, Mississauga ON L4Z 3L5
Tel: 905-890-5161; *Fax:* 905-890-2607
ca@cosmeticsalliance.ca
www.cosmeticsalliance.ca
www.youtube.com/user/CCTFA
www.linkedin.com/company/cosmeticsalliance
www.facebook.com/CosmeticsAlliance
twitter.com/cosm_alliance
To encourage trust & confidence in the Canadian cosmetic industry & in the safety, efficacy & quality of its products; To be the princiapal voice of the personal care industry, including cosmetic-like drug products & cosmetic-like natural health products (NHP), interfacing on a timely basis with governemtn & elected representatives, to ensure development & effective representationof industry positions on all regulatory issues; To have the personal care industry perceived by consumers at large as being socially concerned, responsible & involved with Canadian society
John Coyne, Chair
Darren Praznik, President & CEO

Door & Hardware Institute in Canada
#201, 2800 - 14th Ave., Markham ON L3R 0E4
Tel: 416-492-6502; *Fax:* 416-491-1670
info@dhicanada.ca
www.dhicanada.ca
twitter.com/dhicanada
To serve Canadian members as the professional development, information, advocate & certification resource for the total distribution process in the architectural openings industry
Scott Suppes, President
Carolyne Vigon, Executive Director

Fédération québécoise des revêtements de sol (FQRS) / Québec Institute of Floor Covering
#403, 2030, boul Pie-IX, Montréal QC H1V 2C8
Tél: 514-355-8001; *Téléc:* 514-355-4159
fqrs@spg.qc.ca
www.fqrs.ca
Regrouper les gens de l'industrie des revêtements de sol pour les aider dans les différents domaines
Pierre Hébert, Président

Fenestration Association of BC (FEN-BC)
#101, 20351 Duncan Way, Langley BC V3A 7N3
Tel: 778-571-0245; *Fax:* 866-253-9979
info@fen-bc.org
www.fen-bc.org
To represent the interests of businesses engaged in the fenestration industry in BC
Zana Gordon, Executive Director

Fenestration Canada
#210, 65 Overlea Blvd., Toronto ON M4H 1P1
Tel: 613-424-7239; *Fax:* 866-605-0657
info@fenestrationcanada.ca
www.fenestrationcanada.ca
To represents its members in all aspects of the window & door manufacturing industry, including formulating & promoting high standards of quality in manufacturing, design, marketing, distribution, sales, & application of all types of window & door products
Erin Roberts, Executive Director
Asif Ahmed, Deputy Director

International Sanitary Supply Association Canada
PO Box 10009, 910 Dundas St. West, Whitby ON L1P 1P7
Tel: 905-665-8001; *Toll-Free:* 866-684-8273
info@issa-canada.com
www.issa-canada.com
www.linkedin.com/company/issacanada
www.facebook.com/ISSACanada1
twitter.com/ISSAShowCanada
To provide a high degree of professionalism, technical knowledge & business ethics within the membership; To promote greater public awareness, appreciation & understanding of the sanitation industry
Mike Nosko, Executive Director
Tracy MacDonald, Manager, Operations

The Metal Working Association of New Brunswick (MWANB) / Association des entreprises métallurgiques du Nouveau-Brunswick
PO Box 7129, #12, 567 Coverdale Rd., Riverview NB E1B 4T8
Tel: 506-861-9071; *Fax:* 506-857-3059
nb@cme-mec.ca
www.mwanb.com
To be a voice for the metal working sector in New Brunswick & to provide a forum for members to network & discuss opportunities
Corey MacDonald, President
Scott Black, Vice President

National Floor Covering Association (NFCA) / Association nationale des revêtements de sol
#2, 19299 - 94th Ave., Surrey BC V4N 4E6
Tel: 604-371-0137; *Fax:* 604-881-4744
info@nfca.ca
www.nfca.ca
www.facebook.com/728769117577150
twitter.com/nfca4
To unite the Canadian regional & provincial associations in a spirit of cooperation; To improve & enhance the floorcovering industry; To share information & ideas; To undertake & support programs that will improve communications at all levels of the industry
Chris Maskell, Chief Executive Officer
Thomas Foreman, Executive Director

Organization of Canadian Nuclear Industries (OCNI)
#219, 1550 Kingston Rd., Pickering ON L1V 1C3
Tel: 905-839-0073; *Fax:* 905-839-7085
hello@ocni.ca
www.ocni.ca
www.youtube.com/user/OCINuclear
www.linkedin.com/company/organization-of-canadian-nuclear-in
dustries
www.facebook.com/623976057618324
twitter.com/theoci
To promote the Canadian nuclear industry for the benefit of its members & to offer services that enable members to be successful in the domestic & global nuclear industry
Ron Oberth, President & CEO

Sous-Traitance Industrielle Québec (STIQ)
#900, 1080, côte du Beaver Hall, Montréal QC H2Z 1S8
Tél: 514-875-8789; *Ligne sans frais:* 888-875-8789
info@stiq.com
www.stiq.com
Normand Voyer, Vice-président executive

Tire & Rubber Association of Canada (TRAC) / L'Association canadienne du pneu et du caoutchouc
260 Holiday Inn Dr., #A19, Cambridge ON N3C 4E8
Tel: 519-249-0366; *Fax:* 519-249-0401
info@tracanada.ca
www.tracanada.ca
www.linkedin.com/company/tire-and-rubber-association-of-cana
da
To upgrade & maintain good industry / government working relations; To explore ways of improving industry competitiveness & efficiency; To promote safety in members' products, in their use & in the workplace; To promote expansion & profitability of Canadian rubber manufacturing units; To enhance standing of Canadian rubber industry worldwide; To provide members with industry marketing statistics
Glenn Maidment, President

Toronto Japanese Association of Commerce & Industry
PO Box 104, #122, 20 York Mills Rd., Toronto ON M2P 2C2
Tel: 416-360-0235; *Fax:* 416-360-0236
office@torontoshokokai.org
www.torontoshokokai.org

To promote business relations between Canada & Japan through the activities of the members of the Japanese School of Toronto Shokokai Inc.
Tetsuo Komuro, President
Yukio Arita, Executive Director & Secretary

Truss Plate Institute of Canada (TPIC)
tpic.ca
To serve the needs of manufacturers of truss plates & wood trusses
Augusto Vertolli, P.Eng., President

Marine Trades

Boating BC Association
#130, 10691 Shellbridge Way, Richmond BC V6X 2W8
Tel: 604-248-8906; *Fax:* 604-270-3644
info@boatingbc.ca
www.boatingbc.ca
www.youtube.com/channel/UCyvMWT5_eNm_0LBJFbXiZSw
www.linkedin.com/company/boating-bc-association
www.facebook.com/BoatingBC
twitter.com/boatingbc
To act as the voice of the BC recreational marine industry
Don Prittie, President
Lisa Geddes, Executive Director
Mike Short, First Vice-President & Treasurer

British Columbia Maritime Employers Association (BCMEA)
#500, 349 Railway St., Vancouver BC V6A 1A4
Tel: 604-688-1155; *Fax:* 604-684-2397
www.bcmea.com
www.linkedin.com/company/1556948
www.facebook.com/BCMEA
twitter.com/editorbcmea
To respond to the needs of members; To represent the interests of members; To provide labour relations services to British Columbia's waterfront employers
Terry Duggan, President & Chief Executive Officer
Mike Leonard, Senior Vice President, Employee Relations & Dispatch
John Beckett, Vice President, Training, Safety, & Recruitment
Eleanor Marynuik, Vice President, Human Resources

Canadian Marine Industries & Shipbuilding Association (CMISA) / Association de la construction navale du Canada
#301, 200 Catherine St., Ottawa ON K2P 2K9
Tel: 613-701-7048
info@cmisa.ca
www.cmisa.ca
www.linkedin.com/company/canadian-marine-industry-and-shipb
uilders-association
Represents the interests of the Canadian shipbuilding, ship repair & associated marine equipment & services industries
Colin Cooke, President & CEO

Canadian Marine Industry Foundation (CMIF) / Fondation de l'industrie maritime canadienne (FMIC)
#340, 300 Sparks St., Ottawa ON K1R 7S3
Tel: 613-233-8779
info@cmif-fimc.ca
cmif-fimc.ca
www.linkedin.com/company/canadian-marine-industry-foundatio
n-fondation-de-l-industrie-maritime-canadienne
To raise awareness of the marine industry so it can better compete for skilled labour, trades & accredited professionals; To inform & educate the wider public on the marine & its benefits
Marc-André Poisson, Contact

Canadian Navigation Society (CNS)
c/o Canadian Aeronautics & Space Institute, #104, 350 Terry Fox Dr., Kanata ON K2K 2W5
Tel: 613-591-8787; *Fax:* 613-591-7291
www.casi.ca/canadian-navigation-society
To advance the science, technologies, & applications of navigation
Susan Skone, Society Chair

The Great Lakes Marine Heritage Foundation
55 Ontario St., Kingston ON K7L 2Y2
Tel: 613-542-2261; *Fax:* 613-542-0043
marmus@marmuseum.ca
www.marmuseum.ca
Doug Cowie, Manager

National Marine Manufacturers Association Canada (NMMA)
#8, 14 McEwan Dr., Bolton ON L7E 1H1
Tel: 905-951-4048
www.nmma.ca

To promote & advocate for boating with government; To provide value added services to foster the financial success of the marine industry
Sara Anghel, President
Jim Wielgosz, Director, Provincial & Federal Government Relations

Marketing

American Marketing Association (AMA)
130 East Randolph St., 22nd Fl., Chicago IL 60601 USA
Tel: 312-542-9000; *Fax:* 312-542-9001
www.ama.org
www.linkedin.com/company/american-marketing-association
www.facebook.com/AmericanMarketing
twitter.com/AMA_Marketing
To urge & assist the personal & professional development of members; To advance the science & ethical practice of the marketing discipline

Association of Internet Marketing & Sales (AIMS)
#650, 99 Spadina Ave., Toronto ON M5V 3P8
admin@aimscanada.com
www.aimscanada.com
www.linkedin.com/groups/2239
www.facebook.com/153321404762068
twitter.com/AIMS_Canada
To assist business professionals to leverage the internet in their daily business
Bruce Powell, Member, Executive Board

Atlantic Publishers Marketing Association (APMA)
1484 Carlton St., Halifax NS B3H 3B7
Tel: 902-420-0711; *Fax:* 902-423-4302
www.atlanticpublishers.ca
www.facebook.com/AtlanticBooksToday
twitter.com/abtmagazine
To promote the growth & development of Canadian-owned publishing houses based in Atlantic Canada; To provide a common platform for publishers & individuals involved in Atlantic Canada's publishing industry to share ideas & information; To represent members to all levels of government; To liaison with associations & organizations to further the interests of the Canadian publishing industry; To promote the sale of publications by publishers
Carolyn Guy, Executive Director
Chris Benjamin, Managing Editor

British Columbia Cranberry Marketing Commission (BCCMC)
PO Box 162, Stn. A, Abbotsford BC V2T 6Z5
Tel: 604-897-9252
cranberries@telus.net
www.bccranberries.com
www.instagram.com/bccranberries
www.facebook.com/bccranberries
twitter.com/BCcranberries
To regulate cranberry farming in BC

British Columbia Egg Marketing Board
#250, 32160 South Fraser Way, Abbotsford BC V2T 1W5
Tel: 604-556-3348; *Fax:* 604-556-3410
bcemb@bcegg.com
www.bcegg.com
www.youtube.com/user/BCEggProducers
www.facebook.com/bcegg
twitter.com/bceggs
To regulate British Columbia's egg farming industry
Richard King, Chair

British Columbia Hog Marketing Commission
PO Box 8000-280, Abbotsford BC V2S 6H1
Tel: 604-287-4647; *Fax:* 604-820-6647
info@bcpork.ca
bcpork.ca
Geraldine Auston, Contact

British Columbia Milk Marketing Board
#200, 32160 South Fraser Way, Abbotsford BC V2T 1W5
Tel: 604-556-3444; *Fax:* 604-556-7717
info@milk-bc.com
www.milk-bc.com
To promote, control & regulate the production, transportation, packing, storing & marketing of milk, fluid milk & manufactured milk products within British Columbia
Ben Janzen, Chair
Robert Delage, General Manager

British Columbia Vegetable Marketing Commission (BCVMC)
#207, 15252- 32nd Ave., Surrey BC V3S 0R7
Tel: 604-542-9734; *Fax:* 604-542-9735
tom@bcveg.com
www.bcveg.com
Tom Demma, General Manager
David Taylor, Chair

Canadian Agri-Marketing Association (CAMA)
22 Guyers Dr., RR#3, Port Elgin ON N0H 2C7
Tel: 519-389-6552
info@cama.org
www.cama.org
To promote the exchange & application of agricultural marketing ideas; To encourage high professional standards of agricultural marketing in Ontario
Mary Thornley, Executive Director

Canadian Agri-Marketing Association (Alberta) (CAMA)
22 Guyers Dr., RR#3, Port Elgin ON N0H 2C7
Alberta@cama.org
www.cama.org/chapters/alberta
To increase knowledge of ideas related to agri-marketing; To promote high professional standards of agricultural marketing
Teresa Faulk, President, CAMA Alberta

Canadian Agri-Marketing Association (Manitoba)
210 - 1600 Kenaston Blvd., Winnipeg MB R3P 0Y4
Tel: 204-799-2019; *Fax:* 204-257-5651
camamb@mts.net
www.cama.org/manitoba/ManitobaHome.aspx
To promote excellence in agrimarketing
Barbara Chabih, President

Canadian Agri-Marketing Association (Saskatchewan)
PO Box 4005, Regina SK S4P 3R9
Tel: 306-262-0733
camask@sasktel.net
www.cama.org/saskatchewan/saskatchewanHome.aspx
To operate as a networking organization for all sectors of Saskatchewan's agricultural industry
Lesley Kelly, President

Canadian Hotel Marketing & Sales Executives (CHMSE)
26 Avonhurst Rd., Toronto ON M9A 2G8
Tel: 416-252-9800; *Fax:* 416-252-7071
info@chmse.com
www.chmse.com
www.linkedin.com/groups/3020813
twitter.com/CHMSE
To be the leading association in providing professional development opportunities to sales & marketing executives within the Canadian hospitality industry
Shelley Macdonald, Executive Director

Canadian Marketing Association (CMA) / Association canadienne du marketing (ACM)
#603, 55 University Ave., Toronto ON M5J 2H7
Tel: 416-391-2362; *Toll-Free:* 800-267-8805
info@thecma.ca
www.the-cma.org
www.youtube.com/user/canadianmarketing
www.linkedin.com/groups/47336
www.facebook.com/cdnmarketing
twitter.com/Cdnmarketing
To be the pre-eminent marketing association in Canada representing the integration & convergence of all marketing disciplines, channels & technologies
John Wiltshire, President & CEO

Canadian Produce Marketing Association (CPMA) / Association canadienne de la distribution de fruits et légumes
162 Cleopatra Dr., Ottawa ON K2G 5X2
Tel: 613-226-4187; *Fax:* 613-226-2984
question@cpma.ca
www.cpma.ca
www.linkedin.com/company/can-produce-marketing-association
twitter.com/CPMA_ACDFL
To increase the market for fresh fruits & vegetables in Canada, by encouraging cooperation & information exchange in all segments, at the domestic & international level
Ron Lemaire, President

Marketing Research & Intelligence Association (MRIA) / L'Association de la recherche et de l'intelligence marketing (ARIM)
#1102, 21 St Clair Ave. East, Toronto ON M4T 1L9
Toll-Free: 855-561-4286
info@mria-arim.ca
mria-arim.ca
www.linkedin.com/company/marketing-research-and-intelligence-association
www.facebook.com/MRIAARIM
twitter.com/MRIAARIM
To benefit the public & its members by developing & delivering ethical, professional practice standards, promoting the industry & advocating for public policy that balances the need for research with privacy & consumer rights
Lee Robinson, Officer, Compliance

Multicultural Marketing Society of Canada
Toronto ON
Gautam Nath, Founder

Natural Products Marketing Council
PO Box 890, Truro NS B2N 5G6
Tel: 902-893-6511; *Fax:* 902-893-6573
www.novascotia.ca
To assure the orderly marketing of natural products
Elizabeth Crouse, General Manager
Ken Peacock, Chair

New Brunswick Egg Marketing Board (NBEMB) / L'Office de commercialisation des oeufs de Nouveau Brunswick
#101, 275 Main St., Fredericton NB E3A 1E1
www.nbegg.ca

North American Farmers' Direct Marketing Association, Inc. (NAFDMA)
62 White Loaf Rd., Southampton MA 01073 USA
Tel: 413-244-5374
nafdma.com
To promote the farm direct marketing & agritourism industry
Charlie Touchette, Executive Director

North Shore Forest Products Marketing Board
PO Box 386, Bathurst NB E2A 3Z3
Tel: 506-548-8958
nsfpmb@nb.aibn.com
www.forestrysyndicate.com
To negotiate with industry & government on behalf of the private wood producers of the regulated area for fair prices for the products of the woodlots & to promote improved forest management
Patrick Doucet, General Manager

Nova Scotia Wool Marketing Board
c/o Natural Products Marketing Council, NS Dept. of Agriculture, PO Box 190, Halifax NS B3J 2M4
To foster the production of high-quality wool in Nova Scotia, & the effective marketing of this product

Ontario Farm Fresh Marketing Association (OFFMA)
2002 Vandorf Sideroad, Aurora ON L4G 7B9
Tel: 905-841-9278; *Fax:* 905-726-3369
info@ontariofarmfresh.com
ontariofarmfresh.com
www.instagram.com/ontariofarmfresh
www.facebook.com/OntarioFarmFresh
twitter.com/OFFMA
To assist members in marketing skills & to provide knowledge & leadership to grow the farm fresh experience
Leslie Forsythe, President
Nicole Judge, Vice President

Ontario Flue-Cured Tobacco Growers' Marketing Board (OFCTGMB)
4B Elm St., Tillsonburg ON N4G 0C4
Tel: 519-842-3661; *Fax:* 519-842-7813
otb@ontarioflue-cured.com
www.ontarioflue-cured.com
To administer & enforce the provisions of Regulation 207/09 (Tobacco - Plan) & Regulation 208/09 (Tobacco - Powers of Local Board), made under the Farm Products Marketing Act; To control & regulate the production & marketing of tobacco, within the limits imposed by the Farm Products Marketing Act

Ontario Pork Producers' Marketing Board (OPPMB)
655 Southgate Dr., Guelph ON N1G 5G6
Tel: 519-767-4600; *Fax:* 519-829-1769
Toll-Free: 877-668-7675
comm@ontariopork.on.ca
www.ontariopork.on.ca
www.youtube.com/user/ontarioporkrecipes
twitter.com/ontariopork

To foster a vibrant business environment for pork producers
Ken Ovington, General Manager
Stacey Ash, Manager, Communications & Consumer Marketing

Ontario Sheep Farmers
130 Malcolm Rd., Guelph ON N1K 1B1
Tel: 519-836-0043; Fax: 519-836-2531
admin@ontariosheep.org
www.ontariosheep.org
To represent all aspects of the sheep, lamb, & wool industry in
Ontario; To improve the marketing of sheep & enhance
producers' returns; To provide the public with safe, quality lamb
& related products
Jennifer MacTavish, General Manager

Prince Edward Island Hog Commodity Marketing Board
#209, 420 University Ave., Charlottetown PE C1A 7Z5
Tel: 902-892-4201; Fax: 902-892-4203
peipork@hotmail.com
www.peipork.pe.ca
www.youtube.com/user/SwineTV
twitter.com/porkisyummy
To provide information to the pork production industry of Prince
Edward Island; To voice the concerns of hog farmers
Tim Seeber, Executive Director
Paul Larsen, Chair

Prince Edward Island Marketing Council
PO Box 1600, Charlottetown PE C1A 7N3
Tel: 902-569-7575; Fax: 902-569-7745
To administer the Natural Products Marketing Act under which
commodity boards & groups
Ian MacIssac, Secretary & General Manager

Saskatchewan Turkey Producers' Marketing Board (STPMB)
1438 Fletcher Rd., Saskatoon SK S7M 5T2
Tel: 306-931-1050; Fax: 306-931-2825
saskaturkey@sasktel.net
To manage the supply managed system in Saskatchewan,
which includes negotiating the province's quota levels with the
CTMA, negotiating price levels with local processors and
developing a long-term strategic focus for Saskatchewan's
turkey industry
Rose Olson, Executive Director

Mental Health

Alberta Psychiatric Association (APA)
#600, 900 - 6th Ave. SW, Calgary AB T2P 3K2
Tel: 403-244-4487; Fax: 403-244-2340
info@albertapsych.org
www.albertapsych.org
Arlie Fawcett, President

Association des médecins-psychiatres du Québec (AMPQ) / Québec Psychiatrists' Association
CP 216, Succ. Desjardins, Montréal QC H5B 1G8
Tél: 514-350-5128; Télec: 514-350-5198
www.ampq.org
Promouvoir les intérêts professionnels et économiques de ses
membres
Karine J. Igartua, Présidente
Guillaume Dumont, Secrétaire

Canadian Alliance on Mental Illness & Mental Health (CAMIMH)
#702, 141 Laurier Ave. West, Ottawa ON K1P 5J3
Tel: 613-237-2144; Fax: 613-237-1674
www.camimh.ca
www.facebook.com/CAMIMHACMMSM
twitter.com/CAMIMH_ACMMSM
An alliance of mental health organizations comprised of health
care providers and organizations representing persons with
mental illness and their families and caregivers

Canadian Art Therapy Association (CATA) / L'association canadienne d'art thérapie
PO Box 658, Stn. Main, Parksville BC V9P 2G7
admin@canadianarttherapy.org
www.canadianarttherapy.org
www.instagram.com/cata_photos_acat
www.linkedin.com/company/canadian-art-therapy-association----
association-canadienne-d'art-thérapie-cata----acat-
www.facebook.com/CATAarttherapy
twitter.com/cata_art
To promote the development & maintenance of professional
standards of art therapy training, registration, research &
practice in Canada; To heighten awareness of art therapy as an
important mental health discipline
Amanda Gee, President

Nicole Le Bihan, Vice-President
Waqas Yousafzai, Treasurer

Canadian Association for Suicide Prevention (CASP) / L'Association canadienne pour la prévention du suicide (ACPS)
PO Box 53082, Stn. Rideau Centre, Ottawa ON K1N 1C5
Tel: 613-702-4446; Fax: 613-209-4932
casp@suicideprevention.ca
www.suicideprevention.ca
www.facebook.com/CanadianAssociationforSuicidePrevention
twitter.com/casp_ca
To reduce the suicide rate; To minimize the harmful
consequences of suicide
Julie Kathleen Campbell, Executive Director
Karen Letofsky, President

Canadian Institute of Stress (CIS)
150 York St., Toronto ON M5H 3S5
Tel: 416-236-4218
info@stresscanada.org
www.stresscanada.org
To provide programs & tools for individuals & workplaces to
handle stress
Richard Earle, Managing Director

Canadian Mental Health Association (CMHA) / Association canadienne pour la santé mentale (ACSM)
#500, 250 Dundas St. West, Toronto ON M5T 2Z5
Tel: 416-646-5557
info@cmha.ca
www.cmha.ca
www.instagram.com/cmhanational
www.facebook.com/CMHA.ACSM.National
twitter.com/CMHA_NTL
To promote mental health as well as support the resilience &
recovery of people experiencing mental illness, through
advocacy, education, research & service
Margaret Eaton, National Chief Executive Officer
Jordan Frisen, National Director, Workplace Mental Health
Greg Kyllo, National Director, Program Innovation
Ariel Shneer, National Director, Fund Development

Canadian Psychiatric Association (CPA) / Association des psychiatres du Canada
#701, 141 Laurier Ave. West, Ottawa ON K1P 5J3
Tel: 613-234-2815; Fax: 613-234-9857
Toll-Free: 800-267-1555
cpa@cpa-apc.org
www.cpa-apc.org
www.linkedin.com/company/canadian-psychiatric-association
www.facebook.com/cpa.apc
twitter.com/CPA_APC
To forge a strong, collective voice for Canadian psychiatrists &
to promote an environment that fosters excellence in the
provision of clinical care, education & research
Katie Hardy, Chief Executive Officer
Ann Miller, Director, Finance
Rob Cornforth, Manager, Communications

Canadian Psychoanalytic Society (CPS) / Société canadienne de psychanalyse (SCP)
7000 Côte-des-Neiges Rd., Montréal QC H3S 2C1
Tel: 514-738-6105; Fax: 514-738-6393
www.psychoanalysis.ca
To promote psychoanalysis treatments & professionals
Jorge Palacios-Boix, President

Canadian Psychological Association (CPA) / Société canadienne de psychologie (SCP)
#702, 141 Laurier Ave. West, Ottawa ON K1P 5J3
Tel: 613-237-2144; Fax: 613-237-1674
Toll-Free: 888-472-0657
cpa@cpa.ca
www.cpa.ca
www.youtube.com/user/CPAVideoChannel
www.facebook.com/146082642130174
twitter.com/CPA_SCP
To improve the health & welfare of Canadians by promoting
psychological research, education & practice
Karen R. Cohen, Chief Executive Officer
Lisa Votta-Bleeker, Deputy CEO & Director, Science Directorate
Phil Bolger, Chief Financial Officer
Seán Kelly, Director, Events, Membership & Association
Development

Centre de ressources et d'intervention pour hommes abusés sexuellement dans leur enfance (CRIPHASE) / Resource and Intervention Center for Men Sexually Abused during their Childhood
#100, 8105, rue de Gaspé, Montréal QC H2P 2J9
Tél: 514-529-5567; Télec: 514-529-0571
info@criphase.org
www.criphase.org
www.facebook.com/168619389848314
Alice Charasse, Coordinatrice

Child & Parent Resource Institute (CPRI)
600 Sanatorium Rd., London ON N6H 3W7
Tel: 519-858-2774; Fax: 519-858-3913
Toll-Free: 877-494-2774
TTY: 519-858-0257
www.cpri.ca
To enhance the quality of life of children & youth with complex
mental health or developmental challenges; to assist their
families so these children & youth can reach their full potential

Children's Mental Health Ontario (CMHO) / Santé Mentale pour Enfants Ontario (SMEO)
#2305, 180 Dundas St. West, Toronto ON M5G 1Z8
Tel: 416-921-2109; Fax: 416-921-7600
info@cmho.org
www.cmho.org
www.linkedin.com/company/children's-mental-health-ontario
www.facebook.com/kidsmentalhealth
twitter.com/kidsmentalhlth
To promote, support & strengthen a sustainable system of
mental health services for children, youth & their families
Kimberly Moran, Chief Executive Officer

Crisis Services Canada (CSC) / Services de crises du Canada
439 University Ave., Toronto ON M5G 1Y8
Toll-Free: 833-456-4566
www.crisisservicescanada.ca
www.linkedin.com/company/18350091
www.facebook.com/CrisisServicesCanada
twitter.com/crisiscanada
To strengthen regional services; To close gaps in mental health
& suicide prevention support across the country
Stephanie MacKendrick, Chief Executive Officer
Matthew Little, Chief Financial Officer
Jason Chare, Director, Clinical Operations

Fédération des familles et amis de la personne atteinte de maladie mentale (FFAPAMM) / Federation of Families & Friends of Persons with a Mental Illness
#203, 1990, rue Cyrille-Duquet, Québec QC G1N 4K8
Tél: 418-687-0474; Télec: 418-687-0123
Ligne sans frais: 800-323-0474
info@ffapamm.com
www.ffapamm.com
Défendre et promouvoir les intérêts de ses membres; de les
soutenir dans leur développement; de sensibiliser l'opinion
publique aux problèmes reliés à la maladie mentale; de créer
des programmes de communication et d'éducation
Hélène Fradet, Directrice générale

Fondation Jeunes en Tête
#804, 55, av du Mont-Royal ouest, Montréal QC H2T 2S6
Tél: 514-529-1000
info@fondationjeunesentete.org
www.fondationjeunesentete.org
www.instagram.com/jeunesentete
www.linkedin.com/company/fondation-québec-jeunes
www.facebook.com/fondationjeunesentete
twitter.com/JeunesEnTete
Pour mettre des services cliniques en place et les maintenir;
prévenir les maladies mentales
Mélanie Boucher, Directrice générale

The LifeLine Canada Foundation (TLC) / La Fondation LIfeLine Canada
PO Box 21040, Stn. Orchard Park, Kelowna BC V1Y 9N8
thelifelinecanada.ca
www.facebook.com/theLifelineCanada
twitter.com/TheLifeLineCan
To advocate for positive mental health & suicide prevention
across Canada & around the world

Mental Health Commission of Canada (MHCC) / Commission de la santé mentale du Canada (CSMC)
#1210, 350 Albert St., Ottawa ON K1R 1A4
Tel: 613-683-3755; Fax: 613-798-2989
mhccinfo@mentalhealthcommission.ca
www.mentalhealthcommission.ca
www.instagram.com/themhcc
www.linkedin.com/company/mental-health-commission-of-canad
a
www.facebook.com/theMHCC
twitter.com/mhcc_
To suggest improvements to the mental health system on a national level
Louise Bradley, President & CEO
Ed Mantler, Vice-President, Programs & Priorities
Michel Rodrigue, Vice-President, Organizational Performance & Public Affairs
Robert Thomas, Vice-President & CFO, Corporate Services

Mental Health Foundation
9942 - 108 St., 6th Fl., Edmonton AB T5K 2J5
Tel: 780-342-7718
mentalhealthfoundation.ca
www.instagram.com/mentalhealthab
www.facebook.com/mentalhealthab
twitter.com/MentalHealthAB
To ensure that all individuals in Alberta have access to mental health care; To promote mental health research & education
Mark Korthuis, President & CEO

Mental Illness Caregivers Association of Canada
PO Box 5065, 19 Colonnade Rd., Ottawa ON K2G 4V8
Tel: 613-860-7800
info@micaontario.com
www.micaontario.com
www.facebook.com/MICAOntario
twitter.com/MICAONTARIO
To help members manage the effects of mental illness &/or addiction through the provision of education & support
Paul McIntyre, President

Mood Disorders Association of Ontario (MDAO)
#602, 36 Eglinton Ave. West, Toronto ON M4R 1A1
Tel: 416-486-8046; Fax: 416-486-8127
Toll-Free: 888-486-8236
info@mooddisorders.ca
www.mooddisorders.ca
www.instagram.com/mooddisordersassociation
www.facebook.com/MoodDisordersAssociationON
twitter.com/mooddisorderson
To provide information, education & support to those affected by depression & manic depression, their families & friends; To develop & maintain a network of supportive self-help groups; To improve the quality of life of people who experience mood disorders, their families & friends; To advocate for a flexible & responsive system of care
Ann Marie MacDonald, Executive Director

Mood Disorders Society of Canada (MDSC) / La Société pour les troubles de l'humeur du Canada
46 Hope Cres., Belleville ON K8P 4S2
Tel: 613-921-5565
info@mdsc.ca
www.mdsc.ca
www.youtube.com/user/MDSofC
www.linkedin.com/company/mood-disorders-society-of-canada
www.facebook.com/MoodDisordersSocietyCanada
twitter.com/MoodDisordersCa
To ensure that issues related to mood disorders are understood & considered in the setting of research priorities, the development of treatment strategies, & the creation of government programs & policies
John Starzynski, President

Ontario Psychological Association (OPA)
#403, 21 St. Clair Ave. East, Toronto ON M4T 1L8
Tel: 416-961-5552; Fax: 416-961-5516
opa@psych.on.ca
www.psych.on.ca
www.facebook.com/ONPsych
twitter.com/onpsych
To advance the practice & science of psychology in Ontario communities; To promote the highest ethical standards in the profession
Diana Velikonja, President
Richard Morrison, Chief Executive Officer

L'Ordre des psychologues du Québec (OPQ)
#510, 1100, av Beaumont, Montréal QC H3P 3H5
Tél: 514-738-1881; Téléc: 514-738-8838
Ligne sans frais: 800-363-2644
info@ordrepsy.qc.ca
www.ordrepsy.qc.ca
twitter.com/ordrepsy
Assurer la protection du public; contrôler l'exercice de la profession par ses membres; veiller à la qualité des services dispensés par ses membres; favoriser le développement de la compétence professionnelle, le respect des normes déontologiques et l'accessibilité aux services psychologiques
Christine Grou, Présidente

Saskatchewan Psychiatric Association
Saskatoon SK
sask-psychiatrists.tripod.com
To increase psychiatric knowledge in Saskatchewan

Schizophrenia Society of Canada (SSC) / Société canadienne de schizophrénie
#100, 4 Fort St., Winnipeg MB R3C 1C4
Tel: 204-786-1616; Fax: 204-783-4898
Toll-Free: 800-263-5545
info@schizophrenia.ca
www.schizophrenia.ca
www.facebook.com/SchizophreniaSocietyCanada
twitter.com/SchizophreniaCa
To improve the quality of life for those affected by schizophrenia & psychosis; To advocate on behalf of individuals & families affected by schizophrenia for improved treatment & services
Chris Summerville, D. Min, CPRP, Chief Executive Officer

Woori Maum
Toronto ON
woorimaum.toronto@gmail.com
www.woorimaumtoronto.com
www.facebook.com/woorimaumtoronto
To raise awareness of mental health issues within the Korean-Canadian community; To reduce the stigma surrounding persons with mental illness in the Korean-Canadian community; To serve as a liaison between Korean-Canadian mental health professionals & community members in need
Marianne Noh, Chair

Your Life Counts (YLC)
Seaway Mall, 800 Niagara St. North, #GG5B, Welland ON L3C 5Z4
Tel: 289-821-4199
info@yourlifecounts.org
www.yourlifecounts.org
www.youtube.com/user/YOURLIFECOUNTSTV
www.facebook.com/YourLifeCounts
twitter.com/yourlifecounts
To work with youth, families, veterans & emergency services to support trauma, addiction & overwhelming life situations that may lead to thoughts of suicide
S. Ruaraidh Butler, Founder & CEO

Youth Mental Health Canada (YMHC)
51 Stuart St., Hamilton ON L8L 1B5
Tel: 647-952-9642
admin@youthmentalhealth.ca; admin@ymhc.ngo
ymhc.ngo
www.instagram.com/youth_mental_health
www.facebook.com/YMHECanada
twitter.com/YMHCanada
To raise awareness of youth mental health, especially in relation to the educational system; To advocate for young people with mental health issues; To develop mental health & wellness education tools & resources; To promote you, family & community engagement on mental health education, support, advocacy & change; To be a leader on social media platforms including Facebook, Twitter, Instagra, Youtube & TikTok
Sheryl Boswell, Executive Director

Military & Veterans

Air Cadet League of Canada / Ligue des cadets de l'air du Canada
#201, 1505 Laperriere Ave., Ottawa ON K1Z 7T1
Tel: 613-729-1941; Fax: 613-725-3777
Toll-Free: 877-422-6359
leaguehq@aircadetleague.com
aircadetleague.com
www.youtube.com/user/AirCadetLeague
www.linkedin.com/company/air-cadet-league-of-canada
www.facebook.com/Air.Cadet.League.of.Canada
twitter.com/AirCadetLeague

To promote & encourage a practical interest in aeronautics among young people; To assist those intending to pursue a career in aviation
Donald A. Berrill, CD, President
Pierre Forgues, Executive Director

Army Cadet League of Canada (ACLC) / Ligue des cadets de l'armée du Canada
#201, 1505 Laperriere Ave., Ottawa ON K1Z 7T1
Fax: 613-941-3744
Toll-Free: 877-276-9223
national@armycadetleague.ca
www.armycadetleague.ca
www.facebook.com/armycadetleague
twitter.com/ArmyCadetLeague
To provide accommodation, transportation, & financial support for the army cadets; To promote the corps & assists in recruitment
Robert Gill, Executive Director

Army, Navy & Air Force Veterans in Canada (ANAVETS) / Les Anciens combattants de l'armée, de la marine et des forces aériennes au Canada
#2, 6 Beechwood Ave., Ottawa ON K1L 8B4
Tel: 613-744-0222; Fax: 613-744-0208
anavets@storm.ca
www.anavets.ca
To unite veterans & their supporters to maintain entitlements & benefits; To provide a fraternal milieu for members by acquiring & operating clubs & homes; To strive to promote patriotism in Canada, & nurture cooperation & unity within the British Commonwealth
Deanna Fimrite, Secretary-Treasurer

Canadian Aboriginal Veterans & Serving Members Association (CAV)
34 Kingham Pl., Victoria BC V9B 1L8
Tel: 250-900-5768
national-president@nationalalliance.ca
canadianaboriginalveterans.ca

Canadian Association of Veterans in United Nations Peacekeeping (CAVUNP) / Association Canadienne des Vétérans des Forces de la Paix pour les Nations Unies
PO Box PO Box 46026, RPO Beacon Hill, 2339 Ogilvie Rd., Gloucester ON K1J 9M7
Tel: 613-746-3302
cavunp@rogers.com
www.cavunp.org
To promote & enhance the traditions of peace support operations, for which Canada is renowned, through activities such as public speaking, assistance to schools or civic bodies, & participation in joint efforts with organizations that share the objectives of the association
Richard W. Wright, National President
Robert George, CD, National Vice-President
Ronald R. Griffis, Chair, Board of Directors
Wayne R. MacCulloch, National Immediate Past President

Canadian Battlefields Foundation
c/o Canadian War Museum, 1 Vimy Pl., Ottawa ON K1R 1C2
Tel: 613-731-7767
cbf.fccb@gmail.com
www.canadianbattlefieldsfoundation.ca
www.facebook.com/220483754647284
twitter.com/CBFFCCB
To act with Le Mémorial to educate the international public with respect to Canada's role in the Second World War & to educate Canadians through providing scholarships, bursaries & prizes to carry on research into military history; to raise & disburse funds to support these activities.
H.G. Needham, Treasurer
Charles Belzile, President
Antonio Lamer, Honorary Patron

Canadian Corps Association
2 Carleton St. South, Thorold ON L2V 5C2

The Canadian Corps of Commissionaires / Le Corps Canadien des Commissionnaires
#201, 100 Gloucester St., Ottawa ON K2P 0A4
Tel: 613-688-0710; Fax: 613-688-0719
Toll-Free: 877-322-6777
info@commissionaires.ca
commissionaires.ca
www.linkedin.com/company/commissionaires-canada
www.facebook.com/CommissionairesCanada
twitter.com/Commissionaires
To create meaningful employment opportunities for former members of the Canadian Forces, the Royal Canadian Mounted Police & others who wish to contribute to the security & well-being of Canadians

Mark Watson, Chief of Staff

Canadian Peacekeeping Veterans Association (CPVA)
PO Box 905, Kingston ON K7L 4X8

Tel: 506-627-6437
info@cpva.ca
www.cpva.ca

To assist Canadians who have served on peacekeeping missions
Donald MacPherson, President

Commonwealth War Graves Commission - Canadian Agency (CWGC) / Commission des sépultures de guerre du Commonwealth - Agence canadienne (CSGC)
#1412, 66 Slater St., Ottawa ON K1A 0P4

Tel: 613-992-3224; *Fax:* 613-995-0431
enquiries@cwgc.org
www.cwgc-canadianagency.ca/index.php

To ensure Commonwealth War Burials in the Americas (including the Caribbean) are marked & maintained; To ensure maintenance of memorials to the missing; To keep records & registers; To discharge Commission duties for Commonwealth war graves in the Americas (comprising some 3,350 cemeteries & over 20,000 commemorations)
David Kettle, Secretary General

Conference of Defence Associations (CDA) / Conférence des associations de la défense
#900, 75 Albert St., Ottawa ON K1P 5E7

Tel: 613-236-9903
cdacanada.ca
twitter.com/CDAInstitute

To place before people of Canada problems of defence & the well-being of Canada's Armed Forces
Matthew Overton, Executive Director
Meghan Fitzpatrick, Director, Research
Valerie Aji, Financial Officer

Korea Veterans Association of Canada Inc., Heritage Unit (KVA) / Association canadienne des vétérans de la Corée (ACVC)

www.kvacanada.com

To promote awareness of Canada's role in the Korean War; To represent veterans & their families
Dave Davidson, Chair, Membership

Military Collectors Club of Canada (MCC of Canada)
1442 - 26A St. SW, Calgary AB T3C 1K8

Tel: 204-669-0871
militarycollectorsclubofcanada@yahoo.ca
www.mccofc.ca

To serve as the focal point for collectors of all types of military artifacts, including medals, badges, artwork, military arms, vehicles or any other militaria-related item
Doug Styles, President
Garry Milne, Vice President
Martin Urquhart, Secretary-Treasurer

National Council of Veteran Associations (NCVA) / Conseil national des associations d'anciens combattants au Canada (CNAAC)
2827 Riverside Dr., Ottawa ON K1V 0C4

Tel: 613-731-3821; *Fax:* 613-731-3234
Toll-Free: 800-465-2677
ncva@waramps.ca
www.ncva-cnaac.ca
twitter.com/NCVACanada

To provide a voice on issues which are of significant interest to the Veterans' community
Brian N. Forbes, Chair

The Naval Association of Canada / L'Association Navale du Canada

noacexdir@msn.com
www.navalassoc.ca
www.facebook.com/navalassn
twitter.com/navalassn

To maintain active interest in the Maritime affairs of Canada; To oversee 12 member branches in major cities from coast to coast
Bill Conconi, President
David Soule, Executive Director

Navy League of Canada / Ligue navale du Canada
#201, 1505 Laperriere Ave., Ottawa ON K1Z 7T1

Toll-Free: 800-375-6289
info@navyleague.ca
navyleague.ca
www.facebook.com/navyleaguecanada
twitter.com/NavyLeagueCA

To promote an interest in maritime affairs generally throughout Canada; To prepare, publish & disseminate information &

encourage debate relating to the role & importance of maritime matters in the interests of Canada; To promote, organize, sponsor, support & encourage the education & training of the youth of the country through Cadet movements & other youth groups with a maritime orientation; To hold conferences, symposia & meetings for the discussion & exchange of views in matters relating to the objects of The League; To raise funds as may be deemed necessary, for the welfare & benefit of seamen, for their dependents & for Seamen's Homes, Hostels & other institutions in Canada, including the establishment, operation & maintenance thereof; To co-operate with any kindred society having either in whole or in part comparable objects to The League
Matt Waterman, National President

New Brunswick Signallers Association (NB Sigs)
c/o 3 ASG Signal Squadron, CFB Gagetown, PO Box 17000, Stn. Forces, Oromocto NB E2V 4J5

Tel: 506-357-7314
admin@nbsigs.net
www.nbsigs.net

Al Lustig, President

Princess Patricia's Canadian Light Infantry Association
PO Box 10500, Stn. Forces, Edmonton AB T5J 4J5

Tel: 780-973-4011
secretary@ppliassoc.ca
ppcliassoc.ca

To support the interests of the Regiment
Paul Hale, President

Royal Canadian Air Force Association / Association de l'Aviation royale canadienne
PO Box 2460, Stn. D, Ottawa ON K1P 5W6

Tel: 613-232-2303; *Toll-Free:* 866-351-2322
contact@airforce.ca
www.rcafassociation.ca
www.facebook.com/RCAFAssociationARC
twitter.com/RCAFAssociation

To promote a viable well-equipped air force & a strong Canadian aerospace industry
Dean Black, National Executive Director

The Royal Canadian Legion (RCL) / La Légion royale canadienne
Dominion Command, 86 Aird Pl., Ottawa ON K2L 0A1

Tel: 613-591-3335; *Fax:* 613-591-9335
Toll-Free: 888-556-6222
info@legion.ca
www.legion.ca
www.youtube.com/user/RCLDominionCommand
www.linkedin.com/company/royalcanadianlegion
www.facebook.com/CanadianLegion
twitter.com/RoyalCdnLegion

To serve veterans, ex-military & military members, their families, communities & Canada
Larry Murray, Grand President
Thomas D. Irvine, Dominion President
Mark Barham, Dominion Treasurer
Steven Clark, National Executive Director

Royal Canadian Military Institute (RCMI)
426 University Ave., Toronto ON M5G 1S9

Tel: 416-597-0286; *Fax:* 416-597-6919
Toll-Free: 800-585-1072
info@rcmi.org
www.rcmi.org

To promote the navy, army & air force art, science, literature & interests; promotion of good fellowship & esprit de corps amongst the officers of the various branches of the services; to maintain of a clubhouse for the accommodation, recreation, enlightenment, convenience & entertainment of its members.
Chris Corrigan, Executive Director

Royal Canadian Mounted Police Veterans' Association / Association des anciens de la Gendarmerie royale du Canada
PO Box 8900, 1 Sandridge Rd., Ottawa ON K1G 3J2

Toll-Free: 877-251-1771
contact@rcmpva.org
rcmpva.org

Ralph Mahar, Executive Officer

Royal Canadian Naval Benevolent Fund (RCNBF) / Caisse de bienfaisance de la marine Royale Canadienne
#9, 6 Beechwood Ave., Ottawa ON K1L 8B4

Tel: 613-236-7389; *Toll-Free:* 888-557-8777
rcnbf@rcnbf.com
www.rcnbf.ca
www.facebook.com/rcnbf
twitter.com/rcnbf_fbmrc

To relieve distress & promote the well-being of individuals who have served in the Naval Forces of Canada & their dependants

Ukrainian War Veterans Association of Canada (UWVA)
145 Evans Ave., Toronto ON M8Z 5X8

Tel: 416-925-2770
www.unfcanada.ca/uwva

To promote national unity & maintain Ukrainian identity; To support the Ukrainian National Federation of Canada

Veterans Transition Network (VTN) / Réseau de transition des vétérans (RTV)
#622, 470 Granville St., Vancouver BC V6C 1V5

Tel: 604-559-8155; *Toll-Free:* 844-236-8387
vtncanada.org
www.instagram.com/vtncanada
www.facebook.com/VTNCanada
twitter.com/VTNCanada

To deliver mental health services to veterans across the country
Oliver Thorne, Executive Director
Paul Whitehead, Ph.D., CCC, R.P, National Clinical Director

Mines & Mineral Resources

Association de l'exploration minière de Québec (AEMQ) / Quebec Mineral Exploration Assocation (QMEA)
#203, 132, av du Lac, Rouyn-Noranda QC J9X 4N5

Tél: 819-762-1599; *Téléc:* 819-762-1522
info@aemq.org
www.aemq.org
www.facebook.com/AEMQ1975
twitter.com/AEMQ_

Développer, défendre et promouvoir l'exploration minière au Québec
Philippe Cloutier, Président
Valerie Fillion, Directrice générale

Association for Mineral Exploration British Columbia (AMEBC)
#800, 889 West Pender St., Vancouver BC V6C 3B2

Tel: 604-689-5271; *Fax:* 604-681-2363
info@amebc.ca
www.amebc.ca
www.linkedin.com/company/association-for-mineral-exploration-bc
www.facebook.com/Association.for.Mineral.Exploration.BC
twitter.com/ame_bc

To promote & assist development & growth of mining of mineral exploration in BC
Edie Thome, President & CEO
Jonathan Buchanan, Director, Communications & Public Affairs
Simone Hill, Director, Member Relations & Events

Association minière du Québec (AMQ) / Québec Mining Association (QMA)
Place de la Cité - Tour Belle Cour, #720, 2590, boul Laurier, Québec QC G1V 4M6

Tél: 418-657-2016; *Téléc:* 418-657-2154
amq@amq-inc.com
www.amq-inc.com

Promouvoir le développement de l'industrie des mines, de la métallurgie et des industries connexes; défendre les intérêts généraux de ses membres; soutenir les efforts de ses membres quant au bien-être, à la sécurité et à la prévention des accidents au travail
Josée Méthot, Présidente-directrice générale
Katie Deneault, Directrice, Service-conseil en ressources humaines
Mathieu St-Amant, Directeur, Communications stratégiques

Association of Applied Geochemists (AEG)
PO Box 26099, 72 Robertson Rd., Ottawa ON K2H 9R0

Tel: 613-828-0199; *Fax:* 613-828-9288
office@appliedgeochemists.org
www.appliedgeochemists.org

To promote interest in the applications of geochemistry to mineral & petroleum exploration, resource evaluation & related fields
Pim van Geffen, Business Manager

Canada's Oil Sands Innovation Alliance (COSIA)
#1700, 520 - 5th Ave. SW, Calgary AB T2P 3R7

Tel: 403-444-5282
info@cosia.ca
www.cosia.ca
www.linkedin.com/company/cosia
www.facebook.com/676634536088575
twitter.com/COSIA_ca

To drive the growth of Canada's oil sands & improve environmental performance

Wes Jickling, Chief Executive

Canadian Copper & Brass Development Association (CCBDA)
#210, 65 Overlea Blvd., Toronto ON M4H 1P1
Tel: 416-391-5599; *Fax:* 416-391-3823
Toll-Free: 877-640-0946
library@copperalliance.ca
www.coppercanada.ca
To promote, foster & stimulate use of products of Canadian copper & brass industry; To represent & support the primary produers fabricators, manufacturers & consumers of copper & copper alloys in Canada, by increasing industry & public awareness of copper's capabilites & advantages compared to other metals & materials & by providing technical services related to copper's use
Stephen Knapp, Executive Director

Canadian Mineral Analysts (CMA) / Analystes des minéraux canadiens
c/o John Gregorchuk, 444 Harold Ave. West, Winnipeg MB R2C 2E2
Tel: 204-224-1443
www.canadianmineralanalysts.com
To promote communication among analysts in the mining industry & persons engaged in analytical procedures & the development of methods
John Gregorchuk, Managing Secretary
Sean Murry, Treasurer

Chamber of Mines of Eastern British Columbia
215 Hall St., Nelson BC V1L 5X4
Tel: 250-352-5242
chamberofmines@netidea.com
cmebc.com
www.facebook.com/1665420907007129
To act as advocate for the mining industry in British Columbia; To provide a collective voice on behalf of prospectors & miners; To provide information on exploration & mining; To educate the public through accessibility to mineral museum & library
David Johnston Jr., President
Brad Gretchev, Curator

Coal Association of Canada (CAC)
#150, 205 - 9th Ave. SE, Calgary AB T2G 0R3
Tel: 403-262-1544; *Fax:* 403-265-7604
Toll-Free: 800-910-2625
info@coal.ca
www.coal.ca
twitter.com/coalcanada
To promote coal as a vital energy source that is abundant, safe, reliable, environmentally & economically acceptable, despite its major faults
Ann Marie Hann, President
Michelle Mondeville, Director, Communications and Stakeholder Relations

East Kootenay Chamber of Mines
#201, 16 - 11th Ave. South, Cranbrook BC V1C 2P1
Tel: 250-464-9559; *Fax:* 250-426-8755
ekcm2@shaw.ca
www.ekcm.org
www.facebook.com/EastKootenayChamberOfMines
To promote mining iterests in south-eastern British Columbia
Jason Jacob, President

Mineralogical Association of Canada (MAC) / Association minéralogique du Canada
490, rue de la Couronne, Québec QC G1K 9A9
Tel: 418-653-0333; *Fax:* 418-653-0777
office@mineralogicalassociation.ca
www.mineralogicalassociation.ca
To promote & advance knowledge of mineralogy & the allied disciplines of petrology, crystallography, mineral deposits, & geochemistry
Johanne Caron, Manager, Business

Mining Association of British Columbia (MABC)
#730, 800 West Pender St., Vancouver BC V6C 2V6
Tel: 604-681-4321
www.mining.bc.ca
www.linkedin.com/company/mining-association-of-bc
www.facebook.com/MABCMining
twitter.com/ma_bc
To speak on behalf of mineral producers; To represent the interests of British Columbia's mining industry; To communicate with senior government decision-makers, communities, NGOs, First Nations, & the media; To act as the industry's voice regarding issues such as environmental regulations, taxation, infrastructure demands, labour issues, health & safety, & international trade
Michael Goehring, President & CEO
Lindsay Kislock, Vice-President, Corporate Affairs

Mining Association of Canada (MAC) / Association minière du Canada
#1100, 275 Slater St., Ottawa ON K1P 5H9
Tel: 613-233-9392; *Fax:* 613-233-8897
communications@mining.ca
www.mining.ca
twitter.com/theminingstory
To represent the interests of member companies engaged in mineral exploration, extraction & refining; To work with governments on public policy pertaining to minerals
Pierre Gratton, President & CEO
Justyna Laurie-Lean, Vice-President, Environment & Regulatory Affairs
Cynthia Waldmeier, Director, Communications

Mining Association of Manitoba Inc. (MAMI)
#700, 305 Broadway Ave., Winnipeg MB R3C 3J7
Tel: 204-989-1890
www.mines.ca
www.linkedin.com/company/the-mining-association-of-manitoba-inc-
To represent mining & exploration companies in Manitoba
Lovro Paulic, Chair

Mining Association of Nova Scotia (MANS)
7744 St. Margaret's Bay Rd., Ingramport NS B3Z 3Z8
Tel: 902-820-2115
info@tmans.ca
tmans.ca
www.facebook.com/MiningNS
twitter.com/MiningNS
To represent mining & quarrying companies in Nova Scotia involved in exploration, discovery, development, production & reclamation as well as consultants & suppliers to the industry; To promote mining as a corporate industry creating wealth & long-term stable employment, with responsible environmental & social attitudes
Sean Kirby, Executive Director

Mining Industry NL
Prince Charles Bldg., PO Box 21463, #W280, 120 Torbay Rd., St. John's NL A1A 2G8
Tel: 709-722-9542; *Fax:* 709-722-8588
info@miningnl.com
www.miningnl.com
To represent all sectors of the mineral industry in the province; to be a central contact for government, media & the public
Ed Moriarity, Executive Director
Jennifer Kelly, Communications Advisor

Mining Society of Nova Scotia
88 Leeside Dr., Sydney NS B1R 1S6
Tel: 902-567-2147; *Fax:* 902-567-2147
www.miningsocietyns.ca
To provide services in order to help & improve the mining industry
Bob MacDonald, President

Northwest Territories & Nunavut Chamber of Mines
PO Box 2818, #103, 5102 - 50 Ave., Yellowknife NT X1A 3S8
Tel: 867-873-5281; *Fax:* 780-669-5681
info@miningnorth.com
www.miningnorth.com
www.facebook.com/miningnorth
twitter.com/MiningNorth
To support responsible & sustainable mining exploration & development in the Northwest Territories & Nunavut
Tom Hoefer, Executive Director

Ontario Mining Association (OMA)
#1201, 5775 Yonge St., Toronto ON M2M 4J1
Tel: 416-364-9301; *Fax:* 416-364-5986
info@oma.on.ca
www.oma.on.ca
www.youtube.com/user/miningontario
twitter.com/OntMiningAssoc
To help improve the competitiveness of the Ontario mineral industry
Chris Hodgson, President

Prospectors & Developers Association of Canada (PDAC) / Association canadienne des prospecteurs & entrepreneurs
#800, 170 University Ave., Toronto ON M5H 3B3
Tel: 416-362-1969
info@pdac.ca
www.pdac.ca
www.youtube.com/user/ThePDAC
www.linkedin.com/company/thepdac
www.facebook.com/thePDAC
twitter.com/the_PDAC
To protect & promote the interests of the Canadian mineral exploration & development sector

Lisa McDonald, Executive Director
Jeff Killeen, Director, Policy/Programs, Finance/Taxation, Securities, Geoscience & Healt
Nicole Sampson, Director, Convention
Lesley Williams, Director, Policy/Programs, Indigenous/Regulatory, Sustainable Dev. & Int'l.

Saskatchewan Mining Association (SMA)
#1500, 2002 Victoria Ave., Regina SK S4P 0R7
Tel: 306-757-9505; *Fax:* 306-569-1085
info@saskmining.ca
www.saskmining.ca
twitter.com/SaskMiningAssoc
To ensure the safe & profitable development of mineral resources in Saskatchewan; To act as the voice of the mining industry throughout the province; To promote understanding of the development of mineral resources in Saskatchewan
Neil McMillan, President
Pamela Schwann, Executive Director

Yukon Chamber of Mines (YCM)
3151B - 3rd Ave., Whitehorse YT Y1A 1G1
Tel: 867-667-2090; *Fax:* 867-668-7127
info@yukonminers.ca
www.yukonminers.ca
www.facebook.com/yukonminers
twitter.com/yukonminers
To provide services to members, with a focus on the mining industry; To promote responsible exploration & sustainable mining practices
Sue Craig, President
Samson Hartland, Executive Director

Yukon Mine Training Association (YMTA)
2099 - 2nd Ave., Whitehorse YT Y1A 1B5
Tel: 867-633-6463; *Toll-Free:* 877-986-4637
info@ymta.org
ymta.org
To maximize employment opportunities emerging from the growth of the mining and related resource sectors in the North for First Nations and other Yukoners.
P. Jerry Asp, Chair
Sascha Weber, Executive Director

Multiculturalism

Affiliation of Multicultural Societies & Service Agencies of BC (AMSSA)
#205, 2929 Commercial Dr., Vancouver BC V5N 4C8
Tel: 604-718-2780; *Fax:* 604-298-0747
Toll-Free: 888-355-5560
amssa@amssa.org
www.amssa.org
www.facebook.com/amssabc
twitter.com/amssabc
To provide leadership in advocacy & education in British Columbia for anti-racism, human rights & social justice; To support members in serving immigrants, refugees & culturally diverse communities
Katie Rosenberger, Executive Director
Tracy Wideman, Program Director

African Canadian Social Development Council (ACSDC)
#107B, 2238 Dundas St. West, Toronto ON M6R 3A9
Tel: 647-352-5775
www.acsdc.net
www.facebook.com/AfricanCanadianSDC
twitter.com/acsdc_1
To promote social, economic & cultural development within the continental African community in Canada
Kayode (Kay) Alabi, Executive Director/CEO

The Atlantic Jewish Council
#508, 5670 Spring Garden Rd., Halifax NS B3J 1H6
Tel: 902-422-7491; *Fax:* 902-425-3722
atlanticjewishcouncil@theajc.ns.ca
theajc.ns.ca
www.flickr.com/photos/atlanticjewishcouncil
www.facebook.com/AtlanticJewishCouncil
Jon M. Goldberg, Executive Director

Australian and New Zealand Association (ANZA)
261A Beach Rd., 199541 Singapore
info@anzaclub.org
www.anzaclub.org
www.facebook.com/anzaclubvancouver
twitter.com/anzaclub
To foster friendly relations between British Columbia, Canada, Australia & New Zealand

B'nai Brith Canada (BBC)
Toronto ON

Tel: 416-633-6224; Toll-Free: 844-218-2624
info@bnaibrith.ca
www.bnaibrith.ca
www.instagram.com/bnaibrithcanada
www.facebook.com/bnaibrithcanada
twitter.com/bnaibrithcanada

To bring men & women of the Jewish faith together in fellowship to serve the Jewish community through combating anti-Semitism, bigotry & racism in Canada & abroad; To carry out activities which ensure the security & survival of the State of Israel & Jewish communities worldwide
Michael Mostyn, Chief Executive Officer

Baltic Federation in Canada

balticfederation.ca

To provide political representation for its member organizations of Estonian, Latvian & Lithuanian Canadians
Andris Kesteris, President

Black Cultural Society for Nova Scotia
10 Cherry Brook Rd., Cherry Brook NS B2Z 1A8

Tel: 902-434-6223; Fax: 902-434-2306
Toll-Free: 800-465-0767
contact@bccns.com
www.bccns.com
www.facebook.com/188265867860941

To create among members of the Black community an awareness of their past, their heritage & identity; to provide programs & activities to explore, learn about, understand & appreciate Black history, achievements & experiences in Canadian life.
Leslie Oliver, President

Canadian Arab Federation (CAF) / La Fédération Canado-Arabe
1057 McNicoll Ave., Toronto ON M1W 3W6

Tel: 416-493-8635; Fax: 416-493-9239
Toll-Free: 866-886-4675
info@caf.ca
www.caf.ca

To represent Canadian Arabs on issues related to public policy; To protect civil liberties & the equality of human rights

The Canadian Doukhobor Society (CDS)
215 - 33 Ave. South, Creston BC V0G 1G1

Tel: 250-204-2931
spirit-wrestlers.com/CDS

To promote brotherhood, universal peace & the spiritual growth of our members
Beth Terriff, Secretary-Treasurer
Alex Wishlow, President

Canadian Ethnic Media Association (CEMA)
24 Tarlton Rd., Toronto ON M5P 2M4

Tel: 416-488-0048
canadianethnicmedia.com

To promote & preserve the value of the ethnic media in Canada; To advance understanding of Canada's cultural diversity
Madeline Ziniak, Contact

Canadian Ethnic Studies Association (CESA) / Société canadienne d'études ethniques (SCÉE)
c/o University of Calgary, Social Science, #909, 2500 University Dr. NW, Calgary AB T2N 1N4

Tel: 403-220-7372
cesa@ucalgary.ca
www.cesa-scee.ca

To encourage scholarly debate about theoretical & practical issues in Canadian ethnic studies
Evangelia Tastsoglou, President

Canadian Ethnocultural Council (CEC) / Conseil ethnoculturel du Canada
#102, 2904 Hwy. 7 West, Vaughan ON L4K 0K4

Tel: 613-230-3867
cec@web.ca
www.ethnocultural.ca
www.youtube.com/user/EthnoCanada

To represent a cross-section of ethnocultural groups across Canada
Dominic Campione, President

Canadian Institute for Jewish Research (CIJR) / Institut canadien de recherche sur le Judaïsme (ICRJ)
PO Box 175, Stn. H, Montréal QC H3G 2K7

Tel: 514-486-5544; Fax: 514-486-8284
Toll-Free: 855-303-5544
cijr@isranet.org
www.isranet.org
www.facebook.com/CanadianInstituteforJewishResearch
twitter.com/cijr

To increase public understanding of Jewish Israel & general Jewish world issues

Canadian Polish Congress (CPC) / Congrès canadien polonais (CCP)
3055 Lake Shore Blvd. West, Toronto ON M8V 1K6

Tel: 416-532-2876; Fax: 416-532-5730
kongres@kpk.org
kpk.org
www.facebook.com/Canadian.Polish.Congress
twitter.com/CanPolCongress

To represent Polish-Canadians & to defend their interests; To coordinate & support the work of Polish-Canadian organizations in Canada; To foster Polish culture & assist Polish immigrants; To inform Canadians about Poland's contribution to culture & to maintain liaisons with Poland
Janusz Tomczak, President
Dominik Roszak, General Secretary
Marcin Lewandowski, Treasurer

Canadian Race Relations Foundation (CRRF)
#225, 6 Garamond Crt., Toronto ON M3C 1Z5

Tel: 416-703-4164; Fax: 416-441-2752
Toll-Free: 888-240-4936
info@crrf-fcrr.ca
www.crr.ca
linkedin.com/company/the-canadian-race-relations-foundation
www.facebook.com/699059076842903
twitter.com/CRRF

To eliminate racism and all forms of racial discrimination, and promote Canadian identity, belonging and the mutuality of citizenship rights and responsibilities for a more harmonious Canada.
Anita Bromberg, Executive Director

Canadian Slovak League
#6, 259 Traders Blvd. East, Mississauga ON L4Z 2E5

Tel: 905-507-8004
administrator@kanadskyslovak.ca
www.kanadskyslovak.ca

To promote Christian, democratic values, lead the members towards good citizenship & loyalty to Canada, educate the members about the Canadian history & structure of the Canadian system; To promote & build the spirit of cooperation & friendship among the league members; To promote sport, cultural, & social activities that help to achieve better understanding of Canadians & Slovaks; To enrich Canada's multicultural heritage by promoting the Slovak heritage, traditions, & values. Branches in Toronto, Montreal, Ottawa, Welland, Windsor, St. Catharines, Kitchener, Sarnia, & Calgary.
Maria Dinga, Secretary
Paul Carnogursky, Website Administrator
Julius Behul, Editor, Kanadsky Slovák

Canadian Tibetan Association of Ontario (CTAO)
40 Titan Rd., Toronto ON M8Z 2J8

Tel: 416-410-5606; Fax: 416-410-5606
www.ctao.org

To represent Tibetans in Ontario; To serve the needs of the Tibetan community in the province; To promote cross-cultural understanding
Tsering Tsomo, President
Ngawang Diki, Coordinator, Cultural

Canadian Zionist Federation (CZF) / La fédération sioniste canadienne
#315, 4600 Bathurst St., Toronto ON M2R 3V2

Tel: 416-636-7655
czf.national@czfmontreal.org
www.canadianzf.ca

To promote the Zionist ideal among the Jewish population in Canada; To assist in strengthening the Jewish State of Israel; To enrich Canadian Jewish life through the provision of Jewish education & information on Israel & Zionism, through the promotion of Aliyah & activities among Jewish youth in Canada

The Centre for Israel & Jewish Affairs (CIJA)

info@cija.ca
www.cija.ca
www.facebook.com/cijainfo
twitter.com/cijainfo

To act as decision-making body of the Jewish community in Canada; To act on behalf of Canadian Jewish community on issues & concerns affecting Jews in Canada & around the world; To foster interaction between interests & needs of Jewish community in Canada & Canadian society at large on a broad range of political, charitable & social justice issues
Joel Reitman, Co-Chair
Jeffrey Rosenthal, Co-Chair
Shimon Koffler Fogel, President & CEO

Centre multiethnique de Québec (CMQ)
200, rue Dorchester, Québec QC G1K 5Z1

Tél: 418-687-9771; Téléc: 418-687-9063
info@centremultiethnique.com
www.centremultiethnique.com
www.facebook.com/371879376223670

D'accueillir les immigrantes et immigrants de toutes catégories afin de faciliter leur établissement en Canada; De soutenir leur adaptation et leur intégration à la société québécoise et de favoriser leurs accès à de meilleures conditions socio-économiques
Karine Verreault, Directrice

Chinese Canadian National Council (CCNC) / Conseil national des canadiens chinois
#507, 302 Spadina Ave., Toronto ON M5T 2E7

Tel: 416-977-9871

To promote the rights of all individuals, in particular, those of Chinese Canadians & to encourage their full & equal participation in Canadian society; to create an environment in Canada in which the rights of all individuals are fully recognized & protected; to promote understanding & cooperation between Chinese Canadians & all other ethnic, cultural, & racial groups in Canada; to encourage & develop in persons of Chinese descent, a desire to know & respect their historical & cultural heritage, & to educate them in adopting a creative & positive attitude towards the Chinese Canadian contribution to society & the Chinese Canadian heritage
Victor Wong, Executive Director

Clans & Scottish Societies of Canada (CASSOC)
c/o Secretary, #78, 24 Fundy Bay Blvd., Toronto ON M1W 3A4

Tel: 416-492-1623
info@cassoc.ca
www.cassoc.ca
www.facebook.com/clansandscottishsocieties

To foster the organization of & cooperation between Scottish associations, federations, clans, societies & groups through initiation & coordination of projects & undertakings; To advance Scottish cultural heritage in Canada
William R. Petrie, Chair
Jo Ann M. Tuskin, Secretary

Cypriot Federation of Canada / Fédération chypriote du Canada
6 Thorncliff Park Dr., Toronto ON M4H 1H1

Tel: 416-696-7400; Fax: 416-696-9465
cypriotfederation@rogers.com
cypriotfederation.ca
www.facebook.com/115174616903533

To co-ordinate activities relating to ethnicity, community, education & culture
Christine Amygdalidis, President
Petros Mina, General Secretary

Czech & Slovak Association of Canada
PO Box 1507, Manotick ON K4M 1B2

www.cssk.ca
www.facebook.com/CSSKVAN

To develop the highest standards of citizenship in Canadians of Czech or Slovak origin by encouraging, carrying on & participating in activities of national, patriotic, cultural & humanitarian nature; To act in matters affecting status rights & welfare of Canadians of Czech or Slovak origin; To cultivate in members appreciation of their mother tongue, cultural heritage & historical traditions; To promote growth of spirit in toleration, understanding & goodwill between all ethnic elements in Canada; To conduct research & encourage studies
Milos Suchma, President

Estonian Central Council in Canada (EKN)
310 Bloor St. West, Toronto ON M5S 1W4

estoniancentralcouncil@gmail.com
www.estoniancouncil.ca
www.facebook.com/estoniancouncil

To help further the interests & development of the Estonian community in Canada
Marcus Kolga, President

Federation of Canada-China Friendship Associations (FCCFA)
159 Oakmount Rd. SW, Calgary AB T2V 4X3

federation.tripod.com
www.facebook.com/fccfa1

To work with students from the Peoples' Republic of China studying in Canada; To take groups to China; To welcome delegations coming from China; To promote cultural exchanges
Gary Levy, President

Federation of Canadian Turkish Associations (FCTA) / Kanada Türk Dernekleri Federasyonu
#15, 1170 Sheppard Ave. West, Toronto ON M3K 2A3
Tel: 647-955-1923; Fax: 647-776-3111
info@turkishfederation.ca
www.turkishfederation.ca
www.facebook.com/TurkishFederation
To support & encourage activities that deal with important cultural, economic, educational, historical, social & religious issues that relate to the Turkish Community in Canada

Federation of Chinese Canadian Professionals (Ontario) (FCCP)
Coral Place, 55 Glenn Hawthorne Blvd., Mississauga ON L5R 3S6
Tel: 905-890-3235; Fax: 905-568-5293
www.fccpontario.com
To foster the promotion, cooperation, & growth among Chinese Canadian Professionals from various disciplines, including: accounting, architecture, biomedical, chiropractic, dental, education, engineering, information technology, legal, medical, pharmacy, & physiotherapy
Sue Chen, President

Federation of Chinese Canadian Professionals (Québec) (FCCP Québec) / Fédération des professionnels chinois canadiens (Québec)
PO Box 5388, Stn. B, Montréal QC H3B 3K5
Tel: 514-954-3160
To promote the well-being of Chinese Canadian professionals in Québec; To liaise & cooperate with Chinese Canadian professionals in other parts of Canada & throughout the world; To provide a strong voice for the group
Howard Tan, President
John Chen, Vice-President
Renee Chin, Treasurer

Federation of Danish Associations in Canada / Fédération des associations danoises du Canada
secretary@danishfederation.ca
www.danishfederation.ca
To promote cooperation among Danish Canadian organizations; To promote preservation & understanding of Danish tradition & heritage
Rolf Buschardt Christensen, President
Ed Kuhlman, Vice-President
Aase Christensen, Secretary
Sune Overgaard, Treasurer

Finnish Canadian Cultural Federation / Fédération culturelle finno-canadienne
Toronto ON
To act as non-political coordinator between associations, congregations, clubs & other groups of Finnish ethnic background; To promote Finland & Canadians of Finnish origin; To promote Canada & its Finnish ethnic community in Finland; To support Annual Finnish Canadian Grand Festival

German-Canadian Congress (Manitoba) Inc.
#58, 81 Garry St., Winnipeg MB R3C 4J9
Tel: 204-989-8300; Fax: 204-989-8304
info@gccmb.ca
www.gccmb.ca
www.facebook.com/German.Canadian.Congress
To cultivate & promote language, culture, customs & traditions of German Canadians within the scope of Canadian multiculturalism
Björn Meinhardt, President

Goethe-Institut (Toronto)
North Tower, PO Box 136, #201, 100 University Ave., Toronto ON M5J 1V6
Tel: 416-593-5257; Fax: 416-593-5145
info@toronto.goethe.org
www.goethe.de/toronto
www.facebook.com/GoetheToronto
twitter.com/GoetheToronto
To provide cultural programs, international cultural cooperation, German language teaching, & library & information services
Uwe Rau, Director

Greater Vancouver Japanese Canadian Citizens' Association (GVJCAA)
#200, 6688 Southoaks Cres., Burnaby BC V5E 4M7
Tel: 604-777-5222; Fax: 604-777-5223
gvjcca@gmail.com
jccabulletin-geppo.ca/about-2/jcca-bulletin
www.instagram.com/bulletin_geppo
twitter.com/bulletin_geppo
To represent the Japanese Canadian community in Vancouver & the surrounding area
Derek Iwanaka, President

Hellenic Canadian Congress of BC (HCC(BC))
PO Box 129, 4500 Arbutus St., Vancouver BC V6J 4A2
Tel: 604-780-2460
info@helleniccongressbc.ca
www.helleniccongressbc.ca
www.facebook.com/124766634268645
Fosters education, communication, and cooperation between Hellenic Canadians and other ethnic groups, and promotes the development of just and equitable policies and legislation concerning all citizens.
Jimmy Sidiropoulos, President

Holocaust Education Centre
Lipa Green Centre, Sherman Campus, 4600 Bathurst St., 4th Fl., Toronto ON M2R 3V2
Tel: 416-631-5689
neuberger@ujafed.org
www.holocaustcentre.com
twitter.com/Holocaust_Ed
Carson Phillips, Ph.D, Managing Director
Rachel Libman, Manager, Public Programs
Mary Siklos, Manager, Operations
Anna Skorupsky, Librarian

Hungarian Canadian Cultural Centre
141 Sunrise Ave., Toronto ON M4A 1A9
Tel: 416-654-4926
office@hccc.org
www.hccc.org
www.facebook.com/HungarianCanadianCulturalCentre
To preserve & showcase Hungarian heritage in the Canadian mosaic

Icelandic National League of North America (INLNA)
#103, 94 - 1st Ave., Gimli MB R0C 1B1
Tel: 204-642-5897; Fax: 204-642-9382
inl@mymts.net
inlofna.org
www.facebook.com/IcelandicNationalLeagueofNorthAmerica
twitter.com/inlna1
To foster & promote good citizenship among people of Icelandic descent; to foster & strengthen a mutual understanding of kinship, language, literature & cultural bonds among people of Icelandic origin & descent in North America & the people of Iceland; To cooperate with organizations which have similar purposes & objectives; To actively support various cultural & ethnic developments including education, history, publishing & the arts
Stefan Jonasson, President

Igbo Union of Canada
#206, 415 Oakdale Rd., Toronto ON M3N 1W7
Tel: 647-968-9191
info@montrealhelem.org
www.igbounioncanada.com
www.facebook.com/IgboUnionOfCanada
twitter.com/igbounion
To unite Igbo people in Canada & support traditional Igbo fellowship

Immigrant Welcome Centre (MISA)
#A114, 740 Robron Rd., Campbell River BC V9W 6J7
Tel: 250-830-0171; Fax: 250-830-1010
Toll-Free: 855-805-0171
www.immigrantwelcome.ca
www.facebook.com/157900677578942
twitter.com/immigrantcentre
To develop services & programs that provide an on-going opportunity for immigrants & their families to learn skills to adapt to Canadian society; To sponsor opportunities to celebrate cultural diversity & learn about the issues of cultural acceptance, network & support other agencies as the provide services to the multicultural community

International Organization of Ukrainian Communities: Fourth Wave
#2, 15 Canmotor Ave., Toronto ON M8Z 4E4
Tel: 647-334-3899
fourthwave@hotmail.com
www.4th-wave.org
www.facebook.com/4thwavecanada

To contribute to the strengthening & development of the Ukrainian community in Canada; To develop & promote Ukrainian national heritage as an element of the Canadian multicultural environment; To liaise with Ukrainian in Ukraine to promote mutual achievements of Ukrainian Canadians in science, technology, culture & business; To provide social support to Ukrainian Canadians who are in need

Iranian Canadian Congress (ICC)
#900, 45 Sheppard Ave. East, Toronto ON M2N 5W9
Tel: 647-539-4344
info@iccongress.ca
www.iccongress.ca
www.instagram.com/iccongress.ca
www.linkedin.com/company/iranian-canadian-congress-icc-
www.facebook.com/ICCongress
twitter.com/ICCongress
To improve the lives of Iranian-Canadians by promoting & protecting their rights & interests
Soudeh Ghasemi, President

Iranian Women's Organization of Ontario (IWOO)
1761 Sheppard Ave. East, Toronto ON M2J 0A5
Tel: 416-496-9566
info@iwontario.com
iwontario.com
www.instagram.com/iwontario
www.linkedin.com/company/iranian-women's-organization-of-ontario
www.facebook.com/IranianWomenOrganizationofOntario
twitter.com/iwontario
To improve the life of the Iranian women & families
Noushin Khavarian, Coordinator, Programs & Services

Irish Canadian Cultural Association of New Brunswick (ICCA NB)
c/o Patricia O'Leary-Coughlan, 189 Carlisle Rd., Douglas NB E3A 7M8
info@newirelandnb.ca
www.newirelandnb.ca
To recognize & honour the contributions made by our ancestors to Canada by holding an annual Irish Festival, promoting an Irish Studies program at universities & sponsoring Irish cultural & social programs & events
Patricia O'Leary-Coughlan, Contact

Italian Cultural Institute (Istituto Italiano di Cultura)
496 Huron St., Toronto ON M5R 2R3
Tel: 416-921-3802; Fax: 416-962-2503
iicToronto@esteri.it
www.iictoronto.esteri.it
www.youtube.com/user/IICCulturalToronto
www.facebook.com/iictoronto
twitter.com/IICToronto
To promote Italian culture & language in its many expressions in a spirit of vital interaction with the host country; To provide information on Italy's cultural heritage & contemporary cultural production
Alessandro Ruggera, Acting Director
Carlo Settembrini, Technical Manager
Tiziana Miano, Assistant to the Director

Jamaica Association of Montréal Inc.
4065, rue Jean-Talon ouest, Montréal QC H4P 1W6
Tel: 514-737-8229
www.jam-montreal.com
www.facebook.com/JamaicaAssociationOfMontrealInc
To provide educational, cultural & social activities for the Jamaican community

Jamaican Canadian Association (JCA)
995 Arrow Rd., Toronto ON M9M 2Z5
Tel: 416-746-5772; Fax: 416-746-7035
info@jcaontario.org
jcaontario.org
www.instagram.com/jcaontario
www.facebook.com/JamaicanCanadianAssociation
twitter.com/JCA_Ontario
To provide social interaction among members & to facilitate desirable relations with Canadian society; To represent the Caribbean community on public matters; To respond to the diverse social service needs of members; To facilitate economic, social & cultural integration of Caribbean people within Canadian society
Adaoma Patterson, President

Japanese Canadian Association of Yukon (JCAY)
jcayukon@gmail.com
info.jcayukon.org/intro-e.html

Jewish Federations of Canada - UIA (JFC-UIA)
#421, 4600 Bathurst St., Toronto ON M2R 3V3
Tel: 416-636-7655
info@jfcuia.org
www.jewishcanada.org
www.youtube.com/user/JewishFedofCanada
www.facebook.com/JewishFederationsofCanadaUIA
twitter.com/jfcuia
To raise money for Canadian Jewish organizations & to promote their efforts
Nikki Holland, President & CEO

Jewish Heritage Centre of Western Canada Inc. (JHC)
123 Doncaster St., #C140, Winnipeg MB R3N 2B2
Tel: 204-477-7460; *Fax:* 204-477-7465
jewishheritage@jhcwc.org
www.jhcwc.org
The Jewish Heritage Centre comprises The Jewish Historical Society of Western Canada, Marion & Ed Vickar Jewish Museum of Western Canada, Freeman Family Foundation Holocaust Education Centre & Genealogical Institute
Belle Jarniewski, Executive Director
Stan Carbone, Director, Programmes & Exhibits

Latvian Canadian Cultural Centre (LCCC)
4 Credit Union Dr., Toronto ON M4A 2N8
Tel: 416-759-4900; *Fax:* 416-759-9311
office@latviancentre.org
www.latviancentre.org
www.facebook.com/143970339032047
To acquire, maintain & operate a Centre; to foster & sustain the Latvian heritage & cultural tradition; to provide social & cultural exchange with the various cultural communities in Canada; to provide facilities for meetings, concerts, dances, seminars, theatre & film shows & similar social/recreational activities for the general public & members
Sylvia Shedden, President & CEO

Latvian National Federation in Canada (LNAK) / Fédération nationale lettone au Canada
4 Credit Union Dr., Toronto ON M4A 2N8
Tel: 416-755-2353
lnak@lnak.org
www.lnak.net/eng
www.facebook.com/latviannationalfederationincanada
To represent the interests of Latvian Canadians at the city, provincial & federal levels; To maintain contact with other Canadian non-governmental organizations & expedite projects both in Canada & in Latvia
Peteris Brauns, Chair
Ilze Maksina, Administrator

The Latvian Relief Society of Canada
4 Credit Union Dr., Toronto ON M4A 2N8
dvkvbirojs@gmail.com
www.daugavasvanagi.ca
To provide financial assistance to Latvian-Canadians who demonstrate financial need; To encourage Latvian-Canadian youth to pursue post-secondary education

League of Ukrainian Canadian Women (LUCW)
#204, 2282 Bloor St. West, Toronto ON M6S 1N9
Tel: 416-763-8907
info@lucw.ca
www.lucw.ca
www.facebook.com/LeagueOfUkrainianCanadianWomen
To support the development & sustainment of a strong Ukrainian community in Canada; To promote Ukraine's right to protect its national independence & security in the European family of nations

League of Ukrainian Canadians
9 Plastics Ave., Toronto ON M8Z 4B6
Tel: 416-516-8223; *Fax:* 416-516-4033
luc@lucorg.com
www.lucorg.com
www.facebook.com/LeagueofUkrainianCanadians
To aid Ukrainian people living in Canada & in Ukraine; To contribute to the growth & development of a prosperous Ukrainian community in Canada
Orest Steciw, President

The Lithuanian Canadian Community (LCC) / La Communauté lithuanienne du Canada
1 Resurrection Rd., Toronto ON M9A 5G1
Tel: 416-533-3292; *Fax:* 416-533-2282
klb@on.aibn.com
www.klb.org
To promote, maintain & encourage the survival of the Lithuanian culture & language in Canada & abroad
Kazimieras Deksnys, President

Maltese-Canadian Society of Toronto, Inc. (MCST)
3132 Dundas St. West, Toronto ON M6P 2A1
Tel: 416-767-3645
The organization strives for the betterment of the Maltese community in Toronto. It also preserves & promotes the Maltese language & culture in Canada.

Mizrachi Organization of Canada
#316, 4600 Bathurst St., Toronto ON M2R 3V2
Tel: 416-630-9266
mizrachi@mizrachi.ca
www.mizrachi.ca
www.facebook.com/mizrachicanada
twitter.com/MizrachiCanada
To coordinate Zionist-oriented programming for the Orthodox Jewish communities in Canada; To raise funds for educational & social welfare institutions in Israel
Elan Mazer, National Director

Multicultural Association of Northwestern Ontario (MANWO)
511 East Victoria Ave., Thunder Bay ON P7C 1A8
Tel: 807-622-4666; *Fax:* 807-622-7271
Toll-Free: 800-692-7692
manwoyc@tbaytel.net
To promote the concept of multiculturalism; to provide information, training & resources on citizenship, multiculturalism & race relations.

Multicultural Association of Nova Scotia (MANS) / Association multiculturelle de la Nouvelle-Écosse
1113 Marginal Rd., Halifax NS B3H 4P7
Tel: 902-423-6534; *Fax:* 902-422-0881
To develop & influence multicultural policy & to promote equality; To create a sense of belonging & respect for all cultures
Sylvia Parris, Vice-President

Multicultural Council of Windsor & Essex County (MCC)
245 Janette Ave., Windsor ON N9A 4Z2
Tel: 519-255-1127; *Fax:* 519-255-1435
contact@themcc.com
www.themcc.com
www.youtube.com/user/MCCWEC
www.facebook.com/MultiCulturalCl
twitter.com/MultiCulturalCl
To create a harmonious multicultural society
Pat Reid Crichton, President

Multicultural History Society of Ontario (MHSO)
#307, 901 Lawrence Ave. West, Toronto ON M6A 1C3
Tel: 416-979-2973; *Fax:* 416-979-7947
info@mhso.ca
www.mhso.ca
www.youtube.com/user/MulticulturalHistory
www.facebook.com/multiculturalhistorysociety
To work with communities, schools, cultural agencies, & institutions to preserve, record, & make accessible archival & other material which demonstrate the role of immigration & ethnicity in shaping the culture & economic growth of Ontario & Canada. Library is located at St. Michael's College, University of Toronto.
Carl Thorpe, Executive Director
Elizabeth Price, Development Manager

National Association of Japanese Canadians (NAJC)
180 McPhillips St., Winnipeg MB R3E 2J9
Tel: 204-943-2910
national@najc.ca
najc.ca
To promote & develop a strong Japanese Canadian identity, thereby strengthening local communities & the national organization; To strive for equal rights & liberties for all persons & racial & ethnic minorities in particular
Lorene Oikawa, President

National Congress of Italian-Canadians (NCIC) / Congrès national des italo-canadiens
#202, 340 Falstaff Ave., Toronto ON M6L 3E8
Tel: 416-531-9964
info@canadese.org
www.facebook.com/pg/ncictoronto
To promote Italian language & culture among Italian-Canadians

National Council of Trinidad & Tobago Organizations in Canada (NCTTOC)
66 Oakmeadow Blvd., Toronto ON M1E 4G5
Tel: 416-283-9672; *Fax:* 416-283-9672
To provide a national focus for representing the concerns of Trinidad & Tobago Nationals; to advocate on behalf of Trinidad & Tobago Nationals & their families in Canada; to develop & maintain a system of communication, information sharing & networking among Trinidad & Tobago organizations; to provide information, referrals, advocacy & support to new arrivals from Trinidad & Tobago
Emmanuel Dick, Contact

New Brunswick African Association Inc.
NB
nbaa.ca
To support the African community in New Brunswick
Andrew Gbongbor, President

New Brunswick Multicultural Council (NBMC) / Conseil multiculturel du Nouveau-Brunswick (CMNB)
#200, 494 Queen St., Fredericton NB E3B 1B6
Tel: 506-453-1091
www.nb-mc.ca
www.facebook.com/cmnb.nbmc
twitter.com/nbmc_cmnb
To represent multicultural & multi-racial interests of all member associations; to encourage development & formation of new associations; to encourage member associations in their multicultural, inter-cultural & inter-racial programs & activities
Alex LeBlanc, Executive Director

North Shore Multicultural Society (NSMS)
#207, 123 - 15th St. East, North Vancouver BC V7L 2P7
Tel: 604-988-2931; *Fax:* 604-988-2960
office@nsms.ca
www.nsms.ca
To assist immigrant families to settle & integrate into Canadian society; To work with community agencies & schools in making services more accessible to North Shore newcomers
Vera Radyo, President
Elizabeth Jones, Executive Director
Stacie Letham, Director, Operations

Pacific Peoples' Partnership (PPP)
#407, 620 View St., Victoria BC V8W 1J6
Tel: 250-381-4131; *Fax:* 250-388-5258
info@pacificpeoplespartnership.org
www.pacificpeoplespartnership.org
To promote increased understanding of social justice, environment, development, health & other issues of importance to the people of the Pacific Islands; To support equitable, environmentally sustainable development & social justice in the region
April Ingham, Executive Director
Siobhan Powlowski, Deputy Director

Peel Multicultural Council (PMC)
6630 Turner Valley Rd., Mississauga ON L5N 2P1
Tel: 905-819-1144; *Fax:* 905-542-3950
pmc@peelmc.com
www.peelmc.com
www.youtube.com/peelpmc
www.linkedin.com/company/2823166
www.facebook.com/peelmulticulturalcouncil
To promote a harmonious multicultural society by increasing communication & by building bridges of understanding between ethocultural groups, institutions & the community; To facilitate the settlement & integration of newcomers to Canada
Naveed Chaudhry, Executive Director
Raj Jhajj, President
Atma Gill, Vice President
Baljinder Sekhon, Secretary
Eric Wen, Treasurer

Polish Alliance of Canada (PAC)
www.polishalliance.ca
To promote Polish history, culture & interests
Teresa Szramek, President

Polish-Jewish Heritage Foundation of Canada
#61, 396 Woodsworth Rd., Toronto ON M2L 2T9
www.pjhftoronto.ca
To preserve the unique heritage of Polish Jews & to actively foster better understanding & cooperation between Polish & Jewish communities in Canada
Peter Jassem, Chair

Regina Multicultural Council (RMC)
2054 Broad St., Regina SK S4P 1Y3
Tel: 306-757-5990; *Fax:* 306-352-1977
admin.rmc@sasktel.net
reginamulticulturalcouncil.ca
www.instagram.com/mosaicyqr
www.facebook.com/RMCMosaic
twitter.com/RMCMosaic
To promote recognition of cultural diversity in Saskatchewan; To recognize, foster & promote the development of multilingualism & to promote positive cross-cultural relations
John Findura, Interim President
Holly Paluck, Secretary

Richmond Multicultural Community Services (RMCS)
#210, 7000 Minoru Blvd., Richmond BC V6Y 3Z5
Tel: 604-279-7160; *Fax:* 604-279-7168
info@rmcs.bc.ca
www.rmcs.bc.ca
www.facebook.com/richmondmulticulturalcommunityservices
twitter.com/rmcs_1985
To foster intercultural harmony through leadership, education, collaboration, & service delivery; To assist immigrants & refugees with settlement, integration needs & multicultural/diversity training.
Parm Grewal, Executive Director
Ashok Rattan, Coordinator, Settlement Program
Yoshimi Vanrenen, Executive Assistant

Serbian National Shield Society of Canada
#303, 1900 Sheppard Ave. East, Toronto ON M2J 4T4
Tel: 416-496-7881; *Fax:* 416-493-0335
To promote & inform about interests & heritage of Canadian Serbs
Diane Dragasevich, Contact

South Okanagan Immigrant & Community Services (SOICS)
508 Main St., Penticton BC V2A 5C7
Tel: 250-492-6299; *Fax:* 250-490-4684
admin@soics.ca
www.soics.ca
www.facebook.com/soics.penticton
To build a community based upon mutual respect & full participation of people of all backgrounds through education, client advocacy & community programs
Helen Greaves, President
Doug Holmes, Vice President

Turkish Community Heritage Centre of Canada (TCHHC)
#35B, 234-10520 Yonge St., Richmond Hill ON L4C 3C7
Tel: 416-644-9909
info@TurkishCommunityCentre.org
www.turkishcommunitycentre.org
www.facebook.com/178208095522790
twitter.com/tchcc
Provides and maintains a community centre for the Canadian Turkish community.
Musabay Figen, President

UJA Federation of Greater Toronto
4600 Bathurst St., Toronto ON M2R 3V2
Tel: 416-635-2883
info@jewishtoronto.com
www.jewishtoronto.com
www.youtube.com/user/UJAFederation
www.facebook.com/UJAFederationToronto
twitter.com/UJAFederation
To preserve & strengthen Jewish life in Toronto, Canada & Israel, through philanthropic, volunteer & professional leadership; The UJA is committed to social justice on behalf of the Jewish poor & vulnerable locally & internationally, to strengthening ties with Israel & its people, to supporting Israel's struggle to meet its social welfare needs, to combatting antisemitism in all its forms around the world, to nurturing shared values with Canadians of all faiths, to promoting Jewish education, to building a vibrant Jewish communal life. The following Pillars identify main areas of focus for UJA: Jewish Education & Identity; Strategic Planning & Community Engagement; Integrated Development; Operations & Corporate Relations; Business & Finance
Adam Minsky, President & CEO

Ukrainian Canadian Congress (UCC) / Congrès des ukrainiens canadiens
#203, 952 Main St., Winnipeg MB R2W 3P4
Tel: 204-942-4627; *Fax:* 204-947-3882
Toll-Free: 866-942-4627
ucc@ucc.ca
www.ucc.ca
www.instagram.com/ukrcancongress
www.linkedin.com/company/ukrainian-canadian-congress
www.facebook.com/ukrcancongress
twitter.com/ukrcancongress
To protect, promote & enhance cultural identity of Ukrainians throughout Canada & beyond; To maintain, develop & enhance Ukrainian culture & language as integral elements of Canada's multicultural mosaic; To encourage participation of Ukrainian Canadians in cultural, social, economic & political life in Canada; To advance communication, understanding & mutual respect between Ukrainian Canadians & other ethnocultural communities; To foster sense of unity, cohesiveness & cooperation among member organizations
Alexandra Chyczij, President

Ukrainian Canadian Research & Documentation Centre (UCRDC) / Centre canadien-ukrainien de recherches et de documentation
620 Spadina Ave., Toronto ON M5S 2H4
Tel: 416-966-1819; *Fax:* 416-966-1820
info@ucrdc.org
www.ucrdc.org
www.facebook.com/261703763950638
To collect, store & promote information pertaining to Ukrainian historical events & Ukrainian Canadian experiences
Jurij Darewych, Chair & President

Ukrainian Democratic Youth Association (ODUM)
3029 Bloor St. West, Toronto ON M8X 1C5
www.odum.org
To unite Ukrainian Canadians & other Ukrainians across North America

Ukrainian National Federation of Canada (UNF) / Fédération nationale Ukrainienne du Canada
#210, 145 Evans Ave., Toronto ON M8Z 5X8
Tel: 416-925-2770
info@unfcanada.ca
www.unfcanada.ca
www.facebook.com/unfcanada
To unite Ukrainian Canadians while promoting good Canadian citizenship; To represent the interests & needs of the Ukrainian Canadian community; To inform Canadians about Ukrainian history & culture while strengthening the place of the Ukrainian community in Canadian society at large
Olya Grod, Executive Director

Ukrainian Self-Reliance League of Canada (CYC)
3338 Lake Shore Blvd. West, Toronto ON M8W 1M9
Tel: 905-546-6356
info@usrl-cyc.org
www.usrl-cyc.org
To preserve Canadian heritage while advancing Ukrainian Canadian culture; To enhance the future growth of the Ukrainian Orthodox Church of Canada
Peter Kondra, President

Ukrainian Women's Association of Canada (UWAC)
#204, 145 Evans Ave., Toronto ON M8Z 5X8
info@uwac-national.ca
uwac-national.ca
To support the continual growth of the Ukrainian Orthodox Church of Canada; To preserve, develop, & nurture Ukrainian heritage; To foster & encourage cooperation within Canadian society; To support education of Ukrainian Canadian youth in church schools, Ukrainian schools & bilingual schools; To maintain the growth of the Ukrainian Museum of Canada of the UWAC
Olya Sheweli, President

Ukrainian Youth Association of Canada (UYA)
9 Plastics Ave., Toronto ON M8Z 4B6
Tel: 416-537-2007; *Fax:* 416-516-4033
ky-canada@cym.org
cym.org/ca
www.facebook.com/CYM.Canada
To encourage Ukrainian children & youth to discover their Ukrainian heritage; To promote Ukrainian traditions & language; To emphasize the development of Christian ethics & leadership skills
Yuri Broda, President

Urban Alliance on Race Relations (UARR)
#1001, 2 Carlton St., Toronto ON M5B 1J3
Tel: 416-703-6607; *Fax:* 416-703-4415
info@urbanalliance.ca
www.urbanalliance.ca
To promote a stable & healthy multiracial environment in the community, by creating awareness of current issues, assisting institutions to develop solid policies & practices, & promoting full participation by the community to dismantle barriers to equal opportunity
Nigel Barriffe, President
Malika Mendez, Vice President
Ilaneet Goren, Secretary
Tam Goossen, Treasurer

Vietnamese Canadian Federation (VCF) / Fédération vietnamienne du Canada
www.vietfederation.ca
To provide focal point for activities of the Vietnamese community in the National Capital Region & across Canada; To serve as resource centre on Vietnamese culture & issues related to resettlement & integration of Vietnamese refugees & immigrants in Canada; To maintain solidarity among the Vietnamese associations across Canada; To harmonize their activities for a better achievement of their common objectives; To work for the preservation & development of Vietnamese culture & for the

enrichment of Canadian culture; To foster the spirit of mutual help & community responsibility

Native Peoples

Aboriginal Agricultural Education Society of British Columbia (AAESBC)
PO Box 1186, Stn. Main, 7410 Dallas Dr., Kamloops BC V2C 6H3
Tel: 778-469-5040; *Fax:* 778-469-5030
info@aljamcommunitycollege.com
www.aljamcommunitycollege.com/who-we-are
To provide culturally appropriate & respectful training for First Nations agricultural businesses

Aboriginal Coalition to End Homelessness (ACEH)
465 Swift St., Victoria BC V8W 1S2
admin@aboriginalhomelessness.ca
aboriginalhomelessness.ca
To work to end Aboriginal homelessness in Victoria and on Vancouver Island, BC
Fran Hunt-Jinnouchi, Executive Director

Aboriginal Friendship Centres of Saskatchewan
115 Wall St., Saskatoon SK S7K 6C2
Tel: 306-955-0762; *Fax:* 306-955-0972
www.afcs.ca
www.facebook.com/AFCSK
twitter.com/afcsk
To promote the goals and objectives of member Friendship Centres; To represent & advocate for member Friendship Centres at all tiers of gov't
Laurie Bouvier, Executive Director

Aboriginal Head Start Association of British Columbia (AHSABC)
PO Box 20158, Duncan BC V9L 0C2
Tel: 250-858-4543; *Fax:* 250-743-2478
www.ahsabc.com
To promote excellence in Aboriginal early childhood learning programs across British Columbia
Joan Gignac, Executive Director

Aboriginal Veterans Society of Alberta
#304, 12308 - 111 Ave., Edmonton AB T5M 2N4
Tel: 780-475-9508
admin@aboriginalveterans.com
www.aboriginalveterans.com
To unite Aboriginal veterans to advocate for & support one another; To ensure Aboriginal veterans receive appropriate recognition & respect

Aboriginal Women's Association of Prince Edward Island
PO Box 145, 312 Sweetgrass Trail, Lennox Island PE C0B 1P0
Tel: 902-831-3059; *Fax:* 902-831-3027
info@awapei.org
www.awapei.org
www.facebook.com/193334154037222
twitter.com/awapei1
To address issues of concern to Aboriginal women on Prince Edward Island; To improve the educational, social & economic well being of Aboriginal women
Alma MacDougall, President

Alberta Aboriginal Women's Society
PO Box 5168, Stn. Main, Peace River AB T8S 1R8
Tel: 780-624-3416; *Fax:* 780-624-3409
Toll-Free: 877-622-3416
aaws@telusplanet.net
www.facebook.com/telusplanet.net
Ruth Kidder, President
Debra Schapansky, Coordinator, Project

Alberta Native Friendship Centres Association (ANFCA)
10336 - 121 St. NW, Edmonton AB T5N 1K8
Tel: 780-423-3138; *Fax:* 780-425-6277
info@anfca.com
www.anfca.com
To promote the betterment of friendship centres; To assist friendship centres in meeting the needs of the urban Indigenous population
Joanne Mason, Executive Director

Alliance autochtone du Québec / Native Alliance of Québec
21, rue Brodeur, Gatineau QC J8Y 2P6
Tél: 819-770-7763; *Téléc:* 819-770-6070
info@aaqnaq.com
www.aaqnaq.com

Promouvoir et représenter les intérêts des Autochtones (Indiens, Inuits et Métis) qui vivent à l'extérieur des réserves au Québec
Danielle Bédard, Président Grand Chef

Assembly of First Nations (AFN) / Assemblée des Premières Nations (APN)
#1600, 55 Metcalfe St., Ottawa ON K1P 6L5
Tel: 613-241-6789; *Fax:* 613-241-5808
Toll-Free: 866-869-6789
www.afn.ca
www.youtube.com/user/afnposter
www.linkedin.com/company/assembly-of-first-nations
www.facebook.com/AssemblyofFirstNations
twitter.com/AFN_Updates
To act as an advocate for First Nations on many issues, including Aboriginal & Treaty Rights, economic development, education, languages & literacy, health, housing, social development, justice, land claims & the environment
Perry Bellegarde, National Chief
Marlene Poitras, Regional Chief, Alberta
Terry Teegee, Regional Chief, British Columbia
Kevin Hart, Regional Chief, Manitoba
Roger Augustine, Regional Chief, New Brunswick & Prince Edward Island
Norman Yakeleya, Regional Chief, Northwest Territories
Paul Prosper, Regional Chief, Nova Scotia & Newfoundland
RoseAnne Archibald, Regional Chief, Ontario
Ghislain Picard, Regional Chief, Québec & Labrador
Bobby Cameron, Regional Chief, Saskatchewan
Kluane Adamek, Regional Chief, Yukon
Janice Ciavaglia, Chief Executive Officer

Assembly of Manitoba Chiefs
#200, 275 Portage Ave., Winnipeg MB R3B 2B3
Tel: 204-956-0610; *Fax:* 204-956-2109
Toll-Free: 888-324-5483
info@manitobachiefs.com
www.manitobachiefs.com
www.youtube.com/channel/UCjz23-aYRtfN4cQsdNz-0cA
www.facebook.com/AssemblyMBChiefs
twitter.com/amcmbchiefs
To promote & preserve Aboriginal and treaty rights while striving to improve the quality of life of the First Nation citizens in Manitoba.
Arlen Dumas, Grand Chief
Jasmine Tara, Officer, Communications

Association for Native Development in the Performing & Visual Arts (ANDPVA)
#10, 160 Baldwin St., Toronto ON M5T 3K7
Tel: 416-829-3229; *Fax:* 416-535-9331
andpva.ca
www.facebook.com/andpva
To coordinate & develop programs that will encourage Indigenous peoples & communities to become more actively involved in the arts; To act as liaison for Native groups & individuals who are seeking funds for specific arts projects
Millie Knapp, Executive Director

Association of Iroquois & Allied Indians
387 Princess Ave., London ON N6B 2A7
Tel: 519-434-2761; *Fax:* 519-675-1053
Toll-Free: 888-269-9593
www.aiai.on.ca
www.linkedin.com/company/aiai
www.facebook.com/aiai.pto
twitter.com/AIAI_Comms
To advocate for the political interests of seven member nations in Ontario; To promote & protect the inherent rights, languages, cultures, laws & lands of its members
Joel Abram, Grand Chief
Gord Peters, Deputy Grand Chief
Ira Timothy, Coordinator, Communications
Geoff Stonefish, Office Manager

British Columbia Assembly of First Nations (BCAFN)
1004 Landooz Rd., Prince George BC V2K 5S3
bcafn.ca
twitter.com/bcafn
To advocate for & implement Aboriginal Title Rights & Treaty Rights through exercising inherent laws & jurisdiction
Terry Teegee, Regional Chief
Vanessa West, Chief of Staff

British Columbia Association of Aboriginal Friendship Centres (BCAAFC)
551 Chatham St., Victoria BC V8T 1E1
Tel: 250-388-5522; *Fax:* 250-388-5502
Toll-Free: 800-990-2432
admin@bcaafc.com
www.bcaafc.com
www.facebook.com/BCAAFC
twitter.com/bcaafc

To promote the betterment of Aboriginal Friendship Centres in British Columbia by acting as a unifying body for the Centres; To establish & maintain communications between Aboriginal Friendship Centres, other associations, & government
Leslie Varley, Executive Director

British Columbia Native Women's Association
144 Briar Ave., Kamloops BC V2B 1C1
Tel: 250-554-4556; *Fax:* 250-554-4573
bcnwa.weebly.com
www.instagram.com/bcnwa_
www.facebook.com/BC.NativeWomen
twitter.com/BCNWA_
To promote the well-being of Aboriginal women & girls in British Columbia
Anna Thomas, President
Crystle Phillips, Coordinator, ASETS

Canadian Aboriginal & Minority Supplier Council (CAMSC)
#101, 282 Richmond St. East, Toronto ON M5A 1P4
Tel: 416-941-0004; *Fax:* 416-941-9282
info@camsc.ca
www.camsc.ca
www.linkedin.com/company/camsc
www.facebook.com/CAMSCorg
twitter.com/camsc_org
To economically empower Aboriginal & visible minority communities through business development & employment; To identify & certify Aboriginal & minority-owned businesses, & to integrate them into the supply chain of major corporations in Canada
Cassandra Dorrington, President

Canadian Association for the Study of Indigenous Education (CASIE) / Association canadienne pour l'etude de l'education des autochtones (ACÉFÉ)
c/o Canadian Society for the Study of Education, #204, 260 Dalhousie St., Ottawa ON K1N 7E4
Tel: 613-241-0018; *Fax:* 613-241-0019
www.casieaceea.org
To promote Indigenous education in Canada
Mark Aquash, President

Canadian Council for Aboriginal Business (CCAB) / Conseil canadien pour le commerce autochtone
#202, 2 Berkeley St., Toronto ON M5A 4J5
Tel: 416-961-8663; *Fax:* 416-961-3995
info@caab.com
www.ccab.com
www.instagram.com/ccab_national
www.linkedin.com/company/ccab-national
www.facebook.com/CanadianCouncilforAboriginalBusiness
twitter.com/ccab_national
To promote full participation of Aboriginal communities in the Canadian economy
Tabatha Bull, President & CEO
Ken Montour, Director, Membership
Kathryn Wash, Director, Human Resources

Canadian Indigenous Nurses Association (CINA)
50 Driveway, Ottawa ON K2P 1E2
Tel: 613-724-4677; *Toll-Free:* 866-724-3049
info@indigenousnurses.ca
www.indigenousnurses.ca
To work with & on behalf of Aboriginal nurses to promote the development & practice of Aboriginal nursing in order to improve the health of Aboriginal people
Lea Bill, RN BScN, President
Juanita Rickard, RN BScN, Vice-President

Canadian Native Friendship Centre (CNFC)
11728 - 95 St., Edmonton AB T5G 1L9
Tel: 780-760-1900; *Fax:* 780-760-1900
www.cnfc.ca
www.facebook.com/CNFCEdmonton
To support Aboriginal Peoples living in an urban environment; To promote self-determined activities; To strive for equal access to & participation in Canadian society while honouring the distinctiveness of Aboriginal culture
Ron Walker, Executive Director

Centre d'amitié Eenou de Chibougamau
95, rue Jaculet, Chibougamau QC G8P 2G1
Tél: 418-748-7667; *Téléc:* 418-748-6954
info@eenoukamikw.ca
cefc.ca
www.facebook.com/eenoukamikw
Centre social pour les Autochtones de la région; centre d'exposition pour les artisans cri
Cindy Morrison, Présidente
Jo-Ann Toulouse, Directice générale

Chiefs of Ontario
#400, 468 Queen St. East, Toronto ON M5A 1T7
Tel: 416-597-1266; *Fax:* 416-597-8365
Toll-Free: 877-517-6527
www.chiefs-of-ontario.org
vimeo.com/chiefsofontario
www.facebook.com/ChiefsofOntario
twitter.com/chiefsofontario
To enable the political leadership to discuss regional, provincial & national priorities affecting First Nation people in Ontario & to provide a unified voice on these issues.
RoseAnne Archibald, Ontario Regional Chief
Julia Candlish, Director, Education
Scott Cavan, Director, Communications
Amy Lickers, Director, Economic & Sustainable Community Development

Commission de la santé et des services sociaux des Premières Nations du Québec et du Labrador / First Nations of Quebec & Labrador Health & Social Services Commission (FNQLHSSC)
#102, 250, Place Chef Michel-Laveau, Wendake QC G0A 4V0
Tél: 418-842-1540; *Téléc:* 418-842-7045
info@cssspnql.com
www.cssspnql.com
www.youtube.com/user/CSSSPNQL
www.facebook.com/cssspnql
Accompagner les Premières Nations au Québec dans l'atteinte de leurs objectifs en matière de santé, de mieux-être, de culture et d'autodétermination
Marjolaine Sioui, Directrice générale

Confederacy of Mainland Mi'kmaq (CMM)
PO Box 1590, 57 Martin Cresc., Truro NS B2N 5V3
Tel: 902-895-6385; *Fax:* 902-893-1520
Toll-Free: 877-892-2424
www.cmmns.com
To proactively promote and assist Mi'kmaw communities' initiatives toward self determination and enhancement of community.
Donald M. Julien, Executive Director

Congress of Aboriginal Peoples (CAP) / Congrès des Peuples Autochtones
867 St Laurent Blvd., Ottawa ON K1K 3B1
Tel: 613-747-6022; *Fax:* 613-747-8834
Toll-Free: 888-997-9927
reception@abo-peoples.org
www.abo-peoples.org
www.facebook.com/CongressAboPeoples
twitter.com/CAPChief
To represent approximately 3/4 million Aboriginal people living off-reserve in Canada
Elmer St. Pierre, National Chief
Jim Devoe, Chief Executive Officer

Council of Yukon First Nations (CYFN)
2166 - 2nd Ave., Whitehorse YT Y1A 4P1
Tel: 867-393-9200; *Fax:* 867-668-6577
reception@cyfn.net
www.cyfn.ca
www.facebook.com/CouncilofYukonFirstNations
To be the central political organization for the First Nation people of the Yukon & manage intergovernmental relations between First Nations, Yukon Government, & the Government of Canada
Peter Johnston, Grand Chief
Shadelle Chambers, Executive Director

Dene Nation of Northwest Territories
PO Box 2338, Yellowknife NT X1A 2P7
Tel: 867-873-4081; *Fax:* 867-920-2254
Toll-Free: 866-511-4081
admin@denenation.com
www.denenation.com
www.facebook.com/DeneNation
To support Dene territories & communities in protecting Dene rights & interests including those arising from Dene land use & occupation & Treaties

Federation of Saskatchewan Indian Nations
Asimakaniseekan Askiy Reserve, #100, 103A Packham Ave., Saskatoon SK S7N 4K4
Tel: 306-665-1215; *Fax:* 306-244-4413
info@fsin.com
www.fsin.com
www.linkedin.com/company/federation-of-sovereign-indigenous-nations
www.facebook.com/FSINations
twitter.com/fsinations
To honour the spirit & intent of the First Nations Treaties & their rights; to foster the economic, educational & social endeavours of the First Nation people & adherence to democratic procedure & civil law.

Bobby Cameron, Chief

Femmes autochtones du Québec inc. (FAQ) / Québec Native Women Inc.
CP 1989, Kahnawake QC J0L 1B0
Tél: 450-632-0088; *Télec:* 450-632-9280
Ligne sans frais: 800-363-0322
info@faq-qnw.org
www.faq-qnw.org
www.facebook.com/FAQQNW
twitter.com/FAQQNW
Appuyer les efforts des femmes autochtones pour l'amélioration de leurs conditions de vie par la promotion de la non-violence, de la justice et de l'égalité des droits et de les soutenir dans leur engagement au sein de leur communauté
Viviane Michel, Présidente
Carole Bussière, Directrice générale

First Nations Breast Cancer Society
#309, 1333 East 7th Ave., Vancouver BC V5N 1R6
Tel: 604-875-0779; *Fax:* 604-872-4390
echoes@fnbreastcancer.bc.ca
Offers breast cancer education and support to First Nations women.
Jacqueline Davis, President

First Nations Confederacy of Cultural Education Centres
#302, 666 Kirkwood Ave., Ottawa ON K1Z 5X9
Tel: 613-728-5999; *Fax:* 613-728-2247
communications@fnccec.ca
www.fnccec.com
www.facebook.com/FNCCEC
To advocate for the recovery, maintenance, enhancement & preservation of First Nations languages, cultures & traditions
Claudette Commanda, Executive Director

First Nations Lands Advisory Board (LAB)
c/o Robert Louie, Chairman, 2220 Horizon Dr. East, Kelowna BC V1Z 3L4
Tel: 250-769-2804; *Fax:* 250-769-3228
landsadvisoryboard.ca
To assist First Nations in implementing land governance over their reserve lands & resources
Robert Louie, LL.B., OC, Chairman

First Nations Lands Management Resource Centre (LABRC)
PO Box 1022, Sutton West ON L0E 1R0
Tel: 888-985-5711; *Fax:* 866-817-2394
webadmin@labrc.com
labrc.com
www.facebook.com/FNLMRC
To support First Nations in exercising their inherent right to govern their lands & resources
Austin Bear, Chair
Meko Nicholas, Executive Director

First Nations Summit Society (FNS)
#1200, 100 Park Royal South, West Vancouver BC V7T 1A2
Tel: 604-926-9903; *Fax:* 604-926-9923
Toll-Free: 866-990-9939
fns.bc.ca
www.linkedin.com/company/first-nations-summit-society
twitter.com/FNSummit
To provide First Nations in British Columbia an opportunity to address issues of common concern, including Treaty negotiations, with the governments of Canada and B.C.
Howard Grant, Executive Director
Colin Braker, Director, Comminication

Gitxsan Treaty Office (GTO)
PO Box 229, Hazelton BC V0J 2N0
Fax: 250-842-6709
Toll-Free: 866-842-6780
www.gitxsan.com
www.facebook.com/GitxsanDevelopmentCorporation
To support the Gitxsan people in their treaty & other negotiations, & in their economic & social initiatives

Grand Council of the Crees / Grand Conseil des Cris
2, rue Lakeshore, Nemaska QC J0Y 3B0
Tel: 819-673-2600; *Fax:* 819-673-2606
cree@cra.qc.ca
www.gcc.ca
www.linkedin.com/companies/grand-council-of-the-crees
www.facebook.com/gcccra
twitter.com/gcccra
To represent the Cree people; To foster, promote, protect & assist in preserving the way of life, values & traditions of the Cree people of Quebec.
Abel Bosum, Grand Chief
Bill Namagoose, Executive Director

Gunn Métis Local Council #55 (GML55)
PO Box 2057, Stony Plain AB T7Z 1X6
Tel: 780-591-5050
lacsteannemetis@zoho.com
lacsteannemetis.com
To honour our Ancestors by restoring collective histroy & culture; To act on behalf of members regarding industrial development in traditional territories; To develop necessary infrastructre to provide services to members

Indigenous Bar Association
c/o Anne Chalmers, 70 Pineglen Cres., Ottawa ON K2G 0G8
www.indigenousbar.ca
To recognize & respect the spiritual basis of our Indigenous laws, customs & traditions; To promote the advancement of legal & social justice for Indigenous peoples in Canada; To promote reform of policies & laws affecting Indigenous peoples in Canada; To foster public awareness within the legal community, the Indigenous community & the general public in respect of legal & social issues of concern to Indigenous peoples in Canada; To provide a forum & network amongst Indigenous lawyers
Scott Robertson, President
Anne Chalmers, Administrative Support

Indigenous Clean Energy Social Enterprise (ICE)
c/o The Delphi Group, 428 Gilmour St., Ottawa ON K2P 0R8
Tel: 613-562-2005
info@aboriginalpower.ca
indigenouscleanenergy.com
To advance Indigenous inclusion in Canada's energy futures economy through leadership & collaboration with energy companies, utilities, governments, development firms, cleantech innovators, the academic sector & capital markets
Troy Jerome, Co-Chair
Gordon Planes, Co-Chair
Kim Scott, Co-Chair

Indigenous Literary Studies Association (ILSA)
indigenouslsa@gmail.com
www.indigenousliterarystudies.org
www.facebook.com/IndigenousLiteraryStudiesAssociation
To promote the continued production & teaching of Indigenous literature
Keavy Martin, President

Indigenous Women's Business Network (IWBN)
#40, 5957 - 152 St., Surrey BC V3S 3K4
info@indigenouswomenbc.com
www.indigenouswomenbc.com
twitter.com/iwbn_bc
To provide support & resources for female Indigenous entrepreneurs in British Columbia
Nicole McLaren, Founding Director & Chair

Indspire
Six Nations of the Grand River, PO Box 5, #100, 50 Generations Dr., Ohsweken ON N0A 1M0
Tel: 519-445-3021; *Fax:* 866-433-3159
Toll-Free: 855-463-7747
communications@indspire.ca
indspire.ca
www.youtube.com/user/Indspire
www.linkedin.com/company/indspire
www.facebook.com/Indspire
twitter.com/Indspire
To ecourage & support Indigenous education & achievement for the enrichment of the individuals, their families & communities, & Canada
Roberta Jamieson, President & CEO
Rose Goulais, Officer, Donor Services
Amanda Charles, Officer, Communications & Media Relations

Inuit Art Foundation (IAF) / Fondation d'art Inuit
1655 Dupont St., Toronto ON M6P 3T1
Tel: 647-498-7717
contact@inuitartfoundation.org
www.inuitartfoundation.org
www.instagram.com/inuitartfoundation
www.facebook.com/inuitartfoundation
twitter.com/InuitArtFdn
To facilitate the creative expression of Inuit artists; To foster an increased understanding of this expression in a local & global context; To assist in the marketing of Inuit art; To promote Inuit art through exhibits, publications & public events
Heather Igloliorte, President
Alysa Procida, Executive Director

Inuit Tapiriit Kanatami (ITK)
#1101, 75 Albert St., Ottawa ON K1P 5E7
Tel: 613-238-8181; *Fax:* 613-234-1991
Toll-Free: 866-262-8181
info@itk.ca
www.itk.ca
www.youtube.com/inuitofcanada
www.facebook.com/inuittapiriitkanatami
twitter.com/ITK_CanadaInuit
To protect & advance Inuit rights, interest & culture in Canada
Natan Obed, President
Elizabeth Ford, Executive Director

Keewatinook Fishers of Lake Winnipeg (KFLW)
PO Box 57, Dallas MB R0C 0S0
To inform fishers; To help make decisions that benefit Keewatinook Fishers

Labrador Native Women's Association
PO Box 542, Stn. B, Happy Valley-Goose Bay NL A0P 1S0
Tel: 709-896-5071; *Fax:* 709-896-5071
www.exec.gov.nl.ca/exec/wpo/aboriginalwomen

Madii Lii
PO Box 70, Hazelton BC V0J 1Y0
camp.madiilii@gmail.com
www.madiilii.com
vimeo.com/user31647885
www.facebook.com/694143797308168
twitter.com/madii_lii
To prohibit LNG pipelines, enact Territorial Management Plan & construct permanent camp on Madii Lii territory
Richard Wright, Spokesperson

Makivik Corporation / Société Makivik
PO Box 179, Kuujjuaq QC J0M 1C0
Tel: 819-964-2925; *Toll-Free:* 877-625-4845
www.makivik.org
www.facebook.com/538773409574381
A non-profit organization owned by the Inuit of Nunavik, the Corporation promotes the social & economic interests of the Inuit people; receives, administers & invests Inuit compensation funds received under the James Bay & Northern Québec Agreement, & promotes the political, social & economic development of the Nunavik region. Offices in Kuujjuaq, Montreal, Ottawa, Quebec City
Charlie Sr, Watt, President
Andy Pirti, Treasurer
Adamie Padlayat, Corporate Secretary

Manitoba Association of Friendship Centres (MAC)
#102, 150 Henry Ave., Winnipeg MB R3B 0J7
Tel: 204-942-6299
info@friendshipcentres.ca
www.friendshipcentres.ca
www.facebook.com/FriendshipCentres
To assist friendship centres in communication, funding & training
Ryan Paradis, B.Sc., M.C.P., Executive Director

Manitoba Indian Cultural Education Centre (MICEC)
119 Sutherland Ave., Winnipeg MB R2W 3C9
Tel: 204-942-0228; *Fax:* 204-947-6564
info@micec.com
www.micec.com
www.facebook.com/micec.mb
twitter.com/micec
To promote awareness & understanding of Indigenous cultures of Mantioba; To maintain, expand & promote the cultural interests of Manitoba First Nations; To advance the interests of First Nation Peoples

Manitoba Keewatinowi Okimakanak Inc. (MKO)
#1601, 275 Portage Ave., Winnipeg MB R3B 2B3
Tel: 204-927-7500; *Fax:* 204-927-7509
Toll-Free: 800-442-0488
wpgreception@mkonorth.com
mkonation.com
www.facebook.com/MKONorth
twitter.com/MKO_North
To act as a collective voice for citizens of member Nations on issues of inherent, Treaty, aboriginal & human rights; Sub-office in Thompson MB
Garrison Settee, Grand Chief
Kelvin Lynxleg, Executive Director
Michael Hutchinson, Officer, Communications

Skeena Watershed Conservation Coalition (SWCC)
PO Box 70, Hazelton BC V0J 1Y0
Tel: 205-842-2494
info@skeenawatershed.com
skeenawatershed.com
www.facebook.com/Skeenawatershed
twitter.com/SkeenaWatershed
Cultivating a sustainable future & thriving wild salmon
ecosystem; Protecting our culture & Northern B.C.'s Sacred
Headwaters
Shannon McPhail, Executive Director

Stó:lo Research & Resource Management Centre
10 - 7201 Vedder Rd., Chilliwack BC V2R 4G5
Tel: 604-824-2420; *Toll-Free:* 800-565-6004
admin@stolonation.bc.ca
www.srrmcentre.com
To offer high quality culturally & scientifically sound services
David Schaepe, Ph.D., Director

Stó:lo Service Agency
7201 Vedder Rd., Chilliwack BC V2R 4G5
Tel: 604-858-3366; *Fax:* 604-824-5126
Toll-Free: 800-565-6004
www.stolonation.bc.ca
www.facebook.com/stolonation
twitter.com/stolo_services
To support, empower, & ensure the well-being of citizens of
member Nations; To provide leadership & deliver quality
services
Willy Hall, Executive Director

Tecumseh Community Development Corporation
Aamjiwnaang First Nation, 560 Williams Dr., Sarnia ON 7H5
N7T
Tel: 519-332-5151; *Fax:* 519-332-6196
Toll-Free: 888-433-1533
info@tcdc.on.ca
www.tcdc.on.ca
www.facebook.com/TecumsehCDC
To make available financial & management services for the
development of local First Nation economies
Phyllis George, General Manager

Teslin Tlingit Council (TTC)
PO Box 133, Teslin YT Y0A 1B0
Tel: 867-390-2532
admin@ttc-teslin.com
www.ttc-teslin.com
To govern the five clans of the Teslin Tlingit; To foster healthy
Tlingit citizens & a healthy Tlingit lifestyle
Richard Sidney, Nha Shade Heni (Chief)
Jade McGinty, Coordinator, Communications

2-Spirited People of the First Nations (TPFN)
#105, 145 Front St. East, Toronto ON M5A 1E3
Tel: 416-944-9300; *Fax:* 416-944-8381
www.2spirits.com
www.instagram.com/2spirits_com
www.facebook.com/2spiritsTO
To create a place where Aboriginal 2-Spirited people can grow &
learn together as a community, fostering a positive,
self-sufficient image, honouring our past & building a future; to
work together toward bridging the gap between the 2-Spirited,
Lesbian, Gay, Bisexual & Transgendered community & our
Aboriginal identity
Keith McCrady, Executive Director

Union of British Columbia Indian Chiefs
#401, 312 Main St., Vancouver BC V6A 2T2
Tel: 604-684-0231; *Fax:* 604-684-5726
Toll-Free: 800-793-9701
ubcic@ubcic.bc.ca
www.ubcic.bc.ca
www.youtube.com/UBCIC
www.facebook.com/UBCIC
twitter.com/UBCIC
To settle land claims & Aboriginal rights in BC; To improve the
social, economic, health, & education of Aboriginal people in BC;
To provide a political voice for Aboriginal people in BC
Stewart Phillip, President

Union of Nova Scotia Indians (UNSI)
#304, 201 Churchill Dr., Membertou NS B1S 0H1
Tel: 902-539-4107; *Fax:* 902-564-2137
rec@unsi.ns.ca
www.unsi.ns.ca
To promote welfare & progress of Native people in Nova Scotia;
to liaise with all Native people on relevant issues; to defend &
advise on Native rights; to cooperate with Native & non-Native
agencies & organizations to the benefit of Nova Scotia Native
people
Douglas Brown, Executive Director

Union of Ontario Indians (UOI)
Nipissing First Nation, PO Box 711, North Bay ON P1B 8J8
Tel: 705-497-9127; *Fax:* 705-497-9135
Toll-Free: 877-702-5200
info@anishinabek.ca
www.anishinabek.ca
www.youtube.com/user/AnishinabekNation
www.facebook.com/AnishinabekNation
twitter.com/anishnabn
To represent 40 First Nations throughout the province of Ontario
from Golden Lake in the east, Sarnia in the south, Thunder Bay
& Lake Nipigon in the north
Glen Hare, Grand Council Chief

United Native Nations Society
678 Hastings St. East, Vancouver BC V6A 1R1
Tel: 604-688-1821
To advocate for & represent the interests of 90,000 off-reserve
Indigenous people in British Columbia

Whaka Pimadiziiwii Pinaysiiwigamic Inc.
715 Main St., Winnipeg MB R3B 3N7
Tel: 902-436-5101; *Fax:* 902-436-5655
Toll-Free: 877-884-0808
thunderbirdhousewpg@gmail.com
thunderbirdhouse.ca
www.instagram.com/thunderbirdwpg
www.facebook.com/CircleofLifeThunderbirdHouse
twitter.com/ThunderbirdWPG
To provide a space where Indigenous teachings & ceremonies
can be shared for the healing of all our relations
Richelle Scott, Co-chair
David Morrison, Co-chair

Yá thi Néné Land & Resource Office
PO Box 310, Fond du Lac SK S0J 0W0
Tel: 306-686-2250; *Fax:* 306-686-2252
admin@yathinene.com
yathinene.ca
www.facebook.com/YathiNene
To promote & advance the environmental, social, cultural &
economic health & wellbeing of the Athabasca Basin
Communities & their residents
Stacy Howat, Executive Administrative Assistant

Yukon Aboriginal Women's Council
#202, 307 Jarvis St., Whitehorse YT Y1A 2H3
Tel: 867-667-6162; *Fax:* 867-668-7539
yawc@northwestel.net
yawc.ca
www.facebook.com/YukonAboriginalWomensCouncil
To advocate on behalf of Aboriginal women in the Yukon and
Northern B.C.; To support Aboriginal women in leadership
positions; To promote the importance& preservation of
Aboriginal values & way of life
Terri Tzabo, President
Stephanie Brown, Coordinator, Communications

Naturalists

Avicultural Advancement Council of Canada (AACC)
77 Long Island Cres., Unionville ON L3P 7M1
www.aacc.ca
To establish & maintain a national association of interested
societies & individuals to promote the advancement of aviculture
in Canada; To represent the Canadian avicultural community
internationally; To disseminate information; to support
recognized expert aviculturalists; To assist all levels of
government in preparing informed legislation & policy relating to
aviculture; To establish standards for the exhibition of birds in
Canada; To provide a national identification leg band registry; To
establish an avian species preservation program in Canada
Jeremy Faria, President
Gary D'Ornellas, Ring Registrar

British Columbia Waterfowl Society
5191 Robertson Rd., Delta BC V4K 3N2
Tel: 604-946-6980
www.reifelbirdsanctuary.com/bcws.html
To encourage conservation of wetlands; To spur public
awareness on importance of estuaries; To
operate George C. Reifel Migratory Bird Sanctuary
Jack Bates, President
Kathleen Fry, Manager

**Canadian Biomaterials Society (CSB) / Société
canadienne des biomatériaux (SCB)**
www.biomaterials.ca
To develop biomaterials science, technology & education in
Canadian industries, universities & governments
Diego Mantovani, Representative, International Union of
Societies - Biomaterials Science/Engineeri

Ze Zhang, Representative, International Union of Societies -
Biomaterials Science/Engineeri
Rosalind Labow, Treasurer
Lauren Flynn, Secretary

Federation of British Columbia Naturalists (FBCN)
c/o Parks Heritage Centre, 1620 Mount Seymour Rd., North
Vancouver BC V7G 2R9
bcnature.ca
To protect biodiversity, species at risk, & natural areas
throughout British Columbia; To present a unified voice on
conservation & environmental issues
Betty Davison, Office Manager

Jack Miner Migratory Bird Foundation, Inc.
360 RR#3 West, Kingsville ON N9Y 2E5
Tel: 519-733-4034; *Fax:* 519-733-0932
info@jackminer.ca
www.jackminer.ca
www.instagram.com/Jackminer1865
www.facebook.com/JackMinerMigratoryBirdSanctuary
twitter.com/JM_Sanctuary
The sanctuary provides food, shelter & protection to migratory
water fowl, tags birds & tracks migration patterns
Mary E. Baruth, Executive Director

Natural History Society of Newfoundland & Labrador
PO Box 1013, St. John's NL A1C 5M3
naturenl@naturenl.ca
naturenl.ca
www.facebook.com/128262310581874
To promote the enjoyment & protection of all wildlife and natural
history resources in the Province of Newfoundland & Labrador &
surrounding waters.
Dave Innes, Secretary

Nature Alberta
Percy Page Centre, 11759 Groat Rd., 3rd Fl., Edmonton AB
T5M 3K6
Tel: 780-427-8124; *Fax:* 780-422-2663
info@naturealberta.ca
naturealberta.ca
www.youtube.com/user/naturealberta
www.facebook.com/NatureAB
twitter.com/naturealberta
To encourage Albertans to increase knowledge & understanding
of natural history & ecological processes; To provide a unified
voice for naturalists on conservation issues; To organize field
meetings, conferences, nature camps, research symposia, &
other activities
Brian Ilnicki, Executive Director

Nature Canada / Canada Nature
#300, 240 Bank St., Ottawa ON K2P 1X4
Tel: 613-562-3447; *Toll-Free:* 800-267-4088
communications@naturecanada.ca
naturecanada.ca
www.youtube.com/user/NatureCanada1
www.linkedin.com/company/nature-canada
www.facebook.com/NatureCanada
twitter.com/NatureCanada
To protect & conserve wildlife & habitats throughout Canada
Graham Saul, Executive Director
Jodi Joy, Director, Development

Nature Manitoba
#401, 63 Albert St., Winnipeg MB R3B 1G4
Tel: 204-943-9029; *Fax:* 204-943-9029
info@naturemanitoba.ca
www.naturemanitoba.ca
www.facebook.com/naturemanitoba
To foster the popular & scientific study of nature; To preserve
the natural environment; To act as a voice for people interested
in the outdoors & natural history
Jack Dubois, President

Nature NB
#110, 924 Prospect St., Fredericton NB E3B 2T9
Tel: 506-459-4209; *Fax:* 506-459-4209
nbfn@nb.aibn.com
www.naturenb.ca
www.facebook.com/naturenb
twitter.com/NatureNB
To preserve wildlife & protect its natural habitat; to promote a
public interest in & a knowledge of natural history; to promote,
encourage & cooperate with organizations & individuals who
have similar interests & objectives; to consider matters of
environmental concern.
Danielle Smith, Executive Director

Nature Nova Scotia (Federation of Nova Scotia Naturalists)
c/o Nova Scotia Museum of Natural History, 1747 Summer St., Halifax NS B3H 3A6

Tel: 902-798-3329
info@naturens.ca
www.naturens.ca
www.facebook.com/NatureNS

To support the interests of naturalists clubs; To represent naturalists clubs throughout Nova Scotia
Bob Bancroft, President
Patrick Kelly, Secretary
Jean Gibson Collins, Treasurer

Nature Québec
#207, 870, av de Salaberry, Québec QC G1R 2T9

Tél: 418-648-2104; *Téléc:* 418-648-0991
conservons@naturequebec.org
www.naturequebec.org
www.linkedin.com/company/2794658
www.facebook.com/naturequebec
twitter.com/NatureQuebec

Regrouper les individus et les sociétés oeuvrant en sciences naturelles et en environnement; Maintenir des processus écologiques essentiels; Préserver la diversité génétique; Utiliser soutenablement des espèces et des écosystèmes
Christian Simard, Directeur général

Nature Saskatchewan
#206, 1860 Lorne St., Regina SK S4P 2L7

Tel: 306-780-9273; *Fax:* 306-780-9263
Toll-Free: 800-667-4668
info@naturesask.ca
www.naturesask.ca
www.instagram.com/naturesaskatchewan
www.facebook.com/NatureSask
twitter.com/naturesask

To foster appreciation & understanding for the natural environment; To document & protect the biological diversity of Saskatchewan; To preserve the natural eco-systems of the province
Jordan Ignatiuk, Executive Director
Lacey Weekes, Manager, Conservation & Education
Melissa Ranalli, Manager, Species at Risk
Becky Quist, Office Coordinator

Ontario Nature
#612, 214 King St. West, Toronto ON M5H 3S6

Tel: 416-444-8419; *Fax:* 416-444-9866
Toll-Free: 800-440-2366
info@ontarionature.org
www.ontarionature.org
www.youtube.com/user/ONNature
www.facebook.com/OntarioNature
twitter.com/ontarionature

Ontario Nature is a conservation organization that protects wild species & spaces through conservation, education & public engagement. Ontario Nature is a charitable organization representing more than 30,000 members & supporters, & more than 150 member groups from across Ontario. Since it was established as the Federation of Ontario Naturalists in 1931, Ontario Nature has been a champion for nature in Ontario.
Caroline Schultz, Executive Director

Society of Canadian Ornithologists (SCO) / Société des ornithologistes du Canada (SOC)
c/o Darroch Whitaker, PO Box 128, Rocky Harbour NL A0K 4N0

www.sco-soc.ca
www.facebook.com/sco.soc
twitter.com/SCO_SOC

To support research to understand & conserve Canadian birds; To represent Canadian ornithologists
Colllen Barber, President
Darroch Whitaker, Membership Secretary

Nursing

Academy of Canadian Executive Nurses (ACEN)
#400, 331 Cooper St., Ottawa ON K2P 0G5

Tel: 613-235-3033
www.acen.ca

To advance nursing practice, education, research, & leadership; To work in partnership with other national organizations to influence health policy & set direction of healthcare in Canada to assure quality of care to Canadians
Marcy Saxe-Braithwaite, President

Alberta Gerontological Nurses Association (AGNA)
PO Box 67040, Stn. Meadowlark, Edmonton AB T5R 5Y3

info@agna.ca
www.agna.ca
twitter.com/AGNAtweets

To promote a high standard of nursing care & related health services for older adults; To enhance professionalism in the practice of gerontological nursing
Jason Woytas, President

British Columbia College of Nursing Professionals (BCCNP)
900 - 200 Granville St., Vancouver BC V6C 1S4

Tel: 604-742-6200; *Fax:* 604-899-0794
Toll-Free: 866-880-7101
info@bccnp.ca
www.bccnp.ca

To provide safe & appropriate nursing practice through the regulation of nursing professionals; To protect the public by setting standards of practice & evaluating nursing education programs
Cynthia Johansen, Chief Executive Officer

British Columbia Nurses' Union (BCNU) / Syndicat des infirmières de la Colombie-Britannique
4060 Regent St., Burnaby BC V5C 6P5

Tel: 604-433-2268; *Fax:* 604-433-7945
Toll-Free: 800-663-9991
www.bcnu.org
www.youtube.com/user/TheBCNursesUnion
www.facebook.com/OurNursesMatter
twitter.com/BCNursesUnion

To defend nurses' individual rights & the rights of the nursing profession as a whole; To protect & advance the well-being of members & the community at large
Christine Sorenson, President
Aman Grewal, Vice-President

Canadian Association for the History of Nursing (CAHN) / Association canadienne pour l'histoire du nursing
School of Nursing, University of Ottawa, 451 Smyth Rd., Ottawa ON K1H 8M5

www.cahn-achn.ca

To promote interest in the history of nursing; To develop scholarship in the field
Sandra Harrison, President

Canadian Association of Foot Care Nurses (CAFCN)
c/o Audrey Wall, President, 780 Niagara Stone Rd., RR#4, Niagara-on-the-Lake ON L0S 1J0

secretary@cafcn.ca
www.cafcn.ca
www.facebook.com/CAFCN

To advance the practice of foot care through a collaborative & networking process for all individuals providing foot care
Audrey Wall, President

Canadian Association of Nephrology Nurses & Technologists (CANNT) / Association canadienne des infirmières et infirmiers et technologues de néphrologie (ACITN)
#310, 4 Cataraqui St., Kingston ON K7K 1Z7

Tel: 519-652-6767; *Fax:* 519-652-5015
Toll-Free: 877-720-2819
cannt@cannt.ca
cannt-acitn.ca
www.facebook.com/160999717295820
twitter.com/CANNT1

To improve the care of renal patients through support of educational opportunities for association members; To evaluate the performance & competence of nephrology nurses & technologists against the CANNT Standards of Practice
Janice MacKay, President

Canadian Association of Neuroscience Nurses (CANN) / Association canadienne des infirmiers et infirmières en sciences neurologiques (ACIISN)
PO Box 47143, Creekside AB T3P 0A0

info@cann.ca
www.cann.ca
www.facebook.com/CANNInfo
twitter.com/CANNinfo

To prevent illness & to improve health outcomes for people with, or at risk for, neurological disorders; To establish standards of practice for neuroscience nurses
Aline Bourgoin, President
Trudy Robertson, Vice-President & Secretary
Suzanne Basiuk, Treasurer

Canadian Association of Nurses in HIV/AIDS Care (CANAC) / Association canadienne des infirmières et infirmiers en sidologie
Attn: J. Reinhart, 333 Sherbourne St., 2nd Fl., Toronto BC M5A 2S5

canachq@gmail.com
www.canac.org
www.facebook.com/CANAC.ACIIS

To foster excellence in HIV/AIDS nursing; To promote the health, rights & dignity of persons affected by HIV/AIDS & to preventing the spread of HIV infection
Vera Caine, President

Canadian Association of Nurses in Oncology (CANO) / Association canadienne des infirmières en oncologie (ACIO)
#301, 750 West Pender St., Vancouver BC V6C 2T7

Tel: 604-874-4322; *Fax:* 604-874-4378
cano@malachite-mgmt.com
www.cano-acio.ca
www.youtube.com/user/CANOACIO
www.facebook.com/336467099484
twitter.com/CANO_ACIO

To advocate for improved cancer care for all Canadians
Reanne Booker, President
Dana Cooper, Interim Executive Director

Canadian Council of Cardiovascular Nurses (CCCN) / Conseil canadien des infirmières et infirmiers en nursing cardiovasculaire (CCINC)
#202, 300 March Rd., Ottawa ON K2K 2E2

Tel: 613-406-3548; *Fax:* 613-595-1155
info@cccn.ca
www.cccn.ca
www.facebook.com/124535634406687

To promote & maintain high standards of cardiovascular nursing through education, research, health promotion, strategic alliances & advocacy
David Miriguay, Executive Director

Canadian Council of Practical Nurse Regulators (CCPNR)

Tel: 902-388-4789
ed@ccpnr.ca
www.ccpnr.ca

To ensure the safety of the public through the regulation of Licensed / Registered Practical Nurses

Canadian Federation of Mental Health Nurses (CFMHN) / Fédération canadienne des infirmières et infirmiers en santé mentale
#109, 1 Concorde Gate, Toronto ON M3C 3N6

Tel: 416-426-7029; *Fax:* 416-426-7280
www.cfmhn.ca
twitter.com/CFMHN

To serve as the voice of psychiatric & mental health (PMH) nursing; To develop & implement standards of psychiatric & mental health nursing practice; To address mental health issues; To examine government policy; To work with national or international groups with similar professional interests; To provide educational & networking resources for members
Florence Budden, President
Doug Rosser, General Manager

Canadian Gerontological Nursing Association (CGNA) / Association canadienne des infirmières et infirmiers en gérontologie
PO Box 64009, Stn. Royal Bank Plaza, Toronto ON M5J 2T6

cgna.net
www.linkedin.com/company/cdngeronursingassoc
twitter.com/cgna_ca

To promote gerontological nursing practice standards & educational programs in gerontological nursing; To promote the health of elderly persons; To promote networking opportunities; To support & disseminate gerontological nursing research; To represent members to government, education, professional & other appropriate bodies

Canadian Holistic Nurses Association (CHNA) / Association canadienne des infirmières en soins holistiques

info@chna.ca
www.chna.ca
www.youtube.com/channel/UCVcJogJOsOwRRF10YYmlc8Q
www.linkedin.com/company/canadian-holistic-nurses-association
www.facebook.com/CHNA.ca

To further the development of holistic nursing practice; To promote CHNA standards of practice
Connie McDonald, President
Danielle Dawe, Secretary

Canadian Nurse Continence Advisors Association (CNCA)
c/o Jennifer Skelly, St. Joseph's Healthcare, King Campus, 2757 King St. East, Hamilton ON L8G 5E4
Tel: 905-573-4823
www.cnca.ca
To protect the quality standard associated with being an NCA
Jennifer Skelly, President

Canadian Nurses Association (CNA) / Association des infirmières et infirmiers du Canada
50 Driveway, Ottawa ON K2P 1E2
Tel: 613-237-2133; *Fax:* 613-237-3520
Toll-Free: 800-361-8404
cna@cna-aiic.ca
www.cna-aiic.ca
www.youtube.com/user/CNAVideos
www.facebook.com/cnf.fiic
twitter.com/theCNF
To advance the discipline of nursing; To advocate for public policy that incorporates the principles of primary health care & respects the principles, conditions & spirit of the Canada Health Act; To advance the regulation of Registered Nurses in the interest of the public; To advance international health policy & development in Canada
Mike Villeneuve, CEO
Donna Dewar, Chief Operating Officer

Canadian Nurses Foundation (CNF) / Fondation des infirmières et infirmiers du Canada
50 Driveway, Ottawa ON K2P 1E2
Tel: 613-680-0879; *Toll-Free:* 844-204-0124
info@cnf-fiic.ca
www.cnf-fiic.ca
www.facebook.com/CNF.FIIC
twitter.com/theCNF
To advance nursing knowledge & improve health care by providing scholarships, awards, & research grants to nurses & nursing students in Canada
Christine Rieck Buckley, Chief Executive Officer
Annette Martin, Director, Development

Canadian Nurses Protective Society (CNPS) / Société de protection des infirmières et infirmiers du Canada (SPIIC)
#510, 1545 Carling Ave., Ottawa ON K1Z 8P9
Fax: 613-237-6300
Toll-Free: 844-469-2677
info@cnps.ca
www.cnps.ca
www.linkedin.com/company/the-canadian-nurses-protective-society
www.facebook.com/CNPS.SPIIC
twitter.com/CNPS_SPIIC
To offer legal liability protection related to nursing practice to eligible Registered Nurses
Chantal Léonard, CEO

Canadian Occupational Health Nurses Association (COHNA) / Association canadienne des infirmières et infirmiers en santé du travail (ACIIST)
PO Box 25058, Stn. Deer Park, Red Deer AB T4R 2M2
info@cohna-aciist.ca
www.cohna-aciist.ca
To promote national standards for the occupational health nursing practice; To advance the profession by providing a national forum for the exchange of ideas & concerns; To enhance the profile of occupational health nurses; To improve the health & safety of workers; To contribute to the health of the community by providing quality health services to workers; To encourage continuing education
Carmen Skelton, President
Anne Masters-Boyne, Vice President

Canadian Orthopaedic Nurses Association (CONA) / Association canadienne des infirmières et infirmiers en orthopédie
7714 - 80 Ave., Edmonton AB T6C 0S4
www.cona-nurse.org
www.facebook.com/CONAnurses
To foster professional growth of the membership in the assessment, treatment & rehabilitation of individuals with neuromuscular & skeletal alterations; To promote nursing research related to orthopaedics
Maureen Sly-Havey, President

Canadian Vascular Access Association (CVAA) / Association canadienne d'Accès Vasculaire
PO Box 68030, 753 Main St. East, Hamilton ON L8M 3M7
Fax: 888-243-9307
Toll-Free: 888-243-9307
cvaa@cvaa.info
www.cvaa.info
www.instagram.com/cvaacanada
www.facebook.com/165776480198722
twitter.com/CVAACanada
To establish & promote standards of intravenous therapy to enhance patient care & safety
Kristie Naayer, President
Melissa Stark, Executive Director

The College & Association of Registered Nurses of Alberta (CARNA)
11120 - 178 St., Edmonton AB T5S 1P2
Tel: 780-451-0043; *Fax:* 780-452-3276
Toll-Free: 800-252-9392
carna@nurses.ab.ca
www.nurses.ab.ca
www.youtube.com/carnavideo
www.facebook.com/albertarns
twitter.com/albertarns
To set nursing practice standards & to ensure Albertans receive safe, competent & ethical nursing services
Dennie Hycha, President

College of Licensed Practical Nurses of Alberta (CLPNA)
13163 - 146 St., Edmonton AB T5L 4S8
Tel: 780-484-8886; *Fax:* 780-484-9069
Toll-Free: 800-661-5877
info@clpna.com
www.clpna.com
www.youtube.com/clpna
www.linkedin.com/company/college-of-licensed-practical-nurses-of-alberta-clpna-
www.facebook.com/CLPNA
twitter.com/clpna
To regulate & lead the profession in a manner that protects & serves the public through excellence in Practical Nursing
Linda L. Stanger, Chief Executive Officer

College of Licensed Practical Nurses of Manitoba (CLPNM)
463 St. Anne's Rd., Winnipeg MB R2M 3C9
Tel: 204-663-1212; *Fax:* 204-663-1207
Toll-Free: 877-663-1212
info@clpnm.ca
www.clpnm.ca
To license Practical Nurses in Manitoba; To carry out its activities & govern its members in a manner that serves & protects the public interest
Jennifer Breton, Executive Director
Buffie Babb, Business Manager

College of Licensed Practical Nurses of Newfoundland & Labrador (CLPNNL)
209 Blackmarsh Rd., St. John's NL A1E 1T1
Tel: 709-579-3843; *Fax:* 709-579-8268
Toll-Free: 888-579-2576
info@clpnnl.ca
www.clpnnl.ca
To regulate the practice of Licensed Practical Nurses in Newfound & Labrador; To promote safety & protection of the general public through the provision of safe, competent & ethical nursing care
Wanda Wadman, Chief Executive Officer/Registrar

College of Licensed Practical Nurses of Nova Scotia (CLPNNS)
Starlite Gallery, #302, 7071 Bayers Rd., Halifax NS B3L 2C2
Tel: 902-423-8517; *Fax:* 902-425-6811
Toll-Free: 800-718-8517
www.clpnns.ca
To represent licensed practical nurses within the health care system; To protect the public by providing safe, competent nursing care
Ann Mann, Executive Director

College of Licensed Practical Nurses of PEI
#204, 155 Belvedere Ave., Charlottetown PE C1A 2Y9
Tel: 902-566-1512
www.clpnpei.ca
To represent practical nurses within the health care system
Dawn Rix-Moore, Executive Director
Kimberley Jay, Registrar

College of Nurses of Ontario (CNO) / Ordre des infirmières et infirmiers de l'Ontario
101 Davenport Rd., Toronto ON M5R 3P1
Tel: 416-928-0900; *Fax:* 416-928-6507
Toll-Free: 800-387-5526
www.cno.org
www.youtube.com/user/cnometrics
www.linkedin.com/company/college-of-nurses-of-ontario
www.facebook.com/collegeofnurses
twitter.com/collegeofnurses
To protect the public's right to quality nursing services by providing leadership to the nursing profession in self-regulation
Anne Coghlan, Executive Director & CEO
Elizabeth Horlock, Director, Human Resources
Deborah Jones, Director, Communications

College of Registered Nurses of Manitoba (CRNM)
890 Pembina Hwy., Winnipeg MB R3M 2M8
Tel: 204-774-3477; *Fax:* 204-775-6052
Toll-Free: 800-665-2027
registration@crnm.mb.ca
www.crnm.mb.ca
www.facebook.com/collegeofrnsmb
To regulate the practice of registered nurses; To advance the quality of nursing to protect the public interest
Katherine Stansfield, Executive Director
Tammy Murdoch, Manager, Registration Services
Kristin Hancock, Manager, Communications

College of Registered Psychiatric Nurses of Alberta
#201, 9711 - 45 Ave., Edmonton AB T6E 5V8
Tel: 780-434-7666; *Fax:* 780-436-4165
Toll-Free: 877-234-7666
crpna@crpna.ab.ca
www.crpna.ab.ca
To protect & serve the public interest by ensuring members provide safe, competent & ethical practice; To address the needs of members & the public through education, regulation, & advocacy
Mary Haase, President
Barbara Lowe, Executive Director

College of Registered Psychiatric Nurses of Manitoba (CRPNM)
1854 Portage Ave., Winnipeg MB R3J 0G9
Tel: 204-888-4841; *Fax:* 204-888-8638
www.crpnm.mb.ca
To ensure that members of the profession provide safe & effective psychiatric nursing services to the public of Manitoba, in accordance with the Registered Psychiatric Nurses Act
Laura Panteluk, Executive Director

Community Health Nurses of Canada (CHNC) / Infirmières et infirmiers en santé communautaire au Canada (IISCC)
PO Box 64009, Stn. Royal Bank Plaza, Toronto ON M5J 2T6
Tel: 705-527-1014
info@chnc.ca
www.chnc.ca
www.instagram.com/chnc_iiscc
www.linkedin.com/company/chnc-iiscc
www.facebook.com/CHNCIISCC
twitter.com/chnc_iiscc
To act as the voice of community health nurses across Canada; To advocate for the role of community health nurses; To identify & address social & environmental determinants of health by promoting healthy public policy; To encourage a publicly funded, universal health system; To respond to issues which affect community health nurses; To advance practice excellence; To strengthen leadership in community health nursing
Ann Manning, Executive Director

Corporation des infirmières et infirmiers de salle d'opération du Québec (CIISOQ)
CP 63, 10, Place du Commerce, Brossard QC J4W 3L7
info@ciisoq.ca
www.ciisoq.ca
www.facebook.com/ciisoq
Promotion de l'excellence des soins dispensés par l'infirmière en soins périopératoires
Mireille Bélanger, Présidente

Fédération de la santé du Québec - CSQ (FSQ-CSQ)
9405, rue Sherbrooke est, Montréal QC H1L 6P3
Tél: 514-356-8888; *Téléc:* 514-667-5590
www.fsq.lacsq.org
www.instagram.com/lacsq
www.facebook.com/lacsq
twitter.com/csq_centrale
Représentation de ses membres, donne aux syndicats une structure politique et fournit, en collaboration avec la CSQ, des services aux membres en matière de relations de travail, de professionnel, de négociation et de formation

Claire Montour, Présidente

Fédération interprofessionnelle de la santé du Québec (FIQ)
1234, av Papineau, Montréal QC H2K 0A4
Tél: 514-987-1141; *Téléc:* 514-987-7273
Ligne sans frais: 877-987-7273
www.fiqsante.qc.ca
www.youtube.com/FIQSante
www.facebook.com/FIQSante
twitter.com/FIQSante
Améliorer les conditions de travail des infirmières, infirmiers et cardiorespiratoires; s'associer aux luttes des femmes et être présente dans les débats concernant les orientations du système de santé
Nancy Bédard, Présidente

Gerontological Nurses Association of British Columbia (GNABC)
c/o 328 Nootka St., New Westminster BC V3L 4X4
gnabc@shaw.ca
gnabc.com
To promote a high standard of nursing care & related health services for older adults; To enhance professionalism in the practice of gerontological nursing
Lilian MacTaggart, President

Gerontological Nursing Association of Ontario (GNAO)
PO Box 64009, Stn. Royal Bank Plaza, Toronto ON M5J 2T6
info@gnaontario.org
www.gnaontario.org
www.facebook.com/GerontologicalNursingAssociationOntario
twitter.com/GNAOntario
To promote a high standard of nursing care & related health services for older adults; To enhance professionalism in the practice of gerontological nursing
Julie Rubel, President
Gwen Harris, Treasurer

Infirmiers et infirmières sans frontières (IISF) / Nurses Without Borders (NWB)
#2401, 15, boul La Fayette, Longueuil QC J4K 0B2
Tél: 514-797-2005
info@iisf.ca
iisf.ca
www.linkedin.com/company/iisf-nwb-eesf
To support health projects abroad by bringing together health professionals from all over the world
Mario Brûlé, President

Manitoba Gerontological Nursing Association (MGNA)
MB
info@mgna.ca
mgna.ca
To promote a high standard of nursing care & related health services for older adults; To enhance professionalism in the practice of gerontological nursing
Victoria Marek, President

Manitoba Nurses' Union (MNU) / Syndicat des infirmières du Manitoba
#301, 275 Broadway, Winnipeg MB R3C 4M6
Tel: 204-942-1320; *Fax:* 204-942-0958
Toll-Free: 800-665-0043
manitobanurses.ca
www.youtube.com/user/mbnursesunion
www.facebook.com/ManitobaNurses
twitter.com/ManitobaNurses
To represent & support all categories of licensed nurses in Manitoba; To safeguard the role of nurses in the health care system of Manitoba
Sandi Mowat, President
Monica Girouard, Director, Operations
Eric Jorgensen, Director, Labour Relations
Wes Payne, Director, Communications & Government Relations

Manitoba Operating Room Nurses Association (MORNA)
MB
www.ornac.ca/en/morna
To promote professional standards for perioperative nursing practice
Kim Goodman, President

National Emergency Nurses Association (NENA) / Association des infirmières et infirmiers d'urgence
144, 8485 Young Rd., Chilliwack BC V2P 7Y7
nena.ca
www.facebook.com/NationalEmergencyNursesAssociation
twitter.com/NENACanada
To represent the Canadian emergency nursing profession

Jean Harsch, President

New Brunswick Nurses Union (NBNU) / Syndicat des infirmières et infirmiers du Nouveau-Brunswick (SIINB)
103 Woodside Lane, Fredericton NB E3C 2R9
Tel: 506-453-0829; *Fax:* 506-453-0828
Toll-Free: 800-442-4914
nbnu1@nbnu.ca
www.nbnu.ca
www.facebook.com/212365802133370
twitter.com/NBNU_SIINB
To enhance the social, economic, & general work life of nurses; To advocate for nurses & quality health care
Paula Doucet, President
Matt Hiltz, Executive Director

New Brunswick Operating Room Nurses (NBORN)
NB
To represent operating room nurses in New Brunswick
Laura Astle, President

Newfoundland & Labrador Nurses' Union (NLNU) / Syndicat des infirmières de Terre-Neuve et du Labrador
PO Box 416, 229 Major's Path, St. John's NL A1C 5J9
Tel: 709-753-9961; *Fax:* 709-753-1210
Toll-Free: 800-563-5100
info@nlnu.ca
www.nlnu.ca
www.youtube.com/user/RNUNL
www.facebook.com/rnunl
twitter.com/rnu_nl
John Vivian, Executive Director
Karyn Whelan, Communications Specialist

Newfoundland & Labrador Operating Room Nurses Association (N&LORNA)
NL
To enhance patient care by providing members with professional growth opportunities; To promote perioperative nursing practice standards
Joanne Peddle, President

Nova Scotia Gerontological Nurses Association (NSGNA)
PO Box 33101, Stn. Quinpool, Halifax NS B3L 4T6
To promote a high standard of nursing care & related health services for older adults; To enhance professionalism in the practice of gerontological nursing

Nova Scotia Nurses' Union (NSNU)
150 Garland Ave., Dartmouth NS B3B 0A7
Tel: 902-469-1474; *Fax:* 902-466-6935
Toll-Free: 800-469-1474
www.nsnu.ca
www.youtube.com/user/NSNursesUnion
To represent Registered Nurses & Licensed Practical Nurses working in acute & long term care, with the VON & Canadian Blood Services
Janet Hazelton, President
Jean Candy, Executive Director
Cindy Herbert, Director, Finance & Operations

Nurses Association of New Brunswick (NANB) / Association des infirmières et infirmiers du Nouveau-Brunswick (AIINB)
165 Regent St., Fredericton NB E3B 7B4
Tel: 506-458-8731; *Fax:* 506-459-2838
Toll-Free: 800-442-4417
www.nanb.nb.ca
www.facebook.com/1704804403067899
twitter.com/nanb_aiinb
To act as the professional voice & regulatory body of nursing in New Brunswick; To protect the public by maintaining standards for nursing education & practice
Brenda Kinney, President

Ontario Nurses' Association (ONA) / Association des infirmières et infirmiers de l'Ontario
#400, 85 Grenville St., Toronto ON M5S 3A2
Tel: 416-964-8833; *Fax:* 416-964-8864
Toll-Free: 800-387-5580
onamail@ona.org
www.ona.org
www.youtube.com/OntarioNurses
www.facebook.com/OntarioNurses
twitter.com/ontarionurses
To improve the socio-economic welfare of members
Vicki McKenna, President
Beverly Mathers, Chief Executive Officer

Operating Room Nurses Association of Canada (ORNAC) / Association des infirmières et infirmiers de salles d'opération du Canada
PO Box 307, Bath ON K0H 1G0
Toll-Free: 888-608-2828
info@ornac.ca
www.ornac.ca
www.facebook.com/491656354213298
twitter.com/ornacanada
To promote operating nursing for the betterment of surgical patient care
Cathleen Ferguson, President

Operating Room Nurses Association of Nova Scotia (ORNANS)
NS
www.ornans.ca
To address issues concerning nursing practice & standards; To provide educational opportunities to members; To promote the exchange of information among perioperative nurses
Jennifer Radtke-Jardine, President

Operating Room Nurses Association of Ontario (ORNAO)
ON
info@ornao.org
www.ornao.org
To represent registered nurses working in the perioperative nursing field in Ontario
Linda Whyte, President

Operating Room Nurses of Alberta Association (ORNAA)
AB
info@ornaa.org
www.ornaa.org
To ensure quality perioperative nursing practice; To promote the professional growth of members
Darlene Rikley, President
Sandi Burton, Secretary

Ordre des infirmières et infirmiers auxiliaires du Québec (OIIAQ)
531, rue Sherbrooke est, Montréal QC H2L 1K2
Tél: 514-282-9511; *Téléc:* 514-282-0631
Ligne sans frais: 800-283-9511
oiiaq@oiiaq.org
www.oiiaq.org
Favoriser le développement professionnel des infirmières et infirmiers auxiliaires du Québec pour viser l'excellence dans l'exercice professionnel et tendre à une plus grande humanisation des soins
Régis Paradis, Président et directeur général

Ordre des infirmières et infirmiers du Québec (OIIQ)
4200, rue Molson, Montréal QC H1Y 4V4
Tél: 514-935-2501; *Téléc:* 514-935-1799
Ligne sans frais: 800-363-6048
www.oiiq.org
www.flickr.com/photos/ordreinf/sets
www.linkedin.com/company/ordre-des-infirmi-res-et-infirmiers-du-qu-bec
www.facebook.com/OIIQSante
twitter.com/OIIQ
Assurer la protection du public; contrôler l'exercice de la profession par ses membres
Luc Mathieu, Président

Perioperative Registered Nurses Association of British Columbia (PRNABC)
4774 Hill Ave., Prince George BC V2M 0A5
www.prnabc.ca
To promote quality perioperative nursing; To provide educational & professional development opportunities
Catherine Kruger, President
Leenta Nel, Treasurer

Prince Edward Island Gerontological Nursing Association (PEIGNA)
PE
www.peigna.org
To promote a high standard of nursing care & related health services for older adults; To enhance professionalism in the practice of gerontological nursing
Eileen Larkin, President

College of Pharmacists of Manitoba
200 Tache Ave., Winnipeg MB R2H 1A7
Tel: 204-233-1411; *Fax:* 204-237-3468
info@cphm.ca
cphm.ca
To administer the Manitoba Pharmaceutical Act; To give license to & monitors pharmacists in the province, setting standards of practice & investigating complaints
Wendy Clark, President
Susan Lessard-Friesen, Registrar

Council for Continuing Pharmaceutical Education (CCPE) / Conseil de formation pharmaceutique continue (CFPC)
#350, 3333 boul de la Côte-Vertu, Montréal QC H4R 2N1
Tel: 514-333-8362; *Fax:* 514-333-1119
Toll-Free: 888-333-8362
info@ccpe-cfpc.org
www.ccpe-cfpc.com
To provide educational programs to establish improved professional standards within the Canadian pharmaceutical industry; To better meet the needs & expectations of our internal & external stakeholders in the healthcare industry
Jim Shea, General Manager

Innovative Medicines Canada
#1220, 55 Metcalfe St., Ottawa ON K1P 6L5
Tel: 613-236-0455
info@imc-mnc.ca
www.innovativemedicines.ca
www.linkedin.com/company/rx&d
twitter.com/innovativemeds
To discover new medicines that improve the quality of health care available for every Canadian
Michael Tremblay, Chair
Elaine Campbell, Interim President

National Association of Pharmacy Regulatory Authorities (NAPRA) / Association nationale des organismes de réglementation de la pharmacie
#1800, 130 Albert St., Ottawa ON K1P 5G4
Tel: 613-569-9658; *Fax:* 613-569-9659
info@napra.ca
www.napra.ca
To provide national leadership in the pursuit of pharmacy regulatory excellence
Adele Fifield, Executive Director

New Brunswick College of Pharmacists (NBCP) / Ordre des pharmaciens du Nouveau-Brunswick
#200, 686 St. George Blvd., Moncton NB E1E 2C6
Tel: 506-857-8957; *Fax:* 506-857-8838
Toll-Free: 800-463-4434
info@nbpharmacists.ca
www.nbpharmacists.ca
To protect the public by regulating the profession of pharmacy in New Brunswick
Sam Lanctin, Registrar
Karen DeGrace, Communications Manager

New Brunswick Pharmacists' Association (NBPA) / Association des pharmaciens du Nouveau-Brunswick (APNB)
#410, 212 Queen St., Fredericton NB E3B 1A8
Tel: 506-459-6008; *Fax:* 506-453-0736
Toll-Free: 888-358-2345
nbpa@nbnet.nb.ca
www.nbpharma.ca
www.facebook.com/NBPharmacists
twitter.com/PharmacistsNB
To advance the profession of pharmacy in New Brunswick; To represent the interests of members & the profession of pharmacy
Janet MacDonnell, Interim Executive Director

Nova Scotia College of Pharmacists (NSCP)
#800, 1801 Hollis St., Halifax NS B3J 3N4
Tel: 902-422-8528; *Fax:* 902-422-0885
info@nspharmacists.ca
www.nspharmacists.ca
To govern the practice of pharmacy in Nova Scotia to benefit the health & well being of the public
Beverley Zwicker, Registrar & CEO

Ontario College of Pharmacists (OCP)
483 Huron St., Toronto ON M5R 2R4
Tel: 416-962-4861; *Fax:* 416-847-8200
Toll-Free: 800-220-1921
communications@ocpinfo.com
www.ocpinfo.com
www.linkedin.com/company/ontario-college-of-pharmacists
www.facebook.com/ocpinfo
twitter.com/ocpinfo

To administer the Regulated Health Professions Act; To regulate the practice of pharmacy, in accordance with standards of practice; To ensure that members provide quality pharmaceutical service & care to the public
Regis Vaillancourt, President

Ontario Pharmacists' Association (OPA)
#600, 155 University Ave., Toronto ON M5H 3B7
Tel: 416-441-0788; *Fax:* 416-441-0791
Toll-Free: 877-341-0788
mail@opatoday.com
www.opatoday.com
To promote excellence in the practice of pharmacy & the wellness of patients; To act as the voice of pharmacists throughout Ontario
Justin J. Bates, Chief Executive Officer
Amedeo Zottola, CFO & COO

Ordre des pharmaciens du Québec (OPQ)
#301, 266, rue Notre-Dame ouest, Montréal QC H2Y 1T6
Tél: 514-284-9588; *Téléc:* 514-284-3420
Ligne sans frais: 800-363-0324
ordrepharm@opq.org
www.opq.org
www.youtube.com/user/ordrepharmaciensqc
www.facebook.com/OrdredespharmaciensduQuebec
twitter.com/ordrepharmaQc
Protection du public en matières de services pharmaceutiques
Bertrand Bolduc, Président
Manon Lambert, Directrice générale et secrétaire

Pharmacists Manitoba
#201, 90 Garry St., Winnipeg MB R3C 4H1
Tel: 204-956-6680; *Fax:* 204-956-6686
Toll-Free: 800-677-7170
www.pharmacistsmb.ca
www.instagram.com/pharmacistsmb
www.facebook.com/216330955878273
twitter.com/PharmacistsMB
To act as the voice of pharmacists in Manitoba on economic & professional issuess
Brenna Shearer, Chief Executive Officer
Jill Ell, Chief Operating Officer

Pharmacy Association of Nova Scotia (PANS)
#225, 170 Cromarty Dr., Dartmouth NS B3B 0G1
Tel: 902-422-9583; *Fax:* 902-422-2619
pans@pans.ns.ca
pans.ns.ca
www.youtube.com/pharmacyassocns
www.facebook.com/PharmacyNS
twitter.com/pharmacyns
To advance the professional, academic, & commercial aspects of pharmacy & pharmacists throughout Nova Scotia; To represent the interests of Nova Scotia's pharmacists; To improve public health in Nova Scotia
Allison Bodnar, CEO
Michele MacNeil, Administrative & Membership Coordinator

The Pharmacy Examining Board of Canada (PEBC) / Le Bureau des examinateurs en pharmacie du Canada (BEPC)
717 Church St., Toronto ON M4W 2M4
Tel: 416-979-2431; *Fax:* 416-599-9244
pebcinfo@pebc.ca
www.pebc.ca
To establish qualifications for pharmacists; To provide for examinations of those qualifications
Kaye Moran, President
Dinah Santos, Vice-President

Prince Edward Island College of Pharmacy (PEICP)
PO Box 208, 584 Main St., Cornwall PE C0A 1H0
Tel: 902-658-2780; *Fax:* 902-658-2528
info@pepharmacists.ca
www.pepharmacists.ca
To prescribe qualifications, grant authorization & monitor adherence to established standards, so as to promote high standards & safeguard the public with regard to pharmaceutical service
Michelle Wyand, Registrar

Saskatchewan College of Pharmacy Professionals (SCPP)
#100, 1964 Park St., Regina SK S4N 7M5
Tel: 306-584-2292; *Fax:* 306-584-9695
info@saskpharm.ca
saskpharm.ca
To regulate pharmacists, pharmacies, & drugs in Saskatchewan; To register pharmacists who meet the education & training qualifications specified in "The Pharmacy Act, 1996"; To issue permits to operate pharmacies
Marilyn Younghans, President

Rod Amaya, Vice-President
Jeana Wendel, Registrar

Photography

Canadian Association for Photographic Art (CAPA) / L'Association canadienne d'art photographique
PO Box 357, Logan Lake BC V0K 1W0
Tel: 250-523-2378
webmanager@capacanada.ca
capacanada.ca
To promote the advancement of photography as an art form in Canada
Rod Trider, President

Canadian Association of Professional Image Creators (CAPIC) / Association canadienne de photographes et illustrateurs de publicité
#200, 60 Atlantic Ave., Toronto ON M6K 1X9
Tel: 416-462-3677; *Toll-Free:* 888-252-2742
info@capic.org
capic.org
www.facebook.com/CAPICnational
twitter.com/followCAPIC
To safeguard & promote the rights of photographers, illustrators & digital artists who work in the Canadian communications industry
Hai Au Bui, President
Sasha Sobrino, General Manager

Photographic Historical Society of Canada (PHSC)
PO Box 11703, 4335 Bloor St. West, Toronto ON M9C 2A5
Tel: 416-691-1555; *Fax:* 416-693-0018
info@phsc.ca
phsc.ca
www.facebook.com/PHSCPhotographicHistoricalSocietyofCanada
To facilitate the sharing of photographic knowledge; To help research & preserve Canada's photographic heritage
Clint Hyrorijiw, President

Professional Photographers of Canada (PPOC) / Photographes Professionnels du Canada
209 Light St., Woodstock ON N4S 6H6
Tel: 519-537-2555; *Fax:* 519-537-5573
Toll-Free: 888-643-7762
info@ppoc.ca
www.ppoc.ca
www.facebook.com/PPOCNational
twitter.com/ppoc_national
To promote excellence in professional imaging; To elevate professional standards & ethics; To act as a voice for the photographic profession on legal matters & legislative issues
Tanya Thompson, Executive Director

Planning & Development

Alberta Professional Planners Institute (APPI)
PO Box 3099, Sherwood Park AB T8H 2T1
Tel: 780-435-8716; *Fax:* 780-452-7718
Toll-Free: 888-286-8716
admin@albertaplanners.com
www.albertaplanners.com
www.facebook.com/groups/33730560446
twitter.com/_appi
To expand the depth & enhance the credibility of the association; To promote professional growth of practicing planners throughout Alberta, the Northwest Territories, & Nunavut; To maximize membership potential; To provide an effective level of service to the membership
MaryJane Alanko, Executive Director
Vicki Hackl, Office Manager

Atlantic Planners Institute (API) / Institut des Urbanistes de l'atlantique (IVA)
PO Box 63, 5707 St. Peters Rd., St. Peters PE C0A 2A0
Tel: 902-704-2401
executivedirector@atlanticplanners.org
www.atlanticplanners.org
To represent professional planners in New Brunswick, Prince Edward Island, Nova Scotia, Newfoundland & Labrador
Michelle MacDonald, Executive Director

Canadian Association of Certified Planning Technicians (CACPT)
Roseland Plaza, PO Box 91507, 3023 New St., Burlington ON L7R 4L6

Tel: 905-578-4681
assistant@cacpt.org
cacpt.org
www.facebook.com/CACPTech
twitter.com/CACPTech

To maintain high standards for Planning Technicians & other related planning professionals
George Zajac, Executive Director

Canadian Institute of Planners (CIP) / Institut canadien des urbanistes (ICU)
#1112, 141 Laurier Ave. West, Ottawa ON K1P 5J3

Tel: 613-237-7526; *Toll-Free:* 800-207-2138
communications@cip-icu.ca
www.cip-icu.ca
www.instagram.com/cdnplanners
www.linkedin.com/company/canadian-institute-of-planners
www.facebook.com/cdnplanners
twitter.com/CIP_ICU

To advance professional planning excellence, through the delivery of membership & public services in Canada & abroad
Beth McMahon, Chief Executive Officer
Valérie Broadfoot, Manager, Operations

Canadian Urban Institute (CUI)
#500, 30 Patrick St., Toronto ON M5T 3A3

Tel: 416-365-0816; *Fax:* 416-365-0650
cui@canurb.org
www.canurb.org
www.facebook.com/canurb
twitter.com/canurb

To achieve healthy urban development
Peter Halsall, Executive Director
Ariana Cancelli, Planner & Researcher
Lisa Cavicchia, Program Director
Navf Dhaliwal, Director, Fiance

Manitoba Professional Planners Institute (MPPI)
137 Bannatyne Ave., 2nd Fl., Winnipeg MB R3B 0R3

Toll-Free: 844-305-6774
info@mppi.mb.ca
www.mppi.mb.ca

To handle membership applications & services & to enforce the Code of Professional Conduct
Marilyn Steranka, Executive Director

Muniscope (ICURR)
#704, 789 Don Mills Rd., Toronto ON M3C 1T5

Fax: 647-345-7004
www.muniscope.ca
twitter.com/muniscope

To support local & regional governments, as well as private & non-profit companies through subsidized information & networking services; To act as a national resource on municipal issues, with subscription-based research & library services available on economic development, finance and taxation, housing & infrastructure, transportation, planning & sustainability
Mathieu Rivard, Executive Director
Mark Rose, Manager, Information Services

Ontario Professional Planners Institute (OPPI) / Institut des planificateurs professionnels de l'Ontario
#201, 234 Eglinton Ave. East, Toronto ON M4P 1K5

Tel: 416-483-1873; *Fax:* 416-483-7830
Toll-Free: 800-668-1448
info@ontarioplanners.ca
www.ontarioplanners.ca
www.youtube.com/user/OntarioPlanners
www.linkedin.com/company/3068747
www.facebook.com/OntarioProfessionalPlannersInstitute
twitter.com/OntarioPlanners

To act as the voice of Ontario's planning profession; To provide leadership on policies related to planning & development
Andrea Bourrie, President
Mary Ann Rangam, Executive Director
Robert Fraser, Director, Finance & Administration
Loretta Ryan, Director, Public Affairs
Brian Brophey, Registrar & Director, Member Relations

Ordre des urbanistes du Québec (OUQ)
#410, 85, rue St-Paul ouest, Montréal QC H2Y 3V4

Tél: 514-849-1177; *Téléc:* 514-849-7176
info@ouq.qc.ca
www.ouq.qc.ca
www.facebook.com/666855766761080

Assurer la protection du public dans l'exercice de la profession par ses membres et la promotion de la pratique de l'urbanisme au Québec

---

Karina Verdon, Directrice générale

Planning Institute of British Columbia (PIBC)
#1750, 355 Burrard St., Vancouver BC V6C 2G8

Tel: 604-696-5031; *Fax:* 604-696-5032
Toll-Free: 866-696-5031
info@pibc.bc.ca
www.pibc.bc.ca

To promote orderly use of land, buildings & natural resources; To maintain high standard of professional competence; To protect rights & interests of those engaged in the planning profession
Dave Crossley, Executive Director

Provincial Association of Resort Communities of Saskatchewan (PARCS)
PO Box 52, Elbow SK S0H 1J0

Tel: 306-545-6253; *Fax:* 306-854-4412
parcs@sasktel.net
www.parcs-sk.com

To promote the interests of resort communities in Saskatchewan; To promote fair & equitable policies & procedures for all resort communities
Shirley Gange, President
Lynne Saas, Contact, Member Serivvces

Saskatchewan Professional Planners Institute (SPPI)
#505, 2300 Broad St., Regina SK S4P 1Y8

Tel: 306-584-3879
info@sppi.ca
sppi.ca
www.facebook.com/SaskPlanning
twitter.com/SaskPlanning

To promote & maintain professionalism in planning field
Marilyn Steranka, Executive Director

Urban Development Institute Pacific Region
#200, 602 West Hastings St., Vancouver BC V6B 1P2

Tel: 604-669-9585; *Fax:* 604-689-8691
www.udi.bc.ca
www.youtube.com/UDIPacific
www.linkedin.com/company/urban-development-institute—-pacifi
c-region
www.facebook.com/UDIBC
twitter.com/udibc

To promote wise, efficient & productive urban growth; To be an effective voice of the land development & property management industry at all levels of government; To serve as a forum for the exchange of knowledge, experience & research on land use planning & development
Anne McMullin, President & CEO
Jeff Fisher, Vice-President
Elsie Edillor, Manager, Finance

Police

Association of Black Law Enforcers (ABLE)
#6, 467 Edgeley Blvd., Vaughan ON L4K 4E9

Tel: 647-792-1081; *Toll-Free:* 855-265-1322
ableorg.ca@gmail.com
ableorg.ca

To address the news & cocerns of Black & other racial minorities in policing & the community
Jacqueline Edwards, President

Canadian Association of Police Educators (CAPE) / Association canadienne des intervenants en formation policière (ACIFP)
c/o Wayne Jacobsen, 1430 Victoria Ave. East, Brandon MB R7A 2A9

Tel: 204-725-8700
cape.educators@gmail.com
cape-educators.ca
www.facebook.com/593948850654424

To promote law enforcement training & education through the guidance of research, program development, knowledge transfer, network facilitation & collaborative training initiatives; to provide advice & input on national & regional law enforcement training & educations trends/needs; to promote a commitment to training
Catherine Wareham, Secretary
Wayne Jacobsen

Canadian Association of Police Governance (CAPG) / Association canadienne des commissions de police
#204, 78 George St., Ottawa ON K1N 5W1

Tel: 613-344-2384; *Fax:* 613-344-2385
communications@capg.ca
capg.ca

To improve the effectiveness of civilian bodies that govern local police services
Mary Anne Silverthorn, President
Sandy Smallwood, Vice-President
Micki Ruth, Treasurer
Brian Boudreau, Secretary
Jennifer Malloy, Executive Director

Canadian Police Association (CPA) / Association canadienne des policiers (ACP)
#100, 141 Catherine St., Ottawa ON K2P 1C3

Tel: 613-231-4168; *Fax:* 613-231-3254
cpa-acp@cpa-acp.ca
www.cpa-acp.ca
www.facebook.com/CanadianPoliceAssociation
twitter.com/stamatakiscpa

To promote the interests of police personnel & the public they serve; To provide a collective support network for Member Associations; To advocate for adequate & equitable resources for policing; To identify key national issues impacting Member Associations, and facilitate their resolution; To liaise with the international policing community on issues affecting Canadian police personnel
Tom Stamatakis, President

Canadian Search Dog Association (CSDA)
PO Box 37103, Stn. Lynnwood Postal Outlet, Edmonton AB T5R 5Y2

calgary.csda@outlook.com
canadiansearchdog.com
www.facebook.com/156258481071770

To generate a group of trained search workers & search dogs to aid the RCMP & other tasking agencies in the search for lost or missing persons

International Police Association - Canada (IPA Canada)
179 Greak Oak Trail, Binbrook ON L0R 1C0

www.ipa.ca

To encourage contact in social & cultural activities among members throughout the world

National Police Federation (NPF) / Fédération de la Police Nationale (FPN)
#2201, 150 Metcalfe St., Ottawa ON K2P 1P1

info@npf-fpn.com
npf-fpn.com
www.linkedin.com/company/nationalpolicefederation
www.facebook.com/nationalpolicefederation
twitter.com/NPFFPN1

To provide representation to promote & enhance the rights of members
Brian Sauve, President
Michael Brennan, Chief Administrative Officer
Don Armstrong, Director, Finance

Ontario Association of Chiefs of Police (OACP)
#605, 40 College St., Toronto ON M5G 2J3

Tel: 416-926-0424; *Fax:* 416-926-0436
Toll-Free: 800-816-1767
oacpadmin@oacp.ca
www.oacp.on.ca
www.youtube.com/OACPOfficial
www.facebook.com/OACPOfficial
twitter.com/OACPOfficial

The Association coordinates police training & education. It advocates on behalf of its membership, expressing concerns & priorities to the government, public & to any other bodies.
Ron Bain, Executive Director
Joe Couto, Director, Government Relations & Communications
Sharon Seepersad, Manager, Administration/Member Services
Jennifer Evans, President

Ontario Provincial Police Association (OPPA)
119 Ferris Lane, Barrie ON L4M 2Y1

Fax: 705-721-4867
www.oppa.ca

To represent members in negotiations with the Ontario government; to promote safe & healthy work environments
Jim Christie, President
Martin Bain, Vice-President

Prince Edward Island Police Association (PEIPA)
PE

www.peipolice.com

To help members of the community become more familiar with the Prince Edward Island Police force; To promote the public's role in crime prevention; To support Youth Development; To speak for Prince Edward Island's municipal police officers
Ron MacLean, Corporal, President
Jason Blacquiere, Vice-President West
John Flood, Vice-President East

Toronto Police Association (TPA) / Association de la police de Toronto
#200, 2075 Kennedy Rd., Toronto ON M1T 3V3
Tel: 416-491-4301; *Fax:* 416-494-4948
information@tpa.ca
www.tpa.ca
www.instagram.com/tpaca1
www.facebook.com/TPAca
twitter.com/TPAca
To promote & advance the health, safety & economic well-being of the membership
Brian Callanan, Vice President

Politics

Alberta Advantage Party (AAP)
#559, 9768 - 170th St., Edmonton AB T5T 5L4
www.albertaadvantageparty.net
www.facebook.com/ABAdvantageParty
Marilyn Burns, Party Leader
David Inscho, President

Alberta Liberal Party
PO Box 94098, Stn. Elbow River, Edmonton AB T2S 0S4
Tel: 780-414-1124
office@albertaliberal.com
www.albertaliberal.com
www.youtube.com/albertaliberalcaucus
www.facebook.com/ablib
twitter.com/abliberal
To elect Liberals to the Legislative Assembly of Alberta; To enunciate & promote liberal principles & policies; To initiate & maintain effective electoral constituencies
Vacant, Party Leader
Pete Helfric, President

Alberta Party
PO Box 1045, Stn. Main, Edmonton AB T5J 2M1
Tel: 587-930-7933
info@albertaparty.ca
www.albertaparty.ca
www.youtube.com/user/TheAlbertaParty
www.facebook.com/albertaparty
twitter.com/AlbertaParty
Jacquie Fenske, Party Leader

Animal Protection Party of Canada
#101, 221 Broadview Ave., Toronto ON M4M 2G3
Tel: 416-462-9541; *Fax:* 416-462-9647
www.animalprotectionparty.ca
www.facebook.com/AnimalProtectionParty
twitter.com/AnimalProtectCA
To promote a principle of just & equitable human progress that respects, protects & enhances the environment & the lives of animals
Liz White, Leader
Stephen Best, Chief Agent
Jordan Reichert, Deputy Leader

Atlantica Party Association of Nova Scotia
#505, 5264 Morris St., Halifax NS B3J 1B5
www.atlanticaparty.ca
www.facebook.com/AtlanticaPartyNS
twitter.com/AtlanticaParty
To eliminate government monopolies, corporate welfare, & some regulations; To reduce taxes; To introduce not-for-profit charter schools in Nova Scotia
Jonathan Dean, Party Leader

BC Citizens First Party
#101, 1120 Comox St., Vancouver BC V6E 1K5
Tel: 604-355-4069
bccitizensfirst.ca
www.facebook.com/bccitizensfirst
twitter.com/BCCitizensFirst
To advocate for the government's prioritization of British Columbia's Canadian citizens before overseas citizens & corporations
Laura-Lynn Tyler Thompson, Party Leader

BC First Party
1311 Marwalk Cres., Campbell River BC V9W 5V9
Tel: 778-348-0747
www.bcfirst.ca
www.youtube.com/user/TheBCFirstParty
twitter.com/bcfirst
John Horgan, Party Leader

BC New Republican Party
#1107, 11871 Horseshoe Way, Richmond BC V7A 5H5
Tel: 778-985-6000; *Fax:* 604-200-5177
Wei Chen, Party Leader

BC Progressive Party
2283 King George Blvd., Surrey BC V4A 5A4
Tel: 604-835-7503
Trevor Bolin, Leader

BC Vision
12127 - 101B Ave., Surrey BC V3V 7X6
Tel: 604-328-5511; *Fax:* 604-998-4480
bcvision.net
To promote an equal platform for all British Columbians
Jagmohan Bhandari, Party Leader

Beaver Party of Canada (BPOC) / Parti Castor du Canada (PCDC)
392 Cariboo Dr., Nanaimo BC V9R 7E1
Tel: 250-755-1183
info@beaverparty.ca
www.beaverparty.ca
To become a majority government in the Canadian parliament by: 17% flat taxes & increased GDP funding (1% Canadian Space Agency, 3% defence, 7% education including free post-secondary & 12% health care); restorative justice & prison reform, starting with automatic parole, education & implementing 24/7 court services; & environmental protection policies (Clean Water Act & Environment & Climate Change Plan & Policy)
Jasper Jacobs, Leader
Wayne Whiting, Chief Agent
Leona Whiting, Records Officer

Bloc pot
CP 52558, Montréal QC H2R 3C5
Tél: 514-927-1768
blocpot@blocpot.qc.ca
blocpot.qc.ca
www.facebook.com/partiblocpot
twitter.com/blocpot
Jean-Patrick Berthiaume, Chef intérimaire

Bloc québécois (BQ)
#402, 3750, boul Crémazie est, Montréal QC H2A 1B6
Tél: 514-526-3000; *Téléc:* 514-526-2868
Ligne sans frais: 888-448-1880
info@bloc.org
www.blocquebecois.org
www.youtube.com/user/blocquebecois
www.facebook.com/blocquebecois
twitter.com/blocquebecois
Yves-François Blanchet, Chef

British Columbia Action Party
#2205, 13700 Mayfield Pl., Richmond BC V6V 2E4
Tel: 604-244-9645
info@bcactionparty.com
www.bcactionparty.ca
twitter.com/BCActionParty
To achieve a socially progressive & fiscally sound government that takes into account the needs of all British Columbians
Vacant, Leader

British Columbia Conservative Party
#327, 1434 Ironwood St., Campbell River BC V9W 5T5
Tel: 250-434-2550; *Toll-Free:* 866-800-9025
info@bcconservative.ca
www.bcconservative.ca
www.facebook.com/BCConservativeParty
Trevor Bolin, Leader
Justin K. Greenwood, President

British Columbia Excalibur Party
PO Box 1425, Kaslo BC V0G 1M0
Tel: 604-226-5825; *Fax:* 604-756-0346
Michael Halliday, Party Leader

British Columbia Liberal Party
PO Box 28131, Vancouver BC V6C 3T7
Tel: 604-606-6000; *Fax:* 604-632-0253
Toll-Free: 800-567-2257
contact@bcliberals.com
www.bcliberals.com
www.youtube.com/user/BCLiberals
www.facebook.com/BCLiberals
twitter.com/bcliberals
Shirley Bond, Interim Leader
Paul Barbeau, President

British Columbia Libertarian Party (BCLP)
#703, 1180 Falcon Dr., Coquitlam BC V3E 2K7
Tel: 604-944-2845
info@libertarian.bc.ca
www.libertarian.bc.ca
To advocate civil liberties & private property rights, including ending coercive taxation & changing the policies on legalized cannabis to authorize an open, free market with a ban on sales to minors

Donald Wilson, Leader
Clayton Welwood, President

British Columbia Marijuana Party
307 Hastings St. West, Vancouver BC V6B 1H6
Tel: 604-683-1750
Marc Emery, Party Leader

British Columbia Party
7665 Sapperton Ave., Burnaby BC V3N 4C9
Tel: 604-220-3742
John Horgan, Leader

British Columbia Peoples Party
767 - 6th St., New Westminster BC V3L 3C6
Tel: 778-688-7187
Maxime Bernier, Leader

British Columbia Refederation Party
#573, 7360 - 137th St., Surrey BC V3W 1A3
Tel: 604-593-4833
info.bcr@bcrefed.com
www.bcrefed.com
www.facebook.com/bcrefed
To advocate for direct democracy & reform to Canadian federalism
Dale Marcell, President

British Columbia Social Credit Party
1182 Nootka St., Vancouver BC V5K 4E7
Tel: 604-253-9293; *Fax:* 604-253-9293
Carrol Woolsey, Chairperson

Canadian Economic Party
#509, 47 Thorncliffe Park Dr., Toronto ON M4H 1J5
Tel: 647-609-0035
globaleconomicparty@gmail.com
To end poverty & homelessness in Canada
Stephen Harper, Party Leader

Canadian Political Science Association (CPSA) / Association canadienne de science politique (ACSP)
#204, 260 Dalhousie St., Ottawa ON K1N 7E4
Tel: 613-562-1202; *Fax:* 613-241-0019
cpsa-acsp@cpsa-acsp.ca
cpsa-acsp.ca
twitter.com/cpsa_acsp
To encourage & develop political science & its relationship with other disciplines
Silvina Danesi, Executive Director

Canadians' Choice Party (CCP)
#1, 927 Danforth Ave., Toronto ON M4J 1L8
Tel: 416-925-8858
canadianschoice@gmail.com
www.canadianschoice.ca
www.youtube.com/CanadiansChoiceParty
www.facebook.com/canadians.choice
twitter.com/CanadiansChoice
Bahman Yazdanfar, Party Leader

Cascadia Party of British Columbia
PO Box 28527, Stn. Willingdon Heights, Burnaby BC V5C 6J4
Tel: 604-970-4568
To advocate for sovereignty & monetary reform
Troy Gibbons, Party Leader

Changement intégrité pour notre Québec (CINQ)
210, boul Laurette-Théorêt, Sainte-Marthe-sur-le-Lac QC J0N 1P0
info@cinqleparti.org
cinqleparti.org
www.instagram.com/cinqleparti
www.facebook.com/CinqLeParti
Éric Emond, Chef

Christian Heritage Party of British Columbia
PO Box 724, Telkwa BC V0J 2X0
Tel: 250-846-5432
info@chpbc.ca
www.chpbc.ca
To advocate in favour of establishing a constitution to govern the province of British Columbia
Laura-Lynn Tyler Thompson, Party Leader
Dan Stuart, President

Christian Heritage Party of Canada (CHP) / Parti de l'héritage du Canada
PO Box 4958, Stn. E, Ottawa ON K1S 5J1
Fax: 613-248-0909
Toll-Free: 888-868-3247
info@chp.ca
www.chp.ca
www.youtube.com/user/christianheritage
www.facebook.com/CHP.ca.Canada
twitter.com/CHPCanada
To provide true Christian leadership & uphold biblical principles in federal legislation; To attain the leadership of the federal government of Canada through the existing democratic process
Rod Taylor, National Leader
Dave Bylsma, President

Citoyens au pouvoir du Québec
#201, 2500, Jean-Perrin, Québec QC G2C 1X1
Tél: 418-802-8480; Ligne sans frais: 833-248-6936
info@citoyensaupouvoir.ca
citoyensaupouvoir.ca
www.facebook.com/particitoyensaupouvoir
twitter.com/citoyensq

Stéphane Blais, Chef

Coalition Avenir Québec (CAQ)
#50, 1260 rue Mill, Montréal QC H3K 2B4
Tél: 514-800-6000; Téléc: 514-800-0081
Ligne sans frais: 866-416-2960
info@coalitionavenirquebec.org
coalitionavenirquebec.org
www.youtube.com/c/COALITIONAVENIRQUÉBEC
www.facebook.com/coalitionavenir
twitter.com/coalitionavenir

François Legault, Chef

Communist Party of BC (CPCBC)
706 Clark Dr., Vancouver BC V5L 3J1
Tel: 604-254-9836
info@cpcbc.ca
cpcbc.ca

Kimball Cariou, Party Leader

Communist Party of Canada (CPC) / Parti Communiste du Canada
Central Committee, 290A Danforth Ave., Toronto ON M4K 1N6
Tel: 416-469-2446
info@cpc-pcc.ca
www.communist-party.ca
flickr.com/photos/communist-party-of-canada
www.facebook.com/CommunistPartyOfCanada
twitter.com/compartycanada
To establish a socialist society in Canada, in which the principal means of producing & distributing wealth will be the common property of society as a whole
Liz Rowley, Party Leader

Communist Party of Canada (Alberta) (CPC-A)
PO Box 68112, Stn. Bonnie Doon, Edmonton AB T6C 4N6
Tel: 780-934-7893
office@communistparty-alberta.ca
www.communistparty-alberta.ca

Naomi Rankin, Party Leader

Communist Party of Canada (Manitoba) (CPC-M)
387 Selkirk Ave., Winnipeg MB R2W 2M3
Tel: 204-586-7824
cpc-mb@changetheworldmb.ca

Frank Komarniski, Party Leader

Communist Party of Canada (Marxist-Leninist) (CPC(ML)) / Parti communiste du Canada (marxiste-léniniste)
National Headquarters, PO Box 666, Stn. C, Montréal QC H2L 4L5
Tel: 613-792-4475
office@cpcml.ca
www.cpcml.ca
To attain communism & the complete emancipation of the working class; To ensure that all people have claims on the society by virtue of being human
Anna Di Carlo, Party Leader

Communist Party of Canada (Ontario) (CPCO)
290A Danforth Ave., Toronto ON M4K 1N6
Tel: 416-469-2446
info@communistpartyontario.ca
www.communistpartyontario.ca
www.facebook.com/ONCommunists
twitter.com/oncommunists

Drew Garvie, Party Leader

Conservative Party of Canada / Parti conservateur du Canada
#1720, 130 Albert St., Ottawa ON K1P 5G4
Tel: 866-808-8407; Toll-Free: 866-808-8407
www.conservative.ca
www.youtube.com/cpcpcc
www.facebook.com/cpcpcc
twitter.com/CPC_HQ
To provide Canadians with an alternative to the Liberal Party; To develop innovative & practical new policy ideas
Erin O'Toole, Leader
Rob Batherson, President
Candice Bergen, Deputy Leader

Cultural Action Party (British Columbia)
#1, 1032 Arlington Cres., North Vancouver BC V7R 1K9
Tel: 604-813-6030

Brad Saltzberg, Party Leader

Équipe autonomiste
820, rue Saint-Jean-Bosco, Québec QC G1V 2W7
Tél: 438-220-9469
info@equipeautonomiste.ca
equipeautonomiste.ca
www.facebook.com/EquipeAutonomiste
twitter.com/Autonomistes

Stéphane Pouleur, Chef

Federal Liberal Association of Nunavut
c/o Liberal Party of Canada, #920, 350 Albert St., Ottawa ON K1P 6M8
Toll-Free: 888-542-3725
assistance@liberal.ca
www.liberal.ca/ridings/nunavut
To represent the Liberal Party in Nunavut
Morgan Breitkreutz, Riding Chair

For British Columbia
#603, 548 Dallas Rd., Victoria BC V8V 1B3
Tel: 250-507-5797
4bcparty@gmail.com
4bcparty.wixsite.com/home
Shirley Bond, Interim Leader

Freedom Party of Ontario (FPO)
240 Commissioners Rd. West, London ON N6J 1Y1
Tel: 519-681-3999; Fax: 519-681-2857
Toll-Free: 800-830-3301
feedback@freedomparty.on.ca
www.freedomparty.on.ca
www.youtube.com/fpontario
twitter.com/fpontario
To provide a capitalist political alternative in Ontario; To form an elected government in Ontario, based on the principles of fundamental rights & freedoms
Paul McKeever, Leader
Robert Metz, President

Go Vegan
PO Box 67679, Toronto ON M5T 3M1
Tel: 416-648-3275
planetvegan@hotmail.com

Paul Figueiras, Party Leader

The Green Party of Alberta
PO Box 45066, Stn. Brentwood, #319, 3630 Brentwood Rd. NW, Calgary AB T2L 1Y4
info@greenpartyofalberta.ca
greenpartyofalberta.ca
www.facebook.com/GreenPartyOfAlberta
twitter.com/greenpartyab
To encourage the development of an attitude that everyone is part of the land; To encourage strict control of all forms of pollution; To promote programs teaching consensus & facilitation; To facilitate the process of all interested community members becoming involved in education, both learning & teaching, guided by the long-term sustainability of the Earth community; To create the opportunity for Albertans to become involved in the strategic planning process
Cass Romyn, President
Brian Deheer, Vice-President
Kris Enders, Chief Financial Officer

Green Party of Canada (GPC) / Parti vert du Canada
PO Box 997, Stn. B, Ottawa ON K1P 5R1
Tel: 613-562-4916; Fax: 613-706-1424
Toll-Free: 866-868-3447
info@greenparty.ca
www.greenparty.ca
www.youtube.com/user/canadiangreenparty
www.facebook.com/GreenPartyofCanada
twitter.com/canadiangreens

To promote a platform that includes debt reduction, eco-jobs, saving Canada's forests, supporting small business, use of soft energies, sovereignty for First Nations & a guarantee of full rights for women
Annamie Paul, Party Leader

The Green Party of Manitoba
PO Box 26023, Stn. Maryland, 120 Sherbrook St., Winnipeg MB R3G 3R3
Tel: 204-488-2831; Toll-Free: 866-742-4292
info@greenparty.mb.ca
www.greenparty.mb.ca
www.youtube.com/user/GreenPartyofManitoba
www.facebook.com/GreenPartyofManitoba
twitter.com/Green_Party_MB
James R. Beddome, Party Leader
David Nickarz, President

Green Party of New Brunswick / Parti Vert du Nouveau Brunswick
#102, 403 Regent St., Fredericton NB E3B 3X6
Toll-Free: 888-662-8683
www.greenpartynb.ca
www.youtube.com/user/GPVNB
www.facebook.com/GPNB.PVNB
twitter.com/greenpartynb

Marco Morency, Leader

Green Party of Nova Scotia
PO Box 36044, 5665 Spring Garden Rd., Halifax NS B3J 3S9
Tel: 902-252-3995; Toll-Free: 877-707-5775
gpns@greenpartyns.ca
greenpartyns.ca
www.facebook.com/NSGreens
twitter.com/NSGreens
Thomas Trappenberg, Party Leader
Jessica Alexander, Deputy Leader

The Green Party of Ontario (GPO) / Parti Vert d'Ontario
PO Box 1132, Stn. F, #035, 67 Mowat Ave., Toronto ON M4Y 2T8
Tel: 416-977-7476; Fax: 416-977-5476
Toll-Free: 888-647-3366
admin@gpo.ca
www.gpo.ca
Mike Schreiner, Party Leader
Jaymini Bhikha, Executive Director
Nav Dhaliwal, Director of Communications & Press Secretary
Candice Lepage, Director of the Leader's Office
Craig Cantin, Director of Development

Green Party of Prince Edward Island
81 Prince St., Charlottetown PE C1A 4R3
Toll-Free: 855-734-7336
info@greenparty.pe.ca
www.greenparty.pe.ca
www.facebook.com/GreenPartyPEI
twitter.com/PEIgreens
Peter Bevan-Baker, Party Leader
Martin Ruben, Party Leader

Greens of British Columbia (GPBC)
PO Box 8088, Stn. Central, Victoria BC V8W 3R7
Fax: 250-590-4537
Toll-Free: 888-473-3686
info@bcgreens.ca
www.bcgreens.ca
www.instagram.com/GreenPartyBC
www.facebook.com/BCGreens
twitter.com/BCGreens
To form healthy communities with diverse economies by involving the citizens of British Columbia in the political process; To offer voters in British Columbia fiscal responsibility, socially progressive policies & environmental sustainability
Sonia Furstenau, Party Leader

International Political Science Association (IPSA) / Association internationale de science politique (AISP)
#331, 1590, av Docteur-Penfield, Montréal QC H3G 1C5
Tel: 514-848-8717; Fax: 514-848-4095
info@ipsa.org
www.ipsa.org
www.linkedin.com/company/international-political-science-association-ipsa-
www.facebook.com/ipsa.aisp
twitter.com/ipsa_aisp
To promote the advancement of political science through the collaboration of scholars in different parts of the world
Guy Lachapelle, Secretary General
Helen Milner, President

Mathieu St-Laurent, Manager, Membership Services & External Relations

The Island Party of Prince Edward Island
PE

theislandparty@yahoo.com
theislandpartypei.ca
twitter.com/IslandPartyPEI

Sonny Gallant, Interim Party Leader

The Liberal Party of Canada (LPC) / Le Parti Libéral du Canada (PLC)
#920, 350 Albert St., Ottawa ON K1P 6M8

Fax: 613-235-7208
Toll-Free: 888-542-3725
assistance@liberal.ca
www.liberal.ca
www.youtube.com/user/liberalvideo
www.linkedin.com/company/liberal-party-of-canada
www.facebook.com/LiberalCA
twitter.com/Liberal_party

To seek a common ground of understanding among the people of the provinces & territories of Canada; To advocate liberal philosophies, principles & policies; To promote the election of candidates of the Liberal Party to the Parliament of Canada
Justin Trudeau, Prime Minister & Party Leader
Suzanne Cowan, National President
Azam Ishmael, National Director
Mira Ahmad, National Vice-President, English
Elise Bartlett, National Vice-President, French

The Liberal Party of Canada (British Columbia) (LPCBC) / Parti libéral du Canada (Colombie-Britannique)
#460, 580 Hornby St., Vancouver BC V6C 3B6

Tel: 604-664-3777; *Fax:* 877-411-6511
Toll-Free: 888-542-3725
bcinfo@liberal.ca
bc.liberal.ca
www.facebook.com/LPCBC
twitter.com/lpcbc

Gabe Garfinkel, Party Chair
Glen Krueger, Vice-Chair

The Liberal Party of Canada (Manitoba)
Molgat Place, 635 Broadway, winnipeg MB R3C 0X1

Tel: 888-542-3725; *Fax:* 204-284-1492
Toll-Free: 888-542-3725
manitoba.liberal.ca
www.facebook.com/LPCMB.PLCMB
twitter.com/liberalpartymb

Alexander Gilroy, Chair
Tanjit Nagra, Vice-Chair
Nora Fien, Secretary

Liberal Party of Canada (Ontario) (LPC(O)) / Parti libéral du Canada (Ontario)
4910 Yonge St., Toronto ON M2N 5N5

Tel: 416-222-1542; *Fax:* 416-921-3880
Toll-Free: 800-361-3881
ontario@liberal.ca
ontario.liberal.ca
www.facebook.com/LPCO.PLCO
twitter.com/lpc_o

Tyler Banham, President
Mike Rosati, Director, Operations

Liberal Party of Canada in Alberta (LPC(A))
#706, 10025 - 106th St. NW, Edmonton AB T5J 1G4

Toll-Free: 888-542-3725
alberta@liberal.ca
alberta.liberal.ca
www.facebook.com/lpcalberta
twitter.com/lpca

Eleanor Olszewski, Chair
Devin Demerse, Vice-Chair
Brian Gold, Secretary

Liberal Party of Newfoundland & Labrador / Parti libéral de Terre-Neuve et du Labrador
#102, 1 Crosbie Pl., St. John's NL A1B 3Y8

Tel: 709-754-1813; *Toll-Free:* 888-971-6991
info@nlliberals.ca
nlliberals.ca
www.youtube.com/nlliberals
www.facebook.com/nlliberals
twitter.com/nlliberals

Andrew Furey, Premier

Liberal Party of Nova Scotia
PO Box 723, #1400, 5151 George St., Halifax NS B3J 2T3

Tel: 902-429-1993; *Fax:* 902-423-1624
office@liberal.ns.ca
www.liberal.ns.ca
www.youtube.com/nsliberalparty
www.facebook.com/NSLiberalParty
twitter.com/NSLiberal

Stephen McNeil, Leader
Joseph Khoury, President

Liberal Party of Prince Edward Island / Parti libéral de l'Ile du Prince Édouard
PO Box 2559, #121, 161 St Peter's Rd., Charlottetown PE C1A 8C2

Tel: 902-368-3449; *Fax:* 902-368-3687
Toll-Free: 877-740-3449
officialagent@liberalpei.ca
www.liberalpei.ca
www.facebook.com/PEILiberals
twitter.com/peiliberalparty

Scott Barry, President
Jonathan Gallant, Vice-President
Emily MacDonald, Vice-President

The Libertarian Party of Canada
#409, 207 Bank St., Ottawa ON K2P 2N2

Tel: 613-288-9089
www.libertarian.ca
www.linkedin.com/company/libertarian-party-of-canada
www.facebook.com/libertarianCDN
twitter.com/libertarianCDN

Timothy Moen, Party Leader
Coreen Corcoran, President

Manitoba Liberal Party (MLP)
635 Broadway, Winnipeg MB R3C 0X1

Tel: 888-542-3725; *Fax:* 204-284-1492
Toll-Free: 800-567-5746
executive.director@manitobaliberals.ca
www.manitobaliberals.ca
www.youtube.com/user/manitobaliberals
www.facebook.com/manitobaliberals

Dougald Lamont, Leader
Alexander Gilroy, Chair

Manitoba Party
PO Box 46051, Stn. Westdale, Winnipeg MB R3R 3S3

Tel: 204-421-4597
admin@manitoba.party
www.manitoba.party
www.facebook.com/Manitoba.Party

Brian Pallister, Party Leader

Marijuana Party / Parti Marijuana
5535, av Bourbonnière, Montréal QC H1X 2N3

Tel: 514-725-8103
info@marijuanaparty.ca
www.marijuanaparty.ca

Blair T. Longley, Leader

Multicultural Party of Ontario
7336 Rainham Rd., Dunnville ON N1A 1Z3

Tel: 416-970-2713
multiculturalpartyofontario.webs.com

To promote multiculturalism & provide support for Canadian communities; To preserve language & culture
Wasyl Luczkiw, Party Leader

The National Citizens Coalition / Coalition nationale des citoyens inc.
#501, 27 Queen St. East, Toronto ON M5C 2M6

Tel: 416-869-3838; *Fax:* 416-869-1891
ncc@nationalcitizens.ca
www.nationalcitizens.ca
www.facebook.com/nationalcitizens
twitter.com/NatCitizens

To promote free markets, individual freedom & responsibility under limited government & a strong defence
Peter Coleman, President & CEO
Alexander Brown, Digital Content & Communications Manager
Miriam Alford, Vice President Finance and Administration

New Brunswick Liberal Association
715 Brunswick St., Fredericton NB E3B 1H8

Tel: 506-453-3950; *Fax:* 506-453-2476
Toll-Free: 800-442-4902
www.nbliberal.ca
www.youtube.com/user/NBLiberalTV
www.facebook.com/nbla.alnb
twitter.com/NBLA_ALNB

Roger Melanson, Interim Leader

New Democratic Party (NDP) / Nouveau Parti Démocratique
Federal Office, #300, 279 Laurier West, Ottawa ON K1P 5J9

Tel: 613-236-3613; *Fax:* 613-230-9950
Toll-Free: 866-525-2555
TTY: 866-776-7742
www.ndp.ca
www.youtube.com/user/NDPCanada
www.facebook.com/NDP.NPD
twitter.com/NDP

To offer Canadians an alternative political vision based on the principles of democratic socialism; To protect & expand programs such as Medicare & the Old Age Pension through prudent & effective government, & through a truly fair tax system
Jagmeet Singh, Party Leader
Mathieu Vick, President

New People's Choice Party of Ontario
#623, 783 Bathurst St., Toronto ON M5S 0A8

Tel: 416-805-3917
www.thenewpeopleschoiceparty.com

To advocate for a better democracy by addressing issues such as affordable housing, health care & environmental conservationism
Daryl Christoff, Party Leader

None of the Above Direct Democracy Party (NOTA)
1048 Springwater Cres., Mississauga ON L5V 1G4

Tel: 905-501-0010; *Fax:* 905-501-0010
info@nota.ca
www.nota.ca
www.facebook.com/NoneOfTheAboveX
twitter.com/NoneOfTheAboveX

Greg Vezina, Party Leader

Northern Ontario Party (NOP)
76 Oswald St., Thunder Bay ON P7A 6T1

northernontarioparty@hotmail.com
www.northernontarioparty.org
www.facebook.com/groups/446952978836960
twitter.com/VoteNOP

Shawn Poirier, Party Leader
Kenneth Jones, President

Northwest Territories Federal Liberal Association
PO Box 965, Stn. Main, Yellowknife NT X1A 2N8

nwtfla.membership@gmail.com
nwt.liberal.ca
www.facebook.com/NWTFLA

Frederick Haultain, Leader
Charles Blyth, Chair

Nova Scotia Progressive Conservative Association
#1003, 1660 Hollis St., Halifax NS B3J 1V7

Tel: 800-595-8679; *Fax:* 902-423-2465
Toll-Free: 800-595-8679
www.pcparty.ns.ca
www.youtube.com/user/pcnovascotia
www.facebook.com/nspcparty
twitter.com/nspc

To form a fiscally responsible, socially progressive government
Julie Chaisson, President
David MacGregor, Executive Vice-President

Ontario Alliance
PO Box 121, Stn. A, Toronto ON M9C 4V2

Tel: 416-620-5574

William Cook, Party Leader

Ontario Liberal Party (OLP)
#306, 344 Bloor St. West, Toronto ON M5S 3A7

Toll-Free: 800-268-7250
info@ontarioliberal.ca
www.ontarioliberal.ca
www.youtube.com/OntarioLiberalTV
www.linkedin.com/groups/3410725
www.facebook.com/OntarioLiberalParty
twitter.com/OntLiberal

Steven Del Duca, Leader
Brian Johns, President

Ontario Moderate Party
21567 McCowan Rd., Mount Albert ON L0G 1M0

Tel: 416-712-4557
ontariomoderate@gmail.com
www.ontariomoderate.com

Yuri Duboisky, Party Leader
Ihor Nesterenko, President

Ontario Party
58 Sundance Cres., Toronto ON M1G 2M2

Tel: 647-996-1508

Jason Tysick, Party Leader
Joel Charbonneau, President

Ontario Progressive Conservative Party
59 Adelaide St. East, 4th Fl., Toronto ON M5C 1K6
Tel: 416-861-0020; *Fax:* 416-861-9593
Toll-Free: 800-903-6453
www.ontariopc.ca
www.youtube.com/user/ontariopcparty
www.facebook.com/OntarioPC
twitter.com/OntarioPCParty
Doug Ford, Party Leader
Brian Patterson, President

Ontario Provincial Confederation of Regions Party
274 Stone Rd., RR#2, Renfrew ON K7V 3Z5
Tel: 613-432-2725

Murray Reid, Party Leader

Ontario Social Reform Party
#42, 8500 Torbram Rd., Brampton ON L6T 5C6
Tel: 416-821-6644
onsocialreform@gmail.com
www.ontariosocialreformparty.ca
www.facebook.com/onsocialreform
Bradley J. Harness, Party Leader

Parti 51
QC
info@parti51.com
parti51.com
www.youtube.com/c/Parti51Québec
www.facebook.com/1182102545161015

Parti communiste du Québec (PCQ)
5359 av du Parc, #C, Montréal QC H2V 4G9
pccpcq@gmail.com
www.particommunisteduquebec.ca
www.facebook.com/pcq1965
Unifier avec la classe ouvrière et les couches populaires pour que s'installe le pouvoir populaire dans le but de construire le socialisme
Pierre Fontaine, Chef

Parti communiste révolutionnaire (PCR) / Revolutionary Communist Party (RCP)
#303, 9697, boul Saint-Laurent, Montréal QC H3L 2N1
Tél: 514-563-1487
info@pcr-rcp.ca
www.pcr-rcp.ca
Créer un nouveau parti communiste révolutionnaire qui dirigera la lutte pour renverser le système capitaliste pourri dans lequel nous vivons, mettre fin à toute forme d'exploitation et d'oppression et conduire la société vers le socialisme et le communisme

Parti conservateur du Québec / Conservative Party of Québec
CP 133, Succ. Mont-Royal, Montréal QC H3P 3B9
Tél: 514-700-1934
info@pcquebec.ca
www.particonservateurquebec.org
Adrien Pouliot, Chef

Parti culinaire du Québec
8109, rue Saint-Denis, Montréal QC H2P 2G7
particulinaireduquebec@gmail.com
www.facebook.com/particulinaireduquebec
Jean-Louis Thémistocle, Chef

Parti libéral du Québec (PLQ) / Québec Liberal Party (QLP)
254, rue Queen, Montréal QC H3C 2N8
Tél: 514-288-4364; *Téléc:* 514-288-9455
Ligne sans frais: 800-361-1047
info@plq.org
www.plq.org
www.youtube.com/PartiLiberalduQuebec
www.facebook.com/liberalquebec
twitter.com/LiberalQuebec
Dominique Anglade, Chef du Parti
Linda Caron, President

Parti libre
27A, av Hochar, Saint-Sauveur QC J0R 1R4
Tél: 438-938-4802
partilibre69@gmail.com
partilibrecanada.org
Michel Leclerc, Chef

Parti marxiste-léniniste du Québec (PMLQ)
1360, rue Ontario est, Montréal QC H2L 1S1
Tél: 514-522-5872
permanence@pmlq.qc.ca
www.pmlq.qc.ca
Pierre Chénier, Chef du Parti

Parti québécois (PQ)
#325, 4115, rue Ontario est, Montréal QC H1V 1J7
Tél: 514-526-0020; *Téléc:* 514-526-0272
Ligne sans frais: 800-363-9531
info@pq.org
pq.org
www.instagram.com/partiquebecois
www.facebook.com/lepartiquebecois
twitter.com/PartiQuebecois
Réaliser démocratiquement la souveraineté du Québec pour s'épanouir comme peuple francophone, pour ne plus être minoritaire, pour mettre fin au gaspillage, pour se doter d'une politique économique qui répond aux intérêts du Québec; donner au Québec une place dans le monde
Paul St-Pierre-Plamondon, Chef

Parti Vert du Québec (PVQ) / Green Party of Québec
A-3729, rue Wellington, Montréal QC H4G 1V1
Tél: 514-612-3365
communications@pvq.qc.ca
pvq.qc.ca
www.youtube.com/channel/UCzJIsW5xc2DjHwJFhCXmJOg
www.linkedin.com/company/parti-vert-du-québec
www.facebook.com/partivert
twitter.com/partivertqc
Alex Tyrrell, Chef

Pauper Party of Ontario
1069A Windham Rd. 13, Simcoe ON N3Y 4K6
Tel: 519-753-5122

John Turmel, Party Leader

People's Alliance of New Brunswick
#206, 127 Main St., Fredericton NB E3A 1C6
Tel: 506-455-3015
office@peoplesalliance.ca
www.peoplesalliance.ca
www.facebook.com/AGNBPANB
twitter.com/PANB_AGNB
Kris Austin, Party Leader

The Peoples Political Party
#14, 81 Charles St. East, Toronto ON M4Y 1V2
Tel: 647-745-2768
thepeoplespoliticalparty@yahoo.ca
Maxime Bernier, Interim Leader

The Platinum Party of Employers Who Think & Act to Increase Awareness
PO Box 8068, Stn. Central, Victoria BC V8W 3R7
Tel: 250-483-7717
www.platinumparty.org
To ensure that the Government of British Columbia has in place the procedures necessary to maintain a legitimate position of authority over the commercial sector in BC
Espavo Sozo, Interim Party Leader
Antonio Ferreira, Deputy Leader

Progressive Canadian Party / Parti Progressiste Canadien
218 Twyford St., Ottawa ON K1V 0V9
Tel: 613-738-8946
info@pcparty.org
www.pcparty.org
Joe Hueglin, Leader
Dorian Baxter, President

Progressive Conservative Association of Prince Edward Island
PO Box 578, 30 Pond St., #B, Charlottetown PE C1A 7L1
Tel: 902-916-1770; *Fax:* 902-628-6428
info@peipc.ca
peipc.ca
www.facebook.com/peipcparty
twitter.com/PEIPCParty
To form a government that is socially progressive
Dennis King, Party Leader
Charles Blue, President

Progressive Conservative Party of Manitoba
23 Kennedy St., Winnipeg MB R3C 1S5
Tel: 204-594-4080
pcmanitoba@pcmanitoba.com
www.pcmanitoba.com
www.facebook.com/PCManitoba
twitter.com/PC_Manitoba
Brian Pallister, Party Leader

Progressive Conservative Party of New Brunswick / Le Parti Progressiste-Conservateur de Nouveau-Brunswick
#215, 364 York St., Fredericton NB E3B 3P7
Tel: 506-453-3456; *Fax:* 506-444-4713
info@pcnb.org
www.pcnb.ca
www.facebook.com/PCNBca
twitter.com/pcnbca
Blaine Higgs, Party Leader
Claude Williams, President

Progressive Conservative Party of Saskatchewan
3928 Gordon Rd., Regina SK S4S 6Y3
Tel: 306-565-5580; *Fax:* 306-565-5580
www.pcsask.ca
www.facebook.com/PCPSASK
Ken Grey, Party Leader

Pro-Life Alberta Political Association
12 Spruce Ct. SW, Calgary AB T3C 3B3
Toll-Free: 855-398-8486
prolifealberta@gmail.com
prolifealberta.com
Jeremy Fraser, Party Leader
Murray Ruhl, President

Québec en marche
#4, 2680, rue Hochelaga, Montréal QC H2K 1J7
Henriot Gingras, Chef

Québec solidaire
#010, 533, rue Ontario est, Montréal QC H2L 1N8
Tél: 514-278-9014; *Téléc:* 514-270-4379
Ligne sans frais: 866-278-9014
info@quebecsolidaire.net
quebecsolidaire.net
www.facebook.com/Quebecsolidaire
twitter.com/quebecsolidaire
Gaétan Châteauneuf, Chef

Reform Party of Alberta
PO Box 25156, Stn. Deer Park, Red Deer AB T4R 2M2
Tel: 403-358-0377
info@reformalberta.com
www.reformalberta.com
Randy Thorsteinson, Party Leader

Rhinoceros Party
125, rang des Bouleaux, Saint-Donat-de-Rimouski QC G0K 1L0
Tel: 581-624-2530
Sébastien Corriveau, Leader

Rural BC Party
PO Box 152, Houston BC V0J 1Z0
Tel: 250-845-8555
ruralbcparty@gmail.com
www.ruralbc.ca
twitter.com/ruralbcparty
To represent citizens in rural British Columbia
Jonathan Van Barneveld, Leader

Saskatchewan Liberal Party
720 Sweeney St., Regina SK S4T 6H6
Tel: 888-380-7044; *Fax:* 888-380-7044
Toll-Free: 888-380-7044
contact@saskliberals.ca
saskliberals.ca
www.facebook.com/saskliberals
twitter.com/SaskLiberals
Robert Rudachyk, Leader
Brian Allan, President

Saskatchewan Party
6135 Rochdale Blvd., Regina SK S4X 2R1
Tel: 306-359-1638; *Fax:* 306-359-9832
info@saskparty.com
www.saskparty.com
www.youtube.com/user/SaskatchewanParty
www.facebook.com/SaskParty
twitter.com/SaskParty
Scott Moe, Party Leader

Socialist Party of Canada (SPC) / Parti Socialiste du Canada
PO Box 31024, Victoria BC V8N 6J3
Tel: 416-877-2343
spc@worldsocialism.org
www.worldsocialism.org/canada
To promote the establishment of socialism - a system of society based upon the common ownership & democratic control of the means & instruments for producing & distributing wealth by & in the interest of society as a whole

Sammy Shaltout, Leader

Stop Climate Change
434 Hillcrest Ave., Peterborough ON K9J 6H6
Tel: 705-743-2939
E. Kenneth Ranney, Party Leader

Trillium Party of Ontario
95 Cousins Dr., Aurora ON L4G 1B5
Tel: 289-319-1220; Fax: 905-953-9469
www.trilliumontario.ca
www.facebook.com/TrilliumPartyON
twitter.com/trilliumpartyON
To prioritize policies that will benefit the citizens of Ontario
Bob Yaciuk, Party Leader

United Conservative Association
#203, 2915 - 21st St. NE, Calgary AB T2E 7T1
Toll-Free: 888-465-2660
info@unitedconservative.ca
www.unitedconservative.ca
Jason Kenney, Party Leader

Unparty: The Consensus-Building Party
5675 - 47th Ave., Delta BC V4K 1R5
Tel: 778-896-3571
To promote consensus government over adversarial party politics
Michael Donovan, Party Leader

Vancouver Island Party
PO Box 36064, Victoria BC V9A 1J5
Toll-Free: 844-933-4847
www.vanisleparty.com
To advocate for the needs of Vancouver Island's residents
Vacant, Party Leader

Voie du peuple
QC
voiedupeuple.wixsite.com/voiedupeuple
www.facebook.com/PartiVoieduPeuple
Marc Alarie, Chef

Western Independence Party of Saskatchewan (WIPSK)
PO Box 263, Endeavour SK S0A 0W0
Tel: 306-547-4738
Neil Fenske, Party Leader

Wildrose Independence Party of Alberta
7133 - 77th Ave., Edmonton AB T6B 0B5
Tel: 403-774-7393
contact@freedomconservativeparty.ca
Paul Hinman, Leader

Your Political Party of BC (YPP)
#313, 2040 York Ave., Vancouver BC V6J 1E7
Tel: 604-805-3547
ypp@yppofbc.com
www.yourbc.ca
www.instagram.com/yppofbc
www.facebook.com/yppbc
twitter.com/yppofbc
To advocate for more transparency & accountability in government
James Filippelli, Party Founder & Leader

Yukon Green Party
PO Box 31603, Whitehorse YT Y1A 3R3
Tel: 867-633-3392; Fax: 867-633-3392
yukongreenparty@gmail.com
www.yukongreenparty.ca
Frank de Jong, Party Leader

Yukon Liberal Party
PO Box 183, 108 Elliott St., Whitehorse YT Y1A 6C4
info@ylp.ca
www.ylp.ca
www.facebook.com/yukonliberals
twitter.com/YukonLiberal
Emily Farrell, President
Monica Nordling, Vice-President
Clarence Timmons, Treasurer
Kim Stavert, Secretary

Yukon Party
Whitehorse YT Y1A 2C6
Tel: 867-393-7104
www.yukonpartycaucus.ca
www.facebook.com/yukonparty
Currie Dixon, Party Leader
Melanie Brais, President

Poultry & Eggs

Alberta Egg Producers' Board (EFA)
#101, 90 Freeport Blvd. NE, Calgary AB T3J 5J9
Tel: 403-250-1197; Fax: 403-291-9216
Toll-Free: 877-302-2344
info@eggs.ab.ca
eggs.ab.ca
www.facebook.com/EggFarmersAlberta
twitter.com/EFA_AB_eggs
To provide effective promotion, control & regulation of the marketing of eggs in Alberta
Susan Gal, General Manager
David Webb, Manager, Marketing & Communications

British Columbia Broiler Hatching Egg Producers' Association (BCBHEC)
PO Box 191, Abbotsford BC V4X 3R2
Tel: 604-864-7556
association@bcbhec.com
www.bcbhec.com
To establish a better understanding & appreciation with the public & other interested parties regarding the industry; to stimulate & encourage improvements related to sales & scientific development in the field; to promote the exchange of ideas in an effort to find solutions to problems in the broiler hatching egg industry; to encourage economical plans to assists producers; & to provide better contact with hatcheries, feed suppliers, processors, & broiler growers.
Bryan Brandsma, President

British Columbia Turkey Farms
#106, 19329 Enterprise Way, Surrey BC V3S 6J8
Tel: 604-534-5644; Fax: 604-534-3651
info@bcturkey.com
www.bcturkey.com
To represent BC's registered turkey farms; To work closely with all industry partners to promote safe, quality & nutritious turkey products
Michel Benoit, General Manager & Marketing
Nancy Samson, Executive Assistant & Administration

Canadian Hatching Egg Producers (CHEP) / Producteurs d'oufs d'incubation du Canada (POIC)
21 Florence St., Ottawa ON K20 0W6
Tel: 613-232-3023; Fax: 613-232-5241
info@chep-poic.ca
www.chep-poic.ca
To ensure that our members produce enough hatching eggs to meet the needs of the broiler industry
Jack Greydanus, Chair
Giuseppe Caminiti, General Manager

Chicken Farmers of Canada (CFC) / Les Producteurs de poulet du Canada
#1007, 350 Sparks St., Ottawa ON K1R 7S8
Tel: 613-241-2800; Fax: 613-241-5999
info@chicken.ca
www.chickenfarmers.ca
www.youtube.com/user/chickenfarmers1
www.facebook.com/chickenfarmers
twitter.com/theinsidecoop
To build an evidence-based, consumer driven Canadian chicken industry that provides opportunities for profitable growth for all stakeholders
Michael Laliberté, Executive Director
Lisa Riopelle, Senior Officer, Human Resources & Administration
Lisa Bishop-Spencer, Manager, Brand & Communications
Jan Rus, Manager, Market Information & Systems

Chicken Farmers of Prince Edward Island
4701 Baldwin Rd., RR#6, Cardigan PE C0A 1G0
Tel: 902-838-4108; Fax: 902-838-4108
peipoultry@pei.sympatico.ca
Janet Murphy Hilliard, General Manager

Éleveurs de volailles du Québec
#250, 555, boul Roland-Therrien, Longueuil QC J4H 4G1
Tél: 450-679-0530; Téléc: 450-679-5375
evq@upa.qc.ca
volaillesduquebec.qc.ca
A pour mission l'étude, la défense et le développement des intérêts économiques, sociaux et moraux de ses membres; Favorise et stimule la mobilisation et la participation de ses membres tout en les consultant et en les informant; Développe et renforce la mise en marché collective des poulets et des dindons produits au Québec, en mettant en place des services garantissant le fonctionnement optimal du plan conjoint et des autres outils de mise en marché
Pierre-Luc Leblanc, Président

Fédération des producteurs d'oeufs de consommation du Québec (FPOCQ)
Maison de l'UPA, #320, 555, boul Roland-Therrien, Longueuil QC J4H 4E7
Tél: 450-679-0530; Téléc: 450-679-0855
www.oeuf.ca
www.facebook.com/lesoeufs
Favoriser le développement durable de l'industrie québécoise des oeufs et ce par: le respect de l'environnement et le bien-être des animaux; en procurant un revenu équitable aux intervenants du secteur; en répondant aux attentes des consommateurs avec des oeufs et produits de haute qualité
Serge Lefebvre, Président

Ontario Hatcheries Association (OHA)
39 William St., Elmira ON N3B 1P3
Tel: 519-669-3350
info@ontariohatcheries.ca
www.ontariohatcheries.ca
To serve as the voice of hatcheries & associated service & supply companies in Ontario
Susan Fitzgerald, Executive Director

Turkey Farmers of Canada (TFC) / Les éleveurs de dindon du Canada (ÉDC)
Bldg. One, #202, 7145 West Credit Ave., Mississauga ON L5N 6J7
Tel: 905-812-3140; Fax: 905-812-9326
www.turkeyfarmersofcanada.ca
www.facebook.com/TastyTurkey
twitter.com/tastyturkey
To develop & strengthen the Canadian Turkey market through an effective supply management systems that stimulates growth & profitability for stakeholders
Mark Davies, Chair

Printing Industry & Graphic Arts

British Columbia Printing & Imaging Association (BCPIA)
PO Box 75218, Stn. White Rock, Surrey BC V4A 0B1
Tel: 604-542-0902
www.bcpia.org
To be the voice of the BC printing industry & its employees; to provide services & benefits which encourage fellowship, education, community involvement & high standards in business conduct
Marilynn Knoch, Executive Director

Canadian Printing Industries Association (CPIA) / Association canadienne de l'imprimerie (ACI)
#3, 1750 The Queensway, Toronto ON M9C 5H5
admin@cpia-aci.ca
www.cpia-aci.ca
www.linkedin.com/company/canadian-printing-industries-association
To advance the quality of management in the printing & allied trades; to offer services through a network of local & related organizations including representations to various sectors; to enhance the image & profile of the industry
Richard Kouwenhoven, Chair
Tracey Preston, Administrator

Canadian Printing Ink Manufacturers' Association (CPIMA)
ON
Tel: 905-665-9310; Fax: 647-439-1572
www.cpima.org
To exchange information that will be of benefit to members, the ink industry & the printing industry
Steve Marshall, President
Michelle Connolly, Executive Director

Ontario Printing & Imaging Association (OPIA)
#135, 3-1750 The Queensway, Toronto ON M9C 5H5
Tel: 905-602-4441; Fax: 905-602-9798
info.ontarioprinting@gmail.com
www.ontarioprinting.net
To provide leadership for a successful printing & imaging industry in Ontario
Tracey Preston, President

Printing & Graphics Industries Association of Alberta (PGIA)
PO Box 61229, RPO Kensington, Calgary AB T2N 4S6
Tel: 403-281-1421; Fax: 403-225-1421
info@pgia.ca
www.pgia.ca
To be committed to the advancement of a healthy, effective & ethical graphic arts industry by providing leadership in the development of imaged communications

Christoph Bruehl, President

Printing Equipment & Supply Dealers' Association of Canada (PESDA)
11 Alderbrook Pl., Bolton ON L7E 1V3
Tel: 416-524-1954
www.pesda.com
To promote & advance the interests of the printing equipment, consumables & related services industries in Canada
Patrick D'Souza, President
Bob Kirk, General Manager

Saskatchewan Graphic Arts Industries Association (SGAIA)
PO Box 7152, Saskatoon SK S7K 4J1
Tel: 306-373-3202; *Fax:* 306-373-3246
info@sgaia.ca
sgaia.ca
To promote the interests of Saskatchewan's printing & allied industries; To increase the influence of graphic arts industry to the government & the general business community; To promote programs for the graphic arts industry at universities & technical institutions
Don Breher, Executive Director

Society of Graphic Designers of Canada (GDC) / Société des designers graphiques du Canada
Arts Court, 2 Daly Ave., Ottawa ON K1N 6E2
Tel: 613-567-5400; *Fax:* 613-564-4428
Toll-Free: 877-496-4453
info@gdc.net
www.gdc.net
www.instagram.com/gdcnational
www.linkedin.com/company/society-of-graphic-designers-of-canada
www.facebook.com/GDCNational
twitter.com/GDCNational
To maintain a defined, recognized & competent body of graphic designers; To promote high standards of graphic design for benefit of Canadian industry, commerce, public service & education
Melanie MacDonald, Executive Director

Prisoners & Ex-Offenders

Canadian Association of Elizabeth Fry Societies (CAEFS) / Association canadienne des sociétés Elizabeth Fry (ACSEF)
#701, 151 Slater St., Ottawa ON K1P 5H3
Tel: 613-238-2422; *Fax:* 613-232-7130
Toll-Free: 800-637-4606
admin@caefs.ca
www.caefs.ca
www.facebook.com/CAEFSNATIONALOFFICE
twitter.com/CAEFS
To work with & on behalf of women & girls involved with the justice system, in particular criminalized women; To offer services & programs to women in need, advocating for reforms & offering fora within which the public may be informed about & participate in all aspects of the justice system as it affects women
Emilie Coyle, Executive Director

Canadian Coalition Against the Death Penalty (CCADP) / Coalition canadien contre la peine de mort
80 Lillington Ave., Toronto ON M1N 3K7
Tel: 416-693-9112; *Fax:* 416-693-9112
info@ccadp.org
www.ccadp.org
www.youtube.com/ccadpmedia
www.facebook.com/70610338689
To provide information about abuses of the death penalty internationally; To ensure Canada does not return to the death penalty
Tracy Lamourie, Director & Founder
Dave Parkinson, Director & Founder

The John Howard Society of British Columbia
763 Kingsway, Vancouver BC V5V 3C2
Tel: 604-872-5651; *Fax:* 604-872-8737
info@johnhowardbc.ca
www.johnhowardbc.ca
To prevent crime & reform the justice system through alternative programming
Tim Veresh, Executive Director

The John Howard Society of Canada / Société John Howard du Canada
809 Blackburn Mews, Kingston ON K7P 2N6
Tel: 613-384-6272; *Fax:* 613-384-1847
national@johnhoward.ca
johnhoward.ca
www.facebook.com/JohnHowardSocietyCanada
twitter.com/JohnHoward_Can
To promote effective, just, & humane responses to the causes & consequences of crime; To assist individuals who have come into conflict with the law; To advocate for change in the criminal justice process; To educate the community on matters involving prison conditions, criminal law & its applications today
Catherine Latimer, Executive Director

Operation Springboard
#800, 2 Carlton St., Toronto ON M5B 1J3
Tel: 416-977-0089; *Fax:* 416-977-2840
info@springboardservices.ca
www.springboardservices.ca
www.youtube.com/user/OperationSpringboard
www.linkedin.com/company/springboard-services
www.facebook.com/OperationSpringboard
twitter.com/OpSpringboard
To design & provide services & programs that effectively reintegrate offenders into the community as responsible individuals; To develop crime prevention strategies; To promote community involvement in design & provision of services along with continuous effort to encourage understanding & support; To bring forward recommendations that will improve effectiveness of the criminal justice system.
Margaret Stanowski, Executive Director
Anna Peters, Director, Finance, IT & Facilities

St. Leonard's Society of Canada (SLSC) / Société St-Léonard du Canada
#208, 211 Bronson Ave., Ottawa ON K1R 6H5
Tel: 613-233-5170
info@stleonards.ca
www.stleonards.ca
www.facebook.com/SLSCanada
twitter.com/StLeonards_Can
To promote programs that promote responsible community living & safer communities
Anita Desai, Executive Director

Seventh Step Society of Canada
#2017, 246 Stewart Green SW, Calgary AB T3H 3C8
Tel: 403-650-1902
seventh@7thstep.ca
www.7thstep.ca
Self-help organization dedicated to help adult & young offenders to become useful & productive members of society; to provide follow-up to those who wish to use organization as means to maintain freedom
Patrick Graham, Executive Director

Public Health

Doctors of the World Canada / Médecins du Monde Canada (MDMC)
#100, 560, boul Crémazie est, Montréal QC H2P 1E8
Tel: 514-281-8998; *Fax:* 514-523-1861
Toll-Free: 833-896-8998
info@medecinsdumonde.ca
doctorsoftheworld.ca
www.instagram.com/medecinsdumondeca
www.linkedin.com/company/médecins-du-monde-canada
www.facebook.com/doctorsoftheworldcanada
twitter.com/mdmcanada
To promote & defend access to health for all, both in Canada & abroad

Publishing

Alberta Weekly Newspapers Association (AWNA)
3228 Parsons Rd. NW, Edmonton AB T6N 1M2
Tel: 780-434-8746; *Fax:* 780-438-8356
Toll-Free: 800-282-6903
info@awna.com
www.awna.com
To assist members to publish high quality community newspapers; To serve advertisers by providing information about the markets of community newspapers in Alberta
Dennis Merrell, Executive Director

The Alcuin Society
PO Box 3216, Vancouver BC V6B 3X8
info@alcuinsociety.com
www.alcuinsociety.com
www.flickr.com/photos/alcuinsociety
www.facebook.com/alcuinsociety
twitter.com/alcuin
To sponsor educational programs; Yo publish a journal; To offer awards & citations for excellence in book arts
Howard Greaves, Chair

Association des libraires du Québec (ALQ)
483, boul St-Joseph est, Montréal QC H2J 1J8
Tél: 514-526-3349; *Téléc:* 514-526-3340
info@alq.qc.ca
www.alq.qc.ca
Regrouper, pour leur bénéfice mutuel, les libraires engagées dans la vente au détail au Québec et celles engagées dans la vente du livre en langue française au Canada; fournir des services, faire des études, fournir de l'information, tenir des réunions et des rencontres et contribuer à des programmes pour le bénéfice et l'amélioration de ses membres; encourager la vente au détail du livre au Québec; encourager la communication et la collaboration entre les éditeurs, les distributeurs et les autres participants de l'industrie du livre; aider les libraires à encourager la lecture; lutter contre toute forme de censure
Katherine Fafard, Directrice générale

Association nationale des éditeurs de livres (ANEL)
2514, boul Rosemont, Montréal QC H1Y 1K4
Tél: 514-273-8130; *Ligne sans frais:* 866-900-2635
info@anel.qc.ca
anel.qc.ca
anel.qc.ca/blogue
www.facebook.com/Associationnationaledesesediteursdelivres
twitter.com/ANEL_QE
Soutenir le développement d'une industrie nationale de l'édition québécoise et canadienne de langue française; établir entre ses membres des rapports de bonne confraternité; étudier et défendre les intérêts tant généraux que politiques et économiques de ses membres; étudier toute question relative à la profession et diffuser l'information auprès de ses membres; constituer une représentation réelle et efficace de la profession à toute les instances pertinentes
Richard Prieur, Directeur général

Association of Book Publishers of British Columbia (ABPBC)
#600, 402 West Pender St., Vancouver BC V6B 1T6
Tel: 604-684-0228
admin@books.bc.ca
books.bc.ca
To encourage writing, publishing, distribution & promotion of books written by BC & Canadian authors; To cooperate with other associations & organizations to further the reading & studying of books; To work for the development & maintenance of strong competitive book publishing houses owned & controlled in BC & Canada; To further professional training for individuals engaged in book publishing
Heidi Waechtler, Executive Director
Monica Miller, Project Coordinator

Association of Canadian Publishers (ACP) / Association des éditeurs canadiens
#306, 174 Spadina Ave., Toronto ON M5T 2C2
Tel: 416-487-6116; *Fax:* 416-487-8815
admin@canbook.org
www.publishers.ca
twitter.com/CdnPublishers
To encourage writing, publishing, distribution & promotion of books written by Canadian authors in particular, & reading & study of books in general; To represent the members at international book fairs; To facilitate the exchange of information & professional expertise among members; To promote Canadian books; To expand Canadian-owned publishers' domestic & international market share
Kate Edwards, Executive Director
Madeline McCaffrey, Manager, Programs
Jazz Cook, Coordinator, Membership Services

Association of Canadian University Presses (ACUP) / Association des presses universitaires canadiennes (APUC)
542 King Edward Ave., Ottawa ON K1N 6N5
acup-apuc.ca
To support scholarly publishing by university presses in Canada
Lara Mainville, President

Association of English Language Publishers of Québec (AELAQ) / Association des éditeurs de langue anglaise du Québec
#3, 1200, av Atwater, Montréal QC H3Z 1X4
Tel: 514-932-5633
admin@aelaq.org
www.aelaq.org
To raise the profile of English-language books published in Québec
Julia Kater, Executive Director

Association of Manitoba Book Publishers (AMBP)
#404, 100 Arthur St., Winnipeg MB R3B 1H3
Tel: 204-947-3335; *Fax:* 204-956-4689
To promote Manitoba publishing industry
Michelle Peters, Executive Director

Association québécoise des salons du livre (AQSL)
#100, 60, rue St-Antoine, Trois-Rivières QC G9A 0C4
Ligne sans frais: 888-542-2075
info@aqsl.org
www.aqsl.org
De promouvoir du livre, du périodique et de la lecture; De défendre les intérêts des Salons membres et favorise la recherche, la documentation, les contacts professionnels, la création et la diffusion du livre
Julie Brosseau, Présidente

Book & Periodical Council (BPC)
#107, 192 Spadina Ave., Toronto ON M5T 2C2
Tel: 416-975-9366; *Fax:* 416-975-1839
publicity@thebpc.ca
www.thebpc.ca
To increase the level of awareness & the use of Canadian materials by the general public & in educational systems at all levels; To ensure the public has an adequate & representative range of Canadian books & periodicals in sales outlets, library systems & educational institutions; To strengthen book & periodical distribution systems; To support the development of new & existing Canadian-owned companies & encourage their growth & expansion; To improve market conditions & contractual arrangements as well as promotion & publicity given to Canadian writers & their work; To encourage the development of writing & publishing projects of social & cultural importance; To improve the cultural & economic climate in which the Canadian book & periodical industries exist; To discourage expansion of foreign ownership in all sectors of the book & periodical publishing industries
Annie McClelland, Executive Director

Book Publishers Association of Alberta (BPAA)
Percy Page Centre, 2nd Fl., 11759 Groat Rd. NW, Edmonton AB T5M 2K6
Tel: 780-424-5060; *Fax:* 780-424-7943
www.bookpublishers.ab.ca
www.facebook.com/ABbookpub
To work for maintenance & growth of strong book publishing houses owned & controlled in Alberta; To speak for common interests of constituent members; To liaise & cooperate with other associations for the good of the Canadian publishing industry
Kieran Leblanc, Executive Director

British Columbia & Yukon Community Newspapers Association (BCYCNA)
9 West Broadway, Vancouver BC V5Y 1P1
Tel: 604-669-9222; *Fax:* 604-684-4713
Toll-Free: 866-669-9222
info@bccommunitynews.com
www.bccommunitynews.com
www.linkedin.com/company/220705
To encourage excellence in the publishing of community newspapers; To promote the welfare & interests of the community newspaper industry; To improve standards in journalism & newspaper publishing; To facilitate the exchange of information among members; To develop & promote programs & services that benefit members
George Affleck, General Manager
Kerry Slater, Manager, Special Projects
Cora Schupp, Manager, Accounting & Community Classifieds

Canadian Bookbinders & Book Artists Guild (CBBAG) / Guilde canadienne des relieurs et des artisans du livre
#82809, 467 Parliament St., Toronto ON M5A 3Y2
cbbag@cbbag.ca
www.cbbag.ca
www.facebook.com/CanadianBookbindersandBookArtistsGuild
To create a spirit of community among hand workers in the book arts & those who love books; To promote greater awareness of the book arts; To increase educational opportunities; To foster excellence through exhibitions, workshops, lectures & publications

Jose Villa-Arce, President

Canadian Booksellers Association (CBA)
c/o Retail Council of Canada, #800, 1881 Yonge St., Toronto ON M4S 3C4
Toll-Free: 888-373-8245
To promote a high standard of business methods & ethics among members; To define & expand the role of booksellers within the Canadian publishing process; To provide professional advice to prospective & practising booksellers
Darryl Julott, Contact

Canadian Children's Book Centre (CCBC)
#200, 425 Adelaide St. West, Toronto ON M5V 3C1
Tel: 416-975-0010; *Fax:* 365-214-0108
info@bookcentre.ca
bookcentre.ca
www.instagram.com/kidsbookcentre
www.facebook.com/kidsbookcentre
twitter.com/kidsbookcentre
To promote the reading, writing & illustrating of Canadian books for young readers, providing programs, publications & resources for teachers, librarians, authors, illustrators, publishers, booksellers & parents
Rose Vespa, Executive Director
Amanda Halfpenny, Coordinator, Events & Programs
Meghan Howe, Coordinator, Library

Canadian Circulations Audit Board Inc. (CCAB) / Office canadien de vérification de la diffusion
Div. of BPA International, #450, 111 Queen St. East, Toronto ON M5C 1S2
Tel: 416-487-2418; *Fax:* 416-487-6405
www.bpaww.com
To issue standardized statements of data reported by a member; to verify the figures shown in these statements by auditors' examination of any & all records considered by the corporation to be necessary; to disseminate these data for the benefit of any individual or company requiring such information
Tim Peel, Vice-President

Canadian News Media Association
#200, 37 Front St. East, Toronto ON M5E 1B3
Tel: 416-923-3567; *Fax:* 416-923-7206
Toll-Free: 877-305-2262
info@newsmediacanada.ca
nmc-mic.ca
To be the national voice of the print & digital media industry in Canada
John Hinds, President & CEO

Canadian Publishers' Council (CPC)
#6060, 3080 Yonge St., Toronto ON M4N 3N1
www.pubcouncil.ca
twitter.com/pubcouncil_ca
To represent the interests of 18 companies who publish books & other media for elementary & secondary schools, colleges & universities, professional & reference, retail & library markets
David Swail, Executive Director

Canadian University Press (CUP) / Presse universitaire canadienne
cup.ca
www.youtube.com/user/CUPonline
www.facebook.com/canadianuniversitypress
twitter.com/canunipress
To elevate the standard of post-secondary student journalism; To foster communication among post-secondary student newspapers; To provide a national press service for post-secondary student newspapers; To provide facilities for the dissemination of news of importance to post-secondary students
Jacob Dube, President
Caitlin Dutt, Communications Officer

Connexions Information Sharing Services
Tel: 416-988-9586
mailroom@connexions.org
www.connexions.org
www.facebook.com/ConnexionsOnline
twitter.com/connexi0ns
To connect people working for social justice with information, ideas, groups & the history of social change movements

Hebdos Québec
#345, 2250, boul Daniel-Johnson, Laval QC H7T 2L1
Tél: 514-861-2088
communications@hebdos.com
www.hebdos.com
www.facebook.com/hebdosqc
twitter.com/HebdosQuebec
Favoriser et stimuler le développement du secteur des hebdomadaires en offrant à ses membres divers services en matière de recherche, de marketing et de formation; projeter une image crédible de la presse hebdomadaire, de la défendre, et de la rendre plus visible et plus accessible
Gilber Paquette, Directeur général

International Board on Books for Young People - Canadian Section (IBBY - Canada) / Union internationale pour les livres de jeunesse
c/o Canadian Children's Book Centre, #200, 425 Adelaide St. West, Toronto ON M5V 3C1
Tel: 416-975-0010; *Fax:* 416-975-8970
info@ibby-canada.org
www.ibby-canada.org
www.facebook.com/ibbycanada
To promote the belief that all children everywhere should have the ability to read a wide & rich selection of books at the level of their needs & interests; To build bridges of understanding & tolerance through children's books
Yvette Ghione, Co-President
Patti McIntosh, Co-President
Theo Heras, Vice-President

The Literary Press Group of Canada (LPG)
#401, 234 Eglinton Ave. East, Toronto ON M4P 1K5
Tel: 416-483-1321; *Fax:* 416-483-2510
www.lpg.ca
www.facebook.com/lpgcanada
twitter.com/LPGCanada
To advocate on behalf of members; To foster the survival, growth & maintenance of strong Canadian-owned & controlled literary book publishing houses; To help members with the selling & distribution of their books
Laura Rock Gaughan, Executive Director
Mandy Bayrami, Manager, Marketing

Livres Canada Books
#504, 1 Nicholas St., Ottawa ON K1N 7B7
Tel: 613-562-2324; *Fax:* 613-562-2329
info@livrescanadabooks.com
www.livrescanadabooks.com
www.linkedin.com/company/livres-canada-books
www.facebook.com/LivresCanadaBooks
twitter.com/livresCAbooks
To defend the interests of Canadian book publishers by providing market intelligence products & services, information & resources on digital publishing, as well as financial, promotion & logisitical support; To administer the Foreign Rights Marketing Assistance Program, a component of the Canada Book Fund, as well as mentoring programs & other funding initiatives
Robert Dees, Chair
François Charette, Executive Director

Magazines Canada
PO Box 201, #604, 555 Richmond St. West, Toronto ON M5V 3B1
Tel: 416-504-0274; *Fax:* 416-504-0437
Toll-Free: 877-238-8354
info@magazinescanada.ca
www.magazinescanada.ca
www.youtube.com/user/magazinescanada
www.linkedin.com/company/magazines-canada
twitter.com/magscanada
To represent Canadian-owned magazines with Canadian content
Melanie Rutledge, Executive Director
Evan Dickson, Director, Business Developmen
Brianne DiAngelo, Director, Communications & Public Engagement

Manitoba Community Newspapers Association (MCNA)
943 McPhillips St., Winnipeg MB R2X 2J9
Tel: 204-947-1691; *Fax:* 204-947-1919
Toll-Free: 800-782-0051
www.mcna.com
To serve community newspaper publishers in Manitoba; To act as the industry voice for the issues of community newspaper publishers; To encourage high standards in publishing
Vanessa Gensiorek, Manager, Member Services & Administration
Tanis Hutchinson, Manager, Display Ad Sales

National Magazine Awards Foundation (NMAF) / Fondation nationale des prix du magazine canadien
#3500, 2 Bloor St. East, Toronto ON M4W 1A8
Tel: 416-422-1358
staff@magazine-awards.com
www.magazine-awards.com
www.youtube.com/magazineawards
www.linkedin.com/groups/4002310
www.facebook.com/190062084384867
twitter.com/magawards

To recognize & promote excellence in the content & creation of Canadian print & digital publications through an annual program of awards & national publicity efforts
Barbara Gould, Managing Director

National NewsMedia Council (NNC)
#200, 37 Front St. East, Toronto ON M5E 1B3
Tel: 416-340-1981; *Toll-Free:* 844-877-1163
info@mediacouncil.ca
www.mediacouncil.ca
www.facebook.com/CANMediaCouncil
twitter.com/CANmediacouncil
To promote ethical practice in the news media industry; To serve as a forum for complains against its member news organizations; To represent the rights of the public in regards to free speech & freedom of the media
John Fraser, Executive Chair
Patricia Perkel, Executive Director
Brent Jolly, Director, Communications

News Media Canada / Médias d'Info Canada
#200, 37 Front St. East, Toronto ON M5E 1B3
Tel: 416-923-3567; *Fax:* 416-923-7206
Toll-Free: 877-305-2262
info@newsmediacanada.ca
nmc-mic.ca
www.instagram.com/newsmediacanada
www.linkedin.com/company/newspapers-canada
www.facebook.com/newsmediacanada
twitter.com/NewsMediaCanada
To ensure the continuance of a free press to serve readers effectively, by combining the experience, expertise & dedication of members; To increase the profile & effectiveness of Canada's news media industry
John Hinds, President & Chief Executive Officer

Newspapers Atlantic / Journaux Atlantiques
2882 Gottingen St., Halifax NS B3K 3E2
Tel: 902-832-4480; *Fax:* 902-832-4484
Toll-Free: 877-842-4480
info@newspapersatlantic.ca
newspapersatlantic.ca
To promote excellence, credibility, & the economic well-being of member community newspapers throughout Atlantic Canada
Inez Forbes, President
Mike Kierstead, Executive Director

Ontario Community Newspapers Association (OCNA)
#200, 37 Front St. East, Toronto ON M5E 1B3
Tel: 416-923-7724
www.ocna.org
www.facebook.com/171125688577
twitter.com/OCNAAdReach
To support members with information about the Ontario community newspaper industry & market; To improve the competitive position of the industry
Dave Adsett, President
John Willems, Secretary-Treasurer
Caroline Medwell, Executive Director
Karen Shardlow, Coordinator, Member Services
Kelly Gorven, Coordinator, Member Services
Lucia Shepherd, Coordinator, Accounting/Newsprint

Periodical Marketers of Canada (PMC)
120 Sinnott Rd., Toronto ON M1L 4N1
Tel: 613-783-7547
info@periodical.ca
www.periodical.ca
To represent Canadian wholesalers; To promote Canadian magazines

Québec Community Newspaper Association (QCNA) / Association des journaux régionaux du Québec (AJRQ)
#207, 189, boul Hymus, Pointe-Claire QC H9R 1E9
Tel: 514-697-6330; *Fax:* 514-697-6331
info@qcna.qc.ca
www.qcna.org
To promote Québec community English media; To serve as clearinghouse for information; To promote good journalism among members; To enhance the role of the media as social catalysts; To represent members to pertinent government departments; To interact with other provincial & national newspaper associations in Canada; To help members better their financial condition
Richard Tardif, Executive Director

Regroupement des éditeurs canadiens-français (RECF)
#402, 450, rue Rideau, Ottawa ON K1N 5Z4
Tél: 613-562-4507; *Téléc:* 613-562-3320
Ligne sans frais: 888-320-8070
info@recf.ca
www.recf.ca
www.facebook.com/RECF.ca
twitter.com/RECF_
Former une plate-forme d'échanges et un front commun pour mener des actions concertées pertinentes à l'ensemble des éditeurs canadiens-français, tant sur le plan des politiques que de la promotion, la distribution et le développement de marchés
Marc Haentjens, Président
Serge Patrice Thibodeau, Vice-Président
Catherine Voyer-Léger, Directrice générale
Safiatou Ali, Administratrice
Anne Molgat, Secrétaire
Brigitte Bergeron, Trésorière

Saskatchewan Publishers Group (SPG)
#324, 1831 College Ave., Regina SK S4P 4V5
Tel: 306-780-9808; *Fax:* 306-780-9811
info@skbooks.com
www.skbooks.com
twitter.com/SaskBooks
To promote the Saskatchewan book publishing industry; To provide a forum for sharing information & ideas; To speak for the common interests of its members; To undertake specific projects, programs & studies; To work closely with other publishing & cultural organizations across Canada
Brenda Niskala, Executive Director
Jillian Bell, Chief Financial Officer

Saskatchewan Weekly Newspapers Association (SWNA)
#14, 401 - 45th St. West, Saskatoon SK S7L 5Z9
Tel: 306-382-9683; *Fax:* 306-382-9421
Toll-Free: 800-661-7962
www.swna.com
www.facebook.com/sask.newspaper
twitter.com/swnainfo
To assist persons to issue press releases, buy advertising, & place classifieds in member newspapers in central Saskatchewan & the Northwest Territories
Steve Nixon, Executive Director

Société de développement des périodiques culturels québécois (SODEP)
#716, 460, rue Sainte-Catherine ouest, Montréal QC H3B 1A7
Tél: 514-397-8669; *Téléc:* 514-397-6887
info@sodep.qc.ca
www.sodep.qc.ca
www.facebook.com/sodep.qc.ca
twitter.com/cultureenrevues
Travailler à l'essor et au rayonnement des revues culturelles; établir et entretenir des liens avec le milieu de l'enseignement, les bibliothèques, les médias et les maisons de distribution; représenter et promouvoir les intérêts professionnels, éthiques et économiques des éditeurs; favoriser les échanges internationaux
Éric Perron, Président
Daniel Sernine, Vice-président
Francine Bergeron, Directrice générale
Marnie Mariscalchi, Secrétaire-trésorier

Toronto Press & Media Club
#101, 1755 Rathburn Rd. East, Mississauga ON L4W 2M8
info@torontopressclub.net
www.torontopressclub.net
www.facebook.com/TorontoPressAndMediaClub
Ed Patrick, President

Real Estate

Alberta Building Officials Association
12010 - 111 Avenue, Edmonton AB T5G 0E6
www.aboa.ab.ca
To improve standards of building inspection; To be a discussion forum for shared issues and concerns; To assist in education of building inspectors in various fields
Ryan Nixon, President
Brian Boddez, Director, Membership

Alberta Real Estate Association (AREA)
#217, 3332 - 20 St. SW, Calgary AB T2T 6T9
Tel: 403-228-6845; *Toll-Free:* 800-661-0231
www.albertarealtor.ca
To protect the interests of realtors & real estate boards in Alberta
Brad Mitchell, CEO

Alberta West Realtors' Association
162 Athabasca Ave., Hinton AB T7V 2A5
Tel: 780-865-7511; *Fax:* 780-865-7517
admin.awra@shaw.ca
www.abwra.com
To provide its members with quality structure and services
Karen Spencer-Miller, President

Annapolis Valley Real Estate Board
1 Hwy. 1, Aylesford NS B0P 1C0
Tel: 902-847-9336; *Fax:* 902-847-9869
avreb@eastlink.ca

Cathy Simpson, Executive Officer

Appraisal Institute of Canada (AIC) / Institut canadien des évaluateurs (ICE)
#403, 200 Catherine St., Ottawa ON K2P 2K9
Tel: 613-234-6533; *Fax:* 613-234-7197
Toll-Free: 888-551-5521
info@aicanada.ca
www.aicanada.ca
www.linkedin.com/company/appraisal-institute-of-canada
www.facebook.com/AppraisalInstitute.Canada
twitter.com/aic_canada
To grant professional designations in real estate appraisal (Accredited Appraiser Canadian Institute (AACI) & Canadian Residential Appraiser (CRA)); To strive to maintain high standards in real estate appraisal to protect the public interest
Keith Lancastle, Chief Executive Officer
Glenda Cardinal, Director, Finance & Administration
Paul Hébert, Director, Communications
Shelley Poirier, Director, Professional Practice

The Appraisal Institute of Canada - Alberta (AIC-AB)
#245, 495 - 36 St. NE, Calgary AB T2A 6K3
Tel: 403-207-7892; *Fax:* 403-207-7857
aic.alberta@shawlink.ca
www.aicanada.ca/province-alberta/alberta
To maintain professional ethics & standards in real estate valuation; to qualify real estate appraisers in Alberta, Nunavut & the Northwest Territories
Sanjit Singh, President
Christine Vandelinder, Executive Director

The Appraisal Institute of Canada - British Columbia (AIC-BC)
#210, 10451 Shellbridge Way, Richmond BC V6X 2W8
Tel: 604-284-5515; *Fax:* 604-284-5514
Toll-Free: 888-707-8287
info@appraisal.bc.ca
www.aicanada.ca/province-british-columbia/british-columbia
To represent, promote & support members as leaders in the counselling, analysis & evaluation of real property. Chapters: Fraser Valley, Nanaimo, Okanagan, Vancouver, Kamloops, The North, Victoria, & Kootenay.
Steve Blacklock, President
Christina Dhesi, Executive Director

The Appraisal Institute of Canada - Manitoba (AIC-MB)
5 Donwood Dr., Winnipeg MB R2G 0V9
Tel: 204-771-2982; *Fax:* 204-654-9583
mbaic@mts.net
www.aicanada.ca
To maintain professional ethics & standards in real estate valuation; to qualify real estate appraisers in the province
Dan Diachun, President
Pamela Wylie, Executive Director

The Appraisal Institute of Canada - Newfoundland & Labrador (AIC-NL)
PO Box 1571, Stn. C, St. John's NL A1C 5P3
Tel: 709-759-5769
naaic@nf.aibn.com
www.aicanada.ca/province-newfoundland-labrador
To promote the appraisal profession throughout Newfoundland & Labrador.
Greg Bennett, President
Sherry House, Executive Director

The Appraisal Institute of Canada - Ontario (AIC-ON)
#108, 16 Four Seasons Place, Toronto ON M9B 6E5
Tel: 416-695-9333; *Fax:* 877-413-4081
info@oaaic.on.ca
www.aicanada.ca/ontario
To serve the public interest by advancing high standards in the analysis & valuation of real property matters by enhancing the professional competence of its members. Chapters: Credit Valley, Hamilton-Niagara, Huronia, Kingston, London, North Bay, Oshawa/Durham, Ottawa, Peterborough/Lindsay, Sudbury & Sault Ste. Marie, Thunder Bay, Toronto, Waterloo/Wellington, Windsor, York.
Robin Jones, President

Bonnie Prior, Executive Director

The Appraisal Institute of Canada - Prince Edward Island (AIC-PEI)
PO Box 1796, Charlottetown PE C1A 7N4
Tel: 902-368-3355; Fax: 902-368-3582
peiaic@bellaliant.net
www.aicanada.ca/province-prince-edward-island
To promote the appraisal profession throughout Prince Edward Island; to assist members, those wishing to become members & the public
Boyce Costello, President
Suzanne Pater, Executive Director

The Appraisal Institute of Canada - Saskatchewan (AIC-SK)
#505, 2300 Broad St., Regina SK S4P 1Y8
Tel: 306-352-4195
skaic@sasktel.net
sk.aicanada.ca
To assist members, those hoping to become appraisers & the public
Wanda Styre, President
Marilyn Sterdnica, Executive Director

Association des propriétaires du Québec inc. (APQ) / Quebec Landlords Association (QLA)
10720, boul St-Laurent, Montréal QC H3L 2P7
Tél: 514-382-9670; Téléc: 514-382-9676
Ligne sans frais: 888-382-9670
www.apq.org
www.youtube.com/user/assoproprietaires
www.facebook.com/141154527095
twitter.com/apquebec
Défendre les droits et les intérêts des propriétaires de logements locatifs du Québec

L'Association du Québec de l'Institut canadien des évaluateurs (AQICE) / The Appraisal Institute of Canada - Québec (AIC-QC)
#400, 200 Catherine St., Ottawa ON K2P 2K9
Tél: 613-234-6533; Ligne sans frais: 888-551-5521
aqice@aicanada.ca
www.aicanada.ca/province-quebec
La mission de l'Institut canadien des évaluateurs est de protéger l'intérêt du public en s'assurant que ses membres offrent des services d'expert-conseil selon des normes élevées de pratique professionnelle
Daniel Pinard, President
Nicole Laflèche Anderson, Executive Director

Association of Battlefords Realtors
8916 - 19th Ave., North Battleford SK S9A 2V9
Tel: 306-445-6300; Fax: 306-445-9020
bfords.realestate@sasktel.net
To advance & promote interest of those engaged in real estate as brokers, agents, valuators, examiners & experts; To increase public confidence in & respect for those engaged in real estate
Rick Cann, Executive Officer

Association of Regina Realtors
1854 McIntyre St., Regina SK S4P 2P9
Tel: 306-791-2700; Fax: 306-781-7940
www.reginarealtors.com
www.facebook.com/ReginaREALTORS
twitter.com/ReginaREALTORS
To serve Regina through professional real estate services & community involvement
Gord Archibald, CEO

Association of Saskatchewan Realtors (ASR)
1705 McKercher Dr., Saskatoon SK S7H 5N6
Tel: 306-373-3350; Fax: 306-373-5377
Toll-Free: 877-306-7732
info@saskatchewanrealestate.com
www.saskatchewanrealestate.com
www.linkedin.com/company/854852
www.facebook.com/SaskREALTORS
twitter.com/saskREALTORS
To represent real estate boards & their realtor members on government affairs & provincial issues; To develop standards of professional practice; To administer training; To provide information to members, governments & the public; To provide support services to members; To register brokers & salespeople; To develop special projects for the educational benefit of all registrants in Saskatchewan
Bill Madder, Chief Executive Officer
Jacqueline Zabolotney, Director, Learning
Renee Greene, Manager, Marketing & Communications
Sharon Hiebert, Coordinator, Member Services

Bancroft District Real Estate Board
PO Box 1522, 69 Hastings St. North, Bancroft ON K0L 1C0
Tel: 613-332-3842; Fax: 613-332-3842

Barrie & District Association of REALTORS Inc.
30 Mary St., Barrie ON L4N 1S8
Tel: 705-739-4650
www.barrie.realtors.ca
www.linkedin.com/company/barrie-&-district-association-of-realtors-inc-
www.facebook.com/BDARInc
twitter.com/barrierealtors
To provide continuing education, Multiple Listing Service (MLS), statistical information & many other services to its members; To promote a high standard of business practices

BC Northern Real Estate Association
2609 Queensway, Prince George BC V2L 1N3
Tel: 250-563-1236; Fax: 250-563-3637
inquiries@bcnreb.bc.ca
bcnreb.bc.ca
twitter.com/bcnreb
Alexandra Goseltine, Executive Officer

Brampton Real Estate Board (BREB)
#401, 60 Gillingham Dr., Brampton ON L6X 0Z9
Tel: 905-791-9913; Fax: 905-791-9430
info@breb.org
www.breb.org
www.youtube.com/user/TheBREBTV
www.facebook.com/theBREB
To help members achieve their real estate related goals
Gerry Verdone, Executive Officer

Brandon Real Estate Board (BREB)
312 - 10th St., Brandon MB R7A 4G1
Tel: 204-727-4672; Fax: 204-727-8331
info@breb.mb.ca
www.breb.mb.ca
To provide real estate support for Realtors in Brandon
Mandy King, President
Marlee Murray, President-Elect
Warren Neufeld, Treasurer

Brantford Regional Real Estate Association Inc. (BRREA)
106 George St., Brantford ON N3T 2Y4
Tel: 519-753-0308; Fax: 519-753-8638
brantfordreb@rogers.com
www.brrea.com
www.youtube.com/BRREAssociation
www.linkedin.com/company/brantford-regional-real-estate-association
www.facebook.com/BrantfordRegionalRealEstateAssociation
twitter.com/_BRREA
To provide real estate support for realtors working in Brantford
Viktoria Tumilowicz, Executive Officer

British Columbia Northern Real Estate Board
2609 Queensway, Prince George BC V2L 1N3
Tel: 250-563-1236; Fax: 250-563-3637
inquiries@bcnreb.bc.ca
boards.mls.ca/bcnreb
Dorothy Friesen, President

British Columbia Real Estate Association (BCREA)
#1425, 1075 West Georgia St., Vancouver BC V6E 3C9
Tel: 604-683-7702; Fax: 604-683-8601
Toll-Free: 844-288-7702
bcrea@bcrea.bc.ca
www.bcrea.bc.ca
twitter.com/bcrea
To promote the interests of & advocate for the real estate profession; To secure public support & trust in the profession; To promote property rights & real estate related issues; To ensure high standards of ethics & professionalism through ongoing education of realtors
Darlene Hyde, Chief Executive Officer
Corinne Caldwell, Chief Operating Officer

Building Owners & Managers Association - Canada
PO Box 61, #1801, 1 Dundas St. West, Toronto ON M5G 1Z3
Tel: 416-214-1912; Fax: 416-214-1284
info@bomacanada.ca
www.bomacanada.ca
www.linkedin.com/company/boma-canada
www.facebook.com/BOMACanada
twitter.com/BOMA_CAN
To represent the Canadian commerical real estate industry on matters of national concern; To develop a strong communications network between local associations; To promote professionalism of members through education programs & effective public relations activity

Benjamin Shinewald, President & CEO

Building Owners & Managers Association Toronto
#1800, 1 Dundas St. West, Toronto ON M5G 1Z3
Tel: 416-596-8065; Fax: 416-596-1085
info@bomatoronto.org
www.bomatoronto.org
www.youtube.com/user/BOMAtoronto
www.linkedin.com/company/boma-toronto
www.facebook.com/bomatoronto
To represent the interests & concerns of building owners & managers in the commercial & office space industry in the Greater Toronto Area
Susan Allen, President & CEO
Bala Gnanam, Director, Sustainable Building Operations & Strategic Partnerships
Aaron Therrien, Senior Manager, Member Services
Thomas Catania, Manager, Sponsorship
Teresa Champagnie-Bent, Manager, Awards
Fawzia Karim, Manager, Accounting
Kseniia Khudorozhkova, Office Administrator

Calgary Real Estate Board Cooperative Limited (CREB)
300 Manning Rd. NE, Calgary AB T2E 8K4
Tel: 403-263-0530; Fax: 403-218-3688
info@creb.com
www.creb.com
Alan Tennant, Chief Executive Officer

Cambridge Association of Realtors Inc.
2040 Eagle St. North, Cambridge ON N3H 0A1
Tel: 519-623-3660; Fax: 519-623-8253
cambridge-admin@rogers.com
cambridgeassociationofrealtors.com
www.facebook.com/CambridgeAssociationOfRealtors
twitter.com/CamRealtors

Canadian National Association of Real Estate Appraisers (CNAREA)
PO Box 157, Qualicum Beach BC V9K 1S7
Fax: 866-836-6369
Toll-Free: 888-399-3366
hq@cnarea.ca
www.cnarea.ca
To certify & regulate real property appraisers in Canada; To raise the standards of the real property appraising profession; To protect consumers
Steven G. Coull, Chief Executive Officer
James Carty, National President
Michel Beaudoin, National Vice-President
Robert B. Fraser, National Treasurer
Johnathan Carty, National Secretary

The Canadian Real Estate Association (CREA) / Association canadienne de l'immeuble
200 Catherine St., 6th Fl., Ottawa ON K2P 2K9
Tel: 613-237-7111; Fax: 613-234-2567
Toll-Free: 800-842-2732
info@crea.ca
www.crea.ca
www.youtube.com/user/CREACHANNEL
www.linkedin.com/company/creaaci
www.facebook.com/CREA.ACI
twitter.com/CREA_ACI
To enhance member professionalism, competency & profitability; To advocate government policies which improve the industry's market environment & enhance individual rights with respect to the ownership of real property
Michael Bourque, Chief Executive Officer

Central Alberta Realtors Association
4922 - 45th St., Red Deer AB T4N 1K6
Tel: 403-343-0881; Fax: 403-347-9080
office@CARAssociation.ca
www.rdreb.ca
www.facebook.com/243909398990726
twitter.com/CaraRedDeer
Allan Melbourne, President
Larry Westgard, Executive Officer

Chambre immobilière Centre du Québec Inc.
445, rue Brock, Drummondville QC J2B 1E2
Tél: 819-477-1033; Téléc: 819-474-7913
Ligne sans frais: 877-546-8320
chambre@cgocable.ca
www.immobiliercentreduquebec.com
Nathalie Bisson, Présidente

Chambre immobilière de l'Abitibi-Témiscamingue Inc. (CIAT)
#203, 33, av Horne, Rouyn-Noranda QC J9X 4S1
Tél: 819-762-1777; *Téléc:* 819-762-4030
ciat@cablevision.qc.ca
www.ciat.qc.ca

Robert Brière, Président
Gilles Langlais, Directeur général

Chambre immobilière de l'Estrie inc.
19, rue King ouest, Sherbrooke QC J1H 1N4
Tél: 819-566-7616; *Téléc:* 819-566-7688
info@mon-toit.net
www.mon-toit.net
Promouvoir et protéger les intérêts de l'industrie immobilière du Québec afin que les Chambres et les membres accomplissent avec succès leurs objectifs d'affaires.
Johanne Beaudoin, Directrice

Chambre immobilière de l'Outaouais
106, boul Sacré-Coeur, Gatineau QC J8X 1E1
Tél: 819-771-5221; *Téléc:* 819-771-8715
info@avecunagent.com
www.avecunagent.com
www.facebook.com/104740336281495
twitter.com/avecuncourtier
De fournir à ses membres les outils nécessaires pour réussir
Chantal Legault, Directrice générale

Chambre immobilière de la Haute Yamaska Inc. (CIHY) / Haute Yamaska Real Estate Board
#3, 45, rue Centre, Granby QC J2G 5B4
Tél: 450-378-6702; *Téléc:* 450-375-5268
administration.cihy@videotron.ca
Offrir des services de formation et d'information pour les agents immobiliers.
Lise Desrochers, Directrice générale

Chambre immobilière de la Mauricie Inc. / Trois-Rivières Real Estate Board
1275, boul des Forges, Trois-Rivières QC G8Z 1T7
Tél: 819-379-9081; *Téléc:* 819-379-9262
info@cimauricie.com
www.cimauricie.com
www.facebook.com/cimauricie
Lise Girardeau, Directrice générale

Chambre immobilière de Lanaudière Inc.
#101, 216 rue Beaudry nord, Joliette QC J6E 6A6
Tél: 450-759-8511; *Téléc:* 450-759-6557
cil@immobilierlanaudiere.com
www.immobilierlanaudiere.com
www.linkedin.com/company/immobilierlanaudiere
www.facebook.com/chambreimmobilierelanaudiere
Louise Renaud, Directrice générale

Chambre immobilière de Québec
990, av Holland, Québec QC G1S 3T1
Tél: 418-688-3362
info@ciq.qc.ca
www.ciq.qc.ca
www.linkedin.com/company/chambre-immobili-re-de-qu-bec
www.facebook.com/118843518140424
Promouvoir et protéger les intérêts de l'industrie immobilière du Québec afin que les Chambres et les membres accomplissent avec succès leurs objectifs d'affaires.
Martine Bélanger, Directrice générale

Chambre immobilière de Saint-Hyacinthe Inc.
CP 667, Saint-Hyacinthe QC J2S 7P5
Tél: 450-799-2210; *Téléc:* 450-799-2230
chimmob@cgocable.ca
www.chambreimmobilieresthyacinthe.com
Promouvoir et protéger les intérêts de l'industrie immobilière du Québec afin que les Chambres et les membres accomplissent avec succès leurs objectifs d'affaires.
Pierre Tanguay, Président

Chambre immobilière des Laurentides (CIL)
570, boul des Laurentides, Piedmont QC J0R 1K0
Tél: 450-240-0006; *Ligne sans frais:* 800-263-3511
info@cilaurentides.ca
www.cilaurentides.ca
www.facebook.com/OptionLaurentides
De promouvoir et à développer des intérêts professionnels, économiques et sociaux de ses membres
Francine Soucy, Présidente
Daniel Vandal, Directrice générale

Chambre immobilière du Grand Montréal / Greater Montréal Real Estate Board
600, ch du Golf, Ile-des-Soeurs QC H3E 1A8
Tél: 514-762-2440; *Ligne sans frais:* 888-762-2440
cigm@cigm.qc.ca
www.cigm.qc.ca
De protéger les intérêts commerciaux de ses membres afin de développer leur succès
Éric Charbonneau, Directeur général

Chambre immobilière du Saguenay-Lac St-Jean Inc. (CISL)
#140, 2655, boul du Royaume, Jonquière QC G7S 4S9
Tél: 418-548-8808; *Téléc:* 418-548-2588
info@immobiliersaguenay.com
www.immobiliersaguenay.com
www.facebook.com/immobilier.saguenay
Regrouper les membres afin de leur fournir des services, assurer la qualité de leur travail, défendre et promouvoir leurs intérêts; protéger et promouvoir le commerce de l'immobilier et encourager l'accès à la propriété; offrir de la formation et du perfectionnement dans le domaine immobilier afin d'assurer et de garantir le professionnalisme de l'industrie; faciliter au public en général l'accès à l'information dans le domaine immobilier
Carlos Cordeiro, Directeur général

Chatham-Kent Real Estate Board
252 Wellington St. West, Chatham ON N7M 1K1
Tel: 519-352-4351
ckreb@mnsi.net
boards.mls.ca/chatham
www.facebook.com/153823918039312
Jamie Winkler, President

Chilliwack & District Real Estate Board
#1, 8433 Harvard Pl., Chilliwack BC V2P 7Z5
Tel: 604-792-0912
admin@cadreb.com
www.cadreb.com
twitter.com/ChilliwackREB
To serve the real estate needs of Chilliwack, Sardis, Rosedale, Agassiz, Harrison Hot Springs, & Hope
Steve Lerigny, Executive Officer

Cornwall & District Real Estate Board
407B Pitt St., Cornwall ON K6J 3R3
Tel: 613-932-6457; *Fax:* 613-932-1687
www.mls-cornwall.com
Dani Tedesco-Derouchie, Executive Officer

Durham Region Association of REALTORS (DRAR)
#14, 50 Richmond St. East, Oshawa ON L1G 7C7
Tel: 905-723-8184; *Fax:* 905-723-7531
Reception@DurhamRealEstate.org
www.durhamrealestate.org
twitter.com/DurhamRENews
To pursue excellence & professionalism in real estate through commitment & service
Nancy Shaw, Executive Officer

Fort McMurray Realtors Association
9909 Sutherland St., Fort McMurray AB T9H 1V3
Tel: 780-791-1124; *Fax:* 780-743-4724
eo@fmreb.ca
boards.mls.ca/fortmcmurray
Katie Ekroth, President
Andrew Weir, Director

Fraser Valley Real Estate Board
15463 - 104 Ave., Surrey BC V3R 1N9
Tel: 604-930-7600; *Fax:* 604-588-0325
Toll-Free: 877-286-5685
mls@fvreb.bc.ca
www.fvreb.bc.ca
www.linkedin.com/company/fraser-valley-real-estate-board
www.facebook.com/FVREB
twitter.com/FVREB
To provide the most efficient real estate marketing service
John Barbisan, President

Grande Prairie & Area Association of Realtors (GPAAR)
10106 - 102 St., Grande Prairie AB T8V 2V7
Tel: 780-532-3508; *Fax:* 780-539-3515
eo@gpaar.ca
www.grandeprairie-mls.ca
www.facebook.com/GPAAR
Susan Rankin, President

Greater Moncton Real Estate Board Inc.
541 St. George Blvd., Moncton NB E1E 2B6
Tel: 506-857-8200; *Fax:* 506-857-1760
www.monctonrealestateboard.com

To provide its members with the strcuture & services to enhance REALTOR professionalism, standards of business practice and ethics in meeting the real estate needs of the community.
Kerry Rakuson, Executive Officer

Guelph & District Real Estate Board
400 Woolwich St., Guelph ON N1H 3X1
Tel: 519-824-7270
info@gdar.ca
www.gdar.ca
www.linkedin.com/company/guelph-&-district-association-of-realt
ors-r-
www.facebook.com/AssociationofREALTORS
twitter.com/_gdar_

Hamilton-Burlington & District Real Estate Board (HBDREB)
505 York Blvd., Hamilton ON L8R 3K4
Tel: 905-529-8101; *Fax:* 905-529-4349
info@rahb.ca
www.rahb.ca
To pursue excellence & professionalism in real estate through commitment & service
George O'Neill, Chief Executive Officer

Huron Perth Association of Realtors
#6, 55 Lorne Ave. East, Stratford ON N5A 6S4
Tel: 519-271-6870; *Fax:* 519-271-3040
www.hpar.ca
To maintain a professional standard among its members in order to better serve the public
Gwen Kirkpatrick, Executive Officer

Institute of Municipal Assessors (IMA)
#206, 10720 Yonge St., Richmond Hill ON L4C 3C9
Tel: 905-884-1959; *Fax:* 905-884-9263
Toll-Free: 877-877-8703
info@theima.ca
www.assessorsinstitute.ca
The IMA is the largest Canadian professional association representing members that practice in the field of Property Assessment & related Property Taxation functions
Rose McLean, President
Mario Vittiglio, Executive Director

Kamloops & District Real Estate Association (KADREA)
#101, 418 St Paul St., Kamloops BC V2C 2J6
Tel: 250-372-9411
www.kadrea.com
Bobbi Campbell, Contact

Kawartha Lakes Real Estate Association
31 Kent St. East, Lindsay ON K9V 2C3
Tel: 705-324-4515
www.kawarthalakes-mls.ca
www.facebook.com/184458454969478
To provide its members with resources that allow them to grow within the profession
Susan Schell, Executive Officer

Kingston & Area Real Estate Association
720 Arlington Park Pl., Kingston ON K7M 8H9
Tel: 613-384-0880; *Fax:* 613-384-0863
info@karea.ca
www.karea.ca
Adam Rayner, President

Kootenay Real Estate Board (KREB)
#208, 402 Baker St., Nelson BC V1L 4H8
Tel: 250-352-5477; *Fax:* 250-352-7184
Toll-Free: 877-295-9375
info@kar.realtor
www.kreb.ca
www.facebook.com/217611504946687
To promote interest in real estate markets in all aspects through service to members & the public
Chuck Bennett, President
Bruce Seitz, Vice-President
Jazz McPherson, Director
Trevor Koot, Executive Officer

Lethbridge & District Association of Realtors
516 - 6 St. South, Lethbridge AB T1J 2E2
Tel: 403-328-8838; *Fax:* 403-328-8906
eo@ldar.ca
www.ldar.ca
To provide real estate information on the Lethbridge area; to serve as a forum to network & build connections within the real estate community.

London & St. Thomas Association of Realtors
342 Commissioners Rd. West, London ON N6J 1Y3
Tel: 519-641-1400; *Fax:* 519-641-4613
info@lstar.ca
www.lstar.ca
www.youtube.com/user/LSTARMembers
www.facebook.com/LSTAR.REALTORS
twitter.com/LSTARtweets
To provide its members with the necessary tools that enable them to deliver excellent service to the community
Betty Doré, Executive Vice President
Joanne Shannon, Director, Administration

Manitoba Building Officials Association
PO Box 2063, Winnipeg MB R3C 3R4
Tel: 204-832-1512; *Fax:* 204-897-8094
info@mboa.mb.ca
www.mboa.mb.ca
To promote building safety through training & awareness in order to help their members
Rick Grimshaw, President

Manitoba Real Estate Association (MREA)
1873 Inkster Blvd., Winnipeg MB R2R 2A6
Tel: 204-772-0405; *Fax:* 204-775-3781
Toll-Free: 800-267-6019
www.realestatemanitoba.com
To represent the interest of Manitoba's licensed realtors
David Salvatore, Chief Executive Officer
Jill Johnston, Director, Operations
Caroline Duheme, Reception

Medicine Hat Real Estate Board Co-operative Ltd.
403 - 4th St. SE, Medicine Hat AB T1A 0K5
Tel: 403-526-2879; *Fax:* 403-526-0307
randeen.bray@shaw.ca
www.mhreb.ca
Dione Todd, President
Randeen Bray, Executive Officer

Mississauga Real Estate Board (MREB)
#1, 3450 Ridgeway Dr., Mississauga ON L5L 0A2
Tel: 905-608-6732; *Fax:* 905-608-9988
membership@mreb.ca
www.mreb.ca
To foster professionalism in the REALTOR community to ensure that clients are dealing with knowledgeable, proficient REALTORS who specialize in local market; To represent its members & keep them informed about events involving real estate so that they are able to provide knowledgable service to the public
Ray Dubash, Executive Officer
Gay Napper, Manager, Events & Membership Services
Avi Gaitonde, Manager, Finance & Accounting
Sidra Kamal, MLS Administrator

New Brunswick Association of Real Estate Appraisers (NBAREA) / Association des évaluateurs immobiliers du Nouveau-Brunswick (AEIN-B)
#204, 403 Regent St., Fredericton NB E3B 3X6
Tel: 506-450-2016; *Fax:* 506-450-3010
nbarea@nb.aibn.com
www.nbarea.org
To enhance the profession & to protect the public
Andrew Leech, President

New Brunswick Building Officials Association (NBBOA) / L'Association des officiels de la construction du Nouveau-Brunswick
Prospect Plaza Inc., PO Box 30033, Stn. B, Fredericton NB E3B 0H8
Tel: 506-470-3375; *Fax:* 506-450-4924
admin@nbboa.ca
www.nbboa.ca
www.facebook.com/NBBOA
twitter.com/THENBBOA
To achieve & maintain the highest levels of professionalism in membership, education & qualifications, legislative interpretation, building inspection service, building & construction safety.
Amy Poffenroth, President
Tracy Battilana, Executive Assistant

New Brunswick Real Estate Association (NBREA) / L'Association des agents des immobiliers du Nouveau-Brunswick
#1, 22 Durelle St., Fredericton NB E3C 1N8
Tel: 506-459-8055; *Fax:* 506-459-8057
Toll-Free: 800-762-1677
info@nbrea.ca
nbrea.ca
www.facebook.com/NBREALTORS
twitter.com/NBREALTORS

To strengthen & promote standards of professionalism in the real estate industry
Jamie Ryan, Chief Executive Officer
Jane Girard, Financial Officer
Caroyln Cameron, Registrar

Newfoundland & Labrador Association of Realtors (NLAR)
28 Logy Bay Rd., St. John's NL A1A 1J4
Tel: 709-726-5110; *Fax:* 709-726-4221
Toll-Free: 855-726-5110
reception@nlar.ca
www.nlar.ca
www.linkedin.com/company/newfoundland-and-labrador-associa
tion-of-realtors
www.facebook.com/NLAREALTORS
twitter.com/_NLAR
Bill Stirling, Chief Executive Officer

Niagara Association of REALTORS (NAR)
116 Niagara St., St Catharines ON L2R 4L4
Tel: 905-684-9459; *Fax:* 905-684-4778
www.niagararealtor.ca
www.pinterest.com/niagararealtors
www.linkedin.com/company/niagara-association-of-realtors
www.facebook.com/NiagaraRealtors
twitter.com/NiagaraREALTORS
To provide members with the structure & services to facilitate the marketing of real estate; To ensure a high standard of business practices & ethics; To effectively serve the real estate needs of the members
Stephen Oliver, President

North Bay Real Estate Board
926 Cassells St., North Bay ON P1B 4A8
Tel: 705-472-6812; *Fax:* 705-472-0529
admin@nbreb.com
www.nbreb.com
To represent real estate agents and member offices in North Bay
Susan Nosko, President

Northumberland Hills Association of Realtors
#14, 975 Elgin St. West, Cobourg ON K9A 5J3
Tel: 905-372-8630; *Fax:* 905-372-1443
districtrealestate@bellnet.ca
boards.mls.ca/northumberland

Nova Scotia Association of REALTORS (NSAR)
#100, 7 Scarfe Ct., Dartmouth NS B3B 1W4
Tel: 902-468-2515; *Fax:* 902-468-2533
Toll-Free: 800-344-2001
nsrealtors.ca
www.linkedin.com/company/nova-scotia-association-of-realtors
www.facebook.com/nsarREALTORS
twitter.com/nsarREALTORS
To provide Realtors with services & representation to enable them to best serve the public in real estate transactions
Roger Boutilier, Chief Executive Officer
Bonnie Wigg, Director, MLSr & Member Services
Nicole Kreiger, Director, Education

Nova Scotia Real Estate Appraisers Association (NSREAA)
#602, 5670 Spring Garden Rd., Halifax NS B3J 1H6
Tel: 902-422-4077; *Fax:* 902-422-3717
nsreaa@nsappraisal.ns.ca
nsreaa.ca
The Association regulates the practice of real estate appraisal in Nova Scotia, establishes & promotes the interests of appraisers, develops & maintains high standards of knowledge & best practices in the field, develops & enforces professional ethics, promotes public awareness of the profession, & encourages studies in real estate appraisal.
Carla Dempsey, President
Davida Mackay, Executive Director & Registrar

The Oakville, Milton & District Real Estate Board
125 Navy St., Oakville ON L6J 2Z5
Tel: 905-844-6491; *Fax:* 905-844-6699
info@omdreb.on.ca
www.omdreb.on.ca
www.youtube.com/user/omdreb
www.linkedin.com/company/the-oakville-milton-and-district-real-
estate-board-omdreb
www.facebook.com/OMDREB
twitter.com/OMDREB_Official
To represent its members & provide them with services to help further their career
Marta Sponder, Executive Officer

Okanagan Mainline Real Estate Board (OMREB)
#112, 140 Commercial Dr., Kelowna BC V1X 7X6
Tel: 250-491-4560; *Fax:* 250-491-4580
admin@omreb.com
www.omreb.com
www.facebook.com/okanaganmainlineREB
twitter.com/OMREB1
Lynette Keyowski, Chief Executive Officer
Karen Maeers, Chief Operating Officer
Sonja Harkness, Manager, Professionalism & Technology

Ontario Building Officials Association Inc. (OBOA) / Association de l'Ontario des officers en bâtiment inc.
#8, 200 Marycroft Ave., Woodbridge ON L4L 5X4
Tel: 905-264-1662; *Fax:* 905-264-8696
admin@oboa.on.ca
www.oboa.on.ca
www.youtube.com/user/OBOA1956
www.linkedin.com/groups/4469807
www.facebook.com/oboa.ontariocanada
To foster & cooperate in the establishment of uniform regulations relating to the fire protection & structural adequacy of buildings & the safety & health of the occupants; To promote the understanding & uniform interpretation & enforcement of these regulations & their companion documents; To provide assistance in the development & improvement of these regulations & their companion documents; To promote a close liaison & interchange of ideas on these regulations with related associations, the building industry, government & the consumer public
Aubrey LeBlanc, CAO
Michael T. Leonard, Coordinator, Membership, Training, Administration & Registrations

Ontario Real Estate Association (OREA)
99 Duncan Mill Rd., Toronto ON M3B 1Z2
Tel: 416-445-9910; *Fax:* 416-445-2644
Toll-Free: 800-265-6732
info@orea.com
www.orea.com
www.youtube.com/OREAinfo
www.linkedin.com/company/ontario-real-estate-association
www.facebook.com/OREAinfo
twitter.com/oreainfo
To represent the vocational interests of members; To advocate for a better working environment; To communicate with members & the public; To develop educational opportunities for the betterment of the real estate profession; To develop programs to assist members in providing quality services to the public; To develop & administer the educational courses required for registration to trade in real estate on behalf of The Real Estate Council of Ontario
Tim Hudak, Chief Executive Officer

Orangeville & District Real Estate Board (ODREB)
228 Broadway Ave., Orangeville ON L9W 1K5
Tel: 519-941-4547
www.odreb.com
twitter.com/odrebrealtors
David Grime, President

Organisme d'autoréglementation du courtage immobilier du Québec (OACIQ) / Québec Real Estate Association
#2200, 4905, boul Lapinière, Brossard QC J4Z 0G2
Tél: 450-462-9800; *Téléc:* 450-676-7801
Ligne sans frais: 800-440-7170
info@oaciq.com
www.oaciq.com
www.linkedin.com/company/organisme-d-autor-glementation-du-
courtage-immobilier-du-qu-bec-oaciq
www.facebook.com/oaciq
twitter.com/OACIQ
Protéger le public par l'encadrement des activités professionnelles de tous les courtiers et agents immobiliers exerçant au Québec
Michel Léonard, Président du conseil

Ottawa Real Estate Board (OREB) / Chambre d'immeuble d'Ottawa
1826 Woodward Dr., Ottawa ON K2C 0P7
Tel: 613-225-2240; *Fax:* 613-225-6420
Admin@oreb.ca
www.ottawarealestate.org
twitter.com/OREB1

Parry Sound & Area Association of REALTORS
47A James St., Parry Sound ON P2A 1T6
Tel: 705-746-4020; *Fax:* 705-746-2955
psreb@vianet.ca
www.parrysoundrealestateboard.ca
To set a high standard of practice & ethics for its members so that they may better serve the public

Peterborough & the Kawarthas Association of Realtors Inc. (PKAR)
PO Box 1330, 273 Charlotte St., Peterborough ON K9J 7H5
Tel: 705-745-5724; *Fax:* 705-745-9377
info@peterboroughrealestate.org
www.peterboroughrealestate.org
www.linkedin.com/company/peterborough-and-the-kawarthas-association-of-realtorsr-inc-
www.facebook.com/PtboRealtors
twitter.com/pkarrealestate
Mike Heffernan, President

Portage La Prairie Real Estate Board
39 Royal Rd., Portage la Prairie MB R1N 1T9
Tel: 204-857-4111

Powell River Sunshine Coast Real Estate Board
PO Box 307, Powell River BC V8A 5C2
Tel: 604-485-6944; *Fax:* 604-485-6944
Geri Powell, Board Administrator

Prince Albert & District Association of Realtors
615 Branion Dr., Prince Albert SK S6V 2R9
Tel: 306-764-8755; *Fax:* 306-763-0555
pareb@sasktel.net
www.princealbertrealtors.ca
To support realtors in the Prince Albert Real Estate community
Candy Marshall, Executive Officer

Prince Edward Island Real Estate Association (PEIREA)
75 St. Peter's Rd., Charlottetown PE C1A 5N7
Tel: 902-368-8451; *Fax:* 902-894-9487
office@peirea.com
www.peirea.com
To promote the real estate profession; to provide information & services to members, & to the public
Mary Jane Webster, President
Ritchie Simpson, Secretary-Treasurer

Professional Iranian Canadian Real Estate Association (PICRA)
#235, 6021 Yonge St., Toronto ON M2M 3W2
info@picra.ca
picra.ca
www.instagram.com/picra.ca
www.facebook.com/picra
To facilitate & promote co-operation & networking among Iranian Canadian Real Estate professionals; To advance members' professional careers
Shervin Zeinalian, President

Quinte & District Association of REALTORS Inc.
PO Box 128, 51 Cannifton Rd. North, Cannifton ON K0K 1K0
Tel: 613-969-7873; *Fax:* 613-962-1851
ExecOfficer@Quinte-mls.com
www.quinte-mls.com
twitter.com/quinte_REALTORS
Jamie Troke, President

Real Estate Board of Greater Vancouver
2433 Spruce St., Vancouver BC V6H 4C8
Tel: 604-730-3000; *Fax:* 604-730-3100
Toll-Free: 800-304-0565
www.rebgv.org
www.youtube.com/user/rebgv
www.facebook.com/rebgv
twitter.com/rebgv
Robert K. Wallace, CEO

Real Estate Board of the Fredericton Area Inc. (FREB)
544 Brunswick St., Fredericton NB E3B 1H5
Tel: 506-458-8163; *Fax:* 506-459-8922
www.frederictonrealestateboard.com
To serve the needs of its' members by providing cost effective tools, services & information necessary to foster professionalism
Bradley Thomas, President
Sharon Watts, Executive Officer

Real Estate Institute of Canada (REIC) / Institut canadien de l'immeuble (ICI)
#208, 5407 Eglinton Ave. West, Toronto ON M9C 5K6
Tel: 416-695-9000; *Fax:* 416-695-7230
Toll-Free: 800-542-7342
infocentral@reic.ca
www.reic.ca
www.instagram.com/reicnational
www.linkedin.com/company/real-estate-institute-of-canada
www.facebook.com/reicnational
twitter.com/reicnational
To advance opportunities for persons involved in real estate; To offer certification & designation for real estate professionals

---

Stephen Ashworth, Chief Executive Officer
Hafeeza Bassirullah, Director, Education & Training
Kristina Fixter, Director, Marketing & Communications
Li Liu, Director, Finance
Shelley Barfoot-O'Neill, Manager, Membership Services

Real Property Association of Canada
TD North Tower, PO Box 147, #4030, 77 King St. West, Toronto ON M5K 1H1
Tel: 416-642-2700; *Fax:* 416-642-2727
Toll-Free: 855-732-5722
info@realpac.ca
www.realpac.ca
www.youtube.com/user/REALpacVideos
www.linkedin.com/company/realpac
twitter.com/realpac_news
To represent the real estate industry's point of view to government at all levels on legislative & regulatory matters
Michael Brooks, Ph.D., Chief Executive Officer
Carolyn Lane, COO & Vice-President, Member Engagement

Realtors Association of Edmonton
14220 - 112 Ave., Edmonton AB T5M 2T8
Tel: 780-451-6666; *Fax:* 780-452-1135
Toll-Free: 888-674-7479
www.ereb.com
www.facebook.com/REALTORSAssociationOfEdmonton
twitter.com/RAEinfo
Michael Thompson, President & CEO
Ron Hutchinson, Executive Vice-President

REALTORS Association of Grey Bruce Owen Sound (RAGBOS)
517 - 10 St., Lower Level, Hanover ON N4N 1R4
Tel: 519-364-3827
www.ragbos.ca
To provide a web-based multiple listing service for its members
Dawn Lee McKenzie, President

Realtors Association of Lloydminster & District
#203, 5009 - 48th St., Lloydminster AB T9V 0H7
Tel: 780-875-6939; *Fax:* 780-875-5560
lloydreb@telus.net
rald.realtyserver.com
Chris Hassall, President

Realtors Association of South Central Alberta (RASCA)
PO Box 997, 3 Royal Rd. East, Brooks AB T1R 1B8
Tel: 403-793-1666
www.facebook.com/115618335134095
Karen Bertamini, President

Renfrew County Real Estate Board (RCREB)
197 Pembroke St. East, Pembroke ON K8A 3J6
Tel: 613-735-5840; *Fax:* 613-735-0405
www.renfrewcountyrealestateboard.com
www.facebook.com/RCREB
To promote standard practices among its members in order to unify & strengthen their abilities
Sue Martin, Executive Officer

Rideau-St. Lawrence Real Estate Board
#12, 1275 Kensington Pkwy., Brockville ON K6V 6C3
Tel: 613-342-3103; *Fax:* 613-342-1637
rideau@bellnet.ca

Saint John Real Estate Board Inc.
#100, 55 Drury Cove Rd., Saint John NB E2K 2Z8
Tel: 506-634-8772; *Fax:* 506-634-8775
www.sjrealestateboard.ca
www.facebook.com/SaintJohnRealEstateBoard
twitter.com/SJ_REALTORS
To provide services to & set standards for members; To preserve & promote the MLS marketing system to benefit buyers & sellers of real estate property
Sheila Henry, President

Sarnia-Lambton Real Estate Board (SLREB)
555 Exmouth St., Sarnia ON N7T 5P6
Tel: 519-336-6871; *Fax:* 519-344-1928
www.mls-sarnia.com
www.facebook.com/152351484834475
David Burke, Executive Officer

Saskatchewan Building Officials Association Inc. (SBOA)
PO Box 1671, Prince Albert SK S6V 5T2
Tel: 306-445-1733; *Fax:* 306-445-1739
membership@sboa.sk.ca
www.sboa.sk.ca
Dan Knutson, President
Todd Russell, Secretary-Treasurer

Saskatoon Region Association of REALTORS (SRAR)
1705 McKercher Dr., Saskatoon SK S7H 5N6
Tel: 306-343-3459; *Fax:* 306-343-1420
info@srar.ca
www.srar.ca
To represent the real estate interests of its members & the public; To provide services & programs to enhance the professionalism, competency & effectiveness of its members; To advocate public policy towards improving the real estate market environment
Jason Yochim, Chief Executive Officer
Trevor Schmidt, Chief Operating Officer
Sean Cummings, Director, Education & Communications

Sault Ste Marie Real Estate Board (SSMREB)
372 Albert St. East, Sault Ste Marie ON P6A 2J6
Tel: 705-949-4560; *Fax:* 705-949-5935
www.saultstemarierealestate.ca
www.facebook.com/SaultSteMarieRealEstateBoard
Andrea Gagne, Executive Officer

Simcoe & District Real Estate Board
191 Queensway West, Simcoe ON N3Y 2M8
Tel: 519-426-4454; *Fax:* 519-426-9330
www.norfolk-mls.ca
www.facebook.com/sdreb

South Okanagan Real Estate Board (SOREB)
#103, 3310 Skaha Lake Rd., Penticton BC V2A 6G4
Tel: 250-492-0626; *Fax:* 250-493-0832
www.soreb.org
www.facebook.com/151180668308444
twitter.com/soreb1
To pursue excellence & professionalism in real estate, through quality education & high ethical standards; To protect the interest of the membership & the public

Southern Georgian Bay Association of REALTORS
243 Ste. Marie St., Collingwood ON L9Y 2K6
Tel: 705-445-7295
info@sgbREALTORS.com
www.sgbrealtors.com
To deliver MLS & real estate services
Sandy Raymer, Executive Officer

Tillsonburg District Real Estate Board
#202, 1 Library Lane, Tillsonburg ON N4G 4W3
Tel: 519-842-9361; *Fax:* 519-688-6850
tburgreb@bellnet.ca
www.tburgreb.ca
To provide its members with the tools they need to best serve the public
Frank Catry, President

Toronto Real Estate Board (TREB)
1400 Don Mills Rd., Toronto ON M3B 3N1
Tel: 416-443-8100
membership@trebnet.com
www.trebhome.com
www.youtube.com/TREBChannel
www.linkedin.com/company/treb
www.facebook.com/TorontoRealEstateBoard
twitter.com/TREBhome
Gurcharan Bhaura, President

Vancouver Island Real Estate Board (VIREB)
6374 Metral Dr., Nanaimo BC V9T 2L8
Tel: 250-390-4212; *Fax:* 250-390-5014
info@vireb.com
www.vireb.com
www.linkedin.com/pub/vancouver-island-real-estate-board/4a/92
6/332
www.facebook.com/vancouverislandrealestateboard
twitter.com/vireb
To provide cost-effective tools, services & information necessary to foster professionalism & maintain the realtor's position as the primary focus in the real estate industry
Janice Stromar, President
Bill Benoit, CAE, CRAE, Executive Officer

Victoria Real Estate Board (VREB)
3035 Nanaimo St., Victoria BC V8T 4W2
Tel: 250-385-7766; *Fax:* 250-385-8773
info@vreb.org
www.vreb.org
To promote & enhance the use of the real estate services that its members provide to the public
David Corey, Executive Officer

Windsor-Essex County Real Estate Board
3020 Deziel Dr., Windsor ON N8W 5H8
Tel: 519-966-6432; *Fax:* 519-966-4469
www.windsorrealestate.com
www.youtube.com/wecrealtors
www.facebook.com/wecrealtors
twitter.com/wecrealtors
Norm Langlois, President

Winnipeg Real Estate Board (WREB)
1240 Portage Ave., Winnipeg MB R3G 0T6
Tel: 204-786-8854; *Fax:* 204-784-2343
info@winnipegrealtors.ca
www.winnipegrealtors.ca
www.youtube.com/user/winnipegrealtors
To serve members & to promote the benefits of organized real estate
Marina R. James, Chief Executive Officer

Woodstock-Ingersoll & District Real Estate Board
#6, 65 Springbank Ave. North, Woodstock ON N4S 8V8
Tel: 519-539-3616; *Fax:* 519-539-1975
admin@widreb.ca
woodstockingersolldistrictrealestateboard.com
www.facebook.com/widreb1
Nicole Bowman, Executive Officer

Yellowknife Real Estate Board
#201, 5204 - 50th Ave., Yellowknife NT X1A 1E2
Tel: 867-920-4624; *Fax:* 867-873-6387
boards.mls.ca/yellowknife

Yorkton Real Estate Association Inc. (YREA)
41 Broadway St. West, Yorkton SK S3N 0L6
Tel: 306-783-3067; *Fax:* 306-782-3231
yrea@sasktel.net
To promote a high level of professionalism among members by providing leadership in the real estate industry & in the community
Judy Pfeifer, Executive Officer
Ron Skinner, President

Yukon Real Estate Association
#10, 35 Lewes Blvd., Whitehorse YT Y1A 4S5
Tel: 867-633-5565; *Fax:* 867-667-7005
admin@yrea.ca
www.yrea.ca
To promote interest in marketing of real estate in all its aspects & to advance & improve relations of members of society with public

Recreation, Hobbies & Games

Aéroclub des cantons de l'est
Aéroport Roland-Désourdy, 101, rue du Ciel, Bromont QC V6B 3X9
Tél: 514-862-1216
www.facebook.com/AeroclubDesCantonsDeLEst
Marc Arsenault, Contact

Air Currency Enhancement Society (ACES)
c/o Bud Bernston, 13 Casavechia Ct., Dartmouth NS B2X 3G7
www.soaraces.ca
www.youtube.com/user/soaraces
www.facebook.com/AirCurrencyEnhancementSociety
twitter.com/soaraces
To promote & improve standards in aviation
Robert Francis, Chairman
Patrick Dalton, Contact, Communications

Alberta Camping Association (ACA)
Percy Page Centre, 11759 Groat Rd., Edmonton AB T5M 3K6
Tel: 403-477-5443
info@albertacamping.com
www.albertacamping.com
www.facebook.com/AlbertaCampingAssociation
twitter.com/Alberta_Camping
To promote & coordinate organized camping in Alberta by providing camp information & leadership direction as well as promoting high standards of camp programs & activities for all populations; to take a leading role in the recognition & promotion of professional standards for organized camps in Alberta
Gerrit Leewes, President
Gwen Dell'Anno, Executive Director

Alberta Recreation & Parks Association (ARPA)
11759 Groat Rd., Edmonton AB T5M 3K6
Tel: 780-415-1745; *Fax:* 780-451-7915
Toll-Free: 877-544-1747
arpa@arpaonline.ca
arpaonline.ca
www.youtube.com/channel/UCWpGvr7VoeGnxXeivhcuETQ
www.linkedin.com/company/alberta-recreation-and-parks-association
www.facebook.com/arpaonline
twitter.com/arpaonline
To promote accessibility to recreation & parks & their benefits to Albertans; To work toward economic sustainability, natural resource protection, & conservation within provincial parks & natural environments
Bill Wells, Chief Executive Officer
Steve Allan, Director, Finance & Operations
Anna Holtby, Coordinator, Communications

Alberta Whitewater Association (AWA)
85 Valley Meadow Close, Calgary AB T3B 5M1
Tel: 403-479-8017
admin@albertawhitewater.ca
www.albertawhitewater.ca
www.facebook.com/alberta.whitewater
To encourage whitewater paddlesport activities
Sara Jordan, President
Matthew Corbet, Vice-President
Liam McGowan, Treasurer

All Terrain Vehicle Association of Nova Scotia (ATVANS)
PO Box 46020, Stn. Novalea, Halifax NS B3K 5V8
Tel: 902-241-3200; *Toll-Free:* 877-288-4244
admin@atvans.org
www.atvans.org
To represent the interest of ATV'ers to Government, Land owners, other recreation user groups and the general public and educate, inform and organize ATV'ers to preserve and expand ATV recreational opportunities to promote safe family activities.
Vince Sawler, President
Barry Barnet, Executive Director

Assiniboine Park Conservancy
55 Pavilion Cres., Winnipeg MB R3P 2N7
Tel: 204-927-6001
info@assiniboinepark.ca
www.zoosociety.com
www.instagram.com/assiniboineparkzoo
www.facebook.com/assiniboineparkzoo
twitter.com/assiniboinepark
To redevelop & manage the Park's operations & ongoing financial viability
Hartley Richardson, Chair
Margaret Redmond, President & CEO

Association des camps du Québec inc. (ACQ) / Québec Camping Association
CP 1000, Succ. M, 4545, av Pierre-de Coubertin, Montréal QC H1V 3R2
Tél: 514-252-3113; *Téléc:* 514-252-1650
Ligne sans frais: 800-361-3586
info@camps.qc.ca
www.camps.qc.ca
www.instagram.com/campsduquebec
www.facebook.com/130062375961
Assurer le développement, la promotion et la qualité des camps de vacances; s'assurer de la formation du personnel des camps
Eric Beauchemin, Directeur

Bike Ottawa
PO Box 248, Stn. B, Ottawa ON K1P 6C4
info@bikeottawa.ca
www.bikeottawa.ca
www.facebook.com/BikeOttawa
twitter.com/BikeOttawa
To promote cycling as fun, healthy, safe, economical, & environmentally-friendly transportation & recreation
Heather Shearer, President

Boating Ontario
15 Laurier Rd., Penetanguishene ON L9M 1G8
Tel: 705-549-1667; *Fax:* 705-549-1670
Toll-Free: 888-547-6662
info@boatingontario.ca
www.boatingontario.ca
www.facebook.com/BoatingOntario
twitter.com/boatingontario
To promote recreational boating throughout Ontario
Rick Layzell, Chief Executive Officer

British Columbia Camping Association
BC
info@bccamping.org
bccamping.org
www.facebook.com/BCCampingassociation
To facilitate the development of organized camping in order to provide educational, character-building & constructive recreational experiences for all people; to develop awareness & appreciation of the natural environment
Margo Dunnet, President
Stephanie Mikalishen, Secretary
Conor Lorimer, Treasurer

British Columbia Recreation & Parks Association (BCRPA)
#301, 470 Granville St., Vancouver BC V6C 1V5
Tel: 604-629-0965; *Fax:* 604-629-2651
Toll-Free: 866-929-0965
bcrpa@bcrpa.bc.ca
www.bcrpa.bc.ca
twitter.com/bcrpa
To establish & sustain healthy lifestyles & communities in British Columbia
Darryl Condon, President
Holly-Ann Burrows, Manager, Communication
Sandra Couto, Manager, Finance
Sara Ferguson, Clerk

The Bruce Trail Conservancy
PO Box 857, Hamilton ON L8N 3N9
Tel: 905-529-6821; *Fax:* 905-628-8081
Toll-Free: 800-665-4453
info@brucetrail.org
www.brucetrail.org
www.facebook.com/TheBruceTrailConservancy
twitter.com/BruceTrail_BTC
To secure, develop & manage the Bruce Trail as a public footpath along the Niagara Escarpment from Queenston to Tobermory, thereby promoting preservation of the escarpment's ecological & cultural integrity & fostering an appreciation of its natural beauty. The Bruce Trail, designated as a UNESCO World Biosphere Reserve, is Canada's oldest & longest footpath.
Leah Myers, Interim CEO

Campground Owners Association of Nova Scotia (COANS)
c/o Tourism Industry Association of Nova Scotia, 2089 Maitland St., Halifax NS B3K 2Z8
Tel: 902-496-7474
www.campingnovascotia.com
To provide the best camping experience possible throughout our diverse province; To improve standards at all the province's campgrounds; to provide leadership to this important segment of the provincial economy
Jennifer Falkenham, General Manager

Camping Association of Nova Scotia & PEI (CANSPEI)
c/o Sports Nova Scotia, 5516 Spring Garden Rd., 4th Fl., Halifax NS B3J 1G6
Tel: 902-220-3280
info@canspei.ca
canspei.ca
www.facebook.com/CANSPEI
twitter.com/CANSPEI
To support & serve the development of summer residential & organized camping in Nova Scotia & Prince Edward Island
Derek Mitchell, Executive Director

Canada's National Firearms Association (NFA)
PO Box 49090, Edmonton AB T6E 6H4
Tel: 780-439-1394; *Fax:* 780-439-4091
Toll-Free: 877-818-0393
info@nfa.ca
nfa.ca
www.youtube.com/c/CanadasNationalFirearmsAssociation
www.facebook.com/NFACANADA
twitter.com/CanadasNFA
To support hunting & sport shooting rights in Canada
Sheldon Clare, National President
Bill Rantz, Trasurer

Canadian Aerophilatelic Society (CAS) / La société canadienne d'aérophilatélie (SCA)
203A Woodfield Dr., Nepean ON K2G 4P2
www.aerophilately.ca
To represent Canadian aerophilatelists nationally & internationally
Steve Johnson, President
Brian Wolfenden, Secretary-Treasurer

Canadian Association of Numismatic Dealers (CAND) / Association canadienne des marchands numismatiques
c/o Dawn Bell, Executive Secretary, 1141 Main St., Moncton NB E1C 1H8
Tel: 506-333-7778
email@cand.org
www.cand.org
To ensure professionalism by members of the association
Michael Findlay, President
Yvon Chicoine, Vice-President
Mike Walsh, Secretary-Treasurer
Dawn Bell, Executive Secretary

Canadian Association of Wooden Money Collectors (CAWMC)
c/o Ross Kingdon, 12 Peter St., RR#1, Grand Valley ON L0N 1G0
www.nunet.ca/cawmc
Norm Belsten, Contact

Canadian Boating Federation / Fédération nautique du Canada
142, rue Saint-Philippe, Salaberry-de-Valleyfield QC J6S 3H4
Tel: 450-377-4122
info@cbfnc.ca
www.cbfnc.ca
Norm Woods, President

Canadian Bridge Federation (CFB) / La Fédération canadienne incorporée de bridge
c/o Ina Demme, 99 Ellis St., Nobleton ON L0G 1N0
Tel: 416-706-8550; Fax: 905-832-7184
cbf.ca
www.facebook.com/Canadian.Bridge.Federation
To conduct grassroot bridge events in Canada; To select & subsidize teams to World Championships
Niel Kimelman, President
Ina Demme, Executive Assisstant

Canadian Camping Association (CCA) / Association des camps du Canada (ACC)
info@ccamping.org
www.ccamping.org
www.facebook.com/CanadianCampingAssociation
twitter.com/ccampingorg
To develop & promote organized camping for all populations across Canada; To further the interests & welfare of children, youth & adults through camping; To encourage high standards in camping
Stéphane Richard, President

Canadian Casting Federation
c/o Toronto Sportsmen's Association, #66, 2700 Dufferin St., Toronto ON M6B 4J3
Tel: 416-487-4477; Fax: 416-487-4478
info@torontosportsmens.ca
www.torontosportsmens.ca/Casting.html
To teach casting skills, covering fly, bait & spinning

Canadian Correspondence Chess Association (CCCA) / L'Association canadienne des échecs par correspondance (ACEC)
c/o Manny Migicovsky, 1669, Country Rte 4, RR#1, L'Orignal QC K0B 1K0
Tel: 613-632-3166
ccca@cogeco.ca
correspondencechess.com/ccca
To promote chess playing via mail & e-mail both nationally & internationally
Manny Migicovsky, President

Canadian Federation of Outfitter Associations (CFOA) / Fédération canadienne des associations des pourvoiries
3137, rue Laberge, Québec QC G1X 4B5
Tel: 418-877-5191
info@goabc.org
www.canada-outfitters.com
To be the voice of the professional outfitting
Dominic Dugré, Président

Canadian Flag Association (CFA) / Association canadienne de vexillologie (ACV)
409 - 60C Line, Orangeville ON L9W 0A9
cfa.acv@gmail.com
cfa-acv.tripod.com
www.facebook.com/317266027131
To gather, organize & disseminate flag information with particular emphasis on flags having some association with Canada; To promote vexillology; To encourage & facilitate exchange of ideas between flag scholars, flag makers, flag collectors, flag designers & flag historians

Kevin Harrington, President

Canadian International DX Club (CIDX)
PO Box 67063, Stn. Lemoyne, Saint-Lambert QC J4R 2T8
cidxclub@yahoo.com
www.cidx.ca
To serve radio enthusiasts throughout the world

Canadian Paper Money Society (CPMS)
Attn: Dick Dunn, PO Box 562, Pickering ON L1V 2R7
info@cpmsonline.com
www.cpmsonline.ca
To encourage & support historical studies of banks & other paper money issuing authorities in Canada, to preserve their history & statistical records, & through research & publishing the results thereof, ensure that information, documents & other evidence of Canada's financial development will be preserved
Dick Dunn, Secretary-Treasurer

Canadian Parks & Recreation Association (CPRA) / Association canadienne des parcs et loisirs
PO Box 83069, 1180 Walkley Rd., Ottawa ON K1V 2M5
Tel: 613-523-5315
info@cpra.ca
www.cpra.ca
www.linkedin.com/in/cpra-acpl
www.facebook.com/168910893249240
twitter.com/CPRA_ACPL
To advocate on the benefits of parks & recreation services
CJ Noble, Executive Director

Canadian Parks & Wilderness Society (CPAWS) / Société pour la nature et les parcs du Canada (SNAP)
#600, 100 Gloucester St., Ottawa ON K2P 0A4
Tel: 613-569-7226; Fax: 613-569-7098
Toll-Free: 800-333-9453
info@cpaws.org
cpaws.org
www.youtube.com/cpawsnational
www.facebook.com/cpaws
twitter.com/cpaws
To act as the Canadian voice for public wilderness protection
Sandra Schwartz, National Executive Director
Tracy Walden, Director, Communications & Development

Canadian Racing Pigeon Union Inc.
261 Tillson Ave., #C, Tillsonburg ON N4G 5X2
Tel: 519-842-9771; Fax: 519-842-8809
Toll-Free: 866-652-5704
secretary@crpu.ca
www.crpu.ca
www.facebook.com/226183050750688
To promote the sport of pigeon racing in Canada
Jeff Hall, President
Denise Luscher, Administrator

Canadian Senior Pro Rodeo Association (CSPRA)
PO Box 393, Carseland AB T0J 0M0
Tel: 403-875-3242
info@canadaseniorrodeo.com
www.canadianseniorrodeo.com
To allow individuals over 40 to compete in rodeo events across Canada & North America

Canadian Stamp Dealers' Association (CSDA) / Association canadienne des négociants en timbres-poste (ACNTP)
PO Box 81, Stn. Lambeth, London ON N6P 1P9
director@csdaonline.com
www.csdaonline.com
www.facebook.com/214870458990
Angelo E. Komatsoulis, President
John Sheffield, Executive Director

Canadian Toy Collectors' Society Inc. (CTCS) / Société canadienne des collectionneurs de jouets
#245, 91 Rylander Blvd., Unit 7, Toronto ON M1B 5M5
ctcsweb@hotmail.com
www.ctcs.org
www.facebook.com/468396576552495
To promote interest in the collection & display of all types of toys, childhood memorabilia & literature; To acquire, maintain & house a collection of toys & to restore & preserve Canadian toys of historic significance
David Tozer, President

Chess Federation of Canada / Fédération canadienne des échecs
PO Box 85015, Stn. Brant Plaza, Burlington ON L7R 4K3
Tel: 289-337-0561
info@chess.ca
www.chess.ca
www.facebook.com/163031117086480
twitter.com/ChessCanada
To coordinate chess play across Canada
Vlad Drkulec, President
Robert Gillanders, Executive Director

Climb Yukon Association
YT
info@climbyukon.net
www.climbyukon.net
To develop to the climbing community in Yukon as a recreational opportunity for adults & youth; To raise awareness of & address access & safety concerns

Cycle Toronto
#307, 720 Bathurst St., Toronto ON M5S 2R4
Tel: 416-644-7188
www.cycleto.ca
www.facebook.com/cycletoronto
twitter.com/cycletoronto
Cycle Toronto is a member-supported organization that advocates for a healthy, safe, cycling-friendly city for all.
Jared Kolb, Executive Director

Federation of Ontario Cottagers' Associations (FOCA)
#201, 159 King St., Peterborough ON K9J 2R8
Tel: 705-749-3622; Fax: 705-749-6522
info@foca.on.ca
www.foca.on.ca
www.facebook.com/foca.on.ca
To ensure a healthy future for waterfront Ontario; To support the interests of Ontario's cottagers
Terry Rees, Executive Director

Fédération québécoise de camping et de caravaning inc. (FQCC)
#100, 1560, rue Eiffel, Boucherville QC J4B 5Y1
Tél: 450-650-3722; Téléc: 450-650-3721
Ligne sans frais: 877-650-3722
info@fqcc.ca
www.fqcc.ca
www.youtube.com/user/LaFQCC
www.facebook.com/LaFQCC
twitter.com/lafqcc
Unir les adepts du camping et du caravaning; Entreprendre et coordonner des actions relatives au camping et au caravaning
Michel Quintal, Président
André Rivest, Directeur général

Fédération québécoise des échecs (FQE) / Québec Chess Federation
4545, rue Pierre-de-Coubertin, Montréal QC H1V 0B2
Tél: 514-252-3034; Téléc: 514-251-8038
info@fqechecs.qc.ca
www.fqechecs.qc.ca
www.facebook.com/eqechecs
twitter.com/fqechecs
Promouvoir l'étude, l'enseignement et la pratique du jeu d'échecs au Québec
Richard Bérubé, Directeur Général

Fédération québécoise des jeux récréatifs (FQJR)
4545, av Pierre-de Coubertin, Montréal QC H1V 0B2
Tél: 514-252-3032
info@quebecjeux.org
www.quebecjeux.org
www.youtube.com/user/FQJRJeux
www.facebook.com/355560369062
De promouvoir des sports de loisirs et jeux
Dominic Robitaille, Président

Guide Outfitters Association of British Columbia (GOABC)
#103, 19140 - 28th Ave., Surrey BC V3S 6M3
Tel: 604-541-6332; Fax: 604-541-6339
info@goabc.org
www.goabc.org
www.instagram.com/guideoutfittersassociationofbc
www.facebook.com/GOABC1966
twitter.com/GOABC
To market the Canadian northwest as the premier hunting destination in Canada while endorsing the responsible, sustainable & ethical use of wildlife as a recreational resource
Dale Drown, General Manager

Halifax North West Trails Association (HNWTA)
c/o 27 Warwick Lane, Halifax NS B3M 4J3

Tel: 902-443-5051
info@halifaxnorthwesttrails.ca
www.halifaxnorthwesttrails.ca
www.facebook.com/124497311008207
twitter.com/HalifaxNWTrails

To promote the creation, protection and maintenance of trails within the Halifax Mainland North area.
Todd Beal, Chair

Hike Ontario
262 Lavender Dr., Ancaster ON L9K 1E5

Tel: 905-277-4453; *Toll-Free:* 800-894-7249
info@hikeontario.com
www.hikeontario.com
www.youtube.com/takeahikeontario
www.facebook.com/hikeontario
twitter.com/HikeOntario

To act as the voice for hikers & walkers in Ontario; To encourage hiking, walking & trail development in Ontario; To promote trail maintenance, best practices, & safe hiking; To enhance environmental awareness, conservation & sustainable trails
Tom Friesen, President
Stacey Hodder, Secretary
Roma Juneja, Treasurer

Manitoba Camping Association (MCA)
Manitoba Camping Association Sunshine Fund, 545 Telfer St. South, Winnipeg MB R3G 2Y4

Tel: 204-784-1134
sunshinefund@mbcamping.ca
www.mbcamping.ca
www.facebook.com/sunshinefundmb
twitter.com/SunshineFundMB

To act as a coordinating body for organized camping in Manitoba; To promote organized camping as an educational and recreational experience
Liz Kovach, Executive Director
Kelly Giddings, Coordinator, Outdoor Learning & Member Services
Sydney Kazina, Coordinator, Sunshine Fund

Model Aeronautics Association of Canada Inc. (MAAC) / Modélistes Aéronautiques Associés du Canada
#9, 5100 South Service Rd., Burlington ON L7L 6A5

Tel: 905-632-9808; *Fax:* 905-632-3304
Toll-Free: 855-359-6222
office@maac.ca
www.maac.ca
www.facebook.com/FlyMAAC

To foster, enhance, assist, aid & engage in scientific development; To provide central organization to record & disseminate information relating to model aeronautics; To guide & direct national model aviation activities; To direct technical organization of national & international model aircraft contests
Peter Schaffer, President

National Association of Watch & Clock Collectors, Inc. (NAWCC)
514 Poplar St., Columbia PA 17512-2130 USA

Tel: 717-684-8261; *Fax:* 717-684-0878
info@nawcc.org
www.nawcc.org
www.youtube.com/c/NationalWatchClockMuseum
www.linkedin.com/company/nawcc-inc-
www.facebook.com/nawcc
twitter.com/museumoftime

To stimulate interest in timepieces; To collect & preserve horological materials & information; To work with others in exhibiting timepieces; To encourage timepiece collection; To disseminate information on timepieces; To facilitate timepiece markets
Tom Wilcox, Executive Director

Newfoundland & Labrador Camping Association
c/o Malcolm Turner, President, 27 Earle Dr., Pasadena NL A0L 1K0

Tel: 709-686-2363

To facilitate the development of organized camping in order to provide educational, character-building & constructive recreational experiences for all people; to develop awareness & appreciation of the natural environment
Malcolm Turner, President

Northwest Territories Recreation & Parks Association (NWTRPA)
PO Box 841, 4908 - 49th St., Yellowknife NT X1A 2N6

Tel: 867-669-8375; *Fax:* 867-669-6971
admin@nwtrpa.org
www.nwtrpa.org
www.facebook.com/260257614047483

To promote recreation by supporting leaders, communities & partners through training, advocacy & networking
Sheena Tremblay, Executive Director
Kaila Jefferd-Moore, Membership & Communications Coordinator

Nova Scotia Trails Federation (NSTF)
5516 Spring Garden Rd., 4th Fl., Halifax NS B3J 1G6

Tel: 902-425-5454; *Fax:* 902-425-5606
info@nstrails.com
nstrails.com
www.facebook.com/nstrails
twitter.com/NSTrails

To promote the development & responsible use of recreational trails for the benefit & enjoyment of all Nova Scotians & visitors to the province
Heather Stilwell, Managing Director

Ontario Camps Association (OCA)
70 Martin Ross Ave., Toronto ON M3J 2L4

Tel: 416-485-0425; *Fax:* 416-485-0422
Toll-Free: 844-485-0425
info@ontariocamps.ca
www.ontariocamps.ca
www.facebook.com/OntarioCampsAssociation
twitter.com/OCACamps

To promote youth camping throughout Ontario; To maintain high standards for organized camping; To advocate on issues which impact members

Ontario Numismatic Association (ONA)
c/o Dave Bawcutt, PO Box 40033, RPO Waterloo Sq., Waterloo ON N2J 4V1

membership@the-ona.ca
the-ona.ca

Scott Douglas, President

Ontario Parks Association (OPA)
7856 - 5th Line South, RR#4, Milton ON L9T 2X8

Tel: 905-864-6182; *Fax:* 905-864-6184
Toll-Free: 866-560-7783
opa@ontarioparksassociation.ca
www.ontarioparksassociation.ca

To develop & protect parks & green spaces in Ontario
Paul Ronan, Executive Director
Shelley May, Office Manager

Ontario Recreation Facilities Association (ORFA)
#102, 1 Concorde Gate, Toronto ON M3C 3N6

Tel: 416-426-7062; *Fax:* 416-426-7385
Toll-Free: 800-661-6732
info@orfa.com
www.orfa.com

To provide leadership for the recreation facility profession in Ontario; To promote the professional operation of recreation facilities throughout the province
Steve Hardie, RRFA, CIT, CPT, President & Chair
John Milton, Chief Administrative Officer
Remo Petrongolo, Director, Business Development
Terry Piche, RRFA, CIT, Director, Technical
Hubie Basilio, Coordinator, Public Relations & Communications
Rebecca Russell, Facilities Librarian

Ontario Research Council on Leisure (ORCOL) / Conseil Ontarien de Recherche en Loisir
c/o Recreation & Leisure Studies, Faculty of Applied Health Sciences, University of Waterloo, Waterloo ON N2L 3G1

ahsweb@healthy.uwaterloo.ca
www.orcol.uwaterloo.ca

To disseminate research about leisure & recreation, including culture, tourism, fitness, & sports
Bryan Smale, President
Don Reid, Treasurer

Ontario Trails Council (OTC) / Conseil des Sentiers de l'Ontario
PO Box 500, Deseronto ON K0K 1X0

www.ontariotrails.on.ca
www.youtube.com/user/ontrails
www.facebook.com/OntarioTrails
twitter.com/ontrails

To promote the creation, development, preservation, management & use of an integrated, recreational, multi-seasonal trail network in Ontario; To show interest in all types of trails for non-motorized & motorized (where applicable) use in all seasons; To acquire & convert Ontario's abandoned railway

rights-of-way to linear greenways for year-round recreational activities for the people of Ontario
Patrick Connor, CAE, Executive Director
Paul Ronan, Chair, Education Program

Ontario Vintage Radio Association (OVRA)
ON

www.ovra.ca

To preserve Canada's radio history, literature & equipment; to serve as a forum for members to exchange information & continue the legacy of the original club.

Outdoor Recreation Council of British Columbia (ORC)
47 West Broadway, Vancouver BC V5Y 1P1

Tel: 604-873-5546
outdoorrec@orcbc.ca
www.orcbc.ca

To advise industry & government in the development & implementation of outdoor recreation & conservation plans for BC; to contribute to the coordination of regional outdoor recreation by assisting in the establishment of a provincial network of outdoor recreationists to address recreational use conflicts & to advise government & industry on local & regional needs for noncompetitive outdoor recreation; to encourage active participation by the residents of BC in outdoor recreation activities; to promote the quality & diversity of outdoor recreation opportunities in BC by working cooperatively with government, industry, business & the public.
Dennis Webb, Chair
Jeremy McCall, Executive Director

Outward Bound Canada
Centre for Green Cities, #404, 550 Bayview Ave., Toronto ON M4W 3X8

Fax: 705-382-5959
Toll-Free: 888-688-9273
info@outwardbound.ca
www.outwardbound.ca
www.youtube.com/user/OutwardBoundCanada
www.linkedin.com/company/outward-bound-canada
www.facebook.com/outwardboundcanada
twitter.com/OutwardBoundCan

To promote self-reliance, care & respect for others, responsibility to community & concern for the environment
Sarah Wiley, Executive Director

Parks & Recreation Ontario (PRO) / Parcs et loisirs de l'Ontario
#302, 1 Concorde Gate, Toronto ON M3C 3N6

Tel: 416-426-7142; *Fax:* 416-426-7371
Toll-Free: 877-422-9838
pro@prontario.org
www.prontario.org
www.facebook.com/PROntario
twitter.com/prontario

To enhance the quality of life, health & well-being of people, their communities & their environments; To advocate provincially for parks & recreation issues; To provide networking as well as multi-discipline professional development opportunities
Cathy Denyer, Chief Executive Officer

Rando Québec
4545, av Pierre-de Coubertin, Montréal QC H1V 0B2

Tél: 514-252-3157
info@randoquebec.ca
www.randoquebec.ca
www.facebook.com/RandoQC

Promotion de la marche et de la randonnée pedestre; support au développement de lieux de marche
Jean-Luc Caillaud, Directeur général
Émilie Saulnier-Burelle, Directrice, Communication et marketing

Recreation & Parks Association of the Yukon (RPAY)
4061 - 4th Ave., Whitehorse YT Y1A 1H1

Tel: 867-668-3010; *Fax:* 867-668-2455
rpay@klondiker.com
www.rpay.org
www.facebook.com/goRPAY
twitter.com/RPAY1

To promote, encourage and foster the growth and development of all areas of recreation throughout the Yukon Territory.
Ian Spencer, President
Anne Morgan, Executive Director

Recreation Facilities Association of British Columbia (RFABC)
PO Box 53590, Stn. Broadmead, Victoria BC V8X 5K2

Toll-Free: 877-285-3421
info@rfabc.com
www.rfabc.com

To promote safe & successful operating standards for community centres, swimming pools, arenas, stadiums, & parks in British Columbia; To encourage professionalism among recreation facility operators
Dwayne Kalynchuk, Executive Director
Dan Pagely, Manager, Business & Marketing
Don Chow, Manager, Communications

Recreation New Brunswick
70 Melissa St., Fredericton NB E3A 6W1
Tel: 506-459-1929; *Fax:* 506-450-6066
info@recreationnb.ca
www.recreationnb.ca
www.instagram.com/recreationnb
www.facebook.com/RecreationNB
twitter.com/RecreationNB
To develop a professional organization for members; To enhance the image of recreation to government & the general public; To develop liaisons with other recreation groups; To affect legislation in the field of recreation & parks
Chris Gallant, Executive Director
Michelle DeCourcey, Coordinator, Project Development
Peter Morrison, Coordinator, Training & Services

Recreation Newfoundland & Labrador
PO Box 8700, St. John's NL A1B 4J6
Tel: 709-729-3892; *Fax:* 709-729-3814
info@recreationnl.com
www.recreationnl.com
www.facebook.com/455370901173112
To promote, foster & develop recreation; to provide a full range of services to enrich the concept of leisure throughout Newfoundland & Labrador; to enable individual citizens to improve their quality of life.
Dawn Sharpe, President
Gary Milley, Executive Director

Recreation Nova Scotia (RNS)
#309, 5516 Spring Garden Rd., Halifax NS B3J 1G6
Tel: 902-425-1128; *Fax:* 902-422-8201
www.recreationns.ns.ca
www.linkedin.com/company/recreation-nova-scotia
www.facebook.com/RecreationNovaScotia
twitter.com/recreationns
To build healthier futures through programs & services that promote the benefits of recreation
Rhonda Lemire, Executive Director
Rae Gunn, President

Roller Sports Canada / Sports à roulettes du Canada
1 Bancroft Cres., Whitby ON L1R 2E6
Tel: 905-666-9343
rollersports@hotmail.com
rollersports.ca

Tim Macri, Treasurer

Royal Canadian Numismatic Association (RCNA)
#432, 5694 Hwy. 7 East, Markham ON L3P 1B4
Tel: 647-401-4014; *Fax:* 905-472-9645
info@rcna.ca
www.rcna.ca
www.facebook.com/TheRCNA
To encourage & promote education in the science of numismatics, through the study of coins, paper money, medals, tokens & all other numismatic items, with special emphasis on material pertaining to Canada
Robert Forbes, President

The Royal Philatelic Society of Canada (RPSC) / La Société royale de philatélie du Canada (SRPC)
PO Box 69080, Stn. St Clair, Toronto ON M4T 3A1
Tel: 416-921-2077; *Fax:* 416-921-1282
Toll-Free: 888-285-4143
info@rpsc.org
www.rpsc.org
www.facebook.com/Royal.Philatelic.Society.Canada
To promote the hobby of stamp collecting; To use stamps & postal history in education for youths & adults
Ed Kroft, President
Sam Chiu, Vice-President

Saskatchewan Association of Recreation Professionals (SARP)
88 Saskatchewan St. East, Moose Jaw SK S6H 0V4
Tel: 306-693-7277; *Fax:* 306-988-8839
office@sarponlin.ca
www.sarp-online.ca
www.facebook.com/165792676792454
To be committed to supporting & being the voice of professionals working in the field of recreation in Saskatchewan
Nicole Goldsworthy, Chair

Saskatchewan Camping Association (SCA)
3950 Castle Rd., Regina SK S4S 6A4
Tel: 306-586-4026; *Fax:* 306-790-8634
To promote the development of quality organized camping in Saskatchewan; To act as the voice for leaders of organized camps throughout Saskatchewan
Donna Wilkinson, Executive Director

Saskatchewan Parks & Recreation Association (SPRA)
#100, 1445 Park St., Regina SK S4N 4C5
Tel: 306-780-9231; *Fax:* 306-780-9257
Toll-Free: 800-563-2555
office@spra.sk.ca
www.spra.sk.ca
To stimulate & advance parks, recreation & leisure activities, facilities, & programs in Saskatchewan
Todd Shafer, Chief Executive Officer

Sunbeam Sportscar Owners Club of Canada (SSOCC)

Trail Riders of the Canadian Rockies
PO Box 6742, Stn. D, Calgary AB T2P 2E6
Tel: 403-874-4408
admin@trail-rides.ca
trailridevacations.com
www.facebook.com/18917401782454O
To encourage travel on horseback through the Canadian Rockies; to foster the maintenance & improvement of old trails & the building of new trails; to promote good fellowship among those who visit & live in the Canadian Rockies; to encourage the appreciation of outdoor life & the study & conservation of mountain ecology; to assist in every way possible to ensure the preservation of the National Parks of Canada for the use & enjoyment of the public; to cooperate with other organizations with similar aims
Robert Vanderzweerde, Secretary-Treasurer

Trans Canada Trail Foundation (TCTF) / Fondation du sentier transcanadian
#300, 321, rue de la Commune ouest, Montréal QC H2Y 2E1
Tel: 514-485-3959; *Fax:* 514-485-4541
Toll-Free: 800-465-3636
info@tctrail.ca
www.tctrail.ca
www.youtube.com/user/TheTransCanadaTrail
www.linkedin.com/company/trans-canada-trail
www.facebook.com/transcanadatrail
twitter.com/TCTrail
To promote & coordinate the planning, designing & building of a continuous, shared-use recreation trail that winds its way through every Province & Territory
Jane Murphy, National Director of Trail
Gay Decker, Director of Communications
Amparo Jardine, Director of Development

Velo Halifax Bicycle Club
PO Box 125, Dartmouth NS B2Y 3Y2
cycling@chebucto.ns.ca
www.velohalifax.com
Terry Walker, President

Vintage Road Racing Association (VRRA)
info@vrra.ca
www.vrra.ca
www.facebook.com/groups/18352114680
To promote & maintain the sport & traditions of racing classic & vintage machines

YMCA Canada
#601, 1867 Younge St., Toronto ON M4S 1Y5
Tel: 416-967-9622; *Fax:* 416-967-9618
www.ymca.ca
www.facebook.com/YMCACanada
twitter.com/YMCA_Canada
To help grow all persons in spirit, mind & body, & in a sense of responsibility to each other & the global community; To foster & stimulate the development of strong member associations & advocate on their behalf regionally, nationally & internationally
Peter Dinsdale, President & CEO
Kathryn Ross, Chief Financial Officer
Angela de Burger, Manager, External Communications & Marketing

Yukon Outdoors Club (YOC)
4061 - 4th Ave., Whitehorse YT Y1A 1H1
yukonoutdoorsclub@gmail.com
www.yukonoutdoorsclub.ca
To co-ordinate trips that promote the enjoyment of the outdoors

YWCA Canada / Association des jeunes femmes chrétiennes du Canada
104 Edward St., 1st Fl., Toronto ON M5G 0A7
Tel: 416-962-8881; *Fax:* 416-962-8084
national@ywcacanada.ca
www.ywcacanada.ca
www.instagram.com/ywcacanada
www.facebook.com/ywcacanada
twitter.com/YWCA_Canada
To coordinate the YWCA movement in Canada, & advocate for the equity & equality rights of women; To raise awareness on the prevention of violence against women, end homelessness for women & the need for universal, accessible & quality child care & economic equality
Maya Roy, Chief Executive Officer
Raine Liliefeldt, Director, Member Services & Development

Recycling

Association of Alberta Coordinated Action for Recycling Enterprises
5212 - 49 St., Leduc AB T9E 7H5
Tel: 780-980-0035; *Fax:* 780-980-0232
Toll-Free: 866-818-2273
www.albertacare.org
To support waste management & recycling activities at the community level in Alberta
Linda McDonald, Executive Director

Automotive Recyclers Association of Manitoba (ARM)
PO Box 43049, Stn. Kildonan Place, Winnipeg MB R2C 5G5
Tel: 204-654-2726
www.arm.mb.ca
To provide quality recycled auto parts; To serve its customers & communities; To help the environment
Alec Gilman, President

New Brunswick Solid Waste Association (NBSWA) / l'Association des déchets solides du Nouveau-Brunswick (ADSNB)
32 Wedgewood Dr., Rothesay NB E2E 3P7
Tel: 506-849-4218; *Fax:* 506-847-1369
Toll-Free: 877-777-4218
nbswa@nbnet.nb.ca
To promote environmentally friendly solid waste management practices in New Brunswick

Reproductive Issues

Action Canada for Sexual Health & Rights / Action Canada pour la santé et les droits sexuels
501 - 240 Bank St., Ottawa ON K2P 1X4
Tel: 613-241-4474; *Toll-Free:* 888-642-2725
info@actioncanadashr.org
www.actioncanadashr.org
www.instagram.com/actioncanadaSHR
www.facebook.com/actioncanadashr
twitter.com/actioncanadashr
To advance sexual & reproductive health & rights in Canada & abroad through public education & awareness; To provide support for the delivery of programs & services in Canada
Sandeep Prasad, Executive Director

Birthright International / Accueil Grossesse
777 Coxwell Ave., Toronto ON M4C 3C6
Tel: 416-469-4789; *Fax:* 416-469-1772
Crisis Hot-Line: 800-550-4900
contact@birthright.org
www.birthright.org
To provide non-judgmental support to women facing an unplanned pregnancy, helping them carry their baby to term

Canadian Fertility & Andrology Society (CFAS) / Société canadienne de fertilité et d'andrologie
#301, 1719, rue Grand Trunk, Montréal QC H3K 1M1
Tel: 514-524-9009; *Fax:* 514-524-2163
info@cfas.ca
www.cfas.ca
To speak on behalf of interested parties in the field of assisted reproductive technologies & research in reproductive sciences
Eileen McMahon, President
Jason Hitkari, Vice-President
Simon Phillips, Treasurer
Goldie Gill, Executive Director

Fédération du Québec pour le planning des naissances (FQPN)
#335, 469, rue Jean-Talon ouest, Montréal QC H3N 1R4
Tél: 514-866-3721; Téléc: 514-866-1100
info@fqpn.qc.ca
www.fqpn.qc.ca
www.facebook.com/FQPN.Qc
twitter.com/_FQPN_

Promouvoir les droits des femmes dans le domaine de la santé, particulièrement la reproduction et la sexualité; promouvoir l'accès à une information critique et fiable, la liberté de choix et le consentement des femmes face à leur propre corps

Fertility Matters Canada (FMC)
PO Box 30013, Moncton QC E1C 0N2
Tel: 514-853-4401; Toll-Free: 800-263-2929
info@fertilitymatters.ca
www.iaac.ca
www.instagram.com/fertility_canada
www.facebook.com/fertilitymatterscanada
twitter.com/fertilitymattrs

To offer assistance, support & education to individuals with infertility concerns; To increase the awareness & understanding of the causes, treatments & the emotional impact of infertility through the development of educational programs
Sara R. Cohen, President
Carolynn Dubé, Executive Director

Life's Vision Manitoba Inc.
618 Muriel St., Winnipeg MB R2Y 0Y2
Tel: 204-233-8047; Fax: 204-233-0523
Toll-Free: 877-233-8048
lifecollective.io
www.facebook.com/244844832240237
twitter.com/LifesVision1

To engage in non-sectarian educational activities in order to encourage & promote among the general public an understanding & awareness of the dignity & worth of each individual human life, whatever its state & circumstances; To foster respect for all human life

Natural Family Planning Association
#205, 3050 Yonge St., Toronto ON M4N 2K4
Tel: 416-481-5465
www.naturalfamilyplanning.ca

To promote the Billings Ovulation Method of natural family planning which is based on an awareness of a woman's physical systems to gauge optimum fertility state

Newfoundland & Labrador Right to Life Association
PO Box 5427, 195 Freshwater Rd., St. John's NL A1C 5W2
Tel: 709-579-1500; Fax: 709-579-1600
Toll-Free: 877-997-5433
centreforlife@centreforlife.ca
www.centreforlife.ca

To promote a pro-life culture
Linda Holden, President

Ontario Coalition for Abortion Clinics (OCAC)
PO Box 3, 427 Bloor St. West, Toronto ON M5S 1X7
Tel: 416-969-8463
ocac88@gmail.com
ocac-choice.com
www.facebook.com/OCAC88
twitter.com/OCAC25

To work for reproductive rights & access to abortions

Options for Sexual Health (OPT)
3550 East Hastings St., Vancouver BC V5K 2A7
Tel: 604-731-4252; Fax: 604-731-4698
info@optbc.org
www.optionsforsexualhealth.org
www.facebook.com/optbc
twitter.com/optbc

To promote optimal sexual health for all British Columbians by supporting reproductive choice, reducing unplanned pregnancy, & providing quality education, information & clinical services
Michelle Fortin, Executive Director
Ashleigh Turner, Director, Communications

Planned Parenthood - Newfoundland & Labrador Sexual Health Centre (NLSHC)
47 St. Clare Ave., St. John's NL A1C 2J9
Tel: 709-579-1009; Fax: 709-726-2308
Toll-Free: 877-666-9847
pp.nlshc@gmail.com
www.plannedparenthoodnlshc.com
www.instagram.com/plannedparenthoodnlshc
www.facebook.com/PlannedParenthoodNL
twitter.com/NLSexualHealth

To promote positive sexual health attitudes & practices throughout Newfoundland & Labrador; To support & respect individual choice

Shannon Driscoll, Executive Director

The Right to Life Association of Toronto & Area
#302, 120 Eglinton Ave. East, Toronto ON M4P 1E2
Tel: 416-483-7869
www.righttolife.to
www.facebook.com/righttolifeto

To uphold the right to life as the basic human right on which all others depend; to provide information & services to that end

Sexual Health Centre Saskatoon (PPSC)
210 - 2 Ave. North, Saskatoon SK S7K 2B5
Tel: 306-244-7989; Fax: 306-652-4034
info@shcsaskatoon.ca
www.sexualhealthcentresaskatoon.ca

To provide sexuality, contraception, & reproduction information, resources, & support services for members of the community
Jillian Arkles Schwandt, Executive Director

Sexuality Education Resource Centre Manitoba (SERC)
#200, 226 Osborne St. North, Winnipeg MB R3C 1V4
Tel: 204-982-7800; Fax: 204-982-7819
www.serc.mb.ca
www.youtube.com/user/sercmbca
www.facebook.com/sercmb
twitter.com/serc_mb

To promote universal access to comprehensive, reliable information & services on sexuality & related health issues by fostering awareness, understanding & support through education
Nicole Chammartin, Executive Director

Signal Hill
PO Box 45076, Stn. Langley Crossing, Langley BC V2Y 0C9
Tel: 604-532-0023; Fax: 604-532-0094
Toll-Free: 877-774-4625
www.thesignalhill.com
www.youtube.com/thesignalhill
www.facebook.com/thesignalhill

To offer education about life issues, women's health & human rights; To promote the value of human life
Derek Scott, Executive Director

World Organization Ovulation Method Billings Inc.
1506 Dansey Ave., Coquitlam BC V3K 3J1
Tel: 604-936-4472; Fax: 604-936-5690
www.woomb.ca

To teach fertility awareness & natural family planning

Research & Scholarship

AllerGen NCE Inc.
Michael DeGroote Centre for Learning & Discovery, McMaster University, #3120, 1280 Main St. West, Hamilton ON L8S 4K1
Tel: 905-525-9140; Fax: 905-524-0611
info@allergen-nce.ca
www.allergen-nce.ca

To support research, capacity building activities & networking regarding allergic disease in Canada; To reduce the mortality & socio-economic impacts of allergy, asthma & related immune diseases
Diana Royce, President & CEO
Judah Denburg, Scientific Director
Kim Wright, Director, Communications & Knowledge Mobilization

American Musicological Society (AMS)
20 Cooper Sq., 2nd Fl., New York NY 10003 USA
Tel: 212-992-6340; Fax: 212-995-4022
Toll-Free: 877-679-7648
ams@ams-net.org
www.ams-net.org
www.youtube.com/user/amsformusicology
www.linkedin.com/company/american-musicological-society
www.facebook.com/AMS.musicology
twitter.com/AMS_musicology

To advance research in the various fields of music as a branch of learning & scholarship
Siovahn Walker, Executive Director
Katie VanDerMeer, Office Manager

ArcticNet Inc.
Pavillon Alexandre-Vachon, Université Laval, #4081, 1045, av de la Médecine, Québec QC G1V 0A6
Tel: 418-656-5830; Fax: 418-656-2334
arcticnet@arcticnet.ulaval.ca
www.arcticnet.ulaval.ca
twitter.com/arcticnet

To study the impacts of climate change in the coastal Canadian Arctic; To engage Inuit organizations, northern communities, universities, research institutes, industry, government & international agencies as partners in the scientific process

Martin Fortier, Executive Director
Louis Fortier, Scientific Director

Association for Canadian Studies (ACS) / Association d'études canadiennes (AEC)
#850, 1980, rue Sherbrooke ouest, Montréal QC H3H 1E8
Tel: 514-925-3096; Fax: 514-925-3095
general@acs-aec.ca
acs-aec.ca
www.linkedin.com/company/acs-aec
www.facebook.com/acs.aec.canadianstudies
twitter.com/Canadianstudies

To initiate & support activities in the areas of research, teaching, communications & the training of students in Canadian studies, especially in interdisciplinary & multidisciplinary perspectives; To strive to raise public awareness of Canadian issues
Jack Jedwab, President & CEO
James Ondrick, Director, Programs & Administration

AUTO21 Network of Centres of Excellence
401 Sunset Ave., Windsor ON N9B 3P4
Tel: 519-253-3000; Fax: 519-971-3626
info@auto21.ca
www.auto21.ca
www.youtube.com/user/AUTO21NCE
www.linkedin.com/groups/2804256
www.facebook.com/AUTO21
twitter.com/auto21nce

To partner the public & private sectors in applied automotive R&D
Peter Frise, CEO & Scientific Director
Michelle Watters, COO & Executive Director
Stephanie Campeau, Director, Public Affairs & Communications

Canada Media Fund (CMF)
#4, 50 Wellington St. East, Toronto ON M5E 1C8
Tel: 416-214-4400; Fax: 416-214-4420
Toll-Free: 877-975-0766
info@cmf-fmc.ca
www.cmf-fmc.ca
www.facebook.com/cmf.fmc
twitter.com/cmf_fmc

To provide funding to Canada's television & digital media industries through the following two streams: Experimental & Convergent.
Louis L. Roquet, Chair
Valerie Creighton, President & CEO
Stéphane Cardin, Vice-President, Industry & Public Affairs
Sandra Collins, Vice-President & CFO, Operations

Canadian Anthropology Society (CASCA) / Société canadienne d'Anthropologie
c/o Karli Whitmore, #301, 125, rue Dean de la Londe, Baie d'Urfe QC H9X 3TB
www.cas-sca.ca
www.facebook.com/132028862261
twitter.com/CASCATweet

To promote anthropology in Canada
Martha Radice, President
Udo Krautwurst, Treasurer
Charles Menzies, Secretary

Canadian Association of Aesthetic Medicine (CAAM) / L'association canadienne de médecine esthétique
#220, 445 Mountain Hwy., North Vancouver BC V7J 2L1
Tel: 604-988-0450; Fax: 604-929-0871
info@caam.ca
www.caam.ca

CAAM is the face of aesthetic medicine in Canada, comprising of a multidisciplinary group of aesthetic physicians from various backgrounds and interests.
Susan Roberts, Executive Director

Canadian Carbonization Research Association (CCRA)
c/o Ted Todoschuk, PO Box 2460, 1330 Burlington St. East, Hamilton ON L8N 3J5
Tel: 905-548-4796; Fax: 905-548-4653
www.cancarb.ca

To fund coke & coal research in Canada for benefit of member companies
Ted Todoschuk, Contact

Canadian Committee of Byzantinists
Talbot College, Univ. of Western Ontario, London ON N6A 3K7
Tel: 519-661-3045; Fax: 519-850-2388

To network among Canadian Byzantinists; To promote communications & exchange of information; To promote Byzantine Studies in Canada
Geoffrey Greatrex, President

Canadian Federation for the Humanities & Social Sciences (CFHSS) / Fédération Canadienne des Sciences Humaines
#300, 275 Bank St., Ottawa ON K2P 2L6
Tel: 613-238-6112; *Fax:* 613-238-6114
info@ideas-idees.ca
www.ideas-idees.ca
www.youtube.com/user/IdeasIdees
www.linkedin.com/company/canadian-federation-for-the-humanities-and-social-sciences
www.facebook.com/ideas.idees
twitter.com/ideas_idees
To support and advance Canada's research in the humanities & social science fields
Camille Ferrier, Communications Officer

Canadian Institute for Advanced Research (CIFAR) / Institut canadien de recherches avancées (ICRA)
#1400, 180 Dundas St. West, Toronto ON M5G 1Z8
Tel: 416-971-4251; *Fax:* 416-971-6169
Toll-Free: 888-738-1113
info@cifar.ca
www.ciar.ca
www.linkedin.com/company/canadian-institute-for-advanced-research
www.facebook.com/CIFAR
twitter.com/cifar_news
To stimulate leading-edge research projects vital to Canada's future prosperity.
Alan Bernstein, President/CEO

Canadian Institute for Mediterranean Studies (CIMS) / Institut canadien d'études méditerranéennes
c/o Carr Hall, Department of Italian Studies, University of Toronto, 100 St Joseph St., Toronto ON M5S 1J4
sites.utoronto.ca/cims
To study all aspects of Mediterranean culture & civilization, past & present
Mario Crespi, Executive Director

Canadian Institute for Research in Nondestructive Examination (CINDE)
135 Fennell Ave. West, Hamilton ON L8N 3T2
Tel: 905-387-1655; *Fax:* 905-574-6080
Toll-Free: 800-964-9488
www.cinde.ca
www.facebook.com/297023083473
To foster, coordinate & disseminate results of research, development & application of new or advanced NDE techniques in Canada; to promote technology transfer by encouraging collaboration between universities, research organizations & industrial or governmental users; to raise the profile of NDE research in Canada by publicizing the need for & economic benefits arising from advances in NDE
Larry Côté, President and CEO

Canadian Institute of Ukrainian Studies (CIUS) / Institut canadien d'études ukrainiennes
#4-30, Pembina Hall, University of Alberta, Edmonton AB T6G 2H8
Tel: 780-492-2972; *Fax:* 780-492-4967
cius@ualberta.ca
www.cius.ca
www.facebook.com/canadian.institute.of.ukrainian.studies
To develop Ukrainian scholarship in Canada; To organize research in Ukrainian & Ukrainian-Canadian studies
Volodymyr Kravchenko, Director

Canadian Mathematical Society (CMS) / Société mathématique du Canada
#209, 1725 St Laurent Blvd., Ottawa ON K1G 3V4
Tel: 613-733-2662
office@cms.math.ca
www.cms.math.ca
www.facebook.com/canmathsoc
To promote & advance the discovery, learning & application of mathematics
Yvette Roberts, Manager, Finance & Operations
Denise Charron, Manager, Memberships & Publications
Sarah Watson, Manager, Meetings & Events

Canadian Nautical Research Society (CNRS) / Société canadienne pour la recherche nautique
PO Box 34029, Ottawa ON K2J 5B1
Tel: 613-476-1177
www.cnrs-scrn.org
www.facebook.com/cnrs.scrn
twitter.com/CanNautResSoc
To stimulate & promote nautical research in Canada; To enhance Canada's understanding of its maritime heritage; To foster communication in nautical affairs, to organize meetings & to cooperate with other agencies promoting nautical research

Michael Moir, President

Canadian Network of Northern Research Operators (CNNRO)
c/o L. Fishback, Churchill Northern Studies Centre, PO Box 610, Churchill MB R0B 0E0
cnnro.ca
To promote excellence in & advance the collective interests of Canada's northern research operators
LeeAnn Fishback, Chair
Rodd Laing, Director, Communications

Canadian Numismatic Research Society (CNRS)
PO Box 1351, Victoria BC V8W 2W7
www.nunet.ca/cnrs.htm
To promote research & study of numismatics
Ronald Greene, Secretary/Treasurer

Canadian Operational Research Society (CORS) / Société canadienne de recherche opérationelle (SCRO)
PO Box 2225, Stn. D, Ottawa ON K1P 5W4
info@cors.ca
www.cors.ca
To advance the theory & practice of OR in Canada; To stimulate & promote contacts between people interested in the subject
Michael Pavlin, President
Marko Bijvank, Secretary

Canadian Philosophical Association (CPA) / Association canadienne de philosophie (ACP)
PO Box 68, Stn. P, Toronto ON M5S 2S6
administration@acpcpa.ca
www.acpcpa.ca
www.facebook.com/acpcpa.ca
twitter.com/acp_cpa
To advance the discipline of philosophy in Canada
Louise Morel, Executive Director
Judy Pelham, Secretary
Patrice Philie, Treasurer
Eric Dayton, English Editor, Dialogue: Canadian Philosophical Review
Mathieu Marion, Éditeur Francophone, Dialogue: Revue canadienne de philosophie

Canadian Photonic Industry Consortium (CPIC) / Consortium photonique de l'industrie canadienne
Université Laval, Pavillion d'optique-photonique, #2111, 2375, rue de la Terrasse, Québec QC G1V 0A6
Tel: 418-951-4729
info@photonscanada.ca
photonscanada.ca
To assist Canadian companies to optimize operations & to improve profits by facilitating & accelerating the application of photonic technologies that improve quality, productivity & profitability

Canadian Quaternary Association / Association canadienne pour l'étude du Quaternaire
www.canqua.com
twitter.com/canqua_org
To study & advance knowledge of the quaternary period
Matthew Peros, President
Duane Froese, Vice-President
Jeannine-Marie St-Jacques, Secretary-Treasurer

Canadian Research Institute for the Advancement of Women (CRIAW) / Institut canadien de recherches sur les femmes (ICREF)
#201, 240 Catherine St., Ottawa ON K2P 2G8
Tel: 613-422-2188
www.criaw-icref.ca
www.facebook.com/criaw.icref
twitter.com/criawicref
To advance the position of women in society through feminist & women-centred research; To encourage, coordinate & communicate research about the reality of women's lives & ensure an equal place for women & their experiences in the body of knowledge about Canada; To recognize & affirm the diversity of women's experiences; To demystify the research process & promote connections between research, social action & social change; To facilitate communication among feminist researchers & research organizations world-wide
Priti Gami Shah, President
Jacqueline Neapole, Executive Director
Pat Hendrick, Finance Officer

Canadian Society for Aesthetics (CSA) / Société canadienne d'esthétique (SCE)
www.csa-sce.ca
To keep aesthetic theorists in close touch with the creative & critical practices that are the basis of their discipline; To increase awareness of aesthetic issues among Canadian citizens &

develop the intellectual & conceptual resources for dealing with them

Canadian Society for Eighteenth-Century Studies (CSECS) / Société canadienne d'étude du dix-huitième siècle (SCEDS)
c/o Department of French, University of Manitoba, 427 Fletcher Argue Bldg., Winnipeg MB R3T 2N2
Tel: 204-474-9206
www.csecs.ca
To sustain, in Canada, interest in eighteenth-century civilization in Europe & the New World; to encourage, from a wide interdisciplinary base, research on the eighteenth-century; to make known to eighteenth-century specialists the work done in this area in Canada.
Armelle St-Martin, President
Isabelle Tremblay, Secretary
Julie Murray, Treasurer

Canadian Sociological Association (CSA) / Société canadienne de sociologie
PO Box 98014, 2126 Burnhamthorpe Rd. West, Mississauga ON L5L 5V4
Tel: 416-660-4378
office@csa-scs.ca
www.csa-scs.ca
www.linkedin.com/groups/3188569
www.facebook.com/CanadianSociologicalAssociation
twitter.com/csa_sociology
To promote research, publication & teaching of sociology in Canada
Sherry Fox, Executive Director

Canadian Water Network (CWN) / Réseau canadien de l'eau
University of Waterloo, 200 University Ave. West, Waterloo ON N2L 3G1
Tel: 519-888-4567; *Fax:* 519-883-7574
info@cwn-rce.ca
www.cwn-rce.ca
www.linkedin.com/company/canadian-water-network
www.facebook.com/CanadianWaterNetwork
twitter.com/CdnWaterNetwork
To create a national partnership in innovation that promotes environmentally responsible stewardship & opportunities with respect to Canada's water resources resulting in sustained prosperity & improved quality of life for Canadians.
Bernadette Conant, Executive Director
Mark Servos, Scientific Director

Cancer Research Society / Société de recherche sur le cancer
#402, 625, av Président-Kennedy, Montréal QC H3A 3S5
Tel: 514-861-9227; *Fax:* 514-861-9220
Toll-Free: 888-766-2262
info@src-crs.ca
www.cancerresearchsociety.ca
www.facebook.com/recherchecancer
To fund research on all types of cancer to help prevent, detect, & treat this disease
Max Fehlmann, President & CEO
Paul Gauthier, Director, Finance & Administration
Réginald Godin, Development Advisor, Major Gift & Planned Giving
Carolyne Lord, Director, Communications & Marketing

Centre for Research on Latin America & The Caribbean (CERLAC)
8th Fl., Kaneff Tower, York University, 4700 Keele St., Toronto ON M3J 1P3
Tel: 416-736-5237; *Fax:* 416-736-5688
cerlac@yorku.ca
www.yorku.ca/cerlac
To offer an interdisciplinary research unit concerned with economic development, political & social organization & cultural contributions of Latin America & the Caribbean; To build academic & cultural links between these regions & Canada; To inform researchers, policy advisors & public on matters concerning the regions; To assist in development of research & teaching institutions that directly benefit people of the regions
Alan Durston, Director

Classical Association of Canada (CAC) / Société canadienne des études classiques (SCEC)
c/o Guy Chamberland, Thornloe College at Laurentian University, Laurentian University, Sudbury ON P3E 2C6
www.cac-scec.ca
To advance the study of the civilizations of the Roman & Greek worlds; To promote teaching of classical civilizations & languages in Canadian schools; To encourage research in classical studies
Guy Chamberland, Secretary

Commission canadienne pour la théorie des machines et des mécanismes (CCToMM) / Canadian Committee for the Theory of Machines & Mechanisms

Faculté de génie mécanique, Université du Nouveau Brunswick, CP 4400, Fredericton NB E3B 5A3

Tél: 506-458-7454; Téléc: 506-453-5025
www.cctomm.mae.carleton.ca

Promouvoir le développement dans le domaine des machines et des mécanismes par la recherche théorique et expérimentale et leurs applications pratiques.
Marc Arsenault, Secrétaire général
Scott Nokleby, Responsable des communications

FPInnovations

570, boul Saint-Jean, Montréal QC H9R 3J9

Tel: 514-630-4100
info@fpinnovations.ca
web.fpinnovations.ca
www.linkedin.com/company/fpinnovations
www.facebook.com/fpinnovations
twitter.com/fpinnovations

To develop & assist with the implementation of innovative & safe forest operational solutions; To improve sustainable forest operations in Canada; To provide members with knowledge & technology, based on research, to conduct cost-competitive, quality forest operations
Stéphane Renou, President & CEO

GEOIDE Network

Pavillon Louis-Jacques-Casault, Cité Universitaire, #2306, 1055, av du Séminaire, Québec QC G1V 0A6

Tel: 418-656-7758; Fax: 418-656-2611
info@geoide.ulaval.ca
www.geoide.ulaval.ca

To consolidate & strengthen the Canadian geomatics industry, while making optimum use of Canada's research & development resources
Chantal Arguin, President
Nicholas Chrisman, Scientific Director

Great Lakes Institute for Environmental Research (GLIER)

401 Sunset Ave., Windsor ON N9B 3P4

Tel: 519-253-3000; Fax: 519-971-3616
glier@uwindsor.ca
www.uwindsor.ca/glier

Multidisciplinary facility with members from many disciplines, including biology, geology, chemistry, engineering, marine biology, molecular biology, genetics and ecology.
Brian Fryer, Contact

Humanist Association of Canada / Association humaniste du Canada

#900, 251 Laurier Ave. West, Ottawa ON K1P 5J6

Toll-Free: 877-486-2671
info@humanistcanada.ca
www.humanistcanada.ca
www.instagram.com/humanist_canada
www.facebook.com/secularhumanismcanada
twitter.com/CanadaHumanist

To bring together people who share a non-theistic view of the world; To educate the public about humanism & its ethics & values
Martin Frith, President

Institute for Research on Public Policy (IRPP) / Institut de recherche en politiques publiques

#200, 1470, rue Peel, Montréal QC H3A 1T1

Tel: 514-985-2461; Fax: 514-985-2559
irpp@irpp.org
irpp.org
www.youtube.com/user/IRPP1972
www.linkedin.com/company/institute-for-research-on-public-polic
y
www.facebook.com/IRPP
twitter.com/irpp

To improve public policy in Canada by generating research, providing insight & sparking debate contributing to the public policy decision-making process & strengthen the quality of public policy decisions made by Canadian governments, citizens, institutions & organizations
Graham Fox, President & CEO

Institute for Stuttering Treatment & Research & the Communication Improvement Program (ISTAR, CIP)

College Plaza, #1500, 8215 - 112 St., Edmonton AB T6G 2C8

Tel: 780-492-2619; Fax: 780-492-8457
istar@ualberta.ca
www.istar.ualberta.ca
www.youtube.com/user/RehabMedicineUofA
www.facebook.com/UofARehabMedicine
twitter.com/ISTAR_UofA

To provide treatment solutions to adults & children who stutter; to conduct research regarding stuttering.
Holly Lomheim, Clinic Director

Institute of Urban Studies (IUS)

University of Winnipeg, 515 Portage Ave., Winnipeg MB R3B 2E9

Tel: 204-982-1140; Fax: 204-943-4695
ius@uwinnipeg.ca
www.uwinnipeg.ca/ius

To undertake policy-oriented research in the field of Urban Studies; To serve as a resource centre for the community; To provide educational services to the University community & the community-at-large
Jino Distasio, Director
Scott McCullough, Assistant Director

International Council for Canadian Studies (ICCS) / Conseil international d'études canadiennes (CIEC)

PO Box 64016, Stn. Holland Cross, #8, 1620 Scott St., Ottawa ON K1R 6K7

Tel: 613-789-7834; Fax: 613-789-7830
www.iccs-ciec.ca
twitter.com/ICCS_CIEC

To promote scholarly study, research, teaching & publication about Canada in all disciplines & all countries; To enhance communications among its members to facilitate & develop such scholarly activities; To disseminate research results & to publicize researchers' activities in the area of Canadian Studies; To encourage the development of an international community of Canadianists
Munroe Eagles, President
Jane Koustas, Treasurer

International Council for Central & East European Studies (Canada) (ICCEES) / Conseil international d'études de l'Europe centrale et orientale (Canada)

c/o Gabriele Freitag, General Secretary, Schaperstrase 30 D-10719, Berlin Germany

www.iccees.org
www.facebook.com/ICCEES.org
twitter.com/icceesorg

To foster study of East European affairs & to encourage dissemination of this knowledge among specialists; To create an international community of scholars
Georges Mink, President
Andrii Krawchuk, Vice-President & Canadian Contact
Gabriele Freitag, General Secretary

International Council for the Exploration of the Sea (ICES)

H.C. Andersens Blvd. 44-46, Copenhagen VDK-1553 Denmark

info@ices.dk
www.ices.dk

To coordinate research & monitor activities to understand the marine environment & resources & man's impact upon them, including the identification of priority marine contaminants, their distribution, transport & effects; To provide advice regarding marine resources & pollution to member governments & international regulatory commissions; To publish & disseminate the results of research
Alain Vezina, ICES Delegate, Canada
Arran McPhersen, ICES Delegate, Canada

International Geographical Union - Canadian Committee

igu-online.org

To promote international programs in geography within Canada; To promote activities within IGU programs relevant to Canada & to coordinate Canadian participation; To formulate Canadian position & advise the National Research Council on Canadian participation in IGU activities

Mathematics of Information Technology & Complex Systems (MITACS)

Technology Enterprise Facility, University of British Columbia, #301, 6190 Agronomy Rd., Vancouver BC V6T 1Z3

Tel: 604-822-9189; Fax: 604-822-3689
mitacs@mitacs.ca
www.mitacs.math.ca
www.linkedin.com/company/mitacs
www.facebook.com/MITACS
twitter.com/DiscoverMITACS

MITACS leads Canada's effort in the generation, application and commercialization of new mathematical tools and methodologies within a world-class research program. The network initiates and fosters linkages with industrial, governmental, and not-for-profit organizations that require mathematical technologies to deal with problems of strategic importance to Canada. MITACS is driving the recruiting, training, and placement of a new generation of highly mathematically skilled personnel that is vital to Canada's future social and economic wellbeing. Offices in Vancouver, Toronto, Montréal, St. John's & Fredericton.
Arvind Gupta, CEO & Scientific Director

The M.S.I. Foundation

12230 - 106 Ave. NW, Edmonton AB T5N 3Z1

Tel: 780-421-7532; Fax: 780-425-4467
info@msifoundation.ca
www.msifoundation.ca

To foster & support research into any aspect of the provision of medical & allied health services to the people of Alberta
Lisa Petermann, Chairperson

Ontario Centres of Excellence (OCE)

#300, 325 Front St. West, Toronto ON M5V 2Y1

Tel: 416-861-1092; Fax: 416-971-7164
Toll-Free: 866-759-6014
www.oce-ontario.org
www.youtube.com/ocediscovery
www.linkedin.com/company/ontario-centres-of-excellence
www.facebook.com/OCEInnovation
twitter.com/oceinnovation

To create new jobs, products, services, technologies & businesses by creating partnerships between industry & academia
Claudia Krywiak, President & CEO
Narinder Dehal, Vice-President, Finance & Operations
Ketaki Desai, Vice-President, Business Development

Ontario Public Interest Research Group (OPIRG) / Groupe de recherche d'intérêt public de l'Ontario

North Borden Building, #101, 563 Spadina Ave., Toronto ON M5S 2J7

Tel: 416-978-7770; Fax: 416-971-2292
opirg.toronto@utoronto.ca
www.opirg.org

To be committed to the struggle for social & environmental justice; To provide an alternative to the information provided by the academic community, government & business; To offer an analysis of environmental & social issues aimed at motivating change & placing issues in the broader social, economic & political perspective
Sarom Rho, Director

Pulp & Paper Technical Association of Canada (PAPTAC) / Association technique des pâtes et papiers du Canada

#1070, 740, rue Notre-Dame ouest, Montréal QC H3C 3X6

Tel: 514-392-0265; Fax: 514-392-0369
tech@paptac.ca
www.paptac.ca

To provide means for the interchange of knowledge & expertise among its members; to improve the skill levels & effectiveness of present & future employees through training & education; to provide technical & practical information on pulp & paper manufacture & use
Greg Hay, Executive Director

The Royal Canadian Geographical Society (RCGS) / La Société géographique royale du Canada (SGRC)

50 Sussex Dr., Ottawa ON K1M 2K1

Tel: 613-745-4629; Fax: 613-744-0947
rcgs@rcgs.org
www.rcgs.org
twitter.com/RCGS_SGRC

To impart a broader knowledge of Canada, including its environmental, economic, & social challenges, as well as its natural & cultural heritage
John Geiger, Chief Executive Officer
Aaron Kylie, Editor-in-Chief

Royal Canadian Institute (RCI)
#9, 6 Queen's Park Cres. West, Toronto ON M5S 3H2
Tel: 416-977-2983
information@rciscience.ca
www.rciscience.ca
www.youtube.com/rciscience
www.facebook.com/rciscience
twitter.com/RCIScience
To increase public understanding of science; To create an
environment in which science can flourish & be appreciated
Susan MacDonald, President

The Royal Society of Canada (RSC) / La Société royale du Canada
Walter House, 282 Somerset West, Ottawa ON K2P 0J6
Tel: 613-991-6990; *Fax:* 613-991-6996
info@rsc-src.ca
rsc-src.ca
www.youtube.com/user/RSCSRC1
www.facebook.com/RSCTheAcademies
twitter.com/rsctheacademies
To promote learning & research in the arts, humanities &
sciences in Canada; in its role as a National Academy, to draw
on the breadth of knowledge & expertise of its members to
recognize & honour distinguished accomplishments; To advise
on the state of scholarship & culture across Canada; To inform
the public on noteworthy social, scientific & ethical questions of
the day
Darren Gilmour, Executive Director

Scottish Studies Foundation Inc.
c/o Catherine McKenzie Jansen, PO Box 45069, 2482 Yonge St., Toronto ON M4P 3E3
admin@scottishstudies.com
www.scottishstudies.com
www.facebook.com/scottishstudies
twitter.com/ScottishStudies
To promote interest in Scottish history, literature & culture
Kevin James, Chair
Catherine McKenzie Jansen, Membership Secretary

Shevchenko Scientific Society of Canada
516 The Kingsway, Toronto ON M9A 3W6
ntsh.ca@gmail.com
www.ntsh.ca
www.facebook.com/1594608770752854
twitter.com/NtshCanada
To promote scholarly research & publication; To advance
education in the field of Ukrainian & Ukrainian Canadian studies
Daria Darewych, President

Society for the Study of Egyptian Antiquities (SSEA) / Société pour l'Étude de l'Égypte Ancienne
PO Box 19004, Stn. Walmer, 360A Bloor St. West, Toronto ON M5S 3C9
Tel: 437-333-7781
info@thessea.org
www.thessea.org
www.facebook.com/SocietyfortheStudyofEgyptianAntiquities
To stimulate interest in Egyptology; To assist with research &
training in the field; To sponsor & promote archaeological
expeditions to Egypt
Mark B. Trumpour, National President

Stem Cell Network (SCN) / Réseau de cellules souches
#301, 1919 Riverside Dr., Ottawa ON K1H 1A2
Tel: 613-402-3974
info@stemcellnetwork.ca
www.stemcellnetwork.ca
vimeo.com/stemcellnetwork
www.facebook.com/CanadianStemCellNetwork
twitter.com/StemCellNetwork
To investigate the immense therapeutic potential of stem cells
for the treatment of diseases currently incurable by conventional
approaches
Cate Murray, Executive Director & COO
Shannon Sethuram, Director, Finance & Research
Administration
Lisa Willemse, Director, Communications & Public Affairs

Technion Canada
#206, 970 Lawrence Ave. West, Toronto ON M6A 3B6
Tel: 416-789-4545; *Fax:* 416-789-0255
Toll-Free: 800-935-8864
info@technioncanada.org
www.technioncanada.org
www.facebook.com/CanadianTechnion
To support Technion Israel Institute of Technology; To promote
exchange of scientific information between Israel & Canada,
scholarships, research, etc.
Marvin Ostin, President

Association des restaurateurs du Québec (ARQ) / Québec Restaurant Association
5880, boul Louis-H. Lafontaine, Montréal QC H1M 2T2
Tél: 514-527-9801; *Téléc:* 514-527-3066
Ligne sans frais: 800-463-4237
arqc@arqc.qc.ca
www.restaurateurs.ca
www.facebook.com/167396323369138
twitter.com/ARQ_resto
Fournir à l'ensemble des restaurateurs du Québec des services
complets d'information, de formation, d'escomptes,
d'assurances et de représentation gouvernementale
Alain Mailhot, Président directeur général

British Columbia Restaurant & Food Services Association (BCRFA)
#600, 890 West Pender St., Vancouver BC V6C 1J9
Tel: 604-669-2239
info@bcrfa.com
www.bcrfa.com
www.linkedin.com/company/bc-restaurant-&-foodservices-association-bcrfa-
www.facebook.com/BCRFA
twitter.com/BCRFA
To be the voice of the restaurant & food services industry in
British Columbia
Ian Tostenson, President & CEO

Canadian Culinary Federation (CCFCC) / Fédération Culinaire Canadienne
admin@culinaryfederation.ca
www.culinaryfederation.ca
www.instagram.com/culinaryfederation
www.facebook.com/CulinaryFederation
twitter.com/culinaryfed
To promote a Canadian food culture both nationally &
internationally; To encourage professional excellence among
chefs & cooks throughout Canada
Ryan Marquis, President

Manitoba Restaurant & Food Services Association (MRFA)
#5, 130 Marion St., Winnipeg MB R2H 0T4
Tel: 204-783-9955
info@mrfa.mb.ca
mrfa.mb.ca
www.instagram.com/manitobarestaurants
www.facebook.com/ManitobaRFA
www.facebook.com/ManitobaRFA
To lobby government & other regulatory bodies on issues
affecting restaurant & food services businesses; To present
educational seminars & social programs; To provide member
services such as insurance programs & credit card savings; To
represent the restaurant & food service industry effectively
through a large membership
Shaun Jeffrey, Executive Director

Restaurants Canada
1155 Queen St. West, Toronto ON M6J 1J4
Tel: 416-923-8416; *Fax:* 416-923-1450
Toll-Free: 800-387-5649
info@restaurantscanada.org
www.restaurantscanada.org
www.instagram.com/restaurantscanada
www.linkedin.com/company/canadian-restaurant-and-foodservices-association
www.facebook.com/RestaurantsCanada
twitter.com/RestaurantsCA
To create a favourable business environment & deliver tangible
value to members in all sectors of Canada's foodservice industry
Roy Little, Interim President
Troy Taylor, Vice-President, Operations
Lauren van den Berg, National Vice-President, Government
Relations
Christopher Barry, Director, Membership
Roberto Sarjoo, Director, Marketing & Communications

Société des chefs, cuisiniers et pâtissiers du Québec (SCCPQ)
#200, 3115, rue Pinière, Montréal QC J6X 4P7
Tél: 514-528-1083; *Ligne sans frais:* 833-528-1083
bureau-national@sccpq.ca
www.sccpq.ca
www.youtube.com/user/sccpq
www.facebook.com/sccpq
twitter.com/SCCPQ
Mise en valeur et émulation de la profession; reconnaissance
professionnelle au niveau national
Bruno Gagné, Président national
René Derrien, Secrétaire

Association des détaillants en alimentation du Québec (ADA) / Québec Food Retailers' Association
#900, 2120, rue Sherbrooke est, Montréal QC H2K 1C3
Tél: 514-982-0104; *Téléc:* 514-849-3021
Ligne sans frais: 800-363-3923
info@adaq.qc.ca
www.adaq.qc.ca
vimeo.com/adaquebec
www.facebook.com/ADAQuebec
twitter.com/ADAquebec
Représenter et défendre les intérêts professionnels,
socio-politiques et économiques de tous les détaillants du
Québec, et ce, quels que soient leur bannière et le type de
surface qu'ils opèrent
Daniel Choquette, Président
Florent Gravel, Président-directeur général

Association Québécoise des dépanneurs en alimentation (AQDA)
#501, 1, av Holiday, Montréal QC H9R 5N3
Tél: 514-240-3934; *Téléc:* 514-630-6989
info@acda-aqda.ca
www.acda-aqda.ca
Michel Gadbois, Président

Atlantic Convenience Store Association (ACSA)
#163, 103-287 Lacewood Dr., Halifax NS B3M 3Y7
Tel: 902-880-9733
theacsa.ca
twitter.com/theacsa
To represent convenience store retailers in the Atlantic
provinces
Mike Hammoud, President

Canadian Gift Association / Association canadienne de cadeaux
42 Voyager Ct. South, Toronto ON M9W 5M7
Tel: 416-679-0170; *Fax:* 416-679-0175
Toll-Free: 800-611-6100
info@cangift.org
www.cangift.org
www.youtube.com/user/cgtassoc
www.facebook.com/CanGift
twitter.com/cangift
To create & manage sales opportunities for the gift industry
Keir Graaten, Chair

Canadian Sporting Goods Association (CSGA) / Association canadienne d'articles de sport (ACAS)
#1272, 10 - 225 The East Mall, Toronto ON M9B 0A9
Toll-Free: 844-350-9902
info@csga.ca
www.csga.ca
www.instagram.com/csgahub
linkedin.com/company/canadian-sporting-goods-association
www.facebook.com/211952635634448
twitter.com/CSGAHub
To conduct quality trade shows; To provide forum responsive to
the professional needs of its members; To initiate programs
designed to stimulate sports activity participation as considered
feasible
Julian Savory, President & CEO

Conseil québécois du commerce de détail (CQCD) / Retail Council of Québec
#300, 630, rue Sherbrooke ouest, Montréal QC H3A 1E4
Tél: 514-842-6681; *Téléc:* 514-842-7627
Ligne sans frais: 800-364-0566
cqcd@cqcd.org
www.cqcd.org
www.linkedin.com/company/cqcd-detaillants
www.facebook.com/cqcd.org
twitter.com/CQCD_Express
Promouvoir, représenter et valoriser le secteur du commerce de
détail au Québec et les détaillants qui en font partie afin
d'assurer le sain développement et la prospérité du secteur
Léopold Turgeon, Président-directeur général

Convenience Industry Council of Canada (CICC) / Conseil Canadien de l'Industrie des Dépanneurs (CCID)
Toll-Free: 888-686-2823
info@convenienceindustry.ca
convenienceindustry.ca
www.linkedin.com/company/convenience-industry-council-of-canada
www.facebook.com/ConvenienceCan
twitter.com/ConvenienceCan
To represent the diverse needs of the convenience store
industry at the municipal, provincial, federal level

Anne Kothawala, President & CEO
Carmina Jimenez, Manager, Communications & Events

Direct Sellers Association of Canada (DSA) / Association de ventes directes du Canada
#250, 180 Attwell Dr., Toronto ON M9W 6A9
Tel: 416-679-8555; *Fax:* 416-679-1568
info@dsa.ca
www.dsa.ca
www.instagram.com/dsacanada
www.linkedin.com/company/direct-sellers-association-of-canada
www.facebook.com/DSACanada
twitter.com/dsacanada
To represent companies that manufacture & distribute goods & services through independent sales contractors, away from a fixed retail location; To encourage strong consumer protection, through Codes of Ethics & Business Practices; To engage in discussion with government & industry; To act as the voice of the direct selling industry to government in pursuit of better business opportunities for Canadian entrepreneurs.
Peter Maddox, President
Cathy Sampaio-Lepiane, Manager, Communications & Research
Tara Wallbridge, Manager, Operations & Member Services

Neighbourhood Pharmacy Association of Canada
#2003, 365 Bloor St. East, Toronto ON M4W 3L4
Tel: 416-226-9100; *Fax:* 416-226-9185
info@neighbourhoodpharmacies.ca
www.neighbourhoodpharmacies.ca
To ensure a strong chain drug store sector access to high quality products & health care services to Canadians
Sandra Hanna, Chief Executive Officer
Karl Frank, Chair

Ontario Convenience Store Association (OCSA)
#217, 466 Speers Rd., Oakville ON L6K 3W9
Tel: 905-845-9152; *Fax:* 905-849-9947
ontariocstores.ca
twitter.com/ontariocstores
To represent convenience store retailers in Ontario
Dave Bryans, Chief Executive Officer

Pool & Hot Tub Council of Canada (PHTCC) / Conseil canadien des piscines et spas
#17, 5775 Atlantic Dr., Mississauga ON L4W 4P3
Tel: 905-670-3714; *Fax:* 905-670-3069
Toll-Free: 800-879-7066
office@poolcouncil.ca
www.poolcouncil.ca
www.facebook.com/poolcouncil
twitter.com/PHTCC_TC
To promote the image & sales of the pool, spa & hot tub industry throughout Canada; To promote & enhance consumer awareness of the industry's products; To encourage & promote increased health & safety standards within the industry; To support efforts to improve pool, hot tub & spa equipment facilities, services & products; To promote & advance the common interests of members

Retail Council of Canada (RCC) / Conseil canadien du commerce de détail
#800, 1881 Yonge St., Toronto ON M4S 3C4
Tel: 416-922-6678; *Fax:* 416-922-8011
Toll-Free: 888-373-8245
info@retailcouncil.org
www.retailcouncil.org
www.youtube.com/user/RetailCouncil
www.linkedin.com/company/retail-council-of-canada
www.facebook.com/retailcouncil
twitter.com/RetailCouncil
To be the best at delivering the services our retail members value most; To serve, promote & represent the diverse needs of Canada's retailing industry to the highest standards of quality
Greg Hicks, Chair
Diane J. Brisebois, CAE, President & CEO

Surrey Board of Trade (SBOT)
#101, 14439 - 104 Ave., Surrey BC V3R 1M1
Tel: 604-581-7130; *Fax:* 604-588-7549
Toll-Free: 866-848-7130
info@businessinsurrey.com
www.businessinsurrey.com
www.linkedin.com/company/surrey-board-of-trade
www.facebook.com/SurreyBoardofTrade
twitter.com/SBofT
To provide advocacy, resources, experience & networking to members & fosters best business practices to ensure growth & prosperity of members
Anita Huberman, Chief Executive Officer

Safety & Accident Prevention

Alberta Fire Chiefs Association (AFCA)
AB
Tel: 780-719-7939; *Fax:* 780-892-3333
www.afca.ab.ca
William Purdy, Executive Director

Alberta Safety Council
4831 - 93 Ave., Edmonton AB T6B 3A2
Tel: 780-462-7300; *Fax:* 780-462-7318
Toll-Free: 800-301-6407
info@safetycouncil.ab.ca
www.safetycouncil.ab.ca
www.linkedin.com/company/the-alberta-safety-council
www.facebook.com/Albertasafety
twitter.com/ABSafetycouncil
To create awareness & provide educational & training programs to citizens of Alberta on how to maintain a safe environment at home, in traffic, at work & at play
Keri Abel, Program Director, Children's Programs
Mark Dobbelsteyn, Program Director, Traffic Safety
Linda Knowles, Program Director, COR/Workplace

Association des chefs en sécurité incendie du Québec (ACSIQ) / Québec Association of Fire Chiefs
5, rue Dupré, Beloeil QC J3G 3J7
Tél: 450-464-6413; *Téléc:* 450-467-6297
Ligne sans frais: 888-464-6413
administration@acsiq.qc.ca
www.acsiq.qc.ca
Regrouper les personnes détanant un poste de commande dans le domaine de la prévention et de la lutte contre les incendies
Sylvain Mireault, Directeur général

Association paritaire pour la santé et la sécurité du travail - Administration provinciale
#10, 1220, boul Lebourgneuf, Québec QC G2K 2G4
Tél: 418-624-4801
apssap@apssap.qc.ca
apssap.qc.ca
Supporter la prise en charge paritaire de la prévention en matière de santé, de sécurité et d'intégrité physique des personnes du secteur de l'Administration provinciale
Marie Leclerc, Directrice générale

Association paritaire pour la santé et la sécurité du travail du secteur affaires sociales
#600, 7400, bou. des Galeries d'Anjou, Montréal QC H1M 3M2
Tél: 514-253-6871; *Téléc:* 514-253-1443
Ligne sans frais: 800-361-4528
asstsas.qc.ca
www.linkedin.com/in/asstsas
www.facebook.com/asstsas
Pour promouvoir la santé et à assurer la formation et l'information du public
Diane Parent, Directrice générale

Association sectorielle services automobiles
#150, 8, rue de la Place-du-Commerce, Brossard QC J4W 3H2
Tél: 450-672-9330; *Téléc:* 450-672-4835
Ligne sans frais: 800-363-2344
info@autoprevention.org
www.autoprevention.org
www.youtube.com/autoprevention
twitter.com/AutoPrevention
Aider les travailleurs et les employeurs du secteur des services automobiles à prendre en charge la santé et la sécurité au travail, afin d'éliminer les risques d'accidents et de maladies professionnelles
Sylvie Mallette, Directrice Générale

Board of Canadian Registered Safety Professionals (BCRSP) / Conseil canadien des professionnels en securité agréés
#100, 6700 Century Ave., Mississauga ON L5N 6A4
Tel: 905-567-7198; *Fax:* 905-567-7191
Toll-Free: 888-279-2777
info@bcrsp.ca
www.bcrsp.ca
www.linkedin.com/company/board-of-canadian-registered-safety-professionals
www.facebook.com/OfficialBCRSP
www.twitter.com/bcrsp
To protect & promote occupational health & safety, environmental safety, & public safety, through the registration of qualified health & safety professionals committed to a code of ethics
David S. Johnston, Chair
Nicola Wright, Executive Director

Canada Safety Council (CSC) / Conseil canadien de la sécurité (CCS)
1020 Thomas Spratt Pl., Ottawa ON K1G 5L5
Tel: 613-739-1535; *Fax:* 613-739-1566
csc@safety-council.org
canadasafetycouncil.org
www.linkedin.com/company/canada-safety-council
www.facebook.com/canada.safety
twitter.com/CanadaSafetyCSC
To minimize avoidable death & injury & to raise awareness & interest in safety measures
Gareth Jones, President

Canadian Association of Fire Chiefs (CAFC) / Association canadienne des chefs de pompiers (ACCP)
#700, 1 Rideau St., Ottawa ON K1N 8S7
Toll-Free: 800-775-5189
www.cafc.ca
www.linkedin.com/in/canadian-association-of-fire-chiefs-82ba05
2a
To lead & represent the Canadian Fire Service on public safety issues with the vision of being nationally recognized as the fire service voice of authority
Tina Saryeddine, Executive Director
Anabel Therrien, Coordinator, Communication & Administration

Canadian Association of Road Safety Professionals (CARSP) / Association canadienne des professionnels de la sécurité routière (ACPSER)
St Catharines ON
info@casp.ca
www.carsp.ca
twitter.com/CARSPInfo
To preserve & share professional experience regarding road safety; To promote research & professional development; To & facilitates communication & cooperation among road safety groups & agencies
Brenda Suggett, Executive Director

Canadian Automatic Sprinkler Association (CASA)
#302, 315 Renfrew Dr., Markham ON L3R 9S7
Tel: 905-477-2270; *Fax:* 905-477-3611
info@casa-firesprinkler.org
www.casa-firesprinkler.org
www.linkedin.com/groups/3904166
twitter.com/CASAFS
To advance the fire sprinkler art as applied to the conservation of life & property from fire
John Galt, President

Canadian Centre for Occupational Health & Safety (CCOHS) / Centre canadien d'hygiène et de sécurité au travail (CCHST)
135 Hunter St. East, Hamilton ON L8N 1M5
Tel: 905-572-2981; *Fax:* 905-572-2206
Toll-Free: 800-668-4284
clientservices@ccohs.ca
www.ccohs.ca
www.facebook.com/CCOHS
twitter.com/ccohs
To promote the total well-being—physical, psychological & mental health—of working Canadians by providing information, training, education, management systems & solutions that support health, safety & wellness programs
Anne Tennier, President & CEO
Kimberly Pirhonen, Chief Financial Officer

Canadian Fire Safety Association (CFSA)
#210, 2800 - 14th Ave., Markham ON L3R 0E4
Tel: 416-492-9417; *Fax:* 416-491-1670
operations@canadianfiresafety.com
canadianfiresafety.com
twitter.com/CFSA_CANADA
To promote fire safety through seminars, safety training courses, scholarships & regular meetings
Scott Pugsley, President
David Petrie, Administrator

Canadian Radiation Protection Association (CRPA) / Association canadienne de radioprotection (ACRP)
PO Box 83, Carleton Place ON K7C 3P3
Tel: 613-253-3779; *Fax:* 888-551-0712
secretariat@crpa-acrp.ca
www.crpa-acrp.ca
To develop scientific knowledge for protection from the harmful effects of radiation; To encourage research; To assist in the development of professional standards in the discipline
Ed Waller, President
Mojgan Soleimani, Treasurer

Canadian Security Association (CANASA) / L'Association canadienne de la sécurité
National Office, #201, 50 Acadia Ave., Markham ON L3R 0B3
Tel: 905-513-0622; *Fax:* 905-513-0624
Toll-Free: 800-538-9919
info@canasa.org
www.canasa.org
www.linkedin.com/company/canadian-security-association
www.facebook.com/canasanews
twitter.com/CANASA_News
To act as the national voice of the security industry; To promote & protect the interests of members; To increase public awareness of the security industry's effectiveness in reducing risk; To develop & promote programs consistent with the needs of members; To develop & promote programs which will lead to the reduction of false dispatches & improved response; To influence regulations affecting the members
Patrick Straw, Executive Director

Canadian Society of Air Safety Investigators (CSASI)
139 West 13th Ave., Vancouver BC V5Y 1V8
avsafe@shaw.ca
www.beyondriskmgmt.com/csasi.htm
To improve air safety through investigation
Barbara M. Dunn, President

Canadian Society of Safety Engineering, Inc. (CSSE) / Société canadienne de la santé et de la sécurité, inc.
PO Box 51031, RPO Eglinton Sq., Toronto ON M1L 4T2
Tel: 437-374-4340; *Toll-Free:* 844-945-0403
info@csse.org
www.csse.org
www.linkedin.com/groups/1558517
www.facebook.com/CSSESafety
twitter.com/csse
To be the voice of safety in Canada
Deirdre O'Reilly, President
Elizabeth Shelton, Chief Executive Officer

Centre patronal de santé et sécurité du travail du Québec (CPSSTQ) / Employers Center for Occupational Health & Safety of Quebec
#1000, 500, rue Sherbrooke ouest, Montréal QC H3A 3C6
Tél: 514-842-8401; *Téléc:* 514-842-9375
reception@centrepatronalsst.qc.ca
www.centrepatronalsst.qc.ca
www.linkedin.com/company/centre-patronal-de-santé-et-sécurité
-du-travail-du-québec
www.facebook.com/CPSSTQ
twitter.com/CPSSTQ
Fournir de l'information et de la formation en SST aux entreprises regroupées par les associations patronales membres du Centre patronal
Daniel Zizian, Président-directeur général

Coalition to Oppose the Arms Trade (COAT)
541 McLeod St., Ottawa ON K1R 5R2
Tel: 613-231-3076
overcoat@rogers.com
coat.ncf.ca
To actively oppose the arms trade and support the anti-war movement.
Richard Sanders, Coordinator

Council of Canadian Fire Marshals & Fire Commissioners (CCFMFC) / Conseil canadien des directeurs provinciaux et des commissaires des incendies
c/o 491 McLeod Hill Rd., Fredericton NB E3A 6H6
Tel: 506-453-1208; *Fax:* 506-457-0793
CCFMFC@rogers.com
www.ccfmfc.ca
To contribute to a reduction in the number of fire deaths
Duane McKay, President
Harold Pothier, Vice-President
Philippa Gourley, Secretary-Treasurer

Council of Private Investigators - Ontario (CPIO)
#300, 10 Milner Business Court, Toronto ON M1B 3C6
Tel: 647-777-8418; *Fax:* 647-777-8301
info@cpiontario.ca
www.cpi-ontario.com
www.facebook.com/1469094056636753
twitter.com/CPIO2014
To represent the interests of private investigators in Ontario
Brian Sartorelli, President
Lloyd Vaughan, Chief Executive Vice-President
Penny Hill, Administrator

Federal Association of Security Officials (FASO) / Association fédérale des représentants de la sécurité
PO Box 2384, Stn. D, Ottawa ON K1P 5W5
Fax: 613-773-5787
Toll-Free: 888-330-3276
info@faso-afrs.ca
faso-afrs.ca
To enhance the performance & career development of federal security officers through enhancing the security function in government & improving the professionalism of security officers.
Claude J.G. Levesque, President

Fédération Québécoise des Intervenants en Sécurité Incendie (FQISI)
QC
Tél: 514-990-1338
info@fqisi.org
www.fqisi.org
www.facebook.com/FQISI.org
Aider à promouvoir la prévention des incendies; aider, soutenir et susciter des efforts en vue de réduire les pertes de vie; favoriser le perfectionnement en vue de combattre plus efficacement les incendies; promouvoir l'éducation populaire en général sur la protection et la prévention des incendies; faire des recommandations auprès des corps politiques et gouvernementaux
Denis Meunier, Président
Pascal Parent, Directeur Éxécutif

Fire Prevention Canada (FPC)
PO Box 37009, 3332 McCarthy Rd., Ottawa ON K1V 0W0
Tel: 613-247-9207
info.fiprecan@gmail.com
www.fiprecan.ca
To work with the public & private sectors to achieve fire safety through education
Peter Adamakos, National Manager

Industrial Accident Victims Group of Ontario (IAVGO)
55 University Ave., 15th Fl., Toronto ON M5J 2H7
Tel: 416-924-6477; *Fax:* 416-924-2472
Toll-Free: 877-230-6311
www.iavgo.org
www.facebook.com/167369409975545
To provide free services to injured workers in Ontario including legal advice, legal representation, public legal education, advocacy training & community development

Institut de recherche Robert-Sauvé en santé et en sécurité du travail (IRSST) / Robert Sauvé Occupational Health & Safety Research Institute
505, boul de Maisonneuve ouest, Montréal QC H3A 3C2
Tel: 514-288-1551
communications@irsst.qc.ca
www.irsst.qc.ca
www.youtube.com/user/IRSST
www.linkedin.com/company/irsst
www.facebook.com/IRSSTQC
twitter.com/IRSST
Contribuer par la recherche et le développement à l'amélioration de la santé et de la sécurité des travailleurs et plus spécifiquement, à l'élimination à la source des dangers pour leur santé, leur sécurité et leur intégrité physique ainsi qu'à la réadaptation des travailleurs victimes d'accidents ou de maladies professionnelles; fournir au Réseau public québécois de la prévention en santé et en sécurité du travail - composé de CSST, des Centres locaux de services communautaires, des Régies de la santé et des services sociaux et des associations sectorielles paritaires - les services et l'expertise nécessaires à leur action; diffuser les connaissances issues de ces recherches et de ces expertises auprès des milieux de travail et en favoriser le transfert; accorder des bourses d'études supérieures en santé et en sécurité du travail; agir comme laboratoire de référence au Québec, dans le domaine de l'hygiène industrielle
Lyne Sauvageau, Présidente-directrice générale

International Council on Global Privacy & Security, By Design
admin@gpsbydesign.org
www.gpsbydesign.org
To promote the development of technologies that embed privacy-protecting measures during design & production; To collaborate with organizations & governments to innovate systems that will protect both privacy & public safety; To provide people around the world with technologies that keep society safe & secure without compromising the privacy of individuals
Ann Cavoukian, Founder & Chair
George Tomko, Director, Research & Technology

Manitoba Association of Fire Chiefs (MAFC)
PO Box 1208, Portage la Prairie MB R1N 3J9
Tel: 204-857-6249
mb.firechiefs@mymts.net
mafc.ca
Martin Haller, President

MultiPrévention
#150, 2405, boul Fernand-Lafontaine, Longueuil QC J4N 1N7
Tél: 450-442-7763; *Téléc:* 450-442-2332
info@multiprevention.org
multiprevention.org
www.linkedin.com/company/multiprevention
www.facebook.com/MultiPreventionSanteSecurite
L'union rejoindre de sécurité pour les secteurs de la santé et sécurité:métallique, électricité, vêtements & gravures
Nathalie Laurenzi, Directrice générale

MultiPrévention ASP: Association paritaire pour la santé et la sécurité au travail des secteurs: métal, électrique, habillement et imprimerie
#150, 2405 boul Fernand-Lafontaine, Longueuil QC J4N 1N7
Tél: 450-442-7763; *Téléc:* 450-442-2332
multiprevention.org
www.facebook.com/MultiPrévention-214272358763722/
Marie-Josée Ross, Conseillère en gestion
Caroline Godin, Conseiller technique

Ontario Association of Fire Chiefs (OAFC)
#22, 520 Westney Rd. South, Ajax ON L1S 6W6
Tel: 905-426-9865; *Fax:* 905-426-3032
Toll-Free: 800-774-6651
info@oafc.on.ca
www.oafc.on.ca
www.flickr.com/photos/96578349@N02
www.linkedin.com/company/ontario-association-of-fire-chiefs
www.facebook.com/570718659627505
twitter.com/ONFireChiefs
To provide a voice for matters relating to the management & delivery of fire & emergency services in Ontario; To represent fire chief officers in Ontario
Richard Boyes, Executive Director

Ontario Industrial Fire Protection Association (OIFPA)
193 James St. South, Hamilton ON L8P 3A8
Tel: 905-527-0700; *Fax:* 905-527-6254
oifpa@interlynx.net
www.oifpa.org
To unite individuals with a concern for fire protection within Ontario's industrial community

Ontario Safety League (OSL) / Ligue de sécurité de l'Ontario
#212, 2595 Skymark Ave., Mississauga ON L4W 4L5
Tel: 905-625-0556; *Fax:* 905-625-0677
info@osl.org
www.ontariosafetyleague.com
Safety through education with an emphasis on traffic & child safety
Brian J. Patterson, President & General Manager

Opération Nez rouge / Operation Red Nose
Maison Couillard, Université Laval, 2539, rue Marie-Fitzbach, Québec QC G1V 0A6
Tél: 418-653-1492; *Téléc:* 418-653-3315
Ligne sans frais: 800-463-7222
info@operationnezrouge.com
www.operationnezrouge.com
www.youtube.com/user/OperationNezrouge
www.facebook.com/OperationNezrouge
twitter.com/ORNose
Service de chauffeur privé gratuit & bénévole offert pendant la période des Fêtes à tout automobiliste qui a consommé de l'alcool, our qui ne se sent pas en état de conduire son véhicule
Jean-Philippe Giroux, Directeur général
Monique Mailhot, Directrice, Administration et finances

Préventex - Association paritaire du textile et de la bonneterie
1936, rue Rossignol, Brossard QC J4X 2C6
Tél: 450-671-6925; *Téléc:* 450-671-9267
www.preventex.qc.ca
Amener les employeurs et les travailleurs du secteur à prendre charge activement de la prévention des accidents du travail et des maladies professionnelles
Lise Laplante, Directrice générale

Prévibois
Place Iberville II, #210, 1175, av Lavigerie, Québec QC G1V 4P1
Tél: 418-657-2267; *Téléc:* 418-651-4622
Ligne sans frais: 888-632-9326
previbois.com
De soutenir et d'accompagner les entreprises dans l'amélioration continue de la santé et de la sécurité du travail
Éric Dunn, Président-directeur général

Radiation Safety Institute of Canada / Institut de radioprotection du Canada
National Education Centre - Toronto, #760, 100 Sheppard Ave. East, Toronto ON M2N 6N5
Tel: 416-650-9090; *Fax:* 416-650-9920
Toll-Free: 800-263-5803
info@radiationsafety.ca
www.radiationsafety.ca
www.linkedin.com/company/radiation-safety-institute-of-canada
www.facebook.com/RadiationSafetyInstitute
twitter.com/RSICanada
To be an independent source for knowledge about radiation safety in the environment, the community & the workplace
Natalia Mozayani, Interim President & CEO
Bruce Sylvester, Chief Financial Officer

Safety Services Manitoba (SSM)
#3, 1680 Notre Dame Ave., Winnipeg MB R3H 1H6
Tel: 204-949-1085; *Fax:* 204-956-2897
Toll-Free: 800-661-3321
registrar@safetyservicesmanitoba.ca
www.safetyservicesmanitoba.ca
www.linkedin.com/in/gotosafetyservicesmanitoba
www.facebook.com/SafetyServicesManitoba
twitter.com/SafetyServMB
To prevent accidental injury or occupational illness in Manitoba by providing effective safety & health programs
Judy Murphy, President & CEO
Anita Zubricki, Director, Marketing

Safety Services New Brunswick (SSNB) / Services de Sécurité Nouveau-Brunswick
#204, 440 Wilsey Rd., Fredericton NB E3B 7G5
Tel: 506-458-8034; *Fax:* 506-444-0177
Toll-Free: 877-762-7233
info@safetyservicesnb.ca
www.safetyservicesnb.ca
www.facebook.com/motorcyclecourse
twitter.com/safetynb
To promote traffic, occupational & public safety issues & practices through safety training courses & programs, educational material, public information, safety campaigns & conferences.
Bill Walker, President & CEO
Jim Arsenault, Director of OSH & Traffic Training

Safety Services Newfoundland & Labrador
1076 Topsail Rd., Mount Pearl NL A1N 5E7
Tel: 709-754-0210; *Fax:* 709-754-0010
info@safetyservicesnl.ca
safetyservicesnl.ca
www.facebook.com/303428916390762
twitter.com/SafetyNL
Safety Services Newfoundland Labrador is dedicated to the prevention of injuries and fatalities; represents all the major sectors of the province's industry, business, government departments, volunteer organizations and many individuals who have a personal interest in safety, both on and off the job.

Safety Services Nova Scotia (SSNS)
#1, 201 Brownlow Ave., Dartmouth NS B3B 1W2
Tel: 902-454-9621; *Fax:* 902-454-6027
Toll-Free: 866-511-2211
www.linkedin.com/company/saftey-services-nova-scotia
www.facebook.com/SafetyNS
twitter.com/SafetyNS
To develop & provide quality safety & health services, education & training programs to improve the quality of life of Nova Scotians
Tanya Pulley Mailhot, Chair
Brad Doell, Vice-Chair & Secretary

Saskatchewan Safety Council
445 Hoffer Dr., Regina SK S4N 6E2
Tel: 306-757-3197; *Fax:* 306-569-1907
sasksafety.org
www.flickr.com/sasksafetycouncil
www.facebook.com/sasksafetycouncil
twitter.com/SkSafetyCouncil
To inform the public in order that they are able to make sound decisions regarding their safety
Kevin Mooney, President

Jeff Peters, Treasurer
Ryan Jacobson, Secretary

Workplace Safety & Prevention Services (WSPS)
5110 Creekbank Rd., Mississauga ON L4W 0A1
Tel: 905-614-1400; *Fax:* 905-614-1414
Toll-Free: 877-494-9777
customercare@wsps.ca
www.wsps.ca
www.youtube.com/user/WSPSpromo
www.linkedin.com/company/workplace-safety-&-prevention-services
www.facebook.com/wsps.news
twitter.com/WSPS_NEWS
To meet the health & safety needs of businesses in the agricultural, manufacturing & service industries; To provide programs, products & services for the prevention of injury & illness
Lynn Brownell, President & CEO

Scientific

Alberta Society of Professional Biologists (ASPB)
#370, 105 - 12 Ave. East, Calgary AB T2G 1A1
Tel: 403-264-1273
pbiol@aspb.ab.ca
www.aspb.ab.ca
www.linkedin.com/company/alberta-society-of-professional-biologists
twitter.com/albertabiology
To promote excellence in the practice of biology; To provide a voice for professional biologists in Alberta
Jennifer Sipkens, Executive Director

Association des microbiologistes du Québec (AMQ)
5094A, av Charlemagne, Montréal QC H1X 3P3
Tél: 514-728-1087
amq@microbiologistes.ca
www.microbiologistes.ca
De regrouper les microbiologistes du Québec oeuvrant principalment en environnement, en alimentaire et en pharmaceutique; d'étudier, de protéger et de développer les intérêts économiques, sociaux et professionnels des microbiologistes et de promouvoir l'essor de la microbiologie en général
Patrick D. Paquette, Président

Association of Canadian Ergonomists (ACE) / L'Association canadienne d'ergonomie
#2, 555 Hall Ave. East, Renfrew ON K7V 4M7
Fax: 613-432-6840
Toll-Free: 888-432-2223
info@ace-ergocanada.ca
ergonomicscanada.ca
www.facebook.com/ACEergocanada
twitter.com/ace_ergo
To advance human factors / ergonomics through encouraging a high quality of practice, education & research; To facilitate communication among members; To represent the discipline; To increase awareness of human factors / ergonomics; To identify resources
Jennifer Kenny, President
Kayla Wright, Executive Director

Association of Professional Biology (APB)
#300, 1095 McKenzie Ave., Victoria BC V8P 2L5
Tel: 250-483-4283; *Fax:* 250-483-3439
info@professionalbiology.com
professionalbiology.com
www.linkedin.com/in/probio
twitter.com/BIOLOGYAPBWORLD
To represent biology professionals who are practicing in Western Canada; To promote the professional practice of applied biology
Isabelle Houde, Manager & Registrar, Operations

Biophysical Society of Canada (BSC) / La société de biophysique du Canada
BC
www.biophysicalsociety.ca
www.linkedin.com/company/biophysical-society-of-canada
www.facebook.com/biophysicalsocietyofcanada
twitter.com/BiophysCanada
To promote biophysical research & education; To encourage cross-feeding of ideas between the physical & biological sciences; To foster & support scientific meetings, workshops & discussions in biophysics; To represent Canadian biophysics & biophysicists
Zoya Leonenko, President

BioScience Association Manitoba
1000 Waverley St., Winnipeg MB R3T 0P3
Tel: 204-272-5095; *Fax:* 204-272-2961
info@biomb.ca
www.biomb.ca
www.facebook.com/BioscienceMB
To represent the bioscience industry in Manitoba; To provide services for companies in the industry; To promote economic development
Tracey Maconachie, President

BIOTECanada
#600, 1 Nicholas St., Ottawa ON K1N 7B7
Tel: 613-230-5585
info@biotech.ca
www.biotech.ca
www.linkedin.com/company/biotecanada
twitter.com/biotecanada
To provide a unified voice fostering an environment that responds to the needs of the biotechnology industry & research community, both nationally & internationally
Andrew Casey, President & CEO

Canadian Association of Palynologists (CAP) / Association canadienne des palynologues
c/o Dr. Mary A. Vetter, Luther College, University of Regina, Regina SK S4S 0A2
www.scirpus.ca/cap/cap.shtml
To advance all aspects of palynology in Canada
Francine McCarthy, President
Mary A. Vetter, Secretary-Treasurer
Florin Pendea, Editor, CAP Newsletter

Canadian Association of Physicists (CAP) / Association canadienne des physiciens et physiciennes (ACP)
555 King Edward Ave., 3rd Fl., Ottawa ON K1N 7N5
Tel: 613-562-5614; *Fax:* 613-562-5615
membership@cap.ca
www.cap.ca
www.linkedin.com/company/canadian-association-of-physicists-association-canadienne-des-physiciens-et-physiciennes
www.facebook.com/CanadianAssociationOfPhysicists
twitter.com/CAPhys
To serve as a platform for physicists to meet & exchange information, ideas & knowledge; To increase awareness & visibility of physics & Canadian physicists; To encourage Canadians to study physics; To address science policy & funding issues in the physics field
Francine Ford, Executive Director

Canadian Association of Science Centres (CASC) / L'Association canadienne des centres de sciences (ACCS)
100 Ramsey Lake Rd., Sudbury ON P3E 5S9
Tel: 705-522-6825; *Fax:* 705-522-1677
info@casc-accs.com
www.canadiansciencecentres.ca
www.linkedin.com/company/canadian-association-of-science-centres
www.facebook.com/CASC.ACCS
twitter.com/CASC_ACCS
To assist members in contributing to a creative & prosperous Canada through science engagement; To represent Canada's science centres & science-related museums before government; To find solutions to challenges affecting science centres in Canada
Marianne Mader, Executive Director

Canadian Astronomical Society (CASCA) / Société canadienne d'astronomie
100 Viaduct Ave. West, Victoria BC V9E 1J3
casca@casca.ca
www.casca.ca
Robert Thacker, President
Sara Ellison, Vice-President
Leslie Sage, Press Officer

Canadian Botanical Association (CBA) / Association botanique du Canada (ABC)
PO Box 160, Aberdeen SK S0K 0A0
Tel: 306-253-4654; *Fax:* 306-253-4744
www.cba-abc.ca
www.instagram.com/canbotanical
www.facebook.com/586530314800139
twitter.com/canbotanical
To represent Canadian Botany & botanists nationally & internationally; To respond quickly & professionally on matters that are of concern to Canadian botanists
Nicole Fenton, President
Line Rochefort, Vice-President
Deborah Metsger, Secretary

Shelley Hepworth, Treasurer

Canadian College of Physicists in Medicine (CCPM) / Collège canadien des physiciens en médecine
#202, 300 March Rd., Kanata ON K2K 2E2
Tel: 613-599-3491; *Fax:* 613-595-1155
www.ccpm.ca
To identify, through certification, individuals who have acquired & maintained a standard of knowledge & skill essential to the practice of medical physics, in order to serve the public
Cheryl Duzenli, President
Andrew Kerr, Registrar
Nancy Barrett, Executive Director

Canadian Federation of Earth Sciences (CFES) / Fédération canadienne des sciences de la Terre (FCST)
Dept. of Earth Sciences, University of Ottawa, #15025, FSS Hall, Ottawa ON K1N 6N5
www.cfes-fcst.ca
www.facebook.com/CFESciences
twitter.com/CFESciences
To promote coordination & cooperation in activities in Canadian geoscientific education; To advise on science policy involving the earth sciences; To provide an informed opinion to the public of Canada on matters of public concern
Iain Samson, President

Canadian Hydrographic Association (CHA) / Association canadienne d'hydrographie
#1205, 4900 Yonge St., Toronto ON M2N 6A6
Tel: 416-512-5815
www.hydrography.ca
To advance the development of hydrography & associated activities in Canada; To further the knowledge & professional development of members; To enhance & demonstrate the public need for hydrography; To help the development of hydrographic sciences in developing countries; To embrace the disciplines of marine cartography, hydrographic surveying, offshore exploration, marine geodesy & tidal studies
Rob Hare, National President
Kirsten Greenfield, National Secretary
Christine Delbridge, National Treasurer

Canadian Institute of Food Science & Technology (CIFST) / Institut canadien de science et technologie alimentaires (ICSTA)
#305, 3390 South Service Rd., Burlington ON L7N 3J5
Toll-Free: 844-755-6679
cifst@cifst.ca
www.cifst.ca
www.linkedin.com/groups/7472160
www.facebook.com/CIFST/
twitter.com/cifst_icsta
To advance food science & technology; To act as a voice for scientific issues related to the Canadian food industry
Robert Kowal, President
Constance Wrigley-Thomas, Executive Director

Canadian Medical & Biological Engineering Society (CMBES) / Société canadienne de génie biomédical inc. (SCGB)
1485 Laperriere Ave., Ottawa ON K1Z 7S8
Tel: 613-728-1759; *Fax:* 613-729-6206
secretariat@cmbes.ca
www.cmbes.ca
twitter.com/cmbesociety
To advance the theory & practice of medical device technology; To advance individuals who are engaged in interdisciplinary work involving medicine, engineering & the life sciences; To represent the interests of biomedical & clinical engineering to government agencies
Mike Capuano, President
Andrew Ibey, Vice-President

Canadian Meteorological & Oceanographic Society (CMOS) / Société canadienne de météorologie et d'océanographie (SCMO)
PO Box 3211, Stn. D, Ottawa ON K1P 6H7
Tel: 613-990-0300
cmos@cmos.ca
www.cmos.ca
www.facebook.com/cmos.scmo.canada
twitter.com/cmos_scmo
To advance meteorology & oceanography in Canada
Gordon Griffith, Executive Director
Doug G. Steyn, Director, Publications
Sheila Bourque, Director, Education & Outreach
Qing Liao, Office Manager

Canadian Physiological Society (CPS) / Société canadienne de physiologie
c/o Department of Physiology, University of Toronto, Toronto ON M5S 1A8
www.cpsscp.ca
To disseminate & discuss scientific information of interest to researchers in physiology & biological sciences
Graham Collingridge, President

Canadian Phytopathological Society (CPS) / Société Canadienne de Phytopathologie (SCP)
c/o Vikram Bisht, PO Box 1149, 65 - 3 Ave. NE, Carman MB R0G 0J0
Tel: 204-745-0260; *Fax:* 204-745-5690
phytopath.ca
www.facebook.com/111761558875337
twitter.com/phytopathca
To encourage & support research, education, & dissemination of knowledge on the nature, cause, & control of plant diseases; To promote communication among plant pathologists; To broaden educational opportunities for members
Dilantha Fernando, President
Vikram Bisht, Membership Secretary

Canadian Science & Technology Historical Association (CSTHA) / Association pour l'histoire de la science et de la technologie au Canada (AHSTC)
PO Box 8502, Stn. T, Ottawa ON K1G 3H9
cstha-ahstc.ca
To foster the study of Canada's scientific & technological heritage through research, publication, teaching & preservation of artifacts & records
William Knight, President
Erich Weidenhammer, Secretary

Canadian Science Policy Centre (CSPC) / Centre sur les politiques scientifiques canadiennes (CSPC)
#301, 1595 - 16th Avenue, Richmond Hill ON L4B 3N9
Tel: 905-709-7453
info@sciencepolicy.ca
www.sciencepolicy.ca
www.youtube.com/user/sciencepolicycentre
www.linkedin.com/company/canadian-science-policy-centre
www.facebook.com/canadiansciencepolicy
twitter.com/sciencepolicy
To organize a non-partisan, pan-Canadian network of experts to discuss science, technology & innovation policy
Mehrdad Hariri, President & CEO

Canadian Society for Analytical Sciences & Spectroscopy
90 Bader Lane, Kingston ON K7L 3N6
Tel: 613-533-2619; *Fax:* 613-533-6669
www.csass.org
To organize programs of scientific & general interest for the educational benefit of members & the public; To organize annual scientific conferences & workshops on various aspects of pure & applied spectroscopy in the chemical, biological, geochemical & metallurgical sciences
Diane Beauchemin, President
Lu Yang, Treasurer

Canadian Society for Molecular Biosciences (CSBM) / Société Canadienne pour Biosciences Moléculaires
contact@csmb-scbm.ca
www.csmb-scbm.ca
www.instagram.com/csmb_scbm
www.facebook.com/CSMB.SCBM
twitter.com/CSMB_SCBM
Tarik Möröy, President
Imogen Coe, Vice-President

Canadian Society for the History & Philosophy of Science (CSHPS) / Société Canadienne d'Histoire et Philosophie des Sciences (SCHPS)
c/o Dr. Paul Bartha, Department of Philosophy, University of of BC, 1866 Main Mall, #E370, Vancouver BC V6T 1Z1
www.yorku.ca/cshps1
twitter.com/cshpsnews
To explore all aspects of science, past & present
Alan Richardson, President
Paul Bartha, Secretary-Treasurer

The Canadian Society for the Weizmann Institute of Science (CSWIS)
#235, 4823, rue Sherbrooke ouest, Montréal QC H3Z 1G7
Tel: 514-342-0777; *Toll-Free:* 855-337-9611
www.weizmann.ca
www.youtube.com/user/WeizmannCanada
www.linkedin.com/company/weizmann-canada
www.facebook.com/weizmanncanada
twitter.com/WeizmannCanada

To marshal Canadian support for the Weizmann Institute of Science in Rehovot, Israel; to help build & maintain scientific facilities; to acquire costly up-to-date research equipment & instrumentation; to set up endowments for research centres; to establish professional chairs & scholarships
Jeffrey I. Cohen, Chair
Susan Stern, National Executive Director & CEO
Lorie Blumer, National Manager, Communications

Canadian Society of Exploration Geophysicists (CSEG)
#570, 400 - 5th Ave. SW, Calgary AB T2P 0L6
Tel: 403-262-0015; *Fax:* 403-262-7383
office@cseg.ca
www.cseg.ca
www.linkedin.com/company/csegeo
www.facebook.com/csegonline
twitter.com/csegonline
To promote the science of geophysics
Jim Racette, Managing Director

Canadian Society of Forensic Science (CSFS)
PO Box 37040, 3332 McCarthy Rd., Ottawa ON K1V 0W0
Tel: 613-738-0001; *Fax:* 613-738-1987
csfs@bellnet.ca
www.csfs.ca
www.facebook.com/csfscanada
To promote the study of forensic science; To maintain professional standards in the discipline of forensic science
Kimberly Nugent, President
Nelson Lafreniere, Secretary
Louise Cloutier, Treasurer

Canadian Society of Microbiologists (CSM) / Société canadienne des microbiologistes
c/o Rofail Conference and Management Services, 17 Dossetter Way, Ottawa ON K1G 4S3
Tel: 613-421-7229; *Fax:* 613-421-9811
info@csm-scm.org
www.csm-scm.org
twitter.com/CSM_SCM
To advance microbiology in all its aspects; To facilitate interchange of ideas between microbiologists
Janet Hill, President
Mohan Babu, Secretary-Treasurer

Canadian Society of Pharmacology & Therapeutics (CSPT) / Société de pharmacologie du Canada
info@pharmacologycanada.org
www.pharmacologycanada.org
To promote research & education in the disciplines of pharmacology & experimental therapeutics
Kerry Goralski, President
Bruce Carleton, Vice-President
Brad Urquhart, Treasurer

Canadian Society of Plant Biologists (CSPP) / Société canadienne de biologie végétale (SCPV)
c/o Dr. Harold Weger, Dept. of Biology, Univ. of Regina, 3737 Wascana Pkwy., Regina ON S4S 0A2
secretary@cspb-scbv.ca
cspb-scbv.ca
www.linkedin.com/groups/4092532
twitter.com/cspbscbv
To promote the teaching & public awareness of plant physiology in Canada
Daphne Goring, President
Harold Weger, Coordinator, Membership

Canadian Society of Soil Science (CSSS) / Société canadienne de la science du sol (SCSS)
Business Office, PO Box 637, Pinawa MB R0E 1L0
Tel: 204-229-2327
sheppards@ecomatters.com
csss.ca
www.linkedin.com/company/canadian-society-of-soil-science
www.facebook.com/CSSS.Soils
twitter.com/CSSS_Soils
To be actively engaged in land use, soils research & classification
Nathan Basiliko, PhD, President
Amanda Dichon, PhD, Secretary
Edith Olson, Treasurer

Canadian Space Society (CSS) / Société spatiale canadienne
Bldg. E, PO Box 70009, Stn. Rimrock Plaza, 1115 Lodestar Rd., Toronto ON M3J 0H3
www.css.ca
www.linkedin.com/company/canadian-space-society
www.facebook.com/CanadianSpaceSociety
twitter.com/cdnspacesociety

To conduct technical & outreach projects; To promote the involvement of Canadians in human exploration and space development
Kevin Shortt, President
Marc Fricker, Vice-President
Gary McQueen, Treasurer

Citizen Scientists
1749 Meadowvale Rd., Toronto ON M1B 5W8
info@citizenscientists.ca
www.citizenscientists.ca
To monitor local watersheds, foster local environmental stewardship, and educate volunteers and the public.

Geological Association of Canada (GAC) / Association géologique du Canada (AGC)
c/o Dept. of Earth Sciences, Memorial Univ. of Newfoundland, #ER4063, Alexander Murray Bldg., St. John's NL A1B 3X5
Tel: 709-864-7660; *Fax:* 709-864-2532
gac@mun.ca
gac.ca
www.linkedin.com/company/geological-association-of-canada
www.facebook.com/gac.agc
twitter.com/GAC_AGC
To advance the wise use of geoscience in academic, professional & public circles
Dène Tarkyth, President
Kathryn Bethune, Vice-President
James Conliffe, Secretary-Treasurer
Michael Michaud, Chair, Finance
Roger Paulen, Chair, Publications

H.R. MacMillan Space Centre Society (HRMSC)
1100 Chestnut St., Vancouver BC V6J 3J9
Tel: 604-738-7827; *Fax:* 604-736-5665
info@spacecentre.ca
www.spacecentre.ca
www.youtube.com/user/MacMillanSpaceCentre
www.facebook.com/MacMillanSpaceCentre
twitter.com/AskAnAstronomer
To promote education concerning astronomy
Raylene Marchand, Interim Executive Director
Lisa McIntosh, Director, Learning

Institute of Textile Science (ITS) / Institut des sciences textiles
www.textilesciences.com
To promote the dissemination & interchange of knowledge concerning textile science; To encourage research & development related to textile science & technology, including the establishment & granting of awards
Lena Horne, Ph.D, President
Vincent Deregnaucourt, Membership Secretary

International Association of Hydrogeologists - Canadian National Chapter (IAH-CNC) / Internationale association des hydrogeologists (AIC)
c/o WESA, 3108 Carp Rd., Carp ON K0A 1L0
Tel: 613-839-3053
www.iah.ca
To advance the science of hydrogeology & exchange hydrogeologic information internationally
Diana Allen, President

International Association of Science & Technology for Development (IASTED)
Bldg B6, #101, 2509 Dieppe Ave. SW, Calgary AB T3E 7J9
Tel: 403-288-1195; *Fax:* 403-247-6851
calgary@iasted.com
www.iasted.org
www.linkedin.com/in/iastedconferences
www.facebook.com/IASTED
twitter.com/IASTED_Calgary
To further economic development by promoting science & technology

International Oceans Institute of Canada (IOIC)
c/o Dalhousie Univ., PO Box 15000, 6414 Coburg Rd., Halifax NS B3H 4R2
Tel: 902-494-1977; *Fax:* 902-494-1334
ioi@dal.ca
internationaloceaninstitute.dal.ca
To promote responsible management of the world's oceans & sustainable development of marine resources; To protect the integrity of the ocean environment; To promote sustainable resource development; To improve the quality of ocean-dependent human life, including health & safety of maritime communities; To further these objectives, all aspects of the ocean environment are pursued - resource management & development, marine environmental quality, ocean law & policy, high seas management, coastal zone management, marine

transportation, ocean science & technology, tourism & recreation, ocean industries & maritime boundary delimitation
Michael J.A. Butler, Director

Microscopical Society of Canada (MSC) / Société de Microscopie du Canada (SMC)
info@msc-smc.org
msc-smc.org
www.linkedin.com/company/microscopical-society-of-canada—société-de-microscopie-du-canada
www.facebook.com/microscopicalsocietyofcanada
Marek Malac, President
Stefano Rubino, Treasurer
Jeff Fraser, Secretary

MindFuel
#260, 3512 - 33 St. NW, Calgary AB T2L 2A6
Tel: 403-220-0077; *Fax:* 403-284-4132
info@mindfuel.ca
mindfuel.ca
To increase science literacy by creating innovative programs for all Albertans
Cassy Weber, CEO
Alma Abugov, Director, Development & Community Engagement

North Pacific Marine Science Organization (PICES)
c/o Institute of Ocean Sciences, PO Box 6000, Sidney BC V8L 4B2
Tel: 250-363-6366; *Fax:* 250-363-6827
secretariat@pices.int
www.pices.int
To promote & coordinate marine research in the northern North Pacific & adjacent seas especially northward of 30 degrees North; To advance scientific knowledge about the ocean environment, global weather & climate change, living resources & their ecosystems & the impacts of human activities; To promote the collection & rapid exchange of scientific information on these issues
Sonia Batten, Executive Secretary

Nova Scotian Institute of Science (NSIS)
Reference & Research Services, Killam Memorial Library, PO Box 15000, 6225 University Ave., Halifax NS B3H 4R2
nsis.chebucto.org
www.facebook.com/NSInstituteofScience
To provide a forum for scientists & those interested in science
Sherry Niven, President

Ontario Kinesiology Association (OKA)
#100, 6700 Century Ave., Mississauga ON L5N 6A4
Tel: 905-567-7194; *Fax:* 905-567-7191
info@oka.on.ca
www.oka.on.ca
www.instagram.com/onkinesiology
www.linkedin.com/company/ontario-kinesiology-association
www.facebook.com/ontariokinesiologyassociation
twitter.com/ONKinesiology
To promote the application of the science of human movement to other professionals & to the community; To uphold the standards of the profession of kinesiology; To assist kinesiologists in the performance of their duties & responsibilities
Devon Blackburn, President

Royal Astronomical Society of Canada (RASC) / Société royale d'astronomie du Canada
#203, 4920 Dundas St. West, Toronto ON M9A 1B7
Tel: 416-924-7973; *Fax:* 416-924-2911
Toll-Free: 888-924-7272
nationaloffice@rasc.ca
www.rasc.ca
www.facebook.com/theRoyalAstronomicalSocietyofCanada
twitter.com/rasc
To promote the advancement of astronomy across Canada
Robyn Foret, President
Phil Groff, Executive Director

Science Atlantic / Science Atlantique
Dept. of Psychology & Neuroscience, Dalhousie University, PO Box 15000, Halifax NS B3H 4R2
Tel: 902-494-3421
admin@scienceatlantic.ca
www.scienceatlantic.ca
twitter.com/scienceatlantic
To advance science & technology through education & public awareness & the promotion of scientific literacy education & research throughout the region
David McCorquodale, Chair
Lois Whitehead, Executive Director

Society of Toxicology of Canada (STC) / Société de toxicologie du Canada
PO Box 55094, Montréal QC H3G 2W5
stcsecretariat@mcgill.ca
www.stcweb.ca
www.facebook.com/societyoftoxicologyofcanada
twitter.com/scitox
To promote acquisition, facilitate dissemination & encourage utilization of knowledge in the science of toxicology
Geraldine Delbès, President
Adam Socha, Secretary

Southern Ontario Seismic Network (SOSN)
c/o University of Western Ontario, London ON N6A 5B7
Tel: 519-661-3605; *Fax:* 519-661-3198
www.gp.uwo.ca
To obtain information on the seismicity and seismic hazards of a region of southern Ontario in which a number of nuclear power facilities are located.
R.F. Mereu, Administrator

Statistical Society of Canada (SSC) / Société statistique du Canada
#219, 1725 St. Laurent Blvd., Ottawa ON K1G 3V4
Tel: 613-627-3530; *Fax:* 613-733-1386
info@ssc.ca
www.ssc.ca
To promote the development & use of statistics & probability; To ensure that decisions that affect society are based upon valid & appropriate statistics & interpretation; To encourage high standards for statistical education & practice
Shirley Mills, Executive Director

Youth Science Canada (YSC) / Sciences jeunesse Canada (SJC)
PO Box 297, Pickering ON L1V 2R4
Tel: 416-341-0040; *Fax:* 866-613-2542
Toll-Free: 866-341-0040
info@youthscience.ca
youthscience.ca
www.youtube.com/c/YouthScienceCanada
www.facebook.com/ysc.sjc
twitter.com/ysc_sjc
To assist Canadian youth to develop skills & knowledge for excellence in science & technology
Reni Barlow, Executive Director

Senior Citizens

Active Aging Canada (ACA) / Vieillir activement Canada (VAC)
PO Box 143, Stn. Main, Shelburne ON L9V 3L8
Tel: 519-925-1676; *Toll-Free:* 800-549-9799
info@activeagingcanada.ca
www.activeagingcanada.ca
www.youtube.com/c/ActiveAgingCanada
www.facebook.com/183968216963904
twitter.com/ActiveAgingCda
To encourage older Canadians to maintain & enhance their well-being & independence through a lifestyle that embraces daily physical activities
Patricia Clark, Executive Director

AdvantAge Ontario
#700, 7050 Weston Rd., Woodbridge ON L4L 8G7
Tel: 905-851-8821; *Fax:* 905-851-0744
www.advantageontario.ca
To support members in the provision of quality non-profit long term care, seniors' community services, & housing
Lisa Levin, Chief Executive Officer
Chris Noone, Manager, Communications & Member Services

Advocacy Centre for the Elderly (ACE)
#701, 2 Carlton St., Toronto ON M5B 1J3
Tel: 416-598-2656; *Fax:* 416-598-7924
www.advocacycentreelderly.org
To provide legal services to low income senior citizens
Graham Webb, Executive Director

Alberta Continuing Care Association (ACCA)
8861 - 75 St. NW, Edmonton AB T6C 4G8
Tel: 780-435-0699; *Fax:* 780-436-9785
info@ab-cca.ca
www.ab-cca.ca
www.facebook.com/229402317246598
twitter.com/ACCAssoc
To represent owners & operators of long term care & designated assisted living facilities & home care
Tammy Leach, Chief Executive Officer
Heather Aggus, Director, Marketing & Communications

Alberta Council on Aging
PO Box 62099, Edmonton AB T5M 4B5
Tel: 780-423-7781; Fax: 780-425-9246
Toll-Free: 888-423-9666
info@acaging.ca
www.acaging.ca
www.facebook.com/albertacouncilonaging
twitter.com/acaging
To define the needs of aging & the aged & to bring the current needs to the attention of government or voluntary agencies & to take action where appropriate; To identify & encourage relevant areas of research & systematic compilation of information affecting aging; to encourage & develop discussion on all problems affecting aging; To inform government at any level on the potential impact of policies & legislation on the aging; to print, publish, distribute & sell publications related to aging; To foster interagency liaison & cooperation
Ron Rose, President
Donna Durand, Executive Director

British Columbia Seniors Living Association (BCSLA)
#300, 3665 Kingsway, Vancouver BC V5R 5W2
Tel: 604-689-5949; Fax: 604-689-5946
Toll-Free: 888-402-2722
info@bcsla.ca
www.bcsla.ca
Marlene Williams, Director, Membership Services

Canadian Association for Long Term Care (CALTC)
info@caltc.ca
www.caltc.ca
www.facebook.com/caltc.ca
twitter.com/CALTC_CA
To ensure the delivery of quality care to vulnerable citizens of Canada

Canadian Association on Gerontology (CAG) / Association canadienne de gérontologie (ACG)
c/o Department of Occupational Science & Occupational Therapy, #160, 500 University Ave., Toronto ON M5G 1V7
Toll-Free: 855-224-2240
www.cagacg.ca
www.linkedin.com/company/canadian-association-on-gerontology
www.facebook.com/CdnAssocGero
twitter.com/cagacg
To develop the theoretical & practical understanding of individual & population aging through multidisciplinary research, practice, education & policy analysis in gerontology; To seek the improvement of the conditions of life of elderly people in Canada
Laura Kadowaki, President
Anthony Lombardo, Executive Director
Andrea Rochon, Secretary-Treasurer

CARP
70 Jefferson Ave., Toronto ON M6K 1Y4
Toll-Free: 888-363-2279
support@carp.ca
www.carp.ca
www.facebook.com/CARP
twitter.com/CARPAdvocacy
To promote the rights & quality of life of Canadians as they age through advocacy, education, information & CARP-recommended services & programs
Moses Znaimer, President

LA Centre for Active Living
55 Rankin Cres., Toronto ON M6P 4E4
Tel: 416-452-4875
www.loyolaarrupecentre.com
www.facebook.com/LACentreforActiveLiving
twitter.com/lacseniors
To serve the emotional & physical needs of people 55+; To provide & promote independent community living in an inclusive fashion; To allow seniors to live actively with dignity & confidence
Sandra Cardillo, Executive Director

Council for Black Aging / Le Conseil Des Personnes Agées De La Communauté Noire De Montréal
8606, rue Centrale, Montréal QC H4C 1M8
Tel: 514-935-4951
The Council for Black Aging works as an advocate for the needs of Black seniors, undertaking activities designed to advance the interests of Black elders, keeping Black seniors better informed of issues relating to the availability of health and social services, and developing a unique day centre and a nursing home for Black elders.

Fédération des aînées et aînés francophones du Canada (FAAFC)
#300, 450 rue Rideau, Ottawa ON K1N 5Z4
Tél: 613-564-0212; Téléc: 613-564-0212
info@faafc.ca
www.faafc.ca
www.youtube.com/user/LaFAAFC
Défendre les droits des personnes à la retraite; Défendre les droits des préretraités; Programmes intergénérationnels; Protection de la langue et la culture française
Roger Doiron, Président
Jean-Luc Racine, Directeur général
Michel Vézina, Premier vice-président, Saskatchewan
André Faubert, Deuxième vice-présidente, Québec
Richard Martin, Trésorier, Terre-Neuve & Labrador
Mélina Gallant, Secrétaire, Ile-du-Prince-Édouard
Marie-Christine Aubrey, Administratrice, Territoire du Nord-Ouest
Louis Bernardin, Administrateur, Manitoba
Roland Gallant, Administrateur, Nouveau-Brunswick
Charles Gaudet, Administrateur, Nouvelle-Écosse
Claire Grisé, Administratrice, Colombie-Britannique
Germaine Lehodey, Administratrice, Alberta
Francine Poirier, Administratrice, Ontario
Roxanne Thibaudeau, Administratrice, Yukon

HelpAge Canada / Aide aux aînés Canada
#205, 1300 Carling Ave., Ottawa ON K1Z 7L2
Tel: 613-232-0727; Fax: 613-232-7625
Toll-Free: 800-648-1111
info@helpagecanada.ca
helpagecanada.ca
www.youtube.com/channel/UCeQtJt1-UgTWEar0AYz9LVw
www.facebook.com/helpagecanada
twitter.com/helpageca
To meet the needs of poor or destitute elderly people in Canada & the developing world
Gregor Sneddon, Executive Director

National Pensioners Federation (NPF) / Fédération nationale des retraités
2186 Stanfield Rd., Mississauga ON L4Y 1R5
Tel: 905-706-5806
info@npfmail.ca
www.nationalpensionersfederation.ca
www.youtube.com/user/npfederation
www.facebook.com/NPFederation
twitter.com/npfederation
To act as an advisory body providing central contacts, facilities for research, surveys, uniform objectives & a national expansion of the pensioners movement; To stimulate public interest in the welfare of senior citizens by means of adequate pensions & social security that will provide comfortable housing & decent living; To protect the rights & interests of pensioners & prospective pensioners; To prevent discrimination & undue delay in granting pensions; To project a social friendly fellowship among the pensioners of Canada
Trish McAuliffe, President

New Brunswick Association of Nursing Homes, Inc. (NBANH) / Association des foyers de soins du Nouveau-Brunswick, inc. (AFSNB)
#206, 1133 Regent St., Fredericton NB E3B 3Z2
Tel: 506-460-6262; Fax: 506-460-6253
info@nbanh.com
www.nbanh.com
www.facebook.com/afsnb.nbanh
twitter.com/NBANH_AFSNB
To assist members in the provision of quality & efficient care to their residents
Jodi Hall, Executive Director
Michelle Pellerin, Office Manager

New Brunswick Senior Citizens Federation Inc. (NBSCF) / Fédération des citoyen(ne)s aîné(e)s du Nouveau-Brunswick inc. (FCANB)
PO Box 23, #214, 451 Paul St., Dieppe NB E1A 6W8
Tel: 506-857-8242; Fax: 506-857-0315
Toll-Free: 800-453-4333
horizons@nbnet.nb.ca
www.nbscf.ca
www.facebook.com/238798849533942
To promote the general welfare & leadership of New Brunswick's senior citizens regardless of language, race, colour, sex, or creed; To elevate the social, moral, & intellectual standing of NB's senior citizens; To provide information, coordination, communication, & advocating services to members
Lise Guignard, Provincial Office Manager
Isabelle Hébié, Administrative Assistant

New Brunswick Special Care Home Association Inc.
c/o Jan Seely, 2081 Rte. 845, Bayswater NB E5S 1J7
Tel: 506-738-2917; Toll-Free: 866-441-4340
www.nbscha.com
To assist members in delivering quality, cost effective long term care for seniors & special needs adults
Jan Seely, President

Older Adult Centres' Association of Ontario (OACAO) / Association des centres pour aînés de l'Ontario
PO Box 65, Caledon East ON L7C 3L8
Tel: 905-584-8125; Fax: 905-584-8126
Toll-Free: 866-835-7693
admin@oacao.org
www.oacao.org
www.facebook.com/oacao
twitter.com/theoacao
To ensure that seniors in Ontario have opportunities & choices that lead to healthy, active lifestyles
Sue Hesjedahl, Executive Director

Ontario Association of Residents' Councils (OARC)
#201, 80 Fulton Way, Richmond Hill ON L4B 1J5
Tel: 905-731-3710; Fax: 905-731-1755
Toll-Free: 800-532-0201
info@ontarc.com
www.residentscouncils.ca
www.youtube.com/channel/UC9zqu513DgytE8UBLjWo05w
twitter.com/OARCnews
To represent the views of residents on issues that affect the quality of their lives in long term care facilities & to promote & support the role & development of Residents' Councils
Dee Lender, Executive Director
Julie Garvey, Manager, Administration & Finance

Ontario Society of Senior Citizens' Organizations (OSSCO) / La société des organisations des citoyens aînés de l'Ontario (COAAO)
#404, 345 Wilson Ave., Toronto ON M3H 5W1
Tel: 416-785-8570; Fax: 416-785-7361
Toll-Free: 800-265-0779
info@ossco.org
www.ossco.org
www.linkedin.com/company/osscolearning
www.facebook.com/OSSCOlearning
twitter.com/OSSCOlearning
To improve the quality of life for Ontario's seniors by encouraging seniors' involvement in all aspects of society, by keeping them informed of current issues & by focusing on programs to benefit an aging population
Elizabeth Macnab, Executive Director

Prince Edward Island Senior Citizens Federation Inc. (PEISCF)
#214, 40 Enman Cres., Charlottetown PE C1E 1E6
Tel: 902-368-9008; Fax: 902-368-9006
Toll-Free: 877-368-9008
peiscf@pei.aibn.com
www.peiscf.com
To advance the education opportunities for seniors on PEI; To improve the quality of life for seniors by advising government & other decision making bodies regarding seniors' concerns; To improve the quality of life for seniors; to increase societal understanding of seniors & the aging process through positive role modelling
Linda Jean Nicholson, Executive Director

Réseau FADOQ / Québec Federation of Senior Citizens
4545, av Pierre-de Coubertin, Montréal QC H1V 0B2
Tél: 514-252-3017; Ligne sans frais: 800-544-9058
info@fadoq.ca
www.fadoq.ca
www.youtube.com/user/ReseauFADOQ
www.facebook.com/reseaufadoq
twitter.com/ReseauFADOQ
Promouvoir un concept positif du vieillissement; encourager le maintien et l'amélioration de la qualité de vie et de l'autonomie des aînés; initier et soutenir l'organisation d'activités physiques et de loisirs; redonner aux aînés une nouvelle fierté en les revalorisant à leurs propres yeux comme à ceux de la société; remettre entre les mains des aînés la gestion de leurs affaires
Gisèle Tassé-Goodman, Président

Road Scholar
11 Ave. de Lafayette, Boston MA 02111 USA
Tel: 978-323-4141; *Fax:* 877-426-2166
Toll-Free: 800-454-5768
contact@roadscholar.org
www.roadscholar.org
www.youtube.com/user/roadscholarorg
www.linkedin.com/company/road-scholar
www.facebook.com/rsadventures
twitter.com/roadscholarorg
To develop, manage & facilitate educational experiences for older adults through cooperative partnership with educational agents; To balance education & travel in an environment of comradeship & respect; To continue to experiment with pilot projects to reach broader populations of older adults; To be a "learner-centered" organization that responds to the learning needs of older adults; To use new methods of reaching out to an ever more diverse multicultural Canada; To promote cost-effective educational opportunities to an ever widening group of older adults
Jim Moses, President & CEO

Seniors Association of Greater Edmonton (SAGE)
15 Sir Winston Churchill Sq., Edmonton AB T5J 2E5
Tel: 780-423-5510; *Fax:* 780-426-5175
info@mysage.ca
www.mysage.ca
www.facebook.com/438132792913806
twitter.com/sageYEG
To enhance the quality of life of older persons through service, innovation, & advocacy
Barb Burton, President
Karen McDonald, Executive Director

United Senior Citizens of Ontario Inc. (USCO)
3033 Lakeshore Blvd. West, Toronto ON M8V 1K5
Tel: 416-252-2021; *Fax:* 416-252-5770
Toll-Free: 888-320-2222
office@uscont.ca
www.uscont.ca
www.facebook.com/uscont
twitter.com/USCONTseniors
To further the interests & promote the welfare of the senior population in Ontario; To provide for an exchange of ideas for member groups; To assist in the formation of senior citizens clubs
Susanne Robarts, President

Service Clubs

Big Brothers Big Sisters of Canada (BBBSC) / Les Grands Frères Grandes Soeurs du Canada
Toronto Eaton Centre, Galleria L1, #110A, 220 Yonge St., Toronto ON M5B 2H1
Tel: 905-639-0461; *Toll-Free:* 800-263-9133
www.bigbrothersbigsisters.ca
www.youtube.com/bbbscanada
www.linkedin.com/company/big-brothers-big-sisters-of-canada
www.facebook.com/bigbrothersbigsistersofcanada
twitter.com/bbbsc
To provide leadership to member agencies as they develop programs to meet the changing needs of young people
W. Matthew Chater, President & CEO
Sameer Ali, Vice-President, Strategy & Operations

British Columbia Lions Society for Children with Disabilities (BCLS)
3981 Oak St., Vancouver BC V6H 4H5
Tel: 604-873-1865; *Fax:* 604-873-0166
Toll-Free: 800-818-4483
info@eastersealsbcy.ca
www.eastersealsbcy.ca
www.facebook.com/EasterSealsBCY
twitter.com/EasterSealsBCY
To provide as many services as possible to children with disabilities; To enhance the lives of children with special needs; To give children with disabilities self-esteem, self-confidence & a sense of independence

Canadian Federation of Junior Leagues (CFJL) / Fédération canadienne des jeunes ligues
c/o Junior League of Halifax, PO Box 8011, Stn. A, Halifax NS B3K 5L8
www.cfjl.org
To promote a strong national presence in Canada & increase the international impact of the Association of Junior Leagues International; To promote voluntarism, develop the potential of women & improve the community through effective action, leadership & trained volunteers
Susan Simpson, National Coordinator
Dianne Kokesh, Treasurer

Canadian Progress Club / Club progrès du Canada
#435, 10 - 8550 Torbram Rd., Brampton ON L6T 0H7
Tel: 647-546-3601; *Fax:* 888-937-9826
Toll-Free: 877-944-4726
progressclub@rogers.com
www.progressclub.ca
www.linkedin.com/company/canadian-progress-club-national
www.facebook.com/CanadianProgressClub
twitter.com/ProgressClub
To assist those in need as well as creating & preserving a spirit of friendship that is sincere; To advance the best interests of the community in which that club is located
Chris Yonke, President

Club Optimiste de Rivière-du-Loup inc.
CP 1344, Rivière-du-Loup QC G5R 4L9
Tél: 418-862-8454; *Téléc:* 418-862-3366
service@optimiste.org
www.optimiste.org
Les clubs Optimistes inspirent le meilleur chez les jeunes depuis 1919 en rencontrant les besoins des jeunes de toutes les collectivités du monde. Ils organisent des projets de service communautaire positifs qui visent à tendre la main à la jeunesse.
Jean-Louis Dorval, Trésorier

Kin Canada
PO Box 3460, 1920 Rogers Dr., Cambridge ON N3H 5C6
Tel: 519-653-1920; *Fax:* 519-650-1091
Toll-Free: 800-742-5546
kinhq@kincanada.ca
www.kincanada.ca
www.facebook.com/kincanada
twitter.com/kincanada
To enrich communities through service, while embracing national pride, positive values, personal development & lasting friendships; To support Cystic Fibrosis research & care in Canada
Grant Ferron, Executive Director

Kin Canada Foundation / Fondation Kin Canada
PO Box 3460, 1920 Rogers Dr., Cambridge ON N3H 5C6
Toll-Free: 800-742-5546
info@kincanadafoundation.ca
www.kincanadafoundation.ca
www.facebook.com/kincanadafoundation
To support Kin, Kinsmen & Kinette clubs across Canada; To function as the official charitable organization of Kin Canada
Keith Hodgson, Chair

Kiwanis International (Eastern Canada & the Caribbean District)
30 Brant Ave., Brantford ON N3T 3G6
Tel: 519-304-2768
district@kiwanisecc.org
www.kiwanisecc.org
To strengthen communities & help disadvantaged individuals & children

Kiwanis International (Western Canada District)
#122, 350 - 55 Salisbury Way, Sherwood Park AB T8B 0A9
Tel: 780-436-3390
WeCanSect@gmail.com
www.ikiwanis.ca
www.facebook.com/KiwanisWesternCanada
twitter.com/wecankiwanis

Last Post Fund (LPF) / Fonds du Souvenir
#401, 505 René-Lévesque Blvd. West, Montréal QC H2Z 1Y7
Tel: 514-866-2727; *Fax:* 514-866-1471
Toll-Free: 800-465-7113
info@lastpost.ca
www.lastpostfund.ca
www.facebook.com/lastpostfund
twitter.com/lastpostfund
To ensure that no war veterans, or certain other persons who meet the wartime service eligibility criteria, are denied a funeral & burial due to lack of funds
Raymond Mikkola, President
Edouard Pahud, Executive Director

Soroptimist Foundation of Canada
www.soroptimistfoundation.ca
To provide bursaries, scholarships & fellowships to Canadian students & Canadian schools, colleges & universities for the advancement of education & in particular to further the appreciation of social needs, & the study of community, national & international problems
Colleen Penrowley, Chair
Margot Rutherford, Treasurer
Dianne Nielsen, Secretary

Variety - The Children's Charity (Ontario)
3701 Danforth Ave., Toronto ON M1N 2G2
Tel: 416-699-7167; *Fax:* 416-699-5752
TTY: 416-699-8147
info@varietyvillage.on.ca
www.varietyvillage.ca
To improve the quality of life for children with disabilities & to promote their integration into society
Karen Stintz, President & CEO

Variety - The Children's Charity of BC
4300 Still Creek Dr., Burnaby BC V5C 6C6
Tel: 604-320-0505; *Toll-Free:* 800-310-5437
info@variety.bc.ca
www.variety.bc.ca
www.youtube.com/user/VarietyBC
www.facebook.com/variety.bc.ca
twitter.com/VarietyBC
To raise funds throughout the province of B.C. for the benefit of B.C.'s children with special needs; To provide funds for capital costs; To create new centres or improve existing facilities & purchase specialized equipment
Kristy Gill, Executive Director

Variety - The Children's Charity of Manitoba, Tent 58 Inc.
440 Don Ave., #A, Winnipeg MB R3L 0S4
Tel: 204-982-1050; *Fax:* 204-475-3198
admin@varietymanitoba.com
www.varietymanitoba.com
www.youtube.com/user/varietymanitoba
www.facebook.com/varietymanitoba
twitter.com/Varietymanitoba
Jeff Liba, Chief Executive Officer

Variety Club of Northern Alberta, Tent 63
#1205 Energy Square, 10109 - 106th St., Edmonton AB T5J 3L7
Tel: 780-448-9544; *Fax:* 780-448-9289
Raises funds for the children of Northern Alberta who have disabilities or are disadvantaged
Sue McEachern, Executive Director

Variety Club of Southern Alberta
1811 4th St. SW, Calgary AB
Tel: 403-466-1630
info@varietyalberta.ca
www.varietyalberta.ca
www.facebook.com/VarietyAlberta
To support children who are facing physical, developmental, emotional, or learning challenges, through education, advocacy, & community outreach; To create supportive, ability diverse communities that address safe, inclusive, & accessible environments
Jana Hands, CEO
Larry Horeczy, COO

Social Response/Social Services

Action-Haïti
PO Box 99043, Stn. Tremblay, Longueuil QC J4N 0A5
Tel: 450-464-1629
action-haiti.jimdofree.com
Antonio Di Lalla, Président

Agincourt Community Services Association (ACSA)
#100, 4155 Sheppard Ave. East, Toronto ON M1S 1T4
Tel: 416-321-6912; *Fax:* 416-321-6922
info@agincourtcommunityservices.com
www.agincourtcommunityservices.com
www.linkedin.com/company/agincourt-community-services-association
www.facebook.com/AgincourtCommunityServices
twitter.com/AginComServices
To address a variety of issues including systemic poverty, hunger, housing, homelessness, unemployment, accessibility and social isolation in the Scarborough community.
Lee Soda, Executive Director
Vinitha Gengatharan, Chair

Aide internationale à l'enfance
#300, 840, rue Raoul-Jobin, Québec QC G1N 1S7
Tél: 418-653-2409; *Téléc:* 418-653-3262
Ligne sans frais: 877-653-2409
amie@amie.ca
www.amie.ca
www.facebook.com/LAMIE.aide.internationale.enfance
Répondre aux besoins fondamentaux des enfants des pays en développement; Sensibiliser la société aux droits et aux besoins
André Jalbert, Président-directeur général

**Aide internationale pour l'enfance (AIPE) /
Children's Care International (CCI)**
#314, 150, rue Grant, Longueuil QC J4H 3H6
Tel: 514-871-1086
communications@aipe-cci.org
www.aipe-cci.org
To fight against child exploitation around the world
Eloïse Savoie, General Manager

**Alberta Association of Marriage & Family Therapy
(AAMFT)**
Calgary AB
Tel: 403-598-2814
www.aamft.ab.ca
To protect the interests of marriage & family therapists; To
provide individual marriage & family therapy; To provide
educational seminars for therapists
Amy Cote, President

**Alberta College of Social Workers (ACSW) /
Association des travailleurs sociaux de l'Alberta**
#550, 10707 - 100 Ave. NW, Edmonton AB T5J 3M1
Tel: 780-421-1167; *Fax:* 780-421-1168
Toll-Free: 800-661-3089
www.acsw.ab.ca
www.facebook.com/AlbertaCollegeofSocialWorkers
twitter.com/ACSWsocialwork
To promote, regulate & govern the profession of social work in
the Province of Alberta; To advocate for skilled & ethical social
work practices & for policies, programs & services that
promote the profession & protect the best interests of the public
Lynn Labrecque King, Executive Director & Registrar

Alberta Family Mediation Society (AFMS)
#1650, 246 Stewart Green SW, Calgary AB T3H 3C8
Tel: 403-233-0143; *Toll-Free:* 877-233-0143
info@afms.ca
www.afms.ca
To advocate for the resolution of family conflict through
mediation by qualified professionals
Gordon Andreiuk, Chair

ALIGN Association of Community Services
**Bonnie Doon Mall, #255, 8330 - 82nd Ave., Edmonton AB
T6C 4E3**
Tel: 780-428-3660; *Fax:* 780-428-3844
info@alignab.ca
www.alignab.ca
twitter.com/alignalberta
To strengthen & represent the interests of member agencies; To
develop & advocate for conditions & practices that improve
quality of services for vulnerable children & families
Rhonda Barraclough, Executive Director

**Alternative Dispute Resolution Atlantic Institute /
Institut de médiation et d'arbitrage de l'Atlantique**
PO Box 123, Halifax NS B3J 2M4
admin@adratlantic.ca
adratlantic.wildapricot.org
www.facebook.com/adratlantic
To assist ADR users in using alternative dispute resolution
strategies
Wendy Scott, President
Ron Pizzo, Vice President

Les Amis de la Saint-Camille
381, rue Raoul, Saint-Colomban QC J5K 2C4
Tél: 450-565-8290
info@amis-st-camille.org
www.amis-st-camille.org
Informer la population canadienne à la situation en santé
mentale en Afrique noire et à la solution contemporaine apportée
par la St-Camille

Applegrove Community Complex
60 Woodfield Rd., Toronto ON M4L 2W6
Tel: 416-461-8143; *Fax:* 416-461-5513
applegrove@applegrovecc.ca
www.applegrovecc.ca
www.facebook.com/99742456574
To provide social service programs for infants, children, teens,
adults and seniors living in the Queen-Greenwood area of
Toronto.
Susan Fletcher, Executive Director
Ann McKechnie, Chair

Architecture sans frontières Québec (ASFQ)
201, rue Sainte-Catherine est, Montréal QC H2X 1L2
Tél: 514-868-1767
info@asf-quebec.org
www.asf-quebec.org
www.youtube.com/channel/UCrfEAiivf9hiHqsQsxTCpBg
www.linkedin.com/company/architectes-de-l'urgence-et-de-la-co
opération
www.facebook.com/architecturesansfrontieres
twitter.com/quebecasf
Renforcer les capacités des communautés dans le besoin en
engageant le secteur de l'architecture
Bruno Demers, Directeur général

**Association de médiation familiale du Québec
(AMFQ)**
4800, ch Queen Mary, Montréal QC H3W 1W9
Tél: 514-990-4011; *Téléc:* 514-733-9081
Ligne sans frais: 800-667-7559
info@mediationquebec.ca
www.mediationquebec.ca
www.facebook.com/mediationquebec.ca
twitter.com/Amfqinfo
L'Association de médiation familiale du Québec a pour mission
de développer et promouvoir la médiation familiale et les
médiateurs familiaux accrédités, au Québec et à l'étranger
Jean-François Chabot, Présidente
Gerald Schoel, Trésorier
José Mongeau, Secrétaire

**Association des services de réhabilitation sociale
du Québec inc. (ASRSQ) / Association of Social
Rehabilitation Agencies of Québec Inc.**
2000, boul St-Joseph est, Montréal QC H2H 1E4
Tél: 514-521-3733; *Téléc:* 514-521-3753
info@asrsq.ca
www.asrsq.ca
www.facebook.com/asrsq
Promouvoir la participation des citoyens dans l'administration de
la justice, la prévention du crime et la réhabilitation des
délinquants adultes
Nicole Quesnel, Présidente
Solange Bastille, Vice-présidente
Guy Pellerin, Secrétaire
Sylvie Brunet-Lusignan, Trésorier

**Association internationale pour le partenariat
entreprises-ONG - Canada**
369, rue de la Couronne, Québec QC G1K 6E9
Tél: 418-524-5609
info@aipeo.org
www.aipeo.org
www.facebook.com/16696091684779
Lutter contre la pauvreté et l'exclusion des femmes dans les
actions de développement économique; Lutter contre le
chômage des jeunes africains de la francophonie et
d'encourager la remise en action et la prise en main de cette
jeunesse

**The Association of Social Workers of Northern
Canada (ASWNC) / L'Association des travailleurs
sociaux du Nord canadien (ATSNC)**
PO Box 31006, Yellowknife NT Y1A 5P7
Tel: 867-699-7964
ed@socialworknorth.com
www.socialworknorth.com
www.facebook.com/1601328100089021
To represent social workers practicing in Canada's three
Territories in the far north - Nunavut, the Northwest Territories &
the Yukon Territory

**Association québécoise des personnes de petite
taille (AQPPT) / Association of Little People of
Quebec**
#308, 6300, av du Parc, Montréal QC H2V 4H8
Tél: 514-521-9671; *Téléc:* 514-521-3369
info@aqppt.org
www.aqppt.org
www.facebook.com/AQPPT
Promouvoir des intérêts et défendre les droits des personnes de
petite taille et faciliter leur intégration scolaire, sociale et
professionnelle.
Normande Gagnon, Co-fondatrice

**Association québécoise Plaidoyer-Victimes (AQPV) /
Quebec Association for Victim Advocacy (QAVA)**
#201, 4305, rue d'Iberville, Montréal QC H2H 2L5
Tél: 514-526-9037; *Téléc:* 514-526-9951
aqpv@aqpv.ca
www.aqpv.ca
www.facebook.com/aqpv

Défense des droits et des intérêts des victimes d'actes criminels
par la discussion, la sensibilisation, la formation, la concertation
et la recherche
Marie-Hélène Blanc, Directrice générale

Battlefords United Way Inc.
#203, 891 - 99th St., North Battleford SK S9A 0N8
Tel: 306-445-1717
buw@sasktel.net
www.battlefordsunitedway.ca
To improve lives & build community by engaging individuals &
mobilizing collective action
Brendon Boothman, Chair
Jana Blais, Treasurer

BC Society of Transition Houses (BCSTH)
#325, 119 West Pender St., Vancouver BC V6B 1S5
Tel: 604-669-6943; *Fax:* 604-682-6962
Toll-Free: 800-661-1040
info@bcsth.ca
bcsth.ca
www.instagram.com/bcsocietyoftransitionhouses
www.linkedin.com/company/bc-society-of-transition-houses
www.facebook.com/BCSTH
twitter.com/BCSTH
To educate, promote & advocate on issues of violence against
women; to support an organization that provides or seeks to
provide shelter &/or services to women & their children who
experience violence
Shabna Ali, Executive Director

Bereaved Families of Ontario (BFO)
PO Box 10015, Stn. Watline, Mississauga ON L4Z 4G5
info@bereavedfamilies.net
www.bereavedfamilies.net
To create programs, services & resources to support bereaved
families; To be committed to self-help & mutual aid, with a focus
on families who have experienced the death of a child
Carolyn Baltaz, Chair
Lloyd Lindsay, Vice-Chair

Birchmount Bluffs Neighbourhood Centre (BBNC)
93 Birchmount Rd., Toronto ON M1N 3J7
Tel: 416-396-4310; *Fax:* 416-396-4314
contact@bbnc.ca
www.bbnc.ca
www.facebook.com/birchmountbluffs
twitter.com/bbncentre
To provide programs and supports and foster social inclusion
within the community, with a focus on individuals that face a
barrier to service.
Enrique Robert, Executive Director

**Block Parent Program of Canada (BPPCI) /
Programme Parents-Secours du Canada**
**PO Box 7, 50 Dunlop St. East, Lower Level, Barrie ON L4M
6J9**
Tel: 705-792-4245
lindapatterson100@gmail.com
www.blockparent.ca
www.facebook.com/blockparent
To provide immediate assistance through a safety network; To
offer supporting community education programs
Linda Patterson, President

Block Watch Society of British Columbia
891 Mt. Bulman Pl., Vernon BC V1B 2Z4
Toll-Free: 877-602-3358
blockwatch@blockwatch.com
blockwatch.com
To build safe neighbourhoods across British Columbia; To
encourage bonds among local residents & businesses to create
a crime free area through community participation; To assist in
the reduction of crime; To improve relations between police &
communities
Regan Borisenko, President
Gabriel Pelletier, Vice-President

Brant United Way (BUW)
125 Morrell St., Brantford ON N3T 4J9
Tel: 519-752-7848; *Fax:* 519-752-7913
info@brantunitedway.org
www.brantunitedway.org
www.facebook.com/BrantUnitedWay
twitter.com/brantunitedway
To help people in their time of need
Sherry Haines, Executive Director

British Columbia Association of Family Resource Programs
#332, 505-8840 - 210th St., Langley BC VIM 2Y2

Tel: 778-590-0045
info@frpbc.ca
www.frpbc.ca
www.instagram.com/frpbc
www.facebook.com/frpbc
twitter.com/frpbc

To raise awareness of the importance of community-based Family Resources Programs
Sherry Sinclair, Executive Director
Nicky Logins, Vice-President
Ramsay Malange, Research Director

British Columbia Association of Social Workers (BCASW) / Association des travailleurs sociaux de la Colombie-Britannique
#402, 1755 West Broadway, Vancouver BC V6J 4S5

Tel: 604-730-9111; *Fax:* 604-730-9112
Toll-Free: 800-665-4747
bcasw@bcasw.org
www.bcasw.org

To support & promote the profession of social work; To advocate for social justice
Dianne Heath, Executive Director

British Columbia Council for Families (BCCF)
#208, 1847 West Broadway, Vancouver BC V6J 1Y6

Tel: 604-678-8884; *Fax:* 604-678-8886
bccf@bccf.ca
www.bccf.ca
www.linkedin.com/company/bc-council-for-families
www.facebook.com/BCFamilies
twitter.com/BC_Families

To strengthen, encourage & support families through information, education, research & advocacy
Joseph Dunn, Executive Director

British Columbia Federation of Foster Parent Associations (BCFFPA)
#208, 20641 Logan Ave., Langley BC V3A 7R3

Tel: 604-544-1110; *Fax:* 604-544-2223
Toll-Free: 800-663-9999
office@bcfosterparents.ca
www.bcfosterparents.ca

To be the collective voice for all foster parents & to promote fostering; To act as a channel of communication between authorized child welfare agencies & foster parents concerning children & foster children in particular

British Columbia Society for Male Survivors of Sexual Abuse (BCSMSSA)
3126 West Broadway, Vancouver BC V6K 2H3

Tel: 604-682-6482; *Fax:* 604-684-8883
www.bc-malesurvivors.com

To provide treatment & support services to male survivors of sexual abuse & support for their families & partners; To acquire & develop education material & gather statistics; To establish new programs for male survivors within British Columbia or assist other agencies in setting up programs through training & consultation; To advocate for male survivors with government & the general population
Daniel Kline, Executive Director

BullyingCanada Inc.
PO Box 27009, Stn. Atl Superstore, 471 Smythe St., Fredericton NB E3B 9M1

Fax: 866-780-3592
Toll-Free: 877-352-4497
headoffice@bullyingcanada.ca
www.bullyingcanada.ca
www.facebook.com/bullyingcanada
twitter.com/bullyingcanada

To offer information, help & support to everyone involved in bullying; To undertake anti-bullying initiatives, including school workshops & a 24/7 support line
Rob Benn-Frenette, O.N.B., Co-Executive Director
Katie Thompson, Co-Executive Director

Campbell River & District United Way
PO Box 135, Campbell River BC V9W 5A7

Tel: 250-702-2911
bvbayly@uwcnvi.ca

To raise & distribute funds to member agencies that are providing support and services to residents in the Campbell River area

Canada Beyond the Blue (BTB)
info@canadabeyondtheblue.com
www.canadabeyondtheblue.com
www.instagram.com/canadabtb
www.facebook.com/CanadaBTB
twitter.com/CanadaBTB

To offer a support community to police families

Canada Without Poverty / Canada Sans Pauvreté
#100, 334 MacLaren St., Ottawa ON K2P 0M6

Tel: 613-789-0096; *Fax:* 613-566-3449
Toll-Free: 800-810-1076
info@cwp-csp.ca
cwp-csp.ca
www.instagram.com/cwp_csp
www.facebook.com/CanadaWithoutPoverty
twitter.com/CWP_CSP

To eradicate poverty in Canada by promoting income & social security for all Canadians, & by promoting poverty eradication as a human rights obligation.
Leilani Farha, Executive Director

Canadian Alliance to End Homelessness (CAEH)
PO Box 15062, Rpo Aspenwoods, Calgary AB T3H 0N8

Tel: 587-216-5615
info@caeh.ca
caeh.ca
www.youtube.com/user/TheCAEH
www.facebook.com/endinghomelessness
twitter.com/CAEHomelessness

To prevent & end homelessness in Canada
Tim Richter, President & CEO

Canadian Association for Safe Supply (CASS)
#204, 634 East Georgia St., Vancouver BC V6A 2A1

Tel: 778-227-9914
unitedforsafesupply@gmail.com
www.safesupply.ca
www.facebook.com/CASSafeSupply
twitter.com/canadian_safe

To increase access & supply to legal, regulated substances of known potency

Canadian Association for the Prevention of Discrimination & Harassment in Higher Education (CAPDHHE) / L'association canadienne pour la prévention de la discrimination et du harcèlement en milieu d'enseignement supérieur (ACPDHMES)
c/o University of British Columbia, Vancouver BC V6T 1Z2

Tel: 604-822-4859; *Fax:* 604-822-3260
amlong@ubc.ca
capdhhe.org

To provide professional development for individuals employed at colleges & universities in the area of discrimination & harassment
Milé Komlen, President
Sonya Nigam, Vice President

Canadian Association of Sexual Assault Centres (CASAC) / Association canadienne des centres contre les agressions à caractère sexuel (ACCCACS)
Vancouver BC

Tel: 604-876-2622; *Fax:* 604-876-8450
casac01@shaw.ca
www.casac.ca

To work for an end to violence against women & toward women's equality; To provide a national voice for anti-rape workers

Canadian Association of Social Workers (CASW) / Association canadienne des travailleurs sociaux (ACTS)
#402, 383 Parkdale Ave., Ottawa ON K1Y 4R4

Tel: 613-729-6668; *Fax:* 613-729-9608
Toll-Free: 855-729-2279
casw@casw-acts.ca
www.casw-acts.ca
www.facebook.com/casw.acts
twitter.com/casw_acts

To represent Canadian professional social workers; To strengthen & advances the social work profession in Canada; To preserve excellence within the profession
Fred Phelps, MSW, RSW, CAE, Executive Director

Canadian Career Development Foundation (CCDF) / Fondation canadienne pour le développement de carrière (FCDC)
#202, 119 Ross Ave., Ottawa ON K1Y 0N6

Tel: 613-729-6164; *Fax:* 613-729-3515
Toll-Free: 877-729-6164
information@ccdf.ca
www.ccdf.ca
www.linkedin.com/company/ccdf-fcdc
twitter.com/CCDFFCDC

To advance the understanding & practice of career development
Sareena Hopkins, Executive Director
Donnalee Bell, Managing Director

Canadian Centre for Abuse Awareness
120 Harry Walker Pkwy. North, Newmarket ON L3Y 7B2

Tel: 905-727-4357; *Toll-Free:* 800-379-8858
info@abusehurts.ca
www.newmakeit.com
www.instagram.com/abusehurts
www.facebook.com/abusehurtscom

To reduce the incidence & impact of abuse through education & public awareness
Ellen Campbell, Chief Executive Officer & Founder

Canadian Centre for Victims of Torture (CCVT)
194 Jarvis St., 2nd Fl., Toronto ON M5B 2B7

Tel: 416-363-1066; *Fax:* 416-363-2122
www.ccvt.org
www.facebook.com/ccvt.toronto
twitter.com/ccvt_toronto

To offer support & arrange medical, legal & social care for torture victims & their families; To increase public awareness in Canada & abroad of torture & its effects upon survivors & their families
Mulugeta Abai, Executive Director

Canadian Council for Refugees (CCR) / Conseil canadien pour les réfugiés
#301, 6839, rue Drolet, Montréal QC H2S 2T1

Tel: 514-277-7223; *Fax:* 514-277-1447
info@ccrweb.ca
www.ccrweb.ca
www.youtube.com/ccrwebvideos
www.facebook.com/ccrweb
twitter.com/ccrweb

To be committed to the rights & protection of refugees in Canada & around the world & to the settlement of refugees & immigrants in Canada
Janet Dench, Executive Director
Marisa Berry Méndez, Director, Settlement Policy
Colleen French, Coordinator, Communications & Networking

Canadian Counselling & Psychotherapy Association (CCPA) / L'Association canadienne de counseling et de psychothérapie (ACCP)
#202, 245 Menten Pl., Ottawa ON K2H 9E8

Tel: 613-237-1099; *Fax:* 613-237-9786
Toll-Free: 877-765-5565
www.ccpa-accp.ca
www.facebook.com/CCPA.ACCP
twitter.com/ccpa_accp

To enhance the counselling profession in Canada; To promote policies & practices which support the provision of accessible, competent & accountable counselling services throughout the human lifespan, & in a manner sensitive to the pluralistic nature of society
Jenny Rowett, President
Barbara MacCallum, Chief Executive Officer

Canadian Feed The Children (CFTC)
#123, 6 Lansing Sq., Toronto ON M2J 1T5

Tel: 416-757-1220; *Fax:* 416-757-3318
Toll-Free: 800-387-1221
contact@canadianfeedthechildren.ca
www.canadianfeedthechildren.ca
www.youtube.com/user/canadianfeed
www.linkedin.com/company/canadian-feed-the-children
www.facebook.com/CanadianFeedTheChildren
twitter.com/cdnfeedchildren

To alleviate the impact of poverty on children; To work with local partners overseas & in Canada to enhance the well-being of children & the self-sufficiency of their families & communities
Jacquelyn Wright, President & CEO

Canadian Friends of Peace Now (Shalom Achshav) (CFPN)
#517, 119-660 Eglinton Ave. East, Toronto ON M4G 2K2

Tel: 416-322-5559; *Fax:* 416-322-5587
Toll-Free: 866-405-5387
info@peacenowcanada.org
www.peacenowcanada.org
www.facebook.com/CanadianFriendsofPeaceNow

CFPN supports Peace Now, a peace movement in Israel that sponsors dialogue between Israelis & Palestinians, & advocates a 2-state solution for co-existence. CFPN organizes lectures in Canada & sponsors visits by Israeli & Palestinian peace activists. It is a registered charity, BN: 119147320RR0001.
David Brooks, Co-Chair, Ottawa
Gabriella Goliger, Co-Chair, Ottawa
Sheldon Gordon, Chair, Toronto
Stephen Scheinberg, Chair, Montréal

Canadian Grandparents' Rights Association (CGRA)
#207, 14980 - 104 Ave., Surrey BC V3R 1M9
Tél: 604-585-8242; *Fax:* 604-585-8241
Toll-Free: 866-585-8242
www.CanadianGrandparentsRightsAssociation.com
Promotes, supports, and assists Grandparents and their families in maintaining or re-establishing family ties and family stability where the family has been disrupted; especially those ties between grandparents and grandchildren.

Canadian Lyford Cay Foundation
c/o Stern Cohen LLP, attn: Laura Gay, 45 St Clair Ave. West, 14th Fl., Toronto ON M4V 1L3
Fax: 416-967-4372
Toll-Free: 877-265-2942
info@lyfordcayfoundation.org
www.lyfordcayfoundation.org
www.facebook.com/LyfordCayFoundations
To enhance & enrich the Bahamas & the lives of its people

Canadians Concerned About Violence in Entertainment (C-CAVE)
info@c-cave.com
www.c-cave.com
To provide public education on research findings related to media violence through popular culture, commodities marketed primarily to children, adolescents & adults

Career Professionals of Canada (CPC)
Toll-Free: 866-896-8768
info@careerprocanada.ca
careerprocanada.ca
www.linkedin.com/groups/1942226
www.facebook.com/groups/careerprocanada
twitter.com/CareerProCanada
To support the Canadian labour market; To create opportunities for members to gain contacts & credibility in the field
Sharon Graham, Executive Director

Carrefour de solidarité internationale (CSI)
165, rue Moore, Sherbrooke QC J1H 1B8
Tél: 819-566-8595
info@csisher.com
www.csisher.com
www.facebook.com/carrefour.solidarite.internationale
Solidarité internationale et d'éducation à la citoyenneté mondiale pour l'égalité, la justice sociale et l'environnement
Étienne Doyon, Directeur général

Carrefour international bas-laurentien pour l'engagement social (CIBLES)
60, rue de l'Évêché ouest, Rimouski QC G5L 4H6
Tél: 418-723-1880
info@cibles.org
cibles.org
www.instagram.com/ciblesbsl
www.facebook.com/cibles.org
Développement et soutien de projets axés sur l'environnement, le vivre-ensemble et la justice sociale
Sarah Charland-Faucher, Coordonnatrice

Centraide Abitibi Témiscamingue et Nord-du-Québec
1009, 6e rue, Val-d'Or QC J9P 3W4
Tél: 819-825-7139; *Téléc:* 819-825-7155
courrier@centraide-atnq.qc.ca
centraide-rcoq.org
www.instagram.com/centraide_atnq
www.linkedin.com/company/centraide-atnq
www.facebook.com/Centraide.ATNQ
Mélanie Perreault, Directrice générale

Centraide Bas St-Laurent
#303, 1555, boul Jacques Cartier, Mont-Joli QC G5H 2W1
Tél: 418-775-5555; *Téléc:* 418-775-5525
www.centraidebsl.org
www.facebook.com/Centraidebsl
Organisme sans but lucratif de lutte à la pauvreté et de soutien aux personnes démunies
Eve Lavoie, Directrice générale

Centraide Centre du Québec
154, rue Dunkin, Drummondville QC J2B 5V1
Tél: 819-477-0505; *Téléc:* 819-477-6719
Ligne sans frais: 888-477-0505
bureau@centraide-cdq.ca
www.centraide-cdq.ca
www.facebook.com/CentraideCentreDuQuebec
twitter.com/centraide_cdq
Rassembler les personnes et les ressources du Centre-du-Québec afin de contribuer au développement social de la communauté et d'améliorer la qualité de vie de ses membres les plus vulnérables et ce, en lien avec les organismes communautaires.
Isabelle Dionne, Directrice générale

Centraide du Grand Montréal / Centraide of Greater Montréal
493, rue Sherbrooke ouest, Montréal QC H3A 1B6
Tél: 514-288-1261; *Téléc:* 514-350-7282
info@centraide-mtl.org
www.centraide-mtl.org
www.youtube.com/user/CentraideMtl
www.facebook.com/centraide.du.grand.montreal
twitter.com/centraidemtl
To maximize financial & volunteer resources in order to promote mutual aid, social commitment & self-reliance as effective means of improving the quality of life of the community & especially of its neediest members
Lili-Anna Peresa, Présidente et directrice générale

Centraide Duplessis
#101, 185, rue Napoléon, Sept-Iles QC G4R 4R7
Tél: 418-962-2011
administration@centraideduplessis.org
www.centraideduplessis.org
www.facebook.com/centraide.duplessis
Denis Miousse, Directeur général

Centraide Estrie
1150, rue Belvédère sud, Sherbrooke QC J1H 4C7
Tél: 819-569-9281; *Téléc:* 819-569-5195
reception.centraide@qc.aibn.com
www.centraideestrie.com
www.youtube.com/channel/UCM2Tm-5MS5gAlJ4UWEfg5jA
www.facebook.com/Centraide-Estrie-177152949010458
Vise à soutenir les organismes bénévoles et communautaires engagés directement auprès des clientèles les plus démunies et vulnérables
Claude Forgues, Directeur général

Centraide Gaspésie Iles-de-la-Madeleine
#216, 230, rte du Parc, Sainte-Anne-des-Monts QC G4V 2C4
Tél: 418-763-2171
mejcentraide@globetrotter.net
www.centraidegim.ca
www.facebook.com/centraide.gaspesie
Soulager la misère et la souffrance humaine
Stéphan Boucher, Directeur général

Centraide Gatineau-Labelle-Hautes-Laurentides
CP 154, 343, rue de la Madone, Mont-Laurier QC J9L 3G9
Tél: 819-623-4090; *Téléc:* 819-623-7646
bureau@centraideglhl.ca
www.maregioncentraide.ca
www.facebook.com/Centraide.Gatineau.Labelle.Hautes.Laurentides
Laure Voilquin, Directrice générale

Centraide Haute-Côte-Nord/Manicouagan
#301, 858, rue de Puyjalon, Baie-Comeau QC G5C 1N1
Tél: 418-589-5567; *Téléc:* 418-295-2567
www.centraidehcnmanicouagan.ca
Carole Lemieux, Directrice générale

Centraide KRTB-Côte-du-Sud
100, 4e av, La Pocatière QC G0R 1Z0
Tél: 418-856-5105; *Téléc:* 418-856-4385
centraideportage@bellnet.ca
www.facebook.com/CentraideKrtbCoteDuSud
D'aider les gens, d'affecter les ressources en fonction des besoins, d'améliorer la qualité de vie de chacun et de renforcer le soutien communautaire
Sylvain Roy, Directeur général

Centraide Lanaudière
674, rue St-Louis, Joliette QC J6E 2Z6
Tél: 450-752-1999
www.centraide-lanaudiere.com
www.facebook.com/275362692481275
Promouvoir l'entraide, le partage et l'engagement bénévole et communautaire
Nicole Campeau, Directrice générale

Centraide Laurentides
#107, 880, boul Michèle-Bohec, Blainville QC J7C 5E2
Tél: 450-436-1584; *Téléc:* 450-951-2772
www.centraidelaurentides.org
www.youtube.com/user/centraidelaurentides
www.facebook.com/CentraideLaurentides
twitter.com/CentraideLauren
Contribuer, par la promotion du partage et de l'engagement bénévole et communautaire, à la construction d'une société d'entraide vouée à l'amélioration de la qualité de vie des personnes en difficulté
Suzanne M. Piché, Directrice générale

Centraide Mauricie
90, rue Des Casernes, Trois-Rivières QC G9A 1X2
Tél: 819-374-6207; *Téléc:* 819-374-6857
centraide.mauricie@centraidemauricie.ca
www.centraidemauricie.ca
www.linkedin.com/company/centraide-mauricie
www.facebook.com/centraide.mauricie
twitter.com/centraidem
Travailler à un changement social pour une société plus juste, plus humaine et plus démocratique à travers la promotion de l'entraide, la solidarité et l'engagement bénévole afin de répondre aux besoins socio-économiques de notre communauté
Julie Colbert, Directrice générale

Centraide Outaouais
74, boul Montclair, Gatineau QC J8Y 2E7
Tél: 819-771-7751; *Téléc:* 819-771-0301
Ligne sans frais: 800-325-7751
information@centraideoutaouais.com
www.centraideoutaouais.com
www.youtube.com/user/centraideoutaouais
www.facebook.com/CentraideOutaouais
twitter.com/CentraidOuais
Mobiliser le gens et rassembler les ressources pour améliorer la qualité de vie de personnes plus vulnérables et contribuer au développement de collectivités solidaires
Nathalie Lepage, Directrice générale

Centraide Québec et Chaudière-Appalaches
550, ch Sainte-Foy, Québec QC G1S 2J5
Tél: 418-660-2100
centraide@centraide-quebec.com
www.centraide-quebec.com
www.youtube.com/user/CentraideQuebec
www.linkedin.com/company/centraide-qu-bec-et-chaudi-re-appalaches
www.facebook.com/centraidequebec
twitter.com/CentraideQc
Levées de fonds et attribution de subventions à 201 organismes communautaires pour aider les personnes les plus démunies
Bruno Marchand, Président/Directeur général

Centraide Richelieu-Yamaska
320, av de la Concorde nord, Saint-Hyacinthe QC J2S 4N7
Tél: 450-773-6679; *Téléc:* 450-773-4734
Ligne sans frais: 844-773-6679
bureau@centraidery.org
www.centraidery.org
www.facebook.com/Centraiderichelieuyamaska
twitter.com/centraidery
D'améliorer les conditions de vie les plus démuni(e)s de son territoire
Daniel Laplante, Directeur général

Centraide Saguenay-Lac St-Jean
#107, 475, boul Talbot, Chicoutimi QC G7H 4A3
Tél: 418-543-3131; *Téléc:* 418-543-0665
info@centraideslsj.ca
www.centraidesaglac.ca
Rassembler et développer des ressources financières et bénévoles afin d'aider les diverses communautés du Saguenay-Lac-St-Jean à organiser et à promouvoir l'entraide, l'engagement social et la prise en charge afin d'améliorer la qualité de vie de sa collectivité et de ses membres les plus démunis et les plus vulnérables
Martin St-Pierre, Directeur général
Johanne Bouchard, Secrétaire

Centraide sud-ouest du Québec
#161, 11, rue de l'Église, Salaberry-de-Valleyfield QC J6T 1J5
Tél: 450-371-2061; *Téléc:* 450-377-2309
centraide@oricom.ca
www.centraidesudouest.org
www.facebook.com/195796617125646
Grâce à votre don, il y a du changement possible. En effet, la misère qu'elle soit physique, morale, psychologique ou matérielle peut toucher tout le monde, peu importe la classe

sociale. Donner à Centraide Sud-Ouest, c'est susciter un changement positif dans notre communauté
Steve Hickey, Directeur général

Centre Amitié de Solidarité Internationale de la Région des Appalaches (CASIRA)
37, rue Notre Dame ouest, Thetford Mines QC G6G 1J1
Tél: 418-338-6211; *Téléc:* 418-338-3288
info@casira.org
www.casira.org
www.facebook.com/AmistadCASIRA
Recrute des Canadiens pour du travail bénévole à l'étranger, principalement en Amérique latine
Renée Blais, Présidente

Centre de solidarité internationale Corcovado (CSI)
83, rue Gamble ouest, Rouyn-Noranda QC J9X 2R3
Tél: 819-797-8800
csi@csicorcovado.org
www.csicorcovado.org
www.facebook.com/CSI.Corcovado
Soutenir et de développer des projets d'aide internationale; Sensibiliser à la solidarité internationale; Promouvoir la consommation responsable
Denise Trudel, Responsable, librairie solidaire

Centre de solidarité internationale du Saguenay-Lac-Saint-Jean (CSI-SLSJ)
CP 2127, 27, rue Saint-Joseph, Alma QC J9X 2R3
Tél: 418-668-5211; *Téléc:* 418-668-5638
info@centresolidarite.ca
www.centresolidarite.ca
www.instagram.com/centresolidarite.slsj
www.facebook.com/centresolidarite
Sabrina Gauvreau, Directrice générale

Centre for Suicide Prevention (CSP)
#320, 105 - 12 Ave. SE, Calgary AB T2G 1A1
Tel: 403-245-3900; *Fax:* 403-245-0299
Crisis Hot-Line: 403-266-4357
www.suicideinfo.ca
suicideinfo.tumblr.com
www.linkedin.com/company/centre-for-suicide-prevention
www.facebook.com/centreforsuicideprevention
twitter.com/cspyyc
To educate people about the risk of suicide & suicide prevention
Mara Grunau, Executive Director
Hilary Sirman, Director, Impact & Engagement
Crystal Walker, Coordinator, Communications

Certified Listeners Society
#314, 1235 Fairview St., Burlington ON L7S 2K9
info@certifiedlisteners.org
certifiedlisteners.org
www.linkedin.com/company/certified-listeners-society
www.facebook.com/CertifiedListeners
twitter.com/cert_listeners
To provide around-the-clock early-stage emotional support to anyone who needs it
Alejandro Cuellar, Contact

The Child Abuse Survivor Monument Project (CASMP)
274 Rhodes Ave., Toronto ON M4L 3A3
Tel: 416-469-4764; *Fax:* 416-963-8892
mci@irvingstudios.com
www.irvingstudios.com/child_abuse_survivor_monument
www.youtube.com/user/ChildAbuseMonument
www.facebook.com/ChildAbuseMonument
twitter.com/ChildAbuseMnumt
To build a memorial monument for & by survivors of child abuse to assist with the personal & social healing of the ravages of child abuse
Michael C. Irving, Artistic Director

Child Care Advocacy Association of Canada (CCAAC) / Association canadienne pour la promotion des services de garde à l'enfance (ACPSGE)
Impact Hub, 123 Slater St., 6th Fl., Ottawa ON K1P 5H2
Tel: 613-212-0065; *Toll-Free:* 866-620-2753
info@ccnow.ca
timeforchildcare.ca
www.facebook.com/childcarenowcanada
twitter.com/Child_Care_Now
To work toward expanding the child care system & improving its quality; To advocate for the development of an affordable, comprehensive, high-quality, not-for-profit child care system that is supported by public funds & accessible to every Canadian family who wishes to use it

Child Welfare League of Canada (CWLC) / Ligue pour le bien-être de l'enfance du Canada (LBEC)
492 Somerset St. West, Ottawa ON K1R 5J8
Tel: 613-235-4412; *Fax:* 613-235-7616
info@cwlc.ca
www.cwlc.ca
www.facebook.com/CWLC.LBEC
To be a voice for vulnerable children in Canada; To promote the well-being of children, youth, & families who are vulnerable
Lesley Hill, Board Chair
Rachel Gouin, Executive Director

Christie-Ossington Neighbourhood Centre (CONC)
854 Bloor St. West, Toronto ON M6G 1M2
Tel: 416-534-8941; *Fax:* 416-534-8704
www.conccommunity.org
To improve the quality of life in the Christie Ossington community by working in collaboration with residents, community institutions, agencies, local businesses and stakeholders to create a safe and healthy community.
Lynn Daly, Executive Director

The Citizens Foundation Canada (TCF)
#200, 2010 Winston Park Dr., Oakville ON L6H 5R7
Tel: 289-291-7701; *Fax:* 289-291-7601
tcf@tcfcanada.org
tcfcanada.org
www.instagram.com/tcfpak
www.facebook.com/citizensfoundationcanada
twitter.com/TCFCan
To fund education for underprivileged children in Pakistan
Sajid Salman, President
Hyder Zach Masum, Secretary
Zulfiqar Ahmad, Treasurer
Sumera Bukhari, Manager, Office & Administration

Clowns sans frontières
#203, 105 rue Ontario Est, Montréal QC H2X 1G9
Tél: 514-495-1287
contact@clownssansfrontieres.ca
www.clownssansfrontieres.ca
www.youtube.com/channel/UCQWUO8JZx69GPWRlnazRPMw
www.facebook.com/ClownsSansFrontieres
twitter.com/csf_canada
Organise des spectacles et des ateliers gratuits pour offrir un soutien moral et émotionnel aux populations victimes de la guerre, de la misère ou de l'exclusion
Katel Le Fustec, Directrice générale et artistique

Comité pour les droits humains en Amérique latine (CDHAL)
1425, boul René-Lévesque ouest, 3e étage, Montréal QC H3G 1T7
Tél: 514-257-1246
info@cdhal.org
www.cdhal.org
www.youtube.com/user/CDHALQuebec
www.facebook.com/CDHAL.montreal
twitter.com/CDHAL
La défense et la promotion des droits humains en réciprocité avec les mouvements sociaux et les communautés d'Amérique latine
Thérèse Guay, Présidente

Community Action Resource Centre (CARC)
1652 Keele St., Toronto ON M6M 3W3
Tel: 416-652-2273; *Fax:* 416-652-8992
www.communityarc.ca
www.facebook.com/CommunityActionResourceCentre
twitter.com/communityarc
To build the capacity of communities by mobilizing resources & providing supportive social services, for the empowerment of individuals & groups with a focus on serving the most vulnerable and disadvantaged.

Community Social Services Employers' Association (CSSEA)
Two Bentall Centre, PO Box 232, #800, 555 Burrard St., Vancouver BC V7X 1M8
Tel: 604-687-7220; *Fax:* 604-687-7266
Toll-Free: 800-377-3340
cssea@cssea.bc.ca
www.cssea.bc.ca
To strive for excellence & innovation in human resources & labour relations
Gentil Mateus, Chief Executive Officer
Thomas Marshall, Director, Communications

Confédération des organismes familiaux du Québec (COFAQ)
3965, rue Sainte-Catherine est, Montréal QC H1W 2G7
Tél: 514-521-4777
famille@cofaq.qc.ca
cofaq.qc.ca
www.facebook.com/CofaqFamille
Représenter les familles et revendiquer leurs droits auprès des diverses instances publiques et privées; Promouvoir des projets innovateurs et le développement d'expertises satisfaisant aux besoins des familles et leurs organisations; Réaliser des activités de soutien auprès des membres
Mohammed Barhone, Président
Marie Simard, Directrice générale

Conflict Resolution Saskatchewan
PO Box 3765, Regina SK S4P 3N8
Tel: 306-565-3939; *Fax:* 306-586-6711
Toll-Free: 866-565-3938
admin@conflictresolutionsk.ca
www.conflictresolutionsk.ca

Conseil national des chômeurs et chômeuses (CNC)
3734, av du Parc, Montréal QC H2X 2J1
cnc@lecnc.com
www.aranb.ca
www.youtube.com/user/sanschemisenational
www.facebook.com/ConseilNationaldesChomeursetChomeuses
twitter.com/le_cnc
Défense et à la promotion des droits des chômeurs et chômeuses, et plus largement des travailleurs et travailleuses avec ou sans emploi
Pierre Céré, Porte-Parole
Milan Bernard, Conseiller

Cooper Institute / L'Institut Cooper
81 Prince St., Charlottetown PE C1A 4R3
Tel: 902-894-4573; *Fax:* 902-368-7180
www.cooperinstitute.ca
www.facebook.com/156027014448502
To promote programs focused on livable income for all, food sovereignty & cultural diversity & inclusion; To conduct research & popular education projects on provincial, national & international level
Joe Byrne, President

COSTI Immigrant Services
1710 Dufferin St., Toronto ON M6E 3P2
Tel: 416-658-1600; *Fax:* 416-658-8537
info@costi.org
www.costi.org
To provide educational, social & employment support to help immigrants in the greater Toronto area attain self-sufficiency in Canadian society. Services are provided in over 60 languages.
Bruno M. Suppa, President
Mario J. Calla, Executive Director

Cowichan United Way
1 Kenneth Place, Duncan BC V9L 5G3
Tel: 250-748-1312; *Fax:* 250-748-7652
Toll-Free: 877-748-1312
office@cowichan.unitedway.ca
www.cowichan.unitedway.ca
www.facebook.com/UnitedWayCowichan
twitter.com/uwcowichan
To fundraise for charities; To provide guidance & counsel to charitable organization; To take leadership role in raising awareness of community needs
Mike Murphy, President
Heather Gardiner, Interim Advisor

CPA Sans Frontières (CPASF)
#800, 5, Place Ville Marie, Montréal QC H3B 2G2
Tél: 514-288-3256; *Ligne sans frais:* 800-363-4688
cpasf@cpaquebec.com
www.cdhal.org
www.linkedin.com/company/cpa-sans-frontieres-canada
www.facebook.com/CPASansFrontieres
Contribuer positivement au mieux-être de populations dans le besoin, à l'extérieur de nos frontières
Sophie Raymond, Directrice générale

Cyclo Nord-Sud
8717, 8è Av, Montréal QC H1Z 2X4
Tél: 514-843-0077; *Téléc:* 514-270-9190
Ligne sans frais: 888-843-0077
info@cyclonordsud.org
cyclonordsud.org
www.instagram.com/cyclo_nord_sud
www.linkedin.com/company/cyclo-nord-sud
www.facebook.com/cyclonordsud
Promotion du développement durable visant le respect de la biosphère et des personnes qui l'habitent

Marie-Lys Turcotte, Présidente

Davenport-Perth Neighbourhood & Community Health Centre (DPNCHC)
1900 Davenport Rd., Toronto ON M6N 1B7
Tel: 416-656-8025; *Fax:* 416-656-1264
info@dpnchc.ca
dpnchc.com
The Davenport-Perth Neighbourhood Centre (DPNC) is a multi-service agency located in the west end of Toronto dedicated to encouraging people to work together and take action to improve the political, social, economic, spiritual and cultural life of the whole community.
Wade Hilier, President

Dejinta Beesha Multi-Service Centre
8 Taber Rd., Toronto ON M9W 3A4
Tel: 416-743-1286; *Fax:* 416-743-1233
info@dejinta.org
dejinta.org
To provide settlement, integration, recreation, health, employment, education, & social services to the community; Offering services in English, French, Italian, Arabic, Somali, & Kiswahili
Mohamed Gilao, Executive Director

Delta Family Resource Centre
#5, 2972 Islington Ave., Toronto ON M9L 2K6
Tel: 416-747-1172; *Fax:* 416-747-7415
contactus@dfrc.ca
www.dfrc.ca
www.facebook.com/deltafamilycentre
twitter.com/DeltaFamilyRC
To support the needs of families & children within the community; Offering services in English, Spanish, Italian, Hindi, Punjabi, Laotian, Gujarati, Somali, Cantonese, Tamil, Mandarin, Thi, Ewe, Twi, Urdu, Dari & Ga
Rosalyn Miller, Executive Director

DESI
2330, rue Notre-Dame ouest, Montréal QC H3J 2Y2
Tél: 514-904-3093; *Ligne sans frais:* 888-330-3603
info@ong-desi.qc.ca
ong-desi.qc.ca
www.linkedin.com/company/ongdesi
www.facebook.com/DESI.cooperation.internationale
Regroupe des retraités et préretraités qui mettent bénévolement leur expertise au service de communautés dans les pays en développement
Pierre Mathieu, Président

Distress Centres Ontario (DCO)
#1016, 30 Duke St. West, Kitchener ON N2H 3W5
Tel: 416-486-2242; *Fax:* 519-342-0970
info@dcontario.org
www.dcontario.org
To transfer best practices between member centres; To promote, support & sustain member agencies
Colleen Gallagher, Chair
Neta Gear, Executive Director

Dixon Hall
58 Sumach St., Toronto ON M5A 3J7
Tel: 416-863-0499; *Fax:* 416-863-9981
info@dixonhall.org
www.dixonhall.org
www.facebook.com/DixonHallToronto
twitter.com/dixon_hall
To create opportunities for people of all ages to dream, to achieve and to live full and rewarding lives.
Kate Stark, Executive Director

Doorsteps Neighbourhood Services
#106, 200 Chalkfarm Dr., Toronto ON M3L 2H7
Tel: 416-243-5480; *Fax:* 416-243-7406
www.doorsteps.ca
To focus on community education, prevention, & the enhancement of resiliency of individuals & communities
Carol Thames, Executive Director

Dying with Dignity (DWD) / Mourir dans la dignité
#802, 55 Eglinton Ave. East, Toronto ON M4P 1G8
Tel: 416-486-3998; *Fax:* 416-486-5562
Toll-Free: 800-495-6156
info@dyingwithdignity.ca
www.dyingwithdignity.ca
www.youtube.com/user/DWDCanada
www.facebook.com/DWDCanada
twitter.com/DWDCanada
To improve the quality of dying for all Canadians in accordance with their own wishes, values & beliefs
Helen Long, Chief Executive Officer
Cameron Dunkin, Chief Operating Officer

Edmonton Social Planning Council (ESPC)
#200, 10544 - 106 St., Edmonton AB T5H 2X6
Tel: 780-423-2031; *Fax:* 780-425-6244
info@edmontonsocialplanning.ca
www.edmontonsocialplanning.ca
www.facebook.com/edmontonspc
twitter.com/edmontonspc
To deepen community understanding of social planning issues, influence policy, & spark collaborative actions that lead to positive social change
Susan Morrissey, Executive Director
John Kolkman, Research Associate
Sandra Ngo, Research Coordinator

Elder Mediation Canada (EMC)
www.fmc.ca/mediation/elder-mediation
To advance the practice of elder mediation in Canada; To improve the qualifications & effectiveness of mediators
Judy McCann-Beranger, Chair

Family & Community Support Services Association of Alberta (FCSSAA)
Belmead Professional Bldg., #106, 8944 - 182 St., Edmonton AB T5T 2E3
Tel: 780-415-4790; *Fax:* 780-415-4793
assistant@fcssaa.org
www.fcssaa.org
To advocate on behalf of local communities & programs to the general public, municipal governments, regional services, provincial & national agencies, & authorities; To educate individuals, communities, boards, & staff
Arnold Hanson, President
Deb Teed, Executive Director
Judy Macknee, Executive Assistant

Family Mediation Canada (FMC) / Médiation Familiale Canada
PO Box 46003, Stn. Quail Ridge, Kelowna BC V1V 0B1
Tel: 778-674-4362; *Toll-Free:* 877-269-2970
admin@fmc.ca
www.fmc.ca
To improve the provision for cooperative conflict resolution in areas such as separation & divorce, child welfare, adoption, parent & teen counselling, age-related issues & wills & estates
Judy McCann-Beranger, President

Family Mediation Manitoba (FMM)
PO Box 2369, Winnipeg MB R3C 4A6
Tel: 204-989-5330; *Fax:* 204-694-7555
contact@familymediationmanitoba.ca
www.familymediationmanitoba.ca
To promote the use of mediation as apreferred method of dispute resolution in family matters
Karen Burwash, President

Family Service Canada (FSC) / Services à la famille - Canada
#501, 151 City Centre Dr., Mississauga ON L5B 1M7
Tel: 905-270-5626
www.familyservicecanada.org
To promote families as the primary source of nurturing & development of individuals, their relationship in families & communities, through promoting & ensuring the best policies & services for families in Canada.
Chuck MacLean, Chair

Family Service Toronto (FST)
#202, 128A Sterling Rd., Toronto ON M6R 2B7
Tel: 416-595-9618
www.familyservicetoronto.org
www.youtube.com/user/FamilyServiceToronto
www.linkedin.com/company/family-service-toronto
www.facebook.com/FamilyServiceToronto
twitter.com/FamilyServiceTO
To help individuals & families affected by socio-economic circumstances or mental health issues
Ted Betts, President
Margaret Hancock, Executive Director

Fédération des associations de familles monoparentales et recomposées du Québec (FAFMRQ) / Federation of Single-Parent Family Associations of Québec
584, rue Guizot est, Montréal QC H2P 1N3
Tél: 514-729-6666; *Téléc:* 514-729-6746
fafmrq.info@videotron.ca
www.fafmrq.org
www.facebook.com/215273325165435
twitter.com/FAFMRQ
Travailler à améliorer les conditions socio-économiques des familles monoparentales et recomposées du Québec
Sylvie Lévesque, Directrice générale

Fédération des centres d'action bénévole du Québec (FCABQ)
#102, 1855, rue Rachel est, Montréal QC H2H 1P5
Tél: 514-843-6312; *Téléc:* 514-843-6485
Ligne sans frais: 800-715-7515
info@fcabq.org
www.fcabq.org
www.facebook.com/fcabq
twitter.com/FCABQ
Promouvoir l'action bénévole au Québec; former un centre d'action bénévole; organiser la semaine de l'action bénévole
Fimba Tankoano, Directeur général

The 519 Church St. Community Centre
519 Church St., Toronto ON M4Y 2C9
Tel: 416-392-6874; *Fax:* 416-392-0519
info@the519.org
www.the519.org
www.youtube.com/The519Toronto
www.facebook.com/The519
twitter.com/the519
To act as a meeting place & focal point for the diverse downtown Toronto community; To respond to the needs of the local neighbourhood and the broader Lesbian, Gay, Bisexual, Transsexual, Transgender, and Queer community
Maura Lawless, Executive Director

Flemingdon Neighbourhood Services
#104, 10 Gateway Blvd., Toronto ON M3C 3A1
Tel: 416-424-2900; *Fax:* 416-424-3455
info@fnservices.org
www.fnservices.org
To enhance the over-all quality of life for residents of Flemingdon Park and the City of Toronto by increasing access to information and community resources for our clients through advocacy, empowerment and education.
John Carey, Executive Director

La Fondation des Auberges du coeur
Tour sud, #17, 4246, rue Juean-Talon est, Montréal QC H1S 1J8
Tél: 514-523-3659; *Téléc:* 514-523-2109
Ligne sans frais: 866-992-6387
info@aubergesducoeur.com
www.aubergesducoeur.com
www.instagram.com/fondationdesaubergesducoeur
www.facebook.com/LaFondationdesAubergesducoeur
Défendre l'existence & l'autonomie des ressources communautaires d'hébergement pour jeunes adolescents & jeunes adultes en difficulté ou sans abri; Agir comme porte-parole des jeunes sans abri; Favoriser entre les maisons, les jeunes & les partenaires des communautés d'appartenance de chacune des Auberges des échanges sur les besoins des jeunes
Michèle Noël, Directeur général

Fondation Paul Gérin-Lajoie
#900, 465, rue Saint-Jean, Montréal QC H2Y 2R6
Tél: 514-288-3888; *Téléc:* 514-288-4880
Ligne sans frais: 800-363-2687
fpgl@fondationpgl.ca
fondationpgl.ca
www.instagram.com/fondation_pgl
www.facebook.com/fondationpaulgerinlajoie
twitter.com/fondation_pgl
Contribuer à l'amélioration des conditions de vie des populations par une éducation de qualité
Hervé Pilon, Directeur général par intérim

Food Banks Canada / Banques alimentaires Canada
#203, 5090 Explorer Dr., Mississauga ON L4W 4T9
Tel: 905-602-5234; *Fax:* 905-602-5614
Toll-Free: 877-535-0958
www.foodbankscanada.ca
www.instagram.com/foodbankscanada
www.facebook.com/FoodBanksCanada
twitter.com/foodbankscanada
To act as the voice for the hungry in Canada; To find short term & long term solutions for Canadians who are assisted by food banks
Chris Hatch, Chief Executive Officer
Chris Ferraz, Chief Administrative Officer
Sylvie Pelletier, Chief Marketing & Communications Officer
Mahen Kandasamy, Director, Finance

Foster Parent Support Services Society (FPSS)
#145, 735 Goldstream Ave., Victoria BC V9B 2X4
Tel: 778-430-5459; *Fax:* 778-430-5463
Toll-Free: 888-922-8437
admin@fpsss.com
www.fpsss.com
www.facebook.com/fpsssociety
twitter.com/FPSSSociety

To provide meaningful & accessible support, education & networking services which will continually enhance the skills and abilities of foster parents to deliver the best care possible to the children in their homes
Diane Daigle, Chair

Foundation Mères du Monde en Santé (MMS) / Healthy Mothers of the World
208, ch du Club-Marin, Montréal QC H3E 1V5
Tel: 438-872-4662
info@fondationmms.org
www.fondationmms.org
www.instagram.com/fondationmms
www.facebook.com/fondationMMSfoundation
twitter.com/FondationMMS
To reduce maternal mortality in Africa through medical missions addressing obstetric fistula
Jacques Corcos, President

Fred Victor Centre
59 Adelaide St. East, 6th Fl., Toronto ON M5C 1K6
Tel: 416-364-8228; *Fax:* 416-364-4728
www.fredvictor.org
To offer a continuum of community services, housing options and advocacy for adults who are experiencing homelessness, marginalization and poverty; over 150 beds and spaces are available across 6 sites and programs; in 2015, Community Resource Connections of Toronto integrated with Fred Victor
Mark Aston, Executive Director

Frontiers Foundation (FF/OB) / Fondation Frontière
419 Coxwell Ave., Toronto ON M4L 3B9
Tel: 416-690-3930; *Fax:* 416-690-3934
www.frontiersfoundation.ca
www.facebook.com/66661443145
To implement the enduring relief of human poverty throughout Canada & also abroad in tangible advancement projects
Marco A. Guzman, Executive Director

Good Jobs for All Coalition
Toronto ON
Tel: 416-937-9378
communications@goodjobsforall.ca
goodjobsforall.ca
twitter.com/goodjobsforall
To be an alliance of community, labour, social justice, youth and environmental organizations in the Toronto region
Preethy Sivakumar, Coordinator

Goodwill Industries of Alberta
8761 - 51 Ave., Edmonton AB T6E 5H1
Tel: 780-944-1414; *Toll-Free:* 866-927-1414
media@goodwill.ab.ca
www.goodwill.ab.ca
www.instagram.com/goodwill_ab
www.facebook.com/GoodwillAB
twitter.com/goodwillab
To help persons with disabilities & disadvantages; To build a strong future through rehabilitation & training
Larry Brownoff, Chair
Dale Monaghan, President & CEO

GRAND Society
c/o #509, 14 Spadina Rd., Toronto ON M5R 3M4
Tel: 416-513-9404
To provide emotional support to grandparents who have been denied access to their grandchildren; To make the public & professionals aware of this problem; To influence provincial family law to recognize the rights of grandparents
Joan Brooks, President

Grande Prairie & Region United Way
#213, 11330 - 106 St., Grande Prairie AB T8V 7X9
Tel: 780-532-1105; *Fax:* 780-532-3532
info@unitedwayabnw.org
www.gpunitedway.org
www.youtube.com/user/GrowUnitedBreakfast
www.facebook.com/UnitedWayABNW
twitter.com/UnitedWayABNW
To bring people together to strengthen the community; To strengthen the capacity of community & other local agencies to bring about positive change
Brenda Yamkowy, Executive Director

Groupe d'économie solidaire du Québec (GESQ)
CP 357, Succ. Place d'Armes, Montréal QC H2Y 3H1
w4.uqo.ca/gesq
www.facebook.com/GESQ1
René Lachapelle, Président

Habitat for Humanity Canada (HFHC) / Habitat pour l'Humanité Canada
#403, 477 Mount Pleasant Rd., Toronto ON M4S 2L9
Tel: 416-644-0988; *Fax:* 416-646-0574
Toll-Free: 800-667-5137
habitat@habitat.ca
habitat.ca
www.youtube.com/c/HabitatforHumanityCanada
www.linkedin.com/company/habitatcanada
www.facebook.com/HabitatCanada
twitter.com/HabitatCanada
To provide affordable & adequate housing for God's people in need by mobilizing local communities, volunteers & material & financial resources in wide-ranging, inclusive partnerships; To support, encourage, facilitate & empower those affiliates to build affordable homes in partnership with needy families
Julia Deans, President & CEO

Harbourfront Community Centre (HCC)
627 Queen's Quay West, Toronto ON M5V 3G3
Tel: 416-392-1509; *Fax:* 416-392-1512
hcc@harbourfrontcc.ca
www.harbourfrontcc.ca
To advocate for provision of necessary services to the community, provide a range of responsive programs and services in an atmosphere of belonging and meet the needs of a diverse and changing multicultural community.
Leona Rodall, Executive Director

Human Concern International (HCI)
PO Box 3984, Stn. C, Ottawa ON K1Y 4P2
Tel: 613-742-5948; *Toll-Free:* 800-587-6424
info@humanconcern.org
www.humanconcern.org
www.youtube.com/user/HumanConcernInt
www.facebook.com/HCICanada
twitter.com/humanconcernint
To help alleviate human suffering by investing in humanity, through long-term development projects for sustainability, & emergency relief assistance during times of dire need
Kaleem Akhtar, Executive Director
Garnayl Abdi, Program Officer

The Identification Clinic
#101, 260 Wyse Rd., Dartmouth NS B3A 1N3
Tel: 902-292-4587
theidclinic@gmail.com
www.theidclinic.org
www.facebook.com/theidentificationclinic
twitter.com/theidclinic
To assist homeless & disadvantaged individuals in the Halifax area acquire pieces of standard identification
Darren Greer, Founder/Coordinator

Imagine Canada
#700, 65 St Clair Ave. East, Toronto ON M4T 2Y3
Tel: 416-597-2293; *Fax:* 416-597-2294
Toll-Free: 800-263-1178
info@imaginecanada.ca
imaginecanada.ca
www.instagram.com/imaginecanada
www.linkedin.com/company/imagine-canada
www.facebook.com/ImagineCanada
twitter.com/ImagineCanada
To support Canada's charities, non-profit organizations & socially conscious businesses
Bruce MacDonald, President & CEO
Cathy Barr, Ph.D., Vice-President, Policy, Research & Standards
Bill Harper, Vice-President, Finance & Operations

InformOntario (IO)
c/o 3010 Forest Glade Dr., Windsor ON N8R 1L5
Tel: 519-990-9436
info@informontario.on.ca
www.informontario.on.ca
To ensure that all persons have access to human services information
Marcus Logan, President
Barbara McLachlan, Coordinator

Initiatives of Change Association (Canada) (IoFc) / Association Initiatives et Changement (Canada)
#8, 30 Cleary Ave., Ottawa ON K2A 4A1
Tel: 613-230-7197; *Fax:* 613-230-7198
admin.ca@iofc.org
ca.iofc.org
To transform society through changes in human motivations & behaviour, starting with oneself
Karen Bamboyne, Co-Chair & Secretary
Firyal Mohamed, Co-Chair
Lorne Braun, Treasurer

Institute of Cultural Affairs International (ICAI) / Institut des Affaires Culturelles International
c/o ICA Canada, #405, 401 Richmond St. West, Toronto ON M5V 3A8
Tel: 416-691-2316; *Fax:* 416-691-2491
icai@ica-international.org
ica-international.org
www.facebook.com/icainternational
twitter.com/icai
To be engaged in human development activities globally by promoting global ecological perspectives, facilitating organizational change, enabling sustainable development efforts, & advancing lifelong learning & training
Lisseth Lorenz, President
Archana Deshmukh, Secretary
Seva Gandhi, Treasurer

International Social Service Canada (ISSC) / Service Social International Canada (SSIC)
#201, 1376 Bank St., Ottawa ON K1H 7Y3
Tel: 613-733-9938; *Fax:* 613-733-4868
www.issc-ssic.ca
www.facebook.com/533898289965867
twitter.com/ISS_SSICanada
To provide linkages to social service organizations worldwide; To help resolve individual & family problems resulting from the movement of people across national borders
Sylvie J. Lapointe, Executive Director

Jane Finch Community & Family Centre
#108, 440 Jane St., Toronto ON M3N 2K4
Tel: 416-663-2733; *Fax:* 416-663-3816
admin@janefinchcentre.org
www.janefinchcentre.org
www.facebook.com/people/Jane-Finch-Centre/1518951464
To operate with a strong commitment to social justice, community engagement, & collaboration
Michelle Dagnino, Executive Director

Jewish Family & Child (JFCS)
4600 Bathurst St., 1st Fl., Toronto ON M2R 3V3
Tel: 416-638-7800; *Fax:* 416-638-7943
info@jfandcs.com
www.jfandcs.com
www.youtube.com/user/jewishfamilyandchild
www.linkedin.com/company/jewish-family-&-child
www.facebook.com/JFandCS
To support the healthy development of individuals, families & communities in the Greater Toronto Area through prevention, protection, counselling, education & advocacy services, within the context of Jewish values
Brian Prousky, Executive Director

Kids First Parent Association of Canada
4819 Albert St., Burnaby BC V5C 2H2
Tel: 604-291-0088
info@kidsfirstcanada.org
kidsfirstcanada.org
www.facebook.com/KidsFirstParentsAssoci
To lobby to protect their right & choice to raise children in a family setting; To provide support to anyone wanting to further this cause in other communities
Helen Ward, President

Kids Help Phone (KHP) / Jeunesse j'écoute
#300, 439 University Ave., Toronto ON M5G 1Y8
Fax: 416-586-0651
Toll-Free: 800-268-3062
info@kidshelpphone.ca
kidshelpphone.ca
www.facebook.com/KidsHelpPhone
twitter.com/kidshelpphone
To offer free, anonymous services, including professional counselling, information, referrals, & volunteer-led text-based, for young people, in both English & French

Lakeland United Way
Marina Mall, PO Box 8125, #3, 901 - 10 St., Cold Lake AB T9M 1N1
Tel: 780-826-0045; *Fax:* 780-639-2699
www.lakelandunitedway.com
Ajaz Quraishi, President

Lakeshore Area Multi-Service Project (LAMP)
185 - 5th St., Toronto ON M8V 2Z5
Tel: 416-252-6471; *Fax:* 416-252-4474
www.lampchc.org
www.facebook.com/LAMPHEALTHC
To offer community health centre services in South Etobicoke, Toronto West
Russ Ford, Executive Director

Leprosy relief (Canada) Inc. (LR) / Secours aux lepreux (Canada) inc. (SLC)
#305, 1805, rue Sauvé ouest, Montréal QC H4N 3H4
Tel: 514-744-3199; *Fax:* 514-744-9095
Toll-Free: 866-744-3199
info@slc-lr.ca
slc-lr.ca
twitter.com/SlcLrCanada
An organization dedicated to fighting and increasing awareness of leprosy and tuberculosis.
Paul E. Legault, Prèsident
Maryse Legault, Director
Marie Gilbert, Secretaire
Christiane Beauvois, Trèsorière

Little People of Ontario (LPO)
108 Rosedale Heights Dr., Toronto ON M4T 1C6
Tel: 647-849-9844
info@lpo.on.ca
www.littlepeopleofontario.com
To provide support & information to little people, as well as their families & friends; To raise awareness about dwarfism
Allan Redford, President

Lloydminster & District United Way
4419 - 52nd Ave., Lloydminster AB T9V 0Y8
Tel: 780-875-3743; *Fax:* 780-875-3793
lloydminsterunitedway@telusplanet.net
www.lloydminster.unitedway.ca
To strengthen the community by supporting local agencies

Manitoba Association of Women's Shelters (MAWS)
PO Box 389, Winkler MB R6W 4A6
Tel: 204-430-4346
Crisis Hot-Line: 877-977-0007
maws@maws.mb.ca
maws.mb.ca
www.facebook.com/MAWSManitoba
To eliminate violence against women; To provide support to member shelters for abused women & their children; To share information & resources with its member shelters, increase training of staff & increase services for clients
Cristin Smook, Co-Chair
Joyce Schrader, Co-Chair

Manitoba College of Registered Social Workers (MIRSW)
#101, 2033 Portage Ave., Winnipeg MB R3J 0K6
Tel: 204-888-9477; *Fax:* 204-831-6359
admin@mcsw.ca
www.mcsw.ca
To certify members; To act as the regulatory arm of the social work profession; To encourage ethical standards of practice to protect the public
Liz McLeod, President

Mediate BC Society
#177, 800 Hornby St., Vancouver BC V6Z 2C5
Tel: 604-684-1300; *Fax:* 604-684-1306
Toll-Free: 877-656-1300
info@mediatebc.com
www.mediatebc.com
To provide practical, accessible & affordable mediation & dispute resolution choices
Monique Steensma, CEO
Melanie Carfantan-Mclachlan, Executive Director

Mediation Yukon Society
PO Box 31102, Whitehorse YT Y1A 5P7
mediationyukon@gmail.com
mediationyukon.com
To encourage alternate methods for dispute resolution
Christiane Boisjoly, Mediator

La Mine d'Or, entreprise d'insertion sociale
542, 3e rue, Chibougamau QC G8P 1N9
Tél: 418-748-4183
dglaminedor@outlook.com
Organisme sans but lucratif, qui a pour mission l'insertion sociale & professionnelle des personnes en situation d'exclusion; offre une passerelle aux participants vers le marché du travail, la formation ou d'autres alternatives
France Bureau, Présidente

Mouvement ATD Quart Monde Canada / ATD Fourth World Movement Canada
6747, rue Drolet, Montréal QC H2S 2T1
Tél: 514-279-0468
atdcanada@atdquartmonde.ca
www.atdquartmonde.ca
www.facebook.com/AtdQMCanada
twitter.com/ATDCanada

Développer un courant de refus de la misère en donnant la priorité aux plus pauvres, dans le respect des droits et de la dignité de la personne; contribuer à l'action du Mouvement dans le monde

Neepawa & District United Way
PO Box 1545, Neepawa MB R0J 1H0
Tel: 204-476-3410
unitedwayneepawa@mymts.net
www.neepawaunitedway.org
Local United Way Chapter raising funds to help community organization

New Brunswick Association of Food Banks (NBAFB) / Association des banques alimentaires du Nouveau-Brunswick (ABANB)
#234, 1127 Main St., Moncton NB E1C 1H1
Tel: 506-227-5801
info@nbafb-abanb.ca
www.nbafb-abanb.net
www.facebook.com/NBAssociationofFoodBanks
To support member agencies in their efforts to alleviate hunger; To serve as a provincial voice for same
Laurie Stewart, President

New Brunswick Association of Social Workers (NBASW) / Association des travailleurs sociaux du Nouveau-Brunswick
PO Box 1533, Stn. A, Fredericton NB E3B 5G2
Tel: 506-459-5595; *Fax:* 506-457-1421
Toll-Free: 877-495-5595
nbasw@nbasw-atsnb.ca
www.nbasw-atsnb.ca
www.facebook.com/NBASW
twitter.com/NBSocialWorkers
To regulate the profession of social work; To protect the public; To set standards; To promote the profession
Miguel LeBlanc, Executive Director

Newfoundland & Labrador Association of Social Workers (NLASW) / Association des travailleurs sociaux de Terre-Neuve et Labrador
PO Box 39039, 177 Hamlyn Rd., St. John's NL A1E 5Y7
Tel: 709-753-0200; *Fax:* 709-753-0120
registration@nlasw.ca
www.nlasw.ca
To ensure excellence in social work in Newfoundland & Labrador; To take appropriate action on issues of social concern; To disseminate information & provide opportunities for continuing education; To provide consultation to agencies involved in training for or delivering human services; To promote the development & the enhancement of social service delivery system suited to the needs of Newfoundlanders
Lisa Crockwell, Executive Director

Non-Smokers' Rights Association (NSRA) / Association pour les droits des non-fumeurs
#221, 720 Spadina Ave., Toronto ON M5S 2T9
Tel: 416-928-2900; *Fax:* 416-928-1860
www.nsra-adnf.ca
To promote public health by stopping illness & death due to tobacco, including second-hand smoke
Lorraine Fry, Executive Director

North York Community House
Lawrence Square Mall, #226, 700 Lawrence Ave., Toronto ON M6A 3B4
Tel: 416-784-0920
www.nych.ca
www.youtube.com/user/nychonline
www.facebook.com/nychonline
twitter.com/nychonline
To assist newcomers settle, integrate and become vibrant members of our community; to help residents improve their economic conditions; and to help build strong neighbourhoods.
Shelley Zuckerman, Executive Director

Northumberland United Way
#700, 600 William St., Cobourg ON K9A 3A5
Tel: 905-372-6955; *Fax:* 905-372-4417
Toll-Free: 800-833-0002
office@nuw.unitedway.ca
www.mynuw.org
www.youtube.com/user/NlandUnitedWay
www.facebook.com/northumberlandunitedway
twitter.com/nlanduw
To raise & allocate funds in an efficient manner & to promote the effective delivery of services in response to current & emerging social needs in Northumberland County
Lynda Kay, CEO

Nova Scotia Association of Black Social Workers (NSABSW)
1018 Main St., Dartmouth NS B2W 4X9
Tel: 902-407-8809; *Fax:* 902-434-6544
nsabsw@gmail.com
nsabsw.ca
www.instagram.com/absw_ns
www.facebook.com/1479035692341552
To promote the advancement & professional development of Black Social Workers & Human Service Workers in Nova Scotia; To provide educational programs & financial assistance to individuals of African descent studying social work or working in the social services field
Veronica Marsman-Murphy, President
Crystal John, Vice-President
Germaine Howe-Bundy, Treasurer
Chanae Parsons, Secretary

Nova Scotia College of Social Workers (NSCSW)
#700, 1888 Brunswick St., Halifax NS B3J 3J8
Tel: 902-429-7799; *Fax:* 902-429-7650
www.nscsw.org
www.facebook.com/NSCSW
twitter.com/NSCSW
To promote & regulate the practice of social work so the members can provide a high standard of service that respects diversity, promotes social justice & enhances the worth, self-determination & potential of individuals, families & communities
Alec Stratford, Executive Director

One Parent Families Association of Canada (OPFA) / Association des familles uniparentales du Canada
PO Box 628, Pickering ON L1V 3T3
Toll-Free: 877-773-7714
oneparentfamilies@gmx.com
oneparentfamilies.net
To develop & provide a broad comprehensive program for the enlightenment & guidance of single parents & their children on the special problems they encounter & for assistance on the various readjustments involved

Ontario Association for Family Mediation (OAFM)
#204, 2167 Victoria Park Ave., Toronto ON M1R 1V5
Tel: 416-740-6236; *Toll-Free:* 844-989-3026
www.oafm.on.ca
twitter.com/OAFMEDIATION
To promote family mediation as a dispute resolution process for separating couples & for families in conflict
Mary-Ane Popescu, Executive Director

Ontario Association for Marriage & Family Therapy (OAMFT)
PO Box 693, Tottenham ON L0G 1W0
Tel: 905-936-3338; *Fax:* 905-936-9192
Toll-Free: 800-267-2638
admin@oamft.com
rmft.oamft.com
To serve members of the association, the profession of marriage & family therapy, & the public; To uphold the Code of Ethics of the American Association for Marriage & Family Therapy & high professional standards; To advocate for members & communities
Ron Mellish, President
Donna Chamberlain, Administrator

Ontario Association of Children's Aid Societies (OACAS) / Association ontarienne des sociétés de l'aide à l'enfance
#308, 75 Front St. East, Toronto ON M5E 1V9
Tel: 416-987-7725; *Fax:* 416-366-8317
Toll-Free: 800-718-7725
reception@oacas.org
www.oacas.org
www.linkedin.com/company/ontario-association-of-children-s-aid
-societies
twitter.com/our_children
To provide leadership for the achievement of excellence in the protection of children & in the promotion of their well-being within their families & communities
Nicole Bonnie, Chief Executive Officer

Ontario Association of Interval & Transition Houses (OAITH)
PO Box 27585, Stn. Yorkdale Mall, Toronto ON M6A 3B8
Tel: 416-977-6619
info@oaith.ca
www.oaith.ca
www.youtube.com/user/OAITH
www.facebook.com/OAITH
To work towards social change by ensuring that the voices of abused women are heard; To remove barriers to equality for women & children

Marlene Ham, Executive Director

Ontario Association of Social Workers (OASW) / Association des travailleuses et travailleurs sociaux de l'Ontario (ATTSO)
410 Jarvis St., Toronto ON M4Y 2G6
Tel: 416-923-4848; *Fax:* 416-923-5279
info@oasw.org
www.oasw.org
www.linkedin.com/company/ontario-association-of-social-workers
www.facebook.com/ontarioassociationofsocialworkers
twitter.com/oasw_info
To act as the voice of social workers in Ontario
Joan MacKenzie Davies, Executive Director

Ontario Coalition for Better Child Care (OCBCC) / Coalition Ontarienne pour de meilleurs services éducatifs à l'enfance
#206, 489 College St., Toronto ON M6G 1A5
Tel: 416-538-0628; *Fax:* 416-538-6737
Toll-Free: 800-594-7514
info@childcareontario.org
www.childcareontario.org
www.facebook.com/OCBCC
twitter.com/ChildCareON
To advocate on behalf of Ontario's non-profit, licensed child care programs
Sheila Olan-MacLean, President
Christine Sbardella, Vice President
Lynn Poole-Cotnam, Treasurer

Ontario Coalition of Rape Crisis Centres (OCRCC) / Coalition des centres anti-viol de l'Ontario
Toronto ON M5S 1A8
Tel: 416-597-1171
Crisis Hot-Line: 416-597-8808
www.sexualassaultsupport.ca
To work for prevention & eradication of sexual assault; To help implement legal, social & attitudinal changes regarding sexual assault; To provide mechanism for communication, education & mobilization to alleviate political & geographical isolation of rape crisis centres in Ontario; To encourage, direct & generate research into sexual violence; To work with the Canadian Association of Sexual Assault Centres to develop national policies & to liaise with other provincial organizations addressing similar issues
Jacqueline Benn-John, President

Ontario Community Justice Association (OCJA)
Tel: 416-304-1974
www.facebook.com/OntarioCommunityJusticeAssociation
twitter.com/OCJA1979
To promote community justice through support to service providers; to endorse service provision that embraces inclusivity and human rights; to advocate for the presence & accessibility of community justice programs
Gemma Napoli, President
Amy Roy, Representative, Public Relations

Ontario Community Support Association (OCSA) / Association ontarienne de soutien communautaire
#1400B, 180 Dundas St. West, Toronto ON M5G 1Z8
Tel: 416-256-3010; *Fax:* 416-256-3021
Toll-Free: 800-267-6272
website@ocsa.on.ca
www.ocsa.on.ca
www.facebook.com/OntarioCommunitySupportAssociation
twitter.com/OCSAtweets
To support & represent the common goals of community-based, not-for-profit health & social service organizations which assist individuals to live at home in their own community
Deborah Simon, Chief Executive Officer

Ontario Municipal Social Services Association (OMSSA) / Association des services sociaux des municipalités de l'Ontario
#606, 30 Duncan St., Toronto ON M5V 2C3
Tel: 416-479-1491
info@omssa.com
www.omssa.com
www.linkedin.com/company/omssa
www.facebook.com/theOMSSA
twitter.com/theOMSSA
To promote high standards of competency within the profession to ensure quality delivery of human services in communities; To improve social policies & programs in the areas of affordable housing, homelessness prevention, children's services & social assistance; To act as the voice for Consolidated Municipal Service Managers in Ontario
Doug Ball, Executive Director

The Ontario Trillium Foundation / La Fondation Trillium de l'Ontario
800 Bay St., 5th Fl., Toronto ON M5S 3A9
Tel: 416-963-4927; *Fax:* 416-963-8781
Toll-Free: 800-263-2887
TTY: 416-963-7905
otf@otf.ca
www.otf.ca
www.youtube.com/user/trilliumfoundation1
www.facebook.com/ONTrillium
twitter.com/ONTrillium
To work with others to make strategic investments to build healthy & sustainable communities in Ontario
Andrea Cohen Barrack, Chief Executive Officer

Open Door Group
#300, 30 East 6 Ave., Vancouver BC V5T 1J4
Tel: 604-876-0770; *Fax:* 604-873-1758
Toll-Free: 866-377-3670
info@opendoorgroup.org
www.opendoorgroup.org
www.facebook.com/OpenDoorGroup
To assist psychiatrically, emotionally & socially disadvantaged people to develop the necessary skills to lead more satisfying lives
Tom Burnell, Chief Executive Officer
Naomi Bullock, Executive Director, Program Management & Development
Alona Puehse, Executive Director, Corporate Development
Christine Buchanan, Director, Diversity & Disability Services
Katrina Welsh, Director, Human Resources
Joey Alain, Director, Information Technology
Cora David, Financial Controller

Ordre des travailleurs sociaux et des thérapeutes conjugaux et familiaux du Québec (OTSTCFQ)
#800, 255, boul Crémazie est, Montréal QC H2M 1L5
Tél: 514-731-3925; *Téléc:* 514-731-6785
Ligne sans frais: 888-731-9420
info@otstcfq.org
otstcfq.org
www.linkedin.com/company/otstcfq
www.facebook.com/OTSTCFQ
twitter.com/otstcfq
De soutenir et d'encadrer l'exercice professionnel des travailleurs sociaux et des thérapeutes conjugaux et familiaux

Parent Finders Ottawa
ON
Tel: 613-730-8305
pfncr@yahoo.com
parentfindersottawa.com
www.facebook.com/120530528033309
To assist adult adoptees / foster persons & birth relatives to obtain background information from adoption files kept in social services departments; To assist in search & reunion; To promote a feeling of openness about the adoption experience & a better understanding about the longing for a reunion between adult adoptees & birth relatives

Parent Support Services Society of BC (PSSS)
#204, 5623 Imperial St., Burnaby BC V5J 1G1
Tel: 604-669-1616; *Fax:* 604-669-1636
Toll-Free: 877-345-9777
office@parentsupportbc.ca
www.parentsupportbc.ca
www.youtube.com/user/ParentSupportBC
www.facebook.com/ParentSupportBC
twitter.com/PSS_BC
To protect the safety & well-being of children & promote the health of all families
Carol Madsen, Executive Director

Parents-secours du Québec inc. (PSQI)
#203, 17, rue Fusey, Trois-Rivières QC G8T 2T3
Tél: 819-374-5541; *Ligne sans frais:* 800-588-8173
info@parentssecours.ca
www.parentssecours.ca
www.youtube.com/user/ParentsSecours
www.facebook.com/262687173759603
Parents-Secours du Québec inc. (PSQI) est un organisme à but non lucratif qui assure la sécurité et la protection des enfants et des aînés-es en offrant un réseau de foyers-refuges sécuritaires tout en contribuant à promouvoir la prévention par l'information et l'éducation.
Pierre Chalifoux, Directeur général

People, Words & Change (PWC) / Monde des mots
Heartwood House, #202, 404 MacArthur Ave., Ottawa ON K1K 1G8
Tel: 613-234-2494; *Fax:* 613-241-4170
dee@pwc-ottawa.ca
pwc-ottawa.ca
www.facebook.com/PeopleWordsChange
To help English-speaking adults in Ottawa to improve literacy, numeracy, or basic computer skills
Dee Sullivan, Executive Director & Education Counsellor

PFLAG Canada Inc.
#243, 1554 Carling Ave., Ottawa ON K1Z 7M4
Fax: 888-959-4128
Toll-Free: 888-530-6777
operations@pflagcanada.ca
www.pflagcanada.ca
www.facebook.com/PFLAGCA
twitter.com/pflagcanada
To support individuals with questions & concerns about sexual orientation or gender identity; To make Canada a more accepting place for persons of all gender identities & sexual orientations
Bev Belanger, President
Donny Potts, Vice-President
Daniel Snoek, Treasurer
Louis Duncan-He, Director, Marketing
Omid Ravazi, Director, Communications
Ross Wicks, Director, Governance

Plan International Canada Inc.
#300, 245 Eglinton Ave. East, Toronto ON M4P 0B3
Tel: 416-920-1654; *Fax:* 416-920-9942
Toll-Free: 800-387-1418
info@plancanada.ca
plancanada.ca
www.youtube.com/user/plancanadavideos
www.linkedin.com/company/plan-canada
www.facebook.com/PlanCanada
twitter.com/PlanCanada
To help children, their families, & communities in developing countries; To raise funds through sponsorship program & implement programs in health, education & community development overseas
Tanjina Mirza, Co-CEO & Chief Programs Officer
Sarah Kramer, Co-CEO & Chief Operating Officer
Ian Burdett, Vice-President, Finance
Jennifer Fry, Vice-President, Communications & Public Engagement

Portage Plains United Way
PO Box 953, 20 Saskatchewan Ave. East, Portage la Prairie MB R1N 3C4
Tel: 204-857-4440; *Fax:* 204-239-1740
info@portageplainsuw.ca
www.portageplainsuw.ca
www.facebook.com/353759031400503
twitter.com/PortagePlainsUW
To unite the community & enhance the quality of life for those in need
Mandy Dubois, Executive Director
Jennifer Sneesby, Office Manager

Powell River & District United Way
PO Box 370, #205, 4750 Joyce Ave., Powell River BC V8A 5C2
Tel: 604-485-2791
admin@unitedwayofpowellriver.ca
www.unitedwayofpowellriver.ca
www.facebook.com/322827261966
twitter.com/PRUnitedway
Ashley Hull, President

Prince Edward Island Association of Social Workers (PEIASW) / Association des travailleurs sociaux de l'Ile-du-Prince-Édouard
81 Prince St., Charlottetown PE C1A 4R3
Tel: 902-368-7337; *Fax:* 902-368-7180
contact@peiasw.ca
peiasw.ca
To acknowledge & promote the work of social workers in Prince Edward Island; To advance the social work profession throughout the province, to ensure well-being for residents
Kelly MacWilliams, President

Québec Association of Marriage & Family Therapy (QAMFT) / Association québécoise pour la thérapie conjugale et familiale
#200, 360, av Victoria, Westmount QC H3Y 2L5
Tel: 514-949-5688
To promote understanding, research & education in the field of couple & family therapy & to ensure that public needs are met by practitioners of the highest quality

Andrew Sofin, President

Ralph Thornton Centre
765 Queen St. East, Toronto ON M4M 1H3
Tel: 416-392-6810
info@ralphthornton.org
www.ralphthornton.org
www.youtube.com/user/ralphthorntoncentre
To create a supportive environment in which the Riverdale community responds to issues and needs.
Paula Fletcher, President
John Campey, Executive Director

Reena
927 Clark Ave. West, Thornhill ON L4J 8G6
Tel: 905-889-6484; *Fax:* 905-889-3827
info@reena.org
www.reena.org
www.facebook.com/ReenaFoundation
twitter.com/ReenaFoundation
To integrate developmentally disabled people towards independent living within community, with emphasis on Judaic programming
Lorne Sossin, Chair
Bryan Keshen, President & CEO

Renfrew County United Way
224 Pembroke St. West, Pembroke ON K8A 5N2
Tel: 613-735-0436; *Fax:* 613-735-2663
Toll-Free: 888-592-2213
info@renfrewcountyunitedway.ca
www.renfrewcountyunitedway.ca
www.facebook.com/182315931870874
To identify & address the needs of our community by organizing the resources of community members to care for one another
Shelley Rolland-Porucks, Chair
Gail Logan, Executive Director

The Right to Die Society of Canada (RTDSC) / Société Canadienne pour le Droit de Mourir (SCDM)
145 Macdonell Ave., Toronto ON M6R 2A4
Tel: 416-535-0690; *Toll-Free:* 866-535-0690
info@rightodie.ca
www.righttodie.ca
To work with legislators, policy makers & the public to expand the range of humane options for people who are suffering intolerably from incurable conditions & who want a self-directed dying; To work with sufferers to expand their awareness of the options that are legal & may be appropriate for them
Ruth von Fuchs, President & Secretary

Ronald McDonald House Charities of Canada (RMHC) / Oeuvres pour enfants Ronald McDonald du Canada
1 McDonald's Place, Toronto ON M3C 3L4
Tel: 416-446-3493; *Fax:* 416-446-3588
Toll-Free: 800-387-8808
rmhc@ca.mcd.com
www.rmhccanada.ca
www.instagram.com/rmhccanada
www.facebook.com/RMHCCanada
twitter.com/rmhccanada
To help children in need by improving the physical & emotional quality of life for children with serious illnesses, disabilities &/or chronic conditions, allowing them to lead happier, healthier & more productive lives
Cathy Loblaw, President & CEO
Kate Horton, Executive Director
Roxanna Kassam Kara, National Director

Rooftops Canada / Abri International
#313, 720 Spadina Ave., Toronto ON M5S 2T9
Tel: 416-366-1445; *Fax:* 416-366-3876
info@rooftops.ca
rooftops.ca
www.facebook.com/RooftopsCanadaAbri
To provide technical expertise & leadership to help create low-cost housing & settlements in the developing world
Pamela Hine, President
Barry Pinsky, Executive Director

Saskatchewan Association of Social Workers (SASW) / Association des travailleurs sociaux de la Saskatchewan
Edna Osborne House, 2110 Lorne St., Regina SK S4P 2M5
Tel: 306-545-1922; *Fax:* 306-545-1895
Toll-Free: 877-517-7279
sasw@accesscomm.ca
www.sasw.ca
To conduct the work of a professional regulator; To act as the voice of social workers in Saskatchewan; To develop & maintain standards of knowledge, skill, conduct & competence among members to serve & protect the public interest

Kirk Englot, President

Scadding Court Community Centre (SCCC)
707 Dundas St. West, Toronto ON M5T 2W6
Tel: 416-392-0335; *Fax:* 416-392-0340
www.scaddingcourt.org
www.facebook.com/people/Scadding-Court/100001939237499
twitter.com/scadding_court
To support and foster the well being of individuals, families, and community groups by providing and encouraging both local and international opportunities for recreation, education, athletics, community participation and inclusive social interaction.
Kevin Lee, Executive Director

Sex Information & Education Council of Canada (SIECCAN) / Conseil d'information et éducation sexuelles du Canada
#400, 235 Danforth Ave., Toronto ON M4K 1N2
Tel: 416-466-5304
info@sieccan.org
www.sieccan.org
To ensure that all Canadians have access to sexual health information, education & health services; To share knowledge & information with health professionals, policymakers & educators
Alex McKay, Executive Director

Social Planning & Research Council of BC (SPARC BC)
4445 Norfolk St., Burnaby BC V5G 0A7
Tel: 604-718-7733; *Fax:* 604-736-8697
Toll-Free: 888-718-7794
info@sparc.bc.ca
www.sparc.bc.ca
To promote the social, economic & environmental well-being of citizens & communities; to advocate the principles of social justice, equality & the dignity & worth of all people in our multicultural society; to conduct research & planning for public information, education & citizen participation in developing social policies & programs
Lorraine Copas, Executive Director
Irene Willsie, President

Social Planning Council of Ottawa (SPCO) / Conseil de planification sociale d'Ottawa
790 Bronson Ave., Ottawa ON K1S 4G4
Tel: 613-236-9300; *Fax:* 613-236-7060
office@spcottawa.on.ca
www.spcottawa.on.ca
To provide the residents of Ottawa-Carleton with the means to exercise informed leadership on issues affecting their social & economic well-being
Diane Urquhart, Executive Director

Social Planning Council of Winnipeg
#300, 207 Donald St., Winnipeg MB R3C 1M5
Tel: 204-943-2561; *Fax:* 204-942-3221
info@spcw.mb.ca
www.spcw.mb.ca
www.linkedin.com/company/social-planning-council-of-winnipeg
twitter.com/spcw1919
To identify & define social planning issues, needs & resources in the community; to develop & promote policy & program options to policy-makers; to support community groups & the voluntary human service sector; to raise community awareness of social issues & human service needs, social policy options & service delivery alternatives; to serve as a link between the three levels of government & community neighbourhoods
Dennis Lewycky, Executive Director

Social Planning Toronto (SPT)
#1001, 2 Carlton St., Toronto ON M5B 1J3
Tel: 416-351-0095; *Fax:* 416-351-0107
info@socialplanningtoronto.org
www.socialplanningtoronto.org
www.linkedin.com/company/social-planning-toronto
www.facebook.com/SocialPlanningToronto
twitter.com/planningtoronto
To promote community-based, social policy, planning & civic participation at both the local & city-wide levels through analysis & action-oriented research on social issues.
Winston Tinglin, Interim Executive Director
Maria Serrano, Director, Operations

SOS Children's Villages Canada / SOS Villages d'Enfants Canada
#240, 44 By Ward Market Sq., Ottawa ON K1N 7A2
Tel: 613-232-3309; *Toll-Free:* 800-767-5111
info@soschildrensvillages.ca
www.soschildrensvillages.ca
www.youtube.com/user/soscanada1
www.facebook.com/SOSChildrensVillagesCanada
twitter.com/SOSCV_Canada

To assist SOS-Children's Villages in Canada & abroad through financial & operating support; To care for orphaned, abandoned & other children in need of long-term placement; To create opportunities for children to become happy, stable, responsible members of society
Thomas Bauer, President & CEO

Springtide Resources
#220, 215 Spadina Ave., Toronto ON M5T 2C7
Tel: 416-968-3422; *Fax:* 416-968-2026
info@womanabuseprevention.com
www.springtideresources.org
www.facebook.com/springtide.resources
twitter.com/Springtide_VAW
To increase public awareness of the many aspects of violence against women & its effect on children; to change the social conditions that subject women to abuse by providing training & resources proactively.
Marsha Sfeir, Executive Director

Swift Current United Way
Swift Current Business Centre, 145 1st Ave. NE, Swift Current SK S9H 2B1
Tel: 306-773-4828
unitedway@sasktel.net
www.swiftcurrentunitedway.ca
www.instagram.com/swiftunitedway
www.facebook.com/swiftunitedway
twitter.com/swiftunitedway
To strengthen the social & economic conditions of the community; To improve the lives of all residents of Swift Current & Southern Saskatchewan
Stacey Schwartz, Executive Director

Syme-Woolner Neighbourhood & Family Centre (SWNFC)
#3, 2468 Eglinton Ave. West, Toronto ON M6M 5E2
Tel: 416-766-4634; *Fax:* 416-766-8162
swoolner@symewoolner.org
www.symewoolner.org
To create in the community a sense of belonging, to enable individuals, families and groups to support each other and build a better future.
Mark Neysmith, Executive Director

Thompson Crisis Centre
PO Box 1226, Thompson MB R8N 1P1
Tel: 204-677-9668
Crisis Hot-Line: 877-977-0007
tcc9668@mymts.net
www.thompsoncrisiscentre.org
To provide immediate assistance through a walk-in facility & a 24-hour emergency telephone service; To provide a safe place for the women & their children who are victims of physical/emotional abuse; To provide services to women & their children needing longer term support
Harlie Pruder, Chair

Thompson, Nicola, Cariboo United Way
177 Victoria St., Kamloops BC V2C 1Z4
Tel: 250-372-9933; *Fax:* 250-372-5926
Toll-Free: 855-372-9933
office@unitedwaytnc.ca
www.unitedwaytnc.ca
www.youtube.com/unitedwaytnc
www.linkedin.com/company/thompson-nicola-cariboo-united-way
www.facebook.com/unitedwaytnc
twitter.com/unitedwaytnc
To enable all citizens to join in a community wide effort to fund & provide in consort with others, effective delivery of health & social services & programs in response to the needs of the community
Danalee Baker, Executive Director

Toronto Community Foundation (TCF)
#1603, 33 Bloor St. East, Toronto ON M4W 3H1
Tel: 416-921-2035; *Fax:* 416-921-1026
info@tcf.ca
www.tcf.ca
To connect philanthropic individuals & families to charitable organizations in Toronto
Aneil Gokhale, Director, Philanthropy
Nicole Lilauwala, Development Coordinator

Unison Benevolent Fund / Unison fonds de bienfaisance
55 St. Clair Ave. West, Toronto ON M4V 2Y7
Tel: 416-479-0675; *Toll-Free:* 855-986-4766
assistance@unisonfund.ca
unisonfund.ca
www.instagram.com/unisonfund
www.facebook.com/UnisonFund
twitter.com/unisonfund

To provide counselling & emergency relief to the music community in Canada
Amanda Power, Executive Director
Louise Bérubé, Director, Allocations & Services

United Generations Ontario (UGO) / Générations Unies Ontario
#604B, 1185 Eglinton Ave. East, Toronto ON M3C 3C6
Tel: 416-426-7115; *Fax:* 416-426-7388
info@intergenugo.org
To promote programs that bring young & old together in a spirit of cooperation, mutual support, shared affection & regard; to empower people to take a constructive part in the life of their own communities & to create a vital volunteer exchange in caring & sharing

United Way Alberta Northwest
#213, 11330 106 St., Grande Prairie AB T8V 7X9
Tel: 780-532-1105
info@unitedwayabnw.org
www.unitedwayabnw.org
www.youtube.com/user/GrowUnitedBreakfast
www.facebook.com/UnitedWayABNW
twitter.com/UnitedWayABNW
To change community conditions & improve the lives of people in need
Sheldon Rowe, Chair
Brenda Yamkowy, Executive Director
Jodie Johnson, Director, Resource Development
Marnie Young, Director, Resource Development
Joanne Cousins, Administrator

United Way Central & Northern Vancouver Island
#9, 327 Prideaux St., Nanaimo BC V9R 2N4
Tel: 250-591-8731; *Fax:* 250-591-7340
info@uwcnvi.ca
www.uwcnvi.ca
www.youtube.com/user/UnitedWayCNVI
www.linkedin.com/company/united-way-central-&-northern-vancouver-island
www.facebook.com/UWCNVI
twitter.com/UWCNVI
To improve lives by engaging individuals & mobilizing collective action
Signy Madden, Executive Director

United Way Elgin-St. Thomas
#103, 10 Mondamin St., St Thomas ON N5P 2V1
Tel: 519-631-3171; *Fax:* 519-631-9253
www.stthomasunitedway.ca
www.facebook.com/UnitedWayElginStThomas
To be a leader in improving the quality of life for all people in Elgin County.
James Todd, President
Melissa Schneider, Campaign/Communications Coordinator

United Way for the City of Kawartha Lakes (UWVC)
50 Mary St. West, Lindsay ON K9V 2N6
Tel: 705-878-5081; *Fax:* 705-878-0475
office@ckl.unitedway.ca
www.ckl-unitedway.ca
www.facebook.com/UWCKL
twitter.com/unitedwayckl
To promote the organized capacity of people & groups in the City of Kawartha Lakes to care for each other
Penny Barton Dyke, Executive Director

United Way Greater Toronto
26 Wellington St. East, 12th Fl., Toronto ON M5E 1S2
Tel: 416-777-2001; *Fax:* 416-777-0962
TTY: 866-620-2993
www.instagram.com/unitedwaytyr
www.linkedin.com/company/unitedwaytyr
www.facebook.com/unitedwaytyr
twitter.com/unitedwaytyr
To meet urgent human needs & improve social conditions by mobilizing the community's volunteer & financial resources in a common cause of caring
Vince Timpano, Chair
Daniele Zanotti, President & CEO

United Way Niagara
63 Church St., #LC1, St Catharines ON L2R 3C4
Tel: 905-688-5050
info@unitedwayniagara.org
www.unitedwayniagara.org
twitter.com/UWNiagara
To improve live & build community by engaging individuals & mobilizing collective action
Frances Hallworth, Executive Director

United Way of Brandon & District Inc.
Scotia Towers, 201 - 1011 Rosser Ave., Brandon MB R7A 0L5
Tel: 204-571-8929; *Fax:* 204-727-8939
office@brandonuw.ca
www.brandonuw.ca
www.facebook.com/UnitedWayBrandon
Cynamon Mychasiw, CEO

United Way of Burlington & Greater Hamilton
177 Rebecca St., Hamilton ON L8R 1B9
Tel: 905-527-4543; *Fax:* 905-527-5152
uway@uwaybh.ca
www.uwaybh.ca
www.youtube.com/user/UnitedWayBH
www.facebook.com/unitedwaybh
twitter.com/UnitedWayBH
To empower a diverse community to achieve positive social development
Jeff Vallentin, CEO

United Way of Calgary & Area
#600, 105 - 12 Ave SE, Calgary AB T2G 1A1
Tel: 403-231-6265; *Fax:* 403-355-3135
uway@calgaryunitedway.org
www.calgaryunitedway.org
www.instagram.com/unitedwaycgy
www.linkedin.com/companies/united-way-of-calgary-and-area
www.facebook.com/calgaryunitedway
twitter.com/UnitedWayCgy
To invest in 250 programs offered by 130 agencies in Calgary, Airdrie, Cochrane, High River, Okotoks & Strathmore
Lucy Miller, President

United Way of Cambridge & North Dumfries
#2, 135 Thompson Dr., Cambridge ON N1T 2E4
Tel: 519-621-1030; *Fax:* 519-621-6220
www.uwcambridge.on.ca
www.youtube.com/user/UWcambridge
www.facebook.com/UWCND
twitter.com/uwcambridge
To enhance the quality of life in Cambridge & North Dumfries by caring for & contributing to community needs
Ron Dowhaniuk, CEO

United Way of Canada - Centraide Canada
#900, 116 Albert St., Ottawa ON K1P 5G3
Tel: 613-236-7041; *Fax:* 613-236-3087
Toll-Free: 800-267-8221
info@unitedway.ca
www.unitedway.ca
www.youtube.com/UnitedWayofCanada
www.linkedin.com/company/united-way-centraide-canada
www.facebook.com/UnitedWayCentraide
twitter.com/UWCCanada
To create opportunities for a better life for all; To inspire Canadians to make a lasting difference in their communities
Dan Clement, Interim President & CEO

United Way of Cape Breton
245 Charlotte St., Sydney NS B1P 6W4
Tel: 902-562-5226; *Fax:* 902-562-5721
www.unitedwaycapebreton.com
www.facebook.com/UnitedWayOfCapeBreton
To improve the quality of life of Cape Breton's residents
Lynne McCarron, Executive Director

United Way of Central Alberta
4811 - 48th St., Red Deer AB T4N 1S6
Tel: 403-343-3900; *Fax:* 403-309-3820
info@caunitedway.ca
www.caunitedway.ca
To improve lives & build community by engaging individuals & mobilizing collective action
Robert J. Mitchell, Chief Executive Officer

United Way of Chatham-Kent County
PO Box 606, 425 McNaughton Ave. West, Chatham ON N7M 5K8
Tel: 519-354-0430; *Fax:* 519-354-9511
info@uwock.ca
uwock.ca
www.youtube.com/user/UnitedWayChathamKent
www.facebook.com/UnitedWayofChathamKent
twitter.com/UnitedWayCK
To build the organized capacity of people to care for one another
Alison Patrick, President
Karen Kirkwood-Whyte, CEO

United Way of Cochrane-Timiskaming
PO Box 984, Timmins ON P4N 7H6
Tel: 705-268-9696
www.facebook.com/85026973282

To promote the organized capacity of people to care for one another
Jennifer Gorman, Coordinator, Resource Development

United Way of Cumberland County
PO Box 535, #206, 16 Church St., Amherst NS B4H 4A1
Tel: 902-667-2203; *Fax:* 902-667-3819
www.amherst.unitedway.ca
Curt Gunn, President

United Way of Durham Region
345 Simcoe St. South, Oshawa ON L1H 4J2
Tel: 905-436-7377; *Toll-Free:* 866-463-6910
www.unitedwaydr.com
To strengthen the Durham region communities & improve the quality of life of its residents
Cindy Murray, Chief Executive Officer
Robert Howard, Director, Campaign & Communications
Karie Stephenson, Manager, Finance & Office
Michele Watson, Manager, Information Services Program
Jessica Hanson, Manager, Communications & Data
Barb Fannin, Coordinator, Community Investment

United Way of East Kootenay
PO Box 657, 930 Baker St., Cranbrook BC V1C 4J2
Tel: 250-426-8833; *Fax:* 250-426-5455
office@cranbrook.unitedway.ca
www.cranbrook.unitedway.ca
www.facebook.com/ourunitedway
To ensure the effective raising & allocation of charitable funds for community based social services that are in the best interest of the community
Donna Brady Fields, Executive Director

United Way of Estevan
PO Box 611, Estevan SK S4A 2A5
Tel: 306-634-7375
admin@unitedwayestevan.com
www.unitedwayofestevan.com
www.facebook.com/unitedwayestevan
twitter.com/uwestevan
To strengthen the community
Christa Morhart, President

United Way of Fort McMurray
The Redpoll Centre, #200, 10010 Franklin Ave., Fort McMurray AB T9H 2K6
Tel: 780-791-0077
info@fmunitedway.com
fmunitedway.com
www.youtube.com/user/fmunitedwaycampaign
www.facebook.com/142299649181047
twitter.com/FMUnitedWay
To provide effective support for social health & welfare services in the community of Fort McMurray
Ben Dutton, President
Diane Shannon, Executive Director
Russell Thomas, Director, Communications & Community Impact

United Way of Greater Moncton & Southeastern New Brunswick (UWGMSENB) / Centraide de la région du Grand Moncton et du Sud-Est du NB Inc. (CGMSENB)
22 Church St., #T210, Moncton NB E1C 0P7
Tel: 506-858-8600; *Fax:* 506-858-0584
office@moncton.unitedway.ca
www.gmsenbunitedway.ca
www.flickr.com/photos/unitedwaygmsenb
twitter.com/unitedwaygmsenb
To strengthen Southeastern New Brunswick's communities
Debbie McInnis, Executive Director

United Way of Greater Saint John Inc.
#301, 28 Richmond St., Saint John NB E2L 3B2
Tel: 506-658-1212; *Fax:* 506-633-7724
contactus@unitedwaysaintjohn.com
www.unitedwaysaintjohn.com
www.youtube.com/UnitedWaySJ
www.facebook.com/21724743048
twitter.com/SJUnitedWay
Wendy MacDermott, Executive Director

United Way of Greater Simcoe County
1110 Hwy. 26, Midhurst ON L9X 1N6
Tel: 705-726-2301; *Fax:* 705-726-4897
info@uwsimcoemuskoka.ca
www.unitedwaygsc.ca
www.youtube.com/user/UnitedWaySimcoeCty
www.facebook.com/UWSimcoeMuskoka
twitter.com/UWSimcoeMuskoka
To improve quality of life & build community by helping those most in need

Dale Biddell, CEO

United Way of Guelph, Wellington & Dufferin
85 Westmount Rd., Guelph ON N1H 5J2
Tel: 519-821-0571; *Fax:* 519-821-7847
www.unitedwayguelph.com
www.linkedin.com/company/united-way-of-guelph-&-wellington
www.facebook.com/unitedwayguelph
twitter.com/uwguelph
To meet the needs of the community & improve lives
Ken Dardano, Executive Director

United Way of Haldimand-Norfolk
PO Box 472, 45 Kent St. North, Simcoe ON N3Y 4L5
Tel: 519-426-5660; *Fax:* 519-426-0017
reception@unitedwayhn.on.ca
www.unitedwayhn.on.ca
www.facebook.com/Unitedwayofhn
twitter.com/UnitedWayofHN
To improve people's lives & to strengthen the community
Brittany Burley, Executive Director

United Way of Halifax Region
Royal Bank Bldg., 46 Portland St., 7th Fl., Dartmouth NS
B2Y 1H4
Tel: 902-422-1501; *Fax:* 902-423-6837
www.unitedwayhalifax.ca
www.linkedin.com/company/united-way-of-halifax-region
www.facebook.com/UnitedWayHalifaxRegion
twitter.com/UWHalifax
To strengthen neighbourhoods & communities by providing
programs & services that link people & resources, encourage
participation & increase giving
Sara Napier, President & CEO

United Way of Halton Hills
PO Box 286, Georgetown ON L7G 4Y5
Tel: 905-877-3066; *Fax:* 905-877-3067
office@unitedwayofhaltonhills.ca
www.unitedwayofhaltonhills.ca
To provide leadership in the raising & allocation of funds to meet
human needs & to improve social conditions in the community
Janet Foster, Executive Director

United Way of Kingston, Frontenac, Lennox &
Addington
417 Bagot St., Kingston ON K7K 3C1
Tel: 613-542-2674; *Fax:* 613-542-1379
uway@unitedwaykfla.ca
www.unitedwaykfla.ca
www.youtube.com/unitedwaykfla
www.facebook.com/unitedwaykfla
twitter.com/unitedwaykfla
To strengthen the community by supporting social service &
health agencies
Bhavana Varma, President & CEO

United Way of Kitchener-Waterloo & Area
Marsland Centre, #801, 20 Erb St. West, Waterloo ON N2L
1T2
Tel: 519-888-6100
info@uwaykw.org
www.uwaykw.org
www.youtube.com/user/UwayKW
www.facebook.com/uwaykw
twitter.com/UnitedWayKW
To improve quality of life in the community
Ingrid Pregel, President
Jan Varner, CEO

United Way of Lanark County
15 Bates Dr., Carleton Place ON K7C 4J8
Tel: 613-253-9074; *Fax:* 888-249-9075
www.lanarkunitedway.com
www.linkedin.com/company/united-way-of-lanark-county
www.facebook.com/UnitedWayLanarkCounty
twitter.com/UWLanarkCounty
To mobilize people to strengthen the community & enact social
change
Fraser Scantlebury, Executive Director

United Way of Leeds & Grenville
PO Box 576, 42 George St., Brockville ON K6V 5V7
Tel: 613-342-8889; *Fax:* 613-342-8850
info@uwlg.org
www.uwlg.org
www.youtube.com/user/UnitedWayLeedsGrenv
www.facebook.com/UnitedWayLG
To unite people to improve quality of life & build healthy
communities
Melissa Hillier, Executive Director

United Way of Lethbridge & South Western Alberta
1277 - 3 Ave. South, Lethbridge AB T1J 0K3
Tel: 403-327-1700; *Fax:* 403-317-7940
together@lethbridgeunitedway.ca
www.lethbridgeunitedway.ca
www.facebook.com/unitedwaylethy
twitter.com/unitedwaylethy
To build a better community by organizing the capacity of people
to care for one another
Jeff McLarty, Executive Director

United Way of London & Middlesex
409 King St., London ON N6B 1S5
Tel: 519-438-1721; *Fax:* 519-438-9938
www.unitedwaylm.ca
www.linkedin.com/company/unitedwaylm
www.facebook.com/unitedwaylm
twitter.com/unitedwaylm
To exercise leadership in coordinating people & organizations to
assist those in need in our community
Kelly Ziegner, Chief Executive Officer
Suzanne Bembridge, Director, Finance & Operations

United Way of Milton
PO Box 212, 1 Chris Hadfield Way, Milton ON L9T 4N9
Tel: 905-875-2550; *Fax:* 905-875-2402
campaign@miltonunitedway.ca
www.miltonunitedway.ca
www.youtube.com/unitedwaymilton
www.linkedin.com/groups/2558626
www.facebook.com/UnitedWayMilton
twitter.com/unitedwaymilton
To serve the people of the Milton area by working with
recognized charitable agencies to ensure human services that
enhance the quality of life in the community
Kate Holmes, CEO

United Way of Morden & District Inc.
PO Box 758, 379 Stephen St., Morden MB R6M 1A7
Tel: 204-822-6992
mordendistrictuw@gmail.com
www.unitedwaymorden.com
To partner with charitable agencies & organizations to improve
the lives of residents in Morden & the surrounding area
Lisa Gander, President

United Way of North Okanagan Columbia Shuswap
3304 - 30th Ave., Vernon BC V1T 2C8
Tel: 250-549-1346; *Fax:* 250-549-1357
Toll-Free: 866-448-3489
unitedwaynocs@shaw.ca
www.unitedwaynocs.com
www.facebook.com/2264112340037024
twitter.com/unitedwaynocs
To promote a healthy, caring inclusive community; To strenghten
our community's capacity to address social issues
Linda Yule, Executive Director

United Way of Northern BC
1600 - 3rd Ave., Prince George BC V2L 3G6
Tel: 250-561-1040; *Fax:* 250-562-8102
info@unitedwaynbc.ca
www.unitedwaynbc.ca
www.facebook.com/unitedwaynorthernbc
twitter.com/unitedwaynbc
To promote the organized capacity of persons to care for one
another through voluntarism, leadership & education; To ensure
the effective raising & allocation of charitable funds for
community-based social services; To foster the effective
provision of services that are in the best interest of the
community
Sotirios Korogonas, Chair
Roberta Squire, Chief Executive Officer

United Way of Oakville (UWO)
#200, 466 Speers Rd., Oakville ON L6K 3W9
Tel: 905-845-5571; *Fax:* 905-845-0166
info@uwoakville.org
www.uwoakville.org
www.youtube.com/user/UnitedWayofOakville
www.linkedin.com/company/united-way-oakville
www.facebook.com/UnitedWayOakville
twitter.com/uwoakville
To bring people & resources together to strengthen the Oakville
community
John Armstrong, Chair
Brad Park, Chief Executive Officer
Tara Neal, Office Administrator

United Way of Oxford
#447 Hunter St., Woodstock ON N4S 4G7
Tel: 519-539-3851
info@unitedwayoxford.ca
www.unitedwayoxford.ca
www.youtube.com/channel/UCup-8AJZ2pJFCCeZbJ4t87w
www.facebook.com/UnitedWayOxford
twitter.com/UnitedWayOxford
To build strong communities & help improve the lives of
residents, especially those affected by poverty, mental health
issues, or other social challenges
Kelly Gilson, Executive Director
Anne Wismer, Manager, Operations

United Way of Perth-Huron
32 Erie St., Stratford ON N5A 2M4
Tel: 519-271-7730; *Fax:* 519-273-9350
Toll-Free: 877-818-8867
info@perthhuron.unitedway.ca
www.perthhuron.unitedway.ca
www.youtube.com/user/UnitedWPH
www.linkedin.com/groups/3966504
www.facebook.com/UWPH1
twitter.com/UnitedWayPH
To improve people's lives & meet the needs of the community by
mobilizing agencies, individuals, & resources
Ryan Erb, Executive Director
Carolynne Champagne, Vice-President, Resource Development
& Communications
Jeanine Clarke, Director, Finance & Property
Susan Faber, Director, Communications & Community
Information

United Way of Peterborough & District
277 Stewart St., Peterborough ON K9J 3M8
Tel: 705-742-8839; *Fax:* 705-742-9186
office@uwpeterborough.ca
www.uwpeterborough.ca
www.facebook.com/15103169591
twitter.com/UnitedWayPtbo
To improve lives & build community by engaging individuals &
mobilizing collective action; to provide resources, services &
programs for community leadership
Jim Russell, CEO

United Way of Pictou County
PO Box 75, 342 Stewart St., New Glasgow NS B2H 5E1
Tel: 902-755-1754; *Fax:* 902-755-0853
info@pictoucountyunitedway.ca
www.pictoucountyunitedway.ca
www.facebook.com/UWPictouCounty
twitter.com/UWPictouCo
To strengthen communities by facilitating programs & services
that link people & resources; encourage participation; increase
giving
Jessica Smith, Executive Director

United Way of Prince Edward Island / Centraide PEI
PO Box 247, 180 Kent St., 2nd Fl., Charlottetown PE C1A
7K4
Tel: 902-894-8202; *Fax:* 902-894-9643
Toll-Free: 877-902-4438
info@peiunitedway.com
www.peiunitedway.com
www.youtube.com/channel/UCQAZJYD21v35hI9ggOoAJ9w
www.linkedin.com/company/united-way-of-pei
www.facebook.com/UWPEI
twitter.com/uwpei
To provide funds needed to meet community needs & build
stronger communities
Andrea MacDonald, Chief Executive Officer

United Way of Quinte
PO Box 815, Belleville ON K8N 5B5
Tel: 613-962-9531; *Fax:* 613-962-4165
www.unitedwayofquinte.ca
www.facebook.com/UnitedWayofQuinte
twitter.com/unitedwayquinte
To provide leadership in a collaborative endeavor with our
member agencies & others to increase the capacity of our
community to respond to human service needs
Danny Nickle, Chair
Judi Gilbert, Executive Director
Tambra Patrick-MacDonald, Director, Finance & Administration

United Way of Regina
1440 Scarth St., Regina SK S4R 2E9
Tel: 306-757-5671; *Fax:* 306-522-7199
www.unitedwayregina.ca
www.instagram.com/unitedwayregina
www.facebook.com/UnitedWayRegina
twitter.com/unitedwayregina

To mobilize individuals, agencies & resources to improve lives & strengthen the community
Robyn Edwards-Bentz, CEO
Tanya Murray, Director, Operations

United Way of Sarnia-Lambton
PO Box 548, 420 East St. North, Sarnia ON N7T 6Y5
Tel: 519-336-5452; *Fax:* 519-383-6032
info@theunitedway.on.ca
www.theunitedway.on.ca
To generate resources enabling the community to respond to human care priorities in Sarnia-Lambton
Dave Brown, Executive Director

United Way of Saskatoon & Area
#100, 506 - 25 St. East, Saskatoon SK S7K 4A7
Tel: 306-975-7700
office@unitedwaysaskatoon.ca
www.unitedwaysaskatoon.ca
www.facebook.com/UnitedWaySaskatoonAndArea
twitter.com/UnitedWayStoon
To improve social conditions & build a strong community
Jocelyn Zurakowski, Interim CEO

United Way of Sault Ste Marie & District
7A Oxford St., Sault Ste Marie ON P6B 1R7
Tel: 705-256-7476; *Fax:* 705-759-5899
uwssm@ssmunitedway.ca
www.ssmunitedway.ca
www.facebook.com/unitedwaysault
To improve the health, well-being, & quality of life of individuals & families in the community; To fight against poverty & address community issues
Gary Vipond, CEO

United Way of South Eastern Alberta
928 Allowance Ave., Medicine Hat AB T1A 7G7
Tel: 403-526-5544; *Fax:* 403-526-5244
www.utdway.ca
www.facebook.com/UnitedWaySEAB
twitter.com/UnitedWaySEAB
Melissa Fandrick, Coordinator, Community Investment

United Way of Stormont, Dundas & Glengarry / Centraide de Stormont, Dundas & Glengarry
PO Box 441, Stn. Case Postale, Cornwall ON K6H 5T2
Tel: 613-932-2051; *Fax:* 613-932-7534
info@unitedwaysdg.com
www.unitedwaysdg.com
www.facebook.com/209841445745076
twitter.com/unitedwaysdg
To improve lives & build community by supporting agencies, programs & services in the area
Nolan Quinn, President
Lori Greer, Executive Director
Stephanie Lalonde, Coordinator, Campaign & Communication

United Way of the Alberta Capital Region
15132 Stony Plain Rd., Edmonton AB T5P 3Y3
Tel: 780-990-1000; *Fax:* 780-990-0203
united@myunitedway.ca
www.myunitedway.ca
www.youtube.com/uwacr
www.facebook.com/myUnitedWay
twitter.com/myunitedway
To bring people & resources together to build caring, vibrant communities
Rob Yager, President & CEO

United Way of the Central Okanagan & South Okanagan/Similkameen
#202, 1456 St. Paul St., Kelowna BC V1Y 2E6
Tel: 250-860-2356; *Fax:* 250-868-3206
info@unitedwaycso.com
unitedwaycso.com
www.youtube.com/user/UnitedWayCSO
www.facebook.com/unitedwaycso
twitter.com/UnitedWayCSO
To increase the organized capacity of people in our community to care for one another
Shelley Gilmore, Executive Director

United Way of the Fraser Valley (UWFV)
Sweeney Neighbourhood Centre, #208, 33355 Bevan Ave., Abbotsford BC V2S 0E7
Tel: 604-852-1234; *Fax:* 604-852-2316
Toll-Free: 888-251-7777
info@uwfv.bc.ca
www.facebook.com/unitedwayfraservalley
twitter.com/unitedwayfv
To promote the organized capacity of people to care for one another
Wayne Green, Executive Director

United Way of the Lower Mainland
4543 Canada Way, Burnaby BC V5G 4T4
Tel: 604-294-8929; *Fax:* 604-293-0220
www.uwlm.ca
www.youtube.com/user/UnitedWayVancouver
www.linkedin.com/groups/4196396
www.facebook.com/UnitedWayoftheLowerMainland
twitter.com/uwlm
Michael McKnight, President & CEO

United Way of Trail & District
803B Victoria St., Trail BC V1R 3T3
Tel: 250-364-0999; *Fax:* 250-364-1564
www.traildistrictunitedway.com
To raise funds which are allocated to 26 affiliated non-profit organizations
Jodi LeSergent, President

United Way of Windsor-Essex County
300 Giles Blvd. East, #A1, Windsor ON N9A 4C4
Tel: 519-258-0000; *Fax:* 519-258-2346
info@weareunited.com
www.weareunited.com
www.facebook.com/unitedway.windsoressex
twitter.com/UnitedWayWE
To bring people & resources together to improve the community
Lorraine Goddard, CEO

United Way of Winnipeg / Winnipeg Centraide
580 Main St., Winnipeg MB R3B 1C7
Tel: 204-477-5360; *Fax:* 204-453-6198
info@unitedwaywinnipeg.mb.ca
www.unitedwaywinnipeg.ca
www.youtube.com/user/uwaywinnipeg
www.facebook.com/unitedwaywinnipeg
twitter.com/unitedwaywpg
To support & strengthen the organized capacity of people to care for one another
Marilyn McLaren, Chair

United Way/Centraide (Central NB) Inc.
#1A, 385 Wilsey Rd., Fredericton NB E3B 5N6
Tel: 506-459-7773; *Fax:* 506-451-1104
office@unitedwaycentral.com
www.unitedwaycentral.com
www.facebook.com/148382218531358
twitter.com/JessieUnitedWay
To be a leader in helping to create & sustain a caring & healthy community
Blair McLaughlin, President
Jeff Richardson, Executive Director

United Way/Centraide Ottawa (UW/CO)
363 Coventry Rd., Ottawa ON K1K 2C5
Tel: 613-228-6700; *Fax:* 613-228-6730
info@unitedwayottawa.ca
www.unitedwayottawa.ca
www.youtube.com/user/unitedwayottawa
www.linkedin.com/company/united-way-centraide-ottawa
www.facebook.com/unitedwayottawa
twitter.com/UnitedWayOttawa
To bring people & resources together to build a strong, healthy, safe community for all; to build & support a network of high priority, results-oriented community services; to offer leadership in bringing the community together; to excel in fundraising; to invest resources & charitable funds in partnership with the community; to inform & engage community stakeholders
Michael Allen, President/CEO

United Way/Centraide Sudbury & District
105 Elm St., #E6, Sudbury ON P3C 1T3
Tel: 705-560-3330
www.unitedwaysudbury.com
www.facebook.com/UWSudNip
twitter.com/UWSudNip
To increase the organized capacity of people to care for one another through effective fundraising & allocation of these funds
Michael Cullen, Executive Director

Vanier Institute of The Family (VIF) / Institut Vanier de la famille
94 Centrepointe Dr., Ottawa ON K2G 6B1
Tel: 613-228-8500
info@vanierinstitute.ca
www.vanierinstitute.ca
www.facebook.com/vanierinstitute
twitter.com/vanierinstitute
To understand how families in Canada interact with, have an impact on, & are affected by social, economic, environmental, & cultural forces
Nora Spinks, Chief Executive Officer

Victims of Violence (VOV)
#340, 117 Centrepointe Dr., Ottawa ON K2G 5X3
Tel: 613-233-0052; *Fax:* 613-233-2712
Toll-Free: 888-606-0000
vofv@victimsofviolence.on.ca
www.victimsofviolence.on.ca
www.facebook.com/2050474295177768
twitter.com/victimsofviolen
To provide long term support & guidance to victims of violent crime & their families; To provide aide to families of missing children
Gary Rosenfeldt, Executive Director

Volunteer Canada / Bénévoles Canada
#201, 309 Cooper St., Ottawa ON K2P 0G5
Tel: 613-231-4371; *Fax:* 613-231-6725
Toll-Free: 800-670-0401
info@volunteer.ca
volunteer.ca
www.youtube.com/VolunteerCanada
www.facebook.com/VolunteerCanada
twitter.com/VolunteerCanada
To support volunteerism & civic participation through special projects & programs
Paula Speevak, President & CEO

Volunteer Grandparents (VIP)
#203, 2101 Holdom Ave., Burnaby BC V5B 0A4
Tel: 604-736-8271; *Fax:* 604-294-6814
info@volunteergrandparents.ca
www.volunteergrandparents.ca
To support & encourage multigenerational relationships & the concept of extended family by matching screened volunteers (50+) with families with children between the age of 3-14
Stephen Sjoberg, President

The War Amputations of Canada / Les Amputés de guerre du Canada
2827 Riverside Dr., Ottawa ON K1V 0C4
Tel: 613-731-3821; *Fax:* 613-731-3234
Toll-Free: 800-465-2677
communications@waramps.ca
www.waramps.ca
www.youtube.com/warampsofcanada
www.facebook.com/TheWarAmps
twitter.com/thewaramps
To provide a wide range of assistance to all Canadian war amputees & child amputees; To promote the advancement of prosthetics through grants to facilities undertaking research in field of prosthetics
David Saunders, Chief Operating Officer
Danita Chisholm, Executive Director, Communications

Warden Woods Community Centre
74 Firvalley Ct., Toronto ON M1L 1N9
Tel: 416-694-1138; *Fax:* 416-694-1161
www.wardenwoods.com
www.flickr.com/photos/80046247@N07
www.facebook.com/wardenwoodscc
twitter.com/WardenWoodsCC
Warden Woods is a charitable community centre in Scarborough offering programmes to families, seniors, youth.
Ginelle Skerritt, Executive Director

Weyburn & District United Way
PO Box 608, Weyburn SK S4H 2K7
www.weyburnunitedway.com
To improve lives & strengthen the community
Sandra Alexander, Executive Director

Winkler & District United Way
PO Box 1528, Winkler MB R6W 4B4
Tel: 204-325-6321
unitedwaywinkler@gmail.com
www.unitedwaywinkler.com
www.facebook.com/609225769188170
To serve & improve the community
Lori Penner, President

Yorkton & District United Way Inc.
180 Broadway St. West, #A, Yorkton SK S3N 0M6
To unite & facilitate community fundraising; To strengthen the community

Standards & Testing

Canadian Evaluation Society (CES) / Société canadienne d'évaluation
#2, 555 Hall Ave. East, Renfrew ON K7V 4M7
Fax: 613-432-6840
Toll-Free: 855-251-5721
secretariat@evaluationcanada.ca
www.evaluationcanada.ca
www.linkedin.com/groups/8172963
www.facebook.com/ces.sce
twitter.com/CES_SCE

To advance evaluation for its members & the public; To establish & maintain CES as the recognized national organization which represents the evaluation community; To provide a forum for the advancement of theory & practice of evaluation; To develop competencies, ethics, & standards to improve the practice of evaluation; To advocate for high-quality evaluation with practitioners, local chapters, nationally & internationally; To promote the use of evaluation in society
Sarah Farina, President

Canadian General Standards Board (CGSB) / Office des normes générales du Canada (ONGC)
Place Du Portage III, #6B1, 11, rue Laurier, Gatineau QC K1A 1G6
Tel: 819-956-0425; *Fax:* 819-956-1634
Toll-Free: 800-665-2472
ncr.cgsb-ongc@tpsgc-pwgsc.gc.ca
www.tpsgc-pwgsc.gc.ca/ongc-cgsb

To develop standards, through accreditation with the Standards Council of Canada; To offer conformity assessment services, including product certification & registration of quality & environmental management systems, conforming to ISO standards
Begonia Lojk, Acting Director

Canadian Institute for NDE
135 Fennell Ave. West, #E006A, Hamilton ON L8N 3T2
Tel: 905-387-1655; *Fax:* 905-574-6080
Toll-Free: 800-964-9488
info@cinde.ca
www.cinde.ca
www.facebook.com/297023083473

To advance scientific, engineering, technical knowledge in the field of nondestructive testing; To gather & disseminate information relating to nondestructive testing useful to individuals & beneficial to the general public; To promote nondestructive testing through courses of instruction, lectures, meetings, publications, conferences, etc.
Glenn Tubrett, Chief Executive Officer

Canadian Standards Association (CSA)
178 Rexdale Blvd., Toronto ON M9W 1R3
Tel: 416-747-4000; *Fax:* 416-747-2473
Toll-Free: 800-463-6727
member@csagroup.org
www.csagroup.org
www.youtube.com/user/csastandards
www.linkedin.com/company/459949
www.facebook.com/CSA-Group-113511338721494
twitter.com/CSA_Group

To develop new standards & codes to meet needs, such as public health & safety & the facilitation of trade; To contribute to the global harmonization of standards; To serve government, industry, business, & consumers in Canada & the worldwide marketplace
David Weinstein, President & CEO
Robert J. Falconi, VP, Gen. Counsel & Corp. Secretary
Esteban De Bernardis, Executive Vice-President
Vikki Dunn, Executive Vice-President, Strategic Marketing & Communications

Steel & Metal Industries

Aluminium Association of Canada (AAC) / Association de l'aluminium du Canada
#1600, 1010, rue Sherbrooke ouest, Montréal QC H3A 2R7
Tel: 514-288-4842; *Fax:* 514-288-0944
Toll-Free: 844-288-4842
info@aluminium.ca
aluminium.ca
www.linkedin.com/company/aluminum-association-of-canada
www.facebook.com/1490941977666347
twitter.com/AAC_aluminium

To be a representative for the Canadian aluminium industry; To enhance its presence in industrial sectors, especially road & mass transit infrastructure & the automotive industry
Jean Simard, President & CEO

Canadian Foundry Association (CFA) / Association des fonderies canadiennes (AFC)
339 Booth St., Ottawa ON K1R 7K1
Tel: 613-789-4894
info@foundryassociation.ca
www.foundryassociation.ca

To assist & represent the membership in dealing with government on industry specific issues; To communicate information to the industry, which will assist its members in strengthening their own competitive position & ensuring a strong Canadian foundry industry
Fiona Cook, Executive Director

Canadian Institute of Steel Construction (CISC) / Institut canadien de la construction en acier (ICCA)
#102, 445 Apple Creek Blvd., Markham ON L3R 9X7
Tel: 905-604-3231
info@cisc-icca.ca
www.cisc-icca.ca
www.instagram.com/cisc_icca
www.linkedin.com/company/ciscicca
www.facebook.com/CISCWeAreSteel
twitter.com/cisc_icca

To promote good design & safety, together with efficient & economical use of steel as a means of expanding the construction markets for structural steel, joists & platework
Ed Whalen, President

Canadian Sheet Steel Building Institute (CSSBI) / Institut canadien de la tôle d'acier pour le bâtiment (ICTAB)
#2A, 652 Bishop St. North, Cambridge ON N3H 4V6
Tel: 519-650-1285; *Fax:* 519-650-8081
info@cssbi.ca
www.cssbi.ca
www.facebook.com/CSSBI652
twitter.com/cssbi

To make steel the material of choice for building construction in Canada; To develop industry standards
Meredith Perez, Manager, Marketing

Canadian Skills Training & Employment Coalition
#800, 234 Eglinton Ave. East, Toronto ON M4P 1K7
Tel: 416-480-1797; *Fax:* 416-480-2986
general@cstec.ca
www.cstec.ca
www.vimeo.com/user8234365
www.linkedin.com/company/canadian-steel-trade-and-employment-congress

To provide a forum for communication among steel companies, steelworkers, & governments to work for the betterment of the industry & its workforce
Ken Delaney, Executive Director

Canadian Steel Construction Council (CSCC) / Conseil canadien de la construction en acier
#102, 445 Apple Creek Blvd., Markham ON L3R 9X7

To represent the manufacturers of steel products, including: open-web steel joists, steel platework, corrugated steel pipe, sheet steel & steel fasteners; To promote the use of steel in construction through research & engineering

Canadian Steel Producers Association (CSPA) / Association canadienne des producteurs d'acier (ACPA)
#420, 270 Albert St., Ottawa ON K1P 5G8
Tel: 613-238-6049
info@canadiansteel.ca
www.canadiansteel.ca
www.linkedin.com/company/breakwater-communications-and-government-affairs
www.facebook.com/220022834730294
twitter.com/CSPA_ACPA

To represent the steel producers that melt & pour steel in Canada
Catherine Cobden, President

Corrugated Steel Pipe Institute (CSPI) / Institut pour tuyaux de tôle ondulée
#2A, 652 Bishop St. North, Cambridge ON N3H 4V6
Tel: 519-650-8080; *Fax:* 519-650-8081
info@cspi.ca
www.cspi.ca

To promote & encourage general & wider use of corrugated steel pipe for drainage & other uses across Canada; to initiate & support research, marketing, promotion, public relations & advertising programs designed to broaden the markets for CSP products; to cooperate with public & private agencies engaged in the formulation of specifications & designs for drainage & other underground structures; to provide the industry & the public with documented experience & up-to-date technical information on CSP products & their proper use & application; to enhance,

through responsible public relations practices, the reputation & image of the Canadian CSP industry; to cooperate with allied industry & government authorities; to encourage & participate in educational endeavours in colleges & universities.
Ray Wilcock, Executive Director

Nickel Institute
Brookfield Place, #2700, 161 Bay St., Toronto ON M5J 2S1
Tel: 416-591-7999; *Fax:* 416-572-2201
www.nickelinstitute.org
www.youtube.com/user/NickelInstitute
www.linkedin.com/company/nickelinstitute
twitter.com/NickelInstitute

To provide information for nickel users, designers, specifiers, educators & others interested in nickel-containing materials & their applications
Hudson Bates, President
Gerry Schuetz, Chief Financial Officer
Clare Richardson, Director, Communications & Member Services

Ontario Sheet Metal Contractors Association (OSM)
#26, 30 Wertheim Ct., Richmond Hill ON L4B 1B9
Tel: 905-886-9627; *Fax:* 905-886-9959
shtmetal@bellnet.ca
www.osmca.org

To negotiate & administer all provincial collective agreements between OSM, the Ontario Sheet Metal Workers' & Roofers' Conference & the Sheet Metal Workers International Association.
Kim Crossman, President
Wayne Peterson, Executive Director

Reinforcing Steel Institute of Ontario (RSIO)
PO Box 30104, RPO New Westminster, Thornhill ON L4J 0C6
Tel: 416-239-7746; *Fax:* 416-239-7745
rsio@rebar.org
www.rebar.org

To promote reinforced concrete as a building material

Surveying & Mapping

Alberta Land Surveyors' Association (ALSA)
#1000, 10020 - 101A Ave., Edmonton AB T5J 3G2
Tel: 780-429-8805; *Fax:* 888-459-1664
Toll-Free: 800-665-2572
info@alsa.ab.ca
www.alsa.ab.ca

To regulate the practice of land surveying
Brian Munday, Executive Director
Rosalind Broderick, Registrar

Association of British Columbia Land Surveyors (ABCLS)
#301, 2400 Bevan Ave., Sidney BC V8L 1W1
Tel: 250-655-7222; *Fax:* 250-655-7223
office@abcls.ca
www.abcls.ca

To protect the public interest & the integrity of the survey system in British Columbia by regulating & governing the practice of land surveying in the province
R. Chad Rintoul, Chief Administrative Officer
Kelly Stofer, Secretary & Registrar

Association of Canada Lands Surveyors / Association des arpenteurs des terres du Canada
100E, 900 Dynes Rd., Ottawa ON K2C 3L6
Tel: 613-723-9200; *Fax:* 613-723-5558
communications@acls-aatc.ca
www.acls-aatc.ca
www.linkedin.com/company/association-of-canada-lands-surveyors
www.facebook.com/associationofcanadalandssurveyors
twitter.com/aclsaatc

To establish & maintain standards of qualification for Canada Lands Surveyors; to regulate Canada Lands Surveyors; To establish & maintain standards of conduct, knowledge & skill among members of the Association & permit holders; To govern the activities of members of the Association & permit holders; To cooperate with other organizations for the advancement of surveying; To perform the duties & exercise the powers that are imposed or conferred on the Association by the Act
Jim Christie, President

Association of Manitoba Land Surveyors
#202, 83 Gary St., Winnipeg MB R3C 4J9
Tel: 204-943-6972; *Fax:* 204-957-7602
amls@mymts.net
www.amls.ca

To license qualified persons becoming commissioned land surveyors; To protect public interests concerning land boundary matters
Lori Klos, Executive Officer
W.W. (Bill) Shepherd, Registrar

Association of New Brunswick Land Surveyors (ANBLS) / Association des arpenteurs-géomètres du Nouveau-Brunswick (AA-GN-B)
#312, 212 Queen St., Fredericton NB E3B 1A8
Tel: 506-458-8266; *Fax:* 506-458-8267
anbls@nb.aibn.com
www.anbls.nb.ca
To regulate & govern the practice of land surveying in New Brunswick; To develop & maintain standards of knowledge, skill & professional ethics
Doug Morgan, Executive Director

Association of Newfoundland Land Surveyors (ANLS)
67 Majors Path, St. John's NL A1A 5B5
Tel: 709-722-2031; *Fax:* 709-722-4104
www.surveyors.nf.ca
To establish & maintain standards of knowledge, skill & professional conduct in the practice of land surveying, in order to serve & protect the public interest in Newfoundland; To regulate & govern the practice of land surveying in the province
Robert Way, President
Paula Baggs, Executive Director

Association of Nova Scotia Land Surveyors (ANSLS)
325A Prince Albert Rd., Dartmouth NS B2Y 1N5
Tel: 902-469-7962; *Fax:* 902-469-7963
ansls@accesswave.ca
www.ansls.ca
www.facebook.com/TheANSLS
twitter.com/The_ANSLS
To establish & maintain standards of professional ethics among its members, student members & holders of a certificate of authorization, in order that the public interest may be served & protected; & knowledge & skills among its members, student members & holders of a certificate of authorization; To regulate the practice of professional land surveying & govern the profession in accordance with the Act, the regulations & the by-laws; To communicate & cooperate with other professional organizations for the advancement of the best interests of the surveying profession
Fred Hutchinson, Executive Director

Association of Ontario Land Economists
#1000, 30 St Patrick St., Toronto ON M5T 3A3
admin@aole.org
www.aole.org
To continue attracting membership-quality professionals engaged in land economics pursuits; To broaden & enrich the professional development of members; To promote & maintain high ethical work standards throughout our membership; To make submissions to government for improvements in law & public administration bearing on land economics
Andrea Calla, President
Kari Norman, Administrator

Association of Ontario Land Surveyors (AOLS)
1043 McNicoll Ave., Toronto ON M1W 3W6
Tel: 416-491-9020; *Fax:* 416-491-2576
Toll-Free: 800-268-0718
info@aols.org
www.aols.org
www.youtube.com/user/AOLSTUBE
www.linkedin.com/groups/4083207
www.facebook.com/288456831275733
twitter.com/_AOLS
To be responsible for the licensing & governance of professional land surveyors, in accordance with the Surveyors Act
Blain Martin, Executive Director
William Buck, Registrar

Association of Prince Edward Island Land Surveyors (APEILS)
PO Box 20100, Charlottetown PE C1A 9E3
Tel: 902-394-3121
info@apeils.ca
www.apeils.ca
To regulate the practice of land surveying in PEI
RObert Wakelin, President
John Mantha, Vice-President
Sheldon Chisholm, Secretary/Treasurer

Canadian Cartographic Association (CCA) / Association canadienne de cartographie
c/o Byron Moldofsky, 177 Brookdale Ave., Toronto ON M5M 1P4
Tel: 416-489-5307
treasurer@cca-acc.org
www.cca-acc.org
www.facebook.com/177748108946882
twitter.com/CdnCarto
To promote interest in cartographic materials; To encourage research in the field of cartography; To advance education in cartography
Monica Lloyd, President
Byron Moldofsky, Treasurer

Canadian Geophysical Union (CGU) / Union géophysique canadienne (UGC)
c/o Dept. of Earth & Planetary Sciences, 3450 University St., Montréal QC H3A 0E8
Tel: 514-398-6767
info@cgu-ugc.ca
www.cgu-ugc.ca
www.facebook.com/442350399250129
twitter.com/CGU_UGC
To bring together & promote the geophysical sciences; To provide a focus for geophysicists at Canadian universities, government agencies, & industry in fields of study encompassing the composition & processes of the whole earth, including hydrology, space studies, & geology
Richard Petrone, President
Laura Brown, Treasurer
Jeffrey McKenzie, Secretary

Canadian Institute of Quantity Surveyors (CIQS)
#19, 90 Nolan Ct., Markham ON L3R 4L9
Tel: 905-477-0008; *Fax:* 905-477-6774
www.ciqs.org
www.linkedin.com/company/ciqs
www.facebook.com/canadianinstituteofquantitysurveyors
twitter.com/CIQS_Official
To represent the quantity surveying & construction estimating profession in Canada
Sheila Lennon, Executive Director

Ordre des arpenteurs-géomètres du Québec (OAGQ) / Québec Land Surveyors Association
Iberville Quatre, #350, 2954, boul Laurier, Québec QC G1V 4T2
Tél: 418-656-0730; *Téléc:* 418-656-6352
Ligne sans frais: 800-243-6490
oagq@oagq.qc.ca
www.oagq.qc.ca
La protection du public et le contrôle de la profession

Professional Surveyors Canada (PSC) / Géomètres professionnels du Canada (GPC)
#101B, 900 Dynes Rd., Ottawa ON K2C 3L6
Tel: 613-695-8333; *Toll-Free:* 800-241-7200
info@psc-gpc.ca
www.psc-gpc.ca
www.linkedin.com/in/pscgpc
www.facebook.com/ProfessionalSurveyorsCanada
twitter.com/PSC_GPC
To foster cooperation amongst surveyors in Canada; To advocate for an integrated Canadian surveying profession
Helen Derry, BFA, Adminstrative Coordinator
Ria van der Veen, BCS, Executive Assistant & Registrar

Saskatchewan Land Surveyors' Association (SLSA)
#7, 2010 - 7th Ave., Regina SK S4R 1C2
Tel: 306-352-8999; *Fax:* 306-352-8366
info@slsa.sk.ca
www.slsa.sk.ca
To uphold the stewardship & standards of the legal survey profession in Saskatchewan; To regulate & govern members in the practice of professional land surveying & professional surveying; To ensure the competency of members; To administer the profession to protect the public
Mike Waschuk, President
Carla Stadnick, Executive Director

Taxation

Canadian Property Tax Association, Inc. (CPTA) / Association canadienne de taxe foncière, inc
#816, 5863 Leslie St., Toronto ON M2H 1J8
Tel: 416-493-3276
cpta2@bellnet.ca
www.cpta.org
twitter.com/CPTA_ACTF

To facilitate the exchange of information about industrial & commercial property tax issues throughout Canada
Shawna Burke, President
Louise Leclair, Managing Director

Canadian Tax Foundation (CTF) / Foundation canadienne de fiscalité (FCF)
#1400, 145 Wellington St. West, Toronto ON M5J 1H8
Tel: 416-599-0283; *Fax:* 416-599-9283
Toll-Free: 877-733-0283
www.ctf.ca
www.linkedin.com/groups/4000744
twitter.com/cdntaxfdn
To create a greater understanding of the Canadian tax system; To improve the Canadian tax system
Heather L. Evans, Executive Director & CEO
Judy Singh, Librarian

Canadian Taxpayers Federation (CTF)
#265, 438 Victoria Ave. East, Regina SK S4N 0N7
Tel: 306-352-7199; *Fax:* 306-205-8339
Toll-Free: 800-667-7933
admin@taxpayer.com
taxpayer.com
www.youtube.com/taxpayerdotcom
www.facebook.com/TaxpayerDOTcom
twitter.com/taxpayerdotcom
To advocate for the common interest of taxpayers; To effect public policy change
Scott Hennig, President & CEO
Melanie Harvie, Executive Vice-President
Shannon Morrison, Vice-President, Operations

Ontario Municipal Tax & Revenue Association (OMTRA)
#119, 14845 - 6 Yonge St., Aurora ON L4G 6H8
webmaster@omtra.ca
www.omtra.ca
www.facebook.com/278364522173943
twitter.com/omtra1
To bring those persons in the municipal field of tax collecting into helpful association with each other; To promote improved standards of ethics & efficiency in tax collection methods & procedures; To consider, resolve, & recommend amendments to Provincial Acts which may improve the tax billing & collection administration; To encourage submissions & disseminate information of interest to its members; To encourage & assist in the development of educational training programs for collection personnel; To cooperate with other municipal associations; To foster good public relations
Maureen Zabiuk, President

Telecommunications

Canadian Call Management Association (CAM-X)
#10, 24 Olive St., Grimsby ON L3M 2B6
Tel: 905-309-0224; *Fax:* 905-309-0225
Toll-Free: 800-896-1054
info@camx.ca
www.camx.ca
www.facebook.com/118064931573806
twitter.com/CAM-XAssociation
To promote the welfare of the message-handling industry & related services through the encouragement & maintenance of high standards of ethics & services; the exchange of information & the rendering of mutual aid & assistance between member organizations
Linda Osip, Executive Director

Canadian Independent Telephone Association (CITA) / Association canadienne du téléphone indépendant
c/o Creative Events Management, #205, 1402 Queen St., Alton ON L7K 0C3
Tel: 519-940-0935; *Fax:* 519-940-1137
www.cita.ca
To promote the increase & improvement of telephone service in Canada; To promote & protect the common business interest of members; To produce & distribute literature; To represent the industry before regulatory bodies, either federal or provincial
Margi Taylor, General Manager

Canadian Internet Registration Authority (CIRA)
#306, 350 Sparks St., Ottawa ON K1R 7S8
Tel: 613-237-5335; *Fax:* 800-285-0517
www.cira.ca
www.youtube.com/ciranews
www.linkedin.com/groups/2456714
www.facebook.com/cira.ca
twitter.com/ciranews
To operate the dot-ca internet country code.

Byron Holland, President & CEO

Canadian Wireless Telecommunications Association (CWTA) / Association canadienne des télécommunications sans fil (ACTS)
#300, 80 Elgin St., Ottawa ON K1P 6R2
Tel: 613-233-4888; *Fax:* 613-233-2032
info@cwta.ca
www.cwta.ca
twitter.com/CWTAwireless
The authority on wireless issues, trends & developments in Canada; represents cellular, PCS, messaging, mobile radio, fixed wireless & mobile satellite service providers as well as companies that develop & produce products & services for the industry.
Robert Ghiz, President & CEO
Ursula Grant, Vice-President, Industry & Consumer Affairs

Frequency Co-ordination System Association (FCSA) / Association pour la coordination des fréquences
#700, 1 Nicholas St., Ottawa ON K1N 7B7
Tel: 613-241-3080; *Fax:* 613-241-9632
www.fcsa.ca
To operate & administer computerized Microwave Information & Coordination System (MICS); To provide cost-effective, timely & high quality centralized administrative & technical services to allow members to be able to effectively plan & coordinate frequencies for microwave communication systems on national basis
Peter Lin, General Manager & Secretary-Treasurer

Halifax Regional CAP Association (HRCAP)
Halifax NS
Tel: 902-293-8122
admin@halifaxcap.ca
www.halifaxcap.ca
www.facebook.com/HRCAP
twitter.com/hrcap
To deliver quality service to communities through their locally operated Community Access Program (CAP) sites.
Paul Hudson, Chair

Information & Communication Technologies Association of Manitoba (ICTAM)
#412, 435 Ellice Ave., Winnipeg MB R3B 1Y6
Tel: 204-944-0533; *Fax:* 204-957-5628
info@ictam.ca
www.ictam.ca
www.linkedin.com/company/2050183
www.facebook.com/ICTAMMB
twitter.com/ICTAM
To provide programming, advocacy & collaboration to the information & communication technologies industry in Manitoba, in order to accelerate growth, prosperity & sustainability
Kathy Knight, CEO
Tammy Zagari, Chief Financial Officer

Nova Scotia & Prince Edward Island Pioneers
21 Snair Lane, Queensland NS B0J 1T0
acadianpioneers@gmail.com
www.telecompioneers.ca/contact-us/nova-scotia-and-pei
To act as a corporate-based volunteer organization
Tanya Snair, President

Ontario Pioneers
ON
Tel: 905-451-5607; *Fax:* 905-453-3996
Sheila O'Donoghue, Manager

SaskTel Pioneers
2121 Saskatchewan Dr., 2nd Fl., Regina SK S4P 3Y2
Tel: 306-777-2515; *Fax:* 306-777-2831
Toll-Free: 866-944-4442
sasktel.pioneers@sasktel.com
www.sasktelpioneers.com
twitter.com/sasktelpioneers
To unite current & former telecom industry employees, their partners, & their families
Judi Livingstone, President

Telecommunities Canada Inc.
c/o President, #318, 210-1600 Kenaston Blvd., Winnipeg MB R3P 0Y4
www.tc.ca
To ensure that all Canadians are able to participate in community-based communications & electronic information services by promoting and supporting local community network initiatives; to represent & promote Canadian community networking movement at the national & international level
Clarice Leader, President

TelecomPioneers of Alberta
AB
Tel: 403-329-3462
Stan Mills, Manager

TelecomPioneers of Canada
c/o Darrell Liebrecht, 2121 Saskatchewan Dr., 2nd Fl., Regina SK S4P 3Y2
Toll-Free: 866-944-4442
sasktel.pioneers@sasktel.com
www.telecompioneers.ca
To serve as a network of current & former telecom industry employees, their partners, & their families; To improve the quality of life in Canada's communities
Darrell Liebrecht, Director

Television

Alliance québécoise des techniciens de l'image et du son (AQTIS)
#300, 533, rue Ontario est, Montréal QC H2L 1N8
Tél: 514-844-2113; *Téléc:* 514-844-3540
Ligne sans frais: 888-647-0681
info@aqtis.qc.ca
www.aqtis.qc.ca
Bernard Arseneau, Président
Jean-Claude Rocheleau, Directeur général

Independent Production Fund (IPF) / Fonds indépendant de production
#1709, 2 Carlton St., Toronto ON M5B 1J3
Tel: 416-977-8966; *Fax:* 416-977-0694
info@ipf.ca
ipf.ca
To support the production of Canadian dramatic television series by independent producers through financial investment.
Charles Ohayon, Chair
Andra Sheffer, Executive Director
Carly McGowan, Program Manager

Shaw Rocket Fund
#210, 2421 - 37th Ave., Calgary AB T2E 6Y7
www.rocketfund.ca
www.facebook.com/rocketfund
twitter.com/RocketFund
To provide funding for children's programming
Annabel Slaight, Chair
Agnes Augustin, President & Treasurer

Tenants & Landlords

Action Dignité de Saint-Léonard
9089A, boul Viau, Saint-Léonard QC H1R 2V6
Tél: 514-251-2874
Groupe de défense des droits des locataires

Association des locataires de l'Île-des-Soeurs (ALIS/NITA) / Nuns' Island Tenants Association
CP 63008, 40, Place du Commerce, Verdun QC H3E 1V6
Tél: 514-767-1003
Défense des droits des locataires

Comité d'action des citoyennes et citoyens de Verdun
3972, rue de Verdun, Verdun QC H4G 1K9
Tél: 514-769-2228; *Téléc:* 514-769-0825
www.cacv-verdun.org
Soutien les personnes les plus démunies afin qu'elles améliorent leurs conditions de vie dans une optique de prise en charge
Chantal Lamarre, Directrice

Comité d'action Parc Extension (CAPE)
#03, 419, rue St-Roch, Montréal QC H3N 1K2
Tél: 514-278-6028; *Téléc:* 514-278-0900
D'améliorer les conditions de vie de tous les citoyens / citoyennes du quartier Parc Extension
Denis Giraldeau, Coordonnateur

Comité des citoyens et citoyennes du quartier Saint-Sauveur
301, rue Carillon, Québec QC G1K 5B3
Tél: 418-529-6158; *Téléc:* 418-529-9455
cccqss@bellnet.ca
www.cccqss.org
www.facebook.com/CCCQSS

Comité logement de Lacine-Lasalle
426, rue St-Jacques ouest, Lachine QC H8R 1E8
Tél: 514-544-4294; *Téléc:* 514-366-0505
logement.lachine-lasalle@videotron.ca
Daniel Chainey, Responsable

Comité logement du Plateau Mont-Royal
#328, 4450, rue St-Hubert, Montréal QC H2J 2W9
Tél: 514-527-3495; *Téléc:* 514-527-6653
clplateau@yahoo.ca
sites.google.com/site/comitelogementplateau

Comité logement Rosemont
#R-145, 5350, rue Lafond, Montréal QC H1X 2X2
Tél: 514-597-2581; *Téléc:* 514-524-9813
info@comitelogement.org
www.comitelogement.org
www.facebook.com/comitelogement
Défendre et promouvoir les droits des locataires du quartier Rosemont
Martine Poitras, Coordonnatrice

Conseil communautaire Notre-Dame-de-Grâce / Notre-Dame-de-Grâce Community Council
#204, 5964, av Notre-Dame-de-Grâce, Montréal QC H4A 1N1
Tél: 514-484-1471
ndgcc@ndg.ca
www.ndg.ca
Halah Al-Ubaidi, Directrice générale

POPIR-Comité logement (St-Henri, Petite Bourgogne, Ville Émard, Côte St-Paul)
4017, rue Notre-Dame ouest, Montréal QC H4C 1R3
Tél: 514-935-4649; *Téléc:* 514-935-4067
info@popir.org
popir.org
twitter.com/lepopir
Antoine Morneau-Sénéchal, Organisateur Communautaire

Tourism & Travel

Alberta Country Vacations Association (ACVA)
Claresholm AB
Toll-Free: 866-217-2282
www.facebook.com/Alberta.Country.Vacations
twitter.com/acvatweets
To promote ranch & farm holidays in Alberta; To act as the voice of country vacation businesses in Alberta; To assist members of the association to be strong & profitable organizations

Alberta Hotel & Lodging Association
2707 Ellwood Dr. SW, Edmonton AB T6X 0P7
Tel: 780-436-6112; *Fax:* 780-436-5404
Toll-Free: 888-436-6112
www.ahla.ca
www.linkedin.com/company/alberta-hotel-&-lodging-association
www.facebook.com/171333316227097
twitter.com/ABHotelAssoc
To enhance the image, the quality & efficiency of the hotel industry in Alberta
Dave Kaiser, President & CEO

Algoma Kinniwabi Travel Association (AKTA)
334 Bay St., Sault Ste Marie ON P6A 1X1
Tel: 705-254-4293; *Fax:* 705-254-4892
Toll-Free: 800-263-2546
info@algomacountry.com
www.algomacountry.com
www.youtube.com/user/OntarioAlgomaCountry
www.facebook.com/algomacountry
twitter.com/AlgomaCountry
To promote the Algoma Country region to the travelling public
Lori Johnson, President

Almaguin-Nipissing Travel Association
PO Box 351, Stn. Regional Information Centre, North Bay ON P1B 8H5
Tel: 705-474-6634; *Toll-Free:* 800-387-0516
To market Ontario's Near North as a four-seasons family-oriented outdoor vacation destination on behalf of the organized tourist industry

Association Hôtellerie Québec (AHQ)
#100, 450, ch de Chambly, Longueuil QC J4H 3L7
Tél: 579-721-6215; *Téléc:* 579-721-3663
Ligne sans frais: 877-769-9776
info@hotelleriequebec.org
www.hotelleriequebec.org
www.facebook.com/HoteliersQuebecAHQ
Regrouper les établissements hôteliers pour les représenter, défendre leurs intérêts et leurs fournir des services et ce, tout en collaborant au développement de la qualité de la profession hôtelière et de l'industrie touristique en général
Benoit Sirard, Président

Association of Canadian Travel Agencies (ACTA) / Association canadienne des agences de voyages
#226, 2560 Matheson Blvd. East, Mississauga ON L4W 4Y9
Tel: 905-282-9294; *Fax:* 905-282-9826
Toll-Free: 888-257-2282
info@acta.ca
www.acta.ca
www.linkedin.com/company/association-of-canadian-travel-agencies-acta
www.facebook.com/ACTACanada
twitter.com/actacanada
To provide leadership for the retail travel professional
Wendy Paradis, President
Heather Craig-Peddie, Vice-President, Advocacy & Member Relations
Marco Pozzobon, Director, Marketing, Communications & Partnerships
Maggie Santos, Director, Education & Certification

Association of Canadian Travel Agencies - Atlantic
PO Box 21007, Quispamsis NB E2E 4Z4
Tel: 888-257-2282; *Fax:* 855-349-0658
actaatlantic@acta.ca
www.acta.ca
To represent & defend the interests of the retail travel services industry; To serve as the focal point for the retail travel services industry; To support initiatives designed to create & maintain a healthy business & legislative environment
Lorie Cohen Hackett, Regional Manager

Association of Canadian Travel Agents - Alberta & NWT
PO Box 21058, Stn. Terwilligar, 584 Riverbend SW NW, Edmonton AB T6R 2V4
Tel: 780-437-2555; *Fax:* 855-349-0658
Toll-Free: 888-257-2282
www.acta.ca
To represent the retail travel sector of Canada's tourism industy, with a focus on travel agents in Alberta & the Northwest Territories
Anthony Tonkinson, Regional Chair
Barbara Sutherland, Regional Manager

Association of Canadian Travel Agents - British Columbia & Yukon
c/o Association of Canadian Travel Agencies, #226, 2560 Matheson Blvd. East, Mississauga ON L4W 4Y9
Toll-Free: 888-257-2282
www.acta.ca
To promote the interests of the retail travel sector in British Columbia & Yukon
Liz Fleming, Regional Chair

Association of Canadian Travel Agents - Manitoba & Nunavut
c/o Association of Canadian Travel Agencies, #226, 2560 Matheson Blvd. East, Mississauga ON L4W 4Y9
Toll-Free: 888-257-2282
actambsk@acta.ca
www.acta.ca
To promote & represent the retail travel field in Manitoba & Nunavut
Mary Jane Hiebert, Regional Chair

Association of Canadian Travel Agents - Ontario
#226, 2560 Matheson Blvd. East, Mississauga ON L4W 4Y9
Tel: 905-282-9294; *Fax:* 855-349-0658
Toll-Free: 888-257-2282
www.acta.ca
To represent the retail travel sector of Canada's tourism industry, with a focus on Ontario travel agents
Fiona Bowen, Regional Manager
Mike Foster, Regional Chair

Association of Canadian Travel Agents - Québec / Association des agents de voyages du Québec
CP 76063, Mascouche QC J7K 3N9
Tél: 514-357-0890; *Téléc:* 855-349-0658
Ligne sans frais: 888-257-2282
www.acta.ca
Défense des droits et intérêts de l'industrie du voyage
Manon Martel, Directeur régional

Association touristique régionale de Charlevoix
495, boul de Comporté, La Malbaie QC G5A 3G3
Tél: 418-665-4454; *Téléc:* 418-665-3811
Ligne sans frais: 800-667-2276
info@tourisme-charlevoix.com
www.tourisme-charlevoix.com
www.youtube.com/user/TourismeCharlevoix
www.facebook.com/tourismecharlevoix
twitter.com/gocharlevoix
Acceuil, promotion, développement de Charlevoix en tourisme

Association touristique régionale du Saguenay-Lac-Saint-Jean / Tourism Saguenay-Lac-Saint-Jean
#100, 412, boul Saguenay est, Chicoutimi QC G7H 7Y8
Tél: 418-543-3536; *Téléc:* 418-543-1805
Ligne sans frais: 855-253-8387
admin@tourismesaglac.net
www.saguenaylacsaintjean.ca
www.facebook.com/TourismeSaguenayLacSaintJean
Au service et à l'écoute de ses membres et de l'industrie touristique régionale dans son ensemble, elle est une organisation de concertation dont les principales activités visent à développer et promouvoir la qualité de l'expérience touristique, à assurer l'accueil des clientèles touristique et la mise en marché de la destination.
Julie Dubord, Directrice générale
Marie-Eve Claveau, Directrice, Développement de la destination
Julie Chiasson, Directrice, Marketing et de la promotion de la destination

Associations touristiques régionales associées du Québec (ATRAQ) / Québec Regional Tourist Associations Inc.
#330, 1575, boul de l'Avenir, Laval QC H7S 2N5
Tél: 450-686-8358; *Téléc:* 450-686-9630
Ligne sans frais: 877-686-8358
information@atrassociees.com
www.atrassociees.com
www.youtube.com/user/ATRassociees
www.facebook.com/ATRassociees
twitter.com/atrassociees
Regrouper l'ensemble des associations touristiques régionales oeuvrant au Québec en vue de les représenter et défendre leurs intérêts collectifs; les promouvoir et leur offrir des services; contribuer ainsi au développement de l'industrie touristique québécoise
François-G. Chevrier, Président-Directeur général

British Columbia Lodging & Campgrounds Association (BCLCA)
#209, 3003 St. John's St., Port Moody BC V3H 2C4
Tel: 778-383-1037; *Fax:* 604-945-7606
www.bclca.com
www.instagram.com/travelinbc
www.facebook.com/TravellinginBritishColumbia
twitter.com/TravellinginBC
To promote the public's utilization of member lodging & campground businesses; To monitor & make representation to governments on legislation affecting the interests of British Columbia's lodging & campground businesses; To speak for the membership on matters of general or specific interest; To encourage members to strive for excellence in accommodation & service
Joss Penny, Executive Director

Cambridge Tourism
750 Hespeler Rd., Cambridge ON N3H 5L8
Tel: 519-622-2336; *Fax:* 519-622-0177
Toll-Free: 800-749-7560
visit@cambridgechamber.com
www.cambridgetourism.com
www.pinterest.com/cambridgeon
www.facebook.com/249977815059176
To develop tourism initiatives & build partnerships that pool ideas & resources to promote Cambridge as a viable travel destination, generating greater economic impact for the city & other tourism stakeholders.

Camping in Ontario
#6, 1915 Clements Rd., Pickering ON L1W 3V1
Tel: 289-660-2192; *Fax:* 289-660-2146
Toll-Free: 877-672-2226
info@campinginontario.ca
www.campinginontario.ca
www.facebook.com/CampInOntario
twitter.com/CampInOntario
To support & improve the operation of private campgrounds in Ontario by establishing standards, disseminating information & by representation in the tourist industry & at all levels of government
Alexandra Anderson, Executive Director

Camping Québec
#700, 2001, rue de la Métropole, Longueuil QC J4G 1S9
Tél: 450-651-7396; *Téléc:* 450-651-7397
Ligne sans frais: 800-363-0457
www.campingquebec.com
Défendre les intérêts de nos membres; offrir des services de publications et promotion, des activitées, des escomptes sur achats et programmes divers.
Natasha Bouchard, Présidente

Canadian Recreational Vehicle Association (CRVA) / Association canadienne du véhicule récréatif
#300, 1100 Burloak Dr., Burlington ON L7L 6B2
Tel: 905-315-3156
www.crva.ca
www.instagram.com/canadianrvassociation
www.facebook.com/canadianrvassociation
twitter.com/canadianrvassn
To promote recreational vehicle lifestyle
Shane Devenish, Executive Director

Canadian Tourism Research Institute
255 Smyth Rd., Ottawa ON K1H 8M7
Tel: 613-526-3280; *Fax:* 613-526-4857
Toll-Free: 866-711-2262
ctri@conferenceboard.ca
www.conferenceboard.ca
To provide data & economic models for the travel & tourism industry in Canada

Canadian Vacation Ownership Association (CVOA)
Toll-Free: 844-544-2862
membershipservices@canadianvoa.org
canadianvoa.org
www.facebook.com/CVOANews
To raise a better understanding of the value of the vacation ownership product; To ensure fair & ethical treatment by all industry participants, through legislation or industry self-management; To educate & inform within the membership & outwardly to the public
Greg Crist, President & CEO

Cariboo Chilcotin Coast Tourism Association
#204, 350 Barnard St., Williams Lake BC V2G 4T9
Tel: 250-392-2226; *Fax:* 250-392-2838
Toll-Free: 800-663-5885
info@landwithoutlimits.com
www.landwithoutlimits.com
www.youtube.com/user/TheCCCTA
www.facebook.com/CaribooChilcotinCoast
twitter.com/CarChiCoa
To promote tourism products of the Cariboo Chilcotin Coast region of BC. Products & services include, access to an extensive image bank, travel guide & DVD, familiarization tour assistance, itinerary planning assistance, property inspection/recommendations, regional knowledge.
Amy Thacker, CEO

Central Nova Tourist Association (CNTA)
65 Treaty Trail, Millbrook NS B6L 1W3
Tel: 902-893-8782; *Fax:* 902-893-2269
Toll-Free: 800-895-1177
info@centralnovascotia.com
www.centralnovascotia.com
www.facebook.com/62069285284
To contribute to the Central Nova area becoming the most important tourist destination in Nova Scotia, resulting in new tourism initiatives & strengthened businesses by working as a team dedicated to effective communication & production of our community
Joyce Mingo, Executive Director

Centre mondial d'excellence des destinations (CED) / World Centre of Excellence for Destinations (WCED)
PO Box 8888, Stn. Centreville, 1290, Saint-Denis St., #AB-9200, Montréal QC H2X 3J7
Tel: 514-871-1115
info@ced.travel
www.ced.travel
www.facebook.com/CEDTravel
twitter.com/CEDTravel
To guide destinations worldwide toward excellence by supporting efforts to foster sustainable development & increasing their ability to generate economic, social & cultural benefits

Economic Development Winnipeg Inc. (EDW)
#810, 1 Lombard Pl., Winnipeg MB R3B 0X3
Tel: 204-954-1997; *Fax:* 204-942-4043
wpginfo@economicdevelopmentwinnipeg.com
www.economicdevelopmentwinnipeg.com
www.youtube.com/user/EDWinnipeg
www.facebook.com/EDWinnipeg
twitter.com/EDWinnipeg
To act as Winnipeg's economic development & tourism services agency, by marketing the city & providing related economic development & tourism services
Dayna Spiring, President & CEO
Greg Dandewich, Senior Vice-President
Ryan Kuffner, Vice-President
Nike Bello, Director, Finance

Fondation Tourisme Jeunesse / Youth Travel Foundation
#220, 5450, ch de la Côte-des-Neiges, Montréal QC H3T 1Y6
Tél: 514-731-1015; *Ligne sans frais:* 866-754-1015
info@ftj-ytf.org
ftj-ytf.org
www.linkedin.com/company/ftjytf
www.facebook.com/FTJYTF
twitter.com/FTJYTF
Rendre accessible le tourisme aux jeunes, en développant divers outils et services, notamment par le biais des bureaux d'information voyages et des auberges de jeunesse du Québec
Jacques Perreault, Directeur général

Fredericton Tourism
11 Carleton St., Fredericton NB E3B 3T1
Tel: 506-460-2041; *Fax:* 506-460-2474
Toll-Free: 888-888-4768
tourism@fredericton.ca
www.tourismfredericton.ca
www.youtube.com/user/FrederictonTourism
www.facebook.com/FrederictonTourism
twitter.com/FredTourism
To develop & run a variety of cultural programs largely focused in the Historic Garrison District; to operate 2 municipal Visitor Information Centres, Lighthouse on the Green, & River Valley Crafts retail shop.
Ken Forrest, Director, Growth & Community Planning

The Georgian Triangle Tourist Association & Tourist Information Centre
45 St Paul St., Collingwood ON L9Y 3P1
Tel: 705-445-7722; *Fax:* 705-444-6158
Toll-Free: 888-227-8667
info@georgiantriangle.com
www.georgiantriangle.com
www.facebook.com/114000537662
twitter.com/SGeorgianBay
To promote tourism & convention industries in the Georgian Triangle

Hospitality Newfoundland & Labrador (HNL)
#102, 71 Goldstone St., St. John's NL A1B 5C3
Tel: 709-722-2000; *Fax:* 709-722-8104
Toll-Free: 800-563-0700
hnl@hnl.ca
hnl.ca
www.facebook.com/HospitalityNL
twitter.com/hospitalitynl
To develop & promote tourism & hospitality industry throughout Newfoundland & Labrador.
Carol-Ann Gilliard, Chief Executive Officer

Hotel Association of Canada Inc. (HAC) / Association des hôtels du Canada
#1206, 130 Albert St., Ottawa ON K1P 5G4
Tel: 613-237-7149; *Fax:* 613-237-8928
info@hotelassociation.ca
www.hotelassociation.ca
www.linkedin.com/company/hotel-association-of-canada
twitter.com/hotelassoc
To represent members both nationally & internationally; To provide cost-effective services which stimulate & encourage a free market accommodation industry; To bring prosperity to the hotel & lodging industry in Canada
Susie Grynol, President & CEO
Alana Baker, Senior Director, Policy & Public Affairs
Alla Drigola, Director, Government Relations & Public Affairs

Hotel Association of Nova Scotia (HANS)
PO Box 473, Stn. M, Halifax NS B3J 2P8
To make Nova Scotia a year-round travel destination; To act as the official voice of the collective member hotels; To provide support for appropriate advisory boards & committees; To develop & encourage a coordinated joint marketing effort

Hotel Association of Prince Edward Island
c/o Murphy Hospitality Group, 96 Kensington Rd., Charlottetown PE C1A 5J4
Tel: 902-566-3137

Kevin Murphy, President

Institut de tourisme et d'hôtellerie du Québec (ITHQ)
3535, rue Saint-Denis, Montréal QC H2X 3P1
Tél: 514-282-5111; *Ligne sans frais:* 800-282-5111
info@ithq.qc.ca
www.ithq.qc.ca/institut
www.instagram.com/ithqofficiel
www.linkedin.com/school/ithq
www.facebook.com/ITHQofficiel
twitter.com/ithqofficiel

L'ITHQ est la plus importante école de gestion hôtelière au Canada spécialisée en tourisme, hôtellerie, restauration et sommellerie
Liza Frulla, Directrice générale

Klondike Visitors Association (KVA)
PO Box 389, Dawson City YT Y0B 1G0
Tel: 867-993-5575; *Fax:* 867-993-6415
Toll-Free: 877-465-3006
kva@dawson.net
www.dawsoncity.ca
www.facebook.com/dawsoncity
To respond to visitor information requests & liaises with municipal & territorial governments to encourage Tourism-related initiatives; to promote Dawson City, Yukon & the Klondike Region as a year-round tourist destination.
Gary Parker, Executive Director

Kootenay Rockies Tourism
1905 Warren Ave., Kimberley BC V1A 1S2
Tel: 250-427-4838; *Fax:* 250-427-3344
Toll-Free: 800-661-6603
info@kootenayrockies.com
www.krtourism.ca
www.youtube.com/kootrock
www.linkedin.com/company/kootenay-rockies-tourism
www.facebook.com/KootRock
twitter.com/kootrock
To coordinate & execute tourism marketing initiatives of private sector partners.
Kathy Cooper, CEO & Travel Trade Manager

Muskoka Tourism
1342 Hwy. 11 North, Kilworthy ON P0E 1G0
Tel: 705-689-0660; *Fax:* 705-689-9118
Toll-Free: 800-267-9700
info@muskokatourism.ca
www.discovermuskoka.ca
www.youtube.com/user/MuskokaTourism
www.facebook.com/discovermuskoka
twitter.com/DiscoverMuskoka
To market the region's tourism resources to the public, media & group tour travel markets
Michael Lawley, Executive Director

Niagara Falls Tourism (NFT)
6815 Stanley Ave., Niagara Falls ON L2G 3Y9
Tel: 905-356-6061; *Fax:* 905-356-5567
Toll-Free: 800-563-2557
www.niagarafallstourism.com
www.youtube.com/user/niagarafallstourism
www.facebook.com/niagarafallstourismcanada
twitter.com/nfallstourism
To develop the tourism industry in Niagara Falls & bring economic development returns for the region
Noel Buckley, Executive Director

North of Superior Tourism Association (NOSTA)
#2, 605 Victoria Ave. East, Thunder Bay ON P7C 1B1
Tel: 807-346-1130; *Fax:* 807-346-1135
Toll-Free: 800-265-3951
info@northofsuperior.org
www.northofsuperior.org
www.facebook.com/northofsuperior
twitter.com/northosuperior
To market the tourism opportunities for vacationing in Northwestern Ontario.
Tim Lukinuk, President

Northeastern Ontario Tourism
#401, 2009 Long Lake Rd., Sudbury ON P3E 6C3
Tel: 705-522-0104; *Toll-Free:* 800-465-6655
www.northeasternontario.com
www.facebook.com/northeasternontario
twitter.com/NeOntario

Northern British Columbia Tourism Association (NBCTA)
1274 - 5th Ave., Prince George BC V2L 3L2
Tel: 250-561-0432
www.travelnbc.com
To promote & develop the tourism industry of northern British Columbia
Anthony Everett, CEO

Northern Frontier Visitors Association (NFVA)
#4, 4807 - 49th St., Yellowknife NT X1A 3T5
Tel: 867-873-4262; *Fax:* 867-873-3654
Toll-Free: 877-881-4262
info@northernfrontier.com
www.northernfrontier.com
To promote the Northern Frontier Region as an attractive area for tourism; to foster, encourage & assist in any way the growth

of tourism into & within the Northern Frontier Region; to increase awareness within the Northern Frontier Region of the potential tourism holds as a viable, clean, labour intensive industry.

Northern Rockies Alaska Highway Tourism Association (NRAHTA)
PO Box 6850, #300, 9523 - 100th St., Fort St John BC V1J 4J3
Tel: 250-785-2544; *Fax:* 250-785-4424
Toll-Free: 888-785-2544
info@hellonorth.com
www.hellonorth.com
To coordinate opportunites for sustainable tourism growth & development by fostering memorable year round visitor experiences; promoting social & economic benefits to members & wider community.

Northwest Ontario Sunset Country Travel Association
PO Box 647W, Kenora ON P9N 3X6
Tel: 807-468-5853; *Toll-Free:* 800-665-7567
info@ontariossunsetcountry.ca
www.ontariossunsetcountry.ca
sunsetcountry.tumblr.com
www.facebook.com/SunsetCountry
twitter.com/Sunset_Country
To develop, promote & advertise through cooperation, coordination & communication with clients & organizations for the betterment of tourism in Sunset Country & the province.
Gerry Cariou, Executive Director

Northwest Territories Tourism (NWTT)
PO Box 610, Yellowknife NT X1A 2N5
Tel: 867-873-5007; *Toll-Free:* 800-661-0788
info@spectacularnwt.com
www.spectacularnwt.com
www.instagram.com/spectacularnwt
www.facebook.com/spectacularnwt
twitter.com/spectacularnwt
To support the development of a strong tourism sector in the Northwest Territories for the benefit of tourists, residents & communities; To promote pan-territorial tourism; To act as a voice for the tourism industry; To preserve the integrity of the cultural & natural heritage of the Northwest Territories
Brian Desjardins, Executive Director
Ron Ostrom, Director, Marketing
Julie Warnock, Coordinator, Communications
Margo Thorne, Officer, Finance

Nunavut Tourism
PO Box 1450, Iqaluit NU X0A 0H0
Toll-Free: 866-686-2888
info@nunavuttourism.com
www.nunavuttourism.com
www.youtube.com/nunavuttourism
www.facebook.com/nunavuttourism
twitter.com/NunavutTourism
To represent the tourism industry for the private sector in Nunavut; To promote & market Nunavut tourism products

Office du tourisme et des congrès de Québec (OTCQ) / Québec City & Area Tourism & Convention Board
399, rue Saint-Joseph est, Québec QC G1K 8E2
Tél: 418-641-6654; *Téléc:* 418-641-6578
Ligne sans frais: 877-783-1608
www.quebecregion.com
www.instagram.com/quebecregion
www.facebook.com/QuebecRegion
twitter.com/quebecregion
Organisme responsable de la mise en marché de la région touristique de Québec
Gabriel Savard, Directeur général
Daniel Gagnon, Directeur, Communication et publicité

Ontario East Tourism Association (OETA)
PO Box 730, #200, 104 St. Lawrence St., Merrickville ON K0G 1N0
Tel: 613-269-4113; *Fax:* 613-659-4306
Toll-Free: 800-567-3278
support@realontario.ca
www.realontario.ca
To encourage visitation to Eastern Ontario by means of cooperative tourism marketing
Rose Bertoia, Executive Director
John Bonser, President

Tourisme Laval
480, promenade du Centropolis, Laval QC H7T 3C2
Tél: 450-682-5522; *Téléc:* 450-682-7304
info@tourismelaval.com
www.tourismelaval.com
www.youtube.com/user/tourismelaval
www.facebook.com/tourismelaval
twitter.com/TourismeLaval
De promouvoir Laval comme destination touristique
Geneviève Roy, Directrice générale
Yves Legault, Président

Tourisme Mauricie
CP 100, Shawinigan QC G9N 8S1
Tél: 819-536-3334; *Téléc:* 819-536-3373
Ligne sans frais: 800-567-7603
info@tourismemauricie.com
www.tourismemauricie.com
www.youtube.com/tourismemauricie
www.facebook.com/tourismemauricie
twitter.com/mauricie
De promouvoir la ville de Maurice comme une destination
touristique
André Nollet, Directeur général

Tourisme Montérégie
#10, 8940, boul Leduc, Brossard QC J4Y 0G4
Tél: 450-466-4666; *Téléc:* 450-466-7999
Ligne sans frais: 866-469-0069
info@tourisme-monteregie.qc.ca
www.tourisme-monteregie.qc.ca
www.facebook.com/tourisme.monteregie
twitter.com/tourmonteregie
Josée Juliener, Directrice générale
François Trépanier, Directeur, Communications

**Tourisme Montréal/Office des congrès et du
tourisme du Grand Montréal / Greater Montréal
Convention & Tourism Bureau**
CP 979, Montréal QC H3C 2W3
Tél: 514-873-2015; *Téléc:* 514-864-3838
Ligne sans frais: 877-266-5687
info@tourisme-montreal.org
www.tourism-montreal.org
www.youtube.com/user/TourismeMontreal
www.facebook.com/Montreal
twitter.com/montreal
De promouvoir Montréal comme une destination touristique
populaire
Yves Lalumière, Président et directeur général

Tourisme Iles-de-la-Madeleine
128, ch Principal, Cap-aux-Meules QC G4T 1C5
Tél: 418-986-2245; *Téléc:* 418-986-2327
Ligne sans frais: 877-624-4437
info@tourismeilesdelamadeleine.com
www.tourismeilesdelamadeleine.com
www.youtube.com/TourismeIDM
www.facebook.com/tourismeilesdelamadeleine
twitter.com/ATRIM
Regrouper les entreprises de l'industrie touristique de l'archipel
afin d'accroître les efforts de développement et de promotion
Michel Bonato, Directeur général

**Travel & Tourism Research Association (Canada
Chapter) (TTRA)**
canada@ttra.com
ttra.com/canada-chapter/about
Anna Moran, President

Travellers' Aid Society of Toronto (TAS)
13 Mountalan Ave., Toronto ON M4J 1H3
Tel: 416-366-7788; *Fax:* 416-466-6552
TAID668@gmail.com
www.travellersaid.ca
To provide a base of needed information for travellers as well as
shelter & other help in crisis situations

Vancouver, Coast & Mountains Tourism Region
#270, 1651 Commercial Dr., Vancouver BC V5l 3Y3
Tel: 604-739-9011; *Fax:* 604-739-0153
Toll-Free: 800-667-3306
info@vcmbc.com
www.604pulse.com
www.facebook.com/vcmbc
twitter.com/vcmbc
To create tourist experineces for travellers
Kevan Ridgway, President & CEO
Doleen Dean, Visitor Services

**Wilderness Tourism Association of the Yukon
(WTAY)**
#4, 1114 - 1st Ave., Whitehorse YT Y1A 1A3
Tel: 867-668-3369; *Fax:* 867-668-3370
info@wtay.com
wtay.com
To represent the wilderness & adventure tourism industry in
Yukon; To provide marketing, advocacy, research, consultation,
referral & education resources
Felix Geithner, President

Trade

**Asia Pacific Foundation of Canada (APFC) /
Fondation Asie Pacifique du Canada**
#900, 675 Hastings St. West, Vancouver BC V6B 1N2
Tel: 604-684-5986; *Fax:* 604-681-1370
info@asiapacific.ca
www.asiapacific.ca
www.linkedin.com/company/522469
www.facebook.com/asiapacificfoundationofcanada
twitter.com/AsiaPacificFdn
To bring together people & knowledge to provide the most
current & comprehensive research, analysis & information on
Canada's transpacific relations; To promote dialogue on
economic, security, political & social issues, helping to influence
public policy & foster informed decision-making in the Canadian
public, private & non-governmental sectors
Stewart Beck, President & CEO

Beef Cattle Research Council (BCRC)
#180, 6815 - 8th St. NE, Calgary AB T2E 7H7
Tel: 403-275-8558; *Fax:* 403-274-5686
info@beefresearch.ca
www.beefresearch.ca
www.youtube.com/beefresearch
www.facebook.com/BeefResearch
twitter.com/BeefResearch
Canada's national industry-led funding agency for beef research.
Andrea Brocklebank, Research Manager
Reynold Bergen, Science Director

Brazil-Canada Chamber of Commerce (BCCC)
#1600, 401 Bay St., Toronto ON M5H 2Y4
Tel: 416-998-7199
info@brazcanchamber.org
brazcanchamber.org
www.instagram.com/brazcanchamber
www.linkedin.com/groups/2098563
www.facebook.com/brazcanchamber
twitter.com/brazcanchamber
To promote Brazillian-Canadian professionals & businesses; To
facilitate business & trade between Canada & Brazil
Carolina Mangabeira Albernaz, Director, Business Development
& Operations

British Canadian Chamber of Trade & Commerce
#708, 872 Sheppard Ave. West, Toronto ON M3H 5V5
Tel: 416-816-9154
www.bcctc.ca
www.linkedin.com/groups/2493645
twitter.com/bcctc
To foster reciprocal trading between Canada & the U.K.
Thomas O'Carroll, Vice-President, Central
Idalia Obregón, Executive Director

Business Council of British Columbia
#960, 1050 Pender St. West, Vancouver BC V6E 3S7
Tel: 604-684-3384; *Fax:* 888-488-5376
info@bcbc.com
bcbc.com
www.linkedin.com/company/business-council-of-british-columbia
www.facebook.com/businesscouncilbc
twitter.com/BizCouncilBC
To build a competitive & growing economy that provides
opportunities for all who invest, work & live in British Columbia
Greg D'Avignon, President & CEO
Jock Finlayson, Executive VP & Chief Policy Officer
Ken Peacock, Chief Economist & Vice-President

**Canada - Albania Business Council (CABC) /
Conseil Commercial Canada - Albanie**
#701, 165 University Ave., Toronto ON M5H 3B8
Tel: 416-979-1875; *Fax:* 416-979-0825
canadaalbaniabusinesscouncil.ca
To help encourage businesses to invest in & trade with Albania
Robert Baines, Executive Director
Abby Badwi, Chairman, Board of Directors

**Canada China Business Council (CCBC) / Conseil
commercial Canada Chine**
#1501, 330 Bay St., Toronto ON M5H 2S8
Tel: 416-954-3800; *Fax:* 416-954-3806
ccbc@ccbc.com
www.ccbc.com
www.linkedin.com/company/canada-china-business-council
twitter.com/canada_china
To build business success in China & Canada by offering service
& support, from direct operational support in China, to trade &
investment advocacy on its members' behalf
Peter Kruyt, Chair
Sarah Kutulakos, Executive Director

Canada New Zealand Business Council
Auckland New Zealand
www.canada-nz.org.nz
To stimulate & promote trade, investment, communication,
services & interaction between New Zealand & Canada

**Canada Organic Trade Association (COTA) /
Association pour le commerce des produits
biologiques (ACPB)**
#210, 4 Florence St., Ottawa ON K2P 0W7
Tel: 613-482-1717; *Fax:* 613-482-2920
www.ota.com/canada-ota
www.linkedin.com/company/organic-trade-association
www.facebook.com/OrganicTrade
twitter.com/OrganicTrade
To promote & protect the growth of organic trade in Canada; To
benefit organic farmers, consumers, the environment & the
economy; To provide information on ingredients, sourcing,
certification, marketing, imports & exports, & a range of other
concerns
Tia Loftsgard, Executive Director

**Canada-Arab Business Council (CABC) / Conseil de
commerce canado-arabe (CCCA)**
#700, 1 Rideau St., Ottawa ON K1N 8S7
Tel: 613-670-5853
om@c-abc.ca
www.c-abc.ca
www.linkedin.com/company/canada-arab-business-council
www.facebook.com/451940824838113
twitter.com/cdaarabbusiness
To promote trade & business relations between Arab countries
in the MENA region & Canada
Cathy Seguin, Acting President & Executive Director

Canada-ASEAN Business Council (CABC)
Oxley Bizhub, #08-47, 71 Ubi Rd. 1, 408732 Singapore
www.canasean.com
www.linkedin.com/company/canada-asean-business-council
www.facebook.com/CABC2017
twitter.com/CAN_ASEAN
To encourage trade & investment between Canada & ASEAN
countries
Greg Ross, Executive Director

**Canada-India Business Council (C-IBC) / Conseil de
commerce Canada-Inde**
#604, 80 Richmond St. West, Toronto ON M5H 2A4
Tel: 416-214-5947; *Fax:* 416-214-9081
info@canada-indiabusiness.com
www.canada-indiabusiness.com
www.linkedin.com/company/canada-india-business-council
www.facebook.com/172590773300148
twitter.com/CanadaIndia1
To promote trade & investment between Canada & India by
fostering direct contacts between Canadian & Indian business
people; To advise the Canadian government with respect to
policies & programs affecting Canada's relations with India; To
serve as a forum for exchange of information & views between
business executives of Canada & India on issues of importance
to both countries; To provide information & advice to companies
of both countries with respect to trade & investment matters in
either country
Victor Thomas, President & CEO

Canada-Sri Lanka Business Council (CSLBC)
58 Sundial Cres., Toronto ON M4A 2J8
Tel: 416-445-5390; *Fax:* 416-363-4601
cslbcbiz@rogers.com
www.cslbc.ca
To promote trade, investment, technological exchange, tourism
& industrial cooperation between Canada & Sri Lanka
Upali Obeyesekere, President
Ganesan Sugumar, Vice President
Mohan Perera, General Secretary

Canadian Armenian Business Council Inc. (CABC) / Conseil commercial canadien-arménien inc.
#102, 2425, boul de Salaberry, Montréal QC H3M 1L2
To promote & serve the Armenian business community; To act as a marketing tool for North American Armenian businesses
Paul Nahabedian, President

Canadian Association of Importers & Exporters / Association canadienne des importateurs & exportateurs
#400, 3601 Hwy. 7 East, Markham ON L3R 0M3
Toll-Free: 866-616-2243
info@iecanada.com
www.iecanada.com
www.linkedin.com/groups/1853004
To be the voice of Canadian importers & exporters; To support Canadian importers & exporters so that they remain profitable & competitive in a global market
Donald McArthur, President

Canadian Association of Regulated Importers (CARI) / Association canadienne des importateurs règlementés
1545 Carling Ave., Ottawa ON K1Z 8P9
Tel: 613-738-1729
www.cariimport.org
To ensure the right & ability for importers to do business like other businesses & to create one voice for commodities on the import control list or otherwise controlled by regulations

Canadian Colombian Professional Association (CCPA)
info@ccpassociation.com
www.ccpassociation.com
www.linkedin.com/company/canadian-colombian-professional-association
www.facebook.com/CadColPA
twitter.com/SomosCCPA
To support the integration of Hispanic professionals into the Canadian workforce; To facilitate the exchange of information among Canadian Hispanic groups & professionals
Cindy Pesantez, President
Néstor Paez, Treasurer

Canadian Council for the Americas (CCA) / Conseil Canadien pour les Amériques
TD Centre, PO Box 1175, 77 King St. West, Toronto ON M5K 1P2
Tel: 416-367-4313
info@ccacanada.com
www.ccacanada.com
www.youtube.com/CCATorontoOffice
www.linkedin.com/company/canadian-council-for-the-americas
twitter.com/CCACanada
To address Canadian political & economic issues, particularly trade & investment; To foster stronger economic ties between Canada & the regions of Latin America & the Caribbean
Kenneth N. Frankel, President

Canadian Council for the Americas - British Columbia (CCA-BC)
1295 Johnston St., Vancouver BC V6H 3R9
Tel: 604-868-8678
info@cca-bc.com
www.cca-bc.com
www.linkedin.com/company/cca-bc-canadian-council-for-the-americas----british-columbia
To increase business & trade between British Columbia & Latin America
André Nudelman, Chair

Electronics Import Committee (EIC)
PO Box 189, Stn. Don Mills, Toronto ON M3C 2S2
Tel: 416-595-5333
info@iecanada.com
www.iecanada.com
To represent members' interests before government & regulatory bodies
Joy Nott, President

Global Automakers of Canada (GAC) / Constructeurs mondiaux d'automobiles du Canada (CMAC)
PO Box 20, #701, 1 Concorde Gate, Toronto ON M3C 3N6
Tel: 416-595-8251; Fax: 416-595-2864
auto@globalautomakers.ca
www.globalautomakers.ca
To represent before federal, provincial, & territorial governments the interests of members engaged in the manufacturing, importation, distribution, & servicing of light-duty vehicles
David C. Adams, President

Groupe export agroalimentaire Québec - Canada (GEAQC) / Agri-Food Export Group Québec - Canada
1971, rue Léonard-De Vinci, Sainte-Julie QC J3E 1Y9
Tél: 450-649-6266; Téléc: 450-461-6255
Ligne sans frais: 800-563-9767
info@groupexport.ca
www.groupexport.ca
www.linkedin.com/company/1742471
Développer des services adaptés aux besoins réels de nos membres afin d'augmenter leurs ventes sur les marchés internationaux; faciliter l'accès aux programmes gouvernementaux dont nous avons la gestion
André A. Coutu, Président-directeur général
Francine Lapointe, Directrice, Programme et affaires gouvernemntale

Hong Kong Trade Development Council
Office Tower, Convention Plaza, #38F, 1 Harbour Rd., Wanchai Hong Kong
hktdc@hktdc.org
www.hktdc.org
www.youtube.com/user/HKTDC
www.linkedin.com/company/hong-kong-trade-development-council
twitter.com/hktdc
To promote external trade in goods & services; To create & facilitate opportunities in international trade for Hong Kong companies; To strengthen Hong Kong as the global trade platform of Asia; To assist manufacturers, traders & service providers through marketing opportunities, trade contacts, market knowledge & competitive skills

Indo-Canada Chamber of Commerce (ICCC) / Chambre de commerce Indo-Canada
924 The East Mall, Toronto ON M9B 6K1
Tel: 416-224-0090; Fax: 416-916-0086
iccc@iccconline.org
www.iccconline.org
www.linkedin.com/groups/96776
www.facebook.com/ICCCONLINE
twitter.com/Indocanadacc
To promote Indo-Canadian professionals & businesses; To facilitate business & trade between Canada & India & the Indian diaspora throughout the world; To highlight Indo-Canadian contributions in the economic, cultural & social fabric of Canada
Kanwar Dhanjal, President

Indonesia Canada Chamber of Commerce (ICCC)
c/o Canada Centre, World Trade Centre 5, 15th Fl., Jl. Jend. Sudirman kav 29-31, Jakarta 12920 Indonesia
secretariat@iccc.or.id
www.iccc.or.id
www.facebook.com/767769153320680
twitter.com/ID_ICCC
To promote trade & investment between Canada & Indonesia.
Wely Kustono, Chief Operating Officer
Karina Sherlen, Vice Executive Director

International Cheese Council of Canada (ICCC)
c/o Welch LLP, 100-123 Slater St., Ottawa ON K1P 5H2
To act as the representative voice of Canadian importers of cheese, with respect to the activities of the federal & provincial governments & agencies & all other bodies affecting the commercial interests of cheese importers in Canada; To monitor & analyze all developments relating to the importation of cheese into Canada; To contribute to the formulation, revision & amendment of government policy relating to the commercial regulatory framework within which Canadian cheese importers operate their businesses; To promote the commercial interests of members in a public relations capacity; To liaise with other industry & trade associations working in cheese-related sectors
Amesika Baëta, Director, Member Relations & Development

Ontario Association of Trading Houses (OATH)
PO Box 43086, Toronto ON M2N 6N1
Tel: 416-223-2028; Fax: 416-223-5707
info@oath.on.ca
www.oath.on.ca
linkedin.com/company/ontario-association-of-trading-houses
To develop & expand international trade; To help Canadian companies to increase their international trade & investment

Saskatchewan Trade & Export Partnership (STEP)
PO Box 1787, #320, 1801 Hamilton St., Regina SK S4P 3C6
Tel: 306-787-9210; Fax: 306-787-6666
Toll-Free: 888-976-7875
inquire@sasktrade.sk.ca
www.sasktrade.com
www.youtube.com/user/SaskTrade
twitter.com/SaskTrade
To work in partnership with Saskatchewan exporters & emerging exporters to maximize commercial success in global ventures;

To deliver custom export solutions & market intelligence to member companies; To coordinate international development projects
Chris Dekker, President & Chief Executive Officer
Brad Michnik, Senior Vice President, Trade Development
Angela Krauss, Vice President, Marketing & Membership Development

Trade Facilitation Office Canada / Bureau de promotion du commerce Canada
#400, 130 Slater St., Ottawa ON K1P 6E2
Tel: 613-233-3925; Fax: 613-233-7860
Toll-Free: 800-267-9674
info@tfocanada.ca
www.tfocanada.ca
www.linkedin.com/company/tfo-canada
twitter.com/TFOcan
To help improve the economic well-being of developing countries through increased integration into the global economy
Steven Tipman, Executive Director

World Trade Centre Montréal (WTCM)
#6000, 380, rue St-Antoine ouest, Montréal QC H2Y 3X7
Tél: 514-871-4002; Téléc: 514-849-3813
Ligne sans frais: 877-590-4040
wtcmontreal@ccmm.qc.ca
www.btmm.qc.ca/en/international
Appuyer, former et conseiller les entreprises, associations, institutions et organismes de développement économiques dans leurs démarches sur les marchés internationaux
Michel Leblanc, Président et chef de la direction
Lise Aubin, Vice-présidente, Exploitation & Administration

Visual Art, Crafts, Folk Arts

Alberta Craft Council (ACC)
10186 - 106 St., Edmonton AB T5J 1H4
Tel: 780-488-6611; Fax: 780-488-8855
Toll-Free: 800-362-7238
acc@albertacraft.ab.ca
www.albertacraft.ab.ca
www.youtube.com/user/albertacraftcouncil
www.facebook.com/albertacraftcouncil
twitter.com/abcraftcouncil
To stimulate, develop & support craft in Alberta through communication, education, exhibition, & participation
Tom McFall, Executive Director
Tara Owen, Chair

Art Dealers Association of Canada Inc. (ADAC) / Association des marchands d'art du Canada
#301, 250 Consumers Rd., Toronto ON M2J 4V6
Tel: 416-934-1583
info@ad-ac.ca
www.ad-ac.ca
www.facebook.com/ArtDealersAssociationofCanada
twitter.com/ADAC_AMAC
To promote & encourage public awareness of visual arts in Canada & abroad
Joseph Rumi, President

Artists in Stained Glass (AISG)
c/o Elizabeth Steinebach, PO Box 302, Parry Sound ON P2A 2X4
www.aisg.on.ca
To encourage the development of stained glass as a contemporary art form, in Ontario & throughout Canada
Robert Brown, President

The Canadian Art Foundation
#330, 215 Spadina Ave., Toronto ON M5T 2C7
Tel: 416-368-8854; Fax: 416-368-6135
Toll-Free: 800-222-4762
info@canadianart.ca
www.canadianart.ca
vimeo.com/channels/canadianart
www.facebook.com/canadianart
twitter.com/canartca
To foster & support the visual arts in Canada & to celebrate artists & their creativity with a program of events, lectures, competitions, publications & educational initiatives.
Debra Campbell, Co-Chair
Gabe Gonda, Co-Chair

Canadian Association of Professional Conservators (CAPC) / Association canadienne des restaurateurs professionnels (ACRP)
c/o Canadian Museums Association, #400, 280 Metcalfe St., Ottawa ON K2P 1R7
Fax: 613-233-5438
info@capc-acrp.ca
capc-acrp.ca

To foster high standards within the conservation profession through accreditation; To facilitate public access to professional conservators
Fionana Graham, President
Stephanie Porto, Vice-President
Jane Dosman, Treasurer

Canadian Crafts Federation (CCF) / Fédération canadienne des métiers d'art (FCMA)
PO Box 1231, Fredericton NB E3B 5C8
Tel: 506-462-9560
info@canadiancraftsfederation.ca
canadiancraftsfederation.ca
www.instagram.com/CCFFCMA
www.facebook.com/craftsmetiersdart
twitter.com/CCFFCMA
To represent provincial & territorial crafts councils & the Canadian crafts sector; To advance & promote the vitality & excellence of Canadian crafts nationally & internationally to the benefit of Canadian craftspeople & the community at large
Maegen Black, Director

Canadian Guild of Crafts / Guilde canadienne des métiers d'art
#400, 1356, rue Sherbrooke ouest, Montréal QC H3G 1J1
Tel: 514-849-6091; *Fax:* 514-849-7351
Toll-Free: 866-477-6091
info@laguilde.com
laguilde.com
www.instagram.com/laguildemtl
www.facebook.com/LaGuildeMTL
To preserve, encourage & promote Canadian crafts; To organize & sponsor exhibitions of the work of recognized & promising artists in the fields of arts & crafts; To educate interested groups about Canadian & native crafts through tours & lectures
Michelle Joannette, Executive Director

Canadian Quilters' Association (CQA) / Association canadienne de la courtepointe (ACC)
33 Baronwood Ct., Brampton ON L6V 3H6
administration@canadianquilter.com
www.canadianquilter.com
www.instagram.com/Canadian_quilters
www.facebook.com/canadianquilters
twitter.com/cqaquiltcanada
To promote a greater understanding, appreciation & knowledge of the art, techniques & heritage of patchwork, appliqué & quilting; To promote the highest standards of workmanship & design in both traditional & innovative work the fostering of a climate of cooperation amongst quiltmakers across the country
Heather Black, President

Canadian Society of Painters in Water Colour (CSPWC) / Société canadienne de peintres en aquarelle (SCPA)
80 Birmingham St., #B3, Toronto ON M8V 3W6
Tel: 416-533-5100
info@cspwc.com
cspwc.com
To promote the use of experimentation with water-based media; To encourage new artists
Jean Pederson, President
Anita Cotter, Administrator

Conseil des arts de Montréal (CAM)
Édifice Gaston Miron, 1210, rue Sherbrooke est, Montréal QC H2L 1L9
Tél: 514-280-3580
artsmontreal@ville.montreal.qc.ca
www.artsmontreal.org
www.facebook.com/ArtsMontreal
twitter.com/ConseilArtsMtl
Soutenir, encourager et harmoniser les initiatives d'ordre artistique et culturel sur le territoire de la ville de Montréal
Nathalie Maillé, Directrice générale
Tania Orméjuste, Directrice, Communications et des initiatives territoriales
France Laroche, Directrice, Finances et de l'administration

Conseil des métiers d'art du Québec (ind.) (CMA) / Québec Crafts Council (Ind.)
Marché Bonsecours, #400, 390, rue St-Paul est, Montréal QC H2Y 1H2
Tél: 514-861-2787; *Téléc:* 514-861-9191
Ligne sans frais: 855-515-2787
info@metiersdart.ca
www.metiers-d-art.qc.ca
Pour distribuer les créations métiers d'art auprès des grossistes canadiens et étrangers.
Patrice Bolduc, Adjoint du directeur général

Craft Council of British Columbia (CCBC)
Granville Island, 1386 Cartwright St., Vancouver BC V6H 3R8
Tel: 604-687-6511
contact_us@craftcouncilbc.ca
www.cabc.net
pinterest.com/craftcouncilbc
www.linkedin.com/company/craft-council-of-bc
www.facebook.com/CraftCouncilbc
twitter.com/CraftCouncilBC
To develop excellence in crafts
Raine McKay, Executive Director

Craft Council of Newfoundland & Labrador
Devon House, 59 Duckworth St., St. John's NL A1C 1E6
Tel: 709-753-2749; *Fax:* 709-753-2766
info@craftcouncil.nl.ca
www.craftcouncil.nl.ca
www.flickr.com/photos/craftcouncilnl
www.facebook.com/CraftCouncilNL
twitter.com/CraftCouncilNL
To produce high quality work; To assist & advise members in wide variety of craft-related areas
Rowena House, Executive Director

Embroiderers' Association of Canada, Inc. (EAC)
c/o Membership Director, 168 Kroeker Ave., Steinbach MB R5G 0L8
www.eac.ca
To preserve traditional techniques & promote new challenges in embroidery through education & networking; to offer courses in embroidery & certifies teachers.
Beryl Burnett, President
Dianna Thorne, Treasurer

Manitoba Crafts Council (MCC)
#1, 329 Cumberland Ave., Winnipeg MB R3B 1T2
Tel: 204-615-3951
mcc@c2centreforcraft.ca
c2centreforcraft.ca
www.instagram.com/manitobacraft
www.facebook.com/ManitobaCraftCouncil
twitter.com/ManitobaCraft
To promote the development & appreciation of fine craft; To facilitate a supportive environment in which fine, contemporary craft may flourish
Keith Oliver, President
Jessica Hodgson, Coordinator, Administration & Communications

The Metal Arts Guild of Canada (MAGC)
151 Marion St., Toronto ON M6R 1E6
communications@metalartsguild.ca
www.metalartsguild.ca
twitter.com/MAGcanada
To be committed to the exchange of information & ideas encouraging appreciation for the metal arts; To promote & develop the metal arts; To further education in the metal arts; To encourage members to experiment with all the forms that metal takes
Delane Cooper, President

New Brunswick Crafts Council / Conseil d'artisanat du Nouveau-Brunswick
PO Box 1231, Stn. A, Fredericton NB E3B 5C8
Tel: 506-450-8989; *Fax:* 506-457-6010
Toll-Free: 866-622-7238
info@nbcraftscouncil.ca
www.nbcraftscouncil.ca
www.facebook.com/2411474486
To provide opportunities & support to members by developing, promoting & fostering an appreciation of excellence in craft.
Natalie Landry, Executive Director
Kim Bent, President

Nova Scotia Designer Crafts Council (NSDCC)
1113 Marginal Rd., Halifax NS B3H 4P7
Tel: 902-423-3837; *Fax:* 902-422-0881
office@nsdcc.ns.ca
www.nsdcc.ns.ca
www.youtube.com/user/nsdcc
www.facebook.com/NSDCC
twitter.com/NSDCC
To encourage & promote the craft movement in Nova Scotia; to increase public awareness & appreciation of craft products & activities
Susan Hanrahan, Executive Director

Ontario Crafts Council
1106 Queen St. West, Toronto ON M6J 1H9
Tel: 416-925-4222; *Fax:* 416-925-4223
info@craftontario.com
www.craftontario.com
www.facebook.com/CraftOntario
twitter.com/craftontario
To have craft recognized as a valuable part of life & the excellence of Ontario craft & craftspeople acknowledged across Canada & around the world
Janna Hiemstra, Executive Director

PAVED Arts
424 - 20th St. West, Saskatoon SK S7M 0X4
Tel: 306-652-5502
www.pavedarts.ca
www.instagram.com/pavedarts
www.facebook.com/pavedarts
twitter.com/PAVEDArts
To advance knowledge & practices in the arts community, in fields such as photography, audio, video, electronic & digital; To help artists & independent producers make & exhibit thier work
Alex Rogalski, Executive Director
David LaRiviere, Artistic Director
Lenore Maier, Technical Coordinator
Devin McAdam, Production Manager

Prince Edward Island Crafts Council (PEICC)
PO Box 20071, Stn. Sherwood, Charlottetown PE C1A PE3
Tel: 902-892-5152; *Fax:* 902-628-8740
info@peicraftscouncil.com
peicraftscouncil.com
www.facebook.com/peicraftscouncil
twitter.com/PECraftsCouncil
To promote the making & acceptance of quality handcrafted items through the provision of programs & services
Suzanne Scott, President
Laura Cole, Executive Director

Quesnel & District Arts Council (QDCAC)
500 North Star Rd., Quesnel BC V2J 5P6
www.quesnelarts.ca
To increase & broaden opportunities for the region's citizens to enjoy & participate in arts, culture & heritage activities
Bernice Heinzelman, Contact

Royal Canadian Academy of Arts (RCA) / Académie royale des arts du Canada
50 Sussex Dr., Toronto ON K1M 2K1
Tel: 416-408-2718; *Fax:* 416-408-2286
Info@rca-arc.ca
rca-arc.ca
www.facebook.com/canada.rca.arc
To celebrate the achievements of visual artists across Canada; To encourage emerging artists; To facilitate the exchange of ideas about visual culture for the benefit of all Canadians
Taylor Boileau Davidson, Administrator

Saskatchewan Craft Council (SCC)
813 Broadway Ave., Saskatoon SK S7N 1B5
Tel: 306-653-3616
saskcraftcouncil@sasktel.net
www.saskcraftcouncil.org
www.facebook.com/SKCraftCouncil
www.twitter.com/skcraftcouncil
To promote & advance fine craft in Saskatchewan
Carmen Milenkovic, Executive Director

Sculptors Society of Canada (SSC) / Société des sculpteurs du Canada
19 Mill St., Toronto ON M5A 3R3
Tel: 647-435-5858
cansculpt@gmail.com
www.sculptorssocietyofcanada.org
www.facebook.com/sculptorssocietyofcanada
To promote Canadian sculpture; to provide encouragement to sculptors through public exhibitions & discussions in Canada & other countries
Judi Michelle Young, President

Society of Canadian Artists (SCA) / Société des artistes canadiens (SAC)
24 Lorindale Ave., Toronto ON M5M 3C2
Tel: 647-919-6864
info@societyofcanadianartists.com
societyofcanadianartists.com
www.instagram.com/society_of_canadian_artists
www.facebook.com/SocietyofCanadianArtist
twitter.com/SocCanArtists
To promote recognition of its member-artists through exhibitions, seminars, workshops, travelling shows
Kathy Hildebrandt, President
Marissa Sweet, Vice-President

Visual Arts Nova Scotia (VANS)
1113 Marginal Rd., Halifax NS B3H 4P7
Tel: 902-423-4694; *Fax:* 902-422-0881
Toll-Free: 866-225-8267
vans@visualarts.ns.ca
www.visualarts.ns.ca
www.facebook.com/VisualArtsNovaScotia
twitter.com/visualartsns
To promote a better understanding of arts & artists in Nova Scotia; To provide practical assistance to artists; To act in an advisory capacity to public & private interests
Becky Welter-Nolan, Executive Director

Women

Act To End Violence Against Women
#209, 390 Steeles Ave. West, Thornhill ON L4J 6X2
Tel: 905-695-5372; *Fax:* 905-695-5375
Toll-Free: 866-333-5942
info@acttoendvaw.org
www.facebook.com/acttoendvaw
Works locally, nationally & internationally to strengthen the effectiveness of women in the Jewish community & society; to foster the emotional well-being of children; to perpetuate Jewish values & secure world Jewry. Programs include ending violence towards women, sexual assault awareness, emergency housing for women & children, & advocacy to end child poverty in Canada. Offices in Toronto & Montréal, & chapters in Toronto, Montréal, B.C., Windsor & Winnipeg.
Penny Krowitz, Executive Director

Alberta Women's Institutes (AWI)
AB
awi.athabascau.ca
To help discover, stimulate & develop leadership among women
Evelyn Ellerman, Contact

Alliance des femmes de la francophonie canadienne (AFFC)
Place de la francophonie, #302, 450, rue Rideau, Ottawa ON K1N 5Z4
Tél: 613-241-3500
info@affc.ca
www.affc.ca
www.facebook.com/AFFCfemmes
twitter.com/AFFCfemmes
Favorise l'autonomie des femmes canadiennes-françaises sur tous les plans; assure le respect des droits des femmes francophones vivant en milieu minoritaire; soutien le développement de l'action collective et politique des femmes au Canada français; souligne la spécificité des femmes francophones auprès des instances gouvernementales, des diverses associations et du grand public
Soukaina Boutiyeb, Directrice générale

Association féminine d'éducation et d'action sociale (AFEAS) / Feminine Association for Education & Social Action
5999, rue de Marseille, Montréal QC H1N 1K6
Tél: 514-251-1636; *Téléc:* 514-251-9023
info@afeas.qc.ca
www.afeas.qc.ca
twitter.com/afeas1966
Avec ses Activités femmes d'ici organisées sur tout le territoire québécois, l'Afeas informe ses membres, suscite des échanges et des débats et les incite à participer davantage aux différentes structures de la société

Association of Canadian Women Composers (ACWC) / L'Association des femmes compositeurs canadiennes (AFCC)
c/o Canadian Music Centre, 20 St Joseph St., Toronto ON M4Y 1J9
acwcafcc@gmail.com
acwc.ca
twitter.com/ACWComposers
To build on the achievements of & further encourage Canadian women & women-identified composers; To develop & provide a body of well-researched, catalogued & preserved arcival material to be accesible to students, researchs & performers
Carol Ann Weaver, Chair

British Columbia Women's Institutes (BCWI)
PO Box 36, 4395 Mountain Rd., Barriere BC V0E 1E1
Tel: 250-672-0259; *Fax:* 250-672-0259
info@bcwi.org
www.bcwi.ca
www.youtube.com/user/BCWomensInstitute
www.facebook.com/185390304847227
twitter.com/bcwi

To help discover, stimulate & develop leadership among women; to assist, encourage & support women to become knowledgeable & responsible citizens; to ensure basic human rights for women & to work towards their equality; to be a strong voice through which matters of utmost concern can reach the decision makers; to network with organizations sharing similar objectives; to promote the improvement of agricultural & other rural communities & to safeguard the environment

Canadian Association of Women Executives & Entrepreneurs (CAWEE) / Association canadienne des femmes cadres et entrepreneurs
#1600, 401 Bay St., Toronto ON M5H 2Y4
Tel: 416-756-0000; *Fax:* 416-756-0000
contact@cawee.net
www.cawee.net
www.linkedin.com/groups/2294616
www.facebook.com/CAWEEnet
To provide an environment for successful businesswomen to grow & develop, both professionally & personally, through business & community involvement
Heather Freed, President
Marylou Heenan, Director, Policy & Administration
Judi Hughes, Director, Membership
Susan Ward, Director, Community Outreach

Canadian Board Diversity Council (CBDC) / Conseil canadien pour la diversité administrative (CCDA)
#502, 180 Bloor St. West, Toronto ON M5S 2V6
Tel: 416-361-1475
inquiries@boarddiversity.ca
www.boarddiversity.ca
www.linkedin.com/company/882730
twitter.com/diverseboards
To conduct research on diversity on Canadian corporate boards; To provide governance education programming; to educate members & the governance community onboard diversity best practices & principles; To build a network of business leaders who are committed to diversity
Sherri Stevens, Owner & CEO

The Canadian Federation of Business & Professional Women's Clubs (CFBPWC) / Fédération canadienne des clubs des femmes de carrières commerciales et professionnelles (FCCFCCP)
bpwcanada@bpwcanada.com
www.bpwcanada.com
www.instagram.com/canadabpw
www.linkedin.com/in/bpwcanada
www.facebook.com/canadabpw
To develop & encourage women to pursue business, the professions & industry; To work toward the improvement of economic, employment & social conditions for women; To work for high standards of service in business, the professions, industry & public life; To stimulate interest in federal, provincial & municipal affairs; To encourage women to participate in the business of government at all levels; To encourage & assist women & girls to acquire further education & training
Karin Gorgerat, President
Katherine Wentzell, First Vice-President
Kristine Flynn, Secretary
Janet Riehm, Treasurer

Canadian Hadassah-WIZO (CHW)
#209, 638A Sheppard Ave. West, Toronto ON M3H 2S1
Tel: 416-477-5964; *Fax:* 416-977-5965
Toll-Free: 855-477-5964
info@chw.ca
www.chw.ca
www.youtube.com/user/CHWOrganization
www.linkedin.com/company/chw
www.facebook.com/CanadianHadassahWIZO
twitter.com/CHWdotCA
To extend material & moral support of Jewish women of Canada to needy individuals in Hadassah-WIZO welfare institutions in Israel; To encourage Jewish & Hebrew culture in Canada
Alina Ianson, Executive Director

Canadian Women's Foundation / Fondation canadienne des femmes
#302, 1920 Yonge St., Toronto ON M4S 3E2
Tel: 416-365-1444; *Fax:* 416-365-1745
Toll-Free: 866-293-4483
TTY: 416-365-1732
info@canadianwomen.org
canadianwomen.org
www.youtube.com/user/CanadianWomenFdn
www.linkedin.com/company/the-canadian-women%27s-foundation
www.facebook.com/CanadianWomensFoundation
www.twitter.com/cdnwomenfdn

To raise money to research, fund & share the best approaches to ending violence against women & transitioning low-income women out of poverty
Paulette Senior, President & CEO

Centre des femmes de Montréal / Women's Centre of Montréal
3585, rue Saint-Urbain, Montréal QC H2X 2N6
Tel: 514-842-1066; *Téléc:* 514-842-1067
cfmwcm@centredesfemmes.com
www.centredesfemmesmtl.org
D'offrir des services à caractère professionnel et éducatif, de même que des services de conseil et d'orientation pour aider les femmes à s'aider elles-mêmes
Johanne Bélisle, Directrice générale

Centre for Women in Business (CWB)
c/o Mount Saint Vincent University, Margaret Norrie McCain Centre, #411, 166 Bedford Hwy, Halifax NS B3M 2J6
Tel: 902-457-6449; *Fax:* 902-443-4687
Toll-Free: 888-776-9022
cwb@msvu.ca
www.centreforwomeninbusiness.ca
www.youtube.com/user/CentreWomenBusiness
www.linkedin.com/company/1539340
www.facebook.com/centreforwomeninbusiness
twitter.com/cwb_ns
To help women entrepreneurs begin, develop & advance their businesses
Tanya Priske, Executive Director

Comité condition féminine Baie-James
#203, 552 - 3e rue, Chibougamau QC G8P 1N9
Tel: 418-748-4408; *Téléc:* 418-748-2486
ccfbj@tlb.sympatico.ca
ccfbj.com
A pour mission l'amélioration des conditions de vie des Jamésiennes
Gérald Lemoine, Présidente

Congress of Black Women of Canada (CBWC)
To improve the lives of Black women & their families in local & national communities

Federated Women's Institutes of Canada (FWIC) / Fédération des instituts féminins du Canada
PO Box 209, 359 Blue Lake Rd., St George ON N0E 1N0
Tel: 519-448-3873; *Fax:* 519-448-3506
info@fwic.ca
www.fwic.ca
www.facebook.com/WomensInstitutes
twitter.com/fwicanada
To act as a united voice for Women's Institutes of Canada; To promote Canadian women, families & community living

Federated Women's Institutes of Ontario (FWIO)
552 Ridge Rd., Stoney Creek ON L8J 2Y6
Tel: 905-662-2691; *Fax:* 905-930-8631
www.fwio.on.ca
twitter.com/fwiontario
To assist & encourage women to become more knowledgeable & responsible citizens; To promote & develop good family life skills; To help discover, stimulate & develop leadership; To help identify & resolve need in the community
Kim Sauder, Executive Administrator
Andrea Morrison, Manager, Program & Communications

Fédération des femmes du Québec (FFQ)
#319, 469, rue Jean-Talon ouest, Montréal QC H3N 1R4
Tél: 514-876-0166
info@ffq.qc.ca
www.ffq.qc.ca
www.flickr.com/photos/laffq
www.facebook.com/FFQMMF
twitter.com/LaFFQ
Pour défendre les droits et intérêts des femmes
Gabrielle Bouchard, Présidente

Federation of Medical Women of Canada (FMWC) / Fédération des femmes médecins du Canada
1021 Thomas Spratt Pl., Ottawa ON K1G 5L5
Tel: 613-569-5881; *Fax:* 613-249-3906
Toll-Free: 844-215-8455
fmwcmain@fmwc.ca
www.fmwc.ca
www.facebook.com/FMWC1
twitter.com/fmwcanada
To ensure the professional, social & personal advancement of women physicians; To promote the well-being of women in the medical profession & in society at large
Clover Hemans, President

The Group Halifax
Halifax NS

info@thegrouphalifax.com
thegrouphalifax.com
www.linkedin.com/groups/2403135
www.facebook.com/TheGroupHalifax
twitter.com/TheGroupHalifax

A Halifax Metro-based business networking association with the aim of bringing together professionals in different sectors and industries to develop new skills, expand business networks, and promote the growth of their businesses.

Immigrant Women Services Ottawa (IWSO) / Services pour femmes immigrantes d'Ottawa
#400, 219 Argyle St., Ottawa ON K2P 2H4

Tel: 613-729-3145; *Fax:* 613-729-9308
infomail@immigrantwomenservices.com
www.immigrantwomenservices.com
www.facebook.com/immigrantwomenservicesottawa
twitter.com/ImmigrantWomen

To empower & enable immigrant women in the Ottawa region to participate in the elimination of all forms of abuse against women; to raise awareness among immigrant women who are abused, in order to break down their isolation & enable them to advocate on their own behalf; to develop a crisis service for immigrant women who are abused to give them full access to mainstream resources; to develop cross-cultural training for shelters & mainstream agencies regarding the special needs of immigrant women in order to ensure that existing services are accessible & appropriate to them & their families; to educate immigrant communities to work toward ending violence against women.

Manitoba Women's Institutes (MWI)
1129 Queens Ave., Brandon MB R7A 1L9

Tel: 204-726-7135; *Fax:* 204-726-6260
mbwi.ca
www.facebook.com/557282304320877

Focuses on personal development, the family, agriculture, rural development & community action, locally & globally
Joni Swidnicki, Executive Administrator

MATCH International Women's Fund
1404 Scott St., Ottawa ON K1Y 4M8

Fax: 613-798-0990
Toll-Free: 855-640-1872
info@matchinternational.org
www.matchinternational.org
www.youtube.com/user/MATCHIntCentre
www.facebook.com/matchinternational
twitter.com/MATCHIntFund

To encourage sustained development in the global South, through a focus on women's rights & empowerment; To support women in the global South in executing their ideas regarding women's rights & equality; To advance women's rights through international cooperation
Jessica Tomlin, Executive Director

Na'amat Canada Inc.
#212, 5555 av Westminster, Montréal QC H4W 2J2

Tel: 514-488-0792; *Fax:* 514-487-6727
Toll-Free: 888-278-0792
naamat@naamatcanada.org
www.naamat.ca
www.facebook.com/NaamatCanada
twitter.com/NaamatCanada

To support social programs in Canada & Israel; To help protect women, children & families in both nations; To support the state of Israel
Doris Wexler-Charow, President
Vivian Reisler, Executive Vice-President

National Association of Women & the Law (NAWL) / Association nationale de la femme et du droit (ANFD)
234 St Patrick St., Ottawa ON K1N 5K3

Tel: 613-241-7570
info@nawl.ca
nawl.ca
twitter.com/NAWL_ANFD

To promote the equality rights of women through legal education, research & law reform advocacy; To improve the legal status of women in Canada through law reform; To dismantle barriers to all women's equality
Sandeep Prasad, Interim Project Director

The National Council of Women of Canada (NCWC) / Le Conseil national des femmes du Canada
PO Box 67099, Ottawa ON K2A 4E4

Tel: 613-712-4419
presncwc@gmail.com
www.ncwcanada.com
www.facebook.com/thencwc

To bring together groups of women, & of women & men, to work towards improving the quality of life in Canada through: developing NCWC policy based on research & analysis of issues; providing information to NCWC members & the general public on current issues; recommending & working towards change in government laws, regulations, & administrative processes; cooperating with other groups in developing & advancing common policies & objectives

Native Women's Association of the Northwest Territories
Post Office Building, 2nd Fl., PO Box 2321, Yellowknife NT X1A 2P7

Tel: 867-873-5509; *Fax:* 867-873-3152
Toll-Free: 866-459-1114
nativewomensnwt.com
www.facebook.com/NativeWomensAssociationOfTheNwt

To provide training & education programs for native women in the Western Arctic
Marilyn Napier, Executive Director

New Brunswick Women's Institute (NBWI)
681 Union St., Fredericton NB E3A 3N8

Tel: 506-454-0798; *Fax:* 506-451-8949
nbwi@nb.aibn.com
www.nbwi.ca
www.facebook.com/284295801781170

To help discover, stimulate & develop leadership among women; to assist, encourage & support women to become knowledgeable & responsible citizens; to ensure basic human rights for women & work towards their equality; to network with other organizations sharing similar objectives; to promote the improvement of agricultural & other rural communities & to safeguard the environment

Newfoundland & Labrador Women's Institutes
c/o Arts & Culture Centre, PO Box 1854, St. John's NL A1C 5P9

Tel: 709-753-8780; *Fax:* 709-753-8708
nlwi@nfld.com
www.nlwi.ca

To encourage women to work together to expand their skills, broaden their interests, plan meetings, workshops & conferences, & strengthen the quality of life for themselves, their families & their communities
Barbara Taylor, Executive Officer

NSERC Chairs for Women in Science & Engineering
350 Albert St., Ottawa ON K1A 1H5

Tel: 613-944-6240; *Fax:* 613-996-2589
cwse-cfsg@nserc-crsng.gc.ca
www.nserc-crsng.gc.ca

To encourage women in Canada to enter careers in science, engineering, mathematics & computer sciences; To encourage women in Canada to attain high levels of professional achievement in these fields; To serve as an information centre for & about women in these fields; To make people aware of Canadian women scientists & engineers & of career opportunities available to them; To provide a forum for discussion of subjects of interest to members

The Older Women's Network (OWN) / Réseau des femmes aînées
115 The Esplanade, 1st Fl., Toronto ON M5E 1Y7

Tel: 416-214-1518
info@olderwomensnetwork.org
olderwomensnetwork.org
www.facebook.com/OlderWomensNetwork

To initiate & support discussion on issues relevant to the well-being of older women; To develop & support legislation to expand opportunities for housing, economic security & optimum health; To monitor the media in order to encourage a more realistic & positive portrayal of older women; To support the efforts of young women to achieve equal opportunity, freedom from discrimination, abuse & exploitation, & the right to reproductive choice; To support the needs of children; To liaise with movements for social justice in Canada & abroad

Prince Edward Island Business Women's Association (PEIBWA)
#25, 25 Queen St., Charlottetown PE C1A 4A2

Tel: 902-892-6040; *Fax:* 902-892-6050
Toll-Free: 866-892-6040
office@peibwa.org
www.peibwa.org
www.instagram.com/peibwa
www.linkedin.com/company/2715049
www.facebook.com/PEIBWA
twitter.com/peibwa

To assist women in business & help them to succeed by providing services & programs
Hannah Bell, Executive Director
Shannon Pratt, Program Manager

Prince Edward Island Women's Institute (PEIWI)
#105, 40 Enman Cres., Charlottetown PE C1E 1E6

Tel: 902-368-4860; *Fax:* 902-368-4439
wi@gov.pe.ca
www.peiwi.ca
www.facebook.com/PEIWomensInstitute

To help discover, stimulate & develop leadership among women; To assist, encourage & support women to become knowledgeable & responsible citizens; To ensure basic human rights for women & to work towards their equality; To be a strong voice through which matters of utmost concern can reach the decision makers; To network with organizations sharing similar objectives; To promote the improvement of agricultural & other rural communities & to safeguard the environment
Jacquie Laird, President

The Prosperity Project (TPP)
#1202, 595 Bay St., Toronto ON M5G 2C2

info@canadianprosperityproject.ca
canadianprosperityproject.ca
www.instagram.com/cdnprosperity
www.linkedin.com/company/canadian-prosperity
www.facebook.com/CanadianProsperity
twitter.com/ca_prosperity

To mitigate the impacts of the COVID-19 pandemic on women
Pamela Jeffery, Founder

Québec Women's Institutes (QWI)
177, Rg Ste-Anne, Saint-Chrysostome QC J0S 1G0

Toll-Free: 877-781-9293
info@qwi.la
www.qwi.la
www.facebook.com/QuebecWomensInstitute

To help discover, stimulate & develop leadership among women; To assist, encourage & support women to become knowledgeable & responsible citizens; To ensure basic human rights for women & to work toward their equality; To be a strong voice through which matters of utmost concern can reach the decision makers; To promote the improvement of agricultural & other rural communities & to safeguard the environment
Norma Sherrer, President
Pat Clarke, Treasurer

Réseau des femmes d'affaires du Québec inc. (RFAQ) / Business Women's Network
#200, 476, rue Jean-Neveu, Longueuil QC J4G 1N8

Tél: 514-521-2441; *Ligne sans frais:* 800-332-2683
info@rfaq.ca
www.rfaq.ca
www.youtube.com/user/RFAQinc
www.facebook.com/RFAQc
twitter.com/ReseauRFAQ

Afin d'encourager et de promouvoir les femmes à devenir des leaders dans les instances sociales, politiques et économiques
Ruth Vachon, Présidente/Directrice générale

Réseau Femmes Québec (RFQ)
#134, 911, rue Jean-Talon est, Montréal QC H2R 1V5

Tél: 514-484-2375

Ruth Vachon, Présidente

Saskatchewan Women's Institute (SWI)
SK

saskatchewan@fwic.ca
www.facebook.com/436313276575974

To help discover, stimulate & develop leadership among women; To assist, encourage & support women to become knowledgeable & responsible citizens; To ensure basic human rights for women & to work towards their equality; To be a strong voice through which matters of the utmost concern can reach the decision makers; To promote the improvement of agricultural & other rural communities & to safeguard the environment

Society for Canadian Women in Science & Technology (SCWIST) / Société des canadiennes dans la science et la technologie
#311, 525 Seymour St., Vancouver BC V6B 3H7

Tel: 604-893-8657
resourcecentre@scwist.ca
scwist.ca
www.linkedin.com/company/scwist
www.facebook.com/SCWIST
twitter.com/SCWIST

To promote equal opportunities for women in scientific, technical & engineering careers; To educate public about careers in science & technology particularly to improve social attitudes on the stereotyping of careers in science; To assist educators by providing current information on careers & career training in sciences & scientific policies
Paloma Corvalan, President

Transition House Association of Nova Scotia (THANS)
#204, 6169 Quinpool Rd., Halifax NS B3L 4P8
Tel: 902-429-7287; Fax: 902-429-0561
coordinator@thans.ca
thans.ca
www.facebook.com/transitionhouseassociationns
twitter.com/thans_ns
To provide transitional services to women (& their children) experiencing violence & abuse, including culturally relevant services to Mi'kmaw people
Shiva Nourpanah, Provincial Coordinator

Women Business Owners of Manitoba (WBOM)
#338, 23-845 Dakota St., Winnipeg MB R2M 5M3
Tel: 204-775-7981; Fax: 204-897-8094
info@wbom.ca
www.wbom.ca
www.instagram.com/WBOManitoba
www.facebook.com/WomenBusinessOwnersOfManitoba
twitter.com/WBOManitoba
To connect, support & inspire excellence amongst women in the entrepreneurial community in Manitoba
Lucy Camara, President
Tracy Ducharme, Vice-President

Women in Communications & Technology (WCT) / Les femmes en communications et technologie (FCT)
7 Bayview Rd., Ottawa ON K1Y 2C5
Tel: 613-706-0607; Fax: 613-706-0612
Toll-Free: 800-361-2978
info@wct-fct.com
www.wct-fct.com
linkedin.com/company/canadian-women-in-communications
www.facebook.com/WomeninCommunicationsandTechnology
twitter.com/wctfct
To advance the role of women in the communications, media & information, & technology sectors
Joanne Stanley, Executive Director

Women's Art Association of Canada (WAAC)
23 Prince Arthur Ave., Toronto ON M5R 1B2
Tel: 416-922-2060
administration@womensartofcanada.ca
womensartofcanada.ca
www.instagram.com/WomensArtofCan
www.facebook.com/WomensArtofCan
twitter.com/WomensArtofCan
To provide scholarships for the arts through the following schools & colleges: The Royal Conservatory of Music of Toronto; The Ontario College of Art; The Faculty of Music, University of Toronto; The National Ballet School; Sheridan College
Maggie Broda, President
Cal Lorimer, Executive Office Manager

Women's Executive Network (WXN) / Réseau des femmes exécutives (RFE)
150 King St. West, Toronto ON M5S 2V6
Tel: 416-361-1475; Fax: 416-361-1652
Toll-Free: 866-465-3996
membership@wxnetwork.com
www.wxnetwork.com
www.instagram.com/wxnetwork
www.linkedin.com/company/women%27s-executive-network
www.facebook.com/WXNevents
www.twitter.com/wxn
To recognize & advance executive-minded women in the workplace
Sherri Stevens, Owner & CEO

Women's Healthy Environments Network (WHEN)
The Centre for Social Innovation, #400, 215 Spadina Ave., Toronto ON M5T 2C7
Tel: 416-928-0880; Fax: 416-644-0116
office@womenshealthyenvironments.ca
www.womenshealthyenvironments.ca
www.facebook.com/WHENonlinex
twitter.com/WHENonline
To provide a forum for communication; To conduct research on issues relating to women in their environments of planning, health, ecology, workplace design, community development & urban & rural sociology & economy
Cassie Barker, Executive Director

Women's Institutes of Nova Scotia (WINS)
#207, 90 Research Dr., Bible Hill NS B6L 2R2
Tel: 902-843-9467; Fax: 902-896-7276
novascotiawi@eastlink.ca
www.gov.ns.ca/agri/wins

To provide women with opportunities to enhance their lives through community service & involvement, education & leadership development

Women's International League for Peace & Freedom (WILPF)
www.wilpfvancouver.ca
To unite women throughout the world into a force working to put an end to war; To promote the participation of women in all aspects of international & regional disarmament & peace processes
Marlene LeGates, President

Women's Legal Education & Action Fund (LEAF) / Fonds d'action et d'éducation juridiques pour les femmes (FAEJ)
#1420, 180 Dundas St. West, Toronto ON M5G 1Z8
Tel: 416-595-7170; Fax: 416-595-7191
Toll-Free: 888-824-5323
info@leaf.ca
leaf.ca
www.instagram.com/leafnational
www.facebook.com/LEAFFAEJ
twitter.com/LEAFNational
To promote equality for women, primarily by using the gender equality provisions of the Canadian Charter of Rights & Freedoms; To sponsor test cases before the Canadian courts, human rights commissions & government agencies on behalf of women; To provide public education on the issue of gender equality
Megan Stephens, Executive Director & General Counsel
Rosel Kim, Staff Lawyer
Kat Owens, Project Director
Grace Hitimana, Manager, Finance & Human Resources

Women's Network PEI
PO Box 233, 40 Enman Cres., Charlottetown PE C1A 7K4
Tel: 902-368-5040; Fax: 902-368-5039
Toll-Free: 888-362-7373
www.wnpei.org
www.facebook.com/wnpei
To strengthen & support the efforts of PEI women to improve their status in society
Michelle MacCallum, Executive Director

Women's Shelters Canada (WSC) / Hébergement femmes Canada (HFC)
#1501, 85 Albert St., Ottawa ON K1P 6A4
Tel: 613-680-5119; Fax: 613-695-1148
info@endvaw.ca
endvaw.ca
www.facebook.com/endvawnetwork
To provide a unified Canadian voice on violence against women; To help increase awareness so that policies, legislation & regulations are informed by the knowledge of members
Lise Martin, Executive Director

Writers & Editors

Association de la presse francophone (APF) / Association of Francophone Newspapers
267, rue Dalhousie, Ottawa ON K1N 7E3
Tél: 613-241-1017; Téléc: 613-241-6313
admin@apf.ca
www.apf.ca
www.facebook.com/Associationdelapressefrancophone
twitter.com/apf_journaux
Promouvoir l'existence d'une presse communautaire écrite en langue française aussi vigoureuse et aussi répandue que possible dans les communautés de langue française à l'extérieur du Québec; Contribuer à l'amélioration de sa qualité et de son rayonnement; défendre énergiquement les principes de la liberté de parole et de la presse écrite
Linda Lauzon, Directrice générale

Canadian Association of Journalists (CAJ) / L'Association canadienne des journalistes
PO Box 117, Stn. F, Toronto ON MRY 2L4
Tel: 647-968-2393
www.caj.ca
www.linkedin.com/company/canadian-association-of-journalists
www.facebook.com/CdnAssocJournalists
twitter.com/CAJ
To promote excellence in journalism; to encourage & promote investigative journalism
Brent Jolly, President

Canadian Authors Association (CAA)
#203, 6 West St. North, Orillia ON L3V 5B8
Tel: 705-325-3926
admin@canadianauthors.org
canadianauthors.org

To promote & protect Canadian authors & their works; To act as a voice for writers
Anita Purcell, Executive Director

Canadian Farm Writers' Federation (CFWF)
PO Box 250, Ormstown QC J0S 1K0
Fax: 450-829-2226
Toll-Free: 877-782-6456
secretariat@cfwf.ca
www.cfwf.ca
To serve the interests of agricultural journalists
Lisa Guenther, President
Tamara Leigh, Vice-President
Hugh Maynard, Secretary-Treasurer
Christina Franc, Administrator

Canadian Freelance Guild (CFG)
c/o CWA Canada, #301, 2200 Prince of Wales Dr., Ottawa ON K2E 6Z9
Tel: 613-820-9777; Toll-Free: 877-486-4292
canadianfreelanceguild.ca
www.linkedin.com/company/cmg-freelance
www.facebook.com/canadianfreelanceguild
twitter.com/cf_guild
To create a network for freelance workers to gain access to work & professional development opportunities
Don Genova, Organizer & Chair, Transition Commitee
Katherine Lapointe, Digital Media Organizer
Nasr Ahmed, Associate Membership Coordinator

Canadian Journalism Foundation (CJF) / La Fondation pour le journalisme canadien
#401, 595 Bay St., Toronto ON M5G 2C2
Tel: 416-955-0394
www.cjf-fjc.ca
www.facebook.com/cjffjc
twitter.com/cjffjc
To honour outstanding achievements in the field of journalism in Canada through grants, awards & scholarships; To promote & support programs & seminars at or in conjunction with qualified educational institutions in journalism
Natalie Turvey, President & Executive Director
Wendy Kan, Director, Programming
Josh Gurfinkel, Director, Operations

Canadian Society of Children's Authors, Illustrators & Performers (CANSCAIP) / La société canadienne des auteurs, illustrateurs et artistes pour enfants
#503, 720 Bathurst St., Toronto ON M5S 2R4
Tel: 416-515-1559
office@canscaip.org
www.canscaip.org
www.facebook.com/CANSCAIP.org
twitter.com/CANSCAIP
To promote the growth of children's literature by establishing the rapport with teachers, librarians & children; To establish communication between publishers & society; to encourage the development of new writers, illustrators & performers
Sharon Jennings, President

The Crime Writers of Canada (CWC)
#4C, 240 Westwood Rd., Guelph ON N1H 7W9
info@crimewriterscanada.com
www.crimewriterscanada.com
To promote Canadian crime writing
Vicki Delany, Chair

CWA / SCA Canada Inc.
#301, 2200 Prince of Wales Dr., Ottawa ON K2E 6Z9
Tel: 613-820-9777; Toll-Free: 877-486-4292
info@cwa-scacanada.ca
canadianfreelanceguild.ca
www.facebook.com/cwacanada
twitter.com/cwacanada1
To advance the interests of members, improve their lives & support equal job opportunities & human rights; To raise professional standards & ethical business & journalistic practices
Martin O'Hanlon, President
Katherine Lapointe, Digital Media Organizer
Nasr Ahmed, Associate Membership Coordinator

Écrivains Francophones d'Amérique
1995, rue Sherbrooke ouest, Montréal QC H3A 1H9
Tél: 514-318-2590
lesecrivainsfrancophones@yahoo.ca
ecrivainsfrancophones.com
www.facebook.com/111361458891464
Grouper en association les écrivains de langue française, de nationalité canadienne, domiciliés ou non au Canada, auteurs d'un ou de plusieurs livres publiés au Canada ou ailleurs par des éditeurs homologués; servir et défendre les intérêts de la littérature canadienne; prendre toutes les mesures nécessaires

ou opportunes pour assurer le respect de la propriété littéraire de ses membres.
Gino Levesque, Responsable

Editors' Association of Canada (EAC) / Association canadienne des réviseurs (ACR)
#1507, 180 Dundas St. West, Toronto ON M5G 1Z8
Tel: 416-975-1379; *Fax:* 416-975-1637
Toll-Free: 866-226-3348
info@editors.ca
www.editors.ca
www.instagram.com/editorscanada
www.linkedin.com/groups/1858228
www.facebook.com/EditorsReviseursCanada
twitter.com/editorscanada
To promote & maintain standards of professional editing & publishing; To set guidelines to help editors secure fair pay & good working conditions; To foster networking among editors; To cooperate with other publishing associations in areas of common concern
Natasha Bood, Executive Director

Federation of British Columbia Writers (FBCW)
#412, 1641 Lonsdale Ave., Vancouver BC V7M 2J5
Tel: 250-741-6514
membership@bcwriters.ca
www.bcwriters.ca
www.facebook.com/bcwriters
twitter.com/bcwriters
To develop, support, inform, & promote writers in British Columbia; To foster a community for writing in British Columbia
Ann Graham Walker, President
Shaleeta Harrison, Executive Director

The League of Canadian Poets (LCP)
#1519, 2 Carleton St., Toronto ON M5B 1J3
Tel: 416-504-1657; *Fax:* 416-504-0096
info@poets.ca
poets.ca
www.facebook.com/canadianpoets
twitter.com/CanadianPoets
To develop the art of poetry; To enhance the status of poets & nurture a professional poetic community; To facilitate the teaching of Canadian poetry at all levels of education; To enlarge the audience for poetry by encouraging publication, performance & recognition of poetry nationally & internationally; To uphold freedom of expression
Lesley Fletcher, Executive Director
Nicole Brewer, Coordinator, Administration & Communications

Manitoba Writers' Guild Inc. (MWG)
#218, 100 Arthur St., Winnipeg MB R3B 1H3
Tel: 204-944-8013
info@mbwriter.mb.ca
www.mbwriter.mb.ca
www.facebook.com/mbwriters
twitter.com/mbwriters
To provide services & support writers in Manitoba
Melanie Matheson, Executive Director

The Ontario Poetry Society (TOPS)
#710, 65 Spring Garden Ave., Toronto ON M2N 6H9
www.theontariopoetrysociety.ca
To establish a democratic organization for members to unite in friendship for emotional support & encouragement in all aspects of poetry, including writing, editing, performing & publishing
Fran Figge, President
Mel Sarnese, Vice-President
Bunny Iskov, Treasurer
Joan Sutcliffe, Secretary

Québec Writers' Federation (QWF) / Fédération des Écrivaines et Écrivains du Québec
#3, 1200, av Atwater, Westmount QC H3Z 1X4
Tel: 514-933-0878
admin@qwf.org
www.qwf.org
www.facebook.com/quebecwritersfederation
twitter.com/OfficialQWF
To encourage & support English-language writing in Québec to ensure a lasting place for English literature in the province's cultural scene
Christopher Diraddo, President
Julie Barlow, Vice-President
Jason Camlot, Treasurer
Lori Schubert, Executive Director

Saskatchewan Writers Guild (SWG)
PO Box 3986, Regina SK S4P 3R9
Tel: 306-757-6310; *Fax:* 306-565-8554
Toll-Free: 800-667-6788
info@skwriter.com
www.skwriter.com
www.facebook.com/skwritersguild
twitter.com/SKWritersGuild
To promote excellence in writing by Saskatchewan writers; To advocate for Saskatchewan writers; To promote the teaching of Saskatchewan & Canadian literature & instruction in the art of writing at all levels of education; To improve public access to writers & their work; To develop professionalism in the business of writing; To improve the economic status of Saskatchewan writers
Judith Silverthorne, Executive Director
Tracy Hamon, Program Manager
Leah MacLean-Evans, Executive Assistant

Science Writers & Communicators of Canada
PO Box 75, Stn. A, Toronto ON M5W 1A2
Toll-Free: 800-796-8595
office@sciencewriters.ca
sciencewriters.ca
www.linkedin.com/company/science-writers-and-communicators-of-canada
www.facebook.com/SWCCanada
twitter.com/SWC_Can
To foster excellence in science communication; To increase public awareness of Canadian science & technology
Terry Lavender, President
Nikki Berreth, General Manager

Société professionnelle des auteurs et des compositeurs du Québec (SPACQ)
#500, 33, rue Milton, Montréal QC H2X 1V1
Tél: 514-845-3739; *Ligne sans frais:* 866-445-3739
info@spacq.qc.ca
www.spacq.qc.ca
www.linkedin.com/company/spacq
www.facebook.com/SPACQ
twitter.com/SPACQ
Défendre les droits et les intérêts moraux, professionnels et économiques des auteurs et des compositeurs, ainsi que les droits qui se rapportent aux oeuvres, auprès des autorités gouvernementales
Alexandre Alonso, Directeur général
Jean-Richard Lefebvre, Responsable, Services aux membres et Communications

Union des écrivaines et écrivains québécois (UNEQ)
3492, av Laval, Montréal QC H2X 3C8
Tél: 514-849-8540; *Téléc:* 514-849-6239
Ligne sans frais: 888-849-8540
ecrivez@uneq.qc.ca
www.uneq.qc.ca
www.facebook.com/152536222994
twitter.com/Ecrivains_QC
Élaborer des politiques et administrer des programmes en vue de favoriser le développement de la littérature québécoise et sa diffusion au Québec comme à l'étranger, en vue également de faire reconnaître la profession d'écrivain de telle sorte que les intérêts moraux, sociaux et économiques des auteurs soient respectés
Danièle Simpson, Présidente
Francis Farley-Chevrier, Directeur général

Writers' Alliance of Newfoundland & Labrador (WANL)
Haymarket Square, #208, 223 Duckworth St., St. John's NL A1C 6N1
Tel: 709-739-5215; *Toll-Free:* 866-739-5215
wanl@nf.aibn.com
wanl.ca
www.facebook.com/writersalliance
twitter.com/WANL
To enhance the quality of writing in Newfoundland & Labrador through such programmes as workshops, meetings, readings; to encourage & develop public awareness & appreciation for the work of writers in Newfoundland & Labrador
Alison Dyer, Executive Director

Writers' Federation of New Brunswick (WFNB)
#151, 527 Dundonald St., Fredericton NB E3B 1X5
Tel: 506-260-3564
info@wfnb.ca
www.wfnb.ca
www.facebook.com/writersfederation
twitter.com/WritersNB
To promote New Brunswick writing; To assist writers of New Brunswick at all stages of their development by providing services; to uphold the right to free artistic expression; to provide

additional educational services to schools & libraries; to contribute to the enhancement of literary arts

Writers' Federation of Nova Scotia (WFNS)
1113 Marginal Rd., Halifax NS B3H 4P7
Tel: 902-423-8116; *Fax:* 902-422-0881
contact@writers.ns.ca
www.writers.ns.ca
www.facebook.com/WritersFedNS
twitter.com/WFNS
To foster creative & professional writing; To provide advice & assistance to writers; To encourage greater public recognition of Nova Scotia writers
Jonathan Meakin, Executive Director
Robin Spittal, Officer, Communications & Development
Linda Hudson, Officer, Arts Education

The Writers' Guild of Alberta (WGA)
Percy Page Centre, 11759 Groat Rd., Edmonton AB T5M 3K6
Tel: 780-422-8174; *Fax:* 780-422-2663
Toll-Free: 800-665-5354
mail@writersguild.ab.ca
www.writersguild.ab.ca
www.facebook.com/groups/writersguildofalberta
twitter.com/WritersGuildAB
To provide a meeting ground & collective voice for the writers of Alberta; To promote excellence in writing in Alberta
Carol Holmes, Executive Director

The Writers' Trust of Canada
#600, 460 Richmond St. West, Toronto ON M5V 1Y1
Tel: 416-504-8222; *Fax:* 416-504-9090
Toll-Free: 877-906-6548
info@writerstrust.com
www.writerstrust.com
www.facebook.com/writerstrust
twitter.com/writerstrust
To provide support to writers through various programs & awards; To celebrate the talents & achievements of Canada's writers; To explore & introduce to future generations the traditions that will enrich Canada's common literary heritage & strengthen its cultural foundations
Charlie Foran, Executive Director
James Davies, Program Director
Katrina Afonso, Manager, Communications
Julia Yu, Manager, Events

The Writers' Union of Canada (TWUC)
#600, 460 Richmond St. West, Toronto ON M5V 1Y1
Tel: 416-703-8982; *Fax:* 416-504-9090
info@writersunion.ca
www.writersunion.ca
www.facebook.com/thewritersunionofcanada
twitter.com/twuc
To unite writers for the advancement of their common interests; To foster writing in Canada; To maintain relations with publishers; To exchange information among members; To safeguard the freedom to write & to publish; To advance good relations with other writers & their organizations in Canada & all parts of the world
John Degen, Executive Director

Youth

Black Community Resource Centre (BCRC)
#497, 6767, ch de la Côte-des-Neiges, Montréal QC H3S 2T6
Tel: 514-342-2247; *Fax:* 514-342-2283
info@bcrcmontreal.com
bcrcmontreal.com
To help English-speaking visible minority youth achieve their full potential

Centre Afrika
1644, rue St-Hubert, Montréal QC H2L 3Z3
Tél: 514-843-4019; *Téléc:* 514-849-4323
centreafrika@centreafrika.com
www.centreafrika.com
www.facebook.com/centreafrika
Activités sociales & culturelles et activités spirituelles / religieuses

ERS Training & Development Corporation (ERS) / Corporation pour la formation et le développement ERS
#810, 5250, rue Ferrier, Montréal QC H4P 1L4
Tel: 514-731-3419; *Fax:* 514-731-4999
info@erstraining.ca
www.erstraining.ca
www.linkedin.com/company/e-r-s-training-and-development-corporation
www.facebook.com/ERStraininganddevelopment

To promote development & training; To identify the needs of youth; To develop & promote training skills & employment readiness; To seek out & put in place programs for the improvement of youth circumstances; To implement programs so that all may achieve full potential
Peter L. Clement, President & CEO
Susana Semen, Office Manager

Force Jeunesse
#322, 1000, rue Saint-Antoine ouest, Montréal QC H3C 3R7
Tél: 514-384-8666; *Téléc:* 514-384-6442
info@forcejeunesse.qc.ca
www.forcejeunesse.qc.ca
www.facebook.com/ForceJeunesse
twitter.com/FORCEJEUNESSE
Force Jeunesse est un regroupement de jeunes travailleurs issus de différents milieux dont le principe fondateur est l'équité

intergénérationnelle; agit concrètement en revendiquant des mesures qui améliorent la situation économique et sociale des jeunes.
Jonathan Plamondon, Président

Head & Hands / A deux mains
5833, rue Sherbrooke ouest, Montréal QC H4A 1X4
Tel: 514-481-0277; *Fax:* 514-481-2336
info@headandhands.ca
www.headandhands.ca
www.youtube.com/user/HeadandHands
www.facebook.com/headandhands
twitter.com/headandhands
To offer medical, social & legal services with an approach that is harm-reductive, holistic & non-judgmental
Jon McPhedran Waitzer, Director
Juniper Belshaw, Contact, Fundraising and Development

Richelieu International (RI)
#400, 301, promenade Moodie, Ottawa ON K2H 9C4
Téléc: 514-355-4159
Ligne sans frais: 800-267-6525
international@richelieu.org
www.linkedin.com/company/richelieu-international
www.richelieu.org
www.facebook.com/RichelieuInternational
A pour mission l'épanouissement de la personalité de ses membres & au développement de leurs aptitudes personnelles & collectives; la promotion de la langue française; aider la jeunesse
Monique Banville, Présidente

SECTION 4
BROADCASTING

The listings in this section are arranged by province, then city within province, except the Major Broadcasting Companies, which are arranged alphabetically by company name.

CANADIAN ALMANAC & DIRECTORY
RÉPERTOIRE ET ALMANACH CANADIEN

Major Broadcasting Companies

591987 B.C. Ltd.
Owned by: YTV Canada Inc.*
Corus Quay, 25 Dockside Dr., Toronto, ON M5A 0B5
www.corusent.com
591987 B.C. Ltd. is a subsidiary of Corus Entertainment Inc., via YTV Canada Inc., that owns & operates the following TV stations: CHEX & CKWS.

591989 B.C. Ltd.
Owned by: Corus Radio Company*
170 Queen St., Kingston, ON K7K 1B2
Tel: 613-544-2340; Fax: 613-544-5508
www.corusent.com
591989 B.C. Ltd. owns & operates radio stations throughout Ontario.

Access Communications Co-operative Limited
Old Name: Regina Cablevision Co-operative Ltd.
2250 Park St., Regina, SK S4N 7K7
Tel: 306-569-3510; Fax: 306-565-5395
Toll-Free: 866-363-2225
www.myaccess.ca
www.instagram.com/myaccessca,
www.facebook.com/myaccessca, twitter.com/myaccessca
Access Communications offers internet access, television & cable, telephone, home security & web hosting services to communities in Saskatchewan.
Doreen Polischuk, Chair

Accessible Media Inc. (AMI)
Old Name: National Broadcast Reading Service (NBRS)
#200, 1090 Don Mills Rd., Toronto, ON M3C 3R6
Tel: 416-422-4222; Fax: 416-422-1633
Toll-Free: 866-509-4545
info@ami.ca
www.ami.ca
www.youtube.com/user/AccessibleMedia
www.facebook.com/AccessibleMediaInc,
twitter.com/AccessibleMedia
A not-for-profit provider of accessible media.
David Errington, President & CEO

Ag-Com Productions Ltd.
19 McLeod Rd., Emerald Park, SK S4L 1B7
Tel: 306-781-2424; Fax: 306-781-2849
info@agcomdirect.com
agcomproductions.com
Ag-Com is an agricultural broadcast company.

Anthem Sports & Entertainment
Old Name: Anthem Media Group
#1410, 181 University Ave., Toronto, ON M5H 3M7
contact@anthemse.com
www.anthemse.com
www.linkedin.com/company/anthem-media-group-inc-
Anthem is a global media platform involved in a range of media from television to online subscription streaming services. These include: AXS TV; Fight Network; IMPACT Wrestling; Game TV; Game+; Pursuit Channel; & HDNET Movies.
Leonard Asper, President & CEO

Arctic Radio
316 Green St., Flin Flon, MB R8A 0H2
Tel: 204-687-3469; Fax: 204-687-6786
Operates 3 FM Radio stations in Northern Manitoba.

Bayshore Broadcasting Corporation
PO Box 280, 270 - 9th St. East, Owen Sound, ON N4K 5P5
Tel: 519-376-2030; Fax: 519-371-4242
Toll-Free: 866-384-0501
news@bayshorebroadcasting.ca
www.bayshorebroadcasting. ca
www.facebook.com/newsbayshore, twitter.com/newsbayshore
Bayshore Broadcasting Corporation is an independent broadcaster. It operates radio stations in Grey, Bruce, Simcoe & Huron counties in southern Ontario.

Bell Media Inc.
Old Name: CTVglobemedia; Bell Globemedia; Baton Broadcasting
Headquarters
299 Queen St. West, Toronto, ON M5V 2Z5
Tel: 416-384-8000
bellmediapr@bellmedia.ca
www.bellmedia.ca
www.linkedin.com/company/bell-media-,
www.facebook.com/BellMediainc, twitter.com/BellMediapr

Bell Media's subsidiaries are Bell Media TV & Bell Media Radio, which in turn own assets such as CTV, CTV Two, the former CHUM Limited radio properties & 30 specialty cable television channels. In 2013, Bell Media acquired Astral Media & its assets, dissolving the company. In 2021, Groupe V Média Inc. amalgamated with Bell Media.
Wade Oosterman, President

Bell Media Radio
Also known as: iHeartRadio
Owned by: Bell Media Inc.*
299 Queen St. West, Toronto, ON M5V 2Z5
Tel: 416-384-8000
bellmediapr@bellmedia.ca
www.bellmedia.ca/radio
Bell Media Radio owns 44 stations across Canada, including the former CHUM Radio Network.
Wade Oosterman, President, Bell Media

Bell Media TV
Owned by: Bell Media Inc.*
299 Queen St. West, Toronto, ON M5V 2Z5
Tel: 416-384-8000
bellmediapr@bellmedia.ca
www.bellmedia.ca
Bell Media TV owns the CTV network of television channels, including 35 stations, as well as CTV Two. The company also owns 27 specialty channels.
Wade Oosterman, President, Bell Media

Blackburn Radio Inc.
#101, 700 Richmond St., London, ON N6A 5C7
Tel: 519-679-8680
blackburnradio.com
www.linkedin.com/company/blackburn-radio-inc
Blackburn Radio is an AM-FM radio broadcaster that operates 13 stations in Wingham, Sarnia, London, Chatham, Leamington & Windsor.
Ron Dann, President

Blue Ant Media
#200, 130 Merton St., Toronto, ON M4S 1A4
Tel: 416-646-4434; Fax: 416-646-4444
feedback@blueantmedia.ca
blueantmedia.ca
www.linkedin.com/company/blue-ant-media,
twitter.com/blueantmedia
Blue Ant Media is a producer, distributor, channel operator & gaming video content company. The company owns channels including A.Side, BBC Earth, Cottage Life, HIFI, Love Nature, Makeful, Smithsonian Channel & T+E.
Michael MacMillan, Co-Founder & Chief Executive Officer
Robb Chase, Chief Financial Officer

Byrnes Communications Inc.
2148 Country Club Dr., Burlington, ON L7M 4A8
info@byrnesmedia.com
byrnesmedia.com
Chris Byrnes, President

Canadian Broadcasting Corporation (CBC)
Société Radio-Canada
Also known as: CBC/Radio-Canada Enterprise Communications
Head Office
PO Box 3220 C, 181 Queen St., Ottawa, ON K1Y 1E4
Tel: 613-288-6000
cbc.ca
www.instagram.com/cbc, www.facebook.com/cbc,
twitter.com/cbc
Other information: TTY: 613-288-6455
CBC/Radio-Canada is Canada's national public broadcaster. Services are offered on radio, television, the internet, as well as through its record & music distribution service & wireless WAP & SMS messaging services.
Michael Goldbloom, Chair
Catherine Tait, President & CEO
Carol Najm, Vice-President & CFO
Michel Bissonnette, Executive Vice-President, Radio-Canada
Daniel Boudreau, Executive Vice-President, Media Technology & Infrastructure Services
Barbara Williams, Executive Vice-President, CBC

Canadian Broadcasting Corporation - Canadian Broadcasting Centre
Société Radio-Canada
Owned by: Canadian Broadcasting Corporation*

PO Box 500 A, 250 Front St. West, Toronto, ON M5W 1E6
Tel: 416-205-3311
Toll-Free: 866-306-4636
cbcinput@cbc.ca
www.cbc.ca
Other information: TTY: 416-205-6688
The CBC is a Canadian crown corporation & serves as Canada's national public radio & television broadcaster; in French, the CBC is called la Société Radio-Canada (SRC), & the corporation also operates Radio Canada International (RCI); offers programming in English, French & 8 Aboriginal languages on radio & in 9 languages on RCI; provides regional & local television programming in both official languages; broadcasts locally produced programs in English & native languages for people living in the far north; primarily funded by federal statutory grants.
Michael Goldbloom, Chair
Catherine Tait, President & CEO

Channel Zero Inc.
2844 Dundas St. West, Toronto, ON M6P 1Y7
Tel: 416-492-1595
www.chz.com
www.linkedin.com/company/channel-zero-inc-
Channel Zero is a media company that owns several television stations including CHCH in Ontario. Channel Zero also owns the specialty channels Rewind, Silver Screen Classics & Halla Bol Kids TV.
Romen Podzyhun, Chair & Chief Executive Officer
C.J. Millar, President & COO
Geoff Thrasher, General Manager, Sales,
geoff.thrasher@chz.com

Cogeco Communications Inc.
Owned by: Cogeco Inc.*
#3301, 1, Place Ville-Marie, Montréal, QC H3B 3N2
Tel: 514-764-4600
www.cogeco.ca
Cogeco Communications offers broadband services through Cogeco Connexion in Canada & Atlantic Broadband in the United States.
Philippe Jetté, President & CEO, Cogeco Inc. & of Cogeco Communications Inc.

Cogeco Connexion Inc.
Old Name: Cogeco Cable Inc.
Détenteur: Cogeco Communications Inc.*
#1700, 5 Place Ville-Marie, Montréal, QC H3B 0B3
Tél: 514-764-4700
www.cogeco.ca
www.linkedin.com/company/cogeco-connexion,
twitter.com/cogeco
Cogeco Connexion operates in Quebec & Ontario under as Cogeco Cable.
Frédéric Perron, President

Cogeco Inc.
#3301, 1, Place Ville-Marie, Montréal, QC H3B 3N2
Tel: 514-764-4600
www.cogeco.ca
www.linkedin.com/company/cogeco-inc,
www.facebook.com/Cogeco, twitter.com/Cogeco
Cogeco is telecommunications company providing television & radio broadcasting services in Québec & Ontario. It owns & operates 18 radio stations in Québec through its subsidiary Cogeco Media Inc.
Philippe Jetté, President & CEO, Cogeco Inc. & of Cogeco Communications Inc.

Cogeco Media Inc.
Old Name: Cogeco Diffusion Inc.
Owned by: Cogeco Inc.*
#1100, 800, rue de la Gauchetière ouest, Montréal, QC H5A 1M1
Tel: 514-787-7799
web@cogecomedia.com
www.cogecomedia.com
www.linkedin.com/company/cogeco-media
Cogeco Media owns & operates 23 radio stations in Québec.
Caroline Paquet, President

Connelly Communications Corp.
c/o CJKL-FM, 5 Kirkland St., Kirkland Lake, ON P2N 1N9
Tel: 705-567-3366; Fax: 705-567-6101
cjkl@cjklfm.com
www.cjklfm.com
Connelly Communications owns CJKL-FM & CJTT-FM.
Robin Connelly, President, robin@cjklfm.com

---

* For details on this company see listing in Major Broadcasting Companies section; † French language station

Corus Entertainment Inc.
Corporate Head Office
Corus Quay, 25 Dockside Dr., Toronto, ON M5A 0B5
Tél: 416-479-7000; Fax: 416-479-7006
www.corusent.com
Corus Entertainment is a media & entertainment company. It has 33 specialty television channels & 15 regular television stations. It also owns 39 radio stations across Canada.
Doug Murphy, President & CEO

Corus Radio Inc.
Owned by: Corus Entertainment Inc.
Corus Quay, 25 Dockside Dr., Toronto, ON M5A 0B5
Tél: 416-479-7000; Fax: 416-960-5437
www.corusent.com/about/our-brands/radio

CTV News Channel
Old Name: CTV Newsnet
Owned by: Bell Media Inc.
PO Box 9 O, Toronto, ON M4A 2M9
Tél: 416-384-5000
Toll-Free: 866-690-6179
newschannel@ctv.ca
www.ctvnews.ca/ctv-news-channel
Other information: Toll-Free TTY: 800-461-1542
A 24-hour television headline news specialty channel.

Dauphin Broadcasting Co. Ltd.
1735 Main St. South, Dauphin, MB R7N 2V4
Tél: 204-638-3230; Fax: 204-638-8257
730ckdm.com
Operates 730 CKDM, a community radio station serving the local area.

DERYtelecom
Détenteur: Cogeco Connexion Inc.
CP 1154, La Baie, QC G7B 3P3
Ligne san frais: 866-544-3358
servicesaguenay@derytelecom.ca
www.derytele.ca
www.youtube.com/user/DERYtelecom,
www.facebook.com/derytelecom
DERYtelecom is primarily a cable television & internet distributor but it also owns six local television stations across Québec.

Dougall Media
87 Hill St. North, Thunder Bay, ON P7A 5V6
Tél: 807-346-2600; Fax: 807-345-9923
www.dougallmedia.com
Dougall Media owns radio stations, television stations & a newspaper, all of which serve the Thunder Bay area.

Durham Radio Inc.
#207, 1200 Airport Blvd., Oshawa, ON L1J 8P5
Tél: 905-571-0949; Fax: 905-571-1150
Toll-Free: 855-432-7625
www.powerofradio.ca
www.linkedin.com/company/durham-radio-inc.
Durham Radio Inc. owns several radio stations in Oshawa, Hamilton & Caledonia, including CHKX-FM, CHTG-FM, CJKX-F, CKDO-AM & CKGE-FM.
Douglas Kirk, President

EastLink
PO Box 8660 A, Halifax, NS B3K 5M3
Tél: 902-484-2800
Toll-Free: 877-813-1727
www.eastlink.ca
www.linkedin.com/company/eastlink,
www.facebook.com/eastlink, twitter.com/eastlink
EastLink is a privately held telecommunications company operating in Atlantic Canada, Ontario & Alberta.
Lee Bragg, Chief Executive Officer

EastLink TV
Owned by: EastLink
PO Box 8660 A, Halifax, NS B3K 5M3
Tél: 902-484-2800
Toll-Free: 888-345-1111
www.eastlink.ca/cable-digital-tv/community-tv
EastLink TV provides services to clients & operates community TV channels in Nova Scotia, Prince Edward Island, Ontario & Alberta.
Lee Bragg, Chief Executive Officer, Eastlink Inc.

Evanov Communications Inc.
5312 Dundas St. West, Toronto, ON M9B 1B3
Tél: 416-213-1035
info@evanov.ca
evanov.ca
www.linkedin.com/company/evanovcommunications

Owns several radio stations spread across Central & Atlantic Canada; promotes independent radio broadcasting.
Paul Evanov, President & CEO

Fairchild Media Group
3248 Cambie St., Vancouver, BC V5Z 2W4
Tel: 604-295-1313; Fax: 604-295-1300
www.fairchildgroup.com
Fairchild Media Group owns & operates Fairchild TV, Talentvision & Fairchild Radio.
Thomas Fung, Chair & Founder

Fairchild Radio Group Ltd.
Owned by: Fairchild Media Group
#26-29, 151 Esna Park Dr., Markham, ON L3R 3B1
Tel: 905-415-6265; Fax: 905-415-6294
www.fairchildradio.com
www.youtube.com/user/fairchildradiotor,
www.facebook.com/fairchildradiotoronto
Chinese Canadian multicultural radio network with stations in Toronto, Vancouver & Calgary. Provides program schedules & internet simulcasting.

Global Television Network
Also known as: Global
Owned by: Corus Entertainment Inc.
81 Barber Greene Rd., Toronto, ON M3C 2A2
Tél: 416-446-5460
www.globaltv.com
www.youtube.com/c/GlobaltvEntertainment
www.facebook.com/globaltv, twitter.com/globaltv

Golden West Broadcasting Ltd.
Radio Head Office
#201, 125 Centre Ave., Altona, MB R0G 0B0
Tél: 204-324-6464
goldenwest.ca
Golden West has 44 radio stations across Manitoba, Saskatchewan, Alberta & Ontario.
Elmer Hildebrand, Chief Executive Officer

Groupe Remstar Média
Remstar Media Group
#602, 355, rue Ste-Catherine ouest, Montréal, QC H3B 1A5
Tél: 514-284-7587
auditoire@remstarmedia.ca
remstarmedia.ca
Groupe Remstar Média owns two French-language specialty channeles, Elle Fictions & Max.
Maxime Rémillard, President

Groupe TVA inc.
Old Name: Corporation Télé-Métropole inc.
Détenteur: Quebecor Media inc.
1600, boul de Maisonneuve est, Montréal, QC H2L 4P6
Tél: 514-526-9251; Téléc: 514-599-5502
www.groupetva.ca
www.linkedin.com/company/groupe-tva
Groupe TVA est une entreprise de communication intégrée active dans les secteurs de la diffusion, de la production de produits audiovisuels, de la publication de magazines, de l'édition ainsi que de la distribution de films.
France Lauzière, Présidente & chef de la direction
Martin Picard, Vice-président et Chef de l'exploitation du contenu

Harvard Broadcasting Inc.
1900 Rose St., Regina, SK S4P 0A9
Tel: 306-546-6200
www.harvardbroadcasting.com
www.linkedin.com/company/harvard-broadcasting
Harvard Broadcasting owns & operaters 13 radio stations throughout Western Canada.
Cam Cowie, Senior Vice-President & COO,
ccowie@harvardbroadcasting.com

Hollywood Suite Inc.
#200, 186 St George St., Toronto, ON M5R 2N3
info@hollywoodsuite.ca
hollywoodsuite.ca
www.linkedin.com/company/hollywood-suite-inc-,
www.facebook.com/HollywoodSuite, twitter.com/hollywoodsuite
The company owns the Hollywood Suite, a group of four specialty television channels.
Jay Switzer, Owner

ICI Radio-Canada
Old Name: Société Radio-Canada
Détenteur: Canadian Broadcasting Corporation

CP 6000, 1400, boul René-Lévesque est, Montréal, QC H3C 3A8
Tél: 514-597-6000
Ligne san frais: 866-306-4636
ici.radio-canada.ca
www.facebook.com/radiocanada.info,
twitter.com/iciradiocanada
Autre information: ATS: 514-597-6013
ICI Radio-Canada est le radiodiffuseur public national du Canada et l'une des plus grandes institutions culturelles du pays. Avec ses 28 services offerts sur des plateformes comme la radio, la télévision, Internet, la radio par satellite, l'audio numérique, sans compter son service de distribution de disques et de musique et ses services de messagerie sans fil WAP et SMS, CBC/Radio-Canada est maintenant accessible aux Canadiens à leur convenance.
Catherine Tait, Présidente-Directrice générale,
CBC/Radio-Canada
Michel Bissonnette, Executive Vice-President, Radio-Canada

Inuit Broadcasting Corporation (IBC)
Administrative Office
#310, 309 Cooper St., Ottawa, ON K2P 0G5
Tel: 613-235-1892; Fax: 613-230-8824
info@inuitbroadcasting.ca
inuitbroadcasting.ca
www.facebook.com/inuit.broadcasting.9,
twitter.com/Johnnylemming
The IBC produces Inuit television programming in 5 production centres across Nunavut. It is a founding member of Television Northern Canada & the Aboriginal Peoples Television Network.
Manitok Thompson, Chief Executive Officer
Malakie Kilabuk, Director, Operations
Lana Paris, Director, Finance

Jim Pattison Broadcast Group
460 Pemberton Terrace, Kamloops, BC V2C 1T5
Tel: 250-372-3322; Fax: 250-374-0445
info@pattisonmedia.com
pattisonmedia.com
Jim Pattison Broadcast Group is a private western Canada broadcasting company.
Rod Schween, President
Ryan Beck, Director, Finance
Mike Jean, Director, Sales, Metro Markets

Klondike Broadcasting Ltd.
#203, 4103 - 4th Ave., Whitehorse, YK Y1A 1H6
Tel: 867-668-6100; Fax: 867-668-4209
Toll-Free: 800-661-0530
info@ckrw.com
www.ckrw.com
Operates CKRW-FM in Whitehorse, YK.

Le5 Communications
#301, 336 Pine St., Sudbury, ON P3C 1X8
Tel: 705-222-8306; Fax: 705-222-2805
leloupfm.com
www.facebook.com/leloupfm
Le5 Communications owns & operates three radio stations in Northern Ontario. The company also owns the newspapers L'Express de Timmins & Le Voyageur.
Paul Lefebvre, Propriétaire, plefebvre@leloupfm.com

Leclerc Communication Inc.
#505, 815, boul Lebourgneuf, Québec, QC G2J 0C1
Tel: 418-688-0919
commentaires@leclerccommunication.ca
www.leclerccommunication.ca
www.facebook.com/LeclercCommunication
Leclerc Communication owns & operates radio stations in Québec & Montréal.
Jean-François Leclerc, Co-owner,
jf.leclerc@leclerccommunication.ca
Nicolas Leclerc, Co-owner,
nicolas.leclerc@leclerccommunication.ca

Mainstream Broadcasting Corporation
#150, 13571 Commerce Pkwy., Richmond, BC V6V 2R2
Tel: 604-263-1320
adm@am1320.com
www.am1320.com
Mainstream Broadcasting Corporation is a British Columbia radio company serving the Chinese-speaking community & 12 other languages.

Maritime Broadcasting System (MBS)
Old Name: Eastern Broadcasting Limited
90 Lovett Lake Ct., Halifax, NS B3S 0H6
Tel: 902-425-1225; Fax: 902-423-2093
mail@mbsradio.com
www.mbsradio.com

---

* For details on this company see listing in Major Broadcasting Companies section; † French language station

MBS Radio is a private broadcasting company with 24 radio stations serving Nova Scotia, New Brunswick & Prince Edward Island.

My Broadcasting Corporation (MBC)
Also known as: myFM
PO Box 961, 321B Raglan St. South, Renfrew, ON K7V 4H4
Tel: 613-432-6936; Fax: 613-432-1086
www.mybroadcastingcorp.com
The company owns & operates a number of small-market radio stations in Ontario.
Jon Pole, President & Co-Founder
Andrew Dickson, Executive Vice-President & Co-Founder

Newfoundland Broadcasting Co. Ltd.
PO Box 2020, 446 Logy Bay Rd., St. John's, NL A1C 5S2
Tel: 709-722-5015; Fax: 709-726-5017
ntv.ca
www.facebook.com/NTVNewsNL, twitter.com/NTVNewsNL
Reaches 8 million households across Canada via digital cable & satellite
G. Scott Sterling, President & CEO

Odyssey Television Network, Inc.
#300, 437 Danforth Ave., Toronto, ON M4K 1P1
Tel: 416-462-1200; Fax: 416-462-1818
info@odysseytv.ca
odysseytv.ca
The network operates Greek-language television channels.

OKâlaKatiget Society
PO Box 160, Nain, NL A0P 1L0
Tel: 709-922-2187; Fax: 709-922-2293
okradio@oksociety.com
www.oksociety.com
www.facebook.com/302939923049908
Other information: Alt. Email: oktv@oksociety.com
The Society, a non-profit charitable organization, provides communication services to people on the North Coast & the Lake Melville region of Labrador.
Arlene Ikkusek, Executive Director

Peace River Broadcasting Corporation Ltd.
PO Box 300, 9807 - 100th Ave., Peace River, AB T8S 1T5
Tel: 780-624-2535; Fax: 780-624-5424
Toll-Free: 800-610-3610
Peace River Broadcasting Corporation Ltd. owns radio stations in Alberta, including CKHL-FM, CKKX-FM & CKYL-FM.

Quebecor Media Inc.
612, rue St-Jacques, Montréal, QC H3C 4M8
Tél: 514-380-1999
www.quebecor.com
www.linkedin.com/company/quebecor-media-inc/,
twitter.com/quebecor
Quebecor est l'une des plus importantes entreprises de médias au Canada, active dans la télédistribution, téléphonie, accès Interet, et l'édition de journaux, magazines, et livres; Vidéotron; Groupe TVA inc.; Distribution Select.
Pierre Karl Péladeau, Président et Chef de la direction

Quinte Broadcasting Co. Ltd.
PO Box 488, 10 South Front St., Belleville, ON K8N 5B2
Tel: 613-969-5555; Fax: 613-969-8122

Radio 1540 Ltd.
622 College St., 4th Fl., Toronto, ON M6G 1B6
Tel: 416-531-9991; Fax: 416-531-5274
info@chinradio.com
www.chinradio.com
www.facebook.com/chinradiocanada,
twitter.com/chinradiocanada
Lenny Lombardi, President

Radio Canada International (RCI)
Détenteur: Canadian Broadcasting Corporation*
1400, boul René-Lévesque est, Montréal, QC H2L 2M2
Tél: 514-597-7461
info@rcinet.ca
www.rcinet.ca
www.facebook.com/rcinet, twitter.com/rcinet
Autre information: Tèle Français: 514-597-7094
RCI has live radio in English, French, Spanish, Portuguese, Arabic, Mandarin & Russian around the world. Its mandate is to increase awareness of Canadian values, as well as its social, economic & cultural activities to specific geographic areas as determined in consultation with the government of Canada. RCI also has the complementary mandate of addressing these same topics to new immigrants to Canada.
Soleïman Mellali, Editor-in-Chief

Rawlco Radio Ltd.
Corporate Office
715 Saskatchewan Cres. West, Saskatoon, SK S7M 5V7
Tel: 306-934-2222
www.rawlco.com
Rawlco Radio Ltd. is a Saskatchewan company with 7 radio stations.
Kent Newson, Vice-President & General Manager, Rawlco Calgary, 403-385-4000
Tom Newton, Vice-President & General Manager, Rawlco Regina, 306-525-0000
Kristy Werner, Vice-President & General Manager, News Talk Radio
Ryan Zimmerman, Vice-President, FM Programming, Saskatchewan

RNC MÉDIA, Inc.
Also known as: Radio Nord
Old Name: Radio-Nord Communications Inc.
#1405, 1, carré Westmount, Montréal, QC H3Z 2P9
Tél: 514-866-8686; Téléc: 514-866-8056
info@rncmedia.ca
www.rncmedia.ca
Radiodiffusion (WOW, 919 Sports, Radio X); télédiffusion (TVA Gatineau-Ottawa et Abitibi-Témiscamingue; Noovo Gatineau-Ottawa et Abitibi-Témiscamingue); programmation de haute qualité et services de publicité.
Robert Ranger, Président et chef de la direction

Rock 95 Broadcasting Ltd
Also known as: Central Ontario Broadcasting
#10, 431 Huronia Rd., Barrie, ON L4N 9B3
Tel: 705-725-7304; Fax: 705-792-7858
rock95.com
www.instagram.com/rock95barrie
www.facebook.com/Rock95Barrie, twitter.com/rock95barrie
Doug Bingley, President

Rogers Communications Inc.
333 Bloor St. East, 10th Fl., Toronto, ON M4W 1G9
Tel: 416-935-7777
www.rogers.com
www.linkedin.com/company/rogers-communications,
www.facebook.com/rogers, twitter.com/AboutRogers
Rogers Communications Inc. is national telecommunications company offering radio & television services. It operates over 50 radio stations across & a number of television channels including OMNI Television, City, Sportsnet, OLN, FX & TSC. It also owns Rogers Publishing Ltd., Rogers Telecom Inc., Rogers Bank, Rogers Cable & Rogers Wireless.
Joe Natale, President & CEO

Rogers Media Inc.
Also known as: Rogers Sports & Media
Owned by: Rogers Communications Inc.*
Rogers Bldg., 333 Bloor St. East, Toronto, ON M4W 1G9
Tel: 416-935-7777; Fax: 416-935-7627
contact.rsm@rci.rogers.com
www.rogerssportsandmedia.com
www.linkedin.com/company/rogers-sports-and-media,
twitter.com/rsmcanada
Rogers Media has 64 AM & FM radio stations across Canada. Television properties include Toronto multicultural television broadcasters OMNI.1 (CFMT) & OMNI.2, televised & electronic shopping service, TSC, Sportsnet & manages two digital television services.
Jordan Banks, President

Saskatoon Media Group
Old Name: Hildebrand Communications; 629112 Saskatchewan Ltd.
366 - 3rd Ave. South, Saskatoon, SK S7K 1M5
Tel: 306-244-1975
reception@saskatoonmediagroup.com
saskatoonmediagroup.com
www.facebook.com/Saskatoonmediagroup
Operates the following radio stations in Saskatoon: CJWW-AM, CKBL-FM & CJMK-FM.
Tim Kostuik, General Manager, Sales

SaskTel
Also known as: Saskatchewan Telecommunications Holding Corporation
2121 Saskatchewan Dr., Regina, SK S4P 3Y2
Toll-Free: 800-727-5835
corporate.comments@sasktel.com
www.sasktel.com
www.linkedin.com/company/sasktel, www.facebook.com/sasktel,
twitter.com/sasktel

SaskTel is a crown corporation telecommunications company that offers telephone, internet, digital TV (maxTV), cell phone & wireless data services, among others.
Doug Burnett, President & CEO
Jim Dundas, Chief Information Officer
Charlene Gavel, Chief Financial Officer

Seneca College
1750 Finch Ave. East, Toronto, ON M2J 2X5
Tel: 416-491-5050
www.senecacollege.ca
www.linkedin.com/school/seneca-college,
www.facebook.com/senecacollege, twitter.com/senecacollege
Home of SayRadio, a not-for-profit instructional radio station.
David Agnew, President, president@senecacollege.ca

Shaw Communications Inc.
Also known as: Shaw Cablesystems G.P.
Old Name: Capital Cable Television
Headquarters
Owned by: Corus Entertainment Inc.*
#900, 630 - 3rd Ave. SW, Calgary, AB T2P 4L4
Tel: 403-750-4500; Fax: 403-750-4469
Toll-Free: 888-472-2222
www.shaw.ca
www.linkedin.com/company/shaw-communications,
www.facebook.com/shaw, twitter.com/shawinfo
Shaw Communications Inc. is a communications company providing cable television, internet & telecommunications services.
Brad Shaw, Executive Chair & Chief Executive Officer
Paul McAleese, President

Stingray Group Inc.
Old Name: Stingray Digital Group Inc.
730, rue Wellington, Montréal, QC H3C 1T4
Tel: 514-664-1244; Fax: 514-664-1143
Toll-Free: 888-956-4562
info@stingray.com
www.stingray.com
www.linkedin.com/company/stingray, twitter.com/stingray
Stingray Group Inc. is an international, multiplatform service that provides music entertainment for a number of different mediums in 156 countries. In 2018, Stingray acquired Newfoundland Capital Corporation Limited & Newcap Radio.
Eric Boyko, Founder, President & CEO
Jean-Pierre Trahan, Chief Financial Officer

Super Channel Entertainment Network
Also known as: Super Channel
Old Name: Super Channel
#200, 5324 Calgary Trail, Edmonton, AB T6H 4J8
marketing@superchannel.ca
www.superchannel.ca
www.facebook.com/superchannel, twitter.com/superchannel
Super Channel is a network of four channels that airs made-for-TV movies & television series, as well as documentaries & niche programming.
Don McDonald, President & CEO

Télé Inter-Rives Itée
Inter-Riverbank Television
Détenteur: Groupe TVA inc.*
15, rue de la Chute, Rivière-du-Loup, QC G5R 5B7
Tél: 418-867-8080; Fax: 418-867-4710
nousjoindre@cimt.ca
cimt.teleinterrives.com
www.facebook.com/cimtnouvelles, twitter.com/cimt_nouvelles
Tele Inter-Rives Ltd. dirige 4 stations de télévision régionales dans l'est du Québec; CKRT-TV, CIMT-DT, CHAU et CFTF.

Télé-Québec
Also known as: Société de télédiffusion du Québec
905, av de Lorimier, Montréal, QC H2K 3V9
Tél: 514-521-2424; Téléc: 514-864-1970
info@telequebec.tv
www.telequebec.tv
www.instagram.com/telequebec, www.facebook.com/teleqc,
twitter.com/telequebec
La Société a pour objet d'exploiter une entreprise de télédiffusion éducative et culturelle afin d'assurer, par tout mode de diffusion, l'accessibilité de ses produits au public.
Télé-Québec est une société publique de production et de diffusion, desservant plus de 92 % de la population québécoise à travers son réseau riche de 17 émetteurs, alimenté par un lien satellite portant sa programmation de Montréal.
Marie Collin, Présidente-directrice générale

---

* For details on this company see listing in Major Broadcasting Companies section; † French language station

TLN Media Group Inc. (TMG)
Also known as: TLN
Old Name: Telelatino Network Inc.
901 Lawrence Ave. West, 2nd Fl., Toronto, ON M6A 1C3
Tel: 416-744-8200
info@tlnmediagroup.com
www.tln.ca
www.linkedin.com/company/telelatino-network-inc-,
www.facebook.com/tlntelevision, twitter.com/tlntv
TMG consists of the following channels: Mediaset Italia,
EuroWorld Sport, Univision Canada, Telelatino & Soccer
Television.
Aldo DiFelice, President

Touch Canada Broadcasting Inc.
4510 MacLeod Trail South, Calgary, AB T2G 0A4
Tel: 403-276-1111; *Fax:* 403-276-1114
www.shinefm.com
Touch Canada Broadcasting owns & operates Christian radio
stations in Alberta.

TVOntario (TVO)
PO Box 200 Q, Toronto, ON M4T 2T1
Tel: 416-484-2600
Toll-Free: 800-613-0513
asktvo@tvo.org
tvo.org
www.youtube.com/c/tvo, www.facebook.com/TVO,
twitter.com/tvo
TVO is an educational broadcaster that also offers online
learning resources.
Jeffrey Orridge, Chief Executive Officer
John Ferri, Vice-President, Current Affairs & Documentaries

Vista Radio Ltd.
Old Name: Vista Broadcast Group
Corporate Head Office
#201, 910 Fitzgerald Ave., Courtenay, BC V9N 2R5
Tel: 250-338-1133
info@vistaradio.ca
www.vistaradio.ca
www.linkedin.com/company/vista-radio-ltd
Vista owns 49 stations across 7 regions in Alberta, BC, NWT &
Ontario.
Gary Russell, Vice-President, grussell@vistaradio.ca

Wawatay Communications Society
PO Box 1180, 16 - 5th Ave., Sioux Lookout, ON P8T 1B7
Tel: 807-737-2951; *Fax:* 807-737-3224
Toll-Free: 800-243-9059
sales@wawatay.on.ca
wawataynews.ca
Wawatay Communications Society is a community-driven native
organization providing news media in support of indigenous
languages & cultures in northern Ontario.
John Gagnon, Publisher & CEO

Wawatay Radio Network
*Owned by: Wawatay Communications Society**
PO Box 1180, 16 - 5th Ave., Sioux Lookout, ON P8T 1B7
Tel: 807-737-2951; *Fax:* 807-737-3224
Toll-Free: 800-243-9059
wawataynews.ca
The Wawatay Radio Network is a network of radio stations
across northern Ontario.
Jerry Sawanas, Senior Broadcaster

Westman Communications Group
Also known as: Westman Cable
Old Name: Westman Cable TV
1906 Park Ave., Brandon, MB R7B 0R9
Tel: 204-725-4300; *Fax:* 204-726-0853
Toll-Free: 800-665-3337
info@westmancom.com
westmancom.com
www.linkedin.com/company/westmancom,
www.facebook.com/westmancom, twitter.com/westmancom
Westman is a telecommunications company offering television,
internet & phone services to southwestern Manitoba. The
company also owns & operates two radio stations in the
Brandon, MB, area through its subsidiary Riding Mountain
Broadcasting Ltd.: CKLQ-AM & CKLF-FM (Star 94.7).
David Baxter, President & CEO

Wild TV Inc.
11263 - 180th St., Edmonton, AB T5S 0B4
marekting@wildtv.ca
wildtv.ca

WildBrain Ltd.
Old Name: DHX Media Ltd.
Corporate Headquarters
#505, 5657 Spring Garden Rd., Halifax, NS B3J 3R4
Tel: 902-423-0260; *Fax:* 902-422-0752
halifax@wildbrain.com
www.wildbrain.com
www.linkedin.com/company/wildbrain,
www.facebook.com/WildBrainHQ, twitter.com/wildbrainhq
WildBrain creates children & youth programming. In 2013, it
acquired Family Channel, Disney XD & Disney Junior after
Astral Media merged with Bell Media.
Eric Ellenbogen, Chief Executive Officer
Josh Scherba, President
Aaron Ames, Chief Financial Officer

YTV Canada Inc. (YTV)
*Owned by: Corus Entertainment Inc.**
Corus Quay, 25 Dockside Dr., Toronto, ON M5A 0B5
info@ytv.com
www.ytv.com
www.youtube.com/user/ytv

ZoomerMedia Ltd.
70 Jefferson Ave., Toronto, ON M6K 1Y4
Tel: 416-363-7063
www.zoomermedia.ca
www.linkedin.com/company/zoomermedia-limited,
www.facebook.com/ZoomerMedia
Moses Znaimer, Founder, President & CEO
Terenca Chan, Chief Financial Officer, t.chan@zoomermedia.ca

AM Radio Stations

Alberta

Calgary: **CBR** (Freq: 1010)
Owned by: Canadian Broadcasting Corporation*
PO Box 2640, Calgary, AB T2P 2M7
Tel: 403-521-6340, *Toll-Free:* 800-461-9219
calgarynewstips@cbc.ca
www.cbc.ca/calgary
www.instagram.com/cbccalgary, www.facebook.com/cbccalgary,
twitter.com/cbccalgary
Other information: Daybreak Alberta: 888-711-7111

Calgary: **CFAC-AM (Sportsnet 960)** (Freq: 960)
Owned by: Rogers Media Inc.*
#240, 2723 - 37 Ave. NE, Calgary, AB T1Y 5R8
Tel: 403-246-9696
www.sportsnet.ca/960
www.facebook.com/sportsnet960, twitter.com/sportsnet960
Kelly Kirch, Program Director, kelly.kirch@rci.rogers.com

Calgary: **CFFR-AM (600 News)** (Freq: 660)
Owned by: Rogers Media Inc.*
535 - 7th Ave. SW, Calgary, AB T2P 0Y4
Tel: 403-291-0000
www.660news.com
www.facebook.com/660news, twitter.com/660NewsTraffic

Calgary: **CHQR-AM (News Talk 770)** (Freq: 770)
Owned by: Corus Radio Company*
#200, 3320 - 17th Ave. SW, Calgary, AB T3E 0B4
Tel: 403-716-6500
globalnews.ca/radio/newstalk770
www.facebook.com/NewsTalk770Calgary,
twitter.com/NewsTalk770
John Vos, Director, Talk & Talent

Calgary: **CJLI-AM (The Light)** (Freq: 700)
Owned by: Touch Canada Broadcasting Inc.*
4510 Macleod Trail South, Calgary, AB T2G 0A4
Tel: 403-403-1111, *Fax:* 780-469-5335
am700@shinefm.com
www.cjli.ca
www.facebook.com/AM700TheLight

Calgary: **CKMX-AM (Funny 1060 AM)** (Freq: 1060)
Owned by: Bell Media Inc.*
#300, 1110 Centre St. NE, Calgary, AB T2E 2R2
Tel: 403-240-5800
www.iheartradio.ca/funny/funny-1060
www.instagram.com/funny1060am,
www.facebook.com/Funny1060AM, twitter.com/Funny1060AM
Stewart Meyers, General Manager,
stewart.meyers@bellmedia.ca

Drumheller: **CKDQ-AM (910 CFCW)** (Freq: 910)
Owned by: Stingray Group Inc.*
PO Box 1480, 515 Hwy. 10 East, Drumheller, AB T0J 0Y0
Tel: 403-823-3384, *Fax:* 403-823-7241
910cfcw.com
www.facebook.com/910cfcw, twitter.com/910CFCW
Jared Waldo, Station Manager, jwaldo@newcap.ca

Edmonton: **CBX** (Freq: 740)
Owned by: Canadian Broadcasting Corporation*
Edmonton City Centre, #125, 10062 - 102 Ave., Edmonton,
AB T5J 2Y8
Tel: 780-468-2300
www.cbc.ca/edmonton
www.instagram.com/cbcedmonton,
www.facebook.com/cbcedmonton, twitter.com/CBCEdmonton

Edmonton: **CFCW-AM** (Freq: 840)
Owned by: Stingray Group Inc.*
2394 West Edmonton Mall (Entrance 55), 8882 - 170th St.,
Edmonton, AB T5T 4M2
Tel: 780-468-3939, *Fax:* 780-435-0844
www.cfcw.com
www.youtube.com/user/790CFCWAM,
www.facebook.com/840CFCW, twitter.com/840CFCW
Neil Cunningham, Station Manager, ncunningham@newcap.ca

Edmonton: **CFRN-AM (TSN 1260)** (Freq: 1260)
Owned by: Bell Media Inc.*
#100, 18520 Stony Plain Rd., Edmonton, AB T5S 2E2
Tel: 780-486-2800, *Toll-Free:* 888-243-1945
www.tsn1260.ca
www.facebook.com/TSN1260, twitter.com/TSN1260
Rob Vavrek, Program Director, rob.vavrek@bellmedia.ca

Edmonton: **CHED-AM (630 CHED)** (Freq: 630)
Owned by: Corus Radio Company*
5204 - 84th St., Edmonton, AB T6E 5N8
Tel: 780-440-6300
www.630ched.com
www.instagram.com/630ched, www.facebook.com/630ched,
twitter.com/630ched
Syd Smith, Program Director, SSmith@630ched.com

Edmonton: **CHQT-AM (iNews 880)** (Freq: 880)
Owned by: Corus Radio Company*
5204 - 84 St., Edmonton, AB T6E 5N8
Tel: 780-440-6300
www.inews880.com
www.facebook.com/880edmonton, twitter.com/880edmonton
Syd Smith, Program Director, ssmith@630ched.com

Edmonton: **CJCA-AM (The Light)** (Freq: 930)
Owned by: Touch Canada Broadcasting Inc.*
5316 Calgary Trail NW, Edmonton, AB T6H 4J8
Tel: 780-466-4930, *Fax:* 780-469-5335
am930@shinefm.com
www.cjca.ca
www.facebook.com/AM930TheLight

High River: **CHRB-AM** (Freq: 1140)
Owned by: Golden West Broadcasting Ltd.*
11 - 5th Ave. SE, High River, AB T1V 1G2
Tel: 403-652-2472, *Toll-Free:* 866-652-2472
www.highriveronline.com
www.facebook.com/120693441344363, twitter.com/AM_1140

Lethbridge: **CRLC The Kodiak** (Freq: Online radio
station)
3000 College Dr. South, Lethbridge, AB T1K 1L6
Tel: 403-320-3354
news@lethbridgecampusmedia.ca
lethbridgecampusmedia.ca
twitter.com/CRLCTheKodiak
Ray Burgess, Station Manager

Wetaskiwin: **CKJR-AM** (Freq: 1440)
Owned by: Stingray Group Inc.*
5214A - 50th Ave., Wetaskiwin, AB T9A 0S8
Tel: 780-352-0144, *Fax:* 780-352-5656
www.w1440.com
Larry Donohue, Program Director, 780-490-2487,
ldonohue@newcap.com
Kelly Walter, Program Director, 780-437-9209,
kwalter@newcap.ca

---

* For details on this company see listing in Major Broadcasting Companies section; † French language station

British Columbia

100 Mile House: **CKBX-AM (Country 840 AM)** (Freq: 840)
Owned by: Vista Radio Ltd.*
#3, 407 Alder Ave., 100 Mile House, BC V0K 2E0
www.mycariboonow.com
Gary Russell, Regional Manager, grussell@vistaradio.ca

Ashcroft: **CINL-AM (Radio NL)** (Freq: 1340)
Owned by: Stingray Group Inc.*
Ashcroft, BC
www.radionl.com

Burns Lake: **CFLD-AM (Moose FM)** (Freq: 760)
Owned by: Vista Radio Ltd.*
Burns Lake, BC
www.mybulkleylakesnow.com

Clearwater: **CHNL-AM-1 (Radio NL)** (Freq: 1400)
Owned by: Stingray Group Inc.*
Clearwater, BC
www.radionl.com

Dawson Creek: **CJDC-AM** (Freq: 890)
Owned by: Bell Media Inc.*
901 - 102 Ave., Dawson Creek, BC V1G 2B6
Tel: 250-782-3341
www.iheartradio.ca/cjdc-890
www.facebook.com/196127377070136
Terry Shepherd, General Manager,
terry.shepherd@bellmedia.ca

Elkford: **CJEV-AM (Mountain Radio)** (Freq: 1340)
Owned by: CJPR-FM
Elkford, BC
Tel: 403-562-2806, *Fax:* 403-562-8114
mountain.requests@newcap.ca
www.mountainradiofm.com

Fort St. James: **CIFJ-AM (Valley Country)** (Freq: 1480)
Owned by: CIVH-AM (Valley Country)
Fort St. James, BC
www.mynechakovalleynow.com

Fraser Lake: **CIFL-AM (Valley Country)** (Freq: 1450)
Owned by: CIVH-AM (Valley Country)
Fraser Lake, BC
www.mynechakovalleynow.com

Granisle: **CFBV-AM-2 (Moose FM)** (Freq: 1480)
Owned by: CFBV-AM (The Peak)
Granisle, BC
www.mybulkleylakesnow.com

Invermere: **CKIR-AM** (Freq: 870)
Owned by: CKXR-FM (EZ Rock)
Invermere, BC
salmonarm.myezrock.com

Kamloops: **CHNL-AM (Radio NL)** (Freq: 610)
Owned by: Stingray Group Inc.*
611 Lansdowne St., Kamloops, BC V2C 1Y6
Tel: 250-372-2292, *Fax:* 250-372-2293
info@radionl.com
www.radionl.com
www.facebook.com/radionlkamloops, twitter.com/RadioNLNews
Garth Buchko, General Manager, gbuchko@radionl.com

Kelowna: **CKFR-AM** (Freq: 1150)
Owned by: Bell Media Inc.*
435 Bernard Ave., Kelowna, BC V1Y 6N8
Tel: 250-860-8600
news@am1150.ca
www.iheartradio.ca/am-1150
www.facebook.com/AM1150, twitter.com/am1150
Ken Kilcullen, General Manager, ken.kilcullen@bellmedia.ca

Merritt: **CJNL-AM (Radio NL)** (Freq: 1230)
Owned by: Stingray Group Inc.*
Merritt, BC
www.radionl.com

Osoyoos: **CJOR-AM (EZ Rock)** (Freq: 1240)
Owned by: Bell Media Inc.*
#203, 8309 Main St., Osoyoos, BC V0H 1V0
Tel: 250-495-7226
osoyoos.myezrock.com
www.facebook.com/EZRockOsoyoos, twitter.com/ezrockosoyoos
Janet Burley, General Manager & Manager, Sales,
janet.burley@bellmedia.ca

Penticton: **CKOR-AM (EZ Rock)** (Freq: 800)
Owned by: Bell Media Inc.*
33 Carmi Ave., Penticton, BC V2A 3G4
Tel: 250-492-2800
www.iheartradio.ca/ez-rock/ez-rock-penticton
www.facebook.com/EZRock800, twitter.com/ezrockpenticton
Mark Burley, Program Director, mark.burley@bellmedia.ca
Janet Burley, General Manager/Sales Manager,
janet.burley@bellmedia.ca

Port Hardy: **CFNI-AM (1240 Coast AM)** (Freq: 1240)
Owned by: Vista Radio Ltd.*
7035 A Market St., Port Hardy, BC V0N 2P0
Tel: 250-949-6500
www.mytriportnow.com
www.facebook.com/theport1240, twitter.com/ThePort1240

Richmond: **CHMB-AM** (Freq: 1320)
Owned by: Mainstream Broadcasting Corporation*
#150, 13571 Commerce Pkwy., Richmond, BC V6V 2R2
Tel: 604-263-1320, *Fax:* 604-261-0310
adm@am1320.com
am1320.com
www.youtube.com/user/AM1320CHMB
www.facebook.com/am1320, twitter.com/AM1320chmb
Raymond Chow, Program Director,
raymondchow@am1320.com

Richmond: **CISL-AM** (Freq: 650)
Owned by: Stingray Group Inc.*
#20, 11151 Horseshoe Way, Richmond, BC V7A 4S5
Tel: 604-241-2100, *Fax:* 604-272-0917
www.cisl650.com
www.facebook.com/cisl650, twitter.com/CISL650
Sherri Pierce, Station Manager, spierce@newcap.ca

Richmond: **CJVB-AM** (Freq: 1470)
Owned by: Fairchild Radio Group Ltd.*
Aberdeen Centre, #2090, 4151 Hazelbridge Way, Richmond, BC V6X 4J7
Tel: 604-295-1234, *Fax:* 604-295-1201
sales@am1470.com
www.am1470.com
www.facebook.com/am1470fm961
Other information: News, Email: news@am1470.com

Smithers: **CFBV-AM (Moose FM)** (Freq: 870)
Owned by: Vista Radio Ltd.*
1139 Queen St., Smithers, BC V0J 2N0
Tel: 250-847-2521, *Fax:* 250-847-9411
www.mybulkleylakesnow.com
Alissa Angel, Sales Manager, aangel@vistaradio.ca

Terrace: **CFTK-AM (EZ Rock)** (Freq: 590)
Owned by: Bell Media Inc.*
4625 Lazelle Ave., Terrace, BC V8G 1S4
Tel: 250-635-6316, *Toll-Free:* 888-556-8742
www.iheartradio.ca/ez-rock/ez-rock-terrace
www.facebook.com/NorthEZRock, twitter.com/EZRockNorth
Brian Langston, General Manager, brian.langston@bellmedia.ca

Vancouver: **CBU** (Freq: 690)
Owned by: Canadian Broadcasting Corporation*
PO Box 4600, Vancouver, BC V6B 4A2
Tel: 604-662-6000
www.cbc.ca/bc

Vancouver: **CFTE-AM** (Freq: 1410)
Owned by: Bell Media Radio*
#500, 969 Robson St., Vancouver, BC V6Z 1X5
Tel: 604-871-9000, *Fax:* 604-871-2901
programming@tsn1040.ca
www.tsn.ca/radio/vancouver-1040-i-1410
www.facebook.com/teamradiovancouver, twitter.com/TEAM1040

Vancouver: **CHMJ-AM (AM 730)** (Freq: 730)
Owned by: Corus Radio Company*
#2000, 700 West Georgia St., Vancouver, BC V7Y 1K9
Tel: 604-681-7511, *Fax:* 604-331-2722
www.am730.ca
www.facebook.com/am730traffic, twitter.com/am730traffic
Larry Gifford, Program Director

Vancouver: **CKNW-AM (News Talk 980)** (Freq: 980)
Owned by: Corus Radio Company*
#2000, 700 West Georgia St., Vancouver, BC V7Y 1K9
Tel: 604-331-2711, *Fax:* 604-331-2722
Toll-Free: 877-399-9898
www.cknw.com
www.instagram.com/cknw980, www.facebook.com/cknw980,
twitter.com/cknw
Larry Gifford, Program Director

Vancouver: **CKST-AM** (Freq: 1040)
Owned by: Bell Media Radio*
#500, 969 Robson St., Vancouver, BC V6Z 1X5
Tel: 604-871-9000, *Fax:* 604-871-2901
programming@tsn1040.ca
www.tsn.ca/radio/vancouver-1040-i-1410
www.facebook.com/TSNRadioVancouver, twitter.com/TSN1040

Vancouver: **CKWX-AM (News 1130)** (Freq: 1130)
Owned by: Rogers Media Inc.*
2440 Ash St., Vancouver, BC V5Z 4J6
Tel: 604-873-2599, *Fax:* 604-873-0877
www.news1130.com
www.facebook.com/news1130, twitter.com/news1130
Diana Davies, Manager, Sales

Victoria: **CFAX-AM** (Freq: 1070)
Owned by: Bell Media Radio*
1420 Broad St., Victoria, BC V8W 2B1
Tel: 250-386-1070
cfaxnews@cfax1070.com
www.iheartradio.ca/cfax-1070
www.facebook.com/cfax1070, twitter.com/cfax1070

Williams Lake: **CKWL-AM (The Wolf)** (Freq: 570)
Owned by: Vista Radio Ltd.*
83 South First Ave., Williams Lake, BC V2G 1H4
Tel: 250-392-6551, *Fax:* 250-392-4142
www.thewolfonline.ca
www.facebook.com/164187966948000

Manitoba

Boissevain: **CJRB-AM** (Freq: 1220)
Owned by: Golden West Broadcasting Ltd.*
PO Box 1220, 420 South Railway, Boissevain, MB R0K 0E0
Tel: 204-534-6000, *Fax:* 888-765-7039
cjrb@goldenwestradio.com
www.discoverwestman.com/cjrb

Brandon: **CKLQ-AM** (Freq: 880)
Owned by: Westman Communications Group*
624 - 14th St. East, Brandon, MB R7A 7E1
Tel: 204-726-8888, *Toll-Free:* 888-221-0880
qcountry@cklq.mb.ca
qcountryfm.ca
www.youtube.com/user/880CKLQ,
www.facebook.com/cklq.qcountry, twitter.com/QCountry91_5

Cross Lake: **CFNC-AM** (Freq: 1490)
PO Box 129, Cross Lake, MB R0B 0J0
Tel: 204-676-2331, *Fax:* 204-676-2911

Dauphin: **CKDM-AM** (Freq: 730)
Owned by: Dauphin Broadcasting Co. Ltd.*
1735 Main St. South, Dauphin, MB R7N 2V4
Tel: 204-638-3230, *Fax:* 204-638-8257
Toll-Free: 866-997-2536
ckdm.news@730ckdm.ca
730ckdm.ca
www.facebook.com/730CKDM
Allan Truman, General Manager, allan.truman@730ckdm.com

Portage la Prairie: **CFRY-AM** (Freq: 920)
Owned by: Golden West Broadcasting Ltd.*
PO Box 130, 2390 Sisson Dr., Portage la Prairie, MB R1N 3B2
Tel: 204-239-5111, *Toll-Free:* 866-239-5111
www.portageonline.com
twitter.com/cfry_portage

Steinbach: **CHSM-AM** (Freq: 1250)
Owned by: Golden West Broadcasting Ltd.*
#105, 32 Brandt St., Steinbach, MB R5G 2J7
Tel: 204-326-3737, *Toll-Free:* 866-326-3737
www.steinbachonline.com
www.facebook.com/153028841424047, twitter.com/am1250radio

Winkler: **CFAM-AM** (Freq: 950)
Owned by: Golden West Broadcasting Ltd.*
PO Box 399, 1st St., 277-A, Winkler, MB R6W 4A6
Tel: 204-324-6464, *Toll-Free:* 800-355-7065
www.pembinavalleyonline.com/radio/cfam
www.facebook.com/243829332352635

Winnipeg: **CBW** (Freq: 990)
Owned by: Canadian Broadcasting Corporation*
541 Portage Ave., Winnipeg, MB R3B 2G1
Tel: 204-788-3222
www.cbc.ca/manitoba
Gabriela Kilmes, Manager, Communications, Marketing & Brand,
gabriela.klimes@cbc.ca

* For details on this company see listing in Major Broadcasting Companies section; † French language station

Winnipeg: CFRW-AM (Freq: 1290)
Owned by: Bell Media Radio*
1445 Pembina Hwy., Winnipeg, MB R3T 5C2
Tel: 204-780-1290
live@tsn1290.ca
www.tsn.ca/Winnipeg
www.facebook.com/TSN1290, twitter.com/TSN1290Radio
Chris Brooke, Program Director

Winnipeg: CHFC (Freq: 1230)
Owned by: Canadian Broadcasting Corporation*
c/o CBC Winnipeg, 541 Portage Ave., Winnipeg, MB R3B 2G1
Tel: 204-788-3205
Other information: TTY: 866-220-6045

Winnipeg: CJOB-AM (AM 680) (Freq: 680)
Owned by: Corus Radio Company*
#200, 1440 Jack Blick Ave., Winnipeg, MB R3G 0L4
Tel: 204-786-2471
www.cjob.com
www.facebook.com/680cjob, twitter.com/680cjob
Kim Lawson, Executive Produccer
Steve Dubois, General Sales Manager

Winnipeg: CKJS-AM (Freq: 810)
Owned by: Evanov Communications Inc.*
520 Corydon Ave., Winnipeg, MB R3L 0P1
Tel: 204-477-1221
ckjs.com

New Brunswick

Campbellton: CKNB-AM (Freq: 950)
Owned by: Maritime Broadcasting System*
74 Water St., Campbellton, NB E3N 1B1
Tel: 506-753-4415, Fax: 506-789-9505
cknb@mbsradio.com
95cknb.ca
www.facebook.com/95CKNB

Fredericton: CKHJ-AM (KHJ) (Freq: 1260)
Owned by: Bell Media Inc.*
206 Rookwood Ave., Fredericton, NB E3B 2M2
Tel: 506-454-2444
www.iheartradio.ca/kh
www.instagram.com/countrykhj,
www.facebook.com/CountryKHJ, twitter.com/CountryKHJ

Saint John: CFBC-AM (Freq: 930)
Owned by: Maritime Broadcasting System*
226 Union St., Saint John, NB E2L 1B1
Tel: 506-658-5100
www.cfbc.am

Sussex: CJCW-AM (Freq: 590)
Owned by: Maritime Broadcasting System*
PO Box 5900, Sussex, NB E0E 1P0
Tel: 506-432-2529, Fax: 506-433-4900
590cjcw.com
www.facebook.com/590CJCW

Newfoundland & Labrador

Baie Verte: CKIM (VOCM) (Freq: 1240)
Owned by: Stingray Group Inc.*
Baie Verte, NL
Tel: 709-489-2192, Fax: 709-489-8626
www.vocm.com
twitter.com/vocmnews

Clarenville: CKVO-AM (VOCM) (Freq: 710)
Owned by: Stingray Group Inc.*
Clarenville, NL
Tel: 709-466-1399, Fax: 709-596-8626
www.vocm.com
Mike Murphy, General Manager, mmurphy@newcap.ca
Mike Campbell, Program Director, mcampbell@newcap.ca

Corner Brook: CFCB-AM (Freq: 570)
Owned by: Stingray Group Inc.*
345 O'Connell Dr., Corner Brook, NL A2H 7V3
Tel: 709-634-4570, Fax: 709-634-4081
onair@cfcbradio.com
www.cfcbradio.com
www.facebook.com/108849352471861, twitter.com/CFCBRadio
Dave Hillier, Station Manager, dhillier@newcap.ca

Gander: CBG-AM (Freq: 1400)
Owned by: Canadian Broadcasting Corporation*
98 Sullivan Ave., Gander, NL A1V 1S2
Tel: 709-256-4311, Fax: 709-651-2021
www.cbc.ca/nl

Gander: CKGA (VOCM) (Freq: 650)
Owned by: Stingray Group Inc.*
PO Box 650, Gander, NL A1B 1X2
Tel: 709-651-3650, Fax: 709-651-2542
www.vocm.com
David Hillier, Station Manager, dhillier@newcap.ca
Dean Clarke, Program Director, dean.clarke@vocm.com

Grand Falls-Windsor: CBT-AM (Freq: 540)
Owned by: Canadian Broadcasting Corporation*
2 Harris Ave., Grand Falls-Windsor, NL A2A 2Y2
Tel: 709-489-2102, Fax: 709-489-1055
centralmorning@cbc.ca
www.cbc.ca/nl
Denise Wilson, Senior Managing Director, Atlantic Canada,
denise.wilson@cbc.ca
Peter Gullage, Executive Producer, Newfoundland & Labrador,
peter.gullage@cbc.ca
Nadine Antle, Regional Manager, Communications, Marketing &
Brand, 902-420-4223, Nadine.Antle@cbc.ca

Grand Falls-Windsor: CKCM-VOCM (Freq: 620)
Owned by: Stingray Group Inc.*
35A Grenfell Heights, Grand Falls-Windsor, NL A2A 2K2
Tel: 709-489-2192, Fax: 709-489-8626
www.vocm.com
twitter.com/vocmnews
David Hillier, Contact

Marystown: CHCM-AM (VOCM) (Freq: 740)
Owned by: Stingray Group Inc.*
PO Box 560, Marystown, NL A0E 2M0
Tel: 709-279-2560, Fax: 709-279-2800
www.vocm.com
Russell Murphy, Station Manager, rmurphy@newcap.ca

Mount Pearl: VOAR (Freq: 1210)
1041 Topsail Rd., Mount Pearl, NL A1N 5E9
Tel: 709-745-8627, Toll-Free: 888-740-8627
voar@voar.org
www.voar.org
www.flickr.com/photos/69531297@N02,
www.facebook.com/VOARRadio, twitter.com/voarRadio
Sherry Griffin, Station Manager

Port aux Basques: CFGN-AM (Freq: 1230)
Owned by: Stingray Group Inc.*
Port aux Basques, NL A2N 1C6
Tel: 709-643-2191, Fax: 709-643-5025
cfsx@vocm.com
www.cfsxradio.com
Katherine Hogan, Station Manager, khogan@newcap.ca

St. John's: CBN-AM (Freq: 640)
Owned by: Canadian Broadcasting Corporation*
PO Box 12010 A, St. John's, NL A1B 3T8
Tel: 709-576-5000, Fax: 709-576-5234
www.cbc.ca/nl
Other information: Phone, CBC Radio One Newsroom:
709-576-5225
Denise Wilson, Senior Managing Director, Atlantic Canada,
denise.wilson@cbc.ca
Peter Gullage, Executive Producer, Newfoundland & Labrador,
peter.gullage@cbc.ca
Nadine Antle, Regional Manager, Communications, Marketing &
Brand, 902-420-4223, Nadine.Antle@cbc.ca

St. John's: CBY
Owned by: Canadian Broadcasting Corporation*
PO Box 12010 A, St. John's, NL A1B 3T8
Tel: 709-576-5225, Fax: 709-576-5234
radionews@cbc.ca
www.cbc.ca/nl
www.facebook.com/cbcnl, twitter.com/CBCNL

St. John's: CJYQ (Freq: 930)
Owned by: Stingray Group Inc.*
PO Box 8590, 391 Kenmount Rd, St. John's, NL A1B 3P5
Tel: 709-726-5590, Fax: 709-726-4633
email@930kixxcountry.ca
www.930kixxcountry.ca
www.facebook.com/930kixxcountry, twitter.com/930kixxcountry
Mike Murphy, Station Manager, mmurphy@newcap.ca
Mike Campbell, Program Director, mcampbell@newcap.ca

St. John's: VOCM-AM (Freq: 590)
Owned by: Stingray Group Inc.*
PO Box 8-590, 391 Kenmount Rd., St. John's, NL A1B 3P5
Tel: 709-726-5590, Fax: 709-726-4633
www.vocm.com
www.facebook.com/590VOCM, twitter.com/590vocm
Mike Murphy, Station Manager, mmurphy@newcap.ca
Mike Campbell, Program Director, mcampbell@newcap.ca

St. John's: VOWR (Freq: 800)
PO Box 26006, St. John's, NL A1E 0A5
Tel: 709-579-9233
vowr@vowr.org
www.vowr.org

Stephenville: CFSX-AM (Freq: 870)
VOCM Affiliate
Owned by: Stingray Group Inc.*
60 West St., Stephenville, NL A2N 1C6
Tel: 709-643-2191, Fax: 709-643-5025
cfsx@vocm.com
www.cfsxradio.com
www.facebook.com/109059929132227, twitter.com/cfsxradio
Katherine Hogan, Sales Manager, 709-214-0258,
khogan@newcap.ca
Dave Hillier, Station Manager, dhillier@newcap.ca

Northwest Territories

Inuvik: CHAK (Freq: 860)
Owned by: Canadian Broadcasting Corporation*
100 Mackenzie Rd., Inuvik, NT X0E 0T0
Tel: 867-920-5400
www.cbc.ca/north
Kerry Fraser, Communications Manager

Yellowknife: CFYK (Freq: 1340)
Owned by: Canadian Broadcasting Corporation*
PO Box 160, Yellowknife, NT X1A 2N2
Tel: 867-920-5400
www.cbc.ca/north

Nova Scotia

Digby: CKDY-AM (Freq: 1420)
Owned by: CKEN-FM
PO Box 1420, 53 Sydney St., Digby, NS B0V 1A0
Tel: 902-245-2111, Fax: 902-245-9720
www.avrnetwork.com
www.facebook.com/avrnetwork

Middleton: CKAD-AM (Freq: 1350)
Owned by: CKEN-FM
PO Box 550, 10 Bridge St., Middleton, NS B0S 1P0
Tel: 902-825-3429, Fax: 902-825-6009
www.avrnetwork.com
www.facebook.com/avrnetwork

Sydney: CBI (Freq: 1140)
Owned by: Canadian Broadcasting Corporation*
500 George St., Sydney, NS B1P 1K6
Tel: 902-539-5050, Fax: 902-539-1562
www.cbc.ca
Denise Wilson, Senior Managing Director, Atlantic Canada,
denise.wilson@cbc.ca

Sydney: CJCB-AM (Freq: 1270)
Owned by: Maritime Broadcasting System*
318 Charlotte St., Sydney, NS B1P 1C8
Tel: 902-564-5596, Fax: 902-564-1873
www.cjcbradio.com
www.facebook.com/1270cjcb
Other information: News & Sports Phone: 902-539-3000

Windsor: CFAB-AM (Freq: 1450)
Owned by: Maritime Broadcasting System*
PO Box 278, 169A Water St., Windsor, NS B0N 2T0
Tel: 902-798-2111, Fax: 902-798-8140
www.avrnetwork.com
www.facebook.com/avrnetwork

Nunavut

Iqaluit: CFFB (Freq: 1230)
Owned by: Canadian Broadcasting Corporation*
PO Box 490, Iqaluit, NU X0A 0H0
Tel: 867-979-6100
cbc.ca/north
Kerry Fraser, Communications Manager

* For details on this company see listing in Major Broadcasting Companies section; † French language station

Ontario

Belleville: **CJBQ-AM** (Freq: 800)
Owned by: Quinte Broadcasting Co. Ltd.*
PO Box 488, 10 Front St. South, Belleville, ON K8N 5B2
Tel: 613-969-5555, *Fax:* 613-969-8122
www.cjbq.com
www.facebook.com/800CJBQ
John Spitters, News Director, johnspitters@rock107.ca
Jack Miller, Sports Director, jack@mix97.com

Brantford: **CKPC-AM** (Freq: 1380)
Owned by: Evanov Communications Inc.*
571 West St., Brantford, ON N3R 7C5
Tel: 519-759-1000, *Fax:* 519-753-1470
info@arisebrantford.com
arise1380.com
www.facebook.com/Arise1380, twitter.com/Arise1380

Guelph: **CJOY-AM** (Freq: 1460)
Owned by: 591989 B.C. Ltd.*
75 Speedvale Ave. East, Guelph, ON N1E 6M3
Tel: 519-824-7000
cjoy.com
www.facebook.com/1460CJOY, twitter.com/CJOYradio

Hamilton: **CHAM-AM (Funny 820)** (Freq: 820)
Owned by: Bell Media Inc.*
#401, 883 Upper Wentworth St., Hamilton, ON L9A 4Y6
Tel: 905-574-1150, *Fax:* 905-575-6429
www.iheartradio.ca/funny/funny-820
www.facebook.com/funny820, twitter.com/Funny820
Bob Harris, General Manager, Bell Radio Hamilton,
bob.harris@bellmedia.ca
Mike Nabuurs, Brand Director & Host,
mike.nabuurs@bellmedia.ca

Hamilton: **CHML-AM (AM900)** (Freq: 900)
Owned by: Corus Radio Company*
875 Main St. West, Hamilton, ON L8S 4R1
Tel: 905-521-9900, *Fax:* 905-540-2452
news@900chml.com
www.900chml.com
www.facebook.com/am900chml, twitter.com/am900chml
Jeff Storey, Program Director, jstorey@900chml.com

Hamilton: **TSN 1150** (Freq: 1150)
Owned by: Bell Media Inc.*
#401, 883 Upper Wentworth St., Hamilton, ON L9A 4Y6
Tel: 905-574-1150, *Fax:* 905-575-6429
www.tsn.ca/radio/hamilton-1150
www.facebook.com/1150CKOC, twitter.com/TSN1150
Bob Harris, General Manager, Bell Radio Hamilton,
bob.harris@bellmedia.ca

Kitchener: **CKGL-AM (570 News)** (Freq: 570)
Owned by: Rogers Media Inc.*
230 The Boardwalk, 2nd Floor, Kitchener, ON N2N 0B1
Tel: 519-743-2611
news570@rogers.com
www.570news.com
www.facebook.com/570News, twitter.com/570News

London: **CFPL-AM (AM980)** (Freq: 980)
Owned by: Corus Radio Company*
#222, 380 Wellington St., London, ON N6A 5B5
Tel: 519-931-6000
news@am980.ca
www.am980.ca
www.facebook.com/amn980london, twitter.com/am980News
Trudy Shaw, Program Director, tshaw@am980.ca

London: **CJBK-AM (Newstalk 1290)** (Freq: 1290)
Owned by: Bell Media Inc.*
743 Wellington Rd. South, London, ON N6C 4R5
Tel: 519-686-2525
www.iheartradio.ca/newstalk-1290-cjbk
www.facebook.com/1290cjbk, twitter.com/CJBK
Don Mumford, General Manager, don.mumford@bellmedia.ca

London: **CKSL-AM (Funny 1410)** (Freq: 1410)
Owned by: Bell Media Inc.*
743 Wellington Rd. South, London, ON N6C 4R5
Tel: 519-686-2525
www.iheartradio.ca/funny/funny-1410
www.facebook.com/Funny1410, twitter.com/funny1410am
Don Mumford, General Manager, don.mumford@bellmedia.ca

Markham: **CHKT-AM** (Freq: 1430)
Owned by: Fairchild Radio Group Ltd.*
#26-29, 151 Esna Park Dr., Markham, ON L3R 3B1
Tel: 905-415-6265, *Fax:* 905-415-6292
www.am1430.com

North Bay: **CKAT-AM (Country 600)** (Freq: 600)
Owned by: Rogers Media Inc.*
273 Main St. East, North Bay, ON P1B 1B2
Tel: 705-474-2000
www.country600.com
www.facebook.com/600ckat, twitter.com/country600ckat

Oakville: **CJMR-AM** (Freq: 1320)
284 Church St., Oakville, ON L6J 7N2
Tel: 905-271-1320, *Fax:* 905-845-9171
contact@cjmr1320.ca
www.cjmr1320.ca
twitter.com/CJMR1320

Oakville: **CJYE-AM** (Freq: 1250)
284 Church St., Oakville, ON L6J 7N2
Tel: 905-845-2821, *Fax:* 905-842-1250
contact@joy1250.ca
www.joy1250.ca
www.facebook.com/joy1250, twitter.com/JOY1250
Michael H. Caine, Founder

Oshawa: **CKDO-AM** (Freq: 1580)
Owned by: Durham Radio Inc.*
#207, 1200 Airport Blvd., Oshawa, ON L1J 8P5
Tel: 905-571-0949, *Fax:* 905-571-1150
www.ckdo.ca
www.facebook.com/ckdoradio, twitter.com/CKDORadio
Steve Kassay, Vice-President, Programming, steve@kx96.fm

Ottawa: **CFGO-AM** (Freq: 1200)
Owned by: Bell Media Radio*
87 George St., Ottawa, ON K1N 9H7
Tel: 613-750-1200, *Fax:* 613-739-4040
Toll-Free: 877-670-1200
webmaster@tsn1200.ca
www.tsn1200.ca
www.facebook.com/TSN1200, twitter.com/TSN1200
John Rodenburg, Sports Director,
John.Rodenburg@bellmedia.ca

Ottawa: **CFRA-AM** (Freq: 580)
Owned by: Bell Media Radio*
87 George St., Ottawa, ON K1N 9H7
Tel: 613-789-2486, *Toll-Free:* 800-580-2372
www.iheartradio.ca/580-cfra
www.facebook.com/580CFRA, twitter.com/CFRAOttawa
Steve Winogron, Program Director,
Steve.Winogron@bellmedia.ca

Ottawa: **CIWW-AM (1310 News)** (Freq: 1310)
Owned by: Rogers Media Inc.*
2001 Thurston Dr., Ottawa, ON K1G 6C9
Tel: 613-736-2001
tips1310@rogers.com
www.1310news.com
www.facebook.com/1310news, twitter.com/1310news
Glennis Lane, Senior Editor, glennis.lane@rci.rogers.com

Owen Sound: **CFOS-AM** (Freq: 560)
Owned by: Bayshore Broadcasting Corporation*
PO Box 270, 270 - 9th St. East, Owen Sound, ON N4K 5P5
Tel: 519-376-2030, *Fax:* 519-371-4242
info@bayshorebroadcasting.ca
www.560cfos.ca
www.facebook.com/560cfos

Sarnia: **CHOK-AM** (Freq: 1070)
Owned by: Blackburn Radio Inc.*
1415 London Rd., Sarnia, ON N7S 1P6
Tel: 519-542-5500, *Toll-Free:* 866-464-1070
chok.com
www.youtube.com/user/Country1039,
www.facebook.com/chokradio, twitter.com/CHOKsarnia

St Catharines: **CKTB-AM (Newstalk 610)** (Freq: 610)
Owned by: Bell Media Inc.*
12 Yates St., St Catharines, ON L2R 5R2
Tel: 905-684-1174, *Toll-Free:* 877-610-2582
newsroom@610cktb.com
www.iheartradio.ca/610cktb
www.facebook.com/610CKTB, twitter.com/610CKTB
Bob Harris, General Manager, bob.harris@bellmedia.ca

Timmins: **CHIM-AM** (Freq: 1710)
226 Delnite Rd., Timmins, ON P4N 7C2
Tel: 705-264-2150
info@chimfm.com
www.chimfm.com
Roger de Brabant, General Manager, roger@chimfm.com

Toronto: **CFMJ-AM (640 Toronto)** (Freq: 640)
Owned by: Corus Radio Company*
Corus Quay, 25 Dockside Dr., Toronto, ON M5A 0B5
Tel: 416-479-7000
www.640toronto.com
www.facebook.com/640toronto, twitter.com/am640
Nathan Smith, Brand Director

Toronto: **CFRB-AM (Newstalk 1010)** (Freq: 1010)
Owned by: Bell Media Inc.*
250 Richmond St. West, 3rd Fl., Toronto, ON M5V 1W4
Tel: 416-384-8000
news@newstalk1010.com
www.iheartradio.ca/newstalk-1010
www.facebook.com/newstalk1010, twitter.com/newstalk1010
Mike Bendixen, Program Director,
mike.bendixen@newstalk1010.com

Toronto: **CFTR-AM (680 News)** (Freq: 680)
Owned by: Rogers Media Inc.*
1 Ted Rogers Way, Toronto, ON M4Y 3B7
Tel: 416-413-3930
680info@680news.com
www.680news.com
www.facebook.com/680News, twitter.com/680news

Toronto: **CFZM-AM** (Freq: 740)
Owned by: ZoomerMedia Ltd.*
70 Jefferson Ave., Toronto, ON M6K 1Y4
Tel: 416-544-0740, *Toll-Free:* 866-740-4740
zoomerradio.ca
www.facebook.com/zoomerradio, twitter.com/zoomerradio

Toronto: **CHIN-AM** (Freq: 1540)
Owned by: Radio 1540 Ltd.*
622 College St., 4th Fl., Toronto, ON M6G 1B6
Tel: 416-870-1540, *Fax:* 416-531-5274
info@chinradio.com
www.chinradio.com
www.facebook.com/chinradiocanada,
twitter.com/chinradiocanada
Other information: Business Office: 416-531-9991

Toronto: **CHUM-AM (TSN Radio 1050)** (Freq: 1050)
Owned by: Bell Media Radio*
299 Queen St. West, Toronto, ON M5V 2Z5
Tel: 416-870-1050, *Toll-Free:* 855-591-6876
live@tsn1050.ca
www.tsn.ca/toronto
www.facebook.com/TSN1050, twitter.com/TSN1050Radio

Toronto: **CIAO-AM** (Freq: 530)
Owned by: Evanov Communications Inc.*
5312 Dundas St. West, Toronto, ON M9B 1B3
Tel: 416-213-1035
info@evanovradio.com
am530.ca

Toronto: **CJCL-AM (Sportsnet 590 The Fan)** (Freq: 590)
Owned by: Rogers Media Inc.*
1 Ted Rogers Way, Toronto, ON M4Y 3B7
Tel: 416-935-0590
contact@sportsnet590.ca
www.sportsnet.ca/590
www.facebook.com/fan590, twitter.com/fan590

Toronto: **S@Y Radio** (Freq: closed circuit)
Owned by: Seneca College*
70 The Pond Rd., Toronto, ON M3J 3M6
Tel: 416-491-5050
info@sayradio.ca
www.sayradio.ca
www.facebook.com/senecaradio, twitter.com/sayradio

Toronto: **The Scope** (Freq: 1280 (online))
#201, 55 Gould St., Toronto, ON M5B 1E9
Tel: 416-904-6889
admin@thescopeatryerson.ca
www.thescopeatryerson.ca
www.facebook.com/289318544428603,
twitter.com/ScopeatRyerson
Jacky Tuinstra Harrison, Station Manager

---

* For details on this company see listing in Major Broadcasting Companies section; † French language station

†*Windsor:* **CBEF** (Freq: 1550)
Détenteur: **Canadian Broadcasting Corporation***
825, promenade Riverside Ouest, Windsor, ON N9A 5K9
Tél: 519-255-3411, *Téléc:* 519-255-3573
ici.radio-canada.ca

Windsor: **CKLW-AM** (Freq: 800)
Owned by: Bell Media Radio*
1640 Ouellette Ave., Windsor, ON N8X 1L1
Tel: 519-258-8888
newscentre@am800cklw.com
www.iheartradio.ca/am800
www.instagram.com/am800cklw, www.facebook.com/am800,
twitter.com/am800cklw
Eric Proksch, Vice President/General Manager,
Eric.Proksch@bellmedia.ca
Keith Chinnery, Program Director, Keith.Chinnery@bellmedia.ca

Windsor: **CKWW-AM** (Freq: 580)
Owned by: Bell Media Radio*
1640 Ouellette Ave., Windsor, ON N8X 1L1
Tel: 519-258-8888
info@am580radio.com
www.iheartradio.ca/am-580
www.facebook.com/AM580Radio, twitter.com/AM580
Other information: Detroit Switchboard: 888-902-6222

Wingham: **CKNX-AM** (Freq: 920)
Owned by: Blackburn Radio Inc.*
PO Box 300, 215 Carling Terrace, Wingham, ON N0G 2W0
Tel: 519-357-1310, *Fax:* 519-357-1897
Toll-Free: 800-265-3030
cknx.ca
www.facebook.com/CKNXAM920, twitter.com/CKNXRadio

Québec

†*Laval:* **CJLV-AM** (Radio Laval) (Freq: 1570)
Laval, QC
www.1570.ca

†*Montréal:* **CFMB-AM** (Freq: 1280)
Détenteur: **Evanov Communications Inc.***
5877, av Papineau, Montréal, QC H2G 2W3
Tél: 514-790-0251, *Téléc:* 514-483-1362
info@cfmb.ca
cfmb.ca
www.facebook.com/cfmb1280mtl

Montréal: **CJAD-AM** (Freq: 800)
Owned by: Bell Media Inc.*
1717 René-Lévesque Blvd. East, Montréal, QC H2L 4T9
Tel: 514-989-2523
www.iheartradio.ca/cjad
www.facebook.com/cjad800, twitter.com/CJAD800
Chris Bury, Contact, Programming, cbury@cjad.com

Montréal: **CJLO-AM** (Freq: closed circuit)
Owned by: Concordia Student Broadcasting Corporation
7141, rue Sherbrooke ouest, #CC-430, Montréal, QC H4B 1R6
Tel: 514-848-8663, *Fax:* 514-848-7450
feedback@cjlo.com
www.cjlo.com
www.facebook.com/cjlo1690am, twitter.com/CJLO1690AM
Michael Sallot, Station Manager, manager@cjlo.com

†*Montréal:* **CJWI-AM** (Freq: 1410)
3390, boul Crémazie Est, Montréal, QC H2A 1A4
Tél: 514-790-2726, *Téléc:* 514-287-3299
info@cpam1610.com
www.cpam1610.com

†*Montréal:* **CKAC-AM** (Radio Circulation 730) (Freq: 730)
Détenteur: **Cogeco Media Inc.***
Place Bonaventure, #1100, 800, rue de la Gauchetière Ouest, Montréal, QC H5A 1M1
Tél: 514-787-0730
www.radiocirculation.net

Montréal: **CKGM-AM** (Freq: 690)
Owned by: Bell Media Radio*
1717, boul Rene-Levesque est, Montréal, QC H2L 4T9
Tel: 514-931-4487
www.tsn.ca/Montreal
www.facebook.com/TSN690Montreal, twitter.com/TSN690
Chris Bury, Program Director

†*Rimouski:* **CAJT-AM** (Radio étudiante) (Freq: closed circuit)
Cégep de Rimouski, 60, rue de l'Évêché ouest, Rimouski, QC G5L 4H6
Tél: 418-723-1880, *Téléc:* 418-724-4961
Ligne sans frais: 800-463-0617
information.scolaire@cegep-rimouski.qc.ca
www4.cegep-rimouski.qc.ca
www.facebook.com/RadioCajt

Saskatchewan

Estevan: **CJSL-AM** (Freq: 1280)
Owned by: Golden West Broadcasting Ltd.*
#200, 1236 - 5th St., Estevan, SK S4A 0Z6
Tel: 306-634-1280, *Toll-Free:* 800-824-0743
discoverestevan.com
www.facebook.com/168180086627809

†*Gravelbourg:* **CBKF-1** (Freq: 690)
Détenteur: **CBKF-FM (Première Chaîne)**
Gravelbourg, SK

Kindersley: **CFYM-AM** (Freq: 1210)
Owned by: CJYM-AM
Kindersley, SK
Tel: 306-463-2692, *Toll-Free:* 866-463-2692
www.cjym.com

Melfort: **CKJH-AM** (Freq: 750)
Owned by: Jim Pattison Broadcast Group*
611 Main St. North, Melfort, SK S0E 1A0
Tel: 306-752-2587, *Fax:* 306-752-5932
info@yourtownnews.ca
www.ck750.com
twitter.com/CK750am

Moose Jaw: **CHAB-AM** (Freq: 800)
Owned by: Golden West Broadcasting Ltd.*
1704 Main St. North, Moose Jaw, SK S6J 1L4
Tel: 306-694-0800, *Toll-Free:* 800-820-1768
discovermoosejaw.com
www.facebook.com/800CHAB, twitter.com/800CHAB

North Battleford: **CJNB-AM** (1050 CJN) (Freq: 1050)
Owned by: Jim Pattison Broadcast Group*
1711 - 100th St., North Battleford, SK S9A 0W7
Tel: 306-445-2477
cjnbnews@jpbg.ca
www.cjnb.com
www.facebook.com/cjnbcjns
Karl Johnston, General Manager, karl.johnston@jpbg.ca

Prince Albert: **CKBI-AM** (900 CKBI) (Freq: 900)
Owned by: Jim Pattison Broadcast Group*
1316 Central Ave., Prince Albert, SK S6V 7R4
Tel: 306-763-7421
www.ckbi.com
www.facebook.com/900ckbi, twitter.com/ckbi
Karl Johnston, General Manager, karl.johnston@jpbg.ca

Regina: **CJME-AM** (Freq: 980)
Owned by: Rawlco Radio Ltd.*
#210, 2401 Saskatchewan Dr., Regina, SK S4P 4H8
Tel: 306-525-0000
reginanews@rawlco.com
www.cjme.com
www.facebook.com/980cjme, twitter.com/cjmenews

Regina: **CKRM-AM** (Freq: 620)
Owned by: Harvard Broadcasting Inc.*
1900 Rose St., Regina, SK S4P 0A9
Tel: 306-546-6200, *Fax:* 306-781-7338
Toll-Free: 866-767-0620
news@620ckrm.com
www.620ckrm.com
www.youtube.com/user/620ckrm, www.facebook.com/620ckrm,
twitter.com/620ckrm
Other information: News Room: 306-546-6298
Jason Huschi, General Manager,
jasonh@harvardbroadcasting.com
Grant Biebrick, Program Director,
gbiebrick@harvardbroadcasting.com

Rosetown: **CJYM-AM** (Freq: 1330)
Owned by: Golden West Broadcasting Ltd.*
PO Box 490, 208 Hwy. 4, Rosetown, SK S0L 2V0
Tel: 306-882-2686, *Toll-Free:* 800-667-5313
cjymnews@goldenwestradio.com
www.cjym.com

†*Saskatoon:* **CBKF-2** (Freq: 860)
Détenteur: **CBKF-FM (Première Chaîne)**
Saskatoon, SK

Saskatoon: **CJWW-AM** (Freq: 600)
Owned by: Saskatoon Media Group*
366 - 3rd Ave. South, Saskatoon, SK S7K 1M5
Tel: 306-244-1975
info@cjwwradio.com
www.cjwwradio.com
www.facebook.com/cjwwradio, twitter.com/600cjww

Saskatoon: **CKOM-AM** (Freq: 650)
Owned by: Rawlco Radio Ltd.*
715 Saskatchewan Cres. West, Saskatoon, SK S7M 5V7
Tel: 306-934-2222
ckomnews@rawlco.com
www.ckom.com
www.facebook.com/650ckom, twitter.com/ckomnews

Swift Current: **CJSN-AM** (Freq: 1490)
Owned by: Golden West Broadcasting Ltd.*
134 Central Ave. North, Swift Current, SK S9H 0L1
Tel: 306-773-4605, *Toll-Free:* 800-821-8073
cmr@goldenwestradio.com
www.swiftcurrentonline.com
www.facebook.com/CountryMusicRadio, twitter.com/CKSW_570

Swift Current: **CKSW-AM** (Freq: 570)
Owned by: Golden West Broadcasting Ltd.*
134 Central Ave. North, Swift Current, SK S9H 0L1
Tel: 306-773-4605, *Toll-Free:* 800-821-8073
cmr@goldenwestradio.com
www.swiftcurrentonline.com
www.facebook.com/CountryMusicRadio, twitter.com/CKSW_570

Weyburn: **CFSL-AM** (Freq: 1190)
Owned by: Golden West Broadcasting Ltd.*
305 Souris Ave., Weyburn, SK S4H 0C6
Tel: 306-848-1190
discoverweyburn.com
www.facebook.com/111247462239648,
twitter.com/AM1190Weyburn

Yorkton: **CJGX-AM** (Freq: 940)
Owned by: Harvard Broadcasting Inc.*
120 Smith St. East, Yorkton, SK S3N 3V3
Tel: 306-782-2256, *Fax:* 306-783-4994
ykt-reception@harvardbroadcasting.com
www.gx94radio.com
www.youtube.com/user/GX94radio,
www.facebook.com/GX94Radio, twitter.com/GX94Radio
Angie Norton, General Manager,
anorton@harvardbroadcasting.com

FM Radio Stations

Alberta

Airdrie: **CFIT-FM** (Air 106.1) (Freq: 106.1)
Owned by: Golden West Broadcasting Ltd.*
#30, 105 Main St. North, Airdrie, AB T4B 0R3
Tel: 403-217-1061, *Toll-Free:* 866-945-1061
air106@goldenwestradio.com
www.discoverairdrie.com
www.facebook.com/AIR1061, twitter.com/AIR1061FM

Athabasca: **CKBA-FM** (The River 94.1) (Freq: 94.1)
Owned by: Stingray Group Inc.*
#1, 4902 - 49th St., Athabasca, AB T9S 1C2
Tel: 780-675-5301, *Fax:* 780-675-4938
www.941theriver.ca
www.facebook.com/941theriver, twitter.com/river941
Wray Betts, Station Manager, wbetts@newcap.ca

Athabasca: **CKUA-FM-10** (Freq: 98.3)
Owned by: CKUA Radio Network
Athabasca, AB
Toll-Free: 800-494-2582
www.ckua.com

Banff: **CJAY-FM-1** (Freq: 95.1)
Owned by: CJAY-FM (CJAY 92)
Banff, AB
www.cjay92.com

Banff/Canmore: **CKUA-FM-14** (Freq: 104.3)
Owned by: CKUA Radio Network
Banff/Canmore, AB
Toll-Free: 800-494-2582
www.ckua.com

Blairmore: **CJPR-FM (Mountain Radio)** (Freq: 94.9)
Owned by: Stingray Group Inc.*
PO Box 840, 13213 - 20th Ave., 2nd Fl., Blairmore, AB T0K 0E0
Tel: 403-562-2806, *Fax:* 403-562-8114
mountain.requests@newcap.ca
www.mountainradiofm.com
Barb Kelly, Station Manager, bkelly@newcap.ca
Jenn Dalen, Program Director, jdalen@newcap.ca

Bonnyville: **CFNA-FM (Country 99 FM)** (Freq: 99.7)
Owned by: Vista Radio Ltd.*
#102, 5316 - 54 Ave., Bonnyville, AB T9N 2C9
Tel: 780-573-1745, *Fax:* 780-573-1746
www.mylakelandnow.com
www.facebook.com/country99, twitter.com/country99fm
Donnie Atkinson, General Manager, Sales,
datkinson@vistaradio.ca

Bonnyville: **CJEG-FM (101.3 Kool FM)** (Freq: 101.3)
Owned by: Stingray Group Inc.*
PO Box 8251, 4816 - 50th Ave., Bonnyville, AB T9N 2J5
Tel: 780-812-3058, *Fax:* 780-812-3363
www.1013koolfm.com
www.facebook.com/kool1013, twitter.com/Kool101dot3
Lisa Fielding, Station Manager, 780-812-7315,
lfielding@newcap.ca
Cash Kaye, Program Director, cashk@newcap.ca
Melissa Kelman, Marketing Consultant, mkelman@newcap.ca

Brooks: **CIBQ-FM (Q 105.7)** (Freq: 105.7)
Owned by: Stingray Group Inc.*
#8, 403 - 2nd Ave. West, Brooks, AB T1R 0S3
Tel: 403-362-3418
q1057@newcap.ca
www.q1057.ca
www.facebook.com/Q1057, twitter.com/Q1057
John Petrie, Station Manager, jpetrie@newcap.ca

Brooks: **CIXF-FM (101.1 The One)** (Freq: 101.1)
Owned by: Stingray Group Inc.*
#8, 403 - 2nd Ave. West, Brooks, AB T1R 0S3
Tel: 403-362-3418, *Fax:* 403-362-8168
www.theonebrooks.com
www.facebook.com/theonebrooks, twitter.com/theonebrooks
John Petrie, Station Manager, jpetrie@newcap.ca
Jeff Murray, Program Director, jmurray@newcap.ca

Calgary: **CBR-FM** (Freq: 102.1)
Owned by: Canadian Broadcasting Corporation*
1724 Westmount Blvd. NW, Calgary, AB T2N 3G7
Tel: 403-521-6000
www.cbc.ca/calgary

Calgary: **CFGQ-FM (Q107 Calgary)** (Freq: 107.3)
Owned by: Corus Radio Company*
#200, 3320 - 17th Ave. SW, Calgary, AB T3E 0B4
Tel: 403-716-6500, *Fax:* 403-444-4319
www.q107fm.ca
www.instagram.com/q107calgary
www.facebook.com/Q107calgary, twitter.com/q107calgary
Phil Kallsen, Program Director

Calgary: **CFXL-FM (XL 103 FM)** (Freq: 103.1)
Owned by: Stingray Group Inc.*
#100, 1110 Centre St. NE, Calgary, AB T2E 2R2
Tel: 403-271-6366, *Fax:* 403-278-6772
feedback@xl103calgary.com
www.xl103calgary.com
www.facebook.com/xl103, twitter.com/xl103calgary
Vinka Dubroja, General Manager, vdubroja@newcap.ca
Al Tompson, Program Director, al@xl103calgary.com

Calgary: **CHFM-FM (95.9 CHFM)** (Freq: 95.9)
Owned by: Rogers Media Inc.*
535 - 7th Ave. SW, Calgary, AB T2P 0Y4
Tel: 403-246-9696
www.959chfm.com
www.facebook.com/959chfm, twitter.com/959chfm

Calgary: **CHKF-FM** (Freq: 94.7)
Owned by: Fairchild Radio Group Ltd.*
#109, 2723 - 37th Ave. NE, Calgary, AB T1Y 5R8
Tel: 403-717-1940, *Fax:* 403-717-1945
www.facebook.com/fairchildcal
www.fm947.com
www.facebook.com/fairchildcal

Calgary: **CHUP-FM** (Freq: 97.7)
Owned by: Rawlco Radio Ltd.*
#110, 6807 Railway St. SE, Calgary, AB T2H 3A8
Tel: 403-385-4000
www.softrock977.com
www.facebook.com/softrock977, twitter.com/softrock977
Kent Newson, General Manager & Program Director,
knewson@rawlco.com

Calgary: **CIBK-FM (98.5 Virgin Radio)** (Freq: 98.5)
Owned by: Bell Media Inc.*
#300, 1110 Centre St. NE, Calgary, AB T2E 2R2
Tel: 403-240-5800
calgaryweb@virginradio.ca
calgary.virginradio.ca
www.instagram.com/virginradiocalgary,
www.facebook.com/virginradiocalgary,
twitter.com/VirginRadioYYC
Stewart Meyers, General Manager,
stewart.meyers@bellmedia.ca

Calgary: **CJAQ-FM (Jack 96.9)** (Freq: 96.9)
Owned by: Rogers Media Inc.*
535 - 7th Ave. SW, Calgary, AB T2P 0Y4
Tel: 403-250-9797
www.jack969.ca
www.facebook.com/jack969calgary, twitter.com/jack969calgary

Calgary: **CJAY-FM (CJAY 92)** (Freq: 92.1)
Owned by: Bell Media Inc.*
#300, 1110 Centre St. NE, Calgary, AB T2E 2R2
Tel: 403-240-5800
www.cjay92.com
www.facebook.com/CJAY92, twitter.com/CJAY92
Stewart Meyers, General Manager,
stewart.meyers@bellmedia.ca

Calgary: **CJSI-FM (Shine FM)** (Freq: 88.9)
Owned by: Touch Canada Broadcasting Inc.*
4510 Macleod Trail South, Calgary, AB T2G 0A4
Tel: 403-276-1111, *Fax:* 780-469-5335
88.9promotions@shinefm.com
www.cjsi.ca
www.facebook.com/88.9shinefm, twitter.com/889shinefm

Calgary: **CJSW-FM** (Freq: 90.9)
#312, MacEwan Hall, University of Calgary, Calgary, AB T2N 1N4
Tel: 403-220-3902, *Fax:* 403-289-8212
office@cjsw.com
www.cjsw.com
www.myspace.com/cjsw, www.facebook.com/CJSWFM,
twitter.com/cjsw
Myke Atkinson, Station Manager, 403-220-3904,
manager@cjsw.com
Joe Burima, Program Director, 403-220-3903,
programming@cjsw.com
Whitney Ota, Music Director, 403-220-3085, music@cjsw.com
Marc Affeld, News Director, 403-220-8033, news@cjsw.com

Calgary: **CKMP-FM (90.3 Amp Radio)** (Freq: 90.3)
Owned by: Stingray Group Inc.*
#100, 1110 Centre St. NE, Calgary, AB T2E 2R2
Tel: 403-271-6366, *Fax:* 403-278-6772
feedback@ampcalgary.com
www.youtube.com/user/903ampradio
www.facebook.com/ampcalgary, twitter.com/ampcalgary
Vinka Dubroja, Station Manager, vdubroja@newcap.ca
Al Tompson, Program Director, al@xl103calgary.com

Calgary: **CKRY-FM (Country 105)** (Freq: 105.1)
Owned by: Corus Radio Company*
#200, 3320 - 17th Ave. SW, Calgary, AB T3E 0B4
Tel: 403-716-6500, *Fax:* 403-444-4366
www.country105.com
www.instagram.com/country105calgary,
www.facebook.com/country105, twitter.com/country105_fm
Phil Kallsen, Program Director

Calgary: **CKUA-FM-1** (Freq: 93.7)
Owned by: CKUA Radio Network
Calgary, AB
www.ckua.com

Calgary: **CKWD-FM (Wild 95.3)** (Freq: 95.3)
Owned by: Jim Pattison Broadcast Group*
#600, 222 - 58th Ave. SW, Calgary, AB T2H 2S3
Tel: 403-536-3866
www.wild953.com
www.instagram.com/wild953calgary
www.facebook.com/wild953calgary, twitter.com/wild953calgary
Jamie Wall, General Manager, jamie.wall@jpbg.ca

Calgary: **CMRU** (Freq: Online radio station)
Mount Royal University, 4825 Richard Rd. SW, Calgary, AB T3E 6K6
Tel: 403-440-6119, *Fax:* 403-440-6563
cmrubroadcast@gmail.com
www.cmru.ca
www.facebook.com/cmrubroadcast, twitte.com/CMRUbroadcast
Jillian Hunter, Station Manager

Camrose: **CFCW-FM (98.1 CAM FM)** (Freq: 98.1)
Owned by: Stingray Group Inc.*
5708 - 48th Ave., Camrose, AB T4V 0K1
Tel: 780-672-8255, *Fax:* 780-672-4678
www.981camfm.com
www.facebook.com/981CAMFM, twitter.com/981camfm
Neil Cunningham, Station Manager, ncunningham@newcap.ca

Canmore: **CHMN-FM (Mountain FM)** (Freq: 106.5)
Owned by: Rogers Media Inc.*
749 Railway Ave., Canmore, AB T1W 1P2
Tel: 403-678-2222, *Fax:* 403-678-6844
www.mountainfm.ca
www.facebook.com/106.5mountainfm,
twitter.com/1065MountainFM

Cold Lake: **CJXK-FM (K-Rock)** (Freq: 95.3)
Owned by: Stingray Group Inc.*
B-5412 - 55th St., Cold Lake, AB T9M 1R5
Tel: 780-594-2459, *Fax:* 780-594-3001
news@k-rock953.com
www.953krock.com
www.facebook.com/953KRock, twitter.com/953Krock
Kelli Wispinski, Station Manager, kwispinski@newcap.ca

Drayton Valley: **CIBW-FM (Big West Country)** (Freq: 92.9)
Owned by: Jim Pattison Broadcast Group*
PO Box 929, 5164 - 52nd Ave., Drayton Valley, AB T7A 1V3
Tel: 780-542-9290, *Toll-Free:* 888-884-2448
www.bigwestcountry.ca
www.facebook.com/167537829943069,
twitter.com/bigwestcountry

Drumheller: **CHOO-FM (99.5 Drum FM)** (Freq: 99.5)
Owned by: Golden West Broadcasting Ltd.*
105 South Railway Ave., Drumheller, AB T0J 0Y0
Tel: 403-823-9936, *Toll-Free:* 877-823-9936
drumfm@goldenwestradio.com
www.drumhelleronline.com
www.facebook.com/995drumfm, twitter.com/995drumfm

Drumheller/Hanna: **CKUA-FM-13** (Freq: 91.3)
Owned by: CKUA Radio Network
Drumheller/Hanna, AB
Toll-Free: 800-494-2582
www.ckua.com

Edmonton: **CBX-FM** (Freq: 90.9)
Owned by: Canadian Broadcasting Corporation*
10062 - 102 Ave., Edmonton, AB T5J 2Y8
Tel: 780-462-7500
www.cbc.ca/edmonton

Edmonton: **CFBR-FM (100.3 The Bear)** (Freq: 100.3)
Owned by: Bell Media Inc.*
#100, 18520 Stony Plain Rd., Edmonton, AB T5S 2E2
Tel: 780-486-2800
www.thebearrocks.com
www.instagram.com/thebearrocks,
www.facebook.com/TheBearRocks, twitter.com/1003TheBear
Pat Cardinal, General Manager, patrick.cardinal@bellmedia.ca

Edmonton: **CFMG-FM (104.9 Virgin Radio)** (Freq: 104.9)
Owned by: Bell Media Inc.*
#100, 18520 Stony Plain Rd., Edmonton, AB T5S 2E2
Tel: 780-486-2800
www.iheartradio.ca/virginradio/edmonton
www.instagram.com/virginradioedmonton,
www.facebook.com/virginradioedmonton,
twitter.com/virginradioyeg

Edmonton: **CFWE-FM** (Freq: 98.5)
13245 - 146th St., Edmonton, AB T5L 4S8
Tel: 780-455-2700, *Fax:* 780-455-7639
www.cfweradio.ca
www.facebook.com/CFWE.FM, twitter.com/cfweradio
Bert Crowfoot, General Manager, bert@cfweradio.ca

---

* For details on this company see listing in Major Broadcasting Companies section; † French language station

Edmonton: **CHBN-FM (Kiss 91.7)** (Freq: 91.7)
Owned by: Rogers Media Inc.*
5915 Gateway Blvd., Edmonton, AB T6H 2H3
Tel: 780-423-2005, Fax: 780-437-5129
www.kiss917.com
www.instagram.com/kissedmonton
www.facebook.com/kissedmonton, twitter.com/kissedmonton

Edmonton: **CIRK-FM** (Freq: 97.3)
Owned by: Stingray Group Inc.*
West Edmonton Mall, #2394, 8882 - 170th St., Edmonton, AB T5T 4M2
Tel: 780-437-4996, Fax: 780-435-0844
www.k-rock973.com
www.facebook.com/K97Edmonton, twitter.com/k97
Neil Cunningham, General Manager, ncunningham@newcap.ca
John Roberts, Program Director, jroberts@newcap.ca

Edmonton: **CISN-FM (CISN Country 103.9)** (Freq: 103.9)
Owned by: Corus Radio Company*
5204 - 84 St., Edmonton, AB T6E 5N8
Tel: 780-440-6300, Fax: 780-469-5937
www.cisnfm.com
www.facebook.com/cisncountry, twitter.com/cisncountry
Greg Johnson, Program Director

Edmonton: **CJNW-FM** (Freq: 107)
Owned by: Harvard Broadcasting Inc.*
Centre 104, #700, 5241 Calgary Trail, Edmonton, AB T6H 5G8
Tel: 780-435-3023, Fax: 780-988-2387
www.hot107.ca
www.instagram.com/hot107edmonton
www.facebook.com/hot107edmonton,
twitter.com/HOT107Edmonton

Edmonton: **CJRY-FM (Shine FM)** (Freq: 105.9)
Owned by: Touch Canada Broadcasting Inc.*
5316 Calgary Trail NW, Edmonton, AB T6H 4J8
Tel: 780-466-4930, Fax: 780-469-5335
105.9promotions@shinefm.com
www.cjry.ca
www.facebook.com/1059ShineFM, twitter.com/1059shinefm
Johnny Rocket, Program Director, johnny.rocket@ShineFM.com

Edmonton: **CJSR-FM** (Freq: 88.5)
#0-09 Students Union Bldg., University of Alberta, Edmonton, AB T6G 2J7
Tel: 780-492-2577, Fax: 780-492-3121
admin@cjsr.com
www.cjsr.com
www.facebook.com/cjsr885, twitter.com/CJSR
Sarah Edwards, Station Manager

Edmonton: **CKER-FM (World FM)** (Freq: 101.7)
Owned by: Rogers Media Inc.*
5915 Gateway Blvd., Edmonton, AB T6H 2H3
Tel: 780-424-2222, Fax: 780-437-5129
www.worldfm.ca
www.facebook.com/1017WorldFm, twitter.com/1017worldfm

Edmonton: **CKNG-FM (92.5 The Chuck)** (Freq: 92.5)
Owned by: Corus Radio Company*
5204 - 84th St. NW, Edmonton, AB T6E 5N8
Tel: 780-440-6300, Fax: 780-469-5937
www.925thechuck.ca
www.instagram.com/925thechuck
www.facebook.com/925thechuck, twitter.com/925thechuck
Greg Johnson, Program Director

Edmonton: **CKNO-FM (Now! 102.3)** (Freq: 102.3)
Owned by: Jim Pattison Broadcast Group*
#102, 9894 - 42nd Ave. NW, Edmonton, AB T6E 5V5
Tel: 403-536-3866
www.1023nowradio.com
www.facebook.com/nowradio, twitter.com/1023nowradio
Jamie Wall, General Manager, jamie.wall@jpbg.ca
Mark Hunter, Program Director, mark.hunter@jpbg.ca

Edmonton: **CKRA-FM (96.3 Capital FM)** (Freq: 96.3)
Owned by: Stingray Group Inc.*
West Edmonton Mall, #2394, 8882 - 170th St., Edmonton, AB T5T 4M2
Tel: 780-437-4996, Fax: 780-435-0844
info@963capitalfm.com
www.963capitalfm.com
www.facebook.com/963capitalfm, twitter.com/capitalfm
Neil Cunningham, General Manager, ncunningham@newcap.ca
John Roberts, Program Director, jroberts@newcap.ca

Edmonton: **CKUA-FM** (Freq: 94.9)
Owned by: CKUA Radio Network
9804 Jasper Ave. NW, Edmonton, AB T5J 0C5
Tel: 780-428-7595, Fax: 780-428-7624
Toll-Free: 800-494-2582
www.ckua.com
www.facebook.com/CKUARadio, twitter.com/ckuaradio
Ken Regan, Chief Executive Officer
Katrina Ingram, Chief Operations Officer

Edson: **CFXE-FM (The Eagle)** (Freq: 94.3)
Owned by: Stingray Group Inc.*
PO Box 7800, 422 - 50th St., 2nd Fl., Edson, AB T7E 1T1
Tel: 780-723-4461, Fax: 780-723-3765
feedback@theeagle.ca
www.theeagle.ca
www.facebook.com/theeagleradio, twitter.com/theeagleradio
Dave Schuck, General Manager, dave@theeagle.ca

Edson: **CKUA-FM-8** (Freq: 103.7)
Owned by: CKUA Radio Network
Edson, AB
Toll-Free: 800-494-2582
www.ckua.com

†*Falher:* **CKRP-FM** (Freq: 95.7; 102.9; 90.3)
CP 718, Falher, AB T0H 1M0
Tél: 780-837-2346, Ligne sans frais: 866-837-2346
programmation@ckrp.ca
www.ckrp.ca
www.facebook.com/CkrpFm

Fort McMurray: **CJOK-FM (Country 93.3)** (Freq: 93.3)
Owned by: Rogers Media Inc.*
9912 Franklin Ave., Fort McMurray, AB T9H 2K5
Tel: 780-743-2246
rock979.news@rci.rogers.com
www.country933.com
www.facebook.com/country933, twitter.com/Country933
Rick Walters, General Manager
John Knox, Program Director

Fort McMurray: **CKUA-FM-11** (Freq: 96.7)
Owned by: CKUA Radio Network
Fort McMurray, AB
Toll-Free: 800-494-2582
www.ckua.com

Fort McMurray: **CKYX-FM (97.9 ROCK)** (Freq: 97.9)
Owned by: Rogers Media Inc.*
9912 Franklin Ave., Fort McMurray, AB T1B 4Y2
Tel: 403-548-7581
www.979rock.ca
www.facebook.com/979rock, twitter.com/979rock

Fort Saskatchewan: **CKFT-FM (Mix 107.9 FM)** (Freq: 107.9)
Owned by: Golden West Broadcasting Ltd.*
#200, 9940 - 99th Ave., Fort Saskatchewan, AB T8L 4G8
Tel: 780-998-1079, Toll-Free: 855-997-1079
fortsaskonline.com
www.youtube.com/FortSaskOnline, twitter.com/Mix1079FortSask

Fort Vermilion: **CIAM-FM** (Freq: 92.7; 104.3; 95.5; 94.1; 102.9)
PO Box 609, Fort Vermilion, AB T0H 1N0
Tel: 780-927-2426, Fax: 780-927-2427
Toll-Free: 866-927-2426
info@ciamradio.com
www.ciamradio.com

Fox Creek: **CFFC-FM** (Freq: 92.1)
Owned by: CKKX-FM
Fox Creek, AB

Fox Creek: **CFXW-1 (98.1 The Rig)** (Freq: 98.1)
Owned by: CFXW-FM
Fox Creek, AB
Tel: 780-778-5101, Fax: 780-778-5137
www.therig.ca

Grande Cache: **CFXG-FM (The Eagle)** (Freq: 93.3)
Owned by: CFXE-FM 94.3
Grande Cache, AB
Tel: 780-723-4461, Fax: 780-723-3765
feedback@theeagle.ca
www.theeagle.ca
www.facebook.com/theeagleradio, twitter.com/theeagleradio

Grande Prairie: **CFGP-FM (97.7 ROCK)** (Freq: 97.7)
Owned by: Rogers Media Inc.*
#200, 9835 - 101 Ave., Grande Prairie, AB T8V 5V4
Tel: 780-539-9700, Fax: 780-532-1600
www.977rock.ca
www.facebook.com/977rockgp, twitter.com/977rockgp
Other information: News Phone: 780-532-1044

Grande Prairie: **CFRI-FM (104.7 2Day FM)** (Freq: 104.7)
Owned by: Vista Radio Ltd.*
#1, 11002 - 104 Ave., Grande Prairie, AB T8V 7W5
Tel: 780-357-3733, Fax: 780-830-7815
www.mygrandeprairienow.com

Grande Prairie: **CIKT-FM (Q99)** (Freq: 98.9)
Owned by: Jim Pattison Broadcast Group*
#202, 9817 - 101st Ave., Grande Prairie, AB T8V 0X6
Tel: 780-882-6612, Fax: 780-538-1266
www.q99live.com
www.instagram.com/q99live, www.facebook.com/q99live,
twitter.com/q99livefm

Grande Prairie: **CJXX-FM (Big Country)** (Freq: 93.1)
Owned by: Jim Pattison Broadcast Group*
#202, 9817 - 101st Ave., Grande Prairie, AB T8V 0X6
Tel: 780-532-0840, Fax: 780-538-1266
www.bigcountryxx.com
www.instagram.com/bigcountry931fm,
www.facebook.com/bigcountry931, twitter.com/bigcountry931

Grande Prairie: **CKUA-FM-4** (Freq: 100.9)
Owned by: CKUA Radio Network
Grande Prairie, AB
Toll-Free: 800-494-2582
www.ckua.com

High Level: **CKHL-FM (River Country)** (Freq: 102.1)
Owned by: Peace River Broadcasting Corp.*
Fahlman Bldg., PO Box 3759, #201, 9812 - 100th Ave., 2nd Fl,, High Level, AB T0H 1Z0
Tel: 780-926-4531, Fax: 780-926-4564
reception@rivercountry.fm
www.rivercountry.fm
Chris Black, General Manager, 780-618-4230

High Prairie: **CKVH-FM (Prairie FM)** (Freq: 93.5)
Owned by: Stingray Group Inc.*
PO Box 2219, 4833 - 52nd Ave., High Prairie, AB T0G 1E0
Tel: 780-523-5120, Fax: 780-523-3360
feedback@prairiefm.ca
www.prairiefm.ca
www.facebook.com/935PrairieFM, twitter.com/prairiefm
Wray Betts, Station Manager, wbetts@newcap.ca
Dave Schuck, General Manager, dschuck@newcap.ca

High River: **CFXO-FM (SUN Country 99.7)** (Freq: 99.7)
Owned by: Golden West Broadcasting Ltd.*
11 - 5th Ave. SE, High River, AB T1V 1G2
Tel: 403-652-2472, Toll-Free: 866-652-2472
www.highriveronline.com
www.facebook.com/197265794075, twitter.com/suncountry997

Hinton: **CFXH-FM (The Eagle)** (Freq: 97.5)
Owned by: CFXE-FM 94.3
#102, 506 Carmichael Lane, Hinton, AB T7V 1S4
Fax: 780-865-7792
feedback@theeagle.ca
www.theeagle.ca
www.facebook.com/theeagleradio, twitter.com/theeagleradio

Hinton: **CKUA-FM-7** (Freq: 102.5)
Owned by: CKUA Radio Network
Hinton, AB
Toll-Free: 800-494-2582
www.ckua.com

Jasper: **CFXP-FM (The Eagle)** (Freq: 95.5)
Owned by: CFXE-FM 94.3
Jasper, AB
Tel: 780-723-4461, Fax: 780-723-3765
feedback@theeagle.ca
www.theeagle.ca
www.facebook.com/theeagleradio, twitter.com/theeagleradio

La Crete: **CKLA-FM** (Freq: 92.1)
Owned by: CKYL
La Crete, AB

---

*For details on this company see listing in Major Broadcasting Companies section; † French language station

Lac La Biche: **CILB-FM (Big Dog 103.5)** (Freq: 103.5)
Owned by: Stingray Group Inc.*
PO Box 86, #201, 10107 - 102nd Ave., Lac La Biche, AB T0A 2C0
Tel: 780-623-3744, *Fax:* 780-623-3740
www.1035bigdog.com/
www.facebook.com/1035BigDog, twitter.com/BigDog1035
Chad Tabish, General Manager, ctabish@newcap.ca
Rick Flumian, Station Manager, rflumian@newcap.ca
Kurt Price, Program Director, kprice@newcap.ca

Lacombe: **CJUV-FM (Sunny 94 FM)** (Freq: 94.1)
Owned by: L.A. Radio Group Inc.
4720 Hwy. 2A, Lacombe, AB T4L 1H4
Tel: 403-786-0194, *Fax:* 403-786-0199
onair@sunny94.com
sunny94.com
www.facebook.com/SUNNY94FM, twitter.com/Sunny94FM
Troy Schaab, President & Co-owner

Lake Louise: **CJAY-FM-2** (Freq: 97.5)
Owned by: CJAY-FM (CJAY 92)
Lake Louise, AB
www.cjay92.com

Lethbrdge: **CJOC-FM** (Freq: 94.1)
Owned by: Vista Radio Ltd.*
#400, 220 - 3rd Ave. South, Lethbrdge, AB T1J 0G9
Tel: 403-388-2910, *Fax:* 403-388-4648
www.mylethbridgenow.com/cjoc-fm
www.facebook.com/10752dayFM, twitter.com/10752dayFM

Lethbrdge: **CKBD-FM (2day FM)** (Freq: 98.1)
Owned by: Vista Radio Ltd.*
#400, 220 - 3rd Ave. South, Lethbrdge, AB T1J 0G9
Tel: 403-388-2910, *Fax:* 403-388-4648
www.mylethbridgenow.com
www.facebook.com/9812dayfm, twitter.com/9812dayFM

Lethbridge: **CFRV-FM (Kiss 107.7)** (Freq: 107.7)
Owned by: Rogers Media Inc.*
1015 - 3rd Ave. South, Lethbridge, AB T1J 0J3
Tel: 403-320-1220, *Fax:* 403-380-1539
www.kiss1077.ca
www.facebook.com/kiss1077lethbridge, twitter.com/kiss1077

Lethbridge: **CHLB-FM (Country 95.5)** (Freq: 95.5)
Owned by: Jim Pattison Broadcast Group*
#220, 410 - 7th St. South, Lethbridge, AB T1J 2G6
Tel: 403-329-0955
www.country95.fm
www.instagram.com/country955,
www.facebook.com/todayscountry955, twitter.com/country95

Lethbridge: **CJBZ-FM (B-93.3)** (Freq: 93.3)
Owned by: Jim Pattison Broadcast Group*
#220, 410 - 7th St. South, Lethbridge, AB T1J 2G6
Tel: 403-329-0955, *Fax:* 403-329-0165
info@b93.fm
www.b93.fm
www.facebook.com/allhitsb93, twitter.com/allhitsb93

Lethbridge: **CJRX-FM (106.7 ROCK)** (Freq: 106.7)
Owned by: Rogers Media Inc.*
1015 - 3rd Ave. South, Lethbridge, AB T1J 0J3
Tel: 403-320-1220, *Fax:* 403-380-1539
www.1067rock.ca
www.instagram.com/1067Rock, www.facebook.com/1067ROCK,
twitter.com/1067ROCK

Lethbridge: **CKUA-FM-2** (Freq: 99.3)
Owned by: CKUA Radio Network
Lethbridge, AB
Toll-Free: 800-494-2582
www.ckua.com

Lloydminster: **CKLM-FM (106.1 The Goat)** (Freq: 106.1)
Owned by: Vista Radio Ltd.*
Atrium Centre, 5012 - 49th St., 2nd Fl., Lloydminster, AB T9V 0K2
Tel: 780-875-5400, *Fax:* 780-875-4628
www.mylloydminsternow.com
www.youtube.com/thegoat1061,
www.facebook.com/1061TheGoat, twitter.com/1061thegoat

Lloydminster: **CKSA-FM (Lloyd 95.9)** (Freq: 95.9)
Owned by: Stingray Digital Group Inc.*
5026 - 50th St., Lloydminster, AB T9V 1P3
Tel: 780-875-3321, *Fax:* 780-875-4704
Toll-Free: 800-565-2572
Lloyd@newcap.ca
www.959lloydfm.com
www.facebook.com/959LLOYDFM, twitter.com/lloydfm
Chad Tabish, General Manager, ctabish@newcap.ca
Dean Martin, Creative Director, dmartin@newcap.ca

Lloydminster: **CKUA-FM-15** (Freq: 97.5)
Owned by: CKUA Radio Network
Lloydminster, AB
Toll-Free: 800-494-2582
www.ckua.com

Martin Mountain: **CHSL-FM (92.7 Lake FM)** (Freq: 92.7)
Owned by: Stingray Group Inc.*
#103, 228 - 3rd Ave NW, Martin Mountain, AB T0G 2A1
Tel: 780-849-2569, *Fax:* 780-849-4833
onair@lakefm.ca
www.lakefm.ca
www.facebook.com/927LAKEFM, twitter.com/927LakeFM
Wray Betts, Station Manager, wbetts@newcap.ca

Medicine Hat: **CJCY-FM (102.1 CJCY)** (Freq: 102.1)
Owned by: Rogers Media Inc.*
#107, 7 Strachan Bay SE, Medicine Hat, AB T1B 4Y2
Tel: 403-548-7681
info@cjcyfm.com
www.cjcyfm.com
twitter.com/cjcyfm
Other information: News Email: news@cjcyfm.com

Medicine Hat: **CJLT-FM (Praise FM)** (Freq: 93.7)
Owned by: Vista Radio Ltd.*
#206, 1741 Dunmore Rd. SE, Medicine Hat, AB T1A 1Z8
Tel: 403-529-9599, *Fax:* 403-488-5050
www.937praisefm.com
www.facebook.com/937praisefm, twitter.com/937praisefm

Medicine Hat: **CKMH-FM (105.3 ROCK)** (Freq: 105.3)
Owned by: Rogers Media Inc.*
#107, 7 Strachan Bay SE, Medicine Hat, AB T1B 4Y2
Tel: 403-548-7581
www.1053rock.ca
www.facebook.com/1053rock, twitter.com/1053rock

Medicine Hat: **CKUA-FM-3** (Freq: 97.3)
Owned by: CKUA Radio Network
Medicine Hat, AB
Toll-Free: 800-494-2582
www.ckua.com

Okotoks: **CFXL-FM** (Freq: 100.9)
Owned by: Golden West Broadcasting Ltd.*
PO Box 1889, 22 Elizabeth St., Bay 3, Okotoks, AB T1S 1B7
Tel: 403-995-9611, *Toll-Free:* 866-995-9611
theeagle1009@goldenwestradio.com
www.theeagle1009.com
www.facebook.com/296045543680, twitter.com/TheEagle1009

Okotoks: **CLUV-FM (100.9 The Eagle)** (Freq: 100.9)
Owned by: Golden West Broadcasting Ltd.*
PO Box 1889, 22 Elizabeth St., Bay 3, Okotoks, AB T1S 1B7
Tel: 403-995-9611, *Toll-Free:* 866-995-9611
theeagle1009@goldenwestradio.com
okotoksonline.com
www.facebook.com/296045543680, twitter.com/TheEagle1009

Peace River: **CKKX-FM** (Freq: 106.1)
Owned by: Peace River Broadcasting Corp.*
PO Box 300, 9807 - 100th Ave., Peace River, AB T8S 1T5
Tel: 780-624-2535, *Fax:* 780-624-5424
Toll-Free: 800-610-3610
reception@rivercountry.fm
www.kix.fm
www.facebook.com/kixfm, twitter.com/KIXFM

Peace River: **CKUA-FM-5** (Freq: 96.9)
Owned by: CKUA Radio Network
Peace River, AB
Toll-Free: 800-494-2582
www.ckua.com

Peace River: **CKYL-FM (River Country)** (Freq: 94.9)
Owned by: Peace River Broadcasting Corp.*
PO Box 300, 9807 - 100th Ave., Peace River, AB T8S 1T5
Tel: 780-624-2535, *Fax:* 780-624-5424
Toll-Free: 800-610-3610
reception@rivercountry.fm
www.rivercountry.fm
www.facebook.com/RiverCountry949,
twitter.com/RiverCountry949
Chris Black, General Manager, 780-681-4230

Pincher Creek: **CJPV-FM (Mountain Radio)** (Freq: 92.7)
Owned by: CJPR-FM
Pincher Creek, AB
Tel: 403-562-2806, *Fax:* 403-562-8114
www.mountainradiofm.com

Red Deer: **CFDV-FM (The Drive)** (Freq: 106.7)
Owned by: Jim Pattison Broadcast Group*
2840 Bremner Ave., 2nd Fl., Red Deer, AB T4R 1M9
Tel: 403-343-7105, *Fax:* 403-343-2573
rock@1067thedrive.fm
www.1067thedrive.fm
www.facebook.com/1067thedrive, twitter.com/1067thedrive
Bryn James, General & Sales Manager, bryn.james@jpbg.ca

Red Deer: **CHUB-FM (Big 105.5 FM)** (Freq: 105.5)
Owned by: Jim Pattison Broadcast Group*
2840 Bremner Ave., Red Deer, AB T4R 1M9
Tel: 403-343-7105, *Fax:* 403-343-2573
www.big105.fm
www.facebook.com/big105reddeer, twitter.com/big105

Red Deer: **CIZZ-FM (Zed 98.9)** (Freq: 98.9)
Owned by: Stingray Group Inc.*
PO Box 5339, 4920 - 59th St., Red Deer, AB T4N 6W1
Tel: 403-348-0955, *Fax:* 403-346-1230
zed99@newcap.ca
www.zed99.com
www.facebook.com/ZED989, twitter.com/zed99reddeer
Jared Waldo, General Manager, jwaldo@newcap.ca
Jeff Murray, Program Director, jmurray@newcap.ca

Red Deer: **CKGY-FM (KG Country)** (Freq: 95.5)
Owned by: Stingray Group Inc.*
PO Box 5339, 4920 - 59th St., Red Deer, AB T4N 6W1
Tel: 403-348-0955, *Fax:* 403-346-1230
www.kgcountry.ca
www.facebook.com/KGCountry955, twitter.com/kgreddeer
Jared Waldo, General Sales Manager, jwaldo@newcap.com
Jenn Dalen, Program Director, jdalen@newcap.ca

Red Deer: **CKIK-FM (KRAZE 101.3)** (Freq: 101.3)
Owned by: Harvard Broadcasting Inc.*
#103, 6751 - 52nd Ave., Red Deer, AB T4N 4K8
Tel: 403-358-3100, *Fax:* 403-309-8311
onair@kraze1013.com
kraze1013.com
www.facebook.com/kraze1013, twitter.com/kraze1013

Red Deer: **CKRD-FM (Shine FM)** (Freq: 90.5)
Owned by: Touch Canada Broadcasting Inc.*
#13, 7619 - 50th Ave., Red Deer, AB T4P 1M6
Tel: 403-356-9052, *Fax:* 780-469-5335
90.5promotions@shinefm.com
www.ckrd.ca
www.facebook.com/905shinefm, twitter.com/905ShineFM
Jon Ramer, Program Director, jon.ramer@shinefm.com

Red Deer: **CKUA-FM-6** (Freq: 107.7)
Owned by: CKUA Radio Network
Red Deer, AB
Toll-Free: 800-494-2582
www.ckua.com

Redcliff: **CFMY-FM (My 96 FM)** (Freq: 96.1)
Owned by: Jim Pattison Broadcast Group*
10 Boundary Rd., Redcliff, AB T0J 2P0
Tel: 403-548-8282, *Fax:* 403-548-8270
my96fm@jpbg.ca
www.my96fm.com
www.instagram.com/my96fm, www.facebook.com/my96fm,
twitter.com/my96fm

Redcliff: **CHAT-FM (Chat 94.5)** (Freq: 94.5)
Owned by: Jim Pattison Broadcast Group*
10 Boundary Rd., Redcliff, AB T0J 2P0
Tel: 403-548-8282, *Fax:* 403-548-8270
chat945@jpbg.com
www.chat945.com
www.facebook.com/chat94.5, twitter.com/chat945

---

* For details on this company see listing in Major Broadcasting Companies section; † French language station

Rocky Mountain House: CHBW-FM (B-94) (Freq: 94.5)
Owned by: Jim Pattison Broadcast Group*
4814B - 49th St., Rocky Mountain House, AB T4T 1S8
www.yourb94.ca
www.facebook.com/YourB94

Siksika: CHDH-FM (Freq: 97.7)
Siksika, AB
www.siksikamedia.com

Spirit River: CKUA-FM-12 (Freq: 99.5)
Owned by: CKUA Radio Network
Spirit River, AB
Toll-Free: 800-494-2582
www.ckua.com

St Paul: CHSP-FM (97.7 The Spur) (Freq: 97.7)
Owned by: Stingray Group Inc.*
#201, 4341 - 50th Ave., St Paul, AB T0A 3A3
Tel: 780-645-4425, Fax: 780-645-2383
www.977thespur.com
www.facebook.com/97.7TheSpur, twitter.com/977thespur1
Chad Tabish, General Manager, ctabish@newcap.ca
Kurt Price, Program Director, kprice@newcap.ca
Kevin Bernhardt, Marketing Consultant, kbernhardt@newcap.ca

Stettler: CKSQ-FM (Q93.3) (Freq: 93.3)
Owned by: Stingray Group Inc.*
PO Box 2050, 4812A - 50th St., Stettler, AB T0C 2L0
Tel: 403-742-1400, Fax: 403-742-0660
Q933@newcap.ca
www.q933.ca
www.facebook.com/Q933, twitter.com/Q933Country
Vicki Leuck, General & Sales Manager, vleuck@newcap.ca

Wabasca: CHSL-FM-1 (Lake FM) (Freq: 94.3)
Owned by: CHSL-FM 92.7
Wabasca, AB
Tel: 780-849-2569, Fax: 780-849-4833
onair@lakefm.ca
www.lakefm.ca
www.facebook.com/927LAKEFM, twitter.com/927LakeFM

Wainwright: CKKY-FM (Freq: 101.9)
Owned by: Stingray Group Inc.*
1037 - 2nd Ave., 2nd Fl., Wainwright, AB T9W 1K7
Tel: 780-842-4311, Fax: 780-842-4636
www.krock1019.com
www.facebook.com/Krock1019, twitter.com/Krock1019
Chad Tabish, General Manager, ctabish@newcap.ca
Hugh Macdonald, Station/Sales Manager,
hmacdonald@newcap.ca
Kurt Price, Alberta Radio Group - East: Program Director,
kprice@newcap.ca

Wainwright: CKWY-FM (93.7 Wayne FM) (Freq: 93.7)
Owned by: Stingray Group Inc.*
1037 - 2nd Ave., 2nd Fl., Wainwright, AB T9W 1K7
Tel: 780-842-4311, Fax: 780-842-4636
www.waynefm.com
www.facebook.com/waynefm, twitter.com/waynefm
Chad Tabish, General Manager, ctabish@newcap.ca
Hugh MacDonald, Station/Sales Manager,
hmacdonald@newcap.ca
Kurt Price, Program Director, kprice@newcap.ca

Westlock: CKWB-FM (97.9 The Range) (Freq: 97.9)
Owned by: Stingray Group Inc.*
#17, 10030 - 106th St., Westlock, AB T7P 2K4
Tel: 780-349-4421, Fax: 780-349-6259
www.979therange.ca
www.facebook.com/979TheRange, twitter.com/979therange
Wray Betts, General Manager, wbetts@newcap.ca
Stuart McIntosh, Program Director, smcintosh@newcap.ca

Whitecourt: CFXW-FM (96.7 The Rig) (Freq: 96.7)
Owned by: Stingray Group Inc.*
PO Box 2288, 5036 - 50th Ave., Whitecourt, AB T7S 1N4
Tel: 780-778-5137, Fax: 780-778-5137
www.therig.ca
www.facebook.com/967TheRig, twitter.com/RigRadio
Dave Schuck, General Manager, 780-723-4461,
dschuck@newcap.ca
Stuart McIntosh, Program Director, smcintosh@newcap.ca

Whitecourt: CIXM-FM (Freq: 105.3)
Owned by: Jim Pattison Broadcast Group*
4912A - 50th Ave., Whitecourt, AB T7S 1P4
Tel: 780-706-1053, Fax: 780-706-1017
info@xm105fm.com
www.xm105fm.com
www.facebook.com/cixm1053, twitter.com/XM1053FM
Neil Shewchuk, Station Manager & Sales Manager,
neil@xm105fm.com

Whitecourt: CKUA-FM-9 (Freq: 107.1)
Owned by: CKUA Radio Network
Whitecourt, AB
Toll-Free: 800-494-2582
www.ckua.com

British Columbia

100 Mile House: CFFM-FM-3 (The Goat) (Freq: 99.7)
Owned by: CFFM-FM (The Rush)
#3, 407 Alder Ave., 100 Mile House, BC V0K 2E0
Tel: 250-395-3848
www.mycariboonow.com

Abbotsford: CKQC-FM (Country 107.1) (Freq: 107.1)
Owned by: Rogers Media Inc.*
#318, 31935 South Fraser Way, Abbotsford, BC V2T 5N7
Tel: 604-853-4756, Fax: 604-853-1071
Toll-Free: 866-468-1071
country1071.com
www.instagram.com/country107.1,
www.facebook.com/Country1071, twitter.com/country1071

Abbotsford: CKSR-FM (Star FM) (Freq: 98.3)
Owned by: Rogers Media Inc.*
#318, 31935 South Fraser Way, Abbotsford, BC V2T 5N7
Tel: 604-795-5711, Fax: 604-853-1071
Toll-Free: 866-782-7983
www.starfm.com
www.instagram.com/983starfm, www.facebook.com/983starfm,
twitter.com/983StarFM

Barrys Bay: CHBY-FM (Moose FM) (Freq: 106.5)
Owned by: Vista Radio Ltd.*
41 Bay St., Barrys Bay, BC K0J 1B0
Tel: 613-756-1881
www.mybarrysbaynow.com
www.facebook.com/1065moosefm, twitter.com/1065moosefm
Drew Hosick, Program Director, dhosick@vistaradio.ca

Burnaby: CJSF-FM (Freq: 90.1)
#TC216, Simon Fraser University, Burnaby, BC V5A 1S6
Tel: 778-782-3727, Fax: 778-782-3695
cjsfmgr@sfu.ca
www.cjsf.ca
www.facebook.com/cjsfradio, twitter.com/CJSF
Magnus Thyrold, Station Manager
David Swanson, Program Coordinator, cjsfprog@sfu.ca

Burns Lake: CJFW-FM-5 (Freq: 92.9)
Owned by: CJFW-FM
Burns Lake, BC

Campbell River: CIQC-FM (99.7 2day FM) (Freq: 99.7)
Owned by: Vista Radio Ltd.*
470 - 13th Ave., Campbell River, BC V9W 7J4
Tel: 250-287-7106, Fax: 250-287-7170
www.mycampbellrivernow.com/2day-fm
www.facebook.com/9972dayfm, twitter.com/9972DayFM_CR
Andrew Davis, Program Director

Castlegar: CKQR-FM (The Goat) (Freq: 99.3)
Owned by: Vista Radio Ltd.*
#101, 2032 Columbia Ave., Castlegar, BC V1N 2W7
Tel: 250-365-7600, Fax: 250-365-8480
Toll-Free: 877-560-1010
www.mykootenaynow.com
twitter.com/GOATFM

Chetwynd: CHET-FM (Freq: 94.5)
PO Box 214, Chetwynd, BC V0C 1J0
Tel: 250-788-9452, Fax: 250-788-9402
Toll-Free: 800-788-5330
info@peacefm.ca
www.peacefm.ca
www.facebook.com/178391508895881, twitter.com/Peace_FM
Leo Sabulsky, General Manager, leo@peacefm.ca

Christina Lake: CKGF-1-FM (93.3 The Goat) (Freq: 93.3)
Owned by: CKQR-FM
Christina Lake, BC

Courtenay: CFCP-FM (98.9 the Goat) (Freq: 98.9)
Owned by: Vista Radio Ltd.*
#201A, 910 Fitzgerald Ave., Courtenay, BC V9N 2R5
Tel: 250-334-2421, Fax: 250-334-1977
www.mycomoxvalleynow.com/the-goat
www.facebook.com/989TheGoat, twitter.com/989theGOAT

Courtenay: CKLR-FM (97.3 The Eagle) (Freq: 97.3)
Owned by: Jim Pattison Broadcast Group*
801B - 29th St., Courtenay, BC V9N 7Z5
Tel: 250-703-2200, Fax: 250-703-9611
info@973theeagle.com
www.973theeagle.com
www.instagram.com/973theeaglepics
www.facebook.com/973fmtheeagle, twitter.com/theeagle973
Kent Wilson, Program Director, kent.wilson@jpbg.ca

Cranbrook: CFSM-FM (107.5 2Day FM) (Freq: 107.5)
Owned by: Vista Radio Ltd.*
205A Cranbrook St. North, Cranbrook, BC V1C 3R1
Tel: 250-464-4100, Fax: 250-464-4101
www.myeastkootenaynow.com
www.facebook.com/10752dayFM, twitter.com/10752dayFM

Cranbrook: CHBZ-FM (Total Country) (Freq: 104.7)
Owned by: Jim Pattison Broadcast Group*
19 - 9th Ave. South, Cranbrook, BC V1C 2L9
Tel: 250-426-2224, Fax: 250-426-5520
www.b104.ca
www.facebook.com/b104totalcountry, twitter.com/b104country
Matt Van Boeyen, Program Director, leo@thedrivefm.ca

Cranbrook: CHDR-FM (102.9 The Drive) (Freq: 102.9)
Owned by: Jim Pattison Broadcast Group*
19 - 9th Ave. South, Cranbrook, BC V1C 2L8
Tel: 250-426-2224
info@thedrivefm.ca
www.thedrivefm.ca
www.facebook.com/thedrive1029
Marvin Perry, General Manager

Crawford Bay: CBTE-FM (Freq: 89.9)
Owned by: Canadian Broadcasting Corporation
Crawford Bay, BC

Crawford Bay: CKKC-1-FM (Freq: 101.9)
Owned by: CKKC-FM (Kootenays EZ Rock)
Crawford Bay, BC
kootenays.myezrock.com

Creston: CKCV-FM (Juice FM) (Freq: 94.1)
Owned by: Vista Radio Ltd.*
PO Box 1910 A, #208, 1230 Canyon St., Creston, BC V0B 1G5
Tel: 250-428-9160, Fax: 250-428-0507
www.mycrestonnow.com
www.facebook.com/941juicefm, twitter.com/941juicefm
Mike Johnston, General Manager, mjohnston@vistaradio.ca

Dawson Creek: CHAD-FM (Freq: 104.1)
#5, 1017- 103 Ave., Dawson Creek, BC V1G 2G6
Tel: 250-784-2002, Fax: 250-784-2002
info@peacefm.ca
peacefm.ca
Leo Sabulsky, General Manager

Dawson Creek: CHRX-FM-1 (Sun FM) (Freq: 95.1)
Owned by: CHRX-FM (Sun FM)
Dawson Creek, BC
www.peacesunfm.com

Duncan: CJSU-FM (JUICE FM) (Freq: 89.7)
Owned by: Vista Radio Ltd.*
5380 Trans Canada Hwy., Duncan, BC V9L 6W4
Tel: 250-746-0897, Fax: 250-748-1517
www.mycowichanvalleynow.com/juice-fm
www.facebook.com/897juicefm, twitter.com/897juicefm
Rob Alexander, Program Director, ralexander@vistaradio.ca

Egmont: CIEG-FM (Freq: 107.5)
Owned by: CISQ-FM
Egmont, BC

Enderby: CKIZ-FM-1 (Freq: 93.9)
Owned by: CKIZ-FM (107.5 Kiss FM)
Enderby, BC

Enderby: CKXR-FM-2 (Freq: 104.3)
Owned by: CKXR-FM (EZ Rock)
Enderby, BC
salmonarm.myezrock.com

For details on this company see listing in Major Broadcasting Companies section; † French language station

Fort Nelson: **CKRX-FM (102.3 The Bear)** (Freq: 102.3)
Owned by: Bell Media Inc.*
5152 Liard St., Fort Nelson, BC V0C 1R0
Tel: 250-774-2525
www.1023thebear.com
www.facebook.com/The.BEAR.CKRX
Ken Johnson, Station Manager, ken.johnson@bellmedia.ca

Fort St John: **CHRX-FM (Sun FM)** (Freq: 98.5)
Owned by: Bell Media Inc.*
10532 Alaska Rd., Fort St John, BC V1J 1B3
Tel: 250-785-6634
www.iheartradio.ca/sun-fm/peace-sun-fm
www.facebook.com/PeaceSunFM,
twitter.com/PeaceSunFMmusic
Terry Shepherd, General Manager,
terry.shepherd@bellmedia.ca

Fort St John: **CKFU-FM** (Freq: 100.1)
9924 - 101 Ave., Fort St John, BC V1J 2B2
Tel: 250-787-7100
reception@moosefm.ca
energeticcity.ca/moosefm

Fort St John: **CKNL-FM (101.5 The Bear)** (Freq: 101.5)
Owned by: Bell Media Inc.*
10532 Alaska Rd., Fort St John, BC V1J 1B3
Tel: 250-785-6634
www.iheartradio.ca/101-5-the-bear
www.facebook.com/1015thebear, twitter.com/1015thebear
Terry Shepherd, General Manager,
terry.shepherd@bellmedia.ca
Dave Lewis, Creative Director, dave.lewis@bellmedia.ca
Andre Da Costa, News Director, andre.dacosta@bellmedia.ca

Fort St. James: **CIRX-FM-3 (94X)** (Freq: 94.7)
Owned by: CIRX-FM (94X)
Fort St. James, BC

Gibsons: **CISC-FM** (Freq: 107.5)
Owned by: CISQ-FM (Mountain FM)
Gibsons, BC
www.mountainfm.com
Joe Polito, Manager

Gold River: **CJGR-FM (100.1 2day FM)** (Freq: 100.1)
Owned by: Vista Radio Ltd.*
Gold River, BC

Golden: **CKGR-FM (106.3 EZ Rock)** (Freq: 106.3)
Owned by: Bell Media Inc.*
PO Box 1403, 825 - 10th Ave. South, Golden, BC V0A 1H0
Tel: 250-344-7177, Fax: 250-344-7233
golden.myezrock.com
www.facebook.com/EZRockGolden

Grand Forks: **CKGF-FM (Juice FM)** (Freq: 102.3)
Owned by: CJUI-FM
Grand Forks, BC

Grand Forks: **CKGF-FM (The Goat)** (Freq: 96.7)
Owned by: Vista Radio Ltd.*
Grand Forks, BC

Hazelton: **CJFW-FM-8** (Freq: 101.9)
Owned by: CJFW-FM
Hazelton, BC

Hope: **CFSR-FM** (Freq: 100.5)
Owned by: CKSR-FM
Hope, BC

Houston: **CFBV-FM-1 (The Peak)** (Freq: 106.5)
Owned by: CFBV-AM (The Peak)
Houston, BC
thepeak@thepeak.ca
www.thepeak.ca

Houston: **CJFW-FM-7** (Freq: 105.5)
Owned by: CJFW-FM
Houston, BC

Invermere: **CJAY-FM-3** (Freq: 99.7)
Owned by: CJAY-FM (CJAY 92)
Invermere, BC
www.cjay92.com

Kamloops: **CFBX-FM** (Freq: 92.5)
Thompsons Rivers University, 900 McGill Rd., House 8,
Kamloops, BC V2C 0C8
Tel: 250-377-3988
radio@tru.ca
www.theX.ca
www.facebook.com/345643872210945, twitter.com/CFBXRadio
Brant Zwicker, Station Manager, bzwicker@tru.ca

Kamloops: **CIFM-FM (98.3 CIFM)** (Freq: 98.3)
Owned by: Jim Pattison Broadcast Group*
460 Pemberton Terrace, Kamloops, BC V2C 1T5
Tel: 250-372-3322, Fax: 250-374-0445
www.98.3cifm.com
www.instagram.com/983cifm, www.facebook.com/983cifm,
twitter.com/983cifm
Rod Schween, President & General Manager,
rschween@jpbg.ca
Cheryl Blackwell, Director, Radio Programming & Operations,
cheryl.blackwell@jpbg.ca

Kamloops: **CJKC-FM (Country 103)** (Freq: 103.1)
Owned by: Stingray Group Inc.*
611 Lansdowne St., Kamloops, BC V2C 1Y6
Tel: 250-571-1031, Fax: 250-372-2263
info@radionl.com
www.country103.ca
www.facebook.com/Country103, twitter.com/Country103CJKC
Garth Buchko, General Manager, gbuchko@radionl.com

Kamloops: **CKBZ-FM (B-100)** (Freq: 100.1)
Owned by: Jim Pattison Broadcast Group*
460 Pemberton Terrace, Kamloops, BC V2C 1T5
Tel: 250-372-3322, Fax: 250-374-0445
www.b100.ca
www.instagram.com/b100kamloops,
www.facebook.com/b100kamloops, twitter.com/kamloopsb100
Rod Schween, President & General Manager,
rschween@jpbg.com

Kamloops: **CKRV-FM (97.5 The River)** (Freq: 97.5)
Owned by: Stingray Group Inc.*
611 Lansdowne St., Kamloops, BC V2C 1Y6
Tel: 250-372-2197, Fax: 250-372-2293
info@975river.com
www.975river.com
www.facebook.com/161321237228076, twitter.com/ckrvfm
Garth Buchko, General Manager, gbuchko@radionl.com

Kaslo: **CKZX-FM-1** (Freq: 95.3)
Owned by: CKKC-FM (Kootenays EZ Rock)
Kaslo, BC
kootenays.myezrock.com

Kelowna: **CBTK-FM** (Freq: 88.9)
Owned by: Canadian Broadcasting Corporation*
243 Lawrence Ave., Kelowna, BC V1Y 6L2
Tel: 250-861-3781
www.cbc.ca/bc

Kelowna: **CHSU-FM (99.9 Sun FM)** (Freq: 99.9)
Owned by: Bell Media Inc.*
435 Bernard Ave., Kelowna, BC V1Y 6N8
Tel: 250-860-8600
webmaster@thesun.net
www.iheartradio.ca/sun-fm/99-9-sun-fm
www.facebook.com/99.9SUNFM, twitter.com/999SUNFM
Ken Kilcullen, General Manager, ken.kilcullen@bellmedia.ca

Kelowna: **CILK-FM (101.5 EZ Rock)** (Freq: 101.5)
Owned by: Bell Media Inc.*
435 Bernard Ave., Kelowna, BC V1Y 6N8
Tel: 250-860-8600, Fax: 250-860-8856
kelownainfo@myezrock.com
kelowna.myezrock.com
www.facebook.com/101.5EZrockKelowna,
twitter.com/1015ezrock
Ken Kilcullen, General Manager, ken.kilcullen@bellmedia.ca

Kelowna: **CKKO-FM (K963)** (Freq: 96.3)
Owned by: Stingray Group Inc.*
1601 Bertram St., Kelowna, BC VIY 2G5
Tel: 250-861-5693, Fax: 250-469-9963
www.k963.ca
www.instagram.com/k963classicrock,
www.facebook.com/K96.3fm, twitter.com/K963ClassicRock
Peter Angle, General Manager, pangle@newcap.ca
David Larsen, Program Director, dlarsen@newcap.ca

Kelowna: **CKLZ-FM (Power 104 FM)** (Freq: 104.7)
Owned by: Jim Pattison Broadcast Group*
3805 Lakeshore Rd., Kelowna, BC V1W 3K6
Tel: 250-763-1047, Fax: 250-762-2141
info@power104.fm
www.power104.fm
www.instagram.com/power104, www.facebook.com/power104,
twitter.com/power104

Kelowna: **CKOO-FM** (Freq: 103.9)
Kelowna, BC
Steve Huber, General Manager, shuber@vistaradio.ca

Kelowna: **CKQQ-FM (Beach Radio)** (Freq: 103.1)
Owned by: Jim Pattison Broadcast Group*
3805 Lakeshore Rd., Kelowna, BC V1W 3K6
Tel: 250-762-3331
www.beachradiokelowna.com
www.instagram.com/1031beachradio,
www.facebook.com/1031beachradio,
twitter.com/1031beachradio

Keremeos: **CIGV-FM-1** (Freq: 98.9)
Owned by: CIGV-FM
Keremeos, BC

Kitimat: **CJFW-FM-1** (Freq: 92.9)
Owned by: CJFW-FM
Kitimat, BC

Lillooet: **CHLS-FM** (Freq: 100.5)
415 Main St., Lillooet, BC V0K 1V0
Tel: 250-256-7561
radiolillooet@gmail.com
radiolillooet.ca

Mackenzie: **CHMM-FM** (Freq: 103.5)
PO Box 547, Mackenzie, BC V0J 2C0
Tel: 250-997-6277, Fax: 250-997-6222
chmm1035@gmail.com
www.chmm.ca

Masset: **CJFW-FM-4** (Freq: 92.9)
Owned by: CJFW-FM
Masset, BC

Merritt: **CKMQ-FM (Q101.1 FM)** (Freq: 101.1)
Owned by: Stingray Group Inc.*
#201, 2196 Quilchena Ave., Merritt, BC V1K 1A4
Tel: 250-378-4288
www.q101.ca
www.facebook.com/140846484203, twitter.com/Q101Merritt

Nakusp: **CKBS-FM** (Freq: 103.1)
Owned by: CKKC-FM (Kootenays EZ Rock)
Nakusp, BC
kootenays.myezrock.com

Nanaimo: **CHLY-FM** (Freq: 101.7)
c/o The Radio Malaspina Society, #2, 34 Victoria Rd.,
Nanaimo, BC V9R 5B8
Tel: 250-716-3410, Toll-Free: 855-740-1017
www.chly.ca
www.facebook.com/Radio.Malaspina, twitter.com/chlyradio
Bob Simpson, Executive Director & Interim Station Manager,
programdirector@chly.ca

Nanaimo: **CHWF-FM (106.9 The Wolf)** (Freq: 106.9)
Owned by: Jim Pattison Broadcast Group*
4550 Wellington Rd., Nanaimo, BC V9T 2H3
Tel: 250-758-1131, Fax: 250-758-4644
info@1069thewolf.com
www.1069thewolf.com
www.facebook.com/1069thewolf, twitter.com/1069thewolf
Other information: News Phone: 250-758-2467
Rob Bye, General Manager, rob.bye@jpbg.ca

Nanaimo: **CKWV-FM (102.3 The Wave)** (Freq: 102.3)
Owned by: Jim Pattison Broadcast Group*
4550 Wellington Rd., Nanaimo, BC V9T 2H3
Tel: 250-758-1131, Fax: 250-758-4644
info@1023thewave.com
www.1023thewave.com
www.facebook.com/1023thewave, twitter.com/1023thewave
Other information: News Phone: 250-758-2467
Rob Bye, General Manager, rob.bye@jpbg.ca

Nelson: **CHNV-FM (103.5 Juice FM)** (Freq: 103.5)
Owned by: Vista Radio Ltd.*
312 Hall St., Nelson, BC V1L 1Y8
Tel: 250-352-1902, Fax: 250-352-0301
www.mynelsonnow.com/juicefm
www.facebook.com/1035juicefm, twitter.com/1035juicefm

*For details on this company see listing in Major Broadcasting Companies section; † French language station

Steve Huber, General Manager, shuber@vistaradio.ca
John Helm, Programming Director, john@thegoatrocks.ca

Nelson: CJLY-FM (Freq: 93.5; 96.5)
308A Hall St., Nelson, BC V1L 1Y8
Tel: 250-352-9600, Fax: 250-352-9653
km@kootenaycoopradio.com
www.kootenaycoopradio.com
twitter.com/cjly

New Denver: CKZX-FM (Freq: 93.5)
Owned by: CKKC-FM (Kootenays EZ Rock)
New Denver, BC
kootenays.myezrock.com
Lee Sterry, Operations Manager

Oliver: CJOR-FM (EZ Rock) (Freq: 102.9)
Owned by: CJOR-AM (EZ Rock)
Oliver, BC
osoyoos.myezrock.com

Parksville: CHPQ-FM (The Lounge 99.9) (Freq: 99.9)
Owned by: Jim Pattison Broadcast Group*
PO Box 1370, 166 Island Hwy. East, Parksville, BC V9P 2X2
Tel: 850-248-4211, Fax: 250-248-4210
info@thelounge999.com
www.thelounge999.com
Rob Bye, General Manager, rob.bye@jpbg.ca

Parksville: CIBH-FM (88.5 The Beach) (Freq: 88.5)
Owned by: Jim Pattison Broadcast Group*
PO Box 1370, 166 Island Hwy. East, Parksville, BC V9P 2H3
Tel: 250-248-4211, Fax: 250-248-4210
info@885thebeach.com
www.885thebeach.com
www.facebook.com/885thebeach
Rob Bye, General Manager, rbye@jpbg.ca

Pemberton: CISP-FM (Freq: 104.5)
Owned by: CISQ-FM (Mountain FM)
Pemberton, BC
www.mountainfm.com
Gary Miles, President
Joe Polito, Manager

Pender Harbour: CIPN-FM (Freq: 104.7)
Owned by: CISQ-FM (Mountain FM)
Pender Harbour, BC
www.mountainfm.com

Penticton: CIGV-FM (Freq: 100.7)
Owned by: Stingray Group Inc.*
#201, 1301 Main St., Penticton, BC V2A 5E9
Tel: 250-493-6767, Fax: 250-493-2851
okanagancountry.com
www.facebook.com/Country1007, twitter.com/country1007
Peter Angle, General Manager, pangle@newcap.ca
Casey Clarke, Program Director, cclarke@newcap.ca

Penticton: CJMG-FM (Sun FM) (Freq: 97.1)
Owned by: Bell Media Inc.*
33 Carmi Ave., Penticton, BC V2A 3G4
Tel: 250-487-4487
www.sunonline.ca
www.instagram.com/971sunfm,
www.facebook.com/97.1SUNFM, twitter.com/971sunfm
Mark Burley, Brand Director, mark.burley@bellmedia.ca

Port Alberni: CJAV-FM (93.3 The Peak) (Freq: 93.3)
Owned by: Jim Pattison Broadcast Group*
3296 - 3rd Ave., Port Alberni, BC V9Y 4E1
Tel: 250-723-2455, Fax: 250-723-0797
info@933thepeak.com
www.933thepeak.com
www.facebook.com/933thepeak, twitter.com/933thepeak
David Wiwchar, Operations Manager, david.wiwchar@jpbg.ca

Port Alice: CFPA-FM (1240 Coast AM) (Freq: 100.3)
Owned by: CFNI-AM (1240 Coast AM)
Port Alice, BC
www.mytriportnow.com/coast-am

Powell River: CFPW-FM (95.7 Coast FM) (Freq: 95.7)
Owned by: Vista Radio Ltd.*
#103, 7074 Westminster St., Powell River, BC V8A 1C5
Tel: 604-485-4207, Fax: 604-485-4210
www.mypowellrivernow.com/coast-fm
www.facebook.com/957coastfm, twitter.com/957CoastFM
Allison Mandzuk, General Manager, GSM - The Coast Group,
amandzuk@vistaradio.ca
Rob Alexander, Program director, Regional Cluster,
ralexander@vistaradio.ca

Powell River: CJMP-FM (Freq: 90.1)
4476 Marine Ave., Powell River, BC V8A 2K2
Tel: 604-483-1712
onair@cjmp.ca
cjmp.ca
www.facebook.com/CJMP90.1FM, twitter.com/cjmpfm

Prince George: CBYG-FM (Freq: 91.5)
Owned by: Canadian Broadcasting Corporation*
#1, 890 Victoria St., Prince George, BC V2L 5P1
Tel: 250-562-2888
www.cbc.ca/bc

Prince George: CFUR-FM (Freq: 88.7)
3333 University Way, Prince George, BC V2N 4Z9
Tel: 250-960-7664
www.cfur.ca
www.facebook.com/CFURradio
Fraser Hayes, Station Manager, fhayes@cfur.ca

Prince George: CIRX-FM (94.3 The Goat) (Freq: 94.3)
Owned by: Vista Radio Ltd.*
#101, 2977 Ferry Ave., Prince George, BC V2N 1L3
Tel: 250-564-2524, Fax: 250-562-6611
www.myprincegeorgenow.com
twitter.com/943theGOAT

Prince George: CJCI-FM (Country 97 FM) (Freq: 97.3)
Owned by: Vista Radio Ltd.*
#101, 2977 Ferry Ave., Prince George, BC V2N 1L3
Tel: 250-564-2524, Fax: 250-562-6611
www.97fm.ca

Prince George: CKDV-FM (93.3 The Drive) (Freq: 99.3)
Owned by: Jim Pattison Broadcast Group*
1810 - 3rd Ave., 2nd Fl., Prince George, BC V2M 1G4
Tel: 250-564-8861, Fax: 250-562-8768
www.993thedrive.com
www.instagram.com/993thedrive,
www.facebook.com/993thedrive, twitter.com/993thedrive
Mike Clotildes, General Manager, mike.clotildes@jpbg.ca

Prince George: CKKN-FM (The River 101.3) (Freq: 101.3)
Owned by: Jim Pattison Broadcast Group*
1810 - 3rd Ave., 2nd Fl., Prince George, BC V2M 1G4
Tel: 250-564-8861, Fax: 250-562-8768
www.1013theriver.com
www.facebook.com/ckkn1013theriver, twitter.com/1013theriver
Mike Clotildes, General Manager, mike.clotildes@jpbg.ca

Prince Rupert: CHTK-FM (EZ Rock) (Freq: 99.1)
Owned by: Bell Media Inc.*
#230, 215 Cowbay Rd., Prince Rupert, BC V8J 1A8
Tel: 250-635-6316
www.iheartradio.ca/ez-rock/ez-rock-prince-rupert
www.facebook.com/NorthEZRock, twitter.com/EZRockNorth
Brian Langston, General Manager, brian.langston@bellmedia.ca

Prince Rupert: CJFW-FM-2 (Freq: 101.9)
Owned by: CJFW-FM
Prince Rupert, BC

Princeton: CIGV-FM-2 (Freq: 98.1)
Owned by: CIGV-FM
Princeton, BC

Quesnel: CFFM-FM-2 (The Goat) (Freq: 94.9)
Owned by: CFFM-FM (The Rush)
#502, 410 Kinchant St., Quesnel, BC V2J 7J5
Tel: 250-992-7046, Fax: 250-992-2354
www.mycariboonow.com

Quesnel: CKCQ-FM (The Wolf) (Freq: 100.3)
Owned by: Vista Radio Ltd.*
#502, 410 Kinchant St., Quesnel, BC V2J 7J5
Tel: 250-992-7046, Fax: 250-992-2354
www.thewolfonline.ca

Revelstoke: CKCR-FM (EZ Rock) (Freq: 106.1)
Owned by: Bell Media Inc.*
PO Box 1420, #207, 555 Victoria Rd., Revelstoke, BC V0E 2S0
Tel: 250-837-2149
www.revelstoke.myezrock.com
www.facebook.com/revelstokeezrock
Gord Leighton, General Manager, gord.leighton@bellmedia.ca

Richmond: CHKG-FM (Freq: 96.1)
Owned by: Fairchild Radio Group Ltd.*
Aberdeen Centre, #2090, 4151 Hazelbridge Way, Richmond, BC V6X 4J7
Tel: 604-295-1234, Fax: 604-295-1201
www.fm961.com
www.youtube.com/fairchildradiovan,
www.facebook.com/am1470fm961

Richmond: CHLG-FM (LG 104.3) (Freq: 104.3)
Owned by: Stingray Group Inc.*
#20, 11151 Horseshoe Way, Richmond, BC V7A 4S5
Tel: 604-241-2100, Fax: 604-272-0917
www.lg1043.com
www.instagram.com/lg1043fm, www.facebook.com/lg1043,
twitter.com/lg1043
Sherri Pierce, General Manager, spierce@newcap.ca
Paul Sereda, Program Director, psereda@newcap.ca

Richmond: CKZZ-FM (Z95.3) (Freq: 95.3)
Owned by: Stingray Group Inc.*
#20, 11151 Horseshoe Way, Richmond, BC V7A 4S5
Tel: 604-241-2100, Fax: 604-272-0917
www.z953.ca
www.instagram.com/z953fm,
www.facebook.com/z953vancouver, twitter.com/Z953VAN
Sherri Pierce, General Manager, spierce@newcap.ca
Jason Manning, Program Director, jmanning@newcap.ca

Rock Creek: CKGF-3-FM (103.7 Juice FM) (Freq: 103.7)
Owned by: CJUI-FM (103.9 Juice FM)
Rock Creek, BC

Salmon Arm: CKXR-FM (EZ Rock 91.5) (Freq: 91.5)
Owned by: Bell Media Inc.*
PO Box 69, 360 Ross St., Salmon Arm, BC V1E 4N2
Tel: 250-832-2161
www.iheartradio.ca/ez-rock/ez-rock-salmon-arm
www.instagram.com/915ezrock, www.facebook.com/myezrock,
twitter.com/MyEzRock

Sandspit: CJFW-FM-3 (Freq: 92.9)
Owned by: CJFW-FM
Sandspit, BC

Sechelt: CKAY-FM (The Coast) (Freq: 91.7)
Owned by: Vista Radio Ltd.*
#1, 1877 Field Rd., Sechelt, BC V0N 3A1
Tel: 604-741-9170, Toll-Free: 855-451-9170
www.mycoastnow.com
www.facebook.com/917coastfm, twitter.com/917coastfm
Rob Alexander, Regional Program Director,
ralexander@vistaradio.ca

Sechelt: CKKS-FM (Freq: 104.7)
Owned by: CISQ-FM (Mountain FM)
Sechelt, BC
www.mountainfm.com

Smithers: CJFW-FM-6 (Freq: 92.9)
Owned by: CJFW-FM
Smithers, BC

Sorrento: CKXR-FM-1 (Freq: 102.1)
Owned by: CKXR-FM (EZ Rock)
Sorrento, BC
salmonarm.myezrock.com

Squamish: CISQ-FM (Mountain FM) (Freq: 107.1)
Owned by: Rogers Media Inc.*
#202, 40147 Glenalder Place, Squamish, BC V8B 0G2
Tel: 604-892-1021, Fax: 604-892-6383
Toll-Free: 888-429-2724
www.mountainfm.com
www.instagram.com/mountainfmradio,
www.facebook.com/adventurestation, twitter.com/mountainfm

Summerland: CHOR-FM (EZ Rock) (Freq: 98.5)
Owned by: Bell Media Inc.*
#200, 9901 Main St., Summerland, BC V0H 1Z0
Tel: 250-494-0333
www.iheartradio.ca/ez-rock/ez-rock-summerland
www.facebook.com/EZRock98.5, twitter.com/EZRockSland
Mark Burley, Brand Director, mark.burley@bellmedia.ca
Janet Burley, General Manager/Sales Manager,
janet.burley@bellmedia.ca

---

* For details on this company see listing in Major Broadcasting Companies section; † French language station

Terrace: **CJFW-FM** (Freq: 103.1)
Owned by: Bell Media Inc.*
4625 Lazelle Ave., Terrace, BC V8G 1S4
Tel: 250-635-6316
www.cjfw.ca
www.facebook.com/cjfwfm, twitter.com/cjfwfm

Terrace: **CKTK-FM (EZ Rock)** (Freq: 97.7)
Owned by: Bell Media Inc.*
4625 Lazelle Ave., Terrace, BC V8G 1S4
Tel: 250-635-6316
kitimat.myezrock.com
www.facebook.com/NorthEZRock, twitter.com/EZRockNorth
Brian Langston, General Manager, blangston@astral.com

Trail: **CHRT-FM (The Goat)** (Freq: 104.1)
Owned by: Vista Radio Ltd.*
Trail, BC

Trail: **CJAT-FM (Kootenays EZ Rock)** (Freq: 95.7)
Owned by: Bell Media Inc.*
1560 - 2nd Ave., Trail, BC V1R 1M4
Tel: 250-368-5510
kootenays.myezrock.com
www.facebook.com/EZRockKootenayBoundary,
twitter.com/ezrockkootenays
Nicole Beetstra, General Manager, 250-368-5510,
nicole.beetstra@bellmedia.ca

Trail: **CKKC-FM (Kootenays EZ Rock)** (Freq: 106.9)
Owned by: Bell Media Inc.*
1560 - 2nd Ave., Trail, BC V1R 1M4
Tel: 250-368-5510
kootenays.myezrock.com
www.facebook.com/ezrockkootenayboundary,
twitter.com/ezrockkootenays

†*Vancouver:* **CBUF-FM** (Freq: 97.7)
Détenteur: **Canadian Broadcasting Corporation***
700, rue Hamilton, Vancouver, BC V6B 4A2
Tél: 604-662-6135
www.radio-canada.ca
Pierre Guerin, Directeur des services francais dans l'ouest,
204-788-3237, pierre.guerin@radio-canada.ca

Vancouver: **CBU-FM** (Freq: 105.7)
Owned by: Canadian Broadcasting Corporation*
700 Hamilton St., Vancouver, BC V6B 4A2
Tel: 604-662-6000
cbc.ca/bc

Vancouver: **CBUX-FM** (Freq: 90.9)
Owned by: Canadian Broadcasting Corporation*
700, rue Hamilton, Vancouver, BC V6B 4A2
Tel: 604-662-6135
www.radio-canada.ca/regions/colombie-britannique
Pierre Guérin, Directeur des services français, Régions de
l'Ouest, pierre.guerin@radio-canada.ca

Vancouver: **CFBT-FM** (Freq: 94.5)
Owned by: Bell Media Radio*
#500, 969 Robson St., Vancouver, BC V6Z 1X5
Tel: 604-871-9000
www.iheartradio.ca/virginradio/vancouver
www.instagram.com/virginradiovancouver,
www.facebook.com/VirginRadioVancouver,
twitter.com/VirginRadioVan

Vancouver: **CFMI-FM (Rock 101)** (Freq: 101.1)
Owned by: Corus Radio Company*
#2000, 700 West Georgia St., Vancouver, BC V7Y 1K9
Tel: 604-331-2808, *Fax:* 604-331-2722
www.rock101.com
www.instagram.com/rock101van,
www.facebook.com/rock101van, twitter.com/rock101van
Dustin Collins, Program Director, dustin.collins@corusent.com

Vancouver: **CFOX-FM** (Freq: 99.3)
Owned by: Corus Radio Company*
#2000, 700 West Georgia St., Vancouver, BC V7Y 1K9
Tel: 604-684-7221, *Fax:* 604-331-2722
www.cfox.com
www.instagram.com/cfoxvan, www.facebook.com/cfoxvan,
twitter.com/cfoxvan
Dustin Collins, Program Director

Vancouver: **CFRO-FM** (Freq: 102.7)
#110, 360 Columbia St., Vancouver, BC V6A 4J1
Tel: 604-684-8494
www.coopradio.org

Vancouver: **CHQM-FM** (Freq: 103.5)
Owned by: Bell Media Radio*
#500, 969 Robson St., Vancouver, BC V6Z 1X5
Tel: 604-871-9000
www.iheartradio.ca/qmfm
www.instagram.com/1035qmfm, www.facebook.com/1035qmfm,
twitter.com/QMFM

Vancouver: **CITR-FM** (Freq: 101.9)
#233, 6138 Sub Blvd., Vancouver, BC V6T 1Z1
Tel: 604-822-8648, *Fax:* 604-882-9364
stationmanager@citr.ca
www.citr.ca
www.youtube.com/user/CiTR1019fm,
www.facebook.com/CiTR101.9, twitter.com/CiTRradio
Brenda Grunau, Station Manager

Vancouver: **CJAX-FM (Jack 96.9)** (Freq: 96.9)
Owned by: Rogers Media Inc.*
2440 Ash St., Vancouver, BC V5Z 4J6
Tel: 604-872-2557
www.jack969.com
www.instagram.com/jack969van,
www.facebook.com/jack969van, twitter.com/jack969van

Vancouver: **CJJR-FM (JRfm 93.7)** (Freq: 93.7)
Owned by: Jim Pattison Broadcast Group*
#300, 1401 West 8th Ave., Vancouver, BC V6H 1C9
Tel: 604-731-7772
www.jrfm.com
www.instagram.com/jrfm, www.facebook.com/937jrfm,
twitter.com/jrfm

Vancouver: **CKPK-FM (102.7 The Peak)** (Freq: 102.7)
Owned by: Jim Pattison Broadcast Group*
#300, 1401 West 8th Ave., Vancouver, BC V6H 1C9
Tel: 604-731-6111
www.thepeak.fm
www.instagram.com/thepeakvancouver,
www.facebook.com/thepeak, twitter.com/thepeak
Other information: Advertising Phone: 604-730-6553

Vanderhoof: **CIRX-FM-2 (94.7 The Goat)** (Freq: 95.9)
Owned by: CIRX-FM (94X)
Vanderhoof, BC

Vernon: **CICF-FM (105.7 Sun FM)** (Freq: 105.7)
Owned by: Bell Media Inc.*
2800 - 31 St., Vernon, BC V1T 5H4
Tel: 250-545-9222
www.iheartradio.ca/sun-fm/105-7-sun-fm
www.facebook.com/105.7SUNFM
Gord Leighton, General Manager, gord.leighton@bellmedia.ca

Vernon: **CKIZ-FM (Beach Radio 107.5)** (Freq: 107.5)
Owned by: Jim Pattison Broadcast Group*
3313 - 32nd Ave., Vernon, BC V1T 2E1
Tel: 250-545-2141
www.beachradiovernon.ca
www.instagram.com/1075beachradio,
www.facebook.com/1075beachradio,
twitter.com/1075beachradio
Bryan Ford, Contact, Sales, bryan.ford@jpbg.ca

Victoria: **CFUV-FM** (Freq: 101.9)
University of Victoria, PO Box 3035, Victoria, BC V8W 3P3
Tel: 250-721-8607
director@uvic.ca
cfuv.uvic.ca
vimeo.com/user7758198, www.facebook.com/CFUV101.9,
twitter.com/CFUV
Randy Gelling, Station Manager, 250-721-8607,
cfuvman@uvic.ca

Victoria: **CHBE-FM (107.3 Kool FM)** (Freq: 107.3)
Owned by: Bell Media Radio*
1420 Broad St., Victoria, BC V8W 2B1
Tel: 250-382-1073
www.iheartradio.ca/kool-107-3
www.instagram.com/1073koolfm,
www.facebook.com/1073KOOLFM, twitter.com/1073Koolfm
Robin Haggar, Program Director

Victoria: **CHTT-FM (Kiss 103.1)** (Freq: 103.1)
Owned by: Rogers Media Inc.*
817 Fort St., Victoria, BC V8W 1H6
Tel: 250-382-0900, *Fax:* 250-382-4358
www.kiss1031.ca
www.instagram.com/kiss_1031,
www.facebook.com/kiss1031victoria, twitter.com/kiss1031

Victoria: **CIOC-FM (Ocean 98.5)** (Freq: 98.5)
Owned by: Rogers Media Inc.*
817 Fort St., Victoria, BC V8W 1H6
Tel: 250-382-0900, *Fax:* 250-382-4358
www.ocean985.com
www.instagram.com/ocean985, www.facebook.com/ocean985,
twitter.com/ocean985

Victoria: **CJZN-FM (The Zone)** (Freq: 91.3)
Owned by: Jim Pattison Broadcast Group*
2750 Quadra St., Victoria, BC V8T 4E8
Tel: 250-475-6611, *Fax:* 250-475-6626
www.thezone.fm
www.instagram.com/thezone913,
www.facebook.com/thezone.fm, twitter.com/thezone913
Rob Bye, General Manager, rob.bye@jpbg.ca

Victoria: **CKKQ-FM (100.3 The Q!)** (Freq: 100.3)
Owned by: Jim Pattison Broadcast Group*
2750 Quadra St., Victoria, BC V8T 4E8
Tel: 250-475-0100, *Fax:* 250-475-3299
Toll-Free: 800-717-1003
www.theq.fm
www.facebook.com/theq.fm, twitter.com/theqdotfm
Rob Bye, General Manager, rob.bye@jpbg.ca

Whistler: **CISW-FM** (Freq: 102.1)
Owned by: CISQ-FM (Mountain FM)
#126, 4295 Blackcomb Way, Whistler, BC V0N 1B4
Tel: 604-905-1691, *Fax:* 604-892-6383
www.mountainfm.com
www.instagram.com/mountainfmradio,
www.facebook.com/adventurestation, twitter.com/MountainFM

Williams Lake: **CFFM-FM (The Goat)** (Freq: 97.5)
Owned by: Vista Radio Ltd.*
83 South First Ave., Williams Lake, BC V2G 1H4
Tel: 250-392-6551, *Fax:* 250-392-4142
www.mycariboonow.com
www.facebook.com/RushFM

Manitoba

Brandon: **CIWM-FM** (Freq: 91.5)
Owned by: CICY-FM
Brandon, MB

Brandon: **CJJJ-FM** (Freq: 106.5)
1430 Victoria Ave. East, Brandon, MB R7A 2A9
Tel: 204-725-8700
cj-106.assiniboine.net
twitter.com/cj106fm
Jill Ferguson, Contact, 204-725-8700

Brandon: **CKLF-FM (Star 94.7)** (Freq: 94.7)
Owned by: Westman Communications Group*
624 - 14th St. East, Brandon, MB R7A 7E1
Tel: 204-726-8888, *Toll-Free:* 866-727-7827
starfm@starfm.ca
starfm.ca
www.youtube.com/user/StarFMBrandon,
www.facebook.com/starfmbrandon, twitter.com/StarfmBrandon

Brandon: **CKXA-FM (101.1 The Farm)** (Freq: 101.1)
Owned by: Bell Media Inc.*
2940 Victoria Ave., Brandon, MB R7B 3Y3
Tel: 204-728-1150
www.iheartradio.ca/101-the-farm
www.facebook.com/1011thefarm, twitter.com/1011TheFarm
Mark Maheu, General Manager, mark.maheu@bellmedia.ca

Brandon: **CKX-FM (96.1 BOB FM)** (Freq: 96.1)
Owned by: Bell Media Inc.*
2940 Victoria Ave., Brandon, MB R7B 3Y3
Tel: 204-728-1150
www.961bobfm.ca
www.facebook.com/961bobfmbrandon, twitter.com/BOBFM961
Mark Maheu, General Manager, mark.maheu@bellmedia.ca

Flin Flon: **CFAR-FM** (Freq: 102.9)
Owned by: Arctic Radio*
316 Green St., Flin Flon, MB R8A 0H2
Tel: 204-687-3469, *Fax:* 204-687-6786
cfarcopy@arcticradio.ca
flinflononline.com
www.facebook.com/CFAR1029

---

* For details on this company see listing in Major Broadcasting Companies section; † French language station

Portage La Prairie: **CJPG-FM (Mix 96.5)** (Freq: 96.5)
Owned by: Golden West Broadcasting Ltd.*
PO Box 130, 2390 Sissons Dr., Portage La Prairie, MB R1N 3B2
Tel: 204-239-5111, *Toll-Free:* 866-239-5111
www.portageonline.com
www.facebook.com/Mix96.5FM, twitter.com/Mix_96

Portage la Prairie: **CFRY-FM** (Freq: 93.1)
Owned by: CFRY
Portage la Prairie, MB

Pukatawagan: **CFPX-FM** (Freq: 98.3)
PO Box 321, Pukatawagan, MB R0B 1G0
Tel: 204-553-2155, *Fax:* 204-553-2158

†*Saint-Boniface:* **CKXL-FM** (Freq: 91.1)
340, boul Provencher, Saint-Boniface, MB R2H 0G7
Tél: 204-233-4243, *Téléc:* 204-233-3646
Ligne sans frais: 866-894-3691
info@envol91.mb.ca
www.envol91.mb.ca
www.youtube.com/user/Envol91FM,
www.facebook.com/envol91, twitter.com/Envol91
Annick Boulet, Directrice générale, direction@envol91.mb.ca

Steinbach: **CILT-FM (Mix 96)** (Freq: 96.7)
Owned by: Golden West Broadcasting Ltd.*
#105, 32 Brandt St., Steinbach, MB R5G 2J7
Tel: 204-326-3737
mix@steinbachonline.com
www.steinbachonline.com
www.facebook.com/MIX96.7FM, twitter.com/mix967fm

The Pas: **CITP-FM** (Freq: 92.7)
Owned by: CICY-FM
The Pas, MB

The Pas: **CJAR-FM** (Freq: 102.9)
Owned by: Arctic Radio*
PO Box 2980, 130 - 3rd St. West, The Pas, MB R9A 1R7
Tel: 204-623-5307, *Fax:* 204-623-5337
cjar@arcticradio.ca
thepasonline.com
www.facebook.com/CJ1240

Thompson: **CBWK-FM** (Freq: 100.9)
Owned by: Canadian Broadcasting Corporation*
7 Selkirk Ave., Thompson, MB R8N 0M4
www.cbc.ca/manitoba
www.facebook.com/cbcmanitoba, twitter.com/CBCManitoba

Thompson: **CHTM-FM** (Freq: 102.9)
Owned by: Arctic Radio*
103 Cree Rd., Thompson, MB R8N 0B9
Tel: 204-778-7361, *Fax:* 204-778-5252
chtm@arcticradio.ca
thompsononline.ca
www.facebook.com/102.9CHTM

Winkler: **CJEL-FM (The Eagle 93.5)** (Freq: 93.5)
Owned by: Golden West Broadcasting Ltd.*
PO Box 399, 277 - 1st, Winkler, MB R6W 4A6
Tel: 204-331-9300, *Fax:* 888-765-7039
Toll-Free: 800-355-7065
www.pembinavalleyonline.com
www.facebook.com/Eagle935FM, twitter.com/Eagle935FM

Winkler: **CKMW-FM** (Freq: 88.9)
Owned by: Golden West Broadcasting Ltd.*
PO Box 339, 277 - 1st, Winkler, MB R6W 4A6
Tel: 204-325-9506, *Fax:* 888-765-7039
Toll-Free: 800-355-7065
www.pembinavalleyonline.com
www.facebook.com/country889fm, twitter.com/Country889FM

†*Winnipeg:* **CBW-FM** (Freq: 98.3)
Détenteur: Canadian Broadcasting Corporation*
607, rue Langevin, Winnipeg, MB R2H 2W2
Tél: 204-788-3235, *Téléc:* 204-788-3245
www.cbc.ca/manitoba
Sylvie Laurencelle-Vermette, Chef des communications

Winnipeg: **CFEQ-FM (Classical 107 FM)** (Freq: 107.1)
Owned by: Golden West Broadcasting Ltd.*
#2, 20 St. Mary's Rd., Winnipeg, MB R2H 1H1
Tel: 204-256-2525, *Toll-Free:* 855-346-1071
info@classic107.com
classic107.com
www.youtube.com/channel/UCqsKhZ6bKTKaQ2J7Q05yX6Q,
www.facebook.com/classic107, twitter.com/Classic107FM
Fin Paterson, Station Manager

Winnipeg: **CFPG-FM (Peggy 99.1)** (Freq: 99.1)
Owned by: Corus Radio Company*
#200, 1440 Jack Blick Ave., Winnipeg, MB R3G 0L4
Tel: 204-786-2471
www.peggy991.com
www.instagram.com/peggy991, www.facebook.com/peggy991,
twitter.com/peggy991
Don Kollins, Program Director

Winnipeg: **CFQX-FM (QX104)** (Freq: 104.4)
Owned by: Jim Pattison Broadcast Group*
177 Lombard Ave., 3rd Fl., Winnipeg, MB R3B 0W5
Tel: 204-944-1031, *Fax:* 204-989-5291
www.qx104fm.com
www.facebook.com/qx104, twitter.com/qx104winnipeg
Heidi Rasmussen, General Manager, heidi.rasmussen@jpbg.ca

Winnipeg: **CFWM-FM** (Freq: 99.9)
Owned by: Bell Media Radio
1445 Pembina Hwy., Winnipeg, MB R3T 5C2
Tel: 204-477-5120
www.999bobfm.com
www.facebook.com/999BOBFM, twitter.com/999BOBFM
Mark Maheu, General Manager, mark.maheu@bellmedia.ca
David Drake, Program Director, david.drake@bellmedia.ca

Winnipeg: **CHIQ-FM (94.3 The Drive)** (Freq: 94.3)
Owned by: Jim Pattison Broadcast Group*
177 Lombard Ave., 3rd Fl., Winnipeg, MB R3B 0W5
Tel: 204-944-1031, *Fax:* 204-989-5291
www.943thedrive.ca
www.instagram.com/943thedrive
www.facebook.com/943thedrive, twitter.com/943thedrive
Heidi Rasmussen, General Manager, heidi.rasmussen@jpbg.ca

Winnipeg: **CHVN-FM** (Freq: 95.1)
Owned by: Golden West Broadcasting Ltd.*
#1, 741 St. Mary's Rd., Winnipeg, MB R2M 3N5
Tel: 204-452-9602, *Toll-Free:* 866-951-2486
info@chvnradio.com
www.chvnradio.com
www.facebook.com/chvn951, twitter.com/chvn951

Winnipeg: **CHWE-FM** (Freq: 106.1)
Owned by: Evanov Communications Inc.*
520 Corydon Ave., Winnipeg, MB R3L 0P1
Tel: 204-477-1221
info@energy106.ca
energy106.ca
www.instagram.com/energy106fm,
www.facebook.com/energy106fm, twitter.com/energy106fm
Adam West, Program Director, 204-477-1221,
awest@evanovwpg.com

Winnipeg: **CICY-FM** (Freq: 105.5)
1507 Inkster Blvd., Winnipeg, MB R2X 1R2
Tel: 204-772-8255
www.ncifm.com
www.facebook.com/ncifm, twitter.com/NCIWakeUpCrew

Winnipeg: **CITI-FM (92.1 CITI)** (Freq: 92.1)
Owned by: Rogers Media Inc.*
#4, 166 Osborne St., Winnipeg, MB R3L 1Y8
Tel: 204-788-3400
www.921citi.ca
www.instagram.com/921citi, www.facebook.com/921citi,
twitter.com/921citi

Winnipeg: **CJKR-FM (Power 97)** (Freq: 97.5)
Owned by: Corus Radio Company*
#200, 1440 Jack Blick Ave., Winnipeg, MB R3G 0L4
Tel: 204-786-2471
www.power97.com
www.instagram.com/power97, www.facebook.com/Power97,
twitter.com/power97wpg
Don Kollins, Program Director

Winnipeg: **CJUM-FM** (Freq: 101.5)
University of Manitoba, #308, University Centre, Winnipeg, MB R3T 2N2
Tel: 204-474-7027, *Fax:* 204-269-1299
cjum@cjum.com
www.umfm.com
www.youtube.com/user/CJUMVids,
www.facebook.com/umfm1015, twitter.com/UMFM
Jared McKetiak, Station Manager, jared@umfm.com
Michael Elves, Program Director, michael@umfm.com

Winnipeg: **CKMM-FM (103.1 Virgin Radio)** (Freq: 103.1)
Owned by: Bell Media Inc.*
1445 Pembina Hwy., Winnipeg, MB R3T 5C2
Tel: 204-477-5120
winnipeg.virginradio.ca
www.instagram.com/virginradiowinnipeg,
www.facebook.com/VirginRadioWinnipeg,
twitter.com/VirginRadioWPG
Mark Maheu, General Manager, mark.maheu@bellmedia.ca

Winnipeg: **CKUW-FM** (Freq: 95.9)
University of Winnipeg, #4CM11, 515 Portage Ave., Winnipeg, MB R3B 2E9
Tel: 204-786-9782, *Fax:* 204-783-7080
ckuw@uwinnipeg.ca
www.ckuw.ca
www.facebook.com/119731854749489, twitter.com/ckuw
Rob Schmidt, Station Manager, manager@ckuw.ca

Winnipeg: **CKY-FM (Kiss 102.3)** (Freq: 102.3)
Owned by: Rogers Media Inc.*
#4, 166 Osborne St., Winnipeg, MB R3L 1Y8
Tel: 204-780-3400
www.kiss1023.ca
www.instagram.com/kiss1023wpg
www.facebook.com/kiss1023wpg, twitter.com/kiss1023rfm

New Brunswick

†*Balmoral:* **CIMS-FM** (Freq: 103.9)
CP 2561, Balmoral, NB E8E 2W7
Tél: 506-826-1040, *Téléc:* 506-826-2400
info@cimsfm.ca
cimsfm.com
www.facebook.com/RadioRestigouche
Pierre Bourque, Directeur général

Bathurst: **CKBC-FM (Max 104.9)** (Freq: 104.9)
Owned by: Bell Media Inc.*
#1, 640 St. Peter Ave., Bathurst, NB E2A 2Y7
Tel: 506-547-1360
www.iheartradio.ca/max-104-9
www.facebook.com/MAX104.9, twitter.com/Max1049bathurst
Jamie Robichaud, General Manager,
jamie.robichaud@bellmedia.ca

†*Bathurst:* **CKLE-FM** (Freq: 92.9)
#301, 270, av Douglas, Bathurst, NB E2A 1M9
Tél: 506-546-4600, *Téléc:* 506-546-6611
superstation@ckle.fm
www.ckle.fm
www.facebook.com/CKLEFM

†*Caraquet:* **CJVA-FM** (Freq: 94.1)
Détenteur: CKLE-FM
Caraquet, NB
superstation@ckle.fm
www.ckle.fm
www.facebook.com/cklefm
Armand Roussy, Directeur

†*Edmundston:* **CFAI-FM** (Freq: 101.1; 105.1)
17, rue Costigan, Edmundston, NB E3V 1W7
Tél: 506-737-5060, *Téléc:* 506-737-5084
radio@cfai.fm
www.cfai.fm
www.facebook.com/cfaifm, twitter.com/cfaifm
Michelle Daigle, Directrice, direction@cfai.fm

†*Edmundston:* **CJEM-FM** (Freq: 92.7)
64, rue Rice, Edmundston, NB E3V 1T2
Tél: 506-735-3351, *Téléc:* 506-739-5803
cjem@cjemfm.com
cjemfm.com
Serge Parent, Président/Directeur général, 506-735-3351,
serge@cjemfm.com

†*Edmundston:* **CKMV-FM** (Freq: 92.7)
64, rue Rice, Edmundston, NB E3V 1T2
Tél: 506-735-3351, *Téléc:* 506-739-5803
cjem@cjemfm.com
cjemfm.com
Murillo Soucy, Directeur général, direction@cjemfm.com

Fredericton: **CBZF-FM** (Freq: 99.5)
Owned by: Canadian Broadcasting Corporation*
1160 Regent St., Fredericton, NB E3B 5G4
Tel: 506-451-4000
www.cbc.ca/nb

---

* For details on this company see listing in Major Broadcasting Companies section; † French language station

Fredericton: **CFRK-FM (New Country 92.3)** (Freq: 92.3)
Owned by: Stingray Group Inc.*
495A Prospect St., Fredericton, NB E3B 9M4
Tel: 506-455-3602, *Fax:* 506-455-3602
www.newcountry923.com
www.facebook.com/newcountry923, twitter.com/NewCountry923
Kenton Dunphy, Station Manager, kdunphy@newcap.ca
Rod Martens, Program Director, rmartens@newcap.ca

Fredericton: **CFXY-FM (105.3 The Fox)** (Freq: 105.3)
Owned by: Bell Media Inc.*
206 Rookwood Ave., Fredericton, NB E3B 2M2
Tel: 506-451-9111
www.foxrocks.ca
www.instagram.com/105thefox, www.facebook.com/105thefox, twitter.com/105thefox

Fredericton: **CHSR-FM** (Freq: 97.9)
PO Box 4400, #223, 21 Pacey Dr., Fredericton, NB E3B 5A3
Tel: 506-453-4985
stationmanager@chsrfm.ca
chsrfm.ca
www.facebook.com/238304316821, twitter.com/CHSR979
Tim Rayne, Station Manager

Fredericton: **CIBX-FM (106.9 Capital FM)** (Freq: 106.9)
Owned by: Bell Media Inc.*
206 Rookwood Ave., Fredericton, NB E3B 2M2
Tel: 506-454-2444
www.capitalfm.ca
www.facebook.com/1069capitalfm, twitter.com/1069capital

Fredericton: **CIHI-FM (Up! 93.1)** (Freq: 93.1)
Owned by: Stingray Group Inc.*
495A Prospect St., Fredericton, NB E3B 9M4
Tel: 506-455-0923, *Fax:* 506-455-3602
www.up931.com
www.facebook.com/Up931, twitter.com/up931
Kenton Dunphy, Station Manager, kdunphy@newcap.ca
Rod Martens, Program Director, rmartens@newcap.ca

Fredericton: **CIXN-FM** (Freq: 96.5)
#10, 1010 Hanwell Rd., Fredericton, NB E3B 6A4
Tel: 506-454-9600, *Fax:* 506-454-0991
welcome@joyfm.ca
www.joyfm.ca
www.facebook.com/JoyFm965

Fredericton: **CJPN-FM** (Freq: 90.5)
715, rue Priestman, Fredericton, NB E3B 5W7
Tel: 506-454-2576, *Fax:* 506-453-3958
direction@cjpn.ca
www.cjpn.ca
www.facebook.com/Cjpn905Fm, twitter.com/cjpnfm

Grand Falls: **CIKX-FM (K93)** (Freq: 93.5)
Owned by: Bell Media Inc.*
399 Broadway Blvd., Grand Falls, NB E3Z 2K5
Tel: 506-473-9393, *Fax:* 506-473-3893
www.k93.ca
www.instagram.com/k935fm, www.facebook.com/k93fans, twitter.com/k935

Kedgwick: **CFJU-FM** (Freq: 90.1)
PO Box 1043, Kedgwick, NB E8B 1Z9
Tel: 506-235-9000, *Fax:* 506-235-9001
cfjufm@rogers.com
www.cfju.ca
twitter.com/CFJU_FM
Lucille Thériault, Directrice-Animatrice

McLeod Hill: **CKTP-FM** (Freq: 95.7)
1036 McLeod Hill Rd., McLeod Hill, NB E3G 6J7
Tel: 506-474-2795, *Fax:* 506-206-3301
info@957thewolf.ca
www.cktpradio.com
www.facebook.com/957WOLF, twitter.com/957wolf

Miramichi: **CFAN-FM (99.3 The River)** (Freq: 99.3)
Owned by: Maritime Broadcasting System*
396 Pleasant St., Miramichi, NB E1V 1X3
Tel: 506-622-3311, *Fax:* 506-627-0335
www.993theriver.com
www.facebook.com/187522916587

Miramichi: **CHHI-FM (95.9 Sun FM)** (Freq: 95.9)
Owned by: Stingray Group Inc.*
202 Pleasant St., Miramichi, NB E1V 1Y5
Tel: 506-622-3969, *Fax:* 506-622-3970
info@959sunfm.com
959sunfm.com
www.instagram.com/959sunfm, www.facebook.com/959sunfm, twitter.com/959sunfm
Dan Fagan, Station Manager/Sales Manager, dfagan@newcap.ca
Steve Power, Program Director, steve.power@newcap.ca

†*Moncton:* **CBAF-FM** (Freq: Radio-Canada Première Chaîne 88.5 MHz (FM) à Moncton; 102.3 FM à Fredericton/Saint-Jean; 105.7 FM à Allardville; 91.5 FM à Campbellton; 100.3 FM à Edmunston; 90.3 FM à Lamèque/Caraquet; et 91.7 FM à Bon Accord.)
Détenteur: **Canadian Broadcasting Corporation***
#15, 165, rue Main, Moncton, NB E1C 1B8
Tél: 506-853-6666, *Ligne sans frais:* 800-561-7010
infoacadie@radio-canada.ca
ici.radio-canada.ca/acadie
Richard Simoens, Directeur, Radio-Canada Acadie

†*Moncton:* **CBAL-FM** (Freq: 98.3; 95.3; 101.9; 88.1)
Détenteur: **Canadian Broadcasting Corporation***
#15, 165, rue Main, Moncton, NB E1C 1B8
Tél: 506-853-6666, *Ligne sans frais:* 800-561-7010
www.icimusique.ca
Richard Simoens, Directeur

Moncton: **CBAM** (Freq: 106.1)
Owned by: Canadian Broadcasting Corporation*
#15, 165 Main St., Moncton, NB E1C 1B8
Tel: 506-853-6666
www.cbc.ca/nb
twitter.com/cbcnb
Darrow MacIntyre, Executive Producer, News, New Brunswick
Denise Wilson, Senior Managing Director, Atlantic Canada

Moncton: **CFQM-FM (MAX FM)** (Freq: 103.9)
Owned by: Maritime Broadcasting System*
1000 St. George Blvd., Moncton, NB E1E 4M7
Tel: 506-858-1220
1039maxfm.com
www.facebook.com/monctonsgreatesthits

†*Moncton:* **CHOY-FM (Choix 99)** (Freq: 99.9)
Détenteur: **Maritime Broadcasting System***
Moncton, NB E1E 4M7
Tél: 506-384-2469
choix999.com
www.facebook.com/Choix99

Moncton: **CJMO-FM (C103)** (Freq: 103.1)
Owned by: Stingray Group Inc.*
Moncton Industrial Park, 27 Arsenault Ct., Moncton, NB E1E 4J8
Tel: 506-858-5525, *Fax:* 506-858-5539
c103@c103.com
www.c103.com
www.youtube.com/user/C103Moncton, www.facebook.com/c103moncton, twitter.com/c103
Dan Fagan, General Manager, dfagan@newcap.ca
Adam McLaren, Program Director, amclaren@newcap.ca

Moncton: **CJXL-FM (XL Country)** (Freq: 96.9)
Owned by: Stingray Group Inc.*
Moncton Industrial Park, 27 Arsenault Ct., Moncton, NB E1E 4J8
Tel: 506-858-5525, *Fax:* 506-858-5539
reception@xl96.com
www.xl96.com
www.instagram.com/xlcountry969, www.facebook.com/xl969, twitter.com/xlcountry969
Dan Fagan, General Manager, dfagan@newcap.ca
Adam McLaren, Program Director, amclaren@newcap.ca

Moncton: **CKCW-FM (K94.5)** (Freq: 94.5)
Owned by: Maritime Broadcasting System*
1000 St. George Blvd., Moncton, NB E1E 4M7
Tel: 506-858-1220
k945.ca
www.facebook.com/k945moncton, twitter.com/K945Moncton
Krysta Janssen, Manager, Operations

Moncton: **CKOE-FM** (Freq: 107.3)
3030 Mountain Rd., Moncton, NB E1G 2W8
Tel: 506-384-1009, *Fax:* 506-383-9699
info@ckoefm.com
www.ckoefm.com
twitter.com/ckoefm

Jim Houssen, Station Manager

Pokemouche: **CKRO-FM** (Freq: 97.1)
142 Rte 113, Pokemouche, NB E8P 1K7
Tel: 506-336-9706, *Fax:* 506-336-9058
info@ckro.ca
www.ckro.ca
www.facebook.com/radiockro
Donald Noël, Directeur

Riverview: **CITA-FM** (Freq: 105.9)
#4, 645 Pinewood Rd., Riverview, NB E1B 5J9
Tel: 506-872-2901, *Fax:* 506-872-2234
Toll-Free: 855-330-0335
harvestersoffice@gmail.com
www.citafm.com
www.facebook.com/318492205878
Jeff Lutes, Contact, jeff@jefflutes.com

Sackville: **CHMA-FM** (Freq: 106.9)
62 York St., Sackville, NB E4L 1E2
Tel: 506-364-2221
chma@mta.ca
chmafm.wordpress.com
www.facebook.com/8928370874, twitter.com/chmaFM
Pierre Malloy, Station Manager

Saint John: **CBD-FM** (Freq: 91.3)
Owned by: Canadian Broadcasting Corporation*
PO Box 2358, Saint John, NB E2L 3V6
Tel: 506-632-7710
www.cbc.ca/nb
Denise Wilson, Senior Managing Director, Atlantic Canada, denise.wilson@cbc.ca
Darrow MacIntyre, Executive Producer, News, New Brunswick
Steven Webb, Executive Producer, Saint John
Nadine Antle, Regional Manager, Manager, Communications, Marketing & Brand, 902-420-4223
Mary-Pat Schutta, Senior Manager, New Brunswick

Saint John: **CFMH-FM** (Freq: 107.3)
Thomas J Condon Student Centre, University of New Brunswick Saint John, #235, 100 Tucker Park Rd., Saint John, NB E2L 4L5
Tel: 506-648-5667, *Fax:* 506-648-5541
cfmh@unbsj.ca
localfm.ca
www.facebook.com/localfm, twitter.com/local1073fm
Brian Cleveland, Station Manager, brian@cfmh.ca

Saint John: **CHNI-FM (Rock 88.9)** (Freq: 88.9)
Owned by: Stingray Group Inc.*
#137, 1 Market Sq., Saint John, NB E2L 4Z6
Tel: 506-635-6500, *Fax:* 506-635-6505
www.rock889.ca
www.facebook.com/rock889, twitter.com/Rock889FM
Jay McNeil, Station Manager, jay.mcneil@newcap.ca
Rod Martens, Program Director, rmartens@newcap.ca

Saint John: **CHSJ-FM** (Freq: 94.1)
Owned by: Acadia Broadcasting Ltd.
58 King St., Saint John, NB E2L 1G4
Tel: 506-633-3323, *Fax:* 506-644-3485
news@radioabl.ca
www.country94.ca
www.facebook.com/country94, twitter.com/country94chsj

Saint John: **CHWV-FM** (Freq: 97.3)
Owned by: Acadia Broadcasting Ltd.
58 King St., Saint John, NB E2L 1G4
Tel: 506-633-3323, *Fax:* 506-644-3485
mail@thewave.ca
www.thewave.ca
www.facebook.com/973thewave, twitter.com/973thewave

Saint John: **CINB-FM** (Freq: 96.1)
PO Box 96, Saint John, NB E2L 3X1
Tel: 506-657-9600
staff@newsongfm.com
newsongfm.com
www.facebook.com/NewSongFM, twitter.com/NewSongfm
Don Mabee, Station Manager

Saint John: **CIOK-FM (K-100)** (Freq: 100.5)
Owned by: Maritime Broadcasting System*
226 Union St., Saint John, NB E2L 1B1
Tel: 506-658-5100
www.k100.ca
www.facebook.com/k100fm, twitter.com/K100_FM

* For details on this company see listing in Major Broadcasting Companies section; † French language station

Saint John: **CJRP-FM** (Freq: 103.5)
77 King St. East, Saint John, NB E2L 1G9
Tel: 506-657-1035, *Fax:* 888-573-8961
cjrpfm.com
Graham Brown, Contact, graham@saintjohnradio.fm

Saint John: **CJYC-FM (Kool 98)** (Freq: 98.9)
Owned by: Maritime Broadcasting System*
226 Union St., Saint John, NB E2L 1B1
Tel: 506-658-5100
kool98.fm
www.facebook.com/KOOL98SaintJohn, twitter.com/KOOL98FM
Kelly O'Neill, General Manager, Sales

Shédiac: **CJSE-FM** (Freq: 89.5, 101.7, 107.5)
51, ch Cornwall, Shédiac, NB E4P 8T8
Tel: 506-532-0080, *Fax:* 506-532-0120
cjse@cjse.ca
www.cjse.ca
www.facebook.com/CJSEFM89, twitter.com/cjsefm
Patricia Bourque-Chevarie, Directrice générale par intérim

St Stephen: **CHTD-FM** (Freq: 98.1)
Owned by: Acadia Broadcasting Ltd.
112 Milltown Blvd., St Stephen, NB E3L 1G6
Tel: 506-466-1000, *Fax:* 506-466-4500
mail@thetide.ca
www.thetide.ca
www.facebook.com/346408628831, twitter.com/TheTide981

Woodstock: **CJCJ-FM (CJ104)** (Freq: 104.1)
Owned by: Bell Media Inc.*
#2, 131 Queen St., Woodstock, NB E7M 2M8
Tel: 506-325-3030, *Fax:* 506-325-3031
cj104@bellmedia.ca
www.cj104.com
www.facebook.com/cj104fm, twitter.com/cj104fm

Newfoundland & Labrador

Argentia: **CFOZ-FM** (Freq: 100.3)
Owned by: CHOZ-FM
Argentia, NL

Bonavista: **CJOZ-FM** (Freq: 92.1)
Owned by: CHOZ-FM
Bonavista, NL
Brian O'Connell, Station Manager

Carbonear: **CHVO-FM (Kixx Country 103.9)** (Freq: 103.9)
Owned by: Stingray Group Inc.*
1 CHVO Dr., Carbonear, NL A1Y 1A2
Tel: 709-596-1560, *Fax:* 709-596-8626
info@kixxcountry.ca
www.kixxcountry.ca
www.facebook.com/kixxcountry, twitter.com/kixxcountry

Churchill Falls: **CFLC-FM** (Freq: 97.9)
Owned by: CFLN-FM (Big Land - Labrador's FM)
Churchill Falls, NL

Clarenville: **CKLN-FM (Kixx Country 103.9)** (Freq: 97.1)
Owned by: CHVO-FM
Clarenville, NL

Clarenville: **VOCM-FM1 (100.7 K-Rock)** (Freq: 100.7)
Owned by: Stingray Group Inc.*
Clarenville, NL
Tel: 709-726-5590, *Fax:* 709-726-4633
email@krockrocks.com
www.k-rock975.com
www.facebook.com/975krock, twitter.com/975krock

Corner Brook: **CFLN-FM (Big Land - Labrador's FM)** (Freq: 97.9)
Owned by: Stingray Group Inc.*
345 O'Connell Dr., Corner Brook, NL A2H 7V3
Tel: 709-570-1163, *Fax:* 709-726-4633
Toll-Free: 800-356-4570
info@bigland.fm
www.bigland.fm
twitter.com/biglandfm
Mike Murphy, Station Manager, mmurphy@newcap.ca
Mike Campbell, Program Director, mcampbell@newcap.ca

Corner Brook: **CKOZ-FM** (Freq: 92.3)
Owned by: CHOZ-FM
Corner Brook, NL
www.ozfm.com

Corner Brook: **CKXX-FM (K-Rock 103.9)** (Freq: 103.9)
Owned by: Stingray Group Inc.*
345 O'Connell Dr., Corner Brook, NL A2H 7V3
Tel: 709-634-4570, *Fax:* 709-634-4081
www.k-rock1039.com
www.facebook.com/1039krock
Dave Hillier, General Manager, dhillier@newcap.ca
Mike Payne, Program Director, mike.payne@vocm.com

Deer Lake: **CFDL-FM** (Freq: 97.9)
Owned by: CFCB
Deer Lake, NL
Tel: 709-634-4570, *Fax:* 706-634-4081
onair@cfcbradio.com
www.cfcbradio.com

Gander: **CKXD-FM (98.7 K-ROCK)** (Freq: 98.7)
Owned by: Stingray Group Inc.*
PO Box 650, Gander, NL A1V 1X2
Tel: 709-651-3650, *Fax:* 709-651-2542
OnAir@987krock.com
www.987krock.com
www.youtube.com/user/987Krock,
www.facebook.com/233634473362049, twitter.com/987krock
David Hillier, Station Manager, dhillier@newcap.ca

Grand Falls-Windsor: **CKMY-FM** (Freq: 95.9)
Owned by: CHOZ-FM
Grand Falls-Windsor, NL
www.ozfm.com

Grand Falls-Windsor: **CKXG-FM (102.3 K-Rock)** (Freq: 102.3; 101.3)
Owned by: Stingray Group Inc.*
35A Grenfell Heights, Grand Falls-Windsor, NL A2A 2K2
Tel: 709-489-2192, *Fax:* 709-489-8626
onair@krocknl.com
www.krocknl.com
www.facebook.com/krock.grandfallswindsor,
twitter.com/krockgfw
David Hillier, General Manager, dhillier@newcap.ca
Richard King, Program Director, rking@vocm.com

Happy Valley-Goose Bay: **CFGB-FM** (Freq: 89.5)
Owned by: Canadian Broadcasting Corporation*
12 Loring Dr., Happy Valley-Goose Bay, NL A0P 1C0
Tel: 709-896-2911, *Fax:* 709-896-8900
labradormorning@cbc.ca
www.cbc.ca/nl
Denise Wilson, Senior Managing Director, Atlantic Canada, denise.wilson@cbc.ca

Labrador City: **CBDQ-FM** (Freq: 96.3)
Owned by: Canadian Broadcasting Corporation*
500 Vanier Ave., Labrador City, NL A2V 2W7
Tel: 709-944-3616, *Fax:* 709-944-5472
labradormorning@cbc.ca
www.cbc.ca/nl
Denise Wilson, Senior Managing Director, Atlantic Canada, denise.wilson@cbc.ca
Peter Gullage, Executive Producer, Newfoundland & Labrador, peter.gullage@cbc.ca
Nadine Antle, Regional Manager, Communications, Marketing & Brand, 902-420-4223, Nadine.Antle@cbc.ca

Marystown: **CIOZ-FM** (Freq: 96.3)
Owned by: CHOZ-FM
Marystown, NL
www.ozfm.com

Nain: **OKâlaKatiget Society Radio** (Freq: 99.9)
Owned by: OKâlaKatiget Society*
PO Box 160, Nain, NL A0P 1L0
Tel: 709-922-2187, *Fax:* 709-922-2293
okradio@oksociety.com
www.oksociety.com

Northwest River: **CFLN-1-FM** (Freq: 95.9)
Owned by: CFLN-FM
Northwest River, NL
www.bigland.fm

Springdale: **CKCM-1FM (VOCM)** (Freq: 89.3)
Owned by: Stingray Group Inc.*
Springdale, NL
Tel: 709-489-2192, *Fax:* 709-489-8626
www.vocm.com
twitter.com/vocmnews

St Andrews: **CFCVFM** (Freq: 97.7)
Owned by: CFSX-AM
St Andrews, NL
Tel: 709-643-2192, *Fax:* 709-643-5025
www.cfsxradio.com

St Anthony: **CFNN-FM (CFCB 97.9)** (Freq: 97.9)
Owned by: CFCB
St Anthony, NL
www.cfcbradio.com

St. John's: **CBN-FM** (Freq: 106.9)
Owned by: Canadian Broadcasting Corporation*
95 University Ave., St. John's, NL A1B 1Z4
Tel: 709-576-5000
www.cbc.ca/nl
Denise Wilson, Senior Managing Director, Atlantic Canada, denise.wilson@cbc.ca

St. John's: **CHMR-FM** (Freq: 93.5)
Memorial University, PO Box A-119, St. John's, NL A1C 5S7
Tel: 709-864-4777, *Fax:* 709-864-7688
chmr@mun.ca
www.mun.ca/chmr
www.facebook.com/chmrfmnewsdepartment,
twitter.com/chmrmunradio
Kathy Rowe, Station Manager

St. John's: **CHOZ-FM** (Freq: 94.7)
Owned by: Newfoundland Broadcasting Co. Ltd.*
446 Logy Bay Rd., St. John's, NL A1C 5S2
Tel: 709-273-2255
ozfm.com
www.facebook.com/officialozfm, twitter.com/officialozfm

St. John's: **CKIX-FM (Hits FM)** (Freq: 99.1)
Owned by: Stingray Group Inc.*
PO Box 8-590, 391 Kenmount Rd., St. John's, NL A1B 3P5
Tel: 709-726-5590, *Fax:* 709-726-4633
hitsmail@991hitsfm.com
www.991hitsfm.com
www.instagram.com/991hitsfm, www.facebook.com/991hitsfm,
twitter.com/hitsfm
Mike Murphy, General Manager, mmurphy@newcap.ca
Mike Campbell, Program Director, mcampbell@newcap.ca

St. John's: **CKSJ-FM** (Freq: 101.1)
#201, 95 Bonaventure Ave., St. John's, NL A1B 2X5
Tel: 709-754-6748, *Fax:* 709-754-6749
onair@coast1011.com
www.coast1011.com
www.facebook.com/coast1011, twitter.com/coast1011

St. John's: **VOCM-FM (97.5 K-Rock)** (Freq: 97.5)
Owned by: Stingray Group Inc.*
PO Box 8590, 391 Kenmount Rd., St. John's, NL A1B 3P5
Tel: 709-726-5590, *Fax:* 709-726-4633
email@krockrocks.com
www.k-rock975.com
www.facebook.com/975krock, twitter.com/975krock

Stephenville: **CIOS-FM** (Freq: 98.5)
Owned by: CHOZ-FM
Stephenville, NL
www.ozfm.com

Stephenville: **CKXX-FM-1** (Freq: 95.9)
Owned by: CKXX-FM
60 West St., Stephenville, NL

Wabush: **CFLW-FM (Big Land FM)** (Freq: 94.7)
Owned by: CFLN-FM (Big Land - Labrador's FM)
Wabush, NL
www.bigland.fm

Northwest Territories

Hay River: **CJCD-FM-1 (100.1 Moose FM)** (Freq: 100.1)
Owned by: CJCD-FM (Mix 100)
Hay River, NT
Toll-Free: 867-873-4663
www.myyellowknifenow.com

†*Yellowknife:* **CIVR-FM** (Freq: 103.5)
CP 456, 5106, 48e rue, Yellowknife, NT X1A 2P2
Tél: 867-766-5172
civr@radiotaiga.ca
www.radiotaiga.ca
www.facebook.com/299660494713, twitter.com/radiotaiga

---

* For details on this company see listing in Major Broadcasting Companies section; † French language station

Yellowknife: **CJCD-FM (100.1 Moose FM)** (Freq: 100.1)
Owned by: Vista Radio Ltd.*
PO Box 218, 5114 - 49th St., Yellowknife, NT X1A 2N2
Tel: 867-920-4636, *Fax:* 867-920-4033
www.myyellowknifenow.com

Yellowknife: **CKLB-FM** (Freq: 101.9)
PO Box 2193, Yellowknife, NT X1A 2P6
Tel: 320-295-7700
ask@cklbradio.com
cklbradio.com
www.facebook.com/cklbradio.radioclb, twitter.com/cklbradio
Deneze Nakehk'o, Director of Radio,
deneze.nakehko@cklbradio.com

Nova Scotia

Amherst: **CKDH-FM** (Freq: 101.7)
Owned by: Maritime Broadcasting System*
PO Box 670, Amherst, NS B4H 4B8
Tel: 902-667-3875
1017ckdh.com
www.facebook.com/101.7CKDH

Antigonish: **CFXU-FM** (Freq: 93.3)
St. Francis Xavier University, PO Box 948, Antigonish, NS B2G 2W5
Tel: 902-867-2410
cfxu@stfx.ca
radiocfxu.ca
cfxuandu.tumblr.com, www.facebook.com/CFXUTheFox,
twitter.com/CFXUradio
Rory Macleod, Station Manager

Antigonish: **CJFX-FM (989 XFM)** (Freq: 98.9)
c/o Atlantic Broadcasters Limited, PO Box 5800, 5663 Hwy #7, Antigonish, NS B2G 2L9
Tel: 902-863-4580, *Fax:* 902-863-6300
Toll-Free: 800-350-2539
www.989xfm.ca
www.facebook.com/989XFM, twitter.com/989xfm
Ken Farrell, General Manager

Bridgewater: **CKBW-FM** (Freq: 98.1)
Owned by: Acadia Broadcasting Ltd.
#200, 135 North St., Bridgewater, NS B4V 2V7
Tel: 902-543-2401, *Fax:* 902-543-1208
ckbw@ckbw.com
ckbw.ca
www.facebook.com/CKBWRadio, twitter.com/ckbwradio

†*Cheticamp:* **CKJM-FM** (Freq: 106.1)
CP 699, Cheticamp, NS B0E 1H0
Tél: 902-224-1242, *Téléc:* 902-224-1770
Ligne sans frais: 877-828-1242
info@ckjm.ca
www.ckjm.ca
www.facebook.com/radiockjm, twitter.com/RadioCKJM
Angus LeFort, Directeur général, angus@ckjm.ca

Dartmouth: **CKHY-FM** (Freq: 105.1)
Owned by: Acadia Broadcasting Ltd.
Westphal Plaza, #2035, 100 Main St., Dartmouth, NS B2X 1R5
Tel: 902-429-1035
info@jewel105.com
jewel105.com
www.facebook.com/jewel105hfx, twitter.com/jewel105hfx
Scott Pettigrew, Station Manager, pettigrew.scott@radioabl.ca

Dartmouth: **CKHZ-FM** (Freq: 103.5)
Owned by: Acadia Broadcasting Ltd.
Westphal Plaza, #2035, 100 Main St., Dartmouth, NS B2X 1R5
Tel: 902-429-1035
news@hotcountry1035.com
hotcountry1035.com
www.facebook.com/hotcountry1035, twitter.com/HotCountry1035
Scott Pettigrew, Station Manager, pettigrew.scott@radioabl.ca

Eastern Passage: **CFEP-FM** (Freq: 105.9)
PO Box 196, Eastern Passage, NS B3G 1M5
Tel: 902-469-9231, *Fax:* 902-463-1935
info@seasidefm.com
www.seasidefm.com
www.facebook.com/seasidefmradio, twitter.com/seasidefm

†*Halifax:* **CBAX-FM** (Freq: 91.5)
5600 Sackville St., Halifax, NS B3J 1L2
Tél: 902-420-8311
ici.radio-canada.ca

Halifax: **CBHA-FM** (Freq: 90.5)
Owned by: Canadian Broadcasting Corporation*
#100, 7067 Chebucto Rd., Halifax, NS B3L 4R5
Tel: 902-420-8311, *Fax:* 902-420-4357
Toll-Free: 866-306-4636
www.cbc.ca/ns
Other information: Phone, CBC Radio One Newsroom, Halifax:
902-420-4100
Denise Wilson, Senior Managing Director, Atlantic Canada,
denise.wilson@cbc.ca
Chantal Bernard, Senior Officer, Communications, 709-576-5161

Halifax: **CBH-FM** (Freq: 102.7)
Owned by: Canadian Broadcasting Corporation*
#100, 7067 Chebucto Rd., Halifax, NS B3L 4R5
Tel: 902-420-8311
www.cbc.ca/ns
Denise Wilson, Senior Managing Director, Atlantic Canada,
denise.wilson@cbc.ca

Halifax: **CFLT-FM (Jack 92.9)** (Freq: 92.9)
Owned by: Rogers Media Inc.*
6080 Young St., 9th Fl., Halifax, NS B3K 5L2
Tel: 902-493-7200
www.jack929.com
www.instagram.com/jack929hfx, www.facebook.com/jack929hfx,
twitter.com/jack929hfx

Halifax: **CFRQ-FM (Q104)** (Freq: 104.3)
Owned by: Stingray Group Inc.*
#200, 3770 Kempt Rd., Halifax, NS B3K 4X8
Tel: 902-453-4004, *Fax:* 902-453-3120
halifaxreception@newcap.ca
www.q104.ca
www.facebook.com/141967777087, twitter.com/q104halifax
Ken Geddes, General Manager, kgeddes@newcap.ca
Trevor Wallworth, Program Director, twallworth@newcap.ca

Halifax: **CHFX-FM (FX101.9)** (Freq: 101.9)
Owned by: Maritime Broadcasting System*
90 Lovett Lake Ct., Halifax, NS B3S 0H6
Tel: 902-422-1651
www.fx1019.ca
www.facebook.com/FX101.9

Halifax: **CHNS-FM (89.9 The Wave)** (Freq: 89.9)
Owned by: Maritime Broadcasting System*
90 Lovett Lake Ct., Halifax, NS B3S 0H6
Tel: 902-422-1651
899thewave.fm
www.facebook.com/89.9TheWave, twitter.com/899TheWave

Halifax: **CIOO-FM** (Freq: 100.1)
2900 Agricola St., Halifax, NS B3K 6A7
Tel: 902-453-2524
www.iheartradio.ca/c100-fm
www.facebook.com/C100FM, twitter.com/C100FM
Trent McGrath, General Manager, 902-493-2731,
trent.mcgrath@bellmedia.ca
Brad Muir, Program Manager, brad.muir@bellmedia.ca

Halifax: **CJCH-FM** (Freq: 101.3)
Owned by: Bell Media Radio*
2900 Agricola St., Halifax, NS B3K 6A7
Tel: 902-453-2524
www.iheartradio.ca/virginradio/halifax
www.instagram.com/VirginRadioHali,
www.facebook.com/VIRGINRadioHali,
twitter.com/VirginRadioHali
Trent McGrath, General Manager, trent.mcgrath@bellmedia.ca

Halifax: **CJNI-FM (News 95.7)** (Freq: 95.7)
Owned by: Rogers Media Inc.*
6080 Young St., 9th Fl., Halifax, NS B3K 5L2
Tel: 902-493-7200
www.news957.com
www.facebook.com/news957, twitter.com/news957

Halifax: **CKDU-FM** (Freq: 88.1)
Student Union Bldg., 6136 University Ave., Halifax, NS B3H 4J2
Tel: 902-494-6479
info@ckdu.ca
www.ckdu.ca
www.youtube.com/user/CKDUFM,
www.facebook.com/CKDU88.1FM, twitter.com/CKDU881FM
Gianna Lauren, Station Coordinator, gianna@ckdu.ca

Halifax: **CKUL-FM (Mix 96.5)** (Freq: 96.5)
Owned by: Stingray Group Inc.*
#200, 3770 Kempt Rd., Halifax, NS B3K 4X8
Tel: 902-453-4004, *Fax:* 902-453-3120
www.mix965.ca
www.youtube.com/user/radio965hhalifax,
www.facebook.com/mix965halifax, twitter.com/mix965hfx
Ken Geddes, General Manager, kgeddes@newcap.ca
Trevor Wallworth, Program Director, twallworth@newcap.ca

Inverness: **CJFX-FM** (Freq: 102.5)
Owned by: CJFX-FM
Inverness, NS

Kentville: **CKEN-FM (AVR)** (Freq: 97.7)
Owned by: Maritime Broadcasting System*
PO Box 310, 29 Oakdene Ave., Kentville, NS B4N 1H5
Tel: 902-678-2111, *Fax:* 902-678-9894
www.avrnetwork.com
www.facebook.com/avrnetwork

Kentville: **CKWM-FM (Magic)** (Freq: 94.9)
Owned by: Maritime Broadcasting System*
PO Box 310, 29 Oakdene Ave., Kentville, NS B4N 1H5
Tel: 902-678-2111, *Fax:* 902-678-9894
www.magic949.ca
www.facebook.com/250425211647226

New Glasgow: **CKEC-FM (94.1 East Coast FM)** (Freq: 94.1)
Owned by: Hector Broadcasting Co. Ltd.
PO Box 519, 84 Provost St., New Glasgow, NS B2H 5E7
Tel: 902-752-4200, *Fax:* 902-755-2468
info@ecfm.ca
ecfm.ca
www.facebook.com/10388345939, twitter.com/941ECFM
Michael Freeman, Vice-President/General Manager
Doulas Freeman, CEO

New Glasgow: **CKEZ-FM** (Freq: 97.9)
Owned by: Hector Broadcasting Co. Ltd.
PO Box 519, 84 Provost St., New Glasgow, NS B2H 5E7
Tel: 902-752-4200, *Fax:* 902-755-2468
classicrock979.ca
www.facebook.com/Classicrock979, twitter.com/ROCKEZ979

New Minas: **CIJK-FM (89.3 K-Rock)** (Freq: 89.3)
Owned by: Stingray Group Inc.*
#3, 8794 Commercial St., New Minas, NS B4N 3C5
Tel: 902-365-8930, *Fax:* 902-365-3566
info@893krock.com
www.893krock.com
www.instagram.com/893krock, www.facebook.com/893krock,
twitter.com/893krock
Ken Geddes, General Manager, kgeddes@newcap.ca
Melanie Sampson, Program Director, msampson@newcap.ca

Port Hawkesbury: **CIGO-FM (The Hawk)** (Freq: 101.5)
Owned by: Acadia Broadcasting Ltd.
#201, 609 Church St., Port Hawkesbury, NS B9A 2X4
Tel: 902-625-1220, *Fax:* 902-625-2664
1015thehawk@radioabl.ca
www.1015thehawk.com
www.youtube.com/user/1015_The_Hawk,
www.facebook.com/1015TheHawk, twitter.com/1015_The_Hawk
Eric Whynot, Station Manager, whynot.eric@radioabl.ca

†*Saulnierville:* **CIFA-FM** (Freq: 104.1)
CP 8, Saulnierville, NS B0W 2Z0
Tél: 902-769-2432, *Téléc:* 902-769-3101
info@cifafm.com
cifafm.com
www.facebook.com/radiocifa
Ghislain Boudreau, Directeur général

Shelburne: **CJLS-FM-2** (Freq: 96.3)
Owned by: CJLS-FM
Shelburne, NS

Shelburne: **CKBW-FM-2** (Freq: 93.1)
Owned by: CKBW-FM
Shelburne, NS

Sydney: **CBI-FM** (Freq: CBC Radio 2; 105.1)
Owned by: Canadian Broadcasting Corporation*
500 George St., Sydney, NS B1P 1K6
Tel: 902-539-5050
www.cbc.ca/ns

---

* For details on this company see listing in Major Broadcasting Companies section; † French language station

Sydney: **CHER-FM (MAX FM)** (Freq: 98.3)
Owned by: Maritime Broadcasting System*
318 Charlotte St., Sydney, NS B1P 1C8
Tel: 902-564-5596, *Fax:* 902-562-1873
983maxfm.com
www.facebook.com/max983fm
Dwayne Keller, Manager, Operations

Sydney: **CHRK-FM (The Giant)** (Freq: 101.9)
Owned by: Stingray Group Inc.*
#300, 500 Kings St., Sydney, NS B1S 1B1
Tel: 902-270-1019, *Fax:* 902-270-3566
info@giant1019.com
www.giant1019.com
www.instagram.com/1019thegiant,
www.facebook.com/1019TheGiant, twitter.com/1019thegiant
Rob Redshaw, General Manager, rredshaw@newcap.ca
Daryl Stevens, Program Director, dstevens@newcap.ca

Sydney: **CKCH-FM (103.5 The Eagle)** (Freq: 103.5)
Owned by: Stingray Group Inc.*
#300, 500 Kings Rd., Sydney, NS B1S 1B1
Tel: 902-563-1035, *Fax:* 902-270-3566
info@eagle1035.com
www.eagle1035.com
www.instagram.com/1035theeagle,
www.facebook.com/1035TheEagle, twitter.com/1035theeagle
Robert Redshaw, General Manager/ Sales Manager,
rredshaw@newcap.ca
Jay Bedford, Program Director, jbedford@newcap.ca
Daryl Stevens, Operations Manager, dstevens@newcap.ca

Sydney: **CKPE-FM (The Cape)** (Freq: 94.9)
Owned by: Maritime Broadcasting System*
318 Charlotte St., Sydney, NS B1P 1C8
Tel: 902-564-5596, *Fax:* 902-564-1873
949thecape.com
www.facebook.com/thecape949
Dwayne Keller, Manager, Operations

Truro: **CKTO-FM (Big Dog 100.9 FM)** (Freq: 100.9)
Owned by: Bell Media Inc.*
187 Industrial Ave., Truro, NS B2N 6V3
Tel: 902-893-6060
www.bigdog1009.ca
www.instagram.com/bigdogtruro,
www.facebook.com/bigdogfanpage, twitter.com/bigdogtruro

Truro: **CKTY-FM (Cat Country 99.5 FM)** (Freq: 99.5)
Owned by: Bell Media Inc.*
187 Industrial Ave., Truro, NS B2N 6V3
Tel: 902-893-6060
www.iheartradio.ca/cat-country-99-5
www.facebook.com/catcountry995, twitter.com/catcountrytruro

Weymouth: **CKDY-FM-1** (Freq: 103.3)
Owned by: CKEN-FM
Weymouth, NS

Yarmouth: **CJLS-FM** (Freq: 95.5)
Owned by: Acadia Broadcasting Ltd.
#201, 328 Main St., Yarmouth, NS B5A 1E4
Tel: 902-742-7175, *Fax:* 902-742-3143
cjls@radioabl.ca
www.cjls.com
www.facebook.com/186605881367192, twitter.com/CJLSRadio
Jim Grattan, Production Manager

†*Iqaluit:* **CFRT-FM** (Freq: 107.3)
CP 880, Iqaluit, NU X0A 0H0
Tél: 867-979-1073
www.cfrt.ca
www.facebook.com/1302764337094882,
twitter.com/CFRT1073FM
Pascal Auger, Directeur du produit

Iqaluit: **CKIQ-FM** (Freq: 99.9)
PO Box 417, Iqaluit, NU X0A 0H0
Fax: 877-490-2547
Toll-Free: 877-445-2547
icefmiqaluit@gmail.com
www.icefm.ca
www.facebook.com/208026069253058
Glenn Craig, Station Manager

Rankin Inlet: **CBQR-FM** (Freq: 105.1)
Owned by: Canadian Broadcasting Corporation*
PO Box 130, Rankin Inlet, NU X0C 0G0
www.cbc.ca/north

Alliston: **CIMA-FM (myFM)** (Freq: 92.1)
Owned by: My Broadcasting Corporation*
63 Tupper St. West, Alliston, ON L9R 1E4
Tel: 705-530-6936
www.southsimcoetoday.ca
www.facebook.com/921myfm, twitter.com/myfm921
Jon Fee, General Manager, 705-530-6936

Arnprior: **CFMP-FM (Oldies)** (Freq: 107.7)
Owned by: CHMY-FM (myFM)
**Kenwood Corporate Centre, #50, 160 William St. West,
Arnprior, ON K7S 3W4**
Tel: 613-623-7772
arnpriortoday.ca
www.facebook.com/1077oldies, twitter.com/Oldies1077
Lynn Grinstead, General Manager, lynng@mbcmedia.ca

Aylmer: **CHPD-FM** (Freq: 105.9)
16 Talbot St. East, Aylmer, ON N5H 1H4
Tel: 519-773-8555, *Fax:* 519-773-8606
www.mcson.org

Bancroft: **CHMS-FM (Moose FM)** (Freq: 97.7)
Owned by: Vista Radio Ltd.*
PO Box 1240, 30674 Hwy. 28E, Bancroft, ON K0L 1C0
Tel: 613-332-1423, *Fax:* 613-332-0841
www.mybancroftnow.com
www.facebook.com/MooseFMBancroft,
twitter.com/moosefmchms

Barrie: **CFJB-FM** (Freq: 95.7)
Owned by: Rock 95 Broadcasting Ltd.*
#10, 431 Huronia Rd., Barrie, ON L4N 9B3
Tel: 705-725-7304, *Fax:* 705-792-7858
rock95.com

Barrie: **CHAY-FM (93.1 Fresh)** (Freq: 93.1)
Owned by: Corus Radio Company*
PO Box 937, 1125 Bayfield St. North, Barrie, ON L4M 4Y6
Tel: 705-737-3511
www.931freshradio.ca
www.instagram.com/931freshradio,
www.facebook.com/931freshradionews,
twitter.com/931freshradio
Dave Blezard, Contact, Programming, dave@931freshradio.ca

Barrie: **CIQB-FM** (Freq: 101.1)
Owned by: 591989 B.C. Ltd.*
1125 Bayfield St. North, Barrie, ON L4M 4Y6
Tel: 705-726-1011
1011bigfm.com
www.facebook.com/1011bigfm, twitter.com/1011bigfm
Mark Cameron, Program Director, mark@fm96.com

Barrie: **CJLF-FM (Life 100.3)** (Freq: 100.3)
#111, 115 Bell Farm Rd., Barrie, ON L4M 5G1
Tel: 705-735-3370, *Fax:* 705-735-3301
www.lifeonline.fm
Scott Jackson, Station Manager
Janice Baird, CFO & Office Manager

Barrie: **CKMB-FM** (Freq: 107.5)
Owned by: Rock 95 Broadcasting Ltd.*
#10, 431 Huronia Rd., Barrie, ON L4N 9B3
Tel: 705-725-7304, *Fax:* 705-792-7858
1075koolfm.com
www.facebook.com/koolfmbarrie, twitter.com/KoolFMBarrie

Belleville: **CHCQ-FM** (Freq: 100.1)
497 Dundas St. West, Belleville, ON K8P 1B6
Tel: 613-966-0955
www.cool100.fm
www.instagram.com/cool100fm, www.facebook.com/cool100.1,
twitter.com/cool100fm
John Sherratt, President & Owner, johns@cool100.ca

Belleville: **CIGL-FM (Mix 97)** (Freq: 97.1)
Owned by: Quinte Broadcasting Co. Ltd.*
PO Box 488, 10 Front St. South, Belleville, ON K8N 5B2
Tel: 613-969-5555, *Fax:* 613-969-8122
info@mix97.com
mix97.com
www.facebook.com/mix97fm, twitter.com/MIX97radio

Belleville: **CJLX-FM (91X)** (Freq: 91.3)
PO Box 4200, Belleville, ON K8N 5B9
Tel: 613-969-0923, *Fax:* 613-966-0923
contact@91x.fm
www.91x.fm
www.youtube.com/user/91xfm, www.facebook.com/91xfm,
twitter.com/91xfm
Other information: Newsroom, Phone: 613-966-6797

Belleville: **CJOJ-FM** (Freq: 95.5)
497 Dundas St. West, Belleville, ON K8P 1B6
Tel: 613-966-0955
www.955hitsfm.ca
www.instagram.com/955hitsfm, www.facebook.com/955hitsfm,
twitter.com/955hitsfm
John Sherratt, President & Owner, johns@cool100.ca

Belleville: **CJTN-FM (Rock 107)** (Freq: 107.1)
Owned by: Quinte Broadcasting Co. Ltd.*
PO Box 488, 10 Front St. South, Belleville, ON K8N 5B2
Tel: 613-969-5555, *Fax:* 613-969-8122
info@rock107.ca
www.rock107.ca
www.facebook.com/rock107quintesbestrock,
twitter.com/ROCK107fm

Bracebridge: **CFBG-FM (Moose FM)** (Freq: 99.5)
Owned by: Vista Radio Ltd.*
3A Taylor Dr., Bracebridge, ON P1L 1S6
Tel: 705-645-2218, *Fax:* 705-645-5798
www.mymuskokanow.com
www.facebook.com/159641740741946

Bracebridge: **CJMU-FM (Country 102)** (Freq: 102.3)
Owned by: Bayshore Broadcasting Corporation*
111 Manitoba St., Bracebridge, ON P1L 2B6
Tel: 705-640-5375
info@country102.ca
www.country102.ca
www.facebook.com/country102fm, twitter.com/country102onair

Brantford: **CFWC-FM** (Freq: 93.9)
271 Greenwich St., Brantford, ON N3S 2X9
Tel: 519-759-2339, *Fax:* 226-381-0940
info@brant939.faithfm.org
brantford.faithfm.org
www.facebook.com/faithfmBrantford
Peter Jackson, Station Manager

Brantford: **CKPC-FM** (Freq: 92.1)
Owned by: Evanov Communications Inc.*
571 West St., Brantford, ON N3R 7C5
Tel: 519-759-1000, *Fax:* 519-753-1470
lite92.ca
www.facebook.com/lite1067, twitter.com/lite1067fm

Brighton: **CIYM-FM (Oldies)** (Freq: 100.9)
Owned by: My Broadcasting Corporation*
PO Box 1522, Brighton, ON K0K 1H0
Tel: 613-475-6936
www.brightontoday.ca
www.facebook.com/1009oldies, twitter.com/oldies1009
Rob Mise, Regional Manager, 613-475-6936

Brockville: **CFJR-FM** (Freq: 104.9)
Owned by: Bell Media Radio*
601 Stewart Blvd., Brockville, ON K6V 5V9
Tel: 613-345-1666
webmaster@1049jrfm.com
www.iheartradio.ca/104-9-jr-fm
www.facebook.com/1049JRfm, twitter.com/1049JRfm
Greg Hinton, Vice President/General Manager,
greg.hinton@bellmedia.ca

Brockville: **CJPT-FM** (Freq: 103.7)
Owned by: Bell Media Radio*
601 Stewart Blvd., Brockville, ON K6V 5T4
Tel: 613-345-1666, *Toll-Free:* 800-495-1037
webmaster@bob.fm
www.iheartradio.ca/bob-fm
www.facebook.com/1037BOBFM, twitter.com/1037BOB_FM
Greg Hinton, Vice President/General Manager,
greg.hinton@bellmedia.ca

Caledonia: **CHTG-FM (The Grand)** (Freq: 92.9)
Owned by: Durham Radio Inc.*
#4, 282 Argyle St. South, Caledonia, ON N3W 1K8
Tel: 289-284-1070
www.929thegrand.fm
www.facebook.com/929thegrand, twitter.com/929thegrand
Steve Kassay, Vice-President, Programming

---

* For details on this company see listing in Major Broadcasting Companies section; † French language station

Campbellford: **CKOL-FM** (Freq: 93.7)
PO Box 551, Campbellford, ON K0L 1L0
Tel: 705-653-1089
ckol-radio@bell.net
ckol.webs.com
www.facebook.com/CKOLRadio, twitter.com/CKOLfm

Chatham-Kent: **CFCO-FM** (Freq: 630 AM; 92.9 FM)
Owned by: Blackburn Radio Inc.*
117 Keil Dr. South, Chatham-Kent, ON N7M 3H3
Tel: 519-354-2200, Fax: 519-354-2880
info@country929.com
country929.com
www.youtube.com/Country929fm,
www.facebook.com/country929cfco, twitter.com/Country929

Chatham-Kent: **CKSY-FM** (Freq: 94.3)
Owned by: Blackburn Radio Inc.*
117 Keil Dr. South, Chatham-Kent, ON N7M 3H3
Tel: 519-354-2200, Fax: 519-354-2880
cksyfm.com
www.youtube.com/user/cksyfm943
www.facebook.com/943CKSY, twitter.com/943cksy

Chatham-Kent: **CKUE-FM** (Freq: 95.1)
Owned by: Blackburn Radio Inc.*
117 Keil Dr. South, Chatham-Kent, ON N7M 3H3
Tel: 519-354-2200
chatham.coolradio.ca
www.facebook.com/CoolRadioCanada
twitter.com/coolradiocanada

Cobourg: **CHUC-FM** (Freq: 107.9)
Owned by: My Broadcasting Corporation*
PO Box 520, Cobourg, ON K9A 4L3
Tel: 905-372-5401
classicrock1079.ca
www.facebook.com/classicrock1079,
twitter.com/1079classicrock
York Bell-Smith, Program Director, 905-372-5401

Cobourg: **CKSG-FM** (myFM) (Freq: 93.3)
Owned by: My Broadcasting Corporation*
PO Box 520, Cobourg, ON K9A 4L3
Tel: 905-372-5401
newsnorthumberland@mbcmedia.ca
www.gonorthumberland.ca
www.facebook.com/933myFM, twitter.com/933myFM
Tommy West, Manager, tommyw@MBCmedia.ca

Cochrane: **CFIF-FM** (Moose FM) (Freq: 101.1)
Owned by: Vista Radio Ltd.*
22B - 5th Ave., Cochrane, ON P0L 1C0
Tel: 705-272-6467, Fax: 705-272-2520
Shane Button, Regional Program Director,
sbutton@moosefm.com

Cochrane: **CHPB-FM** (Moose FM) (Freq: 98.1)
Owned by: Vista Radio Ltd.*
22B - 5th Ave., Cochrane, ON P0L 1C0
Tel: 705-272-6467, Fax: 705-272-2520
www.mycochranenow.com
www.facebook.com/moosechpb, twitter.com/moosefmchpb
Shane Button, Regional Program Director,
sbutton@moosefm.com

Collingwood: **CHGB-FM** (Max FM) (Freq: 97.7)
Owned by: Bayshore Broadcasting Corporation*
9937 Hwy. 26, Collingwood, ON L9Y 0Y4
Tel: 705-422-0970
info@977maxfm.ca
www.977maxfm.ca
www.facebook.com/977maxfm, twitter.com/977maxfm
Tara Orme-Latreille, Manager, Sales,
torme@bayshorebroadcasting.ca

Collingwood: **CKCB-FM** (95.1 The Peak FM) (Freq: 95.1)
Owned by: 591989 B.C. Ltd.*
186 Hurontario St., Collingwood, ON L9Y 4T4
Tel: 705-446-9510
news@thepeakfm.com
thepeakfm.com
www.youtube.com/user/thepeakfm, twitter.com/thepeakfm
Deb James, Brand Director

Cornwall: **CFLG-FM** (104.5 Fresh) (Freq: 104.5)
Owned by: Corus Radio Company*
709 Cotton Mill St., Cornwall, ON K6H 7K7
Tel: 613-932-5180, Fax: 613-938-0355
www.1045freshradio.ca
www.facebook.com/1045freshradio, twitter.com/1045freshradio

Bill Halman, Program Director, bill.halman@corusent.com

†*Cornwall:* **CHOD-FM** (Freq: 92.1)
#202, 1111, ch Montréal, Cornwall, ON K6H 1E1
Tél: 613-936-2463
chodfm@chodfm.ca
chodfm.ca
www.facebook.com/457850440922218, twitter.com/CHODFM
Marc Charbonneau, Responsable, marc@chodfm.ca

Cornwall: **CJSS-FM** (Boom 101.9) (Freq: 101.9)
Owned by: Corus Radio Company*
709 Cotton Mill St., Cornwall, ON K6H 7K7
Tel: 613-932-5180, Fax: 613-938-0355
Toll-Free: 866-732-1019
www.boom1019.com
www.instagram.com/boomcornwall
www.facebook.com/boomcornwall, twitter.com/boomcornwall
Bill Halman, Program Director, bill.halman@corusent.com

Dryden: **CKDR-FM** (Freq: 92.7)
Owned by: Acadia Broadcasting Ltd.
122 King St., Dryden, ON P8N 1C2
Tel: 807-223-2355, Fax: 807-223-5090
Toll-Free: 800-465-7200
ckdr@radioabl.ca
www.ckdr.net
www.facebook.com/CKDR.Dryden, twitter.com/ckdrnews

Elliot Lake: **CKNR-FM** (Moose FM) (Freq: 94.1)
Owned by: Vista Radio Ltd.*
144 Ontario Ave., Elliot Lake, ON P5A 1Y3
Tel: 705-848-3608, Fax: 705-848-1378
www.myalgomamanitoulinnow.com
www.facebook.com/166739240015143,
twitter.com/moosefmcknr

Espanola: **CJJM-FM** (Moose FM) (Freq: 99.3)
Owned by: Vista Radio Ltd.*
#2, 90 Gray St., Espanola, ON P5E 1G1
Tel: 705-869-0578, Fax: 705-869-0578
www.myespanolanow.com
www.facebook.com/moose.espanola, twitter.com/moosefmcjjm
Peter Hobbs, Regional Manager, phobbs@vistaradio.ca

Exeter: **CKXM-FM** (Freq: 90.5)
Owned by: My Broadcasting Corporation*
#6, 145 Thames Rd. West, Exeter, ON N0M 1S3
Tel: 519-235-3000
www.exetertoday.ca
www.facebook.com/1057myfm, twitter.com/905myFM
Darren Boyle, General Manager, Sales, 519-235-3000

Fort Frances: **CFOB-FM** (The Border) (Freq: 93.1)
Owned by: Acadia Broadcasting Ltd.
210 Scott St., Fort Frances, ON P9A 1G7
Tel: 807-274-5341
info@931theborder.ca
www.b93.ca
www.facebook.com/931TheBorder, twitter.com/B93FortFrances
Other information: U.S Line: 218-283-4420

Gananoque: **CJGM-FM** (myFM) (Freq: 99.9)
Owned by: My Broadcasting Corporation*
PO Box 9, Gananoque, ON K7G 2T6
Tel: 613-382-6936
www.gananoquenow.com
www.facebook.com/999myfm, twitter.com/999myFM
Terri-Lynn Bayford, General Manager, Sales, 613-382-6936,
terri-lynnb@mbcmedia.ca

Goderich: **CHWC-FM** (Freq: 104.9)
Owned by: Bayshore Broadcasting Corporation*
300 Suncoast Dr., #E, Goderich, ON N7A 4N7
Tel: 519-612-1149, Fax: 519-612-1050
info@country1049.ca
www.country1049.ca
www.facebook.com/country1049
Steve Howard, Manager, Sales

Goderich: **CIYN-FM-1** (Freq: 99.7)
Owned by: CIYN-FM (myFM)
Goderich, ON
Tel: 519-565-2675
shorelinetoday.ca

Guelph: **CFRU-FM** (Freq: 93.3)
University Centre, Level 2, University of Guelph, Guelph, ON
N1G 2W1
Tel: 519-824-4120
info@cfru.ca
www.cfru.ca
www.facebook.com/groups/2221470650, twitter.com/cfru_radio
Vish Khanna, Station Manager

Guelph: **CIMJ-FM** (Magic 106.1) (Freq: 106.1)
Owned by: 591989 B.C. Ltd.*
75 Speedvale Ave. East, Guelph, ON N1E 6M3
Tel: 519-824-7000, Fax: 519-824-4118
magic106.com
www.facebook.com/Magic1061, twitter.com/magic1061

Haliburton: **CFZN-FM** (Moose FM) (Freq: 93.5)
Owned by: Vista Radio Ltd.*
PO Box 960, 152 Highland St., Haliburton, ON K0M 1S0
Tel: 705-457-3897, Fax: 705-457-3827
www.myhaliburtonnow.com
Dave Newman, Regional Program Director,
dnewman@vistaradio.ca

Haliburton: **CKHA-FM** (Freq: 100.9)
PO Box 1125, Haliburton, ON K0M 1S0
Tel: 705-457-1009, Fax: 705-457-9522
canoefmadmin@bellnet.ca
www.canoefm.com
www.facebook.com/canoefm
Roxanne Casey, Station Manager, roxanne@canoefm.com

Hamilton: **CHKX-FM** (Freq: 94.7)
Owned by: Durham Radio Inc.*
589 Upper Wellington St., Hamilton, ON L9A 3P8
Tel: 905-388-8911, Fax: 905-388-7947
Toll-Free: 855-667-1947
www.kx947.fm
www.youtube.com/user/kx947fm, www.facebook.com/KX947,
twitter.com/KX947
Bill Toffan, Program Director, bill@kx947.fm
Steve Macaulay, General Manager, Sales, stevemc@kx96.fm

Hamilton: **CING-FM** (95.3 Fresh) (Freq: 95.3)
Owned by: Corus Radio Company*
875 Main St. West, Hamilton, ON L8S 4R1
Tel: 905-521-9900, Fax: 905-521-1691
www.953freshradio.ca
www.instagram.com/953freshradio
www.facebook.com/953freshradio, twitter.com/953freshradio
Wayne Williams, Program Director,
wayne.williams@corusent.com

Hamilton: **CIOI-FM** (Freq: 101.5)
#F111, 135 Fennell Ave., Hamilton, ON L8N 3T2
Tel: 905-575-2175, Fax: 905-575-2420
www.1015thehawk.ca
www.facebook.com/thehawkfm, twitter.com/1015TheHawk
Les Palango, Station Manager, les.palango@mohawkcollege.ca

Hamilton: **CJXY-FM** (Freq: 107.9)
Owned by: Corus Radio Inc.*
875 Main St. West, Hamilton, ON L8S 4R1
Tel: 905-521-9900
y108.ca
www.facebook.com/y108rocks, twitter.com/y108rocks
Tammy Cole, Program Director, tammy.cole@corusent.com

Hamilton: **CKLH-FM** (102.9 K-Lite FM) (Freq: 102.9)
Owned by: Bell Media Inc.*
#401, 883 Upper Wentworth St., Hamilton, ON L9A 4Y6
Tel: 905-574-1150
www.iheartradio.ca/k-lite
www.facebook.com/1029klite, twitter.com/1029klite
Bob Harris, General Manager, Bell Radio Hamilton,
bob.harris@bellmedia.ca
Sarah Cummings, Brand Director,
sarah.cummings@bellmedia.ca

Hamilton: **wave.fm** (Freq: Closed circuit)
589 Upper Wellington, Hamilton, ON L9A 3P8
Tel: 905-388-8911, Fax: 905-388-7947
www.wave.fm
www.youtube.com/user/wave947,
www.facebook.com/waveonlineradio,
twitter.com/waveonlineradio
Steve Macaulay, Vice-President, Sales, stevemc@kx96.fm

---

* For details on this company see listing in Major Broadcasting Companies section; † French language station

Hanover: CFBW-FM (Bluewater Radio) (Freq: 91.3)
267 - 10th St., Hanover, ON N4N 1P1
Tel: 519-364-0200, *Fax:* 519-364-5175
Toll-Free: 855-364-0200
info@bluewaterradio.ca
www.bluewaterradio.ca
twitter.com/bluewaterradio
Andrew McBride, Station Manager, 519-370-9090

Hawkesbury: CKHK-FM (Freq: 107.7)
Owned by: Evanov Communications Inc.*
1320 Main St. East, Hawkesbury, ON K6A 1C5
Tel: 613-446-0925
hotcountry1077.ca
www.facebook.com/hotcountry1077fm,
twitter.com/1077hotcountry

Hearst: CHYK-FM-3 (Freq: 92.9)
Owned by: CHYK (Le Loup 104.1)
Hearst, ON

†**Hearst:** CINN-FM (Freq: 91.1)
CP 2648, Hearst, ON P0L 1NO
Tél: 705-372-1011, *Téléc:* 705-362-7411
Ligne sans frais: 866-362-5168
www.cinnfm.com
www.facebook.com/cinndirection, twitter.com/CINNFM
Steve McInnis, Directeur général, direction@cinnfm.com

Huntsville: CFBK-FM (Moose FM) (Freq: 105.5)
Owned by: Vista Radio Ltd.*
7 John St., Huntsville, ON P1H 1G1
Tel: 705-789-4461, *Fax:* 705-789-1269
www.mymuskokanow.com
www.facebook.com/moosefm1055

Huntsville: CJLF-FM-3 (Freq: 98.9)
Owned by: CJLF-FM (Life 100.3)
Huntsville, ON
www.lifeonline.fm

Kapuskasing: CHYX-FM (Freq: 93.7)
Owned by: CHYK (Le Loup 104.1)
Kapuskasing, ON

Kapuskasing: CKAP-FM (Moose FM) (Freq: 100.9)
Owned by: Vista Radio Ltd.*
#2A, 22 Queen St., Kapuskasing, ON P5N 1G8
Tel: 705-335-2379, *Fax:* 705-337-6391
Toll-Free: 866-505-2379
www.mykapuskasingnow.com
www.facebook.com/MooseCKAP, twitter.com/moosefmckap

†**Kapuskasing:** CKGN-FM (Freq: 89.7 Kapuskasing et
94.7 Smooth Rock Falls)
77, ch Brunelle nord, Kapuskasing, ON P5N 2M1
Tél: 705-335-5915, *Téléc:* 705-335-3508
ckgn-fm@nt.net
www.ckgn.ca
www.facebook.com/197086727069227
Claude Chabot, Directeur général, claudechabot@ckgn.ca

Kapuskasing: CKHT-FM (Moose FM) (Freq: 94.5)
Owned by: CKAP-FM (Moose FM)
#2A, 22 Queen St., Kapuskasing, ON P5N 1G8
Tel: 705-335-2379, *Fax:* 705-337-6391
Toll-Free: 866-505-2379
moose1009@moosefm.com
www.moosefm.com/ckht

Kemptville: CKVV-FM (Juice FM) (Freq: 97.5)
Owned by: Vista Radio Ltd.*
#3, 4 Industrial Rd., Kemptville, ON K0G 1J0
Tel: 613-258-1786, *Fax:* 613-258-1786
www.fm975kemptville.com
www.facebook.com/975juicefm, twitter.com/975juicefm
Tracy Lamoureux, General Manager & General Sales Manager,
tlamoureux@vistaradio.ca

Kenora: CJRL-FM (89.5 The Lake) (Freq: 89.5)
Owned by: Acadia Broadcasting Ltd.
301 - 1st Áve. South, Kenora, ON P9N 1W2
Tel: 807-468-3181
comments@895thelake.ca
www.cjrl.ca
www.facebook.com/895theLake, twitter.com/895thelakenews

Kenora: CKQV-FM (Q104) (Freq: 103.3)
Owned by: Golden West Broadcasting Ltd.*
619 Lakeview Dr., Kenora, ON P9N 3P6
Tel: 807-468-1045, *Toll-Free:* 855-468-1045
www.kenoraonline.com
www.facebook.com/q104fm, twitter.com/q104kenora

Killaloe: CHCR-FM (Freq: 102.9; 104.5)
PO Box 195, Killaloe, ON K0J 2A0
Tel: 613-757-0657, *Fax:* 613-757-0818
radio@chcr.org
www.chcr.org
www.facebook.com/FriendsOfChcr

Kincardine: CIYN-FM (Freq: 95.5)
Owned by: My Broadcasting Corporation*
756 Queen St., Kincardine, ON N2Z 2Y2
Tel: 519-396-7770, *Fax:* 519-396-7771
shorelinetoday.ca
twitter.com/ShorelineOldies
Gord Dougan, General Manager, Sales

Kingston: CFLY-FM (Freq: 98.3)
Owned by: Bell Media Radio*
#10, 993 Princess St., Kingston, ON K7L 1H3
Tel: 613-544-1380
www.iheartradio.ca/98-3-fly-fm
www.facebook.com/983FLYFM, twitter.com/983FLYFM
Greg Hinton, Vice President/General Manager,
greg.hinton@bellmedia.ca

Kingston: CFMK-FM (Freq: 96.3)
Owned by: 591989 B.C. Ltd.*
170 Queen St., Kingston, ON K7K 1B2
Tel: 613-544-2340, *Fax:* 613-544-5508
963bigfm.com
www.facebook.com/963bigfm, twitter.com/963bigfm
Peter Mayhew, General Manager, Sales,
peter.mayhew@corusent.com

Kingston: CFRC-FM (Freq: 101.9)
**Lower Carruthers Hall, Queen's University, 62 - 5th Field
Company Lane, Kingston, ON K7L 3N6**
Tel: 613-533-2121
cfrcops@ams.queensu.ca
www.cfrc.ca
www.youtube.com/user/CFRC1019,
www.facebook.com/cfrcradio, twitter.com/CFRC
Kristiana Clemens, Operations Officer

Kingston: CIKR-FM (K-Rock) (Freq: 105.7)
Owned by: Rogers Media Inc.*
#301, 863 Princess St., Kingston, ON K7L 5N4
Tel: 613-549-1057, *Fax:* 613-549-5302
www.krock1057.ca
www.instagram.com/krock1057, www.facebook.com/krock1057,
twitter.com/krock1057

Kingston: CKLC-FM (98.9 The Drive) (Freq: 98.9)
Owned by: Bell Media Radio*
PO Box 1380, #10, 993 Princess St., Kingston, ON K7L 1H3
Tel: 613-544-1380
onair@989thedrive.com
www.iheartradio.ca/98-9-the-drive
www.facebook.com/989THEDRIVE, twitter.com/989THEDRIVE

Kingston: CKVI-FM (Freq: 91.9)
235 Frontenac St., Kingston, ON K7L 3S7
Tel: 613-544-7864
www.thecave.ca
www.facebook.com/91.9CaveRadio

Kingston: CKWS-FM (Freq: 104.3)
Owned by: 591989 B.C. Ltd.*
170 Queen St., Kingston, ON K7K 1B2
Tel: 613-544-2340, *Fax:* 613-544-5508
1043freshradio.ca
www.facebook.com/1043freshradio, twitter.com/1043freshradio
Peter Mayhew, General Manager, Sales,
peter.mayhew@corusent.com

Kingston: CKXC-FM (Country 93.5) (Freq: 93.5)
Owned by: Rogers Media Inc.*
#301, 863 Princess St., Kingston, ON K7L 5N4
Tel: 613-549-1057
www.country935.ca
www.instagram.com/country935,
www.facebook.com/country935fm, twitter.com/country935fm

Kirkland Lake: CJKL-FM (Freq: 101.5)
Owned by: Connelly Communications Corp.*
PO Box 430, Kirkland Lake, ON P2N 3J4
Tel: 705-567-3366, *Fax:* 705-567-6101
cjkl@cjklfm.com
www.cjklfm.com
www.facebook.com/CJKLFM
Other information: News Phone: 705-567-6200
Robin Connelly, Manager & Program Director, robin@cjklfm.com

Kitchener: CHYM-FM (96.7 CHYM) (Freq: 96.7)
Owned by: Rogers Media Inc.*
#230, 1 The Boardwalk, Kitchener, ON N2N 0B1
Tel: 519-743-2611
www.chymfm.com
www.facebook.com/chym967, twitter.com/chym967
Christa Hicks, Program & Promotions Director
Mike Collins, Manager, Sales

Kitchener: CIKZ-FM (Country 106.7) (Freq: 106.7)
Owned by: Rogers Media Inc.*
#230, 1 The Boardwalk, Kitchener, ON N2N 0B1
Tel: 519-743-2611
www.country1067.com
www.instagram.com/country1067,
www.facebook.com/country1067, twitter.com/country1067
Dave Bossy, Production/Creative Director

Kitchener: CJDV-FM (Freq: 107.5)
Owned by: 591989 B.C. Ltd.*
#210, 50 Sportsworld Crossing Rd., Kitchener, ON N2P 0A4
Tel: 519-772-1212, *Fax:* 519-772-1213
1075daverocks.com
www.instagram.com/1075daverocks
www.facebook.com/1075daverocks, twitter.com/1075daverocks
Scot Turner, Program Director, Scot.Turner@corusent.com

Kitchener: CJIQ-FM (Freq: 88.3)
299 Doon Valley Dr., Kitchener, ON N2G 4M4
Tel: 519-748-3533
www.cjiqfm.com
www.facebook.com/883cjiq, twitter.com/CJIQFM
Brian Clemens, Station Manager, music@cjiq.fm

Kitchener: CJTW-FM (Freq: 94.3)
#207, 659 King St. East, Kitchener, ON N2G 2M4
Tel: 519-575-9090, *Fax:* 519-575-9119
info@faithfm.org
kitchener.faithfm.org
www.facebook.com/943FaithFM
Dave MacDonald, General Manager

Kitchener: CKBT-FM (91.5 The Beat) (Freq: 91.5)
Owned by: Corus Radio Company*
#210, 50 Sportsworld Crossing Rd., Kitchener, ON N2P 0A4
Tel: 519-772-1212, *Fax:* 519-772-1213
www.915thebeat.com
www.instagram.com/915thebeat
www.facebook.com/915thebeat, twitter.com/915thebeat
Steve Kennedy, Program Director,
steve.kennedy@corusent.com

Kitchener: CKWR-FM (Freq: 98.5)
1446 King St. East, Kitchener, ON N2G 2N7
Tel: 519-886-9870, *Fax:* 519-886-0090
general@ckwr.com
www.ckwr.com
www.facebook.com/HANSCKWR
Henning Grumme, Contact, hgrumme@ckwr.com

Leamington: CHYR-FM (Freq: 96.7)
Owned by: Blackburn Radio Inc.*
100 Talbot St. East, Leamington, ON N8H 1L3
Tel: 519-326-6171
mix967.ca
www.facebook.com/mix967, twitter.com/themix967

Lindsay: CKLY-FM (Freq: 91.9)
Owned by: Bell Media Radio*
249 Kent St. West, Lindsay, ON K9V 2Z3
Tel: 705-324-9103, *Fax:* 705-324-4149
www.iheartradio.ca/91-9-bob-fm
www.facebook.com/919bobfm, twitter.com/919bobfm
Steve Fawcett, General Manager, Steve.Fawcett@bellmedia.ca

London: CBBL-FM (Freq: 100.5)
Owned by: Canadian Broadcasting Corporation
London, ON
www.cbc.ca

---

* For details on this company see listing in Major Broadcasting Companies section; † French language station

London: **CBCL-FM** (Freq: 93.5)
Owned by: Canadian Broadcasting Corporation*
208 Piccadilly St., London, ON N6A 1S1
Tel: 519-667-1990
www.cbc.ca/radio

London: **CFHK-FM (103.1 Fresh)** (Freq: 103.1)
Owned by: Corus Radio Company*
#222, 380 Wellington St., London, ON N6A 5B5
Tel: 519-931-6000, Fax: 519-679-1967
www.1031freshradio.ca
www.instagram.com/1031freshradio
www.facebook.com/1031freshradio, twitter.com/1031freshradio
Brad Gibb, Brand Director

London: **CFPL-FM (FM96)** (Freq: 95.9)
Owned by: Corus Radio Company*
#222, 380 Wellington St., London, ON N6A 5B5
Tel: 519-931-6000, Fax: 519-679-1967
www.fm96.com
www.instagram.com/fm96rocks,
www.facebook.com/fm96london, twitter.com/fm96rocks
Brad Gibb, Brand Director

London: **CHJX-FM** (Freq: 99.9)
#100, 120 Wellingston St., London, ON N6B 2K6
Tel: 519-679-2459, Fax: 519-679-8014
info@london.faithfm.org
faithfm.org/london
www.facebook.com/faithfm.org, twitter.com/999FaithFM
Dave Wettlaufer, General Manager, davew@faithfm.org

London: **CHRW-FM** (Freq: 94.9)
Western University, #250, University Community Centre, London, ON N6A 3K7
Tel: 519-661-3601
chrwgm@chrwradio.ca
chrwradio.ca
www.youtube.com/user/chrwradio,
www.facebook.com/chrwradio, twitter.com/chrwradio
Grant Stein, Station Manager
Allison Brown, Program Director, chrwpd@chrwradio.ca
Ed von Aderkas, News, Sports & Spoken Word Director,
chrwnd@chrwradio.ca

London: **CHST-FM (Jack 102.3)** (Freq: 102.3)
Owned by: Rogers Media Inc.*
1 Communications Rd., London, ON N6J 4Z1
Tel: 519-690-0102
www.jack1023.com
www.facebook.com/jack1023ldn, twitter.com/jack1023ldn
Al Smith, Program Director, al@jack1023.com
Pete Travers, Program Director, 519-690-0102
Gerry Derikx, Creative Director, gerry@jack1023.com

London: **CIQM-FM (97.5 Virgin Radio)** (Freq: 97.5)
Owned by: Bell Media Inc.*
743 Wellington Rd. South, London, ON N6C 4R5
Tel: 519-686-2525
london.virginradio.ca
www.instagram.com/virginradiolondonca,
www.facebook.com/VirginRadioLondonCA,
twitter.com/VirginRadioLON
Don Mumford, General Manager, don.mumford@bellmedia.ca

London: **CIXX-FM** (Freq: 106.9)
PO Box 7005, London, ON N5Y 5R6
Tel: 519-453-2810
www.fanshawemedia.ca
www.youtube.com/user/1069TheX,
www.facebook.com/1069TheX, twitter.com/1069TheX

London: **CJBX-FM (BX93)** (Freq: 92.7)
Owned by: Bell Media Inc.*
743 Wellington Rd. South, London, ON N6C 4R5
Tel: 519-685-2525
www.bx93.com
www.instagram.com/bx93london,
www.facebook.com/BX93London, twitter.com/bx93
Don Mumford, General Manager, don.mumford@bellmedia.ca

Markham: **CHKT-FM** (Freq: 88.9)
Owned by: Fairchild Radio Group Ltd.*
#26-29, 151 Esna Park Dr., Markham, ON L3R 3B1
Tel: 905-415-6265, Fax: 905-415-6292
www.am1430.com

Midland: **CICZ-FM** (Freq: 104.1)
355 Cranston Cres., Midland, ON L4R 4L3
Tel: 705-720-1991, Fax: 705-526-3060
1041thedock.com
www.facebook.com/1041thedock, twitter.com/1041thedock

Mora Austin, General Manager, mora.austin@larchecom.com

Milton: **CJML-FM (myFM)** (Freq: 101.3)
Owned by: My Broadcasting Corporation*
315 Steeles Ave. East, Milton, ON L9T 1Y2
Tel: 289-627-1995
news1013@mbcmedia.ca
www.miltonnow.ca
www.facebook.com/miltonmyFM, twitter.com/1013myFM
Hilary Montbourquette, General Manager, Sales, 289-627-1995

Mississauga: **CFRE-FM** (Freq: 91.9)
University of Toronto, Mississauga, #131, 3359 Mississauga Rd., Mississauga, ON L5L 1C6
Tel: 905-828-2088
info@cfreradio.com
www.cfreradio.com
www.youtube.com/user/cfreradio, www.facebook.com/cfreradio,
twitter.com/cfreradio
Monique Swaby, Station Manager, monique@cfreradio.com

Napanee: **CKYM-FM (myFM)** (Freq: 88.7)
Owned by: My Broadcasting Corporation*
11 Market Sq., Napanee, ON K7R 1J4
Tel: 613-354-4554, Fax: 613-354-3661
www.napaneetoday.ca
www.facebook.com/887myfm, twitter.com/887myFM
Rebecca Wilkinson, General Manager, 613-354-4554

New Liskeard: **CJTT-FM** (Freq: 104.5)
Owned by: Connelly Communications Corp.*
PO Box 1058, 55 Whitewood Ave., New Liskeard, ON P0J 1P0
Tel: 705-647-7334, Fax: 705-647-8660
cjtt@cjttfm.com
www.cjttfm.com
www.facebook.com/1045cjttfm

Neyaashiinigmiing: **CHFN-FM** (Freq: 100.1)
67 Community Centre Rd., Neyaashiinigmiing, ON N0H 2T0
Tel: 519-534-1003, Fax: 519-534-4916
chfn@ymail.com
www.nawash.ca/chfn-100-1
www.facebook.com/137257499685779
Waylynne Elliott, Contact

Niagara Falls: **CFLZ-FM (101.1 More FM)** (Freq: 101.1)
Owned by: Byrnes Communications Inc.*
#202, 4673 Ontario Ave., Niagara Falls, ON L2E 3R1
Tel: 905-356-6710
hello@101morefm.ca
www.101morefm.ca
www.facebook.com/101morefm, twitter.com/101morefm

Niagara Falls: **CJED-FM (The River)** (Freq: 105.1)
Owned by: Byrnes Communications Inc.*
#202, 4673 Ontario Ave., Niagara Falls, ON L2E 3R1
Tel: 905-356-6710
www.105theriver.ca
www.facebook.com/1051TheRiverNiagara,
twitter.com/TheRiver105

North Bay: **CFXN-FM (Moose FM)** (Freq: 106.3)
Owned by: Vista Radio Ltd.*
118 Main St. East, North Bay, ON P1B 1A8
Tel: 705-475-9991
www.mynorthbaynow.com
www.facebook.com/moosecfxn, twitter.com/themoose1063
Peter Hobbs, Regional Manager, phobbs@vistaradio.ca

North Bay: **CHUR-FM (Kiss 100.5)** (Freq: 100.5)
Owned by: Rogers Media Inc.*
273 Main St. East, North Bay, ON P1B 8K8
Tel: 705-479-2000
www.kissnorthbay.com
www.instagram.com/kissnorthbay,
www.facebook.com/kissnorthbay, twitter.com/kissnorthbay

North Bay: **CKFX-FM (101.9 ROCK)** (Freq: 101.9)
Owned by: Rogers Media Inc.*
273 Main St. East, North Bay, ON P1B 1B2
Tel: 705-474-2000
www.1019rock.ca
www.facebook.com/1019rock, twitter.com/1019rock

North Bay: **CRFM-FM** (Freq: 89.9)
Canadore College, 100 College Dr., North Bay, ON P1B 8K9
Tel: 705-474-7601
www.ThePanther.ca
www.facebook.com/233056936793545, twitter.com/panthertweet

Orangeville: **CKMO-FM (myFM)** (Freq: 101.5)
Owned by: My Broadcasting Corporation*
45 Mill St., #B, Orangeville, ON L9W 2M4
Tel: 226-790-6936
news1015@mbcmedia.ca
www.orangevilletoday.ca
www.facebook.com/1015Orangeville, twitter.com/1015myFM

Orillia: **CICX-FM** (Freq: 105.9)
Owned by: Bell Media Inc.*
25 Ontario St., Orillia, ON L3V 6H1
Tel: 705-722-5429, Fax: 705-326-1816
www.iheartradio.ca/kicx-106
www.instagram.com/kicx106, www.facebook.com/kicx106,
twitter.com/kicx106

Orillia: **CISO-FM (Sunshine)** (Freq: 89.1)
Owned by: Bayshore Broadcasting Corporation*
#2, 490 West St. North, Orillia, ON L3V 5E8
Tel: 705-325-9786, Fax: 705-325-2600
Toll-Free: 888-536-9786
info@891maxfm.ca
www.891maxfm.ca
www.facebook.com/891maxfm, twitter.com/891maxfm
Rob Wiltshire, Manager, Sales,
rwiltshire@bayshorebroadcasting.ca

Oshawa: **CJKX-FM** (Freq: 95.9)
Owned by: Durham Radio Inc.*
#207, 1200 Airport Blvd., Oshawa, ON L1J 8P5
Tel: 905-428-9600, Fax: 905-571-1150
www.kx96.fm
www.youtube.com/user/kx96fm,
www.facebook.com/KX96Country, twitter.com/kx96
Steve Kassay, Vice-President, Programming, steve@kx96.fm

Oshawa: **CKGE-FM (The Rock)** (Freq: 94.9)
Owned by: Durham Radio Inc.*
#207, 1200 Airport Blvd., Oshawa, ON L1J 8P5
Tel: 905-571-0949, Fax: 905-579-1150
www.therock.fm
www.youtube.com/c/949TheRockToronto,
www.facebook.com/949TheRockToronto
Steve Kassay, Vice-President, Programming, steve@kx96.fm

Ottawa: **CBOF-FM** (Freq: 90.7)
Owned by: Canadian Broadcasting Corporation*
181, rue Queen, Ottawa, ON K1Y 1E4
Tel: 613-288-6000
ici.radio-canada.ca/ottawa-gatineau
Marco Dubé, Directeur, Radio-Canada Ottawa-Gatineau,
613-288-6705, Fax: 613-288-6703,
Marco.Dube@radio-canada.ca
Chantal Jolicoeur, Chef de la programmation et des affaires
publiques, 613-288-6547, Fax: 613-288-6703,
chantal.jolicoeur@radio-canada.ca

Ottawa: **CBO-FM** (Freq: 91.5)
Owned by: Canadian Broadcasting Corporation*
PO Box 3220 C, Ottawa, ON K1Y 1E4
Tel: 613-288-6000
cbcnewsottawa@cbc.ca
www.cbc.ca/ottawa
Ruth Zowdu, Executive Producer, Radio Current Affairs & local
programming

Ottawa: **CBOQ-FM** (Freq: 103.3)
Owned by: Canadian Broadcasting Corporation*
PO Box 3220 C, Ottawa, ON K1Y 1E4
Tel: 613-288-6000
www.cbc.ca/ottawa

†*Ottawa:* **CBOX-FM** (Freq: 102.5)
Détenteur: **Canadian Broadcasting Corporation***
181, rue Queen, Ottawa, ON K1Y 1E4
Tél: 613-288-6000
www.icimusique.ca
Marco Dubé, Directeur, Radio-Canada Ottawa-Gatineau,
Marco.Dube@radio-canada.ca

Ottawa: **CHEZ-FM (106.1 CHEZ)** (Freq: 106.1)
Owned by: Rogers Media Inc.*
2001 Thurston Dr., Ottawa, ON K1G 6C9
Tel: 613-750-4636
www.chez106.com
www.instagram.com/1061chez, www.facebook.com/1061chez,
twitter.com/1061chez

---

* For details on this company see listing in Major Broadcasting Companies section; † French language station

Ottawa: CHRI-FM (Freq: 99.1)
#3, 1010 Thomas Spratt Pl., Ottawa, ON K1G 5L5
Tel: 613-247-1440, Fax: 613-247-7128
Toll-Free: 866-247-1440
chri@chri.ca
www.chri.ca
www.youtube.com/user/CHRIradio
www.facebook.com/chriradio, twitter.com/CHRIRadio

Ottawa: CHUO-FM (Freq: 89.1)
#0038, 65 University Pvt., Ottawa, ON K1N 9A5
Tel: 613-562-5965
prog@chuo.fm
chuo.fm
www.instagram.com/chuo891fm, www.facebook.com/chuofm,
twitter.com/chuofm
Erin Flynn, Station Manager, erin@chuo.fm

Ottawa: CIHT-FM (Hot 89.9) (Freq: 89.9)
Owned by: Stingray Group Inc.*
#100, 6 Antares Dr., Ottawa, ON K2E 8A9
Tel: 613-723-8990, Fax: 613-723-7016
www.hot899.com
www.facebook.com/ottawahot899, twitter.com/newhot899
Scott Broderick, General Manager, sbroderick@newcap.ca
Josie Fenech, Program Director, josie@hot899.com

Ottawa: CILV-FM (Live 88.5) (Freq: 88.5)
Owned by: Stingray Group Inc.*
#100, 6 Antares Dr., Phase 1, Ottawa, ON K2E 8A9
Tel: 613-688-8888, Fax: 613-723-7016
www.live885.com
www.youtube.com/live885, www.facebook.com/live885,
twitter.com/Live885fm
Scott Broderick, Station Manager, sbroderick@newcap.ca
Dan Youngs, Program Director, dyoungs@newcap.ca

Ottawa: CISS-FM (Kiss 105.3) (Freq: 105.3)
Owned by: Rogers Media Inc.*
2001 Thurston Dr., Ottawa, ON K1G 6C9
Tel: 613-736-2001
www.kissottawa.com
www.instagram.com/kissottawa, www.facebook.com/kissottawa,
twitter.com/kissottawa

Ottawa: CJLL-FM (CHIN) (Freq: 97.9)
Owned by: Radio 1540 Ltd.*
1391 Wellington St. West, Ottawa, ON K1Y 2X1
Tel: 613-244-0979, Fax: 613-244-3858
Toll-Free: 866-697-0979
chinottawa@chinradio.com
www.chinradioottawa.com
www.youtube.com/chinradioottawa,
www.facebook.com/chinradioottawa,
twitter.com/CHINRadioottawa
Francesco Di Candia, General Manager

Ottawa: CJMJ-FM (Freq: 100.3)
Owned by: Bell Media Radio*
87 George St., Ottawa, ON K1N 9H7
Tel: 613-789-2486
Majic100Webmaster@bellmedia.ca
www.iheartradio.ca/majic-100-3
www.facebook.com/Majic100, twitter.com/MAJIC100Ottawa
Ian March, Program Director, ian.march@bellmedia.ca

Ottawa: CJOT-FM (Boom 99.7) (Freq: 99.7)
Owned by: Corus Radio Company*
1504 Merivale Rd., Ottawa, ON K2E 6Z5
Tel: 613-225-1069
www.boom997.com
www.instagram.com/boom997fm, www.facebook.com/boom99.7,
twitter.com/boomottawa
Eric Stafford, Brand Director, eric.stafford@corusent.com

Ottawa: CJWL-FM (Freq: 98.5)
Owned by: Evanov Communications Inc.*
127 York St., Ottawa, ON K1N 5T4
Tel: 613-241-9850, Fax: 613-241-9852
info@lite985.com
lite985.ca
www.facebook.com/lite985, twitter.com/lite985

Ottawa: CKBY-FM (Country 101.1) (Freq: 101.1)
Owned by: Rogers Media Inc.*
2001 Thurston Dr., Ottawa, ON K2J 6C9
Tel: 613-736-2001
www.country1011.com
www.instagram.com/country1011fm,
www.facebook.com/country1011, twitter.com/country1011fm

Ottawa: CKCU-FM (Freq: 93.1)
University Centre, Carleton University, #517, 1125 Colonel
By Dr., Ottawa, ON K1S 5B6
Tel: 613-520-2898, Fax: 613-520-4060
info@ckcufm.com
www.ckcufm.com
www.facebook.com/CKCUFM, twitter.com/ckcufm
Matthew Croiser, Station Manager, 613-520-2600,
manager@ckcufm.com

Ottawa: CKDJ-FM (Freq: 107.9)
Algonquin College, 1385 Woodroffe Ave., Ottawa, ON K2G
1V8
Tel: 613-750-2535
ckdj@algonquincollege.com
www.ckdj.net
www.youtube.com/user/ckdj1079video
www.facebook.com/CKDJ1079, twitter.com/ckdj1079

Ottawa: CKKL-FM (Freq: 93.9)
Owned by: Bell Media Radio*
87 George St., Ottawa, ON K1N 9H7
Tel: 613-789-2486
www.iheartradio.ca/new-country-94
www.instagram.com/newcountry94,
www.facebook.com/NewCountry94, twitter.com/newcountry94
Ian March, Program Director

Ottawa: CKQB-FM (JUMP!) (Freq: 106.9)
Owned by: Corus Radio Company*
1504 Merivale Rd., Ottawa, ON K2E 6Z5
Tel: 613-225-1069, Fax: 613-226-3381
Toll-Free: 800-754-1069
www.jumpradio.ca
www.instagram.com/jumpottawa
www.facebook.com/jumpottawa, twitter.com/jumpottawa
Eric Stafford, Brand Director, eric.stafford@corusent.com

Owen Sound: CIXK-FM (Mix 106.5) (Freq: 106.5)
Owned by: Bayshore Broadcasting Corporation*
PO Box 270, 270 - 9th St. East, Owen Sound, ON N4K 5P5
Tel: 519-376-2030, Fax: 519-371-4242
info@bayshorebroadcasting.ca
www.mix106.ca
www.facebook.com/mix1065owensound,
twitter.com/Mix1065OnAir

Owen Sound: CJLF-FM-1 (Freq: 90.1)
Owned by: CJLF-FM (Life 100.3)
Owen Sound, ON
www.lifeonline.fm

Owen Sound: CKYC-FM (Country 93) (Freq: 93.7)
Owned by: Bayshore Broadcasting Corporation*
PO Box 270, 270 - 9th St. East, Owen Sound, ON N4K 5P5
Tel: 519-376-2030, Fax: 519-371-4242
info@country93.ca
www.country93.ca
www.facebook.com/country937

Parry Sound: CKLP-FM (Moose FM) (Freq: 103.3)
Owned by: Vista Radio Ltd.*
#301, 60 James St., Parry Sound, ON P2A 1T5
Tel: 705-746-2163, Fax: 705-746-4292
www.myparrysoundnow.com
www.facebook.com/moosecklp, twitter.com/moosefmcklp

Pembroke: CHVR-FM (Star 96) (Freq: 96.7)
Owned by: Bell Media Inc.*
595 Pembroke St. East, Pembroke, ON K8A 3L7
Tel: 613-735-9670
www.iheartradio.ca/star-96
www.facebook.com/star96fm
Richard Gray, General Manager, richard.gray@bellmedia.ca
Tracy McBride, Sales Manager, tracy.mcbride@bellmedia.ca

Pembroke: CIMY-FM (myFM) (Freq: 104.9)
Owned by: My Broadcasting Corporation*
Victoria Centre, 84 Isabella St., Pembroke, ON K8A 5S5
Tel: 613-735-6936
www.pembroketoday.ca
www.facebook.com/1049myfm, twitter.com/1049myFM

†**Penetanguishene:** CFRH-FM (Freq: 88.1)
CP 5099, Penetanguishene, ON L9M 2G3
Tél: 705-549-8288, Téléc: 705-549-6463
vaguefm@vaguefm.ca
vaguefm.ca
www.facebook.com/radiocfrh
Mélanie Bouchard, Gérante, mbouchard@lacle.ca

Peterborough: CFFF-FM (Freq: 92.7)
Trent University, 715 George St. North, Peterborough, ON
K9H 3T2
Tel: 705-741-4011
Info@TrentRadio.cadio.ca
www.trentu.ca/org/trentradio
Other information: Studio: 705-748-4761
John K. Muir, General Manager

Peterborough: CJMB-FM (Freq 90.5) (Freq: 90.5)
Owned by: My Broadcasting Corporation*
Peterborough, ON
Tel: 705-876-7773
newsptbo@mbcmedia.ca
www.ptbotoday.ca/freq-905
www.facebook.com/Freq905, twitter.com/FreqPtbo

Peterborough: CJWV-FM (Freq: 96.7)
Owned by: My Broadcasting Corporation*
#1, 360 George St. North, Peterborough, ON K9H 7E7
Tel: 705-876-7773, Fax: 705-876-1917
newsptbo@mbcmedia.ca
www.ptbotoday.ca/oldies-96-7
www.facebook.com/Oldies967fm

Peterborough: CKPT-FM (Freq: 99.7)
Owned by: Bell Media Radio*
PO Box 177, 59 George St. North, Peterborough, ON K9J
6Y8
Tel: 705-742-8844, Fax: 705-742-1417
www.iheartradio.ca/energy-99-7
www.facebook.com/Energy997, twitter.com/energy997
Steve Fawcett, General Manager, steve.fawcett@bellmedia.ca

Peterborough: CKQM-FM (Freq: 105.1)
Owned by: Bell Media Radio*
PO Box 177, 59 George St. North, Peterborough, ON K9J
6Y8
Tel: 705-742-8844
www.iheartradio.ca/country-105
www.facebook.com/Country105Peterborough,
twitter.com/Country1051
Steve Fawcett, General Manager, 705-742-8844,
steve.fawcett@bellmedia.ca
Brian Young, Program Director, brian.young@bellmedia.ca

Peterborough: CKRU-FM (Freq: 100.5)
Owned by: 591989 B.C. Ltd.*
743 Monaghan Rd., Peterborough, ON K9J 5K2
Tel: 705-742-0451, Fax: 705-742-7274
1005freshradio.ca
www.instagram.com/1005freshradio
www.facebook.com/1005freshradio, twitter.com/1005freshradio
Rob Seguin, Program Manager, rob.seguin@corusent.com

Peterborough: CKWF-FM (The Wolf 101.5) (Freq:
101.5)
Owned by: 591989 B.C. Ltd.*
743 Monaghan Rd., Peterborough, ON K9J 5K2
Tel: 705-742-0451, Fax: 705-742-7274
thewolf.ca
www.facebook.com/thewolf1015, twitter.com/thewolfca
Rob Seguin, Program Director & Brand Manager

Port Elgin: CFPS-FM (The Bruce) (Freq: 97.9)
Owned by: Bayshore Broadcasting Corporation*
382 Goderich St., Port Elgin, ON N0H 2C1
Tel: 519-832-9800, Fax: 519-832-9808
info@rockthebruce.ca
www.rockthebruce.ca
www.facebook.com/rockthebruce, twitter.com/rockthebruce

Port Elgin: CIYN-FM-2 (Freq: 90.9)
Owned by: CIYN-FM (myFM)
Port Elgin, ON
Tel: 613-396-7770
shorelinetoday.ca

Prescotty: CKPP-FM (Coast FM) (Freq: 107.9)
Owned by: Vista Radio Ltd.*
119 King St. West, Prescotty, ON K0E 1T0
Tel: 613-925-9779
www.myprescottnow.com
www.facebook.com/1069coastfm, twitter.com/1079coastfm
Tracy Lamoureux, General Manager & General Sales Manager,
tlamoureux@vistaradio.ca

Red Lake: CKDR-5 (Freq: 97.1)
Owned by: CKDR-FM
Red Lake, ON

For details on this company see listing in Major Broadcasting Companies section; † French language station

Renfrew: **CHMY-FM** (Freq: 96.1)
Owned by: My Broadcasting Corporation*
PO Box 961, Renfrew, ON K7V 4H4
Tel: 613-432-6936, *Fax:* 613-432-1086
www.renfrewtoday.ca
www.facebook.com/961myfm, twitter.com/961myFM
Bob Dillabough, General Manager, Sales, 613-432-6936

Sarnia: **CBEG-FM** (Freq: 90.3)
Owned by: Canadian Broadcasting Corporation
Sarnia, ON
Sandra Porteous, Managing Editor, Radio & Television,
519-255-3563
David Daigneault, Executive Producer, Radio & Television,
519-255-3410

Sarnia: **CFGX-FM** (Freq: 99.9)
Owned by: Blackburn Radio Inc.*
1415 London Rd., Sarnia, ON N7S 1P6
Tel: 519-542-5500, *Toll-Free:* 888-258-1999
foxfm.com
www.youtube.com/foxfmsarnia, www.facebook.com/foxfmsarnia,
twitter.com/foxfmsarnia

Sarnia: **CHKS-FM** (Freq: 106.3)
Owned by: Blackburn Radio Inc.*
1415 London Rd., Sarnia, ON N7S 1P6
Tel: 519-542-5500, *Toll-Free:* 877-464-1064
k106fm.com
www.youtube.com/user/k1063fm, www.facebook.com/K1063,
twitter.com/k1063sarnia

Sault Ste Marie: **CHAS-FM** (Kiss 100.5) (Freq: 100.5)
Owned by: Rogers Media Inc.*
642 Great Northern Rd., Sault Ste Marie, ON P6B 4Z9
Tel: 705-759-9200
www.kisssoo.com
twitter.com/kis_soo
Gary Creighton, Contact, Programming,
gary.creighton@rci.rogers.com

Sault Ste Marie: **CJQM-FM** (Country 104.3) (Freq:
104.3)
Owned by: Rogers Media Inc.*
642 Great Northern Rd., Sault Ste Marie, ON P6B 4Z9
Tel: 705-759-9200, *Fax:* 705-946-3575
www.country1043.com
www.facebook.com/country1043, twitter.com/country1043
Gary Creighton, Contact, Programming,
gary.creighton@rci.rogers.com

Shelburne: **CFDC-FM** (Country 105) (Freq: 104.9)
Owned by: Bayshore Broadcasting Corporation*
710 Industrial Rd., #B, Shelburne, ON L9V 2Z4
Tel: 519-925-0925
info@country105.ca
www.country105.ca
www.facebook.com/country105fm, twitter.com/Country105OnAir
Adam Ward, Manager, Sales, 519-925-0925,
award@bayshorebroadcasting.ca

Simcoe: **CHCD-FM** (myFM) (Freq: 98.9)
Owned by: My Broadcasting Corporation*
PO Box 98, Simcoe, ON N3Y 4K8
Tel: 519-426-7700
www.norfolktoday.ca
www.facebook.com/989norfolkmyFM, twitter.com/myFM989

Simcoe: **CKNC-FM** (Oldies 99.7) (Freq: 99.7)
Owned by: My Broadcasting Corporation*
PO Box 98, Simcoe, ON N3Y 4K8
Tel: 519-426-7700
www.norfolktoday.ca/oldies-99-7
Alan Duthie, General Manager, 519-426-7700

London: **CICO-DT-18** (Channel: 18)
Owned by: TVOntario*
London, ON
tvo.org

Sioux Lookout: **CKDR-2** (Freq: 97.1)
Owned by: CKDR-FM
Sioux Lookout, ON

Sioux Lookout: **CKWT-FM** (Freq: 89.9)
Owned by: Wawatay Radio Network*
PO Box 1180, 16 - 5th Ave., Sioux Lookout, ON P8T 1B7
Tel: 807-737-2951, *Fax:* 807-737-3224
Toll-Free: 800-243-9059
wawataynews.ca

Smiths Falls: **CJET-FM** (Jack 92.3) (Freq: 92.3)
Owned by: Rogers Media Inc.*
69 Beckwith St. North, Smiths Falls, ON K7A 2B1
Tel: 613-283-4630, *Fax:* 613-283-7243
923jackfm.com
www.facebook.com/jack923sf, twitter.com/jack923sf
Mark Hunter, General Sales Manager, 613-736-2001
Kalum Figura, Retail Sales Manager, 613-736-2001

St Catharines: **CFBU-FM** (Freq: 103.7)
c/o 500 Glenridge Ave., St Catharines, ON L2S 3A1
Tel: 905-688-2644
pd@cfbu.ca
www.cfbu.ca
www.facebook.com/brockradio103.7, twitter.com/cfbu1037
Deborah Cartmer, Program Director

St Catharines: **CHRE-FM** (Niagara's EZ Rock) (Freq:
105.7)
Owned by: Bell Media Inc.*
12 Yates St., St Catharines, ON L2R 5R2
Tel: 905-688-1057
www.1057ezrock.com
www.instagram.com/1057ezrock
www.facebook.com/1057ezrock, twitter.com/1057ezrock
Bob Harris, General Manager, bob.harris@bellmedia.ca

St Catharines: **CHTZ-FM** (HTZ-FM) (Freq: 97.7)
Owned by: Bell Media Inc.*
12 Yates St., St Catharines, ON L2R 5R2
Tel: 905-688-0977
www.htzfm.com
www.instagram.com/977HTZFM,
www.facebook.com/977HTZFM, twitter.com/977HTZFM
Bob Harris, General Manager, bob.harris@bellmedia.ca

St Thomas: **CKZM-FM** (myFM) (Freq: 94.1)
Owned by: My Broadcasting Corporation*
**Grand Central Place, #2, 300 Talbot St., St Thomas, ON N5P
4E2**
Tel: 519-633-6936
news941@mbcmedia.ca
www.stthomastoday.ca
www.facebook.com/941myfm, twitter.com/myFM_News941
Samantha Wakefield, General Manager, 519-633-6936

Stratford: **CHGK-FM** (2day FM) (Freq: 107.7)
Owned by: Vista Radio Ltd.*
376 Romeo St. South, Stratford, ON N5A 4T6
Tel: 519-271-2450, *Fax:* 519-271-3102
www.mystratfordnow.com
www.facebook.com/10772dayfm, twitter.com/10772dayfm
Kevin Fell, Regional Program Director, kfell@vistaradio.ca

Stratford: **CJCS-FM** (Freq: 1240)
Owned by: Vista Radio Ltd.*
376 Romeo St. South, Stratford, ON N5A 4T9
Tel: 519-271-2450, *Fax:* 519-271-3102
www.mystratfordnow.com
twitter.com/1240CJCS

Strathroy: **CJMI-FM** (myFM) (Freq: 105.7)
Owned by: My Broadcasting Corporation*
85 Zimmerman St. South, Strathroy, ON N7G 0A3
Tel: 519-246-6936
www.strathroytoday.ca
www.facebook.com/1057myfm, twitter.com/News1057
David McAllan, General Manager, 519-246-6936

Sturgeon Falls: **CFSF-FM** (Moose FM) (Freq: 99.3)
Owned by: Vista Radio Ltd.*
#1m 159 Main St., Sturgeon Falls, ON P2B 1P1
Tel: 705-475-9991
www.mywestnipissingnow.com
www.facebook.com/moosecfsf, twitter.com/moosefmcfsf
Peter Hobbs, Regional Manager, phobbs@vistaradio.ca

†*Sturgeon Falls:* **CHYQ-FM** (Le Loup) (Freq: 97.1)
Détenteur: **Le5 Communications***
300, rue King, Sturgeon Falls, ON P3B 3A1
Tél: 705-893-8306, *Téléc:* 705-893-0520
leloupfm.com
www.facebook.com/leloupfm

†*Sudbury:* **CBBK-FM** (Freq: 90.9)
Détenteur: **Canadian Broadcasting Corporation***
15, rue Mackenzie, Sudbury, ON P3C 4Y1
Tél: 705-688-3200, *Téléc:* 705-688-3220
Ligne sans frais: 800-461-1138
www.icimusique.ca
Robert McMillan, Responsable de l'affectation,
robert.mcmillan@radio-canada.ca

Sudbury: **CBBS-FM** (Freq: 90.1)
Owned by: Canadian Broadcasting Corporation*
15 MacKenzie St., Sudbury, ON P3C 4Y1
Tel: 705-688-3200
www.cbc.ca/sudbury
Fiona Christensen, Managing Editor, 705-688-3232

†*Sudbury:* **CBBX-FM** (Freq: 90.9)
Détenteur: **Canadian Broadcasting Corporation***
15 MacKenzie St., Sudbury, ON P3C 4Y1
Tél: 705-688-3200
www.icimusique.ca

Sudbury: **CBCS-FM** (Freq: 99.9)
Owned by: Canadian Broadcasting Corporation*
15 MacKenzie St., Sudbury, ON P3C 4Y1
Tel: 705-688-3200, *Fax:* 705-688-3220
Toll-Free: 866-306-4636
www.cbc.ca/sudbury
Other information: Phone, Sudbury News: 705-688-3240;
Toll-Free: 800-461-1138
Fiona Christensen, Managing Editor, 705-688-3232

†*Sudbury:* **CBON-FM** (Freq: 98.1)
Détenteur: **Canadian Broadcasting Corporation***
15 MacKenzie St., Sudbury, ON P3C 4Y1
Tél: 705-688-3200, *Ligne sans frais:* 800-641-1138
www.radio-canada.ca/regions/ontario
www.facebook.com/fm1017.ca, twitter.com/Fm1017Info

Sudbury: **CHNO-FM** (Rewind 103.9) (Freq: 103.9)
Owned by: Stingray Group Inc.*
493B Barrydowne Rd., Sudbury, ON P3A 3T4
Tel: 705-560-8323, *Fax:* 705-560-7765
news@rewind1039.ca
www.rewind1039.ca
www.facebook.com/rewind1039sudbury,
twitter.com/Rewind_1039
Mike Cameron, General Manager, mcameron@newcap.ca
Rick Tompkins, Program Director, rtompkins@newcap.ca

†*Sudbury:* **CHYC-FM** (Le Loup) (Freq: 98.9)
Détenteur: **Le5 Communications***
#301, 336, rue Pine, Sudbury, ON P3C 1X8
Tél: 705-222-8306, *Téléc:* 705-222-2805
leloupfm.com
www.facebook.com/leloupfm
Paul Lefebvre, Propriétaire, plefebvre@leloupfm.com

Sudbury: **CIGM-FM** (Hot 93.5) (Freq: 93.5)
Owned by: Stingray Group Inc.*
493B Barrydowne Rd, Sudbury, ON P3A 3T4
Tel: 705-560-8323, *Fax:* 705-560-7765
info@hot935.ca
www.hot935.ca
www.instagram.com/thenewhot935,
www.facebook.com/thenewhot93.5, twitter.com/TheNewHot935
Mike Cameron, Station Manager, mcameron@newcap.ca
Rick Tompkins, Program Director, rtompkins@newcap.ca

Sudbury: **CJMX-FM** (Kiss 105.3) (Freq: 105.3)
Owned by: Rogers Media Inc.*
880 Lasalle Blvd., Sudbury, ON P3A 1X5
Tel: 705-566-1053
www.kisssudbury.com
www.facebook.com/1053EZRock, twitter.com/kisssudbury
Nick Liard, News Director, sudbury.news@rci.rogers.com

Sudbury: **CJRQ-FM** (92.7 ROCK) (Freq: 92.7)
Owned by: Rogers Media Inc.*
880 Lasalle Blvd., Sudbury, ON P3A 1X5
Tel: 705-566-4480, *Fax:* 705-560-7232
www.instagram.com/927rocksudbury,
www.facebook.com/927rocksudbury, twitter.com/927rocksudbury
Other information: News, Phone: 705-560-7440
Kevin Britton, Contact, Programming/Music,
kevin.britton@rci.rogers.com

Sudbury: **CJTK-FM** (Freq: 95.5)
2150 Lasalle Blvd., Sudbury, ON P3A 2A7
Tel: 705-674-2585, *Fax:* 705-688-1081
Toll-Free: 888-674-2585
mail@kfmradio.ca
www.cjtk.com
www.facebook.com/8680749692
Curtis L. Belcher, Contact

---

* For details on this company see listing in Major Broadcasting Companies section; † French language station

Sudbury: **CKLU-FM** (Freq: 96.7)
935 Ramsey Rd., Sudbury, ON P3E 2C6
Tel: 705-673-6538
traffic@cklu.ca
www.facebook.com/ckluradio, twitter.com/CKLURadio

Thunder Bay: **CBQ-FM** (Freq: 101.7)
Owned by: Canadian Broadcasting Corporation*
213 Miles St. East, Thunder Bay, ON P7C 1J5
Tel: 807-625-5000
www.cbc.ca/thunderbay

Thunder Bay: **CBQT-FM** (Freq: 88.3)
Owned by: Canadian Broadcasting Corporation*
213 East Miles St., Thunder Bay, ON P7C 1J5
Tel: 807-625-5000
www.cbc.ca/thunderbay
Sandra Porteus, Deputy Managing Director, Ontario

Thunder Bay: **CBQX-FM** (Freq: 98.7)
Owned by: Canadian Broadcasting Corporation*
213 East Miles St., Thunder Bay, ON P7C 1J5
Tel: 807-625-5000, Fax: 807-625-5035
www.cbc.ca/thunderbay
twitter.com/CBCTBay
Susan Porteus, Deputy Managing Director, Ontario,
Sandra.Porteus@cbc.ca

Thunder Bay: **CFNO-FM** (Freq: 93.1; 100.7; 107.1)
Owned by: Dougall Media*
87 Hill St. North, Thunder Bay, ON P7A 5V6
Toll-Free: 888-621-1989
info@cfno.fm
cfno.fm
Brad Hilgers, Program Director, bhilgers@dougallmedia.com

Thunder Bay: **CFQK-FM** (Freq: 103.5; 104.5)
Owned by: Dougall Media*
87 Hill St. North, Thunder Bay, ON P7A 5V6
Tel: 807-346-2600, Fax: 807-345-9923
energy@Energyfm.fm
www.energyfm.fm
www.facebook.com/energy103104
Brad Hilgers, Program Director, bhilgers@dougallmedia.com

Thunder Bay: **CJOA-FM** (Freq: 95.1)
#42, 63 Carrie St., Thunder Bay, ON P7A 4J2
Tel: 807-344-9525, Fax: 807-344-9525
fm95@cjoa.ca
www.cjoa.org
www.facebook.com/Cjoa95.1FmChristianRadioThunderBayOntario

Thunder Bay: **CJSD-FM** (Freq: 94.3)
Owned by: Dougall Media*
87 Hill St. North, Thunder Bay, ON P7A 5V6
Tel: 807-346-2600, Fax: 807-345-9923
rock@rock94.com
rock94.com
www.facebook.com/943rock
Brad Hilgers, Program Director, bhilgers@dougallmedia.com

Thunder Bay: **CJUK-FM** (Freq: 99.9)
Owned by: Acadia Broadcasting Ltd.
#200, 180 Park Ave., Thunder Bay, ON P7B 6J4
Tel: 807-344-2000
magic@magic999.ca
www.magic999.ca
www.instagram.com/magic999tbay,
www.facebook.com/magicthunderbay,
twitter.com/magicthunderbay
Scott Pettigrew, Station Manager

Thunder Bay: **CKPR-FM** (Freq: 91.5)
Owned by: Dougall Media*
87 Hill St. North, Thunder Bay, ON P7A 5V6
Tel: 807-346-2600
ckpr.com
www.facebook.com/915CKPROfficial
Brad Hilgers, Program Director, bhilgers@dougallmedia.com

Tillsonburg: **CJDL-FM** (Country 107.3) (Freq: 107.3)
Owned by: Rogers Media Inc.*
77 Broadway St., Tillsonburg, ON N4G 3P5
Tel: 519-842-4281, Fax: 519-842-4284
www.country1073.ca
www.facebook.com/country1073, twitter.com/country1073

Tillsonburg: **CKOT-FM** (Easy 101.3) (Freq: 101.3)
Owned by: Rogers Media Inc.*
77 Broadway St., Tillsonburg, ON N4G 4H3
Tel: 519-842-4281, Fax: 519-842-4284
info@easy101.com
www.easy1013.ca
www.instagram.com/easy1013, www.facebook.com/easy1013,
twitter.com/easy1013

Timmins: **CHMT-FM** (Moose FM) (Freq: 93.1)
Owned by: Vista Radio Ltd.*
49 Cedar St. South, Timmins, ON P4N 2G5
Tel: 705-267-6070, Fax: 705-267-6095
www.mytimminsnow.com
www.facebook.com/moosetimmins, twitter.com/themoose931
Shane Button, Regional Program Director,
sbutton@moosefm.com

†*Timmins:* **CHYK-FM** (Le Loup) (Freq: 104.1)
Détenteur: Le5 Communications*
136, 3e av, Timmins, ON P4N 1C6
Tél: 705-269-8307, Téléc: 705-269-8305
leloupfm.com
www.facebook.com/leloupfm
Paul Lefebvre, Propriétaire

Timmins: **CJQQ-FM** (92.1 ROCK) (Freq: 92.1)
Owned by: Rogers Media Inc.*
260 - 2nd Ave., Timmins, ON P4N 8A4
Tel: 705-264-2351, Fax: 705-264-2984
www.921rock.ca
www.instagram.com/921rock, www.facebook.com/921rock,
twitter.com/921rocktimmins

Timmins: **CKGB-FM** (Kiss 99.3) (Freq: 99.3)
Owned by: Rogers Media Inc.*
260 - 2nd Ave., Timmins, ON P4N 8A4
Tel: 705-264-2351, Fax: 705-264-2984
www.kisstimmins.com
www.facebook.com/kisstimmins, twitter.com/kisstimmins

Toronto: **CBLA-FM** (Freq: 99.1)
Owned by: Canadian Broadcasting Corporation*
PO Box 500 A, Toronto, ON M5W 1E6
Tel: 416-205-3311, Toll-Free: 866-306-4636
www.cbc.ca/toronto
www.facebook.com/radiocbc, twitter.com/cbcradio
Cathy Perry, Managing Director, 416-205-3689

Toronto: **CBL-FM** (Freq: 94.1)
Owned by: Canadian Broadcasting Corporation*
PO Box 500 A, Toronto, ON M5W 3G7
Tel: 416-205-3311, Toll-Free: 866-306-4636
www.cbc.ca/toronto
Cathy Perry, Managing Director, 416-205-3689

Toronto: **CFIE-FM** (Freq: 106.5)
PO Box 87 E, Toronto, ON M6H 4E1
Tel: 416-703-1287, Fax: 416-703-4328
www.aboriginalvoices.com

Toronto: **CFMX-FM** (Freq: 103.1)
Owned by: ZoomerMedia Ltd.*
70 Jefferson Ave., Toronto, ON M6K 1Y4
Tel: 416-367-5353, Fax: 416-367-1742
classicalfm.ca
www.facebook.com/thenewclassical, twitter.com/classical963fm

Toronto: **CFMZ-FM** (Freq: 96.3)
Owned by: ZoomerMedia Ltd.*
70 Jefferson Ave., Toronto, ON M6K 1Y4
Tel: 416-367-5353, Fax: 416-367-1742
classicalfm.ca
www.facebook.com/thenewclassical, twitter.com/classical963fm

Toronto: **CFNY-FM** (102.1 The Edge) (Freq: 102.1)
Owned by: Corus Radio Company*
Corus Quay, 25 Dockside Dr., Toronto, ON M5A 0B5
Tel: 416-479-7000
www.edge.ca
www.instagram.com/1021theedge, www.facebook.com/102edge,
twitter.com/the_edge
Tammy Cole, Program Director

Toronto: **CFXJ-FM** (93-5 The Move) (Freq: 93.5)
Owned by: Stingray Group Inc.*
2 St Clair Ave. West, 2nd Fl., Toronto, ON M4V 1L6
Tel: 416-482-0973, Fax: 416-486-5696
www.935themove.com
www.facebook.com/935TheMoveTO,
twitter.com/935TheMoveTO
Lorie Russell, General Manager, lrussell@newcap.ca

Paul Parhar, Program Director, pparhar@newcap.ca

Toronto: **CHBM-FM** (Boom 97.3) (Freq: 97.3)
Owned by: Stingray Group Inc.*
2 St Clair Ave. West, 20th Fl., Toronto, ON M4V 1L5
Tel: 416-482-0973, Fax: 416-486-5696
info@boom973.com
www.boom973.com
www.facebook.com/boom973Toronto, twitter.com/boom973
Lorie Russell, General Manager, lrussell@newcap.ca
Troy McCallum, Program Director, tmccallum@boom973.com

Toronto: **CHFI-FM** (98.1 CHFI) (Freq: 98.1)
Owned by: Rogers Media Inc.*
1 Ted Rogers Way, Toronto, ON M4Y 3B7
Tel: 416-764-2000, Fax: 416-935-8260
www.chfi.ca
www.instagram.com/981chfi, www.facebook.com/981chfi,
twitter.com/981chfi

Toronto: **CHIN-FM** (Freq: 100.7)
Owned by: Radio 1540 Ltd.*
622 College St., 4th Fl., Toronto, ON M6G 1B6
Tel: 416-870-1007, Fax: 416-531-5274
info@chinradio.com
www.chinradio.com
www.facebook.com/chinradiocanada,
twitter.com/chinradiocanada
Other information: Business Office: 416-531-9991

Toronto: **CHRY-FM** (Freq: 105.5)
**York University, Student Centre, #413, 4700 Keele St.,
Toronto, ON M3J 1P3**
Tel: 416-736-5293
chry@yorku.ca
www.chry.ca
www.youtube.com/user/CHRYRadio,
www.facebook.com/chryradio, twitter.com/chryradio

Toronto: **CHUM-FM** (Freq: 104.5)
Owned by: Bell Media Radio*
299 Queen St. West, Toronto, ON M5V 2Z5
Tel: 416-384-8000
www.iheartradio.ca/chum-fm
www.instagram.com/1045chumfm,
www.facebook.com/1045CHUMFM, twitter.com/1045CHUMFM

Toronto: **CIDC-FM** (Freq: 103.5)
Owned by: Evanov Communications Inc.*
5312 Dundas St. West, Toronto, ON M9B 1B3
Tel: 416-213-1035
info@z1035.com
z1035.com
www.facebook.com/Z103.5toronto, twitter.com/Z1035Toronto

Toronto: **CILQ-FM** (Q107 Toronto) (Freq: 107.1)
Owned by: Corus Radio Company*
Corus Quay, 25 Dockside Dr., Toronto, ON M5A 0B5
Tel: 416-479-7000
www.q107.com
www.instagram.com/q107toronto,
www.facebook.com/Q107toronto, twitter.com/q107toronto
Tammy Cole, Brand Director

Toronto: **CIND-FM** (Freq: 88.1)
Owned by: Rock 95 Broadcasting Ltd.*
20 Hanna Ave., Toronto, ON M6K 3E7
Tel: 416-588-7595
info@indie88.com
indie88.com
www.youtube.com/c/Indie88Toronto,
www.facebook.com/indie88toronto, twitter.com/Indie88Toronto
Megan Bingley, General Manager, megan@indie88.com

Toronto: **CIRR-FM** (Freq: 103.9)
Owned by: Evanov Communications Inc.*
5312 Dundas St. West, Toronto, ON M9B 1B3
Tel: 416-213-1035
proudfm.com
www.facebook.com/1039ProudFM
Sheila Koenig, Creative Director, sheila@evanovradio.com

Toronto: **CIRV-FM** (Freq: 88.9)
1087 Dundas St. West, Toronto, ON M6J 1W9
Tel: 416-537-1088, Fax: 416-537-2463
info@cirvfm.com
www.cirvfm.com

* For details on this company see listing in Major Broadcasting Companies section; † French language station

Toronto: **CIUT-FM** (Freq: 89.5)
89.5 Tower Rd., 3rd Fl., Toronto, ON M5S 0A2
Tel: 416-978-0909
ciutoutreach@gmail.com
www.ciut.fm
www.youtube.com/user/CIUTFM
www.facebook.com/CIUT895FM, twitter.com/CIUT895FM
Ken Stowar, Station Manager & Program Director,
ken.stowar@ciut.fm

†*Toronto:* **CJBC-FM** (Freq: 90.3)
Détenteur: **Canadian Broadcasting Corporation***
CP 500 A, Toronto, ON M5W 1E6
Tél: 416-205-3311
www.icimusique.ca

Toronto: **CJRT-FM** (Freq: 91.1)
#100, 4 Pardee Ave., Toronto, ON M6K 3H5
Tel: 416-595-0404, *Fax:* 416-959-9413
info@jazz.fm
www.jazz.fm
www.youtube.com/jazzfm91, www.facebook.com/jazzfm91,
twitter.com/JAZZFM91
Bernard Webber, Chair
Ross Porter, President & CEO

Toronto: **CKDX-FM** (Freq: 88.5)
Owned by: Evanov Communications Inc.*
5312 Dundas St. West, Toronto, ON M9B 1B3
Tel: 416-213-1035, *Fax:* 416-234-8572
info@885thejewel.com
jewel885.com
www.facebook.com/jewel885, twitter.com/Jewel885

Toronto: **CKFM-FM (99.9 Virgin Radio)** (Freq: 99.9)
Owned by: Bell Media Inc.*
299 Queen St. West, Toronto, ON M5V 2Z5
Tel: 416-922-9999
toronto.virginradio.ca
www.instagram.com/VirginRadioToronto,
www.facebook.com/VirginRadioToronto,
twitter.com/VirginRadioTO

Toronto: **CKHC-FM** (Freq: 96.9)
205 Humber College Blvd., Toronto, ON M9W 5L7
Tel: 416-675-6622
radio.humber.ca
www.instagram.com/radiohumber
www.facebook.com/RadioHumber, twitter.com/RadioHumber
Dean Sinclair, General Manager, Dean.Sinclair@Humber.ca

Toronto: **CKIS-FM (Kiss 92.5)** (Freq: 92.5)
Owned by: Rogers Media Inc.*
1 Ted Rogers Way, Toronto, ON M4Y 3B7
Tel: 416-935-8200
www.kiss925.com
www.instagram.com/kiss925, www.facebook.com/kiss925,
twitter.com/kiss925

Toronto: **CSCR-FM** (Freq: 90.3)
**University of Toronto Scarborough, 1265 Military Trail,
Toronto, ON M1C 1A4**
Tel: 416-287-7051
stationmanager@fusionradio.ca
www.fusionradio.ca
www.instagram.com/fusion_radio
www.facebook.com/FusionRadioCSCR, twitter.com/fusionradio
Rudolf Ray, Station Manager

Waterloo: **CFCA-FM** (Freq: 105.3)
Owned by: Bell Media Radio*
#207, 255 King St. North, Waterloo, ON N2J 4V2
Tel: 519-884-4470
www.iheartradio.ca/virginradio/kitchener
www.instagram.com/virginradiokitchener
www.facebook.com/VirginRadioKW, twitter.com/VirginRadio_KW
Paul Fisher, Vice President/General Manager,
paul.fisher@bellmedia.ca

Waterloo: **CKKW-FM (KFUN 99.5)** (Freq: 99.5)
Owned by: Bell Media Radio*
#207, 255 King St. North, Waterloo, ON N2J 4V2
Tel: 519-884-4470
www.iheartradio.ca/kfun-99-5
www.instagram.com/995kfun, www.facebook.com/KFUN995,
twitter.com/995KFUN
Paul Fisher, Vice-President & General Manager, Bell Media
Radio, Kitchener & London, paul.fisher@bellmedia.ca

Waterloo: **CKMS-FM** (Freq: 100.3)
#2, 108 King St. North, Waterloo, ON N2J 2X6
office@soundfm.ca
soundfm.ca

Wawa: **CJWA-FM** (Freq: 107.1)
PO Box 1447, 55 Broadway Ave., Wawa, ON P0S 1K0
Tel: 705-856-4555, *Fax:* 705-856-1520
Rick Labbe, President, ceojjam@bellnet.ca

Welland: **CRNC-FM** (Freq: 90.1)
300 Woodlawn Rd., Welland, ON L3C 7L3
Tel: 905-735-2211
theheat90.1@gmail.com
broadcasting.niagaracollege.ca/content/Radio/CRNCTheHeat.as
px
www.facebook.com/901FMTHEHEAT,
twitter.com/901FMTHEHEAT
Devin Jorgensen, Program Director

Windsor: **CBE-FM** (Freq: 89.9)
Owned by: Canadian Broadcasting Corporation*
825 Riverside Dr. West, Windsor, ON N9A 5K9
Tel: 519-255-3411
www.cbc.ca/windsor
Shawna Kelly, Managing Editor, Local News & Programs,
519-255-3563

Windsor: **CBEW-FM** (Freq: 97.5)
Owned by: Canadian Broadcasting Corporation*
825 Riverside Dr. West, Windsor, ON N9A 5K9
Tel: 519-255-3456, *Toll-Free:* 866-812-3624
windsor@cbc.ca
www.cbc.ca/windsor
www.facebook.com/CBCWindsor, twitter.com/CBCWindsor
Other information: Windsor Morning: 519-255-3400

Windsor: **CIDR-FM** (Freq: 93.9)
Owned by: Bell Media Radio*
1640 Ouellette Ave., Windsor, ON N8X 1L1
Tel: 519-258-8888
www.iheartradio.ca/93-9-the-river
www.instagram.com/939theriver,
www.facebook.com/939theriverradio, twitter.com/939theriver
Sloane Cummings, Production Director

Windsor: **CIMX-FM** (Freq: 88.7)
Owned by: Bell Media Radio*
1640 Ouellette Ave., Windsor, ON N8X 1L1
Tel: 519-258-8888
www.iheartradio.ca/89x
www.instagram.com/theofficial89x,
www.facebook.com/89XFANS, twitter.com/TheOfficial89X

Windsor: **CJAM-FM** (Freq: 99.1)
**University of Windsor, 401 Sunset Ave., Windsor, ON N9B
3P4**
Tel: 519-971-3606, *Fax:* 519-971-3605
www.cjam.ca
www.instagram.com/cjamfm, www.facebook.com/cjamfm,
twitter.com/CJAMFM
Vernon Smith, Station Manager, statcjam@gmail.com

Wingham: **CKNX-FM** (Freq: 101.7)
Owned by: Blackburn Radio Inc.*
PO Box 300, 215 Carling Terrace, Wingham, ON N0G 2W0
Tel: 519-357-1310, *Fax:* 519-357-1897
Toll-Free: 800-265-3030
1017theone.ca
www.facebook.com/1017TheOne, twitter.com/1017theOne

Woodstock: **CIHR-FM (Heart FM)** (Freq: 104.7)
Owned by: Byrnes Communications Inc.*
223 Norwich Ave., Woodstock, ON N4S 3V8
Tel: 519-537-1047, *Fax:* 519-537-8600
www.heartfm.ca
Scott Lunn, General Manager, 519-320-8730, scott.lunn@bci.fm

Woodstock: **CJFH-FM** (Freq: 94.3)
1038 Parkinson Rd., Woodstock, ON N4S 7W3
Tel: 519-539-2304, *Fax:* 519-539-2011
www.hopefm.ca
Chris Gordon, Music Director, newmusic@hopefm.ca

Woodstock: **CKDK-FM (Country 104)** (Freq: 103.9)
Owned by: Corus Radio Company*
290 Dundas St., Woodstock, ON N4S 1B2
Tel: 519-931-6000, *Toll-Free:* 877-643-1039
www.country104.com
www.instagram.com/country104,
www.facebook.com/country104, twitter.com/country104
Brad Gibb, Program Director, brad.gibb@corusent.com

Charlottetown: **CBCT-FM** (Freq: 96.1)
Owned by: Canadian Broadcasting Corporation*
PO Box 2230, Charlottetown, PE C1A 8B9
Tel: 902-629-6400, *Fax:* 902-629-6518
Other information: Phone, News: 902-629-6402
Denise Wilson, Senior Managing Director, Atlantic Canada,
denise.wilson@cbc.ca
Donna Allen, Executive Producer, Prince Edward Island News
Nadine Antle, Regional Manager, Partnerships,
Communications, Brand, & Promot, 902-420-4223
Chantal Bernard, Senior Officer, Communications,
Chantal.Bernard@cbc.ca

Charlottetown: **CFCY-FM** (Freq: 630)
Owned by: Maritime Broadcasting System*
5 Prince St., Charlottetown, PE C1A 4P4
Tel: 902-892-1066, *Fax:* 902-566-1338
cfcy.fm
www.facebook.com/951fmcfcy, twitter.com/cfcy

Charlottetown: **CHLQ-FM (Q93)** (Freq: 93.1)
Owned by: Maritime Broadcasting System*
5 Prince St., Charlottetown, PE C1A 4P4
Tel: 902-892-1066, *Fax:* 902-566-1338
q93.fm
www.facebook.com/Q93ROCKS, twitter.com/Q93ROCKS

Charlottetown: **CHTN-FM (Ocean 100)** (Freq: 100.3;
99.9; 89.9)
Owned by: Stingray Group Inc.*
176 Great George St., Charlottetown, PE C1A 4K9
Tel: 902-569-1003, *Fax:* 902-569-8693
www.ocean1003.com
www.facebook.com/ocean100, twitter.com/ocean100
Jennifer Evans, General Manager, jevans@newcap.ca

Charlottetown: **CKQK-FM (Hot 105.5)** (Freq: 105.5)
Owned by: Stingray Group Inc.*
176 Great George St., Charlottetown, PE C1A 4K9
Tel: 902-569-1003, *Fax:* 902-569-8693
www.hot1055fm.com
www.instagram.com/thenewhot1055,
www.facebook.com/Hot1055, twitter.com/thehot1055
Jennifer Evans, General Manager, jevans@newcap.ca
Matt MacLeod, Program Director, mmacleod@newcap.ca

Elmira: **CKQK-FM-1 (Hot 105.5)** (Freq: 103.7)
Owned by: Stingray Group Inc.*
Elmira, PE
Tel: 902-569-1003, *Fax:* 902-569-8693
www.hot1055fm.com

St Edwards: **CKQK-FM-2 (Hot 105.5)** (Freq: 91.1)
Owned by: Stingray Group Inc.*
St Edwards, PE
Tel: 902-569-1003, *Fax:* 902-569-8693
www.hot1055fm.com

Akwesasne: **CKON-FM** (Freq: 97.3)
#2, 22 Hilltop Dr., Akwesasne, QC H0H 1A0
Tel: 613-575-2100, *Fax:* 613-575-2566
frontdesk@ckonfm.com
www.ckonfm.com
www.facebook.com/452385308168295, twitter.com/ckonradio
Reen Cook, News Director

†*Alma:* **CFGT-FM (Planète 104.5)** (Freq: 104.5)
Détenteur: **Cogeco Media Inc.***
460, rue Sacré-Coeur ouest, Alma, QC G8B 1L9
Tél: 418-662-6888
alma.planeteradio.ca
www.facebook.com/205430152830652

Amos: **CHOW-FM** (Freq: 105.3)
42, 1re ave Est, Amos, QC J9T 1H2
Tel: 819-732-6991, *Fax:* 819-732-6988
info@radioboreale.com
www.radioboreale.com
www.facebook.com/362476834435, twitter.com/CHOW1053
Guylaine Belley, Coordonnatrice,
coordonnatrice@radioboreale.com

---

* For details on this company see listing in Major Broadcasting Companies section; † French language station

†*Amqui:* CFVM-FM (Rouge FM) (Freq: 99.9)
Détenteur: **Bell Media Inc.***
111, av Gaétan-Archambault, Amqui, QC G5J 2K1
Tél: 418-629-2025
www.iheartradio.ca/rouge-fm/rouge-fm-amqui
www.instagram.com/rougefm, www.facebook.com/999Rougefm,
twitter.com/999Rougefm
André Émond, Directeur Général et Directeur des Ventes

†*Asbestos:* CJAN-FM (Freq: 99.3)
1, rue Hilaire, Asbestos, QC J1T 0A3
Tél: 819-879-5439, Téléc: 819-879-7922
info@fm993.ca
fm993.ca
www.facebook.com/133076530207940

Baie-Comeau: CBMI-FM (Freq: 93.7)
Owned by: CBVE-FM
Baie-Comeau, QC
www.cbc.ca/montreal

†*Baie-Comeau:* CBSI-FM-24 (Freq: 106.1)
Détenteur: **Canadian Broadcasting Corporation**
Baie-Comeau, QC
www.radio-canada.ca/regions/quebec

†*Baie-Comeau:* CHLC-FM (Freq: 97.1)
907, rue de Puyjalon, Baie-Comeau, QC G5C 1N3
Tél: 418-589-3771, Téléc: 418-589-9086
chlcfm97@globetrotter.net
www.chlc.com
www.facebook.com/217028048325739
Georges Daviault, Directeur Général,
direction971-1005@globetrotter.net

Baie-Saint-Paul: CHOX-FM-1 (Freq: 94.1)
Owned by: CHOX-FM
Baie-Saint-Paul, QC

†*Cap-aux-Meules:* CFIM-FM (Freq: 92.7)
CP 8192, Cap-aux-Meules, QC G4T 1R3
Tél: 418-986-5233, Téléc: 418-986-5319
administration@cfim.ca
www.cfim.ca
Charles Eugene Cyr, Directeur général, direction@cfim.ca

†*Carleton:* CIEU-FM (Freq: 94.9; 106.1)
1645, boul Perron Est, Carleton, QC G0C 1J0
Tél: 418-364-7094, Téléc: 418-364-3150
administration@cieufm.com
www.cieufm.com
www.facebook.com/cieufm
Claude Roy, Directeur général, direction@cieufm.com

†*Chandler:* CJMC-FM (Freq: 100.3)
#101, 141, rue Commercial Ouest, Chandler, QC G0C 1K0
Tél: 418-689-0963
direction@bleufm.ca
www.bleufm.ca
www.facebook.com/bleuFM.ca

†*Châteauguay:* CHAI-FM (Freq: 101.9)
25, boul St-Francis, Châteauguay, QC J6J 1Y2
Tel: 450-698-3131, Fax: 450-698-3339
chai@videotron.ca
www.1019fm.net
www.facebook.com/171051749593931, twitter.com/chai1019fm
Sylvain Poirier, Directeur général

†*Chibougamau:* CKXO-FM (Planète) (Freq: 93.5)
Détenteur: **Cogeco Media Inc.***
359, 3e rue, Chibougamau, QC G8P 1N4
Tél: 418-748-3931
chibougamau.planeteradio.ca
www.facebook.com/Planete935

†*Chicoutimi:* CBJ-FM (Freq: 93.7)
Détenteur: **Canadian Broadcasting Corporation***
500, rue des Sagueneens, Chicoutimi, QC G7H 6N4
Tél: 418-696-6666
saguenay@radio-canada.ca
ici.radio-canada.ca/saguenay-lac-saint-jean
www.facebook.com/icisaguenaylacsaintjean,
twitter.com/icisaglac

†*Chicoutimi:* CFIX-FM (Rouge FM) (Freq: 96.9)
Détenteur: **Bell Media Inc.***
**CP 8390, 267, rue Racine est, 2ième étage, Chicoutimi, QC
G7H 5C2**
Tél: 418-543-9797, Ligne sans frais: 800-463-7919
saguenay.rougefm.ca
www.facebook.com/969Rougefm, twitter.com/969Rougefm

†*Chicoutimi:* CJAB-FM (Énergie 94.5) (Freq: 94.5)
Détenteur: **Bell Media Inc.***
CP 8390, Chicoutimi, QC G7H 5C2
Tél: 418-545-9450
www.iheartradio.ca/energie/energie-saguenay
www.facebook.com/saguenay945, twitter.com/energie645

†*Chicoutimi:* CKYK-FM (KYK Radio X) (Freq: 95.7)
Détenteur: **Cogeco Media Inc.***
#160, 345, rue des Sagueneéns, Chicoutimi, QC G7H 6K9
Tél: 418-543-8912
www.957kyk.com
www.facebook.com/957KYK

†*Dégelis:* CFVD-FM (Plaisir 95.5) (Freq: 95.5)
Détenteur: **Arsenal Media**
654, 6e rue est, Dégelis, QC G5T 1Y1
Tél: 418-853-3370, Téléc: 418-853-3321
plaisir955@arsenalmedia.com
plaisir955.com
www.facebook.com/90319881621

†*Dolbeau-Mistassini:* CHVD-FM (Planète) (Freq:
100.3)
Détenteur: **Cogeco Media Inc.***
1975, boul Wallberg, Dolbeau-Mistassini, QC G8L 1J5
Tél: 418-276-3333
dolbeau-mistassini.planeteradio.ca
www.facebook.com/115354181826762

†*Drummondville:* CHRD-FM (Rouge FM) (Freq: 105.3)
Détenteur: **Bell Media Inc.***
2070, rue Raphaël-Nolet, Drummondville, QC J2C 5G6
Tél: 819-475-1480
drummondville.rougefm.ca
www.facebook.com/1053Rougefm, twitter.com/rougefm1053

†*Drummondville:* CJDM-FM (Énergie 92.1) (Freq:
92.1)
Détenteur: **Bell Media Inc.***
2070, rue Raphaël-Nolet, Drummondville, QC J2C 5G6
Tél: 819-475-1480
www.iheartradio.ca/energie/energie-drummondville
www.facebook.com/drummondville921, twitter.com/921energie

Essipit: CHME-FM (Freq: 94.9)
34, rue de la Réserve, Essipit, QC G0T 1K0
Tel: 418-233-2700, Fax: 418-233-3326
Toll-Free: 800-661-2701
chme@B2B2C.ca
chme949.jimdo.com
www.facebook.com/174431196087
Claudine Roussel, Directrice générale

Fermont: CBMR-FM (Freq: 105.1)
Owned by: Canadian Broadcasting Corporation
Fermont, QC
www.cbc.ca/radio

†*Fermont:* CFMF-FM (Freq: 103.1)
20, Place Daviault, Fermont, QC G0G 1J0
Tél: 418-287-5147
infocfmf@diffusionfermont.ca
www.cfmf.ca
www.facebook.com/79719726630, twitter.com/cfmf1031
Karl Gangné Côté, Directeur de station et programmation,
dp@diffusionfermont.ca

Forestville: CFRP-FM (Freq: 100.5)
Forestville, QC

†*Fort-Coulonge:* CHIP-FM (Freq: 101.7)
CP 820, Fort-Coulonge, QC J0X 1V0
Tél: 819-683-3155, Téléc: 819-683-3211
Ligne sans frais: 888-775-3155
admin@chipfm.com
www.chipfm.com
www.facebook.com/chipfm
François Carrier, General Manager, dg@annexef.com

†*Gaspé:* CHGM-FM (Freq: 99.3)
Détenteur: **CHNC**
155 rue de la Reine, Gaspé, QC G4X 2R1
Tél: 418-368-1150

†*Gaspé:* CJRG-FM (Freq: 94.5)
162, rue Jacques Cartier, Gaspé, QC G4X 1M9
Tél: 418-368-3511, Téléc: 418-368-1663
Ligne sans frais: 866-360-3511
www.radiogaspesie.ca
www.facebook.com/radiogaspesie
Jacques Chartier, Directeur général,
jacques.chartier@radiogaspesie.ca

†*Gatineau:* CFTX-FM (Pop) (Freq: 96.5)
Détenteur: **RNC MÉDIA, Inc.***
171A, rue Jean-Proulx, Gatineau, QC J8Z 1W5
Tél: 819-770-1040
popradio.ca
www.facebook.com/POP965

†*Gatineau:* CHLX-FM (Wow) (Freq: 97.1)
Détenteur: **RNC MÉDIA, Inc.***
171, rue Jean-Proulx, Gatineau, QC J8Z 1W5
Tél: 819-770-1040
wow971.ca
www.facebook.com/WOW971, twitter.com/wow_971

†*Gatineau:* CIMF-FM (Rouge FM) (Freq: 94.9)
Détenteur: **Bell Media Inc.***
15, rue Taschereau, Gatineau, QC J8Y 2V6
Tél: 819-243-5555
gatineau.rougefm.ca
www.facebook.com/949rougefm, twitter.com/949rougefm

†*Gatineau:* CKOF-FM (104,7) (Freq: 104.7)
Détenteur: **Cogeco Media Inc.***
150, rue d'Edmonton, Gatineau, QC J8Y 3S6
Tél: 819-561-8801, Téléc: 819-561-3333
www.fm1047.com
www.facebook.com/1047fm.Outaouais, twitter.com/1047_fm

Gatineau: CKTF-FM (Énergie 104.1) (Freq: 104.1)
Owned by: Bell Media Inc.*
15, rue Taschereau, Gatineau, QC J8Y 2V6
Tél: 819-243-5555
www.iheartradio.ca/energie/energie-gatineau-ottawa
www.instagram.com/energie1041,
www.facebook.com/gatineauottawa1041,
twitter.com/energie1041

†*Havre-Saint-Pierre:* CBSI-FM-7 (Freq: 92.5)
Détenteur: **Canadian Broadcasting Corporation**
Havre-Saint-Pierre, QC
www.radio-canada.ca/regions/quebec

†*Hâvre-Saint-Pierre:* CILE-FM (Freq: 95.1)
992, rue du Bouleau, Hâvre-Saint-Pierre, QC G0G 1P0
Tél: 418-538-2453, Téléc: 418-538-3870
info@cilemf.com
www.cilemf.com

†*Joliette:* CJLM-FM (O 103.5) (Freq: 103.5)
Détenteur: **Arsenal Media**
540, rue St-Thomas, Joliette, QC J6E 3R4
Tél: 450-756-1035
o1035.ca
www.facebook.com/O1035

†*Jonquière:* CKAJ-FM (Freq: 92.5)
3877, boul Harvey, 2e étage, Jonquière, QC G7X 0A6
Tél: 418-546-2525, Téléc: 418-546-2528
ckaj@ckaj.org
www.ckaj.org
www.facebook.com/ckajfm, twitter.com/ckaj925
Johanne Tremblay, Directrice générale

Kahnawake: CKRK-FM (K103 Kahnawake) (Freq:
103.7)
PO Box 1050, Kahnawake, QC J0L 1B0
Tel: 450-638-1313, Fax: 450-638-4009
www.k103radio.com
www.facebook.com/139720622747580

Kuujjuaq: CKUJ-FM (Freq: 97.3)
PO Box 1082, Kuujjuaq, QC J0M 1C0
Tel: 819-964-2921

L'Annonciation: CFLO-FM-1 (Freq: 101.9)
Owned by: CFLO-FM
L'Annonciation, QC

†*La Baie:* CILM-FM (O 98.3) (Freq: 98.3)
Détenteur: **Arsenal Media**
993, rue Bagot, La Baie, QC G7B 2N6
Tél: 418-545-2577
o983@arsenalmedia.com
o983.ca
www.facebook.com/983saguenay

†*La Pocatière:* CHOX-FM (Freq: 97.5)
#50, 601 - 1e rue Poiré, La Pocatière, QC G0R 1Z0
Tél: 418-856-1310, Téléc: 418-856-3747
chox@chox97.com
www.chox97.com
www.facebook.com/377928410603, twitter.com/CHOXFM975

---

* For details on this company see listing in Major Broadcasting Companies section; † French language station

†*La Tuque:* **CFLM-FM (O 97.1)** (Freq: 97.1)
Détenteur: **Arsenal Media**
537, rue Commerciale, La Tuque, QC G9X 3A7
Tél: 819-523-4575
o971@arsenalmedia.com
o971.ca
www.facebook.com/o971LaTuque

Lac-Etchemin: **CFIN-FM** (Freq: 100.5)
201, rue Claude-Bilodeau, Lac-Etchemin, QC G0R 1S0
Tel: 418-625-3737, *Fax:* 418-625-3730
www.cfin-fm.com
Sylvie Lamontagne, Coordonnatrice

†*Lac-Mégantic:* **CFJO-FM-1** (Freq: 101.9)
Détenteur: **CFJO-FM**
Lac-Mégantic, QC
www.o973.com
www.facebook.com/182494896930, twitter.com/o973

†*Lac-Mégantic:* **CJIT-FM (Plaisir 106.7)** (Freq: 106.7)
Détenteur: **Arsenal Media**
5605, rue Papineau, Lac-Mégantic, QC G6B 0C8
Tél: 819-583-1067
plaisir1067@attractionradio.com
plaisir1067.com

†*Laval:* **CFGL-FM (Rhythme Montréal)** (Freq: 105.7)
Détenteur: **Cogeco Media Inc.***
#100, 2830, boul St-Martin est, Laval, QC H7E 5A1
Tél: 450-664-4647, *Téléc:* 450-664-4138
Ligne sans frais: 877-984-6336
www.rythmefm.com/montreal
www.youtube.com/user/rythmefm
www.facebook.com/104523882938940,
twitter.com/rythmefm1057
Jean-Luc Meilleur, Directeur général et vice-président, stations
régionales de Cogeco Diffusion

Listuguj: **CFIC-FM** (Freq: 105.1)
PO Box 304, Listuguj, QC G0C 2R0
Tel: 418-788-5166, *Fax:* 418-788-3524
www.105hotcountry.com
Jake Dedan, General Manager

Listuguj: **CHRQ-FM** (Freq: 106.9)
PO Box 180, Listuguj, QC G0C 2R0
Tel: 418-788-2121, *Fax:* 418-788-2653
chrq1069@globetrotter.net

Longueuil: **CHAA-FM** (Freq: 103.3)
91, rue St-Jean, Longueuil, QC J4H 2W8
Tel: 450-646-6800, *Fax:* 450-646-7378
info@fm1033.ca
www.fm1033.ca
www.instagram.com/fm1033, www.facebook.com/fm1033,
twitter.com/fm1033
Eric Tetreault, Directeur, admin@fm1033.ca

†*Maniwaki:* **CFOR-FM** (Freq: 99.3)
139, rue Principal sud, Maniwaki, QC J9E 1Z8
Tél: 819-441-0993, *Téléc:* 819-441-3488
cfor993@b2b2c.ca
www.cforfm.com
Laure Voilquin, Directrice commerciale

†*Maniwaki:* **CHGA-FM** (Freq: 97.3)
158, rue Laurier, Maniwaki, QC J9E 2K7
Tél: 819-449-9730, *Téléc:* 819-449-7331
Ligne sans frais: 866-767-9730
reception@chga.fm
www.chga.qc.ca
www.facebook.com/chga.fm, twitter.com/RadioChga
Gisèle Danis, Directrice générale, gdanis@chga.fm

Maniwaki: **CKWE-FM** (Freq: 103.9)
PO Box 309, Maniwaki, QC J9E 3C9
Tel: 819-449-5097, *Fax:* 819-449-2327
ckwe.radio@gmail.com
www.ckwe1039.fm
www.youtube.com/channel/UCsrPL8A9vOZnFK_-kcXApuw,
www.facebook.com/CKWE103.9Radio,
twitter.com/CKWERADIO

†*Mashteuiatsh:* **CHUK-FM** (Freq: 107.3)
1491, rue Ouiatchouan, Mashteuiatsh, QC G0W 2H0
Tél: 418-275-4684, *Téléc:* 418-275-7964
chuk@chukfm.ca
www.chukfm.ca

†*Matagami:* **CHEF-FM** (Freq: 99.9)
CP 39, Matagami, QC J0Y 2A0
Tél: 819-739-9990, *Téléc:* 819-739-6003
chef99fm@lino.com
www.chef99.ca
Marie-Eve C. Gallant, Directrice générale,
meve.chef99fm@lino.com

†*Matane:* **CBGA-FM** (Freq: 102.1)
Détenteur: **Canadian Broadcasting Corporation***
303, av Saint-Jérôme, Matane, QC G4W 3A8
Tél: 418-562-0290
nouvelles.matane@radio-canada.ca
ici.radio-canada.ca

†*Matane:* **CHOE-FM (O 95.3)** (Freq: 95.3)
Détenteur: **Arsenal Media**
800, av du Phare ouest, Matane, QC G4W 1V7
Tél: 418-562-8181
studiochoe@attractionradio.com
o953.ca
www.facebook.com/o953matane

†*Matane:* **CHRM-FM (Plaisir 105.3)** (Freq: 105.3)
Détenteur: **Arsenal Media**
800, av du Phare ouest, Matane, QC G4W 1V7
Tél: 418-562-4141, *Téléc:* 418-562-0778
studioplaisir1053@attraction.ca
plaisir1053.com
www.facebook.com/Plaisir1053

†*Mont-Laurier:* **CFLO-FM** (Freq: 104.7)
456, rue du Pont, Mont-Laurier, QC J9L 2R9
Tél: 819-623-6610, *Téléc:* 819-623-7406
Ligne sans frais: 888-623-6610
www.cflo.ca
www.facebook.com/178411675560925
Dominic Bell, Directeur général, 819-623-6610, dbell@cflo.ca

†*Montréal:* **CBF-FM** (Freq: 95.1)
Détenteur: **Canadian Broadcasting Corporation***
1400, boul René-Lévesque Est, Montréal, QC H2L 2M2
Tél: 514-597-6000, *Téléc:* 514-597-5545
Ligne sans frais: 866-306-4636
ici.radio-canada.ca

†*Montréal:* **CBFX-FM** (Freq: 100.7)
Détenteur: **Canadian Broadcasting Corporation***
CP 6000 Centre-ville, Montréal, QC H3C 3A8
Tél: 514-597-6000, *Téléc:* 514-597-5545
Ligne sans frais: 866-306-4636
www.icimusique.ca
www.youtube.com/user/musiqueRC,
www.facebook.com/icimusique, twitter.com/icimusique
Guylaine Picard, Réalisatrice-coordonnatrice

†*Montréal:* **CBME-FM** (Freq: 88.5)
Détenteur: **Canadian Broadcasting Corporation***
CP 6000, Montréal, QC H3C 3A8
Tél: 514-597-6000
www.cbc.ca/montreal
Shelagh Kinch, Directrice général, Anglais service

Montréal: **CBM-FM** (Freq: 93.5)
Owned by: Canadian Broadcasting Corporation*
1400, boul René-Lévesque Est, Montréal, QC H2L 2M2
Tel: 514-597-6000, *Fax:* 514-597-5545
Toll-Free: 866-306-4636
www.cbc.ca/montreal

†*Montréal:* **CHMP-FM (l'actualité 98,5)** (Freq: 98.5)
Détenteur: **Cogeco Media Inc.***
#1100, 800, rue de la Gauchetière ouest, Montréal, QC H5A 1M1
Tél: 514-789-0985
www.985fm.ca
www.facebook.com/985fm, twitter.com/le985fm
Autre information: Sports URL: www.985sports.ca; Twitter:
twitter.com/985Sports

Montréal: **CHOM-FM** (Freq: 97.7)
Owned by: Bell Media Inc.*
1717, boul René-Lévesque est, Montréal, QC H2L 4T9
Tél: 514-529-3200
www.iheartradio.ca/chom
www.instagram.com/chom977, www.facebook.com/CHOM977,
twitter.com/CHOM977
André Lallier, Program Director, andre.lallier@bellmedia.ca

†*Montréal:* **CIBL-FM** (Freq: 101.5)
#201, 2, rue Ste-Catherine est, Montréal, QC H2X 1K4
Tél: 514-526-2581, *Téléc:* 514-285-2814
www.cibl1015.com
www.facebook.com/CIBLRadioMontreal, twitter.com/CIBLmedia
Gilles Labelle, Directeur général

Montréal: **CINQ-FM** (Freq: 102.3)
5212, boul St-Laurent, Montréal, QC H2T 1S1
Tél: 514-495-2597, *Fax:* 514-495-2429
cinqfm@radiocentreville.com
www.radiocentreville.com
www.facebook.com/150733819960, twitter.com/fmcentreville
Marc De Roussan, Directeur général

Montréal: **CIRA-FM** (Freq: 91.3)
#199, 4020, rue Saint-Ambroise, Montréal, QC H4C 2C7
Tél: 514-382-3913, *Fax:* 514-858-0965
Toll-Free: 855-212-2020
auditoire@radiovm.com
www.radiovm.com
www.facebook.com/RadioVilleMarie
Raynald Gagné, Directeur général

†*Montréal:* **CISM-FM** (Freq: 89.3)
CP 6128 Centre-Ville, Montréal, QC H3C 3J7
Tél: 514-343-7511
info@cism893.ca
www.cism.umontreal.ca
www.facebook.com/cism893, twitter.com/cism893
Jarrett Mann, Directeur général, jmann@cism893.ca

Montréal: **CITE-FM (Rouge FM)** (Freq: 107.3)
Owned by: Bell Media Inc.*
1717, boul René-Lévesque est, Montréal, QC H2L 4T9
Tél: 514-529-3200
montreal.rougefm.ca
www.instagram.com/107.3_rouge,
www.facebook.com/1073rougefm, twitter.com/1073rouge

Montréal: **CJFM-FM (Virgin Radio 96)** (Freq: 95.9)
Owned by: Bell Media Inc.*
1717, boul René-Lévesque est, Montréal, QC H2L 4T9
Tél: 514-529-3200
montreal.virginradio.ca
www.instagram.com/virginradiomontreal,
www.facebook.com/VirginRadioMontreal,
twitter.com/VirginRadioMTL

†*Montréal:* **CJPX-FM (WKND FM)** (Freq: 99.5)
Détenteur: **Leclerc Communication Inc.***
#100, 1260 rue Mill, Montréal, QC H3K 2B4
Tél: 514-871-0995
reception@leclerccommunication.ca
montreal.wknd.fm
www.facebook.com/wknd995

†*Montréal:* **CKBE-FM (The Beat)** (Freq: 92.5)
Détenteur: **Cogeco Media Inc.***
Place Bonaventure, #1100, 800, rue de la Gauchetière ouest, Montréal, QC H5A 1M1
Tél: 514-767-9250, *Téléc:* 514-787-7979
www.thebeat925.ca
www.youtube.com/user/925thebeatofmontreal,
www.facebook.com/TheBeatofMontreal, twitter.com/thebeat925
Sam Zniber, Program Director

Montréal: **CKDG-FM** (Freq: 105.1)
4865 Jean-Talon St. West, Montréal, QC H4P 1W7
Tél: 514-273-2481, *Fax:* 514-273-3707
info@mikefm.ca
mikefm.ca
www.facebook.com/1051Mike

†*Montréal:* **CKLX-FM (91.9 Sport)** (Freq: 91.9)
Détenteur: **RNC MÉDIA, Inc.***
#250, 200, av Laurier ouest, Montréal, QC H2T 2N8
Tél: 514-790-0919
919sport.ca
www.facebook.com/919sport, twitter.com/919sports

†*Montréal:* **CKMF-FM (Énergie 94.3)** (Freq: 94.3)
Détenteur: **Bell Media Inc.***
1717, boul René-Lévesque Est, Montréal, QC H2L 4T9
Tél: 514-529-3200, *Téléc:* 514-529-9308
www.iheartradio.ca/energie/energie-montreal
www.facebook.com/montreal943, twitter.com/943energie

---

* For details on this company see listing in Major Broadcasting Companies section; † French language station

†*Montréal:* **CKOI-FM** (Freq: 96.9)
Détenteur: **Cogeco Media Inc.***
#1100, 800, rue de la Gauchetière ouest, Montréal, QC H5A 1M1
Tél: 514-789-2564, *Téléc:* 514-787-7982
www.ckoi.com
www.youtube.com/c/ckoi969fm, www.facebook.com/969CKOI, twitter.com/ckoi
Jean-Sébastien Lemire, Directeur de la programmation

Montréal: **CKUT-FM** (Freq: 90.3)
3647 University St., Montréal, QC H3A 2B3
Tel: 514-448-4041
programming@ckut.ca
www.ckut.ca
www.facebook.com/RadioCKUT, twitter/ckut

†*Natashquan:* **CKNA-FM** (Freq: 104.1)
29, ch d'en Haut, Natashquan, QC G0G 2E0
Tél: 418-726-3284, *Téléc:* 418-726-3367
ckna@globetrotter.net
pages.globetrotter.net/ckna

†*New Carlisle:* **CHNC-FM** (Freq: 107.1)
CP 610, New Carlisle, QC G0C 1Z0
Tél: 418-752-2215, *Téléc:* 418-752-6939
Ligne sans frais: 866-470-0462
radiochnc@globetrotter.net
www.radiochnc.com
www.youtube.com/user/CHNCFM
www.facebook.com/115816745122190, twitter.com/radiochnc
Brigitte Paquet, Directrice générale, brigitte@radiochnc.com

Pikogan: **CKAG-FM** (Freq: 100.1)
30, rue David Kistabish, Pikogan, QC J9T 3A3
Tel: 819-727-3237, *Fax:* 819-727-4432
ckagfm@cableamos.com
www.ckagfm.com

†*Plessisville:* **CKYQ-FM** (Hit Country) (Freq: 95.7)
Détenteur: **Arsenal Media**
1646, av St-Laurent, Plessisville, QC G6L 2P6
Tel: 819-362-3737
hitcountry@arsenalmedia.com
hitcountry.com/hit-country-957
www.facebook.com/HitCountry957

†*Pohénégamook:* **CFVD-FM-2** (Freq: 92.1)
Détenteur: **CFVD-FM**
Pohénégamook, QC

†*Port-Menier:* **CJBE-FM** (Freq: 90.1)
CP 15, Port-Menier, QC G0G 2Y0
Tél: 418-535-0292, *Téléc:* 418-535-0497

Québec: **CBVE-FM** (Freq: 104.7)
Owned by: Canadian Broadcasting Corporation*
888, rue Saint-Jean, Québec, QC G1R 5H6
Tel: 418-654-1341, *Fax:* 418-656-8557
Toll-Free: 866-954-1341
www.cbc.ca/montreal

†*Québec:* **CBV-FM** (Freq: 106.3)
Détenteur: **Canadian Broadcasting Corporation***
CP 18800, Québec, QC G1K 9L4
Tel: 418-654-1341, *Ligne sans frais:* 866-954-1341
nouvelles.quebec@radio-canada.ca
ici.radio-canada.ca

†*Québec:* **CBV-FM** (Freq: 106.3)
Détenteur: **Canadian Broadcasting Corporation***
CP 18800, Québec, QC G1K 9L4
Tel: 418-654-1341, *Ligne sans frais:* 866-954-1341
www.radio-canada.ca

Québec: **CBVX-FM** (Freq: 95.3)
Owned by: Canadian Broadcasting Corporation*
888, rue Saint-Jean, Québec, QC G1R 5H6
Tel: 418-654-1341, *Fax:* 418-656-8557
nouvelles.quebec@radio-canada.ca
www.icimusique.ca

†*Québec:* **CFEL-FM** (blvd 102.1) (Freq: 102.1)
Détenteur: **Leclerc Communication Inc.***
#505, 815, boul Lebourgneuf, Québec, QC G2J 0C1
Tel: 418-529-1021
studio@blvd.fm
www.blvd.fm
www.facebook.com/BLVD1021, twitter.com/blvd1021
Pierre-Luc Gilbert, Directeur des ventes,
pl.gilbert@leclerccommunication.ca

†*Québec:* **CFOM-FM** (M-FM) (Freq: 102.9)
Détenteur: **Cogeco Media Inc.***
1305, ch Ste-Foy - 4e étage, Québec, QC G1S 4Y5
Tél: 418-694-1029, *Ligne sans frais:* 877-394-1029
www.m1029.com
www.facebook.com/mfm1029, twitter.com/mfm1029
Richard Renaud, Directeur général

†*Québec:* **CHIK-FM** (Énergie 98.9) (Freq: 98.9)
Détenteur: **Bell Media Inc.***
900, rue d'Youville, 1e étage, Québec, QC G1R 3P7
Tél: 418-687-9900, *Téléc:* 418-687-3106
www.iheartradio.ca/energie/energie-quebec
www.instagram.com/energie989
www.facebook.com/quebec989, twitter.com/energie989

†*Québec:* **CHOI-FM** (CHOI Radio X) (Freq: 98.1)
Détenteur: **RNC MÉDIA, Inc.***
#300, 1134, Grande-Allée ouest, Québec, QC G1S 1E5
Tél: 418-687-9810, *Ligne sans frais:* 877-440-2464
live@radiox.com
radiox.com/choi981
www.facebook.com/radioxquebec, twitter.com/CHOIRadioX

†*Québec:* **CHXX-FM** (Vibe) (Freq: 100.9)
Détenteur: **RNC MÉDIA, Inc.***
#300, 1134 Grande-Allée ouest, Québec, QC G1S 1E5
Tél: 418-670-1009
live@lavibe.fm
lavibe.fm
www.facebook.com/100.9QC

Québec: **CHYZ-FM** (Freq: 94.3)
Pavillon Maurice-Pollack, l'Université Laval, #0236, 2305, rue de l'université, Québec, QC G1V 0A6
Tel: 418-656-7007
info@chyz.ca
www.chyz.ca
www.youtube.com/chyz943fm, www.facebook.com/chyz943, twitter.com/chyz943
Jean-Philippe Lessard, Directeur général, dg@chyz.ca

Québec: **CION-FM** (Freq: 90.9; 102.5; 106.7)
3196, ch Sainte-Foy, Québec, QC G1X 1R4
Tel: 418-659-9090, *Fax:* 418-650-3306
Toll-Free: 800-447-2466
cionfm@radiogalilee.qc.ca
www.radiogalilee.com
Denis Veilleux, Directeur

†*Québec:* **CITF-FM** (Rouge FM) (Freq: 107.5)
Détenteur: **Bell Media Inc.***
900, rue d'Youville, 1e étage, Québec, QC G1R 3P7
Tel: 418-687-9900, *Téléc:* 418-687-3106
quebec.rougefm.ca
www.instagram.com/107.5_rouge
www.facebook.com/1075rougefm, twitter.com/1075rouge

†*Québec:* **CJEC-FM** (WKND FM) (Freq: 91.9)
Détenteur: **Leclerc Communication Inc.***
#505, 815, boul Lebourgneuf, Québec, QC G2J 0C1
Tel: 418-688-0919
quebec.wknd.fm
www.facebook.com/wknd919, twitter.com/wknd919
Pierre-Luc Gilbert, Directeur des ventes,
pl.gilbert@leclerccommunication.ca

†*Québec:* **CJMF-FM** (FM93) (Freq: 93.3)
Détenteur: **Cogeco Media Inc.***
1305, ch Ste-Foy, Québec, QC G1S 4Y5
Tél: 418-687-9330, *Téléc:* 418-687-9718
www.fm93.com
www.facebook.com/fm93quebec, twitter.com/fm93quebec

†*Québec:* **CKIA-FM** (Freq: 88.3)
#200, 335, rue Saint-Joseph, Québec, QC G1K 3B4
Tél: 418-529-9026
www.ckiafm.org
www.facebook.com/115737995163836
Lorinne Larouche, Coordonnatrice aux opérations

†*Québec:* **CKRL-FM** (Freq: 89.1)
405, 3e av, Québec, QC G1L 2W2
Tél: 418-640-2575, *Téléc:* 418-640-1588
programmation@ckrl.qc.ca
www.ckrl.qc.ca
www.facebook.com/CKRL891, twitter.com/CKRL891
Dany Fortin, Directeur général, direction@ckrl.qc.ca

†*Radisson:* **CIAU-FM** (Freq: 103.1)
CP 285, Radisson, QC J0Y 2X0
Tél: 819-638-7033, *Téléc:* 819-638-1031
ciaufm@lino.com
www.ciaufm.ca

†*Rimouski:* **CBRX-FM** (Freq: 101.5)
Détenteur: **Canadian Broadcasting Corporation***
185, boul René-Lepage est, Rimouski, QC G5L 1P2
Tél: 418-723-2217, *Téléc:* 418-723-6126
www.icimusique.ca
Josée Bouchard, Rédactrice en chef, Est du Québec,
josee.bouchard@radio-canada.ca

†*Rimouski:* **CIKI-FM** (Énergie 98.7) (Freq: 98.7)
Détenteur: **Bell Media Inc.***
#502, 287, rue Pierre-Saindon, Rimouski, QC G5L 9A7
Tél: 418-723-2323
www.iheartradio.ca/energie/energie-rimouski
www.facebook.com/nrj987, twitter.com/NRJ987

†*Rimouski:* **CJBR-FM** (Freq: 89.1)
Détenteur: **Canadian Broadcasting Corporation***
185, boul René-Lepage, Rimouski, QC G5L 1P2
Tél: 418-723-2217
www.radio-canada.ca/radio

†*Rimouski:* **CJOI-FM** (Rouge FM) (Freq: 102.9)
Détenteur: **Bell Media Inc.***
#502, 287, rue Pierre-Saindon, Rimouski, QC G5L 9A7
Tél: 418-723-2323
www.iheartradio.ca/rouge-fm/rouge-fm-rimouski
www.facebook.com/1029rougefm, twitter.com/1029rouge

†*Rimouski:* **CKMN-FM** (Freq: 96.5)
323, Montée industrielle et commerciale, Rimouski, QC G5M 1A7
Tél: 418-722-2566, *Téléc:* 418-724-7815
secretariat@ckmn.fm
www.ckmn.fm
www.facebook.com/CKMN.FM

Rivière-au-Renard: **CJRE-FM** (Freq: 97.9)
Owned by: CJRG-FM
Rivière-au-Renard, QC

†*Rivière-du-Loup:* **CIBM-FM** (Freq: 107.1)
64, rue Hôtel-de-Ville, Rivière-du-Loup, QC G5R 1L5
Tél: 418-867-1071, *Téléc:* 418-867-4940
www.cibm107.com
www.facebook.com/140168673893
Daniel St-Pierre, Directeur de la programmation,
dstpierre@cibm107.com

†*Rivière-du-Loup:* **CIEL-FM** (Freq: 103.7)
64, rue Hôtel-de-Ville, Rivière-du-Loup, QC G5R 1L5
Tél: 418-862-8241, *Téléc:* 418-867-4940
www.ciel103.com
www.facebook.com/208658131206
Clermont Labrie, Contrôleur, clabrie@ciel103.com
Daniel St-Pierre, Directeur de la programmation,
dstpierre@ciel103.com

†*Roberval:* **CHRL-FM** (Planète) (Freq: 99.5)
Détenteur: **Cogeco Media Inc.***
568, boul St-Joseph, Roberval, QC G8H 2K6
Tél: 418-275-1831
roberval.planeteradio.ca
www.facebook.com/176702051800

Rouyn-Noranda: **CHIC-FM** (Freq: 88.7)
PO Box 2185, 120, 9e Rue, Rouyn-Noranda, QC J9X 5A6
Tel: 819-797-4242, *Fax:* 819-797-3803
887@chicfm.org
chicfm.org
Richard Dubé, Responsable, Technique et informatique

†*Rouyn-Noranda:* **CHLM-FM** (Freq: 90.7)
70, av Principal, Rouyn-Noranda, QC J9X 4P2
Tél: 819-762-8155, *Ligne sans frais:* 877-666-8155
abitibi@radio-canada.ca
www.radio-canada.ca/regions/abitibi
Serge Cossette, Chef des services français,
Abitibi-Témiscamingue, serge.cossette@radio-canada.ca

Rouyn-Noranda: **CJMM-FM** (Énergie 99.1/Énergie 92.5) (Freq: 99.1)
Owned by: Bell Media Inc.*
191, av Murdoch, Rouyn-Noranda, QC J9X 1E3
Tel: 819-797-2566, *Fax:* 819-797-1664
Toll-Free: 866-991-0925
www.iheartradio.ca/energie/energie-rouyn
www.facebook.com/rouyn991, twitter.com/energie991

---

* For details on this company see listing in Major Broadcasting Companies section; † French language station

Saguenay: **CBJE-FM** (Freq: 102.7FM)
Owned by: CBVE-FM
Saguenay, QC

www.cbc.ca/radio

†*Saguenay:* **CBJX-FM** (Freq: 100.9FM)
Détenteur: **Canadian Broadcasting Corporation***
500, rue des Saguenéens, Saguenay, QC G7H 6N4
Tél: 418-696-6600
www.radio-canada.ca/regions/saguenay-lac

Saint-Augustin: **CJAS-FM** (Freq: 93.5)
PO Box 100, 558 rue Principal, Saint-Augustin, QC G0G 2R0
Tel: 418-947-2239, *Fax:* 418-947-2664
cjasradio@gmail.com
www.lnscommunityradio.com/CJAS
Lorette Gallibois, General Manager

Saint-Gabriel-de-Brandon: **CFNJ-FM** (Freq: 99.1)
245, rue Beauvilliers, Saint-Gabriel-de-Brandon, QC J0K 2N0
Tel: 450-835-3437, *Fax:* 450-835-3581
Toll-Free: 888-935-3437
info@cfnj.net
www.cfnj.net

†*Saint-Georges:* **CKRB-FM** (Freq: 103.5)
CP 100, Saint-Georges, QC G5Y 5C4
Tél: 418-228-1460, *Téléc:* 418-228-0096
Ligne sans frais: 866-535-1035
studio@coolfm.biz
www.coolfm.biz
www.facebook.com/1035CoolFm, twitter.com/InfoRadioBeauce
Roger Quirion, Directeur des Opérations,
rogerquirion@radiobeauce.com

†*Saint-Hilarion:* **CIHO-FM** (Freq: 96.3)
315, ch Cartier nord, Saint-Hilarion, QC G0A 3V0
Tél: 418-457-3333, *Téléc:* 418-457-3518
studio@cihofm.com
www.cihofm.com
www.facebook.com/1016193666699027, twitter.com/cihofm
Gervais Desbiens, Directeur général, direction@cihofm.com

†*Saint-Hyacinthe:* **CFEI-FM (Boom FM)** (Freq: 106.5)
Détenteur: **Bell Media Inc.***
2596, boul Casavant ouest, Saint-Hyacinthe, QC J2S 7R8
Tél: 450-774-6486, *Ligne sans frais:* 877-220-2666
www.boomfm.ca
www.facebook.com/radioboom, twitter.com/radioboomfm

†*Saint-Jean-sur-Richelieu:* **CFZZ-FM (Boom FM)**
(Freq: 104.1)
Détenteur: **Bell Media Inc.***
104, rue Richelieu, Saint-Jean-sur-Richelieu, QC J3B 6X3
Tél: 450-346-0104
www.iheartradio.ca/boom/boom-1041
www.youtube.com/user/BoomFM10651041,
www.facebook.com/radioboom, twitter.com/radioboomfm

†*Saint-Jérôme:* **CHPR-FM (Cime)** (Freq: 102.1)
Détenteur: **Cogeco Media Inc.***
#102, 300, rue Marie-Victorin, Saint-Jérôme, QC J7Y 2G8
Tél: 450-431-2463, *Téléc:* 450-504-5601
lachutehawkesbury.cime.fm
www.instagram.com/cime_fm, www.facebook.com/cime.fm,
twitter.com/cime10391013

†*Saint-Jérôme:* **CIME-FM (Le Rhythme des Laurentides)** (Freq: 101.3; 103.9)
Détenteur: **Cogeco Media Inc.***
#102, 300, rue Marie-Victorin, Saint-Jérôme, QC J7Y 2G8
Tél: 450-431-2463, *Téléc:* 450-504-5601
www.cime.fm
www.facebook.com/cime.fm, twitter.com/CIMEfm
Joanne Leboeuf, Directrice générale

†*Saint-Jérôme:* **CJLA-FM (Cime)** (Freq: 104.9)
Détenteur: **Cogeco Media Inc.***
#102, 300, rue Marie-Victorin, Saint-Jérôme, QC J7Y 2G8
Tél: 450-431-2463, *Téléc:* 450-504-5601
lachutehawkesbury.cime.fm
www.instagram.com/cime_fm, www.facebook.com/cime.fm,
twitter.com/cime10391013

†*Saint-Rémi:* **CHOC-FM** (Freq: 104.9)
93, rue Lachapelle est, Saint-Rémi, QC J0L 2L0
Tél: 450-454-5500, *Téléc:* 450-454-9435
www.chocfm.com

Sainte-Perpétue: **CHOX-FM-2** (Freq: 101.1)
Owned by: CHOX-FM
Sainte-Perpétue, QC

†*Salaberry-de-Valleyfield:* **CKOD-FM** (Freq: 103.1)
#103, 249, rue Victoria, Salaberry-de-Valleyfield, QC J6T 1A9
Tél: 450-373-0103, *Téléc:* 450-854-8103
fm103@ckod.qc.ca
www.ckod.qc.ca
www.facebook.com/CKODFM103, twitter.com/ckodfm
Robert Brunet, Propriétaire

†*Senneterre:* **CIBO-FM** (Freq: 100.5)
121, 1ère rue Est, Senneterre, QC J0Y 2M0
Tél: 819-737-2222, *Téléc:* 819-737-8599
cibo.fm@cableamos.com
cibofm.wix.com/radio
www.youtube.com/user/cibofm, www.facebook.com/cibofm,
twitter.com/cibofm

†*Sept-Iles:* **CBSI-FM** (Freq: 98.1)
Détenteur: **Canadian Broadcasting Corporation***
#30, 350, rue Smith, Sept-Iles, QC G4R 3X2
Tél: 418-968-0720, *Ligne sans frais:* 800-463-1731
cbsi@radio-canada.ca
ici.radio-canada.ca/cote-nord

†*Sept-Iles:* **CIPC-FM (O 99.1)** (Freq: 99.1)
Détenteur: **Arsenal Media**
#400, 106, rue Napoléon, Sept-Iles, QC G4R 3L7
Tél: 418-962-3838
o991.ca
www.facebook.com/o991cipc

Sept-Iles: **CKAU-FM** (Freq: 90.1; 104.5)
100, boul des Montagnais, Sept-Iles, QC G4R 4K2
Tel: 418-927-2476
www.ckau.com
www.facebook.com/ckaufm
Reginald Volant, Directeur Général, 418-927-2476

†*Sept-Iles:* **CKCN-FM (Plaisir 94.1)** (Freq: 94.1)
Détenteur: **Arsenal Media**
#400, 106, rue Napoléon, Sept-Iles, QC G4R 3L7
Tél: 418-962-3838
plaisir941.com
www.facebook.com/Plaisir941

Sherbrooke: **CFAK-FM** (Freq: 88.3)
2500, boul de Université, Sherbrooke, QC J1K 2R1
Tel: 819-821-8000, *Fax:* 819-821-7930
info.cfak883@usherbrooke.ca
cfak883.usherbrooke.ca
www.facebook.com/CFAK883, twitter.com/CFAK883
Serge Langlois, Directeur général, dg.cfak883@usherbrooke.ca

†*Sherbrooke:* **CFGE-FM (Rhythme Sherbrooke)**
(Freq: 93.7; 98.1)
Détenteur: **Cogeco Media Inc.***
4020, boul de Portland, Sherbrooke, QC J1L 2V6
Tél: 819-822-0937, *Téléc:* 819-562-1666
www.rythmefm.com/estrie
www.facebook.com/130198797025166, twitter.com/rythmefm937

†*Sherbrooke:* **CFLX-FM** (Freq: 95.5)
67, rue Wellington Nord, Sherbrooke, QC J1H 5A9
Tél: 819-566-2787, *Téléc:* 819-566-7331
commentaire@cflx.qc.ca
www.cflx.qc.ca
twitter.com/cflx955

†*Sherbrooke:* **CIMO-FM (Énergie 106.1)** (Freq: 106.1)
Détenteur: **Bell Media Inc.***
#200, 2185, rue King ouest, Sherbrooke, QC J1J 2G2
Tél: 819-347-1414, *Téléc:* 819-347-1061
www.iheartradio.ca/energie/energie-estrie
www.facebook.com/estrie1061, twitter.com/1061energie

†*Sherbrooke:* **CITE-FM-1 (Rouge FM)** (Freq: 102.7)
Détenteur: **Bell Media Inc.***
#200, 2185, rue King ouest, Sherbrooke, QC J1L 2E4
Tél: 819-347-1414, *Téléc:* 819-566-1011
estrie.rougefm.ca
www.instagram.com/102.7_rouge,
www.facebook.com/1027rougefm, twitter.com/1027rouge

Sherbrooke: **CJMQ-FM** (Freq: 88.9)
184 Queen St., Sherbrooke, QC J1M 1J9
Tel: 819-822-1838
cjmqnews@yahoo.ca
www.cjmq.fm
www.facebook.com/87230649091
David Teasdale, Station Manager, 819-570-2094,
dteasdale77@yahoo.ca
Maureen Dillon, Program & Music Director, 819-822-1838

†*Sherbrooke:* **CKOY-FM** (Freq: 107.7)
Détenteur: **Cogeco Media Inc.***
4020, boul Portland, Sherbrooke, QC J1L 2V6
Tél: 819-822-0937, *Téléc:* 819-562-1666
www.fm1077.ca
www.facebook.com/1077fm, twitter.com/fm1077

†*Sorel-Tracy:* **CJSO-FM** (Freq: 101.7)
52, rue du Roi, Sorel-Tracy, QC J3P 4M7
Tél: 450-743-2772, *Téléc:* 450-743-0293
Ligne sans frais: 888-489-1017
administration@fm1017.ca
www.fm1017.ca
www.facebook.com/fm1017.ca, twitter.com/Fm1017Info
Jean-Marc Belzile, Président et directeur-général

†*Squatec:* **CFVD-FM-3** (Freq: 92.1)
Détenteur: **CFVD-FM**
Squatec, QC

†*St-Georges:* **CHJM-FM** (Freq: 99.7)
CP 100, St-Georges, QC G5Y 5C4
Tél: 418-227-0997, *Téléc:* 418-228-0096
studio@radiobeauce.com
www.mix997.com
www.facebook.com/mix997, twitter.com/MIX997

†*Ste-Marie-de-Beauce:* **CHEQ-FM (O 101.5)** (Freq: 101.5)
Détenteur: **Arsenal Media**
373, rte Cameron, Ste-Marie-de-Beauce, QC G6E 3E2
Tél: 418-387-1015
o1015@attraction.ca
o1015.ca
www.facebook.com/cheqfm
Chantal Baribeau, Directrice générale, cbaribeau@fm1015.ca

†*Témiscaming:* **CKVM-FM-1** (Freq: 92.1)
Détenteur: **CKVM-FM**
Témiscaming, QC

†*Thetford Mines:* **CKLD-FM (Plaisir 105.5)** (Freq: 105.5)
Détenteur: **Arsenal Media**
216, rue Notre-Dame ouest, Thetford Mines, QC G6G 1J6
Tél: 418-335-7533
plaisir1055@attractionradio.com
plaisir1055.com
www.facebook.com/113218588716902

†*Trois-Rivières:* **CHEY-FM (Rouge FM)** (Freq: 94.7)
Détenteur: **Bell Media Inc.***
#260, 1500, rue Royale, Trois-Rivières, QC G9A 6J4
Tél: 819-378-1023
mauricie.rougefm.ca
www.facebook.com/947Rougefm, twitter.com/947rougefm
Marc Thibault, Directeur de la programmation,
marc.thibault@bellmedia.ca

†*Trois-Rivières:* **CIGB-FM (Énergie 102.3)** (Freq: 102.3)
Détenteur: **Bell Media Inc.***
#260, 1500, rue Royal, Trois-Rivières, QC G9A 6J4
Tél: 819-378-1023
www.iheartradio.ca/energie/energie-mauricie
www.youtube.com/user/NRJquebec,
www.facebook.com/nrj1023, twitter.com/nrjmauricie

†*Trois-Rivières:* **CJEB-FM (Rythme Mauricie)** (Freq: 100.1)
Détenteur: **Cogeco Media Inc.***
#1200, 1350, rue Royale, Trois-Rivières, QC G9A 4J4
Tél: 819-691-1001, *Téléc:* 819-374-3222
www.rythmefm.com/mauricie
www.youtube.com/user/rythmefm,
www.facebook.com/104523882938940,
twitter.com/rythmefm1001
Daniel Brouillette, Directeur général

†*Trois-Rivières:* **CKOB-FM** (Freq: 106.9)
Détenteur: **Cogeco Media Inc.***
#1200, 1350, rue Royale, Trois-Rivières, QC G9A 4J4
Tél: 819-374-3556, *Téléc:* 819-374-3222
www.fm1069.ca
www.facebook.com/fm1069, twitter.com/fm1069

†*Val d'Or:* **CJMV-FM (Énergie 102.7)** (Freq: 102.7)
Détenteur: **Bell Media Inc.***
1610, 3e Avenue, Val d'Or, QC J9P 1V8
Tél: 819-825-2568, *Téléc:* 819-825-2840
www.iheartradio.ca/energie/energie-val-d-or
www.facebook.com/valdor1027, twitter.com/energie1027

---

* For details on this company see listing in Major Broadcasting Companies section; † French language station

†*Val-d'Or:* CHGO-FM (Capitale Rock) (Freq: 104.3)
Détenteur: **Cogeco Media Inc.***
1729, 3e av, Val-d'Or, QC J9P 1W3
Tél: 819-825-1043, *Téléc:* 819-825-1041
www.capitalerock.ca
www.facebook.com/CapitaleRock

†*Val-d'Or:* CJGO-FM (Capitale Rock) (Freq: 102.1)
Détenteur: **Cogeco Media Inc.***
1729, 3e av, Val-d'Or, QC J9P 1W3
Tél: 819-825-1043, *Téléc:* 819-825-1041
www.capitalerock.ca
www.facebook.com/CapitaleRock

†*Victoriaville:* CFDA-FM (Plaisir 101.9) (Freq: 101.9)
Détenteur: **Arsenal Media**
55, rue St-Jean Baptiste, Victoriaville, QC G6P 6T3
Tél: 819-752-2785
plaisir1019@attraction.ca
plaisir1019.com
www.facebook.com/114831865223346

†*Victoriaville:* CFJO-FM (O 97.3) (Freq: 97.3)
Détenteur: **Arsenal Media**
55, rue St-Jean-Baptiste, Victoriaville, QC G6P 4E1
Tél: 819-752-2785
o973.ca
www.facebook.com/182494896930

†*Ville-Marie:* CKVM-FM (Freq: 93.1)
62, rue Ste-Anne, Ville-Marie, QC J9V 2B7
Tél: 819-629-2710, *Téléc:* 819-622-0716
www.ckvmfm.com
www.facebook.com/ckvmfm

Windsor: CIAX-FM (Freq: 98.3)
49, 6e av, Windsor, QC J1S 1T2
Tél: 819-845-2692
unitewindsor@qc.aira.com
www.ciaxfm.net
www.facebook.com/185450771483585

Saskatchewan

†*Bellegarde:* CBKF-FM-4 (Freq: 91.9)
Détenteur: **CBKF-FM (Première Chaîne)**
Bellegarde, SK

Carlyle Lake: CIDD-FM (Freq: 97.7)
Carlyle Lake, SK

Peterborough: CJLF-FM-2 (Freq: 89.3)
Owned by: CJLF-FM (Life 100.3)
Peterborough, ON
www.lifeonline.fm

Carrot River: CJVR-FM-3 (Freq: 99.7)
Owned by: CJVR-FM (CJVR Country)
Carrot River, SK

Dafoe: CJVR-FM-1 (Freq: 100.3)
Owned by: CJVR-FM (CJVR Country)
Dafoe, SK

Estevan: CHSN-FM (Sun 102) (Freq: 102.3)
Owned by: **Golden West Broadcasting Ltd.***
#200, 1236 - 5th St., Estevan, SK S4A 0Z6
Tel: 306-634-1280, *Toll-Free:* 800-824-0743
discoverestevan.com
www.facebook.com/153908414691570, twitter.com/Sun102FM

Estevan: CKSE-FM (Freq: 106.1)
Owned by: **Golden West Broadcasting Ltd.***
#200, 1236 - 5th St., Estevan, SK S4A 0Z6
Tel: 306-636-6106
1061FM@DiscoverEstevan.com
discoverestevan.com
www.facebook.com/1061Ckse, twitter.com/1061FMCKSE

Hudson Bay: CFMQ-FM (Freq: 98.1)
PO Box 1272, Hudson Bay, SK S0E 0Y0
Tel: 306-865-3065, *Fax:* 306-865-2227
cfmq@sasktel.net

Humboldt: CHBO-FM (107.5 Bolt FM) (Freq: 107.5)
Owned by: **Golden West Broadcasting Ltd.***
PO Box 2888, 640 - 10th St., Humboldt, SK S0K 2A0
Tel: 306-682-2255, *Toll-Free:* 855-476-0155
boltfm@discoverhumboldt.com
www.discoverhumboldt.com
www.facebook.com/107.5Humboldt, twitter.com/1075BoltFM

La Ronge: CBKA-FM (Freq: 105.9)
Owned by: Canadian Broadcasting Corporation*
308 La Ronge Ave., La Ronge, SK S0J 1L0
Tel: 306-347-9540
www.cbc.ca/sask

La Ronge: CJLR-FM (Freq: 89.9)
Napoleon T. Gardiner Broadcast Centre, 712 Finlayson St.,
La Ronge, SK S0J 1L0
Tel: 306-425-4003, *Fax:* 306-425-3123
reception@mbcradio.com
www.mbcradio.com
twitter.com/mbcradionews
Deborah A. Charles, CEO, deb@mbcradio.com

Meadow Lake: CFDM-FM (Freq: 105.7)
PO Box 8168, Flying Dust Reserve, Meadow Lake, SK S9X
1T8
Tel: 306-236-1445, *Fax:* 306-236-2861
cfdmradio@hotmail.com
cfdm.sasktelwebhosting.com

Meadow Lake: CJNS-FM (Freq: 102.3)
Owned by: **Jim Pattison Broadcast Group***
Meadow Lake, SK
www.cjns.ca

Melfort: CJVR-FM (CJVR Country) (Freq: 105.1)
Owned by: **Jim Pattison Broadcast Group***
611 Main St. North, Melfort, SK S0E 1A0
Tel: 306-752-2587, *Fax:* 306-752-5932
info@cjvr.com
www.cjvr.com
www.facebook.com/105CJVR, twitter.com/105CJVR
Ken Singer, Vice-President, k.singer@cjvr.com
Linda Rheaume, Station Manager, linda@cjur.com

Moose Jaw: CILG-FM (Country 100) (Freq: 100.7)
Owned by: **Golden West Broadcasting Ltd.***
1704 Main St. North, Moose Jaw, SK S6J 1L4
Tel: 306-694-0800, *Toll-Free:* 800-820-1768
discovermoosejaw.com
www.facebook.com/Country100, twitter.com/country100fm

Moose Jaw: CJAW-FM (Mix 103) (Freq: 103.9)
Owned by: **Golden West Broadcasting Ltd.***
1704 Main St. North, Moose Jaw, SK S6J 1L4
Tel: 306-694-0800, *Toll-Free:* 800-820-1768
discovermoosejaw.com
www.facebook.com/mix103moosejaw, twitter.com/mix103

Nipawin: CJNE-FM (Freq: 94.7)
PO Box 220, Nipawin, SK S0E 1E0
Tel: 306-862-9478, *Fax:* 306-862-2334
www.cjnefm.com
twitter.com/CJNEFM
Norman Rudock, Owner, norm.cjne@sasktel.net

†*North Battleford:* CBKF-FM-5 (Freq: 96.9FM)
Détenteur: **CBKF-FM (Première Chaîne)**
North Battleford, SK

North Battleford: CJCQ-FM (Q98) (Freq: 97.9)
Owned by: **Jim Pattison Broadcast Group***
1711 - 100th St., North Battleford, SK S9A 0W7
Tel: 306-445-2477
cjnbnews@jpbg.ca
www.q98.ca
www.facebook.com/q98allhitmusic
Karl Johnston, General Manager, karl.johnston@jpbg.ca

North Battleford: CJHD-FM (93.3 The Rock) (Freq:
93.3)
Owned by: **Jim Pattison Broadcast Group***
1711 - 100th St., North Battleford, SK S9A 0W7
Tel: 306-445-2477, *Toll-Free:* 888-242-1303
cjnbnews@jpbg.ca
www.933therock.ca
www.facebook.com/933therock
Karl Johnston, General & Station Manager,
karl.johnston@jpbg.ca

Prince Albert: CFMM-FM (Power 99 FM) (Freq: 99.1)
Owned by: **Jim Pattison Broadcast Group***
1316 Central Ave., 2nd Fl., Prince Albert, SK S6V 6P5
Tel: 306-763-7421, *Toll-Free:* 800-667-9000
www.power99fm.com
www.facebook.com/power99fmradio, twitter.com/power99fm
Karl Johnston, General Manager, karl.johnston@jpbg.ca

Prince Albert: CHQX-FM (XFM) (Freq: 101.5)
Owned by: **Jim Pattison Broadcast Group***
1316 Central Ave., Prince Albert, SK S6V 6P5
Tel: 306-763-7421
www.xfmrocks.com
www.facebook.com/xfm1015, twitter.com/xfmrocks

†*Prince Albert:* CKSF-FM (Freq: 90.1)
Détenteur: **CBKF-FM (Première Chaîne)**
Prince Albert, SK

†*Regina:* CBKF-FM (Première Chaîne) (Freq: 97.7)
Détenteur: **Canadian Broadcasting Corporation***
CP 540, 2440, rue Broad, Regina, SK S4P 4A1
Tél: 306-347-9540
saskatchewan@radio-canada.ca
www.radio-canada.ca/saskatchewan
www.facebook.com/radiocanadasaskatchewan,
twitter.com/RC_Saskatchewan

Regina: CBK-FM (Freq: 96.9)
Owned by: Canadian Broadcasting Corporation*
2440 Broad St., Regina, SK S4P 4A1
Tel: 306-347-9540
www.cbc.ca/sask
www.facebook.com/cbcsask, twitter.com/cbcsask
Other information: Radio phone: 306-347-9541
Lenora Sturge, Communications Officer

Regina: CBK-FM (CBC Radio 2; 96.9FM)
Owned by: Canadian Broadcasting Corporation*
2440 Broad St., Regina, SK S4P 0A5
Tel: 306-347-9540
www.cbc.ca/sask
Paul Dederick, Managing Editor, paul.dederick@cbc.ca

Regina: CFWF-FM (Freq: 104.9)
Owned by: **Harvard Broadcasting Inc.***
1900 Rose St., Regina, SK S4P 0A9
Tel: 306-546-6200, *Fax:* 306-781-7338
www.thewolfrocks.com
www.facebook.com/thewolfrocks, twitter.com/thewolfrocks
Jason Huschi, General Manager,
jasonh@harvardbroadcasting.com

Regina: CHBD-FM (Big Dog 92.7) (Freq: 92.7)
Owned by: **Bell Media Inc.***
#100, 4303 Albert St. South, Regina, SK S4S 3R6
Tel: 306-337-2850
www.bigdog927.com
www.instagram.com/bigdog927
www.facebook.com/BigDogRegina, twitter.com/BigDog927regina
David Fisher, General Manager, david.fisher@bellmedia.ca

Regina: CHMX-FM (Freq: 92.1)
Owned by: **Harvard Broadcasting Inc.***
1900 Rose St., Regina, SK S4P 0A9
Tel: 306-936-6200, *Fax:* 306-781-7338
www.my921.ca
www.facebook.com/my921
Jason Huschi, General Manager,
jasonh@harvardbroadcasting.com

Regina: CIZL-FM (Freq: 98.9)
Owned by: **Rawlco Radio Ltd.***
#210, 2401 Saskatchewan Dr., Regina, SK S4P 4H8
Tel: 306-525-0000
www.z99.com
www.facebook.com/z99regina, twitter.com/z99regina

Regina: CJTR-FM (Freq: 91.3)
PO Box 334 Main, Regina, SK S4P 3A1
Tel: 306-525-7274, *Fax:* 306-525-9741
radius@cjtr.ca
www.cjtr.ca
www.facebook.com/cjtrfm, twitter.com/CJTR_Radio
Karl Valiaho, President

Regina: CKCK-FM (Freq: 94.5)
Owned by: **Rawlco Radio Ltd.***
#210, 2401 Saskatchewan Dr., Regina, SK S4P 4H8
Tel: 306-525-0000
www.jack945.com
www.facebook.com/jackregina, twitter.com/jackregina

Rosetown: CKVX-FM (Mix 104.9) (Freq: 104.9)
Owned by: **Golden West Broadcasting Ltd.***
PO Box 490, 208 Hwy. 4, Rosetown, SK S0L 2V0
Tel: 306-882-2686, *Toll-Free:* 800-667-5313
cjymnews@goldenwestradio.com
www.westcentralonline.com
www.facebook.com/324448833194, twitter.com/Mix104FM

* For details on this company see listing in Major Broadcasting Companies section; † French language station

Saskatoon: **CFCR-FM** (Freq: 90.5)
PO Box 7544, Saskatoon, SK S7K 4L4
Tel: 306-664-6678
cfcr@cfcr.ca
www.cfcr.ca
www.youtube.com/CFCRSASKATOON,
twitter.com/CFCRSASKATOON
Neil Bergen, Station Manager, manager@cfcr.ca

Saskatoon: **CFMC-FM** (Freq: 95.1)
Owned by: Rawlco Radio Ltd.*
715 Saskatchewan Cres. West, Saskatoon, SK S7M 5V7
Tel: 306-934-2222
www.c95.com
www.facebook.com/c95saskatoon

Saskatoon: **CJDJ-FM** (Freq: 102.1)
Owned by: Rawlco Radio Ltd.*
715 Saskatchewan Cres. West, Saskatoon, SK S7M 5V7
Tel: 306-934-2222
www.rock102rocks.com
www.facebook.com/rock102rocks, twitter.com/rock102twits

Saskatoon: **CJMK-FM** (Freq: 98.3)
Owned by: Saskatoon Media Group*
366 - 3rd Ave. South, Saskatoon, SK S7K 1M5
Tel: 306-244-1975
www.98cool.ca
www.facebook.com/98cool, twitter.com/98coolfm

Saskatoon: **CKBL-FM** (Freq: 92.9)
Owned by: Saskatoon Media Group*
366 - 3rd Ave. South, Saskatoon, SK S7K 1M5
Tel: 306-244-1975
thebull@929thebullrocks.com
www.thebull.ca
www.facebook.com/929thebull, twitter.com/929thebull

Swift Current: **CIMG-FM (The Eagle 94.1)** (Freq: 94.1)
Owned by: Golden West Broadcasting Ltd.*
134 Central Ave. North, Swift Current, SK S9H 0L1
Tel: 306-773-4605, Toll-Free: 800-821-8073
eaglecontrol@goldenwestradio.com
www.swiftcurrentonline.com
www.facebook.com/164908956862679,
twitter.com/theeagle94one

Swift Current: **CKFI-FM (Magic 97.1)** (Freq: 97.1)
Owned by: Golden West Broadcasting Ltd.*
134 Central Ave. North, Swift Current, SK S9H 0L1
Tel: 306-773-4605, Toll-Free: 800-821-8073
www.swiftcurrentonline.com
www.facebook.com/122248154511534, twitter.com/magic97sc

Waskesiu: **CJVR-FM-2** (Freq: 106.3)
Owned by: CJVR-FM (CJVR Country)
Waskesiu, SK

Weyburn: **CKRC-FM (Magic 103.5)** (Freq: 103.5)
Owned by: Golden West Broadcasting Ltd.*
305 Souris Ave., Weyburn, SK S4H 0C6
Tel: 306-848-1190, Toll-Free: 800-821-9642
discoverweyburn.com
www.facebook.com/105410576167749, twitter.com/magic1035

Yorkton: **CFGW-FM** (Freq: 94.1)
Owned by: Harvard Broadcasting Inc.*
120 Smith St. East, Yorkton, SK S3N 3V3
Tel: 306-782-9410, Fax: 306-783-4994
ykt-reception@harvardbroadcasting.com
www.foxfmonline.ca
www.youtube.com/user/foxfmyorkton,
www.facebook.com/MoreFoxFM, twitter.com/MOREFOXFM
Angie Norton, General Manager,
anorton@harvardbroadcasting.com

†*Zenon Park:* **CBKF-FM-3** (Freq: 93.5FM)
Détenteur: **CBKF-FM (Première Chaîne)**
Zenon Park, SK

Yukon Territory

Whitehorse: **CFWH-FM** (Freq: 94.5)
Owned by: Canadian Broadcasting Corporation*
3103 - 3rd Ave., Whitehorse, YT Y1A 2A2
Tel: 867-668-8400
cbcnorth@cbc.ca
www.cbc.ca/north
Kerry Fraser, Manager, Communications

Whitehorse: **CHON-FM** (Freq: 98.1; 90.5)
#6, 4230A - 4th Ave., Whitehorse, YT Y1A 1K1
Tel: 867-668-6629, Fax: 867-668-6612
nnby@nnby.net
www.nnby.net
www.facebook.com/366402063425924, twitter.com/CHONNews

Whitehorse: **CIAY-FM** (Freq: 100.7)
91806 Alaska Hwy., Whitehorse, YT Y1A 5B7
Tel: 867-393-2429, Fax: 867-393-2439
info@lifewhitehorse.com
lifewhitehorse.com

Whitehorse: **CKRW-FM (The Rush)** (Freq: 610)
Owned by: Klondike Broadcasting Ltd.*
#203, 4103 - 4th Ave., Whitehorse, YT Y1A 1H6
Tel: 867-668-6100, Fax: 867-668-4209
Toll-Free: 800-661-0530
info@ckrw.com
www.ckrw.com
Eva Bidrman, General Manager, eva@ckrw.com

Television Stations

Alberta

Athabasca: **CFRN-TV-12** (Channel: 13)
Owned by: CFRN-TV
Athabasca, AB

Bonnyville: **CKSA-TV-2** (Channel: 9)
Owned by: CKSA-TV
Bonnyville, AB

Calgary: **CBRT-DT** (Channel: 9; 21)
Owned by: Canadian Broadcasting Corporation*
PO Box 2640, Calgary, AB T2P 2M7
Tel: 403-521-6000, Fax: 403-521-6079
www.cbc.ca/calgary
twitter.com/cbccalgary
Other information: Phone, TV Newsroom: 403-521-6055
Alan Thorgeirson, Director, Calgary Centre, 403-521-6252
Suzanne Waddell, Manager, Communications, 403-521-6207,
suzanne.waddell@cbc.ca

Calgary: **CFCN-DT** (Channel: 29)
Owned by: Bell Media TV*
80 Patina Rise SW, Calgary, AB T3H 2W4
Tel: 403-240-5600
calgarynews@ctv.ca
calgary.ctvnews.ca

Calgary: **CICT-TV** (Channel: 7)
Owned by: Global Television Network*
222 - 23rd St. NE, Calgary, AB T2E 7N2
Tel: 403-235-7777
calgary@globalnews.ca
globalnews.ca/calgary
www.facebook.com/globalcalgary, twitter.com/globalcalgary

Calgary: **CJCO-DT (Omni)** (Channel: 38)
Owned by: Rogers Media Inc.*
Calgary, AB
www.omnitv.ca/ab
www.facebook.com/omnitelevision, twitter.com/omnitelevision

Calgary: **CKAL-DT (City Calgary)** (Channel: 5)
Owned by: Rogers Media Inc.*
535 - 7th Ave. SW, Calgary, AB T2P 0Y4
Tel: 403-508-2222
www.citytv.com/calgary
www.instagram.com/city_tv, www.facebook.com/citytv,
twitter.com/city_tv

Drumheller: **CFCN-TV-1** (Channel: 12)
Calgary
Owned by: CFCN-TV
Drumheller, AB

†*Edmonton:* **CBXFT-DT** (Channel: 47)
Détenteur: **Canadian Broadcasting Corporation**
CP 555, Edmonton, AB T5J 2P4
Tél: 780-468-7500, Ligne sans frais: 888-680-2432
nouvelles.alberta@radio-canada.ca
www.radio-canada.ca/alberta

Edmonton: **CBXT-DT** (Channel: 42)
Owned by: Canadian Broadcasting Corporation*
PO Box 555, Edmonton, AB T5J 2P4
Tel: 780-468-7500
www.cbc.ca/edmonton
www.facebook.com/cbcedmonton, twitter.com/CBCEdmonton
Neill Fitzpatrick, Executive Producer, 780-468-7527

Edmonton: **CFRN-DT** (Channel: 12)
Owned by: Bell Media TV*
18520 Stony Plain Rd., Edmonton, AB T5S 1A8
Tel: 780-483-3311
edmonton.ctvnews.ca
www.facebook.com/CTVEdmonton, twitter.com/ctvedmonton

Edmonton: **CHDI-FM (Sonic 102.9)** (Channel: 102.9)
Owned by: Rogers Media Inc.*
5915 Gateway Blvd., Edmonton, AB T6H 2H3
Tel: 780-423-2005, Fax: 780-437-5129
www.sonic1029.com
www.instagram.com/sonic1029, www.facebook.com/sonic1029,
twitter.com/sonic1029

Edmonton: **CITV-DT**
Owned by: Global Television Network*
5325 Allard Way, Edmonton, AB T6H 5B8
Tel: 780-436-1250
edmonton@globalnews.ca
globalnews.ca/edmonton
www.facebook.com/globaledmonton, twitter.com/globaledmonton

Edmonton: **CJEO-DT (Omni)** (Channel: 44)
Owned by: Rogers Media Inc.*
Edmonton, AB
www.omnitv.ca/ab
www.facebook.com/omnitelevision, twitter.com/omnitelevision

Edmonton: **CKEM-DT (City Edmonton)** (Channel: 57)
Owned by: Rogers Media Inc.*
5915 Gateway Blvd., Edmonton, AB T5J 5A3
Tel: 780-424-2222
www.citytv.com/edmonton

Fort McMurray: **Shaw Spotlight - Fort McMurray**
(Channel: 10)
Owned by: Shaw Communications Inc.*
#200, 208 Beacon Hill Dr., Fort McMurray, AB T9H 2J6
shawspotlightftmcmurray@sjrb.ca
www.shawspotlight.ca

Jasper: **CFRN-TV-11** (Channel: 11)
Owned by: CFRN-TV
Jasper, AB

Lac La Biche: **CFRN-TV-5** (Channel: 2)
Edmonton
Owned by: CFRN-TV
Lac La Biche, AB

Lethbridge: **CFCN-TV-5** (Channel: 13)
Owned by: CFCN-TV
Lethbridge, AB

Lethbridge: **CISA-DT** (Channel: 7)
Owned by: Global Television Network*
1401 - 28th St. North, Lethbridge, AB T1H 6H9
Tel: 403-329-2903
lethbridge@globalnews.ca
globalnews.ca/lethbridge
www.facebook.com/globallethbridge, twitter.com/globalleth

Lethbridge: **CJIL-TV** (Channel: 17)
450 - 31 St. North, Lethbridge, AB T1H 3Z3
Tel: 403-380-3399, Fax: 403-380-7490
info@miraclechannel.ca
www.miraclechannel.ca
www.youtube.com/cjiltv, www.facebook.com/115781708437573,
twitter.com/miraclechannel
Leon Fontaine, Chief Executive Officer

Lethbridge: **Shaw Spotlight - Lethbridge** (Channel: 9)
Owned by: Shaw Communications Inc.*
#101, 1232 - 3rd Ave. South, Lethbridge, AB T1J 0J9
shawspotlightlethbridge@sjrb.ca
www.shawspotlight.ca

* For details on this company see listing in Major Broadcasting Companies section; † French language station

Lloydminster: **CITL-TV (CTV)** (Channel: 4)
Owned by: Stingray Group Inc.*
5026 - 50th St., Lloydminster, AB T9V 1P3
Tel: 780-875-3321, *Fax:* 780-875-4704
Toll-Free: 800-565-2572
tvag@newcap.ca
citltv.ca
www.youtube.com/user/Newcaptv/videos,
www.facebook.com/NewcapTelevision,
twitter.com/NewcapTVNews
Chad Tabish, General Manager, ctabish@newcap.ca
Bob Cameron, Program Director, bcameron@newcap.ca

Lloydminster: **CKSA-TV** (Channel: 2; CBC affiliate)
Owned by: Stingray Group Inc.*
5026 - 50th St., Lloydminster, AB T9V 1P3
Tel: 780-875-3321, *Fax:* 780-875-4704
cksatv.ca
www.youtube.com/user/Newcaptv,
www.facebook.com/NewcapTelevision,
twitter.com/NewcapTVNews
Chad Tabish, General Manager, ctabish@newcap.ca
Bob Cameron, Program Director, bcameron@newcap.ca

Lougheed: **CFRN-TV-7** (Channel: 7)
Edmonton
Owned by: CFRN-TV
Lougheed, AB

Medicine Hat: **CFCN-TV-8** (Channel: 8)
Calgary
Owned by: CFCN-TV
Medicine Hat, AB

Medicine Hat: **Shaw Spotlight - Medicine Hat**
(Channel: 10)
Owned by: Shaw Communications Inc.*
954 Factory St. SE, Medicine Hat, AB T1A 8A5
shawspotlightmedicinehat@sjrb.ca
www.shawspotlight.ca

Peace River: **CFRN-TV-2** (Channel: 3)
Edmonton
Owned by: CFRN-TV
Peace River, AB

Red Deer: **CFRN-TV-6** (Channel: 8)
Edmonton
Owned by: CFRN-TV
Red Deer, AB

Red Deer: **Shaw Spotlight - Red Deer** (Channel: 10)
Owned by: Shaw Media Inc.*
4761 - 62nd St., Red Deer, AB T4N 2R4
shawspotlightreddeer@sjrb.ca
www.shawspotlight.ca

Redcliff: **CHAT-TV** (Channel: 6)
Owned by: Jim Pattison Broadcast Group*
10 Boundary Rd. SE, Redcliff, AB T0J 2P0
Tel: 403-548-8282, *Fax:* 403-548-8270
chatnews@jpbg.ca
www.chattelevision.ca
www.facebook.com/chattv, twitter.com/chattelevision
Other information: Alt. Email: chattv.promotions@jbpg.ca

Rocky Mountain House: **CFRN-TV-10** (Channel: 12)
Edmonton
Owned by: CFRN-TV
Rocky Mountain House, AB

Waterton Park: **CFCN-TV-17** (Channel: 6)
Calgary
Owned by: CFCN-TV
Waterton Park, AB

Wetaskiwin: **EastLink TV - Wetaskiwin** (Channel: 10)
Owned by: EastLink TV*
Wetaskiwin, AB
eastlinktvgp@eastlink.ca
eastlinktv.com

Whitecourt: **CFRN-TV-3** (Channel: 12)
Edmonton
Owned by: CFRN-TV
Whitecourt, AB

British Columbia

100 Mile House: **CFJC-TV-6** (Channel: 5)
Kamloops
Owned by: CFJC-TV
100 Mile House, BC

100 Mile House: **CITM-TV** (Channel: 3)
Owned by: CHAN-DT
100 Mile House, BC

Apex Mountain: **CHNJ-TV-1** (Channel: 11)
Vancouver
Owned by: CHAN-DT
Apex Mountain, BC

Blue River: **CH2531** (Channel: 13)
Owned by: CHAN-DT
Blue River, BC

Burnaby: **CHAN-DT** (Channel: 8; 22)
Owned by: Global Television Network*
7850 Enterprise St., Burnaby, BC V58 1V7
Tel: 778-945-9399
tips@globaltvbc.com
globalnews.ca/bc
www.facebook.com/globalbc, twitter.com/globalbc

Burnaby: **KVOS-TV** (Channel: 12)
#218, 4259 Canada Way, Burnaby, BC V5G 1H3
Tel: 604-681-1212, *Fax:* 604-736-4510
metvnetwork.com
www.facebook.com/KVOSTV
Jacky Nelson, Contact, jnelson@kvos.com

Campbell River: **Shaw Spotlight - Campbell River**
(Channel: 4)
Owned by: Shaw Communications Inc.*
500 Robron Rd., Campbell River, BC V9W 5Z2
shawspotlightnvipr@sjrb.ca
www.shawspotlight.ca

Castlegar: **Shaw Spotlight - Castlegar** (Channel: 10)
Owned by: Shaw Communications Inc.*
1951 Columbia Ave., Castlegar, BC V2N 2W8
shawspotlightwestkootenay@sjrb.ca
www.shawspotlight.ca

Celista: **CHBC-TV-6** (Channel: 3)
Kelowna
Owned by: CHBC-TV
Celista, BC

Chase: **CFJC-TV-8** (Channel: 11)
Kamloops
Owned by: CFJC-TV
Chase, BC

Chilliwack: **CHAN-TV-1** (Channel: 11)
Vancouver
Owned by: CHAN-DT
Chilliwack, BC

Clinton: **CFJC-TV-4** (Channel: 9)
Kamloops
Owned by: CFJC-TV
Clinton, BC

Courtenay: **CHAN-TV-4** (Channel: 13)
Vancouver
Owned by: CHAN-DT
Courtenay, BC

Courtenay: **Shaw Spotlight -
Courtenay-Comox-Powell River** (Channel: 4)
Owned by: Shaw Communications Inc.*
1591 McPhee Ave., Courtenay, BC V9N 3A6
shawspotlightnvipr@sjrb.ca
www.shawspotlight.ca

Cranbrook: **Shaw Spotlight - Cranbrook** (Channel:
10)
Owned by: Shaw Communications Inc.*
720 Kootenay St. North, Cranbrook, BC V1C 3V2
shawspotlighteastkootenay@sjrb.ca
www.shawspotlight.ca

Creston: **CKTN-TV-4** (Channel: 12)
Vancouver
Owned by: CHAN-DT
Creston, BC

Dawson Creek: **CJDC-TV** (Channel: 5; CBC affiliate)
Owned by: Bell Media Inc.*
901 - 102 Ave., Dawson Creek, BC V1G 2B6
Tel: 250-782-3341, *Fax:* 250-782-3154
www.cjdctv.com
www.facebook.com/CJDCTVDawsonCreek, twitter.com/cjdctv
Other information: News Phone: 250-782-6397
Terry Shepherd, General Manager,
terry.shepherd@bellmedia.ca

Enderby: **CHBC-TV-5** (Channel: 4)
Kelowna
Owned by: CHBC-TV
Enderby, BC

Fort St John: **Shaw Spotlight - Fort St John**
(Channel: 10)
Northern BC
Owned by: Shaw Communications Inc.*
#204, 9817 - 100th Ave., Fort St John, BC V1J 1Y4
shawspotlightnorthbc@sjrb.ca
www.shawspotlight.ca

Grand Forks: **CISR-TV-1** (Channel: 7)
Vancouver
Owned by: CHAN-DT
Grand Forks, BC

Granisle: **CH2798** (Channel: 7)
Vancouver
Owned by: CHAN-DT
Granisle, BC

Hixon: **CKPG-TV-1** (Channel: 10)
Prince George
Owned by: CKPG-TV
Hixon, BC

Houston: **CFHO-TV** (Channel: 8)
Vancouver
Owned by: CHAN-DT
Houston, BC

Hudson's Hope: **CJDC-TV-1** (Channel: 11)
Dawson Creek
Owned by: CJDC-TV
Hudson's Hope, BC

Kamloops: **CFJC-TV** (Channel: 4)
Owned by: Jim Pattison Broadcast Group*
460 Pemberton Terrace, Kamloops, BC V2C 1T5
Tel: 250-372-3322
www.cfjctv.com
www.instagram.com/cjfc_today, www.facebook.com/cjfctoday,
twitter.com/cfjc_today

Kamloops: **CHKM-TV** (Channel: 6)
Vancouver
Owned by: CHAN-DT
Kamloops, BC

Kamloops: **Shaw Spotlight - Kamloops** (Channel: 10)
Owned by: Shaw Communications Inc.*
23, 700 Tranquille Rd., Kamloops, BC V2B 3J2
shawspotlightthompsonvalley@sjrb.ca
www.shawspotlight.ca

Kelowna: **CHBC-DT** (Channel: 27)
Owned by: Global Television Network*
342 Leon Ave., Kelowna, BC V1Y 6J2
Tel: 250-762-4535, *Toll-Free:* 888-762-4535
okanagan@globalnews.ca
globalnews.ca/okanagan
www.facebook.com/globalokanagan, twitter.com/globalokanagan

Kelowna: **CHKL-DT** (Channel: 24)
Vancouver
Owned by: CHAN-DT
Kelowna, BC

Kelowna: **Shaw Spotlight - Kelowna** (Channel: 11)
Owned by: Shaw Communications Inc.*
2350 Hunter Rd., Kelowna, BC V1X 7H6
Tel: 250-979-6540, *Fax:* 250-979-6550
shawspotlightokanagan@sjrb.ca
www.shawspotlight.ca

Lillooet: **CFDF-TV-2** (Channel: 13)
Vancouver
Owned by: CHAN-DT
Lillooet, BC

---

* For details on this company see listing in Major Broadcasting Companies section; † French language station

Logan Lake: **CH2518** (Channel: 18)
Vancouver
Owned by: CHAN-DT
Logan Lake, BC

Lytton: **CILY-TV-2** (Channel: 8)
Vancouver
Owned by: CHAN-DT
Lytton, BC

Mackenzie: **CIMK-TV-1** (Channel: 9)
Vancouver
Owned by: CHAN-DT
Mackenzie, BC

Mackenzie: **CKPG-TV-4** (Channel: 6)
Prince George
Owned by: CKPG-TV
Mackenzie, BC

Malakwa: **CFFI-TV-2** (Channel: 11)
Vancouver
Owned by: CHAN-DT
Malakwa, BC

McBride: **CH2013** (Channel: 4)
Owned by: CHAN-DT
McBride, BC

Merritt: **CFJC-TV-3** (Channel: 8)
Kamloops
Owned by: CFJC-TV
Merritt, BC

Nakusp: **CJNP-TV-3** (Channel: 7)
Vancouver
Owned by: CHAN-DT
Nakusp, BC

Nanaimo: **Shaw Spotlight - Nanaimo** (Channel: 4)
Owned by: Shaw Communications Inc.*
4316 Boban Dr., Nanaimo, BC V9T 6A7
shawspotlightnanaimo@sjrb.ca
www.shawspotlight.ca

Nanaimo: **Shaw Spotlight - Nanaimo - Parksville**
(Channel: 4)
Owned by: Shaw Communications Inc.*
4316 Boban Dr., Nanaimo, BC V9T 6A7
shawspotlightnanaimo@sjrb.ca
www.shawspotlight.ca

Nelson: **CKTN-TV-3** (Channel: 3)
Vancouver
Owned by: CHAN-DT
Nelson, BC

New Denver: **CH5668 / CH5669** (Channel: 3; 6)
Vancouver
Owned by: CHAN-DT
New Denver, BC

Nicola Valley: **CFJC-TV-12** (Channel: 10)
Kamloops
Owned by: CFJC-TV
Nicola Valley, BC

Olalla: **CHKC-TV-5** (Channel: 11)
Vancouver
Owned by: CHAN-DT
Olalla, BC

Oliver: **CKKM-TV** (Channel: 3)
Owned by: CHAN-DT
Oliver, BC

Peachland: **CIPL-TV** (Channel: 9)
Vancouver
Owned by: CHAN-DT
Peachland, BC

Penticton: **CHBC-TV-7** (Channel: 7)
Kelowna
Owned by: CHBC-TV
Penticton, BC

Penticton: **CHKL-DT-1** (Channel: 30)
Vancouver
Owned by: CHAN-DT
Penticton, BC

Penticton: **Shaw Spotlight - Penticton**
Owned by: Shaw Media Inc.*
1372 Fairview Rd., Penticton, BC V2A 5Z8
shawspotlightokanagan@sjrb.ca
www.shawspotlight.ca

Port Alberni: **CHEK-TV-3** (Channel: 11)
Victoria
Owned by: CHEK-TV
Port Alberni, BC

Port Alberni: **Shaw Spotlight - Port Alberni** (Channel:
4)
Owned by: Shaw Communications Inc.*
4278 - 8th Ave., Port Alberni, BC V9Y 7S8
shawspotlightportalberni@sjrb.ca
www.shawspotlight.ca

Prince George: **CIFG-TV** (Channel: 12)
Vancouver
Owned by: CHAN-DT
Prince George, BC

Prince George: **CKPG-TV** (Channel: 2)
Owned by: Jim Pattison Broadcast Group*
1810 - 3rd Ave., 2nd Fl., Prince George, BC V2M 1G4
Tel: 250-564-8861
www.ckpg.com
www.instagram.com/ckpgnews, www.facebook.com/ckpgnews,
twitter.com/ckpgnews

Prince George: **Shaw Spotlight - Prince George**
(Channel: 10)
Northern BC
Owned by: Shaw Communications Inc.*
2519 Queensway St., Prince George, BC V2L 1N1
shawspotlightnorthbc@sjrb.ca
www.shawspotlight.ca

Prince Rupert: **CFTK-TV-1** (Channel: 6)
Terrace
Owned by: CFTK-TV
Prince Rupert, BC

Pritchard: **CFJC-TV-19** (Channel: 2)
Kamloops
Owned by: CFJC-TV
Pritchard, BC

Pritchard: **CHKM-TV-1** (Channel: 9)
Vancouver
Owned by: CHAN-DT
Pritchard, BC

Quesnel: **CFJC-TV-11** (Channel: 7)
Kamloops
Owned by: CFJC-TV
Quesnel, BC

Quesnel: **CITM-TV-2** (Channel: 8)
Vancouver
Owned by: CHAN-DT
Quesnel, BC

Quesnel: **CKPG-TV-5** (Channel: 13)
Prince George
Owned by: CKPG-TV
Quesnel, BC

Revelstoke: **CHKL-TV-3** (Channel: 7)
Vancouver
Owned by: CHAN-DT
Revelstoke, BC

Rimrock: **CKRR-TV-2** (Channel: 11)
Vancouver
Owned by: CHAN-DT
Rimrock, BC

Salmon Arm: **CFSA-TV-1** (Channel: 13)
Vancouver
Owned by: CHAN-DT
Salmon Arm, BC

Salmon Arm: **CHBC-TV-4** (Channel: 9)
Kelowna
Owned by: CHBC-TV
Salmon Arm, BC

Santa Rosa: **CISR-TV** (Channel: 68)
Vancouver
Owned by: CHAN-DT
Santa Rosa, BC

Savona: **CFSC-TV-1** (Channel: 13)
Vancouver
Owned by: CHAN-DT
Savona, BC

Smithers: **CFHO-TV-1** (Channel: 13)
Vancouver
Owned by: CHAN-DT
Smithers, BC

Spences Bridge: **CJNA-TV-2** (Channel: 7)
Vancouver
Owned by: CHAN-DT
Spences Bridge, BC

Squamish: **CHAN-TV-3** (Channel: 7)
Vancouver
Owned by: CHAN-DT
Squamish, BC

Surrey: **CHNU-DT** (Channel: 66)
Owned by: ZoomerMedia Ltd.*
#204, 5668 - 192nd St., Surrey, BC V3S 2V7
Tel: 604-576-6880
audience@joytv10.ca
www.joytv.ca
www.facebook.com/JoytvBC, twitter.com/JoytvBC

Taghum: **CKTN-TV-2** (Channel: 23)
Vancouver
Owned by: CHAN-DT
Taghum, BC

Terrace: **CFTK-TV** (Channel: 3; CBC affiliate)
Owned by: Bell Media Inc.*
4625 Lazelle Ave., Terrace, BC V8G 1S4
Tel: 250-635-6316, *Fax:* 250-638-6320
www.cftktv.com
www.facebook.com/230113003717168
Other information: News Telephone: 250-638-6325
Brian Langston, General Manager, brian.langston@bellmedia.ca

Trail: **CKTN-TV** (Channel: 8)
Vancouver
Owned by: CHAN-DT
Trail, BC

†*Vancouver:* **CBUFT-DT** (Channel: 26)
Détenteur: **Canadian Broadcasting Corporation***
CP 4600, Vancouver, BC V6B 2R5
Tél: 604-662-6000, *Téléc:* 604-662-6161
www.radio-canada.ca/colombie-britannique-et-yukon

Vancouver: **CBUT-DT** (Channel: 2)
Owned by: Canadian Broadcasting Corporation*
PO Box 4600, Vancouver, BC V6B 4A2
Tel: 604-662-6000
www.cbc.ca/bc

Vancouver: **CHNM-DT (Omni)** (Channel: 42)
Owned by: Rogers Media Inc.*
Vancouver, BC
www.omnitv.ca/bc
www.facebook.com/omnitelevision, twitter.com/omnitelevision

Vancouver: **CIVT-DT** (Channel: 32)
Owned by: Bell Media TV*
#500, 969 Robson St., Vancouver, BC V6Z 1X5
Tel: 604-608-2868, *Fax:* 604-608-2698
bccomments@ctv.ca
bc.ctvnews.ca
www.facebook.com/CTVBCNews, twitter.com/CTVVancouver

Vancouver: **CKVU-DT (City Vancouver)** (Channel: 10)
Owned by: Rogers Media Inc.*
180 West 2nd Ave., Vancouver, BC V5Y 3T9
Tel: 604-876-1344, *Toll-Free:* 888-336-9978
www.citytv.com/vancouver
www.instagram.com/city_tv, www.facebook.com/citytv,
twitter.com/city_tv
Manuel Fonseca, Contact, Programming,
manuel.fonseca@rci.rogers.com

---

* For details on this company see listing in Major Broadcasting Companies section; † French language station

Vancouver: **Novus TV (NVTV 4)** (Channel: 4)
Owned by: Novus Entertainment Inc.
#300, 112 East 3rd Ave., Vancouver, BC V5T 1C8
Tel: 778-724-1371, Fax: 604-685-7832
communitychannel@novusnow.ca
www.novuscommunitytv.ca
www.youtube.com/user/NovusTV, www.facebook.com/NVTV4,
twitter.com/novustv

Vavenby: **CKVA-TV-1** (Channel: 8)
Vancouver
Owned by: CHAN-DT
Vavenby, BC

Vernon: **CHBC-DT-2** (Channel: 20)
Kelowna
Owned by: CHBC-TV
Vernon, BC

Vernon: **CHKL-DT-2** (Channel: 22)
Vancouver
Owned by: CHAN-DT
Vernon, BC

Vernon: **Shaw Spotlight - Vernon**
Owned by: Shaw Communications Inc.*
2924 - 28th Ave., Vernon, BC V1T 8W6
shawspotlightokanagan@sjrb.ca
www.shawspotlight.ca

Victoria: **CHEK-TV** (Channel: 6)
780 Kings Rd., Victoria, BC V8T 5A2
Tel: 250-383-2435, Fax: 250-384-7766
info@cheknews.ca
www.cheknews.ca
www.facebook.com/cheknews, twitter.com/CHEK_News

Victoria: **Shaw Spotlight - Victoria - Duncan**
Owned by: Shaw Communications Inc.*
861 Cloverdale Ave., Victoria, BC V8X 4S7
shawspotlightsvi@sjrb.ca
www.shawspotlight.ca

Whistler: **Shaw Spotlight - Squamish/Whistler**
(Channel: 10)
Owned by: Shaw Communications Inc.*
#214, 4368 Main St., Whistler, BC V8E 1B6
shawspotlightseatosky@sjrb.ca
www.shawspotlight.ca

Williams Lake: **CFJC-TV-5** (Channel: 8)
Kamloops
Owned by: CFJC-TV
Williams Lake, BC

Williams Lake: **CITM-TV-1** (Channel: 13)
Vancouver
Owned by: CHAN-DT
Williams Lake, BC

Manitoba

Flin Flon: **CKYF-TV** (Channel: 13)
Owned by: CKY-DT
Flin Flon, MB

McCreary: **CKX-TV-3** (Channel: 11)
Owned by: CKX-TV
McCreary, MB

The Pas: **CKYP-TV** (Channel: 12)
Owned by: CKY-DT
The Pas, MB

Thompson: **CKYT-TV** (Channel: 9)
Owned by: CKY-DT
Thompson, MB

Thompson: **Shaw Spotlight - Thompson** (Channel: 11)
Owned by: Shaw Communications Inc.*
50 Selkirk Ave., Thompson, MB R8N 0M7
shawspotlightthompson@sjrb.ca
www.shawspotlight.ca

†*Winnipeg:* **CBWFT-TV** (Channel: 51)
Détenteur: **Canadian Broadcasting Corporation***
541, rue Portage, Winnipeg, MB R3C 2H1
Tél: 204-788-3262, Téléc: 204-788-3245
manitoba@radio-canada.ca
www.radio-canada.ca/manitoba

Winnipeg: **CBWT-DT** (Channel: 27)
Owned by: Canadian Broadcasting Corporation*
541 Portage Ave., Winnipeg, MB R3B 2H1
Tel: 204-788-3222
www.cbc.ca/manitoba
Other information: TTY: 866-220-6045
John Bertrand, Director, Manitoba Centre

Winnipeg: **CHMI-DT (City Winnipeg)** (Channel: 57)
Owned by: Rogers Media Inc.*
8 Forks Market Rd., Winnipeg, MB R3C 4Y3
Tel: 204-947-9613
www.citytv.com/winnipeg

Winnipeg: **CKND-DT** (Channel: 9)
Owned by: Global Television Network*
201 Portage Ave., 30th Fl., Winnipeg, MB R3C 1A7
Tel: 204-235-8545
winnipeg@globalnews.ca
globalnews.ca/winnipeg
www.facebook.com/globalwinnipeg, twitter.com/globalwinnipeg

Winnipeg: **CKY-DT** (Channel: 5)
Owned by: Bell Media TV*
#400, 345 Graham Ave., Winnipeg, MB R3C 5S6
Tel: 204-788-3300, Fax: 204-943-3112
winnipegnews@ctv.ca
winnipeg.ctvnews.ca
www.facebook.com/ctvnewswinnipeg, twitter.com/ctvwinnipeg
Other information: TTY: 800-461-1542
Karen Mitchell, News Director, karen.mitchell@bellmedia.ca
Tara Vosbourgh, Human Resources Manager,
tara.vosbourgh@bellmedia.ca

Winnipeg: **Shaw Spotlight - Winnipeg** (Channel: 9)
Owned by: Shaw Communications Inc.*
22 Scurfield Blvd., Winnipeg, MB R3Y 1S5
shawspotlightwinnipeg@sjrb.ca
www.shawspotlight.ca

New Brunswick

†*Beresford:* **Rogers TV - Bathurst (Français)**
(Channel: 9)
Détenteur: **Rogers Media Inc.***
1247, rue Principale, Beresford, NB E8K 1A1
Tél: 506-549-6657, Téléc: 506-546-8886
Ligne sans frais: 888-307-8862
www.rogerstv.com
Wayne Aubie, Producteur, 506-549-6659

Boiestown: **CKLT-TV-2** (Channel: 7)
Owned by: CKLT-DT
Boiestown, NB

Chatham: **CKAM-TV-2** (Channel: 10)
Moncton
Owned by: CKCW-TV
Chatham, NB

Doaktown: **CKAM-TV-4** (Channel: 10)
Moncton
Owned by: CKCW-TV
Doaktown, NB

†*Edmundston:* **CIMT-DT-1** (Channel: 4)
Détenteur: CIMT-DT
121, rue de l'Église, Edmundston, NB E3V 1J9
Tél: 506-353-0237
cimt.teleinterrives.com

Edmunston: **CFTF-DT-1** (Channel: 42)
Owned by: CFTF-DT
Edmunston, NB
www.cftf.ca

†*Edmunston:* **Rogers TV - Edmunston (Français)**
(Channel: 10)
Détenteur: **Rogers Media Inc.***
35, rue Court, Edmunston, NB E3V 1S4
Tél: 506-739-4533, Téléc: 506-735-1801
Ligne sans frais: 888-307-8862
www.rogerstv.com
Guy Couturier, Producteur, 506-739-4533

Fredericton: **CBAT-DT** (Channel: 31)
Owned by: Canadian Broadcasting Corporation*
1160 Regent St., Fredericton, NB E3B 5G4
Tel: 506-451-4000, Toll-Free: 866-306-4636
www.cbc.ca/nb
Other information: Phone, CBC News: 506-451-4044

Denise Wilson, Senior Managing Director, Atlantic Canada
Nadine Antle, Regional Manager, Communications, Marketing & Brand, 902-420-4223
Mary-Pat Schutta, Senior Manager, New Brunswick Programs

Fredericton: **CHNB-DT-1** (Channel: 44)
Owned by: CHNB-DT
Fredericton, NB

Fredericton: **Rogers TV - Fredericton** (Channel: 10)
Owned by: Rogers Media Inc.*
377 York St., Fredericton, NB E3B 3P6
Tel: 506-462-3642, Fax: 506-452-2846
www.rogerstv.com
Terri Willis, Supervising Producer, 506-452-3659

†*Kedgwick:* **CHAU-DT-11** (Channel: 27)
Détenteur: CHAU-DT
Kedgwick, NB

Miramichi: **CHNB-TV-13** (Channel: 40)
Owned by: CHNB-DT
Miramichi, NB

Miramichi: **Rogers TV - Miramichi** (Channel: 10)
Owned by: Rogers Media Inc.*
454 King George Hwy., Miramichi, NB E1V 1M1
Tel: 506-778-3009, Fax: 506-778-3035
Toll-Free: 888-307-8862
www.rogerstv.com
Terri Willis, Supervising Producer, 506-462-3659

†*Moncton:* **CBAFT-DT** (Channel: 11)
Détenteur: **Canadian Broadcasting Corporation***
#15, 165, rue Main, Moncton, NB E1C 1B8
Tél: 506-853-6666, Ligne sans frais: 800-561-7010
www.radio-canada.ca/acadie
Richard Simoens, Directeur

Moncton: **CHNB-DT-3** (Channel: 27)
Owned by: CHNB-DT
Moncton, NB

Moncton: **CKCW-DT** (Channel: 29)
Owned by: Bell Media TV*
Moncton, NB
atlantic.ctvnews.ca

Moncton: **Rogers TV - Moncton** (Channel: 10)
Owned by: Rogers Media Inc.*
70 Assomption Blvd., Moncton, NB E1C 1A1
Tel: 506-388-8405, Fax: 506-388-8622
Toll-Free: 888-307-8862
www.rogerstv.com
Charles Oslcamp, Supervising Producer, 506-388-8671

Newcastle: **CKAM-TV-1** (Channel: 10)
Moncton
Owned by: CKCW-TV
Newcastle, NB

Saint John: **CHNB-DT** (Channel: 12)
Owned by: Global Television Network*
1 Germain St., #A500B, Saint John, NB E2L 4V1
Tel: 506-642-6488, Fax: 506-652-5965
newbrunswick@globalnews.ca
globalnews.ca/new-brunswick
www.facebook.com/globalnb, twitter.com/global_nb

Saint John: **CKLT-DT** (Channel: 9)
Owned by: CTV News Channel*
Red Rose Tea Building, #3, 12 Smythe St., Saint John, NB E2L 5G5
Tel: 506-658-1010, Fax: 506-658-1208
atlanticnews@bellmedia.ca
atlantic.ctvnews.ca

Saint John: **Rogers TV - Saint John** (Channel: 10)
Owned by: Rogers Media Inc.*
55 Waterloo St., Saint John, NB E2L 4V9
Tel: 506-657-8862, Fax: 506-646-5116
Toll-Free: 888-307-8862
www.rogerstv.com
Terri Willis, Supervising Producer, 506-462-3659

†*Saint-Quentin:* **CHAU-DT-2** (Channel: 31)
Détenteur: CHAU-DT
Saint-Quentin, NB

St Stephen: **CHNB-TV-12** (Channel: 21)
Owned by: CHNB-DT
St Stephen, NB

---

* For details on this company see listing in Major Broadcasting Companies section; † French language station

St. John's: **Rogers TV - St. John's** (Channel: 9)
Owned by: Rogers Inc.*
541 Kenmount Rd., St. John's, NB A1B 1W2
Tel: 709-753-7175, *Fax:* 709-753-7541
www.rogerstv.com
Linda Lambe, Regional Station Manager, 705-753-7349

Woodstock: **CHNB-TV-11** (Channel: 38)
Owned by: CHNB-DT
Woodstock, NB

Newfoundland & Labrador

Corner Brook: **Rogers TV - Corner Brook** (Channel: 9)
Owned by: Rogers Media Inc.*
4 Mt. Bernard Ave., Corner Brook, NL A2H 6T2
Tel: 709-634-0525, *Fax:* 709-639-1890
www.rogerstv.com
Roger Robinson, Regional Station Manager, 709-651-2652

Gander: **Rogers TV - Gander** (Channel: 9)
Owned by: Rogers Media Inc.*
141 Airport Blvd., Gander, NL A1V 1T5
Tel: 709-651-2652, *Fax:* 709-256-2797
www.rogerstv.com
Roger Robinson, Regional Station Manager, 709-651-2652

Grand Falls-Windsor: **Rogers TV - Grand Falls-Windsor** (Channel: 9)
Owned by: Rogers Media Inc.*
9 Hardy Ave., Grand Falls-Windsor, NL A2A 2K2
Tel: 709-489-3346, *Fax:* 709-489-1030
www.rogerstv.com
Roger Robinson, Regional Station Manager, 709-651-2652

St. John's: **CBNT-DT** (Channel: 8)
Owned by: Canadian Broadcasting Corporation*
PO Box 12010 A, St. John's, NL A1B 3T8
Tel: 709-576-5000
www.cbc.ca/nl
www.facebook.com/cbcnl, twitter.com/cbcnl
Denise Wilson, Senior Managing Director, Atlantic Canada, denise.wilson@cbc.ca
Nadine Antle, Regional Manager, Communications, Marketing & Brand, 902-420-4223, Nadine.Antle@cbc.ca

St. John's: **CJON-DT** (Channel: 6)
Owned by: Newfoundland Broadcasting Co. Ltd.*
446 Logy Bay Rd., St. John's, NL A1C 5S2
Tel: 709-722-5015, *Fax:* 709-726-5107
web@ntv.ca
ntv.ca
www.facebook.com/ntvnewsnl, twitter.com/ntvnewsnl

Northwest Territories

Yellowknife: **CFYK-DT** (Channel: 8)
Owned by: Canadian Broadcasting Corporation*
PO Box 160, Yellowknife, NT X1A 2N2
Tel: 867-920-5400
www.cbc.ca/north

Nova Scotia

Amherst: **EastLink TV - Amherst** (Channel: 10)
Owned by: EastLink TV*
PO Box 99 Main, 289 Willow St., Amherst, NS B4H 3Y6
Tel: 902-660-3588, *Toll-Free:* 902-667-0344
eastlinktv.com

Antigonish: **CIHF-TV-15** (Channel: 21)
Owned by: CIHF-TV
Antigonish, NS

Antigonish: **EastLink TV - Antigonish** (Channel: 5)
Owned by: EastLink TV*
4038 Old River Rd., Antigonish, NS B2G 2H6
Tel: 902-735-3588, *Toll-Free:* 902-863-5442
eastlinktv.com

Aylesford: **EastLink TV - Aylesford** (Channel: 13)
Owned by: EastLink TV*
PO Box 217, 1257 Victoria Rd., Aylesford, NS B0P 1C0
Tel: 902-847-3404, *Fax:* 902-847-1808
eastlinktv.com

Blockhouse: **EastLink TV - Bridgewater** (Channel: 10)
Owned by: EastLink TV*
PO Box 62, 140 Cornwall Rd., Blockhouse, NS B0J 1E0
Tel: 902-530-3588, *Fax:* 902-624-6194
eastlinktv.com

Bridgewater: **CIHF-TV-6** (Channel: 9)
Owned by: CIHF-DT
Bridgewater, NS

Dingwall: **CJCB-TV-3** (Channel: 9)
Sydney
Owned by: CJCB-TV
Dingwall, NS

Halifax: **CBHT-DT** (Channel: 39)
Owned by: Canadian Broadcasting Corporation*
#100, 7067 Chebucto Rd., Halifax, NS B3L 4R5
Tel: 902-420-8311, *Toll-Free:* 866-306-4636
www.cbc.ca/ns
www.facebook.com/CBCNovaScotia, twitter.com/cbcns
Andrew Cochran, Managing Director, Maritimes
Kathy Large, Program Manager, Nova Scotia
Chantal Bernard, Senior Communications Officer, 902-420-4306

Halifax: **CIHF-DT** (Channel: 8)
Owned by: Global Television Network*
2110 Gottingen St., Halifax, NS B3K 3B3
Tel: 902-481-7400, *Toll-Free:* 800-733-0592
halifax@globalnews.ca
globalnews.ca/halifax
www.facebook.com/globalhalifax, twitter.com/globalhalifax

Halifax: **CJCH-DT** (Channel: 9)
Owned by: Bell Media TV*
PO Box 1653, Halifax, NS B3J 2Z4
Tel: 902-453-4000
atlanticnews@bellmedia.ca
atlantic.ctvnews.ca
www.facebook.com/ctvnewsatlantic, twitter.com/CTVAtlantic

Halifax: **Coast TV**
Owned by: Coast Cable
PO Box 8660 A, Halifax, NS B3K 5M3
Tel: 604-886-8565, *Fax:* 604-886-8936
coasttv@coastcable.com
www.coastcable.com/CoastTV.aspx

Inverness: **CJCB-TV-1** (Channel: 6)
Sydney
Owned by: CJCB-TV
Inverness, NS

Liverpool: **EastLink TV - Liverpool** (Channel: 8)
Owned by: EastLink TV*
PO Box 449, 4130 Highway #3, Liverpool, NS B0T 1K0
Tel: 902-356-3588, *Toll-Free:* 902-354-2246
eastlinktv.com

Lower Sackville: **EastLink TV** (Channel: 10)
Halifax Region
Owned by: EastLink TV*
367 Sackville Dr., Lower Sackville, NS B4C 2R7
Tel: 902-446-3588, *Fax:* 902-453-5714
eastlinktv.com
Rhonda Ann MacDonald, Manager, 902-252-1052

Mulgrave: **CIHF-TV-16** (Channel: 28)
Owned by: CIHF-TV
Mulgrave, NS

New Glasgow: **CIHF-TV-8** (Channel: 34)
Owned by: CIHF-TV
New Glasgow, NS

New Glasgow: **EastLink TV - New Glasgow** (Channel: 10)
Owned by: EastLink TV*
PO Box 157, 111 Park St., New Glasgow, NS B2H 5B7
Tel: 902-695-3588, *Toll-Free:* 902-695-3021
eastlinktv.com

New Minas: **EastLink TV - New Minas** (Channel: 5)
Owned by: EastLink TV*
PO Box 4000, 1001 How Ave., New Minas, NS B4N 4S8
Tel: 902-681-0027, *Fax:* 902-681-6470
eastlinktv.com

Sheet Harbour: **CJCH-TV-5** (Channel: 2)
Halifax
Owned by: CJCH-TV
Sheet Harbour, NS

Shelburne: **CIHF-TV-9** (Channel: 10)
Owned by: CIHF-TV
Shelburne, NS

Shelburne: **EastLink TV - Shelburne** (Channel: 8)
Owned by: EastLink TV*
PO Box 1090, 1530 Jordan Branch Rd., Shelburne, NS B0T 1W0
Tel: 902-875-1267, *Fax:* 902-875-4219
eastlinktv.com

Sydney: **CIHF-TV-7** (Channel: 11)
Owned by: CIHF-TV
Sydney, NS

Sydney: **CJCB-TV** (Channel: 4)
Owned by: Bell Media TV*
1283 George St., Sydney, NS B1P 1N7
Tel: 902-562-5511, *Fax:* 902-562-9714
atlantic.ctvnews.ca

Sydney: **EastLink TV - Sydney** (Channel: 10)
Owned by: EastLink TV*
61 Melody Lane, Sydney, NS B1P 3K4
Tel: 902-539-9611, *Fax:* 866-976-7727
eastlinktv.com

Truro: **CIHF-TV-4** (Channel: 18)
Owned by: CIHF-TV
Truro, NS

Truro: **EastLink TV - Truro** (Channel: 4)
Owned by: EastLink TV*
69 Walker St., Truro, NS B2N 4A8
Tel: 902-843-3588, *Toll-Free:* 902-843-3067
eastlinktv.com

Windsor: **EastLink TV - Windsor** (Channel: 8)
Owned by: EastLink TV*
PO Box 640, 19 Sanford Dr., Windsor, NS B0N 2T0
Tel: 902-798-8315, *Fax:* 902-798-0327
eastlinktv.com

Wolfville: **CIHF-TV-5** (Channel: 20)
Owned by: CIHF-TV
Wolfville, NS

Yarmouth: **CIHF-TV-10** (Channel: 45)
Owned by: CIHF-TV
Yarmouth, NS

Yarmouth: **CJCH-TV-7** (Channel: 40)
Halifax
Owned by: CJCH-TV
Yarmouth, NS

Yarmouth: **EastLink TV - Yarmouth** (Channel: 5)
Owned by: EastLink TV*
25 Shaw Ave., Yarmouth, NS B5A 4C4
Tel: 902-881-3588, *Fax:* 902-742-6259
eastlinktv.com

Ontario

Barrie: **CKVR-DT** (Channel: 10)
Owned by: Bell Media TV*
33 Beacon Rd., Barrie, ON L4N 9J9
Tel: 705-734-3300, *Fax:* 705-733-0302
Toll-Free: 800-461-5820
barrieinbox@ctv.ca
barrie.ctvnews.ca
www.facebook.com/ctvbarrie, twitter.com/ctvbarrienews
Other information: TTY: 800-721-9110
Ruth Anderson, News Director, ruth.anderson@bellmedia.ca

Barrie: **Rogers TV - Barrie** (Channel: 10)
Owned by: Rogers Media Inc.*
1 Sperling Dr., Barrie, ON L4M 6B8
Tel: 705-737-4660, *Fax:* 705-737-0778
Toll-Free: 866-615-5527
www.rogerstv.com
Bev Daoust, Production Administrator, 705-81245120

Belleville: **CICO-DT-53** (Channel: 26)
Owned by: TVOntario*
Belleville, ON
tvo.org

Belleville: YourTV - Belleville (Channel: 700)
Owned by: Cogeco Connexion Inc.*
Belleville, ON

www.yourtv.tv/belleville
www.facebook.com/yourtvquinte, twitter.com/yourtvquinte

Borden: Rogers TV - Borden & Alliston (Channel: 65)
Owned by: Rogers Media Inc.*
Borden, ON

Tel: 705-737-4660

Kevin Kelly, Supervising Producer, 705-812-4539

Brantford: Rogers TV - Brantford (Channel: 20)
Owned by: Rogers Media Inc.*
23 Harris Ave., Brantford, ON N3R 7W5

Tel: 519-759-7711, Fax: 519-759-2629
Toll-Free: 888-410-2020
www.rogerstv.com

Jeremy Parking, Supervising Producer, 519-894-8160

Brockville: YourTV - Brockville/Prescott (Channel: 700)
Owned by: Cogeco Connexion Inc.*
Brockville, ON

www.yourtv.tv/brockville
www.facebook.com/yourtvbkville, twitter.com/yourtvbkville

Burlington: YourTV - Burlington/Oakville (Channel: 700)
Owned by: Cogeco Connexion Inc.*
Burlington, ON

www.yourtv.tv/burlington-oakville
www.youtube.com/c/YourTVHalton,
www.facebook.com/yourtvhalton, twitter.com/yourtvhalton

Chapleau: CITO-TV-4 (Channel: 9)
Owned by: CITO-TV
Chapleau, ON

Chatham: CICO-DT-59 (Channel: 34)
Owned by: TVOntario*
Chatham, ON

tvo.org

Chatham: YourTV - Chatham (Channel: 700)
Owned by: Cogeco Connexion Inc.*
Chatham, ON

www.yourtv.tv/chatham
www.facebook.com/yourtvck, twitter.com/yourtvck

Cloyne: CICO-DT-92 (Channel: 44)
Owned by: TVOntario*
Cloyne, ON

tvo.org

Cobourg: YourTV - Cobourg/Port Hope (Channel: 700)
Owned by: Cogeco Connexion Inc.*
Cobourg, ON

yourtv.cobourg-port-hope@cogeco.com
www.yourtv.tv/cobourg-port-hope
www.facebook.com/yourtvnland, twitter.com/yourtvnland

Collingwood: Rogers TV - Collingwood (Channel: 53)
Owned by: Rogers Media Inc.*
4 Sandford Fleming Dr., Collingwood, ON L9Y 4V9

Tel: 705-445-2120, Fax: 705-445-9949
Toll-Free: 866-615-5527
www.rogerstv.com

Bev Daoust, Production Administrator

Cornwall: CJOH-TV-8 (Channel: 8)
Owned by: CJOH-DT
Cornwall, ON

Cornwall: YourTV - Cornwall (Channel: 700)
Owned by: Cogeco Connexion Inc.*
Cornwall, ON

www.yourtv.tv/cornwall
www.facebook.com/yourtvcornwall, twitter.com/yourtvcornwall

Deseronto: CJOH-TV-6 (Channel: 6)
Owned by: CJOH-DT
Deseronto, ON

Dryden: Shaw Spotlight - Dryden (Channel: 10)
Owned by: Shaw Communications Inc.*
75 Queen St., Dryden, ON P8N 1A1

shawspotlightdryden@sjrb.ca
www.shawspotlight.ca

Elliot Lake: CICI-TV-1 (Channel: 3)
Owned by: CICI-TV
Elliot Lake, ON

Elliot Lake: EastLink TV - Elliot Lake
Owned by: EastLink TV*
Elliot Lake, ON

elliotlake@eastlinktv.com
eastlinktv.com

Fergus: YourTV - Fergus (Channel: 700)
Owned by: Cogeco Connexion Inc.*
Fergus, ON

www.yourtv.tv/fergus

Georgina: Rogers TV - Georgina (Channel: 10)
Owned by: Rogers Media Inc.*
Georgina, ON

www.rogerstv.com

Jim Anderson, Executive Producer, 905-476-1406

Goderich: EastLink TV - Goderich
Owned by: EastLink TV*
Goderich, ON

eastlinktv.com

Guelph: Rogers TV - Guelph (Channel: 20)
Owned by: Rogers Media Inc.*
130 Silvercreek Pkwy., Guelph, ON N1H 7Y5

Tel: 519-824-1900, Fax: 519-824-4210
Toll-Free: 888-410-2020
www.rogerstv.com

Jen Schmidt, Production Administrator

Hamilton: Cable 14 (TV Hamilton Ltd.) (Channel: 14)
Owned by: Cogeco Connexion Inc.*
150 Dundurn St. South, Hamilton, ON L8P 4K3

Tel: 905-523-1414
info@cable14.com
www.cable14.com
www.linkedin.com/company/cable-14-hamilton,
www.facebook.com/cable14hamilton, twitter.com/cable14

Hamilton: CHCH-DT (Channel: 11)
Owned by: Channel Zero Inc.*
PO Box 2230 A, 163 Jackson St. West, Hamilton, ON L8N 3A6

Tel: 905-522-1101, Fax: 905-523-8011
contact@chch.com
www.chch.com
twitter.com/CHCHTV

Hanover: EastLink TV - Hanover
Owned by: EastLink TV*
Hanover, ON

Fax: 519-291-5935
Toll-Free: 866-286-3484
midwest@eastlinktv.com
eastlinktv.com

Hawkesbury: NousTV - Hawkesbury (Channel: 11)
Owned by: Cogeco Connexion Inc.*
Hawkesbury, ON

nous.tv/hawkesbury-en
Other information: French, URL: nous.tv/hawkesbury-fr

Hearst: CITO-TV-3 (Channel: 4)
Owned by: CITO-TV
Hearst, ON

Kapuskasing: CITO-TV-1 (Channel: 10)
Owned by: CITO-TV
Kapuskasing, ON

Kapuskasing: EastLink TV - Kapuskasing
Owned by: EastLink TV*
Kapuskasing, ON

kapuskasing@eastlinktv.com
eastlinktv.com

Kearns: CITO-TV-2 (Channel: 11)
Owned by: CITO-TV
Kearns, ON

Keewatin: Shaw Spotlight - Kenora (Channel: 10)
Owned by: Shaw Communications Inc.*
102 - 10th St., Keewatin, ON P0X 1C0

shawspotlightkenora@sjrb.ca
www.shawspotlight.ca

Kincardine: Rogers TV - Kincardine (Channel: 6)
Owned by: Rogers Media Inc.*
Kincardine, ON

www.rogerstv.com

Bev Daoust, Production Administrator, 705-812-4512

Kingston: CKWS-DT (Channel: 10)
Owned by: 591987 B.C. Ltd.*
170 Queen St., Kingston, ON K7K 1B2

Tel: 613-544-2340, Fax: 613-544-5508
newswatch@corusent.com
globalnews.ca/kingston
twitter.com/ckws_tv

Kingston: YourTV - Kingston (Channel: 700)
Owned by: Cogeco Connexion Inc.*
Kingston, ON

www.yourtv.tv/kingston
www.facebook.com/yourtvkingston, twitter.com/yourtvkingston

Kirkland Lake: EastLink TV - Kirkland Lake
Owned by: EastLink TV*
Kirkland Lake, ON

kirklandlake@eastlink.ca
eastlinktv.com

Kitchener: CICO-DT-28 (Channel: 28)
Owned by: TVOntario*
Kitchener, ON

tvo.org

Kitchener: CKCO-DT (Channel: 13)
Owned by: Bell Media TV*
864 King St. West, Kitchener, ON N2G 1E8

Tel: 519-578-1314
viewermail@kitchener.ctv.ca
kitchener.ctvnews.ca
www.facebook.com/ctvkitchener, twitter.com/CTVKitchener

Kitchener: Rogers TV - Kitchener/Cambridge/Waterloo (Channel: 20)
Owned by: Rogers Media Inc.*
85 Grand Crest Pl., Kitchener, ON N2G 4A8

Tel: 519-893-4400, Fax: 519-893-5861
www.rogerstv.com

Jen Schmidt, Production Administrator

Listowel: EastLink TV - Listowel
Owned by: EastLink TV*
Listowel, ON

Fax: 519-291-5935
Toll-Free: 866-286-3484
midwest@eastlinktv.com
eastlinktv.com

London: Rogers TV - London (Channel: 13)
Owned by: Rogers Media Inc.*
800 York St., London, ON N6A 5B1

Tel: 519-675-1313, Fax: 519-660-7597
www.rogerstv.com

Jeremy Parking, Supervising Producer, 519-894-8160

London: Rogers TV - St Thomas (Channel: 13)
Owned by: Rogers Media Inc.*
800 York St., London, ON N6A 5B1

Tel: 226-984-8186
www.rogerstv.com

Jeremy Parking, Supervising Producer, 519-894-8160

London: Rogers TV - Strathroy-Caradoc (Channel: 13)
Owned by: Rogers Media Inc.*
800 York St., London, ON N6A 5B1

Tel: 226-984-8186
www.rogerstv.com

Jeremy Parking, Supervising Producer, 519-894-8160

Midland: Rogers TV - Midland (Channel: 53)
Owned by: Rogers Media Inc.*
527 Len Self Blvd., Midland, ON L4R 5N6

Tel: 705-526-7905
www.rogerstv.com

Bev Daoust, Production Administrator, 705-812-4512

Niagara Falls: YourTV - Niagara (Channel: 700)
Owned by: Cogeco Connexion Inc.*
Niagara Falls, ON

www.yourtv.tv/niagara
www.facebook.com/yourtvniagara, twitter.com/yourtvniagara

For details on this company see listing in Major Broadcasting Companies section; † French language station

North Bay: **CKNY-TV** (Channel: 10)
Owned by: Bell Media TV*
245 Oak St. East, North Bay, ON P1B 8P8
Tel: 705-476-3111, Fax: 705-495-4474
Toll-Free: 877-303-6288
northernontario.ctvnews.ca
www.facebook.com/ctvnorthernontario,
twitter.com/CTVNorthernNews

North Bay: **YourTV - North Bay** (Channel: 700)
Owned by: Cogeco Connexion Inc.*
North Bay, ON
northbaynews@cogeco.com
www.yourtv.tv/northbay
www.facebook.com/yourtvnorthbay, twitter.com/yourtvnorthbay

Oil Springs: **CKCO-TV-3** (Channel: 42)
Kitchener
Owned by: CKCO-TV
Oil Springs, ON

Orangeville: **Rogers TV - Dufferin-Caledon** (Channel: 63)
Owned by: Rogers Media Inc.*
70 C-Line, Orangeville, ON L9W 6E2
Fax: 519-941-6091
Toll-Free: 866-880-3994
www.rogerstv.com
Willy Jong, Supervising Producer, 416-915-0160

Orillia: **Rogers TV - Orillia** (Channel: 10)
Owned by: Rogers Media Inc.*
Orillia, ON
www.rogerstv.com
Kevin Kelly, Supervising Producer, 705-812-4539

Oshawa: **Rogers TV - Durham Region** (Channel: 10; 63)
Owned by: Rogers Media Inc.*
301 Marwood Dr., Oshawa, ON L1H 1J4
Tel: 905-436-4120, Fax: 905-579-5559
www.rogerstv.com
Jim Anderson, Supervising Producer, 905-476-1406

†*Ottawa:* **CBOFT-DT** (Channel: 9)
Détenteur: **Canadian Broadcasting Corporation***
CP 3220 C, Ottawa, ON K1Y 1E4
Ligne sans frais: 866-306-4636
affairespubliques.ottawagatineau@radio-canada.ca
www.radio-canada.ca/ottawa-gatineau
Marco Dubé, Directeur, Marco.Dube@radio-canada.ca

Ottawa: **CBOT-DT** (Channel: 25)
Owned by: Canadian Broadcasting Corporation*
PO Box 3220 C, Ottawa, ON K1Y 1E4
Tel: 613-288-6000
www.cbc.ca/ottawa

Ottawa: **CICO-DT-24** (Channel: 24)
Owned by: TVOntario*
Ottawa, ON
tvo.org

Ottawa: **CJOH-DT** (Channel: 13)
Owned by: Bell Media TV*
87 George St., Ottawa, ON K1N 9H7
Tel: 613-224-1313, Fax: 888-770-2192
ctvottawa@ctv.ca
ottawa.ctvnews.ca
www.facebook.com/CTVNewsOttawa, twitter.com/ctvottawa

Ottawa: **Rogers TV - Ottawa** (Channel: 22)
Owned by: Rogers Media Inc.*
475 Richmond Rd., Ottawa, ON K2A 3Y8
Tel: 613-728-2222, Fax: 613-728-9793
www.rogerstv.com
Gavin Lumsden, Supervising Producer, 613-759-8542

†*Ottawa:* **Rogers TV - Ottawa (Français)** (Channel: 23)
Détenteur: **Rogers Media Inc.***
475, ch Richmond, Ottawa, ON K2A 3Y8
Tél: 613-728-2222, Téléc: 613-728-9793
www.tvrogers.com
Gavin Lumsden, Superviseur de la programmation, 613-759-8542

Owen Sound: **Rogers TV - Grey County** (Channel: 53)
Owned by: Rogers Media Inc.*
1360 - 20th St. East, Owen Sound, ON N4K 5T7
Tel: 519-376-2832, Fax: 519-376-5216
Toll-Free: 866-615-5527
www.rogerstv.com
Mark Perry, Supervising Producer, 519-376-2832

Peterborough: **CHEX-DT** (Channel: 12)
Owned by: 591987 B.C. Ltd.*
743 Monaghan Rd., Peterborough, ON K9J 5K2
Tel: 705-742-0451
globalnews.ca/peterborough
www.facebook.com/GlobalPeterborough,
twitter.com/chexnewswatch

Peterborough: **YourTV - Peterborough/Lindsay** (Channel: 700)
Owned by: Cogeco Connexion Inc.*
1111 Goodfellow Rd, Peterborough, ON K9J 7M6
Tel: 705-743-8602
yourtv.ptbo@cogeco.com
www.yourtv.tv/peterborough
www.facebook.com/yourtvptbo, twitter.com/yourtvptbo

Port Elgin: **EastLink TV - Port Egin**
Owned by: EastLink TV*
Port Elgin, ON
Fax: 519-291-5935
Toll-Free: 866-286-3484
midwest@eastlinktv.com
eastlinktv.com

Sarnia: **YourTV - Sarnia** (Channel: 700)
Owned by: Cogeco Connexion Inc.*
Sarnia, ON
www.yourtv.tv/sarnia
www.facebook.com/yourtvsarnia, twitter.com/yourtvsarnia

Sault Ste Marie: **Shaw Spotlight - Sault Ste Marie** (Channel: 10)
Owned by: Shaw Communications Inc.*
23 Manitou Dr., Sault Ste Marie, ON P6B 6GN
shawspotlightssm@sjrb.ca
www.shawspotlight.ca

Sault Ste. Marie: **CHBX-TV** (Channel: 2; 11)
Owned by: Bell Media TV*
119 East St., Sault Ste. Marie, ON P6A 3C7
Tel: 705-759-8232, Fax: 705-759-7783
newsforthenorth@ctv.ca
northernontario.ctvnews.ca

Simcoe: **EastLink TV - Simcoe** (Channel: 5)
Owned by: EastLink TV*
21 Donly Dr., Simcoe, ON N3Y 4W3
Tel: 519-426-3090, Fax: 519-426-0162
simcoe@eastlinktv.com
eastlinktv.com

Smiths Falls: **YourTV - Smiths Falls/Perth/North Grenville** (Channel: 700)
Owned by: Cogeco Connexion Inc.*
Smiths Falls, ON
www.yourtv.tv/smiths-falls
www.facebook.com/yourtvsfalls, twitter.com/yourtvsfalls

Straford: **Rogers TV - Stratford** (Channel: 20)
Owned by: Rogers Media Inc.*
32 Erie St., Straford, ON N5A 2M4
Tel: 519-271-5202, Fax: 519-271-1787
Toll-Free: 888-410-2020
www.rogerstv.com
Jeremy Parking, Supervising Producer, 519-894-8160

Sturgeon Falls: **EastLink TV - Sturgeon Falls**
Owned by: EastLink TV*
Sturgeon Falls, ON
sturgeonfalls@eastlinktv.com
eastlinktv.com

Sudbury: **CICI-TV** (Channel: 5)
Owned by: Bell Media TV*
699 Frood Rd., Sudbury, ON P3C 5A3
Tel: 705-674-8301, Fax: 705-674-2706
Toll-Free: 866-389-6288
northernontario.ctvnews.ca
www.facebook.com/ctvnorthernontario,
twitter.com/CTVNorthernNews

Sudbury: **EastLink TV - Sudbury** (Channel: 10)
Owned by: EastLink TV*
PO Box 4500, #15, 500 Barrydowne Rd., Sudbury, ON P3A 5W1
Tel: 705-560-6397, Fax: 705-560-7891
sudbury@eastlinktv.com
eastlinktv.com

Thunder Bay: **CHFD-TV** (Channel: 4)
87 North Hill St., Thunder Bay, ON P7A 5V6
Tel: 807-346-2600, Fax: 807-345-9923
www.ckprthunderbay.com
www.facebook.com/CkprThunderBayTv,
twitter.com/ckprthunderbay

Thunder Bay: **CICO-DT-9** (Channel: 9)
Owned by: TVOntario*
Thunder Bay, ON
tvo.org

Thunder Bay: **CKPR-DT** (Channel: 2; CBC affiliate)
87 North Hill St., Thunder Bay, ON P7A 5V6
Tel: 807-346-2600, Fax: 807-345-9923
www.ckprthunderbay.com

Thunder Bay: **Shaw Spotlight - Thunder Bay** (Channel: 10)
Owned by: Shaw Media Inc.*
1635 Paquette Rd., Thunder Bay, ON P7B 2J2
shawspotlightthunderbay@sjrb.ca
www.shawspotlight.ca

Timmins: **CITO-TV** (Channel: 3)
Owned by: Bell Media TV*
681 Pine St. North, Timmins, ON P4N 7L6
Tel: 705-264-4211, Fax: 705-264-3266
Toll-Free: 800-797-6288
northernontario.ctvnews.ca

Timmins: **EastLink TV - Timmins** (Channel: 3)
Owned by: EastLink TV*
PO Box 1429, 865 Mountjoy St. South, Timmins, ON P4N 7N2
Tel: 705-267-3000, Fax: 705-264-0121
timmins@eastlinktv.com
eastlinktv.com

†*Toronto:* **CBLFT-DT** (Channel: 25)
Détenteur: **Canadian Broadcasting Corporation***
Société Radio-Canada, CP 500 A, Toronto, ON M5W 1E6
Tél: 416-205-2887, Ligne sans frais: 800-551-2985
www.radio-canada.ca/ontario
twitter.com/RC_TV

Toronto: **CBLT-DT** (Channel: 5)
Owned by: Canadian Broadcasting Corporation*
PO Box 500 A, Toronto, ON M5W 1E6
Tel: 416-205-3311
www.cbc.ca/toronto
Other information: Phone, Television Newsroom: 416-205-2500
Susan Marjetti, Managing Director, 416-205-5791
Don loi, Team Manager, Broadcast Sales, 416-205-2732

Toronto: **CFMT-DT (Omni)**
Owned by: Rogers Media Inc.*
33 Dundas St. East, Toronto, ON M5B 1B8
Tel: 416-260-0060, Fax: 416-764-3245
www.omnitv.ca
www.facebook.com/omnitelevision, twitter.com/omnitelevision

Toronto: **CFTO-DT** (Channel: 9)
Owned by: Bell Media TV*
PO Box 9 O, Toronto, ON M4A 2M9
Tel: 416-384-5000, Toll-Free: 800-668-0060
toronto.ctvnews.ca
www.instagram.com/ctvtoronto, www.facebook.com/ctvtoronto,
twitter.com/ctvtoronto
Other information: TTY: 1-800-461-1542

Toronto: **CHEX-TV-2**
Owned by: 591987 B.C. Ltd.*
81 Barber Greene Rd., Toronto, ON M3C 2A2
Tel: 705-742-0451
globalnews.ca/durham
www.facebook.com/globaldurham, twitter.com/globaldurham

Toronto: **CICA-DT** (Channel: 19)
Owned by: TVOntario*
PO Box 200 Q, Toronto, ON M4T 2T1
tvo.org

Toronto: **CITY-DT (City Toronto)** (Channel: 57)
Owned by: **Rogers Media Inc.***
33 Dundas St. East, Toronto, ON M5B 1B8
Tel: 416-599-2489
www.citytv.com
www.instagram.com/city_tv, www.facebook.com/citytv,
twitter.com/city_tv

Toronto: **CJMT-DT (Omni)** (Channel: 44)
Owned by: **Rogers Media Inc.***
33 Dundas St. East, Toronto, ON M5B 1B8
Tel: 416-260-0060, Fax: 416-764-3245
www.omnitv.ca
www.facebook.com/omnitelevision, twitter.com/omnitelevision

†*Toronto:* **TFO**
CP 3005 F, Toronto, ON M4Y 2M5
Tél: 416-968-3536, Téléc: 416-968-8203
Ligne sans frais: 800-387-8435
vos_questions@tfo.org
www.3.tfo.org
www.youtube.com/tfocanada, www.facebook.com/TFOCanada,
twitter.com/TFOCanada
Glenn O'Farrell, Président et chef de la direction,
gofarrell@tfo.org

Uxbridge: **Rogers TV - Uxbridge/Scugog** (Channel: 10)
Owned by: **Rogers Media Inc.***
Uxbridge, ON
www.rogerstv.com
Jim Anderson, Supervising Producer, 905-476-1406

Wawa: **CHBX-TV-1** (Channel: 7)
Owned by: **CHBX-TV**
Wawa, ON

Windsor: **CBET-TV** (Channel: 9)
Owned by: **Canadian Broadcasting Corporation***
825 Riverside Dr. West, Windsor, ON N9A 5K9
Tel: 519-255-3411, Toll-Free: 866-306-4636
www.cbc.ca/windsor
Other information: Phone, Windsor Newsroom: 519-255-3456
Shawna Kelly, Managing Director, 519-255-3563

Windsor: **CICO-DT-32** (Channel: 19)
Owned by: **TVOntario***
Windsor, ON
tvo.org

Woodstock: **Rogers TV - Woodstock** (Channel: 13)
Owned by: **Rogers Media Inc.***
21 Ridgeway Circle, Woodstock, ON N4V 1C9
Tel: 519-533-5550, Fax: 519-533-5560
www.rogerstv.com
Jeremy Parking, Supervising Producer, 519-894-8160

Prince Edward Island

Charlottetown: **CBCT-DT** (Channel: 13)
Owned by: **Canadian Broadcasting Corporation***
PO Box 2230, 430 University Ave., Charlottetown, PE C1A 8B9
Tel: 902-629-6400, Toll-Free: 866-306-4636
www.cbc.ca/pei
www.facebook.com/142551811174
Other information: Phone, CBC News Compass: 902-629-6403;
Toll-Free: 800-671-2228
Denise Wilson, Senior Managing Director, Atlantic Canada
Donna Allen, Executive Producer, News, Prince Edward Island
Nadine Antle, Regional Manager, Partnerships,
Communications, Brand, & Promot, 902-420-4223

Charlottetown: **CHNB-DT-14** (Channel: 42)
Owned by: **CHNB-DT**
Charlottetown, PE

Charlottetown: **EastLink TV** (Channel: 10)
PEI Region
Owned by: **EastLink TV***
100 Cable Ct., Charlottetown, PE C1B 1A9
Tel: 902-367-3588, Toll-Free: 902-569-4731
eastlinktv.com
Bruce MacLean, Regional Manager, 902-569-0115

Québec

†*Alma:* **NousTV - Alma** (Channel: 13; HD 555)
Détenteur: **Cogeco Connexion Inc.***
590, rue Collard ouest, Alma, QC G8B 1N2
Tél: 418-668-3310
noustv.alma@cogeco.com
nous.tv/alma
www.facebook.com/noustvalma

Baie-Comeau: **CFTF-DT-5** (Channel: 9)
Owned by: **CFTF-DT**
Baie-Comeau, QC
www.cftf.ca

†*Baie-Comeau:* **NousTV - Baie-Comeau** (Channel: 6; HD 555)
Détenteur: **Cogeco Connexion Inc.***
323, boul Lasalle, Baie-Comeau, QC G4Z 2L5
Tél: 418-296-9505
noustv.baie-comeau@cogeco.com
nous.tv/baie-comeau
www.facebook.com/169339079809759

Baie-Saint-Paul: **CFTF-DT-10** (Channel: 26)
Owned by: **CFTF-DT**
Baie-Saint-Paul, QC
www.cftf.ca

†*Baie-Saint-Paul:* **CIMT-DT-4** (Channel: 13)
Détenteur: **CIMT-DT**
Baie-Saint-Paul, QC
cimt.teleinterrives.com

Baie-Saint-Paul: **CKRT-DT-1** (Channel: 36)
Owned by: **CKRT-DT**
Baie-Saint-Paul, QC
www.ckrt.ca

†*Baie-Saint-Paul:* **TVCO - Charlevoix**
Détenteur: **DERYtelecom***
74, Ambroise-Fafard, Baie-Saint-Paul, QC G3Z 2J6
Tél: 418-435-5134, Téléc: 418-435-6479
info@tvco.qc.ca
tvcotv.com

†*Berthierville:* **CTRB Cable 9**
Détenteur: **DERYtelecom***
501, rue Montcalm, Berthierville, QC J0K 1A0
Tél: 450-836-5103, Téléc: 450-836-6412
tvcberthierville@hotmail.com
www.ctrb.tv

Cabano: **CFTF-DT-3** (Channel: 12)
Owned by: **CFTF-DT**
Cabano, QC
www.cftf.ca

†*Cabano:* **CIMT-DT-8** (Channel: 23)
Détenteur: **CIMT-DT**
Cabano, QC
cimt.teleinterrives.com

Cabano: **CKRT-DT-4** (Channel: 21)
Owned by: **CKRT-DT**
Cabano, QC
www.ckrt.ca

Carleton: **CFTF-DT-11** (Channel: 44)
Owned by: **CFTF-DT**
Carleton, QC
www.cftf.ca

†*Carleton:* **CHAU-DT** (Channel: 4)
Détenteur: **Télé Inter-Rives ltée***
349, boul Perron, Carleton, QC G0C 1J0
Tél: 418-364-3344, Téléc: 418-364-7168
nousjoindre@chautva.com
cimtchau.ca
www.facebook.com/CHAUNouvelles

†*Chandler:* **CHAU-DT-4** (Channel: 6)
Détenteur: **CHAU-DT**
Chandler, QC

†*Chicoutimi:* **CJPM-DT** (Channel: 6)
Détenteur: **Groupe TVA inc.**
1, rue Mont Ste-Claire, Chicoutimi, QC G7H 5G3
Tél: 418-549-2576, Téléc: 418-549-1130
Ligne sans frais: 800-267-2576
tva.canoe.ca/stations/cjpm

†*Chicoutimi:* **CKTV-DT** (Channel: 12)
Détenteur: **Canadian Broadcasting Corporation***
500, rue des Saguenéens, Chicoutimi, QC G7H 6N4
Tél: 418-696-6600, Ligne sans frais: 800-463-9857
www.radio-canada.ca/saguenay-lac-saint-jean
Michel Gagné, Chef des services français,
michel.gagne-SAG@radio-canada.ca

Chicoutimi: **MAtv** (Channel: 9; HD 609)
Owned by: **Vidéotron ltée**
1, rue de Mont Ste-Claire, Chicoutimi, QC G7H 5G3
Tel: 418-541-5920, Fax: 418-541-5939
saguenay@matv.ca
matv.ca
www.facebook.com/matv, twitter.com/MAtv

†*Cloridorme:* **CHAU-DT-8** (Channel: 11)
Détenteur: **CHAU-DT**
Cloridorme, QC

Dégelis: **CKRT-DT-2** (Channel: 25)
Owned by: **CKRT-DT**
Dégelis, QC
www.ckrt.ca

†*Drummondville:* **NousTV - Drummondville** (Channel: 3; HD 555)
Détenteur: **Cogeco Connexion Inc.***
1970, boul Lemire, Drummondville, QC J2B 6X5
Tél: 819-477-3978
noustv.drummondville@cogeco.com
nous.tv/drummondville
www.facebook.com/noustvdrummondville

Forestville: **CFTF-DT-4** (Channel: 4)
Owned by: **CFTF-DT**
Forestville, QC
www.cftf.ca

Gaspé: **CFTF-DT-9** (Channel: 30)
Owned by: **CFTF-DT**
Gaspé, QC
www.cftf.ca

†*Gaspé:* **CHAU-DT-6** (Channel: 7)
Détenteur: **CHAU-DT**
Gaspé, QC

†*Gatineau:* **CFGS-DT (Noovo Gatineau-Ottawa)** (Channel: 34)
Détenteur: **RNC MÉDIA, Inc.***
171A, rue Jean-Proulx, Gatineau, QC J8Z 1W5
noovogatineau.ca

†*Gatineau:* **CHOT-DT (TVA Gatineau-Ottawa)** (Channel: 40)
Détenteur: **RNC MÉDIA, Inc.***
171A, rue Jean-Proulx, Gatineau, QC J8Z 1W5
tvagatineau.ca
www.facebook.com/tvagatineauottawa

Gatineau: **MAtv** (Channel: 9; HD 609)
Owned by: **Vidéotron ltée**
190, rue d'Edmonton, Gatineau, QC J8Y 3S6
Tel: 819-771-7373, Fax: 819-771-7011
montreal@matv.ca
matv.ca
www.facebook.com/matv, twitter.com/MAtv

Granby: **MAtv** (Channel: 9; HD 609)
Owned by: **Vidéotron ltée**
611, rue Cowie, Granby, QC J2G 3X4
Tel: 450-574-3252, Fax: 450-372-5464
granby@matv.ca
matv.ca
www.facebook.com/matv, twitter.com/MAtv

†*Jonquière:* **CFRS-DT** (Channel: 13)
Détenteur: **Bell Media Inc.***
2303, rue Sir Wilfrid-Laurier, Jonquière, QC G7X 5Z2
Tél: 418-542-4551, Téléc: 418-542-7217
Ligne sans frais: 855-390-6100
noovo.ca

†*L'Anse-à-Valleau:* **CHAU-DT-9** (Channel: 12)
Détenteur: **CHAU-DT**
L'Anse-à-Valleau, QC

---

* For details on this company see listing in Major Broadcasting Companies section; † French language station

†*La Baie:* Télévision DERYtélécom
Détenteur: **DERYtelecom***
#102, 93 rue Bagot, La Baie, QC G7B 2N6
Tél: 418-544-0403
info@tvdl.tv
www.tvdl.tv
www.youtube.com/user/TVDLDERY,
www.facebook.com/tvdl.labaie

Lac-Mégantic: **Télé locale Axion** (Channel: 11; 111)
Owned by: Cable Axion inc.
4764, rue Laval, Lac-Mégantic, QC G6B 1C7
Fax: 418-387-6915
Toll-Free: 866-552-9466
cable11@axion.ca
www.axion.ca/communaute/presentation.php
Yannick Marceau, Coordinateur et journaliste

Les Escoumins: **CFTF-DT-8** (Channel: 33)
Owned by: CFTF-DT
Les Escoumins, QC
www.cftf.ca

†*Les Escoumins:* **CIMT-DT-7** (Channel: 35)
Détenteur: **CIMT-DT**
Les Escoumins, QC
cimt.teleinterrives.com

†*Magog:* **NousTV - Magog** (Channel: 3; HD 555)
Détenteur: **Cogeco Connexion Inc.***
15, rue Saint-Patrice ouest, Magog, QC J1X 1V8
Tél: 819-843-3370
noustv.magog@cogeco.com
nous.tv/magog
www.facebook.com/302930703092590

†*Matane:* **NousTV - Matane** (Channel: 4; HD 555)
Détenteur: **Cogeco Connexion Inc.***
63, rue Brillant, Matane, QC G4W 3P6
Tél: 418-562-4468
noustv.matane@cogeco.com
nous.tv/matane
www.facebook.com/NousvMatane

†*Montmagny:* **NousTV - Montmagny** (Channel: 6; HD 555)
Détenteur: **Cogeco Connexion Inc.***
190, 6e av, Montmagny, QC G5V 0C3
Tél: 418-248-5698
noustv.montmagny@cogeco.com
nous.tv/montmagny

†*Montréal:* **CBFT-DT** (Channel: 19)
Détenteur: **Canadian Broadcasting Corporation***
Maison de Radio-Canada, CP 6000 Centre-ville, Montréal, QC H3C 3A8
Tél: 514-597-6000, *Téléc:* 514-597-5545
Ligne sans frais: 866-306-4636
www.radio-canada.ca/montreal
twitter.com/RC_TV
Helen Evans, Directrice générale

Montréal: **CBMT-DT** (Channel: 21)
Owned by: Canadian Broadcasting Corporation*
PO Box 6000, Montréal, QC H3C 3A8
Tél: 514-597-6000, *Fax:* 514-597-6354
www.cbc.ca/montreal
Shelagh Kinch, Managing Director, English Services,
shelagh.kinch@cbc.ca

Montréal: **CFJP-DT** (Channel: 35)
Owned by: Bell Media Inc.*
85, rue St-Paul ouest, Montréal, QC H2Y 3V4
Tel: 514-390-6100, *Fax:* 514-390-6056
noovo.ca

†*Montréal:* **CFTM-DT** (Channel: 10)
Détenteur: **Groupe TVA inc.***
1600, boul de Maisonneuve est, Montréal, QC H2L 4P2
www.tvanouvelles.ca/regional/tva-montreal
www.facebook.com/ReseauTVA, twitter.com/tvareseau

†*Montréal:* **CIVA-DT** (Channel: 12)
c/o Télé-Québec
Détenteur: **Télé-Québec***
905, av de Lorimier, Montréal, QC H2K 3V9
Tél: 514-521-2424, *Téléc:* 514-873-7464
info@telequebec.tv
www.telequebec.tv

†*Montréal:* **CIVB-DT** (Channel: 22)
c/o Télé-Québec
Détenteur: **Télé-Québec***
905, av de Lorimier, Montréal, QC H2K 3V9
Tél: 514-521-2424, *Téléc:* 514-873-7464
info@telequebec.tv
www.telequebec.tv

†*Montréal:* **CIVB-DT-1** (Channel: 31)
c/o Télé-Québec
Détenteur: **CIVB-DT**
1000, rue Fullum, Montréal, QC H2K 3L7
Tél: 514-521-2424, *Téléc:* 514-864-1970
info@telequebec.tv
www.telequebec.tv

†*Montréal:* **CIVC-DT** (Channel: 45)
c/o Télé-Québec
Détenteur: **Télé-Québec***
905, av de Lorimier, Montréal, QC H2K 3V9
Tél: 514-521-2424, *Téléc:* 514-873-7464
info@telequebec.tv
www.telequebec.tv

†*Montréal:* **CIVF-DT** (Channel: 12)
c/o Télé-Québec
Détenteur: **Télé-Québec***
905, av de Lorimier, Montréal, QC H2K 3V9
Tél: 514-521-2424, *Téléc:* 514-873-7464
info@telequebec.tv
www.telequebec.tv

†*Montréal:* **CIVG-DT** (Channel: 9)
c/o Télé-Québec
Détenteur: **Télé-Québec***
905, av de Lorimier, Montréal, QC H2K 3V9
Tél: 514-521-2424, *Téléc:* 514-873-7464
info@telequebec.tv
www.telequebec.tv

†*Montréal:* **CIVK-DT** (Channel: 15)
c/o Télé-Québec
Détenteur: **Télé-Québec***
905, av de Lorimier, Montréal, QC H2K 3V9
Tél: 514-521-2424, *Téléc:* 514-873-7464
info@telequebec.tv
www.telequebec.tv

†*Montréal:* **CIVK-DT-1** (Channel: 32)
c/o Télé-Québec
Détenteur: **CIVK-DT**
1000, rue Fullum, Montréal, QC H2K 3L7
Tél: 514-521-2424, *Téléc:* 514-864-1970
info@telequebec.tv
www.telequebec.tv

†*Montréal:* **CIVK-DT-2** (Channel: 40)
c/o Télé-Québec
Détenteur: **CIVK-DT**
1000, rue Fullum, Montréal, QC H2K 3L7
Tél: 514-521-2424, *Téléc:* 514-864-1970
info@telequebec.tv
www.telequebec.tv

†*Montréal:* **CIVK-DT-3** (Channel: 35)
c/o Télé-Québec
Détenteur: **CIVK-DT**
1000, rue Fullum, Montréal, QC H2K 3L7
Tél: 514-521-2424, *Téléc:* 514-864-1970
info@telequebec.tv
www.telequebec.tv

†*Montréal:* **CIVM-TV** (Channel: 26)
c/o Télé-Québec
Détenteur: **Télé-Québec***
905, av de Lorimier, Montréal, QC H2K 3V9
Tél: 514-521-2424, *Téléc:* 514-873-7464
info@telequebec.tv
www.telequebec.tv

†*Montréal:* **CIVO-DT** (Channel: 30)
c/o Télé-Québec
Détenteur: **Télé-Québec***
905, av de Lorimier, Montréal, QC H2K 3V9
Tél: 514-521-2424, *Téléc:* 514-873-7464
info@telequebec.tv
www.telequebec.tv

†*Montréal:* **CIVP-DT** (Channel: 23)
c/o Télé-Québec
Détenteur: **Télé-Québec***
905, av de Lorimier, Montréal, QC H2K 3V9
Tél: 514-521-2424, *Téléc:* 514-873-7464
info@telequebec.tv
www.telequebec.tv

†*Montréal:* **CIVQ-DT** (Channel: 15)
c/o Télé-Québec
Détenteur: **Télé-Québec***
905, av de Lorimier, Montréal, QC H2K 3V9
Tél: 514-521-2424, *Téléc:* 514-873-7464
info@telequebec.tv
www.telequebec.tv

†*Montréal:* **CIVS-DT** (Channel: 24)
c/o Télé-Québec
Détenteur: **Télé-Québec***
905, av de Lorimier, Montréal, QC H2K 3V9
Tél: 514-521-2424, *Téléc:* 514-873-7464
info@telequebec.tv
www.telequebec.tv

†*Montréal:* **CIVV-DT** (Channel: 8)
c/o Télé-Québec
Détenteur: **Télé-Québec***
905, av de Lorimier, Montréal, QC H2K 3V9
Tél: 514-521-2424, *Téléc:* 514-873-7464
info@telequebec.tv
www.telequebec.tv

Montréal: **CKMI-DT** (Channel: 15)
Owned by: Global Television Network*
1010, rue Saint Catherine ouest, Montréal, QC H3B 5L1
Tél: 514-521-4323
montreal@globalnews.ca
globalnews.ca/montreal
www.facebook.com/globalmontreal, twitter.com/global_montreal

Montréal: **MAtv** (Channel: 9; HD 609)
Owned by: Vidéotron ltée
1475, rue Alexandre-DeSève, niveau 4D, Montréal, QC H2L 2V4
Tél: 514-985-8408, *Fax:* 514-985-8404
montreal@matv.ca
matv.ca
www.facebook.com/matv, twitter.com/MAtv

†*Percé:* **CHAU-DT-5** (Channel: 13)
Détenteur: **CHAU-DT**
Percé, QC

†*Port-Daniel:* **CHAU-DT-3** (Channel: 10)
Détenteur: **CHAU-DT**
Port-Daniel, QC

†*Québec:* **CBVT-DT** (Channel: 25)
Détenteur: **Canadian Broadcasting Corporation***
CP 18800, Québec, QC G1K 9L4
Tél: 418-654-1341, *Ligne sans frais:* 866-954-1341
nouvelles.quebec@radio-canada.ca
www.radio-canada.ca/quebec
Jean François Rioux, Directeur région de Québec

†*Quebec:* **CFAP-DT** (Channel: 39)
Détenteur: **Bell Media Inc.***
#335, 330, rue De St-Vallier est, Quebec, QC G9K 9C5
Tél: 418-624-2222, *Téléc:* 418-624-8930
Ligne sans frais: 855-390-6100
noovo.ca

†*Québec:* **CFCM-DT** (Channel: 4)
Détenteur: **Groupe TVA inc.***
Québec, QC
www.tvanouvelles.ca/regional/tva-quebec

Québec: **MAtv** (Channel: 9; HD 609)
Owned by: Vidéotron ltée
#1200, 1000, av Myrand, Québec, QC G1V 2W3
Tel: 418-522-8289, *Fax:* 418-522-7237
quebec@matv.ca
matv.ca
www.facebook.com/matv, twitter.com/MAtv

†*Rimouski:* **CFER-TV** (Channel: 5; 11)
Détenteur: **Groupe TVA inc.***
Rimouski, QC
www.tvanouvelles.ca/regional/tva-est-du-quebec
www.facebook.com/tvaestduquebec

For details on this company see listing in Major Broadcasting Companies section; † French language station

†*Rimouski:* **CJBR-DT** (Channel: 45)
Détenteur: **Canadian Broadcasting Corporation***
185, boul René-Lepage est, Rimouski, QC G5L 1P2
Tél: 418-723-2217, *Téléc:* 418-723-6126
cjbr@radio-canada.ca
www.radio-canada.ca/est-du-quebec
Denis Langlois, Premier chef des services français,
denis.langlois@radio-canada.ca

Rimouski: **CJPC-DT** (Channel: 18)
Owned by: CFTF-DT
Rimouski, QC
www.cftf.ca

†*Rimouski:* **NousTV - Rimouski** (Channel: 4; HD 555)
Détenteur: **Cogeco Connexion Inc.***
384, av de la Cathédrale, Rimouski, QC G5L 5L1
Tél: 418-724-5737
noustv.rimouski@cogeco.com
nous.tv/rimouski
www.facebook.com/268586003243317

†*Rivière-au-Rénard:* **CHAU-DT-7** (Channel: 4)
Détenteur: **CHAU-DT**
Rivière-au-Rénard, QC

†*Rivière-du-Loup:* **CFTF-DT** (Channel: 29)
Détenteur: **Télé Inter-Rives ltée***
103, rue des Équipements, Rivière-du-Loup, QC G5R 5W7
Tél: 418-862-2909, *Téléc:* 418-862-8147
nouvelles@cftf.ca
cftf.teleinterrives.com
www.facebook.com/cftf.ca, twitter.com/cftf5

Rivière-du-Loup: **CFTF-DT-6** (Channel: 11)
Owned by: CFTF-DT
Rivière-du-Loup, QC
www.cftf.ca

†*Rivière-du-Loup:* **CIMT-DT** (Channel: 9)
Détenteur: **Télé Inter-Rives ltée***
15, rue de la Chute, Rivière-du-Loup, QC G5R 5B7
Tél: 418-867-1341, *Téléc:* 418-867-4710
nousjoindre@cimt.ca
cimt.teleinterrives.com
www.facebook.com/cimtnouvelles, twitter.com/cimt_nouvelles

†*Rivière-du-Loup:* **CIMT-DT-6** (Channel: 41)
Détenteur: **CIMT-DT**
Rivière-du-Loup, QC
cimt.teleinterrives.com

†*Rivière-du-Loup:* **CKRT-DT** (Channel: 7)
Détenteur: **Télé Inter-Rives ltée***
15, rue de la Chute, Rivière-du-Loup, QC G5R 5B7
Tél: 418-867-1341, *Téléc:* 418-867-4710
info@ckrt.ca
www.ckrt.ca

†*Rivière-du-Loup:* **CKRT-DT** (Channel: 7; possédé à
Télé Inter-Rives ltée)
Détenteur: **Canadian Broadcasting Corporation***
15, rue de la Chute, Rivière-du-Loup, QC G5R 5B7
Tél: 418-867-8080

Rivière-du-Loup: **CKRT-DT-3** (Channel: 13)
Owned by: CKRT-DT
Rivière-du-Loup, QC
www.ckrt.ca

Rivière-du-Loup: **MAtv** (Channel: 9; HD 609)
Owned by: Vidéotron ltée
55, rue de l'Hôtel-de-Ville, Rivière-du-Loup, QC G5R 1L4
Tel: 418-867-1479, *Fax:* 418-867-2829
riviereduloup@matv.ca
matv.ca
www.facebook.com/matv, twitter.com/MAtv

†*Rouyn-Noranda:* **CFEM-DT (TVA
Abitibi-Témiscamingue)** (Channel: 13)
Détenteur: **RNC MÉDIA, Inc.***
380, av Murdoch, Rouyn-Noranda, QC J9X 1G5
nouvelles@rncmedia.ca
tvaabitibi.ca
www.facebook.com/tvaabitibi

†*Rouyn-Noranda:* **CFVS-DT (Noovo
Abitibi-Témiscamingue)** (Channel: 15)
Détenteur: **RNC MÉDIA, Inc.***
380, av Murdoch, Rouyn-Noranda, QC J9X 1G5
noovoabitibi.ca
Francis Beauvais, Directeur général

Rouyn-Noranda: **TVC9** (Channel: 9)
Owned by: Cablevision du Nord de Québec inc.
155, av du Portage, Rouyn-Noranda, QC J9X 7H3
Toll-Free: 800-567-6353
tvc9rn@cablevision.ca
tvc9.cablevision.qc.ca
Geneviève Bélisle, Directrice
Benoit Paquin, Coordinateur, TVC9 Rouyn-Noranda

†*Saint-Georges:* **NousTV - Saint-Georges** (Channel:
9; HD 555)
Détenteur: **Cogeco Connexion Inc.***
15010, boul Lacroix, Saint-Georges, QC G5Y 1R7
Tél: 418-228-9828
noustv.beauce-appalaches@cogeco.com
nous.tv/saint-georges
www.facebook.com/166288396785088

†*Saint-Hyacinthe:* **NousTV - Saint-Hyacinthe**
(Channel: 3; HD 555)
Détenteur: **Cogeco Connexion Inc.***
16900, av Bourdages sud, Saint-Hyacinthe, QC J2T 4P7
Tél: 450-774-1087, *Téléc:* 450-774-3373
noustv.saint-hyacinthe@cogeco.com
nous.tv/saint-hyacinthe

†*Saint-Raymond:* **CJSR - Portneuf**
Détenteur: **DERYtelecom***
240, Côte Joyeuse, Saint-Raymond, QC G3L 4A7
Tél: 418-337-4925, *Téléc:* 418-337-4991
www.cjsr3.com
www.facebook.com/cjsr.latvcportneuvoise

†*Saint-Urbain:* **CIMT-DT-5** (Channel: 38)
Détenteur: **CIMT-DT**
Saint-Urbain, QC
cimt.teleinterrives.com

Saint-Urbain: **CKRT-DT-5** (Channel: 35)
Owned by: CKRT-DT
Saint-Urbain, QC
www.ckrt.ca

†*Sainte-Adèle:* **NousTV - Laurentides** (Channel: 4; HD
555)
Détenteur: **Cogeco Connexion Inc.***
421, boul Sainte-Adèle, Sainte-Adèle, QC J8B 2N1
Tél: 450-745-4003
noustv.laurentides@cogeco.com
nous.tv/laurentides
www.facebook.com/nousTVLaurentides

†*Sainte-Marguerite-Marie:* **CHAU-DT-1** (Channel: 3)
Détenteur: **CHAU-DT**
Sainte-Marguerite-Marie, QC

Sainte-Marie: **Télé locale Axion** (Channel: 11; 150)
Owned by: Cable Axion inc.
166, Notre-Dame nord, Sainte-Marie, QC G6E 3Z9
Fax: 418-387-6915
Toll-Free: 866-552-9466
cable11@axion.ca
www.axion.ca/communaute/presentation.php
Yannick Marceau, Coordinateur et journaliste

†*Salaberry-de-Valleyfield:* **NousTV -
Salaberry-de-Valleyfield** (Channel: 13; HD 555)
Détenteur: **Cogeco Connexion Inc.***
13, rue Saint-Urbain, Salaberry-de-Valleyfield, QC J6S 4M6
Tél: 450-377-1373
noustv.valleyfield@cogeco.com
nous.tv/salaberry-de-valleyfield
www.facebook.com/189329871133292

†*Sept-Iles:* **CFER-TV-2** (Channel: 5)
Détenteur: **CFER-TV**
410, av Évangéline, Sept-Iles, QC G4R 2N5
Tél: 418-968-6011, *Téléc:* 418-968-5665
tva.canoe.ca/stations/cfer

Sept-îles: **CFTF-DT-7** (Channel: 7)
Owned by: CFTF-DT
Sept-îles, QC
www.cftf.ca

†*Sept-îles:* **NousTV - Sept-îles** (Channel: 5; HD 555)
Détenteur: **Cogeco Connexion Inc.***
410, av Évangéline, Sept-îles, QC G4R 2N5
Tél: 418-962-3508
noustv.sept-iles@cogeco.com
nous.tv/sept-iles
www.facebook.com/169339079809759

Sherbrooke: **CFKS-DT** (Channel: 30)
Owned by: Bell Media Inc.*
3720, boul Industriel, Sherbrooke, QC J1L 1Z9
Tel: 819-565-9232, *Fax:* 819-822-4205
Toll-Free: 855-390-6100
noovo.ca

†*Sherbrooke:* **CHLT-DT** (Channel: 7)
Détenteur: **Groupe TVA inc.***
Sherbrooke, QC
www.tvanouvelles.ca/regional/tva-sherbrooke
www.facebook.com/TVASherbrooke

†*Sherbrooke:* **CKSH-DT** (Channel: 9)
Détenteur: **Canadian Broadcasting Corporation***
#350, 1335, rue King ouest, Sherbrooke, QC J1J 2B8
Tél: 819-620-0000, *Téléc:* 819-823-0453
www.radio-canada.ca
Stéphane Laberge, Chef des services français,
stephane.laberge@radio-canada.ca

Sherbrooke: **MAtv** (Channel: 9; HD 609)
Owned by: Vidéotron ltée
#182, 3330, rue King Ouest, Sherbrooke, QC J1L 1C9
Tel: 819-820-7830, *Fax:* 819-820-7834
sherbrooke@matv.ca
matv.ca
www.facebook.com/matv, twitter.com/MAtv

Sorel-Tracy: **MAtv** (Channel: 9; HD 609)
Owned by: Vidéotron ltée
254, ch des Patriotes, Sorel-Tracy, QC J3P 6K7
Tel: 450-742-0113, *Fax:* 450-742-1018
soreltracy@matv.ca
matv.ca
www.facebook.com/matv, twitter.com/MAtv

†*Thetford Mines:* **NousTV - Thetford Mines** (Channel:
9; HD 555)
Détenteur: **Cogeco Connexion Inc.***
39, 10e rue sud, Thetford Mines, QC G6G 7X6
Tél: 418-338-2079
noustv.beauce-appalaches@cogeco.com
nous.tv/thetford-mines
www.facebook.com/166288396785088

†*Tracadie:* **CHAU-DT-10** (Channel: 9)
Détenteur: **CHAU-DT**
Tracadie, QC

†*Trois Rivières:* **NousTV - Mauricie** (Channel: 11; HD
555)
Détenteur: **Cogeco Connexion Inc.***
4141, boul Saint-Jean, Trois Rivières, QC G9B 2M8
Tél: 819-693-8353
noustv.mauricie@cogeco.com
nous.tv/mauricie
www.facebook.com/176585479076008

Trois-Pistoles: **CFTF-DT-2** (Channel: 17)
Owned by: CFTF-DT
Trois-Pistoles, QC
www.cftf.ca

†*Trois-Pistoles:* **CIMT-DT-2** (Channel: 13)
Détenteur: **CIMT-DT**
Trois-Pistoles, QC
cimt.teleinterrives.com

Trois-Pistoles: **CKRT-DT-6** (Channel: 19)
Owned by: CKRT-DT
Trois-Pistoles, QC
www.ckrt.ca

Trois-Rivière: **MAtv** (Channel: 9; HD 609)
Owned by: Vidéotron ltée
#101, 190, rue Fusey, Trois-Rivière, QC G8T 2V8
Tel: 819-375-9888, *Fax:* 819-375-8950
capdelamadeleine@matv.ca
matv.ca
www.facebook.com/matv, twitter.com/MAtv

†*Trois-Rivières:* **CFKM-DT** (Channel: 34)
Détenteur: **Bell Media Inc.***
926, rue Notre Dame Centre, Trois-Rivières, QC G9A 4W8
Tél: 819-377-6053, *Ligne sans frais:* 855-390-6100
noovo.ca

†*Trois-Rivières:* **CHEM-DT** (Channel: 8)
Détenteur: **Groupe TVA inc.***
Trois-Rivières, QC
www.tvanouvelles.ca/regional/tva-trois-rivieres

---

* For details on this company see listing in Major Broadcasting Companies section; † French language station

Trois-Rivières: **CKTM-DT** (Channel: 28)
Owned by: Canadian Broadcasting Corporation*
#101, 225, rue des Forges, Trois-Rivières, QC G9A 2G7
Tel: 819-694-0114, *Toll-Free:* 877-695-6556
www.radio-canada.ca/mauricie
Nancy Sabourin, Chef des services français,
Nancy.sabourin@radio-canada.ca

Val-d'Or: **TVC9** (Channel: 9)
Owned by: Cablevision du Nord de Québec inc.
45, boul Hôtel de Ville, Val-d'Or, QC J9P 2M5
Toll-Free: 800-567-6353
tvc9.cablevision.qc.ca
www.facebook.com/255688484493841
Geneviève Geneviève, Directrice
Pierre-Luc Létourneau, Coordinateur, TVC9 Val-d'Or,
pletourneau@cablevision.ca

†*Ville de Saint-Gabriel:* **CTB TV** (Channel: 3)
Détenteur: **DERYtelecom***
160, rue de Lanaudière, Ville de Saint-Gabriel, QC J0K 2N0
Tél: 450-835-1114
ctbtv.ca

Saskatchewan

Carlyle Lake: **CIEW-TV** (Channel: 7)
Owned by: CFQC-DT
Carlyle Lake, SK

Colgate: **CKCK-TV-1** (Channel: 12)
Owned by: CKCK-TV
Colgate, SK

Fort Qu'appelle: **CKCK-TV-7** (Channel: 7)
Owned by: CKCK-DT
Fort Qu'appelle, SK

Golden Prairie: **CKMC-TV-1** (Channel: 10)
Owned by: CKCK-DT
Golden Prairie, SK

Maple Creek: **CHAT-TV-2** (Channel: 6)
Medicine Hat
Owned by: CHAT-TV
Maple Creek, SK

Meadow Lake: **CITL-TV-3** (Channel: 3)
Lloydminster
Owned by: CITL-TV
Meadow Lake, SK

Moose Jaw: **CKMJ-TV** (Channel: 7)
Owned by: CKCK-DT
Moose Jaw, SK

North Battleford: **CFQC-TV-2** (Channel: 6)
Owned by: CFQC-DT
North Battleford, SK

Pivot: **CHAT-TV-1** (Channel: 4)
Medicine Hat
Owned by: CHAT-TV
Pivot, SK

Prince Albert: **CIPA-TV** (Channel: 9)
Owned by: Bell Media TV*
#104, 2805 - 6th Ave. East, Prince Albert, SK S6V 6Z6
Tel: 306-922-6066, *Fax:* 306-763-3041
cipa@ctv.ca
saskatoon.ctvnews.ca
www.facebook.com/ctvsaskatoon, twitter.com/ctvsaskatoon

Prince Albert: **Shaw Spotlight - Prince Albert**
(Channel: 10)
Owned by: Shaw Media Inc.*
2990 - 2nd Ave. West, #A, Prince Albert, SK S6V 7E9
shawspotlightsask@sjrb.ca
www.shawspotlight.ca
Lisa Risom, Contact, lisa.risom@sjrb.ca

†*Regina:* **CBKFT-DT** (Channel: 13)
Détenteur: **Canadian Broadcasting Corporation***
2440, rue Broad, Regina, SK S4P 4A1
Tél: 306-347-9540
saskatchewan@radio-canada.ca
www.radio-canada.ca/saskatchewan
www.facebook.com/cbcsask, twitter.com/cbcsask

Regina: **CBKT-DT** (Channel: 9)
Owned by: Canadian Broadcasting Corporation*
2440 Broad St., Regina, SK S4P 4A1
Tel: 306-347-9540
www.cbc.ca/sask
www.facebook.com/cbcsask, twitter.com/cbcsask

Regina: **CFRE-DT** (Channel: 11)
Owned by: Global Television Network*
370 Hoffer Dr., Regina, SK S4N 7A4
Tel: 306-775-4000
regina@globalnews.ca
globalnews.ca/regina
www.facebook.com/globalreginanews, twitter.com/globalregina

Regina: **City Saskatchewan**
Owned by: Rogers Media Inc.*
PO Box 3464 Main, Regina, SK S4P 3J8
Tel: 306-779-2726
www.citytv.com/saskatchewan
www.instagram.com/city_tv, www.facebook.com/citytv,
twitter.com/city_tv

Regina: **CKCK-DT** (Channel: 2)
Owned by: Bell Media TV*
PO Box 2000, #1 Highway East, Regina, SK S4P 3E5
Tel: 306-569-2000
ckck@ctv.ca
regina.ctvnews.ca
www.facebook.com/ctvregina, twitter.com/ctvregina

Saskatoon: **CFQC-DT** (Channel: 8)
Owned by: Bell Media TV*
216 - 1 Ave. North, Saskatoon, SK S7K 3W3
Tel: 306-665-8600
cfqcnews@ctv.ca
saskatoon.ctvnews.ca

Saskatoon: **CFSK-DT** (Channel: 4)
Owned by: Global Television Network*
218 Robin Cres., Saskatoon, SK S7L 7C3
Tel: 306-665-6969, *Fax:* 306-665-6069
saskatoon@globalnews.ca
globalnews.ca/saskatoon
www.facebook.com/globalsaskatoon,
twitter.com/globalsaskatoon

Saskatoon: **Shaw Spotlight - Saskatoon** (Channel: 10)
Owned by: Shaw Communications Inc.*
2326 Hanselman Ave., Saskatoon, SK S7L 5Z3
shawspotlightsask@sjrb.ca
www.shawspotlight.ca

Stranraer: **CFQC-TV-1** (Channel: 3)
Owned by: CFQC-DT
Stranraer, SK

Swift Current: **CKMC-TV** (Channel: 12)
Owned by: CKCK-DT
Swift Current, SK

Willow Bunch: **CKCK-TV-2** (Channel: 6)
Owned by: CKCK-TV
Willow Bunch, SK

Wynyard: **CIWH-TV** (Channel: 12)
Owned by: CFQC-DT
Wynyard, SK

Cable Companies

Alberta

Calgary: **Shaw Direct**
Owned by: Shaw Communications Inc.*
**c/o Shaw Communications Inc., #900, 630 - 3rd Ave. SW,
Calgary, AB T2P 4L4**
Toll-Free: 888-554-7827
www.shawdirect.ca
www.facebook.com/ShawDirectSatellite

Calgary: **Shaw Pay-Per-View Limited**
Owned by: Shaw Direct
**c/o Shaw Communications Inc., #900, 630 - 3rd Ave. SW,
Calgary, AB T2P 4L4**
www.shaw.ca/tv/channels

Rainbow Lake: **Rainbow Lake Cable TV**
PO Box 149, Rainbow Lake, AB T0H 2Y0
Tel: 780-956-3934
admin@rainbowlake.ca
rainbowlake.ca

British Columbia

Campbell River: **Nimpkish Valley Communications Ltd.**
Campbell River, BC
Tel: 250-283-2521

Fort St James: **Fort St. James TV & Radio Society**
PO Box 1536, Fort St James, BC
Tel: 250-996-2246
fsjtv.ca
Dave Birdi, President

Logan Lake: **Logan Lake TV Society**
PO Box 56, 3 Watertower, Logan Lake, BC V0K 1W0
Tel: 250-523-6411
admin@lltvs.ca
www.lltvs.ca

Riondel: **Riondel Cable Society**
PO Box 59, 232 Fowler Ave., Riondel, BC V0B 2B0
Tel: 250-225-3433, *Fax:* 250-225-3443
riondelcable@bluebell.ca
bluebell.ca

Salmon Arm: **Mascon Communications Corp.**
PO Box 3386, 4901 Auto Rd. SE, Salmon Arm, BC V1E 4S2
Tel: 250-832-6000, *Fax:* 250-832-5575
Toll-Free: 866-832-6020
info@masconcable.ca
mascon.ca
www.facebook.com/MasconCable, twitter.com/masconcable

Valemount: **Valemount Entertainment Society**
#211, 99 Gorse St., Valemount, BC V0E 2Z0
Tel: 250-566-8288
tv@vctv.ca
vctv.ca
www.youtube.com/user/ValemountCommunityTV,
www.facebook.com/ValemountCommunityTV
Michael Peters, Station Manager

Vancouver: **Novus Entertainment Inc.**
#300, 112 East 3rd St., Vancouver, BC V5T 1C8
Tel: 604-642-6688, *Fax:* 604-685-7832
customerservice@novusnow.ca
www.novusnow.ca
www.facebook.com/novusnow, twitter.com/Novusnow
Doug Holman, Co-President & CFO
Donna L. Robertson, Co-President & CLO

Newfoundland & Labrador

Burgeo: **Burgeo Broadcasting System**
147 Reach Rd., Burgeo, NL A0M 1A0
Tel: 709-886-2935, *Fax:* 709-886-1243
www.burgeonl.com/businesses.htm
Dave MacDonald, Contact

Labrador City: **Community Recreation Rebroadcasting Service Association**
208 Amherst Ave., Labrador City, NL A2V 2Y5
Tel: 709-944-7676, *Fax:* 709-944-7675
info@crrstv.net
crrs.net

Northwest Territories

Deline: **Great Bear Co-operative Association Ltd.**
PO Box 159, Deline, NT X0E 0G0
Tel: 867-589-3361, *Fax:* 867-589-4517
manager@greatbear.coop
arctic-coop.com

Fort McPherson: **Tetlit Service Co-operative Ltd.**
PO Box 27, Fort McPherson, NT X0E 0J0
Tel: 867-952-2417, *Fax:* 867-952-2602
manager@tetlit.coop
arctic-coop.com

---

* For details on this company see listing in Major Broadcasting Companies section; † French language station

Nova Scotia

Canning: **Cross Country TV Ltd.**
PO Box 310, Canning, NS B0P 1H0
Tel: 902-678-2395, Fax: 902-678-2455
office@corp.xcountry.tv
www.xcountry.tv
www.facebook.com/500987776755322

Reserve Mines: **Seaside Communications**
PO Box 4558, 1318 Grand Lake Rd., Reserve Mines, NS B1E
1L2
Tel: 902-539-6250, Fax: 902-539-2597
csr@seaside.ns.ca
www.seaside.ns.ca
www.facebook.com/SeasideCommunicationsInc,
twitter.com/Seaside_Cable

Nunavut

Arctic Bay: **Taqqut Co-operative Ltd.**
PO Box 29, Arctic Bay, NU X0A 0A0
Tel: 867-439-9934, Fax: 867-439-8765
manager@taqqut.coop
arctic-coop.com

Arviat: **Padlei Co-operative Association Ltd.**
PO Box 90, Arviat, NU X0C 0E0
Tel: 867-857-2933, Fax: 867-857-2762
manager@padlei.coop
arctic-coop.com

Baker Lake: **Sanavik Co-operative Association Ltd.**
PO Box 69, Baker Lake, NU X0C 0A0
Tel: 867-793-2912, Fax: 867-793-2594
manager@sanavik.coop
arctic-coop.com

Cambridge Bay: **Ikaluktutiak Co-operative Ltd.**
PO Box 38, Cambridge Bay, NU X0B 0C0
Tel: 867-983-2201, Fax: 867-983-2085
manager@ikaluktutiak.coop
arctic-coop.com

Chesterfield Inlet: **Pitsiulak Co-operative
Association Ltd.**
PO Box 43, Chesterfield Inlet, NU X0C 0B0
Tel: 867-898-9975, Fax: 867-898-9056
manager@pitsiulak.coop
arctic-coop.com

Coral Harbour: **Katudgevik Co-operative
Association Ltd.**
PO Box 201, Coral Harbour, NU X0C 0C0
Tel: 867-925-9969, Fax: 867-925-8308
manager@katudgevik.coop
arctic-coop.com

Gjoa Haven: **Qikiqtaq Co-operative Association Ltd.**
PO Box 120, Gjoa Haven, NU X0E 1J0
Tel: 867-360-7271, Fax: 867-360-6018
manager@qikiqtaq.coop
arctic-coop.com

Kugluktuk: **Kugluktuk Co-operative Ltd.**
PO Box 279, Kugluktuk, NU X0E 0E0
Tel: 867-982-4231, Fax: 867-982-3070
manager@kugluktuk.coop
arctic-coop.com

Naujaat: **Naujat Co-operative Ltd.**
PO Box 70, Naujaat, NU X0C 0H0
Tel: 867-462-9943, Fax: 867-462-4152
manager@naujat.coop
arctic-coop.com

Qikiqtarjuaq: **Tulugak Co-operative Society Ltd.**
PO Box 8, Qikiqtarjuaq, NU X0A 0B0
Tel: 867-927-8031, Fax: 867-927-8044
manager@tulugak.coop
arctic-coop.com

Rankin Inlet: **Kissarvik Co-operative Association
Limited**
PO Box 40, Rankin Inlet, NU X0C 0G0
Tel: 867-645-2801, Fax: 867-645-2280
manager@kissarvik.coop
arctic-coop.com

Whale Cove: **Issatik Co-operative Ltd.**
PO Box 60, Whale Cove, NU X0C 0J0
Tel: 867-896-9956, Fax: 867-896-9087
manager@issatik.coop
arctic-coop.com

Ontario

Ancaster: **Compton Communications**
Owned by: Rogers Communications Inc.*
PO Box 10209, RPO Meadowlands Mall, Ancaster, ON L9K
1P3
Tel: 905-985-8171, Fax: 905-985-0010
Toll-Free: 844-985-8171
customerservice@compton.net
www.compton.net

Ancaster: **Kincardine Cable TV Ltd.**
Owned by: Rogers Communications Inc.*
PO Box 10209, RPO Meadowlands Mall, Ancaster, ON L9K
1P3
Tel: 519-559-7159, Toll-Free: 800-265-3064
kctv@tnt21.com
www.tnt21.com

Aurora: **Robust Computers**
#1, 15450 Yonge St., Aurora, ON L4G 0K1
Tel: 905-773-7046, Toll-Free: 877-976-2878
info@robustcomputers.com
robustcomputers.com
twitter.com/RobustComputers

Chatham: **ATOP Broadband Corp.**
800 Richmond St., Chatham, ON N7M 5J5
Tel: 905-851-5348, Toll-Free: 855-601-9437
info@atoptv.com
atoptv.com
Robert Socci, Owner

Chatham: **TekSavvy Solutions Inc.**
800 Richmond St., Chatham, ON N7M 5J5
Tel: 519-360-1575, Toll-Free: 877-779-1575
sales@teksavvy.com
www.teksavvy.com
www.linkedin.com/company/teksavvy_solutions_inc,
www.facebook.com/TekSavvySolutionsInc,
twitter.com/TekSavvyBuzz
Marc Marc, Chief Executive Officer

Clifford: **Wightman Telecom**
PO Box 70, 100 Elora St. North, Clifford, ON N0G 1M0
Tel: 519-327-8012, Fax: 519-327-8010
Toll-Free: 888-477-2177
questions@wightman.ca
wightman.ca
www.youtube.com/c/WightmanTelecomMinto,
www.facebook.com/wightmantelecom, twitter.com/wightmantel

Dublin: **CABLE TV**
PO Box 118, 123 Ontario St., Dublin, ON N0K 1E0
Tel: 226-302-2341, Fax: 519-345-2873
cabletv@ezlink.ca
www.ezlink.ca

Fenelon Falls: **Cable Cable Inc.**
Owned by: Rogers Communications Inc.*
16 Cable Rd., Fenelon Falls, ON K0M 1M0
Tel: 705-887-6433, Fax: 705-887-2580
Toll-Free: 866-887-6434
hello@cablecable.net
www.cablecable.net
www.facebook.com/cablecable, twitter.com/cablecableinc
Tony Fiorini, President, Tony@cablecable.net

Moose Factory: **Moose Factory Cable Inc.**
PO Box 339, Moose Factory, ON P0L 1W0
Tel: 705-658-5137, Fax: 705-658-5335
www.creecable.com

Norwich: **Nor-Del Cablevision**
PO Box 340, Norwich, ON N0J 1P0
Tel: 519-879-6527, Fax: 519-879-6387
Toll-Free: 800-563-1954
nordel@nor-del.com
www.nor-del.com

Toronto: **Academy of Canadian Cinema & Television**
#9, 411 Richmond St. East, Toronto, ON M5A 3S5
Tel: 416-366-2227, Fax: 416-366-8454
Toll-Free: 800-644-5194
communications@academy.ca
www.academy.ca
www.instagram.com/thecdnacademy,
www.facebook.com/TheCdnAcademy,
twitter.com/TheCdnAcademy
John Young, Chair
Beth Janson, Chief Executive Officer

Toronto: **Beanfield Metroconnect**
#418, 77 Mowat Ave., Toronto, ON M6K 3E3
Tel: 416-532-1555
info@beanfield.com
www.beanfield.com
www.linkedin.com/company/beanfield-technologies,
www.facebook.com/beanfieldtechnologies, twitter.com/beanfield

Toronto: **Comwave Networks Inc.**
61 Wildcat Rd., Toronto, ON M3J 2P5
Tel: 416-663-9600, Toll-Free: 877-474-6638
www.comwave.net
Yuval Barzakay, Chief Executive Officer

Toronto: **Rogers Cable Inc.**
Owned by: Rogers Communications Inc.*
333 Bloor St. East, 10th Fl., Toronto, ON M4W 1G9
Toll-Free: 877-559-5202
www.rogers.com
Other information: TTY: 800-668-9286
Joe Natale, President & CEO, Rogers Communications Inc.

Toronto: **Shaw Broadcast Services**
Owned by: Shaw Communications Inc.*
#1500, 121 Bloor St. East, Toronto, ON M4W 3M5
Toll-Free: 800-268-2943
shawbroadcastsupport@sjrb.ca
www.shawbroadcast.com

Toronto: **Tbaytel**
#418, 77 Mowat Ave., Toronto, ON M6K 3E3
Tel: 807-623-4400, Toll-Free: 800-264-9501
customercare@tbaytel.net
www.tbaytel.net
www.linkedin.com/company/tbaytel, www.facebook.com/tbaytel,
twitter.com/tbaytel
Dan Topatigh, President & CEO
Michael Coffey, Chief Financial Officer

Toronto: **VMedia Inc.**
Toronto, ON
Toll-Free: 855-333-8269
sales@vmedia.ca
www.vmedia.ca
www.instagram.com/vmediainc, www.facebook.com/VMediaTV,
twitter.com/VMediaTV

Woodstock: **Execulink Telecom Inc.**
1127 Ridgeway Rd., Woodstock, ON N4V 1E3
Toll-Free: 866-706-1942
customercare@execulinktelecom.ca
www.execulink.ca
www.linkedin.com/company/execulinktelecom,
www.facebook.com/ExeculinkTelecom, twitter.com/Execulink
Ian Stevens, President & CEO

Québec

†*Chisasibi:* **Kinwapt Cable Inc.**
CP 420, Chisasibi, QC J0M 1E0
Tél: 819-855-2191, Téléc: 819-855-3186

†*Fermont:* **Coopérative de la télévision
communautaire de Fermont**
20, place Daviault, Fermont, QC G0G 1J0
Tél: 418-287-5443, Téléc: 418-287-5776
info@diffusionfermont.ca
diffusionfermont.ca
www.facebook.com/Diffusionfermont

†*Havre-Saint-Pierre:* **Radio Télévision
Communautaire Hâvre-St-Pierre**
992, rue du Bouleau, Havre-Saint-Pierre, QC G0G 1P0
Tél: 418-538-2451
info@cilemf.com
rtccable.com
www.facebook.com/143063915709007, twitter.com/CILEMF

---

* For details on this company see listing in Major Broadcasting Companies section; † French language station

†*Lourdes-de-Blanc-Sablon:* **Coopérative de câblodistribution de Brest**
1147, boul Dr.-Camille-Marcoux, Lourdes-de-Blanc-Sablon, QC G0G 1W0
Tél: 418-461-2003, *Téléc:* 418-461-2703

†*Magog:* **Cable Axion inc.**
250, ch de l'Axion, Magog, QC J1X 6J2
Tél: 819-843-0611, *Téléc:* 819-868-4249
Ligne sans frais: 866-552-9466
info@axion.ca
www.axion.ca
www.youtube.com/user/cableaxion,
www.facebook.com/AxionCable

†*Matane:* **Télécable Multivision inc.**
655, ch de la Greve, Matane, QC G4W 7A1
Tél: 418-562-1950, *Ligne sans frais:* 888-562-1950
tmi@cgocable.ca

Montréal: **Distribuel Communications Limited**
740, rue Notre-Dame ouest, Montréal, QC H3C 1J2
Toll-Free: 877-810-2877
info@distribuel.ca
www.distribuel.ca
www.linkedin.com/company/distribuel,
www.facebook.com/Distribuel, twitter.com/Distribuel
Matt Stein, Chief Executive Officer
Gerry Vanderpost, Chief Financial Officer

†*Montréal:* **Vidéotron**
Détenteur: **Quebecor Media inc.***
612, rue St-Jacques, Montréal, QC H3C 4M8
Tél: 514-281-1711, *Ligne sans frais:* 877-512-0911
videotron.com
www.youtube.com/user/Videotron, www.facebook.com/videotron,
twitter.com/videotron
Jean-François Pruneau, Président et Chef de la direction
Philippe Cloutier, Vice-président principal et Chef de la direction financière

†*Pessamit:* **Télécâble Pessamit**
20, rue Messek, Pessamit, QC G0H 1B0
Tél: 418-567-4443, *Téléc:* 418-567-3292
pessamit.org

†*Québec:* **Coopérative de câblodistribution de l'arrière-pays**
20860, boul Henri-Bourassa, Québec, QC G2N 1P7
Tél: 418-849-7125, *Téléc:* 418-849-7125
Ligne sans frais: 866-749-7125
info@ccapcable.com
www.ccapcable.com
www.facebook.com/ccapcable
Sandra Fournier, Présidente, sandra.fournier@ccap.coop
Stéphane Arseneau, Directeur général, 418-849-7125,
stephane.arseneau@ccap.coop
Marco Gonzalez, Directeur, Opérations,
marco.gonzalez@ccap.coop

Sanikiluaq: **Mitiq Co-operative Association Ltd.**
PO Box 217, Sanikiluaq, QC X0A 0W0
Tel: 867-266-8860, *Fax:* 867-266-8844
manager@mitiq.coop
arctic-coop.com

†*Sherbrooke:* **Groupe Transvision Réseau**
#105, 175, rue Queen, Sherbrooke, QC J1M 1K1
Tél: 819-563-1001, *Téléc:* 819-563-3116
support@gtvr.com
www.gtvr.com

†*Ste-Catherine-de-la-Jacques-Cartier:* **Coopérative câblodistribution Ste-Catherine-Fossambault**
130, rue Désiré-Juneau,
Ste-Catherine-de-la-Jacques-Cartier, QC G3N 2X3
Tél: 418-875-1118, *Téléc:* 418-875-1971
reception@coopscjc.com
coopcscf.com
www.facebook.com/coopcscf

†*Val-D'Or:* **Cablevision du Nord de Québec inc. une Division de Bell Aliant**
45, boul de Hôtel de Ville, Val-D'Or, QC J9P 2M5
Tél: 819-825-5133, *Ligne sans frais:* 800-567-6353
www.cablevision.qc.ca
Bernard Gauthier, Président

†*Warwick:* **Cablovision Warwick inc.**
3, rue de l'Hôtel-de-ville, Warwick, QC J0A 1M0
Tél: 819-358-5858, *Téléc:* 819-358-5592
service@cablovision.com
www.cablovision.com
www.facebook.com/Cablovision

Saskatchewan

Ile-a-la-Crosse: **Ile a la Crosse Communications Society Inc.**
PO Box 480, Ile-a-la-Crosse, SK S0M 1C0
Tel: 306-833-2173, *Fax:* 306-833-2042
ilex@sasktel.net
Nathan Favel, Chief Executive Officer

Imperial: **Imperial Cable System**
310 Royal St., Imperial, SK S0G 2J0
Tel: 306-963-2220, *Fax:* 306-963-2445
town.imperial@sasktel.net
imperial.ca/municipal-services

Limerick: **Village of Limerick**
PO Box 129, 106 Main St., Limerick, SK S0H 2P0
Tel: 306-263-2020, *Fax:* 306-263-2013
rm73@sasktel.net

Rouleau: **Rouleau Cable TV**
PO Box 250, Rouleau, SK S0G 4H0
Tel: 306-776-2270, *Fax:* 306-776-2482
Shawn Duncan, President

Yukon Territory

Dawson City: **Dawson City Cable**
c/o City Office, PO Box 308, 1336 Front St., Dawson City, YT Y0B 1G0
Tel: 867-993-7400, *Fax:* 867-993-7434
www.cityofdawson.ca

Whitehorse: **Northwestel Cable Inc.**
PO Box 2727, Whitehorse, YT Y1A 4Y4
Tel: 867-668-5300, *Fax:* 867-668-7079
Toll-Free: 888-423-2333
customerservice@nwtel.ca
www.nwtel.ca
www.youtube.com/user/NorthwestelTV,
www.facebook.com/Northwestel, twitter.com/northwestel
Curtis Shaw, President

Specialty Broadcasters

ABC Spark
Owned by: Corus Entertainment Inc.*
info@abcspark.com
www.abcspark.ca

Adult Swim
Owned by: Corus Entertainment Inc.*
info@cartoonnetwork.ca
www.adultswim.ca

Cartoon Network
Owned by: Corus Entertainment Inc.*
info@cartoonnetwork.ca
www.cartoonnetwork.ca
www.facebook.com/cartoonnetworkCAN

Cinépop
Détenteur: **Bell Media Inc.***
www.cinepop.ca
www.facebook.com/cinepop

Cooking Channel
Owned by: Corus Entertainment Inc.*
feedback@cookingchannel.ca
www.cookingchannel.ca

Country Music Television Inc.
Owned by: Corus Entertainment Inc.*
info@cmtcanada.com
www.cmt.ca

Crave
Owned by: Bell Media Inc.*
Toll-Free: 888-272-8388
help@crave.ca
www.crave.ca
www.facebook.com/cravecanada, twitter.com/CraveCanada

Crime & Investigation
Owned by: Corus Entertainment Inc.*
Toll-Free: 866-977-3663
feedback@crimeandinvestigation.ca
www.crimeandinvestigation.ca

DejaView
Owned by: Corus Entertainment Inc.*
Toll-Free: 866-977-3663
feedback@dejaviewtv.ca
www.dejaviewtv.ca

DIY Network Canada
Owned by: Corus Entertainment Inc.*
Toll-Free: 866-967-4488
feedback@diy.ca
www.diy.ca
www.facebook.com/DIYNetwork, twitter.com/DIYNetwork

DTOUR
Owned by: Corus Entertainment Inc.*
feedback@dtourtv.com
www.dtourtv.com

Évasion
Détenteur: **Groupe TVA inc.***
www.qub.ca/tvaplus/evasion
www.facebook.com/Evasion.tv

Food Network Canada
Owned by: Corus Entertainment Inc.*
feedback@foodnetwork.ca
www.foodnetwork.ca
www.youtube.com/user/foodnetworkcanada,
www.facebook.com/foodnetworkcanada,
twitter.com/foodnetworkca

FX
Owned by: Rogers Media Inc.*
www.fxnowcanada.ca
www.youtube.com/user/fxnowcanada,
www.facebook.com/FXCanadaTV, twitter.com/fx_canada

FXX
Owned by: Rogers Media Inc.*
www.fxnowcanada.ca

History
Owned by: Corus Entertainment Inc.*
www.history.ca
www.youtube.com/c/HISTORYCanada,
www.facebook.com/HistoryCanada,
twitter.com/HistoryTVCanada

Home & Garden Television Canada
Owned by: Corus Entertainment Inc.*
feedback@hgtv.ca
www.hgtv.ca
www.instagram.com/hgtvcanada, www.facebook.com/hgtv.ca,
twitter.com/hgtvcanada

Ici ARTV
Détenteur: **Canadian Broadcasting Corporation***
ici.artv.ca
www.facebook.com/iciartv, twitter.com/iciartv
Gilbert Morin, Directeur général

Leafs Nation Network
Owned by: Rogers Communications Inc.*
leafsnation.mapleleafs.com

Lifetime
Owned by: Corus Entertainment Inc.*
feedback@mylifetimetv.ca
www.mylifetimetv.ca

MovieTime
Owned by: Corus Entertainment Inc.*
feedback@movietimetv.ca
www.movietimetv.ca

National Geographic
Owned by: Corus Entertainment Inc.*
Toll-Free: 866-447-8353
feedback@nationalgeographic.ca
www.natgeotv.com/ca

National Geographic Wild
Owned by: Corus Entertainment Inc.*
Toll-Free: 866-447-8353
feedback@nationalgeographic.ca
www.natgeotv.com/ca/wild
www.facebook.com/natgeowild, twitter.com/natgeowild

---

* For details on this company see listing in Major Broadcasting Companies section; † French language station

The News Forum
thenewsforum.ca
www.linkedin.com/company/thenewsforum
www.facebook.com/YourNewsForum,
twitter.com/thenewsforum_
Tore Stautland, Chief Executive Officer

OWN
Owned by: Corus Entertainment Inc.*
owninfo@corusent.com
www.owntv.ca
www.facebook.com/OWNCanada

RFD-TV Canada
Owned by: Wild TV Inc.
wildtv.ca/rfdcanada
www.facebook.com/RFDTVCanada

Showcase Television Inc.
Owned by: Corus Entertainment Inc.*
Toll-Free: 866-977-3663
feedback@showcase.ca
www.showcase.ca
www.youtube.com/c/showcaseca
www.facebook.com/showcasetv, twitter.com/ShowcaseTV

Slice
Owned by: Corus Entertainment Inc.*
info@slice.ca
www.slice.ca
www.youtube.com/c/slicetv, www.facebook.com/Slice,
twitter.com/slice_tv

Sportsnet 360
Owned by: Rogers Media Inc.*
now.sportsnet.ca/channel/sportsnet-360

Stingray Classica
Owned by: Stingray Group Inc.*
support@stingrayclassica.com
classica.stingray.com
www.youtube.com/c/StingrayClassica,
www.facebook.com/StingrayClassica

Stingray Country
Owned by: Stingray Group Inc.*
info@stingray.com
country.stingray.com

Stingray iConcerts
Owned by: Stingray Group Inc.*
info@stingrayiconcerts.com
iconcerts.stingray.com
www.facebook.com/StingrayiConcerts

Stingray Juicebox
Owned by: Stingray Group Inc.*
info@stingray.com
juicebox.stingray.com

Stingray Karaoke
Owned by: Stingray Group Inc.*
karaoke.stingray.com
www.youtube.com/c/StingrayKaraoke,
www.facebook.com/stingraykaraoke, twitter.com/stingraykaraoke

Stingray Loud
Owned by: Stingray Group Inc.*
info@stingray.com
loud.stingray.com

Stingray Music
Owned by: Stingray Group Inc.*
music.stingray.com
www.youtube.com/c/StingrayMusic,
www.facebook.com/stingray.music, twitter.com/stingraymusic

Stingray Naturescape
Owned by: Stingray Group Inc.*
info@stingray.com
www.stingray.com/stingray-naturescape

Stingray Retro
Owned by: Stingray Group Inc.*
info@stingray.com
retro.stingray.com

Stingray Vibe
Owned by: Stingray Group Inc.*
info@stingray.com
vibe.stingray.com

Treehouse TV
Owned by: Corus Entertainment Inc.*
info@treehousetv.com
www.treehousetv.com
www.youtube.com/c/TreehouseDirect,
www.facebook.com/Treehouse

VRAK TV
Owned by: Bell Media Inc.*
www.noovo.ca/vrak
www.facebook.com/vraktv, twitter.com/vraktv

Wild TV
wildtv.ca
www.youtube.com/wildtv, www.facebook.com/WildTV,
twitter.com/WildTV

Alberta

Edmonton: The Cowboy Channel Canada
Owned by: Wild TV Inc.*
11263 - 180th St., Edmonton, AB T5S 0B4
customerservice@thecowboychannel.com
www.thecowboychannel.com
www.facebook.com/CowboyChannel,
twitter.com/Cowboy_Channel

Edmonton: Ginx eSports TV Canada
Owned by: Super Channel Entertainment Network*
#200, 5324 Calgary Trail, Edmonton, AB T6H 4J8
marketing@superchannel.ca
www.superchannel.ca

Edmonton: Super Channel Fuse
Owned by: Super Channel Entertainment Network*
#200, 5324 Calgary Trail, Edmonton, AB T6H 4J8
marketing@superchannel.ca
www.superchannel.ca

Edmonton: Super Channel Heart & Home
Owned by: Super Channel Entertainment Network*
#200, 5324 Calgary Trail, Edmonton, AB T6H 4J8
marketing@superchannel.ca
www.superchannel.ca

Edmonton: Super Channel Vault
Owned by: Super Channel Entertainment Network*
#200, 5324 Calgary Trail, Edmonton, AB T6H 4J8
marketing@superchannel.ca
www.superchannel.ca

Edmonton: Water Television Network
Owned by: Wild TV Inc.*
11263 - 180th St., Edmonton, AB T5S 0B4
Tel: 780-444-1518
contact@thewaterchannel.ca
thewaterchannel.ca
www.facebook.com/thewaterchannelcanada

British Columbia

Burnaby: Knowledge Network Corporation
4355 Mathissi Pl., Burnaby, BC V5G 4S8
Tel: 604-431-3222, *Fax:* 604-431-3387
Toll-Free: 877-456-6988
info@knowledge.ca
www.knowledge.ca
www.facebook.com/bcknowledgenetwork, twitter.com/kpassiton

Richmond: Fairchild Television Ltd.
Owned by: Fairchild Media Group*
Aberdeen Centre, #3300, 4151 Hazelbridge Way, Richmond,
BC V6X 4J7
Tel: 604-295-1313, *Fax:* 604-295-1300
info@fairchildtv.com
www.fairchildtv.com
www.linkedin.com/company/fairchild-television,
www.facebook.com/fairchildtv

Richmond: Talentvision TV
Owned by: Fairchild Media Group*
Aberdeen Centre, #3300, 4151 Hazelbridge Way, Richmond,
BC V6X 4J7
Tel: 604-295-1328, *Fax:* 604-295-1399
info@talentvisiontv.com
www.talentvisiontv.com

Vancouver: Daystar Television Canada
PO Box 9550, Vancouver, BC V6B 4G3
Toll-Free: 800-829-1185
partners.canada@daystar.com
www.daystar.com

Vancouver: OUTtv Network Inc.
73 East 6th Ave., Vancouver, BC V5T 1J3
hello@outtvgo.com
outtv.ca
www.youtube.com/c/outtv, www.facebook.com/outtv,
twitter.com/outtv

Vancouver: Shaw Multicultural Channel
Owned by: Shaw Communications Inc.*
Shaw Tower, #900, 1067 West Cordova St., Vancouver, BC
V6C 3T5
Tel: 604-629-4270
smc@shaw.ca
www.multicultural.shaw.ca
www.facebook.com/ShawMulticulturalChannel,
twitter.com/ShawMulChannel

Victoria: Hansard TV
612 Government St., Victoria, BC V8V 1X4
Tel: 250-387-3681, *Fax:* 250-356-5095
hansard.services@leg.bc.ca
www.leg.bc.ca/documents-data/broadcasts-and-webcasts

Manitoba

Winnipeg: Aboriginal Peoples Television Network
339 Portage Ave., Winnipeg, MB R3B 2C3
Tel: 204-947-9331, *Fax:* 204-947-9307
Toll-Free: 888-330-2786
info@aptn.ca
www.aptn.ca
www.youtube.com/c/aptnca, www.facebook.com/aptntv,
twitter.com/APTN

Newfoundland & Labrador

Nain: OKâlaKatiget Society Television
Owned by: OKâlaKatiget Society*
PO Box 160, Nain, NL A0P 1L0
Tel: 709-922-2187, *Fax:* 709-922-2293
oktv@oksociety.com
www.oksociety.com

St. John's: House of Assembly Channel
Confederation Bldg., PO Box 8700, St. John's, NL A1B 4J6
Tel: 709-729-7448, *Fax:* 709-729-6699
tvcontrolroom@gov.nl.ca
www.assembly.nl.ca

Northwest Territories

Yellowknife: CBC North
Owned by: Canadian Broadcasting Corporation (CBC)*
5002 Forrest Dr., Yellowknife, NT X1A 2A9
Tel: 867-920-5400
www.cbc.ca/news/canada/north
www.facebook.com/CBCNorth, twitter.com/CBCNorth

Nova Scotia

Dartmouth: Toon-A-Vision
38 Pleasant St., Dartmouth, NS B2Y 3P2
info@toonavision.ca
www.toonavision.ca
www.facebook.com/ToonAvision, twitter.com/toonavisiontv

**Halifax: Legislative Television Broadcast &
Recording Services**
CIBC Bldg., PO Box 1617, 1809 Barrington St., #B103,
Halifax, NS B3J 3K8
Tel: 902-424-6420, *Fax:* 902-424-0604
ltv@novascotia.ca
nslegislature.ca/legislative-business/legislative-tv
William Hirtle, Manager

---

* For details on this company see listing in Major Broadcasting Companies section; † French language station

Ontario

Burlington: Yes TV
1295 North Service Rd., Burlington, ON L7R 4X5
Tel: 905-331-7333, Fax: 905-332-7481
contactus@yestv.com
www.yestv.com
www.instagram.com/yestvcanada, www.facebook.com/sayyestv,
twitter.com/yestvcanada
Glenn Stewart, Chief Operating Officer, 905-331-7333,
gstewart@yestv.com

Markham: Asian Television Network Ltd.
330 Cochrane Dr., Markham, ON L3R 8E4
Tel: 905-948-8199, Fax: 905-948-8108
atn@asiantelevision.com
www.asiantelevision.com
Shan Chandrasekar, President & CEO

Mississauga: TSC
Owned by: Rogers Communications Inc.*
59 Ambassador Dr., Mississauga, ON L5T 2P9
Fax: 877-202-0877
Toll-Free: 888-202-0888
customerservice@tsc.ca
www.tsc.ca
www.youtube.com/shoptsc, www.facebook.com/ShopTSC,
twitter.com/shoptsc
Other information: TTY: 800-263-2900
Anne Martin-Vachon, President

Oakville: The Weather Network
2655 Bristol Circle, Oakville, ON L6H 7W1
Tel: 905-829-1159; Toll-Free: 877-666-6761
www.theweathernetwork.com
www.youtube.com/user/TheWeatherNetwork,
www.facebook.com/theweathernetworkCAN,
twitter.com/weathernetwork

Ottawa: CPAC
PO Box 81099, Ottawa, ON K1P 1B1
Fax: 613-567-2741
Toll-Free: 877-287-2722
comments@cpac.ca
www.cpac.ca
www.youtube.com/user/cpac, www.facebook.com/CPACTV,
twitter.com/cpac_tv

Toronto: A.Side TV
Owned by: Blue Ant Media*
#200, 130 Merton St., Toronto, ON M4S 1A4
Tel: 416-646-4431, Fax: 416-646-4444
feedback@blueantmedia.ca
tv.ontheaside.com

Toronto: AMI-tv
Owned by: Accessible Media Inc.*
#200, 1090 Don Mills Rd., Toronto, ON M3C 3R6
feedback@ami.ca
www.ami.ca/tv

Toronto: Animal Planet
Owned by: Bell Media Inc.*
9 Channel Nine Ct., Toronto, ON M1S 4B5
www.ctv.ca/animal-planet
www.facebook.com/AnimalPlanetCanada
twitter.com/animalplanetca

Toronto: BBC Earth
Owned by: Blue Ant Media*
#200, 130 Merton St., Toronto, ON M4S 1A4
Tel: 416-646-4431, Fax: 416-646-4444
feedback@blueantmedia.ca
bbcearth.ca
www.facebook.com/bbcearth, twitter.com/BBCEarthCanada

Toronto: BBC First
Owned by: Blue Ant Media*
#200, 130 Merton St., Toronto, ON M4S 1A4
Tel: 416-646-4431, Fax: 416-646-4444
feedback@blueantmedia.ca
bbcfirst.ca
www.facebook.com/BBCFirstCanada

Toronto: BNN Bloomberg
Owned by: Bell Media Inc.*
299 Queen St. West, Toronto, ON M5V 2Z5
Tel: 416-384-6600
www.bnnbloomberg.ca
Noah Zivitz, Managing Editor, noah.zivitz@bellmedia.ca

Toronto: CBC News Network
Owned by: Canadian Broadcasting Corporation*
PO Box 500 A, Toronto, ON M5W 1E6
Tel: 416-205-2130, Toll-Free: 866-306-4636
www.cbc.ca/news
www.facebook.com/newscbc, twitter.com/cbcnews
Other information: TTY: 866-220-6045

Toronto: CIII-DT
Owned by: Global Television Network*
81 Barber Greene Rd., Toronto, ON M3C 2A2
Tel: 416-446-5460
viewercontacttoronto@globaltv.com
globalnews.ca/toronto
www.facebook.com/globaltoronto, twitter.com/globalnewsto

Toronto: Cottage Life
Owned by: Blue Ant Media*
#200, 130 Merton St., Toronto, ON M4S 1A4
Tel: 416-646-4431, Fax: 416-646-4444
feedback@blueantmedia.ca
tv.cottagelife.com
www.facebook.com/cottagelife, twitter.com/cottagelife

Toronto: CP24
Owned by: Bell Media Inc.*
299 Queen St. West, Toronto, ON M5V 2Z5
Tel: 416-384-2700, Fax: 416-384-6554
sales@cp24.com
www.cp24.com
www.instagram.com/cp24breakingnews,
www.facebook.com/CP24Toronto, twitter.com/CP24

Toronto: CTV Comedy Channel
Owned by: Bell Media Inc.*
299 Queen St. West, Toronto, ON M5V 2Z5
www.ctv.ca/comedy
www.youtube.com/c/CTVComedy,
www.facebook.com/CTVComedy, twitter.com/CTVComedy

Toronto: CTV Drama Channel
Owned by: Bell Media Inc.*
299 Queen St. West, Toronto, ON M5V 2Z5
www.ctv.ca/drama

Toronto: CTV Life Channel
Owned by: Bell Media Inc.*
299 Queen St. West, Toronto, ON M5V 2Z5
ctvlifechannel@gmail.com
www.ctv.ca/life
www.facebook.com/CTVLifeChannel, twitter.com/CTVLife

Toronto: CTV Sci-Fi Channel
Owned by: Bell Media Inc.*
299 Queen St. West, Toronto, ON M5V 2Z5
www.ctv.ca/sci-fi
www.youtube.com/c/CTVSciFi, www.facebook.com/CTVSciFi,
twitter.com/CTVSciFi

Toronto: The Discovery Channel
Owned by: Bell Media Inc.*
9 Channel Nine Ct., Toronto, ON M1S 4B5
www.ctv.ca/discovery
www.facebook.com/discoverycanada,
twitter.com/discoverycanada

Toronto: Discovery Science
Owned by: Bell Media Inc.*
9 Channel Nine Ct., Toronto, ON M1S 4B5
www.ctv.ca/discovery-science
twitter.com/DiscoverySciCa

Toronto: Disney Junior
Owned by: Corus Entertainment Inc.*
Corus Quay, 25 Dockside Dr., Toronto, ON M5A 0B5
Tel: 416-479-7000
info@disneyjunior.ca
www.disneyjunior.ca

Toronto: Disney XD
Owned by: Corus Entertainment Inc.*
Corus Quay, 25 Dockside Dr., Toronto, ON M5A 0B5
info@disneyxd.ca
www.disneyxd.ca

Toronto: documentary
Owned by: Canadian Broadcasting Corporation*
PO Box 500 A, Toronto, ON M6W 1E6
Toll-Free: 866-306-4636
www.cbc.ca/documentarychannel
www.youtube.com/c/CBCdocs, www.facebook.com/cbcdocs,
twitter.com/cbcdocs
Other information: TTY: 866-220-6045

Toronto: E!
Owned by: Bell Media Inc.*
299 Queen St. West, Toronto, ON M5V 2Z5
eonline@bellmedia.ca
www.eonline.com/ca
www.youtube.com/user/EonlineCanada,
www.facebook.com/eonlinecanada, twitter.com/EOnlineCanada

Toronto: ESPN Classic Canada
Owned by: Bell Media Inc.*
9 Channel Nine Ct., Toronto, ON M1S 4B5
www.tsn.ca/espn-classic

Toronto: EuroWorld Sport
Owned by: TLN Media Group Inc.*
901 Lawrence Ave. West, 2nd Fl., Toronto, ON M6A 1C3
Tel: 416-744-8200
info@tlntv.com
euroworldsport.ca

Toronto: The Family Channel Inc.
Owned by: WildBrain Ltd.*
c/o WildBrain Television, Queen's Quay Terminal, #550, 207
Queen's Quay West, Toronto, ON M5J 1A7
info@family.ca
www.family.ca
www.instagram.com/family_channel,
www.facebook.com/FamilyChannel, twitter.com/Family_Channel
Other information: TTY: 844-258-7458

Toronto: Family Chrgd
Owned by: Disney XD*
c/o WildBrain Television, Queen's Quay Terminal, #550, 207
Queen's Quay West, Toronto, ON M5J 1A7
www.chrgd.ca
Other information: TTY: 844-258-7458

Toronto: Family Jr.
Owned by: WildBrain Ltd.*
c/o WildBrain Television, Queen's Quay Terminal, #550, 207
Queen's Quay West, Toronto, ON M5J 1A7
info@family.ca
www.familyjr.ca
www.youtube.com/c/FamilyJr, www.facebook.com/FamilyJrTV
Other information: TTY: 844-258-7458

Toronto: FEVA TV
#605, 4576 Yonge St., Toronto, ON M2N 6N4
www.fevatv.com
www.facebook.com/FEVATV, twitter.com/fevatv

Toronto: Game+
Owned by: Anthem Sports & Entertainment*
#1410, 181 University Ave., Toronto, ON M5H 3M7
Tel: 416-987-7841
www.gameplusnetwork.com
twitter.com/GamePlusNetwork

Toronto: The GameTV Corporation
Owned by: Anthem Sports & Entertainment*
#230, 171 East Liberty St., Toronto, ON M6K 3P6
www.igametv.com
www.facebook.com/GameTV, twitter.com/GameTVCanada

Toronto: History2
Owned by: Corus Entertainment Inc.*
121 Bloor St. East, Toronto, ON M4S 3M5
Toll-Free: 866-447-8353
feedback@historytelevision.ca
www.history.ca

Toronto: Hollywood Suite 2000s Movies
Owned by: Hollywood Suite Inc.*
#200, 186 St George St., Toronto, ON M5R 2N3
info@hollywoodsuite.ca
hollywoodsuite.ca

Toronto: Hollywood Suite 70s Movies
Owned by: Hollywood Suite Inc.*
#200, 186 St George St., Toronto, ON M5R 2N3
info@hollywoodsuite.ca
hollywoodsuite.ca

---

* For details on this company see listing in Major Broadcasting Companies section; † French language station

Toronto: Hollywood Suite 80s Movies
Owned by: Hollywood Suite Inc.*
#200, 186 St George St., Toronto, ON M5R 2N3
info@hollywoodsuite.ca
hollywoodsuite.ca

Toronto: Hollywood Suite 90s Movies
Owned by: Hollywood Suite Inc.*
#200, 186 St George St., Toronto, ON M5R 2N3
info@hollywoodsuite.ca
hollywoodsuite.ca

Toronto: HPItv Canada
555 Rexdale Blvd., Toronto, ON M9W 5L2
Tel: 416-675-8886, Fax: 416-213-2130
Toll-Free: 888-675-8886
support@hpibet.com
www.hpibet.com/About/HPItv
twitter.com/hpibet

Toronto: HPItv International
555 Rexdale Blvd., Toronto, ON M9W 5L2
Tel: 416-675-8886, Fax: 416-213-2130
Toll-Free: 888-675-8886
support@hpibet.com
www.hpibet.com/About/HPItv
twitter.com/hpibet

Toronto: HPItv West
555 Rexdale Blvd., Toronto, ON M9W 5L2
Tel: 416-675-8886, Fax: 416-213-2130
Toll-Free: 888-675-8886
support@hpibet.com
www.hpibet.com/About/HPItv
twitter.com/hpibet

Toronto: Investigation Discovery
Owned by: Bell Media Inc.*
9 Channel Nine Ct., Toronto, ON M1S 4B5
www.ctv.ca/investigation-discovery
www.facebook.com/InvestigationDiscovery,
twitter.com/IDdiscoveryCa

Toronto: Love Nature
Owned by: Blue Ant Media*
130 Merton St., Toronto, ON M4S 1A4
Tel: 416-646-4431, Fax: 416-646-4444
feedback@blueantmedia.ca
tv.lovenature.com
www.youtube.com/c/lovenature,
www.facebook.com/LoveNatureCanada
Daniela Santia, Contact, Publicity/Media,
daniela.santia@blueantmedia.ca

Toronto: Makeful
Owned by: Blue Ant Media*
#200, 130 Merton St., Toronto, ON M4S 1A4
Tel: 416-646-4431, Fax: 416-646-4444
feedback@blueantmedia.ca
tv.bemakeful.com
www.youtube.com/c/bemakeful, www.facebook.com/bemakeful

Toronto: Mediaset Italia
Owned by: TLN Media Group Inc.*
901 Lawrence Ave. West, 2nd Fl., Toronto, ON M6A 1C3
Tel: 416-744-8200
info@tlntv.com
mediasetitalia.ca

Toronto: Mediaset TGCOM 24
Owned by: TLN Media Group Inc.*
901 Lawrence Ave. West, 2nd Fl., Toronto, ON M6A 1C3
Tel: 416-744-8200
info@tlntv.com
tgcom24.ca

Toronto: MEGA Cosmos Canada
Owned by: Odyssey Television Network, Inc.*
#300, 437 Danforth Ave., Toronto, ON M4K 1P1
info@odysseytv.ca
odysseytv.ca

Toronto: MTV Canada
Owned by: Bell Media Inc.*
299 Queen St. West, Toronto, ON M5V 2Z5
www.ctv.ca/mtv
www.facebook.com/MTVCanada, twitter.com/mtvcanada

Toronto: MTV2
Owned by: Bell Media Inc.*
299 Queen St. West, Toronto, ON M5V 2Z5
www.mtv.ca
www.facebook.com/mtv2, twitter.com/MTV2

Toronto: Much
Owned by: Bell Media Inc.*
299 Queen St. West, Toronto, ON M5V 2Z5
Fax: 416-384-6824
contactmuch@bellmedia.ca
www.ctv.ca/much
www.youtube.com/c/MuchOfficial, twitter.com/Much
Other information: TTY: 416-340-7207

Toronto: National Geographic Channel HD
Owned by: Corus Entertainment Inc.*
121 Bloor St. East, Toronto, ON M4S 3M5
Toll-Free: 866-447-8353
feedback@nationalgeographic.ca
www.natgeotv.com/ca/hd

Toronto: NBA TV Canada
Owned by: Rogers Communications Inc.*
#500, 50 Bay St., Toronto, ON M5J 2L2
Tel: 416-366-3865
www.nba.com/raptors

Toronto: Nickelodeon
Owned by: Corus Entertainment Inc.*
Corus Quay, 25 Dockside Dr., Toronto, ON M5A 0B5
Tel: 416-479-7000
info@nickcanada.com
www.nickcanada.com

Toronto: Odyssey
Owned by: Odyssey Television Network, Inc.*
#300, 437 Danforth Ave., Toronto, ON M4K 1P1
info@odysseytv.ca
odysseytv.ca

Toronto: OLN
Owned by: Rogers Media Inc.*
545 Lake Shore Blvd., Toronto, ON M5V 1A3
Tel: 416-260-0060
www.oln.ca

Toronto: One
Owned by: ZoomerMedia Ltd.*
64 Jefferson Ave., Toronto, ON M6K 1Y4
Tel: 416-368-3194, Fax: 416-368-9774
Toll-Free: 888-321-2567
www.onetv.ca
www.facebook.com/onetvca, twitter.com/OneTVca

Toronto: Ontario Legislature Broadcast & Recording Service
Legislative Bldg., Queen's Park, #453, 111 Wellesley St. West, Toronto, ON M7A 1A2
Tel: 416-325-7900, Fax: 416-325-7916
www.ola.org

Toronto: Rewind
Owned by: Channel Zero Inc.*
PO Box 6143 A, Toronto, ON M5W 1P6
Tel: 416-492-1595, Fax: 416-492-9539
info@watchrewind.com
www.watchrewind.com
Www.facebook.com/watchrewind, twitter.com/watchrewind

Toronto: Salt & Light Catholic Media Foundation
#300, 250 Davisville Ave., Toronto, ON M4S 1H2
Tel: 416-971-5353, Fax: 41-697-1673
Toll-Free: 888-302-7181
info@saltandlighttv.org
slmedia.org
www.youtube.com/c/SaltandLightMedia,
www.facebook.com/saltandlighttv, twitter.com/saltandlighttv
Alan J. Fogarty, Chief Executive Officer

Toronto: Silver Screen Classics
Owned by: Channel Zero Inc.*
2844 Dundas St. West, Toronto, ON M6P 1Y7
Tel: 416-492-1595, Fax: 416-492-9539
info@silverscreenclassics.com
www.silverscreenclassics.com

Toronto: Smithsonian Channel
Owned by: Blue Ant Media*
#200, 130 Merton St., Toronto, ON M4S 1A4
Tel: 416-646-4431, Fax: 416-646-4444
feedback@blueantmedia.ca
www.smithsonianchannel.ca
www.youtube.com/user/smithsoniantvcanada,
www.facebook.com/SmithsonianChannelCanada,
twitter.com/smithsoniantvca

Toronto: The Sports Network
Owned by: Bell Media Inc.*
9 Channel Nine Ct., Toronto, ON M1S 4B5
www.tsn.ca
www.youtube.com/user/TSNCanada, www.facebook.com/TSN,
twitter.com/TSN_Sports

Toronto: Sportsnet
Owned by: Rogers Media Inc.*
1 Mount Pleasant Rd., Toronto, ON M4Y 3A1
Toll-Free: 888-451-6363
feedback@sportsnet.rogers.com
www.sportsnet.ca
www.youtube.com/c/sportsnet, www.facebook.com/sportsnet,
twitter.com/sportsnet

Toronto: Starz
Owned by: Bell Media Inc.*
c/o Bell Media, 299 Queen St. West, Toronto, ON M5V 2Z5
Toll-Free: 800-565-6684
www.starz.ca
www.facebook.com/STARZCA, twitter.com/StarzCA

Toronto: T+E
Owned by: Blue Ant Media*
#200, 130 Merton St., Toronto, ON M4S 1A4
Tel: 416-646-4434, Fax: 416-646-4444
feedback@blueantmedia.ca
www.tandetv.com
www.youtube.com/travelandescape, www.facebook.com/TETV,
twitter.com/teontv
Daniela Santia, Contact, Publicity/Media,
Daniela.Santia@blueantmedia.ca

Toronto: Telebimbi
Owned by: TLN Media Group Inc.*
901 Lawrence Ave. West, 2nd Fl., Toronto, ON M6A 1C3
Tel: 416-744-8200
info@tlntv.com
telebimbi.ca

Toronto: TeleNiños
Owned by: TLN Media Group Inc.*
901 Lawrence Ave. West, 2nd Fl., Toronto, ON M6A 1C3
Tel: 416-744-8200
info@tlntv.com
teleninos.ca

Toronto: TLN
Owned by: TLN Media Group Inc.*
901 Lawrence Ave. West, 2nd Fl., Toronto, ON M6A 1C3
Tel: 416-744-8200
info@tlnmediagroup.com
www.tln.ca
www.facebook.com/TLNTelevision, twitter.com/tlntv

Toronto: Univision Canada
Owned by: TLN Media Group Inc.*
901 Lawrence Ave. West, 2nd Fl., Toronto, ON M6A 1C3
Tel: 416-744-8200
info@tlnmediagroup.com
univision.ca
www.linkedin.com/showcase/univision-canada,
www.facebook.com/UnivisionCanada,
twitter.com/univisioncanada

Toronto: Vision TV
Owned by: ZoomerMedia Ltd.*
64 Jefferson Ave., Toronto, ON M6K 1Y4
Tel: 416-368-3194, Fax: 416-368-9774
Toll-Free: 888-321-2567
audience@visiontv.ca
www.visiontv.ca
www.facebook.com/visiontelevision, twitter.com/visiontv
Other information: TTY: 416-216-6311

Toronto: W Network Inc.
Owned by: Corus Entertainment Inc.*
Corus Quay, 35 Dockside Dr., Toronto, ON M5A 0B5
www.wnetwork.com
www.instagram.com/w_network, www.facebook.com/wnetwork,
twitter.com/w_network

---

* For details on this company see listing in Major Broadcasting Companies section; † French language station

Québec

†*Montréal:* **AMI-télé**
Détenteur: **Accessible Media Inc.***
#1500, 625, boul René-Lévesque ouest, Montréal, QC H3B 1R2
Ligne sans frais: 844-398-0947
amitele@ami.ca
www.amitele.ca/new_tele
www.youtube.com/c/AMItélé1, www.facebook.com/amitele, twitter.com/Amitele1

†*Montréal:* **Canal D**
Détenteur: **Bell Media Inc.***
1717, boul René-Lévesque est, Montréal, QC H2L 4T9
Tél: 514-983-3330, *Ligne sans frais:* 800-361-5194
www.noovo.ca/canal-d
www.facebook.com/CanalD

Montréal: **Canal Indigo**
Owned by: Vidéotron
612, rue St-Jacques ouest, 4e étage, Montréal, QC H3C 4M8
info@canalindigo.com
www.canalindigo.com

†*Montréal:* **Canal Vie**
Détenteur: **Bell Media Inc.***
1717, boul René-Lévesque est, Montréal, QC H2L 4T9
canalvie@bellmedia.ca
www.noovo.ca/canal-vie
www.facebook.com/canalvie, twitter.com/CanalVie

†*Montréal:* **ELLE Fictions**
Détenteur: **Groupe Remstar Média***
#602, 355, rue Ste-Catherine ouest, Montréal, QC H3B 1A5
Tél: 514-284-2222
ellefictions.ca
www.facebook.com/ELLEFictions

†*Montréal:* **Historia**
Détenteur: **Corus Entertainment Inc.***
#1000, 4200, boul St-Laurent, Montréal, QC H2W 2R2
Tél: 514-904-4099, *Ligne sans frais:* 855-904-4099
auditoirehistoria@corusmedia.com
www.historiatv.com
www.facebook.com/historiatv

†*Montréal:* **Max**
Détenteur: **Groupe Remstar Média***
#602, 355, rue Ste-Catherine ouest, Montréal, QC H3B 1A5
Tél: 514-284-2222
maxtele.ca
www.facebook.com/MAX.chainetv, twitter.com/Max_chainetv

†*Montréal:* **MétéoMédia**
1755, boul René-Lévesque est, Montréal, QC H2K 4P6
Tél: 514-597-0232, *Téléc:* 514-597-0426
www.meteomedia.com
www.youtube.com/c/meteomedia
www.facebook.com/meteomedia, twitter.com/meteomedia

†*Montréal:* **RDI - Le réseau de l'information**
Détenteur: **Canadian Broadcasting Corporation***
CP 6000, Montréal, QC H3C 3A8
Tél: 514-597-5000
ici.radio-canada.ca/rdi
www.youtube.com/user/RadioCanadainfo,
www.facebook.com/radiocanada.info,
twitter.com/RadioCanadaInfo

†*Montréal:* **Le Réseau des Sports**
Détenteur: **Bell Media Inc.***
#300, 1755, boul René-Lévesque est, Montréal, QC H2K 4P6
Tél: 514-599-2244, *Téléc:* 514-599-2299
Ligne sans frais: 888-737-6363
info@rds.ca
www.rds.ca
www.youtube.com/user/rdsca, www.facebook.com/RDS, twitter.com/rdsca
Gerry Frappier, Président et directeur général

†*Montréal:* **Savoir média**
1121, av de Lorimier, Montréal, QC H2K 3V9
Tél: 514-509-2222, *Téléc:* 514-509-2299
Ligne sans frais: 888-640-2626
info@savoir.media
savoir.media
www.facebook.com/savoir.media, twitter.com/savoir_media
Marie Collin, Présidente
Nadine Dufour, Directrice générale, ndufour@savoir.media

†*Montréal:* **Séries+**
Détenteur: **Corus Entertainment Inc.***
#1000, 4200, boul St-Laurent, Montréal, QC H2W 2R2
Tél: 514-904-4099, *Ligne sans frais:* 855-904-4099
auditoireseriesplus@corusmedia.com
www.seriesplus.com
www.youtube.com/c/SériesPlusTV,
www.facebook.com/seriesplus

†*Montréal:* **TV5 Québec Canada**
460, rue Saint-Paul est, Montréal, QC H2Y 3V1
Tél: 514-522-5322
info@tv5.ca
tv5quebeccanada.ca
www.linkedin.com/company/tv5-qu-bec-canada,
www.facebook.com/TV5.ca, twitter.com/TV5ca

Marie-Philippe Bouchard, Présidente/Directrice générale

†*Montréal:* **TV5 Unis**
460, rue Saint-Paul est, Montréal, QC H2Y 3V1
info@tv5.ca
www.tv5unis.ca
www.youtube.com/c/UnisCanada, www.facebook.com/unistv

†*Montréal:* **Z**
Détenteur: **Bell Media Inc.***
1717, boul René-Lévesque Est, Montréal, QC H2L 4T9
Tél: 514-938-3330, *Ligne sans frais:* 800-361-5194
www.noovo.ca/z
www.facebook.com/ztele

†*Québec:* **Assemblée nationale du Québec - Canal de l'Assemblée**
Édifice Jean-Antoine-Panet, 1020, rue des Parlementaires, Québec, QC G1A 1A3
Tél: 418-643-1992, *Téléc:* 418-644-3593
Ligne sans frais: 866-337-8837
diffusion.debats@assnat.qc.ca
www.assnat.qc.ca

†*Saguenay:* **CJPM-DT**
Détenteur: **Groupe TVA inc.***
Saguenay, QC
www.tvanouvelles.ca/regional/tva-saguenay-lac-st-jean

Saskatchewan

Emerald Park: **The Rural Channel**
Owned by: Ag-Com Productions Ltd.*
19 McLeod Rd., Emerald Park, SK S4L 1B7
Tel: 780-444-1518
www.theruralchannel.com
www.facebook.com/TheRuralChannel,
twitter.com/TheRuralChannel

Regina: **Saskatchewan Legislative Network**
2405 Legislative Dr., Regina, SK S4S 0B3
Tel: 306-787-7722
helpdesk@legassembly.sk.ca
www.legassembly.sk.ca

* For details on this company see listing in Major Broadcasting Companies section; † French language station

SECTION 5

BUSINESS & FINANCE

The listings in this section are arranged alphabetically unless otherwise indicated below.

CANADIAN ALMANAC & DIRECTORY
RÉPERTOIRE ET ALMANACH CANADIEN

Major Accounting Firms

Baker Tilly Canada Cooperative
#4, 180 Northfield Dr. West
Waterloo, ON N2L 0C7

info@bakertilly.ca
www.bakertilly.ca
www.facebook.com/BakerTillyCanada; twitter.com/bakertillycan;
www.linkedin.com/company/baker-tilly-canada

Former Name: Collins Barrow National Cooperative
Incorporated
Ownership: An independent member of Baker Tilly
International, UK
Executives:
Ted Verkade, Chief Executive Officer, Baker Tilly International
Affiliated Companies:
Baker Tilly CK, LLP
Baker Tilly Durham LLP
Baker Tilly GWD
Baker Tilly Gatineau Inc.
Baker Tilly HKC Kapuskasing
Baker Tilly HMA LLP
Baker Tilly KDN LLP
Baker Tilly Montréal S.E.N.C.R.L/LLP
Baker Tilly Nova Scotia Inc.
Baker Tilly Ottawa LLP
Baker Tilly REO LLP
Baker Tilly Revelstoke
Baker Tilly Rockies LLP
Baker Tilly SGB LLP
Baker Tilly SK LLP
Baker Tilly SNT LLP
Baker Tilly Sarnia LLP
Baker Tilly Trillium LLP
Baker Tilly Vaughan LLP
Baker Tilly Victoria Ltd.
Baker Tilly WM LLP
Baker Tilly Windsor LLP
Offices:
Dartmouth
#201, 130 Eileen Stubbs Ave.
Dartmouth, NS B3B 2C4
Tel: 902-404-4000
Vaughan
#600, 3300 Hwy. 7 West
Vaughan, ON L4K 4M3

BDO Canada LLP
#500, 20 Wellington St. East
Toronto, ON M5E 1C5

Tel: 416-865-0111; *Fax:* 416-367-3912
info@bdo.ca
www.bdo.ca
www.youtube.com/c/BDOCanada;
www.facebook.com/BDOCanada; twitter.com/BDO_Canada;
www.linkedin.com/company/bdo-canada

Former Name: BDO Dunwoody LLP
Ownership: Private. A member of BDO International Limited,
UK
Year Founded: 1921
Number of Employees: 4,300+
Revenues: $682,900,000 Year End: 20191231
Profile: BDO is of Canada's largest accounting firms, focusing
on independent businesses & community-based organizations.
The firm provides a full range of business advisory services.
Executives:
Pat Kramer, Chief Executive Officer; pkramer@bdo.ca
Everett Chubbs, Chief Information Officer; echubbs@bdo.ca
Alicia DeFreitas, Chief Human Resources Officer;
adefreitas@bdo.ca
Mary Parkes, Chief Financial Officer; mparkes@bdo.ca
Neil Shankman, Chief Marketing Officer; nshankman@bdo.ca
Dave Simkins, Chief Operating Officer; dsimkins@bdo.ca
Affiliated Companies:
BDO Canada Limited
Offices:
Alexandria
55 Anik St.
Alexandria, ON K0C 1A0 Canada
Tel: 613-525-1585; *Fax:* 613-525-1436
alexandria@bdo.ca
Alliston
#13-14, 169 Dufferin St. South
Alliston, ON L9R 1E6 Canada
Tel: 705-435-5585; *Fax:* 705-435-5587
alliston@bdo.ca
Altona
#1, 45 - 4th Ave. NE
Altona, MB R0G 0B1 Canada
Tel: 204-324-8653; *Fax:* 204-324-1629
pembinavalley@bdo.ca

Athabasca
4917- 49 St.
Athabasca, AB T9S 1C5 Canada
Tel: 780-675-2397; *Fax:* 780-461-8800
athabasca@bdo.ca
Barrie
#201, 15 Sperling Dr.
Barrie, ON L4M 6K9 Canada
Tel: 705-797-3999
barriesred@bdo.ca
Barrie - Lakeshore Dr.
#300, 300 Lakeshore Dr.
Barrie, ON L4N 0B4 Canada
Tel: 705-726-6331; *Fax:* 705-722-6588
barrie@bdo.ca
Barrie - Sperling Dr.
#201, 15 Sperling Dr.
Barrie, ON L4M 6K9 Canada
Tel: 705-797-3999
barriesred@bdo.ca
Bedford
#101, 1496 Bedford Hwy.
Bedford, NS B4A 1E5 Canada
Tel: 902-444-5540; *Fax:* 902-444-5539
bedford@bdo.ca
Boissevain
PO Box 60
316 South Railway St.
Boissevain, MB R0K 0E0 Canada
Tel: 204-534-6040; *Fax:* 204-534-6042
boissevain@bdo.ca
Bracebridge
#1, 239 Manitoba St.
Bracebridge, ON P1L 1S2 Canada
Tel: 705-645-5215; *Fax:* 705-645-8125
bracebridge@bdo.ca
Brandon
148 - 10th St.
Brandon, MB R7A 4E6 Canada
Tel: 204-727-0671; *Fax:* 204-726-4580
brandon@bdo.ca
Brantford
#1, 505 Park Rd. North
Brantford, ON N3R 7K8 Canada
Tel: 519-759-8320; *Fax:* 519-759-8421
brantford@bdo.ca
Bridgewater
#102, 215 Dominion St.
Bridgewater, NS B4V 2K7 Canada
Tel: 902-543-7373; *Fax:* 902-543-9941
bridgewater@bdo.ca
Burlington
#400, 3115 Harvester Rd.
Burlington, ON L7N 3N8 Canada
Tel: 905-639-9500; *Fax:* 905-633-4939
burlington@bdo.ca
Calgary
#620, 903 - 8 Ave. SW
Calgary, AB T2P 0P7 Canada
Tel: 403-266-5608; *Fax:* 403-233-7833
calgary@bdo.ca
Cambridge
#107, 231 Shearson Cres.
Cambridge, ON N1T 1J5 Canada
Tel: 519-622-7676; *Fax:* 519-622-7870
cambridge@bdo.ca
Cardston
259 Main St.
Cardston, AB T0K OKO Canada
Tel: 403-653-4137
cardston@bdo.ca
Charlottetown
PO Box 2158
#200, 155 Belvedere Ave.
Charlottetown, PE C1A 8B9 Canada
Tel: 902-892-5365; *Fax:* 902-892-0383
Chatham
PO Box 1195
155 Thames St.
Chatham, ON N7M 5L8 Canada
Tel: 519-352-4130; *Fax:* 519-352-2744
chatham@bdo.ca
Cobourg
PO Box 627
204 Division St.
Cobourg, ON K9A 3P7 Canada
Tel: 905-372-6863; *Fax:* 905-372-6650
cobourg@bdo.ca
Collingwood
#100, 40 Huron St.
Collingwood, ON L9Y 4R3 Canada
Tel: 705-445-4421; *Fax:* 705-445-6691
collingwood@bdo.ca

Corner Brook
#300, 50 Main St.
Corner Brook, NL A2H 1C4 Canada
Tel: 709-634-1590; *Fax:* 709-634-1599
Cornerbrook@bdo.ca
Cornwall
PO Box 644
113 Second St. East
Cornwall, ON K6H 1Y5 Canada
Tel: 613-932-8691; *Fax:* 613-932-7591
cornwall@bdo.ca
Cranbrook
#200, 35 - 10 Ave. South
Cranbrook, BC V1C 2M9 Canada
Tel: 250-426-4285; *Fax:* 250-426-8886
cranbrook@bdo.ca
Dryden
PO Box 3010
37 King St.
Dryden, ON P8N 1B4 Canada
Tel: 807-223-5321; *Fax:* 807-223-2978
dryden@bdo.ca
Edmonton
9897 - 34th Ave. NW
Edmonton, AB T6E 5X9 Canada
Tel: 780-461-8000; *Fax:* 780-461-8000
edmonton@bdo.ca
Embrun
PO Box 128
991 Limoges Rd.
Embrun, ON K0A 1W0 Canada
Tel: 613-443-5201; *Fax:* 613-443-2538
embrun@bdo.ca
Erickson
PO Box 214
19 - 1st St. SW
Erickson, MB R0J 0P0 Canada
Tel: 204-636-2925; *Fax:* 204-636-7789
erickson@bdo.ca
Essex
180 Talbot St. South
Essex, ON N8M 1B6 Canada
Tel: 519-776-6488; *Fax:* 519-776-6090
essex@bdo.ca
Exeter
#2, 145 Thames Rd. West
Exeter, ON N0M 1S3 Canada
Tel: 519-235-0281; *Fax:* 519-235-3367
exeter@bdo.ca
Fort Frances
375 Scott St.
Fort Frances, ON P9A 1H1 Canada
Tel: 807-274-9848; *Fax:* 807-274-5142
fortfrances@bdo.ca
Fraser Valley
#303, 15127 - 100th Ave.
Fraser Valley, BC V3R 0N9 Canada
Tel: 604-496-5080; *Fax:* 604-496-5081
fraservalley@bdo.ca
Gatineau
#200, 160, boul de l'Hopital
Gatineau, QC J8T 8J1 Canada
Tel: 819-561-1422; *Fax:* 819-561-2415
gatineau@bdo.ca
Grande Prairie
#200, 9805 - 97th St.
Grande Prairie, AB T8V 8B9 Canada
Tel: 780-539-7075; *Fax:* 780-538-1890
grandeprairie@bdo.ca
Grenville
289, rue Principale
Grenville, QC J0V 1V0 Canada
Tel: 819-242-8157; *Fax:* 819-242-0535
grenville@bdo.ca
Guelph
512 Woolwich St.
Guelph, ON N1H 3X7 Canada
Tel: 519-824-5410; *Fax:* 519-824-5497
Toll-Free: 877-236-4835
guelph@bdo.ca
Hanover
485 - 10th St.
Hanover, ON N4N 1R2 Canada
Tel: 519-364-3790; *Fax:* 519-364-5334
hanover@bdo.ca
Harrow
37 King St. West
Harrow, ON N0R 1G0 Canada
Tel: 519-738-2236; *Fax:* 519-738-3326
harrow@bod.ca

Huntsville
4 Elm St.
Huntsville, ON P1H 1L1 Canada
Tel: 705-789-4469; *Fax:* 705-789-1079
huntsville@bdo.ca
Invermere
Bldg. 2
906 - 8th Ave., Lower Level
Invermere, BC V0A 1K0 Canada
Tel: 250-342-3383; *Fax:* 250-342-0248
invermere@bdo.ca
Kamloops
#300, 275 Landsdowne St.
Kamloops, BC V2C 6J3 Canada
Tel: 250-372-9505; *Fax:* 250-374-6323
kamloops@bdo.ca
Kelowna
#400, 1631 Dickson Ave.
Kelowna, BC V1Y 0B5 Canada
Tel: 250-763-6700; *Fax:* 250-763-4457
kelowna@bdo.ca
Kenora
#300, 301 First Ave. South
Kenora, ON P9N 4E9 Canada
Tel: 807-468-5531; *Fax:* 807-468-9774
kenora@bdo.ca
Kincardine
970 Queen St.
Kincardine, ON N2Z 2Y2 Canada
Tel: 519-396-3425; *Fax:* 519-396-9829
kincardine@bdo.ca
Kitchener
#201, 150 Caroline St. South
Kitchener, ON N2L 0A5 Canada
Tel: 519-576-5220; *Fax:* 519-576-5471
kitchenerwaterloo@bdo.ca
Lacombe
5820B Hwy. 2A
Lacombe, AB T4L 2G5 Canada
Tel: 780-782-3361; *Fax:* 780-782-3070
lacombe@bdo.ca
Langley
#220, 19916 - 64th Ave.
Langley, BC V2Y 1A2 Canada
Tel: 604-534-8691; *Fax:* 604-534-8900
langley@bdo.ca
Lethbridge
#600, 400 - 4th Ave. South
Lethbridge, AB T1J 4E1 Canada
Tel: 403-328-5292; *Fax:* 403-328-9534
lethbridge@bdo.ca
Lindsay
PO Box 358
165 Kent St. West
Lindsay, ON K9V 4S3 Canada
Tel: 705-324-3579; *Fax:* 705-324-0774
lindsay@bdo.ca
Liverpool
50 Water St.
Liverpool, NS B0T 1K0 Canada
Tel: 902-354-5706; *Fax:* 902-354-2467
liverpool@bdo.ca
London
#300, 633 Colborne St.
London, ON N6B 2V3 Canada
Tel: 519-672-8940; *Fax:* 519-672-5562
london@bdo.ca
MacGregor
78 Hampton St.
MacGregor, MB R0H 0R0 Canada
Tel: 204-685-2323; *Fax:* 204-685-2341
macgregor@bdo.ca
Manitou
330 Main St.
Manitou, MB R0G 1G0 Canada
pembinavalley@bdo.ca
Manotick
PO Box 978
5494 Manotick Main St.
Manotick, ON K4M 1A8 Canada
Tel: 613-692-3501; *Fax:* 613-692-2874
manotick@bdo.ca
Markham
#300, 60 Columbia Way
Markham, ON L3R 0C9 Canada
Tel: 905-946-1066; *Fax:* 905-946-9524
markham@bdo.ca
Marystown
PO Box 488
170 McGettigan Blvd.
Marystown, NL A0E 2M0 Canada
Tel: 709-279-7878; *Fax:* 709-279-7883
Marystown@bdo.ca

Minnedosa
39 Main St. South
Minnedosa, MB R0J 1E0 Canada
Tel: 204-867-2957; *Fax:* 204-867-5021
minnedosa@bdo.ca
Mississauga
#1700, 1 City Centre Dr.
Mississauga, ON L5B 1M2 Canada
Tel: 905-270-7700; *Fax:* 905-671-7915
mississauga@bdo.ca
Mitchell
PO Box 792
235 St. George St.
Mitchell, ON N0K 1N0 Canada
Tel: 519-348-8412; *Fax:* 519-348-4300
mitchell@bdo.ca
Montréal - Cremazie
#805, 1100, boul Cremazie est
Montréal, QC H2P 2X2 Canada
Tel: 514-729-3221; *Fax:* 514-593-8711
northmontreal@bdo.ca
Montréal - Gauchetiere
#200, 1000, rue de la Gauchetiere ouest
Montréal, QC H3B 4W5 Canada
Tel: 514-931-0841; *Fax:* 514-931-9491
montreal@bdo.ca
Montréal - Sherbrooke
#2600, 1002, rue Sherbrooke
Montréal, QC H3A 3L6 Canada
Tel: 514-845-8657; *Fax:* 514-845-9985
Mount Forest
PO Box 418
191 Main St. South
Mount Forest, ON N0G 2L0 Canada
Tel: 519-323-2351; *Fax:* 519-323-3661
mountforest@bco.ca
Nakusp
PO Box 1078
87 - 3rd Ave.
Nakusp, BC V0G 1R0 Canada
Tel: 250-265-4750; *Fax:* 250-265-3220
nakusp@bdo.ca
Newmarket
Gates of York Plaza
#2, 17310 Yonge St.
Newmarket, ON L3Y 7R8 Canada
Tel: 905-898-1221; *Fax:* 905-898-0028
Toll-Free: 866-275-8836
newmarket@bdo.ca
North Bay
#301, 101 McIntyre St. West
North Bay, ON P1B 2Y5 Canada
Fax: 705-495-2001
Toll-Free: 800-461-6324
northbay@bdo.ca
Norwich
PO Box 190
8 Stover St. North
Norwich, ON N0J 1P0 Canada
Tel: 519-863-3126; *Fax:* 519-863-3756
norwich@bdo.ca
Orangeville
77 Broadway Ave.
Orangeville, ON L9W 1K1
Tel: 519-938-8630; *Fax:* 519-372-0189
orangeville@bdodebthelp.ca
Orillia
PO Box 670
19 Front St. North
Orillia, ON L3V 4R6 Canada
Tel: 705-325-1386; *Fax:* 705-325-6649
orillia@bdo.ca
Oshawa
Oshawa Executive Centre
#502, 419 King St. West
Oshawa, ON L1J 2K5 Canada
Tel: 905-576-3430; *Fax:* 905-436-9138
oshawa@bdo.ca
Ottawa - St. Laurent Blvd.
#100, 1730 St-Laurent Blvd.
Ottawa, ON K1G 5L1 Canada
Tel: 613-739-8221; *Fax:* 613-739-1517
ottawa@bdo.ca
Ottawa - Slater St.
275 Slater St., 20th Fl.
Ottawa, ON K1P 5H9 Canada
Tel: 613-237-9331; *Fax:* 613-237-9779
ottawagsl@bdo.ca

Owen Sound
PO Box 397
1717 - 2nd Ave. East
Owen Sound, ON N4K 6V4 Canada
Tel: 519-376-6110; *Fax:* 519-376-4741
owensound@bdo.ca
Pembina Valley
Stanley Business Centre
PO Box 1357
3-23111 PTH 14
Winkler, MB R6W 4B3 Canada
Tel: 204-325-4787; *Fax:* 204-325-8040
pembinavalley@bdo.ca
Penticton
#102, 100 Front St.
Penticton, BC V2A 1H1 Canada
Tel: 250-492-6020; *Fax:* 250-492-8110
penticton@bdo.ca
Peterborough
PO Box 1018
#202, 201 George St. North
Peterborough, ON K9J 7A5 Canada
Tel: 705-742-4271; *Fax:* 705-742-3420
Toll-Free: 888-369-6600
peterborough@bdo.ca
Petrolia
PO Box 869
4495 Petrolia Line
Petrolia, ON N0N 1R0 Canada
Tel: 519-882-3333; *Fax:* 519-882-2703
petrolia@bdo.ca
Picture Butte
325 Highway Ave.
Picture Butte, AB T0K 1V0 Canada
Tel: 403-732-4469; *Fax:* 403-732-5071
picturebutte@bdo.ca
Port Elgin
PO Box 1390
625 Mill St.
Port Elgin, ON N0H 2C0 Canada
Tel: 519-832-2049; *Fax:* 519-832-5659
portelgin@bdo.ca
Portage La Prairie
480 Saskatchewan Ave. West
Portage La Prairie, MB R1N 0M4 Canada
Tel: 204-857-2856; *Fax:* 204-239-1664
portagelaprairie@bdo.ca
Québec
Édifice Le Delta 3
#650, 2875, boul Laurier
Québec, QC G1V 2M2 Canada
Tel: 418-658-6915; *Fax:* 418-658-4008
quebecity@bdo.ca
Red Deer
Millenium Centre
#600, 4909 - 49th St.
Red Deer, AB T4N 1V1 Canada
Fax: 403-343-3070
Toll-Free: 800-661-1269
reddeer@bdo.ca
Red Lake
PO Box 234
#207, 14 Discovery Rd.
Red Lake, ON P0V 2M0 Canada
Tel: 807-727-3227; *Fax:* 807-727-1172
redlake@bdo.ca
Revelstoke
PO Box 2100
#202, 103 - 1st St. East
Revelstoke, BC V0E 2S0 Canada
Tel: 250-837-5225; *Fax:* 250-837-7170
revelstoke@bdo.ca
Ridgetown
211 Main St. East
Ridgetown, ON N0P 2C0 Canada
Tel: 519-674-5418; *Fax:* 519-674-5410
ridgetown@bdo.ca
Rimbey
PO Box 1080
5059 - 50th Ave.
Rimbey, AB T0C 2J0 Canada
Tel: 780-843-2208; *Fax:* 780-843-4611
rimbey@bdo.ca
Rockland
#5, 2784 Laurier St.
Rockland, ON K4K 1A2 Canada
Tel: 613-446-6497; *Fax:* 613-446-7117
rockland@bdo.ca

Saint-Claude
c/o Caisse Populaire St. Claude Ltée
76 First St.
St-Claude, MB R0G 1Z0 Canada
Tel: 204-379-2332; *Toll-Free:* 800-268-3337
stclaude@bdo.ca

St. John's
PO Box 8505
#200, 53 Bond St.
St. John's, NL A1B 3N9 Canada
Tel: 709-279-7878; *Fax:* 709-579-2120
stjohns@bdo.ca

Salmon Arm
#201, 571 - 6th St. NE
Salmon Arm, BC V1E 1R6 Canada
Tel: 250-832-7171; *Fax:* 250-832-2429
salmonarm@bdo.ca

Sarnia
Kenwick Place
PO Box 730
250 Christina St. North
Sarnia, ON N7T 7V3 Canada
Tel: 519-336-9900; *Fax:* 519-332-4828
sarnia@bdo.ca

Sault Ste Marie
PO Box 1109
747 Queen St. East
Sault Ste Marie, ON P6A 2A8 Canada
Tel: 705-945-0990; *Fax:* 705-942-7979
ssm@bdo.ca

Shediac
343 Main St., #B
Shediac, NB E4P 2B3 Canada
Tel: 506-533-9082; *Fax:* 506-532-9068
shediac@bdo.ca

Sherbrooke
2986, ch. Sainte-Catherine
Sherbrooke, QC J1N 3X9 Canada
Tel: 819-566-8064; *Fax:* 819-566-8020

Sioux Lookout
PO Box 1239
#1A, 76 1/2 Front St.
Sioux Lookout, ON P8T 1B8 Canada
Tel: 807-737-1500; *Fax:* 807-737-4443
siouxlookout@bdo.ca

Slave Lake
PO Box 297
#303, Lakeland Centre
Slave Lake, AB T0G 2A0 Canada
Tel: 780-849-3622; *Fax:* 780-849-3625
slavelake@bdo.ca

Squamish
PO Box 168
#202, 38147 Cleveland Ave.
Squamish, BC V8B 0A2 Canada
Tel: 604-892-9424; *Fax:* 604-892-9356
squamish@bdo.ca

Stratford
380 Hibernia St.
Stratford, ON N5A 5W3 Canada
Tel: 519-271-2491; *Fax:* 519-271-4013
stratford@bdo.ca

Strathroy
425 Caradoc St. South, #E
Strathroy, ON N7G 2P5 Canada
Tel: 519-245-1913; *Fax:* 519-245-5987
strathroy@bdo.ca

Sudbury
#4, 754 Falconbridge Rd.
Sudbury, ON P3A 5X5 Canada
Tel: 705-671-3336; *Fax:* 705-671-9552
Toll-Free: 877-820-0404
sudbury@bdo.ca

Summerside
PO Box 1347
107 Walker Ave.
Summerside, PE C1N 4K2 Canada
Tel: 902-436-2171; *Fax:* 902-436-0960
summerside@bdo.ca

Thunder Bay
1095 Barton St.
Thunder Bay, ON P7B 5N3 Canada
Tel: 807-625-4444; *Fax:* 807-623-8460
thunderbay@bdo.ca

Toronto - Wellington St. West
TD Bank Tower
PO Box 131
#3600, 66 Wellington St. West
Toronto, ON M5K 1H1 Canada
Tel: 416-865-0200; *Fax:* 416-865-0887
toronto@bdo.ca

Treherne
274 Railway Ave.
Treherne, MB R0G 2V0 Canada
Tel: 204-723-2454
treherne@bdo.ca

Uxbridge
#1, 1 Brock St. East
Uxbridge, ON L9P 1P6 Canada
Tel: 905-852-9714; *Fax:* 905-852-9898
uxbridge@bdo.ca

Vancouver
Cathedral Place
#600, 925 West Georgia St.
Vancouver, BC V6L 3L2 Canada
Tel: 604-688-5421; *Fax:* 604-688-5132
vancouver@bdo.ca

Vernon
#202, 2706 - 30th Ave.
Vernon, BC V1T 2B6 Canada
Tel: 250-545-2136; *Fax:* 250-545-3364
vernon@bdo.ca

Victoria
#500, 1803 Douglas St.
Victoria, BC V8T 5C3 Canada
Tel: 250-383-0426; *Fax:* 250-383-1091
victoria@bdo.ca

Virden
PO Box 1900
255 Wellington St. West
Virden, MB R0M 2C0 Canada
Tel: 204-748-1200; *Fax:* 204-748-1976
Toll-Free: 866-236-7656
virden@bdo.ca

Vulcan
122 Centre St.
Vulcan, AB T0L 2B0 Canada
Tel: 403-485-2923; *Fax:* 403-485-6098
vulcan@bdo.ca

Walkerton
PO Box 760
121 Jackson St.
Walkerton, ON N0G 2V0 Canada
Tel: 519-881-1211; *Fax:* 519-881-3530
walkerton@bdo.ca

Wetaskiwin
#103, 4725 - 56 St.
Wetaskiwin, AB T9A 3M2 Canada
Tel: 780-352-0808; *Fax:* 780-352-2970
wetaskiwin@bdo.ca

Whistler
#202, 1200 Alpha Lake Rd.
Whistler, BC V0N 1B1 Canada
Tel: 604-932-3799; *Fax:* 604-932-3764
whistler@bdo.ca

Whitehorse
202 - 9016 Quartz Rd.
Whitehorse, YT Y1A 2Z5 Canada
Tel: 867-667-7907; *Fax:* 867-668-3087
whitehorse@bdo.ca

Wiarton
PO Box 249
663 Berford St.
Wiarton, ON N0H 2T0 Canada
Tel: 519-534-1520; *Fax:* 519-534-3454
wiarton@bdo.ca

Windsor
Building 100
3630 Rhodes Dr.
Windsor, ON N8W 5A4 Canada
Tel: 519-944-6993; *Fax:* 519-944-6116
windsor@bdo.ca

Wingham
PO Box 1420
47 Alfred St. West
Wingham, ON N0G 2W0 Canada
Tel: 519-357-3231; *Fax:* 519-357-3230
wingham@bdo.ca

Winnipeg
Wawanesa Bldg.
#700, 200 Graham Ave.
Winnipeg, MB R3C 4L5 Canada
Tel: 204-956-7200; *Fax:* 204-926-7201
winnipeg@bdo.ca

Woodstock
94 Graham St.
Woodstock, ON N4S 6J7 Canada
Tel: 519-539-2081; *Fax:* 519-539-2571
woodstock@bdo.ca

Crowe MacKay LLP
#1100, 1177 West Hastings St.
Vancouver, BC V6E 4T5

Toll-Free: 844-522-7693
contactus@crowemackay.ca
www.crowe.com/ca/crowemackay
www.facebook.com/CroweMackay; twitter.com/CroweMacKay;
www.linkedin.com/company/crowemackay
Former Name: MacKay LLP
Ownership: A member of Crowe Global
Year Founded: 1969
Profile: Services provided include bookkeeping, audit &
accounting, taxation, corporate financing, executive financial
planning, microcomputer support, management consulting,
business investigation, valuation & litigation support, solvency &
restructuring, & international affiliations.
Executives:
Stefan Ferris, CEO, West Coast Offices, Managing Director;
stefan.ferris@crowemackay.ca
Bill Gill, Chief Operating Officer; bill.gill@crowemackay.ca
Affiliated Companies:
Crowe MacKay & Company Ltd.
Branches:
Calgary
Elveden House
#1700, 717 - 7th Ave. SW
Calgary, AB T2P 0Z3
Tel: 403-294-9292; *Fax:* 403-294-9262
Toll-Free: 866-599-9292
calgary@crowemackay.ca
Edmonton
Maulife Place
#2410, 10180 - 101st St.
Edmonton, AB T5J 3S4
Tel: 780-420-0626; *Fax:* 780-425-8780
Toll-Free: 800-622-5293
edmonton@crowemackay.ca
Kelowna
#500, 1620 Dickson Ave.
Kelowna, BC V1Y 9Y2
Tel: 250-763-5021; *Fax:* 250-763-3600
Toll-Free: 866-763-5021
kelowna@crowemackay.ca
Regina
#202, 2022 Cornwall St.
Regina, SK S4P 2K5
Tel: 306-347-2244
regina@crowemackay.ca
Sechelt
PO Box 1610
#200, 5710 Teredo St.
Sechelt, BC V0N 3A0
Tel: 604-697-9271; *Fax:* 604-885-3779
Toll-Free: 866-599-9292
sunshinecoast@crowemackay.ca
Surrey
#200, 5455 - 152nd St.
Surrey, BC V3S 5A5
Tel: 604-591-6181; *Fax:* 604-591-5676
wco@crowemackay.ca
Whitehorse
#200, 303 Strickland St.
Whitehorse, YT Y1A 2J9
Tel: 867-667-7651; *Fax:* 867-668-3797
whitehorse@crowemackay.ca
Yellowknife
PO Box 727
5103 - 51st St.
Yellowknife, NT X1A 2N5
Tel: 867-920-4404; *Fax:* 867-920-4135
Toll-Free: 866-920-4404
yellowknife@crowemackay.ca

Crowe Soberman LLP
#1100, 2 St Clair Ave. East
Toronto, ON M4T 2T5

Tel: 416-964-7633
www.crowe.com/ca/crowesoberman
Other Contact Information: Employment, Email:
hr@crowesoberman.com
www.youtube.com/user/CroweSoberman
www.facebook.com/crowesoberman;
twitter.com/crowesoberman;
www.linkedin.com/company/crowe-soberman
Former Name: Soberman LLP Chartered Accountants
Ownership: A member of Crowe Global
Year Founded: 1958
Profile: The firm provides services in accounting, auditing,
business valuation, corporate & personal bankruptcy, corporate
finance, corporate workout & turnaround strategies, due
diligence, ElderCare, estates & trusts, financial consulting,
forensic investigation litigation support, management services,

mergers & acquisitions, succession planning & tax (domestic & international), claims valuation & media services.
Executives:
Susan Hodkinson, Chief Operating Officer, HR Consulting Practice, Partner; susan.hodkinson@crowesoberman.com

Deloitte LLP
Bay Adelaide East
#200, 8 Adelaide St. West
Toronto, ON M5H 0A9

Tel: 416-601-6150; *Fax:* 416-601-6151
www2.deloitte.com/ca/en.html
www.youtube.com/c/DeloitteCA;
www.instagram.com/deloittecanada;
www.facebook.com/DeloitteCanada; twitter.com/deloittecanada;
www.linkedin.com/company/deloitte-canada
Former Name: Deloitte & Touche LLP
Also Known As: Deloitte Canada
Ownership: Private partnership; Deloitte in Canada is a member firm of Deloitte Touche Tohmatsu.
Year Founded: 1861
Number of Employees: 11,908
Revenues: $2,821,000,000 Year End: 20201231
Profile: Deloitte LLP provides auditing, tax, financial advisory, & consulting services. Deloitte's offices in Québec operate under the corporate name Deloitte S.E.N.C.R.L./s.r.l., a Quebec limited liability partnership.
Executives:
Anthony Viel, LLM, BEC, MAF, Chief Executive Officer; anviel@deloitte.ca
Linda Blair, Chief Experience Officer, Ontario, Managing Partner; lblair@deloitte.a
Tim Christmann, Chief Strategy & Innovation Officer; tchristmann@deloitte.ca
Iseo Pasquali, Chief Business & Financial Officer; ipasquali@deloitte.ca
Marc Perron, Chief Client Officer; mperron@deloitte.ca
Van Zorbas, Chief Culture & People Officer; vzorbas@deloitte.ca
Branches:
Alma
Complexe Jacques Gagnon
#110, 100, rue St-Joseph sud
Alma, QC G8B 7A6 Canada
Tel: 418-669-6969; *Fax:* 418-668-2966
Amos
#200, 101, av 1ère est
Amos, QC J9T 1H4 Canada
Tel: 819-732-8273; *Fax:* 819-732-9143
Bécancour
#107, 4825, rue Bouvet
Bécancour, QC G9H 1X5
Tel: 819-233-3355; *Fax:* 819-691-1213
Brossard
#200, 4605-A, boul Lapinière
Brossard, QC J4Z 3T5 Canada
Tel: 450-618-4270; *Fax:* 450-618-6420
Burlington
#200, 1005 Skyview Dr.
Burlington, ON L7P 5B1 Canada
Tel: 905-315-6770; *Fax:* 905-315-6700
Calgary
#700, 850 - 2nd St. SW
Calgary, AB T2P 0R8 Canada
Tel: 403-267-1700; *Fax:* 403-264-2871
Charlottetown
49 Pownal St.
Charlottetown, PE C1A 3W2
Tel: 506-455-4111
Chicoutimi
#400, 901, boul Talbot
Chicoutimi, QC G7H 0A1 Canada
Tel: 418-549-6650; *Fax:* 418-549-4694
Dolbeau-Mistassini
110, 8e av
Dolbeau-Mistassini, QC G8L 1Y9 Canada
Tel: 418-276-0133; *Fax:* 418-276-8559
Drummondville
212, rue Heriot
Drummondville, QC J2C 1J8 Canada
Tel: 819-477-6311; *Fax:* 819-477-9572
Edmonton
Manulife Place
#1500, 10180 - 101st St.
Edmonton, AB T5J 4K1 Canada
Tel: 780-421-3611; *Fax:* 780-421-3782
Farnham
149, rue Desjardins est
Farnham, QC J2N 2W6 Canada
Tel: 450-293-5327; *Fax:* 450-293-2817

Fredericton - Knowledge Park
10 Knowledge Park Dr.
Fredericton, NB E3C 2M7 Canada
Tel: 506-455-4111
Fredericton - Queen St.
#103, 334 Queen St.
Fredericton, NB E3B 1B2 Canada
Tel: 506-457-9091; *Fax:* 506-458-9358
Gatineau
#405, 200, rue Montcalm
Gatineau, QC JBY 3B5 Canada
Tel: 819-770-3221; *Fax:* 819-770-9662
Granby
190, rue Déragon
Granby, QC J2G 5H9 Canada
Tel: 450-372-3347; *Fax:* 450-372-8643
Halifax
Purdy's Wharf Tower II
#1500, 1969 Upper Water St.
Halifax, NS B3J 3R7 Canada
Tel: 902-422-8541; *Fax:* 902-423-5820
Havre-Saint-Pierre
902A, av Acara
Havre-Saint-Pierre, QC G0G 1P0 Canada
Tel: 418-538-1265; *Fax:* 418-538-1576
Hawkesbury
300 McGill St.
Hawkesbury, ON K6A 1P8 Canada
Tel: 613-632-4178; *Fax:* 613-632-7703
Jonquière
Complexe A E Fortin
2266, boul René-Lévesque
Jonquière, QC G7S 6C5 Canada
Tel: 418-542-9523; *Fax:* 418-542-8814
Kanata
#400, 515 Legget Dr.
Kanata, ON K2K 3G4 Canada
Tel: 613-254-6899; *Fax:* 613-599-4369
Kitchener
195 Joseph St.
Kitchener, ON N2G 1J6 Canada
Tel: 519-650-7600; *Fax:* 519-650-7601
La Sarre
226, 2e rue est
La Sarre, QC J9Z 2G9 Canada
Tel: 819-333-2392; *Fax:* 819-333-2517
Langley
#600, 8621 - 201 St.
Langley, BC V2Y 0G9
Tel: 604-534-7477; *Fax:* 604-534-4220
Laval
Les Tours Triomphe
#210, 2540, boul Daniel-Johnson
Laval, QC H7T 2S3 Canada
Tel: 514-978-3500; *Fax:* 514-382-4984
London
One London Place
#700, 255 Queen's Ave.
London, ON N6A 5R8 Canada
Tel: 519-679-1880; *Fax:* 519-640-4625
Matane
750, av du Phare ouest
Matane, QC G4W 3W8 Canada
Tel: 418-566-2637; *Fax:* 418-566-2839
Moncton
816 Main St.
Moncton, NB E1C 1E6 Canada
Tel: 506-389-8073; *Fax:* 506-632-1210
Montréal
La Tour Deloitte
#500, 1190, av des Canadiens-de-Montréal
Montréal, QC H3B 0M7 Canada
Tel: 514-393-7115; *Fax:* 514-390-4100
Ottawa
#1600, 100 Queen St.
Ottawa, ON K1P 5T8 Canada
Tel: 613-236-2442; *Fax:* 613-236-2195
Prince Albert
#767, 801 - 15th St. East
Prince Albert, SK S6V 0C7
Tel: 306-763-7411; *Fax:* 306-763-0191
Québec
#350, 801 Grande-Allée ouest
Québec City, QC G1S 4Z4 Canada
Tel: 418-624-3333; *Fax:* 418-624-0414
Regina
Bank of Montreal Bldg.
2103 - 11th Ave., 9th Floor
Regina, SK S4P 3Z8 Canada
Tel: 306-585-5200; *Fax:* 306-757-4753

Rimouski
#402, 287, rue Pierre-Saindon
Rimouski, QC G5L 8V5 Canada
Tel: 418-724-4136; *Fax:* 418-724-3807
Rouyn-Noranda
155, av Dallaire
Rouyn-Noranda, QC J9X 4T3 Canada
Tel: 819-762-5764; *Fax:* 819-797-1471
Saint John
Brunswick House
PO Box 6549
44 Chipman Hill, 7th Fl.
Saint John, NB E2L 4R9 Canada
Tel: 506-632-1080; *Fax:* 506-632-1210
St Catharines
25 Corporate Park Dr., 3rd Fl.
St Catharines, ON L2S 3W2 Canada
Tel: 905-323-6000; *Fax:* 905-323-6001
Saint-Hyacinthe
850, boul Casavant ouest
Saint-Hyacinthe, QC J2S 7S3
Tel: 450-774-4000; *Fax:* 450-774-1709
St. John's
#1000, 5 Springdale St.
St. John's, NL A1E 0E4 Canada
Tel: 709-576-8480; *Fax:* 709-576-8460
Saskatoon
#400, 122 - 1st Ave. South
Saskatoon, SK S7K 7E5 Canada
Tel: 306-343-4400; *Fax:* 306-343-4480
Sept-Iles
#200, 421, av Arnaud
Sept-Iles, QC G4R 3B3 Canada
Tel: 418-962-2513; *Fax:* 418-968-6422
Shawinigan
#303, 1785, av Saint-Marc
Shawinigan, QC G9N 2H6 Canada
Tel: 819-538-1721; *Fax:* 819-538-1882
Sherbrooke
Cité du Parc
#300, 1802, rue King ouest
Sherbrooke, QC J1J 0A2 Canada
Tel: 819-823-1616; *Fax:* 819-564-8078
St-Félicien
1180, boul Sacré-Cour
St-Félicien, QC G8K 0B5 Canada
Tel: 418-679-4711; *Fax:* 418-679-8723
Toronto
#200, 8 Adelaide St. W
Toronto, ON M5H 0A9 Canada
Tel: 416-601-6150; *Fax:* 416-601-6151
Trois-Pistoles
546A, rue Jean Rioux
Trois-Pistoles, QC G0L 4K0 Canada
Tel: 418-851-2232; *Fax:* 418-851-4244
Trois-Rivières
1500, rue Royale
Trois-Rivières, QC G9A 5L9 Canada
Tel: 819-691-1212; *Fax:* 819-691-1213
Val-d'Or
#200, 1740 - 3e av
Val-d'Or, QC J9P 1W4
Tel: 819-825-4101; *Fax:* 819-825-1155
Vancouver - Granville St.
939 Granville
Vancouver, BC V7Z 1L3 Canada
Tel: 604-669-4466; *Fax:* 604-685-0395
Vancouver - West Georgia St.
#1500, 885 W. Georgia St.
Vancouver, BC V6C 3E8 Canada
Tel: 604-669-4466; *Fax:* 604-685-0395
Vaughan
#500, 400 Applewood Cres.
Vaughan, ON L4K 0C3 Canada
Tel: 416-601-6150; *Fax:* 416-601-6151
Victoria
#420, 1515 Douglas St.
Victoria, BC V8W 2G4
Tel: 250-978-4400; *Fax:* 250-374-0497
Windsor
#200, 150 Ouellette Pl.
Windsor, ON N8X 1L9 Canada
Tel: 519-967-0388; *Fax:* 519-967-0324
Winnipeg
#2300, 360 Main St.
Winnipeg, MB R3C 3Z3 Canada
Tel: 204-942-0051; *Fax:* 204-947-9390

Ernst & Young LLP (EY)
Ernst & Young Tower
100 Adelaide St. West
Toronto, ON M5H 0B3

Tel: 416-864-1234; Fax: 416-864-1174
www.ey.com/en_ca
www.youtube.com/c/ernstyoung; www.facebook.com/EY;
twitter.com/EYCanada;
www.linkedin.com/company/ernstandyoung

Ownership: A division of Ernst & Young Global Limited, UK.
Year Founded: 1864
Profile: The following services are offered: assurance & advisory business services; corporate finance; tax; & other services. It is affiliated with Ernst & Young Orenda Corporate Finance Inc.
Executives:
Jad Shimaly, Chair, CEO
Affiliated Companies:
Ernst & Young Orenda Corporate Finance Inc.
Branches:
Calgary
Calgary City Centre
#2200, 215 - 2nd St. SW
Calgary, AB T2P 1M4
Tel: 403-290-4100; Fax: 403-290-4265
Dieppe
11 Englehart St.
Dieppe, NB E1A 7Y7
Tel: 506-853-3097; Fax: 506-859-7190
Note: The Dieppe office of the firm LeBlanc Nadeau Bujold merged with Ernst & Young in Sept., 2009.
Edmonton
EPCOR Tower
#1400, 10423 - 101st St.
Edmonton, AB T5H 0E7
Tel: 780-423-5811; Fax: 780-428-8977
Fredericton
#110, 527 Queen St.
Fredericton, NB E2B 3T2
Tel: 506-455-8181; Fax: 506-455-8141
Halifax
RBC Waterside Centre
#500, 1871 Hollis St.
Halifax, NS B3J 0C3
Tel: 902-420-1080; Fax: 902-420-0503
Kitchener
515 Riverbend Dr.
Kitchener, ON N2K 3S3
Tel: 519-744-1171; Fax: 519-744-9604
London
One London Place
#1800, 255 Queens Ave.
London, ON N6A 5S7
Tel: 519-672-6100; Fax: 519-438-5785
Montréal
#2300, 900, boul de Maisonneuve Ouest
Montréal, QC H3A 0A8
Tel: 514-875-6060; Fax: 514-879-2600
Ottawa
#1200, 99 Bank St.
Ottawa, ON K1P 6B9
Tel: 613-232-1511; Fax: 613-232-5324
Québec City
Delta III
#410, 2875 boul Laurier
Québec, QC G1V 0C7
Tel: 418-524-5151; Fax: 418-524-0061
Saint John
Red Rose Tea Bldg.
12 Smythe St., 5th Fl.
Saint John, NB E2L 5G5
Tel: 506-634-7000; Fax: 506-634-2129
St. John's
Fortis Place
#800, 5 Springdale St.
St. John's, NL A1E 0E4
Tel: 709-726-2840; Fax: 709-726-0345
Saskatoon
#1200, 410 - 22nd St. E
Saskatoon, SK S7K 5T6
Tel: 306-934-8000; Fax: 306-653-5859
Toronto
EY Tower
100 Adelaide St. W
Toronto, ON M5H 0B3
Tel: 416-864-1234; Fax: 416-864-1174
Vancouver
Pacific Centre
700 West Georgia St.
Vancouver, BC V7Y 1C7
Tel: 604-891-8200; Fax: 604-643-5422

Victoria
#706, 880 Douglas St.
Victoria, BC V8W 2B7
Tel: 250-294-8370; Fax: 250-294-8371
Waterloo
Evolv1
#300, 420 Wes Graham Way
Waterloo, ON N2L 0J6
Winnipeg
Commodity Exchange Tower
#2700, 360 Main St.
Winnipeg, MB R3C 4G9
Tel: 204-947-6519; Fax: 204-956-0138

Grant Thornton LLP
200 King St. West, 20th Fl.
Toronto, ON M5H 3T4

Tel: 416-366-4240
generalinquiries@ca.gt.com
www.grantthornton.ca
www.youtube.com/c/GrantThorntonLLPCanada;
twitter.com/GrantThorntonCA;
www.linkedin.com/company/grantthorntoncanada

Ownership: Private. Member of Grant Thornton International Ltd.
Year Founded: 1939
Revenues: $1-10 billion
Executives:
Kevin Ladner, FCPA, CA, CBV, CEO, Executive Partner; kevin.ladner@ca.gt.com
Jim Copeland, CA, CMC, Chief Operating Officer, Central Canada, Regional Managing Partner; jim.copeland@ca.gt.com
Sharon Healy, Chief People & Culture Officer; sharon.healy@ca.gt.com
Michelle Wettlaufer, CPA, CA, CMA, Chief Financial Officer; michelle.wettlaufer@ca.gt.com
Norm Raynard, CPA, CA, CBV, Regional Managing Partner, Western Canada; norm.raynard@ca.gt.com
Michele Williams, FCA, BBA, Regional Managing Partner, Atlantic Canada; michele.williams@ca.gt.com
Affiliated Companies:
Grant Thornton Debt Solutions
Grant Thornton Poirier Limited
Raymond Chabot Grant Thornton LLP/RCGT
Branches:
Abbotsford
#201, 2752 Allwood St.
Abbotsford, BC V2T 3R7
Tel: 604-854-3733; Fax: 604-854-6433
Antigonish
#204, 220 Main St.
Antigonish, NS B2G 2C2
Tel: 902-863-4587; Fax: 902-863-0917
Barrie
#400, 85 Bayfield St.
Barrie, ON L4M 3A7
Tel: 705-728-3397; Fax: 705-728-2728
Bathurst - Main St.
Harbourview Pl.
#500, 275 Main St.
Bathurst, NB E2A 1A9
Tel: 506-546-6616; Fax: 506-548-5622
Bow Island
105 - 5th Ave. West
Bow Island, AB T0K 0G0
Tel: 403-545-2217; Fax: 403-526-0908
Bridgewater
Dawson Centre
197 Dufferin St., 4th Fl.
Bridgewater, NS B4V 2G9
Tel: 902-543-8115; Fax: 902-543-7707
Brooks
#6, 500 Cassils Rd. East
Brooks, AB T1R 1M6
Tel: 403-362-5292; Fax: 403-526-0908
Calgary
Centrium Pl.
#1100, 332 - 6th Ave. SW
Calgary, AB T2P 0B2
Tel: 403-260-2500; Fax: 403-260-2571
Camrose
#201, 4870 - 51st St.
Camrose, AB T4V 1S1
Tel: 780-672-9217; Fax: 780-672-9216
Toll-Free: 310-8888
Castlegar
#4, 615 Columbia Ave.
Castlegar, BC V1N 1G9
Tel: 250-365-7745; Fax: 250-365-8027

Charlottetown - Fitzroy St.
PO Box 187
#410, 98 Fitzroy St.
Charlottetown, PE C1A 7K4
Tel: 902-892-6547; Fax: 902-566-5358
Corner Brook
#201, 4 Herald Ave.
Corner Brook, NL A2H 4B4
Tel: 709-634-4382; Fax: 709-634-9158
Courtenay
951 Fitzgerald Ave.
Courtenay, BC V9N 2R6
Tel: 250-338-1394; Fax: 250-338-1969
Toll-Free: 877-338-1394
Digby
Basin Place
PO Box 848
68 Water St.
Digby, NS B0V 1A0
Tel: 902-245-2553; Fax: 902-245-6161
Duncan
823 Canada Ave.
Duncan, BC V9N 1V2
Tel: 250-746-4406; Fax: 250-746-1950
Toll-Free: 888-746-4406
Edmonton - Jasper Ave. NW
Scotia Place 2
#1701, 10060 Jasper Ave. NW
Edmonton, AB T5J 3R8
Tel: 780-422-7114; Fax: 780-426-3208
Essex
14 Victoria Ave.
Essex, ON N8M 1M3
Tel: 519-776-4869; Fax: 519-776-4913
Foremost
119 Main St.
Foremost, AB T0K 0X0
Tel: 403-527-8114; Fax: 403-526-0908
Fort Macleod
2115 - 2nd Ave.
Fort Macleod, AB T0L 0Z0
Tel: 403-527-8114; Fax: 403-526-0908
Fredericton - Queen St.
PO Box 1054
570 Queen St., 4th Fl.
Fredericton, NB E3B 5C2
Tel: 506-458-8200; Fax: 506-453-7029
Gander
PO Box 348
30 Roe Ave.
Gander, NL A1V 1W7
Tel: 709-651-4100; Fax: 709-256-2957
Georgetown
35 Main St. South
Georgetown, ON L7G 3G3
Tel: 905-877-5155; Fax: 905-877-5905
Toll-Free: 866-554-2030
Grand Falls
381 McCormick St.
Grand Falls, NB E3Z 3E8
Tel: 506-475-9440; Fax: 506-475-9449
Grand Falls - Windsor
PO Box 83
5B Harris Ave.
Grand Falls-Windsor, NL A2A 2J3
Tel: 709-489-6622; Fax: 709-489-6625
Halifax
#0100, 1675 Grafton St.
Halifax, NS B3J 0E9
Tel: 902-421-1734; Fax: 902-420-1068
Hamilton
33 Main St. East
Hamilton, ON L8N 4K5
Tel: 905-523-7732; Fax: 905-572-9333
Kelowna
#200, 1633 Ellis St.
Kelowna, BC V1Y 2A8
Tel: 250-712-6800; Fax: 250-712-6850
Kentville
15 Webster St.
Kentville, NS B4N 1H4
Tel: 902-678-7307; Fax: 902-679-1870
Kirkland Lake
#3, 32 Prospect Ave.
Kirkland Lake, ON P2N 2V4
Tel: 705-567-5205; Fax: 705-567-6504
Toll-Free: 855-567-5205
Langley
#320, 8700 - 200th St.
Langley, BC V2Y 0G4
Tel: 604-455-2600; Fax: 604-455-2609

London
#406, 140 Fullarton St.
London, ON N6A 5P2
Tel: 519-672-2930; Fax: 519-672-6455
London - Wharncliffe
145 Wharncliffe Rd. South
London, ON N6A 5K4
Tel: 519-672-3154; Fax: 519-672-7983
Maple Creek
Lifestyle Financial Services Bldg.
101 Maple St.
Maple Creek, SK S0N 1N0
Tel: 403-527-8114; Fax: 403-526-0908
Markham
#200, 15 Allstate Pkwy.
Markham, ON L3R 5B4
Tel: 416-607-2656; Fax: 905-475-8906
Marystown
PO Box 518
2 Queen St.
Marystown, NL A0E 2M0
Tel: 709-279-2300; Fax: 709-279-2340
Medicine Hat
#101, 2248 - 13th Ave. SE
Medicine Hat, AB T1A 8G6
Tel: 403-527-8114; Fax: 403-526-0908
Midland
600 Hugel Ave.
Midland, ON L4R 1W4
Tel: 705-527-6555; Fax: 705-528-7050
Miramichi
135 Henry St.
Miramichi, NB E1V 2N5
Tel: 506-622-0637; Fax: 506-622-5174
Mississauga
#501, 201 City Centre Dr.
Mississauga, ON L5B 2T4
Tel: 416-369-7076; Fax: 905-804-0509
Moncton - Main St.
PO Box 1005
#500, 633 Main St.
Moncton, NB E1C 8P2
Tel: 506-857-0100; Fax: 506-857-0105
Montague
PO Box 70
1 Bailey Dr.
Montague, PE C0A 1R0
Tel: 902-838-4121; Fax: 902-838-4802
Nanaimo
30 Front St.
Nanaimo, BC V9R 5H7
Tel: 250-753-2544; Fax: 250-754-1903
Nelson
513 Victoria St.
Nelson, BC V1L 4K7
Tel: 250-352-3165; Fax: 250-352-7166
New Glasgow
Aberdeen Business Centre
PO Box 427
#270, 610 East River Rd.
New Glasgow, NS B2H 5E5
Tel: 902-752-8393; Fax: 902-752-4009
New Liskeard
PO Box 2170
17 Wellington St.
New Liskeard, ON P0J 1P0
Tel: 705-647-8100; Fax: 705-647-7026
North Bay
#400, 222 McIntyre St. West
North Bay, ON P1B 2Y8
Tel: 705-472-6500; Fax: 705-472-7760
Oyen
Oyen Liquor Mart Building
301 Main St.
Oyen, AB T0J 2J0
Tel: 403-527-8114; Fax: 403-526-0908
Penticton
#201, 99 Padmore Ave. East
Penticton, BC V2A 7H7
Tel: 250-493-0600; Fax: 250-493-4709
Perth-Andover
#2, 15 Station St.
Perth-Andover, NB E7H 4Y2
Tel: 506-273-2276; Fax: 506-273-2033
Peterborough
362 Queen St.
Peterborough, ON L9H 3J6
Tel: 705-743-5020; Fax: 705-743-5081
Port Alberni
4594 Merrifield Rd.
Port Alberni, BC V9Y 6R4
Tel: 250-723-0300; Toll-Free: 888-754-9551

Port Colborne
PO Box 336
222 Catharine St., #B
Port Colborne, ON L3K 5W1
Tel: 905-834-3651; Fax: 905-834-5095
Port Hawkesbury
#104, 609 Church St.
Port Hawkesbury, NS B9A 2X3
Tel: 902-625-5383; Fax: 902-625-5242
Prince Albert
321 Marquis Rd. East
Prince Albert, SK S6V 5K2
Tel: 306-764-3552; Fax: 306-764-3771
Regina
#200, 533 Victoria Ave.
Regina, SK S4N 0P8
Tel: 306-352-1397; Fax: 306-347-8570
Rosthern
1004 - 6th St.
Rosthern, SK S0K 3R0
Tel: 306-232-5211; Fax: 306-232-5508
Saint John - Germain St.
Brunswick Sq. Office Tower
#1100, 1 Germain St.
Saint John, NB E2L 4V1
Tel: 506-634-2900; Fax: 506-634-4569
St Catharines
#200, 80 King St.
St Catharines, ON L2R 7G1
Tel: 905-682-8363; Fax: 905-682-2191
St Catharines - Hannover
#B201, 110 Hannover Dr.
St Catharines, ON L2W 1A4
Tel: 905-685-9400; Fax: 905-685-5991
St. John's
#300, 15 International Pl.
St. John's, NL A1A 0L4
Tel: 709-778-8800; Fax: 709-722-7892
Salmon Arm
PO Box 697
541 - 6th St. NE
Salmon Arm, BC V1E 4N8
Tel: 250-832-7192; Fax: 250-832-5377
Toll-Free: 877-832-7192
Saskatoon
#4, 130 Robin Cres.
Saskatoon, SK S7L 6M7
Tel: 306-934-3944; Fax: 306-934-3409
Summerside
Royal Bank Bldg.
PO Box 1660
220 Water St.
Summerside, PE C1N 2V5
Tel: 902-436-9155; Fax: 902-436-6913
Sydney
George Place
#200, 500 George St.
Sydney, NS B1P 1K6
Tel: 902-562-5581; Fax: 902-562-0073
Thunder Bay
#300, 979 Alloy Dr.
Thunder Bay, ON P7B 5Z8
Tel: 807-345-6571; Fax: 807-345-0032
Toll-Free: 807-345-6571
Timmins
Pine Plaza
#322, 119 Pine St. South, 3rd Fl.
Timmins, ON P4N 2K3
Tel: 705-264-9486; Fax: 705-567-6504
Toll-Free: 855-567-5205
Toronto West
#400, 295 The West Mall
Toronto, ON M9C 4Z4
Tel: 416-599-7255; Fax: 416-599-7268
Trail
1440 Bay Ave.
Trail, BC V1R 4B1
Tel: 250-368-6445; Fax: 250-368-8488
Truro - Prince St.
733 Prince St.
Truro, NS B2N 1G7
Tel: 902-893-1150; Fax: 902-893-9757
Vancouver
Grant Thornton Pl.
#1600, 333 Seymour St.
Vancouver, BC V6B 0A4
Tel: 604-687-2711; Fax: 604-685-6569
Vancouver South
#410, 1200 West 73rd Ave.
Vancouver, BC V6P 6G5
Tel: 604-435-5655; Fax: 604-435-1913

Victoria
#650, 1675 Douglas St.
Victoria, BC V8W 2G5
Tel: 250-383-4191; Fax: 250-381-4623
Toll-Free: 855-383-8994
Waterloo
#6, 60 Bathurst Dr.
Waterloo, ON N2V 2A9
Tel: 519-579-0700; Fax: 519-579-2894
Wetaskiwin
5108 - 51st Ave.
Wetaskiwin, AB T9A 0V2
Tel: 780-352-1679; Fax: 780-352-2451
Weyburn
206 Hill Ave.
Weyburn, SK S4H 1M5
Tel: 306-842-8123; Fax: 306-842-8171
Toll-Free: 877-211-8123
Windsor
#203, 2510 Ouellette Ave.
Windsor, ON N8X 1L4
Tel: 519-966-4626; Fax: 519-966-9206
Winnipeg
94 Commerce Dr.
Winnipeg, MB R3P 0Z3
Tel: 204-944-0100; Fax: 204-957-5442
Toll-Free: 800-446-4794
Woodstock
#101, 318 Connell St.
Woodstock, NB E7M 5E2
Tel: 506-324-8040; Fax: 506-325-2262
Yarmouth
PO Box 297
328 Main St.
Yarmouth, NS B5A 4B2
Tel: 902-742-7842; Fax: 902-742-0224

KPMG
Bay Adelaide Centre
#4600, 333 Bay St.
Toronto, ON M5H 2S5

Tel: 416-777-8500; Fax: 416-777-8818
home.kpmg/ca/en/home.html
www.youtube.com/user/KPMGCanada;
www.facebook.com/KPMGCareersCA;
twitter.com/kpmg_canada;
www.linkedin.com/company/kpmg-canada

Ownership: Private
Year Founded: 1860
Number of Employees: 8,000
Assets: $500m-1 billion Year End: 20200930
Revenues: $1,796,000,000 Year End: 20200930
Executives:
Elio Luongo, Chief Executive Officer, Senior Partner
Kristy Carscallen, Canadian Managing Partner, Audit
Jonathan Kallner, Canadian Managing Partner, Clients &
Markets
Lucy Lacovelli, Canadian Managing Partner, Tax
Mary Lou Maher, Canadian Managing Partner, Quality & Risk
Management
Silvia Montefiore, Canadian Managing Partner, Business
Enablement & Operations
Benjie M. Thomas, Canadian Managing Partner, Advisory
Services
Branches:
Abbotsford
32575 Simon Ave.
Abbotsford, BC V2T 4W6 Canada
Tel: 604-854-2200; Fax: 604-853-2756
Calgary
#3100, 205 - 5th Ave. SW
Calgary, AB T2P 4B9 Canada
Tel: 403-691-8000; Fax: 403-691-8008
Chilliwack
#200, 9123 Mary St.
Chilliwack, BC V2P 4H7 Canada
Tel: 604-793-4700; Fax: 604-793-4747
Edmonton
Commerce Pl.
#2200, 10175 - 101St.
Edmonton, AB T5J 0H3 Canada
Tel: 780-429-7300; Fax: 780-429-7379
Fort St John
#102, 9705 - 100th Ave.
Fort St John, BC V1J 1Y3 Canada
Tel: 250-787-1989; Fax: 250-563-5693
Fredericton
Frederick Sq., TD Tower
#700, 77 Westmorland St.
Fredericton, NB E3B 6Z3 Canada
Tel: 506-452-8000; Fax: 506-450-0072

Halifax
  Purdy's Wharf, Tower One
  #1500, 1959 Upper Water St.
  Halifax, NS B3J 3N2 Canada
  Tel: 902-429-6000; Fax: 902-423-1307
Hamilton
  Commerce Place
  #700, 21 King St. West
  Hamilton, ON L8P 4X9 Canada
  Tel: 905-523-8200; Fax: 905-523-2222
Kamloops
  560 Victoria St.
  Kamloops, BC V2C 2B1 Canada
  Tel: 250-372-5581; Fax: 250-828-2928
Kanata
  #101, 750 Palladium Dr.
  Kanata, ON K2V 1C7 Canada
  Tel: 613-212-5764; Fax: 613-591-7607
Kelowna
  #200, 3200 Richter St.
  Kelowna, BC V1W 5K9 Canada
  Tel: 250-979-7150; Fax: 250-763-0044
Kingston
  #400, 863 Princess St.
  Kingston, ON K7L 5N4 Canada
  Tel: 613-549-1550; Fax: 613-549-6349
Langley
  8506 - 200th St.
  Langley, BC V2Y 0M1 Canada
  Tel: 604-455-4000; Fax: 604-881-4988
Lethbridge
  Lethbridge Centre Tower
  #500, 400 - 4th Ave. South
  Lethbridge, AB T1J 4E1 Canada
  Tel: 403-380-5700; Fax: 403-380-5760
London
  #1400, 140 Fullarton St.
  London, ON N6A 5P2 Canada
  Tel: 519-672-4880; Fax: 519-672-5684
Moncton
  Place Marven's
  One Factory Lane
  Moncton, NB E1C 9M3 Canada
  Tel: 506-856-4400; Fax: 506-856-4499
Montréal
  #1500, 600 boul de Maisonneuve ouest
  Montréal, QC H3A 0A3 Canada
  Tel: 514-840-2100; Fax: 514-840-2187
North Bay
  PO Box 990
  #300, 925 Stockdale Rd.
  North Bay, ON P1B 9N5 Canada
  Tel: 705-472-5110; Fax: 705-472-1249
Ottawa
  #1800, 150 Elgin St.
  Ottawa, ON K2P 2P8
  Tel: 613-212-5764; Fax: 613-212-2896
Prince George
  #400, 177 Victoria St.
  Prince George, BC V2L 5R8 Canada
  Tel: 250-563-7151; Fax: 250-563-5693
  Toll-Free: 888-665-5595
Québec
  #600, 500, Grande-Allée est
  Québec, QC G1R 2J9 Canada
  Tel: 418-577-3400; Fax: 418-577-3440
Quesnel
  #101, 455 McLean St.
  Quesnel, BC V2J 2P3 Canada
  Tel: 250-992-5547; Fax: 250-992-5372
Regina
  McCallum Hill Centre, Tower II
  1874 Scarth St., 20th Fl.
  Regina, SK S4P 0S3 Canada
  Tel: 306-791-1200; Fax: 306-757-4703
Saint John
  Harbour Bldg.
  PO Box 2388
  133 Prince William St.
  Saint John, NB E2L 2B5 Canada
  Tel: 506-634-1000; Fax: 506-633-8828
St Catharines
  #620, 80 King St.
  St Catharines, ON L2R 3H6 Canada
  Tel: 905-685-4811; Fax: 905-682-2008
St. John's
  TD Place
  #1010, 140 Water St.
  St. John's, NL A1C 6H6 Canada
  Tel: 709-733-5000; Fax: 709-800-0929

Saskatoon
  River Centre
  #500, 475 - 2nd Ave. South
  Saskatoon, SK S7K 1P4 Canada
  Tel: 306-934-6200; Fax: 306-934-6233
Sault Ste Marie
  #200, 111 Elgin St.
  Sault Ste Marie, ON P6A 6L6 Canada
  Tel: 705-949-5811; Fax: 705-949-0911
Sudbury
  Claridge Executive Centre
  #400, 144 Pine St.
  Sudbury, ON P3C 1X3 Canada
  Tel: 705-675-8500; Fax: 705-675-7586
Vancouver - Burnaby
  #2401, 4710 Kingsway
  Burnaby, BC V5H 4M2 Canada
  Tel: 604-527-3600; Fax: 604-527-3636
Vancouver - Dunsmuir St.
  777 Dunsmuir St.
  Vancouver, BC V7Y 1K3 Canada
  Tel: 604-691-3000; Fax: 604-691-3031
Vaughan
  Yonge Corporate Centre
  #1400, 100 New Park Pl
  Vaughan, ON L4K 0J3 Canada
  Tel: 416-228-7000; Fax: 416-228-7123
Vernon
  Credit Union Bldg.
  3205 - 32 St., 3rd Fl.
  Vernon, BC V1T 9A2 Canada
  Tel: 250-503-5300; Fax: 250-545-6440
Victoria
  St. Andrew's Square II
  800 - 730 View St.
  Victoria, BC V8W 3Y7 Canada
  Tel: 250-480-3500; Fax: 250-480-3539
Waterloo
  115 King St. South
  Waterloo, ON N2J 5A3 Canada
  Tel: 519-747-8800; Fax: 519-747-8811
Windsor
  Greenwood Centre
  #618, 3200 Deziel Dr.
  Windsor, ON N8W 5A5 Canada
  Tel: 519-251-3500; Fax: 519-251-3530
Winnipeg
  #2000, One Lombard Place
  Winnipeg, MB R3B 0X3 Canada
  Tel: 204-957-1770; Fax: 204-957-0808

MNP LLP
#2000, 330 - 5th Ave. SW
Calgary, AB T2P 0L4

Tel: 403-444-0150
www.mnp.ca
www.youtube.com/c/mnpllpcanada; www.facebook.com/mnpllp;
twitter.com/mnp_llp; www.linkedin.com/company/mnp
Former Name: Meyers Norris Penny
Year Founded: 1945
Number of Employees: 1,040
Profile: MNP is a leading Western Canadian chartered accountancy & business advisory firm. In addition to traditional accounting services like taxation & assurance, MNP offers business services including corporate financing, human resource consulting, business & strategic planning, succession planning, valuations support, information technology consulting, self-employment training, & agricultural advisory services.
Executives:
Jason Tuffs, CPA, CA, Chief Executive Officer; jason.tuffs@mnp.ca
Jeremy Cole, FCPA, FCA, CBV, Executive Vice-President, GTA & Quebec; jeremy.cole@mnp.ca
Tanya Knight, CPA, CA, Executive Vice-President, Clients & Services; tanya.knight@mnp.ca
Diana Render, CPA, CA, Executive Vice-President, Atlantic Canada & Ontario outside of the GTA; diana.render@mnp.ca
Darren Turchansky, CPA, CA, Executive Vice-President, British Columbia, Vancouver, Regional Managing Partner; darren.turchansky@mnp.ca
Sean Wallace, CPA, CA, Executive Vice-President, Prairies; sean.wallace@mnp.ca
Adel Elassal, Chief Information Officer; adel.elassal@mnp.ca
Affiliated Companies:
MNP Corporate Finance Inc.
MNP Ltd
Branches:
Abbotsford
  #300, 32988 South Fraser Way
  Abbotsford, BC V2S 2A8
  Tel: 604-853-9471; Fax: 604-850-3672
  Toll-Free: 877-853-9471

Airdrie
  #311, 401 Coopers Blvd. SW
  Airdrie, AB T4B 4J3
  Tel: 403-912-6235; Fax: 403-912-6332
Arkona
  PO Box 188
  7285 Arkona Rd.
  Arkona, ON N0M 1B0
  Tel: 519-828-3901; Fax: 519-828-3903
Brandon
  1401 Princess Ave.
  Brandon, MB R7A 7L7
  Tel: 204-727-0661; Fax: 204-726-1543
  Toll-Free: 800-446-0890
Brockville
  PO Box 459
  #200, 7 King St. W
  Brockville, ON K6V 5V6
  Tel: 613-342-8424; Fax: 613-342-1714
Brooks
  PO Box 1690
  239 - 1st St. W
  Brooks, AB T1R 1C5
  Tel: 403-362-4498
Burlington
  1122 International Blvd., 6th Fl.
  Burlington, ON L7L 6Z8
  Tel: 905-333-9888; Fax: 905-333-9583
Calgary - 640 - 5th Ave. SW
  #1500, 640 - 5th Ave. SW
  Calgary, AB T2P 3G4
  Tel: 403-263-3385; Fax: 403-269-8450
  Toll-Free: 877-500-0792
Cambridge
  #600, 73 Water St. North
  Cambridge, ON N1R 7L6
  Tel: 519-623-3820; Fax: 519-622-3144
Campbell River
  #201, 990 Cedar St.
  Campbell River, BC V9W 7Z8
  Tel: 250-287-2131; Fax: 250-287-2134
Chilliwack
  #1, 45780 Yale Rd.
  Chilliwack, BC V2P 2N4
  Tel: 604-792-1915; Fax: 604-795-6526
  Toll-Free: 800-444-4070
Clinton
  PO Box 1149
  54 King St.
  Clinton, ON N0M 1L0
  Tel: 519-606-8550; Fax: 519-606-8553
Cornwall
  709 Cotton Mill St.
  Cornwall, ON K6H 7K7
  Tel: 613-932-3610; Fax: 613-938-3215
Courtenay
  467 Cumberland Rd.
  Courtenay, BC V9N 2C5
  Tel: 250-338-5464; Fax: 250-338-0609
Dauphin
  PO Box 6000
  32 - 2nd Ave. SW
  Dauphin, MB R7N 2V5
  Tel: 204-638-6767; Fax: 204-638-8634
  Toll-Free: 877-500-0790
Deloraine
  PO Box 528
  201 Broadway St. North
  Deloraine, MB R0M 0M0
  Tel: 204-747-2842; Fax: 204-747-2856
Drumheller
  PO Box 789
  365 Second St. East
  Drumheller, AB T0J 0Y0
  Tel: 403-823-7800; Fax: 403-823-8914
  Toll-Free: 877-932-3387
Duncan
  372 Coronation Ave.
  Duncan, BC V9L 2T3
  Tel: 250-748-3761; Fax: 250-746-1712
Edmonton
  #1600, 10235 - 101 St. North
  Edmonton, AB T5J 3G1
  Tel: 780-451-4406; Fax: 780-454-1908
  Toll-Free: 800-661-7778
Estevan
  #100, 1219 - 5th St.
  Estevan, SK S4A 0Z5
  Tel: 306-634-2603; Fax: 306-634-8706

Fort Frances
1100 Scott St.
Fort Frances, ON P9A 1J6
Tel: 807-274-9861; Fax: 807-274-8329
Toll-Free: 800-274-8329
Fort McMurray
9707 Main St.
Fort McMurray, AB T9H 1T5
Tel: 780-791-9000; Fax: 780-791-9047
Toll-Free: 866-465-1155
Fort St. John
10611 - 102 St.
Fort St. John, BC V1J 5L3
Tel: 250-785-8166; Fax: 250-785-5660
Grande Prairie
#700, 9909 - 102 St.
Grande Prairie, AB T8V 2V4
Tel: 780-831-1700; Fax: 780-539-9600
Toll-Free: 888-831-2870
Halifax - Dartmouth
#200, 100 Venture Run
Dartmouth, NS B3B 0H9
Tel: 902-835-7333; Fax: 204-835-5297
Toll-Free: 800-495-5909
Humboldt
PO Box 2590
2424 Westwood Dr.
Humboldt, SK S0K 2A0
Tel: 306-682-2673; Fax: 306-682-5910
Toll-Free: 877-500-0789
Kamloops
#220, 301 Victoria St.
Kamloops, BC V2C 2A3
Tel: 250-374-5908; Fax: 250-374-5946
Toll-Free: 877-374-5901
Kelowna
#600, 1628 Dickson Ave.
Kelowna, BC V1Y 9X1
Tel: 250-763-8919; Fax: 250-763-1121
Toll-Free: 877-766-9735
Kenora
315 Main St. South
Kenora, ON P9N 1T4
Tel: 807-468-3338; Fax: 807-468-1418
Toll-Free: 866-381-3338
Kingston - John Counter
#201, 1473 John Counter Blvd.
Kingston, ON K7M 8Z6
Tel: 613-544-2903; Fax: 613-544-6151
Kingston - Princess St.
#410, 27 Princess St.
Kingston, ON K7L 1A3
Tel: 613-546-3111; Fax: 613-546-4089
Lacombe
#201, 4711 - 49B Ave.
Lacombe, AB T4L 1K1
Tel: 403-782-7790; Fax: 403-782-7703
Langley
#580, 8621 - 201 St.
Langley, BC V2Y 0G9
Tel: 604-371-1352; Fax: 604-608-4990
Leduc
#200, 5019 - 49th Ave.
Leduc, AB T9E 6T5
Tel: 780-986-2626; Fax: 780-986-2621
Lethbridge
3425 - 2nd Ave. South
Lethbridge, AB T1J 4V1
Tel: 403-329-1552; Fax: 403-329-1540
Toll-Free: 800-661-8097
Lloydminster
#401, 4908 - 42nd St.
Lloydminster, SK S9V 0E5
Tel: 306-825-9855; Fax: 306-825-9640
London
#700, 495 Richmond St.
London, ON N6A 5A9
Tel: 519-679-8550; Fax: 519-679-1812
Maple Creek
PO Box 1357
728 Pacific Ave.
Maple Creek, SK S0N 1N0
Tel: 306-662-3127; Fax: 306-662-2654
Maple Ridge
#201, 11939 - 224 St.
Maple Ridge, BC V2X 6B2
Tel: 604-463-8831; Fax: 604-463-0401
Markham
#700, 3100 Steeles Ave. East
Markham, ON L3R 8T3
Tel: 416-596-1711; Fax: 416-596-7894
Toll-Free: 877-251-2922

Medicine Hat
666 - 4th St. SE
Medicine Hat, AB T1A 0K9
Tel: 403-527-4441; Fax: 403-526-6218
Toll-Free: 877-500-0786
Melfort
PO Box 2020
601 Main St.
Melfort, SK S0E 1A0
Tel: 306-752-5800; Fax: 306-752-5933
Minnedosa
PO Box 989
#A, 110 Main St. S
Minnedosa, MB R0J 1E0
Tel: 204-867-5550
Mississauga - Burnhamthorpe Rd. West
#900, 50 Burnhamthorpe Rd. West
Mississauga, ON L5B 3C2
Tel: 416-626-6000; Fax: 416-626-8650
Mississauga - Matheson Blvd.
#5, 267 Matheson Blvd. E
Mississauga, ON L4Z 1X8
Tel: 905-629-3200; Fax: 905-629-3056
Toll-Free: 866-320-8922
Mississauga North
#102, Longside Dr.
Mississauga, ON L5W 0G7
Tel: 905-607-9777
Montréal
1155, boul René-Lévesque ouest, 23e étage
Montréal, QC H3B 2K2
Tel: 514-861-9724; Fax: 514-861-9446
Toll-Free: 888-861-9724
Moosomin
PO Box 670
715 Main St.
Moosomin, SK S0G 3N0
Tel: 306-435-3347; Fax: 306-435-2494
Toll-Free: 877-500-0789
Nanaimo
MNP Place
#400, 345 Wallace St.
Nanaimo, BC V9R 5B6
Tel: 250-753-8251; Fax: 250-754-3999
Neepawa
PO Box 760
251 Davidson St.
Neepawa, MB R0J 1H0
Tel: 204-476-2326; Fax: 204-476-3663
Toll-Free: 877-500-0785
Oshawa
#100, 850 Champlain Ave.
Oshawa, ON L1J 8C3
Tel: 905-579-5531; Fax: 905-579-4624
Ottawa - Carling Ave.
#800, 1600 Carling Ave.
Ottawa, ON K1Z 1G3
Tel: 613-691-4200; Fax: 613-726-9009
Ottawa - Hinton Ave.
#100, 7 Hinton Ave. N
Ottawa, ON K1Y 4P1
Tel: 613-271-3700
Parkhill
263 Parkhill Main St.
Parkhill, ON N0M 2K0
Tel: 519-294-0883; Fax: 519-459-2848
Peace River
9913 - 98 Ave.
Peace River, AB T8S 1J5
Tel: 780-624-3252; Fax: 780-624-8758
Port Moody
#601, 205 Newport Dr.
Port Moody, BC V3H 5C9
Tel: 604-949-2088; Fax: 604-949-0509
Portage la Prairie
780 Saskatchewan Ave. W
Portage la Prairie, MB R1N 0M7
Tel: 204-239-6117; Fax: 204-857-3972
Toll-Free: 866-939-6117
Prince Albert
#101, 1061 Central Ave.
Prince Albert, SK S6V 4V4
Tel: 306-764-6873; Fax: 306-763-0766
Toll-Free: 855-667-3310
Prince George
#400, 550 Victoria St.
Prince George, BC V2L 2K1
Tel: 250-596-1111; Fax: 250-596-4908
Prince George
#500, 299 Victoria St.
Prince George, BC V2L 5B8
Tel: 250-564-1111; Fax: 250-562-4950

Quesnel
360 St. Laurent Ave.
Quesnel, BC V2J 5A3
Tel: 250-992-5411
Red Deer
4922 - 53 St.
Red Deer, AB T4N 2E9
Tel: 403-346-8878; Fax: 403-341-5599
Toll-Free: 877-500-0779
Regina
Royal Bank Bldg.
#900, 2010 - 11 Ave.
Regina, SK S4P 0J3
Tel: 306-790-7900; Fax: 306-790-7990
Toll-Free: 877-500-0780
Rimbey
PO Box 317
4714 - 50 Ave.
Rimbey, AB T0C 2J0
Tel: 403-843-4666; Fax: 403-843-4616
St Catharines
#101, 63 Church St.
St Catharines, ON L2R 3C4
Tel: 905-641-0846; Fax: 905-641-3083
Sarnia
#G, 1315 Michigan Ave.
Sarnia, ON N7S 4M6
Tel: 519-542-5372; Fax: 519-542-0718
Saskatoon
#800, 119 - 4 Ave. South
Saskatoon, SK S7K 5X2
Tel: 306-665-6766; Fax: 306-665-9910
Toll-Free: 877-500-0778
Shaunavon
PO Box 897
424 Centre St.
Shaunavon, SK S0N 2M0
Tel: 306-297-3888; Fax: 306-297-2128
Souris
PO Box 927
25 Crescent Ave. West
Souris, MB R0K 2C0
Tel: 204-483-3903; Fax: 204-483-2489
Stratford
#1B, 61 Lorne Ave.
Stratford, ON N5A 6S4
Tel: 519-272-0000; Fax: 519-272-0030
Strathroy
6 Front St. W
Strathroy, ON N7G 1X4
Tel: 519-245-4690; Fax: 519-245-1998
Sudbury
1970 Paris St.
Sudbury, ON P3E 3C8
Tel: 705-523-0272; Fax: 705-523-8454
Toll-Free: 800-581-7510
Surrey
#301, 15303 - 31 Ave.
Surrey, BC V3Z 6X2
Tel: 604-536-7614; Fax: 604-538-5356
Toll-Free: 800-761-7772
Swan River
PO Box 146
359 Kelsey Trail
Swan River, MB R0L 1Z0
Tel: 204-734-2599; Fax: 204-734-3184
Toll-Free: 866-468-0259
Swift Current
50 - 1st Ave NE
Swift Current, SK S9H 4W4
Tel: 306-773-8375; Fax: 306-773-7735
Toll-Free: 877-500-0762
Sydney - 15 Dorchester St.
Commerce Tower
PO Box 1
#500, 15 Dorchester St.
Sydney, NS B1P 6G9
Tel: 902-539-3900; Fax: 902-564-6062
Sydney - 50 Dorchester St.
50 Dorchester St.
Sydney, NS B1P 5Z1
Tel: 902-539-2263; Fax: 902-539-7434
Taber
4713 - 55 St.
Taber, AB T1G 1W6
Tel: 403-223-3581; Fax: 403-223-8695
Terrace
#201, 4630 Lazelle Ave.
Terrace, BC V8G 1S6
Tel: 250-635-4925; Fax: 250-635-4975

Thunder Bay
#210, 1205 Amber Dr.
Thunder Bay, ON P7B 6M4
Tel: 807-623-2141; *Fax:* 807-622-1282
Toll-Free: 866-623-2141
Timmins - Riverside Dr.
2185 Riverside Dr.
Timmins, ON P4R 0A1
Tel: 705-264-9484; *Fax:* 705-264-0788
Toronto
#300, 111 Richmond St. West
Toronto, ON M5H 2G4
Tel: 416-596-1711; *Fax:* 416-596-7894
Toll-Free: 877-251-2922
Truro
#301, 640 Prince St.
Truro, NS B2N 1G4
Tel: 902-897-9291; *Fax:* 902-897-9293
Vancouver
MNP Tower
#2200, 1021 West Hastings St.
Vancouver, BC V6E 0C3
Tel: 604-685-8408; *Fax:* 604-685-8594
Toll-Free: 877-688-8594
Vanderhoof
PO Box 410
#200, 2375 Burrard Ave.
Vanderhoof, BC V0J 3A0
Tel: 250-567-3155; *Fax:* 250-567-3872
Vernon
#100, 2903 - 35 Ave.
Vernon, BC V1T 2S7
Tel: 778-475-5678; *Fax:* 778-475-5618
Toll-Free: 877-475-5678
Victoria - Douglas St.
#701, 1803 Douglas St.
Victoria, BC V8T 5C3
Tel: 250-388-6554; *Fax:* 250-388-6555
Victoria - Fort St.
#300, 888 Fort St.
Victoria, BC V8W 1H8
Tel: 778-265-8883; *Fax:* 778-265-8879
Virden
PO Box 670
590 Seventh Ave. South
Virden, MB R0M 2C0
Tel: 204-748-1340; *Fax:* 204-748-3294
Waterloo
#3, 139 Northfield Dr. West
Waterloo, ON N2L 5A6
Tel: 519-725-7700; *Fax:* 519-725-7708
Toll-Free: 866-464-0740
Weyburn
#301, 117 - 3rd St. NE
Weyburn, SK S4H 0W3
Tel: 306-842-8915; *Fax:* 306-842-1966
Williams Lake
336 Mart St.
Williams Lake, BC V2G 4N1
Tel: 778-412-4200; *Fax:* 778-412-4199
Winnipeg
True North Square
#1200, 242 Hargrave St.
Winnipeg, MB R3C 0T8
Tel: 204-775-4531; *Fax:* 204-783-8520
Toll-Free: 877-500-0795

PricewaterhouseCoopers LLP, Canada
PwC Tower
#2600, 18 York St.
Toronto, ON M5J 0B2
Tel: 416-863-1133; *Fax:* 416-365-8215
www.pwc.com/ca
www.youtube.com/user/PwCCanada;
www.facebook.com/pwccanada; twitter.com/pwc_canada;
www.linkedin.com/company/pwc-canada
Also Known As: PwC Canada
Ownership: Private. A subsidiary of PricewaterhouseCoopers,
London, UK
Number of Employees: 7,300
Profile: PricewaterhouseCoopers Canada is a member firm of
PricewaterhouseCoopers International Limited. The firm helps
businesses solve problems by providing an extensive selection
of services, which are divided into four areas (Assurance,
Consulting, Deals & Tax).
Executives:
Nicolas Marcoux, Chief Executive Officer
Chris Dulny, Chief Innovation Officer
Kristian Knibutat, Chief Operations Officer
Alaina Tennison, Chief Financial Officer
Lana Paton, National Managing Partner, Business Units
Matthew Wetmore, National Managing Partner, Industries &
Regions

Branches:
Brossard
#300, 4255, boul Lapinière
Brossard, QC J4Z 0C7
Tel: 450-678-4255; *Fax:* 450-678-1700
Calgary
Suncor Energy Centre
#3100, 111 - 5th Ave. SW
Calgary, AB T2P 5L3
Tel: 403-509-7500; *Fax:* 403-781-1825
Edmonton
#1501, 10088 - 102nd Ave. NW
Edmonton, AB T5J 3N5
Tel: 780-441-6700; *Fax:* 780-441-6776
Gatineau
#101, 900, boul de la Carrie
Gatineau, QC J8Y 6T5
Tel: 819-643-7476; *Fax:* 819-776-0347
Halifax
#400, 1601 Lower Water St.
Halifax, NS B3J 3P6
Tel: 902-491-7400; *Fax:* 902-422-1166
London
#300, 465 Richmond St.
London, ON N6A 5P4
Tel: 519-640-8000; *Fax:* 519-640-8015
Montréal - René-Lévesque ouest
#2500, 1250, boul René-Lévesque ouest
Montréal, QC H3B 2G4
Tel: 519-205-5000; *Fax:* 514-876-1502
Ottawa
#800, 99 Bank St.
Ottawa, ON K1P 1E4
Tel: 613-237-3702; *Fax:* 613-237-3963
Québec
Place de la Cité Tour Cominar
#1700, 2640, boul Laurier
Québec, QC G1V 5C2
Tel: 418-522-7001; *Fax:* 418-522-5663
Saint John
Brunswick House
#300, 44 Chipman Hill
Saint John, NB E2L 2A9
Tel: 506-632-1810; *Fax:* 506-632-8997
St. John's
#200, 125 Kelsey Dr.
St. John's, NL A1B 0L2
Tel: 709-722-3883; *Fax:* 709-722-5874
Saskatoon
#600, 128 - 4th Ave. South
Saskatoon, SK S7K 1M8
Tel: 306-668-5900; *Fax:* 306-652-1315
Surrey
#1400, 13450 - 102nd Ave.
Surrey, BC V3T 5X3
Tel: 604-495-9990; *Fax:* 604-495-8930
Vancouver
PwC Place
#1400, 250 Howe St.
Vancouver, BC V6C 3S7
Tel: 604-806-7000; *Fax:* 604-806-7806
Vaughan
200 Apple Mill Rd.
Vaughan, ON L4K 0J8
Tel: 905-326-6800; *Fax:* 905-326-5339
Victoria
#525, Fort St.
Victoria, BC V8W 1E8
Tel: 250-298-5260; *Fax:* 250-298-5265
Waterloo
#201, 95 King St. South
Waterloo, ON N2J 5A2
Tel: 519-570-5700; *Fax:* 519-570-5730
Windsor
#300, 245 Ouellette Ave.
Windsor, ON N9A 7J4
Tel: 519-985-8900; *Fax:* 519-258-5457
Winnipeg
Richardson Bldg.
#2300, Lombard Pl.
Winnipeg, MB R3B 0X6
Tel: 204-926-2400; *Fax:* 204-944-1020

Richter
#1100, 1981, av McGill College
Montréal, QC H3A 0G6
Tel: 514-934-3400; *Fax:* 514-934-3408
Toll-Free: 888-805-1793
info@richter.ca
www.richter.ca
www.facebook.com/Richtercanada; twitter.com/Richtercanada;
www.linkedin.com/company/richter
Former Name: Richter Usher & Vineberg

Ownership: Private
Year Founded: 1926
Profile: Aboriginal advisory services, audit, corporate finance,
financial reorganization, management consulting, professional
search, risk management, tax, valuations & litigation support, &
wealth management services are provided.
Executives:
Tasso Lagios, Managing Partner; tlagios@richter.ca
Branches:
Toronto
Bay Wellington Tower
#3510, 181 Bay St.
Toronto, ON M5J 2T3
Tel: 416-488-2345; *Fax:* 416-488-3765
Toll-Free: 888-805-1793

Welch LLP
123 Slater St., 3rd Fl.
Ottawa, ON K1P 5H2
Tel: 613-236-9191; *Fax:* 613-236-8258
www.welchllp.com
www.youtube.com/user/WelchLLP; www.facebook.com/welchllp;
twitter.com/welchllp; www.linkedin.com/company/welchllp
Former Name: Welch & Company LLP
Ownership: An independent member firm of BKR International,
New York, New York, USA
Year Founded: 1918
Number of Employees: 300
Profile: The firm serves business, government, & not-for-profit
clients. Taxation, accounting, auditing, personal financial
planning & wealth management services are provided.
Partners:
Jim McConnery, CPA, CA, TEP, Managing Partner;
jmcconnery@welchllp.com
Don Scott, FCPA, FCA, Director, Tax Services, Ottawa, Tax
Partner; dscott@welchllp.com
Branches:
Belleville
525 Dundas St. East
Belleville, ON K8N 1G4
Tel: 613-966-2844; *Fax:* 613-966-2206
Campbellford
PO Box 1209
57 Bridge St. East
Campbellford, ON K0L 1L0
Tel: 705-653-3194; *Fax:* 705-653-1703
Cornwall
36 - 2nd St. East
Cornwall, ON K6H 1Y3
Tel: 613-932-4953; *Fax:* 613-932-1731
Gatineau
101, 259, boul St-Joseph
Gatineau, QC J8Y 6T1
Tel: 819-771-7381; *Fax:* 819-771-3089
Napanee
36 Bridge St. East
Napanee, ON K7R 1J8
Tel: 613-354-2169; *Fax:* 613-354-2160
Pembroke
PO Box 757
270 Lake St.
Pembroke, ON K8A 6X9
Tel: 613-735-1021; *Fax:* 613-735-2071
Picton
#112, 19-35 Bridge St.
Picton, ON K0K 2T0
Tel: 613-476-3283; *Fax:* 613-476-1627
Renfrew
101 Raglan St. North
Renfrew, ON K7V 1N7
Tel: 613-432-8399; *Fax:* 613-432-9154
Toronto
#1070, 36 Toronto St.
Toronto, ON M5C 2C5
Tel: 647-288-9200; *Fax:* 647-288-7600
Trenton
67 Ontario St.
Trenton, ON K8V 2G8
Tel: 613-392-1287; *Fax:* 613-392-5456
Tweed
PO Box 807
63 Victoria St. North
Tweed, ON K0K 3J0
Tel: 613-478-5051; *Fax:* 613-478-3069

Accounting Firms by Province
Alberta

Airdrie: Padgett Business Services Airdrie
#230, 52 Gateway Dr. NE
Airdrie, AB T4B 0J6

Tel: 403-948-7759
info@padgettairdrie.ca
www.padgettairdrie.com

Bonnyville: Ross & Sylvestre LLP Chartered Professional Accountants
PO Box 6279
4114 - 50 Ave.
Bonnyville, AB T9N 2G8

Tel: 780-826-4469; *Fax:* 780-826-3705
www.rsgroupcpa.com

Calgary: ALW Partners LLP
129 - 17 Ave. NE
Calgary, AB T2E 1L7

Tel: 403-230-2454
generalmail@alw.ca
www.alw.ca
Other Contact Information: Alternate Phone: 403-230-4660

Calgary: Arthur O. Solheim, LLP
#102, 811 Manning Rd. NE
Calgary, AB T2E 7L4

Tel: 403-235-2040; *Fax:* 403-272-8326

Calgary: Brander & Company
5520 - 2nd St. SW
Calgary, AB T2H 0G9

Tel: 403-244-2900; *Fax:* 403-244-5580
info@branderco.ca
www.branderco.ca

Calgary: Brown Economic Consulting Inc.
#216, 5718 - 1A St. SW
Calgary, AB T2H 0E8

Tel: 403-571-0115; *Fax:* 403-571-0932
Toll-Free: 800-301-8801
info@browneconomic.com
www.browneconomic.com
Other Contact Information: Help Line, Toll-Free Phone:
1-888-232-2778

Calgary: Buchanan Barry LLP
#800, 840 - 6th Ave. SW
Calgary, AB T2P 3E5

Tel: 403-262-2116; *Fax:* 403-265-0845
mailbox@buchananbarry.ca
www.buchananbarry.ca
Other Contact Information: Alternate Email:
admin@buchananbarry.ca

Calgary: Bultmann & Company
#117, 5723 - 10th St. NE
Calgary, AB T2E 8W7

Tel: 403-250-8522; *Fax:* 403-250-8524
bultco.ca

Calgary: Calvista LLP
#1635, 1632 - 14th Ave. NW
Calgary, AB T2N 1M7

Tel: 403-777-2299; *Fax:* 403-777-4201
www.calvista.ca
www.facebook.com/CalvistaLLP; twitter.com/CalvistaLLP

Calgary: Catalyst LLP
#250, 200 Quarry Park Blvd. SE
Calgary, AB T2C 5E3

Tel: 403-296-0082; *Fax:* 403-296-0088
inquire@thecatalystgroup.ca
www.thecatalystgroup.ca
www.facebook.com/Catalystyyc; twitter.com/Catalyst_yyc

Calgary: CompassTAX Chartered Accountants
#510, 906 - 12th Ave. SW
Calgary, AB T2R 1K7

Tel: 403-531-2200; *Fax:* 403-263-1826
Toll-Free: 866-531-2281
www.compasstax.ca
twitter.com/CompassTAXLLP

Calgary: David Wallace Professional Corp.
#205, 259 Midpark Way SE
Calgary, AB T2X 1M2

Tel: 587-316-8045
www.davidwallaceprofessionalcorp.ca

Calgary: DLA LLP
#525, 6700 Macleod Trail SE
Calgary, AB T3H 0L3

Tel: 403-217-5925; *Fax:* 403-217-5934
info@dlallp.com
www.dlallp.com

Calgary: Don Akins Chartered Accountant
431B - 41st Ave. NE
Calgary, AB T2E 2N4

Tel: 403-777-0388; *Fax:* 403-777-0385
da.ofc@donakinsca.com
www.donakinsca.com

Calgary: D.W. Robart Professional Corporation
540 - 5th Ave. SW
Calgary, AB T2P 0M2

Tel: 403-266-2611

Calgary: Flood & Associates Consulting Ltd.
840 - 6 Ave. SW
Calgary, AB T2P 3E5

Tel: 403-263-1523

Calgary: Geib & Company Professional Corporation
#1020, 10201 Southport Rd. SW
Calgary, AB T2W 4X9

Tel: 403-259-4519; *Fax:* 403-255-0745
info@geibco.com
www.geibco.com

Calgary: GGT Chartered Professional Accountants
#230, 5010 Richard Rd. SW
Calgary, AB T3E 6L1

Tel: 403-475-8033; *Fax:* 403-475-0931
info@ggtcpa.com
www.ggtcpa.com

Calgary: Hamilton & Rosenthal Chartered Accountants
Mission Square Bldg.
#210, 2424 - 4th St. SW
Calgary, AB T2S 2T4

Tel: 403-266-2175; *Fax:* 403-514-2211
admin@hamrose.com
www.hamrose.com

Calgary: Kapasi & Associates Chartered Professional Accountants
#940, 396 - 11th Ave. SW
Calgary, AB T2R 0C5

Tel: 403-228-4974; *Fax:* 403-228-6823
www.kapasi.ca
www.facebook.com/427824810990599

Calgary: Kenway Mack Slusarchuk Stewart LLP (KMSS)
#1500, 333 - 11 Ave. SW
Calgary, AB T2R 1L9

Tel: 403-233-7750
info@kmss.ca
www.kmss.ca

Calgary: Kirk Wormley Professional Corporation (KW)
#806, 7015 Macleod Trail SW
Calgary, AB T2H 2K6

Tel: 403-266-5607; *Fax:* 403-201-0248
www.kirkwormley.ca
Other Contact Information: Employment Email:
accountingcareer@shaw.ca

Calgary: Masone & Company Ltd.
103 - 2308 Centre St. North
Calgary, AB T2E 2T7

Tel: 403-204-1544; *Fax:* 403-204-1545
www.masoneandcompany.com
www.facebook.com/masoneandcompany;
twitter.com/Masoneandco

Calgary: The Matthews Group LLP
#804, 322 - 11 Ave. SW
Calgary, AB T2R 0C5

Tel: 403-229-0066; *Fax:* 403-229-2817
info@matthewsgrp.com
www.matthewsgrp.com

Calgary: Minor & Associates
#104, 9705C Horton Rd. SW
Calgary, AB T2V 2X5

Tel: 403-509-3290; *Fax:* 403-509-3288
www.minorandassociates.ca
twitter.com/MinorCPA

Calgary: Mitchell-Jones Taxation Services Inc. (MJT)
#350, 5010 Richard Rd. SW
Calgary, AB T3E 6L1

Tel: 403-265-8545; *Fax:* 403-265-8554
clientinfo@mjtaxation.com
www.mjtaxation.com

Calgary: Prospera Chartered Accountants
Willow Park Centre
#404, 10325 Bonaventure Dr. SE
Calgary, AB T2J 7E4

Tel: 403-252-5858; *Fax:* 403-259-8416
info@partnersinprosperity.ca
www.partnersinprosperity.ca

Calgary: Quadrant Chartered Accountants & Business Valuators
816 - 13th Ave. SW
Calgary, AB T2R 0L2

Tel: 403-457-4477; *Fax:* 403-457-4059
info@quadrantaccounting.ca
quadrantaccounting.ca
www.facebook.com/QuadrantAccounting;
twitter.com/QuadrantCA

Calgary: Quon & Associates, & Anchor Accounting Services Ltd.
3700 - 19th St. NE, Bay 1
Calgary, AB T2E 6V2

Tel: 403-250-5111; *Fax:* 403-291-0412
service@quonassociates.com
www.quonassociates.com
www.facebook.com/QuonAssociates;
twitter.com/QuonAssociates

Calgary: Roberts & Company Professional Accountants LLP
#102, 2411 - 4th St. NW
Calgary, AB T2M 2Z8

Tel: 403-282-8889; *Fax:* 403-282-5880
info@robertsco.ca
www.robertsco.ca

Calgary: Schwartz & Company Chartered Professional Accountants
#212, 280 Midpark Way SE
Calgary, AB T2X 1J6

Tel: 403-234-9080; *Fax:* 403-775-0595
info@schwartzcpa.ca
www.schwartzcpa.ca

Calgary: SCP LLP
#810, 734 - 7 Ave. SW
Calgary, AB T2P 3P8

Tel: 403-261-9933; *Fax:* 403-262-3917
firm@scp-ca.com
www.scp-ca.com

Calgary: The Small Business Group of Companies
#101, 11500 - 29th St. SE
Calgary, AB T2Z 3W9

Tel: 403-257-6235; *Fax:* 403-257-6258
Toll-Free: 855-489-3546
info@smallbusinesscompanies.ca
smallbusinesscompanies.ca
www.youtube.com/user/smallbusinesscompany;
www.facebook.com/smallbusinesscalgary

Calgary: Stephen R. Sefcik Professional Corp.
#212, 20 Sunpark Plaza SE
Calgary, AB T2X 3T2

Tel: 403-255-6296
www.sefcikassociate.ca

Calgary: Vanessa A. Brown Professional Corporation
Touchstone Corporate Centre
#308, 222 - 58th Ave. SW
Calgary, AB T2H 2S3

Tel: 403-229-1996
info@vabrown.ca
www.vabrown.ca

Calgary: Vertefeuille Rempel Chartered Accountants
#504, 304 - 8th Ave. SW
Calgary, AB T2P 1C2

Tel: 403-294-0733; *Toll-Free:* 877-794-0733
www.vertrempel.com

Calgary: **Weller & Zimaro Chartered Accountants**
2915 - 15th St. NE
Calgary, AB T2E 1T7

Tel: 403-769-1958; *Fax:* 403-769-1978
admin@wzaccountants.ca
www.wzaccountants.ca
www.facebook.com/WZCharteredAccountants;
twitter.com/wz_accountants

Cochrane: **W. Callaway Professional Corporation**
PO Box 61
Site 5, RR#1
Cochrane, AB T4C 1A1

Tel: 403-932-5433; *Fax:* 403-932-5577
www.wcallaway.com

Edmonton: **Bernhard Brinkmann Chartered Accountant**
PO Box 82090, Stn. Yellowbird
Edmonton, AB T6J 7E6

Tel: 780-434-2756
bhbrinkmann@brinkmann.ca
www.nk.ca:8443/~aboo/brinkmann/contact.html

Edmonton: **Donnelly & Co. LLP**
#100, 15023 - 123rd Ave.
Edmonton, AB T5V 1J7

Tel: 780-488-7071; *Fax:* 780-488-4650
donnellyco.ab.ca

Edmonton: **Givens LLP**
McLennan Ross Bldg.
#201, 12220 Stony Plain Rd.
Edmonton, AB T5N 3Y4

Tel: 780-482-7337; *Fax:* 780-482-7423
Toll-Free: 844-382-7337
edmonton@givens.ca
www.givens.ca
www.facebook.com/Givensaccounting

Edmonton: **King & Company**
#1201, Energy Sq.
10109 - 106th St. NW
Edmonton, AB T5J 3L7

Tel: 780-423-2437; *Fax:* 780-426-5861
www.kingco.ca

Edmonton: **Kingston Ross Pasnak LLP**
9Triple8 Bldg.
#1500, 9888 Jasper Ave.
Edmonton, AB T5J 5C6

Tel: 780-424-3000; *Fax:* 780-429-4817
www.krpgroup.com

Edmonton: **Koehli Wickenberg Chartered Accountants**
9771 - 54th Ave.
Edmonton, AB T6E 5J4

Tel: 780-466-6204; *Fax:* 780-466-6262
info@kwbllp.com
www.kwbllp.com
www.facebook.com/KWBEdmonton;
twitter.com/KWB_Edmonton

Edmonton: **Liu & Associates LLP**
#300, 10534 - 124th St. NW
Edmonton, AB T5N 1S1

Tel: 780-429-1047; *Fax:* 780-423-5076
Toll-Free: 866-212-1318
liuandassociates.com
Other Contact Information: Calgary, Fax: 403-261-6869
www.facebook.com/liuandassociates; twitter.com/LiuLLP

Edmonton: **Padgett Business Services Edmonton NW**
12203 - 107th Ave.
Edmonton, AB T5M 1Y9

Tel: 780-482-7297
padgettnw.com
www.facebook.com/padgettnw; twitter.com/Padgett_NW

Edmonton: **Padgett Edmonton South**
11708 - 170 St.
Edmonton, AB T5S 1J7

Tel: 780-434-7146; *Fax:* 780-434-7697
padgettedmonton.ca

Edmonton: **Romanovsky & Associates, Chartered Accountants**
10260 - 112th St.
Edmonton, AB T5K 1M4

Tel: 780-447-5830; *Fax:* 780-451-6291
Toll-Free: 800-861-5830
www.romanovsky.com

Edmonton: **SVS Group LLP**
#100, 17010 - 103rd Ave.
Edmonton, AB T5S 1K7

Tel: 780-486-3357; *Fax:* 780-486-3320
www.svsgroup.ca
twitter.com/SVSGroupLLP

High River: **Muth & Co. LLP**
PO Box 5039
318 Centre St. SE
High River, AB T1V 1M3

Tel: 403-652-4272; *Fax:* 403-652-2339
reception@mcollp.com
www.mcollp.com

Innisfail: **Baker Tilly Rockies LLP**
PO Box 6401
#202A, 4911 - 50th St.
Innisfail, AB T4G 1T2

Tel: 403-227-4444
innisfail@bakertilly.ca
www.bakertilly.ca/en/innisfail-alberta

Leduc: **Luchak Luchak Sosnowski Chartered Professional Accountants (LLS)**
4716 - 51 Ave.
Leduc, AB T9E 6Y8

Tel: 780-986-8383; *Fax:* 780-986-4499
Toll-Free: 888-986-8383
contact@lls.team
lls.team
www.facebook.com/LuchakLuchakSosnowski

Lethbridge: **Avail LLP**
#100, 530 - 8th St. South
Lethbridge, AB T1J 2J8

Tel: 403-382-6800; *Fax:* 403-327-8990
Toll-Free: 800-665-5034
www.availcpa.com
www.facebook.com/AvailCPA; twitter.com/AvailCPA

Lethbridge: **Blanchette Van Dyk Valgardson Logue (BVVL)**
#801B, 3 Ave. South
Lethbridge, AB T1J 0H8

Tel: 403-317-4500; *Fax:* 403-317-4501
admin@bvvl.ca
www.bvvl.ca

Red Deer: **Pivotal LLP**
Gasoline Alley Business Centre
#201, 33 McKenzie Cres.
Red Deer, AB T4S 2H4

Tel: 403-347-2226; *Fax:* 403-343-6140
Toll-Free: 877-347-2226
office@pivotalcpa.ca
www.pivotalcpa.ca
www.facebook.com/pivotalcpa; twitter.com/pivotalcpa

Slave Lake: **Nash Giroux, LLP**
PO Box 129
Slave Lake, AB T0G 2A0

Tel: 780-849-3977; *Fax:* 780-849-3244
www.nashgirouxllp.ca
www.facebook.com/nashgiroux

St Paul: **Desjardins & Company**
5008 - 51st Ave.
St Paul, AB T0A 3A0

Tel: 780-645-5516; *Fax:* 780-645-6010

Stettler: **Gitzel & Company**
PO Box 460
4912 - 51st St.
Stettler, AB T0C 2L0

Tel: 403-742-4431; *Fax:* 403-742-1266
Toll-Free: 877-742-4431
gitzel.ca

Stony Plain: **Hawkings Tinney LLP**
PO Box 3188, Stn. Main
#101, 5300 - 50th St.
Stony Plain, AB T7Z 1T8

Tel: 780-963-2727; *Fax:* 780-963-1294
hawkings.com

Sundre: **Valerie L. Burrell Prof. Corp.**
Corner Brook Bldg.
PO Box 1963
#201, 101 - 6th St. SW
Sundre, AB T0M 1X0

Tel: 403-638-3116; *Fax:* 403-638-9166
info@valbpc.com
www.valbpc.com

Vegreville: **Wilde & Company Chartered Professional Accountants**
PO Box 70
4902 - 50th St.
Vegreville, AB T9C 1R1

Tel: 780-632-3673; *Fax:* 780-632-6133
Toll-Free: 800-808-0998
office@wildeandco.com
www.wildeandco.com
www.facebook.com/173231086093970

Wainwright: **Hall & Company Chartered Professional Accountants**
#3, 2802 - 15th Ave.
Wainwright, AB T9W 0A4

Tel: 780-842-6106; *Fax:* 780-842-5540
Toll-Free: 888-842-6106
www.hallco.ca

British Columbia

Burnaby: **Kanester Johal LLP Chartered Professional Accountants**
#208, 3993 Henning Dr.
Burnaby, BC V5C 6P7

Tel: 604-451-8300; *Fax:* 604-451-8301
info@kjca.com
www.kjca.com

Burnaby: **Kemp Harvey Burnaby Chartered Professional Accountants Inc.**
PO Box 30567, Stn. Brentwood
#153, 4664 Lougheed Hwy.
Burnaby, BC V5C 3Z6

Tel: 604-291-1470; *Fax:* 604-291-0264
burnaby@kempharvey.com
www.kempharvey.com/index.php/burnaby
www.facebook.com/kempharveygroup.ca;
twitter.com/KempHarveyGroup

Campbell River: **Chase Sekulich Chartered Professional Accountants**
#400, 10th Ave.
Campbell River, BC V9W 4E3

Tel: 250-287-8331; *Fax:* 250-287-7224
Toll-Free: 866-317-8331
office@chasesekulich.com
www.chasesekulich.com
Other Contact Information: Bankruptcy URL:
www.bankruptcytrusteebc.ca

Campbell River: **Eidsvik & Co.**
#303, 1100 Island Hwy.
Campbell River, BC V9W 8C6

Tel: 250-286-6629; *Fax:* 250-286-6779

Castlegar: **Craig M. Gutwald Inc.**
880 Waterloo Rd.
Castlegar, BC V1N 4K8

Tel: 250-365-0434; *Fax:* 250-365-0469
www.gutwald.ca

Coquitlam: **Kemp Harvey Kok de Roca-Chan Inc.**
#210, 1140 Austin Ave.
Coquitlam, BC V3K 3P5

Tel: 604-937-3444; *Fax:* 604-937-3422
coquitlam@kempharvey.com
www.kempharvey.com/index.php/coquitlam
www.facebook.com/kempharveygroup.ca;
twitter.com/KempHarveyGroup

Coquitlam: **Rise Advisors CPA**
566 Lougheed Hwy., 2nd Fl.
Coquitlam, BC V3K 3S3

Tel: 604-936-4377; *Fax:* 604-936-8376
info@riseadvisors.ca
riseadvisors.ca
www.facebook.com/riseadvisors

Duncan: **Palmer Leslie Chartered Professional Accountants**
#301, 394 Duncan St.
Duncan, BC V9L 3W4

Tel: 250-748-1426; *Fax:* 250-748-2805
Toll-Free: 800-818-5703
www.palmerleslie.ca

Grand Forks: Kemp Harvey Burch Kientz Inc.
PO Box 2020
619 Central Ave.
Grand Forks, BC V0H 1H0
Tel: 250-442-2121; *Fax:* 250-442-5825
grandforks@kempharvey.com
www.kempharvey.com/index.php/grand-forks
www.facebook.com/kempharveygroup.ca;
twitter.com/KempHarveyGroup

Kamloops: Campbell & Company
#401, 153 Seymour St.
Kamloops, BC V2C 2C7
Tel: 250-374-1241; *Fax:* 250-828-6828
ca@campbellco.ca
www.campbellco.ca

Kamloops: Sandra J. Crocker
PO Box 28043
328 Seymour St.
Kamloops, BC V2C 0C9
Tel: 250-372-0071; *Fax:* 250-374-0066
Toll-Free: 855-588-0029
sandra@sjcrockerinc.com
sjcrockerinc.com

Kamloops: Tenisci Piva LLP
261A Victoria St.
Kamloops, BC V2C 2A1
Tel: 250-372-7655; *Fax:* 250-372-2118
tp@teniscipiva.com
www.teniscipiva.com

Kelowna: Chun & Company
#202, 3320 Richter St.
Kelowna, BC V1W 4V5
Tel: 250-860-8687
www.chun.ca
www.facebook.com/CHUNandCompany;
twitter.com/CHUNandCo

Kelowna: Kemp Harvey Kelowna Chartered Professional Accountants Inc.
#203, 1740 Gordon Dr.
Kelowna, BC V1Y 3H2
Tel: 250-763-8029; *Fax:* 250-763-5155
kelowna@kempharvey.com
www.kempharvey.com/index.php/delivery
www.facebook.com/kempharveygroup.ca;
twitter.com/KempHarveyGroup

Kelowna: Wahl & Associates
#203, 1441 Ellis St.
Kelowna, BC V1Y 2A3
Tel: 250-762-3362; *Fax:* 250-762-3409
info@wahlcga.com
www.wahlcga.com/contact.html

Lantzville: KMA Chartered Accountants Ltd.
PO Box 70
7190 Lantzville Rd.
Lantzville, BC V0R 2H0
Tel: 250-390-4131
www.kmacpa.ca

Maple Ridge: Choquette & Company Accounting Group
10662 - 240A St.
Maple Ridge, BC V2W 2B1
Tel: 604-463-8202; *Fax:* 604-463-8210
Toll-Free: 800-667-9254
www.choquetteco.com
www.facebook.com/ChoquetteCompany;
twitter.com/ChoquetteCo

Maple Ridge: EPR Maple Ridge Langley
22377 Dewdney Trunk Rd.
Maple Ridge, BC V2X 3J4
Tel: 604-467-5561; *Fax:* 604-467-1219
www.eprcpa.ca

Nanaimo: Church Pickard Chartered Accountants
25 Cavan St.
Nanaimo, BC V9R 2T9
Tel: 250-754-6396; *Fax:* 250-754-8177
Toll-Free: 866-754-6396
mail@churchpickard.com
www.churchpickard.com

Nanaimo: Dougan Irwin & Associates
Long Lake Plaza
#3, 4890 Rutherford Rd., 2nd Fl.
Nanaimo, BC V9T 4Z4
Tel: 250-754-1291; *Fax:* 604-681-5373
info@douganirwin.ca
www.douganirwin.ca

Nelson: Carmichael, Toews, Irving Inc.
247 Baker St.
Nelson, BC V1L 4H4
Tel: 250-354-4451; *Fax:* 250-354-4427
admin@nelsoncpa.ca
www.cti-cga.com

New Westminster: McDonald & Co.
631 Carnavon St.
New Westminster, BC V3M 1E3
Tel: 604-521-8885; *Fax:* 604-521-3611
mcdonald9@direct.ca

North Vancouver: Clearline Chartered Professional Accountants
#203, 1133 Lonsdale Ave.
North Vancouver, BC V7M 2H4
Tel: 604-639-0909; *Fax:* 778-375-3109
we_are@clearlinecpa.ca
www.clearlinecpa.ca
twitter.com/clearlinecpa

North Vancouver: Gray & Associates, Chartered Accountants
#201, 1075 West 1st St.
North Vancouver, BC V7P 3T4
Tel: 604-990-0550; *Fax:* 604-990-0509
Toll-Free: 800-990-0550
info@grayandassociates.ca
grayandassociates.ca
www.facebook.com/grayandassociatesCPAs;
twitter.com/GrayNAssociates

North Vancouver: L.R. Brager & Associates
Griffin Centre
#210, 901 - 3rd St. West
North Vancouver, BC V7P 3P9
Tel: 604-998-4069; *Fax:* 604-243-6990
bragercpa.com

North Vancouver: Weir & Company Chartered Professional Accountants LLP
#201, 1343 Lonsdale Ave.
North Vancouver, BC V7M 2H7
Tel: 604-986-9440; *Fax:* 604-986-9442
cas@weirllp.com
www.weirllp.com

Osoyoos: Kemp Harvey Craig Inc.
PO Box 1039
8901 Main St.
Osoyoos, BC V0H 1V0
Tel: 250-495-3223; *Fax:* 250-495-3559
osoyoos@kempharvey.com
www.kempharvey.com/index.php/3436-2
www.facebook.com/kempharveygroup.ca;
twitter.com/KempHarveyGroup

Penticton: HLW Chartered Professional Accountants Inc.
502 Ellis St.
Penticton, BC V2A 4M3
Tel: 250-492-8821; *Fax:* 250-492-8288
info@hlw-cpa.com
hlw-cpa.com
www.facebook.com/hlwaccountants

Penticton: Kemp Harvey Kemp Thompson Inc.
445 Ellis St.
Penticton, BC V2A 4M1
Tel: 250-492-8200; *Fax:* 250-492-6921
penticton@kempharvey.com
www.kempharvey.com/index.php/penticton
www.facebook.com/kempharveygroup.ca;
twitter.com/KempHarveyGroup

Port Moody: Gregory, Yick & Associates
#402, 130 Brew St.
Port Moody, BC V3H 0E3
Tel: 604-939-2929; *Fax:* 604-936-4002
gregorywhittle.ca
www.facebook.com/356687374350264

Prince George: Terlesky Braithwaite Janzen LLP
180 Victoria St.
Prince George, BC V2L 2J2
Tel: 250-564-2014; *Fax:* 250-564-5613
Toll-Free: 888-564-2014
www.tbjcga.com

Prince George: Tony Tiani & Company Inc.
#200, 411 Quebec St.
Prince George, BC V2L 1W5
Tel: 250-564-0400
www.tiani.ca
www.facebook.com/832768153464962

Revelstoke: Baker Tilly Revelstoke
PO Box 2910
#201, 200 Campbell Ave.
Revelstoke, BC V0E 2S0
Tel: 250-837-4400; *Fax:* 250-837-4494
revelstoke@bakertilly.ca
www.bakertilly.ca/en/revelstoke-british-columbi a

Richmond: BC Sun & Associates Inc.
#708, 6081 No. 3 Rd.
Richmond, BC V6Y 2B2
Tel: 604-270-4610; *Fax:* 604-270-4618
info@bcsun.ca
bcsun.ca
www.facebook.com/BCSUN.ca

Richmond: Bruce Dunn & Company Inc., Chartered Accountants
#200, 5760 Minoru Blvd.
Richmond, BC V6X 2A9
Tel: 604-241-8824; *Fax:* 604-241-8800
info@brucedunn.ca
www.brucedunn.ca

Richmond: Campbell Saunders, Ltd.
Mazda Bldg.
#6080, 8171 Ackroyd Rd.
Richmond, BC V6X 3K1
Tel: 604-821-9882; *Fax:* 604-821-9870
receptionrmd@csvan.com
www.csvan.com

Richmond: Greig Sheppard Ltd.
5090 - 8171 Ackroyd Rd.
Richmond, BC V6X 3K1
Tel: 604-270-7601; *Fax:* 604-270-3314
cga@greigsheppard.com
www.greigsheppard.com

Richmond: Jerry's Accounting Ltd.
#530, 130 - 8191 Westminster Hwy.
Richmond, BC V6X 1A7
Tel: 604-273-7789
jerryky@shaw.ca
www.jerryaccounting.com

Smithers: VanderGaag & Bakker, Chartered Professional Accountants
PO Box 2680
1076 Main St.
Smithers, BC V0J 2N0
Tel: 250-847-2257; *Fax:* 250-847-5102
Toll-Free: 888-499-2257
www.bvcga.com

Surrey: David Pel & Company Inc.
#102, 10715 - 135A St.
Surrey, BC V3T 4E3
Tel: 604-585-1255; *Fax:* 604-585-8525
info@dpelcga.com
davidpelandcompany.com
www.facebook.com/DavidPelCo

Surrey: Heming, Wyborn & Grewal (HWG)
#200, 17618 - 58th Ave.
Surrey, BC V3S 1L3
Tel: 604-576-9121; *Fax:* 604-576-2890
hwgca@hwgca.com
www.hwgca.com

Surrey: Luckett Wenman & Associates (LWA)
#204, 10252 City Pkwy.
Surrey, BC V3T 4C2
Tel: 604-584-3566; *Fax:* 604-584-0629
Toll-Free: 866-584-3566
contact@lwatax.com
www.lwatax.com
twitter.com/lwatax

Surrey: Sharma & Associates
#1, 13018 - 84th Ave.
Surrey, BC V3W 1L2
Tel: 604-597-5612; *Fax:* 604-590-5808
info@sharmacga.com
www.sharmacpa.ca

Surrey: Van Wensem & Vukets Chartered
Professional Accountants
#201, 19292 - 60th Ave.
Surrey, BC V3S 3M2
Tel: 604-510-4900
www.smallbiztax.ca

Terrace: Kemp Harvey Demers Inc.
4734 Park Ave.
Terrace, BC V8G 1W1
Tel: 250-638-8705; *Fax:* 250-638-0600
terrace@kempharvey.com
www.kempharvey.com/index.php/3432-2
www.facebook.com/kempharveygroup.ca;
twitter.com/KempHarveyGroup

Vancouver: Arbutus Group Chartered Professional
Accountants
#1440, 1188 West Georgia St.
Vancouver, BC V6E 4A2
Tel: 604-688-6191
info@arbutusgroupcpa.com
www.arbutusgroupcpa.com

Vancouver: Baker Tilly WM LLP
#900, 400 Burrard St.
Vancouver, BC V6C 3B7
Tel: 604-684-6212; *Fax:* 604-688-3497
vancouver@bakertilly.ca
www.bakertilly.ca/en/vancouver-british-columbia

Vancouver: BBA Accounting Group Inc.
#1760, 650 West Georgia St.
Vancouver, BC V6B 4N8
Tel: 604-685-9843; *Fax:* 604-685-9856
van@bbagroup.ca
www.bbagroup.ca
www.facebook.com/BBAgroup; twitter.com/BBAGroup

Vancouver: BCJ Group
4946 Fraser St.
Vancouver, BC V5W 2Y8
Tel: 604-431-0445; *Fax:* 604-428-0099
info@bcjgroup.ca
www.bcjgroup.ca
www.facebook.com/bcjgroup

Vancouver: Bench
Vancouver, BC
Toll-Free: 888-760-1940
help@bench.co
bench.co
www.instagram.com/benchaccounting;
www.facebook.com/BenchAccounting; twitter.com/bench

Vancouver: Bing C. Wong & Associates Ent. Ltd.
4919 Main St.
Vancouver, BC V5W 2R2
Tel: 604-682-7561

Vancouver: Buckley Dodds LLP
#1140, 1185 West Georgia St.
Vancouver, BC V6E 4E6
Tel: 604-688-7227; *Fax:* 604-681-7716
info@buckleydodds.com
www.buckleydodds.com

Vancouver: Cawley, Curran, Wong & Associates
601 West Broadway Ave., #M9
Vancouver, BC V5Z 4C2
Tel: 604-731-1191; *Fax:* 604-731-3511
bcawley@ccwcpa.ca
www.cawley.ca

Vancouver: Concert CPA
#600, 450 SW Marine Dr.
Vancouver, BC V5X 0C3
Tel: 604-683-0333; *Fax:* 604-683-2346
inquiries@concertcpa.ca
www.concertcpa.ca

Vancouver: D+H Group LLP
1333 West Broadway St., 10th Fl.
Vancouver, BC V6H 4C1
Tel: 604-731-5881; *Fax:* 604-731-9923
info@dhgroup.ca
www.dhgroup.ca
www.facebook.com/37001994848; twitter.com/dhgroup_recruit

Vancouver: Dale Matheson Carr-Hilton Labonte LLP
(DMCL)
#1500, 1140 West Pender St.
Vancouver, BC V6E 4G1
Tel: 604-687-4747; *Fax:* 604-689-2778
info@dmcl.ca
www.dmcl.ca
www.facebook.com/DMCLCPA; twitter.com/dmclcpa

Vancouver: David Lin, Certified General Accountant
5728 East Blvd.
Vancouver, BC V6M 4M4
Tel: 604-267-0381
www3.telus.net/davidlin

Vancouver: Davidson & Co.
Pacific Centre
PO Box 10372
#1200, 609 Granville St.
Vancouver, BC V7Y 1G6
Tel: 604-687-0947
davidson@davidson-co.com
www.davidson-co.com
www.facebook.com/DavidsonAndCompany

Vancouver: Desai & Associates
#201, 5990 Fraser St.
Vancouver, BC V5W 2Z7
Tel: 604-321-9992; *Fax:* 604-321-9998
info@desaiassociates.ca
www.desaiassociates.ca

Vancouver: EPR North Vancouver
#219, 700 Marine Dr. North
Vancouver, BC V7M 1H3
Tel: 604-987-8101; *Fax:* 604-987-1794
www.eprnv.ca
www.facebook.com/EPRNV

Vancouver: Equity Business Services Inc.
#200, 1892 West Broadway Ave.
Vancouver, BC V6J 1Y9
Tel: 604-874-9080; *Fax:* 604-874-9080
www.equityinc.ca

Vancouver: Galloway Botteselle & Company (GBCO)
Maple Place Professional Centre
#300, 2000 West 12th Ave.
Vancouver, BC V6J 2G2
Tel: 604-736-6581; *Fax:* 604-736-0152
vancouver@porterhetu.com
gbco.ca
www.facebook.com/gbco.cpas; twitter.com/GBCo_CPA

Vancouver: Greenberg Associates
5329 West Blvd.
Vancouver, BC V6M 3W4
Tel: 604-264-5170
greenbergassociates.ca

Vancouver: Hirji, Lum & Orr, Chartered Professional
Accountants
601 West Broadway, #M3
Vancouver, BC V5Z 4C2
Tel: 604-738-8299; *Fax:* 604-728-8296
www.hloca.com

Vancouver: Horizon Chartered Professional
Accountants Ltd.
PO Box 11517
#1400, 650 West Georgia St.
Vancouver, BC V6B 4N8
Tel: 604-697-7777; *Fax:* 604-697-7778
admin@horizoncpa.ca
www.horizoncpa.ca

Vancouver: The International Accounting Group
(TIAG)
2590 West King Edward Ave.
Vancouver, BC V6L 1T6
www.tiagnet.com
vimeo.com/taglawtiag; www.facebook.com/tiagalliance;
twitter.com/tiagnet

Vancouver: James Stafford Chartered Professional
Accountants
#350, 1111 Melville St.
Vancouver, BC V6E 3V6
Tel: 604-669-0711; *Fax:* 604-669-0754
info@jamesstafford.ca
www.jamesstafford.ca

Vancouver: Lancaster & David, Chartered
Accountants
PO Box 10133, Stn. Pacific Centre
#510, 701 West Georgia St.
Vancouver, BC V7Y 1C6
Tel: 604-717-5526; *Fax:* 604-717-5560
Toll-Free: 877-668-5263
admin@lancasteranddavid.ca
www.lancasteranddavid.ca

Vancouver: LLN Partners LLP Chartered
Professional Accountants
659-G Moberly Rd.
Vancouver, BC V5Z 4B2
Tel: 604-872-8883; *Fax:* 604-872-8889
info@LLNpartners.ca
www.llnpartners.ca
Other Contact Information: Employment Email:
careers@LLNpartners.ca

Vancouver: Lohn Caulder LLP
1500 West Georgia St., 3rd Fl.
Vancouver, BC V6G 2Z6
Tel: 604-687-5444; *Fax:* 604-688-7228
info@lohncaulder.com
www.lohncaulder.com
www.facebook.com/LohnCaulderLLP;
twitter.com/LohnCaulderLLP

Vancouver: Maharaj & Company Chartered
Professional Accountants
#210, 1080 Mainland St.
Vancouver, BC V6B 2T4
Tel: 604-270-2703
www.mhrj.com
Other Contact Information: Calgary Phone: 403-668-0794;
Edmonton Phone: 780-628-2968; Mobile Phone: 604-889-5329
www.facebook.com/maharajco; twitter.com/maharajco

Vancouver: Manning Elliott
1050 West Pender St., 11th Fl.
Vancouver, BC V6J 3S7
Tel: 604-714-3600; *Fax:* 604-714-3669
info@manningelliott.com
www.manningelliott.com
www.facebook.com/ManningElliott; twitter.com/ManningElliott

Vancouver: McLean Bartok Edwards
#840, 475 West Georgia St.
Vancouver, BC V6B 4M9
Tel: 604-683-4533; *Fax:* 604-683-2585
info@mcleanbartok.ca
www.mcleanbartok.ca

Vancouver: MCPA Services Inc.
#605, 815 Hornby St.
Vancouver, BC V6Z 2E6
Tel: 604-681-8835
info@mcpa.ca
www.mcpa.ca

Vancouver: Mew & Company Chartered Professional
Accountants
#418, 788 Beatty St.
Vancouver, BC V6B 2M1
Tel: 604-688-9198; *Fax:* 604-688-9192
www.mewco.ca
www.facebook.com/MewandCo; twitter.com/mewandco

Vancouver: N.I. Cameron Inc.
#400, 889 West Pender St.
Vancouver, BC V6C 3B2
Tel: 604-669-9631; *Fax:* 604-669-1848
info@nicameroninc.com
www.nicameroninc.com

Vancouver: Quantum Accounting Services Inc.
#110, 828 West 8th Ave.
Vancouver, BC V5Z 1E2
Tel: 604-662-8985; *Fax:* 604-662-8986
www.qas.bc.ca

Vancouver: Renaissance Group Chartered
Accountants Ltd.
#1460, 1075 West Georgia St.
Vancouver, BC V6E 3C9
Tel: 604-629-9600; *Fax:* 604-629-9601
info@rgroup.ca
www.rgroup.ca

Vancouver: **Rolfe, Benson LLP Chartered Professional Accountants**
#1500, 1090 West Georgia St.
Vancouver, BC V6E 3V7
Tel: 604-684-1101; *Fax:* 604-684-7937
admin@rolfebenson.com
www.rolfebenson.com

Vancouver: **Sandhu & Company, CPA**
#101, 2529 Kingsway
Vancouver, BC V5R 5H3
Tel: 604-322-7576
info@sandhutax.com
www.sandhutax.com

Vancouver: **Smythe LLP**
#700, 355 Burrard St.
Vancouver, BC V6C 2G8
Tel: 604-687-1231; *Fax:* 604-688-4675
info@smythecpa.com
www.smythecpa.com
twitter.com/smythecpa

Vancouver: **Stan W. Lee Chartered Professional Accountant**
North Tower
#628, 650 West 41st Ave.
Vancouver, BC V5Z 2M9
Tel: 604-291-6016; *Fax:* 604-291-2018
stan@stanwleeca.com
www.stanwleeca.com

Vancouver: **Strategex Group**
#520, 900 West Hastings St.
Vancouver, BC V6C 1E5
Tel: 604-688-2355; *Fax:* 604-688-2315
info@strategexgroup.ca
www.strategexgroup.ca
www.instagram.com/strategexgroup;
www.facebook.com/StrategexVancouver;
twitter.com/StrategexVan

Vancouver: **Theresa Ko, Chartered Accountant**
2066 Qualicum Dr.
Vancouver, BC V5P 2M2
Tel: 604-327-2069; *Fax:* 604-324-1762
www3.telus.net/public/tkoinc

Vancouver: **Tompkins Wozny LLP**
#206, 698 Seymour St.
Vancouver, BC V6B 3K6
Tel: 604-681-7703; *Fax:* 604-681-7713
info@twmca.com
www.twmca.com

Vancouver: **Trout Lake Group**
Vancouver, BC
Tel: 604-569-4444; *Fax:* 604-569-5060
info@troutlakegroup.ca
troutlakegroup.com

Vancouver: **Vohora LLP**
#1010, 777 Hornby St.
Vancouver, BC V6Z 1S4
Tel: 604-251-1535; *Fax:* 604-541-9845
Toll-Free: 800-281-5214
www.vohora.ca

Vancouver: **WDM Chartered Professional Accountants**
#420, 1501 West Broadway Ave.
Vancouver, BC V6J 4Z6
Tel: 604-734-3247; *Fax:* 604-734-4802
info@wdmca.com
www.wdmca.com

Vancouver: **Wolrige Mahon LLP**
Commerce Place
#900, 400 Burrard St.
Vancouver, BC V6C 3B7
Tel: 604-684-6212; *Fax:* 604-688-3497
info@wm.ca
www.wolrigemahon.com
www.facebook.com/WolrigeMahonLLP;
twitter.com/WolrigeMahonLLP

Vancouver: **Wong, Robinson & Co. Chartered Professional Accountants**
1708 - West 6th Ave.
Vancouver, BC V6J 5E8
Tel: 604-739-9500; *Fax:* 604-739-9394
info@wongrobinson.com
www.wongrobinson.com

Vernon: **Clark Robinson**
3109 - 32nd Ave.
Vernon, BC V1T 2M2
Tel: 250-545-7264; *Fax:* 250-542-5116
info@clarkrobinson.com
clarkrobinson.com
www.facebook.com/1966863250219430;
twitter.com/CR_Accountants

Vernon: **Kemp Harvey Laidman-Betts Inc.**
#206, 3334 - 30th Ave.
Vernon, BC V1T 2C8
Tel: 250-545-1544; *Fax:* 250-260-3641
vernon@kempharvey.com
www.kempharvey.com/index.php/3419-2
www.facebook.com/kempharveygroup.ca;
twitter.com/KempHarveyGroup

Victoria: **Baker Tilly Victoria Ltd.**
#540, 645 Fort St.
Victoria, BC V8W 1G2
Tel: 250-386-0500; *Fax:* 250-386-6151
victoria@bakertilly.ca
www.bakertilly.ca/en/victoria-british-columbia

Victoria: **Burkett & Co. Chartered Accountants**
#200, 3561 Shelbourne St.
Victoria, BC V8P 4G8
Tel: 250-370-9718; *Fax:* 250-370-9179
accountants@burkett.ca
www.burkett.ca

Victoria: **Feil & Co.**
#200, 888 Fort St.
Victoria, BC V8W 1H8
Tel: 250-382-6177; *Fax:* 250-385-0154
email@feilnco.com
www.feilnco.com

Victoria: **MH Stimpson & Associates Ltd.**
Shamrock Professional Centre
#202, 830 Shamrock St.
Victoria, BC V8X 2V1
Tel: 250-590-5211; *Fax:* 250-590-8575
stimpsoncpa.ca

Victoria: **Padgett Business Services - Victoria Capital Region**
#5, 4011 Quadra St.
Victoria, BC V8X 1K1
Tel: 250-744-3854; *Fax:* 250-744-3856
www.countbeans.com
Other Contact Information: Paytrak Phone: 250-708-0070
www.youtube.com/PadgettAccounting;
www.facebook.com/PadgettAccounting; twitter.com/PadgettBC

West Kelowna: **Expatax Services Ltd.**
1837 Olympus Way
West Kelowna, BC V1Z 3H9
Tel: 778-755-0754
www.expatax.ca

West Kelowna: **WK Group LLP**
#1, 2429 Dobbin Rd.
West Kelowna, BC V4T 2L4
Tel: 250-768-3400
info@wkgroup.ca
wkgroup.ca
www.facebook.com/WKGroupAccountants

Whistler: **Gershon & Co. Accounting & Tax Ltd.**
#207A, 4368 Main St.
Whistler, BC V0N 1B4
Tel: 604-938-1892; *Fax:* 604-938-1892
info@gershonandco.com
gershonandco.com
www.facebook.com/whistler.accounting;
twitter.com/Mark_Gershon

Whistler: **Gordon J. Wiber & Associates Inc.**
#10, 1006 Lynham Rd.
Whistler, BC V0N 1B1
Tel: 604-935-1114; *Fax:* 604-935-1154
www.whistlerca.com

Manitoba

Carman: **Nakonechny & Power Chartered Accountants Ltd.**
PO Box 880
31 Main St. South
Carman, MB R0G 0J0
Tel: 204-745-2061; *Fax:* 204-745-6322
admin@nakandpow.com
www.nakandpow.com

St Pierre-Jolys: **Pro Vue Business Group Chartered Professional Accountants Inc.**
PO Box 339
476 Sabourin St.
St Pierre-Jolys, MB R0A 1V0
Tel: 204-433-7964; *Fax:* 204-433-7996
www.dgfillion.com

Stonewall: **EPR Stonewall**
#2, 278 Main St.
Stonewall, MB R0C 2Z0
Tel: 204-467-5566
carol@eprstonewall.com
www.epr.ca

Swan River: **PKHC Chartered Professional Accountants**
PO Box 1660
100 - 4th Ave. North
Swan River, MB R0L 1Z0
Tel: 204-734-9331; *Fax:* 204-734-4785
Toll-Free: 800-743-8447
pkhc@pkhc.ca
www.pkhc.ca

Thompson: **Kendall & Pandya**
118 Cree Rd.
Thompson, MB R8N 0C1
Tel: 204-778-7312

Winnipeg: **Baker Tilly HMA LLP**
#701, 330 Portage Ave.
Winnipeg, MB R3C 0C4
Tel: 204-989-2229; *Fax:* 204-944-9923
Toll-Free: 866-730-4777
winnipeg@bakertilly.ca
www.bakertilly.ca/en/winnipeg-m anitoba

Winnipeg: **Booke & Partners**
#500, 5 Donald St.
Winnipeg, MB R3L 2T4
Tel: 204-284-7060; *Fax:* 204-284-7105
www.bookeandpartners.ca

Winnipeg: **Bulat & Poustie Chartered Professional Accountants**
1700 Ness Ave.
Winnipeg, MB R3J 3Y1
Tel: 204-831-1700; *Fax:* 204-831-7812
www.bandp.ca

Winnipeg: **Chochinov Curry LLP**
#1250, 363 Broadway Ave.
Winnipeg, MB R3C 3N9
porterhetu.com/firms/chochinov-curry-llp

Winnipeg: **Craig & Ross Chartered Professional Accountants**
#1515, 1 Lombard Place
Winnipeg, MB R3B 0X3
Tel: 204-956-9400; *Fax:* 204-956-9424
info@craigross.com
www.craigross.com

Winnipeg: **The Exchange Chartered Accountants LLP (ECA)**
#1, 554 St. Mary's Rd.
Winnipeg, MB R2M 3L5
Tel: 204-943-4584; *Fax:* 204-957-5195
info@exg.ca
www.exg.ca

Winnipeg: **F.H. Black & Company Chartered Professional Accountants Inc.**
36 Roslyn Rd.
Winnipeg, MB R3L 0G6
Tel: 204-949-9113; *Fax:* 204-949-0497
www.fhblack.com

Winnipeg: Fort Group Chartered Professional
Accountants Inc.
219 Fort St.
Winnipeg, MB R3C 1E2
Tel: 204-942-0861; *Fax:* 204-947-6834
www.fortgroupcpa.ca
www.facebook.com/fortgroupcpa; twitter.com/FortGroupCPA

Winnipeg: Frostiak & Leslie Chartered Professional
Accountants Inc.
#200, 1700 Corydon Ave.
Winnipeg, MB R3N 0K1
Tel: 204-487-4449; *Fax:* 204-488-8658
reception@cafinancialgroup.com
www.cafinancialgroup.com

Winnipeg: KWB Chartered Accountants Inc.
#800, 125 Garry St.
Winnipeg, MB R3C 3P2
Tel: 204-982-3878; *Fax:* 204-982-3888
www.kwb.ca

Winnipeg: Lazer Grant LLP Chartered Accountants
& Business Advisors
#300, 309 McDermot Ave.
Winnipeg, MB R3A 1T3
Tel: 204-942-0300; *Fax:* 204-957-5611
Toll-Free: 800-220-0005
www.lazergrant.ca

Winnipeg: M Group Chartered Professional
Accountants LLP
710 Corydon Ave.
Winnipeg, MB R3M 0X9
Tel: 204-992-7200; *Fax:* 204-992-7208
info@mgroup.ca
www.mgroup.ca
www.facebook.com/122828771117017; twitter.com/Mgroupca

Winnipeg: Magnus Chartered Accountants
#430, 5 Donald St.
Winnipeg, MB R3L 2T4
Tel: 204-942-4441
BMM@MagnusLLP.ca
www.magnusllp.ca

Winnipeg: McLenehan & Associates Chartered
Professional Accountants
#205, 3657 Robin Blvd.
Winnipeg, MB R3R 0E2
Tel: 204-505-3113; *Fax:* 204-505-3121
success@mclenehan.com
www.mclenehan.com
www.facebook.com/MikeMcLenehanCGA

Winnipeg: Nachtigal Burgess LLP Certified General
Accountants (NB)
#222, 530 Kenaston Blvd.
Winnipeg, MB R3N 1Z4
Tel: 204-334-8972

Winnipeg: Pope & Brookes LLP
#300, 530 Kenaston Blvd.
Winnipeg, MB R3N 1Z4
Tel: 204-487-7957; *Fax:* 204-487-1243
advice@popebrookes.ca
www.popebrookes.ca

Winnipeg: Rawluk & Robert Chartered Professional
Accountants
226 St. Mary's Rd.
Winnipeg, MB R2H 1J3
Tel: 204-237-6053; *Fax:* 204-231-1461
www.accountants.mb.ca

Winnipeg: RDK Chartered Accountant Ltd.
5 Whitkirk Place
Winnipeg, MB R3R 2A2
Tel: 204-885-5280; *Fax:* 204-831-6670
www.rdkca.com
www.facebook.com/RDKCA

Winnipeg: Reid & Associates Chartered
Professional Accountants Inc.
1741 Portage Ave.
Winnipeg, MB R3J 0E5
Tel: 204-784-4590; *Fax:* 204-784-4599
Toll-Free: 877-784-4590
information@reidaccountants.com
www.reidaccountants.com

Winnipeg: Scarrow & Donald LLP
#100, 5 Donald St.
Winnipeg, MB R3L 2T4
Tel: 204-982-9800; *Fax:* 204-474-2886
sd@scarrowdonald.mb.ca
www.scarrowdonald.mb.ca

New Brunswick

Bathurst: EPR Bathurst /Péninsule
#100, 1935 St. Peter Ave.
Bathurst, NB E2A 7J5
Tel: 506-548-1984
eprbathurst.ca

Campbellton: Allen, Paquet & Arseneau LLP
PO Box 519
207 Roseberry St.
Campbellton, NB E3N 3G9
Tel: 506-789-0820; *Fax:* 506-759-7514
info.campbellton@apallp.com
www.apallp.com

Dieppe: Boudreau Albert Savoie & Associates
#101, 654, boul Malenfant
Dieppe, NB E1A 5V8
Tél: 506-857-0262; *Téléc:* 506-857-0232
info@bascpa.ca
www.bascpa.ca

Dieppe: EPR Robichaud CPA, CA Inc.
#301, 1040 Champlain St.
Dieppe, NB E1A 8L8
Tel: 506-855-3098; *Fax:* 506-855-3099
info@eprrobichaud.ca
www.eprrobichaud.ca
www.facebook.com/EPRRobichaud; twitter.com/eprrobichaud

Fredericton: AC Bringloe Feeney LLP
#100, 168 Dundonald St.
Fredericton, NB E3B 0Y8
Tel: 506-458-8326
www.acgca.ca

Fredericton: Bringloe Feeney LLP
#100, 168 Dundonald St.
Fredericton, NB E3B 0Y8
Tel: 506-458-8326

Fredericton: EPR Daye Kelly & Associates
31 Ashton Ct.
Fredericton, NB E3C 0H8
Tel: 506-458-8620; *Fax:* 506-450-8286
info@dayekelly.com
dayekelly.com

Fredericton: Nicholson & Beaumont Chartered
Accountants
328 King St.
Fredericton, NB E3B 1E3
Tel: 506-458-9815; *Fax:* 506-459-7575
info@nicholsonbeaumont.com
www.nicholsonbeaumont.com
Other Contact Information: Alternate Phone: 506-459-7575
www.facebook.com/nicholsonbeaumont

Quispamsis: Steeves Porter Hétu & Associates P.C.
Inc.
158 Millennium Dr.
Quispamsis, NB E2E 6E6
Tel: 506-847-7471; *Fax:* 506-847-3151
sph@steevesporterhetu.com
www.steevesporterhetu.com

Riverview: AC Stevenson & Partners CPA LLP
548 Pine Wood Rd.
Riverview, NB E1B 5J9
Tel: 506-387-4044
sp@partnersnb.ca
www.acgca.ca

Saint John: Beers Neal LLP
#301, 53 King St.
Saint John, NB E2L 1G5
Tel: 506-632-9020; *Fax:* 506-632-9030
www.beersneal.ca

Saint John: Curry & Betts
#201, 541 Rothesay Ave.
Saint John, NB E2J 2C6
Tel: 506-635-8181; *Fax:* 506-633-5943
info@curry-betts.ca
www.currybetts.ca

Saint John: Green Webber Company (GWC)
#200, 53 King St.
Saint John, NB E2L 1G5
Tel: 506-632-3000; *Fax:* 506-632-1007
www.gwco.ca

Saint John: Padgett Business Services New
Brunswick
221 Loch Lomond Rd.
Saint John, NB E2J 1Y5
Tel: 506-642-4464; *Fax:* 506-652-2780
padgettnb@padgettnb.com
www.padgettnb.com

Saint John: Teed Saunders Doyle & Co. Chartered
Accountants
39 Canterbury St.
Saint John, NB E2L 2C6
Tel: 506-636-9220; *Fax:* 506-634-8208
tsdsj@tsdca.com
www.teedsaundersdoyle.com

St. Stephen: L K Toombs CPA & Associates P.C.
Inc.
#207, 73 Milltown Blvd.
St. Stephen, NB E3L 1G5
Tel: 506-466-3291
lktpc@nb.aibn.com
www.acgca.ca

Sussex: Turnbull & Kindred Certified General
Accountants
PO Box 4608
44 Moffett Ave.
Sussex, NB E4E 5L8
Tel: 506-433-4202; *Fax:* 506-432-6569
tkcga.com
www.facebook.com/TurnbullKindred;
twitter.com/TurnbullKindred

Tracadie-Sheila: Mallet & Aubin CGA
3653, rue Principale
Tracadie-Sheila, NB E1X 1E2
Tél: 506-395-1013; *Téléc:* 506-395-6911
info@malletaubin.ca
malletaubin.ca

Woodstock: Lenehan McCain & Associates
#200, 389 Connell St.
Woodstock, NB E7M 5G5
Tel: 506-325-2101; *Fax:* 506-325-9675
info@lenehanmccain.ca
www.lenehanmccain.ca

Newfoundland & Labrador

Corner Brook: J. Pike & Company Ltd.
PO Box 1031
98 Broadway
Corner Brook, NL A2H 6J3
Tel: 709-639-7774; *Fax:* 709-639-7775

Gander: Sweetapple Accounting Group Ltd.
115 Armstrong Blvd.
Gander, NL A1V 2P2
Tel: 709-256-8682; *Fax:* 709-256-4051
dsweetapple@fms.nf.net
www.sweetappleaccounting.ca

Mount Pearl: EPR Kirby & Company
970 Topsail Rd.
Mount Pearl, NL A1N 3K2
Tel: 709-726-0000; *Fax:* 709-726-2200
info@eprkirby.com
www.kirbygroup.ca/eprkirby

Mount Pearl: Feltham & Associates Chartered
Professional Accountants
#202, 39 Commonwealth Ave.
Mount Pearl, NL A1N 1W7
Tel: 709-364-7300; *Fax:* 709-364-7731
accounting@feltham-associates.ca
feltham-associates.ca
www.facebook.com/124975570879426;
twitter.com/debrafelthamCGA

St. John's: Bussey Porter Hétu
#6, 1 Duffy Place
St. John's, NL A1B 4M6
Tel: 709-747-3615
www.porterhetu.com/nl_bussey.html

St. John's: **Harris Ryan Chartered Professional Accountants**
#202, 120 Stavanger Dr.
St. John's, NL A1A 5E8
Tel: 709-726-8324; *Fax:* 709-726-4525
hrcas@harrisryan.com
www.harrisryan.com

St. John's: **Jody Murphy, Chartered Accountant**
235 Majors Path
St. John's, NL A1A 5A1
Tel: 709-738-3271

St. John's: **Noseworthy Chapman Chartered Accountants**
#201, 516 Topsail Rd.
St. John's, NL A1E 2C5
Tel: 709-364-5600; *Fax:* 709-368-2146
info@noseworthychapman.ca
www.noseworthychapman.ca

Northwest Territories

Yellowknife: **Avery Cooper & Co.**
Laurentian Bldg.
PO Box 1620
4918 - 50th St.
Yellowknife, NT X1A 2P2
Tel: 867-873-3441; *Fax:* 867-873-2353
Toll-Free: 800-661-0787
www.averycooper.com
www.facebook.com/averycooperandco

Yellowknife: **EPR Yellowknife Professional Accounting Corporation**
PO Box 20072
#410, 4921 - 49th St.
Yellowknife, NT X1A 3X8
Tel: 867-669-0242; *Fax:* 867-669-7242
www.epryellowknife.ca

Nova Scotia

Amherst: **The AC Group of Independent Accounting Firms Limited**
c/o McIsaac Darragh Chartered Accountants
PO Box 217
11 Princess St.
Amherst, NS B4H 3Z2
Tel: 902-661-1027; *Fax:* 902-667-0884
admin@acgca.ca
www.acgca.ca
www.facebook.com/64587206840; twitter.com/ACG_CAs

Amherst: **Jorgensen & Bickerton Inc.**
31 Church St.
Amherst, NS B4H 3A7
Tel: 902-667-9339; *Toll-Free:* 877-667-9339
info@jorgensenbickerton.ca
www.jorgensenandbickerton.com

Amherst: **McIsaac Darragh Chartered Professional Accountants**
PO Box 217
11 Princess St.
Amherst, NS B4H 3Z2
Tel: 902-661-1027; *Fax:* 902-667-0884
contact@mcisaacdarragh.ca
www.acgca.ca

Antigonish: **MacDonald & Murphy Inc.**
#101, 155 Main St.
Antigonish, NS B2G 2B6
Tel: 902-867-1820
admin@macdonaldandmurphy.ca
www.acgca.ca

Bedford: **Darrell B. Cochrane & Associates Inc.**
4 Sedgewick Pl.
Bedford, NS B4A 0G5
Tel: 902-430-4796
www.porterhetu.com/ns_cochrane.html

Bedford: **Etter Macleod & Associates Inc.**
117 Brentwood Dr.
Bedford, NS B4A 3S3
Tel: 902-456-1031
porterhetu.com/firms/etter-macleod-associates-inc

Bridgewater: **AC Belliveau Veinotte Inc.**
PO Box 29
11 Dominion St.
Bridgewater, NS B4V 2W6
Tel: 902-543-4278
bridgewater@bvca.ca
www.acgca.ca

Dartmouth: **AC Hunter Tellier Belgrave Adamson**
#24, 260 Brownlow Ave.
Dartmouth, NS B3B 1V9
Tel: 902-468-1949
service@achtba.ca
www.acgca.ca

Dartmouth: **Baker Tilly Nova Scotia Inc.**
#201, 130 Eileen Stubbs Ave.
Dartmouth, NS B3B 2C4
Tel: 902-404-4000; *Fax:* 902-404-3099
infoNS@bakertilly.ca
www.bakertilly.ca/en/dartmouth-nova-scotia

Dartmouth: **Chassé & Associates Inc.**
24-260 Brownlow Ave.
Dartmouth, NS B3B 1V9
Tel: 902-468-0282

Dartmouth: **McNeil Porter Hétu**
344 Prince Albert Rd.
Dartmouth, NS B2Y 1N6
Tel: 902-464-9300
porterhetu.com/firms/mcneil-porter-hetu

Digby: **Sanford & Associates Chartered Professional Accountants Inc.**
PO Box 2410
95 Water St.
Digby, NS B0V 1A0
Tel: 902-245-6400; *Fax:* 902-245-6406
info@sanfordfinancial.ca
www.sanfordfinancial.ca
Other Contact Information: Mobile Phone: 902-308-9466

Halifax: **Green Landers Limited**
#201, 273 Bedford Hwy.
Halifax, NS B3M 2K5
Tel: 902-481-8144; *Fax:* 902-481-8143
www.greenlanders.ca

Halifax: **Howatt Group Chartered Professional Accountants**
#710, 1741 Brunswick St.
Halifax, NS B3J 3X8
Tel: 902-442-9300; *Fax:* 902-425-7827
info@howattgroup.ca
www.howattgroup.ca

Halifax: **Lyle Tilley Davidson Chartered Accountants**
#720, 1718 Argyle St.
Halifax, NS B3J 3N6
Tel: 902-423-7225; *Fax:* 902-422-3649
info@ltdca.com
www.ltdca.com

Sydney: **MGM & Associates Chartered Accountants**
PO Box 1
Sydney, NS B1P 6G9
Tel: 902-539-3900; *Fax:* 902-564-6062
www.mgm.ca

Wolfville: **Bishop & Company Chartered Professional Accountants Inc.**
PO Box 2104
#102, 24 Harbourside Dr.
Wolfville, NS B4P 2N5
Tel: 902-542-7665; *Fax:* 902-542-4554
info@bcica.ca
www.acgca.ca

Ontario

Almonte: **Colby McGeachy Professional Corporation**
PO Box 970
14 Mill St., 2nd Fl.
Almonte, ON K0A 1A0
Tel: 613-256-6415; *Fax:* 613-256-7569
Toll-Free: 866-259-2878
almonte@porterhetu.com
www.colbymcgeachy.com
Other Contact Information:
www.linkedin.com/company/10968970
www.youtube.com/user/colbymcgeachy;
www.facebook.com/ColbyMcGeachyPC;
twitter.com/ColbyMcGeachyPC

Ancaster: **Brownlow Partners Chartered Accountants**
259 Wilson St. East
Ancaster, ON L9G 2B8
Tel: 905-648-0404
info@brownlowcas.com
www.brownlowcas.com

Aurora: **Millard Foster Thibeault Youell PC**
#101, 15449 Yonge St.
Aurora, ON L4G 1P3
Tel: 905-727-1325; *Fax:* 905-727-1159
www.mfty.ca

Bancroft: **Rose Stone & Bains CPAs Professional Corporation**
PO Box 1209
294 Hastings St. North
Bancroft, ON K0L 1C0
Tel: 613-332-0834; *Fax:* 613-332-4154
Toll-Free: 800-333-0834
bancroft@porterhetu.com
www.bancroftaccountants.com

Barrie: **Powell Jones LLP Chartered Accountants**
121 Anne St. South
Barrie, ON L4N 7B6
Tel: 705-728-7461; *Fax:* 705-728-8317
Toll-Free: 888-828-7461
info@powelljones.ca
www.powelljones.ca

Barrie: **Rumley Holmes LLP**
#7, 301 Bryne Dr.
Barrie, ON L4N 8V4
Tel: 705-722-4272; *Fax:* 705-722-9852
Toll-Free: 866-922-5844
rhpartners.ca
www.facebook.com/RumleyHolmes.Accounting;
twitter.com/rumleyholmes

Belleville: **Soden & Co.**
25 Campbell St.
Belleville, ON K8N 1S6
Tel: 613-968-3495

Brampton: **Buttar & Associates Inc.**
Jaipur Chrysler Centre
#1, 470 Chrysler Dr.
Brampton, ON L6S 0C1
Tel: 905-866-6543; *Fax:* 905-866-6566
accounting.buttar.ca

Brampton: **Calvin G. Vickery, Chartered Accountant**
#100, 197 County Court Blvd.
Brampton, ON L6W 4P6
Tel: 905-451-5530
www.vickery.ca

Brampton: **Kenneth Bell CA Business Advisory Group**
#34, 18 Regan Rd.
Brampton, ON L7A 1C2
Tel: 905-453-0844; *Fax:* 905-453-1530
www.kenbell.ca

Brampton: **M W Mirza, Chartered Accountant**
#304, 2250 Bovaird Dr. East
Brampton, ON L6R 0W3
Tel: 647-866-1285; *Fax:* 647-723-7516
info@mwmca.ca
mwmca.ca

Brampton: **SMCA Professional Corporation**
#200, 197 County Court Blvd.
Brampton, ON L6W 4P6
Tel: 905-451-4034; *Toll-Free:* 888-524-4844
www.smca.ca

Brantford: **D.M. Austin, CPA, CA, LPA**
#12, 340 Henry St.
Brantford, ON N3S 7V9
Tel: 519-751-4353; *Fax:* 519-751-4350
www.dmaustin-ca.com

Brantford: **Millards**
PO Box 367
96 Nelson St.
Brantford, ON N3T 5N3
Tel: 519-759-3511; *Fax:* 519-759-7961
www.millards.com

Burlington: **Bateman MacKay**
#102, 5096 South Service Rd.
Burlington, ON L7L 5H4
Tel: 905-632-6400; *Fax:* 905-639-2285
Toll-Free: 866-236-9585
www.batemanmackay.com

Burlington: **The Cino Group Inc.**
#6, 185 Plains Rd. East
Burlington, ON L7T 2C4
Tel: 905-632-8400; *Fax:* 905-632-4501
info@thecinogroup.ca
www.thecinogroup.com
www.facebook.com/thecinogroup; twitter.com/The_Cino_Group

Burlington: **Prapavessis Jasek**
#205, 3380 South Service Rd.
Burlington, ON L7N 3J5
Tel: 905-634-8999; *Fax:* 905-634-5057
www.pj.on.ca

Burlington: **SB Partners LLP**
#301, 3600 Billings Ct.
Burlington, ON L7N 3N6
Tel: 905-632-5978; *Fax:* 905-632-9068
Toll-Free: 866-823-9990
www.sbpartners.ca
www.facebook.com/SBPartners; twitter.com/sbpartnersllp

Burlington: **Scott, Pichelli & Easter Ltd.**
#109, 3600 Billings Ct.
Burlington, ON L7N 3N6
Tel: 905-632-5853; *Fax:* 905-632-6113
www.bankruptcy-trustees.ca
www.facebook.com/ScottAndPichelliLtd

Burlington: **Stevenson & Lehocki LLP Chartered Accountants**
310 Plains Rd. East
Burlington, ON L7T 4J2
Tel: 905-632-0640; *Fax:* 905-632-0645
www.stevensonlehocki.com

Cambridge: **Graham Mathew Professional Corporation**
PO Box 880
150 Pinebush Rd.
Cambridge, ON N1R 5X9
Tel: 519-623-1870; *Fax:* 519-623-9490
www.gmpca.com

Carleton Place: **Kelly Huibers McNeely Professional Corporation (KHMPC)**
9 Emily St.
Carleton Place, ON K7C 1R9
Tel: 613-963-1430; *Fax:* 613-686-3960
Toll-Free: 866-999-1339
acctg@khmpc.ca
www.khmpc.ca

Chatham: **Baker Tilly CK, LLP**
62 Keil Dr. South
Chatham, ON N7M 3G8
Tel: 519-351-2024; *Fax:* 519-351-8831
chatham@bakertilly.ca
www.bakertilly.ca/en/chatham-ontario

Chatham: **EPR Rieger Bray Hohl**
#100, 40 Centre St.
Chatham, ON N7M 5W3
Tel: 519-436-0556; *Fax:* 519-436-1291
Toll-Free: 800-563-1865
info@eprchatham.com
www.eprchatham.com
twitter.com/EprChatham

Chatham: **Gilhula & Grant**
141 Grand Ave. East
Chatham, ON N7L 1W1
Tel: 519-352-3470

Collingwood: **Baker Tilly SGB LLP**
PO Box 130
115 Hurontario St.
Collingwood, ON L9Y 3Z4
Tel: 705-445-2020; *Fax:* 705-444-5833
collingwood@bakertilly.ca
www.bakertilly.ca/en/collingwood-ontario

Concord: **Gary A. Freedman + Associates, Chartered Accountant**
#1, 70 Villarboit Cres.
Concord, ON L4K 4C7
Tel: 905-669-7950; *Fax:* 905-669-7951
www.freedman.ca

Concord: **Miller, Saperia & Company**
#418, 1600 Steeles Ave. West
Concord, ON L4K 4M2
Tel: 905-660-6840; *Fax:* 905-660-6729
www.millersaperia.com

Concord: **Starkman, Salsberg & Feldberg Chartered Accountants**
#316, 1600 Steeles Ave. West
Concord, ON L4K 4M2
Tel: 905-669-9900; *Fax:* 905-669-9901
www.starkmansalsbergfeldberg.com

Courtice: **Baker Tilly Durham LLP**
#200, 1748 Baseline Rd. West
Courtice, ON L1E 2T1
Tel: 905-579-5659; *Fax:* 905-579-8563
durham@bakertilly.ca
www.bakertilly.ca/en/courtice-ontario

Elmvale: **Ian Vasey Professional Corporation**
42 Queen St.
Elmvale, ON L0L 1P0
Tel: 705-322-2440; *Fax:* 705-322-1462
www.ianvaseycga.ca

Grimsby: **Southcott Davoli Professional Corporation**
76 Main St. West
Grimsby, ON L3M 4G1
Tel: 905-945-4942; *Fax:* 905-945-0306

Guelph: **Bairstow, Smart & Smith LLP**
100 Gordon St.
Guelph, ON N1H 4H6
Tel: 519-822-7670; *Fax:* 519-822-6997
bss@bssllp.ca
www.bssllp.ca

Guelph: **Baker Tilly GWD**
#113, 450 Speedvale Ave. West
Guelph, ON N1H 7Y6
Tel: 519-822-7670; *Fax:* 519-822-6997
gwd@bakertilly.ca
www.bakertilly.ca/en/guelph-ontario

Guelph: **Caissa LLP**
#8, 350 Speedvale Ave. West
Guelph, ON N1H 7M7
Tel: 519-821-1555
caissa.ca

Guelph: **Robinson, Lott & Brohman LLP**
#103, 197 Hanlon Creek Blvd.
Guelph, ON N1C 0A1
Tel: 519-822-9933; *Fax:* 519-822-9212
Toll-Free: 866-822-9992
info@rlb.ca
www.rlb.ca
Other Contact Information: Human Resources, Email: hr@rlb.ca
www.facebook.com/RLB.LLP; twitter.com/rlbllp

Guelph: **Weiler & Company**
#3, 512 Woolwich St.
Guelph, ON N1H 3X7
Tel: 519-837-3111; *Fax:* 519-837-1049
Toll-Free: 888-239-3111
info@weiler.ca
www.weiler.ca

Hamilton: **BC&C Professional Corporation**
1 Main St. East, 3rd Fl.
Hamilton, ON L8N 1E7
Tel: 905-570-1370; *Fax:* 905-570-1212
www.bccpc.ca

Hamilton: **Padgett Business Services of Hamilton**
1051 Main St. East
Hamilton, ON L8M 1N5
Tel: 905-549-4418
info@padgetthamilton.com
www.padgetthamilton.com
www.facebook.com/162791240399073;
twitter.com/PadgettHamEast

Hamilton: **Taylor Leibow LLP, Accountants & Advisors**
105 Main St. East, 7th Fl.
Hamilton, ON L8N 1G6
Tel: 905-523-0000; *Fax:* 905-523-4681
hamilton@taylorleibow.com
www.taylorleibow.com
www.youtube.com/user/taylorleibowllp;
www.facebook.com/taylorleibow/info; twitter.com/TaylorLeibow

Kanata: **Johnson & Associates Accounting Services Inc.**
#503, 300 March Rd.
Kanata, ON K2K 2E2
Tel: 613-599-9788; *Fax:* 613-249-3884
info@cfo4u.ca
www.cfo4u.ca

Kapuskasing: **Baker Tilly HKC Kapuskasing**
2 Ash St.
Kapuskasing, ON P5N 3H4
Tel: 705-337-6411; *Fax:* 705-335-6563
kapuskasing@bakertilly.ca
www.bakertilly.ca/en/kapuskasing-ontario

Kenora: **Claudette M. Edie, CGA PC**
685 Lakeview Dr.
Kenora, ON P9N 3P6
Tel: 807-468-8899
www.porterhetu.com/on_edie.html

Kingston: **Davies & Associates CPA Professional Corporation**
Clock Tower Plaza
819 Norwest Rd.
Kingston, ON K7P 2N4
Tel: 613-389-8177; *Fax:* 613-389-7789
Toll-Free: 888-715-3555
info@daviescpa.com
daviescpa.com

Kingston: **Randy E. Brown CPA, CGA**
#18, 745 Gardiners Rd.
Kingston, ON K7M 3Y5
Tel: 613-542-0151
rbrown@porterhetu.com
www.porterhetu.com/on_brown.html

Kingston: **Tierney Simpson Prytula Chartered Professional Accountants**
1159 Clyde Ct.
Kingston, ON K7P 2E4
Tel: 613-634-0880; *Fax:* 613-634-3993
www.tspaccountants.ca

Kitchener: **YNC LLP**
6 Charles St. West
Kitchener, ON N2G 1H2
Tel: 519-772-0125; *Fax:* 519-772-0428
info@yncllp.ca
www.yncllp.ca

London: **Baker Tilly Trillium LLP**
#18, 540 Clarke Rd.
London, ON N5V 2C7
www.bakertilly.ca/en/london-ontario

London: **Burghout Chartered Accountant**
932 Norton Cres.
London, ON N6J 2Y9
Tel: 519-852-2418

London: **Davis Martindale LLP**
373 Commissioners Rd. West
London, ON N6J 1Y4
Tel: 519-673-3141; *Fax:* 519-645-1646
Toll-Free: 800-668-2167
info@davismartindale.com
www.davismartindale.com
www.facebook.com/DavisMartindale; twitter.com/davismartindale

London: **MacNeill Edmundson**
82 Wellington St.
London, ON N6B 2K3
Tel: 519-660-6060
info@meb.on.ca
www.meb.on.ca

London: **Michael A. King, Chartered Accountant**
#502, 383 Richmond St.
London, ON N6A 3C4
Tel: 519-679-8391; *Fax:* 519-679-1446
www.michaelkingca.ca

Markham: **Applebaum, Commisso LLP Chartered Professional Accountants (ACCPA)**
#400, 2800 - 14th Ave.
Markham, ON L3R 0E4
Tel: 905-477-6996; *Fax:* 905-477-9381
info@applebaum-commisso.com
www.applebaum-commisso.com
Other Contact Information: Toronto, Phone: 416-494-4892

Markham: Cooper Bick Chen LLP, Chartered
Accountants (CBCCA)
#202, 1001 Denison St.
Markham, ON L3R 2Z6
Tel: 905-475-6795; Fax: 905-475-1654
www.cbcca.ca

Markham: Copland Chartered Accountant
Professional Corporation
#301, 325 Renfrew Dr.
Markham, ON L3R 9S8
Tel: 905-477-1300
enquire@copland-ca.com
www.copland-ca.com

Markham: DFK Canada Inc.
#210, 2800 - 14th Ave.
Markham, ON L3R 0E4
Tel: 416-491-2886; Fax: 416-491-1670
info@dfk.ca
www.dfk.ca

Markham: Eigenmacht Crackower Chartered
Accountants Professional Corporation
#202, 345 Renfrew Dr.
Markham, ON L3R 9S9
Tel: 905-305-9722; Fax: 905-305-9502
www.eigenmachtcrackower.com
Other Contact Information: Alt. Phone: 416-607-6468
www.facebook.com/378000208950842

Markham: Harris & Partners, LLP
#300, 8920 Woodbine Ave.
Markham, ON L3R 9W9
Tel: 905-477-0363; Fax: 905-477-3735
Toll-Free: 877-401-8004
info@harrisandpartners.com
www.harrisandpartners.com

Markham: HSM LLP Chartered Accountants
West Tower
#200, 675 Cochrane Dr.
Markham, ON L3R 0B8
Tel: 905-470-7090; Fax: 905-470-7449
info@hsmllpcas.com
hsmllpcas.com

Markham: Jack R. Cayne, CGA
#303, 7321 Victoria Park Ave.
Markham, ON L3R 2Z8
Tel: 905-752-1300

Markham: Kestenberg, Rabinowicz & Partners LLP
2797 John St.
Markham, ON L3R 2Y8
Tel: 905-946-1300
enquiries@krp.ca
www.krp.ca

Markham: Kraft Berger LLP
#300, 3160 Steeles Ave. East
Markham, ON L3R 3Y2
Tel: 905-475-2222; Fax: 905-475-9360
Toll-Free: 888-563-6868
accountants@kbllp.ca
www.kbllp.ca

Markham: Kreston GTA LLP
8953 Woodbine Ave.
Markham, ON L3R 0J9
Tel: 905-474-5593; Fax: 905-474-5591
info@krestongta.com
www.krestongta.com
www.facebook.com/krestongta; twitter.com/KrestonGTA

Markham: Larry Silverberg Chartered Accountant
#226, 7181 Woodbine Ave.
Markham, ON L3R 1A3
Tel: 905-475-1000; Fax: 905-475-1001
www.larry.ca

Markham: Mark Feldstein & Associates
#12, 20 Crown Steel Dr.
Markham, ON L3R 9X9
Tel: 647-503-5299; Fax: 905-474-2441
markfeldstein.ca
Other Contact Information: Alternate URL: toronto-accountant.ca
www.facebook.com/markfeldsteintaxhelp;
twitter.com/TorontoTax

Markham: Rebecca Ling Chartered Accountant
Professional Corporation
#220, 3160 Steeles Ave. East
Markham, ON L3R 4G9
Tel: 905-305-9200

Markham: The Sheldon Group
#220, 60 Renfrew Dr.
Markham, ON L3R 0E1
Tel: 905-475-5400; Fax: 905-475-4246
Toll-Free: 855-475-5400
letstalk@thesheldongroup.ca
www.thesheldongroup.ca
www.youtube.com/SheldonGroupTaxFirms

Markham: Valuation Support Partners Ltd.
West Tower
#220, 675 Cochrane Dr.
Markham, ON L3R 0B8
Tel: 905-305-8775
vspltd.ca

Markham: Wasserman Forensic Investigative
Services Inc.
Liberty Square, HSBC Tower
#1008, 3601 Hwy. #7 East
Markham, ON L3R 0M3
Tel: 905-948-8643; Fax: 905-948-8638
info@wassermaninvestigations.com
www.wassermaninvestigations.com

Markham: WEI CPA
#406, 2800 - 14th Ave.
Markham, ON L3R 0E4
Tel: 416-628-9423; Fax: 647-438-5835
www.tax-depot.ca
www.facebook.com/WEICPATORONTO; twitter.com/weicpafirm

Markham: Williams & Partners Chartered
Accountants LLP
East Tower
#505, 675 Cochrane Dr.
Markham, ON L3R 0B8
Toll-Free: 855-888-9913
info@williamsandpartners.com
www.williamsandpartners.com

Markham: Williams & Partners Forensic
Accountants Inc.
East Tower
#505, 675 Cochrane Dr.
Markham, ON L3R 0B8
Toll-Free: 855-888-9937
info@wpfa.ca
www.wpforensicaccountants.com

Milton: Bensen Professional Corporation
377 Scott Blvd.
Milton, ON L9T 0T1
Tel: 905-699-2317
www.bensencpa.ca

Milton: Fonseca & Fonseca Professional
Corporation
#1, 751 Main St. East
Milton, ON L9T 3Z3
Tel: 905-876-4332; Fax: 905-876-0513
info@cpafonseca.com
www.cpafonseca.com

Milton: Mercer & Mercer
245 Commercial St.
Milton, ON L9T 2J3
Tel: 905-876-1144; Fax: 905-876-4209
mail@mercerandmercer.com
www.mercerandmercer.com
twitter.com/MercerMercerCPA

Mississauga: Aneja Professional Corporation
Chartered Accountants
#14, 6980 Maritz Dr.
Mississauga, ON L5W 1Z3
Tel: 905-564-9100; Fax: 905-874-8221
info@csaca.ca
www.aneja.ca

Mississauga: Bimal Shah Professional Corporation
#14, 5484 Tomken Rd.
Mississauga, ON L4W 2Z6
Tel: 905-629-2653; Fax: 905-629-8701
info@shah-cga.com
www.mississaugaaccountants.ca

Mississauga: Bolton & Dignan, Chartered
Accountants
6509 Mississauga Rd., #D
Mississauga, ON L5N 1A6
Tel: 905-858-5006; Fax: 905-858-3392

Mississauga: Brockman & Partners Forensic
Accountants Inc.
#430, 5925 Airport Rd.
Mississauga, ON L4V 1W1
Tel: 905-671-0045; Fax: 905-671-9728
www.brockmanandpartners.ca
Other Contact Information: Pager: 416-715-7147

Mississauga: Clarkson Rouble LLP
#102, 2576 Matheson Blvd. East
Mississauga, ON L4W 5H1
Tel: 905-629-4047; Fax: 905-629-3070
office@crllp.ca
ww.crllp.ca

Mississauga: Dean & Associates Accounting
#215, 2550 Argentia Rd.
Mississauga, ON L5N 5R1
Tel: 647-273-3094; Fax: 905-247-0338
accounting@deanandassociates.ca
www.deanandassociates.ca

Mississauga: Expertax Financial Services Inc.
#200, 5660 McAdam Rd.
Mississauga, ON L4Z 1T2
Tel: 905-276-1154
info@experttax.ca
www.experttax.ca
www.facebook.com/ExpertaxFinancialServicesInc;
twitter.com/ExpertaxInfo

Mississauga: H&A eDiscovery Inc.
#302, 2680 Matheson Blvd. East
Mississauga, ON L4W 0A5
Tel: 416-233-5577
info@haediscovery.com
www.haediscovery.com
Other Contact Information: Employment Email:
careers@haediscovery.com

Mississauga: Hufton Valvano Grover Philipp LLP
(HVGP)
#100, 1599 Hurontario St.
Mississauga, ON L5G 4S1
Tel: 905-891-5339; Fax: 905-891-1513
www.hvgp.ca

Mississauga: Laurel L. Stultz (LLS)
#211, 1425 Dundas St. East
Mississauga, ON L4X 2W4
Tel: 905-602-0001; Fax: 905-602-7721
info@certifiedgeneralaccountant.ca
www.certifiedgeneralaccountant.ca
Other Contact Information: Cell: 416-996-3919

Mississauga: MacGillivray Partners, LLP
#600, 6605 Hurontario St.
Mississauga, ON L5T 0A3
Tel: 905-696-0707; Fax: 905-696-0760
www.macgillivray.com

Mississauga: Madan Chartered Accountant
Professional Corporation
#20, 145 Traders Blvd.
Mississauga, ON L4Z 3L3
Tel: 905-268-0150; Fax: 905-507-9193
madanca.com
www.instagram.com/madanaccounting;
www.youtube.com/user/allanmadan;
www.facebook.com/MadanCharteredAccountant;
twitter.com/Madan_CA

Mississauga: McCann & Roque Chartered
Accountants
#31, 3075 Ridgeway Dr.
Mississauga, ON L5L 5M6
Tel: 905-997-3333
info@mrcas.ca
www.mrcas.ca

Mississauga: MDP LLP
#200, 4230 Sherwoodtowne Blvd.
Mississauga, ON L4Z 2G6
Tel: 905-279-7500; Fax: 905-279-9300
mdp@mdp.on.ca
www.mdp.on.ca

Mississauga: Padgett Business Services
Mississauga North West
#9, 6655 Kitimat Rd.
Mississauga, ON L5N 6J4
Tel: 905-858-9050; Fax: 905-858-1895
www.padgettmississauga.ca

Mississauga: Padgett Business Services
Mississauga South
#208, 1077 North Service Rd.
Mississauga, ON L4Y 1A6
Tel: 905-949-4388; *Fax:* 905-949-9220
www.padgettmiss.ca

Mississauga: Parker Simone LLP
#201, 129 Lakeshore Rd. East
Mississauga, ON L5G 1E5
Tel: 905-271-7977; *Fax:* 905-271-7677
www.parker-simone.com

Mississauga: S+C Partners LLP
#204, 6465 Millcreek Dr.
Mississauga, ON L5N 5R3
Tel: 905-821-9215; *Fax:* 905-821-8212
Toll-Free: 866-965-1435
info@scpllp.com
scpllp.com

Mississauga: SJ Chartered Accountants
#4-101, 2600 Skymark Ave.
Mississauga, ON L4W 5B2
Tel: 905-625-1223; *Fax:* 905-625-1224
info@jainfinancial.com
www.jainfinancial.com

Mississauga: Steve Manias, CPA, CA
#103, 6711 Mississauga Rd.
Mississauga, ON L5N 2W3
Tel: 905-858-5559
www.stevemanias.ca

Mississauga: TMFD Financial Professional
Corporation, Chartered Professional Accountants
#218, 350 Burnhamthorpe Rd. West
Mississauga, ON L5B 3J1
Fax: 905-273-9260
Toll-Free: 833-507-6863
info@tmfd.ca
tmfd.ca
www.facebook.com/tmfdca; twitter.com/tmfdca

Nepean: Jack R. Bowerman, CA - Professional
Corporation
#10, 28 Concourse Gate
Nepean, ON K2E 7T7
Tel: 613-723-8202; *Fax:* 613-723-1216
Toll-Free: 800-282-1879
info@jrbowerman.com
www.jrbowerman.com

Newmarket: Accountable Solutions Accounting
Professional Corporation
#202, 227 Eagle St.
Newmarket, ON L3Y 1J8
Tel: 905-479-2126; *Fax:* 905-235-4476
Toll-Free: 888-508-9885
support@accountablesolutions.ca
www.accountablesolutions.ca

Niagara Falls: Padgett Niagara
6260 Colborne St.
Niagara Falls, ON L2J 1E6
Tel: 905-374-6622
www.padgettniagara.com
www.facebook.com/padgett.niagara; twitter.com/PadgettNiagara

Niagara-on-the-Lake: Bridgman & Durksen
1 Henegan Rd.
Niagara-on-the-Lake, ON L0S 1J0
Tel: 905-468-1659; *Fax:* 905-468-2055
info@bridgmananddurksen.com
www.bridgmananddurksen.com

Norland: ABECK Accounting Tax & Computer
Services Inc.
PO Box 34
7524 Hwy. 35
Norland, ON K0M 2L0
Tel: 705-454-2418; *Fax:* 705-454-2422
info@abeckacctg.com
www.abeckacctg.com

Oakville: Bazar McBean LLP
440 Inglehart St. North
Oakville, ON L6J 3J6
Tel: 905-338-0330; *Fax:* 416-739-0538
mail@bazarmcbean.com
www.bazarmcbean.com

Oakville: CMR Wong Chartered Professional
Accountant
#12, 1200 Speers Rd.
Oakville, ON L6L 2X4
Tel: 905-845-1408; *Fax:* 905-845-5931
www.rickywong.ca

Oakville: Glenn Graydon Wright LLP Chartered
Professional Accountants
#310, 690 Dorval Dr.
Oakville, ON L6K 3W7
Tel: 905-845-6633; *Fax:* 905-845-6064
info@ggw.net
www.ggw.net
Other Contact Information: Alternate URL:
www.oakvilleaccountingfirm.ca
www.facebook.com/GlennGraydonWrightLLP;
twitter.com/GGW_LLP

Orléans: Pyndus & Associates Ltd.
1813 Woodhaven Heights
Orléans, ON K1E 2W3
Tel: 613-834-5054; *Fax:* 613-837-1591
pyndus.associates@sympatico.ca
www3.sympatico.ca/cpyndus

Ottawa: Andrews & Co. Chartered Accountants
540 Lacolle Way
Ottawa, ON K4A 0N9
Tel: 613-837-8282; *Fax:* 613-837-7482
info@andrews.ca
www.andrews.ca
www.facebook.com/Andrews540; twitter.com/andrewsco_cpa

Ottawa: Baker Tilly Ottawa LLP
#400, 301 Moodie Dr.
Ottawa, ON K2H 9C4
Tel: 613-820-8010; *Fax:* 613-820-0465
ottawa@bakertilly.ca
www.bakertilly.ca/en/ottawa-ontario

Ottawa: Charles Ghadban Accounting (CGA)
#105, 1400 St. Laurent Blvd.
Ottawa, ON K1K 4H4
Tel: 613-234-7856; *Fax:* 613-234-7838
cgatax.com
www.facebook.com/766094163430457;
twitter.com/charlesghadban

Ottawa: Gary G. Timmons, Chartered Accountant
#105, 2442 St. Joseph Blvd.
Ottawa, ON K1C 1G1
Tel: 613-830-0200; *Fax:* 613-702-4464
www.gtimmons.com
www.pinterest.com/gtimmonson;
www.facebook.com/571271199648443; twitter.com/gtimmonson

Ottawa: Ginsberg Gluzman Fage & Levitz, LLP
(GGFL)
287 Richmond Rd.
Ottawa, ON K1Z 6X4
Tel: 613-728-5831; *Fax:* 613-728-8085
info@ggfl.ca
www.ggfl.ca
www.facebook.com/GGFLCharteredProfessionalAccountants;
twitter.com/GGFLca

Ottawa: Jerome & Company Professional
Corporation
#2D, 160 Terence Matthews Cres.
Ottawa, ON K2M 0B2
Tel: 613-599-4224; *Fax:* 613-482-3737
www.smallbizottawa.ca
www.facebook.com/131193766930669

Ottawa: Logan Katz LLP
#105, 6 Gurdwara Rd.
Ottawa, ON K2E 8A3
Tel: 613-228-8282
letsgetstarted@logankatz.com
www.logankatz.com
www.facebook.com/logankatzllp; twitter.com/LoganKatz_LLP

Ottawa: Parker Prins Lebano Chartered Professional
Accountants (PPL)
1796 Courtwood Cres.
Ottawa, ON K2C 2B5
Tel: 613-727-7474; *Fax:* 613-727-3715
enquiries@ppl-ca.com
www.parkerprinslebano.com

Ottawa: R. Schlessinger Professional Corporation
332 Gilmour St.
Ottawa, ON K2P 0R3
Tel: 613-235-1807; *Fax:* 613-235-2253
www.schlessinger.ca

Ottawa: Robertson Sharpe & Associates
#2, 200 Colonnade Rd.
Ottawa, ON K2E 7M1
Tel: 613-727-3845; *Fax:* 613-727-7075
www.robertson-sharpe.com

Ottawa: Smith & West Chartered Professional
Accountants
#206, 460 West Hunt Club Rd.
Ottawa, ON K2E 0B8
Tel: 613-425-8871; *Fax:* 613-425-4089
www.smithandwestcpa.com

Ottawa: Surgeson Carson Associates Inc.
#8, 99 Fifth Ave.
Ottawa, ON K1S 5K4
Tel: 613-567-6434; *Fax:* 613-567-0752
www.surgesoncarson.com
www.facebook.com/SOLUTIONSFORDEBT;
twitter.com/OttMoneyHelp

Pembroke: Leach Bradbury Chartered Professional
Accountants
141 Lake St., #A
Pembroke, ON K8A 5L8
Tel: 613-735-3092; *Fax:* 613-735-2637
Toll-Free: 800-368-0747
leabra@lb-ca.ca
www.lb-ca.ca
www.facebook.com/LeachBradbury

Peterborough: Baker Tilly KDN LLP
272 Charlotte St.
Peterborough, ON K9J 2V4
Tel: 705-742-3418; *Fax:* 705-742-9775
peterborough@bakertilly.ca
www.bakertilly.ca/en/peterborough-ontario

Peterborough: Jon S. Thornton, Chartered
Accountant
PO Box 2402
294 Rink St.
Peterborough, ON K9J 7Y8
Tel: 705-742-2308; *Fax:* 705-748-4824
www.thorntonca.com

Peterborough: Peterborough CGAs
313 Stewart St.
Peterborough, ON K9J 3N2
Tel: 705-745-8643; *Fax:* 705-745-6358
peterboroughcpas.com

Peterborough: Rosborough Accounting &
Consulting
457 Water St.
Peterborough, ON K9H 3M2
Tel: 705-652-6347
www.porterhetu.com/on_rosborough.html
Other Contact Information: Alternate Phone: 705-652-8891

Pickering: Michael Evans, Chartered Accountant
#6, 1730 McPherson Ct.
Pickering, ON L1W 3E6
Tel: 905-420-9637; *Fax:* 905-420-0910
www.gtaaccountant.com

Port Perry: 1st Financial Centre
269 Queen St.
Port Perry, ON L9L 1B9
Tel: 905-985-1926; *Toll-Free:* 877-775-3948
www.1fc.ca

Port Perry: Garett Hazelwood, Chartered
Professional Accountant
119 Perry St.
Port Perry, ON L9L 1B8
Tél: 905-985-7171
www.porterhetu.com/on_hazelwood.html

Prescott: Durand & Associates
290 George St.
Prescott, ON K0E 1T0
Tel: 613-925-0145; *Fax:* 613-925-2790
info@durandandassociates.ca
www.durandandassociates.ca

Renfrew: MacKillican & Associates, Chartered
Professional Accountants
620 Barnet Blvd.
Renfrew, ON K7V 0A8
Tel: 613-432-3664; *Fax:* 613-432-8424
www.mackillicans.com

Richmond Hill: Bansal & Giga Chartered
Accountants
#303, 9011 Leslie St.
Richmond Hill, ON L4B 3B6
Tel: 289-807-1393

Richmond Hill: David Burkes - Chartered
Accountant
#201, 30 East Beaver Creek Rd.
Richmond Hill, ON L4B 1J2
Tel: 905-882-0497; *Fax:* 905-882-0499
www.burkes.ca

Richmond Hill: Edwin Law, CA, CFP, Licensed
Public Accountant
#17, 175 West Beaver Creek Rd.
Richmond Hill, ON L4B 3M1
Tel: 416-986-7700
www.edwinlaw.ca

Richmond Hill: Hennick Herman, LLP
#600, 100 York Blvd.
Richmond Hill, ON L4B 1J8
Tel: 416-494-2606; *Fax:* 905-707-0458
general@hh-llp.ca
www.hh-llp.ca

Richmond Hill: inNumbers, Inc.
65A West Beaver Creek Rd.
Richmond Hill, ON L4B 1K4
Tel: 905-882-3137; *Toll-Free:* 877-820-7313
info@innumbers.ca
innumbers.ca
www.facebook.com/innumbers.ca; twitter.com/inNumbersInc

Richmond Hill: J. Michael Mulholland CA
#200, 30 Via Renzo Dr.
Richmond Hill, ON L4S 0B8
Tél: 416-496-9425
mm@jmmulholland.ca
www.jmmulholland.ca

Richmond Hill: Orvitz, Barnartt & Diamond, CPA
Professional Corp.
#6A, 10 West Pearce St.
Richmond Hill, ON L4B 1B6
Tel: 905-889-1549; *Fax:* 905-889-2054
www.obd-cpa.ca

Richmond Hill: Truster Zweig LLP
#200, 500 Hwy. 7 East
Richmond Hill, ON L4B 1J1
Tel: 416-222-5555; *Fax:* 905-707-1322
ashleyb@trusterzweig.com
www.trusterzweig.com

Richmond Hill: Willington Martin Professional
Corporation
#200, 30 Via Renzo Dr.
Richmond Hill, ON L4S 0B8
Tel: 416-848-1585
www.inbalance.org

Sarnia: Baker Tilly Sarnia LLP
1350 L'Heritage Dr.
Sarnia, ON N7S 6H8
Tel: 519-542-7725; *Fax:* 519-542-8321
sarnia@bakertilly.ca
www.bakertilly.ca/en/sarnia-ontario

Sarnia: Jamieson Accounting Services Ltd.
1360A L'Heritage Dr.
Sarnia, ON N7S 6H8
Tel: 519-332-6757
www.jamiesonaccounting.com
www.facebook.com/jamiesonaccounting

Sarnia: TurnerMoore LLP
316 George St.
Sarnia, ON N7T 4P4
Tel: 519-344-1271; *Fax:* 519-344-1268
www.turnermoore.com

St Catharines: Durward Jones Barkwell & Company
LLP (DJB)
#300, 20 Corporate Park Dr.
St Catharines, ON L2S 3W2
Tel: 905-684-9221; *Fax:* 905-684-0566
Toll-Free: 866-219-9431
stcath@djb.com
djb.com
www.facebook.com/djbaccounting; twitter.com/DJB_accounting

St Catharines: Finucci PC
433B St. Paul St.
St Catharines, ON L2R 3N4
Tel: 905-682-2406
www.finuccipc.com

St Thomas: Graham Scott Enns LLP
450 Sunset Dr.
St Thomas, ON N5R 5V1
Tel: 519-633-0700; *Fax:* 519-633-7009
www.grahamscottenns.com

Stouffville: Joe Nemni Financial Services Inc.
33 Katherine Cres.
Stouffville, ON L4A 1K4
Tel: 905-640-0065
www.joenemni.com

Sudbury: Baker Tilly SNT LLP
1174 St Jerome St.
Sudbury, ON P3A 2V9
Tel: 705-560-5592; *Fax:* 705-560-8832
snt-sudbury@bakertilly.ca
www.bakertilly.ca/en/sudbury-ontario

Sutton: Goodwin Porter Hétu
PO Box 1088
101 High St.
Sutton, ON L0E 1R0
Tel: 905-722-8587; *Fax:* 905-722-6519
goodwinph.ca
Other Contact Information: Alternate Phone: 289-470-5008

Thornhill: Ernest H. Wolkin, Chartered Accountant
#500A, 300 John St.
Thornhill, ON L3T 5W4
Tel: 905-882-2100
info@wolkin.ca
www.wolkin.ca

Thornhill: Prasad & Company LLP
7699 Yonge St.
Thornhill, ON L3T 1Z5
Tel: 416-226-9840; *Fax:* 416-226-9179
Toll-Free: 888-550-8227
www.prasadcpa.com
www.facebook.com/PrasadandCompanyLLP;
twitter.com/Prasad_and_Co

Toronto: Adams & Miles LLP Chartered Professional
Accountants
#501, 2550 Victoria Park Ave.
Toronto, ON M2J 5A9
Tel: 416-502-2201; *Fax:* 416-502-2210
solution@adamsmiles.com
www.adamsmiles.com
www.facebook.com/AdamsMilesLLP;
twitter.com/AdamsMilesLLP

Toronto: Alan I. Stern, Chartered Accountant
#6, 4646 Dufferin St.
Toronto, ON M3H 5S4
Tel: 416-209-8318
info@sternca.com
www.sternca.com

Toronto: Allain, Isabella & McLean LLP
#205, 5401 Eglinton Ave. West
Toronto, ON M9C 5K6
Tel: 416-620-7740; *Fax:* 416-920-0023

Toronto: Allan W. Leppik, Chartered Accountant,
Professional Corporation
#2, 1 Rowanwood Ave.
Toronto, ON M4W 1Y5
Tel: 416-822-6744
www.leppikaccounting.com
twitter.com/aleppik1

Toronto: Allen Herblum Professional Corporation
Chartered Accountants
#302, 4141 Yonge St.
Toronto, ON M2P 2A8
Tel: 416-250-7224; *Fax:* 416-733-4579
info@charteredaccountants.ca
www.charteredaccountants.ca

Toronto: Bass Murphy & Partners Chartered
Accountants LLP
885 Progress Ave., #LPH1
Toronto, ON M1H 3G3
Tel: 416-431-3030; *Fax:* 416-431-3340
www.bassmurphy.com

Toronto: Bay Street CPA Professional Corporation
#201, 49 Elm St.
Toronto, ON M5G 1H1
Tel: 647-931-2425
info@baystreetcpa.com
baystreetcpa.com
www.facebook.com/326300544373926

Toronto: BDCA Professional Corporation
#960, 200 Yorkland Blvd.
Toronto, ON M2J 5C1
Tel: 416-490-1042
info@bdca.ca
www.bdca.ca
www.facebook.com/BDCAProfessionalCorporation

Toronto: Bennett Gold LLP, Chartered Accountants
#900, 150 Ferrand Dr.
Toronto, ON M3C 3E5
Tel: 416-449-2249; *Fax:* 416-449-4133
www.bennettgold.ca

Toronto: Brian Borts CPA, CA
892 Bathurst St.
Toronto, ON M5R 3G3
Tel: 416-588-4474; *Fax:* 416-588-8771
Toll-Free: 877-282-6274
taxinfo@brianborts.com
www.brianborts.com

Toronto: Brief Rotfarb Wynberg Cappe LLP
#402, 3845 Bathurst St.
Toronto, ON M3H 3N2
Tel: 416-635-9080; *Fax:* 416-635-0462
info@brwc.com
www.brwc.com

Toronto: Cadesky & Associates LLP
Atria III
#1001, 2225 Sheppard Ave. East
Toronto, ON M2J 5C2
Tel: 416-498-9500; *Fax:* 416-498-9501
taxpros@cadesky.com
www.cadesky.com
Other Contact Information: Employment Email:
careers@cadesky.com

Toronto: Canham Rogers Chartered Accountants
#500, 2 Lansing Sq.
Toronto, ON M2J 4P8
Tel: 416-494-8000; *Fax:* 416-494-8032
www.canhamrogers.com

Toronto: Chaplin & Burd Chartered Professional
Accountants, LLP
#320, 1200 Markham Rd.
Toronto, ON M1H 3C3
Tel: 416-290-6455; *Fax:* 416-290-5190
www.chaplinburd.com

Toronto: Chaplin & Co. Chartered Accountants
#710, 1110 Finch Ave. West
Toronto, ON M3J 2T2
Tel: 416-667-7060; *Fax:* 416-663-3746
ca@chaplinco.com
www.chaplinco.com

Toronto: Chapman Matten Welton Winter LLP
Chartered Accountants (CMWW)
PO Box 79
#6010, 3080 Yonge St.
Toronto, ON M4N 3N1
Tel: 416-488-6275
mail@cmww.ca
www.cmww.ca

Toronto: Cholkan & Stepczuk LLP
#300, 1 Eva Rd.
Toronto, ON M9C 4Z5
Tel: 416-695-9500; Fax: 416-695-3837
Toll-Free: 800-363-9500
www.c-s.ca

Toronto: Clark & Horner LLP
Dynamic Funds Tower
PO Box 181
#2601, 1 Adelaide St. East
Toronto, ON M5C 2V9
Tel: 416-861-0431; Fax: 416-861-0587
info@clarkandhorner.com
www.clarkandhorner.com

Toronto: Clarke Henning LLP
#801, 10 Bay St.
Toronto, ON M5J 2R8
Tel: 416-364-4421; Fax: 416-367-8032
ch@clarkehenning.com
www.clarkehenning.com

Toronto: ConnectCPA
#220, 140 Yonge St.
Toronto, ON M5C 1X6
Tel: 647-560-3350; Toll-Free: 855-596-3342
admin@ConnectCPA.ca
www.connectcpa.ca
www.instagram.com/connectcpa
www.facebook.com/ConnectCPA; twitter.com/Connect_CPA

Toronto: Cooper & Company Ltd.
#108, 1120 Finch Ave. West
Toronto, ON M3J 3H7
Tel: 416-665-3383; Fax: 416-665-0897
info@cooperco.ca
www.cooperco.ca

Toronto: Cooper, Green & Warren LLP
#100, 1370 Don Mills Rd.
Toronto, ON M3B 3N7
Tel: 416-510-1777; Fax: 416-510-1709
www.cgwca.com

Toronto: CPA4IT Inc.
478 Richmond St. West
Toronto, ON M5V 1Y2
Toll-Free: 800-465-7532
customerservice@ca4it.com
www.cpa4it.ca
www.facebook.com/CPA4IT; twitter.com/cpa4it_ca

Toronto: Craig & Company Chartered Accountant
#203, 5468 Dundas St. West
Toronto, ON M9B 6E3
Tel: 416-259-5161; Fax: 416-259-7224
www.craigco.ca

Toronto: Cusimano Professional Corporation, Chartered Professional Accountant
#201, 185 Bridgeland Ave.
Toronto, ON M6A 1Y7
Tel: 416-849-4000; Fax: 416-849-0009
Toll-Free: 877-624-4001
www.cusimanopc.com
twitter.com/cusimanopc

Toronto: D. Jae Gold Entertainment Accountants
#806, 920 Yonge St.
Toronto, ON M4M 3C7
Tel: 416-944-3376; Fax: 416-944-3893
infogold@ggca.com
www.rocknrollaccountant.com
twitter.com/accountant_e

Toronto: Darryl H. Hayashi, CA Professional Corporation
953 O'Connor Dr.
Toronto, ON M4B 2S7
Tel: 416-751-7653; Fax: 416-751-8032
www.darrylhayashi.ca

Toronto: DCY Professional Corporation Chartered Accountants
50 Valleybrook Dr.
Toronto, ON M3B 2S9
Tel: 416-510-8888; Fax: 416-510-2699
dcy@dcy.ca
dcy.ca
www.facebook.com/DCYPCCA

Toronto: DNTW Toronto LLP
#703, 45 Sheppard Ave. East
Toronto, ON M2N 5W9
Tel: 416-924-4900; Fax: 416-924-9377
dntwtoronto.com

Toronto: Duff & Phelps
Bay Adelaide Centre
333 Bay St., 14th Fl.
Toronto, ON M5H 2R2
Tel: 416-364-9700
www.duffandphelps.com

Toronto: Duff & Phelps Corp.
Bay Adelaide Centre
333 Bay St., 14th Fl.
Toronto, ON M5H 2R2
Tel: 416-364-9700
www.duffandphelps.com

Toronto: Edmondson Ball Davies LLP, Chartered Accountants
#501, 10 Milner Business Ct.
Toronto, ON M1B 3C6
Tel: 416-293-5560; Fax: 416-293-5377
www.ebdcas.com

Toronto: Edward & Manning LLP
#407, 170 The Donway West
Toronto, ON M3C 2G3
Tel: 416-621-9998
info@emllp.ca
emllp.ca

Toronto: Ernst & Young Orenda Corporate Finance Inc.
Ernst & Young Tower
100 Adelaide St. West
Toronto, ON M5H 0B3
Tel: 416-864-1234; Fax: 416-864-1174
www.ey.com/en_ca/strategy-transactions

Toronto: Fedder Gurau & Staniewski Chartered Professional Accountants
#508, 245 Fairview Mall Dr.
Toronto, ON M2J 4T1
Tel: 416-222-3221; Fax: 416-222-2034
office@fgsaccountants.com
www.fgsaccountants.com

Toronto: Fruitman Kates LLP Chartered Professional Accountants
1055 Eglinton Ave. West
Toronto, ON M6C 2C9
Tel: 416-920-3434; Fax: 416-920-7799
info@fruitman.ca
www.fruitman.ca

Toronto: Fuller Landau LLP
151 Bloor St. West, 12th Fl.
Toronto, ON M5S 1S4
Tel: 416-645-6500; Fax: 416-645-6501
info.tor@fullerlandau.com
www.fullerllp.com
www.facebook.com/FullerLandauLLP

Toronto: G&G Partnership LLP
15 Coldwater Rd.
Toronto, ON M3B 1Y8
Tel: 416-441-9292; Fax: 416-441-2766
info@ggca.com
www.ggca.com

Toronto: Gardner Zuk Dessen, Chartered Accountants
265 Rimrock Rd.
Toronto, ON M3J 3C6
Tel: 416-631-9800; Fax: 416-631-9183

Toronto: Gary Booth Chartered Professional Accountants, Chartered Accountants
#406, 555 Burnhamthorpe Rd.
Toronto, ON M9C 2Y3
Tel: 416-626-2727; Fax: 416-621-7136
admin@garybooth.com
www.garybooth.com

Toronto: GCSE LLP
#1900, 4950 Yonge St.
Toronto, ON M2N 6K1
Tel: 416-512-6000; Fax: 416-512-9800
info@gcsellp.com
gcsellp.com

Toronto: GLM CPA LLP
#6, 201 Wicksteed Ave.
Toronto, ON M4G 0B1
Tel: 416-499-9099
info@glmcpa.ca
www.glmcpa.ca

Toronto: GO LLP Chartered Professional Accountants
#710, 200 Yorkland Blvd.
Toronto, ON M2J 5C1
Tel: 416-490-1600; Fax: 416-490-1606
info@gollp.com
www.gollp.com
www.facebook.com/343753092471506

Toronto: Goodman & Associates LLP
#200, 45 St. Clair Ave. West
Toronto, ON M4V 1K6
Tel: 416-967-3444
info@goodmancpa.ca
www.goodmancpa.ca

Toronto: Hasnain Panju CA Professional Corporation
#102-103, 716 Gordon Baker Rd.
Toronto, ON M2H 3B4
Tel: 416-756-9562; Fax: 416-756-3118
www.hasnainkpanju.com

Toronto: Hema Murdock CPA, CA
1312 Danforth Ave.
Toronto, ON M4J 1M9
Tel: 416-696-6653
hemamurdock.ca

Toronto: Hilborn LLP
#3100, 401 Bay St.
Toronto, ON M5H 2Y4
Tel: 416-364-1359; Fax: 416-364-9503
info@hilbornca.com
www.hilbornca.com
Other Contact Information: Employment Email:
careers@hilbornca.com

Toronto: Hogg, Shain & Scheck
#1800, 2235 Sheppard Ave. East
Toronto, ON M2J 5B5
Tel: 416-557-5853; Fax: 416-499-4449
consult@hss-ca.com
www.hss-ca.com
www.facebook.com/HoggShainScheck;
twitter.com/HoggShainScheck

Toronto: Ilavsky Chartered Accountants
#5700, 100 King St. West
Toronto, ON M5X 1C7
Tel: 416-690-1597; Fax: 416-690-0617
contact@ilavskyaccounting.ca
www.ilavskyaccounting.ca
www.facebook.com/ilavskyca; twitter.com/ilavskyca

Toronto: Innes Robinson, Chartered Professional Accountants
#100, 2005 Sheppard Ave. East
Toronto, ON M2J 5B4
Tel: 416-590-1728; Fax: 416-590-1576
innesrobinson.ca

Toronto: Jake Kuperhause - Chartered Accountant
#504, 55 Eglinton Ave. East
Toronto, ON M4P 1G8
Tel: 416-932-2665; Fax: 416-932-9100
www.jakekuperhause.com

Toronto: Jones & Cosman Chartered Professional Accountants
25 Laidlaw St.
Toronto, ON M6K 1X3
Tel: 647-872-9957
www.jonescosman.com
Other Contact Information: Alternate Phone: 416-629-1469
www.facebook.com/jonescosman

Toronto: JRPC Chartered Accountant Toronto
56 Shaftesbury Ave.
Toronto, ON M4T 1A3
Tel: 416-487-3000
www.professionalcorporation.ca
Other Contact Information: Alternate URL: www.jrpctaxes.com

Toronto: **Kanish & Partners LLP**
#1203, 1200 Bay St.
Toronto, ON M5R 2A5

Tel: 416-975-9292; Fax: 416-975-9275
kp@kanish-partners.com
www.kanish-partners.com

Toronto: **Kapadia LLP**
#1, 265 Rimrock Rd.
Toronto, ON M3J 3C6

Tel: 416-635-8025; Fax: 416-638-6815
info@kapadiallp.com
www.kapadiallp.com

Toronto: **Kay & Warburton Chartered Professional Accountants (KWCA)**
#403, 225 Richmond St. West
Toronto, ON M5V 1W2

Tel: 416-977-2416; Fax: 416-977-8549
info@kwca.com
www.kwca.com

Toronto: **Kelly Porter Hétu**
475 Queen St. East
Toronto, ON M5A 1T9

Tel: 416-955-0060; Fax: 416-955-0061
info@kellyporterhetu.com
kellyporterhetu.com

Toronto: **Kenneth Michalak**
1576 Bloor St. West
Toronto, ON M6P 1A4

Tel: 416-588-2808; Fax: 416-588-3634
Toll-Free: 866-258-4788
www.kjmcga.com

Toronto: **KJ Accounting Services**
1 Yonge St.
Toronto, ON M5E 1E5

www.kjaccounting.ca
www.facebook.com/CanadaTax; twitter.com/canada_tax_info

Toronto: **Klingbaum Barkin LLP**
The Madison Centre
#1906, 4950 Yonge St.
Toronto, ON M2N 6K1

Tel: 416-512-1221
www.klingbaumbarkin.com

Toronto: **Kopstick Osher Chartered Accountants, LLP**
970 Lawrence Ave. West
Toronto, ON M6A 3B6

Tel: 416-256-7748

Toronto: **Koster, Spinks & Koster LLP (KSK)**
4 Glengrove Ave. West
Toronto, ON M4R 1N4

Tel: 416-489-8100; Fax: 416-489-9194
info@ksk.ca
www.ksk.ca

Toronto: **Kriens-LaRose, LLP**
37 Main St.
Toronto, ON M4E 2V5

Tel: 416-690-6800; Fax: 416-690-9919
www.krienslarose.com

Toronto: **Kudlow & McCann Chartered Professional Accountants**
#401, 21 St. Clair Ave. East
Toronto, ON M4T 1L9

Tel: 416-924-4780; Fax: 416-924-5332
www.kudlowmccann.com

Toronto: **Kwan Chan Law Chartered Accountants Professional Corporation**
#910, 4950 Yonge St.
Toronto, ON M2N 6K1

Tel: 416-226-6668

Toronto: **Lipton LLP**
#600, 245 Fairview Mall Dr.
Toronto, ON M2J 4T1

Tel: 416-496-2900; Fax: 416-496-0559
Toll-Free: 877-869-2900
info@liptonllp.com
www.liptonllp.com
twitter.com/LiptonLLP

Toronto: **LP Tax & Accounting Services Inc.**
#200, 1287 St. Clair Ave. West
Toronto, ON M6E 1B8

Tel: 416-656-9650
info.lptax@gmail.com
www.lptax.ca

Toronto: **M. Schwab Accounting Services Ltd.**
94 Cumberland St.
Toronto, ON M5R 1A3

Tel: 416-324-9933

Toronto: **Marlies Y. Hendricks, CPA**
4899 Dundas St. West
Toronto, ON M9A 1B2

Tel: 416-766-3941; Fax: 416-766-3946
www.ha-accounting.com

Toronto: **McCarney Group LLP**
#1510, 20 Bay St.
Toronto, ON M5J 2N8

Tel: 416-362-0515; Fax: 416-362-0539
info@mgca.com
www.mgca.com

Toronto: **MDS LLP Chartered Accountants**
#601, 40 University Ave.
Toronto, ON M5J 1T1

Tel: 416-599-7255; Fax: 416-599-7268
mds@mdsca.com
www.mdsca.com

Toronto: **Mehl & Reynolds LLP**
Yorkdale Pl.
#200, 1 Yorkdale Rd.
Toronto, ON M6A 3A1

Tel: 416-787-0681; Fax: 416-787-7630
webhome.idirect.com/~gmr

Toronto: **Michael Argue Chartered Accountant**
#108, 150 Consumers Rd.
Toronto, ON M2J 1P9

Tel: 416-490-8544; Fax: 705-727-1518
www.argueca.com

Toronto: **Michael Atlas, Chartered Accountant**
Richmond-Adelaide Centre
#2500, 120 Adelaide St. West
Toronto, ON M5H 1T1

Tel: 416-860-9175
matlas@taxca.com
www.taxca.com
Other Contact Information: For urgent matters outside of business hours, mobile phone: 416-949-7111
www.facebook.com/MichaelAtlasCPA; twitter.com/_matlas

Toronto: **MSI Spergel Inc.**
#200, 505 Consumers Rd.
Toronto, ON M2J 4V8

Tel: 416-497-1660; Fax: 416-494-7199
Toll-Free: 310-4321
www.youtube.com/user/msiSpergelinc;
www.facebook.com/spergelinc; twitter.com/msispergelinc

Toronto: **Myers Tsiofas Norheim LLP**
#812, 330 Bay St.
Toronto, ON M5H 2S8

Tel: 416-868-9017; Fax: 416-868-9256
office@mtnllp.ca
www.mtnllp.ca

Toronto: **Nevcon Accounting Services**
PO Box 43541
1531 Bayview Ave.
Toronto, ON M4G 3B0

Tel: 416-487-7996; Fax: 416-487-7996
Toll-Free: 888-463-8366
info@nevcon.com
www.nevcon.com
Other Contact Information: Alt. Phone: 705-702-0175
twitter.com/NevconAccount

Toronto: **Nicholas Sider, Chartered Professional Accountant**
#303, 344 Bloor St. West
Toronto, ON M5S 3A7

Tel: 416-913-9243; Fax: 416-406-4805
ns@torontotaxaccountant.com
www.torontotaxaccountant.com

Toronto: **Ozden & Cheung Chartered Accountants Professional Corporation**
#202, 640 Bloor St. West
Toronto, ON M6G 1K9

Tel: 416-588-8933; Fax: 647-776-7700
info@ozdencheung.com
www.ozdencheung.com

Toronto: **Pinto Professional Corporation**
#700, 1235 Bay St.
Toronto, ON M5R 3K4

Tel: 416-513-1012; Fax: 416-981-8625
contact@pintocpa.ca
www.pintocpa.ca

Toronto: **Prentice Yates & Clark**
#700, 15 Toronto St.
Toronto, ON M5C 2E3

Tel: 416-366-9256; Fax: 416-366-9171
Toll-Free: 800-265-7818
www.pyc.net

Toronto: **Renée S. Karn, Certified General Accountant**
86 Acton Ave.
Toronto, ON M3H 4H1

Tel: 416-499-0012
info@reneekarn.com
www.reneekarn.com

Toronto: **Reydman & Associates Professional Corporation**
#103, 38 Niagara St.
Toronto, ON M5V 3X1

Tel: 416-777-1500; Fax: 416-777-0880
info@reydman.com
www.reydman.com

Toronto: **Ring Chartered Accountant**
443C Queen St. East
Toronto, ON M5A 1T6

Tel: 416-482-2477; Fax: 416-482-2752
www.ringca.ca
Other Contact Information: Alternate Phone: 416-482-2478

Toronto: **Rita Zelikman Chartered Accountant Professional Corporation**
#301, 1137 Centre St.
Toronto, ON L4J 3M6

Tel: 416-644-4788; Fax: 416-644-4790
www.ritazelikman.com
Other Contact Information: Cell Phone: 416-271-2234

Toronto: **Robert Gore & Associates Chartered Professional Accountants**
1238 Kingston Rd.
Toronto, ON M1N 1P3

Tel: 416-699-8070; Fax: 416-694-3373
info@goreca.com
www.goreca.com

Toronto: **Robin Taub Financial Consulting**
1210 Eglinton Ave. West
Toronto, ON M6C 2E3

Tel: 416-256-4498; Fax: 416-256-4604
robintaub.com

Toronto: **Rosen & Associates Limited**
#802, 90 Adelaide St. West
Toronto, ON M5H 3V9

Tel: 416-363-4515; Fax: 416-363-4849
h.gammon@rosen-associates.com
www.rosen-associates.com

Toronto: **Rosenswig McRae Thorpe LLP**
#800, 36 Toronto St.
Toronto, ON M5C 2C5

Tel: 416-977-6600
admin@rmtcpa.ca
www.rmtcpa.ca
www.facebook.com/RMTCPA; twitter.com/rmtCPA

Toronto: **Roxana Rodriguez Tax & Accounting**
247 Westmount Ave.
Toronto, ON M6E 3M9

Tel: 647-556-0014

Toronto: **RSM Canada LLP**
RSM Place
#700, 11 King St. West
Toronto, ON M5H 4C7

Tel: 416-480-0160; *Fax:* 416-480-2646
Toll-Free: 855-420-8473
inquiries@rsmcanada.com
www.rsmcanada.com
www.facebook.com/RSMCanada1; twitter.com/RSM_Canada

Toronto: **RSP LLP**
#200, 2000 Steeles Ave. West
Toronto, ON L4K 3E9

Tel: 416-798-4997; *Fax:* 905-660-3064
info@rsp.ca
www.rsp.ca
twitter.com/rspllp

Toronto: **Rumanek & Company Ltd.**
#714, 1280 Finch Ave. West
Toronto, ON M3J 3K6

Tel: 416-665-3328
www.rumanek.com
rumanek.com/blog; www.youtube.com/user/trusteeinbankruptcy

Toronto: **RZN, LLP**
#625, 4211 Yonge St.
Toronto, ON M2P 2A9

Tel: 416-636-7500; *Fax:* 416-636-6545
Toll-Free: 877-871-4258
mail@rznaccountants.com
www.rznaccountants.com

Toronto: **Sam Seidman, Chartered Accountant**
629 Sheppard Ave. West
Toronto, ON M3H 2S3

Tel: 416-398-1700; *Fax:* 416-398-6226
help@samseidman.com
samseidman.com
Other Contact Information: Alternate URL: torontoaccountant.ca
www.facebook.com/torontoaccountant;
twitter.com/Sam_CA_Toronto

Toronto: **Sandor M. Feld Chartered Accountant**
#319, 3089 Bathurst St.
Toronto, ON M6A 2A4

Tel: 416-789-4846; *Fax:* 416-789-5123
info@sfeldca.com
accountant-toronto.com

Toronto: **Schwartz Levitsky Feldman LLP/SRL (SLF)**
RioCan Yonge Eglinton Centre
PO Box 2434
#1500, 2300 Yonge St.
Toronto, ON M4P 1E4

Tel: 416-785-5353; *Fax:* 416-785-5663
slf.ca

Toronto: **Schwartz Levitsky Feldman Valuations Inc.**
RioCan Yonge Eglinton Centre
PO Box 2434
#1500, 2300 Yonge St.
Toronto, ON M4P 1E4

Tel: 416-785-5353; *Fax:* 416-785-5663
slf.ca/our-services/business-valuations

Toronto: **Segal LLP**
#500, 2005 Sheppard Ave. East
Toronto, ON M2J 5B4

Tel: 416-391-4499; *Fax:* 416-391-3280
Toll-Free: 800-206-7307
www.segalllp.com
www.facebook.com/SegalLLP

Toronto: **Serbinski & Associates Inc.**
183 Sheppard Ave. West
Toronto, ON M2N 1M9

Tel: 416-733-0300; *Fax:* 416-352-6004
Toll-Free: 888-878-2937
mtscpa@serbinski.com
www.serbinski.com

Toronto: **SF Partnership, LLP**
#400, 4950 Yonge St.
Toronto, ON M2N 6K1

Tel: 416-250-1212; *Fax:* 416-250-1225
general@sfgroup.ca
www.sfgroup.ca
www.facebook.com/SFPartnership

Toronto: **Shrigley Battrick Chartered Professional Accountants**
#600, 36 Toronto St.
Toronto, ON M5C 2C5

Tel: 416-368-2834; *Fax:* 416-360-0278
info@shrigleybattrick.com
shrigleybattrick.com

Toronto: **Silver + Goren Chartered Professional Accountants**
#107, 40 Wynford Dr.
Toronto, ON M3C 1J5

Tel: 647-694-8000
info@silvergoren.com
silvergoren.com

Toronto: **Sims & Company Chartered Accountant Professional Corporation**
346 Forman Ave.
Toronto, ON M4S 2S7

Tel: 416-481-9101; *Fax:* 416-481-7693
www.simsandcompany.com

Toronto: **Sloan Partners LLP**
#6, 4646 Dufferin St.
Toronto, ON M3H 5S4

Tel: 416-665-7735; *Fax:* 416-649-7725
info@sloangroup.ca
www.sloangroup.ca
www.facebook.com/SloanGroup

Toronto: **Sone Rovet Chasson, LLP**
#406, 1220 Sheppard Ave. East
Toronto, ON M2K 2S5

Tel: 416-498-7200; *Fax:* 416-498-6877
general@srcllp.ca
www.srcllp.ca
www.facebook.com/SRCLLP; twitter.com/SRCLLP

Toronto: **Sonny Jackson Chartered Accountant Professional Corporation**
Toronto, ON

Tel: 647-828-6652
contact@sonnyjackson.com
www.sonnyjackson.com

Toronto: **SRJ Chartered Accountants Professional Corporation**
#1400, 330 Bay St.
Toronto, ON M5H 2S8

Tel: 647-725-2537; *Fax:* 416-981-7979
info@srjca.com
www.srjca.com

Toronto: **Stern Cohen LLP**
45 St. Clair Ave. West, 14th Fl.
Toronto, ON M4V 1L3

Tel: 416-967-5100; *Fax:* 416-967-4372
Toll-Free: 877-265-2942
www.sterncohen.com
twitter.com/SternCohenLLP

Toronto: **Stewart & Kett Financial Advisors Inc.**
Citicorp Place
#911, 123 Front St. West
Toronto, ON M5J 2M2

Tel: 416-362-6322; *Fax:* 416-362-6302
ckett@stewartkett.com
www.stewartkett.com

Toronto: **Tator, Rose & Leong, Chartered Accountants**
#603, 160 Eglinton Ave. East
Toronto, ON M4P 3B5

Tel: 416-924-1404; *Fax:* 416-964-3383
email@tarole.ca
www.tarole.ca

Toronto: **Trowbridge Professional Corporation**
#1201, 1 King St. West
Toronto, ON M5H 1A1

Tel: 416-214-7833; *Fax:* 416-214-1281
info@trowbridge.ca
www.trowbridge.ca
www.instagram.com/trowbridge_tax; twitter.com/trowbridge_tax

Toronto: **UHY McGovern Hurley LLP**
#800, 251 Consumers Rd.
Toronto, ON M2J 4R3

Tel: 416-496-1234; *Fax:* 416-496-0125
info@uhymh.com
www.uhymh.com

Toronto: **V.B. Sharma Professional Corporation, Chartered Accountants**
#200, 3390 Midland Ave.
Toronto, ON M1V 5K3

Tel: 416-292-4431; *Fax:* 416-292-7247
info@vbsharma.ca
www.vbsharma.ca

Toronto: **Vincent Zaffino Chartered Accountants**
#301, 155 University Ave.
Toronto, ON M5H 3B7

Tel: 416-363-3031
www.facebook.com/VincentZaffinoCA

Toronto: **Walsh & Company**
#218, 105 Gordon Baker Rd.
Toronto, ON M2H 3P8

Tel: 416-494-3404; *Toll-Free:* 888-372-1210
info@walshco.ca
www.walshco.ca

Toronto: **Williamson Accounting Inc.**
#203, 211 Consumers Rd.
Toronto, ON M2J 4G8

Tel: 416-444-8747
info@williamsonaccounting.ca
www.williamsonaccounting.ca

Toronto: **Yale & Partners LLP**
#400, 20 Holly St.
Toronto, ON M4S 3E8

Tel: 416-485-6000; *Fax:* 416-485-1105
office@yaleandpartners.ca
www.yaleandpartners.ca

Toronto: **Young & Grunier Chartered Accountants**
945 Mt. Pleasant Rd.
Toronto, ON M4P 2L7

Tel: 416-484-4844; *Fax:* 416-484-3717
mail@ygca.com
www.ygca.com

Toronto: **Zeifmans LLP**
201 Bridgeland Ave.
Toronto, ON M6A 1Y7

Tel: 416-256-4000; *Fax:* 416-256-4001
info@zeifmans.ca
www.zeifmans.ca
Other Contact Information: Alternate Fax: 416-256-4001
www.facebook.com/Zeifmans-156011321212569;
twitter.com/zeifmansllp

Trenton: **Wilkinson & Company LLP**
PO Box 400
71 Dundas St. West
Trenton, ON K8V 5R6

Tel: 613-392-2592; *Fax:* 613-392-8512
Toll-Free: 888-713-7283
www.wilkinson.net

Unionville: **Jeffrey G. Greenfield & Associates Chartered Accountants**
#115, 4591 Hwy. 7
Unionville, ON L3R 1M6

Tel: 647-557-2074

Vaughan: **Baker Tilly Vaughan LLP**
#600, 3300 Hwy. 7 West
Vaughan, ON L4K 4M3

Tel: 416-213-2600; *Fax:* 905-669-8705
vaughan@bakertilly.ca
www.bakertilly.ca/en/vaughan-ontario

Vaughan: **Domenic Galati, CGA**
#510, 3100 Steeles Ave. West
Vaughan, ON L4K 3R1

Tel: 416-745-0245
www.galaticga.com
Other Contact Information: Alt. Phone: 905-482-0140

Vaughan: **Fazzari + Partners LLP Chartered Professional Accountants**
#901, 3300 Hwy. 7
Vaughan, ON L4K 4M3

Tel: 905-738-5758; *Fax:* 905-660-7228
info@fazzaripartners.com
fazzaripartners.com
www.facebook.com/fazzaripartners; twitter.com/fazzaripartners

Vaughan: **KT Partners LLP**
#49, 100 Bass Pro Mills Dr.
Vaughan, ON L4K 5X1

Tel: 416-642-2616; Fax: 416-642-2617
info@ktpartners.ca
www.ktpartners.ca
www.facebook.com/156012181131711;
twitter.com/KTPartnersllp

Walkerton: **Padgett Business Services Mid-Western Ontario**
740 Southline, RR#2
Walkerton, ON N0G 2V0

Tel: 519-506-4523; Fax: 519-881-4941
info@biz-coach.ca
www.biz-coach.ca
Other Contact Information: Alternate Phone: 519-881-4523; Cell Phone: 519-881-7498

Waterloo: **Clarke Starke & Diegel LLP (CSD)**
7 Union St. East
Waterloo, ON N2J 1B5

Tel: 519-579-5520; Fax: 519-570-3611
www.csdca.ca

Waterloo: **Transport Financial Services Ltd.**
105 Bauer Pl.
Waterloo, ON N2L 6B5

Tel: 519-886-8070; Fax: 519-886-5214
Toll-Free: 800-461-5970
www.tfsgroup.com

Whitby: **Copetti & Co.**
601 Brock St.
Whitby, ON L1N 4L1

Tel: 905-666-2111
www.copetti.ca
www.facebook.com/412816585809266; twitter.com/KimCopetti

Winchester: **Baker Tilly REO LLP**
PO Box 390
475 Main St.
Winchester, ON K0C 2K0

Tel: 613-744-2854; Fax: 613-744-2586
winchester@bakertilly.ca
www.bakertilly.ca/en/winchester-ontario

Windsor: **Baker Tilly Windsor LLP**
#200, 325 Devonshire Rd.
Windsor, ON N8Y 2L3

Tel: 519-258-5800; Fax: 519-256-6152
windsor@bakertilly.ca
www.bakertilly.ca/en/windsor-ontario

Windsor: **mbsp LLP Chartered Accountants**
Chrysler Building
#301, 1 Riverside Dr. West
Windsor, ON N9A 5K3

Tel: 519-252-1163; Fax: 519-252-5893
www.mbsp.ca

Windsor: **Roth Mosey & Partners LLP**
#300, 3100 Temple Dr.
Windsor, ON N8W 5J6

Tel: 519-977-6410; Fax: 519-977-7083
info@roth-mosey.com
www.roth-mosey.com

Woodbridge: **Rashid & Quinney Chartered Accountants**
#401, 216 Chrislea Rd.
Woodbridge, ON L4L 8S5

Tel: 905-856-2677; Fax: 905-856-2679

Woodstock: **Adam Shaw CPA Professional Corporation**
569 Dundas St.
Woodstock, ON N4S 1C6

Tel: 519-537-7474
www.adamjshaw.ca
www.facebook.com/535463363288967

Woodstock: **Micacchi Warnick & Company, Chartered Professional Accountants**
#2, 35 Perry St.
Woodstock, ON N4S 3C4

Tel: 519-539-6109; Fax: 519-421-1339
Toll-Free: 877-539-6109
www.mwcopc.com

Prince Edward Island

Charlottetown: **Arsenault & Crozier**
PO Box 20055, Stn. Sherwood
45 Maple Hills Ave.
Charlottetown, PE C1A 9E3

Tel: 902-892-0519; Fax: 902-892-1090
www.arsenaultcrozier.ca

Charlottetown: **Arsenault Best Cameron Ellis**
PO Box 455
#100, 18 Queen St.
Charlottetown, PE C1A 7L1

Tel: 902-368-3100; Fax: 902-566-5074
office@abce.ca
www.acgca.ca
www.facebook.com/64587206840; twitter.com/ACG_CAs

Charlottetown: **Fitzpatrick & Co.**
#201, 127 St. Peters Rd.
Charlottetown, PE C1A 5P3

Tel: 902-628-9000; Fax: 902-628-8808
info@fitzandco.ca
fitzandco.ca
www.facebook.com/FitzYourBiz; twitter.com/FitzYourBiz

Charlottetown: **Mella & Shea Chartered Professional Accountants**
51 Queen St.
Charlottetown, PE C1A 4A5

Tel: 902-628-4455; Fax: 902-628-1347
info@mellashea.ca
www.mellashea.ca

Charlottetown: **MRSB Group**
139 Queen St.
Charlottetown, PE C1A 8C3

Tel: 902-368-2643; Fax: 902-566-5633
www.mrsbgroup.com
www.facebook.com/mrsbgroup; twitter.com/mrsb_group

Stratford: **Bradley Handrahan Chartered Professional Accountants**
25 Stratford Rd.
Stratford, PE C1B 1T4

Tel: 902-628-2242; Fax: 902-367-3756
info@bhcpa.ca
www.bhcpa.ca

Summerside: **Peter M. Baglole, Chartered Professional Accountant**
740 Water St. East
Summerside, PE C1N 5X1

Tel: 902-436-1663; Fax: 902-436-1604
www.baglole.ca

Summerside: **Sharon R. O'Halloran CPA Inc.**
#2, 359 Water St.
Summerside, PE C1N 0G2

Tel: 902-859-4430
sharonohalloran.ca
www.facebook.com/SharonOHalloranCGAInc

Quebec

Blainville: **Marcil Girard**
#200, 1340, boul Curé Labelle
Blainville, QC J7C 2P2

Tel: 450-430-7526
info@marcilgirard.com
www.marcilgirard.com
www.youtube.com/marcilgirard;
www.facebook.com/248568805187038

Chicoutimi: **Michel Tremblay CPA**
644, rue Albanel
Chicoutimi, QC G7J 1N8

Tél: 418-545-7343; Téléc: 418-545-8194
micheltremblaycpa.com

Drummondville: **Groupe RDL Drummondville inc.**
1320, boul Lemire
Drummondville, QC J2C 7W5

Tel: 819-445-0400; Fax: 819-445-1050
info.drummondville@grouperdl.ca
www.grouperdl.ca

Gatineau: **Baker Tilly Gatineau Inc.**
#105, 290, boul St-Joseph
Gatineau, QC J8Y 3Y3

Tel: 819-770-0009; Fax: 819-965-0152
gatineau@bakertilly.ca
www.bakertilly.ca/en/gatineau-quebec

Joliette: **Martin, Boulard & Associés, s.e.n.c.r.l.**
#200, 37, Place Bourget sud
Joliette, QC J6E 5G1

Tél: 450-759-2825
info@mba.qc.ca
www.mba.qc.ca

Longueuil: **Dubé & Tétreault, CPA, S.E.N.C.R.L.**
#200, 3065, ch de Chambly
Longueuil, QC J4L 1N3

Tél: 450-442-0944; Téléc: 450-442-2166
dt-cpa@dube-tetreault.com
www.dube-tetreault.com

Lévis: **Lemieux Nolet Comptables Agréés SENCRL**
#310, 1610, boul Alphonse-Desjardins
Lévis, QC G6V 0H1

Tél: 418-833-1054
courrier@lemieuxnolet.ca
lemieuxnolet.ca
www.facebook.com/lemieuxnolet

Mirabel: **Lévesque Comptables Professionels Agréés inc.**
#400, 12450, rue de l'Avenir
Mirabel, QC J7J 2J1

Tél: 450-437-8969; Téléc: 450-437-8996
info@levesquecpa.ca
levesquecpa.ca

Montréal: **A. Bertucci, Chartered Professional Accountant**
1445, rue Lambert Closse
Montréal, QC H3H 1Z5

Tel: 514-932-3229; Fax: 514-932-4634
www.abertucci.com

Montréal: **Accountatax Inc./Comptataxe inc.**
147, rue Spring Garden
Montréal, QC H9B 2T7

Tel: 514-685-7394; Fax: 514-685-7141
Toll-Free: 877-685-7394
www.accountatax.ca

Montréal: **Accuracy Canada**
#1120, 1 Place Ville Marie
Montréal, QC H3B 2A7

Tél: 514-788-6550
accuracy.canada@accuracy.com
www.accuracy.com

Montréal: **Baker Tilly Montréal S.E.N.C.R.L/LLP**
#200, 606, rue Cathcart
Montréal, QC H3B 1K9

Tel: 514-866-8553; Fax: 514-866-8469
montreal@bakertilly.ca
www.bakertilly.ca/en/montreal-quebec

Montréal: **Beauchemin Trépanier Comptables professionnels agréés inc.**
69, rue Sherbrooke ouest
Montréal, QC H2X 1X2

Tél: 514-847-0182; Téléc: 514-849-9082
info@bt-cpa.ca
www.bt-cpa.ca

Montréal: **Brunet, Roy, Dubé, Comptables agréés**
#1200, 7100, rue Jean-Talon
Montréal, QC H1M 3S3

Tél: 514-255-1001; Téléc: 514-255-1002
brd-cpa.com
www.facebook.com/BRDCPA

Montréal: **Crowe BGK Corporate Finance Inc.**
4150, rue Ste-Catherine Ouest, 6è étage
Montréal, QC H3Z 2Y5

Tel: 514-908-3600; Fax: 514-908-3630
admin@crowebgk.com
crowebgk.com/services/mergers-and-acquisitions

Montréal: **Crowe BGK LLP**
4150, rue Ste-Catherine Ouest, 6è étage
Montréal, QC H3Z 2Y5

Tel: 514-908-3600; Fax: 514-908-3630
admin@crowebgk.com
www.crowebgk.com
www.facebook.com/crowebgk

Montréal: **DNTW Chartered Accountants, LLP**
#200, 4420, ch. de la Côte de Liesse
Montréal, QC H4N 2P7

Tel: 514-739-3606; Fax: 514-739-9226
montreal.help@dntw.com
www.dntw.com

Montréal: FL Fuller Landau SENCRL
Place du Canada
200, 1010, rue de la Gauchetiere ouest
Montréal, QC H3B 2S1
Tél: 514-875-2865; *Téléc:* 514-866-0247
Ligne sans frais: 888-355-6697
info@flmontreal.com
www.flmontreal.com
www.facebook.com/fl.llp; twitter.com/fl_llp

Montréal: Gestion-Pro Molige
6455, rue Christophe-Colomb
Montréal, QC H2S 2G5
Tel: 514-274-6831; *Fax:* 514-274-8128
info@gpmolige.com
www.gpmolige.com

Montréal: Goldsmith Hersh S.E.N.C.R.L.
#190, 8200, boul Decarie
Montréal, QC H4P 2P5
Tel: 514-933-8611; *Fax:* 514-933-1142
info@gmhca.com
www.gmhca.com

Montréal: Gosselin & Associés inc.
7930 - 20e av
Montréal, QC H1Z 3S7
Tél: 514-376-4090; *Téléc:* 514-376-4099
info@gosselin-ca.com
www.gosselin-ca.com

Montréal: Le Groupe Belzile Tremblay Inc.
#610, 5650, rue d'Iberville
Montréal, QC H2G 2B3
Tel: 514-384-3620; *Fax:* 514-384-3710
bt@belziletremblay.ca
www.belziletremblay.ca

Montréal: Hardy, Normand & Associés, S.E.N.C.R.L.
#200, 7875, boul Louis-H.-Lafontaine
Montréal, QC H1K 4E4
Tél: 514-355-1550; *Téléc:* 514-355-1559
hn@hardynormand.com
www.hardynormand.com
twitter.com/hardynormand

Montréal: Info Comptabilité Plus (ICP)
#201, 2035, Côte de Liesse
Montréal, QC H4N 2M5
Tel: 514-337-2677; *Fax:* 514-337-1594
info@infocplus.com
infocplus.com

Montréal: James Kromida, Comptable Professionnel
Agréé/James Kromida, Chartered Professional
Accountant
750, av Sainte-Croix
Montréal, QC H4L 3Y2
Tel: 514-747-3413; *Fax:* 514-747-0799
www.kromida.com
www.facebook.com/kromida22; twitter.com/JamesKromida

Montréal: JDM Consultation Inc.
#203, 759, carré Victoria
Montréal, QC H2Y 2J7
Tel: 514-844-4536; *Fax:* 514-849-8647
www.menegakis.ca

Montréal: LCA CPA LLP
#240, 5000, rue Jean-Talon ouest
Montréal, QC H4P 1W9
Tel: 514-276-9499; *Fax:* 514-738-8770
info@lcacpa.ca
www.lcacpa.ca

Montréal: Levy Pilotte S.E.N.C.R.L./Levy Pilotte LLP
#700, 5250, boul Décarie
Montréal, QC H3X 3Z6
Tél: 514-487-1566; *Téléc:* 514-488-5145
contact@levypilotte.com
www.levypilotte.com
www.facebook.com/levypilottellp; twitter.com/levypilotteca

Montréal: Martel Desjardins
Édifice de la Banque Nationale de Paris
#1640, 1981, av McGill College
Montréal, QC H3A 2Y1
Tel: 514-849-2793; *Fax:* 514-849-7104
md@marteldesjardins.com
www.marteldesjardins.ca

Montréal: Martin & Cie
1100, rue Notre-Dame
Montréal, QC H8S 2C4
Tel: 514-637-7887; *Fax:* 514-637-3566
c.martin@martin-cie.com
www.martin-cie.com

Montréal: Mazars Harel Drouin, LLP
#1200, 215, rue Saint-Jacques
Montréal, QC H2Y 1M6
Tel: 514-845-9253; *Fax:* 514-845-3859
contact@mazars.ca
www.mazars.ca
www.youtube.com/user/MazarsGroup
www.facebook.com/MazarsGroup; twitter.com/MazarsGroup

Montréal: MCA Consulting Group
5240-B, rue Saint Denis
Montréal, QC H2J 2M2
Tel: 514-277-8081; *Fax:* 514-276-9150
info@groupemca.com
www.groupemca.com

Montréal: Padgett Business Service of Quebec Inc.
3974, rue Notre Dame
Montréal, QC H4C 1R1
Tel: 514-369-3868; *Fax:* 514-807-3528
info@padgett.org
www.padgett.org

Montréal: Padgett Business Services (West Island - East)
2945, av André
Montréal, QC H9P 1K7
Tel: 514-684-8086; *Fax:* 514-684-0884
www.padgettwestisland.com

Montréal: Padgett Montréal
#402, 1100, boul Crémazie est
Montréal, QC H2P 2X2
Tel: 514-324-5321; *Toll-Free:* 866-530-5321
padgettmontreal.com

Montréal: Petrie Raymond LLP
#1000, 255, boul Crémazie est
Montréal, QC H2M 1L5
Tel: 514-342-4740; *Téléc:* 514-737-4049
info@petrieraymond.com
www.petrieraymond.qc.ca

Montréal: Porter Hétu International (Québec) inc. (PHIQ)
#100, 790, boul Marcel-Laurin
Montréal, QC H4L 2M6
Tel: 514-744-1500
accueil@phiq.ca
phiq.ca
www.facebook.com/porterhetuintqcinc;
twitter.com/PhiqStLaurent

Montréal: PSB Boisjoli Inc.
#400, 3333, boul Graham
Montréal, QC H3R 3L5
Tél: 514-341-5511; *Téléc:* 514-342-0589
info@psbboisjoli.ca
www.psbboisjoli.ca
www.facebook.com/PSBBoisjoli; twitter.com/psbboisjoli

Montréal: Riccio CPA Inc.
#201, 167, rue Fleury ouest
Montréal, QC H3L 1T6
Tél: 514-381-7017
www.porterhetu.com/qc_riccio.html

Montréal: RSW Accounting & Consulting/RSW
Comptabilité & Conseil
Place du Parc
#1900, 300, rue Léo-Pariseau
Montréal, QC H2X 4B5
Tel: 514-842-3911; *Toll-Free:* 866-842-3911
rsw.ca

Montréal: Stamos CPA Inc.
800, av Ste. Croix
Montréal, QC H4L 3Y2
Tel: 514-744-1100; *Téléc:* 514-744-2200
www.stamosporterhetu.com

Montréal: UHY Victor LLP
#400, 759, carré Victoria
Montréal, QC H2Y 2J7
Tel: 514-282-1836; *Fax:* 514-282-6640
www.uhyvictor.com
blog.uhyvictor.com; www.facebook.com/232042816878082;
twitter.com/UHYVictorNews

Montréal: Waked Group
#209, 100, boul Alexis Nihon
Montréal, QC H4M 2N7
Tel: 514-875-6400; *Fax:* 514-861-6301
info@waked.com
www.waked.ca

Montréal: Xen Accounting/Xen Comptabilité
1001, rue Lenoir, #B-442
Montréal, QC H4C 2Z6
Tel: 514-397-0215; *Fax:* 438-300-3030
Toll-Free: 855-692-4062
info@xenaccounting.com
www.xenaccounting.com
www.facebook.com/xenaccounting; twitter.com/XenAccounting

Plessisville: Groupe RDL Thetford/Plessis inc.
2284, rue de la Coopérative
Plessisville, QC G6L 1X2
Tel: 819-362-3203; *Fax:* 819-362-3456
info.plessisville@grouperdl.ca
www.grouperdl.ca

Québec: Blouin, Julien, Potvin S.E.N.C.R.L.
#300, 2795, boul Laurier
Québec, QC G1V 4M7
Tel: 418-651-0405; *Fax:* 418-651-0285
groupe@bjpcpa.ca
www.bjpcpa.ca

Québec: Brassard Carrier, Comptables
Professionnels Agréés
#200, 1651, ch Ste-Foy
Québec, QC G1S 2P1
Tél: 418-682-2929; *Téléc:* 418-682-0282
info@groupebca.com
www.groupebca.com

Québec: Cauchon Turcotte Thériault Latouche,
comptables professionnels agréés, S.E.N.C.R.L.
#200, 5800, boul des Galeries
Québec, QC G2K 2K7
Tél: 418-658-8808; *Téléc:* 418-658-3136
equipe@cttlca.com
www.cttlca.com

Québec: Choquette Corriveau, Chartered
Professional Accountants
Place Iberville I
#300, 1195, av Lavigerie
Québec, QC G1V 4N3
Tel: 418-658-5555; *Fax:* 418-658-1010
info@choquettecorriveau.com
www.choquettecorriveau.com

Québec: Dallaire Forest Kirouac S.E.N.C.R.L. (DFK)
#580, 1175, av Lavigerie
Québec, QC G1V 4P1
Tel: 418-650-2266; *Téléc:* 418-650-2529
Ligne sans frais: 877-650-2266
www.dfk.qc.ca
www.facebook.com/dfkcomptable

Québec: Gariépy, Gravel, Larouche, Blouin CPA,
S.E.N.C.R.L.
#230A, 3333, rue du Carrefour
Québec, QC G1C 5R9
Tel: 418-666-3704; *Fax:* 418-666-6913
www.gglbca.com

Québec: Groupe RDL Québec inc.
#401, 1305, boul Lebourgneuf
Québec, QC G2K 2E4
Tel: 418-622-6666; *Fax:* 418-627-4193
info.quebec@grouperdl.ca
www.grouperdl.ca

Québec: Laberge Lafleur Brown S.E.N.C.R.L.
Place de la Cité
#1060, 2590, boul Laurier
Québec, QC G1V 4M6
Tél: 418-659-7265; *Téléc:* 418-659-5937
webquebec@rcgt.com
www.llbcpa.ca

Québec: Malenfant Dallaire, S.E.N.C.R.L.
Place de la Cité
#872, 2600, boul Laurier
Québec, QC G1V 4W2
Tel: 418-654-0636; *Fax:* 418-654-0639
maldal@malenfantdallaire.com
www.malenfantdallaire.com

Québec: **Mallette S.E.N.C.R.L.**
#200, 3075, ch des Quatre-Bourgeois
Québec, QC G1W 5C4
> Tél: 418-653-4431; Téléc: 418-656-0800
> Ligne sans frais: 877-444-1206
> info.quebec@mallette.ca
> www.mallette.ca
> www.youtube.com/user/mallettecomptables;
> www.facebook.com/mallette.ca

Québec: **Roy, Labrecque, Busque, Blanchet CPA Inc.**
#160, 5055, boul Wilfrid-Hamel
Québec, QC G2E 2G6
> Tel: 418-871-0013; Fax: 418-871-0162
> www.rlbb.ca

Repentigny: **Villeneuve Venne S.E.N.C.R.L.**
#200, 10, boul Brien
Repentigny, QC J6A 4R7
> Tél: 450-585-5503; Téléc: 450-654-6414
> vvrep@vvbkr.com
> www.vvbkr.com

Saint-Hubert: **Hébert Turgeon CPA inc.**
7695, ch de Chambly
Saint-Hubert, QC J3Y 5K2
> Tel: 450-676-0624; Fax: 450-676-7677
> www.htcpa.ca
> www.facebook.com/509382199420997

Saint-Rémi: **Lefaivre Labrèche Gagné, s.e.n.c.r.l.**
151, rue Perras
Saint-Rémi, QC J0L 2L0
> Tél: 450-454-3974; Téléc: 450-454-7320
> info@groupellg.com
> www.lefaivre-labreche.com

Sainte-Émélie-de-l'Énergie: **Gestion Tellier St-Germain**
2801, ch des Sept-Chutes
Sainte-Émélie-de-l'Énergie, QC J0K 2K0
> Tel: 450-886-3762
> ghislaine@gestionrg.qc.ca

Shawville: **Peter B. Smith, CPA, S.E.N.C.**
PO Box 869
389, rue Main
Shawville, QC J0X 2Y0
> Tel: 819-647-2403
> info@thetaxsmith.com
> www.thetaxsmith.com
> www.facebook.com/TheTaxSmith-151121438267171;
> twitter.com/TheTaxSmith

Victoriaville: **Groupe RDL**
c/o Groupe RDL Victoriaville SENCRL
450, boul des Bois-Francs nord
Victoriaville, QC G6P 1H3
> Tel: 819-758-1544; Fax: 819-758-6467
> info@grouperdl.ca
> www.grouperdl.ca
> Other Contact Information: Alternate Fax: 819-752-3836;
> Alternate Email: info.victo@grouperdl.ca; Human Resources,
> Email: rh@grouperdl.ca
> www.youtube.com/grouperdl; www.facebook.com/grouperdl

Victoriaville: **Groupe RDL Victoriaville SENCRL**
450, boul des Bois-Francs nord
Victoriaville, QC G6P 1H3
> Tel: 819-758-1544; Fax: 819-758-6467
> info.victo@grouperdl.ca
> www.grouperdl.ca

Ville Saint-Lauren: **Porter Hétu International**
#100, 790 Marcel-Laurin
Ville Saint-Lauren, QC H4M 2M6
> admin@porterhetucpa.com
> www.porterhetu.ca

Saskatchewan

Esterhazy: **Miller Moar Grodecki Kreklewich & Chorney, Chartered Professional Accountants**
Bank of Montreal Bldg.
PO Box 820
420 Main St.
Esterhazy, SK S0A 1X0
> Tel: 306-745-6611; Fax: 306-745-2899
> esterhazyoffice@millerandco.ca
> millerandco.ca

Rosetown: **Rosetown Accounting Services**
PO Box 1718
219 Main St.
Rosetown, SK S0L 2V0
> Tel: 306-882-2227; Fax: 306-882-2247
> admin.ras2003@sasktel.net
> www.rosetownaccounting.com

Saskatoon: **Baker Tilly SK LLP**
#201, 500 Spadina Cres.
Saskatoon, SK S7K 4H9
> Tel: 306-242-4281; Fax: 306-242-4429
> saskatoon@bakertilly.ca
> www.bakertilly.ca/en/saskatoon-saskatchewan

Saskatoon: **Buckberger Baerg & Partners LLP**
#210, 616 Main St.
Saskatoon, SK S7H 0J6
> Tel: 306-657-8999; Fax: 306-933-2250
> info@bbllp.ca
> www.bbllp.ca

Saskatoon: **Byron J. Reynolds, Chartered Accountant**
PO Box 32029, Stn. Erindale
Saskatoon, SK S7S 1N8
> Tel: 306-384-1130; Fax: 306-373-6431
> www.byronjreynolds.ca

Saskatoon: **Diehl Accounting**
611 - 47th St. East
Saskatoon, SK S7K 7V6
> Tel: 306-384-5451; Fax: 306-384-5771
> info@diehlaccounting.ca
> www.diehlaccounting.ca

Saskatoon: **DNTW Saskatoon**
#104, 1640 Idylwyld Dr. North
Saskatoon, SK S7L 1B1
> Tel: 306-242-5822; Fax: 306-242-5343
> saskatoon.help@dntw.com
> www.dntw.com

Saskatoon: **Hounjet Tastad Harpham**
#207, 2121 Airport Dr.
Saskatoon, SK S7L 6W5
> Tel: 306-653-5100; Fax: 306-653-5141
> www.hth-accountants.ca

Saskatoon: **Lizée Gauthier, CGA**
473 - 2nd Ave. North
Saskatoon, SK S7K 2C1
> Tel: 306-653-4444

Saskatoon: **Salamon Ratzlaff Groenwold**
#215, 728 Spadina Cres. East
Saskatoon, SK S7K 3H2
> Tel: 306-665-8890; Fax: 306-665-8894
> www.salamonratzlaffgroenwold.ca

Saskatoon: **Stewart, Gee & Murray CPA LLP**
#700, 230 - 22nd St. East
Saskatoon, SK S7K 0E9
> Tel: 306-653-7800; Fax: 306-653-7801
> www.sgmcpa.ca

Saskatoon: **Twigg & Company Chartered Professional Accountants**
650 Regency Center
333 - 25th St. East
Saskatoon, SK S7K 0L4
> Tel: 306-244-0808; Fax: 306-244-0004
> twigg.ca@sasktel.net
> www.twiggandcompany.com

Saskatoon: **Virtus Group**
The King George Building
#200, 157 - 2nd Ave. North
Saskatoon, SK S7K 2A9
> Tel: 306-653-6100; Fax: 306-653-4245
> Toll-Free: 855-825-8494
> virtus.saskatoon@virtusgroup.ca
> www.virtusgroup.ca
> www.instagram.com/virtusgroupllp
> www.facebook.com/VirtusGroupLLP; twitter.com/VirtusGroupLLP

Domestic Banks: Schedule I

B2B Bank
PO Box 279, Stn. Commerce Ct.
#600, 199 Bay St.
Toronto, ON M5L 0A2
> Toll-Free: 800-263-8349
> questions@b2bbank.com
> b2bbank.com
> Other Contact Information: GIC Deposits, Toll-Free Fax:
> 888-946-3448; Broker Mortgages, Toll-Free Fax: 866-947-7405
> twitter.com/b2b_bank

Former Name: Sun Life Trust Company; B2B Trust
Ownership: Private. A subsidiary of Laurentian Bank of Canada, Montréal, QC
Year Founded: 1991
Assets: 43,000,000,000 Year End: 20161231
Revenues: 915,451,000 Year End: 20161231

The Bank of Nova Scotia (BNS)/La Banque de Nouvelle-Écosse
Scotia Plaza
44 King St. West
Toronto, ON M5H 1H1
> Tel: 416-701-7200; Toll-Free: 800-472-6842
> email@scotiabank.com
> www.scotiabank.com
> Other Contact Information: TTY: 800-645-0288
> www.youtube.com/user/Scotiabank
> www.facebook.com/scotiabank; twitter.com/scotiabank

Also Known As: Scotiabank
Ownership: Public
Year Founded: 1832
Number of Employees: 86,932
Assets: $915,000,000,000 Year End: 20171231
Revenues: $27,000,000,000 Year End: 20171231

BMO Financial Group (BMO)
First Canadian Place
100 King St. West
Toronto, ON M5X 1B5
> Toll-Free: 844-837-9228
> feedback@bmo.com
> www.bmo.com
> www.youtube.com/bmocommunity;
> www.facebook.com/BMOcommunity; twitter.com/bmo

Also Known As: Bank of Montréal
Ownership: Public
Year Founded: 1817
Number of Employees: 46,000+
Assets: $710,000,000,000 Year End: 20191031
Revenues: $20,700,000,000 Year End: 20191031

BMO Private Banking
119, rue St-Jacques ouest
Montréal, QC H2Y 1L6
> Toll-Free: 855-834-2558
> www.bmo.com/privatebanking
> Other Contact Information: TTY: 866-889-0889

Former Name: BMO Harris Private Banking
Ownership: A member of BMO Financial Group
Number of Employees: 45,513

Bridgewater Bank
#150, 926 - 5th Ave. SW
Calgary, AB T2P 0N7
> Tel: 403-817-7000; Toll-Free: 866-243-4301
> customer.experience@bridgewaterbank.ca
> bridgewaterbank.ca
> www.facebook.com/BridgewaterBankCanada;
> twitter.com/bridgewaterbank

Former Name: Bridgewater Financial Services Ltd.
Ownership: Private. A wholly owned subsidiary of Alberta Motor Association
Year Founded: 1997
Number of Employees: 200+
Assets: $1-10 billion

Canadian Imperial Bank of Commerce (CIBC)/Banque Canadienne Impériale de Commerce
Commerce Court
PO Box 1, Stn. Commerce Court
199 Bay St.
Toronto, ON M5L 1A2
> Tel: 416-980-3096; Fax: 416-980-7012
> Toll-Free: 800-465-2422
> www.cibc.com
> Other Contact Information: Credit Cards, Toll-Free:
> 800-465-4653; Mobile Banking Support: 877-433-2422; TTY:
> 877-331-3338
> www.facebook.com/CIBC; twitter.com/cibc

Ownership: Public
Year Founded: 1961

Number of Employees: 44,000+
Assets: $565,300,000,000 Year End: 20191031
Revenues: $16,280,000,000 Year End: 20191031

Canadian Tire Bank
PO Box 3000
Welland, ON L3B 5S5
Toll-Free: 866-681-2837
www.myctfs.com
Other Contact Information: Credit Card Customer Service:
800-459-6415
Ownership: A subsidiary of Canadian Tire Financial Services Ltd.
Number of Employees: 1400

Canadian Western Bank (CWB)/Banque Canadienne de l'Ouest
Canadian Western Bank Place
#3000, 10303 Jasper Ave.
Edmonton, AB T5J 3X6
Tel: 780-423-8888; *Fax:* 780-423-8897
comments@cwbank.com
www.cwbank.com
Other Contact Information: Investor Relations, Email:
investorrelations@cwbank.com; Group URL:
www.cwbankgroup.com
www.instagram.com/canadianwesternbank;
www.facebook.com/cwbcommunity; twitter.com/CWBcommunity
Also Known As: Canada's Western Bank
Ownership: Public. A part of the Canadian Western Bank Group
Year Founded: 1984
Number of Employees: 2278
Assets: 31,424,235,000 Year End: 20191231
Revenues: 861,604,000 Year End: 20191231

Coast Capital Savings Federal Credit Union
Also listed under: Credit Unions/Caisses Populaires
Corporate Head Office
#800, 9900 King George Blvd.
Surrey, BC V3T 0K7
Tel: 604-517-7000; *Toll-Free:* 888-517-7000
info@coastcapitalsavings.com
www.coastcapitalsavings.com
www.instagram.com/coast_capital;
www.facebook.com/coastcapitalsavings;
twitter.com/Coast_Capital
Ownership: Member-owned
Year Founded: 2000
Number of Employees: 2,000+
Assets: $21,000,000,000

CS Alterna Bank
319 McRae Ave., 2nd Fl.
Ottawa, ON K1Z 0B9
Toll-Free: 866-560-0120
www.alternabank.ca
Other Contact Information: Lost or Stolen Cards, Toll-Free:
888-807-4101; QTrade/Alterna Wealth: 855-731-3901
www.facebook.com/alternabank; twitter.com/alternabank
Also Known As: Alterna Bank
Ownership: A wholly owned subsidiary of Alterna Savings & Credit Union Limited
Year Founded: 2000
Assets: 5,608,317,000 Year End: 20181231
Revenues: 113,138,000 Year End: 20181231

Digital Commerce Bank/Banque de commerce digital
736 Meridian Rd. NE
Calgary, AB T2A 2N7
Toll-Free: 844-836-6040
customersupport@dcbank.ca
www.dcbank.ca
www.instagram.com/dc.bank;
www.facebook.com/DirectCashBank
Former Name: DirectCash Bank
Also Known As: DCBank
Ownership: Private.
Year Founded: 2007
Assets: $58,943,125 Year End: 20190630

Duo Bank of Canada
#810, 33 Yonge St.
Toronto, ON M5E 1G4
Toll-Free: 888-331-6133
www.duobank.com
Other Contact Information: Walmart Mastercard:
www.walmartrewardsmc.ca
Former Name: Walmart Canada Bank
Ownership: Private.
Year Founded: 2019

Equitable Bank
#700, 30 St Clair Ave. West
Toronto, ON M4V 3A1
Tel: 416-515-7000; *Fax:* 416-515-7001
Toll-Free: 866-407-0004
customerservice@eqbank.ca
www.equitablebank.ca
Former Name: The Equitable Trust Company
Also Known As: EQ Bank
Ownership: A wholly owned subsidiary of Equitable Group Inc.
Year Founded: 1970
Number of Employees: 795
Assets: $25,037,145,000 Year End: 20181231
Revenues: $165,626,000 Year End: 20181231

Exchange Bank of Canada (EBC)
Toronto, ON
Toll-Free: 888-223-3934
www.ebcfx.com
Other Contact Information: Trading Desk, Toll-Free:
888-729-9716
www.facebook.com/ExchangeBankofCanada; twitter.com/ebcfx
Ownership: A subsidiary of Currency Exchange International, Orlando, FL, USA
Year Founded: 2016
Number of Employees: 50

First Nations Bank of Canada
#300, 224 - 4th Ave. South
Saskatoon, SK S7K 5M5
Tel: 306-955-6739; *Toll-Free:* 888-454-3622
fnbc.service@fnbc.ca
www.fnbc.ca
www.facebook.com/FNBC.Social; twitter.com/fnbc_bank
Ownership: Private. Over 80% Aboriginal owned & controlled
Year Founded: 1996
Number of Employees: 61
Assets: $672,170,000 Year End: 20191031
Revenues: $2,633,000 Year End: 20191031

General Bank of Canada (GBC)
#100, 11523 - 100th Ave. NW
Edmonton, AB T5K 0J8
Tel: 780-443-5626; *Fax:* 780-443-5628
Toll-Free: 877-443-5620
info@generalbank.ca
www.generalbank.ca
Ownership: A subsidiary of Firstcan Management Inc.
Year Founded: 2005
Assets: 1,813,764,000 Year End: 20181231

Haventree Bank
PO Box 1160, Stn. TD
Toronto, ON M5K 1P2
Tel: 647-277-0051; *Fax:* 416-342-0587
Toll-Free: 855-272-0051
clientaccounts@haventreebank.com
www.haventreebank.com
Other Contact Information: Technical Information:
mortgageservicing@haventreebank.com; Privacy:
privacyofficer@haventreebank.com
Former Name: Equity Financial Trust Company; Equity Transfer & Trust Company
Ownership: Private.
Year Founded: 2018

Home Bank/Banque Home
#2300, 145 King St. West
Toronto, ON M5H 1J8
Toll-Free: 855-263-2265
customerservice@homebank.ca
www.homebank.ca
Other Contact Information: Residential Mortgage Service,
Toll-Free: 855-767-3031
www.facebook.com/hometrustco
Former Name: CFF Bank; MonCana Bank of Canada
Ownership: A wholly owned subsidiary of Home Trust Company
Year Founded: 2011

HomeEquity Bank
#300, 1881 Yonge St.
Toronto, ON M4S 3C4
Tel: 416-925-4757; *Fax:* 416-925-9938
Toll-Free: 866-522-2447
info@heb.ca
www.homeequitybank.ca
www.facebook.com/HomeEquityBank
Ownership: A wholly owned subsidiary of HOMEQ Corporation
Year Founded: 2009
Assets: 4,095,861,000 Year End: 20190930

Laurentian Bank of Canada/Banque Laurentienne du Canada
1981 Mcgill College Ave., 20th Fl.
Montréal, QC H3G 0E5
Tel: 514-252-1846; *Toll-Free:* 800-252-1846
www.laurentianbank.ca
Other Contact Information: TTY: 866-262-2231; Media:
514-284-4500, ext. 40015
www.youtube.com/user/banquelaurentienne;
www.facebook.com/BLaurentienne; twitter.com/BLaurentienne
Ownership: Public
Year Founded: 1846
Number of Employees: 3,667
Assets: $44,353,000,000 Year End: 20191031
Revenues: $968,510,000 Year End: 20191031

Manulife Bank of Canada
PO Box 1602, Stn. Waterloo
#500MA, 500 King St. North
Waterloo, ON N2J 4C6
Tel: 519-747-7000; *Toll-Free:* 877-765-2265
manulife_bank@manulife.com
www.manulifebank.ca
Other Contact Information: Advisor Support Centre, Toll-Free:
800-567-9170; Email: advisorbank@manulife.com
www.facebook.com/manulifebank; twitter.com/manulifebank
Ownership: Private. A wholly-owned subsidiary of The Manufacturers Life Insurance Company
Year Founded: 1993
Number of Employees: 200+
Assets: $25,200,000,000 Year End: 20181231
Revenues: $413,000,000 Year End: 20181231

National Bank of Canada (NBC)/Banque Nationale du Canada(BNC)
National Bank Tower
800, rue Saint-Jacques
Montréal, QC H3B 4L2
Ligne sans frais: 888-835-6281
www.nbc.ca
www.instagram.com/nationalbankofcanada;
www.facebook.com/nationalbanknetworks;
twitter.com/nationalbank
Former Name: The Provincial Bank of Canada; The Mercantile Bank of Canada
Ownership: Public
Year Founded: 1859
Number of Employees: 21,600+
Assets: $246,000,000,000 Year End: 20191031
Revenues: $6,609,000,000 Year End: 20191031

Peoples Bank of Canada
#1400, 888 Dunsmuir St.
Vancouver, BC V6C 3K4
Tel: 778-309-4860; *Toll-Free:* 833-309-4860
www.peoplestrust.com
Other Contact Information: Current Mortgages: 877-462-3788,
pbccustomercare@paradigmquest.com; New Mortgages:
877-441-1984, residentialmortgages@peoplesbank.ca
Ownership: Private. Division of Peoples Group
Year Founded: 2019

President's Choice Financial
PO Box 201
25 York St.
Toronto, ON M5J 2V5
Toll-Free: 866-246-7262
www.pcfinancial.ca
www.facebook.com/PCFinancial; twitter.com/PCFinancial
Also Known As: President's Choice Bank; PC Bank
Ownership: Wholly owned subsidiary of Loblaw Companies Limited
Year Founded: 1998

RFA Bank of Canada
#2401, 1 Yonge St.
Toronto, ON M5E 1E5
Tel: 647-259-7873; *Fax:* 647-259-7874
Toll-Free: 877-416-7873
rfa.ca
Former Name: Street Capital Bank of Canada
Ownership: A wholly owned subsidiary of RFA Capital Holdings Inc.
Year Founded: 2007
Number of Employees: 160

Rogers Bank
350 Bloor St. East, 3rd Fl.
Toronto, ON M4W 1A9
Tel: 705-522-7412; *Toll-Free:* 855-775-2265
www.rogersbank.com
Ownership: A wholly owned subsidiary of Rogers Communications Inc.
Year Founded: 2013

Assets: $378,242,000 Year End: 20190331

Royal Bank of Canada (RBC)
South Tower
200 Bay St., 14th Fl.
Toronto, ON M5J 2S5

Tel: 416-955-7802; *Fax:* 416-955-7800
www.rbc.com
www.facebook.com/rbc; twitter.com/RBC
Also Known As: RBC Financial Group
Year Founded: 1869
Number of Employees: 80,000
Assets: $1,212,853,000 Year End: 20191031
Revenues: $11,500,000 Year End: 20191031

Tangerine Bank
3389 Steeles Ave. East
Toronto, ON M2H 0A1

Toll-Free: 888-826-4374
clientservices@tangerine.ca
www.tangerine.ca
Other Contact Information: French, Toll-Free Phone:
844-826-4374
www.youtube.com/user/TangerineBank;
www.facebook.com/TangerineBank; twitter.com/TangerineBank
Former Name: ING Bank of Canada; ING DIRECT Canada
Also Known As: Tangerine
Ownership: A subsidiary of The Bank of Nova Scotia
Year Founded: 1997
Number of Employees: 1245
Assets: $38,000,000,000

The Toronto-Dominion Bank
TD Centre
PO Box 1
Toronto, ON M5K 1A2

Tel: 416-982-8222; *Toll-Free:* 866-222-3456
www.td.com
www.youtube.com/tdcanada; www.instagram.com/TD_Canada;
www.facebook.com/TDCanada; twitter.com/td_canada
Also Known As: TD Bank; TD Canada Trust
Ownership: Public. Part of TD Bank Financial Group
Year Founded: 1855
Number of Employees: 85,000
Assets: $100 billion + Year End: 20191031
Revenues: $9,292,000,000 Year End: 20191031

UNI Coopération Financière
Also listed under: Credit Unions/Caisses Populaires
Édifice Martin-J.-Légère
CP 5554
295, boul St-Pierre ouest
Caraquet, NB E1W 1B7

Tél: 506-726-4725; *Ligne sans frais:* 833-292-4576
uni.communaute@uni.ca
www.uni.ca
www.instagram.com/unicooperation;
www.facebook.com/unicooperation; twitter.com/UNIcooperation
Also Known As: Fédération des caisses populaires acadiennes
ltée
Ownership: A subsidiary of the Desjardins Group
Year Founded: 1946
Number of Employees: 1,000
Assets: $4,400,000,000

Vancity Community Investment Bank
PO Box 13133, Stn. Terminal
Vancouver, BC V6B 6K1

Tel: 604-708-7800; *Toll-Free:* 888-708-7800
info@vancitycommunityinvestmentbank.ca
www.vancitycommunityinvestmentban k.ca
Other Contact Information: TTY: 1-888-702-7702
Former Name: Citizens Bank of Canada
Ownership: A wholly-owned subsidiary of Vancouver City
Savings Credit Union
Year Founded: 1997

VersaBank
#2002, 140 Fullarton St.
London, ON N6A 5P2

Tel: 519-645-1919; *Fax:* 519-645-2060
Toll-Free: 866-979-1919
versabank.com
twitter.com/VersaBank
Former Name: Pacific & Western Bank of Canada
Ownership: Public. A subsidiary of Pacific & Western Credit
Corp.
Year Founded: 1979
Assets: $1,943,885,000 Year End: 20201031
Revenues: $19,405,000 Year End: 20201031

Wealth One Bank of Canada
#1002, 5160 Yonge St.
Toronto, ON M2N 6L9

Toll-Free: 866-392-1088
help@wealthonecanada.com
www.wealthonebankofcanada.com
Ownership: Public
Year Founded: 2016
Assets: 291,468,000

Foreign Banks: Schedule II

Amex Bank of Canada
PO Box 3204, Stn. F
Toronto, ON M1W 3W7

Tel: 905-474-0870; *Toll-Free:* 800-869-3016
www.americanexpress.com/canada
Other Contact Information: Toll-Free TTY: 866-549-6426
www.instagram.com/amexcanada;
www.youtube.com/user/AmericanExpressCAD;
www.facebook.com/AmericanExpressCanada;
twitter.com/amexcanada
Ownership: A wholly owned subsidiary of American Expess
Travel Related Services Company, Inc., New York, USA
Year Founded: 1853
Number of Employees: 1,600
Assets: $3,778,405,000 Year End: 20181231

Bank of China (Canada)
#600, 50 Minthorn Blvd.
Markham, ON L3T 7X8

Tel: 905-771-6886; *Fax:* 905-771-8555
Toll-Free: 844-669-5566
boccanada@ca.bocusa.com
www.bankofchina.com/ca
Other Contact Information: VIP Customer Service:
gmb@ca.bocusa.com
Ownership: Wholly owned subsidiary of the Bank of China
Limited, Beijing, China.
Year Founded: 1992

Cidel Bank Canada
60 Bloor St. West, 9th Fl.
Toronto, ON M4W 3B8

Tel: 416-925-5504; *Fax:* 416-925-8192
www.cidel.com
Ownership: Part of Cidel Bank & Trust, Barbados.

Citco Bank Canada
#2700, 2 Bloor St. East
Toronto, ON M4W 1A8

Tel: 416-966-9200; *Fax:* 647-426-5300
toronto-bank@citco.com
www.citco.com/global-reach/canada
Ownership: Part of the Citco Group of Companies.

Citibank Canada
Citigroup Place
#1900, 123 Front St. West
Toronto, ON M5J 2M3

Tel: 416-947-5500; *Fax:* 416-639-4878
Toll-Free: 888-834-2484
www.citibank.com/canada
www.youtube.com/citi; www.instagram.com/citi;
www.facebook.com/citi; twitter.com/citi
Ownership: Subsidiary of Citigroup Inc., New York, NY, USA
Year Founded: 1982
Number of Employees: 1,700+
Assets: $1-10 billion

CTBC Bank Corp. (Canada)
1518 West Broadway
Vancouver, BC V6J 1W8

Tel: 604-683-3882
service@ctbcbank.ca
www.ctbcbank.ca
Former Name: CTC Bank of Canada
Ownership: Private. Subsidiary of CTBC Bank Co., Ltd., Taipei,
Taiwan.
Year Founded: 1999
Number of Employees: 10,001

Habib Canadian Bank
#1B, 918 Dundas St. East
Mississauga, ON L4Y 4H9

Tel: 905-276-5300; *Fax:* 905-276-5400
Toll-Free: 855-824-2242
info@habibcanadian.com
www.habibcanadian.com
www.facebook.com/HabibCanadianBank
Ownership: Private. Foreign. Wholly owned by Habib Bank of
AG Zurich, Switzerland.
Year Founded: 1967

HSBC Bank Canada
#300, 885 West Georgia St.
Vancouver, BC V6C 3E9

Tel: 604-525-4722; *Toll-Free:* 888-310-4722
info@hsbc.ca
www.hsbc.ca
Other Contact Information: Vancouver Media Contact, Phone:
604-641-2973
www.youtube.com/user/HSBCCanada; twitter.com/HSBC_CA
Ownership: Subsidiary of HSBC Holdings plc, London, UK.
Year Founded: 1981
Number of Employees: 7,500
Assets: $94,700,000,000 Year End: 20191231
Revenues: $715,000,000 Year End: 20191231

ICICI Bank Canada
Don Valley Business Park
#1200, 150 Ferrand Dr.
Toronto, ON M3C 3E5

Toll-Free: 888-424-2422
customercare.ca@icicibank.com
www.icicibank.ca
Ownership: Wholly owned subsidiary of ICICI Bank Limited,
Mumbai, India.

Industrial & Commercial Bank of China (Canada)
West Tower, Bay Adelaide Centre
#3710, 333 Bay St.
Toronto, ON M5H 2R2

Tel: 416-366-5588; *Fax:* 416-607-2030
Toll-Free: 877-779-5588
info@icbk.ca
www.icbk.ca
Former Name: The Bank of East Asia (Canada)
Ownership: Private. Parent is Industrial & Commercial Bank of
China Limited, Beijing.
Year Founded: 1991

J.P. Morgan Bank Canada
TD Bank Tower
#4500, 66 Wellington St. West
Toronto, ON M5K 1E7

Tel: 416-981-9200
www.jpmorgan.com/ca
Ownership: A subsidiary of JPMorgan Chase & Co.

KEB Hana Bank of Canada
#1101, 4950 Yonge St.
Toronto, ON M2N 6K1

Tel: 416-222-5200
www.kebcanada.com
Former Name: Korea Exchange Bank of Canada
Ownership: Wholly owned subsidiary of Hana Financial Group,
Seoul, Republic of Korea.
Year Founded: 1981

SBI Canada Bank
#106, 77 City Centre Dr.
Mississauga, ON L5B 1M5

Tel: 905-896-6563; *Fax:* 905-896-6545
scicmiss@sbicanada.com
ca.statebank/home
Former Name: State Bank of India (Canada)
Ownership: Wholly owned subsidiary of State Bank of India.
Year Founded: 1982
Number of Employees: 45+
Assets: $100-500 million
Revenues: $1-5 million

Shinhan Bank Canada
#B2, 5095 Yonge St.
Toronto, ON M2N 6Z4

Tel: 416-250-3500; *Fax:* 416-250-3507
www.shinhan.ca
Ownership: Wholly owned subsidiary of Shinhan Bank, Seoul,
Korea.
Year Founded: 2009
Assets: $509,383,000 Year End: 20191231

Société Générale (Canada)
#1800, 1501, av McGill College
Montréal, QC H3A 3M8

Tél: 514-841-6000
americas.societegenerale.com
www.youtube.com/societegenerale;
www.instagram.com/societegenerale;
www.facebook.com/societegenerale; twitter.com/societegenerale
Ownership: Wholly owned subsidiary of Société Générale
Group, Paris, France.
Year Founded: 1974

UBS Bank (Canada)
#800, 154 University Ave.
Toronto, ON M5H 3Z4

Tel: 416-343-1800
www.ubs.com/ca/en
Ownership: Foreign. Public. Subsidiary of UBS AG, Zürich, Switzerland.

Foreign Banks: Schedule III

Bank of America National Association
#400, 181 Bay St.
Toronto, ON M5J 2V8

www.bankofamerica.com
Ownership: Branch of Bank of America, Charlotte, NC, USA.

The Bank of New York Mellon, Toronto Branch
1 York St., 6th Fl.
Toronto, ON M5J 0B6

Tel: 416-775-5914
www.bnymellon.com/ca/en.html
Former Name: Mellon Bank, N.A., Canada Branch
Also Known As: BNY Mellon
Ownership: Foreign. Branch of The Bank of New York Mellon Financial Corporation, New York City, New York.
Year Founded: 2007

Barclays Bank PLC, Canada Branch
Bay Adelaide Centre
333 Bay St., 49th Fl.
Toronto, ON M5H 2R2

Tel: 416-863-8900
corporatecommunicationsamericas@barclays.com
www.barclays.com/contact/ca .html
Ownership: Subsidiary of Barclays Bank PLC, London, UK.

BNP Paribas (Canada)
2001, boul Robert-Bourassa
Montréal, QC H3A 2A6

Tél: 514-285-6000
contact@ca.bnpparibas.com
www.bnpparibas.ca
Former Name: Banque Nationale de Paris (Canada)
Ownership: Foreign. Wholly owned subsidiary of BNP Paribas, Paris, France
Year Founded: 1961
Assets: $1-10 billion

Capital One Bank (Canada Branch)
PO Box 503, Stn. D
Toronto, ON M1R 5L1

Toll-Free: 800-481-3239
www.capitalone.ca
Other Contact Information: TTY: 800-219-1009; Complaints: ombudsman@capitalone.com
www.instagram.com/capitaloneca;
www.youtube.com/CapitalOneCanada;
www.facebook.com/CapitalOneCanada;
twitter.com/CapitalOneCA
Ownership: Foreign. Part of Capital One Services, Inc., McLean, VA, USA.

China Construction Bank Toronto Branch (CCBTO)
#3650, 181 Bay St.
Toronto, ON M5J 2T3

Tel: 647-777-7700; *Fax:* 647-777-7739
enquiry@ca.ccb.com
ca.ccb.com/toronto/en/gywm.html
Ownership: Foreign. Branch of China Construction Bank, Beijing, China.
Year Founded: 2014

Citibank, N.A.
Citigroup Place
#1900, 123 Front St. West
Toronto, ON M5J 2M3

Tel: 416-947-5500; *Fax:* 416-639-4878
Toll-Free: 888-834-2484
www.citibank.com/canada
www.youtube.com/citi; www.facebook.com/citi; twitter.com/citi
Ownership: Branch of Citibank, New York, NY, USA

Comerica Bank, Canada Branch
South Tower, Royal Bank Plaza
PO Box 61
#2210, 200 Bay St.
Toronto, ON M5J 2J2

Tel: 416-367-3113
www.comerica.com
Ownership: Foreign. Branch of Comerica Bank, Detroit, Michigan, USA.

Crédit Agricole Corporate & Investment Bank
#1900, 2000, av McGill College
Montréal, QC H3A 3H3

Tel: 514-982-6200; *Fax:* 514-982-6298
info-ca@ca-cib.com
www.ca-cib.com/our-global-markets/americas/canada
www.facebook.com/CreditAgricoleCIB; twitter.com/CA_CIB_EN
Also Known As: Crédit Agricole CIB
Ownership: Office of Crédit Agricole Corporate & Investment Bank, Paris, France.

Credit Suisse AG, Toronto Branch
PO Box 301
#2900, One First Canadian Place
Toronto, ON M5X 1C9

Tel: 416-352-4500; *Fax:* 416-352-4680
www.credit-suisse.com/ca/en.html
Ownership: Part of Credit Suisse Group, Zurich, Switzerland.

Deutsche Bank AG, Canada Branch
Commerce Court West
PO Box 263, Stn. Commerce Court
#4700, 199 Bay St.
Toronto, ON M5L 1E9

Tel: 416-682-8000; *Fax:* 416-682-8383
www.db.com/canada
Other Contact Information: Alternate Phone: 416-682-8400
twitter.com/DeutscheBank
Ownership: Foreign. Branch of Deutsche Bank AG, Frankfurt, Germany.

Fifth Third Bank, National Association
#1253, 70 York St.
Toronto, ON M5J 1S9

Tel: 416-645-8373
www.53.com
Ownership: Foreign. Branch of Fifth Third Bank, Cincinnati, Ohio, USA

First Commercial Bank
#100, 5611 Cooney Rd.
Richmond, BC V6X 3J6

Tel: 604-207-9600; *Fax:* 604-207-9638
i908a@firstbank.com.tw
www.firstbank.com.tw
Ownership: Foreign. Branch of First Commercial Bank, Taiwan.

JPMorgan Chase Bank, National Association
TD Bank Tower
66 Wellington St. West
Toronto, ON M5K 1E7

www.chase.com/online/canada/canada-home-en.htm
Other Contact Information: Alternate URL: www.jpmorgan.com
Former Name: The Chase Manhattan Bank; Morgan Guaranty Trust Co. of New York; Sears Bank Canada
Ownership: Branch of J.P. Morgan Chase & Co. Inc., Chicago, IL, USA.

M&T Bank
TD Canada Trust Tower, Brookfield Place
PO Box 209
#2520, 161 Bay St.
Toronto, ON M5J 2S1

Tel: 416-214-2301; *Fax:* 416-363-0768
www.mtb.com
www.facebook.com/MandTBank; twitter.com/mandt_bank
Ownership: Subsidiary of M&T Bank, Buffalo, NY.

Mega International Commercial Bank (Canada)
Madison Centre
#1002, 4950 Yonge St.
Toronto, ON M2N 6K1

Tel: 416-947-2800; *Fax:* 416-947-9964
icbcca@megaicbc.com
www.megabank.com.tw/abroad/canada/canada01.asp
Former Name: International Commercial Bank of Cathay (Canada)
Ownership: Wholly owned subsidiary of Mega International Commercial Bank Co., Ltd., Taipei City, Taiwan.

Mizuho Bank, Ltd., Canada Branch (MHCB)
PO Box 29
#1102, 100 Yonge St.
Toronto, ON M5C 2W1

www.mizuhogroup.com/bank/locations/office-subsidiaries
Former Name: Mizuho Corporate Bank (Canada); Mizuho Bank (Canada)
Ownership: Foreign. Branch of Mizuho Corporate Bank, Ltd., Tokyo, Japan.
Year Founded: 2000

MUFG Bank, Ltd., Canada Branch
#1800, South Tower, Royal Bank Plaza
200 Bay St.
Toronto, ON M5J 2J1

Tel: 416-865-0220
www.bk.mufg.jp/global/globalnetwork/americas
Former Name: Bank of Tokyo-Mitsubishi UFJ (Canada)
Ownership: Foreign. A member of Mitsubishi UFJ Financial Group (MUFG), Tokyo, Japan.
Year Founded: 1996

Natixis Canada Branch
#2811, 1800, av McGill College
Montréal, QC M3A 3J6

Tel: 438-333-0491; *Fax:* 438-333-0498
NatixisCIBAmericas@natixis.com
cib.natixis.com
Ownership: Office of Natixis, Paris, France.

The Northern Trust Company, Canada Branch
#1910, 145 King St. West
Toronto, ON M5H 1J8

Toll-Free: 800-636-5775
www.northerntrust.com
www.youtube.com/user/NorthernTrustVideos;
www.facebook.com/ntcareers; twitter.com/NorthernTrust
Ownership: Part of Northern Trust Canada. Branch of Northern Trust Company, Chicago, USA

PNC Bank Canada Branch
The Exchange Tower
PO Box 462
#2140, 130 King St. West
Toronto, ON M5X 1E4

Toll-Free: 800-669-1518
pnc.com/en/corporate-and-institutional/international-services/canada.html
Former Name: National City Bank - Canada Branch
Also Known As: PNC Business Credit
Ownership: Owned by PNC Financial Services Group, Inc., Pittsburgh, Pennsylvania.
Year Founded: 1852

Rabobank Canada
Bay Adelaide Centre, East Tower
#3720, 22 Adelaide St. West
Toronto, ON M5H 4E3

Tel: 647-258-2020; *Fax:* 416-941-9750
canada@rabobank.com
www.rabobank.com/en/locate-us/americas/canada.html
Ownership: Cooperative. Foreign. Branch of Rabobank Nederland, Netherlands
Year Founded: 1997

Silicon Valley Bank (SVB)
#4410, 161 Bay St.
Toronto, ON M5J 2S1

Tel: 416-417-7888
www.svb.com/canada
Other Contact Information:
www.instagram.com/siliconvalleybank;
www.youtube.com/user/SVBFinancialGroup;
medium.com/@svb_financial
www.facebook.com/SVBFinancialGroup;
twitter.com/SVB_Financial
Ownership: Part of the SVB Financial Group.
Year Founded: 2019

Société Générale (Canada Branch)
#1800, 1501, av McGill College
Montréal, QC H3A 3M8

Tél: 514-841-6000
americas.societegenerale.com
www.youtube.com/societegenerale;
www.instagram.com/societegenerale;
www.facebook.com/societegenerale;
twitter.com/SocieteGenerale
Ownership: A branch of Société Générale Group, Paris, France

State Street Bank & Trust Company, Canada Branch
Also listed under: Trust Companies
#1100, 30 Adelaide St. East
Toronto, ON M5C 3G6

Tel: 416-362-1100; *Fax:* 647-775-5966
Toll-Free: 888-287-8639
www.statestreet.com/ca
Also Known As: State Street Trust Company Canada
Ownership: Part of State Street Corporation
Year Founded: 1990

Sumitomo Mitsui Banking Corporation, Canada Branch (SMBC)
Ernst & Young Tower
PO Box 172
#1400, 222 Bay St.
Toronto, ON M5K 1H6

Tel: 416-368-4766
www.smbcgroup.com
Former Name: Sakura Bank (Canada); The Sumitomo Bank of Canada
Ownership: Private. Foreign. Wholly owned subsidiary of Sumitomo Mitsui Banking Corporation, Tokyo, Japan.
Year Founded: 2001

United Overseas Bank Limited (UOB)
Vancouver Centre
#2400, 650 West Georgia St.
Vancouver, BC V6B 4N9

Tel: 604-662-7055; *Fax:* 604-662-3356
UOB.Vancouver@uobgroup.com
www.uobgroup.com
Also Known As: UOB Vancouver Branch
Ownership: Foreign. Branch of United Overseas Bank Limited, Singapore.
Year Founded: 1987

U.S. Bank National Association, Canada Branch
Adelaide Centre
#2300, 120 Adelaide St. West
Toronto, ON M5H 1T1

Toll-Free: 866-274-5898
intouchwithus@usbank.com
www.usbankcanada.com
Other Contact Information: Customer Service, Toll-Free: 800-588-8065; Email: account.coordinators@usbank.com; Technical Help Desk, Toll-Free: 877-332-7461
Ownership: Part of U.S. Bank, Minneapolis, MN, USA.
Year Founded: 2000

Wells Fargo Bank, National Association, Canadian Branch/Société financière Wells Fargo Canada
#2200, 22 Adelaide St.
Toronto, ON M5H 4E3

financial.wellsfargo.com/canada/en/index.html
Also Known As: Wells Fargo Financial Corporation Canada
Ownership: Branch of Wells Fargo & Company, San Francisco, CA, USA.

Foreign Bank Representative Offices

Agricultural Bank of China Limited (ABC)
#2220, 510 West Georgia St.
Vancouver, BC V6B 0M3

Tel: 604-682-8468
www.abchina.com
Also Known As: ABC Vancouver Rep-Office
Ownership: Office of Agricultural Bank of China Limited, Beijing, China

Attijariwafa Bank
2198, boul René-Lévesque ouest
Montréal, QC H3H 2T8

www.attijariwafabank.com
Ownership: Office of Société Nationale d'Investissement (SNI), Morocco.

Banco Base, S.A., Institución de Banca Múltiple
#2500, 120 Adelaide St. West
Toronto, ON M5H 1T1

Tel: 416-943-1603
www.bancobase.com
www.youtube.com/user/BancoBASEoficial;
twitter.com/banco_base
Also Known As: Banco BASE Representative Office
Ownership: Office of Banco Base, S.A., Madrid, Spain

Banco Santander Totta, SA
1110 Dundas St. West
Toronto, ON M6J 1X2

Tel: 416-538-7111
www.santandertotta.pt
www.facebook.com/santandertotta
Ownership: Office of Banco Santander Totta, SA, Lisbon, Portugal.

Bank of Communications Co., Ltd.
#2460, 22 Adelaide St. West
Toronto, ON M5H 4E3

www.bankcomm.com.hk
Ownership: Office of Bank and Communications Co. Ltd., China

Banque Centrale Populaire du Maroc
2208, boul René-Lévesque ouest
Montréal, QC H3H 1R6

Tel: 514-281-1855; *Fax:* 514-281-1974
www.groupebcp.com
Ownership: Office of Banque Centrale Populaire du Maroc, Casablanca, Morocco

Banque Degroof Petercam Luxembourg S.A.
#300, 288, rue St-Jacques
Montréal, QC H2Y 1N1

www.degroofpetercam.com

Banque Marocaine du Commerce Extérieur S.A.
#200, 370, rue Jean-Talon est
Montréal, QC H2R 1T3

www.bankofafrica.ma
Also Known As: BMCE Bank
Ownership: Office of Banque Marocaine du Commerce Extérieur S.A., Casablanca, Morocco, in partnership with Desjardins Group, Montréal, QC

Banque Transatlantique S.A.
Complexe Desjardins
150, rue Sainte-Catherine ouest, 27è étage
Montréal, QC H5B 1E4

Tel: 514-985-4137
btmontreal@banquetransatlantique.com
www.banquetransatlantique.com
Ownership: Part of the Crédit Mutuel group (CIC), Paris, France

Caixa Economica Montepio Geral
1286 Dundas St. West
Toronto, ON M6J 1X7

www.bancomontepio.pt
Ownership: A part of the Montepio group, Lisbon, Portugal

Caixa Geral de Depósitos, S.A.
#100, 425 University Ave.
Toronto, ON M5G 1T6

www.cgd.pt
Ownership: Office of Caixa Geral de Depósitos, Lisbon, Portugal

CaixaBank, S.A.
#1220, 401 Bay St.
Toronto, ON M5H 2Y4

Tel: 416-350-9696
www.caixabank.com

Crédit Industriel et Commercial S.A. (CIC)
Complexe Desjardins
150, rue Sainte-Catherine ouest, 27è étage
Montréal, QC H5B 1E4

btmontreal@banquetransatlantique.com
www.cic.fr
Ownership: A part of the Crédit Mutuel group (CIC), Paris, France

Doha Bank
First Canadian Place
#5600, 100 King St. West
Toronto, ON M5X 1C9

Tel: 647-255-3130; *Fax:* 647-255-3129
qa.dohabank.com
Ownership: Office of Doha Bank, Ad Dawha, Qatar
Year Founded: 2013

JN Bank Limited
1390 Eglinton Ave. West
Toronto, ON M6C 2E4

Tel: 416-784-9657; *Fax:* 416-784-4388
jnbstoronto@jnbs.com
www.jnbank.com
Other Contact Information: Alternate Phone (Brampton, ON): 905-965-3824
Former Name: Jamaica National Overseas (Canada) Ltd.
Also Known As: JNBS Representative Office (Toronto)
Ownership: Office of Jamaica National Building Society, Kingston, Jamaica

Landesbank Baden-Württemberg
#1101, 110 Yonge St.
Toronto, ON M5C 1T4

www.lbbw.de
Ownership: Office of Landesbank Baden-Württemberg, Germany

MetaBank
Picore Centre I
#300, 1315 Pickering Pkwy.
Pickering, ON L1V 7G5

www.metabank.com

National Bank of Pakistan
#3700, 100 King St. West
Toronto, ON M5X 1C9

Tel: 416-644-5097; *Fax:* 416-644-8801
operations@nbpusa.com
www.nbp.com.pk
Ownership: Office of National Bank of Pakistan, Karachi, Pakistan.

Savings Banks

AcceleRate Financial
PO Box 1860, Stn. Main
Winnipeg, MB R3C 3R1

Tel: 204-954-9543; *Fax:* 204-954-9805
Toll-Free: 888-954-9543
info@acceleratefinancial.ca
www.acceleratefinancial.ca
Other Contact Information: After Hours, Toll-Free: 800-567-8111
Ownership: A division of Access Credit Union
Year Founded: 2010

Achieva Financial
PO Box 2729, Stn. Main
Winnipeg, MB R3C 4B3

Tel: 204-925-6824; *Fax:* 204-231-5096
Toll-Free: 877-224-4382
info@achieva.mb.ca
achieva.mb.ca
www.facebook.com/AchievaMB; twitter.com/AchievaMB
Ownership: A division of Cambrian Credit Union
Year Founded: 1998

ATB Financial
#2100, 10020 - 100th St. NW
Edmonton, AB T5J 0N3

Toll-Free: 800-332-8383
atbinfo@atb.com
www.atb.com
Other Contact Information: Investor Services, Toll-Free: 888-282-3863
www.instagram.com/atbfinancial;
www.youtube.com/user/ATBFinancialVids;
www.facebook.com/ATBFinancial; twitter.com/ATBFinancial
Former Name: Alberta Treasury Branches
Ownership: Crown. 100% owned by the Provincial Government of Alberta
Year Founded: 1938
Number of Employees: 5,000+
Assets: $55,801,456,000 Year End: 20200331
Revenues: $1-10 billion Year End: 20200331

EQ Bank
#700, 30 St Clair Ave. West
Toronto, ON M4V 3A1

Tel: 416-551-3449; *Toll-Free:* 844-437-2265
contact@eqbank.ca
www.eqbank.ca
www.facebook.com/EQBank; twitter.com/EQBank
Ownership: A wholly owned subsidiary of Equitable Bank, which is wholly owned by Equitable Group Inc.
Year Founded: 2016

Hubert Financial
233 Main St.
Selkirk, MB R1A 1S1

Fax: 204-785-7649
Toll-Free: 855-448-2378
hubert@happysavings.ca
www.happysavings.ca
Ownership: A division of Sunova Credit Union Ltd.

MAXA Financial
220 - 10th St., #C
Brandon, MB R7A 4E8

Toll-Free: 866-366-6292
info@maxafinancial.com
www.maxafinancial.com
Ownership: A division of Westoba Credit Union Limited

Motive Financial (CDF)
#3000, 10303 Jasper Ave. NW
Edmonton, AB T5J 3X6

Toll-Free: 877-441-2249
info@motivefinancial.com
www.motivefinancial.com
www.facebook.com/motivefncl; twitter.com/MotiveFncl
Former Name: Canadian Direct Financial
Ownership: A division of Canadian Western Bank

Outlook Financial
PO Box 2, Stn. Main
Winnipeg, MB R3C 2G1
Tel: 204-958-7333; *Fax:* 204-958-8655
Toll-Free: 877-958-7333
save@outlookfinancial.com
www.outlookfinancial.com
Ownership: A division of Assiniboine Credit Union Limited

Boards of Trade & Chambers of Commerce

International Chambers & Business Councils

Belgian Canadian Business Chamber (BCBC)
PO Box 508, 161 Bay St., 27th Fl., Toronto ON M5J 2S1
Tel: 416-816-9154
www.belgiumconnect.com
Xavier Van Overmeire, President
Martin Cloutier, Vice-President
Anne Popoff, Vice-President & Events Director
Pierre Boutquin, Treasurer
Idalia Obregón, Executive Director & Board Secretary

Brazil-Canada Chamber of Commerce (BCCC)
#1600, 401 Bay St., Toronto ON M5H 2Y4
Tel: 416-998-7199
info@brazcanchamber.org
brazcanchamber.org
www.instagram.com/brazcanchamber
Carolina Mangabeira Albernaz, Director, Business Development
& Operations

British Canadian Chamber of Trade & Commerce
#708, 872 Sheppard Ave. West, Toronto ON M3H 5V5
Tel: 416-816-9154
www.bcctc.ca
Thomas O'Carroll, Vice-President, Central
Idalia Obregón, Executive Director

Canada China Business Council (CCBC) / Conseil commercial Canada Chine
#1501, 330 Bay St., Toronto ON M5H 2S8
Tel: 416-954-3800; *Fax:* 416-954-3806
ccbc@ccbc.com
www.ccbc.com
Peter Kruyt, Chair
Sarah Kutulakos, Executive Director

Canada China Business Council
#300, 1055 West Hastings St., Vancouver BC V6E 2E9
Tel: 604-681-8838

Canada China Business Council
759, rue du Square-Victoria, #RC4, Montréal QC H2Y 2K3
Tel: 514-842-7837; *Fax:* 514-800-2189

Canada Eurasia Russia Business Association (CERBA)
1 First Canadian Place, #1600, 100 King St. West, Toronto ON M5X 1G5
Tel: 416-862-4403; *Fax:* 416-862-7661
info@cerbanet.org
www.cerbanet.org
Affiliation(s): CERBA Kazakhstan; CERBA Russia; CERBA Uzbekistan
Gilles Breton, National Chair
Katherine Balabanova, National Coordinator

Canada-Arab Business Council (CABC) / Conseil de commerce canado-arabe (CCCA)
#700, 1 Rideau St., Ottawa ON K1N 8S7
Tel: 613-670-5853
om@c-abc.ca
www.c-abc.ca
Affiliation(s): Canadian Chamber of Commerce
Cathy Seguin, Acting President & Executive Director

Canada-ASEAN Business Council (CABC)
Oxley Bizhub, #08-47, 71 Ubi Rd. 1, 408732 Singapore
www.canasean.com
Greg Ross, Executive Director

Canada-Finland Chamber of Commerce
c/o Finnish Credit Union, 191 Eglinton Ave. East, Toronto ON M4P 1K1
Tel: 416-486-1533; *Fax:* 416-486-1592
info@canadafinlanddcc.com
www.canadafinlanddcc.com
Lauri Asikainen, President

Canada-India Business Council (C-IBC) / Conseil de commerce Canada-Inde
#604, 80 Richmond St. West, Toronto ON M5H 2A4
Tel: 416-214-5947; *Fax:* 416-214-9081
info@canada-indiabusiness.com
www.canada-indiabusiness.com
Victor Thomas, President & CEO

Canada-Poland Chamber of Commerce of Toronto
#102, 2680 Matheson Blvd. East, Mississauga ON L4W 0A5
info@canada-poland.com
www.canada-poland.com
www.instagram.com/canadapolandchamber
Wojciech Sniegowski, President

Canadian Council for the Americas (CCA) / Conseil Canadien pour les Amériques
TD Centre, PO Box 1175, 77 King St. West, Toronto ON M5K 1P2
Tel: 416-367-4313
info@ccacanada.com
www.ccacanada.com
www.youtube.com/CCATorontoOffice
Kenneth N. Frankel, President

Canadian Council for the Americas - British Columbia (CCA-BC)
1295 Johnston St., Vancouver BC V6H 3R9
Tel: 604-868-8678
info@cca-bc.com
www.cca-bc.com
André Nudelman, Chair

Canadian German Chamber of Industry & Commerce Inc. (CGCIC) / Deutsch-Kanadische Industrie- und Handelskammer
#1500, 480 University Ave., Toronto ON M5G 1V2
Tel: 416-598-3355; *Fax:* 416-598-1840
info@germanchamber.ca
kanada.ahk.de
Goetz Milcke, Vice-President, Finance & Administration

Canadian Slovenian Chamber of Commerce (CSCC)
4200 South Service Rd., Burlington ON L7L 4X5
Tel: 905-632-6400; *Fax:* 905-639-2285
info@canslo.com
www.canslo.com
Simon Pribac, Executive Director

Chambre de commerce Canada-Pologne
5570, rue Waverly, Montréal QC H2T 2Y1
Tel: 514-278-7617

Chambre de commerce Canado-Suisse (Québec) Inc. (SCCCQ) / Swiss Canadian Chamber of Commerce (Québec) Inc.
#152, 3450, rue Drummond, Montréal QC H3G 1Y4
Tel: 514-937-5822
www.cccsqc.ca
Marie Habre, Présidente

Chambre de commerce Canado-Tunisienne (CCCT) / Tunisian Canadian Chamber of Commerce
#810, 276, rue Saint-Jacques, Montréal QC H2Y 1N3
Tél: 514-847-1281
info@cccantun.com
www.cccantun.ca
Abdeljelil Ouanès, Président

Chambre de commerce et d'industrie française au canada (CCIFC) / French Chamber of Commerce
#2B, 1455, rue Drummond, Montréal QC H3G 1W3
Tél: 514-281-1246; *Téléc:* 514-289-9594
info@ccifcmtl.ca
www.ccifcmtl.ca
Sandrine Perreault, Directrice générale

Danish Canadian Chamber of Commerce (DCCC)
Toronto ON
Tel: 416-923-1811; *Fax:* 416-962-3668
Martin Damm Jensen, Chairman

European Union Chamber of Commerce in Canada (EUCCAN)
#201F, 622 College St., Toronto ON M6G 1B6
Tel: 416-598-7087
info@euccan.com
euccan.com
Stephen Klus, President

Indo-Canada Chamber of Commerce (ICCC) / Chambre de commerce Indo-Canada
924 The East Mall, Toronto ON M9B 6K1
Tel: 416-224-0090; *Fax:* 416-916-0086
iccc@iccconline.org
www.iccconline.org
Kanwar Dhanjal, President

Indonesia Canada Chamber of Commerce (ICCC)
c/o Canada Centre, World Trade Centre 5, 15th. Fl., Jl. Jend. Sudirman kav 29-31, Jakarta 12920 Indonesia
secretariat@iccc.or.id
www.iccc.or.id
Wely Kustono, Chief Operating Officer
Karina Sherlen, Vice Executive Director

International Chamber of Commerce (ICC) / Chambre de Commerce Internationale
#33, 43, av du Président Wilson, Paris 75116 France
icc@iccwbo.org
www.iccwbo.org
www.youtube.com/user/iccwbo1919
Affiliation(s): United Nations; World Trade Organization
John W.H. Denton, Secretary General
Paul Polman, Chair

Ireland-Canada Chamber of Commerce (ICCC)
121 Decarie Circle, Toronto ON M9B 3J6
info@icccto.com
www.icccto.com
Rob McDonnell, President

Italian Chamber of Commerce in Canada (ICCC)
#1150, 550, rue Sherbrooke ouest, Montréal QC H3A 1B9
Tel: 514-844-4249; *Fax:* 514-844-4875
info.montreal@italchamber.qc.ca
italchamber.qc.ca
Carmine D'Argenio, President
Danielle Virone, Executive Director

Italian Chamber of Commerce of Ontario (ICCO)
#201F, 622 College St., Toronto ON M6G 1B6
Tel: 416-789-7169; *Fax:* 416-789-7160
trade@italchambers.ca
www.italchambers.ca
www.instagram.com/italchambers
Tony Altomare, Co-President
Patrick Pelliccione, Co-President
Corrado Paina, Executive Director

The Swedish-Canadian Chamber of Commerce (SCCC)
#2109, 2 Bloor St. West, Toronto ON M4W 3E2
Tel: 416-925-8661
info@sccc.ca
www.sccc.ca
Marie Larsson, Executive Director

Swiss Canadian Chamber of Commerce (Ontario) Inc. (SCCC)
756 Royal York Rd., Toronto ON M8Y 2T6
Tel: 416-236-0039; *Fax:* 416-551-1011
sccc@swissbiz.ca
www.swissbiz.ca
Alexandra Soriano, President

World Chambers Federation (WCF)
33-43, av du Président Wilson, Paris 75116 France
wcf@iccwbo.org
iccwbo.org/chamber-services/world-chambers-federation
Affiliation(s): Specialized div. of International Chamber of Commerce
Peter Bishop, Chair

Chambers of Mines

Alberta Chamber of Resources
Sun Life Place, #800, 10123 - 99 St. NW, Edmonton AB T5J 3H1
Tel: 780-420-1030; *Fax:* 780-425-4623
admin@acr-alberta.com
www.acr-alberta.com
Neil Shelly, Executive Director
Amanda Rose, Communications Officer

Chamber of Mines of Eastern British Columbia
215 Hall St., Nelson BC V1L 5X4
Tel: 250-352-5242
chamberofmines@netidea.com
cmebc.com
David Johnston Jr., President
Brad Gretchev, Curator

East Kootenay Chamber of Mines
#201, 16 - 11th Ave. South, Cranbrook BC V1C 2P1
Tel: 250-464-9559; *Fax:* 250-426-8755
ekcm2@shaw.ca
www.ekcm.org

Jason Jacob, President

Mining Association of Nova Scotia (MANS)
7744 St. Margaret's Bay Rd., Ingramport NS B3Z 3Z8
Tel: 902-820-2115
info@tmans.ca
tmans.ca

Affiliation(s): Mining Association of Canada
Sean Kirby, Executive Director

Northwest Territories & Nunavut Chamber of Mines
PO Box 2818, #103, 5102 - 50 Ave., Yellowknife NT X1A 3S8
Tel: 867-873-5281; *Fax:* 780-669-5681
info@miningnorth.com
www.miningnorth.com

Affiliation(s): Mining Association of Canada; Canadian Institute of Mining, Metallurgy & Petroleum
Tom Hoefer, Executive Director

Yukon Chamber of Mines (YCM)
3151B - 3rd Ave., Whitehorse YT Y1A 1G1
Tel: 867-667-2090; *Fax:* 867-668-7127
info@yukonminers.ca
www.yukonminers.ca

Affiliation(s): Mining Association of Canada
Sue Craig, President
Samson Hartland, Executive Director

Provincial & Territorial Boards of Trade & Chambers of Commerce

Alberta Chambers of Commerce (ACC)
#1808, 10025 - 102A Ave., Edmonton AB T5J 2Z2
Tel: 780-425-4180; *Fax:* 780-429-1061
Toll-Free: 800-272-8854
tacorn@abchamber.ca
www.abchamber.ca

Affiliation(s): Canadian Chamber of Commerce
Shawna Miller, Chair
Ken Kobly, President & CEO

Atlantic Chamber of Commerce (ACC) / Chambre de commerce de l'Atlantique
PO Box 2291, Windsor NS B0N 2T0
Tel: 902-698-0265; *Fax:* 902-678-7420
info@atlanticchamber.ca
www.atlanticchamber.ca
www.linkedin.com/company/atlantic-chamber-of-commerce
Sheri Somerville, Chief Executive Officer
Tracy Beaver, Manager, Administrative Services

Atlantic Provinces Chambers of Commerce
270 Rookwood Ave., Fredericton NB E3B 2M2
Tel: 902-698-0265

Atlantic Provinces Chambers of Commerce
910 Main St., Moncton NB E1C 1G6
Tel: 506-857-3980

British Columbia Chamber of Commerce
#705, 750 West Pender St., Vancouver BC V6C 2T8
Tel: 604-683-0700; *Fax:* 604-683-0416
bccc@bcchamber.org
bcchamber.org
www.youtube.com/user/bcchamberofcom
Dan Baxter, Interim Chief Executive Officer
Rosaline Chan, Director, Finance & Administration

Chambre de commerce française au Canada - Section Québec
#2048, 140 Grande allée est, Québec QC G1R 5P7
Tél: 418-265-0284; *Téléc:* 418-522-0045
info@ccfcquebec.ca
www.ccifcquebec.ca

Jonathan Decherf, Président

Chambre de commerce Latino-américaine du Québec (CCLAQ)
#102, 5333, av Casgrain, Montréal QC H2T 1X3
Tél: 514-400-8969
info@cclaq.ca
www.cclaq.ca

Oscar Ramirez, Président

Chambre de commerce Québec-Afrique (CHAQUA)
671, rue Saint-Jean, Québec QC G1R 1P7
Tél: 581-998-4813
info@chaqua.org
chaqua.org

Charles Moumouni, Président

Fédération des chambres de commerce du Québec (FCCQ)
#1100, 555, boul René-Lévesque ouest, Montréal QC H2Z 1B1
Tél: 514-844-9571; *Téléc:* 514-844-0226
Ligne sans frais: 800-361-5019
info@fccq.ca
www.fccq.ca

Stéphane Forget, Président-directeur général

The Manitoba Chambers of Commerce
227 Portage Ave., Winnipeg MB R3B 2A6
Tel: 204-948-0100; *Fax:* 204-948-0110
Toll-Free: 877-444-5222
www.mbchamber.mb.ca
www.youtube.com/TheManitobaChambers
Chuck Davidson, President & CEO

New Brunswick Chamber of Commerce (NBCC)
1, ch Canada, Edmundston NB E3V 1T6
Tel: 506-737-1868; *Fax:* 506-737-1862

Northwest Territories Chamber of Commerce
NWT Commerce Place, #13, 4802 - 50th Ave., Yellowknife NT X1A 1C4
Tel: 867-920-9505; *Fax:* 867-873-4174
admin@nwtchamber.com
www.nwtchamber.com

Trevor Wever, President

Ontario Chamber of Commerce (OCC)
#2105, 180 Dundas St. West, Toronto ON M5G 1Z8
Tel: 416-482-5222; *Fax:* 416-482-5879
info@occ.on.ca
occ.ca
www.youtube.com/user/OntarioChamber
Rocco Rossi, President & CEO
Victor Korchenko, Vice-President, Finance

Ontario Gay & Lesbian Chamber of Commerce
#118, 2 College St., Toronto ON M5G 1K3
Tel: 416-646-1600
info@oglcc.com
www.oglcc.com

Sadhisha Ambagahawita, President

Saskatchewan Chamber of Commerce
#200, 2221 Cornwall St., Regina SK S4P 2L1
Tel: 306-352-2671; *Fax:* 306-781-7084
info@saskchamber.com
www.saskchamber.com
www.youtube.com/user/SaskChamber
Steve McLellan, Chief Executive Officer

Yukon Chamber of Commerce (YCC)
#205, 2237 - 2 Ave., Whitehorse YT Y1A 0K7
Tel: 867-667-2000; *Fax:* 867-667-2001
office@yukonchamber.com
www.yukonchamber.com

Peter Turner, President

Alberta

Airdrie Chamber of Commerce
#102, 150 Edwards Way NW, Airdrie AB T4B 4B9
Tel: 403-948-4412; *Fax:* 403-948-3141
info@airdriechamber.ab.ca
www.airdriechamber.ab.ca

Marilyne Aalhus, Executive Director

Alberta Beach & District Chamber of Commerce
PO Box 280, Alberta Beach AB T0E 0A0
Tel: 780-924-3255; *Fax:* 780-924-3257
www.albertabeachchamber.com

Bert Pyper, President

Alix Chamber of Commerce
c/o Village of Alix, PO Box 87, 4849 50th St., Alix AB T0C 0B0
Tel: 403-747-2444
www.villageofalix.ca

Catherine Hepburn, President

Athabasca & District Chamber of Commerce (ADCofC)
PO Box 3074, Athabasca AB T9S 2B9
www.athabascachamber.org

Affiliation(s): Canadian Chambers of Commerce

Barrhead & District Chamber of Commerce
PO Box 4524, Barrhead AB T7N 1A4
admin@barrheadchamberofcommerce.com
barrheadchamberofcommerce.com

Dave Sawatzky, President

Bashaw & District Chamber of Commerce
PO Box 645, Bashaw AB T0B 0H0
Tel: 780-372-3087
bashawcc@gmail.com
www.enjoybashaw.com

Dustin Hemingson, Chair

Beaverlodge Chamber of Commerce
PO Box 303, Beaverlodge AB T0H 0C0
Tel: 780-354-8785
beavercc@telus.net
www.beaverlodgechamber.ca

Callie Balderston, President

Beiseker & District Chamber of Commerce
PO Box 277, Beiseker AB T0M 0G0
Tel: 403-947-3875

Iris Balson, Contact

Berwyn & District Chamber of Commerce
PO Box 144, Berwyn AB T0H 0E0
Tel: 780-618-9675

Blackfalds & District Chamber of Commerce
PO Box 249, Blackfalds AB T0M 0J0
Tel: 403-885-2386; *Fax:* 403-885-2386
info@blackfaldslive.ca
www.blackfaldslive.ca

Bluffton & District Chamber of Commerce
PO Box 38, Bluffton AB T0C 0M0
Tel: 403-843-6805; *Fax:* 403-843-3392
blufftonabchamber@gmail.com

Bonnyville & District Chamber of Commerce
PO Box 6054, Hwy. 28 West, Bonnyville AB T9N 2G7
Tel: 780-826-3252; *Fax:* 780-826-4525
admin@bonnyvillechamber.com
www.bonnyvillechamber.com

Tom Allan, President

Bow Island / Burdett District Chamber of Commerce
PO Box 1001, Bow Island AB T0K 0G0
Tel: 403-545-6222; *Fax:* 403-545-6042
chamber@bowislandchamber.com
www.bowislandchamber.com

Bernice Deleenheer, President
Chandra Lane, Vice-President

Boyle & District Chamber of Commerce
PO Box 496, Boyle AB T0A 0M0
Tel: 780-689-2465; *Fax:* 780-689-2082
boylechamber.blogspot.ca

Bragg Creek Chamber of Commerce
PO Box 216, Bragg Creek AB T0L 0K0
Tel: 403-949-0004
info@visitbraggcreek.com
visitbraggcreek.com

Suzanne Jackett, President
Marcella Campbell, Treasurer

Breton & District Chamber of Commerce
PO Box 850, Breton AB T0C 0P0
Tel: 780-696-4888

Brooks & District Chamber of Commerce
PO Box 400, 403 - 2 Ave. West, Brooks AB T1R 1B4
Tel: 403-362-7641; *Fax:* 403-362-6893
manager@brookschamber.ab.ca
www.brookschamber.ab.ca
Karen Vogelaar, Executive Director
Michelle Gietz, President

Calgary Chamber of Commerce
#600, 237 - 8th Ave. SE, Calgary AB T2G 5C3
Tel: 403-750-0400
info@calgarychamber.com
www.calgarychamber.com

Rob Hawley, Chair
Adam Legge, President & CEO
Rebecca Wood, Director, Member Services

Camrose Chamber of Commerce
5402 - 48 Ave., Camrose AB T4V 0J7
Tel: 780-672-4217; *Fax:* 780-672-1059
www.camrosechamber.ca
Sharon Anderson, Executive Director
Tanya Fox, President

The Canadian Chamber of Commerce
PO Box 38057, Calgary AB T3K 5G9
Tel: 403-271-0595; *Fax:* 613-238-7643

Cardston & District Chamber of Commerce
PO Box 1212, 490 Main St., Cardston AB T0K 0K0
Tel: 403-795-1032; *Fax:* 403-653-2644
info@cardstonchamber.com
www.cardstonchamber.com
Michael Meeks, President
Angela Adams, Treasurer

Caroline & District Chamber of Commerce
PO Box 90, Bay 2, 5040 - 49 Ave., Caroline AB T0M 0M0
Tel: 403-722-4066; *Fax:* 403-722-4002
ccoc@telus.net
www.carolinechamber.ca
Shannon Fagnan, Manager

Carstairs Chamber of Commerce
PO Box 968, Carstairs AB T0M 0N0
Tel: 403-337-3710
carstairschamber@gmail.com
www.carstairschamber.ca

Claresholm & District Chamber of Commerce
PO Box 1092, Claresholm AB T0L 0T0
Tel: 403-625-3395
www.claresholmchamber.ca
Russell Sawatzky, President

Coaldale & District Chamber of Commerce
PO Box 1117, 1401 - 20 Ave., Coaldale AB T1M 1M9
Tel: 403-345-2358; *Fax:* 403-345-2339
info@coaldalechamber.com
www.coaldalechamber.com
Everett Duerksen, President

Cochrane & District Chamber of Commerce
PO Box 996, Cochrane AB T4C 1B1
Tel: 403-932-0320; *Fax:* 403-541-0915
c.business@cochranechamber.ca
www.cochranechamber.ca
Bill Popplewell, President

Cold Lake Regional Chamber of Commerce
4009 50th St., Cold Lake AB T9M 1P1
Tel: 780-594-4747
www.coldlakechamber.com
Trevor Benoit, President
Sherri Bohme, Executive Director

Consort & District Chamber of Commerce
PO Box 335, Consort AB T0C 1B0
Tel: 403-577-3644
Donna Ward, President

Coronation Chamber of Commerce
PO Box 960, Coronation AB T0C 1C0
Tel: 403-578-4580
Jodi Shipton, President

Cremona Water Valley & District Chamber of Commerce
PO Box 356, Cremona AB T0M 0R0
Tel: 403-637-2030
info@cremonawatervalley.com
www.cremonawatervalley.com
Linda Newsome, President

La Crete & Area Chamber of Commerce
PO Box 1088, #1, 10500 - 100 St., La Crete AB T0H 2H0
Tel: 780-928-2278; *Fax:* 780-928-2234
admin@lacretechamber.com
lacretechamber.com
Larry Neufeld, Manager

Crossfield Chamber of Commerce
PO Box 1490, 1005 Ross St., Crossfield AB T0M 0S0
Tel: 403-813-5133; *Fax:* 403-946-0157
info@crossfieldchamber.org
www.crossfieldchamber.org
Karen Postill, President

Crowsnest Pass Chamber of Commerce
PO Box 706, 12707 - 20th Ave., Blairmore AB T0K 0E0
Tel: 403-562-7108; *Fax:* 403-562-7493
Toll-Free: 888-562-7108
office@crowsnestpasschamber.ca
www.crowsnestpasschamber.ca
Affiliation(s): Alberta Chamber of Commerce
Sacha Anderson, President
Tim May, Treasurer
Claire Rogers, Secretary

Delburne & District Chamber of Commerce
PO Box 254, Delburne AB T0M 0V0
Tel: 403-749-3606; *Fax:* 403-749-2800
www.delburne.ca

Shelly Nicholson, Director

Devon & District Chamber of Commerce
#104, 32 Athabasca Ave., Devon AB T9G 1G2
Tel: 780-987-5177; *Fax:* 780-987-3303
devoncc@telus.net
www.devonchamber.ca
John Fairhead, President

Diamond Valley Chamber of Commerce
PO Box 61, Turner Valley AB T0L 2A0
Tel: 403-819-4994
info@diamondvalleychamber.ca
diamondvalleychamber.ca
Bev Geier, President

Didsbury Chamber of Commerce
1811 - 20 St., Didsbury AB T0M 0W0
Tel: 403-335-3265; *Fax:* 403-335-4399
www.didsburychamber.ca
Margo Ward, President

Drayton Valley & District Chamber of Commerce (DVDCC)
PO Box 5318, #112, 4302 50 St., Drayton Valley AB T7A 1R5
Tel: 780-542-7578; *Fax:* 780-542-2688
www.draytonvalley.ca/chamber-of-commerce/
Heather Yakimchuk, President

Drumheller & District Chamber of Commerce (DDCC)
60 - 1st Ave. West, Drumheller AB T0J 0Y0
Tel: 403-823-8100; *Fax:* 403-823-4469
chamberinfo@drumhellerchamber.com
www.drumhellerchamber.com
Landon Bosch, President
Heather Bitz, Executive Director

Eckville & District Chamber of Commerce
PO Box 609, Eckville AB T0M 0X0

Edgerton & District Chamber of Commerce
PO Box 337, Edgerton AB T0B 1K0
Tel: 780-755-3006

Edmonton Chamber of Commerce
World Trade Centre, Sun Life Place, #600, 9990 Jasper Ave., Edmonton AB T5J 1P7
Tel: 780-426-4620; *Fax:* 780-424-7946
info@edmontonchamber.com
www.edmontonchamber.com
www.youtube.com/edmontonchamber
Janet M. Riopel, President & CEO

Edson & District Chamber of Commerce
221-55 St., Edson AB T7E 1L5
Tel: 780-723-4918; *Fax:* 780-723-5545
edsonchamber@gmail.com
www.edsonchamber.com
Kathy Arndt, Chamber Manager

Elk Point Chamber of Commerce
PO Box 639, Elk Point AB T0A 1A0
Tel: 780-724-3810; *Fax:* 780-724-2762
www.elkpoint.ca/chamber-of-commerce
Vicki Brooker, Secretary

Evansburg & Entwistle Chamber of Commerce
PO Box 598, Evansburg AB T0E 0T0
Tel: 780-727-3526; *Fax:* 780-727-3526
info@partnersonthepembina.com
www.partnersonthepembina.com
Eric Karlzen, President
Al Hagman, Vice-President

Fairview & District Chamber of Commerce
Lancaster Place, #111, 10316 - 109 St., Fairview AB T0H 0L0
Tel: 780-835-5999; *Fax:* 780-835-5991
director@fairviewchamber.com
www.fairviewchamber.com
Debie Knudsen, Executive Director

Falher Chamber of Commerce
PO Box 814, 11 Central Ave. SW, Falher AB T0H 1M0
Tel: 780-837-2364
Affiliation(s): Falher & Area Economic Development & Tourism

Foremost & District Chamber of Commerce
PO Box 272, Foremost AB T0K 0X0
Tel: 403-867-3077; *Fax:* 403-867-2700
www.foremostalberta.com

Fort Macleod & District Chamber of Commerce
PO Box 178, Fort MacLeod AB T0L 0Z0
Tel: 587-220-5335
fmchamber1888@gmail.com
www.fort-macleod-chamber.com
Andrew Beusekom, Vice-President

Fort McMurray Chamber of Commerce
#105, 9912 Franklin Ave., Fort McMurray AB T9H 2K5
Tel: 780-743-3100; *Fax:* 780-790-9757
www.fortmcmurraychamber.ca
Nick Sanders, President

Fort Saskatchewan Chamber of Commerce
PO Box 3072, 10030 - 99 Ave., Fort Saskatchewan AB T8L 2T1
Tel: 780-998-4355; *Fax:* 780-998-1515
chamber@fortsaskchamber.com
www.fortsaskchamber.com
Affiliation(s): Alberta Chamber of Commerce; Canadian Chamber of Commerce
Lisa Makin, President
Dione Chambers, Executive Director

Fort Vermilion & Area Board of Trade
PO Box 456, Fort Vermilion AB T0H 1N0
Tel: 780-927-3505
www.fortvermilionboardoftrade.ca

Fox Creek Chamber of Commerce
PO Box 774, 105 Campground Rd., Fox Creek AB T0H 1P0
Tel: 780-622-2670; *Fax:* 780-622-2677
office@foxcreekchamber.ca
foxcreekchamber.ca
Corbett Fertig, President

Grande Cache Chamber of Commerce
PO Box 1342, 4600 Pine Plaza, Grande Cache AB T0E 0Y0
Tel: 780-501-4461
gcc@grandecachechamber.com
www.grandecachechamber.com
Affiliation(s): Alberta Chamber of Commerce; Canadian Chamber of Commerce
Rick Bambrick, Acting President

Grande Prairie & District Chamber of Commerce
Centre 2000, #217, 11330 - 106 St., Grande Prairie AB T8V 7X9
Tel: 780-532-5340; *Fax:* 780-532-2926
info@gpchamber.com
www.grandeprairiechamber.com
Dan Pearcy, CEO

Grimshaw & District Chamber of Commerce
PO Box 919, Grimshaw AB T0H 1W0
Tel: 780-617-4654
info@grimshawchamber.com
www.grimshawchamber.com
Daryl Billings, President
Joan Billings, Secretary

Hanna & District Chamber of Commerce
PO Box 2248, Hanna AB T0J 1P0
Tel: 403-854-4004
info@hannachamber.ca
www.hannachamber.ca
Will Warwick, President

High Level & District Chamber of Commerce
10803 - 96 St., High Level AB T0H 1Z0
Tel: 780-926-2470; *Fax:* 780-926-4017
info@highlevelchamber.com
www.highlevelchamber.com
Margaret Carroll, President

High Prairie & Area Chamber of Commerce
PO Box 3600, #107, 4806 - 53rd Ave., High Prairie AB T0G 1E0
Tel: 780-507-1565
office@hpchamber.net
www.hpchamber.net
Affiliation(s): Alberta Chamber of Commerce; Canadian Chamber of Commerce
Tracy Sherkawi, President

High River & District Chamber of Commerce
PO Box 5244, #6, 28 - 12 Ave. SE, High River AB T1V 1M4
Tel: 403-652-3336; *Fax:* 403-652-2627
hrdcc@telus.net
www.hrchamber.ca
Steve Muth, President
Lynette McCracken, Executive Director

Hinton & District Chamber of Commerce
309 Gregg Ave., Hinton AB T7V 2A7
Tel: 780-865-2777; Fax: 780-865-1062
info@hintonchamber.com
www.hintonchamber.com
Brian LeBerge, President
Natalie Charlton, Executive Director

Innisfail & District Chamber of Commerce
5202 50 St., Innisfail AB T4G 1S1
Tel: 403-227-1177; Fax: 403-227-6749
Carla Gabert, Manager

Irma & District Chamber of Commerce
PO Box 284, Irma AB T0B 2H0
Tel: 780-754-3996

Jasper Park Chamber of Commerce
Robson House, PO Box 98, 409 Patricia St., Jasper AB T0E 1E0
Tel: 780-852-4621
admin@jpcc.ca
www.jasperparkchamber.ca
Rusty Noble, President
Pattie Pavlov, General Manager

Kainai Chamber of Commerce
PO Box 350, Stand Off AB T0L 1Y0
Tel: 403-737-8124; Fax: 403-737-2116

Killam & District Chamber of Commerce
PO Box 189, Killam AB T0B 2L0
Tel: 780-385-7050

Lac La Biche & District Chamber of Commerce
PO Box 804, 10307 100 St., Lac La Biche AB T0A 2C0
Tel: 780-623-2818; Fax: 780-623-7217
info@llbchamber.ca
www.llbchamber.ca
Affiliation(s): Alberta Chamber of Commerce
Rik Nikoniuk, President

Lacombe & District Chamber of Commerce
6005 - 50 Ave., Lacombe AB T4L 1K7
Tel: 403-782-4300; Fax: 403-782-4302
info@lacombechamber.ca
www.lacombechamber.ca
Monica Bartman, Executive Director

Langdon & District Chamber of Commerce
PO Box 18, Langdon AB T0J 1X0
Tel: 403-936-5524
www.langdonchamber.com
Affiliation(s): Alberta Chamber of Commerce; Canadian Chamber of Commerce
Al Schule, President

Leduc Regional Chamber of Commerce
6420 - 50th St., Leduc AB T9E 7K9
Tel: 780-986-5454; Fax: 780-986-8108
info@leduc-chamber.com
www.leduc-chamber.com
www.instagram.com/leducchamber
Jennifer Garries, Executive Director
Jessica Roth, Coordinator, Communications & Marketing

Legal & District Chamber of Commerce
PO Box 338, Legal AB T0G 1L0
Tel: 780-961-7634
www.legalchamberofcommerce.ca
Affiliation(s): Greater Edmonton Regional Chambers of Commerce
Ken Evans, President
Carol Tremblay, Secretary & Treasurer

Lethbridge Chamber of Commerce
#200, 529 - 6 St. South, Lethbridge AB T1J 2E1
Tel: 403-327-1586; Fax: 403-327-1001
office@lethbridgechamber.com
www.lethbridgechamber.com
www.youtube.com/lethchamber
Karla Pyrch, Executive Director

Lloydminster Chamber of Commerce
4419 - 52 Ave., Lloydminster AB T9V 0Y8
Tel: 780-875-9013; Fax: 780-875-0755
info@lloydminsterchamber.com
www.lloydminsterchamber.com
www.youtube.com/user/LloydminsterChamber
Serena Sjodin, Executive Director

Magrath & District Chamber of Commerce
PO Box 1165, Magrath AB T0K 1J0
www.magrathchamber.com

Affiliation(s): Alberta Chamber of Commerce; Canadian Chamber of Commerce
Jay Mackenzie, President

Mallaig Chamber of Commerce
PO Box 144, Mallaig AB T0A 2K0
Tel: 780-635-3952

Mannville & District Chamber of Commerce
PO Box 54, Mannville AB T0B 2W0
Tel: 780-763-6455; Fax: 780-763-6451
Hinton Erin, Secretary

Marwayne & District Chamber of Commerce
PO Box 183, Marwayne AB T0B 2X0
Tel: 780-847-2538
Sharon Kneen, President

McLennan Chamber of Commerce
PO Box 90, McLennan AB T0H 2L0
Tel: 780-324-3300
mclennanchamber@serbernet.com
mclennan.ca/town-a-government/businesses/chamber-of-commerce
Louis Gagne, President

Medicine Hat & District Chamber of Commerce
413 - 6th Ave. SE, Medicine Hat AB T1A 2S7
Tel: 403-527-5214; Fax: 403-527-5182
info@medicinehatchamber.com
www.medicinehatchamber.com
Affiliation(s): Alberta Chamber of Commerce; Canadian Chamber of Commerce
Khrista Vogt, President
Lisa Kowalchuk, Executive Director

Millet & District Chamber of Commerce
PO Box 389, Millet AB T0C 1Z0
Tel: 780-387-4554; Fax: 780-387-4459

Morinville & District Chamber of Commerce
10113 - 100 Ave., Morinville AB T8R 1P8
Tel: 780-939-9462
www.morinvillechamber.com
Simon Boersma, President

Nanton & District Chamber of Commerce
PO Box 711, Nanton AB T0L 1R0
Tel: 403-646-2111
info@nantonchamber.com
www.nantonchamber.com
Pam Woodall, President
Simon Hunt, Vice-President

Okotoks & District Chamber of Commerce
PO Box 1053, 4-87 Elizabeth St., Okotoks AB T1S 1B1
Tel: 403-938-2848; Fax: 403-995-3338
ceo@okotokschamber.ca
www.okotokschamber.ca
Cheryl Actemichuk, Executive Director

Olds & District Chamber of Commerce
PO Box 4210, Olds AB T4H 1P8
Tel: 403-556-7070; Fax: 403-556-1515
chamber@oldsalberta.com
www.oldsalberta.com
Barb Babiak, Executive Director

Onoway & District Chamber of Commerce
PO Box 723, Onoway AB T0E 1V0
Tel: 780-918-6847
info@onowaychamber.ca
www.onowaychamber.ca
Janet Fluet, Administration Officer
Ed Gallagher, President

Oyen & District Chamber of Commerce
PO Box 718, Oyen AB T0J 2J0
Tel: 403-664-1001

Peace River & District Chamber of Commerce
PO Box 6599, 9309 - 100 St., Peace River AB T8S 1S4
Tel: 780-624-4166; Fax: 888-525-4423
www.peaceriverchamber.com
www.instagram.com/pr_chamber
Shelly Shannon, President
George Brothers, General Manager

Picture Butte & District Chamber of Commerce
PO Box 517, Picture Butte AB T0K 1V0
Tel: 403-732-4302

Pigeon Lake Regional Chamber of Commerce (PLRCC)
Box 6, Site 6, RR#2 Westerose, Westerose AB T0C 2V0
Tel: 780-586-6263
www.pigeonlakechamber.ca
Affiliation(s): Alberta Chambers of Commerce

Pincher Creek & District Chamber of Commerce
Ranchland Mall, PO Box 2287, #4, 1300 Hewetson Ave., Pincher Creek AB T0K 1W0
Tel: 403-627-5199
www.pincher-creek.com

Ponoka & District Chamber of Commerce
PO Box 4188, 4205 Highway 2A, Ponoka AB T4J 1R6
Tel: 403-783-3888; Fax: 403-783-3886
chamberp@telus.net
www.ponokalive.ca
Andrew Middleton, President
Kori Hart, Vice-President

Provost & District Chamber of Commerce
PO Box 637, Provost AB T0B 3S0
Tel: 780-753-6643
provost.ca/economic-development/chamber-of-commerce

Raymond Chamber of Commerce
PO Box 1435, Raymond AB T0K 2S0
Tel: 403-330-9057

Red Deer Chamber of Commerce
3017 Gaetz Ave., Red Deer AB T4N 5Y6
Tel: 403-347-4491; Fax: 403-343-6188
rdchamber@reddeerchamber.com
www.reddeerchamber.com
Bradley Williams, President
Tim Creedon, Executive Director

Redwater & District Chamber of Commerce
PO Box 322, Redwater AB T0A 2W0
Tel: 780-217-7496
Affiliation(s): Alberta Chamber of Commerce; Canadian Chamber of Commerce

Rimbey Chamber of Commerce
PO Box 87, 5025 50 Ave., Rimbey AB T0C 2J0
Tel: 403-392-6521
rimbeychamber@gmail.com
www.rimbeychamberofcommerce.com
Carrie Vaartstra, Executive Director

Rocky Mountain House & District Chamber of Commerce
PO Box 1374, 5406 - 48 St., Rocky Mountain House AB T4T 1B1
Tel: 403-845-5450; Fax: 403-845-7764
Toll-Free: 800-565-3793
rmhcofc@rockychamber.org
www.rockychamber.org
Affiliation(s): AB Chamber of Commerce; Canadian Chamber of Commerce
Colleen Dwyer, President
Cindy Taschuk, Executive Director

St. Albert & District Chamber of Commerce
71 St. Albert Trail, St Albert AB T8N 6L5
Tel: 780-458-2833; Fax: 780-458-6515
chamber@stalbertchamber.com
www.stalbertchamber.com
Barry Bailey, Chair
Lynda Moffat, President & CEO

St Paul & District Chamber of Commerce
PO Box 887, 4802 - 50 Ave., St Paul AB T0A 3A0
Tel: 780-645-5820; Fax: 780-645-5820
www.stpaulchamber.ca
Affiliation(s): Alberta Chambers of Commerce
Kevin Bernhardt, President
Linda Sallstrom, Executive Director

Sexsmith & District Chamber of Commerce
PO Box 146, Sexsmith AB T0H 3C0
Tel: 780-933-2044
sexsmithchamber@gmail.com
www.sexsmithchamber.com
Shirley Roth, Contact

Sherwood Park & District Chamber of Commerce
100 Ordze Ave., Sherwood Park AB T8B 1M6
Tel: 780-464-0801; Fax: 780-449-3581
Toll-Free: 866-464-0801
www.sherwoodparkchamber.com
www.youtube.com/user/ChamberSherwoodPark
Todd Banks, Executive Director

Slave Lake & District Chamber of Commerce
PO Box 190, Slave Lake AB T0G 2A0
Tel: 780-849-3222; *Fax:* 780-849-6894
sldcc@telus.net
www.slavelakechamber.com
Laurie Renauer, Executive Director

Smoky Lake & District Chamber of Commerce
PO Box 635, Smoky Lake AB T0A 3C0
Tel: 780-656-3532; *Fax:* 866-898-2608
www.smokylakechamber.com
Noel Simpson, Vice-President

Smoky River Regional Chamber of Commerce
PO Box 814, 11 Centre Ave. SW, Falher AB T0H 1M0
Tel: 780-837-8311
www.smokyriverchamber.ca
Affiliation(s): Alberta Chamber of Commerce; Canadian
Chamber of Commerce
Val Viens, President

Spruce Grove & District Chamber of Commerce
PO Box 4210, 99 Campsite Rd., Spruce Grove AB T7X 3B4
Tel: 780-962-2561; *Fax:* 780-962-4417
info@sprucegrovechamber.com
www.sprucegrovechamber.com
Brenda Johnson, President & CEO
Devyn Smith, Office Administrator

**Stettler Regional Board of Trade & Community
Development**
6606 - 50th Ave., Stettler AB T0C 2L2
Tel: 403-742-3181; *Fax:* 403-742-3123
Toll-Free: 877-742-9499
info@stettlerboardoftrade.com
www.stettlerboardoftrade.com
www.youtube.com/user/StettlerBoardofTrade
Matt Dorsett, President
Stacey Benjamin, Executive Director

Stony Plain & District Chamber of Commerce
4815 - 44 Ave., Stony Plain AB T7Z 1V5
Tel: 780-963-4545; *Fax:* 780-963-4542
info@stonyplainchamber.ca
www.stonyplainchamber.ca
Penny Gould, Executive Director

Strathmore & District Chamber of Commerce
PO Box 2222, 129 2nd Ave., Strathmore AB T1P 1K2
Tel: 403-901-3175; *Fax:* 403-901-3175
info@strathmoredistrictchamber.com
strathmoredistrictchamber.com
Terri Kinsman, President

Sundre Chamber of Commerce
600 Main Ave. East, Sundre AB T0M 1X0
Tel: 403-638-3245
scoc@telus.net
www.sundrechamber.ca
Mike Beaukaboom, President

Swan Hills Chamber of Commerce
PO Box 540, Swan Hills AB T0G 2C0
Tel: 780-333-5333
town@townofswanhills.com
www.townofswanhills.com
Janis Smith, Secretary

Sylvan Lake Chamber of Commerce
PO Box 9119, Sylvan Lake AB T4S 1S6
Tel: 403-887-3048; *Fax:* 403-887-3061
info@sylvanlakechamber.com
www.sylvanlakechamber.com
Denise Williams, Executive Director

Taber & District Chamber of Commerce
4702 - 50 St., Taber AB T1G 2B6
Tel: 403-223-2265; *Fax:* 403-223-2291
taberchamber@gmail.com
destinationtaber.com
Bruce Warkentin, President

Thorhild Chamber of Commerce
PO Box 384, Thorhild AB T0A 3J0
Tel: 780-699-3773

Thorsby & District Chamber of Commerce
PO Box 197, Thorsby AB T0C 2P0
Tel: 780-903-1695
Mitch Williams, President

Three Hills & District Chamber of Commerce
PO Box 277, Three Hills AB T0M 2A0
Tel: 403-425-0086
info@threehillschamber.ca
threehillschamber.ca
Tiffannie Patterson, President

Tofield & District Chamber of Commerce
PO Box 967, Tofield AB T0B 4J0
www.tofieldchamber.com
Affiliation(s): Alberta Chambers of Commerce
Greg Litwin, President
Jeff Edwards, Vice-President
Dan Hillyer, Secretary
Calvin Andringa, Treasurer

Trochu Chamber of Commerce
PO Box 771, Trochu AB T0M 2C0
Tel: 403-442-7980
Laurie Klassen, President

Valleyview & District Chamber of Commerce
PO Box 1020, Valleyview AB T0H 3N0
Tel: 780-524-4535
info@valleyviewchamber.ca
www.valleyviewchamber.ca
Justin Jasper, President

Vegreville & District Chamber of Commerce
PO Box 877, #106, 4925 - 50 Ave., Vegreville AB T9C 1R9
Tel: 780-632-2771; *Fax:* 780-632-6958
vegchamb@telus.net
www.vegrevillechamber.com
Darcie Sabados, President
Elaine Kucher, General Manager

Vermilion & District Chamber of Commerce
4606 - 52 St., Vermilion AB T9X 0A1
Tel: 780-853-6593; *Fax:* 780-853-1740
vermilionchamber@gmail.com
www.vermilionchamber.ca
Robert Ernst, President

Viking Economic Development Committee (VEDC)
PO Box 369, Viking AB T0B 4N0
Tel: 780-336-3466
info@viking.ca
www.townofviking.ca
Allan Harvey, Manager

Vilna & District Chamber of Commerce
PO Box 542, Vilna AB T0A 3L0
Tel: 780-636-3615
Affiliation(s): Alberta Chamber of Commerce; Canadian
Chamber of Commerce

Vulcan & District Chamber of Commerce
PO Box 385, Vulcan AB T0L 2B0
www.vulcanchamber.ca
Dwayne Hill, Chair
Tony Scott, Vice-Chair

Wabamun District Chamber of Commerce Society
PO Box 300, Wabamun AB T0E 2K0
Tel: 780-892-4773
wabamun.chamber@xplornet.com
Vicki Specht, President

Wainwright & District Chamber of Commerce
PO Box 2997, #203, 1006 - 4th Ave., Wainwright AB T9W 1S9
Tel: 780-842-4910; *Fax:* 780-842-6061
exec@wdchamber.com
www.wdchamber.com
Stephanie Evans, President
Kelsey Robinson, Executive Director

**Waterton Park Chamber of Commerce & Visitors
Association**
PO Box 55, Waterton Park AB T0K 2M0
Tel: 403-859-2224; *Fax:* 403-859-2650
info@mywaterton.ca
www.mywaterton.ca
Rod Kretz, President

Westlock & District Chamber of Commerce
PO Box 5917, Westlock AB T7P 2P7
Tel: 780-349-4444

Wetaskiwin Chamber of Commerce (WCC)
6420 - 50 St., Leduc AB T9E 7K9
Tel: 780-312-0657; *Fax:* 780-986-8108
info@wetaskiwinchamber.ca
www.wetaskiwinchamber.ca
Wayne Di Lallo, President
Allan Halter, Secretary

Joe Letourneau, Treasurer

Whitecourt & District Chamber of Commerce
Synergy Business Centre, PO Box 1011, 4907 - 52 Ave.,
Whitecourt AB T7S 1N9
Tel: 780-778-5363; *Fax:* 780-778-2351
manager@whitecourtchamber.com
www.whitecourtchamber.com
Affiliation(s): Alberta Chamber of Commerce
Rand Richards, President

Worsley Chamber of Commerce
PO Box 181, Worsley AB T0H 3W0
Tel: 780-685-3943; *Fax:* 780-685-2115

British Columbia

Abbotsford Chamber of Commerce (ACOC)
207 - 32900 South Fraser Way, Abbotsford BC V2S 5A1
Tel: 604-859-9651; *Fax:* 604-850-6880
www.abbotsfordchamber.com
Allan Asaph, Executive Director

Alberni Valley Chamber of Commerce
2533 Port Alberni Hwy., Port Alberni BC V9Y 8P2
Tel: 250-724-6535; *Fax:* 250-724-6560
office@avcoc.com
www.avcoc.com
Neil Malbon, President
Mike Carter, Executive Director

Armstrong-Spallumcheen Chamber of Commerce
PO Box 118, 3550 Bridge St., Armstrong BC V0E 1B0
Tel: 250-546-8155
manager@aschamber.com
aschamber.com
pinterest.com/asvisitorcentre
Fran Stecyk, President

Ashcroft & District Chamber of Commerce
PO Box 741, Ashcroft BC V0K 1A0
www.ashcroftbc.ca

Bamfield Chamber of Commerce
Bamfield BC V0R 1B0
Tel: 250-728-3006
info@bamfieldchamber.com
www.bamfieldchamber.com
Affiliation(s): Pacific Rim Tourism Association

Barriere & District Chamber of Commerce
PO Box 1190, Barriere BC V0E 1E0
Tel: 250-672-9221
Affiliation(s): Canadian Chamber of Commerce

Boundary Country Regional Chamber of Commerce
PO Box 379, Midway BC V0H 1M0
Tel: 250-442-7263
info@boundarychamber.com
www.boundarychamber.com
Kathy Wright, Executive Director

Bowen Island Chamber of Commerce
PO Box 199, 432 Cardena Rd., Bowen Island BC V0N 1G0
Tel: 604-947-9024

Burnaby Board of Trade (BBOT)
#201, 4555 Kingsway, Burnaby BC V5H 4T8
Tel: 604-412-0100; *Fax:* 604-412-0102
admin@bbot.ca
www.bbot.ca
www.youtube.com/user/burnabyboardoftrade
Paul Holden, CEO

Burns Lake & District Chamber of Commerce
Heritage Centre, PO Box 339, 540 Hwy. 16, Burns Lake BC
V0J 1E0
Tel: 250-692-3773; *Fax:* 250-692-3701
info@burnslakechamber.com
burnslakechamber.com
www.instagram.com/visitburnslake
Greg Brown, President

Cache Creek Chamber of Commerce
PO Box 460, Cache Creek BC V0K 1H0
Tel: 250-457-0068
cachecreekhusky@gmail.com
www.cachecreekvillage.com

Campbell River & District Chamber of Commerce
900 Alder St., Campbell River BC V9W 2P6
Tel: 250-287-4636; *Fax:* 250-286-6490
admin@campbellriverchamber.ca
www.campbellriverchamber.ca
www.youtube.com/user/CampbellRiverChamber

Colleen Evans, President & CEO

Castlegar & District Chamber of Commerce (CDCoC)
1995 - 6th Ave., Castlegar BC V1N 4B7
Tel: 250-365-6313; *Fax:* 250-365-5778
info@castlegar.com
www.castlegar.com
Jane Charest, President

Central Coast Chamber of Commerce (CCCC)
PO Box 40, Denny Island BC V0T 1B0
Tel: 250-957-2656
ccccexec@gmail.com
www.dennyislandbc.ca/chamber-of-commerce.php
Ana Santos, President

Chambre de commerce francophone de Vancouver (CCFC)
1555, 7e av ouest, Vancouver BC V6J 1S1
Tél: 604-601-2124
info@ccfvancouver.com
ccfvancouver.com
Daniel Wang, Président

Chase & District Chamber of Commerce
PO Box 592, 400 Shuswap Ave., Chase BC V0E 1M0
Tel: 250-679-8432; *Fax:* 250-679-3120
admin@chasechamber.com
www.chasechamber.com
Carmen Miller, President

Chemainus & District Chamber of Commerce
PO Box 575, #102, 9799 Waterwheel Cres., Chemainus BC V0R 1K0
Tel: 250-246-3944; *Fax:* 250-246-3251
chamber@chemainus.bc.ca
www.chemainus.bc.ca
Jeanne Ross, Chamber Coordinator
Amy Fieldon, Coordinator, Visitor Centre

Chetwynd & District Chamber of Commerce
PO Box 870, 5217 North Access Rd., Chetwynd BC V0C 1J0
Tel: 250-788-3345; *Fax:* 250-788-3655
manager@chetwyndchamber.ca
www.chetwyndchamber.ca
Tonia Richter, Executive Director
Carmen Westgate, President

Chilliwack Chamber of Commerce
#201, 46093 Yale Rd., Chilliwack BC V2P 2L8
Tel: 604-793-4323
info@chilliwackchamber.com
www.chilliwackchamber.com
www.youtube.com/user/ChilliwackChamber
Kirk Dzaman, President
Fieny van den Boom, Executive Director

Christina Lake Chamber of Commerce
1675 Hwy. 3, Christina Lake BC V0H 1E2
Tel: 250-447-6161; *Fax:* 250-447-6161
tourism@christinalake.com
www.christinalake.com

Clearwater & District Chamber of Commerce
209 Dutch Lake Rd., Clearwater BC V0E 1N2
Tel: 250-674-2646; *Fax:* 250-674-3693
www.clearwaterbcchamber.com

Cloverdale & District Chamber of Commerce
5748 - 176 St., Cloverdale BC V3S 4C8
Tel: 604-574-9802; *Fax:* 604-574-9122
info@cloverdalechamber.ca
www.cloverdalechamber.ca
John Gibeau, President

Columbia Valley Chamber of Commerce (CVCC)
PO Box 1019, 651 Hwy. 93/85, Invermere BC V0A 1K0
Tel: 250-342-2844; *Fax:* 250-342-3261
info@cvchamber.ca
www.cvchamber.ca
Affiliation(s): British Columbia Chamber of Commerce
Susan E. Clovechok, Executive Director

Comox Valley Chamber of Commerce (CVCC)
2040 Cliffe Ave., Courtenay BC V9N 2L3
Tel: 250-334-3234; *Fax:* 250-334-4908
Toll-Free: 888-357-4471
events@comoxvalleychamber.com
www.comoxvalleychamber.com
Kevin East, Chair
Dianne Hawkins, CEO

Cowichan Lake District Chamber of Commerce
PO Box 824, 125C South Shore Rd., Lake Cowichan BC V0R 2G0
Tel: 250-749-3244; *Fax:* 250-749-0187
lcchamber@shaw.ca
www.cowichanlake.ca
www.instagram.com/cowichanlakechamber
Affiliation(s): BC Chamber of Commerce; Canadian Chamber of Commerce

Cranbrook & District Chamber of Commerce
Cranbrook & District Chamber of Commerce, PO Box 84, Cranbrook BC V1C 4H6
Tel: 250-426-5914; *Fax:* 250-426-3873
Toll-Free: 800-222-6174
info@cranbrookchamber.com
www.cranbrookchamber.com
David Struthers, President
David Hull, Executive Director

Creston Valley Chamber of Commerce
PO Box 268, 121 Northwest Blvd. (Hwy. 3), Creston BC V0B 1G0
Tel: 250-428-4342; *Fax:* 250-428-9411
Toll-Free: 866-528-4342
info@crestonvalleychamber.com
www.crestonvalleychamber.com
Rob Schepers, President
Jim Jacobsen, Executive Director

Cumberland Chamber of Commerce
PO Box 250, 2680 Dunsmuir Ave., Cumberland BC V0R 1S0
Tel: 250-336-8313; *Toll-Free:* 866-301-4636
chamber@cumberlandbc.org
cumberlandbc.org
Affiliation(s): North By Northwest Tourism Association of BC

Dawson Creek & District Chamber of Commerce
10201 - 10th St., Dawson Creek BC V1G 3T5
Tel: 250-782-4868; *Fax:* 250-782-2371
info@dawsoncreekchamber.ca
www.dawsoncreekchamber.ca
Affiliation(s): BC Chamber of Commerce
Anjula Benjamin, President
Kathleen Connolly, Executive Director

Dease Lake & District Chamber of Commerce
PO Box 338, Dease Lake BC V0C 1L0
Tel: 250-771-3900; *Fax:* 250-771-3900

Delta Chamber of Commerce
6201 - 60 Ave., Delta BC V4K 4E2
Tel: 604-946-4232; *Fax:* 604-946-5285
admin@deltachamber.ca
www.deltachamber.ca
www.youtube.com/user/DeltaChamber
Ian Tait, Executive Director
Dave Hamilton, Chair

Discovery Islands Chamber of Commerce
PO Box 790, Quathiaski Cove BC V0P 1N0
chamber@discoveryislands.ca
www.discoveryislands.ca/chamber
Michael Lynch, President

Duncan-Cowichan Chamber of Commerce (DCCC)
381 Trans-Canada Hwy., Duncan BC V9L 3R5
Tel: 250-748-1111; *Fax:* 250-746-8222
chamber@duncancc.bc.ca
www.duncancc.bc.ca
Sonja Nagel, Executive Director

Elkford Chamber of Commerce
PO Box 220, 4A Front St., Elkford BC V0B 1H0
Tel: 250-425-5725
info@elkfordchamberofcommerce.com
www.elkfordchamberofcommerce.com

Enderby & District Chamber of Commerce
702 Railway St., Enderby BC V0E 1V0
Tel: 250-838-6727; *Fax:* 250-838-0123
Toll-Free: 877-213-6509
www.enderbychamber.com
Corinne Van De Crommenacker, General Manager
Lynne Holmes, President

Esquimalt Chamber of Commerce
#103, 1249 Esquimalt Rd., Victoria BC V9A 3P2
Tel: 250-590-2125
admin@esquimaltchamber.ca
esquimaltchamber.ca
Chris Edley, President

Falkland Chamber of Commerce
PO Box 92, Hwy. 97, Falkland BC V0E 1W0
Tel: 250-379-2780

Fernie Chamber of Commerce
102 Hwy. #3, Fernie BC V0B 1M5
Tel: 250-423-6868; *Fax:* 250-423-3811
Toll-Free: 877-433-7643
members@ferniechamber.com
www.ferniechamber.com
Affiliation(s): Economic Development Association of BC
Sheila Byers, President
Patty Vadnais, Executive Director

Fort Nelson & District Chamber of Commerce
PO Box 196, 5500 Alaska Hwy., Fort Nelson BC V0C 1R0
Tel: 250-774-2956; *Fax:* 250-774-2958
info@fortnelsonchamber.com
www.fortnelsonchamber.com
Kim Eglinski, President
Bev Vandersteen, Executive Director

Fort St. James Chamber of Commerce
PO Box 1164, 115 Douglas Ave., Fort St James BC V0J 1P0
Tel: 250-996-7023; *Fax:* 250-996-7047
fsjchamb@fsjames.com
www.fortstjameschamber.ca

Fort St. John & District Chamber of Commerce
#100, 9907 - 99 Ave., Fort St John BC V1J 1V1
Tel: 250-785-6037; *Fax:* 250-785-6050
info@fsjchamber.com
www.fsjchamber.com
Lilia Hansen, Executive Director
Tony Zabinsky, President

Fraser Lake Chamber of Commerce
c/o Village of Fraser Lake, PO Box 430, 210 Carrier Cres., Fraser Lake BC V0J 1S0
Tel: 250-699-6257; *Fax:* 250-699-6469
www.fraserlake.ca
Teresa Findlay, President

Gabriola Island Chamber of Commerce
PO Box 249, #6, 480 North Rd., Gabriola BC V0R 1X0
Tel: 250-247-9332
giccmanager@shaw.ca
www.adventuregabriola.ca
Affiliation(s): Tourism Association of Vancouver Island
Gloria Hatfield, President
Tammie Hennigar, Manager

Galiano Island Chamber of Commerce
PO Box 73, Galiano Island BC V0N 1P0
Tel: 250-539-2233
www.galianoisland.com
Richard Dewinetz, President

Gibsons & District Chamber of Commerce
PO Box 1190, #20, 900 Gibsons Way, Gibsons BC V0N 1V0
Tel: 604-886-2325; *Fax:* 604-886-2379
staff@gibsonschamber.com
www.gibsonschamber.com
William Baker, President & Treasurer
Chris Nicholls, Executive Director

Gold River Chamber of Commerce
PO Box 39, Gold River BC V0P 1G0
Tel: 250-285-2724
www.goldriver.ca

Greater Kamloops Chamber of Commerce
615 Victoria St., Kamloops BC V2C 2B3
Tel: 250-372-7722; *Fax:* 250-828-9500
mail@kamloopschamber.ca
www.kamloopschamber.ca
Deb McClelland, Executive Director

Greater Langley Chamber of Commerce
#207, 8047 - 199 St., Langley BC V2Y 0E2
Tel: 604-371-3770; *Fax:* 604-371-3731
info@langleychamber.com
www.langleychamber.com
Scott Johnstone, President
Lynn Whitehouse, Executive Director

Greater Nanaimo Chamber of Commerce
2133 Bowen Rd., Nanaimo BC V9S 1H8
Tel: 250-756-1191; *Fax:* 250-756-1584
info@nanaimochamber.bc.ca
www.nanaimochamber.bc.ca
Kim Smythe, CEO
David Littlejohn, Chair
Justin Schley, Treasurer

Greater Vernon Chamber of Commerce (GVCC)
#102, 2901 - 32nd St., Vernon BC V1T 5M2
Tel: 250-545-0771; *Fax:* 250-545-3114
info@vernonchamber.ca
www.vernonchamber.ca
Affiliation(s): Canadian Chamber of Commerce
Dan Rogers, General Manager
Tracy Cobb-Reeves, President

Greater Victoria Chamber of Commerce (GVCC)
#100, 852 Fort St., Victoria BC V8W 1H8
Tel: 250-383-7191; *Fax:* 250-385-3552
chamber@victoriachamber.ca
www.victoriachamber.ca
www.youtube.com/user/victoriachamber
Bruce Carter, CEO
Frank Bourree, Chair
Sang-Kiet Ly, Treasurer

Greater Westside Board of Trade
2372 Dobbin Rd., West Kelowna BC V4T 2H9
Tel: 250-768-3378; *Fax:* 250-768-3465
admin@gwboardoftrade.com
www.gwboardoftrade.com
Craig Garries, President

Harrison Agassiz Chamber of Commerce
PO Box 429, Harrison Hot Springs BC V0M 1K0
info@harrison.ca
www.harrison.ca
Robert Reyerse, President

Hope & District Chamber of Commerce
PO Box 588, 519 - 6 Ave., #J, Hope BC V0X 1L0
Tel: 604-249-1246
info@hopechamber.net
hopechamber.net
Stephen Au-Yeung, President

Houston Chamber of Commerce
PO Box 396, 3289 Hwy. 16, Houston BC V0J 1Z0
Tel: 250-845-7640; *Fax:* 250-845-3682
info@houstonchamber.ca
www.houstonchamber.ca
Jean Marr, President

Kaslo & Area Chamber of Commerce
PO Box 329, Kaslo BC V0G 1M0
Toll-Free: 866-276-3212
thekaslochamber@gmail.com
www.kaslochamber.com
John Addison, President

Kelowna Chamber of Commerce
544 Harvey Ave., Kelowna BC V1Y 6C9
Tel: 250-861-3627; *Fax:* 250-861-3624
info@kelownachamber.org
www.kelownachamber.org
Affiliation(s): BC Chamber of Commerce
Tom Dyas, President
Caroline Grover, Chief Executive Officer

Kicking Horse Country Chamber of Commerce (KHCCC)
PO Box 1320, #500, 10 North Ave., Golden BC V0A 1H0
Tel: 250-344-7125; *Fax:* 250-344-6688
Toll-Free: 800-622-4653
www.goldenchamber.bc.ca
Ruth Hamilton, Manager
Michele La Point, President

Kimberley & District Chamber of Commerce (KBSCC)
253 Wallinger Ave., Kimberley BC V1A 1Z2
Tel: 250-427-3666
info@kimberleychamber.com
www.kimberleychamber.com
Mike Guarnery, Manager

Kitimat Chamber of Commerce
PO Box 214, 2109 Forest Ave., Kitimat BC V8C 2G7
Tel: 250-632-6294; *Fax:* 250-632-4685
Toll-Free: 800-664-6554
info@kitimatchamber.ca
www.kitimatchamber.ca
Wendy Kraft, Chair
Trish Parsons, Executive Director

Kootenay Lake Chamber of Commerce
PO Box 120, Crawford Bay BC V0B 1E0
Tel: 250-227-9655
info@kootenaylake.bc.ca
www.kootenaylake.bc.ca
Gina Medhurst, Chair

Ladysmith Chamber of Commerce
PO Box 598, 33 Roberts St., Ladysmith BC V9G 1A4
Tel: 250-245-2112; *Fax:* 250-245-2124
www.ladysmithcofc.com
Affiliation(s): Cowichan Regional Valley
Alana Newton, President

Lake Country Chamber of Commerce
Winfield Professional Building, #106, 3121 Hill Rd., Lake Country BC V4V 1G1
Tel: 250-766-5670
manager@lakecountrychamber.com
www.lakecountrychamber.com
Kirbey Lockhart, President
Kimberley Kristiansen, Manager

Likely & District Chamber of Commerce
PO Box 29, Likely BC V0L 1N0
Tel: 250-790-2127
www.likely-bc.ca
Lisa Kraus, President

Lillooet & District Chamber of Commerce
PO Box 650, Lillooet BC V0K 1V0
Tel: 250-256-3578; *Fax:* 250-256-4882
info@lillooetchamberofcommerce.com
www.lillooetchamberofcommerce.com
Bob Sheridan, Co-President
Bain Gair, Co-President & Secretary-Treasurer

Lumby Chamber of Commerce
PO Box 534, 1882 Vernon St., Lumby BC V0E 2G0
Tel: 250-547-2300; *Fax:* 250-547-2300
www.monasheetourism.com
Stephanie Sexsmith, Executive Director

Lytton & District Chamber of Commerce
PO Box 460, 400 Fraser St., Lytton BC V0K 1Z0
Tel: 250-455-2523
info@lyttonchamber.com
lyttonchamber.com
Affiliation(s): Thompson Okanagan Tourism Association
Bernie Fandrich, President

Mackenzie Chamber of Commerce
PO Box 880, 88 Centennial Dr., Mackenzie BC V0J 2C0
Tel: 250-997-5459; *Fax:* 250-997-6117
office@mackenziechamber.bc.ca
www.mackenziechamber.bc.ca
Affiliation(s): Retail Merchants Association of BC
Debbie Wallace, President

Maple Ridge Pitt Meadows Chamber of Commerce
12492 Harris Rd., Pitt Meadows BC V3Y 2J4
Tel: 604-457-4599; *Fax:* 604-457-4598
info@ridgemeadowschamber.com
www.ridgemeadowschamber.com
www.instagram.com/pmmrchamber
Affiliation(s): BC Chamber Executive; Canadian Chamber of Commerce; Southwestern BC Tourism
Andrea Madden, Executive Director

Mayne Island Community Chamber of Commerce (MICCC)
PO Box 2, Mayne Island BC V0N 2J0
executiveofficer@mayneislandchamber.ca
www.mayneislandchamber.ca
Toby Snelgrove, Chair
Lauren Underhill, Executive Officer

McBride & District Chamber of Commerce
PO Box 2, McBride BC V0J 2E0
Tel: 250-569-3366; *Fax:* 250-569-3276
Toll-Free: 866-569-3366
www.mcbridechamber.ca
Brenda Molendyk, Chair

Merritt & District Chamber of Commerce
City Hall, 2185 Voght St., Merritt BC V1K 1B8
Tel: 250-378-5634; *Fax:* 250-378-6561
www.merrittchamber.com
Etelka Gillespie, Manager

Mission Regional Chamber of Commerce
34033 Lougheed Hwy., Mission BC V2V 5X8
Tel: 604-826-6914; *Fax:* 604-826-5916
info@missionchamber.bc.ca
www.missionchamber.bc.ca
www.youtube.com/TheMissionChamber
Kristin Parsons, Executive Director

Nakusp & District Chamber of Commerce
PO Box 387, 92 - 6th Ave. NW, Nakusp BC V0G 1R0
Tel: 250-265-4234; *Fax:* 250-265-3808
Toll-Free: 800-909-8819
nakusp@telus.net
www.nakusparrowlakes.com
Affiliation(s): Destination British Columbia
Cedra Eichenauer, Office Manager

Nelson & District Chamber of Commerce
91 Baker St., Nelson BC V1L 4G8
Tel: 250-352-3433; *Fax:* 250-352-6355
Toll-Free: 877-663-5706
info@discovernelson.com
www.discovernelson.com
Affiliation(s): British Columbia Chamber of Commerce; Canadian Chamber of Commerce
Ed Olthof, President

New Westminster Chamber of Commerce
#201, 309 6th St., New Westminster BC V3L 3A7
Tel: 604-521-7781; *Fax:* 604-521-0057
nwcc@newwestchamber.com
www.newwestchamber.com
Lizz Kelly, CEO

North Shuswap Chamber of Commerce
3871 Squilax-Anglemont Rd., #B, Scotch Creek BC V0E 1M5
Tel: 250-955-2113
info@northshuswapbc.com
www.northshuswapbc.com

North Vancouver Chamber of Commerce (NVCC)
1250 Lonsdale Ave., Vancouver BC V7M 2H6
Tel: 604-987-4488; *Fax:* 604-987-8272
www.nvchamber.ca
www.instagram.com/nvchamber
Louise Ranger, Chief Executive Officer
Misha Wilson, Manager, Membership

Parksville & District Chamber of Commerce
PO Box 99, Parksville BC V9P 2G3
Tel: 250-248-3613; *Fax:* 250-248-5210
info@parksvillechamber.com
www.parksvillechamber.com
www.youtube.com/user/ParksvilleChamber1
Kim Burden, Executive Director
Linda Tchorz, Manager, Member Services
Lynda Schneider, Bookkeeper
Patti Lee, Manager, Visitor Centre

Peachland Chamber of Commerce
5684 Beach Ave., Peachland BC V0H 1X6
Tel: 250-767-2422
peachlandchamber@gmail.com
www.chamberpeachland.com
Patrick Van Minsel, Executive Director

Pemberton & District Chamber of Commerce
PO Box 370, Pemberton BC V0N 2L0
Tel: 604-894-6477; *Fax:* 604-894-5571
info@pembertonchamber.com
www.pembertonchamber.com
Affiliation(s): Vancouver Board of Trade
Garth Phare, President
Shirley Henry, Secretary-Treasurer

Pender Harbour & District Chamber of Commerce
Madeira Park, PO Box 265, Madeira Park BC V0N 2H0
Tel: 604-883-2561; *Fax:* 604-883-2561
Toll-Free: 877-873-6337
chamber@penderharbour.ca
www.penderharbour.ca
Leonard Lee, President

Pender Island Chamber of Commerce
PO Box 164, 4605 Bedwell Harbour Rd., Pender Island BC V0N 2M0
Tel: 250-999-6371
info@penderislandchamber.com
www.penderislandchamber.com
Mamie Hutt Temoana, President

Penticton & Wine Country Chamber of Commerce
553 Vees Dr., Penticton BC V2A 8S3
Tel: 250-492-4103
admin@penticton.org
www.penticton.org
Brandy Maslowski, Executive Director
Jason Cox, President

Port Hardy & District Chamber of Commerce
PO Box 249, 7250 Market St., Port Hardy BC V0N 2P0
Tel: 250-949-7622; *Fax:* 250-949-6653
Toll-Free: 866-427-3901
phccadm@cablerocket.com
www.porthardychamber.com
statigr.am/visitporthardy
Todd Landon, President
Carly Pereboom, Executive Director

Port McNeill & District Chamber of Commerce
PO Box 129, Port McNeill BC V0N 2R0
Tel: 250-230-9952
portmcneillchamber@gmail.com
www.portmcneill.net
Gaby Wickstrom, President
Cheryl Jorgenson, Manager

Port Renfrew Chamber of Commerce
PO Box 39, Port Renfrew BC V0S 1K0
Tel: 250-858-7665
www.renfrewchamber.com
Dan Hager, President

Powell River Chamber of Commerce
6807 Wharf St., Powell River BC V8A 2T9
Tel: 604-485-4051
office@powellriverchamber.com
www.powellriverchamber.com
Jack Barr, President
Kim Miller, General Manager

Prince George Chamber of Commerce (PGCOC)
890 Vancouver St., Prince George BC V2L 2P5
Tel: 250-562-2454; *Fax:* 250-562-6510
chamber@pgchamber.bc.ca
www.pgchamber.bc.ca
www.youtube.com/channel/UCzQhi2Ttff84-lkN_Vb6NkQ
Christie Ray, CEO

Prince Rupert & District Chamber of Commerce (PRDCC)
#100, 515 3rd Ave., Prince Rupert BC V8J 1L9
Tel: 250-624-2296; *Fax:* 250-624-6105
info@princerupertchamber.ca
www.princerupertchamber.ca
Jamie Gerrie, Manager, Finance & Administration
Simone Clark, Manager, Communications

Princeton & District Chamber of Commerce
PO Box 540, 105 Hwy. 3 East, Princeton BC V0X 1W0
Tel: 250-295-3103; *Fax:* 250-295-3255

Qualicum Beach Chamber of Commerce
PO Box 159, 124 West 2nd Ave., Qualicum Beach BC V9K 1S7
Tel: 250-752-0960
chamber@qualicum.bc.ca
www.qualicum.bc.ca
www.instagram.com/QualicumBeachVIC
Affiliation(s): Oceanside Tourism Association
Oura Giakoumakis, Chair
Evelyn Clark, CEO

Quesnel & District Chamber of Commerce
335 East Vaughan St., Quesnel BC V2J 2T1
Tel: 250-992-7262
qchamber@quesnelbc.com
quesnelchamber.com
William Lacy, President
Amber Gregg, Manager

Radium Hot Springs Chamber of Commerce
PO Box 225, Radium Hot Springs BC V0A 1M0
Tel: 250-347-9331; *Fax:* 250-347-9127
Toll-Free: 888-347-9331
chamber@RadiumHotSprings.com
www.RadiumHotSprings.com
www.youtube.com/tourismradium
Kent Kebe, Manager

Revelstoke Chamber of Commerce
PO Box 490, 301 Victoria Rd. West, Revelstoke BC V0E 2S0
Tel: 250-837-5345; *Toll-Free:* 800-487-1493
revelstokechamber.com
Judy Goodman, Executive Director

Richmond Chamber of Commerce
North Tower, #202, 5811 Cooney Rd., Richmond BC V6X 3M1
Tel: 604-278-2822; *Fax:* 604-278-2972
rcc@richmondchamber.ca
www.richmondchamber.ca
www.youtube.com/user/RichmondchamberBC

Affiliation(s): Tourism Richmond; Sister Chamber - Kent, Washington
Matt Pitcairn, President & CEO

Saanich Peninsula Chamber of Commerce (SPCOC)
10382 Pat Bay Hwy., North Saanich BC V8L 5S8
Tel: 250-656-3616; *Fax:* 250-656-7111
info@peninsulachamber.ca
www.peninsulachamber.ca
Craig Norris, President
Denny Warner, Executive Director

Salmo & District Chamber of Commerce
PO Box 400, 100 - 4th St., Salmo BC V0G 1Z0
Tel: 250-357-2596
salmoch@telus.net
discoversalmo.ca/Chamber.aspx
Dave Reid, President

Salmon Arm & District Chamber of Commerce (SACC)
PO Box 999, #101, 20 Hudson Ave. NE, Salmon Arm BC V1E 4P2
Tel: 250-832-6247; *Fax:* 250-832-8382
admin@sachamber.bc.ca
www.sachamber.bc.ca
Corryn Grayston, General Manager

Salt Spring Island Chamber of Commerce (SSI Chamber)
121 Lower Ganges Rd., Salt Spring Island BC V8K 2T1
Tel: 250-537-4223; *Fax:* 250-537-4276
Toll-Free: 866-216-2936
chamber@saltspringchamber.com
www.saltspringchamber.com
Janet Clouston, Executive Director

Sechelt & District Chamber of Commerce
PO Box 360, #102, 5700 Cowrie St., Sechelt BC V0N 3A0
Tel: 604-885-0662; *Fax:* 604-885-0691
sdcoc9@telus.net
www.secheltchamber.bc.ca
Kim Darwin, President
Colleen Clark, Executive Director

Seton Portage/Shalalth District Chamber of Commerce
PO Box 2067, Seton Portage BC V0N 3B0
Tel: 250-259-8268
Ray Klassen, Vice-President

Sicamous & District Chamber of Commerce
PO Box 346, #3, 446 Main St., Sicamous BC V0E 2V0
Tel: 250-836-0002; *Fax:* 250-836-4368
info@sicamouschamber.bc.ca
www.sicamouschamber.bc.ca

Similkameen Chamber of Commerce
PO Box 490, Keremeos BC V0X 1N0
Tel: 250-499-5225

Slocan District Chamber of Commerce (SDCC)
PO Box 448, New Denver BC V0G 1S0
chamber@slocanlake.com
slocanlakechamber.com
Jessica Rayner, Manager

Smithers District Chamber of Commerce
PO Box 2379, Smithers BC V0J 2N0
Tel: 250-847-5072; *Fax:* 250-847-3337
Toll-Free: 800-542-6673
info@smitherschamber.com
www.smitherschamber.com
Affiliation(s): Northern BC Tourism Association
Heather Gallagher, Manager

Sooke Chamber of Commerce
Seaview Business Centre, #1A, 6631 Sooke Rd., Sooke BC V9Z 0A3
Tel: 250-642-6112
info@sookeregionchamber.com
www.sookeregionchamber.com
Aline Doiron, Office Manager

South Cariboo Chamber of Commerce
PO Box 2312, #2, 385 Birch Ave., 100 Mile House BC V0K 2E0
Tel: 250-395-6124; *Fax:* 250-395-8974
manager@southcariboochamber.org
www.southcariboochamber.org
Affiliation(s): Canadian Chamber of Commerce
Leon Chretien, Chair

South Cowichan Chamber of Commerce (SCCC)
#368, 2720 Mill Bay Rd., Mill Bay BC V0R 2P1
Tel: 250-743-3566; *Fax:* 250-743-5332
www.southcowichanchamber.org
Dave Shortill, President

South Okanagan Chamber Of Commerce
PO Box 1414, 6237 Main St., Oliver BC V0H 1T0
Tel: 250-498-6321; *Fax:* 250-498-3156
Toll-Free: 866-498-6321
manager@sochamber.ca
www.sochamber.ca
www.youtube.com/user/SouthOKChamber
Denise Blashko, Executive Director

South Shuswap Chamber of Commerce
2405B Centennial Dr., Blind Bay BC V0E 1H2
Tel: 250-515-0002
membership@southshuswapchamber.com
www.southshuswapchamber.com
Karen Brown, General Manager

South Surrey & White Rock Chamber of Commerce
#22, 1480 Foster St., White Rock BC V4B 3X7
Tel: 604-536-6844; *Fax:* 604-536-4994
admin@sswrchamber.ca
www.sswrchamberofcommerce.ca
Affiliation(s): BC Tourism
Ritu Khanna, Executive Director

Sparwood & District Chamber of Commerce
PO Box 1448, 141 Aspen Dr., Sparwood BC V0B 2G0
Tel: 250-425-2423; *Toll-Free:* 877-485-8185
administrator@sparwoodchamber.bc.ca
www.sparwoodchamber.bc.ca
Marjorie Templin, President
Norma McDougall, Manager

Squamish Chamber of Commerce
Squamish Adventure Centre, #102, 38551 Loggers Lane, Squamish BC V8B 0H2
Tel: 604-815-4990
admin@squamishchamber.com
www.squamishchamber.com
www.youtube.com/spiritofsquamish
Louise Walker, Executive Director

Stewart-Hyder International Chamber of Commerce
PO Box 306, Stewart BC V0T 1W0
Tel: 250-636-9224; *Fax:* 250-636-2199

Summerland Chamber of Commerce
PO Box 130, 15600 Hwy. 97, Summerland BC V0H 1Z0
Tel: 250-494-2686; *Fax:* 250-494-4039
membership@summerlandchamber.com
www.summerlandchamber.com
www.youtube.com/user/scedt
Affiliation(s): Thompson/Okanagan Tourism Association; Penticton & Wine Country Chamber of Commerce; South Okanagan Chamber of Commerce
Kelly Marshall, President
Christine Petkau, Executive Director

Surrey Board of Trade (SBOT)
#101, 14439 - 104 Ave., Surrey BC V3R 1M1
Tel: 604-581-7130; *Fax:* 604-588-7549
Toll-Free: 866-848-7130
info@businessinsurrey.com
www.businessinsurrey.com
Anita Huberman, Chief Executive Officer

Tahsis Chamber of Commerce
PO Box 278, 36 Rugged Mountain Rd., Tahsis BC V0P 1X0
Tel: 250-934-6425
www.villageoftahsis.com

Terrace & District Chamber of Commerce
3224 Kalum St., Terrace BC V8G 2N1
Tel: 250-635-2063
admin@terracechamber.com
www.terracechamber.com
Michelle Taylor, Executive Director

Texada Island Chamber of Commerce
PO Box 249, Vananda BC V0N 3K0
Tel: 604-413-0994
Affiliation(s): British Columbia Chamber of Commerce; Canadian Chamber of Commerce
Karen May, President

Tofino-Long Beach Chamber of Commerce
PO Box 249, Tofino BC V0R 2Z0
Tel: 250-725-3153
info@tofinochamber.org
www.tofinochamber.org

Jennifer Steven, President

Trail & District Chamber of Commerce
#200, 1199 Bay Ave., Trail BC V1R 4A4
Tel: 250-368-3144; Fax: 250-368-6427
www.trailchamber.bc.ca
Audry Durham, Executive Director

Tri-Cities Chamber of Commerce Serving Coquitlam, Port Coquitlam & Port Moody
1209 Pinetree Way, Coquitlam BC V3B 7Y3
Tel: 604-464-2716; Fax: 604-464-6796
info@tricitieschamber.com
www.tricitieschamber.com
Michael Hind, CEO

Ucluelet Chamber of Commerce (UCOC)
PO Box 428, 1604 Peninsula Rd., Ucluelet BC V0R 3A0
Tel: 250-726-4641; Fax: 250-726-4611
info@ucluletinfo.com
www.ucluelet.ca
Sally Mole, Executive Director

Valemount & Area Chamber of Commerce (VACC)
PO Box 690, Valemount BC V0E 2Z0
Tel: 250-566-0061; Fax: 250-566-0061
info@valemountchamber.com
www.valemountchamber.com
Christine Latimer, Chair

Vanderhoof Chamber of Commerce
PO Box 126, 2353 Burrard Ave., Vanderhoof BC V0J 3A0
Tel: 250-567-2124; Fax: 250-567-3316
Toll-Free: 800-752-4094
info@vanderhoofchamber.com
www.vanderhoofchamber.com
Affiliation(s): BC Chamber of Commerce
Joe Von Doellen, President
Spencer Siemens, Executive Director

Wells & District Chamber of Commerce
PO Box 123, Wells BC V0K 2R0
Tel: 250-994-2323; Fax: 250-994-3331
Toll-Free: 877-451-9355
wells.ca/profile/wells-district-chamber-commerce

West Shore Chamber of Commerce
2830 Aldwynd Rd., Victoria BC V9B 3S7
Tel: 250-478-1130; Fax: 250-478-1584
www.westshore.bc.ca
Julie Lawlor, Executive Director

West Vancouver Chamber of Commerce
2235 Marine Dr., West Vancouver BC V7V 1K5
Tel: 604-926-6614; Fax: 604-926-6647
info@westvanchamber.com
www.westvanchamber.com
Leagh Gabriel, Executive Director

Whistler Chamber of Commerce
#201, 4230 Gateway Dr., Whistler BC V0N 1B4
Tel: 604-932-5922; Fax: 604-932-3755
www.whistlerchamber.com
www.youtube.com/channel/UCphpSBZQmhRux_-jalEtcwQ
Val Litwin, Chief Executive Officer
Grant Cousar, Chair

Williams Lake & District Chamber of Commerce
1660 South Broadway, Williams Lake BC V2G 2W4
Tel: 250-392-5025; Toll-Free: 877-967-5253
info@williamslakechamber.com
www.williamslakechamber.com
Affiliation(s): BC Chamber of Commerce; Canadian Chamber of Commerce; Cariboo Chilcotin Coast Tourism Association
Angela Sommer, President
Claudia Blair, Executive Director

Zeballos Board of Trade
c/o Village of Zeballos, PO Box 127, Zeballos BC V0P 2A0
Tel: 250-761-4229; Fax: 250-761-4331
adminzeb@recn.ca
www.zeballos.com

Manitoba

Altona & District Chamber of Commerce
Golden West Building, PO Box 329, 125 Centre Ave. East, Altona MB R0G 0B0
Tel: 204-324-8793; Fax: 204-324-1314
chamber@shopaltona.com
www.shopaltona.com
Stephanie Harris, General Manager

Arborg Chamber of Commerce
c/o Town of Arborg, PO Box 159, Arborg MB R0C 0A0
www.townofarborg.com
Owen Eyolfson, Chair

Ashern & District Chamber of Commerce
PO Box 582, Ashern MB R0C 0E0
info@ashern.ca
www.ashern.ca

Assiniboia Chamber of Commerce (MB) (ACC)
PO Box 42122, Stn. Ferry Road, 1867 Portage Ave., Winnipeg MB R3J 3X7
Tel: 204-774-4154; Fax: 204-774-4201
info@assiniboiacc.mb.ca
www.assiniboiacc.mb.ca
Ernie Nairn, Executive Director

Beausejour & District Chamber of Commerce
PO Box 224, Beausejour MB R0E 0C0
Tel: 204-268-3502
beausejourchamber@gmail.com
ourhomeyourhome.ca
Liz Pasieczka, Executive Director

Birtle & District Chamber of Commerce
PO Box 278, Birtle MB R0M 0C0
Tel: 204-842-3234

Blue Water Chamber of Commerce
PO Box 204, St Georges MB R0E 1V0
Tel: 204-367-9970
bluewaterchamber@hotmail.com
Diane Dube, President

Boissevain & District Chamber of Commerce
PO Box 734, Boissevain MB R0K 0E0
Tel: 204-534-6488
admin@boissevain.ca
www.boissevain.ca
Ken Hole, President

Brandon Chamber of Commerce
1043 Rosser Ave., Brandon MB R7A 0L5
Tel: 204-571-5340; Fax: 204-571-5347
info@brandonchamber.ca
brandonchamber.ca
Carolynn Cancade, General Manager
Samantha Chapman, Office Coordinator
Matthew May, Coordinator, Member Relations & Marketing
Krista Powell, Coordinator, Events

Brazil-Canada Chamber of Commerce
Winnipeg MB

Carberry & District Chamber of Commerce
PO Box 101, Carberry MB R0K 0H0
Tel: 204-834-6616
www.townofcarberry.ca
Stuart Olmstead, President

Carman & Community Chamber of Commerce
PO Box 249, Carman MB R0G 0J0
Tel: 204-750-3050
ccchamber@gmail.com
www.carmanchamber.ca
Affiliation(s): Manitoba Chamber of Commerce
Kate Petrie, President
Nikki Bartley, Executive Director

Chambre de commerce de Notre Dame
PO Box 107, Notre Dame de Lourdes MB R0G 1M0
Tel: 204-248-2073; Fax: 204-248-2847
Lise Deleurme, President

La chambre de commerce de Saint-Malo & District
CP 328, Saint-Malo MB R0A 1T0
www.iadorestmalo.ca
Aggie Gosselin, Présidente

Chambre de commerce francophone de Saint-Boniface (CCFSB) / St-Boniface Chamber of Commerce
CP 204, Saint-Boniface MB R2H 3B4
Tél: 204-235-1406; Téléc: 204-237-4618
info@ccfsb.mb.ca
www.ccfsb.mb.ca
Paulette Desaulniers, Executive Director

Churchill Chamber of Commerce
PO Box 176, Churchill MB R0B 0E0
Tel: 204-675-2022; Fax: 204-675-2021
Toll-Free: 888-389-2327
churchillchamber@mts.net
churchillchamberofcommerce.ca

Crystal City & District Chamber of Commerce
PO Box 56, Crystal City MB R0K 0N0
Tel: 204-873-2427; Fax: 204-873-2656
chamberofcommerce@crystalcitymb.ca
www.crystalcitymb.ca
Doug Treble, Contact
Mike Webber, Contact

Cypress River Chamber of Commerce
PO Box 261, Cypress River MB R0K 0P0
Tel: 204-743-2119; Fax: 204-743-2339
www.cypressriver.ca
Jim Cassels, President

Dauphin & District Chamber of Commerce
100 Main St. South, Dauphin MB R7N 1K3
Tel: 204-622-3140; Fax: 204-622-3141
coordinator@dauphinchamber.ca
www.dauphinchamber.ca
Joanne Vandepoele, President

Deloraine & District Chamber of Commerce
c/o Town of Deloraine, PO Box 387, Deloraine MB R0M 0M0
Tel: 204-747-2572; Fax: 204-747-2927
deloraine.org/business/chamber-of-commerce
Shirley Bell, President

Elie Chamber of Commerce
PO Box 175, Elie MB R0H 0H0
Tel: 204-353-2392; Fax: 204-353-2286

Elkhorn Chamber of Commerce
PO Box 141, Elkhorn MB R0M 0N0
www.elkhornchamberofcommerce.ca
Mark Humphries, President

Eriksdale & District Chamber of Commerce
PO Box 434, Eriksdale MB R0C 0W0
Tel: 204-739-2606
www.eriksdale.ca
Keith Lundale, President

Falcon, West Hawk & Caddy Lakes Chamber of Commerce (FWHLCC)
PO Box 187, Falcon Beach MB R0E 0N0
Tel: 204-349-3134; Fax: 204-349-3134
falconwesthawkchamber.com
Affiliation(s): Canadian Chamber of Commerce

Fisher Branch & District Chamber of Commerce
PO Box 566, Fisher Branch MB R0C 0Z0
Tel: 204-372-8585
fisherchamber@gmail.com
www.fisherbranchchamber.com
Wayne Smith, President

Flin Flon & District Chamber of Commerce
#235, 35 Main St., Flin Flon MB R8A 1J7
Tel: 204-687-4518
flinflonchamber@mymts.net
www.flinflondistrictchamber.com
Dianne Russell, President
Karen MacKinnon, President Elect

Gillam Chamber of Commerce
c/o Town of Gillam, PO Box 100, 323 Railway Ave., Gillam MB R0B 0L0
Tel: 204-652-3150; Fax: 204-652-3199
www.townofgillam.com
Alex Muzyczka, President

Grandview & District Chamber of Commerce
PO Box 28, Grandview MB R0L 0Y0
Tel: 204-546-2626
www.grandviewmanitoba.com
Pierce Cairns, President
Robyn Dingwall, Secretary & Treasurer

Grunthal & District Chamber of Commerce
PO Box 451, Grunthal MB R0A 0R0
Tel: 204-371-1081
grunthal.ca/chamber.php
Tim Driedger, Interim President

Hamiota Chamber of Commerce
PO Box 403, Hamiota MB R0M 0T0
Tel: 204-764-3050; Fax: 204-764-3055
www.hamiota.com/chamber_commerce.html
Larry Oakden, President
Bonnie Michaudville, Secretary

Hartney & District Chamber of Commerce
PO Box 224, Hartney MB R0M 0X0
Tel: 204-858-2098

Headingley Chamber of Commerce
#1, 126 Bridge Rd., Headingley MB R4H 1G9
Tel: 204-837-5766; *Fax:* 204-831-7207
hello@headingleychamber.ca
www.headingleychamber.ca
Affiliation(s): Central Plains Development Corporation; White Horse Plains Development Corporation; Headingley Heritage Centre
Graham Hawryluk, President
John Van Massenhoven, Secretary
Dave White, Executive Director

Killarney & District Chamber of Commerce
433 Broadway Ave., Killarney MB R0K 1G0
Tel: 204-523-4202

Lac du Bonnet & District Chamber of Commerce
PO Box 598, Lac du Bonnet MB R0E 1A0
Tel: 204-340-0497
ldbchamberofcommerce@gmail.com
www.lacdubonnetchamber.com
Affiliation(s): Manitoba Chambers of Commerce
Jennifer Hudson Stewart, Administrator

Landmark & Community Chamber of Commerce
PO Box 469, Landmark MB R0A 0X0
Tel: 204-355-5323
Evan Rodgers, President

Leaf Rapids Chamber of Commerce
PO Box 26, Leaf Rapids MB R0B 1W0
Tel: 204-473-2491; *Fax:* 204-473-2284

MacGregor Chamber of Commerce
PO Box 685, MacGregor MB R0H 0R0
Tel: 204-685-2390
Jason McKelvy, President

Melita & District Chamber of Commerce
PO Box 666, Melita MB R0M 1L0
Tel: 204-522-3278
www.melitamb.ca
Darren Stewart, President

Minnedosa Chamber of Commerce
PO Box 857, Minnedosa MB R0J 1E0
Tel: 204-867-2951; *Fax:* 204-867-3641
minnedosachamber@gmail.com
www.discoverminnedosa.ca
Brad Ross, President

Morden & District Chamber of Commerce
#100, 379 Stephen St., Morden MB R6M 1V1
Tel: 204-822-5630
execdirector@mordenchamber.com
www.mordenchamber.com
Candace Olafson, Executive Director

Morris & District Chamber of Commerce
141 Main St. South, Morris MB R0G 1K0
Tel: 204-712-6162
info@morrischamberofcommerce.com
www.morrischamberofcommerce.com
Bruce Third, President
Andy Anderson, Secretary

Neepawa & District Chamber of Commerce
PO Box 726, 282 Hamilton St., Neepawa MB R0J 1H0
Tel: 204-476-5292; *Fax:* 204-476-5231
info@neepawachamber.com
www.neepawachamber.com

Niverville Chamber of Commerce
PO Box 157, Niverville MB R0A 1E0
Tel: 204-388-5340
chamber@niverville.com
www.niverville.com
Dawn Harris, Coordinator

Oakville & District Chamber of Commerce
PO Box 263, Oakville MB R0H 0Y0
Tel: 204-267-2730; *Fax:* 888-552-9910
oakvillechamberoffice@gmail.com
Sian Taris, President

The Pas & District Chamber of Commerce
PO Box 996, 1559 Gordon Ave., The Pas MB R9A 1L1
Tel: 204-623-7256; *Fax:* 204-623-2589
tpchamber@mailme.com
www.thepaschamber.com
Shirley Barbeau, Office Manager

Pinawa Chamber of Commerce
PO Box 544, Pinawa MB R0E 1L0
www.pinawachamber.com
Steffen Bunge, President

Plum Coulee & District Chamber of Commerce
PO Box 392, Plum Coulee MB R0G 1R0
Tel: 204-829-2317; *Fax:* 204-829-2319
rmofrhineland.com
Moira Porte, President

Portage la Prairie & District Chamber of Commerce
56 Royal Rd. North, Portage la Prairie MB R1N 1V1
Tel: 204-857-7778; *Fax:* 204-856-5001
info@portagechamber.com
www.portagechamber.com
Affiliation(s): Canadian Chamber of Commerce
Dave Omichinski, President
Cindy McDonald, Executive Director

Rivers & District Chamber of Commerce
PO Box 795, Rivers MB R0K 1X0
Tel: 204-328-7316
riverschamber@gmail.com
riversdaly.ca/chamber-of-commerce/
Jean Young, Contact

Riverton & District Chamber of Commerce
PO Box 238, Riverton MB R0C 2R0
Tel: 204-378-2376
www.rivertoncanada.com
Clif Evans, Chair

Roblin & District Chamber of Commerce
PO Box 160, 147 Main St., Roblin MB R0L 1P0
Tel: 204-937-3194
rdcoc@mts.net
www.roblinmanitoba.com/index.php?pageid=BUSCOC
Kevin Arthur, President

Rossburn & District Chamber of Commerce
PO Box 579, Rossburn MB R0J 1V0
Tel: 204-859-0050; *Fax:* 204-859-3313
rossburn.chamber@live.ca
Tony White, President

Russell & District Chamber of Commerce
PO Box 155, Russell MB R0J 1W0
Tel: 204-773-2456
chamber@mrbgov.com
www.russellbinscarth.com
Jennifer Seib, President

St. Pierre Chamber of Commerce
PO Box 71, St Pierre Jolys MB R0A 1V0
Tel: 204-377-4384
sundowng@mts.net
www.stpierrejolys.com
Robert Bruneau, President

La Salle & District Chamber of Commerce
10 A Principale St., La Salle MB R0G 0A2
Tel: 204-801-3492
lasallechamber@gmail.com
www.lasallechamber.ca
Allyson Demski, Office Manager

Selkirk & District Chamber of Commerce
City of Selkirk Civic Centre, 200 Eaton Ave., Selkirk MB R1A 0W6
Tel: 204-482-7176; *Fax:* 204-482-5448
info@selkirkbiz.ca
www.selkirkanddistrictchamber.ca
Sheri Skalesky, Executive Director

Shoal Lake & District Chamber of Commerce
PO Box 176, Shoal Lake MB R0J 1Z0
Tel: 204-759-2215
Tracey Myhill, President

Souris & Glenwood Chamber of Commerce
PO Box 939, Souris MB R0K 2C0
Tel: 204-483-2070
sourischamber@gmail.com
Affiliation(s): Manitoba Chamber of Commerce
Darci Semeschuk, President

Ste Rose & District Chamber of Commerce
PO Box 688, Ste Rose du Lac MB R0L 1S0
Tel: 204-447-2621; *Fax:* 204-447-3024

Steinbach Chamber of Commerce
284 Reimer Ave., #D4, Steinbach MB R5G 0R5
Tel: 204-326-9566; *Fax:* 204-346-3638
info@steinbachchamber.com
www.steinbachchamber.com
Cameron Bergen, President
Linda Peters, Executive Director

Stonewall & District Chamber of Commerce
PO Box 762, Stonewall MB R0C 2Z0
Tel: 204-467-8377
info@stonewallchamber.com
www.stonewallchamber.com
Stephanie Duncan, Director

Swan Valley Chamber of Commerce
1500 Main St., Swan River MB R0L 1Z0
Tel: 204-734-3102
info@swanvalleychamber.com
www.swanvalleychamber.com
Naomi Neufeld, President

Teulon Chamber of Commerce
PO Box 235, Teulon MB R0C 3B0
Tel: 204-886-3910
www.teulon.ca
Jan Lambourne, Chair
Linda Lamoureux, Secretary

Thompson Chamber of Commerce
City Centre Mall, PO Box 363, Thompson MB R8N 1N2
Tel: 204-677-4155; *Toll-Free:* 888-307-0103
commerce@mts.net
www.thompsonchamber.ca
Paula Yanko, Office Manager

Treherne Chamber of Commerce
Treherne MB
Ross McKellar, President

Virden Community Chamber of Commerce
PO Box 899, 425 - 6th Ave. South, Virden MB R0M 2C0
Tel: 204-851-1551
info@virdenchamber.ca
www.virdenchamber.ca
Affiliation(s): Virden Wallace Community Development Corp.; Virden Employment Skills Centre Inc., Virden Agricultural Society; Virden Indoor Rodeo
Dave Wowk, President

Wasagaming Chamber of Commerce
PO Box 621, Onanole MB R0J 1N0
discoverclearlake@gmail.com
www.discoverclearlake.com
Scott Gowler, President
Bob Bickerton, Treasurer

Winkler & District Chamber of Commerce
185 Main St., Winkler MB R6W 1B4
Tel: 204-325-9758; *Fax:* 204-325-8290
www.winklerchamber.com
Ryan Hildebrand, President
Tanya Chateauneuf, Executive Director
Dianne Friesen, Manager

Winnipeg Chamber of Commerce (WCC) / Chambre de commerce de Winnipeg
#100, 259 Portage Ave., Winnipeg MB R3B 2A9
Tel: 204-944-8484; *Fax:* 204-944-8492
info@winnipeg-chamber.com
www.winnipeg-chamber.com
www.youtube.com/wpgchamber
Dave Angus, President & Chief Executive Officer
Maxine Kashton, Vice-President, Finance & Operations
Karen Weiss, Vice-President, Membership & Marketing

New Brunswick

Albert County Chamber of Commerce
PO Box 3051, Hillsborough NB E4H 4W5
accofc@gmail.com
www.albertcountychamber.com
David Briggs, President
Janine Underhill, Secretary

Bouctouche Chamber of Commerce / Chambre de commerce de Bouctouche
PO Box 2104, Bouctouche NB E4S 2J2
Tel: 506-743-2411; *Fax:* 506-743-8991
chambouc@nb.aibn.com
www.bouctouche.ca/en/business/chamber-of-commerce

Campbellton Regional Chamber of Commerce / Chambre de commerce régional de Campbellton
41A Water St., Campbellton NB E3N 1A6
Tel: 506-759-7856
crcc@nbnet.nb.ca
Affiliation(s): NB Chamber of Commerce; Atlantic Chamber of Commerce

Central Carleton Chamber of Commerce
PO Box 805, Hartland NB E7P 3K4
Tel: 506-375-4888; *Fax:* 506-375-8007
info@ccchamber.ca
www.ccchamber.ca
Richard Orser, President

Centreville Chamber of Commerce
836 Central St., Centreville NB E7K 2E7
Tel: 506-276-3674; *Fax:* 506-276-9891
Robert Taylor, President

Chambre de commerce de Collette
60, rue des Arbres, Collette NB E4Y 1G4
Tél: 506-775-2898; *Téléc:* 506-622-0477
Maurice Desroches, Président

Chambre de commerce de la région d'Edmundston
1, ch Canada, Edmundston NB E3V 1T6
Tél: 506-737-1866; *Téléc:* 506-737-1862
info@ccedmundston.com
www.ccedmundston.com
www.flickr.com/photos/ccedmundston
Affiliation(s): Chambre de commerce du Nouveau-Brunswick; Chambre de commerce des Provinces Atlantiques; Chambre de commerce du Canada; Chambre de commerce Internationale
Marc Long, Directeur général

Chambre de commerce de la region de Cap-Pelé
CP 1219, Cap-Pelé NB E4N 3B1
Tél: 506-332-0118
chambre_de_commerce@rogers.com
www.cap-pele.com
Albert E. LeBlanc, Président
Gilles Haché, Secrétaire

Chambre de commerce de Rogersville / Rogersville Chamber of Commerce
#5, 11101, rue Principale, Rogersville NB E4Y 2N2
Tél: 506-775-0823; *Téléc:* 506-775-0826

Chambre de Commerce de Saint Louis de Kent
83A rue Beauséjour, Saint-Louis-de-Kent NB E4X 1A6
Tel: 506-876-3475; *Fax:* 506-876-3477

Chambre de commerce de Saint-Quentin Inc.
144D, rue Canada, Saint-Quentin NB E8A 1G7
Tél: 506-235-3666; *Téléc:* 506-235-1804
www.saintquentinnb.com
Pascale Bellavance, Présidente
Sandra Aubut, Secrétaire

Chambre de commerce de Shippagan inc.
227, boul J.D. Gauthier, Shippagan NB E8S 1N2
Tél: 506-336-3347
info@cdcshippagan.com
www.shippagan.ca
Marie-Lou Noël, Présidente

Chambre de commerce des Iles Lamèque et Miscou inc.
CP 2075, Lamèque NB E8T 3N5
Tél: 506-344-3222; *Téléc:* 506-344-3266
www.cclamequemiscou.ca
Eugène Chiasson, Président

Chambre de commerce du Grand Tracadie-Sheila
#4104, rue Principale, Tracadie-Sheila NB E1X 1B8
Tél: 506-394-4028
www.ccgts.ca
Rebecca Preston, Directrice générale

Chambre de commerce et du tourisme du Grand Caraquet
1-39, boul St-Pierre ouest, Caraquet NB E1W 1B6
Tél: 506-727-2931; *Téléc:* 506-727-3191
info@chambregrandcaraquet.com
www.chambregrandcaraquet.com
Claude L'Espérance, Président
Véronique Savoie, Directrice générale

Chambre de commerce Kent-Sud
27, ch Michel, Grand-Digue NB E4R 4V9
Tél: 506-861-1454
www.kentsud.ca
Jacques Robichaud, Président

Eastern Charlotte Chamber of Commerce (ECCC)
#2, 21 Main St., St George NB E5C 3H9
Tel: 506-456-3951; *Fax:* 506-755-6174
Dorothy Gaudet, President
Irene Wright, Secretary

Florenceville-Bristol Chamber of Commerce
#1, 8696 Main St., Florenceville-Bristol NB E7L 1Y7
Tel: 506-392-0900; *Fax:* 506-392-5211
chamber@florencevillebristol.ca
www.florencevillebristol.ca/html/chamber.html
Doug Thomson, Treasurer

Fredericton Chamber of Commerce / La Chambre de Commerce de Fredericton
PO Box 275, #200, 364 York St., Fredericton NB E3B 4Y9
Tel: 506-458-8006; *Fax:* 506-451-1119
fchamber@frederictonchamber.ca
www.frederictonchamber.ca
Stephen Hill, President
Krista Ross, Chief Executive Officer

Gagetown & Area Chamber of Commerce
c/o Village Office, 68 Babbit St., Gagetown NB E5M 1C8
Tel: 506-488-3567

Grand Manan Tourism Association & Chamber of Commerce
PO Box 1310, Grand Manan NB E5G 4E9
Tel: 506-662-3442; *Toll-Free:* 888-525-1655
info@grandmanannb.com
www.grandmanannb.com
Patricia Brown, Secretary & Treasurer

Greater Bathurst Chamber of Commerce / Chambre de commerce du Grand Bathurst
Keystone Bldg., #101, 270 Douglas Ave., Bathurst NB E2A 1M9
Tel: 506-546-8100; *Fax:* 506-548-2200
info@bathurstchamber.ca
www.bathurstchamber.ca
Affiliation(s): Canadian Chamber of Commerce
Mitch Poirier, General Manager
Bernard Cormier, President
Linda Rogers, Treasurer

Greater Moncton Chamber of Commerce (GMCC) / Chambre de commerce du Grand Moncton
#200, 1273 Main St., Moncton NB E1C 0P4
Tel: 506-857-2883
info@gmcc.nb.ca
www.gmcc.nb.ca
www.youtube.com/user/GreaterMonctonCham
Carol O'Reilly, CEO
Scott Lewis, Chair

Greater Sackville Chamber of Commerce (GSCC)
87 Main St., Sackville NB E4L 4A9
Tel: 506-364-8911
gscc@eastlink.ca
greatersackvillechamber.com
Gwen Zwicker, Executive Administrator

Greater Shediac Chamber of Commerce / Chambre de commerce du Grand Shediac
#301, 290 Main St., Shediac NB E4P 2E3
Tel: 506-532-7000; *Fax:* 506-532-6156
www.greatershediacchamber.com
Ronald Cormier, President

Greater Woodstock Chamber of Commerce
#2, 220 King St., Woodstock NB E7M 1Z8
Tel: 506-325-9049; *Fax:* 506-328-4683
info@gwcc.ca
www.gwcc.ca
Lance Minard, President

Hampton Area Chamber of Commerce (HACC)
#7, 27 Centennial Rd., Hampton NB E5N 6N3
Tel: 506-832-2559; *Fax:* 506-832-2807
hacc@nbnet.nb.ca

Kent Centre Chamber of Commerce
#1, 9235 rue Main, Richibucto NB E4W 4B4
Tel: 506-523-7870; *Fax:* 506-523-7850
www.kentcentre.com
Jody Pratt, President & Treasurer

Mactaquac Country Chamber of Commerce
PO Box 1163, Nackawic NB E6G 2N1
Tel: 506-575-9622; *Fax:* 506-575-2035
mccc@mactaquaccountry.com
www.mactaquaccountry.com
Melanie Sloat, President
Marc Jesmer, Secretary

Miramichi Chamber of Commerce (MCC)
PO Box 342, #2, 120 Newcastle Blvd., Miramichi NB E1N 3A7
Tel: 506-622-5522; *Fax:* 506-622-5959
mirchamber@nb.aibn.com
www.miramichichamber.com
www.instagram.com/miramichichamber
Affiliation(s): New Brunswick Chamber of Commerce; Atlantic Provinces Chamber of Commerce; Canadian Chamber of Commerce
Jason Harris, President
Joyce Buckley, Executive Director

Oromocto & Area Chamber of Commerce
Oromocto Mall, PO Box 20124, Oromocto NB E2V 2R6
Tel: 506-446-6043; *Fax:* 506-446-6925
oromoctochamber@nb.aibn.com
www.oromoctochamber.com
Beth Crowell, President

Saint John Region Chamber of Commerce
40 King St., Saint John NB E2L 1G3
Tel: 506-634-8111; *Fax:* 506-632-2008
info@TheChamberSJ.com
www.sjboardoftrade.com
www.youtube.com/SJBoardofTrade1
David Duplisea, CEO

St. Andrews Chamber of Commerce
252 Water St., #C, St Andrews NB E5B 1B5
Tel: 506-529-3555
www.standrewsbythesea.ca
Jeff Holmes, President

St. Martins & District Chamber of Commerce
#2, 73 Main St., St Martins NB E5R 1B4
Tel: 506-833-2010
stmartinschamber@gmail.com
www.stmartinscanada.com
Eric Bartlett, President
Jackie Bartlett, Secretary

St. Stephen Area Chamber of Commerce
73 Milltown Blvd., St Stephen NB E3L 1G5
Tel: 506-466-7703; *Fax:* 506-466-7753
chamber.ststephen@nb.aibn.com
www.ststephenchamber.com
Affiliation(s): Atlantic Chamber of Commerce; Canadian Chamber of Commerce
Jeremy Barham, President

Sussex & District Chamber of Commerce
#2, 66 Broad St., Sussex NB E4E 5L2
Tel: 506-433-1845; *Fax:* 506-433-1886
sdcc@nb.aibn.com
sdccinc.org
Affiliation(s): Atlantic Provinces Chambers of Commerce
Paul Bedford, President
Pam Kaye, Administrator

Valley Chamber of Commerce / Chambre de commerce de la Vallée
#200, 131 Pleasant St., Grand Falls NB E3Z 1G6
Tel: 506-473-1905; *Fax:* 506-475-7779
gfcocgs@nbnet.nb.ca
www.chambrevallee.ca
Christine Levesque, General Manager

Washademoak Region Chamber of Commerce
3359 Lower Cambridge Rd., Cambridge-Narrows NB E4C 4P9
Tel: 506-488-8091
David Craw, President

Newfoundland and Labrador

Baie Verte & Area Chamber of Commerce
PO Box 578, Baie Verte NL A0K 1B0
Tel: 709-532-4204; *Fax:* 709-532-4252
bvachamber@nf.aibn.com
www.bvachamber.com
Lloyd Hayden, President
Kira Rideout, Business Administrator

Bay St. George Chamber of Commerce
35 Carolina Ave., Stephenville NL A2N 3P8
Tel: 709-643-5854; *Fax:* 709-643-6398
www.bsgcc.org
Tom Rose, President

Bonavista Area Chamber of Commerce (BACC)
PO Box 280, Bonavista NL A0C 1B0
Tel: 709-468-7747; *Fax:* 709-468-2495
www.bacc.ca
Neal Tucker, President

Burin Peninsula Chamber of Commerce
PO Box 728, Marystown NL A0E 2M0
Tel: 709-567-3340; *Fax:* 855-749-6880
burinpeninsulachamber@outlook.com
burinpeninsulachamber.com
Loretta Lewis, President
Lisa MacLeod, Business Manager

Channel Port Aux Basques & Area Chamber of Commerce
PO Box 1389, Channel-Port-aux-Basques NL A0M 1C0
Tel: 709-695-3688
pabchamber@nf.aibn.com

Clarenville Area Chamber of Commerce
#203, 293 Memorial Dr., Clarenville NL A5A 1R5
Tel: 709-466-5800; *Fax:* 709-466-5803
Toll-Free: 866-466-5800
info@clarenvilleareachamber.com
www.clarenvilleareachamber.com
Jason Strickland, President
Ina Marsh, Office Manager

Conception Bay Area Chamber of Commerce
105 Church Rd., #A, Conception Bay South NL A1X 6K6
Tel: 709-834-5670; *Fax:* 709-834-5760
info@cbachamber.com
www.cbachamber.com
Margo Murphy, President

Deer Lake Chamber of Commerce
#3, 44 Trans Canada Hwy., Deer Lake NL A8A 2E4
Tel: 709-635-3260; *Fax:* 709-635-4077
info@deerlakechamber.com
www.deerlakechamber.com
Affiliation(s): Newfoundland Chambers of Commerce
Tina Barry-Keith, Treasurer
Roseann White, President

Exploits Regional Chamber of Commerce
PO Box 272, 2B Mill Rd., Grand Falls-Windsor NL A2A 2J7
Tel: 709-489-7512; *Fax:* 709-489-7532
info@exploitschamber.com
www.exploitschamber.com
Kris Spurrell, President

Gander & Area Chamber of Commerce (GACC)
109 Trans Canada Hwy., Gander NL A1V 1P6
Tel: 709-256-7110; *Fax:* 709-256-4794
chambergeneral@ganderchamber.nf.ca
www.ganderchamber.nf.ca
Debby Yannakidis, Chair
Hazel Bishop, Executive Director

Greater Corner Brook Board of Trade (GCBBT)
PO Box 475, 11 Confederation Dr., Corner Brook NL A2H 6E6
Tel: 709-634-5831; *Fax:* 709-639-9710
www.gcbbt.com
Chris Noseworthy, President

Irish Loop Chamber of Commerce
PO Box 114, Trepassey NL A0A 4B0
Tel: 709-438-1189; *Fax:* 709-438-2405
info@IrishLoopChamber.com
irishloopchamber.com
Derrick Thompson, Interim President

Labrador North Chamber of Commerce (LNCC)
PO Box 460, Stn. B, 6 Hillcrest Rd., Happy Valley-Goose Bay NL A0P 1E0
Tel: 709-896-8787; *Fax:* 709-896-8039
Toll-Free: 877-920-8787
www.chamberlabrador.com
Sterling Peyton, President
Brian Fowlow, Chief Executive Officer

Labrador Straits Chamber of Commerce
PO Box 179, Forteau NL A0K 2P0
Tel: 709-931-2073; *Fax:* 709-931-2073

Labrador West Chamber of Commerce
PO Box 273, 118 Humphrey Rd., Labrador City NL A2V 2K5
Tel: 709-944-3723; *Fax:* 709-944-4699
lwc@crrstv.net
www.labradorwestchamber.ca
Alice Regular, President

Lewisporte & Area Chamber of Commerce
395B Main St., Lewisporte NL A0G 3A0
Tel: 709-535-2500; *Fax:* 709-535-2482

Mount Pearl-Paradise Chamber of Commerce
365 Old Placentia Rd., Mount Pearl NL A1N 0G7
Tel: 709-364-8513; *Fax:* 709-364-8500
info@mppcc.ca
www.mtpearlparadisechamber.com
David Mercer, President

Pasadena Chamber of Commerce
c/o Town of Pasadena, 18 Tenth Ave., Pasadena NL A0L 1K0
Tel: 709-686-2075; *Fax:* 709-686-2507
info@pasadena.ca
www.pasadena.ca/chamber.html

Placentia Area Chamber of Commerce (PACC)
1 O'Reilly St., Placentia NL A0B 2Y0
Tel: 709-227-0003
www.placentiachamber.ca
Gerry Sullivan, President
Eugene Collins, Executive Director

St Anthony & Area Chamber of Commerce
PO Box 650, St Anthony NL A0K 4S0
Tel: 709-454-6667
stanthonyandareachamber@yahoo.ca
www.town.stanthony.nf.ca/chamber.php
Agnes Patey, Coordinator

Springdale & Area Chamber of Commerce
PO Box 37, 393 Little Bay Rd., Springdale NL A0J 1T0
Tel: 709-673-3837
info@springdalechamber.com
www.springdalechamber.com
Glenn Seabright, President
Cassandra Caines, Secretary

Straits-St. Barbe Chamber of Commerce
c/o Straits-St. Barbe Community, PO Box 203, Plum Point NL A0K 4A0

Northwest Territories

Fort Simpson Chamber of Commerce
PO Box 244, Fort Simpson NT X0E 0N0
Tel: 867-695-6538; *Fax:* 867-695-3551
fscofc@gmail.com
www.fortsimpsonchamber.ca
Kirby Groat, President

Hay River Chamber of Commerce
10K Gagnier St., Hay River NT X0E 1G1
Tel: 867-874-2565; *Fax:* 867-874-3631
www.hayriverchamber.com
Janet-Marie Fizer, President

Inuvik Chamber of Commerce
PO Box 3039, Inuvik NT X0E 0T0
inuvikchamber.com
Lee Smallwood, President

Norman Wells & District Chamber of Commerce
PO Box 400, Norman Wells NT X0E 0V0
Tel: 867-587-6609
www.normanwellschamber.com
Peter Spilchak, President

Thebacha Chamber of Commerce
PO Box 628, Fort Smith NT X0E 0P0
info@thebachachamber.ca
www.fortsmith.ca/business/chamber-commerce
Janie Hobart, President

Yellowknife Chamber of Commerce
#21, 4802 - 50th Ave., Yellowknife NT X1A 1C4
Tel: 867-920-4944; *Fax:* 867-920-4640
admin@ykchamber.com
www.ykchamber.com
Daneen Everett, Executive Director

Nova Scotia

Amherst & Area Chamber of Commerce
PO Box 283, Amherst NS B4H 3Z4
Tel: 902-667-8186; *Fax:* 902-667-1452
info@amherstchamber.ca
amherstchamberns.ca
Wayne Bishop, Acting Chair

Annapolis Valley Chamber of Commerce (EKCC)
PO Box 314, 66 Cornwallis St., Kentville NS B4N 3X1
Tel: 902-678-4634
coordinator@annapolisvalleychamber.ca
annapolisvalleychamber.ca
Sue Hayes, President
Judy Rafuse, Executive Director

Antigonish Chamber of Commerce
#6, 188 Main St., Antigonish NS B2G 2B9
Tel: 902-863-6308; *Fax:* 902-863-2656
contact@antigonishchamber.com
www.antigonishchamber.com
Dan Fougere, President

Avon Chamber of Commerce
PO Box 2188, Windsor NS B0N 2T0
Tel: 902-799-1185
info@avonchamberofcommerce.ca
www.avonchamberofcommerce.ca
Jeffrey Barrett, President
Joanna Gould-Thorpe, Vice-President

Barrington & Area Chamber of Commerce
Box 1, Comp 7, Barrington NS B0W 1E0
Tel: 902-723-0091
barringtonchamberofcommerce@gmail.com
www.barringtonareachamber.com
Kathy Johnson, Coordinator

Bridgetown & Area Chamber of Commerce (BACC)
PO Box 467, Bridgetown NS B0S 1C0
www.bridgetownareachamber.com
Jennifer D'Aubin, President
Gerry Bezanson, Secretary

Bridgewater & Area Chamber of Commerce (BACC)
373 King St., Bridgewater NS B4V 1B1
Tel: 902-543-4263
www.bridgewaterchamber.com
Dan Hennessey, Executive Director

Brier Island Chamber of Commerce
PO Box 74, Westport NS B0V 1H0
Harold Graham, President

Chambre de commerce de Clare / Clare Chamber of Commerce
CP 35, Pointe-de-l'Église NS B0W 1M0
Tél: 902-769-5312; *Téléc:* 902-769-5500
contact@commercedeclare.ca
www.commercedeclare.ca
Marcel Saulnier, Président

Chester Municipal Chamber of Commerce
4171 Hwy. 3, RR#2, Chester NS B0J 1J0
Tel: 902-275-4709; *Fax:* 902-275-4629
Admin@ChesterAreaNS.ca
www.chesterns.com
Anthony Smith, Chair

East Hants & District Chamber of Commerce (EHDCC)
Parker Place Mall, Upper Level, 8 Old Enfield Rd., Enfield NS B2T 1C9
Tel: 902-883-1010; *Fax:* 902-883-7862
info@ehcc.ca
www.ehcc.ca
Pat Mills, President

Halifax Chamber of Commerce
#100, 32 Akerley Blvd., Dartmouth NS B3B 1N1
Tel: 902-468-7111; *Fax:* 902-468-7333
info@halifaxchamber.com
www.halifaxchamber.com
Cynthia Dorrington, Chair

Mahone Bay & Area Chamber of Commerce
PO Box 59, Mahone Bay NS B0J 2E0
Tel: 902-624-6151; *Fax:* 902-624-6152
Toll-Free: 888-624-6151
info@mahonebay.com
www.mahonebay.com
Sue Bourinot, Chair

Northeast Highlands Chamber of Commerce
PO Box 125, Ingonish NS B0C 1L0
Tel: 902-285-2289; *Fax:* 902-285-2295
Ian Green, President

Pictou County Chamber of Commerce
#3C, 115 MacLean St., New Glasgow NS B2H 4M5
Tel: 902-755-3463
info@pictouchamber.com
www.pictouchamber.com
Jack Kyte, Executive Director

Pugwash & Area Chamber of Commerice
PO Box 239, Pugwash NS B0K 1L0
Tel: 902-243-2275
info@pugwash.biz
pugwash.biz
Lee Fleming, Manager, Member Services

Sheet Harbour & Area Chamber of Commerce & Civic Affairs
PO Box 239, Sheet Harbour NS B0J 3B0
sheetharbourchamber.com
Robert Moser, President

Shelburne & Area Chamber of Commerce
PO Box 1150, Shelburne NS B0T 1W0
Tel: 902-875-2384
shelburnechamber@gmail.com
www.shelburnechamber.ca
Elizabeth Rhuland, President
Ron Chute, Treasurer

South Queens Chamber of Commerce
PO Box 1378, Liverpool NS B0T 1K0
Tel: 902-350-1826
www.southqueenschamber.com
Barry Tomalin, President
Sherri Elliott, Treasurer
Mallory Plummer, Secretary

Springhill & Area Chamber of Commerce
PO Box 1030, Springhill NS B0M 1X0
Tel: 902-597-8614
www.springhillchamber.ca
Marcie Meekins, Secretary

Strait Area Chamber of Commerce
The Professional Centre, #205, 609 Church St., Port Hawkesbury NS B9A 2X4
Tel: 902-625-1588; *Fax:* 902-625-5985
www.straitareachamber.ca
Affiliation(s): Atlantic Provinces Chamber of Commerce
Amanda Mombourquette, Executive Director

Sydney & Area Chamber of Commerce (SACC)
275 Charlotte St., Sydney NS B1P 1C6
Tel: 902-564-6453; *Fax:* 902-539-7487
www.sydneyareachamber.ca
Adrian White, Executive Director

Truro & Colchester Chamber of Commerce
605 Prince St., Truro NS B2N 1G2
Tel: 902-895-6328; *Fax:* 902-897-6641
oa@tcchamber.ca
www.trurocolchesterchamber.com
Sherry Martell, Executive Director
Trish Petrie, Office Administrator

Yarmouth & Area Chamber of Commerce (YCC)
PO Box 532, Yarmouth NS B5A 4B4
Tel: 902-742-3074; *Fax:* 902-749-1383
info@yarmouthchamberofcommerce.com
www.yarmouthchamberofcommerce.com
Chris Atwood, President
Neil Rogers, 1st Vice-President
Angie Greene, 2nd Vice-President

Nunavut

Baffin Regional Chamber of Commerce (BRCC)
Building 987-C, PO Box 59, Iqaluit NU X0A 0H0
Tel: 867-979-4654; *Fax:* 867-979-2929
www.baffinchamber.ca
Chris West, Executive Director

Iqaluit Chamber of Commerce
PO Box 1107, Iqaluit NU X0A 0H0
Tel: 867-979-4095; *Fax:* 867-979-2929

Kivalliq Chamber of Commerce
PO Box 819, Rankin Inlet NU X0C 0G0
Tel: 867-645-2823; *Fax:* 867-645-2082
Paul Delany, Contact

Kugluktuk Chamber of Commerce
11 Coronation Dr., Kugluktuk NU X0B 0E0
Tel: 867-982-3232; *Fax:* 867-982-3229
Ken Brandly, Executive Director

Ontario

Aguasabon Chamber of Commerce
PO Box 40, 1 Selkirk Ave., Terrace Bay ON P0T 2W0
Tel: 807-825-3315
bdi@terracebay.ca
www.asuperiorchamber.com
Sylvie LeBlanc, President

Alexandria & District Chamber of Commerce
PO Box 1058, Alexandria ON K0C 1A0
Tel: 613-525-0588
alexandriachamber.ca
Michael Madden, President

Alliston & District Chamber of Commerce
PO Box 32, 60B Victoria St. West, Alliston ON L9R 1T9
Tel: 705-435-7921; *Fax:* 705-435-0289
www.adcc.ca
www.youtube.com/user/AllistonChamber
Crystal Kellard, Executive Director

Amherstburg Chamber of Commerce
PO Box 101, 268 Dalhousie St., Amherstburg ON N9V 2Z3
Tel: 519-736-2001; *Fax:* 519-736-9721
amherstburgchamber@gmail.com
www.amherstburgchamber.com
Monica Bunde, General Manager

Arthur & District Chamber of Commerce
PO Box 519, 146 George St., Arthur ON N0G 1A0
Tel: 519-848-5603; *Fax:* 519-848-4030
achamber@wightman.ca
www.arthurchamber.ca
Corey Bilton, President

Atikokan Chamber of Commerce
PO Box 997, 214 Main St. West, Atikokan ON P0T 1C0
Tel: 807-597-1599; *Fax:* 807-597-2726
Toll-Free: 888-334-2332
info@atikokanchamber.com
www.atikokanchamber.com
Affiliation(s): Canadian Chamber of Commerce
Ange Sponchia, General Manager

Aurora Chamber of Commerce
#321, 6 - 14845 Yonge St., Aurora ON L4G 6H8
Tel: 905-727-7262; *Fax:* 905-841-6217
info@aurorachamber.on.ca
www.aurorachamber.on.ca
Sandra Ferri, Executive Director

Bancroft & District Chamber of Commerce, Tourism & Information Centre
PO Box 539, 8 Hastings Heritage Way, Bancroft ON K0L 1C0
Tel: 613-332-1513; *Fax:* 613-332-2119
Toll-Free: 888-443-9999
chamber@bancroftdistrict.com
www.bancroftdistrict.com
Greg Webb, General Manager

Bayfield & Area Chamber of Commerce
PO Box 2065, Bayfield ON N0M 1G0
Tel: 519-565-2499; *Toll-Free:* 800-565-2499
info@villageofbayfield.com
www.villageofbayfield.com

Beaverton District Chamber of Commerce
PO Box 29, Beaverton ON L0K 1A0
Tel: 705-426-2051
chamber@beavertononlakesimcoe.com
www.beavertononlakesimcoe.com
Affiliation(s): Ontario Chamber of Commerce
Rossie Baillie, President

Belleville & District Chamber of Commerce (BCC)
5 Moira St., Belleville ON K8P 2S3
Tel: 613-962-4597; *Fax:* 613-962-3911
Toll-Free: 888-852-9992
info@bellevillechamber.ca
www.bellevillechamber.ca
Richard Davis, President
Bill Saunders, CEO

Black River-Matheson Chamber of Commerce
PO Box 518, Matheson ON P0K 1N0
chamber@brmchamberofcommerce.org
www.brmchamberofcommerce.org

Blenheim & District Chamber of Commerce
PO Box 1353, Blenheim ON N0P 1A0
Tel: 519-676-6555
blenheimontario.com/chamber-of-commerce
Frank Vercouteren, President
Betty Russell, Secretary

Blind River Chamber of Commerce (BRCC)
PO Box 998, Blind River ON P0R 1B0
Tel: 705-356-5715; *Fax:* 705-356-5720
chamber@blindriver.com
www.brchamber.ca
Affiliation(s): Algoma Kinniwabi Travel Association
Alex Solomon, President
Garnet Young, Treasurer

Blue Mountains Chamber of Commerce
PO Box 477, 3 Grey St., Thornbury ON N0H 2P0
Tel: 519-599-1200
info@bluemountainschamber.ca
www.bluemountainschamber.ca

Steve Simon, President

Bobcaygeon & Area Chamber of Commerce
PO Box 388, 21 Canal St. East, Bobcaygeon ON K0M 1A0
Tel: 705-738-2202; *Fax:* 705-738-1534
Toll-Free: 800-318-6173
www.bobcaygeon.org
Affiliation(s): Kawartha Lakes Associated Chambers of Commerce
Kent Leckie, President

Bracebridge Chamber of Commerce
#1, 3 Ecclestone Dr., Bracebridge ON P1L 1S4
Tel: 705-645-5231; *Toll-Free:* 866-645-8121
chamber@bracebridgechamber.com
www.bracebridgechamber.com
Brenda Rhodes, Executive Director
Marny Mowat, Office Manager

Brighton-Cramahe Chamber of Commerce
Brighton Community Resource Centre, 1 Young St., Brighton ON K0K 1H0
Tel: 613-475-2775
info@brightonchamber.ca
www.brightonchamber.ca
Burke Friedrichkeit, President

Brockville & District Chamber of Commerce
#1, 3 Market St. West, Brockville ON K6V 7L2
Tel: 613-342-6553; *Fax:* 613-342-6849
info@brockvillechamber.com
www.brockvillechamber.com
Laura Good, President
Pam Robertson, Executive Director

Burlington Chamber of Commerce
#201, 414 Locust St., Burlington ON L7S 1T7
Tel: 905-639-0174; *Fax:* 905-333-3956
info@burlingtonchamber.com
www.burlingtonchamber.com
www.youtube.com/user/BurlingtonChamber
Bruce Nicholson, Chair
Keith Hoey, President

Caledon Chamber of Commerce
12598 Hwy. 50 South, Bolton ON L7E 1T6
Tel: 905-857-7393; *Fax:* 905-857-7405
www.caledonchamber.com
Affiliation(s): Canadian Chamber of Commerce; Ontario Chamber of Commerce
Warren Darnley, Chair

Caledonia Regional Chamber of Commerce
PO Box 2035, 1 Grand Trunk Lane, Caledonia ON N3W 2G6
Tel: 905-765-0377
info@caledonia-chamber.com
www.caledonia-chamber.com
Krista Damant, President
Barb Martindale, Executive Director

Cambridge Chamber of Commerce
750 Hespler Rd., Cambridge ON N3H 5L8
Tel: 519-622-2221; *Fax:* 519-622-0177
Toll-Free: 800-749-7560
cchamber@cambridgechamber.com
www.cambridgechamber.com
www.youtube.com/thecambridgechamber
Greg Durocher, President & CEO

The Canadian Chamber of Commerce
#901, 55 University Ave., Toronto ON M5J 2H7
Tel: 416-868-6415; *Fax:* 416-868-0189

Carleton Place & District Chamber of Commerce & Visitor Centre
170 Bridge St., Carleton Place ON K7C 2V7
Tel: 613-257-1976; *Fax:* 613-257-4148
www.cpchamber.com
Donna MacDonald, Chair

Cayuga & District Chamber of Commerce
PO Box 118, Cayuga ON N0A 1E0
Tel: 905-772-5954
info@cayugachamber.ca
cayugachamber.ca
John Edelman, President

Centre Wellington Chamber of Commerce
400 Tower St. South, Fergus ON N1M 2P7
Tel: 519-843-5140
chamber@cwchamber.ca
www.cwchamber.ca
Roberta Scarrow, Executive Director

Chamber of Commerce Niagara Falls, Canada
4056 Dorchester Rd., Niagara Falls ON L2E 6M9
Tel: 905-374-3666; *Fax:* 905-374-2972
info@niagarafallschamber.com
www.niagarafallschamber.com
www.youtube.com/user/NFChamber
Anna Pierce, Chair
Dolores Fabiano, Executive Director

Chamber of Commerce of Brantford & Brant (BRCC)
77 Charlotte St., Brantford ON N3T 2W8
Tel: 519-753-2617; *Fax:* 519-753-0921
www.brantfordbrantchamber.com
Allan Lovett, President
Charlene Nicholson, CEO

Chatham-Kent Chamber of Commerce
54 - 4th St., Chatham ON N7M 2G2
Tel: 519-352-7540
www.chatham-kentchamber.ca
G.A. (Gail) Antaya, President & CEO

Chesley & District Chamber of Commerce
PO Box 406, 106 - 1st Ave. South, Chesley ON N0G 1L0
Tel: 519-363-9837

Collingwood Chamber of Commerce
#102, 115 Hurontario St., Collingwood ON L9Y 2L9
Tel: 705-445-0221
info@collingwoodchamber.com
www.collingwoodchamber.com
Affiliation(s): Canadian Chamber of Commerce; Ontario
Chamber of Commerce
John Alsop, President
Trish Irwin, General Manager & CEO

Cornwall & Area Chamber of Commerce
#100, 113 - 2nd St. East, Cornwall ON K6J 1Y5
Tel: 613-933-4004
info@cornwallchamber.com
www.cornwallchamber.com
Denis Carr, President
Lezlie Strasser, Executive Manager

Dryden District Chamber of Commerce (DDCC)
284 Government St., Hwy. 17, Dryden ON P8N 2P3
Tel: 807-223-2622; *Fax:* 807-223-2626
Toll-Free: 800-667-0935
chamber@drytel.net
www.drydenchamber.ca
Affiliation(s): Sunset County Travel Association; Patricia
Regional Tourist Council; Kenora District Camp Owners
Association
Stafanie Armstrong, Chair
Gwen Kurz, Manager

Dufferin Board of Trade
246372 Hockley Rd., Mono ON L9W 6K4
Tel: 519-941-0490; *Fax:* 519-941-0492
office@dufferinbot.ca
dufferinbot.ca
www.youtube.com/TheChamberGDACC
Affiliation(s): Ontario Chamber of Commerce; Canadian
Chamber of Commerce
Ron Munro, CEO

Dunnville Chamber of Commerce
231 Chestnut St., Dunnville ON N1A 2H2
Tel: 905-774-3183; *Fax:* 905-774-9281
dunnvillecoc@rogers.com
www.dunnvillechamberofcommerce.ca
Sandy Passmore, Office Manager

East Gwillimbury Chamber of Commerce (EGCOC)
PO Box 1099, #100, 19027 Leslie St., Sharon ON L0G 1V0
Tel: 905-478-8447
egcoc@egcoc.org
www.egcoc.org

Elliot Lake & District Chamber of Commerce
PO Box 81, Elliot Lake ON P5A 2J6
Tel: 705-848-3974; *Fax:* 705-848-7121
www.elliotlakechamber.com
Todd Stencill, General Manager

Emo Chamber of Commerce
c/o Township of Emo, PO Box 520, 39 Roy St., Emo ON P0W 1E0
Tel: 807-482-2580; *Fax:* 807-482-2741
www.emo.ca
Dave Goodman, Vice-President
Mary Goodman, Treasurer

Englehart & District Chamber of Commerce
PO Box 171, Englehart ON P0J 1H0
englehartchamber.weebly.com
Wayne Stratton, President

Fenelon Falls & District Chamber of Commerce
PO Box 28, 15 Oak St., Fenelon Falls ON K0M 1N0
Tel: 705-887-3409; *Fax:* 705-887-6912
info@fenelonfallschamber.com
www.fenelonfallschamber.com
www.youtube.com/channel/UCl3SxaMNk5V0hzAMYFuDIXg
Grant Allman, President

Flamborough Chamber of Commerce (FCC)
#227, 7 Innovation Dr., Flamborough ON L9H 7H9
Tel: 905-689-7650; *Fax:* 905-689-1313
admin@flamboroughchamber.ca
flamboroughchamber.ca
Affiliation(s): Ontario & Canadian Chamber of Commerce
Arend Kersten, Executive Director

Fort Frances Chamber of Commerce (FFCC)
#102, 240 - 1st St. East, Fort Frances ON P9A 1K5
Tel: 807-274-5773; *Fax:* 807-274-8706
Toll-Free: 800-820-3678
thefort@fortfranceschamber.com
www.fortfranceschamber.com
Affiliation(s): Ontario Chamber of Commerce; Canadian
Chamber of Commerce
Jennifer Greenhalgh, President

Georgina Chamber of Commerce
430 The Queensway South, Keswick ON L4P 2E1
Tel: 905-476-7870; *Fax:* 905-476-6700
Toll-Free: 888-436-7446
admin@georginachamber.com
www.georginachamber.com
Robin Smith, Chair

Geraldton Chamber of Commerce
PO Box 128, Geraldton ON P0T 1M0
Tel: 807-854-0895
chamber@geraldtonchamber.com
www.geraldtonchamber.com

Gogama Chamber of Commerce
PO Box 73, Gogama ON P0M 1W0

Grand Bend & Area Chamber of Commerce
PO Box 248, #1, 81 Crescent St., Grand Bend ON N0M 1T0
Tel: 519-238-2001; *Toll-Free:* 888-338-2001
info@grandbendchamber.ca
grandbendchamber.ca
Susan Mills, Manager

Gravenhurst Chamber of Commerce/Visitors Bureau
275 Muskoka Rd. South, Gravenhurst ON P1P 1J1
Tel: 705-687-4432; *Fax:* 705-687-4382
info@gravenhurstchamber.com
www.gravenhurstchamber.com
Bob Collins, President
Danielle Millar, Executive Director

Greater Arnprior Chamber of Commerce (GACC)
#111, 16 Edward St. South, Arnprior ON K7S 3W4
Tel: 613-623-6817; *Fax:* 613-623-6826
info@gacc.ca
www.gacc.ca
Pamela Cox, President
Cheryl Sparling, Administrative Assistant

Greater Barrie Chamber of Commerce
97 Toronto St., Barrie ON L4N 1V1
Tel: 705-721-5000; *Fax:* 705-726-0973
admin@barriechamber.com
barriechamber.com
www.youtube.com/barriechamber
Rod Jackson, CEO

Greater Fort Erie Chamber of Commerce
#1, 660 Garrison Rd., Fort Erie ON L2A 6E2
Tel: 905-871-3803; *Fax:* 905-871-1561
info@forteriechamber.com
www.forteriechamber.com
Rick Phibbs, President
Karen Audet, Operations Manager

Greater Innisfil Chamber of Commerce (GICC)
8034 Yonge St., #B, Innisfil ON L9S 1L6
Tel: 705-431-4199; *Fax:* 705-431-6628
manager@innisfilchamber.com
www.innisfilchamber.com
Affiliation(s): Alcona Business Association; South Innisfil
Business & Community Association; Cookstown Chamber of
Commerce; 400 Industrial Group

Mary-Ellen Madeley, Manager
Shannon MacIntyre, President

Greater Kingston Chamber of Commerce (GKCC)
945 Princess St., Kingston ON K7L 3N6
Tel: 613-548-4453; *Fax:* 613-548-4743
info@kingstonchamber.on.ca
www.kingstonchamber.on.ca
www.youtube.com/channel/UC1Pmf1i3uKXFF7PM_3_5cAA
Martin Sherris, CEO

Greater Kitchener & Waterloo Chamber of Commerce
PO Box 2367, 80 Queen St. North, Kitchener ON N2H 6L4
Tel: 519-576-5000; *Fax:* 519-742-4760
admin@greaterkwchamber.com
www.greaterkwchamber.com
www.youtube.com/user/GreaterKWChamber
Ian McLean, President & CEO

Greater Niagara Chamber of Commerce (GNCC)
#103, 1 St. Paul St., St Catharines ON L2R 7L2
Tel: 905-684-2361; *Fax:* 905-684-2100
info@gncc.ca
www.gncc.ca
Mishka Balsom, President & CEO

Greater Oshawa Chamber of Commerce
#100, 44 Richmond St. West, Oshawa ON L1G 1C7
Tel: 905-728-1683; *Fax:* 905-432-1259
info@oshawachamber.com
www.oshawachamber.com
www.youtube.com/oshawachamber
Affiliation(s): Ontario Chamber of Commerce; Canadian
Chamber of Commerce
Natalie Sims, President
Nancy Shaw, CEO & General Manager

Greater Peterborough Chamber of Commerce (GPCC)
175 George St. North, Peterborough ON K9J 3G6
Tel: 705-748-9771; *Fax:* 705-743-2331
Toll-Free: 887-640-4037
info@peterboroughchamber.ca
www.peterboroughchamber.ca
www.youtube.com/user/PeterboroughChamber
Stuart Harrison, President & CEO

Greater Sudbury Chamber of Commerce / Chambre de commerce du Grand Sudbury
#100, 40 Elm St., Sudbury ON P3C 1S8
Tel: 705-673-7133; *Fax:* 705-673-1951
cofc@sudburychamber.ca
www.sudburychamber.ca
Debbi Nicholson, President & Chief Executive Officer

Grey Highlands Chamber of Commerce
774310 Hwy. 10, Flesherton ON N0C 1E0
Tel: 226-910-1393; *Toll-Free:* 888-986-4612
info@greyhighlandschamber.com
greyhighlandschamber.com
Aakash Desai, President
Ann Detar, Office Administrator

Grimsby & District Chamber of Commerce
33 Main St. West, Grimsby ON L3M 3H1
Tel: 905-945-8319; *Fax:* 905-945-1615
www.grimsbychamber.ca
www.youtube.com/channel/UCN036EfnmnpKPG2rWqEICqA
Marion Thorp, President

Guelph Chamber of Commerce (GCC)
PO Box 1268, 111 Farquhar St., Guelph ON N1H 3N4
Tel: 519-822-8081; *Fax:* 519-822-8451
chamber@guelphchamber.com
www.guelphchamber.com
www.youtube.com/user/GuelphChamberComerc1
Affiliation(s): Guelph Business Enterprise Centre; Guelph
Partnership for Innovation
Kithio Mwanzia, President & CEO

Hagersville & District Chamber of Commerce
PO Box 1090, Hagersville ON N0A 1H0
Tel: 905-768-0422; *Fax:* 289-282-0105
Robert C. Phillips, President

Haliburton Highlands Chamber of Commerce (HHCofC)
PO Box 670, 195 Highland St., #L1, Haliburton ON K0M 1S0
Tel: 705-457-4700; *Fax:* 705-457-4702
admin@haliburtonchamber.com
www.haliburtonchamber.com
Jerry Walker, President
Autumn Smith, Chamber Manager

Halton Hills Chamber of Commerce
8 James St., Halton Hills ON L7G 2H3
Tel: 905-877-7119
tourism@haltonhillschamber.on.ca
www.haltonhillschamber.on.ca
Kathleen Dills, General Manager

Hamilton Chamber of Commerce (HCC)
Plaza Level, 120 King St. West, Hamilton ON L8P 4V2
Tel: 905-522-1151; *Fax:* 905-522-1154
hcc@hamiltonchamber.ca
www.hamiltonchamber.ca
Keanin Loomis, President & CEO

Hanover Chamber of Commerce
214 - 10th St., Hanover ON N4N 1N7
Tel: 519-364-5777; *Fax:* 519-364-6949
info@hanoverchamber.ca
www.hanoverchamber.ca
Curtis Schmalz, President

Harrow & Colchester Chamber of Commerce
PO Box 888, Harrow ON N0R 1G0
www.harrowchamber.ca
Murdo Mclean, President

Havelock, Belmont, Methuen & District Chamber of Commerce
PO Box 779, Havelock ON K0L 1Z0
Tel: 705-778-7873; *Fax:* 866-822-2182
havelockchamber@hotmail.com
www.havelockchamber.com
Phil Higgins, President

Hawkesbury & Region Chamber of Commerce / Chambre de Commerce de Hawkesbury et région
PO Box 36, #35A, 151 Main St. East, Hawkesbury ON K6A 2R4
Tel: 613-632-8066
info@hawkesburycommerce.ca
www.hawkesburycommerce.ca
Bonnie Jean-Louis, Coordinator

Hearst, Mattice - Val Côté & Area Chamber of Commerce
PO Box 987, #60, 9th St., Hearst ON P0L 1N0
Tel: 705-362-5880
info@hearstcommerce.ca
hearstcommerce.ca
Lise Joanis, President

Huntsville, Lake of Bays Chamber of Commerce
37 Main St. East, Huntsville ON P1H 1A1
Tel: 705-789-4771; *Fax:* 705-789-6191
chamber@huntsvillelakeofbays.on.ca
huntsvillelakeofbays.on.ca
Kelly Haywood, Executive Director

Huron Chamber of Commerce - Goderich, Central & North Huron
56 East St., Goderich ON N7A 1N3
Tel: 519-440-0176; *Fax:* 519-440-0305
Toll-Free: 855-440-0176
info@huronchamber.ca
www.huronchamber.ca
www.instagram.com/huronchamber
Gerry Rogers, Chair
Heather Boa, Operations Manager

Huron East Chamber of Commerce
c/o Ralph Laviolette, PO Box 433, Seaforth ON N0K 1W0
Tel: 519-440-6206
www.huroneastcc.ca
Ralph Laviolette, Secretary

Ingersoll District Chamber of Commerce
132 Thames St. South, Ingersoll ON N5C 2T4
Tel: 519-485-7333; *Fax:* 519-485-6606
ingersollchamber.com
Robin Schultz, President
Ann Campbell, General Manager

Iroquois Falls & District Chamber of Commerce
723 Synagogue Ave., Iroquois Falls ON P0K 1G0
Tel: 705-232-4656; *Fax:* 705-232-4656
office@iroquoisfallschamber.com
www.iroquoisfallschamber.com
Gabrielle Rivers, Business Executive

Kapuskasing & District Chamber of Commerce
25 Millview Rd., Kapuskasing ON P5N 2X6
Tel: 705-335-2332; *Fax:* 705-335-2359
info@kapchamber.ca
www.kapchamber.ca
Martin Proulx, President

Kawartha Chamber of Commerce & Tourism
PO Box 537, 12 Queen St., Lakefield ON K0L 2H0
Tel: 705-652-6963; *Fax:* 705-652-9140
Toll-Free: 888-565-8888
www.kawarthachamber.ca
www.instagram.com/kawarthachamber
Kris Keller, President
Sherry Boyce-Found, General Manager

Kenora & District Chamber of Commerce (KDCC)
PO Box 471, Kenora ON P9N 3X5
Tel: 807-467-4646; *Fax:* 807-468-3056
kenorachamber@kmts.ca
www.kenorachamber.com
Carlee Hakenson, Manager

Kincardine & District Chamber of Commerce
777B Queen St., Kincardine ON N2Z 2Y2
Tel: 519-396-9333; *Fax:* 519-396-5529
kincardine.cofc@bmts.com
www.kincardinechamber.com
Matt Smith, President
Jackie Pawlikowski, Office Manager

King Chamber of Commerce
PO Box 381, Schomberg ON L0G 1T0
Tel: 905-717-7199; *Fax:* 416-981-7174
info@kingchamber.ca
kingchamber.ca
Tom Allen, President
Helen Neville, Administrator

Kirkland Lake District Chamber of Commerce (KLCC)
PO Box 966, 23 Government Rd. East, Kirkland Lake ON P2N 3L1
Tel: 705-567-5444; *Fax:* 705-567-1666
kirklandchamber@ntl.sympatico.ca
www.kirklandlakechamberofcommerce.com
Affiliation(s): Ontario Chamber of Commerce
Chantal Ayotte, President

LaCloche Foothills Chamber of Commerce
PO Box 4311, 91 Barber St., Espanola ON P5E 1S4
Tel: 705-869-7671
www.laclochefoothillschamber.com
Cheryl Kay, President

Leamington District Chamber of Commerce
PO Box 321, Leamington ON N8H 3W3
Tel: 519-326-2721; *Fax:* 519-326-3204
www.leamingtonchamber.com
Wendy Parsons, General Manager

Lincoln Chamber of Commerce
PO Box 493, 4961 King St., #T2, Beamsville ON L0R 1B0
Tel: 905-563-5044; *Fax:* 905-563-7098
info@lincolnchamber.ca
www.lincolnchamber.ca
Cathy McNiven, Executive Director

Lindsay & District Chamber of Commerce
180 Kent St. West, Lindsay ON K9V 2Y6
Tel: 705-324-2393; *Fax:* 705-324-2473
info@lindsaychamber.com
www.lindsaychamber.com
Marlene Morrison Nicholls, President
Colleen Collins, Administrative Officer

London Chamber of Commerce
#101, 244 Pall Mall St., London ON N6A 5P6
Tel: 519-432-7551; *Fax:* 519-432-8063
info@londonchamber.com
www.londonchamber.com
Jeff Macoun, President
Gerry MacCartney, CEO

Longlac Chamber of Commerce
PO Box 877, Longlac ON P0T 2A0
info@longlacchamber.com
www.longlacchamber.com
Vaughn Arsenault, President

Lucknow & District Chamber of Commerce
PO Box 313, Lucknow ON N0G 2H0
Tel: 519-357-8454
info@lucknowchamber.ca
www.lucknowchamber.ca
Morten Jakobsen, President

Lyndhurst Seeleys Bay & District Chamber of Commerce
PO Box 89, Lyndhurst ON K0E 1N0
Tel: 613-331-2063
lsbchamber@hotmail.com
www.lyndhurstseeleysbaychamber.com
Mel Magalas, President

Madoc & District Chamber of Commerce
PO Box 669, 20 Davidson St., Madoc ON K0K 2K0
Tel: 613-473-1616
madocchamber@gmail.com
www.centrehastings.com/business/chamber-of-commerce/
Leigh Anne Lavender, Coordinator

Manitouwadge Economic Development Corporation
c/o Township of Manitouwadge, 1 Mississauga Dr., Manitouwadge ON P0T 2C0
Tel: 807-826-3227; *Fax:* 807-826-4592
Toll-Free: 877-826-7529
www.manitouwadge.ca
Karen Robinson, Economic Development Assistant

Marathon & District Chamber of Commerce
PO Box 988, Marathon ON P0T 2E0
Tel: 807-229-1340
marathonchamber@live.ca
www.marathon.ca
Affiliation(s): Northwestern Ontario Associated Chambers of Commerce
Greg Vallance, President

Maxville & District Chamber of Commerce
PO Box 279, Maxville ON K0C 1T0
www.maxvillechamber.ca
Deirdre Hill, President

Meaford Chamber of Commerce (MDCC)
16 Trowbridge St. West, Meaford ON N4L 1N2
Tel: 519-538-1640; *Fax:* 519-538-5493
Toll-Free: 888-632-3673
info@meafordchamber.ca
www.meafordchamber.ca
Dan White, President

Millbrook & District Chamber of Commerce
PO Box 271, 46 King St. East, Millbrook ON L0A 1G0
Tel: 705-932-7007
www.millbrook.ca
Karen Irvine, Office Manager

Milton Chamber of Commerce
#104, 251 Main St. East, Milton ON L9T 1P1
Tel: 905-878-0581; *Fax:* 905-878-4972
info@miltonchamber.ca
www.miltonchamber.ca
www.youtube.com/miltonchamber
Scott McCammon, President & CEO

Minto Chamber of Commerce
PO Box 864, Harriston ON N0G 1Z0
Tel: 519-510-7400
info@mintochamber.on.ca
www.mintochamber.on.ca
John Burgess, President

Mississippi Mills Chamber of Commerce
PO Box 1244, Almonte ON K0A 1A0
Tel: 613-216-5177
admin@mississippimills.com
www.mississippimills.com

Mount Forest District Chamber of Commerce
514 Main St. North, Mount Forest ON N0G 2L0
Tel: 519-323-4480; *Fax:* 519-323-1557
chamber@mountforest.ca
www.mountforest.ca
David Ford, President

Muskoka Lakes Chamber of Commerce
PO Box 536, 3181 Muskoka Rd. 169, Bala ON P0C 1A0
Tel: 705-762-5663; *Fax:* 705-762-5664
info@muskokalakeschamber.com
www.muskokalakeschamber.com
www.youtube.com/user/MuskokaLksCC
Jane Templeton, Manager

Napanee & District Chamber of Commerce
Napanee Business Centre, 47 Dundas St. East, Napanee ON K7R 1H7
Tel: 613-354-6601; *Toll-Free:* 877-354-6601
inquiry@napaneechamber.ca
www.napaneechamber.ca
Brad Way, President

New Clarence-Rockland Chamber of Commerce
#201, 8710 County Rd. 17, Rockland ON K4K 1T2
Tel: 613-761-1954; *Fax:* 866-648-2769
info@ccclarencerockland.com
ccclarencerockland.com
Melinda Raymond, President

Newcastle & District Chamber of Commerce
PO Box 11, 20 King Ave. West, Newcastle ON L1B 1H7
info@newcastle.on.ca
www.newcastle.on.ca
Marilia Hjorngaard, President

Newmarket Chamber of Commerce
470 Davis Dr., Newmarket ON L3Y 2P3
Tel: 905-898-5900; *Fax:* 905-853-7271
info@newmarketchamber.ca
www.newmarketchamber.ca
Dave Peters, Chair
Debra Scott, President & CEO

Niagara-on-the-Lake Chamber of Commerce
PO Box 1043, 26 Queen St., Niagara-on-the-Lake ON L0S 1J0
Tel: 905-468-1950; *Fax:* 905-468-4930
tourism@niagaraonthelake.com
www.niagaraonthelake.com
Janice Thomson, Executive Director

North Bay & District Chamber of Commerce
205 Main St. East, North Bay ON P1B 1B2
Tel: 705-472-8480; *Fax:* 705-472-8027
Toll-Free: 888-249-8998
www.nbdcc.ca
Patti Carr, Executive Director

North Grenville Chamber of Commerce
PO Box 1047, 509 Kernahan St., Kemptville ON K0G 1J0
Tel: 613-258-4838
www.northgrenvillechamber.com
Mark Thornton, Chair

North Perth Chamber of Commerce
580 Main St. West, Listowel ON N4W 1A8
Tel: 519-291-1551; *Fax:* 519-291-4151
npchamber.com
Virginia Dunbar, President
Sharon D'Arcey, General Manager

Northumberland Central Chamber of Commerce
The Chamber Bldg., 278 George St., Cobourg ON K9A 3L8
Tel: 905-372-5831
nccofc.ca
Peter Dounoukos, Chair
Kevin Ward, President & CEO

Northwestern Ontario Associated Chambers of Commerce (NOACC)
#102, 200 Syndicate Ave. South, Thunder Bay ON P7E 1C9
Tel: 807-624-2626; *Fax:* 807-622-7752
www.noacc.ca
Affiliation(s): Ontario Chamber of Commerce
Nathan Lawrence, President

Oakville Chamber of Commerce
#200, 700 Kerr St., Oakville ON L6K 3W5
Tel: 905-845-6613; *Fax:* 905-845-6475
info@oakvillechamber.com
www.oakvillechamber.com
www.instagram.com/oakvillechamber
Affiliation(s): Ontario Chamber of Commerce; Burlington Chamber of Commerce; Milton Chamber of Commerce; Halton Hills Chamber of Commerce; AmCham; Bronte Village Business Improvement Area; Downtown Oakville Business Improvement Area; Kerr Village Business Improvement Area
Caroline Hughes, Chair

1000 Islands Gananoque Chamber of Commerce
215 Stone St. South, Gananoque ON K7G 2V4
Tel: 613-382-7744
info@1000islandsganchamber.com
www.1000islandsganchamber.com
Affiliation(s): Travel Media Association of Canada
Michael Smith, President

Orillia & District Chamber of Commerce
150 Front St. South, Orillia ON L3V 4S7
Tel: 705-326-4424; *Fax:* 705-327-7841
www.orillia.com
Affiliation(s): Canadian Chamber of Commerce
Susan Lang, Managing Director

Orléans Chamber of Commerce / Chambre de commerce d'Orléans
#217W, 255 Centrum Blvd., Orléans ON K1E 3W3
Tel: 613-824-9137; *Fax:* 613-824-0090
www.orleanschamber.ca
www.instagram.com/orleanschamber
Affiliation(s): National Capital Business Alliance
Stella Ronan, Manager, Operations

Oro-Medonte Chamber of Commerce (OMCC)
148 Line 7 South, Oro ON L0L 2E0
Tel: 705-487-7337; *Fax:* 705-487-0133
info@oromedontecc.com
www.oromedontecc.com
George Wodoslawsky, President
Nadia Fitzgerald, Executive Director

Ottawa Chamber of Commerce (OCC)
328 Somerset St. West, Ottawa ON K2P 0J9
Tel: 613-236-3631; *Fax:* 613-236-7498
www.ottawachamber.ca
Ian Faris, President & CEO
Alexandra Walsh, Director, Membership Services
Kenny Leon, Director, Communications

Otter Valley Chamber of Commerce
PO Box 160, Straffordville ON N0J 1Y0
Tel: 519-550-0088
Val Donnell, President

Owen Sound & District Chamber of Commerce
PO Box 1028, #266, 1051 2nd Ave. East, Owen Sound ON N4K 6K6
Tel: 519-376-6261; *Fax:* 519-376-5647
www.oschamber.com
Peter Reesor, Chief Executive Officer

Paris & District Chamber of Commerce
PO Box 130, Paris ON N3L 3E7
Tel: 226-208-1159
info@pariscoc.ca
www.pariscoc.ca
Joanne Forrest, President
Hayley Williams, Coordinator

Parry Sound Area Chamber of Commerce
21 William St., Parry Sound ON P2A 1V2
Tel: 705-746-4213
info@parrysoundchamber.ca
www.parrysoundchamber.ca
Andrew Ryeland, President
Heather Murch, Manager, Member Services

Perth & District Chamber of Commerce
66 Craig St., Perth ON K7H 1Y5
Tel: 613-267-3200; *Fax:* 613-267-6797
welcome@perthchamber.com
perthchamber.com
Affiliation(s): Canadian Chamber of Commerce; Ontario Chamber of Commerce
Amber Hall, Manager

Pointe-au-Baril Chamber of Commerce
PO Box 67, Pointe-au-Baril-Station ON P0G 1K0
Tel: 705-366-2331
Affiliation(s): Rainbow County Travel Association

Port Colborne-Wainfleet Chamber of Commerce
76 Main St. West, Port Colborne ON L3K 3V2
Tel: 905-834-9765; *Fax:* 905-834-1542
office@pcwchamber.com
www.pcwchamber.com

Port Hope & District Chamber of Commerce
58 Queen St., Port Hope ON L1A 3Z9
Tel: 905-885-5519; *Fax:* 905-885-1142
info@porthopechamber.com
www.porthopechamber.com
Doug Blundell, President
Bree Nixon, Manager

Port Sydney/Utterson & Area Chamber of Commerce
#4, 15 South Mary Lake Rd., Port Sydney ON P0B 1L0
Tel: 705-385-1117; *Fax:* 705-385-9753
www.portsydneycoc.com
Karen MacInnes, President

Prince Edward County Chamber of Tourism & Commerce (PECCTAC)
116 Main St., Picton ON K0K 2T0
Tel: 613-476-2421; *Fax:* 613-476-7461
Toll-Free: 800-640-4717
www.pecchamber.com
Affiliation(s): Bay of Quinte Tourist Council; Business Improvement Area Association; Canadian Chamber of Commerce; Ontario Chamber of Commerce; Picton Business Improvement Association; Prince Edward County Federation of Agriculture; Wellington & District Business Association
Emily Cowan, Executive Director

Quinte West Chamber of Commerce (QWCC)
97 Front St., Trenton ON K8V 4N6
Tel: 613-392-7635; *Fax:* 613-392-8400
Toll-Free: 800-930-3255
info@quintewestchamber.ca
www.quintewestchamber.ca
Cindy Dow, President

Rainy River & District Chamber of Commerce
PO Box 458, Atwood Ave., Rainy River ON P0W 1L0
rrdcoc@gmail.com
rainyriverchamber.ca
Paul Carousol, President

Ramara & District Chamber of Commerce
2297 Hwy. 12, Brechin ON L0K 1B0
Tel: 705-484-2141
info@ramarachamber.com
www.ramarachamber.com
Roger Selman, President

Red Lake District Chamber of Commerce
PO Box 430, 137 Howey St., Red Lake ON P0V 2M0
Tel: 807-727-3722; *Fax:* 807-727-3285
redlakechamber@shaw.ca
Colin Knudsen, President
LaMar Weaver, Vice-President
Cathy Majewski, Second Vice-President

Renfrew & Area Chamber of Commerce
161 Raglan St. South, Renfrew ON K7V 1R2
Tel: 613-432-7015; *Fax:* 613-432-8645
info@renfrewareachamber.ca
www.renfrewareachamber.ca
Kent Tubman, President

Richmond Hill Chamber of Commerce (RHCOC)
376 Church St. South, Richmond Hill ON L4C 9V8
Tel: 905-884-1961; *Fax:* 905-884-1962
info@rhcoc.com
www.rhcoc.com
www.youtube.com/user/richmondhillchamber
Affiliation(s): Toronto Board of Trade
Bryon Wilfert, Chair
Elio Fulan, Executive Director

Rideau Chamber of Commerce
PO Box 247, Manotick ON K4M 1A3
Tel: 613-692-6262
drvmc2003@yahoo.com
rideauchamber.com
Affiliation(s): Ontario Chamber of Commerce
Victoria Clarke, President

Ridgetown & South East Kent Chamber of Commerce
PO Box 522, Ridgetown ON N0P 2C0
Tel: 519-359-6597
ridgetownchamber@gmail.com
www.ridgetown.com
Charlie Mitton, President

St Thomas & District Chamber of Commerce
#115, 300 South Edgeware Rd., St Thomas ON N5P 4L1
Tel: 519-631-1981; *Fax:* 519-631-0466
mail@stthomaschamber.on.ca
www.stthomaschamber.on.ca
Affiliation(s): Ontario Chamber of Commerce; Canadian Chamber of Commerce
Bob Hammersley, President & CEO

Sarnia Lambton Chamber of Commerce
556 North Christina St., Sarnia ON N7T 5W6
Tel: 519-336-2400; *Fax:* 519-336-2085
info@sarnialambtonchamber.com
www.sarnialambtonchamber.com
www.youtube.com/user/SarniaLambtonChamber
Shirley de Silva, President & CEO

Sauble Beach Chamber of Commerce
672 Main St., Sauble Beach ON N0H 2G0
manager@saublebeach.com
www.saublebeach.com

Saugeen Shores Chamber of Commerce
559 Goderich St., Port Elgin ON N0H 2C4
Tel: 519-832-2332; *Fax:* 519-389-3725
Toll-Free: 800-387-3456
portelgininfo@saugeenshores.ca
www.saugeenshoreschamber.com

Joanne Robbins, General Manager

Sault Ste Marie Chamber of Commerce (SSMCOC)
#1, 369 Queen St. East, Sault Ste Marie ON P6A 1Z4
Tel: 705-949-7152; *Fax:* 705-759-8166
info@ssmcoc.com
www.ssmcoc.com

Paul A. Johnson, President
Rory Ring, CEO

Scugog Chamber of Commerce
PO Box 1282, 237 Queen St., Port Perry ON L9L 1A0
Tel: 905-985-4971; *Fax:* 905-985-7698
Toll-Free: 877-820-3595
scugogchamber.ca
Affiliation(s): Joint Chambers of Durham Region; Durham
Network for Excellence; Tourism Durham; Tourist Association of
Durham Region; Durham Home & Small Business Association
Julie Curran, Chair

Simcoe & District Chamber of Commerce
Chamber Plaza, 95 Queensway West, Simcoe ON N3Y 2M8
Tel: 519-426-5867; *Fax:* 519-428-7718
www.simcoechamber.on.ca
Ian Swinton, President
Yvonne Di Pietro, General Manager

Sioux Lookout Chamber of Commerce
PO Box 577, 11 First Ave. South, Sioux Lookout ON P8T 1A8
Tel: 807-737-1937; *Fax:* 807-737-1778
chamber@siouxlookout.com
www.siouxlookout.com
Alana Vincent, President

Small Business Centre (SBC)
316 Rectory St., 3rd Fl., London ON N5W 3V9
Tel: 519-659-2882; *Fax:* 519-659-7050
info@sbcentre.ca
www.sbcentre.ca
www.youtube.com/user/SBCLondon
Steve Pellarin, Executive Director

Smiths Falls & District Chamber of Commerce
Town Hall, 77 Beckwith St. North, Smiths Falls ON K7A 2B8
Tel: 613-283-1334; *Fax:* 613-283-4764
info@smithsfallschamber.ca
www.smithsfallschamber.ca
Rebecca White, Marketing Coordinator
Ashley Lennox, Office Co-ordinator

South Dundas Chamber of Commerce
PO Box 288, 91 Main St., Morrisburg ON K0C 1X0
Tel: 613-543-3982; *Fax:* 613-543-2971
www.southdundaschamber.ca
Carl McIntyre, President

South Grenville Chamber of Commerce
PO Box 2000, 107 King St. West, Prescott ON K0E 1T0
Tel: 613-213-1043
southgrenvillechamber@gmail.com
www.southgrenvillechamber.ca
Penny Harland, Secretary

South Huron Chamber of Commerce
483 Main St. South, Exeter ON N0M 1S1
Tel: 226-423-3028
www.shcc.on.ca
Stephen Boles, President

South Stormont Chamber of Commerce
PO Box 489, Ingleside ON K0C 1M0
Tel: 613-537-8344
info@sscc.on.ca
www.sscc.on.ca
Carol Delorme, President

Southeast Georgian Bay Chamber of Commerce
45 Lone Pine Rd., Port Severn ON L0K 1S0
Tel: 705-756-4863; *Fax:* 705-756-4863
info@segbay.ca
www.segbay.ca
Marianne Braid, Manager

Southern Georgian Bay Chamber of Commerce / Chambre de Commerce de la Baie Georgienne Sud
208 King St., Midland ON L4R 3L9
Tel: 705-526-7884
info@sgbchamber.ca
southerngeorgianbay.ca
Denise Hayes, General Manager

Southern Georgian Bay Chamber of Commerce
(May-Oct.) Town Dock, 2 Main St., Penetanguishene ON L9M 2G2
Tel: 705-549-2232; *Fax:* 705-549-3743
ticinfo@penetanguishene.ca
www.penetanguishene.ca/en/discover/tourist-information-centre.asp

Stoney Creek Chamber of Commerce
21 Mountain Ave. South, Stoney Creek ON L8G 2V5
Tel: 905-664-4000; *Fax:* 905-664-7228
admin@chamberstoneycreek.com
www.chamberstoneycreek.com
www.youtube.com/ChamberStoneyCreek
Arnold Strub, Executive Director

Stratford & District Chamber of Commerce
55 Lorne Ave. East, Stratford ON N5A 6S4
Tel: 519-273-5250; *Fax:* 519-273-2229
info@stratfordchamber.com
www.stratfordchamber.com
Affiliation(s): Chamber of Commerce Executives of Canada
Brad Beatty, General Manager

Strathroy & District Chamber of Commerce
137 Frank St., Strathroy ON N7G 2R8
Tel: 519-245-7620; *Fax:* 519-245-9422
info@sdcc.on.ca
www.sdcc.on.ca
Kathy Manness, General Manager

Tavistock Chamber of Commerce
PO Box 670, Tavistock ON N0B 2R0
Tel: 519-301-2118
tavistockchamber@gmail.com
Bob Routly, Secretary

Temagami & District Chamber of Commerce
PO Box 57, 7 Lakeshore Dr., Temagami ON P0H 2H0
Tel: 705-569-3344; *Toll-Free:* 800-661-7609
info@temagamiinformation.com
temagamiinformation.com
Penny St. Germain, Treasurer

Temiskaming Shores & Area Chamber of Commerce (TSACC)
PO Box 811, 883356 Hwy. 65 East, New Liskeard ON P0J 1P0
Tel: 705-647-5771; *Fax:* 705-647-8633
Toll-Free: 866-947-5753
info@tsacc.ca
www.tsacc.ca
Lois Weston-Bernstein, Manager

Thunder Bay Chamber of Commerce (TBCC)
#102, 200 Syndicate Ave. South, Thunder Bay ON P7E 1C9
Tel: 807-624-2626; *Fax:* 807-622-7752
chamber@tbchamber.ca
www.tbchamber.ca
Affiliation(s): Northwestern Ontario Associated Chambers of
Commerce; Ontario Chamber of Commerce; Canadian Chamber
of Commerce
Charla Robinson, President

Tilbury Chamber of Commerce
PO Box 1239, Tilbury ON N0P 2L0
Tel: 519-682-0202; *Fax:* 519-682-2391
tilburychamber@gmail.com
www.tilburychamber.com
Jay Dillon, President
Natalie Whittal, Executive Director

Tillsonburg District Chamber of Commerce
20 Oxford St., Tillsonburg ON N4G 2G1
Tel: 519-688-3737
www.tillsonburgchamber.ca
Andrew Burns, President
Suzanne Renken, CEO

Timmins Chamber of Commerce / Chambre de commerce de Timmins
PO Box 985, 76 McIntyre Rd., Timmins ON P4N 7H6
Tel: 705-360-1900; *Fax:* 705-360-1193
info@timminschamber.on.ca
www.timminschamber.on.ca
www.youtube.com/TimminsChamber
Kurt Bigeau, President
Keitha Robson, Chief Administrative Officer

Tobermory & District Chamber of Commerce
PO Box 250, 7420 Hwy. 6, Tobermory ON N0H 2R0
Tel: 519-596-2452
chamber@tobermory.org
www.tobermory.com
Affiliation(s): Central Bruce Peninsula Chamber of Commerce;
South Bruce Peninsula Chamber of Commerce; Manitoulin

Chamber of Commerce; Manitoulin Tourism Association; Sauble
Beach Chamber of Commerce
Neda Sarbakhsh, President
Kathy Rehorek, Coordinator

Top of Lake Superior Chamber of Commerce
PO Box 402, Nipigon ON P0T 2J0
Tel: 807-887-3188
chamber@topoflakesuperior.com
www.topoflakesuperior.com
Dan Bevilacqua, President

Trent Hills & District Chamber of Commerce
PO Box 376, 51 Grand Rd., Campbellford ON K0L 1L0
Tel: 705-653-1551; *Fax:* 705-653-1629
Toll-Free: 888-653-1556
tourism@trenthillschamber.ca
www.trenthillschamber.ca
Nancy Allanson, Executive Director

Tweed Chamber of Commerce
255 Metcalf St., Tweed ON K0K 3J0
Tel: 613-473-2151
info@tweedchamber.com
www.tweedchamber.com
Roseann Trudeau, President

Upper Ottawa Valley Chamber of Commerce
177 Alexander St., Pembroke ON K8A 4L8
Tel: 613-732-1492
manager@uovchamber.com
www.upperottawavalleychamber.com
www.youtube.com/user/UOVCC
Lorraine MacKenzie, Contact

Uxbridge Chamber of Commerce
PO Box 810, 2 Campbell Dr., Uxbridge ON L9P 0A3
info@uxcc.ca
www.uxcc.ca
Kevin Alexander, President

Vaughan Chamber of Commerce (VCC)
#2, 25 Edilcan Dr., Vaughan ON L4K 3S4
Tel: 905-761-1366; *Fax:* 905-761-1918
info@vaughanchamber.ca
www.vaughanchamber.ca
Brian Shifman, President & CEO
Lori Suffern, Office Manager

Walkerton Business Improvement Area
PO Box 1344, 101 Durham St., Walkerton ON N0G 2V0
Tel: 519-881-3413; *Fax:* 519-881-4009
info@walkertonbia.ca
walkertonbia.ca
Affiliation(s): Ontario Chamber of Commerce
Christine Brandt, Chamber Manager
Dwayne Kaster, President
Trent Heipel, Vice-President

Wallaceburg & District Chamber of Commerce
152 Duncan St., Wallaceburg ON N8A 4E2
Tel: 519-627-1443; *Fax:* 519-627-1485
Toll-Free: 888-545-0558
info@wallaceburgchamber.com
www.wallaceburgchamber.com
Karen Debergh, President

Wasaga Beach Chamber of Commerce
PO Box 394, 550 River Rd. West, Wasaga Beach ON L9Z 1A4
Tel: 705-429-2247; *Fax:* 705-429-1407
Toll-Free: 866-292-7242
info@wasagainfo.com
www.wasagainfo.com
Affiliation(s): Canadian Chamber of Commerce; Ontario
Chamber of Commerce
Trudie McCrea, Office Manager

The Welland/Pelham Chamber of Commerce / La Chambre de commerce de Welland/Pelham
32 East Main St., Welland ON L3B 3W3
Tel: 905-732-7515; *Fax:* 905-732-7175
www.wellandpelhamchamber.com
www.youtube.com/user/WellandPelhamChamber
Jeff Neill, President
Dolores Fabiano, Executive Director

Wellesley & District Board of Trade
c/o Wendy Sauder, Wellesley Service Centre, 1220 Queens
Bush Rd., Wellesley ON N0B 2T0
Tel: 519-656-3494
wellesleyboardoftrade@gmail.com
wellesleyboardoftrade.com
Kim Heinmiller, President

West Elgin Chamber of Commerce
PO Box 276, Rodney ON N0L 2C0
Tel: 519-785-0916
Mike Madeira, President

West Grey Chamber of Commerce
PO Box 671, 144 Garafraxa St. South, Durham ON N0G 1R0
Tel: 519-369-5750
westgreychamber@gmail.com
westgreychamber.ca
Affiliation(s): Durham Business Improvement Association
Nella Monaco-Wells, President

West Lincoln Chamber of Commerce
PO Box 555, 288 Station St., Smithville ON L0R 2A0
Tel: 905-957-1606; *Fax:* 905-957-4628
www.westlincolnchamber.com
Ivan Carruthers, President
Pamela Haire, Administrator

West Nipissing Chamber of Commerce / Chambre de commerce de Nipissing Ouest
173 King St., Sturgeon Falls ON P2B 1R6
Tel: 705-753-5672; *Fax:* 705-580-5672
admin@westnipissingchamber.ca
www.westnipissingchamber.ca
Michelle Schenk, Office Manager & Program Coordinator

West Ottawa Board of Trade
#140, 555 Legget Dr., Kanata ON K2K 2X3
Tel: 613-592-8343; *Fax:* 613-592-1157
info@westottawabot.com
www.westottawabot.com
www.youtube.com/user/KanataChamber
Rosemary Leu, Executive Director

Westport & Rideau Lakes Chamber of Commerce
PO Box 157, Westport ON K0G 1X0
Tel: 613-273-2929; *Fax:* 613-273-2929
wrlcc14@gmail.com
www.therideaucalls.ca
Marty Hawkins, Co-Chair
Ken Rose, Co-Chair

Whitby Chamber of Commerce (WCC)
209 Dundas St. East, Whitby ON L1N 7H8
Tel: 905-668-4506; *Fax:* 905-668-1894
info@whitbychamber.org
www.whitbychamber.org
Brenda Bemis, Office Manager
Natalie Prychitko, Chief Executive Officer
Heather Bulman, Manager, Marketing & Communications

Whitchurch-Stouffville Chamber of Commerce
6176 Main St., Stouffville ON L4A 2S5
Tel: 905-642-4227; *Fax:* 905-642-8966
www.stouffvillechamber.ca
Danny Huang, Chair
Harry Renaud, Executive Director

Wiarton South Bruce Peninsula Chamber of Commerce
PO Box 68, #2, 402 William St., Wiarton ON N0H 2T0
Tel: 519-534-4545
info@wiartonchamber.ca
www.wiartonchamber.ca
Affiliation(s): Wiarton BIA
Paul Deacon, President

Windsor-Essex Regional Chamber of Commerce
2575 Ouellette Place, Windsor ON N8X 1L9
Tel: 519-966-3696; *Fax:* 519-966-0603
www.windsorchamber.org
Jeffrey MacKinnon, Chair
Matt Marchand, President & CEO

Woodstock District Chamber of Commerce
447 Hunter St., Woodstock ON N4S 4G7
Tel: 519-539-9411; *Fax:* 519-456-1611
info@woodstockchamber.ca
www.woodstockchamber.ca
www.youtube.com/woodstockonchamber
Kim Whitehead, General Manager

Zurich & District Chamber of Commerce
PO Box 189, Zurich ON N0M 2T0
zurichontario.com

Prince Edward Island

Chambre de commerce acadienne et francophone de l'Île-du-Prince-Édouard
CP 7, Wellington PE C0B 2E0
Tel: 902-854-3439; *Téléc:* 902-854-3099
www.rdeeipe.net/ccaflipe

Raymond Arsenault, Coordonnateur

Eastern Prince Edward Island Chamber of Commerce
PO Box 1593, Montague PE C0A 1R0
Tel: 902-838-3131
info@epeicc.ca
www.epeicc.ca
Marie LaVie, Managing Director

Greater Charlottetown & Area Chamber of Commerce
PO Box 67, #230, 134 Kent St., Charlottetown PE C1A 7K2
Tel: 902-628-2000; *Fax:* 902-368-3570
www.charlottetownchamber.com
Affiliation(s): Atlantic Provinces Chamber of Commerce
Pam Williams, President
Penny Walsh McGuire, Executive Director
Angela Smith, Office Manager

Greater Summerside Chamber of Commerce (GSCC)
#10, 263 Heather Moyse Dr., Summerside PE C1N 5P1
Tel: 902-436-9651; *Fax:* 902-436-8320
info@summersidechamber.com
www.summersidechamber.com
www.instagram.com/summersidechamber
Jan Sharpe, Executive Director

Kensington & Area Chamber of Commerce
PO Box 234, Kensington PE C0B 1M0
Tel: 902-836-3209; *Fax:* 902-836-3206
info@kensingtonchamber.ca
kensingtonchamber.ca
www.youtube.com/user/KtownChamber
Patricia Bennett, President
Jessica Caseley, Coordinator, Membership & Events

South Shore Chamber of Commerce
PO Box 127, Crapaud PE C0A 1J0
Tel: 902-437-2510
www.southshorechamberpei.ca
Cathie Thomas, Administrator

Québec

The Canadian Chamber of Commerce
#560, 999, boul de Maisonneuve ouest, Montréal QC H3A 3L4
Tel: 514-866-4334; *Fax:* 514-866-7296

Canadian German Chamber of Industry & Commerce Inc.
#200, 410, rue St-Nicolas, Montréal QC H2Y 2P5
Tel: 514-844-3051; *Fax:* 514-844-1473
info.montreal@germanchamber.ca

Chambre de commerce au Coeur de la Montérégie (CCCM)
319, ch de Chambly, Marieville QC J3M 1N9
Tél: 450-460-4019; *Téléc:* 450-460-2362
info@coeurmonteregie.com
www.coeurmonteregie.com
Véronique Côté, Directrice générale

Chambre de commerce Baie-des-Chaleurs
114-B, av Grand-Pré, Bonaventure QC G0C 1E0
Tél: 418-534-0050; *Téléc:* 418-534-4747
www.ccbdc.ca
Maurice Quesnel, Directeur général

Chambre de commerce Bellechasse-Etchemins
159-B, boul Bégin, Sainte-Clare QC G0R 2V0
Tél: 418-563-1131
ccb-e.ca
Yvon Laflamme, Président

Chambre de Commerce Bois-des-Filion - Lorraine
CP 72012, Bois-des-Filion QC J6Z 4N9
Tél: 450-818-3481
info@ccbdfl.com
www.ccbdfl.com
Michel Bourgeois, Co-Président
Michel Limoges, Co-Président

Chambre de commerce d'industrie Les Moulins
2500, boul des Enterprises, Terrebonne QC J6X 4J8
Tél: 450-966-1536
info@ccimoulins.com
www.ccimoulins.com
Affiliation(s): Chambre de commerce du Canada; Chambre de commerce du Québec; Chambre de commerce régionale de Lanaudière; Réseau canadien de centres de services aux entreprises; Centre local de développement économique des Moulins (CLDEM); Centre local d'emploi de Terrebonne; Société de développement touristique des Moulins; Conseil de développement bioalimentaire de Lanaudière.
Lucie Lecours, Directrice générale

Chambre de commerce de Beauceville
CP 5142, Beauceville QC G5X 2P5
Tél: 418-774-1020
info@chambredecommercedebeauceville.com
www.chambredecommercedebeauceville.com
Affiliation(s): Chambre de commerce du Québec; Chambre du commerce du Canada
François Veilleux, Président

Chambre de commerce de Brandon
151, rue Saint-Gabriel, Saint-Gabriel QC J0K 2N0
Tél: 450-835-2105; *Téléc:* 450-835-2991
info@cc-brandon.com
cc-brandon.com
Affiliation(s): Chambre de commerce du Québec
Marc-André Forest, Président

Chambre de Commerce de Cap-des-Rosiers
1127, boul de Cap-des-Rosiers, Cap-des-Rosiers QC G4X 6G3

Chambre de commerce de Carleton
629, boul Perron, Carleton QC G0C 1J0
Tél: 418-364-1004

Chambre de commerce de Charlevoix
#209, 11, rue Saint-Jean-Baptiste, Baie-Saint-Paul QC G3Z 1M1
Tél: 418-760-8648
info@creezdesliens.com
www.creezdesliens.com
Johanne Côté, Directrice générale

Chambre de commerce de Chibougamau
#4, 600 - 3e rue, Chibougamau QC G8P 1P1
Tél: 418-748-4827; *Téléc:* 418-748-6179
info@ccchibougamau.com
www.chibougamauchapais.com
Affiliation(s): Chambre de Commerce du Québec et du Canada
Mélanie Hébert, Coordonnatrice

Chambre de commerce de Cowansville et région
#100-B, 104, rue du Sud, Cowansville QC J2K 2X2
Tél: 450-266-1665; *Téléc:* 450-266-4117
info@cccr.quebec
cccr.quebec
Hélène Paquette, Présidente
Hélène Sactouris, Directrice générale

Chambre de commerce de Disraéli
CP 5008, Disraéli QC G0N 1E0
chambrecommercedisraeli@gmail.com
chambrecommercedisraeli.com
Catherine Morency, Présidente

Chambre de commerce de Ferme-Neuve
125, 12e rue, Ferme-Neuve QC J0W 1C0
Tél: 819-587-3882
ch.comm.fn@tlb.sympatico.ca
www.municipalite.ferme-neuve.qc.ca/Chambre_de_commerce.asp

Chambre de Commerce de Fermont
CP 419, #6C, 299, Le Carrefour, Fermont QC G0G 1J0
Tél: 418-287-3000

Chambre de commerce de Forestville
40, rte 138 ouest, Forestville QC G0T 1E0
Tél: 418-587-1585
chcommforestville@cgocable.ca

Chambre de commerce de Gatineau
#100, 45, rue de Villebois, Gatineau QC J8T 8J7
Tél: 819-243-2246; *Téléc:* 819-243-3346
ccgatineau@ccgatineau.ca
www.ccgatineau.ca
Anne-Marie Proulx, Directrice générale

Chambre de commerce de l'Est de la Beauce
Saint-Prosper QC
Tél: 418-594-1219
ccest.beauce@hotmail.com

Chambre de commerce de l'Est de Montréal
#100, 5600, rue Hochelaga, Montréal QC H1N 3L7
Tél: 514-354-5378; *Téléc:* 514-354-5340
info@ccemontreal.ca
www.ccemontreal.ca
Carl Poulin, Président-directeur général par intérim

Chambre de commerce de l'Est de Portneuf
CP 4031, #2, rue de la Fabrique, Pont-Rouge QC G3H 3R4
Tél: 418-873-4085; *Téléc:* 418-873-4599
ccep@portneufest.com
www.portneufest.com

Karine Lacroix, Directrice

Chambre de commerce de l'Ile d'Orléans (CCIO)
490, côte du Pont, Saint-Pierre-Ile-d'Orléans QC G0A 4E0
Tél: 418-828-0880; *Téléc:* 418-828-2335
ccio@videotron.ca
cciledorleans.com

Affiliation(s): Chambre de commerce de Québec
Sylvie Ann Tremblay, Directrice générale

Chambre de commerce de l'Ouest-de-l'Ile de Montréal / West Island Chamber of Commerce
#106, 1870, boul des Sources, Pointe-Claire QC H9R 5N4
Tél: 514-697-4228; *Téléc:* 514-697-2562
info@ccoim.ca
www.ccoim.ca

Joseph Huza, Directeur exécutif

Chambre de commerce de la grande région de Saint-Hyacinthe
780, av de L'Hôtel-de-ville, Saint-Hyacinthe QC J2S 5B2
Tél: 450-773-3474; *Téléc:* 450-773-9339
chambre@chambrecommerce.ca
www.chambrecommerce.ca

Pierre Rhéaume, Directeur général

Chambre de commerce de la Haute-Gaspésie
96, boul Sainte-Anne ouest, Sainte-Anne-des-Monts QC G4V 1R3
Tél: 418-763-2200
info@cchautegaspesie.com
www.cchg.qc.ca

Steve Ouimet, Président

Chambre de commerce de la Haute-Matawinie
521, rue Brassard, Saint-Michel-des-Saints QC J0K 3B0
Tél: 450-833-1334; *Téléc:* 450-833-1334
infocchm@satelcom.qc.ca
www.haute-matawinie.com

France Chapdelaine, Directrice générale

Chambre de Commerce de la Jacques-Cartier
4517, rte de Fossambault, RR#3,
Ste-Catherine-de-la-Jacques-Cartier QC G0A 3M0
Tél: 418-875-4103

Chambre de commerce de la MRC de L'Assomption
#635, boul Iberville, Repentigny QC J6A 2C5
Tél: 450-581-3010; *Téléc:* 450-581-5069
info@ccmla.ca
www.ccmrclassomption.ca

Benoit Delisle, Président
Alain Bienvenu, Directeur général

Chambre de commerce de la MRC de la Matapédia
#403, 123, rue Desbiens, Amqui QC G5J 3P9
Tél: 418-629-5765; *Téléc:* 418-629-5530
information@ccmrcmatapedia.qc.ca
www.ccmrcmatapedia.qc.ca

Affiliation(s): Fédération des Chambres de commerce du Québec
Pierre Langlois, Directeur général

Chambre de commerce de la MRC de Rivière-du-Loup
298, boul Armand-Thériault, Rivière-du-Loup QC G5R 4C2
Tél: 418-862-5243; *Téléc:* 418-862-5136
info@monreseaurdl.com
www.ccmrcrdl.com

Karine Malenfant, Directrice générale

Chambre de commerce de la région d'Acton
Édifice de la Gare, 980, rue Boulay, Acton Vale QC J0H 1A0
Tél: 450-546-0123; *Téléc:* 450-546-2709
ccracton@cooptel.qc.ca
www.chambredecommerce.info

Alain Giguère, Président

Chambre de commerce de la région de Weedon
280, 9e av, Weedon QC J0B 3J0
Tél: 819-560-8555

Affiliation(s): Chambre de Commerce du Québec

Chambre de commerce de Lac-Brome
CP 3654, #316, 1, rue Knowlton, Lac-Brome QC J0E 1V0
Tél: 450-242-2870
info@cclacbrome.com
www.cclacbrome.com

Suzanne Gregory, Directrice générale

Chambre de commerce de Lévis
#225, 5700, rue J.B.-Michaud, Lévis QC G6V 0B1
Tél: 418-837-3411; *Téléc:* 418-837-8497
cclevis@cclevis.ca
www.cclevis.com

Stéphane Thériault, Directeur général

Chambre de commerce de Manicouagan
22, Place la Salle, 2e étage, Baie-Comeau QC G4Z 1K3
Tél: 418-296-2010; *Téléc:* 418-296-5397
info@ccmanic.qc.ca
www.ccmanic.qc.ca

Dave Prévéreault, Directeur général

Chambre de commerce de Mont-Laurier
CP 64, Mont-Laurier QC J9L 3G9
Tél: 819-623-3642; *Téléc:* 819-623-5220
Ligne sans frais: 855-623-3642
info@ccmont-laurier.com
www.ccmont-laurier.com

Éric Tourangeau, Président
Jocelyn Girouard, Vice-Présidente
Audrey Lebel, Directrice générale

Chambre de commerce de Montmagny
#121, 6, rue St-Jean-Baptiste est, Montmagny QC G5V 1J7
Tél: 418-248-3111; *Téléc:* 418-241-5779
www.ccmontmagny.com

Chambre de commerce de Mont-Tremblant
#205, local 101, rue Lacasse, Mont-Tremblant QC J8E 3G6
Tél: 819-425-8441; *Téléc:* 819-425-7949
ccmt@ccm-t.ca
www.ccm-t.ca

France Paré, Présidente
Isabelle Plouffe, Directrice générale

Chambre de commerce de Port-Cartier
CP 82, Port-Cartier QC G5B 2G7
Tél: 418-766-3110; *Téléc:* 418-766-6367
ccportcartier@globetrotter.net
www.ccportcartier.ca

Jean-Marie Potvin, Président

Chambre de commerce de Rawdon
3874, rue Queen, Rawdon QC J0K 1S0
Tél: 450-834-2282; *Téléc:* 450-834-3084
ccdrawdon@gmail.com
www.chambrecommercerawdon.ca

Francis Martin, Président

Chambre de commerce de Saint-Côme
1661A, rue Principale, Saint-Côme QC J0K 2B0
Tél: 450-883-2730
tourisme@stcomelanaudiere.ca
www.stcomelanaudiere.com

Marie-Marthe Venne, Présidente par intérim

Chambre de commerce de Sainte-Adèle
1370, boul de Sainte-Adèle, Sainte-Adèle QC J8B 2N5
Tél: 450-229-2644; *Téléc:* 450-229-1436
chambredecommerce@sainte-adele.net
www.sainte-adele.net

Guy Goyer, Directeur général

Chambre de commerce de Saint-Georges
#310, 8585, boul Lacroix, Saint-Georges QC G5Y 5L6
Tél: 418-228-7879; *Téléc:* 418-228-8074
reception@ccstgeorges.com
www.ccstgeorges.com

Affiliation(s): Chambre de commerce du Québec; Chambre de commerce du Canada
Nathalie Roy, Directrice générale

Chambre de commerce de Ste-Julienne
1799, rte 125, Sainte-Julienne QC J0K 2T0
Tél: 819-831-3551; *Téléc:* 819-831-3551

Nicole Bourgie, Secrétaire

Chambre de commerce de Ste-Justine
167, rte 204, Sainte-Justine QC G0R 1Y0
Tél: 418-383-3207; *Téléc:* 418-383-3223
chambredecommercestejustine@sogetel.net
www.ccstejustine.ca

Bruno Turcotte, Président

Chambre de commerce de Sept-Iles
#237, 700, boul Laure, Sept-Iles QC G4R 1Y1
Tél: 418-968-3488; *Téléc:* 418-968-3432
ccsi@globetrotter.net
www.ccseptiles.com

Emilie Paquet, Directrice générale

Chambre de commerce de Sherbrooke
#202, 9, rue Wellington sud, Sherbrooke QC J1H 5C8
Tél: 819-822-6151; *Téléc:* 819-822-6156
info@ccsherbrooke.ca
www.ccsherbrooke.ca

Affiliation(s): La jeune chambre de commerce de Sherbrooke
Louise Bourgault, Directrice générale

Chambre de commerce de St-Côme-Linière (CCSCL)
1614, 6e rue, Saint-Côme-Linière QC G0M 1J0
Tél: 418-685-2630; *Téléc:* 418-685-2630
chambredecommerce@stcomeliniere.com
www.stcomeliniere.com/c_ccommerce.php

Chambre de commerce de St-Frédéric
850, rue de l'Hôtel-de-Ville, Saint-Frédéric QC G0N 1P0
commerce@st-frederic.com
www.saint-frederic.com

Cathy Poulin, Directrice générale

Chambre de commerce de St-Jean-de-Dieu
32, rue Principale sud, Saint-Jean-de-Dieu QC G0L 3M0
Tél: 418-963-3529
chambredecommercestjean@outlook.com

Émilie Lebel, Directrice générale

Chambre de commerce de St-Jules-de-Beauce
169, Rang 3, Saint-Jules QC G0N 1R0
Tél: 418-397-1870

Dominic Paré, Présidente

Chambre de commerce de St-Léonard
8370, boul Lacordaire, Saint-Léonard QC H1R 3Y6
Tél: 514-325-4232; *Téléc:* 514-955-8544
info@saintleonardenaffaires.com
saintleonardenaffaires.com

Salvatore Andricciola, Président

Chambre de commerce de Tring-Jonction
CP 1012, Tring-Jonction QC G0N 1X0
Tél: 418-426-2135
c_de_commerce_tring@hotmail.com
www.tringjonction.qc.ca

Richard Lagueux, Vice-président

Chambre de commerce de Valcourt et Région
980, rue St-Joseph, Valcourt QC J0E 2L0
Tél: 450-532-3263; *Téléc:* 450-532-5855
info@valcourtregion.com
www.valcourtregion.com

Affiliation(s): Chambre de commerce régionale de l'Estrie
Pierre Bonneau, Président

Chambre de commerce de Val-d'Or (CCVD)
#200, 921 - 3e av, Val-d'Or QC J9P 1T4
Tél: 819-825-3703; *Téléc:* 819-825-8599
info@ccvd.qc.ca
www.ccvd.qc.ca
www.youtube.com/user/CCVDCom

Marcel H. Jolicoeur, Président
Hélène Paradis, Directrice générale

Chambre de commerce des Jardins de Napierville
780, rue Notre-Dame, Saint-Rémi QC J0L 2L0
Tél: 450-615-0512; *Ligne sans frais:* 844-467-6734
info@ccjdn.com
www.ccjdn.com

Daniel Dagenais, Président

Chambre de commerce des Iles-de-la-Madeleine (CCIM)
Édifice Fernand Cyr, #103, 735, ch Principal,
Cap-aux-Meules QC G4T 1G8
Tél: 418-986-4111; *Téléc:* 418-986-4112
info@ccim.qc.ca
www.ilesdelamadeleine.com

Marius Arseneault, Président

Chambre de commerce du grand de Châteauguay
#100, 15, boul Maple, Châteauguay QC J6J 3P7
Tél: 450-698-0027; *Téléc:* 450-698-0088
info@ccgchateauguay.ca
www.ccgchateauguay.ca

Isabelle Poirier, Directrice générale

Chambre de commerce du Grand Joliette
500, boul Dollard, Joliette QC J6E 4M4
Tél: 450-759-6363; *Téléc:* 450-759-5012
info@ccgj.qc.ca
www.ccgj.qc.ca
www.youtube.com/user/CCGJoliette

Pascale Lapointe-Manseau, Directrice générale

Chambre de commerce du Grand St-Donat
536A, rue Principale, Saint-Donat-de-Montcalm QC J0T 2C0
Tél: 819-216-2273
ccgsdonat@gmail.com

Chambre de commerce du Haut-Richelieu
Centre Ernest-Thuot, 75, 5e av, Saint-Jean-sur-Richelieu QC J2X 1T1
Tél: 450-346-2544; Téléc: 450-346-3812
info@ccihr.ca
www.ccihr.ca
Stéphane Legrand, Directeur général

Chambre de commerce du Haut-Saint-François
221, St-Jean ouest, East Angus QC J0B 1R0
Tél: 819-832-4950; Téléc: 819-832-4950
info@chambredecommercehsf.com
www.chambredecommercehsf.com
Guy Boulanger, Président
Nancy Grenier, Directrice générale

Chambre de commerce du Montréal métropolitain / Chamber of Commerce of Metropolitan Montréal
#6000, 380, rue Saint-Antoine ouest, Montréal QC H2Y 3X7
Tél: 514-871-4000; Téléc: 514-871-1255
info@ccmm.ca
www.ccmm.ca
Michel Leblanc, Président et chef de la direction

Chambre de commerce du Témiscouata
CP 1726, #201, 3, rue de l'Hôtel-de-Ville,
Témiscouata-sur-le-Lac QC G0L 1X0
Tél: 418-714-2263
info@cctemiscouata.com
www.cctemiscouata.com
Martine Lemieux, Directrice générale

Chambre de commerce du Transcontinental
CP 2004, Rivière-Bleue QC G0L 2B0
Tél: 418-893-5504; Téléc: 418-893-2889
cctrans@sympatico.ca
pages.globetrotter.net/cctrans
Sylvain Lafrance, Président

Chambre de commerce Duparquet
CP 369, Duparquet QC J0Z 1W0
Tél: 819-948-2030
Jasmine Therrien, Secrétaire

Chambre de commerce East Broughton
CP 916, East Broughton QC G0N 1G0
Tél: 418-351-0143

Chambre de commerce et d'entrepreneuriat des Sources (CCES)
CP 599, Danville QC J0A 1A0
Tél: 819-839-2742; Téléc: 819-839-2347
Isabelle Lodge, Présidente
Kathy Breton, Secrétaire

Chambre de commerce et d'industrie Beauharnois-Valleyfield-Haut Saint-Laurent
#400, 100, rue Sainte-Cécile, Salaberry-de-Valleyfield QC J6T 1M1
Tél: 450-373-8789; Téléc: 450-373-8642
info@ccibvhsl.ca
www.ccibv.ca
Sylvie Villemure, Directrice générale

Chambre de commerce et d'industrie Berthier-D'Autray
557, rue de Montcalm, Berthierville QC J0K 1A0
Tél: 450-836-4689; Téléc: 450-836-6483
info@cciba.org
www.cciba.org
Jean-François Laporte, Président

Chambre de commerce et d'industrie d'Abitibi-Ouest (CCAO)
364-A, rue Principale, La Sarre QC J9Z 1Z5
Tél: 819-333-9836; Téléc: 819-333-5737
ccao@ccao.qc.ca
www.ccao.qc.ca
Stéphanie Bédard, Directrice générale

Chambre de commerce et d'industrie d'Argenteuil
540, rue Berry, Lachute QC J8H 1S5
Tél: 450-562-1947; Téléc: 450-562-1896
info@cciargenteuil.com
www.cciargenteuil.com
Marguerite Varin, Présidente

Chambre de commerce et d'industrie de Dolbeau-Mistassini
#110, 1201, rue des Érables, Dolbeau-Mistassini QC G8L 1C2
Tél: 418-276-6638; Téléc: 418-276-9518
info@ccidm.ca
www.ccidm.ca
Audrey Jobin, Directrice générale

Chambre de commerce et d'industrie de Drummond (CCID)
CP 188, 234, rue Saint-Marcel, Drummondville QC J2B 6V7
Tél: 819-477-7822
info@ccid.qc.ca
www.ccid.qc.ca
www.youtube.com/channel/UCoFAI0FERsHBU6CITMR1_Ug
Alain Côté, Directeur général

Chambre de commerce et d'industrie de la MRC de Maskinongé
396, av Ste-Élisabeth, Louiseville QC J5V 1M8
Tél: 819-228-8582; Téléc: 819-498-8323
Ligne sans frais: 866-900-8582
info@ccimm.ca
www.ccimm.ca
Geneviève Scott Lafontaine, Directrice générale

Chambre de commerce et d'Industrie de la région de Coaticook (CCIRC)
#22, 150, rue Child, Coaticook QC J1A 2B3
Tél: 819-849-4733; Téléc: 819-849-9683
info@ccircoaticook.ca
www.ccircoaticook.ca
Caroline Thibeault, Présidente

Chambre de commerce et d'industrie de la région de Richmond
CP 3119, Richmond QC J0B 2H0
Tél: 819-826-5854
info@ccrichmond.com
www.ccrichmond.com
Hélène Tousignant, Présidente
Ginette Coutu-Poirier, Trésorière

Chambre de commerce et d'industrie de la Rive-Sud
#101, 85, rue Saint-Charles ouest, Longueuil QC J4H 1C5
Tél: 450-463-2121; Téléc: 450-463-1858
info@ccirs.qc.ca
www.ccirs.qc.ca
Hélène Bergeron, Codirectrice générale
Stéphanie Brodeur, Codirectrice générale

Chambre de commerce et d'industrie de la Vallée-du-Richelieu
#203, 230, rue Brébeuf, Beloeil QC J3G 5P3
Tél: 450-464-3733; Téléc: 450-446-4163
www.ccivr.com
Julie La Rochelle, Directrice générale

Chambre de commerce et d'industrie de Laval (CCIL)
#200, 1555, boul Chomedey, Laval QC H7V 3Z1
Tél: 450-682-5255; Téléc: 450-682-5735
info@ccilaval.qc.ca
www.ccilaval.qc.ca
Chantal Provost, Présidente-directrice générale

Chambre de commerce et d'industrie de Malartic (CCIM)
#160, 866, rue Royale, Malartic QC J0Y 1Z0
Tél: 819-757-3338
info@ccimalartic.com
www.ccimalartic.com
Claudette Jolin, Directrice

Chambre de commerce et d'industrie de Maniwaki & Vallée de la Gatineau (CCIM)
186, rue King, Maniwaki QC J9E 3N6
Tél: 819-449-6627; Téléc: 819-449-7667
Ligne sans frais: 866-449-6728
info@ccmvg.com
www.ccmvg.com
Kim Lafond, Administratrice

Chambre de commerce et d'industrie de Mirabel
#300, 11700, de L'Avenir, Mirabel QC J7J 0G7
Tél: 450-433-1944
www.ccimirabel.com
Steve Raymond, Président

Chambre de commerce et d'industrie de Montréal-Nord (CRIMN)
#207, 5835, boul Léger, Montréal QC H1G 6E1
Tél: 514-329-4453; Téléc: 514-329-5318
www.ccimn.qc.ca
Palmina Panichella, Directrice générale

Chambre de commerce et d'industrie de Québec
#600, 900, boul René-Lévesque est, Québec QC G1R 2B5
Tél: 418-692-3853; Téléc: 418-694-2286
info@cciquebec.ca
www.cciquebec.ca
www.youtube.com/channel/UC6knYpzSAWYkHtfTqnIV6SA
Affiliation(s): Chambre de commerce du Canada
Alain Aubut, Président et chef de la direction

Chambre de commerce et d'industrie de Roberval
CP 115, Roberval QC G8H 2N4
Tél: 418-275-3504; Téléc: 418-275-6895
info@ccroberval.ca
www.ccroberval.ca
Affiliation(s): Chambre de Commerce du Québec; Chambre de Commerce du Canada
Serge Taillon, Président
Jeannot Tremblay, Coordonnateur

Chambre de commerce et d'industrie de Rouyn-Noranda (CCIRN)
70, av du Lac, Rouyn-Noranda QC J9X 4N4
Tél: 819-797-2000; Téléc: 819-762-3091
reseau@ccirn.qc.ca
www.ccirn.qc.ca
Julie Bouchard, Vice-présidente exéc. & Directrice générale

Chambre de commerce et d'industrie de Shawinigan
1635, 105e av, Shawinigan QC G9P 1M8
Tél: 819-536-0777; Téléc: 819-536-0039
info@ccishawinigan.ca
www.ccishawinigan.ca
Mario Lamontagne, Président
Martin St-Pierre, Directeur général

Chambre de commerce et d'industrie de Sorel-Tracy
67, rue George, Sorel-Tracy QC J3P 1C2
Tél: 450-742-0018; Téléc: 450-742-7442
www.ccstm.qc.ca
www.youtube.com/channel/UC2_SG-MoqKsusKJulFD6m5w
Sylvain Dupuis, Directeur général

Chambre de commerce et d'industrie de St-Joseph-de-Beauce
CP 5042, Saint-Joseph-de-Beauce QC G0S 2V0
Tél: 418-397-5980
admin@ccstjoseph.com
ccstjoseph.com
Annie Thibeault, Coordonnatrice

Chambre de commerce et d'industrie de St-Laurent-Mont-Royal
#101, 5255, boul Henri-Bourassa, Montréal QC H4R 2M6
Tél: 514-333-5222; Téléc: 514-333-0937
info@ccsl-mr.com
www.ccsl-mr.com
Sylvie Séguin, Directrice générale

Chambre de commerce et d'industrie de Thetford Mines (CCITM)
81, rue Notre-Dame ouest, Thetford Mines QC G6G 1J4
Tél: 418-338-4551; Téléc: 418-335-2066
www.ccitm.com
Louis Thivierge, Directeur général

Chambre de commerce et d'industrie de Varennes (CCIV)
2102, Marie-Victorin, #B, Varennes QC J3X 1R4
Tél: 450-652-4209; Téléc: 450-652-4244
info@cciv.ca
www.cciv.ca
Marie-Claude Lévesque, Directrice générale

Chambre de commerce et d'industrie des Bois-Francs et de l'Érable
122, rue de l'Acqueduc, Victoriaville QC G6P 1M3
Tél: 819-758-6371; Téléc: 819-758-4604
ccibf@ccibf.qc.ca
www.ccibf.qc.ca
www.youtube.com/ChambreCCIBFE
Josée Desharnais, Directrice générale

Chambre de commerce et d'industrie du bassin de Chambly (CCIB)
929, boul de Périgny, Chambly QC J3L 5H5
Tél: 450-658-7598; *Téléc:* 450-658-3569
info@ccibc.qc.ca
www.ccibc.qc.ca

Serge Gélinas, Directeur général

Chambre de Commerce et d'Industrie du Centre-Abitibi
644, 1e av ouest, Amos QC J9T 1V3
Tél: 819-732-8100; *Téléc:* 819-732-8131
info@ccica.ca
ccica.ca

Joanne Breton, Directrice générale

Chambre de commerce et d'industrie du Coeur-du-Québec
17905, boul des Acadiens, Bécancour QC G9H 1M4
Tél: 819-294-6010; *Téléc:* 819-294-6020
Ligne sans frais: 877-994-6010
info@ccicq.ca
www.ccicq.ca

Chantal Lafond, Présidente

Chambre de commerce et d'industrie du Haut St-Maurice
547-C, rue Commerciale, La Tuque QC G9X 3A7
Tél: 819-523-9933; *Téléc:* 819-523-9939
cchsm@lino.com
www.ccihsm.ca

Mélanie Ricard, Présidente
Manon Côté, Directrice générale

Chambre de commerce et d'industrie du secteur Normandin
1048, rue St-Cyrille, Normandin QC G8M 4R9
Tél: 418-274-2004; *Téléc:* 418-274-7171
ccinormandin@hotmail.com

Nicole Bilodeau, Directrice générale

Chambre de commerce et d'industrie du Sud-Ouest de Montréal
#32, 410, av Lafleur, Montréal QC H8R 3H6
Tél: 514-365-4575; *Téléc:* 514-365-0487
info@ccisom.ca
www.ccisom.ca

Affiliation(s): Chambre de commerce du Canada; Fédération des Chambres de commerce du Québec
Bernard Blanchet, Directeur général

Chambre de commerce et d'industrie Lac-Saint-Jean-Est
640, rue Côté-Ouest, Alma QC G8B 7S8
Tél: 418-662-2734; *Téléc:* 418-669-2220
cci@ccilacsaintjeanest.com
www.ccilacsaintjeanest.com

Kathleen Voyer, Directrice générale

Chambre de commerce et d'industrie Magog-Orford
355, rue Principale ouest, Magog QC J1X 2B1
Tél: 819-843-3494; *Téléc:* 819-769-0292
info@ccimo.qc.ca
www.ccimagogorford.com

Louise Côté, Coprésidente
Éric Graveson, Coprésident

Chambre de commerce et d'industrie MRC de Deux-Montagne (CCI2M)
67A, boul Industriel, Saint-Eustache QC J7R 5B9
Tél: 450-491-1991; *Téléc:* 450-491-1648
info@chambrecommerce.com
www.chambrecommerce.com

Affiliation(s): Chambre de Commerce du Québec
Mélanie Laroche, Directrice générale

Chambre de commerce et d'industrie Nouvelle-Beauce (CCINB)
700, rue Notre-Dame nord, #C, Sainte-Marie QC G6E 2K9
Tél: 418-387-2006; *Ligne sans frais:* 866-387-2006
info@ccinb.ca
www.ccinb.ca

Nancy Labbé, Directrice générale

Chambre de commerce et d'industrie Rimouski-Neigette
#101, 125, rue de l'Évêché ouest, Rimouski QC G5L 4H4
Tél: 418-722-4494; *Téléc:* 418-722-4494
info@ccrimouski.com
www.ccrimouski.com

Chantal Pilon, Présidente

Chambre de commerce et d'industrie secteur Saint-Félicien inc.
CP 34, 1209, boul Sacré-Coeur, Saint-Félicien QC G8K 2P8
Tél: 418-679-2097

Marco Dallaire, Vice-président

Chambre de commerce et d'industrie St-Jérôme (CCISJ)
#20, 236, rue de Parent, Saint-Jérôme QC J7Z 1Z7
Tél: 450-431-4339; *Téléc:* 450-431-1677
www.ccisj.qc.ca

Michel Métivier, Directeur général

Chambre de commerce et d'industrie Thérèse-De Blainville (CCITB)
#202, 141, rue St-Charles, Sainte-Thérèse QC J7E 2A9
Tél: 450-435-8228; *Téléc:* 450-435-0820
info@ccitb.ca
www.ccitb.ca
www.youtube.com/user/CCITB85

Cynthia Kabis, Directrice générale

Chambre de commerce et d'industrie Vaudreuil-Soulanges
450, rue Aimé-Vincent, 2e étage, Vaudreuil-Dorion QC J7V 5V5
Tél: 450-424-6886; *Téléc:* 450-424-4989
info@ccivs.ca
www.ccivs.ca

Nadine Lachance, Directrice générale

Chambre de commerce et d'industries de Trois-Rivières
CP 1045, #200, 225, rue des Forges, Trois-Rivières QC G9A 5K4
Tél: 819-375-9628; *Téléc:* 819-375-9083
info@ccitr.net
www.ccitr.net

Marie-Pier Matteau, Directrice générale

Chambre de Commerce et d'Industries Saguenay - Le Fjord
201 - 365, rue Racine est, Chicoutimi QC G7H 1S6
Tél: 418-543-5941
info@ccisf.ca
www.ccisf.ca

Sandra Rossignol, Directrice générale

Chambre de commerce et de tourisme de Gaspé
27, boul de York est, Gaspé QC G4X 2K9
Tél: 418-368-8525
info@cctgaspe.org
cctgaspe.org

Olivier Nolleau, Directeur général

Chambre de commerce et de tourisme de la Vallée de Saint-Sauveur/Piedmont
30, rue Filion, Saint-Sauveur QC J0R 1R0
Tél: 450-227-2564; *Téléc:* 450-227-6480
Ligne sans frais: 877-528-2553
info@valleesaintsauveur.com
www.valleesaintsauveur.com

Pierre Urquhart, Directeur général

Chambre de commerce et de tourisme de St-Adolphe-d'Howard
c/o Imagine Coiffure, #201, 1937, ch du Village, Saint-Adolphe-d'Howard QC J0T 2B0
Tél: 819-327-3845
www.st-adolphe.com

Michèle Nihoul, Présidente

Chambre de commerce et industrie Mont-Joli-Mitis
CP 183, 1553, boul Jacques-Cartier, Mont-Joli QC G5H 3K9
Tél: 418-775-4366
info@ccimontjolimitis.com
www.ccimontjolimitis.com

Pierre-Luc Harrison, Président

Chambre de commerce Haute-Yamaska et Région (CCHYR)
650, rue Principale, Granby QC J2G 8L4
Tél: 450-372-6100; *Téléc:* 450-696-1119
info@cchyr.ca
www.cchyr.ca

Sylvain Perron, Président

Chambre de commerce Kamouraska-L'Islet (CCKL)
#208, 1000 - 6e av, La Pocatière QC G0R 1Z0
Tél: 418-856-6227; *Téléc:* 418-856-6462
Ligne sans frais: 877-856-6227
cckl@qc.aira.com
www.cckl.org

Élizabeth Hudon, Présidente

Chambre de commerce LGBT du Québec (CCLGBTQ) / The Québec LGBT Chamber of Commerce
#303.3, 372, rue Sainte-Catherine ouest, Montréal QC H3B 1A2
Tél: 514-522-1885
info@cclgbtq.org
www.cclgbtq.org

Steve Foster, Président

Chambre de commerce Mont-Saint-Bruno (CCMSB)
CP 123, Saint-Bruno QC J3V 4P8
Tél: 450-653-0585; *Téléc:* 450-653-6967
info@ccstbruno.ca

Affiliation(s): Chambre de commerce du Québec; Chambre de commerce du Canada
Daniel Tousignant, CGA, Président
Denis Lamothe, Directeur général

Chambre de commerce MRC du Rocher-Percé
#121-2, 129, boul René-Levesque ouest, Chandler QC G0C 1K0
Tél: 418-689-6998
ccrocherperce@gmail.com
www.ccrocherperce.org

Sandrine Rampeneaux, Présidente

Chambre de commerce Notre-Dame-du-Nord
3, rue Principale sud, Notre-Dame-du-Nord QC J0Z 3B0
Tél: 819-723-2586

Chambre de commerce région de Matane
CP 518, Matane QC G4W 3P5
Tél: 418-562-9344
info@ccmatane.com
www.ccmatane.com

Marc Charest, Président

Chambre de commerce région de Mégantic
4336, rue Laval, Lac-Mégantic QC G6B 1B8
Tél: 819-583-5392
info@ccrmeg.com
www.ccrmeg.com

Marc-Olivier Gagnon, Président

Chambre de commerce régionale de St-Raymond (CCRSR)
#100, 1, av St-Jacques, Saint-Raymond QC G3L 3Y1
Tél: 418-337-4049; *Téléc:* 418-337-8017
ccrsr@cite.net
www.ccrsr.qc.ca

Jean-François Drolet, Président

Chambre de commerce régionale de Windsor
CP 115, Windsor QC J1S 2L7
Tél: 819-434-5936
info@ccrwindsor.com
www.ccrwindsor.com

Serge Ranger, Président

Chambre de commerce Ste-Émélie-de-l'Énergie
400, rue St-Michel, Sainte-Émélie-de-l'Énergie QC J0K 2K0
Tél: 450-886-1658

Chambre de commerce Saint-Lin-Laurentides
#101, 704, rue St-Isidore, Saint-Lin-Laurentides QC J5M 2V2
Tél: 450-439-3704; *Téléc:* 450-439-2066
André Corbeil, Président

Chambre de commerce secteur ouest de Portneuf
150, rue Joseph, Saint-Marc-des-Carrières QC G0A 4B0
Tél: 418-268-5447
ccsop@portneufouest.com
www.portneufouest.com

Pascal Lemercier, Communication et services aux membres

Chambre de commerce St-Félix de Valois
5306, rue Principale, Saint-Félix-de-Valois QC J0K 2M0
Tél: 450-889-8161; *Téléc:* 450-889-1590
ccst-flx@stfelixdevalois.qc.ca
www.stfelixdevalois.qc.ca

Johanne Dufresne, Directrice générale

Chambre de commerce St-Jean-de-Matha
185, rue Laurent, Saint-Jean-de-Matha QC J0K 2S0
Tél: 450-886-0599; *Téléc:* 450-886-3123
info@chambrematha.com
www.chambrematha.com

Steve Adam, Président par intérim
Mélanie Paquin, Directrice

Chambre de commerce St-Martin de Beauce
CP 2022, 131, 1e av est, Saint-Martin QC G0M 1B0
Tél: 418-382-5549
chambre@st-martin.qc.ca
www.st-martin.qc.ca
Affiliation(s): Chambre de commerce du Québec; Chambre de
commerce du Canada
Pascal Bergeron, Président

Chambre de commerce Témis-Accord
1E, rue Notre-Dame, Ville-Marie QC J9V 1W3
Tél: 819-629-2918
dg@temis-accord.com
www.temis-accord.com
Véronic Girard, Co-Présidente
Alexandre Touzin, Co-Président

**Chambre de commerce Témiscaming-Kipawa
(CCTK)**
CP 442, 15, rue Principale, Kipawa QC J0Z 2H0
Tél: 819-627-6160
cctk.info@gmail.com
www.temiscaming.net
Guylaine Létourneau, Présidente

Chambre de commerce Vallée de la Missisquoi
Rte 245, Bolton Centre QC J0E 1G0
Tél: 450-292-4217; Téléc: 450-292-4224

Chambre de commerce Vallée de la Petite-Nation
185, rue Henri-Bourassa, Papineauville QC J0V 1R0
Tél: 819-427-8450
direction.ccvpn@videotron.ca
www.ccvpn.org
Jean Careau, Directeur général

Jeune chambre de commerce de Montréal (JCCM)
#700, 1435, rue Saint-Alexandre, Montréal QC H3A 2G4
info@jccm.org
www.jccm.org
Sandrine Archambault, Directrice générale

Jeune chambre de commerce de Québec
#249, 4600, boul Henri-Bourassa, Québec QC G1H 3A5
Tél: 418-622-6937
jccq@jccq.qc.ca
www.jccq.qc.ca
www.youtube.com/user/JeunechambredeQuebec
Justine Audy, Présidente
Virginie Gourdeau, Directrice générale par intérim

**Jewish Chamber of Commerce / Chambre de
commerce juive**
1, carré Cummings, Montréal QC H3W 1M6
Tél: 514-345-2645
info@jccmontreal.com
www.jccmontreal.com
Elana Minz, Director

**Organisme de développement d'affaires
commerciales et économiques (ODACE)**
924, rue King est, Sherbrooke QC J1G 1E2
Tél: 819-565-7991; Téléc: 819-565-3160
info@odace.quebec
www.odace.quebec
Louis Longchamps, Directeur général

Pontiac Chamber of Commerce
131A, rue Victoria, Shawville QC J0X 2Y0
Tel: 819-647-2312; Toll-Free: 855-647-2312
info@pontiacchamberofcommerce.ca
www.pontiacchamberofcommerce.ca
Mireille Alary, President

**Regroupement des jeunes chambres de commerce
du Québec (RJCCQ)**
#1100, 555, boul René-Lévesque ouest, 11e étage, Montréal
QC H2Z 1B1
Tél: 514-933-7595
info@rjccq.com
rjccq.com
www.youtube.com/user/RJCCQ
Guillaum Dubreuil, Président

Saskatchewan

Assiniboia & District Chamber of Commerce (SK)
PO Box 1803, Assiniboia SK S0H 0B0
Tel: 306-642-5553; Fax: 306-642-3529
www.assiniboia.net/business/chamber_of_commerce.html
Glen Hall, Chief Administration Officer

Battlefords Chamber of Commerce
PO Box 1000, Hwy. 16 & 40 East, North Battleford SK S9A
3E6
Tel: 306-445-6226; Fax: 306-446-0188
b.chamber@sasktel.net
www.battlefordschamber.com
Affiliation(s): Institution of Association Executives; Tourism
Industry Association of Saskatchewan
Brendon Bootman, President
Linda Machniak, Executive Director

Big River Chamber of Commerce
PO Box 159, Big River SK S0J 0E0
Tel: 306-469-2124; Fax: 306-469-4409

Biggar & District Chamber of Commerce
PO Box 489, 202 - 3rd Ave. West, Biggar SK S0K 0M0
Tel: 306-948-3317; Fax: 306-948-5134
townofbiggar.com

Blaine Lake & District Chamber of Commerce
c/o Blaine Lake Town Office, PO Box 10, Blaine Lake SK S0J
0J0
Tel: 306-497-2531; Fax: 306-497-2511
blainelakecofc@sasktel.net
www.blainelake.ca/business/chamber.html

Buffalo Narrows Chamber of Commerce
PO Box 430, Buffalo Narrows SK S0M 0J0
Tel: 306-235-7442; Fax: 306-235-4416

Choiceland & District Chamber of Commerce
c/o Town of Choiceland, PO Box 279, 115 - 1st St. East,
Choiceland SK S0J 0M0
Tel: 306-428-2070; Fax: 306-428-2071

Coronach Community Chamber of Commerce
PO Box 577, Coronach SK S0H 0Z0
Tel: 306-267-2077; Fax: 306-267-2047
Affiliation(s): Saskatchewan Chamber of Commerce
J. Marshall, President
S. Nelson, Secretary

Cut Knife Chamber of Commerce
PO Box 629, Cut Knife SK S0M 0N0
Tel: 306-398-2060; Fax: 306-398-2062

Debden & District Chamber of Commerce
PO Box 91, Debden SK S0J 0S0
Tel: 306-724-4414; Fax: 306-724-2220
www.debden.net
Rhonda Peterson, President
Amelie Patrick, Secretary

Eastend & District Chamber of Commerce
PO Box 534, Eastend SK S0N 0T0
Tel: 306-295-4070; Fax: 306-295-3883

Eatonia & District Chamber of Commerce
PO Box 370, Eatonia SK S0L 0Y0
Tel: 306-967-2582; Fax: 306-967-2267

Esterhazy & District Chamber of Commerce
PO Box 490, Esterhazy SK S0A 0X0
Tel: 306-745-5405; Fax: 306-745-6797

Estevan Chamber of Commerce
#2, 322 - 4th St., Estevan SK S4A 0T8
Tel: 306-634-2828; Fax: 306-634-6729
admin@estevanchamber.ca
www.estevanchamber.ca
Jackie Wall, Executive Director

Foam Lake & District Chamber of Commerce
PO Box 238, Foam Lake SK S0A 1A0
Tel: 306-272-4191
Jim Kurtz, President

Fort Qu'Appelle & District Chamber of Commerce
PO Box 1273, Fort Qu'Appelle SK S0G 1S0
Tel: 306-332-7930
FQChamber@hotmail.com

Fox Valley Chamber of Commerce
c/o Delia Hughes, PO Box 72, Fox Valley SK S0N 0V0
Delia E. Hughes, Contact

Goodsoil & District Chamber of Commerce
PO Box 157, Goodsoil SK S0M 1A0
Tel: 306-238-4747; Fax: 306-238-4633

Gravelbourg Chamber of Commerce
PO Box 5, Gravelbourg SK S0H 1X0
Tel: 306-648-7559
gravelbourgchamber@gmail.com
gravelbourg.ca

Fred Hundersmarck, President

Greater Saskatoon Chamber of Commerce
#104, 202 - 4th Ave. North, Saskatoon SK S7K 0K1
Tel: 306-244-2151; Fax: 306-244-8366
chamber@saskatoonchamber.com
www.saskatoonchamber.com
Affiliation(s): Enterprise Centre; Leadership Saskatoon; Raj
Manek Mentorship Program; Saskatchewan Agrivision
Corporation; Saskatchewan Economic Development Authority;
Saskatchewan Young Professionals & Entrepreneurs;
Saskatoon Aboriginal Employment & Business Opportunities
Inc., Saskatoon Air Services; Saskatoon Regional Economic
Development Authority; Tourism Saskatoon; United Way of
Saskatoon; Vision 2000
Kent Smith-Windsor, Executive Director

Herbert & District Chamber of Commerce
PO Box 700, Herbert SK S0H 2A0
Tel: 306-784-2588

Hudson Bay Chamber of Commerce
PO Box 730, Hudson Bay SK S0E 0Y0
www.townofhudsonbay.com
Corinne Reine, President
Janice Dyck, Secretary

Humboldt & District Chamber of Commerce
PO Box 1440, Humboldt SK S0K 2A0
Tel: 306-682-4990; Fax: 306-682-5203
admin@humboldtchamber.ca
www.humboldtchamber.ca
www.youtube.com/user/humboldtchamber
Debra Nyczai, Executive Director

Kamsack & District Chamber of Commerce
PO Box 817, Kamsack SK S0A 1S0
Tel: 306-542-3553; Fax: 306-542-3553

Kenaston & District Chamber of Commerce
PO Box 70, Kenaston SK S0G 2N0
www.kenaston.ca/pages/chamber.htm
Susan Anbolt, Sec.-Treas.
Mary Lou Whittles, President

Kerrobert Chamber of Commerce
433 Manitoba Ave., Kerrobert SK S0L 1R0
Tel: 306-834-5423
kerrobertchamber@sasktel.net
www.kerrobertsk.com
Darryl Morris, President

Kindersley Chamber of Commerce
PO Box 1537, 605 Main St., Kindersley SK S0L 1S0
Tel: 306-463-2320; Fax: 306-463-2312
kindersleychamber@sasktel.net
www.kindersleychamber.com
Heather Wall, Office Manager

Kinistino & District Chamber of Commerce
PO Box 803, Kinistino SK S0J 1H0
Tel: 306-864-2244; Fax: 306-864-2244

Kipling Chamber of Commerce
PO Box 700, Kipling SK S0G 2S0
Tel: 306-736-9065; Fax: 306-736-2962
www.townofkipling.ca/business/chamber-of-commerce
Buck Bright, Secretary
Tammy Frater, Chair

Landis & District Chamber of Commerce
PO Box 400, Landis SK S0K 2K0
Tel: 306-658-2100; Fax: 306-658-4455

Langenburg & District Chamber of Commerce
PO Box 610, Langenburg SK S0A 2A0
Tel: 306-743-2231; Fax: 306-743-2873

Lumsden & District Chamber of Commerce
PO Box 114, Lumsden SK S0G 3C0
Tel: 306-731-2862

Macklin Chamber of Commerce
PO Box 642, Macklin SK S0L 2C0
Tel: 306-753-9394; Fax: 306-753-2849
www.macklinchamber.com
Christy Veller, President

Maidstone & District Chamber of Commerce
PO Box 208, Maidstone SK S0M 1M0
Tel: 306-893-2373; Fax: 306-893-4378
maidstonechamberofcommerce@gmail.com

Maple Creek Chamber of Commerce
PO Box 1766, Maple Creek SK S0N 1N0
Tel: 306-662-8119; *Fax:* 306-662-4005
info@maplecreekchamber.ca
www.maplecreekchamber.ca
Blaine Filthaut, President

Meadow Lake & District Chamber of Commerce
PO Box 847, Meadow Lake SK S9X 1Y6
Tel: 306-236-4061; *Fax:* 306-236-4031
Affiliation(s): Northwest Regional Economic Development
Authority

Melfort & District Chamber of Commerce
PO Box 2002, 102 Spruce Haven Rd., Melfort SK S0E 1A0
Tel: 306-752-4636; *Fax:* 306-752-9505
melfortchamber@sasktel.net
www.melfortchamber.com
Warren Salen, President

Melville & District Chamber of Commerce
PO Box 429, 76 Halifax Ave., Melville SK S0A 2P0
Tel: 306-728-4177
melvillechamber@sasktel.net
www.melvillechamber.com
Joe Kirwan, President

Moose Jaw & District Chamber of Commerce
88 Saskatchewan St. East, Moose Jaw SK S6H 0V4
Tel: 306-692-6414; *Fax:* 306-694-6463
chamber@mjchamber.com
www.mjchamber.com
Rob Clark, CEO
Heather Bergdahl, Office Administrator

Moosomin Chamber of Commerce
PO Box 819, Moosomin SK S0G 3N0
Tel: 306-435-2445
www.moosomin.com/chamber
Kevin Weedmark, Secretary
Janelle Davidson, Treasurer

Nipawin & District Chamber of Commerce
PO Box 177, Nipawin SK S0E 1E0
Tel: 306-862-5252; *Fax:* 306-862-5350
nipawin.chamber@sasktel.net
www.nipawinchamber.ca
Mark Knox, President

Norquay & District Chamber of Commerce
PO Box 327, Norquay SK S0A 2V0
Tel: 306-594-2101; *Fax:* 306-594-2347
www.norquay.ca
Kevin Ebert, President

Outlook & District Chamber of Commerce
PO Box 431, Outlook SK S0L 2N0
Tel: 306-867-9580; *Fax:* 306-867-9559
outlookchamber@gmail.com
outlookchamber.webs.com
Justin Turton, Executive President
Ken Fehr, Executive Treasurer

Paradise Hill Chamber of Commerce
c/o Village of Paradise Hill, PO Box 270, Paradise Hill SK
S0M 2G0
Tel: 306-344-2206
www.paradisehill.ca
George Palen, President

Prince Albert & District Chamber of Commerce
3700 - 2nd Ave. West, Prince Albert SK S6W 1A2
Tel: 306-764-6222; *Fax:* 306-922-4727
chamberpa@sasktel.net
www.princealbertchamber.com
Affiliation(s): Canadian Chamber of Commerce; Saskatchewan
Chamber of Commerce
Gordon Jahn, Chair
Larry Fladager, CEO

Radville Chamber of Commerce
PO Box 799, Radville SK S0C 2G0
Tel: 306-869-2610

Redvers Chamber of Commerce
PO Box 249, Redvers SK S0C 2H0
Tel: 306-452-8844
redverschamberofcommerce@gmail.com
www.redvers.ca
Kim Krainyk, Contact

Regina & District Chamber of Commerce
2145 Albert St., Regina SK S4P 2V1
Tel: 306-757-4658; *Fax:* 306-757-4668
info@reginachamber.com
www.reginachamber.com
www.youtube.com/ReginaChamber
Affiliation(s): Canadian Chamber of Commerce; Saskatchewan
Chamber of Commerce
John Hopkins, CEO
Nadia Williamson, Chair

Riverbend District Chamber of Commerce
PO Box 397, Radisson SK S0K 3L0
Tel: 306-827-4801; *Fax:* 306-827-2218
riverbendchamber.weebly.com
Gerald Wiebe, President

La Ronge & District Chamber of Commerce
PO Box 1493, La Ronge SK S0J 1L0
chamber@laclarongechamber.ca
www.laclarongechamber.ca
Matthew Klassen, President
Lynnette Merriman, Treasurer

Rosetown & District Chamber of Commerce
PO Box 744, Rosetown SK S0L 2V0
Tel: 306-882-1300
rosetownchamber@gmail.com
www.rosetownchamber.com
Kimiko Shimoda, President

St. Walburg Chamber of Commerce
PO Box 501, St Walburg SK S0M 2T0
Tel: 306-248-4681
info@stwalburg.com
www.stwalburg.com
Ali Schmidt, President

Shaunavon Chamber of Commerce
PO Box 1048, Shaunavon SK S0N 2M0
Tel: 306-297-7383
shaunavonchamber@hotmail.com
www.shaunavon.com/?p=980
Joanne Gregoire, President
Kathy Wilkins, Vice-President

Spiritwood Chamber of Commerce
PO Box 267, Spiritwood SK S0J 2M0
Tel: 306-883-2426

Swift Current & District Chamber of Commerce
145 - 1st Ave. NE, Swift Current SK S9H 2B1
Tel: 306-773-7268; *Fax:* 306-773-5686
info@swiftcurrentchamber.ca
www.swiftcurrentchamber.ca
Affiliation(s): Saskatchewan Chamber of Commerce; Canadian
Chamber of Commerce
Clayton Wicks, CEO

Tisdale & District Chamber of Commerce
PO Box 219, 520 93rd Ave., Tisdale SK S0E 1T0
Tel: 306-873-4257
tisdalechamber@sasktel.net
tisdalechamber.ca
Rachelle Casavant, Executive Director

Unity & District Chamber of Commerce
PO Box 834, Unity SK S0K 4L0
Tel: 306-228-2688; *Fax:* 306-228-4229
www.townofunity.com
Helena Long, President
Kristine Moon, Treasurer

Vonda Chamber of Commerce
c/o Vonda Hometown Insurance Brokers, PO Box 285,
Vonda SK S0K 4N0
Tel: 306-221-0559

Waskesiu Chamber of Commerce
PO Box 216, Waskesiu Lake SK S0J 2Y0
Tel: 306-663-5140; *Fax:* 306-663-5448
wakesiuchamber@sasktel.net
www.waskesiulake.ca
George Wilson, Manager

Watrous & District Chamber of Commerce
PO Box 906, Watrous SK S0K 4T0
Tel: 306-946-3353; *Fax:* 306-946-3966

Watson & District Chamber of Commerce
PO Box 686, Watson SK S0K 4V0
Tel: 306-287-3659; *Fax:* 306-287-3601

Weyburn Chamber of Commerce
11 - 3rd St. NE, Weyburn SK S4H 0W5
Tel: 306-842-4738; *Fax:* 306-842-0520
www.weyburnchamber.com
Affiliation(s): Saskatchewan Chamber of Commerce
Rodney Gill, President

Wynyard & District Chamber of Commerce
PO Box 508, Wynyard SK S0A 4T0
Tel: 306-554-3363; *Fax:* 306-554-3851

Yorkton Chamber of Commerce
PO Box 1051, Yorkton SK S3N 2X3
Tel: 306-783-4368; *Fax:* 306-786-6978
info@yorktonchamber.com
www.chamber.yorkton.sk.ca
Affiliation(s): Saskatchewan Economic Developers Association
Joel Martinuk, President
Juanita Polegi, Executive Director

Yukon Territory

Dawson City Chamber of Commerce
PO Box 1006, 1102 Front St., Dawson City YT Y0B 1G0
Tel: 867-993-5274; *Fax:* 867-993-6817
office@dawsoncitychamberofcommerce.ca
www.dawsoncitychamberofcommerce.ca
Dick Van Nostrand, President

St. Elias Chamber of Commerce
PO Box 5419, Haines Junction YT Y0B 1L0
Tel: 867-634-2916
kluaneridin@yknet.ca
Paula Pawlovich, President

Silver Trail Chamber of Commerce
PO Box 268, Mayo YT Y0B 1M0
Tel: 867-332-1770
Anne Leckie, Secretary

Teslin Regional Chamber of Commerce
PO Box 181, Teslin YT Y0A 1B0

Watson Lake Chamber of Commerce
c/o Town Office, PO Box 590, 710 Adela Trail, Watson Lake
YT Y0A 1C0
Tel: 867-536-8000; *Fax:* 867-536-7522
www.watsonlakechamber.com
Rick Harder, President

Whitehorse Chamber of Commerce (WCC)
#101, 302 Steele St., Whitehorse YT Y1A 2C5
Tel: 867-667-7545; *Fax:* 867-667-4507
business@whitehorsechamber.ca
www.whitehorsechamber.ca
Affiliation(s): Yukon Chamber of Commerce; Tourism Industry
Association of Yukon
Rick Karp, President

Credit Unions/Caisses Populaires

1st Choice Savings & Credit Union Ltd.
1320 - 3rd Ave. South
Lethbridge, AB T1J 0K5
Tel: 403-320-4600; *Fax:* 403-320-4608
Toll-Free: 866-803-0733
info@1stchoicesavings.ca
www.1stchoicesavings.ca
www.instagram.com/1stchoicesavings
www.facebook.com/1stchoicesavings; twitter.com/1stchoiceCU
Former Name: St. Patrick's Credit Union Ltd.; Southland Credit
Union
Ownership: Public
Year Founded: 2001
Assets: $613,406,102 Year End: 20181231
Revenues: $20,359,569 Year End: 20181231

ABCU Credit Union Ltd.
5007 - 50th Ave.
Beaumont, AB T4X 1E7
Tel: 780-929-8561; *Fax:* 780-929-2999
Toll-Free: 888-929-7511
general@abcu.ca
www.abcu.ca
www.instagram.com/abcu_cu
www.facebook.com/ABCUCreditUnion; twitter.com/abcu_cu
Assets: $295,303,198 Year End: 20201231
Revenues: Under $1 million Year End: 20201231

Acadian Credit Union
PO Box 250
15089 Cabot Trail
Cheticamp, NS B0E 1H0
Tel: 902-224-2055; *Fax:* 902-224-3510
Toll-Free: 877-477-7724
mdisite@acadian.creditu.net
www.acadiancreditu.ca
www.facebook.com/AcadianCU; twitter.com/AcadianCU
Former Name: Cheticamp Credit Union
Ownership: Member-owned
Year Founded: 1935
Number of Employees: 21
Assets: $10-50 million

Accent Credit Union Ltd.
PO Box 520
78 Main St.
Quill Lake, SK S0A 3E0
Tel: 306-382-4155; *Fax:* 306-383-2622
info@accentcu.ca
www.accentcu.ca
Year Founded: 2010

Access Credit Union
Stanley Business Centre
PO Box 1418
#2 - 23111 PTH #14
Winkler, MB R6W 4B4
Tel: 204-325-4351; *Toll-Free:* 800-264-2926
www.accesscu.ca
www.instagram.com/accesscreditunion;
www.facebook.com/AccessCreditUnion; twitter.com/AccessCred
Year Founded: 1950
Assets: $2,858,574,067 Year End: 20191231

Adjala Credit Union Limited
PO Box V1
7320 St. James Lane
Colgan, ON L0G 1W0
Tel: 905-936-2761
info@adjalacu.com
www.adjalacu.com
Year Founded: 1946

Advance Savings Credit Union (ASCU)
141 Weldon St.
Moncton, NB E1C 5W1
Tel: 506-853-8881; *Fax:* 506-856-8492
www.advancesavings.ca
Former Name: Rexton Credit Union; Royal Credit Union; Trico Credit Union
Ownership: Member-owned
Year Founded: 2006
Assets: $50-100 million

Affinity Credit Union
PO Box 1330
Saskatoon, SK S7K 3P4
Tel: 306-934-4000; *Fax:* 306-934-5490
Toll-Free: 866-863-6237
questions@affinitycu.ca
www.affinitycu.ca
www.facebook.com/affinitycu; twitter.com/Affinity_CU
Former Name: St. Mary's Credit Union Limited
Ownership: Member-owned
Year Founded: 1949
Assets: $5,667,555,000 Year End: 20181231
Revenues: $190,991,000 Year End: 20181231

Airline Financial Credit Union Limited
#310, 2720 Britannia Rd. East
Mississauga, ON L4W 2P7
Tel: 905-673-7262; *Fax:* 905-676-8437
Toll-Free: 800-392-5005
info@airlinecreditunion.com
www.airlinecreditunion.ca
Former Name: Airline (Malton) Credit Union Limited
Ownership: Member-owned
Year Founded: 1950
Assets: $10-50 million

Aldergrove Credit Union
3661 - 248th St.
Aldergrove, BC V4W 2B5
Tel: 604-857-9220
hello@aldergrovecu.ca
www.aldergrovecu.ca
www.facebook.com/AldergroveCreditUnion
Former Name: Otter Farmers' Institute Credit Union
Year Founded: 1954
Number of Employees: 125
Assets: $855,620,113

Alterna Savings & Credit Union Limited
319 McRae Ave., 1st Fl.
Ottawa, ON K1Z 0B9
Tel: 613-560-0100; *Toll-Free:* 877-560-0100
www.alterna.ca
Other Contact Information: Qtrade/Alterna Wealth Line,
Toll-Free: 855-731-3901
www.youtube.com/user/AlternaSavings;
www.facebook.com/AlternaSavings; twitter.com/alternasavings
Former Name: Ottawa Women's Credit Union Limited; Civil Service Co-operative Credit Society Ltd.; Metro Credit Union
Also Known As: Alterna Savings
Ownership: Member-owned. Part of the Alterna Financial Group.
Year Founded: 2005
Number of Employees: 600+
Assets: $1-10 billion

Assiniboine Credit Union Limited (ACU)
Corporate Office
PO Box 2, Stn. Main
200 Main St., 6th Fl.
Winnipeg, MB R3C 2G1
Tel: 204-958-8588; *Fax:* 204-958-7348
Toll-Free: 877-958-8588
cu@assiniboine.mb.ca
www.assiniboine.mb.ca
www.facebook.com/298221280375663;
twitter.com/myassiniboine
Ownership: Member-owned
Year Founded: 1943
Number of Employees: 500
Assets: $1-10 billion

Auto Workers' Community Credit Union Limited
PO Box 158
322 King St. West
Oshawa, ON L1H 7L1
Tel: 905-728-5187; *Toll-Free:* 800-268-8771
www.awccu.ca
www.instagram.com/awccu; www.facebook.com/awccu
Also Known As: AWCCU Financial
Ownership: Member-owned
Year Founded: 1938
Revenues: $100-500 million

Bay Credit Union Limited
142 South Algoma St.
Thunder Bay, ON P7B 3B8
Tel: 807-345-7612; *Fax:* 807-345-8939
Toll-Free: 877-249-7076
info@baycreditunion.com
baycreditunion.com
www.instagram.com/baycreditunion;
www.facebook.com/BayCreditUnionLimited;
twitter.com/baycreditunion
Ownership: Member-owned

Bay St Lawrence Credit Union
3019 Bay St. Lawrence Rd.
St Margaret Village, NS B0C 1R0
Tel: 902-383-2003; *Fax:* 902-383-4002
Ownership: Member-owned
Year Founded: 1937
Number of Employees: 4
Revenues: $621568

Bayview Credit Union
#400, 57 King St.
Saint John, NB E2L 1G5
Tel: 506-634-7910; *Fax:* 506-634-7449
www.bayviewnb.com
Other Contact Information: BayLine Telephone Banking,
Toll-Free Phone: 800-342-8255
www.facebook.com/BayviewCU; twitter.com/bayviewcu
Ownership: Member-owned
Year Founded: 1938
Number of Employees: 115
Assets: $397,228,421 Year End: 20181231
Revenues: $13,649,475 Year End: 20181231

Beaubear Credit Union
PO Box 764
376 Water St.
Miramichi, NB E1V 3V4
Tel: 506-622-4532; *Fax:* 506-622-5008
www.beaubear.ca
www.facebook.com/BeaubearCU; twitter.com/BeaubearCU
Ownership: Member-owned
Year Founded: 1938
Assets: $59,233,306 Year End: 20181213
Revenues: $2,228,288 Year End: 20181213

Belgian-Alliance Credit Union
1177 Portage Ave.
Winnipeg, MB R3G 0T2
Tel: 204-927-0460
info@bacumail.ca
www.belgianalliancecu.mb.ca
Former Name: Alliance Credit Union; Adanac Credit Union Ltd; Communicators Credit Union; Progress Vera Credit Union
Year Founded: 2008
Assets: $221,514,287 Year End: 20191231

Bengough Credit Union Ltd.
260 Main St.
Bengough, SK S0C 0K0
Toll-Free: 877-803-0505
info@bengough.cu.sk.ca
www.bengough.cu.sk.ca
Year Founded: 1943
Assets: $67,485,211 Year End: 20191231

Biggar & District Credit Union Ltd.
302 Main St.
Biggar, SK S0K 0M0
Tel: 306-948-3352; *Fax:* 306-948-2053
www.biggarcu.com
www.facebook.com/BiggarCU
Ownership: Member-owned
Assets: $192,244,787 Year End: 20181231
Revenues: $5-10 million Year End: 20181231

Blackville Credit Union
128 Main St.
Blackville, NB E9B 1P1
Tel: 506-843-2219; *Fax:* 506-843-6773
Ownership: Member-owned
Year Founded: 1936

Blue Shore Financial
1250 Lonsdale Ave.
North Vancouver, BC V7M 2H6
Tel: 604-982-8000; *Fax:* 604-985-6810
Toll-Free: 888-713-6728
info@blueshorefinancial.com
www.blueshorefinancial.com
www.youtube.com/c/Blueshorefinancial;
www.facebook.com/blueshorefinancial;
twitter.com/blueshorenews
Former Name: North Shore Credit Union
Year Founded: 1941
Assets: $4,841,084,000 Year End: 20201231

Bow Valley Credit Union Limited
PO Box 876
212 - 5th Ave. West
Cochrane, AB T4C 1A9
Toll-Free: 800-207-0068
www.bowvalleycu.com
www.facebook.com/BowValleyCU
Ownership: Member-owned
Assets: $363,744,315 Year End: 20190831

Bruno Savings & Credit Union Limited
PO Box 158
511 Main St.
Bruno, SK S0K 0S0
Tel: 306-369-2901; *Fax:* 306-369-2225
brunocu.com
Ownership: Member-owned
Assets: $82,851,412 Year End: 20191231

Buduchnist Credit Union (BCU)
2280 Bloor St. West
Toronto, ON M6S 1N9
Fax: 416-763-4512
Toll-Free: 800-461-5941
info@buduchnist.com
www.buduchnist.com
Other Contact Information: Help Desk, Email:
help@buduchnist.com; Branch Operations, Email:
operations@buduchnist.com
www.facebook.com/BCUFinancial
Ownership: Member-owned
Year Founded: 1952

Bulkley Valley Credit Union
PO Box 3637
3872 - 1st Ave.
Smithers, BC V0J 2N0
Tel: 250-847-3255; *Fax:* 250-847-3012
infoadmin@bvcu.com
www.bvcu.com
www.facebook.com/BulkleyValleyCreditUnion
Year Founded: 1941
Assets: $474,524,860 Year End: 20201231

Caisse Desjardins Ontario
#310, 1173, ch Cyrville
Ottawa, ON K1J 7S6
Tél: 613-747-4800; *Téléc:* 613-747-2691
www.desjardins.com/ca/your-credit-union/ontario/index.jsp
Ownership: A subsidiary of the Desjardins Group
Year Founded: 1946

Caisse Groupe Financier/Caisse Financial Group
Corporate Office
#400, 205 Provencher Blvd.
Winnipeg, MB R2H 0G4
Tél: 204-237-8988; *Téléc:* 204-233-6405
Ligne sans frais: 866-926-0706
info@caisse.biz
www.caisse.biz
www.facebook.com/caissefinancialgroup
Former Name: Fédération des caisses populaires du Manitoba inc.
Also Known As: Caisse Populaire Groupe Financier Ltée
Ownership: Member-owned
Year Founded: 2010
Number of Employees: 250
Assets: $1-10 billion

Caisse populaire Alliance limitée
PO Box 3500
1870 Bond St.
North Bay, ON P1B 4V6
Tel: 705-474-5634; *Fax:* 705-474-5326
support@acpol.com
www.caissealliance.com
www.facebook.com/174831179214242
Former Name: L'Alliance des caisses populaires de l'Ontario limitée
Ownership: Member-owned.
Year Founded: 1979
Number of Employees: 240
Assets: $500m-1 billion
Revenues: $10-50 million

Caisse populaire d'Alban limitée
PO Box 40
#21 Delamere Rd.
Alban, ON P0M 1A0
Tel: 705-857-2082; *Fax:* 705-857-3181
www.caissealliance.com/en/caisses/alban
Ownership: Member-owned

Caisse populaire de Bonfield limitée
230 Yonge St.
Bonfield, ON P0H 1E0
Tel: 705-776-2831; *Fax:* 705-776-1023
www.caissealliance.com/en/caisses/bonfield
Ownership: Member-owned

Caisse populaire de Clare
Administration Office
CP 99
1726, route 1
Church Point, NS B0W 1M0
Tél: 902-769-5312; *Téléc:* 902-769-5500
Ligne sans frais: 888-273-3488
cpcinfo@caissepopclare.com
www.caissepopclare.com
twitter.com/caissepopclare
Former Name: Caisse populaire de Saulnierville
Ownership: Member-owned
Assets: $50-100 million

Caisse populaire de Hearst limitée
PO Box 698
908 Prince St.
Hearst, ON P0L 1N0
Tel: 705-362-4308; *Toll-Free:* 888-362-4308
caissepopulairedehearst@gmail.com
www.caissepopulairedehearst-en.com
www.facebook.com/CaissepopulairedeHearst
Ownership: Member-owned

Caisse populaire de Mattawa limitée
PO Box 519
370 Main St.
Mattawa, ON P0H 1V0
Tel: 705-744-5561; *Fax:* 705-744-5168
www.caissealliance.com/en/caisses/mattawa
Ownership: Member-owned

Caisse populaire de Mattice limitée
PO Box 178
249 King St.
Mattice, ON P0L 1T0
Tel: 705-364-4441; *Fax:* 705-364-2013
www.caissealliance.com/en/caisses/mattice

Ownership: Member-owned

Caisse populaire de Noëlville limitée
87 David St. North
Noëlville, ON P0M 2N0
Tel: 705-898-2350; *Fax:* 705-898-3265
www.caissealliance.com/en/caisses/noelville
Ownership: Member-owned

Caisse populaire de Timmins limitée
45 Mountjoy St. North
Timmins, ON P4N 8H7
Tel: 705-268-9724; *Fax:* 705-268-6858
www.caissealliance.com/en/caisses/timmins
www.facebook.com/caissetimmins
Ownership: Member-owned

Caisse populaire de Verner limitée
PO Box 119
1 Principale St. East
Verner, ON P0H 2M0
Tel: 705-594-2388; *Fax:* 705-594-9423
Toll-Free: 855-590-2388
www.caissealliance.com/en/caisses/verner
Ownership: Member-owned

Caisse populaire Kapuskasing limitée
Main Branch & Administration Office
36 Riverside Dr.
Kapuskasing, ON P5N 1A6
Tel: 705-335-6161; *Fax:* 705-335-2707
adjointe.cpkap@gmail.com
www.en.cpkap.com
www.facebook.com/cpkap
Ownership: Member-owned

Caisse populaire North Bay limitée
630 Cassells St.
North Bay, ON P1B 4A2
Tel: 705-474-5650; *Fax:* 705-474-5687
www.caissealliance.com/en/caisses/north-bay
Ownership: Member-owned

Caisse populaire St. Charles limitée
15 King St. East
St Charles, ON P0M 2W0
Tel: 705-867-2002; *Fax:* 705-867-5710
www.caissealliance.com/en/caisses/st-charles
Ownership: Member-owned

Caisse populaire Sturgeon Falls limitée
241 King St.
Sturgeon Falls, ON P2B 1S1
Tel: 705-753-2970; *Fax:* 705-753-2986
www.caissealliance.com/en/caisses/sturgeon-falls
Ownership: Member-owned

Cambrian Credit Union Ltd.
225 Broadway
Winnipeg, MB R3C 5R4
Tel: 204-925-2600; *Toll-Free:* 888-695-8900
ccuinfo@cambrian.mb.ca
www.cambrian.mb.ca
Other Contact Information: Lost or Stolen Member Cards,
Toll-Free: 888-277-1043
www.facebook.com/CambrianCreditUnion;
twitter.com/CambrianCU
Ownership: Member-owned
Year Founded: 1959
Assets: $1-10 billion

Canadian Credit Union Association (CCUA)(ACCF)
#2301A, 20 Queen St. West
Toronto, ON M5H 3R3
Tel: 416-232-1262; *Fax:* 416-232-9196
Toll-Free: 800-649-0222
inquiries@ccua.com
www.cucentral.ca
Other Contact Information: Alt. Emails: conferences@ccua.com;
webinars@ccua.com
www.facebook.com/CCUA.ACCF; twitter.com/CCUA_ACCF
Former Name: Credit Union Central of Canada
Ownership: Owned by the provincial credit union centrals
Year Founded: 1953
Number of Employees: 46
Assets: 9,014,099 Year End: 20181231
Revenues: 21,054,286 Year End: 20181231

Cape Breton Credit Union
135 Reserve St.
Glace Bay, NS B1A 4W3
Tel: 902-849-7610; *Fax:* 902-842-0911
cbcu.ca
Former Name: Coady Credit Union; Steel Centre Credit Union
Ownership: Member-owned

Year Founded: 2017
Number of Employees: 24

Carpathia Credit Union
952 Main St., 3rd Fl.
Winnipeg, MB R2W 3P4
Tel: 204-989-7400; *Fax:* 204-989-7715
info@carpathiacu.mb.ca
www.carpathiacu.mb.ca
www.facebook.com/CarpathiaCU; twitter.com/CarpathiaCU
Ownership: Member-owned
Year Founded: 1940
Assets: $500,780,503 Year End: 20181231
Revenues: $17,152,436 Year End: 20181231

Casera Credit Union
1300 Plessis Rd.
Winnipeg, MB R2C 2Y6
Tel: 204-958-6300; *Fax:* 204-222-6766
Toll-Free: 866-211-9233
talktous@caseracu.ca
www.caseracu.ca
www.facebook.com/CaseraCU; twitter.com/caseracu
Also Known As: Transcona Credit Union
Ownership: Member-owned
Year Founded: 1951
Assets: $421,920,017 Year End: 20191231

CCEC Credit Union
2248 Commercial Dr.
Vancouver, BC V5N 4B5
Tel: 604-254-4100; *Fax:* 604-254-6558
Toll-Free: 866-254-4100
info@ccec.bc.ca
www.ccec.bc.ca
www.instagram.com/cceccreditunion;
www.facebook.com/CCECCreditUnion;
twitter.com/cceccreditunion
Ownership: Cooperative
Year Founded: 1976

Central 1 Credit Union
British Columbia Regional Office
1441 Creekside Dr.
Vancouver, BC V6J 4S7
Tel: 604-734-2511; *Fax:* 604-734-5055
Toll-Free: 800-661-6813
communications@central1.com
www.central1.com
www.youtube.com/c/Central1; www.instagram.com/central1_;
www.facebook.com/Central1CreditUnion; twitter.com/Central1_
Former Name: Credit Union Central of British Columbia
Ownership: Member credit unions
Year Founded: 1944
Number of Employees: 500
Assets: $17,864,000,000 Year End: 20191231
Revenues: $33,000,000 Year End: 20191231

Chinook Financial
#200, 2850 Sunridge Blvd. NE
Calgary, AB T1Y 6G2
www.chinookfinancial.com
www.facebook.com/ChinookFinancial; twitter.com/chinookFin
Ownership: Member-owned. A division of Connect First Credit Union
Assets: $5,690,380,000 Year End: 20181031
Revenues: $121,100,000 Year End: 20181031

Churchbridge Credit Union
PO Box 260
103 Vincent Ave. East
Churchbridge, SK S0A 0M0
Tel: 306-896-2544; *Toll-Free:* 877-890-2797
info@churchbridge.cu.sk.ca
www.churchbridgecu.com
Year Founded: 1945
Assets: $179,605,832 Year End: 20191231

Citizens Credit Union
179 Sunbury Dr.
Fredericton Junction, NS E5L 1R5
Tel: 506-368-9000; *Fax:* 506-368-9003
Toll-Free: 800-963-4848
www.citizenscreditunion.com
Ownership: Member-owned
Year Founded: 1997

Coast Capital Savings Federal Credit Union
Also listed under: Domestic Banks: Schedule I

Corporate Head Office
#800, 9900 King George Blvd.
Surrey, BC V3T 0K7

Tel: 604-517-7000; Toll-Free: 888-517-7000
info@coastcapitalsavings.com
www.coastcapitalsavings.com
www.instagram.com/coast_capital;
www.facebook.com/coastcapitalsavings;
twitter.com/Coast_Capital

Ownership: Member-owned
Year Founded: 2000
Number of Employees: 2,000+
Assets: $21,000,000,000

Coastal Community Credit Union
#220, 59 Wharf St.
Nanaimo, BC V9R 2X3

Toll-Free: 888-741-1010
service@cccu.ca
www.cccu.ca

Other Contact Information: 1-888-741-4040 (Telephone Banking
Toll-Free); 1-800-567-8111 (Lost Member Card, Canada & the
USA); 1-800-567-8111 (Lost MasterCard, Canada & the USA)
www.facebook.com/CoastalCommunityCU; twitter.com/cccu

Ownership: Member-owned
Year Founded: 1946
Number of Employees: 600+
Assets: $1-10 billion

Coastal Financial Credit Union
Administration Office
2 Collins St.
Yarmouth, NS B5A 3C3

Tel: 902-742-7322; Fax: 902-742-7476
www.coastalfinancial.ca

www.facebook.com/coastalfinancialns; twitter.com/coastalcu

Ownership: Member-owned
Year Founded: 2001
Number of Employees: 53
Assets: $100-500 million

Columbia Valley Credit Union
PO Box 720
511 Main St.
Golden, BC V0A 1H0

Tel: 250-344-2282; Fax: 250-344-2117
Toll-Free: 888-298-1777
www.cvcu.bc.ca

Other Contact Information: Telephone Banking: 844-344-7968;
Loans Phone: 250-344-7024

Ownership: Member-owned
Year Founded: 1955
Assets: $158,317,959 Year End: 20191231
Revenues: $4,926,919 Year End: 20191231

Community Credit Union
150 McGettigan Blvd.
Marystown, NL A0E 2M0

Tel: 709-279-3510; Fax: 709-279-3721
admin@ccunl.ca
www.ccunl.ca

Ownership: Member-owned
Assets: $68,700,000

**Community Credit Union of Cumberland Colchester
Limited**
33 Prince Arthur St.
Amherst, NS B4H 1V7

Tel: 902-667-7541; Fax: 902-667-1779
Toll-Free: 866-318-7541
www.communitycreditunion.ns.ca

Other Contact Information: MemberDirect Assistance, Toll-Free
Phone: 888-273-3488
www.facebook.com/CommunityCreditUnionOfCumberlandColch
ester; twitter.com/co_credit_union

Former Name: Amherst Credit Union; Colchester Credit Union
Ownership: Member-owned
Year Founded: 1999
Assets: $98,180,886
Revenues: $4,296,990

Community First Credit Union Limited
289 Bay St.
Sault Ste Marie, ON P6A 1W7

Tel: 705-942-1000; Fax: 705-946-2363
Toll-Free: 866-942-2328
www.communityfirst-yncu.com
www.facebook.com/communityfirst;
twitter.com/ItsCommunity1st

Ownership: Member-owned. A division of Your Neighbourhood
Credit Union Ltd.
Year Founded: 1948

Community Savings Credit Union
Central City Tower
#1600, 13450 - 102nd Ave.
Surrey, BC V3T 5X3

Tel: 604-654-2000; Toll-Free: 888-963-2000
info@comsavings.com
www.comsavings.com
www.instagram.com/comsavings;
www.facebook.com/CommunitySavings;
twitter.com/ComSavings

Former Name: IWA & Community Credit Union
Year Founded: 1944
Assets: $609,645,900 Year End: 20200630

Compass Credit Union
1016 Rosser Ave.
Brandon, MB R7A 0L6

Toll-Free: 866-922-7771
info@compasscu.ca
www.compasscu.ca

Ownership: Member-owned
Year Founded: 2018

Comtech Fire Credit Union
#102, 220 Yonge St.
Toronto, ON M5B 2H1

Tel: 416-598-1197; Fax: 416-598-0171
Toll-Free: 800-209-7444
member_services@comtechcu.com
www.comtechcu.com
www.facebook.com/comtechfirecu; twitter.com/comtechfirecu

Former Name: Communication Technologies Credit Union
Limited
Ownership: Member-owned
Year Founded: 1940
Number of Employees: 14
Assets: $50-100 million

Concentra Bank
333 - 3rd Ave. North
Saskatoon, SK S7K 2M2

Tel: 306-956-5100; Toll-Free: 800-788-6311
clientsupport@concentra.ca
www.concentra.ca
twitter.com/concentrabank

Former Name: Concentra Financial; Concentra Financial
Corporate Banking; CUCORP Financial Services
Ownership: Private
Year Founded: 1997
Number of Employees: 250+
Assets: $9,436,734,000 Year End: 20191231
Revenues: $257,951,000 Year End: 20191231

Conexus Credit Union
PO Box 1960, Stn. Main
Regina, SK S4P 4M1

Toll-Free: 800-667-7477
www.conexus.ca
www.youtube.com/user/ConexusCU;
www.facebook.com/conexuscu; twitter.com/Conexus_CU

Former Name: Assiniboia Credit Union Ltd.
Number of Employees: 1,000
Assets: $6,260,155,000 Year End: 20181231
Revenues: $232,539,000 Year End: 20181231

Connect First Credit Union
#200, 2850 Sunridge Blvd. NE
Calgary, AB T1Y 6G2

Toll-Free: 844-753-7900
www.connectfirstcu.com
www.youtube.com/user/FCFCommunications

Ownership: Member-owned
Year Founded: 2014
Number of Employees: 700+
Assets: $5,787,591,000 Year End: 20191031

Consolidated Credit Union Ltd.
305 Water St.
Summerside, PE C1N 1C1

Tel: 902-436-9218; Fax: 902-436-7979
shickey@consolidated.creditu.net
www.consolidatedcreditu.com
www.facebook.com/consolidatedcreditunion

Ownership: Member-owned
Assets: $202,296,785 Year End: 20181231
Revenues: $7,444,748 Year End: 20181231

Copperfin Credit Union Ltd.
346 - 2nd St. South
Kenora, ON P9N 1G5

Tel: 807-467-4400; Fax: 807-468-3500
Toll-Free: 888-710-6664
contact@copperfin.ca
www.copperfin.ca
www.instagram.com/copperfincu;
www.facebook.com/CopperfinCreditUnion

Former Name: Superior Credit Union Limited; Lakewood Credit
Union Ltd.
Ownership: Member-owned
Year Founded: 1954

Cornerstone Credit Union Ltd.
PO Box 455
1202 - 100th St.
Tisdale, SK S0E 1T0

Tel: 306-873-2616; Fax: 306-873-4322
Toll-Free: 855-875-2255
connect@cornerstonecu.com
www.cornerstonecu.com

Other Contact Information: Cornerstone Connect Telephone
Assistance, Toll-Free: 855-875-2255
www.youtube.com/user/CornerstoneCUSK;
www.facebook.com/cornerstonecusk;
twitter.com/CornerstoneCUSK

Former Name: Tisdale Credit Union Ltd.
Ownership: Private. Member-owned
Year Founded: 1943
Assets: $1,039,182,000 Year End: 20181231
Revenues: $42,033,000 Year End: 20181231

Creative Arts Financial
625 Church St., 1st Fl.
Toronto, ON M4Y 2G1

Tel: 416-642-6749; Toll-Free: 877-643-3660
contact@creativeartsfinancial.com
www.creativeartsfinancial.com
www.facebook.com/CreativeArtsFinancial

Former Name: Creative Arts Savings & Credit Union
Ownership: A division of FirstOntario Credit Union
Year Founded: 2008

The Credit Union
422 William St.
Dalhousie, NB E8C 2X2

Tel: 506-684-5697; Fax: 506-684-2438
info@thecreditu.ca
www.thecreditu.ca

Former Name: Dalhousie Industrial Credit Union
Ownership: Member-owned

Credit Union Atlantic (CUA)
#350, 7105 Chebucto Rd.
Halifax, NS B3L 4W8

Tel: 902-492-6500; Fax: 902-492-6501
Toll-Free: 800-474-4282
www.cua.com

Other Contact Information: Teleservice: 902-493-4800;
TeleService, Toll-Free: 800-963-4848; MasterCard Inquiries:
800-561-7849; Lost MasterCards: 800-567-8111
www.facebook.com/CUAbanking; twitter.com/cuatlantic

Ownership: Member-owned
Year Founded: 1948
Assets: $625,000,000 Year End: 20191231

Credit Union Central Alberta Limited
#350N, 8500 Macleod Trail South
Calgary, AB T2H 2N1

Tel: 403-258-5900; Fax: 403-253-7720
email@albertacentral.com
www.albertacentral.com
www.youtube.com/user/AlbertaCreditUnions;
www.facebook.com/ABcreditunions; twitter.com/ABCreditUnion

Ownership: Owned by the credit unions of Alberta
Number of Employees: 230
Assets: $3,232,093,000 Year End: 20181231
Revenues: $56,369,000 Year End: 20181231

Credit Unions of Atlantic Canada
Halifax Office
PO Box 9200
6074 Lady Hammond Rd.
Halifax, NS B3K 5N3

Tel: 902-453-0680; Fax: 902-455-2437
Toll-Free: 800-668-2879
atlanticcreditunions.ca
twitter.com/AtlCreditUnions

Former Name: Credit Union Central of New Brunswick; Credit
Union Central of Prince Edward Island; Credit Union Central of
Nova Scotia
Also Known As: Atlantic Central; Atlantic Credit Unions
Ownership: Member-owned

Year Founded: 2011
Number of Employees: 1,364
Assets: $6,000,000,000 Year End: 20190930

Creston & District Credit Union
PO Box 215
140 - 11th Ave. North
Creston, BC V0B 1G0
Tel: 250-428-5351; Fax: 250-428-5302
Toll-Free: 866-857-2802
cdcu@cdcu.com
www.cdcu.com

Year Founded: 1951
Assets: $144,267,264 Year End: 20191231

Crossroads Credit Union Ltd.
PO Box 2006
113 - 2nd Ave. East
Canora, SK S0A 0L0
Tel: 306-563-5641; Toll-Free: 877-535-1299
reception@crossroadscu.ca
www.crossroadscu.ca
Other Contact Information: TeleService, Toll-Free Phone:
877-535-1299
www.facebook.com/CrossroadsCU; twitter.com/CrossroadsCU
Former Name: Canora Credit Union
Ownership: Member-owned
Year Founded: 1959
Assets: $272,217,797 Year End: 20181231
Revenues: $10,188,865 Year End: 20181231

Cypress Credit Union Ltd.
PO Box 1060
110 Jasper St.
Maple Creek, SK S0N 1N0
Tel: 306-662-2683; Fax: 306-662-3859
Toll-Free: 877-353-6311
contactus@cypresscu.sk.ca
www.cypresscu.sk.ca
Assets: $207,614,633 Year End: 20191231

Desjardins Gestion d'actifs/Desjardins Asset Management
Tour Sud
CP 153, Stn. Desjardins
1, complexe Desjardins
Montréal, QC H5B 1B3
Tel: 514-350-8686; Téléc: 514-285-3120
Ligne sans frais: 877-353-8686
info@desjardinsgestiondactifs.com
www.desjardinsgestiondactifs.com
Ownership: A subsidiary of the Desjardins Group.

Diamond North Credit Union
PO Box 2074
100 - 1st St. West
Nipawin, SK S0E 1E0
Tel: 306-862-4651; Fax: 306-862-9611
www.diamondnorthcu.com
www.facebook.com/DiamondNorthCreditUnion;
twitter.com/diamondnorth
Former Name: Arctic Credit Union Ltd.
Ownership: Member-owned
Year Founded: 2006
Assets: $464,639,000 Year End: 20181231
Revenues: $18,972,000 Year End: 20181231

Dodsland & District Credit Union Ltd.
PO Box 129
201 - 2nd Ave.
Dodsland, SK S0L 0V0
Tel: 306-356-2155; Fax: 306-356-2202
Toll-Free: 866-67403328
www.dodslandcreditunion.com
Year Founded: 1961
Assets: $119,405,479 Year End: 20191231

Dominion Credit Union
94 Commercial St.
Dominion, NS B1G 1B4
Tel: 902-849-8648; Fax: 902-842-0273
dominioncreditunion.ca
www.facebook.com/DominionCU
Ownership: Member-owned
Year Founded: 1934

DUCA Financial Services Credit Union Ltd.
Corporate Office
5290 Yonge St.
Toronto, ON M2N 5P9
Tel: 416-223-8502; Fax: 416-221-2293
Toll-Free: 866-900-3822
duca.info@duca.com
duca.com
www.youtube.com/user/DUCAFSCU;
www.facebook.com/DUCACU; twitter.com/DUCACU
Former Name: Virtual One Credit Union; Duca Community
Credit Union; Canadian General Tower Employees (Galt) Credit
Union
Ownership: Member-owned
Year Founded: 1954
Number of Employees: 100
Assets: $500m-1 billion
Revenues: $10-50 million

Dundalk District Credit Union Limited
PO Box 340
79 Proton St. North
Dundalk, ON N0C 1B0
Tel: 519-923-2400; Fax: 519-923-2950
info@dundalkcu.ca
www.dundalkcu.ca
www.facebook.com/1217174918372387
Year Founded: 1943
Assets: $50,767,9895 Year End: 20200831

Eagle River Credit Union
Head Office /L'Anse au Loup Branch
PO Box 29
8 Branch Rd.
L'Anse au Loup, NL A0K 3L0
Tel: 709-927-5524; Fax: 709-927-5759
Toll-Free: 877-377-3728
erinfo@ercu.ca
www.eaglerivercu.com
Ownership: Member-owned
Year Founded: 1984
Number of Employees: 45
Assets: $10-50 million
Revenues: Under $1 million

East Coast Credit Union
Administrative Office
155 Ochterloney St., 3rd & 4th Fl.
Dartmouth, NS B2Y 1C9
Tel: 902-464-7100; Fax: 902-464-7123
info@eastcoastcu.ca
www.eastcoastcu.ca
Other Contact Information: Port Hawkesbury Admin. Office,
Phone: 902-625-5610
www.facebook.com/EastCoastCU; twitter.com/EastCoastCU
Former Name: Bergengren Credit Union
Ownership: Member-owned
Year Founded: 2003
Assets: 769,786,090 Year End: 20181231

East Kootenay Community Credit Union (EKC)
920 Baker St.
Cranbrook, BC V1C 1A5
Tel: 250-426-6666; Fax: 250-426-7370
Toll-Free: 866-960-6666
www.ekccu.ca
www.facebook.com/EKCCU
Year Founded: 1950

EasternEdge Credit Union
31 Corey King Dr.
Mount Pearl, NL A1N 0A5
Tel: 709-739-2920; Fax: 709-739-3728
Toll-Free: 800-716-7283
www.easternedgecu.com
www.facebook.com/easternedgecreditunion
Former Name: NewTel Credit Union
Ownership: Member-owned
Year Founded: 1976
Assets: $10-50 million

ECU
#6, 51 Ardelt Ave.
Kitchener, ON N2C 2S9
Tel: 519-742-3500; Fax: 519-742-6072
info@myecu.ca
www.ecusolutions.com
www.instagram.com/ecuspeaks;
www.youtube.com/user/EducationCreditUnion;
www.facebook.com/ecuspeaks; twitter.com/ecuspeaks
Former Name: Education Credit Union
Ownership: A division of Windsor Family Credit Union Limited
Year Founded: 1972

Encompass Credit Union
Administration Office
502 - 10th St.
Wainwright, AB T9W 1P4
Tel: 780-842-3391; Fax: 780-842-2855
Toll-Free: 877-842-1774
askus@encompasscu.ca
www.encompasscu.ca
www.facebook.com/encompasscu; twitter.com/EncompassCU
Former Name: Wainwright Credit Union Ltd.; Wetaskiwin Credit
Union
Ownership: Member-owned
Year Founded: 2015
Number of Employees: 70
Assets: $100-500 million
Revenues: $10-50 million

Enderby & District Financial
PO Box 670
703 Mill Ave.
Enderby, BC V0E 1V0
Tel: 250-838-6841; Fax: 250-838-9756
www.enderbyfinancial.com
www.facebook.com/EnderbyDistrictFinancial
Ownership: Member-owned. A division of First West Credit
Union

The Energy Credit Union
Head Office
#810, 2 Carlton St.
Toronto, ON M5B 1J3
Tel: 416-238-5606; Fax: 647-689-3065
Toll-Free: 888-942-2522
theenergycu.com
www.theenergycu.com
Former Name: The Toronto Electrical Utilities Credit Union
Limited
Ownership: Member-owned
Year Founded: 1941
Number of Employees: 8

The Energy Credit Union (TECU)
#212, 305 Milner Ave.
Toronto, ON M1B 3V4
Tel: 416-238-5606; Fax: 647-689-3065
Toll-Free: 888-942-2522
www.theenergycu.com
Former Name: Lasco Employees' Credit Union; Southlake
Regional Health Centre Employees' Credit Union; Canadian
Transportation Employees' Credit Union
Ownership: Member-owned
Year Founded: 1939

Entegra Credit Union
Corporate Office
540 St Anne's Rd.
Winnipeg, MB R2M 5R7
Tel: 204-949-7744; Fax: 204-949-9099
info@entegra.ca
www.entegra.ca
Former Name: Holy Spirit Credit Union
Year Founded: 1960
Number of Employees: 82
Assets: $100-500 million

Envision Credit Union
6470 - 201st St.
Langley, BC V2Y 2X4
Tel: 604-539-7300
contact@envisionfinancial.ca
www.envisionfinancial.ca
www.flickr.com/photos/83890812@N06/;
www.youtube.com/user/envisionfinancial;
www.facebook.com/envisionfinancial.ca; twitter.com/EnvisionFin
Also Known As: Envision Financial
Ownership: Member-owned. A division of First West Credit
Union
Year Founded: 1946
Number of Employees: 779
Assets: $1-10 billion
Revenues: $100-500 million

Equity Credit Union
Whitetail Centre
#1, 299 Kingston Rd.
Ajax, ON L1Z 0K5
Tel: 905-426-1389; Fax: 905-428-1590
Toll-Free: 800-263-9793
info@equitycu.com
www.equitycu.com
www.facebook.com/EquityCU; twitter.com/EquityCU
Former Name: Equity Financial Services; Unilever Employees
Credit Union Limited
Ownership: Member-owned

Évangéline-Central Credit Union
37 Mill Rd.
Wellington, PE C0B 2E0

Tel: 902-854-2595; *Fax:* 902-854-3210
evangeline@eccu.ca
www.eccu.ca

Former Name: Evangeline Credit Union; Central Credit Union Limited
Ownership: Member-owned
Year Founded: 2012
Number of Employees: 36
Assets: $160,094,572 Year End: 20181231
Revenues: $5,644,272 Year End: 20181231

Fédération des caisses Desjardins du Québec
100, rue des Commandeurs
Lévis, QC G6V 7N5

Ligne sans frais: 866-835-8444
www.desjardins.com

Former Name: Fédération des Caisses Populaires Desjardins du Québec

Finnish Credit Union Limited
191 Eglinton Ave. East
Toronto, ON M4P 1K1

Tel: 416-486-1533; *Fax:* 416-486-1592
Toll-Free: 800-668-7242
mail@finnishcu.com
www.finnishcu.com

Ownership: Member-owned
Year Founded: 1958

First Calgary Financial
#200, 2850 Sunridge Blvd. NE
Calgary, AB T1Y 6G2

Tel: 403-520-8000; *Fax:* 403-276-5299
Toll-Free: 866-923-4778
www.firstcalgary.com

Other Contact Information: Client Contact Centre, Toll-Free: 866-923-4778
www.facebook.com/firstcalgary; twitter.com/FirstCalgary

Former Name: First Calgary Savings & Credit Union Limited
Ownership: Member-owned. A division of Connect First Credit Union
Year Founded: 1987
Assets: $5,690,380,00 Year End: 20181031
Revenues: $159,562,000 Year End: 20181031

First Credit Union
4448A Marine Ave.
Powell River, BC V8A 2K2

Tel: 604-485-6206; *Fax:* 604-485-7112
Toll-Free: 800-393-6733
info@firstcu.ca
www.firstcu.ca

Other Contact Information: Member Services, Email: memberservice@firstcu.ca; Lending, Email: lending@firstcu.ca; Wealth Management, Email: wealth @firstcu.ca
www.facebook.com/firstcugroup; twitter.com/firstcugroup

Former Name: Powell River Credit Union Financial Group
Also Known As: First Credit Union & Insurance
Year Founded: 1939
Number of Employees: 46
Assets: $442,408,336 Year End: 20181231
Revenues: $13,123,532 Year End: 20181231

First West Credit Union
6470 - 201st St.
Langley, BC V2Y 2X4

Tel: 604-501-4260
communications@firstwestcu.ca
www.firstwestcu.ca
www.flickr.com/photos/62967987@N02; twitter.com/firstwestcu

Ownership: Member-owned
Year Founded: 2010
Assets: 10,300,000,000
Revenues: 312,000,000

FirstOntario Credit Union Limited
#301, 970 South Service Rd.
Stoney Creek, ON L8E 6A2

Fax: 905-574-6202
Toll-Free: 800-616-8878
www.firstontariocu.com
www.facebook.com/FirstOntarioCreditUnion; twitter.com/FirstOntarioCU

Former Name: Rochdale Credit Union Limited; Avestel Family Savings Credit Union Limited; Family Savings & Credit Union Limited
Ownership: Member-owned
Year Founded: 1940
Number of Employees: 300
Assets: $500m-1 billion

Flin Flon Credit Union
36 Main St.
Flin Flon, MB R8A 1J6

Tel: 204-687-6620; *Fax:* 204-687-4110
service@ffcu.ca
www.ffcu.ca

Other Contact Information: Automated Telephone Banking, Toll-Free: 888-949-0226
www.instagram.com/flinfloncreditunion;
www.facebook.com/169147003224623

Former Name: Alpha Credit Union Society Limited
Year Founded: 1940
Assets: $60,223,405 Year End: 20191231

Foam Lake Savings & Credit Union Limited
PO Box 160
402 Main St.
Foam Lake, SK S0A 1A0

Tel: 306-272-3385; *Toll-Free:* 877-722-3528
info@foamlakecu.com
foamlakecu.com

Year Founded: 1941
Assets: $138,347,826 Year End: 20191231

Fort York Community Credit Union Limited
St. Joseph's Health Centre, Sunnyside East Wing
#207, 30 The Queensway
Toronto, ON M6R 1B5

Tel: 416-530-6474; *Fax:* 416-530-6763
fyinfo@fortyork.com
www.fortyork.com

Year Founded: 1950

Frontline Credit Union
365 Richmond Rd.
Ottawa, ON K2A 0E7

Tel: 613-729-4312; *Fax:* 613-729-5075
Toll-Free: 877-542-9249
www.frontlinecu.com

Former Name: Ottawa Fire Fighters' Credit Union Ltd.
Year Founded: 1948

Fusion Credit Union
PO Box 340
505 Main St. North
Dauphin, MB R7N 2V2

Toll-Free: 877-226-7957
info@fusioncu.com
fusioncu.com
www.instagram.com/fusion_cu; www.facebook.com/FusionCU;
twitter.com/fusioncu_mb

Former Name: Vanguard-Catalyst Credit Union; Dauphin Plains Credit Union; Ethelbert Credit Union; Roblin Credit Union
Ownership: Member-owned
Year Founded: 2018

G&F Financial Group
7375 Kingsway
Burnaby, BC V3N 3B5

Tel: 604-517-5100
inquiry@gffg.com
www.gffg.com
www.facebook.com/GFFGcu; twitter.com/gffg

Also Known As: Gulf & Fraser Fishermen's Credit Union
Ownership: Member-owned
Year Founded: 1941
Number of Employees: 175
Assets: $1-10 billion

Ganaraska Financial Credit Union
17 Queen St.
Port Hope, ON L1A 2Y8

Tel: 905-885-8134; *Fax:* 905-885-8298
info@ganaraskacu.com
www.ganaraskacu.com

Former Name: Ganaraska Credit Union
Year Founded: 1945

Glace Bay Central Credit Union
598 Main St.
Glace Bay, NS B1A 4X8

Tel: 902-849-7512; *Fax:* 902-842-9201
gbccu.ca
www.facebook.com/GlaceBayCentralCreditUnion;
twitter.com/GBCentralCU

Ownership: Member-owned
Year Founded: 1932
Assets: $10-50 million

Grand Forks Credit Union (GFCU)
PO Box 2500
447 Market Ave.
Grand Forks, BC V0H 1H0

Tel: 250-442-5511; *Fax:* 250-442-5644
Toll-Free: 866-442-5511
info@gfcu.com
www.gfcu.com
www.instagram.com/gfcu_1949;
www.facebook.com/grandforkscu

Year Founded: 1949
Assets: $276,211,519 Year End: 20201231

Greater Vancouver Community Credit Union
1801 Willingdon Ave.
Burnaby, BC V5C 5R3

Tel: 604-298-3344; *Fax:* 604-421-8949
info@gvccu.com
www.gvccu.com

Year Founded: 1940
Assets: $240,078,549 Year End: 20191231

Hamilton Sound Credit Union
PO Box 272
Hwy. 330
Carmanville, NL A0G 1N0

Tel: 709-534-2224; *Fax:* 709-534-2227
www.hscunl.ca
www.facebook.com/141787892554975; twitter.com/HSCUNL

Ownership: Member-owned
Year Founded: 1991
Number of Employees: 20
Assets: $46,959,065 Year End: 20181231
Revenues: $2,647,077 Year End: 20181231

Health Care Credit Union Ltd.
London Health Sciences Centre, Zone E
PO Box 5010, Stn. B
800 Commissioners Rd. East, #ELL302
London, ON N6A 5W9

Tel: 519-685-8353; *Fax:* 519-685-8153
info@healthcarecu.ca
www.healthcarecu.ca

Year Founded: 1949

Healthcare & Municipal Employees Credit Union (HMECU)
209 Limeridge Rd. East
Hamilton, ON L9A 2S6

Tel: 905-575-8888; *Fax:* 905-575-3104
Toll-Free: 866-808-2888
supprt@hmecu.com
www.hmecu.com
www.instagram.com/hmecu; www.facebook.com/hmecu;
twitter.com/hmecu

Heritage Credit Union
#100, 630 - 17th St.
Castlegar, BC V1N 4G7

Tel: 250-365-7232; *Fax:* 250-365-2913
hcu@heritagecu.ca
www.heritagecu.ca

Former Name: Castlegar Savings Credit Union
Ownership: Member-owned
Year Founded: 1948
Assets: $201,632,231 Year End: 20191231

Heritage Savings & Credit Union Inc. (HSCU)
318 Merritt Ave.
Chatham, ON N7M 3G1

Tel: 519-351-0600; *Fax:* 519-351-0660
www.heritagecreditunion.ca

Former Name: Municipal Employees (Chatham) Credit Union Ltd.
Ownership: Member-owned
Year Founded: 1952

IC Savings
5300 Dundas St. West
Toronto, ON M9B 1B2

Tel: 416-784-9885; *Fax:* 416-784-9881
mail@icsavings.ca
www.icsavings.ca
www.facebook.com/ICSavings; twitter.com/ICSavings

Ownership: Member-owned
Year Founded: 2000

Innovation Credit Union
PO Box 1090, Stn. Main
198 - 1st Ave. NE
Swift Current, SK S9H 3X3
Tel: 306-778-1700; *Toll-Free:* 866-446-7001
www.innovationcu.ca
www.instagram.com/innovationcu;
www.facebook.com/innovationcu; twitter.com/InnovationCU
Ownership: Member-owned
Year Founded: 2007

iNova Credit Union
6175 Almon St.
Halifax, NS B3K 1T8
Tel: 902-453-1145; *Fax:* 902-453-0370
Toll-Free: 800-665-1145
www.inovacreditunion.coop
www.facebook.com/inovacu; twitter.com/inovacu
Former Name: Nova Scotia Postal Employees Credit Union
Ownership: Member-owned
Assets: $35,048,298 Year End: 20181231
Revenues: $1,381,723 Year End: 20181231

Integris Credit Union
1598 - 6th Ave.
Prince George, BC V2L 5B5
Tel: 250-612-3456; *Fax:* 250-612-3451
Toll-Free: 866-554-3456
welcome@integriscu.ca
www.integriscu.ca
www.instagram.com/integriscu; www.facebook.com/integriscu;
twitter.com/IntegrisCU
Former Name: Prince George Savings Credit Union; Nechako
Valley Credit Union; Quesnel & District Credit Union
Year Founded: 2004
Assets: $789,592,261 Year End: 20151231
Revenues: $27,000,368 Year End: 20151231

Interior Savings Credit Union
#300, 678 Bernard Ave.
Kelowna, BC V1Y 6P3
Tel: 250-869-8200; *Fax:* 250-762-9581
info@interiorsavings.com
www.interiorsavings.com
Other Contact Information: Member Service Centre Toll-Free
Phone: 855-220-2580
www.youtube.com/user/interiorsavingscu
www.facebook.com/InteriorSavings; twitter.com/interiorsavings
Ownership: Member-owned
Assets: 2,509,785,000 Year End: 20171231
Revenues: 78,446,000 Year End: 20171231

Island Savings Credit Union
#300, 499 Canada Ave.
Duncan, BC V9L 1T7
Tel: 250-748-4728; *Fax:* 250-748-8831
Toll-Free: 888-597-1083
contact@islandsavings.ca
www.islandsavings.ca
www.youtube.com/user/IslandSavingsBank;
www.facebook.com/IslandSavings; twitter.com/Island_Savings
Ownership: Member-owned. A division of First West Credit
Union.
Year Founded: 1951
Number of Employees: 300
Assets: $500m-1 billion

Kawartha Credit Union Limited
Corporate Office
PO Box 116, Stn. Main
14 Hunter St. East
Peterborough, ON K9J 6Y5
Tel: 705-748-0510; *Toll-Free:* 855-670-0510
info@kawarthacu.com
www.kawarthacu.com
Other Contact Information: Contact Centre, Email:
contact.centre@kawarthacu.com
www.facebook.com/kawarthacu; twitter.com/kawarthacu
Former Name: Pedeco (Brockville) Credit Union Limited; Unity
Savings & Credit Union Limited
Ownership: Member-owned
Year Founded: 1952

Kerrobert Credit Union Ltd.
PO Box 140
445 Atlantic Ave.
Kerrobert, SK S0L 1R0
Tel: 306-834-2611; *Fax:* 306-834-5558
www.kerrobertcreditunion.ca

Year Founded: 1963
Assets: $57,217,663 Year End: 20191231

Khalsa Credit Union (Alberta) Limited
#604, 4656 Westwinds Dr. NE
Calgary, AB T3J 3Z5
Tel: 403-285-0707; *Fax:* 403-285-0771
info@kcufinancial.com
www.kcufinancial.com
Year Founded: 1995
Assets: $1-5 million
Revenues: $1-5 million

Kindred Credit Union
1265 Strasburg Rd.
Kitchener, ON N2R 1S6
Tel: 519-746-1010; *Fax:* 519-746-1045
Toll-Free: 888-672-6728
info@kindredcu.com
www.kindredcu.com
www.facebook.com/kindredcu; twitter.com/kindredcu
Former Name: Mennonite Savings and Credit Union
Ownership: Member-owned

Kingston Community Credit Union Ltd. (KCCU)
18 Market St.
Kingston, ON K7L 1W8
Tel: 613-549-3901; *Fax:* 613-549-6593
kccu@kccu.ca
www.kccu.ca
www.facebook.com/KCCU.Kingston; twitter.com/KingstonCCU
Ownership: Member-owned
Assets: $100-500 million

Kootenay Savings Credit Union
1199 Cedar Ave.
Trail, BC V1R 4B8
Tel: 250-368-2647; *Fax:* 250-368-3754
Toll-Free: 888-368-5728
www.kscu.com
Other Contact Information: Collections Department Toll-Free
Phone: 866-540-8210
www.facebook.com/KootenaySavings;
twitter.com/KootenaySavings
Ownership: Member-owned
Year Founded: 1969
Number of Employees: 200
Assets: $1,205,926,000 Year End: 20181231
Revenues: $39,179,000 Year End: 20181231

Korean (Toronto) Credit Union Limited
#202, 721 Bloor St. West
Toronto, ON M6G 1L5
Tel: 416-535-4511; *Fax:* 416-535-9323
info@koreancu.com
www.koreancu.com
Ownership: Member-owned
Year Founded: 1976

Korean Catholic Church Credit Union Limited
849 Don Mills Rd., 2nd Fl.
Toronto, ON M3C 1W1
Tel: 416-447-7788; *Fax:* 416-447-5297
www.kcccu.ca
Ownership: Member-owned

Ladysmith & District Credit Union
PO Box 430
330 - 1st Ave.
Ladysmith, BC V9G 1A3
Tel: 250-245-2247; *Fax:* 250-245-5913
Toll-Free: 888-899-2247
info@ldcu.ca
www.ldcu.ca
www.instagram.com/ladysmithcreditunion;
www.facebook.com/LadysmithCreditUnion;
twitter.com/ladysmithcu
Also Known As: LDCU
Year Founded: 1944
Assets: $191,125,107 Year End: 20191231

LaFleche Credit Union Ltd.
PO Box 429
105 Main St.
Lafleche, SK S0H 2K0
Tel: 306-472-5215; *Fax:* 306-472-5545
www.laflechecu.com
www.facebook.com/286462581402451
Ownership: Member-owned
Year Founded: 1938
Number of Employees: 15
Assets: 70,000,000 Year End: 20181031

LaHave River Credit Union
29 North St.
Bridgewater, NS B4V 2V7
Tel: 902-543-3921; *Fax:* 902-543-3947
lahaverivercreditunion.ca
www.facebook.com/LahaveRiverCreditUnion
Ownership: Member-owned
Assets: $10-50 million

Lake View Credit Union
800 - 102nd Ave.
Dawson Creek, BC V1G 2B2
Tel: 250-782-4871; *Fax:* 250-782-5828
lvcu@lvcu.ca
www.lakeviewcreditunion.com
www.instagram.com/lvcucommunity;
www.facebook.com/lvcucommunity; twitter.com/lvcucommunity
Ownership: Private
Year Founded: 1943
Assets: $318,680,759 Year End: 20191231

Lakeland Credit Union (LCU)
PO Box 8057
5016 - 50th Ave.
Bonnyville, AB T9N 2J3
Tel: 780-826-3377; *Fax:* 780-826-6322
www.lakelandcreditunion.com
www.facebook.com/LakelandCreditUnion;
twitter.com/LakelandCU
Year Founded: 1940
Assets: $641,708,473 Year End: 20201031

Leading Edge Credit Union
Corporate Office
PO Box 70
27 Grand Bay Rd., 2nd Fl.
Grand Bay East, NL A0N 1K0
Tel: 709-695-7065; *Fax:* 709-695-7078
www.lecu.ca
www.facebook.com/LeadingEdgeCU; twitter.com/Leadingedgecu
Former Name: Codroy Valley Credit Union; Brook Street Credit
Union
Ownership: Member-owned
Assets: $121,827,954 Year End: 20181231
Revenues: $5,140,915 Year End: 20181231

Legacy Financial
#200, 2850 Sunridge Blvd. NE
Calgary, AB T1Y 6G2
Toll-Free: 844-753-7900
info@legacysavings.com
legacysavings.com
www.facebook.com/LegacySavings
Former Name: Legacy Savings & Credit Union Ltd.; Calgary
Firefighters Credit Union; Calgary Terminal Credit Unions
Ownership: A division of Connect First Credit Union
Year Founded: 1941

Libro Credit Union Limited
217 York St., 4th Fl.
London, ON N6A 5P9
Tel: 519-672-0130; *Fax:* 519-672-7831
Toll-Free: 800-265-5935
www.libro.ca
Other Contact Information: Lost or Stolen Cards Toll-Free
Phone: 800-567-8111
www.instagram.com/librocu; www.facebook.com/librocreditunion;
twitter.com/LibroCU
Former Name: Libro Financial Group; United Communities CU;
Kellogg Employees CU; St. Willibrod CU; St. Willibrod
Community CU; Hald-Nor Community CU
Ownership: Member-owned
Year Founded: 1951
Number of Employees: 625
Assets: $1-10 billion
Revenues: $500m-1 billion

L.I.U.N.A. Local 183 Credit Union Limited
#108, 1263 Wilson Ave.
Toronto, ON M3M 3G2
Tel: 416-242-6643; *Fax:* 416-242-7852
info@local183cu.ca
www.local183cu.ca
Year Founded: 1978

Luminus Financial Services & Credit Union Limited
Corporate Office
1 Yonge St.
Toronto, ON M5E 1E5
Tel: 416-366-5534; *Fax:* 416-366-6225
Toll-Free: 877-782-7639
inquiries@luminusfinancial.com
www.luminusfinancial.com
www.facebook.com/ClearlyLuminus; twitter.com/clearlyLuminus

Former Name: Starnews Credit Union
Also Known As: Luminus Financial
Ownership: Member-owned
Year Founded: 2011
Assets: $50-100 million

Mainstreet Credit Union Limited
40 Keil Dr. South
Chatham, ON N7M 3G8
Tel: 519-436-4590; *Fax:* 519-436-5451
Toll-Free: 800-592-9592
www.mainstreetcu.ca
www.facebook.com/MainstreetCreditUnion;
twitter.com/MainSt_CUCA
Former Name: Lambton Financial CU; Unigasco CU; Sydenham Community CU; Goderich Community CU
Ownership: Member-owned
Year Founded: 1952

Malpeque Bay Credit Union
PO Box 428
1 Commercial St.
Kensington, PE C0B 1M0
Tel: 902-836-3030; *Fax:* 902-836-5659
www.malpequebaycreditu.com
Ownership: Member-owned
Assets: $125,016,127 Year End: 20181231
Revenues: $5,730,918 Year End: 20181231

Me-Dian Credit Union
303 Selkirk Ave.
Winnipeg, MB R2W 2L8
Tel: 204-943-9111; *Fax:* 204-942-3698
Toll-Free: 866-295-6819
info@mediancu.mb.ca
www.mediancu.mb.ca
www.instagram.com/mediancreditunion;
www.facebook.com/mediancu; twitter.com/MedianCU
Former Name: Métis Credit Union of Manitoba
Year Founded: 1978
Assets: $50,998,059 Year End: 20191231

Meridian Credit Union
Centre Tower
3280 Bloor St. West, 7th Fl.
Toronto, ON M8X 2X3
Tel: 416-597-4400; *Toll-Free:* 866-592-2226
www.meridian.ca
www.instagram.com/meridiancreditunion;
www.youtube.com/user/MeridianBanking;
www.facebook.com/MeridianCreditUnion;
twitter.com/MeridianCU
Former Name: Desjardins Credit Union; HEPCOE Credit Union Limited; NIAGARA Credit Union
Ownership: Member-owned
Year Founded: 2005
Number of Employees: 1,100
Assets: $29,960,114,000 Year End: 20191231

Momentum Credit Union
698 King St. East
Hamilton, ON L8M 1A3
Tel: 905-529-9445; *Fax:* 905-529-9016
info@momentumcu.ca
www.momentumcu.ca
www.facebook.com/MomentumCU; twitter.com/momentumcu
Former Name: Hamilton Community Credit Union Limited; Twin Oak Credit Union Limited
Ownership: Member-owned
Number of Employees: 15

Morell Credit Union
29 Park St.
Morell, PE C0A 1S0
Tel: 902-961-2735
www.morellcreditu.com
Ownership: Member-owned
Assets: $36,876,288 Year End: 20181231
Revenues: $1,240,422 Year End: 20181231

Motor City Community Credit Union Limited
6701 Tecumseh Rd. East
Windsor, ON N8T 1E8
Tel: 519-944-7455; *Fax:* 519-944-1322
info@mcccu.com
www.mcccu.com
www.facebook.com/MotorCityCommunityCU;
twitter.com/MotorCityCCU
Ownership: Member-owned
Assets: $100-500 million

Mount Lehman Credit Union
5889 Mount Lehman Rd.
Mount Lehman, BC V4X 1V7
Tel: 604-856-7761; *Fax:* 604-856-1429
info@mtlehman.com
www.mtlehman.com
www.facebook.com/MtLehmanCreditUnion
Year Founded: 1942
Assets: $63,223,030 Year End: 20191231

Mountain View Financial
#401, 6501 - 51st St.
Olds, AB T4H 1Y6
Toll-Free: 844-648-6466
www.mountainviewfinancial.com
www.instagram.com/mountainviewfin;
www.facebook.com/MountainViewFinancial;
twitter.com/MountainViewFin
Former Name: Mountain View Credit Union Ltd.
Ownership: Member-owned. A division of Connect First Credit Union
Year Founded: 1977

Mouvement des caisses Desjardins du Québec/Desjardins Group
Also listed under: Insurance Companies
100, rue des Commandeurs
Lévis, QC G6V 7N5
Tél: 418-835-8444; *Ligne sans frais:* 866-835-8444
www.desjardins.com
www.youtube.com/user/desjardinsgroup;
www.instagram.com/desjardinsgroup;
www.facebook.com/desjardinsgroup; twitter.com/desjardinsgroup
Ownership: Private
Year Founded: 1901
Number of Employees: 47,000+
Assets: $100 billion +
Revenues: $1-10 billion

Moya Financial Credit Union Limited
725 Browns Line
Toronto, ON M8W 3V7
Tel: 416-252-1742; *Fax:* 416-255-3871
Toll-Free: 888-728-1742
main@moyafinancial.ca
www.moyafinancial.ca
www.instagram.com/moyafinancial;
www.facebook.com/MoyaFinancial;
twitter.com/MoyaFinancialCU
Ownership: Private
Year Founded: 2016

Nelson & District Credit Union
PO Box 350
501 Vernon St.
Nelson, BC V1L 5R2
Tel: 250-352-7207; *Fax:* 250-352-9663
Toll-Free: 877-352-7207
www.nelsoncu.com
Year Founded: 1950
Assets: $239,712,8896 Year End: 20191231

New Brunswick Teachers' Association Credit Union
PO Box 752
650 Montgomery St.
Fredericton, NB E3B 5R6
Tel: 506-452-1724; *Fax:* 506-452-1732
Toll-Free: 800-565-5626
nbtacu@nbtacu.nb.ca
www.nbtacu.nb.ca
Other Contact Information: Lost or Stolen Cards, Toll-Free Phone: 800-567-8111
twitter.com/NBTACreditUnion
Also Known As: NBTA Credit Union
Ownership: Member-owned
Year Founded: 1971
Number of Employees: 12
Assets: $10-50 million

New Community Credit Union
321 - 20th St. West
Saskatoon, SK S7M 0X1
Tel: 306-653-1300; *Fax:* 306-653-4711
info@newcommunity.cu.sk.ca
www.newcommunitycu.com
www.facebook.com/520885604664443
Former Name: New Community Savings & Credit Union Ltd.
Year Founded: 1939
Assets: $115,727,071 Year End: 20191231

New Ross Credit Union
PO Box 32
56 Forties Rd.
New Ross, NS B0J 2M0
Tel: 902-689-2949; *Fax:* 902-689-2597
www.newrosscreditu.ca
www.facebook.com/NewRossCreditUnionLtd
Ownership: Member-owned
Year Founded: 1956

New Waterford Credit Union
3462 Plummer Ave.
New Waterford, NS B1H 1Z6
Tel: 902-862-6453; *Fax:* 902-862-9206
www.newwaterfordcreditunion.com
www.facebook.com/newwaterfordcreditunion
Ownership: Member-owned
Year Founded: 1933
Number of Employees: 14
Assets: $10-50 million

Nexus Community Savings
PO Box 876
97 Duke St.
Dryden, ON P8N 2Z5
Tel: 807-223-5358; *Fax:* 807-223-5576
Toll-Free: 800-465-7225
www.nlcu.on.ca
Former Name: Nexus Community Credit Union Limited
Ownership: A division of Alterna Savings and Credit Union Limited
Year Founded: 2016

Niverville Credit Union
PO Box 430
62 Main St.
Niverville, MB R0A 1E0
Tel: 204-388-4747; *Fax:* 204-388-9970
Toll-Free: 855-500-6593
info@nivervillecu.mb.ca
www.nivervillecu.mb.ca
www.facebook.com/nivervillecu
Year Founded: 1949
Assets: $410,665,842 Year End: 20200930

North Peace Savings & Credit Union (NPSCU)
10344 - 100th St.
Fort St John, BC V1J 3Z1
Toll-Free: 877-787-0361
www.npscu.ca
www.facebook.com/NPSCU; twitter.com/npscu
Ownership: Private
Year Founded: 1947

North Sydney Credit Union
97 King St.
North Sydney, NS B2A 3S1
Tel: 902-794-2535; *Fax:* 902-794-9888
www.northsydneycreditunion.com
Other Contact Information: Alternate Phone: 902-794-2536
www.facebook.com/NorthSydneyCreditUnion;
twitter.com/northsydneycu
Ownership: Member-owned
Year Founded: 1937
Assets: $10-50 million

North Valley Credit Union Limited
PO Box 1389
516 Main St.
Esterhazy, SK S0A 0X0
Tel: 306-745-6615; *Fax:* 306-745-2858
Toll-Free: 866-533-6828
info@northvalley.cu.sk.ca
northvalleycu.com
www.facebook.com/1006180149415972
Former Name: Esterhazy Credit Union Limited
Ownership: Member-owned
Year Founded: 1998

Northern Birch Credit Union
Estonian House
#305, 958 Broadview Ave.
Toronto, ON M4K 2R6
Tel: 416-465-4659
info@northernbirchcu.com
www.northernbirchcu.com
www.facebook.com/NorthernBirchCU;
twitter.com/northernbirchcu
Former Name: Latvian Credit Union; Estonian Credit Union
Ownership: Member-owned
Year Founded: 2020

Northern Credit Union Limited
PO Box 2200
280 McNabb St.
Sault Ste Marie, ON P6A 5N9
Tel: 705-253-9868; *Toll-Free:* 866-413-7071
www.northercu.com
www.instagram.com/northerncreditunion/
www.facebook.com/NorthernCreditUnion; twitter.com/northerncu
Former Name: Espanola & District Credit Union Limited;
Saugeen Community Credit Union Limited
Ownership: Member-owned
Year Founded: 1957
Assets: $500m-1 billion

Northern Savings Credit Union
138 - 3rd Ave. West
Prince Rupert, BC V8J 1K8
Tel: 250-627-3600; *Fax:* 250-627-3602
Toll-Free: 800-330-9916
www.northsave.com
Other Contact Information: Mortgages, Toll-Free Phone:
866-910-9101; Investments: 877-418-3029.
www.facebook.com/northsave
Ownership: Member-owned

Noventis Credit Union Limited
PO Box 1139
34 Centre St.
Gimli, MB R0C 1B0
Toll-Free: 844-826-6500
info@noventis.ca
noventis.ca
www.instagram.com/noventiscu/
www.facebook.com/NoventisCU; twitter.com/NoventisCU
Former Name: Eriksdale Credit Union Limited
Ownership: Member-owned
Year Founded: 1972
Assets: $962,498,576 Year End: 20191231
Revenues: $24,746,475 Year End: 20191231

OMISTA Credit Union
151 Cornhill St.
Moncton, NB E1C 6L3
Tel: 506-857-3222; *Fax:* 506-857-2235
cornhillstreet@omista.com
www.omista.com
www.facebook.com/OMISTACU; twitter.com/omistacu
Ownership: Member-owned
Number of Employees: 20171231
Assets: $240,000,000

Ontario Educational Credit Union Limited
PO Box 360
#101, 6435 Edwards Blvd.
Mississauga, ON L5T 2P7
Tel: 905-795-1637; *Fax:* 905-795-0625
Toll-Free: 800-463-3602
www.oecu.on.ca
Year Founded: 1962

Ontario Provincial Police Association Credit Union Limited
123 Ferris Lane
Barrie, ON L4M 2Y1
Tel: 705-726-5656; *Fax:* 705-726-1449
Toll-Free: 800-461-4288
contactus@oppacu.com
www.oppacu.com
Also Known As: O.P.P.A Credit Union
Year Founded: 1971

Osoyoos Credit Union
PO Box 360
8312 Main St.
Osoyoos, BC V0H 1V0
Tel: 250-495-6522; *Fax:* 250-495-3363
contact@ocubc.com
ocubc.com
www.facebook.com/osoyooscreditunion;
twitter.com/OsoyoosCU
Ownership: Member-owned
Year Founded: 1946
Number of Employees: 21
Assets: $146,532,155 Year End: 20191231

Ottawa Police Credit Union Limited
#206, 474 Elgin St.
Ottawa, ON K2P 2J6
Tel: 613-236-1222; *Fax:* 613-567-3760
www.opcu.com
Other Contact Information: Telephone Banking: 613-567-6911
Former Name: Ottawa-Carleton Police Credit Union Limited
Ownership: Private.
Year Founded: 1955

Revenues: $10-50 million

PACE Savings & Credit Union Limited (PCU)
#1, 8111 Jane St.
Vaughan, ON L4K 4L7
Tel: 905-738-8900; *Fax:* 905-738-8283
Toll-Free: 800-433-9122
pace.info@pacecu.ca
pacecu.ca
Other Contact Information:
www.youtube.com/user/PACECreditUnion
www.facebook.com/PACEcreditunion; twitter.com/PACECU
Former Name: ETCU Financial Credit Union; Peoples Credit
Union; McMaster Savings & Credit Union; North York
Community Credit Union
Ownership: Member-owned
Year Founded: 1984
Assets: $50-100 million
Revenues: $5-10 million

Parama Lithuanian Credit Union Limited
Lithuanian House
1573 Bloor St. West
Toronto, ON M6P 1A6
Tel: 416-532-1149; *Fax:* 416-532-5595
info@parama.ca
www.parama.ca
www.facebook.com/ParamaCreditUnion
Also Known As: Parama Credit Union
Year Founded: 1952
Number of Employees: 30
Assets: $100-500 million

PenFinancial Credit Union Limited
247 East Main St.
Welland, ON L3B 3X1
Tel: 905-735-4801; *Fax:* 905-735-2983
Toll-Free: 866-272-4275
www.penfinancial.com
Other Contact Information: Telephone Banking: 1-877-282-4226
www.youtube.com/user/penfinancialcu;
www.facebook.com/PenFinancial; twitter.com/PenFinancial
Former Name: Fort Erie Community Credit Union Limited;
Cataract Savings & Credit Union; St Catharines Civic
Employees' Credit Union
Ownership: Member-owned
Year Founded: 1951
Assets: $100-500 million

Peterborough Community Savings
PO Box 1600
167 Brock St.
Peterborough, ON K9H 2P6
Tel: 705-748-4481; *Fax:* 705-748-5520
www.pboccu.com
www.facebook.com/54357791226
Former Name: Peterborough Community Credit Union Limited
Ownership: A division of Alterna Savings & Credit Union
Limited
Year Founded: 1939

Pincher Creek Credit Union Ltd.
PO Box 1660
750 Kettles St.
Pincher Creek, AB T0K 1W0
Tel: 403-627-4431; *Fax:* 403-627-5331
info@pinchercreek-creditunion.com
www.pinchercreek-creditunion.com
Ownership: Member-owned
Year Founded: 1944
Number of Employees: 5

The Police Credit Union Ltd.
#222, 105 Gordon Baker Rd.
Toronto, ON M2H 3P8
Tel: 416-226-3353; *Fax:* 416-226-1565
Toll-Free: 800-561-2557
callcentre@tpcu.on.ca
www.tpcu.on.ca
Ownership: Member-owned
Year Founded: 1946

Prairie Centre Credit Union
PO Box 940
Rosetown, SK S0L 2V0
Tel: 306-882-2693; *Fax:* 306-882-3326
rosetown@pccu.ca
www.pccu.ca
Other Contact Information: Lost or Stolen Cards, Toll-Free
Phone: 888-277-1043
Ownership: Member-owned
Year Founded: 1993
Assets: $770,741,844 Year End: 20191231

Prairie Pride Credit Union
PO Box 37
Alameda, SK S0C 0A0
Tel: 306-489-2131; *Fax:* 306-489-2188
info@ppcu.ca
www.prairiepridecu.ca
www.facebook.com/PrairiePrideCU
Former Name: Gainsborough Credit Union Ltd.
Year Founded: 2001
Assets: $109,472,255 Year End: 20191231

Princess Credit Union
22 Fraser Ave.
Sydney Mines, NS B1V 2B7
Tel: 902-736-9204; *Fax:* 902-736-2887
princesscreditunion.ca
Ownership: Member-owned
Year Founded: 1934

Progressive Credit Union
Fredericton Branch
30 Hughes St.
Fredericton, NB E3A 2W3
Tel: 506-458-9145; *Fax:* 506-459-0106
www.progressivecu.nb.ca
www.facebook.com/ProgressiveCU; twitter.com/progressivecu
Former Name: Capital Credit Union; Carleton Pioneer Credit
Union
Ownership: Member-owned
Year Founded: 1949
Assets: $50-100 million

Prospera Credit Union
Corporate Centre
#1900, 13450 - 102nd Ave.
Surrey, BC V3T 5Y1
Tel: 604-517-0100; *Fax:* 604-585-0250
Toll-Free: 877-506-0100
futurestrong.ca
Other Contact Information: TelExpress Telephone
Banking, Toll-Free Phone: 877-506-0100
www.instagram.com/westminstersavings;
www.facebook.com/westminstersavings; twitter.com/wscu
Former Name: Westminster Savings Credit Union
Ownership: Member-owned
Year Founded: 1944
Number of Employees: 900

Provincial Credit Union Ltd.
Main Branch
281 University Ave.
Charlottetown, PE C1A 4M3
Tel: 902-892-4107; *Fax:* 902-368-3567
www.provincialcu.com
Former Name: Metro Credit Union Ltd.; Montague Credit Union;
Stella Maris Credit Union
Ownership: Member-owned
Year Founded: 1968
Assets: $377,330,172$ Year End: 20181231
Revenues: $11,796,948$ Year End: 20181231

Provincial Government Employees Credit Union
#100, 1718 Argyle St.
Halifax, NS B3J 3N6
Tel: 902-424-5712; *Fax:* 902-424-3662
Toll-Free: 888-484-0880
info@provincialemployees.com
www.provincialemployees.com
Other Contact Information: Lost or Stolen Cards, Toll-Free:
800-561-7849
www.facebook.com/provincehouse; twitter.com/PHCU2
Former Name: Province House Credit Union Ltd.
Ownership: Member-owned
Assets: $10-50 million

Public Service Commission Employees Credit Union
450 Cowie Hill Rd.
Halifax, NS B3K 5M1
Tel: 902-490-4813; *Fax:* 902-490-4808
Ownership: Member-owned

Public Service Credit Union Ltd.
403 Empire Ave.
St. John's, NL A1E 1W6
Tel: 709-579-8210; *Fax:* 709-579-8233
Toll-Free: 800-563-6755
pscuadmin@pscu.ca
www.pscu.ca
Other Contact Information: Loan Inquiries, Email:
loans@pscu.ca; Account Clearing, Email: ac@pscu.ca
www.facebook.com/1188269484571125;
twitter.com/CreditPublic
Ownership: Member-owned
Year Founded: 1936

Number of Employees: 18
Assets: 59,109,838 Year End: 20181231
Revenues: 2,436,761 Year End: 20181231

Radius Credit Union
PO Box 339
120 Main St.
Ogema, SK S0C 1Y0

Tel: 306-459-2266; *Fax:* 306-459-2950
info@radius.cu.sk.ca
www.radiuscu.com
www.facebook.com/radiuscreditunion

Year Founded: 1950
Assets: $378,607,850 Year End: 20191231

Rapport Credit Union
#1, 18 Grenville St.
Toronto, ON M4Y 3B3

Tel: 416-314-6772; *Fax:* 416-314-7805
Toll-Free: 888-516-6664
help@rapportcu.ca
www.rapportcu.ca
www.facebook.com/RapportCU; twitter.com/rapportcu
Former Name: Ontario Civil Service Credit Union Limited;
Provincial Alliance Credit Union Limited
Ownership: Cooperative
Year Founded: 2014
Assets: $100-500 million

Raymore Credit Union Ltd.
PO Box 460
121 Main St.
Raymore, SK S0A 3J0

Tel: 306-746-2160; *Fax:* 306-746-5811
Toll-Free: 866-612-2300
info@raymorecu.com
www.raymorecu.com
www.facebook.com/RaymoreCU
Former Name: Dysart Credit Union Ltd.
Ownership: Member-owned
Year Founded: 1949

Reddy Kilowatt Credit Union Ltd.
PO Box 126
885 Topsail Rd.
Mount Pearl, NL A1N 2C2

Tel: 709-737-5624; *Fax:* 709-737-2937
Toll-Free: 800-409-2887
rkcu@reddyk.net
www.reddyk.net
Other Contact Information: TeleService: 800-963-4848; Lost or
Stolen Cards, Toll-Free Phone: 800-567-8111
www.facebook.com/reddykilowattcreditunion
Ownership: Member-owned
Year Founded: 1956
Assets: $80,072,669 Year End: 20181231
Revenues: $3,609,483 Year End: 20181231

Resurrection Credit Union Limited
3 Resurrection Rd.
Toronto, ON M9A 5G1

Tel: 416-532-3400; *Fax:* 416-532-4816
Toll-Free: 877-525-7285
www.rpcul.com
www.facebook.com/RCULithuanianResurrectionCreditUnion
Former Name: Resurrection Parish (Toronto) Credit Union
Limited

Rocky Credit Union Ltd.
5035 - 49th St.
Rocky Mountain House, AB T4T 1C1
Tel: 403-845-2861; *Fax:* 403-845-7295
info@rockycu.com
www.rockycreditunion.com
www.youtube.com/user/myrockycu; www.facebook.com/rockycu
Ownership: Public
Year Founded: 1944
Number of Employees: 45
Assets: $100-500 million
Revenues: $1-5 million

Rosenort Credit Union Limited
PO Box 339
23 Main St.
Rosenort, MB R0G 1W0

Tel: 204-746-2355; *Fax:* 204-746-2541
Toll-Free: 800-265-7925
www.rcu.ca

Year Founded: 1940
Assets: $595,139,774 Year End: 20200930

St Gregor Credit Union Ltd.
PO Box 128
119 Main St.
St Gregor, SK S0K 3X0

Tel: 306-366-2116; *Fax:* 306-366-2032
www.stgregorcu.com
Assets: $161,029,351 Year End: 20191231

St. Joseph's Credit Union
PO Box 159
3552 Hwy. 206
Petit de Grat, NS B0E 2L0

Tel: 902-226-2288; *Fax:* 902-226-9855
www.stjosephscreditu.ca
www.facebook.com/stjosephscreditu
Ownership: Member-owned
Year Founded: 1936
Number of Employees: 12
Assets: $50-100 million

St. Stanislaus - St. Casimir's Polish Parishes Credit Union Ltd.
220 Roncesvalles Ave.
Toronto, ON M6R 2L7

Tel: 416-537-2181; *Fax:* 416-537-5022
Toll-Free: 855-765-2822
info@polcu.com
www.polcu.com
www.facebook.com/PolishCreditUnion; twitter.com/PolishCU
Former Name: Polish (St Catharines) Credit Union Limited
Year Founded: 1945

Sandhills Credit Union
PO Box 249
202 - 1st Ave. West
Leader, SK S0N 1H0

Tel: 306-628-3687; *Fax:* 306-628-3674
info@sandhills.cu.sk.ca
www.sandhillscu.com
Ownership: Member-owned
Assets: $70,026,626 Year End: 20191231

Saskatoon City Employees Credit Union
City Hall
222 - 3rd Ave. North
Saskatoon, SK S7K 0J5

Tel: 306-975-3280; *Fax:* 306-975-7806
info@saskatooncity.cu.sk.ca
www.scecu.com
www.facebook.com/SCECUyxe
Former Name: Saskatoon City Employee Credit Union Ltd.
Year Founded: 1947
Assets: $65,218,965 Year End: 20191231

SaskCentral
PO Box 3030
2055 Albert St.
Regina, SK S4P 3G8

Tel: 306-566-1200; *Fax:* 306-566-1372
Toll-Free: 866-403-7499
www.saskcentral.com
Other Contact Information: Media Inquiries Phone:
306-566-1314
twitter.com/saskcentral
Ownership: Owned by Saskatchewan credit unions
Assets: $2,852,625,000 Year End: 20181231

Servus Credit Union
151 Karl Clark Rd. NW
Edmonton, AB T6N 1H5

Tel: 780-496-2350; *Toll-Free:* 877-378-8728
contact_us@servus.ca
www.servus.ca
Other Contact Information: Financial Planning, Email:
askafinancialplanner@servus.ca; TTY: 780-450-9647
www.instagram.com/servusalberta;
www.facebook.com/ServusCU; twitter.com/servuscu
Ownership: Member-owned
Year Founded: 1938
Assets: $16,317,332,000 Year End: 20190731

Sharons Credit Union
Administration Office & Main Branch
1055 Kingsway
Vancouver, BC V5V 3C7

Tel: 604-873-6490; *Fax:* 604-873-6498
info@sharonscu.ca
www.sharons.ca
Year Founded: 1988
Number of Employees: 30
Assets: $100-500 million

Smiths Falls Community Credit Union Limited
1 Beckwith St. North
Smiths Falls, ON K7A 2B2

Tel: 613-283-3835
Ownership: Member-owned
Year Founded: 1951

Souris Credit Union
PO Box 159
129 Main St.
Souris, PE C0A 2B0

Tel: 902-687-2721; *Fax:* 902-687-3510
www.souriscreditu.com
Ownership: Member-owned
Assets: $62,653,253 Year End: 20181231
Revenues: $2,812,522 Year End: 20181231

Southwest Regional Credit Union
1205 Exmouth St.
Sarnia, ON N7S 1W7

Tel: 519-383-8001; *Fax:* 519-383-8841
info@southwestcu.com
www.southwestcu.com
Year Founded: 1939
Number of Employees: 30

SPARK The Energy Credit Union Limited (SECU)
#117, 400 - 4th Ave. SW
Calgary, AB T2P 2H5

Tel: 403-718-7770; *Fax:* 403-262-4009
Toll-Free: 877-582-6222
spark@sparkcu.ca
sparkcu.ca
www.instagram.com/sparkenergycu;
www.facebook.com/sparkenergycu
Former Name: Shell Employees' Credit Union Limited
Also Known As: SPARK
Ownership: Member-owned
Year Founded: 1953
Assets: $245,903708 Year End: 20191031
Revenues: $8,507,965 Year End: 20191031

Spruce Credit Union
879 Victoria St.
Prince George, BC V2L 2K7

Tel: 250-562-5415; *Fax:* 250-564-9977
Toll-Free: 866-562-5411
info@sprucecu.bc.ca
www.sprucecu.bc.ca
www.facebook.com/sprucecreditunion
Assets: $173,898,532 Year End: 20191231

Squamish Savings
PO Box 1940
Squamish, BC V8B 0B4

Tel: 604-892-8350; *Toll-Free:* 888-826-2489
www.vancity.com/Squamish
Other Contact Information: Telephone Banking: 604-892-8350;
Squamish Insurance Phone: 604-992-8363; Member Services
Toll-Free Phone: 888-826-2489
Former Name: Squamish Credit Union
Ownership: Private. A division of VanCity.
Number of Employees: 3

Steinbach Credit Union (SCU)
333 Main St.
Steinbach, MB R5G 1B1

Tel: 204-326-3495; *Fax:* 204-326-5093
Toll-Free: 800-728-6440
scu@scu.mb.ca
www.scu.mb.ca
Other Contact Information: CUbyPhone: 1-800-511-8776
Ownership: Member-owned
Year Founded: 1941
Assets: $1-10 billion
Revenues: $50-100 million

Stoughton Credit Union Ltd.
PO Box 420
331 Main St.
Stoughton, SK S0G 4T0

Tel: 306-457-2443; *Fax:* 306-457-2511
info@stoughton.cu.sk.ca
www.stoughtoncu.com
www.facebook.com/StoughtonCU; twitter.com/stoughtoncu
Year Founded: 1960

Stride Credit Union
Corporate Office
19 Royal Rd. North
Portage la Prairie, MB R1N 1T9
Tel: 204-856-2700; *Fax:* 204-856-2710
Toll-Free: 877-228-2636
contactus@stridecu.ca
www.stridecu.ca

Year Founded: 2017

Sudbury Credit Union Limited
Corporate Office
PO Box 662
1 Gribble St.
Copper Cliff, ON P0M 1N0
Tel: 705-682-0645; *Fax:* 705-682-1348
info@sudburycu.com
www.facebook.com/154969844621680
Former Name: Northridge Savings & Credit Union; Sudbury
Regional Credit Union; Community Saving & Credit Union
Ownership: Member-owned
Year Founded: 1951
Assets: $100-500 million

Summerland & District Credit Union
PO Box 750
13601 Victoria Rd. North
Summerland, BC V0H 1Z0
Tel: 250-494-7181; *Fax:* 250-494-4261
sdcu@sdcu.com
www.sdcu.com

Ownership: Member-owned
Year Founded: 1944
Number of Employees: 39

Sunova Credit Union Ltd.
233 Main St.
Selkirk, MB R1A 1S1
Tel: 204-813-5786; *Toll-Free:* 833-378-6682
www.sicu.mb.ca
www.instagram.com/sunovacu; www.facebook.com/sunovacu;
twitter.com/SunovaCU
Former Name: South Interlake Credit Union Ltd.
Ownership: Member-owned
Year Founded: 1944
Assets: $1-10 billion

Sunrise Credit Union Ltd.
2305 Victoria Ave., 2nd Fl.
Brandon, MB R7B 4H7
Tel: 204-726-2030; *Fax:* 204-726-3637
info@sunrisecu.mb.ca
www.sunrisecu.mb.ca
www.youtube.com/user/Sunrisecumarketing;
www.instagram.com/sunrisecreditunion;
www.facebook.com/SunriseCreditUnion; twitter.com/sunrisecu
Former Name: Cypress River Credit Union; Hartney Credit
Union; Tiger Hills Credit Union; Turtle Mountain Credit Union;
Virden Credit Union
Ownership: Member-owned
Year Founded: 2008
Assets: $1,323,240,350 Year End: 20191231
Revenues: $48,936,733 Year End: 20191231

Sunshine Coast Credit Union
985 Gibsons Way
Gibsons, BC V0N 1V0
Tel: 604-740-2662; *Toll-Free:* 800-320-4588
inquiries@sunshineccu.net
www.sunshineccu.com
Other Contact Information: Lost or Stolen Cards, Toll-Free:
800-561-7849; Telephone Banking, Toll-Free: 855-590-1136
www.instagram.com/sunshineccu;
www.facebook.com/sunshinecoastcreditunion
Ownership: Member-owned
Year Founded: 1941
Number of Employees: 90
Assets: $761,340,201 Year End: 20191231
Revenues: $3,891,222 Year End: 20191231

Sydney Credit Union
PO Box 1386
95 Townsend St.
Sydney, NS B1P 5K9
Tel: 902-562-5593; *Fax:* 902-539-8448
sydney@sydneycreditunion.com
www.sydneycreditunion.com
www.youtube.com/user/CreditUnionSydney;
www.instagram.com/sydneycreditunion;
www.facebook.com/SydneyCreditUnion;
twitter.com/SydCreditUnion

Ownership: Member-owned
Year Founded: 1935

Assets: $200,960,500 Year End: 20181231
Revenues: $7,688,384 Year End: 20181231

Synergy Credit Union
#101, 4908 - 42nd St.
Lloydminster, SK S9V 0E5
webmail@synergycu.ca
www.synergycu.ca
www.youtube.com/user/SynergyCreditUnion;
www.instagram.com/synergy_cu;
www.facebook.com/SynergyCreditUnion; twitter.com/synergycu
Year Founded: 1942
Assets: $1,421,615,000 Year End: 20191231

Taiwanese-Canadian (Toronto) Credit Union Limited
Metro Square
#305, 3636 Steeles Ave. East
Markham, ON L3R 1K9
Tel: 905-944-0981; *Fax:* 905-944-0982
Toll-Free: 866-889-8893
info@tctcu.com
www.tctcu.com

Also Known As: Taiwanese Credit Union
Ownership: Member-owned
Year Founded: 1978

Talka Credit Union Limited
830 Main St. East
Hamilton, ON L8M 1L6
Tel: 905-544-7125; *Fax:* 905-544-7126
talkacu@talka.ca
www.talka.ca
Former Name: Talka Lithuanian Credit Union Limited; Talka
Hamilton Credit Union
Year Founded: 1955

Tandem Financial Credit Union
44 Main St. East
Milton, ON L9T 1N3
Fax: 905-878-5500
Toll-Free: 800-598-2891
www.tandia.com
www.facebook.com/TandiaFinancialCreditUnion;
twitter.com/tandiatweets
Former Name: Hamilton Teachers' Credit Union Limited;
Prosperity One Credit Union Limited; Halton Community Credit
Union
Also Known As: Tandia
Ownership: Member-owned
Year Founded: 1957
Assets: $50-100 million

Tandia Credit Union Limited
44 Main St. East
Milton, ON L9T 1N3
Fax: 905-878-5500
Toll-Free: 800-598-2891
tandia.com
www.instagram.com/tandiafinancialcreditunion;
www.facebook.com/TandiaFinancialCreditUnion;
twitter.com/tandiatweets
Also Known As: Tandia
Ownership: Member-owned

TCU Financial Group
2615 Quance St., #E
Regina, SK S4V 3B7
Tel: 306-546-7800; *Fax:* 306-525-5019
tcu@tcu.sk.ca
www.tcufinancialgroup.com
Other Contact Information: TeleService Toll-Free Phone:
844-753-4270; Lost or Stolen Member Card or Debit Card
Toll-Free Phone: 877-828-4343
Ownership: Member-owned
Assets: $739,382,055
Revenues: $26,931,821

Teachers Plus Credit Union
#16, 36 Brookshire Ct.
Bedford, NS B4A 4E9
Tel: 902-477-5664; *Fax:* 902-477-4108
Toll-Free: 800-565-3103
www.teachersplus.ca
www.facebook.com/TeachersPlusCU
Former Name: Nova Scotia Teachers Credit Union
Ownership: Member-owned
Year Founded: 1956
Assets: $56,665,307 Year End: 20181231
Revenues: $2,161,232 Year End: 20181231

Thorold Community Credit Union
63 Front St. South
Thorold, ON L2V 0A7
Tel: 905-227-1106; *Fax:* 905-227-1109
www.thoroldcu.com
www.facebook.com/349116621855654

Tignish Credit Union Ltd.
PO Box 40
284 Business St.
Tignish, PE C0B 2B0
Tel: 902-882-2303; *Fax:* 902-882-3733
www.tignishcreditu.com
Ownership: Member-owned
Number of Employees: 37
Assets: $186,229,970 Year End: 20181231
Revenues: $9,253,644 Year End: 20181231

TransCanada Credit Union
450 - 1st St. SW
Calgary, AB T2P 5H1
Tel: 403-920-2664; *Fax:* 403-920-2445
credit_union@transcanada.com
www.transcanadacreditunion.com
Ownership: Member-owned

Turtleford Credit Union Ltd.
PO Box 370
208 Main St.
Turtleford, SK S0M 2Y0
Tel: 306-845-2105; *Fax:* 306-845-3035
info@turtleford.cu.sk.ca
turtleford.cu.sk.ca
www.facebook.com/turtleford.cu
Year Founded: 1972
Assets: $85,510,761 Year End: 20191231

Ukrainian Credit Union Limited (UCU)
#300, 145 Evans Ave.
Toronto, ON M8Z 5X8
Tel: 416-922-4407; *Fax:* 416-762-1803
Toll-Free: 800-461-0777
ucucentre@ukrainiancu.com
www.ukrainiancu.com
www.facebook.com/ucuykc; twitter.com/UCUYKC
Former Name: United Ukrainian Credit Union Limited
Ownership: Member-owned
Year Founded: 2013

UNI Coopération Financière
Also listed under: Domestic Banks: Schedule I
Édifice Martin-J.-Légère
CP 5554
295, boul St-Pierre ouest
Caraquet, NB E1W 1B7
Tél: 506-726-4725; *Ligne sans frais:* 833-292-4576
uni.communaute@uni.ca
www.uni.ca
www.instagram.com/unicooperation;
www.facebook.com/unicooperation; twitter.com/UNIcooperation
Also Known As: Fédération des caisses populaires acadiennes
ltée
Ownership: A subsidiary of the Desjardins Group
Year Founded: 1946
Number of Employees: 1,000
Assets: $4,400,000,000

Union Bay Credit Union
PO Box 158
313 McLeod Rd.
Union Bay, BC V0R 3B0
Tel: 250-335-2122; *Fax:* 250-335-2131
ubcu@ubcu.ca
www.ubcu.ca
Ownership: Member-owned
Year Founded: 1944
Assets: $91,802,037 Year End: 20181231
Revenues: $2,782,566 Year End: 20181231

United Employees Credit Union Limited
964 Eastern Ave.
Toronto, ON M4L 1A6
Tel: 416-461-9257; *Fax:* 416-461-8141
Toll-Free: 800-894-7644
infounited@unitedcu.com
www.unitedcu.com
Year Founded: 1944

Unity Credit Union Ltd.
PO Box 370
120 - 2nd Ave. East
Unity, SK S0K 4L0

Tel: 306-228-2688; *Fax:* 306-228-2185
info@unitycu.ca
www.unitycu.ca
www.instagram.com/UnityCU; www.facebook.com/UnityCU;
twitter.com/UnitySkCU

Year Founded: 1941
Assets: $269,619,716 Year End: 20191231

Valley Credit Union
5680 Hwy. #1
Waterville, NS B0P 1V0

Tel: 902-538-4510; *Fax:* 902-538-4529
vcu.admin@valleycreditunion.com
www.valleycreditunion.com
www.facebook.com/valleycreditunion; twitter.com/valleycu
Ownership: Member-owned
Year Founded: 1994
Assets: $176,705,943 Year End: 20181231
Revenues: $7,207,694 Year End: 20181231

Valley First Credit Union
184 Main St., 1st Fl.
Penticton, BC V2A 8G7

Tel: 250-490-2720
contact@valleyfirst.com
www.valleyfirst.com
Other Contact Information: Telephone Banking Toll-Free Phone:
800-667-8328; Lost or Stolen MasterCard Toll-Free Phone:
800-567-8111
www.youtube.com/user/FirstWestCU;
www.facebook.com/valley.first; twitter.com/Valley_First
Former Name: Valley Field Credit Union
Also Known As: Valley First Financial Group
Ownership: A division of First West Credit Union
Year Founded: 2001
Assets: $1-10 billion

Vancouver City Savings Credit Union
PO Box 2120, Stn. Terminal
Vancouver, BC V6B 5R8

Tel: 604-877-7000; *Toll-Free:* 888-826-2489
www.vancity.com
Other Contact Information: Governance Practice Inquiries,
Email: board_governance@vancity.com
www.youtube.com/vancityca; www.instagram.com/vancitycu;
www.facebook.com/Vancity; twitter.com/Vancity
Also Known As: VanCity Credit Union
Year Founded: 1946
Assets: $1-10 billion

VantageOne Credit Union
Main Branch
3108 - 33rd Ave.
Vernon, BC V1T 2N7

Tel: 250-545-9251; *Fax:* 250-545-1957
Toll-Free: 888-339-8328
www.vantageone.net
Other Contact Information: Memberlink Toll-Free Phone:
855-393-2030
twitter.com/VantageOneCU
Former Name: Vernon & District Credit Union
Ownership: Co-operative. Member-owned.
Year Founded: 1944
Number of Employees: 45
Assets: $367,625,297 Year End: 20181231
Revenues: $11,981,081 Year End: 20181231

Venture Credit Union Limited
Administrative Offices & Glovertown Branch
PO Box 527
4 Station Rd.
Glovertown, NL A0G 2L0

Tel: 709-533-9184; *Fax:* 709-533-9193
www.venturecu.ca
Former Name: First Coastal Credit Union Limited; Tri-Island
Credit Union Limited
Ownership: Member-owned
Assets: $10-50 million

Vermilion Credit Union Ltd.
5019 - 50th Ave.
Vermilion, AB T9X 1A7

Tel: 780-853-2822; *Fax:* 780-853-4361
www.vermillioncreditunion.com
www.youtube.com/user/VermilionCreditUnion;
www.instagram.com/vermilioncreditunion;
www.facebook.com/VermilionCreditUnion;
twitter.com/vermilioncu
Former Name: Vermilion Savings & Credit Union Ltd.
Year Founded: 1943

Assets: $208,225,732 Year End: 20201231

Victory Credit Union
PO Box 340
41 Gerrish St.
Windsor, NS B0N 2T0

Tel: 902-798-1820; *Fax:* 902-798-1255
www.victorycreditunion.ca
www.facebook.com/VictoryCreditUnion; twitter.com/VictoryCU
Ownership: Member-owned
Assets: $54,467,718 Year End: 20181231
Revenues: $1,922,519 Year End: 20181231

Vision Credit Union Ltd.
5007 - 51st St.
Camrose, AB T4V 1S6

Tel: 780-672-1175; *Fax:* 780-672-5996
www.visioncu.ca
Former Name: Battle River Credit Union Ltd.; Horizon Credit
Union Ltd.
Ownership: Member-owned
Year Founded: 2014
Assets: $500m-1 billion

Westoba Credit Union Limited
220 - 10th St.
Brandon, MB R7A 4E8

Tel: 204-729-2050; *Fax:* 204-729-8852
Toll-Free: 877-937-8622
infowcul@westoba.com
www.westoba.com
www.facebook.com/WestobaCU; twitter.com/WestobaCU
Ownership: Member-owned
Year Founded: 1963
Number of Employees: 200
Assets: $500m-1 billion
Revenues: $10-50 million

Weyburn Credit Union Limited
PO Box 1117
205 Coteau Ave.
Weyburn, SK S4H 2L3

Tel: 306-842-6641; *Fax:* 306-842-6620
Toll-Free: 800-667-8842
info@weyburncu.ca
www.weyburncu.ca
Other Contact Information: Touch Tone TeleService:
306-842-1200; Lost or stolen MemberCard or Credit Union
MasterCard: 800-567-8111 (within Canada or Continental USA)
Ownership: Member-owned
Year Founded: 1944
Assets: 735,000,000
Revenues: $50-100 million

Williams Lake & District Credit Union
139 North 3rd Ave.
Williams Lake, BC V2G 2A5

Tel: 250-392-4135; *Fax:* 250-392-4361
info@wldcu.com
www.wldcu.com
www.facebook.com/WLDCUCommunity
Year Founded: 1952
Assets: $333,740,597 Year End: 20191231

Windsor Family Credit Union Limited
3000 Marentette Ave.
Windsor, ON N8X 4G2

Tel: 519-974-3100
www.wfcu.ca
www.facebook.com/WindsorFamilyCreditUnion
Former Name: Hir-Walk Employees' (Windsor) Credit Union
Also Known As: WFCU Credit Union

Winnipeg Police Credit Union Ltd.
300 William Ave.
Winnipeg, MB R3A 1P9

Tel: 204-944-1033; *Fax:* 204-949-0821
Toll-Free: 866-491-7122
info@wpcu.ca
www.wpcu.ca
www.facebook.com/205575229591394
Year Founded: 1949
Assets: $211,695,557 Year End: 20200930

Your Credit Union Limited
14 Chamberlain Ave
Ottawa, ON K1S 1V9

Tel: 613-238-8001; *Toll-Free:* 800-379-7757
info@yourcu.com
www.yourcu.com
www.facebook.com/YourCreditUnion; twitter.com/YourCreditU
Ownership: Member-owned
Year Founded: 1950
Number of Employees: 60

Your Neighbourhood Credit Union Ltd.
Corporate Office
38 Executive Pl.
Kitchener, ON N2P 2N4

Tel: 519-804-9190
info@yncu.com
www.yncu.com
www.facebook.com/YourNCU; twitter.com/YourNCU
Former Name: boomerang CREDIT UNION Limited; Windsor &
Essex Educational Credit Union
Ownership: Member-owned
Year Founded: 1953

Insurance Companies

*Insurance companies are registered to conduct business under
the federal Insurance Companies Act and/or corresponding provincial legislation. Life insurance companies are registered to underwrite life insurance, accident and sickness insurance and
annuity business. Property and casualty insurance companies
are registered to underwrite insurance other than life insurance.
Included in these listings are federally and provincially incorporated insurance companies, reinsurance companies, fraternal
benefit societies and reciprocal exchanges, with the classes of
insurance they offer.
Companies marked with an *are provincially incorporated. For
provincially incorporated companies not listed below, contact the
government agency for each province. For further information,
please see the "Government Quick Reference" guide at the beginning of Section 7, and check under "Insurance."
Classes of insurance listed below include: Accident, Auto, Aircraft, Boiler & Machinery, Credit, Fidelity, Fire, Hail & Crop, Legal
Expense, Liability, Life, Marine, Personal Accident & Sickness,
Property, Reinsurance, Surety, and Theft.*

Accident
American Bankers Life Assurance Company of Florida
Assumption Mutual Life Insurance Company
AssurePro Insurance Company
Ayr Farmers Mutual Insurance Company
Caisse centrale de Réassurance
The Canada Life Assurance Company
Canadian Professional Sales Association
CIGNA Life Insurance Company of Canada
Connecticut General Life Insurance Co.
Continental Casualty Company
CUMIS Life Insurance Company
Desjardins Sécurité financière
Echelon Insurance
Empire Life Insurance Company
FaithLife Financial
Farm Mutual Reinsurance Plan Inc.
Federated Insurance Company of Canada
The Guarantee Company of North America
Life Insurance Company of North America
Noble Insurance
The Nordic Insurance Company of Canada
Northbridge Insurance
OdysseyRe - Canadian Branch
Old Republic Insurance Company of Canada
Optimum Réassurance inc.
PBC Health Benefits Society
Peace Hills General Insurance Company
Promutuel Assurance
Québec Blue Cross
Société de l'assurance automobile du Québec
South Easthope Mutual Insurance Co.
Tradition Mutual Insurance Company
Trillium Mutual Insurance Company
Western Financial Group Inc.
Zurich Canada

Aircraft
AIG Insurance Company of Canada
Allianz Global Risks US Insurance Company
Aviva Canada Inc.
AXA XL Reinsurance
Berkley Canada
Caisse centrale de Réassurance
Canadian Universities Reciprocal Insurance Exchange
Chubb Insurance Company of Canada
Continental Casualty Company
Co-operators General Insurance Company
Desjardins Insurance
Elite Insurance Company
Everest Insurance Company of Canada
Everest Reinsurance Company
Farm Mutual Reinsurance Plan Inc.
General Reinsurance Corporation
Great American Insurance Company
Hannover Rück SE Canadian Branch

Hartford Fire Insurance Company
Heartland Farm Mutual Inc.
Henderson Insurance Inc.
Johnston Meier Insurance Agencies Group
Liberty Mutual Insurance Company
Lloyd's Underwriters
Mitsui Sumitomo Insurance Co., Limited.
OdysseyRe - Canadian Branch
Old Republic Insurance Company of Canada
Omega General Insurance Company
Peace Hills General Insurance Company
The Personal Insurance Company
TD General Insurance Company
Travelers Canada
Wedgwood Insurance Limited
Westport Insurance Corporation

Auto

AIG Insurance Company of Canada
Alberta Motor Association Insurance Co.
Algoma Mutual Insurance Co.
Allianz Global Risks US Insurance Company
Allstate Insurance Company of Canada
L'ALPHA, compagnie d'assurances inc.
Alpine Insurance & Financial Inc.
The American Road Insurance Company
Archway Insurance
Astro Insurance 1000 Inc.
Atlantic Insurance Company Limited
Aviva Canada Inc.
Aviva General Insurance Company
A-WIN Insurance
AXA XL
AXA XL Reinsurance
Axion Insurance Services Inc.
Ayr Farmers Mutual Insurance Company
Bay of Quinte Mutual Insurance Co.
BCM Insurance Company
Belair Insurance Company Inc.
Berkley Canada
Brant Mutual Insurance Company
British Columbia Automobile Association Insurance Agency
Butler Byers Insurance Ltd.
CAA Insurance Company (Ontario)
Caisse centrale de Réassurance
Canadian Northern Shield Insurance Company
Canadian Professional Sales Association
La Capitale assurances générales inc.
Caradoc Townsend Mutual Insurance Company
Carleton-Fundy Mutual Insurance Company
Certas Direct Insurance Company
Chubb Insurance Company of Canada
Coastal Community Insurance Services (2007) Ltd.
The Commonwell Mutual Insurance Group
La Compagnie d'Assurance Missisquoi
Continental Casualty Company
Co-operators General Insurance Company
CorePointe Insurance Company
COSECO Insurance Company
Crowsnest Insurance Agencies Ltd.
CUMIS General Insurance Company
The CUMIS Group Limited
CUMIS Life Insurance Company
Desjardins assurances générales inc
Desjardins Groupe d'assurances générales inc
Desjardins Insurance
DMW Insurance Ltd.
Dufferin Mutual Insurance Company
Dumfries Mutual Insurance Company
Ecclesiastical Insurance Office plc
Echelon Insurance
Economical Mutual Insurance Company
Edge Mutual Insurance Company
Elite Insurance Company
Energy Insurance Group Ltd.
Erie Mutual Insurance Company
Everest Insurance Company of Canada
Everest Reinsurance Company
Farm Mutual Reinsurance Plan Inc.
Federal Insurance Company
Federated Insurance Company of Canada
Fenchurch General Insurance Company
First North American Insurance Company
General Reinsurance Corporation
Gibbs Insurance Service Inc.
Gore Mutual Insurance Company
Great American Insurance Company
Grenville Mutual Insurance Company
Le Groupe Estrie-Richelieu, compagnie d'assurance
Groupe Promutuel, Fédération de sociétés mutuelles d'assurance générale

The Guarantee Company of North America
Halwell Mutual Insurance Company
Hannover Rück SE Canadian Branch
Hartford Fire Insurance Company
Heartland Farm Mutual Inc.
Henderson Insurance Inc.
Howard Mutual Insurance Co.
Howick Mutual Insurance Company
HT&C Mutual Insurance Company
HTM Insurance Company
HUB International Barton Insurance Brokers
HUB International British Columbia
HUB International Manitoba Limited
HUB International Nunavut
HUB International Ontario
HUB International Québec
iA Financial Group
Industrial Alliance Auto & Home Insurance
Insurance Company of Prince Edward Island
Insurance Corporation of British Columbia
Intact Insurance Company of Canada
Jevco Insurance Company
Johnston Meier Insurance Agencies Group
Kent & Essex Mutual Insurance Company
Kirkham Insurance
Lambton Mutual Insurance Company
Lennox & Addington Mutual Insurance Company
Liberty Mutual Insurance Company
Lloyd's Underwriters
Manitoba Public Insurance
McKillop Mutual Insurance Company
Meloche Monnex Inc.
Mennonite Mutual Insurance Co. (Alberta) Ltd.
Middlesex Mutual Insurance Co.
Millennium Insurance Corporation
Mitsui Sumitomo Insurance Co., Limited.
Morgex Insurance
Motors Insurance Corporation
Munich Reinsurance Company of Canada
New Diamond Insurance Services Ltd.
Noble Insurance
The Nordic Insurance Company of Canada
North Blenheim Mutual Insurance Company
North Kent Mutual Fire Insurance Company
Northbridge Insurance
Northern Savings Insurance Services Ltd.
Nova Mutual Insurance Company
Novex Group Insurance
Nuera Insurance inc.
OdysseyRe - Canadian Branch
Old Republic Insurance Company of Canada
Ontario Mutual Insurance Association
Ontario School Boards' Insurance Exchange
Optimum Assurance Agricole inc.
Optimum Général inc.
Optimum Société d'Assurance inc.
Optimum West Insurance Company Inc.
Pafco Insurance Company
PartnerRe
PC Financial Insurance Brokers Inc.
Peace Hills General Insurance Company
Peel Mutual Insurance Company
Pembridge Insurance Company
The Personal General Insurance Inc.
The Personal Insurance Company
Perth Insurance Company
Pilot Insurance Company
The Portage La Prairie Mutual Insurance Company
Primmum Insurance Company
Québec Blue Cross
RBC Insurance
Royal & Sun Alliance Insurance Company of Canada
S&Y Insurance Company
Saskatchewan Government Insurance
Saskatchewan Mutual Insurance Company
Scottish & York Insurance Co. Limited
Security National Insurance Company
Servus Insurance Services - Home & Auto
Sirius America Insurance Company
Société de l'assurance automobile du Québec
South Easthope Mutual Insurance Co.
Stanley Mutual Insurance Company
Suecia Reinsurance Company
TD General Insurance Company
TD Home & Auto Insurance Company
Thomson Jemmett Vogelzang
The Tokio Marine & Nichido Fire Insurance Co., Ltd.
Traders General Insurance Company
Tradition Mutual Insurance Company
Trafalgar Insurance Company of Canada

Travelers Canada
Trillium Mutual Insurance Company
TruShield Insurance Services Ltd.
Unica Insurance Inc.
Unifund Assurance Company
United General Insurance Corporation
Usborne & Hibbert Mutual Fire Insurance Company
Virginia Surety Company, Inc.
The Wawanesa Mutual Insurance Company
Wedgwood Insurance Limited
West Elgin Mutual Insurance Company
West Wawanosh Mutual Insurance Company
Western Assurance Company
Western Financial Group Inc.
Westland Insurance Group Ltd.
Westminster Mutual Insurance Company
Westport Insurance Corporation
Wyatt Dowling Insurance Brokers
Yarmouth Mutual Fire Insurance Company
Zurich Canada

Boiler & Machinery

Affiliated FM Insurance Company
AIG Insurance Company of Canada
Allianz Global Risks US Insurance Company
Allstate Insurance Company of Canada
The American Road Insurance Company
Atlantic Insurance Company Limited
Aviva Canada Inc.
AXA XL
AXA XL Reinsurance
Ayr Farmers Mutual Insurance Company
Bay of Quinte Mutual Insurance Co.
BCM Insurance Company
Belair Insurance Company Inc.
Berkley Canada
Brant Mutual Insurance Company
Caisse centrale de Réassurance
Canadian Farm Insurance Corp.
Caradoc Townsend Mutual Insurance Company
Carleton-Fundy Mutual Insurance Company
Chubb Insurance Company of Canada
The Commonwell Mutual Insurance Group
La Compagnie d'Assurance Missisquoi
Continental Casualty Company
Co-operators General Insurance Company
CUMIS General Insurance Company
Desjardins assurances générales inc
Desjardins Insurance
Dufferin Mutual Insurance Company
Dumfries Mutual Insurance Company
Ecclesiastical Insurance Office plc
Economical Mutual Insurance Company
Edge Mutual Insurance Company
Elite Insurance Company
Energy Insurance Group Ltd.
Erie Mutual Insurance Company
Everest Insurance Company of Canada
Everest Reinsurance Company
Farm Mutual Reinsurance Plan Inc.
Federal Insurance Company
Federated Insurance Company of Canada
Fenchurch General Insurance Company
FM Global
General Reinsurance Corporation
Great American Insurance Company
Grenville Mutual Insurance Company
Le Groupe Estrie-Richelieu, compagnie d'assurance
The Guarantee Company of North America
Halwell Mutual Insurance Company
Hannover Rück SE Canadian Branch
Hartford Fire Insurance Company
Heartland Farm Mutual Inc.
Howick Mutual Insurance Company
HSB BI&I
HUB International Atlantic Limited
Kent & Essex Mutual Insurance Company
Lambton Mutual Insurance Company
Liberty Mutual Insurance Company
Lloyd's Underwriters
MAX Canada Insurance Company
McKillop Mutual Insurance Company
Mitsui Sumitomo Insurance Co., Limited.
Motors Insurance Corporation
Mutuelle d'assurance en Église
My Mutual Insurance
The Nordic Insurance Company of Canada
Novex Group Insurance
OdysseyRe - Canadian Branch
Omega General Insurance Company
Ontario School Boards' Insurance Exchange

Peace Hills General Insurance Company
Peel Mutual Insurance Company
The Personal General Insurance Inc.
The Personal Insurance Company
Promutuel Assurance
Red River Mutual
Saskatchewan Mutual Insurance Company
Scottish & York Insurance Co. Limited
South Easthope Mutual Insurance Co.
Southeastern Mutual Insurance Company
Stanley Mutual Insurance Company
TD General Insurance Company
Temple Insurance Company
Tradition Mutual Insurance Company
Travelers Canada
Trillium Mutual Insurance Company
Usborne & Hibbert Mutual Fire Insurance Company
Virginia Surety Company, Inc.
The Wawanesa Mutual Insurance Company
West Wawanosh Mutual Insurance Company
Western Financial Group Inc.
Westport Insurance Corporation
Wynward Insurance Group
Zurich Canada

Credit
AIG Insurance Company of Canada
The American Road Insurance Company
Assurance-Vie Banque Nationale
Assurant Solutions Canada
Berkley Canada
The Canada Life Assurance Company
Canadian Premier Life Insurance Company
CIGNA Life Insurance Company of Canada
Continental Casualty Company
CUMIS Life Insurance Company
Euler Hermes Canada
Everest Insurance Company of Canada
Everest Reinsurance Company
General Reinsurance Corporation
The Guarantee Company of North America
Novex Group Insurance
Omega General Insurance Company
Peace Hills General Insurance Company
Transatlantic Reinsurance Company
Westport Insurance Corporation
Zurich Canada

Fidelity
Affiliated FM Insurance Company
AIG Insurance Company of Canada
Allstate Insurance Company of Canada
ATB Financial
Atlantic Insurance Company Limited
Aviva Canada Inc.
AXA XL Reinsurance
Ayr Farmers Mutual Insurance Company
Bay of Quinte Mutual Insurance Co.
BCM Insurance Company
Belair Insurance Company Inc.
Berkley Canada
Brant Mutual Insurance Company
Caisse centrale de Réassurance
Canadian Farm Insurance Corp.
Chubb Insurance Company of Canada
La Compagnie d'Assurance Missisquoi
Continental Casualty Company
Co-operators General Insurance Company
CUMIS General Insurance Company
CUMIS Life Insurance Company
Desjardins Insurance
Dufferin Mutual Insurance Company
Ecclesiastical Insurance Office plc
Echelon Insurance
Edge Mutual Insurance Company
Elite Insurance Company
Erie Mutual Insurance Company
Everest Reinsurance Company
Farm Mutual Reinsurance Plan Inc.
Federal Insurance Company
Federated Insurance Company of Canada
General Reinsurance Corporation
Great American Insurance Company
Grenville Mutual Insurance Company
The Guarantee Company of North America
Halwell Mutual Insurance Company
Hannover Rück SE Canadian Branch
Hartford Fire Insurance Company
Heartland Farm Mutual Inc.
Howard Mutual Insurance Co.
Kent & Essex Mutual Insurance Company

Lambton Mutual Insurance Company
Liberty Mutual Insurance Company
Lloyd's Underwriters
MAX Canada Insurance Company
McKillop Mutual Insurance Company
Mitsui Sumitomo Insurance Co., Limited.
The Nordic Insurance Company of Canada
Nova Mutual Insurance Company
Novex Group Insurance
Omega General Insurance Company
Peace Hills General Insurance Company
Peel Mutual Insurance Company
The Personal Insurance Company
Red River Mutual
Saskatchewan Mutual Insurance Company
Scottish & York Insurance Co. Limited
Sirius America Insurance Company
Suecia Reinsurance Company
Swiss Reinsurance Company Canada
TD General Insurance Company
Tradition Mutual Insurance Company
Travelers Canada
Trillium Mutual Insurance Company
West Elgin Mutual Insurance Company
West Wawanosh Mutual Insurance Company
Western Assurance Company
Western Financial Group Inc.
Western Surety Company
Westport Insurance Corporation
Wynward Insurance Group
Zurich Canada

Fire
Affiliated FM Insurance Company
Alberta Motor Association Insurance Co.
Antigonish Farmers' Mutual Insurance Company
Aviva General Insurance Company
British Columbia Automobile Association Insurance Agency
Caisse centrale de Réassurance
Clare Mutual Insurance Company
La Compagnie d'Assurance Missisquoi
Co-operators General Insurance Company
CUMIS General Insurance Company
CUMIS Life Insurance Company
Desjardins Insurance
Echelon Insurance
Federated Insurance Company of Canada
Germania Mutual Insurance Company
Gore Mutual Insurance Company
Le Groupe Estrie-Richelieu, compagnie d'assurance
The Guarantee Company of North America
Hartford Fire Insurance Company
HTM Insurance Company
Lloyd's Underwriters
Mennonite Mutual Insurance Co. (Alberta) Ltd.
The Mutual Fire Insurance Company of British Columbia
Mutuelle d'assurance en Église
My Mutual Insurance
Noble Insurance
North Kent Mutual Fire Insurance Company
OdysseyRe - Canadian Branch
Ontario School Boards' Insurance Exchange
Optimum Assurance Agricole inc.
Peace Hills General Insurance Company
Prince Edward Island Mutual Insurance Company
Promutuel Assurance
Red River Mutual
Security National Insurance Company
Southeastern Mutual Insurance Company
The Tokio Marine & Nichido Fire Insurance Co., Ltd.
Travelers Canada
The Wawanesa Mutual Insurance Company
Western Assurance Company
Western Financial Group Inc.
Wynward Insurance Group
Zurich Canada

Hail & Crop
Agriculture Financial Services Corporation
AIG Insurance Company of Canada
Allianz Global Risks US Insurance Company
Astro Insurance 1000 Inc.
Aviva Canada Inc.
AXA XL Reinsurance
Ayr Farmers Mutual Insurance Company
Berkley Canada
Brant Mutual Insurance Company
Clare Mutual Insurance Company
The Commonwell Mutual Insurance Group
Continental Casualty Company
Co-operative Hail Insurance Company Ltd.

Co-operators General Insurance Company
Dumfries Mutual Insurance Company
Everest Insurance Company of Canada
Everest Reinsurance Company
General Reinsurance Corporation
Great American Insurance Company
The Guarantee Company of North America
Hannover Rück SE Canadian Branch
Hartford Fire Insurance Company
Heartland Farm Mutual Inc.
Henderson Insurance Inc.
Howard Mutual Insurance Co.
HT&C Mutual Insurance Company
Lambton Mutual Insurance Company
Manitoba Agricultural Services Corporation
North Kent Mutual Fire Insurance Company
Northbridge Insurance
OdysseyRe - Canadian Branch
Optimum West Insurance Company Inc.
Palliser Insurance Company Limited
Rain & Hail Insurance Corporation
Saskatchewan Crop Insurance Corporation
Saskatchewan Municipal Hail Insurance Association
Sirius America Insurance Company
Suecia Reinsurance Company
Tradition Mutual Insurance Company
Trillium Mutual Insurance Company
West Elgin Mutual Insurance Company
Western Financial Group Inc.
Westport Insurance Corporation
Yarmouth Mutual Fire Insurance Company

Legal Expense
Allstate Insurance Company of Canada
Aviva Canada Inc.
Belair Insurance Company Inc.
Berkley Canada
CAA Insurance Company (Ontario)
Caisse centrale de Réassurance
La Compagnie d'Assurance Missisquoi
Echelon Insurance
Farm Mutual Reinsurance Plan Inc.
The Guarantee Company of North America
Lloyd's Underwriters
The Nordic Insurance Company of Canada
Novex Group Insurance
Omega General Insurance Company
The Portage La Prairie Mutual Insurance Company
Scottish & York Insurance Co. Limited

Liability
Affiliated FM Insurance Company
AIG Insurance Company of Canada
Allianz Global Risks US Insurance Company
Allstate Insurance Company of Canada
Alpine Insurance & Financial Inc.
The American Road Insurance Company
Amherst Island Mutual Insurance Company
Archway Insurance
Astro Insurance 1000 Inc.
Atlantic Insurance Company Limited
Aviva Canada Inc.
Aviva General Insurance Company
A-WIN Insurance
AXA XL
AXA XL Reinsurance
Ayr Farmers Mutual Insurance Company
Bay of Quinte Mutual Insurance Co.
BCM Insurance Company
Belair Insurance Company Inc.
Berkley Canada
Brant Mutual Insurance Company
CAA Insurance Company (Ontario)
Caisse centrale de Réassurance
Canadian Farm Insurance Corp.
Canadian Northern Shield Insurance Company
Canadian Universities Reciprocal Insurance Exchange
Canassurance Insurance Company
Caradoc Townsend Mutual Insurance Company
Carleton-Fundy Mutual Insurance Company
Certas Direct Insurance Company
Chubb Insurance Company of Canada
The Commonwell Mutual Insurance Group
La Compagnie d'Assurance Missisquoi
Continental Casualty Company
CorePointe Insurance Company
Crowsnest Insurance Agencies Ltd.
Desjardins assurances générales inc
Desjardins Insurance
Dufferin Mutual Insurance Company
Dumfries Mutual Insurance Company

Ecclesiastical Insurance Office plc
Echelon Insurance
Edge Mutual Insurance Company
Elite Insurance Company
Energy Insurance Group Ltd.
Erie Mutual Insurance Company
Everest Insurance Company of Canada
Everest Reinsurance Company
Farm Mutual Reinsurance Plan Inc.
Federal Insurance Company
Federated Insurance Company of Canada
Fenchurch General Insurance Company
General Reinsurance Corporation
Germania Mutual Insurance Company
Gore Mutual Insurance Company
Great American Insurance Company
Grenville Mutual Insurance Company
Le Groupe Estrie-Richelieu, compagnie d'assurance
The Guarantee Company of North America
Halwell Mutual Insurance Company
Hannover Rück SE Canadian Branch
Hartford Fire Insurance Company
Heartland Farm Mutual Inc.
Henderson Insurance Inc.
Howard Mutual Insurance Co.
Howick Mutual Insurance Company
HSB BI&I
HT&C Mutual Insurance Company
HUB International Atlantic Limited
HUB International Manitoba Limited
Kent & Essex Mutual Insurance Company
Lambton Mutual Insurance Company
Lawyers' Professional Indemnity Company
Legacy General Insurance Company
Lennox & Addington Mutual Insurance Company
Liberty Mutual Insurance Company
Lloyd's Underwriters
MAX Canada Insurance Company
McKillop Mutual Insurance Company
Mennonite Mutual Insurance Co. (Alberta) Ltd.
Middlesex Mutual Insurance Co.
Mitsui Sumitomo Insurance Co., Limited.
Motors Insurance Corporation
Munich Reinsurance Company of Canada
Municipal Insurance Association of British Columbia
MUNIX Reciprocal
Mutuelle d'assurance en Église
The Nordic Insurance Company of Canada
North Blenheim Mutual Insurance Company
North Kent Mutual Fire Insurance Company
Northbridge Insurance
Nova Mutual Insurance Company
Novex Group Insurance
OdysseyRe - Canadian Branch
Old Republic Insurance Company of Canada
Omega General Insurance Company
Ontario School Boards' Insurance Exchange
Optimum Général inc.
Optimum Société d'Assurance inc.
Pafco Insurance Company
Peace Hills General Insurance Company
Peel Mutual Insurance Company
The Personal General Insurance Inc.
The Personal Insurance Company
The Portage La Prairie Mutual Insurance Company
Prince Edward Island Mutual Insurance Company
Promutuel Assurance
Québec Blue Cross
Real Estate Insurance Exchange
Red River Mutual
Saskatchewan Mutual Insurance Company
Scottish & York Insurance Co. Limited
Sirius America Insurance Company
Southeastern Mutual Insurance Company
Stanley Mutual Insurance Company
Suecia Reinsurance Company
TD General Insurance Company
TD Home & Auto Insurance Company
Thomson Jemmett Vogelzang
Tradition Mutual Insurance Company
Trans Global Insurance Company
Travelers Canada
Trillium Mutual Insurance Company
Trisura Guarantee Insurance Company
TruShield Insurance Services Ltd.
Unica Insurance Inc.
Usborne & Hibbert Mutual Fire Insurance Company
Virginia Surety Company, Inc.
The Wawanesa Mutual Insurance Company
West Elgin Mutual Insurance Company

West Wawanosh Mutual Insurance Company
Western Assurance Company
Western Financial Group Inc.
Westland Insurance Group Ltd.
Westminster Mutual Insurance Company
Westport Insurance Corporation
Wynward Insurance Group
Yarmouth Mutual Fire Insurance Company
Zurich Canada

Life
ACTRA Fraternal Benefit Society
Alberta Motor Association Insurance Co.
Allianz Life Insurance Company of North America
Alpine Insurance & Financial Inc.
American Bankers Life Assurance Company of Florida
American Health & Life Insurance Company
American Income Life Insurance Company
Archway Insurance
Assumption Mutual Life Insurance Company
Assurance-Vie Banque Nationale
AXA Equitable Life Insurance Company
BMO Life Assurance Company of Canada
British Columbia Automobile Association Insurance Agency
Butler Byers Insurance Ltd.
C Finance Inc.
CAA Insurance Company (Ontario)
Canada Life Assurance Company
Canadian Premier Life Insurance Company
Canadian Professional Sales Association
Canassurance Insurance Company
La Capitale assurances et gestion du patrimoine
La Capitale assureur de l'administration publique inc.
La Capitale Financial Security Insurance Company
CIBC Life Insurance Company Limited
CIGNA Life Insurance Company of Canada
Combined Insurance Company of America
Connecticut General Life Insurance Co.
Co-operators Life Insurance Company
Croatian Fraternal Union of America
The CUMIS Group Limited
CUMIS Life Insurance Company
Desjardins Sécurité financière
DMW Insurance Ltd.
DPB Insurance & Financial Services
Empire Life Insurance Company
The Equitable Life Insurance Company of Canada
FaithLife Financial
Foresters Life Insurance Company
Gerber Life Insurance Company
Goose Insurance Services Inc.
The Grand Orange Lodge of British America Benefit Fund
HUB International Manitoba Limited
Humania Assurance Inc.
iA Financial Group
Independent Order of Foresters
ivari
Johnston Meier Insurance Agencies Group
Knights of Columbus Insurance
Life Insurance Company of North America
Manitoba Blue Cross
Manufacturers Life Insurance Company
Manulife Financial
MD Insurance Agency Limited
Medavie Blue Cross
Metropolitan Tower Life Insurance Company
Munich Reinsurance Company Canada Branch (Life)
New Diamond Insurance Services Ltd.
Nuera Insurance inc.
Optimum Réassurance inc.
The Order of United Commercial Travelers of America
PartnerRe
PBC Health Benefits Society
PC Financial Insurance Brokers Inc.
PPI
PPI Advisory
Primerica Life Insurance Company of Canada
Québec Blue Cross
RBC Insurance
RBC Insurance Company of Canada
RBC Life Insurance Company
Reliable Life Insurance Company
Saskatchewan Blue Cross
SCOR Global Life SE, Canada Branch
Scotia Life Insurance Company
Sun Life Assurance Company of Canada
Sun Life Financial Inc.
Supreme Council of the Royal Arcanum
TD Life Insurance Company
Trans Global Life Insurance Company
Ukrainian Fraternal Society of Canada

Ukrainian National Association
L'Union-Vie, compagnie mutuelle d'assurance
United American Insurance Company
Uv Mutuelle
Vancity Life Insurance Services Ltd.
The Wawanesa Life Insurance Company
Wedgwood Insurance Limited
Western Financial Group Inc.

Marine
AIG Insurance Company of Canada
Allianz Global Risks US Insurance Company
Antigonish Farmers' Mutual Insurance Company
Aviva Canada Inc.
Belair Insurance Company Inc.
Butler Byers Insurance Ltd.
CAA Insurance Company (Ontario)
Canadian Universities Reciprocal Insurance Exchange
Chubb Insurance Company of Canada
Coast Underwriters Limited
Ecclesiastical Insurance Office plc
Elite Insurance Company
Everest Insurance Company of Canada
Farm Mutual Reinsurance Plan Inc.
Federal Insurance Company
Great American Insurance Company
Harlock Murray Underwriting Ltd.
Henderson Insurance Inc.
HUB International Barton Insurance Brokers
HUB International British Columbia
HUB International Nunavut
Johnston Meier Insurance Agencies Group
Lennox & Addington Mutual Insurance Company
MAX Canada Insurance Company
Northbridge Insurance
Northern Savings Insurance Services Ltd.
Pacific Coast Fishermen's Mutual Marine Insurance Company
Peace Hills General Insurance Company
Swiss Reinsurance Company Canada
The Tokio Marine & Nichido Fire Insurance Co., Ltd.
Travelers Canada
Trillium Mutual Insurance Company
Wedgwood Insurance Limited
Western Assurance Company
Zurich Canada

Personal Accident & Sickness
ACTRA Fraternal Benefit Society
AIG Insurance Company of Canada
Alberta Blue Cross
Alberta Motor Association Insurance Co.
Allianz Global Risks US Insurance Company
Allianz Life Insurance Company of North America
Allstate Insurance Company of Canada
American Bankers Life Assurance Company of Florida
American Income Life Insurance Company
Amherst Island Mutual Insurance Company
Archway Insurance
Assumption Mutual Life Insurance Company
Assurance-Vie Banque Nationale
Aviva Canada Inc.
Aviva General Insurance Company
AXA Equitable Life Insurance Company
AXA XL
AXA XL Reinsurance
Ayr Farmers Mutual Insurance Company
Bay of Quinte Mutual Insurance Co.
BCM Insurance Company
Belair Insurance Company Inc.
Berkley Canada
BMO Life Assurance Company of Canada
Brant Mutual Insurance Company
British Columbia Automobile Association Insurance Agency
Butler Byers Insurance Ltd.
C Finance Inc.
CAA Insurance Company (Ontario)
Canada Life Assurance Company
The Canada Life Assurance Company
Canadian Farm Insurance Corp.
Canadian Premier Life Insurance Company
Canadian Professional Sales Association
Canassurance Insurance Company
La Capitale assurances et gestion du patrimoine
La Capitale Financial Security Insurance Company
Caradoc Townsend Mutual Insurance Company
Chubb Insurance Company of Canada
CIBC Life Insurance Company Limited
CIGNA Life Insurance Company of Canada
Combined Insurance Company of America
Connecticut General Life Insurance Co.
Continental Casualty Company

Co-operators General Insurance Company
Co-operators Life Insurance Company
Croatian Fraternal Union of America
The CUMIS Group Limited
CUMIS Life Insurance Company
Desjardins Sécurité financière
DMW Insurance Ltd.
DPB Insurance & Financial Services
Dufferin Mutual Insurance Company
Echelon Insurance
The Economical Insurance Group
Edge Mutual Insurance Company
Elite Insurance Company
Empire Life Insurance Company
Erie Mutual Insurance Company
Everest Reinsurance Company
FaithLife Financial
Federal Insurance Company
Fenchurch General Insurance Company
First North American Insurance Company
Foresters Life Insurance Company
General Reinsurance Corporation
Goose Insurance Services Inc.
Gore Mutual Insurance Company
Great American Insurance Company
Green Shield Canada
Grenville Mutual Insurance Company
The Guarantee Company of North America
Hannover Rück SE Canadian Branch
Hartford Fire Insurance Company
Heartland Farm Mutual Inc.
Howard Mutual Insurance Co.
Howick Mutual Insurance Company
HUB International Ontario
Humania Assurance Inc.
iA Financial Group
Independent Order of Foresters
Intact Financial Corporation
ivari
Kent & Essex Mutual Insurance Company
Lambton Mutual Insurance Company
Legacy General Insurance Company
Lennox & Addington Mutual Insurance Company
Liberty Mutual Insurance Company
Life Insurance Company of North America
Lloyd's Underwriters
Manitoba Blue Cross
Manufacturers Life Insurance Company
McKillop Mutual Insurance Company
Medavie Blue Cross
Mitsui Sumitomo Insurance Co., Limited.
Munich Reinsurance Company Canada Branch (Life)
New Diamond Insurance Services Ltd.
Nova Mutual Insurance Company
Novex Group Insurance
Nuera Insurance inc.
Omega General Insurance Company
Ontario Blue Cross
Ontario Mutual Insurance Association
Optimum Réassurance inc.
The Order of United Commercial Travelers of America
Pafco Insurance Company
PartnerRe
PBC Health Benefits Society
The Personal Insurance Company
Petline Insurance
Petsecure Pet Health Insurance
Primerica Life Insurance Company of Canada
Québec Blue Cross
RBC Insurance
RBC Insurance Company of Canada
RBC Life Insurance Company
Reliable Life Insurance Company
Royal & Sun Alliance Insurance Company of Canada
Saskatchewan Blue Cross
SCOR Global Life SE, Canada Branch
Scotia Life Insurance Company
Security National Insurance Company
The Sovereign General Insurance Company
Suecia Reinsurance Company
Sun Life Assurance Company of Canada
Supreme Council of the Royal Arcanum
TD General Insurance Company
TD Life Insurance Company
Trans Global Insurance Company
Trans Global Life Insurance Company
Transatlantic Reinsurance Company
TruShield Insurance Services Ltd.
Ukrainian National Association
L'Union-Vie, compagnie mutuelle d'assurance

United American Insurance Company
Usborne & Hibbert Mutual Fire Insurance Company
Uv Mutuelle
Vancity Life Insurance Services Ltd.
The Wawanesa Life Insurance Company
West Elgin Mutual Insurance Company
West Wawanosh Mutual Insurance Company
Western Financial Group Inc.
Westport Insurance Corporation
Zurich Canada

Property

Affiliated FM Insurance Company
AIG Insurance Company of Canada
Alberta Motor Association Insurance Co.
Algoma Mutual Insurance Co.
Allianz Global Risks US Insurance Company
Allstate Insurance Company of Canada
L'ALPHA, compagnie d'assurances inc.
Alpine Insurance & Financial Inc.
The American Road Insurance Company
Amherst Island Mutual Insurance Company
Antigonish Farmers' Mutual Insurance Company
Archway Insurance
Astro Insurance 1000 Inc.
Atlantic Insurance Company Limited
Aviva Canada Inc.
Aviva General Insurance Company
A-WIN Insurance
AXA Art Insurance Corporation
AXA XL
AXA XL Reinsurance
Axion Insurance Services Inc.
Ayr Farmers Mutual Insurance Company
Bay of Quinte Mutual Insurance Co.
BCM Insurance Company
Belair Insurance Company Inc.
Berkley Canada
Brant Mutual Insurance Company
British Columbia Automobile Association Insurance Agency
Butler Byers Insurance Ltd.
CAA Insurance Company (Ontario)
Caisse centrale de Réassurance
Canada Guaranty Mortgage Insurance Company
Canadian Farm Insurance Corp.
Canadian Northern Shield Insurance Company
Canadian Professional Sales Association
Canadian Universities Reciprocal Insurance Exchange
Canassurance Insurance Company
La Capitale assurances générales inc.
Caradoc Townsend Mutual Insurance Company
Carleton-Fundy Mutual Insurance Company
Certas Direct Insurance Company
Chicago Title Insurance Company Canada
Chubb Insurance Company of Canada
Clare Mutual Insurance Company
Coastal Community Insurance Services (2007) Ltd.
The Commonwell Mutual Insurance Group
La Compagnie d'Assurance Missisquoi
Continental Casualty Company
Co-operators General Insurance Company
Co-operators Life Insurance Company
CorePointe Insurance Company
COSECO Insurance Company
Crowsnest Insurance Agencies Ltd.
CUMIS General Insurance Company
The CUMIS Group Limited
CUMIS Life Insurance Company
Desjardins assurances générales inc
Desjardins Groupe d'assurances générales inc
Desjardins Insurance
DMW Insurance Ltd.
Dufferin Mutual Insurance Company
Dumfries Mutual Insurance Company
Ecclesiastical Insurance Office plc
Echelon Insurance
The Economical Insurance Group
Economical Mutual Insurance Company
Edge Mutual Insurance Company
Elite Insurance Company
Energy Insurance Group Ltd.
Erie Mutual Insurance Company
Everest Insurance Company of Canada
Everest Reinsurance Company
Federal Insurance Company
Federated Insurance Company of Canada
Fenchurch General Insurance Company
First Canadian Title
First North American Insurance Company
FM Global
FNF Canada

General Reinsurance Corporation
Genworth Financial Mortgage Insurance Company Canada
Germania Mutual Insurance Company
Gibbs Insurance Service Inc.
Gore Mutual Insurance Company
Great American Insurance Company
Grenville Mutual Insurance Company
Le Groupe Estrie-Richelieu, compagnie d'assurance
Groupe Promutuel, Fédération de sociétés mutuelles d'assurance
    générale
The Guarantee Company of North America
Halwell Mutual Insurance Company
Hannover Rück SE Canadian Branch
Hartford Fire Insurance Company
Heartland Farm Mutual Inc.
Henderson Insurance Inc.
Howard Mutual Insurance Co.
Howick Mutual Insurance Company
HSB BI&I
HT&C Mutual Insurance Company
HTM Insurance Company
HUB International Atlantic Limited
HUB International Barton Insurance Brokers
HUB International British Columbia
HUB International Manitoba Limited
HUB International Nunavut
HUB International Ontario
iA Financial Group
Industrial Alliance Auto & Home Insurance
Insurance Company of Prince Edward Island
Intact Financial Corporation
Intact Insurance Company of Canada
Jevco Insurance Company
Kent & Essex Mutual Insurance Company
Kirkham Insurance
Lambton Mutual Insurance Company
Legacy General Insurance Company
Lennox & Addington Mutual Insurance Company
Liberty Mutual Insurance Company
Lloyd's Underwriters
MAX Canada Insurance Company
McKillop Mutual Insurance Company
Meloche Monnex Inc.
Mennonite Mutual Insurance Co. (Alberta) Ltd.
Middlesex Mutual Insurance Co.
Millennium Insurance Corporation
Mitsui Sumitomo Insurance Co., Limited.
Morgex Insurance
Munich Reinsurance Company of Canada
MUNIX Reciprocal
The Mutual Fire Insurance Company of British Columbia
Mutuelle d'assurance en Église
My Mutual Insurance
New Diamond Insurance Services Ltd.
Noble Insurance
The Nordic Insurance Company of Canada
North Blenheim Mutual Insurance Company
North Kent Mutual Fire Insurance Company
Northbridge Insurance
Northern Savings Insurance Services Ltd.
Nova Mutual Insurance Company
Novex Group Insurance
Nuera Insurance inc.
OdysseyRe - Canadian Branch
Old Republic Insurance Company of Canada
Omega General Insurance Company
Ontario Mutual Insurance Association
Ontario School Boards' Insurance Exchange
Optimum Assurance Agricole inc.
Optimum Général inc.
Optimum Société d'Assurance inc.
Optimum West Insurance Company Inc.
Pafco Insurance Company
PartnerRe
PC Financial Insurance Brokers Inc.
Peace Hills General Insurance Company
Peel Mutual Insurance Company
Pembridge Insurance Company
The Personal General Insurance Inc.
The Personal Insurance Company
Perth Insurance Company
Pets Plus Us
Pilot Insurance Company
The Portage La Prairie Mutual Insurance Company
Primmum Insurance Company
Prince Edward Island Mutual Insurance Company
Promutuel Assurance
RBC Insurance
Red River Mutual
Royal & Sun Alliance Insurance Company of Canada

Saskatchewan Government Insurance
Saskatchewan Mutual Insurance Company
Scottish & York Insurance Co. Limited
Security National Insurance Company
Servus Insurance Services - Home & Auto
SGI Canada
Sirius America Insurance Company
South Easthope Mutual Insurance Co.
Southeastern Mutual Insurance Company
The Sovereign General Insurance Company
Stanley Mutual Insurance Company
Stewart Title Guaranty Company
Suecia Reinsurance Company
Swiss Reinsurance Company Canada
TD General Insurance Company
TD Home & Auto Insurance Company
Temple Insurance Company
Thomson Jemmett Vogelzang
The Tokio Marine & Nichido Fire Insurance Co., Ltd.
Traders General Insurance Company
Tradition Mutual Insurance Company
Trafalgar Insurance Company of Canada
Trans Global Insurance Company
Transatlantic Reinsurance Company
Travelers Canada
Trillium Mutual Insurance Company
TruShield Insurance Services Ltd.
Unica Insurance Inc.
Unifund Assurance Company
Usborne & Hibbert Mutual Fire Insurance Company
Virginia Surety Company, Inc.
The Wawanesa Mutual Insurance Company
Wedgwood Insurance Limited
West Elgin Mutual Insurance Company
West Wawanosh Mutual Insurance Company
Western Assurance Company
Western Financial Group Inc.
Westland Insurance Group Ltd.
Westminster Mutual Insurance Company
Westport Insurance Corporation
Wyatt Dowling Insurance Brokers
Wynward Insurance Group
Yarmouth Mutual Fire Insurance Company
Zurich Canada

Reinsurance
Farm Mutual Reinsurance Plan Inc.
Lloyd's Underwriters
Metropolitan Tower Life Insurance Company
Munich Reinsurance Company Canada Branch (Life)
OdysseyRe - Canadian Branch
Old Republic Insurance Company of Canada
Optimum Reassurance inc.
Optimum Réassurance inc.
Promutuel Assurance
RGA Life Reinsurance Company of Canada
SCOR Canada Reinsurance Company
Suecia Reinsurance Company
Swiss Reinsurance Company Canada
The Toa Reinsurance Company of America (Canada Branch)
Transatlantic Reinsurance Company
Travelers Canada
L'Union-Vie, compagnie mutuelle d'assurance

Surety
Affiliated FM Insurance Company
AIG Insurance Company of Canada
Allianz Global Risks US Insurance Company
Allstate Insurance Company of Canada
L'ALPHA, compagnie d'assurances inc.
The American Road Insurance Company
Atlantic Insurance Company Limited
Aviva Canada Inc.
AXA XL
AXA XL Reinsurance
Belair Insurance Company Inc.
Berkley Canada
CAA Insurance Company (Ontario)
Caisse centrale de Réassurance
Canadian Farm Insurance Corp.
Certas Direct Insurance Company
Chicago Title Insurance Company Canada
Chubb Insurance Company of Canada
La Compagnie d'Assurance Missisquoi
Continental Casualty Company
Co-operators General Insurance Company
CorePointe Insurance Company
Desjardins assurances générales inc
Desjardins Insurance
Echelon Insurance
Economical Mutual Insurance Company

Elite Insurance Company
Everest Insurance Company of Canada
Everest Reinsurance Company
Farm Mutual Reinsurance Plan Inc.
Federal Insurance Company
Federated Insurance Company of Canada
Fenchurch General Insurance Company
General Reinsurance Corporation
Great American Insurance Company
The Guarantee Company of North America
Hannover Rück SE Canadian Branch
Hartford Fire Insurance Company
Johnston Meier Insurance Agencies Group
Liberty Mutual Insurance Company
Lloyd's Underwriters
Mitsui Sumitomo Insurance Co., Limited.
The Nordic Insurance Company of Canada
Novex Group Insurance
OdysseyRe - Canadian Branch
Omega General Insurance Company
Peace Hills General Insurance Company
The Personal General Insurance Inc.
The Personal Insurance Company
Promutuel Assurance
Red River Mutual
Scottish & York Insurance Co. Limited
Sirius America Insurance Company
Swiss Reinsurance Company Canada
TD General Insurance Company
Transatlantic Reinsurance Company
Travelers Canada
Trisura Guarantee Insurance Company
The Wawanesa Mutual Insurance Company
Western Assurance Company
Western Financial Group Inc.
Western Surety Company
Westport Insurance Corporation
Wynward Insurance Group
Zurich Canada

Theft
Aviva General Insurance Company
The Commonwell Mutual Insurance Group
La Compagnie d'Assurance Missisquoi
Co-operators General Insurance Company
CUMIS General Insurance Company
CUMIS Life Insurance Company
Federated Insurance Company of Canada
Germania Mutual Insurance Company
Gore Mutual Insurance Company
The Guarantee Company of North America
Hartford Fire Insurance Company
Munich Reinsurance Company of Canada
Mutuelle d'assurance en Église
My Mutual Insurance
North Kent Mutual Fire Insurance Company
Peace Hills General Insurance Company
Prince Edward Island Mutual Insurance Company
Promutuel Assurance
Red River Mutual
Trafalgar Insurance Company of Canada
The Wawanesa Mutual Insurance Company
Western Financial Group Inc.
Wynward Insurance Group
Zurich Canada

Federal and Provincial Insurance Companies

ACTRA Fraternal Benefit Society (AFBS)
1000 Yonge St.
Toronto, ON M4W 2K2
Tel: 416-967-6600; *Fax:* 416-967-4744
Toll-Free: 800-387-8897
info@afbs.ca
www.afbs.ca
www.facebook.com/enrichingcreativelives;
twitter.com/AFBSCanada
Classes of Insurance: Personal Accident & Sickness, Life

Affiliated FM Insurance Company
#200, 100 New Park Place
Vaughan, ON L4K 0H9
Tel: 905-763-5555; *Fax:* 905-763-5556
www.affiliatedfm.ca
twitter.com/AFMInsurance
Classes of Insurance: Liability, Boiler & Machinery, Fidelity,
Property, Fire, Surety

*Agriculture Financial Services Corporation (AFSC)
5718 - 56th Ave.
Lacombe, AB T4L 1B1
Toll-Free: 877-899-2372
info@afsc.ca
www.afsc.ca
Classes of Insurance: Hail & Crop

AIG Insurance Company of Canada
#2200, 120 Bremner Blvd.
Toronto, ON M5J 0A8
Tel: 416-596-3000; *Toll-Free:* 800-387-4481
askaigcanada@aig.com
www.aig.ca
Other Contact Information: Claims Email: can.claims@aig.com
Classes of Insurance: Personal Accident & Sickness, Aircraft,
Auto, Liability, Boiler & Machinery, Credit, Marine, Fidelity,
Property, Surety, Hail & Crop

*Alberta Blue Cross
Blue Cross Place
10009 - 108th St. NW
Edmonton, AB T5J 3C5
Tel: 780-498-8000; *Fax:* 780-425-4627
Toll-Free: 800-661-6995
www.ab.bluecross.ca
Other Contact Information: Travel Plans: 800-661-6995;
Individual Health & Dental Plans: 800-394-1965; Group Sales:
780-498-8500; Switchboard: 780-498-8100
vimeo.com/albertabluecross;
www.facebook.com/AlbertaBlueCross; twitter.com/ABBluecross
Classes of Insurance: Personal Accident & Sickness

*Alberta Motor Association Insurance Co.
PO Box 8180, Stn. South
Edmonton, AB T6H 5X9
Tel: 780-430-5555; *Toll-Free:* 800-222-6400
ama.ab.ca/insurance
Other Contact Information: Insurance, Toll-Free: 800-615-5987;
Insurance Claims, Toll-Free: 888-426-2444
www.facebook.com/AMAInsurance; twitter.com/AMAInsurance
Classes of Insurance: Personal Accident & Sickness, Auto,
Life, Property, Fire

*Algoma Mutual Insurance Co.
131 Main St.
Thessalon, ON P0R 1L0
Tel: 705-842-3345; *Fax:* 705-842-3500
info@amico.ca
amico.ca
Classes of Insurance: Auto, Property

Allianz Global Risks US Insurance Company
#1600, 130 Adelaide St. West
Toronto, ON M5H 3P5
Tel: 416-915-4247; *Fax:* 416-961-5442
AGCSCommunication@agcs.allianz.com
www.agcs.allianz.com/global-offices/c anada
Classes of Insurance: Personal Accident & Sickness, Aircraft,
Auto, Liability, Boiler & Machinery, Marine, Property, Surety, Hail
& Crop

Allianz Life Insurance Company of North America
#700, 2005 Sheppard Ave. East
Toronto, ON M2J 5B4
Tel: 416-502-2500; *Fax:* 416-502-2555
www.allianzlife.com
Classes of Insurance: Personal Accident & Sickness, Life

Allstate Insurance Company of Canada/Allstate du Canada, Compagnie d'assurance
#100, 27 Allstate Pkwy.
Markham, ON L3R 5P8
Tel: 905-477-6900; *Toll-Free:* 800-255-7828
www.allstate.ca
Other Contact Information: Claims Toll-Free Numbers:
800-387-0462 (ON & USA); 800-661-1577 (BC, AB, SK, MB);
800-561-7222 (NS, NB, PE, NL); 800-463-2813 (QC)
www.facebook.com/AllstateCanada; twitter.com/allstate
Classes of Insurance: Personal Accident & Sickness, Legal
Expense, Auto, Liability, Boiler & Machinery, Fidelity, Property,
Surety

*L'ALPHA, compagnie d'assurances inc.
#119, 430, rue Saint-Georges
Drummondville, QC J2C 4H4
Tel: 819-474-7958; *Fax:* 819-477-6139
Toll-Free: 888-525-7428
info@alphaassurances.com
alphaassurances.com
www.youtube.com/user/AlphaAssurances;
www.facebook.com/alphaassurances
Classes of Insurance: Auto, Property, Surety

*Alpine Insurance & Financial Inc.
#123, 8820 Blackfoot Trail SE
Calgary, AB T2J 3J1
Tel: 403-270-8822; Fax: 403-270-0201
Toll-Free: 877-770-8822
calgary.info@alpineinsurance.ca
alpineinsurance.ca
www.instagram.com/alpine_insurance;
www.facebook.com/AlpineInsuranceAlberta
Classes of Insurance: Auto, Liability, Life, Property

American Bankers Life Assurance Company of Florida/American Bankers Compagnie d'Assurance Vie de la Floride
#2000, 5000 Yonge St., 20th Fl.
Toronto, ON M2N 7E9
Tel: 416-733-3360; Fax: 416-733-7826
Toll-Free: 800-561-3232
Classes of Insurance: Accident, Personal Accident & Sickness, Life

American Health & Life Insurance Company
355 Wellington St.
London, ON N6A 3N7
Toll-Free: 800-285-8623
Classes of Insurance: Life

American Income Life Insurance Company
#2100, 40 King St. West
Toronto, ON M5H 3C2
Tel: 416-364-5371; Fax: 416-366-8571
Classes of Insurance: Personal Accident & Sickness, Life

The American Road Insurance Company
c/o CAS Accounting
#2, 1145 Nicholson Rd.
Newmarket, ON L3Y 9C3
Tel: 905-853-0858
Classes of Insurance: Auto, Liability, Boiler & Machinery, Credit, Property, Surety

*Amherst Island Mutual Insurance Company
RR#1
Stella, ON K0H 2S0
Tel: 613-389-2012; Fax: 613-389-9986
Classes of Insurance: Personal Accident & Sickness, Liability, Property

Antigonish Farmers' Mutual Insurance Company
188 Main St.
Antigonish, NS B2G 2B9
Tel: 902-863-3544; Fax: 902-863-0664
Toll-Free: 800-565-3544
reception@antigonishfarmersmutual.ca
www.antigonishfarmersmutual.ca
Classes of Insurance: Marine, Property, Fire

*Apollo Insurance Solutions Ltd.
#210, 111 Water St.
Vancouver, BC V6B 1A7
apollocover.com
www.facebook.com/apolloinsurance; twitter.com/theapollomag

*Archway Insurance
#103, 137 Chain Lake Dr.
Halifax, NS B3S 1B3
Tel: 902-477-2511; Toll-Free: 800-838-2511
www.archwayinsurance.ca
www.instagram.com/archwayinsurance;
www.facebook.com/ArchwayInsurance;
twitter.com/ArchwayInsure
Classes of Insurance: Personal Accident & Sickness, Auto, Liability, Life, Property

*Assumption Mutual Life Insurance Company/Assomption Compagnie Mutuelle d'Assurance-Vie
Assumption Place
PO Box 160
770 Main St.
Moncton, NB E1C 8L1
Tel: 506-853-6040; Fax: 506-853-5428
Toll-Free: 800-455-7337
comments@assumption.ca
www.assumption.ca
Other Contact Information: Group Insurance, Phone: 506-869-9797; Toll-Free: 1-888-869-9797; Individual Insurance, Toll-Free: 1-800-343-5622; Mortgage Loans, Phone: 506-869-9755
Classes of Insurance: Accident, Personal Accident & Sickness, Life

*Assurance-Vie Banque Nationale/National Bank Life Insurance Company
1100, boul Robert-Bourassa, 5e étage
Montréal, QC H3B 2G7
Tél: 514-871-7500; Ligne sans frais: 877-871-7500
www.nbc-insurance.ca
www.facebook.com/BanqueNationaleAssurances
Classes of Insurance: Personal Accident & Sickness, Life, Credit

Assurant Solutions Canada
#2000, 5000 Yonge St., 20th Fl.
Toronto, ON M2N 7E9
Tel: 416-733-3360; Fax: 416-733-7826
Toll-Free: 800-561-3232
www.assurantsolutions.com/canada
Classes of Insurance: Credit

*AssurePro Insurance Company
200 Albert St. North
Regina, SK S4R 5E2
Tel: 306-791-4326; Fax: 306-949-4461
Toll-Free: 866-222-3021
assurepro@caask.ca
www.assurepro.ca
Classes of Insurance: Accident

*Astro Insurance 1000 Inc.
#100, 542 - 7th St.
Lethbridge, AB T1J 2H1
Tel: 403-328-1000; Fax: 403-320-1962
Toll-Free: 800-465-5242
astro@astro-insurance.com
www.astro-insurance.com
www.instagram.com/astroinsurance;
www.facebook.com/astro.ins
Classes of Insurance: Auto, Liability, Property, Hail & Crop

*Atlantic Insurance Company Limited
64 Commonwealth Ave.
Mount Pearl, NL A1N 1W8
Tel: 709-364-5209; Fax: 709-364-5262
Classes of Insurance: Auto, Liability, Boiler & Machinery, Fidelity, Property, Surety

Aviva Canada Inc./Aviva, Compagnie d'Assurance du Canada
#100, 10 Aviva Way
Markham, ON L6G 0G1
Toll-Free: 800-387-4518
Other Contact Information: Claims, Toll-Free: 866-692-8482
www.youtube.com/user/avivacanada;
www.facebook.com/AvivaCanada; twitter.com/avivacanada
Classes of Insurance: Personal Accident & Sickness, Aircraft, Legal Expense, Auto, Liability, Boiler & Machinery, Marine, Fidelity, Property, Surety, Hail & Crop

Aviva General Insurance Company/Compagnie d'assurance générale Aviva
Aviva Canada Inc.
#100, 10 Aviva Way
Markham, ON L6G 0G1
Toll-Free: 800-387-4518
www.aviva.ca
Other Contact Information: Claims: 1-866-692-8482
Classes of Insurance: Personal Accident & Sickness, Auto, Liability, Property, Fire, Theft

*A-WIN Insurance
#800, 1331 Macleod Trail SE
Calgary, AB T2G 0K3
Toll-Free: 866-278-1050
reception@awinins.ca
www.awinins.ca
www.instagram.com/awin_insurance;
www.facebook.com/AWINInsurance; twitter.com/AwinInsurance
Classes of Insurance: Auto, Liability, Property

AXA Art Insurance Corporation
#3020, 100 King St. West
Toronto, ON M5X 1C9
Tel: 416-304-9690; Toll-Free: 877-269-1993
www.axa-art.com/ca
Classes of Insurance: Property

AXA Equitable Life Insurance Company/AXA Equitable assurance-vie
PO Box 14
#606, 55 Town Centre Ct.
Toronto, ON M1P 4X4
Toll-Free: 800-777-6510
us.axa.com

Classes of Insurance: Personal Accident & Sickness, Life

AXA XL
First Canadian Place
#3020, 100 King St. West
Toronto, ON M5X 1C9
Tel: 416-644-3312
axaxl.com
www.youtube.com/user/axaxl; twitter.com/axa_xl
Classes of Insurance: Personal Accident & Sickness, Auto, Liability, Boiler & Machinery, Property, Surety

AXA XL Reinsurance
First Canadian Place
PO Box 310
#3010, 100 King St.
Toronto, ON M5C 1C9
Tel: 416-598-1084; Fax: 416-598-1980
www.axaxl.com
www.youtube.com/user/axaxl
Classes of Insurance: Personal Accident & Sickness, Aircraft, Auto, Liability, Boiler & Machinery, Fidelity, Property, Surety, Hail & Crop

*Axion Insurance Services Inc.
#205, 95 Mural St.
Richmond Hill, ON L4B 3G2
Tel: 905-731-3118; Fax: 905-731-4446
query@axioninsurance.ca
www.axioninsurance.ca
Classes of Insurance: Auto, Property

*Ayr Farmers Mutual Insurance Company
1400 Northumberland St.
Ayr, ON N0B 1E0
Tel: 519-632-7413; Fax: 519-632-8908
Toll-Free: 800-265-8792
info@ayrmutual.com
www.ayrmutual.com
www.facebook.com/AyrMutual; twitter.com/AyrMutual
Classes of Insurance: Accident, Personal Accident & Sickness, Auto, Liability, Boiler & Machinery, Fidelity, Property, Hail & Crop

*Bay of Quinte Mutual Insurance Co.
PO Box 6050
13379 Loyalist Pkwy.
Picton, ON K0K 2T0
Tel: 613-476-2145; Fax: 613-476-7503
Toll-Free: 800-267-2126
info@bayofquintemutual.com
www.bayofquintemutual.com
www.facebook.com/Bayofquintemutual
Classes of Insurance: Personal Accident & Sickness, Auto, Liability, Boiler & Machinery, Fidelity, Property

*BCM Insurance Company
1003 Niagara St.
Welland, ON L3C 1M5
Tel: 905-735-1234; Fax: 905-735-6519
Toll-Free: 800-263-0494
mail@bertieandclinton.com
bcminsurance.com
Classes of Insurance: Personal Accident & Sickness, Auto, Liability, Boiler & Machinery, Fidelity, Property

*Belair Insurance Company Inc./La Compagnie d'Assurance Belair Inc.
#300, 7101, rue Jean-Talon est
Anjou, QC H1M 3T6
Tel: 514-270-9111; Toll-Free: 888-270-9111
service@belairdirect.com
www.belairdirect.com
Other Contact Information: Auto & Home, Toll-Free: 888-280-8549, 888-270-9732; Travel: 877-874-5433; Claims Emergency: 877-270-9124
www.youtube.com/user/belairdirect;
www.instagram.com/belairdirect;
www.facebook.com/belairdirect; twitter.com/belairdirect
Classes of Insurance: Personal Accident & Sickness, Legal Expense, Auto, Liability, Boiler & Machinery, Marine, Fidelity, Property, Surety

Berkley Canada
#1000, 145 King St. West
Toronto, ON M5H 1J8
Tel: 416-304-1178; Fax: 416-304-4108
Toll-Free: 877-304-1178
info@berkleycanada.com
www.berkleycanada.com
Classes of Insurance: Personal Accident & Sickness, Aircraft, Legal Expense, Auto, Liability, Boiler & Machinery, Credit, Fidelity, Property, Surety, Hail & Crop

Indicates Provincially Incorporated Insurance Company

BMO Life Assurance Company of Canada
60 Yonge St.
Toronto, ON M5E 1H5
Tel: 416-596-3900; Fax: 416-596-4143
Toll-Free: 877-742-5244
www.bmo.com/insurance
Classes of Insurance: Personal Accident & Sickness, Life

*Brant Mutual Insurance Company
20 Holiday Dr.
Brantford, ON N3R 7J4
Tel: 519-752-0088; Fax: 519-752-7917
Toll-Free: 800-461-2543
reception@brantmutual.com
www.brantmutual.com
www.facebook.com/brantmutualins
Classes of Insurance: Personal Accident & Sickness, Auto,
Liability, Boiler & Machinery, Fidelity, Property, Hail & Crop

***British Columbia Automobile Association
Insurance Agency**
4567 Canada Way
Burnaby, BC V5G 4T1
Tel: 604-268-5000; Fax: 604-268-5569
Toll-Free: 800-719-2224
info@bcaa.com
www.bcaa.com
Other Contact Information: Claims: 604-268-5260; TeleCentre,
Toll-Free: 877-325-8888; Customer Contact Centre:
604-268-5555
www.facebook.com/BCAA; twitter.com/BCAA
Classes of Insurance: Personal Accident & Sickness, Auto,
Life, Property, Fire

*C Finance Inc.
#200, 205 Provencher Blvd.
Winnipeg, MB R2H 0G4
Tel: 204-231-1170; Fax: 204-231-1445
Toll-Free: 866-741-6797
info@cfinance.biz
www.cfinance.biz
Classes of Insurance: Personal Accident & Sickness, Life

*CAA Insurance Company (Ontario)
60 Commerce Valley Dr. East
Thornhill, ON L3T 7P9
Tel: 905-771-3000; Fax: 905-771-3101
Toll-Free: 866-988-8878
info@caasco.ca
www.caasco.com/insurance
blog.caasco.com; www.facebook.com/CAASouthCentralON;
twitter.com/caasco
Classes of Insurance: Personal Accident & Sickness, Legal
Expense, Auto, Liability, Life, Marine, Property, Surety

Caisse centrale de Réassurance (CCR)
#1010, 150 York St.
Toronto, ON M5H 3S5
Tel: 416-644-0821; Fax: 416-644-0822
info@ccr.fr
www.ccr.fr
Classes of Insurance: Accident, Aircraft, Legal Expense, Auto,
Liability, Boiler & Machinery, Fidelity, Property, Fire, Surety

Canada Guaranty Mortgage Insurance Company
#400, 1 Toronto St.
Toronto, ON M5C 2V6
Tel: 416-640-8924; Fax: 416-640-8948
Toll-Free: 866-414-9109
www.canadaguaranty.ca
Other Contact Information: Underwriting inquiries, Toll-Free:
877-244-8422; Fax: 877-244-8448; Email:
underwriting@canadaguaranty.ca
Classes of Insurance: Property

Canada Life Assurance Company
100 Osborne St. North
Winnipeg, MB R3C 1V3
Tel: 416-597-1456
info@canadalife.com
canadalife.com
Other Contact Information: TTY, Toll-Free Phone: 800-990-6654;
GRS Access URL: www.grsaccess.com
www.facebook.com/CanadaLifeCo; twitter.com/canadalifeco
Classes of Insurance: Personal Accident & Sickness, Life

The Canada Life Assurance Company
100 Osborne St. North
Winnipeg, MB R3C 1V3
Tel: 416-597-1456
info@canadalife.com
www.canadalife.com
Other Contact Information: TTY: 800-855-0511
www.facebook.com/CanadaLifeCo; twitter.com/canadalifeco
Classes of Insurance: Accident, Personal Accident & Sickness,
Credit

*Canadian Farm Insurance Corp. (CFIC)
#205, 101 Riel Dr.
St Albert, AB T8N 3X4
Tel: 780-447-3276; Fax: 780-733-7724
info@cdnfarmins.com
www.cdnfarmins.com
Other Contact Information: 24-hour Livestock Claims Assistance,
Phone: 780-733-7720; Fax: 780-733-7724
Classes of Insurance: Personal Accident & Sickness, Liability,
Boiler & Machinery, Fidelity, Property, Surety

***Canadian Lawyers Insurance
Association/L'Association d'Assurance des Juristes
Canadiens**
#1530, 2002 Victoria Ave.
Regina, SK S4P 0R7
Tel: 306-347-3057
info@clia.ca
www.clia.ca

**Canadian Northern Shield Insurance Company
(CNS)**
#1900, 555 Hastings St. West
Vancouver, BC V6B 4N6
Tel: 604-662-2900; Fax: 604-662-5698
Toll-Free: 800-663-1953
www.cns.ca
Classes of Insurance: Auto, Liability, Property

Canadian Premier Life Insurance Company
#1400, 25 Sheppard Ave. West
Toronto, ON M2N 6S6
Toll-Free: 844-894-0378
www.canadianpremier.ca
Classes of Insurance: Personal Accident & Sickness, Life,
Credit

Canadian Professional Sales Association (CPSA)
#400, 655 Bay St.
Toronto, ON M5G 2K4
Tel: 416-408-2685; Fax: 416-408-2684
Toll-Free: 888-267-2772
www.cpsa.com
www.facebook.com/CanadianProfessionalSalesAssociation;
twitter.com/cpsa
Classes of Insurance: Accident, Personal Accident & Sickness,
Auto, Life, Property

***Canadian Universities Reciprocal Insurance
Exchange (CURIE)**
#901, 5500 North Service Rd.
Burlington, ON L7L 6W6
Tel: 905-336-3366
info@curie.org
www.curie.org
Classes of Insurance: Aircraft, Liability, Marine, Property

*Canassurance Insurance Company
c/o Québec Blue Cross
550, rue Sherbrooke ouest
Montréal, QC H3A 3S3
Tel: 514-286-7684
www.qc.croixbleue.ca
Classes of Insurance: Personal Accident & Sickness, Liability,
Life, Property

***La Capitale assurances et gestion du patrimoine/La
Capitale Insurance & Financial Services**
CP 1500
625, rue Jacques-Parizeau
Québec, QC G1R 2G5
Tél: 418-644-5226; Ligne sans frais: 800-463-4856
www.lacapitale.com
Classes of Insurance: Personal Accident & Sickness, Life

***La Capitale assurances générales inc./La Capitale
General Insurance Inc.**
625, rue Jacques-Parizeau
Québec, QC G1R 2G5
Tél: 418-266-1700; Ligne sans frais: 800-463-4432
www.lacapitale.com
Other Contact Information: Réclamation: 800-461-0770

Classes of Insurance: Auto, Property

***La Capitale assureur de l'administration publique
inc./La Capitale Civil Service Insurer Inc.**
625, rue Jacques-Parizeau
Québec, QC G1R 2G5
Tél: 418-747-7600; Ligne sans frais: 866-227-2606
www.lacapitale.com
Classes of Insurance: Life

**La Capitale Financial Security Insurance
Company/La Capitale sécurité financière**
7150 Derrycrest Dr.
Mississauga, ON L5W 0E5
Fax: 905-795-2316
Toll-Free: 800-268-2835
www.lacapitalefs.com
Classes of Insurance: Personal Accident & Sickness, Life

***Caradoc Townsend Mutual Insurance Company
(CTM)**
22508 Adelaide Rd.
Mount Brydges, ON N0L 1W0
Tel: 519-264-2298; Fax: 519-264-9101
Toll-Free: 877-707-2298
www.ctmins.ca
twitter.com/CTMIns
Classes of Insurance: Personal Accident & Sickness, Auto,
Liability, Boiler & Machinery, Property

*Carleton-Fundy Mutual Insurance Company
1022 Main St.
Sussex, NB E4E 2M3
Tel: 506-432-1535; Fax: 506-433-6788
Toll-Free: 800-222-9550
info@cfmutual.ca
www.cfmutual.ca
twitter.com/fundymutual
Classes of Insurance: Auto, Liability, Boiler & Machinery,
Property

**Certas Direct Insurance Company/Certas Direct,
compagnie d'assurances**
#550, 3 Robert Speck Pkwy.
Mississauga, ON L4Z 2G5
Toll-Free: 877-818-8873
www.desjardinsgeneralinsurance.com
Classes of Insurance: Auto, Liability, Property, Surety

Chicago Title Insurance Company Canada (CTIC)
55 Superior Blvd.
Mississauga, ON L5T 2X9
Tel: 289-562-5216; Fax: 289-562-2478
Toll-Free: 888-868-4853
info@chicagotitle.ca
www.chicagotitle.ca
Other Contact Information: Claims, Email: claims@ctic.ca
www.facebook.com/cticcanada; twitter.com/ctic_ca
Classes of Insurance: Property, Surety

**Chubb Insurance Company of Canada/Chubb du
Canada Compagnie d'Assurance**
PO Box 139, Stn. Commerce Court
#2500, 199 Bay St.
Toronto, ON M5L 1E2
Tel: 416-359-3222; Toll-Free: 800-268-9344
infocanada@chubb.com
www.chubb.com
Other Contact Information: Worldwide Claims, Toll-Free:
800-532-4822; Canadian Claims, Email:
canadaclaims@chubb.com
www.youtube.com/user/ChubbInsurance;
www.facebook.com/ChubbInsurance; twitter.com/ChubbNA
Classes of Insurance: Personal Accident & Sickness, Aircraft,
Auto, Liability, Boiler & Machinery, Marine, Fidelity, Property,
Surety

**CIBC Life Insurance Company Limited/Compagnie
d'Assurance-Vie CIBC Limitée**
33 Yonge St.
Toronto, ON M5E 1G4
Toll-Free: 888-393-1110
www.cibcinsurance.com
Classes of Insurance: Personal Accident & Sickness, Life

CIGNA Life Insurance Company of Canada
#301, 100 Consilium Pl.
Toronto, ON M1H 3E3
Tel: 416-290-6666; Fax: 416-290-0732
Toll-Free: 800-668-7029
www.cigna.com
www.youtube.com/cigna; www.pinterest.com/cignatogether;
www.facebook.com/CIGNA; twitter.com/cigna

Indicates Provincially Incorporated Insurance Company

Classes of Insurance: Accident, Personal Accident & Sickness, Life, Credit

Clare Mutual Insurance Company
3300 Hwy. 1
Belliveau Cove, NS B0W 1J0
Tel: 902-837-4597; *Fax:* 902-837-7745
Toll-Free: 877-818-0887
www.claremutual.com
Classes of Insurance: Property, Fire, Hail & Crop

Coast Underwriters Limited
PO Box 11519
#2690, 650 West Georgia St.
Vancouver, BC V6B 4N7
Tel: 604-683-5631; *Fax:* 604-683-8561
www.coastunderwriters.ca
Classes of Insurance: Marine

*Coastal Community Insurance Services (2007) Ltd.
c/o Coastal Community Credit Union
#220, 59 Wharf St.
Nanaimo, BC V9R 2X3
Toll-Free: 888-741-1010
www.cccu.ca/personal/insurance/home-insurance
Classes of Insurance: Auto, Property

Combined Insurance Company of America/Compagnie d'assurance Combined d'Amérique
PO Box 3720, Stn. MIP
7300 Warden Ave., 3rd Fl.
Markham, ON L3R 0X3
Tel: 905-305-1922; *Fax:* 905-305-8600
Toll-Free: 888-234-4466
www.combinedinsurance.com
Classes of Insurance: Personal Accident & Sickness, Life

*The Commonwell Mutual Insurance Group
336 Angeline St. South
Lindsay, ON K9V 4R8
Tel: 705-234-2146; *Toll-Free:* 855-436-5883
www.thecommonwell.ca
www.instagram.com/thecommonwellinsurance;
www.facebook.com/280185955466883
Classes of Insurance: Auto, Liability, Boiler & Machinery, Property, Hail & Crop, Theft

La Compagnie d'Assurance Missisquoi/The Missisquoi Insurance Company
#1400, 1, Place Ville Marie
Montréal, QC H3B 2B2
Tél: 514-875-5790; *Téléc:* 514-875-9769
Ligne sans frais: 800-361-7573
www.economical.com
Classes of Insurance: Legal Expense, Auto, Liability, Boiler & Machinery, Fidelity, Property, Fire, Surety, Theft

Connecticut General Life Insurance Co. (CGLIC)
c/o CIGNA Life Insurance Company of Canada
#301, 100 Consilium Pl.
Toronto, ON M1H 3E3
Tel: 416-290-6666; *Fax:* 416-290-0732
www.cigna.com
Classes of Insurance: Accident, Personal Accident & Sickness, Life

Continental Casualty Company
#3700, 66 Wellington St. West
Toronto, ON M5K 1J5
Tel: 416-542-7300; *Fax:* 416-542-7310
Toll-Free: 800-268-9399
www.cnacanada.ca
www.facebook.com/cnainsurance; twitter.com/cna_insurance
Classes of Insurance: Accident, Personal Accident & Sickness, Aircraft, Auto, Liability, Boiler & Machinery, Credit, Fidelity, Property, Surety, Hail & Crop

*Co-operative Hail Insurance Company Ltd.
2709 - 13th Ave.
Regina, SK S4P 3A8
Tel: 306-522-8891; *Fax:* 306-352-9130
info@coophail.com
www.facebook.com/412855019540836; twitter.com/coophail
Classes of Insurance: Hail & Crop

Co-operators General Insurance Company
130 Macdonell St.
Guelph, ON N1H 6P8
Fax: 519-823-9944
Toll-Free: 800-265-2662
connect@cooperators.ca
www.cooperators.ca
www.youtube.com/user/CooperatorsInsurance;
www.instagram.com/the_cooperators;
www.facebook.com/TheCooperatorsInsurance;
twitter.com/The_Cooperators
Classes of Insurance: Personal Accident & Sickness, Auto, Boiler & Machinery, Fidelity, Property, Fire, Surety, Hail & Crop, Theft

Co-operators Life Insurance Company
1920 College Ave.
Regina, SK S4P 1C4
Fax: 306-347-6808
Toll-Free: 800-454-8061
phs_individual_life@cooperators.ca
www.cooperators.ca
Other Contact Information: Group Benefits, Toll Free: 800-667-8164; Fax: 306-761-7373; Wealth Management, Email: phs_wealth_mgmt@cooperators.ca
Classes of Insurance: Personal Accident & Sickness, Life, Property

CorePointe Insurance Company (DCIC)
#2, 1145 Nicholson Rd.
Newmarket, ON L3Y 9C3
Tel: 905-853-0858; *Fax:* 905-853-0183
Classes of Insurance: Auto, Liability, Property, Surety

COSECO Insurance Company
5600 Cancross Ct.
Mississauga, ON L5R 3E9
Toll-Free: 800-387-1963
www.coseco.ca
Classes of Insurance: Auto, Property

Croatian Fraternal Union of America
716 Abingdon Ct.
Pickering, ON L1W 3M7
Tel: 416-601-6150; *Fax:* 416-601-6590
info@croatianfraternalunion.org
www.croatianfraternalunion.org
www.youtube.com/channel/UC7FrwBMwojQS8bAlOHKFB0w;
www.facebook.com/croatianfraternalunion
Classes of Insurance: Personal Accident & Sickness, Life

*Crowsnest Insurance Agencies Ltd.
PO Box 88
12731 - 20th Ave.
Blairmore, AB T0K 0E0
Tel: 403-562-8822; *Fax:* 403-562-8239
Toll-Free: 800-361-8658
info@crowsnestinsurance.com
crowsnestinsurance.com
Classes of Insurance: Auto, Liability, Property

CUMIS General Insurance Company
PO Box 5065
151 North Service Rd.
Burlington, ON L7R 4C2
Tel: 905-632-1221; *Toll-Free:* 800-263-9120
www.cumis.com
Classes of Insurance: Auto, Boiler & Machinery, Fidelity, Property, Fire, Theft

The CUMIS Group Limited
PO Box 5065
151 North Service Rd.
Burlington, ON L7R 4C2
Tel: 905-632-1221; *Toll-Free:* 800-263-9120
www.cumis.com
Classes of Insurance: Personal Accident & Sickness, Auto, Life, Property

CUMIS Life Insurance Company
PO Box 5065
151 North Service Rd.
Burlington, ON L7R 4C2
Tel: 905-632-1221; *Toll-Free:* 800-263-9120
www.cumis.com
Classes of Insurance: Accident, Personal Accident & Sickness, Auto, Life, Credit, Fidelity, Property, Fire, Theft

*Desjardins assurances générales inc/Desjardins General Insurance Inc.
PO Box 3500
6300, boul Guillaume-Couture
Lévis, QC G6V 6P9
Tel: 418-835-4850; *Fax:* 877-699-9923
www.desjardinsassurancesgenerales.com
Classes of Insurance: Auto, Liability, Boiler & Machinery, Property, Surety

*Desjardins Groupe d'assurances générales inc (DGAG)/Desjardins General Insurance Group Inc.
6300, boul Guillaume-Couture
Lévis, QC G6V 6P9
Ligne sans frais: 888-277-8726
www.desjardinsassurancesgenerales.com
Other Contact Information: Claims, Toll-Free Phone: 888-776-8343; Payment: 800-463-7282; Customer Relations Centre: 866-835-8975
Classes of Insurance: Auto, Property

Desjardins Insurance
333 First Commerce Dr.
Aurora, ON L4G 8A4
Toll-Free: 877-659-1570
www.desjardinsagents.com
Other Contact Information: Technical support, Toll-Free: 1-844-238-6400
www.facebook.com/DesjardinsInsuranceAgents; twitter.com/DesjardinsAGT
Classes of Insurance: Aircraft, Auto, Liability, Boiler & Machinery, Fidelity, Property, Fire, Surety

*Desjardins Sécurité financière (DFS)/Desjardins Financial Security
200, rue des Commandeurs
Lévis, QC G6V 6R2
Ligne sans frais: 866-647-5013
www.desjardinsassurancevie.com
Other Contact Information: English, URL: www.desjardinslifeinsurance.com
Classes of Insurance: Accident, Personal Accident & Sickness, Life

*DMW Insurance Ltd.
#3, 22 Simona Dr.
Bolton, ON L7E 4K1
Tel: 905-857-2123; *Fax:* 905-951-8829
www.dmwinsuranceltd.com
Classes of Insurance: Personal Accident & Sickness, Auto, Life, Property

*DPB Insurance & Financial Services
#3, 305 Lakeshore Rd. East
Oakville, ON L6J 1J3
Tel: 905-829-3019; *Fax:* 905-829-3088
Toll-Free: 866-811-2711
dpbinsurance.com
Classes of Insurance: Personal Accident & Sickness, Life

*Dufferin Mutual Insurance Company
#4, 802 Main St. East
Shelburne, ON L9V 2Z5
Tel: 519-925-2026; *Fax:* 519-925-3357
Toll-Free: 800-265-9115
info@dufferinmutual.com
dufferinmutual.com
www.facebook.com/DufferinMutual; twitter.com/dufferinmutual
Classes of Insurance: Personal Accident & Sickness, Auto, Liability, Boiler & Machinery, Fidelity, Property

*Dumfries Mutual Insurance Company
1310 Old Hwy. 8
Sheffield, ON L0R 1Z0
Tel: 519-621-4660; *Fax:* 519-740-8732
Toll-Free: 800-265-3573
info@dumfriesmutual.com
www.dumfriesmutual.com
www.facebook.com/DumfriesMutual; twitter.com/DumfriesMutual
Classes of Insurance: Auto, Liability, Boiler & Machinery, Property, Hail & Crop

Ecclesiastical Insurance Office plc/Société des Assurances écclésiastiques
TD West Tower
PO Box 307
#2200, 100 Wellington St. West
Toronto, ON M5K 1K2
Tel: 416-484-4555; *Fax:* 416-484-6352
www.ecclesiastical.ca
Other Contact Information: After-Hours Emergency Claims Toll-Free Phone: 888-693-2253
www.facebook.com/EIOCanada; twitter.com/eiocanada

* Indicates Provincially Incorporated Insurance Company

Classes of Insurance: Auto, Liability, Boiler & Machinery, Marine, Fidelity, Property

Echelon Insurance/Echelon Compagnie d'Assurances Générale
#300, 2680 Matheson Blvd. East
Mississauga, ON L4W 0A5
Tel: 905-214-7880; *Fax:* 905-214-7893
Toll-Free: 800-324-3566
marketing@echeloninsurance.ca
echeloninsurance.ca
Classes of Insurance: Accident, Personal Accident & Sickness, Legal Expense, Auto, Liability, Fidelity, Property, Fire, Surety

The Economical Insurance Group
PO Box 2000
111 Westmount St. South
Waterloo, ON N2J 4S4
Tel: 519-570-8200; *Fax:* 519-570-8389
Toll-Free: 800-265-2180
www.economicalinsurance.com
www.youtube.com/user/EconomicalInsurance
Classes of Insurance: Personal Accident & Sickness, Property

Economical Mutual Insurance Company
PO Box 2000
111 Westmount Rd. South
Waterloo, ON N2J 4S4
Tel: 519-570-8200; *Fax:* 519-570-8389
Toll-Free: 800-265-9996
www.economical.com
Classes of Insurance: Auto, Boiler & Machinery, Property, Surety

*Edge Mutual Insurance Company
PO Box 190
103 Wellington St.
Drayton, ON N0G 1P0
Tel: 519-638-3304; *Fax:* 519-638-3521
pmmutual@pmmutual.on.ca
www.edgemutual.com
Classes of Insurance: Personal Accident & Sickness, Auto, Liability, Boiler & Machinery, Fidelity, Property

Elite Insurance Company
#10 Aviva Way
Markham, ON L6G 0G1
Tel: 416-288-1800; *Toll-Free:* 800-387-4518
aviva.ca
Other Contact Information: Claims, Toll-Free: 866-692-8482
Classes of Insurance: Personal Accident & Sickness, Aircraft, Auto, Liability, Boiler & Machinery, Marine, Fidelity, Property, Surety

Empire Life Insurance Company/Empire Vie
259 King St. East
Kingston, ON K7L 3A8
Tel: 613-548-1881; *Toll-Free:* 877-548-1881
info@empire.ca
www.empire.ca
Other Contact Information: Investment & Individual Insurance: 800-561-1268; Quebec: 888-469-0969; Group Products: 800-267-0215; Email: group.csu@empire.ca
www.instagram.com/empirelife; www.facebook.com/EmpireLife; twitter.com/EmpireLife
Classes of Insurance: Accident, Personal Accident & Sickness, Life

*Energy Insurance Group Ltd. (EIG)
3026 - 5th St. SW
Calgary, AB T2S 2C4
www.eigltd.com
Classes of Insurance: Auto, Liability, Boiler & Machinery, Property

The Equitable Life Insurance Company of Canada
PO Box 1603, Stn. Waterloo
1 Westmount Rd. North
Waterloo, ON N2J 4C7
Tel: 519-886-5110; *Fax:* 519-883-7400
Toll-Free: 800-722-6615
corporatecommunications@equitable.ca
www.equitable.ca
Other Contact Information: HR, Email: hr@equitable.ca
www.facebook.com/EquitableLife; twitter.com/equitablelife
Classes of Insurance: Life

*Erie Mutual Insurance Company
711 Main St. East
Dunnville, ON N1A 2W5
Tel: 905-774-8566; *Fax:* 905-774-6468
Toll-Free: 800-263-6484
eriemutual@eriemutual.com
www.eriemutual.com
www.instagram.com/erie.mutual.insurance;
www.facebook.com/ErieMutualInsurance; twitter.com/ErieMutual
Classes of Insurance: Personal Accident & Sickness, Auto, Liability, Boiler & Machinery, Fidelity, Property

Euler Hermes Canada
#2810, 1155, boul René-Lévesque ouest
Montréal, QC H3B 2L2
Tel: 514-876-9656; *Fax:* 514-876-9658
Toll-Free: 877-509-3224
www.eulerhermes.ca
twitter.com/eulerhermesNA
Classes of Insurance: Credit

Everest Insurance Company of Canada/La Compagnie d'assurance Everest du Canada
Exchange Tower
#2620, 130 King St. West
Toronto, ON M5X 1C7
Tel: 416-487-3900; *Fax:* 416-487-0311
Toll-Free: 877-691-1247
www.everestre.com
Classes of Insurance: Aircraft, Auto, Liability, Boiler & Machinery, Credit, Marine, Property, Surety, Hail & Crop

Everest Reinsurance Company
The Exchange Tower
#2520, 130 King St. West
Toronto, ON M5X 1E3
Tel: 416-862-1228; *Fax:* 416-366-5899
www.everestre.com
Classes of Insurance: Personal Accident & Sickness, Aircraft, Auto, Liability, Boiler & Machinery, Credit, Fidelity, Property, Surety, Hail & Crop

FaithLife Financial
300 - 470 Weber St. North
Waterloo, ON N2L 6J2
Tel: 519-886-4610; *Fax:* 519-886-0350
Toll-Free: 800-563-6237
moreinfo@faithlifefinancial.ca
www.faithlifefinancial.ca
www.facebook.com/FaithLifeFinancial; twitter.com/FaithLifeFin
Classes of Insurance: Accident, Personal Accident & Sickness, Life

*Farm Mutual Reinsurance Plan Inc.
350 Pinebush Rd.
Cambridge, ON N1T 1Z6
Tel: 519-740-6415; *Fax:* 519-740-8852
Toll-Free: 844-554-3673
www.farmmutualre.com
www.facebook.com/FarmMutualRe; twitter.com/farmmutualre
Classes of Insurance: Accident, Aircraft, Legal Expense, Auto, Liability, Boiler & Machinery, Marine, Fidelity, Surety, Reinsurance

Federal Insurance Company
PO Box 139, Stn. Commerce Court
#2500, 199 Bay St.
Toronto, ON M5L 1E2
Tel: 416-359-3222; *Toll-Free:* 800-268-9344
www.chubb.com
Classes of Insurance: Personal Accident & Sickness, Auto, Liability, Boiler & Machinery, Marine, Fidelity, Property, Surety

Federated Insurance Company of Canada
255 Commerce Dr.
Winnipeg, MB R3C 3C9
Tel: 204-786-6431; *Fax:* 204-783-4443
Toll-Free: 800-665-1934
www.federated.ca
Classes of Insurance: Accident, Auto, Liability, Boiler & Machinery, Fidelity, Property, Fire, Surety, Theft

*Fenchurch General Insurance Company (FGIC)
Promontory II
#115, 2655 North Sheridan Way
Mississauga, ON L5K 2P8
Tel: 905-822-2282; *Fax:* 905-822-1282
Toll-Free: 800-515-8908
info@fenchurchgeneral.com
fenchurchgeneral.com
Classes of Insurance: Personal Accident & Sickness, Auto, Liability, Boiler & Machinery, Property, Surety

First Canadian Title (FCT)
2235 Sheridan Garden Dr.
Oakville, ON L6J 7Y5
Tel: 905-287-1000; *Fax:* 905-287-2400
Toll-Free: 800-307-0370
fct.ca
www.facebook.com/FCTCanada; twitter.com/FCT_Canada
Classes of Insurance: Property

First North American Insurance Company
c/o Manulife Financial
500 King St. North
Waterloo, ON N2J 4C6
www.manulife.ca
Classes of Insurance: Personal Accident & Sickness, Auto, Property

FM Global
#200, 100 New Park Pl.
Vaughan, ON L4K 0H9
Tel: 905-763-5555; *Fax:* 905-763-5556
www.fmglobal.com
www.facebook.com/InsurerFMGlobal; twitter.com/FMGlobal
Classes of Insurance: Boiler & Machinery, Property

FNF Canada
55 Superior Blvd.
Mississauga, ON L5T 2X9
Tel: 289-562-0088; *Fax:* 289-562-2494
Toll-Free: 877-526-3232
info@fnf.ca
www.fnf.ca
Other Contact Information: Accounting & Finance, Email: finance@fnf.ca; Marketing, Email: marketing@fnf.ca; Human Resources, Email: hr@fnf.ca
twitter.com/fnf_canada
Classes of Insurance: Property

*Fonds d'assurance responsabilité professionnelle de la Chambre des notaires du Québec
#101, 2045, rue Stanley, 8e étage
Montréal, QC H3A 2V4
Tel: 514-871-4999; *Fax:* 514-879-1781
Toll-Free: 800-465-6534
web@farpcnq.qc.ca
www.farpcnq.qc.ca

*Fonds d'assurance responsabilité professionnelle du Barreau du Québec/Quebec Bar Professional Liability Insurance Fund
#300, 445, boul Saint-Laurent
Montréal, QC H2Y 3T8
Tél: 514-954-3452; *Téléc:* 514-954-3454
assuranceresponsabilite@farpbq.ca
www.assurance-barreau.com

Foresters Life Insurance Company
789 Don Mills Rd.
Toronto, ON M3C 1T9
Toll-Free: 800-828-1540
service@foresters.com
www.foresters.com
www.youtube.com/user/foresters; www.facebook.com/Foresters; twitter.com/weareforesters
Classes of Insurance: Personal Accident & Sickness, Life

General Reinsurance Corporation
PO Box 471
#5705, 1 First Canadian Pl.
Toronto, ON M5X 1E4
Tel: 416-869-0490; *Fax:* 416-360-2020
AskGenRe@genre.com
www.genre.com
www.youtube.com/user/GenRePerspective; twitter.com/Gen_Re
Classes of Insurance: Personal Accident & Sickness, Aircraft, Auto, Liability, Boiler & Machinery, Credit, Fidelity, Property, Surety, Hail & Crop

Genworth Financial Mortgage Insurance Company Canada
#300, 2060 Winston Park Dr.
Oakville, ON L6H 5R7
Toll-Free: 800-511-8888
mortgage.info@genworth.com
www.genworth.ca
www.facebook.com/genworthcanada; twitter.com/GenworthCanada
Classes of Insurance: Property

* Indicates Provincially Incorporated Insurance Company

Gerber Life Insurance Company
PO Box 986, Stn. F
50 Charles St. East
Toronto, ON M4Y 2T2

Toll-Free: 800-518-8884
www.gerberlife.ca
twitter.com/gerberlife

Classes of Insurance: Life

*Germania Mutual Insurance Company
PO Box 30
403 Mary St.
Ayton, ON N0G 1C0

Tel: 519-665-7715; Fax: 519-665-7558
Toll-Free: 888-418-7770
www.germaniamutual.com
www.instagram.com/GermaniaMutual;
www.facebook.com/GermaniaMutual;
twitter.com/germaniamutual

Classes of Insurance: Liability, Property, Fire, Theft

*Gibbs Insurance Service Inc.
PO Box 10
109 Main St.
Barons, AB T0L 0G0

Tel: 403-757-3820; Fax: 403-757-2083
Toll-Free: 888-974-4227
info@gibbsinsurance.ca
www.gibbsinsurance.ca
www.facebook.com/gibbsinsurance.ca

Classes of Insurance: Auto, Property

*Goose Insurance Services Inc.
#380, 825 Homer St.
Vancouver, BC V6B 2W2

Toll-Free: 888-374-6673
support@gooseinsurance.com
www.gooseinsurance.com
www.instagram.com/gooseinsuranceca;
www.facebook.com/gooseinsurance; twitter.com/gooseinsurance

Classes of Insurance: Personal Accident & Sickness, Life

Gore Mutual Insurance Company
PO Box 70
252 Dundas St. North
Cambridge, ON N1R 5T3

Tel: 519-623-1910; Toll-Free: 800-265-8600
www.goremutual.com
www.facebook.com/GoreMutual; twitter.com/GoreMutual

Classes of Insurance: Personal Accident & Sickness, Auto,
Liability, Property, Fire, Theft

The Grand Orange Lodge of British America Benefit Fund
#706, 505 Consumers Rd.
Toronto, ON M2J 4V8

Tel: 416-223-1690; Fax: 416-223-1324
Toll-Free: 800-565-6248
info@orange.ca
orangebenefitfund.ca
www.facebook.com/OrangeBenefitFund

Classes of Insurance: Life

Great American Insurance Company
#800, 330 Bay St.
Toronto, ON M5H 2S8

Tel: 416-368-8200
www.greatamericaninsurancegroup.com
www.youtube.com/user/GAIGroup;
www.facebook.com/GreatAmericanInsuranceGroup;
twitter.com/gaigroup

Classes of Insurance: Personal Accident & Sickness, Aircraft,
Auto, Liability, Boiler & Machinery, Marine, Fidelity, Property,
Surety, Hail & Crop

Green Shield Canada (GSC)
PO Box 1606
8677 Anchor Dr.
Windsor, ON N9A 6W1

Tel: 519-739-1133; Toll-Free: 800-265-5615
www.greenshield.ca
Other Contact Information: Customer Service, Toll-Free:
1-888-711-1119
www.youtube.com/user/GreenShieldCanada;
www.facebook.com/GreenShieldCanada; twitter.com/gsc_1957

Classes of Insurance: Personal Accident & Sickness

*Grenville Mutual Insurance Company
380 Clonnade Dr.
Kemptville, ON K0G 1J0

Tel: 613-258-9988; Fax: 613-258-1142
www.grenvillemutual.com
www.facebook.com/GrenvilleMutual; twitter.com/GrenvilleMutual

Classes of Insurance: Personal Accident & Sickness, Auto,
Liability, Boiler & Machinery, Fidelity, Property

*Le Groupe Estrie-Richelieu, compagnie d'assurance (GER)
770, rue Principale
Granby, QC J2G 2Y7

Tél: 450-378-0101; Ligne sans frais: 800-363-8971
info@estrierichelieu.com
www.estrierichelieu.com

Classes of Insurance: Auto, Liability, Boiler & Machinery,
Property, Fire

*Groupe Promutuel, Fédération de sociétés mutuelles d'assurance générale
#400, 2000, boul Lebourgneuf
Québec, QC G2K 0B6

Ligne sans frais: 866-999-2433
federation@promutuel.ca
www.promutuelassurance.ca
www.youtube.com/user/PromutuelAssurance;
fr.pinterest.com/promutuel;
www.facebook.com/PromutuelAssurance; twitter.com/Promutuel

Classes of Insurance: Auto, Property

The Guarantee Company of North America/La Garantie, Compagnie d'Assurance de l'Amérique du Nord
700 University Ave.
Toronto, ON M5G 0A1

Tel: 416-341-1464; Toll-Free: 844-489-3768
www.theguarantee.com
twitter.com/TheGuaranteeCo

Classes of Insurance: Accident, Personal Accident & Sickness,
Legal Expense, Auto, Liability, Boiler & Machinery, Credit,
Fidelity, Property, Fire, Surety, Hail & Crop, Theft

*Halwell Mutual Insurance Company
535 Hanlon Creek Blvd.
Guelph, ON N1C 0A1

Tel: 519-836-2860; Toll-Free: 800-267-5706
reception@halwellmutual.com
www.halwellmutual.com
www.facebook.com/HalwellMutual; twitter.com/halwellmutual

Classes of Insurance: Auto, Liability, Boiler & Machinery,
Fidelity, Property

Hannover Rück SE Canadian Branch
#400, 220 Bay St.
Toronto, ON M5J 2W4

Tel: 416-607-9712; Fax: 416-867-9728
www.hannover-rueck.com

Classes of Insurance: Personal Accident & Sickness, Aircraft,
Auto, Liability, Boiler & Machinery, Fidelity, Property, Surety, Hail
& Crop

Harlock Murray Underwriting Ltd./Société d'assurance maritime Sunderland Limitée
#130, 960 Quayside Dr.
Bedford, BC V3M 6G2

Tel: 604-669-7745; Fax: 604-669-8595
info@hmumarine.com
hmumarine.com

Classes of Insurance: Marine

Hartford Fire Insurance Company
#2, 1145 Nicholson Rd.
Newmarket, ON L3Y 9C3

Tel: 905-853-0858; Fax: 905-853-0183
Classes of Insurance: Personal Accident & Sickness, Aircraft,
Auto, Liability, Boiler & Machinery, Fidelity, Property, Fire,
Surety, Hail & Crop, Theft

*Heartland Farm Mutual Inc.
100 Erb St. East
Waterloo, ON N2J 1L9

Tel: 519-886-4530; Fax: 519-746-0222
Toll-Free: 800-265-8813
www.heartlandfarmmutual.com
www.facebook.com/196407977125467;
twitter.com/HeartlandMutual

Classes of Insurance: Personal Accident & Sickness, Aircraft,
Auto, Liability, Boiler & Machinery, Fidelity, Property, Hail & Crop

*Henderson Insurance Inc.
807 Thatcher Dr. East
Moose Jaw, SK S6J 0A9

Tel: 306-694-5959; Fax: 306-693-0117
Toll-Free: 888-661-5959
hii@hendersoninsurance.ca
www.hendersoninsurance.ca
www.facebook.com/HendersonInsuranceInc;
twitter.com/HIInsurance

Classes of Insurance: Aircraft, Auto, Liability, Marine, Property,
Hail & Crop

*Howard Mutual Insurance Co.
PO Box 398
20 Ebenezer St. West
Ridgetown, ON N0P 2C0

Tel: 519-674-5434; Fax: 519-674-2029
howardmutual.com
www.facebook.com/HowardMutualInsurance;
twitter.com/howardmutual

Classes of Insurance: Personal Accident & Sickness, Auto,
Liability, Fidelity, Property, Hail & Crop

*Howick Mutual Insurance Company
40592 Amberley Rd., RR#4
Wingham, ON N0G 2W0

Tel: 519-912-1030; Fax: 519-912-1031
Toll-Free: 800-265-3033
info@howickmutual.com
www.howickmutual.com
www.instagram.com/howickmutual;
www.facebook.com/HowickMutualInsurance;
twitter.com/HowickMutual

Classes of Insurance: Personal Accident & Sickness, Auto,
Liability, Boiler & Machinery, Property

HSB BI&I
#2000, 390 Bay St.
Toronto, ON M5H 2Y2

Tel: 416-363-5491; Fax: 416-363-0538
corporate@biico.com
munichre.com/hsbbii/en.html
www.facebook.com/hsbbii; twitter.com/hsb_bii

Classes of Insurance: Liability, Boiler & Machinery, Property

*HT&C Mutual Insurance Company
37868 Zurich-Hensall Rd.
Zurich, ON N0M 2T0

info@htcmutual.ca
www.htcmutual.ca

Classes of Insurance: Auto, Liability, Property, Hail & Crop

*HTM Insurance Company
PO Box 201
1185 Elgin St. West
Cobourg, ON K9A 4K5

Tel: 905-372-0186; Fax: 905-372-1364
Toll-Free: 800-263-3935
info@htminsurance.ca
www.htminsurance.ca

Classes of Insurance: Auto, Property, Fire

*HUB International Atlantic Limited
#500, 77 Germain St.
Saint John, NB E2L 2E8

Tel: 506-635-0760; Fax: 506-634-5641
Toll-Free: 877-635-0760
www.hubinternational.com
www.youtube.com/user/hubinternational;
www.facebook.com/HUBInternationalLimited;
twitter.com/HUBInsurance

Classes of Insurance: Liability, Boiler & Machinery, Property

*HUB International Barton Insurance Brokers
8346 Noble Rd.
Chilliwack, BC V2P 6R5

Tel: 604-703-7070; Fax: 604-703-7092
Toll-Free: 800-668-2112
barton.hubinternational.com
www.youtube.com/user/hubinternational;
www.facebook.com/HUBInternationalLimited;
twitter.com/HUBInsurance

Classes of Insurance: Auto, Marine, Property

*HUB International British Columbia
Head Office
400 - 4350 Still Creek Dr.
Burnaby, BC V5C 0G5

Tel: 604-269-1000; Fax: 604-269-1001
Toll-Free: 800-606-9969
tos.hubinternational.com
www.youtube.com/user/hubinternational;
www.facebook.com/HUBInternationalLimited;
twitter.com/HUBInsurance

Classes of Insurance: Auto, Marine, Property

Indicates Provincially Incorporated Insurance Company

*HUB International Manitoba Limited
#500, 1661 Portage Ave.
Winnipeg, MB R3J 3T7
Tel: 204-988-4800
www.hubinternational.com
www.youtube.com/user/hubinternational;
www.facebook.com/HUBInternationalLimited;
twitter.com/HUBInsurance
Classes of Insurance: Auto, Liability, Life, Property

*HUB International Nunavut
#500, 1661 Portage Ave.
Winnipeg, MB R3J 3T7
Tel: 204-988-4800; Toll-Free: 866-853-6940
www.hubinternational.com
www.facebook.com/HUBNunavut
Classes of Insurance: Auto, Marine, Property

*HUB International Ontario
#700, 2265 Upper Middle Rd. East
Oakville, ON L6H 0G5
Tel: 905-847-5500; Toll-Free: 800-263-2383
www.hubinternational.com/en-ca/offices/ca/ontario/oakville
www.youtube.com/user/hubinternational;
www.facebook.com/HUBInternationalLimited;
twitter.com/HUBInsurance
Classes of Insurance: Personal Accident & Sickness, Auto, Property

*HUB International Québec
8500, boul Decarie, 5e étage
Montréal, QC H4P 2N2
Tél: 514-374-9600
quebec.hubinternational.com
www.youtube.com/user/hubinternational;
www.facebook.com/HUBInternationalLimited;
twitter.com/HUBInsurance
Classes of Insurance: Auto

*Humania Assurance Inc.
1555, rue Girouard ouest
Saint-Hyacinthe, QC J2S 7C8
Téléc: 450-773-6470
Ligne sans frais: 800-773-8404
info@humania.ca
www.humania.ca
www.facebook.com/humaniaassurance
Classes of Insurance: Personal Accident & Sickness, Life

*iA Financial Group/iA Groupe financier
CP 1907, Stn. Terminus
1080, Grand Allée ouest
Québec, QC G1K 7M3
Tél: 418-684-5000; Ligne sans frais: 800-463-6236
ia.ca/individuals
Other Contact Information: Accident Insurance, Phone:
418-684-5405, Fax: 418-688-0705
www.youtube.com/user/IAquebec; www.facebook.com/iacanada;
twitter.com/iacanada
Classes of Insurance: Personal Accident & Sickness, Auto, Life, Property

Independent Order of Foresters
789 Don Mills Rd.
Toronto, ON M3C 1T9
Tel: 416-429-3000; Toll-Free: 800-828-1540
service@foresters.com
www.foresters.com
Other Contact Information: Member Benefits, Toll-Free:
800-444-3043; Unity Life Policy Holders, Email:
clientservice@unitylife.ca, Toll-Free: 800-267-8777
www.youtube.com/c/foresters;
www.instagram.com/forestersfinancial;
www.facebook.com/Foresters; twitter/com/weareforesters
Classes of Insurance: Personal Accident & Sickness, Life

***Industrial Alliance Auto & Home
Insurance/Industrielle Alliance, Assurance auto et
habitation**
#230, 925, Grande Allée ouest
Québec, QC G1S 1C1
Tél: 418-650-4486; Ligne sans frais: 877-700-7778
ia.ca/home-insurance
Other Contact Information: Claims, Toll-Free: 800-481-2424
Classes of Insurance: Auto, Property

***Insurance Company of Prince Edward Island
(ICPEI)**
PO Box 1120
118 Water St.
Charlottetown, PE C1A 1A7
Fax: 902-626-3529
Toll-Free: 866-404-2734
inquiries@icpei.ca
icpei.ca
Other Contact Information: Commercial Property, Toll-Free:
866-321-0010
Classes of Insurance: Auto, Property

*Insurance Corporation of British Columbia (ICBC)
151 West Esplanade
North Vancouver, BC V7M 3H9
Tel: 604-661-2800; Toll-Free: 800-663-3051
www.icbc.com
www.facebook.com/theICBC; twitter.com/icbc
Classes of Insurance: Auto

Intact Financial Corporation
700 University Ave.
Toronto, ON M5G 0A1
Tel: 416-341-1464; Fax: 416-941-5320
Toll-Free: 877-341-1464
info@intact.net
www.intactfc.com
Classes of Insurance: Personal Accident & Sickness, Property

Intact Insurance Company of Canada
700 University Ave.
Toronto, ON M5G 0A1
Tel: 416-341-1464; Fax: 416-344-8030
Toll-Free: 844-489-3768
info@intact.net
www.intact.ca
www.instagram.com/intactinsurance; www.facebook.com/intact;
twitter.com/intactinsurance
Classes of Insurance: Auto, Property

ivari
#500, 5000 Yonge St.
Toronto, ON M2N 7J8
Tel: 416-883-5000; Fax: 416-883-5003
Toll-Free: 800-846-5970
conversation@ivari.ca
ivari.ca
www.instagram.com/ivari_canada;
www.facebook.com/ivaricanada; twitter.com/ivari_canada
Classes of Insurance: Personal Accident & Sickness, Life

**Jevco Insurance Company/La Compagnie
d'Assurances Jevco**
#900, 6925 Century Ave.
Mississauga, ON L5N 7K2
Tel: 905-227-9350; Fax: 905-277-5008
Toll-Free: 800-265-5458
info@jevco.ca
www.jevco.ca
Other Contact Information: 24-Hour Toll-Free Claims Line:
866-864-1112
Classes of Insurance: Auto, Property

*Johnston Meier Insurance Agencies Group
22367 Dewdney Trunk Rd.
Maple Ridge, BC V2X 3J4
Tel: 604-467-4184; Fax: 604-467-9711
Toll-Free: 888-256-4564
info@jmins.com
www.jmins.com
www.instagram.com/johnstonmeierinsurance;
www.facebook.com/JohnstonMeierInsurance;
twitter.com/JohnstonMeier
Classes of Insurance: Aircraft, Auto, Life, Marine, Surety

*Kent & Essex Mutual Insurance Company
PO Box 356
10 Creek Rd.
Chatham, ON N7M 5K4
Tel: 519-352-3190; Fax: 519-352-5344
Toll-Free: 800-265-5206
info@kemutual.com
www.kemutual.com
www.instagram.com/kemutual; www.facebook.com/kemutual;
twitter.com/kemutual
Classes of Insurance: Personal Accident & Sickness, Auto,
Liability, Boiler & Machinery, Fidelity, Property

*Kirkham Insurance
205 - 11th St. South
Lethbridge, AB T1J 4A6
Tel: 403-328-1228; Fax: 403-380-4051
Toll-Free: 800-256-2955
info@kirkhaminsurance.com
kirkhaminsurance.com
www.facebook.com/kirkhaminsurance
Classes of Insurance: Auto, Property

Knights of Columbus Insurance
c/o The Raymond Richer Agency
26 Davis Ct.
Hampton, ON L0B 1J0
Tel: 905-263-4212
www.kofc.org/un/en/insurance
www.youtube.com/knightsofcolumbus;
www.facebook.com/KnightsofColumbus; twitter.com/kofc
Classes of Insurance: Life

*Lambton Mutual Insurance Company
PO Box 520
7873 Confederation Line
Watford, ON N0M 2S0
Tel: 519-876-2304; Fax: 519-876-6626
Toll-Free: 800-561-4136
info@lambtonmutual.com
www.lambtonmutual.com
www.facebook.com/LambtonMutual; twitter.com/lambtonmutual
Classes of Insurance: Personal Accident & Sickness, Auto,
Liability, Boiler & Machinery, Fidelity, Property, Hail & Crop

**Lawyers' Professional Indemnity Company
(LAWPRO)**
PO Box 3
#3101, 250 Yonge St.
Toronto, ON M5B 2L7
Tel: 416-598-5800; Fax: 416-599-8341
Toll-Free: 800-410-1013
service@lawpro.ca
www.lawpro.ca
www.facebook.com/LAWPROinsurance; twitter.com/LAWPRO
Classes of Insurance: Liability

**Legacy General Insurance Company/Compagnie
d'Assurances Générales Legacy**
25 Sheppard Ave. West
Toronto, ON M2N 6S6
Tel: 647-730-1200; Toll-Free: 800-667-2570
www.canadianpremier.ca
Other Contact Information: Credit Unions, Toll-Free Phone:
800-763-1300; Claims: 800-598-6918
Classes of Insurance: Personal Accident & Sickness, Liability,
Property

*Lennox & Addington Mutual Insurance Company
PO Box 174
32 Mill St.
Napanee, ON K7R 3M3
Tel: 613-354-4810; Fax: 613-354-7112
Toll-Free: 800-267-7812
napanee@l-amutual.com
l-amutual.com
www.facebook.com/lamutualinsurance
Classes of Insurance: Personal Accident & Sickness, Auto,
Liability, Marine, Property

**Liberty Mutual Insurance Company/La Compagnie
d'Assurance Liberté Mutuelle**
#900, 181 Bay St.
Toronto, ON M5J 2T3
Fax: 416-307-4372
Toll-Free: 800-461-5079
infocanada@libertymutual.com
www.libertymutual.com
www.facebook.com/libertymutual; twitter.com/libertymutual
Classes of Insurance: Personal Accident & Sickness, Aircraft,
Auto, Liability, Boiler & Machinery, Fidelity, Property, Surety

Life Insurance Company of North America (LINA)
#301, 100 Consilium Pl.
Toronto, ON M1H 3E3
Tel: 416-290-6666
www.cigna.com
Classes of Insurance: Accident, Personal Accident & Sickness,
Life

* Indicates Provincially Incorporated Insurance Company

Lloyd's Underwriters
#2220, 1155, rue Metcalfe
Montréal, QC H3B 2V6

Tel: 514-861-8361; Fax: 514-861-0470
Toll-Free: 877-455-6937
info@lloyds.ca
www.lloyds.com/lloyds/offices/americas/canada
Other Contact Information: Commercial Inquiries, Phone:
514-864-5444
Classes of Insurance: Personal Accident & Sickness, Aircraft,
Legal Expense, Auto, Liability, Boiler & Machinery, Fidelity,
Property, Fire, Surety, Reinsurance

*Manitoba Agricultural Services Corporation (MASC)
Insurance Corporate Office
#400, 50 - 24th St.
Portage la Prairie, MB R1N 3V9

Tel: 204-239-3246; Fax: 204-239-3401
mailbox@masc.mb.ca
www.masc.mb.ca

Classes of Insurance: Hail & Crop

*Manitoba Blue Cross
PO Box 1046, Stn. Main
599 Empress St.
Winnipeg, MB R3C 2X7

Tel: 204-775-0151; Fax: 204-786-5965
Toll-Free: 888-873-2583
www.mb.bluecross.ca
Other Contact Information: Canada, Toll-Free: 888-596-1032;
Claims Fax: 204-772-1231; Sales Fax: 204-786-5965
Classes of Insurance: Personal Accident & Sickness, Life

*Manitoba Public Insurance
PO Box 6300
Winnipeg, MB R3C 4A4

Tel: 204-985-7000; Toll-Free: 800-665-2410
www.mpi.mb.ca
Other Contact Information: TTY: 204-985-8832; Out of Province
Claims, Toll-Free: 800-661-6051
www.instagram.com/mpidrive;
www.youtube.com/user/MBPublicInsurance;
www.facebook.com/mpidrive

Classes of Insurance: Auto

Manufacturers Life Insurance Company/La Compagnie d'Assurance-Vie Manufacturers
500 King St. North
Waterloo, ON N2J 4Z6

Tel: 519-747-7000
www.manulife.ca
Classes of Insurance: Personal Accident & Sickness, Life

Manulife Financial
200 Bloor St. East
Toronto, ON M4W 1E5

Tel: 416-926-3000
www.manulife.ca
www.instagram.com/manulife; www.facebook.com/Manulife;
twitter.com/Manulife
Classes of Insurance: Life

MAX Canada Insurance Company
#710, 50 Queen St. North
Kitchener, ON N2H 6P4

Toll-Free: 877-770-7729
info@maxinsurance.ca
maxinsurance.ca
Classes of Insurance: Liability, Boiler & Machinery, Marine,
Fidelity, Property

*McKillop Mutual Insurance Company
PO Box 819
91 Main St. South
Seaforth, ON N0K 1W0

Tel: 519-527-0400; Fax: 519-527-2777
Toll-Free: 800-463-9204
www.mckillopmutual.com
Classes of Insurance: Personal Accident & Sickness, Auto,
Liability, Boiler & Machinery, Fidelity, Property

MD Insurance Agency Limited
1870 Alta Vista Dr.
Ottawa, ON K1G 6R7

Tel: 613-731-4552; Toll-Free: 800-267-4022
mdm.ca

Classes of Insurance: Life

*Medavie Blue Cross
PO Box 220
644 Main St.
Moncton, NB E1C 8L3

Tel: 506-853-1811; Fax: 506-867-4651
Toll-Free: 800-667-4511
www.medaviebc.ca
Other Contact Information: Group Benefits, Atlantic Provinces &
Ontario: 888-227-3400; Group Benefits, Québec: 888-588-1212
www.youtube.com/MedavieBlueCross; medaviesmallsteps.com;
www.facebook.com/MedavieBlueCross; twitter.com/MedavieBC
Classes of Insurance: Personal Accident & Sickness, Life

Meloche Monnex Inc.
2161 Yonge St.
Toronto, ON M4S 3A6

Toll-Free: 877-777-7136
www.melochemonnex.com
Other Contact Information: Claims, Toll-Free: 877-323-0343; Alt.
URL: www.group.tdinsurance.com
Classes of Insurance: Auto, Property

*Mennonite Mutual Insurance Co. (Alberta) Ltd. (MMI)
#300, 2946 - 32nd St. NE
Calgary, AB T1Y 6J7

Tel: 403-275-6996; Fax: 403-291-6733
Toll-Free: 866-222-6996
office@mmiab.ca
miab.ca
www.facebook.com/MMIMutual
Classes of Insurance: Auto, Liability, Property, Fire

Metropolitan Tower Life Insurance Company (MTLIC)
#1300, 1981 av McGill College
Montréal, QC H3A 3A8

Tel: 514-985-5260; Fax: 514-985-3066
Toll-Free: 800-985-4326
Classes of Insurance: Life, Reinsurance

*Middlesex Mutual Insurance Co.
PO Box 100
15 Meredith Dr.
Ilderton, ON N0M 2A0

Tel: 519-666-0075; Fax: 519-666-0079
Toll-Free: 800-851-4045
www.middlesexmutual.on.ca
www.instagram.com/mmic12371;
www.facebook.com/middlesexmutualinsurance;
twitter.com/middlesexmutual
Classes of Insurance: Auto, Liability, Property

*MIG Insurance
412 Saskatchewan Ave.
Portage la Prairie, MB R1N 0M4

Tel: 204-857-8100; Fax: 204-239-6500
info@miginsurance.ca
www.miginsurance.ca
www.instagram.com/mig.insurance;
www.facebook.com/mig.insurance; twitter.com/MIGInsurance
Classes of Insurance: Auto, Property

*Millennium Insurance Corporation
#200, 2457 Broadmoor Blvd.
Sherwood Park, AB T8H 0Y6

Tel: 780-467-1500; Fax: 780-467-0004
Toll-Free: 866-467-1245
info@millenniuminsurance.ca
www.millenniuminsurance.ca
Other Contact Information: Calgary Phone: 403-265-4576; Fax:
403-265-4578
Classes of Insurance: Auto, Property

Mitsui Sumitomo Insurance Co., Limited. (MS&AD)
c/o Chubb Insurance Company of Canada, Commerce Court
West
PO Box 139, Stn. Commerce Court
#2500, 199 Bay St.
Toronto, ON M5L 1E2

Tel: 416-863-0550
www.ms-ins.com/english/company/network/area03.html#anc-02
Classes of Insurance: Personal Accident & Sickness, Aircraft,
Auto, Liability, Boiler & Machinery, Fidelity, Property, Surety

Motors Insurance Corporation
#101, 8500 Leslie St.
Thornhill, ON L3T 7M8
Classes of Insurance: Auto, Liability, Boiler & Machinery

*Mouvement des caisses Desjardins du Québec/Desjardins Group
100, rue des Commandeurs
Lévis, QC G6V 7N5

Tél: 418-835-8444; Ligne sans frais: 866-835-8444
www.desjardins.com
www.youtube.com/user/desjardinsgroup;
www.instagram.com/desjardinsgroup;
www.facebook.com/desjardinsgroup; twitter.com/desjardinsgroup

Munich Reinsurance Company Canada Branch (Life)
Munich Re Centre
390 Bay St., 27th Fl.
Toronto, ON M5H 2Y2

Tel: 416-359-2200; Fax: 416-361-0305
www.munichre.com/ca/life
www.facebook.com/munichre; twitter.com/munichre
Classes of Insurance: Personal Accident & Sickness, Life,
Reinsurance

Munich Reinsurance Company of Canada
#2200, 390 Bay St.
Toronto, ON M5H 2Y2

Tel: 416-366-9206; Fax: 416-366-4330
Toll-Free: 800-444-5321
info@mroc.com
www.munichre.com/ca/non-life
twitter.com/munichrecanada
Classes of Insurance: Auto, Liability, Property, Theft

*Municipal Insurance Association of British Columbia (MIABC)
#200, 429 West 2nd Ave.
Vancouver, BC V5Y 1E3

Tel: 604-683-6266; Fax: 604-683-6244
Toll-Free: 855-683-6266
askusanything@miabc.org
www.miabc.org
twitter.com/the_miabc
Classes of Insurance: Liability

*MUNIX Reciprocal (MUNIX)
#300, 8616 - 51st Ave.
Edmonton, AB T6E 6E6

Tel: 780-433-4431; Toll-Free: 877-421-6644
www.auma.ca
twitter.com/theauma
Classes of Insurance: Liability, Property

*The Mutual Fire Insurance Company of British Columbia
9366 - 200A St.
Langley, BC V1M 4B3

Tel: 604-881-1250; Toll-Free: 866-417-2272
info@mutualfirebc.com
mutualfirebc.com
twitter.com/mutualfirebc
Classes of Insurance: Property, Fire

*Mutuelle d'assurance en Église (MAE)
1071, rue de la Cathédrale
Montréal, QC H3B 2V4

Tel: 514-395-4969; Fax: 514-861-8921
Toll-Free: 800-567-6586
info@cmae.ca
www.cmae.ca
Classes of Insurance: Liability, Boiler & Machinery, Property,
Fire, Theft

*My Mutual Insurance
3033 Central Ave.
Waldheim, SK S0K 4R0

Tel: 306-945-4666; Toll-Free: 800-261-0360
hello@mymutualinsurance.ca
www.mymutualinsurance.ca
www.facebook.com/MyMutualInsurance;
twitter.com/mymutualins
Classes of Insurance: Boiler & Machinery, Property, Fire, Theft

*New Diamond Insurance Services Ltd.
#128, 6061 No. 3 Rd.
Richmond, BC V6Y 2B2

Tel: 604-278-1811; Fax: 604-279-0616
info@newdiamondfinancial.com
www.newdiamondfinancial.com/insurance
Other Contact Information: Alt. Phone: 604-233-1811
Classes of Insurance: Personal Accident & Sickness, Auto,
Life, Property

The Nordic Insurance Company of Canada
#1500A, 700 University Ave.
Toronto, ON M5G 0A1

Toll-Free: 866-941-5094

---

* Indicates Provincially Incorporated Insurance Company

Classes of Insurance: Accident, Legal Expense, Auto, Liability, Boiler & Machinery, Fidelity, Property, Surety

*North Blenheim Mutual Insurance Company
11 Baird St. North
Bright, ON N0J 1B0

Tel: 519-454-8661; *Fax:* 519-454-8785
Toll-Free: 800-665-6888
info@northblenheim.com
www.northblenheim.com
www.facebook.com/NorthBlenheimMutualInsuranceCo
Classes of Insurance: Auto, Liability, Property

*North Kent Mutual Fire Insurance Company
PO Box 478
29553 St George St.
Dresden, ON N0P 1M0

Tel: 519-683-4484; *Fax:* 519-683-4509
Toll-Free: 888-736-4705
nkm@nkminsurance.com
nkminsurance.com
www.instagram.com/nkminsurance;
www.facebook.com/NKMInsurance; twitter.com/NKMInsurance
Classes of Insurance: Auto, Liability, Property, Fire, Hail & Crop, Theft

Northbridge Insurance
#700, 105 Adelaide St. West
Toronto, ON M5H 1P9

Tel: 416-350-4400; *Toll-Free:* 855-620-6262
info@nbfc.com
www.nbins.com
www.facebook.com/northbridgeins; twitter.com/northbridgeins
Classes of Insurance: Accident, Auto, Liability, Marine, Property, Hail & Crop

*Northern Savings Insurance Services Ltd.
138 - 3rd Ave. West
Prince Rupert, BC V8J 1K8

Tel: 250-627-1123; *Fax:* 250-624-6444
Toll-Free: 800-555-4093
info@northsave.com
www.northsave.com/Insurance
www.faceook.com/northsave
Classes of Insurance: Auto, Marine, Property

*Nova Mutual Insurance Company
35 Talbot St. East
Jarvis, ON N0A 1J0

Toll-Free: 833-829-6682
contactus@novamutual.com
www.novamutual.com
www.instagram.com/novamutual;
www.facebook.com/NovaMutual
Classes of Insurance: Personal Accident & Sickness, Auto, Liability, Fidelity, Property

Novex Group Insurance/ING Novex Compagnie d'Assurance du Canada
700 University Ave.
Toronto, ON M5G 0A1

Tel: 416-941-5221; *Fax:* 416-941-9758
Toll-Free: 866-941-5221
info@intact.net
www.intact.ca/group-insurance
Classes of Insurance: Personal Accident & Sickness, Legal Expense, Auto, Liability, Boiler & Machinery, Credit, Fidelity, Property, Surety

*Nuera Insurance inc.
Bldg. B
#20, 6020 - 2nd St. SE, 2nd Fl.
Calgary, AB T2H 2L8

Toll-Free: 866-683-6444
contact@nuerainsurance.ca
www.nuerainsurance.ca
www.instagram.com/nuerainsuranceinc;
www.facebook.com/nuerainsurance; twitter.com/NueraInsurance
Classes of Insurance: Personal Accident & Sickness, Auto, Life, Property

OdysseyRe - Canadian Branch
#1600, 55 University Ave.
Toronto, ON M5J 2H7

Tel: 416-862-0162; *Fax:* 416-367-3248
www.odysseyre.com
Classes of Insurance: Accident, Aircraft, Auto, Liability, Boiler & Machinery, Property, Fire, Surety, Hail & Crop, Reinsurance

Old Republic Insurance Company of Canada/L'Ancienne République, Compagnie d'Assurance du Ca
PO Box 557
100 King St. West
Hamilton, ON L8N 3K9

Tel: 905-523-5936; *Fax:* 905-528-8338
Toll-Free: 800-530-5446
www.orican.com
Classes of Insurance: Accident, Aircraft, Auto, Liability, Property, Reinsurance

Omega General Insurance Company
#1200, 34 King St. East
Toronto, ON M5C 2X8

Tel: 416-361-1728; *Fax:* 416-361-6113
contactus@omegageneral.com
tillcap.com/omega/overview
Classes of Insurance: Personal Accident & Sickness, Aircraft, Legal Expense, Liability, Boiler & Machinery, Credit, Fidelity, Property, Surety

*Ontario Blue Cross
#610, 185 The West Mall
Toronto, ON M9C 5P1

Tel: 416-640-3444; *Fax:* 416-626-0997
Toll-Free: 866-722-3444
bco.indhealth@ont.bluecross.ca
on.bluecross.ca
Other Contact Information: Travel, Email: bco.travel@ont.bluecross.ca; Tech Support: 800-563-2538
Classes of Insurance: Personal Accident & Sickness

*Ontario Mutual Insurance Association
350 Pinebush Rd.
Cambridge, ON N1T 1Z6

Tel: 519-622-9220; *Fax:* 519-622-9227
information@omia.com
www.omia.com
Classes of Insurance: Personal Accident & Sickness, Auto, Property

*Ontario School Boards' Insurance Exchange (OSBIE)
91 Westmount Rd.
Guelph, ON N1H 5J2

Tel: 519-767-2182; *Fax:* 519-767-0281
Toll-Free: 800-668-6724
info@osbie.on.ca
www.osbie.on.ca
Other Contact Information: Member Services: memberservices@osbie.on.ca; Risk Management: rm@osbie.on.ca; Claims: claims@osbie.on.ca
Classes of Insurance: Auto, Liability, Boiler & Machinery, Property, Fire

*Optimum Assurance Agricole inc./Optimum Farm Insurance Inc.
#422, 25, rue des Forges
Trois-Rivières, QC G9A 6A7

Tél: 819-373-2040; *Téléc:* 819-373-2801
www.groupe-optimum.com
Classes of Insurance: Auto, Property, Fire

Optimum Général inc./Optimum General Inc.
#1500, 425, boul de Maisonneuve ouest
Montréal, QC H3A 3G5

Tél: 514-288-8711; *Téléc:* 514-288-8269
www.optimum-general.com
Classes of Insurance: Auto, Liability, Property

Optimum Reassurance inc./Optimum Reassurance Inc.
#1200, 425, boul de Maisonneuve ouest
Montréal, QC H3A 3G5

Tél: 514-288-1900; *Téléc:* 514-288-8099
www.optimumre.ca
Classes of Insurance: Reinsurance

*Optimum Réassurance inc./Optimum Reassurance Inc.
#1200, 425, boul de Maisonneuve ouest
Montréal, QC H3A 3G5

Tél: 514-288-1900; *Téléc:* 514-288-8099
www.optimumre.ca
Classes of Insurance: Accident, Personal Accident & Sickness, Life, Reinsurance

*Optimum Société d'Assurance inc. (OSA)/Optimum Insurance Company Inc.
#1500, 425, boul de Maisonneuve ouest
Montréal, QC H3A 3G5

Tél: 514-288-8711; *Téléc:* 514-288-8269
www.optimum-general.com
Classes of Insurance: Auto, Liability, Property

*Optimum West Insurance Company Inc.
1700 - 3777 Kingsway
Burnaby, BC V5H 3Z7

Tel: 604-688-1541; *Fax:* 604-688-1527
www.optimum-general.com
Classes of Insurance: Auto, Property, Hail & Crop

The Order of United Commercial Travelers of America (UCT)
#300, 901 Centre St. North
Calgary, AB T2E 2P6

Tel: 403-277-0745; *Fax:* 403-277-6662
Toll-Free: 800-267-2371
www.uct.org
www.youtube.com/user/UCTinAction;
www.flickr.com/photos/uctinaction;
www.facebook.com/UCTinAction
Classes of Insurance: Personal Accident & Sickness, Life

*Ordre des Architectes du Québec
#200, 420, rue McGill
Montréal, QC H2Y 2G1

Tel: 514-937-6168; *Fax:* 514-933-0242
Toll-Free: 800-599-6168
info@oaq.com
www.oaq.com
www.facebook.com/Ordre.architectes.Qc;
twitter.com/OrdreArchiQc

*Ordre des dentistes du Québec (ODQ)
#1640, 800, boul René-Lévesque ouest
Montréal, QC H3B 1X9

Tel: 514-875-8511; *Fax:* 514-393-9248
Toll-Free: 800-361-4887
www.odq.qc.ca
www.youtube.com/webmestreodq;
www.facebook.com/102225303175310;
twitter.com/ordredentistes

*Pacific Coast Fishermen's Mutual Marine Insurance Company
3757 Canada Way
Burnaby, BC V5G 1G5

Tel: 604-438-4240; *Fax:* 604-438-5756
Toll-Free: 888-438-4242
info@mutualmarine.bc.ca
mutualmarine.bc.ca
Other Contact Information: Toll Free (BC only): 888-438-4242
Classes of Insurance: Marine

Pafco Insurance Company
#100, 27 Allstate Pkwy.
Markham, ON L3R 5P8

Tel: 905-513-4000; *Fax:* 905-513-4026
Toll-Free: 877-216-6973
websitecontactus@pafco.ca
www.pafco.ca
Classes of Insurance: Personal Accident & Sickness, Auto, Liability, Property

*Palliser Insurance Company Limited
#103, 3502 Taylor St. East
Saskatoon, SK S7H 5H9

Tel: 306-955-4814; *Fax:* 306-955-1317
Toll-Free: 844-955-4814
info@palliserinsurance.com
palliserinsurance.com
www.facebook.com/PalliserInsurance; twitter.com/palliserins
Classes of Insurance: Hail & Crop

PartnerRe
95 Wellington St. West, 12th Fl.
Toronto, ON M5J 2N7

Tel: 416-861-0033; *Fax:* 416-861-0200
contactus@partnerre.com
partnerre.com
Classes of Insurance: Personal Accident & Sickness, Auto, Life, Property

* Indicates Provincially Incorporated Insurance Company

*PBC Health Benefits Society
PO Box 7000
4250 Canada Way
Vancouver, BC V6B 4E1
Tel: 604-419-2000; *Fax:* 604-419-2990
Toll-Free: 877-722-2583
www.pac.bluecross.ca
Other Contact Information: Fraud Report: 800-661-9675
www.facebook.com/pacificbluecross; twitter.com/pacbluecross
Classes of Insurance: Accident, Personal Accident & Sickness,
Life

*Peace Hills General Insurance Company
#300, 10709 Jasper Ave.
Edmonton, AB T5J 3N3
Tel: 780-424-3986; *Fax:* 780-424-0396
Toll-Free: 800-272-5614
phi@phgic.com
www.peacehillsinsurance.com
twitter.com/PeaceHillsIns
Classes of Insurance: Accident, Aircraft, Auto, Liability, Boiler
& Machinery, Credit, Marine, Fidelity, Property, Fire, Surety,
Theft

*Peel Mutual Insurance Company
103 Queen St. West
Brampton, ON L6Y 1M3
Tel: 905-451-2386; *Toll-Free:* 800-268-3069
www.peelmutual.com
www.facebook.com/peelmutual; twitter.com/PeelMutual
Classes of Insurance: Auto, Liability, Boiler & Machinery,
Fidelity, Property

Pembridge Insurance Company
#100, 27 Allstate Pkwy.
Markham, ON L3R 5P8
Tel: 905-513-4013; *Toll-Free:* 877-736-2743
websitecontactus@pembridge.com
www.pembridge.com
Classes of Insurance: Auto, Property

***The Personal General Insurance Inc./La
Personnelle, assurances générales inc.**
PO Box 3500
6300, boul Guillaume-Couture
Lévis, QC G6V 6P9
Toll-Free: 888-476-8737
www.lapersonnelle.com
Other Contact Information: Claims, Toll-Free: 888-785-5502;
Payment, Toll-Free: 888-277-6481
www.instagram.com/thepersonalinsurance;
www.facebook.com/ThePersonalInsurance;
twitter.com/tpicinsurance
Classes of Insurance: Auto, Liability, Boiler & Machinery,
Property, Surety

**The Personal Insurance Company/La Personnelle,
compagnie d'assurances**
Tour sud
1, Complexe Desjardins, 17e étage
Montréal, QC H5B 1B1
Toll-Free: 888-476-8737
www.thepersonal.com
Other Contact Information: 24/7 Claims Line, Toll-Free:
866-785-5502; Payment Toll-Free Phone: 888-277-6481
www.facebook.com/ThePersonalInsurance;
twitter.com/tpicinsurance
Classes of Insurance: Personal Accident & Sickness, Aircraft,
Auto, Liability, Boiler & Machinery, Fidelity, Property, Surety

Perth Insurance Company
#1500, 5255 Yonge St.
Toronto, ON M2N 6P4
Tel: 416-590-0038; *Fax:* 416-590-0869
Toll-Free: 800-268-8801
www.economical.com/en/perth-insurance
Classes of Insurance: Auto, Property

Petline Insurance
#300, 600 Empress St.
Winnipeg, MB R3G 0R5
Toll-Free: 800-581-0580
info@petlineinsurance.com
www.petlineinsurance.com
Classes of Insurance: Personal Accident & Sickness

Pets Plus Us
#400, 710 Dorval Dr.
Oakville, ON L6K 3Y1
Toll-Free: 800-364-8422
info@petsplusus.com
www.petsplusus.com
Other Contact Information: Claims Toll-Free Fax: 855-456-7387
www.youtube.com/user/PetsPlusUsCA;
www.facebook.com/PetsPlusUsCa; twitter.com/PetsPlusUsCA
Classes of Insurance: Property

Petsecure Pet Health Insurance
#301, 600 Empress St.
Winnipeg, MB R3G 0R5
Toll-Free: 800-268-1169
info@petsecure.com
www.petsecure.com
Other Contact Information: Claims, Toll-Free Fax: 866-501-5580;
Veterinary Toll-Free Fax: 866-501-5581
www.youtube.com/user/petsecure;
www.facebook.com/petsecure; twitter.com/petsecure
Classes of Insurance: Personal Accident & Sickness

*Pilot Insurance Company
#100, 10 Aviva Way
Markham, ON L6G 0G1
Toll-Free: 800-387-4518
www.avivacanada.com
Other Contact Information: Claims, Toll-Free: 866-692-8482
Classes of Insurance: Auto, Property

The Portage La Prairie Mutual Insurance Company
PO Box 340
749 Saskatchewan Ave. East
Portage La Prairie, MB R1N 3B8
Tel: 204-857-3415; *Fax:* 204-239-6655
Toll-Free: 800-567-7721
info@portagemutual.com
www.portagemutual.com
Other Contact Information: Claims, Toll-Free Fax: 866-345-1770
Classes of Insurance: Legal Expense, Auto, Liability, Property

Primerica Life Insurance Company of Canada
#400, 6985 Financial Dr.
Mississauga, ON L5N 0G3
Tel: 905-812-2900; *Fax:* 905-813-5312
plicc_cn@primerica.com
www.primericacanada.ca
www.youtube.com/primerica
Classes of Insurance: Personal Accident & Sickness, Life

**Primmum Insurance Company/Primmum
Compagnie D'Assurance**
#600, 304 The East Mall
Toronto, ON M9B 6E2
Tel: 416-233-7590; *Fax:* 416-233-9171
Toll-Free: 866-466-5276
tdinsurance.com
Other Contact Information: Quotes, Toll-Free: 800-816-9618;
Claims: 866-725-9722; Calgary, Edmonton, & Halifax:
800-268-8955
Classes of Insurance: Auto, Property

*Prince Edward Island Mutual Insurance Company
116 Walker Ave.
Summerside, PE C1N 6V9
Tel: 902-436-2185; *Fax:* 902-436-0148
Toll-Free: 800-565-5441
protect@peimutual.com
www.peimutual.com
www.facebook.com/PEIMutualInsuranceCompany
Classes of Insurance: Liability, Property, Fire, Theft

*Promutuel Assurance
#400, 2000, boul Lebourgneuf
Québec, QC G2K 0B6
Tel: 418-840-9950; *Toll-Free:* 866-999-2433
federation@promutuel.ca
www.promutuelassurance.ca
www.youtube.com/user/PromutuelAssurance;
fr.pinterest.com/promutuel;
www.facebook.com/PromutuelAssurance; twitter.com/Promutuel
Classes of Insurance: Accident, Liability, Boiler & Machinery,
Property, Fire, Surety, Theft, Reinsurance

*Québec Blue Cross/Croix Bleue du Québec
550, rue Sherbrooke ouest, #B-9
Montréal, QC H3A 3S3
Tel: 514-286-7684; *Toll-Free:* 888-822-5383
info@qc.bluecross.ca
qc.bluecross.ca
Other Contact Information: Technical Support: 1-800-563-2538

Classes of Insurance: Accident, Personal Accident & Sickness,
Auto, Liability, Life

Rain & Hail Insurance Corporation
#200, 4303 Albert St.
Regina, SK S4S 3R6
Tel: 306-584-8844; *Fax:* 306-584-3466
Toll-Free: 800-667-8084
regina@rainhail.com
www.rainhail.com/about/canada.html
Classes of Insurance: Hail & Crop

RBC Insurance
Tower 1
6880 Financial Dr.
Mississauga, ON L5N 7Y5
Toll-Free: 866-235-4332
src-nationaloffice@rbc.com
www.rbcinsurance.com
www.facebook.com/RBCInsurance; twitter.com/rbcinsurance
Classes of Insurance: Personal Accident & Sickness, Auto,
Life, Property

RBC Insurance Company of Canada
6880 Financial Dr.
Mississauga, ON L5N 7Y5
Tel: 905-816-2561; *Fax:* 905-813-4719
www.rbcinsurance.com
Classes of Insurance: Personal Accident & Sickness, Life

RBC Life Insurance Company
6880 Financial Dr.
Mississauga, ON L5N 7Y5
Tel: 905-286-5099; *Toll-Free:* 877-519-9501
www.rbcinsurance.com/lifeinsurance
Other Contact Information: New Life Insurance Inquiries,
Toll-Free: 866-223-7113; Existing Life Insurance Inquiries:
800-461-1413
Classes of Insurance: Personal Accident & Sickness, Life

*Real Estate Insurance Exchange (REIX)
4954 Richard Rd. SW
Calgary, AB T3E 6L1
Tel: 403-228-2667; *Fax:* 403-229-3466
Toll-Free: 877-462-7349
info@reix.ca
www.reix.ca
Classes of Insurance: Liability

*Red River Mutual
PO Box 940
245 Centre Ave. East
Altona, MB R0G 0B0
Tel: 204-324-6434; *Fax:* 204-324-1316
Toll-Free: 800-370-2888
info@redrivermutual.com
www.redrivermutual.com
www.youtube.com/user/redrivermutual;
www.instagram.com/redrivermutual;
www.facebook.com/redrivermutual; twitter.com/RedRiverMutual
Classes of Insurance: Liability, Boiler & Machinery, Fidelity,
Property, Fire, Surety, Theft

Reliable Life Insurance Company
PO Box 557
100 King St. West
Hamilton, ON L8N 3K9
Tel: 905-523-5587; *Fax:* 905-528-8338
Toll-Free: 800-465-0661
service@reliablelifeinsurance.com
www.reliablelifeinsurance.com
Classes of Insurance: Personal Accident & Sickness, Life

**RGA Life Reinsurance Company of Canada/RGA
Compagnie de réassurance-vie du Canada**
#2300, 77 King St. West
Toronto, ON M5K 1H6
Tel: 416-682-0000; *Fax:* 416-777-9526
Toll-Free: 800-433-4326
www.rgare.com
www.facebook.com/rgaglobal; twitter.com/RGA_RE
Classes of Insurance: Reinsurance

**Royal & Sun Alliance Insurance Company of Canada
(RSA)**
#800, 18 York St.
Toronto, ON M5J 2T8
Tel: 416-366-7511; *Fax:* 416-367-9869
Toll-Free: 800-268-8406
www.rsagroup.ca
www.facebook.com/RSACanada; twitter.com/rsacanada
Classes of Insurance: Personal Accident & Sickness, Auto,
Property

* Indicates Provincially Incorporated Insurance Company

*S&Y Insurance Company
#100, 10 Aviva Way
Markham, ON L6G 0G1

Toll-Free: 800-387-4518
www.avivacanada.com
Other Contact Information: Claims, Toll-Free: 866-692-8482
Classes of Insurance: Auto

*Saskatchewan Blue Cross
PO Box 4030
516 - 2nd Ave. North
Saskatoon, SK S7K 3T2

Tel: 306-244-1192; Fax: 306-652-5751
Toll-Free: 800-667-6853
www.sk.bluecross.ca
www.instagram.com/skbluecross;
www.facebook.com/saskatchewanbluecross;
twitter.com/SKBlueCross
Classes of Insurance: Personal Accident & Sickness, Life

*Saskatchewan Crop Insurance Corporation (SCIC)
PO Box 3000
484 Prince William Dr.
Melville, SK S0A 2P0

Tel: 306-728-7200; Fax: 306-728-7202
Toll-Free: 888-935-0000
customer.service@scic.gov.sk.ca
www.saskcropinsurance.com
twitter.com/skcropinsurance
Classes of Insurance: Hail & Crop

*Saskatchewan Government Insurance (SGI)
2260 - 11th Ave.
Regina, SK S4P 0J9

Toll-Free: 844-855-2744
sgiinquiries@sgi.sk.ca
www.sgi.sk.ca
www.instagram.com/sgiphotos;
www.youtube.com/user/SGICommunications;
www.facebook.com/SGIcommunity; twitter.com/SGItweets
Classes of Insurance: Auto, Property

*Saskatchewan Municipal Hail Insurance Association (SMHI)
2100 Cornwall St.
Regina, SK S4P 2K7

Tel: 306-569-1852; Fax: 306-522-3717
Toll-Free: 877-414-7644
smhi@smhi.ca
www.smhi.ca
twitter.com/municipalhail
Classes of Insurance: Hail & Crop

Saskatchewan Mutual Insurance Company (SMI)
279 - 3rd Ave. North
Saskatoon, SK S7K 2H8

Tel: 306-653-4232; Fax: 306-664-1957
Toll-Free: 800-667-3067
headoffice@saskmutual.com
www.saskmutual.com
Classes of Insurance: Auto, Liability, Boiler & Machinery,
Fidelity, Property

SCOR Canada Reinsurance Company/SCOR Canada Compagnie de Réassurance
#2800, 199 Bay St.
Toronto, ON M5L 1G1

Tel: 416-869-3670; Fax: 416-365-9393
www.scor.com
twitter.com/SCOR_SE
Classes of Insurance: Reinsurance

SCOR Global Life SE, Canada Branch/SCOR Global Vie Canada
#2010, 1, Place Ville Marie
Montréal, QC H3B 2C4

Tel: 514-989-3200; Fax: 514-989-3249
scorgloballifeamericas@scor.com
www.scorgloballifeamericas.com
Classes of Insurance: Personal Accident & Sickness, Life

Scotia Life Insurance Company/Scotia-Vie Compagnie d'Assurance
100 Yonge St.
Toronto, ON M5C 2W1

Toll-Free: 800-387-9844
www.scotialifefinancial.com
Classes of Insurance: Personal Accident & Sickness, Life

*Scottish & York Insurance Co. Limited
#100, 10 Aviva Way
Markham, ON L6G 0G1

Toll-Free: 800-387-4518
www.avivacanada.com
Other Contact Information: Claims, Toll-Free: 866-692-8482;
TTY 800-855-0511
Classes of Insurance: Legal Expense, Auto, Liability, Boiler &
Machinery, Fidelity, Property, Surety

Security National Insurance Company/Sécurité Nationale compagnie d'assurance
#708, 2161 Yonge St.
Toronto, ON M4S 3A6

Toll-Free: 800-268-8955
www.melochemonnex.com
Classes of Insurance: Personal Accident & Sickness, Auto,
Property, Fire

Servus Insurance Services - Home & Auto
#501, 326 - 11th Ave. SW
Calgary, AB T2R 0C5

Toll-Free: 888-732-1494
servus.johnson.ca
Classes of Insurance: Auto, Property

*SGI Canada
2260 - 11th Ave.
Regina, SK S4P 0J9

inquiries.sk@sgicanada.ca
www.sgicanada.ca
www.facebook.com/SGICANADA; twitter.com/sgi_canada
Classes of Insurance: Property

Sirius America Insurance Company
#1202, 80 Bloor St. West
Toronto, ON M5S 2V1

Tel: 416-928-2430; Fax: 416-928-2459
www.siriusgroup.com
Classes of Insurance: Auto, Liability, Fidelity, Property, Surety,
Hail & Crop

*Société de l'assurance automobile du Québec
CP 19600, Stn. Terminus
333, boul Jean-Lesage
Québec, QC G1K 8J6

Tél: 418-643-7620; *Ligne sans frais:* 800-361-7620
Other Contact Information: Région de Montréal: 514-873-7620
www.youtube.com/user/saaq; www.facebook.com/SAAQQC;
twitter.com/saaq
Classes of Insurance: Accident, Auto

*South Easthope Mutual Insurance Co.
PO Box 33
62 Woodstock St. South
Tavistock, ON N0B 2R0

Tel: 519-655-2011; Fax: 519-655-2021
Toll-Free: 800-263-9987
info@southeasthope.com
www.southeasthope.com
www.facebook.com/southeasthopemutual;
twitter.com/southeasthope
Classes of Insurance: Accident, Auto, Boiler & Machinery,
Property

*Southeastern Mutual Insurance Company
663 Pinewood Rd.
Riverview, NB E1B 5R6

Tel: 506-386-9002; Fax: 506-386-3325
www.semutual.nb.ca
www.instagram.com/semutualnb; www.facebook.com/semutual
Classes of Insurance: Liability, Boiler & Machinery, Property,
Fire

The Sovereign General Insurance Company
#140, 6700 Macleod Trail SE
Calgary, AB T2H 0L3

Tel: 403-298-4200; Toll-Free: 800-661-1652
www.sovereigngeneral.com
www.facebook.com/SovereignInsurance;
twitter.com/SovInsurance
Classes of Insurance: Personal Accident & Sickness, Property

*SSQ Insurance
Head Office
2525, boul Laurier
Québec, QC G1V 2L2

Toll-Free: 800-463-5525
ssq.ca
www.instagram.com/ssq.ca; www.youtube.com/c/SSQGF;
www.facebook.com/SSQ

*Stanley Mutual Insurance Company
32 Irishtown Rd.
Stanley, NB E6B 1B6

Fax: 506-367-3076
Toll-Free: 800-442-9714
info@stanleymutual.com
www.stanleymutual.com
www.facebook.com/stanleymutual
Classes of Insurance: Auto, Liability, Boiler & Machinery,
Property

Stewart Title Guaranty Company
North Tower, Royal Bank Plaza
#2600, 200 Bay St.
Toronto, ON M5J 2J2

Tel: 416-307-3300; Fax: 416-307-3305
Toll-Free: 888-667-5151
inquirycda@stewart.com
www.stewart.ca
Classes of Insurance: Property

Suecia Reinsurance Company
4 Robert Speck Pkwy., 15th Fl.
Mississauga, ON L4Z 1S1

Tel: 416-361-0056
Classes of Insurance: Personal Accident & Sickness, Auto,
Liability, Fidelity, Property, Hail & Crop, Reinsurance

Sun Life Assurance Company of Canada
Corporate Office
1 York St.
Toronto, ON M5J 0B6

Tel: 416-979-9966; Fax: 416-979-4853
www.sunlife.ca
www.facebook.com/SLFCanada; twitter.com/SunLifeCA
Classes of Insurance: Personal Accident & Sickness, Life

Sun Life Financial Inc.
Corporate Office
1 York St.
Toronto, ON M5J 0B6

Tel: 416-979-9966; Toll-Free: 877-786-5433
service@sunlife.ca
www.sunlife.ca
www.youtube.com/user/sunlifefinancial;
www.facebook.com/SLFCanada; twitter.com/SunLifeCA
Classes of Insurance: Life

Supreme Council of the Royal Arcanum
#200, 1 Hunter St. East
Hamilton, ON L8N 3W1

Tel: 905-528-8411; Fax: 905-528-9008
info@royalarcanum
www.royalarcanum.com
www.facebook.com/RoyalArcanumBoston
Classes of Insurance: Personal Accident & Sickness, Life

Swiss Reinsurance Company Canada
150 King St. West, 8th-10th Fl.
Toronto, ON M5H 1J9

Tel: 416-408-0272; Fax: 416-408-4222
Toll-Free: 800-268-7116
www.swissre.ca
www.youtube.com/user/swissretv;
www.instagram.com/swiss_re_group; twitter.com/swissre
Classes of Insurance: Marine, Fidelity, Property, Surety,
Reinsurance

TD General Insurance Company
c/o Meloche Monnex Inc.
50, Place Crémazie, 12e étage
Montréal, QC H2P 1B6

www.tdinsurance.com
www.facebook.com/TDInsurance; twitter.com/TD_Insurance
Classes of Insurance: Personal Accident & Sickness, Aircraft,
Auto, Liability, Boiler & Machinery, Fidelity, Property, Surety

TD Home & Auto Insurance Company/Compagnie d'Assurance Habitation et Auto TD
101 McNabb St.
Markham, ON L3R 4H8

Toll-Free: 866-361-2311
www.tdinsurance.com
Other Contact Information: Client Services, Toll-Free:
866-361-2311; Claims: 866-848-9744
www.facebook.com/TDInsurance; twitter.com/TD_Insurance
Classes of Insurance: Auto, Liability, Property

---

* Indicates Provincially Incorporated Insurance Company

TD Life Insurance Company/TD, Compagnie d'assurance-vie
Richmond Adelaide Centre
120 Adelaide St. West, 2nd Fl.
Toronto, ON M5H 1T1
Toll-Free: 877-397-4187
www.tdinsurance.com
Classes of Insurance: Personal Accident & Sickness, Life

Temple Insurance Company
390 Bay St., 21st Fl.
Toronto, ON M5H 2Y2
Tel: 416-364-2851; Fax: 416-361-1163
Toll-Free: 877-364-2851
munichre.com/temple-insurance/en.html
Classes of Insurance: Boiler & Machinery, Property

*Thomson Jemmett Vogelzang
321 Concession St.
Kingston, ON K7K 2B9
Tel: 613-544-5313; Fax: 613-542-6839
Toll-Free: 800-787-5006
www.johnson.ca
Classes of Insurance: Auto, Liability, Property

The Toa Reinsurance Company of America (Canada Branch)
PO Box 53
#1700, 55 University Ave.
Toronto, ON M5J 2H7
Tel: 416-366-5888; Fax: 416-366-7444
info@toare.com
www.toare.com
Classes of Insurance: Reinsurance

The Tokio Marine & Nichido Fire Insurance Co., Ltd.
c/o Lombard Canada Ltd.
105 Adelaide St. West, 3rd Fl.
Toronto, ON M5H 1P9
Tel: 416-362-6584
www.tokiomarine-nichido.co.jp/en
Classes of Insurance: Auto, Marine, Property, Fire

Traders General Insurance Company/Compagnie d'Assurance Traders Générale
#400, 2206 Eglinton Ave. East
Toronto, ON M1L 4S8
Tel: 416-288-1800; Toll-Free: 800-387-4518
www.avivacanada.com
Other Contact Information: Claims, Toll-Free: 866-692-8482
Classes of Insurance: Auto, Property

*Tradition Mutual Insurance Company
PO Box 10
264 Huron Rd.
Sebringville, ON N0K 1X0
Tel: 519-393-6402; Fax: 519-393-5185
Toll-Free: 877-380-6402
info@traditionmutual.com
www.traditionmutual.com
www.instagram.com/traditionmutual;
www.facebook.com/TraditionInsurance;
twitter.com/traditionmutual
Classes of Insurance: Accident, Auto, Liability, Boiler & Machinery, Fidelity, Property, Hail & Crop

Trafalgar Insurance Company of Canada
#1500-A, 700 University Ave.
Toronto, ON M5G 0A1
Classes of Insurance: Auto, Property, Theft

*Trans Global Insurance Company (TGI)
#275, 16930 - 114 Ave. NW
Edmonton, AB T5M 3S2
Toll-Free: 844-930-6022
transglobalinsurance.ca
Classes of Insurance: Personal Accident & Sickness, Liability, Property

*Trans Global Life Insurance Company (TGLI)
#275, 16930 - 114 Ave. NW
Edmonton, AB T5M 3S2
Toll-Free: 844-930-6022
transglobalinsurance.ca
Classes of Insurance: Personal Accident & Sickness, Life

Transatlantic Reinsurance Company
PO Box 3
#1110, 95 Wellington St. West
Toronto, ON M5J 2N7
Tel: 416-649-5300; Fax: 416-971-8782
www.transre.com

Classes of Insurance: Personal Accident & Sickness, Credit, Property, Surety, Reinsurance

Travelers Canada
165 University Ave.
Toronto, ON M5H 3B9
Tel: 416-362-7231; Toll-Free: 800-268-8447
www.travelerscanada.ca
www.youtube.com/travelersinsurance;
www.facebook.com/travelers; twitter.com/travelers
Classes of Insurance: Aircraft, Auto, Liability, Boiler & Machinery, Marine, Fidelity, Property, Fire, Surety, Reinsurance

*Trillium Mutual Insurance Company
495 Mitchell Rd. South
Listowel, ON N4W 0C8
Tel: 519-291-9300; Fax: 519-291-1800
Toll-Free: 800-265-3020
admin@trilliummutual.com
trilliummutual.com
www.facebook.com/trilliummutual; twitter.com/TrilliumMutual
Classes of Insurance: Accident, Auto, Liability, Boiler & Machinery, Marine, Fidelity, Property, Hail & Crop

Trisura Guarantee Insurance Company
Bay Adelaide Centre
#1610, 333 Bay St.
Toronto, ON M5H 2R2
Tel: 416-214-2555; Fax: 416-214-9597
info@trisura.com
www.trisura.com
Classes of Insurance: Liability, Surety

TruShield Insurance Services Ltd.
105 Adelaide St. West
Toronto, ON M5H 1P9
Toll-Free: 844-429-9480
www.trushieldinsurance.ca
www.facebook.com/TruShieldIns; twitter.com/TruShieldIns
Classes of Insurance: Personal Accident & Sickness, Auto, Liability, Property

Ukrainian Fraternal Society of Canada
235 McGregor St.
Winnipeg, MB R2W 4W5
Tel: 204-586-4482; Fax: 204-589-6411
Toll-Free: 800-988-8372
ufsc.ca
twitter.com/ufsc_insurance
Classes of Insurance: Life

Ukrainian National Association (UNA)
90 Allstate Pkwy.
Markham, ON L3R 6H3
info@unainc.org
unainc.org
www.facebook.com/UkrainianNationalAssociation
Classes of Insurance: Personal Accident & Sickness, Life

*Unica Insurance Inc./Unica assurances
7150 Derrycrest Dr.
Mississauga, ON L5W 0E5
Tel: 905-677-9777; Toll-Free: 800-676-0967
claims@unicainsurance.com
www.unicainsurance.com
Other Contact Information: Alt. Emails:
accounts@unicainsurance.com;
commercial@unicainsurance.com;
underwriting@unicainsurance.com
Classes of Insurance: Auto, Liability, Property

Unifund Assurance Company
PO Box 12049
10 Factory Lane
St. John's, NL A1C 6H5
Fax: 709-737-1580
unifund@unifund.ca
www.unifund.ca
Classes of Insurance: Auto, Property

*L'Union-Vie, compagnie mutuelle d'assurance/The Union Life, Mutual Assurance Company
142, rue Hériot
Drummondville, QC J2C 1J8
Tél: 819-478-1315; Téléc: 819-474-1990
Ligne sans frais: 800-567-0988
info@uvmutuelle.ca
www.uvmutuelle.ca
Classes of Insurance: Personal Accident & Sickness, Life, Reinsurance

United American Insurance Company (UA)
#2100, 40 King St. West
Toronto, ON M5H 3C2
Tel: 416-369-6624; Fax: 416-366-8571
www.unitedamerican.com
www.youtube.com/user/UnitedAmerican1;
www.facebook.com/UnitedAmerican;
twitter.com/United_American
Classes of Insurance: Personal Accident & Sickness, Life

*United General Insurance Corporation
50 Avonlea Ct.
Fredericton, NB E3C 1N8
Tel: 506-460-8820; Fax: 506-453-0882
united.general@ugic.nb.ca
ugicinsurance.com
Classes of Insurance: Auto

*Usborne & Hibbert Mutual Fire Insurance Company
507 Main St. South
Exeter, ON N0M 1S1
Tel: 519-235-0350; Toll-Free: 800-422-3996
usborneandhibbert.ca
www.facebook.com/UandHMutual; twitter.com/usbornehibbert
Classes of Insurance: Personal Accident & Sickness, Auto, Liability, Boiler & Machinery, Property

*Uv Mutuelle/The International Life Insurance Company
142, rue Hériot
Drummondville, QC J2C 1J8
Tél: 819-478-1315; Téléc: 819-474-1990
Ligne sans frais: 800-567-0988
www.uvmutuelle.ca
Classes of Insurance: Personal Accident & Sickness, Life

*Vancity Life Insurance Services Ltd.
PO Box 2120, Stn. Terminal
Vancouver, BC V6B 5R8
Tel: 604-707-4296; Toll-Free: 877-707-4296
vancityinsurance.com
Classes of Insurance: Personal Accident & Sickness, Life

Virginia Surety Company, Inc. (VCS)/Compagnie de Sûreté Virginia Inc.
#1200, 34 King St. East
Toronto, ON M5C 2X8
Tel: 416-361-1728; Fax: 416-361-6113
www.assurant.com
Classes of Insurance: Auto, Liability, Boiler & Machinery, Property

The Wawanesa Life Insurance Company
#400, 200 Main St.
Winnipeg, MB R3C 1A8
Tel: 204-985-3940; Toll-Free: 888-997-9965
life@wawanesa.com
www.wawanesalife.com
Other Contact Information: Group Phone: 204-985-3806; Fax: 204-985-5781; Toll-Free: 800-665-7076; Email: groupcustomerservice@wawanesa.com
Classes of Insurance: Personal Accident & Sickness, Life

The Wawanesa Mutual Insurance Company
191 Broadway
Winnipeg, MB R3C 3P1
Tel: 204-985-3923; Fax: 204-942-7724
life@wawanesa.com
www.wawanesa.com
twitter.com/WawanesaCanada
Classes of Insurance: Auto, Liability, Boiler & Machinery, Property, Fire, Surety, Theft

*Wedgwood Insurance Limited
#102, 85 Thorburn Rd.
St. John's, NL A1B 3M2
Tel: 709-753-3210
info@wedgwoodinsurance.com
wedgwoodinsurance.com
www.facebook.com/WedgwoodIns; twitter.com/wedgwoodins
Classes of Insurance: Aircraft, Auto, Life, Marine, Property

*West Elgin Mutual Insurance Company
PO Box 312
29584 Pioneer Line
Dutton, ON N0L 1J0
Tel: 519-762-3530; Fax: 519-762-3801
Toll-Free: 800-265-7635
www.westelgin.com
www.facebook.com/westelginmutual
Classes of Insurance: Personal Accident & Sickness, Auto, Liability, Fidelity, Property, Hail & Crop

* Indicates Provincially Incorporated Insurance Company

*West Wawanosh Mutual Insurance Company
58 Hamilton St.
Goderich, ON N7A 1P9
Tel: 226-408-5800; *Fax:* 519-612-2540
Toll-Free: 800-265-5595
wawains@wwmic.com
wwmic.com
www.facebook.com/westwawanoshmutual;
twitter.com/WestWawanosh
Classes of Insurance: Personal Accident & Sickness, Auto, Liability, Boiler & Machinery, Fidelity, Property

Western Assurance Company (WA)
Mississauga Gateway Centre
#100, 2 Prologis Blvd.
Mississauga, ON L5W 0G8
Tel: 905-403-3318; *Fax:* 905-403-3319
Toll-Free: 877-263-4442
www.westernassurance.ca
Classes of Insurance: Auto, Liability, Marine, Fidelity, Property, Fire, Surety

*Western Financial Group Inc.
1010 - 24th St. SE
High River, AB T1V 2A7
Toll-Free: 866-843-9378
info@westernfg.ca
www.westernfinancialgroup.ca
www.youtube.com/c/WesternFinancialGroupCa;
www.facebook.com/westernfinancialgroup
Classes of Insurance: Accident, Personal Accident & Sickness, Auto, Liability, Boiler & Machinery, Life, Fidelity, Property, Fire, Surety, Hail & Crop, Theft

Western Surety Company
#2100, 1881 Scarth St.
Regina, SK S4P 4K9
Tel: 306-791-3735; *Fax:* 306-359-0929
Toll-Free: 800-475-4454
wscinfo@westernsurety.ca
www.westernsurety.ca
www.facebook.com/westernsurety; twitter.com/WesternSurety
Classes of Insurance: Fidelity, Surety

*Westland Insurance Group Ltd.
#200, 2121 - 160th St.
Surrey, BC V3Z 9N6
Tel: 604-543-7788; *Toll-Free:* 800-899-3093
contactus@westlandinsurance.ca
www.westlandinsurance.ca
www.instagram.com/westlandinsurance;
www.facebook.com/westland.insurance.canada;
twitter.com/WestlandIns
Classes of Insurance: Auto, Liability, Property

*Westminster Mutual Insurance Company
14122 Belmont Rd.
Belmont, ON N0L 1B0
Tel: 519-644-1663; *Fax:* 519-644-0315
Toll-Free: 800-565-3523
www.wmic.ca
Classes of Insurance: Auto, Liability, Property

Westport Insurance Corporation
150 King St. West, 8th-10th Fl.
Toronto, ON M5H 1J9
Tel: 416-408-0272; *Toll-Free:* 800-268-7116
www.swissre.com
Classes of Insurance: Personal Accident & Sickness, Auto, Liability, Boiler & Machinery, Credit, Fidelity, Property, Surety, Hail & Crop

*Wyatt Dowling Insurance Brokers
138 Regent Ave. West
Winnipeg, MB R2C 1P9
Toll-Free: 866-245-2779
138regent@wyattdowling.ca
wyattdowling.ca
www.facebook.com/wyattdowling
Classes of Insurance: Auto, Property

Wynward Insurance Group
#1240, 1 Lombard Pl.
Winnipeg, MB R3B 0V9
Tel: 204-943-0721; *Fax:* 204-943-6419
Toll-Free: 800-665-3351
info@wynward.com
www.wynward.com
www.facebook.com/Wynward
Classes of Insurance: Liability, Boiler & Machinery, Fidelity, Property, Fire, Surety, Theft

*Yarmouth Mutual Fire Insurance Company
1229 Talbot St. East
St Thomas, ON N5P 1G8
Tel: 519-631-1572; *Fax:* 519-631-8941
Toll-Free: 877-792-3693
office@yarmouthmutual.com
www.yarmouthmutual.com
www.facebook.com/yarmouthmutualinsurance
Classes of Insurance: Auto, Liability, Property, Hail & Crop

Zurich Canada
First Canadian Place
PO Box 290
#5500, 100 King St. West
Toronto, ON M5X 1C9
Tel: 416-586-3000; *Fax:* 416-586-2525
Toll-Free: 800-387-5454
www.zurichcanada.com
twitter.com/zurichcanada
Classes of Insurance: Accident, Personal Accident & Sickness, Auto, Liability, Boiler & Machinery, Credit, Marine, Fidelity, Property, Fire, Surety, Theft

Major Canadian Companies

Agriculture

AG Growth International (AGI)
198 Commerce Dr.
Winnipeg, MB R3P 0Z6
sales@aggrowth.com
www.aggrowth.com
www.facebook.com/aggrowthintl
twitter.com/aggrowthintl
www.linkedin.com/company/aggrowthinternational
Company Type: Public
Ticker Symbol: AFN/TSX
Staff Size: 2,500
Profile: AG Growth International Inc. was created in 1996. The company is involved in the manufacturing of grain handling, conditioning & storage equipment. Products include belt conveyors, augers, grain storage bins & grain aeration equipment.
Tim Close, President & CEO
Jim Rudyk, Chief Financial Officer

AGT Food & Ingredients
6200 East Primrose Green Dr.
Regina, SK S4V 3L7
306-525-4490
Fax: 306-525-4463
info@agtfoods.com
www.agtfoods.com
www.facebook.com/agtfoodsretail
twitter.com/agtfoodsretail
Company Type: Public
Profile: AGT Food & Ingredients was created in 2007, when Agtech Income Fund, the predecessor to Alliance Grain Traders, acquired Saskcan Pulse Trading. The re-branded fund, Alliance Grain Traders Income Fund, converted to a dividend paying corporation in 2009. AGT Food & Ingredients is engaged in the purchase of lentils, peas, beans & chickpeas from farmers & their exportation to more than 120 countries.
Murad Al-Katib, President & CEO

Buhler Industries Inc.
1260 Clarence Ave.
Winnipeg, MB R3T 1T2
204-661-8711
Fax: 204-654-2503
info@buhler.com
www.buhlerindustries.com
www.linkedin.com/company/buhler-industries-inc-
Company Type: Public
Ticker Symbol: BUI/TSX
Staff Size: 800
Profile: Buhler Industries Inc. was established in 1932. The company manufactures & distributes agricultural equipment, such as tractors, augers, front-end loaders & compact implements. Brand names include Versatile, Allied & Farm King.

Canopy Growth
1 Hershey Dr.
Smiths Falls, ON K7A 0A8
855-558-9333
invest@canopygrowth.com
www.canopygrowth.com
twitter.com/canopygrowth
www.linkedin.com/company/canopy-growth-corporation
Company Type: Public
Ticker Symbol: WEED/TSX
Staff Size: 3,250
Profile: Canopy Growth is a marijuana production company.

David Klein, Chief Executive Officer
Rade Kovacevic, President & Chief Product Officer
Mike Lee, Executive Vice-President & CFO

Ceres Global Ag Corp.
#400, 701 Xenia Ave. South
Golden Valley, MN 55416 USA
952-746-6800
info@ceresglobalag.com
ceresglobalagcorp.com
twitter.com/Ceres_Global
www.linkedin.com/company/ceres-global-ag-corp-
Company Type: Public
Ticker Symbol: CRP/TSX
Profile: Ceres Global Ag Corp. provide investors with direct & indirect exposure to global agricultural assets.
Robert Day, President & CEO
Jay Bierley, Chief Financial Officer

Input Capital
#300, 1914 Hamilton St.
Regina, SK S4P 3N6
306-347-3006
Fax: 306-352-4110
investor@inputcapital.com
inputcapital.com
Company Type: Private
Ticker Symbol: INP/TSX
Profile: Input Capital purchases canola from farmers through multi-year contracts. In 2021, it acquired SRG Security Resource Group Inc., a cyber security & physical security company. The agriculture business will be run-off in 1-2 years.
Doug Emsley, President & CEO
Brad Farquhar, Chief Financial Officer

Itafos
#405, 109 North Post Oak Lane
Houston, TX 77024 USA
713-239-2700
www.itafos.com
www.linkedin.com/company/itafos
Company Type: Public
Ticker Symbol: IFOS/TSX.V
Profile: Itafos produces phosphate fetilizers for global markets.
G. David Delaney, Chief Executive Officer
David Brush, Chief Strategy Officer
George Burdette, Chief Financial Officer

Nutrien Ltd.
#500, 122 - 1st Ave. South
Saskatoon, SK S7K 7G3
306-933-8500
800-667-0403
www.nutrien.com
www.facebook.com/nutrienltd
twitter.com/NutrienLTD
www.linkedin.com/company/nutrien
Company Type: Public
Ticker Symbol: NTR/TSX, NYSE
Staff Size: 23,100
Profile: PotashCorp officially merged with Agrium Inc. in January 2018 to create Nutrien. The company produces & distributes over 25 million tonnes of potash, nitrogen & phosphate products for agricultural, industrial & feed customers around the world. It also runs an agriculture retail network that services over 500,000 growers.
Mayo Schmidt, President & CEO
Pedro Farah, Executive Vice-President & CFO
Brent Poohkay, Executive Vice-President & CIO

Village Farms International Inc.
Also Known As: Village Farms
4700 - 80th St.
Delta, BC V4K 3N3
604-940-6012
Fax: 604-398-2001
www.villagefarms.com
www.facebook.com/villagefarms
twitter.com/villagefarms
www.linkedin.com/company/villagefarmsghg
Company Type: Public
Ticker Symbol: VFF/TSX
Staff Size: 1,200
Profile: Village Farms produces, markets & distributes greenhouse-grown bell peppers, tomatoes & cucumbers. Greenhouse facilities are situated in British Columbia & Texas. Products are distributed mainly to retail grocers & fresh food distributors in Canada & the United States.
Michael A. DeGiglio, President & CEO
Stephen C. Ruffini, Executive Vice-President & CFO

Business & Computer Services

Absolute Software Corporation
PO Box 49211, #1400, 1055 Dunsmuir St.
Vancouver, BC V7X 1K8

604-730-9851
Fax: 604-730-2621
800-220-0733
www.absolute.com
Other Communications: USA Headquarters, Austin, Texas,
Phone: 800-220-0733
twitter.com/absolutecorp
www.linkedin.com/company/absolute-software
Company Type: Public
Ticker Symbol: ABT/TSX
Staff Size: 445
Profile: Absolute Software Corporation provides endpoint
security & management for computers & ultra-portable devices.
Christy Wyatt, President & CEO
Steven Gatoff, Chief Financial Officer
Nicko van Someren, Chief Technology Officer

Alithya Group inc.
#701, 366 Adelaide St. West
Toronto, ON M5V 1R9

800-681-4601
info@alithya.com
www.alithya.com
www.facebook.com/Alithya
www.linkedin.com/company/alithya
Company Type: Public
Ticker Symbol: ALYA/TSX
Staff Size: 3,000
Profile: Founded in 1992, Alithya is a digital technology
company offering a wide range of enterprise services such
cloud-based platforms, data & analytics & applications for
businesses. Industries it covers include financial services,
energy, healthcare, transportion, telecoms & more.
In 2021, it acquired R3D Consulting.
Paul Raymond, President & CEO
Claude Rousseau, Chief Operating Officer
Claude Thibault, Chief Financial Officer

Computer Modelling Group Ltd.
3710 - 33rd St. NW
Calgary, AB T2L 2M1

403-531-1300
support@cmgl.ca
www.cmgl.ca
twitter.com/cmg_software
www.linkedin.com/company/computer-modelling-group-ltd
Company Type: Public
Ticker Symbol: CMG/TSX
Staff Size: 200
Profile: Computer Modelling Group Ltd. is a computer software
engineering & consulting company. It serves the oil & gas
industry. Sales & technical support services are situated in
Calgary, Houston, London, Dubai & Caracas.
Ryan Scheider, President & CEO
Sandra Balic, Chief Financial Officer & Vice-President, Finance

Constellation Software Inc. (CSI)
#1200, 20 Adelaide St. East
Toronto, ON M5C 2T6

416-861-2279
Fax: 416-861-2277
info@csisoftware.com
www.csisoftware.com
Company Type: Public
Ticker Symbol: CSU/TSX
Staff Size: 15,000
Profile: Constellation Software's area of expertise is the
acquisition & management of industry specific software
businesses. Specialized software solutions are provided to
customers in more than 100 countries.
Mark Leonard, President & Chair
Bernard Anzarouth, Chief Investment Officer
Jamel Baksh, Chief Financial Officer
Mark Miller, Chief Operating Officer

Critical Control Energy Services Corp.
#800, 140 - 10th Ave. SE
Calgary, AB T2G 0R1

403-705-7500
855-426-6380
info@criticalcontrol.com
criticalcontrol.com
www.facebook.com/CriticalControlTechnologies
twitter.com/ccescanada
www.linkedin.com/company/ccescanada
Company Type: Public
Profile: Critical Control Energy Services provides cloud-based
software for the oil & gas industry, including production data
measurement & management solutions.

Alykhan Mamdani, Chief Executive Officer

Data Communications Management Corp. (DCM)
9195 Torbram Rd.
Brampton, ON L6S 6H2

905-791-3151
Fax: 905-791-3277
800-268-0128
info@datacm.com
www.datacm.com
www.linkedin.com/company/datacm
Company Type: Public
Ticker Symbol: DGI/TSX
Profile: Data Communications Management Corp offers
document management & marketing solution services. Sectors
served include financial, manufacturing, energy, retail &
consumer services, distribution, government & public services,
health care & not-for-profit. Data Communications Management
offers eco-print solutions to ensure its business is conducted in
an environmentally responsible manner.
Richard Kellam, President & CEO
James Lorimer, Chief Financial Officer

Descartes Systems Group Inc.
120 Randall Dr.
Waterloo, ON N2V 1C6

519-746-8110
800-419-8495
info@descartes.com
www.descartes.com
www.facebook.com/descartessystemsgroup
twitter.com/descartessg
www.linkedin.com/company/descartes-systems-group
Company Type: Public
Ticker Symbol: DSG/TSX; DSGX/NASDAQ
Profile: The Descartes Systems Group provides logistics
management solutions that are used by the transportation
logistics, distribution, manufacturing & retail sectors.
Edward J. Ryan, Chief Executive Officer
J. Scott Pagan, President & COO
Allan Brett, Chief Financial Officer
Raimond Diederik, Executive Vice-President, Information
Services
Chris Jones, Executive Vice-President, Marketing & Services
Michael Verhoeve, General Counsel, Corporate Secretary &
Exec. Vice-President, Legal

Docebo Inc.
#701, 366 Adelaide St. West
Toronto, ON M5V 1R9

800-681-4601
www.docebo.com
www.facebook.com/Docebo
twitter.com/docebo
www.linkedin.com/company/docebo
Company Type: Public
Ticker Symbol: DCBO/TSX
Staff Size: 500
Profile: Docebo Inc. is the Canadian entity of Docebo S.p.A., an
Italian software company. It has a multi-product cloud-based
learning suite for large companies.
Claudio Erba, Founder & Chief Executive Officer
Alessio Artuffo, Founder & President
Ian Kidson, Chief Financial Officer

Dye & Durham Limited
#4610, 199 Bay St.
Toronto, ON M5L 1E9

800-268-7580
sales@dyedurham.com
dyedurham.com
www.linkedin.com/company/dyedurhamcorporation
Company Type: Public
Ticker Symbol: DND/TSX
Staff Size: 950
Profile: Dye & Durham provides a cloud-based platform with
various public records for legal & business professionals. It has
offices in Canada, Australia & the United Kingdom.
Matthew Proud, Chief Executive Officer
Dennis Barnhart, President, Canada
Tom Durbin St. George, President, UK
Avjit Kamboj, Chief Financial Officer
John Robinson, Chief Operating Officer
Eric Tong, Chief Information Officer

Enghouse Systems Limited
#800, 80 Tiverton Ct.
Markham, ON L3R 0G4

905-946-3200
Fax: 905-946-3201
info@enghouse.com
www.enghouse.com
Other Communications: Acquisitions, Email:
acquire@enghouse.com

Company Type: Public
Ticker Symbol: ENGH/TSX
Staff Size: 1,750
Profile: Founded in 1984, Enghouse Systems Limited provides
enterprise software solutions. The company's divisions include
Enghouse Interactive, Enghouse Networks & Enghouse
Transportation. The company has offices in Canada, the United
States, the United Kingdom, France, Germany, Sweden, Israel,
Croatia, Denmark, Norway, India, Japan, Hong Kong, Singapore
& Australia.
Stephen J. Sadler, Chair & Chief Executive Officer
Vince Mifsud, President
Lynette Corbett, Chief Administration & Human Resources
Officer
Doug Bryson, Vice-President, Finance & Administration
Todd M. May, Vice-President & General Counsel

Firan Technology Group Corporation (FTG)
250 Finchdene Sq.
Toronto, ON M1X 1A5

416-299-4000
Fax: 416-292-4308
info@ftgcorp.com
www.ftgcorp.com
www.linkedin.com/company/ftg-aerospace
Company Type: Private
Ticker Symbol: FTG/TSX
Profile: FTG Technology Group is a printed circuit board &
precision illuminated display systems manufacturer.
Brad Boume, President & CEO
Jamie Crichton, Vice-President & CFO
jamiecrichton@ftgcorp.com

Intermap Technologies
#400, 8310 South Valley Hwy.
Englewood, CO 80112 USA

303-708-0955
877-837-7246
info@intermap.com
www.intermap.com
twitter.com/intermap
www.linkedin.com/company/intermap-technologies
Company Type: Public
Ticker Symbol: IMP/TSX.V
Staff Size: 180
Profile: Intermap provides elevation information to help
commercial enterprises & government agencies make
location-based decisions. The company's NEXTMap database
provides wide-area digital elevation data & images. Intermap
also provides geospatial services, like custom 3-D mapping.
Patrick A. Blott, Chair & Chief Executive Officer

Kinaxis Inc.
700 Silver Seven Rd.
Ottawa, ON K2V 1C3

613-592-5780
Fax: 613-592-0584
877-546-2947
support@kinaxis.com
www.kinaxis.com
Other Communications: Investor Relations, Email:
ir@kinaxis.com
www.facebook.com/kinaxis
twitter.com/kinaxis
www.linkedin.com/company/kinaxis
Company Type: Public
Ticker Symbol: KXS/TSX
Staff Size: 500
Profile: Kinaxis is a software company whose focus is on
RapidResponse, which is a technology that provides solutions
for supply chain planning, inventory management, order fulfillment,
capacity planning, master scheduling, or sales & operations
planning.
John Sicard, President & CEO
Richard Monkman, CA, CPA, Chief Financial Officer &
Vice-President, Corporate Services

Lightspeed POS Inc.
#300, 700, rue Saint-Antoine est
Montréal, QC H2Y 1A6

514-907-1801
Fax: 514-221-4499
866-932-1801
hi@lightspeedhq.com
www.lightspeedhq.com
www.facebook.com/LightspeedHQ
twitter.com/LightspeedHQ
www.linkedin.com/company/lightspeed-hq
Company Type: Public
Ticker Symbol: LSPD/TSX
Staff Size: 1,800
Profile: Founded in 2005, Lightspeed provides point of sale
services for retail, restaurants & eCommerce businesses.
Dax Dasilva, Founder & Chief Executive Officer

J.P. Chauvet, President
Brandon Nussey, Chief Financial Officer

mdf commerce inc.
Tour est
#255, 1111, rue St-Charles ouest
Longueuil, QC J4K 5G4

450-449-0102
Fax: 450-449-8725
877-677-9088
info@mdfcommerce.com
www.mdfcommerce.com
www.facebook.com/mdf.commerce.inc
twitter.com/mdfcommerce
www.linkedin.com/company/mdfcommerce
Company Type: Public
Ticker Symbol: MDF/TSX
Staff Size: 600
Profile: Established in 1996, mdf commerce delivers
e-commerce solutions to businesses.
Luc Filiatreault, President & CEO
Deborah Dumoulin, Chief Financial Officer
deborah.dumoulin@mdfcommerce.com
Nicolas Vanasse, Chief Legal Officer & Vice-President

NexJ Systems Inc.
#700, 10 York Mills Rd.
Toronto, ON M2P 2G4

416-222-5611
Fax: 416-222-8623
info@nexj.com
www.nexj.com
Other Communications: Investor Relations, Email:
investor.relations@nexj.com
www.facebook.com/nexjsystems
twitter.com/nexj
www.linkedin.com/company/nexj-systems
Company Type: Public
Ticker Symbol: NXJ/TSX
Staff Size: 200 (ap
Profile: NexJ is a provider of cloud-based software, delivering
enterprise customer relationship management (CRM) solutions
for financial services, insurance & healthcare.
Paul O'Donnell, President & CEO
Richard J. Broley, Chief Operating Officer
Rajneesh Sepra, Chief Financial Officer & Senior
Vice-President, Finance

OpenText Corp.
275 Frank Tompa Dr.
Waterloo, ON N2L 0A1

519-888-7111
Fax: 519-888-0677
www.opentext.com
Other Communications: Investor Relations, Email:
investors@opentext.com
twitter.com/opentext
www.linkedin.com/company/opentext
Company Type: Public
Ticker Symbol: OTEX/TSX, NASDAQ
Staff Size: 14,300
Profile: Founded in 1991, OpenText Corp. provides enterprise
content management solutions to assist organizations manage
their information assets.
Mark J. Barrenechea, Chief Executive Officer & CTO
Gordon A. Davies, Chief Legal Officer & Executive
Vice-President, Corporate Development
Madhu Ranganathan, Executive Vice-President & CFO

Quorum Information Technologies Inc.
Also Known As: Quorum Dealer Management
Systems
6020 - 2nd St. SE, #B28
Calgary, AB T2H 2L8

403-777-0036
Fax: 403-777-0039
877-770-0036
investors@quorumdms.com
quoruminformationsystems.com
www.facebook.com/QuorumInformationTechnologies
www.linkedin.com/company/quoruminformationtechnologies
Company Type: Public
Ticker Symbol: QIS/TSX.V
Profile: Quorum develops, markets, implements & supports its
automotive dealership/customer management system,
XSELLERATOR. The company offers the system to franchised,
independent & some non-automotive dealerships in Canada &
the USA.
Maury Marks, President & CEO
Marilyn Bown, Chief Financial Officer
Mike Herenberg, Chief Operating Officer

Real Matters Inc.
#401, 50 Minthorn Blvd.
Markham, ON L3T 7x8

Fax: 905-739-1222
877-739-2212
inquiries@realmatters.com
www.realmatters.com
Company Type: Public
Ticker Symbol: REAL/TSX
Profile: Real Matters is a technology company that provides
services for the mortgage lending & insurance industries through
proprietary platforms, including Solidifi & iv3.
Brian Lang, Chief Executive Officer
Bill Herman, Executive Vice-President & CFO
Ryan Smith, Executive Vice-President & CTO

Shareworks by Morgan Stanley
#1500, 600 - 3rd Ave. SW
Calgary, AB T2P 0G5

403-515-3910
Fax: 403-515-3919
www.shareworks.com
www.facebook.com/ShareworksbyMorganStanley
twitter.com/Shareworks
www.linkedin.com/company/shareworks-by-morgan-stanley
Company Type: Public
Ticker Symbol: SUM/TSX
Profile: Shareworks provides equity administration and related
services for businesses. Shareworks was formed through the
aquisition of Solium Capital Inc. byMorgan Stanely. It combines
Solium's stock administration platform with Morgan Stanley's
Wealth Management business.

Smart Employee Benefits Inc.
5500 Explorer Dr.
Mississauga, ON L4W 5C7

888-939-8885
Fax: 866-521-3784
investor.relations@seb-inc.com
www.seb-inc.com
www.linkedin.com/company/smart-employee-benefits-seb-inc-
Company Type: Public
Ticker Symbol: SEB/TSX.V
Profile: SEB operates a Benefits Division & Technology
Division. The company offers business software with a focus on
company benefits.
John McKimm, President, Chief Information Officer & CEO
Tim Beaulieu, Chief Financial Officer

Sylogist Inc.
#102, 5 Richard Way SW
Calgary, AB T3E 7M8

403-266-4808
Fax: 403-233-0845
info@sylogist.com
www.sylogist.com
Company Type: Public
Ticker Symbol: SYZ/TSX
Profile: Sylogist is a software & technology company that
provides intellectual property solutions to the public & private
sectors.

Tecsys Inc.
#800, 1, Place Alexis Nihon
Montréal, QC H3Z 3B8

514-866-0001
Fax: 514-866-1805
800-922-8649
info@tecsys.com
www.tecsys.com
Other Communications: Investor Relations, Email:
investor@tecsys.com
www.linkedin.com/company/35372
Company Type: Public
Ticker Symbol: TCS/TSX
Staff Size: 350
Profile: Tecsys develops technology in order to create more
efficiency within supply chain management.
Peter Brereton, President & CEO
Mark J. Bentler, Chief Financial Officer

Topicus.com Inc.
#1200, 20 Adelaide St. East
Toronto, ON M5C 2T6

416-861-227
info@topicus.com
topicus.com
Company Type: Public
Ticker Symbol: EMO/TSX.V
Staff Size: 4,500
Profile: Topicus.com is a provider of vertical market software &
platforms in Europe. It builds, manages & acquires
industry-specific software. It operates through two groups:
Topicus & Total Specific Solutions (TSS).

Daan Dijkhuizen, Chief Executive Officer
Han Knooren, Group Chief Executive Officer, Total Specific
Solutions Public
Ramon Zanders, Group Chief Executive Officer, Total Specific
Solutions Blue

VersaPay Corporation
18 King St. East, 18th Fl.
Toronto, ON M5C 1C4

647-258-9380
Fax: 647-436-9284
866-999-8729
www.versapay.com
twitter.com/versapay
www.linkedin.com/company/versapay
Company Type: Public
Ticker Symbol: VPY/TSX.V
Profile: VersaPay Corp provides accounts receivable
automation technology to businesses.
Craig O'Neill, Chief Executive Officer
Carrie Barkes, Chief Financial Officer

Chemicals

5N Plus Inc.
4385, rue Garand
Montréal, QC H4R 2B4

514-856-0644
Fax: 514-856-9611
info@5nplus.com
www.5nplus.com
Other Communications: Investor Relations, Email:
invest@5nplus.com
Company Type: Public
Ticker Symbol: VNP/TSX
Profile: 5N Plus Inc. produces specialty metal & chemical
products, including bismuth, indium, germanium, compound
semiconductor wafers & inorganic chemicals. Manufacturing
facilities & sales offices are located in North America, South
America, Europe & Asia.
Arjang Roshan, President & CEO
Richard Perron, Chief Financial Officer

Chemtrade Logistics Inc.
#300, 155 Gordon Baker Rd.
Toronto, ON M2H 3N5

416-496-5856
Fax: 416-496-9414
866-887-8805
www.chemtradelogistics.com
www.facebook.com/chemtrade
www.linkedin.com/company/chemtrade-logistics
Company Type: Public
Ticker Symbol: CHE.UN/TSX
Profile: Chemtrade provides industrial chemicals & services to
customers around the world. The company also offers industrial
services, such as processing hydrogen sulphide & waste
streams. In 2011, Chemtrade acquired all the businesses of
Marsulex Inc.
Scott Rook, President & CEO
Rohit Bhardwaj, Chief Financial Officer & Vice-President,
Finance

EcoSynthetix
3365 Mainway
Burlington, ON L7M 1A6

905-335-5669
Fax: 289-337-9780
ecosynthetix.com
twitter.com/ecosynthetix
www.linkedin.com/company/ecosynthetix-inc.
Company Type: Public
Ticker Symbol: ECO/TSX
Profile: EcoSynthetix is a renewable chemicals manufacturer of
a family of bio-based products that are used globally as inputs in
the commercial manufacture of a wide range of consumer &
industrial goods.
Jeff MacDonald, Chief Executive Officer
Robert Haire, Chief Financial Officer

Methanex Corporation
Waterfront Centre
#1800, 200 Burrard St.
Vancouver, BC V6C 3M1

604-661-2600
Fax: 604-661-2676
800-661-8851
invest@methanex.com
www.methanex.com
twitter.com/methanex
www.linkedin.com/company/methanex-corporation
Company Type: Public
Ticker Symbol: MX/TSX, NASDAQ
Staff Size: 1,500

Profile: Methanex Corporation is a producer & marketer of methanol. The company supplies major international markets.
John Floren, President & CEO
Ian Cameron, Chief Financial Officer & Senior Vice-President, Finance
Mike Herz, Senior Vice-President, Corporate Development
Vanessa James, Senior Vice-President, Global Marketing & Logistics

PFB Corporation
#300, 2891 Sunridge Way NE
Calgary, AB T1Y 7H7

403-569-4300
mailbox@pfbcorp.com
www.pfbcorp.com
www.facebook.com/plastifabeps
www.linkedin.com/company/pfb-corporation
Company Type: Public
Ticker Symbol: PFB/TSX
Staff Size: 400
Profile: Through its wholly-owned subsidiaries, PFB Corporation manufactures insulating building products based on expanded polystyrene technology. Brands of insulating building products include: Plasti-Fab EPS Product Solutions, Riverbend Timber Framing, Insulspan Structural Insulating Panels Systems, Precision Craft & Advantage ICF Systems. The company serves construction, industrial, commercial & residential markets throughout North America.
Robert Graham, Chief Executive Officer
Red Ortega, Chief Information Officer
Mirko Papuga, Chief Financial Officer

Communications

BCE Inc.
Also Known As: Bell Canada
Bldg. A
1, carrefour Alexander-Graham-Bell
Verdun, QC H3E 3B3

Fax: 514-766-5735
888-932-6666
bcecomms@bce.ca
www.bce.ca
Other Communications: Investor Relations, Email:
investor.relations@bell.ca
Company Type: Public
Ticker Symbol: BCE/TSX, NYSE
Staff Size: 52,000
Profile: Formed in 1970, BCE Inc. is a communications company that provides broadband wireless & wireline communication services. Clients include both residents & businesses across Canada.
Bell Media is a multimedia company, with assets in television, radio & digital media. Bell Media purchased Astral in July 2013.
Mirko Bibic, President & CEO, BCE & Bell Canada
Wade Oosterman, Group President
Blaik Kirby, Group President, Bell Mobility & Bell Residential & Small Business
Michael Cole, Chief Information Officer
Stephen Howe, Chief Technology Officer
Glen LeBlanc, Chief Financial Officer
Bernard le Duc, Chief Human Resources Officer & Executive Vice-President, Corporate Services

C-COM Satellite Systems Inc.
2574 Sheffield Rd.
Ottawa, ON K1B 3V7

613-745-4110
Fax: 613-745-7144
877-463-8886
info@c-comsat.com
www.c-comsat.com
www.facebook.com/ccomsatellite
twitter.com/ccomsatellite
www.linkedin.com/company/c-comsatellitesystemsinc
Company Type: Public
Ticker Symbol: CMI/TSX.V
Profile: Established in 1997, C-COM Satellite Systems Inc. designs, develops & manufactures commercial grade, fully motorized, auto-pointing mobile antennas for the delivery of broadband Internet to remote locations. The company currently has over 7,000 units operating in over 100 countries.
Leslie Klein, President & CEO
lklein@c-comsat.com
Bilal Awada, Chief Technology Officer
bawada@c-comsat.com
Art Slaughter, Chief Financial Officer
aslaughter@c-comsat.com

Cineplex Inc.
1303 Yonge St.
Toronto, ON M4T 2Y9

416-323-6600
Fax: 416-323-6683
investorrelations@cineplex.com
www.cineplex.com
Other Communications: Investor Relations, Phone:
416-323-7262
www.facebook.com/cineplexstore
twitter.com/cineplexmovies
Company Type: Public
Ticker Symbol: CGX/TSX
Staff Size: 13,000
Profile: Cineplex Inc. is a motion picture exhibitor in Canada. The company owns, leases, or has a joint-venture in 162 theatres across the country. It was acquired by U.K.-based Cineworld in 2019.
Ellis Jacob, President & CEO
Dan McGrath, Chief Operating Officer
Gord Nelson, Chief Financial Officer

Cogeco Communications Inc.
#3301, 1, Place Ville-Marie
Montréal, QC H3B 3N2

514-764-4600
corpo.cogeco.com
www.facebook.com/cogeco
www.twitter.com/cogeco
Company Type: Public
Ticker Symbol: CCA/TSX
Staff Size: 3,800
Profile: The cable telecommunications company provides internet, telephone, audio, & analog & digital television.
Philippe Jetté, President & CEO
Zouheir Zouheir, Senior Vice-President & CTO
Patrice Ouimet, Senior Vice-President & CFO

Cogeco Inc.
#3301, 1, Place Ville-Marie
Montréal, QC H3B 3N2

514-764-4600
carriere@cogeco.com
corpo.cogeco.com
www.facebook.com/cogeco
www.twitter.com/cogeco
www.linkedin.com/company/cogeco-inc
Company Type: Public
Ticker Symbol: CGO/TSX
Staff Size: 3,750
Profile: Cogeco a diversified communications company that provides cable distribution & radio broadcasting. Cogeco Connexion is the cable subsidiary, which builds on its cable distribution base by offering Analogue & Digital Television, High Speed Internet & Telephone services.
Philippe Jetté, President & CEO
Patrice Ouimet, Senior Vice-President & CFO

Corus Entertainment Inc.
Corus Quay
25 Dockside Dr.
Toronto, ON M5A 0B5

416-479-7000
Fax: 416-479-7006
866-537-2397
www.corusent.com
Company Type: Public
Ticker Symbol: CJR.B/TSX
Staff Size: 3,300
Profile: The media & entertainment company is engaged in: television broadcasting, specialty television, pay television, specialty radio, digital audio services, advertising, children's animation & children's book publishing. Some of the companies & brands that comprise Corus Entertainment include: W Network, YTV, Treehouse, TELETOON, Nelvana & Kids Can Press.
In April 2016, Corus Entertainment completed its acquisition of Shaw Communications' broadcasting subsidiary Shaw Media Inc.
Doug Murphy, President & CEO
John Gossling, Executive Vice-President & CFO
Sabah Mirza, Executive Vice-President & General Counsel

Lite Access Technologies Inc.
20108 Logan Ave.
Langley, BC V3A 4L6

604-247-4704
info@liteaccess.com
liteaccess.com
www.facebook.com/LiteAccessTechnologies
twitter.com/liteaccess
www.linkedin.com/company/lite-access-technologies-inc
Company Type: Public
Ticker Symbol: LTE/TSX.V

Profile: Founded in 2004, Lite Access Technologies Inc. produces Micro-duct & fibre optic deployment technologies. They serve both private & public deployments.
Chui Wong, Interim Chief Executive Officer
Linda Han, Interim Chief Financial Officer

Optiva Inc.
East Tower
#302, 2233 Argentia Rd.
Mississauga, ON L5N 2X7

905-625-2622
optiva.com
twitter.com/OptivaInc
www.linkedin.com/company/optivainc
Company Type: Public
Ticker Symbol: OPT/TSX
Profile: Optiva Inc. supplies OSS/BSS software & support to telecommunications companies.
John Giere, President & CEO
Shay Assaraf, Chief Marketing Officer
Matthew Halligan, Chief Technology Officer
Ashish Joshi, Chief Financial Officer

Redline Communications Group
302 Town Centre Blvd., 4th Fl.
Markham, ON L3R 0E8

905-479-8344
Fax: 905-479-5331
866-633-6669
info@rdlcom.com
rdlcom.com
Other Communications: Investor Relations, Email:
ir@rdlcom.com
www.facebook.com/rdlcom
twitter.com/rdlcom
www.linkedin.com/company/redline-communications
Company Type: Public
Ticker Symbol: RDL/TSX
Staff Size: 130
Profile: Redline Communications is the creator of powerful wide-area wireless networks for challenging locations.
Ronan McGrath, Interim Chief Executive Officer
Philip Jones, Chief Financial Officer

Rogers Communications Inc.
333 Bloor St. East
Toronto, ON M4W 1G9

investor.relations@rci.rogers.com
investors.rogers.com
Other Communications: Shareholder Inquiries, Phone:
416-682-3800
www.facebook.com/rogers
twitter.com/aboutrogers
www.linkedin.com/company/rogers-communications
Company Type: Public
Ticker Symbol: RCI.B/TSX
Staff Size: 25,300
Profile: The diversified communications & media company, founded in 1987, provides wireless voice & data communications services, as well as cable television, high-speed Internet & telephony services.
Rogers Media provides magazines & trade publications; sports entertainment; television & radio broadcasting; & televised shopping.
Joe Natale, President & CEO
Jordan Banks, President, Sports & Media
Dave Fuller, President, Wireless
Dean Prevost, President, Connected Home & Rogers for Business
Jorge Fernandes, Chief Technology & Infomration Officer
Tony Staffieri, Chief Financial Officer

Score Media & Gaming Inc.
Also Known As: theScore
500 King St. West, 4th Fl.
Toronto, ON M5V 1L9

416-479-8812
Fax: 416-361-2045
hello@thescore.com
scoremediaandgaming.com
www.facebook.com/thescore
twitter.com/theScore_IR
www.linkedin.com/company/thescore
Company Type: Public
Ticker Symbol: SCR/TSX.V
Staff Size: 220
Profile: Score Media & Gaming provides digital media & sports betting products, such as its media app theScore.
John Levy, Chair & Chief Executive Officer
Benjie Levy, President & COO

Shaw Communications Inc.
630 - 3rd Ave. SW
Calgary, AB T2P 4L4

888-472-2222
www.shaw.ca
Other Communications: Investor Relations, Email:
investor.relations@sjrb.ca
www.facebook.com/shaw
twitter.com/shawinfo
www.linkedin.com/company/shaw-communications
Company Type: Public
Ticker Symbol: SJR.B/TSX; SJR/NYSE
Staff Size: 15,000
Profile: Established in 1966, the communications company provides broadband cable television, internet, digital phone, telecommunications services & satellite direct-to-home services. In April 2016, Corus Entertainment completed its acquisition of the company's broadcasting subsidiary Shaw Media Inc.
Bradley Shaw, Executive Chair & Chief Executive Officer
Paul Deverell, President, Consumer
Paul McAleese, President
Trevor English, Executive Vice-President & CFO
Zoran Stakic, Chief Operating Officer & CTO

Stingray Digital Group
730, rue Wellington
Montréal, QC H3C 1T4

info@stingray.com
www.stingray.com
Other Communications: Investor Relations, Email:
investors@stingray.com
twitter.com/stingray
www.linkedin.com/company/stingray
Company Type: Public
Ticker Symbol: RAY.A, RAY.B/TSX
Staff Size: 1,000
Profile: Stingray is a multi-platform music & in-store media solutions provider operating in 156 countries. Stingray's services include music, concerts & shows, karaoke, music videos & TV channels, 4K TV channels & audio channels.
Eric Boyko, Founder, President & CEO
Ian Lurie, President, Radio
Jean-Pierre Trahan, Chief Financial Officer

TELUS Communications Company
510 West Georgia St., 8th Fl.
Vancouver, BC V6B 0M3

Fax: 604-899-9228
800-667-4871
ir@telus.com
www.telus.com
Other Communications: T
www.facebook.com/telus
twitter.com/telus
www.linkedin.com/company/telus
Company Type: Public
Ticker Symbol: T/TSX; TU/NYSE
Staff Size: 78,100
Profile: TELUS is a national telecommunications company. Their services include wireless, data, Internet protocol (IP), voice, television, entertainment & video.
Darren Entwistle, President & CEO
Doug French, Executive Vice-President & CFO
Eros Spadotto, Executive Vice-President, Technology Strategy & Business Transformation

TeraGo Inc.
#800, 55 Commerce Valley Dr. West
Thornhill, ON L3T 7V9

866-837-2461
info@terago.ca
terago.ca
twitter.com/terago_networks
www.linkedin.com/company/terago-networks
Company Type: Public
Ticker Symbol: TGO/TSX
Profile: TeraGo Networks provides the following services to businesses in Canada: voice services, high speed internet, data networking & internet redundancy. TeraGo owns & operates its National Wireless Network.
Matthew Gerber, Chief Executive Officer
David Charron, Chief Financial Officer

Trilogy International Partners LLC
#400, 155 - 108th Ave. NE
Bellevue, WA 98004 USA

425-458-5900
ir@trilogy-international.com
www.trilogy-international.com
Company Type: Public
Ticker Symbol: TRL/TSX
Profile: Trilogy International Partners is a wireless telecommunications company. It operates through its

international, partly owned subsidiaries: 2degrees (New Zealand) & Viva (Bolivia).
Brad Horwitz, Co-Founder & Chief Executive Officer
Erik Mickels, Senior Vice-President & Chief Financial Officer

TVA Group Inc./Groupe TVA
1600, boul de Maisonneuve est
Montréal, QC H2L 4P2

514-526-9251
Fax: 514-599-5502
www.groupetva.ca
www.facebook.com/ReseauTVA
twitter.com/tvareseau
www.linkedin.com/company/tva-group
Company Type: Public
Ticker Symbol: TVA.B/TSX
Staff Size: 1,330
Profile: The integrated communications company provides: broadcasting, publishing, producing & distributing audiovisual products. TVA Group owns French-language television stations, plus a specialty channel. It also publishes French-language magazines. The TVA Films subsidiary serves both Canada's English & French-language markets.
France Lauzière, President & CEO
Anick Dubois, Vice-President, Finance

WildBrain Ltd.
#505, 5657 Spring Garden Rd.
Halifax, NS B3J 3R4

902-423-0260
Fax: 902-422-0752
halifax@wildbrain.com
www.wildbrain.com
www.facebook.com/WildBrainHQ
twitter.com/wildbrainhq
www.linkedin.com/company/wildbrain
Company Type: Public
Ticker Symbol: WILD/TSX
Staff Size: 1,000
Profile: WildBrain produces, distributes & licenses children's entertainment. WILDBRAIN Entertainment is the company's subsidiary.
Eric Ellenbogen, Chief Executive Officer
Josh Scherba, President
Aaron Ames, Chief Financial Officer

Construction

Aecon Group Inc.
#105, 20 Carlson Ct.
Toronto, ON M9W 7K6

416-297-2600
aecon@aecon.com
www.aecon.com
www.facebook.com/AeconGroupInc
twitter.com/aecongroup
www.linkedin.com/company/aecon
Company Type: Public
Ticker Symbol: ARE/TSX
Staff Size: 5,500
Profile: Aecon Group is a construction & infrastructure development company. It serves both public & private sector clients through the provision of engineering, financing, procurement, construction & project management services.
Jean-Louis Servranckx, President & CEO
David Smales, Executive Vice-President & CFO

Badger Infrastructure Solutions Ltd.
ATCO Bldg. II
919 - 11th Ave. SW, 4th Fl.
Calgary, AB T2R 1P3

403-264-8500
Fax: 403-228-9773
corporate@badgerinc.com
www.badgerinc.com
Company Type: Public
Ticker Symbol: BDGI/TSX
Staff Size: 1,875
Profile: Badger Infrastructure Solutions provides non-destructive excavating services. The company has more than 400 hydrovac units that operate from over 80 field offices throughout Canada & the United States. Badger is employed by contractors & facility owners in the petroleum, construction, transportation, engineering, industrial & utility industries.
Paul J. Vanderberg, President & CEO
Darren Yaworsky, CFO & Vice-President, Finance
John G. Kelly, Chief Operating Officer
Tracey Wallace, Chief Human Resources Officer
Leon Walsh, Vice-President, Safety, Health & Environment

Bird Construction Inc.
#400, 5700 Explorer Dr.
Mississauga, ON L4W 0C6

905-602-4122
www.bird.ca
twitter.com/builtbybird
www.linkedin.com/company/bird-construction
Company Type: Public
Ticker Symbol: BDT/TSX
Profile: The organization is a national general contractor in the residential, institutional & industrial markets.
Teri McKibbon, President & CEO
Wayne Gingrich, Chief Financial Officer

DIRTT Environmental Solutions
7303 - 30th St. SE
Calgary, AB T2C 1N6

800-605-6707
hello@dirtt.net
www.dirtt.net
www.facebook.com/dirttenvironmentalsolutions
twitter.com/DIRTT
www.linkedin.com/company/dirtt-environmental-solutions
Company Type: Public
Ticker Symbol: DRT/TSX
Profile: DIRTT (Doing It Right This Time) creates customizable, sustainable architectural interiors.
Kevin O'Meara, Chief Executive Officer
Jeffrey Calkins, Chief Operation Officer
Geoffrey Krause, Chief Financial Officer

Enterprise Group, Inc.
#2, 64 Riel Dr.
St Albert, AB T8N 4A4

780-418-4400
contact@enterprisegrp.ca
www.enterprisegrp.ca
twitter.com/enterprisegrp
Company Type: Public
Ticker Symbol: E/TSX
Staff Size: 300
Profile: Enterprise Group, Inc. is a consolidator of construction services companies operating in the energy, utility & transportation infrastructure industries. Recently acquired companies include: Artic Therm International Ltd., Calgary Tunnelling & Horizontal Augering Ltd. & Hart Oilfield Rentals Ltd.
Leonard D. Jaroszuk, Chair, President & CEO
Warren Cabral, C.A., Chief Financial Officer

Finning International Inc.
Park Place
#1000, 666 Burrard St.
Vancouver, BC V6C 2X8

604-691-6444
Fax: 604-691-6440
888-346-6464
investor_relations@finning.ca
www.finning.com
www.facebook.com/finningca
twitter.com/finningcanada
www.linkedin.com/company/finning
Company Type: Public
Ticker Symbol: FTT/TSX
Staff Size: 13,000
Profile: The company sells, rents & offers customer service for Caterpillar equipment. Business is conducted in Canada, South America & the United Kingdom.
L. Scott Thomson, President & CEO
Greg Palaschuk, Executive Vice-President & CFO
David W. Cummings, Chief Digital Officer
Chad Hiley, Chief Human Resources Officer

Stuart Olson Inc.
#600, 4820 Richard Rd. SW
Calgary, AB T3E 6L1

403-685-7777
info@stuartolson.com
www.stuartolson.com
www.facebook.com/stuartolsoninc
twitter.com/stuartolsoninc
www.linkedin.com/company/stuart-olson-inc-
Company Type: Public
Ticker Symbol: SOX/TSX
Profile: Stuart Olson is a provider of building construction, industrial construction, & related maintenance services operating in western Canada. In 2020, it was acquired by Bird Construction Inc.

Distribution & Retail

Alimentation Couche-Tard Inc.
4204, boul Industriel
Laval, QC H7L 0E3

888-999-9301
www.couche-tard.com
www.facebook.com/couchetardqc
twitter.com/couchetardqc
www.linkedin.com/company/couche-tard

Company Type: Public
Ticker Symbol: ATD.B/TSX
Staff Size: 131,000
Profile: In eastern, central & western Canada, as well as in the United States, Alimentation Couche-Tard operates convenience stores. Some of these stores are motor fuel dispensers. In Canada, the businesses operate under the brands Couche-Tard & Mac's.
Brian Hannasch, President & CEO
Claude Tessier, Chief Financial Officer

Auxly Cannabis Group Inc.
#002, 777 Richmond St. West
Toronto, ON M6J 0C2

647-812-0121
Fax: 647-812-0120
info@auxly.com
auxly.com
Other Communications: Investor Relations phone:
1-833-695-2414
www.facebook.com/auxlygroup
twitter.com/AuxlyGroup
www.linkedin.com/company/auxlygroup

Company Type: Public
Ticker Symbol: XLY/TSX.V
Profile: The company provides cannabis products. It is based in Canada & Uruguay.
Hugo Alves, Chief Executive Officer
Mike Lickver, President
Ian Rapsey, Chief Creative Officer
Brian Schmitt, Chief Financial Officer

BMTC Group Inc./Groupe BMTC Inc.
8500, Place Marien
Montréal, QC H1B 5W8

514-648-9100
Fax: 514-881-4056

Company Type: Public
Ticker Symbol: GBT/TSX
Staff Size: 1,400
Profile: BMTC Group is a holding company. Its subsidiaries include Ameublements Tanguay Inc. & Brault et Martineau Inc. These subsidiaries are engaged in the retail sale of furniture, electronic goods & household appliances in Québec.
Marie-Berthe Des Groseillers, President & CEO

Canadian Tire Corporation, Ltd.
2180 Yonge St.
Toronto, ON M4P 2V8

416-480-3000
www.canadiantire.ca
www.facebook.com/canadiantire
twitter.com/CanTireCorp
www.linkedin.com/company/canadian-tire

Company Type: Public
Ticker Symbol: CTC, CTC.A/TSX
Staff Size: 32,000
Profile: Founded in 1922, the company is engaged in retail, petroleum & financial services. Canadian Tire has 1,700 retail locations.
Greg Hicks, President & CEO
Stephen Brinkley, President, SportChek
P.J. Czank, President, Mark's
T.J. Flood, President, Canadian Tire Retail
John Koryl, President, CTC Digital
Gregory Craig, Executive Vice-President & CFO

CanWel Building Materials Group Ltd.
PO Box 39, #1600, 1100 Mevlville St.
Vancouver, BC V6E 4A6

604-432-1400
Fax: 604-436-6670
canwel.com
www.facebook.com/CanWelBuildingMaterials
www.linkedin.com/company/canwel-building-materials

Company Type: Public
Ticker Symbol: CWX/TSX
Staff Size: 700
Profile: Founded in 1989, CanWel Building Materials Group is involved in the distribution of building materials & related products across Canada. Its divisions include CanWel Treating, CanWel Fibre, California Cascade, Honsador & Lignum Forest Products.
Amar S. Doman, Chair & Chief Executive Officer

Marc Séguin, President
James Code, Chief Financial Officer
Julie Wong, Director, Human Resources

Cervus Equipment Corporation
#6302, 333 - 96th Ave. NE
Calgary, AB T3K 0S3

877-567-0339
www.cervuscorp.com
www.facebook.com/cervusequipment
twitter.com/cervusequipment
www.linkedin.com/company/cervus-equipment

Company Type: Public
Ticker Symbol: CERV/TSX
Profile: Cervus Equipment Corporation acquires & manages authorized agricultural, commercial, industrial & transportation equipment dealerships. Business is conducted in Alberta, Saskatchewan & Manitoba. The corporation also has an investment partnership with a New Zealand based company named Agriturf Limited.
Angela Lekatsas, Presiedent & CEO
Catie Busch, Chief Financial Officer
Scott Johnston, Chief Operating Officer

Colabor Group Inc./Groupe Colabor Inc.
1620, boul de Montarville
Boucherville, QC J4B 8P4

450-449-4911
Fax: 450-449-6180
info@colabor.com
www.colabor.com

Company Type: Public
Ticker Symbol: GCL/TSX
Profile: In 2009, Colabor Group Inc. completed the conversion of Colabor Income Fund to a corporation. The corporation is engaged in the distribution of confectionary products, refrigerated products, frozen foods, food-related products, dry goods, & beauty & care products. Products are marketed & distributed to retail & foodservice markets.
Louis Frenette, President & CEO

DAVIDsTEA INC.
5430, rue Ferrier
Montréal, QC H4P 1M2

438-814-1941
Fax: 514-739-0200
855-702-3006
customerservice@davidstea.com
ir.davidstea.com
Other Communications: Investor Relations, Email:
investors@davidstea.com
www.facebook.com/DAVIDsTEA
twitter.com/davidstea
www.linkedin.com/company/davidstea

Company Type: Public
Ticker Symbol: DTEA/NASDAQ
Profile: Founded in 2008, DAVIDsTEA is an online & retail seller of tea leaves & brewed tea.
Sarah Segal, Chief Brand Officer & CEO
Frank Zitella, Chief Financial Officer & COO

Dollarama Inc.
5905, av Royalmount
Montréal, QC H4P 0A1

514-737-1006
contactus@dollarama.com
www.dollarama.com

Company Type: Public
Ticker Symbol: DOL/TSX
Staff Size: 23,000
Profile: Dollarama Inc. was founded in 1992. It sells general merchandise & seasonal products for $4 or less in more than 1,000 locations across Canada.
Neil Rossy, President & CEO
Johanne Choinière, Chief Operating Officer
Nicolas Hien, Chief Information Officer
J.P. Towner, Chief Financial Officer
jp.towner@dollarama.com

HEXO Corp.
3000 Solandt Rd.
Kanata, ON K2K 2X2

844-406-1852
info@hexo.com
www.hexocorp.com
www.facebook.com/HEXOCorp
twitter.com/hexocorp
www.linkedin.com/company/hexo-corp

Company Type: Public
Ticker Symbol: HEXO/TSX; HEXO/NYSE
Profile: The company markets packaged cannabis goods worldwide. Until 2018 it was a medical cannabis corporation exclusively.
Sebastien St-Louis, Chief Executive Officer

Donald Courtney, Chief Operating Officer
Trent MacDonald, Chief Financial Officer
James McMillan, Chief Development Officer

Hudson's Bay Co.
8925 Torbram Rd.
Brampton, ON L6T 4G1

905-792-4400
800-521-2364
www.hbc.com

Company Type: Public
Ticker Symbol: HBC/TSX
Profile: HBC offers customers a range of retailing categories & shopping experiences primarily in the United States & Canada. The Hudson's Bay Company played a central role in Canadian history as a quasi-government before selling its land to the fledgling Canadian state.
Richard A. Baker, Chief Executive Officer
Michael Culhane, Chief Financial Officer
David Schwartz, Executive Vice-President & General Counsel

Indigo Books & Music Inc.
#400, 468 King St. West
Toronto, ON M5V 1L8

416-364-4499
800-832-7569
InvestorRelations@indigo.ca
www.chapters.indigo.ca
www.facebook.com/ChaptersIndigo
twitter.com/chaptersindigo
www.linkedin.com/company/indigo

Company Type: Public
Ticker Symbol: IDG/TSX
Profile: Indigo Books & Music Inc. is a Canadian retailer of books, gifts & specialty toys. The company is the majority shareholder of the eReading service, Kobo Inc. Stores include Indigo Books & Music, Indigo Books, Gifts, Kids, IndigoSpirit, Chapters, Coles & The World's Biggest Bookstore. The company's online channel is indigo.ca. Indigo Books & Music also founded the Indigo Love of Reading Foundation.
Heather Reisman, Founder, Chair & Chief Executive Officer
Peter Ruis, President
Gil Dennis, Chief Operating Officer
Craig Loudon, Chief Financial Officer & Executive Vice-President, Supply Chain
Bo Parizadeh, Chief Technology Officer

Le Château Inc.
105, boul Marcel-Laurin
Montréal, QC H4N 2M3

888-532-4283
www.lechateau.com
www.facebook.com/lechateaustyle

Company Type: Public
Ticker Symbol: CTU/TSX
Staff Size: 1,600
Profile: Le Château was formed in 1987. It manufactures & retails fashion apparel, accessories & footwear. The brand is sold in 123 retail locations in Canada.
Emilia Di Raddo, President
Johnny Del Ciancio, Vice-President, Finance

Leon's Furniture Limited
Also Known As: LFL Group
45 Gordon Mackay Rd.
Toronto, ON M9N 3X3

416-243-7880
www.lflgroup.ca
www.facebook.com/leonsfurniture
twitter.com/leonsfurniture
www.linkedin.com/company/leon's-furniture

Company Type: Public
Ticker Symbol: LNF/TSX
Staff Size: 10,000
Profile: The A. Leon Company was founded in 1909 as a general merchandise store. Today, through a chain of retail facilities & franchises across Canada, Leon's Furniture Limited is engaged in the sale of home furnishings, electronics & home appliances.
Edward Leon, Chief Executive Officer
Michael J. Walsh, President & COO
Constantine Pefanis, Chief Financial Officer

Longo Brothers Fruit Markets Inc.
Also Known As: Longo's
8800 Huntington Rd.
Vaughan, ON L4H 3M6

800-956-6467
1800@longos.com
investors.mavbeautybrands.com
www.facebook.com/LongosMarkets
twitter.com/LongosMarkets
www.linkedin.com/company/longos

Company Type: Public
Profile: Founded in 1956, Longo's is a chain of supermarkets in southern Ontario. It owns & operates 36 stores. In 2021, Empire Company Limited acquired a 51% interest in the company.
Anthony Longo, President & CEO

LXRandCo, Inc.
7399, boul Saint-Laurent
Montréal, QC H2R 1W7

514-564-4446
800-764-0521
info@lxrco.com
www.lxrco.com
Other Communications: Investor Relations, Email:
investors@lxrco.com
www.facebook.com/LXRandCo

Company Type: Public
Ticker Symbol: LXR/TSX
Profile: The company markets luxury vintage handbags & accessories from such sources as Chanel, Gucci, Ferragamo & beyond.
Camillo di Prata, Interim Chief Executive Officer
Nadine Eap, Chief Financial Officer
Joslyn Paredes, Chief Operating Officer
Laura Swan, Chief Revenue Officer

Namaste Technologies
#2001, 365 Bloor St. East
Toronto, ON M4W 3L4

877-660-2365
info@namastetechnologies.com
www.namastetechnologies.com
Other Communications: Investor Relations, Email:
ir@namastetechnologies.com
www.facebook.com/NamasteTechnologies
twitter.com/namaste_tech
www.linkedin.com/company/namastetechnologies

Company Type: Public
Ticker Symbol: N/TSX.V; NXTTF/OTCQX
Profile: Founded in 2014, Namaste Technologies is an online cannabis retailer.
Meni Morim, Chief Executive Officer
Chad Agate, Chief Technology Officer
Faraaz Jamal, Chief Operating Officer
Slava Klems, Chief Financial Officer

Neighbourly Pharmacy Inc.
#400, 190 Attwell Dr.
Toronto, ON M9W 6H8

neighbourlypharmacy.ca
Other Communications: Invest Relations, Email:
investorrelations@nbly.ca
www.linkedin.com/company/neighbourlypharmacy

Company Type: Public
Ticker Symbol: NBLY/TSX
Staff Size: 1,650
Profile: The company acquires, opens & operates independent pharmacies. It has over 130 pharmacy locations across canada.
Chris Gardner, Chief Executive Officer
Terri Smyth, Chief Financial Officer

Parkland Fuel Corporation
#1800, 240 - 4th Ave. SW
Calgary, AB T2P 4H4

403-567-2500
877-906-6644
investor.relations@parkland.ca
www.parkland.ca
twitter.com/ParklandCorp
www.linkedin.com/company/parklandcorporation

Company Type: Public
Ticker Symbol: PKI/TSX
Profile: Parkland Fuel is engaged in the marketing & distribution of petroleum products. The company serves wholesale, retail, commercial & home heating fuel customers. Brands include: Fas Gas Plus, Race Trac Gas, Bluewave Energy, Great Northern Oil, United Petroleum Products, Columbia Fuels, Neufeld Petroleum & Propane & Island Petroleum.
Parkland Fuel has a Health, Safety & Enviroment Department as well as HSE committees, & it develops risk mitigation programs & emergency response procedures for the handling of transportation fuels in a manner that is safe & healthy for employees & the environment.
Bob Espey, President & CEO
Pierre Magnan, President, International
Donna Sanker, President, Canada
Marcel Teunissen, Chief Financial Officer

Reitmans (Canada) Limited (RCL)
250, rue Sauvé ouest
Montréal, QC H3L 1Z2

514-384-1140
www.reitmanscanadalimited.com
www.facebook.com/reitmans
www.linkedin.com/company/reitmans

Company Type: Public
Ticker Symbol: RET.A/TSX
Profile: Reitmans (Canada) Ltd. is an operator of clothing stores that specialize in women's fashions & accessories. Stores are operated under the following names: Reitmans, Penningtons, Addition Elle, Thyme Maternity, RW&CO. & Hyba. The company has over 400 stores across Canada.
Stephen F. Reitman, President & CEO
Richard Wait, Chief Financial Officer & Executive Vice-President, Finance
Gale Blank, Chief Information Officer

Richelieu Hardware Ltd./Quincaillerie Richelieu Ltée
7900, boul Henri-Bourassa ouest
Montréal, QC H4S 1V4

514-336-4144
Fax: 514-336-9431
800-361-6000
investisseurs@richelieu.com
www.richelieu.com

Company Type: Public
Ticker Symbol: RCH/TSX
Staff Size: 2,200
Profile: Richelieu Hardware manufactures, imports & distributes specialty hardware & complementary design products. The company serves manufacturers & retailers throughout North America.
Richard Lord, President & CEO
Antoine Auclair, Vice-President & CFO
Marjolaine Plante, Vice-President, Human Resources

Rocky Mountain Equipment Alberta Ltd. (RME)
#301, 3345 - 8th St. SE
Calgary, AB T2G 3A4

403-265-7364
Fax: 403-214-5656
855-763-1427
rockymtn.com
www.facebook.com/RockyMountainEquipment
twitter.com/RMEHQ
www.linkedin.com/company/rocky-mountain-dealerships-inc.

Company Type: Public
Staff Size: 800
Profile: RME has a network of full-service dealership branches that sell, rent & lease new & used agriculture & construction equipment. It also provides repair & maintenance services, as well as third-party finance products. Stores are located in Alberta, Saskatchewan & Manitoba.
Garret Ganden, President & CEO
Jerry Schiefelbein, Chief Financial Officer
Jim Wood, Chief Sales & Operations Officer

Shopify Inc.
150 Elgin St., 8th Fl.
Ottawa, ON K2P 1L4

www.shopify.ca
www.facebook.com/shopify
twitter.com/shopify
www.linkedin.com/company/shopify

Company Type: Public
Ticker Symbol: SHOP/TSX; SHOP/NYSE
Staff Size: 1,900
Profile: Shopify is provides an online marketplace.
Tobi Lütke, Founder & Chief Executive Officer
Harley Finkelstein, President
Toby Shannan, Chief Operating Officer
Amy Shapero, Chief Financial Officer

Sleep Country Canada Holdings
7920 Airport Rd.
Brampton, ON L6T 4N8

289-748-0206
Fax: 905-790-9379
investor.relations@sleepcountry.ca
www.sleepcountryir.ca
www.facebook.com/sleepcountrycanada
twitter.com/sleepcountrycan

Company Type: Public
Ticker Symbol: ZZZ/TSX
Staff Size: 1,200
Profile: Sleep Country is a mattress retailer.
David Friesema, Chief Executive Officer
Craig De Pratto, Chief Financial Officer
Sieg Will, Senior Vice-President, Operations

Sunniva Inc.
#400, 355 - 4th Ave. SW
Calgary, AB T2P 0J1

866-786-6482
info@sunniva.com
www.sunnivalife.com
Other Communications: Investor phone: (212) 896-1233

Company Type: Public
Ticker Symbol: SNN/CSE; SNNVF/OTCQX
Profile: The company is a vertically integrated cannabis company operating in California & Canada, which are the two biggest cannabis markets in the world.
Anthony Holler, Chief Executive Officer
David Weinmann, Interim Chief Financial Officer

SunOpta Inc.
#401, 2233 Argentia Rd.
Mississauga, ON L5N 2X7

905-821-9669
info@sunopta.com
www.sunopta.com
Other Communications: Investor Relations, Email:
investors@sunopta.com
twitter.com/sunopta
www.linkedin.com/company/sunopta

Company Type: Public
Ticker Symbol: SOY/TSX; STKL/NASDAQ
Staff Size: 1,400
Profile: SunOpta Inc. is focused upon sourcing, processing & distributing healthy, environmentally responsible products. Products include natural, organic & specialty foods. The company's brands include Sunrich, Sunrise Growers, arbor & SOWN.
Joseph D. Ennen, Chief Executive Officer
Rob Duchscher, Chief Information Officer
Scott Huckins, Chief Financial Officer
David Largey, Chief Quality Officer

TerrAscend Corp.
PO Box 43125, Mississauga, ON L5B 4A7

855-837-7259
www.terrascend.com
www.facebook.com/TerrAscendCorp
twitter.com/terrascendcorp
www.linkedin.com/company/terrascend

Company Type: Public
Ticker Symbol: TER/CSE; TRSSF/OTCQX
Profile: TerrAscend markets cannabis goods & services to global markets where cannabinoid products have been legalized.
Jason Wild, Executive Chair
Jason Marks, Chief Legal Officer
Keith Stauffer, Chief Financial Officer

Uni-Select Inc.
170, boul Industriel
Boucherville, QC J4B 2X3

450-641-2440
Fax: 450-449-4908
questions@uniselect.com
www.uniselect.com
Other Communications: Investor Relations, Email:
investorrelations@uniselect.com
www.linkedin.com/company/uni-select-inc-

Company Type: Public
Ticker Symbol: UNS/TSX
Staff Size: 6,000
Profile: Uni-Select Inc. was founded in 1968. It is a wholesale distributor & marketer of heavy duty tools, equipment, replacement parts & accessories. The company serves the North American automotive industry.
Brian McManus, Executive Chair & Chief Executive Officer
Anthony Pagano, Chief Financial Officer

VIVO Cannabis
180 John St.
Toronto, ON M5H 2N2

416-848-9839
info@vivocannabis.com
www.vivocannabis.com
twitter.com/VIVO_Cannabis
www.linkedin.com/company/vivo-cannabis-inc

Company Type: Public
Ticker Symbol: VIVO/TSX.V
Profile: VIVO Cannabis grows quality cannabis for the medical & adult-use markets.
Richard Fitzgerald, Interim Chief Executive Officer
Michael Bumby, Chief Financial Officer
Carole Chan, Chief Commercial & People Officer
Tim Hayden, Chief Operating Officer

Wajax Corporation
2250 Argentia Rd.
Mississauga, ON L5N 6A5

905-813-8310
Fax: 905-812-7203
info@wajax.com
www.wajax.com
www.facebook.com/wajax
twitter.com/Wajax
www.linkedin.com/company/wajax

Company Type: Public
Ticker Symbol: WJX/TSX
Staff Size: 2,700
Profile: Through its subsidiaries, Wajax is an industrial products & services provider dealing with power systems, mobile equipment & industrial components. Wajax serves the manufacturing, natural resources, utilities, construction & industrial processing sectors. Branches are located throughout Canada.
Mark Foote, President & CEO
Stuart Auld, Chief Financial Officer
sauld@wajax.com
Steven Deck, Chief Operating Officer
Cristian Rodriguez, Vice-President, Environment, Health, Safety & Sustainability
Andrew Tam, General Counsel & Secretary
atam@wajax.com

Electronics & Electrical Equipment

Avante Logixx
#601, 130 Bloor St. West
Toronto, ON M5S 1N5

416-923-6984
info@avantelogixx.com
www.avantelogixx.com
www.linkedin.com/company/avante-logixx

Company Type: Public
Ticker Symbol: XX/TSX.V
Profile: The company provides security services such as static guard, executive protection & alarm response. It also develops security hardware & software.
Craig Campbell, Chief Executive Officer
Steve Rotz, Chief Financial Officer

Ballard Power Systems Inc.
9000 Glenlyon Pkwy.
Burnaby, BC V5J 5J8

604-454-0900
investors@ballard.com
www.ballard.com
twitter.com/ballardpwr
www.linkedin.com/company/ballard-power-systems

Company Type: Public
Ticker Symbol: BLDP/TSX, NASDAQ
Staff Size: 410
Profile: Ballard Power Systems provides clean energy fuel cell products for a range of applications.
Randall MacEwen, President & CEO
Kevin Cowlbow, Senior Vice-President & CTO
Paul Dobson, Senior Vice-President & CFO

Baylin Technologies
#503, 4711 Yonge St.
Toronto, ON M2N 6K8

www.baylintech.com
twitter.com/baylintech
www.linkedin.com/company/baylin-technologies-inc-

Company Type: Public
Ticker Symbol: BYL/TSX
Profile: Baylin Technologies is a wireless techonology company.
Randy Dewey, President & CEO

BlackBerry Limited
2200 University Ave. East
Waterloo, ON N2K 0A7

ca.blackberry.com
Other Communications: Investor Relations, Email:
investor_relations@blackberry.com
www.facebook.com/blackberry
twitter.com/BlackBerry
www.linkedin.com/company/blackberry

Company Type: Public
Ticker Symbol: BB/TSX, NASDAQ
Staff Size: 3,500
Profile: BlackBerry was originally established as Research in Motion Limited (RIM) in 1984. It changed its name in 2013 to coincide with the release of the BlackBerry 10 device. The company designs, manufactures & markets wireless solutions for the mobile communications market.
John Chen, Executive Chair & Chief Executive Officer
Steve Rai, Chief Financial Officer
Nita White-Ivy, Chief Human Resources Officer

Blackline Safety
#100, 803 - 24th Ave. SE
Calgary, AB T2G 1P5

Fax: 403-451-9981
877-869-7212
info@blacklinesafety.com
www.blacklinesafety.com
www.facebook.com/blacklinesafety
twitter.com/blacklinesafety
www.linkedin.com/company/blacklinesafety

Company Type: Public
Ticker Symbol: BLN/TSX
Profile: Blackline Safety produces & markets lone worker monitoring products & wirelessly connected gas detection.
Cody Slater, Chief Executive Officer
Shane Grennan, Chief Financial Officer
Kevin Meyers, Chief Operating Officer

Celestica Inc.
PO Box 42, #1900, 5140 Yonge Street
Toronto, ON M2N 6L7

416-448-5800
888-899-9998
contactus@celestica.com
www.celestica.com
www.facebook.com/celesticainc
twitter.com/celestica_inc
www.linkedin.com/company/celestica

Company Type: Public
Ticker Symbol: CLS/TSX, NYSE
Staff Size: 20,550
Profile: Celestica delivers end-to-end product lifecycle solutions, specializing in electronics manufacturing, engineering & supply chain management services.
Rob Mionis, President & CEO
Mandeep Chawla, Chief Financial Officer
Todd Cooper, Chief Operations Officer
Leila Wong, Chief Human Resources Officer

Drone Delivery Canada
#441, 6-6175 Hwy. 7
Vaughan, ON L4H 0R6

info@dronedeliverycanada.com
dronedeliverycanada.com
www.facebook.com/dronedeliverycanada
twitter.com/dronedeliveryca
www.linkedin.com/company/drone-delivery-canada

Company Type: Public
Ticker Symbol: FLT/TSX.V
Profile: The company's mission is to construct a drone delivery network in Cananada.
Michael Zahra, President & CEO
Manish Arora, Chief Financial Officer

Evertz Microsystems Limited
5292 John Lucas Dr.
Burlington, ON L7L 5Z9

905-335-3700
Fax: 905-335-3573
877-995-3700
sales@evertz.com
evertz.com
Other Communications: Customer Service, Email:
service@evertz.com
twitter.com/evertztv
www.linkedin.com/company/evertz

Company Type: Public
Ticker Symbol: ET/TSX
Staff Size: 1,700
Profile: Evertz Technologies Limited is a high-technology company. It is engaged in the designing, manufacturing & marketing of film production, post production & broadcast equipment to be used in the film & television broadcast industry.
Romolo Magarelli, President & CEO
Doug Moore, Chief Financial Officer
ir@evertz.com

exactEarth Ltd.
Bldg. B
#30, 206 Holiday Inn Dr.
Cambridge, ON N3C 4E8

519-622-4445
Fax: 519-623-8575
info@exactearth.com
www.exactearth.com
twitter.com/exactearth
www.linkedin.com/company/exactearth-ltd

Company Type: Public
Ticker Symbol: XCT/TSX
Profile: exactEarth manufactures Satellite AIS data services for boats.
Peter Mabson, President & CEO
Sean Maybee, Chief Financial Officer

EXFO Inc.
#100, 3400 Waterview Pkwy.
Richardson, TX 75080

972-761-9271
Fax: 972-761-9067
800-663-3936
www.exfo.com
www.facebook.com/exfoinc
twitter.com/exfo
www.linkedin.com/company/exfo

Company Type: Public
Ticker Symbol: EXF/TSX; EXFO/NASDAQ
Staff Size: 1,500
Profile: EXFO Inc. designs & manufactures measurement & monitoring products. The company's test & service assurance solutions are used by the global telecommunications industry.
Philippe Morin, Chief Executive Officer
Pierre Plamondon, Chief Financial Officer & Vice-President, Finance

Hammond Power Solutions Inc. (HPS)
595 Southgate Dr.
Guelph, ON N1G 3W6

519-822-2441
Fax: 519-822-9701
888-798-8882
ir@hammondpowersolutions.com
www.hammondpowersolutions.com
www.facebook.com/hammondpowersolutions
twitter.com/hpstransformers
www.linkedin.com/company/hammond-power-solutions

Company Type: Public
Ticker Symbol: HPS.A/TSX
Profile: Established in 1917, Hammond Power Solutions Inc. engineers & manufactures custom & standard dry-type transformers & related magnetic products. The company's products are used by the global electrical industry.
William G. Hammond, Chair & Chief Executive Officer
Christopher R. Huether, Chief Financial Officer

Helius Medical Technologies Inc.
#100, 642 Newtown Yardley Rd.
Newtown, PA 18940 USA

877-564-0008
www.heliusmedical.com

Company Type: Public
Ticker Symbol: HSM/TSX; HSDT/NASDAQ
Profile: Helius Medical Technologies is a medical device holding company focusing on advancing neurological treatment technologies. The company develops, acquires & licenses noninvasive technologies that amplify the brain's ability to self-heal. NeuroHabilitation, a division of Helius, is developing its signature PoNS device that delivers translingual neurostimulation to alter the function of brain structures.
Dane C. Andreeff, Interim Chief Executive Officer
Joyce LaViscount, Chief Financial Officer & COO
Jonathan Sackier, Chief Medical Officer

Nanotech Security Corp.
#505, 3292 Production Way
Burnaby, BC V5A 4R4

604-678-5775
info@nanosecurity.ca
www.nanosecurity.ca
twitter.com/nts_corp
www.linkedin.com/company/nanotech-security-corp-

Company Type: Public
Ticker Symbol: NTS/TSX.V
Profile: A security technology development company.
Troy Bullock, President & CEO
Clint Landrock, Chief Technology Officer
Monika Russell, Chief Financial Officer

Novanta Inc.
125 Middlesex Turnpike
Bedford, MA 01730 USA

781-266-5700
800-342-3757
info@novanta.com
www.novanta.com
www.facebook.com/novantacorp
twitter.com/Novantainc
www.linkedin.com/company/novanta-inc

Company Type: Public
Ticker Symbol: NOVT/TSX, NASDAQ
Profile: Novanta supplies laser scanning devices & precision motion & optical control technologies. The company serves the medical, scientific, electronics & industrial markets.
Matthijs Glastra, Chief Executive Officer
Robert Buckley, Chief Financial Officer

Opsens Inc.
750, boul du Parc Technologique
Québec, QC G1P 4S3

418-781-0333
Fax: 418-781-0024
opsens.com
www.linkedin.com/company/opsens-inc
Company Type: Public
Ticker Symbol: OPS/TSX
Profile: Opsens is a fiber optic manufacturer. The company is divided into three streams: medical, energy & life science/industrial.
Louis Laflamme, President & CEO
Robin Villeneuve, Chief Financial Officer

POET Technologies Inc.
#1107, 120 Eglinton Ave. East
Toronto, ON M4P 1E2

416-368-9411
Fax: 416-322-5075
www.poet-technologies.com
twitter.com/poettech
www.linkedin.com/company/poet-technologies
Company Type: Public
Ticker Symbol: PTK/TSX.V
Profile: POET Technologies is the developer of an integrated circuit platform.
Suresh Venkatesan, Chief Executive Officer
Vivek Rajgarhia, President & General Manager
Vivek Rajgarhia, Executive Vice-President & Chief Financial Officer

Quarterhill Inc.
#1101, 25 King St. West
Kitchener, ON M5L 2A1

info@quarterhill.com
www.quarterhill.com
Other Communications: Investor Relations, Email:
ir@quarterhill.com
www.linkedin.com/company/quarterhill-inc
Company Type: Public
Ticker Symbol: QTRH/TSX, NASDAQ
Profile: Quarterhill is a technology innovation & licensing company whose patent portfolio applies to products in the communications & consumer electronics markets. Quarterhill was named in 2017 after WiLAN's acquisition of International Road Dynamics & VIZIYA.
Paul Hill, President & CEO
John Rim, Chief Financial Officer

Sangoma Technologies
#100, 100 Renfrew Dr.
Markham, ON L3R 9R6

905-474-1990
Fax: 905-474-9223
info@sangoma.com
www.sangoma.com
Other Communications: Investor Relations, Email:
investorrelations@sangoma.com
www.facebook.com/sangoma
twitter.com/sangoma
www.linkedin.com/company/sangoma
Company Type: Public
Ticker Symbol: STC/TSX
Profile: Founded in 1984, Sangoma is a hardware & software company that works with voice, data & video applications.
William Wignall, President & CEO
David Moore, Chief Financial Officer

Sierra Wireless, Inc.
13811 Wireless Way
Richmond, BC V6V 3A4

604-231-1100
Fax: 604-231-1109
www.sierrawireless.com
Other Communications: Investor Relations, Email:
investor@sierrawireless.com
www.facebook.com/sierrawireless
twitter.com/sierrawireless
www.linkedin.com/company/sierra-wireless
Company Type: Public
Ticker Symbol: SW/TSX; SWIR/NASDAQ
Staff Size: 1,000
Profile: Sierra Wireless, Inc. specializes in wireless solutions. It provides professional services to clients who require expertise in wireless design, integration & carrier certification.
Kent Thexton, President & CEO
Samuel Cochrane, Chief Financial Officer
Philippe Guillemette, Chief Technology Officer

Spectra7 Microsystems Ltd.
#500, 2550 North First Str.
San Jose, CA 95131 USA

408-770-2915
ir@spectra7.com
www.spectra7.com
Other Communications: Sales, Email: sales@spectra7.com
Company Type: Public
Ticker Symbol: SEV/TSX
Profile: Spectra7 is a manufacturer of ultra-thin 4K panels, HD displays & data centres.
Raouf Halim, Chief Executive Officer
Dave Mier, Chief Financial Officer

The Stars Group Inc.
South Tower
#3205, 200 Bay St.
Toronto, ON M5J 2J2

437-371-5742
www.starsgroup.com

Company Type: Public
Profile: The Stars Group provides a full suite of online gaming products & services including casino, poker, sportsbook, platform, lotteries & slot machines.

Titan Medical Inc.
#750, 155 University Ave.
Toronto, ON M5H 3B7

416-548-7522
info@titanmedicalinc.com
titanmedicalinc.com
Other Communications: Investor Relations, Email:
investors@titanmedicalinc.com
www.linkedin.com/company/titan-medical-inc
Company Type: Public
Ticker Symbol: TMD/TSX; TMDI/NASDAQ
Profile: Titan Medical Inc. is focused on the design, development & commercialization of robotic surgical technologies. Titan is currently developing the Enos system, a robotic surgical system.
David J. McNally, President & CEO
Monique L. Delorme, Chief Financial Officer

Vecima Networks Inc.
771 Vanalman Ave.
Victoria, BC V8Z 3B8

250-881-1982
Fax: 250-881-1974
vecima.com

Company Type: Public
Ticker Symbol: VCM/TSX
Profile: Vecima Networks Inc. is a designer, manufacturer & distributor of hardware products with embedded software that supports broadband access to cable, wireless & telephony networks. Principal markets include Broadband Wireless & Converged Wired Solutions.
Sumit Kumar, Chief Executive Officer
Dale Booth, Chief Financial Officer
Colin Howlett, Chief Technology Officer
Clay McCreery, Chief Operating Officer
Peter Torn, General Counsel & Corporate Secretary

Engineering & Management

Calian Group Ltd.
770 Palladium Dr.
Ottawa, ON K2V 1C8

613-599-8600
Fax: 613-599-8650
877-225-4264
info@calian.com
www.calian.com
Other Communications: Investor Relations, Email:
ir@calian.com
www.facebook.com/CalianGroup
twitter.com/caliangroup
www.linkedin.com/company/calian
Company Type: Public
Ticker Symbol: CGY/TSX
Staff Size: 4,400
Profile: Calian Group Ltd. is a consulting firm, focusing on the areas of IT, training, health & systems engineering, & manufacturing services.
Kevin Ford, Chief Executive Officer
Patrick Houston, Chief Financial Officer & Corporate Secretary
Seann Hamer, Chief Technology Officer
Jerry Johnston, Chief Information Officer

CGI Group Inc.
1350, boul René-Lévesque ouest, 15 étage
Montréal, QC H3G 1T4

514-841-3200
Fax: 514-841-3299
www.cgi.com
www.facebook.com/cgigroup
twitter.com/cgi_global
www.linkedin.com/company/cgi
Company Type: Public
Ticker Symbol: GIB.A/TSX; GIB/NYSE
Staff Size: 77,000
Profile: The information technology & business process services firm is engaged in the integration & customization of technologies & software applications, as well as the management of business processes & transactions.
George D. Schindler, President & CEO
Jean-Michel Baticle, President & COO, Canada
François Boulanger, Executive Vice-President & CFO
Julie Godin, Executive Vice-President, Strategic Planning & Corporate Development

Linamar Corporation
287 Speedvale Ave. West
Guelph, ON N1H 1C5

519-836-7550
Fax: 519-824-8479
www.linamar.com
www.facebook.com/linamarcorporation
twitter.com/linamarcorp
www.linkedin.com/company/linamar
Company Type: Public
Ticker Symbol: LNR/TSX
Staff Size: 25,800
Profile: Linamar Corporation develops, designs & produces highly engineered products. Their operating groups are as follows: Industrial, Commercial & Energy; Manufacturing; Skyjack; & Driveline Systems. The company supplies the global vehicle & mobile industrial equipment markets.
Linda Hasenfratz, Chief Executive Officer
Jim Jarrell, President & COO
Dale Schneider, Chief Financial Officer
Mark Stoddart, Chief Technology Officer & Executive Vice-President, Sales & Marketing

SNC-Lavalin Group Inc.
455, boul René-Lévesque ouest
Montréal, QC H2Z 1Z3

www.snclavalin.com
www.facebook.com/snclavalin
twitter.com/snclavalin
www.linkedin.com/company/snc-lavalin_2
Company Type: Public
Ticker Symbol: SNC/TSX
Staff Size: 37,500
Profile: The international engineering & construction organization owns infrastructure, & is engaged in the provision of operation & maintenance services. Examples of services include project financing, project management, procurement, engineering & construction. The group is involved in sectors such as pharmaceuticals, petroleum, agrifood, the environment, transit, power & mining. It plans to be net carbon zero by 2030.
Ian L. Edwards, President & CEO
Jeff Bell, Executive Vice-President & CFO

Stantec Inc.
#400, 10220 - 103rd Ave. NW
Edmonton, AB T5J 0K4

780-917-7000
www.stantec.com
Other Communications: Investor Relations, Email:
investor.relations@stantec.com
www.facebook.com/stantecinc
twitter.com/stantec
www.linkedin.com/company/stantec
Company Type: Public
Ticker Symbol: STN/TSX, NYSE
Staff Size: 22,000
Profile: Stantec Inc. offers professional consulting services for infrastructure & facilities projects in the areas of: planning, project management, project economics, surveying & geomatics, engineering, architecture, landscape architecture, environmental science & interior design.
Gord Johnston, President & CEO
Theresa Jang, Executive Vice-President & CFO
Stuart Lerner, Executive Vice-President & COO

WSP Global Inc.
1600, boul René Lévesque ouest, 11 étage
Montréal, QC H3H 1P9

www.wsp.com
www.facebook.com/WSPglobal
twitter.com/wsp
www.linkedin.com/company/wsp

Company Type: Public
Ticker Symbol: WSP/TSX
Staff Size: 36,000
Profile: WSP is a large engineering company that provides a full range of consulting services. Market segments include energy, environmental, municipal infrastructure, transportation, industrial & building.
Alexandre L'Heureux, President & CEO
Alain Michaud, Chief Financial Officer

Finance

Accord Financial Corp.
#602, 40 Eglinton Ave. East
Toronto, ON M4P 3A2

844-932-9940
financingcanada@accordfinancial.com
www.accordfinancial.com
www.facebook.com/accordfinancialcorp
twitter.com/accordfincorp
www.linkedin.com/company/accord-financial-corporation
Company Type: Public
Ticker Symbol: ACD/TSX
Profile: Through its subsidiaries, Accord Financial provides financial services to small & medium-sized businesses, including: record-keeping, financing, credit investigation, collection services & guarantees.
Simon Hitzig, President & CEO
Stuar Adair, Senior Vice-President & CFO

AGF Management Limited
Toronto Dominion Bank Tower
#3300, 66 Wellington St. West
Toronto, ON M5K 1E9

905-214-8203
Fax: 905-214-8243
800-268-8583
www.agf.com
Other Communications: Toll-Free Fax: 888-329-4243
www.facebook.com/agfinvestments
twitter.com/agf
www.linkedin.com/company/agf-managements
Company Type: Public
Ticker Symbol: AGF.B/TSX
Staff Size: 600
Profile: The independent investment management firm offers products such as mutual funds, pooled funds & mutual fund wrap programs. Assets are managed on behalf of institutional investors & private clients.
AGF Trust is a complementary business. It provides mortgages, loans & GICs through mortgage brokers & financial advisors.
Kevin McCreadie, Chief Executive Officer & Chief Investment Officer
Judy Goldring, President & Group Head, Global Distribution
Adrian Basaraba, Senior Vice-President & CFO
Chris Jackson, Chief Operating Officer

Alaris Equity Partners Income Trust
#250, 333 - 24th Ave. SW
Calgary, AB T2S 3E6

403-221-7302
businessdevelopment@alarisequity.com
www.alarisequitypartners.com
Other Communications: Investor Relations, Email:
ir@alarisequity.com
www.linkedin.com/company/alaris-equity-partners
Company Type: Public
Ticker Symbol: AD.UN/TSX
Profile: Alaris provides alternative financing for private businesses in North America.
Steve King, President & CEO
Darren Driscoll, Chief Financial Officer
Mike Ervin, Chief Legal Officer

Automotive Finco Corp.
#1800, 8 King St. East
Toronto, ON M5B 1C5

647-351-8870
ir@autofincorp.com
autofincocorp.com
Company Type: Public
Ticker Symbol: AFCC/TSX
Profile: Automotive Finco Corp. is a high growth specialty finance company focused on the auto retail sector. Through its investment in Automotive Finance LP, the company focuses on debt-based acquisition financing to auto dealerships in Canada & across the globe.
Kuldeep Billan, Chief Executive Officer
kbillan@autofincocorp.com

Aviva Canada Inc.
#100, 10 Aviva Way
Markham, ON L6G 0G1

800-387-4518
www.aviva.ca
www.facebook.com/AvivaCanada
twitter.com/AvivaCanada
www.linkedin.com/company/aviva-canada
Company Type: Public
Staff Size: 4,000
Profile: Aviva is a property & casualty insurance group providing coverage for homes, vehicles, business & more.
Jason Storah, Chief Executive Officer

Bank of Nova Scotia
Also Known As: Scotiabank
Scotia Plaza
44 King St. West
Toronto, ON M5H 1H1

416-866-6161
Fax: 416-866-3750
800-472-6842
investor.relations@scotiabank.com
www.scotiabank.com
Other Communications: Investor Relations, Email:
investor.relations@scotiabank.com
www.facebook.com/scotiabank
twitter.com/scotiabankhelps
www.linkedin.com/company/scotiabank
Company Type: Public
Ticker Symbol: BNS/TSX, NYSE
Staff Size: 89,800
Profile: Scotiabank's range of services include personal & commercial banking; corporate & investment banking services & products; & wealth management services. Scotiabank has approximately 24 million customers in over 50 countries.
Brian J. Porter, President & CEO
Ignacio "Nacho" Deschamps, Group Head, International Banking & Digital Transformation
Barbara Mason, Group Head & Chief Human Resources Officer

BMO Financial Group (BMO)
Also Known As: Bank of Montreal
First Canadian Place
100 King St. West
Toronto, ON M5X 1A1

416-867-6785
Fax: 416-867-6793
feedback@bmo.com
www.bmo.com
www.facebook.com/BMOcommunity
twitter.com/bmo
www.linkedin.com/company/bank-of-montreal
Company Type: Public
Ticker Symbol: BMO/TSX
Staff Size: 43,300
Profile: Established in 1817 as Bank of Montreal, BMO Financial Group offers a wide range of financial products & services, including retail banking, investment banking & wealth management.
Darryl White, Chief Executive Officer
Tayfun Tuzun, Chief Financial Officer

Builders Capital Mortgage
#260, 1414 - 8th St. SW
Calgary, AB T2R 1J6

403-685-9888
Fax: 403-225-9470
info@builderscapital.ca
builderscapital.ca
Company Type: Public
Ticker Symbol: BCF/TSX
Profile: A mortgage investment firm.
Sandy Loutitt, President & CEO
John Strangway, Chief Financial Officer

Canaccord Genuity Group Inc.
Pacific Centre
PO Box 10337, #2200, 609 Granville St.
Vancouver, BC V7Y 1H2

800-663-1899
investor.relations@canaccordgenuitygroup.
www.canaccordgenuity.com
Other Communications: Investor Relations, Phone:
416-869-7293
Company Type: Public
Ticker Symbol: CF/TSX
Staff Size: 2,000
Profile: Canaccord Genuity Group Inc. was established in 1950. It is an independent, full-service financial services firm. Through its subsidiaries, Canaccord Financial conducts operations in the areas of wealth management & global capital markets. There are over 60 Canaccord offices throughout the world.

Daniel Daviau, President & CEO
Pat Burke, President, Capital Markets

Canaccord Genuity Group Inc.
#3000, 161 Bay St.
Toronto, ON M5J 2S1

416-869-7293
investor.relations@cgf.com
www.canaccordgenuity.com
Company Type: Public
Ticker Symbol: CF/TSX
Profile: Founded in 1950, Canaccord Genuity Group Inc. is a global full-service financial services firm. It works primarily in wealth management & captial markets.
Dan Daviau, President & CEO

Canadian Imperial Bank of Commerce (CIBC)
Commerce Court
199 Bay St.
Toronto, ON M5L 1A2

416-980-2211
800-465-2422
www.cibc.com
Other Communications: French: 888-337-2422; Telex:
065-24116
www.facebook.com/CIBC
twitter.com/cibc
www.linkedin.com/company/cibc
Company Type: Public
Ticker Symbol: CM/TSX
Staff Size: 44,000
Profile: The Canadian Imperial Bank of Commerce was formed in 1961. CIBC provides financial products & services through its three business units: Retail & Business Banking, Wealth Management & Wholesale Banking. Customers include individuals & small business clients, plus corporate & institutional clients. CIBC has over 1,000 branches throughout Canada.
Victor Dodig, President & CEO
Hratch Panossian, Senior Executive Vice-President & CFO

Canadian Western Bank Group (CWB)
#3000, 10303 Jasper Ave.
Edmonton, AB T5J 3X6

780-423-8888
comments@cwbank.com
www.cwbankgroup.com
www.facebook.com/cwbcommunity
twitter.com/cwbcommunity
www.linkedin.com/company/canadian-western-bank
Company Type: Public
Ticker Symbol: CWB/TSX
Staff Size: 2,500
Profile: The federally chartered, Schedule I bank provides personal & commercial banking services across western Canada. Its subsidiaries offer both personal & corporate trust services, as well as personal home & automobile insurance.
Chris H. Fowler, President & CEO
Darrell Jones, Executive Vice-President & CIO
Bogie Ozdemir, Executive Vice-President & Chief Risk Officer
Matt Rudd, Executive Vice-President & CFO
Kelly Blackett, Executive Vice-President, Human Resources & Corporate Communications

Chesswood Group Limited
#603, 1133 Yonge St.
Toronto, ON M4T 2Y7

416-386-3099
Fax: 416-386-3085
info@chesswoodgroup.com
www.chesswoodgroup.com
Other Communications: Investors, Email:
investorrelations@chesswoodgroup.com
Company Type: Public
Ticker Symbol: CHW/TSX
Profile: The financial services company has operating businesses in Canada & the United States.
Barry W. Shafran, President & CEO
Tobias Rajchel, Vice-President, Finance

CI Financial Corp.
2 Queen St. East, 20th Fl.
Toronto, ON M5C 3G7

416-364-1145
800-268-9374
www.cifinancial.com
Company Type: Public
Ticker Symbol: CIX/TSX
Profile: CI Financial Corp. is a diversified wealth management firm & investment fund company. CI operates primarily through Assante Wealth Management (Canada) Ltd. & CI Investments Inc.
Kurt MacAlpine, Chief Executive Officer
Darie Urbanky, President & COO
Amit Muni, Executive Vice-President & Chief Financial Officer

Clairvest Group Inc.
Also Known As: Clairvest
#1700, 22 St Clair Ave. East
Toronto, ON M4T 2S3

416-925-9270
info@clairvest.com
www.clairvest.com
www.linkedin.com/company/clairvest-group-inc.
Company Type: Public
Ticker Symbol: CVG/TSX
Profile: Clairvest Group Inc. is a private equity management firm. The group invests its own capital & that of third parties in businesses with the potential to generate superior returns.
Ken Rotman, Chief Executive Officer & Managing Director
Michael Wagman, President & Managing Director

Clarke Inc.
#106, 145 Hobson's Lake Dr.
Halifax, NS B3S 0H9

902-442-3000
Fax: 416-640-1834
www.clarkeinc.com
Company Type: Public
Ticker Symbol: CKI/TSX
Profile: Clarke Inc. is an activist catalyst investment company, with several wholly-owned operating companies & divisions. The company has a diversified portfolio of investments. Their operating subsidiaries include: Clarke Transport Inc., Clarke Road Transport Inc., Clarke IT Solutions Inc., La Traverse Rivière-du-Loup - St. Siméon Ltée., CIS Shipping International Inc. & Granby Industries.
George Armoyan, President & CEO
Steve Cyr, Vice-President & CFO
scyr@clarkeinc.com
Paola Calce, Vice-President & General Counsel

Cliffside Capital
#200, 11 Church St.
Toronto, ON M5E 1W1

info@cliffsidecapital.ca
www.cliffsidecapital.ca
Company Type: Public
Ticker Symbol: CEP/TSX.V
Profile: The company invests capital in strategic partnerships.
Steve Malone, Chief Executive Officer
Praveen Gupta, Chief Financial Officer

Crown Capital Partners Inc.
#2730, 333 Bay St.
Toronto, ON M5H 2R2

416-640-6715
crowncapital.ca
www.linkedin.com/company/crowncapitalpartnersinc
Company Type: Public
Ticker Symbol: CRWN/TSX
Profile: Crown Capital is a specialty finance company focused on providing capital to middle-market companies that are unwilling or unable to obtain adequate financing from traditional providers.
Christopher A. Johnson, President & CEO
chris.johnson@crowncapital.ca
Brent G. Hughes, Executive Vice-President & Chief Compliance Officer
brent.hughes@crowncapital.ca
Tim Oldfield, Chief Investment Officer & Senior Vice-President
tim.oldfield@crowncapital.ca
Michael Overvelde, Chief Financial Officer & Senior Vice-President, Finance
michael.overvelde@crowncapital.ca

Diversified Royalty Corp.
PO Box 10033, #330, 609 Granville St.
Vancouver, BC V7Y 1A1

604-235-3146
Fax: 604-685-9970
www.diversifiedroyaltycorp.com
Company Type: Public
Ticker Symbol: DIV/TSX
Profile: Diversified Royalty Corp. acquires royalties from businesses & franchisors in North America.
Sean Morrison, President & CEO
sean@diversifiedroyaltycorp.com
Greg Gutmanis, Chief Financial Officer & Vice-President, Acquisitions
greg@diversifiedroyaltycorp.com

Element Fleet Management Corp.
#3600, 161 Bay St.
Toronto, ON M5J 2S1

416-386-1067
www.elementfleet.com
www.facebook.com/elementfleetmanagement
twitter.com/elementfleet
www.linkedin.com/company/element-fleet-management
Company Type: Public
Ticker Symbol: EFN/TSX
Staff Size: 2,500
Profile: Element Fleet Management is an independent equipment finance company specializing in equipment financing solutions for the end-users, distributors & manufacturers of a wide variety of capital equipment.
Jay Forbes, President & CEO
Vito Culmone, Executive Vice-President & CFO
Jim Halliday, Executive Vice-President & COO

EMX Royalty Corp.
#501, 543 Granville St.
Vancouver, BC V6C 1X8

604-688-6390
Fax: 604-688-1157
info@emxroyalty.com
www.emxroyalty.com
www.facebook.com/emxroyaltycorp
twitter.com/emxcorp
www.linkedin.com/company/emx-royalty-corporation
Company Type: Public
Ticker Symbol: EMX/TSX.V, NYSE
Profile: EMX generates royalties through low cost property acquisition & early-stage mineral exploration projects.
David M. Cole, President & CEO
Christina Cepeliauskas, Chief Administrative Officer
Douglas Reed, Chief Financial Officer

Equitable Group Inc.
Also Known As: Equitable Bank
Equitable Bank Tower
#700, 30 St Clair Ave. West
Toronto, ON M4V 3A1

416-515-7000
Fax: 416-515-7001
866-407-0004
customerservice@eqbank.ca
www.equitablebank.ca
Other Communications: Investors, Email:
investor_enquiry@equitablegroupinc.com
www.linkedin.com/company/equitable_bank
Company Type: Public
Ticker Symbol: EQB/TSX
Staff Size: 800
Profile: Through its wholly-owned subsidiary, The Equitable Bank, Equitable Group Inc. offers first mortgage financing & Guaranteed Investment Certificates to depositors. It was founded in 1970 as The Equitable Trust Company.
Andrew Moor, President & CEO
Chadwick Westlake, Senior Vice-President & CFO

Fiera Capital Inc.
#1500, 1981, av McGill College
Montréal, QC H3A 0H5

514-954-3300
Fax: 514-954-9692
800-361-3499
info@fieracapital.com
www.fieracapital.com
www.linkedin.com/company/fiera-capital
Company Type: Public
Ticker Symbol: FSZ/TSX
Staff Size: 800
Profile: Fiera is an independent, full-service, multi-product investment firm.
Jean-Guy Desjardins, Chair & Chief Executive Officer
Jean-Philippe Lemay, President & COO
Lucas Pontillo, Executive Vice-President & CFO

Firm Capital Mortgage Investment Corp. (FCMIC)
163 Cartwright Ave.
Toronto, ON M6A 1V5

416-635-0221
Fax: 416-635-1713
info@firmcapital.com
firmcapital.com
Other Communications: Investor Relations, Email:
ir@firmcapital.com
www.linkedin.com/company/firm-capital-corporation
Company Type: Public
Ticker Symbol: FC/TSX
Profile: Through its mortgage banker, Firm Capital Corporation, Firm Capital Mortgage Investment Trust is a non-bank lender. It provides residential & commercial real estate financing
Eli Dadouch, President & CEO
edadouch@firmcapital.com
Jonathan Mair, Executive Vice-President & COO
jmair@firmcapital.com
Sandy Poklar, Executive Vice-President, Interim CFO & Manging Director, Finance
spoklar@firmcapital.com

First National Financial LP
North Tower
#1200, 100 University Ave.
Toronto, ON M5J 1V6

416-593-1100
Fax: 800-465-0039
416-593-1900
customer@firstnational.ca
www.firstnational.ca
www.linkedin.com/company/first-national-financial-lp
Company Type: Public
Ticker Symbol: FN/TSX
Staff Size: 915
Profile: First National Financial LP is a non-bank mortgage originator that provides single-family & multi-unit residential & commercial mortgage solutions.
Stephen Smith, Chair, Chief Executive Officer & Co-Founder
Moray Tawse, Executive Vice-President & Co-Founder
Jason Ellis, President & COO
Robert Inglis, Chief Financial Officer

Gluskin Sheff + Associates Inc.
Bay Adelaide Centre
#5100, 333 Bay St.
Toronto, ON M5H 2R2

416-681-6000
Fax: 416-681-6060
866-681-6001
questions@gluskinsheff.com
www.gluskinsheff.com
twitter.com/gluskinsheffinc
www.linkedin.com/company/gluskin-sheff---associates
Company Type: Public
Ticker Symbol: GS/TSX
Staff Size: 125
Profile: Gluskin Sheff + Associates Inc. was formed in 1984. The independent, wealth management firm serves institutional investors & private clients of high net worth.
Jeff Moody, President & CEO

Guardian Capital Group Limited
Commerce Court West
PO Box 201, #3100, 199 Bay St.
Toronto, ON M5L 1E8

416-364-8341
Fax: 416-364-2067
800-253-9181
info@guardiancapital.com
www.guardiancapital.com
Company Type: Public
Ticker Symbol: GCG/TSX
Profile: Guardian Capital Group Limited is a diversified financial services company that was established in 1962. Through its businesses, Guardian Capital is involved in the distribution of mutual funds, institutional & high net worth investment management, as well as other financial services.
George Mavroudis, President & CEO
Matthew Turner, Senior Vice-President & Chief Compliance Officer
Donald Yi, Chief Financial Officer

Home Capital Group Inc.
#2300, 145 King St. West
Toronto, ON M5H 1J8

416-360-4663
Fax: 416-363-7611
800-990-7881
investor.relations@hometrust.ca
www.homecapital.com
www.facebook.com/hometrustco
twitter.com/hometrustco
Company Type: Public
Ticker Symbol: HCG/TSX
Staff Size: 750
Profile: Home Capital Group Inc. is a holding company that operates through its principal subsidiary, Home Trust Company. Home Trust offers deposit, mortgage lending, retail credit & credit card issuing services.
Yousry Bissada, President & CEO
Brad Kotush, Executive Vice-President & CFO
Victor DiRisio, Chief Information Officer
Mark Hemingway, General Counsel & Corporate Secretary

IGM Financial Inc.
One Canada Centre
447 Portage Ave.
Winnipeg, MB R3B 3H5

investor.relations@igmfinancial.com
www.igmfinancial.com
www.linkedin.com/company/igm-financial-services-inc
Company Type: Public
Ticker Symbol: IGM/TSX
Profile: IGM Financial Inc. is a managed asset, mutual fund & personal financial services company. Its operating units include

Investment Planning Counsel Inc., Mackenzie Investments, & IG Wealth Management. IGM is a member of the Power Financial Corporation group.
James O'Sullivan, President & CEO
Luke Gould, Executive Vice-President & CFO

IOU Financial Inc.
#100, 600 TownPark Lane
Kennesaw, GA 30144

866-217-8564
ioufinancial.com
www.facebook.com/ioufinancial
twitter.com/ioufinancial
www.linkedin.com/company/iou-financial-inc-
Company Type: Public
Ticker Symbol: IOU/TSX.V
Profile: IOU Financial is a money lending company.
Phil Marleau, Chief Executive Officer
Robert Gloer, President & COO
David Kennedy, Chief Financial Officer

Laurentian Bank of Canada/Banque Laurentienne du Canada
1360, boul René-Lévesque ouest
Montréal, QC H3G 0E7

800-525-1846
www.laurentianbank.ca
www.facebook.com/blaurentienne
twitter.com/blaurentienne
www.linkedin.com/company/banque-laurentienne
Company Type: Public
Ticker Symbol: LB/TSX
Staff Size: 3,000
Profile: Founded in 1846, Laurentian Bank of Canada has operations across the country. It serves both individuals & small & medium-sized businesses. The bank also offers services to independent financial intermediaries through B2B Trust. Laurentian Bank Securities provides full-service brokerage solutions.
Rania Llewellyn, President & CEO

LendingArch Financial Inc.
3553 - 31st St. NW
Calgary, AB T2L 2K7

hello@lendingarch.com
lendingarch.ca
www.facebook.com/lendingarch
www.linkedin.com/company/lendingarch
Company Type: Public
Profile: The company is a digital lending company offering credit cards, auto loans & personal loans.
Paul Hadzoglou, Chief Executive Officer

MCAN Mortgage Corporation
#600, 200 King St. West
Toronto, ON M5H 3T4

416-572-4880
Fax: 416-598-4142
855-213-6226
mcanexecutive@mcanmortgage.com
mcanmortgage.com
www.linkedin.com/company/mcan-mortgage-corporation
Company Type: Public
Ticker Symbol: MKP/TSX
Profile: MCAN Mortgage is an investment corporation that concentrates on a portfolio of mortgages, as well as other types of loans & investments, real estate & marketable securities.
Karen Weaver, President & CEO
Floriana Cipollone, Vice-President & CFO

Mogo Finance Technology Inc.
#2100, 401 West Georgia St.
Vancouver, BC V6B 5A1

604-659-4380
Fax: 604-733-4944
investors@mogo.ca
www.mogo.ca
www.facebook.com/mogomoney
twitter.com/mogomoney
Company Type: Public
Ticker Symbol: MOGO/TSX; MOGO/Nasdaq
Profile: Mogo Finance Technology produces financial products, including loans, mortgages, a Visa Debit card & credit score viewing.
David Feller, Founder, Chief Executive Officer & Chair
Gregory Feller, President & CFO

Mosaic Capital Corporation
#400, 2424 - 4th St. SW
Calgary, AB T2S 2T4

403-218-6500
info@mosaiccapitalcorp.com
mosaiccapitalcorp.com

Company Type: Public
Ticker Symbol: M/TSX.V
Staff Size: 1,150
Profile: Mosaic Capital was formed in May 2011 through a merger with Mosaic Diversified Income Fund & First West Properties Ltd. It owns a portfolio of established businesses.
Mark Gardhouse, President & CEO
Monty Balderston, Chief Financial Officer
Troy Pearce, Chief Operating Officer

National Bank Financial Group
Also Known As: National Bank of Canada
Tour de la Banque Nationale
600, rue de la Gauchetière ouest
Montréal, QC H3B 4L2

investorrelations@nbc.ca
www.nbc.ca
www.facebook.com/nationalbanknetworks
twitter.com/nationalbank
www.linkedin.com/company/national-bank-of-canada
Company Type: Public
Ticker Symbol: NA/TSX
Staff Size: 26,500
Profile: Chartered under the Bank Act of Canada, the National Bank provides comprehensive financial services, including retail, commercial, corporate, international & treasury banking services. Through its subsidiaries, National Bank Financial Group also offers security brokerage, insurance, wealth management, & mutual fund & retirement plan management. There are over 420 branches across Canada.
Louis Vachon, President & CEO
Ghislain Parent, Chief Financial Officer & Executive Vice-President, Finance & Treasury
Julie Lévesque, Executive Vice-President, Information Technology

New Pacific Metals Corp.
#1750, 1066 West Hastings St.
Vancouver, BC V6E 3X1

604-633-1368
Fax: 604-669-9387
info@newpacificmetals.com
newpacificmetals.com
www.linkedin.com/company/new-pacific-metals-corp
Company Type: Public
Ticker Symbol: NUAG/TSX
Profile: New Pacific Metals Corp. is a mining issuer focusing on exploring & developing precious metal properties in Bolivia, China & Canada. Its flagship project is the Silver Sand project in Bolivia.
Mark Cruise, Chief Executive Officer
Jalen Yuan, Chief Financial Officer
David Tingey, Vice-President, Sustainability
Alex Zhang, Vice-President, Exploration

Olympia Financial Group Inc.
#2300, 125 - 9th Ave. SE
Calgary, AB T2G 0P6

403-261-0900
Fax: 403-265-1455
inquiries@olympiafinancial.com
www.olympiafinancial.com
Company Type: Public
Ticker Symbol: OLY/TSX
Profile: Olympia Financial Group conducts most of its operations through its wholly-owned subsidiary Olympia Trust Company, a non-deposit taking trust company. The company has Foreign Exchange, Registered Plans & TFSA, Benefits & ATM divisions.
Rick Skauge, President
Gerhard Barnard, Chief Financial Officer & Vice-President, Financial Services

Partners Value Investments LP
Brookfield Place
#210, 181 Bay St.
Toronto, ON M5J 2T3

416-956-5142
ir@pvii.ca
www.pvii.ca
Company Type: Public
Ticker Symbol: PVF.UN/TSX
Profile: Partners Value Investments Inc. is a investment holding company whose primary investment is with Brookfield Asset Management Inc.
Brian D. Lawson, Chief Executive Officer
Bahir Manios, President
Leslie Yuen, Director, Finance

Pinetree Capital Ltd.
#200, 1965 Queen Street East
Toronto, ON M4L 1H9

416-941-9600
info@pinetreecapital.com
www.pinetreecapital.com
Company Type: Public
Ticker Symbol: PNP/TSX
Profile: Pinetree is a diversified investment, financial advisory & venture capital firm that is focused on investing in early stage micro & small cap companies.
Damien Leonard, Chief Executive Officer
dleonard@pinetreecapital.com
John Bouffard, Chief Financial Officer

Power Financial Corporation
751, carré Victoria
Montréal, QC H2Y 2J3

514-286-7430
800-890-7440
www.powerfinancial.com
www.linkedin.com/company/power-financial-corporation
Company Type: Public
Ticker Symbol: PWF/TSX
Staff Size: 28,400
Profile: A diversified holding & management company that was founded in 1940. It includes the following subsidiaries: IGM Financial Inc., Great-West Lifeco Inc. & Pargesa.
R. Jeffrey Orr, President & CEO
Greogry D. Tretiak, Executive Vice-President & CFO

RF Capital Group Inc.
#200, 145 King St. West
Toronto, ON M5H 1J8

416-687-1300
Other Communications: Investor Relations, Email: investorrelations@gmpcapital.com
Company Type: Public
Ticker Symbol: RCG/TSX
Staff Size: 300
Profile: GMP Capital Inc. is a Canadian independent investment dealer. Through its subsidiaries, GMP Capital is involved in the investment areas of: alternative investments, capital markets & wealth management. Individual, corporate & institutional investor clients are served.
Kish Kapoor, President & CEO
Tim Wilson, Chief Financial Officer

Rifco Inc.
Millenium Centre
#702, 4909 - 49th St.
Red Deer, AB T4N 1V1

403-314-1288
Fax: 403-314-1132
888-303-2001
info@rifco.net
www.rifco.net
twitter.com/rifconation
www.linkedin.com/company/rifco-auto-finance
Company Type: Public
Ticker Symbol: RFC/TSX
Staff Size: 100
Profile: Rifco Inc. is an auto purchase finance company providing motorists with non-traditional financing operating in all provinces, except Saskatchewan & Quebec.
Jeffrey Newhouse, Chief Executive Officer
Warren Van Orman, Chief Financial Officer

Royal Bank of Canada (RBC)
Royal Bank Plaza
PO Box 1, 200 Bay St., 13th Fl.
Toronto, ON M5J 2J5

416-974-5151
Fax: 416-955-7800
888-212-5533
www.rbc.com
www.facebook.com/rbc
twitter.com/RBC
www.linkedin.com/company/rbc
Company Type: Public
Ticker Symbol: RY/TSX, NYSE
Staff Size: 86,000
Profile: The Royal Bank of Canada is engaged in the following services: personal & commercial banking; corporate & investment banking; insurance; wealth management; & transaction processing services. Offices are located in Canada, the United States, & 51 other countries.
David I. McKay, President & CEO
Rod Bolger, Chief Financial Officer
Helena Gottschling, Chief Human Resources Officer
Doug Guzman, Group Head, RBC Wealth Management & RBC Insurance

Sprott Inc.
South Tower, Royal Bank Plaza
#2600, 200 Bay St.
Toronto, ON M5J 2J1

416-943-8099
855-943-8099
invest@sprott.com
sprott.com
Other Communications: Investor Relations, Email: ir@sprott.com
twitter.com/sprott
www.linkedin.com/company/sprott
Company Type: Public
Ticker Symbol: SII/TSX
Profile: Sprott Inc. is an alternative asset management firm, specializing in precious metal & real asset investments. The company operates through its four business units: Sprott Asset Management L.P., Sprott Private Wealth L.P., Sprott Consulting L.P., & Sprott U.S. Holdings Inc.
As of August 2017, the management of most of Sprott mutual & hedge funds was taken over by SPR & Co L.P.
Peter Grosskopf, Chief Executive Officer
Whitney George, President
Kevin Hibbert, Chief Financial Officer & Senior Managing Director

TMX Group Inc.
#300, 100 Adelaide St. West
Toronto, ON M5H 1S3

416-947-4700
Fax: 416-947-4662
888-873-8392
info@tmx.com
www.tmx.com
Other Communications: Investor Relations, Phone:
416-947-4277
www.facebook.com/thetmxgroup
twitter.com/tmxgroup
www.linkedin.com/company/tmx-group
Company Type: Public
Ticker Symbol: X/TSX
Staff Size: 1,400
Profile: TMX Group is headquartered in Toronto, & has offices in: Montréal, Calgary, Vancouver, New York, London, Singapore & Beijing.
The following are key TMX Group companies: Toronto Stock Exchange, TSX Venture Exchange, TMX Trust, TSX Alpha Exchage, Montreal Exchange, Canadian Derivatives Clearing Corporation, TMX Datalinx, TMX Insights, Shorcan & Trayport. These companies offer listing markets, trading markets, clearing facilities, data products, plus other services to the financial sector around the globe.
John McKenzie, Chief Executive Officer
Luc Fortin, President & CEO, Montréal Exchange

Toronto-Dominion Bank
Also Known As: TD Bank Group
Toronto-Dominion Centre
PO Box 1, #15, 66 Wellington St. West
Toronto, ON M5K 1A1

tdshinfo@td.com
www.td.com
www.facebook.com/TDCanada
twitter.com/td_canada
www.linkedin.com/company/td
Company Type: Public
Ticker Symbol: TD/TSX
Staff Size: 85,000
Profile: The Toronto-Dominion Bank & its subsidiaries are known collectively as TD Bank Group. The Group's four key businesses are: Canadian Personal & Commercial Banking; Wealth & Insurance; U.S. Personal & Commercial Banking; & Wholesale Banking. TD has over 26 million customers worldwide.
Bharat Masrani, Group President & CEO
Riaz Ahmed, Group Head & Chief Financial Officer
Ajai Bambawale, Group Head & Chief Risk Officer

Tricon Residential Inc.
#801, 7 St Thomas St.
Toronto, ON M5S 2B7

416-925-7228
Fax: 416-925-7964
triconresidential.com
www.facebook.com/TriconResidential.Home
www.linkedin.com/company/tricon-residential
Company Type: Public
Ticker Symbol: TCN/TSX
Profile: Founded in 1988, the company is a rental housing company. It owns over 31,000 single- & multi-family rental homes in North America.
Gary Berman, President & CEO
Wissam Francis, Executive Vice-President & CFO

VersaBank
#2002, 140 Fullerton St.
London, ON N6A 5P2

519-645-1919
Fax: 519-645-2060
866-979-1919
www.versabank.com
www.facebook.com/VersaBank
twitter.com/versabank
www.linkedin.com/company/versabank
Company Type: Public
Ticker Symbol: VB/TSX
Profile: VersaBank is a Schedule I chartered bank, & is a "branchless" commerical bank.
David R. Taylor, President & CEO

Wilmington Capital Management Inc.
#700, 505 - 3rd St. SW
Calgary, AB T2P 3E6

403-705-8038
Fax: 403-705-8035
www.wilmingtoncapital.com
Company Type: Public
Ticker Symbol: WCM.A, WCM.B/TSX
Profile: Wilmington capital Management is a Candian investment & asset management company focused on investments in the real estate & energy sectors.
Christopher Killi, Managing Partner & Chief Executive Officer
Patrick Craddock, Managing Partner & Vice-President, Finance
Alex Powell, Corporate Secretary

Food, Beverages & Tobacco

A&W Revenue Royalties Income Fund
#300, 171 West Esplanade
North Vancouver, BC V7M 3K9

604-988-2141
Fax: 604-988-5531
investorrelations@aw.ca
www.awincomefund.ca
Company Type: Public
Ticker Symbol: AW.UN/TSX
Profile: A&W Revenue Royalties Income Fund is a limited purpose trust. It invests in A&W Trade Marks Inc., which owns the trade-marks used in the A&W restaurant business in Canada. Through its subsidiary, A&W Trade Marks Inc., A&W Revenue Royalties licences trade-marks for royalty income.
Susan Senecal, President & CEO
Kelly Blankstein, Chief Financial Officer
Don Leslie, Executive Vice-President

Andrew Peller Limited/Andrew Peller Limitée
697 South Service Rd.
Grimsby, ON L3M 4E8

905-643-4131
Fax: 905-643-4944
info@andrewpeller.com
www.andrewpeller.com
Company Type: Public
Ticker Symbol: ADW.A, ADW.B/TSX
Profile: Andrew Peller Limited has wineries in Nova Scotia, Ontario & British Columbia, & also imports wine. The company's wine agencies are Grady Wine Marketing Inc. in British Columbia & The Small Winemaker's Collection Inc. in Ontario. Andrew Peller also owns & operates more than 100 retail locations. Store names include Aisle 43, WineCountry Vintners & Vineyards Estate Wines.
Through its wholly owned subsidiary, Global Vintners Inc., Andrew Peller also produces & markets personal winemaking products.
John E. Peller, President & CEO
Steve Attridge, Chief Financial Officer & Executive Vice-President, IT
Brendan P. Wall, Executive Vice-President, Operations

Big Rock Brewery Inc.
5555 - 76th Ave. SE
Calgary, AB T2C 4L8

403-720-3239
Fax: 403-236-7523
800-242-3107
reception@bigrockbeer.com
bigrockbeer.com
www.facebook.com/bigrockbrewery
twitter.com/bigrockbrewery
Company Type: Public
Ticker Symbol: BR/TSX
Profile: Big Rock Brewery is a brewer whose products are marketed throughout Canada (excluding Quebec).
Wayne Arsenault, President & CEO
Don Sewell, Chief Financial Officer

BioNeutra North America Inc.
9608 - 25th Ave. NW
Edmonton, AB T6N 1J4

780-466-1481
Fax: 780-801-0036
bioneutra.ca
www.facebook.com/BioNeutra
twitter.com/bioneutra
www.linkedin.com/company/bioneutra
Company Type: Public
Ticker Symbol: BGA/TSX
Profile: BioNeutra is a prebiotic & fiber ingredient manufacturer.
Jianhua Zhu, President & CEO
Branko Jankovic, CPA, CA, Chief Financial Officer

Boston Pizza Royalties Income Fund
#100, 10760 Shellbridge Way
Richmond, BC V6X 3H1

604-207-1108
Fax: 604-270-4168
investorrelations@bostonpizza.com
bpincomefund.com
Company Type: Public
Ticker Symbol: BPF.UN/TSX
Profile: Boston Pizza Royalties Income Fund is a limited purpose open-ended trust. There are over 387 stores in the Royalty Pool. Units are traded on the Toronto Stock Exchange. Boston Pizza Royalties Income Fund pays unitholders a monthly distribution.
Jordan Holm, President
Michael E. Harbinson, Chief Financial Officer

Clearwater Seafoods Incorporated
757 Bedford Hwy.
Bedford, NS B4A 3Z7

902-443-0550
Fax: 902-443-8365
investorinquiries@clearwater.ca
www.clearwater.ca
www.facebook.com/clearwaterseafood
twitter.com/clearwatersea
www.linkedin.com/company/clearwater-seafoods-lp
Company Type: Public
Ticker Symbol: CLR/TSX
Staff Size: 2,500
Profile: Clearwater Seafoods supplies wild, eco-labelled seafood, including lobster, clams, scallops, crab, groundfish & coldwater shrimp. Biologists are employed to ensure innovative & sustainable fishing practices. The company has been in business since 1976.
Ian D. Smith, Chief Executive Officer
Teresa Fortney, Chief Financial Officer & Vice-President, Finance

Corby Spirit & Wine Limited
#1100, 225 King St. West
Toronto, ON M5V 3M2

416-479-2400
investors.corby@pernod-ricard.com
corby.ca
twitter.com/corbysw
www.linkedin.com/company/corbysw
Company Type: Public
Ticker Symbol: CSW.A, CSW.B/TSX
Staff Size: 184
Profile: Corby Spirit & Wine is a marketer of distilled spirits, whiskies & liqueurs produced in Canada. The also market imported wines, gin, cognac, scotch, & liqueurs. Its domestic brands include: Wiser's Canadian whiskies & Seagram Coolers; & its international brands include: Jameson Irish whiskey & Wyndham Estate wines, through its affiliation with Pernod Ricard.
Nicolas Krantz, President & CEO
Edward Mayle, Vice-President & CFO
Marc Valencia, General Counsel, Corporate Secretary & Vice-President, Public Affairs

Diamond Estates Wines & Spirits
1067 Niagara Stone Rd.
Niagara-on-the-Lake, ON L0S 1J0

905-685-5673
www.lakeviewwineco.com
www.facebook.com/LakeviewWineCo
twitter.com/LakeviewWineCo
Company Type: Private
Ticker Symbol: DWS/TSX.V
Profile: Diamond Estates Wines and Spirits produces VQA Ontario wines under the brands Lakeview Cellars, EastDell Estates, 20 Bees, FRESH wines & 1914 wines. The vineyard is located in Niagara-on-the-Lake, Ontario.
J. Murray Souter, President & CEO
Thomas Green, Vice-President, Winemaking & Winery Operations

Empire Company Limited
115 King St.
Stellarton, NS B0K 1S0

902-752-8371
Fax: 902-755-6477
www.empireco.ca

Company Type: Public
Ticker Symbol: EMP.A/TSX
Staff Size: 127,000
Profile: The Empire Company Limited is engaged in food retailing, through its majority ownership of Sobeys Inc. Through wholly-owned companies, Empire Company is also involved in real estate.
Michael Medline, President & CEO
Michael Vels, Executive Vice-President & CFO

Freshii Inc.
#101, 1055 Yonge St.
Toronto, ON M4W 2L2

866-337-4265
ir@freshii.com
freshii.inc
Other Communications: Investor Relations, Email:
ir@freshii.com
www.facebook.com/freshii
twitter.com/freshii

Company Type: Public
Ticker Symbol: FRII/TSX
Profile: Freshii is a fast casual restaurant franchise that serves burritos, wraps, bowls, salads & soups.
Matthew Corrin, Founder, Chair & Chief Executive Officer
Adam Corrin, Chief Operating Officer
Paul Hughes, Chief Business Development Officer & General Counsel

George Weston Limited
#700, 22 St Clair Ave. East
Toronto, ON M4T 2S7

416-922-2500
Fax: 416-922-4395
investor@weston.ca
www.weston.ca

Company Type: Public
Ticker Symbol: WN/TSX
Staff Size: 225,000
Profile: George Weston Limited consists of Weston Foods & Loblaws, of which Shoppers Drug Mart is a subsidiary. Weston Foods is involved in the baking & dairy industries. Operated by Loblaw Companies Limited, Loblaws is engaged in food distribution. Loblaws also offers drug store merchandise & general merchandise, as well as financial products & services.
Galen Weston, Chair & Chief Executive Officer
Richard Dufresne, President & CFO
Gordon A.M. Currie, Executive Vice-President & Chief Legal Officer
Rashid Wasti, Executive Vice-President & Chief Talent Officer
Khush Dadyburjor, Chief Strategy Officer

GLG Life Tech Corporation
#100, 10271 Shellbridge Way
Richmond, BC V6X 2W8

604-285-2602
Fax: 604-285-2606
855-454-7587
info@glglifetech.com
www.glglifetech.com
Other Communications: Investor Relations, Email:
ir@glglifetech.com
www.linkedin.com/company/glg-life-tech

Company Type: Public
Ticker Symbol: GLG/TSX; GLGL/NASDAQ
Profile: GLG Life Tech Corporation is a supplier of stevia extracts, a sweetener used in food & beverages. Through its subsidiary, ANOC, GLG Life Tech Corporation markets stevia sweetened beverages & foods to serve the Chinese market.
Luke Zhang, Chair & Chief Executive Officer
Simon Springett, Chief Operating Officer

Goodfood Market Corp.
#4600, rue Hickmore
Montréal, QC H4T 1K2

855-515-5191
chef@makegoodfood.ca
www.makegoodfood.ca
Other Communications: Investor Relations, Email:
ir@makegoodfood.ca
www.facebook.com/goodfoodca
www.linkedin.com/company/goodfood-market

Company Type: Public
Ticker Symbol: FOOD/TSX
Staff Size: 3,100
Profile: Goodfood is an online grocery company that delivers meal solutions & grocery items to customers. It has facilities

located in Québec, Ontario, Alberta & British Columbia. As of 2021, it has over 300,000 subscribers.
Jonathan Ferrari, Chair & Chief Executive Officer
Neil Cuggy, President & COO
Philippe Adam, Chief Financial Officer

GreenSpace Brands
176 St George St.
Toronto, ON M5R 2M7

416-934-5034
www.greenspacebrands.ca

Company Type: Public
Ticker Symbol: JTR/TSX.V
Profile: GreenSpace Brands is in the business of food items, offering dairy products, meat, yogurt & other commodities.
Shawn R. Warren, President & CEO
Justin Guerin, Chief Financial Officer

High Liner Foods Incorporated
PO Box 910, 100 Battery Point
Lunenburg, NS B0J 2C0

902-634-8811
Fax: 902-634-6228
info@highlinerfoods.com
www.highlinerfoods.com
Other Communications: Investor Relations, Email:
investor@highlinerfoods.com
www.linkedin.com/company/high-liner-foods

Company Type: Public
Ticker Symbol: HLF/TSX
Staff Size: 1,100
Profile: High Liner Foods Incorporated specializes in processing & marketing prepared, frozen seafood products. Products are marketed under the following brands: High Liner, Sea Cuisine, Fisher Boy, Royal Sea & Mirabel.
High Liner also sells FPI, Icelandic Seafood, Viking, Samband of Iceland, Seaside & Seastar products to restaurants & institutions. In 2010, the company purchased the American based assets of Viking Seafoods, Inc., & in 2011 Icelandic USA, Inc. & subsidiaries of Icelandic Group hf were also purchased. High Liner Foods Incorporated serves the retail & food service markets throughout Canada, the United States & Mexico.
Rod Hepponstall, President & CEO
Paul A. Jewer, Executive Vice-President & CFO

Keg Royalties Income Fund
10100 Shellbridge Way
Richmond, BC V6X 2W7

416-646-4960
info@kegincomefund.com
www.kegincomefund.com
www.facebook.com/thekegsteakhouseandbar
twitter.com/thekeg
www.linkedin.com/company/the-keg-steakhouse-and-bar

Company Type: Public
Ticker Symbol: KEG.UN/TSX
Profile: The Keg Royalties Income Fund is an unincorporated open-ended, limited purpose trust. The Fund is the owner of The Keg Rights LP, which owns the trademarks, names & other intellectual property used by The Keg Steakhouse + Bar restaurants. The Keg Royalties Income Fund licenses Keg Restaurants Ltd. to use these rights.
David Aisenstat, Chief Executive Officer
Nick Dean, President
Neil Maclean, Executive Vice-President & CFO

Lassonde Industries Inc./Industries Lassonde inc.
755, rue Principale
Rougemont, QC J0L 1M0

866-552-7643
www.lassonde.com
www.facebook.com/IndustriesLassonde
twitter.com/lassondeinc
www.linkedin.com/company/lassonde

Company Type: Public
Ticker Symbol: LAS.A/TSX
Staff Size: 2,700
Profile: Through its subsidiaries, Lassonde Industries develops, manufactures, packages & markets food products. Products include: fruit juices, fruit beverages, canned corn, baked beans, barbecue sauces, dipping sauces, pasta sauces, meat marinades, bruschetta topping, tapenades & fondue bouillon.
Nathalie Lassonde, Chief Executive Officer
Jean Gattuso, President & COO
Eric Gemme, Chief Financial Officer
Caroline Lemoine, Chief Legal Officer & Secretary
Mathieu Simard, Chief Human Resources Officer

Loblaw Companies Limited
1 President's Choice Circle
Brampton, ON L6Y 5S5

800-564-6253
customerservice@loblaws.ca
www.loblaw.ca
www.facebook.com/loblawcompanieslimited
twitter.com/loblawco
www.linkedin.com/company/loblaw-companies-limited

Company Type: Public
Ticker Symbol: L/TSX
Staff Size: 190,000
Profile: Formed in 1956, Loblaw Companies Limited is a food distributor, as weell as a provider of general merchandise, drug store & financial products, & services. The company operates the following grocery stores: Loblaws, The Real Canadian Superstore, Atlantic Superstore, Extra Foods, Independent, No Frills, Valu-mart, Provigo, Wholesale Club, Zehrs, Club Entrepôt, Cash & Carry & Maxi. As of March 2014, Shoppers Drug Mart is a subsidiary of Loblaw.
Galen G. Weston, Chair & President
Jocyanne Bourdeau, President, Discount Division
Ian Freedman, President, Joe Fresh
Jeff Leger, President, Shoppers Drug Mart
Greg Ramier, President, Market Division
Richard Dufresne, Chief Financial Officer

Maple Leaf Foods Inc.
6985 Financial Dr.
Mississauga, ON L5N 0A1

905-285-5898
800-268-3708
investor.relations@mapleleaf.com
www.mapleleaffoods.com
Other Communications: Sustainability, Email:
sustainability@mapleleaf.com

Company Type: Public
Ticker Symbol: MFI/TSX
Staff Size: 13,500
Profile: Maple Leaf Foods' products include fresh & prepared meats, poultry, seafood, fresh & frozen bakery goods, & animal feed. Brands include Maple Leaf, Maple Leaf Prime Naturally, Schneiders, Olivieri, POM, Shopsy's, Mitchell's Gourmet Foods, Ben's, Bon Matin, Burns, Hygrade, Chevalier, New York Bakery & Dempsters. Products are sold to wholesale, retail & industrial customers around the world. Maple Leaf Foods has operations in Canada, the United States, Mexico, the United Kingdom & Asia.
Michael H. McCain, President & CEO
Curtis Frank, President & COO
Randall Huffman, Chief Food Safety & Sustainability Officer
Andreas Liris, Chief Information Officer
Geert Verellen, Chief Financial Officer

Metro Inc.
11011, boul Maurice-Duplessis
Montréal, QC H1C 1V6

514-643-1000
800-361-4681
corpo.metro.ca
www.linkedin.com/company/metro-inc

Company Type: Public
Ticker Symbol: MRU/TSX
Staff Size: 90,000
Profile: Metro Inc. operates a chain of 950 food retail stores in Ontario & Québec, under the following banners: Metro, Metro Plus, Super C & Food Basics. The company also distributes pharmaceutical products under the following banners: Brunet, Jesn Coutu, Metro Pharmacy & Drug Basics.
Eric R. La Flèche, President & CEO
François Thibault, Executive Vice-President & CFO

MTY Food Group Inc./Le Groupe MTY
8210, rte Transcanadienne
Montréal, QC H4S 1M5

514-336-8885
Fax: 514-336-9222
866-891-6633
info@mtygroup.com
mtygroup.com

Company Type: Public
Ticker Symbol: MTY/TSX
Profile: MTY Food Group is an operator & franchisor of quick service restaurants. Examples of brands include Cultures, Country Style, Jugo Juice, Mr. Sub, Vanellis, Thai Express & Timothy's Coffee.
Eric Lefebvre, Chief Executive Officer

North West Company Inc.
77 Main St.
Winnipeg, MB R3C 2R1

204-943-0881
nwc@northwest.ca
www.northwest.ca
www.facebook.com/thenorthwestcompany
www.linkedin.com/company/the-north-west-company
Company Type: Public
Ticker Symbol: NWC/TSX
Staff Size: 6,900
Profile: Through its subsidiaries, The North West Company is engaged in the retail of food & daily products & services to rural communities & urban neighbourhoods. Areas of operations include Canada, Alaska, the Caribbean & the South Pacific.
Edward S. Kennedy, President & CEO
Daniel G. McConnell, President, International Retail
John D. King, Executive Vice-President & CFO
Steve Boily, Vice-President, Information Services

Pizza Pizza Royalty Corp. (PPRC)
500 Kipling Ave.
Toronto, ON M8Z 5E5

416-967-1010
feedback@pizzapizza.ca
www.pizzapizza.ca
Company Type: Public
Ticker Symbol: PZA/TSX
Profile: Established in 2005, Pizza Pizza Royalty Corp. is a limited purpose, open-ended trust. The Fund acquired trademarks & trade names used by Pizza Pizza Limited in its restaurants. There are 725 Pizza Pizza & Pizza Pizza 73 restaurants in the royalty pool.
Paul Goddard, President & CEO
Christine D'Sylva, Chief Financial Officer

Premium Brands Holdings Corporation
#100, 10991 Shellbridge Way
Richmond, BC V6X 3C6

604-656-3100
Fax: 604-656-3170
855-756-3100
investor@premiumbrandsgroup.com
www.premiumbrandsholdings.com
Company Type: Public
Ticker Symbol: PBH/TSX
Staff Size: 8,700
Profile: Premium Brands Holdings owns specialty food businesses with manufacturing & distribution facilities. The corporation also owns proprietary food distribution & wholesale networks. Facilities are located in Quebec, Ontario, Manitoba, Saskatchewan, Alberta, British Columbia & Washington. Some of Premium Brands' businesses include: Harvest, Hempler's, Piller's, Grimm's, McSweeney's, Deli Chef, Hygaard, Audrey's Patisserie, Oberto & Buddy's.
George Paleologou, President & CEO
Will Kalutycz, Chief Financial Officer
Douglas Goss, Q.C., General Counsel & Corporate Secretary

Primo Water Corporation
#400, 4221 West Boy Scout Blvd.
Tampa, FL 33607

primowatercorp.com
Other Communications: Investor Relations, Email:
investorrelations@primowater.com
Company Type: Public
Ticker Symbol: PRMW/TSX, NYSE
Staff Size: 8,880
Profile: A beverage company that focuses upon private-label products & contract manufacturing.
Thomas Harrington, Chief Executive Officer
Marni Morgan Poe, Chief Legal Officer
Jay Wells, Chief Financial Officer

Radient Technologies
8223 Roper Rd.
Edmonton, AB T6E 6S4

780-465-1318
www.radientinc.com
twitter.com/radientinc
www.linkedin.com/company/radient-technologies-inc.
Company Type: Public
Ticker Symbol: RTI/TSX.V;RDDTF/OTCQX
Profile: The company is in the business of micro-wave assisted extraction of various products including rosemary, grapes, senna, algae oil and cubebol.
Harry Kaura, Chief Executive Officer
Prakash Hariharan, Chief Financial Officer
Steven Splinter, Chief Technology Officer

Recipe Unlimited Corporation
199 Four Valley Dr.
Vaughan, ON L4K 0B8

905-760-2244
844-332-1022
investorrelations@recipeunlimited.com
www.recipeunlimited.com
www.linkedin.com/company/recipe-unlimited-corporation
Company Type: Public
Ticker Symbol: RECP/TSX
Staff Size: 9,000
Profile: Recipe Unlimited is the parent company of Swiss Chalet, East Side Mario's, Milestones, Casey's, Montana's, Bier Markt, Kelsey's, Prime Pubs, Harvey's, New York Fries & The Landing Group.
Frank Hennessey, Chief Executive Officer
Ken Grondin, Chief Financial Officer

Restaurant Brands International Inc. (RBI)
130 King Street West
Toronto, ON M5X 1E1

www.rbi.com
Company Type: Public
Ticker Symbol: QSR/TSX
Profile: Restaurant Brands International was created in 2014, after the merger between Tim Hortons & Burger King. The company operates over 27,000 restaurants in over 100 countries. Tim Hortons & Burger King continue to operate independently. In February 2017, the company also bought fried chicken chain Popeyes.
José Cil, Chief Executive Officer
Matthew Dunnigan, Chief Financial Officer
Joshua Kobza, Chief Operating Officer

Rogers Sugar Inc.
4026, rue Notre-Dame est
Montréal, QC H1W 2K3

514-527-8686
csr@lantic.ca
www.lanticrogers.com
Other Communications: Investor Relations, Email:
investors@lantic.ca
Company Type: Public
Ticker Symbol: RSI/TSX
Staff Size: 680
Profile: In 2008, Rogers Sugar Ltd. merged with Lantic Sugar Limited to create Lantic Inc.
In 2011, Rogers Sugar Income Fund converted into a conventional corporation named Rogers Sugar Inc. The successor to Rogers Sugar Income Fund now owns all of the outstanding shares of Lantic Inc., plus the subordinated Lantic notes.
Lantic Inc. uses both the Lantic & Rogers trademarks. Lantic Inc. is engaged in the refining, processing, distributing & marketing of sugar products, such as granulated sugar, sugar cubes, icing sugar, yellow & brown sugars, liquid sugars, specialty sugars & syrups.
John Holliday, President & CEO
Manon Lacroix, Chief Financial Officer & Vice-President, Finance

Saputo Inc.
6869, boul Métropolitain est
Montréal, QC H1P 1X8

514-328-6662
www.saputo.com
www.linkedin.com/company/saputo
Company Type: Public
Ticker Symbol: SAP/TSX
Staff Size: 17,300
Profile: Saputo Inc. is engaged in the production, commercialization & distribution of dairy products & grocery products. The company's brands include: Saputo, Armstrong, La Paulina, Cracker Barrel, Dairyland, Devondale, Neilson, Nutrilait, Scotsburn, Stella, Sungold, Treasure Cave & others. Production facilities are situated in five countries.
Lino A. Saputo, Chair & Chief Executive Officer
Kai Bockmann, President & COO, Company & International Sector
Maxime Therrien, Chief Financial Officer
Gaétane Wagner, Chief Human Resources Officer

Second Cup Ltd.
#630, 5915 Airport Rd.
Mississauga, ON L4V 1T1

Fax: 905-362-1121
855-379-3388
investor@secondcup.com
www.secondcup.com
www.facebook.com/secondcup
twitter.com/secondcup
Company Type: Public
Ticker Symbol: SCU/TSX
Profile: In 2011, the Second Cup Income Fund converted from an income trust structure to a public corporation. Second Cup Ltd. is a large specialty coffee franchisor. It operates 216 cafés throughout Canada.
Steve Pelton, Chief Executive Officer
Ba Linh Le, Chief Financial Officer

SIR Royalty Income Fund
#200, 5360 South Service Rd.
Burlington, ON L7L 5L1

905-681-2997
Fax: 905-681-0394
info@sircorp.com
www.sircorp.com
Other Communications: Investor Relations, Email:
ir@sircorp.com
www.linkedin.com/company/sir-corp
Company Type: Public
Ticker Symbol: SRV.UN/TSX
Profile: Trademarks related to SIR Corp.'s restaurant brands are used under a license agreement with SIR Royalty Limited Partnership. SIR Royalty Income Fund has an investment in SIR Royalty Limited Partnership. The Fund receives distribution income from this investment.
SIR Corp.'s restaurant brands include Jack Astor's Bar & Grill, Canyon Creek Chop House, Scaddabush, REDS & Loose Moose Tap & Grill.
Peter Fowler, Chief Executive Officer
Jeff Good, Chief Financial Officer
Paul J. Bognar, President & Chief Operating Officer

Sportscene Group Inc./Groupe Sportscene inc.
#102, 1180, Place Nobel
Boucherville, QC J4B 5L2

450-641-3011
Fax: 450-641-9742
800-413-2243
sports@cage.ca
www.cage.ca
www.facebook.com/lacagebrasseriesportive
twitter.com/_lacage
Company Type: Public
Ticker Symbol: SPS.A/TSX.V
Profile: Sportscene Group Inc. has been in business since 1984. The company operates the chain of sports-themed resto-bars in Québec, known as La Cage aux Sport. Sportscene is also involved in other business, such as managing real estate holdings, constructing & renovating & organizing sports-related activities.

Swiss Water Decaffeinated Coffee Inc
7750 Beedie Way
Delta, BC V4G 0A5

604-420-4050
800-667-6181
info@swisswater.com
www.swisswater.com
Other Communications: Investor Relations, Email:
investor@swisswater.com
www.facebook.com/SwissWaterProcess
twitter.com/swisswater
www.linkedin.com/company/swiss-water-decaffeinated-coffee
Company Type: Public
Ticker Symbol: SWP/TSX
Profile: SwissWater is in the market of non-caffeinated coffee. It utilize a non-chemical method of purifying the coffee of its caffeine
Frank Dennis, President & CEO
Iain Carswell, Chief Financial Officer

Waterloo Brewing Ltd.
400 Bingemans Centre Dr.
Kitchener, ON N2B 3X9

519-742-2732
Fax: 519-742-9874
800-505-8971
info@waterloobrewing.com
waterloobrewing.com
www.facebook.com/waterloobrewing
twitter.com/waterloobrewing
www.linkedin.com/company/waterloobrewing
Company Type: Public
Ticker Symbol: WBR/TSX
Staff Size: 240
Profile: Waterloo Brewing Ltd., Founded in 1984, is an Ontario craft brewery.
George H. Croft, President & CEO

Forestry & Paper

Acadian Timber Corp.
365 Canada Rd.
Edmunston, NB E3V 1W2

506-373-2345
www.acadiantimber.com
Other Communications: Investor Relations, Email:
ir@acadiantimber.com

Company Type: Public
Ticker Symbol: ADN/TSX
Profile: Acadian Timber supplies primary forest products. Areas of activity are eastern Canada & the northeastern United States. Acadian Timber complies with environmental legislation & regulations & works with government, regulators, communities & stakeholders. The company reports regularly on its environmental performance.
Erika Reilly, President & CEO
Adam Sheparski, Chief Financial Officer
Normand Haché, Senior Vice-President, Marketing & Operations
Kevin Topolniski, Chief Forester

Canfor Corporation
#100, 1700 West 75th Ave.
Vancouver, BC V6P 6G2

604-661-5241
Fax: 604-661-5253
info@canfor.com
www.canfor.com
twitter.com/canforcorp
www.linkedin.com/company/canfor

Company Type: Public
Ticker Symbol: CFP/TSX
Profile: Formed in 1966, Canfor Corporation is an integrated forest products company. Operations are carried out in British Columbia, Alberta, Quebec, Washington state & North & South Carolina.
Don Kayne, President & CEO
Alan Nicholl, Chief Financial Officer & Executive Vice-President, Finance

Canfor Pulp Products Inc. (CPPI)
#100, 1700 West 75th Ave.
Vancouver, BC V6P 6G2

604-661-5241
contactcwpm@canfor.com
www.canfor.com

Company Type: Public
Ticker Symbol: CFX/TSX
Staff Size: 1,200
Profile: In 2011, Canfor Pulp Income Fund converted from an income trust structure to a corporate structure. Canfor Pulp Products Inc. is a producer of northern softwood kraft pulp & kraft paper.
Don Kayne, Chief Executive Officer

Cascades Inc.
404, boul Marie-Victorin
Kingsey Falls, QC J0A 1B0

819-363-5100
info@cascades.com
www.cascades.com
Other Communications: Investor Relations, Email:
investisseur@cascades.com
www.facebook.com/cascades
twitter.com/cascadessd
www.linkedin.com/company/cascades

Company Type: Public
Ticker Symbol: CAS/TSX
Staff Size: 11,700
Profile: Cascades Inc. was founded in 1964. The company is engaged in the production, transformation & marketing of packaging & tissue products. Products are composed mainly of recycled fibres. Cascades operates throughout North America & Europe.
Mario Plourde, President & CEO
Allan Hogg, Vice-President & CFO
Dominic Doré, Chief Supply Chain & Information Officer
Maryse Fernet, Chief Human Resources Officer

Conifex Timber Inc.
PO Box 10070, #980, 700 West Georgia St.
Vancouver, BC V7Y 1B6

604-216-2949
866-301-2949
conifex.com
www.facebook.com/conifex
twitter.com/conifex_bc
www.linkedin.com/company/conifex

Company Type: Public
Ticker Symbol: CFF/TSX
Profile: Conifex Timber Inc. & its subsidiaries are involved in: timber harvesting, reforestation, forest management, sawmilling logs into lumber & wood chips, & lumber finishing. Conifex is

committed to responsible stewardship & its work is guided by an environmental policy. The company's markets are in Canada, the United States, China & Japan.
Ken Shields, Chief Executive Officer
ken.shields@conifex.com
Winny Tang, Chief Financial Officer
jordan.neeser@conifex.com

Domtar Corporation
395, boul de Maisonneuve ouest
Montréal, QC H3A 1L6

514-848-5555
communications@domtar.com
www.domtar.com
Other Communications: Sustainability, Email:
sustainability@domtar.com
www.facebook.com/DomtarEveryday
twitter.com/domtareveryday
www.linkedin.com/company/domtar

Company Type: Public
Ticker Symbol: UFS/TSX
Staff Size: 6,600
Profile: Domtar is a designer, manufacturer & distributor of a variety of communication, speciality & packing papers, market pulp & airlaid nonwovens. It has 13 pulp & paper mills as well as 10 manufacturing & converting facilities.
John D. Williams, President & CEO
Daniel Buron, Exective Vice-President & CFO

Goodfellow Inc.
225, rue Goodfellow
Delson, QC J5B 1V5

450-635-6511
Fax: 450-635-3729
800-361-6503
info@goodfellowinc.com
www.goodfellowinc.com
www.facebook.com/goodfellowinc
www.linkedin.com/company/goodfellowinc

Company Type: Public
Ticker Symbol: GDL/TSX
Profile: Goodfellow Inc. re-manufactures, wholesales & distributes wood & wood by-products, such as: dressed & rough lumber; sawn timber; composite & veneer based wood panel products; & prefinished & unfinished flooring. Customers are served in Canada & internationally.
Patrick Goodfellow, President & CEO
Charles Brisebois, Chief Financial Officer

Hardwoods Distribution Inc. (HDI)
#306, 9440 - 202th St.
Langley, BC V1M 4A6

604-881-1988
Fax: 604-881-1995
www.hardwoods-inc.com

Company Type: Public
Ticker Symbol: HDI/TSX
Profile: In 2011, the Hardwoods Distribution Income Fund was converted to a corporation by way of a plan of arrangement. Hardwoods Distribution Inc. has a 100% ownership interest in Hardwoods Specialty Products LP & Hardwoods Specialty Products US LP. Every distribution centre of Hardwoods Specialty Products has been certified by the Forestry Stewardship Council for Chain of Custody. Hardwoods Distribution Inc. is also a member of the Canadian Green Building Council & the US Green Building Council in support of green building initiatives.
Jason West, Vice-President, Hardwoods Canada

Interfor Corporation
Metrotower II
#1600, 4720 Kingsway
Burnaby, BC V5H 4N2

604-422-3400
Fax: 604-422-3452
info@interfor.com
interfor.com
www.facebook.com/InterforCareers
www.linkedin.com/company/interfor

Company Type: Public
Ticker Symbol: IFP/TSX
Staff Size: 2,900
Profile: Interfor supplies lumber products.
Ian Fillinger, President & CEO
Rick Pozzebon, Senior Vice-President & CFO
Xenia Kritsos, General Counsel & Corporate Secretary

NFI Group Inc.
711 Kernaghan Ave.
Winnipeg, MB R2C 3T4

204-224-1251
www.nfigroup.com
Other Communications: Investor Relations, Email:
investor@nfigroup.com
www.linkedin.com/company/newflyer

Company Type: Public
Ticker Symbol: NFI/TSX
Staff Size: 8,000
Profile: NFI is an independent bus & coach manufacturer operating in 10 countries. Its brands include New Flyer, Alexander Dennis Limited, Plaxton, MCI, ARBOC & NFI Parts. Its vehicles run on a number of drive systems such as diesel, natural gas, diesel-electric hybrid & fully electric.
Paul Soubry, President & CEO
Brian Dewsnup, President, NFI Parts
Chris Stoddart, President, New Flyer & MCI
Pipasu Soni, Chief Financial Officer

Resolute Forest Products Inc.
#5000, 111, boul Robert-Bourassa
Montréal, QC H3C 2M1

514-875-2160
800-361-2888
info@resolutefp.com
www.resolutefp.com
Other Communications: Investor Relations, Email:
ir@resolutefp.com
www.facebook.com/resolutefp
twitter.com/resolutefp
www.linkedin.com/company/resolute-forest-products

Company Type: Public
Ticker Symbol: RFP/TSX
Staff Size: 7,100
Profile: The company offers a range of products such as pulp, tissue, wood & paper. It owns or operates 40 facilities & power generation assets in North America.
Remi G. Lalonde, President & CEO
Patrice Kinguez, President, Tissue Group
Hugues Simon, President, Wood Products
Sylvain A. Girard, Senior Vice-President & CFO
Patrice Kinguez, CIO & Senior Vice-President, Process Improvement

Stella-Jones Inc.
#300, 3100 boul de la Côte-Vertu
Montréal, QC H4R 2J8

514-934-8666
Fax: 514-934-5327
ir@stella-jones.com
www.stella-jones.com
Other Communications: Human Resources, Email:
hr@stella-jones.com

Company Type: Public
Ticker Symbol: SJ/TSX
Staff Size: 2,200
Profile: Stella-Jones specializes in the production & marketing of industrially treated wood products. Products include: treated wood for bridges; pressure treated railway ties; marine & foundation pilings; construction timbers; highway guardrail posts; & wood poles for electrical utilities & telecommunications companies.
Éric Vachon, President & CEO
Silvana Travaglini, Senior Vice-President & CFO

Supremex Inc.
7213, rue Cordner
Montréal, QC H8N 2J7

800-361-6659
info@supremex.com
www.supremex.com
www.facebook.com/supremexinc
twitter.com/supremexinc
www.linkedin.com/company/supremex-inc.

Company Type: Public
Ticker Symbol: SXP/TSX
Profile: Supremex manufactures & markets a variety of envelopes, labels & related mailing products. Environmental accreditations at manufacturing facilities include the Forest Stewardship Council, Environmental Choice & Sustainable Forestry Initiative.
Stewart Emerson, Chief Executive Officer & General Manager, Central Region
Guy Prenevost, Chief Financial Officer

Taiga Building Products Ltd.
#800, 4710 Kingsway
Burnaby, BC V5H 4M2

604-438-1471
Fax: 604-439-4242
800-663-1470
www.taigabuilding.com
Other Communications: Investor Relations, Email:
i.relations@taigabuilding.com
www.linkedin.com/company/taiga-building-products
Company Type: Public
Ticker Symbol: TBL/TSX
Staff Size: 550
Profile: Taiga Building Products Ltd. distributes building products, such as lumber, engineered wood, mouldings, siding, flooring & polyethylene sheeting. It is also involved in the production of treated wood, which reduces the use of timber resources. The company's customers are most often industrial manufacturers & building supply dealers.
Trent Balog, Co-President & CEO
Russell Permann, Co-President & CEO
Mark Schneidereit-Hsu, Chief Financial Officer & Vice-President, Finance & Administration

West Fraser Timber Co. Ltd.
Also Known As: West Fraser
#501, 858 Beatty St.
Vancouver, BC V6B 1C1

604-895-2700
Fax: 604-681-6061
shareholder@westfraser.com
www.westfraser.com
Other Communications: Environmental Inquiries, Email:
trees@westfraser.com
www.facebook.com/westfraserco
www.linkedin.com/company/west-fraser-timber-co-ltd
Company Type: Public
Ticker Symbol: WFG/TSX
Staff Size: 8,000
Profile: West Fraser Timber Co. is an integrated wood products company. From facilities in Canada & the United States, the company produces: plywood, lumber, wood chips, LVL, MDF, pulp & newsprint.
Raymond Ferris, President & CEO
Chris Virostek, Chief Financial Officer & Vice-President, Finance

Western Forest Products Inc. (WFP)
Royal Centre Bldg.
PO Box 11122, #800, 1055 West Georgia St.
Vancouver, BC V6E 3P3

604-648-4500
Fax: 604-681-9584
info@westernforest.com
www.westernforest.com
www.facebook.com/westernforestproducts
twitter.com/wfpcompany
www.linkedin.com/company/western-forest-products
Company Type: Public
Ticker Symbol: WEF/TSX
Staff Size: 2,100
Profile: Western Forest Products is a large woodland operator & lumber producer in the coastal region of British Columbia. Activities include timber harvesting, sawmilling logs into lumber & wood chips, value-added remanufacturing, & reforestation. Customers are served in North America & around the world.
Don Demens, President & CEO
Stephen Williams, Executive Vice-President & CFO

Holding & Other Investment

AcuityAds Holdings Inc.
#1200, 70 University Ave.
Toronto, ON M5J 2M4

416-218-9888
www.acuityads.com
www.facebook.com/acuityads
twitter.com/acuityads
www.linkedin.com/company/acuity-ads-inc
Company Type: Public
Ticker Symbol: AT/TSX
Profile: AcuityAds Holdings Inc. is the parent company of AcuityAds Inc. & is a technology company that provides targeted digital media solutions.
Tal Hayek, Co-Founder & Chief Executive Officer
Nathan Mekuz, Co-Founder & Vice-President, Artificial Intelligence
Jonathan Pollack, Chief Financial Officer

Advent-AWI Holdings Inc.
#719, 550 West Broadway
Vancouver, BC V5Z 0E9

604-428-0028

Company Type: Public
Ticker Symbol: AWI/TSX.V
Profile: Advent-AWI Holdings Inc. is a holding company that, through its subsidiaries, retails cellular & wireless products, accessories & services. Subsidiaries include Am-Call Wireless Inc. & Advent Marketing Inc.
Alice Chiu, President & CEO

Aimia Inc.
#06-128, 777 Bay St.
Toronto, ON M5G 2C8

647-208-2166
www.aimia.com
Company Type: Public
Ticker Symbol: AIM/TSX
Profile: The loyalty program, Aeroplan, is owned by Aimia. Members of the program earn Aeroplan Miles through the company's partners in the retail, travel & financial sectors.
Philip Mittleman, Chief Executive Officer
Michael Lehmann, President
Steven Leonard, Chief Financial Officer

Apollo Healthcare Corp.
1 Apollo Pl.
Toronto, ON M3J 0H2

info@ahcinvestor.com
apollohealthcarecorp.com
Company Type: Private
Ticker Symbol: AHC/TSX
Profile: Apollo Healthcare Corp. owns the Appolo Health & Beauty Inc. companies.

BPLI Holdings Inc.
18 Prescott St.
St. John's, NL A1C 3S4

709-739-9000
800-563-3638
info@bluedrop.com
www.bpli.ca
Company Type: Public
Profile: BPLI is a holding company for its two wholly-owned operating divisions, Blluedrop Training & Simulation Inc. & Bluedrop Learning Networks Inc. Through these companies, it provides full-service eLearning.
In 2021, Rizbollo Holdings Limited acquired BPLI.
Emad Rizkalla, Founder & Chief Executive Officer
Brad Driscoll, Chief Financial Officer

Brookfield Asset Management Inc.
Brookfield Place
#300, 181 Bay St.
Toronto, ON M5J 2T3

416-363-9491
www.brookfield.com
www.linkedin.com/company/brookfield-asset-management
Company Type: Public
Ticker Symbol: BAM.A/TSX
Staff Size: 150,000
Profile: Founded in 1899, Brookfield Asset Management is a global asset manager concentrating on property, infrastructure & renewable power assets. The company offers clients an array of real estate advisory, property & investment services.
Bruce Flatt, Chief Executive Officer

Cymbria Corporation
#500, 150 Bloor St. West
Toronto, ON M5S 2X9

416-963-9353
Fax: 416-963-5060
866-757-7207
www.cymbria.com
info@cymbria.com
Company Type: Public
Ticker Symbol: CYB/TSX.V
Profile: Founded in 2008, Cymbria is an investment company with a concentrated portfolio of global companies, as well as an investment in EdgePoint Wealth Management Inc.
Patrick Farmer, Chair
farmer@edgepointwealth.com

Decisive Dividend Corporation
#201, 1674 Bertram St.
Kelowna, BC V1Y 9G4

250-870-9146
decisivedividend.com
twitter.com/decisivedivcorp
www.linkedin.com/company/decisive-dividend-corporation
Company Type: Public
Ticker Symbol: DE/TSX.V
Profile: Decisive Dividend Corporation is an investment company interested in acquiring North American companies that require an investment of up to $25 million.
James Paterson, Chief Executive Officer
james@decisivedividend.com

Terry Edwards, Chief Operating Officer
terry@decisivedividend.com
Rick Torriero, Chief Financial Officer
rick@decisivedividend.com

Dominion Lending Centres Group (DLCG)
2215 Coquitlam Ave.
Port Coquitlam, BC V3B 1J6

Fax: 604-939-8795
888-806-8080
dlcg.ca
Company Type: Public
Ticker Symbol: FCF/TSX.V
Profile: DLCG is an investment company dealing in equity, debt & other securities of public & private companies.
Gary Mauris, Chief Executive Officer
James Bell, President, Corporate
jbell@dlcg.ca
Eddy Cocciollo, President, DLC Inc.
Rich Spence, President, Mortgage Centre Canada
Geoff Willis, President, Newton Connectivity Systems
Dustan Woodhouse, President, Mortgage Architect's
Geoff Hague, Chief Financial Officer

Dundee Corporation
#2000, 1 Adelaide St. East
Toronto, ON M5C 2V9

416-350-3388
info@dundeecorporation.com
www.dundeecorporation.com
twitter.com/dundeecorptsx
www.linkedin.com/company/dundeecorporation
Company Type: Public
Ticker Symbol: DC.A/TSX
Staff Size: 30
Profile: The asset management company is engaged in real estate & resources. Subsidiaries include Dundee Realty Corporation, Dundee Resources Limited & Dundee Real Estate Asset Management.
Jonathan Goodman, President & CEO
Robert Sellars, Executive Vice-President & CFO
Mark Pereira, Corporate Secretary

ECN Capital Corp.
North Tower, Royal Bank Plaza
#1625, 200 Bay St.
Toronto, ON M5J 2T3

416-646-4710
Fax: 844-402-1074
www.ecncapitalcorp.com
Company Type: Public
Ticker Symbol: ECN/TSX
Staff Size: 445
Profile: ECN Capital is an equipment finance company, operating across North America in three verticals of the equipment finance market: Rail Finance, Commercial & Vendor Finance, & Aviation Finance.
Stephen K. Hudson, Chief Executive Officer
Michael Lepore, Chief Financial Officer

Exchange Income Corporation
#101, 990 Lorimer Blvd.
Winnipeg, MB R3P 0Z9

204-982-1857
Fax: 204-982-1855
www.exchangeincomecorp.ca
twitter.com/exchangeincome
Company Type: Public
Ticker Symbol: EIF/TSX
Staff Size: 4,400
Profile: Exchange Income Corporation was established to invest in profitable companies in Canada & the United States. Cash dividends are distributed each month to shareholders. Exchange Income Corporation owns subsidiaries in the business segments of specialty manufacturing & aviation.
Michael Pyle, Chief Executive Officer
Carmele Peter, President
Darryl Bergman, Chief Financial Officer
Darwin Sparrow, Chief Operating Officer

Fairfax Financial Holdings Limited
#800, 95 Wellington St. West
Toronto, ON M5J 2N7

416-367-4941
Fax: 416-367-4946
www.fairfax.ca
Company Type: Public
Ticker Symbol: FFH/TSX
Staff Size: 38,000
Profile: Through its subsidiaries, the financial services holding company is involved in insurance claims management; property & casualty insurance; & reinsurance & investment management. Subsidiaries include Northbridge Financial, Crum & Forster,

Falcon Insurance, Fairfirst Insurance, Odyssey Group, Group Re, Allied World & more.
V. Prem Watsa, Chair & Chief Executive Officer
Jennifer Allen, Vice-President & CFO
Peter Clarke, Vice-President & COO

Freehold Royalties Ltd.
#1000, 517 - 10th Ave. SW
Calgary, AB T2R 0A8

403-221-0802
Fax: 403-221-0888
888-257-1873
reception@rife.com
www.freeholdroyalties.com
Other Communications: Investors, Email:
investorrelations@freeholdroyalties.com

Company Type: Public
Ticker Symbol: FRU/TSX
Profile: Freehold Royalties acquires & manages a portfolio of non-Crown oil & gas royalties in Canada.
David M. Spyker, President & CEO
David W. Hendry, Chief Financial Officer & Vice-President, Finance

GoldMoney Inc.
#307, 334 Adelaide St. West
Toronto, ON M5V 1R4

647-250-7170
ir@goldmoney.com
www.goldmoney.com
www.facebook.com/goldmoney
twitter.com/Goldmoney
www.linkedin.com/company/goldmoney

Company Type: Public
Ticker Symbol: XAU/TSX
Profile: Goldmoney is a precious metals holding company.
Roy Sebag, Chief Executive Officer
Steve Fray, Chief Financial Officer
Paul Mennega, Chief Operating Officer
Alessandro Premoli, Chief Technology Officer

H&R Real Estate Investment Trust
Also Known As: H&R REIT
#500, 3625 Dufferin St.
Toronto, ON M3K 1N4

416-635-7520
888-635-7717
info@hr-reit.com
www.hr-reit.com

Company Type: Public
Ticker Symbol: HR.UN/TSX
Profile: The organization is an open-ended real estate investment trust. Its portfolio includes retail properties, office properties, single tenant industrial properties & development projects.
Thomas J. Hofstedter, President & CEO
Larry Froom, Chief Financial Officer

IBI Group Inc.
55 St Clair Ave. West, 7th Fl.
Toronto, ON M4V 2Y7

416-596-1930
www.ibigroup.com
www.facebook.com/ibigroup
twitter.com/ibigroup
www.linkedin.com/companies/ibi-group_2

Company Type: Public
Ticker Symbol: IBG/TSX
Staff Size: 3,000
Profile: IBI Group provides plans, designs & other consulting services related to the development of urban land, building facilities, transportation networks & systems technology.
Scott Stewart, Chief Executive Officer
David Thom, President
Stephen Taylor, Chief Financial Officer

James Richardson & Sons Ltd. (JRSL)
3000 One Lombard Pl.
Winnipeg, MB R3B 0Y1

204-953-7970
enquiries@jrsl.ca
www.jrsl.ca

Company Type: Public
Profile: Founded in 1957, JRSL is a private company investing in trade & agri-food business, energy, real estate, financial services, investments & transportation. Its assets are located across North America & the United Kingdom.
Hartley T. Richardson, President & CEO

Jim Pattison Group Inc.
#1800, 1067 West Cordova St.
Vancouver, BC V6C 1C7

604-688-6764
admin@jp-group.com
www.jimpattison.com

Company Type: Public
Staff Size: 48,000
Profile: Founded in 1961, the Jim Pattison Group is a private holding company with investments throughout the world.
Jimmy Pattinson, Chair & Chief Executive Officer

KP Tissue Inc.
#500, 2 Prologis Blvd.
Mississauga, ON L5W 0G8

www.kptissueinc.com

Company Type: Public
Ticker Symbol: KPT/TSX
Staff Size: 2,700
Profile: KP Tissue Inc. a holding company with a limited partnership interest in KPLP (Kruger Products L.P.), a leading tissue products supplier.
Dino Bianco, Chief Executive Officer
Mark Holbrook, Chief Financial Officer
François Paroyan, Corporate Secretary & General Counsel

Labrador Iron Ore Royalty Corporation (LIORC)
PO Box 957, Toronto, ON M5C 2K3

416-362-0066
investor.relations@labradorironore.com
labradorironore.com

Company Type: Public
Ticker Symbol: LIF/TSX
Profile: In 2010, the Labrador Iron Ore Royalty Income Fund converted to the Labrador Iron Ore Royalty Corporation, which holds an equity interest in Iron Ore Company of Canada, directly & through its wholly-owned subsidiary, Hollinger-Hanna Limited.
John F. Tuer, President & CEO
Alan R. Thomas, Chief Financial Officer
Sandra Rosch, Executive Vice-President

Metalla Royalty & Streaming Ltd.
#501, 543 Granville St.
Vancouver, BC V6C 1X8

604-696-0741
Fax: 604-688-1157
info@metallaroyalty.com
www.metallaroyalty.com
twitter.com/metallaroyalty
www.linkedin.com/company/metalla-royalty-and-streaming-ltd.

Company Type: Public
Ticker Symbol: MTA/TSX.V
Profile: Metalla acquires royalties & streams of precious metals, mainly gold & silver.
Brett Heath, President & CEO
Saurabh Handa, Chief Financial Officer

Mount Logan Capital Inc.
#800, 365 Bay St.
Toronto, ON M6H 2V1

info@mountlogancapital.ca
www.mountlogancapital.ca

Company Type: Public
Ticker Symbol: MLC/TSX
Profile: Mount Logan Capital Inc. is focused on natural resource lending.
Edward Goldthorpe, Chief Executive Officer
Edward Gilpin, Chief Financial Officer

Northfield Capital Corporation
#301, 141 Adelaide St. West
Toronto, ON M5H 3L5

416-628-5901
Fax: 416-628-5911
info@northfieldcapital.com
www.northfieldcapital.com

Company Type: Public
Ticker Symbol: NFD.A/TSX.V
Profile: Formed in 1981, the investment company owns interests in diverse business activities. Major oil, gas, & mining holdings include GoldCorp Inc., Osisko Mining Corp., Canada Lithium Corp. & Trimac Transportation Ltd.
Robert D. Cudney, President & CEO
Michael G. Leskovec, Chief Financial Officer

Onex Corporation
161 Bay St.
Toronto, ON M5J 2S1

416-362-7711
investor@onex.com
www.onex.com
www.linkedin.com/company/onex

Company Type: Public
Ticker Symbol: ONEX/TSX

Staff Size: 147,000
Profile: Through Onex Partners & ONCAP families of funds, Onex Corporation makes private equity investments. The company is also engaged in the management of alternative asset platforms, which focuses on real estate & distressed credit.
Gerald W. Schwartz, Chair & Chief Executive Officer

Power Corporation of Canada
751, carré Victoria
Montréal, QC H2Y 2J3

514-286-7400
800-890-7440
www.powercorporation.com
www.linkedin.com/company/power-corporation-of-canada

Company Type: Public
Ticker Symbol: POW/TSX
Staff Size: 30,000
Profile: Power Corporation of Canada, incorporated in 1925, is an international management & holding company with interests primarily focused on companies in the financial services, renewable energy & communications sectors. Its main subsidiary is Power Financial Corp.
R. Jeffrey Orr, President & CEO
Gregory D. Tretiak, Executive Vice-President & CFO

Richards Packaging Income Fund
6095 Ordan Dr.
Mississauga, ON L5T 2M7

905-670-7760
Fax: 905-670-1960
844-670-7760
www.richardspackaging.com

Company Type: Public
Ticker Symbol: RPI.UN/TSX
Staff Size: 485
Profile: Richards Packaging Income Fund is an indirect owner of securities of Richards Packaging Inc. Richards Packaging is a plastic & glass container manufacturer & distributor. The company also distributes metal & plastic closures, as well as injection molded containers & packaging systems.

Senvest Capital Inc.
c/o Investor Relations
#2400, 1000, rue Sherbrooke ouest
Montréal, QC H3B 2G4

senvestcapitalinquries@senvest.com
www.senvest.com

Company Type: Public
Ticker Symbol: SEC/TSX
Staff Size: 24
Profile: Senvest Capital Inc.'s subsidiaries are involved in the asset management, merchant banking, real estate & electronic security sectors.
Victor Mashaal, President
Richard Mashaal, Vice-President

Spackman Equities Group Inc.
Scotia Plaza
#2502, 40 King St. West
Toronto, ON M5H 3Y2

416-956-4926
info@spackmanequities.com
spackmanequities.com

Company Type: Public
Ticker Symbol: SQG/TSX
Profile: Spackman Equities Group is an investment company that selectively invests in growth companies that possess proprietary know-how to technology, primarily in Asia.
Richard Lee, Chair & Interim Chief Executive Officer
Alex Falconer, Chief Financial Officer

Spartan Delta Corp.
#500, 207 - 9th Ave. SW
Calgary, AB T2P 1K3

403-265-8011
info@spartandeltacorp.com
www.spartandeltacorp.com

Company Type: Public
Ticker Symbol: SDE/TSX
Profile: The company is focused on developing, acquiring & optimzing energy assets. In 2021, the company amalgamated with Inception Exploration Ltd.
Fotis Kalantzis, President & CEO
Geri Greenall, Chief Financial Officer
Thanos Natras, Vice-President, Exploration

TerraVest Industries Inc.
4901 Bruce Rd.
Vegreville, AB T9C 1C3

terravestindustries.com

Company Type: Public
Ticker Symbol: TVK/TSX
Staff Size: 700

Profile: TerraVest Capital is an industrial manufacturer that provides investment funds to industries such as the Gas Field Services & Diamond Energy Services.
Dustin Haw, President & CEO
416-855-1928, dshaw@terravestindustires.com
Mitchell Gilbert, Chief Investment Officer
416-364-0064, mitchell.gilbert@terravestcapital.com

United Corporations Limited
165 University Ave., 10th Fl.
Toronto, ON M5H 3B8

416-947-2578
Fax: 416-362-2592
www.ucorp.ca

Company Type: Public
Ticker Symbol: UNC/TSX
Profile: Founded 1929, United Corporations is a closed-end investment corporation that works towards long-term growth through investments in common equities.
Duncan Jackman, Chair & President

Uranium Participation Corporation (UPC)
#1100, 40 University Ave.
Toronto, ON M5J 1T1

416-979-1991
info@uraniumparticipation.com
uraniumparticipation.com

Company Type: Public
Ticker Symbol: U/TSX
Profile: Uranium Participation Corporation was established in 2005. The investment holding company invests in uranium, either in the form of uranium oxide in concentrates or uranium hexafluoride.

Urbana Corporation
#1702, 150 King St. West
Toronto, ON M5H 1J9

416-595-9106
Fax: 416-862-2498
info@urbanacorp.com
www.urbanacorp.com

Company Type: Private
Ticker Symbol: URB.A, URB/TSX
Profile: Urbana Corporation is an investment company with current interests across the financial services sector.
Thomas Caldwell, President & CEO

Wecommerce Holdings Ltd.
Victoria, BC V8W 1K8

hello@wecommerce.co
www.wecommerce.co
www.facebook.com/WeCommerceCo
twitter.com/WeCommerce_co
www.linkedin.com/company/wecommerce-co

Company Type: Public
Ticker Symbol: WE/TSX.V
Staff Size: 130
Profile: Founded in 2019, WeCommerce acquires companies & brands that serve the Shopify partner ecosystem. Its companies include the following: Pixel Union, Out of the Sandbox, Yopify, SuppleApps, Rehash, Foursixty & Stamped.
Chris Sparling, Chief Executive Officer
Alex Persson, President
Evan Brown, Chief Financial Officer
evan@wecommerce.co

Westaim Corporation
#1700, 70 York St.
Toronto, ON M5J 1S9

416-969-3333
Fax: 416-969-3334
info@westaim.com
westaim.com

Company Type: Public
Ticker Symbol: WED/TSX
Profile: Westaim invests, directly & indirectly, through acquisitions, joint ventures & other arrangements.
J. Cameron MacDonald, President & CEO
Robert T. Kittel, Chief Operating Officer
Glenn MacNeil, Chief Financial Officer

Westshore Terminals Investment Corporation
1 Roberts Bank
Delta, BC V4M 4G5

604-646-4491
info@westshore.com
www.westshore.com

Company Type: Public
Ticker Symbol: WTE/TSX
Profile: Westshore Terminals Investment Corporation & its wholly-owned subsidiary, Westshore Terminals Holdings Ltd., operate a coal storage & loading terminal in British Columbia.
Glenn Dudar, Vice-President & General Manager
Greg Andrew, Director, Engineering & Environmental Services

Angela Morfitt, Director, Finance & Corporate Services

Insurance

Co-operators General Insurance Company
130 MacDonell St.
Guelph, ON N1H 6P8

Fax: 519-823-9944
800-265-2662
connect@cooperators.ca
www.cooperators.ca
www.facebook.com/TheCooperatorsInsurance
twitter.com/The_Cooperators
www.linkedin.com/company/the-co-operators

Company Type: Public
Ticker Symbol: CCS/TSX
Staff Size: 4,300
Profile: Co-operators General Insurance Company provides home, automobile, farm & commecial insurance services throughout Canada.
Rob Wesseling, President & CEO
Karen Higgins, Executive Vice-President & CFO
Carol Poulsen, Executive Vice-President & CIO

E-L Financial Corporation Limited
165 University Ave., 10th Fl.
Toronto, ON M5H 3B8

416-947-2578
Fax: 416-362-2592
ww.e-lfinancial.ca

Company Type: Public
Ticker Symbol: ELF/TSX
Profile: The investment & insurance holding company was incorporated in 1968. E-L Financial Corporation consists of two segments, E-L Corporate & Empire Life Insurance Company.
Duncan N.R. Jackman, President & CEO
Scott F. Ewert, Vice-President & CFO

Echelon Financial Holdings Inc.
#200, 2800 Skymark Ave.
Mississauga, ON L4W 5A7

905-602-2150
info@efh.ca
efh.ca

Other Communications: Investor Relations, Email: ir@efh.ca
Company Type: Public
Ticker Symbol: EFH/TSX.V
Profile: EFH Holdings Inc. is a provider of property & casualty insurance. It distributes insurance products through The Insurance Company of Prince Edward Island.
Serge Lavoie, President & CEO
Teddy Chien, Chief Financial Officer

Great-West Lifeco Inc.
100 Osborne St. North
Winnipeg, MB R3C 1V3

204-946-1190
www.greatwestlifeco.com

Company Type: Public
Ticker Symbol: GWO/TSX
Staff Size: 24,500
Profile: The international financial services holding company has interests in life insurance, health insurance, reinsurance, asset management, retirement & investment services. Great-West Lifeco's companies include The Great-West Life Assurance Company, Great-West Life & Anuity Insurance Company, The Canada Life Assurance Compnay & Putnam Investments. Great-West Lifeco & its companies are members of the Power Financial Corporation group of companies.
Paul A. Mahon, President & CEO
David Harney, President & COO, Canada
Jeff Macoun, President & COO
Garry MacNicholas, Executive Vice-President & CFO
Steve Rullo, Executive Vice-President & Global CIO

iA Financial Group
PO Box 1907 Stn. Terminus, , 1080, Grande Allée ouest
Québec, QC G1K 7M3

418-684-5000
800-463-6236
ia.ca
www.facebook.com/iacanada
twitter.com/iacanada
www.linkedin.com/company/industrielle_alliance

Company Type: Public
Ticker Symbol: IAG/TSX
Staff Size: 7,700
Profile: Founded in 1982, iA Financial Group provides a range of financial & insurance products & services, including life & health insurance; automobile & home insurance; RRSPs, savings & retirement plans; securities, mutual & segregated funds; & mortgage loans.
Denis Ricard, President & CEO
Jacques Potvin, Executive Vice-President, Chief Actuary & CFO

Intact Financial Corporation
#1500, 700 University Ave.
Toronto, ON M5G 0A1

416-941-5336
Fax: 416-941-0006
866-778-0774
ir@intact.net
www.intactfc.com
www.linkedin.com/company/intact

Company Type: Public
Ticker Symbol: IFC/TSX
Staff Size: 13,000
Profile: Intact Financial Corporation provides property & casualty insurance in Canada. Products & services are marketed & distributed through Intact Insurance, belairdirect & Grey Power.
Charles Brindamour, Chief Executive Officer
Patrick Barbeau, Executive Vice-President & Chief Operating Officer
Louis Marcotte, Senior Vice-President & Chief Financial Officer

Manulife Financial Corporation
Also Known As: Manufacturers Life Insurance Company
200 Bloor St. East
Toronto, ON M4W 1E5

416-926-3000
www.manulife.com
www.facebook.com/manulife
twitter.com/manulife
www.linkedin.com/company/manulife-financial

Company Type: Public
Ticker Symbol: MFC/TSX, NYSE
Staff Size: 37,000
Profile: Founded in 1887, Manulife Financial provides financial protection services & wealth management products with operations in Asia, Canada & the United States. In the United States, Manulife Financial operates as John Hancock.
Roy Gori, President & CEO
Mike Doughty, President & CEO, Manulife Canada
Philip J. Witherington, Chief Financial Officer

People Corporation
1403 Kenaston Blvd.
Winnipeg, MB R3P 2T5

866-940-3950
info@peoplecorpration.com
www.peoplecorporation.com
www.linkedin.com/company/people-corporation

Company Type: Public
Profile: People Corporation is a national provider of group benefits, group retirement & human resources services. In 2020, it was acquired by Goldman Sachs Merchant Banking.
Laurie Goldberg, Chief Executive Officer
Brevan Canning, President
Dennis Stewner, Chief Financial Officer & Chief Operating Officer

Sagen MI Canada Inc.
#300, 2060 Winston Park Dr.
Oakville, ON L6H 5R7

800-511-8888
investor.sagen.ca
www.facebook.com/sagencanada
twitter.com/sagen
www.linkedin.com/company/sagencanada

Company Type: Public
Ticker Symbol: MIC/TSX
Profile: Sagen MI Canada Inc. provides mortgage default insurance in Canada through its subsidiary, Genworth Financial Mortgage Insurance Company Canada.
Stuart Levings, President & CEO
Philip Mayers, Senior Vice-President & CFO
Craig Sweeney, Senior Vice-President & Chief Risk Officer

Sun Life Financial Inc.
5455, av du Gaspé
Montréal, QC H2T 3B3

877-786-5433
service@sunlife.ca
www.sunlife.ca
Other Communications: Investor Relations, Email:
investor.relations@sunlife.com
www.facebook.com/slfcanada
twitter.com/SunLife
www.linkedin.com/company/sun-life-financial

Company Type: Public
Ticker Symbol: SLF/TSX, NYSE
Staff Size: 23,100
Profile: Sun Life Financial serves both individuals & corporate customers. It offers customers a broad range of protection & wealth management products & services.
Jacques Goulet, President, Sun Life Financial Canada

Alex Guertin, Senior Vice-President & CFO

Trisura Group
Bay Adelaide Centre
#1610, 333 Bay St.
Toronto, ON M5H 2R2

416-214-2555
Fax: 416-214-9597
www.trisura.com/group
twitter.com/trisura
www.linkedin.com/company/trisura-group-ltd
Company Type: Public
Ticker Symbol: TSU/TSX
Profile: Trisura Group, originally Trisura Guarantee Insurance Company, formed Trisura Group as a Canadian insurance holding company in 2017. The group consists of Trisura Guarantee Insurance Company, Trisura International Insurance & Trisura Specialty Insurance Company (U.S.A.). Trisura Group operates in surety, risk solutions & corporate insurance & reinsurance.
David Clare, President & CEO
David Scotland, Chief Financial Officer

Machinery

Exco Technologies Limited
130 Spy Ct., 2nd Fl.
Markham, ON L3R 5H6

905-477-3065
www.excocorp.com
www.linkedin.com/company/exco-technologies-limited
Company Type: Public
Ticker Symbol: XTC/TSX
Staff Size: 4,700
Profile: Exco Technologies Limited serves the automotive, die-cast & extrusion industries by providing innovative technologies.
Darren Kirk, President & CEO
Darren Kirk, Chief Financial Officer & Vice-President, Finance

Kelso Technologies Inc.
13966 - 18B Ave.
Surrey, BC V4A 8J1

903-583-9200
info@kelsotech.com
www.kelsotech.com
www.linkedin.com/company/kelso-technologies-inc-
Company Type: Public
Ticker Symbol: KLS/TSX; KIQ/NYSE
Profile: Kelsotech is a product development company that specializes in the engineering & production of transportation service equipment, including truck tanker equipment, rail wheel cleaning systems, military components, rail emergency kits & suspension for high-performance vehicles.
James (Rik) Bond, President & CEO
bond@kelsotech.com
Anthony (Tony) Andrukaitis, Chief Operating Officer
Richard Lee, Chief Financial Officer
lee@kelsotech.com

Ritchie Bros. Auctioneers
9500 Glenlyon Pkwy.
Burnaby, BC V5J 0C6

778-331-5500
Fax: 778-331-5501
800-663-1739
www.rbauction.com
Other Communications: USA, Toll-Free Phone: 800-663-8457
www.facebook.com/ritchiebros
twitter.com/ritchiebros
www.linkedin.com/company/ritchie-bros
Company Type: Public
Ticker Symbol: RBA/TSX
Staff Size: 2,600
Profile: Founded in 1958, Ritchie Bros. is an industrial auctioneer serving equipment buyers & sellers all over the world. It conducts live, unreserved public auctions with both on-site & online bidding, selling a wide range of used & unused equipment for the construction, mining, transportation, agriculture, oil & gas, lifting & material handling, forestry, as well as other industries.
Ann Fandozzi, Chief Executive Officer
Sharon Driscoll, Chief Financial Officer
Jim Kessler, Chief Operating Officer
Carmen Thiede, Chief Human Resources Officer

Strongco Corporation
1640 Enterprise Rd.
Mississauga, ON L4W 4L4

905-670-5100
Fax: 905-670-7869
800-268-7004
www.strongco.com
www.facebook.com/StrongcoEquip
twitter.com/StrongcoCorp

Company Type: Public
Staff Size: 500
Profile: The large multiline mobile equipment dealer sells, rents & services equipment used in the following sectors: mining, oil & gas, forestry, construction, municipal & waste management. Operations take place in Canada & the United States. In 2020, it was acquired by the Portugal-based company Nors, S.A.
Oliver Nachevski, President & CEO
J. David Wood, Vice-President & CFO

Toromont Industries Limited
PO Box 5511, 3131 Hwy. 7 West
Concord, ON L4K 1B7

416-667-5511
Fax: 416-667-5555
www.toromont.com
Company Type: Public
Ticker Symbol: TIH/TSX
Profile: The company is engaged in the design, engineering & sale of specialized & heavy equipment. Its business segments are the Equipment Group & CIMCO. The Equipment Group includes rental operations. CIMCO is engaged in the engineering & installation of industrial & recreational refrigeration systems. Toromont Industries has implemented environmental practices, such as technology to recycle energy, reduce greenhouse gas emissions & cleanse oil of contaminants.
Scott Medhurst, President & CEO
Paul R. Jewer, Executive Vice-President & CFO
Michael P. Cuddy, Vice-President & Chief Information Officer
Jennifer J. Cochrane, Vice-President, Finance

Westport Fuel Systems Inc.
#101, 1750 West 75th Ave.
Vancouver, BC V6P 6G2

604-718-2000
wfsinc.com
twitter.com/westportdotcom
www.linkedin.com/company/westport-fuel-systems
Company Type: Public
Ticker Symbol: WPRT/TSX, NASDAQ
Staff Size: 1,300
Profile: Westport Innovations Inc. merged with Fuel Systems Solutions Inc. in 2016 to form Westport Fuel Systems Inc. The company is a leading global supplier of proprietary solutions that allow engines to operate on clean-burning fuels such as compressed natural gas (CNG), liquefied natural gas (LNG), hydrogen & renewable natural gas (RNG), helping to reduce greenhouse gas emissions (GHG).
David M. Johnson, Chief Executive Officer
Richard Orazietti, Chief Financial Officer

Manufacturing, Miscellaneous

AirBoss of America Corp.
16441 Yonge St.
Newmarket, ON L3X 2G8

905-751-1188
Fax: 905-751-1101
info@airbossofamerica.com
airboss.com
www.facebook.com/AirBossofAmerica
twitter.com/airbossamerica
www.linkedin.com/company/airboss-of-america
Company Type: Public
Ticker Symbol: BOS/TSX
Staff Size: 1,300
Profile: The company is a developer, manufacturer & seller of rubber compounds & specialty rubber moulded products. Products are used in the industrial, transportation & defense industries.
Gren Schoch, Chair & Chief Executive Officer
Chris Bitsakakis, President & COO
Frank Ientile, Chief Financial Officer

ATS Automation Tooling Systems Inc.
Bldg. 2
730 Fountain St. North
Cambridge, ON N3H 4R7

519-653-6500
Fax: 519-650-6545
info@atsautomation.com
atsautomation.com
Other Communications: Investor Relations, Email:
investor@atsautomation.com
www.facebook.com/atsautomation
twitter.com/atsautomation
www.linkedin.com/company/atsautomation
Company Type: Public
Ticker Symbol: ATA/TSX
Staff Size: 5,000
Profile: Established in 1978, ATS Automation Tooling Systems serves the automation systems needs of companies throughout the world. ATS Automation is also involved in the solar energy

industry, through its solar business in Ontario. Manufacturing takes place in Canada, the United States, Europe, southeast Asia & China.
Andrew Hilder, Chief Executive Officer

Avcorp Industries Inc.
10025 River Way
Delta, BC V4G 1M7

www.avcorp.com
Company Type: Public
Ticker Symbol: AVP/TSX
Profile: Avcorp Industries is a designer & builder for aircraft companies. The company specializes in custom solutions for airframe structures.
Amandeep Kaler, Group Chief Executive Officer
Jessica Gill, Group Vice-President, Human Resources

Brampton Brick Limited
225 Wanless Dr.
Brampton, ON L7A 1E9

905-840-1011
Fax: 905-840-1535
800-462-7425
www.bramptonbrick.com
Other Communications: Sales, Fax: 905-840-6461
www.facebook.com/brampton.brick.ltd
twitter.com/_bramptonbrick
www.linkedin.com/company/brampton-brick-limited
Company Type: Public
Ticker Symbol: BBL.A/TSX
Staff Size: 323
Profile: Brampton Brick Limited manufactures clay brick, concrete masonry products, concrete interlocking paving stones, retaining walls & enviro products. Products are used for residential construction, industrial & institutional building projects. Markets served include Ontario, Québec & the northeastern & midwestern United States.
Universal Resource Recovery operates a waste composting facility in Welland, Ontario.
Jeffrey G. Kerbel, President & CEO
Trevor M. Sandler, Chief Financial Officer & Vice-President, Finance

Carmanah Technologies Corp.
250 Bay St.
Victoria, BC V9A 3K5

carmanah.com
www.facebook.com/CarmanahTechnologies
twitter.com/carmanahtech
www.linkedin.com/company/carmanah-technologies
Company Type: Public
Ticker Symbol: CMH/TSX
Staff Size: 150
Profile: Carmanah Technologies is a manufacturer of renewable & energy-efficient technology solutions, including solar-powered LED lighting, solar power systems (off grid & grid tie), & LED illuminated signage.
Geoff Wilcox, President & CEO

CCL Industries Inc.
#801, 111 Gordon Baker Rd.
Toronto, ON M2H 3R1

416-756-8500
ccl@cclind.com
www.cclind.com
Company Type: Public
Ticker Symbol: CCL.B/TSX
Staff Size: 20,000
Profile: CCL Industries Inc. is engaged in the development & provision of specialty packaging for producers of consumer brands. Products include labelling, plastic tubes & aluminum containers. CCL serves customers in Canada, the United States & Mexico.
Geoffrey T. Martin, President & CEO
Sean Washcuk, Senior Vice-President & CFO

D-Box Technologies Inc.
2172, rue de la Province
Longueuil, QC J4G 1R7

888-442-3269
www.d-box.com
www.facebook.com/dboxmotion
twitter.com/dboxtech
www.linkedin.com/company/d-box-technologies
Company Type: Public
Ticker Symbol: DBO/TSX
Profile: D-Box Technologies manufactures motion systems technology.
Sébastien Mailhot, President & CEO
Robert Desautels, Chief Technology Officer
David Montpetit, Chief Financial Officer

Dorel Industries Inc.
#300, 1255, av Greene
Montréal, QC H3Z 2A4

514-934-3034
www.dorel.com

Company Type: Public
Ticker Symbol: DII.A, DII.B/TSX
Staff Size: 8,200
Profile: Established in 1962, Dorel Industries Inc. designs, manufactures & markets juvenile products, bicycles & home furnishings. The company has facilities in 17 countries & sells its products throughout the world.
Martin Schwartz, President & CEO
Jeffrey Schwartz, Executive Vice-President & CFO
Alan Schwartz, Executive Vice-President, Operations

Dynamic Technologies Group Inc.
RioCan Yonge & Eglinton Center
PO Box 2029, #1820, 20 Eglinton Ave. West
Toronto, ON M4P 1A6

416-366-7227
info@dynamictechgroup.com
dynamictechgroup.com
twitter.com/Dyntechgroup
www.linkedin.com/company/dynamic-tech-group

Company Type: Public
Ticker Symbol: DTG/TSX.V
Staff Size: 400
Profile: Dynamic Technologies Group is a company involved in the design & manufacture of complex engineered products. It produces marquee theme park rides, complex mechanical & structural installations, hydrovac excavation trucks & other complex industrial equipment.
Guy Nelson, Executive Chair & CEO
Jerry Pierson, Chief Operating Officer
Michael Martin, Chief Financial Officer

Hammond Manufacturing Ltd.
394 Edinburgh Rd. North
Guelph, ON N1H 1E5

519-822-2960
Fax: 519-822-0715
www.hammondmfg.com
www.facebook.com/hammondmfg
twitter.com/hammondmfg
www.linkedin.com/company/hammondmfg

Company Type: Public
Ticker Symbol: HMM.A/TSX
Staff Size: 700
Profile: Established in 1917, Hammond Manufacturing caters to the electronic & electrical products industry. Examples of products manufactured by Hammond Manufacturing include: small cases, racks, outlet strips, metallic & non-metallic enclosures, electronic transformers & surge suppressors. Facilities are located in Canada, the United States & Europe.
Robert F. Hammond, Chair & CEO
Alexander Stirling, Chief Financial Officer

Hanwei Energy Services Corp.
#902, 595 Howe St.
Vancouver, BC V6C 2T5

604-685-2239
Fax: 604-677-5579
info@hanweienergy.com
www.hanweienergy.com

Company Type: Public
Ticker Symbol: HE/TSX
Profile: Hanwei Energy Services develops, manufactures & sells high pressure fiberglass reinforced plastic products. Products are used mainly in the global energy sector.
Fulai Lang, Chair, President & CEO
Mary Ma, Chief Financial Officer
mma@hanweienergy.com

Héroux-Devtek Inc.
Tour est
#600, 1111, rue Saint-Charles ouest
Longueuil, QC J4K 5G4

450-679-5450
info@herouxdevtek.com
www.herouxdevtek.com
www.facebook.com/herouxdevtek
twitter.com/HerouxDevtekinc
www.linkedin.com/company/heroux-devtek

Company Type: Public
Ticker Symbol: HRX/TSX
Staff Size: 1,300
Profile: Héroux-Devtek Inc. develops, designs, manufactures, repairs & overhauls systems & components. The company has three divisions: The Landing Gear Division, The Aerostructure Division & The Industrial Division. Products are used in the aerospace market in both the commercial & military sectors, & in the industrial market for power generation & other machinery applications.

Martin Brassard, President & CEO
Stéphane Arsenault, Vice-President & CFO

IBC Advanced Alloys
401 Arvin Rd.
Franklin, IN 46131 USA

317-738-2558
800-423-5612
info@ibcadvancedalloys.com
ibcadvancedalloys.com
www.facebook.com/ibcadvanced
twitter.com/ibcadvanced
www.linkedin.com/company/ibc-advanced-alloys

Company Type: Public
Ticker Symbol: IB/TSX.V; IAALF/OTCQB
Profile: IBC Advanced Alloys manufactures beryllium & copper advanced alloys to serve a variety of industries.
Mark Smith, Chair & Chief Executive Officer
Toni Wendel, Chief Financial Officer & Corporate Secretary

Imaflex Inc.
5710, rue Notre Dame ouest
Montréal, QC H4C 1V2

514-935-5710
Fax: 514-935-0264
877-935-5710
www.imaflex.com
Other Communications: Investor Relations, Email:
johnr@imaflex.com

Company Type: Public
Ticker Symbol: IFX/TSX.V
Profile: Imaflex Inc. manufactures & sells polyethylene films.
Joseph Abbandonato, President & CEO
Giancarlo Santella, Chief Financial Officer

INSCAPE Corporation
67 Toll Rd.
Holland Landing, ON L9N 1H2

905-836-7676
info@myinscape.com
myinscape.com
www.facebook.com/myinscape
twitter.com/myinscape
www.linkedin.com/company/myinscape

Company Type: Public
Ticker Symbol: INQ/TSX
Staff Size: 300
Profile: INSCAPE Corporation designs, manufactures & markets office systems & storage & wall solutions for commercial workplaces. Office & production facilities are located in Canada & the United States.
Eric Ehgoetz, Chief Executive Officer
Jon Szczur, Chief Financial Officer

Magna International Inc.
337 Magna Dr.
Aurora, ON L4G 7K1

905-726-2462
www.magna.com
www.facebook.com/magnainternational
twitter.com/magnaint
www.linkedin.com/company/magna-international

Company Type: Public
Ticker Symbol: MG/TSX; MGA/NYSE
Staff Size: 158,000
Profile: A diversified automotive supplier that designs, develops & manufactures automotive systems, assemblies, modules & components. Magna also engineers & assembles complete vehicles to sell to original equipment manufacturers of cars & trucks. The company's geographic segments are North America, Europe, Asia, South America & Africa.
Donald J. Walker, Chief Executive Officer
Vincent J. Galifi, Executive Vice-President & CFO
Tommy J. Skuditis, Executive Vice-President & COO

McCoy Global Inc.
#201, 9910 - 39th Ave. NW
Edmonton, AB T6E 5H8

780-453-8451
info@mccoyglobal.com
www.mccoyglobal.com
www.linkedin.com/company/mccoy-corporation_2

Company Type: Public
Ticker Symbol: MCB/TSX
Staff Size: 100
Profile: McCoy Global serves the energy industry. The company's two business segments are Energy Products & Services & Mobile Solutions. Operations are based in western Canada & the United States' Gulf Coast.
Jim Rakievich, President & CEO
Lindsay McGill, Vice-President & CFO

Neo Performance Materials
#1740, 121 King St. West
Toronto, ON M5H 3T9

416-367-8588
www.neomaterials.com
www.facebook.com/neoperformancematerials
twitter.com/neo_materials
www.linkedin.com/company/neo-performance-materials

Company Type: Public
Ticker Symbol: NEO/TSX
Profile: Neo Performance Materials provides materials for technology including hard disk drives, fiber optics, cars & vehicles.
Constantine Karayannopoulos, Chief Executive Officer
Rahim Suleman, Chief Financial Officer
Kevin Morris, Chief Operating Officer

Neovasc Inc.
#5138, 13562 Maycrest Way
Richmond, BC V6V 2J7

604-270-4344
Fax: 604-270-4384
info@neovasc.com
www.neovasc.com
www.linkedin.com/company/neovasc-inc.

Company Type: Public
Ticker Symbol: NVCN/TSX
Profile: Neovasc develops medical devices & technology to treat mitral valve disease.
Fred Cohen, President & CEO
Christopher Clark, Chief Financial Officer
Bill Little, Chief Operating Officer

Nexoptic Technology
#1500, 409 Granville St.
Vancouver, BC V6C 1T2

604-669-7330
nexoptic.com
Other Communications: Investor Relations, Email:
look@nexoptic.com
www.facebook.com/nexoptic
twitter.com/nexoptictech
www.linkedin.com/company/nexoptic-technology-corp-

Company Type: Public
Ticker Symbol: NXO/TSX.V
Profile: The company produces optical lenses for binoculars, cameras, computer imaging, medical imaging, mobile devices & telescopes.
Paul McKenzie, Chief Executive Officer
Samantha Shorter, Chief Financial Officer

Omni-Lite Industries Canada Inc.
17210 Edwards Rd.
Cerritos, CA 90703

562-404-8510
800-577-6664
www.omni-lite.com

Company Type: Public
Ticker Symbol: OML/TSX.V
Staff Size: 8,000
Profile: A research & development company that manufactures parts used in cars & aircraft manufacturing.
David Robbins, President & CEO
d.robbins@omni-lite.com
Carl Lueders, Chief Financial Officer
Michael Walker, Vice-President, Research & Development

Pearl River Holdings
#502, 383 Richmond St.
London, ON N6A 3C4

519-645-0267

Company Type: Public
Ticker Symbol: PRH/TSX.V
Profile: A plastic products manufacturer with distribution in China, Australia & the United States.
George Lunick, Chief Executive Officer
george@lunick.ca

Photon Control Inc.
#130, 13500 Verdun Pl.
Richmond, BC V6V 1V2

604-900-3150
855-574-6866
info@photon-control.com
www.photon-control.com
www.linkedin.com/company/photoncontrolinc

Company Type: Public
Ticker Symbol: PHO/TSX
Profile: Photon Control, founded in 1988, is a measurement tool manufacturing company.
Nigel Hunton, President & CEO
Damian Towns, Chief Financial Officer

Pinnacle Renewable Energy
#350, 3600 Lysander Lane
Richmond, BC V7B 1C3

604-270-9613
Fax: 604-270-9914
877-737-4344
sales@pinnaclepellet.com
www.pinnaclepellet.com

Company Type: Public
Profile: Pinnacle creates and distributes wood pellets for power generators. This is considered to be a more environmentally-friendly means of producing renewable power. In 2021, it became an indirect wholly-owned subsidiary of Drax Group plc.
Andrea Johnston, Chief Financial Officer

Reko International Group Inc.
469 Silver Creek Industrial Dr.
Lakeshore, ON N8N 4W2

519-727-3287
Fax: 519-727-6681
rekointl.com
www.facebook.com/rekointernationalgroup
twitter.com/reko_intl
www.linkedin.com/company/reko-international-group-inc

Company Type: Public
Ticker Symbol: REKO/TSX.V
Profile: In business since 1976, Reko International Group Inc. is a designer & manufacturer of customized engineering solutions. The company serves the automotive, rail, military, mining & oil & gas sectors. Business units include Reko Manufacturing Group & Concorde Machine Tool. All divisions are ISO 9001:2008 certified.
Diane Reko, President & CEO

Savaria Corporation
2 Walker Dr.
Brampton, ON L6T 5E1

855-728-2742
info@savaria.com
www.savaria.com
Other Communications: Investor Relations, Email:
investor@savaria.com
www.facebook.com/savariabettermobility
twitter.com/mobilityforlife
www.linkedin.com/company/savaria

Company Type: Public
Ticker Symbol: SIS/TSX
Staff Size: 2,300
Profile: Savaria Corporation is a designer, manufacturer & distributor of elevators, starlifts, & vertical & inclined platform lifts for residential & commercial use. The company also specializes in the conversion & adaptation of wheelchair accessible automotive vehicles. They also provide scooters & motorized wheelchairs.
Marcel Bourassa, President & CEO
Stephen Reitknecht, Chief Financial Officer

Stelco Holdings Inc.
386 Wilcox St.
Hamilton, ON L8L 8K5

905-528-2511
info@stelco.com
www.stelco.com
Other Communications: Investor Relations, Email:
investor.relations@stelco.com

Company Type: Public
Ticker Symbol: STLC/TSX
Staff Size: 2,201
Profile: The company produces steel at its Hamilton Habour & Lake Erie facilities.
Alan Kestenbaum, Chair & Chief Executive Officer
Sujit Sanyal, Chief Operating Officer
Paul Scherzer, Chief Financial Officer

Winpak Ltd.
100 Saulteaux Cres.
Winnipeg, MB R3J 3T3

204-889-1015
Fax: 204-888-7806
info@winpak.com
www.winpak.com
www.linkedin.com/company/winpak

Company Type: Public
Ticker Symbol: WPK/TSX
Staff Size: 2,500
Profile: Manufacturing & distributing packaging materials & related packaging machines are the chief activities of Winpak Ltd. Products are used to protect perishable foods & beverages, as well as in health care applications. The company operates 10 facilities in Canada, the United States & Mexico. Its services are offered in North America, Latin America, the Pacific Rim countries & Europe.
Olivier Muggli, President & CEO

Olivier Muggli, Vice-President & CFO

Mining

49 North Resources
#602, 224 - 4th Ave. South
Saskatoon, SK S7K 5M5

306-653-2692
Fax: 306-664-4483
www.fnr.ca

Company Type: Public
Ticker Symbol: FNR/TSX.V
Profile: 49 North Resources is a resource investment company.
Tom MacNeill, President & CEO
Andrew Davidson, Chief Financial Officer

Abcourt Mines Inc.
475, av de l'Église
Rouyn-Noranda, QC J0Z 1Y1

819-768-2857
Fax: 819-768-5475
abcourt.com

Company Type: Public
Ticker Symbol: ABI/TSX.V
Profile: Abcourt Mines is a gold producer & Canadian exploration company with strategically located mining properties located in Abitibi, Québec.
Renaud Hinse, President & CEO

Aberdeen International Inc.
198 Davenport Rd.
Toronto, ON M5H 2M5

416-861-5812
www.aberdeen.green
www.facebook.com/aberdeenaab
twitter.com/aberdeenaab

Company Type: Public
Ticker Symbol: AAB/TSX
Profile: Aberdeen International is a resource investment corporation & merchant bank. Aberdeen focuses on private, small-cap resource companies.
Christopher Younger, Chief Executive Officer
Ryan Ptolemy, Chief Financial Officer

Abitibi Royalties
2864, ch Sullivan
Val-d'Or, QC J9P 0B9

info@abitibiroyalties.com
www.abitibiroyalties.com
Other Communications: Investor Relations, Toll-Free Phone:
888-392-3857
www.facebook.com/abitibiroyalties
twitter.com/abitibirzz
www.linkedin.com/company/abitibi-royalties-inc

Company Type: Public
Ticker Symbol: RZZ/TSX.V
Profile: The company owns mines in Malartic, Québec & in the Ring of Fire, in Ontario.
Ian Ball, President & CEO
Rico De Vega, Chief Financial Officer

Adventus Mining Corporation
#550, 220 Bay St.
Toronto, ON M5J 2W4

416-306-8201
info@adventusmining.com
www.adventusmining.com
www.linkedin.com/company/adventus-mining-corporation

Company Type: Public
Ticker Symbol: ADZN/TSX.V
Profile: The company is centered upon its El Domo-Curipamba Project as well as its Ecuadorian Exploration Alliance.
Christian Kargl-Simard, President & CEO

African Gold Group
#1600, 100 King St. West
Toronto, ON M5X 1G5

info@africangoldgroup.com
www.africangoldgroup.com
twitter.com/AfricanGoldG
www.linkedin.com/company/african-gold-group

Company Type: Public
Ticker Symbol: AGG/TSX.V
Profile: African Gold Group holds interests in mines in West Africa.
Danny Callow, President & CEO
danny.callow@africangoldgroup.com
Paul Bozoki, Chief Financial Officer

Agnico Eagle Mines Limited
#400, 145 King St. East
Toronto, ON M5C 2Y7

416-947-1212
Fax: 416-367-4681
888-822-6714
info@agnicoeagle.com
www.agnicoeagle.com
www.facebook.com/agnicoeagle
twitter.com/agnicoeagle
www.linkedin.com/company/agnico-eagle-mines

Company Type: Public
Ticker Symbol: AEM/TSX, NYSE
Staff Size: 6,500
Profile: Agnico Eagle Mines Limited is an international gold production company that carries out exploration & development activities. Operations are conducted in Canada, the United States, Mexico & Finland.
Sean Boyd, Chief Executive Officer
David Smith, Chief Financial Officer & Senior Vice-President, Finance
Dominique Girard, Senior Vice-President, Operations, Canada & Europe
Carol Plummer, Senior Vice-President, Sustainability, People & Culture

Alamos Gold Inc.
#3910, 181 Bay St.
Toronto, ON M5J 2T3

416-368-9932
866-788-8801
info@alamosgold.com
alamosgold.com
twitter.com/AlamosGoldInc
www.linkedin.com/company/alamos-gold-inc

Company Type: Public
Ticker Symbol: AGI/TSX, NYSE
Profile: The Canadian-based gold producer owns & operates a mine in Mexico. The mining company also has exploration & development activities in Mexico & Turkey. In April 2015, Alamos acquired AuRico Gold, a mining company whose main asset is located in Sonora, Mexico.
John A. McCluskey, President & CEO
Jamie Porter, Chief Financial Officer
Peter MacPhail, Chief Operating Officer
Christine Barwell, Vice-President, Human Resources

Alexco Resource Corp.
Two Bentall Centre
PO Box 216, #1225, 555 Burrard St.
Vancouver, BC V7X 1M9

604-633-4888
Fax: 604-633-4887
info@alexcoresource.com
www.alexcoresource.com
twitter.com/alexcoresource
www.linkedin.com/company/alexco-resource-corp

Company Type: Public
Ticker Symbol: AXU/TSX, NYSE
Profile: Alexco Resource Corp. holds several mineral properties, including the Bellekeno silver mine in the Keno Hill Silver District of Yukon Territory. Through the company's wholly owned envrionmental services division, the Alexco Environmental Group, remediation, reclamation & mine closure services are also provided.
Clynton R. Nauman, Chief Executive Officer
Brad A. Thrall, President
Michael Clark, Chief Financial Officer & Company Ethics Officer
Alan McOnie, Vice-President, Exploration

Almaden Minerals Ltd.
#210, 1333 Johnston St.
Vancouver, BC V6H 3R9

604-689-7644
Fax: 604-689-7645
info@almadenminerals.com
www.almadenminerals.com

Company Type: Public
Ticker Symbol: AMM/TSX; AAU/NYSE
Profile: Almaden Minerals is an exploration company specializing in the generation of new mineral prospects.
Morgan Poliquin, President & CEO
Korm Trieu, Chief Financial Officer

Almonty Industries
#5700, 100 King St. West
Toronto, ON M5X 1C7

647-438-9766
Fax: 416-628-2516
info@almonty.com
almonty.com
www.facebook.com/almontyindustries
www.linkedin.com/company/almonty

Company Type: Public
Ticker Symbol: AII/TSX
Profile: Almonty is focused on acquiring distressed & underperforming operations & assets in Tungsten markets.
Lewis Black, President & CEO
Mark Gelmon, Chief Financial Officer

Alphamin Resources Corp.
c/o Adansonia Management Services Limited
#1, Perrieri Office Suites, Level 3
La Croisette, Grand Baie, 30517 Mauritius

230-269-4166
alphaminresources.com
Other Communications: Alt. Phone: +243-810-003-943
www.linkedin.com/company/alphamin-resources-corp-afmjf-
Company Type: Public
Ticker Symbol: AFM/TSX.V
Profile: Alphamin is a tin exploration & mining business.
Maritz Smith, Chief Executive Officer
Eoin O'Driscoll, Chief Financial Officer

Altius Minerals Corporation
PO Box 8263 Stn. A, , St. John's, NL A1B 3N4

709-576-3440
Fax: 709-576-3441
877-576-2209
info@altiusminerals.com
altiusminerals.com
twitter.com/altiusminerals
www.linkedin.com/company/altius-minerals-corp
Company Type: Public
Ticker Symbol: ALS/TSX
Profile: Altius Minerals Corporation is a natural resource project generation & royalty business. The company has royalty interest & equity stakes in several natural resource projects.
Brian F. Dalton, President & CEO
Ben Lewis, Chief Financial Officer
Lawrence Winter, Vice-President, Exploration

Alvopetro Energy Ltd.
#1920, 215 - 9th Ave. SW
Calgary, AB T2P 1K3

587-794-4224
info@alvopetro.com
alvopetro.com
twitter.com/alvopetroenergy
www.linkedin.com/company/alvopetro-energy-ltd
Company Type: Public
Ticker Symbol: ALV/TSX
Profile: Alvopetro is involved in resource exploration in Brazil.
Corey Ruttan, President & CEO
Alison Howard, Chief Financial Officer
Andrea Hatzinikolas, Vice-President, Corporate & Legal

Amarillo Gold Corp.
#201, 82 Richmond St. East
Toronto, ON M5C 1P1

416-671-4966
info@amarillogold.com
www.amarillogold.com
www.facebook.com/amarillogold
twitter.com/amarillogold
www.linkedin.com/company/amarillo-gold
Company Type: Public
Ticker Symbol: AGC/TSX.V
Profile: Amarillo Gold is a gold exploration organization, whose main project is in central Brazil.
Mike Mutchler, President & CEO
Hemdat Sawh, Chief Financial Officer

American Lithium
#1507, 1030 West Georgia St.
Vancouver, BC V6E 2Y3

604-428-6128
info@americanlithiumcorp.com
americanlithium.com
www.facebook.com/americanlithium
twitter.com/lithiumamerican
www.linkedin.com/company/american-lithium-corp
Company Type: Public
Ticker Symbol: LI/TSX.V; LIACF/OTCQB
Profile: The company operates in Nevada. In 2021, the company acquired Plateau Energy Metals Inc., which has exploration & development operations in Peru.
Michael Kobler, Chief Executive Officer

Americas Gold & Silver Corporation
#2870, 145 King St. West
Toronto, ON M5H 1J8

416-848-9503
Fax: 866-401-3069
info@americassilvercorp.com
www.americassilvercorp.com
www.facebook.com/AmericasGoldandSilver
twitter.com/americas_gold
www.linkedin.com/company/americas-silver-corporation
Company Type: Public
Ticker Symbol: USA/TSX
Staff Size: 500
Profile: Americas Silver Corporation is a silver producer whose exploring & mining activities are conducted in Mexico.
Darren Blasutti, President & CEO
Daren Dell, Chief Operating Officer
Warren Varga, Chief Financial Officer

Amerigo Resources Ltd.
The Marine Bldg.
#1260, 355 Burrard St.
Vancouver, BC V6C 2G8

604-681-2802
Fax: 604-682-2802
info@amerigoresources.com
www.amerigoresources.com
Company Type: Public
Ticker Symbol: ARG/TSX; ARREF/OTCQX
Profile: Amerigo Resources's wholly owned subsidiary is Minera Valle Central. The company specializes in the production of copper & molybdenum concentrates from tailings from an underground copper mine, known as Codelco's El Teniente mine.
Aurora Davidson, President & CEO
ad@amerigoresources.com
Carmen Amezquita, Chief Financial Officer

Anaconda Mining Inc.
#915, 20 Adelaide St. East
Toronto, ON M5C 2T6

416-304-6622
Fax: 416-363-4567
info@anacondamining.com
www.anacondamining.com
www.facebook.com/anacondamining
twitter.com/anaconda_mining
www.linkedin.com/company/anaconda-mining-inc-anx-
Company Type: Public
Ticker Symbol: ANX/TSX; ANX/OCTQX
Profile: Anaconda is a gold mining & exploration company, whose main project is the Point Rousse Project located in Baie Verte, Newfoundland.
Kevin Bullock, President & CEO
Robert Dufour, Chief Financial Officer
Paul McNeill, Vice-President, Exploration

Anfield Energy Inc.
PO Box 17528 Stn. The Ritz, , Vancouver, BC V6E 0B2
604-669-5762
Fax: 604-608-4804
info@anfieldresources.com
anfieldenergy.com
www.facebook.com/anfieldresources
Company Type: Public
Ticker Symbol: AEC/TSX.V
Profile: Anfield Energy is a uranium development & near-term production company & has 24 recent acquisition projects in Wyoming.
Corey Dias, Chief Executive Officer

Aquila Resources
#520, 141 Adelaide St. West
Toronto, ON M5H 3L5

647-943-5672
info@aquilaresources.com
aquilaresources.com
www.facebook.com/aquilaresources
twitter.com/aquilaresources
www.linkedin.com/company/aquila-resources-inc.
Company Type: Public
Ticker Symbol: AQA/TSX
Profile: A mining company that owns a gold & zinc mine in Michigan.
Guy Le Bel, President & CEO
Stephanie Malec, Chief Financial Officer
Michael Foley, Director, Environment & Infrastructure
Bob Mahin, Director, Exploration

Archon Minerals Ltd.
#2801, 323 Jervis St.
Vancouver, BC V6C 3P8

604-682-3303

Company Type: Public
Ticker Symbol: ACS/TSX.V
Profile: Archon Mines focuses on the exploration of minerals in the Northwest Territories.
Stewart Blusson, President & CEO

Argonaut Gold Inc.
9600 Prototype Ct.
Reno, NV 89521 USA

775-284-4422
Fax: 775-284-4426
info@argonautgold.com
www.argonautgold.com
www.facebook.com/ArgonautGoldInc
twitter.com/Argonaut_Gold
www.linkedin.com/company/argonaut-gold-inc
Company Type: Public
Ticker Symbol: AR/TSX
Staff Size: 900
Profile: Argonaut Gold Inc is a mining company that engages in the exploration, development & production of gold in Mexico. In 2020, Alio Gold Inc. merged with Argonaut, which brought along assets that included its producing San Francisco gold mine.
Peter C. Dougherty, President & CEO
David A. Ponczoch, Chief Financial Officer
Brian Arkell, Vice-President, Exploration

Arianne Phosphate
#200, 393, rue Racine est
Chicoutimi, QC G7H 1T2

418-549-7316
Fax: 418-549-5750
855-549-7316
info@arianne-inc.com
www.arianne-inc.com
www.facebook.com/ariannephosphate
twitter.com/arianne_dan
www.linkedin.com/company/arianne-phosphate-inc-tsx-v-dan
Company Type: Public
Ticker Symbol: DAN/TSX.V; DRRSF/OTC
Profile: Founded in 1997, Arianne is a mineral exploration company focused on developing its Lac à Paul greenfield project.
Brian Ostroff, Chief Executive Officer
Pier-Elise Herbet-Tremblay, Chief Financial Officer
Jean-Sébastien David, Chief Operating Officer

Arizona Gold Corp.
#902, 18 King St. East
Toronto, ON M5C 1C4

416-855-9305
info@arizona-gold.com
www.arizona-gold.com

Company Type: Public
Ticker Symbol: AZG/TSX; AGAUF/OTCQB
Profile: Kerr Mines is a North American gold development & exploration company whose primary focus is its Copperstone property in the Unted States.
Giulio T. Bonifacio, Chief Executive Officer
Dale Found, Chief Financial Officer

Arizona Metals Corp.
#4100, 66 Wellington St. West
Toronto, ON M5K 1B7

www.arizonametalscorp.com
twitter.com/ArizonaCorp
Company Type: Public
Ticker Symbol: AMC/TSX.V
Profile: Arizona Metals Corp. owns 100% of the Kay Mine Property in Yavapai County, AZ & the Sugarloaf Peak Property, La Paz County, AZ.
Marc Pais, President & CEO
Sung Min (Eric) Myung, Chief Financial Officer

Asbestos Corp./Société Asbestos Limitée
840, boul Ouellet
Thetford Mines, QC G6G 7A5

418-338-5195
Fax: 418-338-6069
mail@asbestos-corp.com
www.asbestoscorporation.com
Company Type: Public
Ticker Symbol: AB.H/TSX.V
Profile: Asbestos Corp mines nickel, cobalt, chrome & magnesium minerals in & around Thetford Mines.

Ascendant Resources Inc.
#501, 110 Yonge St.
Toronto, ON M5C 1T4

647-796-0066
Fax: 647-796-0067
info@ascendantresources.com
www.ascendantresources.com
Other Communications: Investor Relations, Toll-Free Phone:
888-723-2413
twitter.com/ascendantres
www.linkedin.com/company/ascendant-resources-inc.
Company Type: Public
Ticker Symbol: ASND/TSX; ASDRF/OTCQX
Profile: Ascendant Resources Inc. is a mining company
operating in its 100%-owned El Mochito zinc-lead-silver mine in
Honduras.
Mark Brennan, Chief Executive Officer
Joao Barros, President
Jason Brooks, Chief Financial Officer
Cliff Hale-Sanders, Executive Vice-President
Sergio Gelcich, Vice-President, Exploration

Ascot Resources Ltd.
#1050, 1095 West Pender St.
Vancouver, BC V6E 2M6

778-725-1060
Fax: 778-725-1070
info@ascotgold.com
www.ascotgold.com
www.facebook.com/ascotresources
twitter.com/ascotgold
www.linkedin.com/company/ascot-resources-ltd
Company Type: Public
Ticker Symbol: AOT/TSX; AOTVF/OTCQX
Profile: The mining company focuses on developing gold in BC.
Derek White, President & CEO
John Kiernan, Chief Operating Officer
Carol Li, Chief Financial Officer
Lars Beggerow, Vice-President, Geoscience & Exploration
Dianna Stoopnikoff, Vice-President, Environmental & Regulatory
Affairs

ATAC Resources Ltd.
#1500, 409 Granville St.
Vancouver, BC V6C 1T2

604-687-2522
info@atacresources.com
atacresources.com
twitter.com/atac_resources
www.linkedin.com/company/atac-resources-ltd
Company Type: Public
Ticker Symbol: ATC/TSX.V
Profile: The exploration company is developing its 100% owned
Rackla Gold Project in the Yukon. The project contains Canada's
only Carlin-Type gold discoveries. For its environmental
standards, ATAC Resources has been the recipient of the Robert
E. Leckie Award for Outstanding Reclamation Practices in
Quartz Exploration & Mining by the Yukon Government.
Graham Downs, President & CEO
Larry Donaldson, Chief Financial Officer
Ian J. Talbot, Chief Operating Officer
Adam Coulter, Vice-President, Exploration

Athabasca Minerals Inc.
Canada Place
#620, 407 - 2nd St. SW
Calgary, AB T2P 2Y3

587-392-5862
Fax: 780-430-9865
info@athabascaminerals.com
athabascaminerals.com
www.facebook.com/amiminerals
twitter.com/AmiMinerals
www.linkedin.com/company/athabasca-minerals-inc
Company Type: Public
Ticker Symbol: ABM/TSX.V
Profile: Athabasca Minerals is a Canadian management &
exploration company specializing in developing & exploring for
aggregates & industrial minerals in Alberta.
Robert Beekhuizen, Chief Executive Officer
Mark Smith, Chief Financial Officer

Atico Mining
#501, 543 Granville St.
Vancouver, BC V6C 1X8

604-633-9022
aticomining.com
twitter.com/aticoaty
www.linkedin.com/company/atico-mining-corporation
Company Type: Public
Ticker Symbol: ATY/TSX.V
Profile: A copper-gold mining company with projects in South
America. Its main location is the El Roble mine in Colombia.
Fernando Ganoza, Chief Executive Officer

Alain Bureau, President
Bill Tsang, Chief Financial Officer

Atlantic Gold
409 Billybell Way
Mooseland, NS B0N 1X0

902-384-2772
Fax: 902-384-2259
communityrelations@atlanticgold.ca
atlanticgold.ca
Company Type: Public
Profile: The mining company owns four projects in Nova Scotia.
In 2019, Atlantic Gold became a St Barbara Limited company.
Andrew Taylor, General Manager

Aura Minerals Inc.
78 SW 7th St.
Miami, FL 33130 USA

305-239-9332
info@auraminerals.com
auraminerals.com
Other Communications: Investor Relations, Email:
ir@auraminerals.com
Company Type: Public
Ticker Symbol: ORA/TSX
Profile: Aura Minerals Inc. is a mid-tier gold & copper production
company focused on the development & operation of gold &
base metal projects in the Americas.
Rodrigo Barbosa, President & CEO
JoÆo Kleber Cardoso, Chief Financial Officer

Aurcana Corporation
#850, 789 West Pender St.
Vancouver, BC V6C 1H2

604-331-9333
Fax: 604-633-9179
866-532-9333
info@aurcana.com
www.aurcana.com
Company Type: Public
Ticker Symbol: AUN/TSX.V
Profile: Aurcana Corporation is a public, junior mining company.
It owns 100% of the Shafter silver mine in Presidio County,
Texas, & has a 92% interest in the La Negra silver, copper, lead
& zinc mine, located in Queretaro State, Mexico.
Kevin Drover, President & CEO
Charles Andrew, Chief Financial Officer
Val Practico, Chief Geologist

Avalon Advanced Materials Inc.
#1901, 130 Adelaide St. West
Toronto, ON M5H 3P5

416-364-4938
Fax: 416-364-5162
office@avalonam.com
www.avalonadvancedmaterials.com
Other Communications: Investor Relations, Email:
ir@avalonam.com
www.facebook.com/avalonadvancedmaterials
twitter.com/avalonadvanced
www.linkedin.com/company/avalon-advanced-materials
Company Type: Public
Ticker Symbol: AVL/TSX; AVLNF/OTCQX
Profile: The mineral development company is focused upon rare
metals deposits in Canada. The Nechalacho Deposit, situated in
the Northwest Territories, is Avalon Rare Metals' flagship project.
Heavy rare earth elements are important for enabling advances
in green energy technology.
Donald S. Bubar, President & CEO
R.J. (Jim) Andersen, Chief Financial Officer & Vice-President,
Finance
William Mercer, Vice-President, Exploration
Mark Wiseman, Vice-President, Sustainability

Avino Silver & Gold Mines Ltd.
#900, 570 Granville St.
Vancouver, BC V6C 3P1

604-682-3701
Fax: 604-682-3600
ir@avino.com
www.avino.com
twitter.com/avino_asm
www.linkedin.com/company/avino-silver-&-gold-mines-ltd
Company Type: Public
Ticker Symbol: ASM/TSX; ASM/NYSE
Profile: Avino is a junior mining company with interests in
Mexico.
David Wolfin, President & CEO
Nathan Harte, Chief Financial Officer
Carlos Rodriguez, Chief Operating Officer

Aya Gold & Silver Inc.
#132, 1320, boul Graham
Montréal, QC H3P 3C8

647-919-2227
ayagoldsilver.com
twitter.com/AyaGoldSilver
www.linkedin.com/company/aya-gold-silver
Company Type: Public
Ticker Symbol: AYA/TSX
Staff Size: 223
Profile: Aya Gold & Silver is a mining company with a primary
interest in developing the Zgounder Silver Mine in Morocco, &
conducting pre-economic assessment studies on the Boumadine
polymetallic deposit.
Benoit La Salle, President & CEO
Ugo Landry-Tolszczuk, Chief Financial Officer

Azarga Uranium Corp.
#1, 15782 Marine Dr.
White Rock, BC V4B 1E6

604-536-2711
info@azargauranium.com
azargauranium.com
twitter.com/azargauranium
Company Type: Public
Ticker Symbol: AZZ/TSX
Profile: Azarga Uranium is a uranium development company
that owns uranium deposits in Colorado, Wyoming &
Kyrgyzstan.
Blake Steele, President & CEO
John Mays, Chief Operating Officer
Dan O'Brien, Chief Financial Officer

Azucar Minerals
#210, 1333 Johnston St.
Vancouver, BC V6H 3R9

604-689-7644
Fax: 604-689-7645
info@azucarminerals.com
www.azucarminerals.com
twitter.com/azucarminerals
www.linkedin.com/company/azucar-minerals-ltd
Company Type: Public
Ticker Symbol: AMZ/TSX.V;AXDDF/OTCQX
Profile: This company's goal is to exploit the El Cobre project on
Mexico's east coast.
Morgan Poliquin, President & CEO
Korm Trieu, Chief Financial Officer

B2Gold Corp.
Park Place
#3400, 666 Burrard St.
Vancouver, BC V6C 2X8

604-681-8371
Fax: 604-681-6209
800-316-8855
investor@b2gold.com
www.b2gold.com
twitter.com/b2goldcorp
Company Type: Public
Ticker Symbol: BTO/TSX; BTG/NYSE
Profile: Founded in 2007, B2Gold Corp. is an international gold
producer that has mines in Nicaragua, plus exploration &
development assets in Columbia, Uruguay & Nicaragua.
Clive T. Johnson, President & CEO
Mike Cinnamond, Chief Financial Officer & Senior
Vice-President, Finance
Tom Garagan, Senior Vice-President, Exploration
William Lytle, Senior Vice-President, Operations

Bacanora Lithium
The Clubhouse
8 St. James's Sq.
London, SW1Y 4JU UK

info@bacanoralithium.com
Other Communications: Advisors: +44-(0)-20-7920-3150
twitter.com/bacanoral
www.linkedin.com/company/bacanora-minerals
Company Type: Public
Ticker Symbol: BCN/TSX.V
Profile: The company's main focus is the Sonora Lithium Project
in Mexico.
Janet Blas, Chief Financial Officer

Barrick Gold Corporation
#3700, 161 Bay St.
Toronto, ON M5J 2S1

416-861-9911
800-720-7415
www.barrick.com
Other Communications: Investor Relations, Email:
investor@barrick.com
www.facebook.com/barrick.gold.corporation
twitter.com/barrickgold
www.linkedin.com/company/barrick-gold-corporation
Company Type: Public
Ticker Symbol: ABX/TSX; GOLD/NYSE
Staff Size: 22,600
Profile: The gold mining company explores, develops &
operates mines in five continents.
Mark Bristow, President & CEO
Graham Shuttleworth, Senior Executive Vice-President & CFO
Catherine Raw, Chief Operating Officer, North America

Batero Gold Inc.
#230, 2 Toronto St.
Toronto, ON M5C 2B5

info@baterogold.com
baterogold.com
Company Type: Public
Ticker Symbol: BAT/TSX
Profile: Batero Gold operates the Batero-Quinchia Project in
Colombia.
Gonzalo de Losada, President & CEO
Rodger Roden, Chief Financial Officer

Bear Creek Mining Corporation
#1400, 400 Burrard St.
Vancouver, BC V6C 3A6

604-685-6269
Fax: 604-685-6268
info@bearcreekmining.com
bearcreekmining.com
Company Type: Public
Ticker Symbol: BCM/TSX.V
Profile: Formed in 2000, Bear Creek Mining Corporation
explores for mineral deposits. The company's focus is in Peru,
where projects include Corani & Santa Ana. These projects
contain silver & by-product base metals.
Anthony Hawkshaw, President & CEO
Paul Tweddle, Chief Financial Officer

Belo Sun Mining Corp.
PO Box 75, #800, 65 Queen St. West
Toronto, ON M5H 2M5

416-309-4395
info@belosun.com
www.belosun.com
Company Type: Public
Ticker Symbol: BSX/TSX
Profile: Belo Sun is a Canadian-based mining company focused
on developing the Volta Grande Gold Project in Brazil.
Peter Tagliamonte, President & CEO
Ian Pritchard, Chief Operating Officer
Ryan Ptolemy, Chief Financial Officer
Stéphane Amireault, Vice-President, Exploration

Bluestone Resources Inc.
#2000, 885 West Georgia St.
Vancouver, BC V6C 3E8

604-757-4715
info@bluestoneresources.ca
bluestoneresources.ca
Company Type: Public
Ticker Symbol: BSR/TSX.V
Profile: Bluestone Resources was founded in 2017 with the
purchase of the Cerro Blanco gold & Mita Geothermal projects in
Guatemala.
Jack Lundin, President & CEO
Peter Hemstead, Chief Financial Officer
David Cass, Vice-President, Exploration

Bonterra Resources Inc.
#2, 2872, ch Sullivan
Val-d'Or, QC J9P 0B9

819-825-8678
Fax: 819-825-1222
info@btrgold.com
btrgold.com
Other Communications: Investor Relations, Email:
ir@btrgold.com
www.facebook.com/bonterraresources
twitter.com/bonterragold
Company Type: Public
Ticker Symbol: BTR/TSX.V
Profile: Bonterra Resources is a gold exploration company
operating in its Gladiator Gold Deposit in Québec.
Pascal Hamelin, Chief Executive Officer

Johnny Oliveira, Chief Financial Officer

Bullman Minerals
#303, 595 Howe St.
Vancouver, BC V6C 2T5

Company Type: Public
Profile: Bullman Minerals Inc. is exploring its Siguiri &
Balandougouba projects in Guinea & Mali.
Peter Yue, Chief Executive Officer

Cadillac Ventures Inc.
#269, 1099 Kingston Rd.
Pickering, ON L1V 1B5

416-203-7722
cadillacventures.com
Company Type: Public
Ticker Symbol: CDC/TSX.V
Profile: Cadillac Ventures owns the Thierry Property copper
development project located outside of Pickle Lake in
norhwestern Ontario. The company also holds assets in Peru,
New Brunswick & Québec.
Norman Brewster, President & CEO

Calibre Mining Corp.
PO Box 49167, #413, 595 Burrard St.
Vancouver, BC V7X 1J1

604-681-9944
Fax: 604-681-9955
calibre@calibremining.com
calibremining.com
twitter.com/calibreminingco
Company Type: Public
Ticker Symbol: CXB/TSX.V
Profile: Calibre Mining is a Canadian-based exploration & mine
development company with gold, silver & copper mineral
exploration projects in the 'Mining Triangle' of northeastern
Nicaragua.
Darren Hall, President & CEO
John Seaberg, Senior Vice-President & CFO
Mark Petersen, Vice-President, Exploration

Callinex Mines
#1555, 555 West Hastings St.
Vancouver, BC V6B 4N6

604-605-0885
info@callinex.ca
callinex.ca
Company Type: Public
Ticker Symbol: CNX/TSX.V
Profile: The company has mining projects in Flin Flon, MB,
Bathurst, NB & Buchans, NL. The Flin Flon project hosts
copper, zinc, gold & silver. The Bathurst project hosts silver.
Max Porterfield, President & CEO
Killian Ruby, Chief Financial Officer

Cameco Corporation
2121 - 11th St. West
Saskatoon, SK S7M 1J3

306-956-6200
Fax: 306-956-6201
www.cameco.com
Other Communications: Investor Inquiries, Phone: 306-956-6294
www.facebook.com/cameco.careers
twitter.com/cameconews
www.linkedin.com/company/cameco-corporation
Company Type: Public
Ticker Symbol: CCO/TSX; CCJ/NYSE
Staff Size: 1,900
Profile: Cameco is engaged in the production of uranium to
generate electricity in nuclear energy plants throughout the
world.
Tim S. Gitzel, President & CEO
Grant E. Isaac, Senior Vice-President & CFO
Brian Reilly, Senior Vice-President & COO
Sean Quinn, Senior Vice-President & Chief Legal Officer
Alice Wong, Senior Vice-President & Chief Corporate Officer

Canagold Resources Ltd.
#810, 625 Howe St.
Vancouver, BC V6C 2T6

604-685-9700
Fax: 604-685-9744
info@canarc.net
canarc.net
twitter.com/CCMGoldLtd
www.linkedin.com/company/canagold-resources
Company Type: Public
Ticker Symbol: CCM/TSX; OTCQX/CRCUF
Profile: Canagold Resources is focused on gold & silver assets
located in North America. The company's main project is New
Polaris gold project in northern British Columbia.
Scott Eldridge, Chief Executive Officer
Garry Biles, President & COO

Philip Yee, Chief Financial Officer
Troy Gill, Vice-President, Exploration

Candente Copper Corp.
#801, 1112 West Pender St.
Vancouver, BC V6E 2S1

604-689-1957
877-689-1964
info@candentecopper.com
www.candentecopper.com
Company Type: Public
Ticker Symbol: DNT/TSX
Profile: Candente Copper Corp. owns 100% of the Cañariaco
Norte Copper Project in northern Peru. The company undertakes
exploration in accordance with the Peruvian Ministry of Energy &
Mines' General Mining Law & regulations.
Joanne C. Freeze, President & CEO
Mark Lotz, Chief Financial Officer

Capstone Mining Corp.
#2100, 510 West Georgia St.
Vancouver, BC V6B 0M3

604-684-8894
Fax: 604-688-2180
866-684-8894
info@capstonemining.com
capstonemining.com
www.facebook.com/capstonemining
twitter.com/capstonemining
www.linkedin.com/company/capstone-mining
Company Type: Public
Ticker Symbol: CS/TSX
Profile: Capstone Mining Corp. operates three producing copper
mines: Pinto Valley, U.S.; Cozamin, Mexico; & Minto, Canada.
Development projects are underway in British Columbia, Chile &
Australia.
In 2011, Capstone Mining acquired Far West Mining Ltd., a
company engaged in the acquisition & exploration of mineral
properties in Chile & Australia.
Darren M. Pylot, President & CEO
Raman Randhawa, Chief Financial Officer

Cartier Resources Inc.
#1000, 1740, ch Sullivan
Val d'Or, QC J9P 7H1

819-874-1331
Fax: 819-874-3113
877-874-1331
info@ressourcescartier.com
ressourcescartier.com
www.facebook.com/cartierresources
twitter.com/cartierress
www.linkedin.com/company/ressources-cartier-resources
Company Type: Public
Ticker Symbol: ECR/TSX-V
Profile: Cartier Resources explores projects in the Abitibi Gold
Belt.
Philippe Cloutier, President & CEO
philippe.cloutier@ressourcescartier.com
Nancy Lacoursière, Chief Financial Officer
nancy.lacoursiere@ressourcescartier.com
Gaétan Lavallière, Vice-President
gaetan.lavalliere@ressourcescartier.com

Centerra Gold Inc.
#1500, 1 University Ave.
Toronto, ON M5J 2P1

416-204-1953
Fax: 416-204-1954
info@centerragold.com
www.centerragold.com
www.facebook.com/CenterraGold
twitter.com/Centerra_Gold
www.linkedin.com/company/centerra-gold-inc-
Company Type: Public
Ticker Symbol: CG/TSX
Profile: Centerra Gold Inc. is engaged in the acquisition,
exploration, development & operation of gold properties in
Central Asia, the former Soviet Union & other emerging markets.
Scott G. Perry, President & CEO
Daniel (Dan) Desjardin, Vice-President & COO
Darren J. Millman, Vice-President & Chief Financial Officer
Yousef Rehman, Vice-President & General Counsel

Century Global Commodities Corporation
#1401, 200 University Ave.
Toronto, ON M5H 3C6

416-977-3188
Fax: 416-977-8002
contact@centuryglobal.ca
centuryglobal.ca
Other Communications: Investor Relations, Email:
ir@centuryglobal.ca
www.facebook.com/CenturyGlobalCommodities

Company Type: Public
Ticker Symbol: CNT/TSX
Profile: Century Global Commodities is a mining company with mineral exploration & development activities focused on iron ore. Its projects are locatd in Quebec & Newfoundland & Labrador.
Sandy Chim, Chair, President & CEO
Bonnie Leung, Chief Financial Officer
Allan Gan, Director, Exploration

Chesapeake Gold Corp.
#201, 1512 Yew St.
Vancouver, BC V6K 3E4

604-731-1094
Fax: 604-731-0209
invest@chesapeakegold.com
www.chesapeakegold.com
www.facebook.com/chesapeakegold
twitter.com/chesapeake_gold
www.linkedin.com/company/chesapeake-gold-corp

Company Type: Public
Ticker Symbol: CKG/TSX.V
Profile: Chesapeake Gold Corp. explores for & develops precious metals projects. The company's focus is upon its 100% owned Metates gold deposit in Durango state, Mexico.
Alan Pangbourne, Chief Executive Officer
P. Randy Reifel, President
Erick J. Underwood, Chief Financial Officer
Alberto Galicia, Vice-President, Exploration

China Gold International Resources Corp. Ltd.
One Bentall Centre
PO Box 27, #660, 505 Burrard St.
Vancouver, BC V7X 1M4

604-609-0598
Fax: 604-688-0598
info@chinagoldintl.com
www.chinagoldintl.com
Other Communications: Investor Relations, Phone:
604-609-0598

Company Type: Public
Ticker Symbol: CGG/TSX; 2099/HKSE
Profile: China Gold International Resources is a mineral development company that operates the CSH Gold Mine, located in Inner Mongolia, as well as the Jiama Copper-Polymetallic Mine, situated in the Tibet Autonomous Region of China. The company's aim is to explore, acquire & develop new projects in China & elsewhere.
Liangyou Jiang, Chief Executive Officer
Yuehe Lu, Chief Financial Officer

Commerce Resources Corp.
#1450, 789 West Pender St.
Vancouver, BC V6C 1H2

604-484-2700
Fax: 604-681-8240
866-484-2700
info@commerceresources.com
www.commerceresources.com
www.facebook.com/commerceresourcesfan
twitter.com/commercescce

Company Type: Public
Ticker Symbol: CCE/TSX.V
Profile: The exploration & development company's focus is upon British Columbia's Upper Fir Tantalum & Niobium Deposit & Québec's Eldor Rare Earth Project.
David Hodge, Chief Executive Officer
Christopher Grove, President
Jody Bellefleur, Chief Financial Officer
Jody Dahrouge, Vice-President, Exploration
Mireille Smith, Manager, Social & Environmental Sustainability

Copper Fox Metals Inc.
#650, 340 - 12th Ave. SW
Calgary, AB T2R 1L5

403-264-2820
Fax: 403-264-2920
844-464-2820
info@copperfoxmetals.com
www.copperfoxmetals.com
Other Communications: Investor Relations, Email:
investor@copperfoxmetals.com

Company Type: Public
Ticker Symbol: CUU/TSX.V
Profile: Copper Fox is a Canadian-based resource development company with a 25% interest in a Joint Venture on the Schaft Creek Project in Northern British Columbia.
Elmer B. Stewart, Chair, President & CEO
Mark T. Brown, Chief Financial Officer

Copper Mountain Mining Corporation
#1700, 700 West Pender St.
Vancouver, BC V6C 1G8

604-682-2992
Fax: 604-682-2993
877-451-2662
cumtn.com

Company Type: Public
Ticker Symbol: CMMC/TSX; C6C/ASX
Profile: The resource company owns 75% of the Copper Mountain Mine, which is located south of Princeton, British Columbia.
Gil Clausen, President & CEO
gil.clausen@cumtn.com
Rod Shier, Chief Financial Officer
rod@cumtn.com
Peter Holbek, Vice-President, Exploration

Cornerstone Capital Resources Inc.
#800, 1730 St Laurent Blvd.
Ottawa, ON K1G 3Y7

343-689-0714
ir@cornerstoneresources.ca
cornerstoneresources.com

Company Type: Public
Ticker Symbol: CGP/TSX.V
Profile: Cornerstone Capital Resources has a diversified portfolio of gold, silver & copper projects in Ecuador & Chile.
H. Brooke Macdonald, President & CEO
David Loveys, Chief Financial Officer

Cornish Metals Inc.
#960, 789 Pender St.
Vancouver, BC V6C 1H2

604-200-6664
Fax: 604-283-1136
877-315-0580
info@cornishmetals.com
www.cornishmetals.com
www.facebook.com/CornishMetals
twitter.com/CornishMetals
www.linkedin.com/company/cornish-metals-inc

Company Type: Public
Ticker Symbol: CUSN/TSX.V
Profile: Cornish Metals, an Associate Company of Osisko, is a mineral exploration company focused on metal assets in the United Kingdom & North America. Its main projects are United Downs in Cornwall, UK & South Crofty.
Richard Williams, President & CEO
Matthew Hird, Chief Financial Officer
Owen Mihalop, Chief Operating Officer

Corsa Coal Corp.
PO Box 260, 1576 Stoystown Rd.
Friedens, PA 15541 USA

724-754-0028
communication@corsacoal.com
www.corsacoal.com

Company Type: Public
Ticker Symbol: CSO/TSX.V
Staff Size: 280
Profile: Corsa Coal Corp. mines, processes & sells metallurgical coal. The company is active in Central & Northern Appalachia.
Peter Merritts, Chief Executive Officer
Kevin M. Harrigan, Chief Financial Officer

Corvus Gold Inc.
#1750, 700 West Pender St.
Vancouver, BC V6C 1G8

604-638-3246
844-638-3246
www.corvusgold.com
twitter.com/corvus_gold

Company Type: Public
Ticker Symbol: KOR/TSX; CORVF/OTCQX
Profile: Corvus Gold is a junior exploration & development gold company with operations in Nevada. Corvus wholly owns two projects: North Bullfrog & Mother Lode.
Jeffrey A. Pontius, President & CEO
Carl Brechtel, Chief Administrative Officer
Peggy Wu, Chief Financial Officer

Critical Elements Lithium Corporation/Corporation Lithium Éléments Critiques
#2101, 1080, côte du Beaver Hall
Montréal, QC H2Z 1S8

514-904-1496
Fax: 514-904-1597
www.cecorp.ca
www.facebook.com/criticalelementslithiumcorporation
twitter.com/crecorp
www.linkedin.com/company/critical-elements-corporation

Company Type: Public
Ticker Symbol: CRE/TSX.V

Profile: Critical Elements Lithium Corporation is a junior mining company. Its flagship project is the Rose Lithium-Tantalum project in James Bay, Québec.
Jean-Sébastien Lavallée, Chief Executive Officer
Steffen Haber, President
Nathalie Laurin, Chief Financial Officer & Secretary

Crystal Peak Minerals Inc.
#550, 2150 South 1300 East
Salt Lake City, UT 84106 USA

801-485-0223
info@crystalpeakminerals.com
crystalpeakminerals.com

Company Type: Public
Ticker Symbol: CPM/TSX.V
Profile: Crystal Peak Minerals Inc. is an exploration-stage pre-revenue potash development company.
Dean Pekeski, Interim Chief Executive Officer
Blake Measom, Chief Financial Officer
Dean Pekeski, Vice-President, Project Development

Cub Energy Inc.
#3300, 205 - 5th Ave. SW
Calgary, AB T2P 2V7

www.cubenergyinc.com

Company Type: Public
Ticker Symbol: KUB/TSX.V
Profile: Cub Energy Inc. is an upstream oil & gas company with 132,500 net acres in the Ukraine.
Patrick McGrath, Interim Chief Executive Officer
Eugene Chaban, Chief Financial Officer
Sergil Panchuk, Chief Operating Officer

Denison Mines Corp.
#1100, 40 University Ave.
Toronto, ON M5J 1T1

416-979-1991
Fax: 416-979-5893
info@denisonmines.com
www.denisonmines.com
www.facebook.com/denisonmines
twitter.com/denisonminesco
www.linkedin.com/company/denison-mines-usa-corp-

Company Type: Public
Ticker Symbol: DML/TSX; DNN/NYSE
Profile: Denison Mines Corp. is a uranium exploration & production company. Its active uranium mines are located in Canada & the United States. Denison Environmental Services (DES) was established to provide mine decommissioning, long-term care & maintenance services to closed mining facilities.
David D. Cates, President & CEO
Mac McDonald, Chief Financial Officer & Executive Vice-President, Finance
David Bronkhorst, Vice-President, Operations

Dexterra Group Inc.
#425, 5915 Airport Rd.
Mississauga, ON L4V 1T1

416-483-5152
dexterra.com
www.linkedin.com/company/dexterra-group

Company Type: Public
Ticker Symbol: DXT/TSX
Staff Size: 1,400
Profile: Dexterra Group's services include northern marine transportation & logistics, mobile structures, matting solutions & camp management & catering. Services are provided to natural resource development projects in Canada's western provinces & northern territories.
John Mac Cuish, CEO & President, Facilities Management
Mark Becker, COO & President, WAFES
Dawn Nigro, President, NRB Modular Solutions
Drew Knight, Chief Financial Officer
Cindy McArthur, Chief Human Resources Officer
Lee-Anne Lyon-Bartley, Executive Vice-President, Health, Safety, Environment & Quality

Dundee Precious Metals Inc.
PO Box 195, #500, 1 Adelaide St. East
Toronto, ON M5C 2V9

416-365-5191
Fax: 416-365-9080
info@dundeeprecious.com
www.dundeeprecious.com

Company Type: Public
Ticker Symbol: DPM/TSX
Profile: Dundee Precious Metals Inc. acquires, explores, develops & mines precious metals properties. The company is active in Armenia, Bulgaria, Serbia & Namibia.
David Rae, President & CEO
Hume Kyle, Executive Vice-President & CFO
Kelly Stark-Anderson, General Counsel & Executive Vice-President, Corporate Affairs

Dynacor Gold Mines Inc.
#1200, 625, boul René-Lévesque ouest
Montréal, QC H3B 1R2

514-393-9000
Fax: 514-393-9002
dyn@dynacor.com
www.dynacor.com
Other Communications: Investor Relations, Email:
investors@dynacor.com
twitter.com/dynacorgold

Company Type: Public
Ticker Symbol: DNG/TSX
Profile: The company operates a gold processing plant in Peru.
Jean Martineau, President & CEO
Léonard Teoli, Vice-President & CFO

East Africa Metals Inc.
777 Dunsmuir St., 17th Fl.
Vancouver, BC V7Y 1K4

604-488-0822
866-488-0822
investors@eastafricametals.com
eastafricametals.com

Company Type: Public
Ticker Symbol: EAM/TSX.V
Profile: The mining company has projects in Ethiopia & Tanzania.
Andrew Lee Smith, President & CEO
Jacqueline Tucker, Chief Financial Officer

Eastern Platinum Limited
Also Known As: Eastplats
#1080, 1188 West Georgia St.
Vancouver, BC V6E 4A2

604-800-8200
Fax: 604-210-4516
info@eastplats.com
eastplats.com

Company Type: Public
Ticker Symbol: ELR/TSX
Profile: Eastern Platinum Limited was established in 2003. The metals mining company has acquired platinum & rhodium deposits in South Africa.
Diana Hu, Chief Executive Officer
Rowland Wallenius, Chief Financial Officer

Eldorado Gold Corporation
Five Bentall Centre
#1188, 550 Burrard St.
Vancouver, BC V6C 2B5

604-687-4018
Fax: 604-687-4026
888-353-8166
info@eldoradogold.com
www.eldoradogold.com
www.facebook.com/eldoradogoldcorp
www.linkedin.com/company/eldorado-gold-corporation

Company Type: Public
Ticker Symbol: ELD/TSX; EGO/NYSE
Staff Size: 4,900
Profile: Eldorado Gold Corporation is an international company that specializes in the exploration & development of gold properties. In 2012, Eldorado Gold Corporation acquired all the issued & outstanding securities of European Goldfields Limited, a company with gold reserves in the European Union.
The gold producer now has properties in Brazil, Greece, Turkey, China & Romania. Industry best practices are implemented in each region in an effort to minimize environmental impacts.
Eldorado Gold acquired Integra Gold in July 2017.
George Burns, President & CEO
Joseph Dick, Executive Vice-President & COO
Philip Yee, Executive Vice-President & CFO

Emerita Resources Corp.
#800, 65 Queen St. West
Toronto, ON M5H 2M5

www.emeritaresources.com
twitter.com/EmeritaRes

Company Type: Public
Ticker Symbol: EMO/TSX.V
Profile: Emerita Resources is an exploration & development company focused on properties in Spain & Brazil.
David Gower, Chief Executive Officer
Joaquin Merino-Marquez, President
Greg Duras, Chief Financial Officer

Endeavour Mining
5 Young St.
London, W8 5EH UK

info@endeavourmining.com
www.endeavourmining.com
Other Communications: +44-203-011-2723
twitter.com/EndeavourMining
www.linkedin.com/company/endeavour-mining

Company Type: Public
Ticker Symbol: EDV/TSX
Staff Size: 4,900
Profile: Endeavour Mining is a senior gold producer with seven producing mines in West Africa. In 2021, the company merged with Teranga Gold Corporation.
Sébastien de Montessus, President & CEO
Mark Morcombe, Executive Vice-President & COO
Joanna Pearson, Executive Vice-President & CFO
Pascal Bernasconi, Executive Vice-President, Public Affairs, Sustainability & Security

Endeavour Silver Corp.
PO Box 10328, #1130, 609 Granville St.
Vancouver, BC V7Y 1G5

604-685-9775
877-685-9775
info@edrsilver.com
www.edrsilver.com
www.facebook.com/edrsilvercorp
twitter.com/edrsilvercorp
www.linkedin.com/company/endeavour-silver-corp

Company Type: Public
Ticker Symbol: EDR/TSX; EXK/NYSE
Profile: The mid-cap silver mining company has resources in Mexico.
Dan Dickson, Chief Executive Officer
Donald Grey, Chief Operating Officer
Christine West, Chief Financial Officer
Luis R. Castro Valdez, Vice-President, Exploration

Energold Drilling Corp.
#1605, 777 Dunsmuir St.
Vancouver, BC V6C 1X8

604-681-9501
hello@energold.com
www.energold.com
www.linkedin.com/company/energold-drilling

Company Type: Public
Profile: Founded in 1991, Energold Drilling serves the international mining sector.
Brian Mittman, Chief Executive Officer
Matthew Freeman, Chief Financial Officer
matthew@energold.com

Energy Fuels Inc.
#308, 82 Richmond St. East
Toronto, ON M5C 1P1

303-974-2140
Fax: 303-974-2141
888-864-2125
info@energyfuels.com
www.energyfuels.com
twitter.com/energy_fuels
www.linkedin.com/company/energy-fuels-resources

Company Type: Public
Ticker Symbol: EFR/TSX
Staff Size: 200
Profile: Energy Fuels focuses upon the development & expansion of uranium & vanadium assets in the United States. The company also has exploration properties in the Athabasca Basin of Saskatchewan.
In 2013, Energy Fuels acquired Strathmore Minerals.
Mark Chalmers, President & CEO
David C. Frydenlund, General Counsel & CFO

Entrée Resources Ltd.
#1650, 1066 West Hastings St.
Vancouver, BC V6E 3X1

604-687-4777
Fax: 604-687-4770
866-368-7330
info@entreeresourcesltd.com
www.entreeresourcesltd.com
twitter.com/entreeresource
www.linkedin.com/company/entreeresourcesltd

Company Type: Public
Ticker Symbol: ETG/TSX; EGI/NYSE
Profile: Entrée Resources is a Canadian mineral exploration company with an interest in an integral part of the Oyu Tolgoi copper-gold mining project in Mongolia.
In May 2017, Entrée Gold Inc. became Entrée Resources Ltd.
Stephen Scott, President & CEO
Duane Lo, Chief Financial Officer
Susan McLeod, Vice-President, Legal Affairs

Equinox Gold Corp.
#1501, 700 West Pender St.
Vancouver, BC V6C 1G8

604-558-0560
833-379-4653
info@equinoxgold.com
www.equinoxgold.com

Company Type: Public
Ticker Symbol: EQX/TSX.V
Profile: Equinox Gold is a multi-asset mining company active in the Aurizona Gold Mine in Brazil & development at the Castle Mountain project in California. In 2021, it acquired Premier Gold Mines, which added projects in Ontario & Mexico.
Christian Milau, Chief Executive Officer
Greg Smith, President
Peter Hardie, Chief Financial Officer
Doug Reddy, Chief Operating Officer
Scott Heffernan, Executive Vice-President, Exploration

Erdene Resource Development Corp.
Metropolitan Place
#1480, 99 Wyse Rd.
Dartmouth, NS B3A 4S5

902-423-6419
info@erdene.com
www.erdene.com
www.linkedin.com/company/erdene-resource-development-corp-

Company Type: Public
Ticker Symbol: ERD/TSX
Profile: Erdene Resource Development Corp. is a resource exploration & development company that has several 100%-owned prospects & deposits in Mongolia, including the company's flagship Khundii Gold Project. The company also has an alliance with Teck Resources Ltd. on a regional copper-gold exploration in the prospective Trans Altai region of southwest Mongolia.
Peter C. Akerley, President & CEO
Bayarmaa Bagabandi, Chief Administrative Officer
Robert Jenkins, Chief Financial Officer
rjenkins@erdene.com
Michael X. Gillis, Vice-President, Exploration & Operations

Ero Copper Corp.
#1050, 625 Howe St.
Vancouver, BC V6C 2T6

604-499-9244
Fax: 604-398-3767
info@erocopper.com
erocopper.com

Company Type: Public
Ticker Symbol: ERO/TSX
Profile: Ero Copper is a mid-tier copper producer with a 99.6% interest in Mineraçao Caraíba S.A. (MMCSA), a Brazilian copper mining company with assets in the MCSA Mining Complex in Bahia State, Brazil.
David Strang, Chief Executive Officer
Makko DeFilippo, President
Wayne Drier, Chief Financial Officer
Michel Richard, Chief Geological Officer
Pablo Mejia-Herrera, Vice-President, Exploration

Euromax Resources
14 Blvd. Partizanski Odredi
Skopje, 1000 Macedonia

info@euromaxresources.mk
www.euromaxresources.com
www.facebook.com/euromaxresources

Company Type: Public
Ticker Symbol: EOX/TSX
Profile: Euromax Resources is a development company focused on building & operating the Ilovica-Shtuka copper & gold projects in Macedonia.
Nicolas Treand, President & Executive Director
Pat Forward, Chief Operating Officer
Nikola Gulev, Chief Financial Officer

Excelsior Mining Corp.
Concord Place
#300, 2999 North 44th St.
Phoenix, AZ 85018 USA

info@excelsiormining.com
www.excelsiormining.com
Other Communications: Investor Relations, Phone:
604-723-1433

Company Type: Public
Ticker Symbol: MIN/TSX
Profile: A copper mining company currently developing a project in Arizona.
Stephen Twyerould, President & CEO
Greg Duschek, Senior Vice-President & CFO

Falco Resources Ltd.
#300, 1100, av des Canadiens-de-Montréal
Montréal, QC H3B 2S2

514-905-3162
info@falcores.com
www.falcores.com
www.facebook.com/falcoresources
twitter.com/falcoresources
www.linkedin.com/company/falco-pacific-resource-group

Company Type: Public
Ticker Symbol: FPC/TSX.V
Profile: Falco Resources is a junior gold resource exploration company with one of the largest claims in the Abitibi region of Québec: with 100% ownership of 74,000 hectares of property.
Luc Lessard, President & CEO
Anthony Glavac, Chief Financial Officer
Ronald Bougie, Vice-President, Engineering & Construction
Hélène Cartier, Vice-President, Environment & Sustainable Development

Fancamp Exploration Ltd.
7290 Gray Ave.
Burnaby, BC V5J 3Z2
604-434-8829
info@fancamp.ca
www.fancampexplorationltd.ca
Company Type: Public
Ticker Symbol: FNC/TSX.V
Profile: Fancamp Exploration Ltd. is a junior mineral exploration company. The company has an inventory of resource properties in Québec, Ontario & New Brunswick, with commodities including gold, base metals, titanium, chromium & iron.
Rajesh Sharma, Interim Chief Executive Officer
Debra Chapman, Chief Financial Officer
Francois Auclair, Vice-President

Filo Mining Corp.
HSBC Bldg.
#2000, 885 West Georgia St.
Vancouver, BC V6C 3E8
604-689-7842
info@filo-mining.com
www.filo-mining.com
Company Type: Public
Ticker Symbol: FIL/TSX.V
Profile: The company is developing its Filo del Sol copper-gold-silver project.
Jamie Beck, President & CEO
Bob Carmichael, Vice-President, Exploration
Jeff Yip, Chief Financial Officer

Fiore Gold Ltd.
#1410, 120 Adelaide St. West
Toronto, ON M5H 1T1
416-639-1426
info@fioregold.com
fioregold.com
www.facebook.com/FioreGoldLtd
twitter.com/fiore_gold
Company Type: Public
Ticker Symbol: F/TSX.V
Profile: Fiore Gold Ltd. is a new company focused on its producing Pan Mine in Nevada. It also has exploration projects in Nevada, Washington & Chile.
Tim Warman, Chief Executive Officer
Ross MacLean, Chief Operating Officer
Barry O'Shea, Chief Financial Officer

First Majestic Silver Corp.
#1800, 925 West Georgia St.
Vancouver, BC V6C 3L2
604-688-3033
Fax: 604-639-8873
866-529-2807
info@firstmajestic.com
www.firstmajestic.com
Other Communications: sales@firstmajestic.com
twitter.com/fmsilvercorp
www.linkedin.com/company/first-majestic-silver-corp-
Company Type: Public
Ticker Symbol: FR/TSX; AG/NYSE
Staff Size: 5,400
Profile: The silver company is focused on production in Mexico. In 2012, First Majestic Silver Corp. acquired Silvermex Resources Inc., a mining company with a portfolio of exploration & production projects in Mexico. In 2017, First Majestic acquired Primero Mining Corp.
Keith Neumeyer, President & CEO
Raymond L. Polman, Chief Financial Officer

First Mining Gold Corp.
#2070, 1188 West Georgia St.
Vancouver, BC V6E 4A2
844-306-8827
info@firstminingfinancial.com
firstmininggold.com
twitter.com/firstmining
www.linkedin.com/company/first-mining-gold-corp
Company Type: Public
Ticker Symbol: FF/TSX; FFMGF/OTCQX
Profile: First Mining Finance is a mineral property 'bank' focused on acquiring, enhancing & monetizing high-quality mineral assets in the Americas.

Dan Wilton, Chief Executive Officer
Ken Engquist, Chief Operating Officer
Andy Marshall, Chief Financial Officer
Andy Marshall, Vice-President, Environment & Community Relations

First Quantum Minerals Ltd.
Three Bantell Centre
#2600, 595 Burrard St.
Vancouver, BC V7X 1L3
416-361-6400
Fax: 416-368-4692
888-688-6577
info@fqml.com
first-quantum.com
www.facebook.com/firstquantumminerals
www.linkedin.com/company/firstquantumminerals
Company Type: Public
Ticker Symbol: FM/TSX
Staff Size: 20,000
Profile: Operations of the mining & metals company include mineral exploration, development, mining, smelting & refining. First Quantum Minerals is engaged in copper & cobalt mining in Africa. The company also has interest in gold & cobalt production.
Hannes Meyer, Chief Financial Officer

Fission Uranium Corp.
#700, 1620 Dickson Ave.
Kelowna, BC V1Y 9Y2
250-868-8140
Fax: 250-868-8493
877-868-8140
info@fissionuranium.com
fissionuranium.com
Other Communications: Investor Relations, Email: ir@fissionuranium.com
twitter.com/fissionuranium
www.linkedin.com/company/fission-energy-corp
Company Type: Public
Ticker Symbol: FCU/TSX; FCUUF/OTCQX
Profile: The company mines & develops uranium in the Athabasca Basin in northern Saskatchewan.
Ross McElroy, President, CEO & Chief Geologist

Focus Graphite
PO Box 116, 945 Princess St.
Kingston, ON K7L 0E9
613-241-4040
Fax: 613-241-8632
info@focusgraphite.com
www.focusgraphite.com
Company Type: Public
Ticker Symbol: FMS.V/TSX
Profile: Focus Graphite Inc. is a mid-tier junior mining development company with its attention geared toward high purity graphite.
Marc Roy, President & CEO
Judith T. Mazvihwa-MacLean, Chief Financial Officer

Foran Mining Corporation
#904, 409 Granville St.
Vancouver, BC V6C 1T2
604-488-0008
ir@foranmining.com
foranmining.com
www.facebook.com/ForanMining
twitter.com/foranmining
www.linkedin.com/company/foran-mining
Company Type: Public
Ticker Symbol: FOM/TSX.V
Profile: Foran Mining Corporation is an exploration & development company focused on zinc & copper resource development in the Hanson Lake VMS Camp in east-central Saskatchewan.
Patrick Soares, Executive Chair & CEO
Tim Thiessen, Chief Financial Officer
Roger March, Vice-President, Exploration

Forsys Metals Corp.
#200, 20 Adelaide St. East
Toronto, ON M5C 2K3
416-818-4035
info@forsysmetals.com
www.forsysmetals.com
Company Type: Public
Ticker Symbol: FSY/TSX
Profile: Forsys Metals is a uranium producer. The company owns 100% of the Namibplaas Uranium Project & the Valencia Uranium Project, which are both located in Namibia, Africa.
Mark Frewin, Interim Chief Executive Officer
Miles Nagamatsu, Chief Financial Officer

Fort St. James Nickel Corp.
#888, 888 Dunsmuir St.
Vancouver, BC V6C 3K4
604-488-3900
Fax: 604-488-3910
office@ftjminerals.com
ftjminerals.com
twitter.com/fortstjamescorp
Company Type: Public
Ticker Symbol: FTJ/TSX.V
Profile: Fort St. James Nickel is a mineral exploration company for properties in North America.
Barry Brown, President

Fortuna Silver Mines Inc.
#650, 200 Burrard St.
Vancouver, BC V6C 3L6
604-484-4085
Fax: 604-484-4029
info@fortunasilver.com
www.fortunasilver.com
Company Type: Public
Ticker Symbol: FVI/TSX; FSM/NYSE
Profile: Fortuna is a silver & base metal producer. Areas of operation are southern Peru & Mexico. In 2016, the company acquired Goldrock Mines Corp.
Jorge Ganoza, President & CEO
Luis D. Ganoza, Chief Financial Officer
Manuel Ruiz-Canejo, Vice-President, Operations
David Volkert, Vice-President, Volkert

Fortune Minerals Limited
617 Wellington St.
London, ON N6A 3R6
519-858-8188
Fax: 519-858-8155
info@fortuneminerals.com
www.fortuneminerals.com
www.linkedin.com/company/fortune-minerals-limited
Company Type: Public
Ticker Symbol: FT/TSX
Profile: The diversified resource company has mineral deposits & exploration projects located in Canada. Projects include the Mount Klappan anthracite metallurgical coal deposit in British Columbia, & the NICO gold, colbalt, bismuth, copper deposit in the Northwest Territories.
Robin E. Goad, President & CEO
Patricia Penney, Interim Chief Financial Officer
Richard P. Schryer, Vice-President, Regulatory & Envrionmental Affairs

Franco-Nevada Corporation
PO Box 285 Stn. Commerce Cour, , #2000, 199 Bay St.
Toronto, ON M5L 1G9
416-306-6300
info@franco-nevada.com
www.franco-nevada.com
Company Type: Public
Ticker Symbol: FNV/TSX, NYSE
Profile: Franco-Nevada Corporation has interests in large gold development & exploration projects.
Paul Brink, President & CEO
Sandip Rana, Chief Financial Officer
Jaosn O'Connell, Senior Vice-President, Energy

Freegold Ventures
PO Box 10351, #888, 700 West Georgia St.
Vancouver, BC V7Y 1G5
604-662-7307
Fax: 604-662-3791
ask@freegoldventures.com
www.freegoldventures.com
Company Type: Public
Ticker Symbol: FVL/TSX
Profile: Freegold Ventures is focussed on the exploration & development of Alaskan gold assets.
J. Kristina Walcott, President & CEO
604-662-7307
Gordon Steblin, Chief Financial Officer
Alvin Jackson, Vice-President, Exploration & Development

Fury Gold Mines Limited
#900, 34 King St. East
Toronto, ON M5C 2X8
844-601-0841
info@furygoldmines.com
furygoldmines.com
twitter.com/FuryGoldMines
www.linkedin.com/company/furygoldmines
Company Type: Public
Ticker Symbol: FURY/TSX, NYSE
Profile: The company is an exploration & development company focused on three mining regions: James Bay, QC; Golden

Triangle, BC; Kitikmeot Region, NT. It was spun out from Auryn Resources in 2020.
Michael Timmins, President & CEO
Lynsey Sherry, Chief Financial Officer
Michael Henrichsen, Senior Vice-President, Exploration

Galane Gold Ltd.
Brookfield Place
#1800, 181 Bay St.
Toronto, ON M5J 2T9

investors@galanegold.com
www.galanegold.com
www.linkedin.com/company/galane-gold-ltd
Company Type: Public
Ticker Symbol: GG/TSX.V
Profile: Galane Gold Ltd. is an unhedged gold producer & explorer with mining operations & exploration tenements in the Republic of Botswana & in South Africa.
Nicholas Brodie, Chief Executive Officer
Gavin Vandervegt, Chief Financial Officer

Galiano Gold Inc.
#1640, 1066 West Hastings St.
Vancouver, BC V6E 3X1

604-683-8193
Fax: 604-683-8194
855-246-7341
info@galianogold.com
www.galianogold.com
Company Type: Public
Ticker Symbol: GAU/TSX, NYSE
Staff Size: 550
Profile: Galiano Gold is a mineral exploration company that operates & manages the Asanko Gold Mine in Ghana, West Africa, which it holds jointly with Gold Fields.
Grey McCunn, Chief Executive Officer
Fausto Di Trapani, Executive Vice-President & CFO
Todd Romaine, Executive Vice-President, Sustainability

Garibaldi Resources Corp.
#1150, 409 Granville St.
Vancouver, BC V62 1T2

604-488-8851
Fax: 604-488-8871
info@garibaldiresources.com
www.garibaldiresources.com
Other Communications: Mexico, Email:
minera_pender@hotmail.com
Company Type: Public
Ticker Symbol: GGI/TSX.V; GGIFF/OTC
Profile: This company operates in British Columbia & Mexico. In June 2019 it began drilling at its sulphide discovery at Nickel Mountain in British Columbia.
Steve Regoci, President & CEO
Barrie Di Castri, Executive Vice-President & CFO

Global Atomic
#1700, 8 King St. East
Toronto, ON M5C 1B5

416-368-3949
855-221-4474
info@globalatomiccorp.com
www.globalatomiccorp.com
twitter.com/atomiccorp
www.linkedin.com/company/global-atomic-corporation
Company Type: Public
Ticker Symbol: GLO/TSX
Profile: The company owns a high-grade, large DASA uranium deposit in Niger. It also has a share in the Turkey-located Befesa Silvermet zinc concentrate production facility.
Stephen Roman, Chair, President & CEO
Ronald S. Halas, Chief Operating Officer
Rein Lehari, Chief Financial Officer

GobiMin Inc.
#2700, 1000, rue Sherbrook ouest
Montréal, QC H3A 3G4

info@gobimin.com
www.gobimin.com

Company Type: Public
Ticker Symbol: GMN/TSX.V
Profile: GobiMin Inc. is engaged in the development & exploration of mineral properties, mainly in the Xinjiang Uygur Autonomous Region of China.
Felipe Tan, Chair, President & CEO
Joyce Ko, Chief Financial Officer & Vice-President, Corporate Affairs

GoGold Resources Inc.
#1301, 2000 Barrington St.
Halifax, NS B3J 3K1

902-482-1998
Fax: 902-442-1898
gogoldresources.com
www.facebook.com/gogoldresources
twitter.com/gogoldresources
www.linkedin.com/company/gogold
Company Type: Public
Ticker Symbol: GGD/TSX
Profile: GoGold Resources is a mineral resource company with active development & exploration properties in Mexico.
Bradley Langille, President & CEO
Dana M. Hatfield, Chief Financial Officer
Anis Nehme, Chief Operating Officer

Gold Springs Resource Corp.
#880, 580 Hornby St.
Vancouver, BC V6C 3B6

778-801-1667
Fax: 604-684-0642
goldspringsresource.com
www.facebook.com/WesternGreatBasin
twitter.com/GoldSpringsGRC
www.linkedin.com/company/gold-springs-resource-corp
Company Type: Public
Ticker Symbol: GRC/TSX; GRCAF/OTCQB
Profile: Gold Springs Resource Corp. is a mineral exploration company focused on the development of its Gold Springs project in Nevada & Utah.
Matias Herrero, President & CEO
Killian Ruby, Chief Financial Officer
Randall L. Moore, Vice-President, Exploration

Gold Standard Ventures Corp.
#610, 815 West Hastings St.
Vancouver, BC V6C 1B4

604-687-2766
Fax: 604-687-3567
info@goldstandardv.com
goldstandardv.com
twitter.com/VenturesCorp
www.linkedin.com/company/gold-standard-ventures-corp
Company Type: Public
Ticker Symbol: GSV/TSX, NYSE
Profile: Gold Standard Ventures is an advanced stage precious metals exploration company focused on Nevada.
Jonathan Awde, President & CEO
Jordan Neeser, Chief Financial Officer
Lawrence Radford, Chief Operating Officer

Gold Terra Resource Corp.
#410, 325 Howe St.
Vancouver, BC V6C 1Z7

604-689-1749
855-737-2684
info@goldterracorp.com
goldterracorp.com
twitter.com/goldterra
Company Type: Public
Ticker Symbol: YGT/TSX.V; YGTFF/OTC
Profile: Gold Terra Resource Corp. is a major project in Yellowknife as well as projects in the Burin Peninsula of Newfoundland.
Gerald Panneton, Executive Chair
gpanneton@goldterracorp.com
David Suda, President & CEO
dsuda@goldterracorp.com
Mark Brown, Chief Financial Officer
Joseph Campbell, Chief Operating Officer
jcampbell@goldterracorp.com

Golden Star Resources Ltd.
#2400, 333 Bay St.
Toronto, ON M5H 2T6

investor@gsr.com
www.gsr.com
www.facebook.com/goldenstarresources
twitter.com/golden_star_res
www.linkedin.com/company/golden-star-resources-ltd.
Company Type: Public
Ticker Symbol: GSC/TSX; GSS/NYSE
Profile: The gold mining company has two operating mines located on the Ashanti Gold Belt of Ghana, West Africa. Golden Star Resources conducts its activities with a long-term commitment to the environment, health & education.
Andrew Wray, President & CEO
Paul Thomson, Chief Financial Officer
Philipa Varris, Executive Vice-President & Head, Sustainability

Golden Valley Mines Ltd.
2864, ch Sullivan
Val-d'Or, QC J9P 0B9

819-824-2808
Fax: 819-824-3379
info@goldenvalleymines.com
www.goldenvalleymines.com
www.facebook.com/goldenvalleymines
twitter.com/goldenvalleyGZZ
www.linkedin.com/company/golden-valley-mines-ltd
Company Type: Public
Ticker Symbol: GZZ/TSX.V
Profile: Golden Valley owns gold, base-metal & energy mineral projects in Québec, Ontario & Saskatchewan.
Glenn Mullan, Chair, President & Chief Executive Officer
Rico De Vega, Chief Financial Officer
Michael Rosatelli, Vice-President, Exploration

Goldgroup Mining Inc.
#1201, 1166 Alberni St.
Vancouver, BC V6E 3Z3

604-682-1943
Fax: 604-682-5596
877-655-6928
info@goldgroupmining.com
www.goldgroupmining.com
Company Type: Public
Ticker Symbol: GGA/TSX
Profile: Goldgroup Mining Inc. is a gold production, development & exploration company with a portfolio of projects in Mexico.
Anthony Balic, Interim Chief Executive Officer & CFO

GoldMining Inc.
#1830, 1030 West Georgia St.
Vancouver, BC V6E 2Y3

Fax: 604-682-3591
855-630-1001
info@goldmining.com
www.goldmining.com
twitter.com/goldmininginc
Company Type: Public
Ticker Symbol: GOLD/TSX.V
Profile: GoldMining Inc. acquires & advances gold mining projects in the Americas.
Alastair Still, Chief Executive Officer
Paulo Pereira, President
Pat Obara, Chief Financial Officer

GoviEx Uranium Inc.
#654, 999 Canada Pl.
Vancouver, BC V6C 3E1

604-681-5529
Fax: 604-682-2060
info@goviex.com
goviex.com
www.facebook.com/GoviEx
twitter.com/goviexuranium
www.linkedin.com/company/goviex
Company Type: Public
Ticker Symbol: GXU/TSX.V
Profile: GoviEx focuses on the development & mining of uranium. It fully owns the Madaouela Project, located in north central Niger.
Daniel Major, Chief Executive Officer
danielm@goviex.com
Lei Wang, Chief Financial Officer

Gowest Gold Ltd.
#1400, 80 Richmond St. West
Toronto, ON M5H 2A4

416-363-1210
Fax: 416-363-2959
877-363-1218
info@gowestgold.com
www.gowestgold.com
Company Type: Public
Ticker Symbol: GWA/TSX.V
Profile: Gowest Gold has interests in the North Timmins Gold Project.
Gregory James Romain, President & CEO
gregr@gowestgold.com
Janet O'Donnell, Chief Financial Officer

Gran Colombia Gold Corp.
PO Box 15, #2400, 401 Bay St.
Toronto, ON M5H 2Y4

416-360-4653
Fax: 416-603-4653
investorrelations@grancolombiagold.com
www.grancolombiagold.com
twitter.com/gcmgold
www.linkedin.com/company/gran-colombia-gold

Tony Young, Chief Financial Officer
Sergio Cattalani, Senior Vice-President, Exploration

Lithium Americas Corp.
#300, 900 West Hastings St.
Vancouver, BC V6C 1E5

778-656-5820
info@lithiumamericas.com
www.lithiumamericas.com
Other Communications: Investor Relations, Email:
ir@lithiumamericas.com
twitter.com/lithiumamericas
www.linkedin.com/company/lithiumamericas
Company Type: Public
Ticker Symbol: LAC/TSX, NYSE
Profile: Lithium Americas is a lithium mining company.
Jonathan Evans, President & CEO
Eduard Epshtein, Chief Financial Officer

Loncor Gold Inc.
1 First Canadian Place
#7070, 100 King St. West
Toronto, ON M5X 1E3

416-361-2510
Fax: 416-366-7722
info@loncor.com
loncor.com
www.facebook.com/LoncorGold
twitter.com/Loncorgold
www.linkedin.com/company/loncor-gold-inc
Company Type: Public
Ticker Symbol: LGDN/TSX
Profile: Loncor Gold is a gold exploration company focused on
the Democratic Republic of the Congo (DRC).
Arnold Kondrat, Chief Executive Officer
Peter Cowley, President
Donat Madilo, Chief Financial Officer

Los Andes Copper Ltd.
#880, 580 Hornby St.
Vancouver, BC V6C 3B6

604-639-3892
Fax: 604-684-0642
info@losandescopper.com
www.losandescopper.com
twitter.com/LosAndesCopper
www.linkedin.com/company/los-andes-copper
Company Type: Public
Ticker Symbol: LA/TSX.V
Profile: Los Andes Copper Ltd. is an exploration & development
company. It holds an interest in a copper-molybdenum deposit in
Chile.
Fernando Porcile, Executive Chair
Antony Amberg, Chief Executive Officer & Chief Geologist
Harry Nijjar, Chief Financial Officer

Lucara Diamond Corp.
#502, 1250 Homer St.
Vancouver, BC V6B 2Y5

604-689-7842
Fax: 604-689-4250
info@lucaradiamond.com
www.lucaradiamond.com
www.facebook.com/lucaradiamond
twitter.com/lucaradiamond
www.linkedin.com/company/lucara-diamond-corp-
Company Type: Public
Ticker Symbol: LUC/TSX
Profile: Lucara Diamond Corp. owns the Karowe diamond mine
in Botswana, which has been in production since 2012.
Eira Thomas, President & CEO
Zara Boldt, Chief Financial Officer

Lumina Gold Corp.
#410, 625 Howe St.
Vancouver, BC V6C 2T6

604-646-1890
Fax: 844-896-8192
info@luminagold.com
luminagold.com
twitter.com/lumina_gold
www.linkedin.com/company/lumina-gold
Company Type: Public
Ticker Symbol: LUM/TSX.V
Profile: Lumina Gold is a Canadian precious & base metals
exploration & development company focused on gold & copper
projects in Ecuador.
Marshall Koval, President & CEO
Martin Rip, Chief Financial Officer

Lundin Gold Inc.
#2000, 885 West Georgia St.
Vancouver, BC V6C 3E8

604-689-7842
888-689-7842
info@lundingold.com
www.lundingold.com
www.facebook.com/lundingold
twitter.com/lundingoldec
www.linkedin.com/company/lundin-gold
Company Type: Public
Ticker Symbol: LUG/TSX
Profile: Lundin Gold's main project is Fruta del Norte in
Ecuador.
Ron F. Hochstein, President & CEO
Alessandro Bitelli, Executive Vice-President & CFO
Nathan Monash, Vice-President, Business Sustainability

Lundin Mining Corporation
PO Box 38, #2200, 150 King St. West
Toronto, ON M5H 1J9

416-342-5560
Fax: 416-348-0303
info@lundinmining.com
www.lundinmining.com
Company Type: Public
Ticker Symbol: LUN/TSX; LUMI/OMX
Staff Size: 7,500
Profile: Lundin Mining Corporation, formed in 1994, is engaged
in the exploration, mining & production of base metal mineral
resources, such as copper, nickel, zinc & lead. Operations are
located in Spain, Portugal & Sweden. The corporation also holds
a development project pipeline & an equity stake in a copper &
cobalt project in the Democratic Republic of Congo.
Marie Inkster, President & CEO
Jinhee Magie, Senior Vice-President & CFO
Peter Richardson, Senior Vice-President & COO
Kristen Mariuzza, Vice-President, Environment & Social
Performance
Ciara Talbot, Vice-President, Exploration

Lupaka Gold Corp.
1569 Dempsey Rd.
North Vancouver, BC V7K 1S8

604-669-7748
info@lupakagold.com
www.lupakagold.com
Company Type: Public
Ticker Symbol: LPK/TSX.V
Profile: Lupaka Gold Corp. is a gold explorer with geographic
diversification & balance through its asset-based resource
projects spread across Peru.
Gordon Ellis, President & CEO
Darryl Jones, Chief Financial Officer

MAG Silver Corp.
#770, 800 West Pender St.
Vancouver, BC V6C 2V6

604-630-1399
866-630-1399
info@magsilver.com
magsilver.com
Company Type: Public
Ticker Symbol: MAG/TSX, NYSE
Profile: MAG Silver Corp. is focused on advancing two
significant projects located within the Mexican Silver Belt.
George Paspalas, President & CEO
Peter Megaw, Chief Exploration Officer
Larry Taddei, Chief Financial Officer

Majestic Gold Corp.
#306, 1688 - 152nd St.
Surrey, BC V4A 4N2

604-560-9060
Fax: 604-560-9062
info@majesticgold.com
www.majesticgold.com
Company Type: Public
Ticker Symbol: MJS/TSX.V
Profile: Majestic Gold Corp. is a gold producer in Shandong
Province, China.
Stephen Kenwood, President & CEO
James Mackie, Chief Financial Officer & Corporate Secretary

Major Drilling Group International Inc.
Also Known As: Major Drilling
#100, 111 St George St.
Moncton, NB E1C 1T7

506-857-8636
866-264-3986
info@majordrilling.com
www.majordrilling.com
Other Communications: Investors Relations, Email:
if@majordrilling.com
www.facebook.com/majordrilling
twitter.com/majordrilling
www.linkedin.com/company/major-drilling-international-inc.
Company Type: Public
Ticker Symbol: MDI/TSX
Staff Size: 2,400
Profile: Major Drilling Group International's drilling operations
are carried out in: Canada, the United States, Central America,
South America, Africa, Armenia, Indonesia & Australia. Drilling
services include geotechnical, environmental drilling, surface &
underground coring, reverse circulation, water-well, shallow gas
& coal-bed methane. The company primarily serves the mining
industry.
Denis Larocque, President & CEO
Ian Ross, Chief Financial Officer

Mako Mining Corp.
Three Bentall Centre
#2833, 595 Burrard St.
Vancouver, BC V7X 1J1

647-203-8793
info@makominingcorp.com
makominingcorp.com
twitter.com/MakoMiningCorp
www.linkedin.com/company/mako-mining-corporation
Company Type: Public
Ticker Symbol: MKO/TSX.V
Profile: The gold & silver mining company has properties in
Mexico & Nicaragua.
Akiba Leisman, Chief Executive Officer
Scott Kelly, Chief Financial Officer
Jesse Muñoz, Chief Operating Officer

Mandalay Resources Corporation
#330, 76 Richmond St. East
Toronto, ON M5C 1P1

647-260-1566
mandalayresources.com
twitter.com/mandalayauag
Company Type: Public
Ticker Symbol: MND/TSX
Profile: Mandalay Resources is a mineral exploration company
focused on copper-silver prospects in northern Chile.
Dominic Duffy, President & CEO
Nick Dwyer, Chief Financial Officer
Belinda Labatte, Chief Development Officer
Toni Streczynski, Vice-President, Processing & Metallurgy

Marathon Gold
#600, 36 Lombart St.
Toronto, ON M5C 2X3

416-861-0851
marathon-gold.com
www.facebook.com/MarathonGoldMOZ
twitter.com/marathongoldmoz
www.linkedin.com/company/marathongoldmoz
Company Type: Public
Ticker Symbol: MOZ/TSX; MGDPF/OTCQX
Profile: Marathon Gold is a gold resource development
company whose main project is the Valentine Gold Project in
central Newfoundland & Labrador.
Matthew Manson, President & CEO
Hannes Portmann, Chief Financial Officer
Tim Williams, Chief Operating Officer

Marimaca Copper Corp.
#1504, Cerro El Plomo 5420
Las Condes, Santiago

marimaca.com
Other Communications: +56-2-2431-7608
twitter.com/Marimaca_Copper
Company Type: Public
Ticker Symbol: MARI/TSX
Profile: Marimaca Copper is a copper-producing company with
a strategy to grow its Chilean copper production through the
discovery, development & operation of 'Coro type' deposits.
Luis Albano Tondo, President & CEO
Petra Decher, Chief Financial Officer
Sergio Rivera, Vice-President

Mason Graphite
#600, 3030, boul Le Carrefour
Laval, QC H7T 2P5

514-289-3580
info@masongraphite.com
www.masongraphite.com
www.facebook.com/masongraphite
www.linkedin.com/company/mason-graphite
Company Type: Public
Ticker Symbol: LLG/TSX.V
Profile: A mining & mineral processing company with its primary focus on the Lac Guéret graphite project located in northeastern Québec.
Pascale Choquet, Interim Chief Financial Officer & Director, Finance & Administration

Maverix Metals Inc.
#575, 510 Burrard St.
Vancouver, BC V6C 3A8

604-449-9290
info@maverixmetals.com
maverixmetals.com
twitter.com/maverixmetals
www.linkedin.com/company/maverix-metals-inc.
Company Type: Public
Ticker Symbol: MMX/TSX; MMX/NYSE
Profile: Founded in 2016, the company is a precious metals royalty & streaming company with 100 royalties in 16 countries.
Dan O'Flaherty, Chief Executive Officer
Ryan McIntyre, President
Matt Fargey, Chief Financial Officer

Mawson Gold Limited
#1305, 1090 West Georgia St.
Vancouver, BC V6E 3V7

604-699-0202
Fax: 604-683-1585
info@mawsonresources.com
mawsongold.com
www.facebook.com/MawsonGold
twitter.com/mawsongold
www.linkedin.com/company/mawson-resources-ltd
Company Type: Public
Ticker Symbol: MAW/TSX
Profile: Mawson Resources Limited is a Nordic exploration company with a focus on the flagship Rajapalot & Rompas gold projects, located in Finland.
Michael Robert Hudson, Chair & Chief Executive Officer
Nick Cook, Chief Geologist
Nick DeMare, Chief Financial Officer

Mazarin Inc.
696, rue Monfette est
Thetford Mines, QC G6G 7G9

418-338-3669
Fax: 418-338-0229
www.mazarin.ca
Company Type: Public
Ticker Symbol: MAZ.H/TSX.V
Profile: Mazarin Inc. mines minerals including dolomite & graphite.
Guy Bérard, President
Mario Simard, Chief Financial Officer

Mega Uranium Ltd.
#401, 217 Queen St. West
Toronto, ON M5V 0R2

416-643-7630
Fax: 416-941-1090
info@megauranium.com
www.megauranium.com
Other Communications: Investor Relations, Email: ir@megauranium.com
Company Type: Public
Ticker Symbol: MGA/TSX
Profile: Mega Uranium is a producer of uranium through the development of projects in Australia.
Richard Patricio, President & CEO
Carmelo Marrelli, Chief Financial Officer
Richard Homsany, Executive Vice-President, Australia
Wendy Warhaft, General Counsel

Metalo Manufacturing Inc. (MMI)
#1400, 141 Adelaide St.
Toronto, ON M5H 3L5

902-233-7255
Fax: 902-835-0585
info@metalo.ca
www.metalo.ca
Company Type: Public
Ticker Symbol: MMI/CSE
Profile: Merchant Pig Iron is the focus of Metalo Manufacturing's investment in the private company Grand River Ironsands.
Francis MacKenzie, President

C. H. (Bert) Loveless, Chief Operating Officer

Midland Exploration
#4000, 1, Place Ville-Marie
Montréal, QC H3B 4M4

450-420-5977
Fax: 450-420-5978
info@midlandexploration.com
www.midlandexploration.com
www.linkedin.com/company/midland-exploration
Company Type: Public
Ticker Symbol: MD/TSX.V
Profile: A gold & mineral mining company.
Gino Roger, President & CEO
Ingrid Martin, Chief Financial Officer
Mario Masson, Vice-President, Exploration

Millennial Lithium
#300, 1455 Bellevue Ave.
West Vancouver, BC V7T 1C3

604-662-8184
Fax: 604-602-1606
info@millenniallithium.com
www.millenniallithium.com
twitter.com/millennialli
Company Type: Public
Ticker Symbol: ML/TSX.V
Profile: The company operates its Pastos Grandes lithium project in Salta Province, Argentina, as well as its Cauchari East project in the same country.
Farhad Abasov, President & CEO
Iain Scarr, Chief Operating Officer & Vice-President, Development & Exploration

Minco Capital Corp.
#2060, 1055 West Georgia St.
Vancouver, BC V6E 3R5

604-888-8002
Fax: 604-888-8030
888-288-8288
pr@mincomining.ca
www.mincocapitalcorp.com
Company Type: Public
Ticker Symbol: MMM/TSX.V
Profile: Minco Capital Corp. is a mineral exploration & development company investment issuer. It holds a 18.2% stake in Minco Silver Corporation, which holds a 90% interest in the Fuwan silver deposit in China & a 51% interest in the Changkeng gold project.
Ken Z. Chai, Chair, President & CEO
Melinda Hsu, Chief Financial Officer

Minco Silver Corporation
PO Box 11176, #2060, 1055 West Georgia St.
Vancouver, BC V6E 3R5

604-688-8002
Fax: 604-688-8030
888-288-8288
pr@mincosilver.ca
www.mincosilver.ca
Other Communications: Beijing Office, Phone: +86-10-5957-5377
Company Type: Public
Ticker Symbol: MSV/TSX
Profile: Minco Silver Corporation acquires & develops silver projects. The company owns a 90% interest in the Fuwan Silver Deposit, which is located in Guangdong China.
Ken Z. Cai, Chair, President & CEO
Melinda Hsu, Chief Financial Officer

Minnova Corp.
#401, 217 Queen Street West
Toronto, ON M5V 0R2

info@minnovacorp.ca
www.minnovacorp.ca
Company Type: Public
Ticker Symbol: MCI/TSX.V
Profile: Minnova Corp. is a gold exploration & production company. The company owns an interest in the PL Gold Mine in central Manitoba.
Gorden Glenn, Chair, President & CEO
gglenn@minnovacorp.ca

Mirasol Resources Ltd.
#1150, 355 Burrard St.
Vancouver, BC V6C 2G8

604-602-9989
contact@mirasolresources.com
mirasolresources.com
twitter.com/MRZ_Mirasol
www.linkedin.com/company/mirasolresources
Company Type: Public
Ticker Symbol: MRZ/TSX.V

Profile: Mirasol Resources is a prospect generator engaged in exploration & discovery in emerging areas in the Americas.
Tim Heenan, President
Matthew Lee, Chief Financial Officer

Monarch Mining Corporation
68, av de la Gare
Saint-Sauveur, QC J0R 1R0

514-840-9709
888-994-4465
info@monarchmining.com
www.monarchmining.com
twitter.com/GBAR_TO
www.linkedin.com/company/monarchmining
Company Type: Public
Ticker Symbol: GBAR/TSX; GBARF/OTCQX
Profile: Monarch is a gold mining, development & exploration company centered on its Abitibi mining camp in Quebec.
Jean-Marc Lacoste, President & CEO
Alain Lévesque, Chief Financial Officer

Monument Mining Limited
#1580, 1100 Melville St.
Vancouver, BC V6E 4A6

604-638-1661
Fax: 604-638-1663
info@monumentmining.com
www.monumentmining.com
Company Type: Public
Ticker Symbol: MMY/TSX.V
Profile: Monument Mining is a Canadian-based gold producer with gold production, gold development stage properties, exploration properties & land positions in Malaysia & Australia.
Cathy Zhai, President & CEO
Hugh A. Bresser, Chief Managing Geologist
Chris Leighton, Interim Chief Financial Officer

Mountain Province Diamonds Inc.
PO Box 216, #1410, 161 Bay St.
Toronto, ON M5J 2S1

416-361-3562
Fax: 416-603-8565
info@mountainprovince.com
www.mountainprovince.com
Company Type: Public
Ticker Symbol: MPVD/TSX, NASDAQ
Profile: Mountain Province Diamonds Inc. is engaged in diamond exploration & development. The Kennady Lake diamond project in the Northwest Territories is being developed by the company, in partnership with De Beers Canada.
Stuart Brown, President & CEO
Perry Ing, Chief Financial Officer
Tom E. McCandless, Vice-President, Exploration

Namibia Critical Metals Inc.
Sun Tower
#802, 1550 Bedford Hwy.
Bedford, NS B4A 1E6

902-835-8760
Fax: 902-835-8761
info@namibiacmi.com
www.namibiacriticalmetals.com
www.facebook.com/NamibiaMetals
twitter.com/NamibiaMetals
www.linkedin.com/company/namibiametals
Company Type: Public
Ticker Symbol: NMI/TSX.V
Profile: Namibia Critical Metals Inc. (formerly Namibia Rare Earths Inc.) operates the Lofdal Project in Namibia which focuses on the heavy rare earth mineral xenotime.
Donald Burton, President
Susanne Willett, Chief Financial Officer
Rainer Ellmies, Vice-President, Exploration

Nevada Copper Corp.
#910, 800 West Pender St.
Vancouver, BC V6C 2V6

775-463-3510
info@nevadacopper.com
nevadacopper.com
twitter.com/NevadaCopper
www.linkedin.com/company/nevada-copper-corp-ncu-
Company Type: Public
Ticker Symbol: NCU/TSX; NEVDF/OTC
Profile: Nevada Copper Corp. owns 100% of a development property in the Walker Lane mineralized belt situated in western Nevada.
Mike Ciricillo, President & CEO
Andre Van Niekerk, Chief Financial Officer
Greg French, Vice-President, Exploration

New Found Gold Corp.
#1430, 800 West Pender St.
Vancouver, BC V6C 2V6

604-562-9664
contact@newfoundgold.ca
newfoundgold.ca
twitter.com/newfoundgold
www.linkedin.com/company/newfound-gold-corp

Company Type: Public
Ticker Symbol: NFG/TSX.V
Profile: Founded in 2015, New Found Gold is an exploration company with projects in Newfoundland & Ontario.
Craig Roberts, Chief Executive Officer
Denis Laviolette, President
Michael Kanevsky, Chief Financial Officer
Greg Matheson, Chief Operating Officer
Ken Rattee, Vice-President, Exploration

New Gold Inc.
Brookfield Place
#3320, 181 Bay St.
Toronto, ON M5J 2T3

416-324-6000
Fax: 416-324-9494
info@newgold.com
www.newgold.com

Company Type: Public
Ticker Symbol: NGD/TSX, NYSE
Profile: The intermediate gold mining company has assets in Canada, the United States, Mexico, Australia & Chile.
Renaud Adams, President & CEO
Robert J. Chausse, Executive Vice-President & CFO
Bethany Borody, Director, Sustainability

Newmont Corp.
#700, 6900 East Layton Ave.
Denver, CO 80237 USA

303-836-7414
Fax: 303-837-5837
www.newmont.com
www.facebook.com/NewmontCorporation
twitter.com/NewmontCorp
www.linkedin.com/company/newmont

Company Type: Public
Ticker Symbol: NGT/TSX
Profile: Newmont has interests in North & South America, Australia & Africa. It is a producer of gold, copper, silver, zinc & lead.
Tom Palmer, President & CEO
Rob Atkins, Chief Operating Officer
Nancy Buese, Chief Financial Officer

NexGen Energy Ltd.
#3150, 1021 West Hastings St.
Vancouver, BC V6E 0C3

604-428-4112
Fax: 604-259-0321
www.nexgenenergy.ca

Company Type: Public
Ticker Symbol: NXE/TSX, NYSE
Profile: The company explores & develops uranium in the Athabasca Basin, located in Saskatchewan.
Leigh Curyer, Chief Executive Officer
Harpreet Dhaliwal, Chief Financial Officer

Nickel 28 Capital Corp.
#401, 4 King St. West
Toronto, ON M5H 1B6

647-846-7765
info@nickel28.com
www.nickel28.com

Company Type: Public
Ticker Symbol: NKL/TSX.V
Profile: This company was formed following Pala Investments Limited's acquisition of Cobalt 27. It focuses on investments in battery metals. It offers exposure to cobalt & nickel for electric vehicles & storage.
Anthony Milewski, Chair
Justin Cochrane, President & CEO

Nickel Creek Platinum Corp.
#3001, 130 Adelaide St. West
Toronto, ON M5H 3P5

416-304-9315
Fax: 416-583-2438
833-304-9315
info@nickelcp.com
www.nickelcreekplatinum.com
twitter.com/nickelcreekptm
www.linkedin.com/company/nickel-creek-platinum

Company Type: Public
Ticker Symbol: NCP/TSX; NCPCF/OTCQX
Profile: Nickel Creek Platinum Corp. is a mining exploration &

development company that wholly owns the Nickel Shäw project in Yukon.
Stuart Harshaw, President & CEO
Joe Romagnolo, Senior Vice-President & CFO

Nickel North Exploration
#890, 580 Hornby St.
Vancouver, BC V6C 2E7

604-551-7892
Fax: 604-899-1240
www.nickelnorthexploration.com
Other Communications: Investor, Email: invest@nickelnorth.com

Company Type: Public
Ticker Symbol: NNX/TSX.V
Profile: Nickel North is focused on its 18,000 hectare Hawk Ridge Project in Quebec.
Yingting Guo, President & CEO
Cathy Wang, Chief Financial Officer

Nighthawk Gold Corp.
#301, 141 Adelaide St. West
Toronto, ON M5H 3L5

647-794-4313
Fax: 416-628-5911
info@nighthawkgold.com
www.nighthawkgold.com
www.facebook.com/nighthawkgoldcorp
twitter.com/nighthawkgold
www.linkedin.com/company/nighthawk-gold-corp

Company Type: Public
Ticker Symbol: NHK/TSX.V
Profile: Nighthawk is a Canadian-based exploration company focused on acquiring & developing gold mineral properties in the Northwest Territories.
Keyvan Salehi, President & CEO
Michael Leskovec, Chief Financial Officer
Richard Roy, Vice-President, Exploration

Niocorp Developments Ltd.
#115, 7000 South Yosemite St.
Centennial, CO 80112 USA

720-639-4647
www.niocorp.com
www.facebook.com/niocorp
twitter.com/NioCorp

Company Type: Public
Ticker Symbol: NB/TSX
Profile: Niocorp is developing North America's only niobium/scandium/titanium project, located near Elk Creek, Nebraska. It operates through its wholly-owned subsidiary, Elk Creek Resources Corp.
Mark A. Smith, Chair, President & CEO
Neal S. Shah, Chief Financial Officer
Scott Honan, Vice-President, Business Development & President, Elk Creek Resources Corp.

Nomad Royalty Company Ltd.
#500, 1275, av des Canadiens-de-Montréal
Montréal, QC H3B 0G4

nomadroyalty.com

Company Type: Public
Ticker Symbol: NSR/TSX
Profile: Nomad is a gold & silver royalty company with a portfolio of 14 royalty & stream assets.
Vincent Metcalfe, Chief Executive Officer
vmetcalfe@nomadroyalty.com
Joseph de la Plante, Chief Information Officer
jdelaplante@nomadroyalty.com
Elif Lévesque, Chief Financial Officer

Noranda Income Fund
First Canadian Place
PO Box 403, #6900, 100 King St. West
Toronto, ON M5X 1E3

info@norandaincomefund.com
www.norandaincomefund.com

Company Type: Public
Ticker Symbol: NIF.UN/TSX
Profile: Noranda Income Fund's main asset is CEZinc., a zinc processing facility in Salaberry-de-Valleyfield, Québec. Canadian Electrolytic Zinc Limited operates & manages the CEZ processing facility. The facility has obtained ISO 9001 & ISO 14001 certification to cover all environmental processes at the plant.
Liana Centomo, Chief Executive Officer
Paul Einarson, Vice-President & CFO
Martin Fillion, Chief Operating Officer

Noront Resources Ltd.
#501, 212 King St. West
Toronto, ON M5H 1K5

416-367-1444
Fax: 416-367-5444
info@norontresources.com
www.norontresources.com
www.facebook.com/norontresources
twitter.com/norontresources
www.linkedin.com/company/noront-resources

Company Type: Public
Ticker Symbol: NOT/TSX.V
Profile: Noront Resources is a mining company with a land position in the Ring of Fire, an emerging multi-metals area in the James Bay Lowlands of Northern Ontario. Their primary project in the region is a high-grade nickle-copper-platinum group element deposit called Eagle's Nest.
In 2015, the company acquired the Cliffs chromite properties & in 2016, the MacDonald Mines.
Alan Coutts, President & CEO
Gregory Rieveley, Chief Financial Officer
Steve Flewelling, Chief Development Officer
Ryan Weston, Vice-President, Exploration

North American Nickel Inc.
c/o 1 First Canadian Place, Bennett Jones LLP
PO Box 130, #3400, 100 King St. West
Toronto, ON M5X 1A4

604-770-4334
833-770-4334
info@northamericannickel.com
www.northamericannickel.com
www.facebook.com/northamericannickel
twitter.com/namericannickel
www.linkedin.com/company/north-american-nickel

Company Type: Public
Ticker Symbol: NAN/TSX.V
Profile: A nickel mining company whose main projects are the Sudbuy Nickel Camp, & more recently, the Maniitsoq nickel-copper-PGE property in Greenland.
Keith Morrison, Chief Executive Officer
Mark Fedikow, President
Sarah-Wenjia Zhu, Chief Financial Officer
Peter Lightfoot, Chief Geologist

Northcliff Resources Ltd.
1040 West Georgia St., 14th Fl.
Vancouver, BC V6E 4H1

604-684-6365
Fax: 604-684-8092
800-667-2114
info@hdimining.com
www.northcliffresources.com

Company Type: Public
Ticker Symbol: NCF/TSX
Profile: The company owns the Sisson Tungsten-Molybdenum Project, which has a tungsten-molybdenum deposit.
Andrew Ing, Interim Chief Executive Officer
Luqman Khan, Interim Chief Financial Officer

Northern Dynasty Minerals Ltd.
1040 West Georgia St., 14th Fl.
Vancouver, BC V6E 4H1

604-684-6365
Fax: 604-684-8092
800-667-2114
info@northerndynasty.com
www.northerndynastyminerals.com

Company Type: Public
Ticker Symbol: NDM/TSX; NAK/NYSE
Profile: Northern Dynasty Minerals Ltd. is a mineral exploration company focused on the Pebble gold-copper-molybdenum project in Alaska.
Ronald Thiessen, President & CEO
Mark Peters, Chief Financial Officer
Bruce Jenkins, Executive Vice-President, Environment & Sustainability

Northern Vertex Mining Corp.
#1650, 1075 West Georgia St.
Vancouver, BC V6E 3C9

604-601-3656
855-633-8798
info@northernvertex.com
www.northernvertex.com
www.facebook.com/NorthernVertexMiningCorp
twitter.com/northern_vertex
www.linkedin.com/company/northern-vertex-mining-corp-nhvcf-

Company Type: Public
Ticker Symbol: NEE/TSX.V
Profile: A mining company that owns 100% of the Moss Mine Gold-Silver Project in Arizona.
Michael Allen, President
David Splett, Chief Financial Officer

Warwick Board, Vice-President, Exploration

NorthWest Copper Corp.
#1900, 1055 West Hastings St.
Vancouver, BC V6E 2E9

604-683-7790
info@northwestcopper.ca
northwestcopper.ca
www.linkedin.com/company/northwestcopper
Company Type: Public
Ticker Symbol: NWST/TSX.V
Profile: NorthWest Copper Corp. was formed in 2021 from the merger of Sun Metals Corp. & Serengeti Resources Inc. It is an exploration & development company with several projects throughout British Columbia.
Peter Bell, President & CEO
James Lang, Chief Geoscientist
Lauren McDougall, Chief Financial Officer
Ian Neill, Vice-President, Exploration

NorZinc Ltd.
PO Box 11644, #1710, 650 West Georgia St.
Vancouver, BC V6B 4N9

604-688-2001
Fax: 604-688-2043
ir@norzinc.com
norzinc.com
twitter.com/norzincltd
www.linkedin.com/company/norzinc
Company Type: Public
Ticker Symbol: NZC/TSX
Profile: The company has its Prairie Creek Mine in the Northwest Territories as well as properties in Newfoundland which it aquired from Paragon Minerals Corporation in 2012.
Rohan Hazelton, President & CEO
Peter Portka, Chief Financial Officer
peter.portka@norzinc.com
Scott Fulton, Vice-President

Nouveau Monde Graphite
331, rue Brassard
Saint-Michel-des-Saints, QC J0K 3B0

450-757-8905
info@nouveaumonde.ca
nouveaumonde.group
www.facebook.com/NouveauMondeGraphite
twitter.com/NYSE_NMG
www.linkedin.com/company/nouveaumondegraphite
Company Type: Public
Ticker Symbol: NOU/TSX.V
Profile: Founded in 2011, the company discovered a lucrative deposit of graphite in 2015 in the Matawinie region of Quebec.
Éric Desaulniers, Founder, President & CEO
Charles-Olivier Tarte, Chief Financial Officer
David Torralbo, Chief Legal Officer & Corporate Secretary
Patrice Boulanger, Vice-President, Sales, Marketing & Business Development
Sylvain Descombes, Vice-President, Construction
Alain Dorval, Vice-President, Process & Metallurgy
Martine Paradis, Vice-President, Engineering & Environment

NovaGold Resources Inc.
#1860, 400 Burrard St.
Vancouver, BC V6C 3A6

604-669-6227
Fax: 604-669-6272
866-669-6227
info@novagold.com
www.novagold.com
www.facebook.com/novagold
twitter.com/novagold
www.linkedin.com/company/novagold
Company Type: Public
Ticker Symbol: NG/TSX, NYSE
Profile: NovaGold is focused on permitting & developing its 50%-owned flagship property, Donlin Gold, one of the world's largest known undeveloped gold deposits. In 2018 Novagold sold its Galore Creek copper-gold-silver project in British Columbia to Newmont.
Gregory A. Lang, President & CEO
David Ottewell, Vice-President & CFO

Novo Resources Corp.
#880, 580 Hornby St.
Vancouver, BC V6C 3B6

www.novoresources.com
www.facebook.com/novoresources
twitter.com/novo_resources
www.linkedin.com/company/novo-resources-corp
Company Type: Public
Ticker Symbol: NVO/TSX
Profile: Novo Resources owns the Beatons Creek Tenements in Western Australia & has the right to earn a 70% interest in the Pilbara Paleoplacer Gold Project in Western Australian.

Quinton Hennigh, Chair & President
Rob Humphryson, Chief Executive Officer
Ronan Sabo-Walsh, Chief Financial Officer

O3 Mining Inc.
#1440, 155 University Ave.
Toronto, ON M5H 3B7

416-363-8653
info@o3mining.ca
o3mining.ca
twitter.com/O3Mining
www.linkedin.com/company/o3-mining
Company Type: Public
Ticker Symbol: OIII/TSX.V
Profile: A gold mining company with projects in Quebec & Ontario.
Jose Vizquerra, President & CEO
Blair Zaritsky, Chief Financial Officer
Louis Gariepy, Vice-President, Exploration

OceanaGold Corp.
99 Melbourne St., Level 3
4101 Australia

info@oceanagold.com
oceanagold.com
Other Communications: Australia, Phone: +61-3-9656-5300
twitter.com/OceanaGold
www.linkedin.com/company/oceana-gold
Company Type: Public
Ticker Symbol: OGC/TSX, ASX
Profile: The gold producer has a portfolio of exploration, development & operating assets in the Asia Pacific region.
Michael Holmes, President & CEO
Scott McQueen, Executive Vice-President & Chief Financial Officer
Craig Feebrey, Executive Vice-President, Exploration & Development
Sharon Flynn, Executive Vice-President, Sustainability

Oceanic Iron Ore Corp.
Three Bentall Centre
#3083, 595 Burrard St.
Vancouver, BC V7X 1L3

604-566-9080
Fax: 604-566-9050
www.oceanicironore.com
Company Type: Public
Ticker Symbol: FEO/TSX.V
Profile: Oceanic is focused on the development of the Ungava Bay iron properties.
Bing Pan, Interim Chief Executive Officer
Chris Batalha, Chief Financial Officer
Eddy Canova, Director, Exploration

Orbit Garant Drilling Inc.
3200, boul Jean-Jacques Cossette
Val-d'Or, QC J9P 6Y6

819-824-2707
Fax: 819-824-2195
866-824-2707
info@orbitgarant.com
orbitgarant.com
www.facebook.com/orbitgarant
www.linkedin.com/company/forage-orbit-garant-inc.-ogd-to-
Company Type: Public
Ticker Symbol: OGD/TSX
Staff Size: 1,100
Profile: The mineral drilling company provides both underground & surface drilling services. Operations are carried out in Canada & internationally.
Éric Alexandre, President & CEO
Daniel Maheu, Chief Financial Officer

Orea Mining Corp.
1090 Hamilton St.
Vancouver, BC V6B 2R9

604-634-0970
Fax: 604-634-0971
888-818-1364
ir@oreamining.com
oreamining.com
www.facebook.com/OreaMining
twitter.com/oreamining
www.linkedin.com/company/oreamining
Company Type: Public
Ticker Symbol: OREA/TSX
Profile: Orea Mining Corp. is a gold exploration & development company operating in French Guiana.
Rock Lefrançois, President & CEO
Andrew Yau, Executive Vice-President & CFO

Orezone Gold
#910, 1111 Melville St.
Vancouver, BC V6E 3V6

778-945-8977
888-673-0663
info@orezone.com
www.orezone.com
twitter.com/orezonec
www.linkedin.com/company/orezone-gold-corporation
Company Type: Public
Ticker Symbol: ORE/TSX.V
Profile: The company has 90% interest in the Bomboré gold deposit in Burkina Faso.
Patrick Downey, President & CEO
Peter Tam, Chief Financial Officer

Orla Mining Ltd.
#202, 595 Howe St.
Vancouver, BC V6C 2T5

604-564-1852
info@orlamining.com
www.orlamining.com
twitter.com/MiningOrla
www.linkedin.com/company/orla-mining-ltd
Company Type: Public
Ticker Symbol: OLA/TSX.V
Profile: Orla Mining operates the Cerro Quema gold project in Panama.
Jason Simpson, President & CEO
Andrew Cormier, Chief Operating Officer
Etienne Morin, Chief Financial Officer
Sylvain Guerard, Senior Vice-President, Exploration

Orosur Mining Inc.
82 Richmond St. East, 1st Fl.
Toronto, ON M5C 1P1

778-373-0100
info@orosur.ca
www.orosur.ca
www.linkedin.com/company/orosur-mining-ltd
Company Type: Public
Ticker Symbol: OMI/TSX
Staff Size: 500
Profile: The exploration company & gold producer is active in Latin America. Orosur Mining's exploration portfolio includes assets in Chile & Uruguay. It also operates a producing gold mine in Uruguay.
Brad George, Chief Executive Officer
Victor Hugo, Chief Financial Officer

Orvana Minerals Corp.
#1710, 70 York St.
Toronto, ON M5J 1S9

416-369-1629
Fax: 416-369-1402
www.orvana.com
Company Type: Public
Ticker Symbol: ORV/TSX
Profile: The Canadian gold & copper mining & exploration company evaluates, develops & mines precious & base metals deposits. Orvana Minerals two main assets are the El Valle-Boinás/Carlés Mines in Northern Spain and mines in the Don Mario district of Eastern Bolivia.
Juan Gavidia, Chief Executive Officer
Nuria Menendez, Chief Financial Officer
nmenendez@orvana.com

Osisko Gold Royalties Ltd.
PO Box 211, #300, 1100, av des Canadiens-de-Montréal
Montréal, QC H3B 2S2

514-940-0670
Fax: 514-940-0669
info@osiskogr.com
osiskogr.com
www.linkedin.com/company/osisko-gold-royalties-ltd
Company Type: Public
Ticker Symbol: OR/TSX; OR/NYSE
Profile: Osisko is an intermediate precious medal royalty company that holds a portfolio of over 130 royalties & streams. Its assets include a 5% stake in the Canadian Malartic mine, a 12.7% interest in Falco Resources Ltd., & a 32.7% interest in Barkerville Gold Mines Ltd.
Sandeep Singh, President & CEO
Frédéric Ruel, Chief Financial Officer & Vice-President, Finance

Osisko Mining
#1440, 155 University Ave.
Toronto, ON M5H 3B7

416-363-8653
Fax: 416-363-9813
info@osiskomining.com
www.osiskomining.com
www.facebook.com/miningosisko
twitter.com/osisko_mining
www.linkedin.com/company/osisko

Company Type: Public
Ticker Symbol: OSK/TSX
Profile: A gold mining company whose main project is in Québec.
John Burzynski, Chief Executive Officer
Mathieu Savard, President
Alix Drapack, Chief Sustainability Officer
Don Njegovan, Chief Operating Officer
Blair Zaritsky, Chief Financial Officer

Pacific Booker Minerals Inc. (PBM)
#1103, 1166 Alberni St.
Vancouver, BC V6E 3Z3

604-681-8556
Fax: 604-687-5995
800-747-9911
info@pacificbooker.bc.ca
www.pacificbooker.com

Company Type: Public
Ticker Symbol: BKM/TSX
Profile: The company owns the Morrison property, a copper-gold-molybdenum mine.
John Plourde, President & CEO
Ruth Swan, Chief Financial Officer
Erik Tornquist, Chief Operating Officer

Pan American Silver Corp.
#1440, 625 Howe St.
Vancouver, BC V6C 2T6

604-684-1175
Fax: 604-684-0147
info@panamericansilver.com
www.panamericansilver.com
www.linkedin.com/company/pan-american-silver-corp.

Company Type: Public
Ticker Symbol: PAAS/TSX, NASDAQ
Staff Size: 6,850
Profile: Pan American Silver, founded in 1994, conducts its mining & exploration activities in Mexico, Bolivia, Peru & Argentina.
Michael Steinmann, President & CEO
Steve Busby, Chief Operating Officer
Robert Doyle, Chief Financial Officer

Panoro Minerals Ltd.
#1610, 700 West Pender St.
Vancouver, BC V6C 1G8

604-684-4246
Fax: 604-684-4200
info@panoro.com
panoro.com

Other Communications: Peru Office, Phone: +51-9-4016-2518
www.linkedin.com/company/panoro-minerals

Company Type: Public
Ticker Symbol: PML/TSX.V, BVL
Profile: Panoro Minerals Ltd. has a portfolio of mineral properties situated in southeastern Peru. The region is known for its copper & gold deposits.
Luqman Shaheen, President & CEO
Shannon Ross, Chief Financial Officer
Luis Vela, Vice-President, Exploration

Parex Resources Inc.
West Tower, Eighth Avenue Place
#2700, 585 - 8th Ave. SW
Calgary, AB T2P 1G1

403-265-4800
Fax: 403-265-8216
info@parexresources.com
parexresources.com

Other Communications: Colombia: +(571)-629-1716
www.linkedin.com/company/parex-resources

Company Type: Public
Ticker Symbol: PXT/TSX
Profile: Oil & natural gas exploration & production are conducted in the Caribbean area & South America. Parex Resources has holdings onshore Trinidad & in Colombia's Llanos Basin.
Imad Mohsen, President & CEO
Kenneth Pinsky, Chief Financial Officer
Ryan W. Fowler, Senior Vice-President, Exploration

Platinum Group Metals Ltd.
#838, 1100 Melville St.
Vancouver, BC V6E 4A6

604-899-5450
Fax: 604-484-4710
866-899-5450
info@platinumgroupmetals.net
www.platinumgroupmetals.net
Other Communications: South Africa Office, Phone:
+27-(11)-782-2186

Company Type: Public
Ticker Symbol: PTM/TSX; PLG/NYSE
Staff Size: 320
Profile: Formed in 2000, & based in Vancouver, British Columbia & Johannesburg, South Africa, Platinum Group Metals Ltd. is engaged in the exploration, construction & operation of mines. The company holds mineral rights in the Bushveld Igneous Complex of South Africa, in addition to two joint ventures with the government of Japan. Platinum Group Metals Ltd.'s focus is upon the development of platinum operations.
R. Michael Jones, President & CEO
Frank Hallam, Chief Financial Officer

Polymet Mining Corp.
#2060, 444 Cedar St.
St Paul, MN 55101 USA

651-389-4100
info@polymetmining.com
polymetmining.com
www.facebook.com/polymet
twitter.com/polymetmining
www.linkedin.com/company/polymet-mining-inc.

Company Type: Public
Ticker Symbol: POM/TSX; PLM/NYSE
Profile: PolyMet Mining Corp. is a mine development company. It controls 100% of the NorthMet copper, nickel, precious metals & ore project, which is located on the Mesabi Range of northeastern Minnesota. The company also owns 100% of a nearby processing facility, known as Erie Plant.
Jon Cherry, President & CEO
Patrick Keenan, Executive Vice-President & Chief Financial Officer
Andrew Ware, Chief Geologist
Bruce Richardson, Vice-President, Corporate Communications & External Affairs

Pretium Resources Inc.
Also Known As: Pretivm
Four Bentall Centre
PO Box 49334, #2300, 1055 Dunsmuir St.
Vancouver, BC V7X 1L4

604-558-1784
877-558-1784
invest@pretivm.com
www.pretivm.com
www.linkedin.com/company/pretium-resources-inc

Company Type: Public
Ticker Symbol: PVG/TSX, NYSE
Profile: Pretium, stylized as Pretivm, is involved in the development of the Brucejack Project, a high-grade undeveloped gold project in northern British Columbia.
Jacques Perron, President & CEO
Matthew Quinlan, Vice-President & CFO
Greg Norton, Vice-President, Environment & Regulatory Affairs

Prime Mining Corp.
#1507, 1030 West Georgia St.
Vancouver, BC V6E 2Y3

604-428-6128
info@primeminingcorp.ca
primeminingcorp.ca
twitter.com/PrimeMiningCorp
www.linkedin.com/company/prime-mining-corp

Company Type: Public
Ticker Symbol: PRYM/TSX.V
Profile: Prime Mining is a mineral exploration company focused on bring to term gold production at the Los Reyes project in Sinaloa, Mexico.
Daniel J. Kunz, Chief Executive Officer
Ian Harcus, Chief Financial Officer
Kerry Sparkes, Executive Vice-President, Exploration

Probe Metals Inc.
Head Office
#1000, 56 Temperance St.
Toronto, ON M5H 3V5

416-777-6703
info@probemetals.com
www.probemetals.com
twitter.com/probemetals

Company Type: Public
Ticker Symbol: PRB.V/TSX
Profile: Probe Metals is a Canadian gold exploration company focused on the acquisition, exploration & development of highly prospective gold properties. The company's key asset is the Val-d'Or East Gold Project.
Probe Metals was formed as a result of the sale of Probe Mines Limited to Goldcorp in March 2015. Goldcorp currently owns a 13.8% stake in the company.
David Palmer, President & CEO
Yves Dessureault, Chief Operating Officer
Carmelo Marrelli, Chief Financial Officer

Puma Exploration
175, rue Légaré
Rimouski, QC G5L 3B9

418-724-0901
Fax: 418-722-0310
info@explorationpuma.com
explorationpuma.com
www.facebook.com/explorationpuma
twitter.com/explorationpuma
www.linkedin.com/company/puma-exploration-inc

Company Type: Public
Ticker Symbol: PUMA/TSX.V
Profile: The company operates its Murray Brook, Turgeon & Nicholas-Denys projects in New Brunswick. It also has an equity interest in BWR Exploration Inc.
Marcel Robillard, Chair, President & CEO
president@explorationpuma.com
Ginette Gosselin Brisson, Chief Financial Officer

Pure Gold Mining
#1900, 1055 West Hastings St.
Vancouver, BC V6E 2E9

604-646-8000
info@puregoldmining.ca
puregoldmining.ca
www.facebook.com/puregoldmining
twitter.com/puregoldredlake
www.linkedin.com/company/pure-gold-mining-inc

Company Type: Public
Ticker Symbol: PGM/TSX.V
Profile: A gold mining company with projects in northwestern Ontario.
Darin Labrenz, President & CEO
Christopher Lee, Chief Geoscientist
Sean Tetzlaff, Chief Financial Officer
Phil Smerchanski, Vice-President, Exploration

QMX Gold Corporation
PO Box 370, 1876, 3e ave
Val d'Or, QC J9P 7A9

Fax: 819-825-3412
877-717-3027
info@qmxgold.ca
www.qmxgold.ca

Company Type: Public
Profile: QMX Gold Corporation is a mining company operating in Val-d'Or, Quebec & Snow Lake, Manitoba. As of 2021, the company is a wholly-owned subsidiary of Eldorado Gold Corporation.
Brad Humphrey, President & CEO
Paul Bozoki, Chief Financial Officer
Andreas Rompel, Vice-President, Exploration

Quaterra Resources Inc.
#1100, 1199 West Hastings St.
Vancouver, BC V6E 3T5

778-898-0057
info@quaterra.com
www.quaterra.com

Company Type: Public
Ticker Symbol: QTA/TSX.V
Profile: The junior mineral exploration company conducts operations in North America.
C. Travis Naugle, Chief Executive Officer
Stephen Goodman, President
Lei Wang, Chief Financial Officer

QuestEx Gold & Copper Ltd.
#500, 666 Burrard St.
Vancouver, BC V6C 3P6

250-768-1511
855-768-1511
info@questex.ca
questex.ca
twitter.com/QuestEx_au_cu
www.linkedin.com/company/questexgoldandcopper

Company Type: Public
Ticker Symbol: QEX/TSX.V
Profile: QuestEx is a mineral exploration company focused on acquiring & advancing mineral properties in the Golden Triangle & Toodoggone areas of British Columbia. The company owns seven projects in British Columbia.
Joseph Mullin, Chief Executive Officer
Tim Thiessen, Chief Financial Officer & Corporate Secretary

Regulus Resources Inc.
#2710, 200 Granville St.
Vancouver, BC V6C 1S4

604-685-6800
info@regulusresources.com
regulusresources.com
twitter.com/IncRegulus
www.linkedin.com/company/regulus-resources-inc-reg-

Company Type: Public
Ticker Symbol: REG/TSX.V
Profile: A mining company whose main project is the Rio Grande porphyry Cu-Au mine located in Argentina.
John Black, Chief Executive Officer
Fernando Pickmann, President & COO
Kevin Heather, Chief Geological Officer
Mark Wayne, Chief Financial Officer

Robex Resources
#100, 437, Grande Allée est
Québec, QC G1R 2J5

581-741-7421
Fax: 581-742-7241
info@robexgold.com
robexgold.com
twitter.com/relation_robex
www.linkedin.com/company/robexgold

Company Type: Public
Ticker Symbol: RBX.V/TSX
Profile: Robex is a junior Canadian mining exploration & development company.
Benjamin Cohen, Chief Executive Officer
Georges Cohen, President
Augustin Rousselet, Chief Operating Officer & Chief Financial Officer

Roxgold Inc.
#500, 360 Bay St.
Toronto, ON M5H 2V6

416-203-6401
Fax: 416-203-0341
info@roxgold.com
www.roxgold.com
www.linkedin.com/company/roxgold-inc-

Company Type: Public
Ticker Symbol: ROXG/TSX
Profile: Roxgold Inc. is a gold exploration company currently investigating three exploration permits in mineral rich Burkina Faso, West Africa.
John Dorward, President & CEO
Paul Criddle, Chief Operating Officer
Vince Sapuppo, Chief Financial Officer
Julien Baudrand, Vice-President, Health, Safety & Sustainability
Paul Weedon, Vice-President, Exploration

Sabina Gold & Silver Corp.
PO Box 220, #1800, 555 Burrard St.
Vancouver, BC V7X 1M9

604-998-4175
Fax: 604-998-1051
info@sabinagoldsilver.com
www.facebook.com/SabinaGoldSilver
twitter.com/BRP_Sabina
www.linkedin.com/company/sabina-gold-&-silver-corp.

Company Type: Public
Ticker Symbol: SBB/TSX
Profile: The precious metals company has flagship projects in Nunavut. Primary assets include: the Back River Gold Project; a royalty on the Hackett River silver & zinc property; & the Wishbone greenstone belt & its potential for gold discoveries.
Bruce McLeod, President & CEO
Elaine Bennett, Chief Financial Officer & Vice-President, Finance
Angus Campbell, Vice-President, Exploration
Matthew Pickard, Vice-President, Environment & Sustainability

Sailfish Royalty Corp.
Sea Meadow House
PO Box 116 Stn. Road Town, , Tortola, VG1110 British Virgin Islands

284-494-6401
sailfishroyalty.com

Company Type: Public
Ticker Symbol: FISH/TSX.V
Profile: A gold royalty company whose portfolio is on the Spring Valley Gold Project in Nevada and San Albino in northern Nicaragua.
Akiba Leisman, Chief Executive Officer
Peter Van Zoost, Chief Financial Officer

Salazar Resources Ltd.
#1305, 1090 West Georgia St.
Vancouver, BC V6E 3V7

604-685-9316
Fax: 604-683-1585
ir@salazarresources.com
www.salazarresources.com
twitter.com/srl_exploration
www.linkedin.com/company/salazar-resources-ltd

Company Type: Public
Ticker Symbol: SRL/TSX.V
Profile: Salazar Resources Ltd. is a mineral exploration & development company focused on the development of prospective areas in Ecuador. Salazar currently owns four projects throughout Ecuador.
Fredy Salazar, President & CEO
Pablo Acosta, Chief Financial Officer
Merlin Marr-Johnson, Executive Vice-President & Corporate Secretary
merlin@salazarresources.com

Sama Resources Inc.
#132, 1320, boul Graham
Montréal, QC H3P 3C8

Fax: 514-747-4276
877-792-6688
info@samaresources.com
samaresources.com

Company Type: Public
Ticker Symbol: SME/TSX.V
Profile: Sama Resources is a resource company focused on exploring the Samapleu Nickel-Copper project in Ivory Coast, West Africa.
Marc-Antoine Audet, Chief Executive Officer
Isabelle Gauthier, Chief Financial Officer

Sandstorm Gold Ltd.
#1400, 400 Burrard St.
Vancouver, BC V6C 3A6

604-689-0234
Fax: 604-689-7317
866-584-0234
info@sandstormgold.com
www.sandstormgold.com
twitter.com/sandstormssl
www.linkedin.com/company/sandstorm-gold

Company Type: Public
Ticker Symbol: SSL/TSX
Profile: Founded in 2008, Sandstorm Gold Ltd. is a commodity streaming company that provides upfront financing to resource companies.
Nolan Watson, President & CEO
Erfan Kazemi, Chief Financial Officer

Santacruz Silver Mining Ltd.
#880, 580 Hornby St.
Vancouver, BC V6C 3B6

www.santacruzsilver.com
www.facebook.com/santacruzsilver
twitter.com/santacruzsilver
www.linkedin.com/company/santacruz-silver-mining

Company Type: Public
Ticker Symbol: SCZ/TSX.V
Profile: Santacruz Silver Mining owns & operates four silver mines in Mexico.
Arturo Préstamo Elizondo, Chair & Chief Executive Officer
Carlos Silva Ramos, Chief Executive Officer

Scorpio Gold Corp.
#1, 15782 Marine Dr.
White Rock, BC V4B 1E6

604-536-2711
scorpio@scorpiogold.com
scorpiogold.com
Other Communications: Investor Relations, Email:
ir@scorpiogold.com

Company Type: Public
Ticker Symbol: SGN/TSX.V
Profile: The precious metals company owns 70% of the Mineral Ridge mine in Esmeralda County, Nevada. It is the full owner of the Goldwedge property in Manhattan, Nevada.
Brian Lock, Chief Executive Officer
block@scorpiogold.com
Dan O'Brien, Chief Financial Officer

Seabridge Gold Inc.
#400, 106 Front St. East
Toronto, ON M5A 1E1

416-367-9292
Fax: 416-367-2711
info@seabridgegold.net
www.seabridgegold.net
www.facebook.com/SeabridgeGold
twitter.com/GoldSeabridge
www.linkedin.com/company/seabridge-gold-inc

Company Type: Public
Ticker Symbol: SEA/TSX; SA/NYSE
Profile: Seabridge Gold's principal assets are the 100% owned Courageous Lake gold project in the Northwest Territories & the 100% owned KSM property near Stewart, British Columbia.
Rudi P. Fronk, Chair & Chief Executive Officer
Jay S. Layman, President & COO
Christopher J. Reynolds, Chief Financial Officer & Vice-President, Finance
R. Brent Murphy, Senior Vice-President, Environmental Affairs

Sherritt International Corporation
East Tower, Bay Adelaide Centre
#4220, 22 Adelaide St. West
Toronto, ON M5H 4E3

416-924-4551
Fax: 416-924-5015
800-704-6698
info@sherritt.com
Other Communications: Investor Relations, Email:
investor@sherritt.com

Company Type: Public
Ticker Symbol: S/TSX
Staff Size: 3,200
Profile: Sherritt International Corporation has interests in nickel & cobalt metals business; thermal coal production & electricity generation; & oil & gas exploration; & development & production. The company conducts its operations in Canada & internationally.
Leon Binedell, President & CEO
Steve Wood, Executive Vice-President & COO
Elvin Saruk, Senior Vice-President, Oil & Gas and Power
Karen Trenton, Senior Vice-President, Human Resources

Sierra Metals Inc.
PO Box 200, #4260, 161 Bay St.
Toronto, ON M5J 2S1

416-366-7777
866-493-9646
info@sierrametals.com
www.sierrametals.com
www.facebook.com/sierrametalsinc
twitter.com/sierrametals
www.linkedin.com/company/sierra-metals-inc-

Company Type: Public
Ticker Symbol: SMT/TSX
Staff Size: 1,300
Profile: Sierra Metals Inc. is a mid-tier precious & base metals producer in Latin America.
Luis Marchese, Chief Executive Officer
Ed Guimaraes, Chief Financial Officer
Alonso Lujan, Vice-President, Exploration

Silver Elephant Mining Corp.
#1610, 409 Granville St.
Vancouver, BC V6C 1T2

604-569-3661
info@silverelef.com
www.silverelef.com
Other Communications: Investor Relations, Email:
ir@silverelef.com

Company Type: Public
Ticker Symbol: ELEF/TSX
Profile: A mining company with projects in Bolivia & Manitoba.
John Lee, Executive Chair
Irina Plavutska, Chief Financial Officer

Silvercorp Metals Inc.
#1750, 1066 West Hastings St.
Vancouver, BC V6E 3X1

604-669-9397
Fax: 604-669-9387
888-224-1881
investor@silvercorp.ca
silvercorp.ca
www.facebook.com/silvercorpmetalssvm
twitter.com/silvercorpsvm
www.linkedin.com/cpmpany/silvercorp-metals-inc

Company Type: Public
Ticker Symbol: SVM/TSX, NYSE
Profile: Silvercorp Metals acquires, explores & mines silver-related properties located in Canada & China. The

company has implemented a range of employee safety measures & environmental protection measures.
Rui Feng, Chair & Chief Executive Officer
Derek Liu, Chief Financial Officer

SilverCrest Metals Inc.
#501, 570 Granville St.
Vancouver, BC V6C 3P1

604-694-1730
Fax: 604-357-1313
866-691-1730
info@silvercrestmetals.com
www.silvercrestmetals.com

Company Type: Public
Ticker Symbol: SIL/TSX
Staff Size: 420
Profile: SilverCrest Metals is an exploration, development & extraction company focused on silver & other precious metals. Its projects are located in Mexico.
N. Eric Fier, Chief Executive Officer
Christopher Ritchie, President
Pierre Beaudoin, Chief Operating Officer
Anne Yong, Chief Financial Officer
Stephany Fier, Vice-President, Exploration & Technical Services

Sirios Resources
#410, 1000, rue St-Antoine ouest
Montréal, QC H3C 3R7

514-510-7961
Fax: 514-510-7964
info@sirios.com
sirios.com
www.facebook.com/RessourcesSirios
www.linkedin.com/company/sirios-resources

Company Type: Public
Ticker Symbol: SOI/TSX.V
Profile: Founded in 1995, the company has multiple projects in Quebec.
Dominique Doucet, President & CEO
Frédéric Sahyouni, Chief Financial Officer

Skeena Resources Ltd.
#650, 1021 West Hastings St.
Vancouver, BC V6E 0C3

604-684-8725
Fax: 604-558-7695
info@skeenaresources.com
skeenaresources.com
www.facebook.com/skeenaresources
twitter.com/skeenaresources

Company Type: Public
Ticker Symbol: SKE/TSX.V
Profile: Skeena Resources is a junior Canadian mining exploration company focused on developing prospective base & precious metal properties in the Golden Triangle region of northwest British Columbia.
Walter Coles, Jr., President & CEO
Andrew MacRitchie, Chief Financial Officer
Shane Williams, Chief Operating Officer
Paul Geddes, Vice-President, Exploration & Resource Development
Justin Himmelright, Vice-President, Sustainability

Soma Gold Corp.
#970, 1050 West Pender St.
Vancouver, BC V6E 3S7

604-259-0302
info@somagoldcorp.com
www.somagoldcorp.com
www.facebook.com/somagoldcorp
twitter.com/SomaGoldCorp

Company Type: Public
Ticker Symbol: SOMA/TSX.V
Profile: Soma Gold has mines in Colombia.
Geoff Hampson, Executive Chair
Javier Cordova Unda, President & CEO
Greg Hayes, Chief Financial Officer

Sombrero Resources Inc.
#600, 1199 West Hastings St.
Vancouver, BC V6E 3T5

778-729-0600
info@sombreroresources.com
www.sombreroresources.com
twitter.com/SombreroRes
www.linkedin.com/company/sombrero-resources

Company Type: Public
Profile: Sombrero Resources is a gold & copper exploration company. It was spun out from Auryn Resources in 2020. Its operations are focused in southeast Peru.
Ivan Bebek, President & CEO
Michael Henrichsen, Chief Geologist
Elizabeth Senez, Interim Chief Financial Officer
Dave Smithson, Vice-President, Exploration

SOPerior Fertilizer Corporation
5213 Durie Rd.
Mississauga, ON L5M 2C6

info@sopfertilizer.com
www.soperiorfertilizer.com
Other Communications: 416-362-8640, Ext. 104
Company Type: Public
Ticker Symbol: SOP/TSX
Profile: SOPerior Fertilizer is a fertilizer producer with projects in Quebec & Utah.
Andrew Squires, Chief Executive Officer
Olga Nikitovic, Chief Financial Officer

Spanish Mountain Gold Ltd.
#1120, 1095 West Pender St.
Vancouver, BC V6E 2M6

604-601-3651
Fax: 604-681-6866
info@spanishmountaingold.com
spanishmountaingold.com
twitter.com/spmtngold

Company Type: Public
Ticker Symbol: SPA/TSX.V; S3Y/FSE
Profile: Spanish Mountain Gold's flagship project is located in south central British Columbia.
Larry Yau, Chief Executive Officer
Sharon Ng, Chief Financial Officer
Judy Stoeterau, Vice-President, Geology

SRHI Inc.
c/o Peterson McVicar LLP
#902, 18 King St. East
Toronto, ON M5C 1C4

647-749-5859
info@srhi.ca
srhi.ca

Company Type: Public
Ticker Symbol: SRHI/TSX
Profile: Sprott Resource Holdings Inc. invests & operates through its subsidiaries in the natural resource sector. Sprott's investments include operations in oil & gas, energy, agriculture & agricultural nutrients, as well as a large position in physical gold bullion.
Terrence Lyons, Interim Chief Executive Officer
Michael Staresinic, President & CFO

SSR Mining Inc.
PO Box 49088, #800, 1055 Dunsmuir St.
Vancouver, BC V7X 1G4

604-689-3846
Fax: 604-689-3847
888-338-0046
www.ssrmining.com
www.linkedin.com/company/ssr-mining-inc

Company Type: Public
Ticker Symbol: SSRM/TSX, NASDAQ
Profile: SSR Mining explores & operates precious metals projects. Operations take place in Canada, the United States, Mexico, Argentina & Peru.
In 2016 Silver Standard acquired Canadian mining company Claude Resources, including its Seabee gold mine in Saskatchewan. In 2020, it merged with Alacer Gold Corp.
Rodney P. Antal, President & CEO
Stewart Beckman, Executive Vice-President & COO
Alison White, Executive Vice-President & CFO

Star Diamond Corp.
#600, 224 - 4th Ave. South
Saskatoon, SK S7K 5M5

306-664-2202
Fax: 306-664-7181
stardiamondcorp@stardiamondcorp.com
stardiamondcorp.com
twitter.com/StarDiamondCorp

Company Type: Public
Ticker Symbol: DIAM/TSX
Profile: Star Diamond Corp. is focused on exploring & developing diamond resouces in Saskatchewan. The company holds 100% of the Fort à la Corne mineral dispositions in central Saskatchewan, as well as an interest in the Buffalo Hills diamond project north of Edmonton.
Ken MacNeill, President & CEO
Greg Shyluk, Chief Financial Officer

Starcore International Mines Ltd.
PO Box 113, #750, 580 Hornby St.
Vancouver, BC V6C 3B6

604-602-4935
investor@starcore.com
starcore.com
Other Communications: Investor Relations, Phone: 866-602-4935, Ext. 211
Company Type: Public
Ticker Symbol: SAM/TSX

Profile: The mining company acquires & develops gold & silver properties. Starcore International Mines is active in Mexico.
Robert Eadie, President & CEO
Gary Arca, Chief Financial Officer

Starr Peak Mining Ltd.
#300, 1055 West Hastings St.
Vancouver, BC V6E 2E9

646-661-0409
info@starrpeakminingltd.com
starrpeakminingltd.com

Company Type: Public
Ticker Symbol: STE/TSX.V
Profile: Starr Peak Mining is an exploration company focused on gold projects in Canada. Its main focus is the NewMetal property in Quebec.
Johnathan More, Chief Executive Officer
Cyrus Driver, Chief Financial Officer
Yves Rougerie, Vice-President, Exploration

Steppe Gold
Shangri-La Office
#1201, Olympic St. 19A
Ulaanbaatar, 14241 Mongolia

steppegold.com
Other Communications: Mongolia: +976-7732-1914
twitter.com/steppegold

Company Type: Public
Ticker Symbol: STGO/TSX
Profile: The precious metals company is focused on its Mongolian projects, such as the ATO project aquired from Centerra Mongolia in 2017.
Matthew Wood, Executive Chair
Batta Tumur-Ochir, President & CEO, Mongolia
Jeremy South, Senior Vice-President & CFO

Stornoway Diamond Corp.
Tour ouest
#400, 1111, rue St-Charles ouest
Longueuil, QC J4K 5G4

450-616-5555
Fax: 450-674-2012
877-331-2232
www.stornowaydiamonds.com
www.facebook.com/swydiamonds
twitter.com/swydiamonds
www.linkedin.com/company/swydiamonds

Company Type: Public
Ticker Symbol: SWY/TSX
Staff Size: 300
Profile: Stornoway is a leading Canadian diamond exploration & development company with 100% ownership of the Renard Diamond Project in Quebec.
Patrick Sévigny, Chief Operating Officer

Strategic Metals Ltd.
#1016, 510 West Hastings St.
Vancouver, BC V6B 1L8

604-687-2522
Fax: 604-688-2578
888-688-2522
www.strategicmetalsltd.com
www.facebook.com/strategicmetals
twitter.com/tsxvsmd

Company Type: Public
Ticker Symbol: SMD/TSX.V
Profile: Strategic Metals is an exploration company, with properties & royalty interests in the Yukon. The company also owns shares of: Silver Range Resources, ATAC Resources Ltd. & Rockhaven Resources Ltd.
W. Douglas Eaton, President & CEO
Larry B. Donaldson, Chief Financial Officer
Ian J. Talbot, Chief Operating Officer

Sulliden Mining Capital
#800, 65 Queen St. West
Toronto, ON M5H 2M5

416-861-2267
info@sulliden.com
sulliden.com

Company Type: Public
Ticker Symbol: SMC/TSX
Profile: Sulliden Mining Capital is focused on the acquisition & development of quality mining projects in the Americas.
Stan Bharti, Interim Chief Executive Officer
Deborah Battiston, Chief Financial Officer

Sun Summit Minerals Corp.
PO Box 35, #704, 595 Howe St.
Vancouver, BC V6C 2T5

778-588-9606
info@sunsummitminerals.com
sunsummitminerals.com

Company Type: Public
Ticker Symbol: SMN/TSX.V
Profile: Sun Summit Minerals is a mineral exploration company. Its main project is the Buck Project, located in central British Columbia.
Robert D. Willis, Chief Executive Officer
Fernando J. Costa, Chief Financial Officer

Superior Gold Inc.
#1410, 70 University Ave.
Toronto, ON M5J 2M4

647-925-1292
www.superior-gold.com
Other Communications: Investor Relations Phone: 647-925-1293
www.linkedin.com/company/superior-gold-inc.
Company Type: Public
Ticker Symbol: SGI/TSX.V
Profile: Superior Gold's main asset is the Australia-based Plutonic Gold mine.
Tamara Brown, Interim Chief Executive Officer
Keith Boyle, Chief Operating Officer
Paul Olmsted, Chief Financial Officer

Surge Copper Corp.
PO Box 10351, #888, 700 West Georgia St.
Vancouver, BC V7Y 1G5

604-718-5454
Fax: 604-646-2054
888-500-4587
info@surgecopper.com
surgecopper.com
Company Type: Public
Ticker Symbol: SURG/TSX.V
Profile: Surge Copper Corp. is a mineral exploration & development company operating its wholly-owned Ootsa copper-gold porphyry project in British Columbia.
Leif Nilsson, Chief Executive Officer
Shane Ebert, President & Vice-President, Exploration
Chantelle Collins, Chief Financial Officer

Tanzanian Gold Corporation
#202, 5626 Larch St.
Vancouver, BC V6M 4E1

844-364-1830
tnxcorporate@tangoldcorp.com
www.tangoldcorp.com
Other Communications: Investor Relations, Email:
investors@tangoldcorp.com
www.facebook.com/tanzaniangold
twitter.com/tanzaniangold
www.linkedin.com/company/tanzanian-gold-corporation
Company Type: Public
Ticker Symbol: TNX/TSX; TRX/NYSE
Profile: Tanzanian Gold Corporation is engaged in the exploration of mineral properties in Tanzania.
Stephen Mullowney, Chief Executive Officer
Michael P. Leonard, Chief Financial Officer

Taseko Mines Limited
1040 West Georgia St., 12th Fl.
Vancouver, BC V6E 4H1

778-373-4533
Fax: 778-373-4534
877-441-4533
investor@tasekomines.com
www.tasekomines.com
www.facebook.com/tasekomines
twitter.com/tasekomines
Company Type: Public
Ticker Symbol: TKO/TSX; TGB/NYSE
Profile: Taseko Mines Limited is a mineral exploration & mining company. The company is engaged in the following main projects in British Columbia: the New Prosperity gold-copper project; the Gibraltar open pit copper mine; the wholly owned Aley niobium project; & the Harmony gold prospect.
Russell Hallbauer, Chief Executive Officer
Stuart McDonald, President
Bryce Hamming, Chief Financial Officer
John McManus, Chief Operating Officer

Teck Resources Limited
Five Bentall Centre
#3300, 550 Burrard St.
Vancouver, BC V6C 0B3

604-699-4000
Fax: 604-699-4750
www.teck.com
Other Communications: Investor Relations, Email:
investors@teck.com
www.facebook.com/teckresourcesltd
twitter.com/teckresources
www.linkedin.com/company/teck-resources-limited
Company Type: Public
Ticker Symbol: TECK.A/TSX; TECK/NYSE

Staff Size: 10,000
Profile: The resource company has business units focused on zinc, copper, steelmaking coal & energy. Teck is building parnerships to confront sustainability challenges in the regions where it operates. The company is committed to increasing awareness of the global health issue of zinc deficiency. Shares are listed on the Toronto & New York stock exchanges.
Donald R. Lindsay, President & CEO
Jonathan Price, Chief Financial Officer & Senior Vice-President, Finance
Peter C. Rozee, Senior Vice-President, Commercial & Legal Affairs

Telson Mining Corporation
#1000, 1111 Melville St.
Vancouver, BC V6E 3V6

604-684-8071
ir@telsonmining.com
www.telsonmining.com
www.facebook.com/telsonmining
twitter.com/telsonmining
www.linkedin.com/company/telson-mining-corp
Company Type: Public
Ticker Symbol: TSN/TSX.V
Profile: Telson Mining Corporation is a junior resource mining company with two Mexican gold, silver & base metal projects, including the Campo Morado mine project in Guerrero & the Tahuehueto project in Durango State.
Ralph Shearing, President & Chief Executive Officer
Omar Garcia Abrego, Chief Financial Officer

Teras Resources Inc.
#206, 6025 - 12th St. SE
Calgary, AB T2H 2K1

403-262-8411
Fax: 403-269-3290
info@teras.ca
teras.ca
www.facebook.com/TerasResources
twitter.com/TerasResources
www.linkedin.com/company/teras-resources
Company Type: Public
Ticker Symbol: TRA/TSX.V
Profile: A gold mining company with projects in California, Montana & Nevada.
Joseph Carrabba, President & CEO
Kuldip Baid, Chief Financial Officer

Tervita Corp.
#1600, 140 - 10th Ave. SE
Calgary, AB T2G 0R1

Fax: 403-261-5612
855-837-8482
info@tervita.com
tervita.com
www.facebook.com/tervita
twitter.com/tervita
www.linkedin.com/company/tervita
Company Type: Public
Ticker Symbol: TEV/TSX
Profile: Tervita provides environmental and waste services to clients. They specilize in oil, gas, industry & mining, offering facilities for such purposes as water, treatment recovery & bioremediation.
John Cooper, President & CEO
Linda Dietsche, Chief Financial Officer
Rob Dawson, Executive Vice-President, Strategy & Corporate Development

THEMAC Resources Group Ltd.
#1500, 409 Granville St.
Vancouver, BC V6C 1T2

info@themacresourcesgroup.com
themacresourcesgroup.com
Other Communications: Investor Relations, Email:
investor@themacresourcesgroup.com
Company Type: Public
Ticker Symbol: MAC/TSX
Profile: THEMAC Resources Group Ltd is a Canadian-based resource company focused on acquiring, exploring & developing natural resource properties, bringing innovation & sustainable approaches to mine development, production & reclamation processes.
Andrew Maloney, Chief Executive Officer
Mark McIntosh, Chief Financial Officer
Jeffrey Smith, Chief Operating Officer

Thor Explorations Ltd.
167 Broadhurst Gardens, 1st Fl.
London, NW6 3AU UK

778-373-0102
info@thorexpl.com
thorexpl.com
twitter.com/thorexpl_thx
www.linkedin.com/company/thor-explorations-ltd
Company Type: Public
Ticker Symbol: THX/TSX.V
Profile: Thor Explorations is a Canadian mineral exploration company engaged in the acquisition & exploration & development of mineral properties in West Africa. The company's Flagship Project is the Segilola Gold Project in Osun State, Nigeria.
Segun Lawson, President & CEO
Ben Hodges, Chief Financial Officer
Louise Porteus, Environmental & Social Manager

Tier One Silver Inc.
#600, 1199 West Hastings St.
Vancouver, BC V6E 3T5

778-729-0600
info@tieronesilver.com
www.tieronesilver.com
twitter.com/TierOneSilver
www.linkedin.com/company/tier-one-silver
Company Type: Public
Profile: The company is a previous metals exploration company with projects focused in Peru. It was spun out from Auryn Resources in 2020.
Peter Dembicki, President & CEO
Michael Henrichsen, Chief Geologist
Elizabeth Senez, Interim Chief Financial Officer
Dave Smithson, Senior Vice-President, Exploration

Tinka Resources Ltd.
#1305, 1090 West Georgia St.
Vancouver, BC V6E 3V7

info@tinkaresources.com
www.tinkaresources.com
www.facebook.com/TinkaResources
twitter.com/tinkaresources
www.linkedin.com/company/tinka-resources
Company Type: Public
Ticker Symbol: TK/TSX.V
Profile: A junior mining company with projects in Peru.
Graham Carman, President & CEO
Nick DeMare, Chief Financial Officer
Alvaro Fernandez-Baca, Vice-President, Exploration

Titan Mining
#555, 999 Canada Pl.
Vancouver, BC V6C 3E1

604-687-1717
info@titanminingcorp.com
www.titanminingcorp.com
twitter.com/titanminingcorp
www.linkedin.com/company/titan-mining-corporation
Company Type: Public
Ticker Symbol: TI/TSX
Profile: Titan Mining has full ownership of its Empire State Mine in New York State, which produces zinc concentrate.
Donald Taylor, Chief Executive Officer
Purni Parikh, President
Michael McClelland, Chief Financial Officer

Torex Gold Resources Inc.
Exchange Tower
#740, 130 King St. West
Toronto, ON M5X 2A2

647-260-1500
Fax: 416-304-4000
info@torexgold.com
torexgold.com
twitter.com/torexgold
www.linkedin.com/company/torex-gold-resources-inc
Company Type: Public
Ticker Symbol: TXG/TSX
Profile: The mining company explores precious metal resources, especially gold. Torex Gold Resources Inc. owns 100% of the Morelos Gold Project, which is situated in the Morelos Gold Belt near Mexico City.
Jody Kuzenko, President & CEO
Andrew Snowden, Chief Financial Officer

Trailbreaker Resources Ltd.
#2110, 650 West Georgia St.
Vancouver, BC V6B 4N9

604-681-1820
Fax: 604-681-1864
info@trailbreakerresources.com
www.trailbreakerresources.com
www.facebook.com/TrailbreakerLtd
twitter.com/TrailbreakerLtd
www.linkedin.com/company/trailbreaker-resources

Company Type: Public
Ticker Symbol: TBK/TSX.V
Profile: Trailbreaker is a mining company.
Daithi Mac Gearait, President & CEO
Lucy Zhang, Chief Financial Officer

Treasury Metals Inc.
The Exchange Tower
PO Box 99, #3680, 130 King St. West
Toronto, ON M5X 1B1

416-214-4654
Fax: 416-599-4959
info@treasurymetals.com
www.treasurymetals.com
twitter.com/treasurymetals
www.linkedin.com/company/treasury-metals-inc.

Company Type: Public
Ticker Symbol: TML/TSX
Profile: The mineral exploration & development company is focused on the acquisition of gold projects in the Americas. Treasury Metals' main focus are the Goliath Gold Project, situated in the Kenora Mining District near Dryden, Ontario, & the Goldcliff Project, located in the Manitou Straits Fault Zone, south of Dryden, Ontario.
Jeremy Wyeth, President & CEO
Orin Baranowsky, Chief Financial Officer
Mac Potter, Manager, Environmental & Community

Trevali Mining Corporation
#1900, 999 West Hastings St.
Vancouver, BC V6C 2W2

778-655-5885
Fax: 604-608-9863
info@trevali.com
www.trevali.com
twitter.com/trevali
www.linkedin.com/company/trevali

Company Type: Public
Ticker Symbol: TV/TSX
Profile: Trevali Mining Corporation has production sites in northern New Brunswick, Burkino Faso, Namibia & in Peru.
Ricus Grimbeeek, President & CEO
Steven Molnar, Chief Legal Officer

Trilogy Metals Inc.
#1150, 609 Granville St.
Vancouver, BC V7Y 1G5

604-638-8088
Fax: 604-638-0644
855-638-8088
info@trilogymetals.com
trilogymetals.com
www.facebook.com/novacopper
twitter.com/trilogy_alaska
www.linkedin.com/company/trilogy-metals-inc.

Company Type: Public
Ticker Symbol: TMQ/TSX, NYSE
Profile: Trilogy Metals is an exploration & development company focusing on the Upper Kobuk Mineral Projects, which are high-grade copper-zinc-lead-gold-silver properties in Northwest Alaska.
Tony Giardini, President & CEO
Elaine M. Sanders, Chief Financial Officer
Richard Gosse, Vice-President, Exploration

TriStar Gold Inc.
#209, 7950 East Acoma Dr.
Scottsdale, AZ 85260 USA

480-794-1244
info@tristargold.com
www.tristargold.com
www.facebook.com/tristargoldinc
twitter.com/tristar_gold
www.linkedin.com/company/tristar-gold-inc-tsg

Company Type: Public
Ticker Symbol: TSG/TSX.V
Profile: TriStar Gold advances mining projects from exploration to production, with a focus on precious metals deposits in the Americas. The company's primary project is the Castelo de Sonhos Gold project in Pará State, Brazil.
Nick Appleyard, President & CEO
Scott Brunsdon, Chief Financial Officer

Turquoise Hill Resources
#3680, 1 Place Ville-Marie
Montréal, QC H3B 3P2

514-848-1567
877-589-4455
info@turquoisehill.com
turquoisehill.com

Company Type: Public
Ticker Symbol: TRQ/TSX, NYSE
Staff Size: 2,615
Profile: Turquoise Hill Resources is an international mining company focused on copper, gold & coal mines in the Asia Pacific region.
Steve Thibeault, Interim Chief Executive Officer
Luke Colton, Chief Financial Officer

Typhoon Exploration
458, boul des Laurentides
Piedmont, QC J0R 1K0

450-622-4066
Fax: 450-622-4337
info@explorationtyphoon.com
explorationtyphon.com
www.linkedin.com/company/exploration-typhon-inc

Company Type: Public
Ticker Symbol: TYP/TSX.V
Profile: This gold company owns 50% of the Fayolle Project in Quebec as well as shares in & full ownership of other properties in the province.
Serge Roy, Chair
Ghislain Morin, President, CEO & Secretary

Ucore Rare Metals Inc.
#106, 210 Waterfront Dr.
Halifax, NS B4A 0H3

902-482-5214
info@ucore.com
ucore.com
www.facebook.com/UcoreRareMetals
twitter.com/ucore

Company Type: Public
Ticker Symbol: UCU/TSX.V; UURAF /OTCQX
Profile: The mining company focuses on developing technology metals.
Pat Ryan, Chief Executive Officer
Peter Manuel, Chief Financial Officer

UEX Corp.
2465 Berton Pl.
North Vancouver, BC V7H 2W9

236-259-1132
Fax: 604-669-1240
uex@uexcorp.com
www.uexcorp.com
www.facebook.com/uexcorporation
twitter.com/uexcorporation
www.linkedin.com/company/uex-corporation

Company Type: Public
Ticker Symbol: UEX/TSX
Profile: UEX is a mineral exploration & development company focusing on the development of existing & new uranium & cobalt deposits in the Athabasca Basin. UEX has four flagship projects: Christie Lake, West Bear, Shea Creek & Horseshoe-Raven.
Roger Lemaitre, President & CEO
Evelyn Abbott, Chief Financial Officer

Unigold Inc.
PO Box 4, #2704, 401 Bay St.
Toronto, ON M5H 2Y4

416-866-8157
unigold@unigoldinc.com
www.unigoldinc.com

Company Type: Public
Ticker Symbol: UGD.V/TSX
Profile: Founded in 1990, Unigold Inc. is a junior natural resource company focused on exploring & developing its gold projects in the Dominican Republic.
Joseph Hamilton, Chair & Chief Executive Officer
Wesley Hanson, Chief Operating Officer
Donna McLean, Chief Financial Officer

Ur-Energy Inc.
#1300, 55 Metcalfe St.
Ottawa, ON K1P 6L5

613-236-3882
Fax: 613-230-6423
www.ur-energy.com
twitter.com/ur_energy

Company Type: Public
Ticker Symbol: URE/TSX; URG/NYSE
Staff Size: 80
Profile: Ur-Energy is a dynamic junior mining company operating the Lost Creek in-situ recovery (ISR) uranium facility in south-central Wyoming.

Jeffrey Klenda, President & CEO
Roger Smith, Chief Financial Officer & Chief Administrative Officer

ValOre Metals Corp.
#1020, 800 West Pender St.
Vancouver, BC V6C 2V6

604-646-4527
contact@valoremetals.com
valoremetals.com

Company Type: Public
Ticker Symbol: VO/TSX.V
Profile: ValOre Metals Corp. (previously Kivalliq Energy Corporation) is a uranium, precious & base metals exploration company.
Jim Paterson, Chair & Chief Executive Officer
Robert J. Scott, Chief Financial Officer
Colin Smith, Vice-President, Exploration

Victoria Gold Corp.
#204, 80 Richmond St. West
Toronto, ON M5H 2A4

416-866-8800
Fax: 416-866-8801
vgcx.com
www.facebook.com/VictoriaGoldCorp
twitter.com/victoriagold

Company Type: Public
Ticker Symbol: VGCX/TSX
Profile: The gold company is engaged in acquisition, exploration & project development. Victoria Gold Corp.'s flagship project is the Eagle Gold Deposit, which is located on the Dublin Gulch property in Yukon. The company continues to explore in Yukon & Nevada.
John McConnell, President & CEO
Mark Ayranto, Chief Operating Officer
Marty Rendall, Chief Financial Officer

Vista Gold Corp.
#5, 7961 Shaffer Pkwy.
Littleton, CO 80127 USA

720-981-1185
Fax: 720-981-1186
866-981-1185
www.vistagold.com
twitter.com/vista_goldcorp
www.linkedin.com/company/vista-gold-corp

Company Type: Public
Ticker Symbol: VGZ/TSX, NYSE
Profile: Founded in 1983, Vista is focused on the development of the Mt. Todd gold project in Northern Territory, Australia.
Frederick H. Earnest, Chief Executive Officer
Douglas Tobler, Chief Financial Officer

Wallbridge Mining Company Limited
129 Fielding Rd.
Lively, ON P3Y 1L7

705-682-9297
Fax: 888-316-4156
info@wallbridgemining.com
wallbridgemining.com
twitter.com/wallbridgewm
www.linkedin.com/company/wallbridgemining

Company Type: Public
Ticker Symbol: WM/TSX
Profile: Wallbridge Mining Company is preparing to develop its 100%-owned gold project at Fenelon Mine in Québec. The company also has interests in large nicle, copper & PGM projects in Sudbudy, ON; as well as in copper & gold projects in Jamaica & British Columbia.
Marz Kord, President & CEO
Brian Penny, Chief Financial Officer
Attila Péntek, Vice-President, Exploration

Wealth Minerals
#2710, 200 Granville St.
Vancouver, BC V6C 1S4

604-331-0096
Fax: 604-408-7499
888-331-0096
info@wealthminerals.com
wealthminerals.com
www.facebook.com/WealthMineralsLtd
twitter.com/Wealthminerals
www.linkedin.com/company/wealth-minerals

Company Type: Public
Ticker Symbol: WML/TSX.V
Profile: The company focuses on its Seven Salars lithium brine project, its Atacama Salar project, its Five Salars project, its Trinity project & its Laguna Verde project, all located in Chile.
Henk van Alphen, Chief Executive Officer
Sead Hamzagic, Chief Financial Officer

Wesdome Gold Mines Ltd.
#1200, 220 Bay St.
Toronto, ON M5J 2W4

416-360-3743
info@wesdome.com
www.wesdome.com

Company Type: Public
Ticker Symbol: WDO/TSX
Staff Size: 130
Profile: Wesdome Gold Mines Ltd. is the owner of the Mishi &
Eagle River gold mining operations in Wawa, Ontario & the
Kiena mining complex, situated in Val d-Or, Québec.
Duncan Middlemiss, President & CEO
Scott Gilbert, Chief Financial Officer
Marc-Andre Pelletier, Chief Operating Officer
Michael Michaud, Vice-President, Exploration

West Vault Mining Inc.
#838, 1100 Melville St.
Vancouver, BC V6E 4A6

604-685-8311
Fax: 604-484-4710
866-899-5450
info@westvaultmining.com
www.westvaultmining.com

Company Type: Public
Ticker Symbol: WVM/TSX.V
Profile: West Vault Mining focuses on exploring & developing
gold in Nevada.
R. Michael Jones, President & CEO
Frank Hallam, Chief Financial Officer
Sandy McVey, Chief Operating Officer

Western Copper & Gold Corporation
#1200, 1166 Alberni St.
Vancouver, BC V6E 3Z3

604-684-9497
Fax: 604-669-2926
888-966-9995
info@westerncopperandgold.com
www.westerncopperandgold.com
www.facebook.com/westerncopperandgold
twitter.com/westerncuandau
www.linkedin.com/company/western-copper-and-gold

Company Type: Public
Ticker Symbol: WRN/TSX, NYSE
Profile: The exploration & development company has gold,
copper & molybdenum resources & reserves. The company is
active in the Yukon, where it owns 100% of the Casino Project.
Paul West-Sells, President & CEO
Varun Prasad, Chief Financial Officer
Cameron Brown, Vice-President, Engineering

Western Resources Corp.
#1205, 789 West Pender St.
Vancouver, BC V6C 1H2

604-689-9378
Fax: 604-620-0775
info@westernresources.com
www.westernresources.com

Company Type: Public
Ticker Symbol: WRX/TSX
Profile: Western Resources Corp., through its wholly-owned
subsidiary Western Potash Corp., has begun developing a
Potash Project called 'Milestone' near Regina, Saskatchewan.
Bill Xue, President & CEO
George Gao, CFO & Senior Vice-President, Corporate Finance

Wheaton Precious Metals Corp.
#3500, 1021 West Hastings St.
Vancouver, BC V6E 0C3

604-684-9648
Fax: 604-684-3123
800-380-8687
info@wheatonpm.com
www.wheatonpm.com
www.facebook.com/wheatonpm
twitter.com/wheaton_pm
www.linkedin.com/company/wheatonpm

Company Type: Public
Ticker Symbol: WPM/TSX, NYSE
Profile: Wheaton Precious Metals (formerly known as Silver
Wheaton prior to May 2017) is engaged in pure precious metal
streaming around the world. The company has streaming
agreements for 23 operating mines & 8 development stage
projects, from which it purchases silver & gold production.
Randy Smallwood, President & CEO
Gary Brown, Senior Vice-President & CFO
Curt Bernardi, Senior Vice-President, Legal & Corporate
Secretary
Patrick Drouin, Senior Vice-President, Investor Relations
Haytham Hodaly, Senior Vice-President, Corporate
Development

White Gold Corp.
Toronto, ON

647-930-1880
whitegoldcorp.ca
Other Communications: Investor Relations, Email:
ir@whitegoldcorp.ca
www.facebook.com/WGOwhitegold
twitter.com/whitegoldcorp
www.linkedin.com/company/whitegoldcorp

Company Type: Public
Ticker Symbol: WGO/TSX.V; WHGOF/OTC
Profile: White Gold is a gold company operating in the White
Gold District of the Yukon. The company owns over 420,000
hectares of quartz claims, including its Golden Saddle & Arc
projects.
David D'Onofrio, Chief Executive Officer
Shawn Ryan, Chief Technical Advisor
Terry Brace, Vice-President, Exploration

Whitecap Resources Inc.
East Tower, Eighth Avenue Place
#3800, 525 - 8th Ave. SW
Calgary, AB T2P 1G1

403-266-0767
Fax: 403-266-6975
info@wcap.ca
www.wcap.ca

Company Type: Public
Ticker Symbol: WCP/TSX
Profile: The oil company's core operating areas include the
Valhalla North Property in Alberta, the Pembina Property in
Alberta, the Fosterton Property in Saskatchewan, & the West
Central Sask Property.
Grant B. Fagerheim, President & CEO
Thanh Kang, Senior Vice-President & CFO
Joel M. Armstrong, Senior Vice-President, Production &
Operations
Darin Dunlop, Vice-President, Engineering
P. Gary Lebsack, Vice-President, Land

Yamana Gold Inc.
North Tower, Royal Bank Plaza
#2200, 200 Bay St.
Toronto, ON M5J 2J3

416-815-0220
Fax: 416-815-0021
888-809-0925
investor@yamana.com
www.yamana.com
www.facebook.com/yamanagoldinc
twitter.com/yamanagoldinc
www.linkedin.com/company/yamana-gold-inc

Company Type: Public
Ticker Symbol: YRI/TSX; AUY/NYSE
Staff Size: 5,100
Profile: Yamana Gold Inc. began operations in 2003. It is
engaged in the exploration & production of gold, copper & other
precious metals. Development projects & operating mines are
located in Canada, Chile, Brazil & Argentina.
Daniel Racine, President & CEO
Jason LeBlanc, Chief Financial Officer & Senior Vice-President,
Finance
Richard Campbell, Senior Vice-President, Human Resources

Yangarra Resources Ltd. (YGR)
#1530, 715 - 5th Ave. SW
Calgary, AB T2P 2X6

403-262-9558
Fax: 403-262-8281
info@yangarra.ca
www.yangarra.ca

Company Type: Public
Ticker Symbol: YGR/TSX.V
Profile: The junior oil & gas company is engaged in exploration,
development & production in central Alberta.
Jim Evaskevich, President & CEO
Lorne Simpson, Vice-President, Operations
James Glessing, Chief Financial Officer
Randall Faminow, Vice-President, Land

Yorbeau Resources Inc.
#503, 110, boul Crémazie ouest
Montréal, QC H2P 1B9

514-384-2202
Fax: 514-384-6399
info@yorbeauresources.com
www.yorbeauresources.com
www.facebook.com/yorbeauresources
twitter.com/yorbeau
www.linkedin.com/company/yorbeau-resources-inc-tsx-yrb
Company Type: Public
Ticker Symbol: YRB/TSX
Profile: Yorbeau Resources is a gold exploration company in
Québec. The majority of its properties are located in the

northwestern area of the province, most notable of which is the
Cadillac-Larder Lake region on the Abitibi Greenstone Belt.
Terry Kocisko, Interim Chief Executive Officer
Georges Bodnar, Jr., President & CFO
Sylvain Lépine, Vice-President, Exploration

ZEN Graphene Solutions Ltd.
#210, 1205 Amber Dr.
Thunder Bay, ON P7B 6M4

844-730-9822
info@zengraphene.com
www.zengraphene.com
twitter.com/zentsxv

Company Type: Public
Ticker Symbol: ZEN/TSX.V
Profile: Zenyatta Ventures is a mineral development company
whose main project is the Albany Graphite Deposit in
northeastern Ontario.
Greg Fenton, Chief Executive Officer
Peter Wood, President
Brian Bosse, Chief Financial Officer

ZincX Resources Corp.
PO Box 11121 Stn. Royal Centre, , #2050, 1055 West Georgia
St.
Vancouver, BC V6E 3P3

604-684-2181
Fax: 604-682-4768
info@zincxresources.com
zincxresources.com

Company Type: Public
Ticker Symbol: ZNX/TSX.V
Profile: The mineral exploration company conducts operations
in British Columbia. ZincX Resources holds the mineral belt
known as the Kechika Trough.
Peeyush Varshney, President & CEO
Praveen Varshney, Chief Financial Officer
Ken MacDonald, Vice-President, Exploration

Oil & Gas

Advantage Oil & Gas Ltd.
Millennium Tower
#2200, 440 - 2nd Ave. SW
Calgary, AB T2P 5E9

403-718-8000
Fax: 403-718-8332
866-393-0393
ir@advantageog.com
www.advantageog.com

Company Type: Public
Ticker Symbol: AAV/TSX, NYSE
Profile: The intermediate oil & natural gas corporation has
properties in western Canada, including the Montney natural gas
resource at Glacier, Alberta.
Andy J. Mah, Chief Executive Officer
Mike Belenkie, President & COO
Craig Blackwood, Chief Financial Officer

Africa Energy Corp
#2000, 885 West Georgia St.
Vancouver, BC V6C 3E8

604-689-7842
Fax: 604-689-4250
info@africaenergycorp.com
www.africaenergycorp.com
twitter.com/africanenergy

Company Type: Public
Ticker Symbol: AFE/TSX.V; AEC/NASDAQ
Profile: This oil & gas company has exploration projects in
Namibia & South Africa.
Garrett Soden, President & CEO
Jeromie Kufflick, Chief Financial Officer
Jan Maier, Vice-President, Exploration

Africa Oil Corp.
#2000, 885 West Georgia St.
Vancouver, BC V6C 3E8

604-806-3575
aoi@namdo.com
africaoilcorp.com

Company Type: Public
Ticker Symbol: AOI/TSX.V
Profile: The oil & gas company has assets in Ethiopia & Kenya.
Through its equity interest in Horn Petroleum Corporation, Africa
Oil Corp. also has assets in Somalia.
Keith C. Hill, President & CEO
Pascal Nicodeme, Chief Financial Officer
Tim Thomas, Chief Operating Officer
Mark Dingley, Vice-President, Operations
Paul Martinez, Vice-President, Exploration

Akita Drilling Ltd.
#1000, 333 - 7th Ave. SW
Calgary, AB T2P 2Z1

403-292-7979
Fax: 403-292-7990
akitainfo@akita-drilling.com
www.akita-drilling.com

Company Type: Public
Ticker Symbol: AKT.A/TSX
Profile: Akita Drilling Ltd. serves the oil & gas industry by providing contract drilling services. Western Canada, Canada's northern territories & Alaska are the principal areas of activity.
Linda Southern-Heathcot, Executive Chair & Chief Executive Officer
Raymond T. Coleman, President, USA Division
Colin A. Dease, President, Canadian Division
Darcy Reynolds, Chief Financial Officer & Vice-President, Finance
darcy.reynolds@akita-drilling.com

Altura Energy Inc.
#2500, 605 - 5th Ave. SW
Calgary, AB T2P 3H5

403-984-5197
Fax: 844-269-8922
info@alturaenergy.ca
www.alturaenergy.ca

Company Type: Public
Ticker Symbol: ATU.VN/TSX
Profile: An oil & gas producer.
David Burghardt, President & CEO
dburghardt@alturaenergy.ca
Tavis Carlson, Chief Financial Officer & Vice-President, Finance
tcarlson@alturaenergy.ca

ARC Resources Ltd.
#1200, 308 - 4th Ave. SW
Calgary, AB T2P 0H7

403-503-8600
Fax: 403-509-6427
888-272-4900
ir@arcresources.com
www.arcresources.com
www.facebook.com/arcresources
twitter.com/arcresources
www.linkedin.com/company/arc-resources-ltd-

Company Type: Public
Ticker Symbol: ARX/TSX
Staff Size: 560
Profile: Founded in 1996, ARC Resources is a conventional oil & gas company focused in western Canada. In 2021, it merged with Seven Generations Energy Ltd. & maintained the ARC name.
Terry Anderson, President & CEO
Kris Bibby, Senior Vice-President & Chief Financial Officer
David Holt, Senior Vice-President & Chief Operating Officer

Arrow Exploration
#1430, 333 - 11th Ave. SW
Calgary, AB T2R 1L9

403-237-5700
info@arrowexploration.ca
arrowexploration.ca

Company Type: Public
Ticker Symbol: AXL/TSX.V
Profile: This oil company has projects in Columbia.
Marshall Abbott, Chief Executive Officer
Joe McFarlane, Chief Financial Officer

Athabasca Oil Corp. (AOC)
#1200, 215 - 9th Ave. SW
Calgary, AB T2P 1K3

403-237-8227
Fax: 403-264-4640
info@atha.com
www.atha.com
www.linkedin.com/company/athabasca-oil-sands-corporation

Company Type: Public
Ticker Symbol: ATH/TSX
Profile: Athabasca Oil Corp. was incorporated in 2006. The oil company is engaged in the development of oil sands resources in northern Alberta's Athabasca region.
Robert Broen, President & CEO
Matt Taylor, Chief Financial Officer

Baytex Energy Corp.
East Tower, Centennial Place
#2800, 520 - 3rd Ave. SW
Calgary, AB T2P 0R3

587-952-3000
Fax: 587-952-3029
800-524-5521
investor@baytexenergy.com
www.baytexenergy.com
twitter.com/BaytexEnergy

Company Type: Public
Ticker Symbol: BTE/TSX, NYSE
Profile: Baytex Energy specializes in the acquisition, development & production of oil & natural gas. The area of operation is the Western Canadian Sedimentary Basin, in addition to a growing presence in the United States.
Edward D. LaFehr, President & CEO
Rodney D. Gray, Executive Vice-President & CFO

Bellatrix Exploration Ltd.
#1920, 800 - 5th Ave. SW, 21st. Fl.
Calgary, AB T2P 3T6

403-266-8670
Fax: 403-264-8163
www.bxe.com
Other Communications: Investor Relations, Email:
investor.relations@bxe.com

Company Type: Public
Ticker Symbol: BXE/TSX, NYSE
Profile: The oil & gas company operates in British Columbia, Alberta & Saskatchewan.
Tom E. Macinnis, Interim Chief Executive Officer
Shane Abel, Chief Financial Officer & Executive Vice-President, Finance

Bengal Energy Ltd.
#1110, 715 - 5th Ave. SW
Calgary, AB T2P 2X6

403-205-2526
Fax: 403-263-3168
info@bengalenergy.ca
bengalenergy.ca
Other Communications: Investors, Email:
investor.relations@bengalenergy.ca

Company Type: Public
Ticker Symbol: BNG/TSX.V
Profile: Bengal Energy is an international oil & gas exploration & production company with its main production facilities in Australia's Copper Basin.
Chayan Chakrabarty, President & CEO
Jerrad Blanchard, Chief Financial Officer

Birchcliff Energy Ltd.
#1000, 600 - 3rd Ave. SW
Calgary, AB T2P 0G5

403-261-6401
Fax: 403-261-6424
info@birchcliffenergy.com
birchcliffenergy.com
www.linkedin.com/company/birchcliff-energy

Company Type: Public
Ticker Symbol: BIR/TSX
Profile: The intermediate oil & gas company is involved in exploration, development & production.
A. Jeffery Tonken, President & CEO
Myles R. Bosman, Chief Operating Officer & Vice-President, Exploration
Bruno P. Geremia, Chief Financial Officer & Vice-President

Bonavista Energy Corporation
900, 207 - 9th Ave. SW
Calgary, AB T2P 1K3

403-213-4300
Fax: 403-262-5184
investor.relations@bonavistaenergy.com
www.bonavistaenergy.com
www.linkedin.com/company/bonavista-energy-corporation

Company Type: Public
Profile: Bonavista Energy is an oil & gas company, formed in 1997, that focuses on select multi-zone regions of Western Canada.
Jason E. Skehar, President & CEO
Bruce Jensen, Chief Operating Officer
Dean Kobelka, Chief Financial Officer & Vice-President, Finance
Colin J. Ranger, Vice-President, Operations
Lynda Robinson, Vice-President, Human Resources & Administration

Bonterra Energy Corp.
#901, 1015 - 4th St. SW
Calgary, AB T2R 1J4

403-262-5307
Fax: 403-265-7488
info@bonterraenergy.com
www.bonterraenergy.com
www.linkedin.com/company/bonterra-energy-corp

Company Type: Public
Ticker Symbol: BNE/TSX
Profile: Bonterra Energy Corp. is engaged in acquiring, exploring & developing oil & natural gas properties. Activities are conducted in Saskatchewan, Alberta & British Columbia.
George F. Fink, Chief Executive Officer
Robb D. Thompson, Chief Financial Officer
Adrian Neumann, Chief Operating Officer

Calfrac Well Services Ltd.
#500, 407 - 8th Ave. SW
Calgary, AB T2P 1E5

866-770-3722
www.calfrac.com
www.facebook.com/calfrac
twitter.com/calfracws
www.linkedin.com/company/calfrac-well-services

Company Type: Public
Ticker Symbol: CFW/TSX
Staff Size: 3900
Profile: Calfrac Well Services Ltd. is engaged in the provision of oilfield services, such as cementing, fracturing & well stimulation services. Operations are situated in western Canada, the United States, Mexico, Argentina & Russia.
Lindsay Link, President & COO
Michael Olinek, Chief Financial Officer
Gordon Milgate, President, Canadian Operating Division

Canacol Energy Ltd.
#2650, 585 - 8th Ave. SW
Calgary, AB T2P 1G1

403-561-1648
canacolenergy.com

Company Type: Public
Ticker Symbol: CNE/TSX; CNE.C/BVC
Profile: The oil & gas company has operations in Colombia & Ecuador.
Charle Gamba, President & CEO
Jason Bednar, Chief Financial Officer
Ravi Sharma, Chief Operating Officer
Mark Teare, Senior Vice-President, Exploration

Canadian Natural Resources Limited (CNRL)
#2100, 855 - 2nd St. SW
Calgary, AB T2P 4J8

403-517-6700
Fax: 403-517-7350
ir@cnrl.com
www.cnrl.com
Other Communications: Investor Relations, Phone:
403-514-7777
www.facebook.com/CanadianNatural
twitter.com/canadiannatural
www.linkedin.com/company/cnrl

Company Type: Public
Ticker Symbol: CNQ/TSX
Staff Size: 10,000
Profile: Canadian Natural Resources Limited is an independent oil & natural gas producer. It is engaged in the exploration, development & production of oil & natural gas. Operations are carried out in western Canada, the North Sea & offshore West Africa.
Tim S. McKay, President
Mark Strainthorpe, Chief Financial Officer & Senior Vice-President, Finance
Darren M. Fichter, Chief Operating Officer, Exploration & Production
Scott Stauth, Chief Operating Officer, Oil Sands

Canadian Spirit Resources Inc. (CSRI)
#900, 140 - 4th Ave. SW
Calgary, AB T2P 3N3

403-539-5005
info@csri.ca
www.csri.ca

Company Type: Public
Ticker Symbol: SPI/TSX.V
Profile: The natural resources company focuses on opportunities in the unconventional gas sector.
Louisa DeCarlo, President & CEO
Sead Hamzagic, Chief Financial Officer

Cardinal Energy Ltd.
#600, 400 - 3rd Ave. SW
Calgary, AB T2P 4H2

403-234-8681
info@cardinalenergy.ca
cardinalenergy.ca

Company Type: Public
Ticker Symbol: CJ/TSX
Profile: Cardinal Energy is an oil focused investment company.
M. Scott Ratushny, Chief Executive Officer
Dale Orton, Chief Operating Officer
Shawn Van Spankeren, Chief Financial Officer
Robert Wollmann, Senior Vice-President, Exploration

Cathedral Energy Services Ltd.
6030 - 3rd St. SE
Calgary, AB T2H 1K2

403-265-2560
Fax: 403-262-4682
866-276-8201
info@cathedralenergyservices.com
www.cathedralenergyservices.com
www.facebook.com/CathedralDrilling
www.linkedin.com/company/cathedral-energy-services
Company Type: Public
Ticker Symbol: CET/TSX
Profile: Founded in 1988, Cathedral Energy Services provides drilling & completions services.
Tom Connors, President & CEO
Ian Graham, Chief Financial Officer

Cenovus Energy Inc.
225 - 6th Ave. SW
Calgary, AB T2P 0M5

403-766-2000
Fax: 403-766-7600
877-766-2066
questions&comments@cenovus.com
www.cenovus.com
www.facebook.com/cenovus
twitter.com/cenovus
www.linkedin.com/company/cenovus-energy
Company Type: Public
Ticker Symbol: CVE/TSX, NYSE
Profile: Cenovus Energy operates oilsand projects located in northern Alberta. Cenovus also has 50% ownership in two refineries in Roxana, Illinois & Borger, Texas. Cenovus Energy employs environmental specialists to analyze land for drilling activities & to develop a plan to reclaim the land. In 2021, it amalgamated with Husky Energy Inc.
Alex Pourbaix, President & CEO
Jeff Hart, Executive Vice-President & CFO

Centaurus Energy Inc.
Dome Tower
#1600, 333 - 7th Ave. SW
Calgary, AB T2P 2Z1

403-264-1915
Fax: 403-266-6016
info@ctaurus.com
www.ctaurus.com
Company Type: Public
Ticker Symbol: CTA/TSX.V
Profile: Centaurus is an independent, Canadian-based, domestic & international upstream oil & gas company whose main business activities include exploration, development & production of crude oil, natural gas liquids & natural gas.
David Tawil, Chief Executive Officer

Cequence Energy Ltd.
#1400, 215 - 9th Ave. SW
Calgary, AB T2P 1K3

403-229-3050
Fax: 403-229-0603
info@cequence-energy.com
www.cequence-energy.com
Company Type: Public
Profile: Cequence is an oil & natural gas company focused developing its Simonette asset in the Alberta Deep Basin.
Todd Brown, Chief Executive Officer
David P. Robinson, Vice-President, Geology

CES Energy Solutions Corp.
#1400, 332 - 6th Ave. SW
Calgary, AB T2P 3J4

403-269-2800
Fax: 403-266-5708
888-785-6695
www.canadianenergyservices.com
Company Type: Public
Ticker Symbol: CEU/TSX
Staff Size: 2001
Profile: CES Energy Solutions is involved in the design & implementation of drilling fluid systems. The company serves the oil & natural gas industry in western Canada & in the United States through its subsidiary, AES Drilling Fluids, LLC.
Thomas Simons, President & CEO

CGX Energy Inc.
#1100, 333 Bay St.
Toronto, ON M5H 2R2

416-364-5569
Fax: 416-364-5400
info@cgxenergy.com
cgxenergy.ca
www.linkedin.com/company/cgx-energy-inc
Company Type: Public
Ticker Symbol: OYL/TSX.V
Profile: The oil & gas exploration company is active in the Guyana - Suriname Basin. CGX Energy is also pursuing the Equatorial Atlantic Margin Play.
Suresh Narine, Executive Chair
Tralisa Maraj, Chief Financial Officer

Condor Petroleum Inc.
#2400, 144 - 4th Ave. SW
Calgary, AB T2P 3N4

403-201-9694
Fax: 403-201-9607
condorpetroleum.com
Company Type: Public
Ticker Symbol: CPI/TSX
Profile: Condor Petroleum Inc. is an international oil & gas company that is engaged in exploration, development & production of oil, natural gas & NGLs in Kazakhstan & Turkey.
Don Streu, President & CEO
Sandy Quilty, Vice-President & CFO
Norman Storm, Managing Director, Kazakhstan

Crescent Point Energy Corp.
#2000, 585 - 8th Ave. SW
Calgary, AB T2P 1G1

403-693-0020
Fax: 403-693-0070
888-693-0020
www.crescentpointenergy.com
Other Communications: Investor Relations, Toll-Free Phone:
855-767-6923
twitter.com/cpg_corp
www.linkedin.com/company/crescent-point-energy
Company Type: Public
Ticker Symbol: CPG/TSX, NYSE
Staff Size: 735
Profile: Formed in 1994, Crescent Point Energy Corp. is an oil & gas producer. The company is engaged in the acquisition of reserves & production in western Canada.
On June 30, 2015, Crescent Point Energy completed the acquisition of Legacy Oil + Gas, an energy production company whose assets lie primarily in Saskatchewan.
Craig Bryksa, President & CEO
Ryan Gritzfeldt, Chief Operating Officer
Ken Lamont, Chief Financial Officer
Mark Eade, Vice-President, General Counsel & Corporate Secretary

Crew Energy Inc.
#800, 250 - 5th St. SW
Calgary, AB T2P 0R4

403-266-2088
Fax: 403-266-6259
www.crewenergy.com
www.linkedin.com/company/crew-energy-inc
Company Type: Public
Ticker Symbol: CR/TSX
Profile: The junior oil & natural gas producer carries out its activities in northeastern British Columbia & central Alberta.
Dale O. Shwed, President & CEO
John G. Leach, Executive Vice-President & CFO
James Taylor, Chief Operating Officer

Crown Point Energy Inc.
PO Box 1562 Stn. M, , Calgary, AB T2P 3B9

403-232-1150
info@crownpointenergy.com
crownpointenergy.com
Company Type: Public
Ticker Symbol: CWV/TSX.V
Profile: Crown Point Energy Inc. is a junior international oil & gas company with a base in two of the largest producing basins in Argentina.
Brian J. Moss, President & CEO
Marisa Tormakh, Chief Financial Officer & Vice-President, Finance

Distinction Energy Corp.
#2300, 333 - 7th Ave. SW
Calgary, AB T2P 2Z1

403-265-6171
Fax: 403-265-6207
info@distinctionenergy.ca
distinctionenergy.ca
Company Type: Public
Profile: Distinction Energy is engaged in the exploration, development & production of oil & natural gas. Operations take place in western Canada.
Patrick Carlson, President & CEO

Divestco Geoscience Ltd.
#2500, 715 - 5th Ave. SW
Calgary, AB T2P 2X6

587-952-8000
Fax: 587-952-8370
888-294-0081
info@divestco.com
www.divestco.com
www.facebook.com/divestco
www.linkedin.com/company/divestco-geoscience
Company Type: Public
Ticker Symbol: DVT/TSX
Profile: Divestco is an exploration services company dedicated to providing a focused offering of products & services to the oil & gas industry worldwide.

Enbridge Inc.
Fifth Avenue Place
#200, 425 - 1st St. SW
Calgary, AB T2P 3L8

403-231-3900
Fax: 403-231-3920
webmaster-corp@enbridge.com
www.enbridge.com
Other Communications: Investor Relations, Email:
investor.relations@enbridge.com
www.facebook.com/enbridge
twitter.com/enbridge
www.linkedin.com/company/enbridge
Company Type: Public
Ticker Symbol: ENB/TSX, NYSE
Staff Size: 11,200
Profile: Enbridge Inc. is engaged in the following businesses: natural gas pipelines; crude oil & liquids pipelines; natural gas distribution. The company's pipeline system is located in Canada & the United States. International activity includes energy projects & renewable energy.
In 2011, Enbridge, through Canadian Acquireco, acquired all the outstanding common shares of Tonbridge Power Inc.
In 2016, it was announced that Enbridge would be acquiring Houston-based Spectra Energy Corp. The new combined company would continue to be known as Enbridge Inc.
Al Monaco, President & CEO
Colin Gruending, Executive Vice-President & CFO

Enerflex Ltd.
#904, 1331 Macleod Trail SE
Calgary, AB T2G 0K3

403-387-6377
800-242-3178
info@enerflex.com
www.enerflex.com
www.facebook.com/enerflexltd
twitter.com/enerflexltd
www.linkedin.com/company/enerflex-ltd-
Company Type: Public
Ticker Symbol: EFX/TSX
Staff Size: 2,000
Profile: Enerflex is a supplier for natural gas compression, oil & gas processing, refrigeration systems & power generation equipment - plus in-house engineering & mechanical services expertise.
Marc Rossiter, President & CEO
Sanjay Bishnoi, Senior Vice-President & CFO

Enerplus Corp.
The Dome Tower
#3000, 333 - 7th Ave. SW
Calgary, AB T2P 2Z1

403-298-2200
Fax: 403-298-2211
investorrelations@enerplus.com
www.enerplus.com
twitter.com/enerpluscorp
www.linkedin.com/company/enerplus
Company Type: Public
Ticker Symbol: ERF/TSX, NYSE
Staff Size: 800
Profile: Enerplus Corp. has a portfolio of oil & natural gas producing properties situated in western Canada & the United States.

Ian C. Dundas, President & CEO
Wade D. Hutchings, Senior Vice-President & COO
Jodine Jenson Labrie, Senior Vice-President & CFO

Ensign Energy Services Inc.
#1000, 400 - 5th Ave. SW
Calgary, AB T2P 0L6

403-262-1361
Fax: 403-262-8215
info@ensignenergy.com
www.ensignenergy.com
Other Communications: Investor Relations, Email:
ir@ensignenergy.com
www.facebook.com/ensignenergy
twitter.com/EnsignEnergyInc
www.linkedin.com/company/ensign-energy-services
Company Type: Public
Ticker Symbol: ESI/TSX
Profile: Ensign Energy Services Inc. is a service contractor that
provides oilfield services throughout the world to the oil & natural
gas industry. Some of Ensign Energy Services's principal
operating subsidiaries include Arctic Ensign Drilling Ltd., Big Sky
Drilling Inc., Encore Coring & Drilling Inc., Opsco Energy
Industries Ltd., Rockwell Servicing Inc. & Gwich'in Ensign
Oilfield Services Inc.
Robert H. Geddes, President & COO
Mike Gray, Chief Financial Officer

Essential Energy Services Ltd.
Livingston Place West
#1100, 250 - 2nd St. SW
Calgary, AB T2P 0C1

403-263-6778
service@essentialenergy.ca
essentialenergy.ca
Company Type: Public
Ticker Symbol: ESN/TSX
Profile: Essential Energy Services Ltd. offers oilfield services to
oil & gas producers in western Canada. In 2011, Essential
Energy Services acquired Technicoil Corporation to strengthen
the company's position as a coil tubing well service provider.
Garnet K. Amundson, President & CEO
Jeff Newman, Chief Financial Officer

Falcon Oil & Gas Ltd.
68 Merrion Sq. South
Dublin, 2 Ireland

info@falconoilandgas.com
falconoilandgas.com
Other Communications: Phone: +353-1-676-8702
Company Type: Public
Ticker Symbol: FO/TSX.V
Profile: Falcon Oil & Gas Ltd. is a global energy company that is
focused on acquiring, exploring & developing large acreage
positions of unconventional & conventional oil & gas resources.
Philip O'Quigley, Chief Executive Officer
Anne Flynn, Chief Financial Officer

Forza Petroleum Limited
First Canadian Centre
#3400, 350 - 7th Ave. SW
Calgary, AB T2P 3N9

info@forzapetroleum.com
www.forzapetroleum.com
twitter.com/ForzaPetroleum
www.linkedin.com/company/forza-petroleum
Company Type: Public
Ticker Symbol: FORZ/TSX
Profile: Founded in 2010, Forza Petroleum is an independent oil
& gas exploration & production company with focus on projects
in Africa & the Middle East.
Vance Querio, Chief Executive Officer
Lindsey Rosebush, Head, Finance

Frontera Energy Corporation
#1100, 333 Bay St.
Toronto, ON M5H 2R2

416-362-7735
Fax: 416-360-7783
ir@fronteraenergy.ca
www.fronteraenergy.ca
Other Communications: Sustainability, Email:
sustainability@fronteraenergy.ca
www.facebook.com/fronteraenergy
twitter.com/fronteraenergy
Company Type: Public
Ticker Symbol: FEC/TSX
Profile: Frontera Energy is engaged in crude oil & natural gas
exploration, primarily in Latin America.
Orlando Cabrales Segovia, Chief Executive Officer
Alejandro Piñero, Chief Financial Officer

Galleon Gold Corp.
TD Canada Trust Tower
#2700, 161 Bay St.
Toronto, ON M5J 2S1

info@galleongold.com
galleongold.com
www.facebook.com/GalleonGold
twitter.com/galleongold
www.linkedin.com/company/galleon-gold-corp
Company Type: Public
Ticker Symbol: GGO/TSX.V
Profile: Galleon Gold Corp. is a junior gold & base metals
exploration company with mineral holdings in Ontario, Quebec &
New Brunswick.
R. David Russell, President & CEO
Sonia Agustina, Chief Financial Officer
Chris Dupont, Vice-President & COO

Gear Energy
Bow Valley Square II
#800, 205 - 5th Ave. SW
Calgary, AB T2P 2V7

403-538-8435
Fax: 403-705-2660
info@gearenergy.com
gearenergy.com
Company Type: Public
Ticker Symbol: GXE/TSX
Profile: Gear Energy is an exploration & production company
focused on heavy oil. In 2016 Gear Energy merged with Striker
Exploration.
Ingram B. Gillmore, President & CEO
David Hwang, Chief Financial Officer & Vice-President, Finance

Gibson Energy Inc.
Also Known As: Gibsons
#1700, 440 - 2nd Ave. SW
Calgary, AB T2P 5E9

403-206-4000
Fax: 403-206-4001
investor.relations@gibsonenergy.com
www.gibsons.com
www.facebook.com/gibsonenergy
www.linkedin.com/company/gibson-energy
Company Type: Public
Ticker Symbol: GEI/TSX
Staff Size: 500
Profile: Gibson Energy Inc. is a midstream energy company that
is engaged in: crude oil transportation; blending & processing
hydrocarbons; marketing & distributing crude oil & refined
products; & providing water disposal & oilfield waste
management services.
In 2011, Gibson Energy Inc. & Palko Environmental Ltd. entered
into an arrangement agreement, providing for the acquisition by
Gibson of all the issued & outstanding common shares of Palko.
Steve Spaulding, President & CEO
Sean Brown, Senior Vice-President & Chief Financial Officer

Gran Tierra Energy Inc.
#900, 520 - 3rd Ave. SW
Calgary, AB T2P 0R3

403-265-3221
Fax: 403-265-3242
info@grantierra.com
www.grantierra.com
www.linkedin.com/company/gran-tierra-energy
Company Type: Public
Ticker Symbol: GTE/TSX, NYSE, LSE
Profile: The company is focused on the exploration & production
of oil & gas in Colombia & Ecuador.
Gary S. Guidry, President & CEO
Ryan Ellson, CFO & Executive Vice-President, Finance
Diego Perez-Claramunt, Vice-President, HSE & Corporate
Social Responsibility
Lawrence West, Vice-President, Exploration

Granite Oil Corp.
#3203, 308 - 4th Ave. SW
Calgary, AB T2P 0H7

587-349-9113
info@graniteoil.ca
www.graniteoil.ca
Company Type: Public
Ticker Symbol: GXO/TSX; GXOCF/OTCQX
Profile: Granite Oil focuses on oil & natural gas exploration in
western Canada.
Michael Kabanuk, President & CEO
John (Jack) Smith, Interim Chief Financial Officer

Headwater Exploration Inc.
#1200, 500 - 4th Ave. SW
Calgary, AB T2P 2V6

587-391-3680
888-429-4511
info@headwaterexp.com
headwaterexp.com
Company Type: Public
Ticker Symbol: HWX/TSX
Profile: Headwater Exploration Inc. is a junior resource
company engaged in the exploration & development of oil & gas
properties. Activities are carried out onshore in New Brunswick &
offshore in the Gulf of St. Lawrence.
Neil Roszell, Chair & Chief Executive Officer
Jason Jaskela, President & COO
Ali Horvath, Chief Financial Officer & Vice-President, Finance
Jonathan Grimwood, Vice-President, Exploration

Hemisphere Energy Corporation
#501, 905 West Pender St.
Vancouver, BC V6C 1L6

604-685-9255
Fax: 604-685-9676
info@hemisphereenergy.ca
www.hemisphereenergy.ca
www.linkedin.com/company/hemisphere-energy-corporation
Company Type: Public
Ticker Symbol: HME/TSX.V
Profile: Hemisphere Energy is an oil & gas company whose
main projects are in southeast Alberta near Jenner & Atlee
Buffalo.
Don Simmons, President & CEO
Ian Duncan, Chief Operating Officer
Dorlyn Evancic, Chief Financial Officer
Andrew Arthur, Vice-President, Exploration
Ashley Ramsden-Wood, Vice-President, Engineering

High Arctic Energy Services Inc.
#500, 700 - 2nd St. SW
Calgary, AB T2P 2W1

403-508-7836
Fax: 780-948-3058
800-668-7143
info@haes.ca
haes.ca
www.facebook.com/HighArcticEnergyServices
www.linkedin.com/company/high-arctic-energy-services
Company Type: Public
Ticker Symbol: HWO/TSX
Profile: Through its subsidiaries, High Arctic Energy Services
specializes in providing oilfield equipment & services. Operations
are carried out in western Canada & in Papua New Guinea.
Mike Maguire, Chief Executive Officer

Imperial Oil Limited
505 Quarry Park Blvd. SE
Calgary, AB T2C 5N1

800-567-3776
contact.imperial@esso.ca
www.imperialoil.ca
www.facebook.com/ImperialOilLimited
twitter.com/imperialoil
www.linkedin.com/company/imperial-oil
Company Type: Public
Ticker Symbol: IMO/TSX
Staff Size: 5,800
Profile: Imperial Oil is a producer of crude oil & natural gas, &
also refines & markets petroleum products. The company aims
to minimize its impact on the air, land & water by investing in
research & technology & adhering to detailed management
systems.
Brad Corson, Chair, President & CEO
Sherri Evers, Senior Vice-President, Commercial & Corporate
Development
Daniel Lyons, Senior Vice-President, Finance & Administration
Ian Laing, Vice-President, General Counsel & Corporate
Secretary

InPlay Oil Corp.
#920, 640 - 5th Ave. SW
Calgary, AB T2P 3G4

587-955-9570
Fax: 587-955-0630
info@inplayoil.com
www.inplayoil.com
Company Type: Private
Ticker Symbol: IPO/TSX
Profile: InPlay Oil is a growth-oriented light oil development &
production company with a focus on large oil in place pools with
low recovery factors, low declines & long line reserves. The
company's primary target is the Cardium Formation in Alberta.
Douglas J. Bartole, President & CEO
Darren Dittmer, Chief Financial Officer
Kevin Yakiwchuk, Vice-President, Exploration

Inter Pipeline Ltd.
#3200, 215 - 2nd St. SW
Calgary, AB T2P 1M4

403-290-6000
Fax: 403-290-6090
866-716-7473
investorrelations@interpipeline.com
interpipeline.com
twitter.com/inter_pipeline
www.linkedin.com/company/inter-pipeline

Company Type: Public
Ticker Symbol: IPL/TSX
Profile: Inter Pipeline Fund was created in 1997. It is involved in natural gas liquids extraction, petroleum storage & transportation.
Christian Bayle, President & CEO
Brent Heagy, Chief Financial Officer
Bernard Perron, Senior Vice-President, Projects & Operations Services

International Petroleum Corp. (IPC)
#2000, 885 West Georgia St.
Vancouver, BC V6C 3E8

604-689-7842
info@international-petroleum.com
www.international-petroleum.com
www.facebook.com/internationalpetroleumcorp
www.linkedin.com/company/internationalpetroleumcorp

Company Type: Public
Ticker Symbol: IPCO/TSX, NASDAQ
Profile: A member of the Lundin Group of Companies, International Petroleum Corp. is an international oil & gas exploration & production company with assets in Canada, Europe & Southeast Asia.
Mike Nicholson, Chief Executive Officer
William Lundin, Chief Operating Officer
Christophe Nerguararian, Chief Financial Officer

Jericho Energy Ventures
#2100, 1055 West Georgia St.
Vancouver, BC V6C 3P3

604-343-4534
jerichoenergyventures.com
twitter.com/JerichoEV
www.linkedin.com/company/jericho-energy-ventures

Company Type: Public
Ticker Symbol: JEV/TSX.V
Profile: Jericho Energy Ventures is an upstream oil & gas production company.
Brian Williamson, President & CEO
Ben Holman, Chief Financial Officer

Journey Energy Inc.
Centre 10
#700, 517 - 10th Ave. SW
Calgary, AB T2R 0A8

403-294-1635
Fax: 403-232-1317
888-294-1635
info@journeyenergy.ca
www.journeyenergy.ca

Company Type: Public
Ticker Symbol: JOY/TSX
Profile: An oil & gas producer working in Western Canada.
Alex G. Verge, President & CEO
Gerald N. Gilewicz, Chief Financial Officer

Jura Energy Corporation
#5100, 150 - 6th Ave. SW
Calgary, AB T2P 3Y7

403-266-6364
info@juraenergy.com
www.juraenergy.com

Company Type: Public
Ticker Symbol: JEC/TSX
Profile: Jura Energy Corporation is an international independent upstream oil & gas company.
Arif Siddiq, Chief Financial Officer

Kelt Exploration
East Tower
#300, 311 - 6th Ave. SW
Calgary, AB T2P 3H2

403-294-0154
Fax: 403-291-0155
keltexploration.com

Company Type: Public
Ticker Symbol: KEL/TSX
Profile: Kelt Exploration is an oil & gas company specializing in the exploration, development & production of crude oil & natural gas resources.
David Wilson, President & CEO
Sadiq Lalani, Vice-President & CFO
Douglas MacArthur, Vice-President, Operations

Patrick Miles, Vice-President, Exploration

Kolibri Global Energy Inc.
#327, 3623 Old Conejo Rd.
Newbury Park, CA 91320 USA

805-484-3613
info@kolibrienergy.com
www.bnkpetroleum.com
www.linkedin.com/company/kolibri-global-energy-inc

Company Type: Public
Ticker Symbol: KEI/TSX
Profile: The company is focused on the exploration for & production of oil & gas. Through its subsidiaries & affiliates, BNK Petroleum Inc. is the owner & operator of shale gas properties located in the United States, Spain, Poland & Germany.
Wolf E. Regener, President & CEO
Gary W. Johnson, Vice-President & Chief Financial Officer

Leucrotta Exploration Inc.
#700, 639 - 5th Ave. SW
Calgary, AB T2P 0M9

403-705-4525
Fax: 403-705-4526
info@leucrotta.ca
www.leucrotta.ca

Company Type: Public
Ticker Symbol: LXE/TSX.V
Profile: Luecrotta is a Montney focused producer whose main project is located in the Dawson-Sunrise area, in Northeast British Columbia.
Robert J. Zakresky, President & CEO
Nolan Chicoine, Chief Financial Officer & Vice-President, Finance
Terry Trudeau, Chief Operating Officer & Vice-President, Operations
R.D. (Rick) R.D. (Rick), Senior Vice-President, Exploration
Peter Cochrane, Vice-President, Engineering
Helmut R. Eckert, Vice-President, Land

Macro Industries Inc.
PO Box 6781, Fort St John, BC V1J 4J2

250-785-0033
Fax: 250-785-0073
office@macroindustries.ca
www.macroenterprises.ca

Company Type: Public
Ticker Symbol: MCR/TSX.V
Profile: Macro Industries specializes in construction & maintenance of small- to mid-inch pipelines, facilities & gathering systems.
Frank Miles, President & CEO
frank@macroindustries.ca

MEG Energy Corp. (MEG)
600 - 3rd Ave. SW, 25th Fl.
Calgary, AB T2P 0R3

403-770-0446
Fax: 403-264-1711
www.megenergy.com

Company Type: Public
Ticker Symbol: MEG/TSX
Staff Size: 400
Profile: The Canadian oil sands company focuses upon sustainable in situ development & production. The area of activity is Alberta's Southern Athabasca oil sands region. MEG Energy Corp. also owns interests in Stonefell Terminal & Access Pipeline.
The company strives to meet environmental regulations & look beyond compliance, by implementing technology & environmental programs to mitigate impacts on land, air, water & wildlife.
Derek Evans, President & CEO
Eric Toews, Chief Financial Officer
Chi-Tak Yee, Chief Operating Officer
Lyle Yuzdepski, General Counsel & Vice-President, Legal

New Zealand Energy Corp. (NZEC)
14 Connett Rd.
Bell Block, 4312 New Zealand

info@newzealandenergy.com
www.newzealandenergy.com

Company Type: Public
Ticker Symbol: NZ/TSX.V
Profile: New Zealand Energy Corp. is focused on the production, development & exploration of oil & natural gas prospects in New Zealand.
Michael Adams, Chief Executive Officer
Jenny Wells, Chief Financial Officer

North American Construction Group
#27287 - 100th Ave.
Acheson, AB T7X 6H8

780-960-7171
Fax: 780-969-5599
businessdevelopment@nacg.ca
nacg.ca

Other Communications: Investor Relations, Email: ir@nacg.ca
www.facebook.com/North.American.Construction.Group

Company Type: Public
Ticker Symbol: NOA/TSX, NYSE
Profile: North American Construction Group Inc. provides services in the pipeline, piling, heavy construction & mining sectors. Large oil, natural gas & resource companies are the main recipients of these services. The principal area of activity is the Canadian oil sands.
Martin Ferron, President & CEO
Jason Veenstra, Executive Vice-President & CFO
David G. Kallay, Vice-President, Health, Safety, Environment & Human Resources

NuVista Energy Ltd.
#2500, 525 - 8th Ave. SW
Calgary, AB T2P 1G1

403-538-8500
Fax: 403-538-8505
investor.relations@nuvistaenergy.com
www.nuvistaenergy.com

Company Type: Public
Ticker Symbol: NVA/TSX
Profile: Nuvista Energy is a Canadian oil & gas company that acquires, explores & develops oil & gas properties. The company is active in the Western Canadian Sedimentary Basin.
Jonathan A. Wright, President & CEO
Ross L. Andreachuk, Chief Financial Officer & Vice-President, Finance
Mike Lawford, Chief Operating Officer

NXT Energy Solutions Inc.
#302, 3320 - 17th Ave. SW
Calgary, AB T3E 0B4

403-264-7020
Fax: 403-264-6442
nxt_info@nxtenergy.com
www.nxtenergy.com

Company Type: Public
Ticker Symbol: SFD/TSX
Profile: NXT Energy is a publically traded company that provides a unique geophysical service to the upstream oil & gas industry using its proprietary gravity-based Stress Field Detection remote-sensing survey system.
George Liszicasz, President & CEO
Eugene Woychyshyn, Chief Financial Officer & Vice-President, Finance

Obsidian Energy Ltd.
#200, 207 - 9th Ave. SW
Calgary, AB T2P 1K3

403-777-2500
866-693-2707
www.obsidianenergy.com
Other Communications: Investors, Email:
investor_relations@obsidianenergy.com
www.linkedin.com/company/obsidian-energy-ltd

Company Type: Public
Ticker Symbol: OBE/TSX; OBELF/OTCQX
Staff Size: 200
Profile: Obsidian Energy is an oil & gas producer.
Stephen E. Loukas, Interim President & CEO
Peter D. Scott, Sneior Vice-President & CFO

Ovintiv Inc.
#1700, 370 - 17th St.
Denver, CO 80202 USA

303-623-2300
Fax: 303-623-2400
800-374-2955
general.inquiries@ovintiv.com
www.ovintiv.com
Other Communications: Canada Operations, Phone:
888-568-6322
twitter.com/ovintiv
www.linkedin.com/company/ovintiv

Company Type: Public
Ticker Symbol: OVV/TSX, NYSE
Staff Size: 2,000
Profile: The company is engaged in producing natural gas, oil & natural gas liquids. In 2019, it changed names from Encana Corporation & moved its head office from Calgary, AB to Denver, CO.
Doug Suttles, Chief Executive Officer
Brendan McCracken, President
Corey Code, Executive Vice-President & CFO
Greg Givens, Executive Vice-President & COO

Pan Orient Energy Corp.
#1505, 505 - 3rd St. SW
Calgary, AB T2P 3E6

403-294-1770
Fax: 403-294-1780
www.panorient.ca

Company Type: Public
Ticker Symbol: POE/TSX.V
Profile: The junior oil & natural gas company has principal properties located in: Thailand, Indonesia & the Canadian oil sands.
Jeff Chisholm, Chief Executive Officer
Bill Ostlund, Chief Financial Officer

Paramount Resources Ltd.
#2800, 421 - 7th Ave. SW
Calgary, AB T2P 4K9

403-290-3600
www.paramountres.com

Company Type: Public
Ticker Symbol: POU/TSX
Staff Size: 497
Profile: The oil & natural gas exploration, development & production company carries out its operations in western Canada. In 2011, Paramount Resources Ltd. completed the acquisition of ProspEx Resources Ltd.
James Riddell, President & CEO
Paul Kinvig, Chief Financial Officer

Pason Systems Inc.
6130 - 3rd St. SE
Calgary, AB T2H 1K4

403-301-3400
Fax: 403-301-3499
877-255-3158
canada@pason.com
www.pason.com
Other Communications: Investor Relations, Email:
investorrelations@pason.com
www.facebook.com/PasonInnovates
twitter.com/pasoninnovates
www.linkedin.com/company/pason-systems

Company Type: Public
Ticker Symbol: PSI/TSX
Profile: Pason Systems Inc. specializes in the design & manufacture of data management systems. These systems are used by the oilfield industry on land based & offshore drilling & service rigs. Operations are located in Canada, the United States, Mexico, South America & Australia.
Jon Faber, President & CEO
Celine Boston, Chief Financial Officer

Pembina Pipeline Corporation
#4000, 585 - 8th Ave. SW
Calgary, AB T2P 1G1

403-231-7500
Fax: 403-237-0254
888-428-3222
investor-relations@pembina.com
www.pembina.com

Company Type: Public
Ticker Symbol: PPL/TSX; PBA/NYSE
Staff Size: 2,600
Profile: In 2010, Pembina converted from an income trust to a corporation. Pembina Pipeline Corporation is an energy transportation & service provider that has over 9,100 kilometres of pipeline. Areas of activity are in British Columbia & Alberta
Michael (Mick) Dilger, President & CEO
Scott Burrows, Senior Vice-President & CFO

Perpetua Resources Corp.
PO Box 429, 13181 Hwy. 55
Donnelly, ID 83615 USA

208-901-3060
Fax: 208-325-9273
community@perpetua.us
perpetuaresources.com
twitter.com/Perpetua_Idaho
www.linkedin.com/company/perpetuaresources

Company Type: Public
Ticker Symbol: PPTA/TSX
Profile: Perpetua Resources Corp. owns the Stibnite Gold Project in central Idaho.
Stephen Quin, President & CEO
Darren Morgans, Chief Financial Officer
Liz Monger, Corporate Secretary & Manager, Investor Relations

Perpetual Energy Inc.
#3200, 605 - 5th Ave. SW
Calgary, AB T2P 3H5

403-269-4400
Fax: 403-269-4444
800-811-5522
www.perpetualenergyinc.com

Company Type: Public
Ticker Symbol: PMT/TSX
Profile: Established in 2010, Perpetual Energy Inc. operates as an independent natural gas company.
Susan L. Riddell Rose, President & CEO
W. Mark Schewitzer, Chief Financial Officer & Vice-President, Finance

PetroFrontier Corp.
#900, 903 - 8th Ave. SW
Calgary, AB T2P 0P7

403-718-0366
info@petrofrontier.com
petrofrontier.com

Company Type: Public
Ticker Symbol: PFC/TSX.V
Profile: PetroFrontier Corp. is a junior energy company focusing on developments in the Wabasca & Cold Lake areas of Alberta.
Kelly Kimbley, President & CEO
Robert Gillies, Chief Financial Officer & Vice-President, Finance
Ulrich Wirth, Vice-President, Exploration

Petroshale Inc.
#3230, 421 - 7th Ave. SW
Calgary, AB T2P 4K9

403-266-1717
info@petroshaleinc.com
www.petroshaleinc.com

Company Type: Public
Ticker Symbol: PSH/TSX.V
Profile: Petroshale is an oil & gas exploration company that focuses on exploration in the North Dakota Bakken/Three Forks area.
Jacob Roorda, President & CEO
Richard Kessy, Chief Operating Officer
Scott Pittman, Chief Financial Officer

Petroteq Energy Inc.
c/o DLA Piper, 1 First Canadian Place
PO Box 367, #6000, 100 King St. West
Toronto, ON M5X 1E2

800-979-1897
info@petroteq.energy
www.petroteq.com
www.facebook.com/petroteqenergy
twitter.com/petroteqenergy
www.linkedin.com/company/petroteqenergy

Company Type: Public
Ticker Symbol: PQE/TSX
Profile: Petroteq Energy is a Canadian-registered holding company focused on the development & implementation of proprietary technologies for the environmentally safe exraction of heavy oils, oil shale deposits & shallow oil deposits.
Aleksandr Blyumkin, Interim Chief Executive Officer
Donald Clark, Chief Geologist
Mark Korb, Chief Financial Officer
Vladimir Podlipskiy, Chief Technology Officer

Petrus Resources Ltd.
#2400, 240 - 4th Ave. SW
Calgary, AB T2P 4H4

403-984-4014
Fax: 403-984-2717
www.petrusresources.com

Company Type: Public
Ticker Symbol: PRQ/TSX
Profile: An oil & gas company with developments in Alberta.
Neil Korchinski, President & CEO
403-930-0889, kgray@petrusresources.com

Peyto Exploration & Development Corp.
#300, 600 - 3rd Ave. SW
Calgary, AB T2P 0G5

403-261-6081
Fax: 403-451-4100
www.peyto.com

Company Type: Public
Ticker Symbol: PEY/TSX
Profile: Peyto Exploration & Development is engaged in the exploration for & the production of unconventional natural gas in Alberta's Deep Basin.
Darren Gee, President & CEO
Jean-Paul (JP) Lachance, Chief Operating Officer & Vice-President, Engineering
Kathy Turgeon, Vice-President & CFO
David Thomas, Vice-President, Exploration

PHX Energy Services Corp.
#1400, 250 - 2nd St. SW
Calgary, AB T2P 0C1

403-543-4466
Fax: 403-543-4485
investor@phxtech.com
www.phxtech.com

Company Type: Public
Ticker Symbol: PHX/TSX
Staff Size: 900
Profile: PHX Energy Services' Canadian operations are carried out through Phoenix Technology Service LP. American operations are conducted through PHX Energy Services' wholly owned subsidiary, Phoenix Technology Services USA Inc. PHX Energy Services also has sales offices in Peru, Colombia, Albania & Russia.
John M. Hooks, Chair & Chief Executive Officer
Mike Buker, President
Cameron M. Ritchie, Chief Financial Officer & Senior Vice-President, Finance

Pieridae Energy Ltd.
#3100, 308 - 4th Ave. SW
Calgary, AB T2P 0H7

403-261-5900
Fax: 403-261-5902
info@pieridaeenergy.com
pieridaeenergy.com
www.facebook.com/PieridaeEnergy
twitter.com/pieridaeenergy
www.linkedin.com/company/pieridae-energy-canada-ltd-

Company Type: Public
Ticker Symbol: PEA/TSX
Profile: Pieridae Energy is an infrastructure development company focused on liquefied natural gas opportunities.
Alfred Sorensen, Chief Executive Officer
Rob Dargewitcz, Chief Financial Officer
Darcy Reding, Chief Operating Officer

Pine Cliff Energy Ltd.
#850, 1015 - 4th St. SW
Calgary, AB T2R 1J4

403-269-2289
Fax: 587-393-1693
info@pinecliffenergy.com
www.pinecliffenergy.com

Company Type: Public
Ticker Symbol: PNE/TSX.V
Profile: Pine Cliff Energy Ltd. is a company engaged in the exploration, development & production of natural gas, crude oil & natural gas liquids.
Philip B. Hodge, President & CEO
Alan MacDonald, Chief Financial Officer & Corporate Secretary
Terry L. McNeill, Chief Operating Officer

Pipestone Energy Corp.
#3700, 888 - 3rd St. SW
Calgary, AB T2P 5C5

587-392-8411
Fax: 587-392-8421
pipestonecorp.com
Other Communications: Investor Relations, Email:
ir@pipestonecorp.com

Company Type: Public
Ticker Symbol: PIPE/TSX.V
Profile: Pipestone Energy Corp was formed in January 2019 through the merger of Pipestone Oil Corp. & Blackbird Energy Inc.
Paul Wanklyn, President & CEO
Dustin Hoffman, Chief Operating Officer
Craig Nieboer, Chief Financial Officer

Prairie Provident Resources Inc.
#1100, 640 - 5th Ave. SW
Calgary, AB T2P 3G4

403-292-8000
Fax: 403-292-8001
info@ppr.ca
www.ppr.ca

Company Type: Public
Ticker Symbol: PPR/TSX
Profile: Prairie Provident Resources is engaged in the exploration & development of oil & natural gas. Operations are primarily focused in the Western Canadian Sedimentary Basin in Alberta.
Mim M. Lai, Interim Chief Executive Officer
Gjoa Taylor, Vice-President, Land

PrairieSky Royalty Ltd.
#1700, 350 - 7th Ave. SW
Calgary, AB T2P 3N9

587-293-4000
Fax: 587-293-4001
general.inquiries@prairiesky.com
www.prairiesky.com
Other Communications: Investor Relations, Email:
investor.relations@prairiesky.com

Company Type: Public
Ticker Symbol: PSK/TSX
Profile: Prairiesky Royalty buys & sells fee simple mineral title & gross overriding royalty lands in Western Canada.

Andrew Phillips, President & CEO
Cameron Proctor, Chief Operating Officer
Pamela Kazeil, Chief Financial Officer & Vice-President, Finance

Precision Drilling Corporation
#800, 525 - 8th Ave. SW
Calgary, AB T2P 1G1

403-716-4500
info@precisiondrilling.com
www.precisiondrilling.com
www.facebook.com/precisiondrilling
www.linkedin.com/company/precision-drilling
Company Type: Public
Ticker Symbol: PD/TSX; PDS/NYSE
Staff Size: 3,500
Profile: Precision Drilling Corporation is an oilfield services company that provides drilling, well servicing & strategic support services to customers.
Kevin A. Neveu, President & CEO
Carey T. Ford, Senior Vice-President & CFO
Gene C. Stahl, Chief Marketing Officer

Questerre Energy Corporation
#1650, 801 - 6th Ave. SW
Calgary, AB T2P 3W2

403-777-1185
Fax: 403-777-1578
info@questerre.com
www.questerre.com
Company Type: Public
Ticker Symbol: QEC/TSX
Profile: Questerre Energy Corporation is an independent energy company focused on unconventional oil & gas projects.
Michael R. Binnion, President & CEO
Jason D'Silva, Chief Financial Officer
John Brodylo, Vice-President, Exploration
Rick Tityk, Vice-President, Land

Reconnaissance Energy Africa Ltd.
Also Known As: ReconAfrica
PO Box 48326 Stn. Bentall, , Vancouver, BC V7X 1A1
admin@reconafrica.com
reconafrica.com
Other Communications: Investor Relations, Email:
investors@reconafrica.com
www.facebook.com/ReconAfrica
twitter.com/Recon_Africa
www.linkedin.com/company/reconnaissance-energy-africa-ltd
Company Type: Public
Ticker Symbol: RECO/TSX.V
Profile: ReconAfrica is an oil & gas exploration & development company focused on operations in northeast Namibia & northwest Botswana.
Scot Evans, Chief Executive Officer
Carlos Escribano, Chief Financial Officer

SDX Energy
Head Office
38 Welbeck St.
London
www.sdxenergy.com
Other Communications: UK phone: +44-(0)-203-219-5640
twitter.com/sdxenergy
www.linkedin.com/company/sdx-energy-plc
Company Type: Public
Ticker Symbol: SDX/AIM
Profile: SDX Energy has projects in Egypt & Morocco.
Mark Reid, Chief Executive Officer
Nicholas Box, Chief Financial Officer

SECURE Energy Services Inc.
Brookfield Place
#2300, 225 - 6th Ave. SW
Calgary, AB T2P 1N2

403-984-6100
www.secure-energy.com
www.facebook.com/secureenergyservicesinc
twitter.com/secure_ses
www.linkedin.com/company/secure-energy-inc
Company Type: Public
Ticker Symbol: SES/TSX
Profile: The energy services company provides specialized services to upstream oil & natural gas companies. Secure Energy Services' two divisions are the Processing, Recovery & Disposal Division & the Drilling Division. Operations are carried out in the Western Canadian Sedimentary Basin.
In 2017, SECURE Eergy Services Inc. began the acquisition of Ceiba Energy Services Inc.
Rene Amirault, President & CEO
Chad Magus, Chief Financial Officer
David Mattinson, Executive Vice-President, Environmental Solutions

ShaMaran Petroleum Corp.
#2000, 885 West Georgia St.
Vancouver, BC V6C 3E8

604-689-7842
Fax: 604-689-4250
investor.relations@shamaranpetroleum.com
shamaranpetroleum.com
www.facebook.com/shamaranpetroleumcorp
Company Type: Public
Ticker Symbol: SNM/TSX.V
Profile: The oil exploration & development company is focused upon projects in Kurdistan.
Adel Chaouch, President & CEO

ShawCor Ltd.
25 Bethridge Rd.
Toronto, ON M9W 1M7

416-743-7111
Fax: 416-743-5927
www.shawcor.com
www.linkedin.com/company/shawcor
Company Type: Public
Ticker Symbol: SCL-T/TSX
Staff Size: 5,000
Profile: ShawCor Ltd. is a provider of technology-based products & services for the pipeline & pipe services market, as well as the petrochemical & industrial market. Facilities are located in over twenty countries.
Michael Reeves, President & CEO
Gaston Tano, Chief Financial Officer & Senior Vice-President, Finance

Source Energy
#500, 438 - 11th Ave. SE
Calgary, AB T2G 0Y4

403-262-1312
Fax: 403-800-9101
info@sourceenergyservices.com
sourceenergyservices.com
www.facebook.com/sourceenergyservices
twitter.com/SESLogistics
www.linkedin.com/company/source-energy-services
Company Type: Public
Ticker Symbol: SHLE/TSX
Profile: Source Energy Services is an oil & gas company operating in Western Canada.
Brad Thomson, Chief Executive Officer
Derren Newell, Chief Financial Officer

Stampede Drilling Ltd.
Bow Valley Square IV
#2200, 250 - 6th Ave. SW
Calgary, AB T2P 3H7

403-984-5042
Fax: 403-984-5097
info@stampededrilling.com
www.matrrix.com
www.linkedin.com/company/stampede-drilling
Company Type: Public
Ticker Symbol: SDI/TSX
Profile: Stampede Drilling Ltd. is an oil & gas drilling company in Western Canada, offering oilfield ring drilling.
Lyle Whitmarsh, President & CEO
Terry Kuiper, Chief Operating Officer
Jeff Schab, Chief Financial Officer

STEP Energy Services
Bow Valley Square 2
#1200, 205 - 5th Ave. SW
Calgary, AB T2P 2V7

403-457-1772
info@stepenergyservices.com
www.stepenergyservices.com
www.facebook.com/stepenergyservices
www.linkedin.com/company/step-energy-services
Company Type: Public
Ticker Symbol: STEP/TSX
Profile: STEP Energy Services is an oilfield service company that provides specialized coiled tubing & other pumping/support equipment to service the deep horizontal well market in Western Canada, Texas & Louisiana.
Regan Davis, President & CEO
Michael Kelly, Executive Vice-President & Chief Financial Officer
Steve Glanville, Chief Operating Officer & Vice-President, Operations

Storm Resources Ltd.
#600, 215 - 2nd St. SW
Calgary, AB T2P 1M4

403-817-6145
Fax: 403-817-6146
info@stormresourcesltd.com
stormresourcesltd.com
Company Type: Public
Ticker Symbol: SRX/TSX
Profile: Storm Resources Ltd. is a junior exploration & production company that commenced operations in 2010. The company focuses upon exploring for, acquiring, & developing oil & natural gas reserves in the Grande Prairie region of northwestern Alberta & the Horn River Basin & Umbach areas of northeastern British Columbia. In 2012, Storm Resources Ltd. acquired Bellamont Exploration Ltd.
Brian Lavergne, President & CEO
Michael J. Hearn, Chief Financial Officer
Robert S. Tiberio, Chief Operating Officer
Jamie P. Conboy, Vice-President, Geology

Strad Inc.
#1200, 440 - 2nd Ave. SW
Calgary, AB T2P 5E9

403-232-6900
866-778-2552
www.stradenergy.com
www.facebook.com/stradinc
www.linkedin.com/company/stradinc
Company Type: Public
Ticker Symbol: SDY/TSX
Profile: The company specializes in industrial matting & equipment rentals in North America. Industries it services include pipelines, oil & gas, transmission & distribution & construction.
Andy Pernal, Chief Executive Officer
Lyle Wood, President
Michael Donovan, Chief Financial Officer

Strathcona Resources Ltd.
#1900, 421 - 7th Ave. SW
Calgary, AB T2P 4K9

403-930-3000
877-316-6006
info@strathconaresources.com
www.strathconaresources.com
Company Type: Public
Profile: The company is an oil & gas producer focused on thermal oil, enhanced oil recovery & condensate-rich Montney. It formed from the amalgamation of Cona Resources Ltd. & Strath Resources Ltd. in 2020 following Cona's acquisition of Pengrowth Energy Corporation.
Rob Morgan, President & CEO
Michael Makinson, Senior Vice-President & CFO
Tom Everest, Vice-President, Development

Suncor Energy Inc.
PO Box 2844, 150 - 6th Ave. SW
Calgary, AB T2P 3E3

403-269-8000
Fax: 403-269-3030
www.suncor.com
Other Communications: Investor Relations, Email:
invest@suncor.com
www.facebook.com/suncorenergy
twitter.com/suncor
www.linkedin.com/company/suncor
Company Type: Public
Ticker Symbol: SU/TSX
Staff Size: 12,500
Profile: Suncor Energy Inc. is engaged in natural gas production in western Canada, with a focus on the oil sands. Refinement & marketing operations are carried out in Ontario & Colorado. The company also invests in renewable energy, especially ethanol production & wind power. In March 2016, Suncor completed its acquisition of Canadian Oil Sands, increasing Suncor's stake in the Syncrude project.
Mark Little, President & CEO
Alister Cowan, Executive Vice-President & CFO
Martha Hall Findlay, Chief Sustainability Officer

Surge Energy Inc.
#2100, 635 - 8th Ave. SW
Calgary, AB T2P 3M3

403-930-1010
Fax: 403-930-1011
info@surgeenergy.ca
www.surgeenergy.ca
Other Communications: Investor Relations, Email:
invest@surgeenergy.ca
Company Type: Public
Ticker Symbol: SGY/TSX
Profile: The oil & gas company conducts operations in Manitoba, Alberta & North Dakota.
Paul Colborne, President & CEO
Jared Ducs, Chief Financial Officer

TAG Oil Ltd.
#2040, 885 West Georgia St.
Vancouver, BC V6C 3E8

604-682-6496
Fax: 604-682-1174
info@tagoil.com
www.tagoil.com
Other Communications: Investor Relations, Email: ir@tagoil.com
Company Type: Public
Ticker Symbol: TAO/TSX; TAOIF/OTCQX
Profile: TAG Oil is involved in international oil & gas exploration, development & production focused on Australia & New Zealand.
Toby Pierce, Chief Executive Officer
Suneel Gupta, Vice-President & COO
Barry MacNeil, Chief Financial Officer

Tamarack Valley Energy Ltd.
Jamieson Place
#3300, 308 - 4th Ave. SW
Calgary, AB T2P 0H7

403-263-4440
Fax: 403-263-5551
operations@tamarackvalley.ca
www.tamarackvalley.ca
Other Communications: Investors, Email:
investorrelations@tamarackvalley.ca
Company Type: Public
Ticker Symbol: TVE/TSX
Profile: Tamarack Valley Energy Ltd. is an oil & gas company with operations in the Western Canadian Sedimentary Basin. Assets are located in: the Garrington/Harmattan, Buck Lake, Lochend, Foley Lake & Quaich areas of Alberta; Wilder in northeastern British Columbia; southeast of Lloydminster in Saskatchewan.
Brian Schmidt, President & CEO
Steve Buytels, Chief Financial Officer & Vice-President, Finance
Kevin Screen, Vice-President, Production & Operations

Terrace Energy Corp.
Canadian Office
PO Box 21546, 1424 Commercial Dr.
Vancouver, BC V5L 5G2

604-282-7897
Fax: 604-629-0418
terrace@terraceenergy.net
www.terraceenergy.net
Company Type: Public
Ticker Symbol: TZR/TSX.V
Profile: An oil & gas company with projects in the United States.
Dave Gibbs, President & CEO

Tidewater Midstream & Infrastructure Ltd.
#900, 222 - 3rd Ave. SW
Calgary, AB T2P 0B4

587-475-0210
Fax: 587-475-0211
info@tidewatermidstream.com
www.tidewatermidstream.com
Company Type: Public
Ticker Symbol: TWM/TSX
Profile: Tidewater Midstream & Infrastructure is dedicated to the purchase, sale & transportation of Natural Gas Liquids (NGLs) throughout North America.
Joel A. MacLeod, President & CEO
jmacleod@tidewatermidstream.com
Joel K. Vorra, Chief Financial Officer
jvorra@tidewatermidstream.com

Total Energy Services Inc.
#1000, 734 - 7th Ave. SW
Calgary, AB T2P 3P8

403-216-3939
Fax: 403-234-8731
877-818-6825
general@totalenergy.ca
www.totalenergy.ca
Other Communications: Investor Relations, Email:
investorrelations@totalenergy.ca
Company Type: Public
Ticker Symbol: TOT/TSX
Profile: Total Energy Services Inc. is an energy services company that provides drilling, rental & transportation services, as well as the fabrication, sale, rental & servicing of new & used equipment for oil & gas processing, & gas compression.
In June 2017, Total Energy Services completed its acquisition of Savanna Energy Services Corp.
Daniel Halyk, President & CEO
Yuliya Gorbach, Chief Financial Officer & Vice-President, Finance
Brad Macson, Vice-President, Operations

Touchstone Exploration Inc.
#4100, 350 - 7th Ave. SW
Calgary, AB T2P 3N9

403-750-4400
Fax: 403-266-5794
info@touchstoneexploration.com
www.touchstoneexploration.com
www.facebook.com/touchstoneexploration
twitter.com/touchstoneexp
www.linkedin.com/company/touchstone-exploration-inc-
Company Type: Public
Ticker Symbol: TXP/TSX
Profile: Established in 2010, Touchstone Exploration Inc. is a junior, international oil company focused primarily on the country of Trinidad.
Paul Baay, President & CEO
Scott Budau, Chief Financial Officer
James Shipka, Chief Operating Officer

Tourmaline Oil Corp.
#3700, 250 - 6th Ave. SW
Calgary, AB T2P 3H7

403-266-5992
Fax: 403-266-5952
info@tourmalineoil.com
www.tourmalineoil.com
twitter.com/TourmalineOil
www.linkedin.com/company/tourmaline-oil-corp
Company Type: Public
Ticker Symbol: TOU/TSX
Staff Size: 188
Profile: Formed in 2008, Tourmaline Oil Corp. is an intermediate crude oil & natural gas exploration & production company. The company's operations are conducted in the Western Canadian Sedimentary Basin.
In 2011, Tourmaline Oil Corp. acquired Cinch Energy Corp.
Michael L. Rose, Chair, President & CEO
Brian G. Robinson, Chief Financial Officer & Vice-President, Finance

TransGlobe Energy Corporation
#900, 444 - 5th Ave. SW
Calgary, AB T2P 2T8

403-264-9888
Fax: 403-770-8855
www.trans-globe.com
Other Communications: Investors, Email:
investor.relations@trans-globe.com
twitter.com/TransGlobe_EC
www.linkedin.com/company/transglobe-energy-corp
Company Type: Public
Ticker Symbol: TGL/TSX; TGA/NASDAQ
Profile: TransGlobe Energy acquires, explores & develops oil & gas properties. The Alberta-based oil & gas exploration & development company focuses its production activities in Egypt.
Randall Neely, President & CEO
Geoff Probert, Vice-President & Chief Operating Officer
Edward Ok, Chief Financial Officer & Vice-President, Finance

Trican Well Service Ltd.
#2900, 645 - 7th Ave. SW
Calgary, AB T2P 4G8

403-266-0202
info@trican.ca
www.tricanwellservice.com
Other Communications: Investor Inquiries, Phone: 403-476-6767
www.facebook.com/tricanwellservice
twitter.com/tricanws
www.linkedin.com/company/trican-well-service-ltd-
Company Type: Public
Ticker Symbol: TCW/TSX
Profile: Trican Well Service Ltd. is an international pressure pumping company. It provides products, equipment & services, which are employed in the exploration & development of oil & gas reserves.
Bradley Fedora, President & CEO
Klaas Deemter, Interim Chief Financial Officer
Todd Thue, Chief Operating Officer
Dawn Sweany, Vice-President, Human Resources

Valeura Energy Inc.
Bow Valley Square I
#1200, 202 - 6th Ave. SW
Calgary, AB T2P 2R9

403-237-7102
contact@valeuraenergy.com
www.valeuraenergy.com
Other Communications: Investor Relations, Email:
ir@valeuraenergy.com
www.facebook.com/valeuraenergy
twitter.com/valeuraenergy
www.linkedin.com/company/valeuraenergy
Company Type: Public
Ticker Symbol: VLE/TSX

Profile: Valeura Energy Inc. is an explorer, developer & producer of petroleum & natural gas. Operations take place in western Canada & Turkey.
Sean Guest, President & CEO
Heather Campbell, Chief Financial Officer
Rob Sadownyk, Vice-President, Exploration

Vermilion Energy Inc.
#3500, 520 - 3rd Ave. SW
Calgary, AB T2P 0R3

403-269-4884
Fax: 403-476-8100
866-895-8101
investor_relations@vermilionenergy.com
www.vermilionenergy.com
Other Communications: Sustainability, Email:
sustainability@vermilionenergy.com
www.linkedin.com/company/vermilion-energy
Company Type: Public
Ticker Symbol: VET/TSX, NYSE
Staff Size: 750
Profile: Founded in 1994, Vermilion Energy Inc. specializes in the acquisition, exploration, development & optimization of oil & natural gas producing properties. Activities take place in western Canada, western Europe & Australia.
Curtis Hicks, President
Lars Glemser, Vice-President & CFO
Yvonne Jeffery, Vice-President, Sustainability

Virginia Energy Resources Inc.
#650, 1021 West Hastings St.
Vancouver, BC V6E 0C3

434-432-1065
Fax: 604-558-7695
info@virginiaenergyresources.com
www.virginiaenergyresources.com
Company Type: Public
Ticker Symbol: VUI/TSX.V
Profile: Virginia Energy is a uranium development & exploration company. Its main site is in Virginia, USA.
Walter Coles Sr., Chair & Chief Executive Officer
Karen Allan, Chief Financial Officer
Walter Coles Jr., Executive Vice-President

Westcoast Energy Inc.
Fifth Avenue Place
#200, 425 - 1st St. SW
Calgary, AB T2P 3L8

403-231-3900
Fax: 403-231-3920
noms.wei-pipeline.com
Company Type: Public
Ticker Symbol: W.PR.H/TSX
Profile: Westcoast is a natural gas infrastructure company engaged in gathering & processing; transmitting & storing; & distributing energy resources.
In 2016, Enbridge Inc. acquired Spectra Energy Corp., along with all of its subsidaries (among which Westcoast was included).

Western Energy Services Corp.
#1700, 215 - 9th Ave. SW
Calgary, AB T2P 1K3

403-984-5916
Fax: 403-984-5917
info@wesc.ca
www.wesc.ca
Other Communications: Investor Relations, Email: ir@wesc.ca
Company Type: Public
Ticker Symbol: WRG/TSX
Profile: Western Energy Services Corp. provides contract drilling services & well servicing for oil companies. Operating companies include Horizon Drilling in Canada & Stoneham Drilling Corporation in the United States. Western also provides well servicing through Eagle Well Servicing, & provides rental services through Aero Rental Services.
In March 2017, Western Energy Services annouced the acquisition of Savanna Energy Services Corp.
Alex Macausland, President & CEO
Jeffrey K. Bowers, Chief Financial Officer & Senior Vice-President, Finance

Whitemud Resources Inc.
Bow Valley Square 2
#3030, 205 - 5th Ave. SW
Calgary, AB T2P 2V7

403-266-1985
Fax: 403-263-5053
info@whitemudresources.com
www.whitemudresources.com
Company Type: Public
Ticker Symbol: WMK/TSX.V
Profile: Whitemud Resources develops kaolin deposits.
Stanley Owerko, Chief Executive Officer

David Storoshenko, President
David Koplovich, Chief Financial Officer

Zedcor Inc.
Also Known As: Zedcor Security
#3000, 500 - 4th Ave. SW
Calgary, AB T2P 2V6

403-930-5430
Fax: 403-460-6216
877-511-9332
info@zedcor.ca
zedcorsecurity.ca
www.facebook.com/109482067559169
twitter.com/ZedcorSecure
www.linkedin.com/company/zedcor-security
Company Type: Public
Ticker Symbol: ZDC/TSX.V
Profile: This is also engaged with security & surveillance services.
Todd Ziniuk, President & CEO
tziniuk@zedcor.ca
Amin Ladha, Chief Financial Officer
aladha@zedcor.ca

Zenith Energy
Bankers Court
#1500, 850 - 2nd St. SW, 15th Fl.
Calgary, AB T2P 0R8

587-315-9031
info@zenithenergy.ca
www.zenithenergy.ca
twitter.com/zenithenergyltd
www.linkedin.com/company/zenith-energy-limited
Company Type: Public
Ticker Symbol: ZEE/TSX.V; ZEN/LSE
Profile: Zenith Energy operates the largest onshore oilfield in Azerbaijan. It also holds assets in Italy.
Andrea Cattaneo, President & CEO
Luca Benedetto, Chief Financial Officer

Pharmaceuticals

AbCellera Biologics Inc.
2215 Yukon St.
Vancouver, BC V5Y 0A1

604-559-9005
www.abcellera.com
twitter.com/AbCelleraBio
www.linkedin.com/company/abcellera
Company Type: Public
Ticker Symbol: ABCL/NASDAQ
Staff Size: 200
Profile: AbCellera is a technology company using its platform to identify antibodies its partners can use to develop drugs.
Carl Hansen, Chief Executive Officer
Andrew Booth, Chief Financial Officer
Ester Falconer, Chief Technology Officer
Véronique Lecault, Chief Operating Officer

Acasti Pharma Inc.
#102, 3009, boul de la Concorde est
Laval, QC H7E 2B5

450-686-4555
Fax: 450-686-2505
info@acastipharma.com
www.acastipharma.com
Company Type: Public
Ticker Symbol: ACST/TSX.V
Profile: The company does research & development of active pharmaceutical ingredients used in cardiometabolic medication. In 2021, it plans to merge with Grace Therapeutics, Inc., a biopharmaceutical company with drug delivery technologies for rare & orphan disease treatment.
Jan D'Alvise, President & CEO
Pierre Lemieux, Chief Scientific Officer & COO
Brian D. Ford, Chief Financial Officer

Acerus Pharmaceuticals Corporation
2486 Dunwin Dr.
Mississauga, ON L5L 1J9

416-679-0771
www.aceruspharma.com
Other Communications: Investor Relations, Email:
ir@aceruspharma.com
twitter.com/aceruspharma
www.linkedin.com/company/acerus-pharma
Company Type: Public
Ticker Symbol: ASP/TSX
Profile: The pharmaceutical company develops & markets specific drugs that use a bioadhesive intranasal gel delivery technology. It also owns the dry powder inhaler/nasal dispersion system TriVair.
Edward Gudaitis, President & CEO

Robert Motz, Chief Financial Officer
Christopher Sorli, Chief Medical Officer

AEterna Zentaris Inc.
315 Sigma Dr.
Summerville, SC 29486 USA

843-900-3223
www.zentaris.com
Other Communications: Investor Relations, Email:
ir@aezsinc.com
www.facebook.com/aezsinc
twitter.com/AEZS_inc
www.linkedin.com/company/aeterna-zentaris-inc.
Company Type: Public
Ticker Symbol: AEZS/TSX; AEZS/NASDAQ
Profile: Aeterna Zentaris Inc. is a specialty biopharmaceutical company engaged in developing novel treatments in oncology & endocrinology.
Klaus Paulini, President & CEO
Leslie Auld, Chief Financial Officer & Senior Vice-President

Akumin Inc.
8300 Sunrise Blvd. West
Plantation, FL 33322 USA

844-730-0050
akumin.com
www.facebook.com/AkuminHealth
twitter.com/akuminhealth
www.linkedin.com/company/akumin
Company Type: Public
Ticker Symbol: AKU/TSX
Profile: Akumin Inc. provides diagnostic imaging services including X-Ray, Mammography & Ultrasound.
Riadh Zine-Ei-Abidine, President & CEO
Mohammad Saleem, Chief Financial Officer

Alcanna Inc.
#101, 17220 Stony Plain Rd.
Edmonton, AB T5S 1K6

info@alcanna.com
www.alcanna.com
Other Communications: Investor Relations, Email:
investor@alcanna.com
Company Type: Public
Ticker Symbol: CLIQ/TSX
Profile: Alcanna Inc. is a retailer of highly-regulated controlled substances. It operates 176 retail liquor stores in Alberta & British Columbia. It owns a 63% stake in Nova Cannabis Inc., which operates 53 retail cannabis stores in Alberta & Saskatchewan.
James Burns, Chief Executive Officer
David Gordey, Executive Vice-President & CFO

Aptose Biosciences Inc.
#120, 12770 High Bluff Dr.
San Diego, CA 92130 USA

858-926-2730
www.aptose.com
Other Communications: Investor Relations, Email:
ir@aptose.com
Company Type: Public
Ticker Symbol: APS/TSX; APTO/NASDAQ
Profile: Aptose Biosciences is a clinical-stage biotechnology company that is building a pipeline of oncology therapies to treat life-threatening cancers like acute myeloid leukemia & high-risk myelodysplastic syndromes.
William G. Rice, Chair, President & CEO
Rafael Bejar, M.D., Senior Vice-President & Chief Medical Officer
Jotin Marango, Senior Vice-President, Chief Business Officer & CFO

Aurinia Pharmaceuticals Inc.
#1203, 4464 Markham St.
Victoria, BC V8Z 7X8

250-708-4272
Fax: 250-744-2498
www.auriniapharma.com
Other Communications: Investor Relations, Email:
ir@auriniapharma.com
www.facebook.com/AuriniaPharma
twitter.com/AuriniaPharma
www.linkedin.com/company/aurinia-pharmaceuticals
Company Type: Public
Ticker Symbol: AUP/TSX
Profile: A clinical stage biopharmaceutical development company, focusing on developing therapies in areas of high unmet medical need.
Peter Greenleaf, Chief Executive Officer
Michael Martin, Chief Operating Officer
Joe Miller, Chief Financial Officer
Neil Solomons, Chief Medical Officer

Aurora Cannabis Inc.
#500, 10355 Jasper Ave.
Edmonton, AB T5J 1Y6

855-279-4652
aurora@icrinc.com
www.auroramj.com
Other Communications: Investor Relations, Email:
ir@auroramj.com
twitter.com/aurora_mmj
www.linkedin.com/company/aurora-cannabis-inc
Company Type: Public
Ticker Symbol: ACB/TSX
Staff Size: 2,400
Profile: Aurora Cannabis Inc. is a licensed cannabis producer. The company has several subsidiaries & brands, including CanniMed, MedReleaf, Alta Vie, Whistler Cannabis Co., Aurora Drift & Daily Special.
Miguel Martin, Chief Executive Officer
Glen Ibbott, Chief Financial Officer

Bausch Health Companies Inc.
2150, boul St-Elzéar ouest
Laval, QC H7L 4A8

514-744-6792
Fax: 514-744-6272
800-361-1448
www.bauschhealth.com
twitter.com/bauschhealth
www.linkedin.com/company/bausch-health-companies
Company Type: Public
Ticker Symbol: BHC/TSX, NYSE
Profile: Bausch Health manufactures & markets a range of branded & generic pharmaceuticals, OTC products & medical devices (like contact lenses & ophthalmic surgical equipment). Bausch's brand portfolio includes: Bausch + Lomb, Salix Pharmaceuticals & Ortho Dermatologics.
Joseph C. Papa, Chair & Chief Executive Officer
Sam Eldessouky, Executive Vice-President & Chief Financial Officer

Bellus Health Inc.
275, boul Armand-Frappier
Laval, QC H7V 4A7

450-680-4500
Fax: 450-680-4501
info@bellushealth.com
bellushealth.com
twitter.com/bellushealth
www.linkedin.com/company/bellus-health
Company Type: Private
Ticker Symbol: BLU/TSX, NASDAQ
Profile: Bellus Health is a clinical-stage biopharmaceutical company that is focused on developing novel therapeutics for conditions with high unmet medical need. Its projects include the company's lead drug candidate BLU-5937 for chronic cough.
Roberto Bellini, President & CEO
Ramzi Benamar, Chief Financial Officer
Catherine Bonuccelli, Chief Medical Officer

BioSyent Inc.
#402, 2476 Argentia Rd.
Mississauga, ON L5N 6M1

905-206-0013
Fax: 905-206-1413
888-439-0013
info@biosyent.com
www.biosyent.com
Other Communications: Investor Relations, Email:
investors@biosyent.com
www.linkedin.com/company/biosyent-inc
Company Type: Public
Ticker Symbol: RX/TSX.V
Profile: BioSyent is a specialty pharmaceutical company focused on in-licensing or acquiring innovative products.
René C. Goehrum, Chair, President & CEO
Robert March, Vice-President & CFO

BriaCell Therapeutics Corp.
Bellevue Centre
#300, 235 - 15th St.
West Vancouver, BC V7T 2X1

604-921-1810
Fax: 604-921-1898
info@briacell.com
briacell.com
www.facebook.com/BriaCell
twitter.com/briacell
www.linkedin.com/company/briacell-therapeutics-corp
Company Type: Public
Ticker Symbol: BCT/TSX; BCTXF/OTCQB
Profile: BriaCell Therapeutics is developing immunotherapies to fight cancer, primarily for breast cancer.
William V. Williams, President & CEO
Gadi Levin, Chief Financial Officer

CannTrust Holdings
3280 Langstaff Rd.
Vaughan, ON L4K 5B6

Fax: 844-295-6641
855-794-2266
investor@canntrust.ca
canntrust.ca
twitter.com/canntrust
www.linkedin.com/company/canntrust

Company Type: Public
Ticker Symbol: TRST/TSX
Profile: CannTrust is a federal medical cannabis producer.
Greg Gyatt, Chief Executive Officer
Rob Schenkel, Chief Information Officer

Ceapro
7824 - 51st Ave.
Edmonton, AB T6E 6W2

780-421-4555
Fax: 780-421-1320
info@ceapro.com
ceapro.com
www.facebook.com/CeaproInc
twitter.com/ceaproinc
www.linkedin.com/company/ceapro

Company Type: Public
Ticker Symbol: CZO/TSX
Profile: Ceapro is a Canadian biotechology company that develops & commercializes innovative active ingredients for the human & animal health markets.
Gilles Gagnon, President & CEO
Stacy Prefontaine, Chief Financial Officer

Cipher Pharmaceuticals
#501, 209 Oak Park Blvd.
Oakville, ON L6H 0M2

905-602-5840
info@cipherpharma.com
www.cipherpharma.com

Company Type: Public
Ticker Symbol: CPH/TSX
Profile: Cipher Pharmaceuticals is a specialty pharmaceutical company that develops improved formulations of existing drugs.
Craig Mull, Interim Chief Executive Officer
Diane Gajewczyk, Vice-President, Scientific & Medical Affairs

Claritas Pharmaceuticals, Inc.
#200, 4040 Civic Center Dr.
San Rafael, CA 94903

888-861-2008
info@claritaspharma.com
claritaspharma.com

Company Type: Public
Ticker Symbol: CLAS/TSX.V
Profile: Kalytera is a pharmaceutical company developing a drug, R-107, for treatment of vaccine-resistant strains of COVID-19 & other viral infections. It previously developed CBD & other cannabinoid therapeutics for disease treatment.
Robert Farrell, President & CEO

Covalon Technologies Ltd.
#5, 1660 Tech Ave.
Mississauga, ON L4W 5S7

905-568-8400
Fax: 905-568-5200
877-711-6055
info@covalon.com
www.covalon.com
www.facebook.com/CovalonTechnologies
twitter.com/covalon
www.linkedin.com/company/covalon-technologies-ltd

Company Type: Public
Ticker Symbol: COV/TSX.V
Profile: The company develops technology for the medical industry. Their products are geared towards infection, condition management, tissue repair & more.
Brian Pedlar, Chief Executive Officer
bpedlar@covalon.com
Danny Brannagan, Chief Financial Officer
Val DiTizio, Chief Scientific Officer

Crescita Therapeutics Inc.
#800, 6733 Mississauga Rd.
Mississauga, ON L5N 6J5

905-673-4295
Fax: 905-673-3614
www.crescitatherapeutics.com

Company Type: Public
Ticker Symbol: CTX/TSX
Profile: Crescita is a commercial dermatology company that owns multiple proprietary non-prescription drug delivery platforms. Crescita owns a portfolio of non-prescription skincare products.
Serge Verreault, President & CEO

Jose DaRocha, Chief Financial Officer

CRH Medical Corp.
#200, 322 Water St.
Vancouver, BC V6B 1B6

800-660-2153
info@crhmedcorp.com
www.crhsystem.com

Company Type: Public
Profile: Founded in 2000, CRH Medical focuses on promoting the CRH O'Regan system as a treatment for hemorrhoids. In 2021, it became a wholly owned subsidiary of WELL Health Technologies.
Tushar Ramani, MD, Chief Executive Officer
Richard Bear, Chief Financial Officer

Cronos Group Inc.
#320, 720 King St. West
Toronto, ON M5V 2T3

416-504-0004
info@thecronosgroup.com
thecronosgroup.com

Company Type: Public
Ticker Symbol: CRON/TSX.V
Profile: The Cronos group seeks to fortify & accelerate growth of a network of medicinal marijuana companies in Canada through investments in licensed producers, which include: Peace Naturals, In The Zone, Whistler Medical Marijuana Company (WMMC), ABcann, Hydropothecary & Evergreen Midicinial Supply.
Kurt Schmidt, President & CEO
Jerry Barbato, Chief Financial Officer
Anna Shlimak, Senior Vice-President, Corporate Affairs

Delta 9 Cannabis
#1, 827 Dakota St.
Winnipeg, MB R2M 5M2

855-245-1259
hello@delta9.ca
www.delta9.ca
www.facebook.com/delta9biotech
twitter.com/Delta9BioTech

Company Type: Public
Ticker Symbol: DN/TSX
Profile: The company is in the business of medical cannabis.
Bill Arbuthnot, Chair, President & Co-Founder
John Arbuthnot, Chief Executive Officer & Co-Founder
James Lawson, Chief Financial Officer
Marshall Posner, Chief Marketing Officer
Matthew Sodomsky, Chief Technology Officer

Emerald Green Therapeutics
#210, 800 West Pender St.
Victoria, BC V6C 1J8

Fax: 855-623-3325
800-757-3536
info@emeraldhealth.ca
emeraldhealth.ca
Other Communications: Investor Relations, Email:
invest@emeraldhealth.ca
www.facebook.com/emeraldhealthca
twitter.com/emeraldhealthca
www.linkedin.com/company/emerald-health-therapeutics

Company Type: Public
Ticker Symbol: EMH/TSX.V
Profile: The company produces medical cannabis.
Avtar Dhillon, Executive Chair
Riaz Bandali, President & CEO
Jenn Hepburn, Chief Financial Officer
Moe Jiwan, Chief Operating Officer

Essa Pharma Inc.
#720, 999 West Broadway
Vancouver, BC V5Z 1K5

778-331-0962
www.essapharma.com
twitter.com/essapharma
www.linkedin.com/company/essa-pharma

Company Type: Public
Ticker Symbol: EPIX/NASDAQ
Profile: Essa Pharma Inc. is a pharmaceutical company engaged in the development of small molecule drugs for cancer treatment.
David R. Parkinson, President & CEO
Peter Virsik, Executive Vice-President & COO
Alessandra Cesano, Chief Medical Officer
David S. Wood, Chief Financial Officer

Fennec Pharmaceuticals Inc.
Research Triangle Park
PO Box 13628, 68 T.W. Alexander Dr.
Durham, NC 27709 USA

919-636-4530
Fax: 919-890-0490
info@fennecpharma.com
fennecpharma.com
www.linkedin.com/company/fennec-pharmaceuticals-inc

Company Type: Public
Ticker Symbol: FRX/TSX
Profile: Fennec Pharmaceuticals Inc. is a biotechnology company focused on the development of PEDMARK, which is a unique formulation of Sodium Thiosulfate for the prevention of cisplatin-induced ototoxicity (hearing loss from a chemotherapy drug) in pediatric patients.
Rostislav Raykov, Chief Executive Officer
Robert Andrade, Chief Financial Officer

Green Organic Dutchmen Holdings Ltd.
Bldg. A
#301, 6205 Airport Dr.
Mississauga, ON L4V 1E3

888-603-8463
info@tgod.ca
www.tgod.ca
www.facebook.com/TGODH
twitter.com/grnorganicdutch

Company Type: Public
Ticker Symbol: TGOD/TSX
Profile: The company cultivates cannabis products. It is a holding company which operates through subsidaries.
Sean Bovingdon, Chief Executive Officer & Interim CFO
Michel Gagné, Chief Operating Officer

Hamilton Thorne
#465E, 100 Cummings Centre
Beverly, MA 01915 USA

978-921-2050
Fax: 978-921-0250
800-323-0503
info@hamiltonthorne.com
www.hamiltonthorne.com
Other Communications: Investor Relations, Email:
ir@hamiltonthorne.com
www.facebook.com/HamiltonThorneInc
twitter.com/hamiltonthorne

Company Type: Public
Ticker Symbol: HTL/TSX.V
Profile: The company develops precision lasers & image anaylsis systems. These products are marketed in the fields of fertility, stem cell & development biology research.
David Wolf, President & CEO
Michael Bruns, Chief Financial Officer

Harvest One
#404, 999 Canada Pl.
Vancouver, BC V6C 3E2

604-449-9280
info@harvestone.com
www.harvestone.com
Other Communications: Investor, Email: ir@harvestone.com
twitter.com/harvestoneinc
www.linkedin.com/company/harvest-one-cannabis-inc

Company Type: Public
Ticker Symbol: HVT/TSX.V
Profile: Harvest One is a cannabis company focusing on wellness & lifestyle products.
Gord Davey, President & CEO
Jack Tasse, Chief Financial Officer

HLS Therapeutics, Inc.
#701, 10 Carlson Ct.
Etobicoke, ON M9W 6L2

647-495-9000
Fax: 416-213-0045
www.hlstherapeutics.com
www.linkedin.com/company/hlstherapeutics

Company Type: Public
Ticker Symbol: HLS/TSX
Profile: The company aquires and markets late-stage development pharmaceutical products. They centre around products aimed at the cardiovascular & central nervous systems.
Gilbert Godin, Chief Executive Officer
Tim Hendrickson, Chief Financial Officer

IMV Inc.
#19, 130 Eileen Stubbs Ave.
Halifax, NS B3B 2C4

902-492-1819
Fax: 902-492-0888
www.imv-inc.com
twitter.com/imv_inc
www.linkedin.com/company/imv-inc

Company Type: Public
Ticker Symbol: IMV/TSX
Profile: IMV Inc. is a clinical-stage immuno-oncology company. IMV develops cancer immunotherapies & infectious disease vaccines using its proprietary platform, DPX-Survivac.
Frederic Ors, Chief Executive Officer
Pierre Labbé, Chief Financial Officer
Joanne Schindler, Chief Medical Officer
Annie Tanguay, Senior Vice-President, Quality & Compliance

InMed Pharmaceuticals
#310, 815 West Hastings St.
Vancouver, BC V6C 1B4

604-669-7207
Fax: 778-945-6800
info@inmedpharma.com
www.inmedpharma.com
www.facebook.com/InMedPharma
twitter.com/inmedpharma
www.linkedin.com/company/inmedpharma
Company Type: Public
Ticker Symbol: INM/NASDAQ
Profile: The company is dedicated to the development of medical cannabis.
Eric Adams, President & CEO
Bruce Cowill, Chief Financial Officer
Eric C. Hsu, Senior Vice-President, Pre-Clinical Research & Development
Alexandra D.J. Mancini, Senior Vice-President, Clinical & Regulatory Affairs
Michael Woudenberg, Vice-President, Chemistry, Manufacturing & Controls

Intellipharmaceutics International Inc.
30 Worcester Rd.
Toronto, ON M9W 5X2

416-798-3001
investors@intellipharmaceutics.com
intellipharmaceutics.com
Company Type: Public
Ticker Symbol: IPCI/TSX, NASDAQ
Profile: Intellipharmaceutics International Inc. is engaged in the research, development & commercialization of controlled-release & targeted pharmaceuticals, with a focus on the opioid abuse deterrence segment.
Isa Odidi, Chair, CEO & Co-Chief Scientific Officer
Amina Odidi, President, COO & Co-Chief Scientific Officer

Isodiol International
#2710, 200 Granville St.
Vancouver, BC V6C 1S4

604-409-4409
Fax: 604-608-3348
isodiol.com
www.facebook.com/isodiol
twitter.com/isodiol
www.linkedin.com/company/isodiol
Company Type: Public
Ticker Symbol: ISOL/TSX
Profile: Isodial is a CBD company which offers a variety of products including capsules, coffee, candy & topicals.
Marcos Agramont, Chief Executive Officer
Andrew Alvis, President & Interim CFO

Jamieson Wellness Inc.
#2200, 1 Adelaide St. East
Toronto, ON M5C 2V9

info@jamiesonwellness.com
investors.jamiesonwellness.com
twitter.com/jwel_canada
www.linkedin.com/company/jamieson-wellness
Company Type: Public
Ticker Symbol: JWEL/TSX
Profile: Jamieson is a manufacturer, marketer & distributor of natural health products, including vitamins, minerals & supplements through various brands.
Mark Hornick, President & CEO
Christopher Snowden, Chief Financial Officer
Regan Stewart, Chief Operations & People Officer

Knight Therapeutics Inc.
#1055, 3400, boul de Maisonneuve ouest
Montréal, QC H3Z 3B8

514-484-4483
Fax: 514-481-4166
info@gudknight.com
www.gud-knight.com
www.linkedin.com/company/knight-therapeutics
Company Type: Public
Ticker Symbol: GUD/TSX
Profile: Knight Therapeutics is a specialty pharmaceutical company focused on acquiring, in-licensing, selling & marketing pharmaceutical products.
Jonathan Ross Goodman, Chief Executive Officer

Samira Sakhia, President & COO
Arvind Utchanah, Chief Financial Officer

Leviathan Natural Products
#116, 250 The Esplanade
Toronto, ON M5A 4J6

416-842-8408
info@leviathan-naturals.com
leviathan-naturals.com
Company Type: Public
Ticker Symbol: EPIC/CSE
Profile: The company is in the business of non-psychoactive hemp derived products for health & wellness. It has Canadian, American & Colombian projects.
Martin Doane, Chief Executive Officer

Liminal BioSciences Inc.
#300, 440, boul Armand-Frappier
Laval, QC H7V 4B4

450-781-0115
Fax: 450-781-4477
info@liminalbiosciences.com
liminalbiosciences.com
Other Communications: Investor Relations, Email:
investor@liminalbiosciences.com
twitter.com/LiminalBio
www.linkedin.com/company/liminal-biosciences-inc
Company Type: Public
Ticker Symbol: LMNL/NASDAQ
Staff Size: 275
Profile: Liminal BioSciences offers its technologies for large-scale purification of biologics, drug development, proteomics & the elimination of pathogens to a growing base of industry leaders.
Bruce Pritchard, Chief Executive Officer
Patrick Sartore, President
Murielle Lortie, Chief Financial Officer

Medicure Inc.
#2, 1250 Waverley St.
Winnipeg, MB R3T 6C6

204-487-7412
Fax: 204-488-9823
888-435-2220
info@medicure.com
www.medicure.com
twitter.com/MedicureInc
www.linkedin.com/company/medicure
Company Type: Public
Ticker Symbol: MPH/TSX.V
Profile: Medicure is a specialty pharmaceutical company focused on the development & commercialization of therapeutics for the U.S. hospital market.
Albert D. Friesen, Chair & Chief Executive Officer
Neil Owens, President & COO

Microbix Biosystems Inc.
265 Watline Ave.
Mississauga, ON L4Z 1P3

905-361-8910
800-794-6694
customer.service@microbix.com
microbix.com
Other Communications: Investor Relations, Email:
ir@microbix.com
www.facebook.com/MicrobixBiosystems
www.linkedin.com/company/microbix-biosystems
Company Type: Public
Ticker Symbol: MBX/TSX
Profile: Microbix Biosystems develops antigens & uses proficiency programs to assess the quality of their clinic laboratory tests. Their notable products include LumiSort & Kinytic.
Cameron L. Groome, President & CEO
Jim Currie, Chief Financial Officer

Milestone Pharmaceuticals Inc.
#420, 1111, boul Dr.-Frederik-Philips
Montréal, QC H4M 2X6

514-336-0444
info@milestonepharma.com
milestonepharma.com
twitter.com/milestonepharma
www.linkedin.com/company/milestone-pharmaceuticals
Company Type: Public
Ticker Symbol: MIST/NASDAQ
Profile: Milestone Pharmaceuticals is a biopharmaceutical company developing a new drug, etripamil, for cardiovascular disease treatment.
Joseph Oliveto, President & CEO
Amit Hasija, CFO & Executive Vice-President, Corporate Development
Jeff Nelson, Chief Operating Officer
Francis Plat, Chief Medical Officer

Mountain Valley MD Inc.
#4, 260 Edgeley Blvd.
Vaughn, ON L4K 3Y4

647-725-9755
info@mountainvalleymd.com
ww.mountainvalleymd.com
www.facebook.com/mountainvalleymd
twitter.com/mountainvmd
www.linkedin.com/company/mountain-valley-md
Company Type: Public
Ticker Symbol: MVMD/TSX
Profile: Mountain Valley MD focuses on the areas of cultivation, research and development, and manufacturing across a portfolio of sustainable cannabis assets.
Dennis Hancock, President & CEO
Aaron Triplett, Chief Financial Officer

Neptune Wellness Solutions
#100, 545, promenade du Centropolis
Laval, QC H7T 0A3

450-687-2262
Fax: 450-687-2272
888-664-9166
www.neptunecorp.com
www.facebook.com/NeptuneWellness
twitter.com/neptune_corp
www.linkedin.com/company/neptunewellness
Company Type: Public
Ticker Symbol: NEPT/TSX, NASDAQ
Profile: Neptune Wellness Solutions maintains a portfolio of sustainable plant-based consumer products, including cannabis products & essential oils.
Michael Cammarata, President & CEO
Toni Rinow, Chief Financial Officer

Nuvo Pharmaceuticals Inc.
Also Known As: Miravo Healthcare
#800, 6733 Mississauga Rd.
Mississauga, ON L5N 6J5

905-673-6980
Fax: 905-673-1842
www.miravohealthcare.com
www.linkedin.com/company/nuvo-pharmaceuticals-inc
Company Type: Public
Ticker Symbol: MRV/TSX; MRVFF/OTCQX
Profile: Miravo is a pharmaceutical company that targets areas including pain, allergy & dermatology.
Jesse Ledger, President & CEO
Mary-Jane Burkett, Vice-President & CFO

Oncolytics Biotech Inc.
#210, 1167 Kensington Cres. NW
Calgary, AB T2N 1X7

403-670-7377
info@oncolyticsbiotech.com
www.oncolyticsbiotech.com
www.facebook.com/oncolytics.biotech.inc
twitter.com/oncolytics
Company Type: Public
Ticker Symbol: ONC/TSX
Profile: Oncolytics Biotech Inc. is developing an instravenously delivered immuno-oncolytic virus called REOLYSIN for the treatment of solid tumours.
Matt Coffey, President & CEO
Kirk Look, Chief Financial Officer
Andrew de Guttadauro, Global Head, Business Development
adeguttadauro@oncolytics.ca

OrganiGram Holdings Inc.
35 English Dr.
Moncton, NB E1E 3X3

www.organigram.ca
Other Communications: Investor Relations, Phone:
416-704-9057
www.facebook.com/discoverogi
twitter.com/discoverogi
www.linkedin.com/company/organigram
Company Type: Public
Ticker Symbol: OGI/TSX
Profile: Established in 2013, OrganiGram is a grower, tester & producer of medical cannabis products.
Derrick West, Chief Financial Officer

Resverlogix Corp.
#300, 4820 Richard Rd. SW
Calgary, AB T3E 6L1

403-254-9252
Fax: 403-256-8495
info@resverlogix.com
www.resverlogix.com
twitter.com/resverlogix_rvx
Company Type: Public
Ticker Symbol: RVX/TSX
Profile: A pharmaceutical development company.

Donald McCaffrey, President & CEO
Norman Wong, Chief Scientific Officer & Co-Founder
A. Brad Cann, Chief Financial Officer

Sundial Growers Inc.
Also Known As: Sundial Group
#300, 919 - 11th Ave. SW
Calgary, AB T2R 1P3

844-249-6746
info@sundialgrowers.com
www.sndlgroup.com
Other Communications: Investor Relations, Email:
investors@sundialgrowers.com
twitter.com/sundialcannabis
www.linkedin.com/company/sundialgrowers

Company Type: Public
Ticker Symbol: SNDL/NASDAQ
Staff Size: 400
Profile: Sundial is a licensed Canadian producer of cannabis. Its brands include Top Leaf, Sundial Cannabis, Palmetto & Grasslands.
Zachary George, Chief Executive Officer
Andrew Stordeur, President & COO
Jim Keough, Chief Financial Officer

Supreme Cannabis Company Inc.
178R Ossington Ave.
Toronto, ON M6J 2Z7

416-630-7272
info@supreme.ca
www.supreme.ca
Other Communications: Investor Relations, Email:
ir@supreme.ca
www.facebook.com/TheSupremeFIRE
twitter.com/TheSupremeFIRE
www.linkedin.com/company/the-supreme-cannabis-company

Company Type: Public
Ticker Symbol: FIRE/TSX.V
Profile: Supreme Cannabis is a federally approved medical marijuana company operating a Hybrid Greenhouse.
Beena Goldenberg, President & CEO
Nikhil Handa, Chief Financial Officer
John Griese, Chief Operating Officer

The Valens Company
230 Carion Rd.
Kelowna, BC V4V 2K5

778-755-0052
info@thevalenscompany.com
thevalenscompany.com
www.facebook.com/thevalenscompany
twitter.com/TheValensCo
www.linkedin.com/company/thevalenscompany

Company Type: Public
Ticker Symbol: CVE/TSX.V
Profile: This biotechnology corporation focuses on cannabis processing & formulation.
Tyler Robson, Chair & Chief Executive Officer
Chris Buysen, Chief Financial Officer

Theratechnologies Inc.
2015, rue Peel, 11e étage
Montréal, QC H3A 1T8

514-336-7800
Fax: 514-331-9691
communications@theratech.com
www.theratech.com

Company Type: Public
Ticker Symbol: TH/TSX; THTX/NASDAQ
Profile: Theratechnologies is a specialty pharmaceutical company addressing unmet medical needs among HIV patients.
Paul Lévesque, President & CEO
Philippe Dubuc, Senior Vice-President & CFO

Tilray, Inc.
1100 Maughan Rd.
Nanaimo, BC V9X 1J2

Fax: 888-783-1323
844-845-7291
tilray@tilray.ca
www.tilray.ca
www.facebook.com/tilray
twitter.com/tilray

Company Type: Public
Ticker Symbol: TLRY/TSX
Profile: Tilray is a Health Canada licensed producer of medical cannabis products. In 2021, it merged with Aphria Inc. & continues to use Aphria branding.
Irwin D. Simon, Chief Executive Officer
Carl Merton, Chief Financial Officer

Trillium Therapeutics Inc.
2488 Dunwin Dr.
Mississauga, ON L5L 1J9

416-595-0627
info@trilliumtherapeutics.com
trilliumtherapeutics.com

Company Type: Public
Ticker Symbol: TRIL/TSX, NASDAQ
Profile: The company develops cancer treatment therapies.
Jan Skvarka, President & CEO
Ingmar Bruns, Chief Medical Officer
James Parsons, Chief Financial Officer
james@trilliumtherapeutics.com
Penka Petrova, Chief Development Officer

WeedMD Inc.
250 Elm St.
Aylmer, ON N5H 2M8

Fax: 844-933-3637
844-933-3636
orders@weedmd.com
www.weedmd.com
twitter.com/weedmd

Company Type: Public
Ticker Symbol: WMD/TSX.V
Profile: WeedMD Inc. is the parent of WeedMD Rx Inc. The latter is a producer of adult-use & medical cannabis. The company has a greenhouse in Strathroy, ON.
George Scorsis, Chief Executive Officer
Peter Blecher, Chief Medical Officer
Beth Carreon, Chief Financial Officer

Zenabis Global Ltd.
#400, 1152 Mainland St.
Vancouver, BC V6B 4X2

Fax: 855-936-3291
855-936-2247
service@zenabis.com
www.zenabis.com
twitter.com/zenabis
www.linkedin.com/company/zenabis

Company Type: Public
Ticker Symbol: ZENA/TSX
Profile: Zenabis is a producer of both recreational & medical cannabis.
Shai Altman, President & CEO
Alan Mayo, Chief Quality & Compliance Officer
Eric Rasmussen, Chief Financial Officer
Parbinder Cheema, Senior Vice-President, Operations

Zymeworks Inc.
#540, 1385 West 8th Ave.
Vancouver, BC V6H 3V9

604-678-1388
Fax: 604-737-7077
www.zymeworks.com
twitter.com/zymeworksinc
www.linkedin.com/company/zymeworks

Company Type: Public
Ticker Symbol: ZYME/NYSE
Profile: Zymeworks is a biotherapeutics company with proprietary platforms, including Azymetric, ZymeLink, EFECT & AlbuCore.
Ali Tehrani, President & CEO
Neil Klompas, Chief Financial Officer & Executive Vice-President, Business Operations

Printing & Publishing

Glacier Media Inc.
2188 Yukon St.
Vancouver, BC V5Y 3P1

604-872-8565
info@glaciermedia.ca
www.glaciermedia.ca
Other Communications: Investor Relations, Email:
investors@glaciermedia.ca

Company Type: Public
Ticker Symbol: GVC/TSX
Staff Size: 2,000
Profile: Glacier Media Inc. provides information & related services through print, electronic & online media.
The Business & Professional Information Group consists of organizations such as CD-Pharma, Eco Log, Specialty Technical Publishers & Fundata.
The Newspaper & Trade Information Group is comprised of newspapers such as the Prince George Citizen, The Kamloops Daily News & the Estevan Mercury. Trade information group publications include The Western Producer, The Daily Oil Bulletin, New Technology Magazine, Business in Vancouver, Canadian Cattlemen & The Northern Miner.
Jonathon J.L. Kennedy, President & CEO
jkennedy@glaciermedia.ca

Peter Kvarnstrom, President, Community Media
Mark Melville, President, Glacier Business Information
Orest Smysniuk, Chief Financial Officer
osmysniuk@glaciermedia.ca

GVIC Communications Corp.
389 West 6th Ave.
Vancouver, BC V5Y 1L1

604-638-2451
Fax: 604-879-1483
www.gviccommunicationscorp.ca

Company Type: Public
Profile: GVIC Communications is an information communications company.
Orest Smysniuk, Chief Financial Officer
osmysniuk@gviccommunicationscorp.ca

Pollard Banknote Limited (PBL)
140 Otter St.
Winnipeg, MB R3T 0M8

204-474-2323
Fax: 204-453-1375
winnipeg@pollardbanknote.com
www.pollardbanknote.com
twitter.com/pollardbanknote
www.linkedin.com/company/pollard-banknote

Company Type: Public
Ticker Symbol: PBL/TSX
Profile: Pollard Banknote Limited is a lottery vendor & supplier to the charitable gaming industry. The company manufactures instant tickets, pull tab tickets & bingo paper. Other activities include warehousing, distributing & marketing.
Douglas Pollard, Co-Chief Executive Officer
John Pollard, Co-Chief Executive Officer
Robert Rose, Chief Financial Officer & Executive Vice-President, Finance

Postmedia Network Canada Corp.
365 Bloor St. East
Toronto, ON M4W 3L4

416-383-2300
www.postmedia.com
www.facebook.com/postmedia
twitter.com/postmedianet
www.linkedin.com/company/postmedia-network-inc.

Company Type: Public
Ticker Symbol: PNC.A/TSX
Staff Size: 2,000
Profile: Postmedia Network Canada Corp. is a communications & media publishing & printing company. Publications include the National Post, Windsor Star & Toronto Sun.
Andrew MacLeod, President & CEO
Brian Bidulka, Executive Vice-President & CFO
Mary Anne Lavalle, Executive Vice-President & COO

Quebecor Inc.
612, rue Saint-Jacques
Montréal, QC H3C 4M8

514-380-1999
www.quebecor.com
twitter.com/quebecor
www.linkedin.com/company/quebecor-media-inc

Company Type: Public
Ticker Symbol: QBR.A, QBR.B/TSX
Profile: Quebecor Inc. is a holding company that has a 81% interest in Quebecor Media Inc.
Pierre Karl Péladeau, President & CEO
Hugues Simard, Chief Financial Officer

Thomson Reuters Corp.
333 Bay St.
Toronto, ON M5H 2R2

416-687-7500
thomsonreuters.com
Other Communications: Investor Relations, Email:
investor.relations@tr.com
www.facebook.com/thomsonreuters
twitter.com/thomsonreuters
www.linkedin.com/company/thomson-reuters

Company Type: Public
Ticker Symbol: TRI/TSX, NYSE
Profile: Thomson Reuters is a Mass Media company that provides organizations with information pertaining to finance, governance, intellectual property, legality, tax & accounting. It was founded in Toronto in the 1960s, where its legal domicile offices are still located, although the majority of operations now take place at their location in Times Square, New York.
Steve Hasker, President & CEO
Michael Eastwood, Chief Financial Officer
Kirsty Roth, Chief Operating & Technology Officer

Torstar Corporation
1 Yonge St.
Toronto, ON M5E 1E6

416-869-4010
Fax: 416-869-4183
torstar@torstar.ca.
www.torstar.com
www.linkedin.com/company/torstar-corporation
Company Type: Public
Ticker Symbol: TS.B/TSX
Profile: The media & book publishing company includes: Star Media Group, which features the Toronto Star & digital properties such as toronto.com & thestar.com; & Metroland Media Group, which publishes community & daily newspapers throughout Ontario.
Lorenzo DeMarchi, Interim President & CEO
Jennifer Barber, Chief Financial Officer
Marie E. Beyette, Senior Vice-President, General Counsel & Corporate Secretary

Transcontinental Inc.
#3240, 1, Place Ville-Marie
Montréal, QC H3B 0G1

514-954-4000
Fax: 514-954-4016
communications@tc.tc
transcontinental.com
www.facebook.com/tc.transcontinental
twitter.com/tctranscontinen
www.linkedin.com/company/tc-transcontinental
Company Type: Public
Ticker Symbol: TCL.A/TSX
Staff Size: 8,000
Profile: The company is engaged in the printing & publishing of consumer magazines & community newspapers, as well as direct marketing & distribution of advertising material. Transcontinental Inc. has worked to address environmental issues by implementing programs such as the Transcontinental Paper Purchasing Policy.
François Olivier, President & CEO
Christine Desaulniers, Chief Legal Officer & Corporate Secretary
Donald Lecavalier, Chief Financial Officer
Lynn Martel, Chief Human Resources Officer

Yellow Pages Inc.
1751, rue Richardson
Montréal, QC H3K 1G6

514-934-2611
800-361-6010
www.yellowpages.ca
www.facebook.com/yellowpagesgroup
Company Type: Public
Ticker Symbol: Y/TSX
Staff Size: 700
Profile: Yellow Pages owns & operates properties & publications such as the Yellow Pages print directories, YellowPages.ca, Canada411.ca & RedFlagDeals.com. The company is also involved in digital advertising through Mediative.
David A. Eckert, President & CEO
Franco Sciannamblo, Senior Vice-President & CFO

ZoomerMedia Limited
70 Jefferson Ave.
Toronto, ON M6K 1Y4

416-363-7063
zoomermedia.ca
www.linkedin.com/company/zoomermedia-limited
Company Type: Public
Ticker Symbol: ZUM/TSX.V
Profile: Formed in 1991, ZoomerMedia Limited is a multimedia company that serves the interests of persons 45 years of age & older. The company offers: television, radio, magazines, internet & trade shows. Examples of ZoomerMedia's television properties include Vision TV, ONE & Joytv. Radio properties include Zoomer Radio & The New Classical. ZoomerMedia also publishes Zoomer Magazine on www.everythingzoomer.com. ZoomerMedia's trade show division produces the Zoomer Show.
Moses Znaimer, Founder, President & CEO
Terence Chan, Chief Financial Officer
t.chan@zoomermedia.ca

Real Estate

Allied Hotel Properties Inc. (AHPI)
#300, 515 West Pender St.
Vancouver, BC V6B 6H5

604-669-5335
info@alliedhotels.com
alliedhotels.com
Company Type: Public
Ticker Symbol: AHP/TSX.V
Profile: The company owns, develops & manages Canadian hotels.

Peter Eng, Founder & Chair
Michael Chan, President

Allied Properties Real Estate Investment Trust
Also Known As: Allied Properties REIT
#1700, 134 Peter St.
Toronto, ON M5V 2H2

416-977-9002
Fax: 416-306-8704
info@alliedreit.com
www.alliedreit.com
twitter.com/alliedreit
www.linkedin.com/company/alliedproperties
Company Type: Public
Ticker Symbol: AP.UN/TSX
Profile: Allied Properties REIT is the owner of urban office properties. The organization plans to continue the acquisition of Class I & other office properties. Target markets are in Victoria, Vancouver, Edmonton, Calgary, Winnipeg, Kitchener, Toronto, Ottawa, Montréal & Québec.
Michael R. Emory, President & CEO
Thomas G. Burns, Executive Vice-President & COO
Cecilia C. Williams, Executive Vice-President & CFO

Altus Group Limited
#500, 33 Yonge St.
Toronto, ON M5E 1G4

info@altusgroup.com
www.altusgroup.com
www.facebook.com/AltusGroup
twitter.com/altus_group
www.linkedin.com/company/altus-group
Company Type: Public
Ticker Symbol: AIF/TSX
Staff Size: 2,300
Profile: Altus Group offers real estate consulting & advisory services. The organization's business units are: Research, Valuation & Advisory; Realty Tax Consulting; Cost Consulting & Project Management; ARGUS Software; & Geomatics.
Mike Gordon, Chief Executive Officer
Angelo Bartolini, Chief Financial Officer

American Hotel Income Properties REIT LP
#800, 925 West Georgia St.
Vancouver, BC V6C 3L2

604-630-3134
Fax: 604-630-0790
info@ahipreit.com
www.ahipreit.com
Company Type: Public
Ticker Symbol: HOT.UN/TSX
Profile: American Hotel Income Properties REIT was formed to indirectly own & acquire hotel properties in the United States.
Jonathan Korol, Chief Executive Officer
Chris Cameron, Chief Investment Officer
Anne Yu, Interim Chief Financial Officer

Ansar Financial & Development
#209, 1825 Markham Rd.
Toronto, ON M1B 4Z9

416-646-1271
Fax: 416-646-1271
info@ansarfinancial.com
www.ansarfinancial.com
Company Type: Public
Ticker Symbol: AFD/CSE
Profile: Ansar purchases, develops & sells real estate.
Pervez Nasim, Chair & Chief Executive Officer
Mohammed Jalaluddin, President & COO

Artis Real Estate Investment Trust
Also Known As: Artis REIT
#600, 220 Portage Ave.
Winnipeg, MB R3C 0A5

204-947-1250
Fax: 204-947-0453
www.artisreit.com
www.linkedin.com/company/artis-real-estate-investment-trust
Company Type: Public
Ticker Symbol: AX.UN/TSX
Staff Size: 200
Profile: Artis REIT is an unincorporated closed-ended real estate investment trust whose portfolio is comprised of industrial, retail & office space in Canada & the United States.
Samir Manji, President & CEO
Jaclyn Koenig, Chief Financial Officer
Frank Sherlock, Executive Vice-President

Atrium Mortgage Investment Corporation
Also Known As: Atrium MIC
#900, 20 Adelaide St. East
Toronto, ON M5C 2T6

416-867-1053
Fax: 416-867-1303
info@atriummic.com
www.atriummic.com
www.facebook.com/atriummic
twitter.com/atriummic
linkedin.com/company/atrium-mortgage-investment-corporation
Company Type: Public
Ticker Symbol: AI/TSX
Profile: Atrium Mortgage Investment Corp. is a Canadian non-bank lender that provides financial solutions in both the commercial & residential real estate sectors.
Robert Goodall, President & CEO
Jennifer Scoffield, Chief Financial Officer

Automotive Properties REIT
#300, 133 King St. East
Toronto, ON M5C 1G6

647-789-2440
ir@automotivereit.ca
automotivepropertiesreit.ca
Company Type: Public
Ticker Symbol: ARP.UN/TSX
Profile: Automotive Properties REIT is an open-ended, growth-oriented real estate investment trust that owns income-producing automotive dealership properties in strategic Canadian urban centres.
Milton Lamb, President & CEO
Andrew Kalra, Chief Financial Officer

Becker Milk Co. Ltd.
Also Known As: Beckers Convenience Stores
#400, 305 Milner Ave.
Toronto, ON M1B 3V4

416-291-4441
info@mybeckers.ca
www.mybeckers.ca
Company Type: Public
Ticker Symbol: BEK.B/TSX
Profile: The Becker Milk Company Limited, is engaged in the ownership & management of retail commercial properties, mainly in Ontario.
Geoffrey Pottow, President & CEO

Boardwalk Real Estate Income Trust
Also Known As: Boardwalk REIT
#200, 1501 - 1st St. SW
Calgary, AB T2R 0W1

403-531-9255
www.bwalk.com
www.facebook.com/bwalkcommunity
twitter.com/bwalkcommunity
www.linkedin.com/company/boardwalk-reit
Company Type: Public
Ticker Symbol: BEI.UN/TSX
Staff Size: 1,600
Profile: The open-ended real estate investment trust owns & operates multi-family communities. Boardwalk REIT's portfolio is concentrated in British Columbia, Alberta, Saskatchewan, Ontario & Quebec.
Sam Kolias, Chair & CEO
403-206-6789
Lisa Smandych, Chief Financial Officer
Helen Mix, Vice-President, People

Bridgemarq Real Estate Services Inc.
39 Wynford Dr.
Toronto, ON M3C 3K5

416-510-5800
info@brookfieldres.com
www.bridgemarq.com
Company Type: Public
Ticker Symbol: BRE/TSX
Profile: Brookfield Real Estate Services is involved in the provision of services to residential real estate brokers & their realtors. Cash flow is generated from franchise royalties & service fees from brokers & agents who operate under the brand names: Johnston & Daniel; Royal LePage; & Via Capitale Real Estate Network.
Philip Soper, President & CEO
416-386-6000, phil.soper@bridgemarq.com
Glen McMillan, Chief Financial Officer
416-510-5605, glen.mcmillan@brookfieldres.com

BTB Real Estate Investment Trust/Fonds de placement immobilier BTB
Also Known As: BTB REIT
1411, rue Crescent
Montréal, QC H3G 2B3

514-286-0188
Fax: 514-286-0011
www.btbreit.com

Company Type: Public
Ticker Symbol: BTB.UN/TSX.V
Staff Size: 60
Profile: BTB REIT invests in a portfolio of industrial, commercial, office & retail properties, predominantly in Québec.
Michael Léonard, President & CEO
mleonard@btbreit.com
Mathieu Bolté, Vice-President & CFO
mbolte@btbreit.com

Chartwell Retirement Residences
7070 Derrycrest Dr.
Mississauga, ON L5W 0G5

905-501-9219
Fax: 905-501-0813
855-461-0685
chartwell.com
www.facebook.com/chartwellretirement
www.linkedin.com/company/chartwell-retirement-residences
Company Type: Public
Ticker Symbol: CSH.UN/TSX
Staff Size: 13,000
Profile: Chartwell Retirement Residences owns & manages senior housing properties through its indirect subsidiary Chartwell Master Care LP.
Vlad Volodarski, Chief Executive Officer
Karen Sullivan, President & COO
Sheri Harris, Chief Financial Officer

Choice Properties Real Estate Investment Trust
Also Known As: Choice Properties REIT
The Weston Centre
#700, 22 St Clair Ave. East
Toronto, ON M4T 2S5

416-628-7771
Fax: 416-628-7777
www.choicereit.ca
Other Communications: Investor Relations, Email:
investor@choicereit.ca
Company Type: Public
Ticker Symbol: CHP.UN/TSX
Profile: Choice Properties REIT is an owner & developer of retail & commercial real estate in Canada. Loblaw Companies Ltd. is Choice Properties' principal tenant. In May 2018, Choice Properties REIT acquired Canadian Real Estate Investment Trust (CREIT).
Rael Diamond, President & CEO
Mario Barrafato, Chief Financial Officer

City Office REIT, Inc.
#3210, 666 Burrard St.
Vancouver, BC V6C 2X8

604-806-3366
investorrelations@cityofficereit.com
cioreit.com
Company Type: Public
Ticker Symbol: CIO/NYSE
Profile: CIO is a real estate company that owns & operates office properties in south & western United States metropolitan areas.
James Farrar, Chief Executive Officer
Greg Tylee, President & COO
Anthony Maretic, Chief Financial Officer

Colliers International Canada
200 Granville St., 19th Fl.
Vancouver, BC V6C 2R6

604-681-4111
vancouver.reception@colliers.com
www.collierscanada.com
www.facebook.com/collierscanada
twitter.com/collierscanada
www.linkedin.com/company/colliers
Company Type: Public
Ticker Symbol: CIGI/TSX, NASDAQ
Staff Size: 12,000
Profile: Colliers International is a commercial real estate company involved with real estate management, valuation, consulting, project management, & project marketing & research.
Brian Rosen, President & CEO, Canada

Cominar Real Estate Investment Trust
Complexe Jules-Dallaire
#850, 2820, boul Laurier
Québec, QC G1V 0C1

418-681-8151
Fax: 418-681-2946
info@cominar.com
www.cominar.com
www.facebook.com/FPICominar
www.linkedin.com/company/fpicominar
Company Type: Public
Ticker Symbol: CUF.UN/TSX
Profile: Cominar is a large, diversified real estate investment trust. It ownscommercial property in Québec. The real estate investment trust also has a portfolio of properties in the Atlantic provinces, Ontario & western Canada.
Sylvain Cossette, President & CEO
Antoine Tronquoy, Executive Vice-President & CFO

Crombie Real Estate Investment Trust
Also Known As: Crombie REIT
#200, 610 East River Rd.
New Glasgow, NS B2H 3S2

902-755-8100
800-463-2406
www.crombie.ca
twitter.com/crombiereit
www.linkedin.com/company/crombiereit
Company Type: Public
Ticker Symbol: CRR.UN/TSX
Profile: Crombie REIT is an open-ended real estate investment trust. It owns & manages properties in eight provinces. Crombie's portfolio consists of retail, office & mixed-use properties.
Donald E. Clow, President & CEO
Glenn R. Hynes, Executive Vice-President & COO
Clinton Keay, Chief Financial Officer

Dream Industrial REIT
#301, 30 Adelaide St. East
Toronto, ON M5C 3H1

416-365-3535
Fax: 416-365-6565
industrialinfo@dream.ca
dream.ca/industrial
Company Type: Public
Ticker Symbol: DIR.UN/TSX
Profile: Dream Industrial REIT is a national pure-play industrial REIT primarily made up of high-quality light industrial properties.
Brian Pauls, Chief Executive Officer
Alexander Sannikov, Chief Operating Officer
Lenis Quan, Chief Financial Officer
Joe Iadeluca, Senior Vice-President, Portfolio Management

Dream Office Real Estate Investment Trust
Also Known As: Dream Office REIT
#301, 30 Adelaide St. East
Toronto, ON M5C 3H1

416-365-3535
Fax: 416-365-6565
officeinfo@dream.ca
dream.ca/office
Company Type: Public
Ticker Symbol: D.UN/TSX
Profile: Dream Office REIT is an unincorporated, open-ended real estate investment trust. It owns industrial & office assets throughout Canada.
In 2012, Dream Office (formerly Dundee REIT) acquired Whiterock Real Estate Investment Trust, a provider of office, retail & industrial properties in Canada.
Michael J. Cooper, President & CEO
Deborah Starkman, Chief Financial Officer

Dream Unlimited
#301, 30 Adelaide St. East
Toronto, ON M5C 3H1

416-365-3535
Fax: 416-365-6565
info@dream.ca
dream.ca
Company Type: Public
Ticker Symbol: DRM/TSX
Profile: Dream was founded in 1994 & is now the largest residential developer in Western Canada. The company owns & operates Homes by Dream, Dream Development,& three TSX-listed REITs: Dream Office REIT, Dream Industrial REIT & Dream Global REIT, as well as the TSX-listed Dream Alternatives Trust.
Michael J. Cooper, President & Chief Responsible Officer
P. Jane Gavan, President, Asset Management
Deborah Starkman, Chief Financial Officer

European Residential REIT
#401, 11 Church St.
Toronto, ON M5E 1W1

www.eresreit.com

Company Type: Public
Ticker Symbol: ERE/TSX.V
Profile: European Residential REIT has a portfolio of multi-residential real estate properties, with a leading focus in the Netherlands.
Phillip Burns, Chief Executive Officer
416-354-0167, p.burns@eresreit.com
Stephen Co, Chief Financial Officer
416-306-3009, s.co@eresreit.com

Firm Capital Property Trust
163 Cartwright Ave.
Toronto, ON M6A 1V5

416-635-0221
Fax: 416-635-1713
info@firmcapital.com
Other Communications: Investor Relations, Email:
ir@firmcapital.com
www.linkedin.com/company/firm-capital-corporation
Company Type: Public
Ticker Symbol: FCD.UN/TSX.V
Profile: Firm Capital REIT is a real estate investment & development company.
Eli Dadouch, President & CEO
edadouch@firmcapital.com
Jonathan Mair, Executive Vice-President & COO
jmair@firmcapital.com
Sandy Poklar, Executive Vice-President, Interim CFO & Managing Director, Finance
spoklar@firmcapital.com

First Capital Real Estate Investment Trust
Also Known As: First Capital REIT
#400, 85 Hanna Ave.
Toronto, ON M6K 3S3

416-504-4114
Fax: 416-941-1655
877-504-4114
fcr.ca
www.linkedin.com/company/first-capital-reit
Company Type: Public
Ticker Symbol: FCR.UN/TSX
Staff Size: 350
Profile: First Capital REIT owns, develops & operates shopping centres, anchored by supermarkets & drug stores. Properties are located mainly in metropolitan areas.
Adam E. Paul, President & CEO
Neil Downey, CFO & Executive Vice-President, Enterprise Strategies
Jordan Robins, Executive Vice-President & COO
Maryanne McDougald, Senior Vice-President, Operations

FirstService Corporation
#600, 1255 Bay St.
Toronto, ON M5R 2A9

416-960-9566
Fax: 647-258-0008
www.firstservice.ca
Company Type: Public
Ticker Symbol: FSV/TSX, NASDAQ
Staff Size: 24,000
Profile: FirstService Corporation is involved in residential property management, property improvement services & commercial real estate.
D. Scott Patterson, President & CEO
Jeremy Rakusin, Chief Financial Officer

FRONSAC Real Estate Investment Trust
Also Known As: FRONSAC REIT
106, av Gun
Montréal, QC H9R 3X3

450-536-5328
www.en.fronsacreit.com
Company Type: Public
Ticker Symbol: FRO.UN/TSX.V
Profile: A commericial real estate company specializing in quick service restaurant chains, major Canadian oil companies, coonvenience store chains & other standalone properties located along highways & heavy trafficked areas.
Jason Parravano, President & CEO
Ben Gazith, Chief Financial Officer

Genesis Land Development Corp.
6240, 333 - 96th Ave. NE
Calgary, AB T3K 0S3

403-265-8079
info@genesisland.com
www.genesisland.com
www.facebook.com/genesislandcorp

Company Type: Public
Ticker Symbol: GDC/TSX
Profile: The community development company operates in British Columbia & Alberta. Most of the land is situated in & around Calgary. Activities include land development, single-family & multi-family home building & commercial development & leasing.
Iain Stewart, President & CEO

Granite Real Estate Investment Trust
Also Known As: Granite REIT
Toronto-Dominion Centre
PO Box 159, #4010, 77 King St. West
Toronto, ON M5K 1H1

647-925-7500
ir@graniteit.com
graniteit.com

Company Type: Public
Ticker Symbol: GRT.UN/TSX; GRP.U/NYSE
Profile: Granite REIT is involved in the acquisition, development, selective construction, lease, management & ownership of a predominantly industrial global rental portfolio of properties in North America & Europe.
Kevan Gorrie, President & CEO
Teresa Neto, Chief Financial Officer

Gulf & Pacific Equities Corp.
#800, 1240 Bay St.
Toronto, ON M5R 2A7

416-968-3337
Fax: 416-968-3339
info@www.gpequities.com
www.gpequities.com

Company Type: Public
Ticker Symbol: GUF/TSX.V
Profile: Gulf & Pacific Equities Corp. is focused on the acquisition, management & development of anchored shopping centres in Western Canada.
Anthony Cohen, President & CEO
Greg K.W. Wong, Chief Financial Officer

Halmont Properties Corporation
#400, 51 Yonge St.
Toronto, ON M5E 1J1

416-956-5140

Company Type: Public
Ticker Symbol: HMT/TSX.V
Profile: Halmont Properties Corporation invests directly in real estate & securities of companies with real estate interests.
Heather Fitzpatrick, President

Holloway Lodging Corp.
#106, 145 Hobsons Lake Dr.
Halifax, NS B3S 0H9

902-404-3499
Fax: 902-423-4001
inquiries@hlcorp.ca
hlcorp.ca
www.linkedin.com/company/holloway-lodging-corporation

Company Type: Public
Profile: Holloway Lodging Corporation is focused on select & limited service hotels in tertiary & suburban markets. In 2019, it was acquired by Clarke Inc.
Felix Seiler, Chief Operating Officer

Imperial Equities Inc.
Scotia Pl.
#2151, 10060 Jasper Ave.
Edmonton, AB T5J 3R8

780-424-7227
Fax: 780-425-6379
imperialequities.com

Company Type: Public
Ticker Symbol: IEI/TSX.V
Profile: Imperial Equities Inc. is an industrial landlord focusing on the acquisition, development & re-development of real estate assets.
Sine Chadi, President & CEO
sine@imperialequities.com
Patricia Misutka, Chief Operating Officer
patricia@imperialequities.com

InterRent Real Estate Investment Trust
Also Known As: InterRent REIT
#207, 485 Bank St.
Ottawa, ON K2P 1Z2

613-569-5699
Fax: 888-696-5698
www.interrentreit.com
Other Communications: Investors, Email: investorinfo@interrentreit.com

Company Type: Public
Ticker Symbol: IIP.UN/TSX

Profile: InterRent REIT works to increase unitholder value by acquiring & owning multi-residential properties.
Mike McGahan, Chief Executive Officer
Brad Cutsey, President
Curt Millar, Chief Financial Officer

Killam Apartment Real Estate Investment Trust
Also Known As: Killam Apartment REIT
#100, 3700 Kempt Rd.
Halifax, NS B3K 4X8

902-453-9000
Fax: 902-455-5325
866-453-8900
leasing@killamproperties.com
killamreit.com
www.facebook.com/killamapartments
twitter.com/killamtweets
www.linkedin.com/company/killam-apartments

Company Type: Public
Ticker Symbol: KMP.UN/TSX
Staff Size: 550
Profile: Killam Apartments REIT is a large residential landlord. The company owns, develops & operates multi-family apartments & manufactured home communities. Environmental intiatives at Killam's properties include the increasing use of solar power, reducing heating costs with outdoor controllers & reducing water consumption with water saving kits.
Philip D. Fraser, President & CEO
Robert Richardson, Executive Vice-President

King George Financial Corp.
#750, 510 Burrard St.
Vancouver, BC V6C 3A8

604-687-8882

Company Type: Public
Ticker Symbol: KGF/TSX.V
Profile: A commercial & residential real estate firm.
Dennis Ng, President & CEO

Lakeview Hotel Investment Corp.
Also Known As: Lakeview Hotel REIT
#600, 185 Carlton St.
Winnipeg, MB R3C 3J1

204-947-1161
877-355-3500
info@lakeviewhotels.com
www.lakeviewhotels.com
www.facebook.com/lakeviewhotelsandresorts

Company Type: Public
Ticker Symbol: LHR/TSX.V
Profile: Lakeview Hotel Investment owns & co-manages the Lakeview Inn & Suites & has licensing income from five other hotels through its 49% interest in the "Lakeview Flag".
Keith Levit, President & CEO

Madison Pacific Properties Inc.
389 - 6th Ave. West
Vancouver, BC V5Y 1L1

604-732-6540
info@madisonpacific.ca
madisonpacific.ca

Company Type: Public
Ticker Symbol: MPC/TSX
Profile: Madison Pacific Properties Inc. is a real estate investment & development company. Its properties include rentable industrial & commercial space.
In 2011, Madison Pacific Properties Inc. acquired the shares of MP Western Properties Inc. The shares were acquired for investment purposes.
Marvin Haasen, President & CEO
Bernice Yip, Chief Financial Officer

Mainstreet Equity Corp.
305 - 10th Ave. SE
Calgary, AB T2G OW2

403-215-6060
Fax: 403-266-8867
mainstreet@mainst.biz
www.mainst.biz
www.facebook.com/mainstreetequitycorp
twitter.com/rentmainstreet
www.linkedin.com/company/mainstreet-equity-corp

Company Type: Public
Ticker Symbol: MEQ/TSX
Profile: Mainstreet Equity is engaged in the acquisition & renting of boutique apartments. Business is conducted in Abootsford & Surrey, British Columbia; Calgary, Lethbridge & Edmonton, Alberta; Saskatoon & Regina, Saskatchewan; & Toronto & Mississauga, Ontario.
Bob Dhillon, President & CEO
bdhillon@mainst.biz
Trina Cui, Chief Financial Officer

Melcor Developments Ltd.
#900, 10310 Jasper Ave. NW
Edmonton, AB T5J 1Y8

780-423-6931
866-635-2671
info@melcor.ca
www.melcor.ca
Other Communications: Investor Relations, Email: ir@melcor.ca
twitter.com/melcordev
www.linkedin.com/company/melcor-developments

Company Type: Public
Ticker Symbol: MRD/TSX
Profile: Melcor Developments Ltd. is a real estate development company that was established in 1923. It acquires land to develop & sell for multi-family sites, residential communities & commercial sites. The organization is also the owner, developer & manager of commercial income properties & golf courses.
Darin Rayburn, President & CEO
Naomi Stefura, Chief Financial Officer

Melcor Real Estate Investment Trust
Also Known As: Melcor REIT
#900, 10310 Jasper Ave.
Edmonton, AB T5J 1Y8

780-423-6931
866-635-2671
info@melcorreit.ca
melcorreit.ca
Other Communications: Investor Relations, Email: ir@melcorreit.ca

Company Type: Public
Ticker Symbol: MR.UN/TSX
Profile: The corporation owns, develops & manages commercial properties in western Canada.
Darin Rayburn, President & CEO
Naomi Stefura, Chief Financial Officer

Mongolia Growth Group Ltd.
First Canadian Place
#5600, 100 King St. West, 56th Fl.
Toronto, ON M5X 1C9

289-848-2035
Fax: 866-468-9119
877-644-1186
info@mongoliagrowthgroup.com
mongoliagrowthgroup.com
twitter.com/mongoliagg
www.linkedin.com/company/mongolia-growth-group-ltd

Company Type: Public
Ticker Symbol: YAK/TSX.V
Profile: Mongolia Growth Group Ltd. is a real estate & financial services conglomerate focusing its operations on Mongolia.
Harris Kupperman, Chief Executive Officer
Genevieve Walkden, Chief Financial Officer

Morguard Corporation
#800, 55 City Centre Dr.
Mississauga, ON L5B 1M3

905-281-3800
800-928-6255
info@morguard.com
www.morguard.com
www.linkedin.com/company/morguard

Company Type: Public
Ticker Symbol: MRC/TSX
Staff Size: 1,500
Profile: Morguard Corporation is a real estate & property management company. Through its investment in Morguard REIT, the corporation has a diversified portfolio of residential, office, retail & industrial properties owned or under management. Through Morguard Investments Limited & Morguard Residential, management services to institutional & other investors for residential & commercial real estate are offered.
K. Rai Sahi, Chair & Chief Executive Officer
rsahi@morguard.com
Paul Miatello, Chief Financial Officer
pmiatello@morguard.com
Beverley G. Flynn, Senior Vice-President, General Counsel & Secretary
bflynn@morguard.com
Brian Athey, Vice-President, Development
bathey@morguard.com

Morguard North American Residential Real Estate Inves
Also Known As: Morguard North American Residential REIT
#800, 55 City Centre Dr.
Mississauga, ON L5B 1M3

905-281-3800
800-928-6255
info@morguard.com
www.morguard.com

Company Type: Public
Ticker Symbol: MRG.UN/TSX
Profile: Morguard North American Residential REIT is a publicly traded open-ended real estate investment trust, created in April 2012. The company owns multi-unit residential rental properties across Canada & the United States.
K. Rai Sahi, Chair & Chief Executive Officer
rsahi@morguard.com
Christopher Newman, Chief Financial Officer
cnewman@morguard.com

Morguard REIT
#800, 55 City Centre Dr.
Mississauga, ON L5B 1M3

905-281-3800
800-928-6255
info@morguard.com
www.morguard.com

Company Type: Public
Ticker Symbol: MRT.UN/TSX
Profile: Morguard REIT is a real-estate investment trust with a portfolio of 47 commercial properties in six provinces.
K. Rai Sahi, President & CEO
rsahi@morguard.com
Andrew Tamlin, Chief Financial Officer
atamlin@morguard.com

Mountain China Resorts (Holding) Limited (MCR)
#1000, 595 Burrard St.
Vancouver, BC V7X 1S8
Other Communications: Phone: +86-10-66420868
Company Type: Public
Ticker Symbol: MCG/TSX.V
Profile: Mountain China Resorts (Holding) Limited develops ski resorts in China.
Gang Han, Chief Executive Officer
Yang Shi, Chief Financial Officer

Nexus Real Estate Investment Trust
Also Known As: Nexus REIT
#211, 1540 Cornwall Rd.
Oakville, ON L6J 7W5

416-613-1262
nexusreit.com

Company Type: Public
Ticker Symbol: NXR.UN/TSX
Profile: Nexus REIT was created by the merge of Nobel REIT & Edgefront REIT. The company deals with industrial, office & retail properties in Canada.
Kelly C. Hanczyk, Chief Executive Officer
Robert P. Chiasson, Chief Financial Officer

Plaza Retail REIT
Head Office
96 Main St.
Fredericton, NB E3A 9N6

506-451-1826
Fax: 506-451-1802
info@plaza.ca
plaza.ca
www.linkedin.com/company/plazareit

Company Type: Public
Ticker Symbol: PLZ.UN/TSX
Profile: Plaza Retail REIT is engaged in the acquisition, development & re-development of enclosed mall shopping centres & strip plazas. Operations take place in Ontario, Western Canada, Québec & Atlantic Canada.
Michael Zakuta, President & CEO
michael.zakuta@plaza.ca
Jim Drake, Chief Financial Officer
jim.drake@plaza.ca

Pro Real Estate Investment Trust
Also Known As: Pro REIT
#1000, 2000, rue Mansfield
Montréal, QC H3A 2Z7

514-933-9552
Fax: 514-933-9094
info@proreit.com
proreit.com

Company Type: Public
Ticker Symbol: PRV.UN/TSX
Profile: Pro REIT owns commercial real estate in Québec, Atlantic Canada, Alberta, British Columbia & Ontario.
James Beckerleg, President & CEO
Gordon Lawlor, Executive Vice-President & CFO

Realia Properties Inc.
151 Yonge St.
Toronto, ON M5C 2W7

647-775-8337
realiaproperties.com
Other Communications: Toll-Free Fax: 888-831-2559

Company Type: Public
Ticker Symbol: TSP/TSX.V
Profile: Relia Properties is a Canadian real estate investment company whose focuse is on the southwestern United States.
Eric Fazilleau, Chief Executive Officer
eric.fazilleau@inovalis.com
Kyra Dorn, Chief Fianance Officer
kdorn@hochepartners.com

RioCan Real Estate Investment Trust
Also Known As: RioCan
RioCan Yonge Eglinton Centre
PO Box 2386, #500, 2300 Yonge St.
Toronto, ON M4P 1E4

800-465-2733
inquiries@riocan.com
riocan.com
Other Communications: Investor Relations, Email:
ir@riocan.com

Company Type: Public
Ticker Symbol: REI.UN/TSX
Staff Size: 580
Profile: RioCan owns a portfolio of retail properties throughout Canada & manages neighbourhood shopping centres that are anchored by supermarkets.
Jonathan Gitlin, President & CEO
Franca Smith, Interim Chief Financial Officer

Slate Retail REIT
#200, 121 King St. West
Toronto, ON M5H 3T9

416-644-4264
Fax: 416-947-9366
ir@slateam.com
www.slateretailreit.com
www.linkedin.com/company/slateam

Company Type: Public
Ticker Symbol: SRT.UN/TSX
Profile: Slate Retail REIT provides investors with direct exposure to recovery in Canadian office & U.S. grocery-anchored retail assets.
David Dunn, Chief Executive Officer
Andrew Agatep, Chief Financial Officer
Ramsey Ali, General Counsel

SmartCentres REIT
3200 Hwy. 7
Vaughan, ON L4K 5Z5

905-326-6400
Fax: 905-326-0783
info@smartcentres.com
www.smartcentres.com
twitter.com/smartcentres
www.linkedin.com/company/smartcentres

Company Type: Public
Ticker Symbol: SRU.UN/TSX
Profile: In 2015, Calloway REIT acquired the SmartCentre platform & changed their name to SmartREIT. The company is a REIT that owns & manages over 34 million square feet of retail centres that are principally Walmart-anchored. In 2018, SmartREIT changed its name to SmartCentres REIT.
Peter Forde, President & CEO
Mauro Pambianchi, Chief Development Officer
Peter E. Sweeney, Chief Financial Officer

Summit Industrial Income Real Estate Investment Trust
Also Known As: Summit Industrial Income REIT;
Summit II REIT
#120, 110 Cochrane Dr.
Markham, ON L3R 9S1

905-791-1181
info@summitiireit.com
www.summitiireit.com
www.linkedin.com/company/summit-industrial-income-reit

Company Type: Public
Ticker Symbol: SMU.UN/TSX
Profile: Summit Industrial Income REIT is an open ended mutual fund trust focused on growing & managing a portfolio of light industrial properties across Canada.
Paul Dykeman, Chief Executive Officer
Ross Drake, Chief Financial Officer
Dayna M. Gibbs, Chief Operating Officer

Terra Firma Capital Corporation
#200, 22 St Clair Ave. East
Toronto, ON M4T 2S3

416-792-4700
Fax: 416-792-4711
invest@tfcc.ca
www.tfcc.ca
twitter.com/terrafirmacap
www.linkedin.com/company/terra-firma-capital-corporation

Company Type: Public
Ticker Symbol: TII/TSX.V
Profile: Terra Firma Capital Corporation is a boutique real estate finance company that provides customized debt & equity solutions to the real estate industry.
Glenn Watchorn, President & CEO
gwatchorn@tfcc.ca
Mano Thiyagarajah, Chief Financial Officer & Corporate Secretary
mthiyagarajah@tfcc.ca

True North Commercial REIT
Centre Tower
#1400, 3280 Bloor St. West
Toronto, ON M8X 2X3

416-234-8444
ircommercial@truenorthreit.com
truenorthreit.com

Company Type: Public
Ticker Symbol: TNT.UN/TSX
Profile: True North Commercial REIT is an owner & acquirer of Canadian commercial real estate properties.
Leslie Veiner, Chief Executive Officer
Tracy C. Sherren, President & CFO

Urbanfund Corp.
35 Lesmill Rd.
Toronto, ON M3B 2T3

416-703-1877
Fax: 416-504-9216

Company Type: Public
Ticker Symbol: UFC/TSX.V
Profile: Urbanfund Corp. engages in the development & operation of real estate properties in Canada.
Mitchell Cohen, President & CEO
mcohen@urbanfund.ca

Wall Financial Corporation
#3502, 1088 Burrard St.
Vancouver, BC V6Z 2R9

604-893-7131
Fax: 604-893-7179

Company Type: Public
Ticker Symbol: WFC/TSX
Staff Size: 232
Profile: The corporation is engaged in: real estate development; investment in properties; management of residential rental apartments & hotel properties; & development & construction of residential housing for resale.
Bruno Wall, President

WPT Industrial Real Estate Investment Trust
Also Known As: WPT Industrial REIT
#4000, 199 Bay St.
Toronto, ON M5L 1A9

612-800-8530
ir@wptreit.com
www.wptreit.com

Company Type: Public
Ticker Symbol: WIR.U/TSX
Profile: WPT Industrial REIT is focused on the acquisition & sale of warehouse & distribution properties in the United States.
Scott T. Frederiksen, Chief Executive Officer
stf@wptreit.com
Matthew Cimino, Chief Operating Officer & General Counsel
mcimino@wptreit.com
Judd Gilats, Chief Financial Officer
jgilats@wptreit.com

Services, Miscellaneous

Black Diamond Group Limited
#1000, 440 - 2nd Ave. SW
Calgary, AB T2P 5E9

403-206-4747
Fax: 403-264-9281
888-569-4880
investor@blackdiamondgroup.com
www.blackdiamondlimited.com
www.linkedin.com/company/black-diamond-limited

Company Type: Public
Ticker Symbol: BDI/TSX
Staff Size: 250
Profile: Black Diamond Group was founded in 2003. The corporation provides modular buildings, workforce accommodations & energy services. The group's businesses include: BOXX Modular, Britco, MPA Systems, Black Diamond Camps & Lodging, Black Diamond Energy Services, Black Diamond International & LodgeLink.
Trevor Haynes, Chair, President & CEO
Toby Labrie, Executive Vice-President & CFO
Patrick Melanson, Executive Vice-President & CIO

Boyd Group Services Inc. (BGSI)
1745 Ellice Ave.
Winnipeg, MB R3H 1A6

204-895-1244
Fax: 204-895-1283
info@boydgroup.com
www.boydgroup.com
www.linkedin.com/company/the-boyd-group-inc
Company Type: Public
Ticker Symbol: BYD/TSX
Staff Size: 9,000
Profile: Boyd Group Services controls the Boyd Group Inc. & its subsidiaries, which operate collision repair centers in North America. Trade names include Boyd Autobody & Glass, Assured Automotive & Gerber Collision & Glass. The company is also a retail auto glass operator in the US under several trade names. Through Gerber National Claim Services, it offers glass, emergency roadside & first notice of loss services.
Tim O'Day, President & CEO
Narendra (Pat) Pathipati, Executive Vice-President & CFO

Caldwell Partners International
TD South Tower
PO Box 75, #2410, 79 Wellington St. West
Toronto, ON M5K 1E7

416-920-7702
Fax: 416-922-8646
888-366-3827
www.caldwellpartners.com
twitter.com/caldwellptners
www.linkedin.com/company/the-caldwell-partners
Company Type: Public
Ticker Symbol: CWL/TSX
Profile: Caldwell Partners is a staffing company, with a focus on finding senior executives & directors.
John Wallace, Chief Executive Officer
Chris Beck, President & CFO

Canlan Ice Sports Corp.
Also Known As: Canlan Sports
6501 Sprott St.
Burnaby, BC V5B 3B8

604-736-9152
www.canlansports.com
www.facebook.com/CanlanSports
twitter.com/CanlanSports
www.linkedin.com/company/canlan-sports
Company Type: Public
Ticker Symbol: ICE/TSX
Staff Size: 1,000
Profile: Canlan Sports is an owner-operator & investor in multi-sport recreation facilities. It has 19 sports complexes in Canada the US.
Joey St-Aubin, President & CEO
Mark Faubert, Chief Operating Officer
Ivan Wu, Chief Financial Officer

CareRx Corporation
#2100, 20 Eglinton Ave. West
Toronto, ON M4R 1K8

Fax: 416-927-8405
800-265-9197
info@carerx.ca
www.carerx.ca
www.facebook.com/CareRxCorp
twitter.com/carerxcorp
www.linkedin.com/company/carerxcorp
Company Type: Public
Ticker Symbol: CRRX/TSX
Profile: CareRx is a diversified healthcare services company. Operations include: medical assessments, specialty pharmacy services, surgical centres, physiotherapy, rehabilitation & disability management, homecare & the provision of home medical equipment.
David Murphy, President & CEO

CIBT Education Group Inc.
#1200, 777 West Broadway
Vancouver, BC V5Z 4J7

604-871-9909
Fax: 604-871-9919
info@cibt.net
cibt.net
www.facebook.com/369587237231369
twitter.com/CIBT_Group
www.linkedin.com/company/cibt-education-group-inc.
Company Type: Public
Ticker Symbol: MBA/TSX; MBAIF/OTCQX
Staff Size: 300
Profile: The education management company is the owner & operator of language, business & technical colleges. CIBT Education Group's subsidiaries include Sprott-Shaw Degree College, Sprott-Shaw Community College, King George International College & the CIBT School of Business China.

These subsidiaries enable the CIBT Education Group to offer Western & Chinese accredited business & management degrees, plus programs in college preparation, information technology, English language training, English teacher certification, automotive maintenance, hotel management & tourism.
Toby Chu, President & CEO
Hilbert Ng, Chief Financial Officer

ClearStream Energy Services
#1650, 311 - 6th Ave. SW
Calgary, AB T2P 3H2

587-318-0997
855-410-1112
communications@clearstreamenergy.ca
clearstreamenergy.ca
www.facebook.com/clearstreamenergy
twitter.com/clearstream_cdn
www.linkedin.com/company/clearstream-energy-services
Company Type: Public
Ticker Symbol: CSM/TSX
Staff Size: 3,000
Profile: ClearStream Energy constructs, transports & provides maintenance services to the oil & gas, petrochemical, mining, power, agriculture, forestry, infrastructure & water treament industries.
Yves Paletta, Chief Executive Officer
Randy Watt, Chief Financial Officer
Neil Wotton, Chief Operating Officer

Dialogue Health Technologies Inc.
#200, 390, rue Notre-Dame ouest
Montréal, QC H2Y 1T9

hello@dialogue.co
www.dialogue.co
Other Communications: Investor Relations, Email:
investors@dialogue.co
www.facebook.com/godialogue
twitter.com/godialogue
www.linkedin.com/company/dialogue-md
Company Type: Public
Ticker Symbol: CARE/TSX
Staff Size: 250
Profile: Founded in 2016, Dialogue is a global telemedicine provider. This includes an integrated health platform for organizations that provides wellness reporting, programs & more.
Cherif Habib, Chief Executive Officer
Jean-Nicolas Guillemette, Chief Operating Officer
Navaid Mansuri, Chief Financial Officer
Alexis Smirnov, Chief Technology Officer

EBlock, Inc.
#500, 10 Lower Spadina Ave.
Toronto, ON M5V 2Z2

866-776-9446
info@eblock.ca
eblock.com
www.facebook.com/eblock.inc
twitter.com/eblocksocial
www.linkedin.com/company/eblock-inc.
Company Type: Public
Profile: Founded in 2016, EBlock is an online vehicle auction website.
Jason McClenahan, President & CEO
Andy Bohlin, Chief Financial Officer
John Brasher, Chief Operating Officer
Dmitry Vodiansky, Chief Technology Officer
Jill Murray, Chief People Officer

Evergreen Gaming Corporation
8200 Tacoma Mall Blvd.
Lakewood, WA 98499 USA

425-282-4172
Fax: 425-572-6437
info@evergreengaming.com
evergreengaming.com
Company Type: Public
Ticker Symbol: TNA/TSX.V
Profile: Evergreen Gaming owns four casinos in Washington State.
Tom Marvin, Chief Executive Officer
Laurence Smith, Chief Financial Officer

Extendicare Inc.
#103, 3000 Steeles Ave. East
Markham, ON L3R 4T9

905-470-4000
communications@extendicare.com
www.extendicare.com
twitter.com/extendicare
www.linkedin.com/company/extendicare
Company Type: Public
Ticker Symbol: EXE/TSX

Staff Size: 23,000
Profile: Extendicare Inc. operates senior care facilities. Through its ParaMed Home Health Care division, home health care services are also provided.
Michael Guerriere, President & CEO
David Bacon, Senior Vice-President & Chief Financial Officer

Gamehost Inc.
#104, 548 Laura Ave.
Red Deer, AB T4E 0A5

403-346-4545
Fax: 403-340-0683
877-703-4545
www.gamehost.ca
Company Type: Public
Ticker Symbol: GH/TSX
Profile: Gamehost Inc. is involved in the hotel & gaming business. Operations include the Great Northern Casino, Boomtown Casino & Service Plus Inns & Suites hotel in Alberta. The company also has a 91% controlling interest in Deerfoot Inn & Casino in Calgary.
David J. Will, President & CEO
Elston J. Noren, Chief Operating Officer
Craig M. Thomas, Chief Financial Officer
Darcy J. Will, Vice-President

GDI Integrated Facility Services
695, 90e av
Lasalle, QC H8R 3A4

514-612-8089
info@gdi.com
gdi.com
twitter.com/gdiservices
www.linkedin.com/company/gdi-integrated-facility-services
Company Type: Public
Ticker Symbol: GDI/TSX
Staff Size: 20,000
Profile: GDI Integrated Facility Services provides facility maintenance services across Canada & the U.S. The company specializes in cleaning, energy management & multi-trade services.
Claude Bigras, President & CEO
Stéphane Lavigne, Senior Vice-President & CFO

goeasy Ltd.
#510, 33 City Centre Dr.
Mississauga, ON L5B 2N5

905-272-2788
Fax: 905-272-9886
888-528-3279
www.goeasy.com
www.facebook.com/goeasyltd
twitter.com/goeasyltd
www.linkedin.com/company/goeasyltd
Company Type: Public
Ticker Symbol: GSY/TSX
Staff Size: 2,000
Profile: goeasy Ltd. is a merchandise lease company. The company rents products, such as household furnishings, home entertainment products, electronics, appliances & computers. Customers may have the option to purchase products.
Jason Mullins, President & CEO
jmullins@goeasy.com
Hal Khouri, Executive Vice-President & CFO
hkhouri@goeasy.com
Michael Eubanks, Senior Vice-President & CIO

Great Canadian Gaming Corporation
39 Wynford Dr.
Toronto, ON M3C 3K5

604-303-1000
Fax: 604-516-7155
information@gcgaming.com
gcgaming.com
Other Communications: Information Relations, Email:
ir@gcgaming.com
www.facebook.com/greatcanadiangaming
twitter.com/grtcanadian
www.linkedin.com/company/great-canadian-gaming-corporation
Company Type: Public
Ticker Symbol: GC/TSX
Staff Size: 7,900
Profile: Great Canadian Gaming Corporation is a gaming & entertainment operator. Operations include entertainment facilities, such as casinos, racetracks & show theatres. Business is conducted in New Brunswick, Nova Scotia, Ontario, British Columbia & Washington State.
Terrance Doyle, Interim Chief Executive Officer
Darren Gwozd, Executive Vice-President, Finance

Hut 8 Mining Corp.
#1800, 130 King St. West
Toronto, ON M5X 2A2

info@hut8mining.com
hut8mining.com
www.facebook.com/Hut8Corp
twitter.com/hut8mining
www.linkedin.com/company/hut8mining

Company Type: Public
Ticker Symbol: HUT/TSX, NASDAQ
Staff Size: 30
Profile: Hut 8 is a digital asset mining company. It was the first publicly traded miner on the TSX.
Jaime Leverton, Chief Executive Officer
Shane Downey, Chief Financial Officer
Ronnie Yu, Head, Sustainability

Information Services Corporation
#300, 10 Research Dr.
Regina, SK S4S 7J7

Fax: 306-787-8179
866-275-4721
ask@isc.ca
www.isc.ca

Company Type: Public
Ticker Symbol: ISV/TSX
Staff Size: 300
Profile: Information Services Corporation is responsible for the development, management & administration of: registries of land titles, personal property, corporate & survey registries; geographic information; & access to government services for people & business.
Jeff Stusek, President & CEO
Shawn B. Peters, Executive Vice-President & CFO

K-Bro Linen Inc.
14903 - 137th Ave. NW
Edmonton, AB T5V 1R9

780-453-5218
Fax: 780-455-6676
www.k-brolinen.com

Company Type: Public
Ticker Symbol: KBL/TSX
Staff Size: 2,100
Profile: K-Bro Linen Inc. is involved in the operation of laundry & linen processing facilities. It serves industrial & commercial sectors, such as hospitality & healthcare. Processing facilities are located in Montréal, Québec, Toronto, Calgary, Edmonton, Vancouver & Victoria. Brands include Les Buanderies Dextraze, Buanderie HMR & K-Bro Linen Systems Inc.
Linda McCurdy, President & CEO
Kristie Plaquin, Chief Financial Officer

LifeWorks Inc.
Tower One
#700, 895 Don Mills Rd.
Toronto, ON M3C 1W3

416-445-2700
Fax: 416-445-7989
investors@lifeworks.com
lifeworks.com
twitter.com/LifeWorks
www.linkedin.com/company/lifeworks

Company Type: Public
Ticker Symbol: LWRK/TSX
Staff Size: 6,000
Profile: LifeWorks offers human resource consulting & outsourcing services with a focus on business & wellness.
Stephen Liptrap, President & CEO
Grier Colter, Executive Vice-President & CFO

Liquid Media Group Ltd.
#202, 5626 Larch St.
Vancouver, BC V6M 4E1

www.liquidmediagroup.co
Other Communications: Investor Relations, Email:
pg@liquidmediagroup.co

Company Type: Public
Ticker Symbol: YVR/NASDAQ
Profile: The company provides business solutions for independent IP creators. Services include packaging, finances, delivery & monetization globally.
Ronald Thomson, Chief Executive Officer
Charlie Brezer, President
Andy Wilson, Chief Financial Officer

Loop Industries, Inc.
480, rue Fernand Poitras
Terrebonne, QC J6Y 1Y4

450-951-8555
info@loopindustries.com
www.loopindustries.com
Other Communications: Careers, Email: hr@loopindustries.com
www.facebook.com/Loopindustrie
www.linkedin.com/company/loop-industries

Company Type: Public
Ticker Symbol: LOOP/NASDAQ
Profile: Founded in 2015, Loop Industries is a technology company with proprietary recycling technology.
Daniel Solomita, Chief Executive Officer

MAV Beauty Brands Inc.
#810, 100 New Park Pl.
Vaughan, ON L4K 0H9

416-347-8954
investors.mavbeautybrands.com
Other Communications: Investor Relations, Email:
ir@mavbeautybrands.com
www.linkedin.com/company/mav-beauty-brands

Company Type: Public
Ticker Symbol: MAV/TSX
Staff Size: 100
Profile: MAV is a provider of personal care products. It has four brands: Marc Anthony True Professional; Renpure; Cake Beauty; & The Mane Choice. Its brands cover hair care, body care & beauty products.
Tim Bunch, President & CEO
Niv Majar, Interim CFO & Vice-President, Finance

Medical Facilities Corporation (MFC)
#701, 4576 Yonge St.
Toronto, ON M2N 6N4

416-848-7380
877-402-7162
investors@medicalfc.com
www.medicalfacilitiescorp.ca

Company Type: Public
Ticker Symbol: DR/TSX
Staff Size: 1,250
Profile: Medical Facilities Corporation owns controlling interests in four specialty surgical hospitals in Oklahoma & South Dakota. The corporation also owns interests in an ambulatory surgery center, located in California. The specialty surgical hospitals derive revenue from fees charged for use of the facilities.
Robert O. Horrar, President & CEO
David Watson, Chief Financial Officer
James Rolfe, Chief Development Officer

Mistplay
481, av Viger ouest
Montréal, QC H2Z 1G6

www.mistplay.com
www.facebook.com/mistplayapp
twitter.com/mistplayapp
www.linkedin.com/company/mistplay

Company Type: Public
Profile: Founded in 2015, Mistplay offers mobile video game players a loyalty program.
Henri Machalani, Founder & Chief Executive Officer
Eugene Joannides, Chief Operating Officer
Charles Machalani, Chief Financial Officer

New Look Vision Group Inc./Groupe Vision New Look Inc.
4405, ch du Bois-Franc
Montréal, QC H4S 1A8

infoweb@newlook.ca
www.newlookvision.ca
www.facebook.com/newlook.ca

Company Type: Public
Ticker Symbol: BCI/TSX
Profile: In 2010, Benvest New Look Income Fund was converted into a corporation named New Look Eyewear Inc. The eye care organization operates laboratories & over 390 stores across Canada & Florida.
Antoine Amiel, President & CEO

No Fixed Address Inc. (NFA)
50 Carroll St.
Toronto, ON M4M 3G3

hello@nofixedaddressinc.com
nofixedaddressinc.com
www.facebook.com/nofixedaddressinc
twitter.com/nfainctweets
www.linkedin.com/company/no-fixed-address

Company Type: Public
Profile: NFA is an advertising agency.

Nova Leap Health
#5003, 7071 Bayers Rd.
Halifax, NS B3L 2C2

902-401-9480
novaleaphealth.com

Company Type: Public
Ticker Symbol: NLH/TSX
Profile: The company provides personal home support & care. It is an aquisitive company which strives to grow in North America & beyond.
Chris Dobbin, President & CEO
cdobbin@novaleaphealth.com
Megan Spidle, Chief Financial Officer

Park Lawn Corporation
#1300, 2 St Clair Ave. West
Toronto, ON M4V 1L5

416-231-1462
info@parklawncorp.com
www.parklawncorp.com
www.facebook.com/parklawnlp
www.linkedin.com/company/parklawncorp

Company Type: Public
Ticker Symbol: PLC/TSX
Profile: In 2011, Park Lawn Income Trust converted from an income trust to a corporation. Park Lawn Corporation indirectly holds six cemeteries in the Greater Toronto Area of Ontario, plus a larger, diverse portfolio of properties & businesses in Canada & the USA.
Brad Green, Chief Executive Officer
Jay Dodds, President & Chief Operating Officer
Daniel Millett, Chief Financial Officer
Jeff Parker, Chief Technology Officer

Points International Ltd.
Also Known As: Points
#700, 111 Richmond St. West
Toronto, ON M5H 2G4

416-596-6370
Fax: 416-595-6444
www.points.com
Other Communications: Investor Relations, Email:
ir@points.com
www.facebook.com/pointsfans
twitter.com/pointsloyalty
www.linkedin.com/companies/points

Company Type: Public
Ticker Symbol: PTS/TSX; PCOM/NASDAQ
Staff Size: 260+
Profile: Points International Ltd. owns & operates the loyalty reward management program platform www.Points.com. The platform permits users to redeem, exchange, & trade miles & rewards.
Rob MacLean, Chief Executive Officer
Christopher Barnard, President
Don Dew, Chief Technology Officer
Erick Georgiou, Chief Financial Officer

Profound Medical Corp.
#6, 2400 Skymark Ave.
Mississauga, ON L4W 5K5

647-476-1350
Fax: 647-847-3739
info@profoundmedical.com
profoundmedical.com
www.facebook.com/ProfoundMedical
twitter.com/profoundmedical
www.linkedin.com/company/profound-medical-inc

Company Type: Public
Ticker Symbol: PRN/TSX
Profile: Profound Medical is commercializing TULSA-PRO© technology, to aid in the treatment of prostate-related issues.
Arun Menawat, Chief Executive Officer

Pulse Seismic Inc.
#2700, 421 - 7th Ave. SW
Calgary, AB T2P 4K9

403-237-5559
877-460-5559
www.pulseseismic.com
www.linkedin.com/company/pulse-seismic-inc-

Company Type: Public
Ticker Symbol: PSD/TSX
Profile: Pulse Seismic Inc. is engaged in the acquisition, marketing & licensing of 2D & 3D seismic data. The company's data library covers key areas in the Northwest Territories, Yukon, northeastern British Columbia, Alberta, Saskatchewan, Manitoba & Montana. Pulse Seismic serves the western Canadian energy sector.
Neal Coleman, President & CEO
Pamela Wicks, Chief Financial Officer

Quipt Home Medical Corp.
1019 Town Dr.
Wilder, KY 41076 USA

859-300-6455
quipthomemedical.com

Company Type: Private
Ticker Symbol: QIPT/TSX.V
Profile: Quipt provides home solutions to people who have heart disease & health conditions.
Greg Crawford, Chief Executive Officer

Sienna Senior Living Inc.
#300, 302 Town Centre Blvd.
Markham, ON L3R 0E8

905-477-4006
Fax: 905-415-7623
info@siennaliving.ca
siennaliving.ca
Other Communications: Investor Relations, Email:
investors@siennaliving.ca
www.facebook.com/siennaliving
www.linkedin.com/company/sienna-senior-living

Company Type: Public
Ticker Symbol: SIA/TSX
Staff Size: 13,000
Profile: Sienna Senior Living is a licensed long-term care provider, with operations in Ontario. The corporation owns 41 long-term care facilities & 27 retirement residences. Subsidiaries include Ontario Long Term Care & Preferred Health Care Services.
Nitin Jain, President & CEO
Karen Hon, Chief Financial Officer & Senior Vice-President

Snipp Interactive Inc.
#1700, 666 Burrard St.
Vancouver, BC V6C 2X8

888-997-6477
www.snipp.com
www.facebook.com/snippinc
twitter.com/snippinc
www.linkedin.com/company/snipp

Company Type: Public
Ticker Symbol: SPN/TSX
Profile: Snipp is a global loyalty & promotions company.
Atul Sabharwal, Co-Founder & Chief Executive Officer
Jaisun Garcha, Chief Financial Officer
Wayne Wong, Chief Technology Officer

Spark Power Group Inc.
#1300, 1315 North Service Rd. East
Oakville, ON L6H 1A7

833-775-7697
sparkpowercorp.com
www.facebook.com/sparkpowercorp
twitter.com/sparkpowercorp
www.linkedin.com/company/spark-power-corp-

Company Type: Public
Ticker Symbol: SPG/TSX
Staff Size: 1,350
Profile: Spark Power Group Inc. provides end-to-end electrical contracting, operations & maintenance services & energy sustainability solutions to other businesses through its subsidiary, Spark Power Corp. This includes equipment sales, renewable & on-site facility services & more.
Richard Jackson, President & CEO
Dan Ardila, Vice-President & CFO
dardila@sparkpower.ca
Grayson Swan, Vice-President, Renewables

Spin Master Ltd.
#200, 225 King St. West
Toronto, ON M5V 3M2

800-622-8339
customercare@spinmaster.com
www.spinmaster.com
www.facebook.com/spinmaster
twitter.com/spinmaster
www.linkedin.com/company/spin-master-ltd-

Company Type: Public
Ticker Symbol: TOY/TSX
Staff Size: 985
Profile: Spin Master is a toy manufacturer, founded in 1994. It is the owner of the Air Hoggs brand, Zoobles & Bakugan. It has also launched 2 children's programs, PAW Patrol & Little Charmers.
Max Rangel, President & CEO
Mark Segal, Executive Vice-President & CFO
Ben Varadi, Executive Vice-President & Chief Creative Officer

StorageVault Canada Inc.
100 Canadian Rd.
Toronto, ON M1R 4Z5

877-622-0205
ir@storagevaultcanada.com
www.storagevaultcanada.com

Company Type: Public
Ticker Symbol: SVI/TSX.V
Profile: StorageVault is a self storage centre company.
Steven Scott, Chief Executive Officer
Iqbal Khan, Chief Financial Officer

Superior Plus Corp.
#401, 200 Wellington St. West
Toronto, ON M5V 3C7

416-346-8050
Fax: 416-340-6030
866-490-7587
investor-relations@superiorplus.com
www.superiorplus.com

Company Type: Public
Ticker Symbol: SPB/TSX
Staff Size: 3,000
Profile: Superior Plus Corp. consists of: Specialty Chemical, including manufacturing & selling; Energy Services, involving the distribution of propane & distillates; & Construction Products distribution.
Luc Desjardins, President & CEO
Beth Summers, Executive Vice-President & CFO
Darren Hribar, Senior Vice-President & Chief Legal Officer

TWC Enterprises Ltd.
55 City Centre Dr.
Mississauga, ON L5B 1M3

905-281-3800
Fax: 905-281-5890
www.twcenterprises.ca

Company Type: Public
Ticker Symbol: TWC/TSX
Staff Size: 500
Profile: TWC owns & operates the ClubLink golf clubs & resorts.
K. Rai Sahi, President & CEO
rsahi@morguard.com
Andrew Tamlin, Chief Financial Officer
atamlin@clublink.ca

Vitalis Extraction Technology Inc.
591 Gaston Ave.
Kelowna, BC V1Y 7E6

250-864-0848
info@vitaliset.com
vitaliset.com
www.facebook.com/VitalisET
twitter.com/vitaliset
www.linkedin.com/company/vitalis-extraction-tech

Company Type: Public
Staff Size: 70
Profile: Founded in 2016, Vitalis is an engineering & manufacturing company producing industrial CO_2 extraction systems for cannabis, hemp, pharmaceuticals & other related industries. It has operations in Canada, Australia, Colombia, Denmark, United Kingdom & Serbia.
Joel Sherlock, Founder & Chief Executive Officer

Waste Connections of Canada
610 Applewood Cres., 2nd Fl.
Vaughan, ON L4K 0C3

905-532-7510
www.wasteconnections.com
www.linkedin.com/company/waste-connections-of-canada
Company Type: Public
Ticker Symbol: WCN/TSX, NYSE
Profile: Waste Connections of Canada is a full-service waste management company. It offers non-hazardous solid waste collection & landfill disposal services. The company serves residential, municipal, commercial & industrial customers located in six Canadian provinces & the District of Columbia in the United States.
Waste Connections of Canada rebranded its operations from Progressive Waste Solutions Ltd. in 2017.
Ronald J. Mittelstaedt, Executive Chair
Worthing Jackman, President & CEO
Mary Anne Whitney, Executive Vice-President & CFO

WELL Health Technologies Corp.
#200, 322 Water St.
Vancouver, BC V6B 1B6

www.well.company
www.linkedin.com/company/wellhealthtechnologiescorp
Company Type: Public
Ticker Symbol: WELL/TSX
Profile: Founded in 2010, WELL is a digital health company that owns & operates primary & executive health clinics in Canada &

the US. It also operates a digital electronic medical records business serving clinics & health systems globally.
Hamed Shahbazi, Chair & Chief Executive Officer
Eva Fong, Chief Financial Officer
Michael Frankel, Chief Medical Officer
Amir Javidan, Chief Operating Officer
Arjun Kumar, Chief Information Officer

WOW Unlimited Media Inc.
#200, 2025 West Broadway
Vancouver, BC V6J 1Z6

www.wowunlimited.co
www.facebook.com/wowunlimited

Company Type: Public
Ticker Symbol: WOW/TSX.V
Staff Size: 240
Profile: WOW Unlimited Media Inc. is an animation production company that is responsible for the creation of feature films, shorts & direct to DVD movies. WOW's operating assets include Frederator Networks & Mainframe Studios.
Michael Hirsh, Chief Executive Officer
Neil Chakravarti, President & COO
John Vandervelde, Executive Vice-President & CFO

Steel & Metal

ADF Group Inc.
300, rue Henry-Bessemer
Terrebonne, QC J6Y 1T3

450-965-1911
Fax: 450-965-8558
800-263-7560
infos@adfgroup.com
adfgroup.com
www.facebook.com/ADFgroupinc
www.linkedin.com/company/adf-group-inc
Company Type: Public
Ticker Symbol: DRX/TSX
Staff Size: 500
Profile: ADF Group Inc. specializes in the design & engineering of connections; fabrication & installation of complex steel structures & heavy steel build-ups; & miscellaneous & architectural metalwork. The company serves the non-residential construction market.
Jean Paschini, Chair & Chief Executive Officer
Pierre Paschini, P.Eng., President & COO
Jean-François Boursier, Chief Financial Officer

Bri-Chem Corp.
27075 Acheson Rd.
Acheson, AB T7X 6B1

780-962-9490
Fax: 780-962-9875
info@brichem.com
www.brichem.com

Company Type: Public
Ticker Symbol: BRY/TSX
Profile: Bri-Chem Corp., formed in 1985, is comprised of the Drilling Fluid Division & the Steel Pipe Division. The Drilling Fluid Division supplies drilling fluids to the oil & gas industry, while the Steel Pipe Division manufactures & provides steel pipe for the energy industry.
Don Caron, Chief Executive Officer
Tony Pagnucco, Chief Financial Officer

Excellon Resources Inc.
#200, 10 King St. East
Toronto, ON M5C 1C3

416-364-1130
Fax: 416-324-6745
844-396-7770
info@excellonresources.com
www.excellonresources.com
twitter.com/exn_resources
www.linkedin.com/company/excellon-resources-inc
Company Type: Public
Ticker Symbol: EXN/TSX
Staff Size: 275
Profile: Excellon Resources is a mining company operating in Durango & Zacatecas States, Mexico, as well as Ontario & Quebec, Canada.
Brendan Cahill, President & CEO
Alfred Colas, Chief Financial Officer
Paul Keller, Chief Operating Officer

Kincora Copper Limited
#400, 837 West Hastings St.
Vancouver, BC V6C 3N6

604-283-1722
888-241-5996
www.kincoracopper.com

Company Type: Public
Ticker Symbol: KCC/TSX.V

Profile: Kincora Copper is a mining exploration & development company with a focus in Australia & Mongolia.
Jonathan (Sam) Spring, President & CEO
Yuying Liang, Chief Financial Officer

Martinrea International Inc.
3210 Langstaff Rd.
Vaughan, ON L4K 5B2

416-749-0314
www.martinrea.com
Other Communications: Investor Relations, Email:
investor@martinrea.com
www.facebook.com/MartinreaInternational
twitter.com/MartinreaInt
www.linkedin.com/company/martinreainternational
Company Type: Public
Ticker Symbol: MRE/TSX
Staff Size: 15,000
Profile: Founded in 2001, Martinrea International Inc. specializes in the production of metal parts, assemblies & modules, & fluid management systems. The company supplies the automotive industry & other industrial sectors. Divisions are located in Canada, the United States, Mexico & Europe.
Pat D'Eramo, President & CEO
Fred Di Tosto, Chief Financial Officer

Russel Metals Inc.
6600 Financial Dr.
Mississauga, ON L5N 7J6

905-819-7777
Fax: 905-819-7409
800-268-0750
info@russelmetals.com
www.russelmetals.com
Company Type: Public
Ticker Symbol: RUS/TSX
Staff Size: 3,000
Profile: The metal processor & distributor operates in North America. The company implemented environmental standards & an ongoing audit process.
John G. Reid, President & CEO
Martin J. Juravsky, Executive Vice-President & CFO

Tree Island Steel Ltd.
3933 Boundary Rd.
Richmond, BC V6V 1T8

604-524-3744
Fax: 604-524-2362
800-663-0955
www.treeisland.com
www.linkedin.com/company/tree-island-steel-ltd-
Company Type: Public
Ticker Symbol: TSL/TSX
Staff Size: 450
Profile: Tree Island Steel manufacturers wire & wire products.
Remy Stachowiak, President & COO
Nancy Davies, Chief Financial Officer & Vice-President, Finance
ndavies@treeisland.com

Velan Inc.
7007, ch de la Côte-de-Liesse
Montréal, QC H4T 1G2

514-748-7743
Fax: 514-748-8635
communications@velan.com
www.velan.com
twitter.com/velaninc
www.linkedin.com/company/velan-inc-
Company Type: Public
Ticker Symbol: VLN/TSX
Staff Size: 1,700
Profile: Velan Inc. manufactures industrial steel valves. Manufacturing plants are located in Canada, the United States, Europe & Asia. Velan valves are used in numerous industries, such as oil & gas; chemical & petrochemical; pulp & paper; mining; & power generation. The company also offers aftermarket services. It is ISO 9001 & ISO 14001 certified, among other certifications.
Yves Leduc, Chief Executive Officer
Bruno Carbanaro, President

Textiles, Apparel & Leather

Aritzia Inc.
#118, 611 Alexander St.
Vancouver, BC V6A 1E1

604-251-3132
855-274-8942
service@aritzia.ca
investors.aritzia.com
www.facebook.com/aritzia
twitter.com/aritzia
Company Type: Public
Ticker Symbol: ATZ/TSX

Profile: Aritzia Inc. designs a wide range of women's apparel & accesories for their collection of exclusive brands to sell under the Aritzia banner.
Brian Hill, Founder & Chief Executive Officer
Jennifer Wong, President, Chief Operating Officer & Corporate Secretary
Todd Ingledew, Chief Financial Officer
Dave MacIver, Chief Information Officer

Canada Goose Holdings Inc.
250 Bowie Ave.
Toronto, ON M6E 4Y2

416-780-9850
ir@canadagoose.com
investor.canadagoose.com
www.facebook.com/canadagoose
twitter.com/canadagoose
www.linkedin.com/company/canada-goose-inc
Company Type: Public
Ticker Symbol: GOOS/TSX, NYSE
Profile: Canada Goose is a winter apparel manufacturer.
Dani Reiss, President & CEO
Jonathan Sinclair, Executive Vice-President & CFO
Carrie Baker, President, North America

Gildan Activewear Inc.
600, boul de Maisonneuve ouest 33e étage
Montréal, QC H3A 3J2

514-735-2023
866-755-2023
communications@gildan.com
gildancorp.com
www.facebook.com/gildancorp
twitter.com/gildancorp
www.linkedin.com/company/gildan
Company Type: Public
Ticker Symbol: GIL/TSX, NYSE
Staff Size: 44,000
Profile: Gildan Activewear manufactures & markets activewear, athletic socks & underwear. The company serves both North American & international markets. Brands include: Gildan, Goldtoe, Anvil, Alstyle, Secret, Silks & American Apparel.
Glenn J. Chamandy, President & CEO
Michael R. Hoffman, President, Sales, Marketing & Distribution
Benito Masi, President, Manufacturing
Rhodri Harries, Exec. Vice-Pres., Chief Financial & Administrative Officer

iFabric Corp.
#1, 525 Denison St.
Markham, ON L3R 1B8

905-752-0566
info@ifabriccorp.com
www.ifabriccorp.com
twitter.com/iFabricCorp
www.linkedin.com/company/ifabric-corp.
Company Type: Public
Ticker Symbol: IFA/NEX
Profile: iFabric Corp. develops a wide range of fabrics for use in medical applications, health care, sports & athletic, military, corporate & consumer, bedding, & linens. This is done through their division Intelligent Fabric Technologies (North America) Inc.
Hylton Karon, President & CEO
Hilton Price, Chief Financial Officer

Intertape Polymer Group Inc. (IPG)
#200, 9999, boul Cavendish
Montréal, QC H4M 2X5

info@itape.com
www.intertapepolymer.com
www.facebook.com/intertape
www.twitter.com/ipgtape
www.linkedin.com/company/intertape-polymer-group
Company Type: Public
Ticker Symbol: ITP/TSX
Staff Size: 3,700
Profile: Intertape Polymer Group Inc. develops, manufactures & markets a variety of specialized polyolefin plastic packaging products & systems for industrial & retail use.
Gregory A.C. Yull, President & CEO
Jeffrey Crystal, Chief Financial Officer
Douglas Nalette, Senior Vice-President, Operations
Shawn Nelson, Senior Vice-President, Sales

Roots Canada
1400 Castlefield Ave.
Toronto, ON M6B 4C4

844-762-2343
investors@roots.com
www.roots.com
www.facebook.com/roots
twitter.com/rootscanada
Company Type: Public
Ticker Symbol: ROOT/TSX

Staff Size: 2,200
Profile: Established in 1973, Roots is a manufacturer of apparel, leather goods, accessories & footwear.
Meghan Roach, Chief Executive Officer
Mona Kennedy, Chief Financial Officer

Unisync Corp.
#1328, 885 West Georgia St.
Vancouver, BC V6C 3E8

833-864-7962
www.unisyncgroup.com
www.linkedin.com/company/unisync
Company Type: Public
Ticker Symbol: UNI/TSX
Profile: Unisync Group produces uniforms, worwear & personal protective apparel under the Hammill brand, & corporate uniforms & image apparel under the York brand.
Matt Graham, Chief Executive Officer
mgraham@unisyncgroup.com
Meen Sathish, Chief Technology Officer
msathish@unisyncgroup.com
Richard Smith, Chief Financial Officer
rsmith@unisyncgroup.com

Transportation & Travel

Air Canada
7373, boul Côte-Vertu ouest
Montréal, QC H4S 1Z3

514-422-7849
Fax: 514-422-7877
shareholders.actionnaires@aircanada.ca
www.aircanada.com
Other Communications: Investors, Email:
investors.investisseurs@aircanada.ca
www.facebook.com/aircanada
twitter.com/aircanada
www.linkedin.com/company/air-canada
Company Type: Public
Ticker Symbol: AC/TSX
Staff Size: 33,000
Profile: Founded in 1937, Air Canada is the country's largest domestic & inter national airline, serving 220 airports on six continents. Air Canada serves over 51 million customers annually.
Michael Rousseau, President & CEO
Lucie Guillemette, Executive Vice-President & Chief Commercial Officer
Amos Kazzaz, Executive Vice-President & Chief Financial Officer

Algoma Central Corporation
#600, 63 Church St.
St Catharines, ON L2R 3C4

905-687-7888
inquiry@algonet.com
www.algonet.com
twitter.com/algomacentral
www.linkedin.com/company/algoma-central-corporation
Company Type: Public
Ticker Symbol: ALC/TSX
Staff Size: 1,600
Profile: Algoma Central Corporation is a Canadian-flag ship owner on the Great Lakes - St Lawrence Waterway. The company owns both dry-bulk carriers & product tankers. As well as the operation of vessels, ship & diesel engine repair & fabrication are part of Algoma Central's operations. Algoma Central Corporation also owns Algoma Central Hotels & Algoma Central Properties Inc. These businesses own & manage commercial real estate properties in St Catharines, Waterloo & Sault Ste Marie.
Gregg Ruhl, President & CEO
Peter D. Winkley, Chief Financial Officer

AutoCanada Inc.
#200, 15511 - 123rd Ave. NW
Edmonton, AB T5V 0C3

Fax: 780-447-0651
info@autocan.ca
www.autocan.ca
www.facebook.com/autocan
twitter.com/autocanada
www.linkedin.com/company/autocanada
Company Type: Public
Ticker Symbol: ACQ/TSX
Staff Size: 4,200
Profile: AutoCanada is an automobile dealership group. It operates franchised dealerships in Nova Scotia, New Brunswick, Ontario, Manitoba, Alberta & British Columbia.
Michael Rawluk, President
Mike Borys, Chief Financial Officer
Peter Hong, Chief Strategy Officer & General Counsel

Bombardier Inc.
800, boul René-Lévesque ouest
Montréal, QC H3B 1Y8

514-861-9481
Fax: 514-861-2420
bombardier.com
www.facebook.com/bombardierjets
twitter.com/bombardier
www.linkedin.com/company/bombardier

Company Type: Public
Ticker Symbol: BBD.A, BBD.B/TSX
Staff Size: 60,000
Profile: Manufacturers of railroad equipment, aircraft, aircraft engines & engine parts, aircraft parts & auxiliary equipment, various transportation equipment; Personal credit institutions; Real estate land subdividers & developers.
Éric Martel, President & CEO
Bart Demosky, Senior Vice-President & CFO
Daniel Brennan, Senior Vice-President, People & Sustainability

BRP Inc.
726, rue Saint-Joseph
Valcourt, QC J0E 2L0

450-532-2211
www.brp.com
www.facebook.com/brpinfo
twitter.com/brpnews
www.linkedin.com/company/brp

Company Type: Public
Ticker Symbol: DOO/TSX
Staff Size: 8,700
Profile: BRP designs, manufactures, distributes & markets motorized recreational vehicles & powersports engines.
José Boisjoli, President & CEO
Sébastien Martel, Chief Financial Officer
Martin Langelier, General Counsel & Vice-President, Public Affairs

CAE Inc.
8585, ch de Côte-de-Liesse
Montréal, QC H4T 1G6

514-341-6780
investor.relations@cae.com
www.cae.com
www.facebook.com/cae.inc
twitter.com/cae_inc
www.linkedin.com/company/cae

Company Type: Public
Ticker Symbol: CAE/TSX, NYSE
Staff Size: 10,500
Profile: CAE Inc. serves the civil aviation & defense forces, through the provision of simulation & modelling technologies, as well as integrated training solutions. The company's civil aviation & military training centres are located throughout the world. CAE Inc. has been granted the BOMA Go Green plan certification, & has implemented environmental programs such as the management of residual materials, recycling, pollution prevention & residue exchange.
Marc Parent, President & CEO
Sonya Branco, Chief Financial Officer & Vice-President, Finance

Canadian National Railway Company (CN)
935, rue de La Gauchetière ouest
Montréal, QC H3B 2M9

888-888-5909
www.cn.ca
www.facebook.com/cnrail
twitter.com/cnrailway
www.linkedin.com/company/cn

Company Type: Public
Ticker Symbol: CNR/TSX; CNI/NYSE
Staff Size: 24,500
Profile: Crossing the North American continent with over 21,000 route miles of track, the Canadian National Railway Company serves ports on the Atlantic, Pacific & Gulf coasts.
Jean-Jacques Ruest, President & CEO
Ghislain Houle, Executive Vice-President & CFO
Rob Reilly, Executive Vice-President & COO

Canadian Pacific Railway Limited (CP)
7550 Ogden Dale Rd. SE
Calgary, AB T2C 4X9

888-333-6370
www.cpr.ca
www.facebook.com/canadian.pacific
twitter.com/canadianpacific
www.linkedin.com/company/canadian-pacific-railway

Company Type: Public
Ticker Symbol: CP/TSX, NYSE
Staff Size: 12,000
Profile: The transcontinental carrier operates in North America. Canadian Pacific provides freight transportation services, supply chain expertise & logistics solutions. The company incorporates technology & environmental practices for safety & efficiency.

Keith Creel, President & CEO
Nadeem Velani, Executive Vice-President & CFO

Cargojet Inc.
2281 North Sheridan Way
Mississauga, ON L5K 2S3

800-753-1051
cs@cargojet.com
cargojet.com
twitter.com/CargoJetAirways
www.linkedin.com/company/cargojet-income-fund

Company Type: Public
Ticker Symbol: CJT/TSX
Staff Size: 800
Profile: Cargojet provides overnight air cargo services across North America.
Ajay K. Virmani, President & CEO
John Kim, Chief Financial Officer
Jamie Porteous, Executive Vice-President & Chief Commercial Officer

Chorus Aviation Inc.
#100, 3 Spectacle Lake Dr.
Dartmouth, NS B3B 1W8

902-873-5000
investorsinfo@chorusaviation.ca
chorusaviation.ca

Company Type: Public
Ticker Symbol: CHR.A, CHR.B/TSX
Staff Size: 2,800
Profile: Incorporated in September 2010, Chorus Aviation is the successor to Jazz Air Income Fund. Jazz Aviation LP is wholly owned by Chorus Aviation.
Joseph D. Randell, President & CEO
Jolene Mahody, Executive Vice-President & Chief Strategy Officer
Gary Osborne, Chief Financial Officer
Laurel Clark, Vice-President, Corporate Human Resources

ElectraMeccanica Vehicles Corp.
102 East 1st Ave.
Vancouver, BC V5T 1A4

604-428-7656
info@electrameccanica.com
electrameccanica.com
www.facebook.com/EMVsolo
twitter.com/ElectraMecc

Company Type: Public
Ticker Symbol: SOLO/NASDAQ
Profile: ElectraMeccanica designs & manufactures electric vehicles. Its flagship vehicle is a single-seater called the SOLO.
Paul Rivera, Chief Executive Officer
Isaac Moss, Chief Administrative Officer
isaac.moss@electrameccanica.com
Bal Bhullar, Chief Financial Officer
bal@electrameccanica.com

Helijet International Inc.
Vancouver International Airport
5911 Airport Rd. South
Richmond, BC V7B 1B5

604-273-4688
800-665-4354
emailus@teslaexploration.com
helijet.com
Other Communications: Charter, Email: charters@helijet.com
www.facebook.com/helijet
twitter.com/helijet
www.linkedin.com/company/helijet-international-inc

Company Type: Private
Profile: Helijet launched Canada's first scheduled helicopter service in 1986. The company has operations in Richmond, Vancouver, Victoria, Nanaimo, Prince Rupert & Haida Gwaii. Helijet has a fleet of medium & large helicopters, as well as a medically-equipped & corporate Learjet. The company went private in 2019.
Daniel Sitnam, President & CEO
dsitnam@helijet.com
Frank Inouye, Chief Financial Officer

Logistec Corporation
600, rue de la Gauchetiere ouest
Montréal, QC H3B 4L2

514-844-9381
888-844-9381
info@logistec.com
www.logistec.com
www.facebook.com/logisteccorp
twitter.com/LogistecGroup
www.linkedin.com/company/logisteccorporation

Company Type: Public
Ticker Symbol: LGT.A, LGT.B/TSX
Staff Size: 2,700
Profile: Logistec Corporation & its subsidiaries serve the marine

& industrial sectors. Cargo-handling services are offered at port terminals situated in eastern Canada, the United States & on the Great Lakes. Other services include agency services to foreign ship-owners & operators at Canadian ports, marine transportation services & on-site decontamination services.
Madeleine Paquin, President & CEO
Jean-Claude Dugas, Chief Financial Officer
Ingrid Stefancic, Vice-President, Corporate & Legal Services

Magellan Aerospace Corporation
3160 Derry Rd. East
Mississauga, ON L4T 1A9

905-677-1889
Fax: 905-677-5658
magellan.corporate@magellan.aero
magellan.aero
Other Communications: Investor Relations, Email: ir@magellan.aero
www.linkedin.com/company/magellan-aerospace

Company Type: Public
Ticker Symbol: MAL/TSX
Staff Size: 3,400
Profile: Magellan is engaged in designing, engineering & manufacturing aeroengine & aerostructure assemblies & components. The company serves the aerospace & military markets. Operating units are located in Canada, the United States & the United Kingdom.
Phillip Underwood, President & CEO
Elena Milantoni, Chief Financial Officer
Jim Powell, Vice-President, North American Operations

Mullen Group
#121A, 31 Southridge Dr.
Okotoks, AB T1S 2N3

403-995-5200
Fax: 403-995-5296
866-995-7711
ir@mullen-group.com
www.mullen-group.com

Company Type: Public
Ticker Symbol: MTL/TSX
Profile: Mullen Group serves western Canada's oil & natural gas industry by providing specialized transportation & related services. The company also provides management & financial services as well as technology & systems support to the independently operated businesses that it owns.
Murray K. Mullen, Chair, President & CEO
P. Stephen Clark, Chief Financial Officer
Richard Maloney, Senior Vice-President

TFI International Inc.
#500, 8801, rte Transcanadienne
Saint-Lauren, QC H4S 1Z6

514-331-4000
Fax: 514-337-4200
tfiintl.com
www.linkedin.com/company/tfi-international-inc.

Company Type: Public
Ticker Symbol: TFII/TSX
Staff Size: 16,400
Profile: TFI International is a transportation & logistics industry, operating across North American through its subsidiaries. The company services the package & courier, less-than-truckload, truckload & logistics industries.
Alain Bédard, Chair, President & CEO
David Saperstein, Chief Financial Officer

Titanium Transportation Group, Inc.
32 Simpsons Rd.
Bolton, ON L7E 1G9

905-266-3010
www.ttgi.com

Company Type: Public
Ticker Symbol: TTR/TSX
Staff Size: 1,100
Profile: Titanium Transportation is a trucking, transportation logistics & warehouse company.
Ted Daniel, President
Marilyn Daniel, Chief Operating Officer
marilyn.daniel@ttgi.com

Tornado Global Hydrovacs
#510, 7015 Macleod Trail SE
Calgary, AB T2H 2K6

403-742-6121
877-340-8141
www.tornadotrucks.com
www.facebook.com/TornadoHydrovac
twitter.com/TornadoHydrovac
www.linkedin.com/company/tornadohydrovac

Company Type: Public
Ticker Symbol: TGH/TSX.V
Profile: The company designs & produces hydrovac trucks.
Bill Rollins, President & CEO

Al Robertson, Chief Financial Officer

Transat A.T. Inc.
#600, 300, rue Léo-Pariseau
Montréal, QC H2X 4C2

800-387-2672
customerrelations@transat.com
www.transat.com
www.facebook.com/airtransatcanada
twitter.com/airtransat
www.linkedin.com/company/airtransat

Company Type: Public
Ticker Symbol: TRZ.B/TSX
Staff Size: 2,000
Profile: Transat A.T. is an integrated international tourism company specializing in holiday travel to 60 destinations in 26 countries.
Annick Guérard, President & CEO
Denis Pétrin, Chief Financial Officer & Vice-President, Finance & Administration
Bernard Bussières, Vice-President, General Counsel & Corporate Secretary
Christophe Hennebelle, Vice-President, Human Resources & Corporate Affairs

WestJet Airlines Ltd.
22 Aerial Pl. NE
Calgary, AB T2E 3J1

403-539-7594
Fax: 403-444-2604
888-937-8538
investor_relations@westjet.com
www.westjet.com
Other Communications: TTY: 877-952-0100; Investor Relations, Phone: 877-493-7853
www.facebook.com/westjet
www.twitter.com/westjet
www.linkedin.com/company/westjet

Company Type: Public
Ticker Symbol: WJA/TSX
Staff Size: 14,000
Profile: Founded in 1996, Westjet provides schedules & charter air service toover 100 destinations. Westjet is the second-largest Canadian air carrier, behind Air Canada, & the ninth-largest air carrier in North America.
Edward Sims, President & CEO
Harry Taylor, Executive Vice-President & CFO

Utilities

Algonquin Power & Utilities Corp.
354 Davis Rd.
Oakville, ON L6J 2X1

905-465-4500
Fax: 905-465-4514
investorrelations@apucorp.com
www.algonquinpower.com
twitter.com/aqn_utilities
www.linkedin.com/company/algonquin-power-&-utilities-corp

Company Type: Public
Ticker Symbol: AQN/TSX
Staff Size: 2,200
Profile: Algonquin Power & Utilities Corp. is a renewable energy & regulated utility company. Its operating subsidiaries are Algonquin Power Company & Liberty Utilities. Through these subsidiaries, Algonquin Power & Utilities Corp. invests in sustainable utility distribution businesses as well as hydroelectric, wind, & solar power facilities.
Arun Banskota, President & CEO
Johnny Johnston, Chief Operating Officer
Arthur Kacprzak, Chief Financial Officer
Kirsten Olsen, Chief Human Resource Officer

AltaGas Ltd.
#1700, 355 - 4th Ave. SW
Calgary, AB T2P 0J1

403-691-7575
888-890-2715
www.altagas.ca

Company Type: Public
Ticker Symbol: ALA/TSX
Profile: AltaGas is involved in power, natural gas & the regulated utilities sectors, with a focus on renewable energy sources.
Randy Crawford, President & CEO
Corine Bushfield, Executive Vice-President & Chief Administrative Officer
D. James Harbilas, Executive Vice-President & CFO

ATCO Ltd.
5302 Forand St. SW
Calgary, AB T3E 8B4

403-292-7500
Fax: 403-292-7532
investorrelations@atco.com
www.atco.com
www.facebook.com/atcogroup
twitter.com/atco
www.linkedin.com/company/atco-group

Company Type: Public
Ticker Symbol: ACO.X/TSX
Staff Size: 6,100
Profile: ATCO Ltd. delivers business solutions with companies engaged in the following: utilities, including natural gas & electricity transmission & distribution; energy, including power generation & liquids extraction; logistics & structures, included manufacturing & noise abatement; & technologies.
Nancy C. Southern, Chair & Chief Executive Officer
Dennis DeChamplain, Senior Vice-President & CFO

Atlantic Power Corporation
#155, 3 Allied Dr.
Dedham, MA 02026 USA

617-977-2400
info@atlanticpower.com
www.atlanticpower.com
Other Communications: Investor Relations, Phone: 617-977-2700

Company Type: Public
Profile: Atlantic Power Corporation is a power & infrastructure company. The company's portfolio of assets are located in Canada & the United States. Electricity from Atlantic Power's generation projects are sold to utilities & commercial customers. In 2011, Atlantic Power acquired Capital Power Income L.P.
James J. Moore, Jr., President & CEO
Jamie D'Angelo, Chief Administrative Officer
Brian Dee, Vice-President, Finance

Boralex Inc.
36, rue Lajeunesse
Kingsey Falls, QC J0A 1B0

819-363-6363
Fax: 819-363-6399
info@boralex.com
www.boralex.com
www.facebook.com/BoralexInc
twitter.com/boralexinc
www.linkedin.com/company/boralex

Company Type: Public
Ticker Symbol: BLX, BLX.DB/TSX
Profile: Boralex Inc. is a power producer focusing on hydroelectric, thermal, wind & solar power.
Patrick Lemaire, President & CEO
Bruno Guilmette, Vice-President & CFO

Canadian Solar Inc.
545 Speedvale Ave. West
Guelph, ON N1K 1E6

519-837-1881
Fax: 519-837-2550
www.canadiansolar.com
www.facebook.com/Canadian.Solar.CSIQ
twitter.com/Canadian_Solar
www.linkedin.com/company/canadian-solar-inc-

Company Type: Public
Ticker Symbol: CSIQ/NASDAQ
Staff Size: 12,774
Profile: Founded in 2001, Canadian Solar is a global energy provider working in 20 countries & regions. It has manufacturing facilities in Canada, China, Brazil & South East Asian countries.
Shawn Qu, Chair & Chief Executive Officer
Ismael Guerrero Arias, Corporate Vice-President & President, Energy Business
Yan Zhuang, President, CSI Solar
Huifeng Chang, Senior Vice-President & CFO

Capital Power Corporation
#1200, 10423 - 101st St. NW
Edmonton, AB T5H 0E9

780-392-5100
info@capitalpower.com
www.capitalpower.com
www.facebook.com/capitalpowercommunity
twitter.com/capitalpower
www.linkedin.com/company/capital-power

Company Type: Public
Ticker Symbol: CPX/TSX
Staff Size: 800
Profile: Capital Power Corporation is a power producer with sixteen facilities throughout North America. Capital Power is also developing wind generation projects in Ontario, Alberta & British Columbia.
Brian Vaasjo, President & CEO

Sandra Haskins, Chief Financial Officer & Senior Vice-President, Finance
Kate Chisholm, Q.C., Chief Sustainability Officer & Senior Vice-President, Planning & Stakeholder Relations
Jacquie Pylypiuk, Senior Vice-President, People, Culture & Technology

CU Inc.
Also Known As: Canadian Utilities Limited
5302 Forand St. SW
Calgary, AB T3E 8B4

403-292-7500
Fax: 403-292-7532
www.canadianutilities.com

Company Type: Public
Ticker Symbol: CU/TSX
Staff Size: 5,000
Profile: CU Inc., an ATCO company, is involved in natural gas & electricity transmission & distribution, as well as power generation.
Siegfried W. Kiefer, President & CEO
Dennis A. DeChamplain, Executive Vice-President & CFO

Emera Inc.
1223 Lower Water St.
Halifax, NS B3J 3S8

902-450-0507
888-450-0507
info@emera.com
www.emera.com
Other Communications: Investor Relations, Email: investors@emera.com

Company Type: Public
Ticker Symbol: EMA/TSX
Staff Size: 7,000
Profile: The holding company is involved in the energy sector. Emera Inc.'s investments include Nova Scotia Power Inc., Emera Energy, New Mexico Gas Co., People Gas, Emera New Brunswick, Emera Technologies, Emera Newfoundland & Labrador, Emera Caribbean.
Scott Balfour, President & CEO
Greg Blunden, Chief Financial Officer
Bruce Marchand, Chief Legal & Compliance Officer
Mike Roberts, Chief Human Resources Officer

Etrion Corporation
4, rue du Commerce
Geneva, 1204 Switzerland

info@etrion.com
etrion.com

Company Type: Public
Ticker Symbol: ETX/TSX, OMX
Profile: Etrion Corporation is an independent power producer that owns & operates renewable assets.
Marco A. Northland, Chief Executive Officer
Christian Lacueva, Chief Financial Officer

Fortis Inc.
Fortis Place
PO Box 8837, #1100, 5 Springdale St.
St. John's, NL A1B 3T2

709-737-2800
Fax: 709-737-5307
investorrelations@fortisinc.com
www.fortisinc.com
twitter.com/fortis_na
www.linkedin.com/company/fortis-inc.

Company Type: Public
Ticker Symbol: FTS/TSX
Staff Size: 9,000
Profile: Fortis Inc. is an international distribution utility holding company, which serves gas & electricity customers. The company sold its property division (which included hotels & commercial real estate in Canada) in January 2015.
Barry V. Perry, President & CEO
Jocelyn H. Perry, Executive Vice-President & CFO
James R. Reid, Executive Vice-President & Chief Legal Officer

FuelPositive Corporation
82 Richmond St. East
Toronto, ON M5C 1P1

416-535-8395
Fax: 416-535-4043
eestorcorp.com

Company Type: Public
Ticker Symbol: ESU/TSX.V
Profile: FuelPositive is a provider of electrical energy storage & related technologies.
Ian Clifford, President & CEO
ian.clifford@eeastorcorp.com
Jing Peng, Chief Financial Officer

H2O Innovation Inc.
#340, 330, rue St-Vallier est
Québec, QC G1K 9C5

418-688-0170
Fax: 418-688-9259
888-688-0170
service.ca@h2oinnovation.com
www.h2oinnovation.com
twitter.com/h2o_innovation
www.linkedin.com/company/h2o-innovation

Company Type: Public
Ticker Symbol: HEO/TSX.V
Profile: H2O Innovation is a developer of water treatment solutions. Its clients include municipalities, as well as energy & mining companies.
Frédéric Dugré, President & CEO
Marc Blanchet, Chief Financial Officer

HTC Purenergy Inc.
Also Known As: HTC Extraction Systems
#002, 2305 Victoria Ave.
Regina, SK S4P 0S7

306-352-6132
Fax: 306-545-3262
lpk@htcextraction.com
htcextraction.com

Company Type: Public
Ticker Symbol: HTC/TSX
Profile: The company hemp biomass extraction & formulation company.
Lionel Kambeitz, Chair & Chief Executive Officer
Jeff Allison, Senior Vice-President & Chief Financial Officer

Hydro One Networks Inc.
South Tower
483 Bay St., 8th Fl.
Toronto, ON M5G 2P5

416-345-5000
877-955-1155
customercommunications@hydroone.com
www.hydroone.com
Other Communications: Investor Relations, Email:
investor.relations@hydroone.com
www.facebook.com/hydrooneofficial
twitter.com/hydroone
www.linkedin.com/company/hydro-one

Company Type: Public
Ticker Symbol: H/TSX
Staff Size: 5,400
Profile: Hydro One is the provider of power to the province of Ontario.
In July 2017, Hydro One began the acquisition process of Avista Corporation (a U.S. electricity & natural gas utilities company).
Mark Poweska, President & CEO

Innergex Renewable Energy Inc.
1225, rue Saint-Charles ouest, 10e étage
Longueuil, QC J4K 0B9

450-928-2550
Fax: 450-928-2544
info@innergex.com
www.innergex.com
Other Communications: Vancouver Office, Phone:
604-633-9990, Fax: 604-633-9991
www.facebook.com/Innergex
twitter.com/innergex_ine
www.linkedin.com/company/innergex-energie-renouvelable-inc

Company Type: Public
Ticker Symbol: INE/TSX
Profile: Innergex Renewable Energy develops & operates renewable power generating facilities. Operations are carried out in British Columbia, Ontario, Québec & Idaho, USA. The company focuses upon the wind power, solar power & hydroelectric sectors.
Michel Letellier, President & CEO
Jean-François Neault, Chief Financial Officer
jperron@innergex.com
Jay Sutton, Senior Vice-President, Construction & Engineering
Matt Kennedy, Vice-President, Environment

Keyera Corp.
West Tower, Sun Life Plaza
#200, 144 - 4th Ave. SW
Calgary, AB T2P 3N4

403-205-8300
Fax: 403-205-8318
888-699-4853
ir@keyera.com
www.keyera.com
www.linkedin.com/company/keyera

Company Type: Public
Ticker Symbol: KEY/TSX
Staff Size: 900
Profile: Keyera is engaged in natural gas gathering &

processing. The company also transports, stores & markets natural gas liquids. Activities are conducted in the Western Canada Sedimentary Basin.
Dean Setoguchi, President & CEO
Bradley W. Lock, Senior Vice-President & COO
Eileen Marikar, Senior Vice-President & CFO

MAXIM Power Corp.
Also Known As: MAXIM
#1800, 715 - 5th Ave. SW
Calgary, AB T2P 2X6

403-263-3021
Fax: 403-263-9125
maxim@maximpowercorp.com
maximpowercorp.com
Other Communications: Investor Relations, Email:
investors@maximpowercorp.com

Company Type: Public
Ticker Symbol: MXG/TSX
Profile: MAXIM Power Corp. is an independent power producer. The company is involved in the acquisition, development, ownership & operation of environmentally responsible power projects. Its assets include coal & natural gas powered generators in western Canada, the United States & France.
Bruce Chernoff, Chair & Chief Executive Officer
Robert (Bob) Emmott, Executive Vice-President & COO
Kyle Mitton, Chief Financial Officer & Vice-President, Corporate Development

Northland Power Inc.
30 St Clair Ave. West, 12th Fl.
Toronto, ON M4V 3A1

416-962-6262
investorrelations@northlandpower.ca
www.northlandpower.ca
Other Communications: Investor Relations, Phone:
647-288-1019
twitter.com/northlandpower
www.linkedin.com/company/northland-power-inc-

Company Type: Public
Ticker Symbol: NPI/TSX
Staff Size: 1,150
Profile: Northland Power Inc. is engaged in the development of wind, solar, run-of-river hydro projects & additional power generation opportunities. The company's assets include facilities that produce electricity form natural gas & renewable resources such as biomass, solar & wind.
Mike Crawley, President & CEO
Pauline Alimchandani, Chief Financial Officer
Rachel Stephenson, Chief People Officer

Polaris Infrastructure Inc.
#309, 7 St Thomas St.
Toronto, ON M5S 2B7

647-245-7199
info@polarisinfrastructure.com
polarisinfrastructure.com

Company Type: Public
Ticker Symbol: PIF/TSX
Profile: Polaris Infrastructure Inc. is a renewable energy company that acquires, explores, develops & operates geothermal properties in Latin America.
Marc Murnaghan, Chief Executive Officer
Anton Jelic, Chief Financial Officer

Synex International Inc.
#101, 1444 Alberni St., 4th Fl.
Vancouver, BC V6G 2Z4

604-688-8271
Fax: 604-688-1286
synex.com

Company Type: Public
Ticker Symbol: SXI/TSX
Profile: Synex International Inc. has two wholly owned subsidiary companies: Synex Energy Resources Ltd & Sigma Engineering Ltd. The company covers the development, ownership & operation of electric power facilities & the consulting engineering & environmental services related to the hydroelectric industry.
Daniel Russell, Chief Executive Officer

TC Energy
450 - 1st St. SW
Calgary, AB T2P 5H1

403-920-2000
Fax: 403-920-2200
800-661-3805
www.tcenergy.com
www.facebook.com/TCEnergyCorporation
twitter.com/TCEnergy
www.linkedin.com/company/tcenergy

Company Type: Public
Ticker Symbol: TRP/TSX, NYSE
Staff Size: 7,500

Profile: TC Energy is engaged in the development & operation of energy infrastructure, including natural gas & oil pipelines, power generation & gas storage facilities in North America.
François Poirier, President & CEO
Stan Chapman, Executive Vice-President & President, U.S. Natural Gas Pipelines
Bevin Wirzba, Executive Vice-President & President, Liquids Pipelines
Donald R. Marchand, Executive Vice-President & CFO

Topaz Energy Corp.
#2900, 250 - 6th Ave.
Calgary, AB T2P 3H7

587-747-4830
info@topazenergy.ca
topazenergy.ca

Company Type: Public
Ticker Symbol: TPZ/TSX
Profile: Topaz is a royalty & energy infrastructure company.
Marty Staples, President & CEO
Cheree Stephenson, CFO & Vice-President, Finance

TransAlta Corporation
PO Box 1900 Stn. M, , 110 - 12th Ave. SW
Calgary, AB T2P 2M1

403-267-7110
www.transalta.com
Other Communications: Investor Relations, Email:
investor_relations@transalta.com
www.facebook.com/transalta
twitter.com/transalta
www.linkedin.com/company/transalta

Company Type: Public
Ticker Symbol: TA/TSX
Staff Size: 1,400
Profile: TransAlta Corporation is engaged in coal & gas-fired generation. The company carries out its activities in Canada, the United States, Mexico & Australia.
The company works to limit environmental impact by focusing growth on renewable generation methods. It meets ISO 14001 standards.
John Kousinioris, President & CEO
Todd Stack, Chief Financial Officer & Vice-President, Finance

TransAlta Renewables Inc.
PO Box 1900 Stn. M, , 110 - 12th Ave. SW
Edmonton, AB T2P 2M1

403-267-7110
800-387-3598
investor_relations@transalta.com
www.transalta.com
www.facebook.com/transalta
twitter.com/transalta
www.linkedin.com/company/transalta

Company Type: Public
Ticker Symbol: RNW/TSX
Profile: TransAlta Renewables is a section of TransAlta Corporation, a coal & gas-fired generation provider. The company specializes in renewable power generation facilities.
Todd Stack, President
Brent Ward, Chief Financial Officer

Stock Exchanges

Alpha Exchange Inc.
c/o TMX Group, The Exhange Tower
130 King St. West
Toronto, ON M5X 1J2

Tel: 647-259-0405; *Toll-Free:* 888-873-8392
www.tsx.com/trading/tsx-alpha-exchange
Other Contact Information: Alternate Emails:
businessdevelopment@tmx.com; trading_sales@tmx.com
Also Known As: TSX Alpha Exchange
Ownership: A subsidiary of Alpha Trading Systems Limited Partnership

Alpha Trading Systems Limited Partnership
#300, 100 Adelaide St. West
Toronto, ON M5H 1S3

Tel: 416-947-4700; *Fax:* 416-947-4662
Toll-Free: 877-421-2369
www.tsx.com/trading/tsx-alpha-exchange
Other Contact Information: Alternate Emails:
businessdevelopment@tmx.com; trading_sales@tmx.com;
marketdata@tmx.com

Also Known As: Alpha Group; Alpha
Ownership: A limited partner of TMX Group Limited, Toronto, ON

Canadian Securities Exchange (CSE)
#7210, 100 King St. West
Toronto, ON M5X 1E1

Tel: 416-572-2000; Fax: 416-572-4160
info@thecse.com
thecse.com
Other Contact Information: Alternate Emails:
listings@thecse.com; trading@thecse.com
www.instagram.com/canadiansecuritiesexchange;
www.youtube.com/c/CSETV;
www.facebook.com/CanadianSecuritiesExchange;
twitter.com/CSE_News
Former Name: Canadian National Stock Exchange; Canadian
Trading & Quotation System Inc.
Ownership: Owned & operated by CNSX Markets Inc.
Year Founded: 2004

Canadian Unlisted Board Inc. (CUB)
Toronto Stock Exchange, The Exchange Tower, c/o Trading
Services
130 King St. West
Toronto, ON M5X 1J2

Tel: 416-947-4705
cubadmin@cub.ca
www.cub.ca
Ownership: wholly owned by TSX Venture Exchange
Year Founded: 2000

CanDeal.ca, Inc.
#1200, 50 Bay St.
Toronto, ON M5J 3A5

Toll-Free: 866-422-6332
sales@candeal.com
www.candeal.ca
Other Contact Information: Support Email:
support@candeal.com
twitter.com/CanDeal
Ownership: Partially owned by TMX Group Limited, Toronto,
ON

ICE Futures Canada, Inc.
850A Pembina Hwy.
Winnipeg, MB R3M 2M7

Tel: 204-925-5000; Fax: 204-943-5448
www.theice.com/futures-us
www.facebook.com/IntercontinentalExchange;
twitter.com/ICE_Markets
Former Name: Winnipeg Commodity Exchange Inc.; Winnipeg
Grains & Produce Exchange
Ownership: A wholly owned subsidiary of
IntercontinentalExchange (ICE), Atlanta, GA, USA
Year Founded: 1887

Montréal Exchange Inc. (MX)/Bourse de Montréal Inc.
CP 37
#1800, 1190, av des Canadiens-de-Montréal
Montréal, QC H3B 0G7

Tél: 514-871-2424; Téléc: 514-871-3514
Ligne sans frais: 800-361-5353
info@tmx.com
m-x.ca
Other Contact Information: Alternate Emails:
samsupport@m-x.ca; finances@m-x.ca; marketdata@tmx.com;
reg@m-x.ca; legal@m-x.ca
www.facebook.com/montrealexchange;
twitter.com/MtlExchange
Ownership: A subsidiary of TMX Group Limited, Toronto, ON
Year Founded: 1874

Natural Gas Exchange Inc. (NGX)
#320, 607 - 8th Ave. SW
Calgary, AB T2P 0A7

Tel: 403-508-1300; Toll-Free: 888-NGX-5888
sales-icengx@theice.com
www.theice.com/ngx/overview
Other Contact Information: NGX Help Desk & Operations, Email:
to-icengx@theice.com
Ownership: Wholly owned by Intercontinental Exchange (ICE)
Year Founded: 1994

NEO Exchange Inc.
#400, 155 University Ave.
Toronto, ON M5H 3B7

Tel: 416-933-5900; Toll-Free: 844-567-6424
info@neostockexchange.com
www.neo.inc
Other Contact Information: Listing Inquiries, Email:
neolistingssales@neostockexchange.com; Trading Inquiries:
neoexchangeoperations@neostockexchange.com
www.instagram.com/neo_exchange;
www.youtube.com/c/NEOExchange;
www.facebook.com/theNEOExchange;
twitter.com/neo_exchange

Former Name: Aequitas NEO Exchange Inc.
Also Known As: NEO
Ownership: A subsidiary of Aequitas Innovations Inc., Toronto,
ON
Year Founded: 2014

NEX
Filing Office
PO Box 11633
#2700, 650 West Georgia St.
Vancouver, BC V6B 4N9

Tel: 604-689-3334; Fax: 604-844-7502
Toll-Free: 866-344-5639
nex@tsx.com
apps.tmx.com/en/nex
Former Name: NEX Board
Ownership: A separate board of TSX Venture Exchange, which
is a subsidiary of TMX Group Limited, Toronto, ON
Year Founded: 2003

TMX Group Limited
#300, 100 Adelaide St. West
Toronto, ON M5H 1S3

Tel: 416-947-4700; Fax: 416-947-4662
Toll-Free: 888-873-8392
info@tmx.com
www.tmx.com
Other Contact Information: Investor Relations, Phone:
416-947-4277, Email: tmxshareholder@tmx.com
www.facebook.com/thetmxgroup; twitter.com/TMXGroup
Former Name: TSX Group Inc.; Maple Group Acquisition
Corporation
Assets: $32,359,700,000 Year End: 20191231
Revenues: $806,900,000 Year End: 20191231

The Toronto Stock Exchange (TSX)
The Exchange Tower
PO Box 450
130 King St. West
Toronto, ON M5X 1J2

Tel: 416-947-4700; Toll-Free: 888-873-8392
info@tmx.com
www.tsx.com
Other Contact Information: Alternate Emails:
businessdevelopment@tmx.com; trading_sales@tmx.com;
marketdata@tmx.com;
www.facebook.com/tmxmoney; twitter.com/TMXGroup
Ownership: A subsidiary of TMX Group Limited, Toronto, ON
Year Founded: 1861

TSX Venture Exchange
Head Office
685 Centre St. SW
Calgary, AB T2G 1S5

Tel: 403-218-2800; Fax: 403-237-0450
Toll-Free: 888-873-8392
businessdevelopment@tsx.com
www.tsx.com
Other Contact Information: TMX Equity Trading Account
Management, Email: trading_sales@tsx.com; Compliance &
Disclosure, Email: complianceanddisclosure@tsxventure.com
www.facebook.com/tmxmoney; twitter.com/TMXGroup
Former Name: Canadian Venture Exchange
Ownership: A subsidiary of TMX Group Limited, Toronto, ON

Trust Companies

All Nations Trust Company (ANTCO)
520 Chief Eli LaRue Way
Kamloops, BC V2H 1H1

Tel: 778-471-4110; Fax: 250-372-2585
Toll-Free: 800-663-2959
antco@antco.ca
www.antco.ca
www.facebook.com/102487614784; twitter.com/AllNationsTrust
Ownership: Private. Aboriginal-owned
Year Founded: 1984
Assets: $42,277,013 Year End: 20200331

The Bank of Nova Scotia Trust Company
Scotia Plaza
44 King St. West
Toronto, ON M5H 1H1

Tel: 416-866-6161; Fax: 416-866-3750
scotiawealthmanagement.com/ca/en/home/scotiatrust.html
Also Known As: Scotiatrust
Ownership: Private. Subsidiary of The Bank of Nova Scotia
Year Founded: 1993

BMO Trust Company
First Canadian Place
100 King St. West
Toronto, ON M5X 1A9

Toll-Free: 855-834-2558
www.bmo.com/privatebanking/our-services/trust-estate
Former Name: The Trust Company of Bank of Montréal
Also Known As: Advisor's Advantage Trust (AAT)
Ownership: Wholly owned subsidiary of Bank of Montreal.
Member of BMO Financial Group.

BNY Trust Company of Canada
#650, 1001, boul de Maisonneuve ouest
Montréal, QC H3A 3C8

Tel: 514-228-8640
www.bnymellon.com/ca/en.html
Ownership: Foreign. A wholly owned subsidiary of The Bank of
New York Mellon Financial Corporation, New York City, NY,
USA
Year Founded: 2001

Caledon Trust Company
#2500, 200 Front St. West
Toronto, ON M5V 3K2

Tel: 416-361-4561; Fax: 416-361-0294
www.caledontrust.ca
Other Contact Information: CommonWealth Fund Services Ltd,
URL: www.commonwealthfundservices.com
Ownership: Private

The Canada Trust Company
Toronto Dominion Centre
PO Box 1, Stn. TD Centre
55 King St. West
Toronto, ON M5K 1A2

Tel: 416-216-6868; Toll-Free: 888-222-3456
www.tdcanadatrust.com
www.youtube.com/tdcanada; www.facebook.com/TDCanada;
twitter.com/td_canada
Year Founded: 1855

Canadian Western Trust Co. (CWT)
#300, 750 Cambie St.
Vancouver, BC V6B 0A2

Tel: 604-685-2081; Fax: 604-669-6069
Toll-Free: 800-663-1124
informationservices@cwt.ca
www.cwt.ca
Ownership: A division of Canadian Western Bank. Part of the
Canadian Western Bank Group.

Central 1 Trust Company
c/o Central 1 Credit Union
1441 Creekside Dr.
Vancouver, BC V6J 4S7

Tel: 604-734-2511; Toll-Free: 800-661-6813
communications@central1.com
www.central1.com/trust
Ownership: Subsidiary of Central 1 Credit Union
Assets: $1-10 billion

CIBC Mellon Trust Company
#500, 1 York St.
Toronto, ON M5J 0B6

Tel: 416-643-5000
www.cibcmellon.com
Other Contact Information: Workbench Help Desk:
888-439-2457
www.facebook.com/cibcmellon; twitter.com/cibcmellon
Ownership: Jointly owned by the The Bank of New York Mellon
& Canadian Imperial Bank of Commerce
Year Founded: 1978
Number of Employees: 1,700+
Assets: $100 billion +

CIBC Trust Corporation
#900, 55 Yonge St.
Toronto, ON M5E 1J4

Toll-Free: 866-220-4504
cibc.com/en/private-wealth-management/about-us.html
Ownership: Wholly owned subsidiary of Canadian Imperial
Bank of Commerce

Cidel Trust Company
Vintage Towers
#403, 322 - 11th Ave. SW
Calgary, AB T2R 0C5

Tel: 403-697-6962; Fax: 403-410-9095
www.cidel.com
Ownership: Part of Cidel Bank & Trust, Barbados.

Citco (Canada) Inc.
5151 George St.
Halifax, NS B3J 1M5

Tel: 902-442-4242; *Fax:* 902-442-4258
halifax-fund@citco.com
www.citco.com/our-expertise/services/corporate-an d-trust
Ownership: Part of the Citco Group of Companies.
Assets: 1,645,230,000 Year End: 20181231
Revenues: 31,333,000 Year End: 20181231

Community Trust Company
2350 Matheson Blvd. East
Mississauga, ON L4W 5G9

Tel: 416-763-2291; *Fax:* 416-763-2444
Toll-Free: 800-268-1576
www.communitytrust.ca
Other Contact Information: Investments, Email:
is@communitytrust.ca; Deposit Services, Email:
depositservices@communitytrust.ca
Also Known As: Community Trust
Ownership: Private
Year Founded: 1975
Assets: $1,375,357,000

Computershare Canada
100 University Ave., 8th Fl.
Toronto, ON M5J 2Y1

Tél: 416-263-9200; *Ligne sans frais:* 800-564-6253
www.computershare.com/ca
www.facebook.com/ComputershareCPU;
twitter.com/computershare
Former Name: Montreal Trust
Ownership: Public. Owned by Computershare Limited, listed on the Australian Stock Exchange
Year Founded: 2000

Computershare Trust Company of Canada
100 University Ave., 8th Fl.
Toronto, ON M5J 2Y1

Tel: 416-263-9200
www.computershare.com/ca/en
Ownership: Subsidiary of Computershare Canada

Concentra Trust
333 - 3rd Ave. North
Saskatoon, SK S7K 2M2

Tel: 306-956-5100; *Toll-Free:* 800-788-6311
ExecutorEase@concentra.ca
www.concentra.ca
Ownership: Wholly owned subsidiary of Concentra Financial.
Assets: $1-10 billion

The Effort Trust Company
240 Main St. East
Hamilton, ON L8N 1H5

Tel: 905-528-8956; *Fax:* 905-528-8182
efforttrust.com
Ownership: Private. A wholly owned subsidiary of Effort Corporation
Year Founded: 1978

Fiduciary Trust Company of Canada
#1500, 200 King St. West
Toronto, ON M5H 3T4

Toll-Free: 800-574-3822
contact@ftcc.ca
www.fiduciarytrust.ca
Former Name: Bissett & Associates Investment Management Ltd.
Ownership: A member of the Franklin Templeton Investments family of companies.
Year Founded: 1982

Fiducie Desjardins inc/Desjardins Trust Inc.
1, complexe Desjardins
Montréal, QC H5B 1B2

Tél: 514-286-3100; *Téléc:* 514-286-3198
Ligne sans frais: 800-361-6840
www.fiduciedesjardins.com
Other Contact Information: Programme Immigrants Investisseurs, Phone: 514-499-8440; Toll-Free: 1 800-363-3915; info@immigrantinvestor.com
Ownership: A subsidiary of the Desjardins Group.
Year Founded: 2005

Georgeson Inc.
100 University Ave., 8th Fl.
Toronto, ON M5J 2Y1

Fax: 416-981-9663
Toll-Free: 800-890-1037
www.georgeson.com
Ownership: Private. A Computershare company

Home Trust Company
#2300, 145 King St. West
Toronto, ON M5H 1J8

Tel: 416-775-5000; *Fax:* 416-363-7611
Toll-Free: 877-903-2133
inquiry.htc@hometrust.ca
www.hometrust.ca
www.facebook.com/hometrustco; twitter.com/hometrustco
Ownership: A wholly owned subsidiary of Home Capital Group Inc.
Year Founded: 1977
Number of Employees: 296

HSBC Trust Company (Canada)
885 West Georgia St.
Vancouver, BC V6C 3E8

Toll-Free: 888-310-4722
www.hsbc.ca
Ownership: Private. A wholly owned subsidiary of HSBC Bank Canada
Year Founded: 1972

Industrial Alliance Trust Inc.
CP 1907, Stn. Terminus
1080, Grande Allée ouest
Québec, QC G1K 7M3

Téléc: 418-684-5161
Ligne sans frais: 844-744-4272
iatrust.ca
Former Name: Industrial-Alliance Trust Company
Ownership: Wholly owned subsidiary of iA Financial Group, Québec, QC.
Year Founded: 2000
Assets: $1-10 billion

Investors Group Trust Co. Ltd./La Compagnie de Fiducie du Groupe Investors Ltée
One Canada Centre
447 Portage Ave.
Winnipeg, MB R3B 3H5

Toll-Free: 888-746-6344
www.investorsgroup.com
Other Contact Information: Toll-Free, Quebec: 800-661-4578; TTY: 866-844-5909
www.youtube.com/investorsgroupcanada;
www.facebook.com/InvestorsGroup;
twitter.com/Investors_Group
Ownership: Subsidiary of Investors Group Inc.
Year Founded: 1968

Laurentian Trust of Canada Inc.
#600, 1360, boul René-Lévesque ouest
Montréal, QC H3G 0E5

Tel: 514-252-1846; *Toll-Free:* 800-252-1846
www.laurentianbank.com
Other Contact Information: TTY: 866-262-2231
Ownership: Private. A wholly owned subsidiary of the Laurentian Bank of Canada
Year Founded: 1939
Assets: $500m-1 billion
Revenues: $10-50 million

LBC Trust
#600, 1360, René-Lévesque boul ouest
Montréal, QC H3G 0E5

Toll-Free: 800-252-1846
www.laurentianbank.ca
Ownership: Wholly owned subsidiary of Laurentian Bank

Legacy Private Trust
PO Box 1
#800, 1 Toronto St.
Toronto, ON M5C 2V6

Tel: 416-868-0001; *Fax:* 416-868-6541
info@legacyprivatetrust.com
www.legacyprivatetrust.com
www.facebook.com/LegacyPrivateTrust
Ownership: Private
Year Founded: 2002

Manulife Trust Company
500 King St. North
Waterloo, ON N2J 4C6

Toll-Free: 877-765-2265
manulife_bank@manulife.com
www.manulifebank.ca/manulife-trust.html
Ownership: Wholly owned subsidiary of Manulife Bank of Canada.

MD Private Trust Company
1870 Alta Vista Dr.
Ottawa, ON K1G 6R7

Tel: 613-731-4552; *Toll-Free:* 800-267-4022
www.mdm.ca
www.instagram.com/md_financial_management
Ownership: Private. Subsidiary of MD Physician Services Inc., part of the CMA Group of Companies

Mennonite Trust Limited
PO Box 40
3005 Central Ave.
Waldheim, SK S0K 4R0

Tel: 306-945-2080; *Fax:* 306-945-2225
mtl@mtrust.net
mtrust.net
Year Founded: 1917

Montreal Trust Company of Canada/Montreal Trust Company
44 King St. West
Toronto, ON M5H 1H1

www.scotiabank.com
Ownership: Owned by The Bank of Nova Scotia.
Year Founded: 1889

National Bank Trust
600, rue de la Gauchetière ouest
Montréal, QC H3B 4L2

Tel: 514-871-7100; *Toll-Free:* 800-463-6643
trustservices@nbc.ca
www.nbc.ca/about-us/trust-national-bank.html
Ownership: A wholly owned subsidiary of National Bank of Canada
Year Founded: 1927
Assets: $100 billion +

National Trust Company
44 King St. West
Toronto, ON M5H 1H1

www.scotiabank.com
Ownership: Owned by The Bank of Nova Scotia.

The Northern Trust Company, Canada
#1910, 145 King St. West
Toronto, ON M5H 1J8

Toll-Free: 800-636-5775
www.northerntrust.com
www.youtube.com/user/NorthernTrustVideos;
twitter.com/NorthernTrust
Ownership: Part of Northern Trust Canada. Subsidiary of The Northern Trust Company, Canada Branch, which is a branch of The Northern Trust Company, Chicago

Odyssey Trust Company
United Kingdom Bldg.
#323, 409 Granville St.
Vancouver, BC V6C 1T2

Tel: 587-885-0960
info@odysseytrust.com
www.odysseytrust.com
Ownership: Private
Year Founded: 2017

Olympia Trust Company
#2200, 125 - 9th Ave. SE
Calgary, AB T2G 0P6

Tel: 403-261-0900; *Fax:* 403-261-7523
inquiries@olympiafinancial.com
www.olympiatrust.com
Ownership: Wholly owned subsidiary of Olympia Financial Group Inc.
Year Founded: 1996

Peace Hills Trust Company
Corporate Office
10011 - 109th St., 10th Fl.
Edmonton, AB T5J 3S8

Tel: 780-421-1606; *Fax:* 780-426-6568
pht@peacehills.com
www.peacehills.com
Ownership: Private
Year Founded: 1981
Number of Employees: 120
Assets: $467,527,000 Year End: 20190930
Revenues: $10-50 million Year End: 20190930

Peoples Trust Company
#1400, 888 Dunsmuir St.
Vancouver, BC V6C 3K4

Tel: 604-683-2881; *Fax:* 604-331-3469
Toll-Free: 855-683-2881
www.peoplestrust.com
Ownership: Private. Division of Peoples Group
Year Founded: 1985

SECTION 6
EDUCATION

Arranged by province, and each grouping's the following categories. Each category is further arranged by specific subcategories, as applicable to each province.

Government Agencies

School Boards/Districts/Divisions
Public, Faith-Based/Catholic, French; School Authorities

Schools: Specialized
Charter, First Nations, Home-schooling/based/Distance Education, Special Education

Schools: Independent & Private

Universities & Colleges

Post-Secondary/Technical

Alberta

Government Agencies

Edmonton: Alberta Ministry of Education
228 Legislature Building
10800 - 97 Ave., Edmonton, AB T5K 2B6, Canada
Tel: 780-427-7219
alberta.ca/education.aspx
Hon. Adriana LaGrange, Minister
education.minister@gov.ab.ca
Hon. Demetrios Nicolaides, Minister, Advanced Education
780-427-5777
ae.minister@gov.ab.ca

School Boards/Districts/Divisions

Public

Airdrie: Rocky View School Division
2651 Chinook Winds Dr., Airdrie, AB T4B 0B4
Tel: 403-945-4000; *Fax:* 403-945-4001
rvs@rockyview.ab.ca
www.rockyview.ab.ca
www.facebook.com/RockyViewSchools
twitter.com/rvsed
www.youtube.com/c/RVSchools
Number of Schools: 51 *Grades:* K - 12 *Enrollment:* 26000
Number of Employees: 2,500
Fiona Gilbert, Chair
fgilbert@rockyview.ab.ca
Greg Luterbach, Superintendent, Schools, 403-945-4003
suptoffice@rockyview.ab.ca
Murray Besenski, Associate Superintendent, Schools,
403-945-4015
jkeenan@rockyview.ab.ca
Laurie Copeland, Associate Superintendent, Human Resources,
403-945-4075
lduggan@rockyview.ab.ca
Lori Meyer, Associate Superintendent, Learning, 403-945-4018
lshemko@rockyview.ab.ca
Larry Paul, Associate Superintendent, Business & Operations,
403-945-4008
lpaul@rockyview.ab.ca

Athabasca: Aspen View Regional Division
Also known as: Aspen View Public Schools (AVPS)
3600 - 48th Ave., Athabasca, AB T9S 1M8
Tel: 780-675-7080; *Toll-Free:* 888-488-0288
info@aspenview.org
www.aspenview.org
www.facebook.com/aspenviewschools
www.instagram.com/aspenviewschools
Number of Schools: 14 *Grades:* K - 12 *Enrollment:* 2600
Candy Nikipelo, Chair
Neil O'Shea, Superintendent
Karen Penney, Deputy Superintendent
Ernest Aleixandre, Director, Information Technology Services
Kim Carson, Director, Human Resources
David Kwiatkowski, Director, Facilities & Maintenance
Shannon Smith, Director, Student Services

Barrhead: Pembina Hills Regional Division
Also known as: Pembina Hills School Division
5310 - 49th St., Barrhead, AB T7N 1P3
Tel: 780-674-8500; *Fax:* 780-674-3262
Toll-Free: 877-693-1333
info@pembinahills.ca
www.pembinahills.ca
www.facebook.com/PembinaHillsSchoolDivision
twitter.com/PembinaHills
Number of Schools: 15 schools; 2 outreach; 2 colony *Grades:* 1 -
12; Adult Ed. *Enrollment:* 3800
Jennifer Tuininga, Chair
jennifer.tuininga@pembinahills.ca
David Garbutt, Superintendent, 780-674-8507
david.garbutt@pembinahills.ca
Brent Cooper, Assistant Superintendent, Human Resources,
780-674-8525
brett.cooper@pembinahills.ca
Mark Thiesen, Assistant Superintendent, Education Services,
780-674-8505
mark.thiesen@pembinahills.ca

**Bonnyville: Northern Lights School Division No. 69
(NLSD)**
Also known as: Northern Lights Public Schools
6005 - 50th Ave., Bonnyville, AB T9N 2L4
Tel: 780-826-3145; *Fax:* 780-826-4600
Toll-Free: 888-826-3145
communications@nlsd.ab.ca
www.nlpsab.ca
www.facebook.com/nlpsab
twitter.com/nlpsab
Number of Schools: 27 *Grades:* K-12 *Enrollment:* 6200 *Note:*
This division is an amalgamation of the Lac La Biche School
Division & the Lakeland Public School District.
Arlene Hrynyk, Chair
arlene.hrynyk@nlsd.ab.ca
Rick Cusson, Superintendent, Schools
rick.cusson@nlsd.ab.ca
Bill Driedger, Assoc. Superintendent, Teaching Quality &
Professional Svcs
Jimmi Lou Irvine, Associate Superintendent, Student Services
Terry Moghrabi, Associate Superintendent, Curriculum &
Programming

Brooks: Grasslands Regional Division
Also known as: Grasslands Public Schools
745 - 2nd Ave. East, Brooks, AB T1R 1L2
Tel: 403-793-6700; *Fax:* 403-362-8225
info@grasslands.ab.ca
www.grasslands.ab.ca
www.facebook.com/106850974363632
twitter.com/GPSD6
Number of Schools: 13 schools; 7 Hutterian Brethren Colony
Schools *Grades:* K - 12; Alternative Ed.
Scott Brandt, Superintendent
Rhian Schroeder, Associate Superintendent, Business Services
Sean Beaton, Assistant Superintendent
Katie Graham, Assistant Superintendent
Shane Harahus, Director, Finance, 403-793-6700
Patti Jones, Director, Student Services
patrice.jones@grasslands.ab.ca
Michael Nielsen, Director, Technology, 403-793-6701

Calgary: Calgary Board of Education
Also known as: Calgary School District #19
Education Centre
1221 - 8 St. SW, Calgary, AB T2R 0L4
Tel: 403-817-4000
cbecommunications@cbe.ab.ca
www.cbe.ab.ca
Other Information: 403-817-7955; Trustees: 403-817-7933;
Indigenous Education: 403-817-7607
twitter.com/yyCBEdu
Number of Schools: 246 schools *Grades:* K - 12; Continuing Ed.
Enrollment: 125800 *Number of Employees:* 14,000
Christine Davies, Director, Area 1, 403-777-8710
area1@cbe.ab.ca
Chris Meaden, Director, Area 2, 403-777-8720
area2@cbe.ab.ca
Scott MacNeill, Director, Area 3, 403-777-6820
area3@cbe.ab.ca
Calvin Davies, Director, Area 4, 403-777-6233
area4@cbe.ab.ca
Ann Ard, Director, Area 5, 403-777-8412
area5@cbe.ab.ca
Darlene Unruh, Director, Area 6, 403-777-8780
area6@cbe.ab.ca
Lori Cooper, Director, Area 7, 403-777-8750
area7@cbe.ab.ca
Christopher Usih, Chief Superintendent, Schools, 403-817-7902
chiefsuperintendent@cbe.ab.ca
Dianne Yee, Superintendent, Inclusive Education, 403-817-7901
schoolimprovement@cbe.ab.ca
Joanne Pitman, Superintendent, Research & Strategy,
403-817-7500
schoolimproveement@cbe.ab.ca
Dany Breton, Superintendent, Facilities & Environmental
Services, 403-817-6331
fes@cbe.ab.ca
Rob Armstrong, Superintendent, Human Resources,
403-817-7300
hrcommunications@cbe.ab.ca
Brad Grundy, Superintendent, Finance & Technology Services,
403-817-7400
cbebusinessoperations@cbe.ab.ca

Camrose: Battle River Regional Division
Also known as: Battle River School Division
5402 - 48A Ave., Camrose, AB T4V 0L3
Tel: 780-672-6131; *Fax:* 780-672-6137
www.brrd.ab.ca
www.facebook.com/battleriver31
twitter.com/battleriver31

Number of Schools: 23 *Grades:* K - 12 *Enrollment:* 6700
Karen Belich, Chair
Rita Marler, Superintendent, Schools

**Canmore: Canadian Rockies Regional Division No.
12**
Also known as: Canadian Rockies Public Schools
618 - 7th St., Canmore, AB T1W 2H5
Tel: 403-609-6072; *Fax:* 403-609-6071
www.crps.ca
www.facebook.com/CRPSB
twitter.com/mountainedu
www.instagram.com/canadianrockiespublicschools
Number of Schools: 7 *Grades:* K - 12 *Enrollment:* 2000
Carol Picard, Chair, 403-678-7688
Christopher MacPhee, Superintendent, Schools, 403-609-6070
Debbie McKibbin, Deputy Superintendent
Lisa Blackstock, Director, Learning Services
Steve Greene, Director, Technology, Learning & Facilities

Cardston: Westwind School Division No. 74
P.O. Box 10
445 Main St., Cardston, AB T0K 0K0
Tel: 403-653-4991
inquiries@westwind.ab.ca
www.westwind.ab.ca
www.facebook.com/wwsd74
twitter.com/wwsd74
Number of Schools: 13 *Grades:* Pre-K - 12 *Enrollment:* 4400
Jim Ralph, Chair
Darren Mazutinec, Superintendent
Rob Doig, Assistant Superintendent, Learning Services
Todd Heggie, Assistant Superintendent, Human Resources
Austin Nunn, Assistant Superintendent, Student Services

Dunmore: Prairie Rose Regional Division (PRRD)
Also known as: Prairie Rose School Division
P.O. Box 204
918 - 2nd Ave., Dunmore, AB T0J 1A0
Tel: 403-527-5516; *Fax:* 403-528-2264
communications@prrd8.ca
prrdweb.com
Number of Schools: 17 public schools, 15 colony schools, 1
outreach; 1 Mennonite Alternative *Grades:* JK-12 *Enrollment:*
3380 *Number of Employees:* 645
Roger Clarke, Superintendent, Schools
rogerclarke@prrd8.ca
Reagan Weeks, Deputy Superintendent, Education & Learning
Services
reaganweeks@prrd8.ca
Kal Koch, Assistant Superintendent, Human Resources
kalkoch@prrd8.ca
Derek Beck, Director, Transportation
derekbeck@prrd8.ca
Darrell Drefs, Director, Maintenance Operations
darrelldrefs@prrd8.ca
Camille Quinton, Director, Inclusion
camillequinton@prrd8.ca

Edmonton: Edmonton Public Schools (EPSB)
Centre for Education
1 Kingsway NW, Edmonton, AB T5H 4G9
Tel: 780-429-8000; *Fax:* 780-429-8318
www.epsb.ca
www.facebook.com/EdmontonPublicSchools
twitter.com/EPSBNews
www.linkedin.com/company/edmonton-public-schools
www.YouTube.com/EdPublicSchools
Number of Schools: 213 *Grades:* K - 12 *Enrollment:* 104930
Number of Employees: 9,431 full-time employees
Lorne Parker, Assistant Superintendent, Infrastructure,
780-429-8426
lorne.parker@epsb.ca
Darrel Robertson, Superintendent, Schools, 780-429-8010
darrel.robertson@epsb.ca
Ron MacNeil, Assistant Superintendent, Schools, 780-429-8374
ron.macneil@epsb.ca
Leona Morrison, Assistant Superintendent, Schools,
780-429-8625
leona.morrison@epsb.ca
Kathy Muhlethaler, Assistant Superintendent, Schools,
780-429-8011
kathy.muhlethaler@epsb.ca
Kent Pharis, Assistant Superintendent, Schools, 780-429-8267
kent.pharis@epsb.ca
Mike Suderman, Assistant Superintendent, Schools,
780-429-8177
mike.suderman@epsb.ca
Liz Yule, Assistant Superintendent, Schools, 780-489-8402
liz.yule@epsb.ca

Edson: Grande Yellowhead Public School Division (GYPSD)
3656 - 1st Ave., Edson, AB T7E 1S8
Tel: 780-723-2414; Fax: 780-723-2414
Toll-Free: 800-723-2564
escgypsd@gypsd.ca
www.gypsd.ca
www.facebook.com/gypsd
twitter.com/gypsd77
Number of Schools: 17 *Grades:* Elementary - Secondary *Enrollment:* 5000 *Number of Employees:* 600
Brenda Rosadiuk, Chair, 780-727-4691
Carolyn Lewis, Superintendent, Schools, 780-723-4471, ext. 103
Constantine Kastrinos, Chief Deputy Superintendent, Human Resources, 780-723-4471, ext. 102
Kelly Harding, Assistant Superintendent, Communications & Curriculum, 780-723-4471, ext. 112
Kelly Smith, Assistant Superintendent, Inclusive Learning & Technology, 780-723-4471, ext. 104
Ken Baluch, Managing Director, Facility Services, 780-723-4471, ext. 119

Fort Macleod: Livingstone Range School Division (LRSD)
Also known as: Livingstone Range School Division No. 68
P.O. Box 1810
410 - 20th St., Fort Macleod, AB T0L 0Z0
Tel: 403-625-3356; Fax: 403-553-0370
Toll-Free: 800-310-6579
centraloffice@lrsd.ab.ca
lrsd.ca
www.facebook.com/10268642807043
twitter.com/LRSD_68
Number of Schools: 14 schools; 13 Hutterite colony schools *Grades:* Pre.-12 *Enrollment:* 3600
Darryl Seguin, Superintendent
seguind@lrsd.ab.ca
Jeff Perry, Associate Superintendent, Business Services, 800-310-6579, ext. 227
perryj@lrsd.ab.ca
Chad Kuzyk, Associate Superintendent, Curriculum & Innovation
kuzykc@lrsd.ab.ca
Richard Feller, Associate Superintendent, Learning Services
fellerr@lrsd.ab.ca
Sandy Gould, Administrative Assistant, Human Resources, 403-625-3356
goulds@lrsd.ab.ca

Fort McMurray: Fort McMurray Public School District No. 2833
Also known as: Fort McMurray Public Schools
Clearwater Public Education Centre
231 Hardin St., Fort McMurray, AB T9H 2G2
Tel: 780-799-7900; Fax: 780-743-2655
info@fmpsd.ab.ca
fmpsdschools.ca
www.facebook.com/fmpsd
twitter.com/fmpsd
www.instagram.com/fmpsd
Number of Schools: 12 elementary schools; 4 high schools *Grades:* ECS - 12
Linda Mywaart, Chair
linda.mywaart@fmpsd.ab.ca
Jennifer Turner, Superintendent, Schools
Phil Meagher, Chief Deputy Superintendent, HR & Administration, 780-799-9970
phil.meagher@fmpsd.ab.ca
Allan Kallal, Associate Superintendent, Business & Finance, 780-799-7908
allan.kallal@fmpsd.ab.ca
Annalee Nutter, Associate Superintendent, Education & Administration, 780-743-3101
Jennifer Quigley, Director, Education

Fort Vermilion: Fort Vermilion School Division (FVSD)
Also known as: Fort Vermilion School Division No. 52
P.O. Box 1
5213 River Rd., Fort Vermilion, AB T0H 1N0, Canada
Tel: 780-927-3766; Fax: 780-927-4625
info@fvsd.ab.ca
www.fvsd.ab.ca
Number of Schools: 15 schools & 4 Learning Stores *Grades:* Kindergarten - 12 *Enrollment:* 3406 *Number of Employees:* 508
Michael McMann, Superintendent, Schools, 780-927-3766
mikem@fvsd.ab.ca
Scot Leys, Assistant Superintendent, Operations
scotl@fvsd.ab.ca
Karen Smith, Assistant Superintendent of Learning
karens@fvsd.ab.ca

Norman Buhler, Secretary-Treasurer
normanb@fvsd.ab.ca

Grande Prairie: Grande Prairie School District
10213 - 99th St., Grande Prairie, AB T8V 2H3
Tel: 780-532-4491; Fax: 780-539-4265
info@gppsd.ab.ca
www.gppsd.ab.ca
www.facebook.com/gppsd2357
twitter.com/gppsd2357
www.linkedin.com/company/gppsd2357
Number of Schools: 18 *Grades:* K - 12 *Enrollment:* 8500
John Lehners, Chair, 780-532-4491
john.lehners@gppsd.ab.ca
Sandy MacDonald, Superintendent, Schools
sandy.mcdonald@gppsd.ab.ca
James Robinson, Deputy Superintendent, Schools
james.robinson@gppsd.ab.ca
Geoff Barron, Director, Operations & Maintenance
geoff.barron@gppsd.ab.ca
Kimberly Frykas, Director, System Supports
kimberly.frykas@gppsd.ab.ca
Nancy Gorgichuk, Director, Inclusive Learning
Justin Vickers, Director, Information Technology
justin.vickers@gppsd.ab.ca
Wade Webb, Director, Finance
wade.webb@gppsd.ab.ca

Grande Prairie: Peace Wapiti Public School Division
8611A - 108th St., Grande Prairie, AB T8V 4C5
Tel: 780-532-8133
www.pwsd76.ab.ca
www.facebook.com/PWPSD
twitter.com/PWPSD
Number of Schools: 36 *Grades:* K - 12 *Enrollment:* 5800 *Number of Employees:* 345 teachers; 600 non-teaching staff
Karl Scheers, Chair
Bob Stewart, Superintendent, Schools
Darren Young, Deputy Superintendent
Kevin Elias, Assistant Superintendent
Heather Putio, Assistant Superintendent
Ted Gobin, Director, Transportation
Kellie Lewis, Director, Human Resources & Labour Relations
David Michalko, Director, Facilities

Grimshaw: Peace River School Division (PRSD)
P.O. Box 380
4702 - 51st St., Grimshaw, AB T0H 1W0
Tel: 780-624-3601; Fax: 780-332-1050
peaceriversd@prsd.ab.ca
www.prsd.ab.ca
www.facebook.com/prsd10
twitter.com/prsd10
Number of Schools: 20 *Grades:* K-12 *Enrollment:* 3000
Darren Kuester, Chair, 780-971-2465
Paul Bennett, Superintendent, 780-624-3601
Adam Murray, Assistant Superintendent, Human Resources, 780-624-3650, ext. 10139
Aleeta Ploc, Assistant Superintendent, Learning Supports, 780-624-3650, ext. 10131
Jeff Thompson, Assistant Superintendent, Teaching & Learning, 780-624-3650, ext. 10125

Hanna: Prairie Land Regional Division (PLRD)
P.O. Box 670
101 Palliser Trail, Hanna, AB T0J 1P0
Tel: 403-854-4481; Fax: 403-854-2803
Toll-Free: 800-601-3898
www.plrd.ab.ca
www.facebook.com/plrd25
twitter.com/plrd25
Number of Schools: 13 *Grades:* K-12 *Enrollment:* 1300
Holli Smith, Chair, 403-854-4481
holli.smith@plrd.ab.ca
Cam McKeage, Superintendent, 403-854-4481, ext. 702
cam.mckeage@plrd.ab.ca
Steven Nielsen, Chief Deputy Superintendent, 403-854-4481, ext. 704
steven.nielsen@plrd.ab.ca

High Prairie: High Prairie School Division (HPSD)
P.O. Box 870
4806 - 53th Ave., High Prairie, AB T0G 1E0
Tel: 780-523-3337; Fax: 780-523-4639
Toll-Free: 877-523-3337
news@hpsd.ca
hpsd.ca
www.facebook.com/HPSD48
Number of Schools: 13 *Grades:* K - 12 *Enrollment:* 3200 *Number of Employees:* 550
Steve Adams, Chair
sadams@hpsd.ca

Laura Poloz, Superintendent
lpoloz@hpsd.ca
Margaret Hartman, Deputy Superintendent
mhartman@hpsd.ca
Treva Emter, Assistant Superintendent
temter@hpsd.ca
Sascha Klingsch, Director, Technology
sklingsch@hpsd.ca

High River: Foothills School Division
P.O. Box 5700
#300, 129 - 4th Ave. SW, High River, AB T1V 1M7
Tel: 403-652-3001; Fax: 403-652-4204
info@fsd38.ab.ca
www.fsd38.ab.ca
www.facebook.com/foothills.school.division
www.linkedin.com/school/foothills-school-division
twitter.com/fsd38
Number of Schools: 19 public schools; 3 open campus locations; 3 Hutterite Colony schools *Grades:* Pre K - 12; French Immersion *Enrollment:* 8200 *Number of Employees:* 900
Larry Albrecht, Chair, 403-869-8025
albrechtl@fsd38.ab.ca
Christopher Fuzessy, Superintendent, Schools
superintendent@fsd38.ab.ca
Drew Chipman, Assistant Superintendent, Corporate Services
chipmand@fsd38.ab.ca
Allen Davidson, Assistant Superintendent, Employee Services
davidsona@fsd38.ab.ca
Caroline Roberts, Assistant Superintendent, Learning Services
robertsc@fsd38.ab.ca
Denise Gow, Director, Financial Services, 403-652-6503
gowd@fsd38.ab.ca

Innisfail: Chinook's Edge School Division
4904 - 50th St., Innisfail, AB T4G 1W4
Tel: 403-227-7070; Fax: 403-227-3652
Toll-Free: 800-561-9229
division.office@cesd73.ca
www.cesd73.ca
www.facebook.com/223673484324928
twitter.com/cesd73
Number of Schools: 43 *Enrollment:* 11000 *Number of Employees:* 800 teachers; 650 support staff
Kurt Sacher, Superintendent, Schools
ksacher@cesd73.ca
Karyn Barber, Associate Superintendent, Student Information Services
kbarber@cesd73.ca
Jason Drent, Associate Superintendent, Learning Services
jdrent@cesd73.ca
Ray Hoppins, Associate Superintendent, People Services
rhoppins@cesd73.ca
Shawn Russell, Associate Superintendent, Corporate Services
srussell@cesd73.ca

Lethbridge: Lethbridge School District
433 - 15th St. South, Lethbridge, AB T1J 2Z5
Tel: 403-380-5300
www.lethsd.ab.ca
www.facebook.com/LSD51
twitter.com/LethSchDivision
Number of Schools: 18 *Grades:* K-12 *Enrollment:* 8100 *Number of Employees:* 463 teachers; 338 support staff
Christine Light, Chair, 403-929-3747
Cheryl Gilmore, Superintendent, Schools, 403-380-5301
cheryl.gilmore@lethsd.ab.ca
Morag Asquith, Associate Superintendent, Instructional Services
Christine Lee, Associate Superintendent, Business & Operations, 403-380-5307
Mike Nightingale, Associate Superintendent, Human Resources, 403-380-5321
Mark DeBoer, Director, Finance, 403-380-5308
mark.deboer@lethsd.ab.ca

Lethbridge: Palliser Regional Division
#101, 3305 - 18th Ave. North, Lethbridge, AB T1H 5S1
Tel: 403-328-4111; Fax: 403-380-6890
Toll-Free: 877-667-1234
www.pallisersd.ca
www.facebook.com/PalliserRegionalSchools
twitter.com/PalliserSchools
Number of Schools: 15 community; 17 Hutterian colony; 11 faith-based alternative; 5 outreach; 1 online; 2 alternative *Grades:* Pre - 12 *Enrollment:* 8400
Robert Strauss, Chair
Dave Driscoll, Superintendent
superintendent@pallisersd.ab.ca

Lloydminster: **Lloydminster Public School Division #99 (LPSD)**
5017 - 46th St., Lloydminster, AB T9V 1R4
Tel: 780-875-5541; *Fax:* 780-875-7829
contact@lpsd.ca
www.lpsd.ca
www.facebook.com/LloydPublic
twitter.com/LloydPublic
Number of Schools: 6 elementary schools; 2 middle schools; 1 secondary school; 1 outreach school *Grades:* Pre - 12 *Enrollment:* 3945 *Number of Employees:* 507
Todd Robinson, Director, Education
Scott Wouters, Deputy Director, Education
Trisha Rawlake, Superintendent, Education
scott.wouters@lpsd.ca
Brent Thomas, Superintendent, Education

Medicine Hat: **Medicine Hat School District No. 76**
Also known as: Medicine Hat Public School Division
601 - 1st Ave. SW, Medicine Hat, AB T1A 4Y7
Tel: 403-528-6700; *Fax:* 403-529-5339
info@mhpsd.ca
mhpsd.ca
www.facebook.com/MHPublicSchools
Number of Schools: 11 elementary; 3 secondary; 3 middle *Grades:* K.-12 *Enrollment:* 7000
Catherine Wilson, Chair, 403-528-6726
Mark Davidson, Superintendent
mark.davidson@sd76.ab.ca
Lyle Cunningham, Deputy Superintendent
lyle.cunningham@sd76.ab.ca
Tracy Hensel, Associate Superintendent, Student Services
tracy.hensel@sd76.ab.ca
Corey Sadlemyer, Associate Superintendent, Inclusive Mindset
corey.sadlemyer@sd76.ab.ca
Jason Peters, Associate Superintendent, Universal Design & Learning
jason.peters@sd76.ab.ca

Morinville: **Sturgeon School Division (SSD)**
Also known as: Sturgeon School Division No. 24
Old Name: Morinville School Division
9820 - 104 St., Morinville, AB T8R 1L8, Canada
Tel: 780-939-4341; *Fax:* 780-939-5520
Toll-Free: 888-459-4062
frec@sturgeon.ab.ca
www.sturgeon.ab.ca
www.facebook.com/sturgeonSD
twitter.com/sturgeonschools
Number of Schools: 17 *Grades:* K.-12 *Enrollment:* 5000 *Number of Employees:* 650
Mary Lynne Campbell, Superintendent, 780-939-4341
marylynne.campbell@sturgeon.ab.ca
Terry Jewell, Chair, 780-686-3367
terry.jewell@sturgeon.ab.ca
Ruth Kuik, Associate Superintendent, Education Services, 780-939-4341
rkuik@sturgeon.ab.ca
Lisa Lacroix, Associate Superintendent, People Services, 780-939-4341
lisa.lacroix@sturgeon.ab.ca

Nisku: **Black Gold Regional Division (BGRD)**
1101 - 5th St., 3rd Fl., Nisku, AB T9E 7N3
Tel: 780-955-6025; *Fax:* 780-955-6050
bgsd@blackgold.ca
www.blackgold.ca
www.facebook.com/BlackGoldSchoolDivision
twitter.com/BlackGldSchools
www.youtube.com/c/BlackGoldSchoolDivision
Number of Schools: 31 *Grades:* JK - 12 *Enrollment:* 12250 *Number of Employees:* 660 teachers; 630 support staff
Devonna Klaassen, Chair
devonna.klaassen@blackgold.ca
Bill Romanchuk, Superintendent, 780-955-6025
bill.romanchuk@blackgold.ca
Norm Dargis, Associate Superintendent, Learning Services, 780-955-6025
norm.dargis@blackgold.ca
Calvin Monty, Associate Superintendent, Human Resources & Administration, 780-955-6025
calvin.monty@blackgold.ca
Chelsey Volkman, Associate Superintendent, Business & Finance, 780-955-6049
chelsey.volkman@blackgold.ca

Peace River: **Northland School Division**
P.O. Box 1400
9809 - 77th Ave., Peace River, AB T8S 1V2
Tel: 780-624-2060; *Fax:* 780-624-5914
Toll-Free: 800-362-1360
centralofficestaff@nsd61.ca
www.northland61.ab.ca
www.facebook.com/TheNorthlandSchoolDivision
twitter.com/northland61
Number of Schools: 20 *Grades:* K.-12 *Enrollment:* 2000
Nancy Spencer-Poitras, Superintendent, Schools, 780-624-2060, ext. 6102
nancy.spencerpoitras@nsd61.ca
Wes Oginski, Associate Superintendent, Human Resources, 780-624-2060, ext. 6157
wesley.oginski@nsd61.ca
Cully Robinson, Associate Superintendent, 780-624-2060, ext. 6105
dermod.madden@nsd61.ca
Tim Stensland, Associate Superintendent, 780-742-6333
tim.stensland@nsd61.ca

Ponoka: **Wolf Creek School Division**
6000 Hwy. 2A, Ponoka, AB T4J 1P6
Tel: 403-783-3473; *Fax:* 403-783-3483
info@wolfcreek.ab.ca
www.wolfcreek.ab.ca
www.facebook.com/wolfcreekpublicschools
twitter.com/WCPS72
Number of Schools: 30 *Grades:* K.-12; Special Education
Pamela Hansen, Chair
pamela.hansen@wolfcreek.ab.ca
Jayson Lovell, Superintendent, Schools
Danica Martin, Assistant Superintendent, Inclusive Learning Services
Mark McWhinnie, Assistant Superintendent, Learning Services
Corrine Thorsteinson, Assistant Superintendent, People Services

Red Deer: **Red Deer School District**
4747 - 53rd St., Red Deer, AB T4N 2E6
Tel: 403-343-1405; *Fax:* 403-347-8190
info@rdpsd.ab.ca
www.rdpsd.ab.ca
twitter.com/rdpschools
Number of Schools: 30 *Grades:* K - 12 *Enrollment:* 11100 *Number of Employees:* 1,451
Nicole Buchanan, Chair, 403-596-4611
Chad Erickson, Superintendent, 403-342-3713
Ron Eberts, Associate Superintendent, Learning Services, 403-342-3700
Ron.Eberts@rdpsd.ab.ca
Nicola Golby, Associate Superintendent, Student Services, 403-342-3715
Dan Lower, Associate Superintendent, Learning Services, 403-342-3711
Robert Moltzahn, Associate Superintendent, Human Resource, Payroll & Benefits, 403-342-3720
Della Ruston, Associate Superintendent, System Services, 403-357-3994

Rocky Mountain House: **Wild Rose School Division (WRSD)**
4912 - 43rd St., Rocky Mountain House, AB T4T 1P4
Tel: 403-845-3376; *Fax:* 403-845-4287
Toll-Free: 800-771-0537
contactus@wrsd.ca
www.wrsd.ca
www.facebook.com/WRSD.ca
twitter.com/wildroseschools
Number of Schools: 17 schools *Grades:* K - 12 *Enrollment:* 4700 *Number of Employees:* 470
Brad Volkman, Superintendent, Schools
brad.volkman@wrsd.ca
Greg Wedman, Deputy Superintendent
greg.wedman@wrsd.ca
Kristen Disley, Director, Transportation
kristen.disley@wrsd.ca
Dave Elwood, Director, Human Resources
dave.elwood@wrsd.ca
Darlene Ferris, Director, Wellness & Human Services
darlene.ferris@wrsd.ca
Jaymon Lefebvre, Director, IT Services
jaymon.lefebvre@wrsd.ca
Jen Lefebvre, Director, Instruction
jen.lefebvre@wrsd.ca
Mike Lundstrom, Director, Facilities & Maintenance
mike.lundstrom@wrsd.ca

Sherwood Park: **Elk Island Public Schools (EIPS)**
Central Administration Bldg.
683 Wye Rd., Sherwood Park, AB T8B 1N2
Tel: 780-464-3477; *Fax:* 780-417-8181
Toll-Free: 800-905-3477
www.eips.ca
www.facebook.com/ElkIslandPublicSchools
twitter.com/eips
Number of Schools: 43 *Enrollment:* 17000 *Number of Employees:* 860 full-time equivalent teaching staff; 500 full-time equivalent non-teaching staff
Mark Liguori, Superintendent, Schools
Brent Billey, Associate Superintendent, Human Resources
Sandra Stoddard, Associate Superintendent, Supports for Students

St Albert: **St. Albert School District**
60 Sir Winston Churchill Ave., St Albert, AB T8N 0G4
Tel: 780-460-3712; *Fax:* 780-460-7686
info@spschools.org
www.spschools.org
www.facebook.com/StAlbertPublicSchools
twitter.com/StAlbertPublic
Number of Schools: 10 elementary; 5 junior high; 3 high school *Grades:* K - 12 *Enrollment:* 8600
Glenys Edwards, Chair
glenys.edwards@spschools.org
Krimsen Sumners, Superintendent, Schools
krimsen.sumners@spschools.org
Marianne Barrett, Deputy Superintendent, Program & Planning
marianne.barrett@spschools.org
Michael Brenneis, Associate Superintendent, Finance/Secretary-Treasurer
brenneism@spschools.org
Paul MacLeod, Associate Superintendent, Human Resources
paul.macleod@spschools.org

St Paul: **St. Paul Education Regional Division No.1**
Also known as: St. Paul Education
4313 - 48th Ave., St Paul, AB T0A 3A3
Tel: 780-645-3323; *Fax:* 780-645-5789
st_paul@sperd.ca
www.stpauleducation.ab.ca
www.facebook.com/stpauleducation
twitter.com/StPaulEducation
Number of Schools: 18 *Grades:* K - 12 *Enrollment:* 3900 *Number of Employees:* 255 teaching staff; 378 support staff
Heather Starosielski, Chair, 780-614-5556
starheat@sperd.ca
Glen Brodziak, Superintendent
brodglen@sperd.ca
Patricia Gervais, Assistant Superintendent
gervpatr@sperd.ca
Doug Fedoruk, Director, Facilities & Transportation
fedodoug@sperd.ca
Maria Letawsky, Acting Director, Finance
letamari@sperd.ca
Sha Tichkowsky, Director, Student Supports
tichshal@sperd.ca
Jean Champagne, Secretary-Treasurer, 780-645-3323

Stettler: **Clearview School Division**
P.O. Box 1720
5031 - 50th St., Stettler, AB T0C 2L0
Tel: 403-742-3331; *Fax:* 403-742-1388
www.clearview.ab.ca
Number of Schools: 23 *Grades:* K - 12 *Enrollment:* 2374
Guy Neitz, Chair
gneitz@clearview.ab.ca
Brenda MacDonald, Superintendent, Schools
bmacdonald@clearview.ab.ca
Peter Neale, Associate Superintendent, Business & Finance
pneale@clearview.ab.ca

Stony Plain: **Parkland School Division**
Centre for Education
4603 - 48th St., Stony Plain, AB T7Z 2A8
Tel: 780-963-4010; *Fax:* 780-963-4169
Toll-Free: 800-282-3997
divisionoffice@psd70.ab.ca
www.psd70.ab.ca
www.facebook.com/psd70
twitter.com/psd_70
Number of Schools: 22 *Enrollment:* 9454 *Number of Employees:* 640 teaching staff; 480 support staff
Lorraine Stewart, Chair
lstewart@psd70.ab.ca
Shauna Boyce, Superintendent, Schools
sboyce@psd70.ab.ca
Mark Francis, Deputy Superintendent
mfrancis@psd70.ab.ca

Scott Johnston, Associate Superintendent
sjohnston@psd70.ab.ca
Dianne McConnell, Associate Superintendent
dmcconnell@psd70.ab.ca
Scott McFadyen, Associate Superintendent, Corporate Supports & Services
smcfadyen@psd70.ab.ca

Strathmore: Golden Hills School Division
435A Hwy. #1, Strathmore, AB T1P 1J4
Tel: 403-934-5121; *Fax:* 403-934-5125
Toll-Free: 800-320-3739
www.ghsd75.ca
Number of Schools: 15 regular; 19 Hutterite colonies; 2 Christian; 2 Virtual; 3 outreach; 1 international program *Grades:* ECS - 12 *Enrollment:* 8200
Laurie Huntley, Chair
Bevan Daverne, Superintendent, Schools
Wes Miskiman, Deputy Superintendent, Human Resources
Jeff Grimsdale, Associate Superintendent, Learning Services
Christina Hoover, Director, Learning

Taber: Horizon School Division
6302 - 56th St., Taber, AB T1G 1Z9
Tel: 403-223-3547; *Fax:* 403-223-2999
www.horizon.ab.ca
www.facebook.com/HSD67
twitter.com/horizonsd67
Number of Schools: 16 schools; 19 Hutterian Brethren schools
Enrollment: 3500
Marie Logan, Chair
Wilco Tymensen, Superintendent
wilco.tymensen@horizon.ab.ca
Robbie Charlebois, Assistant Superintendent, Human Services, 403-223-3547, ext. 10122
Amber Darroch, Associate Superintendent, Learner Services, 403-223-3547, ext. 10152

Wainwright: Buffalo Trail Schools Regional Division
Central Office
1041 - 10A St., Wainwright, AB T9W 2R4
Tel: 780-842-6144; *Fax:* 780-842-3255
central_office@btps.ca
www.btps.ca
twitter.com/BTPS28
Number of Schools: 27 *Grades:* K - 12 *Enrollment:* 4200 *Number of Employees:* 575
Lanie Parr, Chair, 780-847-4211
lanie.parr@btps.ca
Rhae-Ann Holoien, Superintendent, Schools
superintendent@btps.ca
Michelle Webb, Deputy Superintendent, Schools, 780-806-2062
James Trodden, Assistant Superintendent, Schools, 780-806-2059

Wetaskiwin: Wetaskiwin Regional Division
Also known as: Wetaskiwin Regional Public Schools (WRPS)
5515 - 47A Ave., Wetaskiwin, AB T9A 3S3
Tel: 780-352-6018; *Fax:* 780-352-7886
Toll-Free: 877-352-8078
wrps@wrps11.ca
www.wrps11.ca
www.facebook.com/wrps11
www.twitter.com/WRPS11
www.youtube.com/c/WetaskiwinRegionalPublicSchools
Number of Schools: 19 *Grades:* Pre-K - 12 *Enrollment:* 4000
Lynn Ware, Chair, 780-352-9619
Peter Barron, Superintendent, Schools, 780-352-4153, ext. 233
Rick Hayes, Associate Superintendent, Personnel, 780-352-4153, ext. 235
Sherri Senger, Associate Superintendent, Business, 780-352-4153, ext. 227

Whitecourt: Northern Gateway Regional Division
Also known as: Northern Gateway Public School (NGPS)
P.O. Box 840
4816 - 49th Ave., Whitecourt, AB T7S 1N8
Tel: 780-778-2800; *Fax:* 780-778-6719
Toll-Free: 800-262-8674
learn@ngps.ca
www.ngps.ca
www.facebook.com/northerngatewaypublicschools
twitter.com/ngpschools
Number of Schools: 16 schools; 4 outreach schools *Grades:* K - 12 *Enrollment:* 5000
Kevin Andrea, Superintendent
kevin.andrea@ngps.ca
Michelle Brennick, Deputy Superintendent
michelle.brennick@ngps.ca
Leslee Jodry, Assistant Superintendent
leslee.jodry@ngps.ca

Catholic

Bonnyville: Lakeland Catholic School District Board
Also known as: Lakeland Catholic Schools
Catholic Education Centre
4810 - 46th St., Bonnyville, AB T9N 1B5
Tel: 780-826-3764; *Fax:* 780-826-7576
lcsd150.ab.ca
www.facebook.com/LakelandCatholicSchoolDivision
twitter.com/LCSD_150
Number of Schools: 8 *Enrollment:* 2500 *Number of Employees:* 196
Joe Arruda, Superintendent
Pamela Guilbault, Deputy Superintendent
Michelle Dargis, Director, Student Learning
Clint Elliott, Director, Technology

Calgary: Calgary Catholic School District
Catholic School Centre
1000 - 5th Ave. SW, Calgary, AB T2P 4T9
Tel: 403-500-2000
inquiries@cssd.ab.ca
www.cssd.ab.ca
Other Information: Communications: 403-500-2763; Trustees: 403-500-2761
www.facebook.com/CalgaryCatholicSchoolDistrict
twitter.com/CCSD_edu
www.instagram.com/CalgaryCatholicSchoolDistrict
Number of Schools: 55 elem.; 41 elem. / jun. high; 3 jun. / sen.; 10 sen. high; 5 jun. high; 2 special ed. *Grades:* K - 12
Enrollment: 58000 *Number of Employees:* 5,488
Bryan Szumlas, Chief Superintendent, 403-500-2769
Narin Kishinchandani, Superintendent, Finance & Business, & Secretary-Treasurer, 403-500-2777
Mary Martin, Chair, Board, 403-500-2761
mary.martin@cssd.ab.ca
Andrea Holowka, Superintendent, Specialized Program Schools, 403-500-2424
Brad MacDonald, Superintendent, Support Services, 403-500-2733
Richard Svoboda, Superintendent, Human Resources, 403-500-2429
Mark Rawlek, Superintendent, Area North Schools, 403-500-2606
John McDonald, Superintendent, Area South Schools, 403-500-2606

Edmonton: Edmonton Catholic Schools (ECSD)
9807 - 106 St., Edmonton, AB T5K 1C2
Tel: 780-441-6000; *Fax:* 780-425-8759
Toll-Free: 888-441-6010
info@ecsd.net
www.ecsd.net
www.facebook.com/EdmontonCatholicSchoolDistrict
twitter.com/EdmCathSchools
www.linkedin.com/company/edmonton-catholic-schools
www.youtube.com/user/EdmontonCatholic
Number of Schools: 95 schools; 8 outreach schools *Grades:* K - 12 *Enrollment:* 44330 *Number of Employees:* 4,253
Laura Thibert, Chair, Board, 780-231-6312
laura.thibert@ecsd.net
Robert Martin, Superintendent, 780-441-6000
superintendent@ecsd.net

Fort McMurray: Fort McMurray Roman Catholic Separate School District (FMCS)
9809 Main St., Fort McMurray, AB T9H 1T7
Tel: 780-799-5700; *Fax:* 780-799-5706
info@fmcsd.ab.ca
www.fmcsd.ab.ca
Other Information: Service Support Centre, Phone: 780-799-5714
www.facebook.com/166299413409478
twitter.com/fmcsd
Number of Schools: 12 *Grades:* K - 12; French Immersion *Enrollment:* 6800
Cathie Langmead, Chair
cl4707@fmcsd.ab.ca
George McGuigan, Superintendent
Monica Mankowski, Deputy Superintendent, Inclusive Education
stsvcs@fmcsd.ab.ca

Grande Prairie: Grande Prairie Roman Catholic Separate School District
Catholic Education Centre
9902 - 101st St., Grande Prairie, AB T8V 2P4
Tel: 780-532-3013; *Fax:* 780-532-3430
cec@gpcsd.ca
www.gpcsd.ca
www.facebook.com/GPCSD
Number of Schools: 13 *Grades:* JK - 12; French Immersion; Outreach *Enrollment:* 5600 *Number of Employees:* 700

Michael Ouellette, Chair
michaelouellette@gpcsd.ca
Karl Germann, Superintendent, Schools
Greg Miller, Assistant Superintendent, Human Resources
Jessie Shirley, Assistant Superintendent, Teaching & Learning
Nicole Macmullin, Director, Finances

Leduc: St. Thomas Aquinas Roman Catholic Separate School Division
Also known as: STAR Catholic Schools
4906 - 50th Ave., Leduc, AB T9E 6W9, Canada
Tel: 780-986-2500; *Fax:* 780-986-8620
Toll-Free: 1-800-583-0688
feedback@starcatholic.ab.ca
www.starcatholic.ab.ca
www.facebook.com/starcatholic
twitter.com/STARCatholic
www.youtube.com/user/starcatholic
Number of Schools: 12 schools; 1 outreach centre *Grades:* Pre-K - 12 *Enrollment:* 4000 *Number of Employees:* 400
Charlie Bouchard, Superintendent, Schools
charlie.bouchard@starcatholic.ab.ca
Laurie Kardynal, Assistant Superintendent, Learning Services
laurie.kardynal@starcatholic.ab.ca
Sean McGuinness, Assistant Superintendent
sean.mcguinness@starcatholic.ab.ca
Ed Latka, Secretary-Treasurer
edward.latka@starcatholic.ab.ca
Clare Ganton, Director, Faith Life & Religious Education
clare.ganton@starcatholic.ab.ca
Chris Manion, Director, Facilities
chris.manion@starcatholic.ab.ca
Ceilidh Osland, Director, Finance & Business
ceilidh.osland@starcatholic.ab.ca
Chris Zarski, Director, Instruction & Staff Development
chris.zarski@starcatholic.ab.ca
Caitlin Kehoe, Manager, Communications
caitlin.kehoe@starcatholic.ab.ca
David McNair, Manager, Technology
david.mcnair@starcatholic.ab.ca
Michelle Lamer, Chair, Board
michelle.lamer@starcatholic.ab.ca

Lethbridge: Holy Spirit Roman Catholic Separate School Division
Also known as: Holy Spirit Catholic School Division
620 - 12B St. North, Lethbridge, AB T1H 2L7
Tel: 403-327-9555; *Fax:* 403-327-9595
contact@holyspirit.ab.ca
www.holyspirit.ab.ca
www.facebook.com/HolySpiritCSD
twitter.com/HolySpiritCSD
www.youtube.com/user/HolySpiritSchools1
Number of Schools: 15 *Grades:* K - 12 *Enrollment:* 5003 *Number of Employees:* 565
Bob Spitzig, Chair
Ken Sampson, Superintendent
sampsonk@holyspirit.ab.ca
Michelle MacKinnon, Deputy Superintendent
Amanda Lindemann, Director, Finance
lindemanna@holyspirit.ab.ca

Lloydminster: Lloydminster Roman Catholic School Division (LCSD)
6611B - 39th St., Lloydminster, AB T9V 2Z4
Tel: 780-808-8585; *Fax:* 780-808-8787
information@lcsd.ca
www.lcsd.ca
www.facebook.com/lcsd89
Number of Schools: 6 *Grades:* K.-12
Paula Scott, Chair
Nigel McCarthy, Director, Education
Melanie Stelmaschuk, Chief Financial Officer

Medicine Hat: Medicine Hat Catholic Separate School Division
Also known as: Medicine Hat Catholic Board of Education
1251 - 1st Ave. SW, Medicine Hat, AB T1A 8B4
Tel: 403-527-2292; *Fax:* 403-529-0917
Toll-Free: 866-864-0013
www.mhcbe.ab.ca
Grades: Pre-K - 12 *Enrollment:* 2800
Dick Mastel, Chair
Dwayne Zarichny, Superintendent, Schools
dwayne.zarichny@mhcbe.ab.ca
Chuck Hellman, Deputy Superintendent
chuck.hellman@mhcbe.ab.ca
Hugh Lehr, Associate Superintendent, Learning Services
hugh.lehr@mhcbe.ab.ca

Okotoks: Christ the Redeemer Catholic Separate School Division
1 McRae St., Okotoks, AB T1S 1B3
Tel: 403-938-2659; *Fax:* 403-938-4575
Toll-Free: 800-737-9383
info@redeemer.ab.ca
www.redeemer.ab.ca
www.facebook.com/CTRcatholic
Number of Schools: 17 *Grades:* K - 12 *Enrollment:* 6200 *Number of Employees:* 540 teachers; 300 support staff
Ron Schreiber, Chair, 403-938-6374
Scott Morrison, Superintendent
smorrison@redeemer.ab.ca
Vincent Behm, Associate Superintendent
vbehm@redeemer.ab.ca
Michael Kilcommons, Associate Superintendent, Corporate Services
mkilcommons@redeemer.ab.ca

Peace River: Holy Family Catholic Regional Division (HFCRD)
10307 - 99th St., Peace River, AB T8S 1R5
Tel: 780-624-3956; *Fax:* 780-624-1154
Toll-Free: 800-285-8712
hfcrd@hfcrd.ab.ca
hfcrd.ab.ca
www.facebook.com/hfcrd
twitter.com/HFCRD37
Number of Schools: 9 *Enrollment:* 2100 *Number of Employees:* 306
Kelly Whalen, Chair
kelly.whalen@hfcrd.ab.ca
Betty Turpin, Superintendent
betty.turpin@hfcrd.ab.ca
Jim Taplin, Assistant Superintendent, Inclusion & Student Support
jim.taplin@hfcrd.ab.ca
Cora Ostermeier, Assistant Superintendent, Human Resources & Learning
cora.ostermeier@hfcrd.ab.ca

Red Deer: Red Deer Catholic Regional Schools
Montfort Centre
5210 - 61st St., Red Deer, AB T4N 6N8
Tel: 403-343-1055; *Fax:* 403-347-6410
info@rdcrs.ca
www.rdcrs.ca
www.facebook.com/RDCRS
twitter.com/rdcrs
www.linkedin.com/company/red-deer-catholic-regional-schools
www.youtube.com/c/RedDeerCatholicRegionalSchools
Number of Schools: 20 *Enrollment:* 10360 *Number of Employees:* 571 teachers; 416 support staff
Kathleen Finnigan, Superintendent, Schools, 403-343-1055, ext. 310125
Dave Khatib, Associate Superintendent, Inclusive Learning, 403-343-1055, ext. 310124
Ryan Ledene, Associate Superintendent, Personnel, 403-343-1055, ext. 310114
ryan.ledene@rdcrs.ca

Sherwood Park: Elk Island Catholic Separate School Division
Also known as: Elk Island Catholic Schools (EICS)
310 Broadview Rd., Sherwood Park, AB T8H 1A4
Tel: 780-467-8896; *Toll-Free:* 800-996-9982
eics@eics.ab.ca
www.eics.ab.ca
www.facebook.com/eics.ab.ca
twitter.com/EICSCatholic
Number of Schools: 18 *Grades:* Pre-K - 12 *Enrollment:* 7800
Shawn Haggarty, Superintendent, Schools, 780-467-8896
Paul Corrigan, Assistant Superintendent, Faith & Wellness, 780-449-6445
Lorraine Court, Assistant Superintendent, Inclusive Learning, 780-449-6445
Brett Cox, Assistant Superintendent, Human Resources, 780-449-6451
Thérèse deChamplain-Good, Assistant Superintendent, Educational Excellence, 587-745-2012

Spruce Grove: Evergreen Catholic Separate School Division
#110, 381 Grove Dr., Spruce Grove, AB T7X 2Y9
Tel: 780-962-5627; *Fax:* 780-962-4664
Toll-Free: 800-825-7152
www.ecsrd.ca
Number of Schools: 11 *Grades:* ECS - 12 *Enrollment:* 4300
Number of Employees: 450
Ron McKay, Chair
rmckay@ecsrd.ca
Mike Paonessa, Superintendent

Dave Dempsey, Deputy Superintendent
Cindy Escott, Associate Superintendent, Learning

St Albert: Greater St. Albert Roman Catholic Separate School Division
Also known as: Greater St. Albert Catholic Schools
Old Name: Greater St. Albert Roman Catholic Separate School District No. 734
6 St Vital Ave., St Albert, AB T8N 1K2
Tel: 780-459-7711; *Fax:* 780-458-3213
www.gsacrd.ab.ca
www.facebook.com/gsacrd
twitter.com/GSACRD
www.youtube.com/user/GSACRD
Number of Schools: 18 *Grades:* K - 12 *Enrollment:* 5500
Noreen Radford, Chair
Joan Crockett, Vice-Chair
jcrockett@gsacrd.ab.ca
David Keohane, Superintendent
dkeohane@gsacrd.ab.ca
Steve Bayus, Deputy Superintendent
sbayus@gsacrd.ab.ca
David Quick, Assistant Superintendent, Learning Services
dquick@gsacrd.ab.ca
Colleen McClure, Interim Associate Superintendent, Student Services
cmcclure@gsacrd.ab.ca
Calvin Wait, Director, Facilities
cwait@gsacrd.ab.ca
Lydia Yeomans, District Principal
lyeomans@gsacrd.ab.ca
Deb Schlag, Secretary-Treasurer
dschlag@gsacrd.ab.ca

Wainwright: East Central Alberta Catholic Separate Schools Regional Division No. 16
Also known as: East Central Catholic Schools (ECCS)
1018 - 1st Ave., Wainwright, AB T9W 1G9
Tel: 780-842-3992; *Fax:* 780-842-5322
www.ecacs.ca
www.facebook.com/EastCentralCatholicSchools
twitter.com/ecacs16
Number of Schools: 7 *Grades:* K - 12 *Enrollment:* 2400 *Number of Employees:* 230
Debra Klein, Chair
Glenn Nowosad, Superintendent
glenn.nowosad@ecacs16.ab.ca
Kelly Ehalt, Assistant Superintendent
kelly.ehalt@ecacs16.ab.ca

Whitecourt: Living Waters Catholic Separate School Division
P.O. Box 1949
4204 Kepler St., Whitecourt, AB T7S 1P6
Tel: 780-778-5666; *Fax:* 780-778-2727
Toll-Free: 888-434-7348
www.livingwaters.ab.ca
Number of Schools: 6 *Grades:* Pre.-12 *Enrollment:* 1800 *Number of Employees:* 200
Jo-Anne Lanctot, Superintendent
Trevor Mitchell, Deputy Superintendent
Courtney Lawrance, Associate Superintendent, Learning

French

Calgary: Conseil scolaire FrancoSud
#230, rue 6940 Fisher SE, Calgary, AB T2H 0W3
Tél: 403-686-6998; *Téléc:* 403-686-2914
Ligne sans frais: 877-245-7686
infoconseil@francosud.ca
francosud.ca
www.facebook.com/csfrancosud
twitter.com/csfrancosud
Number of Schools: 14 *Grades:* Mat. - 12 *Enrollment:* 3300
Erwan Goasdoué, Président, Conseil
erwan.goasdoue@francosud.ca
Lyne Bacon, Directrice générale adjointe, Ressources humaines, 403-686-6998
lyne.bacon@francosud.ca
Daniel Therrien, Directeur général, 403-686-6998
daniel.therrien@francosud.ca
Christian Roux, Directeur général adjoint, Services éducatifs, 403-686-6998
christian.roux@francosud.ca
Valérie Tétrault, Directrice, Services financiers, 403-686-6998
valerie.tetrault@francosud.ca

Edmonton: Conseil scolaire Centre-Nord
Greater North Central Francophone Education Region #2
#322, 8627, rue Marie-Anne-Gaboury (91 St.), Edmonton, AB T6C 3N1
Tél: 780-468-6440; *Téléc:* 780-440-1631
Ligne sans frais: 800-248-6886
conseil@centrenord.ab.ca
www.centrenord.ab.ca
www.facebook.com/conseil.centrenord
twitter.com/CSCNInfo
www.linkedin.com/company/conseil-scolaire-centre-nord
Number of Schools: 19 *Grades:* Élém. - Sec. *Enrollment:* 3670
Number of Employees: 500
Tanya Saumure, Présidente, Conseil
tsaumure@centrenord.ab.ca
Robert Lessard, Directeur général, 780-468-6440
directiongenerale@centrenord.ab.ca
Gisèle Bourque, Directrice générale adjointe, 780-468-6440
gbourque@centrenord.ab.ca
Josée Devaney, Secrétaire-trésorière, 780-468-6440
jdevaney@centrenord.ab.ca
Suzanne Amyotte, Préposée, Comptes payables & recevables, 780-468-6440
samyotte@centrenord.ab.ca
Nathalie Gosselin, Préposée, Paie & Finances, 780-468-6440
ngosselin@centrenord.ab.ca
Martine Ruest, Préposée, Ressources humaines, 780-468-6440
mruest@centrenord.ab.ca
Grégory Djomo, Coordinateur, Communications & Recrutement, 780-468-6440
glucien@centrenord.ab.ca

Saint-Paul: Conseil scolaire Centre-Est
East Central Francophone Education Region #3
P.O. Box 249
4617 - 50th Ave., Saint-Paul, AB T0A 3A0
Tél: 780-645-3888; *Téléc:* 780-645-2045
Ligne sans frais: 866-645-9556
centreest@centreest.ca
centreest.ca/accueil
Number of Schools: 5 *Grades:* Pre-12
Réginald Roy, Président
rroy@centreest.ca
Dolorèse Nolette, Directrice générale
dnolette@centreest.ca
Josée Verreault, Directrice générale adjointe, Services pédagogiques
jverreault@centreest.ca

St Isidore: Conseil scolaire du Nord-Ouest
Northwest Francophone Education Region #1
P.O. Box 1220
#23, 3 av des Compagnons, St Isidore, AB T0H 3B0
Tél: 780-624-8855; *Téléc:* 780-624-8554
Ligne sans frais: 866-624-8855
conseil@csno.ab.ca
csno.ab.ca
www.facebook.com/CSNOno1
twitter.com/CSNO
www.instagram.com/csnoalberta
Number of Schools: 3 *Grades:* K - 12 *Enrollment:* 430 *Number of Employees:* 83
Sylvianne Maisonneuve, Présidente
Brigitte Kropielnicki, Directrice générale
brigittekropielnicki@csno.ab.ca
Rachelle Bergeron, Secrétaire générale
rachellebergeron@csno.ab.ca

First Nations

Brocket: Peigan Board of Education
P.O. Box 130
Brocket, AB T0K 0H0
Tel: 403-965-3910; *Fax:* 403-965-3713
Toll-Free: 877-965-3910
info@piikani.ca
www.piikani.ca
www.facebook.com/peiganboardofeducation
Grades: K - 12
Lisa Crowshoe, Director, Education
director@piikani.ca

Chateh: Dene Tha' First Nation Education Department
P.O. Box 120
Chateh, AB T0H 0S0
Tel: 780-321-3775; *Fax:* 780-321-3886
Toll-Free: 877-336-3842
denetha.ca/programs/education
Number of Schools: 1 *Grades:* KJ - 12; Dene language
Enrollment: 450 *Note:* The Dene Tha' First Nation Education

Department oversees education, counselling, transportation & accommodation for Dene Tha' First Nation band members. They operate the Dene Tha' Community School.
Shane Providence, Councillor, Learning
shane.providence@denetha.ca
Carlito Somera, Principal
carlitos@chateh-education.net

Driftpile: Driftpile Band Education Authority
P.O. Box 240
Driftpile, AB T0G 0V0
Tel: 780-355-3615
education@dpcn.ca
www.dpcn.ca/community/education
Grades: K - 8 *Enrollment:* 75 *Note:* The Driftpile Band operates the Driftpile First Nation Community School.
Tedmann Onyango, Education Director

Duffield: Paul Band Education Authority
P.O. Box 89
Duffield, AB T0E 0N0
Tel: 780-892-2025; *Fax:* 780-892-2019
www.paulfirstnation.com
Grades: K-12 *Note:* Paul Band Education Authority operates the Paul Band First Nation School.
Nicole Callihoo, Director, Education
birk_callihoonicole@hotmail.com

Enoch: Kitaskinaw Education Authority
P.O. Box 90
Enoch, AB T7X 3Y3
Tel: 780-470-5657
info@kitaskinaw.com
www.kitaskinaw.com
Number of Schools: 1 *Grades:* Nursery - 9 *Note:* The Kitaskinaw Education Authority oversees education for the Enoch Cree Nation & operates the Kitaskinaw School.

Fort Vermilion: Tallcree Band Education Authority
P.O. Box 310
Fort Vermilion, AB T0H 1N0
Tel: 780-927-3727
www.tallcreefirstnation.ca
Number of Schools: 2 *Grades:* K - 6 *Enrollment:* 100 *Note:* Chief Tallcree North School & Chief Tallcree South School

Glenevis: Alexis Band Education Authority
P.O. Box 27
Glenevis, AB T0E 0X0
Tel: 780-967-2225; *Fax:* 780-967-5484
www.alexised.ca
Enrollment: 180 *Note:* The Alexis Band operates the Alexis Elementary Junior Senior High School & the Nikoodi Upgrading School.
Toni Letendre, Education Director
toni.letendre@alexised.ca
Jasmine Alexis, Assistant Director
jasmine.alexis@alexised.ca

Goodfish Lake: Whitefish Lake Education Authority
P.O. Box 271
Goodfish Lake, AB T0A 1R0
Tel: 780-636-7000
contact@wfl128.ca
wfl128.ca/education-services

Hobbema: Nipisihkopahk Education Authority (NEA)
P.O. Box 658
Hobbema, AB T0C 1N0
Tel: 780-585-2211; *Fax:* 780-585-3857
Toll-Free: 800-843-7359
www.scnea.com
Number of Schools: 5 *Grades:* 1-12 *Enrollment:* 1000
Kevin Wells, Superintendent
kevinwells@scnea.com

Hythe: Horse Lake First Nation Education Authority
P.O. Box 303
Hythe, AB T0H 2C0
Tel: 780-356-2248; *Fax:* 780-356-3666
Note: Horse Lake First Nation operates the Horse Lake School.

John D'Or Prairie: Little Red River Board of Education
P.O. Box 120
John D'Or Prairie, AB T0H 3X0
Tel: 780-759-3772; *Fax:* 780-759-3890
lrrcn.ab.ca
Number of Schools: 3 *Grades:* Kindergarten - 12; Special Ed. *Enrollment:* 1050 *Note:* The Little Red River Board of Education administers the provision of educational programming for First Nation students of the Little Red River Cree Nation. Cultural programming is part of the students' education. The Board also offers adult upgrading & trades training.

Gordon Breen, Director, Education, 780-759-3912, ext. 1118
gordonb@lrrbe.com
Patsy Johns, Assistant Director, 780-759-3912, ext. 1117
patsyj@lrrbe.com

Kehewin: Kehewin Band Education Department
P.O. Box 30
Kehewin, AB T0A 1C0
Tel: 780-826-6200; *Fax:* 780-826-5919
www.kcec.ca
Number of Schools: 2 *Note:* The Kehewin Band operates the Kehewin Community Education Centre.
Linda Gadwa, Principal
lgadwa@kcec.ca

Kinuso: Swan River First Nation Education Authority
P.O. Box 270
Kinuso, AB T0G 1K0
Tel: 780-775-3536; *Fax:* 780-775-3796
swanriverfirstnation.com/departments/education
Number of Schools: 1
Paula Cardinal, Education Manager

Lac La Biche: Beaver Lake Education Authority
P.O. Box 5000
Lac La Biche, AB T0A 2C0
Tel: 780-623-4549; *Fax:* 780-623-4523
amiskcommunityschool@yahoo.ca
www.beaverlakecreenation.ca
Other Information: Amisk Community School, Phone: 780-623-4548; Fax: 780-623-4659
Number of Schools: 1 *Grades:* Early Childhood Svs.-Jr. Secondary *Note:* The Beaver Lake Education Authority operates the Amisk Community School. The school is led by a nine member management team which is supervised by the Beaver Lake Cree Nation Band Council Education Portfolio Holder.

Lac La Biche: Heart Lake Band #469 Education Authority
P.O. Box 447
Lac La Biche, AB T0A 2C0
Tel: 780-623-2130; *Fax:* 780-623-3505
heartlakefirstnation.com
Note: Heart Lake Band #469 operates the Heart Lake Kohls School.

Maskwacîs: Maskwacîs Education Schools Commission (MESC)
P.O. Box 58
Maskwacîs, AB T0C 1N0
Tel: 780-585-3333; *Fax:* 780-585-3857
Toll-Free: 800-843-7358
info@maskwacised.ca
www.maskwacised.ca
www.facebook.com/MaskwacisEducation
Number of Schools: 11 *Grades:* K - 12 *Note:* The commission is owned & operated by the Ermineskin Cree Nation, Louis Bull Tribe, Montana First Nation & Samson Cree Nation. It serves Maskwacîs Cree & formed in 2016 from the amalgamation of four separate authorities.

Morinville: Alexander First Nation Education Authority
P.O. Box 3449
Morinville, AB T8R 1S3
Tel: 780-939-3551; *Fax:* 780-939-3523
education@alexanderfn.com
alexanderfn.com/programs/education
Note: The Alexander First Nation Education Authority operates the Kipohtakaw Education Centre.
Jody Kootenay, Director, Education, 780-939-3551, ext. 205
Verna Arcand, Assistant Director, Education, 780-939-3551, ext. 204

Morley: Stoney Education Authority
238 East Morley Rd., Morley, AB T0L 1N0
Tel: 403-881-2743; *Fax:* 403-881-4252
www.stoneyeducation.ca
www.facebook.com/StoneyEducation
twitter.com/StoneyEducation
Number of Schools: 3 *Grades:* K - 12; Stoney language *Enrollment:* 1100 *Note:* The Stoney Education Authority, located west of Calgary, Alberta, provides education to members of the Stoney Nakoda First Nation. Education includes cultural programs.
Bill Shade, Superintendent

Rocky Mountain House: Sunchild First Nation Band Education Authority
P.O. Box 1149
Rocky Mountain House, AB T4T 1A8
Tel: 403-989-3476
www.sunchildschool.com
www.facebook.com/sunchildschool
Number of Schools: 1 *Grades:* K - 12
Angie Goodrunning, Director, Education
goodrunning@sunchildschool.com

Saddle Lake: Saddle Lake Education Authority
P.O. Box 130
Saddle Lake, AB T0A 3T0
Tel: 780-726-7609; *Fax:* 780-726-4069
Toll-Free: 800-668-0243
slpssmokesignals.wordpress.com
Number of Schools: 4 *Grades:* Elem.; Sec.
Debra Cardinal, Superintendent, Schools
dcardinal@saddlelake.ca

Siksika: Siksika Board of Education
P.O. Box 1099
Siksika, AB T0J 3W0
Tel: 403-734-4028; *Fax:* 403-734-2505
siksikaed@sboe.ca
siksikaed.com
www.facebook.com/siksikaboardofeducation
Number of Schools: 4 *Grades:* K - 12
Lenora Rabbit Carrier, Superintendent
rabbitcarrierl@sboe.ca
Wanda Calf Robe, Assistant Superintendent
calfrobew@sboe.ca
Lenora Poundmaker, Director, Learning
poundmakerl@sboe.ca

Stand Off: Kainai Board of Education
P.O. Box 240
Stand Off, AB T0L 1Y0
Tel: 403-737-3966; *Fax:* 403-737-2361
kainaied.ca
www.facebook.com/640532316009811
Number of Schools: 5 *Grades:* 1-12
Mike Bruised Head, Chair
Cameron Shade, Superintendent

Tsuu T'ina Sarcee: Tsuu T'ina Nation Board of Education
#250, 9911 Chiila Blvd. SW, Tsuu T'ina Sarcee, AB T2W 6H6
Tel: 403-238-5484
tsuutinanation.com/tsuutina-education-department
Number of Schools: 3 *Grades:* K - 12; Adult Upgrading *Enrollment:* 299
Valerie McDougall, Director, Education, 403-238-5484
vmcdougall@tsuutinaeducation.com

Valleyview: Sturgeon Lake First Nation, Band #154, Education Authority
P.O. Box 5
Valleyview, AB T0H 3N0
Tel: 306-764-5506
www.slfn.ca
Number of Schools: 1 *Grades:* K - 12 *Note:* Sturgeon Lake First Nation Band #154 operates the Sturgeon Lake School.

Wabasca: Bigstone Cree Nation Education Authority
P.O. Box 870
Wabasca, AB T0G 2K0
Tel: 780-891-3825; *Fax:* 780-891-2178
Toll-Free: 877-458-2447
bcnea.info@bigstoneeducation.ca
www.bigstoneeducation.ca
Number of Schools: 1 *Grades:* Elementary *Enrollment:* 247
Note: Bigstone Education Authority Society operates the Bigstone Cree Nation Community School.

Schools: Specialized

Charter

Androssan: New Horizons School
53145 Range Rd., Androssan, AB T8E 2M8, Canada
Tel: 780-467-6409; *Fax:* 780-417-1786
administration@newhorizons.ab.ca
www.newhorizons.ab.ca
Grades: K - 9 *Enrollment:* 200
Don Falk, Superintendent

Calgary: Almadina Language Charter Academy (ALCA)
#210, 1829 - 54 St. SE, Calgary, AB T2B 1N5, Canada
Tel: 403-543-5078; *Fax:* 403-543-5079
www.esl-almadina.com

Number of Schools: 2 *Grades:* ECS - 9 *Enrollment:* 600
Haytham Ghouriri, Board Chair
hghouriri@esl-almadina.com
Yvonne DePeel, Superintendent, 403-543-5078
ydepeel@esl-almadina.com
Suzanne Bedard, Secretary Treasurer, 403-543-5078

Calgary: Calgary Arts Academy Society (CAA)
4931 Grove Hill Rd. SW, Calgary, AB T3E 4G4, Canada
Tel: 403-532-3020; *Fax:* 403-217-0965
info@calgaryartsacademy.com
www.calgaryartsacademy.com
www.facebook.com/203455252638
Number of Schools: 2 *Grades:* K - 9 *Enrollment:* 279
Dale Erickson, Superintendent
derickson@calgaryartsacademy.com
Jan Jordan, Secretary-Treasurer
jjordan@calgaryartsacademy.com
Kevin Loftus, Communications / Registrar
kloftus@calgaryartsacademy.com

Calgary: Calgary Girls' School (CGS)
#203, 610 - 70th Ave. SE, Calgary, AB T2H 2J6, Canada
Tel: 403-252-0702; *Fax:* 403-252-0717
www.calgarygirlsschool.com
twitter.com/CalGirlsSchool
Number of Schools: 2 *Grades:* 4-9 *Enrollment:* 600
Dianne McBeth, Superintendent
dianne.mcbeth@calgarygirlsschool.com
Wendy Juergens, Secretary Treasurer
Wendy.Juergens@calgarygirlsschool.com
Debbie Malone, Library Technologist
Debbie.Malone@calgarygirlsschool.com

Calgary: Connect Charter School (CCS)
5915 Lewis Dr. SW, Calgary, AB T3E 5Z4
Tel: 403-282-2890; *Fax:* 403-282-2896
www.connectcharter.ca
www.facebook.com/connectcharter
twitter.com/connectcharter
www.youtube.com/channel/UCPNG2xEVeXrAqPpiuTFKCGQ
Grades: 4-9 *Enrollment:* 600 *Number of Employees:* 34 teaching staff
Garry McKinnon, Superintendent, 403-282-2890, ext. 232
garry.m@connectcharter.ca
Darrell Lonsberry, Principal, 403-282-2890, ext. 122
darrell.l@connectcharter.ca
Phil Butterfield, Assistant Principal, 403-282-2890, ext. 116
phil.b@connectcharter.ca
Scott Petronech, Assistant Principal & Educational Technologist
scott.p@connectcharter.ca
Myra Penberthy, Secretary-Treasurer
myra.p@connectcharter.ca
Michelle Hodgson, Library Assistant and Outdoor Education Coordinator
michelle.h@connectcharter.ca

Calgary: Foundations for the Future Charter Academy (FFCA)
FFCA Central Office
#240, 688 Heritage Dr. SE, Calgary, AB T2H 1M6
Tel: 403-520-3206; *Fax:* 403-520-3209
board@ffca-calgary.com
www.ffca-calgary.com
Number of Schools: 7 *Grades:* K - 12
Jay Pritchard, Superintendent
Rick Byers, Director, Facilities, 403-520-3206, ext. 157
Judy Gray, Coordinator, School Improvement, 403-520-3206, ext. 152
John Deines, Coordinator, Instruction, 403-520-3206, ext. 162

Calgary: Westmount Charter School Society
728 - 32 St. NW, Calgary, AB T2N 2V9, Canada
Tel: 403-217-3707; *Fax:* 403-249-3422
admin@westmountcharter.com
www.westmountcharter.com
Number of Schools: 2 *Grades:* K-12 *Enrollment:* 880
Joe Frank, Superintendent, 403-217-3707, ext. 1023
joe.frank@westmountcharter.com
Johnathan Liu, Secretary-Treasurer, 403-217-3707, ext. 1020
johnathan.liu@westmountcharter.com

Edmonton: Aurora Charter School
12245 - 131 St., Edmonton, AB T5L 1M8
Tel: 780-454-1855; *Fax:* 780-454-8104
aurorasc@auroraschool.com
www.auroraschool.com
Grades: K - 9 *Enrollment:* 600
Don Wilson, Board Chair
Dale Bischoff, Superintendent
dbischoff@auroraschool.com
Ian Gray, Principal
igray@auroraschool.com

Janet Rockwood, Assistant Principal
jrockwood@auroraschool.com
Georgia Foster, Registrar
gfoster@auroraschool.com
Kathy Holubitsky, Learning Resources
kholubitsky@auroraschool.com

Edmonton: Boyle Street Education Centre (BSEC)
10312 - 105 Ave., Edmonton, AB T5J 1E6, Canada
Tel: 780-428-1420; *Fax:* 780-429-1428
info@bsec.ab.ca
www.bsec.ab.ca
www.facebook.com/BoyleStreedEducationCentre
twitter.com/BoyleStreetEd
www.youtube.com/user/BoyleStreetEd
Grades: 7-12 *Enrollment:* 105

Edmonton: Suzuki Charter School Society
10720 - 54 St., Edmonton, AB T6A 2H9
Tel: 780-468-2598; *Fax:* 780-463-8630
www.suzukischool.ca
Grades: Preschool - 6 *Note:* The charter school provides academics, enriched with music based on the Suzuki Approach.
Lee Lucente, Superintendent
lucentel@suzukischool.ca
Karen Spencer, Principal
spencerk@suzukischool.ca
Dale Szalacsi, Assistant Principal
szalacsid@suzukischool.ca
Heather Christison, Secretary-Treasurer
christison@suzukischool.ca
Allison Elsdon, Library Technician

Medicine Hat: Centre for Academic & Personal Excellence Institute (CAPE)
830A Balmoral St. SE, Medicine Hat, AB T1A 0W9, Canada
Tel: 403-528-2983; *Fax:* 403-528-3048
info@capeisgreat.org
www.capeisgreat.org
www.facebook.com/107913172565986
twitter.com/CAPESchoolMH
Grades: K-9 *Enrollment:* 203 *Number of Employees:* 30 *Note:* CAPE is a public charter school in southeastern Alberta. Personalized integrated program; full day everyday kindergarten; very low student-teacher ratio & high number of support educational assistant; full-time educational psychologist.
Teresa Di Ninno, Superintendent, 403-528-2983
tdininno@capeisgreat.org
Jeney Gordon, Principal, 403-528-2983
jgordon@capeisgreat.org
Cali Berard, Vice-Principal, 403-528-2983
cberard@capeisgreat.org
Linda Krochak, Director, Student Services, 403-528-2983
lkrochak@capeisgreat.org

Stony Plain: Mother Earth's Children's Charter School Society (MECCS)
P.O. Box 11
Site 504, RR#5, Stony Plain, AB T7Z 1X5, Canada
Tel: 780-892-7531; *Fax:* 780-848-2395
admin@meccs.org
www.meccs.org
Grades: K - 9
Ed Wittchen, Superintendent
ed.wittchen@telus.net
Anita LeMoignan, Secretary/Treasurer
alemoignan@meccs.org

Valhalla Centre: Valhalla School Foundation
Also known as: Valhalla Community School
P.O. Box 148
9702 - 100 Ave., Valhalla Centre, AB T0H 3M0, Canada
Tel: 780-356-2370; *Fax:* 780-356-2789
info@valhallacommunityschool.ca
www.valhallacommunityschool.ca
Grades: K - 9

First Nations

Atikameg: Whitefish Lake First Nation School
General Delivery, Atikameg, AB T0G 0C0
Tel: 780-767-3797

Brocket: Napi's Playground Elementary School (NPES)
P.O. Box 10
Brocket, AB T0K 0H0
Tel: 403-965-2121; *Fax:* 403-965-2054
www.piikani.ca
Grades: K - 6 *Number of Employees:* 15
Rudy Schuh, Principal
Principal@piikani.ca

Brocket: Piikani Nation Secondary School
P.O. Box 10
Brocket, AB T0K 0H0
Tel: 403-965-2121; *Fax:* 403-965-2054
www.piikani.ca
Grades: 7 - 12
Rudy Schuh, Principal
Principal@piikani.ca

Cadotte Lake: Woodland Cree First Nation Cadotte Lake School
General Delivery, Cadotte Lake, AB T0H 0N0
Tel: 780-629-3767
Grades: K - 12

Cardston: Kainai High School
P.O. Box 2640
Cardston, AB T0K 0K0
Tel: 403-737-3963; *Fax:* 403-737-2100
khs.kainaied.ca
Annette Bruised Head, Principal

Cardston: Tatsikiisaapo'p Middle School
P.O. Box 250
Cardston, AB T0K OKO
Tel: 403-737-2846
tms.kainaied.ca
Grades: 6 - 8
Ramona Big Head, Principal

Chard: Chipewyan Prairie Dene High School
General Delivery, Chard, AB T0P 1G0
Tel: 780-559-2478

Chateh: Dene Tha' Community School (DTCS)
P.O. Box 30
Chateh, AB T0H 0S0
Tel: 780-321-3940; *Fax:* 780-321-3800
Toll-Free: 877-336-3842
reception@chateh-education.net
www.denetha.ca/education/dtcs/
Grades: K - 10; Dene language *Enrollment:* 150 *Note:* Dene Tha' Community School provides education that follows Alberta's kindergarten to grade 10 curriculum, as well as programs such as an early literacy program, a special education program, & Dene language & culture programs.
Jim Brown, Principal, 780-321-3940
jamesb@chateh-education.net
Virginia Alarcon, Vice-Principal, Junior High, 780-321-3940

Cold Lake: LeGeoff School
P.O. Box 1769
Cold Lake, AB T9M 1P4
Tel: 780-594-7183; *Fax:* 780-594-3577
clfns.com
Grades: K-9 *Enrollment:* 96 *Number of Employees:* 13 *Note:* LeGeoff School is federally administered & funded by the Department of Indian Affairs. The school employs seven federally funded teachers & six Cold Lake First Nations funded positions.
Maryanne Bushore, Principal, 780-594-3733
maryannebushore@kinusoo.ca

Driftpile: Driftpile Community School
P.O. Box 240
Driftpile, AB T0G 0V0, Canada
Tel: 780-355-3615; *Fax:* 780-355-2135
www.driftpilecreenation.com
Grades: K - 8; Cree language *Enrollment:* 75 *Note:* Driftpile Community School offers a full academic program, as well as a Cree language & cultural program with traditional music, folklore, & crafts.
Daisy McGee, Principal
Josephine Willier, Secretary
Janice Chalifoux, Family School Wellness Worker
Leonard Isadore, Contact, Cultural Appreciation

Duffield: Paul Band First Nation School
P.O. Box 63
Duffield, AB T0E 0N0
Tel: 780-892-2675
www.paulfirstnation.com
Ruby Bird, Principal, 780-892-2025
rubybird@paulfirstnation.com

Enilda: Sucker Creek K4-K5 School
P.O. Box 65
Enilda, AB T0G 0W0
Tel: 780-523-5593

Enoch: Kitaskinaw School
P.O. Box 90
Enoch, AB T7X 3Y3

Tel: 780-470-5657; Fax: 780-470-5687
www.kitaskinaw.com
Grades: Nursery - 9 Note: Kitaskinaw School is part of the
Kitaskinaw Education Authority. The school educates members
of the Enoch Cree Nation.
Phyllis Cardinal, Principal
phyllis.cardinal@kitaskinaw.com

Fort Vermillion: Chief Tallcree School North
P.O. Box 310
Fort Vermillion, AB T0H 1N0

Tel: 780-927-4381

Fort Vermillion: Chief Tallcree School South
P.O. Box 310
Fort Vermillion, AB T0H 1N0

Tel: 780-927-3803

Fox Lake: Jean Baptiste Sewepagaham School
P.O. Box 270
Fox Lake, AB T0H 1R0

Tel: 780-659-3820
Grades: K - 12; Cree language Enrollment: 600 Note: Jean
Baptiste Sewepagaham School is one of three schools in the
Little Red River Board of Education. The school serves
members of the Little Red River Cree Nation, located
approximately 125 kilometres east of High Level, Alberta.

Frog Lake: Chief Napeweaw Comprehensive School
General Delivery, Frog Lake, AB T0A 1M0, Canada
Tel: 780-943-3918; Fax: 780-943-2336
www.froglake.ca/education_authority.html
Grades: K - 12 Enrollment: 300
Sherri O'Dell, Principal
sherriodell@froglake.ca

Garden River: Sister Gloria School
P.O. Box 90
Garden River, AB T0H 4G0

Tel: 780-659-3644; Fax: 780-659-3890
Note: The Little Red River Board of Education consists of three
schools, including Sister Gloria School. Sister Gloria School
provides education to First Nation students of the Little Red
River Cree Nation. The Alberta community is situated
approximately 125 kilometres east of High Level.
Garry Wilson, Principal
wilson_garry@hotmail.com

**Glenevis: Alexis Elementary Junior Senior High
School**
P.O. Box 27
Glenevis, AB T0E 0X0

Tel: 780-967-5919; Fax: 780-967-2671
www.alexised.ca/alexis-school-%28es-jr-sr%29.aspx
Loretta Mustus-Duncan, Principal

Glenevis: Nikoodi Upgrading School
P.O. Box 135
Glenevis, AB T0E 0X0

Tel: 780-967-4878; Fax: 780-967-4999

**Goodfish Lake: Pakan Elementary and Junior High
School**
P.O. Box 274
Goodfish Lake, AB T0A 1R0

Tel: 780-636-2525
www.wfl128.ca
Grades: K - 9
Duane Manderscheid, Principal

Hobbema: Kisipatnahk School
P.O. Box 1290
Hobbema, AB T0C 1N0

Tel: 780-585-0035; Fax: 780-585-0039
school@lbschool.com
lbschool.com
www.facebook.com/kisipatnahkschool.louisbull
Grades: K - 9 Enrollment: 212 Number of Employees: 28 Note:
The School is a Cree Cultural School offering instruction in
Maskwacis Cree language.
Patricia Marshall, Principal

Hobbema: Maskwacis Outreach School
P.O. Box 658
Hobbema, AB T0C 1N0

Tel: 780-585-3076; Fax: 780-585-3792
www2.scnea.com/academy/
Enrollment: 139 Note: This four nations joint initiative is being
co-administered by Samson Cree Nation (NEA) and Ermineskin
Cree Nation (MWE) on behalf of the four Hobbema communities.

Sharon Seright, Principal, 780-585-3076
sseright@scnea.com

Hobbema: Meskanahk Ka-Nipa-Wit School
Also known as: Montana School
P.O. Box 129
Hobbema, AB T0C 1N0, Canada
Tel: 780-585-2799; Fax: 780-585-2264
www.montana-education.ca
Grades: K-9 Enrollment: 100
Butch French, Principal
butch@montana-education.ab.ca

Hythe: Horse Lake School
P.O. Box 303
Hythe, AB T0H 2C0

Tel: 780-356-3151

John D'Or Prairie: John D'Or Prairie School
P.O. Box 120
John D'Or Prairie, AB T0H 3X0

Tel: 780-759-3772
Note: John D'Or Prairie School is part of the Little Red River
Board of Education. Education is provided to the Little Red River
Cree Nation, located approximately 865 kilometres north of
Edmonton, Alberta.

Kehewin: Kehewin Community Education Centre
P.O. Box 30
Kehewin, AB T0A 1C0, Canada
Tel: 780-826-6200; Fax: 780-826-5919
kehewincreenation.ca
Grades: K-12
Linda Gadwa, Principal
lrgadwa@yahoo.ca

Kinuso: Swan River First Nation School
P.O. Box 120
Kinuso, AB T0G 1K0

Tel: 780-775-2177; Fax: 780-775-2155
www.swanriverfirstnation.org
Grades: 7 - 12 Enrollment: 40 Number of Employees: 7 Note:
The Swan River First Nation School operates on the Swan River
First Nation Reserve in Kinuso, Alberta.

Lac La Biche: Amisk Community School
P.O. Box 5000
Lac La Biche, AB T0A 2C0

Tel: 780-623-4548; Fax: 780-623-4659
www.beaverlakecreenation.ca
Grades: Early Childhood Svs.-Jr. Secondary Note: Operated by
the Beaver Lake Education Authority, the Amisk Community
School provides education to the Beaver Lake Cree Nation.

Lac La Biche: Heart Lake Kohls School
P.O. Box 447
Lac La Biche, AB T0A 2C0, Canada
Tel: 780-623-2330; Fax: 780-623-3505
Grades: Pre.K-12
David Keffer, Principal
david.keffer@hlks.org

Longview: Chief Jacob Bearspaw School
P.O. Box 116
100 Center St. SW, Longview, AB T0L 1H0
Tel: 403-558-2480; Fax: 403-558-3618
Note: Chief Jacob Bearspaw School, located on the Eden Valley
Reserve in Alberta, is part of the Stoney Education Authority.
Bill Shade, Principal

Mameo Beach: Mimiw-Sakahikan School
P.O. Box 154
Mameo Beach, AB T0C 1X0

Tel: 780-586-3808; Fax: 780-586-3809
www.scnea.com/MSS/
Grades: K - 6
Dianne Crane, Principal

**Maskwacis: Ermineskin Ehpewapahk Alternate
School**
P.O. Box 360
Maskwacis, AB T0C 1N0

Tel: 780-585-2202; Fax: 780-585-2204
www.miyo.ca/alternate/
Grades: 13-19 yrs old
Wendy Solland, Principal

Maskwacis: Ermineskin Elementary School
P.O. Box 420
Maskwacis, AB T0C 1N0

Tel: 780-585-3760; Fax: 780-585-2001
www.miyo.ca/elementary/
www.facebook.com/ermineskinelementaryschool/
Grades: K - 6

Debbie Stockdale, Principal
debbie_stockdale@miyo.ca

Maskwacis: Ermineskin Junior Senior High School
P.O. Box 249
Maskwacis, AB T0C 1N0

Tel: 780-585-3931; Fax: 780-585-2023
www.miyo.ca/juniorhigh
Grades: 7 - 12 Enrollment: 318 Number of Employees: 45
Keith MacQuarrie, Principal
Keith_Macquarrie@miyo.ca

Maskwacis: Nipishkopahk Primary School
P.O. Box 1350
Maskwacis, AB T0C 1N0

Tel: 780-585-2075; Fax: 780-585-2028
www.scnea.com/NPS/
Grades: K - 2
Kathy Kiss, Principal

Maskwacis: Nipisihkopahk Elementary School
P.O. Box 369
Maskwacis, AB T0C 1N0

Tel: 780-585-2244; Fax: 780-585-2084
www.scnea.com/NES/
Grades: 3 - 7 Enrollment: 247
Tracy Larocque, Principal
tlarocque@scnea.com

Maskwacis: Nipisihkopahk Secondary School
P.O. Box 990
Maskwacis, AB T0C 1N0

Tel: 780-585-4449; Fax: 780-585-2259
www.scnea.com/NSS/
Grades: 8 - 12

Morinville: Kipohtakaw Education Centre (KEC)
P.O. Box 3449
Morinville, AB T8R 1S3

Tel: 780-939-3868; Fax: 780-939-3991
Grades: K5 - 12
Gloria Cardinal, Principal

Morley: Morley Community School
P.O. Box 238
Morley, Morley, AB T0L 1N0

Tel: 403-881-2755; Fax: 403-881-2793
sites.google.com/a/stoneyeducation.ca/morley-community-schoo
l
Grades: 6 - 12 Note: The Stoney Education Authority oversees
the Morley Community School. The First Nations school serves
members of the Nakoda First Nation, situated west of Calgary,
Alberta.

Red Earth Creek: Clarence Jaycox School
Bag #4, Red Earth Creek, AB T0G 1X0

Tel: 780-649-2942; Fax: 780-649-2714
www.clarencejaycoxschool.com
Grades: K - 12
LaVina Gillespie, Principal

**Rocky Mountain House: O'Chiese Education
Authority**
P.O. Box 337
Rocky Mountain House, AB T4T 1A3, Canada
Tel: 403-989-3911; Fax: 403-989-2122
ochiese.ca/education/education
Grades: K-12
Lara Jollymore, Principal
lara.jollymore@ochieseeducation.ca

**Rocky Mountain House: O'Chiese First Nation
School**
P.O. Box 337
Rocky Mountain House, AB T4T 1A3

Tel: 403-989-3911; Fax: 403-989-2122
www.ochiese.ca/Education/Education/
Kathy Breaker, Principal

**Rocky Mountain House: Sunchild First Nation
School**
P.O. Box 1149
Rocky Mountain House, AB T4T 1A8

Tel: 403-989-3476; Fax: 403-989-3614
www.sunchildschool.com
Grades: K - 12 Enrollment: 400 Number of Employees: 50 Note:
The Sunchild First Nation School is part of the Sunchild First
Nation Band Education Authority.
Susan Collicutt, Principal
collicutts@yahoo.ca
David Malthouse, Vice-Principal
malthoused@sunchildschool.com

Saddle Lake: Kehew Asiniy School
P.O. Box 159
Saddle Lake, AB T0A 3T0, Canada
Tel: 780-726-2000; *Fax:* 780-726-2002
www.saddlelake.ca

Florence Quinn, Principal

Saddle Lake: Onchamînahos School
P.O. Box 70
Saddle Lake, AB T0A 3T0
Tel: 780-726-3730; *Fax:* 780-726-4141
www.saddlelake.ca
Enrollment: 358 *Number of Employees:* 42
Gloria McGilvery, Principal

Siksika: Chief Old Sun Elementary School
P.O. Box 1070
Siksika, AB T0J 3W0
Tel: 403-734-5300; *Fax:* 403-734-3529
coss@siksikaeducation.org
www.siksikaboardofeducation.com

Siksika: Crowfoot School
P.O. Box 1280
Siksika, AB T0J 3W0
Tel: 403-734-5320
www.siksikaboardofeducation.com
Enrollment: 180 *Number of Employees:* 26
Geraldine Red Gun, Principal

Siksika: Siksika Nation High School
P.O. Box 1220
Siksika, AB T0J 3W0
Tel: 403-734-5400
www.siksikaboardofeducation.com

Stand Off: Aahsaopi Elementary School
P.O. Box 240
Stand Off, AB T0L 1Y0
Tel: 403-737-3808
aes.kainaied.ca

Grades: K - 5 *Number of Employees:* 28
Lauretta Many Bears, Principal, 403-737-3808
Billy Yellow Horn, Librarian

Stand Off: Blood Tribe Youth Ranch Alternate High School
P.O. Box 240
Stand Off, AB T0L 1Y0
Tel: 403-737-2257; *Fax:* 403-737-3520

Stand Off: Kainai Alternate Academy
P.O. Box 419
Stand Off, AB T0L 1Y0
Tel: 403-737-3288
kaa.kainaied.ca

Eric Spencer, Principal, 403-737-3288

Stand Off: Saipoyi Community School
General Delivery, Stand Off, AB T0L 1Y0
Tel: 403-737-3772
scs.kainaied.ca

Grades: K - 5
Marie Shade, Principal

Tsuu T'ina: Tsuu T'ina Bullhead Adult Education Centre (BAEC)
#250 - 9911 Chiila Blvd., Tsuu T'ina, AB T2W 6H6
Tel: 403-974-1400; *Fax:* 409-974-1449
www.tsuutina.ca

Tsuu T'ina Sarcee: Chiila Elementary School
#250, 991 Chiila Blvd. SW, Tsuu T'ina Sarcee, AB T2W 6H6
Tel: 403-238-5484
www.tsuutina.ca
Grades: K4 - 5 *Note:* Chiila Elementary School is part of the Tsuu T'ina Nation Board of Education.

Tsuu T'ina Sarcee: Tsuu T'ina Junior Senior High School
#250, 991 Chiila Blvd. SW, Tsuu T'ina Sarcee, AB T2W 6H6
Tel: 403-251-9555; *Fax:* 403-251-9833
www.tsuutina.ca
Grades: 6 - 12 *Note:* The Tsuu T'ina Nation Board of Education oversees the operations of the Tsuu T'ina Junior Senior High School.

Valleyview: Sturgeon Lake School
Bag 5, Valleyview, AB T0H 3N0
Tel: 780-524-4590; *Fax:* 780-524-3696
www.sturgeonlake.ca/sturgeon_lake_school.html
Grades: K - 12 *Enrollment:* 230 *Note:* The Sturgeon Lake School is part of the Sturgeon Lake First Nation, Band #154, Education

Authority. The First Nation school serves the Sturgeon Lake Cree Nation.

Wabasca: Bigstone Cree Nation Community School Oski Pasikoniwew Kamik
P.O. Box 930
Wabasca, AB T0G 2K0
Tel: 780-891-3830; *Fax:* 780-891-3831
www.bigstone.ca/content/oski-pasikoniwew-kamik-school
Grades: Preschool - 6 *Enrollment:* 247 *Note:* The Bigstone Community School operates under the direction of the Bigstone Cree Nation Education Authority. The school strives to maintain traditional values as its educational foundation.

Hearing Impaired

Edmonton: Alberta School for the Deaf (ASD)
6240 - 113 St. NW, Edmonton, AB T6H 3L2
Tel: 780-439-3323; *Fax:* 780-436-0385
abschdeaf@epsb.ca
asd.epsb.ca
TTY: 780-439-3323
Grades: 1-12 *Note:* Provides educational services for Deaf & Hard of Hearing students in Alberta & beyond.
Sandra Mason, Principal

Distance Education

Didsbury: Northstar Academy Canada
P.O. Box 2220
#103, 1001- 20th Ave., Didsbury, AB T0M 0W0
Tel: 403-335-9587; *Fax:* 403-335-9513
Toll-Free: 877-335-1171
office@nsaschool.ca
www.northstaracademycanada.org
Grades: Secondary *Note:* NorthStar Academy Canada is a Canadian Evangelical Christian community of learners working and studying in an online context.

Schools: Independent & Private

Public

Edmonton: Kate Chegwin School
3119 - 48 St., Edmonton, AB T6L 6P5
Tel: 780-469-0470; *Fax:* 780-463-7844
kchegwin@epsb.ca
katechegwin.epsb.ca

Grades: Jr. High
John Holmes, Principal
john.holmes@epsb.ca

Protestant

Airdrie: Airdrie Koinonia Christian School (AKCS)
77 Gateway Dr., Airdrie, AB T4B 0J6, Canada
Tel: 403-948-5100; *Fax:* 403-948-5563
www.akcs.com
Grades: K-12 *Enrollment:* 300 *Number of Employees:* 36
Earl Driedger, Principal
Dave Kenney, Business Administrator

Bow Island: Cherry Coulee Christian Academy (CCCA)
P.O. Box 10370
Bow Island, AB T0K 0G0, Canada
Tel: 403-545-2107; *Fax:* 403-545-2944
cherrycoulee@shaw.ca
www.cherrycoulee.ca
Grades: K-9
Mike Daniels, Principal

Brant: Brant Christian School
P.O. Box 130
Brant, AB T0L 0L0, Canada
Tel: 403-684-3752; *Fax:* 403-684-3894
brantchristianschool.ca
Grades: K - 12
Rob Cowie, Principal
Susan McLean, Librarian

Brooks: Newell Christian School (NCS)
P.O. Box 100
Hwy. 544, Junction #36, Brooks, AB T1R 1B2, Canada
Tel: 403-378-4448; *Fax:* 403-378-3991
ncsadmin@newellchristianschool.com
www.newellchristianschool.com
Grades: K - 9 *Note:* The Alberta curriculum is taught from a Christian perspective.
Theresa Nagal, Principal

Calgary: Bearspaw Christian School (BCS)
15001 - 69 St. NW, Calgary, AB T3R 1C5, Canada
Tel: 403-295-2566; *Fax:* 403-275-8170
info@bearspawschool.com
www.bearspawschool.com
www.facebook.com/BearspawChristianSchool
twitter.com/BearspawCSchool
Grades: JK - 12 *Enrollment:* 600 *Number of Employees:* 90
Kelly Blake, President & CEO
kblake@bearspawschool.com
Judy Huffman, Principal
jhuffman@bearspawschool.com
Jennifer Lockhart, Vice Principal, Elementary
jlockhart@bearspawschool.com
Lara Melashenko, Vice Principal, Secondary
lmelashenko@bearspawschool.com

Calgary: Bethel Christian Academy
2220 - 39th Ave. NE, Calgary, AB T2E 6P7, Canada
Tel: 403-735-3335
www.facebook.com/1377783089203229
Grades: K.-12
Terry Denny, Principal

Calgary: Calgary Christian School (CCS)
North Bldg.
5029 - 26th Ave. SW, Calgary, AB T3E 0R5, Canada
Tel: 403-242-2896; *Fax:* 403-242-6682
info@calgarychristianschool.com
www.calgarychristianschool.com
www.facebook.com/calgarychristianschool
Grades: Preschool - 12 *Enrollment:* 800 *Note:* Calgary Christian School has an elementary campus & a secondary campus.
Ken DeWyn, Executive Director
Mike Thiesen, Principal, Elementary
Harry Fritschy, Principal, Secondary

Calgary: Eastside Christian Academy (ECA)
1320 Abbeydale Dr. SE, Calgary, AB T2A 7L8
Tel: 403-569-1003; *Fax:* 403-569-7557
admin@ecaab.ca
eastsidechristianacademy.ca
www.facebook.com/122526574470804
Number of Schools: 1 *Grades:* K - 9
Frank Moody, Principal
drmoody52@hotmail.com
Marie Poulin, Career Counsellor
mpoulin@shaw.ca

Calgary: Glenmore Christian Academy (GCA)
16520 - 24th St., Calgary, AB T2Y 4W2, Canada
Tel: 403-254-9050; *Fax:* 403-256-9695
www.gcaschool.ca
www.facebook.com/glenmorechristianacademyalumnae
twitter.com/gcacalgary
Grades: Pre.-9; Special Ed.
Derrick Mohamed, Principal, Junior High
Gwen Uittenbosch, Principal, Elementary

Calgary: Heritage Christian Academy
2003 McKnight Blvd. NE, Calgary, AB T2E 6L2, Canada
Tel: 403-219-3201; *Fax:* 403-219-3210
ibelong@hcacalgary.com
www.hcacalgary.com
www.facebook.com/HCACalgary
twitter.com/HCA_Calgary
Grades: K-12 *Enrollment:* 600
Brenda Giroux, Executive Director
bgiroux@hcacalgary.com
Leslie Olson, Principal

Calgary: Master's Academy & College
4414 Crowchild Trail SW, Calgary, AB T2T 5J4
Tel: 403-242-7034
Academy@masters.ab.ca
Other Information: Academy (K-6): 403-242-7034, ext 200; College (7-12): ext. 260
www.facebook.com/MastersAcademyCollege
Grades: K - 12 *Note:* Master's Academy & College, established in 1997, is known as a school of Profound Learning. Instruction & guidance is provided from a Christian perspective. Master's Academy features Kindergarten to grade 6, & Master's College includes grades 7 to 12.
Tom Rudmik, Founder & Chief Executive Officer
Paul Graham, Chief Operating Officer
Lynda Dyck, Academy Principal
Peter Muller, College Principal
Susan McAllister, College Vice-Principal
Doreen Grey, Coordinator, Research & Development

Calgary: Menno Simons Christian School
7000 Elkton Dr. SW, Calgary, AB T3H 4Y7, Canada
Tel: 403-531-0745; *Fax:* 403-531-0747
office@mennosimons.ab.ca
www.mennosimonschristianschool.ca
Grades: Pre.-9
Philip Knafla, Principal
philip.knafla@pallisersd.ab.ca

Calgary: Trinity Christian School (TCS)
#100, 295 Midpark Way SE, Calgary, AB T2X 2A8, Canada
Tel: 403-254-6682; *Fax:* 403-254-9843
trinity@tcskids.com
www.tcskids.com
Other Information: 403-254-6716 (Phone, Business Office)
Grades: K - 9
Stan Hielema, Principal
stan.hielema@pallisersd.ab.ca
Michelle Duimel, Vice Principal
michelle.duimel@pallisersd.ab.ca
John Unrau, Business Manager
john.unrau@pallisersd.ab.ca
Carol Nudd, Librarian
carol.nudd@pallisersd.ab.ca

Calgary: Tyndale Christian School
18 Hart Estates Blvd., Calgary, AB T2P 2G7
Tel: 403-590-5881
tcs@tyndalecalgary.ca

Champion: Hope Christian School (HSC)
P.O. Box 235
320 - 3rd Ave. North, Champion, AB T0L 0R0
Tel: 403-897-3019; *Toll-Free:* 1-877-897-3131
secretary@hopechristianschool.ca
www.hopechristianschool.ca
Other Information: Home School Office, Phone: 403-897-3799
Grades: 1-12 *Note:* Hope Christian School was established in 1981. It is owned & operated by the Evangelical Free Church of Champion, Alberta. The school offers day school on campus, home education, & HSC online learning.
Dale Anger, Principal & Administrator
Mayruth Guenter, Manager, Day School Office
Sherrill Losey, Manager, Homeschool Office

Coaldale: Coaldale Christian School
2008 - 8 St., Coaldale, AB T1M 1L1, Canada
Tel: 403-345-4055; *Fax:* 403-345-6436
ccsoffic@telusplanet.net
www.coaldalechristianschool.com
Grades: Pre.-12; *Special Ed.*
Joop Harthoorn, Principal

Coalhurst: Calvin Christian School
P.O. Box 26
Coalhurst, AB T0L 0V0, Canada
Tel: 403-381-3030; *Fax:* 403-381-3051
office@ccschool.ca
www.ccschool.ca

Cochrane: Canadian Southern Baptist Seminary & College
200 Seminary View, Cochrane, AB T4C 2G1
Tel: 403-932-6622; *Fax:* 403-932-7049
info@csbs.ca
www.csbs.edu
www.facebook.com/CSBSeminary
twitter.com/csbseminary
www.linkedin.com/company/canadian-southern-baptist-seminary
Rob Blackaby, President, 403-932-6622
rob.blackaby@csbs.ca
Sabine Koster, Director, Finance & Administration, 403-932-6622, ext. 234
sabine.koster@csbs.ca
Barry Nelson, Director, Development, 403-932-6622, ext. 264
barry.nelson@csbs.ca
David Ong, Director, Admissions, 403-932-6622, ext. 251
admissions@csbs.ca
Sherri Watson, Director, Student Services, 403-932-6622, ext. 237
sherri.watson@csbs.ca
Kathleen McNaughton, Registrar, 403-932-6622, ext. 221
kathleen.mcnaughton@csbs.ca

Cold Lake: Lakeland Christian Academy
P.O. Box 8397
Cold Lake, AB T9M 1N2
Tel: 780-639-2077; *Fax:* 780-639-4151
lca@hlvc.org
Grades: K - 12 *Note:* The school offers an individualized academic program & an emphasis on moral values.
Allan Amesman, Contact

Cold Lake: Trinity Christian School
5731 - 50th Ave., Cold Lake, AB T9M 1T1, Canada
Tel: 780-594-2205; *Fax:* 780-594-3737
administration@trinitychristian.ca
www.trinitychristian.ca
Grades: 1-12
Richard Schienbein, Principal

Devon: Devon Christian School
205 Miquelon Ave. West, Devon, AB T9G 1Y1, Canada
Tel: 780-987-4157; *Fax:* 780-987-4156
dcs@devonchristianschool.ca
www.devonchristianschool.ca
Grades: Pre.-9 *Enrollment:* 90
Rhonda Bray, Principal

Didsbury: Koinonia Christian Schools
c/o Koinonia Christian Education Society
P.O. Box 1405
#107, 1001 - 20th Ave., Didsbury, AB T0M 0W0, Canada
Tel: 587-796-1170; *Fax:* 403-335-9513
Toll-Free: 888-242-8635
admin@koinoniaschools.com
www.koinoniaschools.com
Number of Schools: 7 *Grades:* Pre.-12 *Enrollment:* 835 *Note:* Koinona Christian Schools is a system of 7 evangelical, non-denominational schools in Alberta.
Vern Rand, Superintendent
vern.rand@koinonia.ca
Garry Anderson, Associate Superintendent
garryka@gmail.com
Judy Nelson, Business Administrator
jnelson@koinoniaschools.com

Edmonton: Edmonton Bible Heritage Christian School
13054 - 112 St. NW, Edmonton, AB T5E 6E6
Tel: 780-454-3672; *Fax:* 780-488-3672
Grades: 1-9 *Note:* The school offers a home education program & a home education blended program.

Edmonton: Edmonton Christian Schools
Northeast School
5940 - 159 Ave., Edmonton, AB T5Y 0J5
Tel: 780-408-7942; *Fax:* 780-478-1728
ecsne@epsb.ca
www.edmchristian.org
Number of Schools: 3
Krista Mulder, Principal

Campuses
Edmonton Christian West School
14345 McQueen Rd., Edmonton, AB T5N 3L5
Tel: 780-408-7948; *Fax:* 780-452-5669
ecswest@epsb.ca
Darren Oskoboiny, Principal

Edmonton Christian High School
14304 - 109 Ave., Edmonton, AB T5N 1H6
Tel: 780-408-7945; *Fax:* 780-454-0793
ecshs@epsb.ca
Darren Oskoboiny, Principal

Edmonton: Meadowlark Christian School
9825 - 158 St., Edmonton, AB T5P 2X4, Canada
Tel: 780-483-6476; *Fax:* 780-487-8992
meadowlarkChristian@epsb.ca
www.k-9christian.com
Grades: K - 9
Darren Sweeney, Principal

Edmonton: Parkland Immanuel Christian School
21304 - 35 Ave. NW, Edmonton, AB T6M 2P6, Canada
Tel: 780-444-6443; *Fax:* 780-444-6448
info@parklandimmanuel.ca
www.parklandimmanuel.ca
Grades: Pre.-12
John Jagersma, Principal
jjagersma@parklandimmanuel.ca

Edson: Yellowhead Koinonia Christian School
430 - 72 St., Edson, AB T7E 1N3
Tel: 780-723-3850; *Fax:* 780-723-7566
office@ykcschool.com
www.ykcschool.com
Grades: Pre-kindergarten - 12 *Note:* The independent Christian school serves Edson & the surrounding area.
Jason Rand, Principal, 780-693-3775
Glenda Ferguson, Home School Coordinator (West)
Bobbie Luymeson, Home School Coordinator (East)

Fort McMurray: Fort McMurray Christian School
190 Tamarack Way, Fort McMurray, AB T9K 1A1
Tel: 780-743-1079; *Fax:* 780-743-1379
christian.fmpsdschools.ca
www.facebook.com/143827752310999
twitter.com/fmpsd
Grades: K - 8 *Note:* The Fort McMurray Christian School is an interdenominational Christian school that is affiliated with the Association of Independent Schools & Colleges in Alberta as well as Christian Schools International.
Joseph Champion, Principal

Grande Prairie: Grande Prairie Christian School
8202 - 110 St., Grande Prairie, AB T8W 1M3, Canada
Tel: 780-539-4566; *Fax:* 780-539-4748
www.gppsd.ab.ca/school/gpchristian
Grades: Pre.-12 *Enrollment:* 220
Travis Fehler, Principal

Grande Prairie: Hillcrest Christian School
10306 - 102 St., Grande Prairie, AB T8V 2W3, Canada
Tel: 780-539-9161; *Fax:* 780-532-6932
hcsadmin@hcsgp.ca
Grades: Pre.-12

High Level: High Level Christian Academy
P.O. Box 1100
10701 - 100 Ave., High Level, AB T0H 1Z0, Canada
Tel: 780-926-2360; *Fax:* 780-926-3245
www.highlevelchristianacademy.ca
Grades: Pre.-12
Mark Pelley, Principal

Kingman: Cornerstone Christian Academy
P.O. Box 63
Kingman, AB T0B 2MO, Canada
Tel: 780-672-7197; *Fax:* 780-608-1420
www.brsd.ab.ca/school/cornerstonekingman
Grades: Pre.-12; *Special Ed. Note:* Core subjects are taught; Bible Studies.
Steve Ioanidis, Principal
sioanidis@brsd.ab.ca

Lacombe: Central Alberta Christian High School (CACHS)
22 Eagle Rd., Lacombe, AB T4L 1G7, Canada
Tel: 403-782-4535; *Fax:* 403-782-5425
office@cachs.ca
www.cachs.ca
www.facebook.com/167864616645517
Grades: 10-12 *Enrollment:* 105 *Number of Employees:* 8 teaching staff; 4 support staff
Mel Brandsma, Principal
mbrandsma@cachs.ca
Peter Hoekstra, Vice-Principal
phoekstra@cachs.ca
Ann Oudman, Secretary
Wendy Barnes, Business Administrator
wbarnes@cachs.ca

Lacombe: College Heights Christian School (CHCS)
5201 College Ave., Lacombe, AB T4L 1Z6
Tel: 403-782-6212
office@collegeheightschristianschool.ca
www.collegeheightschristianschool.ca
Grades: Early chilhood services - 9 *Note:* Operated by the Seventh-day Adventist Church, the College Heights Christian School offers a spiritually oriented education.
Reo Ganson, Principal
Pastor Myles, Chaplain & Bible Teacher

Lacombe: Lacombe Christian School
5206 - 58 St., Lacombe, AB T4L 1G9, Canada
Tel: 403-782-6531; *Fax:* 403-782-5760
office@lacs.ca
www.lacs.ca
Grades: Pre.-9
M. Folkerts, Principal
mfolkerts@lacs.ca

Lacombe: Parkview Adventist Academy
6940 University Dr., Lacombe, AB T4L 2E7, Canada
Tel: 403-782-3381; *Fax:* 866-931-2652
Toll-Free: 800-661-8129
office@paa.ca
www.paa.ca
www.facebook.com/ParkviewAdventistAcademy
Grades: 10-12 *Enrollment:* 80 *Note:* Christian boarding school.
Dallas Weis, Principal, 403-782-3381, ext. 4110
dallasweis@paa.ca
Rod Jamieson, Vice-Principal, 403-782-3381, ext. 4111
rjamieso@paa.ca

Susanna May, Administrative Assistant, 403-782-3381, ext. 4109

Leduc: Covenant Christian School (CCS)
P.O. Box 3827
Leduc, AB T9E 6M7, Canada
Tel: 780-986-8353; *Fax:* 780-986-8360
www.covenantchristian.ca
Grades: K-9; Special Ed. *Enrollment:* 165 *Note:* Christ-centered education within a curriculum of core subjects.
Gayle Monsma, Principal
gayle.monsma@blackgold.ca

Lethbridge: Immanuel Christian Elementary Schools
Elementary Campus
2010 - 5 Ave. North, Lethbridge, AB T1H 0N5, Canada
Tel: 403-317-7860; *Fax:* 403-317-7862
ices@lethsd.ab.ca
ices.lethsd.ab.ca
twitter.com/ICESLethbridge

Grades: K.-5
Jay Visser, Principal
jay.visser@lethsd.ab.ca
Barbi Wall, Vice-Principal
barbi.wall@lethsd.ab.ca

Campuses
Secondary School Campus
802 - 6 Ave. North, Lethbridge, AB T1H 0S1, Canada
Tel: 403-328-4783; *Fax:* 403-327-6333
icss@lethsd.ab.ca
icss.lethsd.ab.ca
www.facebook.com/icstogether
Grades: 6-12
Jason Ferrie, Business Manager
manager@immanuelcs.ca

Linden: Kneehill Christian School
P.O. Box 370
Linden, AB T0M 1J0
Tel: 403-546-3781; *Fax:* 403-546-3181
Grades: 1-9

Medicine Hat: Cornerstone Christian School
2566 Southview Dr. SE, Medicine Hat, AB T1B 1R2
Tel: 403-529-6169; *Fax:* 403-529-6165
www.cornerstonechristians.ca
www.facebook.com/293343004056497
twitter.com/CCSMedHat
Grades: K - 9
Sandy Sergeant, Principal

Medicine Hat: Higher Ground Christian School
1 Shirley St. SE, Medicine Hat, AB T1A 8N5
Tel: 403-527-2714
www.highergroundchristianschool.ca
Grades: 1 - 9; ESL

Medicine Hat: Medicine Hat Christian School
68 Rice Dr. SE, Medicine Hat, AB T1B 3X2, Canada
Tel: 403-526-3246; *Fax:* 403-528-9048
mhcs@sd76.ab.ca
www.medhatchristianschool.com
twitter.com/medhatchristian
Grades: K-9 *Enrollment:* 195
Shade Holmes, Principal, 403-526-3246, ext. 5102

Mirror: Living Truth Christian School
P.O. Box 89
4803 - 49 Ave., Mirror, AB T0B 3C0
Tel: 403-788-2444; *Fax:* 403-788-2445
ltcs@abchristianschools.ca
www.livingtruthchristian.ca
Grades: 1 - 12

Monarch: Providence Christian School
P.O. Box 240
615 Queen Ave., Monarch, AB T0L 1M0, Canada
Tel: 403-381-4418; *Fax:* 403-381-4428
admin@pcsmonarch.com
www.pcsmonarch.com
www.facebook.com/256229551179711
Grades: K-12
Hugo VanderHoek, Principal

Morinville: Morinville Christian School
10515 - 100 Ave., Morinville, AB T8R 1A2, Canada
Tel: 780-939-2987; *Fax:* 780-939-6646
www.mcfchurch.net/mcs
Grades: 1 - 12
Lou Brunelle, Director, School

Olds: Olds Koinonia Christian School
P.O. Box 4039
Olds, AB T4H 1P7, Canada
Tel: 403-556-4038; *Fax:* 403-556-8770
olds.koinonia@cesd73.ca
www.oldskoinonia.com
Grades: K-12 *Enrollment:* 300
Dwayne Brown, Administrator/Principal
dwaynebrown@cesd73.ca

Ponoka: Ponoka Christian School (PCS)
6300 - 50 St., Ponoka, AB T4J 1V3, Canada
Tel: 403-783-6563; *Fax:* 403-783-6687
office@ponokachristianschool.com
www.ponokachristianschool.com
Grades: Pre.-9
Robert Morris, Principal
bob.morris@ponokachristianschool.com

Red Deer: Destiny Christian School
P.O. Box 30
Site 4, RR#4, Red Deer, AB T4N 5E4, Canada
Tel: 403-343-6510; *Fax:* 403-343-1963
info@destinyschool.ca
www.destinyschool.ca
Grades: Pre.-9
Glenn Mullen, Principal
Marjorie Mullen, Principal

Red Deer: Koinonia Christian School of Red Deer
6014 - 57 Ave., Red Deer, AB T4N 4S9, Canada
Tel: 403-346-1818; *Fax:* 403-347-3013
accounts@koinonia.ca
www.koinonia.ca
Grades: Pre.-12
Vern Rand, Principal

Red Deer: South Side Christian School
P.O. Box 219
Red Deer, AB T4N 5E8, Canada
Tel: 403-886-2266; *Fax:* 403-886-5026
www.southsidechristianschool.ca
www.facebook.com/140592702777091
Grades: Pre.-10 *Note:* Affiliated with the Seventh-day Adventist Church

Rimbey: Rimbey Christian School
P.O. Box 90
4522 - 54th Ave., Rimbey, AB T0C 2J0, Canada
Tel: 403-843-4790; *Fax:* 403-843-3904
office@rimbeychristianschool.com
www.rimbeychristianschool.com
Grades: K - 9 *Enrollment:* 84 *Note:* The Alberta Provincial Program of Studies is taught from a Christian perspective.
Edith Dening, Principal, 403-843-4790
principal@rimbeychristianschool.com

Rocky Mountain House: Rocky Christian School (RCS)
5204 - 54 Ave., Rocky Mountain House, AB T4T 1S5, Canada
Tel: 403-845-3516; *Fax:* 403-845-4370
rocky-christian@wrsd.ca
www.rockycs.com
Grades: K - 9 *Enrollment:* 105 *Note:* The interdenominational school provides a Biblically based curriculum, which reflects Alberta Learning requirements.
Robert Duiker, Principal

Slave Lake: Slave Lake Koinonia Christian
P.O. Box 1548
328 - 2 St. NE, Slave Lake, AB T0G 2A0, Canada
Tel: 780-849-5400; *Fax:* 780-849-5460
admin@slkcs.com
www.slkcs.com
Grades: 1-12
Theresa Nagel, Principal
principal@slkcs.com

Spruce Grove: Living Waters Christian Academy (LWCA)
5 Grove Dr. West, Spruce Grove, AB T7X 3X8, Canada
Tel: 780-962-3331; *Fax:* 780-962-3958
www.lwca.ab.ca
www.facebook.com/lwca.ab.ca
Grades: Pre.-12
Keith Penner, Principal
kpenner@lwca.ab.ca
Savaya Hofsink, Community Resource Director
savaya.hofsink@lwca.ab.ca

Sundre: Olds Mountain View Christian School
Box 2, Site 8, RR#2, Sundre, AB T4H 1P3, Canada
Tel: 403-556-1551; *Fax:* 403-556-5936
principal@omvcs.ca
www.omvcs.ca
Grades: K-12

Sylvan Lake: Lighthouse Christian Academy (LCA)
4290 50 St., Sylvan Lake, AB T4S 0H3
Tel: 403-887-2166; *Fax:* 403-887-5729
www.lighthousechristianacademy.ca
Grades: Pre.-12 *Note:* Private education is offered in a Christian community setting.
Dion Krause, Principal
Rose Plante, Assistant Principal

Taber: Taber Christian School
Taber, AB
Tel: 403-223-4550
taberchristian.horizon.ab.ca
www.facebook.com/HSD67
twitter.com/horizonsd67
Grades: K - 9
John Bronsema, Principal

Taber: Tween Valley Christian School
P.O. Box 4297
Taber, AB T1G 1A0, Canada
Tel: 403-223-9571; *Fax:* 403-223-9594
tvcs.principal@live.ca
tweenvalleychristianschool.weebly.com
Grades: 1-12
Dennis Dyck, Administrator

Three Hills: Prairie Bible Institute (PBI)
P.O. Box 4000
350 - 5th Ave. NE, Three Hills, AB T0M 2N0
Tel: 403-443-5511; *Fax:* 403-443-5540
Toll-Free: 800-661-2425
info@prairie.edu
www.prairie.edu
www.facebook.com/PrairieColleges
twitter.com/prairiecolleges
www.youtube.com/user/PrairieColleges
Number of Employees: 64 employees
Mark Maxwell, President
mark.maxwell@prairie.edu
Glenn Loewen, Dean, 403-443-5511, ext. 3239
glenn.loewen@prairie.edu

Schools
Prairie Christian Academy (PCA)
Elementary School
P.O. Box 68
1025 - 4th St. NE, Three Hills, AB T0M 2A0
Tel: 403-443-4220
pcainfo@ghsd75.ca
www.pca3hills.ca
www.facebook.com/PCA3Hills
twitter.com/pca3hills
Grades: Pre.-6 *Enrollment:* 300 *Note:* Non-denominational, Christian school.

Prairie Christian Academy (PCA)
Secondary School
P.O. Box 68
604 - 3rd St. North, Three Hills, AB T0M 2A0, Canada
Tel: 403-443-4220
pcainfo@ghsd75.ca
www.pca3hills.ca
Grades: 7-12

Catholic

Calgary: Clear Water Academy
2521 Dieppe Ave. SW, Calgary, AB T3E 7J9, Canada
Tel: 403-217-8448; *Fax:* 403-217-8043
administration@clearwateracademy.com
www.clearwateracademy.com
www.facebook.com/147970885245245
Grades: Pre.-12 *Note:* An independent Catholic school.
Darren Forrester, Principal, 403-240-7912
dforrester@clearwateracademy.com
Bill Tomiak, Executive Director, 403-240-7911
btomiak@clearwateracademy.com

First Nations

Ponoka: Mamawi Atosketan Native School
RR#2, Ponoka, AB T4J 1R2
Tel: 403-783-4362; *Fax:* 403-783-3839
mamawiatosketan@xplornet.com
an6440.adventistschoolconnect.org
Grades: K - 12

Special Education

Calgary: Calgary Quest School
3405 Spruce Dr. SW, Calgary, AB T3C 0A5
Tel: 403-253-0003; *Fax:* 403-253-0025
info@calgaryquestschool.com
www.calgaryquestschool.com
Grades: Pre.-12 *Enrollment:* 160 *Note:* Calgary Quest School
offers a program for children with special challenges.
Barbara Pitts, President

Calgary: Foothills Academy
745 - 37th St. NW, Calgary, AB T2N 4T1
Tel: 403-270-9400; *Fax:* 403-270-9438
info@foothillsacademy.com
www.foothillsacademy.org
twitter.com/FoothillsAC
www.linkedin.com/groups/3112702
Grades: 1-12; Special Ed.
Gordon M. Bullivant, Executive Director

Calgary: Janus Academy
2223 Spiller Rd. SE, Calgary, AB T2G 4G9
Tel: 403-262-3333
contact@janusacademy.org
www.janusacademy.org
Other Information: Jr. High & High School Site, Phone:
403-228-5559
www.facebook.com/JanusAcademyYYC
twitter.com/JanusAcademyYYC
www.linkedin.com/company/janus-academy
www.instagram.com/janusacademy
Grades: 1-12; Special Education *Enrollment:* 57 *Note:* Janus
Academy strives to enhance the lives of children with autism.
The program is accredited by Alberta Education & The
Association of Independent Schools & Colleges. Janus Academy
is a registered charity.
Stacey Oliver, Principal
Lorie Abernethy, Executive Director
Paige McNeill, Program Director, Elementary School
Koren Trnka, Program Director, Junior & Senior High School

Calgary: New Heights School & Learning Services
4041 Breskens Dr. SW, Calgary, AB T3E 7M1
Tel: 403-240-1312; *Fax:* 403-769-0633
info@newheightscalgary.com
www.newheightscalgary.com
Grades: Pre.-12
Gary Lepine, Chair

Calgary: Third Academy
North Campus
510 - 77th Ave. SE, Calgary, AB T2H 1C3
Tel: 403-288-5335; *Fax:* 403-288-5804
info@thirdacademy.com
www.thirdacademy.com
Grades: 1-12 *Note:* The Third Academy offers an Individualized
Program Plan that addresses the needs of students with learning
disorders.
Sunil Mattu, LLB (Hons) Law, BEd, Executive Director
S. Lal Mattu, Founder & Ambassador at Large
Rehana Mattu, Principal
Bruce Freeman, Communications Officer & Manager,
Transportation
Sabu Alexander, Chief Accountant

Campuses
South Campus
P.O. Box 4
Site 22, RR#8, Calgary, AB T2J 2T9
Tel: 403-201-6335; *Fax:* 403-201-2036
Joe Smith, Principal

Edmonton: Columbus Academy
#145, 10403 - 172 St., Edmonton, AB T5S 1K9
Tel: 780-440-0708; *Fax:* 780-440-0760
www.upcs.org
Grades: 7-12 *Note:* The school is a special education, private
school in Alberta. Students are referred from social service
agencies, surrounding school jurisdictions, & parents.
Kathy King, Contact
kking@upcs.org

Edmonton: Edmonton Academy
#2, 810 Saddleback Rd. NW, Edmonton, AB T6J 4W4
Tel: 780-482-5449; *Fax:* 780-482-0902
info@edmontonacademy.com
www.edmontonacademy.com
www.facebook.com/edmontonacademyschool
Grades: 3-12 *Note:* Provides specialized teaching for students
with learning disabilities.
Victoria Morisbak, Executive Director
victoria.morisbak@edmontonacademy.com

Jill Melnyk, Principal & Director, Education
jill.melnyk@edmontonacademy.com

Edmonton: Elves Child Development Centre
Elves Special Needs Society
10825 - 142 St., Edmonton, AB T5N 3Y7
Tel: 780-454-5310; *Fax:* 780-454-5889
inquiries@elves-society.com
www.elves-society.com
Grades: Pre.-12 *Note:* The Elves Special Needs Society offers
programs for pre-school & older children, youth & adults with
disabilities & special needs, as well as outreach to students
unable to attend school for extended periods of time.
Barb Tymchak Olafson, Executive Director

Edmonton: Thomas More Academy
Edmonton, AB
Tel: 780-440-0708
abh_admin@boscohomes.ca
www.boscohomes.ca
Grades: K - 12

**Grande Prairie: John Howard Society of Grande
Prairie**
Tabono Centre
#200, 10135 - 101 Ave., Grande Prairie, AB T8V 0Y4, Canada
Tel: 780-532-0373; *Fax:* 780-538-4931
info@johnhowardgp.ca
www.johnhowardgp.ca
www.facebook.com/JohnHowardSocietyOfAlberta
twitter.com/johnhowardab
Note: The Grande Prairie John Howard Society's Tabono Centre
is a learning centre offering arts & culture, health & recreation,
work skills, personal development, academic support, & credit &
family support educational programs.
Penny Mickanuck, Executive Director

Red Deer: Parkland School
6016 - 45 Ave., Red Deer, AB T4N 3M4
Tel: 403-347-3911; *Fax:* 403-342-2677
prkland@shaw.ca
www.parklandschool.org
Grades: 4-19 yrs old; Special Ed. *Number of Employees:* 45
Trudy Lewis, Chief of Educational Services

Independent & Private Schools

Calgary: Akiva Academy
140 Haddon Rd. SW, Calgary, AB T2V 2Y3, Canada
Tel: 403-258-1312; *Fax:* 403-258-3812
office@akiva.ca
www.akiva.ca
Grades: Pre.-6
John Hadden, Principal
johnhadden@akiva.ca
Rabbi Chaim Greenwald, Director of Judaic Studies
rabbigreenwald@akiva.ca

Calgary: Asasa Academy
Northmount Campus
599 Northmount Dr. NW, Calgary, AB T2K 3J6
Tel: 403-285-5677; *Fax:* 403-457-5289
asasaprivateschool.ca
www.facebook.com/1666107586945995
twitter.com/AsasaAcademyYYC
www.linkedin.com/company/asasaacademy
Grades: JK - 6
Jessica Pope, Principal

Campuses
Pinetown Campus
119 Pinetown Pl. NE, Calgary, AB T1Y 5J1
Tel: 403-285-9277; *Fax:* 403-457-5289
Grades: K.

Calgary: Banbury Crossroads Private School
#201, 2451 Dieppe Ave. SW, Calgary, AB T3E 7K1, Canada
Tel: 403-270-7787; *Fax:* 403-270-7486
general@banburycrossroads.com
www.banburycrossroads.com
Grades: K.-12 *Enrollment:* 60 *Number of Employees:* 14 *Note:*
Banbury Crossroads Private School offers self-disciplinary
education to children aged 3 to 18.
Diane Swiatek, Director, 403-703-6787
dswiatek@banburycrossroads.com
Karen Harrison, Principal
karenharrison@banburycrossroads.com
Anne Bransby-Williams, Office Administrator
general@banburycrossroads.com
Kyra Weston, Contact, Marketing
kweston@banburycrossroads.com

Calgary: Calgary Academy
1677 - 93 St. SW, Calgary, AB T3H 0R3, Canada
Tel: 403-686-6444; *Fax:* 403-240-3427
info@calgaryacademy.com
www.calgaryacademy.com
www.facebook.com/wearecalgaryacademy
twitter.com/CalgaryAcademy
www.linkedin.com/company/113463
www.instagram.com/calgaryacademy
Grades: 2-12 *Enrollment:* 625
Peter Istvanffy, President & CEO
Tim Carlson, Principal
Sarah Hoag, Dean, Student Affairs
Paula Chattha, Vice-Principal, Elementary
Karim Dhalla, Vice-Principal, Junior High
Kim Petersen, Vice-Principal, High School

Calgary: Calgary Chinese Alliance School
Calgary Chinese Alliance Church
150 Beddington Blvd. NE, Calgary, AB T3K 2E2, Canada
Tel: 403-274-7046; *Fax:* 403-275-7799
chineseschool@calgarychinesealliance.org
calgarychinesealliance.org
Grades: 1 - 12 *Enrollment:* 500
Alex Hung, President
Mimi Fong, Principal
mimiefong@hotmail.com

Calgary: Calgary Chinese Private School
126 - 2 Ave. SW, Calgary, AB T2P 0B9, Canada
Tel: 403-264-2233; *Fax:* 403-282-9854
ccps@shaw.ca
www.ccpschool.ca
www.facebook.com/CalgaryChinesePrivateSchool
Grades: K-12 *Note:* The Calgary Chinese Private School works
to maintain Chinese heritage & culture in the community.
Henry Chan, President
Thomas Cheuk, Vice-President
Candy Leung, Treasurer
Esther Li, Secretary

**Calgary: Calgary French & International School
(CFIS)**
700 - 77th St. SW, Calgary, AB T3H 5R1, Canada
Tel: 403-240-1500; *Fax:* 403-249-5899
inquiries@cfis.com
www.cfis.com
Grades: Preschool - 12 *Enrollment:* 700 *Number of Employees:*
80 *Note:* Calgary French & International School offers French
Immersion education.
Joanne Weninger, Chair
societyboard@cfis.com
Margaret Dorrance, Head of School, 403-240-1500, ext. 130
mdorrance@cfis.com
Karen MacPherson, Director of Admissions, 403-240-1500, ext.
329
kmacpherson@cfis.com
Amy Murray, Director of Early Childhood Education,
403-240-1500, ext. 113
amurray@cfis.com
Robert Ward, Principal of Elementary Education (4-6),
403-240-1500, ext. 229
rward@cfis.com
Janet Crofton, Director of Finance and Business Operations,
403-240-1500, ext. 135
jcrofton@cfis.com
Nicola (Nikki) Abrioux-Camirand, Principal of Primary Education
(PreK-3), 403-240-1500, ext. 210
ncamirand@cfis.com
Ahmed Amrouche, Principal of Secondary Education (7-12),
403-240-1500, ext. 156
aamrouche@cfis.com

Calgary: Calgary German Language School
Calgary German Language School Society
3940 - 73 St. NW, Calgary, AB T3B 2L9, Canada
info@germanlanguageschoolcalgary.com
www.germanlanguageschoolcalgary.com
Frank Moeller, Principal
moellerfr2@gmail.com
Ines Schiemann, Executive Director

Calgary: Calgary Islamic School (CIS)
Akram Joma'a Campus
2612 - 37th Ave. NE, Calgary, AB T1Y 5L2, Canada
Tel: 403-248-2773; *Fax:* 403-569-6654
www.calgaryislamicschool.com
Grades: K.-12 *Enrollment:* 490 *Note:* Calgary Islamic School
offers the regular curriculum, as well as a Quran recitation &
memorization curriculum, an Arabic language curriculum, an
Islamic Studies curriculum.
Ramy Elhamalawy, Principal
ramy.elhamalawy@pallisersd.ab.ca

Campuses
Omar Bin al-Alkattab Campus
225 - 28 St. SE, Calgary, AB T2A 5K4, Canada
Tel: 587-353-8900; *Fax:* 587-353-8999
info.omar@cislive.ca
obk.calgaryislamicschool.com

Raiha Idrees, Principal

Calgary: Calgary Italian School
Centro Linguistico e culturale italiano di Calgar
416 - 1st Ave. NE, Calgary, AB T2E 0B4, Canada
Tel: 403-264-6349
clcic@shaw.ca
www.italianschoolcalgary.com
Grades: K-12 *Enrollment:* 196 *Number of Employees:* 12
teachers *Note:* A total of 13 courses (9 courses for children & 4
for adults).

Calgary: Calgary Jewish Academy (CJA)
6700 Kootenay St. SW, Calgary, AB T2V 1P7, Canada
Tel: 403-253-3992; *Fax:* 403-255-0842
info@cja.ab.ca
www.cja.ab.ca

Grades: Preschool - 9
Reva Faber, Interim Principal
faberr@cja.ab.ca
Shoshana Kirmayer, Associate Principal
kirmayers@cja.ab.ca
Deborah Sherwood, Office Manager
sherwoodd@cja.ab.ca

Calgary: Calgary Waldorf School
515 Cougar Ridge Dr. SW, Calgary, AB T3H 5G9, Canada
Tel: 403-287-1868; *Fax:* 403-287-3414
info@calgarywaldorf.org
www.calgarywaldorf.org
Grades: Pre. - 9 *Note:* Calgary Waldorf School offers a
Parent-and-Tot program.
Laureen Loree, Principal
Anna Driehuyzen, Pedagogical Administrator
Dinah Clark, Financial Administrator
Cathie Foote, School Administrator
Sandra Langlois, Manager, Admissions & Facility
Barbara Hergert, Library Coordinator

Calgary: The Chinese Academy
John G. Diefenbaker Senior High School
6620 - 4th St. NW, Calgary, AB T2K 1C2, Canada
Tel: 403-777-7663; *Fax:* 403-777-7669
thechineseacademy@gmail.com
www.chineseacademy.ca
Grades: K - 12 *Enrollment:* 1925 *Note:* Kindergarten, Level 1,
begins for children aged 3.5 years at the Sir John A. Macdonald
Junior High School, 6600 - 4th St. NW in Calgary. The goal of
the school is to promote Chinese language & culture. Cantonese
& Mandarin classes, as well as Chinese as a Second Language
for beginners in Cantonese & Mandarin.
Elaine Chan, Principal

Calgary: Chinook Winds Adventist Academy (CWAA)
10101 - 2nd Ave. SW, Calgary, AB T3B 5T2, Canada
Tel: 403-286-5686; *Fax:* 403-247-1623
www.cwaa.net
www.facebook.com/ChinookWindsAdventistAcademy
twitter.com/cwaa_academy
Grades: K - 12 *Note:* The Seventh-day Adventist school also
features music, outdoor education, Bible instruction, & mission
trips for senior high students.
Lara Melashenko, Principal
lmelashenko@cwaa.net
David Elias, Vice Principal
delias@cwaa.net
Brent Wilson, Chaplain
bwilson@cwaa.net
Katie Crews, Librarian
kcrews@cwaa.net

Calgary: Delta West Academy
414 - 11A St. NE, Calgary, AB T2E 4P3, Canada
Tel: 403-290-0767; *Fax:* 403-290-0768
info@deltawestacademy.ca
www.deltawestacademy.ca
twitter.com/DWACalgary
Grades: Pre.-12; Special Ed.
Denise Dutchuk-Smith, B.A., B.Ed., Head of School
ddutchuk-smith@deltawestacademy.ca
C. Tiltmann, Principal, Academic Head
ctiltmann@deltawestacademy.ca

Calgary: Edge School for Athletes
33055 Township Rd. 250, Calgary, AB T3Z 1L4
Tel: 403-246-6432; *Fax:* 403-217-8463
info@edgeschool.com
www.edgeschool.com
www.facebook.com/edgeschool
twitter.com/edgeschool
Grades: 5-12 *Note:* The school prepares student-athletes for
university.
Cameron Hodgson, Chief Executive Officer & Principal,
403-246-6432, ext. 105
chodgson@edgeschool.com
Dale Unruh, Chief Operating Officer
Anne McCaffrey, Director, Admissions, 403-246-6432, ext. 111
amccaffrey@edgeschool.com
Lauren Ritchie, Director, Marketing & Communications,
403-246-6432, ext. 439
lritchie@edgeschool.com
Jaques Ferguson, Director, Sport, 403-246-6432, ext. 447
jferguson@edgeschool.com
Keith Taylor, Principal, 403-246-6432, ext. 110
ktaylor@edgeschool.com

Calgary: Equilibrium School
707 - 14 St. NW, Calgary, AB T2N 2A4, Canada
Tel: 403-283-1111; *Fax:* 403-270-7786
school@equilibrium.ab.ca
www.equilibrium.ab.ca
www.facebook.com/EquilibriumSchool
Grades: 10-12

Calgary: Greek Community School
1 Tamarac Cres. SW, Calgary, AB T3C 3B7, Canada
Tel: 403-246-4553; *Fax:* 403-246-8191
school@calgaryhellenic.com
calgaryhellenic.com/our-school/
Grades: Pre. - 6
Yvonne Paschalis, Principal
greekschoolofcalgaryprincipal@gmail.com

Calgary: Green Learning Academy (GLA)
#150, 7260 - 12 St. SE, Calgary, AB T2H 2S5
Tel: 403-873-1966; *Fax:* 403-873-1967
glainformation@greenlearning.com
www.greenlearning.com
Grades: Pre. - 9

Calgary: Khalsa School Calgary
P.O. Box 2
#RR6 Site 1, Calgary, AB T2M 4L5
Tel: 403-293-7712; *Fax:* 403-293-2245
info@khalsaschoolcalgary.ca
www.khalsaschoolcalgary.ca
Grades: 1 - 9
Beverly Hammond, Principal
beverly.hammond@khalsaschoolcalgary.ca

Calgary: Lycée Louis Pasteur
**4099, boul Garrison sud-ouest, Calgary, AB T2T 6G2,
Canada**
Tél: 403-243-5420; *Téléc:* 403-287-2245
bureau@lycee.ca
www.lycee.ca
www.facebook.com/LyceeLP
twitter.com/LyceeLP
Grades: Pre.-12 *Note:* The Lycée Louis Pasteur is accredited by
both the French Ministry of Education and Alberta Education.
Hervé Gagliardi, Chef d'établissement

Calgary: Maria Montessori Education Centre of Calgary
Building B4
#003, 2452 Battleford Ave. SW, Calgary, AB T3E 7K9
Tel: 403-668-8538; *Fax:* 403-685-2048
mmec.ca
Grades: Toddler - Elem.
Amanda Kershaw, Principal
amanda@mmec.ca

Calgary: Montessori School of Calgary
2201 Cliff St. SW, Calgary, AB T2S 2G4, Canada
Tel: 403-229-1011; *Fax:* 403-229-4474
admissions@msofc.ca
www.montessorischoolofcalgary.com
Grades: Pre. - Elem. *Enrollment:* 100 *Note:* The children at the
Montessori School of Calgary range in age from 2.5 to 12. Both
the Montessori program & the Alberta Programme of Studies are
followed.
Sandy Moser, Principal
sandy.moser@msofc.ca

Calgary: Mountain View Academy (MVA)
#B4, 2452 Battleford Ave. SW, Calgary, AB T3E 7K9, Canada
Tel: 403-217-4346; *Fax:* 403-249-4312
www.mountainviewacademy.ca
www.facebook.com/mtnviewacademy
twitter.com/mtviewacademy
Grades: Preschool - 12
Lenka Popplestone, Principal
lpopplestone@mountainviewacademy.ca
Colleen Ryan, Vice Principal
cryan@mountainviewacademy.ca
Jane Lizotte, Assistant Principal
jlizotte@mountainviewacademy.ca

Calgary: Phoenix Foundation
320 - 19th St. SE, Calgary, AB T2E 6J6
Tel: 403-265-7701; *Fax:* 403-275-7715
info@phoenixfoundation.ca
phoenixfoundation.ca
Grades: K - 12 *Enrollment:* 275 *Number of Employees:* 18-22
Note: Phoenix is a non-profit private school that specializes in
homeschooling.
Robert Straub, Principal

Calgary: Prince of Peace Lutheran School
243209 Garden Rd. NE, Calgary, AB T1X 1E1
Tel: 403-285-2288; *Fax:* 403-285-2855
school@princeofpeace.ca
ppeace.rockyview.ab.ca
Grades: K - 9 *Enrollment:* 395 *Note:* Prince of Peace Lutheran
School is affiliated with Lutheran Church-Canada.
Todd Hennig, Principal

Calgary: The Renert School
14 Royal Vista Link NW, Calgary, AB T3R 0K4
Tel: 587-353-1053
info@renertschool.ca
renertschool.ca
Grades: 1 - 12

Calgary: Renfrew Educational Services
Main School & Administrative Centre
2050 - 21st St. NE, Calgary, AB T2E 6S5, Canada
Tel: 403-291-5038; *Fax:* 403-291-2499
renfrew@renfreweducation.org
www.renfreweducation.org
www.facebook.com/62176705325
Grades: Preschool - Elementary *Enrollment:* 650 *Note:* Renfrew
Educational Services offers specialized educational programs for
preschool & elementary students. The not-for-profit society also
develops programs for children with special needs.
Tom Buchanan, Chair
Janice McTighe, Executive Director
Kim LaCourse, Associate Executive Director
Cathy Gable, Director, Community Services
Mary lou Hill, Director, Education
Bruce Monnery, Director, Finance & Administration

Calgary: River Valley School (RVS)
3127 Bowwood Dr. NW, Calgary, AB T3B 2E7
Tel: 403-246-2275; *Fax:* 403-686-7631
info@rivervalleyschool.ca
www.rivervalleyschool.ca
www.facebook.com/287475947950915
twitter.com/rvssocial
www.linkedin.com/pub/erin-corbett/42/655/4b0
www.flickr.com/photos/69513039@N07
Grades: JK-6 *Enrollment:* 200
Erin Corbett, Head of School

Calgary: Rundle College Society
7379 - 17 Ave. SW, Calgary, AB T3H 3W5
Tel: 403-291-3866; *Fax:* 403-291-5458
contactus@rundle.ab.ca
www.rundle.ab.ca
Grades: K. - 12
Jason B. Rogers, Headmaster

Campuses
Rundle College Primary/Elementary School
7615 - 17 Ave. SW, Calgary, AB T3H 3W5, Canada
Tel: 403-282-8411; *Fax:* 403-282-4460
rundle.ab.ca/schools/college
Grades: K.-6

Rundle College Junior/Senior High School
7375 - 17 Ave. SW, Calgary, AB T3H 3W5, Canada
Tel: 403-250-7180
rundle.ab.ca/schools/college
Grades: 7-12

Rundle College Academy
4330 - 16 St. SW, Calgary, AB T2T 4H9
Tel: 403-250-2965
www.rundle.ab.ca/academy
twitter.com/rundleacademy
Grades: 4-12 *Note:* Rundle College Academy offers a program for students with learning disabilities.

Calgary: **St. John Bosco Private School**
712 Fortalice Cres. SE, Calgary, AB T2A 2E1, Canada
Tel: 403-248-3664; *Fax:* 403-273-8012
school.stdennis.ca

Grades: Pre.-9
Dr. Carol Donaldson, Principal

Calgary: **The School of Alberta Ballet**
West Annex
906 - 12 Ave. SW, 2nd Fl., Calgary, AB T2R 1K7
Tel: 403-245-2274; *Fax:* 403-245-2293
calgarystudios@albertaballet.com
www.schoolofalbertaballet.com
Other Information: Edmonton Studio: 780-702-4725;
edmontonstudios@albertaballet.com
Grades: 7 - 12
Chris George, Managing Director, 403-245-2274, ext. 559
chrisg@albertaballet.com
Edmund Stripe, Artistic Director, 403-245-2274, ext. 731
edmunds@albertaballet.com
Jane Roberts, Academic Principal, 403-245-2274, ext. 711
janer@albertaballet.com

Calgary: **Tanbridge Academy**
P.O. Box 4
Site 22, #RR 8, Calgary, AB T2J 2T9
Tel: 403-259-3443; *Fax:* 403-259-3432
info@tanbridge.com
www.tanbridge.com
Grades: 4 - 9
Linda Choy, Principal

Calgary: **Webber Academy**
1515 - 93rd St. SW, Calgary, AB T3H 4A8, Canada
Tel: 403-277-4700; *Fax:* 403-277-2770
www.webberacademy.ca
Grades: JK - 12 *Note:* Webber Academy is a coeducational, non-denominational university preparatory school.
Dr. Neil Webber, President and Chairman, 403-277-4700, ext. 222
nwebber@webberacademy.ca
Barbara Webber, Vice-President, Administration, 403-277-4700, ext. 223
bwebber@webberacademy.ca
Dianne Lever, Contact, Admissions, 403-277-4700, ext. 225
admissions@webberacademy.ca

Calgary: **West Island College (WIC)**
7410 Blackfoot Trail SE, Calgary, AB T2H 1M5, Canada
Tel: 403-255-5300; *Fax:* 403-252-1434
office@westislandcollege.ab.ca
www.westislandcollege.ab.ca
Other Information: admissions@westislandcollege.ab.ca (E-mail, Admissions)
Grades: 7 - 12 *Note:* West Island College provides pre-university training. Programs include English & French communication skills & the arts.
Carol Grant-Watt, Head of School, 403-255-5300, ext. 238
CarolGrant-Watt@westislandcollege.ab.ca
Gord Goodwin, Principal
GordGoodwin@westislandcollege.ab.ca
Claire Allen, Director, International Studies, 403-255-5300, ext. 302
ClaireAllen@westislandcollege.ab.ca
Scott Bennett, Director, Business Studies, 403-255-5300, ext. 501
scottbennett@westislandcollege.ab.ca
Nicole Tremblay, Director, Professional Development
NicoleTremblay@westislandcollege.ab.ca
Todd Larsen, Director, Co-Curricular Programmes, 403-255-5300, ext. 231
ToddLarsen@westislandcollege.ab.ca
Nicole Bernard, Director, Admissions
NicoleBernard@westislandcollege.ab.ca
Malcolm Rennie, Director, Post-Secondary Placement, 403-255-5300, ext. 286
MalcolmRennie@westislandcollege.ab.ca
John Ralph, Librarian
JohnRalph@westislandcollege.ab.ca

Cold Lake: **Art Smith Aviation Academy**
Acadèmie de l'Aviation Art Smith
Cold Lake, AB
Tel: 780-594-1404; *Fax:* 780-594-1406
artsmithaviationacademy.ca

Grades: K-4 French Immersion; K-8 English
R. Young, Principal
ryoung@artsmithaviationacademy.ca

Edmonton: **Alberta International College (AIC)**
#307, 10621 - 100 Ave. NW, Edmonton, AB T5H 3A3
Tel: 587-524-5644
info@albertainternationalcollege.ca
www.albertainternationalcollege.ca
Grades: 9 - 12

Edmonton: **Coralwood Adventist Academy**
12218 - 135 St. NW, Edmonton, AB T5L 1X1, Canada
Tel: 780-454-2173; *Fax:* 780-455-6946
office@coralwood.org
www.coralwood.org
Grades: K - 12
Michelle Northam, Principal
principal@coralwood.org

Edmonton: **Dante Alighieri Society School of Italian Language and Culture**
c/o Cardinal Léger Junior High School
8808 - 144 Ave. NW, Edmonton, AB T5E 3G7, Canada
Tel: 780-471-6656
www.ladanteedmonton.org
Enrollment: 192 *Number of Employees:* 11 teachers *Note:* Courses are offered for both children & adults.
Aristide Melchionna, Principal
aristidem@shaw.ca

Edmonton: **Edmonton Islamic Academy**
14525 - 127 St., Edmonton, AB T6V 0B3, Canada
Tel: 780-454-4573; *Fax:* 780-454-3498
eia@islamicschool.ca
www.islamicacademy.ca
Grades: K.-9 *Enrollment:* 700
Jawdah Jorf, Principal

Edmonton: **Edmonton Khalsa School**
4504 Millwoods Rd. South, Edmonton, AB T6L 6Y8
edkhalsa@telus.net
www.ihla.ca/IHLA
Grades: K - 6 *Enrollment:* 160

Edmonton: **Edmonton Menorah Academy**
10735 McQueen Rd. NW, Edmonton, AB T5N 3L1, Canada
Tel: 780-451-1848; *Fax:* 780-451-2254
menorahacademy.org
www.facebook.com/menorahacademy
Grades: Pre.-9
Rabbi Rafi Draiman, Head of School
rabbidraiman@menorahacademy.org
Bobbi Scheelar, Director of Communications
bobbi@menorahacademy.org

Edmonton: **German Language School Society of Edmonton**
c/o Rio Terrace School
7608 - 154 St., Edmonton, AB T5R 1R7, Canada
Tel: 780-435-7540
kerstin.buelow@shaw.ca
www.germanschooledmonton.org
Grades: Pre. - 12
Kerstin Buelow, School Director
kerstin.buelow@shaw.ca
Judith Meyers, Administrator
judith.meyers@gmx.de

Edmonton: **Gil Vicente Portuguese School**
Escola Gil Vicente
St. Cecilia Junior High School
8830 - 132nd Ave., Edmonton, AB T5E 0X8
Tel: 780-966-1189
www.gilvicenteedmonton.ca
www.facebook.com/167591875959
Grades: Pre-K-12; Adult *Number of Employees:* 12
Cindy Pereira, Principal, 780-966-1189
cindy.pereira@gilvicenteedmonton.ca

Edmonton: **Headway School Society of Alberta**
3530 - 91 St., Edmonton, AB T6E 6P1, Canada
Tel: 780-466-7733; *Fax:* 780-461-7683
headway@telus.net
www.headwayschool.ca
Grades: K - 12
Jagwinder Singh Sidhu, Principal
headman@telus.net

Edmonton: **Inner City High School**
11205 - 101 St., Edmonton, AB T5G 2A5
Tel: 780-424-9425; *Fax:* 780-426-3386
info@innercity.ca
innercity.ca

Grades: 9 - 12 *Note:* Senior academic and arts based high school. Inner City High School is accredited by Alberta Education

Edmonton: **Ivan Franko School of Ukrainian Studies (IFSUS)**
10611 - 110 Ave., Edmonton, AB T5H 2W9
Tel: 780-439-2320; *Fax:* 780-439-0989
Note: The school teaches Ukrainian courses.
Liliya Sukhy, Director
lsukhy@hotmail.com

Edmonton: **MAC Islamic School**
11342 - 127th St., Edmonton, AB T5M 0T8
Tel: 780-453-2220; *Fax:* 780-453-2233
office@macislamicschool.com
www.macislamicschool.com
www.facebook.com/MacIslamicSchool
Grades: K - 5
Raiha Idrees Ali, Principal

Edmonton: **Newman Theological College**
10012 - 84 St., Edmonton, AB T6A 0B2
Tel: 780-392-2450; *Fax:* 780-462-4013
www.newman.edu
www.facebook.com/NewmanTheologicalCollege
Jason West, President

Edmonton: **Phoenix Academy**
#145, 10403 - 172 St., Edmonton, AB T5S 1K9
Tel: 780-440-0708; *Fax:* 780-440-0760
www.upcs.org
Grades: K-12 *Note:* School for students who struggle with behavioural disorders and learning disabilities.
Kathy King, Principal, 780-440-0708, ext. 224
kking@upcs.org

Edmonton: **Progressive Academy**
13212 - 106 Ave., Edmonton, AB T5N 1A3, Canada
Tel: 780-455-8344; *Fax:* 780-455-1425
info@progressiveacademy.ca
www.progressiveacademy.ca
www.facebook.com/ProAcadEdmonton
Grades: K - 12 *Enrollment:* 172 *Number of Employees:* 40 *Note:* The school offers small classes & the flexibility for students to progress through grades at an advanced pace.
Lisa Sander, Office Administrator, 780-455-8344, ext. 1002
lisa.s@progressiveacademy.ca

Edmonton: **St. George's Hellenic Language School**
10831 - 124 St., Edmonton, AB T5M 0H4, Canada
Tel: 780-452-1455; *Fax:* 780-452-1455
st.georgesgreekschool@gmail.com
www.gocedm.org/greek-school/
Grades: 10-12
Maria Carrozza, Principal

Edmonton: **Solomon College**
#228, 10621 - 100 Ave., Edmonton, AB T5J 0B3, Canada
Tel: 780-431-1515; *Fax:* 780-431-1644
info@solomoncollege.ca
www.solomoncollege.ca
www.facebook.com/SolomonCollege
Grades: 10-12 *Enrollment:* 1000
Ping Ping Lee, Program Director
Ben Lau, General Manager

Edmonton: **Tempo School**
5603 - 148 St., Edmonton, AB T6H 4T7, Canada
Tel: 780-434-1190; *Fax:* 780-430-6209
admin@temposchool.org
www.temposchool.org
Grades: Pre.-12 *Enrollment:* 380
B. Michael, Head, Lower School
R. Slevinsky, Head, Upper School

Edmonton: **Waldorf Independent School of Edmonton**
7114 - 98 St., Edmonton, AB T6E 3M1
Tel: 780-466-3312
info@wese.ca
www.thewise.ca
Grades: K - 4
Mandie Abrams, President
mandie@wese.ca

Neerlandia: **Covenant Canadian Reformed School**
P.O. Box 67
Neerlandia, AB T0G 1R0, Canada
Tel: 780-674-4774; *Fax:* 780-401-3295
ccrs.office@gmail.com
covenantschool.ca

Grades: K - 12; Special Ed. *Enrollment:* 170 *Note:* Students are members of the Canadian Reformed or United Reformed churchesLocation: 3030 Township Rd. 615A, Neerlandia.
J. Meinen, Principal
principal@covenantschool.ca

Okotoks: Edison School
Box 2, Site 11, RR#2, Okotoks, AB T1S 1A2
Tel: 403-938-7670; *Fax:* 403-938-7224
office@edisonschool.ca
www.edisonschool.ca
Grades: K - 12 *Enrollment:* 185 *Note:* Edison School is a fully accredited private school.

Okotoks: Strathcona-Tweedsmuir School
RR#2, Okotoks, AB T1S 1A2
Tel: 403-938-4431; *Fax:* 403-938-4492
advancement@sts.ab.ca
www.sts.ab.ca
www.facebook.com/StrathconaTweedsmuirSchool
twitter.com/STSConnections
www.linkedin.com/groups/3237845
www.youtube.com/user/STSConnections
Grades: 1-12
William Jones, Head of School
wagerj@sts.ab.ca

Ponoka: Woodlands Adventist School
P.O. Box 16
Site 2, RR#3, Ponoka, AB T4J 1R3, Canada
Tel: 403-783-2640; *Fax:* 403-783-2878
woodlands22.adventistschoolconnect.org
Grades: 1 - 8
Andrea Gray, Principal
andrea.a.gray@gmail.com

Spirit River: Northern Lights School
Box 19, Site 4, RR#1, Spirit River, AB T0H 3G0, Canada
Tel: 780-351-2242; *Fax:* 780-351-2280
Grades: 1 - 9 *Note:* The Northern Lights Church of God in Christ Mennonite congregation operates the Northern Lights School.

Stony Plain: St. Matthew Lutheran School
5014 - 53 Ave., Stony Plain, AB T7Z 1R8, Canada
Tel: 780-963-2715; *Fax:* 780-963-7324
school@st-matthew.com
www.stmatthewsschool.ca
Grades: Pre.-9
Rev. Mark Dressler, Principal

Sylvan Lake: Sylvan Meadows Adventist School
P.O. Box 1006B
Sylvan Lake, AB T4S 1X6
Tel: 403-887-5766; *Fax:* 403-887-5766
www.sylvanmeadows.org

Wetaskiwin: Peace Hills Adventist School
RR#3, Stn Main, Wetaskiwin, AB T9A 1X1
Tel: 780-352-8555
peacehillsschool@gmail.com
peace23.adventistschoolconnect.org

Universities & Colleges

Protestant

Edmonton: The King's University
9125 - 50th St., Edmonton, AB T6B 2H3
Tel: 780-465-3500; *Fax:* 780-465-3534
Toll-Free: 800-661-8582
www.kingsu.ca
www.facebook.com/TheKingsUniv
twitter.com/TheKingsU
www.linkedin.com/school/the-king's-university
www.youtube.com/user/TheKingsUC
Full Time Equivalency: 910 *Note:* The King's University is a private Christian university founded in 1979.
Dr. Melanie Humphreys, President

First Nations

Edmonton: Yellowhead Tribal College
Also known as: Yellowhead Tribal Education Centre
10045 - 156th St. NW, Edmonton, AB T5P 2P7
Tel: 780-484-0303; *Fax:* 780-481-7275
Toll-Free: 877-982-3382
admissions@ytced.ca
ytced.ab.ca
www.facebook.com/YTCollege
twitter.com/ytcollege
www.linkedin.com/school/yellowhead-tribal-college
Note: Academic environment that nurtures First Nations cultures & traditions.

Diana Steinhauer, President, 587-525-6149
president@ytced.ca

Maskwacis: Maskwacis Cultural College
P.O. Box 960
Maskwacis, AB T0C 1N0
Tel: 780-585-3925; *Fax:* 780-585-2080
info@mccedu.ca
www.mccedu.ca
www.facebook.com/maskwacisculturalcollege
Note: An Indigenous People's cultural college.
Claudine Louis, President
clouis@mccedu.ca

Distance Education

Athabasca: Athabasca University (AU)
1 University Dr., Athabasca, AB T9S 3A3
Tel: 780-675-6100; *Fax:* 780-675-6437
Toll-Free: 800-788-9041
www.athabascau.ca
www.facebook.com/AthabascaU
twitter.com/Athabascau
www.linkedin.com/school/athabasca
www.youtube.com/user/AthabascaUniversity
Full Time Equivalency: 40000 *Note:* An open university offering any student access to university-level study.
Dr. Neil Fassina, President
Dr. Matthew Prineas, Provost & Vice-President, Academic
provost@athabascau.ca
Deborah Meyers, Vice-President, Finance & Administration
Jennifer Griffin Schaeffer, Chief Information Officer

Faculties
Faculty of Business
Tel: 780-675-6189; *Toll-Free:* 800-468-6531
business-support@athabascau.ca
business.athabascau.ca
www.facebook.com/athabascau.business
twitter.com/AthabascaUBiz
www.linkedin.com/school/athabasca-university-faculty-of-business
www.instagram.com/athabascaubiz
Deborah Hurst, Dean
fbdean@fb.athabascau.ca

Faculty of Health Disciplines
Toll-Free: 800-788-9041
fhdcontact@athabascau.ca
fhd.athabascau.ca/index.php
Margaret Edwards, Dean
marge@athabascau.ca

Faculty of Humanities & Social Sciences
Tel: 780-675-6486
fhss.athabascau.ca
Dr. Veronica Thompson, Dean

Faculty of Science & Technology
Fax: 780-675-6148
Toll-Free: 855-362-2870
fst_success@athabascau.ca
fst.athabascau.ca
www.facebook.com/athabascau.ScienceTech
Dr. Lisa Carter, Dean
lisac@athabascau.ca

Faculty of Graduate Studies
Tel: 780-675-6821; *Fax:* 780-675-6354
Toll-Free: 800-788-9041
fgs@athabascau.ca
fgs.athabascau.ca
Shawn Fraser, Interim Dean
shawnf@athabascau.ca

Centre for Distance Education
Tel: 780-675-6179; *Fax:* 780-675-6170
Toll-Free: 800-788-9041
mde@athabascau.ca
cde.athabascau.ca
Martha Cleveland-Innes, Chair
martic@athabascau.ca

Research Centre
Tel: 780-675-6651; *Fax:* 780-675-6722
Toll-Free: 800-788-9041
research@athabascau.ca
research.athabascau.ca
Rebecca Heartt, Manager, Research Services, 780-675-6275
rebeccah@athabascau.ca

Centre for Learning Accreditation
Tel: 780-675-6348; *Fax:* 780-675-6431
Toll-Free: 800-788-9041
priorlearning.athabascau.ca
Patricia Imbeau, Student Support Administrator

Fran Holler, Mentorship Coordinator

Centre for World Indigenous Knowledge & Research
Tel: 780-428-2064
indigenous@athabascau.ca
indigenous.athabascau.ca
Priscilla Campeau, Chair
pcampeau@athabascau.ca

Universities

Calgary: Alberta University of the Arts
Also known as: AUArts
Old Name: Alberta College of Art & Design (ACAD)
1407 - 14th Ave. NW, Calgary, AB T2N 4R3
Tel: 403-284-7600; *Fax:* 403-289-6682
communications@auarts.ca
www.auarts.ca
www.facebook.com/AlbertaUArts
twitter.com/AlbertaUArts
www.linkedin.com/school/albertauarts
www.youtube.com/c/AlbertaUArts
Full Time Equivalency: 906
Daniel Doz, President & CEO
Alex Link, Interim Dean, Academic Programs

Edmonton: MacEwan University
P.O. Box 1796
Edmonton, AB T5J 2P2
Tel: 780-497-5040; *Fax:* 780-497-5001
Toll-Free: 1-888-497-4622
info@macewan.ca
www.macewan.ca
www.facebook.com/MacEwanUniversity
twitter.com/macewanu
www.linkedin.com/school/macewanuniversity
www.youtube.com/c/macewanuniversity
Annette Trimbee, President

Calgary: University of Calgary
2500 University Dr. NW, Calgary, AB T2N 1N4, Canada
Tel: 403-220-5110
www.ucalgary.ca
www.facebook.com/universityofcalgary
twitter.com/ucalgary
www.linkedin.com/school/university-of-calgary
www.instagram.com/ucalgary
Full Time Equivalency: 33000 *Number of Employees:* 1800 faculty; 3200 staff
Ed McCauley, President & Vice-Chancellor
Dru Marshall, Provost & Vice-President, Academic
Bart Becker, Vice-President, Facilities
Linda Dalgetty, Vice-President, Finance & Services
Ed McCauley, Vice-President, Research
Nuvyn Peters, Vice-President, Advancement
Karen Jackson, General Counsel

Faculties
Faculty of Arts
2500 University Dr. NW, Calgary, AB T2N 1N4
Tel: 403-220-3580; *Fax:* 403-210-6335
ascarts@ucalgary.ca
arts.ucalgary.ca
www.facebook.com/UCalgaryArts
twitter.com/ucalgaryarts
www.instagram.com/ucalgaryarts
Enrollment: 8000 *Number of Employees:* 1000
Richard Sigurdson, Dean, 403-220-6151
sigurdso@ucalgary.ca

Graduate Studies
Earth Sciences
#1010, 2500 University Drive NW, Calgary, AB T2N 1N4
Tel: 403-220-4938; *Fax:* 403-289-7635
graduate@ucalgary.ca
grad.ucalgary.ca
www.facebook.com/UCalgaryFGS
twitter.com/UCalgaryFGS
www.youtube.com/user/UCalgaryGradStudies
Enrollment: 6000
Robin Yates, Vice Provost; Dean
deangrad@ucalgary.ca

Kinesiology
Main Office, #KNB135
376 Collegiate Blvd. NW, Calgary, AB T2N 1N4
Tel: 403-220-5607
kinesiology.ucalgary.ca
www.facebook.com/UofCKinesiology
twitter.com/uofcknes
www.instagram.com/ucalgaryknes
Penny Werthner, Dean
knesdean@ucalgary.ca

Law
2500 University Drive NW, Calgary, AB T2N 1N4
Tel: 403-220-4155; *Fax:* 403-210-3928
law@ucalgary.ca
law.ucalgary.ca
www.facebook.com/UCalgaryLaw
twitter.com/UCalgaryLaw
www.instagram.com/UCalgaryLaw
Ian Holloway, Dean, 403-220-5447
lawdean@ucalgary.ca
Ali Abel, Manager, Marketing & Communications, 403-210-8720
amabel@ucalgary.ca

Nursing
#2259, Professional Faculties
2500 University Dr. NW, Calgary, AB T2N 1N4
Tel: 403-220-6262; *Fax:* 403-284-4803
nursing.ucalgary.ca
www.facebook.com/nursingucalgary
twitter.com/ucalgarynursing
www.youtube.com/ucalgarynursing
Sandra Davidson, Dean

Faculty of Science
Biological Sciences Building
#540, 2500 University Dr. NW, Calgary, AB T2N 1N4
Tel: 403-220-5516; *Fax:* 403-282-9154
scidean@ucalgary.ca
science.ucalgary.ca
www.facebook.com/UofCFacultyofScience
twitter.com/UofC_Science
Enrollment: 4000 *Number of Employees:* 200 Faculty
Bernhard Mayer, Interim Dean, 403-220-5389
bmayer@ucalgary.ca
Gloria Visser-Niven, Director, Marketing and Communications, 403-220-7056
gvissern@ucalgary.ca

Faculty of Social Work
MacKimmie Tower
#301, 2500 University Drive NW, Calgary, AB T2N 1N4
Tel: 403-220-5942; *Fax:* 403-282-7269
socialwk@ucalgary.ca
fsw.ucalgary.ca
www.facebook.com/UCalgarySocialWork
twitter.com/Ucalgary_FSW
Jackie Sieppert, Dean, 403-220-5945
sieppert@ucalgary.ca

Faculty of Veterinary Medicine
3280 Hospital Dr. NW, Calgary, AB T2N 1N4
Tel: 403-210-3961; *Fax:* 403-210-8121
vetmed@ucalgary.ca
vet.ucalgary.ca
twitter.com/Ucalgaryvetmed
www.instagram.com/ucalgaryvetmed
Baljit Singh, Dean, 403-210-3961
baljit.singh1@ucalgary.ca
Collene Ferguson, Manager, Marketing and Communications, 403-210-6615
collene.ferguson@ucalgary.ca

<u>Schools</u>
Cumming School of Medicine
Foothills Campus, Health Sciences Centre
3330 Hospital Dr. NW, Calgary, AB T2N 4N1
Tel: 403-220-6842
cumming.ucalgary.ca
www.facebook.com/UCalgaryMed
twitter.com/UCalgaryMed
www.youtube.com/UCalgaryMedicine
Dr. Jon Meddings, Dean
meddings@ucalgary.ca

Haskayne School of Business
Scurfield Hall
2500 University Dr. NW, Calgary, AB, T2N 1N4
Tel: 403-220-5685; *Fax:* 403-282-0095
haskayne.ucalgary.ca
www.facebook.com/uofchaskayne
twitter.com/haskayneschool
www.youtube.com/user/HaskayneSchool
Enrollment: 5500
Jim Dewald, Dean, 403-220-5689
jim.dewald@haskayne.ucalgary.ca

Schulich School of Engineering
2500 University Dr. NW, #ENC101, Calgary, AB T2N 1N4
Tel: 403-220-5738; *Fax:* 403-284-3697
schulich@ucalgary.ca
schulich.ucalgary.ca
www.facebook.com/schulichengineering
twitter.com/SchulichENGG
www.linkedin.com/school/schulich-school-of-engineering
www.instagram.com/schulichengineer

Enrollment: 5100 *Number of Employees:* 170 Faculty
Sarah McGinnis, Manager, Marketing and Communication
smcginni@ucalgary.ca

School of Continuing Education
2500 University Dr. NW, Calgary, AB T2N 1N4
Tel: 403-220-2866; *Toll-Free:* 866-220-4992
conted@ucalgary.ca
conted.ucalgary.ca
www.facebook.com/uofconted
twitter.com/UCalgaryConted
www.youtube.com/user/UofCConted
Note: Offering two, one-day (7 hours) courses on managing cannabis in the workplace, including policies and case law.
Sheila LeBlanc, Director

Werklund School of Education
Education Tower
#1340, 2750 University Way NW, Calgary, AB T2N 1N4
Tel: 403-220-6794; *Fax:* 403-282-5849
educ.admin@ucalgary.ca
werklund.ucalgary.ca
twitter.com/UCalgaryEduc
Enrollment: 2750 *Number of Employees:* 130
Dianne Gereluk, Dean
dean.werklund@ucalgary.ca
Mary Kate MacIsaac, Senior Manager, Communications
marykate.macisaac@ucalgary.ca

School of Architecture Planning and Landscape
Professional Faculties Bldg.
2500 University Dr. NW, #PF2182, Calgary, AB T2N 1N4
Tel: 403-220-6606
info@sapl.ucalgary.ca
sapl.ucalgary.ca
www.facebook.com/ucalgarysapl
twitter.com/ucalgarysapl
www.linkedin.com/school/ucalgarysapl
www.instagram.com/ucalgarysapl
John L. Brown, Dean, 403-220-6606
brownj@ucalgary.ca
Vita Leung, Manager, Marketing & Communications, 403-220-5323
vita.leung@ucalgary.ca

Edmonton: University of Alberta
116 St. & 85 Ave., Edmonton, AB T6G 2R3
Tel: 780-492-3111
www.ualberta.ca
www.facebook.com/ualberta
twitter.com/ualberta
www.youtube.com/user/UniversityofAlberta
Full Time Equivalency: 40000
Douglas R. Stollery, Chancellor
Bill Flanagan, President
Steven Dew, PhD, Provost & Vice-President, Academic
provost@ualberta.ca
Gitta Kulczycki, Vice-President, Finance & Administration, 780-492-2657
Matthias Ruth, Vice-President, Research & Innovation, 780-492-6378
vpresearch@ualberta.ca
Andrew Sharman, Vice-President, Facilities & Operations
Kelly Spencer, Vice-President, Advancement, 780-492-7400
giving@ualberta.ca
Catherine Swindlehurst, Vice-President, University Relations

<u>Faculties</u>
Faculty of Agriculture, Life & Environmental Sciences (ALES)
2-06 Agriculture Forestry Centre, University of A
Edmonton, AB T6G 2P5
Tel: 780-492-4933; *Fax:* 780-492-8524
questions.ales@ualberta.ca
ualberta.ca/agriculture-life-environment-sciences
www.facebook.com/UAlbertaALES
twitter.com/UofAALES
www.youtube.com/user/TheFacultyofALES
Stanford F. Blade, Dean, 780-492-0102
blade@ualberta.ca

Alberta School of Business
Business Building, University of Alberta
#3-23, 11211 Saskatchewan Drive NW, Edmonton, AB T6G 2R6
Tel: 780-492-7676; *Fax:* 780-492-3325
business.generaloffice@ualberta.ca
www.ualberta.ca/business
www.facebook.com/UAlbertaBiz
twitter.com/UAlbertaBiz
www.linkedin.com/school/UAlbertaBiz
www.youtube.com/user/abbusinessschool
Joseph Doucet, Ph.D., Dean, 780-492-7644

Faculty of Education
Faculty of Education, University of Alberta
11210 - 87 Ave., Edmonton, AB T6G 2G5
Tel: 780-492-3659
educ.info@ualberta.ca
ualberta.ca/education
www.facebook.com/UofAEducation
twitter.com/UAlbertaEd
www.youtube.com/user/EducationUofA
Jennifer Tupper, Dean
jatupper@ualberta.ca

Faculty of Engineering
Donadeo Innovation Centre for Engineering
9211 - 116th St. NW, Edmonton, AB T6G 1H9
Tel: 780-492-0503; *Fax:* 780-492-3973
Toll-Free: 800-407-8354
www.ualberta.ca/engineering
www.facebook.com/UofAEngineering
twitter.com/UAlberta_Eng
www.linkedin.com/school/ualbertaengineering
www.instagram.com/ualberta_engineering
Fraser Forbes, Dean, 780-492-3596
fraser.forbes@ualberta.ca

Faculty of Extension
10230 Jasper Ave., Edmonton, AB T5J 4P6
Tel: 780-492-3116
extweb@ualberta.ca
www.ualberta.ca/extension
www.facebook.com/uaextension
twitter.com/uaextension
www.instagram.com/uaextension
Enrollment: 7000
Maria Mayan, Interim Dean, 780-492-9209
maria.mayan@ualberta.ca

Faculty of Graduate Studies & Research
2-29 Triffo Hall, Killam Centre for Advanced Stud
Edmonton, AB T6G 2E1
Tel: 780-492-3499; *Fax:* 780-492-0692
Toll-Free: 800-758-7136
grad.mail@ualberta.ca
ualberta.ca/graduate-studies
www.facebook.com/UAlbertaFGSR
twitter.com/UAlbertaFGSR
www.instagram.com/ualbertafgsr
Enrollment: 8225
Brooke Milne, Vice-Provost & Dean, 780-492-2816
graddean@ualberta.ca

Faculty of Kinesiology, Sport & Recreation
3-100 University Hall, Van Vliet Complex
Edmonton, AB T6G 2H9
Tel: 780-492-9510; *Fax:* 780-492-2222
infoden@ualberta.ca
www.ualberta.ca/kinesiology-sport-recreation
www.facebook.com/UAlbertaKSR
twitter.com/UAlbertaKSR
www.instagram.com/ualbertaksr
Enrollment: 1140 *Number of Employees:* 53
Kerry Mummery, Dean
kerry.mummery@ualberta.ca

Faculty of Law
111 - 89 Ave., Edmonton, AB T6G 2H5
Tel: 780-492-3122; *Fax:* 780-492-4924
law.studentservices@ualberta.ca
ualberta.ca/law
www.facebook.com/UAlbertaLaw
twitter.com/UAlbertaLaw
www.linkedin.com/school/ualbertalaw
www.youtube.com/user/UofALaw1
David Percy, Interim Dean, 780-492-5590
deanoflaw@ualberta.ca

Faculty of Medicine & Dentistry
Walter C. Mackenzie Health Sciences Centre
#2J2.00, 8440 - 112 St. NW, Edmonton, AB T6G 2R7
Tel: 780-492-6621; *Fax:* 780-492-7303
meddent@ualberta.ca
www.ualberta.ca/medicine
www.facebook.com/UofAMedicineDentistry
twitter.com/UAlberta_FoMD
www.linkedin.com/school/15095830
www.youtube.com/user/FoMDcommsteam
Brenda Hemmelgarn, Dean

Faculty of Nursing
Level 3, Edmonton Clinic Health Academy
11405 - 87 Ave., Edmonton, AB T6G 1C9
Fax: 780-492-2551
Toll-Free: 888-492-8089
www.ualberta.ca/nursing
www.facebook.com/UofANursing
twitter.com/UAlbertaNursing
www.instagram.com/ualbertanursing
Greta Cummings, Dean
greta.cummings@ualberta.ca

Faculty of Pharmacy & Pharmaceutical Sciences
2-35 Medical Sciences
8613 - 114 St., Edmonton, AB T6G 2H7
Tel: 780-492-3362
www.ualberta.ca/pharmacy
twitter.com/ualberta_pharm
www.linkedin.com/school/ualberta-pharmacy
www.instagram.com/ualberta_pharmacy
Neal Davies, Dean
ndavies@ualberta.ca

Faculty of Rehabilitation Medicine
3-48 Corbett Hall
8205 - 114 St., Edmonton, AB T6G 2G4
Tel: 780-492-2903; *Fax:* 780-492-1626
info@rehabmed.ualberta.ca
www.ualberta.ca/rehabilitation
www.facebook.com/UofARehabMedicine
twitter.com/UofARehabMed
www.youtube.com/user/RehabMedicineUofA
Bob Haennel, Ph.D., Dean

Faculty of Native Studies
2-31 Pembina Hall, University of Alberta
Edmonton, AB T6G 2H8
Tel: 780-492-2991; *Fax:* 780-492-0527
nativestudies@ualberta.ca
www.ualberta.ca/native-studies
www.facebook.com/UAlbertaNativeStudies
twitter.com/UANativeStudies
Chris Andersen, Dean, 780-492-8178
chris.andersen@ualberta.ca

Faculty of Science
1-001 CCIS, University of Alberta
Edmonton, AB T6G 2E9
Tel: 780-492-4758; *Fax:* 780-492-7033
Toll-Free: 800-358-8314
www.ualberta.ca/science
www.facebook.com/UAlbertaScience
twitter.com/ualbertascience
www.instagram.com/ualbertascience
Enrollment: 43600
Matina Kalcounis-Ruepell, Dean
dean.science@ualberta.ca

Faculty of Arts
6-5 Humanities Centre
Edmonton, AB T6G 2E5
Tel: 780-492-2787; *Fax:* 780-492-7251
ualberta.ca/arts
www.facebook.com/UofAArts
twitter.com/UofA_Arts
www.youtube.com/user/UofAlbertaArts
Lesley Cormack, Ph.D., Dean, 780.492.4223
artsdean@ualberta.ca
Michael O'Driscoll, Vice-Dean
michael.odriscoll@ualberta.ca
Sheila Graham, Manager, Marketing and Communications,
780.492.3920
sheila.graham@ualberta.ca

Schools
School of Public Health
3-300 Edmonton Clinic Health Academy
11405 - 87 Ave., Edmonton, AB T6G 1C9
Tel: 780-492-9954; *Fax:* 780-492-0364
school.publichealth@ualberta.ca
www.ualberta.ca/public-health
www.facebook.com/UAlbertaSPH
twitter.com/UAlbertaSPH
www.youtube.com/user/SPHUofA
Shanthi Johnson, Dean

School of Library & Information Studies
7-104 Education North
Edmonton, AB T6G 2G5
Tel: 780-492-7625; *Fax:* 780-492-2024
slis@ualberta.ca
ualberta.ca/school-of-library-and-information-studies
www.facebook.com/UAlbertaSLIS
Toni Samek, Chair, 780-492-3932
toni.samek@ualberta.ca

Campuses
Augustana Campus
4901 - 46 Ave., Camrose, AB T4V 2R3
Tel: 780-679-1100; *Fax:* 780-679-1129
augustana.info@ualberta.ca
www.ualberta.ca/augustana
www.facebook.com/UofAAugustana
twitter.com/UofA_Augustana
www.youtube.com/user/AugustanaCampus
Enrollment: 1100
Demetres Tryphonopoulos, Dean & Executive Officer,
780-679-1130
augdean@ualberta.ca
Tia Lalani, Communications Coordinator, 780-679-1157
augcomm@ualberta.ca

Campus Saint-Jean
Également connu sous le nom de: Faculté Saint Jean
8406, rue Marie-Anne-Gaboury, Edmonton, AB T6C 4G9
Tél: 780-465-8700; *Téléc:* 780-465-8760
Ligne sans frais: 800-537-2509
recrutement@csj.ualberta.ca
ualberta.ca/campus-saint-jean
www.facebook.com/ualbertaCSJ
twitter.com/ualberta_csj
www.instagram.com/ualberta_csj
Enrollment: 800
Pierre-Yves Mocquais, Ph.D., Doyen, 780-465-8705
mocquais@ualberta.ca
Victorine Ade Mimbe, Coordonnateur, Relations avec le public,
780-492-0407
Dany Bazira, Coordonnateur, Relations avec le public,
780-485-8638
kezimana@ualberta.ca

St. Joseph's College
University of Alberta
Edmonton, AB T6G 2J5
Tel: 780-492-7681; *Fax:* 780-492-8145
sjcadmin@ualberta.ca
ualberta.ca/st-josephs
www.facebook.com/SJCUofA
twitter.com/sjcuofa
www.instagram.com/SJCUofA
Note: The College, located at the University of Alberta, was
established by the Roman Catholic Archdiocese of Edmonton. It
offers courses in Christian theology & philosophy.
Fr. Terence Kersch, President, 780-492-7681
kersch@ualberta.ca
Shawn W. Flynn, Academic Dean, 780-492-7683
shawn.flynn@ualberta.ca
Sara McKeon, Academic Program Coordinator, 780-492-7682
sjcdean@ualberta.ca

St. Stephen's College
University of Alberta Campus
8810 - 112 St., Edmonton, AB T6G 1J6
Tel: 780-439-7311; *Fax:* 780-433-8875
Toll-Free: 1-800-661-4956
st.stephens@ualberta.ca
ualberta.ca/st-stephens
www.facebook.com/StStephensCollegeUofA
twitter.com/StStephensEdu
Note: A graduate studies college at the University of Alberta
whose program areas include Theology, Counselling, Art
Therapy & Ministry
Frederick Tappenden, Dean & Principal
frederick.tappenden@ualberta.ca
Shelley Westermann, Director, Academic/Administrative
Services, 780-439-7311, ext. 35
westerma@ualberta.ca

Centres & Institutes
Alberta Centre for Sustainable Rural Communities (ACSRC)
Augustana Campus
4901 - 46 Ave., Camrose, AB T4V 2R3
Tel: 780-679-1672
ualberta.ca/augustana/research/centres/acsrc
www.facebook.com/UofA.ACSRC
twitter.com/ACSRC
www.youtube.com/user/AugustanaCampus
Lars K. Hallström, Director, 780-679-1661
lars.hallstrom@ualberta.ca

Centre for Health & Nutrition
4-077 Edmonton Clinic Health Academy
Edmonton, AB T6G 1C9
Tel: 780-492-9415
chaninfo@ualberta.ca
www.ualberta.ca
Kim Raine, Scientific Director
kim.raine@ualberta.ca

Poultry Research Centre
F83 Edmonton Research Station
Edmonton, AB T6G 2E1
Tel: 780-492-6221; *Fax:* 780-492-6471
prc@ualberta.ca
poultry.ualberta.ca
Martin Zuidhof, Academic Leader, 780-248-1655
martin.zuidhof@ualberta.ca

Dairy Research & Technology Centre (DRTC)
F-30 Edmonton Research Station, South Campus
Edmonton, AB T6H 2V5
Tel: 780-491-6013; *Fax:* 780-492-8580
webmaster@ales.ualberta.ca
drtc.ualberta.ca

Canadian Centre for Corporate Social Responsibility
(CCCSR)
Alberta School of Business
Edmonton, AB T6G 2R6
Tel: 780-492-3998; *Fax:* 780-492-3325
cccsr@ualberta.ca
www.ualberta.ca/business/centres/corporate-social-responsibility
P. Devereaux Jennings, Coordinator, 780-492-3998
devereaux.jennings@ualberta.ca

Centre for Applied Business Research in Energy & the
Environment (CABREE)
3-20D Alberta School of Business
Edmonton, AB T6G 2R6
Tel: 780-492-8489
www.ualberta.ca/business
Andrew Leach, Academic Director, 780-492-8489
aleach@ualberta.ca
Kristin Thibault, Centre Research Administrator, 780-248-1650
kristin.thibault@ualberta.ca

Centre for Entrepreneurship & Family Enterprise
4-20B Business Building
Edmonton, AB T6G 2R6
Tel: 780-492-5876; *Fax:* 780-492-2519
www.ualberta.ca/business/centres/family-entrepreneurship
Lloyd Steier, Academic Director
lloyd.steier@ualberta.ca

Technology Commercialization Centre
4-40J Alberta School of Business
Edmonton, AB T6G 2R6
Tel: 780-492-1684; *Fax:* 780-492-3325
www.ualberta.ca/business/centres/technology-commercialization
Mike Lounsbury, Academic Director, 780-492-1684
ml37@ualberta.ca
Tony Briggs, Executive Director, 780-492-4993
tony.briggs@ualberta.ca

Lethbridge: University of Lethbridge
4401 University Dr., Lethbridge, AB T1K 3M4, Canada
Tel: 403-329-2111
www.uleth.ca
www.facebook.com/ulethbridge.ca
twitter.com/ulethbridge
www.linkedin.com/company/university-of-lethbridge
www.youtube.com/user/ulethbridge
Full Time Equivalency: 8956 *Number of Employees:* 1177
Charles Weaselhead, Chancellor
Mike Mahon, Ph.D., President & Vice-Chancellor
mike.mahon@uleth.ca
Andrew Hakin, Provost & Vice-President, Academic
hakin@uleth.ca
Erasmus Okine, Vice-President, Research
erasmus.okine@uleth.ca
Nancy Walker, Vice-President, Finance & Administration
nancy.walker@uleth.ca

Faculties
Faculty of Arts & Science
University Hall
4401 University Dr.,#A570, Lethbridge, AB T1K 3M4
Tel: 403-329-5101
www.uleth.ca/artsci
www.facebook.com/uLethbridgeArtSci
twitter.com/UofArtsci
Matthew Letts, Interim Dean, 403-380-1813
matthew.letts@uleth.ca

Faculty of Education
Turcotte Hall
#421, 4401 University Dr., Lethbridge, AB T1K 3M4
Tel: 403-329-2254; *Fax:* 403-329-2372
edu.sps@uleth.ca
uleth.ca/education
twitter.com/ULethbridgeEdu
Craig Loewen, Dean, 403-329-2051
craig.loewen@uleth.ca

Faculty of Fine Arts
University Centre for the Arts
4401 University Dr., #W620, Lethbridge, AB T1K 3M4
Tel: 403-329-2126; Fax: 403-382-7127
finearts@uleth.ca
uleth.ca/fine-arts
www.facebook.com/ULethbridgeFineArts
twitter.com/UofL_Finearts
www.instagram.com/ulethbridge_finearts
Mary I. Ingraham, Dean, 403-329-2126
finearts.dean@uleth.ca

Faculty of Health Sciences
Markin Hall
4401 University Dr., Lethbridge, AB T1K 3M4
Tel: 403-329-2699; Fax: 403-329-2668
health.sciences@uleth.ca
www.uleth.ca/healthsciences
Robert Wood, Dean
robert.wood@uleth.ca

Schools
Dhillon School of Business
4401 University Dr., #M2060, Lethbridge, AB T1K 3M4
Tel: 403-329-2153; Fax: 403-329-2038
dhillon.advising@uleth.ca
www.uleth.ca/dhillon
www.facebook.com/DhillonBusiness
Enrollment: 1669 Number of Employees: 60 faculty members
Kerry Godfrey, Dean, 403-329-2633
kerry.godfrey@uleth.ca

School of Liberal Education
University Hall
4401 University Dr., #A812, Lethbridge, AB T1K 3M4
Tel: 403-329-2378
liberal.ed@uleth.ca
uleth.ca/liberal-education
Shelly Wismath, Dean, 403-329-2529
wismaths@uleth.ca

St Paul: University nuhelot'ine thaiyots'i
nistameyimâkanak Blue Quills (UnBQ)
P.O. Box 279
3 Airport Rd. North, St Paul, AB T0A 3A0, Canada
Tel: 780-645-4455; Fax: 780-645-5215
Toll-Free: 888-645-4455
inquiries@bluequills.ca
www.bluequills.ca
www.facebook.com/179353185415252
Note: The university is incorporated under federal statute &
governed by seven First Nations (Beaver Lake, Cold Lake, Frog
Lake, Whitefish Lake, Heart Lake, Kehewin, & Saddle Lake).
Vincent Steinhauer, President

Colleges

Calgary: Ambrose University
150 Ambrose Circle SW, Calgary, AB T3H 0L5
Tel: 403-410-2000; Fax: 403-571-2556
registrar@ambrose.edu
ambrose.edu
www.facebook.com/ambroseuniversity
twitter.com/ambrose_uni
www.linkedin.com/school/ambrose-university-college
www.youtube.com/user/AmbroseUniversity
Full Time Equivalency: 900 Note: Ambrose University is a
private Christian university.
Gordon T. Smith, President
gtsmith@ambrose.edu

Calgary: Bow Valley College
345 - 6th Ave. SE, Calgary, AB T2G 4V1
Tel: 403-410-1400; Toll-Free: 866-428-2669
info@bowvalleycollege.ca
bowvalleycollege.ca
www.facebook.com/bowvalleycollege
twitter.com/BowValley
www.linkedin.com/school/bow-valley-college
Full Time Equivalency: 15000
Misheck Mwaba, President & CEO

Calgary: St. Mary's University
14500 Bannister Rd. SE, Calgary, AB T2X 1Z4
Tel: 403-531-9130; Fax: 403-531-9136
admissions@stmu.ca
www.stmu.ab.ca
www.facebook.com/StMarysUniversityCalgary
twitter.com/StMarysUC
www.linkedin.com/school/st-marys-university
www.youtube.com/c/StMarysU
Full Time Equivalency: 700 Note: St. Mary's is a Christian
university.

Gerry Turcotte, President, 403-254-3701
gerry.turcotte@stmu.ca
John Deausy, Vice-President, Finance & CFO, 403-254-3702
john.deausy@stmu.ca
Tara Hyland-Russell, Vice-President, Academic, 403-254-3771
tara.hyland-russell@stmu.ca
Thérèse Takacs, Vice-President, Advancement, 403-254-3139
therese.takacs@stmu.ca

Edmonton: Concordia University of Edmonton
(CUE)
7128 Ada Blvd. NW, Edmonton, AB T5B 4E4
Tel: 780-479-8481; Toll-Free: 866-479-5200
info@concordia.ab.ca
concordia.ab.ca
www.facebook.com/CUEdmonton
twitter.com/cuedmonton
www.linkedin.com/school/concordia-university-of-edmonton
www.youtube.com/user/ConcordiaEdmonton
Full Time Equivalency: 2300
Tim Loreman, President & Vice-Chancellor
Valerie Henitiuk, Vice-President, Academic & Provost

Edmonton: NorQuest College
Downtown Campus, Main Bldg.
10215 - 108th St. NW, Edmonton, AB T5J 1L6
Tel: 780-644-6000; Fax: 780-644-6013
Toll-Free: 866-534-7218
info@norquest.ca
www.norquest.ca
www.facebook.com/NorQuestCollege
twitter.com/NorQuest
www.linkedin.com/school/norquest-college
www.youtube.com/user/NorQuestVids
Carolyn Campbell, President & CEO

Edmonton: Taylor College & Seminary
11525 - 23rd Ave. NW, Edmonton, AB T6J 4T3
Tel: 780-431-5200; Fax: 780-436-9416
Toll-Free: 800-567-4988
info@taylor-edu.ca
www.taylor-edu.ca
www.facebook.com/TaylorUpdates
www.linkedin.com/school/taylor-college-and-seminary
David Williams, President
Ralph Korner, Academic Dean

Fort McMurray: Keyano College
8115 Franklin Ave., Fort McMurray, AB T9H 2H7
Tel: 780-791-4800; Toll-Free: 800-251-1408
www.keyano.ca
www.facebook.com/keyanocollege
twitter.com/keyanocollege
www.linkedin.com/company/keyano-college
www.youtube.com/user/keyanocollege
Trent Keough, President

Campuses
Janvier Learning Center
P.O. Box 85
Janvier, AB T0P 1G0
Tel: 780-559-2047; Fax: 780-559-2999

Gregoire Lake Learning Centre
General Delivery, Anzac, AB, Canada
Tel: 780-334-2559; Fax: 780-334-2559

Conklin Learning Centre
Conklin, AB, Canada
Tel: 780-559-2434;

Fort McKay Learning Centre
General Delivery, Fort McKay, AB T0P 1C0
Tel: 780-828-4433; Fax: 780-828-4434

Grande Prairie: Grande Prairie Regional College
(GPRC)
10726 - 106th Ave., Grande Prairie, AB T8V 4C4
Tel: 780-539-2944; Fax: 888-539-4772
studentinfo@gprc.ab.ca
www.gprc.ab.ca
www.facebook.com/GPRCAB
twitter.com/GPRC_AB
www.linkedin.com/school/grande-prairie-regional-college
www.youtube.com/user/GPRCab
Full Time Equivalency: 2000
Glenn Feltham, Interim President & CEO
Vanessa Sheane, Interim Vice-President, Academics &
Research

Campuses
Fairview Campus
P.O. Box 3000
11235 - 98th Ave., Fairview, AB T0H 1L0
Tel: 780-835-6600; Fax: 888-539-4772

Lac La Biche: Portage College
P.O. Box 417
9531 - 94 Ave., Lac La Biche, AB T0A 2C0, Canada
Tel: 780-623-5580; Fax: 780-623-5519
Toll-Free: 866-623-5551
info@portagecollege.ca
www.portagecollege.ca
www.facebook.com/PortageCollege
twitter.com/PortageCollege
www.linkedin.com/company/portage-college
www.instagram.com/portagecollege
Note: The college offers over 30 programs, including Business,
Environmental Studies, Food Sciences, Health & Wellness,
Human Services, Native Arts & Culture & Trades & Technology.
Continuing education, distance education & academic upgrading
are also offered. The Lac Le Biche location provides
administrative & support services for the school's Boyle heavy
equipment campus.
Randolph Benson, Chair
Trent Keough, President & CEO

Campuses
Cold Lake Campus
Cold Lake Energy Centre
#101, 7825 - 51 St., Cold Lake, AB T9M 0B6
Tel: 780-639-0030; Fax: 780-639-2330
Toll-Free: 866-623-5551
www.portagecollege.ca/Campus-Locations/Cold-Lake
Note: Also provides administrative & support services for the
school's Frog Lake satellite campus.

St. Paul Campus
P.O. Box 1471
5205 - 50 Ave., St Paul, AB T0A 3A0
Tel: 780-645-5223; Fax: 780-645-5162
Toll-Free: 866-623-5551
www.portagecollege.ca/Campus-Locations/St-Paul
Note: Also provides administrative & support services for the
school's Saddle Lake & Goodfish Lake satellite campuses.

Lacombe: Burman University
6730 University Dr., Lacombe, AB T4L 2E5
Tel: 403-782-3381; Toll-Free: 800-661-8129
info@burmanu.ca
www.burmanu.ca
www.facebook.com/burmanuniversity
www.youtube.com/cucvideos
Mark Haynal, President, 403-782-3381, ext. 4147
mhaynal@burmanu.ca

Lethbridge: Lethbridge College
3000 College Dr. South, Lethbridge, AB T1K 1L6
Tel: 403-320-3200; Toll-Free: 800-572-0103
info@lethbridgecollege.ca
www.lethbridgecollege.ca
www.facebook.com/LethbridgeCollege
twitter.com/LethCollege
www.youtube.com/lethbridgecollege
Paula Burns, President & CEO, 403-320-3209
president@lethbridgecollege.ca

Campuses
Claresholm Campus
5202 - 5 St. East, Claresholm, AB T0L 0T0
Tel: 403-625-4231
claresholm@lethbridgecollege.ca

Pincher Creek Campus
732 Kettles St., Pincher Creek, AB T0K 1W0, Canada
Tel: 403-563-7041
pinchercreek@lethbridgecollege.ca

Vulcan County Campus
110 - 1 Ave. South, Vulcan, AB T0L 2B0
Tel: 403-485-1488
vulcancounty@lethbridgecollege.ca

Olds: Olds College
4500 - 50th St., Olds, AB T4H 1R6, Canada
Tel: 403-556-8281; Fax: 403-556-4711
Toll-Free: 1-800-661-6537
info@oldscollege.ca
www.oldscollege.ca
Other Information: Registrar: 403-556-8281
www.facebook.com/olds.college
twitter.com/oldscollege
www.youtube.com/user/OldsCollegeComm
Full Time Equivalency: 1772 Note: Olds College features the
following areas of study: Agriculture; Animal Sciences; Business;
Fashion; Horticulture; Land & Environment; School of Trades; &
Continuing Education.
Leona Staples, Chair
Stuart Cullum, President

School of Continuing Education: Horticulture
Tel: 403-556-4740; *Toll-Free:* 800-661-6537
coned@oldscollege.ca
Note: The Cannabis Production program is a 16-week online program with a one-week field study.

Campuses
Calgary Campus
345 - 6th Ave. SE, Calgary, AB T2G 4V1
Tel: 403-697-6130; *Fax:* 403-697-6131
Toll-Free: 1-800-661-6537
fashioninstitute@oldscollege.ca

Siksika: **Old Sun Community College**
P.O. Box 1250
Siksika, AB T0J 3W0
Tel: 403-734-3862; *Fax:* 403-734-5363
Toll-Free: 888-734-3862
admin@oldsuncollege.net
oldsuncollege.ca
www.facebook.com/109459200589699
Maurice Manyfingers, President, 403-734-3862, ext. 222
maurice.manyfingers@oldsuncollege.ca

Slave Lake: **Northern Lakes College**
1201 Main St. SE, Slave Lake, AB T0G 2A3
Tel: 780-849-8600; *Fax:* 780-849-2570
Toll-Free: 866-652-3456
info@northernlakescollege.ca
www.northernlakescollege.ca
www.facebook.com/StartHereNLC
twitter.com/starthere_nlc
www.linkedin.com/company/start-here-nlc
www.youtube.com/user/YourfutureNLC
Note: Northern Lakes College provides distance learning for students in 30 rural communities in north central Alberta.
Glenn Mitchell, President

Campuses
Grouard Campus
64 Mission St., Grouard, AB T0G 1C0
Tel: 780-751-3200; *Fax:* 780-751-3376

Vermilion: **Lakeland College**
Also known as: Alberta/Saskatchewan Interprovincial Coll.
Vermilion Campus
5707 College Dr., Vermilion, AB T9X 1K5
Tel: 780-853-8400; *Toll-Free:* 800-661-6490
admissions@lakelandcollege.ca
www.lakelandcollege.ca
twitter.com/LakelandCollege
www.linkedin.com/company/lakeland-college-canada
www.youtube.com/user/LakelandCollegeAB
Alice Wainwright-Stewart, President & CEO

Campuses
Lloydminster Campus
2602 - 59 Ave., Lloydminster, AB T9V 3N7
Tel: 780-871-5700; *Toll-Free:* 800-661-6490

Emergency Training Centre
5704 College Dr., Vermilion, AB T9X 1K4
Tel: 780-853-5800

Post Secondary/Technical

First Nations

Stand Off: **Red Crow Community College (RCCC)**
P.O. Box 8858
Stand Off, AB T0L 1Y0
Tel: 403-737-2400; *Fax:* 403-737-2101
Toll-Free: 866-937-2400
www.redcrowcollege.com
Note: Red Crow Community College is a post-secondary institution that offers Diploma, Degree & Masters programs. The College partners with Mount Royal, Lethbridge Community College, SAIT, the University of Lethbridge & the University of Calgary.
Roy Weasel Fat, President

Universities

Calgary: **Mount Royal University**
Lincoln Park Campus
4825 Mount Royal Gate SW, Calgary, AB T3E 6K6
Tel: 403-440-6111; *Fax:* 403-440-5938
Toll-Free: 877-440-5001
aro@mtroyal.ca
www.mtroyal.ca
www.facebook.com/MountRoyal4U
twitter.com/mountroyal4u
www.linkedin.com/school/mount-royal-university
www.youtube.com/user/MountRoyal4U
Enrollment: 11787 *Note:* Offers bachelor's degrees, diplomas, credit & non-credit Continuing Education programs, & Community Service Learning Citation courses.
Alex Pourbaix, Chair
Tim Rahilly, President

Campuses
Springbank Campus
143 MacLaurin Dr., Springbank, AB T3Z 3S4
Tel: 403-288-9551

Colleges

Fort McMurray: **Keyano College**
8115 Franklin Ave., Fort McMurray, AB T9H 2H7
Tel: 780-791-4800; *Toll-Free:* 800-251-1408
info@keyano.ca
www.keyano.ca
www.facebook.com/keyanocollege
twitter.com/keyanocollege
www.linkedin.com/school/keyano-college
www.youtube.com/user/keyanocollege
Dale Mountain, Interim President & CEO

Campuses
Fort Chipewyan Campus
P.O. Box 60
Fort Chipewyan, AB T0P 1B0
Tel: 780-697-3767

Medicine Hat: **Medicine Hat College**
299 College Dr. SE, Medicine Hat, AB T1A 3Y6
Tel: 403-529-3811; *Fax:* 403-504-3517
Toll-Free: 866-282-8394
info@mhc.ab.ca
www.mhc.ab.ca
www.facebook.com/MHCollege
twitter.com/mhcollege
www.youtube.com/user/mhcca
Kevin Shufflebotham, President & CEO
kshufflebotham@mhc.ab.ca
David Petis, Vice-President, Advancement & Community Relations
dpetis@mhc.ab.ca
Wayne Resch, Vice-President, Administration & Finance
wresch@mhc.ab.ca
Sandy Vanderburgh, Interim Vice-President, Academic
svanderburgh@mhc.ab.ca
Irlanda Price, Associate Vice-President, Student Development
iprice@mhc.ab.ca

Campuses
Brooks Campus
200 Horticultural Station Rd. East, Brooks, AB T1R 1E5
Tel: 403-362-1677; *Fax:* 403-362-1474
brooksinfo@mhc.ab.ca

Red Deer: **Red Deer College (RDC)**
P.O. Box 5005
100 College Blvd., Red Deer, AB T4N 5H5
Tel: 403-342-3400; *Fax:* 403-357-3660
Toll-Free: 888-732-4630
inquire@rdc.ab.ca
rdc.ab.ca
www.facebook.com/RedDeerCollege
twitter.com/RedDeerCollege
www.youtube.com/user/TheRdctube
Note: Beginning September 2021, RDC offers degrees as a Polytechnic Institution.
Peter Nunoda, President

Post Secondary/Technical

Banff: **The Banff Centre**
P.O. Box 1020
107 Tunnel Mountain Dr., Banff, AB T1L 1H5
Tel: 403-762-6100; *Fax:* 403-762-6444
www.banffcentre.ca
www.facebook.com/thebanffcentre
twitter.com/thebanffcentre
www.linkedin.com/school/banff-centre
www.youtube.com/c/thebanffcentre
Janice Price, President & CEO

Calgary: **ABM College**
#200, 3880 - 29th St. NE, Calgary, AB T1Y 6B6
Tel: 403-719-4300
info@abmcollege.com
www.abmcollege.com
www.facebook.com/abmcollege1
twitter.com/AbmCollege
Note: Health & Technology College.

Campuses
Toronto Campus
#205, 705 Lawrence Ave. West, Toronto, ON M6A 1B4
Tel: 416-849-4200

Calgary: **Alberta Business & Educational Services (ABES)**
#10, 221 - 18th St. SE, Calgary, AB T2E 6J5
Tel: 403-232-8758
recruiter@abes.ca
abes.ca
www.facebook.com/abescollege
Note: Healthcare & medical service training.

Calgary: **Alberta College of Acupuncture & Traditional Chinese Medicine**
#102, 1910 - 20th Ave. NW, Calgary, AB T2M 1H5
Tel: 403-286-8788; *Toll-Free:* 888-789-9984
admin@acatcm.com
www.acatcm.com
www.facebook.com/acatcm.official
www.youtube.com/c/AlbertaCollegeOfAcupunctureCalgary
Dr. Dennis Lee, Co-President
Dr. Colton Oswald, Co-President

Calgary: **Alberta Health & Safety Training Institute (AHSTI)**
#125, 3510 - 29th St. NE, Calgary, AB T1Y 7E5
Tel: 403-670-5406; *Fax:* 866-202-1822
Toll-Free: 888-670-5406
customerservice@safetyed.ca
www.safetyed.ca

Campuses
Calgary South East Campus
#236, 755 Lake Bonavista Dr. SE, Calgary, AB T2J 0N3
Tel: 403-670-5406; *Toll-Free:* 888-670-5406

Red Deer Campus
Bay 22
7471 Edgar Industrial Bend, Red Deer, AB T4P 3Z5
Tel: 403-348-2422; *Toll-Free:* 888-670-5406

Calgary: **Artists Within Makeup Academy**
#101, 638 - 11th Ave. SW, Calgary, AB T2R 0E2
Tel: 587-891-5828
info@artistswithin.com
www.artistswithin.com
www.facebook.com/artistswithinmakeupacademy

Calgary: **Calgary College of Traditional Chinese Medicine & Acupuncture**
#107/217, 4014 Macleod Trail, Calgary, AB T2G 2R7
Tel: 403-287-8688; *Fax:* 403-287-8660
Toll-Free: 866-676-8688
info@cctcma.com
www.cctcma.com
Note: Offers courses in acupuncture, Chinese herbology, Chinese massage, Qigong & food therapy.
Dr. Frank H. Du, President

Calgary: **Cambrooks College**
1105 - 7th Ave. SW, Calgary, AB T2P 1B2
Tel: 403-764-1414
info@cambrooks.ca
www.cambrooks.ca
Note: Programs in Information Technology, Business, Health, Academic Upgrading or ESL.
Pamela Paul, Program Manager
ppaul@cambrooks.ca

Calgary: **Canadian Institute of Traditional Chinese Medicine (CITCM)**
Two Executive Place
#300, 1824 Crowchild Trail NW, Calgary, AB T2M 3Y7
Tel: 403-520-5289; *Toll-Free:* 888-859-8686
info@citcm.com
citcm.com
www.facebook.com/CITCM

Note: CITCM offers programs including an Acupuncture Diploma program, a fully funded Double Major Acupuncture / Doctor of Traditional Chinese Medicine diploma program & a Bachelor of Traditional Chinese Medicine degree.

Calgary: **Canadian School of Natural Nutrition (CSNN)**
Calgary Campus
1415 - 28th St. NE, Calgary, AB T2A 2P6
Tel: 403-276-1551
info@csnncal.ca
csnn.ca
www.facebook.com/CSNNNational
twitter.com/csnn
www.youtube.com/user/wwwcsnnca

Campuses
Edmonton Campus
Edmonton, AB T6B 2V4
Tel: 780-437-3933
edmonton@csnn.ca
csnn.ca/edmonton
www.facebook.com/csnnedm

London Campus
#108, 747 Hyde Park Rd., London, ON N6H 3S3
Tel: 519-936-1610
london@csnn.ca
csnn.ca/london
www.facebook.com/joni.yungblut.CSNN.London
twitter.com/CSNN_London

Mississauga Campus
#205, 1107 Lorne Park Rd., Mississauga, ON L5H 3A1
Tel: 905-891-0024
mississauga@csnn.ca
csnn.ca/mississauga
www.facebook.com/csnnmississauga

Moncton Campus
#205, 1201 Mountain Rd., Moncton, NB E1C 2T4
Tel: 506-384-2700
moncton@csnn.ca
csnn.ca/moncton
Judy Underhill, Branch Manager

Ottawa Campus
#603, 250 City Centre Ave., Ottawa, ON K1R 6K7
Tel: 613-314-6991
ottawa@csnn.ca
csnn.ca/ottawa
www.facebook.com/csnnottawa
Natalie Rivier, Branch Manager

Richmond Hill Campus
#216, 10909 Yonge St., Richmond Hill, ON L4C 3E3
Tel: 905-737-0284
richmondhill@csnn.ca
csnn.ca/richmondhill

Toronto Campus
#302, 150 Eglinton Ave. East, Toronto, ON M4P 1E8
Tel: 416-482-3772
toronto@csnn.ca
csnn.ca/toronto

Vancouver Campus
#100, 2245 West Broadway, Vancouver, BC V6K 2E4
Tel: 604-730-5611
van@csnn.ca
csnn.ca/vancouver

Vancouver Island Campus
#208, 3045 Douglas St., Victoria, BC V8T 4N2
Tel: 250-668-8663
v.i@csnn.ca
csnn.ca/vancouverisland

Calgary: **Canadian Sport Institute**
Olympic Oval
#125, 2500 University Dr. NW, Calgary, AB T2N 1N4
Tel: 403-202-6809
info@csicalgary.ca
csicalgary.ca
www.facebook.com/CSICalgary
twitter.com/CSICalgary
www.linkedin.com/company/274917
www.youtube.com/user/CSCCalgary

Note: Offers The National Coaching Certification Program (NCCP).

Calgary: **Columbia College Calgary**
802 Manning Rd. NE, Calgary, AB T2E 7N8
Tel: 587-805-0400; *Toll-Free:* 855-228-2022
columbia@columbia.ab.ca
www.columbia.ab.ca
www.facebook.com/ColumbiaCollegeCalgary
Enrollment: 4000 *Number of Employees:* 200 *Note:* Adult education & continuing education. Professional programmes (business management, dental assisting, paramedic, health care aide, practical nurse); ESL; bridging programmes / university preparation; academic upgrading. ISO 9001:2000 certified.

Calgary: **DelMar College of Hair & Esthetics**
Hairstyling & Barbering Campus
5915 - 1A St. SW, Calgary, AB T2H 0G4
Tel: 403-264-8055; *Fax:* 403-264-8050
Toll-Free: 888-264-2422
www.delmarcollege.com
www.facebook.com/DelMarCollegeCalgary
Carla Cavanagh, Owner
Dan Cavanagh, Owner

Campuses
Calgary - Esthetics Campus
5769 - 4th St. SE, Calgary, AB T2H 0P4
Tel: 403-255-6644

Red Deer Campus
4929 - 49th St., Red Deer, AB T4N 1V1
Tel: 403-347-4233

Red Deer - Esthetics Campus
5009 - 49th St., Red Deer, AB T4N 1V4
Tel: 403-347-2070

Calgary: **École Holt Couture - School of Sewing & Design**
2227 - 20th Ave. SW, Calgary, AB T2T 0M4
Tel: 403-244-5460
info@ecoleholtcouture.com
ecoleholtcouture.com
www.facebook.com/ecoleholtcouture
twitter.com/EHCSchool
www.youtube.com/user/ecoleholtcouture

Calgary: **Elevated Learning Academy Inc.**
#305, 4014 MacLeod Trail SE, Calgary, AB T2G 2R7
Tel: 403-802-0933; *Toll-Free:* 888-544-5573
info@elevatedlearningacademy.com
elevatedlearningacademy.com
www.facebook.com/elevatedlearningacademy
www.linkedin.com/company/elevated-learning-academy-inc.
Note: Personal Fitness Training.

Campuses
Edmonton Campus
#209, 10080 Jasper Ave., Edmonton, AB T5J 1V9
Tel: 780-425-0933; *Toll-Free:* 888-544-5573
Note: Personal Fitness Training.

Calgary: **Energy Safety Canada (ESC)**
#150, 2 Smed Lane SE, Calgary, AB T2C 4T5
Tel: 403-516-8000; *Fax:* 403-516-8166
Toll-Free: 800-667-5557
customerservice@energysafetycanada.com
www.energysafetycanada.com
www.facebook.com/EnergySafetyCanada
twitter.com/EnergySafetyCan
www.linkedin.com/company/energy-safety-canada
Note: ESC provides training for the oil & gas industry.
Murray Elliott, President & CEO

Campuses
British Columbia
#2060, 9600 - 93rd Ave., Fort St John, BC V1J 5Z2
Tel: 250-794-0100; *Toll-Free:* 855-436-3676

Genesee
Genesee, AB
Tel: 780-955-7770; *Toll-Free:* 800-667-5557
Note: GPS Coordinates: 53ø20'05.7"N 144ø22'26.4"W

Nisku
1803 - 11th St., Nisku, AB T9E 1A8
Tel: 780-955-7770; *Toll-Free:* 800-667-5557
niskufacility@energysafetycanada.com

Saskatchewan
#208, 117 - 3rd St. NE, Weyburn, SK S4H 0W3
Tel: 306-842-9822; *Toll-Free:* 877-336-3676

Calgary: **Fleet Safety International (FSI)**
#119, 4999 - 43rd St. SE, Calgary, AB T2B 3N4
Tel: 403-283-0077; *Toll-Free:* 866-432-5076
fsionline@fleetsafetyinternational.com
www.fleetsafetyinternational.com
www.facebook.com/fleetsafetyintl
twitter.com/fleet_safety
www.linkedin.com/company/fleet-safety-international
Note: Driver training.

Calgary: **KDM Dental College International Inc.**
#520, 940 - 6th Ave. SW, Calgary, AB T2P 3T1
Tel: 403-264-2744; *Fax:* 403-264-2757
Toll-Free: 800-463-9201
www.kdmdental.com

Campuses
Edmonton Campus
#2101, 10104 - 103rd Ave., Edmonton, AB T5J 0H8
Tel: 780-423-6863; *Fax:* 780-423-6892

Calgary: **L R Helicopters Inc.**
Springbank Airport
135 MacLaurin Dr., Calgary, AB T3Z 3S4
Tel: 403-286-4601; *Fax:* 403-286-4602
Toll-Free: 877-286-4601
info@lrhelicopters.ca
www.lrhelicopters.com
www.facebook.com/130657577011861
twitter.com/lrhelicopters

Calgary: **MCG Career College**
#220, 4774 Westwinds Dr. NE, Calgary, AB T3J 0L7
Fax: 587-317-7401
Toll-Free: 888-261-8999
info@mcgcollege.com
mcgcollege.com
www.facebook.com/mcgcollege
twitter.com/mcg_college
www.linkedin.com/school/mcg-career-college
www.instagram.com/mcgcollege
Note: MCG Career College offers health & wellness career programs.
Debra Stafford, Registrar

Campuses
Cold Lake Campus
Elevation Health
#103, 5605 - 55th St., Cold Lake, AB T9M 1R6

Red Deer Campus
#200, 4806 - 51st Ave., Red Deer, AB T4N 4H3

Calgary: **Medical Reception College Ltd.**
#400, 7015 Macleod Trail South, Calgary, AB T2H 2K6
Tel: 403-400-0999
www.medicalreceptioncollege1ltd.com

Calgary: **Mountain View Helicopters**
402A Otter Bay, Calgary, AB T3Z 3S6
Tel: 403-286-7186
fly@mvheli.com
www.mvheli.com
www.facebook.com/mvheli
www.instagram.com/mvheli
Note: Helicopter training.

Calgary: **MTG Healthcare Academy**
#100, 1324 - 36th Ave. NE, Calgary, AB T2E 8S1
Tel: 403-264-2009; *Fax:* 587-352-2009
Toll-Free: 844-353-0684
mtghealthcare.com

Campuses
Edmonton Campus
6920 Roper Rd. NW, Edmonton, AB T6B 3H9
Tel: 780-863-8236; *Fax:* 780-434-8328

Red Deer Campus
4811 - 48th St., Red Deer, AB T4N 1S6
Tel: 403-986-0684; *Fax:* 403-986-4815

Calgary: **NIWE Academy of Cosmetology & Massage**
Also known as: NIWE Academy
Old Name: National Institute of Wellness & Esthetics
3817 - 37th Ave. NE, Calgary, AB T1Y 7G2
Tel: 403-453-8200
info@niwe.ca
niwe.ca
www.facebook.com/niweacademy
Sangeeta Sharma, President

Calgary: Numa International Institute of Makeup &
Design
6410 - 1A St. SW, Calgary, AB T2H 0G6

Tel: 403-455-6862
info@niimd.com
niimd.com

Kelsey Yule, President & Founder

Calgary: The Southern Alberta Institute of
Technology (SAIT)
1301 - 16th Ave. NW, Calgary, AB T2M 0L4

Tel: 403-284-7248; *Fax:* 403-284-7112
Toll-Free: 877-284-7248
www.sait.ca
www.facebook.com/sait
twitter.com/sait
www.linkedin.com/school/saitca
www.youtube.com/c/saitpolytechnic

David Ross, President & CEO

Campuses
Culinary Campus
#226, 230 - 8th Ave. SW, Calgary, AB T2P 1B5

Tel: 403-284-8612
culinary.campus@sait.ca
culinarycampus.ca

Mayland Heights Campus
NR Buck Crump Bldg.
1940 Centre Ave. NE, Calgary, AB T2E 0A7

Tel: 403-210-4150
transportation.info@sait.ca

Art Smith Aero Centre for Training & Technology
1916 McCall Landing NE, Calgary, AB T2E 9B5

Tel: 403-284-7018
aerocentre@sait.ca

Calgary: Springbank Air Training College
132 MacLaurin Dr., Calgary, AB T3Z 3S4

Tel: 403-288-7700
admin@springbankair.com
www.springbankair.com
www.facebook.com/satcinfo

Jayme Hepfner, President

Camrose: High Velocity Equipment Training College
#201, 5061 - 50th St., Camrose, AB T4V 1R3

Tel: 780-678-6288; *Fax:* 780-678-2274
Toll-Free: 866-963-4766
admin@heavymetaltraining.com
www.heavymetaltraining.com
www.facebook.com/HighVelocityEquipmentTraining

Note: Heavy machinery training school.

Condor: Total Health School of Nutrition
P.O. Box 17
Condor, AB T0M 0P0

Tel: 403-746-5388; *Fax:* 403-746-5377
www.totalhealthschoolofnutrition.com

Note: Offers a Nutritional Counselling diploma program through
distance learning.
Darlene P. Blaney, President

Drumheller: Badlands Community College
420 - 12th St. East, Drumheller, AB T0J 0Y5

Edmonton: A & J Driving School
17527 - 100th Ave., Edmonton, AB T5S 2B8

Tel: 780-486-5090
info@aj-drivingschool.com
aj-drivingschool.com
www.instagram.com/aj.drivingschool

Edmonton: Alberta Academy of Aesthetics
#424, 8882 - 170th St., Edmonton, AB T5T 3J7

Tel: 780-486-7201; *Fax:* 780-486-7504
Toll-Free: 800-661-4675
info@academyofaesthetics.com
academyofaesthetics.com
www.facebook.com/261875777174989

Edmonton: Alberta Caregiving Institute
#277, 3428 - 99th St., Edmonton, AB T6E 5X5

Tel: 780-203-9617; *Toll-Free:* 844-276-4650
admin@albertacaregivinginstitute.com
albertacaregivinginstitute.com
www.facebook.com/135077749864773

Edmonton: Alberta College of Massage Therapy
Administrative Office
4656 - 99th St. NW, Edmonton, AB T6E 5H5

Fax: 888-849-2578
Toll-Free: 877-768-8400
info@acmt.ca
acmt.ca
www.facebook.com/ACMTCA
www.linkedin.com/company/alberta-college-of-massage-therapy
www.instagram.com/acmtca

Note: Offers two massage therapy programs: Spa Massage
Practitioner Certificate & Massage Therapy Diploma.
Ashley Taylor, Academic Director
ashley@acmt.ca

Campuses
Calgary - Kensington Campus
1167 Kensington Cres., Calgary, AB T2N 1X7

Toll-Free: 877-768-8400

Calgary - South Campus
10333 Southport Rd., Calgary, AB T2W 3X6

Toll-Free: 877-768-8400

Edmonton - Downtown Campus
10434 - 122nd St., Edmonton, AB T5N 1M3

Toll-Free: 877-768-8400

Edmonton - Southside Campus
4620 - 99th St., Edmonton, AB T6E 5H5

Toll-Free: 877-768-8400

Fort McMurray Campus
Keyano College
9908 Penhorwood St., Fort McMurray, AB T9H 1L3

Toll-Free: 877-768-8400

Grande Prairie Campus
#200, 11402 - 100th St., Grande Prairie, AB T8V 2N5

Toll-Free: 877-768-8400

Lloydminster Campus
5712 - 44th St., Lloydminster, AB T9V 0B6

Toll-Free: 877-768-8400

Red Deer Campus
4913 - 50th Ave., Red Deer, AB T4N 4A6

Toll-Free: 877-768-8400

Edmonton: Auctioneering College of Canada
P.O. Box 48088
14912 - 128th Ave., Edmonton, AB T5N 5V9

Tel: 780-453-6964; *Toll-Free:* 888-453-6964
www.auctioncollege.ca

Edmonton: Campbell College
Stanley Bldg. #2
#101, 11748 Kingsway Ave., Edmonton, AB T5G 0X5

Tel: 780-448-1850; *Fax:* 780-447-5902
info@campbellcollege.ca
campbellcollege.ca
www.facebook.com/CampbellCollege.ca
twitter.com/CampbellColleg1
www.linkedin.com/company/campbell-college

Note: Administrative Professional Diploma Program.

Campuses
Calgary Campus
#210, 4202 - 17th Ave. SE, Calgary, AB T2A 0T2

Tel: 403-475-2985

Toronto Campus
2300 Sheppard Ave. West, Toronto, ON M9M 3A4

Tel: 416-747-5152

Edmonton: Digital School Technical Design College
10010 - 100th St., Edmonton, AB T5J 0N3

Tel: 780-414-0200
learn@digitalschool.ca
www.digitalschool.ca
www.facebook.com/digitalschool.ca
twitter.com/digital_school
www.linkedin.com/company/digital-school

Note: Digital School is a private vocational career college
specializing in computer-aided drafting & design training.

Edmonton: Edmonton Public Schools Metro
Continuing Education
7835 - 76th Ave. NW, Edmonton, AB T6C 2N1

Tel: 780-428-1111; *Fax:* 780-428-1112
Toll-Free: 877-202-2003
metro@epsb.ca
www.metrocontinuingeducation.ca
www.facebook.com/MetroConEd
twitter.com/MetroConEd
www.linkedin.com/company/metro-continuing-education

Note: Edmonton Public Schools Metro Continuing Education
offers courses in English as a Second Language, academics,
business, computers & personal interest.
Jean Stiles, Director

Edmonton: Est-elle Academy of Hair Design
8004 Gateway Blvd., Edmonton, AB T6E 6A2

Tel: 780-432-7577; *Fax:* 780-433-4799
Toll-Free: 888-432-8828
info@est-elle.ab.ca
www.est-elle.ab.ca
www.facebook.com/EstelleAcademy
twitter.com/estelleacademy

Edmonton: European Institute of Esthetics (EIE)
Esthetic & Laser Training Centre
6724 - 75th St., Edmonton, AB T6E 6T9

reg@eietrainingcentre.ca
www.eietrainingcentre.ca
www.facebook.com/EIETrainingCentre
www.instagram.com/eie_training_centre

Linda Malito, General Manager

Campuses
East Campus
6012 - 82nd Ave. NW, Edmonton, AB T6E 6T9

Toll-Free: 800-557-3223

Note: Esthetics

Edmonton: EvelineCharles Academy
#2047, 8882 - 170th St. NW, Edmonton, AB T5T 4J2

Tel: 780-409-5672
admissions@ecacademy.com
ecacademy.com
www.facebook.com/ECAcademy
twitter.com/ECAcademy

Campuses
Peace River Campus
8801 - 96th St., Peace River, AB T8S 1R6

Tel: 780-409-5672

Edmonton: Excel Academy
10766 - 97th St., Edmonton, AB T5H 4R2

Tel: 780-441-7999
info@excelacademy.ca
excelacademy.ca
www.facebook.com/Excel.Academy.Edmonton

Note: The Excel Academy offers the Health Care Aide &
Community Support Worker Certificate Programs, as well as
other Professional Development courses related to the human
services industry.
Chris Thomson, Director

Edmonton: Gennaro Transport Training
15430 - 131st Ave. NW, Edmonton, AB T5V 0A1

Tel: 780-451-0111; *Fax:* 780-488-3115
info@gennaro.ca
www.gennaro.ca
www.facebook.com/GennaroTransport
www.instagram.com/gennaro_transport

Note: Professional truck driver training.

Edmonton: GRB College of Welding
9712 - 54th Ave. NW, Edmonton, AB T6E 0A9

Tel: 780-436-7342
www.grbwelding.com
twitter.com/GRB_Enterprises

Edmonton: MaKami College
Bonnie Doon Shopping Centre
#137, 8330 - 82nd Ave. NW, Edmonton, AB T6C 4E3

Tel: 780-468-3454; *Fax:* 780-485-6081
info@makamicollege.com
makamicollege.com
www.facebook.com/MaKamiCollege
twitter.com/MaKamiCollege
www.linkedin.com/school/makami-college
www.youtube.com/c/MaKamiCollege

Note: The college offers massage therapy courses.

Campuses
Calgary - Northeast Campus
Marlborough Mall
#1600, 3800 Memorial Dr. NE, Calgary, AB T2A 2K2
Tel: 403-474-0772; Fax: 587-350-7492

Calgary - Southwest Campus
9618 Horton Rd. SW, Calgary, AB T2V 4K8
Tel: 403-474-0772; Fax: 587-350-7492

Edmonton: MC College
Also known as: Marvel College
Corporate Office
#801, 10345 - 107th St., Edmonton, AB T5J 1K3
www.mccollege.ca
www.facebook.com/mccollegegroup
twitter.com/mccollegegroup
www.youtube.com/user/MCCollegeCanada
Note: MC College offers courses in Fashion, Hairstyling, &
Esthetics.
Joe Cairo, President
joe@mccollege.ca
Anna Gemellaro, Director, Education, 780-497-3155
anna@mccollege.ca

Campuses
Calgary Campus
1023 - 7th Ave. SW, Calgary, AB T2P 1A8
Tel: 403-290-0051; Fax: 403-269-3359
Jessica Reddon, Director, 403-290-6992
jreddon@mccollege.ca

Edmonton Campus
#301, 10345 - 107th St. NW, Edmonton, AB T5J 1K3
Tel: 780-429-4407; Fax: 780-951-9591
Analia Rubie, Director
arubie@mccollege.ca

Kelowna Campus
#100, 1875 Spall Rd., Kelowna, BC V1Y 4R2
Tel: 250-861-5828; Fax: 250-763-1747
Nikki McCrimmon, Director
nikki@mccollege.ca

Red Deer Campus
5008 Ross St., Red Deer, AB T4N 1Y3
Tel: 403-342-1110; Fax: 403-342-5210
Janet Davey, Director
jdavey@mccollege.ca

Saskatoon Campus
#228, 21 St. East, Saskatoon, SK S7K 0B9
Tel: 306-664-2474; Fax: 306-653-6883
Vanessa Slater, Director
vslater@mccollege.ca

Winnipeg Campus
575 Wall St., Winnipeg, MB R3G 2T5
Tel: 204-786-5081; Fax: 204-783-7342
Anna McGregor, Director
amcgregor@mccollege.ca

Edmonton: McBride Career Group Inc.
Energy Square
10109 - 106th St NW, 11th Fl., Edmonton, AB T5J 1Z7
Tel: 780-448-1380; Fax: 780-448-1392
edmmcg@mcgcareers.com
www.mcgcareers.com

Campuses
Calgary Campus
602 - 12th Ave. SW, 4th Fl., Calgary, AB T2R 1J3
Tel: 403-777-5627; Fax: 403-777-5655
mcg@mcgcareers.com

Fort Saskatchewan Campus
#2, 9902 - 93rd St., Fort Saskatchewan, AB T8L 4K8
Tel: 587-285-8118; Fax: 587-285-8117
fortsask@mcgcareers.com

High River Campus
#6, 28 - 12th Ave. SE, 2nd Fl., High River, AB T1V 1T2
Tel: 403-601-2660; Fax: 403-601-2627
highriver@mcgcareers.com

Okotoks Campus
#3, 87 Elizabeth St., Okotoks, AB T1S 1B2
Tel: 403-995-4377; Fax: 403-995-3616
okotoks@mcgcareers.com

Red Deer Campus
#210, 4814 - 50th St., Red Deer, AB T4N 1X4
Tel: 403-596-4854; Fax: 403-986-6402
rdmcg@mcgcareers.com

Edmonton: MH Vicars School of Massage Therapy
2828 Calgary Trail, Edmonton, AB T6J 6V7
Tel: 780-491-0574
info@mhvicarsschool.com
www.mhvicarsschool.com
www.facebook.com/MHVicarsSchool
Maryhelen Vicars, President
Sarah Ward, Executive Director
Linda McGeachy, Director, Curriculum

Campuses
Calgary Campus
#101, 200 Country Hills Landing NW, Calgary, AB T3K 5P3
Tel: 403-567-1451
Sarah Ward, Director

Edmonton: Nightingale Academy of Health Services Inc.
Venta Care Centre
13525 - 102nd St., Edmonton, AB T5E 4K3
Tel: 780-886-0619; Fax: 780-478-5284
info@nightingaleacademy.com
nightingaleacademy.com
Clive McNichol, President & CEO

Edmonton: The Northern Alberta Institute of Technology (NAIT)
11762 - 106th St. NW, Edmonton, AB T5G 2R1
Tel: 780-471-6248; Fax: 780-471-8583
Toll-Free: 877-333-6248
asknait@nait.ca
www.nait.ca
www.facebook.com/NAIT
twitter.com/nait
www.linkedin.com/school/nait
www.youtube.com/user/naitvideos
Enrollment: 40000
Laura Jo Gunter, President & CEO, 780-471-7700
president@nait.ca
Sue Fitzsimmons, Vice-President, Academic & Provost,
780-491-3970
sfitz@nait.ca

Campuses
Patricia Campus
12204 - 149th St. NW, Edmonton, AB T5V 1A2
Tel: 780-378-7200

Souch Campus
7110 Gateway Blvd., Edmonton, AB T6E 0E6
Tel: 780-378-1000

Spruce Grove Campus
281 Tamarack Dr., Spruce Grove, AB T7X 0Y1

Edmonton: Pixel Blue College
Empire Bldg.
#200, 10080 Jasper Ave., Edmonton, AB T5J 1V9
Tel: 780-756-3990
info@pixelblue.ca
www.pixelblue.ca
www.facebook.com/PixelBlueCollege
twitter.com/PixelBlueFx
www.instagram.com/madebypbc
Note: Diploma programs offered in art & design, including
graphic design, 3D animation & audio production.
Curtis Greenland, Director, Education

Edmonton: Reeves College
Edmonton City Centre Campus
#500, 10004 Jasper Ave., Edmonton, AB T5J 1R3
Toll-Free: 800-670-4512
www.reevescollege.ca
www.facebook.com/ReevesCollege
twitter.com/ReevesCollege
www.linkedin.com/school/reeves-college
www.youtube.com/c/ReevesCollegeCanada
Note: Reeves College delivers vocational training licensed under
the Private Vocational Schools Act. Programs are offered in the
areas of business, legal, health care, & art & design. The college
has five campus locations across Alberta.

Campuses
Calgary - City Centre Campus
#400, 703 - 6th Ave. SW, Calgary, AB T2P 0T9

Calgary - North Campus
#120, 2886 Sunridge Way NE, Calgary, AB T1Y 7H9

Calgary - South Campus
#9, 6624 Centre St., Calgary, AB T2H 0C6

Edmonton - North Campus
#174, 9450 - 137th Ave. NW, Edmonton, AB T5E 6C2

Edmonton - South Campus
#103, 9910 - 39th Ave. NW, Edmonton, AB T6E 5H8

Lethbridge Campus
#110, 601 - 4th Ave. South, Lethbridge, AB T1J 0N6

Lloydminster Campus
5012 - 49th St., Upper Level, Lloydminster, AB T9V 0K2

Edmonton: Wholistic Health Training & Research Centre
#107, 4990 - 92nd Ave. NW, Edmonton, AB T6B 2V4
Tel: 780-461-6708
info@wholistictraining.com
wholistictraining.com
www.facebook.com/wholistichealthtraining
twitter.com/WHTRCEdmonton
www.instagram.com/wholistichealthtraining
Note: Offers studies in massage therapy, aromatherapy,
acupressure therapy, psychosomatic therapy & other wholistic
modalities.

Fort McMurray: McMurray Aviation
531 Snow Eagle Dr., Fort McMurray, AB T9H 0H8
Tel: 780-791-2182; Fax: 780-790-2364
info@mcmurrayaviation.com
www.mcmurrayaviation.com
www.facebook.com/mcmurrayaviation
www.youtube.com/c/mcmurrayaviation
Note: Flight Training.

Grande Prairie: Adventure Aviation Inc.
11021 - 123rd St., Grande Prairie, AB T8V 7Z3
Tel: 780-539-6968; Fax: 780-532-9661
info@adventureaviation.ca
adventureaviation.ca
www.facebook.com/adventureaviationinc
Note: Flight training. Fort St. John, BC location: 250-785-6966;
fax: 250-787-9661.

Grande Prairie: ONE Beauty Academy
#209, 10001 - 101st Ave., Grande Prairie, AB T8V 0X9
Tel: 780-532-4443
oneacademy.ca

Campuses
Medicine Hat Campus
634 - 2nd St. SE, Medicine Hat, AB T1A 0C9
Tel: 403-527-6822; Fax: 780-486-7504

Grande Prairie: TriTech Safety & Training
11901 - 97th Ave., Grande Prairie, AB T8W 0C7
Tel: 780-539-5353
admin@tritechsafety.ca
tritechsafety.ca
www.facebook.com/TriTechSafety

Leduc: Alberta School of Dog Grooming
5009 - 50th Ave., Leduc, AB T9E 6V9
info@albertaschoolofdoggrooming.com

Lethbridge: Excel Flight Training Inc.
#201, 421 Stubb Ross Rd., Lethbridge, AB T1K 7N3
Tel: 403-329-4887; Fax: 403-329-4872
excelflt@telus.net
flywithexcel.com
www.facebook.com/ExcelFlightTrainingInc
Roland Morton, President

Lethbridge: Gateway Safety Services Ltd.
3804 - 18th Ave. North, Lethbridge, AB T1H 5G3
Tel: 403-328-8496; Fax: 403-320-8446
Toll-Free: 866-922-4283
info@gatewaysafety.ca
www.gatewaysafety.ca
www.facebook.com/gatewaysafetyservices
Note: Certified Business & Driver Safety Training.

Lethbridge: Southern Alberta Institute of Massage (SAIM)
534 - 18th St. South, Lethbridge, AB T1J 3E7
Tel: 403-331-5657
info@southernalbertainstituteofmassage.com
www.southernalbertainstituteofmassage.com

Note: Private institute that teaches a 2,200 Hour Massage Therapy Program.

Campuses
Medicine Hat Campus
340 Maple Ave. SE, Medicine Hat, AB T1A 7L5
Tel: 403-504-9694

Lethbridge: **Training Inc.**
444 - 5th Ave. South, Lethbridge, AB T1J 0T5
Tel: 403-320-5100; *Fax:* 403-320-0567
Toll-Free: 866-380-3480
info@traininginc.ca
traininginc.ca
www.facebook.com/TrainingInc.Services
www.instagram.com/TrainingInc.Services
Note: Offers post-secondary & self-interest programs, industry-specific certification courses & oilfield & safety training.

Campuses
Cardston Campus
58 - 2nd Ave. West, Cardston, AB T0K 0K0
Tel: 403-653-4603; *Fax:* 403-653-4604

Pincher Creek Campus
P.O. Box 1506
715C Main St., Pincher Creek, AB T0K 1W0
Tel: 403-627-1874; *Fax:* 403-627-1878

Lloydminster: **3A Academy & Consulting Ltd.**
#601, 5116 - 50th St., Lloydminster, AB T9V 1M3
Tel: 780-808-2258; *Fax:* 780-871-0578
training@3aacademy.com
3aacademy.com
www.facebook.com/3aacademy
Note: Workplace training services & computer training services.

Lloydminster: **Border City Aviation**
P.O. Box 10963
7054 - 83rd Ave., Lloydminster, AB T9V 3B3
Tel: 780-875-5834; *Fax:* 780-875-5871
info@bordercityaviation.com
www.bordercityaviation.com
www.facebook.com/1667536530146681
Note: Flight training.

Medicine Hat: **Cypress College**
3 - 7th St. SE, Medicine Hat, AB T1A 1J2
Tel: 403-527-4382; *Fax:* 403-526-4388
admissions@cypresscollege.ca
www.cypresscollege.ca
www.facebook.com/cypresscollege.ca
twitter.com/CypressCollege1
Note: Training for computer, business & employment-related skills.
David Martin, President

Campuses
Brooks Campus
716 - 2nd St. West, Brooks, AB T1R 1C4
Tel: 587-270-5042; *Fax:* 403-526-4388
Note: Training for computer, business & employment-related skills.

Medicine Hat Lodge Campus
1051 Ross Glen Dr. SE, Medicine Hat, AB T1B 3T8
Tel: 403-527-4382; *Fax:* 403-526-4388
Note: Training for computer, business & employment-related skills.

Medicine Hat: **Super T Aviation Academy**
#11, 1 Airport Dr. SW, Medicine Hat, AB T1A 5G4
Tel: 403-548-6636
contact-us@supertaviation.ca
www.supertaviation.ca
www.facebook.com/supertaviation
Terri Super, Manager, Operations
tsuper@supertaviation.ca

Olds: **Calgary Flight Training Centre (CFTC)**
#423, 1436 Township Rd. 320, Olds, AB T4H 1T8
Tel: 403-688-2232
info@calgaryflight.com
calgaryflight.com
www.facebook.com/calgaryflight

Penhold: **Sky Wings Aviation Academy**
Hangar 13, Red Deer Regional Airport
P.O. Box 190
Penhold, AB T0M 1R0
Tel: 403-886-5191; *Toll-Free:* 800-315-8097
info@skywings.com
www.skywings.com
www.facebook.com/SkywingsAviationAcademyLtd
Dennis Cooper, Chief Executive Officer

Red Deer: **Alberta Institute of Massage**
#104A, 4315 - 55th Ave., Red Deer, AB T4N 4N7
Tel: 403-346-1018; *Fax:* 403-346-0606
info@aimassage.ca
albertainstituteofmassage.com
www.facebook.com/albertainstituteofmassage

Red Deer: **The Health Care Aide Academy**
#200, 5009 - 49th St., Red Deer, AB T4N 1V4
Tel: 403-967-0309
info@healthcareaideacademy.com
healthcareaideacademy.com
www.facebook.com/healthcareaideacademy

Sexsmith: **Peace River Bible Institute (PRBI)**
P.O. Box 99
Sexsmith, AB T0H 3C0
Tel: 780-568-3962; *Fax:* 780-568-4431
Toll-Free: 800-959-7724
prbi@prbi.edu
www.prbi.edu
www.facebook.com/acollegeforlife
www.instagram.com/prbilife
Note: Interdenominational school that focuses on the basics of evangelical Christianity.
Kim Cairns, President

Sherwood Park: **Emergency Services Academy (ESA)**
161 Broadway Blvd., 2nd Fl., Sherwood Park, AB T8H 2A8
Tel: 780-416-8822; *Fax:* 780-449-4787
info@esacanada.com
www.esacanada.com
www.facebook.com/ESAcanada
www.instagram.com/ESAReady
Note: Fully-accredited programs for Emergency Medical Responder, Emergency Medical Technician / Primary Care Paramedic & Professional Fire Fighter.

Sherwood Park: **International Academy of Esthetics (IAE)**
#122, 150 Chippewa Rd., Sherwood Park, AB T8A 6A2
Tel: 780-449-1225
iaesthetics.com
www.facebook.com/iaesthetics

St Albert: **AB RoadSafe**
26526 Township Rd. 543, St Albert, AB T8T 1M2
Tel: 780-668-9799
www.abroadsafe.com
www.facebook.com/ABRoadSafeSturgeonCounty
Note: AB RoadSafe offers Class 1 & Class 3 truck training, safety training & online training.
Corri McCarty, Office Manager
corri@abroadsafe.com

Sturgeon County: **Synergy Aviation Ltd.**
Synergy Flight Training, Bldg. 38, Villeneuve Air
Sturgeon County, AB T8T 0E3
Tel: 587-416-5647
training@synergyaviation.ca
synergyflighttraining.ca
www.facebook.com/FlySynergyAviation
www.linkedin.com/company/flysynergy
Note: Synergy Aviation Ltd. offers training through Synergy Flight Training Inc. & Centennial Flight Centre.

Campuses
Centennial Flight Centre
Villeneuve Airport, Hangar 42
Sturgeon County, AB T8T 0E3
Tel: 780-451-7676; *Fax:* 780-452-3575
info@centennial.ca
synergyflighttraining.ca
www.facebook.com/centennialflightcentre
Note: Flight training school offering training in Recreational Pilot Permit (RPP), Private Pilot Licence (PPL), Commercial Pilot Licence (CPL), Multi-Engine (ME), & Instrument Rating (IFR).

Wetaskiwin: **Wetaskiwin Air Services Ltd.**
Also known as: Absolute Aviation
6301 - 47th Ave., Wetaskiwin, AB T9A 2G2
Tel: 780-352-5643
info@absoluteaviation.ca
www.absoluteaviation.ca
www.facebook.com/flyabsolute
Note: Flight training.

Whitecourt: **Rotorworks Inc.**
P.O. Box 86
Whitecourt, AB T7S 1N3
Tel: 780-778-6600
info@rotorworks.com
www.rotorworks.com
www.facebook.com/RotorworksInc
www.instagram.com/rotorworks_inc
Note: Helicopter Flight Training.

British Columbia

Government Agencies

Victoria: **British Columbia Ministry of Advanced Education, Skills & Training**
P.O. Box 9885 Prov Govt
Victoria, BC V8W 9T6, Canada
Tel: 250-356-5170; *Fax:* 250-356-5468
AEST.GeneralInquiries@gov.bc.ca
www.gov.bc.ca/aved

Hon. Anne Kang, Minister
AEST.Minister@gov.bc.ca

Victoria: **British Columbia Ministry of Education (BCED)**
Ministry of Education
P.O. Box 9150 Prov Govt
Victoria, BC V8W 9E2
Tel: 250-387-6121; *Fax:* 250-356-0948
Toll-Free: 800-663-7867
EDUC.correspondence@gov.bc.ca
www.gov.bc.ca/bced
TTY: 604-775-0303

Hon. Jennifer Whiteside, Minister, 250-356-8247
educ.minister@gov.bc.ca

School Boards/Districts/Divisions

Public

Abbotsford: **Abbotsford School District (SD34)**
2790 Tims St., Abbotsford, BC V2T 4M7
Tel: 604-859-4891; *Fax:* 604-852-8587
info@abbyschools.ca
www.abbyschools.ca
www.facebook.com/AbbotsfordSD
twitter.com/abbotsfordsd
www.linkedin.com/company/abbotsfordsd
www.instagram.com/abbotsfordsd
Number of Schools: 30 elementary schools; 8 middle schools; 1 middle-secondary schools; 7 secondary schools *Grades:* K - 12 *Enrollment:* 19200 *Number of Employees:* 2,200 *Note:* Also has a virtual school, an Aboriginal education centre, an annual summer school, continuing education courses & an international student program.
Linda Peters, Director, Finance, 604-859-4891, ext. 1287
linda.peters@abbyschools.ca
Stan Petersen, Chair, 778-878-3613
stan.petersen@abbyschools.ca
Ray Velestuk, Secretary-Treasurer, 604-859-4891, ext. 1241
ray.velestuk@abbyschools.ca
Derrin Demaer, Manager, Purchasing, 604-859-4891, ext. 1242
derrin.demaer@abbyschools.ca
Kayla Stuckart, Manager, Communications, 604-859-4891, ext. 1206
kayla.stuckart@abbyschools.ca
Kevin Godden, Superintendent, Schools, 604-859-4891, ext. 1230
kevin.godden@abbyschools.ca
Michele Radomski, Associate Superintendent, Human Resources, 604-859-4891, ext. 1212
Michele.Radomski@abbyschools.ca

Ashcroft: **Gold Trail School District #74**
P.O. Box 250
400 Hollis Rd., Ashcroft, BC V0K 1A0
Tel: 250-453-9151; *Fax:* 250-453-2425
Toll-Free: 1-855-453-9101
district@sd74.bc.ca
www.sd74.bc.ca
twitter.com/sd74news
Number of Schools: 4 elementary; 2 secondary; 3 K-12; 1 rural *Grades:* K - 12 *Enrollment:* 1800 *Number of Employees:* 150 teachers & support staff
Valerie Adrian, Chair, Board, 250-453-9101
vadrian@sd74.bc.ca
Teresa Downs, Superintendent, Schools, 250-453-9151, ext. 234
tdowns@sd74.bc.ca

Lynda Minnabarriet, Secretary-Treasurer, 250-453-9151, ext. 201
lminnabarriet@sd74.bc.ca
Tammy Mountain, District Principal - Aboriginal Education, 250-453-9151, ext. 215
tmountain@sd74.bc.ca
Debby Sansome, Director, Facilities, 250-498-3481, ext. 103
dsansome@sd74.bc.ca
Steve Aie, Manager, Finance, 250-453-9151, ext. 221
saie@sd74.bc.ca
Diana Hillocks, Manager, Human Resources, 250-453-9151, ext. 211
dhillocks@sd74.bc.ca

Burnaby: Burnaby School District #41 (SD41)
Also known as: Burnaby Schools
5325 Kincaid St., Burnaby, BC V5G 1W2
Tel: 604-296-6900; *Fax:* 604-296-6910
inquiries@burnabyschools.ca
burnabyschools.ca
twitter.com/burnabyschools
Number of Schools: 41 elementary schools; 7 community schools; 8 secondary schools *Grades:* K - 12; Community & Continuing Ed. *Enrollment:* 25000 *Number of Employees:* 4,000
Gary Wong, Chair, Board, 604-420-1310
gary.wong@burnabyschools.ca
Russell Horswill, Secretary-Treasurer, 604-296-6900, ext. 661003
russell.horswill@burnabyschools.ca
Gina Niccoli-Moen, Superintendent, Schools & Chief Executive Officer, 604-296-6900, ext. 661001
gina.niccoli-moen@burnabyschools.ca
Roberto Bombelli, Assistant Superintendent, 604-296-6900, ext. 661005
roberto.bombelli@burnabyschools.ca
Heather Hart, Assistant Superintendent, 604-296-6900, ext. 661007
heather.hart@burnabyschools.ca
Wanda Mitchell, Assistant Superintendent, 604-296-6900, ext. 661008
wanda.mitchell@burnabyschools.ca
Richard Per, Assistant Superintendent, 604-296-6900, ext. 661067
richard.per@burnabyschools.ca

Campbell River: Campbell River School District #72
425 Pinecrest Rd., Campbell River, BC V9W 3P2
Tel: 250-830-2300; *Fax:* 250-287-2616
info@sd72.bc.ca
www.sd72.bc.ca
www.facebook.com/190414822472
twitter.com/CRSD72
www.youtube.com/user/schooldistrict72
Number of Schools: 13 elementary; 2 middle; 2 secondary; 3 specialized *Grades:* K - 12; Continuing Ed; ESL *Enrollment:* 5405 *Number of Employees:* 870
Richard Franklin, Board Chair
richard.franklin@sd72.bc.ca
Jeremy Morrow, PhD., Superintendent, Schools; CEO, 250-830-2398
jeremy.morrow@sd72.bc.ca
Nevenka Fair, Assistant Superintendent, Schools, 250-830-2398
nevenka.fair@sd72.bc.ca
Kevin Patrick, Secretary-Treasurer, 250-830-2302
kevin.patrick@sd72.bc.ca
Greg Johnson, District Principal, Alternate Programs & Indigenous Education, 250-923-4902
greg.johnson@sd72.bc.ca
Yves Vachon, Director, Human Resources, 250-830-2310
yves.vachon@sd72.bc.ca
Cathy Fowler, District Teacher Librarian, 250-830-2322
cathy.fowler@sd72.bc.ca

Chilliwack: Chilliwack School District #33
8430 Cessna Dr., Chilliwack, BC V2P 7K4
Tel: 604-792-1321; *Fax:* 604-792-9665
www.sd33.bc.ca
www.facebook.com/chilliwackschooldistrict
twitter.com/ChilliwackSD33
Number of Schools: 20 elementary; 5 middle; 3 secondary; 1 alternative *Grades:* K - 12; Adult Ed. *Enrollment:* 14000 *Number of Employees:* 1800 *Note:* Offers continuing and distance education programs.
Dan Coulter, Board Chair, 604-316-4850
dan_coulter@sd33.bc.ca
Rohan Arul-pragasam, Acting Superintendent, Schools, 604-792-1321
rohan_arul@sd33.bc.ca
Gerry Slykhuis, Secretary-Treasurer, 604-703-1781
gerry_slykhuis@sd33.bc.ca
Kirk Savage, Acting Assistant Superintendent
kirk_savage@sd33.bc.ca

Janet Hall, Acting Assistant Superintendent
janet_hall@sd33.bc.ca
Allan Van Tassel, Director, Facilities & Transportation, 604-792-4327
allan_vantassel@sd33.bc.ca
Tamara Ilersich, Director, Human Resources
tamara_ilersich@sd33.bc.ca
Kevin Josephson, Manager, Finance
kevin_josephson@sd33.ba.ca

Coquitlam: Coquitlam School District #43 (SD43)
550 Poirier St., Coquitlam, BC V3J 6A7
Tel: 604-939-9201; *Fax:* 604-939-7828
information@sd43.bc.ca
www.sd43.bc.ca
www.facebook.com/sd43bc
twitter.com/sd43bc
www.youtube.com/SchoolDistrict43Coquitlam
Number of Schools: 45 elementary schools; 14 middle schools; 9 secondary schools; 3 alternative education programs *Grades:* K - 12 *Enrollment:* 32000 *Number of Employees:* 4,370
Kerri Palmer Isaak, Chair, Board, 604-861-052
kpalmerisaak@sd43.bc.ca
Chris Nicolls, Secretary-Treasurer, 604-939-9201
cnicolls@sd43.bc.ca
Patricia Gartland, Superintendent, Schools & Chief Executive Officer
pgartland@sd43.bc.ca

Courtenay: Comox Valley School District #71
607 Cumberland Rd., Courtenay, BC V9N 7G5
Tel: 250-334-5500; *Fax:* 250-334-5552
info@sd71.bc.ca
www.sd71.bc.ca
www.facebook.com/ComoxValleySchools
twitter.com/ComoxValleySD71
Number of Schools: 15 elementary; 1 middle; 3 secondary; 2 alternative *Grades:* K - 12 *Enrollment:* 8500 *Number of Employees:* 1500 *Note:* Also offers a Learning Resources Centre, a Nala'atsi Program, an International Student Program, an outdoor education centre, French immersion programs, and a school with a Montessori program.
Janice Caton, Board Chair, 250-897-0756
janice.caton@sd71.bc.ca
Dean Lindquist, Superintendent, 250-334-5500
heidi.bell@sd71.bc.ca
Nicole Bittante, Secretary-Treasurer, 250-334-5500
nicole.bittante@sd71.bc.ca
Lynda-Marie Handfield, Director, Human Resources
lynda-marie.handfield@sd71.bc.ca
Bruce Carlos, District Principal, Aboriginal Education, 250-331-4040, ext. 1
bruce.carlos@sd71.bc.ca

Cranbrook: Southeast Kootenay School District #5
#1, 940 Industrial Rd., Cranbrook, BC V1C 4C6
Tel: 250-426-4201; *Fax:* 250-489-5460
cbo.mailing@sd5.bc.ca
www.sd5.bc.ca
Number of Schools: 10 elementary; 7 secondary; 2 alternative *Grades:* K - 12 *Enrollment:* 5485 *Number of Employees:* 600
Silke Yardley, Superintendent; CEO, 250-417-2079
silke.yardley@sd5.bc.ca
Alan Rice, Secretary-Treasurer, 250-417-2054
alan.rice@sd5.bc.ca
Diane Casault, Director, Student Learning & Innovation, 250-417-2053
diane.casault@sd5.bc.ca

Dawson Creek: Peace River South School District #59
11600 - 7th St., Dawson Creek, BC V1G 4R8
Tel: 250-782-8571; *Fax:* 250-782-3204
sbo_Reception@sd59.bc.ca
www.sd59.bc.ca
www.facebook.com/SchoolDistrict59
twitter.com/sd59prs
Number of Schools: 14 elementary; 4 secondary; 1 Montessori; 1 alternative *Grades:* K - 12 *Enrollment:* 3600
Tamara Ziemer, Board Chair, 250-219-5504
tamara_ziemer@sd59.bc.ca
Candace Clouthier, Superintendent; CEO, 250-782-8571, ext. 212
cclouthi@sd59.bc.ca
Melissa Panoulias, Secretary-Treasurer, 250-782-8571
mpanoulias@sd59.bc.ca
Mike Readman, Director, Instruction, 250-782-8571
mreadman@sd59.bc.ca
Wade Simlik, Director, Operations, 250-782-2417
wade_simlik@sd59.bc.ca

Dease Lake: Stikine School District #87
P.O. Box 190
5 Commerical Dr., Dease Lake, BC V0C 1L0, Canada
Tel: 250-771-4440; *Fax:* 250-771-4441
www.sd87.bc.ca
Number of Schools: 1 K-7; 1 K-9; 2 K-12 schools *Grades:* K - 12; Alternative Ed. *Enrollment:* 260 *Number of Employees:* 71
Yvonne Tashoots, Chair, Board
yvonne.tashoots@sd87.bc.ca
Mike Gordon, Superintendent, Schools
mgordon@sd87.bc.ca
Ken Mackie, Secretary-Treasurer
kmackie@sd87.bc.ca
Gerry Brennan, Director, Instruction
gbrennan@sd87.bc.ca

Delta: Delta School District #37
4585 Harvest Dr., Delta, BC V4K 5B4
Tel: 604-946-4101
webmaster@deltasd.bc.ca
https://www.deltasd.bc.ca/
www.facebook.com/deltaschooldistrict
twitter.com/deltasd37
www.instagram.com/deltasd37/
Number of Schools: 24 elementary; 7 secondary *Grades:* K - 12; Adult Ed. *Enrollment:* 15800 *Note:* Also offers the Delta Manor Education Centre, Delta Community College, & Home Quest alternative education centre.
Laura Dixon, Chairperson, 604-999-2053
ldixon@deltasd.bc.ca
Doug Sheppard, Superintendent, 604-952-5340
dsheppard@deltasd.bc.ca
Nancy Gordon, Assistant Superintendent, 604-952-5345
ngordon@deltasd.bc.ca
Brad Bauman, Assistant Superintendent, 604-952-5346
bbauman@deltasd.bc.ca
Nicola Christ, Secretary Treasurer, 604-952-5334
nchrist@deltasd.bc.ca
Robyn Faust, Director, Finance and Management, 604-952-5096
rfaust@deltasd.bc.ca
Jennifer Hill, Manager, Communications & Marketing, 604-952-5397
jhill@deltasd.bc.ca
Neil Stephenson, Director, Learning Services, 604-952-5069
nstephenson@deltasd.bc.ca

Duncan: Cowichan Valley School District #79
2557 Beverly St., Duncan, BC V9L 2X3
Tel: 250-748-0321; *Fax:* 250-748-6591
info@sd79.bc.ca
www.sd79.bc.ca
www.facebook.com/CowichanSchools
twitter.com/TransportSD79
Number of Schools: 17 elementary; 5 secondary; 3 alternative *Grades:* K - 12 *Enrollment:* 8300
Robyn Gray, Superintendent, Schools, 250-748-0321, ext. 215
rgray@sd79.bc.ca
Jason Sandquist, Secretary-Treasurer, 250-748-0321, ext. 208
jsandqui@sd79.bc.ca
Denise Augustine, Director, Aboriginal Education and Learner Engagement, 250-748-0321, ext. 235
daugusti@sd79.bc.ca
Roma Medves, Manager, Human Resources, 250-748-0321, ext. 221
rmedves@sd79.bc.ca
Monroe Grobe, Director, Operations, 250-748-0338, ext. 260
mgrobe@sd79.bc.ca

Fort Nelson: Fort Nelson School District #81
P.O. Box 87
5104 Airport Dr., Fort Nelson, BC V0C 1R0
Tel: 250-774-2591; *Fax:* 250-774-2598
contact@sd81.bc.ca
www.sd81.bc.ca
www.facebook.com/sd81.sbo
Number of Schools: 2 primary; 1 elementary; 1 secondary; 1 K-12 *Grades:* K - 12 *Enrollment:* 871 *Number of Employees:* 100
Linda Dolen, Board Chair, 250-774-4880
ldolen@sd81.bc.ca
Diana Samchuck, Superintendent, 250-774-2591
dsamchuck@sd81.bc.ca
Margaret-Anne Hall, Secretary-Treasurer, 250-774-2591
mhall@sd81.bc.ca
Darryl Low, Supervisor, Maintenance, 250-774-6742
dlow@sd81.bc.ca
Seanah Roper, Coordinator, Literacy Outreach
coordinator@fncls.com

Fort St. John: **Peace River North School District #60**
10112 - 105 Ave., Fort St. John, BC V1J 4S4, Canada
Tel: 250-262-6000; *Fax:* 250-262-6048
www.prn.bc.ca
Other Information: After Hours Emergency: 250-785-6781
www.facebook.com/SD60PRN
twitter.com/sd60
Number of Schools: 9 elementary; 2 middle; 1 secondary; 4
K-12; 3 rural; 2 alternative *Grades:* K - 12 *Enrollment:* 6000
Dave Sloan, Superintendent, 250-262-6017
dsloan@prn.bc.ca
Brenda Hooker, Secretary-Treasurer, 250-262-6009
bhooker@prn.bc.ca
Crystal Jessen, Coordinator, Human Resources, 250-262-6016
hr@prn.bc.ca
Keith MacGillivray, District Principal, Learning Services,
250-262-6075
kmacgillivray@prn.bc.ca

Gibsons: **Sunshine Coast School District #46**
P.O. Box 220
494 South Fletcher Rd., Gibsons, BC V0N 1V0, Canada
Tel: 604-886-8811; *Fax:* 604-886-4652
Toll-Free: 877-886-8811
questions@sd46.bc.ca
www.sd46.bc.ca
www.facebook.com/SD46SC
twitter.com/SSCschools
Number of Schools: 9 elementary; 4 secondary; 1 alternative
Grades: K - 12; Alternative Ed. *Enrollment:* 3150
Pammila Ruth, Chair, Board, 604-886-4483
pruth@sd46.bc.ca
Patrick Bocking, Superintendent, Schools, 604-886-4489
pbocking@sd46.bc.ca
Nicholas Weswick, Secretary-Treasurer, 604-886-4484
nweswick@sd46.bc.ca
Rob Collison, Manager, Facilities & Transportation,
604-886-9870
rcollison@sd46.bc.ca
Tara Sweet, Manager, Human Resources
hr@sd46.bc.ca
Shannon Whittall, Manager, Finance, 604-886-4485
swhittall@sd46.bc.ca

Gold River: **Vancouver Island West School District
#84**
P.O. Box 100
2 Hwy. 28, Gold River, BC V0P 1G0, Canada
Tel: 250-283-2241; *Fax:* 250-283-7352
www.sd84.bc.ca
Number of Schools: 1 elementary; 3 elematary secondary; 1
secondary *Grades:* K - 12 *Enrollment:* 466 *Note:* Also offers
continuing education classes.
Arlaine Fehr, Chair, Board, 250-283-7367
afehr@viw.sd84.bc.ca
Lawrence Tarasoff, Superintendent, Schools;
Secretary-Treasurer, 250-283-2241, ext. 225
ltarasoff@viw.sd84.bc.ca
Annie McDowell, Associate Director, Human Resources,
250-283-2241, ext. 224
amcdowell@viw.sd84.bc.ca
Stephen Larre, District Principal, Student Learning & Staff
Development, 250-283-2241, ext. 233
slarre@viw.sd84.bc.ca

Grand Forks: **Boundary School District #51**
P.O. Box 640
1021 Central Ave., Grand Forks, BC V0H 1H0
Tel: 250-442-8258; *Fax:* 250-442-8800
info@sd51.bc.ca
www.sd51.bc.ca
www.facebook.com/SD51Boundary
twitter.com/sd51boundary
Number of Schools: 7 elementary; 2 secondary; 1 K-9; 1
alternative education *Grades:* K - 12; Alternate Ed.
Cindy Strukoff, Board Chair, 250-447-2609
cindy.strukoff@sd51.bc.ca
Ken Minette, Superintendent, Schools, 250-442-8258
ken.minette@sd51.bc.ca
Miranda Burdock, Secretary-Treasurer, 250-442-8258
miranda.burdock@sd51.bc.ca
Doug Lacey, Director, Instruction, 250-442-8258
doug.lacey@sd51.bc.ca
Dean Higashi, Manager, Operations, 250-442-8258
dean.higashi@sd51.bc.ca
Erin Perkins, Coordinator, Community Literacy, 250-442-2704,
ext. 229
eperkins@cbal.org

Hagensborg: **Central Coast School District #49
(SD49)**
P.O. Box 130
Hagensborg, BC V0T 1H0
Tel: 250-982-2691; *Fax:* 250-982-2319
www.sd49.bc.ca
Number of Schools: 5 *Grades:* K - 12; Aboriginal Ed. *Enrollment:*
200 *Number of Employees:* 60
Nicola Koroluk, Chair, Board, 250-982-0045
nkoroluk@sd49.ca
Helen Zhao, Secretary-Treasurer, 250-982-2691
hzhao@sd49.ca
Cecilia Walkus, Coordinator, Aboriginal Education,
250-982-2691
lwalkus@sd49.ca
Steve Dishkin, Superintendent, Schools, 250-982-2691
sdishkin@sd49.ca

Hope: **Fraser Cascade School District #78**
650 Kawkawa Lake Rd., Hope, BC V0X 1L4
Tel: 604-869-2411; *Fax:* 604-869-7400
enquiry@sd78.bc.ca
www.sd78.bc.ca
Other Information: Agassiz Phone: 604-796-2225
twitter.com/sd78bc
Number of Schools: 4 elementary; 2 elementary-secondary; 1
secondary; 2 alternative *Grades:* K - 12 *Enrollment:* 1815
Linda Kerr, Chair, Board
linda.kerr@sd78.bc.ca
Karen Nelson, PhD., Superintendent, Schools, 604-869-2411,
ext. 103
karen.nelson@sd78.bc.ca
Natalie Lowe, CA, Secretary-Treasurer, 604-869-2411, ext. 101
natalie.lowe@sd78.bc.ca
Dan Landrath, Supervisor, Transportation, 604-796-1042
dan.landrath@sd78.bc.ca
Donna Barner, District Coordinator, Student Support Services,
604-869-2411, ext. 112
donna.barner@sd78.bc.ca
Rod Peters, District Aboriginal Education Coordinator,
604-869-2842, ext. 108
rod.peters@sd78.bc.ca

Invermere: **Rocky Mountain School District #6**
P.O. Box 430
620 - 4th St., Invermere, BC V0A 1K0, Canada
Tel: 250-342-9243; *Fax:* 250-342-6966
www.sd6.bc.ca
www.facebook.com/sd6.bc.ca/
twitter.com/RMSD6
Number of Schools: 1 primary; 9 elementary; 1 middle; 3
secondary; 4 alternative *Grades:* JK - 12 *Enrollment:* 3119
Amber Byklum, Chair, Board, 250-349-5622
amber.byklum@sd6.bc.ca
Paul Carriere, Superintendent, 250-342-4671
paul.carriere@sd6.bc.ca
Dale Culler, Secretary-Treasurer, 250-342-4672
dale.culler@sd6.bc.ca
Cheryl Lenardon, Assistant Superintendent, 250-342-4673
cheryl.lenardon@sd6.bc.ca
Steve Jackson, Director, Operations, 250-342-4676
steve.jackson@sd6.bc.ca

Kamloops: **Kamloops-Thompson School District #73**
1383 - 9th Ave., Kamloops, BC V2C 3X7
Tel: 250-374-0679; *Fax:* 250-372-1183
www.sd73.bc.ca
Number of Schools: 32 elementary; 1 middle; 9 secondary; 3
alternative *Grades:* K - 12; Continuing Ed. *Enrollment:* 14675
Number of Employees: 1,113 full time, part time, and relief
educators; 759 support staff
Kathleen Karpuk, Chair, Board, 250-319-6516
kkarpuk@sd73.bc.ca
Alison Sidow, Superintendent, Schools, 250-374-0679
asidow@sd73.bc.ca
Kelvin Stretch, Secretary-Treasurer, 250-374-0679
kstretch@sd73.bc.ca
Mike Bowden, District Principal - Aboriginal Education,
250-374-0679
mbowden@sd73.bc.ca
Trina Cassidy, Director, Finance, 250-374-0679, ext. 230
tcassidy@sd73.bc.ca
Art McDonald, Director, Facilities & Transportation,
250-851-4420
amcdonald@sd73.bc.ca

Kelowna: **Central Okanagan Public Schools (SD23)**
Also known as: Central Okanagan School District #23
Administrative Offices
1040 Hollywood Rd., Kelowna, BC V1X 4N2
Tel: 250-860-8888; *Fax:* 250-870-5056
schoolboard.office@sd23.bc.ca
www.sd23.bc.ca
www.facebook.com/sd23news
twitter.com/SD23News
Number of Schools: 31 elementary schools; 6 middle schools; 5
secondary schools; 1 alternative school *Grades:* K - 12;
Alternate Ed. *Enrollment:* 22230
Moyra Baxter, Chair, Board, 250-767-6153
moyra.baxter@sd23.bc.ca
Bob McEwan, Director, Human Resources, 250-860-8888
bob.mcewen@sd23.bc.ca
Peter Molloy, Director, Student Support Services, 250-470-3267
brenda-lee.erickson@sd23.bc.ca
Mitch Van Aller, Director, Operations, 250-870-5150
mitch.vanaller@sd23.bc.ca
Ryan Stierman, Secretary-Treasurer, 250-470-3216
Ryan.Stierman@sd23.bc.ca
Lloyd Pendleton, Manager, Purchasing, 250-870-5152
po@sd23.bc.ca
Kevin Kaardal, Superintendent, 250-470-3256
kevin.kaardal@sd23.bc.ca
Terry Beaudry, Deputy Superintendent, 250-470-3225
terry.beaudry@sd23.bc.ca
Vianne Kintzinger, Assistant Superintendent, Central Kelowna,
250-470-3271
jodee.hermiston@sd23.bc.ca
Rick Oliver, Assistant Superintendent, Westside, 250-470-3210
deborah.rouire@sd23.bc.ca
Rhonda Ovelson, Assistant Superintendent, Mission and Lake
Country, 250-470-3227
jan.nicholls@sd23.bc.ca
Jon Rever, Assistant Superintendent, Rutland, 250-470-3288
jody.kirschner@sd23.bc.ca

Langley: **Langley School District #35 (SD35)**
Also known as: Langley Schools
4875 - 222nd St., Langley, BC V3A 3Z7
Tel: 604-534-7891; *Fax:* 604-533-1115
feedback@sd35.b.ca
www.sd35.bc.ca
www.facebook.com/LangleySchoolDistrict
twitter.com/LangleySchools
www.linkedin.com/company/langley-school-district
Number of Schools: 45 *Grades:* K - 12; French Immersion; IB
Enrollment: 21000 *Number of Employees:* 2800
Megan Dykeman, Chair, Board, 604-530-5019
mdykeman@sd35.bc.ca
Gord Stewart, Superintendent, Schools, 778-726-3546
gstewart@sd35.bc.ca
Brian Iseli, Secretary-Treasurer, 604-532-1476
biseli@sd35.bc.ca
Mike Pue, District Principal of Aboriginal Education,
604-534-7891
mpue@sd35.bc.ca

Maple Ridge: **Maple Ridge-Pitt Meadows School
District #42**
22225 Brown Ave., Maple Ridge, BC V2X 8N6
Tel: 604-463-4200; *Fax:* 604-463-4181
contact@sd42.ca
www.sd42.ca
www.facebook.com/MapleRidgePittMeadowsSchoolSD42
twitter.com/sd42news
www.linkedin.com/company/school-district-42-maple-ridge-/
www.instagram.com/mapleridge.pittmeadows42/
Number of Schools: 22 elementary; 6 secondary *Grades:* K - 12
Enrollment: 14754 *Note:* Also offers continuing education at
Riverside Centre and higher education qualifications at Ridge
Meadows College.
Korleen Carreras, Board Chair, 604-463-4200
korleen_carreras@sd42.ca
Sylvia Russell, Superintendent, Schools, 604-466-6228
sylvia_russell@sd42.ca
Flavia Coughlan, Secretary-Treasurer, 604-466-6232
flavia_coughlan@sd42.ca
Rick Delorme, Director, Facilities, 604-463-8918
rick_delorme@sd42.ca
Dana Sirsiris, Director, Human Resources, 604-466-6219
dana_sirsiris@sd42.ca
Bruce Grady, Principal, Aboriginal Education (Acting),
604-466-6265
bruce_grady@sd42.ca
Alixe Alden, Manager, Purchasing and Transportation,
604-466-6236
alixe_alden@sd42.ca

Merritt: Nicola-Similkameen School District #58
P.O. Box 4100 Main
1550 Chapman St., Merritt, BC V1K 1B8
Tel: 250-378-5161; *Fax:* 250-378-6263
Toll-Free: 800-778-3208
twitter.com/sd58connect
Number of Schools: 7 elementary; 2 secondary; 4 alternative
Grades: K - 12 *Enrollment:* 2300
Gordon Comeau, Board Chair, 250-295-8802
gcomeau@365.sd58.bc.ca
Stephen McNiven, Superintendent, Schools, 250-378-5161, ext. 1110
smcniven@365.sd58.bc.ca
Barbara Ross, Secretary-Treasurer, 250-378-5161, ext. 1105
bross@365.sd58.bc.ca
Shelley Oppenheim-Lacerte, District Principal, Aboriginal Education, 250-378-5161, ext. 1111
soppenheim-lacerte@365.sd58.bc.ca

Mission: Mission School District #75
33046 - 4th Ave., Mission, BC V2V 1S5
Tel: 604-826-6286; *Fax:* 604-826-4517
info.sd75@mpsd.ca
www.mpsd.ca
twitter.com/mpsd75
www.youtube.com/missionpublicschools
Number of Schools: 12 elementary; 2 middle; 1 secondary; 1 alternative *Grades:* Pre-K - 12 *Enrollment:* 6311 *Note:* Also provides apprenticeship programs & high education training at Riverside College.
Angus Wilson, Superintendent, Schools, 604-826-6286, ext. 3701
angus.wilson@mpsd.ca
Corien Becker, Secretary-Treasurer, 604-814-3700
corien.becker@mpsd.ca
Joseph Heslip, Acting District Principal - Aboriginal Contact, 604-826-3103
joseph.heslip@mpsd.ca

Nakusp: Arrow Lakes School District #10
P.O. Box 340
98 - 6th Ave. NW, Nakusp, BC V0G 1R0
Tel: 250-265-3638
sd10.bc.ca
Other Information: 250-265-3638, ext. 3301
Number of Schools: 6 *Grades:* K - 12 *Enrollment:* 479
Melissa Teindl, Chair, Board, 250-358-2578
melissa.teindl@sd10.bc.ca
Terry Taylor, Superintendent & Secretary-Treasurer, 250-265-3638, ext. 3304
terry.taylor@sd10.bc.ca
Lorna Newman, PhD., Director, Learning, 250-265-3638, ext. 3320
lorna.newman@sd10.bc.ca
Art Olson, Manager, Operations & Transportation, 250-265-3638, ext. 3331
art.olson@sd10.bc.ca

Nanaimo: Nanaimo Ladysmith Public Schools
Also known as: School District 68
(Nanaimo-Ladysmith)
395 Wakesiah Ave., Nanaimo, BC V9R 3K6
Tel: 250-754-5521; *Fax:* 250-741-5248
communications@sd68.bc.ca
www.sd68.bc.ca
www.facebook.com/NanaimoLadysmithPublicSchools
twitter.com/sd68bc
www.instagram.com/nanaimoladysmith
Number of Schools: 28 elementary; 6 secondary; 1 distributed learning; 1 secondary alternative *Grades:* Pre-K.-12 *Enrollment:* 14400 *Number of Employees:* 2,000
Scott Saywell, Superintendent & CEO, 250-741-5231
Superintendent@sd68.bc.ca
Mark Walsh, Secretary-Treasurer, 250-741-5231
SecretaryTreasurer@sd68.bc.ca
Dale Burgos, Executive Director, Communications/Privacy & Engagement, 250-741-5273
DirectorCommunications@sd68.bc.ca
Laura Tait, Assistant Superintendent (Elementary Programs)
AsstSupElementary@sd68.bc.ca
Don Balcombe, Assistant Superintendent (Secondary Programs)
AsstSupSecondary@sd68.bc.ca

Nelson: Kootenay Lake School District #8
811 Stanley St., Nelson, BC V1L 1N8
Tel: 250-352-6681; *Fax:* 250-352-6686
info@sd8.bc.ca
www.sd8.bc.ca
www.facebook.com/sd8kootenaylk/
twitter.com/SD8KootenayLk

Number of Schools: 14 elementary; 3 secondary; 3 elementary-secondary; 1 middle *Grades:* K - 12 *Enrollment:* 5400 *Note:* Also offers 3 alternative schools.
Lenora Trenaman, Board Chair, 250-229-4633
ltrenaman@sd8.bc.ca
Christine Perkins, EdD., Superintendent; CEO, 250-505-9625
christine.perkins@sd8.bc.ca
Michael McLellan, Secretary-Treasurer; CFO, 250-505-7039
michael.mclellan@sd8.bc.ca
Ben Eaton, Director, Inclusive Education, 250-505-7053
beaton@sd8.bc.ca
Deanna Holitzki, Director, Human Resources, 250-505-7012
dholitzki@sd8.bc.ca

New Aiyansh: Nisga'a School District #92
P.O. Box 240
4702 Huwilp Rd., New Aiyansh, BC V0J 1A0
Tel: 250-633-2228; *Fax:* 250-633-2401
www.nisgaa.bc.ca
www.facebook.com/sd92nisgaa
twitter.com/nisgaa_sd92/
Number of Schools: 3 elementary; 1 secondary *Grades:* K - 12 *Enrollment:* 370
Elsie Davis, Board Chair, 250-621-2399
edavis@nisgaa.bc.ca
Joe Rhodes, Superintendent, Schools, 250-633-2228, ext. 1102
jrhodes@nisgaa.bc.ca
Kory Tanner, Secretary-Treasurer, 250-633-2228, ext. 1105
ktanner@nisgaa.bc.ca
Calvin Morven, Director, Operations, 250-633-2211, ext. 1301
cmorven@nisgaa.bc.ca

New Westminster: New Westminster School District #40
811 Ontario St., New Westminster, BC V3M 0J7
Tel: 604-517-6240; *Fax:* 604-517-6390
info@sd40.bc.ca
newwestschools.ca
www.facebook.com/newwestschools/
twitter.com/NewWestSchools
Number of Schools: 8 elementary; 3 middle; 1 secondary; 3 alternative *Grades:* K - 12 *Enrollment:* 7500
Mark Gifford, Board Chair, 604-838-0444
mgifford@sd40.bc.ca
Karim Hachlaf, Superintendent, Schools, 604-517-6328
khachlaf@sd40.bc.ca
Kim Morris, Secretary-Treasurer, 604-517-6312
kmorris@sd40.bc.ca
Bruce Cunnings, Director, Instruction - Learning Services, 604-517-6369
bcunnings@sd40.bc.ca
Robert Weston, Director, Human Resources, 604-517-6346
rweston@sd40.bc.ca

North Vancouver: North Vancouver School District (NVSD)
Also known as: North Vancouver School District No. 44
Education Services Centre
2121 Lonsdale Ave., North Vancouver, BC V7M 2K6
Tel: 604-903-3444; *Fax:* 604-903-3445
sd44.ca
www.facebook.com/nvsd44
twitter.com/NVSD44
Number of Schools: 25 elementary; 8 secondary *Grades:* K - 12 *Enrollment:* 15822 *Number of Employees:* 2,646 *Note:* Also offers 7 StrongStart centres & an outdoor school.
Christie Sacre, Board Chair, 604-999-2894
csacre@sd44.ca
Mark Pearmain, Superintendent of Schools, 604-903-3449
mpearmain@sd44.ca
Georgia Allison, Secretary-Treasurer, 604-903-3470
gallison@sd44.ca
Brad Baker, District Principal - Indigenous Education, 604-903-3463
bbaker@sd44.ca

Oliver: Okanagan Similkameen School District #53
P.O. Box 1770
6161 Okanagan St., Oliver, BC V0H 1T0
Tel: 250-498-3481; *Fax:* 250-498-4070
general@sd53.bc.ca
www.sd53.bc.ca
twitter.com/ssimilkameen
Number of Schools: 5 elementary; 1 elementary-secondary; 2 secondary; 1 alternative *Grades:* K - 12; Continuing Education *Enrollment:* 2500
Rob Zandee, Chair, Board, 250-498-1333
rzandee@sd53.bc.ca
Beverly Young, Superintendent, Schools, 250-498-3481, ext. 115
byoung@sd53.bc.ca

Subra Paliappa, Secretary-Treasurer, 250-498-3481, ext. 113
spaliapp@sd53.bc.ca
Debby Sansome, Director, Facilities, 250-498-3481, ext. 103
dsansome@sd53.bc.ca
Marcus Toneatto, Director, Learning and Inquiry, 250-498-3481, ext. 117
mtoneatto@sd53.bc.ca
Susan Trower, Manager, Human Resources, 250-498-3481, ext. 102
strower@sd53.bc.ca

Parksville: Qualicum School District #69
P.O. Box 430
100 East Jensen Ave., Parksville, BC V9P 2G5, Canada
Tel: 250-248-4241; *Fax:* 250-248-5767
www.sd69.bc.ca
twitter.com/SD69Qualicum
Number of Schools: 8 elementary; 2 secondary; 2 alternative
Grades: K - 12 *Enrollment:* 4000
Eve Flynn, Chair, Board, 250-240-2845
eflynn@sd69.bc.ca
Keven Elder, Ed.D, Interim Superintendent, Schools, 250-248-4241
kelder@sd69.bc.ca
Ron Amos, Secretary-Treasurer, 250-248-4241
ramos@sd69.bc.ca
Rosie McLeod-Shannon, District Principal, Indigenous Education, 250-954-3041
rmcleods@sd69.bc.ca
Brenda Paul, Director, Human Resources, 250-248-4241

Penticton: Okanagan Skaha School District #67
425 Jermyn Ave., Penticton, BC V2A 1Z4, Canada
Tel: 250-770-7700; *Fax:* 250-770-7730
sd67@summer.com
www.sd67.bc.ca
Number of Schools: 11 elementary; 3 middle; 3 secondary; 3 alternative *Grades:* K - 12 *Enrollment:* 5989 *Number of Employees:* 800
Shelley Clarke, Board Chair, 250-770-7700
boardofeducation@summer.com
Wendy Hyer, Superintendent, 250-770-7700, ext. 6565
whyer@summer.com
Kevin Lorenz, Secretary-Treasurer, 250-770-7700, ext. 6490
klorenz@summer.com
Jason Corday, Director, Instruction - Human Resources, 250-770-7700, ext. 6496
jcorday@summer.com
Doug Gorcak, Director, Facilities, 250-770-7700, ext. 6558
dgorcak@summer.com
Susan Thomson, Director, Instruction - Student Services, 250-770-7700, ext. 6390
sthomson@summer.com

Port Alberni: Alberni School District #70
4690 Roger St., Port Alberni, BC V9Y 3Z4
Tel: 250-723-3565; *Fax:* 250-723-3553
info@sd70.bc.ca
www.sd70.bc.ca
Number of Schools: 13 *Grades:* K - 12 *Enrollment:* 3800
Pam Craig, Chair, Board, 250-724-0683
pcraig@sd70.bc.ca
Greg Smyth, Superintendent, 250-720-2770
gsmyth@sd70.bc.ca
Lindsay Cheetham, Secretary-Treasurer, 250-720-2756
lcheetham@sd70.bc.ca
Laurie Morphet, District Principal, Inclusive Education, 250-720-2764
Jack Hitchings, Director, Instruction - Learning Services, 250-731-5221
jhitchings@sd70.bc.ca
Greg Roe, Director, Operations, 250-723-8821
groe@sd70.bc.ca

Port Hardy: Vancouver Island North School District #85
P.O. Box 90
6975 Rupert St., Port Hardy, BC V0N 2P0, Canada
Tel: 250-949-6618; *Fax:* 250-949-8792
www.sd85.bc.ca
Number of Schools: 7 elementary; 4 secondary *Grades:* K - 12 *Enrollment:* 1340 *Number of Employees:* 230
Leightan Wishart, Chair, Board, 250-949-1949
lwishart@sd85.bc.ca
Carol Robertson, Superintendent, Schools, 250-949-6618, ext. 2236
crobertson@sd85.bc.ca
John Martin, Secretary-Treasurer, 250-949-6618, ext. 2222
jmartin@sd85.bc.ca
Irene Isaac, District Principal, Aboriginal Programs, 250-949-6618, ext. 2233
iisaac@sd85.bc.ca

Darby Gildersleeve, Manager, Operations, 250-949-8155, ext. 2522
dgildersleeve@sd85.bc.ca

Powell River: Powell River School District #47
4351 Ontario Ave., Powell River, BC V8A 1V3, Canada
Tel: 604-485-6271; Fax: 604-485-6435
info@sd47.bc.ca
www.sd47.bc.ca
www.facebook.com/schooldistrict47/
twitter.com/sd47_board
Number of Schools: 6 elementary; 1 secondary; 1 alternative
Grades: K - 12 Enrollment: 2200 Note: Also offer an
Eco/Sustainability Program, an Outdoor Learning Centre, an
Early Years Centre, and a distributed learning centre called
Partners in Education.
Aaron Reid, Board Chair, 604-485-3700
aaron.reid@sd47.bc.ca
Jay Yule, Superintendent, 604-414-2600
jay.yule@sd47.bc.ca
Steve Hopkins, Secretary-Treasurer, 604-414-2604
steve.hopkins@sd47.bc.ca
Don Fairbairn, Director, Instruction, 604-414-2600
don.fairbairn@sd47.bc.ca

Prince George: Prince George School District #57
2100 Ferry Ave., Prince George, BC V2L 4R5, Canada
Tel: 250-561-6800; Fax: 250-561-6801
Toll-Free: 1-800-256-7857
monitors@sd57.bc.ca
www.sd57.bc.ca
Number of Schools: 32 elementary; 8 secondary; 1 Centre for
Learning Alternatives Grades: K - 12 Enrollment: 13000 Number
of Employees: 1800 Note: The Centre for Learning Alternatives
includes continuing education, distance education, and
community alternate programs.
Tim Bennett, Chair, Board, 250-612-9806
tbennett@sd57.bc.ca
Rod Allen, Superintendent, 250-561-6800
rallen@sd57.bc.ca
Darleen Patterson, Secretary-Treasurer, 250-561-6800, ext. 247
dpatterson@sd57.bc.ca
Hannah Brown, Director, Finance, 250-561-6800
hbrown@sd57.bc.ca
Marie St. Laurent, Director, Human Resources, 250-561-6800
mstlaurent@sd57.bc.ca
Kap Manhas, District Administrator, Transportation Services,
250-561-6802
kmanhas@sd57.bc.ca
Madeleine Crandell, Acting Principal, Aboriginal Education,
250-562-4843
mcrandell@sd57.bc.ca

Prince Rupert: Prince Rupert School District #52
634 - 6th Ave. East, Prince Rupert, BC V8J 1X1, Canada
Tel: 250-624-6717; Fax: 250-624-6517
www.rupertschools.ca
twitter.com/RupertSchools
Number of Schools: 5 elementary; 1 middle; 2 secondary
Grades: K - 12 Enrollment: 2937
James Horne, Chair, Board, 250-624-9093
james.horne@sd52.bc.ca
Irene LaPierre, Superintendent, Schools, 250-627-2104
irene.lapierre@sd52.bc.ca
Cam McIntyre, Secretary-Treasurer, 250-627-2103
cam.mcintyre@sd52.bc.ca
Peter Edwards, Director, Finance, 250-627-2108
peter.edwards@sd52.bc.ca
Ian Larocque, Director, Human Resources, 250-627-2107
ian.larocque@sd52.bc.ca
Andrew Samoil, Director, Instruction - Education Innovation,
250-627-2105
andrew.samoil@sd52.bc.ca
James Warburton, Director, Operations, 250-627-2127
james.warburton@sd52.bc.ca
Roberta Edzerza, District Principal - Aboriginal Education,
250-627-2387
roberta.edzerza@sd52.bc.ca

Queen Charlotte: Haida Gwaii School District #50
P.O. Box 69
107 - 3rd Ave., Queen Charlotte, BC V0T 1S0, Canada
Tel: 250-559-8471; Fax: 250-559-8849
Toll-Free: 1-888-771-3131
sd50.bc.ca
Number of Schools: 4 elementary; 2 secondary Grades: Elem. -
Sec.; Aboriginal Ed.
Roeland Denooij, Chair, Board, 250-637-1888
rdenooij@sd50.bc.ca
Joanne Yovanovich, Interim Superintendent, 250-559-8471, ext.
104
jyovanovich@sd50.bc.ca

Shelley Sansome, Secretary-Treasurer, 250-559-8471, ext. 103
ssansome@sd50.bc.ca
Lao Peerless, Supervisor, Maintenance & Transportation,
250-559-8471, ext. 107
lpeerless@sd50.bc.ca

Quesnel: Quesnel School District #28
401 North Star Rd., Quesnel, BC V2J 5K2, Canada
Tel: 250-992-8802; Fax: 250-992-7652
www.sd28.bc.ca
Number of Schools: 12 elementary; 3 secondary; 1 continuing
education Grades: K - 12 Enrollment: 4360
Gloria Jackson, Chair, Board, 250-255-4319
gloriajackson@sd28.bc.ca
Sue-Ellen Miller, Superintendent, Schools, 250-992-8802
sueellenmiller@sd28.bc.ca
Bettina Ketcham, Secretary-Treasurer, 250-992-8802
bettinaketcham@sd28.bc.ca
Perry Lofstrom, Director, Instruction - Human Resources,
250-992-8802
perrylofstrom@sd28.bc.ca
Sue MacDonald, Director, Instruction - Curriculum,
250-992-8802
suemacdonald@sd28.bc.ca
Alison Dodge, District Literacy Resource Teacher, 250-992-0416
alisondodge@sd28.bc.ca

Revelstoke: Revelstoke School District #19
P.O. Box Bag 5800
501 - 11 St., Revelstoke, BC V0E 2S0, Canada
Tel: 250-837-2101; Fax: 250-837-9335
www.sd19.bc.ca
twitter.com/RevelstokeSec
Number of Schools: 3 elementary; 1 secondary Grades: K - 12
Enrollment: 960
Bill MacFarlane, Chair, Board, 250-837-2101
bmacfarlane@sd19.bc.ca
Mike Hooker, Superintendent, Schools, 250-837-2101
mhooker@sd19.bc.ca
Bruce Tisdale, Secretary-Treasurer, 250-837-2101
btisdale@sd19.bc.ca
Greg Kenyon, District Principal, Indigenous Education,
250-837-2173
gkenyon@sd19.bc.ca

Richmond: Richmond School District #38 (SD38)
7811 Granville Ave., Richmond, BC V6Y 3E3
Tel: 604-668-6000
www.sd38.bc.ca
www.facebook.com/RichmondSD38
twitter.com/richmondsd38
www.youtube.com/richmondsd38
Number of Schools: 38 elementary schools; 10 secondary
schools; 1 virtual school Grades: K - 12 Enrollment: 20000 Note:
Offers French Immersion, Montessori, and International
Baccalaureate Programs
Laura Buchanan, Executive Director, Human Resources,
604-668-6000, ext. 6085
lbuchanan@sd38.bc.ca
Frank Geyer, Executive Director, Planning and Development,
604-295-7000
fgeyer@sd38.bc.ca
Robert Laing, Executive Director - Learning and Business
Technology, 604-668-6088
rlaing@sd38.bc.ca
Michael Khoo, Director, Instruction - Continuing Education,
604-668-6123
mkhoo@sd38.bc.ca
Richard Steward, Director, Instruction - Learning Services,
604-668-6093
rsteward@sd38.bc.ca
Roy Uyeno, Secretary-Treasurer, 604-668-6008
ruyeno@sd38.bc.ca
Scott Robinson, Superintendent, Schools, 604-668-6081
srobinson@sd38.bc.ca

Saanichton: Saanich School District #63 (SD63)
2125 Keating Cross Rd., Saanichton, BC V8M 2A5
Tel: 250-652-7300; Fax: 250-652-6421
inquiries@sd63.bc.ca
www.sd63.bc.ca
twitter.com/sd63schools
www.youtube.com/SaanichDistrict63
Number of Schools: 8 elementary schools; 3 middle schools; 3
secondary schools; 3 learning & development centres Grades:
JK - 12 Enrollment: 8000
Tim Dunford, Chair, Board, 250-652-7332
tdunford@sd63.bc.ca
Jason Reid, Secretary-Treasurer, 250-652-7332
jreid@sd63.bc.ca
Dave Eberwein, Superintendent, Schools & Chief Executive
Officer, 250-652-7332
deberwein@sd63.bc.ca

Salmon Arm: North Okanagan-Shuswap School District #83
P.O. Box 129
341 Shuswap St. S.W., Salmon Arm, BC V1E 4N2, Canada
Tel: 250-832-2157; Fax: 250-832-9428
www.sd83.bc.ca
www.facebook.com/sd83schools
twitter.com/sd83schools
Number of Schools: 17 elementary; 3 middle; 5 secondary
Grades: K - 12 Enrollment: 6723
Marianne VanBuskirk, Chair, Board
mvanbusk@sd83.bc.ca
Peter Jory, Superintendent & CEO, 250-804-7822
pjory@sd83.bc.ca
Alana Cameron, Secretary-Treasurer, 250-804-7830
acameron@sd83.bc.ca
Carl Cooper, Director, Instruction - Curriculum and Innovation,
250-832-2157
ccooper@sd83.bc.ca
Gary Greenhough, Director, Finance, 250-804-7832
ggreenho@sd83.bc.ca
Carol-Ann Leidloff, Director, Instruction - Inclusive Education,
250-804-7828
cleidlof@sd83.bc.ca
Ryan Brennan, Assistant Superintendent - Human Resources,
250-804-7841

Salt Spring Island: Gulf Islands School District #64
112 Rainbow Rd., Salt Spring Island, BC V8K 2K3
Tel: 250-537-5548; Fax: 250-537-4200
www.facebook.com/GulfIslandsSecondary
twitter.com/GISecondary
Number of Schools: 1 primary; 3 elementary; 1 middle; 1
secondary; 4 K-12; 1 alternative Grades: K - 12 Enrollment:
1700 Number of Employees: 230 Note: Offers Indigenous
programming, an International Program, a performing arts
academy, as well as late French Immersion programs.
Robert Pingle, Board Chair, 250-537-6292
rpingle@sd64.org
Scott Benwell, PhD., Superintendent, 250-537-5548
sbenwell@sd64.org
Jesse Guy, Secretary-Treasurer, 250-537-5548, ext. 205
jguy@sd64.org
Richard Frost, Director, Facilities and Transportation,
250-537-5723
rfrost@sd64.org
Doug Livingston, Director, Instruction - Learning Services,
250-537-5548
dlivingston@sd64.org

Smithers: Bulkley Valley School District #54
P.O. Box 758
1235 Montreal St., Smithers, BC V0J 2N0
Tel: 250-877-6820; Fax: 250-877-6835
contact-sd54@sd54.bc.ca
www.sd54.bc.ca
Number of Schools: 6 elementary; 2 secondary Grades: K - 12
Note: Also offers the Bulkley Valley Learning Centre (BVLC) at
Northwest Community College (250-877-3218) and Bulkley
Valley Education Connection, a combined elementary and
secondary home school distributed leraning program tailored to
individual students (250-877-6834).
Jennifer Williams, Chair, Board
jwilliams@sd54.bc.ca
Mike McDiarmid, Superintendent, Schools
Cathy van der Mark, Assistant Superintendent
Dave Margerm, Secretary-Treasurer
Tim Bancroft, Director, Facilities & Maintenance, 250-847-2865

Squamish: Sea to Sky School District #48
P.O. Box 250
37866 2nd Ave., Squamish, BC V8B 0A2
Tel: 604-892-5228; Fax: 604-892-1038
tmiller@sd48.bc.ca
sd48seatosky.org
twitter.com/SeatoSkySD48
Number of Schools: 9 elementary; 1 middle; 3 secondary; 2
alternative Grades: K - 12 Enrollment: 4593
Lisa McCullough, Superintendent, 604-892-5228, ext. 113
lmccullough@sd48.bc.ca
Mohammed Azim, Secretary-Treasurer, 604-892-5228, ext. 104
mazim@sd48.bc.ca
Susan Leslie, District Principal, Aboriginal Education,
604-892-5228, ext. 123
sleslie@sd48.bc.ca
Louise Harris, Human Resources Assistant, 604-892-5228, ext.
106
lharris@sd48.bc.ca

Surrey: Surrey Schools (SD36)
Also known as: Surrey School District #36
District Education Centre
14033 - 92nd Ave., Surrey, BC V3V 0B7
Tel: 604-596-7733; *Fax:* 604-596-4197
webmaster@surreyschools.ca
www.surreyschools.ca
www.facebook.com/SurreySchools
twitter.com/Surrey_Schools
www.linkedin.com/company/school-district-36-surrey
Number of Schools: 102 elementary schools; 27 secondary schools; 5 student learning centres; 2 adult education centres *Grades:* K - 12; Adult Ed. *Enrollment:* 71489 *Number of Employees:* 10,989 *Note:* Also offers Aboriginal & online / distace programs, preschool programs, special needs support, choice programs & trades / career courses.
Laurie Larsen, Chair, 778-772-5019
larsen_laurie@surreyschools.ca
Jordan Tinney, Superintendent, Schools & Chief Executive Officer, 604-595-6313
tinney_j@surreyschools.ca
D. Greg Frank, Secretary-Treasurer, 604-595-6300
frank_g@surreyschools.ca
Neher Dhillon, Acting Assistant Superintendent, City Centre, 604-595-6312
dhillon_n@surreyschools.ca
Andrew Holland, Assistant Superintendent, Cloverdale & Clayton, 604-595-6311
holland_a@surreyschools.ca
Christy Northway, Assistant Superintendent, Newton/Fleetwood, 604-595-6311
northway_c@surreyschools.ca
Lynda Reeve, Assistant Superintendent, South Surrey/White Rock, 604-595-6312
reeve_l@surreyschools.ca
Catherine Sereda, Assistant Superintendent, Guildford, 604-595-6311
sereda_c@surreyschools.ca
Jacob Sol, Assistant Superintendent, Panorama/Sullivan, 604-595-6312
sol_j@surreyschools.ca

Terrace: Coast Mountains School District #82
3211 Kenney St., Terrace, BC V8G 3E9
Tel: 250-635-4931; *Toll-Free:* 855-635-4931
cmsd.bc.ca
Number of Schools: 1 primary; 10 elementary; 1 middle; 1 middle/secondary; 2 secondary; 1 K-12; 2 alternative *Grades:* K - 12; Adult Ed. *Enrollment:* 4500 *Number of Employees:* 375 teachers
Shar McCrory, Chair, Board, 250-842-6065
shar.mccrory@cmsd.bc.ca
Katherine McIntosh, Superintendent, Schools, 250-638-4407
katherine.mcintosh@cmsd.bc.ca
Raymond McDonald, Secretary-Treasurer, 250-638-4434
raymond.mcdonald@cmsd.bc.ca
Agnes Casgrain, Director, Instruction - Indigenous Education, 250-638-4464
agnes.casgrain@cmsd.bc.ca
Travis Elwood, Director, Facility Services, 250-638-4405
travis.elwood@cmsd.bc.ca
Cameron MacKay, Director, Human Resources, 250-638-4441
cam.mackay@cmsd.bc.ca

Trail: Kootenay-Columbia School District #20
2001 - 3rd Ave., Trail, BC V1R 1R6, Canada
Tel: 250-368-6434; *Fax:* 250-364-2470
Toll-Free: 888-316-3338
www.sd20.bc.ca
twitter.com/sd20kc/
www.instagram.com/schooldistrict20/
Number of Schools: 6 elementary; 1 elementary/secondary; 2 secondary; 1 alternative *Grades:* K - 12 *Enrollment:* 3700 *Number of Employees:* 650 *Note:* Also offers Early Learning programs in Blueberry Creek, Robson, Fruitvale, and Rossland Summit schools.
Teri Ferworn, Chair, Board, 250-365-3026
tferworn@sd20.bc.ca
Bill Ford, Superintendent, Schools, 250-368-2230
bford@sd20.bc.ca
Natalie Verigin, Secretary-Treasurer, 250-368-2223
natalieverigin@sd20.bc.ca
Kristi Crowe, Director, Instruction, 250-368-2234
kcrowe@sd20.bc.ca
Heather Simm, Director, Operations, 250-365-8331, ext. 801
hsimm@sd20.bc.ca
Katherine Shearer, Director, Instruction, 250-368-2232
kshearer@sd20.bc.ca

Vancouver: Vancouver School Board (VSB)
Also known as: Vancouver School District #39
1580 West Broadway Ave., Vancouver, BC V6J 5K8
Tel: 604-713-5000; *Fax:* 604-713-5049
info@vsb.bc.ca
www.vsb.bc.ca
www.facebook.com/VancouverSchoolBoard
twitter.com/VSB39
www.youtube.com/VanSchoolBoard
Number of Schools: 89 elementary schools; 1 middle schools; 18 secondary schools; 2 adult education centres *Grades:* K - 12; Continuing Ed. *Enrollment:* 50000 *Number of Employees:* 9000
Janet Fraser, Chair, Board, 604-362-1826
janet.fraser@vsb.bc.ca
Mette Hamaguchi, Director, Instruction - Learning Services, 604-713-5202
J. David Green, Secretary-Treasurer, 604-713-5080
Suzanne Hoffman, Superintendent, Schools, 604-713-5100

Vanderhoof: Nechako Lakes School District #91
P.O. Box 129
153 East Connaught St., Vanderhoof, BC V0J 3A0
Tel: 250-567-2284; *Fax:* 250-567-4639
Toll-Free: 800-903-4771
www.sd91.bc.ca
www.facebook.com/SD91BC
twitter.com/sd91bc
www.instagram.com/nechakolakes/
Number of Schools: 9 elementary; 3 secondary; 3 elementary-secondary; 4 alternative *Grades:* K - 12 *Enrollment:* 4500 *Number of Employees:* 600
Steve Davis, Board Chair, 250-597-2284
sdavis@sd91.bc.ca
Manu Madhok, Superintendent, 250-567-2284
mmadhok@mail.sd91.bc.ca
Darlene Turner, Secretary-Treasurer, 250-567-2284
dturner@mail.sd91.bc.ca
Claire McKay, Director, Instruction, 250-996-1600
cmckay@sd91.bc.ca
Leona Prince, District Principal, Aboriginal Education, 250-251-0959
lprince@sd91.bc.ca

Vernon: Vernon School District #22
1401 - 15 St., Vernon, BC V1T 8S8, Canada
Tel: 250-542-3331; *Fax:* 250-549-9200
district_web@sd22.bc.ca
www.sd22.bc.ca
www.facebook.com/SD22Vernon/
twitter.com/SD22Vernon
Number of Schools: 14 elementary; 5 secondary *Grades:* Pre-K. - 12 *Enrollment:* 8200 *Note:* Also offers alternative education, international, and Aboriginal programs.
Robert Lee, Chair, Board
robertlee@sd22.bc.ca
Joe Rogers, Superintendent, 250-549-9226
jrogers@sd22.bc.ca
Sterling Olson, Secretary-Treasurer, 250-549-9226
solson@sd22.bc.ca
Gerry William, PhD, Director, Aboriginal Programs, 250-549-9291
gwilliam@sd22.bc.ca

Victoria: Greater Victoria School District #61
556 Boleskine Rd., Victoria, BC V8Z 1E8
Tel: 250-475-3212; *Fax:* 250-475-6161
community@sd61.bc.ca
www.sd61.bc.ca
Other Information: Alternative Ed., Phone: 250-360-4300;
Continuing Ed: 250-360-4300
www.facebook.com/SD61schools
twitter.com/sd61schools
Number of Schools: 27 elementary; 10 middle; 7 secondary; 1 alternative *Grades:* K - 12; Continuing Ed. *Enrollment:* 20000
Jordan Watters, Board Chair, 778-676-2571
jwatters@sd61.bc.ca
Shelley Green, Superintendent, Schools, 250-475-4162
sgreen@sd61.bc.ca
Deb Whitten, Deputy Superintendent, 250-475-4117
dwhitten@sd61.bc.ca
Greg Kitchen, Associate Superintendent, 250-475-4220
gkitchen@sd61.bc.ca
Colin Roberts, Associate Superintendent, 250-475-4220
croberts@sd61.bc.ca
Katrina Stride, Acting Secretary-Treasurer, 250-475-4106
kstride@sd61.bc.ca
Louise Sheffer, Director, Learning, 250-475-4156
lsheffer@sd61.bc.ca
Ted Pennell, Director, Information Technology, 250-475-4147
tpennell@sd61.bc.ca

Victoria: Sooke School District #62
3143 Jacklin Rd., Victoria, BC V9B 5R1, Canada
Tel: 250-474-9800; *Fax:* 250-474-9825
info@sd62.bc.ca
www.sd62.bc.ca
Number of Schools: 18 elementary; 4 middle; 3 secondary; 1 adult/alternative *Grades:* K - 12; Alternative Learning *Enrollment:* 10600
Ravi Parmar, Chair, Board, 250-893-5685
rparmar@sd62.bc.ca
Scott Stinson, Superintendent, Schools; CEO, 250-474-9811
sstinson@sd62.bc.ca
Harold Cull, Secretary-Treasurer, 250-474-9836
hcull@sd62.bc.ca
Pete Godau, Director, Facilities, 250-474-9840, ext. 203
pgodau@sd62.bc.ca
Dawn Irmscher, Director, Finance, 250-474-9881
dirmscher@sd62.bc.ca

West Vancouver: West Vancouver School District #45
1075 - 21st St., West Vancouver, BC V7V 4A9, Canada
Tel: 604-981-1000; *Fax:* 604-981-1001
info@wvschools.ca
www.sd45.bc.ca
www.facebook.com/westvancouverschools/
twitter.com/WestVanSchools
www.instagram.com/westvancouverschools/
Number of Schools: 14 elementary; 3 secondary *Grades:* K - 12 *Enrollment:* 7118
Carolyn Broady, Chair, Board, 604-981-1000
cbroady@wvschools.ca
Chris Kennedy, Superintendent/CEO, 604-981-1031
ckennedy@wvschools.ca
Julia Leiterman, Secretary-Treasurer, 604-981-1033
jleiterman@wvschools.ca
Liz Hill, Director, Instruction - Learning & Innovation, 604-981-1341
lhill@wvschools.ca
Ian Kennedy, Director, Instruction, 604-981-1156
ikennedy@wvschools.ca
Diane Nelson, Director, Instruction - WV Premier Academy Programs, 604-981-1150
dnelson@wvschools.ca
Florencio De Dios, Director, Facilities, 604-981-1075
fdedios@wvschools.ca

Williams Lake: Cariboo-Chilcotin School District #27
School Administration Office
350 - 2nd Ave. North, Williams Lake, BC V2G 1Z9
Tel: 250-398-3800; *Fax:* 250-398-7871
info@sd27.bc.ca
www.sd27.bc.ca
www.facebook.com/sd27.bc.ca
Number of Schools: 15 elementary; 6 combined elementary-junior secondary; 2 secondary *Grades:* K - 12; Adult Education *Enrollment:* 4600 *Number of Employees:* 1000+ *Note:* Also provide the Graduate Routes Other Ways (GROW) Centre offering adult continuing education, Skyline alternate programs for grades 8-12, distance education for grades K-12, and cross-enrolled courses for grades 10-12.
Willow MacDonald, Board Chair, 250-305-7983
willow.macdonald@sd27.bc.ca
Chris van der Mark, Superintendent, 250-398-3824
jodi.symmes@sd27.bc.ca
Norine Durban, Secretary-Treasurer (Interim), 250-398-3833
carrie.pratt@sd27.bc.ca
Jerome Beauchamp, Director, Instruction - Education Services, 250-398-3811
jerome.beauchamp@sd27.bc.ca

Catholic

Victoria: Island Catholic Schools
#1, 4044 Nelthorpe St., Victoria, BC V8X 2A1
Tel: 250-727-6893; *Fax:* 250-479-5423
info@cisdv.bc.ca
www.cisdv.bc.ca
Number of Schools: 4 elementary schools; 1 secondary school *Grades:* K - 12 *Enrollment:* 1600
Glen Palahicky, Director, Office of Religious Education
gpalahicky@cisdv.bc.ca
Beverly Pulyk, Superintendent, Schools
bpulyk@cisdv.bc.ca

French

Richmond: **Conseil scolaire francophone de la Colombie-Britannique (CSF)**
French Education Authority of British Columbia
Également connu sous le nom de: School District #93
100 - 13511 Commerce Pkwy., Richmond, BC V6V 2J8
Tél: 604-214-2600; *Téléc:* 604-214-9881
Ligne sans frais: 888-715-2200
info@csf.bc.ca
www.csf.bc.ca
www.facebook.com/CSF.Colombie.Britannique
twitter.com/CsFCb
Number of Schools: 35 *Grades:* Élém. - Sec. *Enrollment:* 6000
Number of Employees: 900
Marie-Pierre Lavoie, Présidente, Conseil, 778-977-6274
Mariepierre_lavoie@csf.bc.ca
Michel St-Amant, Directeur général, 604-214-2601
michel_stamant@csf.bc.ca
Kapka Djarova, Directrice, Ressources humaines, 604-214-2614
kapka_djarova@csf.bc.ca
Lucie Pineau, Secrétaire-trésorier, 604-214-2606
lucie_pineau@csf.bc.ca
Pascale Cyr, Coordonnatrice, Relations publiques, 604-214-2617
pascale_cyr@csf.bc.ca

First Nations

Chase: **Neskonlith Education Center**
P.O. Box 318
739 Chief Neskonlith Dr., Chase, BC V0E 1M0
Tel: 250-679-2963; *Fax:* 250-679-2968
neskonlith.org
www.facebook.com/NeskonlithIndianBand

Kamloops: **Secwepemc Cultural Education Society (SCES)**
#219, 345 Chief Alex Thomas Way, Kamloops, BC V2H 1H1
Tel: 250-376-0903; *Fax:* 778-471-7779
scesadministrativeassistant@shaw.ca
www.secwepemc.org
www.facebook.com/sces0903

Savona: **Skeetchestn Indian Band Education**
P.O. Box 178
Savona, BC V0K 2J0
Tel: 250-373-2493; *Fax:* 250-373-2494
Toll-Free: 866-373-2493
education@skeetchestn.ca
www.skeetchestn.ca/education
Grades: K-12; Adult Education
Barb Deneault, Coordinator, Education, 250-373-2493, ext. 218
education@skeetchestn.ca

Schools: Specialized

First Nations

Bella Coola: **Acwsalcta Band School**
P.O. Box 778
834 Four Mile Subdivision, Bella Coola, BC V0T 1C0, Canada
Tel: 250-799-5911; *Fax:* 250-799-5576
www.acwsalcta.ca
twitter.com/Acwsalcta
Grades: K-12 *Enrollment:* 136 *Note:* Acwsalcta School promotes the teaching of Nuxalk cultural skills and values, and promote the use of twenty-first-century technology.
Barry Prong, Principal, 250-799-5911, ext. 201
principal@acwsalcta.ca
Theresa Brook (Qway), Acting Director of Education, 250-799-5911, ext. 209
theresabrook@acwsalcta.ca

Merritt: **Lower Nicola Band School**
181 Nawishaskin Ln., Merritt, BC V1K 1N2, Canada
Tel: 250-378-5157; *Fax:* 250-378-6188
reception@lnib.net
www.lnib.net
Grades: K-6 *Enrollment:* 34 *Note:* As an independent school, the Band School follows the BC Curriculum. Their teachers not only have their BC Teaching Certificates, but have knowledge and deep appreciation of First Nations cultures.
Angie Sterling, Principal
asterling@lnib.net

Hearing Impaired

Burnaby: **BC Provincial School for the Deaf**
c/o Burnaby South Secondary School
5455 Rumble St., Burnaby, BC V5J 2B7
Tel: 604-296-6880; *Fax:* 604-296-6883
bcsd.burnabyschools.ca
TTY: 604-664-8563
Grades: K-12 *Enrollment:* 75
Catherine Bennett, Principal
catherine.bennett@burnabyschools.ca

Special Education

North Vancouver: **Kenneth Gordon Maplewood School**
420 Seymour River Pl., North Vancouver, BC V7H 1S8
Tel: 604-985-5224; *Fax:* 604-985-4562
admissions@kgms.ca
www.kgms.ca
www.facebook.com/KennethGordonMaplewoodSchool
twitter.com/KGM_School
www.instagram.com/kgm_school
Grades: K.-7 *Note:* School for children with language-based learning disabilities.
Dr. James Christopher, Head of School
jchristopher@kgms.ca

Richmond: **Glen Eden Multimodal Centre**
#190, 13151 Vanier Pl., Richmond, BC V6V 2J1
Tel: 604-821-1457; *Fax:* 604-821-1527
glenedenschool@gleneden.org
www.gleneden.org
Grades: K-12 *Note:* Teaches children & adolescents who, because of unique combinations of medical, psychiatric, & developmental problems, are not functioning adequately & have not shown improvement in school based special service programs.
Rick Brennan, Executive Director

Vancouver: **Avenir School**
#207, 877 East Hastings St., Vancouver, BC V6A 3Y1
avenirschool.ca
www.facebook.com/AvenirSchool
twitter.com/AvenirSchoolBC
www.youtube.com/AvenirSchoolBC
Grades: 5 - 12
Martin Hamm, Principal, 604-569-2222
mhamm@avenirschool.ca

Distance Education

Chilliwack: **Fraser Valley Distance Education School (FVDES)**
46361 Yale Rd., Chilliwack, BC V2P 2P8
Tel: 604-701-4910; *Fax:* 604-701-4970
Toll-Free: 800-663-3381
www.fvdes.com
twitter.com/fvdes_news
Grades: K - 12; Adult *Enrollment:* 3000
David Manuel, Principal, 604-701-4915
dmanuel@k12connect.ca
Gordon Bridge, Business Manager, 604-701-4918
gbridge@k12connect.ca

Courtenay: **North Island Distance Education School**
2505 Smith Rd., Courtenay, BC V9J 1T6, Canada
Tel: 250-898-8999; *Fax:* 250-898-8883
Toll-Free: 800-663-7925
principal@nides.bc.ca
www.nides.bc.ca
www.facebook.com/NavigateNIDES
twitter.com/navigatenides
www.youtube.com/user/navigatenides
Grades: K-12; Adult *Enrollment:* 466
Jeff Stewart, Principal
jeff.stewart@sd71.bc.ca

Fort St John: **Northern BC Distance Education School**
10511 - 99 Ave., Fort St John, BC V1J 1V6, Canada
Tel: 250-261-5660; *Fax:* 250-785-1188
Toll-Free: 800-663-9511
info@nbcdes.com
nbcdes.com
www.facebook.com/186605384690919
twitter.com/nbcdes
Grades: K-12 *Enrollment:* 228
Randy Pauls, Principal

Grindrod: **Christian Homelearner's eStreams (CHeS)**
P.O. Box 162
Grindrod, BC V0E 1Y0, Canada
Tel: 877-777-1547; *Fax:* 877-777-1547
info@estreams.ca
www.estreams.ca
Grades: K-12
H. Hunt, Principal

Kelowna: **Heritage Christian Online School**
905 Badke Rd., Kelowna, BC V1X 5Z5, Canada
Tel: 250-862-2376; *Fax:* 250-762-9277
Toll-Free: 877-862-2375
info@onlineschool.ca
www.onlineschool.ca
Grades: K-12 *Enrollment:* 864
Greg Bitgood, Superintendent
gbitgood@onlineschool.ca
Janet Rainbow, Director of Individualized Education
jrainbow@onlineschool.ca
Ted Gerk, Director of Operations
tgerk@onlineschool.ca
Gordon Robideau, Director of Development, Heritage Christian Schools
grobideau@onlineschool.ca
Delayne Cama Moroka, Assistant Director of BC Online School
dcmoroka@bconlineschool.ca

Merritt: **South Central Interior Distance Education School (SCIDES)**
P.O. Box 4700 Main
2475 Merritt Ave., Merritt, BC V1K 1B8, Canada
Tel: 250-378-4245; *Fax:* 250-378-1447
Toll-Free: 800-663-3536
www.scides.com
Grades: K-12 *Enrollment:* 137
Al Mackay-Smith, Principal, 800-663-3536, ext. 1200
amackay@scides.ca

Nelson: **Distance Education School of the Kootenays (DESK)**
811 Stanley St., Nelson, BC V1L 1N8, Canada
Tel: 250-354-4311; *Fax:* 250-505-7007
Toll-Free: 800-663-4614
www.desk.bc.ca
Grades: K-12
Tim Huttemann, Principal
thuttemann@sd8.bc.ca
Ron Kilgour, Vice Principal
rkilgour@sd8.bc.ca

Prince George: **Central Interior Distance Education (CIDES)**
3400 Westwood Dr., Prince George, BC V2N 1S1, Canada
Tel: 250-564-6574; *Fax:* 250-563-5487
Toll-Free: 800-661-7515
www.cides.sd57.bc.ca
Grades: K-12 *Enrollment:* 188
Chris Molcak, Principal, 250-564-6574, ext. 2003
Joyce Chow, Business Manager, 250-564-6574, ext. 2005

Salmon Arm: **Anchor Academy Distributed Learning**
P.O. Box 3015
7201 Hurst Rd., Salmon Arm, BC V1E 4R8
Tel: 250-832-2754; *Fax:* 250-832-4379
Toll-Free: 888-917-3783
anchor@ark.net
www.ark.net
Grades: K-12 *Enrollment:* 595
Melanie Bartusek, Acting Principal
melanie@ark.net

Surrey: **Traditional Learning Academy (DL) (TLA)**
#103, 17688 - 66th Ave., Surrey, BC V3S 7X1, Canada
Tel: 604-575-8596; *Fax:* 604-575-8565
Toll-Free: 800-745-1320
info@schoolathome.ca
www.schoolathome.ca
Grades: K-12 *Enrollment:* 334 *Note:* Christian school.
Karen Gledhill, Principal

Terrace: **North Coast Distance Education (NCDES)**
#2, 3211 Kenney St., Terrace, BC V8G 3E9, Canada
Tel: 250-635-7944; *Fax:* 888-546-0027
Toll-Free: 800-663-3865
www.ncdes.ca
www.facebook.com/165376870170928
www.youtube.com/channel/UCq522BKANJk95EB2bPniH6w
Grades: K-12 *Enrollment:* 220
Cindy Sousa, Principal, 250-638-4467
Cindy.Sousa@cmsd.bc.ca

Rob Wahl, Vice-Principal, 250-638-4478
Rob.Wahl@ncdes.ca

Vancouver: SelfDesign Learning Community
PO Box 74560 RPO Kitsilano, Vancouver, BC V6K 4P4,
Canada
Tel: 604-224-3640; Fax: 604-224-3662
Toll-Free: 877-353-3374
info@selfdesign.org
www.selfdesign.org
www.facebook.com/SelfDesignLearningCommunity
twitter.com/SelfDesignHigh

Grades: K - 12 Enrollment: 652
Brent Cameron, Principal
brentcameron@selfdesign.org

Vancouver: Vancouver Learning Network (VLN)
Also known as: Greater Vancouver Distance Education
530 East 41st Ave., Vancouver, BC V5W 1P3
Tel: 604-713-5520; Fax: 604-713-5528
vln@vsb.bc.ca
vlns.ca
vlnbuzz.wordpress.com

Grades: K-12 Enrollment: 578
Pedro Da Silva, Principal, 604-713-5520
pdasilva@vsb.bc.ca
Jim DStassinopoulos, Vice Principal, 604-713-5534
jstassinop@vsb.bc.ca

Victoria: South Island Distance Education (SIDES)
4575 Wilkinson Rd., Victoria, BC V8Z 7E8, Canada
Tel: 250-704-4979; Fax: 250-479-9870
Toll-Free: 800-663-7610
sides@sides.ca
www.sides.sd63.bc.ca
www.facebook.com/311415469129
twitter.com/SIDESBC
www.linkedin.com/company/930424
www.youtube.com/user/SIDESTV

Grades: K-12 Enrollment: 626
Kevin White, Principal, 250-704-4962
kwhite@sides.ca

Schools: Independent & Private

Public

Summerland: Glenfir School
P.O. Box 1800
7808 Pierre Drive, Summerland, BC V0H 1Z0
Tel: 250-494-0004; Fax: 250-494-0058
Toll-Free: 1-866-494-0005
mtaylor@glenfir.com
www.glenfir.com

Grades: JK-12
Daphne O'Sullivan, Principal
dducharme@glenfir.com

Protestant

Abbotsford: Abbotsford Christian School (ACS)
35011 Old Clayburn Rd., Abbotsford, BC V2S 7L7, Canada
Tel: 604-755-1891; Fax: 604-850-6978
administration@abbotsfordchristian.com
www.abbotsfordchristian.com
www.facebook.com/myacs
www.pinterest.com/AbbyChristianS/
Grades: Pre-School - 12 Enrollment: 1000
Julius Siebenga, Executive Director
jsiebenga@abbotsfordchristian.com
Alvin Scholing, Director of Development
ascholing@abbotsfordchristian.com
Lorraine Child, Financial Administrator
lchild@abbotsfordchristian.com
Roy Van Eerden, Principal, Elementary
rvaneerden@abbotsfordchristian.com
Tym Berger, Principal, Middle School
tberger@abbotsfordchristian.com
Gerry Goertzen, Principal, Secondary
ggoertzen@abbotsfordchristian.com

Abbotsford: Cornerstone Christian School
P.O. Box 520 Main
3970 Gladwin Rd., Abbotsford, BC V2T 6Z7, Canada
Tel: 604-859-7867; Fax: 604-859-7860
admin@cornerstoneschool.ca
www.cornerstoneschool.ca

Grades: K.-9 Enrollment: 176
Cori Richard, Principal
principal@cornerstoneschool.ca

Abbotsford: Mennonite Educational Institute (MEI)
4081 Clearbrook Rd., Abbotsford, BC V4X 2M8
Tel: 604-859-3700; Fax: 604-859-9206
infod@meischools.com
www.meisoc.com
www.facebook.com/MEIschools
twitter.com/meischools
Grades: Pre. - 12 Enrollment: 1774 Note: The British Columbia
curriculum is taught from a Biblical perspective.
Tim Regehr, President
Peter Froese, Superintendent
Ernest Janzen, Principal, Elementary
Dave Loewen, Principal, Chilliwack
David Neufeld, Principal, Secondary
dneufeld@meisoc.com
Heather Smith, Principal, Middle
Jeff Gamache, Vice Principal, Elementary
Rick Thiessen, Principal, Secondary
rthiessen@meisoc.com
Grant Wardle, Vice Principal, Middle
Mr. M. Friesen, Business Adminstrator

Agassiz: Agassiz Christian School
7571 Morrow Rd., Agassiz, BC V0M 1A2, Canada
Tel: 604-796-9310; Fax: 604-796-9519
office@agassizchristianschool.com
www.agassizchristianschool.com
Grades: Pre.-7 Enrollment: 85
John Zuidhof, Principal

Burnaby: Carver Christian High School
7650 Sapperton Ave., Burnaby, BC V3N 4E1
Tel: 604-523-1580; Fax: 604-523-9646
office@carverchristian.org
carverchristian.org
www.facebook.com/carverchristian
twitter.com/carverchristian
Grades: 9 - 12

Burnaby: John Knox Christian School
8260 - 13 Ave., Burnaby, BC V3N 2G5, Canada
Tel: 604-522-1410; Fax: 604-522-4606
info@johnknoxbc.org
www.myjkcs.com
Grades: K.-7 Enrollment: 400
Anne Ferguson, Principal

Campbell River: Campbell River Christian School (CRCS)
250 South Dogwood St., Campbell River, BC V9W 6Y7,
Canada
Tel: 250-287-4266; Fax: 250-287-3130
office@crcs.bc.ca
www.crcs.bc.ca
www.facebook.com/crcs.bc.ca
Grades: K - 12
Neil Steinke, Principal
ns-admin-crcs@uniserve.com

Chetwynd: Peace Christian School
P.O. Box 2050
6189 Dokkie School Rd., Chetwynd, BC V0C 1J0
Tel: 250-788-2044; Fax: 888-615-9510
peacechristianschool@gmail.com
peacechristianschool.ca
www.youtube.com/user/peacechristian
Grades: K-10 Enrollment: 74
S. Lee, Principal

Chilliwack: Cascade Christian School
46420 Brooks Ave., Chilliwack, BC V2P 1C5
Tel: 604-793-7997; Fax: 604-793-7991
office@cascadechristian.ca
www.cascadechristian.ca
www.facebook.com/290056471071316
Grades: K - 9; EU
Ryan Morrow, Principal
rmorrow@cascadechristian.ca

Chilliwack: Mount Cheam Christian School (MCCS)
48988 Yale Rd. East, Chilliwack, BC V2P 6H4, Canada
Tel: 604-794-3072; Fax: 604-794-3078
office@mccs.ca
www.mccs.ca
Grades: K - 12 Enrollment: 360
Jan Neels, Principal
jneels@mccs.ca
Marianne Luteyn, Elementary Coordinator / Special Needs &
Learning Assistance
mluteyn@mccs.ca
Stephan Hoogendijk, Middle School Coordinator
shoogendijk@mccs.ca

Jaap Ter Haar, Secondary Coordinator
jterhaar@mccs.ca
Marry Kardux, Librarian
mkardux@mccs.ca

Chilliwack: Timothy Christian School
50420 Castleman Rd., Chilliwack, BC V2P 6H4, Canada
Tel: 604-794-7114; Fax: 888-794-7114
office@timothychristian.ca
www.timothychristian.ca
Grades: K-12 Enrollment: 287
Jacob Stam, Principal

Chilliwack: Unity Christian School (UCS)
P.O. Box 371
50950 Hack Brown Rd., Chilliwack, BC V4Z 1K9, Canada
Tel: 604-794-7797; Fax: 604-794-7667
general@unitychristian.ca
www.unitychristian.ca
www.facebook.com/289932854352155
twitter.com/UnityChristian1
Grades: Pre. - 12 Note: A Christ-centered education is provided
by Unity Christian School.
Mike Campbell, Principal
mcampbell@unitychristian.ca
Jeanette Berkenbosch, Vice Principal
jberkenbosch@unitychristian.ca

Cranbrook: Kootenay Christian Academy (KCA)
1200 Kootenay St. North, Cranbrook, BC V1C 5X1
Tel: 250-426-0166; Fax: 250-426-0186
info@kcacademy.ca
www.kcacademy.ca
Other Information: KCA Preschool, Phone: 250-489-3426
Grades: Pre.-10; Special Education Note: The Kootenay
Christian Academy is an independent, non-denominational
school. Operated by the Cranbrook Christian Society, the school
offers a biblically directed education. Kootenay Christian
Academy is accredited by the British Columbia Ministry of
Education, & it follows British Columbia's curriculum guidelines.
Heather Wik, Chair
Catharine Kwan, Secretary
Bob Conroy, Treasurer
Des McKay, Principal
dmckay@kcacademy.ca

Dawson Creek: Mountain Christian School (MCS)
9700 - 5th St., Dawson Creek, BC V1G 3L4, Canada
Tel: 250-782-9528; Fax: 250-782-3888
info@mcsed.ca
www.mcsed.ca
www.facebook.com/MountainChristianSchool
Grades: K - 12 Enrollment: 94
Eva Hutchinson, Principal
principal@mcsed.ca

Dawson Creek: Ron Pettigrew Christian School
1761 - 110th Ave., Dawson Creek, BC V1G 4X4
Tel: 250-782-4580
admin@rpschool.ca
www.rpschool.ca
Grades: K - 12 Enrollment: 120 Number of Employees: 10 Note:
Operated by the Dawson Creek Community Christian Education
Society.
Leanie Jacobs, Principal
ljacobs@rpschool.ca

Delta: Delta Christian School
4789 - 53 St., Delta, BC V4K 2Y9, Canada
Tel: 604-946-2514; Fax: 604-946-2589
info@deltachristianschool.org
www.deltachristianschool.org
Grades: K.-7 Enrollment: 169
Bryan Young, Principal
principal@deltachristianschool.org

Duncan: Duncan Christian School
495 Beech Ave., Duncan, BC V9L 3J8
Tel: 250-746-3654; Fax: 250-746-3615
office@duncanchristianschool.ca
www.duncanchristianschool.ca
www.facebook.com/duncanchristianschool
twitter.com/duncancschool
Grades: K - 12 Enrollment: 276
Jeremy Tinsley, Principal

Fort St John: Christian Life School
8923 - 112th Ave., Fort St John, BC V1J 6G2
Tel: 250-785-1437; Fax: 250-785-4852
office@christianlifeschool.ca
www.christianlifeschool.ca
Grades: K - 12 Number of Employees: 19

Garry Jones, Administrator
principal@christianlifeschool.ca

Fort St John: Maccabee Christian School
P.O. Box 6051 Main
Fort St John, BC V1J 4H6, Canada
Tel: 250-772-5010; *Fax:* 250-772-5099
mcbschool95@yahoo.ca

Grades: K-9 *Enrollment:* 33
Karl Oysmueller, Principal

Grindrod: Christian Homelearners eStreams
P.O. Box 162
Grindrod, BC V0E 1Y0
Fax: 877-777-1547
Toll-Free: 877-777-1547
info@estreams.ca
www.estreams.ca

Grades: K - 12 *Note:* Christian Homelearners eStreams is an independent, faith-based community dedicated to providing personalized, educational support.

Houston: Houston Christian School
P.O. Box 237
2161 Caledonia Ave., Houston, BC V0J 1Z0
Tel: 250-845-7736; *Fax:* 250-845-7738
www.houstonchristianschool.ca

Grades: K.-12 *Enrollment:* 131
Marshall Duzan, Principal

Kamloops: Kamloops Christian School
750 Cottonwood Ave., Kamloops, BC V2B 3X2
Tel: 250-376-6900; *Fax:* 250-376-6904
www.kamcs.org
www.facebook.com/KamloopsChristianSchool
twitter.com/KCS_Kamloops

Grades: K.-12
Sandro Cuzzetto, Principal
sandroc@kamcs.org

Kamloops: Our Lady of Perpetual Help School
235 Poplar St., Kamloops, BC V2B 4B9
Tel: 250-376-2343; *Fax:* 250-376-2361
admin@olphschool.ca
www.olphschool.ca

Grades: K.-7 *Enrollment:* 181
Christopher Yuen, Principal

Kelowna: Heritage Christian School (HCS)
907 Badke Rd., Kelowna, BC V1X 5Z5
Tel: 250-862-2377; *Fax:* 250-862-4943
office@heritagechristian.ca
www.heritagechristian.ca
www.facebook.com/heritagechristianschool

Grades: K - 12 *Enrollment:* 340
Paul Kelly, Principal, High School
pkelly@heritagechristian.ca
Steve Cox, Principal, Elementary
scox@heritagechristian.ca
Matt Dorie, Secondary Vice-Principal
mdorie@heritagechristian.ca
Gord Robideau, Director, Development
grobideau@onlineschool.ca

Kelowna: Kelowna Christian School
Middle & High School Campus
2870 Benvoulin Rd., Kelowna, BC V1W 2E3
Tel: 250-861-3238; *Fax:* 250-861-4844
info@kcschool.ca
www.kcschool.ca
www.facebook.com/KCSchool
twitter.com/kcs_kelowna

Grades: 6-12 *Enrollment:* 802
Darren Lewis, Lead Principal
Scott Campbell, Vice-Principal, Middle School, 250-861-3238, ext. 308
scott.campbell@kcschool.ca

Campuses
Preschool & Elementary School Campus
3285 Gordon Dr., Kelowna, BC V1W 3N4
Tel: 250-861-5432; *Fax:* 250-861-5806

Grades: K-5
Dan Hein, Vice-Principal, Elementary, 250-861-5432, ext. 201
dan.hein@kcschool.ca

Kelowna: Kelowna Christian School
2870 Benvoulin Rd., Kelowna, BC V1W 2E3, Canada
Tel: 250-861-3238; *Fax:* 250-861-4844
info@kcschool.ca
www.kcschool.ca
www.facebook.com/KCSchool
twitter.com/kcs_kelowna
www.instagram.com/KelownaChristian

Grades: K.-12 *Enrollment:* 195
Darren Lewis, Lead Principal

Kelowna: Okanagan Christian School
1035 Hollywood Rd. South, Kelowna, BC V1X 4N3
Tel: 250-860-5305; *Fax:* 250-868-9703
info@ocskelowna.com
www.ocskelowna.com

Grades: JK - 12 *Enrollment:* 135 *Note:* Operated by the Seventh-day Adventist Church.
Lawrence McMullen, Principal
principal@ocskelowna.com

Kelowna: Willowstone Academy
4091 Lakeshore Rd., Kelowna, BC V1W 1V7, Canada
Tel: 250-764-3111; *Fax:* 250-764-3129
info@willowstoneacademy.com
www.willowstoneacademy.com

Grades: Pre.-8 *Note:* The school of the First Lutheran Church in Kelowna, BC.
Karine Veldhoen, Chief Learning Officer

Langley: Aldergrove Christian Academy
4057 - 248 St., Langley, BC V4W 1E3, Canada
Tel: 604-856-2577
academy@rosbc.com
www.rosbc.com/christianschool.html

Grades: K - 12; Religious ed.
David Strauss, Principal

Langley: Credo Christian Schools
21846 - 52 Ave., Langley, BC V2Y 2M7, Canada
Tel: 604-530-5396; *Fax:* 604-530-8965
office@credochs.com
www.credochs.com

Grades: K-12 *Enrollment:* 470
H. Moes, Principal, 604-530-1941
h.moes@credochs.com

Langley: Langley Christian School
22702 - 48th Ave., Langley, BC V2Z 2T6
Tel: 604-533-2222; *Fax:* 604-533-7276
elem@langleychristian.com
www.langleychristian.com
www.facebook.com/143371662374567
www.linkedin.com/company/langley-christian-school

Grades: K-12 *Enrollment:* 813
Henry Vanderveen, Superintendent
superintendent@langleychristian.com

Maple Ridge: Maple Ridge Christian School
12140 - 203 St., Maple Ridge, BC V2X 2S5, Canada
Tel: 604-465-4442; *Fax:* 604-465-1685
www.mrcs.ca
www.facebook.com/MapleRidgeChristianSchool
twitter.com/MRCSCommunity

Grades: Pre.-12 *Enrollment:* 322
R. Roxburgh, Principal

Mission: Valley Christian School (VCS)
8955 Cedar St., Mission, BC V4S 1A3, Canada
Tel: 604-826-1388; *Fax:* 604-826-2744
info@valleychristianschool.ca
www.valleychristianschool.ca
www.facebook.com/VCSMission

Grades: K - 12
Ken Keis, Chair, Board of Directors
Bill Humphreys, Principal
Bob Barclay, Business Administrator

Nanaimo: Nanaimo Christian School (NCS)
198 Holland Rd., Nanaimo, BC V9R 6W2
Tel: 250-754-4512; *Fax:* 250-754-4271
admin.ncs@shaw.ca
www.ncsnanaimo.com

Grades: Pre. - 12
James Sijpheer, Executive Principal
Shelley Yates, Preschool Director

North Vancouver: Lions Gate Christian Academy (LGCA)
919 Tollcross Rd., North Vancouver, BC V7H 2G3
Tel: 604-984-8226; *Fax:* 604-984-8254
office@lgca.ca
www.lgca.ca

Grades: K.-12 *Enrollment:* 300 *Note:* Established in 1994, the school offers Christian education for students on the North Shore of British Columbia. The British Columbia curriculum of the Ministry of Education is provided by the Lions Gate Christian Academy.
Adam B. Reid, Principal

Penticton: Penticton Community Christian School
#102, 96 Edmonton Ave., Penticton, BC V2A 2G8, Canada
Tel: 250-493-5233; *Fax:* 250-276-4124
office@pentictonchristianschool.ca
www.pentictonchristianschool.ca

Grades: K-12 *Enrollment:* 54
K. Boehmer, Principal
kboehmer@pentictonchristianschool.ca

Port Alberni: Port Alberni Christian School (PACS)
6211 Cherry Creek Rd., Port Alberni, BC V9Y 8S9, Canada
Tel: 250-723-2700; *Fax:* 250-723-5799
office@portalbernichristianschool.ca
www.portalbernichristianschool.ca

Grades: K-8 *Enrollment:* 36
Mary Walker, Acting Principal

Port Coquitlam: British Columbia Christian Academy (BCCA)
1019 Fernwood Ave., Port Coquitlam, BC V3B 5A8
Tel: 604-941-8426; *Fax:* 604-945-6455
admissions@bcchristianacademy.ca
www.bcchristianacademy.ca
www.facebook.com/bcchristianacademy
twitter.com/BCCASchool

Grades: JK - 12 *Note:* British Columbia Christian Academy is an interdenominational Christian school.
Ian Jarvie, Head Principal
ijarvie@bcchristianacademy.ca
Beth Peters, Elementary Principal
Theresa Lee, Director, Pre-School, Daycare
kidsclub@bcchristianacademy.ca
Doug Dowell, Director, Development & Sports
ddowell@bcchristianacademy.ca
Tracy Tko, Librarian
tko@bcchristianacademy.ca

Prince George: Cedars Christian School
701 North Nechako Rd., Prince George, BC V2K 1A2
Tel: 250-564-0707; *Fax:* 250-564-0729
www.cedars.bc.ca
www.facebook.com/cedarschristian

Grades: Pre.-12 *Note:* Cedars Christian School is a non-denominational school.
Curtis Tuininga, Principal

Prince George: Immaculate Conception School
3285 Cathedral Ave., Prince George, BC V2N 5R2
Tel: 250-964-4362; *Fax:* 250-964-9465
icsoffice@cispg.ca
www.icschool.ca

Grades: K.-7
Kathleen Barth, Principal
kbarth@cispg.ca

Quesnel: North Cariboo Christian School (NCCS)
2876 Red Bluff Rd., Quesnel, BC V2J 6C7
Tel: 250-747-4417; *Fax:* 250-747-4410
office@nccschool.ca
www.nccschool.ca

Grades: K-9 *Enrollment:* 63 *Note:* The North Cariboo Christian School is a non-denominational school.
Andrew Martin, Principal

Richmond: Cornerstone Christian Academy
7890 No. 5 Rd., Richmond, BC V6Y 2V2
Tel: 604-303-9181; *Fax:* 604-303-9187
cca@cebccanada.com
cornerstonechristianacademy.ca

Grades: Pre.-7 *Enrollment:* 198 *Note:* Associated with the Cornerstone Evangelical Baptist Church located on the same property.
Leila Chin, Principal

Richmond: Richmond Christian School (RCS)
Elementary School Campus
5240 Woodwards Rd., Richmond, BC V7E 1H1, Canada
Tel: 604-272-5720; *Fax:* 604-272-7370
info@myrcs.ca
myrcs.ca

Grades: Pre. - 5 *Enrollment:* 470 *Note:* The Richmond Christian Elementary School is an independent school, which offers a Christ-centered curriculum.
Roger Grose, Superintendent
Jason Paul, Principal, Elementary Campus
Cathie Schneck, Vice-Principal

Campuses
Middle School Campus
10200 No. 5 Rd., Richmond, BC V7A 4E5
Tel: 604-274-1122; *Fax:* 604-274-1192

Grades: 6 - 8 *Enrollment:* 235
Bonnie Burton, Principal, Middle Campus
Chris Finch, Vice-Principal

Secondary School Campus
10260 No. 5 Rd., Richmond, BC V7A 4E5
Tel: 604-274-1122; *Fax:* 604-274-1128
Grades: 9 - 12 *Enrollment:* 233

Salmon Arm: **King's Christian School**
350B - 30th St. NE, Salmon Arm, BC V1E 1J2, Canada
Tel: 250-832-5200; *Fax:* 250-832-5201
info@kingschristianschool.com
www.kingschristianschool.com
www.facebook.com/KCSOkanagan
twitter.com/KCSOkanagan
kcsnews.wordpress.com
Grades: K-12 *Enrollment:* 214
Dan Demeter, Principal

Sechelt: **Gibsons Christian School**
5078 Davis Bay Rd., Sechelt, BC V0N 3A2
Tel: 604-885-3628; *Fax:* 604-885-3625
gcs@dccnet.com
www.gibsonschristian.org
Deborah Levy, Principal
gcsprincipal@dccnet.com

Smithers: **Bulkley Valley Christian School (BVCS)**
P.O. Box 3635
3575 - 14th Ave., Smithers, BC V0J 2N0
Tel: 250-847-4238; *Fax:* 250-847-3564
www.bvcs.ca
www.facebook.com/BulkleyValleyChristianSchool
Grades: K./Elem./Sec. *Note:* Bulkley Valley Christian School
offers a program for international students.
Chris Steenhof, Principal
csteenhof@bvcs.ca
Monique Vander Wart, Vice-Principal
mvanderwart@bvcs.ca
Tom Grasmeyer, Director, Development
tgrasmeyer@bvcs.ca

Surrey: **Bibleway Christian Academy (BCA)**
18603 - 60th Ave., Surrey, BC V3S 7P4, Canada
Tel: 604-576-8188; *Fax:* 604-576-1370
www.biblewayacademy.org
Grades: K - 9
Kim Dingwall, President
Terry Tekatch, Principal

Surrey: **Pacific Academy**
10238 - 168 St., Surrey, BC V4N 1Z4, Canada
Tel: 604-581-5353; *Fax:* 604-581-0087
contact@pacificacademy.net
www.pacificacademy.net
www.facebook.com/groups/154091321343008/
Grades: K-12 *Enrollment:* 1450 *Note:* Private Christian School
Paul Horban, Head of School

Surrey: **Regent Christian Academy (RCA)**
15100 - 66A Ave., Surrey, BC V3S 2A6, Canada
Tel: 604-599-8171; *Fax:* 604-599-8175
www.facebook.com/RegentCA
Grades: Preschool - 13 *Enrollment:* 550 *Note:* Regent Christian
Academy is a coeducational school, which offers primary,
middle, high school, English as a Second Language, &
international programs.
Paul Johnson, Principal
pjohnson@regent.bc.ca
Linda Barber, Administrator, Middle Division
lbarber@regent.bc.ca
Allan Visser, Administrator, International Division
avisser@regent.bc.ca
Maureen Sayler, Registrar & Secretary
msayler@regent.bc.ca

Surrey: **Surrey Christian School**
8930 - 162 St., Surrey, BC V4N 3G1, Canada
Tel: 604-498-3233; *Fax:* 604-581-3520
info@surreychristian.com
www.surreychristian.com
www.facebook.com/SurreyChristianSchool
twitter.com/surreychristian
www.youtube.com/user/SurreyChristianFilms
Grades: K - 12 *Enrollment:* 608
A. Stegeman, Principal

Surrey: **White Rock Christian Academy**
2265 - 152 St., Surrey, BC V4A 4P1, Canada
Tel: 604-531-9186; *Fax:* 604-531-1727
Toll-Free: 888-531-9186
wrca@wrca.bc.ca
www.facebook.com/WhiteRockChristianAcademy
twitter.com/w_r_c_a
www.linkedin.com/company/white-rock-christian-academy
Grades: K-12 *Enrollment:* 308
Stephen Hardy, Principal

Surrey: **William of Orange Christian School**
P.O. Box 34090
17790 Hwy. 10, Surrey, BC V3S 8C4, Canada
Tel: 604-576-2144; *Fax:* 604-576-0975
admin@wofo.org
www.credochs.com/wohome.cfm
Grades: K-7 *Enrollment:* 106
J. Siebenga, Principal

Surrey: **Zion Lutheran Christian Church & School**
Also known as: Cloverdale Christian School
5950 - 179 St., Surrey, BC V3S 4J9, Canada
Tel: 604-576-6313; *Fax:* 604-576-1399
www.cloverdalechristianschool.ca/school
Grades: Pre.-7 *Enrollment:* 170
Matthew Beimers, Principal

Terrace: **Centennial Christian School**
3608 Sparks St., Terrace, BC V8G 2V6
Tel: 250-635-6173; *Fax:* 250-635-9385
office@centennialchristian.ca
www.centennialchristian.ca
Grades: K - 12
Edgar Veldman, Principal
principal@centennialchristian.ca

Terrace: **Mountain View Christian Academy**
4506 Lakelse Ave., Terrace, BC V8G 1P4
Tel: 250-635-5518; *Fax:* 250-635-5528
mvcacademy@yahoo.ca
www.mountainviewchristianacademy.net
Grades: K - 12
Gunther Rauschenberger, Principal

Vancouver: **Vancouver Christian School (VCS)**
3496 Mons Dr., Vancouver, BC V5M 3E6, Canada
Tel: 604-435-3113; *Fax:* 604-430-1591
office@vancouverchristian.org
www.vancouverchristian.org
Other Information: 604-523-1580 (Phone, Carver Christian High
School)
Grades: K - 12 *Note:* Vancouver Christian School is an
independent, interdenominational school. Grades nine to twelve
are offered at Carver Christian High School.
Ellen Freestone, Principal
Andrea Wiebe, Vice Principal, Kindergarten - Grade 5
Mrs. Con, Vice Principal, Grades 6 to 8

Vancouver: **West Coast Christian School (WCCS)**
15 North Renfrew St., Vancouver, BC V5K 3N6, Canada
Tel: 604-255-2990; *Fax:* 604-255-2103
office@westcoastchristianschool.ca
www.westcoastchristianschool.ca
Grades: K - 12 *Enrollment:* 100 *Note:* The school is a ministry of
West Coast Christian Fellowship. It offers a Christian approach
to learning.
David Ferguson, Principal
Julie Shettler, Administrative Assistant

Vanderhoof: **Northside Christian School**
3337 Voth Rd., Vanderhoof, BC V0J 3A2
Tel: 250-567-9335; *Fax:* 250-567-9332
admin@thenorthsideschool.ca
www.thenorthsideschool.org
Grades: K - 12 *Enrollment:* 133 *Number of Employees:* 21
Michael Shenk, Principal
michaelshenk@thenorthsideschool.org
Shelly Lee, Office Administration
admin@thenorthsideschool.ca

Vernon: **Pleasant Valley Christian Academy**
1802 - 45th Ave., Vernon, BC V1T 3M7
Tel: 250-545-7852; *Fax:* 250-545-9230
admin@pleasantvalleychristian.com
www.pleasantvalleychristian.com
Grades: K.-8 *Enrollment:* 54 *Note:* Affiliated with the
Seventh-day Adventist Church
Rosemary Fischer, Principal

Vernon: **Vernon Christian School**
6890 Pleasant Valley Rd., Vernon, BC V1B 3R5
Tel: 250-545-7345; *Fax:* 250-545-0254
info@vcs.ca
www.vcs.ca
www.facebook.com/VernonChristianSchool
twitter.com/myvcs
Grades: Pre.-12 *Enrollment:* 350 *Note:* Vernon Christian School
is an interdenominational school. The school's secondary
campus is located at 6920 Pleasant Valley Road.
Matt Driediger, Principal
mdriediger@vcs.ca
Melannie Armanini, Vice-Principal, Secondary Campus
marmanini@vcs.ca
Andy Overend, Vice-Principal, Elementary Campus
aoverend@vcs.ca

Victoria: **Lakeview Christian School**
729 Cordova Bay Rd., Victoria, BC V8Y 1P7
Tel: 250-658-5082; *Fax:* 250-658-5072
www.lakeviewchristianschool.ca
Grades: Pre.-9 *Note:* The Lakeview Christian School is affiliated
with other Seventh-day Adventist Christian schools to provide
Christian education.
Janice Harford, Principal

Victoria: **Lighthouse Christian Academy**
1289 Parkdale Dr., Victoria, BC V9B 4G9, Canada
Tel: 250-474-5311; *Fax:* 250-474-5021
info@lighthousechristianacademy.com
www.lighthousechristianacademy.com
www.facebook.com/133384233375987
Grades: K-9 *Enrollment:* 70
Leland Makaroff, Principal

Victoria: **Pacific Christian School (PCS)**
654 Agnes St., Victoria, BC V8Z 2E7, Canada
Tel: 250-479-4532; *Fax:* 250-479-3511
www.pacificchristian.ca
www.facebook.com/yourPCS
twitter.com/pcsvictoria
pinterest.com/yourpcs
Grades: K-12 *Enrollment:* 900
B. Helmus, Principal
bhelmus@pacificchristian.ca

Williams Lake: **Cariboo Adventist Academy**
1405 South Lakeside Dr., Williams Lake, BC V2G 3A7
Tel: 250-392-4741
office@caa-bc.ca
www.caawl.ca
Grades: K.-12 *Note:* The Cariboo Adventist Academy is
operated by the Seventh-day Adventist Church.
Rob Parker, Principal

Williams Lake: **Maranatha Christian School**
1278 Lakeview Cres., Williams Lake, BC V2G 1A3, Canada
Tel: 250-392-7410; *Fax:* 250-392-7409
maranatha@wlefc.com
www.wlmcs.org
Grades: K-12 *Enrollment:* 155
C. Klaue, Principal

Catholic

Abbotsford: **St. James School**
2767 Townline Rd., Abbotsford, BC V2T 5E1, Canada
Tel: 604-852-1788; *Fax:* 604-850-5376
www.stjameselementary.ca
Grades: K-7 *Enrollment:* 219
Terri Sask, Principal

Abbotsford: **St. John Brebeuf**
2747 Townline Rd., Abbotsford, BC V2T 5E1, Canada
Tel: 604-855-0571; *Fax:* 604-855-0572
www.stjohnbrebeuf.ca
Grades: 8-12 *Enrollment:* 347
Ted Brennan, Principal
tbrennan@stjohnbrebeuf.ca

Burnaby: **Holy Cross Elementary**
1450 Delta Ave., Burnaby, BC V5B 3G2, Canada
Tel: 604-299-3530; *Fax:* 604-299-3534
hcoffice@telus.net
www.holycrosselementary.ca
Grades: K-7 *Enrollment:* 224
Dino Alberti, Principal
dinohc@telus.net

Burnaby: **Our Lady of Mercy School**
7481 - 10 Ave., Burnaby, BC V3N 2S1, Canada
Tel: 604-526-7121; *Fax:* 604-520-3194
office@ourladyofmercy.ca
www.ourladyofmercy.ca

Grades: K-7 *Enrollment:* 240
Neva Grout, Principal

Burnaby: St. Francis de Sales School
6656 Balmoral St., Burnaby, BC V5E 1J1
Tel: 604-435-5311; *Fax:* 604-434-4798
office@sfdsschool.ca
www.sfdsschool.ca
www.facebook.com/sfdsflames
twitter.com/sfdsflames
www.instagram.com/sfdsflames
Grades: K.-7 *Enrollment:* 217 *Note:* St. Francis de Sales is a
Catholic school located in the Highgate region of South Burnaby.
Irene Wihak, Principal

Burnaby: St. Helen's School
3894 Triumph St., Burnaby, BC V5C 1Y7, Canada
Tel: 604-299-2234; *Fax:* 604-299-3565
school.sthelensparish.ca
Grades: K-7 *Enrollment:* 352
Waldemar Sambor, Principal
wsambor@cisva.bc.ca

Burnaby: St. Michael's School
9387 Holmes St., Burnaby, BC V3N 4C3, Canada
Tel: 604-526-9768; *Fax:* 604-540-9799
school@stmichaelschool.ca
www.stmichaelschool.ca
Grades: K-7 *Enrollment:* 216
C. Kennedy, Principal

Burnaby: St. Thomas More Collegiate (STMC)
7450 - 12 Ave., Burnaby, BC V3N 2K1, Canada
Tel: 604-521-1801; *Fax:* 604-520-0725
info@stmc.bc.ca
www.stmc.bc.ca
Grades: 8-12 *Enrollment:* 675 *Number of Employees:* 55
Michel DesLauriers, Principal
mdeslauriers@stmc.bc.ca

Chilliwack: St. Mary's Catholic School
8909 Mary St., Chilliwack, BC V2P 4J4, Canada
Tel: 604-792-7715; *Fax:* 604-792-7031
www.stmarysschoolchwk.com
Grades: K-7 *Enrollment:* 183
M. McDermott, Principal

Coquitlam: Our Lady of Fatima School
315 Walker St., Coquitlam, BC V3K 4C7, Canada
Tel: 604-936-4228; *Fax:* 604-936-4403
info@fatimaschool.ca
www.fatimaschool.ca
Grades: K-7 *Enrollment:* 388 *Note:* Independent, English and
French Immersion School accredited in British Columbia under
the terms of the Independent School Act.
Maria Katsionis, Principal

Coquitlam: Queen of All Saints Elementary School
(QAS)
1405 Como Lake Ave., Coquitlam, BC V3J 3P4, Canada
Tel: 604-931-9071; *Fax:* 604-931-9089
queenofallsaintsschool@shawcable.com
www.queenofallsaintsschool.ca
Grades: K - 7 *Note:* Queen of All Saints Elementary School was
established by the Roman Catholic Archdiocese of Vancouver.
The school belongs to All Saints Parish.
Joan Sandberg, Principal

Coquitlam: Traditional Learning Academy (TLA)
1189 Rochester Ave., Coquitlam, BC V3K 2X3, Canada
Tel: 604-931-7265; *Fax:* 604-931-3432
tlaoffice@traditionallearning.com
www.traditionallearning.com
Other Information: tlaprincipal@traditionallearning.com (E-mail,
Principal)
Grades: K - 12 *Note:* Traditional Learning Academy encourages
students to know the Catholic faith.
Allan Garneau, Administrator

Cranbrook: St. Mary's Catholic Independent School
1701 - 5 St. South, Cranbrook, BC V1C 1K1
Tel: 250-426-5017; *Fax:* 250-426-5076
stmary@shaw.ca
www.stmarysschool.ca
Grades: K.-6 *Enrollment:* 143
Jerelynn MacNeil, Principal
stmprincipal@shaw.ca

Dawson Creek: Notre Dame School
925 - 104th Ave., Dawson Creek, BC V1G 2H8
Tel: 250-782-4923; *Fax:* 250-782-4388
www.notredamedc.org/notre-dame-school
Grades: K.- 7 *Enrollment:* 150
Mrs. Terri Haynal, Principal

Kathy Lear, Principal

Delta: Immaculate Conception School
8840 - 119 St., Delta, BC V4C 6M4, Canada
Tel: 604-596-6116; *Fax:* 604-596-4338
immaculate_conception_school@hotmail.com
www.icdelta.com
Grades: K-7 *Enrollment:* 473
Maurice Jacob, Principal
Fr. Patrick Tepoorten, Pastor

Delta: Sacred Heart School
P.O. Box 10 Main
3900 Arthur Dr., Delta, BC V4K 3N5, Canada
Tel: 604-946-2611; *Fax:* 604-946-0598
office@shsdelta.org
www.shsdelta.net
Grades: K-7 *Enrollment:* 400
Wendell MacCormack, Principal

Duncan: Queen of Angels Catholic School
2085 Maple Bay Rd., Duncan, BC V9L 5L9, Canada
Tel: 250-746-5919; *Fax:* 250-746-8689
qa@cisdv.bc.ca
www.queenofangels.ca
Grades: Pre.-9 *Enrollment:* 416
Kathy Korman, Principal
kkorman@cisdv.bc.ca
Keefer Pollard, Vice-Principal
Lana Durand, Coordinator, Special Education
ldurand@cisdv.bc.ca
Tina Campagne, Secretary
tcampagne@cisdv.bc.ca
Melissa Telfer, Secretary
mtelfer@cisdv.bc.ca

Kelowna: Immaculata Catholic Regional High
School
1493 K.L.O. Rd., Kelowna, BC V1W 3N8
Tel: 250-762-2730; *Fax:* 250-861-3028
irhs.office@cisnd.ca
www.immaculatakelowna.ca
twitter.com/IRHS_Athletics
Grades: 8-12; Religious Education *Enrollment:* 250 *Number of
Employees:* 34 (13 teachers)
Rob Plaxton, B.Ed. M.Ed., Principal
irhs.principal@cisnd.ca
Bruno Oliveira, B.Ed. M.A., Vice-Principal
boliveira@cisnd.ca
Fr. Cerlouie Jimenez, Chaplain
Rhonda Sali, PDP Ed., M.Ed., Coordinator, Religious Education
rsali@cisnd.ca
Paula Despins, Secretary
pdespins@cisnd.ca
Nadine Casorso, Librarian
ncasorso@cisnd.ca

Langley: St. Catherines School
20244 - 32 Ave., Langley, BC V2Z 2E1, Canada
Tel: 604-534-6564; *Fax:* 604-534-4871
lfa@lfabc.org
www.stcatherines.ca
Grades: K-7 *Enrollment:* 229
Diane Little, Principal

Maple Ridge: St. Patrick's School
22589 - 121 Ave., Maple Ridge, BC V2X 3T5, Canada
Tel: 604-467-1571; *Fax:* 604-467-2686
school@stpatsschool.org
www.stpatsschool.org
twitter.com/stpatsmr
Grades: K-7 *Enrollment:* 214
Clive Heah, Principal

North Vancouver: Holy Trinity Elementary School
128 - West 27 St., North Vancouver, BC V7N 2H1, Canada
Tel: 604-987-4454
holyt@telus.net
www.holytrinityschool.ca
Grades: K-7 *Enrollment:* 233
Kevin Smith, Principal
ksmith@cisva.bc.ca

North Vancouver: St. Edmund's School
535 Mahon Ave., North Vancouver, BC V7M 2R7, Canada
Tel: 604-988-7364; *Fax:* 604-988-7350
office@stedmunds.ca
www.stedmunds.ca
Grades: K-7 *Enrollment:* 204
Michael Field, Principal
mfield@stedmunds.ca

North Vancouver: St. Pius X Elementary School
1150 Mount Seymour Rd., North Vancouver, BC V7G 1R6,
Canada
Tel: 604-929-0345; *Fax:* 604-929-5051
www.saintpius.ca
Grades: K-7 *Enrollment:* 227
Fabio Battisti, Principal

North Vancouver: St. Thomas Aquinas Regional
Secondary School
541 Keith Rd. West, North Vancouver, BC V7M 1M5, Canada
Tel: 604-987-4431; *Fax:* 604-987-7816
office@aquinas.org
www.aquinas.org
Grades: 8-12 *Enrollment:* 601
John Campbell, Principal
jcampbell@aquinas.org

Penticton: Holy Cross Elementary School
1298 Main St., Penticton, BC V2A 5G2, Canada
Tel: 250-492-4480; *Fax:* 250-490-4602
www.holyc.com
Grades: K.-7 *Enrollment:* 145
Jeff Brophy, Principal

Port Coquitlam: Archbishop Carney Regional
Secondary School (ACRSS)
1335 Dominion Ave., Port Coquitlam, BC V3B 8G7, Canada
Tel: 604-942-7465; *Fax:* 604-942-5289
office@acrss.org
www.acrss.org
Grades: 8-12 *Enrollment:* 720
Lorraine Paruzzolo, Principal, 604-942-7465, ext. 2
paruzzol@acrss.org

Port Coquitlam: Our Lady of the Assumption School
2255 Fraser Ave., Port Coquitlam, BC V3B 6G8, Canada
Tel: 604-942-5522; *Fax:* 604-942-8313
info@assumptionschool.com
www.assumptionschool.com
Grades: K-7 *Enrollment:* 244
Rosaleen Heffernan, Principal

Powell River: Assumption Catholic School
7091 Glacier St., Powell River, BC V8A 1R8, Canada
Tel: 604-485-9894; *Fax:* 604-485-7984
assump.office@shaw.ca
www.assumpschool.com
Grades: K.-9 *Enrollment:* 186 *Note:* Accredited by the B.C. Min.
of Education. Curriculum includes math, sciences, social studies,
physical education, languages, music, art, drama, & relgion.
Mimi Richardson, Principal

Richmond: St. Joseph the Worker School
4451 Williams Rd., Richmond, BC V7E 1J7, Canada
Tel: 604-277-1115; *Fax:* 604-272-5214
office.sjosw@cisva.bc.ca
stjosephtheworker.ca
Grades: K-7 *Enrollment:* 222
Paul Fraser, Principal
paulfraser.stjo@gmail.com

Richmond: St. Paul's School
8251 St. Alban's Rd., Richmond, BC V6Y 2L2, Canada
Tel: 604-277-4487; *Fax:* 604-277-1810
office@stpaulschool.ca
www.stpaulschool.ca
Grades: K-7 *Enrollment:* 241
Nicole Regush, Principal

Surrey: Cloverdale Catholic School
17511 - 59th Ave., Surrey, BC V3S 1P3
Tel: 604-574-5151; *Fax:* 604-574-5160
office@ccsunited.ca
ccsunited.ca
www.facebook.com/204955139548051
twitter.com/ClovCatholicSch
Grades: Preschool; K.-7 *Enrollment:* 245
Jason Borkowski, Principal
jborkowski@cisva.bc.ca
Janet Mahussier, Librarian
jmahussier@ccsunited.ca

Surrey: Holy Cross Regional High School
16193 - 88 Ave., Surrey, BC V4N 1G3, Canada
Tel: 604-581-3023; *Fax:* 604-583-4795
office@holycross.bc.ca
www.holycross.bc.ca
www.facebook.com/holycrossregionalhighschool
twitter.com/dailycrusader
www.flickr.com/photos/holycrossregionalsecondary
Grades: 8-12 *Enrollment:* 797
Chris Blesch, Principal

Surrey: Our Lady of Good Counsel School
10504 - 139 St., Surrey, BC V3T 4L5, Canada
Tel: 604-581-3154; *Fax:* 604-588-1633
olgcprincipal@shaw.ca
www.olgcschool.ca

Grades: K-7 *Enrollment:* 245
Gerard Wright, Principal

Surrey: St. Bernadette School
13130 - 65B Ave., Surrey, BC V3W 9M1, Canada
Tel: 604-596-1101; *Fax:* 604-596-1550
www.stbernadetteschool.ca

Grades: K-7 *Enrollment:* 227
Kelly Kozack, Principal

Surrey: St. Matthew's Elementary
16065 - 88th Ave., Surrey, BC V4N 1G3
Tel: 604-589-7545
office@stmatthewselementary.ca
www.stmatthewselementary.ca

Grades: K - 3
Deborah Welsh, Principal
welsh@stmatthewselementary.ca

Surrey: Star of the Sea School
15024 - 24 Ave., Surrey, BC V4A 2H8, Canada
Tel: 604-531-6316; *Fax:* 604-531-0171
school@starofthesea.ca
www.staroftheseaschool.ca
twitter.com/StaroftheSeaBC

Grades: K-7 *Enrollment:* 316
Lesya Balsevich, Principal
lbalsevich@starofthesea.bc.ca

Terrace: Veritas School
4836 Straume Ave., Terrace, BC V8G 4G3
Tel: 250-635-3035; *Fax:* 250-635-7588
veritas@cispg.ca
www.veritascatholicschool.ca

Grades: Pre.-9 *Enrollment:* 234
Tamara Berg, Principal
tberg@cispg.ca

Trail: St. Michael's Catholic School
1329 - 4 Ave., Trail, BC V1R 1S3
Tel: 250-368-6151; *Fax:* 250-368-9962
www.smces.ca

Grades: K.-7 *Enrollment:* 179
Julia Mason, Principal
smprincipal@smces.ca

Vancouver: Blessed Sacrament School
École Saint Sacrement
3020 Heather St., Vancouver, BC V5Z 3K3, Canada
Tel: 604-876-7211; *Fax:* 604-876-7280
admin@ess.vancouver.bc.ca
ess.vancouver.bc.ca/moodle

Grades: K - 7

Vancouver: Corpus Christi School
6344 Nanaimo St., Vancouver, BC V5P 4K7, Canada
Tel: 604-321-1117; *Fax:* 604-321-1410
officecc@telus.net
www.corpuschristi-school.ca

Grades: K-7 *Enrollment:* 241
Rosa Natola, Principal

Vancouver: Immaculate Conception School
Vancouver
3745 - 28 Ave. West, Vancouver, BC V6S 1S6, Canada
Tel: 604-224-5012; *Fax:* 604-224-3721
www.icschoolvancouver.com

Grades: K-7 *Enrollment:* 200
Colette Foran, Principal

Vancouver: Little Flower Academy (LFA)
4195 Alexandra St., Vancouver, BC V6J 4C6, Canada
Tel: 604-738-9016; *Fax:* 604-738-5749
lfa@lfabc.org
www.lfabc.org

Grades: 8-12 *Enrollment:* 469
M. DeFreitas, Principal

Vancouver: Notre Dame Regional Secondary School
2880 Venables St., Vancouver, BC V5K 4Z6, Canada
Tel: 604-255-5454; *Fax:* 604-255-2115
scirillo@ndrs.org
www.ndrs.ca

Grades: 8 - 12 *Enrollment:* 620 *Note:* Notre Dame Regional Secondary School is a Catholic school.
Roger DesLauriers, Principal, 604-255-5454
rdeslauriers@ndrs.org
George Oswald, Vice Principal, 604-255-5454
goswald@ndrs.org

Andrew McCracken, Librarian
amccracken@ndrs.org
Maureen Grant, Manager, Office, 604-255-5454
mgrant@ndrs.org

Vancouver: Our Lady of Perpetual Help School
2550 Camosun St., Vancouver, BC V6R 3W6, Canada
Tel: 604-228-8811; *Fax:* 604-224-6822
office@olphbc.ca
www.olphbc.ca

Grades: K-7 *Enrollment:* 406
Lora Clarke, Principal

Vancouver: Our Lady of Sorrows School
575 Slocan St., Vancouver, BC V5K 3X5, Canada
Tel: 604-253-2434; *Fax:* 604-253-1523
ourladyofsorrows1@telus.net
www.ourladyofsorrows.ca

Grades: K-7 *Enrollment:* 231
P. Balletta, Principal

Vancouver: Saint Patrick Elementary School
2850 Quebec St., Vancouver, BC V5T 3A9, Canada
Tel: 604-879-4411; *Fax:* 604-879-3737
www.spev.ca

Grades: K-7 *Enrollment:* 249
M. Boreham, Principal
mboreham@spev.ca

Vancouver: Saint Patrick Regional Secondary School
115 - 11 Ave. East, Vancouver, BC V5T 2C1, Canada
Tel: 604-874-6422; *Fax:* 604-874-5176
administration@stpats.bc.ca
www.stpats.bc.ca
www.facebook.com/129972273748715
twitter.com/StPatsSecVanBC
www.youtube.com/STPCouncil

Grades: 8-12 *Enrollment:* 501
Ralph Gabriele, Principal

Vancouver: St. Andrew's School
450 - 47th Ave. East, Vancouver, BC V5W 2B4, Canada
Tel: 604-325-6317; *Fax:* 604-325-0920
principal@standrewsschool.ca
standrewsschool.ca/wordpress/

Grades: K-7 *Enrollment:* 227
Marian Mailley, Principal

Vancouver: St. Anthony of Padua
1370 - 73rd Ave. West, Vancouver, BC V6P 3E8, Canada
Tel: 604-261-4043; *Fax:* 604-261-4036
office@stanthonyofpaduaschool.ca
www.stanthonyofpaduaschool.ca

Grades: K-7 *Enrollment:* 209
Oscar Pozzolo, Principal

Vancouver: St. Augustine School
2154 West 7th Ave., Vancouver, BC V6K 0E3, Canada
Tel: 604-731-8024; *Fax:* 604-739-1712
info@faithandfoundation.com
www.faithandfoundation.com

Grades: K-7 *Enrollment:* 297
Michael Yaptinchay, Principal

Vancouver: St. Francis of Assisi School
870 Victoria Dr., Vancouver, BC V5L 4E7, Canada
Tel: 604-253-7311; *Fax:* 604-253-7375
sfaoffice@telus.net
www.sfaschool.ca

Grades: K-7 *Enrollment:* 191
Joan Sandberg, Principal

Vancouver: St. Francis Xavier School
428 Great Northern Way, Vancouver, BC V5T 4S5, Canada
Tel: 604-254-2714; *Fax:* 604-254-2514
admin@sfxschool.ca
www.sfxschool.ca

Grades: K-7 *Enrollment:* 327
B. Krivuzoff, Principal

Vancouver: St. Joseph's School
3261 Fleming St., Vancouver, BC V5N 3V6, Canada
Tel: 604-872-5715; *Fax:* 604-872-5700
stjosephsvancouver@telus.net
www.stjoesschool-vancouver.org

Grades: K-7 *Enrollment:* 210
Dierdre O'Callaghan, Principal

Vancouver: St. Jude's School
2953 - 15 Ave. East, Vancouver, BC V5M 2K7, Canada
Tel: 604-434-1633; *Fax:* 604-434-8677
stjude@shawcable.com
stjude.ca
twitter.com/stjudevan

Grades: K-7 *Enrollment:* 221
M. Perry, Principal

Vancouver: St. Mary's School
5239 Joyce St., Vancouver, BC V5R 4G8
Tel: 604-437-1312; *Fax:* 604-437-1193
www.stmary.bc.ca
twitter.com/SMSaints604
www.instagram.com/smsaints604

Grades: K-7 *Enrollment:* 230
Brenda Krivuzoff, Principal

Vancouver: Vancouver College
5400 Cartier St., Vancouver, BC V6M 3A5, Canada
Tel: 604-261-4285
info@vc.bc.ca
www.vc.bc.ca

Grades: K - 12 *Enrollment:* 1000 *Note:* Vancouver College consists of an elementary school, a middle school, & a senior school.
John McFarland, Principal
jmcfarland@vc.bc.ca
Kelly Lattimer, Business Manager
klattimer@vc.bc.ca
Ronith Cogswell, Director, Advancement
rcogswell@vc.bc.ca
Margaret Vossen, Registrar
mvossen@vc.bc.ca

Victoria: St. Andrew's Regional High School
880 Mckenzie Ave., Victoria, BC V8X 3G5, Canada
Tel: 250-479-1414; *Fax:* 250-479-5356
sarhs@cisdv.bc.ca
www.standrewshigh.ca

Grades: 8-12 *Enrollment:* 469
Andrew Keleher, Principal
akeleher@cisdv.bc.ca

Victoria: St. Joseph's Victoria Elementary School
757 Burnside Rd. West, Victoria, BC V8Z 1M9, Canada
Tel: 250-479-1232; *Fax:* 250-479-1907
sjv@cisdv.bc.ca
www.stjosephschool.ca

Grades: K-7 *Enrollment:* 203
Simon Di Castri, Co-Principal
Keefer Pollard, Co-Principal

Victoria: St. Patrick's Elementary School
2368 Trent St., Victoria, BC V8R 4Z3, Canada
Tel: 250-592-6713; *Fax:* 250-592-6717
sp@cisdv.bc.ca
www.stpatrickselem.ca

Grades: K-7 *Enrollment:* 355
Deanne Paulson, Principal

West Vancouver: St. Anthony's School
595 Keith Rd., West Vancouver, BC V7T 1L8, Canada
Tel: 604-922-0011; *Fax:* 604-922-3196
office@saswv.ca
www.saswv.ca

Grades: K-7 *Enrollment:* 204
Laila Maravillas, Principal
principal@saswv.ca

Williams Lake: Sacred Heart Catholic School
455 Pigeon Ave., Williams Lake, BC V2G 4R5, Canada
Tel: 250-398-7770; *Fax:* 250-398-7725
admin@sacredheartwl.com
sacredheartwl.com

Grades: Pre. K - 7 *Enrollment:* 84
Nicholas Iachetta, Principal
principal@sacredheartwl.com

French

Vancouver: L'Ecole Française Internationale Cousteau de Vancouver
Cousteau, The French International School of Vancouver
3657 Fromme Rd., Vancouver, BC V7K 2E6
Tél: 604-924-2457; *Téléc:* 604-924-4483
cousteauschool.hubbli.com

Grades: Pre.-8 *Enrollment:* 143
Annabelle Glas, Principal
principal@cousteauschool.org

First Nations

Iskut: Klappan Independent Day School
P.O. Box 60
Iskut, BC V0J 1K0
Tel: 250-234-3561; *Fax:* 250-234-3563
www.bced.gov.bc.ca
Grades: K.-8 *Enrollment:* 48 *Note:* Serving students of Iskut First
Nation.
Carolyn Doody, Principal
principal@iskut.org

Merritt: Coldwater Band School
P.O. Box 4600
2249 Quilchena Ave., Merritt, BC V1K 1B8
Tel: 250-378-9261; *Fax:* 250-378-9212
Grades: K - 12

Merritt: N'Kwala School (Upper Nicola Band)
P.O. Box 3700
Merritt, BC V1K 1J5
Tel: 250-350-3370; *Fax:* 250-350-3319

Port Hardy: Gwa'sala-'Nakwaxda'xw School
P.O. Box 1799
Port Hardy, BC V0N 2P0, Canada
Tel: 250-949-7743; *Fax:* 250-949-7402
www.gwanak.info
Enrollment: 82 *Note:* Independent First Nation's school
Grace Smith, Education Coordinator
grace.smith176@gmail.com

Special Education

Kelowna: Venture Academy
#338, 101 - 1865 Dilworth Dr., Kelowna, BC V1Y 9T1
Tel: 250-491-4593; *Fax:* 250-491-0251
Toll-Free: 855-281-5813
info@ventureacademy.ca
www.ventureacademy.ca
Grades: 7-12 *Note:* A therapeutic program & boarding school for
troubled teens; also has locations in Alberta & Ontario.
Gordon Hay, B.G.S., Founder
Louise Beard, Executive Director
Jeff Brain, MA, CTS, CEP, Director, Admissions & Program
Development

Maple Ridge: James Cameron School
P.O. Box 157 Del Ctr.
20245 Dewdney Trunk Rd., Maple Ridge, BC V2X 7G1,
Canada
Tel: 604-465-8444; *Fax:* 604-465-4561
jcsadmin@jcs.bc.ca
www.jcs.bc.ca
www.facebook.com/JCS.BC
Grades: 2-7 *Enrollment:* 54
Penny Shepherd-Hill, Principal

New Westminster: PALS Autism School
101 - 3rd St., New Westminster, BC V3L 2P9
Tel: 604-251-7257; *Fax:* 604-251-1627
info@palsautismschool.ca
www.palsautismschool.ca
www.facebook.com/PALSAutismSchool
twitter.com/PALSAutismBC
Grades: K-12; Adult
Andrea Kasunic, Head of School

Vancouver: Eaton Arrowsmith School
#204, 6190 Agronomy Rd., Vancouver, BC V6T 1Z3
Tel: 604-264-8327; *Fax:* 604-222-8327
info@eatonarrowsmith.com
www.eatonarrowsmith.com
www.facebook.com/eatonarrowsmithschool
twitter.com/eatonarrowsmith
Grades: K.-12 *Enrollment:* 100
Howard Eaton, Director
Sarah Cohen, Head of Schools

Campuses
White Rock Campus
#300, 1538 Foster St., White Rock, BC V4B 3X8
Tel: 604-538-1710; *Fax:* 604-538-1709
info@eatonarrowsmith.com
Kelsey Hanna, Principal

Distance Education

Victoria: Regent Christian Online Academy (RCOA)
#105, 4475 Viewmont Ave., Victoria, BC V8Z 6L8
Tel: 250-592-1759; *Fax:* 250-721-0036
Toll-Free: 866-877-1737
regentonline.ca

Grades: K - 12 *Enrollment:* 1100 *Number of Employees:* 85
teachers
Mark Langley, Principal
Carolyn Langley, Business Administrator

Independent & Private Schools

Abbotsford: Dasmesh Punjabi School
5930 Riverside St., Abbotsford, BC V4X 1T8, Canada
Tel: 604-826-1666; *Fax:* 604-820-8924
info@dasmeshschool.com
www.dasmeshschool.com
Grades: K.-12 *Enrollment:* 397
George Peary, Principal

Agassiz: Seabird College
P.O. Box 650
2895 Chowat Rd., Agassiz, BC V0M 1A0
Tel: 604-796-6896; *Fax:* 604-796-3729
www.seabirdisland.ca/page/seabird-college
www.facebook.com/SeabirdIslandBand
twitter.com/SeabirdIsland
Grades: K - 12 *Enrollment:* 162
Dianne Parkinson, Contact
dianneparkinson@seabirdisland.ca

Ahousat: Maaqtusiis School
General Delivery, Ahousat, BC V0R 1A0, Canada
Tel: 250-670-9555; *Fax:* 250-670-9543
maaqtusiis.wordpress.com
Grades: 1-12 *Enrollment:* 217
Rebecca Atleo, Principal

Aldergrove: Fraser Valley Adventist Academy (FVAA)
26026 - 48th Ave., Aldergrove, BC V4W 1J2
Tel: 604-607-3822; *Fax:* 604-856-1002
fvaa@fvaa.net
www.fvaa.ca
www.facebook.com/FVAAeducation
twitter.com/fvaaeducation
Grades: K-12 *Enrollment:* 173 *Note:* Seventh-day Adventist
college preparatory secondary & elementary school.
Karen Wallace, Principal, 604-607-3822, ext. 315
principal@fvaa.ca
Colleen Russell, Business Manager, 604-607-3822, ext. 341
business@fvaa.ca
Joan Septembre, Secretary, Librarian, 604-607-3822, ext. 301
info@fvaa.ca

Alert Bay: T'lisalagi'lakw School
P.O. Box 50
Alert Bay, BC V0N 1A0, Canada
Tel: 250-974-5591; *Fax:* 250-974-2475
Grades: K.-7 *Enrollment:* 46
Michael Kanhai, Principal
michaelk@namgis.bc.ca

Armstrong: North Okanagan Junior Academy (NOJA)
4699 South Grandview Flats Rd., Armstrong, BC V0E 1B5,
Canada
Tel: 250-546-8330; *Fax:* 250-546-8343
info@noja.ca
www.noja.ca
Note: The Academy is operated by the Seventh-day Adventist
Church.
Marilyn Ilchuk, Principal
marilynilchuk@aol.com
Sharon Trussell, Vice Principal
shrbet@shaw.ca

Bowen Island: Island Pacific School
P.O. Box 128
671 Carter Rd., Bowen Island, BC V0N 1G0, Canada
Tel: 604-947-9311; *Fax:* 604-947-9366
info@go.islandpacific.org
www.islandpacific.org
www.facebook.com/islandpacificschool
twitter.com/IPSchool
www.linkedin.com/company/island-pacific-school
www.youtube.com/user/islandpacificschool
Grades: 6-9 *Enrollment:* 52 *Note:* Program elements of the
school's instructional curriculum include language, art, music,
literature, physical education, science, math, design &
technology, & practical reasoning. The Grade 9 curriculum also
includes the Masterworks Program, which is required for
graduation.
Scott Herrington, Head of School

Burnaby: Deer Lake SDA School
Also known as: Deer Lake School
5550 Gilpin St., Burnaby, BC V5G 2H6, Canada
Tel: 604-434-5844; *Fax:* 604-434-5845
office@deerlakeschool.ca
www.deerlakeschool.ca
Grades: K-12 *Enrollment:* 278
Caren Erickson, Principal

Chilliwack: Highroad Academy
46641 Chilliwack Central Rd., Chilliwack, BC V2P 1K3
Tel: 604-792-4680; *Fax:* 604-792-2465
info@highroadacademy.com
www.highroadacademy.com
Grades: K-12 *Enrollment:* 430
Dave Shinness, Principal
dshinness@highroadacademy.com

Chilliwack: John Calvin School
4268 Stewart Rd., Chilliwack, BC V2R 5G3, Canada
Tel: 604-823-6814; *Fax:* 604-823-6791
office@jcss.ca
www.jcss.ca
Grades: K-7 *Enrollment:* 170
Pieter H. Torenvliet, Principal, 604-823-6814

Cobble Hill: Evergreen Independent School
P.O. Box 166
3515 Watson Ave., Cobble Hill, BC V0R 1L0, Canada
Tel: 250-743-2433; *Fax:* 250-743-2570
evergreen@evergreenbc.net
www.evergreenbc.net
Grades: K.-6 *Enrollment:* 63
Alex Gallacher, Co-Administrator
Bridget Moss, Co-Administrator

Comox: Phil & Jennie Gaglardi Academy
1475 Noel Ave., Comox, BC V9M 4H8, Canada
Tel: 250-339-1200; *Fax:* 250-339-1215
office@cvchristian.com
www.pjgaglardiacademy.ca
www.facebook.com/GatewayAcademyComox
Grades: K-9 *Enrollment:* 112
R. Janzen, Principal

Coquitlam: Children of Integrity Montessori Academy
2541 Quay Pl., Coquitlam, BC V3S 3H7, Canada
Tel: 604-461-1223; *Fax:* 604-461-1228
info@childrenofintegrity.com
www.childrenofintegrity.com
Grades: K.-7

Coquitlam: Coquitlam College
516 Brookmere Ave., Coquitlam, BC V3J 1W9, Canada
Tel: 604-939-6633; *Fax:* 604-939-0336
admiss@coquitlamcollege.com
www.coquitlamcollege.com
www.facebook.com/coquitlamcollege
www.youtube.com/user/ccoquitlam
Grades: 11-12 *Enrollment:* 85
Tom Tait, President
Will Eckford, Principal

Coquitlam: Mediated Learning Academy
550 Thompson Ave., Coquitlam, BC V3J 3Z8, Canada
Tel: 604-937-3641; *Fax:* 604-931-5155
info@mediatedlearningacademy.org
www.mediatedlearningacademy.org
Grades: K-12 *Enrollment:* 84 *Note:* The Mediated Learning
Academy is an educational facility for children to learn through
Mediated Learning Experience and "brain-based" teaching.
Kathleen Jeffrey, Principal

Courtenay: Saltwater Waldorf School
2311 Rosewall Cres., Courtenay, BC V9N 8R9
Tel: 250-871-7777
info@saltwaterschool.com
www.saltwaterschool.com
www.facebook.com/cvsws
Grades: Pre. - 6 *Enrollment:* 7 *Number of Employees:* 10
Rebecca Watkin, Principal
Marussia Nesling, Administrator

Duncan: Island Oak High School
P.O. Box 873 Main
5814 Banks Rd., Duncan, BC V9L 3Y2, Canada
Tel: 250-701-0400; *Fax:* 250-701-0410
mail@islandoak.org
islandoak.org
www.tumblr.com/register/follow/islandoak
Grades: 9-12 *Enrollment:* 36
Gary Ward, Principal

Duncan: Queen Margaret's School (QMS)
660 Brownsey Ave., Duncan, BC V9L 1C2, Canada
Tel: 250-746-4185; *Fax:* 250-746-4187
admissions@qms.bc.ca
www.qms.bc.ca
www.facebook.com/240936919190
twitter.com/QMSDuncan
Grades: JK - 12 *Enrollment:* 325 *Number of Employees:* 115
Note: Queen Margaret's School consists of a coeducational
junior school for students from junior kindergarten to grade
seven. The school also consists of an All-Girls High School,
which offers a university preparatory program. An English as a
Second Language Program is available for beginner & advanced
students.
Leigh Taylor, Chair
Wilma Jamieson, Head of School
wjamieson@qms.bc.ca
Sharon Klein, Deputy Head, Education & Senior School Principal
sklein@qms.bc.ca
Susan Cruikshank, Junior School Principal
scruikshank@qms.bc.ca
Celina Mason, Director, Residential Life & Student Support
cmason@qms.bc.ca
Julie Scurr, Director, Finance & Privacy Officer
jascurr@qms.bc.ca
Courtney Gillan, Executive Director, Admissions & Advancement
cgillan@qms.bc.ca

Duncan: Sunrise Waldorf School (SWS)
2148 Lakeside Rd., Duncan, BC V9L 6M3, Canada
Tel: 250-743-7253; *Fax:* 250-743-7245
mail@sunrisewaldorfschool.org
www.sunrisewaldorfschool.org
www.facebook.com/sunrisewaldorf
Grades: K-8 *Enrollment:* 162
J. Canty, Principal

Fernie: Fernie Academy
P.O. Box 2677
451 - 2nd Ave., 2nd Fl., Fernie, BC V0B 1M0, Canada
Tel: 250-423-0212; *Fax:* 250-423-4799
office@thefernieacademy.ca
www.thefernieacademy.ca
Grades: K-12 *Enrollment:* 97
J. Sombrowski, Principal
jsombrowski@fernieacademy.com

Fort Nelson: Chalo School
Mile 293, RR#1, Fort Nelson, BC V0C 1R0, Canada
Tel: 250-774-7651; *Fax:* 250-774-7655
chaloschool@gmail.com
www.chaloschool.bc.ca
Grades: Preschool - 12 *Enrollment:* 200 *Note:* Fort Nelson First
Nation owns & operates Chalo School.
Colette Duperreault-Young, Principal
chaloschool@gmail.com

Fort St James: Nak'albun Elementary School
P.O. Box 1390
Fort St James, BC V0J 1P0, Canada
Tel: 250-996-8441; *Fax:* 250-996-2229
nkbprincipal@hotmail.ca
www.nakalbun.ca
Grades: K - 7 *Enrollment:* 60 *Note:* The elementary school is
operated under the jurisdiction of Nak'azdli Band.
Rick Aucoin, Principal
nkbprincipal@fsjames.com

Fort Ware: Aatse Davie School
P.O. Box 79
Fort Ware, BC V0J 3B0
Tel: 250-471-2002; *Fax:* 250-471-2080
aatse@pris.bc.ca
www.kwadacha.com
www.facebook.com/138180549552045
Grades: K.-12 *Enrollment:* 84 *Note:* The school serves the
Kwadacha First Nation. In addition to the standard humanities &
sciences curriculum, classes in the Tsek'ene language are
taught. Governed by the Kwadacha Education Society.
Andreas Rohrbach, Principal

Kamloops: St. Ann's Academy
205 Columbia St., Kamloops, BC V2C 2S7
Tel: 250-372-5452; *Fax:* 250-372-5257
officeadmin@st-anns.ca
st-anns.ca
Grades: K.-12 *Enrollment:* 480
Shawn Chisholm, Principal
shawn.chisholm@st-anns.ca

Kelowna: Aberdeen Hall Preparatory School
950 Academy Way, Kelowna, BC V1V 3A4
Tel: 250-491-1270; *Fax:* 250-491-1289
info@aberdeenhall.com
www.aberdeenhall.com
www.facebook.com/AberdeenHallPS
twitter.com/aberdeenhallPS
Grades: Pre.-12 *Enrollment:* 320
Christopher H. Grieve, Head of School
christopher.grieve@aberdeenhall.com

Kelowna: Kelowna Waldorf School
429 Collett Rd., Kelowna, BC V1W 1K6
Tel: 250-764-4130; *Fax:* 250-764-4139
info@kelownawaldorf.org
www.kelownawaldorf.org
www.facebook.com/kelownawaldorfschool
Grades: K.-8 *Enrollment:* 128
EveLynn Debusschere, Principal
evelynn@kelownawaldorf.org

Kelowna: St. Joseph Elementary School
839 Sutherland Ave., Kelowna, BC V1Y 5X4
Tel: 250-763-3371; *Fax:* 250-763-2740
sjkoffice@cisnd.ca
www.stjosephkelowna.ca
www.facebook.com/SaintJosephCatholicElementarySchool
Grades: K.-7 *Enrollment:* 250
Lynn Fleck, Principal
lfleck@cisnd.ca

Kelowna: Studio 9 Independent School of the Arts
1180 Houghton Rd., Kelowna, BC V1X 2C9
Tel: 250-868-8816; *Fax:* 250-868-8836
www.studio9.ca
www.facebook.com/Studio9Kelowna
twitter.com/Studio9Kelowna
Grades: K - 12
C. Belliveau, Principal

Kispiox: Kispiox Community School
Also known as: Ans'Payaxw School Society
Old Name: Kispiox Junior Secondary School
1439 Mary Blackwater Dr., Kispiox, BC V0J 1Y4
Tel: 250-842-6148; *Fax:* 250-842-5799
info@kispioxschool.ca
kispioxschool.ca
Grades: K.-7 *Enrollment:* 117
Brian Muldon, Principal
bmuldon@kispioxschool.ca

Kitimat: St. Anthony's School
1750 Nalabila Blvd., Kitimat, BC V8C 1E6
Tel: 250-632-6313; *Fax:* 250-632-6317
staoffice@cispg.ca
www.stanthonysschoolkitimat.com
Grades: K.-9 *Enrollment:* 150 *Number of Employees:* 19
Katja Groves, Principal
staprincipal@cispg.ca

Ladysmith: Stu"ate Lelum Secondary School
P.O. Box 730
Ladysmith, BC V9G 1A5, Canada
Tel: 250-245-3522; *Fax:* 250-245-8263
www.facebook.com/140555322648015
Enrollment: 100
L. Merriman, Principal

Langley: Global Montessori School
19785 - 55A Ave., Langley, BC V3A 3X1
Tel: 604-534-1556; *Fax:* 604-532-4358
info@globalmontessorischool.com
globalmontessorischool.com
Grades: K - 8
Andrea Riegert, Head of School
andrear@globalmontessorischool.com
Karun Kumar, Director of Operations
karunk@globalmontessorischool.com

Langley: King's School
The King's Centre
P.O. Box 28
21783 - 76B Ave., Langley, BC V0X 1T0, Canada
Tel: 604-888-0969; *Fax:* 604-888-0977
school@tkc.edu
www.thekingsschool.org
Grades: K-12 *Enrollment:* 141
P. Thomas, Principal

Langley: Langley Montessori School
21488 Old Yale Rd., Langley, BC V3A 4M8
Tel: 604-532-5667; *Fax:* 604-532-5634
info@langleymontessori.ca
www.langleymontessori.ca
Other Information: Early Learning Centre Phone: 604-533-5664
www.facebook.com/LangleyMontessoriSchool
twitter.com/LangMontessori
Grades: Pre.-7
Kim Nichols, Principal

Langley: Whytecliff Agile Learning Centres
Langley School
20561 Logan Ave., Langley, BC V3A 7R3
Tel: 604-532-1268; *Fax:* 604-532-1269
walc@walc.ca
walc.ca
www.facebook.com/walc.ca
twitter.com/WhytecliffLearn
Grades: 8-12 *Enrollment:* 46 *Note:* Whytecliff Agile Learning
Centres are provincially accredited, independent schools for
boys & girls, aged 13-19, who face personal or behavioural
challenges. Many of the students have dropped out of school, or
have been excluded or expelled.
Angela Butler, Principal

Campuses
Whytecliff Agile Learning Centre - Burnaby
3450 Boundary Rd., Burnaby, BC V5M 4A5
Tel: 604-438-4451; *Fax:* 604-438-5572
Grades: 8-12

Lantzville: Aspengrove School
7660 Clark Dr., Lantzville, BC V0R 2H0
Tel: 250-390-2201; *Fax:* 250-390-2281
cgrunlund@aspengroveschool.ca
aspengroveschool.ca
www.facebook.com/AspengroveSchool
twitter.com/aspengrovenews
www.youtube.com/AspengroveSchool
Grades: JK-12 *Enrollment:* 190 *Note:* Accredited International
Baccalaureate programs for primary and middle years; core
academic subjects, as well as performing arts, physical and
outdoor education, community service.
Zinda Fitzgerald, Head of School

Lax Kw'Alaams: Coast Tsimshian Academy
11 Legaic St., Lax Kw'Alaams, BC V0V 1H0, Canada
Tel: 604-625-3207; *Fax:* 604-625-3425
ctahome@tsimshianacademy.com
www.tsimshianacademy.com
Grades: K-12 *Enrollment:* 152
S. Campbell, Principal

Lillooet: Fountainview Academy
P.O. Box 500
7615 Lytton-Lillooet Hwy., Lillooet, BC V0K 1V0
Tel: 250-256-5400; *Fax:* 250-256-5499
info@fountainview.ca
fountainviewacademy.ca
www.facebook.com/fountainviewacademy
www.youtube.com/user/fountainviewacademy
Grades: 10-12 *Enrollment:* 87
Baird Corrigan, Principal
bcorrigan@fountainview.ca

Lytton: Stein Valley Nlakapamux School
P.O. Box 300
Lytton, BC V0K 1Z0, Canada
Tel: 250-455-2522; *Fax:* 250-455-2512
Grades: K-12 *Enrollment:* 109
C. Holmes, Principal

Maple Ridge: Meadowridge School
12224 - 240th St., Maple Ridge, BC V4R 1N1, Canada
Tel: 604-467-4444; *Fax:* 604-467-4989
www.meadowridge.bc.ca
www.facebook.com/meadowridge
twitter.com/Meadowridge
www.linkedin.com/pub/meadowridge-school/2a/6a7/316
Grades: JK - 12 *Enrollment:* 450
H. Burke, Principal
hburke@meadowridge.bc.ca

Mill Bay: Brentwood College School (BCS)
2735 Mount Baker Rd., Mill Bay, BC V0R 2P1
Tel: 250-743-5521; *Fax:* 250-743-2911
admissions@brentwood.bc.ca
www.brentwood.bc.ca
www.facebook.com/brentwoodcollegeschool
twitter.com/BrentwoodNews/everything-brentwood-2
www.linkedin.com/groups/2561828

Grades: 9 - 12 *Enrollment:* 480 *Number of Employees:* 200
Note: Brentwood College School is a co-educational university prep school.
Bud Patel, Head of School
David Burton, Director of Finance

Mission: Seminary of Christ the King
General Delivery, Mission, BC V2V 4J2
Tel: 604-820-9969; *Fax:* 604-826-8725
frpeterosb@gmail.com
www.sck.ca

Grades: 8 - 12

Nanaimo: Discover Montessori School
1111 Dufferin Cres., Nanaimo, BC V9S 2B5
Tel: 250-760-0615; *Fax:* 250-753-0163
office@dm-school.ca
public.dm-school.ca

Grades: K.-8
Diana Chalmers, Principal

Campuses
Parksville Campus
1223 Smithers Rd., Parksville, BC V9P 2C1
Tel: 250-760-0615

Nanaimo: The High School at Vancouver Island University
Also known as: Malaspina International High School
900 Fifth St., Nanaimo, BC V9R 5S5, Canada
Tel: 250-740-6317; *Fax:* 250-740-6470
highschool@viu.ca
www2.viu.ca/highschool
www.facebook.com/144549182292155
twitter.com/MHS_at_VIU
www.flickr.com/photos/vancouverislanduniversity/
Grades: 10-12 *Enrollment:* 121
T. Lewis, Principal

Nelson: Nelson Waldorf School
3648 Silverking Ski Hill Rd., Nelson, BC V1L 5P9
Tel: 250-352-6919; *Fax:* 250-352-6887
info@nelsonwaldorf.org
www.nelsonwaldorf.org
Grades: K.-8 *Note:* The school offers Waldorf education to children in the West Kootenay area.
Donna Switzer, Principal & Director, Education
donna.switzer@nelsonwaldorf.org
Diana Finley, Vice-Principal
diana.finley@nelsonwaldorf.org
Keitha Patton, Secretary
keitha.patton@nelsonwaldorf.org

Nelson: St. Joseph's School
523 Mill St., Nelson, BC V1L 4S2
Tel: 250-352-3041; *Fax:* 250-352-9188
office@stjosephnelson.ca
www.stjosephnelson.ca
www.facebook.com/St.JosephNelson
Grades: K.-8 *Enrollment:* 122
Marlene Suter, Principal
msuter@cisnd.ca
Yvonne Vulcano, Secretary
yvulcano@cisnd.ca

New Westminster: Purpose Independent Secondary School
Also known as: Purpose Young Adult Learning Centre
40 Begbie St., New Westminster, BC V3M 3L9, Canada
Tel: 604-526-2522; *Fax:* 604-526-6546
info@purposesociety.org
purposesecondary.org
Grades: 10 - 12 *Note:* The program at The Purpose School is designed for students, aged fifteen to nineteen, who are unable to succeed in the traditional school system. A Purpose Secondary School education leads to a Standard Dogwood Diploma.
Phill Esau, Principal
phill.esau@purposesociety.org
Jacquie Robertson, Student Services\Child Care Worker
jacquie.robertson@purposesociety.org

New Westminster: Urban Academy
101 Third St., New Westminster, BC V3L 2P9
Tel: 604-524-2211; *Fax:* 604-524-2711
admin@urbanacademy.ca
www.urbanacademy.ca
www.facebook.com/urbanacademybc
twitter.com/urbanacademybc
www.linkedin.com/company/urban-academy
www.instagram.com/urbanacademybc
Grades: JK-12 *Enrollment:* 115
Cheryle Beaumont, Head of School

North Vancouver: Bodwell High School
955 Harbourside Dr., North Vancouver, BC V7P 3S4, Canada
Tel: 604-924-5056; *Fax:* 604-924-5058
onlineinquiry@bodwell.edu
www.bodwell.edu/highschool
www.facebook.com/bodwell.highschool
www.flickr.com/photos/bodwellcollege/collections
Grades: 8 - 12 *Enrollment:* 450 *Note:* Bodwell High School is a co-educational day & boarding school.
Mark Lewis, B.Ed., M.A., Principal
Cathy Lee, B.S.Sc., M.S.W., Director, Admissions
Stephen Goobie, BSc.(Hons.), B.Ed., M.Ed., Director, Residence

North Vancouver: Brockton School
3467 Duval Rd., North Vancouver, BC V7J 3E8
Tel: 604-929-9201; *Fax:* 604-929-9501
info@brocktonschool.com
www.brocktonschool.com
www.facebook.com/brocktonschool
twitter.com/brockton_school
www.instagram.com/brocktonschool
Grades: JK-12 *Enrollment:* 225
Karen McCulla, Head of School

North Vancouver: North Star Montessori Elementary School
1325 East Keith Rd., North Vancouver, BC V7J 1J3
Tel: 604-980-1205; *Fax:* 604-980-1805
admin@northstarmontessori.ca
northstarmontessori.ca
Grades: Pre. - 8

North Vancouver: Vancouver Waldorf School (VWS)
2725 St Christophers Rd. North, North Vancouver, BC V7K 2B6
Tel: 604-985-7435; *Fax:* 604-985-4948
reception@vws.ca
www.vws.ca
www.facebook.com/vancouverwaldorfschool
twitter.com/vws_waldorf
Grades: Preschool - 12 *Note:* Vancouver Waldorf School integrates the movement arts & artistic activities throughout the curriculum.
Brian Gohlke, Business Manager
Jeffrey Onans, Pedagogical Manager
Feza Sanigok, Development Manager
Fiona Thatcher, Admissions Manager, 604-985-7435, ext. 200
admissions@vws.ca

Oliver: Sen Pok Chin School
1006 McKinney Rd., Oliver, BC V0H 1T8, Canada
Tel: 250-498-2019; *Fax:* 250-498-3096
office@senpokchin.com
www.senpokchin.com
Grades: JK-7 *Enrollment:* 85
R. Laurie, Principal
principal@senpokchin.com

Port Alberni: Haahuupayak School
6000 Santu Dr., Port Alberni, BC V9Y 7M2, Canada
Tel: 250-724-5542; *Fax:* 250-724-7335
ha-ak-sap@hotmail.com
www.haahuupayak.com
Grades: K-6 *Enrollment:* 79
Tricia McAuley, Principal

Port Coquitlam: Hope Lutheran Christian School
Port Coquitlam Campus
3151 York St., Port Coquitlam, BC V3B 4A7, Canada
Tel: 604-942-5322; *Fax:* 604-942-5311
www.hopelcs.ca
www.facebook.com/hopelcs
twitter.com/hopelcs
Grades: K.-6
Susan Eisner, Principal

Campuses
Pitt Meadows Campus
18477 Old Dewdney Trunk Rd., Pitt Meadows, BC V3& 2R9, Canada
Tel: 604-457-4673
Grades: 7-12
Dan Mathew, Principal

Port Hardy: Avalon Adventist Junior Academy
P.O. Box 974
Port Hardy, BC V0N 2P0, Canada
Tel: 250-949-8243; *Fax:* 250-949-6770
avalonacad@hotmail.com
www.aaja.ca
Grades: K - 10
Clifford Wood, Principal
wagonwoody2003@yahoo.ca

Prince George: Sacred Heart School
785 Patricia Blvd., Prince George, BC V2L 3V5
Tel: 250-563-5201; *Fax:* 250-563-5201
shspg@netbistro.com
www.shspg.com
www.facebook.com/sacredheartschoolpg
Grades: K.-7 *Enrollment:* 150 *Number of Employees:* 9
Rebecca Gilbert, Principal
rgilbert@cispg.ca

Prince George: St. Mary's School
1088 Gillett St., Prince George, BC V2M 2V3
Tel: 250-563-7502; *Fax:* 250-563-7818
www.stmaryspg.org
Grades: K.-7 *Enrollment:* 199
Brent Arsenault, Principal
barsenault@cispg.ca
Jacqueline Boyes, Secretary
jboyes@cispg.ca

Prince George: Westside Academy
3791 Hwy. 16 West, Prince George, BC V2N 5P8
Tel: 250-964-9600
office@westsideacademy.ca
www.westsideacademy.ca
Grades: K - 12 *Note:* Westside Academy is a ministry of Westside Family Fellowship.
Donna Rosenbaum, High School Principal
donna.rosenbaum@westsideacademy.ca
Sherry Breck, Elementary Principal
sherry.breck@westsideacademy.ca

Prince Rupert: Annunciation School
627 - 5 Ave. West, Prince Rupert, BC V8J 1V1
Tel: 250-624-5873; *Fax:* 250-627-4486
www.annunciationpr.ca
Grades: K.-8
Laura Lowther, Principal

Quesnel: St. Ann's School
150 Sutherland Ave., Quesnel, BC V2J 2J5
Tel: 250-992-6237; *Fax:* 250-992-6234
office.stanns@shawcable.com
www.stannsschool.ca
Grades: K.-7 *Enrollment:* 71
Tara Milley, Principal

Richmond: BC Muslim School
12300 Blundell Rd., Richmond, BC V6W 1B3, Canada
Tel: 604-270-2511; *Fax:* 604-270-2679
admin@bcmuslimschool.ca
www.bcmuslimschool.ca
Grades: K - 7 *Note:* BC Muslim School offers an accredited Arabic program.
Farida Wahab, Principal

Richmond: Choice School
Main Campus
20451 Westminster Hwy. North, Richmond, BC V6V 1B3
Tel: 604-273-2418; *Fax:* 604-273-2419
info@choiceschool.org
www.choiceschool.org
www.facebook.com/choiceschool.org
twitter.com/RayProbyn
Grades: Pre-K. - 8 *Note:* Choice School offers gifted education to talented & gifted children.
Ray Probyn, Principal

Richmond: Richmond Jewish Day School (RJDS)
8760 No. 5 Rd., Richmond, BC V6Y 2V4
Tel: 604-275-3393; *Fax:* 604-275-9322
info@rjds.ca
www.rjds.ca
www.facebook.com/RichmondJewishDaySchool
twitter.com/myrjds
Grades: Preschool - 7 *Note:* Richmond Jewish Day School incorporates Hebrew & Judaic studies with the British Columbia curriculum.
Abba Brodt, Principal
abrodt@rjds.ca
Mary Jane Brown, Business Manager
mjbrown@rjds.ca

Roberts Creek: Sun Haven Waldorf School
1341 Margaret Rd., Roberts Creek, BC V0N 2W2
Tel: 604-741-0949
office@sunhavenschool.ca
www.sunhaven.ca
www.facebook.com/sunhavenwaldorfschool
Grades: Pre. - 8
Catherine Solomon, School Administrator

Shawnigan Lake: Dwight International School
2371 Shawnigan Lake Rd., Shawnigan Lake, BC V0R 2W5
Tel: 250-929-0506
admissions@dwightcanada.org
dwightinternational.com
www.facebook.com/dwightcanada
twitter.com/dwightcanada
www.linkedin.com/company/dwight-school-canada
Grades: 6-12
Jerry Salvador, Head of School
Christine Bater, Contact, Admissions Office

Shawnigan Lake: Shawnigan Lake School
1975 Renfrew Rd., Shawnigan Lake, BC V0R 2W0
Tel: 250-743-5516; *Fax:* 250-743-6200
info@sls.bc.ca
www.shawnigan.ca
www.facebook.com/shawnigan
twitter.com/shawnigan
www.linkedin.com/groups/830377
www.youtube.com/user/shawnigantube
Grades: 8-12 *Enrollment:* 454
Sara Blair, Headmaster
sblair@shawnigan.ca

Smithers: Ebenezer Canadian Reformed School
P.O. Box 3700
1685 Viewmount Rd. North, Smithers, BC V0J 2N0, Canada
Tel: 250-847-3492; *Fax:* 250-847-3912
office@ebenezerschool.com
www.ebenezerschool.com
Grades: K-12 *Enrollment:* 133
D. Stoffels, Principal

Smithers: Moricetown Elementary School
#2 - 205 Beaver Rd., Smithers, BC V0J 2N1
Tel: 250-847-3166; *Fax:* 250-877-5092
www.moricetown.ca
Grades: Elementary *Enrollment:* 49

Smithers: St. Joseph's School
P.O. Box 454
4054 Broadway Ave., Smithers, BC V0J 2N0
Tel: 250-847-9414; *Fax:* 250-847-9402
stj@cispg.ca
www.stjosephsschool.ca
Grades: K.-7 *Enrollment:* 191
Rosemary McKenzie, Principal

South Hazelton: Gitsegukla Elementary School
21 Seymour Ave., RR#1, South Hazelton, BC V0J 2R0, Canada
Tel: 250-849-5739; *Fax:* 250-849-5276
www.gitsegukla.org
Grades: K-7 *Enrollment:* 60
Tuskasa Sakata, Principal

Squamish: Cedar Valley Waldorf School
P.O. Box 5356
38265 Westway Ave., Squamish, BC V8B 0C2
Tel: 604-898-3287
info@cedarvalleyschool.com
www.cedarvalleyschool.com
www.facebook.com/squamishwaldorf
Grades: Elem.

Surrey: Cornerstone Montessori School
14724 - 84 Ave., Surrey, BC V3S 2M5, Canada
Tel: 604-599-9918; *Fax:* 604-597-0468
corstone@telus.net
cornerstone-montessori.ca
Grades: K-7 *Enrollment:* 121
Rita Gausman, Principal

Surrey: Dogwood School
10752 - 157th St., Surrey, BC V4N 1K6
Tel: 604-581-8111; *Fax:* 604-581-8219
dogwood@SurreySchools.ca
www.surreyschools.ca
twitter.com/Dogwood159
Grades: 3 - 12
Lys Paredes, Principal
Paredes_l@surreyschools.ca

Surrey: Iqra School
14590 - 116A Ave., Surrey, BC V3R 2V1
Tel: 604-583-7530; *Fax:* 604-583-7510
info@iqraschool.com
www.iqraschool.com
Grades: K.-8 *Enrollment:* 434
Randa El-Khatib, Principal

Surrey: Khalsa School (Surrey)
6933 - 124th St., Surrey, BC V3W 3W6, Canada
Tel: 604-591-2248; *Fax:* 604-591-3396
info@khalsaschool.ca
www.khalsaschool.ca
Grades: K.-10 *Enrollment:* 1468

Surrey: Relevant Schools Society
Relevant High School
18620 56 Ave., Surrey, BC V3S 1G1, Canada
Tel: 604-574-4736; *Fax:* 604-576-9746
relevantschool@shawlink.ca
relevantschoolssociety.ca
Number of Schools: 2 *Grades:* 8 - 12 *Note:* Relevant High School is coeducational, non-denominational secondary school.

Schools
Diamond Elementary
18620 56 Ave., Surrey, BC V3S 1G1, Canada
Tel: 604-576-1146; *Fax:* 604-576-9746
diamondschool@shawlink.ca
Grades: K-7 *Enrollment:* 172
Jeanne Zimmerman, Principal

Surrey: Roots & Wings Montessori
Also known as: Roots & Wings Montessori Farm School
15250 - 54A Ave., Surrey, BC V3S 6T4, Canada
Tel: 604-510-2588
admin@rootsandwingsbc.com
www.rootsandwingsbc.com
www.facebook.com/rootsandwingsbc
www.youtube.com/user/rootsandwingsbc
Number of Schools: 3 *Grades:* Pre.; K.-9 *Number of Employees:* 20 *Note:* Primary Montessori for children, ages 3 to 5; childcare, ages 4 months to 5; elementary Montessori farm school, ages 6 to 12; secondary ages 12 to 15.
Kristin Cassie, Principal, 604-961-5713
info@rootsandwingsbc.com
Véronique Bodart, Vice-Principal
bodartv@hotmail.com
Raman Dosanj, Registrar

Campuses
Hazelmere School
Camp McLean
20315 - 16 Ave., Langley, BC V2Z 1W5, Canada
Tel: 604-510-2588
Grades: 1-9 *Note:* The intermediate, senior, & secondary programs are designed for students between the ages of 6 & 15.

Surrey: Southridge School
2656 - 160 St., Surrey, BC V3S 0B7, Canada
Tel: 604-535-5056; *Fax:* 604-535-3676
www.southridge.bc.ca
www.facebook.com/336018147405
twitter.com/SouthridgeNews
Grades: 8-12 *Enrollment:* 680 *Number of Employees:* 103
M. Ayotte, Head of Senior School
mayotte@southridge.bc.ca

Surrey: Surrey Muslim School
#119, 7475 - 135 St., Surrey, BC V3W 0M8
Tel: 604-599-6608; *Fax:* 604-599-6790
administration@surreymuslimschool.ca
www.surreymuslimschool.ca
Grades: K - 7
Ebrahim Bawa, Acting Principal
vp.surreymuslimschool@gmail.com

Tsawwassen: Southpointe Academy
1900 - 56 St., Tsawwassen, BC V4L 2B1, Canada
Tel: 604-948-8826; *Fax:* 604-948-8853
info@spacademy.ca
www.southpointeacademy.ca
www.facebook.com/SouthpointeAcademy
Grades: K-12 *Enrollment:* 425
Bruce Griffioen, Headmaster
bruce.griffioen@spacademy.ca

Vancouver: Canadian College
#200, 1050 Alberni St., Vancouver, BC V6E 1A3, Canada
Tel: 604-688-9366
www.canadiancollege.com
www.facebook.com/Canadian.College
twitter.com/canadiancollege
www.instagram.com/canadiancollege
Enrollment: 300
Lane Clark, CEO
Shaun Macleod, Academic Director

Vancouver: Century High School (CHS)
#200, 1788 West Broadway, Vancouver, BC V6J 1Y1
Tel: 604-730-8138; *Fax:* 604-731-9542
admission@centuryhighschool.ca
www.centuryhighschool.ca
Grades: 8 - 12

Vancouver: Columbia College
438 Terminal Ave., Vancouver, BC V6A 0C1, Canada
Tel: 604-683-8360; *Fax:* 604-682-7191
admin@columbiacollege.ca
www.columbiacollege.ca
www.facebook.com/cc.vancouver.bc
twitter.com/ccvancouver
www.youtube.com/user/ColumbiaCollegeTV
Enrollment: 57 *Note:* A liberal arts college offering 1st & 2nd year university transfer courses, associate degrees, university preparation programmes, adult secondary school completion, & English language instruction geared to international students.
Dr. Trevor Toone, Principal

Vancouver: Core Education & Fine Arts (CEFA)
2946 Commercial Dr., Vancouver, BC V5N 4C9
Tel: 604-879-2332; *Fax:* 604-879-2330
vancouver@cefa.ca
www.cefa.ca
www.facebook.com/cefaearlylearning
Grades: Pre./K.
Natacha V. Beim, Founder

Campuses
Burnaby - Brentwood Campus
4664 Lougheed Hwy., #LM 100, Burnaby, BC V5C 3Z5
Tel: 604-565-3333
brentwood@cefa.ca
cefa.ca/find-school/burnaby-brentwood

Burnaby - Canada Way Campus
4970 Canada Way, Burnaby, BC V5G 1M4
Tel: 604-299-2373; *Fax:* 604-299-2378
cefa.ca/find-school/canada-way
Leanna Rasmussen, Manager
leannarasmussen@cefa.ca

Burnaby - Kingsway Campus
4021 Kingsway, Burnaby, BC V5H 1Y9
Tel: 604-568-8808; *Fax:* 604-299-2378
kingsway@cefa.ca
cefa.ca/find-school/burnaby-kingsway

Coquitlam Campus
#201, 3380 David Ave., Coquitlam, BC V3E 0J5
Tel: 604-474-0877
coquitlam@cefa.ca
cefa.ca/find-school/coquitlam

Kelowna - McKay Campus
#100, 590 McKay Ave., Kelowna, BC V1Y 5A8
Tel: 236-420-3868
kelowna@cefa.ca
cefa.ca/find-school/kelowna-mckay

Langley - Walnut Grove Campus
#100, 19950 - 88th Ave. East, Langley, BC V1M 0A5
Tel: 604-881-2332; *Fax:* 604-881-2338
langley@cefa.ca
cefa.ca/find-school/langley-walnut-grove

Langley - Willowbrook Campus
20510 Langley Bypass, Langley, BC V3A 6K8
Tel: 604-533-2287
willowbrook@cefa.ca
cefa.ca/find-school/langley-willowbrook

New Westminster Campus
725 Carnarvon St., New Westminster, BC V3M 1E6
Tel: 604-777-0053; *Fax:* 604-777-3053
newwestminster@cefa.ca
cefa.ca/find-school/new-westminster

North Vancouver Campus
#402, 935 Marine Dr., North Vancouver, BC V7P 1S3
Tel: 604-929-2332; *Fax:* 604-929-2303
northvancouver@cefa.ca
cefa.ca/find-school/north-vancouver

Richmond - City Centre Campus
7931 Alderbridge Way, #B, Richmond, BC V6X 2A4
Tel: 604-279-1818
richmondcitycentre@cefa.ca
cefa.ca/find-school/richmond-city-centre

Richmond - Crestwood Campus
#120, 13700 International Pl., Richmond, BC V6V 2X8
Tel: 604-273-0118
crestwood@cefa.ca
cefa.ca/find-school/richmond-crestwood

Richmond South Campus
#160, 10811 No. 4 Rd., Richmond, BC V7A 2Z5
Tel: 604-275-2332; *Fax:* 604-288-5065
richmond@cefa.ca
cefa.ca/find-school/richmond

South Surrey - Morgan Crossing Campus
15355 - 24 Ave., #D400, Surrey, BC V4A 2H9
Tel: 604-385-3441
morgancrossing@cefa.ca
cefa.ca/find-school/south-surrey-morgan-crossing

South Surrey - Panorama Campus
#100, 5446 152nd St., Surrey, BC V3S 5J9
Tel: 604-449-2332
southsurrey@cefa.ca
cefa.ca/find-school/surrey-panorama

Surrey - Fleetwood Campus
1 - 16050 Fraser Hwy., Surrey, BC V4N 0G3
Tel: 604-593-2650
fleetwood@cefa.ca
cefa.ca/find-school/surrey-fleetwood

Surrey - Guildford Campus
#100 - 10172 152A St., Surrey, BC V3R 1J7
Tel: 604-589-2332
guildford@cefa.ca
cefa.ca/find-school/surrey-guildford

Vancouver - Cambie Campus
Also known as: CEFA - Early Learning Cambie
8685/8687 Yukon St., Vancouver, BC V5X 4V1
Tel: 604-325-4417
cambie@cefa.ca
cefa.ca/find-school/vancouver-cambie-2
Manpreet Mann, Principal

Vancouver: Crofton House School
3200 - 41 Ave. West, Vancouver, BC V6N 3E1, Canada
Tel: 604-263-3255; *Fax:* 604-263-4941
www.croftonhouse.ca
Grades: Elem./Sec.; girls *Enrollment:* 667
Patricia J. Dawson, Head of School
pdawson@croftonhouse.ca
Susan Mueller, Director of Business Administration
Bill McCracken, Director of Admissions
Patricia Vasseur, Director of Advancement
Ryan Melsom, Director of Communications & Marketing

Vancouver: Fraser Academy
2294 - 10 Ave. West, Vancouver, BC V6K 2H8, Canada
Tel: 604-736-5575; *Fax:* 604-736-5578
info@fraseracademy.ca
www.fraseracademy.ca
www.facebook.com/fraseracademy
twitter.com/fraseracademy
www.youtube.com/fraseracademyschool
Grades: 1-12 *Enrollment:* 250
Maureen Steltman, Head of School
msteltman@fraseracademy.ca
Frans Ang, Business Manager
fang@fraseracademy.ca

Vancouver: King David High School
5718 Willow St., Vancouver, BC V5Z 4S9, Canada
Tel: 604-263-9700; *Fax:* 604-263-4848
kdhs.org
www.facebook.com/kdhsvancouver
twitter.com/KDHSVancouver
Grades: 8-12 *Enrollment:* 140 *Note:* King David High School
(KDHS) is a pluralistic, community, co-educational, Jewish high
school in the Oakridge district of Vancouver.
Russ Klein, Head of School
rklein@kdhs.org

Vancouver: Madrona School Society
Primary & Junior School
2040 West 10th Ave., Vancouver, BC V6J 2B3
Tel: 604-396-1605
www.madronaschool.com
Grades: K-7
Paul Felts, Principal
paul@madronaschool.com

Campuses
Senior School
530 Hornby St., 2nd & 4th Fl., Vancouver, BC V6C 2E7
Tel: 604-499-7303
Grades: 8-10
Eric O'Donnell, Head of School
eric@madronaschool.com
Judy O'Donnell, Director, Admissions
judy@madronaschool.com

Chelsea Chevalier, Vice-Principal, Senior School
chelsea@madronaschool.com

Vancouver: Pacific Spirit School (PSS)
12620 Westminster Hwy., Vancouver, BC V6V 1A1, Canada
Tel: 604-222-1900; *Fax:* 604-222-1934
info@pacificspiritschool.org
www.pacificspiritschool.org
www.facebook.com/Pacificspiritschool
Grades: K-7 *Enrollment:* 227 *Note:* Pacific Spirit School is the
flagship for the New Learning Society, which promotes and
supports the growth of the whole child.
Ingrid Price, Ph.D., Executive Director
Ann-Marie Gasher, B.GS., Business Manager

Vancouver: Pacific Torah Institute (PTI)
5750 Oak St., 4th Fl., Vancouver, BC V6M 2V9
Tel: 604-261-1502; *Fax:* 604-261-1526
office@ptibc.org
www.ptibc.org
Grades: 8-12 *Enrollment:* 16 *Number of Employees:* 12
Rabbi Noam Abramchik, Head, Pacific Torah Institute
rabbia@ptibc.org
Rabbi Aaron Kamin, Dean, Beis Midrash Program
rabbik@ptibc.org
Colin Cameron, Principal, General Studies, 778-998-5471
ccameron@ptibc.org

Vancouver: Pattison High School
981 Nelson St., Vancouver, BC V6Z 3B6
Tel: 604-608-8788; *Fax:* 604-608-8789
info@pattisonhighschool.ca
www.pattisonhighschool.ca
www.facebook.com/pattisonhighschool
twitter.com/pattisonhigh
www.linkedin.com/company/pattison-high-school
www.youtube.com/user/pattisonhigh
Grades: 8-12 *Enrollment:* 170
Daniel Chowne, Principal
principal@pattisonhighschool.ca

Vancouver: Royal Canadian College
8610 Ash St., Vancouver, BC V6P 3M2, Canada
Tel: 604-738-2221; *Fax:* 604-738-2282
info@royalcanadiancollege.com
www.royalcanadiancollege.com
Grades: 8-12 *Enrollment:* 52
Leon King, President

Vancouver: St. George's School
4175 - 29th Ave. West, Vancouver, BC V6S 1V1
Tel: 604-224-1304; *Fax:* 604-224-7066
info@stgeorges.bc.ca
www.stgeorges.bc.ca
www.facebook.com/stgeorgesbc
twitter.com/saintsbc
www.youtube.com/saintscommunications
Grades: 1-12 *Enrollment:* 1150 *Note:* Day and boarding school
for boys
Dr. Tom Matthews, Headmaster
tmatthews@stgeorges.bc.ca
Greg Devenish, Principal - Junior School, 604-222-5892
gdevenish@stgeorges.bc.ca
Shawn Lawrence, Principal - Senior School, 604-221-3618
slawrence@stgeorges.bc.ca
Barry Mitchell, Director of Finance, 604-221-3886
bmitchell@stgeorges.bc.ca

Vancouver: St. John's International
1885 West Broadway, Vancouver, BC V6J 1Y5, Canada
Tel: 604-683-4572; *Fax:* 604-683-4679
info@stjohnsis.com
www.stjohnsis.com
Grades: 8-12 *Enrollment:* 76

Vancouver: St. John's School
2215 - 10 Ave. West, Vancouver, BC V6K 2J1, Canada
Tel: 604-732-4434; *Fax:* 604-732-1074
admissions@stjohns.bc.ca
www.stjohns.bc.ca
www.facebook.com/StJohnsSchoolVancouver
twitter.com/stjohnssociety
Grades: JK - 12 *Enrollment:* 342 *Note:* University prep school
Stephen L.M. Hutchison, Head of School
shutchison@stjohns.bc.ca

Vancouver: Stratford Hall
3000 Commercial Dr., Vancouver, BC V5N 4E2, Canada
Tel: 604-436-0608; *Fax:* 604-436-0616
info@stratfordhall.ca
www.stratfordhall.ca
twitter.com/Stratford_Hall
Grades: K-12 *Enrollment:* 370

J. McConnell, Principal

Vancouver: Torah High School - Vancouver
Schara Tzedeck Synagogue
3476 Oak St., Vancouver, BC V6H 2L8
Tel: 604-736-7607
www.vancouver.torahhigh.org
Grades: 8-12 *Note:* Torah High offers courses in Religious
Studies, Hebrew Language, Philosophy, Political Science,
Nutrition, Arts & Interdisciplinary Studies for students attending
public or private secondary schools. Classes take place at King
David High School.
Rabbi Stephen Berger, Director, Education

Vancouver: Vancouver Hebrew Academy (VHA)
1545 West 62nd Ave., Vancouver, BC V6P 2E8, Canada
Tel: 604-266-1245; *Fax:* 604-264-0648
vha@vhebrewacademy.com
www.vhebrewacademy.com
Grades: Preschool - 10 *Note:* Vancouver Hebrew Academy is an
Orthodox Jewish school which offers Judaic & general studies.
Rabbi Don Pacht, Head of School
dpacht@vhebrewacademy.com
Alaina Smith, Principal, General Studies
asmith@vhebrewacademy.com
Rabbi Eleazar Durden, Principal, Judaic Studies
ejdurden@vhebrewacademy.com
Nancy Scambler, Administrative Secretary

Vancouver: Vancouver Montessori School
8650 Barnard St., Vancouver, BC V6P 5G5, Canada
Tel: 604-261-0315
www.vancouvermontessorischool.com
Grades: Preschool - Elementary *Note:* Preschool (Casa)
programs are available for three to six year old children.
Elementary classes are offered for children from age six to
twelve.
Prasannata Runkel, Principal
Roni (Bamendine) Jones, Administrator, School Operations
Chrystle Williams, Registrar & Administration Assistant

Vancouver: Vancouver Talmud Torah School (VTT)
998 West 26th Ave., Vancouver, BC V5Z 2G1, Canada
Tel: 604-736-7307; *Fax:* 604-736-9754
info@talmudtorah.com
www.talmudtorah.com
Grades: Preschool - 7 *Enrollment:* 500 *Note:* Vancouver Talmud
Torah School is a Jewish day school.
Cathy Lowenstein, Head of School
Leigh Ariel, Principal of Primary Grades
Rabbi Matthew Bellas, Principal of Judaic Studies/School Rabbi
Candice Gartry, Chief Financial Officer
Gaby Lutrin, Director, Preschool
Jessica Neville, Senior Principal, Intermediate Grades & Student
Services
Jennifer Shecter-Balin, Director, Admissions & Communications

Vancouver: West Point Grey Academy (WPGA)
4125 West 8th Ave., Vancouver, BC V6R 4P9
Tel: 604-222-8750; *Fax:* 604-222-8756
info@wpga.ca
www.wpga.ca
Other Information: 604-224-1332 (Phone, Senior School)
www.facebook.com/westpointgreyacademy
twitter.com/wpgadotca
www.linkedin.com/school/west-point-grey-academy
Grades: Pre. - 12 *Enrollment:* 905 *Note:* West Point Grey
Academy demonstrates a belief in Humanism in its community of
Renaissance learners. The pre-kindergarten class is for four
year old children.
Robert Standerwick, Chair
boardchair@wpga.ca
Clive S.K. Austin, Headmaster
headmaster@wpga.ca
Stephen Anthony, Head, Senior School
headmaster@wpga.ca

Vancouver: Westside Montessori Academy
Casa dei Bambini & Elementary School
3075 Slocan St., Vancouver, BC V5M 3E4
Tel: 604-434-9611
media@westsidemontessoriacademy.ca
www.westsidemontessoriacademy.ca
www.facebook.com/WestsideMontessoriAcademy
twitter.com/WesMonAcademy
www.instagram.com/westside_montessori_academy
Grades: Pre.-7 *Enrollment:* 125 *Number of Employees:* 25 *Note:*
Westside Montessori Academy aims to provide a supportive
educational environment designed to help students reach their
full social & academic potential. Located in Vancouver at the
Italian Cultural Centre. General inquiries:
office@westsidemontessoriacademy.ca

Sarah Gatiss-Brown, Co-Founder, Principal & Director, Admissions
info@westsidemontessoriacademy.ca
Lorelei Poulin, Secretary
office@westsidemontessoriacademy.ca
Pamela Woronko, Elementary Principal & Co-Directress, Upper Elementary
pworonko@westsidemontessoriacademy.ca
Catherine Williams, Elementary Vice-Principal & Co-Directress, Upper Elementary
cwilliams@westsidemontessoriacademy.ca

Vancouver: The Westside School
788 Beatty St., Vancouver, BC V6B 2M1
Tel: 604-687-8021; *Fax:* 604-687-8024
www.thewestsideschools.ca
Grades: K - 12
Graham Baldwin, President & Chief Executive Officer

Vancouver: York House School
4176 Alexandra St., Vancouver, BC V6J 2V6, Canada
Tel: 604-736-6551
webmaster@yorkhouse.ca
www.yorkhouse.ca
www.facebook.com/yorkhouseschool
twitter.com/yorkhouseschool
www.youtube.com/yorkhousedotca
Grades: K-12 *Enrollment:* 598
Shelley Lammie, Principal
slammie@yorkhouse.ca

Vernon: St. James School
2700 - 28 Ave., Vernon, BC V1T 1V7
Tel: 250-542-4081; *Fax:* 250-542-5696
sjschoolvern@shaw.ca
www.stjamesvernon.com
Grades: K.-7 *Enrollment:* 106
Paul Rossetti, Principal
principalsjs@shaw.ca

Victoria: Artemis Place Secondary
#103, 2610 Douglas St., Victoria, BC V8T 4M1
artemisplace.org/PlaceForGirls/secondary-school
Grades: 9 - 12

Victoria: Brookes Westshore
Brookes Education Group
1945 Sooke Rd., Victoria, BC V9B 1W2
Tel: 250-929-0506
admissions@westshore.brookes.org
westshore.brookes.org
www.facebook.com/BrookesWestshore
twitter.com/BrookesEdu
www.instagram.com/brookeseducationgroup
Grades: 6-12 *Enrollment:* 300 *Note:* Private co-educational day & boarding school
Andrea Spinner, Head of School & Principal
Linda Bayes, Vice-Principal, Academics
Cathy Mingo, Vice-Principal, Student Life
Terry Downton, Business Manager & Director, Human Resources
tdownton@westshore.brookes.org
Sheri Onushko, Contact
sonushko@westshore.brookes.org
Lucy Kenneally, Director, Global Communications
lkenneally@brookes.org

Victoria: Christ Church Cathedral School (CCCS)
912 Vancouver St., Victoria, BC V8V 3V7, Canada
Tel: 250-383-5125; *Fax:* 250-383-5128
cathedralschool@cathedralschool.ca
cathedralschool.ca
www.facebook.com/ChristChurchCathedralSchool
vimeo.com/cccathedralschool
Grades: K.-8 *Enrollment:* 185 *Note:* Christ Church Cathedral School is an Anglican school for Kindergarten to Grade 8. Junior Kindergarten: 1670 Richardson St., Victoria, V8S 1R4, 250-383-5132.
Stuart Hall, Head of School
stuart.hall@cathedralschool.ca

Victoria: Discovery School
4052 Wilkinson Rd., Victoria, BC V8Z 5A5
Tel: 250-595-7765; *Fax:* 250-595-7712
principal@discoveryschool.ca
www.discoveryschool.ca
Grades: 1 - 12

Victoria: Glenlyon Norfolk School (GNS)
801 Bank St., Victoria, BC V8S 4A8, Canada
Tel: 250-370-6800; *Fax:* 250-370-6840
admissions@mygns.ca
www.mygns.ca
www.facebook.com/mygns
twitter.com/glenlyonnorfolk
www.youtube.com/user/glenlyonnorfolk
Grades: K-12 *Enrollment:* 670
Glenn Zederayko, Head of School
gzederayko@mygns.ca
Chad Holtum, Deputy Head of School
choltum@mygns.ca

Victoria: Maria Montessori Academy
1841 Fairburn Dr., Victoria, BC V8N 1P8, Canada
Tel: 250-479-4746; *Fax:* 250-744-1925
office@mariamontessoriacademy.net
mariamontessoriacademy.net
Grades: Pre.-12 *Enrollment:* 95
Patrick Vincentine, Principal

Victoria: Oak and Orca Bioregional School
2738 Higgins St., Victoria, BC V8T 3N1
Tel: 250-383-6609; *Fax:* 877-544-3427
yj383@victoria.tc.ca
oakandorca.ca
Grades: Pre. - 10

Victoria: St. Margaret's School (SMS)
1080 Lucas Ave., Victoria, BC V8X 3P7, Canada
Tel: 250-479-7171; *Fax:* 250-479-8976
info@stmarg.ca
www.stmarg.ca
www.facebook.com/saintmargarets
twitter.com/st_margarets
www.flickr.com/photos/st_margarets
Grades: K-12 *Enrollment:* 353 *Note:* An independent all-girls school.
Cathy Thornicroft, Head of School, 250-479-7171
Mary Lue Emmerson, Principal, Foundation Years
Megan Hedderick, Principal, Senior Years, 250-479-7171, ext. 2126
Alia Zawacki, Principal, Middle Years

Victoria: St. Michael's University School
3400 Richmond Rd., Victoria, BC V8P 4P5, Canada
Tel: 250-592-2411; *Fax:* 250-592-2812
info@smus.ca
www.smus.ca
www.facebook.com/yoursmus
twitter.com/gosmus
Number of Schools: 3 *Grades:* 9-12 *Enrollment:* 923
Bob Snowden, Head of School
bob.snowden@smus.ca

Victoria: Selkirk Montessori School
2970 Jutland Rd., Victoria, BC V8T 5K2, Canada
Tel: 250-384-3414; *Fax:* 250-384-3449
office@selkirkmontessori.ca
www.selkirkmontessori.ca
www.facebook.com/159664350728103
Grades: K - 8 *Enrollment:* 202
G. Henry, Interim Academic Head

Victoria: West-Mont Montessori School
4075 Metchosin Rd., Victoria, BC V9C 4A4, Canada
Tel: 250-474-2626; *Fax:* 250-478-8944
info@west-mont.ca
www.west-mont.ca
www.facebook.com/westmontschool
twitter.com/west_mont
www.pinterest.com/westmontschool/
Grades: Preschool - 8 *Note:* West-Mont School provides a Montessori preschool to grade three. For students in grades four to seven, an enriched British Columbia curriculum is offered. The school is operated by the Western Communities Montessori Society.
Magnus Hanton, Principal
principal@west-mont.ca
Jason Bowers, Assistant Principal
jasonb@west-mont.ca
Barbara Kennelly, Manager, Business
bkennelly@west-mont.ca
Barb Lewis, Head, Admissions
barbl@west-mont.ca

Waglisla: Bella Bella Community School (BBCS)
General Delivery, Waglisla, BC V0T 1Z0, Canada
Tel: 250-957-2391; *Fax:* 250-957-2691
Brendah@bellabella.net
www.bellabella.ca
www.facebook.com/bbcsbellabellacommunityschool

Grades: K - 12
Jan Gladish, Principal
Jason Cobey, Vice Principal
Frances Brown, Head, Heiltsuk Language Program

West Vancouver: The Anna Wyman School of Dance Arts
1457 Marine Dr., West Vancouver, BC V7T 1B8
Tel: 604-926-6535; *Fax:* 604-926-6912
info@annawyman.com
www.annawyman.com
www.facebook.com/AnnaWymanSchoolOfDanceArts
www.instagram.com/annawymandance
Enrollment: 300 *Number of Employees:* 11 faculty members
Note: The school of dance features two large studios.
Anna Wyman, Founder & Artistic Director
Neil Wortley, Founder, Co-Director & Stage Manager

West Vancouver: Collingwood School
Morven Campus
70 Morven Dr., West Vancouver, BC V7S 1B2
Tel: 604-925-3331; *Fax:* 604-925-3862
jonna.mcguinness@collingwood.org
www.collingwood.org
www.facebook.com/collingwoodschool
twitter.com/collingwoodcavs
www.linkedin.com/groups/3706309
Grades: K-12 *Enrollment:* 1200
Rodger Wright, Headmaster, 604-925-3331, ext. 2295
rodger.wright@collingwood.org

West Vancouver: Mulgrave School
2330 Cypress Bowl Lane, West Vancouver, BC V7S 3H9, Canada
Tel: 604-922-3223; *Fax:* 604-922-3328
admissions@mulgrave.com
www.mulgrave.com
twitter.com/MulgraveSchool
Grades: K-12 *Note:* The coeducational, non-denominational school is an IB World School.
John Wray, Head of School
jwray@mulgrave.com
Gordon MacIntyre, Deputy Head of School
gmacintyre@mulgrave.com
Martin Jones, Principal, Middle School
mjones@mulgrave.com
Karyn Mitchell, Principal, Junior School
kmitchell@mulgrave.com
Morven McClean, Principal, Early Learning Centre
mmcclean@mulgrave.com
Chiara Tabet, Principal, Senior School
ctabet@mulgrave.com
Kelly Chow, Chief Financial Officer
kchow@mulgrave.com
Elizabeth Calderon, Director, Admissions, Communications & Marketing
ecalderon@mulgrave.com
David Dallman, Director, Educational Technology
ddallman@mulgrave.com
Tracey Dixon, Director, Talent Recruitment & Development
tdixon@mulgrave.com
Graham Gilley, Director, Risk & Safety
ggilley@mulgrave.com
Mark Steffens, Director, Community Development
msteffens@mulgrave.com
Laura Walsh, Director, Advancement
lwalsh@mulgrave.com
Mike Lopez, Manager, Facilities
mlopez@mulgrave.com
Kaayla Sinclaire, Coordinator, Office Services
ksinclaire@mulgrave.com

Westbank: Our Lady of Lourdes Elementary School
2547 Hebert Rd., Westbank, BC V4T 2J6, Canada
Tel: 250-768-9008; *Fax:* 250-768-0168
adminolol@telus.net
www.olol-bc.com/olol-bc/
Grades: K-7 *Enrollment:* 132
Diane Letendre, Principal

Westbank: Sensisyusten House of Learning
1920 Quail Lane, Westbank, BC V4T 2H3
Tel: 250-768-2802; *Fax:* 250-768-5462
school@wfn.ca
Grades: K.-6 *Enrollment:* 55
Wayne Peterson, Principal

Whistler: Whistler Secondary Community School
8000 Alpine Way, Whistler, BC V0N 1B8
Tel: 604-905-2581; *Fax:* 604-905-2583
www.whistlersecondary.bc.ca
Grades: Secondary

Bev Oakley, Principal
boakley@sd48.bc.ca

Whistler: Whistler Waldorf School
P.O. Box 1501
7324 Kirkpatrick Way, Whistler, BC V0N 1B0
Tel: 604-932-1885
info@whistlerwaldorf.com
www.whistlerwaldorf.com
www.facebook.com/WhistlerWaldorf
Grades: Pre. K - 8
Aegir Morgan, Principal

Winlaw: The Whole School
P.O. Box 240
5614 Highway #6, Winlaw, BC V0G 2J0
Tel: 250-226-7737
wholeschool@gmail.com
www.wholeschool.ca
Grades: K - 7

Universities & Colleges

Independent & Private Schools

Vancouver: Fairleigh Dickinson University - Vancouver (FDU)
842 Cambie St., Vancouver, BC V6B 2P6
Tel: 604-682-8112; *Fax:* 604-682-8132
Toll-Free: 877-338-8002
vancouver@fdu.edu
www.fdu.edu/campuses/vancouver-campus
Note: Fairleigh Dickinson University is an independent university founded in 1942. FDU has campuses in Teaneck, New Jersey, Madison, New Jersey, Wroxton, England & downtown Vancouver, Canada.
David O'Reilly, Deputy Campus Executive
doreilly@fdu.edu

Universities

Abbotsford: University of the Fraser Valley
33844 King Rd., Abbotsford, BC V2S 7M8
Tel: 604-504-7441; *Fax:* 604-855-7614
Toll-Free: 888-504-7441
info@ufv.ca
www.ufv.ca
www.facebook.com/goUFV
twitter.com/goUFV
www.linkedin.com/school/university-of-the-fraser-valley_2
www.youtube.com/user/goUFV
Full Time Equivalency: 15000
Dr. Andy Sidhu, Chancellor
Dr. Joanne MacLean, President & Vice-Chancellor
presidentsoffice@ufv.ca
Dr. James Mandigo, Provost & Vice-President, Academic, 604-864-4630
james.mandigo@ufv.ca
Betty Poettcker, Chief Financial Officer & Vice-President, Administration
betty.poettcker@ufv.ca
Al Wiseman, University Secretary
al.wiseman@ufv.ca

Faculties
College of Arts
Building B, 3rd Fl., Office B315
Abbotsford, BC V2S 7M8
Tel: 604-851-6351; *Fax:* 604-859-6653
www.ufv.ca/arts
Jacqueline Nolte, Dean of Arts, 604-864-4632
jacqueline.nolte@ufv.ca

Faculty of Science
Building D
#203, 33844 King Rd., Abbotsford, BC V2S 7M8
Tel: 604-504-7441; *Toll-Free:* 888-504-7441
science@ufv.ca
www.ufv.ca/science
Dr. Lucy Lee, Dean, Faculty of Science, 604-851-6346
lucy.lee@ufv.ca

Faculty of Professional Studies
33844 King Rd., Abbotsford, BC V2S 7M8
www.ufv.ca/ps
Dr. Tracy Ryder Glass, Dean, 604-851-6341
tracy.ryderglass@ufv.ca

Faculty of Applied & Technical Studies
Trades & Technology Centre
5579 Tyson Rd., Chilliwack, BC V2R 0H9
Tel: 604-847-5448; *Fax:* 604-824-7931
Toll-Free: 888-504-7441
trades@ufv.ca
www.ufv.ca/trades
John English, Dean, 604-847-5700
john.english@ufv.ca

Faculty of Access & Continuing Education
33844 King Rd., #B309, Abbotsford, BC V2S 7M8
access@ufv.ca
www.ufv.ca/access
Dr. Sue Brigden, Dean, 604-504-7441, ext. 4643
sue.brigden@ufv.ca

Faculty of Health Sciences
Bldg. A
#2451, 45190 Caen Ave., Chilliwack, BC V2R 0N3
Tel: 604-795-2841; *Fax:* 604-858-4773
Toll-Free: 888-504-7441
healthstudies@ufv.ca
www.ufv.ca/health
www.facebook.com/ufvhealth
twitter.com/UFVhealth
www.youtube.com/channel/UCv_sbhjl2CUd60Mbe2fjssg
Alastair Hodges, Dean, 604-702-2600
alastair.hodges@ufv.ca

Schools
Graduate Studies
33844 King Rd., Abbotsford, BC V2S 7M8
Tel: 604-557-4074
graduate.studies@ufv.ca
www.ufv.ca/graduate-studies
Deborah Block, Coordinator, 604-864-4639
deborah.block@ufv.ca

Campuses
Chilliwack Campus
45190 Caen Ave., Chilliwack, BC V2R 0N3, Canada
Tel: 604-792-0025; *Fax:* 604-824-7931

Mission Campus
Heritage Park Centre
33700 Prentis Ave., Mission, BC V2V 7B1, Canada
Tel: 604-557-7603; *Fax:* 604-826-0681

UFV India Office
SD College Chandigarh (SDCC)
Sector 32C, Chandigarh, UT, India
ufv.india@ufv.ca
ufv.in
Other Information: +91 (0) 172-499-2400

Centres & Institutes
Trades & Technology Centre
Canada Education Park
5579 Tyson Rd., Chilliwack, BC V2R 0H9, Canada
Tel: 604-847-5448; *Fax:* 604-824-7931
Toll-Free: 888-504-7441
trades@ufv.ca

UFV Aerospace Centre
Abbotsford Airport
30645 Firecat Ave., Abbotsford, BC V2T 6H5, Canada
Fax: 604-852-7399
Toll-Free: 888-504-7441
aerospace@ufv.ca

Hope Centre
1250 7th Ave., Hope, BC V0X 1L4, Canada
Tel: 604-869-9991; *Fax:* 604-869-7431
Michelle Vandepol, Coordinator
michelle.vandepol@ufv.ca

Clearbrook Centre
32355 Veterans Way, Abbotsford, BC V2T 0B3
Tel: 604-851-6324

Burnaby: Simon Fraser University
8888 University Dr., Burnaby, BC V5A 1S6, Canada
Tel: 778-782-3111
www.sfu.ca
Other Information: Student Services: 778-782-6930
www.facebook.com/simonfraseruniversity
twitter.com/sfu
www.linkedin.com/company/simon-fraser-university
www.youtube.com/user/SFUNews
Full Time Equivalency: 35700 *Number of Employees:* 1000 faculty
Anne E. Giardini, Chancellor
Andrew Petter, President & Vice-Chancellor
Dr. Jonathan Driver, Interim Vice-President, Academic & Provost
Joanne Curry, Vice-President, External Relations

Joy Johnson, Vice-President, Research & International
vpres@sfu.ca
Martin Pochurko, Vice-President, Finance & Administration
pochurko@sfu.ca
Li-Jeen Broshko, Acting University Secretary
gcasst@sfu.ca

Faculties
Faculty of Applied Sciences
Applied Science Bldg.
#9861, 8888 University Dr., Burnaby, BC V5A 1S6
Tel: 778-782-4724; *Fax:* 778-782-5802
fasgen@sfu.ca
sfu.ca/fas.html
www.facebook.com/FAS.SFU
twitter.com/fas_sfu
www.youtube.com/user/fascomms
Eugene Fiume, Dean, 778-782-4936
eugene_fiume@sfu.ca
Amanda Woodhall, Senior Director, 778-782-8786
amanda@sfu.ca

Faculty of Arts and Social Sciences
Academic Quadrangle
#6168, 8888 University Dr., Burnaby, BC V5A 1S6
Tel: 778-782-4414; *Fax:* 778-782-3033
sfu.ca/fass
www.facebook.com/sfufass
twitter.com/sfufass
www.youtube.com/SFUFASS
Enrollment: 12750 *Number of Employees:* 300 faculty
Jane Pulkingham, Dean, 778-782-4415
fassdean@sfu

Beedie School of Business
8888 University Dr., Burnaby, BC V5A 1S6
Tel: 778-782-5567
beedie.sfu.ca/
www.facebook.com/sfubeedie
twitter.com.com/school/sfubeedie
www.linkedin/comchool/sfubeedie
www.instagram.com/sfubeedie
Enrollment: 4000
Ali Dastmalchian, Dean, 778-782-7664
beedie_dean@sfu.ca

Continuing Studies
#2300, 515 West Hastings St., Vancouver, BC V6B 5K3
Tel: 778-782-8000; *Toll-Free:* 844-782-8877
learn@sfu.ca
www.sfu.ca/continuing-studies
www.facebook.com/sfucontinuingstudies
twitter.com/CS_SFU
www.linkedin.com/company/sfu-continuing-studies
www.youtube.com/sfucontinuingstudies
Julia Denholm, Dean, Lifelong Learning, 778-782-5138
csdean@sfu.ca

Faculty of Education
8888 University Dr., Burnaby, AB V5A 1S6
Tel: 778-782-3395
sfu.ca/education.html
www.facebook.com/sfueducation
twitter.com/sfueducation
www.youtube.com/user/sfufacultyofed
Susan O'Neill, Dean, 778-782-3148
eddean@sfu.ca

Graduate Studies & Postdoctoral Fellows
Maggie Benston Student Services Centre
#1100, 8888 University Dr., Burnaby, BC V5A 1S6
Tel: 778-782-3042; *Fax:* 778-782-3080
gradstdy@sfu.ca
sfu.ca/dean-gradstudies.html
www.facebook.com/sfugrad
twitter.com/SFU_GradStudies
Jeff Derksen, Dean
jderksen@sfu.ca

Health Sciences
#11300, Blusson Hall
8888 University Dr., Burnaby, BC V5A 1S6
Tel: 778-782-4821; *Fax:* 778-782-5927
fhs@sfu.ca
www.sfu.ca/fhs.html
Tania Bubela, Dean
fhsdean@sfu.ca

Faculty of Communication, Art and Technology
TASC 2
#7800, 8888 University Dr., Burnaby, BC V5A 1S6
Tel: 778-782-8790
fcataa@sfu.ca
sfu.ca/fcat
www.facebook.com/FCATatSFU
twitter.com/FCATatSFU
www.instagram.com/FCATatSFU
Owen Underhill, Interim Dean, 778-782-2168
fcatdean@sfu.ca

Faculty of Environment
TASC 2
#8800, 8888 University Dr., Burnaby, BC V5A 1S6
Tel: 778-782-8787
fenvsec@sfu.ca
sfu.ca/fenv
www.facebook.com/sfuenv
twitter.com/sfuenv
www.instagram.com/sfuenv
Naomi Krogman, Dean, 778-782-8797
envdean@sfu.ca

Faculty of Science
TASC 2
#9900, 8888 University Dr., Burnaby, BC V5A 1S6
Tel: 778-782-8787
sfu.ca/science
www.facebook.com/sfuscience
twitter.com/sfu_science
www.instagram.com/sfuscience
Paul Kench, Dean, 778-782-7521
scsec@sfu.ca

Schools
School for the Contemporary Arts (SCA)
Goldcorp Centre for the Arts
#2860, 149 West Hastings St., Vancouver, BC V6B 1H4
Tel: 778-782-3363; *Fax:* 778-782-5907
ca@sfu.ca
www.sfu.ca/sca
www.facebook.com/SFUContemporaryArts
twitter.com/SFUContmpryArts
www.instagram.com/sfucontemporaryarts
Arne Eigenfeldt, Interim Director
arne_e@sfu.ca

Centres & Institutes
Centre for Experimental & Constructive Mathematics (CECM)
Shrum Science Building
8888 University Dr., #P8495, Burnaby, BC V5A 1S6
Tel: 778-782-5617; *Fax:* 778-782-5614
cecm.sfu.ca
Michael Monagan, Director, 778-782-4279
John Hebron, System Administrator, 778-782-4279

Centre for Natural Hazards Research
TASC 1 Building
#7201, 8888 University Dr., Burnaby, BC V5A 1S6
Tel: 778-782-5387; *Fax:* 778-782-4198
info-cnhr@sfu.ca
sfu.ca/cnhr
Brent Ward, Co-Director
Glyn Williams-Jones, Co-Director

Centre for Wildlife Ecology (CWE)
Department of Biological Sciences
8888 University Dr., Burnaby, BC V5A 1S6
Tel: 778-782-4282; *Fax:* 778-782-3496
www.sfu.ca/biology/wildberg/NewCWEPage
www.facebook.com/cwesfu
Ron Ydenberg, Director, 778-782-4282
ydenberg@sfu.ca

Institute of Micromachine & Microfabrication Research (IMMR)
8888 University Dr., Burnaby, BC V5A 1S6
Tel: 604-291-3455; *Fax:* 604-291-4951
sfu.ca/engineering/research/research-labs/immr
Ash Parameswaran, Director, 778-782-4951
param@cs.sfu.ca

Centre for Sustainable Development
c/o Department of Sociology & Anthropology
8888 University Dr., AQ 5054, Burnaby, BC V5A 1S6
Tel: 778-782-8787; *Fax:* 778-782-8788
sfu.ca/sustainabledevelopment.html
Yildiz Atasoy, Director, 778-782-5520
yatasoy@sfu.ca

Centre for Tourism & Policy Research (CTPR)
8888 University Dr., Burnaby, BC V5A 1S6
www.sfu.ca/rem/tourism.html
Pascal Haegeli, Contact

Cooperative Resource Management Institute
c/o School of Resource and Environmental Manageme
8888 University Dr., Burnaby, BC V5A 1S6
Tel: 778-782-9246; *Fax:* 778-782-4968
www.sfu.ca/rem/CRMI
Jonathan Moore, Director

Kamloops: Thompson Rivers University
805 TRU Way, Kamloops, BC V2C 0C8
Tel: 250-828-5000; *Fax:* 250-828-5086
admissions@tru.ca
www.tru.ca
www.facebook.com/thompsonriversu
twitter.com/thompsonriversu
www.youtube.com/user/truwebbies
Full Time Equivalency: 20000 *Number of Employees:* 1543 staff;
415 faculty *Note:* With distance-learning, enrollment figures swell
to over 28,000 students.
Nathan Matthew, Chancellor
Brett Fairbairn, President & Vice-Chancellor, 250-828-5001
president@tru.ca
Dr. Christine Bovis-Cnossen, Provost & Vice-President,
Academic
Matt Milovick, Vice-President, Administration & Finance,
250-377-6123
Jeff Sodowsky, Vice-President, Advancement
Paul Michel, Executive Director, Aboriginal Affairs

Faculties
Faculty of Adventure, Culinary Arts & Tourism
805 TRU Way, Kamloops, BC V2C 0C8
Tel: 250-828-5000
adventure@tru.ca
Doug Ellis, Dean
dellis@tru.ca

Faculty of Arts
805 TRU Way, Kamloops, BC V2C 0C8
Tel: 250-371-5566
artsadvising@tru.ca
Richard McCutcheon, Dean, 250-828-5170
rmccutcheon@tru.ca

Faculty of Science
805 TRU Way, Kamloops, BC V2C 0C8
www.tru.ca/science
Dr. Tom Dickinson, Dean, 250-852-7137
tdickinson@tru.ca

Faculty of Education & Social Work
805 TRU Way, Kamloops, BC V2C 0C8
www.tru.ca/edsw

Faculty of Law
805 TRU Way, Kamloops, BC V2C 0C8
Tel: 250-852-7699
lawadmissions@tru.ca
Bradford Morse, Dean
bmorse@tru.ca

Faculty of Student Development
805 TRU Way, Kamloops, BC V2C 0C8

Schools
School of Business & Economics (SoBE)
805 TRU Way, Kamloops, BC V2C 0C8
www.facebook.com/TRUBusinessEcon
twitter.com/TRUBusinessEcon
flickr.com/photos/54437427@N07
Michael Henry, Dean, 250-852-6290
mihenry@tru.ca

School of Nursing
805 TRU Way, Kamloops, BC V2C 0C8
Tel: 250-828-5401; *Fax:* 250-371-5909
nursing@tru.ca
www.tru.ca/nursing
Rani Srivastava, Dean
rsrivastava@tru.ca

School of Trades & Technology
805 TRU Way, Kamloops, BC V2C 0C8
www.tru.ca/trades
Baldev Pooni, Dean, 250-828-5110
bpooni@tru.ca

Campuses
Williams Lake Campus
1250 Western Ave., Williams Lake, BC V2G 1H7, Canada
Tel: 250-392-8000; *Fax:* 250-392-4984
Toll-Free: 800-663-4936
wlmain@tru.ca
www.tru.ca/williamslake.html

100 Mile House Training & Education Centre
#1, 808 Alpine Ave., 100 Mile House, BC V0K 2E0, Canada
Tel: 250-395-3115; *Fax:* 250-395-2894

Robin Bercowski, Coordinator
rbercowski@tru.ca

Ashcroft & Cache Creek Centre
P.O. Box 339
#10, 155 Main St., Lillooet, BC V0K 1V0, Canada
Tel: 250-256-4296; *Fax:* 250-256-4278
Margaret Hohner, Coordinator
mhohner@tru.ca

Barriere Centre
P.O. Box 1407
4629 Barriere Town Rd., Barriere, BC V0E 1E0, Canada
Tel: 250-672-9875; *Fax:* 250-672-9875
Susan Ross, Coordinator
sross@tru.ca

Clearwater Centre
Also known as: North Thompson Community Skills Centre
209 Dutch Lake Rd., Clearwater, BC V0E 1N2, Canada
Tel: 250-674-3530; *Fax:* 250-674-3540
Susan Ross, Coordinator
sross@tru.ca

Lillooet & Lytton Training & Education Centre
P.O. Box 339
#10, 155 Main St., Lillooet, BC V0K 1V0, Canada
Tel: 250-256-4296; *Fax:* 250-256-4278
Margaret Hohner, Coordinator
mhohner@tru.ca

Open Learning Division
BC Centre for Open Learning
805 TRU Way, Kamloops, BC V2C 0C8, Canada
Tel: 250-852-7000; *Fax:* 250-852-6405
Toll-Free: 1-800-663-9711
student@tru.ca

Langley: The Associated Canadian Theological
Schools of Trinity Western University (ACTS)
7600 Glover Rd., Langley, BC V2Y 1Y1, Canada
Tel: 604-513-2044; *Toll-Free:* 888-468-6898
acts@twu.ca
www.actsseminaries.com
www.facebook.com/actsseminaries
twitter.com/ACTSseminaries

Langley: Mennonite Brethren Biblical Seminary - BC
Also known as: MB Biblical Seminary
7600 Glover Rd., Langley, BC V2Y 1Y1
Tel: 604-513-2133; *Toll-Free:* 855-252-3293
langley@mbseminary.ca
www.mbseminary.ca
www.facebook.com/MBSeminary
twitter.com/mbseminary
www.linkedin.com/school/mennonite-brethren-biblical-seminary
www.youtube.com/mbseminary
Bruce Guenther, Associate Dean

Campuses
Mennonite Brethren Biblical Seminary - MB
Also known as: MB Biblical Seminary
500 Shaftesbury Blvd., Winnipeg, MB R3P 2N2
Tel: 204-487-3300; *Toll-Free:* 877-231-4570
winnipeg@mbseminary.ca

Langley: Trinity Western University
7600 Glover Rd., Langley, BC V2Y 1Y1
Tel: 604-888-7511; *Fax:* 604-513-2061
Toll-Free: 888-468-6898
admissions@twu.ca
www.twu.ca
www.facebook.com/trinitywestern
twitter.com/TrinityWestern
www.instagram.com/trinitywestern
Full Time Equivalency: 5000
Mark Husbands, President
president@twu.ca
W. Robert Wood, Provost
Scott Fehrenbacher, Senior Vice-President, External Relations
Jim Poulsen, Vice-President, Finance
Grant McMillan, Registrar, 604-513-2070
grant.mcmillan@twu.ca

Faculties
Faculty of Natural and Applied Sciences
www.twu.ca/academics/faculty-natural-applied-sciences
Ka Yin Leung, Dean
kayin.leung@twu.ca

Faculty of Humanities and Social Sciences
www.twu.ca/faculty-humanities-social-sciences
Todd Martin, Dean

School of the Arts, Media & Culture
www.twu.ca/academics/school-arts-media-culture

David Squires, Dean
david.squires@twu.ca

School of Business
www.twu.ca/academics/school-business
Kevin Sawatsky, Dean
sawatsky@twu.ca

School of Education
www.twu.ca/academics/school-education
Allyson Jule, Dean
allyson.jule@twu.ca

School of Human Kinetics
Tel: 604-513-2162
www.twu.ca/academics/school-human-kinetics
www.facebook.com/trinity.hkin
Blair Whitmarsh, Dean
blair.whitmarsh@twu.ca

School of Nursing
Tel: 604-513-2050; Fax: 604-513-2012
admission@twu.ca
www.twu.ca/academics/school-nursing
Sheryl Reimer-Kirkham, Acting Dean, 604-513-2121, ext. 3239
dean.nursing@twu.ca

School of Graduate Studies
fgs@twu.ca
www.twu.ca/academics/school-graduate-studies
Eve Stringham, Vice Provost, Research & Graduate Studies
stringha@twu.ca

Campuses
Bellingham Campus
143 West Kellogg Rd., Bellingham, WA, USA
Tel: 360-527-0222
info@twubellingham.com
www.twubellingham.com

Richmond Campus
#305, 5900 Minoru Blvd., Richmond, BC V6X 0L9
Tel: 604-513-2193
richmond@twu.ca
Katherine Sayson, Director, Operations
katherine.sayson@twu.ca

Affiliations
Associated Canadian Theological Schools of Trinity Western University (ACTS)
Also known as: ACTS Seminaries
Fosmark Centre
7600 Glover Rd., Langley, BC V2Y 1Y1, Canada
Tel: 604-513-2044; Toll-Free: 888-468-6898
acts@twu.ca
www.actsseminaries.com
Guy Saffold, Executive Director
guy.saffold@twu.ca
Howard G. Andersen, Academic Director
howard.andersen@twu.ca

Canadian Baptist Seminary
7600 Glover Rd., Langley, BC V2Y 1Y1, Canada
Tel: 604-513-2015
canbapseminary@twu.ca
www.canadianbaptistseminary.com
Roger Helland, President
Bernard Mukwavi, Adjunct Professor
Wendell Phillips, Chief Financial Officer
Sarah Last, Office Coordinator

Northwest Baptist Seminary
7600 Glover Rd., Langley, BC V2Y 1Y1, Canada
Tel: 604-888-7592; Fax: 604-637-3212
www.nbseminary.ca
www.facebook.com/nbseminary
twitter.com/nbseminary
Kent Anderson, President
Howard Andersen, Academic Dean
Loren Warkentin, Registrar

Trinity Western Seminary
7600 Glover Rd., Langley, BC V2Y 1Y1, Canada
Tel: 604-888-7511
John Auxier, Associate Dean, 604-888-7511, ext. 3821
auxier@twu.ca

Summit Pacific College
P.O. Box 1700
35235 Straiton Rd., Abbotsford, BC V2S 7E7, Canada
Tel: 604-853-7491; Fax: 604-853-8951
Toll-Free: 800-976-8388
pr@summitpacific.ca
www.summitpacific.ca
www.facebook.com/summitpc
twitter.com/summitpc
www.youtube.com/user/SPCcollege

Note: Formerly Western Pentecostal Bible College
Dr. Dave Demchuk, President
ddemchuk@summitpacific.ca
Melody Deeley, Registrar, 604-851-7225
registrar@summitpacific.ca
Mark Hawkes, Dean of Students, 604-851-7213
deanofstudents@summitpacific.ca
Wilf Hildebrandt, Dean of Education, 604-851-7235
interculturalstudies@summitpacific.ca
Laurence Van Kleek, Librarian, 604-851-7230
librarian@summitpacific.ca

Nanaimo: **Vancouver Island University (VIU)**
Nanaimo Campus
900 - 5th St., Nanaimo, BC V9R 5S5
Tel: 250-753-3245; Toll-Free: 888-920-2221
info@viu.ca
www.viu.ca
www.facebook.com/viuniversity
twitter.com/VIUniversity
www.linkedin.com/school/vancouver-island-university
www.youtube.com/user/viuchannel
Full Time Equivalency: 14500
Dr. Deb Saucier, President & Vice-Chancellor
Dr. Carol Stuart, Provost & Vice-President, Academic
Marlene Kowalski, Chief Financial Officer & Vice-President, Administration
William Litchfield, Associate Vice-President, University Relations
Dan VanderSluis, Associate Vice-President, Human Resources
Marie Armstrong, University Secretary

Campuses
Cowichan Campus
2011 University Way, Duncan, BC V9L 0C7
Tel: 250-746-3500
cowichan.viu.ca

Parksville-Qualicum Campus
100 Jensen Ave. East, Parksville, BC V9P 2G3
Tel: 250-248-2096; Fax: 250-248-9792
pqcampus@viu.ca
www.viu.ca/parksville

Powell River Campus
#100, 7085 Nootka St., Powell River, BC V8A 3C6
Tel: 604-485-2878; Fax: 604-485-2868
Toll-Free: 877-888-8890
pr.viu.ca

North Vancouver: **Capilano University**
2055 Purcell Way, North Vancouver, BC V7J 3H5, Canada
Tel: 604-986-1911; Fax: 604-984-4985
www.capilanou.ca
TTY: 604-990-7848
www.facebook.com/capilanou
twitter.com/CapilanoU
www.linkedin.com/company/capilano-university
www.youtube.com/user/CapilanoUniversity
Full Time Equivalency: 12700
Paul Dangerfield, President & Vice-Chancellor
pdangerfield@capilanou.ca
Laureen Styles, Provost & Vice-President, Academic
laureenstyles@capilanou.ca
Jennifer Ingham, Vice-President, University Relations
jenniferingham@capilanou.ca
Toran Savjord, Vice-President, Strategic Planning
tsavjord@capilanou.ca
Jacqui Stewart, Vice-President, Finance & Administration
jacquistewart@capilanou.ca

Prince George: **University of Northern British Columbia (UNBC)**
3333 University Way, Prince George, BC V2N 4Z9
Tel: 250-960-5555
www.unbc.ca
www.facebook.com/UNBC
twitter.com/UNBC
www.linkedin.com/school/unbc
www.youtube.com/UNBCnews
Full Time Equivalency: 3570 *Number of Employees:* 341 faculty; 502 staff
Dr. Joseph Arthur Gosnell, Chancellor
Dr. Geoff Payne, Interim President & Vice-Chancellor
Dan Ryan, Provost & Vice-President, Academic
Kathy Lewis, Interim Vice-President, Research
Colleen Smith, Interim Vice-President, Finance
Tim Tribe, Vice-President, University Advancement

Faculties
Arts, Social & Health Sciences
3333 University Way, Prince George, BC V2N 4Z9
www.unbc.ca/cashs
Shannon Wagner, Dean
shannon.wagner@unbc.ca

Graduate Programs
3333 University Way, Prince George, BC V2N 4Z9
grad-office@unbc.ca
www.unbc.ca/graduate-programs

Science & Management
3333 University Way, Prince George, BC V2N 4Z9
www.unbc.ca/csam
Erik Jensen, Acting Dean
erik.jensen@unbc.ca

Campuses
Northwest Campus (Terrace)
4837 Keith Ave., Terrace, BC V8G 1K7
Fax: 250-615-5478
Toll-Free: 800-697-7388
northwest@unbc.ca

Northwest Campus (Prince Rupert)
353 - 5th St., Prince Rupert, BC V8J 3L5
Tel: 250-624-2862; Fax: 250-624-9703
Toll-Free: 888-554-6554
northwest@unbc.ca

Peace River-Liard Campus (Fort St John)
P.O. Box 1000
9820 - 120th Ave., Fort St John, BC V1J 6K1
Tel: 250-787-6220; Fax: 250-758-9665
Toll-Free: 800-935-2270
northeast@unbc.ca

South-Central Campus (Quesnel)
100 Campus Way, #S100, Quesnel, BC V2J 7K1
Tel: 250-991-7540; Fax: 250-997-7528
Toll-Free: 800-627-9931
south-central@unbc.ca

Wilp Wilxo'oskwhl Nisga'a (Affiliate Campus)
P.O. Box 70
3001 Ts'oohl Ts'ap Ave., Gitwinksihlkw, BC V0J 3T0
Tel: 250-633-2292; Fax: 250-633-2463
Toll-Free: 800-980-8838

Surrey: **Kwantlen Polytechnic University**
12666 - 72nd Ave., Surrey, BC V3W 2M8
Tel: 604-599-2000; Fax: 604-599-2068
studentinfo@kpu.ca
www.kpu.ca
www.facebook.com/kwantlenu
twitter.com/kwantlenu
www.instagram.com/kwantlenu
Full Time Equivalency: 20000 *Number of Employees:* 1400
George Melville, Chancellor
Alan R. Davis, President & Vice-Chancellor, 604-599-2078
Sandy Vanderburgh, Provost & Vice-President, Academic
sandy.vanderburgh@kpu.ca
Marlyn Graziano, Vice-President, External Affairs
Zena Mitchell, Registrar, 604-599-2463
zena.mitchell@kpu.ca
Keri van Gerven, University Secretary, 604-599-2078
keri.vangerven@kpu.ca

Faculties
Faculty of Arts
Arbutus Building
12666 - 72nd Ave., #A2110, Surrey, BC V3W 2M8
Tel: 604-599-3068; Fax: 604-599-2966
arts@kpu.ca
Diane Purvey, Dean

Faculty of Science and Horticulture
Tel: 604-599-2422
science&horticulture@kpu.ca
www.facebook.com/KPUFSH
twitter.com/kpusciencehort
Elizabeth Worobec, Dean, 604-599-2244
elizabeth.worobec@kpu.ca

Faculty of Health
South Bldg.
#2810, 20901 Langley Bypass, Langley, BC V3A 4H9
Tel: 604-599-2263
www.kpu.ca/health
www.facebook.com/KPUHealth
twitter.com/kpuhealth
Dr. David Florkowski, Dean
david.florkowski@kpu.ca

Faculty of Academic and Career Advancement
Tel: 604-599-2321; Fax: 604-599-2435
www.kpu.ca/aca
Patrick J. Donahoe, Dean
patrick.donahoe@kpu.ca

Faculty of Trades and Technology
Tel: 604-599-2000; Fax: 604-598-6111
www.kpu.ca/trades

Brian Moukperian, Dean, 604-598-6101
brian.moukperian@kpu.ca

Schools
School of Business
Tel: 604-599-3251; Fax: 604-599-3242
business@kpu.ca
www.kpu.ca/business
www.facebook.com/KPUSoB
twitter.com/KPU_business

Wayne Tebb, Dean, 604-599-3252
wayne.tebb@kpu.ca

Wilson School of Design
www.kpu.ca/design

Carolyn Robertson, Dean, 604-599-2673
carolyn.robertson@kpu.ca

School of Continuing and Professional Studies
Tel: 604-599-2020
cps@kpu.ca
Note: The Cannabis Career Training program offers three courses relating to the commercial cannabis industry. Offered online only. Also available; Retail Cannabis Consultant Workshop as a two-day, in-class course. KPU is partnering with the National Institute for Cannabis Health and Education (NICHE).

Campuses
Surrey Campus
12666 - 72 Ave., Surrey, BC V3W 2M8, Canada
Fax: 604-599-2068

Richmond Campus
8771 Lansdowne Rd., Richmond, BC V6X 3X7, Canada

Cloverdale Campus
Also known as: Tech Campus
5500 - 180 St., Surrey, BC V3S 4K5, Canada
Tel: 604-599-2000

Langley Campus
20901 Langley Bypass, Langley, BC V3A 8G9, Canada

Vancouver: Emily Carr University of Art & Design
520 East 1st Ave., Vancouver, BC V5T 0H2, Canada
Tel: 604-844-3800; Fax: 604-844-3801
Toll-Free: 800-832-7788
reception@ecuad.ca
www.ecuad.ca
www.facebook.com/Emily.Carr.University
twitter.com/EmilyCarrU
www.youtube.com/user/EmilyCarrUniversity
Full Time Equivalency: 1898 *Number of Employees:* 70 faculty; 143 administrative staff; 45 technical staff *Note:* Emily Carr University offers art, design, & media degrees, certificates, & courses. Formerly Emily Carr Institute of Art & Design, the school was granted full university status in 2008.
Dr. Gillian Siddall, President & Vice-Chancellor

Vancouver: University Canada West (UCW)
#100, 626 West Pender St., Vancouver, BC V6B 1V9
Tel: 800-288-9502; Toll-Free: 877-431-6887
info@ucanwest.ca
www.ucanwest.ca
www.facebook.com/UniversityCanadaWest
twitter.com/unicanadawest
www.youtube.com/CanadaUniversity
Full Time Equivalency: 800 *Note:* University Canada West (UCW) is an independent university established in 2004. UCW offers programs at their Vancouver campus and Online.
Dr. Arthur Coren, President & Vice-Chancellor

Vancouver: University of British Columbia (UBC)
2329 West Mall, Vancouver, BC V6T 1Z4, Canada
Tel: 604-822-2211
www.ubc.ca
www.facebook.com/universityofbc
twitter.com/ubc
www.linkedin.com/school/the-university-of-british-columbia
www.youtube.com/user/ubc
Full Time Equivalency: 64798 *Number of Employees:* 6,057 faculty + 10,834 staff
Michael Korenberg, Chair
Lindsay Gordon, Chancellor
Santa J. Ono, President, 604-822-8300
presidents.office@ubc.ca
Andrew Szeri, Provist & Vice-President, Academic
provost.vpa@ubc.ca
Gail Murphy, Vice-President, Research, 604-822-4813
gail.murphy@ubc.ca
Peter Smailes, Vice-President, Finance & Operations, 604-822-9625
peter.smailes@ubc.ca

Faculties
Faculty of Applied Science
#5000, 2332 Main Mall, Vancouver, BC
Tel: 604-822-6413
info@apsc.ubc.ca
www.apsc.ubc.ca

James Olson, Dean

Faculty of Arts
Buchanan A240
1866 Main Mall, Vancouver, BC V6T 1Z1
Tel: 604-822-3828; Fax: 604-822-6096
www.arts.ubc.ca

Gage Averill, Dean, 604-822-3751
gage.averill@ubc.ca

Faculty of Dentistry
#350, 2194 Health Sciences Mall, Vancouver, BC V6T 1Z3
Tel: 604-822-5773; Fax: 604-822-4532
www.dentistry.ubc.ca

Dr. Mary MacDougall, Dean
macdougall@dentistry.ubc.ca

Faculty of Education
2125 Main Mall, Vancouver, BC V6T 1Z4
Tel: 604-822-5242
info.educ@ubc.ca
www.educ.ubc.ca

Blye Frank, Dean, 604-822-2049
dean.educ@ubc.ca

Faculty of Forestry
2424 Main Mall, Vancouver, BC V6T 1Z4
Fax: 604-822-8645
www.forestry.ubc.ca

John Innes, Dean, 604-822-6761
john.innes@ubc.ca

Faculty of Graduate & Postdoctoral Studies
#170, 6371 Crescent Rd., Vancouver, BC V6T 1Z2
Tel: 604-822-2848; Fax: 604-822-5802
www.grad.ubc.ca

Susan Porter, Dean, 604-827-5547
susan.porter@ubc.ca

Faculty of Land & Food Systems
248 - 2357 Main Mall, Vancouver, BC V6T 1Z4
Tel: 604-822-1219; Fax: 604-822-2184
www.landfood.ubc.ca

Rickey Yada, Dean, 604-822-1219
dean.landfood@ubc.ca

Faculty of Medicine
#317, 2194 Health Sciences Mall, Vancouver, BC V6T 1Z3
Tel: 604-822-2421; Fax: 604-822-6061
fomdo.reception@ubc.ca
www.med.ubc.ca
www.facebook.com/UBCmed
twitter.com/UBCMedicine
www.youtube.com/user/UBCmedicine

Dermot Kelleher, Dean

Faculty of Pharmaceutical Sciences
2405 Wesbrook Mall, Vancouver, BC V6T 1Z3
pharmsci.ubc.ca
www.facebook.com/ubcpharmacy
twitter.com/ubcpharmacy
www.linkedin.com/company/ubc-faculty-of-pharmaceutical-sciences

Michael Coughtrie, Dean

Faculty of Sciences
2178 - 2207 Main Mall, Vancouver, BC V6T 1Z4
www.science.ubc.ca

Mark MacLachlan, Acting Dean
scidean@science.ubc.ca

Department of Medicine
10th Floor, 2775 Laurel St., Vancouver, BC V5Z 1M9
Tel: 604-875-4045; Fax: 604-875-4886
medicine.ubc.ca
twitter.com/UBCDoM
Note: A partnership between UBC & Canopy Growth is performing clinical trials studying the role of cannabis as a form of treatment for opioid dependency.
Dr. M-J Milloy, PhD, Canopy Growth Professor of Cannabis Science

Department of Botany
Faculty of Science
3200-6270 University Blvd., Vancouver, BC V6T 1Z4
Tel: 604-822-2133; Fax: 604-822-6089
www.botany.ubc.ca
www.facebook.com/ubc.deptbotany
twitter.com/ubcbotany
Note: A collaboration research project between UBC botanist, Jonathan Page, & Aurora Cannabis Inc. examining the evolution

& genetics of cannabis. The research intends to provide useful information for the agriculture & medical industries.
Jon Page, PhD, Adjunct Professor/Chief of Science, Aurora Cannabis Inc., 604-822-0253
jon.page@botany.ubc.ca

Schools
School of Architecture & Landscape Architecture
402 - 6333 Memorial Rd., Vancouver, BC V6T 1Z2
Tel: 604-827-7252
info@sala.ubc.ca
www.sala.ubc.ca

Ron Kellett, Director
rkellett@sala.ubc.ca

School of Audiology & Speech Sciences
2177 Wesbrook Mall, Vancouver, BC V6T 1Z3
Tel: 604-822-5591; Fax: 604-822-6569
inquiry@audiospeech.ubc.ca
www.audiospeech.ubc.ca
www.facebook.com/ubc.sass
twitter.com/UBC_Sass

Jeff Small, Director
director@audiospeech.ubc.ca

School of Community & Regional Planning
433 - 6333 Memorial Rd., Vancouver, BC V6T 1Z2
Tel: 604-822-3276; Fax: 604-822-3787
www.scarp.ubc.ca

Heather Campbell, Director

School of Kinesiology
#210, 6081 University Blvd., Vancouver, BC V6T 1Z1
Tel: 604-822-9192; Fax: 604-822-6842
ubc.kin@ubc.ca
kin.educ.ubc.ca
www.facebook.com/ubckin
twitter.com/ubckin
www.instagram.com/ubckin

Robert Boushel, Director
robert.boushel@ubc.ca

School of Library, Archival & Information Studies
Also known as: iSchool
470 - 1961 East Mall, Vancouver, BC V6T 1Z1
Tel: 604-822-2404; Fax: 604-822-6006
ischool.info@ubc.ca
www.slais.ubc.ca

Luanne Freund, Director
luanne.freund@ubc.ca

School of Music
Music Building
6361 Memorial Rd., Vancouver, BC V6T 1Z2
Tel: 604-822-3113; Fax: 604-822-4884
www.music.ubc.ca

Alexander Fisher, Acting Director
fisher@mail.ubc.ca

School of Nursing
2211 Wesbrook Mall, #T201, Vancouver, BC V6T 2B5
Tel: 604-822-7417; Fax: 604-822-7466
www.nursing.ubc.ca
www.facebook.com/ubcnursing
twitter.com/ubcnursing
www.linkedin.com/company/ubc-school-of-nursing
www.youtube.com/channel/UCTajhpu5yW2p4PjTqbcFbgg
Elizabeth Saewyc, Director
elizabeth.saewyc@ubc.ca

School of Population & Public Health
2206 East Mall, Vancouver, BC V6T 1Z3
Tel: 604-822-2772; Fax: 604-822-4994
info@spph.ubc.ca
www.spph.ubc.ca
www.facebook.com/ubc.spph
twitter.com/ubcspph
www.youtube.com/ubcspph1

Vacant, Director
Chris Lovato, Co-Director
chris.lovato@ubc.ca

School of Journalism
6388 Crescent Rd., Vancouver, BC V6T 1Z2
Tel: 604-822-6688; Fax: 604-822-6707
jrnl.journal@ubc.ca
www.journalism.ubc.ca

Alfred Hermida, Director

School of Social Work
Jack Bell Building
2080 West Mall, Vancouver, BC V6T 1Z2
Tel: 604-822-2255; Fax: 604-822-8656
www.socialwork.ubc.ca

Miu Chung Yan, Director
miu.yan@ubc.ca

Sauder School of Business
2053 Main Mall, Vancouver, BC V6T 1Z2
Tel: 604-822-8500; *Fax:* 604-822-8468
www.sauder.ubc.ca
Robert Helsley, Dean

Peter A. Allard School of Law
1822 East Mall, Vancouver, BC V6T 1Z1
Tel: 604-822-3151
allard.ubc.ca
Catherine Dauvergne, Dean, 604-822-2818
lawdean@allard.ubc.ca

Extended Learning
410 - 5950 University Blvd., Vancouver, BC V6T 1Z3
Tel: 604-822-1444; *Fax:* 604-822-0388
extendedlearning.ubc.ca
Simon Bates, Interim Executive Director

Campuses
UBC Okanagan Campus
3333 University Way, Kelowna, BC V1V 1V7, Canada
Tel: 250-807-8000; *Toll-Free:* 866-596-0767
ok.ubc.ca

UBC Robson Square Campus
800 Robson St., Vancouver, BC V6Z 3B7
Tel: 604-822-3333
robson.info@ubc.ca
www.robsonsquare.ubc.ca
twitter.com/UBCRobsonSquare
pinterest.com/ubcrobsonsquare

Great Northern Way Campus
685 Great Northern Way, Vancouver, BC V5T 0C6
Tel: 778-370-1001; *Fax:* 778-370-1020
Toll-Free: 855-737-2666
admin@thecdm.ca
thecdm.ca
Note: Great Northern Way Campus Trust is jointly owned by UBC, SFU, BCIT, & Emily Carr University. This campus operates The Centre for Digital Media.
Dennis Chenard, Director, Industry Relations
dennis_chenard@thecdm.ca

UBC Vantage College
Orchard Commons
#2001, 6363 Agronomy Rd., Vancouver, BC V6T 1Z4
Tel: 604-827-0337
info@vantagecollege.ubc.ca
www.vantagecollege.ubc.ca
Joanne Fox, Principal

Affiliations
Regent College
5800 University Blvd., Vancouver, BC V6T 2E4, Canada
Tel: 604-224-3245; *Fax:* 604-224-3097
Toll-Free: 1-800-663-8664
reception@regent-college.edu
www.regent-college.edu
Other Information: Regent Bookstore, Toll Free: 1-800-334-3279
www.facebook.com/regentcollege
twitter.com/regentcollege
www.linkedin.com/company/regent-college
www.youtube.com/user/underthegreenroof
Jeffrey P. Greenman, President

St. Mark's College
5935 Iona Dr., Vancouver, BC V6T 1J7, Canada
Tel: 604-822-4463
info@stmarkscollege.ca
www.stmarkscollege.ca
Peter Meehan, Principal
pmeehan@corpuschristi.ca
Gabriel Pillay, Registrar
gpillay@corpuschristi.ca

Carey Theological College
5920 Iona Dr., Vancouver, BC V6T 1J6
Tel: 604-225-5920
registrar@carey-edu.ca
carey-edu.ca
www.facebook.com/carey.edu
twitter.com/carey_edu
www.linkedin.com/company/carey-theological-college

Vancouver School of Theology
6015 Walter Gage Rd., Vancouver, BC V6T 1Z1
Tel: 604-822-9031; *Toll-Free:* 866-822-9031
info@vst.edu
www.vst.edu
www.facebook.com/vst.edu
twitter.com/vst_vancouver
www.youtube.com/user/VSTVancouver
Richard Topping, Principal, 604-822-9808
richardt@vst.edu

Patricia Dutcher-Walls, Dean, 604-822-9804
patdw@vst.edu

Centres & Institutes
Zach Walsh Research Lab
zachary.walsh@ubc.ca
blogs.ubc.ca/walshlab
Note: The Therapeutic, Recreational, & Problematic Substance Use lab focuses on the use of cannabis & psychedelic drugs for therapeutic & recreational purposes, studying their associations to mental health & addictions.
Zach Walsh, PhD, Research Director

Victoria: **Royal Roads University**
2005 Sooke Rd., Victoria, BC V9B 5Y2, Canada
Tel: 250-391-2511; *Fax:* 250-391-2500
Toll-Free: 1-800-788-8028
www.royalroads.ca
www.facebook.com/royalroadsu
twitter.com/royalroads
www.linkedin.com/school/royal-roads-university
www.youtube.com/user/RoyalRoadsUni
Full Time Equivalency: 5300 *Note:* Royal Roads University offers: Doctoral degrees in Social Sciences; Masters degrees in Arts, Business Admin., Science; Bachelor degrees in Arts, Commerce, Science; Graduate Certificates; Graduate Diplomas.
Kathleen Birney, Chair & Chancellor
Philip Steenkamp, President & Vice-Chancellor
Dr. Bill Holmes, Interim Provost & Vice-President, Academic, 250-391-2545

Victoria: **University of Victoria**
3800 Finnerty Rd., Victoria, BC V8P 5C2, Canada
Tel: 250-721-7211; *Fax:* 250-721-7212
Toll-Free: 888-721-8620
www.uvic.ca
Other Information: 250-721-7599;
www.facebook.com/universityofvictoria
twitter.com/uvic
www.linkedin.com/company/university-of-victoria
www.youtube.com/UVic
Full Time Equivalency: 21800 *Number of Employees:* 900 faculty
Shelagh Rogers, Chancellor
Kevin Hall, President & Vice-Chancellor
pres@uvic.ca
Chris Horbachewski, Vice-President, External Relations
eavper@uvic.ca
Gayle Gorrill, B.B.A., C.A., C.B.V., Vice-President, Finance & Operations
vpfo@uvic.ca
Lisa Kalynchuk, PhD, Vice-President, Research
vpr@uvic.ca
Valerie Kuehne, B.Sc.N., M.Ed., M.A., Ph., Vice-President, Academic & Provost
provost@uvic.ca

Faculties
Peter B. Gustavson School of Business
P.O. Box 1700 CSC
Victoria, BC V8W 2Y2
Tel: 250-472-4139; *Fax:* 250-721-6613
gustavson@uvic.ca
uvic.ca/gustavson
www.facebook.com/GustavsonUVic
twitter.com/GustavsonUVic
www.instagram.com/GustavsonUVic
Enrollment: 1100 *Number of Employees:* 122
Saul Klein, Dean, 250-721-6422
bizdean@uvic.ca

University of Victoria Continuing Studies (UVCS)
Continuing Studies Bldg.
3800 Finnerty Rd., 2nd Fl., Victoria, BC V8P 5C2
Tel: 250-472-4747; *Fax:* 250-721-8774
register@uvcs.uvic.ca
continuingstudies.uvic.ca
www.facebook.com/uviccontinuingstudies
Enrollment: 19202
Jo-Anne Clarke, Dean
uvcsdean@uvic.ca

Faculty of Education
MacLaurin Bldg.
3800 Finnerty Rd., #A243, Victoria, BC V8P 5C2
Tel: 250-721-7877; *Fax:* 250-472-5063
adve@uvic.ca
uvic.ca/education
www.facebook.com/UVicEducation
twitter.com/UVicEducation
Ralf St. Clair, Dean, 250-721-7757
edasst@uvic.ca
Wendy Seager, Administrative Officer, 250-721-7863
edao@uvic.ca

Faculty of Engineering
P.O. Box 1700 CSC
3800 Finnerty Rd., Victoria, BC V8W 2Y2
Tel: 250-721-6023; *Fax:* 250-721-8676
engr@uvic.ca
uvic.ca/engineering
www.facebook.com/UVicECS
twitter.com/UVicECS
www.instagram.com/uvicecs
Enrollment: 2900 *Number of Employees:* 89 Faculty
Peter Wild, Acting Dean
engrdean@uvic.ca

Fine Arts
Fine Arts Bldg.
P.O. Box 1700 CSC
#116, 3800 Finnerty Rd., Victoria, BC V8P 5C2
Tel: 250-721-7755; *Fax:* 250-721-7748
fineasst@uvic.ca
www.uvic.ca/finearts
www.facebook.com/uvicfinearts
twitter.com/uvic_finearts
www.youtube.com/user/UVicFineArts
Number of Employees: 150 faculty
Allana Lindgren, Acting Dean, 250-721-7755
finedean@uvic.ca

Graduate Studies
University Centre
P.O. Box 3025 CSC
3800 Finnerty Rd., #A206, Victoria, BC V8W 3P2
Tel: 250-472-4657; *Fax:* 250-472-5420
garo@uvic.ca
uvic.ca/graduatestudies
Grades: 3000
David Capson, Dean, 250-472-5187
graddean@uvic.ca
Cheryl Lawrence, Assistant to the Dean; Office Manager, 250-472-5187
fgsadmin@uvic.ca

Human & Social Development (HSD)
HSD Building
P.O. Box 1700 CSC
3800 Finnerty Rd., #A102, Victoria, BC V8W 2Y2
Tel: 250-721-8050; *Fax:* 250-721-7067
hsdinfo@uvic.ca
uvic.ca/hsd
www.facebook.com/UVicHSD
twitter.com/HSDResearch
Patricia Marck, Dean, 250-721-8050
hsddean@uvic.ca

Humanities
Clearihue Bldg.
P.O. Box 1700
3800 Finnerty Rd., #C305, Victoria, BC V8V 2Y2
Tel: 250-472-4677; *Fax:* 250-472-7059
humsoff@uvic.ca
uvic.ca/humanities
twitter.com/UVicHumanities
www.youtube.com/user/HumanitiesUVic
Annalee Lepp, Acting Dean, 250-472-5556
deanhums@uvic.ca

Faculty of Law
Murray and Anne Fraser Bldg.
P.O. Box 1700 CSC
#102, 3800 Finnerty Rd., Victoria, BC V8W 2Y2
Tel: 250-721-8150; *Fax:* 250-721-6390
weblaw@uvic.ca
www.uvic.ca/law
www.facebook.com/uvicfacultyoflaw
twitter.com/UVicLaw
Susan Breau, Dean, 250-721-8147
lawdean@uvic.ca

Faculty of Science
Elliott Bldg.
#166, 3800 Finnerty Rd., Victoria, BC V8P 5C2
Tel: 250-721-7062
uvic.ca/science
www.facebook.com/uvicscience
twitter.com/uvicscience
www.instagram.com/uvicscience
Number of Employees: 240
Hans-Peter Loock, Dean, 250-721-7062
sciedean@uvic.ca

Faculty of Social Sciences
Business & Economics Bldg.
#456, 3800 Finnerty Rd., Victoria, BC V8P 5C2
Tel: 250-472-5058; *Fax:* 250-472-4583
soscoff@uvic.ca
www.uvic.ca/socialsciences
www.facebook.com/uvicsocialsci
twitter.com/UVicSocialSci
www.youtube.com/user/facultysocialscience
Enrollment: 4900 *Number of Employees:* 370
Ann Stahl, Acting Dean, 250-472-5058
soscdean@uvic.ca

Centres & Institutes
Canadian Institute for Substance Use Research
Technology Enterprise Facility
P.O. Box 1700 CSC
#273, 2300 McKenzie Ave., Victoria, BC V8W 2Y2
Tel: 250-472-5445; *Fax:* 250-472-5321
cisur@uvic.ca
www.uvic.ca/research/centres/cisur
www.facebook.com/UVic.CISUR
twitter.com/UVic_CISUR
www.youtube.com/user/CARBCUVic

Tim Stockwell, Director
timstock@uvic.ca

Centre for Advanced Materials & Related Technology
(CAMTEC)
Elliott Building
#207, 3800 Finnerty Rd., Victoria, BC V8W 2Y2
Tel: 250-721-7736
camtec@uvic.ca
www.camtec.uvic.ca

Alexandre G. Brolo, Director, 250-721-7167
camdir@uvic.ca

Centre for Asia-Pacific Initiatives (CAPI)
Sedgewick Bldg.
P.O. Box 1700 CSC
3800 Finnerty Rd., #C128, Victoria, BC V8W 2Y2
Tel: 250-721-7020; *Fax:* 250-721-3107
capi@uvic.ca
uvic.ca/research/centres/capi
www.facebook.com/uviccapi
twitter.com/CAPIUVic
www.youtube.com/uviccapi

Victor V. Ramraj, Director, 250-721-7024
ramraj@uvic.ca

Centre for Biomedical Research
P.O. Box 1700 CSC
Victoria, BC V8W 2Y2
Tel: 250-472-4067; *Fax:* 250-472-4075
cfbr@uvic.ca
www.uvic.ca/research/centres/biomedical
twitter.com/UVicCBR

Dr. Stephanie Willerth, Acting Director

Centre for Indigenous Research & Community-Led
Engagement (CIRCLE)
P.O. Box 1700 CSC
Victoria, BC V8W 2Y2
Tel: 250-472-5456; *Fax:* 250-472-5450
circle@uvic.ca
www.uvic.ca/research/centres/circle
www.facebook.com/CIRCLE.UVic
twitter.com/CIRCLE_UVic
www.youtube.com/UVic

Charlotte Loppie, Director
loppie@uvic.ca

Colleges

Abbotsford: Summit Pacific College
P.O. Box 1700
35235 Straiton Rd., Abbotsford, BC V2S 7E7, Canada
Tel: 604-853-7491; *Fax:* 604-853-8951
Toll-Free: 1-800-976-8388
pr@summitpacific.ca
www.summitpacific.ca
www.facebook.com/summitpc
twitter.com/summitpc
www.youtube.com/user/SPCcollege
Note: Formerly Western Pentecostal Bible College; Canada Post
does not deliver to this address

Castlegar: Selkirk College
Castlegar Campus
301 Frank Beinder Way, Castlegar, BC V1N 4L3
Tel: 250-365-7292; *Fax:* 250-365-6568
Toll-Free: 888-953-1133
www.selkirk.ca
www.facebook.com/SelkirkCollege
twitter.com/selkirkcollege
www.youtube.com/selkirkcollege
Full Time Equivalency: 2771 *Note:* The regional community
college consists of the following schools: Kootenay School of the
Arts; School of Adult Basic Education & Transitional Training;
School of Business & Aviation; School of Digital Media & Music;
School of Environment & Geomatics; School of Health & Human
Services; School of Hospitality & Tourism; School of Industry &
Trades Training; School of Renewable Resources; School of
University Arts & Sciences & Selkirk International.
Burce LeRose, Chair
Angus Graeme, President & Chief Executive Officer

Campuses
Grand Forks Campus
P.O. Box 968
486 - 72nd Ave., Grand Forks, BC V0H 1H0, Canada
Tel: 250-442-2704; *Fax:* 250-442-2877

Kaslo Centre
P.O. Box 1149
421 Front St., Kaslo, BC V0G 1M0, Canada
Tel: 250-353-2618; *Fax:* 250-353-7121

Kootenay Studio Arts (KSA) Campus
606 Victoria St., Nelson, BC V1L 4K9, Canada
Tel: 250-352-2821; *Fax:* 250-352-1625
Toll-Free: 877-552-2821

Nakusp Centre
P.O. Box 720
311 Broadway, Nakusp, BC V0H 1R0, Canada
Tel: 250-265-4077; *Fax:* 250-265-3195
Other Information: Adult Basic Education: 250-265-3640

Silver King Campus
2001 Silver King Rd., Nelson, BC V1L 1C8, Canada
Tel: 250-352-6601; *Fax:* 250-352-3180
Toll-Free: 866-301-6601

Tenth Street Campus
820 Tenth St., Nelson, BC V1L 3C7, Canada
Tel: 250-352-6601; *Fax:* 250-352-5716
Toll-Free: 866-301-6601

Trail Campus
900 Helena St., Trail, BC V1R 4S6, Canada
Tel: 250-368-5236; *Fax:* 250-368-4983

Courtenay: North Island College
Comox Valley Campus
2300 Ryan Rd., Courtenay, BC V9N 8N6
Tel: 250-334-5000; *Fax:* 250-334-5018
Toll-Free: 800-715-0914
questions@nic.bc.ca
www.nic.bc.ca
www.facebook.com/North.Island.College
John Bowman, President

Campuses
Campbell River Campus
1685 South Dogwood St., Campbell River, BC V9W 8C1
Tel: 250-923-9700; *Fax:* 250-923-9703

Port Alberni Campus
3699 Roger St., Port Alberni, BC V9Y 8E3
Tel: 250-724-8711; *Fax:* 250-724-8700

Mount Waddington Regional Campus
P.O. Box 901
#140, 8950 Granville St., Port Hardy, BC V0N 2P0
Tel: 250-949-7912; *Fax:* 250-949-2617

Vigar Vocational Centre
2780 Vigar Rd., Campbell River, BC V9W 6A3
Tel: 250-923-9794; *Fax:* 250-830-0816

Tebo Vocational Centre
4751 Tebo Ave., Port Alberni, BC V9Y 6X7
Tel: 250-724-8738; *Fax:* 250-723-4573

Ucluelet Centre
P.O. Box 198
#10, 1636 Penninsula Rd., Ucluelet, BC V0R 3A0
Tel: 250-726-2697; *Fax:* 250-726-2698

Cranbrook: College of the Rockies
P.O. Box 8500
2700 College Way, Cranbrook, BC V1C 5L7
Tel: 250-489-2751; *Fax:* 250-489-1790
Toll-Free: 877-489-2687
info@cotr.bc.ca
www.cotr.bc.ca
www.facebook.com/COTR1
twitter.com/cotr_updates
www.linkedin.com/school/college-of-the-rockies
www.youtube.com/user/cotr1

David Walls, President & CEO

Campuses
Creston Campus
P.O. Box 1978
301 - 16th Ave., Creston, BC V0B 1G0
Tel: 250-428-5332; *Fax:* 250-428-4314
creston@cotr.bc.ca
www.cotr.bc.ca/creston

Kim Garety, Campus Manager
kgarety@cotr.bc.ca

Invermere Campus
#2, 1535 - 14th St., RR#4, Invermere, BC V0A 1K4
Tel: 250-342-3210; *Fax:* 250-342-9221
Toll-Free: 866-740-2687
invermere@cotr.bc.ca
www.cotr.bc.ca/invermere
twitter.com/COTRinvermere

Michelle Taylor, Acting Campus Manager
mtaylor2@cotr.bc.ca

Fernie Campus
P.O. Box 1770
342 - 3rd Ave., Fernie, BC V0B 1M0
Tel: 250-423-4691; *Fax:* 250-423-3932
Toll-Free: 866-423-4691
fernie@cotr.bc.ca
www.cotr.bc.ca/fernie

Anita Palmer, Campus Manager
apalmer@cotr.bc.ca

Golden Campus
P.O. Box 376
1305 South 9th St., Golden, BC V0A 1H0
Tel: 250-344-5901; *Fax:* 250-344-5745
golden@cotr.bc.ca
www.cotr.bc.ca/golden
www.facebook.com/cotrgolden
twitter.com/COTR_Golden

Karen Cathcart, Campus Manager
kcathcart@cotr.bc.ca

Kimberley Campus
1850 Warren Ave., Kimberley, BC V1A 1S1
Tel: 250-427-7116; *Fax:* 250-427-3034
kimberley@cotr.bc.ca
www.cotr.bc.ca/kimberley
www.facebook.com/COTRConEd

Cranbrook: College of the Rockies
P.O. Box 8500
2700 College Way, Cranbrook, BC V1C 5L7
Tel: 250-489-2751; *Fax:* 250-489-1790
Toll-Free: 877-489-2687
info@cotr.bc.ca
www.cotr.bc.ca
www.facebook.com/COTR1
twitter.com/cotr_updates
www.linkedin.com/school/college-of-the-rockies
www.youtube.com/user/cotr1
Note: Offers a 26-week Cannabis Retail Specialist program.
Offered online only. Program includes a work placement. Upon
completion, students will recieve a Certificate of Achievement.

Dawson Creek: Northern Lights College
Regional Administration
11401 - 8th St., Dawson Creek, BC V1G 4G2
Tel: 250-782-5251; *Fax:* 250-784-7563
Toll-Free: 866-463-6652
appinfo@nlc.bc.ca
www.nlc.bc.ca
www.facebook.com/nrnlights
twitter.com/nrnlights
www.instagram.com/nrnlights
Bryn Kulmatycki, President & CEO

Campuses
Atlin Campus
Also known as: Atlin Learning Centre
P.O. Box 29
Atlin, BC V0W 1A0
Tel: 250-651-7762; *Fax:* 250-651-7730
Toll-Free: 866-463-6652
Note: The campus offers continuing education in academic & pre-professional studies, development & upgrading, distance education, & industrial & workforce training.
Derrick Mohamed, Principal, Secondary Campus
Brad Martens, Vice-Principal

Chetwynd Campus
P.O. Box 1180
5132 - 50th St., Chetwynd, BC V0C 1J0
Tel: 250-788-2248; *Fax:* 250-788-9706
Toll-Free: 866-463-6652
Note: Programs offered include applied business technology, teacher assistant training, social services worker training, forestry, hospitality & tourism operations, continuing education, adult basic education, university transfer, & adult special education.
David Szucsko, Campus Administrator
dszucsko@nlc.bc.ca

Dawson Creek Campus
11401 - 8 St., Dawson Creek, BC V1G 4G2
Tel: 250-782-5251; *Fax:* 250-784-7563
Toll-Free: 866-463-6652
Note: The campus features technical, academic, trades, & vocational programs.
Lorelee Mathias, Director, Student Services
lmathias@nlc.bc.ca

Dease Lake Campus
P.O. Box 220
Commercial Dr., Lot 10, Dease Lake, BC V0C 1L0
Tel: 250-771-5500; *Fax:* 250-771-5510
Toll-Free: 866-463-6652
Note: The campus serves full-time & part-time vocational and continuing education students in Atlin, Telegraph Creek, Lower Post, Iskut, & Good Hope Lake.
Jacinta Snyder, Head of School, 905-565-8707, ext. 12
jsnyder@rotherglen.com

Fort Nelson Campus
P.O. Box 860
5201 Simpson Trail, Fort Nelson, BC V0C 1R0
Tel: 250-774-2741; *Fax:* 250-774-2750
Toll-Free: 1-866-463-6652
Note: Continuing education programs are provided.
Laurie Dolan, Campus Administrator
ldolan@nlc.bc.ca

Fort St. John Campus
P.O. Box 1000
9820 - 120 Ave., Fort St John, BC V1J 6K1
Tel: 250-785-6981; *Fax:* 250-785-1294
Toll-Free: 866-463-6652
Note: Academic, apprenticeship, career/technical, vocational, & international students students are served by the Fort St. John campus.
Kathy Handley, Campus Administrator
khandley@nlc.bc.ca

Tumbler Ridge Campus
P.O. Box 180
180 Southgate Dr., Tumbler Ridge, BC V0C 2W0
Tel: 250-242-5591; *Fax:* 250-242-3109
Toll-Free: 866-463-6652
Note: Adult basic education is offered in Tumbler Ridge.
Tracy Chong, Co-Head of School
tchong@rotherglen.com
Eileen Lanigan, Co-Head of School
elanigan@rotherglen.com

Langley: Trinity Western Seminary
7600 Glover Rd., Langley, BC V2Y 1Y1
acts@twu.ca
www.twu.ca/academics/trinity-western-seminary
www.facebook.com/trinitywesternseminary

Prince George: College of New Caledonia
3330 - 22nd Ave., Prince George, BC V2N 1P8, Canada
Tel: 250-562-2131; *Fax:* 250-561-5816
Toll-Free: 1-800-371-8111
askcnc@cnc.bc.ca
www.cnc.bc.ca
www.facebook.com/CollegeOfNewCaledonia
twitter.com/cnc_bc_ca
www.linkedin.com/school/college-of-new-caledonia
www.youtube.com/user/CaledoniaCollege
Full Time Equivalency: 5250

Henry Reiser, President
reiserh@cnc.bc.ca

Campuses
Nicholson Campus
2211 Nicholson Ave. South, Prince George, BC V2N 1P8, Canada
Tel: 250-562-2131; *Toll-Free:* 800-371-8111

Lakes District Campus
Also known as: Burns Lake
P.O. Box 5000
545 Hwy. 16 West, Burns Lake, BC V0J 1E0, Canada
Tel: 250-692-1700; *Fax:* 250-692-1750
Toll-Free: 866-692-1943
lksdist@cnc.bc.ca
Corinne George, Regional Principal
georgec3@cnc.bc.ca

Mackenzie Campus
P.O. Box 2110
540 Mackenzie Blvd., Mackenzie, BC V0J 2C0, Canada
Tel: 250-997-7200; *Fax:* 250-997-3779
cncmackenzie@cnc.bc.ca
Shannon Bezo, Regional Principal
bezos@cnc.bc.ca

Quesnel Campus
100 Campus Way, Quesnel, BC V2J 7K1, Canada
Tel: 250-991-7500; *Fax:* 250-991-7523
Toll-Free: 866-680-7550
quesnel@cnc.bc.ca

Nechako Campus
3231 Hospital Rd., Vanderhoof, BC V0J 3A2, Canada
Tel: 250-567-3200; *Fax:* 250-567-3217
nechako@cnc.bc.ca
Troy Morin, Regional Principal
morintr@cnc.bc.ca

Fort St. James Campus
P.O. Box 1557
179 Douglas St., Fort St. James, BC V0J 1P0
Tel: 250-996-7019; *Fax:* 250-996-7014
cncfsj@cnc.bc.ca
Troy Morin, Regional Principal
morintr@cnc.bc.ca

Centres & Institutes
Fraser Lake Learning Centre
298 McMillan Ave., Fraser Lake, BC V0J 1S0
Tel: 250-699-6249; *Fax:* 250-699-6269
cncfl@cnc.bc.ca

John A. Brink Trades & Technology Centre
1727 West Central, Prince George, BC V2N 1P6
Tel: 250-561-5804

Terrace: Coast Mountain College
College Services
5331 McConnell Ave., Terrace, BC V8G 4X2
Tel: 250-635-6511; *Fax:* 250-638-5432
Toll-Free: 1-877-277-2288
www.nwcc.bc.ca
www.facebook.com/coastmountaincollege
twitter.com/cmtncollege
www.instagram.com/coastmountaincollege
Ken Burt, President & CEO

Campuses
Hazelton Campus
P.O. Box 338
4815 Swannell Dr., Hazelton, BC V0J 1Y0, Canada
Tel: 250-842-5291; *Fax:* 250-842-5813

Kitimat Campus
606 Mountainview Sq., Kitimat, BC V8C 2N2, Canada
Tel: 250-632-4766; *Fax:* 250-632-5069

Prince Rupert Campus
353 - 5th St., Prince Rupert, BC V8J 3L6, Canada
Tel: 250-624-6054; *Fax:* 250-624-3923

Queen Charlotte Campus
P.O. Box 67
138 Bay St., Queen Charlotte Village, BC V0T 1S0, Canada
Tel: 250-559-8222; *Fax:* 250-559-8219

Smithers Campus
P.O. Box 3606
3966 - 2nd Ave., Smithers, BC V0J 2N0, Canada
Tel: 250-847-4461; *Fax:* 250-847-4568

Terrace Campus
5331 McConnell Ave., Terrace, BC V8G 4X2, Canada
Tel: 250-635-6511; *Fax:* 250-638-5432

Masset Campus
P.O. Box 559
2151 Tahayghen, Masset, BC V0T 1M0, Canada
Tel: 250-626-3670; *Fax:* 250-626-3680

Victoria: Camosun College
Lansdowne Campus
3100 Foul Bay Rd., Victoria, BC V8P 5J2
Tel: 250-370-3550; *Toll-Free:* 877-554-7555
www.camosun.ca
www.facebook.com/CamosunCollege
twitter.com/camosun
www.youtube.com/user/mycamosun
Full Time Equivalency: 19000 *Number of Employees:* 900
Sherri Bell, President

Schools
School of Continuing Education
continuinged@camosun.ca
Note: Three professional training courses will soon be available through the Continuing Education program.

Campuses
Interurban Campus
Liz Ashton Campus Centre
#226, 4461 Interurban Rd., Victoria, BC V9E 2C1

Victoria: Lester B. Pearson United World College of the Pacific
Also known as: Pearson College UWC
Old Name: Lester B. Pearson College of the Pacific
650 Pearson College Dr., Victoria, BC V9C 4H7
Tel: 250-391-2411
www.pearsoncollege.ca
www.facebook.com/PearsonUWC
twitter.com/PCUWC
www.linkedin.com/groups/49277
www.youtube.com/user/PearsonUWC
Full Time Equivalency: 200
Désirée McGraw, President

Post Secondary/Technical

Colleges

Kelowna: Okanagan College
1000 KLO Rd., Kelowna, BC V1Y 4X2
Tel: 250-862-5480; *Fax:* 250-862-5434
Toll-Free: 866-638-0058
cscentral@okanagan.bc.ca
www.okanagan.bc.ca
www.facebook.com/okanagancollege.ca
twitter.com/OkanaganCollege
www.linkedin.com/company/okanagan-college
www.youtube.com/user/OkanaganCollege
Enrollment: 20000
Jim Hamilton, President
jhamilton@okanagan.bc.ca
Allan Coyle, Interim Vice-President, Students
acoyle@okanagan.bc.ca
Andrew Hay, Vice-President, Education
ahay@okanagan.bc.ca
Curtis Morcom, Vice-President, Employee & Corporate Services
cmorcom@okanagan.bc.ca

School of Continuing Studies
Tel: 250-862-5480
cscentral@okanagan.bc.ca
Note: Okanagan College offers 7 cannabis training courses; including cannabis legislation and quality assurance, botany and plant sciences, business fundamentals, pest management, and more. Okanagan College is partnering with CropHealth and Sunniva.

Campuses
Penticton Campus
583 Duncan Ave. West, Penticton, BC V2A 8E1
Tel: 250-492-4305; *Fax:* 250-490-3950
Toll-Free: 866-510-8899
penticton@okanagan.bc.ca
www.okanagan.bc.ca/southokanagan
www.facebook.com/OCPen
Allan Coyle, Interim Dean

Salmon Arm Campus
2552 10th Ave. NE, Salmon Arm, BC V1E 4N3
Tel: 250-832-2126; *Toll-Free:* 888-831-0341
csshuswap@okanagan.bc.ca
Joan Ragsdale, Regional Dean
jragsdale@okanagan.bc.ca

Vernon Campus
7000 College Way, Vernon, BC V1B 2N5
Tel: 250-545-7291; *Fax:* 250-503-2653
Toll-Free: 800-289-8993
csnorth@okanagan.bc.ca

Jane Lister, Dean

New Westminster: Douglas College
P.O. Box 2503
700 Royal Ave., New Westminster, BC V3L 5B2
Tel: 604-527-5400; *Fax:* 604-527-5095
regoffice@douglascollege.ca
www.douglascollege.ca
www.facebook.com/douglascollege
twitter.com/douglascollege
www.linkedin.com/school/douglas-college
www.youtube.com/user/DouglasCollegeVideo

Enrollment: 25000
Kathy Denton, President & CEO

Campuses
Coquitlam Campus
1250 Pinetree Way, Coquitlam, BC V3B 7X3

Vancouver: Langara College
100 West 49th Ave., Vancouver, BC V5Y 2Z6
Tel: 604-323-5511; *Fax:* 604-323-5555
geninfo@langara.ca
langara.ca
www.facebook.com/langaracollege
twitter.com/langaracollege
www.youtube.com/user/LangaraCollege

Enrollment: 21500
Lane Trotter, President & CEO
ltrotter@langara.ca

Vancouver: Vancouver Community College
Broadway Campus
1155 East Broadway, Vancouver, BC V5T 4V5
Tel: 604-871-7000; *Fax:* 604-871-7100
Toll-Free: 866-565-7820
www.vcc.ca
www.facebook.com/vcc
twitter.com/myVCC
www.linkedin.com/school/vancouver-community-college
www.youtube.com/user/myVCC

Ajay Patel, President

Campuses
Annacis Island Campus
1608 Cliveden Ave., Delta, BC V3M 6P1
Tel: 604-871-7000

Downtown Campus
250 West Pender St., Vancouver, BC V6B 1S9
Tel: 604-871-7000; *Fax:* 604-443-8588
Toll-Free: 866-565-7820

Victoria: Camosun College
Lansdowne Campus
3100 Foul Bay Rd., Victoria, BC V8P 5J2
Tel: 250-370-3550; *Fax:* 250-370-3750
Toll-Free: 877-554-7555
camosun.ca
www.facebook.com/CamosunCollege
twitter.com/camosun
www.linkedin.com/school/camosun-college
www.youtube.com/user/mycamosun

Enrollment: 20400
Sherri Bell, President

Campuses
Interurban Campus
Liz Ashton Campus Centre
#226, 4461 Interurban Rd., Victoria, BC V9E 2C1

Post Secondary/Technical

Abbotsford: BC Helicopters
1404 Townline Rd., Abbotsford, BC V2T 6E1
Tel: 604-639-9090; *Fax:* 604-639-9091
www.bchelicopters.com
www.facebook.com/bchelicopters
www.instagram.com/bchelicopters

Mischa Gelb, Chief Flight Instructor
mischa@bchelicopters.com

Burnaby: Brighton College
#305, 4538 Kingsway, Burnaby, BC V5H 4T9
Tel: 604-430-5608
study@brightoncollege.com
brightoncollege.com
www.facebook.com/brightoncollege
twitter.com/BrightonCol
www.linkedin.com/school/brighton-college
www.youtube.com/user/BrightonColl

Patrick Zhao, President

Burnaby: British Columbia Institute of Technology (BCIT)
3700 Willingdon Ave., Burnaby, BC V5G 3H2
Tel: 604-434-5734; *Toll-Free:* 866-434-1610
www.bcit.ca
www.facebook.com/bcit.ca
twitter.com/bcit
www.linkedin.com/school/bcit
www.instagram.com/lifeatbcit

Enrollment: 48000
Kathy Kinloch, President
Ana Lopez, Vice-President, Human Resources & People Development
Paul McCullough, Vice-President, Advancement
Tom Roemer, Vice-President, Academic

Burnaby: Cambridge College
4800 Kingsway, #OL454, Burnaby, BC V5H 4J2
Tel: 604-438-7246; *Fax:* 604-438-2667
info@cambridgecollege.ca
www.cambridgecollege.ca

Burnaby: CDI College
Collège CDI
Headquarters
#500, 5021 Kingsway, Burnaby, BC V5H 4A5
Toll-Free: 1-800-675-4392
www.cdicollege.com
www.facebook.com/CDICollege
twitter.com/CDICollege
www.linkedin.com/school/cdi-college
www.youtube.com/c/CDICollegeCanada
Note: Graduates of the college are trained to work in the business, technology, & healthcare sectors.

Campuses
Brampton Campus
#101, 2 County Court Blvd., Brampton, ON L6W 3W8

Burnaby Campus
#500, 5021 Kingsway, Burnaby, BC V5H 4A5

Calgary - City Centre Campus
#200, 703 - 6th Ave. SW, Calgary, AB T2P 0T9

Calgary - North Campus
#100, 403 - 33rd St. NE, Calgary, AB T2A 1X5

Calgary - South Campus
Midnapore Mall
#200, 240 Midpark Way SE, Calgary, AB T2X 1N4

Edmonton - City Centre Campus
#200, 10004 Jasper Ave., Edmonton, AB T5J 1R3

Edmonton - North Campus
#174, 9450 - 137th Ave., Edmonton, AB T5E 6C2

Edmonton - South Campus
#101, 4723 - 52nd Ave. NW, Edmonton, AB T6B 3R6

Edmonton - West Campus
176 Mayfield Common, Edmonton, AB T5P 4B3

Laval Campus
#400, 3, place Laval, Laval, QC H7N 1A2

Longueuil Campus
Complexe St-Charles
#120, 1111, rue St-Charles ouest, Longueuil, QC J4K 5G4

Mississauga Campus
#280, 33 City Centre Dr., Mississauga, ON L5B 2N5

Montréal Campus
#700, 416, boul de Maisonneuve ouest, Montréal, QC H3A 1L2

North York Campus
#33, 4950 Yonge St., Toronto, ON M2N 6K1

Pointe-Claire Campus
#500, 1000, boul Saint-Jean, Montréal, QC H9R 5P1

Red Deer Campus
5000 Gaetz Ave., 5th Fl., Red Deer, AB T4N 6C2

Richmond Campus
#180, 4351 No. 3 Rd., Richmond, BC V6X 3A7

Scarborough Campus
#205, 2206 Eglinton Ave. East, Toronto, ON M1L 4S8

St-Leonard Campus
9480, boul Lacordaire, Montréal, QC H1R 0C4

Surrey Campus
#100, 11125 - 124th St., Surrey, BC V3V 4V2

Surrey - South Campus
#105, 15149 - 56th Ave., Surrey, BC V3S 9A5

Vancouver Campus
549 Howe St., 4th Fl., Vancouver, BC V6C 2C2

Winnipeg Campus
280 Main St., Winnipeg, MB R3C 1A9

Burnaby: Pacific Vocational College (PVC)
4064 McConnell Dr., Burnaby, BC V5A 3A8
Tel: 604-421-5255; *Fax:* 604-421-7445
admin@pvc.training
pacificvocationalcollege.ca
Note: Technical training is offered through the following programs: plumbing, sprinklerfitting, steamfitting, gasfitting & cross connection control.

Burnaby: Sprott Shaw College
3216 Beta Ave., Burnaby, BC V5G 4K4
Tel: 778-800-2719; *Fax:* 778-379-0411
www.sprottshaw.com
www.facebook.com/sprottshaw
twitter.com/sprottshaw
www.linkedin.com/school/sprottshaw
www.instagram.com/sprottshaw

Campbell River: Canadian Outdoor Leadership Training (COLT)
Strathcona Park Lodge
P.O. Box 2160
41040 Gold River Hwy., Campbell River, BC V9W 5C5
Tel: 250-286-3122; *Fax:* 250-286-6010
info@colt.bc.ca
coltoutdoorleadership.com
www.facebook.com/COLT.program
www.instagram.com/colt_outdoorleadership

Campbell River: **Discovery Community College**
Campbell River Spirit Square Campus
1130 Shoppers Row, Campbell River, BC V9W 2C8
Tel: 250-287-9850
discoverycommunitycollege.com
www.facebook.com/DiscCommCollege
twitter.com/disccommcollege

Campuses
Courtenay Campus
Comox Valley Seniors Village
4640 Headquarters Rd., Courtenay, BC V9N 7J3
Tel: 250-338-9663

Maple Ridge Campus
22141 - 119th Ave., Maple Ridge, BC V2X 2Y7
Tel: 604-463-1174

Nanaimo Campus
#101, 495 Dunsmuir St., Nanaimo, BC V9R 6B9
Tel: 250-740-0115

Parksville Campus
#201, 160 Corfield Ave. South, Parksville, BC V9P 2H5
Tel: 250-468-7777

Surrey Campus
10040 King George Blvd., Surrey, BC V3T 2W4
Tel: 604-930-9908

Courtenay: **Keystone College**
#4, 2720 Cliffe Ave., Courtenay, BC V9N 2L6
Tel: 250-871-8300
info@keystonecollege.ca
keystonecollege.ca
www.facebook.com/2036267726409719
Note: Founded in 2007, Keystone College offering courses in business, hair, esthetics, hospitality & language.

Campuses
Surrey Campus
#117 & 216, 9801 King George Blvd., Surrey, BC V3T 5H6
Tel: 778-820-2020; *Fax:* 778-820-2021

Kelowna: **Centre for Arts & Technology (CAT)**
#100, 1632 Dickson Ave., Kelowna, BC V1Y 7T2
Toll-Free: 866-860-2787
inquire@digitalartschool.com
www.digitalartschool.com
www.facebook.com/centreforartsandtechnology
www.linkedin.com/company/centre-for-arts-and-technology
www.youtube.com/user/CanDigiSchool

Kelowna: **Kelowna College of Professional Counselling (KCPC)**
#101, 251 Lawrence Ave., Kelowna, BC V1Y 6L2
Tel: 250-717-0412
www.counsellortraining.com
Note: The Kelowna College of Professional Counselling is accredited by the Private Career Training Institutions Agency. Students may earn a Diploma of Applied Psychology & Counselling.
Phillip R. Hay, Executive Director & Registrar
registrar@counsellortraining.com

Langley: **New Directions Vocational Testing & Counselling Services Ltd.**
Also known as: New Directions Langley
#100, 20436 Fraser Hwy., Langley, BC V3A 4G2
Tel: 604-530-0535; *Fax:* 604-532-0561
office@newdir.ca
www.newdirectionsschool.com
Note: New Directions is an English language school funded by Immigration, Refugees & Citizenship Canada.
Yvonne Hopp, President & CEO

Langley: **Roofing Contractors Association of British Columbia (RCABC) Training Centre**
9734 - 201st St., Langley, BC V1M 3E8
Tel: 604-882-9734
training@rcabc.org
www.rcabc.org
www.facebook.com/RoofingCABC
twitter.com/RoofingCABC
Note: Instruction is delivered to the roofing & construction-related industries of British Columbia. Apprenticeship training is provided in the architectural sheet metal & the roof, damp & waterproofing sectors.

Maple Ridge: **Ridge Meadows College**
20575 Thorne Ave., Maple Ridge, BC V2X 9A6
Tel: 604-466-6555; *Fax:* 604-463-5437
rmc@sd42.ca
www.rmcollege.ca

Note: The private college offers certificate programs. General interest courses are available, as well as trades programs, such as Forklift Operator & Building Service Worker.

Merritt: **Nicola Valley Institute of Technology (NVIT)**
4155 Belshaw St., Merritt, BC V1K 1R1
Tel: 250-378-3300; *Fax:* 250-315-0107
Toll-Free: 877-682-3300
info@nvit.bc.ca
www.nvit.ca
www.facebook.com/NVIT83
twitter.com/NVIT83
www.youtube.com/user/MyNVIT
Enrollment: 1500 *Note:* Certificate & diploma programs, adult basic education, collaborative degrees & on-campus, in-community & online delivery
Ken Tourand, President
ktourand@nvit.bc.ca

Campuses
Vancouver Campus
#200, 4355 Mathissi Pl., Burnaby, BC V5G 4S8
Tel: 604-602-9555; *Fax:* 604-412-5496

Nelson: **Kootenay Columbia College of Integrative Health Sciences (KCCIHS)**
#2, 560 Baker St., Nelson, BC V1L 4H9
Tel: 250-352-5887
kootenaycolumbiacollege.com
www.facebook.com/kootenaycolumbiacollege
twitter.com/CollegeKootenay
www.instagram.com/kootenaycolumbiacollege

New Westminster: **Boucher Institute of Naturopathic Medicine**
#230, 435 Columbia St., New Westminster, BC V3L 5N8
Tel: 604-777-9981; *Fax:* 604-777-9982
info@binm.org
binm.org
www.facebook.com/BoucherInstitute
twitter.com/BoucherInst

New Westminster: **Central College**
#200, 60 - 8th St., New Westminster, BC V3M 3P1
Tel: 604-523-2388; *Fax:* 604-523-2389
contact@centralcollegebc.ca
centralcollegebc.ca
www.facebook.com/CentralCollege.ca

Campuses
Downtown Campus
#216, 181 Keefer Pl., Vancouver, BC V6B 6C1
Tel: 604-336-9788

New Westminster: **Hilltop Academy**
#215, 810 Quayside Dr., New Westminster, BC V3M 6B9
Tel: 604-553-0505; *Fax:* 604-357-1133
info@hilltopacademy.ca
www.hilltopacademy.ca
Note: The academy offers a fitness leadership diploma program. Graduates become BC Recreation & Park Association registered weight trainers, personal trainers & group fitness instructors. The academy is a partner of the American Council on Exercise, so students are able to become ACE certified personal trainers.
Kim Bond, Administrator, Senior Education

New Westminster: **Justice Institute of British Columbia (JIBC)**
New Westminster Campus
715 McBride Blvd., New Westminster, BC V3L 5T4
Tel: 604-525-5422; *Fax:* 604-528-5518
Toll-Free: 888-865-7764
infodesk@jibc.ca
www.jibc.ca
www.facebook.com/justiceinstitute
twitter.com/JIBCnews
www.linkedin.com/school/justice-institute-of-british-columbia
www.instagram.com/justiceinstitutebc
Michel Tarko, President & CEO
mtarko@jibc.ca

Campuses
Chilliwack Campus
5470 Dieppe St., Chilliwack, BC V2R 5Y8
Tel: 604-525-5422
www.jibc.ca/jibc-campuses/jibc-chilliwack

Maple Ridge Campus
13500 - 256th St., Maple Ridge, BC V4R 1C9
Tel: 604-525-5422
www.jibc.ca/jibc-campuses/jibc-maple-ridge

Okanagan Campus
825 Walrod St., Kelowna, BC V1Y 2S4
Tel: 604-525-5422
www.jibc.ca/jibc-campuses/jibc-okanagan

Pit Meadows Campus
18200 Ford Rd., Pitt Meadows, BC V3Y 1T6
Tel: 604-525-5422
www.jibc.ca/jibc-campuses/jibc-pitt-meadows

Victoria Campus
810 Fort St., Victoria, BC V8W 1H8
Tel: 604-525-5422
www.jibc.ca/jibc-campuses/jibc-victoria

Centres & Institutes
Fire & Safety Training Centre
13500 - 256th St., Maple Ridge, BC V4R 1C9
Tel: 604-528-5590
fire@jibc.ca
www.jibc.ca/areas-of-study/firefighting
Note: Courses offered on marine & industrial firefighting, emergency response to incidents involving hazardous materials & fire service training from recruit to chief officer.
Keith Boswell, Coordinator
kboswell@jibc.ca

Pitt Meadows Driver Education Centre
18799 Airport Way, Pitt Meadows, BC V3Y 2B4
Tel: 604-528-5807
dec@jibc.ca

New Westminster: **West Coast College of Massage Therapy (WCCMT)**
New Westminster Campus
613 Columbia St., New Westminster, BC V3M 1A7
Tel: 604-520-1844
admissions@collegeofmassage.com
collegeofmassage.com
www.facebook.com/WCCMT
twitter.com/WCCMT
Lori DeCou, Director, Operations

Campuses
WCCMT Victoria Campus (WCCMT)
#100, 818 Broughton St., Victoria, BC V8W 1E4
Tel: 250-381-9800; *Fax:* 250-381-9801
Lindy Lovett, Executive Director, Operations
lindyl@collegeofmassage.com

Canadian College of Massage & Hydrotherapy - Halifax Campus (CCMH)
Mumford Professional Centre
P.O. Box 0180
#180, 6960 Mumford Rd., Halifax, NS B3L 4P1
Tel: 902-484-0158; *Fax:* 902-832-1077
admissions@ccmhhalifax.com
www.ccmhhalifax.com

New Westminster: **Winston College**
1176 - 8th Ave., New Westminster, BC V3M 2R6
Tel: 604-357-8021
info@winstoncollege.com
www.winstoncollege.com
www.facebook.com/WinstonCollege.Burnaby

Port Coquitlam: **All Body Laser Corp. Training Institute**
#140, 2627 Shaughnessy St., Port Coquitlam, BC V3C 0E1
Tel: 604-773-7515
www.allbodylaser.com/training-institute
Note: Specialized training institute in the area of cosmetic medical laser technology & advanced skin care.
Marina Bosnjak, President & CEO

Queen Charlotte: **Canadian Acupressure College**
P.O. Box 65
Queen Charlotte, BC V0T 1S0
Tel: 250-480-6679
cai@islandnet.com
www.acupressureshiatsuschool.com
www.facebook.com/5EAcupressure
twitter.com/cacacupressure
Note: Founded in 1994, the Canadian Acupressure College is a member of the Health Action Network Society, Association of Holistic Health Practitioners, & Natural Health Practitioners of Canada.
Kathy de Bucy, Founder, Administrator & Director

Revelstoke: **Canadian Avalanche Association**
P.O. Box 2759
110 MacKenzie Ave., Revelstoke, BC V0E 2S0
Tel: 250-837-2435; *Fax:* 866-366-2094
www.avalancheassociation.ca

Note: The Canadian Avalanche Association offers an industry training program for avalanche workers. The program is a fully bonded, private, post-secondary educational institution that teaches across Canada.
Joe Obad, Executive Director
jobad@avalancheassociation.ca
Emily Grady, Manager, Industry Training Program
egrady@avalancheassociation.ca

Surrey: **Canadian Health Care Academy**
#202, 10252 City Pkwy., Surrey, BC V3T 4C2
Tel: 604-540-2421; *Fax:* 604-540-8550
info@chcabc.com
www.chcabc.com

Surrey: **Dorset College**
#205, 10114 King George Blvd., Surrey, BC V3T 2W4
Tel: 604-879-8686; *Fax:* 604-874-8686
Toll-Free: 888-272-3333
info@dorsetcollege.bc.ca
www.dorsetcollege.bc.ca

Surrey: **Stenberg College**
#750, 13450 - 102nd Ave., Surrey, BC V3T 5X3
Tel: 604-580-2772; *Fax:* 604-580-2774
Toll-Free: 866-580-2772
stenbergcollege.com
www.facebook.com/StenbergCollege
twitter.com/StenbergCollege
www.linkedin.com/school/stenberg-college
www.youtube.com/user/stenbergcollege
Note: The college offers programs for the following roles: Resident care attendant; community support worker; nursing unit clerk, medical office assistant; institutional aid; veterinary assistant; practical nursing program; automotive technician.
Jeremy Sabell, President

Surrey: **West Coast College of Health Care**
#204, 9648 - 128 St., Surrey, BC V3T 2X9
Tel: 604-951-6644; *Fax:* 604-951-6608
Toll-Free: 1-800-807-8558
admin@westcoastcollege.com
www.westcoastcollege.com
www.facebook.com/westcoastcollegeofhealthcare
Note: West Coast College of Health Care provides health & human services training. Program offered is instruction to become a medical laboratory assistant. The college is designated by the Private Training Institutions Branch of British Columbia. Program is eligible for student loans.

Toronto: **Aveda Institute Canada**
125 King St. East, Toronto, BC M5C 1G6
Tel: 416-803-1426; *Toll-Free:* 877-902-8332
info@avedainstitute.ca
www.avedainstitute.ca
www.facebook.com/AvedaInstitutesToronto
Note: Founded in 1978, the Aveda Institute offers Private Career Training Institutions Agency accredited programs for careers in hair styling or cosmetology.

Vancouver: **Ashton College**
1190 Melville St., 3rd Fl., Vancouver, BC V6E 3W1
Tel: 604-899-0803; *Fax:* 604-899-0830
Toll-Free: 866-759-6006
info@ashtoncollege.ca
www.ashtoncollege.ca
www.facebook.com/AshtonCollege
twitter.com/AshtonCollege
www.linkedin.com/school/ashton-college
www.youtube.com/user/AshtonCommunications
Colin Fortes, President

Vancouver: **Blanche Macdonald Centre**
Uptown Campus, City Square
#100, 555 West 12th Ave., Vancouver, BC V5Z 3X7
Tel: 604-685-0347
info@blanchemacdonald.com
www.blanchemacdonald.com
www.facebook.com/blanchemacdonaldcentre
twitter.com/blancheworld
www.linkedin.com/school/blanche-macdonald-centre
Note: Founded in 1960, the Blanche Macdonald Centre provides training in the areas of fashion design & merchandising, makeup artistry, hair design, nail technology & spa therapy.
Lise Graham, Managing Director
lise@blanchemacdonald.com
Barbara Johnston, Managing Director
barb@blanchemacdonald.com

Campuses
Atelier Campus
#201, 410 Robson St., Vancouver, BC V6B 0H3
Tel: 604-685-5560

Downtown Campus
460 Robson St., Vancouver, BC V6B 2B5
Tel: 604-685-0337

Vancouver: **Body Glamour Institute of Beauty**
1919 Lonsdale Ave., Vancouver, BC V7M 2K3
Tel: 604-904-4111; *Fax:* 604-980-5744
www.bodyglamourinc.com

Vancouver: **Canadian College of English Language**
#450, 1050 Alberni St., Vancouver, BC V6E 1A3
Tel: 604-688-9366
canada-english.com
Note: An English certificate & diploma are offered, as well as English for business lessons & English tutoring.
Lane Clark, Chief Executive Officer
Shaun Macleod, Academic Director

Vancouver: **Canadian College of Shiatsu Therapy (CCST)**
142 Lonsdale Ave., Vancouver, BC V7M 2E8
Tel: 604-904-4187; *Fax:* 604-904-4183
info@shiatsuvancouver.ca
www.shiatsuvancouver.ca
www.facebook.com/100063672995014

Vancouver: **Canadian Institute of Gemmology (CIG)**
P.O. Box 57010
Vancouver, BC V5K 5G6
Tel: 604-530-8569
www.cigem.ca
www.facebook.com/CanadianInstituteOfGemmology

Vancouver: **Canadian Tourism College (CTC)**
Vancouver Campus
#200, 1111 Melville St., Vancouver, BC V6E 3V6
Tel: 604-736-8000; *Fax:* 604-731-9819
Toll-Free: 877-731-9810
reception@tourismcollege.com
www.tourismcollege.com
www.facebook.com/ctcfans
twitter.com/ctourismcollege
www.linkedin.com/school/canadian-tourism-college
www.youtube.com/c/tourismcollege
Note: The Canadian Tourism College was established in 1980 to offer hospitality & tourism education in British Columbia. The college is fully accredited by the Private Career Training Institutions Agency of British Columbia.

Campuses
Surrey Campus
#320, 10362 King George Blvd., Surrey, BC V3T 2W5
Tel: 604-582-1122; *Fax:* 604-583-4092
Toll-Free: 800-668-9301

Vancouver: **Erickson Coaching International**
#8871, 200-375 Water St., Vancouver, BC V6B 0M9
Tel: 604-757-2797; *Toll-Free:* 877-435-1455
info@erickson.edu
erickson.edu
www.facebook.com/EricksonCoachingInternational
twitter.com/EricksonCoaches
www.linkedin.com/company/erickson-coaching-international
www.youtube.com/c/EricksonEdu
Note: Erickson College offers certified professional coach training.
Marilyn Atkinson, PhD, PCC, President
Lawrence McGinnis, LLB, Executive Director

Vancouver: **Fine Art Bartending School Vancouver Ltd.**
Also known as: Fine Art Bartending Vancouver
432 West Pender St., Vancouver, BC V6B 1T5
Tel: 604-873-2811
info@fineartbartending.ca
www.fineartbartending.ca
www.facebook.com/FineArtBartendingVancouver
twitter.com/BartendVanCity
Number of Employees: 3 *Note:* Founded in 1981, Fine Art Bartending offers bartending training & certification. Subjects include mixology, beer & wine service, responsible alcohol service & customer service.

Vancouver: **Gateway College**
#702, 333 Terminal Ave., Vancouver, BC V6A 4C1
Tel: 604-738-0285; *Fax:* 604-738-0994
info@gwcollege.ca
www.gwcollege.ca
www.facebook.com/gwcollegevan
Note: Founded in 1986, the college offers programs that lead to careers such as a health care assistant, a long-term care aide, a nursing assistant, & a dementia professional. Red Cross emergency first aid training is also available.
Gateway College is a member of the following organizations:

Private Career Training Institutes Agency, British Columbia Career Colleges Association, British Columbia Education Quality Assurance, National Association of Career Colleges, & the Better Business Bureau.

Vancouver: **Granville College**
#725, 570 Dunsmuir St., Vancouver, BC V6B 1Y1
Tel: 604-683-8850; *Fax:* 604-682-7115
info@granvillecollege.ca
granvillecollege.ca
www.facebook.com/granvillecollegebc
www.linkedin.com/school/granville-college
www.instagram.com/granvillecollege
Note: Founded in 1993, Granville College offers programs focused on the veterinary & animal care industries, as such vet tech & business administration.

Vancouver: **Native Education College (NEC)**
285 East 5th Ave., Vancouver, BC V5T 1H2
Tel: 604-873-3772; *Fax:* 604-873-9152
info@necvancouver.org
www.necvancouver.org
www.facebook.com/NativeEd
twitter.com/NEC_Vancouver
www.linkedin.com/school/nec-native-education-college
www.youtube.com/c/NativeEducation
Note: The college opened in 1967 to offer developmental, vocational & applied academic programs to Indigenous adult students.
Rose Guerin, Chair
Tammy Harkey, President
tharkey@necvancouver.org

Vancouver: **Rhodes Wellness College**
#280, 1125 Howe St., Vancouver, BC V6Z 2K8
Tel: 604-708-4416; *Fax:* 604-708-4418
Toll-Free: 877-708-4416
admin@rhodescollege.ca
www.rhodescollege.ca
www.facebook.com/RhodesWellnessCollege
twitter.com/wellnesscollege
www.linkedin.com/company/rhodes-wellness-college
Note: Founded in 1996, Rhodes Wellness College offers coaching, counselling & wellness training to certify professional life coaches & counsellors.
Ben Colling, President

Vancouver: **Vancouver Art Therapy Institute**
1575 Johnston St., Vancouver, BC V6H 3R9
Tel: 604-681-8284; *Fax:* 604-331-8262
info@vati.bc.ca
www.vati.bc.ca
www.facebook.com/VancouverArtTherapyInstitute

Vancouver: **Vancouver School of Theology**
6015 Walter Gage Rd., Vancouver, BC V6T 1Z1
Tel: 604-822-9031; *Toll-Free:* 866-822-9031
possibilities@vst.edu
vst.edu
www.facebook.com/vst.edu
www.youtube.com/c/VancouverSchoolofTheology
Enrollment: 200 *Note:* Multi-denominational graduate school educating for the church, service agencies & businesses.
Rev. Dr. Richard Topping, President

Victoria: **Academy of Excellence Hair Design & Aesthetics Ltd.**
303 Goldstream Ave., Victoria, BC V9B 2W4
Tel: 250-386-7843
info@aoevictoria.com
www.academyofexcellencevictoria.com
www.facebook.com/AcademyOfExcellenceHairDesignAesthetics Ltd
Note: Established in 1963, the Academy of Excellence offers career training in hair design & spa therapy.
Lorie Chadsey, Director & Instructor

Victoria: **Canadian College of Performing Arts (CCPA)**
1701 Elgin Rd., Victoria, BC V8R 5L7
Tel: 250-595-9970; *Fax:* 250-595-0779
admin@ccpacanada.com
www.ccpacanada.com
www.facebook.com/canadiancollegeofperformingarts
twitter.com/CCPACanada
www.youtube.com/user/CCPA11
Enrollment: 84 *Note:* Offers a two-year Enriched Performing Arts diploma program & a 21-week Company C Studio Ensemble program.
Caleb Marshall, Managing Artistic Director
director@ccpacanada.com

Victoria: Global Village
Victoria
#200, 1290 Broad St., Victoria, BC M5S 2V6
Tel: 250-384-2199
victoria@gvenglish.com
www.gvenglish.com
www.facebook.com/gvvictoria
www.linkedin.com/school/gvenglish
www.youtube.com/c/GVVictoria

Victoria: Lester B. Pearson United World College
650 Pearson College Dr., Victoria, BC V9C 4H7
Tel: 250-391-2411
info@pearsoncollege.ca
www.pearsoncollege.ca
www.facebook.com/PearsonUWC
twitter.com/PCUWC
www.linkedin.com/company/pcuwc
www.youtube.com/user/PearsonUWC
Grades: Pre-university *Enrollment:* 200
Craig Davis, President
cdavis@pearsoncollege.ca

Winfield: Interior Heavy Equipment Operator School
Also known as: IHE School
#2, 11852 Hwy. 97 North, Winfield, BC V4V 1E3
Tel: 250-766-3853; *Fax:* 877-347-6384
Toll-Free: 866-399-3853
info@iheschool.com
www.iheschool.com
www.facebook.com/iheschool
twitter.com/IHESchool
www.linkedin.com/company/ihecollege
www.instagram.com/ihe_heavy_equipment_training

Campuses
Edmonton Training Site
54231 Hwy. 44, Edmonton, AB T8T 0K7

Innisfail Training Site
36040 Range Rd. 284A, Innisfail, AB T4G 1T8

Winfield Training Site
425 Beaver Lake Rd., Winfield, BC V4V 1S5

Manitoba

Government Agencies

Winnipeg: Manitoba Ministry of Education
Legislative Bldg.
#168, 450 Broadway, Winnipeg, MB R3C 0V8, Canada
Tel: 204-945-3720; *Fax:* 204-945-1291
minedu@leg.gov.mb.ca
www.edu.gov.mb.ca
Hon. Cliff Cullen, Minister
Hon. Wayne Ewasko, Minister, Advanced Education, Skills &
Immigration

School Boards/Districts/Divisions

Public

Altona: Border Land School Division
P.O. Box 390
120 - 9th St. NW, Altona, MB R0G 0B0
Tel: 204-324-6491; *Fax:* 204-324-1664
Toll-Free: 866-324-6491
blsd@blsd.ca
www.blsd.ca
Number of Schools: 17 *Grades:* K - 12; French Immersion
Craig Smiley, Board Chair, 204-324-7510
Krista Curry, CEO & Supertintendent, 204-324-6491, ext. 1010
Carol Braun, Assistant Superintendent, 204-324-6491, ext. 1011

Beausejour: Sunrise School Division
Sunrise Education Center
P.O. Box 1206
344 - 2nd St. North, Beausejour, MB R0E 0C0, Canada
Tel: 204-268-6500; *Fax:* 204-268-6545
Toll-Free: 1-866-444-5559
www.sunrisesd.ca
Other Information: Transportation, Phone: 204-268-2055;
Business, Fax: 204-268-4149
Number of Schools: 19 *Grades:* K - 12; Adult Education
Enrollment: 4600
Don Nichol, Chair, Board, 204-348-2818
trustee.nichol@sunrisesd.ca
Cathy Tymko, Superintendent/CEO
ctymko@sunrisesd.ca
Scott Carleton, Secretary-Treasurer, 204-268-6514
scarleton@sunrisesd.ca

Danielle Erickson, Transportation Manager, 204-444-2498
derickson@sunrisesd.ca
Derrick Ryback, Maintenance Manager, 204-268-6528
dryback@sunrisesd.ca

Birtle: Park West School Division
P.O. Box 68
1126 St. Clare St., Birtle, MB R0M 0C0, Canada
Tel: 204-842-2100; *Fax:* 204-842-2110
Toll-Free: 877-418-5320
pwsdoffice@pwsd.ca
www.pwsd.ca
www.facebook.com/ParkWestSchoolDivision/
twitter.com/ParkWestSD
www.instagram.com/parkwestsd
Number of Schools: 7 elementary; 3 secondary; 5 K-12 *Grades:*
K - 12 *Enrollment:* 1800 *Number of Employees:* 196 teaching;
214 non-teaching
Tiffany Priestley, Chair, Board
tpriestley@pwsd.ca
Stephen David, Superintendent/CEO, 204-842-2117
sdavid@pwsd.ca
Dorelle Fulton, Secretary-Treasurer, 204-842-2112
dfulton@pwsd.ca
Colleen Clearsky, Director, Aboriginal Education, 204-859-2777
cclearsky@pwsd.ca
Rick Hrycak, Supervisor, Transportation, 204-842-2111
rhrycak@pwsd.ca

Brandon: Brandon School Division
1031 - 6th St., Brandon, MB R7A 4K5, Canada
Tel: 204-729-3100; *Fax:* 204-727-2217
info@bsd.ca
www.bsd.ca
www.facebook.com/BrandonSchoolDivision/
twitter.com/BrandonMBSD
www.instagram.com/brandonmbsd/
Number of Schools: 18 elementary; 3 secondary; 1 alternative
Grades: K - 12; French Immersion *Enrollment:* 8388
Linda Ross, Ph.D, Chair, Board, 204-724-9687
ross.linda@bsd.ca
Marc Casavant, Ph.D, Superintendent/CEO
casavant.marc@bsd.ca
Denis Labossiere, Secretary-Treasurer
labossiere.denis@bsd.ca
Caroline Cramer, Director, Facilities and Transportation
cramer.caroline@bsd.ca
Brent Ewasiuk, Director, Management of Information Systems
Technology
ewasiuk.brent@bsd.ca
Yemi Otukoya, Director, Human Resources
otukoya.yemi@bsd.ca
Bob Day, Supervisor, Facilities
day.robert@bsd.ca
Ron Harkness, Supervisor, Transportation, 204-729-3976
harkness.ron@bsd.ca

Carman: Prairie Rose School Division
P.O. Box 1510
45 Main St. South, Carman, MB R0G 0J0
Tel: 204-745-2003; *Fax:* 204-745-3699
Toll-Free: 866-745-2003
prsd@prsdmb.ca
www.prsdmb.ca
Number of Schools: 10 community; 17 Hutterian *Grades:* K - 12
Enrollment: 2300 *Number of Employees:* 395
Elaine L. Owen, Chair
elowen@prsdmb.ca
Terry Osiowy, Superintendent
tosiowy@prsdmb.ca
Ron Sugden, Assistant Superintendent
rsugden@prsdmb.ca
Louise Duncan, Director, Student Services
lduncan@prsdmb.ca

Dauphin: Mountain View School Division
P.O. Box 715
Dauphin, MB R7N 3B3, Canada
Tel: 204-638-3001; *Fax:* 204-638-7250
www.mvsd.ca
twitter.com/MVSD_Schools/
Number of Schools: 9 elementary; 1 middle; 4 secondary; 2 K-12
Grades: K - 12 *Enrollment:* 3200
Leifa Misko, Chair, Board, 204-638-3001
leifa.misko@mvsd.ca
Dan Ward, Superintendent & CEO, 204-638-3001
dan.ward@mvsd.ca
Bart Michaleski, Secretary-Treasurer, 204-638-3001
bart.michaleski@mvsd.ca
Suzanne Cottyn, Coordinator, Curriculum and Assessment,
204-638-3001
suzanne.cottyn@mvsd.ca

Rick Tritthart, Coordinator, Operations, 204-638-3001
rick.tritthart@mvsd.ca

Eriksdale: Lakeshore School Division
P.O. Box 100
23 - 2nd Ave., Eriksdale, MB R0C 0W0, Canada
Tel: 204-739-2101; *Fax:* 204-739-2145
admin@lakeshoresd.mb.ca
www.lakeshoresd.mb.ca
twitter.com/LakeshoreSD
Number of Schools: 10 *Grades:* K - 12 *Enrollment:* 1000 *Number
of Employees:* 270
Jim Cooper, Chair, Board, 204-739-5469
cooperj@lakeshoresd.mb.ca
Darlene Willetts, Superintendent
willetd@lakeshoresd.mb.ca
Marlene Michno, Secretary-Treasurer, 204-739-2101, ext. 1222
michnom@lakeshoresd.mb.ca
Mark Parkes, Director, Operations & Infrastructure,
204-739-2101, ext. 1227
parkesm@lakeshoresd.mb.ca

Flin Flon: Flin Flon School Division
9 Terrace Ave., Flin Flon, MB R8A 1S2, Canada
Tel: 204-681-3413; *Fax:* 204-681-3417
www.ffsd.mb.ca
twitter.com/MBSchoolBoards
Number of Schools: 1 elementary; 1 elementary dual track; 1
secondary; 1 alternative *Grades:* K - 12; Alternative Ed.
Enrollment: 1000
Leslie Fernandes, Chair, Board
lfernandes@ffsd.mb.ca
Tammy Ballantyne, Superintendent
tballantyne@ffsd.mb.ca
Heather Fleming, Secretary-Treasurer
hfleming@ffsd.mb.ca
Steve Lytwyn, Director
slytwyn@ffsd.mb.ca
Brent Osika, Maintenance/Transportation Supervisor
bosika@ffsd.mb.ca

Gimli: Evergreen School Division
P.O. Box 1200
140 Centre Ave. West, Gimli, MB R0C 1B0, Canada
Tel: 204-642-6260; *Fax:* 204-642-7273
www.esd.ca
twitter.com/evergreen_sd
Number of Schools: 1 primary; 4 elementary-middle; 3
secondary *Grades:* K.-12; Continuing Ed. *Enrollment:* 1400
Number of Employees: 260
Ruth Ann Furgala, Board Chair, 204-378-2901
ruthann.furgala@esd.ca
Roza Gray, Superintendent & CEO
roza.gray@esd.ca
Scott Hill, Assistant Superintendent
scott.hill@esd.ca
Gary Thompson, Maintenance Manager
gary.thompson@esd.ca
Amanda Senkowski, Secretary-Treasurer

Gladstone: Pine Creek School Division
P.O. Box 420
25 Brown St., Gladstone, MB R0J 0T0, Canada
Tel: 204-385-2216; *Fax:* 204-385-2825
pcsddo@pinecreeksd.mb.ca
www.pinecreeksd.mb.ca
Number of Schools: 5 elementary; 2 secondary; 7 Hutterian
Colony *Grades:* K - 12 *Enrollment:* 1100
Diedrich Toews, Chair, Board, 204-466-2696
dtoews@pinecreeksd.mb.ca
Donna Miller Fry, Superintendent
dmillerfry@pinecreeksd.mb.ca
Gerri Wygle, Manager, Business and Finance
Donald Hickey, Transportation Supervisor, 866-896-1953
dhickey@pinecreeksd.mb.ca

Killarney: Turtle Mountain School Division
P.O. Box 280
435 Williams Ave., Killarney, MB R0K 1G0, Canada
Tel: 204-523-7531; *Fax:* 204-523-7269
dbo@tmsd.mb.ca
www.tmsd.mb.ca
Number of Schools: 1 elementary / middle school; 2 K - 12
schools; 2 adult ed; 4 Hutterite colony *Grades:* K - 12;
Continuing Ed.
Garth Nichol, Chair, Board
gnichol@tmsd.mb.ca
Tim De Ruyck, Superintendent/CEO
tderuyck@tmsd.mb.ca
Kathy Siatecki, Secretary-Treasurer
ksiatecki@tmsd.mb.ca
Attila Szabo, Transportation Supervisor, 204-534-6269
aszabo@tmsd.mb.ca

Lorette: Seine River School Division (SRSD)
475-A Senez St., Lorette, MB R5K 1E3, Canada
Tel: 204-878-4713; *Fax:* 204-878-4717
www.srsd.mb.ca
twitter.com/seineriversd
Number of Schools: 15 *Grades:* K - 12 *Enrollment:* 4400 *Note:*
Also offers adult learning programs.
Wendy Bloomfield, Chair, Board, 204-269-4270
wbloomfield@srsd.ca
Michael Borgfjord, Superintendent
mborgfjord@srsd.ca
Paul Ilchena, Secretary-Treasurer, 204-878-4713
pilchena@srsd.ca
Jerry Marchadour, Operations Coordinator, 204-878-0274
jmarchadour@srsd.ca

McCreary: Turtle River School Division
P.O. Box 309
808 Burrows Rd., McCreary, MB R0J 1B0, Canada
Tel: 204-835-2067; *Fax:* 204-835-2426
division@trsd.ca
www.trsd.ca
twitter.com/TurtleRiverSD
Number of Schools: 7 *Grades:* K - 12 *Enrollment:* 725 *Number of Employees:* 63 teachers; 52 support staff
Karey Wilkinson, Chair, Board
kwilkinson@trsd.ca
Bev Szymesko, Superintendent, 204-835-2067, ext. 202
bevs@trsd.ca
Shannon Desjardins, Secretary-Treasurer, 204-835-2067, ext. 203
shannon@trsd.ca
Dean Bluhm, Transportation & Maintenance Supervisor, 204-835-2067, ext. 209
deanb@trsd.ca
Steven Hopfner, Information & Communication Technology Director, 204-835-2067, ext. 208
steven@trsd.ca

Minnedosa: Rolling River School Division
P.O. Box 1170
36 Armitage Ave., Minnedosa, MB R0J 1E0, Canada
Tel: 204-867-2754; *Fax:* 204-867-2037
rrsd@rrsd.mb.ca
www.rrsd.mb.ca
twitter.com/RollingRiverSD
Number of Schools: 8 elementary; 4 secondary; 5 Hutterite Colony *Grades:* K - 12 *Enrollment:* 1753
Victoria McKay, Chair, Board
vmckay@rrsd.mb.ca
Mary-Anne Ploshynsky, Superintendent, 204-867-2754, ext. 222
mploshynsky@rrsd.mb.ca
Kathlyn McNabb, Secretary-Treasurer, 204-867-2754, ext. 226
kmcnabb@rrsd.mb.ca
Fred Scott, Maintenance Supervisor, 204-867-2754, ext. 239
fscott@rrsd.mb.ca
Cam Woodcock, Transportation Supervisor, 204-867-2754, ext. 235
cwoodcock@rrsd.mb.ca

Morden: Western School Division
#4, 75 Thornhill St., Morden, MB R6M 1P2, Canada
Tel: 204-822-4448; *Fax:* 204-822-4262
divoff@westernsd.mb.ca
www.westernsd.mb.ca
Number of Schools: 4 *Grades:* K - 12 *Enrollment:* 1700
Brian Fransen, Chair, Board, 204-822-6066
bfransen@westernsd.mb.ca
Stephen Ross, Superintendent
sross@westernsd.mb.ca
Carl Pedersen, Secretary-Treasurer
cpedersen@westernsd.mb.ca
Allan Toews, Supervisor, Operations
atoews@westernsd.mb.ca
Parviz Salimi, Information Technology Director, 204-822-2280
psalimi@westernsd.mb.ca

Morris: Red River Valley School Division
P.O. Box 400
233 Main St., Morris, MB R0G 1K0, Canada
Tel: 204-746-2317; *Fax:* 204-746-2785
inquiries@rrvsd.ca
www.rrvsd.ca
twitter.com/rrvsd1
Number of Schools: 14 *Grades:* K - 12 *Enrollment:* 2196
Charlene Geiler, Chair, Board
cgeiler@rrvsd.ca
Brad Curtis, Superintendent & CEO, 204-746-2317, ext. 2225
bcurtis@rrvsd.ca
Alma Mitchell, Secretary-Treasurer, 204-746-2317, ext. 2226
amitchell@rrvsd.ca

Darren Cameron, Transportation Supervisor, 204-746-2317, ext. 2229
dcameron@rrvsd.ca
Trevor Thiessen, Maintenance Supervisor, 204-746-2317, ext. 2245
tthiessen@rrvsd.ca

Neepawa: Beautiful Plains School Division
P.O. Box 700
213 Mountain Ave., Neepawa, MB R0J 1H0, Canada
Tel: 204-476-2387; *Fax:* 204-476-3606
bpsd@bpsd.mb.ca
www.beautifulplainssd.ca
twitter.com/beautifulplains
Number of Schools: 14 *Grades:* K - 12; *Special Ed. Enrollment:*
1886 *Number of Employees:* 246
Richard Manns, Chair, Board
mannsr@bpsd.mb.ca
Jason Young, Superintendent
jyoung@bpsd.mb.ca
Shannon Bayes, Secretary-Treasurer
sbayes@bpsd.mb.ca
Rhonda Dickenson, Student Services Coordinator
rdickenson@bpsd.mb.ca
Royce Hollier, Technology Coordinator
rhollier@bpsd.mb.ca
Warren Rainka, Transportation Supervisor
wrainka@bpsd.mb.ca

Pinawa: Whiteshell School District
P.O. Box 130
20 Vanier Dr., Pinawa, MB R0E 1L0, Canada
Tel: 204-753-8366; *Fax:* 204-753-2237
ceo@sdwhiteshell.mb.ca
www.sdwhiteshell.mb.ca
Number of Schools: 1 elementary; 1 secondary *Grades:* K - 12
Enrollment: 204
Lorraine Nelson, Chair, Board
nelsonl@sdwhiteshell.mb.ca
Tim Stefanishyn, Superintendent/Secretary-Treasurer
tstef@sdwhiteshell.mb.ca

Portage la Prairie: Portage la Prairie School Division
535 - 3 St. NW, Portage la Prairie, MB R1N 2C4, Canada
Tel: 204-857-8756; *Fax:* 204-239-5998
www.plpsd.mb.ca
twitter.com/PortageSD
Number of Schools: 9 *Grades:* K - 12 *Enrollment:* 3300
Hélène Hoggarth, Chair, Board
hhoggarth@plpsd.mb.ca
Todd Cuddington, Superintendent
tcuddington@plpsd.mb.ca
Jonathan Hyman, Manager, Business and Finance, 204-857-8756
Rochelle Rands, Director, Student Services, 204-857-8756
Parker Garnham, Supervisor, Operations, 204-857-5841, ext. 121
parker_garnham@plpsd.mb.ca

Selkirk: Lord Selkirk School Division (LSSD)
205 Mercy St., Selkirk, MB R1A 2C8, Canada
Tel: 204-482-5942; *Fax:* 204-482-3000
Toll-Free: 866-433-5942
lssd.boardoffice@lssd.ca
www.lssd.ca
www.facebook.com/LordSelkirkSD
twitter.com/lordselkirk_sd
www.instagram.com/lordselkirk_sd/
Number of Schools: 15 *Grades:* K - 12; *Adult Ed. Enrollment:*
5000 *Note:* The schools celebrate the heritage and culture of the region - including the Brokenhead Ojibway Nation, the Scottish pioneers, the French Canadian voyageurs and the Ukrainian settlers. Also offer an adult learning program.
Lena Kublick, Chair, Board, 204-757-2889
lkublick@lssd.ca
Michele Polinuk, Superintendent/CEO
mpolinuk@lssd.ca
Brian Spurrill, Secretary-Treasurer
bspurrill@lssd.ca
Alan Campbell, Manager, Transportation
acampbell@lssd.ca

Souris: Southwest Horizon School Division
Education & Operations
P.O. Box 820
67 Willow Ave. E, Souris, MB R0K 2C0, Canada
Tel: 204-483-5533; *Fax:* 204-483-5535
info@shmb.ca
www.shmb.ca
twitter.com/SWHorizonSD
Number of Schools: 13 *Grades:* K - 12 *Enrollment:* 1555
Janice McDonald, Chair, Board
janicemcdonald@shmb.ca

Carolyn Cory, Superintendent, 204-483-6248
carolyncory@shmb.ca
Kevin Zabowski, Secretary-Treasurer, 204-483-6261
kevinzabowski@shmb.ca
Glynn Warnica, Operations Supervisor, 204-483-6250
glynnwarnica@shmb.ca

Affiliations
Melita
Finance & Payroll
P.O. Box 370
165 North St., Melita, MB R0M 1L0, Canada
Tel: 204-483-6294
www.shmb.ca

Steinbach: Hanover School Division
5 Chrysler Gate, Steinbach, MB R5G 0E2, Canada
Tel: 204-326-6471; *Fax:* 204-326-9901
info@hsd.ca
www.hsd.ca
twitter.com/HanoverSD
Number of Schools: 7 elementary; 3 elementary-middle; 4 middle; 3 middle-secondary; 2 secondary; 1 K-12 *Grades:* K - 12
Enrollment: 8100 *Number of Employees:* 1100
Ron Falk, Chair, Board, 204-688-3277
rfalk@hsd.ca
Randy Dueck, Superintendent/CEO
rdueck@hsd.ca
Kevin Heide, Secretary-Treasurer
kheide@hsd.ca
Bob Proulx, Director, Facilities
bproulx@hsd.ca
Robert Warkentin, Director, Transportation
rwarkentin@hsd.ca
Chris MacKinnon, Technology Services Manager
cmackinnon@hsd.ca
Dave Rushforth, Human Resources Manager
drushforth@hsd.ca
Bob Wiebe, Communications Manager
bobwiebe@hsd.ca

Stonewall: Interlake School Division
192 - 2nd Ave. North, Stonewall, MB R0C 2Z0, Canada
Tel: 204-467-5100; *Fax:* 204-467-8334
isd@isd21.mb.ca
www.isd21.mb.ca
twitter.com/interlakesd
Number of Schools: 2 elementary; 6 elementary/middle; 2 middle; 3 secondary; 9 K-12 *Grades:* K - 12; Continuing Ed.
Enrollment: 2915 *Number of Employees:* 235 FTE teachers; 280 support staff
Fran Frederickson, Chair, Board, 204-467-8454
ffrederickson@isd21.mb.ca
Margaret Ward, Superintendent/CEO, 204-467-5100, ext. 232
mward@isd21.mb.ca
Allen Leiman, Secretary/Treasurer, 204-467-5100, ext. 222
aleiman@isd21.mb.ca
Jaret Thiessen, Transportation Supervisor, 204-467-8730
jthiessen@isd21.mb.ca

Swan Lake: Prairie Spirit School Division
P.O. Box 130
15 Lorne Ave., Swan Lake, MB R0G 2S0, Canada
Tel: 204-836-2147; *Fax:* 204-836-2356
prspirit@mts.net
www.prairiespirit.mb.ca
twitter.com/PSSDBus
Number of Schools: 15 schools; 14 Hutterite Colony *Grades:* K - 12 *Enrollment:* 2479
Jan McIntyre, Chair, Board
jmcintyre@prspirit.org
Keith Murray, Superintendent
kmurray@prspirit.org
Jill Mangin, Secretary-Treasurer
jmangin@prspirit.org
Darryl Mason, Transportation Supervisor
dmason@prspirit.org

Swan River: Swan Valley School Division
John Kastrukoff Building
1481 - 3rd St. North, Swan River, MB R0L 1Z0, Canada
Tel: 204-734-4531; *Fax:* 204-734-2273
www.svsd.ca
www.facebook.com/SVSD.CA/
Number of Schools: 2 elementary; 5 elementary-middle; 1 middle; 1 secondary *Grades:* K - 12; French Immersion
Laurie Evans, Chair, Board
levans@svsd.ca
Jon Zilkey, Superintendent, 204-734-4531
jzilkey@svsd.ca
Brent Rausch, Secretary-Treasurer, 204-734-4531
brausch@svsd.ca

Doug Coulthart, Transportation Supervisor, 204-734-3415
dcoulthart@svsd.ca
Chris Staniland, Maintenance Supervisor, 204-734-4531
cstaniland@svsd.ca

The Pas: Kelsey School Division
P.O. Box 4700
322 Edwards Ave., The Pas, MB R9A 1R4, Canada
Tel: 204-623-6421; *Fax:* 204-623-7704
www.ksd.mb.ca
Number of Schools: 5 *Grades:* K - 12 *Enrollment:* 1733
Vaughn Wadelius, Chair, Board, 204-623-3073
vaughnw@mymts.net
Julia McKay, Superintendent
mckayj@ksd.mb.ca
Jeannette Freese, Secretary-Treasurer
jfreese@ksd.mb.ca
Greg Shepherd, Transportation Supervisor
gshepherd@ksd.mb.ca

Thompson: Mystery Lake School District
408 Thompson Dr. North, Thompson, MB R8N 0C5, Canada
Tel: 204-677-6150; *Fax:* 204-677-9528
sdml@mysterynet.mb.ca
www.mysterynet.mb.ca
Number of Schools: 6 elementary; 1 secondary *Grades:* K - 12
Enrollment: 3169 *Number of Employees:* 207 teaching staff; 94
non-teaching staff
Don Macdonald, Chair, Board
dmacdonald@mysterynet.mb.ca
Lorie Henderson, Superintendent, Educational Services &
Programming
lhenderson@mysterynet.mb.ca
Angèle Bartlett, Superintendent, Human Resources & Policy
abartlett@mysterynet.mb.ca
Kelly Knott, Secretary-Treasurer
kknott@mysterynet.mb.ca
Orest Chychula, Facilities Manager
orestchychula@mysterynet.mb.ca

Virden: Fort La Bosse School Division
P.O. Box 1420
523 - 9th Ave. South, Virden, MB R0M 2C0
Tel: 204-748-2692; *Fax:* 204-748-2436
flbsd@flbsd.mb.ca
www.flbsd.mb.ca
Number of Schools: 10 *Grades:* K - 12 *Enrollment:* 1480
Garry E. Draper, Chair
gdraper@flbsd.mb.ca
Barry Pitz, Superintendent
Vaughn Wilson, Supervisor of Operations
Kent Reid, Secretary-Treasurer
Teresa Sanheim, Administrator of Student Services and
Strategic Initiatives

Winkler: Garden Valley School Division
P.O. Box 1330
750 Triple E Blvd., Winkler, MB R6W 4B3, Canada
Tel: 204-325-8335; *Fax:* 204-325-4132
gvsd@gvsd.ca
www.gvsd.ca
Number of Schools: 4 elementary; 4 elementary-middle; 2
middle; 2 secondary; 1 K-12 *Grades:* K - 12 *Enrollment:* 4374
Laurie Dyck, Chair, Board
laurie.dyck@gvsd.ca
Todd Monster, Superintendent/CEO
todd.monster@gvsd.ca
Terry Penner, Secretary-Treasurer
terry.penner@gvsd.ca
Angela Plett, Transportation Supervisor, 204-325-8335, ext.
2041
angela.plett@gvsd.ca
Davis Wieler, Maintenance Supervisor
davis.wieler@gvsd.ca
Shayne Thomson, Human Resource Manager
shayne.thomson@gvsd.ca

Winnipeg: Frontier School Division
30 Speers Rd., Winnipeg, MB R2J 1L9
Tel: 204-775-9741; *Fax:* 204-775-9940
frontier@fsdnet.ca
www.fsdnet.ca
www.facebook.com/frontierschooldivision
twitter.com/frontiersd
Number of Schools: 41 schools; 21 Adult education sites
Grades: K - 12 *Enrollment:* 6305 *Number of Employees:* 595
teachers; 930 support staff
Linda Ballantyne, Chair, Board
April Krahn, Assistant Superintendent, Indigenous Way of Life
Brian Spurrill, Secretary-Treasurer
brian.spurrill@fsdnet.ca
Reg Klassen, Chief Superintendent

Bradley Hampson, Assistant Superintendent, Technology,
204-775-9741
Jacqueline Connell, Assistant Superintendent, Senior Years &
Career Studies

Winnipeg: Louis Riel School Division (LRSD)
Division scolaire Louis Riel
900 St. Mary's Rd., Winnipeg, MB R2M 3R3
Tel: 204-257-7827; *Fax:* 204-256-8553
www.lrsd.net
www.facebook.com/LouisRielSchoolDivision
twitter.com/louis_riel_sd
www.linkedin.com/company/louis-riel-school-division
Number of Schools: 31 elementary schools; 7 high schools; 1
technical & vocational training schools; 1 learning centre *Grades:*
K - 12 *Enrollment:* 15533 *Number of Employees:* 1,212 teaching
staff; 934 non-teaching staff *Note:* This division is an
amalgamation of the St. Boniface & St. Vital School Divisions.
Sandy Nemeth, Chair, Board, 204-230-6475
Steven Lawrie, Director, Student Support Services
Charles Robert, Director of Facilities
Marna Kenny, Secretary-Treasurer
Christian Michalek, Superintendent, Schools

Winnipeg: Pembina Trails School Division
181 Henlow Bay, Winnipeg, MB R3Y 1M7
Tel: 204-488-1757; *Fax:* 204-487-3667
info@pembinatrails.ca
www.pembinatrails.ca
www.facebook.com/pembinatrails
twitter.com/PembinaTrails
www.linkedin.com/company/9310277
www.youtube.com/user/PembinaTrails
Number of Schools: 35 *Grades:* K - 12 *Enrollment:* 14590
Number of Employees: 1,859
Jamie Glenat, Chair, Board
jglenat@pembinatrails.ca
Nora Wood, Secretary-Treasurer
nwood@pembinatrails.ca
Ted Fransen, Superintendent, Education
tfransen@pembinatrails.ca

Winnipeg: River East Transcona School Division
589 Roch St., Winnipeg, MB R2K 2P7
Tel: 204-667-7130; *Fax:* 204-661-5618
www.retsd.mb.ca
www.facebook.com/retsd
twitter.com/RETSDschools
www.vimeo.com/retsdvideo
Number of Schools: 24 early years schools; 3 early / middle
schools; 8 middle schools; 7 senior schools *Grades:* K - 12
Enrollment: 16500 *Number of Employees:* 3,000
Colleen Carswell, Chair, Board, 204-222-1486
ccarswell@retsd.mb.ca
Vince Mariani, Secretary-Treasurer & Chief Financial Officer
Kelly Barkman, Superintendent & Chief Executive Officer
Jason Drysdale, Assistant Superintendent, Educational Services
& Planning
Tammy Mitchell, Assistant Superintendent, Student Services

Winnipeg: St. James-Assiniboia School Division
(SJASD)
2574 Portage Ave., Winnipeg, MB R3J 0H8
Tel: 204-888-7951; *Fax:* 204-831-0859
inquiries@sjasd.ca
www.sjasd.ca
Other Information: Continuing Ed., Phone: 204-832-9637; Intl.
Program: 204-837-1331
www.facebook.com/St.JamesAssiniboiaSchoolDivision
www.instagram.com/st.james_assiniboiasd
Number of Schools: 15 early years schools; 6 middle years
schools; 5 senior years schools *Grades:* K - 12 *Enrollment:*
8200
Cheryl Smukowich, Chair, Board, 204-885-0054
cheryl.smukowich@sjasd.ca
Michael J. Friesen, Secretary-Treasurer & Chief Finanical Officer
Randy Calvert, Manager, Facilities & Maintenance
Carrol A. Harvey, Manager, Human Resources (Professional
Staff)
Cindy Labaty, Manager, Human Resources (CUPE & MANTE)
Mike Wake, Chief Superintendent
Doreen Cost, Assistant Superintendent, Student Services (K-12)
Jenness Moffatt, Assistant Superintendent, Education &
Administration

Winnipeg: Seven Oaks School Division
830 Powers St., Winnipeg, MB R2V 4E7
Tel: 204-586-8061; *Fax:* 204-589-2504
www.7oaks.org
www.facebook.com/510220119018091
twitter.com/7oaksschooldiv
www.instagram.com/sevenoaksschooldivision
Number of Schools: 24 *Grades:* K - 12 *Enrollment:* 11654
Number of Employees: 1,000

Edward Ploszay, Chair, Board, 204-339-1260
edward.ploszay@7oaks.org
Wayne Shimizu, Secretary-Treasurer
wayne.shimizu@7oaks.org
Brian O'Leary, Superintendent
brian.oleary@7oaks.org
Gwen Birse, Assistant Superintendent, Personnel
gwen.birse@7oaks.org
Verland Force, Assistant Superintendent, Student Services
verland.force@7oaks.org
Matt Henderson, Assistant Superintendent, Curriculum
Matt.henderson@7oaks.org

Winnipeg: Winnipeg School Division (WSD)
1577 Wall St. East, Winnipeg, MB R3E 2S5
Tel: 204-775-0231; *Fax:* 204-772-6464
wsd@wsd1.org
www.winnipegsd.ca
www.facebook.com/WinnipegSD
twitter.com/WinnipegSD
www.linkedin.com/company/winnipeg-school-division
www.instagram.com/winnipegsd
Number of Schools: 78 *Grades:* Pre-K - 12 *Enrollment:* 33000
Number of Employees: 6,000
Chris Broughton, Chair, Board
Paul Kochan, Secretary-Treasurer
Pauline Clarke, Chief Superintendent

Catholic

Winnipeg: Manitoba Catholic Schools Group
Services (MCSGS)
1495 Pembina Hwy., Winnipeg, MB R3T 2C6
Tel: 204-452-2227; *Fax:* 204-453-8236
awcs@archwinnipeg.ca
mbcatholicschools.ca
Number of Schools: 19 *Grades:* K - 12; University
Tannis Scott, Administrative Coordinator, Catholic Schools
tscott@archwinnipeg.ca
Robert Praznik, Superintendent
rpraznik@archwinnipeg.ca

French

Lorette: Division scolaire franco-manitobaine
(DSFM)
1263, ch Dawson, Lorette, MB R5K 0S1
Tél: 204-878-9399; *Téléc:* 204-878-9407
Ligne sans frais: 800-699-3736
dsfm@dsfm.mb.ca
www.dsfm.mb.ca
www.facebook.com/dsfmecole
twitter.com/dsfmecole
Number of Schools: 21 élémentaires; 15 secondaires; 1 autre
Grades: K - 12 *Enrollment:* 5000
Bernard Lesage, Président
bernard.lesage@dsfm.mb.ca
Alain Laberge, Directeur général, 204-878-4424, ext. 211
alain.laberge@dsfm.mb.ca
Rob Dupré, Secrétaire-trésorier
rob.dupre-ollinek@dsfm.mb.ca

First Nations

Birch River: Wuskwi Sipihk Education Authority
P.O. Box 307
Birch River, MB R0L 0E0
Tel: 204-236-4783; *Fax:* 204-236-4779
Number of Schools: 1 *Note:* Wuskwi Sipihk Education Authority
operates the Chief Charles Audy Memorial School.
Seaford Kematch, Director, Education
skematch24@gmail.com

Bloodvein: Miskooseepi Education Authority Inc.
General Delivery, Bloodvein, MB R0C 0J0
Tel: 204-395-2148; *Fax:* 204-395-2189
Stella Keller, Education Director

Cross Lake: Cross Lake Education Authority (CLEA)
P.O. Box 370
Cross Lake, MB R0B 0J0
Tel: 204-676-2917; *Fax:* 204-676-2087
cleamb.ca
Number of Schools: 2
Greg Halcrow, Director, Education
ghalcrow@clea.mb.ca

Ebb & Flow: Ebb & Flow Education Authority
P.O. Box 160
Ebb & Flow, MB R0L 0R0
Tel: 204-448-2438; *Fax:* 204-448-2393
eandf@mts.net

Number of Schools: 1 *Grades:* Elementary - Secondary
Enrollment: 426 *Note:* The Ebb & Flow Education Authority
serves the Ebb & Flow First Nation in Manitoba.

Edwin: Dakota Plains Education Authority
General Delivery, Edwin, MB R0H 0G0
Tel: 204-252-2895; *Fax:* 204-252-2188
www.dakotaplainswahpetonoyate.com

Elphinstone: Keeseekoowenin Education Authority
P.O. Box 250
Elphinstone, MB R0J 0N0
Tel: 204-625-2028; *Fax:* 204-625-2693
www.keeseekoowenin.ca/education-authority
Note: Keeseekoowenin Education Authority operates the
Keeseekoowenin School.

Erickson: Rolling River First Nation
P.O. Box 606
Erickson, MB R0J 0P0
Tel: 204-636-2983; *Fax:* 204-636-2545
Note: Rolling River First Nation operates the Wapi-Penace
School.
Charles Gaywish, Education Director

Fairford: Pinaymootang First Nation Education Authority
General Delivery, Fairford, MB R0C 0X0
Tel: 204-659-5705; *Fax:* 204-659-2068
pinayschool.org
Note: Pinaymootang First Nation operates the Pinaymootang
School.

Fisher River: Fisher River Cree Nation Board of Education
P.O. Box 368
Fisher River, MB R0C 1S0
Tel: 204-645-2283; *Fax:* 204-645-2788
fisherriver.ca/fisher-river-board-of-education
Note: The Fisher River Cree Nation Board of Education operates
the Charles Sinclair School, Fisher River High School & Fisher
River Wee Care Daycare Centre.

Fort Alexander: Sagkeeng Education Authority
P.O. Box 3
Fort Alexander, MB R0E 0P0
Tel: 204-367-4287; *Fax:* 204-367-2129
www.sagkeeng.ca/education-authority
www.facebook.com/sagkeengeducationauthority
Number of Schools: 3 *Grades:* Elementary - Secondary *Note:*
Anicinabe Community School; Sagkeeng Junior High School; &
Sagkeeng Anicinabe High School
Crissy Courchene, Education Director
ecourchene@sfnedu.org

Garden Hill: Garden Hill Education Authority
General Delivery, Garden Hill, MB R0B 0T0
Tel: 204-456-2880; *Fax:* 204-456-2129
Number of Schools: 2 *Grades:* Pre. - 12
David Flett, Education Director

Gillam: Fox Lake First Nation Education Authority
P.O. Box 379
Gillam, MB R0B 0L0
Tel: 204-486-2307; *Fax:* 204-486-2606
www.foxlakecreenation.com

Ginew: Roseau River Anishinabe First Nation
P.O. Box 10
Ginew, MB R0A 2R0
Tel: 204-427-2490; *Fax:* 204-427-2398
Note: Roseau River Anishinabe First Nation operates the Ginew
School.
Marlene Starr, Education Director
mstarr10@hotmail.com

God's Lake Narrows: God's Lake First Nation Education Authority
P.O. Box 284
God's Lake Narrows, MB R0B 0N0
Tel: 204-335-2003
glnschoolboard@yahoo.ca
www.facebook.com/101893194988840
Grades: Pre-K - 9 *Enrollment:* 400 *Note:* God's Lake First Nation
Education Authority operates the God's Lake Narrows First
Nation School.

God's River: Amos Okemow Memorial Education Authority
P.O. Box 103
God's River, MB R0B 0N0
Tel: 204-366-2312; *Fax:* 204-366-2569
Number of Schools: 1 *Grades:* Pre - 11 *Enrollment:* 250 *Note:*
The Amos Okemow Memorial Education Authority serves the

Manto Sipi Cree Nation through operation of the Amos Okemow
Memorial School. To continue their secondary school education,
students must leave the community.
Rex Ross, Director, Education
rrossdirectoreducation@outlook.com

Griswold: Sioux Valley Education Authority
P.O. Box 99
Griswold, MB R0M 0S0
Tel: 204-855-2536; *Fax:* 204-855-2023
svdngovernance.com
www.facebook.com/SiouxValleyEducation
Note: Sioux Valley Education Authority operates the Sioux
Valley High School.
Kevin Nabess, Education Director
kcnabess@hotmail.com

Gypsumville: Dauphin River Education Authority
P.O. Box 140
Gypsumville, MB R0C 1J0
Tel: 204-659-5268; *Fax:* 204-659-5790
www.irtc.ca/dauphin-river-first-nation
Note: Dauphin River Education Authority operates the Dauphin
River School.

Gypsumville: Little Saskatchewan Education Authority
P.O. Box 5050
Gypsumville, MB R0C 1J0
Tel: 204-659-2672; *Fax:* 204-659-5763
Enrollment: 119 *Note:* The Little Saskatchewan Education
Authority operates the Little Saskatchewan H.A.G.M.E. School.
Jerry Sumner, Education Director

Hodgson: Kinonjeoshtegon Education Authority
P.O. Box 359
Hodgson, MB R0C 1N0
Tel: 204-394-2429; *Fax:* 204-394-2431
www.irtc.ca/kinonjeoshtegon-first-nation
Note: The Kinonjeoshtegon Education Authorityoperates the
Lawrence Sinclair Memorial School.

Lac Brochet: Northlands Dene Education Authority
General Delivery, Lac Brochet, MB R0B 2E0
Tel: 204-367-2278; *Fax:* 204-337-2078
Note: The Northlands Dene Education Authority operates the
Petit Casimir Memorial School.
Gerard Butt, Education Director

Little Grand Rapids: Little Grand Rapids Education Authority Inc.
P.O. Box 160
Little Grand Rapids, MB R0B 0V0
Tel: 204-397-2199; *Fax:* 204-397-2102
Grades: K - 12 *Note:* This authority operates the Abbalak
Thunderswift Memorial School.
Margaret Simmons, Director, Education
margaretjsimmons@hotmail.com

Marius: Sandy Bay Education Foundation
P.O. Box 108
Marius, MB R0H 0T0
Tel: 204-843-2431; *Fax:* 204-843-2269
www.sandybayfirstnation.com/education.html
Enrollment: 1000 *Note:* Sandy Bay Education Foundation
operates the Isaac Beaulieu Memorial School.
Rene Roulette, Education Director

Nelson House: Nelson House Education Authority
General Delivery, Nelson House, MB R0B 1A0
Tel: 204-484-2095; *Fax:* 204-484-2257
www.nhea.info
Number of Schools: 2 *Note:* Nelson House Education Authority
operates Nisichawayasihk Neyo Ohtinwak Collegiate &
Otetiskiwin Kiskinwamahtowekamik.
L. Gail Gossfeld-McDonald, Director, Education

Opaskwayak: Opaskwayak Educational Authority Inc.
P.O. Box 10370
Opaskwayak, MB R0B 2J0
Tel: 204-623-7431; *Fax:* 204-623-2870
oca@mts.net
www.opased.com
Note: Opaskwayak Educational Authority Inc. operates the
Oscar Lathlin Collegiate and the Joe A. Ross School.
Beverly Fontaine, Director, Education
bev.fontaine@opased.com

Oxford House: Oxford House First Nation Board of Education
P.O. Box 265
Oxford House, MB R0B 1C0
Tel: 204-538-2051; *Fax:* 204-538-2013
ohboe.net
Number of Schools: 2 *Grades:* Elementary - S4 *Note:* Oxford
House Elementary School & 1972 Memorial High School. The
Oxford House First Nation Board of Education serves the
Bunibonibee Cree Nation of Oxford House, which is situated 600
km north of Winnipeg, Manitoba.
Peter Andrews, Director, Education
peter.andrews@ohboe.net

Peguis: Peguis First Nation School Board
P.O. Box 190
Peguis, MB R0C 3J0
Tel: 204-645-2648; *Fax:* 204-645-2730
Toll-Free: 866-383-2648
Note: Peguis First Nation School Board operates the Peguis
Central School.

Pelican Rapids: Sapotaweyak Education Authority (SEA)
General Delivery, Pelican Rapids, MB R0L 1L0
Tel: 204-587-2115; *Fax:* 204-587-2123
education@ndkms.com
www.ndkms.com/sea.html
Number of Schools: 1 *Grades:* Nursery - 12 *Number of
Employees:* 50 *Note:* The Sapotaweyak Education Authority is
responsible for the provision of education for the Sapotaweyak
Cree Nation, near the towns of Swan River & The Pas in
Manitoba.

Pipestone: Canupawakpa Dakota Nation Education Authority
P.O. Box 146
Pipestone, MB R0M 1T0
Tel: 204-854-2959; *Fax:* 204-854-2525
canupawakpanation.com/index.php/administration/education

Poplar River: Poplar River First Nation Education
P.O. Box 90
Poplar River, MB R0B 0Z0
Tel: 204-244-2113; *Fax:* 204-244-2259
www.prfn.ca/partners

Portage La Prairie: Long Plain First Nation Education Board
P.O. Box 430
Portage La Prairie, MB R1N 3B7
Tel: 204-252-2326; *Fax:* 204-252-2786
lpband.ca/long-plain-school
Enrollment: 200 *Note:* The Long Plain First Nation Education
Board operates the Long Plain School.

Pukatawagan: Pukatawagan Education Authority
P.O. Box 318
Pukatawagan, MB R0B 1G0
Tel: 204-553-2089; *Fax:* 204-553-2419
Note: The Pukatawagan Education Authority operates the
Sakastew School.
Jackie Ferland, Education Director
ferlandjackie@hotmail.com

Red Sucker Lake: Red Sucker Lake Education Authority
General Delivery, Red Sucker Lake, MB R0B 1H0
Tel: 204-469-5039; *Fax:* 204-469-5206
Bernice Monias, Education Director

Scanterbury: Brokenhead Education Authority
2-1100 Waverley St., Scanterbury, MB R3T 3X9
Tel: 204-594-1290
info@mfnerc.com
mfnerc.org/school_auth/brokenhead-education-authority
Nora Murdock, Director of Instructional Services, 204-594-1290,
ext. 2163

Shamattawa: Shamattawa Education Authority
General Delivery, Shamattawa, MB R0B 1K0
Tel: 204-565-2320; *Fax:* 204-565-2320
Note: Shamattawa Education Authority operates the Abraham
Beardy Memorial School.
Roy Miles, Education Director

Shortdale: Tooinaowaziibeeng Education Authority
General Delivery, Shortdale, MB R0L 1W0
Tel: 204-546-3334; *Fax:* 204-546-3090
Note: Tooinaowaziibeeng Education Authority operates the Chief
Clifford Lynxleg Anishinabe School.
Donna Dudek, Director, Education

Split Lake: **Tataskweyak Education Authority**
General Delivery, Split Lake, MB R0B 1P0
Tel: 294-342-2148; *Fax:* 204-342-2240
tataskweyakeducationauthority@gmail.com
Note: Tataskweyak Education Authority operates the Chief Sam Cook Mahmuwee Education Centre.
Alfred Beardy, Director, Education

St Theresa Point: **St. Theresa Point Education Authority**
P.O. Box 520
St Theresa Point, MB R0B 1J0
Tel: 204-462-2131; *Fax:* 204-462-2552
education@stpfirstnation.com
www.stpfirstnation.com/education-authority
Number of Schools: 1 *Enrollment:* 1400
Freddie Wood, Director, Education

Swan Lake: **Swan Lake First Nation Education Authority**
P.O. Box 145
Swan Lake, MB R0G 2S0
Tel: 204-836-2332; *Fax:* 204-836-2317
swanlakefirstnation.com/indian-springs-school
Enrollment: 80 *Note:* Swan Lake First Nation operates the Indian Springs School.
Donovan Mann, Director, Education

Tadoule Lake: **Sayisi Dene First Nation Education Authority**
General Delivery, Tadoule Lake, MB R0B 2C0
Tel: 204-684-2014; *Fax:* 204-684-2187
Note: Sayisi Dene First Nation operates the Peter Yassie Memorial School.
Geoffrey Ndibali, Education Director

Vogar: **Lake Manitoba Education Authority**
P.O. Box 1249
Vogar, MB R0C 3K0
Tel: 204-768-2728; *Fax:* 204-768-2194
Note: The Lake Manitoba Education Authority operates the Lake Manitoba School.
Crystal Missyabit, Education Director

York Landing: **York Factory First Nation Education**
General Delivery, York Landing, MB R0B 2B0
Tel: 204-341-2180; *Fax:* 204-341-2322
www.yffn.ca/departments/education

Schools: Specialized

First Nations

Beulah: **Chan Kagha Otina Dakota Wayawa Tipi School**
P.O. Box 40
Beulah, MB R0M 0B0, Canada
Tel: 204-568-4757
Grades: Pre.-12 *Enrollment:* 137 *Number of Employees:* 10 *Note:* The Chan Kagha Otina Dakota Wayawa Tipi School serves the Birdtail Sioux Dakota Nation. It is part of Manitoba's Frontier School Division.

Birch River: **Chief Charles Thomas Audy Memorial School**
P.O. Box 307
Birch River, MB R0L 0E0, Canada
Tel: 204-236-4783; *Fax:* 204-236-4779
wuskwisipihkschool@gmail.com
Grades: Nursery - 8 *Enrollment:* 37 *Note:* Chief Charles Thomas Audy Memorial School serves the Wuskwi Sipihk First Nation.

Black River: **Little Black River School**
P.O. Box 260
Black River, MB, Canada
Tel: 204-367-4411; *Fax:* 204-367-1414
www.black-river.ca
Note: Members of the Little Black River First Nation are educated at the Little Black River School in O'Hanley, Manitoba. The First Nation community is situated approximately 150 kilometres north of Winnipeg.
Jack Johnson, Program Manager, Special Projects and Alternative Education

Bloodvein: **Miskooseepi School**
General Delivery, Bloodvein, MB R0C 0J0
Tel: 204-395-2012; *Fax:* 204-395-2189
Grades: Pre.-9 *Enrollment:* 163
Irene Rupp, Principal

Brandon: **Sioux Valley High School**
2320 Louis Ave., Brandon, MB R7B 2C6, Canada
Tel: 204-729-2770; *Fax:* 204-727-2054
kcnabess@hotmail.com
Grades: 7 - 12 *Enrollment:* 136
Kevin Nabess, Principal
kcnabess@hotmail.com

Camperville: **Pine Creek Indian Day School**
P.O. Box 130
973 Duck Bay Rd., Camperville, MB R0L 0J0
Tel: 204-524-2318; *Fax:* 204-524-2177
Grades: K-11

Crane River: **Donald Ahmo School**
P.O. Box 91
Crane River, MB R0L 0M0, Canada
Tel: 204-732-2548; *Fax:* 204-732-2753
Grades: K - 8 *Enrollment:* 109 *Note:* The Donald Ahmo School is a band-operated First Nation school which serves the O-Chi-Chak-Ko-Sipi First Nation in Crane River, Manitoba.
Andrew Spence, Principal
bigandy4@hotmail.com

Cross Lake: **Mikisew Middle School**
P.O. Box 128
Cross Lake, MB R0B 0J0, Canada
Tel: 204-676-3030; *Fax:* 204-676-2798
crosslakeeducation.homestead.com/MIKISEW.html
Grades: K, 5-8
Connie McIvor, Principal
cmcivor@clea.mb.ca

Cross Lake: **Otter Nelson River School**
P.O. Box 370
Cross Lake, MB R0B 0J0
Tel: 204-676-2050; *Fax:* 204-676-2464
crosslakeeducation.homestead.com/ONR.html
Grades: Pre.-12 *Enrollment:* 1200 *Number of Employees:* 50 teachers
Irvin Spence, Principal
ispence@clea.mb.ca

Dakota Tipi: **Dakota Tipi School**
2000A Dakota Dr., Dakota Tipi, MB R1N 3P1, Canada
Tel: 204-857-7190
Enrollment: 60 *Note:* Located outside the city of Portage La Prairie, Manitoba, the Dakota Tipi School is a First Nations band operated school. The school serves the Dakota Tipi First Nation.

Dominion City: **Ginew School**
P.O. Box 10
Dominion City, MB R0A 2R0
Tel: 204-427-2490; *Fax:* 204-427-2398
Grades: Pre.-8 *Enrollment:* 126
Teresa Anderson, Principal
ltandersonbrowning@gmail.com

Easterville: **Chemawawin School**
P.O. Box 10
Easterville, MB R0C 0V0, Canada
Tel: 204-329-2115; *Fax:* 204-329-2214
Grades: JK - 12 *Enrollment:* 512 *Note:* Located on the southern shore of Cedar Lake, 300 kilometres north of Winnipeg, Manitoba, the Chemawawin School provides education to the Chemawawin Cree Nation.
Rachel Clarke, Principal
Sandra Lavallee, Vice Principal

Ebb & Flow: **Ebb & Flow School**
P.O. Box 160
Ebb & Flow, MB R0L 0R0, Canada
Tel: 204-448-2012; *Fax:* 204-448-2393
Grades: Pre. - 12 *Enrollment:* 611 *Note:* The Ebb & Flow School is a band-operated school in Manitoba which provides education to the Ebb & Flow First Nation.
Paul Monchka, Principal

Edwin: **Dakota Plains School**
P.O. Box 100
Edwin, MB R0H 0G0, Canada
Tel: 204-252-2895; *Fax:* 204-252-2188
Grades: K - 8 *Enrollment:* 63 *Note:* The Dakota Plains School serves the Dakota Plains Wahpeton Nation.
Jannita Emerson, Principal

Elphinstone: **Keeseekoowenin School**
P.O. Box 129
Elphinstone, MB R0J 0N0
Tel: 204-625-2062; *Fax:* 204-625-2418
keesee@mts.net
keeseekoowenin.wix.com/school
Grades: Pre.-8 *Enrollment:* 57

Audrey Blackbird, Principal
audreyblackbird@keeseekoowenin.com

Erickson: **Wapi-Penace School**
P.O. Box 588 Erickson, MB
Erickson, MB R0J 0P0
Tel: 204-636-7894; *Fax:* 204-636-2545
Grades: Pre. K *Enrollment:* 10
Angeline McKay, Principal

Fairford: **Pinaymootang School**
General Delivery, Fairford, MB R0C 0X0, Canada
Tel: 204-659-2045; *Fax:* 204-659-2270
pinayschoolprin@yahoo.com
kinaabik.tripod.com
Grades: Pre.-12 *Enrollment:* 280
Moti Patram, Principal

Fisher River: **Charles Sinclair School**
P.O. Box 109
Fisher River, MB R0C 1S0
Tel: 204-645-2206; *Fax:* 204-645-2614
www.csschool.mb.ca
www.facebook.com/161435650714825
Grades: Pre - 12 *Enrollment:* 442 *Note:* Part of the Fisher River Board of Education, Charles Sinclair School provides education to the Fisher River Cree Nation.
Delores Bouchey, Principal, 204-645-2206
Warren Woodhouse, Vice-Principal

Fort Alexander: **Sagkeeng Consolidated School**
P.O. Box 5
Fort Alexander, MB R0E 0P0
Tel: 204-367-2588; *Fax:* 204-367-9231
www.sagkeengeducation.org
Grades: K, 4 - 8 *Enrollment:* 347 *Note:* The school operates under the Sagkeeng Education Authority.
Garry Swampy, Principal
garryswampy@yahoo.ca

Garden Lake: **Kistiganwacheeng Elementary School**
General Delivery, Garden Lake, MB R0B 0T0, Canada
Tel: 204-456-2391; *Fax:* 204-456-2350
kistiganwacheengelementaryschool@knet.ca
Grades: K-6 *Enrollment:* 665
Madeline Little, Principal
madlittle194@yahoo.ca

Gillam: **Fox Lake School**
P.O. Box 379
Gillam, MB R0B 0L0
Tel: 204-486-2307; *Fax:* 204-486-2606
Grades: K.-9 *Enrollment:* 32
Russell Sinclair, Principal
r.sinclair@foxlakecreenation.com

God's Lake Narrows: **God's Lake Narrows First Nation School**
P.O. Box 284
God's Lake Narrows, MB R0B 0M0
Tel: 204-335-2003; *Fax:* 204-335-2440
www.glns.ca
Grades: Pre.-9 *Enrollment:* 400
Peter Andrews, Principal
pandrews@glns.ca

God's River: **Amos Okemow Memorial School**
General Delivery, God's River, MB R0B 0N0
Tel: 204-366-2070; *Fax:* 204-366-2105
www.mantosipi.com
Grades: K - 11 *Enrollment:* 229 *Note:* Under the direction of the Amos Okemow Memorial Education Authority, the Amos Okemow Memorial School serves the Manto Sipi Cree Nation. Students must leave the community to continue their secondary school education.
Arthur MacDonald, Principal

Griswold: **Sioux Valley School**
P.O. Box 99
Griswold, MB R0M 0S0
Tel: 204-855-2536; *Fax:* 204-855-3204
svschool@dakotaoyate.com
Grades: Pre. - 6 *Enrollment:* 192
Bernice Ledoux, Principal

Gypsumville: **Little Saskatchewan H.A.G.M.E. School**
P.O. Box 5050
Gypsumville, MB R0C 1J0, Canada
Tel: 204-659-2672; *Fax:* 204-659-5763
saskatchewanlittle@yahoo.ca
Grades: JK-9 *Enrollment:* 36
Patrick Anderson, Principal
patpinay@yahoo.ca

Hodgson: Lawrence Sinclair Memorial School
P.O. Box 359
Hodgson, MB R0C 1N0, Canada
Tel: 204-394-2429; Fax: 204-394-2431
Grades: Nursery - 10 Enrollment: 51 Note: Lawrence Sinclair Memorial School is a band operated school which serves members of the Kinonjeoshtegon First Nation.
Adeline Traverse, Principal
adelinetravers@kinonjeo.com

Island Lake: Garden Hill First Nations High School
General Delivery, Island Lake, MB R0B 0T0, Canada
Tel: 204-456-2886; Fax: 204-456-2894
Grades: 7-12 Enrollment: 472
Wilfred Fiddler, Principal

Lac Brochet: Petit Casimir Memorial School
P.O. Box 60
Lac Brochet, MB R0B 2E0
Tel: 204-337-2278; Fax: 204-337-2078
pcms@gmail.com
www.pcmschool.ca
Grades: K - 8 Enrollment: 248 Note: Petit Casimir Memorial School is a Northlands Dene First Nation School. The Dene culture, heritage, & language are integrated in education.
Gerard Butt, Principal
Gerard.butt@gmail.com
Pierre Bernier, Vice-Principal

Lake Manitoba First Nation: Lake Manitoba School
P.O. Box 1249
Lake Manitoba First Nation, MB R0C 3K0, Canada
Tel: 204-768-2728; Fax: 204-768-2194
Grades: Pre - 8 Enrollment: 218 Note: Lake Manitoba School provides education to the Lake Manitoba First Nation.
Freda Missayabit, Principal
fmissyabit@hotmail.ca

Little Grand Rapids: Abbalak Thunderswift Memorial School
P.O. Box 160
Little Grand Rapids, MB R0B 0V0
Tel: 204-397-2199; Fax: 204-397-2102
Grades: Pre. - 10 Enrollment: 207
Clarence Greene, Principal
cjgreene2003@yahoo.com

Marius: Isaac Beaulieu Memorial School
P.O. Box 108
Marius, MB R0H 0T0
Tel: 204-843-2407; Fax: 204-843-2269
Grades: Pre.-12 Enrollment: 975
Colleen West, Principal
colleenwest@live.ca

Nelson House: Nisichawayasihk Neyo Ohtinwak Collegiate
1A School Rd., Nelson House, MB R0B 1A0, Canada
Tel: 204-484-2602; Fax: 204-484-2612
www.nhea.info/schools.html
Grades: 9-12 Enrollment: 220
Lillian Gail Gossfeld McDonald, Principal
gailm@nhea.info

Nelson House: Otetiskiwin Kiskinwamahtowekamik
1 School Dr., Nelson House, MB R0B 1A0, Canada
Tel: 204-484-2242; Fax: 204-484-2002
www.nhea.info
Grades: Pre.-8 Enrollment: 718
Natalie Tays, Principal
nataliet@nhea.info

Opaskwayak: Joe A. Ross School
P.O. Box 10160
136 Waller Rd., Opaskwayak, MB R0B 2J0
Tel: 204-623-4286; Fax: 204-623-4442
www.joeaross-school.ca
Grades: Pre.-6
Karon McGillivary, Principal
karon.mcgillivary@opased.com

Opaskwayak: Oscar Lathlin Collegiate
P.O. Box 10160
Opaskwayak, MB R0B 2J0
Tel: 204-623-5259; Fax: 204-623-5361
www.oscarlathlincollegiate.ca
Grades: 7 - 12 Enrollment: 452
Ronald E. Constant, Principal
ron.constant@opased.com

Oxford House: 1972 Memorial High School
General Delivery, Oxford House, MB R0B 1C0, Canada
Tel: 204-538-2020; Fax: 204-538-2075
Toll-Free: 1-888-377-8520

Grades: 7 - 13 Enrollment: 310 Note: Under the Oxford House First Nation Board of Education, the 1972 Memorial High School serves the Bunibonibee Cree Nation of Oxford House.
James Forward, Principal
jforwardmusic@yahoo.ca

Oxford House: Oxford House Elementary School
General Delivery, Oxford House, MB R0B 1C0, Canada
Tel: 204-538-2389; Fax: 204-538-5023
Grades: Pre - 6 Enrollment: 453 Note: Under the Oxford House First Nation Board of Education, the Oxford House Elementary School serves the Bunibonibee Cree Nation of Oxford House.
Wilfred Wood, Principal
wilnaniwood_25@yahoo.ca

Pauingassi: Omiishosh Memorial School
P.O. Box 31
Pauingassi, MB R0B 2G0
Tel: 204-397-2219; Fax: 204-397-2379
Grades: Pre. K - 9 Enrollment: 75
Roddy Owens, Education Portfolio
Byron Murdock, Principal
byronmurdock@gmail.com

Peguis First Nation: Peguis Central School
P.O. Box 670
Peguis First Nation, MB R0C 3J0, Canada
Tel: 204-645-2164; Fax: 204-645-2270
www.peguiscentralschool.ca
Grades: Pre - 12 Enrollment: 820 Number of Employees: 82
Jean Malcolm, Principal
jeanmalcolm@peguiscentralschool.ca

Pelican Rapids: Neil Dennis Kematch Memorial School (NDKMS)
General Delivery, Pelican Rapids, MB R0L 1L0, Canada
Tel: 204-587-2045; Fax: 204-587-2341
school@ndkms.com
www.ndkms.com
Grades: Nursery - 12 Enrollment: 392 Note: The Neil Dennis Kematch Memorial School serves the citizens of Sapotaweyak Cree First Nation in a community located approximately 120 kilometres north of Swan River, Manitoba. The school is administered by the Sapotaweyak Education Authority.
Cora Campeau, Principal
coracook@ndkms.com

Pine Falls: Anicinabe Community School
P.O. Box 219
Pine Falls, MB R0E 1M0
Tel: 204-367-2285; Fax: 204-367-9231
Grades: Nursery - 3 Enrollment: 250 Note: Anicinabe Community School serves the Sagkeeng First Nation. It operates under the direction of the Sagkeeng Education Authority.
Rick Fewchuck, Principal
rfewchuck@sagkeengeducation.com

Pine Falls: Sagkeeng Anicinabe High School
P.O. Box 1610
Pine Falls, MB R0E 1M0
Tel: 204-367-2243; Fax: 204-367-4566
www.sagkeengeducation.org
Grades: 8 - 12 Enrollment: 215 Note: The Sagkeeng Education Authority operates the Sagkeeng Anicinabe High School, which educates secondary school students of the Sagkeeng First Nation.
Claude Guimond, Principal
cgmojo@hotmail.com

Pipestone: Wambdi Iyotaka School
P.O. Box 146
Pipestone, MB R0M 1T0, Canada
Tel: 204-854-2975; Fax: 204-854-2933
Grades: Pre.- K Enrollment: 15 Note: The Wambdi Iyotaka School serves members of the Canupawakpa Dakota Nation in Manitoba.
Laura Ellen Elliot, Principal
Wis.cdn.lee@gmail.com

Poplar River: Poplar River School
P.O. Box 120
Poplar River, MB R0B 0Z0
Tel: 204-244-2113; Fax: 204-244-2259
Grades: Pre. K - 9 Enrollment: 254
Roy Hammond, Principal
roy_hammond@hotmail.com

Portage la Prairie: Long Plain School
P.O. Box 430
Portage la Prairie, MB R1N 3B7
Tel: 204-252-2326; Fax: 204-252-2786
Grades: Pre.-9 Enrollment: 267

Isaac Edwards, Principal
ijedw@hotmail.com

Pukatawagan: Sakastew School
P.O. Box 319
Pukatawagan, MB R0B 1G0
Tel: 204-553-2163; Fax: 204-553-2225
Grades: K - 12 Enrollment: 602
Melvin George, Principal
Melvin_george@hotmail.com

Red Sucker Lake: Red Sucker Lake School
General Delivery, Red Sucker Lake, MB R0B 1H0
Tel: 204-469-5302; Fax: 204-469-5436
redsuckerlakeschool@gmail.com
Grades: Pre.-12 Enrollment: 341
Wesley Harper, Principal

Scanterbury: Sergeant Tommy Prince School
P.O. Box 179
Scanterbury, MB R0E 1W0
Tel: 204-766-2636; Fax: 204-766-2809
Grades: K - 12
Robert Moore, Principal
principal@stpschool.ca

Shamattawa: Abraham Beardy Memorial School
General Delivery, Shamattawa, MB R0B 1K0, Canada
Tel: 204-565-2022; Fax: 204-565-2122
Grades: K - 10 Enrollment: 327 Note: Abraham Beardy Memorial School serves the Cree First Nation of Shamattawa.
Lawrence W. Einarsson, Principal
l.einarsson@hotmail.com
Rebecca McCaffery, Vice Principal

Shortdale: Chief Clifford Lynxleg Anishinabe School
General Delivery, Shortdale, MB R0L 1W0, Canada
Tel: 204-546-2641; Fax: 204-546-3120
Grades: Pre. - 7 Enrollment: 63 Number of Employees: 13 Note: Chief Clifford Lynxleg Anishinabe School is located on the Tootinawaziibeeng (Valley River) Reserve, where it provides education to the Tootinaowaziibeeng First Nation.
Donna Dudek, Principal
donnacatagas@yahoo.ca

Split Lake: Chief Sam Cook Mahmuwee Education Centre
P.O. Box 100
Split Lake, MB R0B 1P0, Canada
Tel: 204-342-2134; Fax: 204-342-2139
Grades: Nursery - 12 Enrollment: 713 Note: Chief Sam Cook Mahmuwee Education Centre serves the Tataskweyak Cree Nation. The Tataskweyak reserve is located approximately 150 kilometres northeast of Thompson, Manitoba.
Caroline Flett, Principal, Elementary
flettcaroline@live.com
Thelma Spence, Principal, High School
thelmaspence@hotmail.com

St Theresa Point: St. Theresa Point School
P.O. Box 520
St Theresa Point, MB R0B 1J0, Canada
Tel: 204-462-9179; Fax: 204-462-2341
Grades: Pre - 4 Enrollment: 565
Giselle McDougall, Principal
Gisellemcd2012@yahoo.com

St. Theresa Point: St. Theresa Point High School
P.O. Box 670
St. Theresa Point, MB R0B 1J0
Tel: 204-462-2600; Fax: 204-462-2341
Grades: 5 - 12 Enrollment: 537
Raymond Flett, Principal
raymondflett@hotmail.com

St. Theresa Point: St. Theresa Point Middle School
P.O. Box 350
St. Theresa Point, MB R0B 1J0
Tel: 204-462-2420; Fax: 204-462-2793
Grades: 5 - 8 Enrollment: 327
Roy A. Mason, Principal
Ramason.ca@yahoo.com

Swan Lake: Indian Springs School
P.O. Box 145
Swan Lake, MB R0G 2S0
Tel: 204-836-2332; Fax: 204-836-2317
Toll-Free: 866-786-7841
lssprincipal@mts.net
www.swanlakefirstnation.ca/iss.html
Grades: K - 8 Enrollment: 68
Donovan Mann, Principal

Tadoule Lake: Peter Yassie Memorial School
P.O. Box 77
Tadoule Lake, MB R0B 2C0
Tel: 204-684-2279; *Fax:* 204-684-2130
Grades: Pre. - 8 *Enrollment:* 64 *Note:* Peter Yassie Memorial School is a Sayisi Dene First Nation school.
Geoffrey Ndibali, Principal
gndibali@yahoo.ca

Wasagamack: George Knott School
P.O. Box 82
Wasagamack, MB R0B 1Z0
Tel: 204-457-2485; *Fax:* 204-457-2273
Grades: Pre.-12 *Enrollment:* 575
Randy Harper, Principal
R_harper@live.ca

Waywayseecappo: Waywayseecappo Community School
P.O. Box 9
Waywayseecappo, MB R0J 1S0, Canada
Tel: 204-859-2811; *Fax:* 204-859-2992
Grades: K-8 *Enrollment:* 330 *Note:* The Waywayseecappo Community School is a band operated elementary school, which provides education to members of Manitoba's Waywayseecappo First Nation. The First Nation community is situated approximately thirty-four kilometres east of Russell. Secondary school students from Waywayseecappo First Nation are transported to Russell's Major Pratt School.
Troy Luhowy, Principal

Winnipeg: Lake St. Martin School
1970 Ness Ave., Winnipeg, MB R3J 0Y9, Canada
Tel: 204-942-2270; *Fax:* 204-942-6759
www.facebook.com/168797906499673
Grades: Nursery - 9 *Enrollment:* 109 *Note:* The Lake St. Martin School provides elementary education to the Lake St. Martin First Nation in Manitoba's Interlake Region.
C. Allan Moar, Principal
c.allanmoar@yahoo.ca

Winnipeg: Southeast Collegiate
1301 Lee Blvd., Winnipeg, MB R3T 5W8, Canada
Tel: 204-261-3551; *Fax:* 204-269-7880
secinfo@secollege.ca
www.secollege.ca
Grades: 10-12 *Enrollment:* 163
Sheryl McCorrister, Principal

York Landing: George Saunders Memorial School
General Delivery, York Landing, MB R0B 2B0, Canada
Tel: 204-341-2118; *Fax:* 204-341-2235
gsmschool@hotmail.com
Grades: K-8 *Enrollment:* 99
Lloyd Chubb, Principal

Hearing Impaired

Winnipeg: Manitoba School for the Deaf (MSD)
242 Stradford St., Winnipeg, MB R2Y 2C9
Tel: 204-945-8934; *Fax:* 204-945-1767
principal@msd.ca
www.msd.ca
TTY: 204-945-8934
Grades: JK - 12 *Enrollment:* 100
Ricki Hall, Principal
rhall@msd.ca

Special Education

Brandon: Child & Adolescent Treatment Centre (CATC)
1240 - 10th St., Brandon, MB R7A 7L6
Tel: 204-727-3445; *Fax:* 204-727-3451
Toll-Free: 866-403-5459
www.prairiemountainhealth.ca/child-and-youth-referral-services
Other Information: After Hours Phone: 204-571-7278
Grades: 4-12 *Note:* The CATC provides mental health services to children, including a day program, Crisis Stabilization Unit, Early Intervention Services, & educational services

Portage la Prairie: Gladys Cook Educational Centre
P.O. Box 1342
2 River Rd., Portage la Prairie, MB R1N 3A9
Tel: 204-239-3029; *Fax:* 204-239-3025
Grades: 1-12

St Norbert: Behavioural Health Foundation
P.O. Box 250
35 av de la Digue, St Norbert, MB R3V 1L6, Canada
Tel: 204-269-3430; *Fax:* 204-269-8049
info@bhf.ca
www.bhf.ca

Note: The Behavioural Health Foundation provides long term residential addictions treatment programming for men, women, teens and family units experiencing a variety of addiction problems and co-occurring mental health concerns.
Kerri Whitworth, Contact
kerriw@bhf.ca

Winnipeg: Marymound School
442 Scotia St., Winnipeg, MB R2V 1X4, Canada
Tel: 204-336-5285; *Fax:* 204-338-4690
school@marymound.com
www.marymound.com/main/education/
www.facebook.com/marymoundwpg
twitter.com/marymound
Grades: Elem.-11
Mark Miles, Principal

Winnipeg: St. Amant School
440 River Rd., Winnipeg, MB R2M 3Z9, Canada
Tel: 204-256-4301; *Fax:* 204-257-4349
inquiries@stamant.ca
stamant.ca/programs/st-amant-school
www.facebook.com/StAmantMB
twitter.com/StAmantMB
www.linkedin.com/company/st-amant
www.youtube.com/user/StAmantMB
Grades: K-12
Shirley Labossiere, Acting President & CEO

Distance Education

Winnipeg: Wapaskwa Virtual Collegiate
#200, 1090 Waverley St., Winnipeg, MB R3T 0P4
Tel: 204-594-1290; *Fax:* 204-477-4314
www.wapaskwa.ca
Note: Wapaskwa Virtual Collegiate is under the leadership of the Manitoba First Nations Education Resource Centre (MFNERC). They help First Nation students in Manitoba access new sources of education and learning opportunities to meet all of their graduation or post-secondary requirements.
Allison McDonald, Principal

Schools: Independent & Private

Protestant

Altona: Sunflower Valley Christian School
P.O. Box 2484
Altona, MB R0G 0B0, Canada
Tel: 204-324-1564; *Fax:* 204-327-5505
Grades: 1-9

Arborg: Interlake Mennonite Fellowship School
P.O. Box 388
Arborg, MB R0C 0A0, Canada
Tel: 204-364-2328
Grades: 1-12

Arborg: Lake Center Mennonite Fellowship School
P.O. Box 838
Arborg, MB R0C 0A0
Tel: 204-364-2201; *Fax:* 204-364-2272
Grades: K-9

Arborg: Morweena Christian School (MCS)
P.O. Box 1030
Arborg, MB R0C 0A0
Tel: 204-364-2466; *Fax:* 204-364-3117
info@morweenaschool.org
www.morweenaschool.org
Grades: K - 12 *Enrollment:* 135
Tim Reimer, Principal

Austin: Austin Christian Academy
P.O. Box 460
Austin, MB R0H 0C0, Canada
Tel: 204-637-2303; *Fax:* 204-637-3127
ausaca@mynetset.ca
www.austinchristianacademy.ca
Grades: K.-12 *Enrollment:* 50
Myla Krauskopf, Principal

Austin: Austin Mennonite School
P.O. Box 267
Austin, MB R0H 0C0, Canada
Tel: 204-637-2008
Grades: 1-12

Austin: Edrans Christian School
P.O. Box 1
RR #1, Austin, MB R0H 0C0, Canada
Tel: 204-466-2865; *Fax:* 204-466-2994
www.echurchnet.ca/christian-school/
Grades: K-12

Birnie: Shady Oak Christian School
P.O. Box 14
Birnie, MB R0J 0J0
Tel: 204-966-3477; *Fax:* 204-966-3479
www.shadyoak.net
www.facebook.com/shady.oak.3
Grades: 1 - 9
Joyce Trigger, Director

Brandon: Christian Heritage School
Heritage Campus
2025 - 26 St., Brandon, MB R7B 3Y2
Tel: 204-725-3209; *Fax:* 204-728-9641
office@chsbrandon.ca
www.chsbrandon.ca
Grades: K.-8 *Enrollment:* 152
Kari Tannas, President
Bryan Schroeder, Principal
principal@chsbrandon.ca

Carman: Dufferin Christian School
P.O. Box 1450
Carman, MB R0G 0J0
Tel: 204-745-2278; *Fax:* 204-745-3441
office@dufferinchristian.ca
www.dufferinchristian.ca
Grades: K.-12
Arie Veenendaal, Chair
arieveenendaal@dufferinchristian.ca
Andy Huisman, Principal
andyhuisman@dufferinchristian.ca

Gretna: Mennonite Collegiate Institute
P.O. Box 250
466 Mary St., Gretna, MB R0G 0V0
Tel: 204-327-5891; *Fax:* 204-327-5872
Toll-Free: 877-624-2583
info@mciblues.net
www.mciblues.net
www.facebook.com/156227284431207
Grades: 7-12 *Enrollment:* 140
Darryl Loewen, Principal
darrylloewen@mciblues.net

Grunthal: Mennonite Christian Academy
P.O. Box 149
Grunthal, MB R0A 0R0
Tel: 204-434-9315
Grades: K - 12

Hodgson: Hodgson Christian Academy
P.O. Box 220
Hodgson, MB R0C 1N0, Canada
Tel: 204-372-8483
Grades: 1-12

Horndean: Horndean Christian Day School
P.O. Box 79
Horndean, MB R0G 0Z0
Tel: 204-829-3354
Grades: 1-10

Kane: Kane Christian Academy
P.O. Box 51
RR#1, Lowe Farm, Kane, MB R0G 1E0
Tel: 204-343-2526
Grades: 2 - 8

Killarney: Lakeside Christian School
P.O. Box 894
Killarney, MB R0K 1G0
Tel: 204-523-8240; *Fax:* 204-523-8351
ics@mts.net
www.facebook.com/lcskillarney
Grades: K.-10
Nancy Reimer, Principal

Kleefeld: New Hope Christian School
P.O. Box 120
Kleefeld, MB R0A 0V0
Tel: 204-377-4204
Grades: 1 - 12

Lorette: Daystar Christian Academy
RR#2, Lorette, MB R0A 0Y0
Tel: 204-878-3044
Grades: 1-12

Pine Falls: Christian Faith Academy
P.O. Box 130
Pine Falls, MB R0E 1M0, Canada
Tel: 204-367-2056
Grades: 1 - 12

Plum Coulee: Christ Full Gospel Academy
P.O. Box 107
75 Elm St., Plum Coulee, MB R0G 1R0, Canada
Tel: 204-829-3576
www.christfullgospel.org
www.facebook.com/christfullgospel
twitter.com/ChristFullGF
Grades: K - 12 *Note:* Christ Full Gospel Academy uses the Accelerated Christian Education curriculum.

Plum Coulee: Prairie Mennonite School
P.O. Box 50
Plum Coulee, MB R0G 1R0
Tel: 204-829-3336
Grades: K - 12

Portage La Prairie: Solid Rock Ministries Christian School
124 4th Ave. NE, Portage La Prairie, MB R1N 0E9, Canada
Tel: 204-239-6785; *Fax:* 204-239-6785
Grades: 1 - 10

Portage la Prairie: Lighthouse Christian Academy
P.O. Box 1360
Portage la Prairie, MB R1N 3N9, Canada
Tel: 204-428-5332; *Fax:* 204-428-5386
Grades: K-12

Roblin: Parkland Christian School
P.O. Box 480
Roblin, MB R0L 1P0
Tel: 204-937-2870
Grades: 1-9

Steinbach: Steinbach Christian High School
50 Pth 12 North, Steinbach, MB R5G 1T4
Tel: 204-326-3537; *Fax:* 204-326-5164
info@steinbachchristian.ca
www.steinbachchristian.ca
www.facebook.com/Steinbach.Christian.Schools
www.instagram.com/steinbachchristianschool
Grades: K - 12 *Enrollment:* 340 *Note:* Christian high school with Mennonite affiliation

Stuartburn: Border View Christian Day School
P.O. Box 103
Stuartburn, MB R0A 2B0
Tel: 204-427-2932
Grades: 1-10

Swan River: Community Bible Fellowship Christian School (CBFCS)
P.O. Box 1630
Hwy. #83A South, Swan River, MB R0L 1Z0, Canada
Tel: 204-734-2174; *Fax:* 204-734-5706
cbfchristianschool@gmail.com
www.cbfchristianschool.ca
Grades: JK-8
Jocelyn Beehler, Principal

Winkler: Grace Valley Mennonite Academy
P.O. Box 839
Winkler, MB R6W 4A9, Canada
Tel: 204-829-3301; *Fax:* 204-829-3038
Grades: K-12

Winkler: Valley Mennonite Academy
P.O. Box 139
Grp. 7, RR#1, Winkler, MB R6W 4A1
Tel: 204-325-8172; *Fax:* 204-331-3199
Number of Schools: 2 *Grades:* K - 12 *Enrollment:* 134

Winnipeg: Calvin Christian School
Collegiate Campus
706 Day St., Winnipeg, MB R2C 1B6, Canada
Tel: 204-222-7910; *Fax:* 204-222-8511
calvinchristian.mb.ca
Other Information: 204-338-7981 (Elementary phone);
204-339-3280 (Elementary fax)
twitter.com/ccselementary
Grades: K.-12 *Note:* The school's elementary campus is located at 245 Sutton Ave., Winnipeg, MB R2G 0T1.
Ray Algera, Principal, Collegiate Campus
Hank Vande Kraats, Principal, Elementary Campus

Winnipeg: Christ the King School
12 Lennox Ave., Winnipeg, MB R2M 1A6, Canada
Tel: 204-257-0027; *Fax:* 204-257-2129
office@ctkschool.ca
www.ctkschool.ca
Grades: JK-8
Mike Desautels, Chair
Laura Carreiro, Principal

Winnipeg: Faith Academy
Elementary/High School Campus
437 Matheson Ave., Winnipeg, MB R2W 0E1, Canada
Tel: 204-582-3400; *Fax:* 204-582-2616
elementary.office@faithacademy.ca
www.faithacademy.ca
Grades: K.-4; 9-12 *Note:* Faith Academy is a conservative, evangelical, Christian, revival-based educational institution open to any Manitoba student willing & able to follow the established school guide. The High School campus (highschool.office@faithacademy.ca) is located at the west side of the Matheson Avenue building.
Trevor Warkentin, Principal
trevor.warkentin@faithacademy.ca
Laurie Dyck, Principal, Elementary

Campuses
Middle School Campus
600 Jefferson Ave., Winnipeg, MB R2V 0P2, Canada
Tel: 204-338-6150
middleschool.office@faithacademy.ca
Grades: 5-8
Blair Mensforth, Principal

Pritchard Campus
220 Pritchard Ave., Winnipeg, MB R2W 2J1, Canada
Tel: 204-589-6885; *Fax:* 888-867-6914
Grades: K.-3

Winnipeg: Hosanna Christian School
129 Dagmar St., Winnipeg, MB R3A 0Z3
Tel: 204-944-8237
Grades: N-12

Winnipeg: Immaculate Heart of Mary School
650 Flora Ave., Winnipeg, MB R2W 2S5
Tel: 204-582-5698; *Fax:* 204-586-6698
ihms.mb.ca
Other Information: Alternate Phone: 204-589-2709
www.facebook.com/immaculateheartofmary
twitter.com/ihms_winnipeg
Grades: JK-8
Sr. Anne Pidskalny, S.S.M.I., School Director
Rod Picklyk, Principal

Winnipeg: Immanuel Christian School
215 Rougeau Ave., Winnipeg, MB R2C 3Z9
Tel: 204-661-8937; *Fax:* 204-669-7013
office@immanuelchristian.ca
www.immanuelchristian.ca
Grades: K.-12 *Enrollment:* 181
Rob Dewitt, Chair
Peter Veenendaal, Principal

Winnipeg: The King's School
851 Panet Rd., Winnipeg, MB R2K 4C9, Canada
Tel: 204-989-6581; *Fax:* 204-989-6584
contact@thekingsschool.ca
www.thekingsschool.ca
Grades: Pre.-12 *Enrollment:* 300 *Note:* The King's School is a co-educational school & ministry of Gateway Christian Community Church.
Suzan Zielke, Principal

Winnipeg: Linden Christian School
877 Wilkes Ave., Winnipeg, MB R3P 1B8
Tel: 204-989-6730; *Fax:* 204-487-7068
www.lindenchristian.org
www.facebook.com/LindenChristianSchool
www.instagram.com/lindenchristianschool
Grades: K.-12 *Enrollment:* 800
Garry Nickel, Chair
Robert Charach, Principal
rcharach@lindenchristian.org

Winnipeg: Mennonite Brethren Collegiate Institute (BMCI)
173 Talbot Ave., Winnipeg, MB R2L 0P6
Tel: 204-667-8210; *Fax:* 204-661-5091
mbci.mb.ca
Grades: 6-12
Fred Pauls, Principal

Winnipeg: St. Aidan's Christian School
Aberdeen Campus
418 Aberdeen Ave., Winnipeg, MB R2W 1V7, Canada
Tel: 204-586-6792; *Fax:* 204-582-0155
staidanschool@mts.net
staidansschool.ca
Grades: 6-10 *Enrollment:* 30
Vanessa David, Principal

Campuses
Calvary Temple Campus
400 Hargrave St., Winnipeg, MB, Canada
Tel: 204-944-9674

Winnipeg: Springs Christian Academy
261 Youville St., Winnipeg, MB R2H 2S7
Tel: 204-331-3640; *Fax:* 204-257-1286
www.springschurch.com/sca
www.instagram.com/springschristianacademy
Grades: K.-12 *Enrollment:* 689 *Note:* Affiliated with Springs Church
Darcy Bayne, Principal
dbayne@springs.ca

Winnipeg: Westgate Mennonite Collegiate
86 West Gate, Winnipeg, MB R3C 2E1, Canada
Tel: 204-775-7111; *Fax:* 204-786-1651
www.westgatemennonite.ca
Grades: 7 - 12 *Enrollment:* 315 *Note:* The Christian school is based upon the Anabaptist Mennonite tradition.
Bob Hummelt, Principal

Winnipeg: Winnipeg Mennonite Elementary & Middle School
Bedson Campus
250 Bedson St., Winnipeg, MB R3K 1R7
Tel: 204-885-1032; *Fax:* 204-897-4068
wmems@wmems.ca
www.wmems.ca
www.facebook.com/wmems1981
Grades: K.-8 *Enrollment:* 400
John Sawatzky, Principal
john.sawatzky@wmems.ca

Schools
Winnipeg Mennonite Elementary School - Katherine Friesen Campus
26 Agassiz Dr., Winnipeg, MB R3T 2K7
Tel: 204-261-9637; *Fax:* 204-275-5181
agassiz.office@wmems.ca
Grades: K.-6
David Stoesz, Principal
david.stoesz@wmems.ca

Catholic

Winnipeg: Holy Cross School
300 Dubuc St., Winnipeg, MB R2H 1E4, Canada
Tel: 204-237-4936; *Fax:* 204-237-7433
hcsoffice@holycrossschool.mb.ca
www.holycrossschool.mb.ca
Grades: Pre.-8 *Enrollment:* 410 *Number of Employees:* 27
Alexander Cap, Principal
acap@holycrossschool.mb.ca

Winnipeg: Our Lady of Victory School
249 Arnold Ave., Winnipeg, MB R3L 0W4, Canada
Tel: 204-452-7632; *Fax:* 204-453-3081
olv@shawbiz.ca
www.victoryedu.com
twitter.com/olv_school
Grades: Pre K.-8 *Enrollment:* 117
A. Cap, Principal

Winnipeg: St. Charles Catholic School
331 St. Charles St., Winnipeg, MB R3K 1T6, Canada
Tel: 204-837-1520; *Fax:* 204-837-2326
sec@stccs.ca
www.stccs.ca
Grades: K.-8 *Enrollment:* 206 *Number of Employees:* 33
Dr. Anne Penny, Principal
dr_penny@stccs.ca

Independent & Private Schools

Austin: Pine Creek Colony School
P.O. Box 370
Austin, MB R0H 0C0, Canada
Tel: 204-466-2925
Grades: K.-12

Austin: Pine Creek School
P.O. Box 219
Austin, MB R0H 0C0, Canada
Tel: 204-385-3025
Grades: K-10

Beausejour: Willow Grove School
P.O. Box 59
Beausejour, MB R0E 0C0
Tel: 204-268-4035; *Fax:* 204-268-9452
Grades: 1-9

Cartwright: **Cartwright Community Independent School (CCIS)**
P.O. Box 439
Cartwright, MB R0K 0L0, Canada
Tel: 204-529-2357
www.facebook.com/CCISProud

Grades: 12 (Senior 4)

Cartwright: **Rock Lake School**
P.O. Box 69
Cartwright, MB R0K 0L0
Tel: 204-529-2349; *Fax:* 204-529-2184
Grades: 1 - 9 *Note:* Rock Lake School is a private school established by the Church of God in Christ, Mennonite.

Elie: **Milltown Academy**
P.O. Box 250
Elie, MB R0H 0H0, Canada
Tel: 204-353-4111; *Fax:* 204-353-2729
Grades: K - 12

Elm Creek: **Wingham HB School**
P.O. Box 45
RR #1, Elm Creek, MB R0G 0N0, Canada
Tel: 204-436-3231; *Fax:* 204-436-3230
winghamhbschool.com
Grades: K.-12
James Waldner, Principal
james@winghamhbschool.com

Elma: **Riverside School**
P.O. Box 136
Elma, MB R0E 0Z0
Tel: 204-348-2686; *Fax:* 204-348-7181
Grades: 1 - 9

Elma: **Twin Rivers Country School**
P.O. Box 30
Elma, MB R0E 0Z0, Canada
Tel: 204-426-5611; *Fax:* 204-426-5611
Grades: K - 8

Gladstone: **Prairie View Amish School**
General Delivery, Gladstone, MB R0J 0T0
Grades: 1 - 9

Grandview: **Poplar Grove School**
P.O. Box 70
Grandview, MB R0L 0Y0
Tel: 204-546-2691
Grades: 1-9

Kenville: **Riverdale School**
RR#1, Kenville, MB R0L 0Z0
Tel: 204-539-2660; *Fax:* 204-539-2480
Grades: 1 - 9

Kleefeld: **Wild Rose School**
P.O. Box 167
Kleefeld, MB R0A 0V0
Tel: 204-377-4778; *Fax:* 204-377-4778
Grades: 1-9

Kola: **Kola Community School**
P.O. Box 312
Kola, MB R0M 1B0, Canada
Tel: 204-556-2347; *Fax:* 204-556-2425
kola.flbsd.mb.ca
Grades: 1-9 *Number of Employees:* 4 teachers; 4 administrative; 2 custodial; 1 bus driver *Note:* Provides programming in three combined classrooms with the following divisions: Grade One to Grade Three, Grade Four to Grade Six, & Grade Seven to Grade Nine.
Kristi Wilson, Principal, 204-748-3438

MacGregor: **H.B. Community Baker Colony School**
P.O. Box 40
MacGregor, MB R0H 0R0, Canada
Tel: 204-252-2178; *Fax:* 204-252-2381
Grades: K-12

Neepawa: **Living Hope School**
P.O. Box 2158
Neepawa, MB R0J 1H0, Canada
Tel: 204-966-3274
Grades: 3-12

Pine River: **Pine River Country School**
P.O. Box 242
Pine River, MB R0L 1M0
Tel: 204-263-2001
Grades: 1 - 8

Portage la Prairie: **Airport Colony School**
P.O. Box 967
Portage la Prairie, MB R1N 3C4, Canada
Tel: 204-274-2412
Grades: K-12 *Note:* Location: NE 2-13-8 W, MacDonald, MB.

Portage la Prairie: **Westpark School**
P.O. Box 91
2375 Saskatchewan Ave. West, Portage la Prairie, MB R1N 3B2, Canada
Tel: 204-857-3726
office@westparkschool.com
www.westparkschool.com
www.facebook.com/westparkschool
Grades: K.-12 (Senior 1 - 4) *Enrollment:* 220 *Note:* The school is a ministry of Portage Alliance Church.
Lydia Stoesz, B.Ed., M.Div, Principal

Rosenort: **Prairie View School**
P.O. Box 117
112 River Rd. North, Rosenort, MB R0G 1W0
Tel: 204-746-8837
Grades: 1 - 9

Sinclair: **Stony Creek School**
P.O. Box 5
Sinclair, MB R0M 2A0
Tel: 204-662-4431; *Fax:* 204-662-4539
Grades: 1-9

Sperling: **Silverwinds School**
P.O. Box 130
Sperling, MB R0G 2M0, Canada
Tel: 204-626-3378; *Fax:* 204-626-3397
Grades: K-12

Ste. Anne: **Greenland School**
P.O. Box 22
Grp. 15, RR#1, Ste. Anne, MB R5H 1R1
Tel: 204-355-4922; *Fax:* 204-355-9280
Grades: K-9

Steinbach: **Church of God Sunrise Academy**
P.O. Box 3368
Steinbach, MB R5G 1P6, Canada
Tel: 204-434-6643; *Fax:* 204-326-6681
Grades: K-12

Steinbach: **Countryview School**
P.O. Box 3910
Steinbach, MB R5G 1P9
Tel: 204-326-1481; *Fax:* 204-326-4788
Number of Schools: 1 *Grades:* 2-9 *Enrollment:* 22 *Number of Employees:* 2
Phyllis Wohlgemuth, Principal, 306-326-4968
Tim Wiebe, Vice-Principal, 306-326-1413

Steinbach: **VCFG School**
P.O. Box 3160
Steinbach, MB R5G 1P5
Tel: 204-320-2716; *Fax:* 204-320-2716
Grades: K - 10

Winkler: **New Life Fellowship**
P.O. Box 41
Winkler, MB R6W 4A7
Tel: 204-331-1689
Grades: 1 - 10

Winnipeg: **Al-Hijra Islamic School (AIS)**
410 Desalaberry Ave., Winnipeg, MB R2L 0Y7
Tel: 204-489-1300; *Fax:* 204-489-1323
ais123@mts.net
www.alhijra.ca
Grades: K.-9 *Enrollment:* 185 *Note:* Established in 1996, teaching at Al-Hijra Islamic School includes Arabic, Quranic, & Islamic studies.
Abdo El-Tassi, Board Chair
Abed Moussa, Principal

Winnipeg: **Balmoral Hall School**
630 Westminster Ave., Winnipeg, MB R3C 3S1, Canada
Tel: 204-784-1600
www.balmoralhall.com
TTY: 1-866-373-2611
www.facebook.com/balmoralhall
twitter.com/balmoralhall
www.youtube.com/user/BalmoralHallWinnipeg
Grades: Nursery - 5 *Note:* Balmoral Hall School specializes in education for girls. It also offers a child care program for girls, aged 2 & 3.
Jim Perchaluk, Chair
Joanne Kamins, Head of School
Geneviève Delaquis, Director, Advancement, 204-784-1615

Bin Dong Jiang, Administrator, Day Admissions, 204-784-1608

Winnipeg: **Beautiful Savior Lutheran School (BSLS)**
52 Birchdale Ave., Winnipeg, MB R2H 1R9, Canada
Tel: 204-984-9600; *Fax:* 204-984-9607
admin@bsls.ca
www.bsls.ca
Grades: Nursery - 8 *Note:* Beautiful Savior Lutheran School also offers a daycare program & before & after school care.
Jennifer McCrea, Principal
principal@bsls.ca
Heather Burnett, Director, Child Care Services

Winnipeg: **Casa Montessori and Orff**
1055 Wilkes Ave., Winnipeg, MB R3P 2L7
Tel: 204-487-6167; *Fax:* 204-487-2944
montessoriandorff.ca
Number of Schools: 2 *Grades:* Pre.-6
Fay Sequeira, Co-Founder/Director
Lorraine Barnett, Co-Founder/Director

Winnipeg: **The Collegiate at the University of Winnipeg**
515 Portage Ave., Winnipeg, MB R3B 2E9, Canada
Tel: 204-786-9221; *Fax:* 204-775-1942
collegiate@uwinnipeg.ca
collegiate.uwinnipeg.ca
www.facebook.com/theuniversityofwinnipegcollegiate
twitter.com/Collegiate_UWPG
Grades: 9-12 *Note:* The independent secondary school is a division of The University of Winnipeg.
Robert Bend, Dean, 204-988-7583
r.bend@uwinnipeg.ca
Bonnie Talbot, Associate Dean, 204-786-9243
b.talbot@uwinnipeg.ca
Olaf Johnson, Office Manager, 204-786-9901
o.johnson@uwinnipeg.ca

Winnipeg: **Gray Academy of Jewish Education**
123 Doncaster St., #A100, Winnipeg, MB R3N 2B4
Tel: 204-477-7410; *Fax:* 204-477-7474
info@grayacademy.ca
www.grayacademy.ca
www.facebook.com/MyGrayAcademy
twitter.com/MyGrayAcademy
Grades: JK-12 *Note:* The largest independent Jewish day school in Western Canada. Co-educational. General subjects & Jewish studies programmes.
Rory Paul, Head of School & CEO, 204-477-7425
Dr. Ruth Ashrafi, Director of Judaic Studies, 204-477-7483
Jack Cipilinski, Chief Financial Officer, 204-477-7402
Ashley Morgan, Coordinator of Marketing & Communications, 204-477-7489

Winnipeg: **Holy Ghost School**
319 Selkirk Ave., Winnipeg, MB R2W 2L8
Tel: 204-582-1053; *Fax:* 204-582-4870
schooloffice@holyghost.ca
www.holyghostschool.ca
Grades: K.-8
Fr. Alfred Grzempa, Pastor
J. Siska, Principal

Winnipeg: **Islamic Academy of Manitoba**
Académie islamique du Manitoba
P.O. Box 153
208 Provencher Blvd., Winnipeg, MB R2H 3B4, Canada
Tel: 204-231-4441
ecolesofiyaschool@mts.net
ecolesofiyaschool.weebly.com
Grades: K.-8 *Note:* Program & instruction Arabic, English & French. Daily Qur'an studies. École Sofiya School is IAM's elementary school section for boys & girls. Collège Sofiya is the junior high section for girls in Grades 7 & 8.
Dr. Taib Soufi, Principal

Winnipeg: **The Laureate Academy**
100 Villa Maria Pl., Winnipeg, MB R3V 1A9
Tel: 204-831-7107; *Fax:* 204-885-3217
frontdesk@laureateacademy.com
www.laureateacademy.com
www.facebook.com/168440733271620
Grades: 1-12
Edward T. Scully, President & Co-Founder
Barbara E. Butler, Vice-President & Co-Founder

Winnipeg: **Oholei Torah School**
1845 Mathers Ave., Winnipeg, MB R3N 0N2, Canada
Tel: 204-339-8737; *Fax:* 204-272-8178
oholeitorah@chabadwinnipeg.org
Grades: N.-8
Shawna Cogan, Principal

Winnipeg: Ohr Hatorah School
620 Brock St., Winnipeg, MB R3N 0Z4, Canada
Tel: 204-489-1147; *Fax:* 204-489-5899
principal@ohrhatorah.ca
Grades: N.-4

Winnipeg: Paradise Montessori School
1341 Kenaston Blvd., Winnipeg, MB R3P 2P2
Tel: 204-832-0866; *Fax:* 204-487-3469
www.paradisemontessori.ca
Grades: N-K
Lileena Mendis, Director
lileena@paradisemontessori.ca

Winnipeg: Red River Valley Junior Academy (RRVJA)
56 Grey St., Winnipeg, MB R2L 1V3, Canada
Tel: 204-661-2408; *Fax:* 204-667-1396
mail@rrvja.ca
www.rrvja.ca
Other Information: Admissions: 204-667-2383
Grades: JK-10 *Note:* Red River Valley Junior Academy is owned & operated by the Seventh Day Adventist Church.
Ian Mighty, M.A., B.Ed., PBCE, Admin., Principal
imight@rrvja.ca
Daniel NcGuire, B.Ed., Vice-Principal & Middle Years Specialist
dmcguire@rrvja.ca
Evelyn Mallorca, Administrative Assistant
emallorca@rrvja.ca

Winnipeg: Riverview Montessori
170 Ashland Ave., Winnipeg, MB R3L 1L1, Canada
Tel: 204-475-1039; *Fax:* 204-452-4643
info@riverviewmontessori.ca
www.riverviewmontessori.ca
www.facebook.com/RiverviewMontessori
Grades: Pre./K.
Judy Hurd, Director

Winnipeg: St. Alphonsus School
343 Munroe Ave., Winnipeg, MB R2K 1H2, Canada
Tel: 204-667-6271; *Fax:* 204-663-4187
info@stalphonsusschool.ca
www.stalphonsusschool.ca
www.facebook.com/stalphonsusschool1
twitter.com/stalphonsus1
Grades: K.-8 *Enrollment:* 225
Christine McInnis, Principal
christine.mcinnis@stalphonsusschool.ca

Winnipeg: St. Boniface Diocesan High School
282 Dubuc St., Winnipeg, MB R2H 1E4, Canada
Tel: 204-987-1560; *Fax:* 204-237-9891
admin@sbdhs.net
www.sbdhs.net
www.facebook.com/1763463477216113
twitter.com/SBDHSWpg
Grades: 9-12 *Enrollment:* 150
Jaime Robinson, Principal
jrobinson@sbdhs.net

Winnipeg: St. Edward's School
836 Arlington St., Winnipeg, MB R3E 2E4, Canada
Tel: 204-774-8773; *Fax:* 204-775-0011
www.stedwards.ca
Grades: K.-6 *Enrollment:* 197 *Number of Employees:* 19
Linda Doyle, Principal
lindadoyle@mts.net

Winnipeg: St. Emile School
552 St. Anne's Rd., Winnipeg, MB R2M 3G4, Canada
Tel: 204-989-5020; *Fax:* 204-989-5026
www.stemileschool.ca
Grades: Pre.-8
Luca Macchia, President

Winnipeg: St. Gerard School
40 Foster St., Winnipeg, MB R2L 1V7, Canada
Tel: 204-667-4862; *Fax:* 204-668-7932
stgerard@shaw.ca
www.stgerardschool.net
Grades: Pre.-8
Jean Gilbert, Principal
jgilbert.stgerard@shaw.ca

Winnipeg: St. Ignatius School
239 Harrow St., Winnipeg, MB R3M 2Y3, Canada
Tel: 204-475-1386
school@stignatius.mb.ca
www.stignatius.mb.ca
Grades: Pre.-8
Jeannine Pistawka, Principal

Winnipeg: St. John Brebeuf School
605 Renfrew St., Winnipeg, MB R3N 1J8, Canada
Tel: 204-489-2115; *Fax:* 204-928-7455
schooloffice@sjbcommunity.ca
www.sjbschool.ca
Grades: K.-8 *Enrollment:* 221
Father Mark A. Tarrant, Pastor
matarrant@sjbcommunity.ca
Ms. Carreiro, Principal
carreiro@sjbcommunity.ca

Winnipeg: St. John's-Ravenscourt School
400 South Dr., Winnipeg, MB R3T 3K5
Tel: 204-477-2485; *Fax:* 204-477-2429
info@sjr.mb.ca
www.sjr.mb.ca
www.facebook.com/196987707625
twitter.com/SJR_School
www.linkedin.com/company/st-john%27s-ravenscourt-school
Grades: K.-12 *Enrollment:* 780
Sean Lawton, Chair

Winnipeg: St. Joseph the Worker School
505 Brewster St., Winnipeg, MB R2C 2W6, Canada
Tel: 204-222-1841; *Fax:* 204-222-1769
stjoesch@mymts.net
sjtwschool.ca
Grades: K.-6 *Enrollment:* 129
Judi Pacheco, Principal

Winnipeg: St. Mary's Academy
550 Wellington Cres., Winnipeg, MB R3M 0C1, Canada
Tel: 204-477-0244; *Fax:* 204-453-2417
www.smamb.ca
www.facebook.com/smawinnipeg
twitter.com/SMAwpg
www.linkedin.com/company/st-mary%27s-academy----winnipeg-mb
www.youtube.com/user/SMAWinnipeg
Grades: 7-12 *Enrollment:* 600 *Note:* St. Mary's Academy operates under the direction of the Sisters of the Holy Names of Jesus & Mary.
Connie Yunyk, President
cyunyk@smamb.ca
Michelle Klus, Principal, Senior School
mklus@smamb.ca
Carol-Ann Swayzie, Principal, Junior School
caswayzie@smamb.ca

Winnipeg: St. Maurice School
1639 Pembina Hwy., Winnipeg, MB R3T 2G6, Canada
Tel: 204-453-4020; *Fax:* 204-452-4050
admin@stmaurice.mb.ca
www.stmaurice.mb.ca
Grades: K.-12 *Enrollment:* 585
B. Doiron, Principal
bdoiron@stmaurice.mb.ca

Winnipeg: St. Paul's High School
2200 Grant Ave., Winnipeg, MB R3P 0P8, Canada
Tel: 204-831-2300; *Fax:* 204-831-2340
contact-us@stpauls.mb.ca
www.stpauls.mb.ca
www.facebook.com/stpaulshigh
twitter.com/stpauls
Grades: 9-12 *Enrollment:* 582 *Note:* Jesuit University prep school for boys
Tom Lussier, Principal
Fr. Len Altilia, President

Winnipeg: St. Vital Montessori School
613 St Mary's Rd., Winnipeg, MB R3M 3L8, Canada
Tel: 204-255-0209
stvms@hotmail.com
www.stvitalmontessori.ca
Grades: Pre.

Winnipeg: Twelve Tribes School
90 East Gate, Winnipeg, MB R3C 2C3, Canada
Tel: 204-779-1118
Grades: K - 10

Winnipeg: Winnipeg Montessori School Inc.
1525 Willson Pl., Winnipeg, MB R3T 4H1, Canada
Tel: 204-452-3315; *Fax:* 204-452-3315
wpgmont@winnipegmontessori.com
www.winnipegmontessori.com
Grades: K
Dana Downey, Chair

Winnipeg: Winnipeg South Academy
870 Scotland Ave., Winnipeg, MB R3M 1X8
Tel: 204-452-6547; *Fax:* 204-452-6563
info@kiddiekampus.ca
www.kiddiekampus.ca
Grades: JK-4 *Note:* Founded in 1990, Winnipeg South Academy is a private school that offers an extension of the Montessori philosophy.
Gayle Lavigne, Founder
April Beauregard, Head of School
Suzanne Van Cauwenberghe, Principal

Universities & Colleges

Universities

Brandon: Brandon University
270 - 18th St., Brandon, MB R7A 6A9, Canada
Tel: 204-728-9520; *Fax:* 204-726-4573
communications@brandonu.ca
www.brandonu.ca
www.facebook.com/BrandonUni
twitter.com/brandonuni
www.linkedin.com/school/brandon-university
Full Time Equivalency: 3300
Dr. David Docherty, President & Vice-Chancellor
president@brandonu.ca
Scott J.B. Lamont, Vice-President, Administration & Finance
lamont@brandonu.ca
Dr. Steven Robinson, Vice-President, Academic & Provost
robinsons@brandonu.ca

Faculties
Faculty of Arts
Clark Hall
#101, 270 - 18th St., Brandon, MB R7A 6A9
Tel: 204-727-9790; *Fax:* 204-726-0473
arts@brandonu.ca
www.brandonu.ca/arts
Demetrios P. Tryphonopoulos, Dean
artsdean@brandonu.ca

Faculty of Education
Tel: 204-727-9626
facultyed@brandonu.ca
www.brandonu.ca/education
www.facebook.com/BUeducation
twitter.com/BU_Faculty_Ed
Heather Duncan, Dean
deanofed@brandonu.ca

Faculty of Health Studies
270 - 18th St., Brandon, MB R7A 6A9
Tel: 204-727-7409; *Fax:* 204-571-8568
healthstudies@brandonu.ca
www.brandonu.ca/health-studies
Other Information: 204-571-8569
Dr. John Moraros, Dean
morarosj@brandonu.ca

Faculty of Science
John R. Brodie Science Centre
270 - 18th St., Brandon, MB R7A 6A9
Tel: 204-727-9624; *Fax:* 204-728-7346
science@brandonu.ca
www.brandonu.ca/science
Bernadette Ardelli, Dean
ardellib@brandonu.ca

School of Music
Queen Elizabeth II Music Bldg.
270 - 18th St., Brandon, MB R7A 6A9
Tel: 204-727-7388; *Fax:* 204-728-6839
music@brandonu.ca
www.brandonu.ca/music
Greg Gatien, Dean

Winnipeg: Booth University College
447 Webb Pl., Winnipeg, MB R3B 2P2, Canada
Tel: 204-947-6701; *Fax:* 204-942-3856
Toll-Free: 877-942-6684
admissions@myboothuc.ca
www.boothuc.ca
www.facebook.com/BoothUC
twitter.com/boothuc
Marjory R. Kerr, President
Michael W. Boyce, Dean & Vice-President, Academic, 204-924-4882
michael_boyce@boothuc.ca
Rhonda Friesen, Dean of Students, 204-924-4876
rhonda_friesen@boothuc.ca
Jeremy Perrott, Registrar

Winnipeg: Canadian Mennonite University (CMU)
500 Shaftesbury Blvd., Winnipeg, MB R3P 2N2, Canada
Tel: 204-487-3300; *Fax:* 204-487-3858
Toll-Free: 877-231-4570
info@cmu.ca
www.cmu.ca
www.facebook.com/CMUwpg
twitter.com/CMUwpg
www.youtube.com/cmumedia
Full Time Equivalency: 1750 *Note:* Undergraduate & graduate studies.
Cheryl Pauls, President
Jonathan Dueck, Vice-President, Academic
Terry Schellenberg, Vice-President, External
John Unger, Vice-President, Administration & Finance
Kevin Kilbrei, Director, Communications & Marketing
Lois Nickel, Director, Enrolment
Randy Neufeld, Director, Operations
Dianna Robson, Director, Human Resources
Stephanie Penner, Registrar

Schools
Redekop School of Business
500 Shaftesbury Blvd., Winnipeg, MB R3P 2N2
www.cmu.ca/business.php
Ray Vander Zaag, Director, 204-487-3300, ext. 643
rvanderzaag@cmu.ca

Canadian School of Peacebuilding
500 Shaftesbury Blvd., Winnipeg, MB R3P 2N2
Tel: 204-487-3300; *Fax:* 204-487-3858
Toll-Free: 877-231-4570
csop@cmu.ca
csop.cmu.ca
www.facebook.com/csop.cmu
twitter.com/cmu_csop
Wendy Kroeker, Academic Director
Valerie Smith, Program Director

Community School of Music & the Arts
500 Shaftesbury Blvd., Winnipeg, MB R3P 2N2
Tel: 204-487-3300; *Fax:* 204-487-3858
Toll-Free: 877-231-4570
www.cmu.ca/csma
Verna Wiebe, Director, 204-837-4870
vwiebe@cmu.ca

Graduate School of Theology & Ministry
500 Shaftesbury Blvd., Winnipeg, MB R3P 2N2
www.cmu.ca/academics.php?s=gstm
Karl Koop, Director, 204-487-3300, ext. 630
kkoop@cmu.ca

School of Music
500 Shaftesbury Blvd., Winnipeg, MB R3P 2N2
www.cmu.ca/academics.php?s=music
Janet Brenneman, Dean
jbrenneman@cmu.ca

Winnipeg: University of Manitoba
66 Chancellors Circle, Winnipeg, MB R3T 2N2
Tel: 204-474-8880; *Toll-Free:* 800-432-1960
www.umanitoba.ca
www.facebook.com/umanitoba
twitter.com/umanitoba
www.linkedin.com/company/university-of-manitoba
www.youtube.com/user/YouManitoba
Full Time Equivalency: 29498
Harvey Secter, Chancellor
Dr. David T. Barnard, B.Sc., M.Sc., Ph.D., Dip., President & Vice-Chancellor
John Kearsey, Vice-President, External
Digvir Jayas, Ph.D., Vice-President, Research & International
Dr. Janice Ristock, Vice-President, Academic & Provost
Lynn Zapshala-Kelln, Vice-President, Administration
Jeff Leclerc, University Secretary
jeff.leclerc@umanitoba.ca

Faculties
Faculty of Agricultural & Food Sciences (AFS)
Agriculture Bldg.
#256, 66 Dafoe Rd., Winnipeg, MB R3T 2N2
Tel: 204-474-6026; *Fax:* 204-474-7525
agfoodsci@umanitoba.ca
umanitoba.ca/afs
www.facebook.com/UMFAFS
twitter.com/UM_agfoodsci
www.linkedin.com/company/umfafs
www.instagram.com/um_agfoodsci
Martin Scanlon, Dean, 204-474-9380
agdean@umanitoba.ca

Faculty of Architecture
Russell Bldg.
#201, 84 Curry Pl., Winnipeg, MB R3T 2M6
Tel: 204-474-6578; *Fax:* 204-474-7532
env.design@unmanitoba.ca
umanitoba.ca/faculties/architecture
www.instagram.com/faumanitoba
Jonathan Beddoes, Dean, 204-474-9806
jonathan.beddoes@umanitoba.ca

Faculty of Arts
Fletcher Argue Bldg.
#306A, 15 Chancellors Circle, 3rd Fl., Winnipeg, MB R3T 2N2
Tel: 204-474-9100; *Fax:* 204-474-7590
Toll-Free: 800-432-1960
arts_inquiry@umanitoba.ca
umanitoba.ca/faculties/arts
www.facebook.com/UManitobaArtsFaculty
twitter.com/UMArtsFaculty
www.instagram.com/umartsfaculty
Jeffery Taylor, Dean, 204-474-9271
jeff_taylor@umanitoba.ca

Extended Education
Extended Education Complex
#185, 406 University Crescent, Winnipeg, MB R3T 2N2
Tel: 204-474-8800; *Fax:* 204-474-7661
Toll-Free: 888-216-7011
extended@umanitoba.ca
umextended.ca
www.facebook.com/umextendeded
twitter.com/umextendeded
www.instagram.com/umextended
Gary Hepburn, Dean

Faculty of Education
Education Bldg.
#230, 224 Dysart Rd., Winnipeg, MB R3T 2N2
Tel: 204-474-9004; *Fax:* 204-474-7551
Toll-Free: 800-432-1960
education@umanitoba.ca
umanitoba.ca/faculties/education
www.facebook.com/umfacultyofeducation
twitter.com/um_education
David Mandzuk, Dean, 204-474-9001
deanedu@umanitoba.ca

Price Faculty of Engineering
Engineering & Information Technology Complex
75 Chancellors Circle, #E2-290, Winnipeg, MB R3T 5V6
Tel: 204-474-9809; *Fax:* 204-275-3773
dean_engineering@umanitoba.ca
umanitoba.ca/faculties/engineering
www.facebook.com/umengineering
twitter.com/um_engineering
www.linkedin.com/showcase/umengineering
Jonathan Beddoes, Dean
jonathan.beddoes@umanitoba.ca

Clayton H. Riddell Faculty of Environment, Earth & Resources
Wallace Bldg.
#440, 125 Dysart Rd., Winnipeg, MB R3T 2N2
Tel: 204-474-7252; *Fax:* 204-275-3147
riddell.faculty@umanitoba.ca
umanitoba.ca/faculties/environment
www.facebook.com/UManitobaRiddellFaculty
twitter.com/riddellfaculty
www.linkedin.co/in/riddell-faculty
www.instagram.com/riddellfaculty
Norman Halden, Dean
nm_halden@umanitoba.ca

Faculty of Graduate Studies
University Centre
#500, 65 Chancellors Circle, Winnipeg, MB R3T 2N2
Tel: 204-474-9377; *Fax:* 204-474-7553
graduate.studies@umanitoba.ca
umanitoba.ca/faculties/graduate_studies
www.facebook.com/umgradstudies
twitter.com/umgradstudies
Louise Simard, Acting Dean, 204-474-9887
louise.simard@umanitoba.ca

I.H. Asper School of Business
Drake Centre
#324, 181 Freedman Cres., Winnipeg, MB R3T 5V4
Tel: 204-474-6390; *Fax:* 204-474-7544
asb_info@umanitoba.ca
umanitoba.ca/faculties/management
www.facebook.com/IHAsperSchool
twitter.com/AsperSchool
www.linkedin.com/company/38090617
www.youtube.com/user/aspermedia

Gady Jacoby, Dean
gady.jacoby@umanitoba.ca

Faculty of Law
Robson Hall
#303, 224 Dysart Rd., Winnipeg, MB R3T 2N2
Tel: 204-474-6130; *Fax:* 204-474-7580
lawinfo@umanitoba.ca
law.robsonhall.ca
www.facebook.com/umanitoba.law
twitter.com/robsonhall
www.youtube.com/user/robsonhallvideo
Jonathan Black-Branch, Dean, 204-474-9282
jonathan.black-branch@umanitoba.ca

Faculty of Medicine
260 Brodie Centre
727 McDermot Ave., Winnipeg, MB R3E 3P5
Tel: 204-789-3557; *Fax:* 204-789-3929
umanitoba.ca/faculties/health_sciences/medicine
www.facebook.com/RadyFaculty
twitter.com/UM_RadyFHS
Brian Postl, Dean

Desautels Faculty of Music
Tache Arts Complex
136 Dafoe Rd. West, #T319, Winnipeg, MB R3T 2N2
Tel: 204-474-9310; *Fax:* 204-474-7546
music@umanitoba.ca
umanitoba.ca/faculties/music
www.facebook.com/DesautelsFacultyofMusic
twitter.com/facultyofmusic
www.youtube.com/user/UofMFacultyofMusic
Number of Employees: 32 Faculty
Edward Jurkowski, Dean

Faculty of Science
Machray Hall
#239, 186 Dysart Rd., Winnipeg, MB R3T 2N2
Tel: 204-474-8256; *Fax:* 204-474-7618
sciadv@umanitoba.ca
www.sci.umanitoba.ca
www.facebook.com/umanitobasci
twitter.com/umanitobasci
www.linkedin.com/school/47193353
www.instagram.com/umanitobasci
Stefi Baum, Dean, 204-474-9348
stefi.baum@umanitoba.ca

Faculty of Social Work
Tier Building
#521, 173 Dafoe Road West, Winnipeg, MB R3T 2N2
Tel: 204-474-7050; *Fax:* 204-474-7594
social_work@umanitoba.ca
umanitoba.ca/faculties/social_work
www.facebook.com/umsocialwork
Michael Yellow Bird, Dean

Faculty of Kinesiology and Recreation Management
Frank Kennedy Building
#102, 420 University Crescent, Winnipeg, MB R3T 2N2
Tel: 204-474-9747; *Fax:* 204-474-7634
kinrec@cc.umanitobaca
umanitoba.ca/faculties/health_sciences/medicine
www.facebook.com/umkinrec
twitter.com/umkinrec
www.instagram.com/umkinrec
Enrollment: 567 *Number of Employees:* 28
Douglas A. Brown, Dean, 204-474-8764
douglas.brown@umanitoba.ca

Schools
Dr. Gerald Niznick College of Dentistry
780 Bannatyne Ave., #D113, Winnipeg, MB R3T 2N2
Tel: 204-789-3631; *Fax:* 204-789-3912
info_dent@umanitoba.ca
umanitoba.ca/healthsciences/dentistry
Dr. Anastasia Kelekis-Cholakis, Dean

College of Nursing
Helen Glass Centre for Nursing
89 Curry Pl., Winnipeg, MB R3T 2N2
Tel: 204-474-7452; *Fax:* 204-474-7682
Toll-Free: 800-432-1960
nursing@umanitoba.ca
umanitoba.ca/nursing
www.facebook.com/NursingatUofM
Netha Dyck, Dean
netha.dyck@umanitoba.ca

College of Pharmacy
Apotex Centre
750 McDermot Ave., Winnipeg, MB R3E 0T5
Tel: 204-474-9306; *Fax:* 204-789-3744
pharmacy@umanitoba.ca
umanitoba.ca/faculties/health_sciences/pharmacy

Lalitha Raman-Wilms, Dean
lalitha.raman-wilms@umanitoba.ca

Max Rady College of Medicine
Brodie Centre
#260, 727 McDermot Ave., Winnipeg, MB R3T 2P5
Tel: 204-789-3557; *Fax:* 204-789-3929
umanitoba.ca/faculties/health_sciences/medicine
Brian Postl, Dean, 204-789-3485
Brian.Postl@umanitoba.c

College of Rehabilitation Sciences
College of Rehabilitation Sciences
#R106, 771 McDermot Ave., Winnipeg, MB R3E 0T6
Tel: 204-789-3897; *Fax:* 204-789-3927
umanitoba.ca/rehabsciences/
Reginald Urbanowski, Dean, 204-318-5284
reginald.urbanowski@umanitoba.ca

Affiliations
St. John's College
92 Dysart Rd., Winnipeg, MB R3T 2M5
Tel: 204-474-8531; *Fax:* 204-474-7610
Toll-Free: 1-800-432-1960
stjohns_college@umanitoba.ca
umanitoba.ca/colleges/st_johns
Note: Affiliated with the Anglican Church of Canada, St. John's College is located on the University of Manitoba campus.
Dr. Chris Trott, Warden & Vice-Chancellor, 204-474-8529
christopher.trott@umanitoba.ca
Sherry Peters, Registrar, 204-474-8520
sherry.peters@umanitoba.ca

St. Andrew's College
29 Dysart Rd., Winnipeg, MB R3T 2M5
Tel: 204-474-8895; *Fax:* 204-474-7624
st_andrews@umanitoba.ca
umanitoba.ca/colleges/st_andrews

St. Paul's College
70 Dysart Rd., Winnipeg, MB R3T 2M6
Tel: 204-474-8575; *Fax:* 204-474-7620
stpaulscollege@umanitoba.ca
www.umanitoba.ca/colleges/stpauls
www.facebook.com/stpaulscollegeuniversityofmanitoba
twitter.com/SPC_College
www.linkedin.com/company/st-paul-s-college-university-of-manitoba
www.instagram.com/spc_college
Note: The Roman Catholic College is located on the University of Manitoba campus.
Christopher Adams, Rector, 204-474-8581
rector.stpaulscollege@umanitoba.ca
Dilantha Fernando, Dean of Studies, 204-474-8577
dilantha.fernando@umanitoba.ca

University College
University of Manitoba
#203, 220 Dysart Rd., Winnipeg, MB R3T 2N2
Tel: 204-474-6839; *Fax:* 204-261-0021
Toll-Free: 800-432-1960
flyora.major@umanitoba.ca
umanitoba.ca/colleges/uc

Prairie Theatre Exchange
393 Portage Ave., #Y300, Winnipeg, MB R3B 3H6
Tel: 204-942-7291; *Fax:* 204-942-1774
www.pte.mb.ca
www.facebook.com/PrairieTheatre
twitter.com/PrairieTheatre
www.youtube.com/user/PTEtv
Tracey Loewen, General Manager, 204-925-5251
generalmgr@pte.mb.ca

Winnipeg: University of Winnipeg
515 Portage Ave., Winnipeg, MB R3B 2E9, Canada
Tel: 204-786-7811; *Fax:* 204-783-4996
www.uwinnipeg.ca
www.facebook.com/uwinnipeg
twitter.com/UWinnipeg
www.linkedin.com/school/university-of-winnipeg
www.youtube.com/user/uwinnipeg
Full Time Equivalency: 9072

Faculties
Faculty of Arts
515 Portage Ave., Winnipeg, MB R3B 2E9
arts@uwinnipeg.ca
www.uwinnipeg.ca/arts
twitter.com/uwfacultyofarts
Catherine Taylor, Acting Dean, 204-786-9893
c.taylor@uwinnipeg.ca

Faculty of Business & Economics
515 Portage Ave., Winnipeg, MB R3B 2E9
www.uwinnipeg.ca/fbe
www.facebook.com/uwinnipegFoBE
www.instagram.com/uwinnipegfbe
Hugh Grant, Acting Dean, 204-786-9856
h.grant@uwinnipeg.ca

Faculty of Education
515 Portage Ave., Winnipeg, MB R3B 2E9
Tel: 204-786-9491; *Fax:* 204-772-7980
www.uwinnipeg.ca/education
Ken McCluskey, Dean, 204-786-9470
k.mccluskey@uwinnipeg.ca

Faculty of Graduate Studies
515 Portage Ave., Winnipeg, MB R3B 2E9
Tel: 204-779-8946
gradstudies@uwinnipeg.ca
uwinnipeg.ca/graduate-studies
www.facebook.com/271256406461
twitter.com/UWGradStudies
www.instagram.com/uwpggradstudies
Manish Pandey, Acting Dean
m.pandey@uwinnipeg.ca

Gupta Faculty of Kinesiology & Applied Health
515 Portage Ave., Winnipeg, MB R3B 2E9
kinesiology@uwinnipeg.ca
www.uwinnipeg.ca/kinesiology
Doug Goltz, Acting Dean, 204-786-9748
d.goltz@uwinnipeg.ca

Faculty of Science
515 Portage Ave., Winnipeg, MB R3B 2E9
sciences@uwinnipeg.ca
www.facebook.com/129478117154189
twitter.com/uwsciences
Doug Goltz, Acting Dean, 204-786-9748
d.goltz@uwinnipeg.ca

Schools
The United Centre for Theological Studies (UCTS)
515 Portage Ave., Winnipeg, MB R3B 2E9
www.uwinnipeg.ca/theology
www.facebook.com/unitedcentrefortheologicalstudies
Sandy Peterson, Administrative Officer, Graduate Studies, 204-786-9797
s.peterson@uwinnipeg.ca

Global College
520 Portage Ave., Winnipeg, MB R3B 2E9
Tel: 204-988-7105
global.college@uwinnipeg.ca
www.uwinnipeg.ca/global-college
www.facebook.com/UofWGlobalCollege
Jan Stewart, Executive Director

Richardson College for the Environment
599 Portage Ave., Winnipeg, MB R3B 2G3
Tel: 204-786-9236
www.uwinnipeg.ca/richardson-college
Danny Blair, Contact
d.blair@uwinnipeg.ca

Affiliations
Menno Simons College
520 Portage Ave., Winnipeg, MB R3C 0G2, Canada
Tel: 204-953-3855; *Fax:* 204-783-3699
msc@uwinnipeg.ca
www.mscollege.ca
www.facebook.com/mennosimonscollege
twitter.com/MSCwpg
www.instagram.com/MSCwpg
Note: A college of the Canadian Mennonite University, maintaining an affiliation with the University of Winnipeg. It is located on the campus of the U. of W.
Cheryl Pauls, President
Jonathan Dueck, Academic Dean & Vice-President, Academic

Colleges

Brandon: Assiniboine Community College
1430 Victoria Ave. East, Brandon, MB R7A 2A9
Tel: 204-725-8700; *Fax:* 204-725-8740
Toll-Free: 800-862-6307
info@assiniboine.net
www.assiniboine.net
www.facebook.com/accmanitoba
twitter.com/ACCMB
www.youtube.com/user/ACCManitoba
Number of Employees: 500
Mark Frison, President & CEO

Campuses
Parkland Campus
520 Whitmore Ave. East, Dauphin, MB R7N 2V5
Tel: 204-622-2222; *Fax:* 800-482-2933
parklandinfo@assiniboine.net

Winnipeg Campus
#87, 1313 Border St., Winnipeg, MB R3H 0X4
Tel: 204-694-7111; *Fax:* 800-482-2933
hhs@assiniboine.net

North Hill Campus
1035 - 1st St. North, Brandon, MB R7A 2Y1
Fax: 204-725-8740

Adult Collegiate
725 Rosser Ave., Brandon, MB R7A 0K8
Tel: 204-725-8735; *Fax:* 204-725-8740
adultcollegiate@assiniboine.net

Brandon: Manitoba Emergency Services College
1601 Van Horne Ave. East, Brandon, MB R7A 7K2
Tel: 204-726-6855; *Fax:* 204-726-6847
Toll-Free: 1-888-253-1488
firecomm@gov.mb.ca
firecomm.gov.mb.ca/mesc.html
Note: The college is a broad-based emergency services training organization which offers a full-time program for those interested in a career in the EMS field.

The Pas: University College of the North (UCN)
P.O. Box 3000
436 - 7th St. East, The Pas, MB R9A 1M7
Tel: 204-627-8500; *Fax:* 204-627-8514
Toll-Free: 866-627-8500
info@ucn.ca
www.ucn.ca
www.facebook.com/universitycollegeofthenorth
www.linkedin.com/school/university-college-of-the-north
www.youtube.com/user/UCNTube
Full Time Equivalency: 3500
Doug Lauvstad, President & Vice-Chancellor

Campuses
Thompson Campus
55 UCN Dr., The Pas, MB R8N 1L7
Tel: 204-677-6450; *Toll-Free:* 866-677-6450

Winnipeg: Red River College (RRC)
2055 Notre Dame Ave., Winnipeg, MB R3H 0J9
Tel: 204-632-3960; *Toll-Free:* 888-515-7722
register@rrc.mb.ca
www.rrc.mb.ca
www.facebook.com/redrivercollege
twitter.com/rrc
www.linkedin.com/school/red-river-college
www.youtube.com/c/redrivercollege
Full Time Equivalency: 22000
Fred Meier, President & CEO

Campuses
Interlake & Peguis - Fisher River Campus
P.O. Box 304
825 Manitoba Ave., Selkirk, MB R1A 1T0
Tel: 204-785-5328; *Toll-Free:* 866-946-3241
interlake@rrc.ca
www.rrc.ca/interlake

Portage Campus
32 - 5th St. SE, Portage la Prairie, MB R1N 1J2
Tel: 204-856-1914
portage@rrc.mb.ca
www.rrc.ca/portage

Steinbach Campus
#2, 385 Loewen Blvd., Steinbach, MB R5G 0B3
www.rrc.ca/steinbach

Stevenson Campus
2280 Saskatchewan Ave., Winnipeg, MB R3J 3Y9
www.rrc.ca/stevenson

Winkler Campus
#100, 561 Main St., Winkler, MB R6W 1E8
Tel: 204-325-9672
winkler@rrc.ca
www.rrc.ca/winkler
Other Information: Winkler Community Learning Centre, Phone: 204-325-4997

Winnipeg: Université de Saint-Boniface
200, av de la Cathédrale, Winnipeg, MB R2H 0H7
Tél: 204-233-0210; *Téléc:* 204-237-3240
Ligne sans frais: 888-233-5112
info@ustboniface.ca
ustboniface.ca
www.facebook.com/ustboniface
twitter.com/ustboniface
www.youtube.com/user/ustboniface

Sophie Bouffard, Présidente

Faculties
Faculté des arts
Alexandre Brassard, Dean

Faculté des sciences

Faculté d'éducation
Stéfan Delaquis, Dean

Schools
École technique et professionnelle
etp@ustboniface.ca
ustboniface.ca/etp

Mélanie Cwikla, Directrice

École de travail social
ustboniface.ca/ecole-de-travail-social

Post Secondary/Technical

Protestant

Otterburne: Providence University College
10 College Cres., Otterburne, MB R0A 1G0
Tel: 204-433-7488; *Fax:* 204-433-7158
Toll-Free: 800-668-7768
info@prov.ca
www.prov.ca
www.facebook.com/ProvManitoba
twitter.com/ProvManitoba
www.youtube.com/c/ProvManitoba
Note: Institution for Christian higher education.
Kenton Anderson, President
kenton.anderson@prov.ca

Post Secondary/Technical

Blumenort: United Transportation Driver Training (UTDT)
214 Center Ave., Blumenort, MB R0A 0C0
Tel: 204-326-4200
uniteddrivertraining.ca
www.facebook.com/yourgatewaytotheworld

Campuses
Brandon Campus
132 Industrial Dr., Brandon, MB R7A 7S5
Tel: 204-326-4200

Winkler Campus
425 George Ave., Winkler, MB R6W 3N4
Tel: 204-326-4200

Brandon: H&CO Academy
603 Princess Ave., Brandon, MB R7A 0P2
Tel: 204-727-0358
hcoacademy@hotmail.com
www.hcoacademy.com

Brandon: Systems Beauty College (SBC)
763 - 13th St., Brandon, MB R7A 4R6
Tel: 204-728-8843
info@systemsbeautycollege.ca
www.systemsbeautycollege.ca
www.facebook.com/116195348452283
www.instagram.com/systemsbeautycollege
Number of Employees: 3 *Note:* Training for online Hairstyling,
Hairstyling, & Nail Technology
Donna Pawchuk, Director
systems@hotmail.ca

Richmond Hill: Academy of Learning Career College (AOLCC)
#400, 100 York Blvd., Richmond Hill, MB L4B 1J8
Fax: 855-996-9977
Toll-Free: 855-996-9977
admissions@academyoflearning.com
www.academyoflearning.com
www.facebook.com/academyoflearning
twitter.com/AcademyLearning
www.linkedin.com/school/academy-of-learning-college
www.youtube.com/user/AcademyofLearning09
Note: Computer & business training. Students can choose from
over 30 diploma & certificate programs.

Campuses
Abbotsford Campus
#204, 2692 Clearbrook Rd., Abbotsford, BC V2T 2Y8
Tel: 604-855-3315; *Fax:* 604-855-3365
abbotsford@academyoflearning.com
www.academyoflearning.com/locations/british-columbia/abbotsford

Airdrie Campus
#203, 28 Gateway Dr. NE, Airdrie, AB T4B 0J6
Tel: 587-609-9125; *Fax:* 587-449-8214
admissions.airdrie@academyoflearning.com
www.academyoflearning.com/locations/alberta/airdrie

Belleville Campus
250 Sidney St., Belleville, ON K8P 3Z3
Tel: 613-967-8973; *Fax:* 613-967-4642
academyoflearning1@cogeco.net
www.academyoflearning.com/locations/ontario/belleville

Brampton - East Campus
8740 The Gore Rd., Brampton, ON L6P 0B1
Tel: 905-508-5791; *Fax:* 289-948-1077
info@aolbrampton.ca
aolbrampton.ca
www.facebook.com/aolbramptoncampus
www.instagram.com/aolbrampton

Brampton - West Campus
#306, 7700 Hurontario St., Brampton, ON L6Y 4M3
Tel: 365-788-4080
info@aolmississauga.com
www.academyoflearning.com/locations/ontario/brampton-west

Brooks Campus
212 - 2nd Ave. West, #C, Brooks, AB T1R 1B7
Tel: 403-793-2294; *Fax:* 587-270-0379
admissions.brooks@academyoflearning.com
www.academyoflearning.com/locations/alberta/brooks

Calgary - North East Campus
#260, 495 - 36th St. NE, Calgary, AB T2A 6K3
Tel: 403-569-8973; *Fax:* 403-569-1085
calgaryne@academyoflearning.ab.ca
www.academyoflearning.com/locations/alberta/calgary-north-east

Calgary - South Campus
#220, 8228 Macleod Trail South, Calgary, AB T2H 2B8
Tel: 403-252-8973; *Fax:* 403-252-8993
calgarys@academyoflearning.ab.ca
www.academyoflearning.com/locations/alberta/calgary-south

Charlottetown Campus
55 Grafton St., Charlottetown, PE C1A 1K8
Tel: 902-894-8973

Edmonton - Downtown Campus
10010 - 100th St., Edmonton, AB T5J 0N3
Tel: 780-424-1144; *Fax:* 780-423-8962
edmdtn@academyoflearning.ab.ca
www.academyoflearning.com/locations/alberta/edmonton-downtown

Edmonton - South Campus
5650 - 23rd Ave., Edmonton, AB T6L 6N2
Tel: 780-433-7284; *Fax:* 780-435-6656
edmsouth@academyoflearning.ab.ca
www.academyoflearning.com/locations/alberta/edmonton-south

Edmonton - West Campus
17718 - 64th Ave., Edmonton, AB T5T 4J5
Tel: 780-496-9428; *Fax:* 780-944-9341
westedm@academyoflearning.ab.ca
www.academyoflearning.com/locations/alberta/edmonton-west

Halifax Campus
Mumford Professional Centre
#155, 6960 Mumford Rd., Halifax, NS B3L 4P1
Tel: 902-455-3395
www.academyoflearning.com/locations/nova-scotia/halifax

Hamilton Campus
401 Main St. East, Hamilton, ON L8N 1J7
Tel: 905-777-8553; *Fax:* 289-426-2734
info@aolhamilton.com
aolhamilton.com

High River Campus
#4, 28 - 12th Ave. SE, High River, AB T1V 1T2
Tel: 403-652-2116; *Fax:* 403-652-1492
admissions.highriver@academyoflearning.com
www.academyoflearning.com/locations/alberta/high-river

Kamloops Campus
699 Victoria St., Kamloops, BC V2C 2B3
Tel: 250-372-5429; *Fax:* 250-372-5462
kamloops@academyoflearning.com
www.academyoflearning.com/locations/british-columbia/kamloops

Kelowna Campus
#240A, 1640 Leckie Rd., Kelowna, BC V1X 7C6
Tel: 250-868-3688; *Fax:* 250-868-3511
kelowna@academyoflearning.com
www.academyoflearning.com/locations/british-columbia/kelowna

Kingston Campus
1469 Princess St., Kingston, ON K7M 3E9
Tel: 613-544-8973
admissions@aolkingston.com
www.academyoflearning.com/locations/ontario/kingston
www.facebook.com/AcademyofLearningKingston

Langley Campus
#201, 20621 Logan Ave., Langley, BC V3A 7R3
Tel: 604-532-4040; *Fax:* 604-532-4001
langley@academyoflearning.com
www.academyoflearning.com/locations/british-columbia/langley

Medicine Hat Campus
#115, 3030 - 13th Ave. SE, Medicine Hat, AB T1B 1E3
Tel: 403-526-5833; *Fax:* 403-526-4376
medicinehat@academyoflearning.ab.ca
www.academyoflearning.com/locations/alberta/medicine-hat

Mississauga - East Campus
#4, 1310 Dundas St. East, Mississauga, ON L4Y 2C1
Tel: 905-273-6788
www.academyoflearning.com/locations/ontario/mississauga-east

Mississauga - West Campus
#500, 3660 Hurontario St., Mississauga, ON L5B 3C4
Tel: 905-306-0666; *Fax:* 647-948-5571
info@aolccollege.ca
www.academyoflearning.com/locations/ontario/mississauga-west

Nanaimo Campus
#7, 1551 Estevan Rd., Nanaimo, BC V9S 3Y3
Tel: 250-753-4220; *Fax:* 250-753-4295
nanaimo@academyoflearning.com
www.academyoflearning.com/locations/british-columbia/nanaimo

North Battleford Campus
1492 - 105th St., North Battleford, SK S9A 1T3
Tel: 306-445-8188; *Fax:* 306-445-9133
northbattleford@academyoflearning.com
www.academyoflearning.com/locations/saskatchewan/north-battleford

Ottawa Campus
#217, 1600 Merivale Rd., Ottawa, ON K2G 5J8
Tel: 613-224-8973; *Fax:* 613-224-2669
www.academyoflearning.com/locations/ontario/ottawa-west

Owen Sound Campus
1043 - 2nd Ave. East, Owen Sound, ON N4K 2H8
Tel: 519-371-6188; *Fax:* 519-376-1737
www.academyoflearning.com/locations/ontario/owen-sound

Pine Falls Campus
P.O. Box 250
3 Walnut St., Pine Falls, MB R0E 1M0
Tel: 204-367-2761; *Fax:* 204-367-1217
www.academyoflearning.com/locations/manitoba/pine-falls

Red Deer Campus
2965 Bremner Ave., Red Deer, AB T4R 1S2
Tel: 403-347-6676; *Fax:* 403-347-9097
reddeer@academyoflearning.ab.ca
www.academyoflearning.com/locations/alberta/red-deer

Regina Campus
#205, 2075 Hamilton S., Richmond Hill, ON S4P 2E1
Tel: 306-527-0441; *Fax:* 306-373-8708
www.academyoflearning.com/locations/saskatchewan/regina

Richmond Campus
#200, 4351 - 3rd Rd., Richmond, BC V6X 3A7
Tel: 604-270-3907; *Fax:* 604-270-6109
www.academyoflearning.com/locations/british-columbia/richmond

Saskatoon Campus
1202A Quebec Ave., Saskatoon, SK S7K 1V2
Tel: 306-373-8700; *Fax:* 306-373-8708
admissions@shaw.ca
www.academyoflearning.com/locations/saskatchewan/saskatoon

Selkirk Campus
389 Eveline St., Selkirk, MB R1A 1N7
Tel: 204-785-8223
www.academyoflearning.com/locations/manitoba/selkirk

Steinbach Campus
Clearspring Centre
178 PTH 12, Steinbach, MB R5G 1T7
Tel: 204-326-4188; *Fax:* 204-326-3480

Summerside Campus
10 Slemon Park Dr., Summerside, PE C0B 2B0
Tel: 902-436-9889
www.academyoflearning.com/locations/prince-edward-island/su
mmerside

Surrey Campus
#102, 13753 - 72nd Ave., Surrey, BC V3W 2P2
Tel: 604-598-3555; *Fax:* 604-598-3666
admissionss@bcaol.com
www.academyoflearning.com/locations/british-columbia/surrey

Thunder Bay Campus
#103, 975 Alloy Dr., Thunder Bay, ON P7B 5Z8
Tel: 807-624-2380
www.academyoflearning.com/locations/ontario/thunder-bay

Toronto - Albion & Islington Campus
#201, 1123 Albion Rd., Toronto, ON M9V 1A9
Tel: 416-746-3333
training@academyolrexdale.com
www.academyoflearning.com/locations/ontario/toronto-albion-isli
ngton

Toronto - Bay & Queen Campus
#1000, 401 Bay St., Toronto, ON M5H 2Y4
Tel: 416-969-8845; *Fax:* 416-969-9372
info@aoltoronto.com
aoltoronto.com

Toronto - Downsview Campus
#112, 1280 Finch Ave. West, Toronto, ON M3J 3K6
Tel: 416-767-7679
www.academyoflearning.com/locations/ontario/toronto-downsvie
w

Toronto - Downtown East Campus
#103, 29 Gervais Dr., Toronto, ON M3C 1Y9
Tel: 416-422-5627; *Fax:* 416-422-5628
pape@aollcc.ca
www.academyoflearning.com/locations/ontario/toronto-downtow
n-east

Toronto - Lawrence Campus
3585 Lawrence Ave. East, Toronto, ON M1G 1P4
Tel: 416-499-7994
www.academyoflearning.com/locations/ontario/toronto-lawrence

Toronto - Warden & Sheppard Campus
2190 Warden Ave., #G4, Toronto, ON M1T 1V6
Tel: 416-754-4456; *Fax:* 416-754-3143
www.academyoflearning.com/locations/ontario/toronto-warden-s
heppard

Vancouver Campus
#302, 2555 Commercial Dr., Vancouver, BC V5N 4C1
Tel: 604-876-8600; *Fax:* 604-876-4333
admissionsv@aolvancouver.com

Victoria - Westshore Campus
715 Goldstream Ave., Victoria, BC V9B 2X4
Tel: 250-391-6020; *Fax:* 250-391-6021
westshore@academyoflearning.com

Winnipeg - North Campus
77 Redwood Ave., 2nd Fl., Winnipeg, MB R2W 5J5
Tel: 204-582-9400
www.academyoflearning.com/locations/manitoba/winnipeg-north

Winnipeg - South Campus
297 St Mary's Rd., Winnipeg, MB R2H 1J5
Tel: 204-478-8884; *Fax:* 204-478-5020
winnipegsouth@academyoflearning.com
www.academyoflearning.com/locations/manitoba/winnipeg-south

Winnipeg: Arnold Bros. Transportation Academy
739 Lagimodiere Blvd., Winnipeg, MB R2J 0T8
Tel: 204-231-1183; *Fax:* 204-255-1566
www.arnoldbrosacademy.com

Winnipeg: Commonwealth College
294 William Ave., Winnipeg, MB R3B 0R1
Tel: 204-944-8202
commonwealthcollege.ca
www.facebook.com/commonwealthcollegeca
Note: The college offers diploma programs in business,
hospitality, beauty & health.

Winnipeg: Criti Care EMS
200 Osborne St. North, Winnipeg, MB R3C 1V4
Tel: 204-989-3671
info@criticareems.com
www.criticareems.com

Note: Paramedic & Fire training academy.
Bill Sommers, President & CEO

Winnipeg: European School of Esthetics (ESE)
294 William Ave., Winnipeg, MB R3B 0R1
Tel: 204-944-8202
info@europeanschoolofesthetics.ca
europeanschoolofesthetics.ca
www.facebook.com/europeanschoolofesthetics

Winnipeg: Evolve College of Massage Therapy
Clarion Hotel & Suites
1445 Portage Ave., 5th Fl., Winnipeg, MB R3G 3P4
Tel: 204-772-8999
info@evolvecollege.ca
evolvecollege.ca
www.facebook.com/evolvecollegeofmassage
www.linkedin.com/company/evolve-college-of-massage

Winnipeg: First Class Training Centre Inc.
485 Lucas Ave., Winnipeg, MB R3C 2E6
Tel: 204-632-5302; *Fax:* 204-632-5329
Toll-Free: 855-632-5302
info@firstclasstrainingcentre.com
www.firstclasstrainingcentre.com
www.facebook.com/FirstClassTrainingCentre
www.linkedin.com/company/first-class-training-centre-inc-
Note: First Class is a private training institute for the truck
transport industry. Brandon location: 109150 Zavislak Rd.,
Brandon, 204-727-4781.

Winnipeg: Hua Xia Acupuncture, Massage, Herb College of Canada
2810 Pembina Hwy., #A, Winnipeg, MB R3T 2H8
Tel: 204-452-3654; *Fax:* 204-219-1120
www.mbacuschool.com
Note: The Hua Xia Acupuncture, Massage, Herb College of
Canada offers courses in Traditional Chinese Medicine.

Winnipeg: Manitoba Institute of Trades & Technology (MITT)
130 Henlow Bay, Winnipeg, MB R3Y 1G4
Tel: 204-989-6500; *Fax:* 204-488-4152
mitt.ca
www.facebook.com/MITTcanada
twitter.com/MITTcanada

Enrollment: 1200
Ray Karasevich, President & CEO

Winnipeg: Mid-Ocean School of Media Arts (MOSMA)
1588 Erin St., Winnipeg, MB R3E 2T1
Tel: 204-775-3308; *Fax:* 204-775-9231
info@midoceanschool.ca
www.midoceanschool.ca
www.facebook.com/mosmaofficial
Note: Provides education in audio production.
Carlos Vela, Director

Winnipeg: National Screen Institute
#400, 141 Bannatyne Ave., Winnipeg, MB R3B 0R3
Tel: 204-956-7800; *Fax:* 204-956-5811
Toll-Free: 800-952-9307
info@nsi-canada.ca
nsi-canada.ca
www.facebook.com/nsicanada
twitter.com/nsicanada
Note: Professional training & development for Canadian film &
television writers, directors & producers
Joy Loewen, Chief Executive Officer
joy.loewen@nsi-canada.ca
Ursula Lawson, Manager, Programs & Development
ursula.lawson@nsi-canada.ca
Elise Swerhone, Manager, Programs & Development
elise.swerhone@nsi-canada.ca

Winnipeg: Neeginan College of Applied Technology
#304, 181 Higgins Ave., Winnipeg, MB R3B 3G1
cahrd.com
Note: Neeginan Institute of Applied Technology is CAHRD's
post-secondary, training division. It works in partnership with
industry partners & vocational training institutions to offer
post-secondary programs & training to students.

Winnipeg: Northwest Law Enforcement Academy
#200, 1821 Wellington Ave., Winnipeg, MB R3H 0G4
Tel: 204-953-8300; *Fax:* 204-953-8309
study@northwestlaw.ca
www.northwestlaw.ca

Winnipeg: Operating Engineers Training Institute of Manitoba Inc. (OETIM)
#6, 225 McPhillips St., Winnipeg, MB R3E 2K3
Tel: 204-775-7059; *Fax:* 204-772-6041
Toll-Free: 866-949-0333
oetim@oetim.com
www.oetim.com
www.facebook.com/OETIMtraining
twitter.com/OETIMinc

Winnipeg: Professional Transport Driver Training School
65 Bergen Cutoff Rd., Winnipeg, MB R3C 2E6
Tel: 204-925-1580; *Fax:* 204-925-1587
learn@transportdriver.com
www.transportdriver.com
www.facebook.com/Professional.Training.Driver
Note: Class 1 air brake licence training

Campuses
Brandon Branch
1731B Middleton Ave., Brandon, MB R7C 1A7
Tel: 204-729-0240; *Fax:* 204-729-0244
Darrell Wonnick, Manager

Winnipeg: Robertson College
180 Main St., Winnipeg, MB R3C 1A6
Tel: 204-943-5661; *Fax:* 204-926-8320
Toll-Free: 877-880-8789
info@robertsoncollege.com
www.robertsoncollege.com
www.facebook.com/OfficialRobertsonCollege
twitter.com/RobertsonColleg
www.linkedin.com/school/robertson-college
www.youtube.com/c/RobertsonCollegeSchoolOfNewWork
Enrollment: 5000 *Note:* Specializes in Business, Health Care &
Information Technology education.

Campuses
Brandon Campus
Town Centre
800 Rosser Ave., Brandon, MB R7A 6N5
Tel: 204-900-0969; *Fax:* 204-725-7218
brandoninfo@robertsoncollege.com

Calgary Campus
#100, 2912 Memorial Dr. SE, Calgary, AB T2A 6R1
Tel: 403-920-0070; *Fax:* 403-263-8176
Toll-Free: 866-920-0070
calgaryinfo@robertsoncollege.com

Edmonton Campus
#206, 10145 - 109th St. NW, Edmonton, AB T5J 4Y6
Tel: 780-705-6633; *Fax:* 780-705-8085
Toll-Free: 855-663-0566
edmontoninfo@robertsoncollege.com

Winnipeg: The Salon Professional Academy (TSPA)
#260, 1395 Ellice Ave., Winnipeg, MB R3G 3P2
Tel: 204-772-8772
admissions@tspawinnipeg.com
www.tspawinnipeg.com
www.facebook.com/tspawinnipeg
Note: Courses offered in Hairstyling, Esthetics & Make-up
Artistry.

Winnipeg: Southern Manitoba Academy for Response Training
#113, 1100 Concordia Ave., Winnipeg, MB R2K 4B8
info@smartems.net
smartems.net
Note: Firefighter & EMS Training.

Winnipeg: Wellington College of Remedial Massage Therapies Inc.
435 Berry St., Winnipeg, MB R3J 1N6
Tel: 204-957-2402; *Fax:* 204-957-1578
Toll-Free: 888-957-2402
info@wellingtoncollege.com
www.wellingtoncollege.com
www.facebook.com/wcrmt
Randy Ellingson, Director

Winnipeg: Willis College
#200, 464 Hargrave St., Winnipeg, MB R3A 0X5
Tel: 204-956-4708; *Fax:* 204-947-9881
Toll-Free: 866-579-4154
info@prairieview.ca
prairieview.ca
www.facebook.com/willliscollegewinnipeg

New Brunswick

Government Agencies

Fredericton: New Brunswick Department of Education & Early Childhood Development
Départment de L'Éducation et Dévelopment de la petite enfa
Place 2000
P.O. Box 6000
250 King St., Fredericton, NB E3B 5H1
Tel: 506-453-3678; *Fax:* 506-457-4810
edcommunication@gnb.ca
www.gnb.ca/education
Hon. Dominic Cardy, Minister, 506-453-2523

Fredericton: New Brunswick Department of Post-Secondary Education, Training & Labour
Départment de L'Éducation postsecondaire, Formation et Tr
Chestnut Complex
P.O. Box 6000
470 York St., Fredericton, NB E3B 5H1, Canada
Tel: 506-453-2597; *Fax:* 506-453-3618
dpetlinfo@gnb.ca
www.gnb.ca/petl
Hon. Trevor A. Holder, Minister
dpetlinfo@gnb.ca

School Boards/Districts/Divisions

Public

Fredericton: Anglophone West School District
1135 Prospect St., Fredericton, NB E3B 3B9, Canada
Tel: 506-453-5454; *Fax:* 506-444-5264
Toll-Free: 888-388-4455
asdwinfo@nbed.nb.ca
secure1.nbed.nb.ca/sites/asd-w
twitter.com/ASD_West
Number of Schools: 69 *Grades:* K.-12 *Enrollment:* 22901
Number of Employees: 2915
David McTimoney, Superintendent, 506-444-4034
david.mctimoney@nbed.nb.ca
Karla Deweyert, Director, Education Support Services,
506-462-5180
karla.deweyert@nbed.nb.ca
Karen Kozak, Human Resources Officer (Wellness Coordinator),
506-453-4444
karen.kozak@gnb.ca
Dianne Kay, Director, Curriculum & Instruction, 506-444-4035
dianne.kay@nbed.nb.ca
Shawn Tracey, Director, Finance & Administration,
506-325-4744
shawn.tracey@nbed.nb.ca

Miramichi: Anglophone North School District
78 Henderson St., Miramichi, NB E1N 2R7, Canada
Tel: 506-778-6075; *Fax:* 506-778-6090
asd-n.nbed.nb.ca
twitter.com/asdnnb
Number of Schools: 12 elementary; 10 elementary-middle; 4 middle; 2 middle-secondary; 5 secondary; 1 K-12 *Grades:* K - 12
Enrollment: 8100
Micheal Mortlock, District Education Council Chair
micheal.mortlock@gnb.ca
Mark Donovan, Superintendent, 506-778-6084
mark.donovan@gnb.ca
Connie Daley, Director, Education Support Services,
506-778-6888
connie.daley@nbed.nb.ca
Tim Dunn, Director, Finance and Administration, 506-778-6710
tim.dunn@gnb.ca
Joan MacMillan, Director, Curriculum and Instruction,
506-549-5123
joan.macmillan@gnb.ca
Stewart Stanger, Director, Human Resources, 506-549-5418
stewart.stanger@gnb.ca

Moncton: Anglophone East School District
1077 St. George Blvd., Moncton, NB E1E 4C9, Canada
Tel: 506-856-3222; *Fax:* 506-856-3224
asdeinfo@nbed.nb.ca
web1.nbed.nb.ca/sites/ASD-E
www.facebook.com/anglophoneeast
twitter.com/anglophoneeast
Number of Schools: 12 elementary; 12 elementary-middle; 5 middle; 2 middle-secondary; 5 secondary; 2 K-12 *Grades:* K - 12
Enrollment: 15600 *Number of Employees:* 2500
Harry Doyle, Chair, Board
harry.doyle@nbed.nb.ca

Gregg Ingersoll, Superintendent
gregg.ingersoll@gnb.ca
Krista Allen, Director, Education Support Services
Aubrey Kirkpatrick, Director, Finance and Administration
Todd Silliphant, Director, Human Resources
todd.silliphant@gnb.ca

Saint John: Anglophone South School District
490 Woodward Ave., Saint John, NB E2K 5N3, Canada
Tel: 506-658-5300; *Fax:* 506-658-5399
asdsinfo@nbed.nb.ca
web1.nbed.nb.ca/sites/ASD-S
twitter.com/ASD_South
Number of Schools: 74 *Grades:* K - 12
Robert Fowler, Chair, Board, 506-650-9579
robert.fowler@nbed.nb.ca
Zoë Watson, Superintendent, 506-658-5325
zoe.watson@nbed.nb.ca
Gary Hall, Director, Curriculum & Instruction, 506-658-5633
gary.hall@nbed.nb.ca
John MacDonald, Director, Finance & Administration,
506-643-7313
johna.macdonald@nbed.nb.ca
Susan Moffatt, Acting Director, Human Resources,
506-466-7910
susan.moffatt@nbed.nb.ca
Peter Smith, Director, Education Support Services,
506-658-5303
petert.smith@nbed.nb.ca

French

Dieppe: District scolaire francophone Sud
425, rue Champlain, Dieppe, NB E1A 1P2
Tél: 506-856-3333; *Téléc:* 506-856-3254
Ligne sans frais: 888-268-9088
DSF-SInfo@nbed.nb.ca
francophonesud.nbed.nb.ca
www.facebook.com/francophonesud
twitter.com/francophonesud
Number of Schools: 37 écoles *Enrollment:* 14800 *Number of Employees:* 2000
Paul Demers, Président
paul.demers2@nbed.nb.ca
Monique Boudreau, Directrice générale, 506-856-3225
monique.boudreau2@gnb.ca
Isabelle Savoie, Directrice exécutive de l'apprentissage,
506-856-3081
isabelle.savoie2@gnb.ca
Nathalie Kerry, Directrice exécutive de l'apprentissage
Diane Albert-Ouellette, Directrice de l'amélioration continue
David Després, Directeur des services administratifs et financiers
Sylvie Dallaire, Directrice des ressources humaines

Edmundston: District scolaire francophone Nord-Ouest (DSFNO)
298, rue Martin, Edmundston, NB E3V 5E5, Canada
Tél: 506-737-4567; *Téléc:* 506-737-4568
info@dsfno.ca
www.dsfno.ca
www.facebook.com/DistrictScolaireFrancophoneDuNordOuest
twitter.com/District_sc3
Number of Schools: 18 *Enrollment:* 7318 *Number of Employees:* 880
Francine Cyr, Présidente
Luc Caron, Directeur général
luc.caron@gnb.ca
Louise Morin, Directrice exécutive de l'apprentissage
Dany Desjardins, Directrice des services de soutien à l'apprentissage
Danielle Michaud-Côté, Directrice des services à la petite enfance
Yvan Guérette, Directeur de l'amélioration continue
Martine Mercure-Dumont, Directrice des services administratifs et financiers (DSAF)

Tracadie-Sheila: District scolaire francophone Nord-Est
P.O. Box 3668
3376, rue Principale, Tracadie-Sheila, NB E1X 1G5
Tél: 506-394-3400; *Téléc:* 506-394-3455
www.dsfne.ca
www.facebook.com/dsfne
Number of Schools: 27 primaires; 6 secondaires; 1 m-12
Grades: K - 12 *Enrollment:* 9126 *Number of Employees:* 2000
Ghislaine Foulem, Présidente
Marc Pelletier, Directeur général
Ginette Sonier, Directrice à l'apprentissage - Péninsule acadienne
Gilles Lurette, Directeur à l'apprentissage - Restigouche-Chaleur

Carole Raymond, Directrice des ressources humaines
carole.raymond@gnb.ca
Eloi Doucet, Directeur des services administratifs et financiers
eloi.doucet@gnb.ca

Schools: Specialized

First Nations

Eel Ground: Eel Ground First Nation School
55 Church Rd., Eel Ground, NB E1V 4E6, Canada
Tel: 506-627-4615; *Fax:* 506-627-4621
Grades: K.-8; Mi'kmaq Language *Note:* Eel Ground First Nation School operates as part of School District #16 in Miramichi, New Brunswick. The school provides education to the Eel Ground First Nation, a Mi'kmaq community in northeastern New Brunswick.
Helen Ward, Principal

Eel River Bar: Eel River Bar First Nation Pre-School
Eel River Bar First Nation
P.O. Box 4007
#201, 11 Main St., Eel River Bar, NB E8C 1A1, Canada
Tel: 506-684-1196; *Fax:* 506-684-6282
Grades: Pre-School (K4) *Note:* Eel River Bar First Nation Pre-School is a First Nations band operated school in a Mi'kmaq village on New Brunswick's north shore.

Elsipogtog: Elsipogtog School
356 Big Cove Rd., Elsipogtog, NB E4W 2S6, Canada
Tel: 506-523-8240; *Fax:* 506-523-8235
www.elsipogtogschool.ca
Grades: Pre.-8 *Note:* Part of Miramichi, New Brunswick's School District #16, the Elsipogtog School provides education to the Elsipogtog First Nation.
Stanley Drillen, Acting Principal

Esgenoopetitj: Esgenoôpetitj School
603 Bayview Dr., Esgenoopetitj, NB E9G 2A5, Canada
Tel: 506-776-1206; *Fax:* 506-776-1226
www.burntchurchschool.ca
Grades: K.-8 *Enrollment:* 120 *Note:* The Esgenoopetitj School, located northeast of the City of Miramichi, is part of School District #16. The school serves the Burnt Church First Nation.
Larry Flanagan, Principal
larry.flanagan@nbed.nb.ca

Fredericton: Chief Harold Sappier Memorial Elementary School (CHSMES)
c/o St. Mary's Maliseet First Nation
305 Maliseet Dr., Fredericton, NB E3A 5R8, Canada
Tel: 506-462-9683; *Fax:* 506-462-9686
www.chsmes.ca
Grades: K4-K5; 1-5; Maliseet Language *Note:* In addition to providing elementary education beginning with kindergarten, the Chief Harold Sappier Memorial Elementary School provides education about the Maliseet language & culture.
Allison Brooks, Principal
allison.brooks@nb.aibn.com
Judy Fullarton, Administrative Assistant
chsmesjf@nb.aibn.com

Fredericton: Wulastukw Elementary School
Kingsclear First Nation
712 Church St., Fredericton, NB E3E 1K8
Tel: 506-363-3019; *Fax:* 506-363-4051
www.firstnationhelp.com/wulastukw
Grades: K4; 1-5
Sarah Sacobie, Contact
sacobie_sarah@hotmail.com

Red Bank: Metepanagiag - Red Bank School
1926 MicMac Rd., Red Bank, NB E9E 1B3, Canada
Tel: 506-836-6160; *Fax:* 506-836-2787
metdu@nbnet.nb.ca
metepenagiagschool.ca
twitter.com/met_school
Grades: K4; 1-6
Lori Gillham, Principal
lgillham@metepenagiagschool.ca
Mindy Ward-Wayne, Administrative Assistant

Tobique First Nation: Mah-Sos School
270 Main St., Tobique First Nation, NB E7H 2Y8
Tel: 506-273-5407; *Fax:* 506-273-5436
w8liftr@hotmail.com
firstnationhelp.com/mahsos/
Grades: K4; 1-5
Paula Pirie, Principal

Woodstock First Nation: **Woodstock First Nation Pre-School**
6 Eagles Nest Dr., Woodstock First Nation, NB E7M 4J3
Tel: 506-328-4332; *Fax:* 506-328-2420
www.woodstockfirstnation.com/services/child-development-centr
e/
Number of Schools: 1 *Grades:* K-12 *Note:* The school serves
Woodstock First Nation.
Lisat Sappier, Coordinator, 506-328-4332
Jennifer Pitts, Child & Family Services Director, 506-324-6253

Schools: Independent & Private

Protestant

Fredericton: **Fredericton Christian Academy**
778 MacLaren Ave., Fredericton, NB E3A 3L7
Tel: 506-458-9379; *Fax:* 506-459-6148
office@fcae.ca
www.fcae.ca
www.facebook.com/Frederictonchristianacademy
twitter.com/MeetFCA
Grades: K.-12 *Enrollment:* 180
Jonathan McAloon, Principal
j.mcaloon@dpcs.ca

Moncton: **Moncton Christian Academy (MCA)**
945 St. George Blvd., Moncton, NB E1E 2C9, Canada
Tel: 506-855-5403; *Fax:* 506-857-9016
info@monctonchristian.ca
www.monctonchristian.ca
Grades: K.-12 *Enrollment:* 145 *Number of Employees:* 17 *Note:*
Moncton Christian Academy is an interdenominational school.
Willie Brownlee, Principal
wbrownlee@monctonchristian.ca

Plaster Rock: **Apostolic Christian School**
123 Main St., Plaster Rock, NB E7G 2H2
Tel: 506-356-8690; *Fax:* 506-356-9996
Grades: K.-12
Sanford Goodine, Principal

Rothesay: **Valley Christian Academy (VCA)**
P.O. Box 4722
30 Vincent Rd., Rothesay, NB E2E 5X4, Canada
Tel: 506-848-6373; *Fax:* 506-848-6379
vca@nbnet.nb.ca
www.valleychristianacademy.com
www.facebook.com/valleychristianacademynb
Grades: K - 8 *Note:* Valley Christian Academy is a ministry of
Rothesay Baptist Church. The preschool accepts children as
young as three years of age.
Barry Todd, Principal
principal@bellaliant.com
Linda Hallahan, Vice Principal
principal@bellaliant.com

Somerville: **Somerville Christian Academy (SCA)**
2608 Hwy 103, Somerville, NB E7P 3A9, Canada
Tel: 506-375-4327; *Fax:* 506-375-4406
somervillechristian.ca
Grades: K-5 *Enrollment:* 63
Angela Mabey, Principal

Sussex: **Sussex Christian School**
45 Chapman Dr., Sussex, NB E4E 1M4, Canada
Tel: 506-433-4005; *Fax:* 506-433-3402
info@sussexchristianschool.ca
www.sussexchristianschool.ca
www.facebook.com/sussexcs
twitter.com/sussexcs
Grades: JK-12 *Enrollment:* 67
Marsha Boyd-Mitchell, Principal
mboyd-mitchell@sussexchristianschool.ca

Independent & Private Schools

Rothesay: **Rothesay Netherwood School (RNS)**
40 College Hill Rd., Rothesay, NB E2E 5H1, Canada
Tel: 506-847-8224; *Fax:* 506-848-0851
education@rns.cc
www.rns.cc
www.facebook.com/RNS1877
twitter.com/RNS1877
www.linkedin.com/groups/2665809
Grades: 6-12 *Enrollment:* 285 *Note:* Rothesay Netherwood
School is a day & boarding school.
Dr. David Marr, Chair
Paul McLellan, Head of School, 506-848-0863
paul.mclellan@rns.cc
Robert Beatty, Director, Development & Alumni Affairs,
506-848-1731
rob.beatty@rns.cc

Tammy Earle, Director, Technology & Learning Initiatives,
506-848-1739
tammy.earle@rns.cc
Craig Jollymore, Director, Faculty & Programs
craig.jollymore@rns.cc
Tanya Moran, Director, Finance & Operations, 506-848-0855
tanya.moran@rns.cc
Patrick Nobbs, Director, Enrolment Management, 506-848-0859
patrick.nobbs@rns.cc
Peter Tomilson, Director, Student Life
peter.tomilson@rns.cc
Jackie Sullivan, Manager, Human Resources
jackie.sullivan@rns.cc

Rothesay: **Touchstone Academy**
68A Hampton Rd., Rothesay, NB E2E 5P5
Tel: 506-847-2673; *Fax:* 506-849-9582
www.touchstoneacademy.ca
www.facebook.com/142096802605782
Grades: Pre.-5 *Enrollment:* 77
Angela Prosser, Principal

Universities & Colleges

Universities

Fredericton: **St. Thomas University**
51 Dineen Dr., Fredericton, NB E3B 5G3, Canada
Tel: 506-452-0640; *Fax:* 506-450-9615
Toll-Free: 877-788-4443
admissions@stu.ca
www.stu.ca
www.facebook.com/StThomasUCanada
twitter.com/StThomasU
www.youtube.com/user/UStThomas
Full Time Equivalency: 2095
Robert Harris, Chancellor
Dawn Russell, President & Vice-Chancellor, 506-452-0537
president@stu.ca
Kim Fenwick, Vice-President, Academic & Research,
506-452-0531
vpacademic@stu.ca
Lily Fraser, Vice-President, Finance & Administration,
506-452-0533
vpfa@stu.ca
Jodi Misheal, Vice-President, Advancement & Alumni Relations
jmisheal@stu.ca
Karen Preston, Registrar, 506-452-0400
preston@stu.ca
Kathryn Monti, Director of Admissions, 506-452-0603
monti@stu.ca
Wanda Bearresto, Alumni Affairs Officer, 506-452-0521
wbearresto@stu.ca
Fr. Shawn Daley, Chaplain, 506-440-6014
chaplain@stu.ca

Fredericton: **University of New Brunswick**
P.O. Box 4400
3 Bailey Dr., Fredericton, NB E3B 5A3
Tel: 506-453-4666; *Toll-Free:* 888-895-3344
chooseunb@unb.ca
www.unb.ca
www.facebook.com/uofnb
twitter.com/unb
www.youtube.com/unbtube
Full Time Equivalency: 11000
Dr. Paul Mazerolle, President & Vice-Chancellor
George MacLean, Vice-President, Academic
vpacad@unb.ca
Bob Skillen, Vice-President, Advancement
David MaGee, Vice-President, Research
dmagee@unb.ca
Karen Cunningham, Vice-President, Administration & Finance
Sarah DeVarenne, University Secretary
sdevaren@unb.ca

Faculties
Faculty of Arts
P.O. Box 4400
Fredericton, NB E3B 5A3
Tel: 506-453-4655; *Fax:* 506-453-5102
arts@unb.ca
www.unb.ca/fredericton/arts
Joanne Wright, Dean
jwright@unb.ca

Arts (Saint John)
P.O. Box 5050
Saint John, NB E2L 4L5
Tel: 506-648-5560; *Fax:* 506-648-5947
www.unb.ca/saintjohn/arts

Faculty of Business (Saint John)
P.O. Box 5050
Saint John, NB E2L 4L5
Tel: 506-648-5570; *Fax:* 506-648-5574
Toll-Free: 800-508-6275
business@unb.ca
www.unb.ca/saintjohn/business
Fazley Siddiq, Dean

Faculty of Business Administration
255 Singer Hall
7 Macauley Lane, Fredericton, NB E3B 5A3
Tel: 506-453-4869; *Fax:* 506-453-3561
fba@unb.ca
www.unb.ca/fredericton/business
Devashis Mitra, Dean
dmitra@unb.ca

Faculty of Computer Science
Information Technology Center
P.O. Box 4400
550 Windsor St., ITC-314, Fredericton, NB E3B 5A3
Tel: 506-453-4566; *Fax:* 506-453-3566
fcs@unb.ca
www.cs.unb.ca
www.facebook.com/UNBCS
twitter.com/UNBFCS
Luigi Benedicenti, Dean

Faculty of Education
Marshall d'Avray Hall
#327, 10 Mackay Dr., Fredericton, MB E3B 5A3
Tel: 506-453-3508; *Fax:* 506-453-3569
www.unb.ca/fredericton/education
Sharon Wahl, Dean

Faculty of Engineering
P.O. Box 4400
Fredericton, NB E3B 5A3
Tel: 506-453-4570; *Fax:* 506-453-4569
engineer@unb.ca
www.unb.ca/fredericton/engineering
Chris Diduch, Dean
diduch@unb.ca

Faculty of Forestry & Environmental Management
P.O. Box 4400
Fredericton, NB E3B 5A3
Tel: 506-453-4501; *Fax:* 506-453-3538
www.unb.ca/fredericton/forestry
Van Lantz, Dean

Faculty of Kinesiology
P.O. Box 4400
Fredericton, NB E3B 5A3
Tel: 506-453-4575; *Fax:* 506-453-3511
kin@unb.ca
www.unb.ca/fredericton/kinesiology
www.facebook.com/KinUNB
twitter.com/kinunb
Wayne Albert, Dean
walbert@unb.ca

Faculty of Law
P.O. Box 4400
41 Dineen Dr., Fredericton, NB E3B 5A3
Tel: 506-453-4641
lawgen@unb.ca
www.unb.ca/fredericton/law
Pamela Hackett, Dean
pamela.hackett@unb.ca

Faculty of Nursing
P.O. Box 4400
33 Dineen Dr., Fredericton, NB E3B 5A3
Tel: 506-453-4642; *Fax:* 506-453-4798
nursing@unb.ca
www.unb.ca/fredericton/nursing
Lorna Butler, Dean
lorna.butler@unb.ca

Faculty of Science
P.O. Box 4400
Fredericton, NB E3B 5A3
Tel: 506-453-4586; *Fax:* 506-453-3570
science@unb.ca
www.unb.ca/fredericton/science
Gary Saunders, Acting Dean

Faculty of Science, Applied Science & Engineering (Saint John)
P.O. Box 5050
Saint John, NB E2L 4L5
Tel: 506-648-5615; *Fax:* 506-648-5650
sci-eng@unbsj.ca
www.unb.ca/saintjohn/sase

Schools
School of Graduate Studies
Sir Howard Douglass Hall
P.O. Box 4400
Fredericton, NB E3B 5A3
Tel: 506-453-4673; *Fax:* 506-453-4817
gradschl@unb.ca
www.unb.ca/gradstudies

Drew Rendall, Dean

Campuses
Renaissance College
P.O. Box 4400
Fredericton, NB E3B 5A3
Tel: 506-447-3092; *Fax:* 506-447-3224
rc@unb.ca
www.unb.ca/fredericton/renaissance
www.facebook.com/RenaissanceCollege

Cynthia Stacey, Dean

Saint John Campus
P.O. Box 5050
Saint John, NB E2L 4L5
Tel: 506-648-5500; *Toll-Free:* 877-753-6763
unbsjreg@unbsj.ca

Robert MacKinnon, Vice-President
rmackinn@unb.ca

Affiliations
Maritime College of Forest Technology
1350 Regent St., Fredericton, NB E3C 2G6
Tel: 506-458-0199; *Fax:* 506-458-0679
info@mcft.ca
www.mcft.ca
www.facebook.com/MCFTfredericton
twitter.com/MCFTfredericton
www.youtube.com/user/MCFTVIDEOS

Loretta Phillips, Contact
lphillips@mcft.ca

Fredericton: Yorkville University
#102, 100 Woodside Lane, Fredericton, NB E3C 2R9
Fax: 506-454-1221
Toll-Free: 866-838-6542
www.yorkvilleu.ca
www.facebook.com/YorkvilleUniversity
twitter.com/YorkvilleU
www.youtube.com/user/YorkvilleUniversity
Note: In 2018, the university acquired & amalgamated with the
RCC Institute of Technology.
Rick Davey, President

Campuses
Concord Campus
2000 Steeles Ave. West, Concord, ON L4K 4N1
Note: Electronics & computer networks engineering technology
training & programs
Dr. Rick Davey, President

Toronto Campus
460 Yonge St., Toronto, ON M4Y 1W9
Note: Electronics & computer networks engineering technology
training & programs

New Westminster Campus
88 - 6th St., New Westminster, BC V3L 5B3
Note: Electronics & computer networks engineering technology
training & programs

Moncton: Crandall University
P.O. Box 6004
333 Gorge Rd., Moncton, NB E1C 9L7
Tel: 506-858-8970; *Fax:* 506-863-6460
Toll-Free: 888-968-6228
www.crandallu.ca
www.facebook.com/CrandallUniversity
twitter.com/CrandallU
www.youtube.com/user/CrandallUniversity
Full Time Equivalency: 900 *Note:* Crandall University is an
independent Christian university founded in 1949. They offer
multiple bachelor degrees and professional education and
certificate programs.
Dr. Bruce G. Fawcett, President & Vice-Chancellor

Moncton: Université de Moncton
Campus de Moncton
18, av Antonine-Maillet, Moncton, NB E1A 3E9
Tél: 506-858-4000; *Ligne sans frais:* 1-800-363-8336
info@umoncton.ca
www.umoncton.ca
www.facebook.com/umoncton
twitter.com/campus_moncton
www.youtube.com/UMoncton
Note: Une institution d'enseignement exclusivement de langue
française; campus: Edmunston, Moncton et Shippagan

Jacques Paul Couturier, Recteur et vice-chancelier par intérim
André Samson, Vice-recteur à l'enseignement et à la recherche
Edgar Robichaud, Vice-recteur à l'administration et aux
ressources humaines
Lynne M. Castonguay, Secrétaire générale
Linda Schofield, Directrice générale des relations universitaires

Faculties
Faculté des sciences
Pavillon Rémi-Rossignol, Local R-119
60 rue Notre-Dame-du-Sacré-Coeur, Moncton, NB E1A 3E9
Tél: 506-858-4447; *Téléc:* 506-858-4541
Note: L'Université de Moncton a développé un projet de
recherche institutionnel sur le cannabis pour avancer la
productivité en partenariat avec le gouvernement du Canada,
Génome Atlantique, Génome Canada, la Fondation de
l'innovation du Nouveau-Brunswick & Organigram. La recherche
sera menée par des membres du département de biologie.
Dr David Joly, Directeur de recherche
Dr Martin Filion, Directeur de recherche

Campuses
Campus d'Edmundston
165, boul Hébert, Edmundston, NB E3V 2S8
Tél: 506-737-5051; *Ligne sans frais:* 800-363-8336
info@umce.ca
www.umoncton.ca/umce
www.facebook.com/UdeMEdmundston

Campus de Shippagan
218, boul J.-D.-Gauthier, Shippagan, NB E8S 1P6
Tél: 506-336-3400; *Ligne sans frais:* 800-363-8336
info@umcs.ca
www.umoncton.ca/umcs
www.facebook.com/UdeMCampusdeShippagan
twitter.com/umcs_umoncton
www.youtube.com/user/campusdeshippagan

Sackville: Mount Allison University
62 York St., Sackville, NB E4L 1E2, Canada
Tel: 506-364-2269; *Fax:* 506-364-2272
regoffice@mta.ca
www.mta.ca
www.facebook.com/mountallison
twitter.com/mountallison
www.youtube.com/MountAllison
Full Time Equivalency: 2250 *Number of Employees:* 129
Lynn Loewen, Chancellor
Jean-Paul Boudreau, President & Vice-Chancellor,
506-364-2300
president@mta.ca
Jeff Ollerhead, Provost & Vice-President, Academic & Research,
506-364-2622
provost@mta.ca
Robert Inglis, Vice-President, Finance & Administration,
506-364-2630
Kim Meade, Vice-President, International & Student Affairs
Gloria Jollymore, Vice-President, University Advancement,
506-364-2261
Elizabeth Wells, Dean, Faculty of Arts
deanofarts@mta.ca
Amanda Cockshutt, Dean, Faculty of Science
deanofscience@mta.ca
Nauman Farooqi, Dean, Faculty of Social Sciences
deanofsocialsciences@mta.ca
Chris Parker, Registrar
cparker@mta.ca

St. Stephen: St. Stephen's University
8 Main St., St. Stephen, NB E3L 3E2
Tel: 506-466-1781; *Fax:* 855-466-1783
Toll-Free: 888-225-5778
ssu@ssu.ca
www.ssu.ca
Note: St. Stephen's is an independent Christian university.
Robert J. Cheatley, President
Peter Fitch, Dean of Ministry Studies
Walter Thiessen, Dean of Arts

Colleges

**Bathurst: Collège communautaire du
Nouveau-Brunswick (CCNB)**
P.O. Box 266
725, rue du Collège, Bathurst, NB E2A 3Z6
Tél: 506-547-2063; *Téléc:* 506-547-2741
Ligne sans frais: 855-676-2262
admission@ccnb.ca
ccnb.ca
www.facebook.com/CCNB.officielle
www.linkedin.com/company/ccnb

Pierre Zundel, Président-directeur général

Campuses
Campus de Bathurst
P.O. Box 266
725, rue du Collège, Bathurst, NB E2A 3Z2
Tél: 506-547-2145; *Téléc:* 506-547-7674
Ligne sans frais: 800-552-5483
bathurst@ccnb.ca

Campus de Campbellton
P.O. Box 309
47, av du Village, Campbellton, NB E3N 3G7
Tél: 506-789-2377; *Téléc:* 506-789-2433
Ligne sans frais: 888-648-4111
campbellton@ccnb.ca

Campus de Dieppe
505, rue de Collège, Dieppe, NB E1A 6X2
Tél: 506-856-2200; *Téléc:* 506-856-2847
Ligne sans frais: 800-561-7162

Campus d'Edmundston
P.O. Box 70
35, rue du 15-Août, Edmundston, NB E3V 3K7
Tél: 506-735-2500; *Téléc:* 506-735-2717
Ligne sans frais: 888-695-2262

Campus de la Péninsule acadienne
P.O. Box 2010
218, boul J.-D.-Gauthier, Shippagan, NB E8S 3H1
Tél: 506-336-3073; *Téléc:* 506-336-3075
Ligne sans frais: 866-299-9900

Post Secondary/Technical

Colleges

**Fredericton: New Brunswick Community College
(NBCC)**
284 Smythe St., Fredericton, NB E3B 3C9
Tel: 506-460-6222; *Toll-Free:* 888-796-6222
nbcc@nbcc.ca
nbcc.ca
www.facebook.com/myNBCC
twitter.com/myNBCC
www.linkedin.com/school/nbcc-new-brunswick-community-colleg
e-
www.youtube.com/user/myNBCC

Mary Butler, President & CEO

Campuses
Fredericton Campus
26 Duffie Dr., Fredericton, NB E3B 0R6
Tel: 506-453-3641; *Fax:* 506-453-7944
nbcc.ca/campuses/fredericton

Miramichi Campus
P.O. Box 1053
80 University Ave., Miramichi, NB E1N 3W4
Tel: 506-460-6222; *Fax:* 506-778-6001
nbcc.ca/campuses/miramichi

Enrollment: 500

Moncton Campus
1234 Mountain Rd., Moncton, NB E1C 8H9
Tel: 506-460-6222; *Fax:* 506-856-3288
nbcc.ca/campuses/moncton

Enrollment: 1400

St. Andrews Campus
99 Augustus St., St Andrews, NB E5B 2E9
Tel: 506-460-6222; *Fax:* 506-529-5078
nbcc.ca/campuses/st-andrews

Enrollment: 250

Saint John Campus
950 Grandview Ave., Saint John, NB E2L 3V1
Tel: 506-460-6222; *Fax:* 506-643-2853
nbcc.ca/campuses/saint-john

Enrollment: 1500

Woodstock Campus
100 Broadway St., Woodstock, NB E7M 5C5
Tel: 506-460-6222; *Fax:* 506-328-8426
nbcc.ca/campuses/woodstock

Enrollment: 250

Post Secondary/Technical

Dieppe: Chez Bernard Beauty Academy Inc.
106 Dieppe Blvd., Dieppe, NB E1A 6P8
Tel: 506-857-0192; *Fax:* 506-854-5403
academy@nb.aibn.com
www.chezbernardbeautyacademy.com
www.facebook.com/100063588160031

Sonia LeBlanc, Owner

Dieppe: Medes College
#300, 1040 Champlain St., Dieppe, NB E1A 8L8
Tel: 506-384-3223; Fax: 506-853-3062
Toll-Free: 844-384-3223
reception@medes.ca
medescollege.ca
www.facebook.com/collegemedes
www.instagram.com/medescollege
Note: Programs offered in Esthetics, Nail Technology, Makeup & Electrolysis.
Richard Long, General Manager
richardl@medes.ca

Fredericton: Atlantic Business College (ABC)
1115 Regent St., Fredericton, NB E3B 3Z2
Tel: 506-450-1408
atlantic@abc.nb.ca
abc.nb.ca
www.facebook.com/AtlanticBusinessCollege
Note: Day school programs, continuing education courses, corporate training.

Fredericton: Atlantic College of Therapeutic Massage
University of New Brunswick Campus
2 Peter Kelly Dr., Fredericton, NB E3B 5A3
Tel: 506-451-8188; Fax: 506-451-8402
actmoffice@nb.aibn.com
www.actmonline.com

Campuses
Collège Atlantique de Massage Thérapeutique
1040 Champlain St., Dieppe, NB E1A 8L8
Tél: 506-855-2286; Téléc: 506-855-9251
camt@nb.aibn.com
www.actmonline.com

Fredericton: Atlantic Hairstyling & Aesthetics Academy
Aesthetics Division
440 Brunswick St., Fredericton, NB E3B 1H3
Tel: 506-453-9192; Fax: 506-459-1792
atlantichairstylingacademy@rogers.com
www.atlantichairstyling.com
www.facebook.com/atlantichairstyling

Campuses
Hairstyling Division
23 Sunbury St., Fredericton, NB E3B 3S9
Tel: 506-453-9196

Fredericton: Atlantic School of Reflexology
16A Main St., Fredericton, NB E3A 1B6
Tel: 506-260-0265
asrcourseinfo@gmail.com
www.reflexologyasr.com
www.facebook.com/atlanticschoolofreflexology
Note: Reflexology & holistic bodywork training.

Fredericton: East Coast Trades College Inc.
1080 Brookside Dr., Fredericton, NB E3G 8T8
Tel: 506-454-0867
eastcoasttrades.com

Belinda Sangster, Office Manager
belinda.sangster@eastcoasttrades.com

Fredericton: Majestany Institute
Fredericton Campus
120 Westmorland St., Fredericton, NB E3B 3L5
Tel: 506-458-8070; Fax: 506-457-1708
inquiry@majestany.ca
www.majestany.ca
www.facebook.com/Majestany
Note: Programs offered in aesthetics, hairstyling & nail technology.

Campuses
Saint John Campus
418 Rothesay Ave., Saint John, NB E2J 2C4
Tel: 506-693-4125; Fax: 506-693-4126
saintjohn@majestany.ca

Fredericton: Maritime College of Forest Technology (MCFT)
1350 Regent St., Fredericton, NB E3C 2G6, Canada
Tel: 506-458-0199; Fax: 506-458-0652
info@mcft.ca
mcft.ca
Note: The Maritime College of Forest Technology (MCFT), formerly the Maritime Forest Ranger School (MFRS) Fredericton, New Brunswick was established in April 1946 as a co-operative effort of the provincial governments of New Brunswick and Nova Scotia, and the wood-using industries of the two provinces. The goal was to address the need for skilled forestry workers in the Maritime provinces, and retrain and reintegrate returning World War II veterans. Since this time, MFRS/MCFT has developed one of Canada's Forest Technology diploma programs, and established Atlantic Canada's first Utility Arborist program.
Adrian Pearson, Recruitment Officer
apearson@mcft.ca

Grand Falls: École de coiffure LaFrance
LaFrance School of Hair Design
P.O. Box 7428
651 E.H. Daigle Blvd., Grand Falls, NB E3Z 3E7
Tel: 506-473-7212
www.lafrancehairdesign.com
www.facebook.com/262625849654

Miramichi: Amoura Aesthetics
205 Edward St., Miramichi, NB E1V 2Y7
Tel: 506-622-4331; Fax: 506-836-7969
amouraaesthetics@gmail.com
www.amouraaesthetics.com

Miramichi: Miramichi Health Training Centre
P.O. Box 297
2 Johnson Ave., Miramichi, NB E1N 3A6
Tel: 506-773-7971; Fax: 506-773-6896
mhtcentre@nb.aibn.com
www.healthtrainingcentre.com
Note: Offers CPR training, as well as home support services training.

Moncton: Ally Beauty Academy
#300, 51 Highfield St., Moncton, NB E1C 5N2
Tel: 506-857-8111; Fax: 506-860-3423
allybeautyacademy@gmail.com
allybeautyacademy.ca
www.facebook.com/Allymoncton
Note: Programs include aesthetics, hairstyling & nail technology.
Lynn Savoie, President

Moncton: Brenda's Academy of Professional Dog Grooming
209 Collishaw St., Moncton, NB E1C 7E6
Tel: 506-858-9947; Fax: 506-382-2571
brendas@animalgrooming.ca
www.animalgrooming.ca
www.facebook.com/Brendasacademyofdoggrooming
Brenda Dumesnil, Owner & Instructor

Moncton: Elite Dog Grooming & Academy
45 Colonial Dr., Moncton, NB E1G 2J1
Tel: 506-855-8808
www.elitedoggrooming.com

Moncton: Glamour Paws Grooming Academy
1633 Mountain Rd., Moncton, NB E1G 1A5
Tel: 506-384-3647
glamourpawsgroomingacademy@gmail.com
glamourpawsgroomingacademy.com
www.facebook.com/glamourpawsgroomingacademy

Moncton: L'Institut Jon rayMond
21 Stone Ave., Moncton, NB E1A 3M3
Tel: 506-857-9840; Fax: 506-857-9844
Toll-Free: 877-857-9840
info@jonraymond.com
www.jonraymond.com
www.facebook.com/jonraymondnb
Note: Bilingual Hairstyling & Aesthetics School.
Claudette Guimond, Director

Moncton: McKenzie College
#700, 860 Main St., Moncton, NB E1C 1G2
Tel: 506-384-6460; Toll-Free: 855-888-6053
info@mckenzie.edu
www.mckenzie.edu
www.facebook.com/mckenziecollegemoncton
twitter.com/mckenziecollege
www.linkedin.com/school/mckenzie-college
Dale Ritchie, President

Moncton: Medavie HealthEd
New Brunswick Campus
567 St George Blvd., Moncton, NB E1E 2B9
Fax: 506-389-2198
Toll-Free: 888-798-3888
info@medaviehealthed.com
www.medaviehealthed.com
www.facebook.com/medaviehealthed
twitter.com/medaviehealthed
www.instagram.com/medavie_healthed
Note: Paramedicine training.

Campuses
Nova Scotia Campus
#154, 50 Eileen Stubbs Ave., Dartmouth, NS B3B 0M7
Fax: 902-434-2242
Toll-Free: 888-798-3888
Note: Paramedicine training.

Moncton: Oulton College
4 Flanders Ct., Moncton, NB E1C 0K6
Toll-Free: 888-757-2020
info@oultoncollege.com
oultoncollege.com
www.facebook.com/OultonCollege
www.youtube.com/c/OultonCollegeMoncton
Note: College offering business, human services, health science & information technology programs.

Campuses
Dental Education Campus
5 Pacific Ave., Moncton, NB E1E 1A1
Toll-Free: 888-757-2020

Moncton: Pretty Pooch Dog Grooming
316 Worthington Ave., Moncton, NB E1C 0B7
Tel: 506-382-9393

New Maryland: Labourers' Training Institute of New Brunswick Inc.
36D Bonaccord St., New Maryland, NB E1C 5K7
Tel: 506-383-0395; Fax: 506-383-0065
Toll-Free: 800-332-3985
registrationdesk@ltinb.ca
ltinb.ca
Note: The Labourers' Training Institute provides members with skills training & health & safety training.

Newtown: ECR Heavy Equipment & Construction Training
65 Taylor Rd., Newtown, NB E4G 1N9
Tel: 506-434-4328
ecr4328@gmail.com
ecrheavyequipmenttraining.ca
www.facebook.com/ECRSussex

Saint John: Care-Ed Learning Centre
Also known as: Senior Watch
Senior Watch, Prince Edward Square Mall
#111, 100 Prince Edward St., Saint John, NB E2L 4M5
Tel: 506-634-8906; Toll-Free: 800-561-2463
train@seniorwatch.com
www.care-ed.com
Note: Focus on the preparation of persons seeking a caregiving career as well as support for family caregivers.

Saint John: The Landscape Horticulture Training Institute
P.O. Box 742
Saint John, NB E2L 4B3
Toll-Free: 866-752-6862
lnb@nbnet.nb.ca
landscapenb-pei.ca
www.facebook.com/Landscapenewbrunswick

Saint John: Ready Arc Training & Testing
70 McIlveen Dr., Saint John, NB E2J 4Y7
Tel: 506-696-8336
info@readyarc.ca
www.readyarc.ca
www.facebook.com/ReadyArc
Note: Private Welding School.

Sussex: Versatile Training Solutions
P.O. Box 4591
95 Alton Rd., Sussex, NB E4E 5L8
Tel: 506-433-5832; Fax: 506-433-5530
Toll-Free: 833-927-5832
infovts@nb.aibn.com
versatiletrainingsolutions.com
www.facebook.com/VersatileTrainingSolutions
Note: Safety, evaluation & driver / operator training for individuals in the Emergency Services, Municipal Works, Utilities & Construction & Transportation industries.
Dan Keys, Owner

Newfoundland & Labrador

Government Agencies

St. John's: Newfoundland Department of Education
Confederation Bldg., West Block
P.O. Box 8700
100 Prince Philip Dr., 3rd Fl., St. John's, NL A1B 4J6,
Canada
Tel: 709-729-5097; *Fax:* 709-729-1400
education@gov.nl.ca
www.gov.nl.ca/education
Hon. Tom Osborne, Minister, 709-729-5040

St. John's: Newfoundland Department of
Immigration, Population Growth, & Skills
Confederation Building, 3rd Fl.
P.O. Box 8700
St. John's, NL A1B 4J6
Tel: 709-729-2480
ISL@gov.nl.ca
www.gov.nl.ca/isl
Hon. Gerry Byrne, Minister, 709-729-3580

School Boards/Districts/Divisions

Public

St. John's: Newfoundland & Labrador English
School District
Avalon Regional Office
95 Elizabeth Ave., St. John's, NL A1B 1R6
Tel: 709-758-2372; *Fax:* 709-758-2706
www.nlesd.ca
twitter.com/NLESDCA
Number of Schools: 256 schools; 5 alternate sites *Grades:* K -
12; Alternate Ed. *Enrollment:* 65068 *Number of Employees:*
8,200
Goronwy Price, Chair, Board
goronwyprice@nlesd.ca
Anthony Stack, Director, Education & Chief Executive Officer,
709-758-2381
anthonystack@nlesd.ca
Terry Hall, Assistant Director, Education (Finance - Provincial),
709-758-2382
terryhall@nlesd.ca
Ed Walsh, Associate Director, Education (Human Resources -
Provincial), 709-758-2345
edwalsh@nlesd.ca

Campuses
Labrador Regional Office
P.O. Box 1810 B
16 Strathcona St., Happy Valley-Goose Bay, NL A0P 1E0
Tel: 709-896-2431; *Fax:* 709-896-9638
Number of Schools: 22
Christina White, Assistant Director, Education, 709-896-2431,
ext. 221
christinawhite@nlesd.ca
Janet Wiseman, Senior Officer, Education, 709-896-2431, ext.
233
janetwiseman1@nlesd.ca

Western Regional Office
P.O. Box 368
10 Wellington St., Corner Brook, NL A2H 6G9
Tel: 709-637-4000; *Fax:* 709-634-1828
Number of Schools: 63
Daniel O'Brien, Assistant Director, Education, 709-637-4006
DanielOBrien@nlesd.ca
Robyn Breen, Director, Student Support Services, 709-637-4616
robynbreen@nlesd.ca
Robert George, Manager of Finance & Administration,
709-637-4034
robertgeorge@nlesd.ca
Delores Clarke-Genge, Director of Schools, 709-637-4000
deloresclarkegenge@nlesd.ca
Truman Greenham, Director of Schools, 709-637-4000
paulrose@nlesd.ca
Alfred Paul Rose, Director of Schools, 709-637-4000
paulrose@nlesd.ca

Central Regional Office
203 Elizabeth Dr., Gander, NL A1V 1H6
Tel: 709-256-2547; *Fax:* 709-651-3044
Number of Schools: 78
Andrew Hickey, Assistant Director, Education, 709-256-2547
andrewhickey@nlesd.ca
Maria Antle, Director of Schools, 709-256-2547, ext. 314
mariaantle@nlesd.ca

Kelly Ann Kinden, Director, Human Resources, 709-256-2547,
ext. 226
kellyannkinden@nlesd.ca
Shawn Fowlow, Director of Schools, 709-256-2547, ext. 307
shawnfowlow@nlesd.ca
Donald Perry, Director of Schools, 709-279-7814, ext. 246
cynthiapope@nlesd.ca
Duane Smith, Director of Schools, 709-256-2547, ext. 277
duanesmith@nlesd.ca

French

Saint-Jean: Conseil scolaire francophone provincial
de Terre-Neuve-et-Labrador (CSFP)
#212, 65, ch Ridge, Saint-Jean, NL A1B 4P5
Tél: 709-722-6324; *Téléc:* 709-722-6325
Ligne sans frais: 888-794-6324
conseil@csfp.nl.ca
www.csfp.nl.ca
Number of Schools: 6 *Grades:* Mat. - 12
Kim Christianson, Directrice générale, 709-722-6324
kchristanson@csfp.nl.ca
Peter C. Smith, Directeur général adjoint, Finances &
Administration, 709-722-6747
psmith@csfp.nl.ca
Patricia Greene, Directrice, Services éducatifs, 709-757-2818
pgreene@csfp.nl.ca
Anne-Sophie Haven, Gestionnaire, Comptabilité & Ressources
humaines, 709-722-6324
finances@csfp.nl.ca

First Nations

Sheshatshiu: Innu School Board
Also known as: Mamu Tshishkutamashutau Innu
Education
P.O. Box 539
12 Edwards Dr., Sheshatshiu, NL A0P 1M0
Tel: 709-497-3664; *Fax:* 709-497-3678
admin@innueducation.ca
www.innueducation.ca
twitter.com/InnuSchoolBoard
Number of Schools: 2 K - 12 *Note:* Offers Aboriginal culture and
language curriculum components.
Bart Jack, Co-Chair, Board
Mary Jane Edmonds, Co-Chair, Board
Kanani Davis, Director, Administration & Professional Services
Elena Andrew, Community Director, Education - Sheshatshiu
Katie Rich, Community Director, Education - Natuashish
Clarence Davis, Assistant Director, Programs
Bryn McDonnell, Assistant Director, Finance
Rena Penashue, Assistant Director, Human Resources
Eugene Power, Assistant Director, Student Support

Schools: Specialized

First Nations

Conne River: Se't A'newey Kina'magino'kuom
School
Also known as: St. Anne's School
Miawpukek Mi'kamawey Mawi'omi
P.O. Box 100
Conne River, NL A0H 1J0
Tel: 709-882-2747; *Fax:* 709-882-2528
vpiercey@setaneway.ca
Grades: K-12 *Note:* The Miawpukek Mi'kmaw Mawi'omi of
Conne River operate the Se't A'newey Kina'magino'kuom
school. The curriculum, prescribed by the province of
Newfoundland & Larador, is provided to members of the
community from preschool children to elders. The school also
offers a Mi'kmaq studies program that includes the language &
spiritual & cultural teachings of the Mi'kmaq
Rod Jeddore, Director of Education

Natuashish: Mushuau Innu Natuashish
P.O. Box 189
Natuashish, NL A0P 1A0, Canada
Tel: 709-497-3664; *Fax:* 709-497-3678
info@innueducation.ca
www.innueducation.ca
Grades: K-12
Dave Jackman, Manager K-12
djackman@innueducation.ca

North West River: Sheshatshiu Innu Natuashish
P.O. Box 70
Mackenzie Dr., North West River, NL A0M 1M0, Canada
Tel: 709-497-3533; *Fax:* 709-497-3588
info@innueducation.ca
www.innueducation.ca
Grades: K-12

Clarence Davis, Manager K-12
cdavis@innueducation.ca

Schools: Independent & Private

Independent & Private Schools

Churchill Falls: Eric G. Lambert School
P.O. Box 40
Churchill Falls, NL A0R 1A0, Canada
Tel: 709-925-3371; *Fax:* 709-925-3364
www.ericglambert.ca
Grades: K.-12 *Enrollment:* 156
Steve Power, Principal

St. John's: Lakecrest - St. John's Independent
School
58 Patrick St., St. John's, NL A1E 2S7, Canada
Tel: 709-738-1212; *Fax:* 709-738-1701
www.lakecrest.ca
Grades: K.-9 *Enrollment:* 129
Robert Pittman, Head of School
rpittman@lakecrest.ca

St. John's: St. Bonaventure's College
2A Bonaventure Ave., St. John's, NL A1C 6B3, Canada
Tel: 709-726-0024; *Fax:* 709-726-0148
info@stbons.ca
www.stbonaventurescollege.ca
www.facebook.com/stbonaventures
twitter.com/StBonaventures
Grades: K-12 *Enrollment:* 325 *Note:* Catholic school in the Jesuit
tradition
Cecil Critch, Principal
ccritch@stbonaventurescollege.ca

Universities & Colleges

Universities

St. John's: Memorial University of Newfoundland
(MUN)
P.O. Box 4200
St. John's, NL A1C 5S7
Tel: 709-864-8000
www.mun.ca
www.facebook.com/MemorialUniversity
twitter.com/MemorialU
www.linkedin.com/school/memorial-university-of-newfoundland
www.youtube.com/user/MemorialUVideos
Full Time Equivalency: 18204
Susan Dyer Knight, Chancellor
Dr. Vianne Timmons, President & Vice-Chancellor
Dr. Mark Abrahams, Provost & Vice-President, Academic
Kent Decker, Vice-President, Administration & Finance
Dr. Neil Bose, Vice-President, Research
vp.research@mun.ca
Tom Nault, Registrar
tnault@mun.ca

Faculties
Faculty of Business Administration
Memorial University of Newfoundland
St. John's, NL A1B 3X5
Tel: 709-864-8512
busihelp@mun.ca
business.mun.ca
www.facebook.com/MUNBusiness
twitter.com/MUNBusiness
www.youtube.com/MUNBusiness
Isabelle Dostaler, Dean, 709-864-8851
idostaler@mun.ca

Faculty of Education
Memorial University of Newfoundland
St. John's, NL A1B 3X8
Tel: 709-864-3403; *Fax:* 709-864-4379
muneduc@mun.ca
www.mun.ca/ed
www.facebook.com/MemorialEducation
twitter.com/MUNEducation
Kirk Anderson, Dean, 709-864-8588

Faculty of Engineering & Applied Science
S.J. Carew Bldg.
240 Prince Philip Dr., #EN4019, St. John's, NL A1B 3X5
Tel: 709-864-8812; *Fax:* 709-864-4042
mun.ca/engineering
www.facebook.com/291040487679665
twitter.com/MUN_Engineering
Enrollment: 2000
Greg Naterer, Dean, 709-864-8810
gnaterer@mun.ca

Faculty of Humanities & Social Sciences
A-5015 Arts & Administration Bldg.
St. John's, NL A1C 5S7
Tel: 709-864-8254; Fax: 709-864-2135
hss@mun.ca
www.mun.ca/hss
www.facebook.com/3176895322369092
twitter.com/mun_hss

Jennifer Simpson, Dean
jsimpson@mun.ca

Faculty of Medicine
Tel: 709-864-6358; Fax: 709-864-6365
www.med.mun.ca
www.facebook.com/MUNMedicine
twitter.com/MUNMed
www.youtube.com/user/MUNmedicine
Dr. Margaret Steele, Dean, 709-864-6324
deanofmedicine@med.mun.ca

Faculty of Science
#C-2001, Chemistry / Physics Bldg.
St. John's, NL A1B 3X7
Tel: 709-864-8154; Fax: 709-864-3316
science@mun.ca
mun.ca/science
www.facebook.com/MUNScience
twitter.com/MUN_Science
www.instagram.com/mun_science
Travis Fridgen, Acting Dean, 709-864-8153
deansci@mun.ca

Schools
School of Graduate Studies
230 Elizabeth Ave., St. John's, NL A1C 5S7
sgs@mun.ca
www.mun.ca/sgs
www.facebook.com/mungradstudies
Enrollment: 3800
Aimée Surprenant, Dean, 709-864-2478
deansgs@mun.ca

School of Human Kinetics & Recreation
Physical Education Bldg.
St. John's, NL A1C 5S7
Tel: 709-864-8130
www.mun.ca/hkr
www.facebook.com/SchoolofHumanKineticsandRecreation
twitter.com/MemorialHKR
Linda Rohr, Dean

School of Music
M.O. Morgan Bldg.
7 Phelan Rd., #MU-2000, St. John's, NL A1C 5S7
Tel: 709-864-7486; Fax: 709-864-2666
music@mun.ca
mun.ca/music
www.facebook.com/musicatmun
twitter.com/musicatmemorial
Ian Sutherland, Dean, 709-864-7486
isutherland@mun.ca
Annie Corrigan, Academic Program Administrator, 709-864-7955
acorrigan@mun.ca

School of Nursing
300 Prince Philip Dr., St. John's, NL A1B 3V6
Tel: 709-777-2165
www.mun.ca/nursing
www.facebook.com/Nursing.MemorialU
twitter.com/MUN_Nursing
Alice Gaudine, Dean
agaudine@mun.ca

School of Pharmacy
Health Sciences Centre
St. John's, NL A1B 3V6
Tel: 709-777-8910; Fax: 709-777-7044
pharminfo@mun.ca
www.mun.ca/pharmacy
www.facebook.com/schoolofpharmacy
twitter.com/SchoolofPharm
Shawn Bugden, Dean
shawn.bugden@mun.ca

School of Social Work
General Office
P.O. Box 4200
230 Prince Philip Dr., #J-2000, St. John's, NL A1C 5S7
Tel: 709-864-8165; Fax: 709-864-2408
socialwork@mun.ca
mun.ca/socialwork
www.facebook.com/MUNScwk
twitter.com/MUNScwk

Heather Hair, Associate Dean, Undergraduate Programs,
709-864-2562
hhair@mun.ca

Campuses
Grenfell Campus
P.O. Box 2000
20 University Dr., Corner Brook, NL A2H 6P9
Tel: 709-637-6200; Fax: 709-639-8125
Toll-Free: 866-381-7022
info@grenfell.mun.ca
www.grenfell.mun.ca
www.facebook.com/grenfellcampus
twitter.com/grenfellcampus
www.youtube.com/grenfellcampus

Harlow Campus
The Maltings, St Johns Walk, Old Harlow
Essex, UK
harlow@mun.ca
www.mun.ca/harlow
twitter.com/munharlow
www.linkedin.com/company/munharlow
www.instagram.com/munharlow
Sandra Wright, General Manager
sandra.wright@mun.ca

Affiliations
Queen's College
Faculty of Theology
210 Prince Philip Dr., St. John's, NL A1B 3R6
Tel: 709-753-0116; Toll-Free: 877-753-0116
queens@mun.ca
queenscollegenl.ca
www.facebook.com/1053002811439684
twitter.com/queenscollegenl
The Rev. Dr. David Bell, Dean, Theology, 709-753-0116
dbell@mun.ca

Centres & Institutes
Centre for Innovation in Teaching & Learning (CITL)
G.A. Hickman Bldg., ED-3000
St. John's, NL A1B 3X8
Tel: 709-864-8700; Fax: 709-864-7941
Toll-Free: 866-435-1396
citl.mun.ca
www.facebook.com/citl.memorialu
twitter.com/mun_students
Gavan Watson, Director
gwatson@mun.ca

Fisheries & Marine Institute of Memorial University of Newfoundland (MI)
Also known as: Marine Institute
P.O. Box 4920
155 Ridge Road, St. John's, NL A1C 5R3
Tel: 709-778-0200; Fax: 709-778-0346
Toll-Free: 1-800-563-5799
www.mi.mun.ca
www.facebook.com/marine.institute
twitter.com/marineinstitute
www.linkedin.com/company/3338651
www.youtube.com/marineinstitutepr
Glenn Blackwood, Vice-President of Memorial University (Marine Institute), 709-778-0464

Colleges

Stephenville: College of the North Atlantic (CNA)
432 Massachusetts Dr., Stephenville, NL A2N 2Z6, Canada
Toll-Free: 888-982-2268
info@cna.nl.ca
www.cna.nl.ca
www.facebook.com/CNANewfoundlandLabrador
twitter.com/cna_news
www.youtube.com/user/CNamarketing
Full Time Equivalency: 25000
Bruce Hollett, President
Elizabeth Kidd, Chief Operating Officer
Trudy Barnes, Vice-President, Partnerships, Innovation & Entrepreneurship
Libby Chaulk, Vice-President, Student Engagement
Brian Tobin, Vice-President, Academic Programs & Delivery

Schools
School of Academics
Brenda Tobin, Dean, 709-292-5636
brenda.tobin@cna.nl.ca
Jason Rolls, Dean, Lang Studies & Academics (Qatar)
jason.rolls@cna-qatar.edu.qa

School of Applied Arts
Brenda Tobin, Dean, 709-292-5636
brenda.tobin@cna.nl.ca

School of Business
Mary Vaughan, Dean, 709-649-7970
mary.vaughan@cna.nl.ca
David King, Dean, Qatar
david.king@cna-qatar.edu.qa

School of Engineering Technology
Brent Howell, Dean, 709-637-8608
brent.howell@cna.nl.ca
Michael Walsh, Dean, Qatar
mike.walsh@cna-qatar.edu.qa

School of Health Sciences
Nelson Rodrigues, Dean, 974-495-2342
nelson.rodrigues@cna-qatar.edu.qa
Irene O'Brien, Dean, Qatar
irene.obrien@cna-qatar.edu.qa

School of Industrial Trades
Robin Walters, Dean, 709-744-3012
robin.walters@cna.nl.ca

School of Information Technology
Mary Vaughan, Dean, 709-649-7970
mary.vaughan@cna.nl.ca
Theodore Chiasson, Dean, Qatar
theodore.chiasson@cna-qatar.edu.qa

School of Natural Resources
Brent Howell, Dean, 709-637-8608
brent.howell@cna.nl.ca

School of Tourism
Brenda Tobin, Dean, 709-292-5636
brenda.tobin@cna.nl.ca

Campuses
Baie-Verte Campus
1 Terra Nova Rd., Baie Verte, NL A0K 1B0, Canada
Tel: 709-532-8066; Fax: 709-532-4624
Emily Foster, Campus Administrator, 709-532-8066
emily.foster@cna.nl.ca

Bay St. George Campus - Headquarters
DSB Fowlow Bldg.
P.O. Box 5400
432 Massachussetts Dr., Stephenville, NL A2N 2Z6, Canada
Tel: 709-643-7730; Fax: 709-643-7734
Chris Dohaney, Campus Administrator, 709-643-7916
chris.dohaney@cna.nl.ca

Bonavista Campus
P.O. Box 670
301 Confederation Dr., Bonavista, NL A0C 1B0, Canada
Tel: 709-468-1700; Fax: 709-468-2004

Burin Campus
P.O. Box 370
105 Main St., Burin Bay, NL A0E 1G0, Canada
Tel: 709-891-5600; Fax: 709-891-2256
Toll-Free: 800-838-0976
Stephen Warren, Campus Administrator, 709-891-5613

Carbonear Campus
P.O. Box 60
4 Pike's Lane, Carbonear, NL A1Y 1A7, Canada
Tel: 709-596-6139; Fax: 709-596-2688
Josiah Mullins, Campus Administrator, 709-596-8911
joe.mullins@cna.nl.ca

Clarenville Campus
P.O. Box 308
69 Pleasant St., Clarenville, NL A0E 1J0, Canada
Tel: 709-466-6900; Fax: 709-466-2771
Maisie Caines, Campus Administrator, 709-446-6931
maisie.caines@cna.nl.ca

Corner Brook Campus
P.O. Box 822
41 O'Connell Dr., Corner Brook, NL A2H 6H6, Canada
Tel: 709-637-8530; Fax: 709-634-2126
Chad Simms, Campus Administrator, 709-637-8549
chad.simms@cna.nl.ca

Gander Campus
P.O. Box 395
1 Magee Rd., Gander, NL A1V 1W8, Canada
Tel: 709-651-4800; Fax: 709-651-4854
Fergus O'Brien, Campus Administrator, 709-651-4821
fergus.obrien@cna.nl.ca

Grand Falls-Windsor Campus
P.O. Box 413
5 Cromer Ave., Grand Falls-Windsor, NL A2A 1X3, Canada
Tel: 709-292-5600; Fax: 709-489-4180
Joan Pynn, Campus Administrator, 709-292-5625
joan.pynn@cna.nl.ca

Happy Valley-Goose Bay Campus
P.O. Box 1720 B
219 Hamilton River Rd., Happy Valley-Goose Bay, NL A0P 1E0, Canada
Tel: 709-896-6300; *Fax:* 709-896-3733
Paul Motty, Campus Administrator, 709-896-6312
paul.motty@cna.nl.ca

Labrador West Campus
1600 Nichols-Adam Hwy, Labrador City, NL A2V 0B8, Canada
Tel: 709-944-7210; *Fax:* 709-944-6581
Richard Sawyer, Campus Administrator, 709-944-5895
richard.sawyer@cna.nl.ca

Placentia Campus
P.O. Box 190
1 Roosevelt Ave., Placentia, NL A0B 2Y0, Canada
Tel: 709-227-2037; *Fax:* 709-227-7185
Darrell Clarke, Campus Administrator, 709-227-2037
darrell.clarke@cna.nl.ca

Port-aux-Basques Campus
P.O. Box 760
59 Grand Bay Rd., Port-aux-Basques, NL A0M 1C0, Canada
Tel: 709-695-3343; *Fax:* 709-695-2963
Jan Peddle, Campus Administrator, 709-695-3343
jan.peddle@cna.nl.ca

Prince Philip Drive Campus - St. John's
P.O. Box 1693
1 Prince Philip Dr., St. John's, NL A1C 5P7, Canada
Tel: 709-758-7284; *Fax:* 709-758-7304
Trudy Barnes, Campus Administrator, 709-757-5187
trudy.barnes@cna.nl.ca

Ridge Road Campus
P.O. Box 1150
153 Ridge Rd., St. John's, NL A1C 6L8
Tel: 709-758-7000; *Fax:* 709-758-7304
Paul Forward, Campus Administrator, 709-793-3214
paul.forward@cna.nl.ca

Seal Cove Campus
P.O. Box 19003 Seal Cove
1670 Conception Bay Hwy., Conception Bay South, NL A1X 5C7, Canada
Tel: 709-744-2047; *Fax:* 709-744-3929
Chris Patey, Campus Administrator, 709-744-1041
chris.patey@cna.nl.ca

St. Anthony Campus
P.O. Box 550
83-93 East St., St Anthony, NL A0K 4S0, Canada
Tel: 709-454-3559; *Fax:* 709-454-8808
Cecil Roberts, Campus Administrator, 709-454-2884
cecil.roberts@cna.nl.ca

Qatar Campus
P.O. Box 24449
68 Al Tarafa, Duhail North, Doha, Qatar
Other Information: Int'l Phone: 974-4495-2222; Fax: 974-4495-2200
Shawn Brace, Vice-Pres., Finance & Administration
shawn.brace@cna-qatar.edu.qa

Post Secondary/Technical

Badger: **Central Training Academy**
P.O. Box 400
6 - 3rd Ave., Badger, NL A0H 1A0
Tel: 709-539-5150; *Fax:* 709-539-5145
Toll-Free: 800-563-5153
info@centraltraining.ca
www.centraltraining.ca
Note: The academy provides instruction for excavating, land clearing, road, building, grading & the maintenance of machinery.

Corner Brook: **Academy Canada**
Corner Brook Campus
2 University Dr., Corner Brook, NL A2H 5G4
Tel: 709-637-2100; *Fax:* 709-637-2123
Toll-Free: 800-561-8000
info@academycanada.com
www.academycanada.com
www.facebook.com/AcademyCanada
twitter.com/academycanada
www.linkedin.com/school/academy-canada
www.youtube.com/user/AcademyCanada1
Number of Employees: 153
Michael Barrett, President

Campuses
St. John's - Kenmount Campus
#167, 169 Kenmount Rd., St. John's, NL A1B 3P9
Tel: 709-739-6767; *Fax:* 709-739-6797

St. John's - Harding Campus
#37, 45 Harding Rd., St. John's, NL A1A 5T8
Tel: 709-722-9151; *Fax:* 709-722-9197

Gander: **Gander Flight Training Aerospace**
P.O. Box 355
70 C.L. Dobbin Dr., Gander, NL A1V 1W7
Tel: 709-256-7484; *Fax:* 709-256-7953
Toll-Free: 877-438-2359
admin@gft.ca
evasair.com/gft
www.facebook.com/GanderFlightTraining

Grand Falls-Windsor: **Corona Training Institute**
Excite Bldg.
32 Queensway Business Park, Grand Falls-Windsor, NL A2A 2J3
Tel: 709-489-7825; *Fax:* 709-489-5001
Toll-Free: 888-926-7662
admin@coronacollege.com
www.coronacollege.com
www.facebook.com/coronacollege
twitter.com/coronacollege
Bernice Walker, President & CEO
bwalker@coronacollege.com

Holyrood: **Operating Engineers College (OEC)**
P.O. Box 389 Salmonier Line
Holyrood, NL A0A 2R0
Tel: 709-229-6464; *Fax:* 709-229-6469
Toll-Free: 888-229-6468
oec@oecollege.ca
www.oecollege.ca

Lewisporte: **DieTrac Technical Institute**
P.O. Box 970
82 Premier Dr., Lewisporte, NL A0G 3A0
Tel: 709-535-0550; *Fax:* 709-535-6101
Toll-Free: 888-332-5555
studentservices@dietrac.com
www.dietrac.com
www.facebook.com/dietrac
Note: Offers industrial trades training.

Mount Pearl: **Iron Workers Education & Training Co. Inc.**
Education & Training Centre
7 Kyle Ave., Mount Pearl, NL A1N 4R4
Tel: 709-747-2158; *Fax:* 709-747-1042
info@ironworkerslocal764.com
www.ironworkerslocal764.com
Note: This program follows the Provincial Plan of Training. The Ironworker Generalist Program offers the student both theory & practical exposure to all aspects of the Ironworker trade including structural erection & dismantling, reinforcing, post-tensioning, rigging & cranes.
Stephanie Jones, Office Administrator
sjones@nf.aibn.com

Paradise: **Carpenter Millwright College Inc. (CMC)**
P.O. Box 3040
89 McNamara Dr., Paradise, NL A1L 3W2
Tel: 709-364-5586; *Fax:* 709-364-5587
info@cmcnl.ca
www.carpentermillwrightcollege.ca
www.facebook.com/CarpenterMillwrightCollege

Campuses
Cape Breton
24 Cossitt Heights Dr., Sydney, NS B1P 7E8
Tel: 902-562-5130

New Brunswick
82 Timothy Ave. South, Hanwell, NB E3A 2B8
Tel: 506-450-4024
admin@cmcnb.ca

Nova Scotia & PEI
1000 Sackville Dr., Sackville, NS B4E 0C2
Tel: 902-252-3553; *Fax:* 902-252-3554
admissions@cmcns.ca

St. John's: **Association for New Canadians (ANC)**
ESL Training Centre
148 Elizabeth Ave., St. John's, NL A1B 1S4
Tel: 709-726-6848; *Fax:* 709-726-6841
linc@nfld.net
www.ancnl.ca

Note: The Association for New Canadians is a non-profit organization that offers an ESL Training Centre to support the integration of immigrants & refugees.

St. John's: **Keyin College**
St. John's, NL
Toll-Free: 800-563-8989
info@keyin.com
keyin.com
www.facebook.com/KeyinCollege
twitter.com/KeyinCollege
Note: The college provides industry-directed education.
Craig Tucker, President

Schools
Burin Trade School
P.O. Box 160
Creston, NL A0E 1K0
Tel: 709-279-5090; *Fax:* 709-279-5091

Carbonear Campus
81 LeMarchant St., Carbonear, NL A1Y 1A9
Tel: 709-787-0244; *Fax:* 709-596-0217
Debbie Penney, Counselor
dpenney@keyin.ca

Gander Campus
175 Airport Blvd., Gander, NL A1V 1K6
Tel: 709-651-8560; *Fax:* 709-651-8565

Grand Falls-Windsor Campus
60 Hardy Ave., Grand Falls-Windsor, NL A2A 2P9
Tel: 709-489-8560; *Fax:* 709-489-2535

Lewisporte Campus
Dietrac Technical Institute
P.O. Box 970
82 Premier Dr., Lewisporte, NL A0G 3A0
Tel: 709-535-3946; *Fax:* 709-535-3950

Marystown Campus
P.O. Box 1327
814 Ville Marie Dr., Marystown, NL A0E 2M0
Tel: 709-279-5090; *Fax:* 709-279-5091

Port aux Basques Campus
4-10 High St., #B, Port aux Basques, NL A0M 1C0
Tel: 709-695-5555; *Fax:* 709-695-7161

Springdale Campus
The College Group Inc. Bldg.
83 Little Bay Rd., Springdale, NL A0J 1T0
Tel: 709-673-2809; *Fax:* 709-673-2748

St. John's Campus
644 Topsail Rd., St. John's, NL A1E 2E3
Tel: 709-579-1061; *Fax:* 709-579-6002
Shannon Hannaford, Counselor
shannon@keyin.com

Stephenville Campus
128 Carolina Ave., Stephenville, NL A2N 2S5
Tel: 709-643-6444; *Fax:* 709-643-6083

Centres & Institutes
Stephenville Adult Learning Center
70 Main St., Stephenville, NL A2N 1H8
Tel: 709-643-6444; *Fax:* 709-643-6467

Northwest Territories

Government Agencies

Yellowknife: **Northwest Territories Department of Education, Culture & Employment**
P.O. Box 1320
Yellowknife, NT X1A 2L9, Canada
Tel: 867-767-9352
ecepublicaffairs@gov.nt.ca
www.ece.gov.nt.ca
Hon. R.J. Simpson, Minister
Rj_simpson@gov.nt.ca

School Boards/Districts/Divisions

Public

Behchokò: **Tłı̨chǫ Community Services Agency**
P.O. Box 412
127 Donda Tili, Behchokò, NT X0E 0Y0
Tel: 867-392-6381; *Fax:* 867-392-6389
info@tlicho.ca
www.tlicho.ca
www.facebook.com/Tlicho
vimeo.com/tlicho
Number of Schools: 5

Linsey Hope, Director, Education, 867-392-3000
Linsey_Hope@tlicho.net
Stephanie Bonnar, Curriculum Coordinator, 867-392-3000
stephanie-bonnar@tlicho.net
Arthur Elms, Information and Computer Technology Coordinator, 867-392-3035
arthur_elms@tlicho.net
Carolyne Whenham, Literacy Coordinator, 867-392-3000
carolyne_whenham@tlicho.net
Rosa Mantla, Tlicho Language Culture Coordinator, 867-392-3037
rosa_mantla@tlicho.net

Fort Simpson: Dehcho Divisional Education Council (DDEC)
P.O. Box 376
Fort Simpson, NT X0E 0N0
Tel: 867-695-7300; Fax: 867-695-7359
ddec.ca
Number of Schools: 9 *Grades:* JK - 12 *Enrollment:* 591
Renalyn Pascua-Matte, Chair, Board
Philippe Brulot, Superintendent

Fort Smith: South Slave Divisional Education Council (SSDEC)
Jack Taylor Bldg.
P.O. Box 510
202 McDougal Rd., Fort Smith, NT X0E 0P0
Tel: 867-872-5701; Fax: 867-872-2150
www.facebook.com/SouthSlaveDEC
Number of Schools: 8 *Grades:* K - 12 *Enrollment:* 1300
Ann Pishinger, Chair, Divisional Educational Council
Chris Talbot, Coordinator, Public Affairs, 867-872-5701, ext. 23
ctalbot@ssdec.nt.ca
Joan Duford, Clerk, Finance, 867-872-5701, ext. 25
jduford@ssdec.nt.ca
Curtis Brown, Superintendent, 867-872-5701
cbrown@ssdec.nt.ca

Inuvik: Beaufort Delta Education Council (BDEC)
Bag Service #12, Inuvik, NT X0E 0T0
Tel: 867-777-2332; Fax: 867-777-2469
www.bdec.nt.ca
Number of Schools: 9 *Grades:* K - 12 *Enrollment:* 1382 *Number of Employees:* 200
Darlene Gruben, Chair, Board
dargruben@outlook.com
Jennifer Parrott, Vice-Chair, Board
jparrott01@hotmail.com
Devin Roberts, Assistant Superintendent, 807-777-2332, ext. 508
devin_roberts@bdec.learnnet.nt
Gary McBride, Comptroller, 867-777-2332, ext. 503
gary_mcbride@bdec.learnnet.nt.ca
Lisa Steen, Coordinator, Public Affairs, 867-777-2332, ext. 509
lisa_steen@bdec.learnnet.nt.ca
Frank Galway, Superintendent, Schools, 867-777-2332, ext. 506
frank_galway@bdec.learnnet.nt.ca
Paul Loewen, Assistant Superintendent, 807-777-2332, ext. 510
paul_loewen@bdec.learnnet.nt

Norman Wells: Sahtu Divisional Education Council
P.O. Box 64
Norman Wells, NT X0E 0V0
Tel: 867-587-3450; Fax: 867-587-2551
reception@sahtudec.ca
www.sahtudec.ca
Number of Schools: 5 *Grades:* K - 12
Karen Peachy, Chair, Divisional Education Council
Harry Cassie, Supervisor, Finance
Jessie Jane Campbell, Consultant, Aboriginal Languages
Renee Closs, Superintendent, 867-587-3456
Lorraine Kuer, Assistant Superintendent, 867-587-3458

Yellowknife: Yellowknife Education District #1
P.O. Box 788
5402 - 50th Ave., Yellowknife, NT X1A 2N6, Canada
Tel: 867-766-5050; Fax: 867-873-5051
www.yk1.nt.ca
www.facebook.com/YK1District
twitter.com/yk1_schools
Number of Schools: 8 *Grades:* K-12 *Enrollment:* 2000 *Number of Employees:* 250
Metro Huculak, Superintendent of Education, 867-766-5064
metro.huculak@yk1.nt.ca
Ed Lippert, Assistant Superintendent of Education, 867-766-5057
ed.lippert@yk1.nt.ca
Scott Willoughby, Indiginous Education Coordinator, 867-766-5059
scott.willoughby@yk1.nt.ca

Stacey Scarf, Manager, Personnel Services, 867-766-5058
yk1hr@yk1.nt.ca
Tram Do, Director, Corporate Services, 867-766-5062
tram.do@yk1.nt.ca

Catholic

Yellowknife: Yellowknife Catholic Schools
5124 - 49 St., Yellowknife, NT X1A 2P4
Tel: 867-766-7400; Fax: 867-766-7401
info@ycs.nt.ca
www.ycs.nt.ca
www.facebook.com/297013387110202
twitter.com/ycsnwt
Number of Schools: 3 *Grades:* JK - 12; French Immersion
Enrollment: 1330 *Number of Employees:* 110
Simone Gessler, Superintendent, 867-766-7411
Patrick Sullivan, Assistant Superintendent, Learning, 867-766-7407
Liz Baile, Coordinator, Student Services, 867-766-7405
Chris Cahoon, Assistant Superintendent, Business, 867-766-7404
Erin Currie, Chair, Board, 867-445-1291
erin.currie@ycs.nt.ca

French

Yellowknife: Commission scolaire francophone des Territoires du Nord-Ouest (CSFTNO)
Également connu sous le nom de: Commission scolaire francophone TNO
P.O. Box 1980
#207, 4915 - 48e rue, Yellowknife, NT X1A 2P5
Tél: 867-873-6555; Téléc: 867-873-5644
Ligne sans frais: 866-238-2733
info@csftno.ca
www.csftno.com
www.facebook.com/192939544097519
twitter.com/CSFTNO
Number of Schools: 2 *Grades:* Prémat. - Sec. *Enrollment:* 205
Number of Employees: 35
Simon Cloutier, Président, Conseil
simon.cloutier@csftno.com
Marc Akpoe, Contrôleur financier, 867-873-6555
marc.akpoe@csftno.com
Yvonne Careen, Directrice générale, 867-873-6555
yvonne.careen@csftno.com
Mathieu Gagnon, Coordonnateur, Programmes d'integration scolaires, 867-873-6555
mathieu.gagnon@csftno.com

Schools: Independent & Private

Independent & Private Schools

Yellowknife: Northwest Territories Montessori Society
5212 - 52nd St., Yellowknife, NT X1A 1T9
Tel: 867-669-7987; Fax: 867-873-2526
montess@ssimicro.com
www.ykmontessori.ca
www.facebook.com/groups/48934094227/
Lynda Baillargeon, Executive Director

Universities & Colleges

Colleges

Inuvik: Aurora College
P.O. Box 1008
Inuvik, NT X0E 0T0
Tel: 867-777-7800; Fax: 867-777-2850
Toll-Free: 866-287-2655
www.auroracollege.nt.ca
www.facebook.com/131796776862510
Jeff O'Keefe, Interim President

Thebacha Campus
P.O. Box 600
50 Conibear Cres., Fort Smith, NT X0E 0P0
Tel: 867-872-7500; Fax: 867-872-4511
Toll-Free: 866-266-4966
Dave Porter, Campus Director

Yellowknife/North Slave Campus
P.O. Box 9700
5004 - 54th St., Yellowknife, NT X1A 2R3
Tel: 867-920-3030; Fax: 867-873-0333
Toll-Free: 866-291-4866
Heather McCagg-Nystrom, Vice-President, Community & Extensions

Nova Scotia

Government Agencies

Halifax: Nova Scotia Department of Education & Early Childhood Development
Department of Education and Early Childhood Devel
P.O. Box 578
2021 Brunswick St., Halifax, NS B3J 2S9, Canada
Tel: 902-424-5168; Fax: 902-424-0511
Toll-Free: 888-825-7770
ednet.ns.ca
Hon. Becky Druhan, Minister, 902-424-4236
educmin@novascotia.ca

Halifax: Nova Scotia Department of Labour & Advanced Education
P.O. Box 697
1505 Barrington St., Halifax, NS B3J 2T8
Tel: 902-424-5301; Fax: 902-428-2203
Toll-Free: 844-424-5301
novascotia.ca/lae
Hon. Brian Wong, Minister, 902-424-5301
MIN_LAE@novascotia.ca

School Boards/Districts/Divisions

Public

Berwick: Annapolis Valley Regional Centre for Education (AVRCE)
P.O. Box 340
121 Orchard St., Berwick, NS B0P 1E0
Tel: 902-538-4600; Fax: 902-538-4630
Toll-Free: 800-850-3887
www.avrce.ca
Number of Schools: 40 schools; 2 adult high schools *Grades:* Pre. - 12; Adult Ed. *Enrollment:* 12861 *Number of Employees:* 1,720
Dave Jones, Regional Executive Director, Education, 902-538-4615
executivedirector@avrce.ca
Lesley MacDonald, Director, Human Resources, 902-538-4687
lesley.macdonald@avrce.ca
Jeanne Saulnier, Director, Finance, 902-538-4605
jeanne.saulnier@avrce.ca

Bridgewater: South Shore Regional Centre for Education (SSRCE)
69 Wentzell Dr., Bridgewater, NS B4V 0A2
Tel: 902-543-2468; Fax: 902-541-3060
Toll-Free: 888-252-2217
receptionist@ssrce.ca
ssrce.ca
www.facebook.com/SSRCENS
twitter.com/ssrce_ns
Number of Schools: 26 schools *Grades:* Pre-K - 12 *Enrollment:* 6300
Ashley Gallant, Coordinator, Communications
agallant@ssrce.ca

Dartmouth: Halifax Regional Centre for Education (HRCE)
33 Spectacle Lake Dr., Dartmouth, NS B2Y 4S8
Tel: 902-464-2000
www.hrce.ca
twitter.com/HRCE_NS
www.youtube.com/c/HalifaxRegionalCentreforEducation
Number of Schools: 83 elementary; 17 junior high; 10 senior high; 6 junior/senior high; 1 elementary/junior/senior *Grades:* Pre - 12 *Enrollment:* 53000 *Number of Employees:* 11,500
Elwin LeRoux, Regional Executive Director, Education, 902-464-2000, ext. 2312
Gerard Costard, Acting Director, Operations Services, 902-464-2000, ext. 4122
Alison King, Director, Program & Student Services, 902-464-2000, ext. 2567
Tracy O'Kroneg, Director, Human Resource Services, 902-464-2000, ext. 2323
Susan Tomie, Director, School Administration, 902-464-2000, ext. 2275
Terri Thompson, Director, Financial Services, 902-464-2000, ext. 2241

Port Hawkesbury: **Strait Regional Centre for Education (SRCE)**
#2, 304 Pitt St., Port Hawkesbury, NS B9A 2T9
Tel: 902-625-2191; *Fax:* 902-625-2281
Toll-Free: 800-650-4448
srce@srce.ca
srce.ca
twitter.com/SRCE_NS
Number of Schools: 20 *Grades:* K - 12 *Enrollment:* 5711 *Number of Employees:* 1,008
Paul Landry, Regional Executive Director, Education,
902-625-7065
paul.landry@srce.ca
Chris Grover, Director, Finance, 902-625-7050
chris.grover@srce.ca
Janice Gough, Director, Human Resources, 902-625-7081
janice.gough@srce.ca
Mike Landry, Director, Operations
Darrell LeBlanc, Director, Programs & Student Services,
902-625-7083
darrell.leblanc@srce.ca

Sydney: **Cape Breton-Victoria Regional School Board (CB-VRCE)**
275 George St., Sydney, NS B1P 1J7
Tel: 902-564-8293; *Fax:* 902-564-0123
cbvrce.ca
www.facebook.com/CapeBretonVictoriaRegionalSchoolBoard
twitter.com/CBVRCE_NS
Number of Schools: 54 *Grades:* Elementary - Secondary
Enrollment: 13774 *Number of Employees:* 1067 teachers; 923
support staff; 29 administrators
Darren Googoo, Chair
Susan Kelley, Regional Executive Director, 902-562-6479
susankelley@cbvrce.ca
Lynn Crawford-Carter, Director, Programs & Student Services,
902-562-6480
lcrawford@cbvrce.ca
Nancy Dove, Director, Financial Services, 902-564-8293
ndove@cbvrce.ca
Wendy King, Director, Human Resources Services,
902-562-6486
wking@cbvrce.ca

Truro: **Chignecto-Central Regional Centre for Education**
60 Lorne St., Truro, NS B2N 3K3
Tel: 902-897-8900; *Fax:* 902-897-8989
Toll-Free: 800-770-0008
ccrce.ca
www.facebook.com/CCRCE
twitter.com/ccrce_ns
Number of Schools: 67 *Grades:* K - 12 *Enrollment:* 20000
Number of Employees: 2,700
Gary Adams, Regional Executive Director, Education,
902-897-8910
Aaron Callaghan, Director, Programs & Student Services,
Education Services, 902-897-8950
Valerie Gauthier, Director, Financial Services, 902-897-8920
Jessi Taggart, Director, Human Resources Services,
902-897-8940

Yarmouth: **Tri-County Regional Centre for Education**
79 Water St., Yarmouth, NS B5A 1L4
Tel: 902-749-5696; *Fax:* 902-749-5697
Toll-Free: 800-915-0113
contact@tcrce.ca
www.tcrce.ca
www.facebook.com/TCRCENS
twitter.com/TCRCE_NS
Number of Schools: 22 *Grades:* Primary - 12 *Enrollment:* 5800
Chris Boulter, Regional Executive Director, 902-749-5818
chris.boulter@tcrce.ca
Craig Crosby, Director, Operations, 902-749-5673
craig.crosby@tcrce.ca
Christie Macdonald, Director, Human Resources, 902-749-5684
christie.macdonald@tcrce.ca
Jared Purdy, Director, Programs & Student Services,
902-749-5818
jared.purdy@tcrce.ca
Hilary Arenburg-Gobien, Manager, Finance, 902-749-5683
hilary.arenburg@tcrce.ca

French

Saulnierville: **Conseil scolaire acadien provincial (CSAP)**
P.O. Box 88
Saulnierville, NS B0W 2Z0
Tél: 902-769-5460; *Téléc:* 902-769-5461
Ligne sans frais: 888-533-2727
info@csap.ca
csap.ca
www.facebook.com/CSAPOfficiel
twitter.com/CSAP_Officiel
Number of Schools: 21 *Grades:* Mat. - Sec. *Enrollment:* 6000
Number of Employees: 900
Michel Comeau, Directeur général, 902-769-5458
michel.comeau@csap.ca
Louise Marchand, Présidente du Conseil, 902-226-3744
louise.marchand@csap.ca
Normand DeCelles, Directeur, Ressources humaines,
902-433-7040
normand.decelles@csap.ca
Michel Collette, Directeur, Services éducatifs, 902-433-7047
michel.collette@csap.ca
Janine Saulnier, Directrice, Finances, 902-769-5462
janine.saulnier@csap.ca

First Nations

Eskasoni: **Eskasoni First Nation School Board**
P.O. Box 7959
4645 Shore Rd., Eskasoni, NS B1W 1B8
Tel: 902-379-2507; *Fax:* 902-379-2273
eskasoni@schoolbd.ca
www.schoolbd.ca
Grades: Day Care - Secondary; Mi'kmaq *Enrollment:* 1249 *Note:*
Eskasoni Ksite'taqnk Day Care; Eskasoni Unama'ki Training &
Education Centre; Eskasoni Elementary & Middle School, &
Chief Allison Bernard Memorial High School. Situated on eastern
Cape Breton Island, Eskasoni First Nation is a large Mi'kmaq
community. Education in the community is directed by the
Eskasoni First Nation School Board, which is overseen by the
Eskasoni Band Council.
Elizabeth Cremo, Director, Education, 902-379-3436
elizabethcremo@schoolbd.ca
Justin Denny, Director, Finance
justindenny@schoolbd.ca

Schools: Specialized

First Nations

Chapel Island: **Potlotelewey Kina'matmokuam**
P.O. Box 538
RR#1, Richmond County, Chapel Island, NS B0E 3B0,
Canada
Tel: 902-535-2307; *Fax:* 902-535-3428
Grades: K - 6 *Note:* The school serves the Chapel Island First
Nation.
Shaunna Francis, Principal
sfrancis@potloek.ca

Eskasoni: **Chief Allison Bernard Memorial High School**
P.O. Box 7969
4673 Shore Rd., Eskasoni, NS B1W 1B8, Canada
Tel: 902-379-3000; *Fax:* 902-379-3011
www.eskasonischoolbd.com
Grades: 10 - 12; Mi'kmaq language & culture *Enrollment:* 200
Note: Chief Allison Bernard Memorial High School operates
under the direction of the Eskasoni First Nation School Board.
The First Nation secondary school is situated in the Mi'kmaq
community of Eskasoni in Cape Breton Island. Chief Allison
Bernard Memorial High School follows the Nova Scotia
Curriculum Guide & also offers Mi'kmaq studies.
Newell Johnson, Principal

Eskasoni: **Eskasoni Elementary & Middle School**
P.O. Box 7970
4675 Shore Rd., Eskasoni, NS B1W 1B8, Canada
Tel: 902-379-2825; *Fax:* 902-379-2886
eems@eskasonischool.ca
www.eskasonischool.ca
Grades: K - 9; Mi'kmaq language *Note:* Eskasoni Elementary &
Middle School is a Mi'kmaq First Nation school, which operates
under the direction of the Eskasoni First Nation School Board.
Mi'kmaq immersion classes are offered from kindergarten to
grade 3.
Philomena Moore, Principal
philmoore46@hotmail.com
Cameron Frost, Vice-Principal

Eskasoni: **Eskasoni Ksite'taqnk Day Care**
c/o Eskasoni First Nation School Board
P.O. Box 7959
4645 Shore Rd., Eskasoni, NS B1W 1B8
Tel: 902-379-2017
www.eskasonischoolbd.com/id11.html
Grades: Pre-School *Number of Employees:* 1 coordinator, 6
early childhood educators; 1 cook / day care worker *Note:* The
Eskasoni Ksite'taqnk Day Care operates under the
administration of the Eskasoni First Nation School Board. The
day care offers a Mi'kmaq educational program, taught in the
Mi'kmaq language.
Miranda Bernard, Contact

Eskasoni: **Unama'ki Training & Education Centre**
P.O. Box 7010
Eskasoni, NS B1L 1A1, Canada
Tel: 902-379-2758; *Fax:* 902-379-2586
www.unamakitec.ca
Grades: 9 - 12 *Enrollment:* 75 *Number of Employees:* 1 principal;
1 teaching vice-principal; 5 teachers; 1 guidance counsellor; 1
secretary *Note:* Activities of the Unama'ki Training & Education
Centre are guided by the Eskasoni First Nation School Board.
Michelle Marshall-Johnson, Principal
Joanne MacDonald, Vice-Principal

Indian Brook: **L'nu Sipu'k Kina'matnuokuom**
579 Church St., Indian Brook, NS B0N 1W0
Tel: 902-236-3041; *Fax:* 902-236-3049
Grades: K - 12

Sydney: **Membertou Elementary School**
45 Maillard St., Sydney, NS B1S 2P5
Tel: 902-562-2205; *Fax:* 902-562-4561
www.membertouschool.ca
Grades: Primary - 6 *Note:* Membertou Elementary School's staff
consists of a Mi'kmaw language teacher. The school follows the
curriculum guidelines established by the Nova Scotia
Department of Education.
Sharon Bernard, M.Ed, B.Ed, BACS, Principal
sbernard@membertouschool.ca
Lucy Joe, M.Ed, B.Ed, BA, Vice-Principal
ljoe@membertouschool.ca

Trenton: **Pictou Landing First Nation School**
P.O. Box 116
Site 6, RR#2, Trenton, NS B0K 1X0
Tel: 902-755-9954; *Fax:* 902-752-4916
schooladmin@pictoulandingschool.ca
www.pictoulandingschool.ca
Grades: K - 6 *Note:* The Pictou Landing First Nation School
works in partnership with the Pictou Landing First Nation
community, its Elders, & parents to provide an education that
includes the Mi'kmaw language & culture.
Irene Endicott, Principal
iendicott@pchg.net

Wagmatcook: **Wagmatcookewey School**
P.O. Box 30018
Wagmatcook, NS B0E 3N0, Canada
Tel: 902-295-3491; *Fax:* 902-295-1091
wagmatcookeweyschool.ca
Grades: Primary - 12; Mi'kmaq Studies *Note:* Located on the
Wagmatcook First Nation Reserve in Cape Breton, Nova Scotia,
the Wagmatcookewey School provides education to Mi'Kmaq
First Nation students.
Marjorie Pierro, Principal
marjoriepierro@gmail.com

Whycocomagh: **We'koqma'q Mikmaw School**
P.O. Box 209
15 Reservation Rd., Whycocomagh, NS B0E 3M0, Canada
Tel: 902-756-9000; *Fax:* 902-756-2171
admin@wfns.ca
www.wfns.ca
Grades: K - 12
Joanne Alex, Principal
joanna@wfnes.ca

Special Education

Halifax: **Atlantic Provinces Special Education Authority (APSEA)**
5940 South St., Halifax, NS B3H 1S6, Canada
Tel: 902-424-8500; *Fax:* 902-424-0543
apsea@apsea.ca
www.apsea.ca
TTY: 902-424-8500
www.facebook.com/apseacanada
twitter.com/apseacanada
Note: The Atlantic Provinces Special Education Authority
(APSEA) is an interprovincial cooperative agency established in
1975 by joint agreement among the Ministers of Education of

New Brunswick, Newfoundland, Nova Scotia, and Prince Edward Island.
Lisa Doucet, Superintendent

Schools: Independent & Private

Public

Oxford: Oxford Regional Education Centre
P.O. Box 340
249 Lower Main St., Oxford, NS B0M 1P0
Tel: 902-447-4513; *Fax:* 902-447-4517
www.facebook.com/OxfordRegionalEducationCentreHomeSchool
Duane Starratt, Principal
Carmen Buchanan-Baker, Vice-Principal

Protestant

Bedford: Sandy Lake Academy
435 Hammonds Plains Rd., Bedford, NS B4B 1Y2, Canada
Tel: 902-835-8548; *Fax:* 902-835-9752
principal@sandylakeacademy.ca
www.sandylakeacademy.ca
www.facebook.com/SandyLakeAcademy
twitter.com/SandyLakeAcdmy
Grades: Pre.-12 *Enrollment:* 80 *Note:* A Seventh-day Adventist Christian School
Maureen Westhaver, Principal

Halifax: Halifax Christian Academy
114 Downs Ave., Halifax, NS B3N 1Y6, Canada
Tel: 902-475-1441; *Fax:* 902-477-4922
admissions@halifaxchristianacademy.ca
www.halifaxchristianacademy.ca
www.facebook.com/HalifaxChristianAcademy
twitter.com/HfxChristian
Grades: Pre.-12 *Number of Employees:* 37
Shaun Alspach, Head of School
Will Radford, Vice-Principal, High School
Sue Webber, Vice-Principal, Elementary

Truro: Colchester Christian Academy
P.O. Box 403
Truro, NS B2N 5C5, Canada
Tel: 902-895-6520; *Fax:* 902-893-3727
cca@eastlink.ca
colchesterchristianacademy.ca
Grades: Pre.-12 *Enrollment:* 132
Steve Vanderkwaak, Principal

Tusket: Living Waters Christian Academy
318 Mood Rd., Tusket, NS B0W 3M0, Canada
Tel: 902-648-2676
Grades: Pre.-9 *Enrollment:* 44

Independent & Private Schools

Blockhouse: South Shore Waldorf School & Kindergarten Assoc. (SSWS)
Also known as: South Shore Waldorf
P.O. Box 177
64 School Rd., Blockhouse, NS B0J 1E0
Tel: 902-624-0874; *Fax:* 902-531-3020
sswaldorf@waldorfns.org
www.waldorfns.org
www.facebook.com/SouthShoreWaldorfSchool
twitter.com/SSWaldorfSchool
Grades: K.-6 *Enrollment:* 51 *Number of Employees:* 10
Darlene Eisnor, Office Administrator
darlene.eisnor@waldorfns.org
Caitlin Rooney, Enrollment & Development Coordinator
admin@waldorfns.org
Anne Greer, Board Secretary, 902-688-1857
greerwhite@eastlink.ca

Dartmouth: Newbridge Academy
361 John Savage Ave., Dartmouth, NS B3B 0J3
Tel: 902-252-3339; *Fax:* 902-252-3108
info@newbridgeacademy.ca
www.newbridgeacademy.ca
Grades: Pre.-12 *Enrollment:* 300
Trevor MacEachern, CEO
Jason Wolfe, Headmaster
jason.wolfe@newbridgeacademy.ca

Guysborough: Chedabucto Education Centre / Guysborough Academy
P.O. Box 19
27 Green St., Guysborough, NS B0H 1N0
Tel: 902-533-2288; *Fax:* 902-533-3554
cecga.srsb.ca
Other Information: Alternate Phone: 902-533-4006
Grades: K-12 *Enrollment:* 296
Paul Lang, Principal
paul.landry@srsb.ca

Halifax: Armbrae Academy
1400 Oxford St., Halifax, NS B3H 3Y8, Canada
Tel: 902-423-7920; *Fax:* 902-423-9731
office@armbrae.ns.ca
www.armbrae.ns.ca
www.facebook.com/armbraeacademy
twitter.com/armbrae
www.instagram.com/armbrae
Grades: Pre.-12 *Number of Employees:* 43
Gary O'Meara, Headmaster
head@armbrae.ns.ca

Halifax: Halifax Grammar School
945 Tower Rd., Halifax, NS B3H 2Y2, Canada
Tel: 902-423-9312; *Fax:* 902-423-9315
reception@hgs.ns.ca
www.hgs.ns.ca
www.facebook.com/halifaxgrammarschool
twitter.com/halifaxgrammar
www.linkedin.com/company/halifax-grammar-school
www.youtube.com/halifaxgrammar
Grades: Pre.-12 *Enrollment:* 500
Steven Laffoley, Headmaster
headmaster@hgs.ns.ca

Halifax: Maritime Muslim Academy
6225 Chebucto Rd., Halifax, NS B3L 1K7, Canada
Tel: 902-429-9067; *Fax:* 902-429-0136
admin@maritimemuslimacademy.ca
www.maritimemuslimacademy.ca
Grades: Pre.-12; Islamic studies; Arabic *Enrollment:* 78
Dr. Hadi Salah, Principal

Halifax: Sacred Heart School of Halifax
5820 Spring Garden Rd., Halifax, NS B3H 1X8, Canada
Tel: 902-422-4459; *Fax:* 902-423-7691
info@shsh.ca
www.shsh.ca
www.facebook.com/SacredHeartHalifax
twitter.com/SacredHeartHfx
www.instagram.com/trulysacredheart
Grades: Pre.-12
Anne Wachter, Headmistress
awachter@shsh.ca

Halifax: Shambhala School
5450 Russell St., Halifax, NS B3K 1W9, Canada
Tel: 902-454-6100; *Fax:* 902-454-6157
director@shambhalaschool.org
www.shambhalaschool.org
Grades: Preschool - 12 *Enrollment:* 160 *Note:* This is a non-denominational school, which offers an enriched curriculum.
Steve Mustain, Director

Lunenburg: Class Afloat - West Island College International
P.O. Box 10
97 Kaulbach St., Lunenburg, NS B0J 2C0
Tel: 902-634-1895; *Fax:* 902-634-7155
info@classafloat.com
www.classafloat.com
www.facebook.com/classafloat
twitter.com/classafloat
www.linkedin.com/company/west-island-college-international
Grades: 11-Univ. *Enrollment:* 60 *Note:* Students at Class Afloat sail the world on a classic tall ship, which they themselves sail, while engaged in academic study. Courses are available at the following levels of study: grade 11, 12, & first-year university.
David Jones, President

Tantallon: Crossroads Academy
3650 Hammonds Plains Rd., Tantallon, NS B3Z 4R3, Canada
Tel: 902-826-1805
Grades: Pre.-6

Windsor: King's-Edgehill School
33 King's-Edgehill Lane, Windsor, NS B0N 2T0, Canada
Tel: 902-798-2278; *Fax:* 902-798-2105
kesinfo@kes.ns.ca
www.kes.ns.ca
www.facebook.com/kingsedgehill
twitter.com/kingsedgehill
www.youtube.com/kingsedgehill
Grades: 6-12 *Enrollment:* 282
Joseph Seagram, Headmaster
jseagram@kes.ns.ca

Wolfville: Landmark East School
708 Main St., Wolfville, NS B4P 1G4
Tel: 902-542-2237; *Fax:* 902-542-4147
Toll-Free: 800-565-5887
admissions@landmarkeast.org
www.landmarkeast.org
www.facebook.com/landmarkeast
twitter.com/landmarkeast
www.linkedin.com/company/landmark-east-school
www.youtube.com/lmeschoolcanada
Grades: 3-12 *Enrollment:* 60 *Note:* The international school serves students with learning disabilities. Landmark East has an overall student-teacher ratio of 3:1.
Greg Coldwell, Chair
Karen Fougere, Headmaster
Glen Currie, Director, Students
gcurrie@landmarkeast.org

Universities & Colleges

Universities

Antigonish: St. Francis Xavier University
5005 Chapel Sq., Antigonish, NS B2G 2W5, Canada
Tel: 902-863-3300; *Fax:* 902-867-2329
admit@stfx.ca
www.stfx.ca
Other Information: Admissions: 902-867-2219
www.facebook.com/stfxuniversity
twitter.com/stfxuniversity
www.linkedin.com/company/st.-francis-xavier-university
www.youtube.com/user/stfxbox
Full Time Equivalency: 4200 *Note:* The university is primarily an undergraduate university, offering education in the arts, science, business & information systems, & applied programs.
Kent MacDonald, President & Vice-Chancellor, 902-867-2188
kdmacdon@stfx.ca
Dr. Kevin Wamsley, Vice-President, Academic & Provost
avp@stfx.ca
Murray Kyte, Vice-President, Advancement
Andrew Beckett, Vice-President, Finance & Administration
John Blackwell, Director, Research Grants, 902-867-3733
jblackwe@stfx.ca
Kris MacSween, Manager, Access Services, 902-867-4917
kmacswee@stfx.ca

Faculties
Faculty of Arts
2329 Notre Dame Ave., Antigonish, NS B2G 2W5
Tel: 902-867-2165; *Fax:* 902-867-2793
www.stfx.ca/academics/arts
Karen Brebner, Dean
kbrebner@stfx.ca

Faculty of Science
2329 Notre Dame Ave., Antigonish, NS B2G 2W5
Tel: 902-867-3903; *Fax:* 902-867-2793
www.stfx.ca/academics/science
Note: In December 2017, StFX signed a 3-year research partnership with Cultivator Catalyst Corporation (owner of THC Dispensaries Canada Inc.). The multi-disciplinary agreement offers students research collaboration and training opportunities in the commercial cannabis industry.
Petra Hauf, Dean

Centres & Institutes
Coady International Institute
P.O. Box 5000
4780 Tompkins Lane, Antigonish, NS B2G 2W5
Tel: 902-867-3960; *Fax:* 902-867-3907
Toll-Free: 1-866-820-7835
coady.stfx.ca
www.facebook.com/coady.institute
twitter.com/coadystfx
www.youtube.com/CoadyInstitute
June Webber, Vice-President

Halifax: **Atlantic School of Theology**
660 Francklyn St., Halifax, NS B3H 3B5, Canada
Tel: 902-423-6939; *Fax:* 902-492-4048
www.astheology.ns.ca
www.facebook.com/AtlanticSchoolofTheology
twitter.com/ASTComm
www.youtube.com/user/astheology

Full Time Equivalency: 120
Rev. Neale Bennet, President, 902-423-6939
nbennet@astheology.ns.ca
Rev. Dr. Rob Fennell, Academic Dean, 902-425-3298
rfennell@astheology.ns.ca
Ted Vaughan, Chief Administrative Officer, 902-496-7946
tvaughan@astheology.ns.ca
Cynthia Thomson, Registrar, 902-425-3691
registrar@astheology.ns.ca

Halifax: **Dalhousie University**
P.O. Box 15000
Halifax, NS B3H 4R2
Tel: 902-494-2211; *Fax:* 902-494-1630
communications.marketing@dal.ca
www.dal.ca
www.facebook.com/DalhousieUniversity
twitter.com/Dalnews
www.youtube.com/user/DalhousieU

Full Time Equivalency: 18500 *Note:* Dalhousie University is a comprehensive teaching & research university located in Atlantic Canada. Dalhousie places special emphasis on Ocean Studies & Health Studies & has a growing involvement in Advanced Technical Studies.

Faculties
Faculty of Agriculture
P.O. Box 550
Truro, NS B2N 5E3
Tel: 902-893-6600
dal.ca/faculty/agriculture
www.facebook.com/dalagriculture
Dr. David Gray, Dean, Faculty of Agriculture, 902-893-6720
dean.agriculture@dal.ca

Faculty of Architecture & Planning
P.O. Box 15000
5410 Spring Garden Rd., Halifax, NS B3H 4R2
Tel: 902-494-3971; *Fax:* 902-423-6672
arch.office@dal.ca
www.dal.ca/faculty/architecture-planning.html
www.facebook.com/DalhousieArchitectureandPlanning
John Newhook, Acting Dean, 902-494-3972
Dean.AP@dal.ca

Faculty of Arts & Social Sciences
P.O. Box 15000
Halifax, NS B3H 4R2
Tel: 902-494-1440; *Fax:* 902-494-1957
fass@dal.ca
dal.ca/faculty/arts
www.facebook.com/FASSDal
twitter.com/DAL_FASS
www.instagram.com/dal_fass
Number of Employees: 140 faculty
Roberta Barker, Acting Dean, 902-494-1439
fassdean@dal.ca

Faculty of Computer Science
P.O. Box 15000
6050 University Ave., Halifax, NS B3H 4R2
Tel: 902-494-2093; *Fax:* 902-492-1517
inquiries@cs.dal.ca
dal.ca/faculty/computerscience
www.facebook.com/dalfcs
Andrew Rau-Chaplin, Dean, 902-494-2732
deanfcs@dal.ca

Faculty of Dentistry
P.O. Box 15000
5981 University Ave., Halifax, NS B3H 4R2
Tel: 902-494-2824; *Fax:* 902-494-2527
admissions.dentistry@dal.ca
www.dal.ca/faculty/dentistry
www.facebook.com/daldentistry
Dr. Ben Davis, Dean

Faculty of Engineering
P.O. Box 15000
5248 Morris St., Halifax, NS B3H 4R2
Tel: 902-494-8431; *Fax:* 902-492-0011
dal.ca/faculty/engineering
www.facebook.com/DalhousieEngineering
Number of Employees: 150
John Newhook, Dean, 902-494-6217
deaneng@dal.ca

Faculty of Graduate Studies
Henry Hicks Academic Administration Building
P.O. Box 15000
#314, 6299 South St., Halifax, NS B3H 4R2
Tel: 902-494-2485; *Fax:* 902-494-8797
graduate.studies@dal.ca
www.facebook.com/dalgradstudies
twitter.com/dalgradstudies
Enrollment: 3500
Marty Leonard, Dean
grad.dean@dal.ca

Faculty of Health
P.O. Box 15000
#316, 5968 College St., Halifax, NS B3H 4R2
Tel: 902-494-3327; *Fax:* 902-494-1966
health@dal.ca
dal.ca/faculty/health.html
twitter.com/DalHealth
Enrollment: 3000 *Number of Employees:* 200 faculty + 80 staff
Dr. Brenda Merrit, Dean, 902-494-2345
b.merritt@dal.ca

Faculty of Management
Kenneth C. Rowe Management Building
P.O. Box 15000
#3052, 6100 University Ave., Halifax, NS B3H 4R2
Tel: 902-494-2582; *Fax:* 902-494-1195
dal.ca/faculty/management
www.facebook.com/dalmanagement
twitter.com/dalmanagement
www.youtube.com/dalmanagement
Kim Brooks, Dean, 902-494-7142
kim.brooks@dal.ca

Faculty of Medicine
1459 Oxford St., Halifax, NS B3H 4R2
Tel: 902-494-6592; *Fax:* 902-494-7119
medical.communications@dal.ca
medicine.dal.ca
www.facebook.com/DalhousieMedicalSchool
twitter.com/DalMedSchool
Dr. David Anderson, Dean
dean.medicine@dal.ca

Faculty of Science
Life Sciences Centre
#827, 1355 Oxford St., Halifax, NS B3H 4R2
Tel: 902-494-2373; *Fax:* 902-494-1123
science@dal.ca
dal.ca/faculty/science
twitter.com/ocean_networks
Enrollment: 3900
Chris Moore, Dean, 902-494-3540
dscience@dal.ca

Schools
Rowe School of Business
Kenneth C. Rowe Management Building
P.O. Box 15000
6100 University Ave., Halifax, NS B3H 4R2
Tel: 902-494-7080; *Fax:* 902-494-1107
dal.ca/faculty/management/rsb
www.facebook.com/rowebusiness
twitter.com/rowebusiness
www.linkedin.com/showcase/5236876
www.youtube.com/dalmanagement
Benoit Aubert, Director, 902-494-1884
benoit.aubert@dal.ca

College of Continuing Education
P.O. Box 15000
#2201, 1459 LeMarchant St., Halifax, NS B3H 4R2
Tel: 902-494-2526; *Fax:* 902-494-3662
Toll-Free: 800-565-8867
continuinged@dal.ca
dal.ca/faculty/cce/
Dianne Tyers, Dean

College of Pharmacy
P.O. Box 15000
5968 College St., Halifax, NS B3H 4R2
Tel: 902-494-2378; *Fax:* 902-494-1396
pharmacy@dal.ca
www.dal.ca/faculty/health/pharmacy.html
Susan Mansour, Director, 902-494-3504
susan.mansour@dal.ca

School of Health & Human Performance
P.O. Box 15000
Halifax, NS B3H 4R2
Tel: 902-494-2152; *Fax:* 902-494-5120
Toll-Free: 866-325-4247
hahp@dal.ca
www.dal.ca/faculty/health/health-humanperformance.htm

Dr. Laurene Rehman, Director
laurene.rehman@dal.ca

School of Health Administration
P.O. Box 15000
5850 College St., Halifax, NS B3H 4R2
Tel: 902-494-7097; *Fax:* 902-494-6849
healthadmin@dal.ca
www.dal.ca/faculty/health/health-administration.html
Tanya Packer, Director
tanya.packer@dal.ca

School of Communication Sciences & Disorders
P.O. Box 15000
5850 College St., #2C01, Halifax, NS B3H 4R2
Tel: 902-494-7052; *Fax:* 902-494-5151
scsd@dal.ca
www.dal.ca/faculty/health/scsd.html
Michael Kiefte, Director

School of Information Management
P.O. Box 15000
#4010, 6100 University Ave., Halifax, NS B3H 4R2
Tel: 902-494-3656; *Fax:* 902-494-2451
sim@dal.ca
dal.ca/faculty/management/school-of-information-management
www.facebook.com/SIMDalhousie
twitter.com/dalsimnews
www.linkedin.com/groups/2360751
Sandra Toze, Director, 902-494-2488
stoze@dal.ca

School of Nursing
P.O. Box 15000
5869 University Ave., Halifax, NS B3H 4R2
Tel: 902-494-2535; *Fax:* 902-494-3487
nursing.inquiries@dal.ca
www.dal.ca/faculty/health/nursing.html
Ruth Martin-Misener, Director

School of Occupational Therapy
Forrest Bldg.
#215, 5869 University Ave., Halifax, NS B3H 4R2
Tel: 902-494-8804; *Fax:* 902-494-1229
occupational.therapy@dal.ca
www.dal.ca/faculty/health/occupational-therapy
www.facebook.com/dalsot
Lori Turnbull, Director, 902-494-4243
lturnbul@dal.ca

School of Physiotherapy
P.O. Box 15000
5869 University Ave., Halifax, NS B3H 4R2
Tel: 902-494-2524; *Fax:* 902-494-1941
physiotherapy@dal.ca
www.dal.ca/faculty/health/school-of-physiotherapy

School of Public Administration
P.O. Box 15000
6100 University Ave., Halifax, NS B3H 4R2
Tel: 902-494-3742; *Fax:* 902-494-7023
dalmpa@dal.ca
dal.ca/faculty/management/school-of-administration
www.facebook.com/dalmpa
twitter.com/dalmanagement
www.youtube.com/user/DalManagement

School for Resource & Environmental Studies
Kenneth C. Rowe Management Building
P.O. Box 15000
#5010, 6100 University Ave., Halifax, NS B3H 4R2
Tel: 902-494-3632; *Fax:* 902-494-3728
sres@dal.ca
dal.ca/faculty/management/sres
Michelle Adams, Director, 902-494-4588
adamsm@dal.ca

Schulich School of Law
Weldon Law Bldg.
P.O. Box 15000
6061 University Ave., Halifax, NS B3H 4R2
Tel: 902-494-3495; *Fax:* 902-494-1316
lawinfo@dal.ca
dal.ca/faculty/law
www.facebook.com/SchulichSchoolofLaw
twitter.com/SchulichLaw
www.instagram.com/schulichlaw
Camille Cameron, Dean, 902-494-2114
camillecameron@dal.ca
Joanne Tortola, Director, Finance & Administration, 902-494-2115
joanne.tortola@dal.ca

School of Social Work
P.O. Box 15000
#3201, 1459 LeMarchant St., Halifax, NS B3H 4R2
Tel: 902-494-3760; *Fax:* 902-494-6709
social.work@dal.ca
dal.ca/faculty/health/socialwork
Judy MacDonald, Director, 902-494-1347
judy.macdonald@dal.ca

Centres & Institutes
Centre for the Study of Security & Development
Henry Hicks Building
P.O. Box 15000
#301, 6299 South St., Halifax, NS B3H 4R2
Tel: 902-494-3769; *Fax:* 902-494-3825
centre@dal.ca
dal.ca/sites/cssd
twitter.com/dalcssd
Brian Bow, Director, 902-494-6629
brian.bow@dal.ca

Healthy Populations Institute (HPI)
P.O. Box 15000
1318 Robie St., Halifax, NS B3H 4R2
Tel: 902-494-2240; *Fax:* 902-494-3594
hpi@dal.ca
www.healthypopulationsinstitute.ca
twitter.com/DalHPI
Dr. Sara Kirk, Scientific Director
sara.kirk@dal.ca
Gillian Ritcey, Managing Director
gillian.ritcey@dal.ca

Halifax: NSCAD University (NSCAD)
Also known as: Nova Scotia College of Art & Design
5163 Duke St., Halifax, NS B3J 3J6, Canada
Tel: 902-444-9600; *Fax:* 902-425-2420
admissions@nscad.ca
www.nscad.ca
www.facebook.com/NSCAD
twitter.com/NSCADUniversity
www.youtube.com/user/NSCADAdmissions
Full Time Equivalency: 690
Dianne Taylor-Gearing, President
Ann-Barbara Graff, Vice-President, Academic & Research
abgraff@nscad.ca
Sharon Johnson-Legere, Vice-President, Finance &
Administration
sjohnson@nscad.ca

Halifax: Saint Mary's University
923 Robie St., Halifax, NS B3H 3C3, Canada
Tel: 902-420-5400
helpdesk@smu.ca
www.smu.ca
Other Information: Students Closure/Cancellation Hotline:
902-491-6263
www.facebook.com/smuhalifax
twitter.com/SMUHalifax
www.linkedin.com/school/saint-mary's-university
Full Time Equivalency: 6373 *Note:* Offers a wide range of both
undergraduate & graduate programs.
Dr. Paul D. Sobey, Chancellor
Dr. Robert Summerby-Murray, President
Malcolm Butler, Vice-President, Academic & Research
Gabrielle Morrison, Vice-President, Finance & Administration
Erin Sargeant Greenwood, Vice-President, Advancement

Faculties
Arts
Tel: 902-420-5437; *Fax:* 902-491-8634
smarts@smu.ca
www.smu.ca/academics/faculty-of-arts.html
Margaret MacDonald, Dean

Extended Learning
Atrium Bldg.
#213, 923 Robie St., Halifax, NS B3H 3C3
Tel: 902-420-5492; *Fax:* 902-420-5015
extend@smu.ca
smu.ca/academics/studio/extended-learning.html

Graduate Studies & Research
Atrium Bldg.
#210, 923 Robie St., Halifax, NS B3H 3C3
Tel: 902-420-5089; *Fax:* 902-496-8772
fgsr@smu.ca
Adam J. Sarty, Dean, 902-496-8169
adam.sarty@smu.ca

Science
923 Robie St., Halifax, NS B3H 3C3
Tel: 902-420-5661
advisor.science@smu.ca

Steven M. Smith, Dean, 902-420-5494
dean.science@smu.ca

Schools
Sobey School of Business
Sobey Bldg.
#212, 903 Robie St., Halifax, NS B3H 3C3
Tel: 902-420-5422; *Fax:* 902-420-5892
www.smu.ca/academics/sobey
Harjeet Bhabra, Dean

Centres & Institutes
Centre for Environmental Analysis & Remediation (CEAR)
Science Bldg.
#501, 923 Robie St., Halifax, NS B3H 3C3
Tel: 902-496-8798; *Fax:* 902-496-8104
cear@smu.ca
www.smu.ca/centres-and-institutes/cear
Patricia Granados, Research Instrument Technician,
902-420-5135
patricia.granados@smu.ca

Centre for Occupational Health & Safety
5960 Inglis St., Halifax, NS B3H 3C3
Tel: 902-491-6253; *Fax:* 902-496-8135
cncohs@smu.ca
www.smu.ca/centres-and-institutes/cncohs

Electron Microscopy Centre
Science Bldg.
#422, 923 Robie St., Halifax, NS B3H 3C3
Tel: 902-420-5709; *Fax:* 902-496-8104
www.smu.ca/research/emc
Xiang Yang, Instrument Technician
xiang.yang@smu.ca

Institute for Computational Astrophysics
Department of Astronomy & Physics
Halifax, NS B3H 3C3
Tel: 902-420-5105; *Fax:* 902-496-8218
icaadmin@ap.smu.ca
www.smu.ca/centres-and-institutes/ica
Florence Woolaver, Contact

*Maritime Provinces Spatial Analysis Research Centre
(MP_SpARC)*
Burke Bldg.
#207B, 923 Robie St., Halifax, NS B3H 3C3
Tel: 902-420-5472; *Fax:* 906-496-8772
Greg Baker, Research Instrument Technician
mpsparc@smu.ca

Regional Analytical Facility
Science Bldg.
#422, 923 Robie St., Halifax, NS B3H 3C3
Tel: 905-420-5709; *Fax:* 902-420-5261
www.smu.ca/research/rgc
Xiang Yang, Technician
xiang.yang@smu.ca

Halifax: University of King's College
6350 Coburg Rd., Halifax, NS B3H 2A1, Canada
Tel: 902-422-1271; *Fax:* 902-423-3357
registrar@ukings.ca
www.ukings.ca
www.facebook.com/universityofkingscollege
twitter.com/ukings
www.youtube.com/kingscollegehfx
Full Time Equivalency: 1170
Hon. Kevin Lynch, Chancellor
William Lahey, President & Vice-Chancellor
Julie Green, Registrar, 902-422-1271, ext. 122
julie.green@ukings.ca

Pointe-de-L'Église: Université Sainte-Anne
1695, Rte 1, Pointe-de-L'Église, NS B0W 1M0
Tél: 902-769-2114; *Téléc:* 902-769-2930
Ligne sans frais: 888-338-8337
www.usainteanne.ca
www.facebook.com/usainteanne
twitter.com/usainteanne
www.youtube.com/user/usainteannecom/videos
Full Time Equivalency: 411 *Note:* La seule institution
d'enseignement post-secondaire de langue française en
Nouvelle-Écosse. Programmes: administration des affaires,
éducation, sciences humaines, science pures, programmes
professionnels. Campus: Pointe-de-L'Église, Halifax,
Petit-de-Grat, Saint-Joseph-du Moine, et Tusket
Allister Surette, Recteur et vice-chancelier
Kenneth Deveau, Vice-recteur à l'enseignement et recherche
Éric Tufts, Vice-recteur à l'administration et affaires étudiantes
Hughie Batherson, Vice-recteur au recrutement et aux
partenariats

Campuses
Campus de Halifax
#100, 1190 Barrington St., Halifax, NS B3H 2R4, Canada
Tel: 902-424-2630; *Fax:* 902-424-3607
Daniel Lamy, Directeur
daniel.lamy@usainteanne.ca

Campus de Petit-de-Grat
3433, rte 206, Petit-de-Grat, NS B0E 2L0, Canada
Tel: 902-226-3900; *Fax:* 902-226-3919
Michelle Theriault, Directrice
michelle.theriault@usainteanne.ca

Campus de Saint-Joseph-du-Moine
12521, Cabot Trail, St-Joseph-du-Moine, NS B0E 3A0,
Canada
Tel: 902-244-4100; *Fax:* 902-224-4119
Michel Aucoin, Facilitateur
michel.aucoin@usainteanne.ca

Campus de Tusket
1 Slocomb Cres., Tusket, NS B0W 3M0, Canada
Tel: 902-648-3524; *Fax:* 902-648-3525
Marie-Germaine Chartrand, Directrice
mariegermaine.chartr@usainteanne.ca

Sydney: Cape Breton University
P.O. Box 5300
1250 Grand Lake Rd., Sydney, NS B1P 6L2, Canada
Tel: 902-539-5300; *Fax:* 902-562-0119
Toll-Free: 888-959-9995
registrar@cbu.ca
www.cbu.ca
www.facebook.com/CapeBretonUniversity
twitter.com/cbuniversity
www.linkedin.com/school/cape-breton-university
www.youtube.com/user/capebretonu
Full Time Equivalency: 3500 *Note:* The university is also home
to Unama'ki College which offers Mi'kmaw programs and
services, such as teacher training, court worker certification,
business, Mi'kmaw language, health careers, and natural
resources.
Annette Verschuren, Chancellor
David C. Dingwall, President & Vice-Chancellor
Gordon MacInnis, Vice-President, Finance & Operations,
902-563-1128
gordon_macinnis@cbu.ca
Richard MacKinnon, Interim Vice-President, Academic &
Provost, 902-563-1980
richard_mackinnon@cbu.ca
Debbie Rudderham, Chief Information Officer, 902-563-1446
debbie_rudderham@cbu.ca
Brendan MacDonald, Registrar, 902-563-1853
brendan_macdonald@cbu.ca

Schools
School of Arts & Social Sciences
Tel: 902-563-1258
admissions@cbu.ca
Andrew Parnaby, Dean, 902-563-1286
andy_parnaby@cbu.ca

School of Professional Studies
Tel: 902-563-1368
www.cbu.ca/academic-programs/program/school-of-professional
-studies
Carolin Kreber, Dean, 902-563-1672
carolin_kreber@cbu.ca

School of Science & Technology
Tel: 902-563-1149
cbu.ca/academic-programs/program/school-of-science-and-tech
nology
Rick Pierrynowski, Dean, 902-563-1262
rick_pierrynowski@cbu.ca

Shannon School of Business
Tel: 902-563-1110
www.cbu.ca/academic-programs/program/shannon-school-of-bu
siness
George Karaphillis, Dean, 902-563-1467
george_karaphillis@cbu.ca

Wolfville: Acadia University
15 University Ave., Wolfville, NS B4P 2R6, Canada
Tel: 902-542-2201; *Toll-Free:* 877-585-1121
agi@acadiau.ca
www.acadiau.ca
www.facebook.com/acadiauniversity
twitter.com/acadiau
www.youtube.com/user/AcadiaWebmaster
Full Time Equivalency: 3802
Peter J. Ricketts, President & Vice-Chancellor
Dr. Heather Hemming, Acting Vice-President, Academic
Christopher Callbeck, Vice-President, Finance & Administration

Mark Bishop, Registrar

Faculties
Faculty of Arts

Tel: 902-585-1485; *Fax:* 902-585-1070
arts.acadiau.ca
Barry Moody, Acting Dean of Arts
barry.moody@acadiau.ca

Faculty of Professional Studies
P.O. Box 144
Wolfville, NS B4P 2R6

Tel: 902-585-1597; *Fax:* 902-585-1086
professionalstudies.acadiau.ca
Ann Vibert, Dean, Faculty of Professional Studies

Faculty of Pure & Applied Science

Tel: 902-585-1472; *Fax:* 902-585-1637
dean.science@acadiau.ca
science.acadiau.ca
Suzie Currie, Dean of Pure & Applied Science
suzie.currie@acadiau.ca

Schools
Acadia Divinity College
38 Crowell Dr., Wolfville, NS B4P 2R6, Canada

Tel: 902-585-2210; *Fax:* 902-585-2233
Toll-Free: 866-875-8975
adcinfo@acadiau.ca
acadiadiv.ca
www.facebook.com/acadiadivinitycollege
twitter.com/acadiadiv
www.youtube.com/user/AcadiaDivCollege
Full Time Equivalency: 160
Harry G. Gardner, President, 902-585-2213
harry.gardner@acadiau.ca
Stephen D. McMullin, Academic Dean
stephen.mcmullin@acadiau.ca
Shawna Peverill, Registrar, 902-585-2216
shawna.peverill@acadiau.ca

Colleges

Halifax: **Nova Scotia Community College (NSCC)**
NSCC Admissions
P.O. Box 220
Halifax, NS B3J 2M4

Tel: 902-491-4911; *Fax:* 902-491-3514
Toll-Free: 866-679-6722
admissions@nscc.ca
www.nscc.ca
Other Information: Toll-Free Fax: 1-866-329-6722
TTY: 866-288-7034
www.facebook.com/NovaScotiaCommunityCollege
twitter.com/NSCCNews
www.linkedin.com/school/nova-scotia-community-college
www.youtube.com/c/NovaScotiaCommunityCollege
Full Time Equivalency: 1400
Don Bureaux, President, 902-491-4898
Margaret Champion, Dean, Health & Human Services,
902-491-6764
margaret.champion@nscc.ca
Tom Gunn, Dean, Trades & Transportation, 902-227-5249
tom.gunn@nscc.ca
Terrah Keener, Dean, Access, Education & Language,
902-491-2183
terrah.keener@nscc.ca
Andrew Lafford, Dean, Technology & Environment,
902-401-6159
andrew.lafford@nscc.ca
Scott MacPherson, Dean, Business & Creative Industries
scott.macpherson@nscc.ca

Schools
School of Fisheries
1575 Lake Rd., Shelburne, NS B0T 1W0

Tel: 902-875-8641; *Fax:* 902-875-3797
nssf@nscc.ca
www.nscc.ca/explorenscc/campuses/school-of-fisheries

Campuses
Akerley Campus
21 Woodlawn Rd., Dartmouth, NS B3W 2R7

Tel: 902-491-4900; *Fax:* 902-491-4903
akerley.info@nscc.ca
www.nscc.ca/explorenscc/campuses/akerley
Other Information: Student Services: 902-491-4908

Annapolis Valley Campus & Centre of Geographic Sciences
(AVCCOGS)
RR#1, Elliott Rd., Lawrencetown, NS B0S 1M0

Tel: 902-825-3491; *Fax:* 902-825-2285
avc.info@nscc.ca
www.nscc.ca/explorenscc/campuses/cogs
Other Information: Student Services: 902-825-2930

Burridge Campus
372 Pleasant St., Yarmouth, NS B5A 2L2

Tel: 902-749-3501; *Fax:* 902-749-2402
burridge.info@nscc.ca
www.nscc.ca/explorenscc/campuses/burridge
Other Information: Student Services: 902-742-0760
Mary Thompson, Principal, 902-742-0642
mary.thompson@nscc.ca

Cumberland Campus
P.O. Box 550
1 Main St., Springhill, NS B0M 1X0

Tel: 902-597-3737; *Fax:* 902-597-8548
cumberland.info@nscc.ca
www.nscc.ca/explorenscc/campuses/cumberland
Other Information: Student Services: 902-597-4101
Donald McCormack, Principal
donald.mccormack@nscc.ca

eCampus
P.O. Box 1042
1240 Grand Lake Rd., Sydney, NS B1P 6J7

Toll-Free: 877-491-6774
ecampus.info@nscc.ca
www.nscc.ca/explorenscc/campuses/ecampus

Institute of Technology Campus
5685 Leeds St., Halifax, NS B3K 2T3

Tel: 902-491-6722
itcampus.info@nscc.ca
www.nscc.ca/explorenscc/campuses/institute
Full Time Equivalency: 5200

Ivany Campus
80 Mawiomi Pl., Dartmouth, NS B2Y 0A5

Tel: 902-491-1100; *Fax:* 902-491-1795
www.nscc.ca/explorenscc/campuses/ivany
Other Information: Student Services: 902-491-1305
Kathleen Allen, Principal, 902-223-8857
kathleen.allen@nscc.ca

Kingstec Campus
236 Belcher St., Kentville, NS B4N 0A6

Tel: 902-678-7341
kingstec.info@nscc.ca
www.nscc.ca/explorenscc/campuses/kingstec
Other Information: Student Services: 902-679-7361
Full Time Equivalency: 1750
Jason Clark, Principal, 902-679-7350
jason.clark@nscc.ca

Lunenburg Campus
75 High St., Bridgewater, NS B4V 1V8

Tel: 902-543-4608; *Fax:* 902-543-0190
lunenburg.info@nscc.ca
www.nscc.ca/explorenscc/campuses/lunenburg
Other Information: Student Services: 902-543-2295
Craig Collins, Principal, 902-543-0846
craig.collins@nscc.ca

Marconi Campus
P.O. Box 1042
1240 Grand Lake Rd., Sydney, NS B1P 6J7

Tel: 902-563-2450; *Fax:* 902-563-3440
marconi.info@nscc.ca
www.nscc.ca/explorenscc/campuses/marconi
Other Information: Student Services: 902-563-2464
Fred Tilley, Principal, 902-577-0661
fred.tilley@nscc.ca

Pictou Campus
P.O. Box 820
39 Acadia Ave., Stellarton, NS B0K 1S0

Tel: 902-752-2002; *Fax:* 902-755-7295
pictou.info@nscc.ca
www.nscc.ca/explorenscc/campuses/pictou
Other Information: Student Services: 902-755-7299
Full Time Equivalency: 1675
Maxine Mann, Principal, 902-755-7209
maxine.mann@nscc.ca

Shelburne Campus
P.O. Box 760
1575 Lake Rd., Shelburne, NS B0T 1W0

Tel: 902-875-8640; *Fax:* 905-875-3797
shelburne.info@nscc.ca
www.nscc.ca/explorenscc/campuses/shelburne
Other Information: Student Services: 902-875-8640

Strait Area Campus
226 Reeves St., Port Hawkesbury, NS B9A 2A2

Tel: 902-625-2380; *Fax:* 902-625-0193
strait.info@nscc.ca
www.nscc.ca/explorenscc/campuses/strait
Other Information: Student Services: 902-625-4017

Note: The Nautical Institute is located on the Strait Area
Campus.

Truro Campus
36 Arthur St., Truro, NS B2N 1X5

Tel: 902-893-5385; *Fax:* 902-893-5610
truro.info@nscc.ca
www.nscc.ca/explorenscc/campuses/truro
Other Information: Student Services: 902-893-5346
Full Time Equivalency: 1300
Lech Krzywonos, Principal
lech.krzywonos@nscc.ca

Centres & Institutes
Amherst Learning Centre
147 Albion St. South, Amherst, NS B4H 2X2

Tel: 902-661-3180; *Fax:* 902-661-3170

Aviation Institute - Dartmouth Gate
#100, 375 Pleasant St., Dartmouth, NS B2Y 4N4

Tel: 902-491-1100; *Fax:* 902-491-4989
ivany.info@nscc.ca
www.nscc.ca/explorenscc/campuses/aviation_institute

Nautical Institute
226 Reeves St., Port Hawkesbury, NS B9A 2A2

Tel: 902-625-4228; *Fax:* 902-625-0193
nautical@nscc.ca
www.nscc.ca/explorenscc/campuses/nautical-institute

Post Secondary/Technical

Distance Education

Sydney: **Centre for Distance Education**
Heritage Professional Centre
222 George St., #C, Sydney, NS B1P 1J3

Fax: 866-559-0131
Toll-Free: 866-446-5898
info@cd-ed.com
www.cd-ed.com
www.facebook.com/CentreForDistanceEducation
twitter.com/cd_ed
www.youtube.com/user/CDEDYourOnlineSchool
Note: Online college program offerings in technology, media
design, healthcare, & business.
Rose King, Director of Admissions, 866-446-5898, ext. 226
rking@cd-ed.com

Post Secondary/Technical

Bedford: **CL Douglas Centre for Computer Studies**
1142 Bedford Hwy., Bedford, NS B4A 1B8

Tel: 902-835-8880
www.cldouglas.com
Note: Computer software, network management training.
Paul Cudmore, President

Bedford: **Ravensberg College**
1658 Bedford Hwy. #0200, Bedford, NS B4A 2X9

Tel: 902-482-4704
info@ravensbergcollege.ca
www.ravensbergcollege.ca
www.facebook.com/ravensbergcollege.ca
Note: Ravensberg College offers a two-year Law Enforcement
Foundations Diploma.

Dartmouth: **The Academy of Cosmetology**
#201, 33 Thornhill Dr., Dartmouth, NS B3B 1R9

Tel: 902-469-7788; *Fax:* 902-461-4625
academy@eastlink.ca
www.academyofcosmetology.com
www.facebook.com/123283184396385

Falmouth: **Operating Engineers Training Institute of**
Nova Scotia (OETINS)
P.O. Box 103
296 Grey Mountain Rd., Falmouth, NS B0P 1L0

Tel: 902-798-5070; *Fax:* 902-798-5660
info@trainingforthefuture.ca
trainingforthefuture.ca
www.facebook.com/operatingengineerstraining

Halifax: **Atlantic Flight Attendant Academy Limited**
6148 Quinpool Rd., Halifax, NS B3L 1A3

Tel: 902-422-0339; *Toll-Free:* 877-329-2699
flightattendantschool@gmail.com
flightattend.com
www.facebook.com/100057381433245
Note: Flight Attendant Diploma Program.
Cynthia Sullivan, Director

Halifax: **Eastern College**
Halifax Campus
#111, 6940 Mumford Rd., Halifax, NS B3L 0B7
Tel: 902-423-3933; Fax: 902-423-2042
Toll-Free: 877-297-0777
info@easterncollege.ca
easterncollege.ca
www.facebook.com/EasternCollege
twitter.com/easterncollege
www.linkedin.com/school/eastern-college
Frank Gerencser, Chief Executive Officer
Stuart Bentley, President

Campuses
Fredericton Campus
850 Prospect St., Fredericton, NB E3B 9M5
Tel: 506-454-5166; Fax: 506-455-1653

Moncton Campus
1070 St George Blvd., Moncton, NB E1E 4K7
Tel: 506-856-5166; Fax: 506-854-1653

Saint John Campus
#123, 212 McAllister Dr., Saint John, NB E2J 2S5
Tel: 506-633-5166; Fax: 506-633-1653

Halifax: **Eastern Esthetics Career College**
Bayers Lake Business Park
19 Crane Lake Dr., Halifax, NS B3S 1B5
Tel: 902-450-2160; Fax: 902-450-2165
Toll-Free: 888-859-3434
info@lcneast.com
www.lcneast.com/eastern-esthetics-home
www.facebook.com/easternesthetics
twitter.com/lcncanada
www.instagram.com/lcncanada

Halifax: **The Hair Design Centre School of Cosmetology**
278 Lacewood Dr., Halifax, NS B3M 3N8
Tel: 902-455-0535; Fax: 902-422-1023
info@hairdesigncentre.com
hairdesigncentre.com
www.facebook.com/hdchalifax
www.instagram.com/hdchalifax
Tina Burke, Director, School Operations, 902-422-8323

Halifax: **Maritime Conservatory of Performing Arts**
6199 Chebucto Rd., Halifax, NS B3L 1K7
Tel: 902-423-6995; Fax: 902-423-6029
admin@maritimeconservatory.com
www.maritimeconservatory.com
www.facebook.com/maritimeconservatory
www.instagram.com/maritimeconservatory
Note: Not-for-profit organization offering programs in dance & music.
Janet Bradbury, Dean, Dance
dance.dean@maritimeconservatory.com%u200B
Sibylle Marquardt, Dean, Music
music.dean@maritimeconservatory.com

Halifax: **Nova Scotia College of Early Childhood Education (NSCECE)**
6208 Quinpool Rd., 2nd Fl., Halifax, NS B3L 1A3
Tel: 902-423-7114
www.nscece.ca
www.facebook.com/nscece
Note: NSCECE offers a two-year Early Childhood Education (ECE) diploma program.

Hubbards: **Atlantic Home Building & Renovation Sector Council**
P.O. Box 337
Hubbards, NS B0J 1T0
Toll-Free: 1-800-565-2151
info@ahbrsc.com
www.ahbrsc.com
Note: The Atlantic Home Building & Renovation Sector Council has provided courses to over 7,000 builders, carpenters, renovators, designers, inspectors, labourers, & sub-trade workers.
Michael Montgomery, Executive Director, 902-240-1133

Lower Sackville: **Maritime Business College**
800 Sackville Dr., Lower Sackville, NS B4E 1R8
Tel: 902-463-6700; Toll-Free: 800-550-6516
maritimebusinesscollege.ca
www.facebook.com/MaritimeBusinessCollege

North Sydney: **Hair Masters**
26 Archibald Ave., North Sydney, NS B2A 2W3
www.hairmasters-esthetics.com
Note: Offers courses in Esthetics / Nail Technology, Hair Dressing & Cosmetology.

Angela Iannetti, Owner
angelaiannetti@hotmail.ca

St Anns: **The Gaelic College**
Colaisde Na Gàidhlig
P.O. Box 80
51779 Cabot Trail, St Anns, NS B0C 1H0
Tel: 902-295-3411; Fax: 902-295-2912
info@gaeliccollege.edu
gaeliccollege.edu
www.facebook.com/GaelicCollege
twitter.com/GaelicCollege
www.youtube.com/user/gaeliccollege
Note: Offers programs in Gaelic culture.
Hon. Rodney MacDonald, President & CEO
ceo@gaeliccollege.edu
Jennifer Daisley, Chief Financial Officer
jennifer@gaeliccollege.edu

Sydney: **Cape Breton Business College (CBBC)**
Sydney Campus
315 Jamieson St., Sydney, NS B1N 3B1
Tel: 902-564-2222; Toll-Free: 855-225-6741
info@cbbccareercollege.ca
www.cbbccareercollege.ca

Campuses
Dartmouth Campus
#100, 45 Alderney Dr., Dartmouth, NS B2Y 2N6
Tel: 902-706-5529; Toll-Free: 855-226-4981
Kendra MacEachern, Campus Manager
kendra@cbbc.ns.ca

Halifax Campus
1046 Barrington St., #A, Halifax, NS B3H 2R1
Tel: 902-334-1849; Toll-Free: 855-226-4981

Sydney - Townsend Campus
74 Townsend St., Sydney, NS B1P 5C8
Tel: 902-564-2222

Sydney: **Island Career Academy**
721 Alexandra St., Sydney, NS B1S 2H4
Tel: 902-564-6112; Fax: 902-562-6175
admissions@islandcareeracademy.ca
islandcareeracademy.ca
www.facebook.com/islandcareeracademy

Sydney: **Maritime Environmental Training Institute (METI)**
301 Alexandra St., Sydney, NS B1S 2E8
Tel: 902-539-9766; Toll-Free: 877-800-6384
training@metiatlantic.com
www.metiatlantic.com
www.facebook.com/metiatlantic

Truro: **Commercial Safety College (CSC)**
P.O. Box 848
Truro, NS B2n 5G6
Tel: 902-662-2190; Fax: 902-662-2657
Toll-Free: 800-667-5455
info@safetycollege.ca
safetycollege.ca
www.facebook.com/CommercialSafetyCollege
Note: Private career college specializing in truck driving, bus driving & heavy equipment operation training.

Campuses
Masstown Campus
11490 Hwy. #2, Masstown, NS B0M 1G0

Truro: **Jane Norman College (JNC)**
#1, 60 Lorne St., Truro, NS B2N 3K3
Tel: 902-893-3342
info@janenorman.ca
www.janenorman.ca
www.facebook.com/JaneNormanCollege
Note: Early Childhood Education Diploma; Public School Program Assistant Certificate; Special Education Diploma; Youth Worker Diploma
Kimberly Elliott, Executive Director
Anna MacDonell, CDSA IV, B.A., M.Ed., Program Director
Debbie Connolly, CDSA IV, BBA, Registrar

Waverley: **Nova Scotia Firefighters School (NSFS)**
48 Powder Mill Rd., Waverley, NS B2R 1E9
Tel: 902-861-3823; Fax: 902-860-0255
Toll-Free: 866-861-3832
info@fireschool.ca
fireschool.ca

Wolfville: **Acadia Entrepreneurship Centre**
Acadia University
P.O. Box 142
Wolfville, NS B4P 2R6
Tel: 902-585-1180
entrepreneurship@acadiau.ca
www.acadiaentrepreneurshipcentre.com
www.facebook.com/acadiaEcentre
www.linkedin.com/company/acadia-entrepreneurship-centre

Nunavut

Government Agencies

Iqaluit: **Nunavut Department of Education**
Building 1107, 2nd Fl.
P.O. Box 1000 900
Iqaluit, NU X0A 0H0, Canada
Tel: 867-975-5600; Fax: 867-975-5605
info.edu@gov.nu.ca
www.gov.nu.ca/education

Hon. David Joanasie, Minister

School Boards/Districts/Divisions

Public

Baker Lake: **Kivalliq School Operations**
P.O. Box 90
Baker Lake, NU X0C 0A0
Tel: 867-793-2803; Fax: 867-793-2996
Number of Schools: 12 Grades: K - 12
Leigh Ann Willard, Executive Director
lwillard@gov.nu.ca

Iqaluit: **Iqaluit District Education Authority (IDEA)**
P.O. Box 235
Iqaluit, NU X0A 0H0
Tel: 867-979-5314; Fax: 867-979-0330
admin@iqaluitdea.ca
iqaluitdistricteducationauthority.com
www.facebook.com/423900144325267
Lynda Gunn, Administrator

Kugluktuk: **Kitikmeot School Operations**
P.O. Box 287
Kugluktuk, NU X0A 0E0
Tel: 867-982-7420; Fax: 867-982-3054
Number of Schools: 8 Grades: K - 12
Millie Kuliktana, Executive Director, 867-982-7421
mkuliktana@gov.nu.ca

Pond Inlet: **Qikiqtani School Operations**
P.O. Box 429
Pond Inlet, NU X0A 0S0
Tel: 867-899-7350; Fax: 867-899-7334
Number of Schools: 22 Grades: K - 12
Trudy Pettigrew, Executive Director, 867-899-7335
tpettigrew@gov.nu.ca

French

Iqaluit: **La Commission scolaire francophone du Nunavut (CSFN)**
P.O. Box 11008
113 - 8th Storeys, Iqaluit, NU X0A 1H0
Tél: 867-975-2660; Téléc: 867-975-2046
administration@csfn.ca
www.csfn.ca
www.facebook.com/csfn.ca
twitter.com/csftno

Number of Schools: 1 Grades: Mat. - 12
Nancy Guyon, Présidente, Conseil

Post Secondary/Technical

Arviat: **Nunavut Arctic College**
Head Office
P.O. Box 230
Arviat, NU X0C 0E0, Canada
Tel: 867-857-8600; Fax: 867-857-8619
Toll-Free: 866-988-4636
www.arcticcollege.ca
www.facebook.com/NunavutArcticCollege
twitter.com/NunavutCollege

Sheila Kolola, President

Campuses

Kitikmeot Campus - Cambridge Bay
P.O. Box 54
Cambridge Bay, NU X0B 0C0, Canada
Tel: 867-983-4111; *Fax:* 867-983-4106
Toll-Free: 866-383-4533
kitikmeot@arcticcollege.ca

Kivalliq Campus - Rankin Inlet
P.O. Box 002
Rankin Inlet, NU X0C 0G0, Canada
Tel: 867-645-5500; *Fax:* 867-645-2516
kivalliq@arcticcollege.ca

Nunatta Campus - Iqaluit
P.O. Box 600
Iqaluit, NU X0A 0H0, Canada
Tel: 867-979-7222; *Fax:* 867-979-7103
Toll-Free: 866-979-7222
nunatta@arcticcollege.ca

Centres & Institutes
Nunavut Trades Training Centre
P.O. Box 002
Rankin Inlet, NU X0C 0G0
Tel: 867-645-4871
kivalliq@arcticcollege.ca

Nunavut Research Institute
P.O. Box 1720
Iqaluit, NU X0A 0H0
Tel: 867-979-7280; *Fax:* 867-979-7109
www.nri.nu.ca

Ontario

Government Agencies

Toronto: Ontario Ministry of Colleges & Universities
Ministry of Colleges and Universities
438 University Ave., 5th Floor, Toronto, ON M7A 2A5,
Canada
Tel: 416-325-2929; *Fax:* 416-325-6348
Toll-Free: 800-387-5514
www.ontario.ca/page/ministry-colleges-universities
TTY: 416-325-3408
www.facebook.com/ONtrainandstudy
twitter.com/ONtrainandstudy
www.instagram.com/ONtrainandstudy
Hon. Jill Dunlop, Minister, 416-326-1600
jill.dunlop@pc.ola.org

Toronto: Ontario Ministry of Education
Ministry of Education
315 Front St., 14th Floor, Toronto, ON M7A 1B8
Tel: 416-325-2929; *Fax:* 416-325-6348
Toll-Free: 800-387-5514
information.met@ontario.ca
ontario.ca/page/ministry-education
TTY: 800-268-7095
www.facebook.com/OntarioEducation
twitter.com/ONEducation
www.youtube.com/user/OntarioEDU
Number of Employees: 1700
Hon. Stephen Lecce, Minister, 416-325-2600
minister.edu@ontario.ca

Campuses
Barrie
#9, 20 Bell Farm Rd., Barrie, ON L4M 6E4, Canada
Tel: 705-725-7627; *Toll-Free:* 800-471-0713

London
#207, 217 York St., London, ON N6A 5P9, Canada
Tel: 519-667-1440; *Toll-Free:* 800-265-4221

North Bay/Sudbury
#1103, 199 Larch St., Sudbury, ON P3E 5P9, Canada
Tel: 705-474-7210; *Toll-Free:* 800-461-9570

Ottawa
#504, 1580 Merivale Rd., Ottawa, ON K2G 4B5, Canada
Tel: 613-225-9210; *Fax:* 613-225-2881
Toll-Free: 800-267-1067

Thunder Bay
615 South James St., 1st Fl., Thunder Bay, ON P7E 6P6,
Canada
Tel: 807-474-2980; *Toll-Free:* 800-465-5020

Toronto & Area
Centre Tower
#1610, 3280 Bloor St. West, Toronto, ON M8X 2X3, Canada
Tel: 416-325-6870; *Toll-Free:* 800-268-5755

School Boards/Districts/Divisions

Public

Aurora: York Region District School Board
The Education Centre
P.O. Box 40
60 Wellington St. West, Aurora, ON L4G 3H2, Canada
Tel: 905-727-3141; *Fax:* 905-727-1931
feedback@yrdsb.edu.on.ca
www.yrdsb.ca
twitter.com/yrdsb
Number of Schools: 178 elementary; 33 secondary *Grades:* K -
12 *Enrollment:* 127004 *Number of Employees:* 13301
Corrie McBain, Chair, Board, 416-219-7426
corrie.mcbain@yrdsb.ca
Louise Sirisko, Director, Education, 905-727-0022, ext. 2234
director@yrdsb.ca
Karen Friedman, Associate Director, Education - Schools and
Program, 905-727-0022, ext. 2385
karen.friedman@yrdsb.ca
Clayton La Touche, Associate Director, Education - Schools and
Operations, 905-727-0022, ext. 2316
clayton.latouche@yrdsb.ca
Wanda Muirhead, Chief Financial Officer, 905-727-0022, ext.
2425
wanda.muirhead@yrdsb.ca

Belleville: Hastings & Prince Edward District School
Board (HPEDSB)
156 Ann St., Belleville, ON K8N 3L3, Canada
Tel: 613-966-1170; *Fax:* 613-961-2003
Toll-Free: 800-267-4350
information@hpedsb.on.ca
www.hpedsb.on.ca
twitter.com/HPEschools
www.youtube.com/user/HPESchools
Number of Schools: 33 elementary; 1 K-12; 6 secondary
Grades: K - 12 *Enrollment:* 15000 *Number of Employees:* 1800
teaching and support staff
Shannon Binder, Chair, Board, 613-921-1848
sbinder@hpedsb.on.ca
Sean Monteith, Director, Education; Secretary, Board,
800-267-4350, ext. 62201
directors.office@hpedsb.on.ca
Laina Andrews, Superintendent, Human Resources,
800-267-4350, ext. 62203
hr.services@hpedsb.on.ca
Ken Dostaler, Superintendent, Student Services, 800-267-4350,
ext. 62312
student.services@hpedsb.on.ca
Tina Elliott, Superintendent, Curriculum Services, 800-267-4350,
ext. 62210
curriculum.services@hpedsb.on.ca
Nick Pfeiffer, Superintendent, Business Services; Treasurer,
Board, 800-267-4350, ext. 62280
business.services@hpedsb.on.ca
Kelvin MacQuarrie, Senior Information and Technology Services
Officer, 800-267-4350, ext. 62410
it.services@hpedsb.on.ca

Brantford: Grand Erie District School Board
Education Centre
349 Erie Ave., Brantford, ON N3T 5V3, Canada
Tel: 519-756-6301; *Fax:* 519-756-9181
Toll-Free: 888-548-8878
info@granderie.ca
www.granderie.ca
www.facebook.com/GEDSB
twitter.com/GEDSB
Number of Schools: 58 elementary; 14 secondary *Grades:* JK -
12; Special Ed; Continuing Ed. *Enrollment:* 26681 *Number of
Employees:* 1831 Instructional; 1017 Non-instructional
Greg Anderson, Chair, 519-446-0218
greg.anderson@granderie.ca
Brenda Blancher, Director of Education
Wayne Baker, Superintendent of Education
Lisa Munro, Superintendent of Education
Linda De Vos, Superintendent of Education
Denise Martins, Superintendent of Education
Scott Sincerbox, Superintendent of Education
Liana Thompson, Superintendent of Education
Rafal Wyszynski, Superintendent of Business

Brockville: Upper Canada District School Board
(UCDSB)
225 Central Ave. West, Brockville, ON K6V 5X1, Canada
Tel: 613-342-0371; *Toll-Free:* 1-800-267-7131
inquiries@ucdsb.on.ca
www.ucdsb.on.ca
www.facebook.com/UCDSB
twitter.com/UCDSB
www.youtube.com/uppercanadadsb
Number of Schools: 79 *Grades:* K - 12 *Enrollment:* 27000
Number of Employees: 4200 *Note:* Also offers alternative &
continuing education programs.
John McAllister, Chair, Board, 613-213-4094
john.mcallister@ucdsb.on.ca
Stephen Sliwa, Director, Education, 613-342-0371, ext. 1234
stephen.sliwa@ucdsb.on.ca
Deanna Perry, Superintendent, Schools, 613-342-0371
deanna.perry@ucdsb.on.ca
Bill Loshaw, Acting Superintendent, Schools, 613-342-0371, ext.
1159
bill.loshaw@ucdsb.on.ca
David Coombs, Superintendent, Schools, 613-258-9393
david.coombs@ucdsb.on.ca
Ron Ferguson, Superintendent, Schools, 800-766-8474, ext.
1118
ron.ferguson@ucdsb.on.ca
Susan Rutters, Acting Superintendent, Schools, 613-346-9626
susan.rutters@ucdsb.on.ca
Robert Backstrom, Superintendent, Business, 613-342-0371
robert.backstrom@ucdsb.on.ca
Jeremy Hobbs, Superintendent, Human Resources and
Operational Services, 613-342-0371
jeremy.hobbs@ucdsb.on.ca
Phil Dawes, Superintendent, District Alignment, 613-342-0371
phil.dawes@ucdsb.on.ca

Burlington: Halton District School Board (HDSB)
J.W. Singleton Education Centre
2050 Guelph Line, Burlington, ON L7P 5A8
Tel: 905-335-3663; *Fax:* 905-335-9802
Toll-Free: 877-618-3456
contact@hdsb.ca
www.hdsb.ca
Other Information: New Street Education Centre, Phone:
905-631-6120
www.facebook.com/HaltonDistrictSchoolBoard
twitter.com/HaltonDSB
www.instagram.com/hdsbschools
Number of Schools: 88 elementary schoools; 20 secondary &
alternative schools *Grades:* K - 12 *Enrollment:* 65179 *Number of
Employees:* 2,887 elementary teachers; 1,325 secondary
teachers; 2,164 support staff
Andréa Grebenc, Chair, Board of Trustees, 905-875-9590
grebenca@hdsb.ca
Stuart Miller, Director, Education, 905-335-3665, ext. 3354
millers@hdsb.ca
David Boag, Associate Director, Student Achievement,
905-335-3665, ext. 3354
boagd@hdsb.ca
Debra McFadden, Executive Officer, Human Resources,
905-335-3665, ext. 3274
mcfaddend@hdsb.ca
Marnie Denton, Manager, Communication Services,
905-335-3665, ext. 2227
dentonm@hdsb.ca
Roxana Negoi, Superintendent, Business Services,
905-335-3665, ext. 3261
negoir@hdsb.ca

Chesley: Bluewater District School Board
P.O. Box 190
351 - 1st Ave. North, Chesley, ON N0G 1L0, Canada
Tel: 519-363-2014; *Fax:* 519-370-2909
Toll-Free: 1-800-661-7509
communications@bwdsb.on.ca
www.bwdsb.on.ca
Other Information: Purchasing & Transportation Dept.:
519-364-0605
www.facebook.com/BluewaterDSB
twitter.com/BluewaterDSB
Number of Schools: 39 elementary; 9 secondary *Grades:* JK -
12; Special Ed. *Enrollment:* 16000 *Number of Employees:* 3,000
permanent and casual
Jan Johnstone, Chair, Board, 519-396-1467
jan_johnstone@bwdsb.on.ca
Alana Murray, Director, Education
Rob Cummings, Superintendent, Business Services; Treasurer
Cynthia Lemon, Superintendent, Education - Human Resources
Wendy Kolohon, Superintendent, Education
Paul Hambleton, Superintendent, Education
Lori Wilder, Superintendent of Education

Dryden: Keewatin-Patricia District School Board (KPDSB)
79 Casimir Ave., Dryden, ON P8N 2H4

Tel: 807-468-5571; *Fax:* 807-468-3857
Toll-Free: 877-275-7771
www.kpdsb.on.ca

Number of Schools: 17 elementary; 6 secondary *Grades:* K - 12
Enrollment: 5180 *Number of Employees:* 722 permanent staff;
617 non-permanent staff
Sean Monteith, Director of Education, 807-468-5571, ext. 236
sean.monteith@kpdsb.on.ca
David Penney, Board Chair, 807-934-2757
david.penney@kpdsb.on.ca
Dean Carrie, Superintendent of Business, 807-468-5571, ext. 237
dean.carrie@kpdsb.on.ca
Joan Kantola, Superintendent of Education, 807-468-5571, ext. 225
joan.kantola@kpdsb.on.ca
Caryl Hron, Superintendent of Education, 807-223-5311, ext. 264
caryl.hron@kpdsb.on.ca
Kim Carlson, Facilities Manager, 807-468-5571, ext. 260
kim.carlson@kpdsb.on.ca
Kathleen O'Flaherty, Finance Manager, 807-468-5571, ext. 230
kathleen.oflaherty@kpdsb.on.ca
Arlene Szestopalow, Purchasing & Payables Officer, 807-468-5571, ext. 253
arlene.szestopalow@kpdsb.on.ca
Jocelyn Bullock, Human Resources Manager, 807-468-5571, ext. 267
jocelyn.bullock@kpdsb.on.ca

Fort Frances: Rainy River District School Board
522 Second St. East, Fort Frances, ON P9A 1N4, Canada

Tel: 807-274-9855; *Fax:* 807-274-5078
Toll-Free: 800-214-1753
www.rrdsb.com
www.facebook.com/RRDSB
twitter.com/rrdsb

Number of Schools: 10 elementary; 3 secondary; 1 alternative
Grades: JK - 12
Raymond Roy, Chair, Board, 807-271-4677
raymond.roy@mail.rrdsb.com
Heather Campbell, Director, Education
heather.campbell@mail.rrdsb.com
Laura Mills, Superintendent, Business, 807-274-9855, ext. 4991
laura.mills@mail.rrdsb.com
Andrew Harris, Superintendent, Education
andrew.harris@mail.rrdsb.com
Allan McManaman, Superintendent, Education
allan.mcmanaman@mail.rrdsb.com
Kevin Knutsen, Executive Officer, Employee and Labour Relations
kevin.knutsen@mail.rrdsb.com
Stephen Danielson, Manager, Information Technology Services
stephen.danielson@mail.rrdsb.com
Travis Enge, Manager, Plant Operations & Maintenance
travis.enge@mail.rrdsb.com

Guelph: Upper Grand District School Board (UGDSB)
Main Office
500 Victoria Rd. North, Guelph, ON N1E 6K2

Tel: 519-822-4420; *Fax:* 519-826-9534
Toll-Free: 800-321-4025
inquiry@ugdsb.on.ca
www.ugdsb.ca
www.facebook.com/ugdsb
twitter.com/ugdsb
www.instagram.com/uppergrand

Number of Schools: 65 elementary schools; 11 secondary
schools; 4 continuing education sites *Grades:* K - 12; Continuing
Ed. *Enrollment:* 34000 *Number of Employees:* 3,000
Martha MacNeil, Chair, Board, 519-822-4420
martha.macneil@ugdsb.on.ca
Martha Rogers, Director, Education, 519-822-4420, ext. 721
amy.villeneuve@ugdsb.on.ca
Tracey Lindsay, Superintendent, Program, 519-941-6191, ext. 254
krystyna.gazo@ugdsb.on.ca
Glen Regier, Superintendent, Finance, 519-822-4420, ext. 860
angela.alies@ugdsb.on.ca
Denise Heaslip, Superintendent, Education, 519-822-4420, ext. 745
stephanie.mcnabb@ugdsb.on.ca
Brent McDonald, Superintendent, Education, 519-822-4420, ext. 741
lynne.mcinnis@ugdsb.on.ca
Doug Morrell, Superintendent, Education, 519-822-4420, ext. 749
amanda.creed@ugdsb.on.ca

Gary Slater, Superintendent, Education, 519-822-4420, ext. 850
karen.zorzi@ugdsb.on.ca
Cheryl Van Ooteghem, Superintendent, Education, 519-822-4420, ext. 746
june.pollard@ugdsb.on.ca

Hamilton: Hamilton-Wentworth District School Board (HWDSB)
P.O. Box 2558
20 Education Ct., Hamilton, ON L8N 3L1

Tel: 905-527-5092; *Fax:* 905-521-2544
info@hwdsb.on.ca
www.hwdsb.on.ca
www.facebook.com/hwdsb
twitter.com/hwdsb
www.linkedin.com/company/429568
www.youtube.com/hwdsbtv

Number of Schools: 84 elementary schools; 13 secondary
schools *Grades:* K - 12 *Enrollment:* 49748 *Number of
Employees:* 7,096
Alex Johnstone, Chair, Board, 905-515-7082
ajjohnst@hwdsb.on.ca
Manny Figueiredo, Director, Education, 905-527-5092, ext. 2297
director@hwdsb.on.ca
Peter Sovran, Associate Director, Learning Services, 905-527-5092, ext. 2624
lsheppar@hwdsb.on.ca
Stacey Zucker, Associate Director, Support Services, 905-527-5092, ext. 2500
gmacdona@hwdsb.on.ca
Peggy Blair, Superintendent, Specialized Services, 905-527-5092, ext. 2625
ahewitt@hwdsb.on.ca
Jamie Nunn, Superintendent, Human Resources, 905-527-5092, ext. 2753
ephilipp@hwdsb.on.ca
Sharon Stephanian, Superintendent, Equity & Well-Being, 905-527-5092, ext. 2386
jcravero@hwdsb.on.ca
Bill Torrens, Superintendent, Program, 905-527-5092, ext. 2624
lsheppar@hwdsb.on.ca
Paul Denomme, Superintendent, Student Achievement, 905-527-5092, ext. 2304
khussey@hwdsb.on.ca
Sue Dunlop, Superintendent, Student Achievement, 905-527-5092, ext. 2673
mbaines@hwdsb.on.ca
Jeff Gillies, Superintendent, Student Achievement, 905-527-5092, ext. 2361
tshaver@hwdsb.on.ca
Jane Macpherson, Superintendent, Student Achievement, 905-527-5092, ext. 2626
vaguirre@hwdsb.on.ca
Laura Romano, Superintendent, Student Achievement, 905-527-5092, ext. 2622
jemacdon@hwdsb.on.ca

Kingston: Limestone District School Board (LDSB)
Education Centre
220 Portsmouth Ave., Kingston, ON K7M 0G2

Tel: 613-544-6920; *Fax:* 613-544-6804
Toll-Free: 800-267-0935
inquiries@limestone.on.ca
www.limestone.on.ca

Other Information: Automated Attendant, Phone: 613-544-6925
TTY: 613-548-0279
www.facebook.com/308623265872996
twitter.com/LimestoneDSB
www.youtube.com/LimestoneDSB

Number of Schools: 55 Schools; 5 alternative learning centres
Grades: K - 12; Alternate Ed. *Enrollment:* 19000
Suzanne Ruttan, Chair, Board, 613-353-6439
ruttansu@limestone.on.ca
Debra Rantz, Director, Education, 613-544-6925, ext. 235
rantzd@limestone.on.ca
Patrick Fisher, Supervisor, Financial Services - Procurement & Payments, 613-544-6925, ext. 291
fisherp@limestone.on.ca
Paul Babin, Superintendent, Business Services, 613-544-6925, ext. 338
youngcra@limestone.on.ca
Andre Labrie, Superintendent, Human Resources, 613-544-6925, ext. 230
labriea@limestone.on.ca

Kitchener: Waterloo Region District School Board (WRDSB)
51 Ardelt Ave., Kitchener, ON N2C 2R5

Tel: 519-570-0003
info@wrdsb.ca
www.wrdsb.ca
www.facebook.com/216410025090633
twitter.com/wrdsb
www.instagram.com/wr_dsb

Number of Schools: 105 Elementary Schools; 16 Secondary
Schools *Grades:* K - 12 *Enrollment:* 64883
Jayne Herring, Chair, Board, 519-240-3613
jayne_herring@wrdsb.ca
John Bryant, Director, Education & Secretary, Board, 519-570-0003, ext. 4223
elaine_burns@wrdsb.ca
Matthew Gerard, Superintendent, Business Services & Treasurer, Board, 519-570-0003, ext. 4322
matthew_gerard@wrdsb.ca
Michael R. Weinert, Superintendent, Human Resource Services, 519-570-0003, ext. 4253
michael_weinert@wrdsb.ca
Lila Read, Associate Director, Student Achievement & Well-Being, 519-570-0003, ext. 4219
karen_leishman@wrdsb.ca

Lindsay: Trillium Lakelands District School Board (TLDSB)
P.O. Box 420
300 County Rd. 36, Lindsay, ON K9V 4S4, Canada

Tel: 705-324-6776; *Fax:* 705-328-2036
Toll-Free: 1-888-526-5552
info@tldsb.on.ca
tldsb.ca

Other Information: Muskoka Office, Phone: 705-645-8704
www.facebook.com/TLDSB
twitter.com/TLDSB
www.instagram.com/trillium_lakelands_dsb

Number of Schools: 41 elementary; 7 secondary; 6 adult
education centres *Grades:* K - 12; French Immersion; Adult Ed.
Louise Clodd, Chair, 705-394-8260
louise.clodd@tldsb.on.ca
Larry Hope, Director, Education, 888-526-5552, ext. 22104
Dave Golden, Superintendent, Learning, 888-526-5552, ext. 21256
Paul Goldring, Superintendent, Learning, 888-526-5552, ext. 22115
Jennifer Johnston, Superintendent, Learning, 888-526-5552, ext. 22144
Katherine MacIver, Superintendent, Learning, 888-526-5552, ext. 22146
Tim Ellis, Superintendent, Business Services, 888-526-5552, ext. 22164
Jennifer Anderson, Superintendent, Employee Services, 888-526-5552, ext. 22105

London: Thames Valley District School Board (TVDSB)
1250 Dundas St., London, ON N5W 5P2

Tel: 519-452-2000; *Fax:* 519-452-2395
www.tvdsb.ca
www.facebook.com/TVDSB
twitter.com/TVDSB
https://www.youtube.com/TVDSBVideos

Number of Schools: 132 elementary schools; 27 secondary
schools; 5 adult education centres *Grades:* K - 12; Adult Ed.;
Alternative Ed. *Enrollment:* 77000 *Number of Employees:* 8,193
teachers, principals and support staff
Arlene Morell, Chair, Board, 519-452-2000, ext. 22402
a.morell@tvdsb.ca
Mark Fisher, Director of Education
Jeff Pratt, Associate Director & Treasurer
Gary Keathley, Supervisor, Purchasing
Cathy Lynd, Superintendent, Business
Linda Nicholls, Superintendent, Human Resources
Riley Culhane, Associate Director, Learning Support Services
Karen Edgar, Superintendent, Student Achievement - Culture for Learning
Marion Moynihan, Superintendent, Student Achievement - Information Technology

Marathon: Superior-Greenstone District School Board
P.O. Box Bag A
12 Hemlo Dr., Marathon, ON P0T 2E0

Tel: 807-229-0436; *Fax:* 807-229-1471
boardoffice@sgdsb.on.ca
www.sgdsb.on.ca
www.facebook.com/SGDSBoard
twitter.com/SGDSBoard
www.youtube.com/user/SuperiorGreenstone

Number of Schools: 10 elementary; 5 secondary *Grades:* K - 12
Enrollment: 1413
Nicole Morden-Cormier, Director, Education
nmorden-cormier@sgdsb.on.ca
Charles Bishop, Superintendent, Education
cbishop@sgdsb.on.ca
Cathy Tsubouchi, Superintendent, Business
ctsubouchi@sgdsb.on.ca
Marc Paris, Manager, Plant Services
mparis@sgdsb.on.ca
Brent Harris, Manager, Financial Services
bharris@sgdsb.on.ca
Linda Demers, Coordinator, Business Services
ldemers@sgdsb.on.ca
Matthew Legacy, Coordinator, Maintenance & Safety
mlegacy@sgdsb.on.ca
Jay Lucas, Coordinator, Systems & Information Technology
jlucas@sgdsb.on.ca
Denis Nault, Manager, Human Resources
dnault@sgdsb.on.ca
Christine Dee, Health & Wellness Administrator
cdee@sgdsb.on.ca
Nancy O'Donnell, Indigenous Education Lead
nodonnell@sgdsb.on.ca
Pinky McRae, Chair, Board, 807-229-7787
pmcrae@sgdsb.on.ca

Midhurst: Simcoe County District School Board (SCDSB)
Education Centre
1170 Hwy. 26, Midhurst, ON L9X 1N6, Canada
Tel: 705-728-7570; *Fax:* 705-728-2265
Toll-Free: 1-877-728-1187
info@scdsb.on.ca
www.scdsb.on.ca
Other Information: 905 Calling: 905-729-2265 (Switchboard);
905-729-3600 (Auto)
www.facebook.com/SCDSB
twitter.com/SCDSB_Schools
www.instagram.com/SCDSB
Number of Schools: 87 elementary; 14 secondary; 6 Adult
Learning Centres *Grades:* K - 12; Continuing Ed. *Enrollment:*
50000 *Number of Employees:* 6,000 full-time and part-time staff
Jodi Lloyd, Chair, Board, 705-734-6363, ext. 11008
jlloyd@trustee.scdsb.on.ca
Steve Blake, Director, Education, 705-734-6363, ext. 11223
Stuart Finlayson, Superintendent, Education - Area 1,
705-734-6363, ext. 11397
Douglas Paul, Superintendent, Education - Area 2,
705-734-6363, ext. 11208
Dean Maltby, Superintendent, Education - Area 3A,
705-734-6363, ext. 11811
Dawn Stephens, Superintendent, Education - Area 3B,
705-734-6363, ext. 11357
Daryl Halliday, Superintendent, Education - Area 4,
705-734-6363, ext. 11318
Michael Giffen, Superintendent, Education - Area 5,
705-734-6363, ext. 11638
Hanne Nielsen, Superintendent, Ed. - Learning Centres &
Alternative Education, 705-734-6363, ext. 11427
Brian Jeffs, Superintendent, Business & Facility Services,
705-734-6363, ext. 11259
John Dance, Superintendent, Human Resource Services,
705-734-6363, ext. 11375
Chris Samis, Superintendent, Program & Special Education,
705-734-6363, ext. 11244
Rick Defoe, Chief Information Officer, 705-734-6363, ext. 11205

Mississauga: Peel District School Board
HJA Brown Education Centre
5650 Hurontario St., Mississauga, ON L5R 1C6
Tel: 905-890-1010; *Fax:* 905-890-6747
Toll-Free: 800-668-1146
communications@peelsb.com
peelschools.org
www.facebook.com/peelschools
twitter.com/peelschools
www.youtube.com/peelschools
Number of Schools: 215 elementary schools; 35 secondary
schools *Grades:* K - 12 *Enrollment:* 156701 *Number of
Employees:* 9,711 academic staff; 4,117 business staff
Peter Joshua, Director, Education, 905-890-1010, ext. 2006
Brad MacDonald, Chair, Board, 905-593-3547
brad.macdonald@peelsb.com
Carla Pereira, Director, Communications & Community
Relations, 905-890-1010, ext. 2812
Antoine Haroun, Chief Information Officer, 905-890-1010, ext.
2478
Marlene McAlister, Manager, Purchasing, 905-890-1010, ext.
2127
Adrian Graham, Superintendent, Curriculum & Instruction
Support Services, 905-890-1010, ext. 2343

North Bay: Near North District School Board
P.O. Box 3110
963 Airport Rd., North Bay, ON P1B 8H1, Canada
Tel: 705-472-8170; *Fax:* 705-472-9927
Toll-Free: 800-278-4922
info@nearnorthschools.ca
www.nearnorthschools.ca
www.facebook.com/141124442647950
twitter.com/NearNorthSchool
Number of Schools: 35 elementary; 7 secondary *Grades:* K.-12
Enrollment: 10500 *Note:* Also offers continuing education
programs.
Jackie Young, Director, 705-472-8170, ext. 5012
jackie.Young@nearnorthschools.ca
David Thompson, Chair, 705-474-0442
david.thompson@nearnorthschools.ca
Liz Therrien, Superintendent of Business, 705-472-8170, ext.
5023
Liz.Therrien@nearnorthschools.ca
Jeff Hewitt, Superintendent of Support Services, 705-472-8170,
ext. 5008
Jeffrey.Hewitt@nearnorthschools.ca
Craig Myles, Superintendent of Support Success, 705-472-8170,
ext. 5002
Craig.Myles@nearnorthschools.ca
Roz Bowness, Superintendent of Schools, 705-472-8170, ext.
8256
Roslyn.Bowness@nearnorthschools.ca
Tim Graves, Superintendent of Schools and Programs,
705-472-8170, ext. 7031
Timothy.Graves@nearnorthschools.ca

Ottawa: Ottawa-Carleton District School Board (OCDSB)
133 Greenbank Rd., Ottawa, ON K2H 6L3
Tel: 613-721-1820; *Fax:* 613-820-6968
communications@ocdsb.ca
www.ocdsb.ca
www.facebook.com/OCDSB
twitter.com/OCDSB
www.linkedin.com/company/25512
www.youtube.com/user/TheOCDSB
Number of Schools: 113 elementary schools; 25 secondary
schools; 5 secondary alternate sites *Grades:* JK - 12; Special
Ed. *Enrollment:* 70000 *Number of Employees:* 9,000
Lynn Scott, Chair, Board, 613-832-3813
lynn.scott@ocdsb.ca
Camille Williams Taylor, Director, Education & Secretary, Board,
613-596-8211, ext. 8490
director@ocdsb.ca
Mike Carson, Chief Financial Officer, 613-596-8211, ext. 8881
Sandra Lloyd, Manager, Risk & Supply Chain Management,
613-596-8762
Nadia Towaij, Superintendent, Program & Learning K-12,
613-596-8211, ext. 8573
Peter Symmonds, Superintendent, Learning Support Services,
613-596-8254
Janice McCoy, Superintendent, Human Resources,
613-596-8207

Pembroke: Renfrew County District School Board (RCDSB)
1270 Pembroke St. West, Pembroke, ON K8A 4G4, Canada
Tel: 613-735-0151; *Fax:* 613-735-6315
Toll-Free: 1-800-267-1098
www.rcdsb.on.ca
www.facebook.com/RCDSB
twitter.com/rcdsb
Number of Schools: 21 elementary; 7 secondary; 4 continuing
education centres *Grades:* K - 12 *Enrollment:* 9199 *Note:* Also
offers continuing education programs.
Susan Humphries, Chair, Board, 613-432-8039
humphriess@rcdsb.on.ca
Pino Buffone, Director, Education, 613-735-0151
Jennifer Barnes, Superintendent, Business - Corporate Services,
613-735-0151
Brent McIntyre, Superintendent, Human Resources - Employee
Services, 613-735-0151
Renald Cousineau, Superintendent, Education - Program
Services, 613-735-0151, ext. 3307
Steve Blok, Superintendent, Education - Program Services,
613-735-0151
Jacqueline Poirier, Superintendent, Education - Program
Services, 613-735-0151
Jonathan Laderoute, Communications Manager, 613-735-0151

Peterborough: Kawartha Pine Ridge District School Board
Education Centre
P.O. Box 7190
1994 Fisher Dr., Peterborough, ON K9J 6X6, Canada
Tel: 705-742-9773; *Fax:* 705-742-7801
Toll-Free: 877-741-4577
kpr_info@kprdsb.ca
www.kprschools.ca
twitter.com/kprschools
www.instagram.com/kprschools
Number of Schools: 73 elementary schools; 13 secondary
schools; 3 adult and alternative learning centres *Enrollment:*
32000 *Number of Employees:* 3500
Diane Lloyd, Chair, Board, 705-652-3677
diane_lloyd@kprdsb.ca
Jennifer Leclerc, Director, Education; Secretary of the Board,
705-742-9773, ext. 2005
director_education@kprdsb.ca
Chris Arnew, Superintendent, Education - Business and
Corporate Services, 705-742-9773, ext. 2024
chris_arnew@kprdsb.ca
Jack Nigro, Superintendent - First Nation, Métis, and Inuit
Education, 705-742-9773, ext. 2602
jack_nigro@kprdsb.ca

Sarnia: Lambton Kent District School Board (LKDSB)
Sarnia Education Centre
P.O. Box 2019
200 Wellington St., Sarnia, ON N7T 7L2, Canada
Tel: 519-336-1500; *Fax:* 519-336-0992
Toll-Free: 800-754-7125
info@lkdsb.net
www.lkdsb.net
www.facebook.com/LKDSB
twitter.com/LKDSB
Number of Schools: 51 elementary schools; 12 secondary
schools *Grades:* JK - 12 *Enrollment:* 21000
Jane Bryce, Chair, Board, 519-899-2619
jane.bryce@lkdsb.net
John Howitt, Director, Education, 519-336-1500, ext. 31297
john.howitt@lkdsb.net
Brian McKay, Superintendent, Business, 519-336-1500, ext.
31480
brian.mckay@lkdsb.net
Helen Lane, Superintendent - Indigenous Ed./Leadership &
Equity, 519-336-1500, ext. 31263
helen.lane@lkdsb.net
Angie Barrese, Superintendent, Education - Special Education,
519-354-3770, ext. 31303
angie.barrese@lkdsb.net
Mark Sherman, Superintendent, Ed. - Capital Planning & Pupil
Accommodation, 519-336-1500, ext. 31449
mark.sherman@lkdsb.net
Ben Hazzard, Superintendent, Education - Early
Years/Elementary, 519-336-1500, ext. 31570
ben.hazzard@lkdsb.net
Gary Girardi, Superintendent, Education - Human Resources,
519-336-1500, ext. 31486
gary.girardi@lkdsb.net
Mary Mancini, Superintendent, Education - Student
Success/Secondary, 519-336-1500, ext. 31449
mary.mancini@lkdsb.net

Campuses
Lambton Kent District School Board
Chatham Regional Education Centre
P.O. Box 1000
476 McNaughton Ave. East, Chatham, ON N7M 5L7, Canada
Tel: 519-354-3770; *Fax:* 519-354-0662
Toll-Free: 800-754-7125

Sault Ste Marie: Algoma District School Board
Central Board Office, Education Centre
644 Albert St. East, Sault Ste Marie, ON P6A 2K7, Canada
Tel: 705-945-7111; *Fax:* 705-942-2540
Toll-Free: 1-888-393-3639
comments@adsb.on.ca
www.adsb.on.ca
Number of Schools: 30 elementary; 16 secondary & adult
education centres *Grades:* K - 12 *Enrollment:* 9787 *Number of
Employees:* 2100 permanent and casual *Note:* Also offers
continuing education programs.
Jennifer Sarlo, Chair, Board, 705-942-5805
sarloj@trustee.adsb.on.ca
Lucia Reece, Director, Education, 705-945-7234
Joe Santa Maria, Executive Superintendent, Business and
Operations, 705-945-7233
Joe Maurice, Superintendent, Education, 705-945-7245
Marcy Bell, Superintendent, Education, 705-945-7235
Brent Vallee, Superintendent, Education, 705-945-7297

Frank Palumbo, Superintendent, Human Resources, 705-945-7111

Campuses
Algoma District School Board
Northern Area Office
36 McKinley Ave., Wawa, ON P0S 1K0, Canada
Tel: 705-848-3661; *Fax:* 705-848-9225

Ian Gauld, Coordinator

Algoma District School Board
Eastern Area Office
303 Mississauga Ave., Elliot Lake, ON P5A 1E8, Canada
Tel: 705-848-3661; *Fax:* 705-848-9225

Ian Gauld, Coordinator

Algoma District School Board
Central Plant Office
190 Northern Ave. E., Sault Ste. Marie, ON P6B 4H6, Canada
Tel: 705-945-7308; *Fax:* 705-759-2811

David Steele, Manager

Seaforth: **Avon Maitland District School Board**
Education Centre
62 Chalk St. North, Seaforth, ON N0K 1W0, Canada
Tel: 519-527-0111; *Fax:* 519-527-0222
Toll-Free: 1-800-592-5437
info@ed.amdsb.ca
yourschools.ca
www.facebook.com/AvonMaitlandSchools
twitter.com/yourschools
www.instagram.com/yourschools
Number of Schools: 31 elementary; 9 secondary *Grades:* JK - Secondary; Continuing Ed. *Enrollment:* 16388 *Number of Employees:* 1600 teachers; 900 support staff
Colleen Schenk, Chair, Board, 519-357-1066
colleen.schenk@ed.amdsb.ca
Lisa Walsh, PhD., Director, Education; Secretary, Board, 519-527-0111, ext. 106
lisa.walsh@ed.amdsb.ca
Janet Baird-Jackson, Superintendent, Corporate Services, 519-527-0111, ext. 206
janet.bairdjackson@ed.amdsb.ca
Kim Black, Superintendent, Education - Learning Services, 519-527-0111, ext. 109
kimberley.black@ed.amdsb.ca
Jane Morris, Superintendent, Education - Program, 519-527-0111, ext. 116
jane.morris@ed.amdsb.ca
Paul Langis, Superintendent, Education - Human Resource Services, 519-527-0111, ext. 113
paul.langis@ed.amdsb.ca
Jodie Baker, Superintendent, Education, 519-527-0111, ext. 208
jodie.baker@ed.amdsb.ca
Cheri Carter, Associate Superintendent, Financial Services and Treasurer, 519-527-0111, ext. 207
cheri.carter@ed.amdsb.ca

St. Catharines: **District School Board of Niagara (DSBN)**
191 Carleton St., St. Catharines, ON L2R 7P4
Tel: 905-641-1550
inquiries@dsbn.org
dsbn.org
Other Information: Free Local Phone: 905-563-0909
www.facebook.com/DSBNiagara
twitter.com/dsbn
www.instagram.com/dsbniagara
Number of Schools: 79 elementary; 20 secondary schools *Grades:* JK - 12; Adult Ed. *Enrollment:* 36000 *Number of Employees:* 3,000 teachers; 1,300 support staff
Sue Barnett, Chair, Board, 905-734-7110
sue.barnett@dsbn.org
Warren Hoshizaki, Director, Education & Secretary, Board, 905-641-1550, ext. 54101
Kim Yielding, Chief Communications Officer, 905-641-2929, ext. 54160
Robert Dunn, Manager, Projects & Maintenance, 905-641-2929, ext. 54305
Colin Munro, Manager, Facility Services, 905-641-2929, ext. 54310
Lora Courtois, Superintendent, Human Resources, 905-641-1550, ext. 54131

Sudbury: **Rainbow District School Board**
Also known as: Rainbow Schools
408 Wembley Dr., Sudbury, ON P3E 1P2
Tel: 705-674-3171; *Fax:* 705-674-3167
Toll-Free: 888-421-2661
info@rainbowschools.ca
www.rainbowschools.ca
www.facebook.com/rainbowdsb

Number of Schools: 32 elementary schools; 9 secondary schools *Grades:* K - 12 *Enrollment:* 13517 *Number of Employees:* 1,600
Doreen Dewar, Chair, Board, 705-682-9449
dedward@rainbowschools.ca
Norm Blaseg, Director, Education, 705-674-3171, ext. 7216
Dennis Bazinet, Superintendent, Business, 705-674-3171, ext. 7236
Bruce Bourget, Superintendent, Schools, 705-674-3171, ext. 7213
Judy Noble, Superintendent, Schools, 705-674-3171, ext. 7213
Kathy Wachnuk, Superintendent, Schools, 705-674-3171, ext. 7236

Thunder Bay: **Lakehead District School Board**
Also known as: Lakehead Public Schools
Jim McCuaig Education Centre
2135 Sills St., Thunder Bay, ON P7E 5T2
Tel: 807-625-5100; *Fax:* 807-622-0961
Toll-Free: 888-565-1406
webmaster@lakeheadschools.ca
www.lakeheadschools.ca
www.facebook.com/LakeheadSchools
twitter.com/LakeheadSchools
www.youtube.com/user/LakeheadSchools
Number of Schools: 25 elementary schools; 3 secondary schools; 1 adult education centre *Grades:* K - 12; Adult Ed. *Enrollment:* 8802 *Number of Employees:* 2236
Ellen Chambers, Chair, Board, 807-629-1839
ellen_chambers@lakeheadschools.ca
Ian MacRae, Director, Education, 807-625-5131
imacrae@lakeheadschools.ca
Helen Valnycki, Manager, Human Resources & Payroll, 807-625-5171
helen_valnycki@lakeheadschools.ca
Gerrie Tennant, Supervisor, Purchasing, 807-625-5275
gtennant@lakeheadschools.ca
David Wright, Superintendent, Business, 807-625-5126
david_wright@lakeheadschools.ca
AJ Keene, Superintendent, Education, 807-625-5100
akeene@lakeheadschools.ca
Michelle Probizanski, Superintendent, Education, 807-625-5126
michelle_probizanski@lakeheadschools.ca

Timmins: **District School Board Ontario North East**
P.O. Box 1020
Timmins, ON P4N 7H7
Tel: 705-360-1151; *Fax:* 705-268-7100
Toll-Free: 800-381-7280
comments@dsb1.ca
www.dsb1.ca
Other Information: New Liskeard Office: 705-647-7394 (local)
Number of Schools: 25 elementary; 9 secondary; 1 alternative *Grades:* K - 12; Adult Ed. *Enrollment:* 8105
Bob Brush, Chair, 705-288-4974
bob.brush@dsb1.ca
Lesleigh Dye, Director, Education, 705-360-7689
lesleigh.dye@dsb1.ca
Jim Rowe, Senior Manager of Human Resources
Pearl Fong-West, Superintendent of Business/Finance and Treasurer

---

Toronto: **Toronto District School Board (TDSB)**
5050 Yonge St., Toronto, ON M2N 5N8
Tel: 416-397-3000
generalinquiries@tdsb.on.ca
www.tdsb.on.ca
Other Information: Media Relations, Phone: 416-395-2721
www.facebook.com/toronto.dsb
twitter.com/TDSB
www.youtube.com/user/TDSByt
Number of Schools: 583 *Grades:* K - 12; Adult Ed.; French Immersion *Enrollment:* 247000 *Number of Employees:* 16,360 permanent teachers; 15,500 permanent support staff; 6,350 occasional staff
Alexander Brown, Chair, Board
John Malloy, Director, Education, 416-397-3190
john.malloy@tdsb.on.ca
Carlene Jackson, Associate Director, Operations & Service Excellence, 416-393-8780
Ross Parry, Executive Officer, Government, Public and Community Relations
Jim Spyropoulos, Executive Superintendent, Human Rights and Indigenous Ed.
Shirley Chan, Superintendent, 416-396-9178
shirley.chan@tdsb.on.ca
Peter Chang, Superintendent, 416-394-2032
p.chang@tdsb.on.ca
John Chasty, Superintendent, 416-396-9188
john.chasty@tdsb.on.ca
Curtis Ennis, Superintendent, 416-395-8819
curtis.ennis@tdsb.on.ca

Mike Gallagher, Superintendent, 416-394-2048
mike.gallagher@tdsb.on.ca
Tracy Hayhurst, Superintendent, 416-396-9174
tracy.hayhurst@tdsb.on.ca
Mary Jane McNamara, Superintendent, 416-394-2036
maryjane.mcnamara@tdsb.on.ca
Louie Papathanasakis, Superintendent, 416-395-8809
louie.papathanasakis@tdsb.on.ca
Nadira Persaud, Superintendent, 416-396-9190
nadira.persaud@tdsb.on.ca
Jane Phillips-Long, Superintendent, 416-394-2042
jane.phillips-long@tdsb.on.ca
Audley Salmon, Superintendent, 416-395-8808
audley.salmon@tdsb.on.ca
Kerry-Lynn Stadnyk, Superintendent, 416-396-9192
kerry-lynn.stadnyk@tdsb.on.ca
Sandra Tondat, Superintendent, 416-394-2046
sandra.tondat@tdsb.on.ca

Whitby: **Durham District School Board (DDSB)**
Education Centre
400 Taunton Rd. East, Whitby, ON L1R 2K6
Tel: 905-666-5500; *Fax:* 905-666-6474
Toll-Free: 800-265-3968
ddsb.ca
Other Information: Trustees' Administrative Assistant, Phone: 905-666-6363
TTY: 905-666-6943
www.facebook.com/DurhamDistrictSchoolBoard
twitter.com/durhamdsb
www.instagram.com/durhamschools
Number of Schools: 133 schools *Grades:* K - 12; Special Ed.; Continuing Ed. *Enrollment:* 70000 *Number of Employees:* 7,000 teaching & educational services staff
Norah Marsh, Acting Director, Education, 905-666-6312
Chris Braney, Chairperson, Board of Trustees
Jim Markovski, Acting Associate Director, Academic Services, 905-666-6351
Carla Kisko, Interim Associate Director, Corporate Services, 905-666-6459

Windsor: **Greater Essex County District School Board (GECDSB)**
P.O. Box 210
451 Park St. West, Windsor, ON N9A 6K1
Tel: 519-255-3200; *Toll-Free:* 888-779-7735
www.publicboard.ca
Other Information: Adult & Continuing Education, Phone: 519-253-5006
www.facebook.com/gecdsbcomm
twitter.com/gecdsbpro
www.youtube.com/GECDSBMediaCentre
Number of Schools: 55 elementary schools; 15 secondary schools; 3 agency schools; 1 continuing education program *Grades:* K - 12; Alternative Ed. *Enrollment:* 36000 *Number of Employees:* 4,700
Erin Kelly, Director, Education, 519-255-3200, ext. 10259
director@publicboard.ca
Ron Le Clair, Chair, Board of Trustees, 519-995-2277
ron.leclair@publicboard.ca
Vicki Houston, Superintendent, Human Resources, 519-255-3200, ext. 10254
vicki.houston@publicboard.ca
Todd Awender, Superintendent, School Development and Design, 519-255-3200, ext. 10394
todd.awender@publicboard.ca
Shelley Armstrong, Superintendent, Business, 519-255-3200, ext. 10210
shelley.armstrong@publicboard.ca
Jeff Hillman, Superintendent, Education - School Effectiveness, 519-255-3200, ext. 10316
jeff.hillman@publicboard.ca
Clara Howitt, Superintendent, Education - Program & Professional Learning, 519-255-3200, ext. 10255
clara.howitt@publicboard.ca
Chris Mills, Superintendent, Education - Elementary Staffing, 519-255-3200, ext. 10253
chris.mills@publicboard.ca
Mike Wilcox, Superintendent, Education - Special Education, 519-255-3200, ext. 10223
mike.wilcox@publicboard.ca
Sharon Pyke, Superintendent, Education - Student Well-Being, 519-255-3200, ext. 10222
sharon.pyke@publicboard.ca

Catholic

Aurora: York Catholic District School Board
320 Bloomington Rd. West, Aurora, ON L4G 0M1, Canada
Tel: 905-713-1211; *Fax:* 905-713-1272
communications@ycdsb.ca
www.ycdsb.ca
Other Information: Alternate Phone: 416-221-5051
twitter.com/ycdsb
www.youtube.com/user/YorkCatholicDSB
Number of Schools: 85 elementary; 16 secondary; 1 alternative
education *Grades:* K - 12 *Enrollment:* 54000 *Number of
Employees:* 5000 teaching staff
Dominic Mazzotta, Chair, Board, 905-713-1211, ext. 17130
dominic.mazzotta@ycdsb.ca
Ab Falconi, Director, Education, 905-713-1211, ext. 13000
ab.falconi@ycdsb.ca
Anthony Arcadi, Superintendent, Education - School Leadership,
905-713-1211, ext. 13656
anthony.arcadi@ycdsb.ca
Tina D'Acunto, Superintendent, Education - School Leadership,
905-713-1211, ext. 13130
tina.dacunto@ycdsb.ca
Opiyo Oloya, Superintendent, Education - School Leadership,
905-713-1211, ext. 13625
opiyo.oloya@ycdsb.ca
Eugene Pivato, Superintendent, Education - School Leadership,
905-713-1211, ext. 13133
eugene.pivato@ycdsb.ca
Jennifer Sarna, Superintendent, Education - School Leadership,
905-713-1211, ext. 13663
jennifer.sarna@ycdsb.ca
Laura Sawicky, Superintendent, Education - School Leadership,
905-713-1211, ext. 13123
laura.sawicky@ycdsb.ca
Mary Battista, Superintendent, Education - Curriculum &
Assessment, 905-713-1211, ext. 13656
mary.battista@ycdsb.ca
Marianne Fedrigoni, Superintendent, Education - Exceptional
Learners, 905-713-1211, ext. 11630
marianne.fedrigoni@ycdsb.ca
Nancy Di Nardo, Superintendent, Human Resources,
905-713-1211, ext. 13850
nancy.dinardo@ycdsb.ca
Darlene Clapham, Chief Information Officer, 905-713-1211, ext.
12386
darlene.clapham@ycdsb.ca
Anthony Yeung, Chief Financial Officer; Treasurer, Board,
905-713-1211, ext. 12300
anthony.yeung@ycdsb.ca
Joe McLoughlin, Controller, Plant & Accommodation Services,
905-713-1211, ext. 12387
joe.mcloughlin@ycdsb.ca
Tom Pechkovsky, Coordinating Manager, Planning &
Operations, 905-713-1211, ext. 12374
tom.pechkovsky@ycdsb.ca

Barrie: Simcoe Muskoka Catholic District School Board (SMCDSB)
46 Alliance Blvd., Barrie, ON L4M 5K3
Tel: 705-722-3555; *Fax:* 705-722-6534
info@smcdsb.on.ca
www.smcdsb.on.ca
www.facebook.com/SMCDSB
twitter.com/SMCDSB
Number of Schools: 41 elementary schools; 9 secondary
schools *Grades:* K - 12 *Enrollment:* 21000 *Number of
Employees:* 4,000
Joe Zerdin, Chair, Board, 705-722-3559, ext. 347
jzerdin@smcdsb.on.ca
Brian Beal, Director, Education
directorofeducation@smcdsb.on.ca
Kim Weishar, Superintendent, Education - Elementary,
705-722-3555, ext. 247
Chris Woodcroft, Superintendent, Education - Elementary,
705-722-3555, ext. 321
Lonnie Bolton, Superintendent, Education - Elementary,
705-722-3555, ext. 272
Andy Sendzik, Superintendent, Education - Secondary,
705-722-3555, ext. 228
Suzanne Olimer, Superintendent of Business and Finance,
705-722-3555, ext. 244

Brantford: Brant Haldimand Norfolk Catholic District School Board (BHNCDSB)
Catholic Education Centre
P.O. Box 217
322 Fairview Dr., Brantford, ON N3T 5M8, Canada
Tel: 519-756-6369; *Fax:* 519-756-9913
info@bhncdsb.ca
www.bhncdsb.ca
Other Information: Purchasing: purchasing@bhncdsb.ca;
519-756-9913
twitter.com/bhncdsb
www.youtube.com/user/BHNCDSBvideo
Number of Schools: 28 elementary; 4 secondary *Grades:* K - 12;
Special Ed. *Enrollment:* 10000 *Number of Employees:* 700+
teachers; 300+ non-academic staff
Rick Petrella, Chair, Board, 226-388-1548
rpetrella@bhncdsb.ca
Mike McDonald, Director, Education; Secretary, 519-756-6505,
ext. 223
directorsoffice@bhncdsb.ca
Michelle Shypula, Superintendent, Education, 519-756-6505,
ext. 237
lblasdell@bhncdsb.ca
Leslie Telfer, Superintendent, Education, 519-756-6505, ext. 237
lblasdell@bhncdsb.ca
Scott Keys, Superintendent, Business; Treasurer, 519-756-6505,
ext. 272
lluciani@bhncdsb.ca
Tracey Austin, Manager, Communications & Community
Relations, 519-756-6505, ext. 234
taustin@bhncdsb.ca
Norm Cicci, Manager, Information Technology, 519-756-6505,
ext. 317
ncicci@bhncdsb.ca
Lou Citino, Manager, Facilities & Construction Projects,
519-756-6505, ext. 125
lcitino@bhncdsb.ca
Philip Kuckyt, Manager, Transportation Services, 519-751-7532,
ext. 1
Colleen Oldman, Manager, Human Resources, 519-756-6505,
ext. 235
coldman@bhncdsb.ca
Pat Petrella, Manager, Finance, 519-756-6505, ext. 228
ppetrella@bhncdsb.ca
Terre Slaght, Principal, Continuing Education, 519-756-6505,
ext. 402
tslaght@bhncdsb.ca

Burlington: Halton Catholic District School Board (HCDSB)
Catholic Education Centre
802 Drury Lane, Burlington, ON L7R 2Y2
Tel: 905-632-6300; *Fax:* 905-333-4661
Toll-Free: 800-741-8382
comments@hcdsb.org
www.hcdsb.org
Other Information: Special Education Services, E-mail:
speced@hcdsb.org
www.facebook.com/HCDSB
twitter.com/HCDSB
Number of Schools: 45 elementary schools; 9 secondary
schools; 3 continuing education centres *Grades:* K - 12;
Continuing Ed. *Enrollment:* 35000 *Number of Employees:* 3,500
Vincent Iantonasi, Chair, Board, 905-536-4100
iantomasiv@hcdsb.org
Pat Daly, Director, Education, 905-632-6314, ext. 115
Lisa-Marie Collimore, Chief Officer, Research & Development
Services, 905-632-6314, ext. 370
Wayne Elshof, Manager, Information Technology Services,
905-632-6314, ext. 550
Frederick Thibeault, Senior Manager, Planning Services,
905-632-6314, ext. 107
Andrea Swinden, Manager, Strategic Communications Services,
905-632-6314, ext. 159
Daniel Tkalcic, Manager, Purchasing Services, 905-632-6314,
ext. 132
Camillo Cipriano, Superintendent, Special Education Services,
905-632-6314, ext. 125
Ryan Merrick, Superintendent, Facility Management Services,
905-632-6314, ext. 171
Aaron Lofts, Superintendent, Business Services; Treasurer,
905-632-6314, ext. 131
Joseph O'Hara, Superintendent, Human Resource Services,
905-632-6314, ext. 129
Anna Prkacin, Superintendent, Curriculum Services,
905-632-6314, ext. 123
Jeff Crowell, Superintendent, School Services, 905-632-6314,
ext. 127
Colin McGillicuddy, Superintendent, School Services,
905-632-6314, ext. 124
Lorraine Naar, Superintendent, School Services, 905-632-6314,
ext. 135

Antonia Pinelli, Superintendent, School Services, 905-632-6314,
ext. 181

Burlington: Resource Centre
2333 Headon Forest Dr., Burlington, ON L7M 3X6
Tel: 905-632-4814

Dublin: Huron-Perth Catholic District School Board
P.O. Box 70
87 Mill St., Dublin, ON N0K 1E0, Canada
Tel: 519-345-2440; *Fax:* 519-345-2449
Toll-Free: 800-265-8508
www.huronperthcatholic.ca
www.facebook.com/hpcdsb
twitter.com/hpcdsb
Number of Schools: 16 elementary; 2 secondary *Grades:* K - 12
Enrollment: 4600 *Number of Employees:* 500
Amy Cronin, Chair, Board, 519-887-9158
acronin@hpcdsb.ca
Chris Roehrig, Director, Education, 519-345-2440
croehrig@hpcdsb.ca
Dawne Boersen, Supervisory Officer, 519-345-2440, ext. 8052
dboersen@hpcdsb.ca
Tara Boreham, Supervisory Officer, 519-345-2440, ext. 8051
tboreham@hpcdsb.ca
Mary-Ellen Ducharme, Superintendent, Business, 519-345-2440,
ext. 8065
mducharme@hpcdsb.ca

Fort Frances: Northwest Catholic District School Board
555 Flinders Ave., Fort Frances, ON P9A 3L2, Canada
Tel: 807-274-2931; *Fax:* 807-274-8792
Toll-Free: 888-311-2931
info@tncdsb.on.ca
www.tncdsb.on.ca
www.facebook.com/tncdsb
Number of Schools: 6 elementary *Grades:* K - 8
David Sharp, Chair, Board
dsharp@tncdsb.on.ca
Brendan Hyatt, Director, Education, 807-274-2931, ext. 1222
Jackie Robinson, Superintendent, Education, 807-223-4663, ext.
1033
Colin Drombolis, Manager, Information Systems, 807-274-2931,
ext. 1227
Toby Munro, Manager, Facilities, 807-274-2931, ext. 1231
Seija Van Haesendonck, Senior Manager, Finance,
807-223-4663, ext. 1031

Dryden
Business Office
Suite B, 75 Van Horne Ave., Dryden, ON P8N 2B2, Canada
Tel: 807-223-4663; *Fax:* 807-223-4014
Toll-Free: 877-235-4663
Rick Boisvert, Director, Education, 807-274-2931, ext. 1222
Anne-Marie Fitzgerald, Chair
amfitzgerald@tncdsb.on.ca
Margot Saari, Superintendent of Education, 807-223-4663, ext.
1033
Chris Howarth, Superintendent of Business, 807-223-4663, ext.
1024
Natasha Getson, Curriculum Coordinator, 807-223-4663, ext.
1023
Seija Van Haesendonck, Manager of Finance, 807-223-4663,
ext. 1031

Guelph: Wellington Catholic District School Board
75 Woolwich St., Guelph, ON N1H 6N6
Tel: 519-821-4600; *Fax:* 519-824-3088
generalinquiries@wellingtoncdsb.ca
www.wellingtoncdsb.ca
www.facebook.com/WellingtonCDSB
twitter.com/wellingtoncath
Number of Schools: 18 elementary schools; 3 secondary
schools; 1 alternative education program *Grades:* K - 12;
Alternate Ed. *Enrollment:* 7982 *Number of Employees:* 855
Marino Gazzola, Chair, Board, 519-824-6069
marino.gazzola@wellingtoncdsb.ca
Tamara Nugent, Director, Education, 519-821-4640, ext. 214
tamara.nugent@wellingtoncdsb.ca
Tracy McLennan, Superintendent, Corporate Services &
Treasurer, 519-821-4640, ext. 229
tracy.mclennan@wellingtoncdsb.ca
Brian Capovilla, Superintendent, Human Resources,
519-821-4640, ext. 207
brian.capovilla@wellingtoncdsb.ca
Michael Glazier, Superintendent, Education, 519-821-4640, ext.
244
michael.glazier@wellingtoncdsb.ca
Michelle Sawa, Superintendent, Education, 519-821-4640, ext.
209
michelle.sawa@wellingtoncdsb.ca

Hamilton: Hamilton-Wentworth Catholic District School Board (HWCDSB)
Father Kyran Kennedy Catholic Education Centre
P.O. Box 2012
90 Mulberry St., Hamilton, ON L8N 3R9
Tel: 905-525-2930; *Fax:* 905-525-1724
www.hwcdsb.ca
Other Information: Summer Fax: 905-525-2914; Emergency
Phone: 905-522-6680
www.facebook.com/hwcdsb
twitter.com/HWCDSB
www.instagram.com/hwcdsb
Number of Schools: 48 elementary schools; 7 secondary
schools; 1 adult education centre *Grades:* K - 12; Continuing Ed.
Patrick Daly, Chair, Board, 905-525-2930
dalyp@hwcdsb.ca
D. Hansen, Director, Education, 905-525-2930, ext. 2181
P. Pace-Gubekjian, Associate Director of Corporate Services,
905-525-2930, ext. 2139
A. Romano, Executive Officer, Human Resources,
905-525-2930

Hanover: Bruce-Grey Catholic District School Board
799 - 16th Ave., Hanover, ON N4N 3A1, Canada
Tel: 519-364-5820; *Fax:* 519-364-5882
bruce_grey@bgcdsb.org
www.bgcdsb.org
www.facebook.com/brucegreycdsbpage
twitter.com/BGCDSB
www.youtube.com/user/BruceGreyCatholicDSB
Number of Schools: 11 elementary; 2 secondary *Grades:* K - 12;
Religious Ed. *Enrollment:* 3600 *Number of Employees:* 400
Beverley Eckensweiler, Chair, Board, 519-376-2770
bev_eckensweiler@bgcdsb.ca
Gary O'Donnell, Director, Education, 519-364-5820, ext. 224
Mike Bethune, Superintendent, Education, 519-364-5820, ext. 231
Karyn Bruneel, Superintendent, Education, 519-364-5820, ext. 226
Cathy DeGoey, Superintendent, Education, 519-364-5820, ext. 225
Alecia Lantz, Superintendent, Business, 519-364-5820, ext. 223
Danielle de Boer, Executive Manager, Human Resources,
519-364-5820, ext. 232
Joyce Benninger, Supervisor, Health and Safety, 519-364-5820, ext. 258
Jaime Carter, Supervisor, Financial Services, 519-364-5820, ext. 256
Nancy Fischer, Supervisor, Payroll Services, 519-364-5820, ext. 275
Al Hastie, Supervisor, Facility Services, 519-364-5820, ext. 277

Kemptville: Catholic District School Board of Eastern Ontario
c/o Kemptville Board Office
P.O. Box 2222
2755 Hwy. 43, Kemptville, ON K0G 1J0, Canada
Tel: 613-258-7757; *Fax:* 613-258-7134
Toll-Free: 1-800-443-4562
mail@cdsbeo.on.ca
www.cdsbeo.on.ca
Other Information: hr@cdsbeo.on.ca; religiousod@cdsbeo.on.ca
www.facebook.com/CDSBEO
twitter.com/CDSBEO
www.instagram.com/cdsbeo
Number of Schools: 39 elementary; 10 secondary *Grades:* K - 12 *Enrollment:* 13000 *Number of Employees:* 881 teachers; 560 support staff
Todd Lalonde, Chair, Board, 613-933-6442
todd.lalonde@cdsbeo.on.ca
John Cameron, Director, Education, 613-258-7757, ext. 3077
director@cdsbeo.on.ca
Brent Bovaird, Superintendent, School Effectiveness,
613-258-7757, ext. 3181
judith.beriault@cdsbeo.on.ca
Natalie Cameron, Superintendent, School Effectiveness,
613-933-1720, ext. 3099
karen.oshaughnessy@cdsbeo.on.ca
Norma McDonald, Superintendent, School Effectiveness,
613-258-7757, ext. 3123
karen.hogan@cdsbeo.on.ca

Kenora: Kenora Catholic District School Board
Catholic Education Center
1292 Heenan Pl., Kenora, ON P9N 2Y8, Canada
Tel: 807-468-9851; *Fax:* 807-468-8094
info@kcdsb.on.ca
www.kcdsb.on.ca
www.facebook.com/KenoraCatholic
twitter.com/KCDSB
www.youtube.com/user/KenoraCatholicDSB

Number of Schools: 4 elementary; 1 secondary *Grades:* K - 12
Enrollment: 1453
Teresa Gallik, Chair, Board
tgallik@kcdsb.on.ca
Derek Haime, Director, Education, 807-468-9851, ext. 239
dhaime@kcdsb.on.ca
Michelle Sawa, Superintendent, Instructional Services,
807-468-9851, ext. 232
msawa@kcdsb.on.ca
Paul White, Superintendent, Instructional Services,
807-468-9851, ext. 249
pwhite@kcdsb.on.ca
Alison Smith, Superintendent, Business Services, 807-468-9851,
ext. 225
alsmith@kcdsb.on.ca
Craig Debbo, Manager, Information Technology Services,
807-468-9851, ext. 242
cdebbo@kcdsb.on.ca
Krista Helsel, Manager, Human Resource Services,
807-468-9851, ext. 233
khelsel@kcdsb.on.ca
Andrew Poirier, Manager, Operational Services, 807-468-9851,
ext. 227
apoirier@kcdsb.on.ca

Kitchener: Waterloo Catholic District School Board (WCDSB)
35 Weber St. West, #A, Kitchener, ON N2H 3Z1
Tel: 519-578-3660; *Fax:* 519-578-5291
info@wcdsb.ca
www.wcdsb.ca
www.facebook.com/wcdsb
twitter.com/WCDSBNewswire
www.linkedin.com/company/wcdsb
www.youtube.com/WCDSBTube
Number of Schools: 43 elementary schools; 5 secondary
schools; 4 adult & continuing education campuses *Grades:* JK -
12 *Enrollment:* 36000 *Number of Employees:* 2640
Bill Conway, Chair, Board, 519-241-9574
bill.conway@wcdsb.ca
Loretta Notten, Director, Education & Secretary, Board
loretta.notten@wcdsb.ca
Chris Demers, Chief Information Officer
chris.demers@wcdsb.ca
John Shewchuk, Chief Managing Officer
john.shewchuk@wcdsb.ca
Jeff Admans, Manager, Supply & Administrative Services
jeff.admans@wcdsb.ca
Shesh Maharaj, Executive Superintendent, Corporate Services
shesh.maharaj@wcdsb.ca
Maria Ivankovic, Superintendent, Learning - Adult & Continuing
Education
maria.ivankovic@wcdsb.ca
John Klein, Superintendent, Learning - Program Services
john.klein@wcdsb.ca
Judy Merkel, Superintendent, Learning - Leadership Strategy
judy.merkel@wcdsb.ca
Richard Olson, Superintendent, Learning - Student Success
richard.olson@wcdsb.ca
Laura Shoemaker, Superintendent, Learning - Special Education
laura.shoemaker@wcdsb.ca

L'Orignal: Conseil scolaire de district catholique de l'Est ontarien (CSDCEO)
875, ch de comté 17, L'Orignal, ON K0B 1K0
Tél: 613-675-4691; *Téléc:* 613-675-2921
Ligne sans frais: 800-204-4098
courriel@csdceo.org
csdceo.org
www.facebook.com/csdceo
twitter.com/CSDCEO
Number of Schools: 33 *Grades:* Élém.-Sec. *Enrollment:* 10000
François Bazinet, Président
François Turpin, Directeur, Éducation et Secrétaire,
613-675-4691
Chantal-Christin Gratton, Surintendante, Éducation,
800-204-4098, ext. 256
Martin Lavigne, Surintendant, Affaires et Trésorier,
800-204-4098, ext. 212
Maryse Legault, Surintendante, Éducation, 800-204-4098, ext.
253
Lyne Racine, Surintendante, Éducation, 800-204-4098, ext. 287

London: London District Catholic School Board (LDCSB)
5200 Wellington Rd. South, London, ON N6E 3X8
Tel: 519-663-2088; *Fax:* 519-663-9250
www.ldcsb.ca
www.facebook.com/LDCSBSchools
twitter.com/LDCSB
www.linkedin.com/company/ldcsb
www.instagram.com/ldcsb

Number of Schools: 43 elementary schools; 9 secondary
schools; 1 continuing education centre *Grades:* JK - 12;
Continuing Ed. *Enrollment:* 22000 *Number of Employees:* 3,000
John Jevnikar, Chair, Board, 519-619-9724
jjevnikar@ldscb.ca
Linda Staudt, Director, Education & Secretary, 519-663-2088,
ext. 40002
Linda Wells, Supervisor, Library & Media Services,
519-663-2088, ext. 41018
Debbie Jordan, Superintendent, Business
Jim Vair, Superintendent, Human Resources & General
Counsel, 519-663-2088, ext. 43403
Ana Paula Fernandes, Superintendent, Education
Kathy Furlong, Superintendent, Education, 519-663-2088, ext.
40007
Kelly Holbrough, Superintendent, Education, 519-663-2088, ext.
42203
Vince Romeo, Superintendent, Education, 519-663-2088, ext.
40009

Mississauga: Dufferin-Peel Catholic District School Board (DPCDSB)
40 Matheson Blvd. West, Mississauga, ON L5R 1C5
Tel: 905-890-1221; *Fax:* 905-890-7610
Toll-Free: 800-387-9501
www.dpcdsb.org
www.facebook.com/DPCDSBSchools
twitter.com/DPCDSBSchools
www.linked.com/company/dpcdsb
www.youtube.com/user/DPCDSBVideos
Number of Schools: 125 elementary schools; 26 secondary
schools *Grades:* K - 12; Adult Ed. *Enrollment:* 81000 *Number of
Employees:* 11,000
Sharon Hobin, Chair, Board, 905-301-1210
sharon.hobin@dpcdsb.org
Marianne Mazzorato, Director, Education, 905-890-0708, ext.
24201
Daniel Del Bianco, Associate Director, Corporate Services
Julie Cherepacha, Executive Superintendent, Financial Services
Deb Finegan-Downey, Superintendent, Special Education &
Learning Services
Brian Hester, Superintendent, Financial Services
Stephanie Strong, Superintendent, Human Resources &
Employee Relations
Max Vecchiarino, Superintendent, Policy, Strategy & Global
Learning

Napanee: Algonquin & Lakeshore Catholic District School Board
151 Dairy Ave., Napanee, ON K7R 4B2
Tel: 613-354-2255; *Toll-Free:* 800-581-1116
info@alcdsb.on.ca
www.alcdsb.on.ca
www.facebook.com/alcdsb
twitter.com/ALCDSB
www.youtube.com/user/ALCDSBvid
Number of Schools: 32 elementary; 5 secondary; 2 outdoor
education centres *Grades:* Elementary - Secondary *Enrollment:*
11000 *Number of Employees:* 1,300
David DeSantis, Director, Education, 613-354-6257, ext. 445
Breanne Bradshaw, Superintendent, Finance & Business
Services, 613-354-6257, ext. 475
Michael Faught, Superintendent, Education, 613-354-6257, ext.
439
Darcey French, Superintendent, Education, 613-354-6257, ext.
447
Michele McGrath, Superintendent, Education, 613-354-6257,
ext. 439
Carey Smith-Dewey, Superintendent, Education, 613-354-6257,
ext. 447

North Bay: Conseil scolaire catholique Franco-Nord
681-C, rue Chippewa ouest, North Bay, ON P1B 6G8
Tél: 705-472-1702; *Téléc:* 705-474-3824
information@franco-nord.ca
www.franco-nord.ca
www.facebook.com/CSCFrancoNord
twitter.com/CSCFrancoNord
Number of Schools: 11 élémentaires; 3 secondaires *Grades:*
Élem.-Sec. *Enrollment:* 3400
Ronald Demers, Président
demersr@franco-nord.ca
Monique Ménard, Directrice, Éducation, 705-472-1701, ext. 2360
menardm@franco-nord.ca
Marc Cantin, Surintendant, Affaires, 705-472-1701, ext. 2300
cantinm@franco-nord.ca
Éric Foisy, Surintendant, Éducation, 705-472-1701, ext. 2350
foisye@franco-nord.ca
Serge Levac, Surintendent, Éducation, 705-472-1701, ext. 2350
levacs@franco-nord.ca

North Bay: **Nipissing-Parry Sound Catholic District School Board (NPSC)**
1000 High St., North Bay, ON P1B 6S6, Canada
Tel: 705-472-1201; *Fax:* 705-472-0507
contact@npsc.ca
www.npsc.ca
twitter.com/npsc_schools
Number of Schools: 11 elementary; 1 secondary; 1 continuing ed. *Grades:* K - 12; Adult Ed. *Enrollment:* 2674 *Number of Employees:* 212 teachers
Judy Manitowabi, Chair, Board, 705-472-1201, ext. 31243
manitowj@npsc.ca
Anna Marie Bitonti, Director, Education, 705-472-1201, ext. 31243
bitontia@npsc.ca
Paula Mann, Superintendent, Education, 705-472-1201, ext. 31242
mannp@npsc.ca
Jody Weller, Superintendent, Education, 705-472-1201, ext. 31242
wellerj@npsc.ca
Grace Barnhardt, Superintendent, Business, 705-472-1201, ext. 31225
barnharg@npsc.ca
Connie Vander Wall, Senior Manager, Human Resources, 705-472-1201, ext. 31218
vanderwc@npsc.ca
Danny Russo, Senior Manager, Plant Services and Health & Safety, 705-472-1201, ext. 31202
russod@npsc.ca

Oshawa: **Durham Catholic District School Board (DCDSB)**
650 Rossland Rd. West, Oshawa, ON L1J 7C4
Tel: 905-576-6150; *Fax:* 905-721-8239
Toll-Free: 877-482-0722
www.dcdsb.ca
www.facebook.com/124498987628845
twitter.com/DurhamCatholic
www.youtube.com/DurhamCatholicDSB
Number of Schools: 38 elementary schools; 7 secondary schools; 6 alternative & continuing education sites *Grades:* K - 12; Adult Ed.; Alternative Ed. *Enrollment:* 21150 *Number of Employees:* 2,191
Janice Oldman, Chair, Board, 905-431-8759
Tracy Barill, Director, Education, 905-576-6150, ext. 22317
Ronald Rodriguez, Chief Information Officer, 905-576-6150, ext. 2287
Ryan Putnam, Superintendent, Business Services & Chief Financial Officer, 905-576-6150, ext. 22244
Michael Gray, Superintendent, Human Resources and Administrative Services, 905-576-6150, ext. 22285
Janine Bowyer, Superintendent, Education, 905-576-6150, ext. 22279
Rosemary LeClair, Superintendent, Education, 905-576-6150, ext. 22238
Susie Lee-Fernandes, Superintendent, Education, 905-576-6150, ext. 22254
John Mullins, Superintendent, Education, 905-576-6150, ext. 22250
Mariah O'Reilly, Superintendent, Education, 905-576-6150, ext. 22191

Ottawa: **Conseil des écoles catholiques du Centre-Est (CECCE)**
French Catholic School Board in Ottawa
4000, rue Labelle, Ottawa, ON K1J 1A1
Tél: 613-744-2555; *Téléc:* 613-746-3081
Ligne sans frais: 1-888-230-5131
accueil@ecolecatholique.ca
www.ecolecatholique.ca
www.facebook.com/ecolecatholique
twitter.com/ecolecatholique
ww.linkedin.com/company/1781547
www.instagram.com/ecolecatholique
Number of Schools: 44 écoles élémentaire; 13 écoles secondaires; 1 école pour adultes *Grades:* Mat. - 12; Adultes *Enrollment:* 25500 *Number of Employees:* Plus de 2750 *Note:* Chef de file reconnu pour la transformation de l'expérience d'apprentissage, l'excellence et la bienveillance de ses écoles catholiques et sa synergie avec la communauté, le CECCE est le plus grand réseau canadien d'écoles de langue française à l'extérieur du Québec.
Johanne Lacombe, Présidente, Conseil
lacombej@ecolecatholique.ca
Réjean Sirois, Directeur, Éducation & Secrétaire-trésorier
siroir@ecolecatholique.ca
Laurie-Eve Bergeron, Directrice exécutive, Ressources humaines
bergel@ecolecatholique.ca
Christine Brisson, Directrice exécutive, Services administratifs
brissc@ecolecatholique.ca

Anouar Nemry, Directeur exécutif, Communications et marketing, 613-746-3066
nemrya@ecolecatholique.ca
Philippe Lebel, Directeur adjoint, Communications et marketing, 613-746-3059
lebelp@ecolecatholique.ca

Ottawa: **Ottawa Catholic District School Board**
570 West Hunt Club Rd., Ottawa, ON K2G 3R4, Canada
Tel: 613-224-2222; *Fax:* 613-224-5063
info@ocsb.ca
www.facebook.com/OttCatholicSB
twitter.com/ottcatholicsb
www.instagram.com/ottcatholicsb
Number of Schools: 69 elementary; 1 intermediate; 15 secondary; 1 adult high; 4 continuing education centres *Grades:* K - 12; Continuing Education *Enrollment:* 42800 *Number of Employees:* 4600 full-time equivalent teaching and non-teaching staff
Mark Mullan, Chair, Board, 613-841-4836
mark.mullan@ocsb.ca
Denise Andre, Director, Education; Secretary-Treasurer, 613-224-4455, ext. 2272
director@ocsb.ca
Fred Chrystal, Superintendent, Planning and Facilities, 613-224-4455, ext. 2322
fred.chrystal@ocsb.ca
Mary Donaghy, Superintendent, Student Success - Elementary, 613-224-4455, ext. 2345
mary.donaghy@ocsb.ca
Geoff Edwards, Superintendent, Learning Technologies, 613-224-4455, ext. 2303
geoffrey.edwards@ocsb.ca
Debbie Frendo, Superintendent, Student Success - Intermediate and Secondary, 613-224-4455, ext. 2371
debbie.frendo@ocsb.ca
Stephen McCabe, Superintendent, Human Resources, 613-224-4455, ext. 2402
stephen.mccabe@ocsb.ca
Shelley Montgomery, Superintendent, Leading and Learning, 613-224-4455, ext. 2342
shelley.montgomery@ocsb.ca
Lisa Schimmens, Superintendent, Finance & Administration; Assistant Treasurer, 613-224-4455, ext. 2281
lisa.schimmens@ocsb.ca
Manon Séguin, Superintendent, Special Education and Student Services, 613-224-4455, ext. 2351
manon.seguin@ocsb.ca
Ben Vallati, Superintendent, Continuing and Community Education, 613-224-4455, ext. 2501
ben.vallati@ocsb.ca

Pembroke: **Renfrew County Catholic District School Board (RCCDSB)**
499 Pembroke St. West, Pembroke, ON K8A 5P1, Canada
Tel: 613-735-1031; *Fax:* 613-735-2649
Toll-Free: 800-267-0191
www.rccdsb.edu.on.ca
www.facebook.com/RCCDSB
twitter.com/RCCDSB
Number of Schools: 18 elementary; 2 secondary; 2 alternative secondary *Grades:* K - 12 *Enrollment:* 4600 *Number of Employees:* 525 permanent staff; 300 occaisional staff
David Howard, Chair, Board, 613-687-6593
dhoward@rccdsb.edu.on.ca
Jaimie Perry, Director, Education, 613-735-1031, ext. 202
jperry@rccdsb.edu.on.ca
Elizabeth Burchat, Superintendent, Educational Services, 613-735-1031, ext. 207
eburchat@rccdsb.edu.on.ca
Mary-Lise Rowat, Superintendent, Educational Services, 613-735-1031, ext. 207
mrowat@rccdsb.edu.on.ca
Mark Searson, Superintendent, Educational Services, 613-735-1031, ext. 207
msearson@rccdsb.edu.on.ca
Mary Lynn Schauer, Superintendent, Business Services, 613-735-1031, ext. 311
mschauer@rccdsb.edu.on.ca

Peterborough: **Peterborough Victoria Northumberland & Clarington Catholic District School Board (PVNCCDSB)**
1355 Lansdowne St. West, Peterborough, ON K9J 7M3, Canada
Tel: 705-748-4861; *Fax:* 705-748-9734
Toll-Free: 800-461-8009
geagle@pvnccdsb.on.ca
www.facebook.com/PVNCCDSB
twitter.com/pvnccdsb
www.instagram.com/pvnccdsb
Number of Schools: 30 elementary; 6 secondary *Grades:* K - 12 *Enrollment:* 15000 *Number of Employees:* 948 academic; 315 occasional academic; 557 support staff; 108 administrative; 254 temporary
Michelle Griepsma, Chair, Board, 705-928-4474
mgriepsma@pvnccdsb.on.ca
Michael Nasello, Director, Education; Secretary-Treasurer, 705-748-4861, ext. 1247
mnasello@pvnccdsb.on.ca
Joan Carragher, Superintendent, Learning/Leadership & Human Resource Services, 705-748-4861, ext. 1193
jcarragher@pvnccdsb.on.ca
Laurie Corrigan, Superintendent, Learning/Special Education Services, 705-748-4861, ext. 1213
lcorrigan@pvnccdsb.on.ca
Isabel Grace, Superintendent, Business & Finance/Plant, 705-748-4861, ext. 1251
igrace@pvnccdsb.on.ca
Dawn Michie, Superintendent, Learning/Program, 705-748-4861, ext. 1241
dmichie@pvnccdsb.on.ca
Timothy Moloney, Superintendent, Learning/Student Success, 705-748-4861, ext. 1226
tmoloney@pvnccdsb.on.ca

Sault Ste Marie: **Huron-Superior Catholic District School Board (HSCDSB)**
90 Ontario Ave., Sault Ste Marie, ON P6B 6G7, Canada
Tel: 705-945-5400; *Fax:* 705-945-5575
Toll-Free: 800-267-0754
frontdesk@hscdsb.on.ca
www.hscdsb.on.ca
www.facebook.com/HuronSuperiorCatholicDistrictSchoolBoard
twitter.com/hscdsb
www.youtube.com/user/HSCDSB1
Number of Schools: 16 elementary; 1 secondary; 2 alternative *Grades:* K - 12 *Enrollment:* 5000 *Number of Employees:* 1,000+
Lindsay Liske, Chair, Board, 705-869-1401
lindsay.liske@hscdsb.on.ca
Rose Burton Spohn, Director, Education, 705-945-5600
rose.burtonspohn@hscdsb.on.ca
Joe Chilelli, Superintendent, Education, 705-945-5600
joe.chilelli@hscdsb.on.ca
Maria Esposito, Superintendent, Education, 705-945-5602
maria.esposito@hscdsb.on.ca
Danny Viotto, Superintendent, Education, 705-945-5690
danny.viotto@hscdsb.on.ca
Chris Spina, Superintendent, Business, 705-945-5624
chris.spina@hscdsb.on.ca

Sudbury: **Conseil scolaire catholique du Nouvel-Ontario (CSCNO)**
201, rue Jogues, Sudbury, ON P3C 5L7
Tél: 705-673-5626; *Téléc:* 705-669-1270
Ligne sans frais: 800-259-5567
info@nouvelon.ca
www.nouvelon.ca
www.facebook.com/CSCNouvelOn
twitter.com/CSCNouvelOn
www.instagram.com/cscnouvelontario
Number of Schools: 27 écoles élémentaires, 9 écoles secondaires; 1 centre d'éducation aux adultes *Grades:* Élém. - Sec.; Éducation aux adultes *Enrollment:* 6700
André Bidal, Président, Conseil, 705-524-2177
andre.bidal@nouvelon.ca
Paul E. Henry, Directeur, Éducation et secrétaire-trésorier, 705-673-5626, ext. 274
paul.henry@nouvelon.ca
Tracy Rossini, Directrice exécutive, Apprentissage, 705-673-5626, ext. 214
tracy.rossini@nouvelon.ca
Maryse Barrette, Directrice, Service des finances & des achats, 705-673-5626, ext. 379
maryse.barrette@nouvelon.ca
Daniel Bourgeois, Directeur, Service des ressources humaines, 705-673-5626, ext. 311
daniel.bourgeois@nouvelon.ca
Cathy Modesto, Surintendante, Affaires & Finances, 705-673-5626, ext. 236
cathy.modesto@nouvelon.ca

Tracey-Lynn Foucault, Surintendante, Éducation, 705-673-5626, ext. 231
traceylynn.foucault@nouvelon.ca
Tammy Séguin, Surintendant, Éducation, 705-673-5626, ext. 235
Tammy.seguin@nouvelon.ca

Sudbury: Sudbury Catholic District School Board (SCDSB)
Catholic Education Centre
165A D'Youville St., Sudbury, ON P3C 5E7
Tel: 705-673-5620; *Fax:* 705-673-6670
info@sudburycatholicschools.ca
sudburycatholicschools.ca
www.facebook.com/sudburycatholicschools
twitter.com/sudburycdsb
vimeo.com/sudburycatholicschools
Number of Schools: 13 elementary schools; 5 secondary schools; 1 adult education centre *Grades:* K - 12; French Immersion; Adult Ed. *Enrollment:* 5930 *Number of Employees:* 410 teachers; 29 early childhood educators; 264 support workers
Michael Bellmore, Chair, Board, 705-669-0166
bellmom@sudburycatholicschools.ca
Joanne Bénard, Director, Education & Chief Executive Officer, Board, 705-673-5620, ext. 238
joanne.benard@sudburycatholicschools.ca
Cheryl Ann Corallo, Superintendent, Business & Finance, 705-673-5620, ext. 418
cherylann.corallo@sudburycatholicschools.ca
Rossella Bagnato, Superintendent, School Effectiveness, 705-673-5620, ext. 300
rossella.bagnato@sudburycatholicschools.ca
Nicole Bédard, Superintendent, School Effectiveness, 705-673-5620, ext. 212
nicole.bedard@sudburycatholicschools.ca
Peter Prochilo, Superintendent, School Effectiveness, 705-673-5620, ext. 301
peter.prochilo@sudburycatholicschools.ca

Terrace Bay: Superior North Catholic District School Board (SNCDSB)
17 Cartier Drive, Terrace Bay, ON P0T 2W0, Canada
Tel: 807-825-3209; *Fax:* 807-825-3885
Toll-Free: 1-800-465-3346
www.sncdsb.on.ca
www.facebook.com/sncdsb
twitter.com/sncdsb
Number of Schools: 9 elementary *Grades:* Elementary; Religious Program
Hugh McCorry, Chair, Board
hmccorry@sndsb.on.ca
Maria Vasanelli, Interim Director of Education, 807-825-3209, ext. 1001
mvasanelli@sncdsb.on.ca
Colleen Sheriff, Indigenous Education Lead, 807-829-1260
csheriff@sncdsb.on.ca

Thunder Bay: Conseil scolaire de district catholique des Aurores boréales (CSDCAB)
175, rue High nord, Thunder Bay, ON P7A 8C7
Tél: 807-344-2266; *Téléc:* 807-344-3734
Ligne sans frais: 800-367-0874
info@csdcab.on.ca
www.csdcab.on.ca
www.facebook.com/csdcab
Number of Schools: 9 écoles élémentaires; 1 école secondaire
Grades: Élém. - Sec. *Enrollment:* 652
Sylvie Payeur, Présidente, Conseil, 807-876-4987
spayeur@csdcab.on.ca
Mireille Major Levesque, Directrice, Éducation, 807-983-4043
mmajor@csdcab.on.ca
Lucie Allaire, Directrice, Éducation, 807-343-4050
lallaire@csdcab.on.ca
Jolanta Hausner, Directrice, Service des finances/transport, 807-343-4063
jhausner@csdcab.on.ca
Michel Mercier, Directeur, Service des ressources humaines, 807-343-4077
mmercier@csdcab.on.ca
Carol-Ann van Rassel, Directrice, Service des communications, 807-343-4089
cavanrassel@csdcab.on.ca

Thunder Bay: Thunder Bay Catholic District School Board (TBCDSB)
Catholic Education Centre
459 Victoria Ave. West, Thunder Bay, ON P7C 0A4
Tel: 807-625-1555; *Fax:* 807-623-0431
www.tbcdsb.on.ca
www.facebook.com/tbcdsb
twitter.com/tbc_schools
www.instagram.com/tbcdsb

Number of Schools: 15 elementary schools; 3 senior elementary schools; 2 secondary schools; 8 alternative programs *Grades:* K - 12; Alternate Ed.
Francis Veneruz, Chair, Board, 807-625-1547
fveneruz@tbcschools.ca
Pino Tassone, Director, Education, 807-625-1567
ptassone@tbcschools.ca
Alexandra Frankow, Officer, Communications, 807-625-1587
afrankow@tbcschools.ca
Sheila Chiodo, Supertintendent, Business & Corporate Services, 807-625-1508
schiodo@tbcschools.ca
Allison Sargent, Superintendent, Education (K - 6 Schools), 807-625-1573
asargent@tbcschools.ca
Omer Belisle, Superintendent, Education (Senior Elementary 7 - 8), 807-625-1573
obelisle@tbcschools.ca
Jean-Paul Tennier, Superintendent, Education (9 - 12 Schools), 807-625-1590
jptennier@tbcschools.ca

Timmins: Conseil scolaire catholique de district des Grandes Rivières
896, promenade Riverside, Timmins, ON P4N 3W2
Tél: 705-267-1421; *Téléc:* 705-267-7247
Ligne sans frais: 800-465-9984
cscdgr@cscdgr.education
www.cscdgr.education
www.facebook.com/cscdgr
Number of Schools: 29 élémentaires; 8 secondaires; 3 centres
Grades: Élém-Sec. et adultes *Enrollment:* 6200
Langis Dion, Président
langis.dion@cscdgr.education
Sylvie Petroski, Directrice, Éducation, 705-267-1421, ext. 263
sylvie.petroski@cscdgr.education
Richard Loiselle, Directeur, Communications et d'imputabilité, 705-267-1421, ext. 245
richard.loiselle@cscdgr.education

Timmins: Northeastern Catholic District School Board (NCDSB)
383 Birch St. North, Timmins, ON P4N 6E8, Canada
Tel: 705-268-7443; *Fax:* 705-267-3590
Toll-Free: 877-422-9322
janice.viskovich@ncdsb.on.ca
www.ncdsb.on.ca
www.facebook.com/NCDSB
twitter.com/NECDSB
www.instagram.com/necdsb
Number of Schools: 12 elementary; 1 secondary *Grades:* K - 12
Rick Brassard, Chair, Board, 705-544-8055
rbrassard@ncdsb.on.ca
Tricia Stefanic-Weltz, Director, Education, 705-268-7443
tsweltz@ncdsb.on.ca
Daphne Brumwell, Superintendent, Education, 705-268-7443
dbrumwell@ncdsb.on.ca
Jennifer Dunkley, Superintendent, Education, 705-268-7443
jdunkley@ncdsb.on.ca
Keld Scott, Superintendent, Business, 705-268-7443
kelscott@ncdsb.on.ca
Mélanie Bidal-Mainville, Manager, Human Resources, 705-268-7443, ext. 3204
mbidal@ncdsb.on.ca
Jessica Carriere, Manager, Finance, 705-268-7443, ext. 3208
financedept@ncdsb.on.ca
David Horton, Manager, Plant & Maintenance, 705-268-7443, ext. 3212
dhorton@ncdsb.on.ca
Glen Nakashoji, Manager, Information & Communications Technology Services, 705-268-7443, ext. 3214
gnakashoji@ncdsb.on.ca

Toronto: Conseil scolaire catholique MonAvenir
110, av Drewry, Toronto, ON M2M 1C8
Tél: 416-397-6564; *Téléc:* 416-397-6576
Ligne sans frais: 800-274-3764
commentaires@cscmonavenir.ca
www.cscmonavenir.ca
www.facebook.com/cscmonavenir
twitter.com/cscmonavenir
www.youtube.com/conseilscolairecatholiquemonavenir
Number of Schools: 61 écoles *Grades:* Élém. - Sec. *Enrollment:* 17500
Melinda Chartrand, Présidente, Conseil, 855-506-5002, ext. 1004
mchartrand2@cscmonavenir.ca
André Blais, Directeur, Éducation & Secrétaire-trésorier, 416-397-6564, ext. 73100
ablais@cscmonavenir.ca

Albert Aazouz, Directeur, Service des ressources matérielles, 416-397-6564, ext. 73600
aaazouz@cscmonavenir.ca
Mikale-Andrée Joly, Directrice, Service des relations corporatives, 416-397-6564, ext. 73130
mjoly@cscmonavenir.ca
Abdu-L-Kerim Sandooya, Directeur, Service des ressources informatiques, 416-397-6564, ext. 73700
asandooya@cscmonavenir.ca
Colette Pradeilles, Directrice par intérim, Service des ressources financières, 416-397-6564, ext. 73500
cpradeilles@cscmonavenir.ca
Gabriel Bérard, Directeur adjoint, Ressources humaines, 416-397-6564, ext. 73400
gberard@cscmonavenir.ca
Sébastien Lacroix, Conseiller, Gestion des affaires diocésaines & scolaires, 416-397-6564, ext. 72021
slacroix@cscmonavenir.ca

Toronto: Toronto Catholic District School Board (TCDSB)
80 Sheppard Ave. East, Toronto, ON M2N 6E8
Tel: 416-222-8282; *Fax:* 416-229-5345
webmaster@tcdsb.org
www.tcdsb.org
twitter.com/tcdsb
www.youtube.com/user/TCDSBVid
Number of Schools: 168 elementary; 21 secondary schools; 3 combined elementary & secondary schools *Grades:* K - 12; Adult Ed. *Enrollment:* 91000 *Number of Employees:* 10,000
Note: Also offers night school & summer school.
Joseph Martino, Chair, Board, 416-512-3410
joseph.martino@tcdsb.org
Rory McGuckin, Director, Education, 416-222-8282, ext. 2296
rory.mcguckin@tcdsb.org
Dan Koenig, Associate Director, Academic Services, 416-222-8282, ext. 2294
dan.koenig@tcdsb.org
Lloyd Noronha, Associate Director, Planning & Facilities, 416-222-8282, ext. 2249
lloyd.noronha@tcdsb.org
Shazia Vlahos, Senior Coordinator, Communications, 416-222-8282, ext. 5331
shazia.vlahos@tcdsb.org
Jacqueline Charles, Coordinator, Materials Management, 416-222-8282, ext. 2210
jacqueline.charles@tcdsb.org
Linda Maselli-Jackson, Superintendent, Education & Special Services, 416-222-8282, ext. 2486
Flora Cielli, Superintendent, Schools - Area 1, 416-222-8282, ext. 2732
flora.cifelli@tcdsb.org
Maria Meehan, Superintendent, Schools - Area 2, 416-222-8282, ext. 2732
maria.meehan@tcdsb.org
Shawna Campbell, Superintendent, Schools - Area 3, 416-222-8282, ext. 2267
shawna.campbell@tcdsb.org
Christina Fernandes, Superintendent, Schools - Area 4, 416-222-8282, ext. 2267
christina.fernandes@tcdsb.org
John Wujek, Superintendent, Schools - Area 5, 416-222-8282, ext. 5371
john.wujek@tcdsb.org
John Shanahan, Superintendent, Schools - Area 6, 416-222-8282, ext. 5371
john.shanahan@tcdsb.org
Peter Agular, Superintendent, Schools - Area 7, 416-222-8282, ext. 2263
peter.agular@tcdsb.org
Kevin Malcolm, Superintendent, Schools - Area 8, 416-222-8282, ext. 2263
kevin.malcolm@tcdsb.org

Wallaceburg: St. Clair Catholic District School Board
Catholic Education Centre
420 Creek St., Wallaceburg, ON N8A 4C4, Canada
Tel: 519-627-6762; *Fax:* 519-627-8230
Toll-Free: 1-866-336-6139
www.st-clair.net
www.facebook.com/SCCDSB
twitter.com/sccdsb
Number of Schools: 26 elementary; 2 secondary *Grades:* K - 12
John Van Heck, Chair, Board, 519-627-5746
john.vanheck@sccdsb.net
Deb Crawford, Director, Education, 519-627-6762, ext. 10241
deb.crawford@st-clair.net
Amy Janssens, Associate Director, Corporate Services, 519-627-6762, ext. 10325
amy.janssens@st-clair.net

Laura Callaghan, Superintendent, Education, 519-627-6762, ext. 10282
laura.callaghan@st-clair.net
Lisa Demers, Superintendent, Education, 519-627-6762, ext. 10227
lisa.demers@st-clair.net
Scott Johnson, Superintendent, Education, 519-627-6762, ext. 10282
scott.johnson@st-clair.net
James Duff, Executive Manager, Human Resource Services, 519-627-6762, ext. 10236
james.duff@st-clair.net

Welland: Niagara Catholic District School Board
427 Rice Rd., Welland, ON L3C 7C1, Canada
Tel: 905-735-0240; *Fax:* 905-734-8828
info@ncdsb.com
www.niagaracatholic.ca
www.facebook.com/NiagaraCatholicDSB
twitter.com/niagaracatholic
www.youtube.com/niagaracatholicdsb
Number of Schools: 49 elementary; 8 secondary *Grades:* Pre-K - 12 *Enrollment:* 28697 *Number of Employees:* 1252 teachers; 538 support staff; 73 principals & vice principals; 7 directors & superintendents
Frank Fera, Chair, Board, 905-374-8129
frankfera4@gmail.com
John Crocco, Director, Education; Secretary-Treasurer, 905-735-0240, ext. 220
john.crocco@ncdsb.com
Yolanda Baldasaro, Superintendent, Education, 905-735-0240, ext. 227
yolanda.baldasaro@ncdsb.com
Ted Farrell, Superintendent, Education, 905-735-0240, ext. 230
ted.farrell@ncdsb.com
Lee Ann Forsyth-Sells, Superintendent, Education, 905-735-0240, ext. 229
leeann.forsythsells@ncdsb.com
Frank Iannantuono, Superintendent, Education, 905-735-0240, ext. 228
frank.iannantuono@ncdsb.com
Pat Rocca, Superintendent, Education
Giancarlo Vetrone, Superintendent, Business & Financial Services, 905-735-0240, ext. 232
giancarlo.vetrone@ncdsb.com
Scott Whitwell, Controller, Facilities Services, 905-735-0240, ext. 252

Windsor: Conseil scolaire catholique Providence
7515, promenade Forest Glade, Windsor, ON N8T 3P5
Tél: 519-948-9227; *Téléc:* 519-948-1091
Ligne sans frais: 888-768-2219
www.cscprovidence.ca
www.facebook.com/CscProvidence
twitter.com/CscProvidence
Number of Schools: 23 écoles élémentaires; 7 écoles secondaires; 1 centre de formation continue *Grades:* Élém. - Sec.; Éducation aux adultes *Enrollment:* 10000 *Number of Employees:* 754 enseignants
Doris Sauvé, Président, Conseil, 519-798-3483
SauvDori@CscProvidence.ca
Joseph Picard, Directeur, Éducation & Secrétaire, Conseil
Carolyn Bastien, Surintendante, Affaires & Trésorière, Conseil
Jean-Paul Gagnier, Surintendant, Éducation
Nathalie Sanson, Surintendante, Éducation
Edith St-Armaud, Surintendante, Éducation
Kimberly Fortin, Surintendante adjointe, Éducation
Denis Robert, Surintendant adjoint, Éducation

Windsor: Windsor-Essex Catholic District School Board (WECDSB)
1325 California Ave., Windsor, ON N9B 3Y6
Tel: 519-253-2481; *Fax:* 519-253-8397
www.wecdsb.on.ca
www.facebook.com/WECDSB
twitter.com/wecdsb
www.youtube.com/WECDSBMedia
Number of Schools: 35 elementary schools; 9 secondary schools; 1 adult education program *Grades:* K - 12; Adult Ed. *Enrollment:* 20201 *Number of Employees:* 1,191 teaching staff; 854 support staff
Fulvio Valentinis, Chair, Board, 519-977-5067
fulvio_valentinis@wecdsb.on.ca
Terry Lyons, Director, Education, 519-253-2481, ext. 1201
director@wecdsb.on.ca
Emelda Byrne, Executive Superintendent, Education - Student Achievement, 519-253-2481, ext. 1526
emelda_byrne@wecdsb.on.ca
Dan Fister, Executive Superintendent, Innovation and Experiential, 519-253-2481, ext. 1207
dan_fister@wecdsb.on.ca

Penny King, Executive Superintendent, Business, 519-253-2481, ext. 1247
penny_king@wecdsb.on.ca
Colleen Norris, Superintendent, Human Resources, 519-253-2481, ext. 1122
collen_norris@wecdsb.on.ca
John Ulicny, Superintendent, Human Resources, 519-253-2481, ext. 1525
john_ulicny@wecdsb.on.ca
Melissa Farrand, Superintendent, Education - Student Achievement K - 12, 519-253-2481, ext. 1120
melissa_farrand@wecdsb.on.ca
Joseph Ibrahim, Superintendent, Education - Student Achievement K - 12, 519-253-2481, ext. 1219
joseph_ibrahim@wecdsb.on.ca
Rosemary Lo Faso, Superintendent, Education - Student Achievement K - 12, 519-253-2481, ext. 1203
Rosemary_lofaso@wecdsb.on.ca

French

North Bay: Conseil scolaire public du Nord-Est de l'Ontario
P.O. Box 3600
820, promenade Lakeshore, North Bay, ON P1B 9T5, Canada
Tél: 705-472-3443; *Téléc:* 705-472-5757
Ligne sans frais: 888-591-5656
information@cspne.ca
www.cspne.ca
www.facebook.com/cspne
twitter.com/cspne
Number of Schools: 20 *Grades:* M-12 *Note:* Timmins: 111, av Wilson, (705) 264-1119.
Simon Fecteau, Directeur de l'éducation par intérim, 705-264-1119
simon.fecteau@cspne.ca
Denis Labelle, Président du Conseil
denis.labelle@cspne.ca
Linda Lacroix, Surintendant de l'éducation, 705-472-3443, ext. 233
Linda.lacroix@cspne.ca
Tracy Dottori, Surintendante adjointe des affaires - ressources humaines
tracy.dottori@cspne.ca
Jamie Point, Gestionnaire des technologies de l'information & de la comm., 705-472-3443, ext. 229
jamie.point@cspne.ca

Ottawa: Conseil des écoles publiques de l'Est de l'Ontario (CEPEO)
2445, boul Saint-Laurent, Ottawa, ON K1G 6C3
Tél: 613-742-8960; *Ligne sans frais:* 888-332-3736
info@cepeo.on.ca
www.cepeo.on.ca
www.facebook.com/cepeo
twitter.com/ottawacepeo
www.linkedin.com/company/cepeo
vimeo.com/cepeo
Number of Schools: 43 *Grades:* Mat. - 12; écoles spécialisées *Enrollment:* 17000 *Number of Employees:* 1,850
Denis Chartrand, Président, Conseil
denis.m.chartrand@cepeo.on.ca
Ann Mahoney, Directrice par intérim, Éducation
ann.mahoney@cepeo.on.ca
Simone Rose-Oliver, Surintendant par intérim, Éducation
simone.rose-oliver@cepeo.on.ca
Christian-Charle Bouchard, Surintendant, Éducation
christian-charle.bouchard@cepeo.on.ca
Amine H. Aidouni, Surintendant, Éducation
amine.aidouni@cepeo.on.ca
Sylvie C. R. Tremblay, Surintendant, Éducation
sylvie.tremblay@cepeo.on.ca
Matthieu Vachon, Surintendant, des affaires
stephane.vachon@cepeo.on.ca

Sudbury: Conseil scolaire public du Grand Nord de l'Ontario (CSPGNO)
296, rue Van Horne, Sudbury, ON P3B 1H9
Tél: 705-671-1533; *Téléc:* 705-671-1720
Ligne sans frais: 800-465-5993
information@cspgno.ca
www.cspgno.ca
www.facebook.com/CSPGNO
twitter.com/CSPGNO
Number of Schools: 11 écoles élémentaires; 8 écoles secondaires *Grades:* Élém. - Sec. *Enrollment:* 2318 *Number of Employees:* 673
Jean-Marc Aubin, Président, Conseil, 705-969-4079
jean-marc.aubin@cspgno.ca
Marc Gauthier, Directeur, Éducation, 705-671-1533, ext. 2202
marc.gauthier@cspgno.ca

Carole Brouillard-Landry, Directrice, Services pédagogiques, 705-671-1533, ext. 2230
carole.brouillard-landry@cspgno.ca
Carole Dubé, Directrice, Communications, 705-671-1533, ext. 2233
carole.dube@cspgno.ca
Carole Paquette, Directrice, Services à l'élève, 705-671-1533, ext. 2211
carole.paquette@cspgno.ca
Diane Arbour, Agente, Ressources humaines, 705-671-1533, ext. 2204
diane.arbour@cspgno.ca
Barbara Breault, Surintendante, Éducation, 705-671-1533, ext. 2203
barbara.breault@cspgno.ca
Alain Gélinas, Surintendant, Affaires, 705-671-1533, ext. 2245
alain.gelinas@cspgno.ca

Toronto: Conseil scolaire Viamonde
116, Cornelius Pkwy., Toronto, ON M6L 2K5
Tél: 416-614-0844; *Téléc:* 416-397-2072
Ligne sans frais: 888-583-5383
csviamonde.ca
www.facebook.com/CSViamonde
twitter.com/CSViamonde
www.youtube.com/user/CSViamonde
Number of Schools: 41 écoles élémentaires; 15 écoles secondaires *Grades:* Mat. - 12 *Enrollment:* 13000 *Number of Employees:* 2500
Sylvie A. Landry, Présidente du Conseil, 416-998-9610
landrys@csviamonde.ca
Claire Francoeur, Directrice, Communications & Marketing, 416-465-5772
francoeurc@csviamonde.ca
Martin Bertrand, Directeur, Éducation, 416-614-5929
bertrandm@csviamonde.ca
Miguel Ladouceur, Directeur, Immobilisation & Entretien, 416-614-5917
ladouceurm@csviamonde.ca
Marie-Josée Smith, Directrice, Ressources humaines, 416-614-5895
smithm@csviamonde.ca
Sébastien Fontaine, Surintendant, Éducation, 416-637-5695
fontaines@csviamonde.ca
Jason Rodrigue, Surintendant, Affaires, 905-732-7825
rodriguej@csviamonde.ca

School Authorities

Moose Factory: Moose Factory Island District School Area Board
P.O. Box 160
Moose Factory, ON P0L 1W0, Canada
Tel: 705-658-4571; *Fax:* 705-658-4768
mfidsab.ca/mfidsab
Grades: JK - 8
Marilyn McLeod, Chair, Board
marilyn.mcleod@mfidsab.ca
Gord Daniels, Supervisory Officer
gord.daniels@mfidsab.ca
Kathy Cheechoo, Business Administrator & Treasurer
kathy.cheechoo@mfidsab.ca

Moosonee: James Bay Lowlands Secondary School Board (JBLSSB)
P.O. Box 157
1 Pinew St., Moosonee, ON P0L 1Y0, Canada
Tel: 705-336-2903; *Fax:* 705-336-0234
jblssb.ca
Number of Schools: 1 secondary *Grades:* 9 - 12 *Enrollment:* 180
Harold Gunner, Chair, Board
Tom Steele, Superintendent, Education
tome.steele@jblssb.ca
Brenda Chilton-Jeffries, Business Administrator; Treasurer
Val Hunter, Board Office Clerk

Moosonee: Moosonee District School Area Board
P.O. Box 250
22 2nd St., Moosonee, ON P0L 1Y0, Canada
Tel: 705-336-2300; *Fax:* 705-336-0334
Grades: K-8 *Enrollment:* 275
Kelly Reuben, Chair
Cheryl Wapachee, Secretary-Treasurer & Business Administrator

Oshawa: Campbell Children's School Authority
600 Townline Rd. South, Oshawa, ON L1H 7K6
Tel: 905-576-8403; *Fax:* 905-576-4414
ccs@grandviewkids.ca
campbellchildrensschool.com
Number of Schools: 1 *Grades:* JK - 1 *Enrollment:* 45 *Number of Employees:* 16 *Note:* Hospital-based school authority that serves

local students who live with communication or multiple disabilities and are enrolled in specialized programs.
Janet Harper, Principal
janet.harper@grandviewkids.ca

Ottawa: **Ottawa Children's Treatment Centre School Authority**
Also known as: CHEO School
395 Smyth Rd., Ottawa, ON K1H 8L2
Tel: 613-737-0871; *Fax:* 613-523-5167
Toll-Free: 800-565-4839
www.cheo.on.ca
Number of Schools: 1 *Grades:* K - 3 *Enrollment:* 30 *Note:* The OCTC School provides full-day educational instruction in both English & French to children who have a primary diagnosis of a physical disability & other associated complex needs.

Penetanguishene: **The Protestant Separate School Board of the Town of Penetanguishene (PSSBP)**
P.O. Box 107
#48, 2 Poyntz St., Penetanguishene, ON L9M 1M2, Canada
Tel: 705-549-6422; *Fax:* 705-549-2768
www.pssbp.ca
Number of Schools: 1 *Grades:* JK-8 *Enrollment:* 234 *Note:* Operates the Burkvale Protestant Separate School in Penetanguishene, Ontario
Lynne Cousens, Chair
Tim Overholt, Supervisory Officer
toverholt@pssbp.ca
Sean Turner, Manager, Finance & Treasurer
sturner@pssbp.ca

St Catharines: **Niagara Peninsula Children's Centre School Authority**
Also known as: Niagara Children's Centre School
567 Glenridge Ave., St Catharines, ON L2T 4C2
Tel: 905-688-3550; *Fax:* 905-688-1055
Toll-Free: 800-896-5496
info@niagarachildrenscentre.com
niagarachildrenscentre.com
www.facebook.com/NiagaraChildrensCentre
twitter.com/niagarachildctr
Number of Schools: 1 *Grades:* Special Ed. *Enrollment:* 84 *Note:* The Niagara Children's Centre School Authority provides individualized education & therapeutic programming in small group settings to children & youth 4 - 21 years of age with communication & physical disabilities.
Don Thorpe, Chair, Board
Oksana Fisher, Chief Executive Officer, 905-688-1890, ext. 102

Toronto: **Bloorview School Authority**
150 Kilgour Rd., Toronto, ON M4G 1R8
Tel: 416-424-3831; *Fax:* 416-425-2981
info@bloorviewschool.ca
www.bloorviewschool.ca
www.facebook.com/HBKRH
twitter.com/HBKidsHospital
www.youtube.com/user/PRBloorview
Note: Bloorview School Authority provides school programs to children & youth with special needs.
Dr. Julia Alleyne, Chair, Board
juliaalleyne@bloorviewschool.ca

Waterloo: **KidsAbility School Authority Board**
General Services & Business Office
500 Hallmark Dr., Waterloo, ON N2K 3P5
Tel: 519-886-8886; *Fax:* 519-886-7292
Toll-Free: 888-372-2259
info@kidsability.ca
www.kidsability.ca
www.facebook.com/KidsAbility
twitter.com/kidsability
www.youtube.com/user/KidsAbility1957
Grades: JK *Note:* KidsAbility School Authority Board serves children who have a wide range of special needs. Programs & services include a junior kindergarten program, individual education plans, composite classes, communication classes & language classes.
Ken Bell, Chair, Board, 519-886-8886, ext. 1227
schoolauthoritychair@kidsability.ca
Kelly Lantink, Secretary, Board & Principal, 519-886-8886, ext. 1225
klantink@kidsability.ca
Joanne Cotter, Executive Assistant, 519-886-8886, ext. 1227
jcotter@kidsability.ca

Windsor: **John McGivney Children's Centre School Authority**
John McGivney Children's Centre
3945 Matchette Rd., Windsor, ON N9C 4C2
Tel: 519-282-7281; *Fax:* 519-252-5873
Toll-Free: 800-976-5622
school@jmccentre.ca
www.jmccentre.ca
www.facebook.com/JohnMcGivneyChildrensCentre
twitter.com/JMCCentre
Number of Schools: 1 *Note:* The John McGivney Children's Centre School Authority governs the John McGivney Children's Centre School, formerly known as the Children's Rehabilitation Centre School. The school provides a post-traumatic / post-operative rehabilitation program for students from ages four to fourteen who live in Windsor / Essex County.
Elizabeth Haugh, President
Vince Laframboise, Vice-President
Jessica Sartori, Chief Executive Officer

First Nations

Akwesasne: **Ahkwesahsne Mohawk Board of Education (AMBE)**
169 Akwesasne International Rd., Akwesasne, ON K6H 0G5, Canada
Tel: 613-933-0409; *Fax:* 613-933-9262
www.ambe.ca
www.facebook.com/AhkwesahsneMohawkBoardofEducation
twitter.com/ambe_ca
Number of Schools: 3 *Grades:* K - 8; Alternative Ed. *Note:* The Ahkwesahsne Mohawk Board of Education operates three elementary schools. Since the Ahkwesahsne Mohawk Board of Education does not have a secondary school, there is an agreement with the Upper Canada Public School Board to provide secondary education.
Rosemary Square, Chair, Board
Donna Lahache, Director, Education, 613-933-0409, ext. 1403
donna.lahache@ambe.ca
Owen Benedict, Superintendant, Finance Operations, 613-933-0409, ext. 1404
owen.benedict@ambe.ca

Attawapiskat: **Attawapiskat First Nation Education Authority**
P.O. Box 247
General Delivery, Attawapiskat, ON P0L 1A0, Canada
Tel: 705-997-2232; *Fax:* 705-997-2419
reception.board@afnea.com
www.afnea.com
Number of Schools: 1 elementary; 1 secondary *Grades:* JK - 12; Special Ed. *Enrollment:* 800 *Note:* Kattawapiskak Elementary School & Vezina Secondary School
Travis Koostachin, Chair, Board
Dorothy Hookimaw, Education Director
dorothy.hookimaw@afnea.com

Balmertown: **Keewaytinook Okimakanak Board of Education (KOBE)**
P.O. Box 274
10 Eric Radford Way, Balmertown, ON P0V 1C0
Tel: 807-735-1381; *Fax:* 807-735-3392
Toll-Free: 800-387-3740
www.koeducation.ca
Number of Schools: 5 *Enrollment:* 681
Nora Ignace, Manager
noraignace@edu.knet.ca

Big Trout Lake: **Kitchenuhmaykoosib Education Authority**
General Delivery, Big Trout Lake, ON P0V 1G0
Tel: 807-537-2553; *Fax:* 807-537-2316
kifirstnation@knet.ca
www.bigtroutlake.firstnation.ca
Number of Schools: 1 *Grades:* JK-11; Special Ed. *Enrollment:* 275 *Note:* Aglace Chapman Education Centre. The Kitchenuhmaykoosib Education Authority serves the Kitchenuhmaykoosib Inninnuwug First Nation, formerly known as Big Trout Lake First Nation, located north of Thunder Bay, Ontario. Secondary programs are also available through computer, radio & television.

Christian Island: **Beausoleil Education Department**
Beausoleil Education Department
11 O'Gemaa Miikaan, Christian Island, ON L9M 0A9, Canada
Tel: 705-247-2051; *Fax:* 705-247-2239
chimnissing.ca/education
Number of Schools: 1 elementary *Grades:* JK - 8; Special Ed. *Note:* The Beausoleil Education Department serves the Chippewas of the Beausoleil First Nation by operating the Christian Island Elementary School. For secondary education,

students attend high schools in the Simcoe County District School Board or the Simcoe Muskoka Catholic School Board.
Nancy Assance, Acting Director, Education
n.assance@chimnissing.ca
Makayla Laramey, Administrative Assistant, 705-247-2051, ext. 258
makayla@chimnissing.ca
Connie Howell, Principal - Christian Island Elementary School
principal@chimnissing.ca

Constance Lake: **Constance Lake First Nation Education Authority**
P.O. Box 4000
Constance Lake, ON P0L 1B0, Canada
Tel: 705-463-4511; *Fax:* 705-463-2222
clfn.on.ca/clea
Number of Schools: 3 *Grades:* JK - 12 *Enrollment:* 257 *Note:* Mamawmatawa Holistic Education Center. Located in the District of Cochrane, the Constance Lake First Nation Education Authority provides education to community members of Cree & Ojibway ancestry. The Constance Lake First Nation Education Authority is supported by the Matawa Education Department in Thunder Bay, Ontario. Also offers day care services and adult education.
Lizzie Sutherland, Chairperson
lizzie.sutherland@clfn.on.ca
Bonnie John-George, Day Care Administrator, 705-463-1199, ext. 125
bonnie.joh-george@clfn.on.ca
Ken Neegan, Education Administrator, 705-463-1199, ext. 115
ken.neegan@clfn.on.ca

Dinorwic: **Wabigoon Lake Ojibway Nation Education Authority**
P.O. Box 24
Site 112, Dinorwic, ON P0V 1P0, Canada
Tel: 807-938-6684; *Fax:* 807-938-1166
Number of Schools: 1 *Grades:* JK - 8 *Note:* Wabsnki-Penasi School. Elementary education is provided in a school operated by the Wabigoon Lake Ojibway Nation. Secondary school students are bused to nearby Dryden, Ontario.

Eabamet Lake: **Eabametoong (Fort Hope) First Nation Education Authority**
P.O. Box 294
Eabamet Lake, ON P0T 1L0
Tel: 807-242-1305; *Fax:* 807-242-1313
efnea64@gmail.com
efnea64.com
Other Information: Education Coordinator, Phone: 807-242-1305, ext. 24
Number of Schools: 1 *Grades:* K - 10; Special Ed. *Note:* Eabametoong (Fort Hope) is a fly-in Ojibwe First Nations community located approximately 360 kilometres northeast of Thunder Bay, Ontario. The Education Authority consists of a Board of Directors & a head office staff. The Matawa Education Department in Thunder, Bay, Ontario supports the education authority.
Nancy Waswa, Education Director

Fort Albany: **Mundo Peetabeck Education Authority**
P.O. Box 31
Fort Albany, ON P0L 1H0, Canada
Tel: 705-278-3390; *Fax:* 705-278-1049
Number of Schools: 1 JK - 12 *Enrollment:* 150
Nicole Gillies, Education Director
mundo_peetabeck@yahoo.ca

Fort Severn: **Wasaho Education Authority**
P.O. Box 165
General Delivery, Fort Severn, ON P0V 1W0, Canada
Tel: 807-478-9548; *Fax:* 807-478-2573
Other Information: Alternative phone number: 807-478-9549
Number of Schools: 1 *Note:* The Wasaho Education Authority provides education to members of the Fort Severn First Nation. The Fort Severn First Nation Reserve is situated in northern Ontario, near the mouth of the Severn River.
Moses Kakekaspan, Education Director, 807-478-9548, ext. 25
moseskakekaspan@gmail.com
Sherri Curtis, Principal
Shirley Miles, Social Counsellor

Hudson: **Lac Seul Education Authority**
c/o LSEA
P.O. Box 319
Hudson, ON P0V 1X0, Canada
Tel: 807-582-3499; *Fax:* 807-582-3431
lacseul.firstnation.ca
Number of Schools: 3 *Enrollment:* 97
Jennifer Manitowabi, Education Director
jmanitowabi@lsfn.ca

Kasabonika Lake: **Sineonokway Education Authority**
P.O. Box 33
Kasabonika Lake, ON P0V 1Y0, Canada
Tel: 807-535-2547; *Fax:* 807-535-1152
www.kasabonika.ca
Grades: K - 12 *Enrollment:* 250
Josie Semple, Education Director, 807-535-2547, ext. 236
josies@kasabonika.ca
Eileen Anderson, Assistant Education Director, 807-535-2547,
ext. 244

Kashechewan: **Hishkoonikun Education Authority
(HEA)**
P.O. Box 210
430 Riverside Rd., Kashechewan, ON P0L 1S0, Canada
Tel: 705-275-4538; *Fax:* 705-275-4515
Toll-Free: 1-800-433-4863
Other Information: Alternative phone number: 705-275-1029
www.facebook.com/140558452626096
Number of Schools: 1 elementary; 1 secondary *Grades:* JK - 12
Enrollment: 580 *Number of Employees:* 77 employees
James Wesley, Director, Education

Kejick: **Shoal Lake #40 Education Authority**
c/o Education Authority
P.O. Box 7 Kejick PO Shoa
General Delivery, Kejick, ON P0X 1E0, Canada
Tel: 807-733-2455; *Fax:* 807-733-3900
www.facebook.com/ojibwayheritageschool
Grades: Elementary *Enrollment:* 50
Frances Green, Band Manager
frances.redsky@hotmail.com
Gwen Redsky, Education Director; Principal, Ojibway Heritage
School
gwenredsky.ohs@bimose.ca

Kingfisher Lake: **Kingfisher Lake Education
Authority**
P.O. Box 57
Kingfisher Lake, ON P0V 1Z0, Canada
Tel: 807-532-2067; *Fax:* 807-532-2063
www.kingfisherlake.ca
Grades: Elementary *Enrollment:* 100
Edna Quequish, Education Director, 807-532-2067, ext. 234
ednaq@kingfisherlake.ca

Longlac: **Long Lake #58 First Nations Education
Authority**
P.O. Box 89
Longlac, ON P0T 2A0
Tel: 807-876-4914
www.longlake58fn.ca/education
Number of Schools: 2 *Grades:* JK-12; Special Ed; Ojibwa
language *Enrollment:* 200
Claire Onabigon, Education Director
claireonabigon@58education.com

M'Chigeeng: **West Bay Board of Education**
22 Bebonang St., M'Chigeeng, ON P0P 1G0, Canada
Tel: 705-377-5611; *Fax:* 705-377-5080
Grades: Elem. *Enrollment:* 180
Melvina Corbiere, Education Coordinator

MacDiarmid: **Biinjitiwaabik Zaaging Anishinaabek
Education Authority**
Also known as: Rocky Bay First Nation Education
Authority
Rocky Bay Reserve
501 Spirit Bay Rd., MacDiarmid, ON P0T 2B0
Tel: 807-885-3401; *Fax:* 807-885-1218
www.rockybayfn.ca
Number of Schools: 2 *Grades:* Elem. *Note:* Biinjitiwaabik
Zaaging Anishnaabek Education Authority operates the Rocky
Bay Alternative High School & Biinjitiwaabik Zaaging
Anishnaabek School (Rocky Bay).
Gabrielle Swerdlyk, Education Director
gswerdlyk@rockybayfn.ca

Migisi Sahgaigan: **Eagle Lake First Nation Education
Board**
42 School Rd., Migisi Sahgaigan, ON P0V 3H0
Tel: 807-755-5350; *Fax:* 807-755-2086
sites.google.com/migisischool.com/migisischool
www.facebook.com/migisischool
Grades: Elem. *Note:* Eagle Lake First Nation Education Board
operates the Migisi Sahgaigan School.
Andrew Kivell, Principal & Director, Education
principal@migisi.ca

Mishkeegogamang: **Mishkeegogamang Education
Authority**
c/o Education Services
General Delivery, Mishkeegogamang, ON P0V 2H0
Tel: 807-928-2299; *Fax:* 807-928-2494
missabayschool@live.ca
www.mishkeegogamang.ca/serv-edu.html
Other Information: Alternative number: 807-928-2284
Number of Schools: 2 *Grades:* K - 8 *Enrollment:* 160
Ida Mackuck, Education Director
idamuckuck@gmail.com
Krystle Roundhead, School Receptionist

Morson: **Big Grassy River (Mishkosiminiziibiing)
Education Authority**
Pegamigaabo School
P.O. Box 453
513 Beach Rd., Morson, ON P0W 1J0, Canada
Tel: 807-488-5916; *Fax:* 807-488-5345
Toll-Free: 1-800-265-3379
school@biggrassy.ca
biggrassy.ca/education
Other Information: Alternate Phone: 807-488-5986
Number of Schools: 1 elementary *Grades:* JK - 8; Special Ed.
Enrollment: 61

Muncey: **Chippewas of the Thames First Nation
Board of Education**
324 Chippewa Rd., Muncey, ON N0L 1Y0
Tel: 519-289-0621; *Fax:* 519-289-0633
www.cottfn.com/education
Number of Schools: 1 *Grades:* Elementary *Note:* Chippewas of
the Thames First Nation Board of Education operates the Antler
River Elementary School.
Chantel Fisher, Education Director
cfisher@chippewa-ed.on.ca

Muskrat Dam: **Muskrat Dam First Nation Education
Authority**
c/o Samson Beardy Memorial School
P.O. Box 140
Muskrat Dam, ON P0V 3B0, Canada
Tel: 807-471-2524; *Fax:* 807-471-2649
muskratdamfirstnation@knet.ca
Other Information: Whasa Distant Education Centre, Phone:
807-471-2619
Number of Schools: 1 *Grades:* JK - 8 *Note:* Samson Beardy
Memorial School. The Muskrat Dam First Nation community is
situated approximately 370 kilometres north of Sioux Lookout.
Oji-Cee & English are spoken. The community features an
elementary school, plus the Wahsa Distance Education Centre
to support secondary & post-secondary students attending
schools in towns & cities.
Roy Morris, Education Director & Principal, 807-471-2573, ext.
211
royamorris@knet.ca

Neyaashiinigmiing: **Chippewas of Nawash Unceded
First Nation Board of Education**
6 Harbour Rd., Neyaashiinigmiing, ON N0H 2T0, Canada
Tel: 519-534-0882; *Fax:* 519-534-5138
www.nawash.ca/education
Number of Schools: 1 elementary *Grades:* JK - 8 *Number of
Employees:* 19 *Note:* The board of education serves the
Chippewas of Nawash Unceded First Nation band members of
the Neyaashiinigmiing Indian Reserve No. 27. The reserve is
situated on the eastern shore of the Saugeen (Bruce) Peninsula
in Ontario, approximately 26 kilometres from Wiarton. The
Chippewas of Nawash Unceded First Nation Board of Education
strives to offer a culturally & community based education, based
upon traditional values.
Jessica Keeshig-Martin, Chair, Board
Judy Nadjiwan, Education Administrator, 519-534-0882
nawashed.administrator@gbtel.ca
Jennifer Linklater, Coordinator, Post Secondary
nawashed.postsec@gbtel.ca
Connie Salkey, Coordinator, Secondary Student Services
nawashed.edcounsellor@gbtel.ca
Vanessa M. Keeshig, Administrative Support
nawashed.vkeeshig@gbtel.ca
Debra Chegahno, Principal, Kikendaasogamig Elementary
School
nawashed.principal@gbtel.ca

North Bay: **Anishinabek Education System (AES)**
Also known as: Kinoomaadziwin Education Body
#100, 132 Osprey Miikan, North Bay, ON P1B 8G5
Tel: 705-845-3634; *Fax:* 705-845-3637
aes-keb.com
www.facebook.com/AnishinabekEducation
Grades: JK - 12 *Enrollment:* 2000 *Note:* The AES serves a group
of 23 Anishinabek First Nations in Ontario.

Christine Dokis, Director, Education
christine.dokis@a-e-s.ca

North Spirit Lake: **North Spirit Lake Education
Authority**
General Delivery, North Spirit Lake, ON P0V 2G0
Tel: 807-776-0001; *Fax:* 807-776-0026
nsl.firstnation.ca
Number of Schools: 2 *Grades:* Elem.
Adrian Lawrence, Principal & Education Program Coordinator

Ogoki: **Marten Falls (Ogoki) First Nation Education
Authority**
c/o Education Department
General Delivery, Ogoki, ON P0T 2L0, Canada
Tel: 807-349-2628; *Fax:* 807-349-2511
www.martenfalls.ca/education
Number of Schools: 1 *Grades:* K - 8 *Note:* The Marten Falls
(Ogoki) First Nation Education Authority offers elementary
education in the Cree-Ojibwe community. Members of the First
Nation board in Thunder Bay, Ontario to attend secondary
school. The Matawa Education Department provides educational
support services to the Marten Falls (Ogoki) First Nation
Education Authority.
Sandy Moonias, Acting Education Director
sandyoren@hotmail.com
Gloria Coaster, Principal/1-2 Teacher
hcmsprincipal@gmail.com

Pawitik: **Naotkamegwanning Northwest Angle
Education Authority**
c/o Education Authority
1800 Pawitik St., Pawitik, ON P0X 1L0
Tel: 807-226-5411; *Fax:* 807-226-5389
Grades: K - 12 *Enrollment:* 300
Loranda Kavanaugh, Executive Assistant
Donna Copenace, Acting Education Director

Peawanuck: **Weenusk First Nation Education
Services**
P.O. Box 1
34 Main St., Peawanuck, ON P0L 2H0, Canada
Tel: 705-473-2554; *Fax:* 705-473-2503
Grades: Elementary *Enrollment:* 60
Edmond Hunter, Chief

Pic River First Nation: **Pic River First Nation
Education Authority**
Pic River Children & Family Learning Centre
P.O. Box 156
10 Lynx Rd., Pic River First Nation, ON P0T 1R0, Canada
Tel: 807-229-0198; *Fax:* 807-229-1944
www.picriver.com
Number of Schools: 1 elementary; 1 secondary; 1 early
childhood education *Grades:* K - 12 *Enrollment:* 94
Lisa Michano-Courchene, Director, Education
lisamichano@picriver.com
Stephanie Michano-Drover, Director, Early Childhood Education

Pikangikum: **Pikangikum Education Authority**
c/o Eenchokay Birchstick School
**General Delivery, Pikangikum First Nations, Pikangikum, ON
P0V 2L0, Canada**
Tel: 807-773-5561; *Fax:* 807-773-5958
info@ebs-school.org
www.ebs-school.org/pikangikum-education-authority.html
Number of Schools: 1 *Grades:* K - 12 *Enrollment:* 520 *Number of
Employees:* 60 teachers
Samson Keeper, Chair, Board
Kyle Peters, Director, Education, 807-773-1093
kylepeters57@gmail.com
Daniel Keeper, Assistant Director, Education, 807-773-1093

Sandy Lake: **Sandy Lake Board of Education**
P.O. Box 8
Sandy Lake, ON P0V 1V0, Canada
Tel: 807-774-1135; *Fax:* 807-774-1166
www.sandylake.firstnation.ca/?q=sandy-lake-board-education
Other Information: Alternate Phone: 807-774-1089
Number of Schools: 3 *Grades:* K - 12; Adult Ed. *Enrollment:* 514
Note: The Sandy Lake Board of Education oversees the
management of schools which serve students of Sandy Lake
First Nation.
Troy Kakepetum, Education Director, 807-774-1135
troykakepetum@knet.ca
Fabian Crow, Band Councillor - Education Portfolio,
807-774-3421

Sarnia: **Aamjiwnaang First Nation Education Administration**
Administration Office
978 Tashmoo Ave., Sarnia, ON N7T 7H5, Canada
Tel: 519-336-8410; *Fax:* 519-336-0382
www.aamjiwnaang.ca/education
www.facebook.com/AamjiwnaangEd
Grades: K - 12 *Note:* Formerly Chippewas of Sarnia, the community of Aamjiwnaang First Nation is located in the city limits of Sarnia, Ontario.
Vicki Ware, Education Coordinator

Sioux Lookout: **Windigo Education Authority**
P.O. Box 299
160 Alcona Dr., Sioux Lookout, ON P8T 1A3, Canada
Tel: 807-737-1585; *Fax:* 807-737-3133
www.windigoeducation.on.ca
Number of Schools: 4 elementary-middle *Grades:* JK - 8
Enrollment: 362 *Note:* Windigo Education Authority consists of the following First Nation members: Bearskin Lake First Nation, Cat Lake First Nation, Sachigo Lake First Nation, & Slate Falls Nation. The language of each First Nation community is Ojibway or Oji-Cree. Language and culture programs are offered by WEA.
Brittany Jeffery, Education Director
Rachelle Ningewance, Education Assistant
rningewance@windigo.on.ca
Pamela Hardy, Secondary Student Support Coordinator

Southwold: **Education Department of the Oneida Nation of the Thames**
2113 Elm Ave., Southwold, ON N0L 2G0, Canada
Tel: 519-652-1580; *Fax:* 519-652-3219
oneida.on.ca/life-long-learning-2
Other Information: Standing Stone School phone number:
519-652-3271
Grades: Elementary *Enrollment:* 210
Bette Summers, Life Long Learning Administrator
bette.summers@oneida.on.ca
Brenda Antone, Senior Administrative Assistant
brenda.antone@oneida.on.ca
Debra Bridgman, Principal - Standing Stone School

Thunder Bay: **Matawa Education Department**
20 Lillie St. N, Thunder Bay, ON P7C 5Y2
Tel: 807-768-3300; *Fax:* 807-768-3301
Toll-Free: 888-283-9747
education@matawa.on.ca
matawaeducation.com
Number of Schools: 8 *Grades:* K - 12 *Enrollment:* 700 *Number of Employees:* 56 teachers *Note:* The Matawa Education Department delivers educational support services to local education authorities. Education is provided at local Matawa First Nation schools in a culturally appropriate environment to meet the diverse needs of students. Post-secondary student support services, as well as alternative learning & adult education & training, are also offered.
Brad Battiston, Principal
bbattiston@matawa.on.ca
Sharon Nate, Manager, Education
snate@matawa.on.ca
Georgette O'Nabigon, Coordinator, Post-Secondary Program
gonabigon@matawa.on.ca

Tyendinaga Mohawk Territory: **Tyendinaga Mohawk Education, Culture, & Language Department**
Administration Bldg.
13 Old York Rd., Tyendinaga Mohawk Territory, ON K0K 1X0
Tel: 613-396-3424; *Fax:* 613-396-3627
www.mbq-tmt.org/
Number of Schools: 2 *Grades:* Pre-K - 12 *Note:* Educational programs available for the Mohawks of the Bay of Quinte include the Eksa'okon:'a Child Care Centre, the Tahatikonhsotontie Head Start Program, a Post-Secondary Education Program, a Native Student Liaison Program, an Employment & Training Program, the Ka:nhiote Public Library, & Mohawk Bus Lines. Mohawk language & cultural instruction is part of Tahatikonhsotontie Head Start, an early childhood education program.
Diana Barlow, Good Minds Coordinator, 967-01226716, ext. 102
dianabg@mbq-tmt.org
Angela Maracle, Interim Eksa'okon Centre Manager, 613-967-4401
Mike Hill, Mohawk Bus Lines Manager, 613-396-2000
mbl@mbq.tmt.org
Karen Lewis, Kanhiote Librarian, 613-967-6264
kanhiote@gmail.com
Patti Brinklow, Post-Secondary Education Counsellor, 613-396-3424
pattig@mbq-tmt.org
Kerri Smart, Mohawk Language Teacher, 613-396-6716
kerris@mbq-tmt.org

Lynda Leween, Employment & Training Officer, 613-396-3424, ext. 101
lyndal@mbq-tmt.org

Wallaceburg: **Walpole Island Elementary School**
521 Tecumseh Road, RR#3, Wallaceburg, ON N8A 4K9, Canada
Tel: 519-627-0712; *Fax:* 519-627-8596
walpoleislandfirstnation.ca/education
www.facebook.com/walpoleislandeducation
Grades: JK-8 *Enrollment:* 450 *Note:* The Walpole Island Elementary School is a First Nation operated school which serves members of the Walpole Island First Nation community. School employees are required to have knowledge & understanding of the Anishinaabeg culture. The education program is administered by the Walpole Island First Nation Board of Education. For secondary education, students from Walpole Island First Nation are transported to the nearby communities of Sarnia, Chatham, & Wallaceburg.
Russ Blackbird, Principal
russ.blackbird@walpoleislandschool.org

Wallaceburg: **Walpole Island First Nation Board of Education**
521 Tecumseh Rd., Wallaceburg, ON N8A 4K9
Tel: 519-662-7070; *Fax:* 519-627-8596
Number of Schools: 1 *Grades:* JK - 8 *Note:* Walpole Island Elementary School. Secondary school students from the Walpole Island First Nation community are transported to Chatham, Sarnia & Wallaceburg to attend school.

Weagamow Lake: **North Caribou Lake First Nation Education Authority**
P.O. Box 155
Weagamow Lake, ON P0V 2Y0
Tel: 807-469-1254; *Fax:* 807-469-1351
northcaribaboulakefirstnation@knet.ca
Grades: Elem.
Saul Williams, Education Director

Wikwemikong: **Wikwemikong Board of Education**
34 Henry St., Wikwemikong, ON P0P 2J0
Tel: 705-859-3834; *Fax:* 705-859-2407
info@wbe-education.ca
www.wbe-education.ca
Number of Schools: 7 *Grades:* K - 12 *Enrollment:* 486
Maureen Aiabens, Financial Controller/Manager, 705-859-3834, ext. 224
maiabens@wbe-education.ca
Dominic Beaudry, Education Director, 705-859-3834, ext. 229

Wunnummin Lake: **Wunnumin Lake Education Authority**
P.O. Box 105
Wunnummin Lake, ON P0V 2Z0, Canada
Tel: 807-442-2559; *Fax:* 807-442-2627
www.wunnumin.ca
Grades: Elementary *Enrollment:* 146
Sam Mamakwa, Director
samm@wunnumin.ca

Independent & Private Schools

Toronto: **Toronto Adventist District School Board (TADSB)**
531 Finch Ave. West, Toronto, ON M2R 3X2
Tel: 416-633-0090; *Fax:* 416-633-0467
info@tadsb.com
caasda.com
Number of Schools: 4 *Grades:* K. / Elem. / Sec. *Enrollment:* 850
Travis Afflick, Chair, Board
Norman Brown, Supervising Principal, 416-633-0090, ext. 222
nbrown@tadsb.com

Schools: Specialized

First Nations

Aroland: **Johnny Therriault Memorial School**
c/o Aroland First Nation
P.O. Box 40
Hwy 643, Aroland, ON P0T 1B0
Tel: 807-329-5470; *Fax:* 807-329-5472
arolandfirstnation@yahoo.ca
www.education.matawa.on.ca
Grades: K-9 *Enrollment:* 75 *Note:* The Johnny Therriault School serves the Aroland First Nation School, which is located approximately 350 kilometres northeast of Thunder Bay, Ontario. The school is supported by the Matawa Education Department. Tuition agreements are in place with the Superior-Greenstone District School Board, so that Aroland First Nation students can attend grades 10 to 12 in the communities of Nakina & Geraldton.

Sam Kashkeesh, Chief, Aroland First Nation
Patricia Magiskan, Member, Matawa Regional Committee on Education
Stephanie Ash, Communications Officer, Aroland First Nation, 807-767-4443

Attawapiskat: **J.R. Nakogee Elementary School**
Also known as: Attawapiskat First Nation Elementary
P.O. Box 15
Attawapiskat, ON P0L 1A0
Tel: 705-997-2114; *Fax:* 705-997-2357
www.attawapiskat.org
Grades: JK - 8; Special Ed *Note:* J.R. Nakogee Elementary School is located in the Ontario Cree fly-in only community of Attawapiskat. It is part of the Attawapiskat First Nation Education Authority.

Attawapiskat: **Vezina Secondary School**
P.O. Box 15
Attawapiskat, ON P0L 1A0
Tel: 705-997-2117; *Fax:* 705-997-2357
Grades: 9 - 12 *Note:* Attawapiskat First Nation Education Authority operates the high school on the west coast of James Bay.

Bearskin Lake: **Michikan Lake School**
c/o Michikan Lake School
P.O. Box 78
Bearskin Lake, ON P0V 1E0
Tel: 807-363-1011; *Fax:* 807-363-2519
www.windigoeducation.on.ca/schools/michikan-lake
Grades: JK-8 *Enrollment:* 100 *Note:* Operations of the Michikan Lake School are overseen by the Windigo Education Authority. The school provides elementary education to young people of the Bearskin Lake First Nation. The First Nation community is located about 425 kilometres north of Sioux Lookout, Ontario & offers classes on Aboriginal language and cultures.
Stephanie Petiquan, Principal, 807-363-2570
Jerry Mekanak, Education Director, 807-363-1011

Big Trout Lake: **Aglace Chapman Education Centre**
P.O. Box 168
Big Trout Lake, ON P0V 1G0, Canada
Tel: 807-537-2264; *Fax:* 807-537-1067
Grades: JK-11; Special Ed. *Enrollment:* 275 *Note:* The Kitchenuhmaykoosib Education Authority oversees operations of the Aglace Chapman Education Centre. The centre is located about 270 air miles north of Sioux Lookout, Ontario, where it provides education to the Kitchenuhmaykoosib Inninnuwug First Nation.

Cat Lake: **Lawrence Wesley Education Centre**
c/o Education Authority
P.O. Box 80
122 Back Rd., Cat Lake, ON P0V 1J0
Tel: 807-347-2102; *Fax:* 807-347-2057
www.titotayschool.myknet.org
Grades: JK-8 *Enrollment:* 120 *Note:* The Titotay Memorial School is one of four schools within the Windigo Education Authority. The First Nation School provides elementary education to members of the Cat Lake First Nation. The school is situated about 180 kilometres north of Sioux Lookout, Ontario & offers classes on Aboriginal language & culture.
Ruby Keesiquayash, Principal, 807-347-2294, ext. 1000
Marie Stewart, Education Director

Christian Island: **Christian Island Elementary School**
67 Kate Kegwin St., Christian Island, ON L0K 1C0
Tel: 705-247-2011
www.beausoleil-education.ca
Grades: JK - 8; Special Ed *Note:* Under the Beausoleil First Nation Education Authority, the Christian Island Elementary School provides education to the Chippewas of the Beausoleil First Nation.
Mike Lucas, Principal
m.lucas@beausoleil-education.ca
Sylvia Norton-Sutherland, Native Student Advisor

Constance Lake: **Mamawmatawa Holistic Education Center**
P.O. Box 4000
Constance Lake, ON P0L 1B0
Tel: 705-463-1199; *Fax:* 705-463-2077
www.clfn.on.ca
Grades: Daycare - JK - 12; Adult Education *Enrollment:* 257
Note: The Mamawmatawa Holistic Education Center educates members of the Constance Lake First Nation, who live west of Hearst, Ontario. The school operates under the direction of the Constance Lake First Nation Education Authority.
Zandra Bear-Lowen, Principal
zandra.bear-lowen@clfn.on.ca

Deer Lake: Deer Lake School
P.O. Box 69
Deer Lake, ON P0V 1N0, Canada
Tel: 807-775-2055; *Fax:* 807-775-2148
Toll-Free: 888-751-9225
www.dls.firstnationschools.ca
Grades: K4-K5; 1-9; Special Education *Note:* The Deer Lake School also offers native language instruction.
Ila Mamakeesic, Principal
ilamamakeesic@knet.ca
Myra Mamakeesic, Secretary

Dinorwic: Wabsnki-Penasi School
P.O. Box 24
Site 112, Dinorwic, ON P0V 1P0
Tel: 807-938-6825; *Fax:* 807-938-1166
Grades: JK - 8 *Note:* The First Nation elementary school is part of the Wabigoon Lake Ojibway Nation Education Authority. For secondary school education, students are transported thirty kilometres west to Dryden, Ontario.

Fort Hope: John C. Yesno Education Centre
P.O. Box 297
Fort Hope, ON P0T 1L0, Canada
Tel: 807-242-8421; *Fax:* 807-242-1592
www.facebook.com/jcyschool
Grades: JK-10; Special Ed. *Enrollment:* 280 *Note:* The John C. Yesno Education Centre serves the Eabametoong First Nation. The Ojibwe First Nations community is located on the north shore of northern Ontario's Eabamet Lake. Eabametoong First Nation students continuing their education beyond tenth grade attend schools in Thunder Bay, Sault Ste. Marie, & Sioux Lookout.
Phil Vardy, Acting Principal

Fort Severn: Wasaho First Nations School
P.O. Box 165
Fort Severn, ON P0V 1W0
Tel: 807-478-9548
Grades: JK-8 *Enrollment:* 120 *Note:* The Wasaho First Nations School is part of the Wasaho Education Authority. The school serves members of the Fort Severn First Nation in northern Ontario.
Sherri Curtis, Principal

Lansdowne House: Neskantaga First Nation Education Centre
P.O. Box 106
Lansdowne House, ON P0T 1Z0
Tel: 807-479-1170; *Fax:* 807-479-1178
Grades: JK - 9; Native culture & language *Note:* The Neskantaga First Nation Education Centre is situated in a community approximately 180 kilometres north of Pickle Lake in northern Ontario. The elementary school is a Matawa First Nations community school which receives educational support services from the Matawa Education Department.
Tony Sakanee, Education Director, 807-479-1024
tonysakanee@hotmail.com

Longlac: Migizi Wazisin Elementary School
P.O. Box 240
Martin Rd., Longlac, ON P0T 2A0
Tel: 807-876-4482; *Fax:* 807-876-4128
www.longlake58fn.ca
Grades: JK - 7; Special Ed; Native language *Note:* The Migizi Wazisin Elementary School is located in Long Lake #58 First Nation, an Anishinaabe (Ojibway) First Nation near Geraldton, Ontario. It serves students from both the Long Lake #58 First Nation & the Ginoogaming First Nation. Operations of the elementary school are administered by the Long Lake #58 & Ginoogaming First Nations Education Authority.

Mobert: Netamisakomik Education Centre
P.O. Box 615
Mobert, ON P0M 2J0, Canada
Tel: 807-822-2011; *Fax:* 807-822-2710
www.picmobert.ca
Grades: JK-8
Jacky Craig, Principal
principal@picmobert.ca

Muskrat Dam: Samson Beardy Memorial School
P.O. Box 43
Muskrat Dam, ON P0V 3B0
Tel: 807-471-2524; *Fax:* 807-471-2649
Grades: JK - 8 *Note:* The Samson Beardy Memorial School is a First Nation operated school administered by the Muskrat Dam First Nation Education Authority. Secondary & post-secondary students attend schools outside the remote First Nation community.

Nordegg: Taotha School
P.O. Box 39
Nordegg, ON T0M 2H0
Tel: 403-721-3989; *Fax:* 403-721-2174
Note: The Taotha School is part of the Stoney Education Authority. The school serves members of the Stoney Nakoda First Nation.

Ogoki Post: Henry Coaster Memorial School
General Delivery, Ogoki Post, ON P0T 2L0
Tel: 807-349-2509; *Fax:* 807-349-2511
Grades: JK - 8 *Enrollment:* 90 *Note:* Henry Coaster Memorial School is located in Marten Falls Nation, on the north side of the Albany River in northern Ontario. The First Nation school offers traditional culture & language programming. The elementary school operates with support from the Marten Falls (Ogoki) First Nation Education Authority.
Norma Achneepineskum, A/Education Administrator, 807-349-2628

Ohsweken: Six Nations of the Grand River
P.O. Box 5000
1695 Chiefswood Rd., Ohsweken, ON N0A 1M0, Canada
Tel: 519-445-2201; *Fax:* 519-445-4208
www.sixnations.ca
Number of Schools: 5 *Grades:* 3-8 *Enrollment:* 1328
Kathy Knott

Pikangikum: Eenchokay Birchstick School
General Delivery, Pikangikum, ON P0V 2L0, Canada
Tel: 807-773-5561; *Fax:* 807-773-5958
www.ebs-school.org
Grades: K./Elem./Sec. *Note:* Serving students of the Pikangikum First Nation.
Melanie Doyle, Principal

Sachigo Lake: Martin McKay Memorial School
P.O. Box 51
Sachigo Lake, ON P0V 2P0, Canada
Tel: 807-595-2526; *Fax:* 807-595-1305
www.windigoeducation.on.ca/schools/martin-mckay-memorial
Grades: JK-8; Aboriginal language & culture *Enrollment:* 100
Note: The Martin McKay Memorial School serves students of the Sachigo Lake First Nation. The First Nation community is situated approximately 150 kilometres west of Big Trout Lake, Ontario. Activities of the Sachigo Lake First Nation school are administered by the Windigo Education Authority.
Robin Warner, Principal, 807-595-2526

Sarnia: Aamjiwnaang First Nation Junior Kindergarten
1900 Virgil Ave., Sarnia, ON N7T 8A7
Tel: 519-344-4132; *Fax:* 519-344-6956
Grades: JK *Note:* Under the Aamjiwnaang First Nation Education Administration, education is offered to members of the Aamjiwnaang First Nation.
Kim Henry, Principal
Muriel Joseph-Plain, Supervisor, 519-344-5831

Sault St. Marie: Batchewana Learning Centre
15 Jean Ave., Sault St. Marie, ON P6B 4B1, Canada
Tel: 705-759-7285; *Fax:* 705-759-9982
Toll-Free: 1-866-339-3370
colleen@batchewana.ca
www.batchewana.ca
Elaine McDonagh, Education Director/Principal

Slate Falls: Bimaychikamah School
c/o Bimaychikamah School General Delivery
54 Lakeview Dr., Slate Falls, ON P0V 3C0
Tel: 807-737-5701; *Fax:* 888-431-5617
www.slatefalls.firstnation.ca
Grades: JK-8; Aboriginal language & culture *Enrollment:* 42
Note: Education for members of the Slate Falls Nation is provided by the Bimaychikamah School. The elementary school is situated in the Slate Falls Nation community north of Sioux Lookout, Ontario. Operations of Bimaychikamah School are overseen by the Windigo Education Authority.
Danick Clavel, Principal, 807-737-5701
Chancillor Crane, Education Director

Summer Beaver: Nibinamik First Nation Education Centre
c/o Nibinamik Education Centre General Delivery
P.O. Box 117
Summer Beaver, ON P0T 3B0
Tel: 807-593-2195; *Fax:* 807-593-2198
www.nibinamikeducationcentre.firstnationschools.ca
Grades: K-9 *Enrollment:* 100 *Note:* The Nibinamik First Nation Education Centre is a Matawa First Nations community school which receives educational support services from the Matawa Education Department. The Nibinamik First Nation is located

approximately 185 kilometres northwest of Pickle Lake in northern Ontario & offers classes in Native languages.
Kevin Booth, Principal
Doreen Beaver, Administrative Assistant
doreenbeaver@gmail.com

Whitedog: Mizhakiiwetung Memorial School
General Delivery, Whitedog, ON P0X 1P0, Canada
Tel: 807-927-2000; *Fax:* 807-927-2176
Grades: JK - 12; Alternative Education *Enrollment:* 297 *Note:* Elementary & secondary education is provided to Wabaseemoong First Nation students living in a community situated about 100 kilometres northwest of Kenora, Ontario. The school focuses upon academics as well as cultural education.
Ron R. McDonald, Principal, 807-927-2000, ext. 246

Wiarton: Cape Croker Elementary School
Also known as: Chippewas of Nawash Elementary School
17 School Rd., RR#5, Wiarton, ON N0H 2T0
Tel: 519-534-0719; *Fax:* 519-534-1592
www.nawash.ca/school/
Grades: Pre.- 8 *Note:* Part of the Chippewas of Nawash Unceded First Nation Board of Education, the Cape Croker Elementary School provides a culturally-based education, which includes the history of the Anishnabek, band sovereignty, & communication & language arts in Anishinaabemowin & English.
Judy Nadjiwan, Education Administrator, Board of Education, 519-534-0882
nawashed.administrator@gbtel.ca
Debra Chegahno, Principal, Cape Croker Elementary School, 519-534-0719
nawashed.principal@gbtel.ca
Chastity Jenner, Ojibway Language Resource Teacher
nawashed.nativelanguage@gbtel.ca

Hearing Impaired

Belleville: The Sir James Whitney School for the Deaf
350 Dundas St. West, Belleville, ON K8P 1B2
Tel: 613-967-2823; *Toll-Free:* 800-501-6240
pdsbnet.ca/en/schools/sir-james-whitney
TTY: 613-967-2823
Enrollment: 110
Arnold Potma, Principal

Brantford: The W. Ross Macdonald School for the Blind
350 Brant Ave., Brantford, ON N3T 3J9
Tel: 519-759-0730; *Toll-Free:* 866-618-9092
pdsbnet.ca/en/schools/w-ross-macdonald
twitter.com/WRMSBrantford
Enrollment: 217
Dan Maggiacomo, Principal

London: The Robarts School for the Deaf
1515 Cheapside St., London, ON N5V 3N9
Tel: 519-453-4400
pdsbnet.ca/en/schools/robarts
TTY: 519-453-4400
Linda Wall, Vice Principal

Milton: Ernest C. Drury School for the Deaf
255 Ontario St. South, Milton, ON L9T 2M5
Tel: 905-878-2851
pdsbnet.ca/en/schools/ernest-c-drury
TTY: 905-878-7195
twitter.com/ECDMilton
Cindy Smith, Principal

Special Education

Belleville: Sagonaska Demonstration School
350 Dundas St. West, Belleville, ON K8P 1B2
Tel: 613-967-2830
pdsbnet.ca/en/schools/sagonaska
twitter.com/SagonaskaLD
Enrollment: 120
Tina MacCauley-Gray, Principal

London: Amethyst Demonstration School
1515 Cheapside St., London, ON N5V 3N9
Tel: 519-453-4400
pdsbnet.ca/en/schools/amethyst
twitter.com/AmethystSchool
Sean Gregory, Principal

Milton: Trillium Demonstration School
347 Ontario St. South, Milton, ON L9T 3X9
Tel: 905-878-2851
pdsbnet.ca/en/schools/trillium
TTY: 905-878-7195

Enrollment: 120
Desiree Smith, Principal

Mississauga: Kids CAN Social Centre
Oakwood Academy
2150 Torquay Mews, Mississauga, ON L5N 2M6
Tel: 416-578-8116
www.kidscancentre.com
www.facebook.com/kidscan.charity.9
twitter.com/KidsCANCharity
Grades: JK-8 *Note:* Offers individualized education programs to students with special needs.

Newmarket: Above & Beyond Learning Experience
#202, 1220 Stellar Dr., Newmarket, ON L3Y 7B9
Tel: 705-796-2253; *Fax:* 844-320-4838
Toll-Free: 855-796-2253
able_info@ablearning.org
www.ablearning.org
www.facebook.com/AboveBeyondLearning
www.instagram.com/ablearningexperience
Enrollment: 25
Mikki White, Principal, 705-796-2253, ext. 2
mikki@ablearning.org
Phil White, Vice-Principal

Oakville: Missing Links Academy
P.O. Box 60026
1515 Rebecca St., Oakville, ON L6L 6R4
Tel: 905-876-0055
info@missinglinks.ca
www.missinglinks.ca
Grades: Pre.-8 *Note:* Missing Links fills the gaps to Autism by delivering unique, individualized programming for the education and treatment of children with Autism Spectrum Disorder (ASD) and other exceptionalities.
Am Badwall, Executive Director

Ottawa: Centre Jules-Léger
281, av Lanark, Ottawa, ON K1Z 6R8
Tél: 613-761-9300; *Téléc:* 613-761-9301
Ligne sans frais: 866-390-3670
centrejulesleger.ca
Other Information: ATS: 613-761-9302
Note: Services aux enfants (et leurs familles) en difficultés d'apprentissage, avec ou sans déficit d'attention / hyperactivité, qui sont sourds ou malentendant, qui sont aveugles ou en basse vision, ou qui sont sourds et aveugles.
Ginette Faubert, Surintendante

Thornhill: Giant Steps Toronto Inc.
School
35 Flowervale Rd., Thornhill, ON L3T 4J3
Tel: 905-881-3104; *Fax:* 905-881-4592
info@giantstepstoronto.ca
www.giantstepstoronto.ca
www.facebook.com/GiantStepsToronto
www.instagram.com/giantstepstoronto
Note: Giant Steps is a school & therapy centre for elementary school-aged children with Autism Spectrum Disorder (ASD).
Colleen Smith, Executive Director
csmith@giantstepstoronto.ca
Joanne Scott-Jackson, Director, Development
jscottjackson@giantstepstoronto.ca

Toronto: The Dunblaine School
21 Deloraine Ave., Toronto, ON M5M 2A8
Tel: 416-483-9215; *Fax:* 416-483-0903
info@dunblaineschool.com
www.dunblaineschool.com
Grades: Elem. *Note:* A specialized school for students with learning disabilities.
Charleen Pryke, Principal

Toronto: New Haven Learning Centre
301 Lanor Ave., Toronto, ON M8W 2R1
Tel: 416-259-4445; *Fax:* 416-259-2023
info@newhavencentre.com
www.newhavencentre.com
twitter.com/NewHavenCentre
www.linkedin.com/groups/New-Haven-Learning-Centre-3010708
www.youtube.com/user/NewHavenCentre
Note: Centre of Excellence in the treatment and education of children with autism.
Sandra Hughes, Executive Director, 416-259-4445, ext. 12

Toronto: Reach Toronto
#206, 2238 Dundas St. West, Toronto, ON M5R 3A9
Tel: 416-929-1670
www.reachtoronto.ca
www.facebook.com/ReachToronto
twitter.com/reachtoronto

Note: Reach Toronto is a not-for-profit organization, offering unique programs for adults and youth with ASD and Asperger's Syndrome.

Distance Education

Bayfield: Virtual High School (Ontario) (VHS)
P.O. Box 402
27 Main St. North, Bayfield, ON N0M 1G0
www.virtualhighschool.com
Stephen Baker, Principal, Founder and CEO
Principal@VirtualHighSchool.com
Kim Loebach, Director of Operations; Human Resources
Kimberley.Loebach@VirtualHighSchool.com
Ashley Homuth, School Administrative Head
Ashley.Homuth@VirtualHighSchool.com
Adam Wise, Registrar
Adam.Wise@VirtualHighSchool.com

Clinton: Avon Maitland Distance Education Centre (AMDEC)
P.O. Box 729
165 Princess St. East, Clinton, ON N0M 1L0
Tel: 519-482-5428; *Fax:* 519-482-8795
office@amdec.ca
www.amdec.ca
Other Information: principal@amdec.ca
Grades: Secondary *Note:* The Avon Maitland District e-Learning Centre is a full distance, online secondary school course provider administered by the Avon Maitland District School Board.

Embrun: Ottawa Carleton E-School (OCES)
P.O. Box 277
#201, 993 Notre-Dame St., Embrun, ON K0A 1W0
Tel: 613-443-9522; *Fax:* 613-482-4504
info@ottawacarletone-school.ca
www.ottawacarletone-school.ca
www.facebook.com/myeschool
twitter.com/Canada_eSchool
www.linkedin.com/in/canadaeschool
myskype.info/myeschool
Grades: Secondary *Note:* Accredited Internet high school offering Ontario Secondary School Diploma (OSSD).
Annette Levesque, Director
Carl J. Frizell, Principal

Lindsay: OpenSchool (OS)
230 Angeline St. South, Lindsay, ON K9V 4R2
Tel: 705-328-2925; *Fax:* 705-878-8891
office@openschoolontario.ca
www.openschoolontario.ca
Grades: Secondary *Note:* OpenSchool is a continuous entry online school offering Ontario high school credits "on demand." They are part of the Adult and Continuing Education program with Trillium Lakelands District School Board.

Lindsay: Trillium Lakelands District School Board ~ Virtual Learning Centre (VLC)
230 Angeline St. South, Lindsay, ON K9V 4R2
Tel: 705-328-2925; *Fax:* 705-878-8891
www.virtuallearning.ca
twitter.com/tldsbvlc
Grades: Secondary *Note:* Provides on-line secondary level credit courses that count towards the high school diploma.
Peter Warren, Principal, 705-328-2925
Kim Boldt, Manager/Registrar, 705-328-2925

Sioux Lookout: Wahsa Distance Education Centre
P.O. Box 1118
74 Front St., Sioux Lookout, ON P8T 1B7, Canada
Tel: 807-737-1488; *Fax:* 807-737-1732
Toll-Free: 800-667-3703
Grades: 9-12 *Enrollment:* 950 *Note:* The Wahsa Distance Education Centre allows students in northern Ontario communities across the Sioux Lookout District to complete their secondary school education at home. Courses & services are developed in consultation with First Nation communities. The Centre is operated by the Northern Nishnawbe Education Council.
Darrin Head, Principal
dhead@nnec.on.ca

Toronto: Granton Institute of Technology
263 Adelaide St. West, Toronto, ON M5H 9Z9
Tel: 416-977-3929; *Fax:* 416-977-5612
info@grantoninstitute.com
www.grantontech.com
www.facebook.com/264715466875614
Note: Offers learn-at-home Certificate and Diploma courses.

Toronto: Independent Learning Centre (ILC)
P.O. Box 200 Q
Toronto, ON M4T 2T1
Tel: 416-484-2704; *Fax:* 416-484-2722
Toll-Free: 800-387-5512
www.facebook.com/independentlearningcentre
twitter.com/ILC_CEI
Grades: 9 - 12; OSSD; GED: ESL *Note:* The Independent Learning Centre (ILC) is Ontario's leading provider of accredited distance education and GED Testing.
Lise Leclair, Senior Information Officer, 416-484-2600, ext. 2144
lleclair@tvo.org
Sarah Irwin, Managing Director, 416-484-2600, ext. 2003
sirwin@tvo.org

Independent & Private Schools

Rockland: Canadian International Hockey Academy
8720 County Rd. 17, Rockland, ON K4K 1T2
Fax: 866-739-8652
Toll-Free: 877-244-9199
www.cihacademy.com
Grades: 9 - 12 *Enrollment:* 80 *Note:* Hockey boarding institution providing athletes a tailored education provided by the Upper Canada District School Board (UCDSB).
Randy Stevenson, Headmaster, 613-446-2212, ext. 222
rstevenson@cihacademy.com
Germain Laflèche, Director of Admissions, 613-446-2212, ext. 223
glafleche@cihacademy.com
Claudine Loiselle, Director of Finance, 613-446-2212, ext. 228
cloiselle@cihacademy.com

Schools: Independent & Private

Protestant

Ajax: Faithway Baptist Church School
1964 Salem Rd., Ajax, ON L1T 4V3, Canada
Tel: 905-686-0951; *Fax:* 905-686-1450
faithway@faithway.org
www.school.faithway.org
Grades: K./Elem./Sec. *Enrollment:* 65
L. Homan

Ajax: Pickering Christian School
162 Rossland Rd. East, Ajax, ON L1T 4V2, Canada
Tel: 905-427-3120; 905-427-0211
office@pickeringcs.on.ca
www.pickeringcs.on.ca
www.facebook.com/PickeringCS
www.linkedin.com/company/pickering-christian-school
Grades: JK-8 *Enrollment:* 210 *Number of Employees:* 35
Dr. Paul Douglas Ogborne, Principal
pogborne@pickeringcs.on.ca
Judith Grant, Vice-Principal
jgrant@pickeringcs.on.ca
Nathaniel Ogborne, Vice-Principal
nogborne@pickeringcs.on.ca
Dave Park, Development Director
dpark@pickeringcs.on.ca

Alliston: Alliston Community Christian School (ACCS)
4428 Adjala-Tecumseth Townline, RR#4, Alliston, ON L9R 1V4, Canada
Tel: 705-434-2227; *Fax:* 705-435-0126
info@allistonccs.ca
www.allistonccs.com
Grades: K./Elem. *Enrollment:* 113
John Bronsema, Principal

Amaranth: Dufferin Area Christian School
394016 County Rd. 12, Amaranth, ON L9W 0N2, Canada
Tel: 519-941-4368; *Fax:* 519-941-3748
Grades: Elem.
Jelko Oosterhof, Principal

Ancaster: Hamilton District Christian High
92 Glancaster Rd., Ancaster, ON L9G 3K9, Canada
Tel: 905-648-6655; *Fax:* 905-648-3139
info@hdch.org
hdch.org
www.facebook.com/HDCH.info
twitter.com/HDCH_Info
www.youtube.com/user/HDCHtube
Grades: Sec. *Enrollment:* 448
Nathan Siebenga, Principal

Aylmer: Immanuel Christian School Society
75 Caverly Rd., Aylmer, ON N5H 2P6, Canada
Tel: 519-773-8476; *Fax:* 519-773-8315
office@immanuelchristianschool.net
www.immanuelchristianschool.net
www.facebook.com/ICSAylmer
twitter.com/ICSAylmer

Grades: K./Elem.
Keith Cameron, Principal
k.cameron@immanuelchristianschool.net

Aylmer: Mount Salem Christian School (MSCS)
c/o Evangelical Mennonite Church
6576 Springfield Rd., RR#6, Aylmer, ON N5H 2R5
Tel: 519-765-3555; *Fax:* 519-765-3879
info@mtscs.ca
www.mtscs.ca
www.facebook.com/mountsalemchristianschool
twitter.com/mscsinfo

Grades: JK - 12 *Note:* Mount Salem Christian School is an interdenominational school, using a BEKA curriculum.
Lena Wall, Principal
lwall@mtscs.ca
Anita Thiessen, Secretary
athiessen@mtscs.ca

Barrie: Heritage Christian Academy
79 Ardagh Rd., Barrie, ON L4N 9B6
Tel: 705-733-0112; *Fax:* 705-733-2054

Grades: JK - 12 *Enrollment:* 75
Pastor Brett Penell, Principal

Barrie: Timothy Christian School
750 Essa Rd., Barrie, ON L4N 9E9, Canada
Tel: 705-726-6621; *Fax:* 705-726-8571
tcsgen@timothychristianschool.ca
www.timothychristianschool.ca
twitter.com/tcs_barrie
www.instagram.com/tcs_barrie

Grades: JK-8 *Note:* Timothy Christian School is an interdenominational school.
Rod Berg, Principal
Robin Nibourg, Secretary
Michelle Roberts, Director, Development

Beamsville: Great Lakes Christian High School
4875 King St., Beamsville, ON L0R 1B6, Canada
Tel: 905-563-5374; *Fax:* 905-563-0818
www.glchs.on.ca
www.facebook.com/294769903952932
twitter.com/glchs

Grades: 9-12
Don Rose, Principal & Chief Administrator
drose@glchs.on.ca

Belleville: Belleville Christian School (BCS)
18 Christian School Rd., RR#5, Belleville, ON K8N 4Z5, Canada
Tel: 613-962-7849; *Fax:* 613-962-6440
office@bellevillechristianschool.ca
www.bellevillechristianschool.ca
www.facebook.com/BellevilleChristianSchool

Grades: JK-8
Laurie Tuckey, Director, Learning

Belleville: Quinte Christian High School (QCHS)
138 Wallbridge-Loyalist Rd., Belleville, ON K8N 4Z2, Canada
Tel: 613-968-7870; *Fax:* 613-968-7970
admin@qchs.ca
www.qchs.ca
www.facebook.com/QCHS.CA
twitter.com/quintechristian
www.youtube.com/user/QuinteChristian

Grades: Secondary
John Vanderwindt, Principal
principal@qchs.ca

Bloomingdale: Koinonia Christian Academy
850 Sawmill Rd., Bloomingdale, ON N0B 1K0, Canada
Tel: 519-744-7447; *Fax:* 519-744-6745
kcf@kcf.org
www.kcf.org
www.facebook.com/koinoniabloomingdale
twitter.com/kcf_org

Enrollment: 157
David J. Champion, Principal
dave.champion@kcf.org

Bowmanville: Durham Christian High School
340 West Scugog Lane, Bowmanville, ON L1C 3K2, Canada
Tel: 905-623-5940; *Fax:* 905-623-6258
office@dchs.com
www.dchs.com
www.facebook.com/durhamchristianhighschool
twitter.com/www_dchs_com

Grades: Sec.
Shannon Marcus, Principal
principal@dchs.com

Bowmanville: Knox Christian School
410 North Scugog Ct., Bowmanville, ON L1C 6T1, Canada
Tel: 905-623-5871
office@knoxchristian.com
www.knoxchristian.com
www.facebook.com/knoxchristianschool

Grades: K./Elem. *Enrollment:* 193
Paul Marcus, Principal & COO
principal@knoxchristian.com

Brampton: Canada Christian Academy
22 Abbey Rd., Brampton, ON L6W 2T8
Tel: 905-789-5841; *Fax:* 289-901-0982
info@canadachristianacademy.org
canadachristianacademy.org

Grades: JK - 12
Deepa Patro, Principal

Brampton: John Knox Christian School
82 McLaughlin Rd. South, Brampton, ON L6Y 2C7, Canada
Tel: 905-451-3236; *Fax:* 905-451-3448
info@bramptonjkcs.org
bramptonjkcs.org
www.facebook.com/johnknoxbrampton
twitter.com/JKCSBrampton

Grades: JK-8 *Enrollment:* 300
George Van Kampen, Principal
gvankampen@bramptonjkcs.org

Brantford: Brantford Christian School (BCS)
7 Calvin St., Brantford, ON N3S 3E4, Canada
Tel: 519-752-0433; *Fax:* 519-752-6088
www.bcsbrantford.ca
www.facebook.com/1544451639151540

Grades: JK-8
Justin DeMoor, Principal
Francine Roth, Vice-Principal
Leanna Silver, Vice-Principal

Brantford: Central Baptist Academy (CBA)
300 Fairview Dr., Brantford, ON N3R 2X6, Canada
Tel: 519-754-4806; *Fax:* 519-754-4201
office@cbabrantford.ca
www.cbabrantford.ca

Grades: JK-10
Jordan Butcher, Principal

Breslau: Woodland Christian High School
1058 Spitzig Rd., Breslau, ON N0B 1M0
Tel: 519-648-2114; *Fax:* 519-648-3402
office@woodland.on.ca
www.woodland.on.ca
www.facebook.com/WoodlandCHS
twitter.com/woodlandchs
www.linkedin.com/company/woodland-christian-high-school
www.youtube.com/user/WoodlandCHSVideos

Grades: Sec. *Enrollment:* 194
John VanPelt, Principal
principal@woodland.on.ca

Burlington: Burlington Christian Academy (BCA)
521 North Service Rd. West, Burlington, ON L7P 5C3, Canada
Tel: 905-639-7364; *Fax:* 905-639-1657
office@onlyatbccs.com
onlyatbca.com
www.facebook.com/burlingtonchristianacademy
twitter.com/BCA1975
www.instagram.com/burlingtonchristianacademy

Grades: JK-8 *Enrollment:* 150
Heather Crossing, Principal
heather.crossing@onlyatbccs.com
Doreen Van de Ban, Office Administrator
Teresa Hawton, Head, Primary Division
teresa.hawton@onlyatbccs.com
John Williams, Head, Junior & Senior Division
john.williams@onlyatbccs.com
JD Collier, Head, Junior & Senior Programming
jd.collier@onlyatbccs.com

Burlington: Grace Christian School
607 Dynes Rd., Burlington, ON L7N 2V4, Canada
Tel: 905-634-8015; *Fax:* 905-634-9772
office@graceschool.ca
www.graceschool.ca

Grades: K./Elem. *Enrollment:* 200 *Note:* Grace Christian School was formed as a result of the amalgamation of Covenant Christian School & John Calvin Christian School.
Mike VanderVelde, Principal

Burlington: Trinity Christian School
2170 Itabashi Way, Burlington, ON L7M 5B3, Canada
Tel: 905-634-3052; *Fax:* 905-634-9382
trinity@tcsonline.ca
www.tcsonline.ca
www.facebook.com/TCSBurlington

Grades: JK-8
Sara Flokstra, Interim Principal
sara.flokstra@tcsonline.ca
Christy Mack, Vice-Principal, Learning
christy.mack@tcsonline.ca
Kim Abela, Communication & Office Administrator
Heidi Purvis, Financial Administrator
finance@tcsonline.ca
Audrey McGregor, Curriculum Coordinator
audrey.mcgregor@tcsonline.ca

Caledon: Brampton Christian School (BCS)
12480 Hutchinson Farm Lane, Caledon, ON L7C 2B6
Tel: 905-843-3771; *Fax:* 905-843-2929
admin@bramptoncs.org
www.bramptoncs.org
www.facebook.com/bramptoncs
twitter.com/BramptonCS

Grades: JK - 12
Andy Cabral, Principal
afcabral@bramptoncs.org
Karen Davis, Vice-Principal, Senior High
kdavis@bramptoncs.org
Cathy Doggart, Vice-Principal, Elementary
cdoggart@bramptoncs.org
John Miller, Vice-Principal, Junior High
jmiller@bramptoncs.org

Cambridge: Cambridge Christian School (CCS)
Also known as: Eagles' Nest Christian Preschool
229 Myers Rd., Cambridge, ON N1R 7H3, Canada
Tel: 519-623-2261; *Fax:* 519-623-4042
info@cambridgechristianschool.com
www.cambridgechristianschool.com
www.facebook.com/CambridgeCS

Grades: Pre.-8 *Enrollment:* 241
Scott Beda, Principal
sbeda@cambridgechristianschool.com
Rhonda Kalverda, Advancement Coordinator

Chatham: Chatham Christian High School (CCHS)
475 Keil Dr. South, Chatham, ON N7M 6L8
Tel: 519-352-4980; *Fax:* 519-352-4041
office@chathamchristian.ca
www.chathamchristian.ca
www.facebook.com/ChathamChristianSchool
twitter.com/CK_CCS

Grades: 9-12 *Enrollment:* 140
Marvin Bierling, Head Administrator

Chatham: Chatham Christian School
475 Keil Dr. South, Chatham, ON N7M 6L8
Tel: 519-352-4980; *Fax:* 519-352-4041
www.chathamchristian.ca
www.facebook.com/ChathamChristianSchool
twitter.com/CK_CCS

Grades: JK - 12
Marvin Bierling, Head Administrator
marvinbierling@chathamchristian.ca

Chatham: Eben-Ezer Christian School
485 McNaughton Ave. East, Chatham, ON N7L 2H2, Canada
Tel: 519-354-1142; *Fax:* 519-354-2159
info@eecschatham.com
eecschatham.com

Grades: Elem.
R. Vanderveen, Chair
Lisa DeBoer, Principal

Clinton: Huron Christian School
87 Percival St., Clinton, ON N0M 1L0
Tel: 519-482-7851; *Fax:* 519-482-7448
office@huronchristianschool.ca
www.huronchristianschool.ca

Grades: JK.-8
Heather VanDorp, Chair

Nick Geleynse, Principal
principal@huronchristianschool.ca

Cobourg: Northumberland Christian School
8861 Danforth Rd., Cobourg, ON K9A 4J8, Canada
Tel: 905-372-8766; *Fax:* 905-372-6299
office@northumberlandchristian.ca
ncschool.wixsite.com/ncschool
www.facebook.com/160903610730492
Grades: Pre.-8 *Note:* Northumberland Christian School is an interdenominational school for students in preschool through grade 8.
Ginette Mack, Principal
gmack@northumberlandchristian.ca

Copetown: Rehoboth Christian School (RCS)
P.O. Box 70
198 Inksetter Rd., Copetown, ON L0R 1J0, Canada
Tel: 905-627-5977; *Fax:* 905-628-4422
office@rehoboth.on.ca
www.rehoboth.on.ca
Grades: K.-12 *Note:* Rehoboth Free Reformed Christian School Society of Copetown owns & operates the school. Education is provided with a Reformed Christian view.
Brian Kemper, Principal
principal@rehoboth.on.ca
Herman den Hollander, Elementary Vice-Principal
hdenhollander@rehoboth.on.ca
Dick Naves, Secondary Vice-Principal
dnaves@rehoboth.on.ca

Drayton: Community Christian School (CCS)
P.O. Box 141
35 High St., Drayton, ON N0G 1P0, Canada
Tel: 519-638-2935
office@ccsdrayton.org
www.ccsdrayton.org
Grades: JK-8 *Enrollment:* 97 *Number of Employees:* 12
Ray Verburg, Principal & COO
principal@ccsdrayton.org
Candace Burnett, Office Manager

Dundas: Providence Christian School
542 Ofield Rd. North, Dundas, ON L9H 5E2, Canada
Tel: 905-627-1411; *Fax:* 905-627-8004
office@providencecs.ca
www.providencecs.ca
www.facebook.com/providencecs
twitter.com/DCCS_ca
Grades: Pre.-8 *Enrollment:* 180
Kevin Bouwers, Principal
kbouwers@providencecs.ca
Tina Vandervelde, Office Administrator

Dunnville: Dunnville Christian School
37 Robinson Rd., RR#1, Dunnville, ON N1A 2W1, Canada
Tel: 905-774-5142; *Fax:* 905-774-5519
www.dunnvillechristianschool.ca
www.facebook.com/DunnvilleChristianSchool
Grades: K./Elem. *Enrollment:* 100
Ralph De Boer, Chair
Nicole VanHuizen, Principal
nvanhuizen@dunnvillechristianschool.ca
Marjorie Hoekstra, Director, Development
secretary@dunnvillechristianschool.ca

East Gwillimbury: King Christian School
19740 Bathurst St., East Gwillimbury, ON L9N 0N5, Canada
Tel: 905-853-1881; *Fax:* 905-853-1701
office@kingchristian.ca
www.kingchristian.ca
Grades: K./Elem. *Enrollment:* 220
Sherry Bokma, Principal

Fergus: Emmanuel Christian High School
680 Tower St. South, Fergus, ON N1M 0B1, Canada
Tel: 226-383-7300
office@echs.ca
www.echs.ca
Grades: Sec.
Henk Nobel, Principal
hnobel@echs.ca

Fergus: Maranatha Christian School
8037 Wellington Rd. 19, RR#3 Garafraxa St., Fergus, ON N1M 2W4
Tel: 519-843-3029; *Fax:* 519-843-4711
info@mcsfergus.ca
www.mcsfergus.ca
Grades: Elem. *Enrollment:* 175
R. Hoeksema, Principal
principal@mcsfergus.ca

Fort Erie: Niagara Christian Collegiate (NCC)
2619 Niagara Pkwy., Fort Erie, ON L2A 5M4
Tel: 905-871-6980; *Fax:* 905-871-9260
ncc@niagaracc.com
www.niagaracc.com
Grades: JK - 12
Scott Herron, President
Mark Thiessen, Principal
Chris Baird, Vice-Principal

Georgetown: Halton Hills Christian School
11643 Trafalgar Rd., Georgetown, ON L7G 4S4, Canada
Tel: 905-877-4221; *Fax:* 905-877-1483
office@hh-cs.org
www.haltonhillschristianschool.org
www.facebook.com/HaltonHillsChristianSchool
Grades: Pre.-8 *Enrollment:* 322 *Note:* Formerly known as Georgetown District Christian School
Marianne Vangoor, Principal

Guelph: Elora Road Christian School (ERCS)
5696 Wellington Rd.7, RR #5, Guelph, ON N1H 6J2, Canada
Tel: 519-824-1890; *Fax:* 519-821-3518
school@ercf.ca
www.eloraroad.ca
Grades: JK-8 *Enrollment:* 99
Cindy Westendorp, Principal

Guelph: Guelph Community Christian School
195 College Ave. West, Guelph, ON N1G 1S6, Canada
Tel: 519-824-8860; *Fax:* 519-824-2105
info@guelphccs.ca
www.guelphccs.ca
www.facebook.com/GuelphCommunityChristianSchool
www.instagram.com/guelphccs
Grades: K.-8 *Enrollment:* 188
Tanya Pennings, Interim Principal
tanya.pennings@guelphccs.ca

Guelph: Resurrection Christian Academy
400 Speedvale Ave. East, Guelph, ON N1E 1N9, Canada
Tel: 519-836-5395
www.rcaflames.com
Grades: K./Elem.
Lisa Brombal, Director & Co-Founder
Sue Warren, Director & Co-Founder

Haldimand: Grand River Academy of Christian Education
1691 RR, Haldimand, ON N1A 2W4, Canada

Hamilton: Calvin Christian School (CCS)
547 West 5th St., Hamilton, ON L9C 3P7, Canada
Tel: 905-388-2645; *Fax:* 905-388-2769
www.ccshamilton.com
www.facebook.com/calvinchristianschoolhamilton
twitter.com/ccshamilton
www.youtube.com/user/ccshamilton
Grades: JK-8 *Enrollment:* 450 *Number of Employees:* 16 full-time; 8 part-time
Ted Postma, Principal

Hamilton: Guido de Bres Christian High School
420 Crerar Dr., Hamilton, ON L9A 5K3, Canada
Tel: 905-574-4011; *Fax:* 905-574-8662
office@guidodebres.com
www.guidodebres.com
www.instagram.com/guido_de_bres
Grades: Sec. *Enrollment:* 400
R. Vanoostveen, Principal
principal@guidodebres.com

Hawkesville: Countryside Christian School
3745 Hergott Rd., Hawkesville, ON N0B 1X0, Canada
Tel: 519-699-5793; *Fax:* 519-699-4576
Grades: K./Elem./Sec.
Howard Lichty, Principal

Jarvis: Jarvis Community Christian School
149 Talbot St. East, Jarvis, ON N0A 1J0, Canada
Tel: 519-587-4444; *Fax:* 519-587-2985
office@jdcs.ca
www.jarvisccs.ca
Grades: K.-8 *Enrollment:* 129
Chad Haverkamp, Principal

Jordan: Heritage Christian School
P.O. Box 400
2850 Fourth Ave., Jordan, ON L0R 1S0, Canada
Tel: 905-562-7303; *Fax:* 905-562-0020
heritage@hcsjordan.ca
www.hcsjordan.ca
Grades: K - 12 *Enrollment:* 501
Ben Harsvoort, Principal

Jordan Station: Jordan Christian School
P.O. Box 69
4171 - 15 St. South, Jordan Station, ON L0R 1S0, Canada
Tel: 905-562-4023; *Fax:* 905-562-4024
secretary@ourjcs.ca
www.jordanchristianschool.ca
www.facebook.com/jordanchristianschool
Enrollment: 132
Paul Wagenaar, Principal

Kingston: Kingston Christian School
1212 Woodbine Rd., Kingston, ON K7L 4V2, Canada
Tel: 613-384-9572; *Fax:* 613-384-9580
www.kingstonchristianschool.ca
www.facebook.com/439358032785954
Grades: K./Elem.
Jennifer Shoniker, Principal

Kitchener: Fellowship Christian School
1780 Glasgow St., Kitchener, ON N2N 0A7, Canada
Tel: 519-746-0008; *Fax:* 519-746-4206
www.kwfcs.com
Grades: JK-8
Trevor Long, Principal

Kitchener: Laurentian Hills Christian School (LHCS)
11 Laurentian Dr., Kitchener, ON N2E 1C1
Tel: 519-576-6700; *Fax:* 519-576-2583
lhcs.ws
www.facebook.com/LaurentianHills
Grades: JK-8 *Enrollment:* 275
Ian Timmerman, Principal

Kitchener: Rockway Mennonite Collegiate Inc.
110 Doon Rd., Kitchener, ON N2G 3C8, Canada
Tel: 519-743-5209
rockway.ca
www.facebook.com/RockwayMennonite
twitter.com/RockwayMC
Grades: 7-12 *Enrollment:* 350 *Note:* Rockway Mennonite Collegiate is an inspected & accredited private school, with students from Mennonite congregations & Christian denominations.
Ann Schultz, Principal
Dennis Wikerd, Assistant Principal
David Lobe, Director, Admissions & Recruitment
Christine Rier, Director, Development
Karen Martin Schiedel, Business Manager

Kleinburg: Kleinburg Christian Academy (KCA)
6950 Nashville Rd., Kleinburg, ON L0J 1C0, Canada
Tel: 905-893-7211
www.kleinburgchristian.ca
Grades: JK-8
LeeAnn Major, Principal

Leamington: United Mennonite Educational Institute (UMEI)
614 Mersea Rd. 6, RR#5, Leamington, ON N8H 3V8, Canada
Tel: 519-326-7448; *Fax:* 519-326-0278
office@umei.on.ca
umei.ca
www.facebook.com/umeischool
twitter.com/umei_chs
www.youtube.com/user/umeichristian
Grades: 9-12 *Note:* United Mennonite Educational Institute is a secondary school providing an education that incorporates an Anabaptist / Mennonite world view.
Sonya Bedal, Principal
principal@umei.ca

Lindsay: Heritage Christian School
159 Colborne St. West, Lindsay, ON K9V 5Z8, Canada
Tel: 705-324-8363; *Fax:* 705-324-8372
www.myhcs.ca
www.facebook.com/HeritageChristianSchoolLindsay
Grades: K.-8 *Enrollment:* 102
Lonneke Brown, Principal

Listowel: Listowel Christian School
P.O. Box 151
6020 Line 87, Listowel, ON N4W 3H2
Tel: 519-291-3086; *Fax:* 519-291-3086
office@listowelchristianschool.ca
www.listowelchristianschool.ca
Grades: JK-8
Ed Boelens, Principal

London: Covenant Christian School
7 Howard Ave., London, ON N6P 1B3, Canada
Tel: 519-203-0266
info@ccslondon.org
www.ccslondon.org
Grades: K.-8 *Enrollment:* 110 *Number of Employees:* 8

John Boeringa, Chair
board@ccslondon.org
Shawn Wolski, Principal
principal@ccslondon.org

London: London Christian Academy (LCA)
85 Charles St., London, ON N6H 1H1, Canada
Tel: 519-473-3332; *Fax:* 519-473-9843
www.londonchristianacademy.ca
www.facebook.com/londonchristianacademy
www.youtube.com/user/londoncatv
Grades: JK-8 *Note:* London Christian Academy is an interdenominational Christian school.
Ron Hesman, Principal
principal@londonchristianacademy.ca
Steve Gaunt, Vice-Principal
sgaunt@londonchristianacademy.ca

London: London Christian Elementary School
202 Clarke Rd., London, ON N5W 5E4, Canada
Tel: 519-455-0360; *Fax:* 519-455-6717
info@londonchristian.ca
www.londonchristian.ca
Grades: JK-8 *Enrollment:* 200
Stephen Janssen, Principal
principal@londonchristian.ca

London: London District Christian Secondary School
24 Braesyde Ave., London, ON N5W 1V3, Canada
Tel: 519-455-4360; *Fax:* 519-455-4364
office@ldcss.ca
www.ldcss.ca
Grades: Sec. *Enrollment:* 360
Tim Bentum, Principal

Markham: Peoples Christian Academy (PCA)
245 Renfrew Dr., Markham, ON L3R 6G3
Tel: 416-733-2010
www.peopleschristianacademy.ca
www.facebook.com/181436515199705
Grades: Pre.-12 *Enrollment:* 370

Markham: Wesley Christian Academy
22 Heritage Rd., Markham, ON L3P 1M4, Canada
Tel: 905-201-8461; *Fax:* 905-201-6438
info@wesleyca.com
wesleyca.com
www.facebook.com/wca.elc
twitter.com/wca_elc
Grades: Senior Kindergarten - 8 *Note:* Wesley Christian Academy offers an academic program within the context of Christian principles.
M. Serio, Principal

Metcalfe: Community Christian School (CCS)
2681 Glen St., Metcalfe, ON K0A 2P0
Tel: 613-821-3669; *Fax:* 613-821-6135
info@ccsmetcalfe.ca
www.ccsmetcalfe.ca
Grades: JK - 8 *Enrollment:* 65 *Number of Employees:* 11
Rick Dykstra, Principal
rick.dykstra@communitychristianschool.ca

Milverton: Fair Haven Christian Day School
4184 Line 61, RR#1, Milverton, ON N0K 1M0, Canada
Tel: 519-595-4568
Grades: K.-10
Howard Bean, Principal

Mississauga: Mississauga Christian Academy (MCA)
2720 Gananoque Dr., Mississauga, ON L5N 2R2, Canada
Tel: 905-826-4114; *Fax:* 905-567-5874
info@mississaugachristianacademy.com
www.mississaugachristianacademy.com
www.facebook.com/mississaugachristianacademy
twitter.com/MississaugaCA
Grades: JK-8 *Enrollment:* 127 *Note:* Offers a Before & After School care program.
Daniel Jovin, Principal

Mississauga: Philopateer Christian College
6341 Mississauga Rd., Mississauga, ON L5N 1A5
Tel: 905-814-5181
www.pccprivateschool.com
Grades: Pre.-12 *Enrollment:* 300
Mary Ashun, Principal

Newmarket: Newmarket & District Christian Academy (NDCA)
P.O. Box 297
221 Carlson Dr., Newmarket, ON L3Y 4X1, Canada
Tel: 905-895-1199; *Fax:* 905-895-4353
ndca-office@ndca.ca
www.ndca.ca
Grades: K.-8

Oakville: John Knox Christian School
2232 Sheridan Garden Dr., Oakville, ON L6J 7T1, Canada
Tel: 905-829-8048; *Fax:* 905-829-8056
info@jkcs-oakville.org
www.jkcs-oakville.org
Grades: Elem. *Enrollment:* 395
George Petrusma, Principal
gpetrusma@jkcs-oakville.org

Oakville: King's Christian Collegiate
528 Burnhamthorpe Rd. West, Oakville, ON L6M 4K6, Canada
Tel: 905-257-5464; *Fax:* 905-257-5463
office@kingschristian.net
www.kingschristian.net
Grades: 9-12 *Enrollment:* 470 *Note:* An independent government-inspected and approved Christian high school.
John De Boer, Principal, 905-257-5464, ext. 505
jdeboer@kingschristian.net

Oakville: Oakville Christian School (OCS)
112 Third Line, Oakville, ON L6L 3Z6, Canada
Tel: 905-825-1247; *Fax:* 905-825-3398
admissions@oakvillechristianschool.com
www.oakvillechristianschool.com
Grades: Pre.-8 *Enrollment:* 250
Jeff Kennedy, Principal
jkennedy@oakvillechristianschool.com

Orillia: Orillia Christian School (OCS)
P.O. Box 862
505 Gill St., Orillia, ON L3V 6K8, Canada
Tel: 705-326-0532; *Fax:* 705-327-9856
office@orilliachristianschool.com
www.orilliachristianschool.com
www.facebook.com/250606451725956
Grades: JK-8 *Enrollment:* 120
Donna Veenstra, Principal
principal@orilliachristianschool.com

Oshawa: Immanuel Christian School
849 Rossland Rd. West, Oshawa, ON L1J 8R5
Tel: 905-728-9071; *Fax:* 905-728-0604
www.immanuelschool.ca
www.facebook.com/169017956538053
Grades: K./Elem.
Jasper Hoogendam, Principal

Ottawa: Life Christian Academy
209 Glen Park Dr., Ottawa, ON K1B 5B8
Tel: 613-800-9368
www.lifechristianacademy.ca
www.facebook.com/LifeChristianAcademy
twitter.com/LCA_AVC
Grades: Elem./Sec.
Michael Karpishka, Principal

Ottawa: Ottawa Christian School
255 Tartan Dr., Ottawa, ON K2J 3T1, Canada
Tel: 613-825-3000; *Fax:* 613-825-4008
info@ocschool.org
www.ocschool.org
www.facebook.com/YourOCS
Grades: K.-8 *Enrollment:* 200
Paul Triemstra, Principal

Ottawa: Redeemer Christian High School (RCHS)
82 Colonnade Rd. North, Ottawa, ON K2E 7L2, Canada
Tel: 613-723-9262; *Fax:* 613-723-9321
info@rchs.on.ca
www.rchs.on.ca
www.facebook.com/RedeemerChristianHighSchool
twitter.com/RedeemerCHS
Grades: 9-12 *Note:* Redeemer Christian High School offers a Christ-centered education. The school also provides programs for students with learning disabilities.
Linda Delean, Principal
principal@rchs.on.ca
David Naftel, B.Ed., B.Sc., Vice-Principal
dnaftel@rchs.on.ca

Owen Sound: Timothy Christian School (TCS)
1735 - 4th Ave. West, Owen Sound, ON N4K 4X7, Canada
Tel: 519-371-9151; *Fax:* 519-371-8607
office@tcsowensound.com
www.tcsowensound.com
Grades: JK-8 *Enrollment:* 87 *Number of Employees:* 13
Matt Bittel, Principal
principal@tcsowensound.com

Peterborough: Rhema Christian School
29 County Rd. 4, Peterborough, ON K9L 1B8, Canada
Tel: 705-743-1400; *Fax:* 705-743-1415
office@rhema.ca
www.rhema.ca
www.facebook.com/RhemaCS
twitter.com/rhemaptbo
Grades: JK-8 *Note:* Rhema Christian School is a day school which offers a Christ-centered education.
Sheila May, Principal
Kate Lingard, Office Administrator
Cindy Ferguson, Business Administrator

Picton: Sonrise Christian Academy
58 Johnson St., Picton, ON K0K 2T0, Canada
Tel: 613-476-7883
office@sonrisechristianacademy.com
www.sonrisechristianacademy.com
www.facebook.com/120078748064586
Grades: JK-8 *Enrollment:* 62
Julie Scrivens, Principal
principal@sonrisechristianacademy.com

Prince Albert: Trinity Grace Academy
P.O. Box 3308
14480 Old Simcoe Rd., Prince Albert, ON L9L 1C3, Canada
Tel: 905-985-3741; *Fax:* 905-985-7153
www.trinitygraceacademy.ca
Grades: K.-8
Jessica Bandstra, Office Administrator

Richmond Hill: Richmond Hill Christian Academy Bayview Campus
9711 Bayview Ave., Richmond Hill, ON L4C 9X7, Canada
Tel: 905-770-4055; *Fax:* 905-770-6255
rhca@rogers.com
rhcaweb.ca
Grades: Pre.-8 *Enrollment:* 375 *Note:* Richmond Hill Christian Academy is a non-denominational school & a member of the Association of Christian Schools International. The A Beka curriculum is used.
John Yip, Principal, 647-535-4055
Grace Yip, Administrator, 647-535-4056

Campuses
Hillsview Campus
Richmond Hill Chinese Baptist Church
136 Hillsview Dr., Richmond Hill, ON L4C 1T2, Canada
Tel: 905-737-9055
Grades: JK-3 *Enrollment:* 70

Rosslyn: Thunder Bay Christian School (TBCS)
37 Cooper Rd., Rosslyn, ON P7K 0E2, Canada
Tel: 807-939-1209; *Fax:* 807-939-2843
office@tbaychristianschool.ca
www.tbaychristianschool.ca
Grades: JK-10 *Enrollment:* 165 *Note:* Thunder Bay Christian School is an interdenominational school operated by parents.
Peter Himanen, Principal

Sarnia: Sarnia Christian School
1273 Exmouth St., Sarnia, ON N7S 1W9, Canada
Tel: 519-383-7750; *Fax:* 519-383-6304
info@sarniachristian.com
www.sarniachristian.com
www.facebook.com/SarniaChristian
Grades: K.-8 *Enrollment:* 164
Len Smit, Principal
len.smit@sarniachristian.com

Smithville: Covenant Christian School
P.O. Box 924
6470 Regional Rd. #14, Smithville, ON L0R 2A0, Canada
Tel: 905-957-7796; *Fax:* 905-957-7794
ccs@nace.ca
covenant.nace.ca
www.facebook.com/covenant.nace.ca
Grades: K-8 *Enrollment:* 226 *Note:* Member of the Niagara Association for Christian Education (NACE).
Joyce Koornneef, Principal

Smithville: **Smithville Christian High School**
6488 Smithville Townline Rd., Smithville, ON L0R 2A0, Canada

Tel: 905-957-3255; Fax: 905-957-3431
office@smithvillechristian.ca
www.smithvillechristian.ca
www.facebook.com/smithvillechristian
twitter.com/smthvllechrstn
www.smithvillechristian.blogspot.com
Grades: Sec. Enrollment: 235
Ted Harris, Administrator
tharris@smithvillechristian.ca
Fred Breukelman, Vice-Principal & Athletic Director
fbreukelman@smithvillechristian.ca
Marlene Bergsma, Admissions/International Student Coordinator
mbergsma@smithvillechristian.ca
Lorraine VanderHeide, Office Administrative Assistant
office@smithvillechristian.ca

St Catharines: **Beacon Christian School**
300 Scott St., St Catharines, ON L2N 1J3

Tel: 905-937-7411
mail@beaconchristian.org
www.beaconchristian.org
www.facebook.com/BeaconCS
twitter.com/BeaconChristian
Grades: JK-8 Note: Beacon Christian School is an independent, interdenominational school.
Ralph Pot, Principal
rpot@beaconchristian.org

St Thomas: **Faith Christian Academy**
345 Fairview Ave., St Thomas, ON N5R 6M7, Canada
Tel: 519-633-0943; Fax: 519-633-6848
www.faithchristianacademy.ca
Grades: JK-8
Barry E. Pearce, Principal
bpearce@path2faith.com

Stoney Creek: **John Knox Christian School**
795 Hwy. #8, Stoney Creek, ON L8E 5J3, Canada
Tel: 905-643-2460; Fax: 905-643-5875
johnknox.nace.ca
www.facebook.com/JohnKnoxChristianSchool
Grades: JK-8 Enrollment: 122 Number of Employees: 14 Note: Member of Niagara Association for Christian Education (NACE).
Bonnie Desjardins, Principal
bdesjardins@nace.ca
Kevin Huinink, Executive Director
khuinink@nace.ca

Stouffville: **Stouffville Christian School**
3885 Stouffville Rd., 2nd Fl., Stouffville, ON L4A 3X1, Canada
Tel: 905-887-3330; Fax: 905-887-3355
info@stouffvillechristianschool.com
www.stouffvillechristianschool.com
Grades: JK-8
Dave Burns, Principal

Strathroy: **Strathroy Community Christian School (SCCS)**
7880 Walkers Dr., Strathroy, ON N7G 3H4, Canada
Tel: 519-245-1934; Fax: 519-245-4424
office@sccs.ca
www.sccs.ca
www.facebook.com/221558934557393
Grades: Jr. K.-8 Enrollment: 212 Number of Employees: 21
Ken VanMinnen, Principal
principal@sccs.ca

Toronto: **Alive Christian Academy International**
20 Progress Ave., Toronto, ON M1H 2X3
Tel: 416-439-2480
aca@jciami.com
www.jciami.com/aca/
Grades: Pre.-12 Note: Established by Jesus Christ Is Alive Ministries International.
Elias Sebastian, Principal

Toronto: **Cathedral Christian Academy**
1111 Arrow Rd., Toronto, ON M9N 3B3, Canada
Tel: 416-747-2843; Fax: 416-241-4404
mail@ccaschool.ca
www.ccaschool.ca
Grades: JK - 12

Toronto: **People's Christian Academy**
374 Sheppard Ave. East, Toronto, ON M2N 3B6
Tel: 416-222-3341; Fax: 416-222-3344
info@pca.ca
www.pca.ca
www.facebook.com/181436515199705

Grades: Jr. K.-12 Enrollment: 808
Rev. Reg Andrews, Director, Operations & Ministry

Toronto: **Signet Christian School**
675 Sheppard Ave. East, Toronto, ON M2K 1B6
Tel: 416-750-7515; Fax: 416-750-7720
www.signetchristianschool.com
www.facebook.com/signetschool.ca
Grades: JK-12 Enrollment: 80
Catherine Dumé, Principal

Toronto: **Three Fishes Christian Elementary School**
801 Progress Ave., Toronto, ON M1H 2X4, Canada
Tel: 416-284-9003
3fishes@threefishes.org
www.threefishes.org
Grades: JK - 8 Note: Three Fishes Christian Elementary School offers a Christ-centered & academically demanding program.
Laurel Ann Mirams, Principal
dmirams@sympatico.ca

Toronto: **Timothy Christian School (Rexdale) (TCS)**
28 Elmhurst Dr., Toronto, ON M9W 2J5, Canada
Tel: 416-741-5770; Fax: 416-741-3359
www.timothycs.com
www.facebook.com/TimothyChristianSchool
Grades: JK-8 Enrollment: 100 Note: Timothy Christian School in Rexdale offers a Christ-centred education.
Margareth Lise, Principal

Toronto: **Whitefield Christian Schools**
5808 Finch Ave. East, Toronto, ON M1B 4Y6
Tel: 416-297-1212; Fax: 416-291-4632
office@wcschools.ca
whitefieldchristianschools.ca
Grades: JK-8

Toronto: **Willowdale Christian School**
60 Hilda Ave., Toronto, ON M2M 1V5
Tel: 416-222-1711; Fax: 416-222-1939
office@willowdalechristianschool.org
www.willowdalechristianschool.org
Grades: JK-8 Enrollment: 130
Cathy Sallows, Principal
csallows@willowdalechristianschool.org

Toronto: **The Yorkland School (TYS)**
255 Yorkland Blvd., Toronto, ON M2J 1S3, Canada
Tel: 416-491-7667; Fax: 416-491-3806
admin@yorkland.on.ca
www.yorkland.on.ca
www.facebook.com/ntcschool
Grades: JK - 12 Note: The Yorkland School is the middle & upper school division of the North Toronto Christian School. The school is commited to Biblical principles & values.
Allen Schenk, Principal
aschenk@ntcs.on.ca
Lyne Gagné, Vice Principal
lgagne@ntcs.on.ca
Gordon Cooke, Administrator / Treasurer
gcooke@ntcs.on.ca

Trenton: **Trenton Christian School**
340 Second Dug Hill Rd., Trenton, ON K8V 5P7, Canada
Tel: 613-392-3600
office@trentonchristianschool.com
trentonchristianschool.com
Grades: JK-8
Joe Kuipers, Chair
Allen Bron, Principal
principal@trentonchristianschool.com

Utterson: **Muskoka Christian School**
P.O. Box 150
2483 Old Muskoka Rd., Utterson, ON P0B 1M0, Canada
Tel: 705-385-2847; Fax: 705-385-1756
mcs@muskoka.com
www.muskokachristianschool.com
Grades: JK-8 Note: The school is owned & operated by the Muskoka Association of Christian Education.
Lauralynn Mercer, Principal

Wallaceburg: **Wallaceburg Christian Private School (WCS)**
693 Albert St., Wallaceburg, ON N8A 1Y8, Canada
Tel: 519-627-6013; Fax: 519-627-5051
admin@wallaceburgchristianschool.com
www.wallaceburgchristianschool.com
Grades: JK-8 Note: The school is a member of the Ontario Alliance of Christian Schools & Christian Schools International. It is independent of the Ministry of Education, although the school is registered with the Ministry.

Wheatley: **Old Colony Christian Academy**
21311 Campbell Rd., RR#1, Wheatley, ON N0P 2P0, Canada
Tel: 519-825-9188; Fax: 519-825-9122
Grades: Elem. Enrollment: 252

Williamsburg: **Timothy Christian School (TCS)**
P.O. Box 179
12600 County Rd. 18, Williamsburg, ON K0C 2H0, Canada
Tel: 613-535-2687; Fax: 613-535-1074
office@tcswilliamsburg.ca
www.tcswilliamsburg.ca
www.facebook.com/104962496361440
Grades: JK - 8 Enrollment: 130
Gary Postma, Principal
Principal@tcswilliamsburg.ca

Windsor: **First Lutheran Christian Academy**
3850 Locke St., Windsor, ON N9G 1S1, Canada
Tel: 519-250-7888; Fax: 519-250-7715
flca@mnsi.net
www.flca.ca
Enrollment: 201
Suzanne Eberhard, Principal
Rev. Glenn Stresman, Pastor

Windsor: **Maranatha Christian Academy**
939 Northwood St., Windsor, ON N9E 1A2
Tel: 519-966-7424; Fax: 519-966-9519
www.maranathachristian.ca
www.facebook.com/mcawindsor
Grades: JK - 12
Rob Lofthouse, Principal

Windsor: **Windsor Christian Fellowship Academy**
4490 - 7th Concession, RR#1, Windsor, ON N9A 6J3, Canada
Tel: 519-972-5977; Fax: 519-972-8915
reception@wcf.ca
www.wcf.ca
www.facebook.com/WindsorChristianFellowship
Grades: Elem. Enrollment: 81
Brian Ciaramitaro, CMO
bfc@wcf.ca

Woodbridge: **Credo Christian Private School**
8260 Huntington Rd., RR#1, Woodbridge, ON L4L 1A5, Canada
Tel: 905-851-1620; Fax: 905-851-1620
office@credochristianschool.com
www.credochristianschool.com
Grades: K.-8
Lamberta Maat, Contact

Woodbridge: **TDChristian High School (TDCH)**
Also known as: Toronto District Christian High School
377 Woodbridge Ave., Woodbridge, ON L4L 2V7, Canada
Tel: 905-851-1772; Fax: 905-851-9992
Toll-Free: 855-663-6632
info@tdchristian.ca
www.tdchristian.ca
Grades: 9-12 Enrollment: 405 Number of Employees: 47
William Groot, Principal, 905-851-1772, ext. 213
groot@tdchristian.ca
Patty Schuurman, Vice-President, Admissions, 905-851-1772, ext. 203
schuurman@tdchristian.ca

Wyoming: **John Knox Christian School of Wyoming**
4738 Confederation Line, Wyoming, ON N0N 1T0, Canada
Tel: 519-845-3112; Fax: 519-845-1404
www.wyomingjkcs.com
Grades: K./Elem.
Ymko Boersma, Principal

Catholic

Mississauga: **Holy Name of Mary College School**
2241 Mississauga Rd., Mississauga, ON L5H 2K8
Tel: 905-891-1890; Fax: 905-891-2082
administration@hnmcs.ca
www.holynameofmarycollegeschool.com
Grades: 5-12; Girls
Marilena Tesoro, Head of School
tesoro@hnmcs.ca
Kathryn Anderson, Director of Schools

Mississauga: **Lumen Veritatis Academy**
225 Broadway St., Mississauga, ON L5M 1J1
Tel: 905-813-9215
info@lumenveritatis.ca
www.lumenveritatis.ca
www.facebook.com/lumenveritatisacademy
twitter.com/lvablog
Grades: JK-8 Enrollment: 75

Campuses
Thornhill Campus
191 Wade Gate, Thornhill, ON L4J 5Y4

Tel: 905-597-4933

Richmond Hill: Holy Trinity School
11300 Bayview Ave., Richmond Hill, ON L4S 1L4

Tel: 905-737-1114; *Fax:* 905-737-5187
reception@hts.on.ca
www.hts.on.ca
www.facebook.com/HTSHolyTrinitySchool
twitter.com/HTSRichmondHill
www.linkedin.com/company/holy-trinity-school

Grades: JK - 12 *Enrollment:* 759
Barry Hughes, Head of School

Toronto: De La Salle College 'Oaklands' (DEL)
131 Farnham Ave., Toronto, ON M4V 1H7, Canada

Tel: 416-969-8771; *Fax:* 416-969-9175
info@delasalle.toronto.on.ca
www.delasalleoaklands.ca
www.facebook.com/398396406871450

Grades: Elem./Sec. *Enrollment:* 578
Joseph Pupo, Principal, 416-969-8771, ext. 230
jpupo@delasalleoaklands.org

French

Mississauga: Mississauga Christian French School (MCFS)
1245 Eglinton Ave. West, Mississauga, ON L5V 2M4

Tel: 905-567-4032
administrative.assistant@mcfschool.ca
www.mcfschool.ca

Grades: Pre.-8 *Enrollment:* 120
Marian Guirgius, Principal

Hearing Impaired

Toronto: Yeshivas Nefesh Dovid
77 Stormont Ave., Toronto, ON M5N 2C3

Tel: 416-630-6220
info@nefeshdovid.com
www.nefeshdovid.com

Grades: 9 - 12

Special Education

Brant: The Gregory School for Exceptional Learning
1249 Colborne St. West, Brant, ON N3T 5L7

Tel: 519-449-1650
www.kalyanasupportsystems.com/the-gregory-school-1
www.facebook.com/144244872262082

Note: School for children with special needs that require special programming.
Angeline Savard, Principal

Burlington: Woodview Learning Centre
69 Flatt Rd., Burlington, ON L7R 3X5

Tel: 905-689-4727; *Fax:* 905-689-2474
www.woodview.ca
www.facebook.com/WoodviewWLC
twitter.com/WoodviewWLC

Grades: K.-9 *Note:* The Learning Centre provides individualized learning strategies for students with Autism.
Lindsey Court, Program Coordinator
lcourt@woodview.ca

Campuses
Brantford Office
643 Park Rd. North, Brantford, ON N3T 5L8

Tel: 519-752-5308; *Fax:* 519-752-9102
general@woodview.ca

Hamilton Office
Also known as: Mischa Weisz Centre for Autism Services
1900 Main St. West, Hamilton, ON L8S 4R8

Tel: 905-689-4727; *Fax:* 905-522-4690
wcc@woodview.ca

Mississauga: Good Samaritan School for Exceptional Learners
Also known as: Good Samaritan Private School
6341 Mississauga Rd., Mississauga, ON L5N 1A7

Tel: 905-219-9969

Grades: JK-12; Adult Ed.

Ottawa: Académie de la Capitale
#200, 1010 Morrison Dr., Ottawa, ON K2H 8K7

Tel: 613-721-3872; *Fax:* 613-721-8189
info@acadecap.org
www.acadecap.org
www.facebook.com/acadecap.org
twitter.com/Acadecap

Grades: Pre.-12
Lucie Lalonde, Director

Ottawa: Astolot Educational Centre
#203, 1187 Bank St., Ottawa, ON K1S 3X7

Tel: 613-260-5996
astolot@rogers.com
www.astolot.com

Jennifer Cowan, M.Ed., Principal

Peterborough: Arrowsmith School Peterborough
366 Parkhill Rd. East, Peterborough, ON K9L 1C3

Tel: 705-741-4800; *Fax:* 705-741-1832
peterborough@arrowsmithprogram.ca
www.arrowsmithschool.org/peterborough
www.facebook.com/arrowsmithprogram

Grades: 1-12 *Enrollment:* 40
Robert Gunning, Vice-Principal

Richmond Hill: Academy for Gifted Children
Also known as: P.A.C.E.
12 Bond Cres., Richmond Hill, ON L4E 3K2, Canada

Tel: 905-773-0997; *Fax:* 905-773-4722
www.pace.on.ca

Grades: Elem./Sec. *Enrollment:* 284 *Note:* P.A.C.E. - Programming for Academic & Creative Excellence. A non-denominational, co-ed, private day school, with programmes focussing on basic skills, with a strong emphasis on math & science, accelerated learning & individual instruction.
Barbara Rosenberg, Founder & Principal

Thornhill: Kayla's Children Centre
36 Atkinson Ave., Thornhill, ON L4J 8C9

Tel: 905-673-8554
office@kaylaschildrencentre.org
kaylaschildrencentre.org/school
www.facebook.com/kaylaschildrencentre
www.instagram.com/kaylaschildrencentre

Grades: Pre.-12

Campuses
School Office
36 Atkinson Ave., Thornhill, ON L4J 8C9

Tel: 905-738-5542; *Fax:* 905-738-8047
Pat Resnick, Director, Preschool
patricia@zareinu.org
Sarah Weitz, Office Manager
sarah@zareinu.org

Toronto: Arrowsmith School Toronto
245 St. Clair Ave. West, Toronto, ON M4V 1R3

Tel: 416-963-4962; *Fax:* 416-963-5017
info@arrowsmithschool.com
www.arrowsmithschool.org
www.facebook.com/arrowsmithprogram
twitter.com/ArrowsmithProg
www.linkedin.com/company/arrowsmith-program

Grades: 1-12 *Enrollment:* 75
Barbara Arrowsmith Young, Director

Toronto: Bright Start Academy
#318, 4630 Dufferin St., Toronto, ON M3H 5S4

Tel: 416-514-1415; *Fax:* 416-514-1410
registration@brightstartacademy.info
www.brightstartacademy.info
www.facebook.com/BSAandFTW
twitter.com/bsa_autism
www.instagram.com/brightstartacademyinc

Grades: Pre.-12 *Enrollment:* 25 *Number of Employees:* 10 *Note:* The Academy offers a behaviour & education program for children with autism & learning difficulties.
Allie Offman, Owner & Principal
allie@brightstartacademy.info

Toronto: Brighton School
240 The Donway West, Toronto, ON M3B 2V8

Tel: 416-932-8273; *Fax:* 416-850-5493
www.brightonschool.ca
www.facebook.com/BrightonSchoolToronto
www.instagram.com/torontobrightonschool

Grades: 1-12 *Enrollment:* 65 *Note:* Brighton is a private school for students who learn best in small classes, are one or more years behind academically, have a learning disability or an uneven learning profile.
Kathy Lear, Executive Director
Irene McRae, Principal

Toronto: Don Valley Academy
#408, 4576 Yonge St., Toronto, ON M2N 6N4

Tel: 416-223-7561; *Fax:* 416-223-0065
www.donvalleyacademy.com
www.facebook.com/donvalleyacademy

Grades: 9-12 *Enrollment:* 30 *Note:* Don Valley Academy provides personalized education for gifted students, as well as those with learning difficulties.
Alex J. Evans, Principal

Toronto: Kohai Educational Centre
2010 Yonge St., 3rd Fl., Toronto, ON M4S 1Z9

Tel: 416-489-3636; *Fax:* 416-489-3662
info@kohai.ca
www.kohai.ca
www.facebook.com/Kohai.Educational.Centre
twitter.com/KohaiLIFE
www.instagram.com/kohailife

Grades: Pre.-12 *Note:* Programs & education for students with genetic disorders, behaviour problems, & language disorders.
Barbara Brown, Principal

Toronto: Magnificent Minds
47 Glenbrook Ave., Lower Level, Toronto, ON M6B 2L7

Tel: 647-404-6349
MagnificentMindsToronto@Gmail.com
www.magnificentminds.ca
www.facebook.com/MagnificentMinds
twitter.com/MagMinds
www.pinterest.com/magnificentmind/

Grades: Pre-K-Elem.
Alley Dezenhouse, Principal, Director, Behaviour Therapist

Toronto: Shoore Centre for Learning
801 Eglinton Ave. West, Toronto, ON M5N 1E3

Tel: 416-781-4754; *Fax:* 416-781-0163
info@shoorecentre.com
www.shoorecentre.com
www.facebook.com/222318484489159
twitter.com/ShooreCentre
www.youtube.com/user/ShooreCentre

Grades: 7 - 12
Michael I. Shoore, B.Sc., M.Ed., Director
michael@shoorecentre.com
Tamara Shoore, Principal
tammy@shoorecentre.com

Toronto: The YMCA Academy
Also known as: The Academy
15 Breadalbane St., 3rd Fl., Toronto, ON M4Y 1C2

Tel: 416-928-0124; *Fax:* 416-928-0212
info@ymcaacademy.org
www.ymcaacademy.org
www.facebook.com/ymcaacademy
twitter.com/ymcaacademy
www.youtube.com/user/YMCAAcademy

Grades: Secondary *Note:* The YMCA Academy is a high school for students with learning disabilities, located in downtown Toronto.
Don Adams, Head of School, 416-928-0124, ext. 31401
don.adams@ymcagta.org

Utopia: Renaissance Academy
8058 - 8th Line, Utopia, ON L0M 1T0

Tel: 705-423-9688; *Fax:* 705-423-9788
www.renaissanceacademy.ca

Grades: K-12 *Note:* Renaissance Academy offers residential and day programs, ranging from gifted to life skills.
Giancarlo Marchi, Head of School
gmarchi@renaissanceacademy.ca

Independent & Private Schools

Ajax: Avalon Private High School
#204, 40 Old Kingston Rd., Ajax, ON L1T 2Z7

Tel: 905-683-5299

Grades: 9 - 12
Kathy Greenfield, Principal

Ajax: Jaamiah Aluloom Al-Islamyyah Institute of Islamic Learning
2944 Audley Rd., Ajax, ON L1Z 1T7

Tel: 905-686-4003; *Fax:* 905-686-4428
info@jaamiahajax.com
www.jaamiahajax.com

Enrollment: 400

Amaranth: The Maples Academy
Also known as: The Maples Independent Country School
513047 2nd Line, Amaranth, ON L9W 0S3, Canada

Tel: 519-942-3310; *Fax:* 519-942-8041
info@TheMaplesSchool.com
www.themaplesschool.com
www.facebook.com/154097964653598
twitter.com/TheMaplesSchool
www.pinterest.com/themaplesschool/

Grades: Preschool - 8 *Enrollment:* 120

Greg Playford, Principal
greg.playford@themaplesschool.com

Amherstburg: St. Peter's ACHS College School
6101 County Rd. #20, Amherstburg, ON N0R 1G0
Toll-Free: 888-832-8121
achscanada@gmail.com
achscanada.com

Grades: JK-8; Boys
Peter Thyrring, Headmaster

Aurora: Aurora Montessori School
330 Industrial Pkwy. North, Aurora, ON L4G 4C3, Canada
Tel: 905-841-0065; *Fax:* 905-841-2022
info@auroramontessori.com
www.auroramontessori.com
Grades: Pre.-8 *Note:* Aurora Montessori School & Private School
also offers a toddler program for children from ages 18 months
to 3 years. Casa programs are for children from ages 2.5 to 6
years.
Kane Burg, Principal

Aurora: Aurora Preparatory Academy
81 Industrial Pkwy. North, Aurora, ON L4G 4C4, Canada
Tel: 905-713-1141; *Fax:* 905-713-6340
www.aurora-prep.com
www.facebook.com/APrepAcademy
twitter.com/APrepAcademy
Grades: JK-8
Rhonda Vissers, Principal
vissers@aurora-prep.com

Aurora: La Maison Montessori House
14 Stone Rd., Aurora, ON L4G 6X9
Tel: 905-726-2110
info@lmmh.ca
www.lmmh.ca
Grades: Toddler - Pre.
Anne Martin, Principal

Campuses
Newmarket Campus
1205 Stellar Dr., Newmarket, ON L3Y 7B8
Tel: 905-895-2110
elementary@lmmh.ca
Grades: Elem.

Aurora: St. Andrew's College
15800 Yonge St., Aurora, ON L4G 3H7, Canada
Tel: 905-727-3178; *Fax:* 905-841-6911
info@sac.on.ca
www.sac.on.ca
www.facebook.com/standrewscollege
twitter.com/StAndrews1899
www.youtube.com/StAndrews1899
Grades: 5-12 *Enrollment:* 614 *Note:* All-boys boarding and day
school
Kevin McHenry, Headmaster, 905-727-3178, ext. 226
kevin.mchenry@sac.on.ca
Michael Paluch, Assistant Headmaster, Academics,
905-727-3178, ext. 285
michael.paluch@sac.on.ca
Greg L. Reid, Assistant Headmaster, School Life and
Operations, 905-727-3178, ext. 258
greg.reid@sac.on.ca
Courtenay Shrimpton, Assistant Headmaster, Strategic
Development and Student Life, 905-727-3178, ext. 307
courtenay.shrimpton@sac.on.ca
Sherrill Knight, Director of Human Resources, 905-727-2580,
ext. 230
sherrill.knight@sac.on.ca

**Baden, Region of Waterloo: Canadian Independent
College (CIC)**
3601 Sandhills Rd., Baden, Region of Waterloo, ON N3A 3B9
Tel: 519-634-9255; *Fax:* 519-634-9355
info@cicbaden.ca
www.cicbaden.ca
www.facebook.com/cicbaden
Grades: 9-12 *Enrollment:* 115 *Note:* The CIC has a sister
campus in Accra, Ghana.
Dr. Heather Bohez, B.Sc., N.D., Principal

Belleville: Albert College
160 Dundas St. West, Belleville, ON K8P 1A6
Tel: 613-968-5726; *Fax:* 613-968-9651
Toll-Free: 800-952-5237
info@albertcollege.ca
www.albertcollege.ca
www.facebook.com/Albert.College
twitter.com/AlbertCollege
www.youtube.com/user/AlbertSince1857
Grades: Elem./Sec. *Enrollment:* 298

Heather Kidd, Director, Admission
hkidd@albertcollege.ca

Bolton: Countryside Montessori Private School
1 Loring Dr., Bolton, ON L7E 1Y1, Canada
Tel: 905-951-3359; *Fax:* 905-951-3920
Enrollment: 257

Brampton: Academic Montessori
#1-6, 333 Fairhill Ave., Brampton, ON L7A 3N9
Tel: 905-846-4611; *Fax:* 905-459-3800
www.academicmontessori.com
Grades: Elem.
Peter Sesek, Principal

Brampton: Al-Iman School
#1-4, 253 Summerlea Rd., Brampton, ON L6T 5A8
Tel: 905-799-9231
islamicprivate@bellnet.ca
alimanschool.ca
Grades: JK - 8
Syyed Hamid Ali, Principal

Brampton: Har Tikvah Congregational School
P.O. Box 36023
9893 Torbram Rd., Brampton, ON L6S 6A3
Tel: 905-792-7589
info@hartikvah.org
www.hartikvah.org

Brampton: Khalsa Community School
69 Maitland St., Brampton, ON L6S 3B5, Canada
Tel: 905-791-1750; *Fax:* 905-458-9133
info@khalsacommunityschool.com
www.khalsacommunityschool.com
Grades: K.-9 *Enrollment:* 187
Ripsodhak Singh Grewal, Administrator

Brampton: Khalsa Montessori School
Also known as: KM School
#2, 4535 Ebenezer Rd., Brampton, ON L6P 2P7
Tel: 905-913-0801; *Fax:* 866-566-6069
info@kmschool.org
www.kmschool.org
www.facebook.com/theKMSchool
twitter.com/theKMSchool
Grades: Toddler - Elem.
Harpeet Singh, Principal

**Brampton: Rowntree Montessori Schools - RMS
Academy**
3 Sunforest Dr., Brampton, ON L6Z 2Z2
Tel: 905-790-3838; *Fax:* 905-790-5686
admin@rowntreemontessori.com
rowntreemontessori.com
Grades: Pre.-8 *Enrollment:* 100
J. Harris, Principal
R. Coates-Reid, Vice-Principal

Campuses
Central Park Campus
502 Central Park Dr., Brampton, ON L6S 2C8
Tel: 905-793-6231; *Fax:* 905-793-9020
rowntreemontessori.com/campuses/central-park
Grades: Pre./K./Elem.
M. Penrice, Principal
S. Thawer, Vice-Principal

Downtown Campus
4 Elizabeth St. North, Brampton, ON L6X 1S2
Tel: 905-457-7439; *Fax:* 905-457-2518
rowntreemontessori.com/campuses/downtown
Grades: Pre./K./Elem.
J. Baldassarre, Principal

Mayfield Campus
11613 Bramalea Rd., Brampton, ON L6R 0C2
Tel: 905-499-2595; *Fax:* 905-790-5686
rowntreemontessori.com/campuses/mayfield
Grades: Pre./K./Elem.
T. Rivard, Principal

Brampton: Tall Pines School
8525 Torbram Rd., Brampton, ON L6T 5K4, Canada
Tel: 905-458-6770; *Fax:* 905-458-7967
info@tallpinesschool.com
www.tallpinesschool.com
Grades: K.-8 *Enrollment:* 519 *Note:* Private Montessori &
Progressive school
Elizabeth Szekeres, Registrar
registrar@tallpinesschool.com

Brantford: Braemar House School
36 Baxter St., Brantford, ON N3R 2V8, Canada
Tel: 519-753-2929; *Fax:* 519-753-1235
admin@braemarhouseschool.ca
www.braemarhouseschool.ca
www.facebook.com/BraemarHouseSchool
Grades: JK - 8 *Enrollment:* 92 *Note:* Braemar House School also
offers a Montessori Casa program.
Annette Minutillo, Executive Director

Brantford: Montessori House of Children
85 Charlotte St., Brantford, ON N3T 2X2, Canada
Tel: 519-759-7290; *Fax:* 519-720-0172
mails@montessorihouseofchildren.com
www.montessorihouseofchildren.com
Other Information: admissions@montessorihouseofchildren.com
(Admission inquiries)
Note: Brantford's Montessori House of Children provides
programs for children from 1.5 to 9 years of age.
Nazar Altai, Director
altainazar@yahoo.com

Breslau: St. John's-Kilmarnock School
P.O. Box 179
2201 Shantz Station Rd., Breslau, ON N0B 1M0
Tel: 519-648-2183; *Fax:* 519-648-2186
info@sjkschool.org
www.sjkschool.org
www.facebook.com/sjkschool
twitter.com/sjkschool
www.youtube.com/user/sjkschool
Grades: JK - 12 *Enrollment:* 505
Jeff Aitken, Head of School

Brockville: Fulford Academy
280 King St. East, Brockville, ON K6V 1E2
Tel: 613-341-9330; *Fax:* 613-341-9344
www.fulfordacademy.com
www.facebook.com/fulfordacademy
www.youtube.com/fulfordacademy
Grades: 7 - 10 *Enrollment:* 60 *Note:* Private international
boarding school.
Dr. Thomas Steel, Head of School
tom.steel@fulfordacademy.com

Burlington: Fairview Glen Montessori
3508 Commerce Ct., Burlington, ON L7N 3L7
Tel: 905-634-0781
info@fairviewglen.com
www.fairviewglen.com
Grades: Pre.-6 *Enrollment:* 125
Tammy-Leigh Sage, Director

Burlington: Halton Waldorf School (HWS)
2193 Orchard Rd., Burlington, ON L7L 7J8, Canada
Tel: 905-331-4387; *Fax:* 905-331-3231
info@haltonwaldorf.com
www.haltonwaldorf.com
Grades: Pre.-8 *Enrollment:* 160 *Note:* The school provides
Waldorf education.

**Caledon: King's College School for Bright and
Gifted Children**
16379 The Gore Rd., Caledon, ON L7E 0X4
Tel: 905-880-7645
admissions@kingscollegeschool.ca
www.kingscollegeschool.ca
www.facebook.com/KingsCollegeCaledon
twitter.com/kingscollschool
Grades: 3-12 *Enrollment:* 52
John Eta, Head of School
Barbara Lord, Principal
Sandra Donovan, Director, Admissions
admissions@kingscollegeschool.ca

Cambridge: Montessori School of Cambridge
9 Roseview Ave., Cambridge, ON N1R 4A5
Tel: 519-622-1470; *Fax:* 519-622-4801
montessori@in.on.ca
montessoricambridge.com
www.facebook.com/MontessoriSchoolofCambridge
twitter.com/montessoricamb
Grades: Toddler - Pre.
Marilyn Herriot, Principal

Campbellville: Hitherfield Preparatory School
2439 - 10th Side Rd., Campbellville, ON L0P 1B0, Canada
Tel: 905-854-0890; *Fax:* 905-854-3155
hitherfield.org/www/
twitter.com/HitherfieldInfo
Grades: Elem./Sec. *Enrollment:* 115
Ann J. Scott, Principal, 9058540890, ext. 102

Carp: Venta Preparatory School
2013 Old Carp Rd., Carp, ON K0A 1L0
Tel: 613-839-2175; *Fax:* 613-839-1956
info@ventaprep.com
www.ventapreparatoryschool.com
twitter.com/VentaSchool
Grades: JK - 10 *Note:* Venta Preparatory School is a day &
boarding school. The maximum class size is twelve students.
Marilyn Mansfield, Principal, 613-839-2175, ext. 223
mmansfield@ventaprep.com
Sean Hopper, Executive Director, 613-839-2175, ext. 225
shopper@ventaprep.com
Shaun Quinn, Director, Studies, 613-839-2175, ext. 224
squinn@ventaprep.com
Tanya Kaye, Director, Marketing & Admissions, 613-839-2175,
ext. 240

Cookstown: Thornton Academy
4073 - 4th Line, Cookstown, ON L0L 1L0
Tel: 647-505-2313
www.thorntonacademy.ca
Other Information: 416-888-3483
www.facebook.com/ThorntonAcademySchool
Grades: JK - 12
Pat Wilson, Office Manager

Campuses
Toronto Campus
3445 Sheppard Ave. East, Toronto, ON M1T 3K5
Tel: 647-505-2313
Other Information: 416-888-3483

Cornwall: Islamic Institute Al-Rashid
18345 County Rd. 2, RR#1, Cornwall, ON K6H 5R5, Canada
Tel: 613-931-2895
contact@alrashid.ca
www.alrashid.ca
Grades: Elem./Sec.
M. Mazhar Alam, Principal

Cornwall: Ontario Hockey Academy
1541 Vincent Massey Dr., Cornwall, ON K6H 5R6
Tel: 613-938-5009; *Fax:* 613-937-3422
oha.admissions@gmail.com
www.ontariohockeyacademy.com
www.facebook.com/108238760044
twitter.com/OHAMavericks
Grades: 9 - 12

**Deep River: The Deep River Science Academy
(DRSA)**
P.O. Box 600
20 Forest Ave., Deep River, ON K0J 1P0
Tel: 613-584-4541; *Fax:* 613-584-9597
info@drsa.ca
www.drsa.ca
www.facebook.com/DeepRiverScienceAcademy
twitter.com/DRSA_25
www.pinterest.com/drsa
Grades: 10 - 12 *Enrollment:* 25 *Number of Employees:* 3 *Note:*
The Deep River Science Academy partners with Atomic Energy
of Canada, Ltd. to offer science camps. Students must have
completed a grade 10 or higher science high school credit.
Hhigh school credits are awarded.
Shawna Miller, Executive Director
shawna.miller@drsa.ca
Margo Ingram, Principal

Dundas: Dundas Valley Montessori School
14 Kemp Dr., Dundas, ON L9H 2M9
Tel: 905-627-1073; *Fax:* 289-494-0102
dvms.ca
www.facebook.com/DVMSbook
twitter.com/dvmstweets
Grades: Pre. - Jr. High
Tony Evans, Director
dvms@golden.net

Durham: Edge Hill Country School
RR#1, Durham, ON N0G 1R0
Tel: 519-369-3195
info@edgehill-school.com
www.edgehill-school.com
www.facebook.com/EdgeHillCountrySchool
Grades: K - 8
Lise Gunby, School Administrator

Embrun: Canada eSchool
P.O. Box 277
921 Notre-Dame St., Embrun, ON K0A 1W0
Tel: 613-443-9522; *Fax:* 613-482-4504
info@myeschool.ca
www.canadaeschool.ca
www.facebook.com/myeschool
twitter.com/Canada_eSchool
Enrollment: 1340 *Note:* Canada eSchool supplements students'
education with eLearning technology, accessible anywhere in
the world.
Ron Rambarran, Principal
rrambarran@myeschool.ca
Chrissy Visneskie, Contact
cvisneskie@myeschool.ca

**Fort Frances: Lac La Croix Elementary & High
School**
P.O. Box 640
Fort Frances, ON P9A 3M9, Canada
Tel: 807-485-2402; *Fax:* 807-485-2558
Grades: Elem./9-12

**Fort Frances: Seven Generations Education Institute
School**
Nanicost Complex
P.O. Box 297
1455 Idylwild Dr., Fort Frances, ON P9A 3M6, Canada
Tel: 807-274-2796; *Fax:* 807-274-8761
www.7generations.org
www.facebook.com/115074575204883
Dan Bird

Guelph: Montessori School of Wellington
68 Suffolk St. West, Guelph, ON N1H 2J2
Tel: 519-821-5876; *Fax:* 519-821-3531
montessori.wellington@bellnet.ca
www.montessori-school.ca
Grades: Casa
Glynis Hamilton, Principal

Guelph: Trillium Waldorf School
540 Victoria Rd. North, Guelph, ON N1E 6Z4
Tel: 519-821-5140; *Fax:* 519-821-0453
info@trilliumwaldorfschool.com
www.trilliumwaldorfschool.com
Grades: Pre. K - 8

Hamilton: Columbia International College of Canada
1003 Main St. West, Hamilton, ON L8S 4P3, Canada
Tel: 905-572-7883; *Fax:* 905-572-9332
columbia@cic-totalcare.com
www.cic-totalcare.com
www.facebook.com/53144393827
twitter.com/cic_totalcare
Grades: 7 - 12 *Enrollment:* 1700 *Note:* Private boarding and
university preparatory school.
Ron Rambarran, Principal
principal@cic-totalcare.com

**Hamilton: Hamilton Hebrew Academy Zichron Meir
School**
60 Dow Ave., Hamilton, ON L8S 1W4, Canada
Tel: 905-528-0330; *Fax:* 905-528-0544
school@hamiltonhebrewacademy.ca
www.hamiltonhebrewacademy.ca
Grades: Pre.-8
Rabbi Daniel Green, Dean
dean@hamiltonhebrewacademy.ca
Rabbi Yaakov Morel, Principal
ymorel@hamiltonhebrewacademy.ca

Hamilton: Hamilton Hebrew High (HHH)
125 Cline Ave. South, Hamilton, ON L8S 1X2
Tel: 416-230-0242
info@hcubed.ca
www.hcubed.ca
Grades: 9-12 *Note:* Hamilton Hebrew High offers secondary
school students extra Ontario Secondary School credits with a
Jewish perspective.

Hamilton: Hillfield Strathallan College
299 Fennell Ave. West, Hamilton, ON L9C 1G3
Tel: 905-389-1367; *Fax:* 905-389-6366
www.hsc.on.ca
www.facebook.com/hillfieldstrathallancollege
twitter.com/HillStrath
www.youtube.com/officialHSC
Grades: JK - 12 *Enrollment:* 1000
Marc Ayotte, Head, College

Hamilton: Islamic School of Hamilton (ISH)
1545 Stonechurch Rd. East, Hamilton, ON L8W 3P8, Canada
Tel: 905-383-7786; *Fax:* 905-574-8548
riham@ishcanada.com
www.ishcanada.com
Grades: Pre.-8 *Enrollment:* 170 *Note:* The school also teaches
the Arabic language, Quran, & Islam Studies.
Yousef Kfaween, Principal
principal@ishcanada.com
Husam Hameed, Vice-Principal, Operations
Sabeeha Quader, Vice-Principal, Administration
Riham Balousha, Office Administrator

Hamilton: Lyonsgate Montessori School
86 Homewood Ave., Hamilton, ON L8P 2M4
Tel: 905-525-4283
info@lyonsgate.ca
www.lyonsgate.ca
Grades: Pre.
Rachel Lyons, Principal

Hamilton: Southern Ontario Collegiate
28 Rebecca St., Hamilton, ON L8R 1B4, Canada
Tel: 905-546-1500; *Fax:* 866-875-2619
www.mysoc.ca
Other Information: Alternate Phone: 905-546-1501
Grades: Sec. *Note:* International secondary school specializing
in ESL & University prep.
Susan J. Woods, Principal

Hamilton: Timothy Canadian Reformed School
430 East 25th St., Hamilton, ON L8V 3B4, Canada
Tel: 905-385-3953; *Fax:* 905-385-8073
office@timothyschool.org
www.timothyschool.org
Grades: K.-8 *Note:* The school is affiliated with the Canadian
Reformed Church.
Michael Noot, Principal
mnoot@timothyschool.org

Hamilton: Westdale Children's School
2 Bond St. North, Hamilton, ON L8S 3W1
Tel: 905-529-4678
info@westdalechildrensschool.org
www.westdalechildrensschool.org
Grades: K. *Enrollment:* 10 *Number of Employees:* 3 *Note:* The
school is a developing member of the Waldorf Early Childhood
Association of North America (WECAN) & the curriculum is
based on the philosophy of Rudolf Steiner.
Ursula Bethune, Head Teacher
Christeen Urquhart, Contact, Administration

**Harrowsmith: Canadian Montessori Teacher
Education Institute**
4979 Hwy. 38, Harrowsmith, ON K0H 1V0
Tel: 416-458-8970; *Toll-Free:* 877-416-8970
www.montessori-institute.ca
Daniel Jutras, Director
jutrasdaniel@hotmail.com

Huntsville: Muskoka Montessori School
228 Chub Lake Rd., Huntsville, ON P1H 1S4
Tel: 705-788-3802
info@muskokamontessori.ca
www.muskokamontessori.ca
twitter.com/MiMSy_ca
Grades: Pre. - Jr. High
Timo Bijl, Principal

Innisfil: Kempenfelt Bay School
2145 Innisfil Beach Rd., Innisfil, ON L9S 4B9
Tel: 705-739-4731
www.kempenfeltbayschool.ca
www.facebook.com/KempenfeltBaySchool
Grades: JK-8 *Enrollment:* 175
Christopher White, Head of School
Diane Fitzgerald, Director, Academics & School Life

King: The Country Day School (CDS)
13415 Dufferin St., King, ON L7B 1K5
Tel: 905-833-1220; *Fax:* 905-833-1350
questions@cds.on.ca
www.cds.on.ca
Grades: JK - 12 *Note:* The co-educational school is
non-denominational.
John Liggett, Head of School
David Huckvale, Director, Admission

King City: Villanova College
P.O. Box 133
2480 15th Sideroad, King City, ON L7B 1A4, Canada
Tel: 905-833-1909; *Fax:* 905-833-1915
info@villanovacollege.org
www.villanovacollege.net
www.facebook.com/VillanovaCollege
twitter.com/VC_Online
www.youtube.com/channel/UCGeUZLn6mmQcBpKh33fZ5UQ
Grades: 5-12 *Enrollment:* 450
Paul Paradiso

Kingston: Mulberry Waldorf School
25 Markland St., Kingston, ON K7K 1S2
Tel: 613-542-0669; *Fax:* 613-542-0667
administrator@mulberrywaldorfschool.ca
www.mulberrywaldorfschool.ca
www.facebook.com/MulberryWaldorfSchool
Grades: Elem.
Peelu Hira, Administrator

Kitchener: Carmel New Church School
40 Chapel Hill Dr., Kitchener, ON N2R 1N2
Tel: 519-748-5802
www.carmelnewchurchschool.org
Grades: JK-10
Rev. Brad Heinrichs, Pastor
pastor@carmelnewchurch.org
James Bellinger, Principal
jbellinger@carmelnewchurch.org

Kitchener: Kitchener-Waterloo Montessori School
527 Bridgeport Rd. East, Kitchener, ON N2K 1N6
Tel: 519-742-1051
admin@kwmontessorischool.com
www.kwmontessorischool.com
Grades: K./Elem.
Ann Marie Fear, Principal

Kitchener: St. Jude's School Inc.
888 Trillium Dr., Kitchener, ON N2R 1K4, Canada
Tel: 519-888-0807; *Fax:* 519-884-0316
www.stjudes.com
Grades: 1-8 *Enrollment:* 172 *Note:* Founded in 1980 for students with learning difficulties. Also offers an after-hours Tutoring School

Kitchener: Scholar's Hall
888 Trillium Dr., Kitchener, ON N2R 1K4
Tel: 519-888-6620; *Fax:* 519-884-0316
director@scholarshall.com
www.scholarshall.com
www.facebook.com/scholars.hall
Grades: K - 12

Kitchener: Sunshine Montessori School Kitchener
10 Boniface Ave., Kitchener, ON N2C 1L9, Canada
Tel: 519-744-1423; *Fax:* 519-744-9929
admin@sunshinemontessori.on.ca
www.sunshinemontessori.on.ca
Grades: JK-8 *Enrollment:* 209

Kleinburg: Montessori School of Kleinburg
P.O. Box 445
10515 Hwy. 27, Kleinburg, ON L0J 1C0.
Tel: 905-893-0560; *Fax:* 905-893-8109
admin@msk2002.com
www.msk2002.com
Grades: Pre. - Elem.
Enza Pellegrini, Principal
e.pellegrini@msk2002.com
John Pellegrini, Director
j.pellegrini@msk2002.com

Lakefield: Lakefield College School
4391 County Rd. 29, Lakefield, ON K0L 2H0
Tel: 705-652-3324; *Fax:* 705-652-6320
www.lcs.on.ca
www.facebook.com/LakefieldCollege
twitter.com/LakefieldCS
www.linkedin.com/groups/874867
www.youtube.com/LakefieldCollege
Grades: 9 - 12 *Enrollment:* 365 *Note:* Founded 1879; co-ed boarding and day school, for grades 9-12 and 7-12 respectively; core academics, athletics, and co-curricular arts programmes.
Struan Robertson, Head of School, 705-652-3324, ext. 327
srobertson@lcs.on.ca
John Runza, Assistant Head: School Life, 705-652-3324, ext. 353
jrunza@lcs.on.ca
Tim Rutherford, Chief Financial Officer, 705-652-3324, ext. 325
trutherford@lcs.on.ca

London: Al-Taqwa Islamic Schools
Elementary School
35 Jim Ashton St., London, ON N5V 3H4, Canada
Tel: 519-951-1414; *Fax:* 519-951-1092
Toll-Free: 866-812-9127
ischool@altaqwa.org
www.altaqwa.org
Grades: Elem./Sec. *Enrollment:* 163 *Note:* The elementary school is located at 35 Jim Ashton St.; the secondary school is located at 1697 Trafalgar St., (519) 452-3366,
secondary@altaqwa.org.
Siham Kaloti, Principal

London: London Community Hebrew Day School
536 Huron St., London, ON N5Y 4J5
Tel: 519-439-8419; *Fax:* 519-439-0404
office@lchds.ca
www.lchds.ca
www.facebook.com/130138960416975
Grades: K./Elem.
Carol Marcus, Chair
Linda Latella, Principal

London: London International Academy (LIA)
#361, 365 Richmond St., London, ON N6A 3C2
Tel: 519-433-3388; *Fax:* 519-433-3387
admissions@lia-edu.ca
lia-edu.ca
twitter.com/LondonIntlAcad
Grades: 9 - 12

London: London Islamic School
151 Oxford St. West, London, ON N6H 1S3, Canada
Tel: 519-679-9920; *Fax:* 519-679-6842
www.londonislamicschool.com
Grades: K.-8 *Enrollment:* 260
Omar Hamadache, Principal

London: London Waldorf School
7 Beaufort St., London, ON N6G 1A5
Tel: 519-858-8862
info@londonwaldorf.ca
www.londonwaldorf.ca
www.facebook.com/122238667810381
twitter.com/londonwaldorf
londonwaldorf.wordpress.com
Grades: Pre. - 8 *Enrollment:* 109
Ruth Baer, Business Manager
Rebecca Soltan, Business Manager

London: Matthews Hall Private School
1370 Oxford St. West, London, ON N6H 1W2
Tel: 519-471-1506; *Fax:* 519-471-8647
www.matthewshall.ca
Grades: JK-8
Ric Anderson, Head of School
Jen McKay, Assistant Head
Alana Hepworth, Director, Student Learning

London: Montessori Academy of London
711 Waterloo St., London, ON N6A 3W1
Tel: 519-433-9121; *Fax:* 519-433-8941
reception@montessori.on.ca
www.montessori.on.ca
www.facebook.com/MontessoriAcademyofLondon
twitter.com/MAofLondon
Grades: Pre.-8 *Enrollment:* 350 *Number of Employees:* 41 teachers; 8 administrative staff *Note:* Established in 1968, Montessori Academy provides traditional accredited Montessori education for children aged 18 months through 14 years. The school is accredited by the Canadian Council of Montessori Administrators (CCMA).
Tina Sartori, Executive Director, 519-433-9121, ext. 210
tsartori@montessori.on.ca
Kristen Crouse, Academic Director, 519-433-9121, ext. 222
kcrouse@montessori.on.ca
Victoria Little, Registrar, 519-433-9121, ext. 211
vlittle@montessori.on.ca
Linda Yovanovich, Director, Communications, 519-433-9121, ext. 225
lyovanovich@montessori.on.ca

Campuses
Oxford Central Campus
311 Oxford St. East, London, ON N6A 1V3
Tel: 519-433-1019

Waterloo Central Campus
718 Waterloo St., London, ON N6A 3W1
Tel: 519-433-0341

Westmount South Campus
362 Commissioners Rd. West, London, ON N6J 1Y3
Tel: 519-472-0930

Maple: Chabad Romano Sunday Hebrew School
10500 Bathurst St., Maple, ON L6A 0H2
Tel: 905-303-1880; *Fax:* 905-303-1008
chabad@chabadrc.org
www.chabadrc.org
Rabbi Shlomo Vorovitch, Director, Hebrew School & Programs
sv@chabadrc.org

Maple: Maple Children's Montessori School
#9, 10175 Keele St., Maple, ON L6A 3Y9
Tel: 905-832-6665
www.maplechildrensmontessori.com
Grades: Toddler - Pre.
Gary Carrera, Principal
Mr.carrera@maplechildrensmontessori.com

Markham: Academic Vision
Cosburn Plaza
6061 Hwy. 7 East, #A, Markham, ON L3P 3B2
Tel: 905-471-6273
inquiries@academicvision.ca
academicvision.ca
www.facebook.com/AcademicVisionMarkham
twitter.com/Academic_Vision
Jennifer Hou, Principal & Director

Markham: Aspiration Academy
60 Riviera Dr., Markham, ON L3R 5M1
Tel: 905-752-0988
info@AspirationandDiscoveries.com
aspirationacademy.com

Markham: J. Addison School
2 Valleywood Dr., Markham, ON L3R 8H3
Tel: 905-477-4999
info@addisonschool.com
www.addisonschool.com
www.facebook.com/150702185027644
twitter.com/JAddisonSchool
www.pinterest.com/jaddison2002/
Grades: 9 - 12 *Enrollment:* 100
Lee Venditti, Principal
lvenditti@addisonschool.com

Markham: Learning Has No Limits (LHNL)
#2677, 2 Bur Oak Ave., Markham, ON L6B 1K8
Tel: 647-692-5465
www.facebook.com/learninghasnolimits
Grades: Pre.-12

Markham: Marander Montessori School
5906 - 6th Ave., Markham, ON L3P 3J3
Tel: 905-471-7118; *Fax:* 905-471-9338
marander@rogers.com
www.marandermontessori.com
www.facebook.com/149992325157734
Grades: Toddler - Pre.
Margaret Lee, Principal

Markham: Merit College
HSBC Tower
#808, 3601 Hwy. 7 East, Markham, ON L3R 0M3
Tel: 416-800-4168
info@meritedu.ca
www.meritedu.ca
www.facebook.com/MeritEducation
twitter.com/Merit_Education
www.youtube.com/user/MeritEducation/feed
Grades: 9 - 12
Joe Lu, Principal

Markham: Queens Montessori Academy (QMA)
1151 Denison St., Markham, ON L3R 3Y4
Tel: 905-944-0077; *Fax:* 905-944-0078
queensmontessori@brightpathkids.com
www.queensmontessori.com
Grades: Toddler - Pre.
Jan Sharma, Principal

Markham: Royal Cachet Montessori & Private School
Markham Campus
9921 Woodbine Ave., Markham, ON L6C 1H7
Tel: 905-888-7700; *Fax:* 905-888-6200
info@rcmschool.ca
www.rcmschool.ca
Grades: Pre./K./Elem. *Enrollment:* 110
Kathy Bobotsis, Director

Campuses
Stouffville Campus
160 Mostar St., Stouffville, ON L4A 0Y2
Tel: 905-640-8088; *Fax:* 905-888-6200

Markham: Somerset Academy
7700 Brimley Rd., Markham, ON L3R 0E5, Canada
Tel: 905-940-8990; *Fax:* 905-940-8992
administration@somersetacademy.ca
www.somersetacademy.ca
Grades: JK.-8 *Enrollment:* 172
Cathy Barogianis, Principal

Markham: Town Centre Montessori Private Schools
(TCMPS)
Main Campus
155 Clayton Dr., Markham, ON L3R 7P3, Canada
Tel: 905-470-1200; *Fax:* 905-470-0184
admin@tcmps.com
www.tcmps.com
Grades: 2-12
Marianne Vanderlugt, Director

Campuses
Amarillo Campus
76 Amarillo Ave., Markham, ON L3R 0V3, Canada
Tel: 905-474-3434; *Fax:* 905-474-3113
admin@tcmps.com
Grades: Pre.-1 *Note:* The preschool program accepts children as
young as two years of age.

Milliken Campus
3 Clayton Dr., Markham, ON L3R 8N3, Canada
Tel: 905-470-8178; *Fax:* 905-470-0570
admin@tcmps.com
Grades: Pre. *Note:* The preschool program accepts children as
young as two years of age.

Markham: Town Centre Private High School
(TCPHS)
155 Clayton Dr., Markham, ON L3R 7P3
Tel: 905-470-1200; *Fax:* 905-470-1721
www.tcphs.ca
www.facebook.com/254938157912596
Grades: 9 - 12 *Note:* This is a coeducational school which
provides university bound & advanced placement courses.

Markham: Trillium School
4277 - 14th Ave., Markham, ON L3R 0J2, Canada
Tel: 905-946-1181; *Fax:* 905-946-8267
info@trilliumschool.ca
www.trilliumschool.ca
Grades: K.-12 *Note:* Trillium School is a coeducational,
non-denominational school. It features a Casa program.
Lily Moon, Principal
lmoon@trilliumschool.ca

Markham: Wishing Well Montessori School
#30, 455 Cochrane Dr., Markham, ON L3R 9R4
Tel: 905-470-9751
www.wishingwellschools.com
www.facebook.com/wwsmarkham
Grades: K./Elem.

Merrickville: Fulford Preparatory College
P.O. Box 100
118 Main St. East, Merrickville, ON K0G 1N0
Tel: 613-269-2064
admissions@fulfordprep.com
www.fulfordprep.com
www.facebook.com/344493712305585
www.instagram.com/fulfordpreparatory
Grades: 7 - 10 *Note:* Boarding school for students looking to
complete their secondary school education, ESL skills, and to be
prepared for university or college.
Don Rickers, Headmaster
donr@fulfordprep.com

Mississauga: 3sixty Education
141 Brunel Rd., Mississauga, ON L4Z 1X3
Tel: 647-494-4340; *Fax:* 647-494-4341
Toll-Free: 866-360-2622
info@3sixtyeducation.ca
www.3sixtyeducation.ca
Grades: 9 - 12
Sangeeta Kumar, Principal

Mississauga: ABC Montessori
Elementary Campus
305 Matheson Blvd. East, Mississauga, ON L4Z 1X8
Tel: 905-568-8989
contactus@abcmontessori.com
www.abcmontessori.com
www.facebook.com/abcmontessoriprivateschool
Grades: Pre.-5 *Enrollment:* 140
Raj Vekaria, Principal

Campuses
Cawthra Casa Campus
4300 Cawthra Rd., Mississauga, ON L4Z 1V8
Tel: 905-281-2595; *Fax:* 905-568-0958
Mari Ang, Principal

Matheson Casa & Toddler Campus
285 Matheson Blvd. East, Mississauga, ON L4Z 1X8
Tel: 905-568-1716; *Fax:* 905-568-0958
Rick Kordts, Campus Administrator

Mississauga: Applewood Rainbow Montessori
School
24 Stavebank Rd., Mississauga, ON L5G 2T5
Tel: 905-274-2321; *Fax:* 905-829-0341
info@rainbowmontessori.ca
www.applewoodrainbowmontessori.com
Grades: Pre.-K
Razia Rangooni, Director

Mississauga: Bet Sefer Solel
2399 Folkway Dr., Mississauga, ON L5L 2M6
Tel: 905-820-5915; *Fax:* 905-280-1956
info@solel.ca
www.solel.ca/education/#bet-sefer
Grades: JK-10 *Note:* Bet Sefer Solel is a Reform Jewish school.
Robbin Botnick, President
Arliene Botnick, B.A., M.Ed., Director, Education
amora@solel.ca

Mississauga: Bright Scholars Academy - Cooksville
3180 Kirwin Ave., Mississauga, ON L5A 2K7
Tel: 905-896-4553
www.brightscholars.ca

Campuses
Bright Scholars Academy - Streetsville
24 Falconer Dr., Mississauga, ON L5N 2P7
Tel: 905-826-3595

Bright Scholars Academy - Meadowvale
5920 Montevideo Rd., Mississauga, ON L5N 3J5
Tel: 905-542-1895

Heritage Montessori - Oakville
1289 Marlborough Ct., Oakville, ON L6H 2R9
Tel: 905-842-3061

Mississauga: Bronte College
Senior School Campus
88 Bronte College Ct., Mississauga, ON L5B 1M9
Tel: 905-270-7788; *Fax:* 905-270-7828
info@brontecollege.ca
www.brontecollege.ca
www.facebook.com/brontecollege
twitter.com/brontecollege
www.youtube.com/user/brontecollege
Grades: Pre - 12 *Enrollment:* 550 *Note:* Bronte College of
Canada is a co-educational, international day & boarding school.
The school also offers University of Guelph & Bronte College
first year university courses, an advanced placement program, &
English as a Second Language (ESL).
Diane Finlay, Head of School
W. Johnson, Principal, Junior School

Mississauga: Dewey College
5889 Coopers Ave., Mississauga, ON L4Z 1P9
Tel: 905-897-6668; *Fax:* 905-897-6662
info@deweycollege.ca
deweycollege.ca
Grades: 9 - 12 *Note:* Offers courses from high School OSSD
(9-12 Grades) program to Advanced Placement (AP) program to
English as Second Language program.
Dr. Donna Zhang, Principal

Mississauga: Elpis College
Mississauga Campus
#1, 2155 Dunwin Dr., Mississauga, ON L5L 4M1
Tel: 905-607-7773
info@elpiscollege.ca
elpiscollege.ca
www.facebook.com/elpiscollegecanada
twitter.com/ElpisGlobalEdu
Grades: 9-12
David Jinman Kim, Principal

Campuses
North York Campus
#201, 18 Greenfield Ave., Toronto, ON M2N 3C8
Tel: 416-228-8878
eleducation@hotmail.com
Grades: 9-12

Mississauga: The Erindale Academy (TEA)
1576 Dundas St. West, Mississauga, ON L5C 1E5, Canada
Tel: 905-232-1576
www.teacademy.ca
www.facebook.com/erindaleacademy
Grades: 9-12 *Note:* University preparatory school.
Nash Vadsaria, Principal

Mississauga: Fun to Learn Montessori School
1840 Argentia Rd., Mississauga, ON L5N 1P9
Tel: 905-812-9606; *Fax:* 905-812-9606
info@funtolearn.org
www.funtolearn.org
www.facebook.com/474762045967575
Grades: Toddler - Pre. *Enrollment:* 45 *Number of Employees:* 10
Shahla Ambreen, Director

Mississauga: Golden Orchard Montessori School
1170 Tynegrove Rd., Mississauga, ON L4W 3B2
Tel: 905-629-7555; *Fax:* 905-507-3377
education@goldenorchardmontessori.com
www.goms.ca
Grades: Pre.
Virginia Rajakumar, Principal

Mississauga: Grade Learning
#20, 5225 Orbitor Dr., Mississauga, ON L4W 4Y8
Tel: 905-624-9661; *Fax:* 905-624-9661
Toll-Free: 800-208-3826
office@gradelearning.ca
www.gradelearning.ca
www.facebook.com/gradelearning
twitter.com/gradelearning
www.linkedin.com/company/grade-learning
www.youtube.com/gradelearning
Grades: 9-12

Campuses
Etobicoke Campus
#502, 1243 Islington Ave., Toronto, ON M8X 1Y9
Tel: 416-231-0333; *Fax:* 416-231-0023
etobicoke@gradelearning.ca

Milton Campus
#202, 450 Bronte St. South, Milton, ON L9T 8T2
Tel: 905-693-8484; *Fax:* 905-693-8480
milton@gradelearning.ca

Newmarket Campus
#35, 17665 Leslie St., Newmarket, ON L3Y 3E3
Tel: 905-953-1234; *Fax:* 905-953-1233
newmarket@gradelearning.ca

Richmond Hill Campus
#13-14, 1455 - 16th Ave., Richmond Hill, ON L4B 4W5
Tel: 905-886-6500; *Fax:* 905-886-8952
richmondhill@gradelearning.ca

Toronto Central Campus
#2102, 2300 Yonge St., Toronto, ON M4P 2W6
Tel: 416-482-2272; *Fax:* 416-482-2270
torontocentral@gradelearning.ca

Toronto North Campus
#510, 1315 Finch Ave., Toronto, ON M3J 2G6
Tel: 416-667-1500; *Fax:* 416-667-1502
torontonorth@gradelearning.ca

Weston Campus
#12, 2007 Lawrence Ave. West, Toronto, ON M9N 3V1
Tel: 416-243-2272; *Fax:* 416-243-2262
weston@gradelearning.ca

Mississauga: IQRA Islamic School
5751 Coopers Ave., Mississauga, ON L4Z 1R9, Canada
Tel: 905-507-6688; *Fax:* 905-507-9243
iqraislamicschool@gmail.com
www.iqraislamicschool.com
Grades: 1 - 8 *Enrollment:* 150

Mississauga: ISNA Elementary School
1525 Sherway Dr., Mississauga, ON L4X 1C5, Canada
Tel: 905-272-4303; *Fax:* 905-272-4311
elementary@isnaschools.com
isnaschools.com/elementary-school
Grades: K./Elem.
Obaid Yarkhan, Principal
o.yarkhan@isnaschools.com

Mississauga: ISNA High School
2200 South Sheridan Way, Mississauga, ON L5J 2M4
Tel: 905-403-8406; *Fax:* 905-403-8409
info@isnacanada.com
high.isnaschools.com
twitter.com/ISNAHigh
www.youtube.com/user/ISNAHighTube

Grades: 9-12
S.A. Rasoul, Principal

Mississauga: Kaban Montessori School
2449 Dunwin Dr., Mississauga, ON L5L 1T1
Tel: 905-569-3112
www.kabanmontessori.ca

Grades: Infant - Elem.
Karla Escobedo, Executive Director
karla@kabanmontessori.ca

Mississauga: Kendellhurst Academy
Streetsville Preschool
175 Queen St. South, Mississauga, ON L5M 1L2
Tel: 905-567-1070; Fax: 905-821-0891
info@kendellhurst.com
www.kendellhurst.com

Grades: Pre./K.
Paula Carrasco-Kendell, Director
Cathy Finelli, Administrator, Preschool Division

Campuses
Oakville Campus
#11 & 12, 2460 Neyagawa Blvd., Oakville, ON L6H 7P4
Tel: 905-257-2030
Grades: Pre./K.

Streetsville Grade School
170 Church St., Mississauga, ON L5M 2M3
Tel: 905-813-8000; Fax: 905-821-0891
Grades: JK-8
Tony McConney, Principal

Mississauga: Lakeside Montessori School
1079 Lakeshore Rd. East, Mississauga, ON L5E 1E8
Tel: 905-891-8332
schoolinfo@lakesidemontessorischool.com
www.lakesidemontessorischool.com

Grades: Toddler - Pre.
Carolyn Peto-De Khors, Director

Mississauga: Lynn-Rose Heights Private School
7215 Millcreek Dr., Mississauga, ON L5N 3R3
Tel: 905-567-3553; Fax: 905-567-5318
info@lynnroseheights.org
www.lynnroseheights.com

Grades: Pre.-10 Enrollment: 300

Mississauga: Meadow Green Academy
649 Queensway West, Mississauga, ON L5B 1C2
Tel: 905-273-3344
meadowgreen1@hotmail.com
www.meadowgreenacademy.ca
www.facebook.com/MeadowGreenAcademy
twitter.com/MeadowGreenAc

Grades: Pre.-8 Enrollment: 150
Georganne M. MacKenzie, Director

Campuses
Senior Campus
1884 Lakeshore Rd. West, Mississauga, ON L5J 1J7
Tel: 905-273-3344

Mississauga: Mentor College
Main Campus
40 Forest Ave., Mississauga, ON L5G 1L1, Canada
Tel: 905-271-3393; Fax: 905-271-8367
admin@mentorcollege.edu
www.mentorcollege.edu
www.facebook.com/TEAMandMentor
twitter.com/Mentor_TEAM
www.youtube.com/user/TEAMMentor

Grades: 5-12
Ken Philbrook, Executive Director

Campuses
Primary Campus
56 Cayuga Ave., Mississauga, ON L5G 3S9, Canada
Tel: 905-271-7100; Fax: 905-271-8076
56cayuga@mentorcollege.edu

Grades: JK-4
Barb Philbrook, Principal, Primary Division

Mississauga: Northstar Montessori Private School
4900 Tomken Rd., Mississauga, ON L4W 1J8, Canada
Tel: 905-890-7827; Fax: 905-890-6771
admin@northstarmontessori.com
www.northstarmontessori.com
www.facebook.com/NorthstarMontessoriPrivateSchool
twitter.com/NorthstarMontes

Grades: Pre./Elem. Note: Northstar Montessori offers the following programs: toddlers, pre-Casa, primary, elementary, & junior high. Ages of children range from 18 months to 14 years.
Virginia Ramirez, Principal
Sherry Gosal, Vice-Principal

Rick Ramirez, Manager, Business
Rose Sta. Ana, Office Administrator

Mississauga: Olive Grove School (OGS)
2300 Speakman Dr., Mississauga, ON L5K 1B4
Tel: 905-855-8557; Fax: 905-855-7917
info@olivegroveschool.ca
www.olivegroveschool.ca
www.facebook.com/olivegroveschool
Grades: Pre. - 8 Note: Olive Grove School is a private Islamic School registered by the Ontario Ministry of Education
Mr. Bakbak, Principal

Mississauga: Peel Montessori School
964 Meadow Wood Rd., Mississauga, ON L5J 2S6
Tel: 905-823-6522; Fax: 905-823-5397
info@peelmontessori.com
peelmontessori.com

Grades: Pre.-6 Enrollment: 100
Santina Cowdrey, Principal

Mississauga: Royal School of Canada
#108, 1140 Burnhamthorpe Rd. West, Mississauga, ON L5C 4E9
Tel: 905-279-4567; Fax: 905-279-0969
admissions@royalschoolofcanada.com
royalschoolofcanada.com

Grades: 9 - 12
Scott Headrick, Principal

Mississauga: Safa & Marwa Islamic School
5550 McAdam Rd., Mississauga, ON L4Z 1P1
Tel: 905-566-8533; Fax: 905-823-3938
admin@safaandmarwa.ca
safaandmarwa.ca

Grades: K - 8

Mississauga: St. Jude's Academy
2150 Torquay Mews, Mississauga, ON L5N 2M6
Tel: 905-814-0202; Fax: 905-814-0299
info@stjudesacademy.com
www.stjudesacademy.com
www.facebook.com/392663204140440
twitter.com/stjudesacademy2
www.linkedin.com/company/st.-jude's-academy

Grades: JK-12 Enrollment: 115
Aaron Sawatsky, Head of School

Mississauga: Sherwood Heights School
Erin Mills Campus
3650 Platinum Dr., Mississauga, ON L5M 0Y7, Canada
Tel: 905-569-8999; Fax: 905-569-9034
info@sherwoodheights.com
www.sherwoodheights.com
www.facebook.com/113774888639558
twitter.com/SherwoodHeights

Grades: K./Elem./Sec. Enrollment: 206

Campuses
Kennedy Campus
5870 Kennedy Rd., Mississauga, ON L4Z 4G6, Canada
Tel: 905-712-4343; Fax: 905-569-9034
Grades: K./Elem.

Mississauga: Star Academy
1587 Cormack Cres., Mississauga, ON L5E 2P8
Tel: 905-891-1555; Fax: 905-891-1696
info@staracademy.ca
www.staracademy.ca
www.facebook.com/staracademymississauga
twitter.com/myStarAcademy
www.linkedin.com/company/star-academy

Grades: JK-8 Enrollment: 95
Belinda Bernardo, Principal

Mississauga: TEAM School
Also known as: Tutorial & Educ. Assistance in Mississauga
275 Rudar Rd., Mississauga, ON L5A 1S2, Canada
Tel: 905-279-7200; Fax: 905-279-1561
www.teamschool.com
www.facebook.com/TEAMandMentor
twitter.com/Mentor_TEAM

Grades: 1-12

Mississauga: White Oaks Montessori School Ltd. (WOMS)
Vanier Campus
1200 Vanier Dr., Mississauga, ON L5H 4C7, Canada
Tel: 905-278-4454; Fax: 905-278-5184
admin@woms.ca
www.whiteoaksmontessori.ca
Other Information: 905-855-2321 (Phone, Clarkson Campus)

Grades: Preschool - Elementary Note: White Oaks Montessori School is a fully accredited Canadian Council of Montessori Administrators school. The youngest children are offered toddler programs. Casa programs are provided for children from age three to five. The Clarkson Campus is located at the following address: 1338 Clarkson Road North, Mississauga.
Barbara S. Ward, AMI, Founder & Chief Administrative Officer
Irene Stathoukos, BSc., AMI, Principal
Daniel Ward, Information Technologist

Mount Hope: Grandview Adventist Academy
3975 Hwy. 6, Mount Hope, ON L0R 1W0, Canada
Tel: 905-679-4492; Fax: 905-679-4492
info@grandviewschool.ca
www.grandviewschool.ca
twitter.com/GrandviewSDA

Grades: Elem./Sec. Enrollment: 58
Lisa Clarke, Principal
principal@grandviewschool.ca

Nestor Falls: Mikinaak Onigaming School
P.O. Box 339
Nestor Falls, ON P0X 1K0
Tel: 807-484-2510; Fax: 807-484-2352
Grades: JK - 12 Enrollment: 115 Note: Mikinaak Onigaming School is a band operated school, providing education for the Ojibways of Onigaming First Nation.
Steve Grindrod, Principal

New Hamburg: Our Lady of Mount Carmel Academy
2483 Bleams Rd. East, New Hamburg, ON N3A 3J2
Tel: 519-634-4932; Fax: 519-634-9395
olmc@sspx.ca
fsspx.com/olmc/

Grades: K - 12
Fr. David Sherry, Principal

Newmarket: Or Hadash Religious School, Newmarket
Also known as: Or Hadash Hebrew School
#210, 130 Davis Dr., Newmarket, ON L3Y 2N1
contact@orhadash.org
www.orhadash.org
www.facebook.com/orhadashnewmarket
twitter.com/orhadashnmkt
Note: School of Or Hadash Synagogue, Newmarket. Grades: First grade to B'nei Mitzvah. Minimum required number of students to run school: 6.
Herman Yeger, President, Or Hadash Synagogue
herman@orhadash.org
Howard Lindo, Principal
howard@orhadash.org

Newmarket: Pickering College
16945 Bayview Ave., Newmarket, ON L3Y 4X2
Tel: 905-895-1700; Fax: 905-895-9076
Toll-Free: 877-895-1700
info@pickeringcollege.on.ca
www.pickeringcollege.on.ca
Grades: JK - 12 Enrollment: 400 Note: Day and Boarding School
Peter C. Sturrup, Headmaster
Maria Wolscht, Director of Junior School
Scott Hammell, Director of Senior School

Niagara Falls: Niagara Centre for the Arts Academy
4700 Epworth Circle, Niagara Falls, ON L2E 1C6
Tel: 905-513-1685; Fax: 905-339-2994
info@NiagaraCentreForTheArts.com
academy.niagaracentreforarts.com

Grades: 11-12; adult

Nobleton: The Montessori Country School
Nobleton Campus
P.O. Box 455
6185 - 15th Sideroad, Nobleton, ON L0G 1N0, Canada
Tel: 905-859-4739; Fax: 905-859-5696
www.montessoricountryschool.ca
Grades: Pre.-8 Note: The Montessori Country School offers a toddler program, a Casa program, & an elementary program. Children range in age from 12 months to 12 years.
Sarah Enright, Principal
Joanne Hastie, Vice-Principal

Campuses
Milton Campus
8560 Tremaine Rd., Milton, ON L9T 2Y3, Canada
Tel: 905-864-0590; Fax: 905-859-5696
milton@montessoricountryschool.ca
Amanda Green, Administrator
amandag@mcs-milton.com

Oakville: **Al-Falah Islamic School**
391 Burnhamthorpe Rd. East, Oakville, ON L6H 7B4, Canada
Tel: 905-257-5782; *Fax:* 905-257-0848
office@al-falah.org
www.al-falah.org
twitter.com/Al_FalahSchool
Grades: Elem. *Enrollment:* 215 *Note:* Accredited by the Ontario Min. of Education; curriculum also includes programmes in the arts, computers, phyiscial education, Arabic language, & Quran studies.
Mohsin Chowdhury, Principal, 905-257-5782, ext. 252

Oakville: **Appleby College**
540 Lakeshore Rd. West, Oakville, ON L6K 3P1, Canada
Tel: 905-845-4681; *Fax:* 905-845-9828
info@appleby.on.ca
www.appleby.on.ca
www.facebook.com/applebycollege
twitter.com/applebycollege
www.youtube.com/applebycollege
Grades: 7-12 *Enrollment:* 740 *Note:* Independent, co-educational school for boarding & day students in Grades 7 through 12.
Katrina Samson, Head of School
ksamson@appleby.on.ca
Innes van Nostrand, Principal
ivannostrand@appleby.on.ca

Oakville: **Chisholm Educational Centre**
Also known as: Chisholm Academy
1484 Cornwall Rd., Oakville, ON L6J 7W5, Canada
Tel: 905-844-3240; *Fax:* 905-844-7321
www.chisholmacademy.com
Grades: 7-12 *Note:* Chisholm Academy provides educational services to senior elementary & high school students, including those with special needs. Programs include tutoring & remediation, educational assessments, & counselling services.
Dr. Howard Bernstein, Executive Director
David Jowett, Principal
Sylvia Moyssakos, Vice-Principal & Head, Specialized Academic Services
Dr. Shirley Bryntwick, Director, Professional Services
Adam Bernstein, Manager, Operations & Development

Oakville: **Clanmore Montessori School**
2463 Lakeshore Rd. East, Oakville, ON L6J 1M7
Tel: 905-337-8283
info@clanmore.ca
www.clanmore.ca
www.facebook.com/Clanmore
twitter.com/ClanmoreMontess
www.instagram.com/clanmore
Grades: Pre.-8 *Enrollment:* 110
Leslie Austin, Coordinator, Facility, Policy & Finance
Elaine Delsnyder, Coordinator, Admissions
Anne Mercer, Coordinator, Communications

Oakville: **Dearcroft Montessori School & West Wind Montessori Jr. High**
1167 Lakeshore Rd. East, Oakville, ON L6J 1L3
Tel: 905-844-2114; *Fax:* 905-844-3529
dearcroft@primus.ca
www.dearcroft.com
Grades: JK-8
Gordon Phippen, Principal/Director

Oakville: **Fern Hill School**
Oakville Campus
3300 Ninth Line, Oakville, ON L6H 7A8, Canada
Tel: 905-257-0022; *Fax:* 905-257-2002
admissions@fernhillschool.com
www.fernhillschool.com
Grades: Pre.-8 *Enrollment:* 400 *Number of Employees:* 50 *Note:* Fern Hill School Oakville is a co-educational school for students in preschool to Grade 8. The personalized curriculum is taught in a rotary system by qualified, subject-specific teachers.
Wendy Derrick, Director
Laura Beamish, Director, Admissions
Karen Kusters, Admissions Officer

Campuses
Burlington Campus
801 North Service Rd., Burlington, ON L7P 5B6
Tel: 905-634-8652
enrol@fernhillschool.com
Grades: Pre.-8 *Enrollment:* 180
Celia Stone, Admissions Officer
cstone@fernhillschool.com

Oakville: **Glen Abbey Montessori School (GAMS)**
1081 Glen Valley Rd., Oakville, ON L6M 3K4
Tel: 905-825-2121
info@glenabbeymontessori.com
www.glenabbeymontessori.com

Grades: Pre. *Number of Employees:* 6
Claire Perry, Principal & Administrator

Oakville: **Glenburnie School**
2035 Upper Middle Rd. East, Oakville, ON L6J 7G7, Canada
Tel: 905-338-6236; *Fax:* 905-338-2654
admin.gbs@glenburnieschool.com
www.glenburnieschool.com
www.facebook.com/GlenburnieSchool
twitter.com/GlenburnieSch
www.youtube.com/user/glenburnieschool
Grades: Pre.-8 *Enrollment:* 361
Linda Sweet, Director
lsweet@glenburnieschool.com
Melissa Meevis, Principal
mmeevis@glenburnieschool.com
Sean McCammon, Vice-Principal
smccammon@glenburnieschool.com

Oakville: **MacLachlan College**
337 Trafalgar Rd., Oakville, ON L6J 3H3
Tel: 905-844-0372; *Fax:* 905-844-9369
admissions@maclachlan.ca
www.maclachlan.ca
www.facebook.com/MacLachlanCollege
www.youtube.com/maclachlanc
Grades: Pre.-12 *Enrollment:* 300
Michael Piening, Head of School

Oakville: **Rotherglen School**
Oakville Primary Campus
2045 Sixth Line, Oakville, ON L6H 1X9
Tel: 905-338-3528
rotherglen.com
Grades: Pre.-1 *Enrollment:* 1000 *Note:* The Casa program is designed for children as young as three years of age. The school includes students from age three to six.
Mary Williamson, Head of School, 905-338-3528, ext. 11
mwilliamson@rotherglen.com

Campuses
Oakville Elementary Campus
2050 Neyagawa Blvd., Oakville, ON L6H 6R2, Canada
Tel: 905-849-1897; *Fax:* 905-849-1354
Grades: Pre.-8
Laura Crumb, Head of School, 905-849-1897, ext. 340
lcrumb@rotherglen.com

Erin Mills Campus
3553 South Common Ct., Mississauga, ON L5L 2B3
Tel: 905-820-9445; *Fax:* 905-569-1569
Grades: Pre.-8 *Note:* The Erin Mills campus provides a Montessori program for its students, from Casa to grade eight.

Meadowvale Elementary Campus
929 Old Derry Rd., Mississauga, ON L5L 2B3
Tel: 905-565-8707; *Fax:* 905-565-0485
Grades: Pre.-8

Oakville: **St. Mildred's-Lightbourn School**
1080 Linbrook Rd., Oakville, ON L6J 2L1, Canada
Tel: 905-845-2386
contact@smls.on.ca
www.smls.on.ca
twitter.com/StMildreds
Grades: Pre.-12 *Enrollment:* 600 *Note:* All-girls school
Nancy Richards, Head of School

Oakville: **Shaarei-Beth El Religious School**
186 Morrison Rd., Oakville, ON L6J 4J4
Tel: 905-849-6000
office@sbe.ca
www.sbe.ca
Grades: Pre.-12
Rabbi Stephen Wise, 905-849-6000, ext. 2
rabbi.wise@sbe.ca
Cheryl Wise, Director, Education, 905-849-6000, ext. 15
educator@sbe.ca

Oakville: **Wildwood Academy**
2250 Sheridan Garden Dr., Oakville, ON L6J 7T1
Tel: 905-829-4226; *Fax:* 905-829-2318
admin@wildwoodacademy.com
wildwoodadmin.wixsite.com/wildwood
www.facebook.com/WildwoodAcademy
Grades: 2-8 *Enrollment:* 60 *Number of Employees:* 18 *Note:* Wildwood Academy educates children with a variety of learning abilities through the provision of specialized programming. The school aims to accelerate the academic achievement of students.
Kelley Caston, Principal
kcaston@wildwoodacademy.com
Doris Huber, Office Manager

Orangeville: **Hillcrest School**
7A Little York St., Orangeville, ON L9W 1L8, Canada
Tel: 519-941-5591
Grades: K./Elem./Sec.
Gail P. Hooper, Principal
gail@hillcrestps.com

Oshawa: **College Park Elementary School**
220 Townline Rd. North, Oshawa, ON L1K 2J6, Canada
Tel: 905-723-0163; *Fax:* 905-723-2984
www.cpes.ca
Grades: K.-8 *Enrollment:* 200
Daniel Carley, Principal
dancarley@yahoo.com

Oshawa: **Kingsway College**
1200 Leland Rd., Oshawa, ON L1K 2H4, Canada
Tel: 905-433-1144; *Fax:* 905-433-1156
admissions@kingswaycollege.on.ca
www.kingswaycollege.on.ca
Other Information: Records Fax: 905-433-8078
www.facebook.com/groups/kingswaycollege
twitter.com/kingswayc
www.youtube.com/user/KingswayCollege
Grades: 9-12
Lee Richards, President, 905-433-1144, ext. 217
richardsl@kingswaycollege.on.ca
Jeremy O'Dell, Vice-President, Finance, 905-433-1144, ext. 214
odellj@kingswaycollege.on.ca

Otonabee-South Monaghan: **Kawartha Montessori School**
2247 Burnham Line, Otonabee-South Monaghan, ON K9J 6X7
Tel: 705-748-5437; *Fax:* 705-748-6674
admissions@kawarthamontessori.com
www.kawarthamontessori.com
Grades: Pre.-8
Ugette Vanderpost, Principal
uvanderpost@kawarthamontessori.com

Ottawa: **Abraar School**
70 Fieldrow St., Ottawa, ON K2G 2Y7, Canada
Tel: 613-226-1396; *Fax:* 613-820-1495
info@abraarschool.com
www.abraarschool.com
Grades: JK - 9 *Enrollment:* 212 *Note:* Islamic school. Location: 1085 Grenon Ave., Ottawa.
Mohammed Saleem, Principal

Ottawa: **Ashbury College**
362 Mariposa Ave., Ottawa, ON K1M 0T3
Tel: 613-749-5954; *Fax:* 613-749-9724
info@ashbury.ca
www.ashbury.ca
www.facebook.com/AshburyCollege
twitter.com/ashburycollege
www.linkedin.com/groups/1353977
www.youtube.com/user/ashburycollege
Grades: 4-12 *Enrollment:* 680 *Note:* Boarding school.
Norman Southward, Head of School
Gary Godkin, Head, Senior School
Kendal Young, Head, Junior School
Alex Milroy, Chief Financial Officer
Bruce Mutch, Executive Director, Enrollment & Advancement

Ottawa: **Bishop Hamilton Montessori School**
2199 Regency Terrace, Ottawa, ON K2C 1H2
Tel: 613-596-4013; *Fax:* 613-596-4971
info@bhms.ca
www.bhsmontessori.ca
Grades: Pre.-8 *Enrollment:* 190 *Number of Employees:* 47 *Note:* Bishop Hamilton School is a Christian Montessori school for children from ages 3 months to 14 years.
Renette Sasouni, Director
Jackie Lalumiere, Admissions Director
jlalumiere@bhms.ca
Nancy VanRyswyk, Business Manager
nvanryswyk@bhms.ca
Helen Sousa, Contact, Marketing & Communications
hsousa@bhms.ca

Ottawa: **Elmwood School**
Rockcliffe Park
261 Buena Vista Rd., Ottawa, ON K1M 0V9
Tel: 613-749-6761; *Fax:* 613-741-8210
info@elmwood.ca
www.elmwood.ca
www.facebook.com/ElmwoodSchool
twitter.com/ElmwoodDotCa
pinterest.com/elmwoodschool
Grades: JK - 12; Girls *Enrollment:* 564
Cheryl Boughton, Headmistress

Ottawa: Fern Hill School (Ottawa) Inc.
50 Vaughan St., Ottawa, ON K1M 1X1, Canada
Tel: 613-746-0255; *Fax:* 613-746-7514
www.fernhillottawa.com
Grades: Pre.-8 *Enrollment:* 99 *Note:* Enriched academic
programme; before/after school care & after school
programmes; extended French programme.
Deborah Gutierrez, Principal
principal@fernhillottawa.com

Ottawa: Joan of Arc Academy
2221 Elmira Dr., Ottawa, ON K2C 1H3, Canada
Tel: 613-728-6364; *Fax:* 613-728-2935
info@joanofarcacademy.com
joanofarcacademy.com
www.facebook.com/JoanOfArcAcademy
twitter.com/academyjoa
www.pinterest.com/joanofarcacadem
Grades: JK-8; Girls
Brian Lamb, Head
brian.lamb@joanofarcacademy.com

Ottawa: Kanata Montessori School
355 Michael Cowpland Dr., Ottawa, ON K2M 2C5
Tel: 613-592-2189; *Fax:* 613-592-3705
info@kanata-montessori.com
www.kanatamontessori.com
www.facebook.com/kanatamontessori
twitter.com/KMSMontessori
Grades: Toddler - Jr. High
Jonathan Robinson, Principal
jonathan@kanata-montessori.com

Campuses
North Campus
630 Cameron Harvey Dr., Ottawa, ON K2K 1X7
Tel: 613-592-2189; *Fax:* 613-592-3705

Ottawa: Lycée Claudel
1635, prom Riverside, Ottawa, ON K1G 0E5, Canada
Tél: 613-733-8522; *Téléc:* 613-733-3782
www.claudel.org
Grades: Mat - Terminale *Enrollment:* 1000
Pascale Garrec, Proviseur

Ottawa: OMS Montessori
335 Lindsay St., Ottawa, ON K1G 0L6, Canada
Tel: 613-521-5185; *Fax:* 613-521-6796
info@omsmontessori.com
www.omsmontessori.com
www.facebook.com/omsmontessori
twitter.com/OMSMontessori
www.linkedin.com/company/oms-montessori
Grades: Pre.-6 *Enrollment:* 240 *Number of Employees:* 50+
Gregory Dixon, Head of Schools, 613-521-5185, ext. 101
greg@omsmontessori.com

Ottawa: Ottawa Islamic School
10 Coral Ave., Ottawa, ON K2E 5Z6, Canada
Tel: 613-727-5066; *Fax:* 613-727-8486
info@ottawaislamicschool.org
www.ottawaislamicschool.org
Grades: JK-12 *Enrollment:* 246
Mohamed Sheik, Principal
principal@ottawaislamicschool.org

Ottawa: St-Laurent Academy
Académie St-Laurent
641 Sladen Ave., Ottawa, ON K1K 2S8
Tel: 613-842-8047; *Fax:* 613-842-9956
admin@st-laurentacademy.com
www.st-laurentacademy.com
www.facebook.com/stlaurentacademy
twitter.com/stlaurentacad
www.linkedin.com/company/5162456
www.youtube.com/user/Stlaurentacademy
Grades: Pre.-8 *Enrollment:* 200
Bill Kokkaliaris, CEO & School Director

Ottawa: Torah Day School of Ottawa
1119 Lazard St., Ottawa, ON K2C 2R5, Canada
Tel: 613-274-0110
office@torahday.ca
torahday.ca
www.facebook.com/TorahDayOttawa
Grades: Pre.-8 *Note:* Orthodox Jewish day school offering
general & Judaic studies.
Rabbi Zischa Shaps, Executive Director
rabbi.shaps@torahday.ca
Rabbi Elazar Durden, Principal
rabbi.durden@torahday.ca
Sharon Holzscherer, Vice-Principal, General Studies
sholz@torahday.ca
Debbie Goldstein, Office Manager

Ottawa: Torah High School - Ottawa
21 Nadolny Sachs Private, Ottawa, ON K2A 1R9
Tel: 613-262-6283; *Fax:* 613-798-9839
torahhighottawa.weebly.com
www.facebook.com/NCSYOttawa
Grades: 9-12 *Note:* Torah High offers courses in Religious
Studies, Hebrew Language, Philosophy, Political Science,
Nutrition, Arts & Interdisciplinary Studies for students attending
public or private secondary schools. The school is located at 261
Centrepointe Dr., Ottawa, ON K2G 6E8.
Rabbi Yehuda Simes, Dean & Co-Founder
Gaby Scarowsky, Executive Director
gaby@ncsy.ca

Ottawa: Turnbull School
1132 Fisher Ave., Ottawa, ON K1Z 6P7, Canada
Tel: 613-729-9940; *Fax:* 613-729-1636
info@turnbull.ca
turnbull.ca
www.facebook.com/turnbullschool
Grades: JK-8
Gareth Reid, Director
Buddy Clinch, Principal, Junior School
Craig Dunn, Principal, Senior School
Liz Doran, Head, Academic Studies - Primary Division
Christine Ferris, Head, Academic Studies - Senior Division
Katie Horton, Head, Academic Studies - Junior Division
Steve Fini, Head, Community Engagement
Jody Rantala, Head, Student Life - Senior School
Lorie Roy, Head, Student Life - Junior School
Yvon Carrière, Director, Athletics
Joyce Walker-Steed, Registrar

Ottawa: Westboro Academy
Académie Westboro
200 Brewer Way, Ottawa, ON K1S 5R2
Tel: 613-737-9543; *Fax:* 613-737-7716
Westboro@WestboroAcademy.com
www.westboroacademy.com
www.facebook.com//120750381288847
Grades: JK - 8 *Note:* Westboro Academy is a coeducational
school, which offers an enriched bilingual education.
Marcel Papineau, Principal

Owen Sound: Riverforest Montessori School
1595 - 3rd Ave. West, Owen Sound, ON N4K 4R2, Canada
Tel: 519-371-2313; *Fax:* 519-371-1178
riverforestmontessori@hotmail.com
www.riverforestmontessori.com
Grades: Pre.-6 *Note:* The Casa program is offered for children
from age 2.5 to 6.

Pawitik: Baibombeh Anishinabe School
Whitefish Bay First Nation
General Delivery, Pawitik, ON P0X 1L0
Tel: 807-226-5698; *Fax:* 807-226-1089
Grades: JK - 12 *Note:* Baibombeh Anishinabe School is a band
operated Ojibway school.

Pickering: Blaisdale Montessori School
415 Toynevale Rd., Pickering, ON L1W 2G9, Canada
Tel: 905-509-5005; *Fax:* 905-509-1959
info@blaisdale.com
www.blaisdale.com
Grades: Toddler/Casa/Elementary/Renaissance *Note:* Blaisdale
Montessori School offers programs for ages 12 months to 14
years, including pre-toddler.
Heather Wilson, Principal & Administrator, 905-509-5005, ext.
107
hwilson@blaisdale.com

Campuses
Bowmanville Campus
80 Rhonda Blvd., Bowmanville, ON L1C 3Y9
Tel: 905-697-3064
www.blaisdale.com/bowmanville.html
Grades: 12 mo. - Gr. 6

Milner Campus
231 Milner Ave., Toronto, ON M1S 5E3
Tel: 416-289-2273
www.blaisdale.com/milner-scarb.html
Grades: 12 mo. - Gr. 3

Oshawa Campus
1037 Simcoe St. North, Oshawa, ON L1G 4W3
Tel: 905-721-1933
www.blaisdale.com/oshawa-ajax.html
Other Information: Alternate Phone: 416-607-6297
Grades: 12 mo. - Gr. 8

Rotherglen Campus
403 Kingston Rd., Ajax, ON L1S 6L7
Tel: 905-683-5005
www.blaisdale.com/rotherglen-ajax.html
Grades: 12 mo. - Gr. 8

Village Campus
56 Old Kingston Rd., Ajax, ON L1T 2Z7
Tel: 905-427-5006
www.blaisdale.com/viillage-ajax.html
Grades: 12 mo. - 9 yrs

Westney Campus
20 O'Brien Ct., Ajax, ON L1S 7J8
Tel: 905-426-5665
www.blaisdale.com/westney-ajax.html
Grades: 12 mo. - Gr. 8

Whitby Campus
200 Byron St. South, Ajax, ON L1N 4P6
Tel: 905-665-1516
www.blaisdale.com/whitby-whitby.html
Grades: 12 mo. - 6 yrs

Annex Campus
1340 Rougemount Dr., Pickering, ON L1V 1M9
Tel: 905-509-9989
www.blaisdale.com/rotherglen-ajax.html
Grades: 12 mo. - 6 yrs

**Pickering: Montessori Learning Centre of Pickering
(MLCP)**
401 Kingston Rd., Pickering, ON L1V 1A3, Canada
Tel: 905-509-1722; *Fax:* 905-509-8283
info@montessorilearningcentre.com
www.mlcp.ca
www.facebook.com/MontessoriLearningCentreOfPickering
twitter.com/MontessoriMLCP
Grades: Pre./Elem. *Enrollment:* 200 *Note:* Montessori Learning
Centre of Pickering provides the following programs: infants,
pre-Casa, Casa, & elementary.
Nicola Phillips, Principal

Port Hope: Trinity College School (TCS)
55 Deblaquire St. North, Port Hope, ON L1A 4K7, Canada
Tel: 905-885-3217; *Fax:* 905-885-9690
info@tcs.on.ca
www.tcs.on.ca
www.facebook.com/TCSBears
twitter.com/tcsbears
www.youtube.com/user/TCSBears
Grades: 5-12 *Enrollment:* 555 *Number of Employees:* 71
full-time; 3 part-time *Note:* The school is a coeducational
boarding/day school. The senior school has approximately 450
students. Over 100 students attend the junior school.
Stuart K.C. Grainger, Headmaster
sgrainger@tcs.on.ca

Richmond Hill: Century Private School
11181 Yonge St., Richmond Hill, ON L4S 1L2, Canada
Tel: 905-737-1160
info@centurypscanada.com
www.centurypscanada.com
Grades: Pre.-12 *Note:* Offers preschool, Casa (JK/SK),
elementary, & high school programs.
Marcel Pereira, Director
mperiera@centurypscanada.com
John Elmer, Principal, High School
jelmer@centurypscanada.com
Elizabeth Pereira, Principal, Elementary
bpereira@centurypscanada.com

Richmond Hill: Children's Montessori Academy
201 King Rd., Richmond Hill, ON L4E 2W2
Tel: 905-773-1234
montessorimagic@yahoo.com
www.thechildrensmontessori.com
Lorraine Pinto, Owner

Richmond Hill: Discovery Academy
10030 Yonge St., Richmond Hill, ON L4C 1T8
Tel: 416-302-4085
info@diacademy.ca
www.discoveryacademy.ca
Other Information: Dayschool Phone: 647-727-1737
Grades: 1-12
Marina Blumin, Ph.D., Headmistress

Richmond Hill: Richland Academy
11570 Yonge St., Richmond Hill, ON L4E 3N7
Tel: 905-224-5600; Fax: 905-224-4080
info@richlandacademy.ca
www.richlandacademy.ca
www.facebook.com/richlandacad
twitter.com/richlandacad
www.linkedin.com/company/richland-academy
www.instagram.com/richlandacad
Grades: Pre.-8 Enrollment: 115
Jill Colyer, Head of School
Laura Murgatroyd, Director, Communications & Admissions

Richmond Hill: Richmond Hill Montessori & Elementary School (RHMS)
189 Weldrick Rd. East, Richmond Hill, ON L4C 0A6, Canada
Tel: 905-508-2228; Fax: 905-508-2229
reception@rhms.ca
www.rhms.ca
Number of Schools: 1 Grades: Preschool - 8 Number of Employees: 75 Note: The school's preschool program is Montessori based. The junior program includes three & four year old children. The senior program is designed for children who are four & five year olds.
Walter Ribeiro, Director
w.ribeiro@rhms.ca
Janet Darbey, Registrar
jdarbey@rhms.ca
Dino D'Amato, Principal
ddamato@rhms.ca
Andrea Cudini, Human Resources Manager
hr@rhms.ca
Ashley Travassos, Contact, Marketing & Communications
atravassos@rhms.ca
Rose Chitiz, Administrator
reception@rhms.ca
Claude Rodrigues, Contact, Purchasing & Finance
crodrigues@rhms.ca

Richmond Hill: Toronto Montessori Schools (TMS)
Also known as: TMS School
8569 Bayview Ave., Richmond Hill, ON L4B 3M7
Tel: 905-889-6882; Fax: 905-886-6516
admissions@tmsschool.ca
www.tmsschool.ca
Other Information: tmshr@tmsschool.ca (E-mail, Human Resources)
Grades: Pre.-6 Enrollment: 750

Campuses
Toronto Montessori School (TMS)
Elgin Mills Campus
500 Elgin Mills Rd. East, Richmond Hill, ON L4C 5G1
Tel: 905-780-1002; Fax: 905-780-8981
admissions@tmsschool.ca
Grades: 7-12
Sheila Thomas, Head, Upper School
sthomas@tmsschool.ca

Rosseau: Rosseau Lake College (RLC)
1967 Bright St., Rosseau, ON P0C 1J0, Canada
Tel: 705-732-4351; Fax: 705-732-6319
Toll-Free: 800-265-0569
school.office@rlc.on.ca
www.rosseaulakecollege.com
www.facebook.com/569881713028836
twitter.com/Rosseaulake
Grades: 7 - 12 Enrollment: 90 Note: Rosseau Lake College is a coeducational day & boarding school. The average class size is twelve.
Lance Postma, Head of School

Sandy Lake: Thomas Fiddler Memorial Elementary School
P.O. Box 8
Sandy Lake, ON P0V 1V0, Canada
Tel: 807-744-4491; Fax: 807-774-1324
www.sandylake.firstnation.ca
Grades: JK-6; Special Ed. Enrollment: 400 Number of Employees: 53 Note: The Thomas Fiddler Memorial Elementary School is part of the Sandy Lake Board of Education. The elementary school educates members of Sandy Lake First Nation. From kindergarten to grade four, Thomas Fiddler Memorial Elementary School provides a native immersion program.
Ralph Bekintis, Vice-Principal

Sandy Lake: Thomas Fiddler Memorial High School
P.O. Box 8
Sandy Lake, ON P0V 1V0
Tel: 807-774-1229; Fax: 807-774-1228
www.sandylake.firstnation.ca

Grades: 7 - 10 Enrollment: 124 Note: The activities of Thomas Fiddler Memorial High School are overseen by the Sandy Lake Board of Education. The secondary school serves students of the Sandy Lake First Nation.

Sioux Lookout: Pelican Falls First Nation High School (PFFNHS)
P.O. Box 4127
Sioux Lookout, ON P8T 1J9, Canada
Tel: 807-737-1110; Fax: 807-737-1449
Toll-Free: 800-378-9111
www.nnec.on.ca
Grades: Sec. Enrollment: 143
Solomon Kakagamic, Principal

Smithville: John Calvin Private School
P.O. Box 280
320 Station St., Smithville, ON L0R 2A0, Canada
Tel: 905-957-2341; Fax: 905-957-2342
office@johncalvinschool.com
www.johncalvin.ca
Grades: K./Elem.
George Hofsink, Principal
ghofsink@live.com

St Catharines: Beyond Montessori School
St. George's Anglican Church
P.O. Box 647
83 Church St., St Catharines, ON L0S 1E0
Tel: 905-937-0700
info@beyondmontessori.com
www.beyondmontessori.com
www.facebook.com/208151271840
twitter.com/BMontessoriStC
beyondmontessori.wordpress.com
Grades: Pre.-3 Enrollment: 50 Number of Employees: 12
Natasha Secord, Head of School

St Catharines: Nelephant Montessori School
134 Louth St., St Catharines, ON L2S 2T4
Tel: 905-704-1388; Fax: 905-704-4520
gcns@becon.org
www.nelephant.ca
Grades: Toddler - Casa
Nicole Boulet, Academic Supervisor

St Catharines: Ridley College
P.O. Box 3013
2 Ridley Rd., St Catharines, ON L2R 7C3
Tel: 905-684-1889; Fax: 905-684-8875
admission@ridleycollege.com
www.ridley.on.ca
www.facebook.com/145690058823243
twitter.com/Ridley_College
www.youtube.com/RidleyCollege1889
Grades: K - 12 Enrollment: 625 Note: Ridley College is a university preparatory school, which features both a lower school & an uppper school. Boarding is available. Over 30% of students are international students.
George C. Hendrie, President, Board Chair
Ed Kidd, Headmaster, 905-684-1889
ed_kidd@ridleycollege.com
Stephen Clarke, Deputy Headmaster, 905-684-1889, ext. 2205
stephen_clarke@ridleycollege.com
Jim Parke, Director, Finance & Operations
jim_parke@ridleycollege.com
Andrew T. Weller, Dean of Admissions, 905-684-1889, ext. 2298
andrew_t_weller@ridleycollege.com
Margaret Lech, Assistant Headmaster, Student Affairs
margaret_lech@ridleycollege.com
James Milligan, Assistant Head, Lower School, 905-684-1889, ext. 2296
jim_milligan@ridleycollege.com

St Catharines: Wheatley School of Montessori Education Inc.
497 Scott St., St Catharines, ON L2M 3X3, Canada
Tel: 905-641-3012; Fax: 905-641-1443
mail@wheatleyschool.com
www.wheatleyschool.com
Grades: Pre.-8 Note: The coeducational, non-denominational school provides Montessori programs for children from preschool to grade four. The Wheatley School's preschool program accepts children as young as two years of age. For upper elementary students in grades five to eight, a traditional, enriched program is offered.
Eda Varalli, Principal

St Thomas: St. Thomas Community School
77 Fairview Ave., St Thomas, ON N5R 4X7, Canada
Tel: 519-633-0690; Fax: 519-633-0019
info@stthomaschristian.org
www.stthomaschristian.org

Grades: JK-8 Enrollment: 789
Jason Schouten, Principal

Stouffville: The Progressive Montessori Academy
6411 Main St., Stouffville, ON L4A 1G4
Tel: 416-220-8070
www.thepma.ca
www.facebook.com/ThePMASchool
twitter.com/pma_school
www.instagram.com/thepma
Grades: Pre.-6 Enrollment: 40
Lubna Jaffer, Principal
ljaffer@thepma.ca

Stratford: Nancy Campbell Academy Private Residential & Day High School
45 Waterloo St. South, Stratford, ON N5A 4A8
Tel: 519-272-1900; Toll-Free: 888-641-6224
info@nancycampbell.ca
www.nancycampbell.ca
Grades: 9 - 12 Number of Employees: 40 Note: Nancy Campbell Academy is a not-for-profit, private, residential and day school. NCA is dedicated to providing education through community service and academic excellence. NCA's Aurora campus is a private day school for grades 7 to 12.
Sana Zareey, Vice-Principal
szareey@nancycampbell.ca
Nancy Elliott, Director, Student Placement, 519-272-1900, ext. 1
nelliott@nancycampbell.ca
Cindy Wang, Guidance Counsellor, 519-272-1900, ext. 2
Mehrang Yazdani, Senior Recruiter
myazdani@nancycampbell.ca

Thornhill: Associated Hebrew Schools of Toronto — The Kamin Education Centre
300 Atkinson Ave., Thornhill, ON L4J 8A2, Canada
Tel: 905-889-3998; Fax: 905-889-5183
www.associatedhebrewschools.com/kamin-education-centre
Grades: K./Elem. Enrollment: 1415
Karen Sitnik, Principal

Thornhill: Central Montessori Schools (CMS)
72 Steeles Ave. West, Thornhill, ON L4J 1A1, Canada
Tel: 905-889-0012; Fax: 905-889-0422
www.cmschool.net
Grades: Pre.-6 Enrollment: 900 Note: Central Montessori Schools are co-educational, non-denominational schools.
Tracy Grisdale, Principal

Campuses
Maplehurst Campus
181 Maplehurst Ave., Toronto, ON M2N 3C1
Tel: 416-222-9207

Sheppard Campus
200 Sheppard Ave. East, Toronto, ON M2N 3A9
Tel: 416-222-5940; Fax: 416-222-2546

Willowdale Campus
157 Willowdale Ave., Toronto, ON M2N 4Y3
Tel: 416-250-1022; Fax: 416-250-5191

York Mills Campus
18 Coldwater Rd., Toronto, ON M2N 1Y7
Tel: 416-510-1200; Fax: 416-510-1230

Thornhill: Chabad of Markham Hebrew School
83 Green Lane, Thornhill, ON L3T 6K6
Tel: 905-886-0420
www.chabadmarkham.org
www.facebook.com/chabadofmarkham
Grades: K.-9
Esther Gitlin, Director, Hebrew School

Thornhill: Everest Academy
130 Racco Pkwy., Thornhill, ON L4J 8X9
Tel: 905-881-3335; Fax: 905-756-1111
info@everestacademies.com
www.everestacademies.com
Grades: 1-12
Tim Sim, Principal

Thornhill: Jewish Youth Network Hebrew School (JYN)
#5, 8700 Bathurst St., Thornhill, ON L4J 9J8
Tel: 905-889-7582
www.jewishyouth.ca
www.facebook.com/JewishYouth
Grades: 1-7
Chani Nachlas, Director

Thornhill: Joe Dwek Ohr HaEmet Sephardic School
7026 Bathurst St., Thornhill, ON L4J 8K3
Tel: 905-669-7653; Fax: 905-669-5138
www.jdohss.org

Rabbi Noah Sonenberg, Director, Judaic Studies
nsonenberg@bastoronto.org
Nicky Kagan, Assistant Principal, Yeshivat Or Chaim
nkagan@bastoronto.org
Jonathan Parker, Assistant Principal, Yeshivat Or Chaim
jparker@bastoronto.org

Toronto: Boardwalk Montessori School
1975 B. Queen St. East, Toronto, ON M4L 1J1
Tel: 416-691-6740; Fax: 416-691-9046
office@boardwalkmontessori.com
www.boardwalkmontessori.com

Grades: Toddler - Pre.
Joan Walder, Principal

Toronto: Bond Academy
1500 Birchmount Rd., Toronto, ON M1P 2G5
Tel: 416-266-8878; Fax: 416-266-3898
www.bondacademy.ca
Grades: K./Elem./Sec. Enrollment: 450
John Healey, Principal, Elementary
johnh@web.bondacademy.ca
Jeffrey Farber, Principal, Secondary
jfarber@web.bondacademy.ca

Toronto: Bond International College
1500 Birchmount Rd., Toronto, ON M1P 2G5, Canada
Tel: 416-266-8878; Fax: 416-266-3898
info@bondcollege.com
www.bondcollege.com
Grades: Secondary Note: Bond International College prepares
international students for colleges & universities in Canada, the
United States, the United Kingdom, & Australia.
Jeffrey Farber, Principal

Toronto: Braemar College
229 College St., Toronto, ON M5T 1R4
Tel: 416-487-8138; Fax: 416-487-6165
info@braemarcollege.com
www.braemarcollege.com
Grades: 9 - 12

Toronto: Branksome Hall
10 Elm Ave., Toronto, ON M4W 1N4
Tel: 416-920-9741; Fax: 416-920-5390
attendance@branksome.on.ca
www.branksome.on.ca
www.facebook.com/95081778626
twitter.com/branksomehall
www.linkedin.com/groups./3802471
Grades: JK - 12 Enrollment: 880 Number of Employees: 120
faculty Note: Branksome Hall is an independent day & boarding
school for girls & an International Baccalaureate (IB) World
School.
Karen Jurjevich, Principal, 416-920-6265, ext. 208
Sarah Craig, Head, Junior School, 416-920-6265, ext. 105
scraig@branksome.on.ca
Amanda Kennedy, Head, Middle School, 416-920-6265, ext. 373
akennedy@branksome.on.ca
Joanne Colwell, Head, Senior School, 416-920-6265, ext. 271
jcolwell@branksome.on.ca
Denise Power, Director, Student Life, 416-920-6265, ext. 111
dpower@branksome.on.ca
Julia Drake, Executive Director, Communications & Marketing,
416-920-6265, ext. 103
jdrake@branksome.on.ca
Heather Friesen, Head, Academics, 416-920-6265, ext. 102
hfriesen@branksome.on.ca
Heidi Vesely, Executive Director, Finance & Administration,
416-920-6265, ext. 108
hvesely@branksome.on.ca
Kelly Longmore, Interim Director, Residence, 416-920-6265, ext.
162
klongmore@branksome.on.ca

Toronto: Casa Vera Montessori School
2000 Keele St., Toronto, ON M6M 3Y4
Tel: 416-850-9705; Fax: 416-850-9706
mail@casaverams.com
www.casaverams.com
Grades: Toddler - Casa
Viera Scurova, Principal

Toronto: Centre for Jewish Living & Learning Religious School
Also known as: Lomdim
120 Old Colony Rd., Toronto, ON M2L 2K2
Tel: 416-449-3880
reception@templeemanuel.ca
www.templeemanuel.ca
Note: The school offers progressive Jewish learning for children.
Jennifer Katz, Director
jenn@templeemanuel.ca

Toronto: Children's Garden Junior School (CGS)
670 Eglinton Ave. East, Toronto, ON M4G 2K4, Canada
Tel: 416-423-5017; Fax: 416-423-0727
info@cgsschool.com
www.cgsschool.com
Grades: Pre.-3
Marie Bates, Principal & Founder, 416-423-5017, ext. 24
marie@cgsschool.com
Zandee Toovey, Executive Assistant, 416-423-5017, ext. 44
ztoovey@cgsschool.com

Toronto: Children's Garden Nursery School
1847 Bayview Ave., Toronto, ON M4G 3E4
Tel: 416-488-4298; Fax: 416-488-6499
info@childrensgarden.ca
www.childrensgarden.ca
Grades: Pre-K. Enrollment: 140
Pauline Foulkes, Director
pauline@childrensgarden.ca
Kyra Gurney, Administrator
kyra@childrensgarden.ca

Toronto: La Citadelle International Academy of Arts & Science
15 Mallow Rd., Toronto, ON M3B 1G2
Tel: 416-385-9685; Fax: 416-385-9685
info@lacitadelleacademy.com
www.lacitadelleacademy.com
www.facebook.com/la.citadelle.1
twitter.com/LaCitadelle1
www.youtube.com/channel/UCBAmw50YMGo3VVD-WeJS5bw
Grades: Pre.-12 Enrollment: 230
Alfred Abouchar, Headmaster
Faye Tabbara, Coordinator, Administration & Admission
admin@lacitadelleacademy.com

Toronto: City Academy
#1000, 3080 Yonge St., Toronto, ON M4N 3N1, Canada
Tel: 416-482-2521; Fax: 416-482-2496
info@cityacademy.ca
www.cityacademy.ca
Grades: Sec. Enrollment: 230
Sheila Dever, Principal

Toronto: Community Hebrew Academy of Toronto (CHAT)
Also known as: TanenbaumCHAT
Wallenberg Campus
200 Wilmington Ave., Toronto, ON M3H 5J8, Canada
Tel: 416-636-5984; Fax: 416-636-7717
info@tanenbaumchat.org
tanenbaumchat.org
www.facebook.com/TanenbaumCHAT1
twitter.com/TanenbaumCHAT
www.youtube.com/user/tanenbaumchatchannel
Grades: Sec. Enrollment: 1100 Note: Co-educational high school
of the Greater Toronto Jewish community. Campuses in Toronto
& Vaughan. Programmes include core subjects & Jewish
studies. The Wallenberg Campus is for students living south of
Steeles Ave. in Toronto.
Rabbi Lee Buckman, Head of School
lbuckman@tanenbaumchat.org
Rhona Birenbaum, CFO & Executive Director
rbirenbaum@tanenbaumchat.org
Rabbi Moshe Yeres, Principal, Jewish Studies
myeres@tanenbaumchat.org
Jonathan Levy, Principal
jlevy@tanenbaumchat.org
Rabbi Eli Mandel, Vice-Principal
emandel@tanenbaumchat.org
Bradley Mittelman, Dean of Students
bmittelman@tanenbaumchat.org

Campuses
Kimel Family Education Centre
Joseph & Wolf Lebovic Jewish Community Campus
9600 Bathurst St., Vaughan, ON L6A 3Z8
Tel: 905-787-8772; Fax: 905-787-8773
info@tanenbaumchat.org
tanenbaumchat.org/locations/kimel
Enrollment: 1500 Note: The Kimel Family Education is for
students living north of Steeles Ave. in Vaughan.
Frances Bigman, Director, Advancement, 416-636-5984, ext.
230
fbigman@tanenbaumchat.org
Laurie Wasser, Director, Admissions & Recruitment,
416-636-5984, ext. 291
lwasser@tanenbaumchat.org

Toronto: Cornerstone Montessori Prep School (CMPS)
177 Beverley St., Toronto, ON M5T 1Y7
Tel: 647-493-8660
www.cornerstoneprep.ca
Grades: Pre.-12 Enrollment: 130
Dr. Stephanie Ling, Ph.D., Principal

Campuses
Don Mills Campus
33 Mallard Rd., Toronto, ON M3B 1S4
Tel: 647-977-5584

Toronto: Crescent School
2365 Bayview Ave., Toronto, ON M2L 1A2, Canada
Tel: 416-449-2556
info@crescentschool.org
www.crescentschool.org
Grades: 3-12 Note: Crescent School is a day school for boys.
Michael Fellin, Headmaster

Toronto: Crestwood Preparatory College
217 Brookbanks Dr., Toronto, ON M3A 2T7, Canada
Tel: 416-391-1441; Fax: 416-444-0949
www.crestwood.on.ca
www.facebook.com/109125222250
Grades: Elem./Sec. Enrollment: 280
Vince Pagano, Headmaster

Toronto: Crestwood School
411 Lawrence Ave. East, Toronto, ON M3C 1N9, Canada
Tel: 416-444-5858; Fax: 416-444-2127
www.crestwood.on.ca
Grades: JK-6
Dalia Eisen, Principal
dalia.eisen@crestwood.on.ca

Toronto: Danforth Jewish Circle Children's Jewish Studies Programme (DJC)
#125, 283 Danforth Ave., Toronto, ON M4K 1N2
Tel: 416-580-6303
info@djctoronto.com
djctoronto.com/education/childrens-studies
Grades: JK-7 Note: Jewish studies program emphasizing arts,
music, culture, & film.
Alysse Rich, Principal

Toronto: Darchei Noam Hebrew School
864 Sheppard Ave. West, Toronto, ON M3H 2T5
Tel: 416-638-4783; Fax: 416-638-5852
info@darcheinoam.ca
www.darcheinoam.ca
www.facebook.com/darcheinoam
twitter.com/darcheinoam
Grades: JK-6
Ariel Zaltzman, Director, Youth Education & Programming
ariel@darcheinoam.ca

Toronto: David & Esther Freiman Childhood Education Centre
4588 Bathurst St., Toronto, ON M2R 1W6
Tel: 416-638-1881; Fax: 416-636-5813
Note: Non-denominational education for children aged 18
months to 5 years.

Toronto: Discovering Minds Montessori Preschool
74 Bathurst St., Toronto, ON M5V 2P5
Tel: 416-504-0110; Fax: 416-731-7419
discovering@dmmps.com
www.dmmps.com
www.facebook.com/159824140742150
Grades: Pre.
Guadalupe Rengifo, Director

Toronto: Downtown Jewish Community School (DJCS)
Miles Nadal Jewish Community Centre
750 Spadina Ave., Toronto, ON M5S 2J2
Tel: 416-924-6211; Fax: 416-924-0442
www.djcs.org
www.facebook.com/downtownjewishcommunityschool
Grades: JK-7
Naomi Azrieli, Chair
Belinda Keshen, Principal

Toronto: Downtown Montessori School
City Place Campus
335 Bremner Blvd., Toronto, ON M5V 3V4
Tel: 416-623-1738
downtownmontessori@rogers.com
www.downtownmontessori.ca
Grades: Toddler - Pre.
Elizabeth Ferguson, Director, 416-698-0218

Campuses
Coatsworth Campus
11 Coatsworth Cres., Toronto, ON M4C 5P8
Tel: 416-694-9444

Infinity Place Campus
26 Grand Trunk Cres., Toronto, ON M5J 3A9
Tel: 416-849-3691

Simcoe Place Campus
200 Front St. West, Toronto, ON M5V 3J1
Tel: 416-340-8757

Toronto: The Dragon Academy
35 Prince Arthur Ave., Toronto, ON M5R 1B2
Tel: 416-323-3243; Fax: 416-323-7780
info@dragonacademy.org
www.dragonacademy.org
www.facebook.com/151620228237983
twitter.com/dragonacademy

Grades: 7-12 *Enrollment:* 75
Meg Fox, Ph.D., Founding Principal
megfox@dragonacademy.org

Toronto: Early Childhood Centre at Holy Blossom Temple
Holy Blossom Temple
1950 Bathurst St., Toronto, ON M5P 3K9
Tel: 416-789-3291; Fax: 416-789-9697
templemail@holyblossom.org
www.holyblossom.org/study-limud/preschool
www.facebook.com/holyblossomtemple
twitter.com/holyblossom
www.linkedin.com/groups/4507427
www.youtube.com/user/holyblossomtemple

Grades: Preschool
Jessica Lipinski, Director
jlipinski@holyblossom.org

Toronto: Eastern Canada High School
36 Colville Rd., Toronto, ON M6M 2Yz
Tel: 416-567-4404; Fax: 416-551-7036
www.easterncanadahs.com

Grades: 9 - 12

Toronto: EC English Language Centres Toronto
#400, 124 Eglinton Ave. West, Toronto, ON M4R 2G8, Canada
Tel: 416-488-2200; Fax: 416-488-2225
www.ecenglish.com
www.facebook.com/ecenglish.toronto
twitter.com/ecenglish
www.youtube.com/user/ecwebteam

Jon Chodarcewicz, Director

Campuses
LSC Montréal
#401, 1610 St. Catherine St. West, Montréal, QC H3H 2S2, Canada
Tel: 514-939-9911; Fax: 514-939-2223

Elisa Gazzola, Director

EC Vancouver
#200, 570 Dunsmuir St., Vancouver, BC V6B 1Y1, Canada
Tel: 604-683-1199; Fax: 604-683-6088

Martha Delgadillo, Director

Toronto: Eitz Chaim Schools - Administrative/Patricia Branch
475 Patricia Ave., Toronto, ON M2R 2N1, Canada
Tel: 416-225-1187; Fax: 416-225-3732
patricia@eitzchaim.com
www.facebook.com/130394700748444

Grades: 1-8 *Enrollment:* 800 *Note:* This branch houses the boys school & administrative offices.
Rabbi Shlomo Schwartz, Head of School
sschwartz@eitzchaim.com
Elias Levy, Executive Director
levye@eitzchaim.com

Campuses
Spring Farm Branch
80 York Hill Blvd., Thornhill, ON L4J 2P6, Canada
Tel: 905-764-6633; Fax: 905-764-9577
spring@eitzchaim.com

Grades: Pre.-8 *Note:* This branch houses the girls school.

Viewmount Branch
1 Viewmount Ave., Toronto, ON M5B 1T2, Canada
Tel: 416-789-4366; Fax: 416-785-1384
view@eitzchaim.com

Grades: Pre.-8 *Note:* This branch houses the girls school (grades 1-8); preschool, JK & SK are mixed

Toronto: Ellesmere Montessori School
37 Marchington Circle, Toronto, ON M1R 3M6, Canada
Tel: 416-447-1059; Fax: 416-447-1059

Grades: K./Elem.

Toronto: Ellington Montessori School
40 Cowdray Ct., Toronto, ON M1S 1A1
Tel: 416-759-8363; Fax: 416-759-2162
ellingtonmontessorischool@on.aibn.com
www.ellingtonmontessori.ca

Grades: Toddler - Middle *Note:* Located in the lower level of Wexford United Church.
Deborah Renwick, Principal

Toronto: Etobicoke Montessori School
4 La Rose Ave., Toronto, ON M9P 1A5
Tel: 416-246-9896; Fax: 416-243-2999
info@etobicokemontessorischool.ca
www.etobicokemontessorischool.ca

Grades: Toddler - Pre.
Christina Zentena, Principal

Toronto: Fieldstone School
2999 Dufferin St., Toronto, ON M6B 3T4, Canada
Tel: 416-487-7381; Fax: 416-487-8190
admissions@fieldstonedayschool.org
www.fieldstoneschool.org
www.facebook.com/FDSJK8

Grades: JK - 12 *Enrollment:* 280 *Note:* Cambridge School for students JK to 12
Ginie Wong, Head of School, 416-487-7381, ext. 230
gwong@fieldstonekcschool.org
Kristine Foy, Managing Director, Admissions & International Programme, 416-487-1989, ext. 249
kfoy@fieldstonekcschool.org
Melany Butcher, Admissions Coordinator, 416-487-1989, ext. 248
mbutcher@fieldstonekcschool.org
Sue Johnson, Admissions Contact, 416-487-7381, ext. 224
sjohnson@fieldstonedayschool.org

Toronto: Forest Hill Montessori School
Junior Campus
3180 Bathurst St., Toronto, ON M6A 2A9
Tel: 416-781-4449
info@foresthillmontessorischool.com
www.foresthillmontessorischool.com
www.facebook.com/ForestHillMontessoriSchool
twitter.com/fhms_toronto
www.instagram.com/foresthillmontessorischool

Grades: Pre. - Elem.
Sandra Bosnar-Dale, Director
Erika Lacey, Principal

Campuses
Elementary Campus
585 Cranbrooke Ave., Toronto, ON M6A 2X9

Toronto: FutureSkills High School
#204, 5635 Yonge St., Toronto, ON M2M 3S9
Tel: 416-227-1177; Fax: 416-227-0811
info@futureskills.com
www.futureskills.com

Grades: 9 - 12
Hassan Mirzai, Principal

Toronto: Gan Netivot
470 Glencairn Ave., Toronto, ON M5N 1V8
Tel: 905-771-1234

Grades: Pre.-JK; Orthodox

Toronto: German International School Toronto
980 Dufferin St., Toronto, ON M6H 4B4
Tel: 416-922-6413
www.gistonline.ca
www.facebook.com/175972742449216
www.linkedin.com/company/german-international-school-toronto
Grades: Pre.-8 *Enrollment:* 70 *Note:* German International School Toronto offers students a curriculum that blends German & Ontario educational standards.
Dr. Philipp von Witzendorff, Chair & President
Mark Benkelmann, Principal

Toronto: The Giles School
L'École Giles
80 Scarsdale Rd., Toronto, ON M3C 2C3, Canada
Tel: 416-446-0825; Fax: 416-446-0846
office@gilesschool.ca
www.gilesschool.ca
www.facebook.com/TheGilesSchool

Grades: Pre-K - 12 *Note:* The Giles School is a co-educational school which offers an enriched French immersion program. Students are introduced to a third language in grade one.

Kemp Rickett, Headmaster
kemp_rickett@gilesschool.ca
Caroline Bernaba, Principal
caroline_bernaba@gilesschool.ca
Rosine Dika Balotoken, Manager, Administration
rosine_dika@gilesschool.ca
Bob Spencer, Manager, Special Projects
rgspencer@rogers.com

Toronto: Gradale Academy
159 Roxborough Dr., Toronto, ON M4W 3X8
Tel: 416-917-9409
gradale@bell.net
www.gradaleacademy.com

Grades: Pre.-3 *Enrollment:* 50 *Note:* Gradale Academy also offers classes outdoors at Evergreen Brick Works in Toronto.
Michelle Gradish, Director

Toronto: Great Lakes College of Toronto (GLCT)
323 Keele St., Toronto, ON M6P 2K6, Canada
Tel: 416-763-4121; Fax: 416-763-5225
query@glctschool.com
www.glctschool.com
www.facebook.com/GreatLakesCollegeToronto

Grades: 9-12 *Note:* The school is an international high school which offers a pre-university program. English as a Second Language courses are also provided.
Tom Tidey, B.A., M.Ed., Principal

Campuses
The Canadian Trillium College - Beijing (CTC)
Chaoyang District, Bldg. 3
#608, 108 the 4th North Ring East Rd., Beijing, China
glctbjoffice@glctschool.com.cn
www.ctc-school.com
Other Information: Tel: 010-84833541 / 84833542; Fax: 010-84833540

Grades: 9-12 *Enrollment:* 150 *Note:* Ontario curriculum.
John Holtom, Supervisor Principal
jholtom@glctschool.com

Toronto: Greenwood College School
443 Mount Pleasant Rd., Toronto, ON M4S 2L8
Tel: 416-482-9811; Fax: 416-482-9188
www.greenwoodcollege.com
www.facebook.com/138629896185229
twitter.com/Greenwood_2002
www.linkedin.com/company/501131
www.youtube.com/user/greenwoodcollege

Grades: 7-12 *Enrollment:* 460
Allan Hardy, B.A., B.Ed., M.A.T., Principal
allan.hardy@greenwoodcollege.com

Toronto: Guildwood Village Montessori School (GVMS)
Montessori Village & Education Centre
297 Old Kingston Rd., Toronto, ON M1C 1B4
Tel: 416-266-0424
www.gvmontessori.ca

Grades: Pre.-8 *Enrollment:* 75
Elisa Bourdon, Principal
edeblasibourdon@rogers.com

Toronto: Haadi Elementary School
710 Progress Ave., Toronto, ON M1H-2X3
Tel: 416-628-6252; Fax: 416-490-0317
SchoolAdmin@Haadi.ca
school.haadi.ca

Grades: K - 12

Toronto: Hanson International Academy
#102A, 155 Consumers Rd., Toronto, ON M2J 0A3
Tel: 416-977-8188; Fax: 416-979-9880
info.toronto@canadahanson.com
www.canadahanson.com
www.facebook.com/HansonInt
twitter.com/hansonint
www.instagram.com/hansoncanada

Grades: 9-12

Campuses
Brampton Campus
#111, 44 Peel Centre Dr., Brampton, ON L6T 4B5
Tel: 905-791-7555; Fax: 905-791-5176
info.brampton@canadahanson.com

Vancouver Campus
#218, 810 Quayside Dr., New Westminster, BC V3M 6B9
Tel: 604-553-2835; Fax: 604-553-2835
info.vancouver@canadahanson.com

Toronto: Hashomer Hatzair Canada - Kesher Program
#121, 215 Spadina Ave., Toronto, ON M5T 2C7
Tel: 416-736-1339; *Fax:* 647-693-7359
mail@campshomria.com
www.hashomerhatzair.ca/kesher.html
twitter.com/HavergalCollege
Grades: JK-2 *Note:* Educational program focused on examining Jewish history & culture through arts, dance, & music.
Noga Ron Amit, Office Manager

Toronto: Havergal College
Upper School
1451 Avenue Rd., Toronto, ON M5N 2H9, Canada
Tel: 416-483-3843
info@havergal.on.ca
www.havergal.on.ca
www.facebook.com/HavergalCollege
twitter.com/HavergalCollege
www.youtube.com/user/HavergalCollege
Grades: JK - 12 *Enrollment:* 950 *Note:* University-preparatory day and boarding school for girls, junior kindergarten to grade 12.
Helen-Kay Davy, Principal
poffice@havergal.on.ca
Seonaid Davis, Vice-Principal, Teaching & Learning
sdavis@havergal.on.ca
Maggie Houston White, Executive Director, Enrolment Management (Admissions), 416-482-4724
admissions@havergal.on.ca
Hilary Adamson, Associate Director, Junior School Admission, 416-482-7547
admissions@havergal.on.ca

Campuses
Junior School
460 Rosewell Ave., Toronto, ON M4R 2H5, Canada
Tel: 416-483-3519

Toronto: Hawthorn School for Girls
101 Scarsdale Rd., Toronto, ON M3B 2R2, Canada
Tel: 416-444-3054; *Fax:* 416-449-2891
www.hawthornschool.com
www.facebook.com/HawthornSchool
twitter.com/hawthornschool
Grades: Pre.-12 *Enrollment:* 120
Regina Gutiérrez Cortina, Head of School

Toronto: Head Start Montessori School
260 Yorkland Blvd., Toronto, ON M2J 1R7
Tel: 416-756-7300; *Fax:* 416-756-9019
ifo@headstartmontessori.ca
www.headstartmontessori.ca
Grades: Pre.
Naureen Shah, Principal

Toronto: High Park Day School
291A Jane St., Toronto, ON M6S 3Z3
Tel: 416-645-7440
info@highparkdayschool.com
www.highparkdayschool.com
www.facebook.com/HighParkDaySchoolToronto
twitter.com/HPDS_TO
www.linkedin.com/company/16178689
www.instagram.com/hpds_to
Grades: JK-8
Amanda Dervaitis, Founder & Principal
amanda@highparkdayschool.com
Kristin Palin, Vice-Principal & Director, Admissions
kristin@highparkdayschool.com

Toronto: High Park Gardens Montessori School
35 High Park Gdns., Toronto, ON M6R 1S8, Canada
Tel: 416-763-6097
admin@highparkgardensmontessori.com
www.mildenhallmontessori.com
Grades: Pre.-6 *Enrollment:* 115
Lee Gair, Principal

Toronto: Hillside Montessori School
76 Anglesey Blvd., Toronto, ON M9A 3C1
Tel: 416-695-3466
www.hillsidemontessori.com
Grades: Pre.
Diana Pace-Asciak, Principal
dianapace@sympatico.ca

Toronto: Horizons Secondary School (Toronto) (HSS)
#202, 4632 Yonge St., Toronto, ON M2N 5M1
Tel: 416-966-4009; *Fax:* 416-226-6888
canadahorizons.ca
Grades: 9 - 12
Dr. Martin Reinink, Principal

Toronto: Humberside Montessori School
121 Kennedy Ave., Toronto, ON M6S 2X8
Tel: 416-762-8888; *Fax:* 416-766-1211
www.humbersidemontessori.ca
Grades: Elem./Ungraded
Felix Bednarski, Principal
Molly Galle, Director & Owner

Toronto: Humbervale Montessori School Inc.
1447 Royal York Rd., Toronto, ON M9P 3V8
Tel: 416-244-4001
info@HumbervaleMontessori.ca
humbervalemontessori.ca
Grades: Pre.-JK *Enrollment:* 85
Andrea Heitz, Principal

Toronto: Imperial College of Toronto
20 Queen Elizabeth Blvd., Toronto, ON M8Z 1L8
Tel: 416-251-4970; *Fax:* 416-251-0259
info@imperialcollege.org
www.imperialcollege.org
Grades: 9 - 12
Eileen Crichton, Principal

Toronto: Islamic Foundation School
441 Nugget Ave., Toronto, ON M1S 5E1, Canada
Tel: 416-321-0909; *Fax:* 416-321-1995
www.islamicfoundation.ca
twitter.com/MYIFS
Grades: Elem. *Enrollment:* 327

Schools
Evening School
441 Nugget Ave., Toronto, ON M1S 5E1
Tel: 416-321-0909; *Fax:* 416-321-1995
Grades: Religious Education
Qari Yunus Ingar, Principal, 416-321-0909, ext. 226
yingar@islamicfoundation.ca

Full-Time Hifz School
441 Nugget Ave., Toronto, ON M1S 5E1, Canada
Tel: 416-321-0909
Grades: Religious Education
Qari Yunus Ingar, Principal, 416-321-0909, ext. 226
yingar@islamicfoundation.ca

Summer Hifz & Summer School
441 Nugget Ave., Toronto, ON M1S 5E1, Canada
Tel: 416-321-0909; *Fax:* 416-321-1995
Grades: Religious Education
Uzma Khan, Administrative Assistant, 416-321-3776, ext. 237
ukhan@islamicfoundation.ca
Maulana Abdurrahman Hafejee, Administrative Assistant, 416-321-3776, ext. 237
arhafeje@islamicfoundation.ca

Sunday School
441 Nugget Ave., Toronto, ON M1S 5E1, Canada
Tel: 416-321-0909; *Fax:* 416-321-1995
Grades: Religious Education
Qari Yunus Ingar, Principal, 416-321-0909, ext. 226
yingar@islamicfoundation.ca

Toronto: The Japanese School of Toronto Shokokai Inc.
c/o McMurrich Junior Public Shool
115 Winnona Dr., Toronto, ON M6G 3S8, Canada
Tel: 416-656-4822; *Fax:* 416-658-8931
torohoshomu@bellnet.ca
www.torontohoshuko.ca
Note: This is a Japanese Saturday school

Toronto: The Jewish Heritage School at Congregation Habonim
5 Glen Park Ave., Toronto, ON M6B 4J2
Tel: 416-322-0749
habonimschool@gmail.com
jewishheritageschool.org
Other Information: Synagogue Office: 416-782-7125
Grades: 1-6 *Note:* The school offers Judaic & Hebrew language studies, & Jewish music class.
Yodfat S. Mandil, Principal
Cathy Rechtshaffen, Volunteer Director, School Operations

Toronto: Junior Academy
2454 Bayview Ave., Toronto, ON M2L 1A6
Tel: 416-425-4567; *Fax:* 416-425-7379
www.junioracademy.com
www.facebook.com/465133306867808
Grades: JK - 8
Pat Kendall, Administrator
pk@junioracademy.com
Dianne Johnson, Principal
Julie Stewart, Vice Principal
Cathy Hibbert, Director, Physical Education

Susan Jones, Director, Middle School
Kris Potter, Director, Student Affairs

Toronto: Kew Park Montessori Day School
79 Hiawatha Rd., Toronto, ON M4L 2X7
Tel: 416-694-6273; *Fax:* 416-694-9452
info@kewparkmontessori.com
www.kewparkmontessori.com
Grades: Pre. - Elem.
Tarynn Parry, Co-Principal
Tacha Pearce-Miller, Co-Principal

Toronto: Kingsley Primary School
3962 Bloor St. West, Toronto, ON M9B 1M3, Canada
Tel: 416-233-0150; *Fax:* 416-233-5971
kingsleyprimaryschool@gmail.com
www.kingsleyschool.ca
www.facebook.com/kingsleyschool
twitter.com/kingsleytoronto
Grades: JK-5 *Enrollment:* 30 *Number of Employees:* 7
Louisa Florio, Principal, 416-233-0150

Toronto: Kingsway College School
4600 Dundas St. West, Toronto, ON M9A 1A5, Canada
Tel: 416-234-5073; *Fax:* 416-234-8386
admissions@kcs.on.ca
www.kcs.on.ca
www.facebook.com/KCSMatters
twitter.com/KCSMatters
www.linkedin.com/groups/4030878
www.youtube.com/KCSMatters
Grades: Elem. *Enrollment:* 309
Derek Logan, Head of School

Toronto: Kiosk International College
#104, 40 Wellesley St. East, Toronto, ON M4Y 1G4
Tel: 416-545-1660
info@kiosk.on.ca
highschool.kiosk.on.ca
www.facebook.com/kiosklc
twitter.com/KioskLC
Grades: 9 - 12

Toronto: The Laurel School
44 Upjohn Rd., Toronto, ON M3B 2W1
Tel: 416-510-2500; *Fax:* 855-514-5002
info@laurelschool.ca
www.laurelschool.ca
Grades: Pre.-6 *Enrollment:* 70

Toronto: Leaside Children's House Montessori
839 Millwood Rd., Toronto, ON
Tel: 416-425-0101; *Fax:* 416-778-7753
info@leasidechildrenshouse.com
www.leasidechildrenshouse.com
Grades: Toddler - Pre.
Lillian Nimis, Director

Toronto: Leonardo Da Vinci Academy of Arts & Sciences
100 Allanhurst Dr., Toronto, ON M9A 4K4
Tel: 416-247-6137; *Fax:* 416-247-6138
ldva@ldva.on.ca
www.ldva.on.ca
www.facebook.com/147542175314808
Grades: Pre.-8
Salvatore Ritacca, President & Co-Founder
sr@ldva.on.ca
Dom Tassielli, Treasurer & Co-Founder
dt@ldva.on.ca

Toronto: The Linden School
10 Rosehill Ave., Toronto, ON M4T 1G5, Canada
Tel: 416-966-4406; *Fax:* 416-966-9736
linden@lindenschool.ca
www.lindenschool.ca
twitter.com/TheLindenSchool
Grades: JK-12 *Enrollment:* 120 *Number of Employees:* 29 *Note:* The Linden School provides education for girls.
Janice Gladstone, Principal
janice@lindenschool.ca
Jean Greary, Director, Admissions
jean@lindenschool.ca
Nancy Hurst, Director, Business Administration
nancy@lindenschool.ca

Toronto: Little Feet Little Faces
183 Avenue Rd., Toronto, ON M5R 2J2
Tel: 416-923-8882; *Fax:* 416-923-8802
arts@littlefeetlittlefaces.com
www.littlefeetlittlefaces.com
Grades: Pre.-SK *Enrollment:* 55 *Note:* A private licensed daycare following the Ontario academic curriculum, with an emphasis on the arts.

Ingrid Rea, Creative Director

Toronto: Lycée Français de Toronto (LFT)
2327, rue Dufferin, Toronto, ON M6E 3S5, Canada
Tél: 416-924-1789; Téléc: 416-924-9078
admissions@lft.ca
www.lft.ca

Grades: Pre.-12 Enrollment: 450
M. Dominique Duthel, Proviseur

Toronto: The Mabin School
50 Poplar Plains Rd., Toronto, ON M4V 2M8, Canada
Tel: 416-964-9594; Fax: 416-964-3643
admissions@mabin.com
www.mabin.com
www.facebook.com/113792558651689
Grades: JK-6 Note: The Mabin School provides a full day, non-denominational program for girls & boys.
Nancy Steinhauer, Principal
Michelle Barchuk, Director, Admissions & Communications, 416-964-9594, ext. 247
michellebarchuk@mabin.com

Toronto: Madinatul-Uloom Academy
670 Progress Ave., Toronto, ON M1H 3A4, Canada
Tel: 416-332-9428; Fax: 416-332-0470
info@mua.ca
www.mua.ca
Grades: Elem.-Sec. Enrollment: 358
Nilofar Asif, Principal

Toronto: Madresatul Banaat Almuslimaat Muslim Girl's School
10 Vulcan St., Toronto, ON M9W 1L2
Tel: 416-244-8600; Fax: 416-244-0059
www.muslimgirlsschool.com
Grades: JK-12; Girls Enrollment: 152 Note: Alhamdulillah, Madresatul Banaat Almuslimaat, the first Muslim girls school in Toronto, Ontario, Canada, is a registered, non-profit, charitable organization duly approved and accredited by the Ontario Ministry of Education and Waqf Lillahi Taala.
S. Ataullah Qadri, President/Principal

Schools
Madresatul Atfaal Almuslimeen
Muslim Children's School
10 Vulcan St., Toronto, ON M9W 1L2
Tel: 416-244-8600
www.muslimgirlsschool.com
Grades: JK.-5; Boys & Girls Note: The school provides primary education from JK to grade 5, for boys and girls at the same location (under the same management) as Madresatul Banaat Almuslimaat's, at their junior school.

Toronto: Maria Montessori School
125 Brentcliffe Rd., Toronto, ON M4G 3Y7
Tel: 416-423-9123; Fax: 416-423-7819
www.mariamontessori.ca
Grades: Elem.
Gail Brand, School Administrator

Toronto: McDonald International Academy
920 Yonge St., 2nd Fl., Toronto, ON M4W 3C7, Canada
Tel: 416-322-1502; Fax: 416-322-5775
mia@mcdonaldacademy.com
www.mcdonaldacademy.com
Enrollment: 753
Fraser Rose, Principal

Campuses
North York Campus
#128, 5 Park Home Ave., Toronto, ON M2N 6L4, Canada
Tel: 416-222-6838; Fax: 416-222-6898
Toll-Free: 800-363-1202

Toronto: Metropolitan Preparatory Academy
49 Mobile Dr., Toronto, ON M4A 1H5
Tel: 416-285-0870; Fax: 416-285-0873
www.metroprep.com
twitter.com/MetroPrep
www.youtube.com/MetroPrepAcademy
Grades: 7 - 12 Note: Metropolitan Preparatory Academy offers a middle & high school program for university-oriented students.
William Wayne McKelvey, Principal
Debra McKelvey-Cleveland, Vice Principal & Head, Guidance
dmckelvey@MetroPrep.com
Jason Van Allen, Administrator, Information Technology
jvanallen@metroprep.com

Toronto: Miles Nadal Jewish Community Centre Nursery School
750 Spadina Ave., Toronto, ON M5S 2J2
Tel: 416-924-6211; Fax: 416-924-0442
info@mnjcc.org
www.mnjcc.org
Grades: Preschool Note: Non-denominational education for children aged 2 1/2 - 5 years.
Cathy Indig, Director, Early Childhood Education
cathyi@mnjcc.org

Toronto: Montcrest School
4 Montcrest Blvd., Toronto, ON M4K 1J7, Canada
Tel: 416-469-2008; Fax: 416-469-0934
info@montcrest.ca
www.montcrest.on.ca
www.facebook.com/montcrest
twitter.com/montcrest
Grades: JK-8 Enrollment: 300 Note: Montcrest School is a co-educational, nondenominational school. The school also offers special education classes for students with learning disabilities.
David Thompson, Head of School
dthompson@montcrest.ca

Toronto: Montessori Jewish Day School
55 Yeomans Rd., Toronto, ON M3H 3J7
Tel: 416-784-5071
adminmjds@mjds.ca
www.mjds.ca
www.facebook.com/133140750091854
Grades: Pre.-8 Enrollment: 115
Regina Lulka, Head of School
regina@mjds.ca
Matti Shorr, Director, Administration

Toronto: Morris Winchevsky School: Toronto's Secular Jewish Community School
The Winchevsky Centre
585 Cranbrooke Ave., Toronto, ON M6A 2X9
Tel: 416-789-5502; Fax: 416-789-5981
info@winchevskycentre.org
winchevskycentre.org/school
www.facebook.com/WinchevskyCtr
Grades: K.-8 Note: The school caters to secular, non-traditional, mixed culture, & unaffiliated families.
Lia Tarachansky, Director, Education

Toronto: NAMF Islamic Academy
4140 Finch Ave. East, Toronto, ON M1S 3T9
Tel: 416-299-1969; Fax: 416-299-4890
www.namf.ca
Grades: K - 8

Toronto: National Ballet School (NBS)
400 Jarvis St., Toronto, ON M4Y 2G6
Tel: 416-964-3780; Fax: 416-964-5133
Toll-Free: 800-387-0785
www.nbs-enb.ca
www.facebook.com/NBSENB
twitter.com/NBS_ENB
www.youtube.com/nbsenb
Note: The school offers ballet training, academic instruction, & residential care.
John Petch, Chair
Cathryn Gregor, Executive Director
Mavis Staines, Artistic Director

Toronto: New Oriental International College
#500, 3660 Midland Ave., Toronto, ON M1V 0B8
Tel: 416-291-8829; Fax: 416-291-8859
www.neworientalgroup.org
Note: University preparation courses for international students.

Toronto: Newton's Grove School
1 City View Dr., Toronto, ON M9W 5A5
Tel: 416-745-1328; Fax: 416-745-4168
info@newtonsgroveschool.com
www.newtonsgroveschool.com
www.facebook.com/NewtonsGroveSchool
twitter.com/NGSTalks
Grades: JK - 12 Enrollment: 350
Gabrielle Bush, Director

Toronto: Northern Lights Preparatory College
5075 Yonge St. 8th Fl., Toronto, ON M2N 6C6
Tel: 416-225-0057; Fax: 416-225-4727
info@northernlightscollege.ca
www.northernlightscollege.ca
Grades: K - 12
Robert Eckler, Principal
principal@northernlightscollege.ca

Toronto: Northmount School
26 Mallard Rd., Toronto, ON M3B 1S3, Canada
Tel: 416-449-8823; Fax: 416-449-1244
info@northmount.com
www.northmount.com
Grades: JK-8 Note: Northmount School specializes in the education of boys.
Terence Sheridan, Headmaster

Toronto: Odyssey Montessori School
136 Sorauren Ave., Toronto, ON M6R 2E4
Tel: 416-535-9402; Fax: 647-477-6585
www.odysseymontessori.com
Grades: Casa
Mary Tomazos, Principal
mary@odysseymontessori.com

Toronto: Olivet New Church School
279 Burnhamthorpe Rd., Toronto, ON M9B 1Z6
Tel: 416-239-3054; Fax: 416-239-4935
www.olivetnewchurch.org
Grades: JK-6 Enrollment: 50
Rev. Jared Buss, Pastor

**Toronto: Ontario International College
Collège International de l'Ontario**
#600, 4580 Dufferin St., Toronto, ON M3H 5Y2
Tel: 416-739-1888; Fax: 416-739-1884
adm@oicedu.ca
www.oicedu.ca
www.facebook.com/oicedu
Grades: 9 - 12
Ekaterina Agar, Vice Principal, 416-739-1888, ext. 1600
dean@oicedu.ca

Toronto: Ontario International Institute (OII)
#203, 1001 Sandhurst Circle, Toronto, ON M1V 1Z6
Tel: 416-701-1763; Fax: 905-471-3586
info@oii-edu.ca
www.oii-edu.ca
Grades: 9 - 12 Note: A Government-inspected school, fully authorized by the Ministry of Education to award credits leading to the Ontario Secondary School Diploma (OSSD).
Sami Appadurai, Principal

Toronto: Oraynu Children's School
St. Andrews Junior High School
131 Fenn Ave., Toronto, ON M2P 1X7
Tel: 416-385-3910
info@oraynu.org
www.oraynu.org/school
www.facebook.com/Oraynu
Grades: K.-7 Note: The school is part of the Oraynu Congregation for Humanistic Judaism.
Steven Shabes, Principal
stevenshabes@yahoo.com
Roby Sadler, Coordinator

Toronto: P.T. Montessori School
280 Culford Rd., Toronto, ON M6L 2V3, Canada
Tel: 416-242-3725
ptmontessori@bellnet.ca
www.ptmontessori.com
Grades: Elem. Enrollment: 51

Campuses
Mississauga Campus
2250 Credit Valley Rd., Mississauga, ON L5M 4L9, Canada
Tel: 905-820-7016

Toronto: Petite Maison Montessori School
126 O'Connor Dr., Toronto, ON M4K 2K7
Tel: 416-429-0507; Fax: 416-429-0507
info@petitemaison.ca
www.petitemaison.ca
Grades: Casa - Elem.
Roula Patsavos, Principal

Toronto: Phoenix Montessori School
19 Glen Agar Dr., Toronto, ON M9B 5L5
Tel: 416-695-1212; Fax: 416-695-1095
info@phoenixmontessori.ca
www.phoenixmontessori.ca
Grades: Toddler - Elem.
Lori Priolo, Principal
lpriolo@phoenixmontessori.ca

Toronto: The Prestige School
21 Eddfield Ave., Toronto, ON M2N 2M5
Tel: 647-494-9977
www.prestigeprivateschool.ca
www.facebook.com/prestigeprivateschool
Grades: JK-12 Enrollment: 210
Olga Margold, Principal

Campuses
Richmond Hill Campus
11 Headdon Gate, Richmond Hill, ON L4C 9W9
Tel: 647-556-0588

Toronto: Prince Edward Montessori School
2850 Bloor St. West, Toronto, ON M8X 1B2
Tel: 416-234-9127
info@princeedwardmontessori.com
www.princeedwardmontessori.com
Grades: Pre.-K. *Enrollment:* 100
Bozena Nowicka-Lipa, Director

Campuses
Mississauga Campus
12 Peter St. South, Mississauga, ON L5H 0A1
Tel: 905-891-6912; *Fax:* 905-891-6912

Toronto: Queen's Collegiate
2 Gibbs Rd., Toronto, ON M9B 6L6
Tel: 416-231-9899; *Fax:* 416-231-3936
info@queenscollegiate.com
www.queenscollegiate.com
www.facebook.com/110355299021172
Grades: K - 12
Dr. Jooyon Cho, Principal
jooyon.cho@queenscollegiate.com

Toronto: Robbins Hebrew Academy
Administration Office
1700 Bathurst St., Toronto, ON M5P 3K3
Tel: 416-224-8737; *Fax:* 855-271-2236
info@rhacademy.ca
www.rhacademy.ca
www.facebook.com/RobbinsHebrewAcademy
twitter.com/RobbinsHebrew
Grades: JK-8 *Enrollment:* 600 *Note:* Robbins Hebrew Academy
is a Conservative Jewish day school.
Claire Sumerlus, Head of School
csumerlus@rhacademy.ca
Michael Ferman, Director, Admissions & Alumni
mferman@rhacademy.ca

Toronto: The Rosedale Day School
#426, 131 Bloor St. West, Toronto, ON M5S 1R1
Tel: 416-923-4726; *Fax:* 416-923-7379
office@rds-on.com
www.rds-on.com
Other Information: Admissions Office: 416-923-1336
Grades: JK-8 *Enrollment:* 115
James Lee, Head of School
jlee@rds-on.com

Toronto: Royal St. George's College
120 Howland Ave., Toronto, ON M5R 3B5
Tel: 416-533-9481; *Fax:* 416-533-0028
contactus@rsgc.on.ca
www.rsgc.on.ca
www.facebook.com/RSGC1
twitter.com/RoyalSGC
Grades: Elem./Sec.; Boys *Enrollment:* 426
Stephen Beatty, Headmaster
sbeatty@rsgc.on.ca
David Fitzpatrick, Dean of Students, Senior School
dfitzpatrick@rsgc.on.ca
Jacquie Baby, Administrator, Junior School
jbaby@rsgc.on.ca

Toronto: Sabouhi Academy Of Art & Design
#6303, 6305 Yonge St., Toronto, ON M2M 3X7
Tel: 416-221-2111; *Fax:* 416-221-7274
Info@SabouhiAcademy.com
www.sabouhiacademy.com
www.youtube.com/user/SabouhiAcademy
Grades: 9 - 12

Toronto: St. Clement's School
21 St. Clements Ave., Toronto, ON M4R 1G8, Canada
Tel: 416-483-4835; *Fax:* 416-483-5040
admissions@scs.on.ca
www.scs.on.ca
www.facebook.com/StClementsSchoolToronto
twitter.com/SCS_Clementines
www.instagram.com/stclementsschool
Grades: 1-12 *Enrollment:* 460 *Note:* Independent all-girl's day
school
Martha Perry, Principal, 416-483-4414, ext. 2359
Elena Holeton, Director, Admissions, 416-483-4414, ext. 2227
admissions@scs.on.ca

Toronto: St. Michael's College School
1515 Bathurst St., Toronto, ON M5P 3H4, Canada
Tel: 416-653-3180; *Fax:* 416-653-7704
info@smcsmail.com
www.stmichaelscollegeschool.com
www.facebook.com/smcs1852
twitter.com/smcs1852
www.youtube.com/user/SMCS1852
Grades: 7-12 *Enrollment:* 1100 *Note:* St. Michael's College
School provides Catholic, Liberal Arts education for young men.
Fr. Mario D'Souza, C.S.B., Chair, Board of Directors
Fr. Jefferson Thompson, C.S.B., President
thompson@smcsmail.com
Greg Reeves, Principal
reeves@smcsmail.com
Emile John, Vice-Principal, 416-653-3180, ext. 156
john@smcsmail.com
David Lee, Vice-Principal, 416-653-3180, ext. 179
lee@smcsmail.com
Chris DePiero, Director, Athletics
depieroc@smcsmail.com

Toronto: Salaheddin Islamic School
741 Kennedy Rd., Toronto, ON M1K 2C6, Canada
Tel: 416-264-9495; *Fax:* 416-264-3343
principal@salaheddin.org
www.salaheddin.org
Grades: Elem. *Enrollment:* 185
Laila Maarouf

Toronto: Sathya Sai School of Canada
451 Ellesmere Rd., Toronto, ON M1R 4E5
Tel: 416-297-7970; *Fax:* 416-297-0945
info.sathyasaischool@gmail.com
www.sathyasaischool.ca
Grades: JK-8 *Enrollment:* 200 *Note:* Sathya Sai School seeks to
promote the five human values of Truth, Right Conduct, Peace,
Love, & Non-violence in students through education of
character, along with academics.
Revathi Chennabathni, Ph.D., Principal
rchennabathni@sathyasaischool.ca
Edith Recht, Office Administrator
erecht@sathyasaischool.ca

Toronto: Shmuel Zahavy Cheder Chabad of Toronto
#203, 900 Alness St., Toronto, ON M3J 2H6, Canada
Tel: 416-663-1972; *Fax:* 416-650-9404
www.chabad.org
Note: Students at Shmuel Zahavy Cheder Chabad of Toronto
also receive education in Torah scholarship & classic Jewish
values.
Rabbi Yona Shur, Director
Rabbi Baruch Zaltzman, Principal

Toronto: Sidney Ledson Institute
#107, 220 Duncan Mill Rd., Toronto, ON M3B 3J5, Canada
Tel: 416-447-5355
sidney.ledson@bellnet.ca
www.sidneyledsoninstitute.net
Grades: Pre.-6 *Enrollment:* 50

Toronto: Sterling Hall School of Toronto (SHS)
99 Cartwright Ave., Toronto, ON M6A 1V4, Canada
Tel: 416-785-3410; *Fax:* 416-785-6616
info@sterlinghall.com
www.sterlinghall.com
www.facebook.com/SterlingHallSchool
twitter.com/SHSToronto
vimeo.com/user3297765
Grades: JK-8 *Enrollment:* 310 *Number of Employees:* 65 *Note:*
All-boys independent day school.
Rick Parsons, Principal
rparsons@sterlinghall.com
Kate Sherk, Director, Administration, 416-785-3490, ext. 220
ksherk@sterlinghall.com

Toronto: Sunnybrook School (SBS)
469 Merton St., Toronto, ON M4S 1B4, Canada
Tel: 416-487-5308; *Fax:* 416-487-5381
admissions@sunnybrookschool.ca
www.sunnybrookschool.com
www.facebook.com/154018124624187
Grades: JK.-6 *Enrollment:* 130 *Number of Employees:* 20
Dr. Irene Davy, Ph.D., Director & Principal

Toronto: SuOn International Academy
70 Chartwell Rd., Toronto, ON M8Z 4G6
Tel: 416-255-8808
suon.admi@gmail.com
www.suon.ca
Grades: 9 - 12 *Note:* SuOn International Academy is a private
secondary and university preparatory school.

Toronto: TAIE International Institute
296 Parliament St., Toronto, ON M5A 3A4
Tel: 416-368-2882
taie.ca
www.facebook.com/taie.canada
twitter.com/TAIECanada
Grades: 9 - 12
Raymond Lee, Chief Director of Offices, 416-368-2882
raymondlee@taie.ca

Toronto: Tayyibah Islamic Academy (TIA)
#205, 100 McLevin Ave., Toronto, ON M1B 2V5
Tel: 416-297-7336; *Fax:* 416-297-7930
theprincipal@tayyibahacademy.com
www.tayyibahacademy.com
Grades: K - 12

Toronto: Temple Sinai Hebrew & Religious School
210 Wilson Ave., Toronto, ON M5M 3B1
Tel: 416-487-3281; *Fax:* 416-487-5499
www.templesinai.net
Grades: Pre./Elem. *Note:* The Temple Sinai Congregation of
Toronto also offers a nursery program.
Rayner Conway, Executive Director
rayner@templesinai.net
Carrie Swartz, Director, Congregational Learning
carrie@templesinai.net
Andrea Zecharia, Director, Preschool

Toronto: Tiferes Bais Yaakov
Also known as: Daniel T. Gordon High School for Girls
85 Stormont Ave., Toronto, ON M5N 2C3
Tel: 416-785-4044; *Fax:* 416-785-4046
secretary@tiferesbaisyaakov.com
www.tiferesbaisyaakov.com
Grades: Secondary; Girls *Enrollment:* 150 *Note:* Tiferes Bais
Yaakov is an Orthodox Jewish high school for girls.
Rabbi Yitzchak Feigenbaum, Principal
rabbif@tiferesbaisyaakov.com
Polina Nagla, Principal, General Studies
pnagla@tiferesbaisyaakov.com
Adina Ribacoff, Principal, Judaic Studies
ribacoff@tiferesbaisyaakov.com

Toronto: Torah High School - Toronto
4600 Bathurst St., Toronto, ON M2R 3V2
Tel: 905-761-6279; *Toll-Free:* 866-867-2444
www.torahhigh.org
www.facebook.com/TorahHigh
twitter.com/TorahHigh
www.youtube.com/ncsytube
Grades: 8-12 *Note:* Torah High offers courses in Religious
Studies, Hebrew Language, Philosophy, Political Science,
Nutrition, Arts, & Interdisciplinary Studies for students attending
public or private secondary schools. The school has four
locations in Toronto: Promenade Mall, Prosserman JCC,
Schwartz Reisman Centre, & Village Shul.

Toronto: Toronto Cheder School
3995 Bathurst St., Toronto, ON M3H 5V3, Canada
Tel: 416-636-2987
thetorontocheder@bellnet.com
Enrollment: 200 *Note:* Toronto Cheder School is an Orthodox
school for boys.
Rabbi D. Engel, Principal

Toronto: Toronto Collegiate Institute
#25, 50 Weybright Crt., Toronto, ON M1S 5A8
Tel: 416-289-0051; *Fax:* 866-810-7489
admin@torontoci.com
www.torontoci.com
Grades: 9 - 12

Toronto: Toronto Farsi School
5527 Yonge St., Toronto, ON M2N 1A1
www.torontofarsischool.com
Grades: 9 - 12

Toronto: Toronto French Montessori
53 Cummer Ave., Toronto, ON M2M 2E5
Tel: 416-250-9952; *Fax:* 416-250-9957
admissions@torontofrenchmontessori.com
www.torontofrenchmontessori.ca
www.facebook.com/TorontoFrenchMontessori
Grades: Pre.-8 *Enrollment:* 90
Marie Mousa, Principal
principal@torontofrenchmontessori.com

Toronto: Toronto French School (TFS)
Toronto Campus
306 Lawrence Ave. East, Toronto, ON M4N 1T7, Canada
Tel: 416-484-6533; *Fax:* 416-488-3090
admissions@tfs.ca
www.tfs.ca
www.facebook.com/TorontoFrenchSchoolFB
twitter.com/TFS_Toronto
www.youtube.com/user/torontofrenchschool
Grades: Preschool - 12 *Enrollment:* 1400 *Number of Employees:*
200 *Note:* Toronto French School is a co-educational,
non-denominational school, which offers bilingual education.
Nathalie Mercure, Chair
board@tfs.ca
Mirna Hafez, Head of School
Alain Delaune, Principal, Mississauga School
Heidi Gollert, Principal, Senior School
Mirna Hafez, Principal, Junior School

Toronto: The Toronto Heschel School
819 Sheppard Ave. West, Toronto, ON M3H 2T3, Canada
Tel: 416-635-1876; *Fax:* 416-635-1800
info@torontoheschel.org
www.facebook.com/163617997000292
twitter.com/TorontoHeschel
Grades: Junior Kindergarten - 8 *Enrollment:* 300 *Note:* The
Jewish day school combines the teaching of Judaism with a
general studies curriculum.
Gail Baker, Head of School & Principal
head@torontoheschel.org
Mark Abramsohn, Director, Business Operations
admin@torontoheschel.org
Greg Beiles, Curriculum Consultant
curriculum@torontoheschel.org

Toronto: Toronto International College (TIC)
Collège International de Toronto
Also known as: Toronto International College of
Business
#500, 3550 Victoria Park Ave., Toronto, ON M2H 2N5
Tel: 416-498-9299; *Fax:* 416-493-9166
www.ticedu.ca
Grades: 9 - 12
Yelena Mordovskaya, Dean, 416-498-9299, ext. 5192
dean@ticedu.ca

Toronto: Toronto Prep School
#200, 250 Davisville Ave., Toronto, ON M4S 1H2
Tel: 416-545-1020; *Fax:* 416-545-1456
www.torontoprepschool.com
Grades: 7-12 *Enrollment:* 300
Steve Tsimikalis, B.A., B.Ed., M.E.S., Principal
ftsimikalis@torontoprepschool.com

Toronto: University of Toronto Schools (UTS)
371 Bloor St. West, Toronto, ON M5S 2R7, Canada
Tel: 416-978-3212; *Fax:* 416-978-6775
info@utschools.ca
www.utschools.ca
Other Information: 416-946-7995 (Phone, Admissions);
416-978-7325 (Student Services)
Grades: 7 - 12 *Enrollment:* 640 *Number of Employees:* 65 *Note:*
UTS is a coeducational school, affiliated with the University of
Toronto.
Jim Fleck, Board Chair
UTSBoard@utschools.ca
Rosemary Evans, Principal, 416-946-7936
revans@utschools.ca

Toronto: Upper Canada College (UCC)
200 Lonsdale Rd., Toronto, ON M4V 1W6
Tel: 416-488-1125; *Fax:* 416-484-8611
administration@ucc.on.ca
www.ucc.on.ca
Other Information: Office of Advancement, Phone:
416-488-1125, ext. 2239
Grades: SK - 12 *Note:* The Preparatory School has over 400
boys from Senior Kindergarten to grade seven. The Upper
School offers a five year secondary education.
Russell Higgins, Chair, Board of Governors
Sam McKinney, Principal
principal@ucc.on.ca
Jim Garner, Vice-Principal, Advancement & Strategy
jgarner@ucc.on.ca
Thomas Lindell, Vice-Principal, People & Organizational
Development
tlindell@ucc.on.ca
David McBride, Vice-Principal, Enrolment Management
dmcbride@ucc.on.ca
Patti MacNicol, Chief Administrative Officer
pmacnicol@ucc.on.ca

Julia Kinnear, Academic Dean
jkinnear@ucc.on.ca
Thomas Babits, Head, Primary Division
tbabits@ucc.on.ca
Naheed Bardai, Head, Middle Division
nbardai@ucc.on.ca
Scott Cowie, Head, Senior Division
scowie@ucc.on.ca
Derek Poon, Head, Intermediate Division
dpoon@ucc.on.ca

Toronto: Upper Madison College (UMC)
5075 Yonge St., 5th Fl., Toronto, ON M2N 7H3
Tel: 416-512-1026
info@umcollege.ca
www.umcollege.ca
www.facebook.com/umcollegeca
www.instagram.com/umcollege
Grades: 7-12

Campuses
Montréal Campus
360, rue Mayor, Montréal, QC H3A 1N7
Tel: 514-281-0606

Toronto: Voice Integrative School
50 Gristmill Lane, Toronto, ON M5A 3C4
Tel: 416-691-4639; *Fax:* 416-691-3722
vis@voiceintegrative.com
www.voiceintegrativeschool.com
Grades: 1-8 *Enrollment:* 90
Marie Lardino, B.A., B.Ed., M.Ed., Founder & Director

Toronto: Waldorf Academy
250 Madison Ave., Toronto, ON M4V 2W6
Tel: 416-962-6447; *Fax:* 416-975-5513
info@waldorfacademy.org
waldorfacademy.org
www.facebook.com/waldorfacademy
twitter.com/WALDORFtoronto
www.instagram.com/waldorf_academy
Grades: Pre.-8 *Enrollment:* 240
Dean Husseini, Managing Facilitator
Jennifer Deathe, Contact, Admissions
admissions@waldorfacademy.org
Matthew Denton, Manager, Business Operations

Toronto: Wales College
#518, 4002 Sheppard Ave. East, Toronto, ON M1S 4R5
Tel: 416-299-9966; *Fax:* 416-299-1577
info@walescollege.ca
www.walescollege.ca
Grades: 9 - 12
Juan Federici, Principal

Toronto: William School
#200, 3761 Victoria Park Ave., Toronto, ON M1W 3S3
Tel: 416-491-6888; *Fax:* 416-640-2000
wschool@rogers.com
www.williamschool.ca
Grades: 9 - 12

Toronto: WillowWood School
55 Scarsdale Rd., Toronto, ON M3B 2R3
Tel: 416-444-7644; *Fax:* 416-444-1801
info@willowwoodschool.ca
www.willowwoodschool.ca
Grades: 1-12 *Enrollment:* 250
Fred Howe, Principal

Toronto: Yeshiva Bnei Zion of Bobov
44 Champlain Blvd., Toronto, ON M3H 2Z1, Canada
Tel: 416-633-6332; *Fax:* 416-633-6704
Grades: JK-8; Boys
Rabbi Shlomo Tzvi Frank, Director, Education
schloime.frank@gmail.com

Toronto: Yeshiva Darchei Torah
18 Champlain Blvd., Toronto, ON M3H 2Z1
Tel: 416-782-7974; *Fax:* 416-782-7811
www.darchei.ca
Grades: Secondary *Note:* Yeshiva Darchei Torah is an Orthodox
Jewish high school for boys, with Jewish & secular programs.
Rabbi Eliezer Breitowitz, Rosh Hayeshiva
breitowitz@darchei.ca
Ed McMahon, English Principal
mcmahon@darchei.ca
Jeff Toledano, Executive Director
toledano@darchei.ca

Toronto: Yeshiva Yesodei Hatorah
77 Glen Rush Blvd., Toronto, ON M5N 2T8
Tel: 416-787-1101; *Fax:* 416-787-9044
office@yesodeihatorah.ca

Grades: Pre.-8; Boys *Enrollment:* 450
Rabbi M. Bornstein, Principal

Toronto: Yeshivas Nachalas Zvi
475 Lawrence Ave. West, Toronto, ON M5M 1C6, Canada
Tel: 416-782-8912; *Fax:* 416-787-8517
ynzvitoronto@gmail.com
Grades: 8-12; Religious Orthodox; Boys *Enrollment:* 75
Rabbi Yitzchok Kaplan, Contact

Toronto: The York School
1320 Yonge St., Toronto, ON M4T 1X2, Canada
Tel: 416-926-1325; *Fax:* 416-926-9592
admission@yorkschool.com
www.yorkschool.com
Other Information: 416-646-5275 (Phone, Admissions)
www.facebook.com/theyorkschool
twitter.com/theyorkschool
www.linkedin.com/company/the-york-school
Grades: JK-12 *Enrollment:* 675 *Note:* The York School is
co-educational & non-denominational. It is an International
Baccalaureate World School, which offers PYP, MYP, & Diploma
programs.
Conor Jones, Head of School, 416-926-1325, ext. 5271
cjones@yorkschool.com
David Hamilton, Principal, Senior School, 416-926-1325, ext.
5272
dhamilton@yorkschool.com
Helen Gin, Principal, Middle School, 416-926-1325, ext. 1187
hgin@yorkschool.com
Jennifer Wyatt, Principal, Junior School, 416-926-1325, ext.
5273
jwyatt@yorkschool.com
Katie Leopold, Chief Financial Officer
Rick DeMarinis, Director, Athletics
David Hanna, Director, University Counselling
Elissa Kline-Beber, Director, Student Wellness
Judy MacGowan, Director, Advancement
Justin Medved, Director, Learning, Innovation & Technology
Praveen Muruganandan, Director, Strategic Enrolment
Management
Sarah Charley, Executive Coordinator, Citizenship

Unionville: Montessori North School
4561 Highway 7 East, Unionville, ON L3R 1M4
Tel: 905-475-9341; *Fax:* 416-953-0391
info@montessorinorth.ca
www.montessorinorth.ca
Grades: Toddler - Pre.
Anahita Faroogh, Principal

Unionville: Unionville Montessori School (UMS)
9302 Kennedy Rd., Unionville, ON L6C 1N6, Canada
Tel: 905-474-9888; *Fax:* 905-474-5767
office@unionvillemontessori.com
www.unionvillemontessori.com
Grades: Preschool - 8 *Note:* Unionville Montessori School is a
coeducational, non-denominational school. The Casa program is
available for children from age two to six.

Unionville: Yip's Music & Montessori Elementary
School
100 Lee Ave., Unionville, ON L3R 8G2
Tel: 905-948-9477
www.yips.com
Other Information: Administration Phone: 905-752-0275, ext.
2100
www.facebook.com/YipsCanada
twitter.com/YipsCanada
Grades: Pre.-8
Katherine Kwok, Chief Administrator
katherine@yips.com
Christian Bayly, Principal, Unionville Campus
christian@yips.com

Campuses
Markham Campus
#19, 28 Crown Steel Dr., Markham, ON L3R 0A1
Tel: 905-513-0955
Elsa Lee, Principal
elsa@yips.com

Thornhill Campus
#8, 8100 Yonge St., Thornhill, ON L4J 1W3
Tel: 905-881-9333
Amy Or, Principal
amy.or@yips.com

Vaughan: Beit Rayim Synagogue & School
Joseph & Wolf Lebovic Jewish Community Campus
#244, 9600 Bathurst St., Vaughan, ON L6A 3Z8
Tel: 905-303-5471
admin@beitrayim.org
www.beitrayim.org

Note: Beit Rayim Hebrew School is an egalitarian Conservative Jewish school. Classes meet two days a week: Sunday mornings & Thursday afternoons.
Avivit Yoffe, Principal & Director, Youth Engagement & Education
avivit@beitrayim.org

Vaughan: Casa Dei Bambini Montessori School
#4-6, 661 Chrislea Rd., Vaughan, ON L4L 8A3
Tel: 905-851-8837; *Fax:* 905-851-8839
www.facebook.com/191392617592230
Grades: Pre.-1 *Enrollment:* 75

Vaughan: The Hill Academy
2600 Rutherford Rd., Vaughan, ON L4K 5R1
Tel: 905-303-4530; *Fax:* 905-303-2201
admissions@thehillacademy.com
www.thehillacademy.com
Grades: K - 12
Peter Merrill, Founder & CEO
peter.merrill@thehillacademy.com
Wally Tymkiv, Principal
wtymkiv@thehillacademy.com

Vaughan: Kachol Lavan - The School for Hebrew & Israel Studies
Administration
Schwartz/Reisman Centre
9600 Bathurst St., Vaughan, ON L6A 3Z8
Tel: 905-303-1821
kachol.lavan@srcentre.ca
www.kachol-lavan.com
Note: Classes also offered at 4588 Bathurst St., Toronto; phone: 416-638-1881

Vaughan: King Heights Academy
28 Roytec Rd., Vaughan, ON L4L 8E4
Tel: 905-652-1234; *Fax:* 905-652-9000
info@kingheightsacademy.com
kingheightsacademy.com
Grades: JK-6 *Enrollment:* 150
Elsa Norberto, Director

Vaughan: RoyalCrest Academy
9500 Dufferin St., Vaughan, ON L6A 1S2
Tel: 905-303-7557; *Fax:* 905-303-7107
info@royalcrestacademy.com
www.royalcrestacademy.com
Grades: Pre.-8 *Enrollment:* 250
Brian Drake, Principal
Michelle Johnson, Director, Admissions

Vaughan: Victoria International Ballet Academy
7 Bradwick Dr., Vaughan, ON L4K 2T4
Tel: 905-707-7580
info@victoriaballet.com
www.victoriaballet.com
www.facebook.com/VictoriaBalletAcademy
twitter.com/VictoriaBalletA
www.youtube.com/user/victoriaballet1
Grades: 9 - 12

Vaughn: As-Sadiq Islamic School
9000 Bathurst St., Vaughn, ON L4J 8A7, Canada
Tel: 905-695-1588; *Fax:* 905-695-1590
www.as-sadiqschool.com
Grades: Toddler - 8 *Enrollment:* 165
Fernanda Pires, Principal

Vineland: Niagara Academy
3373 - 1st Ave., Vineland, ON L0R 2E0
Tel: 905-562-0683
www.niagaraacademy.ca
Grades: K - 12

Waterloo: Kitchener Waterloo Bilingual School
Also known as: The K-W Bilingual School
600 Erb St. West, Waterloo, ON N2J 3Z4, Canada
Tel: 519-886-6510; *Fax:* 519-886-4053
bilingualschool@bellnet.ca
www.kwbilingualschool.com
Grades: JK-8
Mona Balea, Principal
m_balea@kwbilingualschool.net
Keesha Dickson, Secretary

Webequie: Simon Jacob Memorial Education Centre
P.O. Box 265
Webequie, ON P0T 3A0, Canada
Tel: 807-353-6491; *Fax:* 807-353-1306
www.webequie.ca/article/education-136.asp
Grades: K-10; Native Language; Special Ed. *Note:* The Simon Jacob Memorial Education Centre is operated by the Webequie First Nation Education Authority.

Mary Gardiner, Principal
Stephanie Jones, Teacher, Special Education
Lois Whitehead, Instuctor, Native Language

Wellandport: Robert Land Academy (RLA)
6727 South Chippawa Rd., Wellandport, ON L0R 2J0, Canada
Tel: 905-386-6203; *Fax:* 905-386-6607
www.robertlandacademy.com
www.facebook.com/robertlandacademy
www.youtube.com/user/robertlandacademy1
Grades: 6 - 12 *Enrollment:* 125 *Note:* Robert Land Academy is a highly structured military boarding school, which provides education for previously under-achieving boys with potential.
Major (retired) G. Scott Bowman, Founder & Headmaster

Whitby: Kendalwood Montessori School
104 Consumers Dr., Whitby, ON L1N 5T3
Tel: 905-665-4766
admin@kendalwoodmontessori.com
www.kendalwoodmontessori.com
www.facebook.com/228602640484301
twitter.com/KendalwoodMont
Grades: Toddler - Elem.
Lisa Jobe, Principal

Whitby: Trafalgar Castle School
401 Reynolds St., Whitby, ON L1N 3W9, Canada
Tel: 905-668-3358; *Fax:* 905-668-4136
www.trafalgarcastle.ca
www.facebook.com/Trafalgarcastle
twitter.com/trafalgarcastle
Grades: 5 - 12 *Note:* The day & boarding school educates young women.
Adam De Pencier, Head of School
depencier.adam@trafalgarcastle.ca
Gillian Martin, Vice Principal, School Life, 905-668-3358, ext. 228
martin.gillian@trafalgarcastle.ca
Tim Southwell, Vice Principal, Academics, 905-668-3358, ext. 229
southwell.tim@trafalgarcastle.ca
Marguerita Dykstra, Director, Finance, 905-668-3358, ext. 232
dykstra.marguerita@trafalgarcastle.ca
Sharon Magor, Director, Marketing & Development
magor.sharon@trafalgarcastle.ca

Whitby: Whitby Montessori & Elementary School
95 Taunton Rd., Whitby, ON L1R 3L3, Canada
Tel: 905-430-8201
welcomecentre@whitbymontessori.ca
www.whitbymontessori.ca
Grades: Pre.-Elem. *Note:* Whitby Montessori & Elementary School educates children from age twelve months to fourteen years.

Willowdale: Montessori Education Centre
80 George Henry Blvd., Willowdale, ON M2J 1E7
Tel: 416-502-1769; *Fax:* 416-502-1769
www.montessoried.ca
Grades: Casa
Imanthi Nanayakkara, Principal
imanthi86@gmail.com

Windsor: A21 Academy
8787 McHugh St., Windsor, ON N8S 0A1
Tel: 519-900-6021
info@a21academy.com
www.axxiacademy.com
twitter.com/a21academy
Grades: Elem.
Kristi Spidalieri, Principal

Windsor: Académie Ste. Cécile International School
925 Cousineau Rd., Windsor, ON N9G 1V8, Canada
Tél: 519-969-1291; *Téléc:* 519-969-7953
info@stececile.ca
academiestececile.ca
twitter.com/OnlyatASCIS
Grades: Pre./Elem./Sec. *Enrollment:* 250 *Note:* Affiliated with the Univ. of Windsor. Programmes include the Ontario Sec. School Programme, the International Bacc. Programme, Advanced Placement; emphasis on music, dance, art, & performing arts, as well as programmes in technology; ESL, FSL & TOEFL courses; summer school.
Thérèse H. Gadoury, Directrice

Campuses
Ste Cécile Child Enrichment Centre
925 Cousineau Rd., Windsor, ON N9G 1V8, Canada
Tél: 519-969-1291
academiestececile.ca

Dance Studio of Académie Ste Cécile
925 Cousineau Rd., Windsor, ON N9G 1V8, Canada
Tél: 519-969-1291
dancestudio@stececile.ca
academiestececile.ca

Windsor: An-Noor Private School
1480 Janette Ave., Windsor, ON N8X 1Z4, Canada
Tel: 519-966-4422; *Fax:* 519-966-5233
annoorprivateschool@gmail.com
www.annoorschool.ca
www.facebook.com/annoorschool
Grades: JK-8 *Enrollment:* 300 *Note:* Provides students with an academic & Islamic education.
Amney Behiry, Acting Principal

Woodbridge: Maple Leaf Montessori Schools Inc.
8142 Islington Ave., Woodbridge, ON L4L 1W6, Canada
Tel: 905-856-3359
info@mlmontessori.org
www.mlmontessori.org
www.facebook.com/mapleleafmontessori
Grades: Pre.-6
Johanna Madeley, Administrator & Founder
johanna@mlmontessori.org
Michael Madeley, Elementary Principal
michael@mlmontessori.org

Wunnummin Lake: Lydia Lois Beardy Memorial School
P.O. Box 108
General Delivery, Wunnummin Lake, ON P0V 2Z0
Tel: 807-442-2575; *Fax:* 807-442-2640
www.llbms.firstnationschools.ca
Grades: Elem./Sec.
Maija Lamminmaki, Principal

Universities & Colleges

Protestant

Toronto: Tyndale University
3377 Bayview Ave., Toronto, ON M2M 3S4
Tel: 416-226-6620; *Fax:* 416-226-6746
Toll-Free: 877-896-3253
contact@tyndale.ca
www.tyndale.ca
www.facebook.com/tyndaleuniversity
twitter.com/tyndaleu
www.youtube.com/c/TyndaleUniversityOfficial
Note: Founded in 1984, Tyndale University is a private Christian university & seminary offering academic programs & degrees in theology.
Marjory Kerr, President
president@tyndale.ca

Universities

Guelph: University of Guelph
50 Stone Rd. East, Guelph, ON N1G 2W1
Tel: 519-824-4120; *Fax:* 519-767-1693
www.uoguelph.ca
www.facebook.com/uofguelph
twitter.com/uofg
www.linkedin.com/company/university-of-guelph
www.youtube.com/uofguelph
Full Time Equivalency: 29614
Martha Billes, Chancellor
Franco Vaccarino, President & Vice-Chancellor
president@uoguelph.ca
Charlotte Yates, Provost & Vice-President (Academic)
Daniel Atlin, Vice-President (External)
Malcolm Campbell, Vice-President (Research)
Don O'Leary, Vice-President (Finance, Administration & Risk)
David Whittle, Chief Information Officer
Ray Darling, Registrar

Faculties
College of Arts
MacKinnon Bldg.
50 Stone Rd. East, Guelph, ON N1G 2W1
www.uoguelph.ca/arts
Other Information: 519-824-4120, ext. 53301
www.facebook.com/UOGCollegeofArts
twitter.com/UoG_ARTS
www.linkedin.com/in/college-of-arts-59381414a
www.instagram.com/uog_arts
Samantha Brennan, Dean, 519-824-4120, ext. 53301
sjbrennan@uoguelph.ca

College of Biological Science (CBS)
Summerlee Science Complex
50 Stone Road East, Guelph, ON N1G 2W1

Tel: 519-824-4120
www.uoguelph.ca/cbs
www.facebook.com/cbsguelph

Enrollment: 4900
Glen Van Der Kraak, Interim Dean, 519-824-4120, ext. 53424
gvanderk@uoguelph.ca
Vanessa Myers, Associate Director, Finance and Operations,
519-824-4120, ext. 53463
vmyers@uoguelph.ca
Emily Perreault, Administrative Officer, 519-824-4120, ext.
53343
emilyp@uoguelph.ca

Gordon S. Lang School of Business & Economics
MacDonald Hall
50 Stone Road East, Guelph, ON N1G 2W1

www.uoguelph.ca/business
www.linkedin.com/groups/3719672
www.youtube.com/user/cmeguelph
Enrollment: 4000 Number of Employees: 74 faculty
Sara Mann, Interim Dean, 519-824-4120, ext. 56118
smann@uoguelph.ca

College of Engineering & Physical Sciences
Summerlee Science Complex
#1313, 50 Stone Road East, Guelph, ON N1G 2W1

Tel: 519-824-4120
kmooibro@uoguelph.ca
www.uoguelph.ca/ceps
twitter.com/UofGCEPS
Enrollment: 3800 Number of Employees: 150 full-time faculty
Mary A. Wells, Dean, 514-824-4120, ext. 53125
mawells@uoguelph.ca

College of Social & Applied Human Sciences (CSAHS)
50 Macdonald St., Guelph, ON N1G 2W1

Tel: 519-824-4120; Fax: 519-766-4797
csahs@uoguelph.ca
csahs.uoguelph.ca
www.facebook.com/CSAHSUoG
twitter.com/CSAHS_UoG
www.youtube.com/user/CSAHSUofG
Gwen Chapman, Dean
csahsdean@uoguelph.ca

Office of Graduate & Postdoctoral Studies (OGPS)
University Centre
50 Stone Rd. East, 3rd Fl., Guelph, ON N1G 2W1

gradonln@uoguelph.ca
www.uoguelph.ca/graduatestudies
Other Information: General Reception: 519-824-4120, ext. 56833
www.facebook.com/uofgGradStudies
twitter.com/uofgGradStudies
www.instagram.com/uofg_gradstudies
Pauline Sinclair, Director, 519-824-4120, ext. 56740
paulines@uoguelph.ca

Ontario Agricultural College (OAC)
Johnston Hall
50 Stone Rd. East, Guelph, ON N1G 2W1, Canada

Tel: 519-824-4120
oacinfo@uoguelph.ca
www.uoguelph.ca/oac
twitter.com/UofGuelphOAC
www.youtube.com/user/UofGuelphOAC
Enrollment: 3700 Number of Employees: 740
Rene Van Acker, Dean, 519-824-4120, ext. 52285
vanacker@uoguelph.ca
Sara Stephens, Administrative Officer, 519-824-4120, ext. 56403
sara.stephens@uoguelph.ca

Ontario Veterinary College (OVC)
50 Stone Rd. East, Guelph, ON N1G 2W1

Fax: 519-837-3230
ovcdean@uoguelph.ca
www.ovc.uoguelph.ca
Other Information: 519-824-4120, ext. 54401
www.facebook.com/OntVetCollege
twitter.com/OntVetCollege
www.youtube.com/user/OntarioVetCollege
Jeffrey Wichtel, Dean, 519-824-4120, ext. 54417
jwichtel@uoguelph.ca
Carol Ann Higgins, Chief Administrative Officer, 519-824-4120,
ext. 54784
chiggins@uoguelph.ca

Schools
School of Environmental Design & Rural Development
50 Stone Road East, Guelph, ON N1G 2W1

Tel: 519-824-4120; Fax: 519-767-1686
sedrd@uoguelph.ca
www.uoguelph.ca/sedrd

Sean Kelly, Director, 519-824-4120, ext. 56870
sean.kelly@uoguelph.ca
Jenn McCreary, Administrative Officer, 519-824-4120, ext.
53353
mccrearj@uoguelph.ca

School of Fine Art & Music (SOFAM)
MacKinnon Building
50 Stone Road East, Guelph, ON N1G 2W1

www.uoguelph.ca/arts/sofam
Martin Pearce, Director, 519-824-4120, ext. 56930
pearcem@uoguelph.ca

School of English & Theatre Studies (SETS)
MacKinnon Building
50 Stone Road East, Guelph, ON N1G 2W1

www.uoguelph.ca/arts/sets
Martha Nandorfy, Interim Director
mnandorf@uoguelph.ca

School of Languages and Literatures (SOLAL)
MacKinnon Building
50 Stone Road East, Guelph, ON N1G 2W1

www.uoguelph.ca/arts/solal
Margot Irvine, Director, 519-824-4120, ext. 53167
mirvine@upguelph.ca

Campuses
Ridgetown Campus
120 Main St. East, Ridgetown, ON N0P 2C0

Tel: 519-674-1500; Toll-Free: 877-674-1610
rcweb@uoguelph
www.ridgetownc.ca
twitter.com/ridgetowncampus
Enrollment: 625 Number of Employees: 45 Note: Offers diploma,
apprenticeship, & certificate programs in subjects related to
agriculture, food, the environment, & rural communities.
Ken McEwan, Director

Centres & Institutes
Advanced Analysis Centre (AAC)
Summerlee Science Complex
50 Stone Rd. East, Guelph, ON N1G 2W1

Fax: 519-767-2044
aac@uoguelph.ca
www.uoguelph.ca/aac
Other Information: 519-824-4120, ext. 56814
Debbie Chan, Manager, 519-824-4120, ext. 56814
dchan@uoguelph.ca
Glen Van Der Kraak, Executive Director, 519-824-4120, ext.
53424
gvanderk@uoguelph.ca

Hamilton: McMaster University
1280 Main St. West, Hamilton, ON L8S 4L8, Canada

Tel: 905-525-9140
www.mcmaster.ca
www.facebook.com/mcmasteruniversity
twitter.com/mcmasteru
www.linkedin.com/company/mcmaster-university
www.youtube.com/mcmastertv
Full Time Equivalency: 31746

Faculties
Engineering
1280 Main Street West, Hamilton, ON L8S 4L7

Tel: 905-525-9140
eng.mcmaster.ca
www.facebook.com/McMasterUEngineering
twitter.com/McMasterEng
www.linkedin.com/school/15102221
www.youtube.com/user/McMasterEngineering
Enrollment: 6338 Number of Employees: 177 faculty members
Ishwar K. Puri, Dean, 905-525-9140, ext. 24900
deaneng@mcmaster.ca
Janet Delsey, Supervisor, Engineering Support Services,
905-525-9140, ext. 24910
delsey@mcmaster.ca

Faculty of Humanities
1280 Main St. West, Hamilton, ON L8S 4L8

humanities@mcmaster.ca
www.humanities.mcmaster.ca
Other Information: 905-525-9140, ext. 27532
www.facebook.com/mcmaster.humanities
twitter.com/mcmasterhum
www.youtube.com/user/mcmasterhumanities
Enrollment: 3000 Number of Employees: 125 Faculty Members
Pamela Swett, Dean, 905-525-9140, ext. 26546
Martin Horn, Associate Dean of Graduate Studies and
Research, 905-525-9140, ext. 26546
Jeff Chuchman, Associate Dean of Finance and Administration,
905-525-9140, ext. 24602
humdfa@mcmaster.ca

Faculty of Science
Burke Science Bldg.
#102, 1280 Main St. West, Hamilton, ON L8S 4K1

Fax: 905-546-9995
science@mcmaster.ca
science.mcmaster.ca
Other Information: 905-525-9140, ext. 22616
www.facebook.com/McMasterScience
twitter.com/McMasterScience
www.linkedin.com/company/mcmaster-faculty-of-science
www.instagram.com/mcmasterscience
Enrollment: 7400 Number of Employees: 200 Full-time faculty
Maureen J. MacDonald, Dean, 905-525-9140, ext. 22615
macdonmj@mcmaster.ca

Faculty of Social Sciences
Kenneth Taylor Hall
#129, 1280 Main St. West, Hamilton, ON L8S 4M4

Fax: 905-525-0844
socscfac@mcmaster.ca
socialsciences.mcmaster.ca
Other Information: 905-525-914, ext. 24727 or 23772
www.facebook.com/McMasterSocialSciences
twitter.com/McMasterSocSci
www.youtube.com/user/McMasterSocSci
Jeremiah Hurley, Dean, 905-525-9140, ext. 26156
deansoc@mcmaster.ca

Department of Peace Studies
Togo Salmon Hall
#721, 1280 Main St. West, Hamilton, ON L8S 4M2

peacestudies@mcmaster.ca
peacestudies.humanities.mcmaster.ca
Other Information: 905-525-9140, ext. 27734
Antoinette Somo, Acting Administrative Coordinator,
905-525-9140, ext. 27734
somoant@mcmaster.ca
Chandrima Chakraborty, Director, 905-525-9140, ext. 23777
peacedir@mcmaster.ca

Schools
DeGroote School of Business
1280 Main Street West, Hamilton, ON L8S 4M4

Tel: 905-525-9140
degroote.mcmaster.ca
www.facebook.com/degrootebiz
twitter.com/DeGrooteBiz
www.linkedin.ca/school/degroote-school-of-business
www.instagram.com/dsbcampus
Leonard Waverman, Dean, 905-525-9140, ext. 24431
deanbus@mcmaster.ca

Arts & Science Program
L.R. Wilson Hall
#3038, 1280 Main St. West, Hamilton, ON L8S 4K1

Tel: 905-525-9140
artsci.mcmaster.ca
www.facebook.com/macartsci
twitter.com/macartsci
Shelley Anderson, Program Administrator, 905-525-9140, ext.
24655
anderso@mcmaster.ca
Jean Wilson, Program Director, 905-525-9140, ext. 24656
wilsonj@mcmaster.ca

Indigenous Studies Program
L.R. Wilson Hall
#1811, 1280 Main St. West, Hamilton, ON L8S 4K1

Fax: 905-540-8443
indigenous.admin@mcmaster.ca
www.indigenous.mcmaster.ca
Other Information: 905-525-9140, ext. 23788
www.facebook.com/indigenous.recruit
twitter.com/MACIndigenous
Chelsea Gabel, Acting Academic Director, 905-525-9140, ext.
23316
gabelc@mcmaster.ca
Carrie McMullin, Program Administrator, 905-525-9140, ext.
23788
indigaa@mcmaster.ca

School of Graduate Studies
Gilmour Hall
#212, 1280 Main St. West, Hamilton, ON L8S 4L8

askgrad@mcmaster.ca
gs.mcmaster.ca
Other Information: 905-525-9140, ext. 23679
www.facebook.com/McMasterGraduateStudies
twitter.com/mcmastersgs
www.youtube.com/user/McMasterSGS
Doug Welch, Vice-Provost & Dean, 905-525-9140, ext. 24205
deangrad@mcmaster.ca

McMaster University Continuing Education
OJN
#386, 1 James St. North, 3rd Fl., Hamilton, ON L8S 4K1
Fax: 905-546-1690
Toll-Free: 800-463-6223
conted@mcmaster.ca
mcmastercce.ca/
Other Information: 905-525-9140, ext. 24321
www.facebook.com/McMaster.Continuing.Education
twitter.com/McMasterContEd
www.linkedin.com/school/15150251
www.youtube.com/user/McMasterContEd
Note: A collaborative program developed by the Peter Boris
Centre for Addictions Research, the Michael G. DeGroote
Centre for Medicinal Cannabis Research, and McMaster
Continuing Education. Offers three courses in an online format:
Fundamentals of Cannabis Science, Therapeutic Applications of
Cannabis, and Risks and Harms of Cannabis.

Affiliations
McMaster Divinity College (MDC)
1280 Main St. West, Hamilton, ON L8S 4K1
Tel: 905-525-9140; *Fax:* 905-577-4782
pcs@mcmaster.ca
www.mcmasterdivinity.ca
www.facebook.com/McMasterDiv
twitter.com/McMasterDiv
www.linked.com/company/mcmasterdiv
www.instagram.com/mcmasterdiv
Stanley E. Porter, President & Dean, 905-525-9140, ext. 23500
princpl@mcmaster.ca
Phil C. Zylla, Vice President Academic, 905-525-9140, ext.
20104
zyllap@mcmaster.ca

Centres & Institutes
AllerGen
Michael DeGroote Centre for Learning & Discovery
#3120, 1280 Main St. West, Hamilton, ON L8S 4K1
Fax: 905-524-0611
info@allergen-nce.ca
www.allergen-nce.ca
Other Information: 905-525-9140, ext. 26502
twitter.com/allergen_nce
Note: Research network focused on allergic disease.
Diana Royce, President & CEO

Biointerfaces Institute
1280 Main St. West, #ETB416, Hamilton, ON L8S 4L8
biointerfaces@mcmaster.ca
biointerfaces.mcmaster.ca
Other Information: 905-525-9140, ext. 20706
www.facebook.com/biointerfacesinstitute
twitter.com/HTBiointerfaces
Note: An instiute for investigating the nature of the
biological/material interface, or biointerface.
John Brennan, Institute Director, 905-525-9140, ext. 27033
brennanj@mcmaster.ca

Bertrand Russell Research Centre
Mills Memorial Library
1280 Main St. West, Hamilton, ON L8S 4L6
russell.mcmaster.ca
Other Information: 905-525-914, ext. 24896
Arlene Duncan, Contact
duncana@mcmaster.ca

Canadian Centre For Electron Microscopy (CCEM)
A. N. Bourns Building
1280 Main St. West, #B161, Hamilton, ON L8S 4M1
Tel: 905-525-9140; *Fax:* 905-521-2773
ccem.mcmaster.ca
twitter.com/CCEMCanada
www.linkedin.com/company/ccemcanada
Brian Langelier, Acting Facility Manager, 905-525-9140, ext.
21269
langelb@mcmaster.ca

CanChild Centre for Childhood Disability Research
Institute for Applied Health Sciences
#408, 1400 Main St. West, Hamilton, ON L8S 1C7
Tel: 905-525-9140; *Fax:* 905-529-7687
canchild@mcmaster.ca
www.canchild.ca
www.facebook.com/canchild.ca
twitter.com/canchild_ca
vimeo.com/canchild
Dr. Jan Willem Gorter, Director

Centre for Advanced Polymer Processing & Design (CAPPA-D)
John Hodgins Engineering Building
#374, 1280 Main St. West, Hamilton, ON L8S 4L7
Tel: 905-525-9140
eng.mcmaster.ca

Michael Thompson, Contact, 905-525-9140, ext. 23213
mthomps@mcmaster.ca

Centre for Emerging Device Technologies (CEDT)
1280 Main St. West, Hamilton, ON L8S 4L7
Tel: 905-525-9140; *Fax:* 905-528-5406
cedt@mcmaster.ca
eng.mcmaster.ca/centre-emerging-device-technologies-cedt-0#
Sarah Novosedlik, Administrator, CEDT, 905-525-1940, ext.
27129
anstets@mcmaster.ca

Centre for Evaluation of Medicines (CEM)
1280 Main St. West, Hamilton, ON L8S 4L8
Tel: 905-525-9140
Mitchell Levine, Director
levinem@mcmaster.ca

Centre for Functional Genomics (CFG)
Michael G. DeGroote Centre for Learning & Discove
1280 Main St. West, Hamilton, ON L8S 4K1
Tel: 905-525-9140; *Fax:* 905-522-6750
fhs.mcmaster.ca/cfg
John Hassell, Director, 905-525-9140, ext. 27217
hassell@mcmaster.ca

Centre for Health Economics & Policy Analysis (CHEPA)
CRL Bldg.
#282, 1280 Main St. West, Hamilton, ON L8S 4K1
Tel: 905-525-9140
chepa@mcmaster.ca
www.chepa.org
twitter.com/CHEPAMcMaster
Jean-Éric Tarride, Director, 905-525-9140, ext. 22122
tarride@mcmaster.ca

Centre for Microbial Chemical Biology (CMCB)
1200 Main St. West, #MDCL-2330, Hamilton, ON L8S 4K1
Tel: 905-525-9140
iidr.mcmaster.ca/cmcb
Tracey Campbell, Research Manager
campbtl@mcmaster.ca

Centre for Minimal Access Surgery (CMAS)
50 Charlton Ave. East, #T2141, Hamilton, ON L8N 4A6
Tel: 905-522-1155; *Fax:* 905-521-6194
info@cmas.ca
www.cmas.ca
www.facebook.com/CMASHamilton
twitter.com/cmashamilton
Marie Fairgrieve, Manager
mfairgri@stjosham.on.ca

Centre for Probe Development & Commercialization
Nuclear Research Bldg.
1280 Main St. West, Hamilton, ON L8S 4K1
cpdc@imagingprobes.ca
imagingprobes.ca
Other Information: 905-525-914, ext. 21212
John Valliant, Founder
Justyna Kelly, Interim Chief Executive Officer
John Thornbaun, Chief Operating Officer
Anne Goodbody, Chief Regulatory Officer

Centre for Spatial Analysis (CSPA)
1280 Main St. West, Hamilton, ON L8S 4M1
Tel: 905-525-9140
research.mcmaster.ca/research-centres/centre-of-spatial-analysis

Centre for Surgical Invention & Innovation (CSII)
39 Charlton Ave. East, Hamilton, ON L8N 1Y3
Tel: 905-522-1155
www.csii.ca
www.facebook.com/174502995911995
twitter.com/CSiiCECR
Debra Vivian, Director, Communications
dvivian@stjosham.on.ca

Centre for Sustainable Archaeology
McMaster Innovation Park
175 Longwood Road West, #B22, Hamilton, ON L8P 0A1
sustarc.mcmaster.ca
twitter.com/SustArchMIP
Scott Martin, Operations Manager, 905-525-9140, ext. 21970
sustarc@mcmaster.ca

Centre for Effective Design of Structures
1280 Main St. West, #JHE-301, Hamilton, ON L8S 4L7
Fax: 905-529-9688
www.eng.mcmaster.ca/centre-effective-design-structures-1
Other Information: 905-525-9140, ext. 24917
Wael El-Dakhakhni, Co-Director, 905-525-9140, ext. 26109
eldak@mcmaster.ca
Michael Tait, Co-Director, 905-525-9140, ext. 26469
taitm@mcmaster.ca

Farncombe Family Digestive Health Research Institute
Heath Sciences Centre
1280 Main St. West, #3N4, Hamilton, ON L8S 4K1
Tel: 905-525-9140
farncombe.mcmaster.ca
twitter.com/FFDHRI

Firestone Institute for Respiratory Health
St. Joseph's Healthcare
50 Charlton Ave. East, Hamilton, ON L8N 4A6
Tel: 905-522-1155
www.firh.ca
Marnie Buchanan, Clinical Manager
mbuchana@stjosham.on.ca

Gilbrea Centre for Studies in Aging
L.R. Wilson Hall
#2025-2028, 1280 Main St. West, Hamilton, ON L8S 4K1
Tel: 905-525-9140; *Fax:* 905-525-4198
gilbrea@mcmaster.ca
gilbrea.mcmaster.ca
www.facebook.com/TheGilbreaCentre
twitter.com/GilbreaCentre
www.linkedin.com/in/gilbreacentre
www.youtube.com/user/TheGilbreaCentre
Meridith Griffin, Acting Director
griffmb@mcmaster.ca

Institute on Globalization & the Human Condition
L.R. Wilson Hall
#2021, 1280 Main St. West, Hamilton, ON L8S 4K1
Fax: 905-577-4667
globalhc@mcmaster.ca
globalization.mcmaster.ca
Other Information: 905-525-9140, ext. 27556
www.facebook.com/instiueonglobalization
twitter.com/mcmaster_IGHC
Petra Rethmann, Director, 905-525-9140, ext. 26259
rethman@mcmaster.ca
Leigh-Ann Sepe, Program Administration, 905-525-9140, ext.
27556
globalhc@mcmaster.ca

McMaster Ancient DNA Centre
Chester New Hall
#524, 1280 Main St. West, Hamilton, ON L8S 4L9
kuchm@mcmaster.ca
adna.mcmaster.ca
Other Information: 905-525-9140, ext. 24807
Hendrik Poinar, Principal Investigator, 905-525-9140, ext. 26331
poinarh@mcmaster.ca

McMaster Centre for Scholarship in the Public Interest (MCSPI)
1280 Main St. West, Hamilton, ON L8S 4L8
Tel: 905-525-9140
mcspi.ca

McMaster Centre for Software Certification
Information Technology Bldg.
#101, 1280 Main St. West, Hamilton, ON L8S 4K1
mcscert@cas.mcmaster.ca
mcscert.ca
Other Information: 905-525-9140, ext. 23362
Richard Paige, Director
paigeri@mcmaster.ca

McMaster Centre for Climate Change
Burke Sciences Bldg.
#323, 1280 Main St. West, Hamilton, ON L8S 4K1
Fax: 905-546-0463
climate@mcmaster.ca
climate.mcmaster.ca
Other Information: 905-525-9140, ext. 23313
www.facebook.com/McMasterClimateCentre
twitter.com/mac_climate
Note: Promotes and facilitates education, research activities and
collaborations to study and model processes of Earth's climate
system and the impacts change on the environment,
ecosystems,water resources and human health.
Altaf Arain, Director, 905-525-9140, ext. 27941
arainm@mcmaster.ca

McMaster eBusiness Research Centre
DeGroote School of Business
1280 Main St. West, #A203, Hamilton, ON L8S 4M4
Tel: 905-525-9140
merc.mcmaster.ca
www.facebook.com/degrootebiz
twitter.com/DeGrooteBiz
www.linkedin.com/groups/3717724/profile
Khaled Hassanein, Director, 905-525-9140, ext. 23956
hassank@mcmaster.ca

McMaster Immunology Research Centre
MDCL
#4010, 1280 Main St. West, Hamilton, ON L8S 4K1
Tel: 905-525-9140; *Fax:* 905-522-6750
mirc.mcmaster.ca
www.facebook.com/169351976425223
twitter.com/MacImmunology
Dr. Carl Richards, Director, 905-525-9140, ext. 22391
richards@mcmaster.ca

McMaster Institute for Automotive Research and Technology (MacAUTO)
1280 Main St. West, Hamilton, ON L8S 4L8
Tel: 905-525-9140

McMaster Institute for Energy Studies (MIES)
1280 Main St. West, Hamilton, ON L8S 4L8
Tel: 905-525-9140
energy.mcmaster.ca
Note: Conducts research in solar, wind, and nuclear energy as well as fuel cell technology.
Kelton Friedrich, Manager, Operations
friedrke@mcmaster.ca

McMaster Institute for Health Equity (MIHE)
L.R. Wilson Hall
#380, 1280 Main St. West, Hamilton, ON L8S 4K1
Tel: 905-525-9140
mihe@mcmaster.ca
mihe.mcmaster.ca

Jim Dunn, Director
jim.dunn@mcmaster.ca

Paul R. MacPherson Institute for Leadership, Innovation & Excellence in Teaching
Mills Library
1280 Main St. West, #L504, Hamilton, ON L8S 4K1
Tel: 905-525-9140
mi@mcmaster.ca
mi.mcmaster.ca
www.facebook.com/MacPhersonInst
twitter.com/McMaster_MI
Lori Goff, Director, 905-525-9140, ext. 24368
midirect@mcmaster.ca

McMaster Institute for Molecular Biology & Medicine (MOBIX)
Health Sciences Centre
1200 Main St. West, #3N4F, Hamilton, ON L8N 3Z5
Tel: 905-525-9140
mobixlab@mcmaster.ca
healthsci.mcmaster.ca/mobix
Galina Kataeva, Manager

McMaster Institute for Music & the Mind (MIMM)
1280 Main St. West, Hamilton, ON L8S 4L8
Tel: 905-525-9140; *Fax:* 905-529-6225
mimm.mcmaster.ca
Laurel Trainor, Director, 905-525-9140, ext. 23007
trainorlab.mcmaster.ca

McMaster Institute for Polymer Production Technology (MIPPT)
1280 Main St. West, Hamilton, ON L8S 4L8
Tel: 905-525-9140
Archie E. Hamielec, Director, 905-525-9140, ext. 24950
hamielec@mcmaster.ca

McMaster Institute for Transportation & Logistics (MITL)
General Science Bldg.
#206, 1280 Main St. West, Hamilton, ON L8S 4K1
mitl@mcmaster.ca
mitl.mcmaster.ca
Other Information: 905-525-9140, ext. 22542
twitter.com/MITLnews
www.youtube.com/user/MITLresearch
Saiedeh N. Razavi, Director

McMaster Manufacturing Research Institute (MMRI)
John Hodgins Engineering Building
1280 Main St. West, Hamilton, ON L8S 4L7
Tel: 905-525-9140
mmri-admin@mcmaster.ca
www.eng.mcmaster.ca
www.facebook.com/McMasterMMRI
twitter.com/MMRI_McMaster
www.linkedin.com/company/9018948
www.instagram.com/mmri.mcmaster
Stephen Veldhuis, Director, 905-525-9140, ext. 27044
veldhu@mcmaster.ca
Jennifer Anderson, Administrator, 905-525-9140, ext. 24285
jeanders@mcmaster.ca

Stem Cell & Cancer Research Institute (SCC-RI)
Michael DeGroote Centre for Learning & Discovery
1280 Main St. West, Hamilton, ON L8S 4K1
Tel: 905-525-9140
sccri@mcmaster.ca
sccri.mcmaster.ca
twitter.com/McMasterSCCRI
Mick Bhatia, Director

Medical Imaging Informatics Research Centre at McMaster (MIIRC@M)
1280 Main St. West, Hamilton, ON L8S 4L8
Tel: 905-521-2100
www.miircam.ca
David A. Koff, Director
david.koff@miircam.ca
Jane Castelli, Project Manager
jane.castelli@miircam.ca

Michael G. DeGroote Institute for Infectious Disease Research
#2235, 1280 Main St. West, Hamilton, ON L8S 4K1
Tel: 905-525-9140; *Fax:* 905-528-5330
iidr@mcmaster.ca
iidr.mcmaster.ca
www.facebook.com/McMasterIIDR
twitter.com/McMasterIIDR
www.youtube.com/user/McMasterIIDR
Dr. Gerry Wright, Director
wrightge@mcmaster.ca
Gina Mannen, Managing Director
manneng@mcmaster.ca

Michael G. DeGroote Institute for Pain Research & Care
MDCL
#2101, 1280 Main St. West, Hamilton, ON L8S 4K1
Tel: 905-525-9140; *Fax:* 905-523-1224
fhs.mcmaster.ca/paininstitute
Dr. Norm Buckley, Scientific Director
buckleyn@mcmaster.ca

Offord Centre for Child Studies
1280 Main St. West, MIP 201A, Hamilton, ON L8S 4K1
Tel: 905-525-9140; *Fax:* 905-574-6665
Toll-Free: 888-541-5437
info@offordcentre.com
offordcentre.com
Ellen Lipman, Director
Deepa Mathew, Administrator, 905-525-9140, ext. 21513

Origins Institute (OI)
Arthur Bourns Building
#241, 1280 Main St. West, Hamilton, ON L8S 4M1
Tel: 905-525-9140; *Fax:* 905-546-1252
origins@mcmaster.ca
origins.mcmaster.ca
Note: Institute focused on the origins of the universe.
Paul Higgs, Director
higgsp@mcmaster.ca

Population Health Research Institute (PHRI)
237 Barton St. East, Hamilton, ON L8L 2X2
Tel: 905-521-2100
information@phri.ca
www.phri.ca
Dr. Salim Yusuf, Executive Director
yusufs@mcmaster.ca

Lewis & Ruth Sherman Centre for Digital Scholarship
Mills Memorial Library
1280 Main St. West, Hamilton, ON L8S 4L8
scdc@mcmaster.ca
scds.mcmaster.ca
Other Information: 905-525-9140, ext. 22077
Andrea Zeffiro, Academic Director, 905-525-9140, ext. 21901
zeffiroa@mcmaster.ca

Statistics Canada Research Data Centre
LR Wilson Hall
1280 Main St. West, 5th Fl., Hamilton, ON L8S 4L6
Tel: 905-525-9140
rdc@mcmaster.ca
rdc.mcmaster.ca
Michael Veall, Academic Director, 905-525-9140, ext. 23829
veall@mcmaster.ca

Steel Research Centre (SRC)
1280 Main St. West, Hamilton, ON L8S 4L8
Tel: 905-525-9140; *Fax:* 905-526-8404
www.eng.mcmaster.ca/mcmaster-steel-research-centre
Joe McDermid, Director, 905-525-9140, ext. 27476
mcdermi@mcmaster.ca

Surgical Outcomes Research Centre (SOURCE)
#202, 39 Charlton Ave. East, Hamilton, ON L8N 1Y3
Tel: 905-523-0019; *Fax:* 905-523-0229
www.fhs.mcmaster.ca/source
Dr. Achilleas Thoma, Director
athoma@mcmaster.ca

Thrombosis & Atherosclerosis Research Institute (TaARI)
David Braley Research Institute
237 Barton St. East, #C5-121, Hamilton, ON L8L 2X2
Tel: 905-521-2100; *Fax:* 905-575-2646
info@taari.ca
www.taari.ca
Annette Rosati, Administrator
annette.rosati@taari.ca

McMaster University Chaplaincy Centre
MUSC
#231, 1280 Main St. West, Hamilton, ON L8S 4L8
chaplain@mcmaster.ca
mcmasterchaplaincy.org
Other Information: 905-525-9140, ext. 24207

McMaster Automotive Resource Center (MARC)
McMaster Innovation Park
#105, 175 Longwood Rd. South, Hamilton, ON L8P 0A1
Tel: 905-667-5500; *Fax:* 905-667-5501
mcmasterinnovationpark.ca

Michael G. DeGroote Centre for Medicinal Cannabis Research (CMCR)
St. Joseph's Healthcare Hamilton
100 West 5th St., Hamilton, ON L8P 3R2
cmcr@mcmaster.ca
cannabisresearch.mcmaster.ca
Other Information: 905-525-9140, ext. 39492
Note: The Centre is dedicated to researching & understanding the medicinal value & potential risks associated with cannabis. The Centre examines the use of medicinal cannabis as treatment for chronic pain as well as anxiety. The Centre is a partnership between McMaster University, St. Joseph's Healthcare Hamilton, the Peter Boris Centre for Addictions Research and the Michael G. DeGroote School of Medicine.
Dr. James MacKillop, Director, 905-522-1155, ext. 39492
jmackill@mcmaster.ca
Dr. Jason Busse, Associate Director, 905-525-9140, ext. 21731
bussejw@mcmaster.ca

Hearst: Université de Hearst
P.O. Box 580
60, 9e rue, Hearst, ON P0L 1N0, Canada
Tél: 705-372-1781; *Téléc:* 705-362-7518
Ligne sans frais: 1-800-887-1781
www.uhearst.ca
www.facebook.com/uhearst
twitter.com/udehearst
www.youtube.com/user/UHearst
Full Time Equivalency: 139
Luc Bussières, Recteur
Marc Bédard, Vice-recteur

Campuses
Kapuskasing
75, rue Queen, Kapuskasing, ON P5N 1H5, Canada
Tél: 705-335-2626; *Téléc:* 705-335-3835
Other Information: 705-335-8561

Timmins
395, boul Thériault, Timmins, ON P4N 0A8, Canada
Tél: 705-267-2144; *Ligne sans frais:* 1-866-467-2144

Centres & Institutes
Centre d'archives de la Grande Zone
60, 9e rue, Hearst, ON P0L 1N0
Tél: 705-372-1781
www.uhearst.ca/archives
www.facebook.com/328927100844018
Danielle Coulombe, Responsable
danielle_coulombe@uhearst.ca

Kingston: Queen's University
99 University Ave., Kingston, ON K7L 3N6, Canada
Tel: 613-533-2000
admission@queensu.ca
www.queensu.ca
www.facebook.com/queensuniversity
twitter.com/queensu
www.linkedin.com/school/queen's-university
www.youtube.com/QueensUCanada
Full Time Equivalency: 25260 *Number of Employees:* 840 full time faculty; 425 clinical medicine faculty; 2,486 other faculty; 9,571 staff
James Leech, Chancellor
Dr. Patrick Deane, Principal & Vice-Chancellor
Sam Hiemstra, Rector

Dr. Mark Green, Provost & Vice-Principal (Academic)
Michael Fraser, Vice-Principal (University Relations)
Donna Janiec, Vice-Principal (Finance & Administration)
Kimberly Woodhouse, Vice-Principal (Research)
Lon Knox, Secretary of the University
S. Pinchin, Interim Registrar

Faculties
Faculty of Arts & Science
Dunning Hall
94 University Ave., Kingston, ON K7L 3N6
Tel: 613-533-2470; *Fax:* 613-533-2467
www.queens.ca/artsci
www.facebook.com/queensartsci
twitter.com/quartsci
www.instagram.com/quartsci
Enrollment: 10100 *Number of Employees:* 450 faculty
Barbara Crow, Dean, 613-533-2446
deanartsci@queensu.ca

Faculty of Education
Duncan McArthur Hall
511 Union St., Kingston, ON K7M 5R7
Tel: 613-533-6205; *Fax:* 613-533-6203
educstudentservices@queensu.ca
educ.queensu.ca
www.facebook.com/QueensEduc
twitter.com/QueensEduc
www.youtube.com/user/QueensEduc
Rebecca Luce-Kapler, Dean, 613-533-6000, ext. 77238
rebecca.luce-kapler@queensu.ca

Faculty of Engineering & Applied Science
Beamish-Munro Hall
#300, 45 Union St., Kingston, ON K7L 3N6
Tel: 613-533-2055; *Fax:* 613-533-6500
engineering.reception@queensu.ca
engineering.queensu.ca
www.facebook.com/QueensEngineer
twitter.com/queensengineer
www.instagram.com/queens_engineer
Enrollment: 25260 *Number of Employees:* 9,571
Kevin Deluzio, Dean, 613-533-2055, ext. 32055
engdean@queensu.ca

Faculty of Health Sciences
Decanal Office
18 Barrie St., Kingston, ON K7L 3N6
Tel: 613-533-2544
healthsci.queensu.ca
www.facebook.com/QueensUHealth
twitter.com/queensuhealth
www.instagram.com/queensuhealth
Dr. Richard Reznick, Dean
richard.reznick@queensu.ca

Faculty of Law
Macdonald Hall
128 Union St., Kingston, ON K7L 3N6
Tel: 613-533-2220; *Fax:* 613-533-6509
law.queensu.ca
www.facebook.com/queensulaw
twitter.com/queensulaw
www.linkedin.com/school/queen'slaw
www.instagram.com/queensulaw
Mark Waltersn, B.A., LLB, D.Phil, Dean, 613-533-6000, ext. 74324
mark.walters@queensu.ca

Schools
Dan School of Drama & Music
Harrison LeCaine Hall
39 Bader Ln., Kingston, ON K7L 3N6
Tel: 613-533-2066
info.danschool@queensu.ca
sdm.queensu.ca
Craig Walker, Director
craig.walker@queensu.ca

Queen's School of Computing
Queen's University, 557 Goodwin Hall
Kingston, ON K7L 2N8
Tel: 613-533-6050; *Fax:* 613-533-6513
cs.queensu.ca
www.facebook.com/QueensComputing
twitter.com/queenscomputing
Hossam Hassanein, Director, 613-533-6052
hossam@cs.queensu.ca

Queen's School of English (QSOE)
Duncan McArthur Hall
511 Union St., #B242, Kingston, ON K7M 5R7
Tel: 613-533-2472
soe@queensu.ca
www.queensu.ca/qsoe
www.facebook.com/qsoecanada
twitter.com/Queens_SoE
Karen Burkett, Associate Director, 613-533-6000, ext. 75531
karen.burkett@queensu.ca

School of Graduate Studies (SGS)
Gordon Hall
#425, 74 Union St., Kingston, ON K7L 3N6
Tel: 613-533-6100; *Fax:* 613-533-6015
grad.studies@queensu.ca
www.queensu.ca/sgs
www.facebook.com/queensgradstudy
twitter.com/queensgradstudy
www.linkedin.com/in/queensgradstudy
Fahim Quadir, Dean, 613-533-6100, ext. 36079
deansgsr@queensu.ca

School of Kinesiology & Health Sciences (SKHS)
SKHS Bldg.
28 Division St., Kingston, ON K7L 3N6
Tel: 613-533-2666; *Fax:* 613-533-2009
skhs.queensu.ca
www.facebook.com/SchoolOfKinesiologyAndHealthStudies
Kyra Pyke, Director

School of Nursing (SON)
Cataraqui Bldg.
92 Barrie St., Kingston, ON K7L 3N6
Tel: 613-533-2668; *Fax:* 613-533-6770
nursing@queensu.ca
nursing.queensu.ca
www.facebook.com/queensschoolofnursing
twitter.com/QueensuSON
www.linkedin.com/groups/8189529
www.instagram.com/queensnursing
Dr. Ema Snelgrove-Clarke, Director
erna.snelgroveclarke@queensu.ca

School of Policy Studies (SPS)
Robert Sutherland Hall
#301, 138 Union St., Kingston, ON K7L 3N6
Tel: 613-533-3020; *Fax:* 613-533-2135
policy@queensu.ca
queensu.ca/sps
www.facebook.com/queenssps
twitter.com/QueensSPS
Warren Mabee, Director, 613-533-3020
mabeew@queensu.ca

School of Rehabilitation Therapy
Louise D. Acton Bldg.
31 George St., Kingston, ON K7L 3N6
Tel: 613-533-6103; *Fax:* 613-533-6776
rehab@queensu.ca
www.rehab.queensu.ca
www.facebook.com/QueensSRT
twitter.com/QueensSRT
Marcia Finlayson, Director

School of Religion
Queen's University, Theological Hall
Kingston, ON K7L 3N6
Tel: 613-533-2109
school.of.religion@queensu.ca
queensu.ca/religion
www.facebook.com/queensreligion
Pamela Dickey Young, Interim Director, 613-533-6000, ext. 74324
youngpd@queensu.ca
Levanna Schonwandt, Departmental Administrator, 613-533-2109
lsb1@queensu.ca

School of Urban & Regional Planning (SURP)
Queen's University, Mackintosh-Corry Hall
Kingston, ON K7L 3N6
Tel: 613-533-6030; *Fax:* 613-533-6122
queensu.ca/surp
twitter.com/QueensSURP
Paul Treitz, Acting Head of Department, 613-533-2903
paul.treitz@queensu.ca

Smith School of Business
Goodes Hall
143 Union St., Kingston, ON K7L 3N6
Toll-Free: 877-533-2330
smith.research@queensu.ca
smith.queensu.ca
www.facebook.com/smithbusiness
twitter.com/smithbusiness
www.instagram.com/smithbusiness
Brenda Brouwer, Interim Dean, 613-533-2305, ext. 32305
brouwerb@queensu.ca

Department of French Studies
Kingston Hall
#300, 103 Stuart St., Kingston, ON K7L 3N6
Tel: 613-533-2090; *Fax:* 613-533-6522
french.undergradquestions@queensu.ca
www.queensu.ca/french
www.facebook.com/dept.french.studies
twitter.com/FrenchStudiesQU
Stéphane Inkel, Interim Director, 613-533-2083
inkels@queensu.ca

Centres & Institutes
Centre for International & Defence Policy (CIDP)
Robert Sutherland Hall
#403, 138 Union St., Kingston, ON K7L 3N6
Tel: 613-533-2381; *Fax:* 613-533-6885
cidp@queensu.ca
www.queensu.ca/cidp
twitter.com/QueensCIDP
Maureen Bartram, Administration Manager, 613-533-2381
m.bartram@queensu.ca

Canadian Institute for Military & Veteran Health Research
Kingston Hall
#301, 103 Stuart St., Kingston, ON K7L 3N6
Tel: 613-533-3329; *Fax:* 613-533-3405
www.cimvhr.ca
www.facebook.com/CIMVHR
twitter.com/CIMVHR_ICRSMV
Dr. David Pedlar, Scientific Director

Institute of Intergovernmental Relations (IIGR)
Robert Sutherland Hall
#412, 138 Union St., Kingston, ON K7L 3N6
Tel: 613-533-2080
iigr@queensu.ca
www.queensu.ca/iigr
www.facebook.com/168924363201700
twitter.com/IIGR_QueensU
Christian Leuprecht, Director, 613-533-2080
christian.leuprecht@queensu.ca
Mary Kennedy, Administrative Secretary
iigr@queensu.ca

Queen's Cancer Research Institute (QCRI)
#302, 10 Stuart St., Kingston, ON K7L 3N6
Tel: 613-533-6507
qcri.queensu.ca
www.facebook.com/qcri.queensu.ca
twitter.com/QueensCRI
David M. Berman, Director
bermand@queensu.ca

Queen's Centre for Energy and Power Electronics Research
Also known as: ePOWER
Walter Light Hall
#108, 19 Union St., Kingston, ON K7L 3N6
Tel: 613-533-3199; *Fax:* 613-533-3395
e.power@queensu.ca
www.queensu.ca/epower
Praveen Jain, Director
praveen.jain@queensu.ca

Health Services and Policy Research Institute (HSPRI)
Abramsky Hall
21 Arch St., 3rd Fl., Kingston, ON K7L 3N6
Tel: 613-533-6387; *Fax:* 613-533-6353
chspr@queensu.ca
healthsci.queensu.ca/research/hspri
Michael Green, Director
michael.green@dfm.queensu.ca

Centre for Law in the Contemporary Workplace (CLCW)
Macdonald Hall
128 Union St., #C521, Kingston, ON K7L 3N6
Tel: 613-533-6000
clcw@queensu.ca
clcw.queenslaw.ca/
www.youtube.com/QueensCLCW
Kevin Banks, Director, 613-533-6000, ext. 79244
banksk@queensu.ca

Centre for Neuroscience Studies (CNS)
Botterell Hall
18 Stuart St., Kingston, ON K7L 3N6
Tel: 613-533-6360; Fax: 613-533-6840
neuroscience.queensu.ca
www.facebook.com/QueensuCNS
twitter.com/QueensU_CNS

Roumen Milev, Director
roumen.milev@queensu.ca
Kelly Moore, Manager
kmm@queensu.ca

Centre for Studies in Primary Care (CSPC)
P.O. Box 8888
220 Bagot St., Kingston, ON K7L 5E9
Tel: 613-533-9300; Fax: 613-533-9302
familymedicine.queensu.ca/research/cspc
twitter.com/CSPC_QueensU

Susan Phillips, Director
susan.phillips@dfm.queensu.ca

Queen's - RMC Fuel Cell Research Centre (FCRC)
Nicol Hall
60 Union St., Kingston, ON K7L 3N6
Tel: 613-533-6579
www.fcrc.ca

Brant A. Peppley, Contact, 613-533-3247
brant.peppley@queensu.ca

GeoEngineering Centre
Ellis Hall, Queen's University
58 University Ave., Kingston, ON K7L 3N6
Fax: 613-533-2128
info@geoeng.ca
geoeng.ca
Other Information: 613-533-6000, ext. 78591
Greg Siemens, Executive Director, 613-541-6000, ext. 6396
greg.siemens@queensu.ca

Centre for Advanced Computing (CAC)
99 University Ave., Kingston, ON K7L 3N6
Tel: 613-533-2561
cac.admin@queensu.ca
cac.queensu.ca

Chris MacPhee, Interim Executive Director
chris.macphee@queensu.ca

John Deutsch Institute for the Study of Economic Policy (JDI)
Dunning Hall
#209, 94 University Ave., Kingston, ON K7L 3N6
Tel: 613-533-2294; Fax: 613-533-6025
jdi.queensu.ca

Christopher Cotton, Director
cotton@econ.queensu.ca

Southern African Research Centre (SARC)
99 University Ave., Kingston, ON K7L 3N6
Tel: 613-533-2000

Surveillance Studies Centre
Department of Sociology
Kingston, ON K7L 3N6
sscqueens.org
twitter.com/sscqueens
Note: Researches developments in surveillance technology.
David Lyon, Director, 613-533-6000, ext. 74489
lyond@queensu.ca

Sudbury Neutrino Observatory Laboratory (SNOLAB)
Creighton Mine #9
1039 Regional Rd. 24, Lively, ON P3Y 1N2
Tel: 705-692-7000; Fax: 705-692-7001
info@snolab.ca
snolab.ca

Nigel Smith, Executive Director
Blaire Flynn, Coordinator, Education & Outreach, 705-692-7000, ext. 2806
Blaire.Flynn@snolab.ca

Queen's University International Centre (QUIC)
Mitchell Hall
#208, 69 Union St, Kingston, ON K7L 3N6
Tel: 613-533-2604; Fax: 613-533-3159
quic@queensu.ca
quic.queensu.ca
www.facebook.com/quic.queensu.ca
twitter.com/quic
www.youtube.com/user/quicatqueens

Sultan Almajil, Director
sultan.almajil@queensu.ca

Centre for Teaching & Learning
Mackintosh-Corry Hall
68 University Ave., #F200, Kingston, ON K7L 3N6
Tel: 613-533-6428
ctl@queensu.ca
queensu.ca/ctl
twitter.com/queensCTL
Sue Fostaty Young, Director, 613-533-6000, ext. 78557
fostatys@queensu.ca

Human Mobility Research Centre (HMRC)
Kingston General Hospital
76 Stuart St., Kingston, ON K7L 2V7
Tel: 613-548-2430; Fax: 613-549-2529
hmrc@queensu.ca
www.queensu.ca/hmrc
Dr. Brian Amsden, Co-Director, Regenerative Medicine
Dr. Ryan Bicknell, Co-Director, Clinical Studies
Dr. Tim Bryant, Co-Director, Biomechanical Design, Rehabilitation & Ergonomic
Dr. James Stewart, Co-Director, Computer Assisted Therapies

Industrial Relations Centre (IRC)
275 Ontario St., 3rd Floor, Kingston, ON K7K 2X5
Tel: 613-533-6628; Toll-Free: 888-858-7838
irc@queensu.ca
irc.queensu.ca
www.facebook.com/QueensIRC
twitter.com/QueensIRC
www.linkedin.com/company/queens-university-irc
www.youtube.com/user/QueensIRC
Stephanie Noel, Director, 613-533-6000, ext. 77088
stephanie.noel@queensu.ca

Bader International Study Centre
Herstmonceux Castle
Hailsham, East Sussex BN27 1RN, UK
welcome@bisc.queensu.ac.uk
queensu.ca/bisc
Other Information: Phone: 44-1323-834444; Fax: 44-1323-834499
www.facebook.com/BaderISC
twitter.com/QueensBISC
www.linkedin.com/groups/3946625
www.instagram.com/QueensBISC
Hugh Horton, Vice-Provost

Community Outreach Centre
Duncan McArthur Hall
511 Union St., A342, Kingston, ON K7M 5R7
Tel: 613-533-6000
www.educ.queensu.ca/coc
Lynda Colgan, Contact, 613-533-6000, ext. 75553
colganl@queensu.ca

Ban Righ Centre
32 Bader Lane, Kingston, ON K7L 3N8
Tel: 613-533-2976
banrighcentre.queensu.ca
www.facebook.com/85116218998
twitter.com/banrighcentre
Susan Belyea, Director, 613-533-6000, ext. 74931
susan.belyea@queensu.ca

Kingston: Royal Military College of Canada (RMCC)
Collège militaire royal du Canada
P.O. Box 17000 Forces
Kingston, ON K7K 7B4
Tel: 613-541-6000; Fax: 613-542-3565
Toll-Free: 1-866-762-2672
liaison@rmc.ca
www.rmc-cmr.ca
twitter.com/CanadianForces
www.youtube.com/user/CanadianForcesVideos
Full Time Equivalency: 2180 Note: Individuals must be a Canadian citizen in possession of the necessary academic qualifications. Applicants must also be one of the following: an MOC ((Military Occupation Classification) qualified member of the Canadian Forces; an applicant for the Regular Officer Training Plan (ROTP) or the Reserve Entry Training Plan (RETP); an employee of the Department of National Defence; or the spouse of a member of the Canadian Forces.
Dr. H.J. Kowal, Principal
principals.office@rmc.ca
LGen Frederick Sutherland, Chair
Karl Michaud, Registrar, 613-541-6000, ext. 6302

Faculties
Continuing Studies
Grazia Scoppio, Dean, 613-541-6000, ext. 6845
scoppio-g@rmc.ca

Engineering
www.rmc-cmr.ca/en/faculty-engineering

D. Bouchard, CD, RMC, BEng, MEng, PhD,, Dean, 613-541-6000, ext. 6371

Graduate Studies & Research
Pat Heffernan, Dean
dgs-des@rmc.ca

Science
Gord Simons, BMath, MSc, PhD, Dean, 613-541-6000, ext. 6419

Social Sciences & Humanities
www.rmc-cmr.ca/en/faculty-social-sciences-humanities
James Denford, CD, BEng, MBA, PhD, Dean, 613-541-6000, ext. 6970
jim.denford@rmc.ca

London: Brescia University College
1285 Western Rd., London, ON N6G 1H2, Canada
Tel: 519-432-8353; Fax: 519-858-5137
brescia@uwo.ca
www.brescia.uwo.ca
www.facebook.com/BresciaUniversityCollege
twitter.com/bresciauc
www.linkedin.com/company/brescia-university-college
www.youtube.com/user/Bresciauniversityc
Note: A women's university affiliated with Western University

London: **Western University**
Also known as: University of Western Ontario
1151 Richmond St., London, ON N6A 3K7, Canada
Tel: 519-661-2111
www.uwo.ca
www.facebook.com/WesternUniversity
twitter.com/westernu
www.linkedin.com/company/westernuniversity
www.youtube.com/user/WesternUniversity
Full Time Equivalency: 34673 Number of Employees: 1,406 full time faculty; 2,465 full time staff
Alan Shepard, President & Vice-Chancellor, 519-661-3745
alan.shepard@uwo.ca
Andrew N. Hrymak, Provost & Vice-President, Academic, 519-661-3110
provostvpa@uwo.ca
Lynn Logan, Vice-President, Operations & Finance, 519-661-3114
llogan2@uwo.ca
Sarah Prichard, Acting Vice-President, Research, 519-661-3812
vpr@uwo.ca

Faculties
Faculty of Arts & Humanities
University College
#2220, 1151 Richmond St., London, ON N6A 3K7
Tel: 519-661-2111
arts@uwo.ca
www.uwo.ca/arts
www.facebook.com/westernuArts
twitter.com/westernuArts
www.youtube.com/user/ArtsUWO
Michael Milde, Dean
Jamy Brodt, Director of Administration
jbrodt@uwo.ca

Faculty of Education
1137 Western Rd., London, ON N6G 1G7
Tel: 519-661-2111; Fax: 519-850-2377
education@uwo.ca
edu.uwo.ca
www.facebook.com/westernuEdu
twitter.com/westernuedu
www.linkedin.com/groups/4413033
Kathy Hibbert, Acting Dean, 519-661-2111, ext. 88557
khibber2@uwo.ca
Pamela Bishop, Associate Dean, Graduate Programs, 519-661-2111, ext. 88879
pbishop@uwo.ca
Perry Klein, Associate Dean, Research, 519-661-2111, ext. 88872
pklein@uwo.ca

Faculty of Engineering
Spencer Engineering Bldg.
London, ON N6A 5B9
Tel: 519-661-2111; Fax: 519-661-3808
contactWE@eng.uwo.ca
eng.uwo.ca
www.facebook.com/westernEng
twitter.com/westernuEng
www.linkedin.com/school/westernueng
www.instagram.com/westernueng
Ken Coley, Dean

Faculty of Health Sciences
Arthur and Sonia Labatt Health Sciences Bldg.
#200, 1151 Richmond St., London, ON N6A 3K7
Tel: 519-661-2111
www.uwo.ca/fhs
www.facebook.com/fhswestern
twitter.com/westernuFHS

Jayne Garland, Dean
fhsdean@uwo.ca

Faculty of Information & Media Studies
FIMS & Nursing Bldg.
London, ON N6A 5B9
Tel: 519-661-3720; Fax: 519-661-3506
fims@uwo.ca
fims.uwo.ca
Other Information: 519-661-3542; Graduate Student Services:
519-661-4017
www.facebook.com/westernuFIMS
twitter.com/westernuFIMS
Number of Employees: 67
Lisa Henderson, Dean, 519-661-2111, ext. 84235
lhende44@uwo.ca

Faculty of Law
1151 Richmond St., London, ON N6A 3K7
Tel: 519-661-3346; Fax: 519-661-3790
law.uwo.ca
Other Information: 519-661-3352 (Legal Clinic)
www.facebook.com/westernuLaw
twitter.com/westernuLaw
Erika Chamberlain, Dean, 519-661-2111, ext. 80036
echambe@uwo.ca

Don Wright Faculty of Music
Talbot College
#210, 1151 Richmond St., London, ON N6A 3K7
music@uwo.ca
music.uwo.ca
Other Information: 519-661-2111, ext. 82043
www.facebook.com/westernuMusic
twitter.com/westernuMusic
Enrollment: 650
Betty Anne Younker, Dean, 519-661-4008, ext. 84008
byounker@uwo.ca
Megan Clements, Director of Administration, 519-661-2111, ext. 85348
mcleme22@uwo.ca

Faculty of Science
North Campus Bldg.
#240, 1151 Richmond St., London, ON N6A 5B7
Fax: 519-661-3703
science@uwo.ca
www.uwo.ca/sci
Other Information: 519-661-2111, ext. 89192
www.facebook.com/scibmsac
twitter.com/westernuScience
www.linkedin.com/company/westernuscience
www.youtube.com/user/westernuscience
Number of Employees: 1215
Matt Davison, Dean, 519-661-2111, ext. 83041
sciad@uwo.ca

Faculty of Social Science
Social Science Centre
London, ON N6A 5C2
Tel: 519-661-2053
social-science@uwo.ca
www.ssc.uwo.ca
www.facebook.com/westernussaco
twitter.com/westernuSocSci
Enrollment: 7160 Number of Employees: 235 full-time faculty
Joan Finegan, Acting Dean, 519-661-2053
socsi-dean@uwo.ca
Linda M Brock, Director of Administration, 519-661-2111, ext. 84956
lbrock@uwo.ca

Schools
School of Graduate & Postdoctoral Studies
1151 Richmond St., London, ON N6A 3K7
Tel: 519-661-2102
grad.uwo.ca

Enrollment: 5000
Linda Miller, Vice-Provost
grad-vp@uwo.ca
Ron Wagler, Director of Administration
ron.wagler@uwo.ca

Schulich School of Medicine & Dentistry
Clinical Skills Building
London, ON N6A 5C1
Tel: 519-661-3459
www.schulich.uwo.ca
www.facebook.com/SchulichMedicineAndDentistry
twitter.com/SchulichMedDent
Dr. John Yoo, Acting Dean

Ivey Business School
1255 Western Rd., London, ON N6G 0N1
Tel: 519-661-3206; Fax: 519-661-3485
ivey.uwo.ca
www.facebook.com/iveybusiness
twitter.com/iveybusiness
www.linkedin.com/school/ivey-business-school
www.instagram.com/iveybusiness
Number of Employees: 100 full-time faculty
Sharon Hodgson, Dean
shodgson@ivey.ca
Stephanie Brooks, Chief Administrative Officer
sbrooks@ivey.ca

Western Continuing Studies (WCO)
Citi Plaza
#240, 355 Wellington St., London, ON N6A 3N7
Tel: 519-661-3658
cstudies@uwo.ca
wcs.uwo.ca
www.facebook.com/westernuCS
twitter.com/westernucs
www.linkedin.com/groups/4206113
www.instagram.com/westernucs
Carolyn Young, Director

Affiliations
Brescia University College
1285 Western Rd., London, ON N6G 1H2
Tel: 519-432-8353; Fax: 519-858-5137
brescia@uwo.ca
www.brescia.uwo.ca
www.facebook.com/BresciaUniversityCollege
twitter.com/bresciauc
www.linkedin.com/company/brescia-university-college
Susan Mumm, Principal
bucprincipal@uwo.ca
Lauretta Frederking, Vice-Principal & Academic Dean,
519-432-8353, ext. 28363
bucdean@uwo.ca

Huron University College
1349 Western Rd., London, ON N6G 1H3
Tel: 519-438-7224; Fax: 519-438-3938
www.huronuc.on.ca
www.facebook.com/huronatwestern
twitter.com/huronatwestern
www.linkedin.com/school/huron-university
www.instagram.com/huronatwestern
Barry Craig, President, 519-438-7224, ext. 237
president@huron.uwo.ca
Jennifer Smuck, Institutional Support Assistant, 519-438-7224, ext. 871
jennifer.smuck@huron.uwo.ca

King's University College
266 Epworth Ave., London, ON N6A 2M3
Tel: 519-433-3491; Toll-Free: 800-265-4406
info@kings.uwo.ca
kings.uwo.ca
www.facebook.com/kingsatwestern
twitter.com/kingsatwestern
www.linkedin.com/school/kingsatwestern
www.instagram.com/kingsatwestern
Full Time Equivalency: 3100
David C. Malloy, Principal
Sauro Camiletti, Vice-Principal; Acedemic Dean, 519-433-3491, ext. 4303

Centres & Institutes
Alan G. Davenport Wind Engineering Group
Faculty of Engineering
London, ON N6A 5B9
Tel: 519-661-3338; Fax: 519-661-3339
info@blwtl.uwo.ca
www.blwtl.uwo.ca

Canadian Centre for Activity & Aging
1490 Richmond St., London, ON N6G 0J4
Tel: 519-661-1603; Fax: 519-661-1612
Toll-Free: 866-661-1603
ccaa@uwo.ca
www.uwo.ca/actage
www.facebook.com/actage
www.youtube.com/user/CCAAUWO

Clara Fitzgerald, Executive Director
cfitzge4@uwo.ca
J.B. Orange, Scientific Director
jborange@uwo.ca

Canadian Research Centre on Inclusive Education
1137 Western Rd., London, ON N6G 1G7
Tel: 519-661-2111
inclusiveeducationresearch.ca
www.facebook.com/westernuEdu
twitter.com/westernuEdu
www.linkedin.com/company/westernuedu
Jacqueline Specht, Director
jspecht@uwo.ca

Centre for the Study of Theory & Criticism
Stevenson Hall
#2157, 1151 Richmond St., London, ON N6A 5B8
Tel: 519-661-3442; Fax: 519-850-2927
theory@uwo.ca
uwo.ca/theory
www.facebook.com/theoryandcriticism
Allan Pero, Director, 519-661-2111, ext. 84705
apero@uwo.ca

Chemical Reactor Engineering Centre (CREC)
London, ON N6A 5B9
Tel: 519-661-2144; Fax: 519-850-2931
www.eng.uwo.ca/crec
Hugo de Lasa, Director, 519-661-2144
hdelasa@eng.uwo.ca

Geotechnical Research Centre
Spencer Engineering Bldg.
#3010C, 1151 Richmond St. North, Toronto, ON N6A 5B9
Tel: 519-661-3344
grcentre@uwo.ca
www.eng.uwo.ca/grc
Enrollment: 72
Cynthia Quintus, Coordinator, 519-661-3344
cquintus@eng.uwo.ca

International Centre for Olympic Studies (ICOS)
Health Science Bldg.
#335, 1151 Richmond St., London, ON N6A 5B9
Tel: 519-661-4113
www.uwo.ca/olympic
Angela Schneider, Director, 519-661-2111, ext. 88527
aschneid@uwo.ca

Robarts Imaging
Imaging Research Laboratories
1151 Richmond St. North, London, ON N6A 5B7
Tel: 519-931-5777; Fax: 519-931-5789
robarts.ca
Janet Wallace, Research Manager, 519-931-5240, ext. 25240
jwallace@robarts.ca

Museum of Ontario Archaeology
1600 Attawandaron Rd., London, ON N6G 3M6
Tel: 519-473-1360; Fax: 519-850-2363
info@archaeologymuseum.ca
www.archaeologymuseum.ca
www.facebook.com/ArchaeologyMuseum
twitter.com/MuseOntArch
www.linkedin.com/company/museum-of-ontario-archaeology
www.instagram.com/museontarch
Rhonda Bathurst, Executive Director
rhonda@archaeologymuseum.ca
Cindy Barrett, Administrative Officer
cindy@archaeologymuseum.ca
Ronald F. Williamson, President, Board of Directors

Lawrence National Centre for Policy & Management
Ivey Business School
1255 Western Rd., London, ON N6G 0N1
Tel: 519-661-4253; Fax: 519-661-4297
lawrence@ivey.ca
www.ivey.uwo.ca/lawrencecentre
Romel Mostafa, Director, 519-661-2111, ext. 84206
rmostafa@ivey.ca

Surface Science Western
P.O. Box 12
999 Collip Circle, #LL31, London, ON N6G 0J3
Tel: 519-661-2173; Fax: 519-661-3709
info@surfacesciencewestern.com
surfacesciencewestern.com
www.facebook.com/surfacesciencewestern
twitter.com/SurfSciWestern
www.linkedin.com/company/surface-science-western
www.youtube.com/user/ssw
Mark Biesinger, Director
biesingr@uwo.ca
Gary Good, Manager, Operations
ggood@uwo.ca

North Bay: Nipissing University
P.O. Box 5002
100 College Dr., North Bay, ON P1B 8L7
Tel: 705-474-3450; *Fax:* 705-474-1947
nuinfo@nipissingu.ca
www.nipissingu.ca
TTY: 877-688-5507
www.facebook.com/NipissingU
twitter.com/NipissingU
www.linkedin.com/school/nipissing-university
www.youtube.com/user/nipissinguniversity
Full Time Equivalency: 5077
Paul Cook, Chancellor
Mike DeGagné, President & Vice-Chancellor
Arja Vainio-Mattila, Provost & Vice-President, Academic &
Research
Cheryl Sutton, Vice-President, Finance & Administration
cheryls@nipissingu.ca

Faculties
Faculty of Arts & Science
Murat Tuncali, Dean
muratt@nipissingu.ca

Faculty of Applied and Professional Studies
Rick Vanderlee, Dean, 705-474-3450, ext. 4240
rickv@nipissingu.ca

Schools
School of Graduate Studies
Jim McAuliffe, Dean, Graduate Studies & Research,
705-474-3450, ext. 4293
jimmc@nipissingu.ca

Schulich School of Education
Carole Richardson, Dean of Education, 705-474-3450, ext. 4268
caroler@nipissingu.ca
Jessica McMillan, Administrator, 705-474-3450, ext. 4264
jessicam@nipissingu.ca

Campuses
Brantford Campus
50 Wellington St., Brantford, ON N3T 2L6
Tel: 519-752-1524; *Fax:* 519-752-8372
brant@nipissingu.ca

Oshawa: University of Ontario Institute of Technology (UOIT)
Also known as: Ontario Tech University
2000 Simcoe St. North, Oshawa, ON L1G 0C5, Canada
Tel: 905-721-8668; *Fax:* 905-721-3178
connect@ontariotechu.ca
ontariotechu.ca
www.facebook.com/ontariotechu
twitter.com/ontariotech_u
www.linkedin.com/school/ontariotech
www.youtube.com/c/OntarioTech
Full Time Equivalency: 10000 *Number of Employees:* 2,000+
Mitch Frazer, Chancellor
Steven Murphy, President & Vice-Chancellor
president@ontariotechu.ca
Lori Livingston, Provost & Vice-President, Academic
provost@ontariotechu.ca
Susan McGovern, Vice-President, External Relations,
905-721-8668, ext. 3135
susan.mcgovern@ontariotechu.ca
Craig Elliott, Chief Financial Officer, 905-721-8668, ext. 3393
craig.elliott@ontariotechu.ca
Cheryl A. Foy, Secretary & General Counsel, 905-721-8668, ext.
3174
cheryl.foy@ontariotechu.ca

Faculties
Business & Information Technology
Tel: 905-721-3190; *Fax:* 905-721-3167
fbit@uoit.ca
www.businessandit.uoit.ca
Pamela Ritchie, Ph.D., Dean, 905-721-8668, ext. 3077
pamela.ritchie@uoit.ca

Education
P.O. Box 385
11 Simcoe St. North, Oshawa, ON L1H 7L7
Tel: 905-721-3181; *Fax:* 905-721-1707
faculty-of-education@uoit.ca
education.uoit.ca
Michael Owen, Dean, 905-721-8668, ext. 5661
michael.owen@uoit.ca

Energy Systems & Nuclear Science
Tel: 905-721-8668; *Fax:* 905-721-3046
nuclear.uoit.ca
Akira Tokuhiro, Ph.D., Dean, 905-721-8668, ext. 3142
akira.tokuhiro@uoit.ca

Engineering & Applied Science
Tel: 905-721-8668
www.engineering.uoit.ca
Tarlochan Sidhu, Dean

Health Sciences
Science Bldg.
#3000, 2000 Simcoe St. North, Oshawa, ON L1H 7K4
Tel: 905-721-3166; *Fax:* 905-721-3179
connect@ontariotechu.ca
healthsciences.ontariotechu.ca
Bernadette Murphy, Interim Dean
bernadette.murphy@ontariotechu.ca

Office of Graduate Studies
#1400, 2000 Simcoe St. North, Oshawa, ON L1H 7K4
Tel: 905-721-8668; *Fax:* 905-721-3062
gradstudies@uoit.ca
gradstudies.uoit.ca
Langis Roy, Dean

Science
Tel: 905-721-3050; *Fax:* 905-721-3304
facultyofscience@uoit.ca
www.science.uoit.ca
Greg Crawford, Ph.D., Dean, 905-721-8668, ext. 3235
greg.crawford@uoit.ca

Social Sciences & Humanities
55 Bond St. East, Oshawa, ON L1H 7K4
Tel: 905-721-3234; *Fax:* 905-721-3372
SSH@uoit.ca
www.socialscienceandhumanities.uoit.ca
Peter Stoett, Dean, 905-721-8668, ext. 5856
peter.stoett@uoit.ca

Ottawa: Carleton University
1125 Colonel By Dr., Ottawa, ON K1S 5B6
Tel: 613-520-7400; *Fax:* 613-520-3847
www.carleton.ca
www.facebook.com/carletonuniversity
twitter.com/Carleton_U
www.youtube.com/user/carletonvideos
Full Time Equivalency: 31202 *Number of Employees:* 939
academic staff; 1167 staff; 810 contract instructors; 1823 TAs;
107 library staff
Yaprak Baltacioglu, Chancellor
Benoit-Antoine Bacon, President & Vice-Chancellor
Jerry Tomberlin, Provost & Vice-President, Academic,
613-520-2600, ext. 3806
jerry.tomberlin@carleton.ca

Faculties
Arts & Social Sciences
Paterson Hall
#330, 1125 Colonel By Dr., Ottawa, ON K1S 5B6
Tel: 613-520-2355; *Fax:* 613-520-4481
fassod@carleton.ca
www.carleton.ca/fass/
twitter.com/cu_fass
www.instagram.com/cu_fass
Enrollment: 9000 *Number of Employees:* 318 faculty and 68
administrative staff *Note:* Bachelor of Arts, Bachelor of Music,
Bachelor of Humanities, Bachelor of Arts Honours, Bachelor of
Arts Combined Honours, MA & PhD programs.
L. Pauline Rankin, Dean, 613-520-2355
paulinerankin@cunet.carleton.ca

Engineering & Design
The Minto Centre
#3010, 1125 Colonel By Dr., Ottawa, ON K1S 5B6
Tel: 613-520-5790; *Fax:* 613-520-7481
info_engdesign@carleton.ca
carleton.ca/engineering-design/
www.facebook.com/CarletonUniFED
twitter.com/CarletonU_Eng
www.instagram.com/carleton_fed
Enrollment: 7200 *Note:* Bachelor of Engineering, Bachelor of
Architectural Studies, Bachelor of Industrial Design, Bachelor of
Information Technology, & Bachelor of Media Production &
Design degrees.
Larry Kostiuk, Dean, 613-520-2600, ext. 3348
larry.kostiuk@carleton.ca

Graduate & Postdoctoral Affairs
Tory Building
#512, 1125 Colonel By Dr., Ottawa, ON K1S 5B6
Tel: 613-520-2525; *Fax:* 613-520-4049
graduate_studies@carleton.ca
gradstudents.carleton.ca
twitter.com/CUGradStudies
www.youtube.com/gradsatcarleton
Patrice Smith, Dean, 613-520-2518
patrice.smith@carleton.ca

Joanne Bree, Director, 613-520-2600, ext. 1464
joanne.bree@carleton.ca

Public Affairs
Loeb Building
1125 Colonel By Dr., #D391, Ottawa, ON K1S 5B6
Tel: 613-520-3741; *Fax:* 613-520-3742
odfpa@carleton.ca
www.carleton.ca/fpa/
www.facebook.com/cufpa
twitter.com/fpacarleton
Enrollment: 7500 *Number of Employees:* 200 faculty members
Note: Bachelor of Journalism, Bachelor of Social Work, Bachelor
of Public Affairs and Policy Management, and, run in tandem
with the Faculty of Arts and Social Sciences, the Bachelor of
Arts; as well as an array of MA and PhD programs, a Master of
Journalism, a Master of Social Work, and the Clayton H. Riddell
Graduate Program in Political Management.
André Plourde, Dean, 613-520-2600, ext. 1858

Science
Herzberg Laboratories, Carleton University
#3230, 1125 Colonel By Dr., Ottawa, ON K1S 5B6
Tel: 613-520-2600; *Fax:* 613-520-4389
odscience@carleton.ca
science.carleton.ca
www.facebook.com/carletonscience
twitter.com/carletonscience
www.linkedin.com/carletonscience
www.instagram.com/carletonscience
Enrollment: 3793 *Note:* Bachelor of Science - variety of
programs, Bachelor of Computer Science - variety of streams,
Bachelor of Health Sciences, Bachelor of Mathematics - variety
of programs, Master of Science , Master of Computer Science,
Master of Health: Science, Technology and Policy, Ph.D. in
Biology, Chemistry, Computer Science, Earth Sciences,
Mathematics, Neuroscience, or Physics.
Charles MacDonald, Dean

Schools
Azrieli School of Architecture & Urbanism
Architecture Building
#202, 1125 Colonel By Dr., Ottawa, ON K1S 5B6
Tel: 613-520-2855; *Fax:* 613-520-2849
architecture@carleton.ca
carleton.ca/architecture/
www.facebook.com/azrielischoolofarchitectureurbanism
twitter.com/carletonu_arch
www.instagram.com/carleton_architecture
Jill Stoner, Director, 613-520-2600, ext. 2862
jill.stoner@carleton.ca
Ellen Perrissoud, Administrative Coordinator, 613-520-2600, ext.
2895
ellen.perrissoud@carleton.ca

School for Studies in Art & Culture (SSAC)
St. Patrick's Building, Carleton University
#423, 1125 Colonel By Dr., Ottawa, ON K1S 5B6
Tel: 613-520-5606; *Fax:* 613-520-3575
ssac@carleton.ca
www.carleton.ca/ssac/
twitter.com/cuweb
Note: Departments of Art History, Film Studies, and Music joined
together to form the School for Studies in Art and Culture.
Brian Foss, Director, 613-520-2600, ext. 3791
brian.foss@carleton.ca
Kristin Guth, School Administrator, 613-520-2600, ext. 3993
kristin.guth@carleton.ca

School of Linguistics & Language Studies (SLALS)
Paterson Hall, Carleton University
#236, 1125 Colonel By Dr., Ottawa, ON K1S 5B6
Tel: 613-520-6612; *Fax:* 613-520-6641
www.carleton.ca/slals/
David Wood, School Director, 613-520-2600, ext. 6684
david_wood@carleton.ca
Tracey Wright, School Administrator, 613-520-2600, ext. 8256
tracey.wright@carleton.ca

Sprott School of Business
Dunton Tower, Carleton University
#810, 1125 Colonel By Dr., Ottawa, ON K1S 5B6
Tel: 613-520-2388; *Fax:* 613-520-2532
info@sprott.carleton.ca
sprott.carleton.ca
twitter.com/SprottSchool
www.linkedin.com/company/35438142
www.youtube.com/user/SprottSchoolCarleton
Enrollment: 2603 *Number of Employees:* 60 faculty members; 31
staff *Note:* Bachelor of Commerce, Bachelor of International
Business, Sprott MBA, PhD in Management, Professional
Programs
Dana Brown, Dean, 613-520-2600, ext. 2810
dana.brown@carleton.ca

Deborah Casselman-Jones, Manager of Operations, Dean's Office, 613-520-2600, ext. 3223
deborah.casselman@carleton.ca

School of Indigenous & Canadian Studies
Dunton Tower, Carleton University
#1206, 1125 Colonel By Dr., Ottawa, ON K1S 5B6
Tel: 613-520-2366; Fax: 613-520-3903
carleton.ca/sics
Note: BA degree in Canadian Studies; BA degree in Indigenous Studies; MA program or Ph.D. program that is run jointly with Trent University.
Anna Hoefnagels, Director, 613-520-2600, ext. 3737
anna.hoefnagels@carleton.ca

School of Computer Science (SCS)
5302 Herzberg Laboratories
1125 Colonel By Dr., Ottawa, ON K1S 5B6
Tel: 613-520-4333; Fax: 613-520-4334
carleton.ca/scs
Note: Undergraduate Programs, Master's degree in Computer Science (MCS), and Doctor in Philosophy (Ph.D) in Computer Science.
Michel Barbeau, Director, 613-520-2600
barbeau@scs.carleton.ca
Mylien Reid, School Administrator, 613-520-2600, ext. 5704
mylien.reid@scs.carleton.ca

Technology, Society, Environment Studies (TSES)
4442 Herzberg Laboratories
1125 Colonel By Dr., Ottawa, ON K1S 5B6
Tel: 613-520-2600; Fax: 613-520-3422
carleton.ca/tses
Dr. John Buschek, Director, 613-520-4483
john_buschek@carleton.ca
Michelle Santoianni, Administrator, 613-520-4461
michelle_santoianni@carleton.ca

School of Industrial Design (SID)
Mackenzie Building, Carleton University
#3470, 1125 Colonel By Dr., Ottawa, ON K1S 5B6
Tel: 613-520-5672; Fax: 613-520-4465
id@carleton.ca
carleton.ca/id
www.facebook.com/carletonSID
Note: Bachelor of Industrial Design, Master of Design
Bjarki Hallgrimsson, Director, 613-520-2600, ext. 5677
bjarki.hallgrimsson@carleton.ca
Anna Kim, Administrator, 613-520-2600, ext. 5591
anna.kim@carleton.ca

School of Information Technology (CSIT)
Azrieli Pavilion, Carleton University
#230, 1125 Colonel By Dr., Ottawa, ON K1S 5B6
Tel: 613-520-5644; Fax: 613-520-6623
info@csit.carleton.ca
www.csit.carleton.ca
Note: The school offers four undergraduate programs under the "Bachelor of Information Technology" in collaboration with Algonquin College; It offers one undergraduate degree under the "Bachelor of Media Production & Design" in collaboration with the School of Journalism
Dr. Chris Joslin, Director, 613-520-2600, ext. 1889
chris.joslin@carleton.ca
Hana Jabi, School Administrator, 613-520-2600, ext. 5644
hana.jabi@carleton.ca

School of Journalism & Communication (SJC)
Richcraft Hall
#4309, 1125 Colonel By Dr., Ottawa, ON K1S 5B6
Tel: 613-520-2600; Fax: 613-520-6690
journalism@carleton.ca
carleton.ca/sjc
www.facebook.com/jschoolcu
twitter.com/jschool_cu
www.instagram.com/jschool_cu
Enrollment: 1900 *Note:* Bachelor of Journalism and Bachelor of Arts in Communication Studies, Master of Journalism, Master of Arts in Communication, and PhD in Communication.
Melanie Leblanc, School Administrator, 613-520-2600, ext. 8469
melanie.leblanc@carleton.ca

Norman Paterson School of International Affairs (NPSIA)
Richcraft Hall
#5206, 1125 Colonel By Dr., Ottawa, ON K1S 5B6
Tel: 613-520-6655
international.affairs@carleton.ca
carleton.ca/npsia
twitter.com/cu_npsia
Note: Master of Arts in International Affairs and Juris Doctor degree (M.A./JD)., Ph.D. Program, Master of Infrastructure Protection and International Security (MIPIS)
Yiagadeesen Samy, Director, 613-520-2600, ext. 1218
yiagadeesen.samy@carleton.ca

Coleen Kornelsen, School Administrator, 613-520-2600, ext. 8067
coleen.kornelsen@carleton.ca

School of Public Policy & Administration (SPPA)
Richcraft Hall
#5224, 1125 Colonel By Dr., Ottawa, ON K1S 5B6
Tel: 613-520-2547; Fax: 613-520-2551
sppa@carleton.ca
carleton.ca/sppa
www.facebook.com/carletonuniversitysppa
twitter.com/carletonSPPA
www.linkedin.com/in/carleton-sppa-55aa4887
www.youtube.com/user/CarletonSPPA
Note: Doctoral degree in Public Policy and masters degree programs in Public Administration, Sustainable Energy Policy, and Philanthropy and Nonprofit Leadership
Graeme Auld, Director, 613-520-2600, ext. 2259
graeme.auld@carleton.ca
Meghan Innes, School Administration, 613-520-2600, ext. 6300
meghan.innes@carleton.ca

School of Social Work
Dunton Tower, Carleton University
#509, 1125 Colonel By Dr., Ottawa, ON K1S 5B6
Tel: 613-520-5601; Fax: 613-520-7496
carleton.ca/socialwork
Sarah Todd, Professor/Director, 613-520-2600, ext. 4498
sarah_todd@carleton.ca
Karen Spencer, School Administrator, 613-520-2600, ext. 5602
karen_spencer@carleton.ca

School of Mathematics & Statistics
Herzberg Laboratories, Carleton University
#4302, 1125 Colonel By Dr., Ottawa, ON K1S 5B6
Tel: 613-520-2600; Fax: 613-520-3536
ms-staff@math.carleton.ca
www.carleton.ca/math
Note: Joint graduate program with the University of Ottawa.
Paul Mezo, Director, 613-520-2600, ext. 2156
ms-dir@math.carleton.ca
Tracie Barkley, Acting School Administrator, 613-520-2600, ext. 2152
tracie.barkley@carleton.ca

Institute for Comparative Studies in Literature, Art & Culture (ICSLAC)
St. Patrick's Building, Carleton University
#201, 1125 Colonel By Dr., Ottawa, ON K1S 5B6
Tel: 613-520-2177; Fax: 613-520-2564
icslac@carleton.ca
www.carleton.ca/icslac
Pascal Gin, Director, 613-520-2600, ext. 1308
pascal.gin@carleton.ca
Dawn Schmidt, Administrator, 613-520-2177
Dawn.Schmidt@carleton.ca

Institute of African Studies (IAS)
Paterson Hall, Carleton University
#439, 1125 Colonel By Dr., Ottawa, ON K1S 5B6
Tel: 613-520-2600; Fax: 613-520-2363
african_studies@carleton.ca
www.carleton.ca/africanstudies
www.facebook.com/180779781960983
twitter.com/ias_carleton
www.youtube.com/user/iasatcarletonu
Note: At the undergraduate level, it provides a Combined Honours and a General program in African Studies in the bachelor of Art (BA) degree, and Honours and a General program in Africa and Globaization in the Bachelor of Global and International Studies (BGInS) degree, and a Minor program in African Studies open to all Collaborative Masters in African Studies. At the graduate level, it offers a Collaborative Masters in African Studies.
Christine Duff, Interim Director, 613-520-2600, ext. 2170
christine_duff@carleton.ca
June C. Payne, Institute Administrator, 613-520-2600, ext. 2220
june_payne@carleton.ca

Institute of Cognitive Science
Dunton Tower, Carleton University
#2221, 1125 Colonel By Dr., Ottawa, ON K1S 5B6
Tel: 613-520-2600
ics@cunet.carleton.ca
www.carleton.ca/ics
www.facebook.com/groups/InstCogSci
twitter.com/CogSciCU
www.linkedin.com/company/10612521
Note: Offers Bachelors, Masters, PBD, and Ph.D. degrees in Cognitive Science
Dr. Jo-Anne LeFevre, Director, 613-520-2600, ext. 2693
jo-anne.lefevre@carleton.ca

Melissa Lett, Main Office & Undergraduate Administrator, 613-520-2600, ext. 2522
melissa.lett@carleton.ca

Institute of Interdisciplinary Studies
Dunton Tower
#1315, 1125 Colonel By Dr., Ottawa, ON K1S 5B6
Tel: 613-520-2368; Fax: 613-520-2301
iis@carleton.ca
www.carleton.ca/iis
twitter.com/IISCarleton
Note: The home of two interdisciplinary programs of study: Childhood and Youth Studies (CHST) and Human Rights and Social Justice (HUMR)
Julie C. Garlen, Co-Director, 613-520-2600, ext. 6044
julie.garlen@carleton.ca
Paul Mkandawire, Co-Director, 613-520-2600, ext. 3101
paul.mkandawire@carleton.ca

Pauline Jewett Institute of Women's & Gender Studies (PJIWGS)
Dunton Tower, Carleton University
#1401, 1125 Colonel By Dr., Ottawa, ON K1S 5B6
Tel: 613-520-6645
lanakeon@cunet.carleton.ca
www.carleton.ca/womensstudies
twitter.com/ccefjcws
www.instagram.com/ccefjcws
Note: Houses the Carleton University - University of Ottawa Joint Chair in Women's Studies.
Ann Cvetkovich, Director, 613-520-2600, ext. 1122
anncvetkovich@cunet.carleton.ca
Lana Keon, Institute Administrator, 613-520-6645
lana.keon@carleton.ca

Institute of Criminology & Criminal Justice
Loeb Building, Carleton University
1125 Colonel By Dr., #C562, Ottawa, ON K1S 5B6
Tel: 613-520-2588; Fax: 613-520-6654
criminology@carleton.ca
www.carleton.ca/criminology
Note: Undergraduate degree in Criminology and Criminal Justice
Nicolas Carrier, Director, 613-520-2600, ext. 4488
Nicolas.Carrier@carleton.ca
Robin Dunbar, Institute Administrator, 613-520-2600, ext. 3767
Robin.Dunbar@carleton.ca

Institute of European, Russian & Eurasian Studies
Richcraft Hall, Carleton University
#3304, 1125 Colonel By Dr., Ottawa, ON K1S 5B6
Tel: 613-520-2600; Fax: 613-520-7501
www.carleton.ca/eurus
www.facebook.com/EURUSCarletonU
twitter.com/EURUSCarletonU
www.linkedin.com/groups/5177876
www.instagram.com/eurus_carleton
Note: Offers a BA degree, an MA degree, a specialization on "Europe and Russia in the World" in the Bachelor of Global and International Studies (BGInS), and a Graduate Diploma (GDip) in European Integration Studies
Jeff Sahadeo, Director, 613-520-2600, ext. 2996
jeff.sahadeo@carleton.ca
Krysia Kotarba, Institute Administrator, 613-520-2600, ext. 2888
krysia.kotarba@carleton.ca

Institute of Political Economy
Dunton Tower, Carleton University
#1501, 1125 Colonel By Dr., Ottawa, ON K1S 5B6
Tel: 613-520-7414; Fax: 613-520-2154
political_economy@carleton.ca
carleton.ca/politicaleconomy
www.facebook.com/PECOCarleton
Note: Offers five different graduate degrees
Cristina Rojas, Director, 613-520-2600, ext. 8858
cristina.rojas@carleton.ca
Donna Coghill, Institute Administrator
donna.coghill@carleton.ca

Institute of Biochemistry
Nesbitt Biology Building, Carleton University
#209, 1125 Colonel By Dr., Ottawa, ON K1S 5B6
Tel: 613-520-2478; Fax: 613-520-3539
biochem@carleton.ca
www.carleton.ca/biochem
Enrollment: 200 *Number of Employees:* 20 faculty members, administrative staff members, 2 lab coordinators
Bruce McKay, Director, 613-520-2600, ext. 3265
bruce.mckay@carleton.ca
Sarah Anne Szaboth, Department Administrator, 613-520-2600, ext. 3892
sarahanne.szaboth@carleton.ca

Institute of Environmental Science
Herzberg Laboratories
#4442, 1125 Colonel By Dr., Ottawa, ON K1S 5B6
Tel: 613-520-2600
carleton.ca/environmentalscience
twitter.com/carletonIEIS
Michelle Santoianni, Administrator, 613-520-2600, ext. 4461
michelle.santoianni@carleton.ca
Steven Cooke, Director, 613-520-2600, ext. 4377
steven.cooke@carleton.ca

Integrated Science Institute
4442 Herzberg Laboratories
1125 Colonel By Dr., Ottawa, ON K1S 5B6
Tel: 613-520-2600
isi.carleton.ca
Note: No longer acceping applications. The last admission was in 2013.
Julia Wallace, Director
julia.wallace@carleton.ca
Michelle Santoianni, Administrator
michelle.santoianni@carleton.ca

Centres & Institutes
Carleton Centre for Community Innovation (3CI)
Dunton Tower
#2104, 1125 Colonel By Dr., Ottawa, ON K1S 5B6
Tel: 613-520-2600
ccci@carleton.ca
www.carleton.ca/3ci
twitter.com/3ci_CU
Note: A reserch centre based at the School of Public Policy and Administration at Carleton University
Frances Abele, Academic Director, 613-520-2600, ext. 2553
frances_abele@carleton.ca

Carleton Centre for Public History (CCPH)
Paterson Hall
#400, 1125 Colonel By Dr., Ottawa, ON K1S 5B6
carleton.ca/ccph
David Dean, Co-Director
david.dean@carleton.ca
John C. Walsh, Co-Director
john_walsh@carleton.ca

Carleton Immersive Media Studio (CIMS)
Visualization & Simulation Bldg.
1125 Colonel By Dr., 4th Fl., Ottawa, ON K1S 5B6
Tel: 613-520-2600
info@cims.carleton.ca
www.cims.carleton.ca
www.facebook.com/thecimslab
twitter.com/thecimslab
www.instagram.com/thecimslab
Note: Affiliated with the Azrieli School of Architecture and Urbanism in the Faculty of Engineering and Design.
Stephen Fai, Director

Carleton Sustainable Energy Research Centre (CSERC)
1125 Colonel By Dr., Ottawa, ON K1S 5B6
Tel: 613-520-2600
www.carleton.ca/cserc
Note: CSERC work to integrate work in sustainable energy done by the Faculty of Engineering and Design and the Faculty of Public Administration, together with other faculties in the sciences, social sciences, economic and business.
James Meadowcroft, Academic Director
james.meadowcroft@carleton.ca

Centre for Conflict Education & Research (CCER)
1125 Colonel By Dr., Ottawa, ON K1S 5B6
Tel: 613-520-2600
www.carleton.ca/ccer
Neil Sargent, Director, 613-520-2600, ext. 8853

Centre for European Studies (CES)
Dunton Tower
#1104, 1125 Colonel By Dr., Ottawa, ON K1S 5B6
Tel: 613-520-2600; *Fax:* 613-520-7483
ces@carleton.ca
www.carleton.ca/ces
www.facebook.com/groups/142734875742998
twitter.com/Cen4EUStudies
Joan DeBardeleben, Co-Director, 613-520-2600, ext. 2886
joan.debardeleben@carleton.ca
Achim Hurrelmann, Co-Director, 613-520-2600, ext. 2294
achim.hurrelmann@carleton.ca
Cathleen Schmidt, Project Manager, 613-520-2600, ext. 1087
cathleen.schmidt@carleton.ca

Centre for Indigenous Research, Culture, Language & Education (CIRCLE)
1125 Colonel By Dr., Ottawa, ON K1S 5B6
circle@carleton.ca
carleton.ca/circle
www.facebook.com/people/Circle-Carleton/100013677578567
Miranda Brady, Co-Director
miranda.brady@carleton.ca
Anna Hoefnagels, Co-Director
anna.hoefnagels@carleton.ca
Kahente Horn-Miller, Co-Director
kahente.hornmiller@carleton.ca
John M.H. Kelly, Co-Director
john.kelly@carleton.ca

Centre for International Migration & Settlement Studies (CIMSS)
2106 Dunton Tower
1125 Colonel By Dr., Ottawa, ON K1S 5B6
Tel: 613-520-2717; *Fax:* 613-520-3676
cimss@carleton.ca
www.carleton.ca/cimss
Adnan Türegün, Executive Director

Centre for Research on Inclusion at Work (CRIW)
Dunton Tower
#322, 1125 Colonel By Dr., Ottawa, ON K1S 5B6
Tel: 613-520-2650
criw@carleton.ca
carleton.ca/criw
Note: A research centre at the Sprott School of Business, focused on conducting and sharing research that advances diversity, equity and inclusion at work.
Luciara Nardon, Co-Director, 613-520-2600, ext. 1802
luciara.nardon@carleton.ca
Merridee Bujaki, Co-Director, 613-520-2600, ext. 2774
merridee.bujaki@carleton.ca

Centre for Trade Policy & Law (CTPL)
Dunton Tower
#2115, 1125 Colonel By Dr., 21st Fl., Ottawa, ON K1S 5B6
Tel: 613-520-6696; *Fax:* 613-520-3981
carleton.ca/ctpl
Phil Rourke, Executive Director, 613-520-2600, ext. 6706
phil.rourke@carleton.ca

Centre for Transnational Cultural Analysis (CTCA)
St. Patrick's Building
#201, 1125 Colonel By Dr., Ottawa, ON K1S 5B6
Tel: 613-520-2600
ctca@carleton.ca
www.carleton.ca/ctca
Note: A research hub based within the Institute for Comparative Studies in Literature, Art and Culture (ICSLAC) at Carleton University.

Centre on Values and Ethics (COVE)
1125 Colonel By Dr., Ottawa, ON K1S 5B6
www.carleton.ca/cove
Stephen Maguire, Executive Director
stephen.maguire@carleton.ca

Geomatics and Cartographic Research Centre (GCRC)
1125 Colonel By Dr., Ottawa, ON K1S 5B6
Tel: 613-520-2600
gcrc.carleton.ca
Note: Research centre in the Department of Geography and Environmental Studies, whose research focuses on the application of geographic information aprocessing and the presentation of socioeconomic data in new and innovative cartographic forms
Fraser Taylor, Director, 613-520-2600, ext. 8232
fraser.taylor@carleton.ca
Amos Hayes, Technical Manager, 613-520-2600, ext. 8179
ahayes@carleton.ca

Max & Tessie Zelikovitz Centre for Jewish Studies
Paterson Hall
#225, 1125 Colonel By Dr., Ottawa, ON K1S 5B6
Tel: 613-520-2600
jewish.studies@carleton.ca
www.carleton.ca/jewishstudies
www.facebook.com/ZelikovitzCentre
twitter.com/ZelikovitzC
Deidre Butler, Director, 613-520-2600, ext. 8106
deidre.butler@carleton.ca
Susan Landau-Chark, Associate Director, 613-520-2600, ext. 1320
prof.sjilc@zoho.com

Ottawa Medical Physics Institute (OMPI)
ompi_aao@physics.carleton.ca
www.physics.carleton.ca/ompi
Dr. Malcolm McEwen, Executive Director
malcolm.mcewen@nrc-cnrc.gc.ca

Ottawa-Carleton Bridge Research Institute (OCBRI)
Minto Building
#3010, 1125 Colonel By Dr., Ottawa, ON K1S 5B6
Tel: 613-520-2600
David Lau, Director, 613-520-2600, ext. 7473
david.lau@carleton.ca

Canadian Health Adaptations, Innovations, & Mobilization Centre (CHAIM)
2304 Health Sciences Building
1125 Colonel By Dr., Ottawa, ON K1S 5B6
Tel: 613-520-2600
carleton.ca/chaimcentre
twitter.com/CHAIM_Centre

Visualization and Simulation Centre (VSIM)
1125 Colonel By Dr., Ottawa, ON K1S 5B6
www.carleton.ca/vsim
Other Information: 613-520-2600, ext. 2496

Center for Applied Cognitive Research (CACR)
B550 Loeb Bldg.
1125 Colonel By Dr., Ottawa, ON K1S 5B6
Tel: 613-520-2600; *Fax:* 613-520-3515
www.carleton.ca/cacr
Jo-Anne LeFevre, Director, 613-520-2600, ext. 4574
jlefevre@connect.carleton.ca

Centre for Indigenous Initiatives
Paterson Hall
#228, 1125 Colonel By Dr., Ottawa, ON K1S 5B6
Tel: 613-520-2600; *Fax:* 613-520-4037
indigenous@carleton.ca
carleton.ca/indigenous
www.facebook.com/cuindigenous
twitter.com/CUIndigenous
Benny Michaud, Assistant Director of Equity Services, 613-520-2600, ext. 1787
benny.michaud@carleton.ca

Discovery Centre
MacOdrum Library, 4th Fl.
1125 Colonel By Dr., Ottawa, ON K1S 5B6
Tel: 613-520-2600; *Fax:* 613-520-2600
discovery.centre@carleton.ca
carleton.ca/discoverycentre
www.facebook.com/CarletonUniversityDiscoveryCentre
twitter.com/CU_Discovery
www.instagram.com/cu_discovery
Alan Steele, Director, 613-520-2600, ext. 1504
Aleksandra Minic, Discovery Centre Coordinator, 613-520-2600, ext. 1503
aleksandra.minic@carleton.ca

Carleton Technology & Training Centre
Carleton Technology and Training Centre
1125 Colonel By Dr., Ottawa, ON K1S 5B6
Tel: 613-520-2600

Minto Centre for Advanced Studies in Engineering
1125 Colonel By Dr., Ottawa, ON K1S 5B6
Tel: 613-520-2600

Educational Development Centre (EDC)
Dunton Tower
#410, 1125 Colonel By Dr., Ottawa, ON K1S 5B6
Tel: 613-520-4433; *Fax:* 613-520-4456
edc@carleton.ca
carleton.ca/edc
twitter.com/CU_Teaching
Note: Provides a range of pedgogical and technological teaching tools and resources to faculty, instructors and teaching assistants.
Jaymie Koroluk, Assistant Director, 613-520-2600, ext. 3118
jaymie.koroluk@carleton.ca

Centre for Initiatives in Education (CIE)
Dunton Tower
#1516, 1125 Colonel By Dr., Ottawa, ON K1S 5B6
Tel: 613-520-2804; *Fax:* 613-520-2515
cie@carleton.ca
www.carleton.ca/cie
twitter.com/carleton_u
Note: Offers accessibility and learning support to individuals from a variety of non-traditional educational backgrounds who experience barriers entering into university for reasons of GPA, learning needs, and former educational experiences
Petra Watzlawik-Li, Director, 613-520-2600, ext. 3740
petra.watzlawikli@carleton.ca

National Wildlife Research Centre
1125 Colonel By Dr., Ottawa, ON K1S 5B6
Tel: 613-520-2600

Canada-India Centre for Excellence in Science, Technology, Trade & Policy (CICE)
Richcraft Hall
#1401R-F, 1125 Colonel By Dr., Ottawa, ON K1S 5B6
Tel: 613-520-2600
india@carleton.ca
www.carleton.ca/india
www.facebook.com/cice.carleton.3
twitter.com/CanadaIndia_CA
Michael Weatherhead, Manager, 613-520-2600, ext. 7873

Ottawa: Dominican University College
Collège Universitaire Dominicain
Also known as: Dominican College of Philosophy & Theology
96 Empress Ave., Ottawa, ON K1R 7G3, Canada
Tel: 613-233-5696; *Fax:* 613-233-6064
info@dominicanu.ca
www.dominicanu.ca
www.facebook.com/DUCOttawa
twitter.com/DUCOttawa

Full Time Equivalency: 2115
André Descôteaux, Chancellor
Maxime Allard, President
Peter Foy, Vice-President, Finance & Administration
Francis Peddle, Vice-President, Academic Affairs
Michel Gourgues, Vice-President, Regent of Studies

Ottawa: Saint Paul University
Université Saint-Paul
223 Main St., Ottawa, ON K1S 1C4, Canada
Tel: 613-236-1393; *Fax:* 613-782-3005
Toll-Free: 1-800-637-6859
www.ustpaul.ca
www.facebook.com/UniversiteSaintPaulUniversity
twitter.com/ustpaul_ca
www.linkedin.com/school/saint-paul-university-cp
www.youtube.com/user/uspottawa

Full Time Equivalency: 820
Chantal Beauvais, Rector
rectrice-rector@ustpaul.ca
Jean-Marc Barrette, Vice-Rector, Academic & Research
jmbarrette@ustpaul.ca
Normand Beaulieu, Vice-Rector, Administration
nbeaulieu@ustpaul.ca

Faculties
Canon Law
canonlaw@ustpaul.ca
ustpaul.ca/canon-law.php
John Renken, Dean
doyendcadean@ustpaul.ca

Faculty of Human Sciences
Tel: 613-236-1393; *Toll-Free:* 800-637-6859
info@ustpaul.ca
ustpaul.ca
Lorraine Ste-Marie, Interim Dean
doyenfsh@ustpaul.ca

Philosophy
info@ustpaul.ca
ustpaul.ca/philosophy
Manal Guirguis-Younger, Dean
doyenfsh@ustpaul.ca

Theology
theology@ustpaul.ca
ustpaul.ca/theology
Yvan Mathieu, Dean
ymathieu@ustpaul.ca

Centres & Institutes
Sophia Research Centre
223 Main St., Ottawa, ON K1S 1C4
Tel: 613-236-1393
ustpaul.ca

Research Centre for the Religious History of Canada
223 Main St., Ottawa, ON K1S 1C4
Tel: 613-236-1393
ustpaul.ca

Ottawa: University of Ottawa
Université d'Ottawa
Also known as: uOttawa
75 Laurier Ave. East, Ottawa, ON K1N 6N5, Canada
Tel: 613-562-5700; *Fax:* 613-562-5323
Toll-Free: 1-877-868-8292
www.uottawa.ca
www.facebook.com/uottawa
twitter.com/uottawa
www.linkedin.com/school/uottawa
www.youtube.com/uOttawa

Full Time Equivalency: 41900 *Number of Employees:* 3187 academic staff; 3043 support staff
Calin Rovinescu, Chancellor
Jacques Frémont, President & Vice-Chancellor
Jill Scott, Provost & Vice-President, Academic
Sylvain Charbonneau, Vice-President, Research
Jacline Nyman, Vice-President, External Relations
Annick Bergeron, Secretary-General

Faculties
Arts
Simard Hall
60 University, Ottawa, ON K1N 6N5
Tel: 613-562-5134
arts@uottawa.ca
arts.uottawa.ca
Other Information: Graduate Studies: 613-562-5439
Kevin Kee, Dean
deanarts@uottawa.ca

Civil Law
Fauteux Hall
57 Louis-Pasteur St., Ottawa, ON K1N 6N5
Tel: 613-562-5162; *Fax:* 613-562-5337
Toll-Free: 877-967-5352
dcivil@uottawa.ca
droitcivil@uottawa.ca
Céline Lévesque, Dean

Common Law
Fauteux Hall
57 Louis Pasteur St., Ottawa, ON K1N 6N5
Tel: 613-562-5794; *Fax:* 613-562-5124
clawgen@uottawa.ca
commonlaw.uottawa.ca
Adam Dodek, Dean

Education
#143, 145 Jean-Jacques-Lussier Private, Ottawa, ON K1N 6N5
Tel: 613-562-5804; *Fax:* 613-562-5963
Toll-Free: 800-860-8577
education@uottawa.ca
www.facebook.com/uOttawaEducation
twitter.com/uOttawaEdu
Richard Barwell, Dean

Engineering
800 King Edward Ave., Ottawa, ON K1N 6N5
Tel: 613-562-5918; *Fax:* 613-562-5187
bacinfo@engineering.uottawa.ca
engineering.uottawa.ca
Jacques Beauvais, Dean

Graduate & Postdoctoral Studies
75 Laurier Ave. East, Ottawa, ON K1N 6N5
www.uottawa.ca/graduate-studies
Claire Turenne Sjolander, Vice-Provost
viceprovost-gps@uottawa.ca

Health Sciences
Montpetit Hall
#232, 125 University, Ottawa, ON K1N 6N5
Tel: 613-562-5853; *Toll-Free:* 877-868-8292
healthsc@uottawa.ca
health.uottawa.ca
Lucie Thibault, Dean

Medicine
451 Smyth Rd., Ottawa, ON K1H 8M5
Tel: 613-562-5800
infomed@uottawa.ca
med.uottawa.ca
Dr. Bernard Jasmin, Dean
jasmin@uottawa.ca

Science
Gendron Hall
30 Marie Curie, Ottawa, ON K1N 6N5
Tel: 613-562-5727; *Fax:* 613-562-5274
infosci@uottawa.ca
science.uottawa.ca
Other Information: Graduate Studies: 613-562-5800
Louis Barriault, Dean

Social Sciences
Social Sciences Building
120 University Private, Ottawa, ON K1N 6N5
Tel: 613-562-5709; *Fax:* 613-562-5311
socialsciences@uottawa.ca
socialsciences.uottawa.ca
Other Information: Graduate Studies: 613-562-5732
Maurice Lévesque, Interim Dean
doyenfssdean@uottawa.ca

Schools
Official Languages and Bilingualism Institute (OLBI)
#130, 70 Laurier Ave. East, Ottawa, ON K1N 6N5
Tel: 613-562-5743; *Fax:* 613-562-5126
olbi@uottawa.ca
www.olbi.uottawa.ca
Jérémie Séror, Director
jseror@uottawa.ca

Teffler School of Management
55 Laurier Ave. East, Ottawa, ON K1N 6N5
Tel: 613-562-5731
info@telfer.uottawa.ca
www.telfer.uottawa.ca
www.facebook.com/Telfer.uOttawa
twitter.com/Telfer_uOttawa
www.youtube.com/user/TelferSchool
Enrollment: 4200 *Number of Employees:* 200 *Note:* Degree programs in business and healthcare management.
François Julien, Dean, 613-562-5800, ext. 5815
julien@telfer.uOttawa.ca

Peterborough: Trent University
1600 West Bank Dr., Peterborough, ON K9J 0G2, Canada
Tel: 705-748-1011; *Toll-Free:* 1-855-698-7368
communications@trentu.ca
www.trentu.ca
www.facebook.com/trentuniversity
twitter.com/TrentUniversity
www.linkedin.com/company/trent-university
www.youtube.com/user/trentUniversity

Full Time Equivalency: 8940
Stephen Stohn, Chancellor
Leo Groarke, President
Jacqueline Muldoon, Provost & Vice-President, Academic
Julie Davis, Vice-President, External Relations & Advancement
Neil Emery, Vice-President, Research & Innovation
Kent Stringham, Acting Vice-President, Finance & Administration

Centres & Institutes
Frost Centre for Canadian Studies & Indigenous Studies
Kerr House, Trail College
#103, 299 Dublin St., Peterborough, ON K9H 7P4
Tel: 705-748-1750; *Fax:* 705-748-1801
frostcentre@trentu.ca
www.trentu.ca/frostcentre
twitter.com/TrentFrostCtr
Heather Nicol, Acting Director
heathernicol@trentu.ca

Trent University Archaeological Research Centre (TUARC)
c/o Department of Anthropology & Archaeology
1600 West Bank Dr., Peterborough, ON K9L 0G2
Tel: 708-748-1011; *Fax:* 705-748-1613
tuarc@trentu.ca
www.trentu.ca/tuarc
Eugene Morin, Director
eugenemorin@trentu.ca

Water Quality Centre (WQC)
1600 West Bank Dr., Peterborough, ON K9L 0G2
Tel: 705-748-1011
www.trentu.ca/wqc
Hayla Evans, Business Manager
hevans@trentu.ca

St Catharines: Brock University
1812 Sir Isaac Brock Way, St Catharines, ON L2S 3A1
Tel: 905-688-5550
www.brocku.ca
www.facebook.com/brockuniversity
twitter.com/brockuniversity
www.linkedin.com/school/brock-university
www.youtube.com/brockuvideo

Full Time Equivalency: 19000 *Number of Employees:* 600 faculty; 6,000 total employment
Shirley Cheechoo, Chancellor
Gervan Fearon, President & Vice-Chancellor
Greg Finn, Provost & Vice-President, Academic
gfinn@brocku.ca
Brian Hutchings, Vice-President, Administration
Tim Kenyon, Vice-President, Research
Geraldine Jones, Registrar
gjones@brocku.ca

Faculties
Faculty of Education
Tel: 905-688-5550; *Fax:* 905-685-4131
brocku.ca/education
www.facebook.com/brockueducation
twitter.com/brockueducation
Michael Owen, Dean, 905-688-5550, ext. 3712
mowen@brocku.ca

Faculty of Humanities
Mackenzie Chown Complex
1812 Sir Isaac Brock Way, #A310, St Catharines, ON L2S 3A1
Tel: 905-688-5550
brocku.ca/humanities
Carol U. Merriam, Dean

Faculty of Social Sciences
Scotiabank Hall
1812 Sir Isaac Brock Way, St Catharines, ON L2S 3A1
Tel: 905-688-5550; Fax: 905-641-5076
brocku.ca/social-sciences
www.facebook.com/BrockUFOSS
twitter.com/BrockUFOSS
Ingrid Makus, Dean, 905-688-5550, ext. 3425
imakus@brocku.ca

Faculty of Mathematics & Sciences
brocku.ca/mathematics-science
www.facebook.com/BrockUFMS
twitter.com/brockuFMS
www.instagram.com/brockufms
Ejaz Ahmed, Dean, 905-688-5550, ext. 3422
dean.fms@brocku.ca

Faculty of Applied Health Sciences
brocku.ca/applied-health-sciences
www.facebook.com/brockfahs
twitter.com/brockfahs
Peter Tiidus, Dean, 905-688-5550, ext. 3385
peter.tiidus@brocku.ca

Faculty of Graduate Studies
Mackenzie Chown Complex
1812 Sir Isaac Brock Way, St Catharines, ON L2S 3A1
Tel: 905-688-5550; Fax: 905-688-0748
gradadmissions@brocku.ca
brocku.ca/graduate-studies
www.facebook.com/BrockGradStudies
twitter.com/BrockGradStudy
Diane Dupont, Interim Dean
ddupont@brocku.ca

Schools
Goodman School of Business
Taro Hall
1812 Sir Isaac Brock Way, St Catharines, ON L2S 3A1
brocku.ca/goodman
www.facebook.com/GoodmanSchool
twitter.com/GoodmanSchool
www.linkedin.com/company/goodman-school-of-business
www.instagram.com/GoodmanSchool
Andrew Gaudes, Dean, 905-688-5550, ext. 4006
agaudes@brocku.ca

Campuses
Hamilton Campus
1842 King St. East, Hamilton, ON L8K 1V7
Tel: 905-547-3555;

Sudbury: Huntington University
935 Ramsey Lake Rd., Sudbury, ON P3E 2C6
Tel: 705-673-4126; Fax: 705-673-6917
Toll-Free: 800-461-6366
info@huntingtonuniversity.com
huntingtonu.ca
www.facebook.com/huntingtonuni
twitter.com/HuntingtonUni
www.instagram.com/huntingtonuniversity
Note: Liberal Arts University specializing in Communication Studies, Ethics, Gerontology, Religious studies and Theology.

Canadian Institute for Studies in Aging (CISA)
935 Ramsey Lake Rd., Sudbury, ON P3E 2C6

Lougheed Teaching & Learning Centre
935 Ramsey Lake Rd., Sudbury, ON P3E 2C6
www.huntingtonu.ca
Lorraine Mercer, Director
lmercer@huntingtonu.ca

Sudbury: Laurentian University (Sudbury) (LU)
Université Laurentienne (Sudbury)
935 Ramsey Lake Rd., Sudbury, ON P3E 2C6, Canada
Tel: 705-675-1151; Toll-Free: 800-461-4030
communications@laurentian.ca
www.laurentian.ca
www.facebook.com/laurentian
twitter.com/laurentianu
www.linkedin.com/school/laurentian-university
www.youtube.com/laurentianuniversity
Full Time Equivalency: 9602 *Note:* Teaching is in French & English. Certain faculties offer parallel programs in both languages.
Robert Haché, President & Vice-Chancellor

Serge Demers, Vice-President & Provost
Lorella Hayes, Vice-President
Rui Wang, Vice-President, Research
Sara Kunto, University Secretary & General Counsel

Faculties
Faculty of Arts
935 Ramsey Lake Rd., Sudbury, ON P3E 2C6
Tel: 705-675-1151
laurentian.ca/faculty/arts
Joël Dickinson, Interim Dean
jdickinson@laurentian.ca

Faculty of Education
935 Ramsey Lake Rd., Sudbury, ON P3E 2C6
Tel: 705-675-1151
laurentian.ca/faculty/education
Lace Marie Brogden, Dean, 705-675-1151, ext. 5151
lbrogden@laurentian.ca

Faculty of Graduate Studies
Parker P-346
Ramsey Lake Rd., Sudbury, ON P3E 2C6
Tel: 705-675-1151
graduatestudies@laurentian.ca
laurentian.ca/faculty/graduate-studies
David Lesbarrères, Dean
dlesbarreres@laurentian.ca

Faculty of Health
935 Ramsey Lake Rd., Sudbury, ON P3E 2C6
Tel: 705-675-1151; Fax: 705-675-4888
laurentian.ca/faculty/health
Céline Larivière, Dean
clariviere@laurentian.ca

Faculty of Management
935 Ramsey Lake Rd., Sudbury, ON P3E 2C6
Tel: 705-675-1151
laurentian.ca/faculty/management
Stephen Havlovic, Dean

Faculty of Medicine
935 Ramsey Lake Rd., Sudbury, ON P3E 2C6
Tel: 705-675-1151
laurentian.ca/faculty-medicine

Faculty of Science, Engineering & Architecture
935 Ramsey Lake Rd., Sudbury, ON P3E 2C6
Tel: 705-675-1151
laurentian.ca/faculty/science

Schools
Bharti School of Engineering
935 Ramsey Lake Rd., #F-232, Sudbury, ON P3E 2C6
Tel: 705-675-1151; Fax: 705-675-4862
Toll-Free: 800-461-4030
bhartiengineering@laurentian.ca
www3.laurentian.ca/engineering
Markus Timusk, Director
mtimusk@laurentian.ca

Goodman School of Mines
935 Ramsey Lake Rd., Sudbury, ON P3E 2C6
Tel: 705-675-1151; Fax: 705-673-6554
goodmanschoolofmines.laurentian.ca
www.facebook.com/goodmanschoolofmines
twitter.com/GSM_LU
www.linkedin.com/school/laurentian-university
Bruce Jago, Executive Director, 705-675-1151, ext. 7222

Harquail School of Earth Sciences
935 Ramsey Lake Rd., Sudbury, ON P3E 2C6
Tel: 705-675-1151
hes@laurentian.ca
hes.laurentian.ca
www.facebook.com/HarquailEarthSciences
twitter.com/harquailes
www.instagram.com/heslaurentian
Douglas K. Tinkham, Director
dtinkham@laurentian.ca

McEwen School of Architecture
85 Elm St., Sudbury, ON P3C 1T5
Tel: 705-673-6500
architecture@laurentian.ca
www3.laurentian.ca/McEwenArchitecture

School of Education
935 Ramsey Lake Rd., Sudbury, ON P3E 2C6
Tel: 705-675-1151
laurentian.ca/dept/school-education
George Sheppard, Director
gsheppard@laurentian.ca

School of the Environment
935 Ramsey Lake Rd., Sudbury, ON P3E 2C6
Tel: 705-675-1151
laurentian.ca/dept/school-environment
Brett Buchanan, Director
bbuchanan@laurentian.ca

School of Human Kinetics
935 Ramsey Lake Rd., Sudbury, ON P3E 2C6
Tel: 705-675-1151
laurentian.ca/dept/school-human-kinetics

School of Indigenous Relations
935 Ramsey Lake Rd., Sudbury, ON P3E 2C6
Tel: 705-675-1151
laurentian.ca/dept/school-indigenous-relations

School of Midwifery
935 Ramsey Lake Rd., Sudbury, ON P3E 2C6
Tel: 705-675-1151
laurentian.ca/dept/midwifery

School of Northern & Community Studies
Arts Bldg.
935 Ramsey Lake Rd., Sudbury, ON P3E 2C6
Tel: 705-675-1151
laurentian.ca/stub-24
Darrel Manitowabi, Director
dmanitowabi@laurentian.ca

School of Nursing
935 Ramsey Lake Rd., Sudbury, ON P3E 2C6
Tel: 705-675-1151
laurentian.ca/dept/school-nursing
Sylvie Larocque, Director

School of Rural & Northern Health
935 Ramsey Lake Rd., Sudbury, ON P3E 2C6
Tel: 705-675-1151
laurentian.ca/dept/school-rural-and-northern-health

School of Social Work
935 Ramsey Lake Rd., Sudbury, ON P3E 2C6
Tel: 705-675-1151
laurentian.ca/dept/school-social-work

School of Speech-Language Pathology
935 Ramsey Lake Rd., Sudbury, ON P3E 2C6
Tel: 705-675-1151
laurentian.ca/dept/speech-therapy

School of Sports Administration
935 Ramsey Lake Rd., Sudbury, ON P3E 2C6
Tel: 705-675-1151
spad@laurentian.ca
laurentian.ca/dept/school-sports-administration
twitter.com/LU_SPAD
Anthony Church, Director
achurch@laurentian.ca

Affiliations
University of Sudbury
Université de Sudbury
Also known as: UofS
Old Name: Collège du Sacré Coeur
935 Ramsey Lake Rd., Sudbury, ON P3E 2C6, Canada
Tel: 705-673-5661; Fax: 705-673-4912
usudreg@usudbury.ca
usudbury.ca
www.facebook.com/usudbury
twitter.com/UofSudbury

Number of Employees: 50
Gérald Michel, Chancellor
Sophie Bouffard, President & Vice-Chancellor
presidentrectrice@usudbury.ca
Sylvie Renault, Registrar & Director, Recruitment & Communications, 705-673-5661, ext. 316
srenault@usudbury.ca
Sarah Noel, Development & Communications Officer, 705-673-5661, ext. 307
snoel@usudbury.ca
Roxanne Langemann, Recruitment Officer, 705-673-5661, ext. 364
rlangemann@usudbury.ca
Marianne Denis, Administrative & Communications Coordinator, 705-673-5661, ext. 316
mdenis3@usudbury.ca

Huntington University
935 Ramsey Lake Rd., Sudbury, ON P3E 2C6
Tel: 705-673-4126; Fax: 705-673-6917
Toll-Free: 800-461-6366
www.huntingtonu.ca
www.facebook.com/huntingtonuni
twitter.com/HuntingtonUni
www.pinterest.com/huniversity
Dr. Kevin McCormick, President & Vice-Chancellor

Thorneloe University at Laurentian University
935 Ramsey Lake Rd., Sudbury, ON P3E 2C6, Canada
Tel: 705-673-1730; *Fax:* 705-673-4979
Toll-Free: 1-866-846-7635
info@thorneloe.ca
www.thorneloe.ca
www.facebook.com/ThorneloeUni
twitter.com/ThorneloeUni
Note: Affiliated with the Anglican Church, Thorneloe University features the departments of Religious Studies, Classical Studies, Theatre Arts, & Women's Studies.
Anne Germond, Chancellor
Robert Derrenbacker, President & Vice-Chancellor
rderrenbacker@laurentian.ca

Centres & Institutes
Centre for Evolutionary Ecology & Ethical Conservation
935 Ramsey Lake Rd., Sudbury, ON P3E 2C6
Tel: 705-675-1151; *Fax:* 705-675-1151
info@ceeec.ca
www.ceeec.ca
Albrecht Schulte-Hostedde, Director

Centre for Humanities Research & Creativity
L-707 R.D. Parker Bldg.
935 Ramsey Lake Rd., Sudbury, ON P3E 2C6
Tel: 705-675-1151
laurentian.ca/research/centres/chrc
Gillian Crozier, Director
gcrozier@laurentian.ca

Centre for Research in Occupational Safety & Health
935 Ramsey Lake Rd., Sudbury, ON P3E 2C6
Tel: 705-675-1151; *Fax:* 705-675-4845
crosh@laurentian.ca
crosh.ca
twitter.com/crosh_crsst
www.instagram.com/crosh_crsst
Sandra Dorman, Director
sdorman@laurentian.ca

Centre for Research in Social Justice & Policy
935 Ramsey Lake Rd., Sudbury, ON P3E 2C6
Tel: 705-675-1151
laurentian.ca/research/centres/CRSJP

Centre for Rural & Northern Health Research
935 Ramsey Lake Rd., Sudbury, ON P3E 2C6
Tel: 705-675-1151; *Fax:* 705-671-3876
cranhr@laurentian.ca
www.cranhr.ca
twitter.com/cranhr
Diana Urajnik, Director
durajnik@laurentian.ca

Cooperative Freshwater Ecology Unit
935 Ramsey Lake Rd., Sudbury, ON P3E 2C6
laurentian.ca/research/centres/cfeu

Evaluating Children's Health Outcomes Research Centre
935 Ramsey Lake Rd., Sudbury, ON P3E 2C6
Tel: 705-675-1151
echo@laurentian.ca
www.echoresearchcentre.com
Nicole Yantzi, Director
nyantzi@laurentian.ca

Institut Franco-Ontarien
935 Ramsey Lake Rd., Sudbury, ON P3E 2C6
laurentian.ca/research/centres/ifo

Institute for Northern Ontario Research & Development
935 Ramsey Lake Rd., Sudbury, ON P3E 2C6
laurentian.ca/institute-northern-ontario-research-and-development
David Robinson, Director

Institute for Sports Marketing
935 Ramsey Lake Rd., Sudbury, ON P3E 2C6
Tel: 705-675-1151; *Fax:* 705-675-1151
sportmarketing.ca
Ann Pegoraro, Director
apegoraro@laurentian.ca

International Centre for Interdisciplinary Research in Law
935 Ramsey Lake Rd., Sudbury, ON P3E 2C6
laurentian.ca/research/centres/icirl
Henri Pallard, Director

International Centre for Interdisciplinary Research in the Human Sciences
935 Ramsey Lake Rd., Sudbury, ON P3E 2C6
laurentian.ca/research/centres/icirhs

International Economic Policy Institute
935 Ramsey Lake Rd., Sudbury, ON P3E 2C6
laurentian.ca

Mineral Exploration Research Centre (MERC)
935 Ramsey Lake Rd., Sudbury, ON P3E 2C6
Tel: 705-675-1151
merc@laurentian.ca
merc.laurentian.ca
www.facebook.com/MineralExplorationResearchCentre
twitter.com/MERC_Geoscience
www.linkedin.com/company/merc-mineral-exploration-research-centre

Mining Innovation, Rehabilitation & Applied Research Corporation (MIRARCO)
935 Ramsey Lake Rd., Sudbury, ON P3E 2C6
Tel: 705-671-3333; *Fax:* 705-675-4838
info@mirarco.org
www.mirarco.org

Sudbury Neutrino Observation Laboratory (SNOLAB)
Creighton Mine #9
1039 Regional Rd. 24, Lively, ON P3Y 1N2
Tel: 705-692-7000; *Fax:* 705-692-7001
info@snolab.ca
www.snolab.ca
Nigel Smith, Executive Director

Sudbury: Thorneloe University
935 Ramsey Lake Rd., Sudbury, ON P3E 2C6
Tel: 705-673-1730; *Fax:* 705-673-4979
Toll-Free: 866-846-7635
info@thorneloe.ca
www.thorneloe.ca
www.facebook.com/ThorneloeUni
twitter.com/ThorneloeUni
Note: Thorneloe offers diplomas, certificates & bachelor degrees. The University is partners with Laurentian University & Cambrian College.

Sudbury: University of Sudbury
935 Ramsey Lake Rd., Sudbury, ON P3E 2C6, Canada
Tel: 705-673-5661
usudreg@usudbury.ca
www.usudbury.ca
www.facebook.com/usudbury
twitter.com/UofSudbury
www.linkedin.com/groups/4419839

Faculties
Folklore et ethnologie
usudbury.ca/fr/folk-folklore-et-ethnologie

Études journalistiques
usudbury.ca/fr/programmes/culture-et-communication

Indigenous Studies
www.usudbury.ca/en/programs/indigenous-studies

Philosophy
www.usudbury.ca/en/programs/philosophy

Religious Studies
www.usudbury.ca/en/programs/religious-studies

Thunder Bay: Lakehead University
955 Oliver Rd., Thunder Bay, ON P7B 5E1, Canada
Tel: 807-343-8110; *Fax:* 807-343-8023
www.lakeheadu.ca
www.facebook.com/lakeheaduniversity
twitter.com/mylakehead
www.linkedin.com/company/lakehead-university
www.youtube.com/lakeheaduniversity
Full Time Equivalency: 8284 *Number of Employees:* 2100
Lyn McLeod, Chancellor
Moira McPherson, President & Vice-Chancellor
David W. Barnett, Provost & Vice-President, Academic
Andrew P. Dean, Vice-President, Research & Innovation
Kathy Pozihun, Vice-President, Administration & Finance
Barbara Eccles, General Counsel & Secretary
Toby Goodfellow, Chief of Staff

Faculties
Business Administration
Ryan Bldg.
#1025, 955 Oliver Rd., Thunder Bay, ON P7B 5E1
Tel: 807-343-8386; *Fax:* 807-343-8443
business@lakeheadu.ca
www.lakeheadu.ca/academics/departments/business
Enrollment: 500
David Richards, Dean, 807-343-8525
david.richards@lakeheadu.ca

Education
Bora Laskin Bldg.
#1016, 955 Oliver Rd., Thunder Bay, ON P7B 5E1
Tel: 807-346-7818; *Fax:* 807-346-7918
www.lakeheadu.ca/academics/departments/education
Wayne Melville, Dean, 807-766-7194
wmelvill@lakeheadu.ca

Engineering
955 Oliver Rd., Thunder Bay, ON P7B 5E1
www.lakeheadu.ca/academics/faculties/engineering
Hassan Naser, Interim Dean, 807-343-8389
hnaser@lakehead.ca
Heather Moynihan, Academic Manager, 807-766-7148
hemoynih@lakehead.ca

Natural Resources Management
Braun Bldg.
955 Oliver Rd., #1001G, Thunder Bay, ON P7B 5E1
Tel: 807-343-8507; *Fax:* 807-343-8116
www.lakeheadu.ca/departments/nrm
Ulf Runesson, Dean, 807-343-8784
ulf.runesson@lakeheadu.ca

Graduate Studies
Forestry Building
#2010, 955 Oliver Rd., Thunder Bay, ON P7B 5E1
Tel: 807-343-8785; *Fax:* 807-346-7705
lakeheadu.ca/programs/faculties/graduate-studies
Chander Shahi, Dean

Northern Ontario School of Medicine
955 Oliver Rd., Thunder Bay, ON P7B 5E1
Tel: 807-766-7300; *Fax:* 807-766-7370
Toll-Free: 800-461-8777
www.nosm.ca
Sarita Verma, Dean, President & CEO

Social Sciences and Humanities
955 Oliver Rd., #BB-1072E, Thunder Bay, ON P7B 5E1
Tel: 807-343-8202; *Fax:* 807-766-7155
lakeheadu.ca/programs/faculties/social-sciences-and-humanities
Betsy Birmingham, Dean, 807-343-8167
ebirming@lakeheadu.ca
Sue Viitala, Administrative Assistant, 807-343-8202
susan.viitala@lakeheadu.ca

Science & Environmental Studies
955 Oliver Rd., #CB 4008, Thunder Bay, ON P7B 5E1
Tel: 807-766-7211; *Fax:* 807-766-7214
lakeheadu.ca/programs/faculties-science-and-environmental-studies
Todd Randall, Dean, 807-343-8289
randall@lakeheadu.ca

Bora Laskin Faculty of Law
PACI Bldg.
955 Oliver Rd., Thunder Bay, ON P7B 5E1
Tel: 807-346-7866; *Fax:* 807-346-7750
www.lakeheadu.ca/programs/departments/law
www.facebook.com/lakeheadlaw
Jula Hughes, Dean

Schools
Kinesiology
Sanders Fieldhouse
955 Oliver Rd., #SB 1021, Thunder Bay, ON P7B 5E1
Tel: 807-343-8544
www.lakeheadu.ca/programs/departments/kinesiology
Ian Newhouse, Director
inewhous@lakeheadu.ca

Nursing
School of Nursing Bldg.
955 Oliver Rd., Thunder Bay, ON P7B 5E1
Tel: 807-343-8395
www.lakeheadu.ca/programs/departments/nursing
Karen McQueen, Director
kmcqueen@lakeheadu.ca

Outdoor Recreation, Parks & Tourism
955 Oliver Rd., #SN 2002, Thunder Bay, ON P7B 5E1
Tel: 807-343-8759; *Fax:* 807-346-7836
www.lakeheadu.ca/programs/departments/outdoor-rec
www.facebook.com/LakeheadORPT
Margaret Johnston, Director

Social Work
955 Oliver Rd., #RC 3004, Thunder Bay, ON P7B 5E1
Tel: 807-343-8576; *Fax:* 807-346-7727
www.lakeheadu.ca/academics/departments/social-work
Natalya Timoshkina, Director, 705-330-4008, ext. 2702
natimosh@lakeheadu.ca

Centres & Institutes
Lakehead University's Centre for Analytical Services (LUCAS)
CASES Bldg.
955 Oliver Rd., #FB2004H, Thunder Bay, ON P7B 5E1
Tel: 807-343-8590
kmaa@lakeheau.ca
lakeheadu.ca/centre/lucas
Francis Appoh, Director, 807-343-8853
fappoh@lakeheadu.ca

Centre for Education and Research on Aging & Health
955 Oliver Rd., Thunder Bay, ON P7B 5E1
Tel: 807-766-7271; *Fax:* 807-766-7222
cerah@lakeheadu.ca
cerah.lakeheadu.ca

Debbie Riddell, Contact
dlamers@lakeheadu.ca

Centre of Excellence for Sustainable Mining & Exploration (CESME)
955 Oliver Rd., #CB4001, Thunder Bay, ON P7B 5E1
Tel: 807-343-8329
lakeheadu.ca/centre/cesme

Peter Hollings, Director
peter.hollings@lakeheadu.ca

Centre for Place and Sustainability Studies
955 Oliver Rd., Thunder Bay, ON P7B 5E1
Tel: 807-766-7193
lakeheadu.ca/programs/departments/education/our-research-innovations

David Greenwood, Director
dgreenwo@lakeheadu.ca
Pauline Sameshima, Associate Director
psameshima@lakeheadu.ca

Centre of Education and Research on Positive Youth Development (CERPYD)
955 Oliver Rd., Thunder Bay, ON P7B 5E1
Tel: 807-343-8196; *Fax:* 807-346-7991
cerpyd@lakeheadu.ca
lakeheadu.ca/centre/cerpyd

Edward Rawana, Director
ed.rawana@lakeheadu.ca

Centre for Research on Safe Driving (CRSD)
955 Oliver Rd., #BB 1043, Thunder Bay, ON P7B 5E1
Tel: 807-766-7256; *Fax:* 807-346-7707
crsd@lakeheadu.ca
lakeheadu.ca/centre/crsd

Hillary Maxwell, Research Coordinator
hmaxwell@lakeheadu.ca

Toronto: Innis College
2 Sussex Ave., Toronto, ON M5S 1J5, Canada
Tel: 416-978-2513; *Fax:* 416-978-5503
registrar.innis@utoronto.ca
innis.utoronto.ca
www.facebook.com/innisregistrar
twitter.com/innisregistrar
Full Time Equivalency: 1480 *Note:* Constituent college of the University of Toronto
Charlie Keil, Principal, 416-978-2510
principal.innis@utoronto.ca
Donald Boere, Assistant Principal & Registrar, 416-978-2513
donald.boere@utoronto.ca

Toronto: Knox College
59 St. George St., Toronto, ON M5S 2E6, Canada
Tel: 416-978-4500; *Fax:* 416-971-2133
knox.college@utoronto.ca
www.knox.utoronto.ca
www.facebook.com/KnoxCollege.CA
twitter.com/knoxcollegeca
Note: Theological college at the University of Toronto affiliated with the Presbyterian Church in Canada

Toronto: Massey College
4 Devonshire Pl., Toronto, ON M5S 2E1, Canada
Tel: 416-978-2896
porter@masseycollege.ca
masseycollege.ca
www.facebook.com/MasseyCollege
twitter.com/MasseyCollege
www.youtube.com/MasseyCollege
Note: A graduate students' residence associated with the University of Toronto.

Toronto: New College
Wilson Hall
40 Willcocks St., Toronto, ON M5S 1C6
Tel: 416-978-2460; *Fax:* 416-978-0554
newcollege.registrar@utoronto.ca
www.newcollege.utoronto.ca

Toronto: OCAD University (OCAD)
Also known as: Ontario College of Art & Design
100 McCaul St., Toronto, ON M5T 1W1, Canada
Tel: 416-977-6000
admissions@ocadu.ca
www.ocadu.ca
www.facebook.com/ocaduniversity
twitter.com/OCAD
www.linkedin.com/school/ocad-university
www.youtube.com/user/ocaduniversity

Full Time Equivalency: 6072
Salah J. Bachir, Chancellor
Sara Diamond, President
sdiamond@ocadu.ca
Carole Beaulieu, Vice-President, Advancement
cbeaulieu@ocadu.ca
Robert Luke, Vice-President, Research & Innovation
rluke@ocadu.ca
Alan Simms, Vice-President, Finance & Administration
asimms@ocadu.ca
Adam Bereza, Director, Academic Relations
abereza@ocadu.ca
Nicky Davis, Director, Human Resources
ndavis@ocadu.ca
Peter Fraser, Director, Finance
pfraser@ocadu.ca
Elisabeth Paradis, University Registrar
eparadis@ocadu.ca

Faculties
Faculty of Art
100 McCaul St., Toronto, ON M5T 1W1
www.ocadu.ca/academics/faculty-of-art.htm
Vladimir Spicanovic, Dean
vspicanovic@ocadu.ca

Faculty of Design
100 McCaul St., Toronto, ON M5T 1W1
www.ocadu.ca/academics/faculty-of-design.htm
Dori Tunstall, Dean
dtunstall@ocadu.ca

Faculty of Liberal Arts & Sciences
100 McCaul St., Toronto, ON M5T 1W1
www.ocadu.ca/academics/faculty-of-las-and-sis.htm
Caroline Langill, Dean

Graduate Studies
100 McCaul St., Toronto, ON M5T 1W1
Tel: 416-977-6000; *Fax:* 647-439-4194
gradstudies@ocadu.ca
www.ocadu.ca/academics/graduate-studies
Ashok Mathur, Dean, 416-977-6000, ext. 3849
amathur@ocadu.ca

Toronto: Ontario Institute for Studies in Education
252 Bloor St. West, Toronto, ON M5S 1V6
Tel: 416-978-0005
www.oise.utoronto.ca
www.facebook.com/OISEUofT
twitter.com/OISEUofT
Glen A. Jones, Dean

Toronto: Ryerson University
350 Victoria St., Toronto, ON M5B 2K3, Canada
Tel: 416-979-5000
inquire@ryerson.ca
www.ryerson.ca
www.facebook.com/ryersonu
twitter.com/ryersonu
www.linkedin.com/company/ryerson-university
www.youtube.com/user/RyersonUTube
Full Time Equivalency: 45313 *Number of Employees:* 900 faculty
Janice Fukakusa, Chancellor
Mohamed Lachemi, President
Saeed Zolfaghari, Interim Provost & Vice-President, Academic
Deborah Brown, Vice-President, Administration & Operations
Denise O'Neil Green, Vice-President, Equity & Community Inclusion
Steven N. Liss, Vice-President, Research & Innovation, 416, ext. 5283
ovpri@ryerson.ca
Ian Mishkel, Vice-President, University Advancement & Alumni Relations
Julia Shin Doi, General Counsel, 416-979-5000, ext. 2992
julia.shindoi@ryerson.ca
Charmaine Hack, Registrar
chack@ryerson.ca

Faculties
Faculty of Arts
Jorgenson Hall
#100, 380 Victoria St., Toronto, ON M5B 2K3
help@arts.ryerson.ca
www.ryerson.ca/arts
Other Information: 416-979-5000, ext. 4040
www.facebook.com/RUFacultyofArts
twitter.com/RUFacultyofArts
www.youtube.com/user/RyersonFacultyofArts
Enrollment: 4570 *Number of Employees:* 200 faculty
Pamela Sugiman, Dean, 416-979-5000, ext. 4040
sugiman@arts.ryerson.ca

Kathleen Kellett, Associate Dean, Undergraduate Studies, 416-979-5000, ext. 6196
kkellett@ryerson.ca
Patrizia Albanese, Associate Dean, Research & Graduate Studies, 416-979-5000, ext. 6526
palbanes@ryerson.ca
Melissa Wong, Director, Operations & Strategic Initiatives, 416-979-5000, ext. 2266
smckenzie@ryerson.ca

Faculty of Communication & Design (FCAD)
Rogers Communication Center
#320, 80 Gould St., Toronto, ON M5B 2K3
Tel: 416-979-5348; *Fax:* 416-979-5285
www.ryerson.ca/fcad
www.facebook.com/ryersonfcad
twitter.com/RyersonFCAD
www.instagram.com/ryersonfcad
Charles Falzon, Dean, 416-979-5012
cfalzon@ryerson.ca
Dan Greenwood, Director, 416-979-5232
dan.greenwood@ryerson.ca

Faculty of Community Services (FCS)
350 Victoria St., Toronto, ON M5B 2K3
Fax: 416-979-5384
ryerson.ca/fcs
Other Information: 416-979-5000, ext. 5034
twitter.com/RyersonFCS
www.instagram.com/ryersonfcs
Lisa Barnoff, Dean, 416-979-5000, ext. 5034
lbarnoff@ryerson.ca
Sarah Bukhari, Administrative Coordinator, 416-979-5000, ext. 4641
sarah.bukhari@ryerson.ca

Faculty of Engineering & Architectural Science (FEAS)
245 Church St., Toronto, ON M5B 1Z2
www.ryerson.ca/feas
twitter.com/RyersonFEAS
www.instagram.com/ryersonfeas
Enrollment: 6100
Thomas Duever, Dean, 416-979-5000, ext. 5140
tom.duever@ryerson.ca
Dorothy Opasinis, Administration Manager, 416-979-5000, ext. 5102
dopasini@ryerson.ca

Research & Innovation
1 Dundas St. West, 11th Fl., Toronto, ON M5G 1Z3
Tel: 416-979-5000
www.ryerson.ca/research
twitter.com/Ryersonresearch
Steven Liss, Vice-President, Research & Innovation
ovpri@ryerson.ca

Faculty of Science
Victoria Bldg.
#740, 285 Victoria St., Toronto, ON M5B 1W1
Tel: 416-979-5251
www.ryerson.ca/science
David Cramb, Dean, 416-979-5000, ext. 5251
david.cramb@ryerson.ca

Lincoln Alexander School of Law
350 Victoria St., Toronto, ON M5B 2K3
Tel: 416-979-5000
law@ryerson.ca
ryerson.ca/law
twitter.com/ryersonulaw
Donna E. Young, Dean

Schools
The G. Raymond Chang School of Continuing Education
Also known as: The Chang School
297 Victoria St., Toronto, ON M5B 1W1
Tel: 416-979-5035
ce@ryerson.ca
continuing.ryerson.ca
www.facebook.com/ChangSchool
twitter.com/changschool
www.linkedin.com/company/changschool
Enrollment: 70000 *Note:* The Chang School is offering an introductory course that provides an overview of the cannabis industry in Canada.
Gary Hepburn, Dean, 416-979-5000, ext. 5005
gary.hepburn@ryerson.ca
Brad Poulos, Instructor

Ted Rogers School of Management
55 Dundas St. West, Toronto, ON M5G 2C5
Tel: 416-979-5000; *Fax:* 416-979-5001
www.ryerson.ca/tedrogersschool
www.facebook.com/TedRogersSchool
twitter.com/TRSMRyersonU
www.linkedin.com/school/ted-rogers-school-of-management
www.youtube.com/user/tedrogersschool
Note: Programs include Accounting & Finance, Business
Technology Management, Economics & Management Science,
Entrepreneurship & Strategy, Hospitality & Tourism
Management, Marketing Management, Retail Management, &
Graduate Programs
Daphne Taras, Dean

Yeates School of Graduate Studies
1 Dundas St. West, 11th Fl., Toronto, ON M5B 2K3
Tel: 416-979-5365
www.ryerson.ca/graduate
www.facebook.com/RyersonGraduate
twitter.com/RyersonGraduate
www.youtube.com/user/RyersonGraduate
Cory Searcy, Vice-Provost & Dean
Rachquel Thompson, Administrative Coordinator
rachquel.thompson@ryerson.ca
Sarah Pratt, Communications and Social Media Coordinator
Sarah.pratt@ryerson.ca

Centres & Institutes
Ryerson Centre for Immigration & Settlement (RCIS)
Kerr Hall South
40 Gould St, #46C, Toronto, ON M5B 1E9
rcis@ryerson.ca
www.ryerson.ca/rcis
twitter.com/rc1s
www.linkedin.com/company/ryersoncis
www.youtube.com/user/rcis01
Usha George, Academic Director
ugeorge@ryerson.ca

Centre for Labour Management Relations (CLMR)
#429, 1 Dundas St. West, Toronto, ON M5G 1Z3
Tel: 416-979-5000
clmr@ryerson.ca
www.ryerson.ca/clmr
Other Information: 416-979-5000, ext. 552379
twitter.com/RyersonCLMR
Tim Bartkiw, Director, 416-979-5000, ext. 2430
tbartkiw@ryerson.ca

Centre for the Study of Commercial Activity (CSCA)
**#1063, 1 Dundas Street West, 10th Floor, Toronto, ON M5G
1Z3**
csca@ryerson.ca
csca.ryerson.ca
Tony Hernandez, Director, 416-979-5000, ext. 557200
thernand@ryerson.ca
Cari Bish, Manager, 416-979-5000, ext. 557201
cbish@ryerson.ca

Ryerson Law Research Centre
350 Victoria St., Toronto, ON M5B 2K3
lawcentre@ryerson.ca
ryerson.ca/lawcentre
Other Information: 416-979-5000, ext. 3024
twitter.com/LawCentreRye
Avner Levin, Academic Director
Aleksandra Acimovic, Coordinator, Administration &
Communication
lawcentre@ryerson

*Ryerson Centre for Cloud and Context-Aware Computing
(RC4)*
#1000, 10 Dundas St. East, Toronto, ON M5B 2K3
Tel: 416-979-5000
rc4@ryerson.ca
rc4.ryerson.ca
www.facebook.com/RyersonRC4
twitter.com/RyersonRC4
www.youtube.com/user/RC4Ryerson

Ryerson University Analytical Centre (RUAC)
#215, 350 Victoria St., Toronto, ON M5B 2K3
Fax: 416-979-5044
smcfadde@ryerson.ca
www.ryerson.ca/ruac
Other Information: 416-979-5000, ext. 7964
Steve Wylie, Director

Toronto: University of Guelph Humber
207 Humber College Blvd., Toronto, ON M9W 5L7
Tel: 416-798-1331; *Fax:* 416-798-3606
info@guelphhumber.ca
www.guelphhumber.ca
www.facebook.com/uoguelphhumber
twitter.com/guelphhumber
www.youtube.com/chooseguelphhumber
John Walsh, Vice-Provost, Chief Academic & Executive Officer
Nancy Birch, Department Head, Library Services
Gabrielle Bernardi-Dengo, Department Head, Finance &
Administration
Julie Gustavel, Department Head, Academic Services
Grant Kerr, Registrar

Toronto: University of Toronto
Also known as: U of T
Old Name: King's College
27 King's College Circle, Toronto, ON M5S 1A1
Tel: 416-978-2011
www.utoronto.ca
Other Information: 416-978-7669;
www.facebook.com/universitytoronto
twitter.com/uoft
www.linkedin.com/company/university-of-toronto
www.youtube.com/user/universitytoronto
Full Time Equivalency: 90077 *Number of Employees:* 21556
Note: Founded in 1827, the University of Toronto has over 700
undergraduate programs across three campuses in the Greater
Toronto Area, & offers the most courses of any University in
Canada. The University contributes to the country's research
landscape in both the scientific & medical fields. The library
network is the largest collection in the country. U of T is home to
more students & faculty than any other in Canada.
Rose M. Patten, O.C., Chancellor
Meric Gertler, PhD., President
Cheryl Regehr, PhD., Vice-President & Provost
David Estok, MA, Vice-President, Communications
Vivek Goel, MD, CM, MSc, SM, FRCPC., Vice-President,
Research & Innovation
Kelly Hannah-Moffat, PhD., Vice-President, Human Resources &
Equity
Scott Mabury, PhD., Vice-President, University Operations
David Palmer, MFA, Vice-President, Advancement
Edward H. Sargent, PhD., Vice-President, International
Andrew Thomson, BA, Chief of Government Relations

Faculties
Faculty of Applied Science & Engineering
44 St. George St., Toronto, ON M5S 2E4
Tel: 416-978-5896
engineering@ecf.utoronto.ca
www.engineering.utoronto.ca
www.facebook.com/uoftengineering
twitter.com/uoftengineering
vimeo.com/uoftengineering
Christopher Yip, Dean, 416-978-3131
dean.engineering@ecf.utoronto.ca

*John H. Daniels Faculty of Architecture, Landscape &
Design*
1 Spadina Cres., Toronto, ON M5S 2J5
Tel: 416-978-5038
enquiry@daniels.utoronto.ca
www.daniels.utoronto.ca
www.facebook.com/UofTDaniels
twitter.com/UofTDaniels
www.youtube.com/user/UofTDaniels
Richard M. Sommer, Dean

Faculty of Arts & Science
Sidney Smith Hall
100 St. George St., Toronto, ON M5S 3G3
Tel: 416-978-3384
ask.artsci@utoronto.ca
www.artsci.utoronto.ca
www.facebook.com/UofTArtSci
twitter.com/uoftartsci
www.instagram.com/uoftartsci
Melanie Woodin, Dean

Faculty of Dentistry
124 Edward St., Toronto, ON M5G 1G6
Tel: 416-864-8113
www.dentistry.utoronto.ca
www.facebook.com/UofTDentistry
twitter.com/UofTDentistry
vimeo.com/dentistry
Daniel Haas, Dean

Faculty of Forestry
33 Willcocks St., Toronto, ON M5S 3B3
Tel: 416-978-5480; *Fax:* 416-978-3834
www.forestry.utoronto.ca
www.facebook.com/uoftforestry
twitter.com/UofTForestry
Robert M. Wright, Dean, 416-978-4713
r.wright@daniels.utoronto.ca

Faculty of Information
Claude Bissell Building
140 St. George St., Toronto, ON M5S 3G6
Tel: 416-978-3234; *Fax:* 416-978-5762
inquire.ischool@utoronto.ca
www.ischool.utoronto.ca
www.facebook.com/iSchoolToronto
twitter.com/UofTInfoFaculty
www.youtube.com/user/iSchoolUofT
Wendy Duff, Dean

Faculty of Law
78 Queen's Park, Toronto, ON M5S 2C5
Tel: 416-978-0210; *Fax:* 416-978-7899
www.law.utoronto.ca
twitter.com/utlaw
www.linkedin.com/company/university-of-toronto-faculty-of-law
www.youtube.com/user/UTorontoLaw
Edward Iacobucci, Dean
deansoffice.law@utoronto.ca

Rotman School of Management
105 St. George St., Toronto, ON M5S 3E6
Tel: 416-978-5703; *Fax:* 416-978-5433
www.rotman.utoronto.ca
www.facebook.com/RotmanSchoolOfManagement
twitter.com/rotmanschool
www.youtube.com/user/RotmanSchool
Tiff Macklem, Dean
tiff.macklem@rotman.utoronto.ca

Faculty of Medicine
Medical Sciences Bldg.
#2109, 1 King's College Circle, Toronto, ON M5S 1A8
Tel: 416-978-6585
discovery.commons@utoronto.ca
medicine.utoronto.ca
www.facebook.com/UofTMedicine
twitter.com/uoftmedicine
www.instagram.com/uoftmedicine
Trevor Young, MD, PhD, FRCPC, FCAHS, Dean

Faculty of Music
Edward Johnson Bldg.
80 Queen's Park, Toronto, ON M5S 2C5
Tel: 416-978-3750; *Fax:* 416-946-3353
www.music.utoronto.ca
www.facebook.com/UofTMusic
twitter.com/UofTMusic
www.instagram.com/UofTMusic
Don McLean, Dean
mclean@utoronto.ca

Lawrence S. Bloomberg Faculty of Nursing
#130, 155 College St., Toronto, ON M5T 1P8
Tel: 416-978-2392
communications.nursing@utoronto.ca
bloomberg.nursing.utoronto.ca
www.facebook.com/UofTNursing
twitter.com/UofTNursing
www.youtube.com/user/uoftnursing
Linda Johnston, Dean
dean.nursing@utoronto.ca

Ontario Institute for Studies in Education (OISE)
Also known as: Faculty of Education
252 Bloor St. West, Toronto, ON M5S 1V6
Tel: 416-978-0005; *Fax:* 416-323-9964
www.oise.utoronto.ca
www.facebook.com/OISEUofT
twitter.com/OISEUofT
Glen A. Jones, Dean, 416-978-8292
gjones@oise.utoronto.ca

Leslie Dan Faculty of Pharmacy
144 College St., Toronto, ON M5S 3M2
Tel: 416-978-2889; *Fax:* 416-978-8511
adm.phm@utoronto.ca
www.pharmacy.utoronto.ca
www.facebook.com/UofTPharmacy
twitter.com/UofTPharmacy
www.instagram.com/uoftpharmacy
Lisa Dolovich, Interim Dean, 416-978-2880
lisa.dolovich@utoronto.ca

Faculty of Kinesiology & Physical Education
55 Harbord St., Toronto, ON M5S 2W6
Tel: 416-978-5909; *Fax:* 416-971-2118
www.kpe.utoronto.ca
www.facebook.com/kperegistraroffice
twitter.com/UofTKPE
www.instagram.com/uoftkpe
Ira Jacobs, Dean
dean.kpe@utoronto.ca

School of Graduate Studies (SGS)
63 St. George St., Toronto, ON M5S 2Z9
Tel: 416-978-6614
graduate.information@utoronto.ca
www.sgs.utoronto.ca
www.facebook.com/GradlifeUofT
twitter.com/UofTGradlife
Joshua Barker, Dean
sgs.dean@utoronto.ca

Factor-Inwentash Faculty of Social Work
246 Bloor St. West, Toronto, ON M5S 1V4
Tel: 416-978-6314; *Fax:* 416-978-7072
socialwork.utoronto.ca
www.facebook.com/PhDSAFIFSW
Dexter Voisin, Dean
dexter.voisin@utoronto.ca

School of the Environment
#1016V, 33 Willcocks St., Toronto, ON M5S 3E8
Tel: 416-978-6526; *Fax:* 416-978-3884
www.environment.utoronto.ca
www.facebook.com/UofTenvironment
twitter.com/UofTenvironment
www.instagram.com/uoftenvironment
Steve Easterbrook, Director
director.environment@utoronto.ca

<u>Schools</u>
Munk School of Global Affairs
Also known as: Munk
315 Bloor St. West, Toronto, ON M5S 0A7
Tel: 416-946-8900
munkschool@utoronto.ca
munkschool.utoronto.ca
www.facebook.com/munkschool
twitter.com/munkschool
vimeo.com/munkschool
Randall Hansen, Interim Director, 416-946-8450
r.hansen@utoronto.ca

Transitional Year Programme
123 St. George St., Toronto, ON M5S 2E8
Tel: 416-978-6832; *Fax:* 416-971-1397
typ.info@utoronto.ca
sites.utoronto.ca/typ
Lance McCready, Interim Director, 416-978-0938
lance.mccready@utoronto.ca

<u>Affiliations</u>
University of Toronto Mississauga (UTM)
Also known as: Erindale College
3359 Mississauga Rd., Mississauga, ON L5L 1C6, Canada
Tel: 905-569-4455
www.utm.utoronto.ca
Other Information: Admissions, Phone: 905-828-5400
www.facebook.com/UTMississauga
twitter.com/UTM
www.linkedin.com/school/university-of-toronto
www.youtube.com/user/UTMississauga
Full Time Equivalency: 14930 *Number of Employees:* 3000
Ulrich Krull, PhD., Vice-President & Principal, 905-828-5211
principal.utm@utoronto.ca

Massey College
4 Devonshire Pl., Toronto, ON M5S 2E1, Canada
Tel: 416-978-2895
porter@masseycollege.ca
www.masseycollege.ca
www.facebook.com/MasseyCollege
twitter.com/MasseyCollege
www.youtube.com/MasseyCollege
Nathalie Des Rosiers, Principal, 416-978-2549
ndesrosiers@masseycollege.ca
Amela Marin, Dean, Fellowships, Programs & Liaisons,
416-978-2891
amarin@masseycollege.ca
Joyee Chau, Bursar, 416-978-8447
jchau@masseycollege.ca

New College
Wetmore Hall
300 Huron St., Toronto, ON M5S 3J6
Tel: 416-978-2460; *Fax:* 416-978-0554
newcollege.registrar@utoronto.ca
www.newcollege.utoronto.ca
www.facebook.com/NewCollegeUofTAlum
twitter.com/newcollegeUofT
Bonnie McElhinny, Principal, 416-978-2461
nc.principal@utoronto.ca
Tara Goldstein, Vice-Principal, 416-946-0291
tara.goldstein@utoronto.ca

University of Toronto Scarborough
1265 Military Trail, Toronto, ON M1C 1A4
Tel: 416-287-8872; *Fax:* 416-287-7528
www.utsc.utoronto.ca
www.facebook.com/UofTScarborough
twitter.com/utsc
www.linkedin.com/school/university-of-toronto
www.youtube.com/user/uoftscarborough
Wisdom Tettey, Vice-President & Principal
principal@utsc.utoronto.ca
William Gough, Vice-Principal, Academic & Dean
H. Bernie Kraatz, Vice-Principal, Research
vpresearch@utsc.utoronto.ca
Desmond Pouyat, Dean, Student Affairs, 416-208-4760
dpouyat@utsc.utoronto.ca
Andrew Arifuzzaman, Chief Administrative Officer, 416-287-7108
arifuzzaman@utsc.utoronto.ca
Lisa Fenton Lemon, Executive Director, Development & Alumni
Relations
Desma Charlemagne-Michel, Director, Human Resource
Services, 416-287-7077
desma.charlemagne.michel@utoronto.ca
Curtis Cole, Registrar & Assistant Dean, Enrolment
Management, 416-287-7527
cole@utsc.utoronto.ca

University College
15 King's College Cir., Toronto, ON M5S 3H7
Tel: 416-978-4428
uc.registrar@utoronto.ca
www.uc.utoronto.ca
Donald Ainslie, Principal, 416-978-7516
donald.ainslie@utoronto.ca

Woodsworth College
119 St. George St., Toronto, ON M5S 1A9
Tel: 416-978-4444; *Fax:* 416-978-4088
wdwregistrar@utoronto.ca
www.wdw.utoronto.ca
www.facebook.com/WoodsworthCollege
twitter.com/WWCollege
Carol Chin, Principal
carol.chin@utoronto.ca
Liza Nassim, Dean, Students, 416-946-7397
liza.nassim@utoronto.ca

St. Michael's College
81 St. Mary St., Toronto, ON M5S 1J4
Tel: 416-926-1300
stmikes.utoronto.ca
www.facebook.com/uStMikes
twitter.com/uStMikes
www.instagram.com/ustmikes
Full Time Equivalency: 4893 *Note:* Fully federated with the
University of Toronto, St. Michael's College has a large Faculty
of Theology. It also features the Canadian Catholic Bioethics
Institute & the Pontifical Institute of Mediaeval Studies.
David Sylvester, President & Vice-Chancellor
Randy Boyagoda, Principal

Trinity College
6 Hoskin Ave., Toronto, ON M5S 1H8
Tel: 416-978-2522; *Fax:* 416-978-2797
registrar@trinity.utoronto.ca
www.trinity.utoronto.ca
Other Information: Bursar's Office, E-mail:
fees@trinity.utoronto.ca
twitter.com/fortrinstudents
Full Time Equivalency: 1700 *Note:* Founded in 1851, it is
Canada's oldest Anglican theological school.
Hon. William C. Graham, Chancellor
Nelson De Melo, Director, Student Services & Registrar,
416-946-7614, ext. 2614
demelo@trinity.utoronto.ca

Victoria University
73 Queen's Park Cres., Toronto, ON M5S 1K7
Tel: 416-585-4508; *Fax:* 416-585-4459
vic.registrar@utoronto.ca
www.vicu.utoronto.ca
www.facebook.com/vicu.utoronto
twitter.com/VicCollege_UofT
Angela Esterhammer, Principal

Knox College
59 St. George St., Toronto, ON M5S 2E6
Tel: 416-978-4500; *Fax:* 416-971-2133
knox.college@utoronto.ca
www.knox.utoronto.ca
www.facebook.com/knoxcollege
twitter.com/knoxcollegeca
www.youtube.com/user/KnoxCollegeCA
Rev. Dr. John Vissers, Principal, 416-978-4511
john.vissers@utoronto.ca
Shawn Stovell, Registrar & Manager, Academic Services,
416-978-4501
knox.registrar@utoronto.ca

Wycliffe College
5 Hoskin Ave., Toronto, ON M5S 1H7
Tel: 416-946-3535
www.wycliffecollege.ca
www.facebook.com/wyclifffetoronto
twitter.com/wycliffe_uoft
www.youtube.com/user/wyclifffeUofT
Rt. Rev. Dr. Stephen Andrews, Principal, 416-946-3521

Regis College
100 Wellesley St. West, Toronto, ON M5S 2Z5
Tel: 416-922-5474; *Fax:* 416-922-2898
inquiries@regiscollege.ca
www.regiscollege.ca
www.facebook.com/RegisCollegeTO
twitter.com/regiscollege
www.youtube.com/user/RegiscollegeToronto
Note: Regis is a Roman Catholic college in the Jesuit tradition. It
is a federated college of the University of Toronto.
Thomas Worcester, President
thomas.worcester@utoronto.ca

Elliott Allen Institute for Theology & Ecology
81 St. Mary's St., Toronto, ON M5S 1J4
Tel: 416-926-1300; *Fax:* 416-926-7294
eaite.contact@utoronto.ca
stmikes.utoronto.ca
Vacant , Director

Innis College
2 Sussex Ave., Toronto, ON M5S 1J5
Tel: 416-978-2513; *Fax:* 416-978-5503
registrar.innis@utoronto.ca
innis.utoronto.ca
www.facebook.com/innisregistrar
twitter.com/innisregistrar
www.youtube.com/user/InnisCollegeVideo
Charlie Keil, Principal, 416-978-2510
principal.innis@utoronto.ca

<u>Centres & Institutes</u>
Asian Institute
1 Devonshire Pl., Toronto, ON M5S 3K7
Tel: 416-946-8900; *Fax:* 416-946-8915
asian.institute@utoronto.ca
www.munk.utoronto.ca/ai
www.facebook.com/AsianInstituteUofT
twitter.com/ai_uoft
www.youtube.com/user/AsianInstituteUofT
Rachel Silvey, Director
ai.director@utoronto.ca

Canadian Institute for Theoretical Astrophysics (CITA)
60 St. George St., 14th Fl., Toronto, ON M5S 3H8
Tel: 416-978-6879; *Fax:* 416-978-3921
office@cita.utoronto.ca
www.cita.utoronto.ca
www.facebook.com/CITA.ICAT
twitter.com/CITA_ICAT
Ue-Li Pen, Interim Director, 416-978-6477
pen@cita.utoronto.ca

Centre for Comparative Literature
c/o Isabel Bader Theatre, 3rd Fl.
93 Charles St. West, Toronto, ON M5S 1K9
Tel: 416-813-4041; *Fax:* 416-813-4040
complit.utoronto.ca
Ann Komaromi, PhD., Acting Director, 416-813-4042
a.komaromi@utoronto.ca

Centre for European, Russian, & Eurasian Studies
Monk School of Global Affairs
1 Devonshire Pl., Toronto, ON M5S 3K7
Tel: 416-946-8900; Fax: 416-946-8915
munkschool.utoronto.ca/ceres
www.facebook.com/CERESMunk
twitter.com/CERESMunk
Note: Part of the Munk School of Global Affairs
Randall Hansen, DPhil., Director, 416-946-8450
r.hansen@utoronto.ca
Joseph Hawker, Research & Programs Coordinator,
416-946-8698
j.hawker@utoronto.ca
Katia Malyuzhinets, Program & Internship Coordinator
katia.malyuzhinets@utoronto.ca

Centre for Industrial Relations & Human Resources
121 St. George St., Toronto, ON M5S 2E8
Tel: 416-978-2927; Fax: 416-978-5696
cir.info@utoronto.ca
www.cirhr.utoronto.ca
twitter.com/CIRHR_UofT
www.instagram.com/CIRHR_UofT
Rafael Gomez, Director
ralph.gomez@utoronto.ca

Centre for Medieval Studies (CMS)
125 Queen's Park, 3rd Fl., Toronto, ON M5S 2C7
Tel: 416-978-4884
medieval.studies@utoronto.ca
medieval.utoronto.ca
Isabelle Cochelin, Interim Director
director.medieval@utoronto.ca

Centre for Reformation & Renaissance Studies (CRRS)
E.J. Pratt Library
#301, 71 Queen's Park Cres. East, Toronto, ON M5S 1K7
Tel: 416-585-4468; Fax: 416-585-4430
crrs.info@vicu.utoronto.ca
crrs.ca
www.facebook.com/crrs.utoronto
twitter.com/CRRS_Toronto
www.instagram.com/crrs.uoft
Ethan Matt Kavaler, Director, 416-585-4461
matt.kavaler@utoronto.ca

Centre for South Asian Studies
1 Devonshire Pl., Toronto, ON M5S 3K7
Tel: 416-946-8900; Fax: 416-946-8915
asian.institute@utoronto.ca
munkschool.utoronto.ca/csas
www.facebook.com/csasut
Christoph Emmrich, PhD., Director, 416-978-6463
christoph.emmrich@utoronto.ca

Centre for the Study of Pain
#300, 155 College St., Toronto, ON M5T 1P8
sites.utoronto.ca/pain
www.facebook.com/UofTPain
twitter.com/UofT_Pain
Robert Bonin, PhD., Interim Director, 416-978-2716
rob.bonin@utoronto.ca
Nancy Mitchell, Administrative Coordinator
nancy.mitchell@utoronto.ca
Renata Musa, Research Officer
renata.musa@utoronto.ca

Centre for Criminology & Sociolegal Studies
14 Queen's Park Cres. West, Toronto, ON M5S 3K9
Tel: 416-978-7124; Fax: 416-978-4195
criminology.utoronto.ca
Audrey Macklin, LLM, Director
audrey.macklin@utoronto.ca

Computing in the Humanities & Social Sciences
#572, 100 St. George St., Toronto, ON M5S 3G3
Tel: 416-978-2535; Fax: 416-978-6519
support@chass.utoronto.ca
www.chass.utoronto.ca

Fields Institute for Research in Mathematical Sciences
222 College St., 2nd Fl., Toronto, ON M5T 3J1
Tel: 416-348-9710; Fax: 416-348-9714
inquiries@fields.utoronto.ca
www.fields.utoronto.ca
www.facebook.com/fieldsinstitute
twitter.com/FieldsInstitute
www.instagram.com/fieldsinstitute
Kumar Murty, PhD., Director, 416-348-9710, ext. 2012
director@fields.utoronto.ca

Centre for Drama, Theatre & Performance Studies (CDTPS)
Also known as: Drama Centre
214 College St., Toronto, ON M5T 2Z9
Tel: 416-978-7980
www.cdtps.utoronto.ca
Other Information: Undergraduate Program: 416-978-8099
www.facebook.com/CDTPS
twitter.com/CDTPS_UofT
www.instagram.com/CDTPS_UofT
Tamara Trojanowska, PhD., Director, 416-978-7982
t.trojanowska@utoronto.ca

University of Toronto Institute for Aerospace Studies (UTIAS)
4925 Dufferin St., Toronto, ON M3H 5T6
Tel: 416-667-7700; Fax: 416-667-7799
www.utias.utoronto.ca
www.facebook.com/UofTIAS
twitter.com/UTIAS
Chris Damaren, PhD., Director, 416-667-7704
damaren@utias.utoronto.ca

Institute for History & Philosophy of Science & Technology (IHPST)
Victoria College
#316, 91 Charles St. West, Toronto, ON M5S 1K7
Tel: 416-978-5397
ihpst.info@utoronto.ca
www.hps.utoronto.ca
Cheryl Misak, DPhil., Acting Director
cheryl.misak@utoronto.ca

Institute for Life Course & Aging
#238, 246 Bloor St. West, Toronto, ON M5S 1V4
Tel: 416-978-0377
aging@utoronto.ca
www.aging.utoronto.ca
www.facebook.com/agingutoronto
twitter.com/lifecourseUofT
Esme Fuller-Thomson, PhD., Director, 416-978-3269
esme.fuller.thomson@utoronto.ca

Women & Gender Studies Institute (WGSI)
Wilson Hall, New College
40 Willcocks St., Toronto, ON M5S 1C6
Fax: 416-946-5561
wg.si@utoronto.ca
www.wgsi.utoronto.ca
www.facebook.com/wgsiuoft
twitter.com/wgsi
Alissa Trotz, PhD., Director, 416-978-8286
wgsi.director@utoronto.ca

Institute of Biomaterials & Biomedical Engineering
Rosebrugh Bldg.
#407, 164 College St., Toronto, ON M5S 3G9
Tel: 416-978-7459
contact.ibbme@utoronto.ca
www.ibbme.utoronto.ca
twitter.com/IBBME_UofT
Warren Chan, PhD., Director, 416-946-0020
warren.chan@utoronto.ca

Institute of Medical Science (IMS)
Medical Sciences Bldg.
#2374, 1 King's College Cir., Toronto, ON M5S 1A8
Tel: 416-946-8286; Fax: 416-971-2253
www.ims.utoronto.ca
www.facebook.com/uoftims
twitter.com/UofTIMS
Mingyao Liu, MSc, MD, Director, 416-946-3002
dir.medscience@utoronto.ca

Knowledge Media Design Institute (KMDI)
#713, 140 St. George St., Toronto, ON M5S 3G6
Tel: 416-978-5634
admin.kmdi@utoronto.ca
www.kmdi.utoronto.ca
www.facebook.com/kmditoronto
twitter.com/kmdi
Sara Grimes, PhD., Director
sara.grimes@utoronto.ca

McLuhan Centre for Culture & Technology
Also known as: The Coach House Institute
39A Queen's Park Cres. East, Toronto, ON M5S 3C3
Tel: 416-978-7026
mcluhan.centre@utoronto.ca
www.mcluhancentre.ca
www.facebook.com/mcluhancentre
twitter.com/McLuhanCHI
Sarah Sharma, PhD., Director
sarah.sharma@utoronto.ca

Dr. Eric Jackman Institute of Child Study
45 Walmer Rd., Toronto, ON M5R 2X2
Tel: 416-934-4526; Fax: 416-934-4565
www.oise.utoronto.ca/jics
Rhonda Martinussen, PhD., Director
rhonda.martinussen@utoronto.ca

Centre for Indigenous Initiatives
563 Spadina Ave., 2nd Fl., Toronto, ON M5S 2J7
Tel: 416-978-2233
indigenous.studies@utoronto.ca
indigenousstudies.utoronto.ca
www.facebook.com/IndigenousUofT
twitter.com/IndigenousUofT
Susan Hill, PhD., Director

Senior College Centre
#412, 256 McCaul St., Toronto, ON M5T 1W5
Tel: 416-978-7553
senior.college@utoronto.ca
seniorcollege.utoronto.ca
Harold L. Atwood, Principal

Joint Centre for Bioethics (JCB)
#754, 155 College St., Toronto, ON M5T 1P8
Tel: 416-978-2709; Fax: 416-978-1911
jcb.info@utoronto.ca
jcb.utoronto.ca
www.facebook.com/uoftjcb
twitter.com/utjcb
Jennifer L. Gibson, Director

Institute for Canadian Music
Edward Johnson Bldg.
80 Queen's Park, Toronto, ON M5S 2C5
Tel: 416-946-8622; Fax: 416-946-3353
sites.utoronto.ca/icm
Robin Elliott, Director
robin.elliott@utoronto.ca

Donnelly Centre for Cellular and Biomolecular Research
#230, 160 College St., Toronto, ON M5S 3E1
Tel: 416-978-8861; Fax: 416-978-8287
www.thedonnellycentre.utoronto.ca
twitter.com/DonnellyCentre
Brenda Andrews, Director
brenda.andrews@utoronto.ca

Cinema Studies Institute
Innis College
2 Sussex Ave., Toronto, ON M5S 1J5
Tel: 416-978-5809; Fax: 416-946-0168
www.cinema.utoronto.ca
Other Information: Undergraduate Office: 416-978-8571
Corinn Columpar, Director
cinema.director@utoronto.ca

Institute of Communication, Culture, Information & Technology (ICCIT)
University of Toronto Mississauga
3359 Mississauga Rd., Toronto, ON L5L 1C6
Tel: 905-569-4489
iccit.utm@utoronto.ca
www.utm.utoronto.ca/iccit
www.facebook.com/ICCITUTM
twitter.com/iccitutm
Anthony Wensley, Director
anthony.wensley@utoronto.ca

Centre for Diaspora & Transnational Studies
#230, 170 St. George St., Toronto, ON M5R 2M8
Tel: 416-946-8464; Fax: 416-978-7045
cdts@utoronto.ca
cdts.utoronto.ca
Kevin Lewis O'Neill, Director

Toronto Nanofabrication Centre (TNFC)
Sandford Fleming Building
10 King's College Rd., #B540, Toronto, ON M5S 3G4
tnfc@utoronto.ca
tnfc.utoronto.ca
Wai Tung Ng, Director

Centre for Ethics
6 Hoskin Ave., Toronto, ON M5S 1H8
Tel: 416-978-6288; Fax: 416-946-8069
ethics@utoronto.ca
ethics.utoronto.ca
Markus D. Dubber, Director
markus.dubber@utoronto.ca

Centre for Forensic Science & Medicine
Medical Science Bldg.
#6231, 1 King's College Circle, Toronto, ON M5S 1A8
Tel: 416-946-0136
www.forensics.utoronto.ca

Michael Pollanen, Director
michael.pollanen@ontario.ca

Centre for the Study of France and the Francophone World
Centre des Études de la France et du Monde Francophone
1 Devonshire Pl., Toronto, ON M5S 3K7
munkschool.utoronto.ca/cefmf

Paul Cohen, Director
p.cohen@utoronto.ca

Centre for Global Change Science
60 St. George St., Toronto, ON M5S 1A7
Tel: 416-978-2933; *Fax:* 416-978-8905
www.cgcs.utoronto.ca

Ana Sousa, Contact
ana@atmosp.physics.utoronto.ca

Institute of Health Policy, Management & Evaluation
#425, 155 College St., Toronto, ON M5T 3M6
Tel: 416-978-4326; *Fax:* 416-978-7350
ihpme@utoronto.ca
ihpme.utoronto.ca
www.facebook.com/IHPMEUofT
twitter.com/ihpmeuoft
www.linkedin.com/groups/2289738
www.instagram.com/ihpmeuoft

Rhonda Cockerill, Acting Director
rhonda.cockerill@utoronto.ca

Jackman Humanities Institute
Jackman Humanities Bldg.
170 St. George St., 10th Fl., Toronto, ON M5R 2M8
Tel: 416-978-7415; *Fax:* 416-946-7434
www.humanities.utoronto.ca

Alison Keith, Director

Impact Centre
#331, 60 St. George St., Toronto, ON M5S 1A7
Tel: 416-978-1457; *Fax:* 416-978-3936
info@imc.utoronto.ca
www.impactcentre.ca

Cynthia Goh, Director
cgoh@imc.utoronto.ca

Centre for Innovation Law & Policy
78 Queen's Park, Toronto, ON M5S 2C5
Tel: 416-946-7549
centre.ilp@utoronto.ca
cilp.law.utoronto.ca

Anthony Niblett, Co-Director
Simon Stern, Co-Director

Lassonde Institute of Mining
#107, 35 St. George St., Toronto, ON M5S 1A4
Tel: 416-316-7155
lassondeinstitute.utoronto.ca

Lesley Warren, Director

McLaughlin Centre
Peter Gilgan Centre for Research & Learning
686 Bay St., 13th Fl., Toronto, ON M5G 0A4
Tel: 416-813-7654
www.mclaughlin.utoronto.ca

Stephen Scherer, Director
stephen.scherer@sickkids.ca
Hin Lee, Program Manager
hin.lee@utoronto.ca

Trudeau Centre for Peace, Conflict & Justice
1 Devonshire Pl., Toronto, ON M5S 3K7
Tel: 416-946-0326
munkschool.utoronto.ca/trudeaucentre

Paola Salardi, Director

Pulp & Paper Centre
#420, 200 College St., Toronto, ON M5S 3E5
Tel: 416-978-3062; *Fax:* 416-971-2106
paper@chem-eng.utoronto.ca
www.pulpandpaper.utoronto.ca

Honghi Tran, Director

Centre for Quantum Information & Quantum Control
cqiqc@physics.utoronto.ca
cqiqc.physics.utoronto.ca

Daniel James, Director
dfvj@physics.utoronto.ca

Tanz Centre for Research in Neurodegenerative Diseases
Krembil Discovery Tower
60 Leonard Ave., #4KD481, Toronto, ON M5T 2S8
Tel: 416-507-6838; *Fax:* 416-603-6435
crnd.director@utoronto.ca
tanz.med.utoronto.ca

Peter St. George-Hyslop, Director

Rotman Institute for International Business (RIIB)
www.rotman.utoronto.ca

Wendy Dobson, Co-Director
dobson@rotman.utoronto.ca
Ig Horstman, Co-Director
ihorstmann@rotman.utoronto.ca

Mark S. Bonham Centre for Sexual Diversity Studies
University College
15 King's College Circle, Toronto, ON M5S 3H7
Tel: 416-978-6276; *Fax:* 416-971-2027
sexual.diversity@utoronto.ca
sds.utoronto.ca
www.facebook.com/BonhamCentreSDS
twitter.com/bonhamcentresds
www.instagram.com/bonhamcentresds

Dana Seitler, Director

Centre for the Study of the United States
Munk School of Global Affairs
1 Devonshire Pl., Toronto, ON M5S 3K7
Tel: 416-946-8972
csus@utoronto.ca
munkschool.utoronto.ca/csus

Nicholas Sammond, Director

Centre for Urban Schooling (CUS)
Ontario Institute for Studies in Education
252 Bloor St. West, Toronto, ON M5S 1V6
Tel: 416-978-0146
cusinquiries@utoronto.ca
cus.oise.utoronto.ca

Tara Goldstein, Contact

Wilson Centre
200 Elizabeth St., #1ES-565, Toronto, ON M5G 2C4
Tel: 416-340-3646; *Fax:* 416-340-3792
www.thewilsoncentre.ca
twitter.com/thewilsoncentre

Dr. Cynthia Whitehead, Director
cynthia.whitehead@utoronto.ca

Centre for Women's Studies in Education (CWSE)
OISE
#2-225, 252 Bloor St. West, Toronto, ON M5S 1V6
Tel: 416-978-2080
cwse@utoronto.ca
www.oise.utoronto.ca/cwse
www.facebook.com/thecwse
twitter.com/CWSEoise

Jamie-Lynn Magnusson, Head

Hughes Lab
Banting and Best Department of Medical Research
#1302, 160 College St., Toronto, ON M5S 3E1
Tel: 416-946-8260; *Fax:* 416-978-8287
t.hughes@utoronto.ca
hugheslab.ccbr.utoronto.ca
Other Information: 416-946-7838
Note: The Hughes lab is part of the Molecular Genetics Department, focusing on genome functions. One of the current studies is focused on cannabinoids.
Timothy R. Hughes, PhD, Research Director
Debashish Ray, Senior Research Associate/Lab Manager
Ally Yang, Senior Research Associate/Lab Manager
Mihai Albu, Senior Research Associate

Toronto: **Victoria University**
73 Queen's Park Cres., Toronto, ON M5S 1K7
Tel: 416-585-4508; *Fax:* 416-585-4459
vic.registrar@utoronto.ca
www.vicu.utoronto.ca
www.facebook.com/vicu.utoronto
twitter.com/VicCollege_UofT

Emmanuel College
#102, 75 Queen's Park Cres., Toronto, ON M5S 1K7, Canada
Tel: 416-585-4539; *Fax:* 416-585-4516
ec.office@utoronto.ca
www.emmanuel.utoronto.ca
Note: Theological college affiliated with the United Church of Canada
Rev. Ralph Carl Wushke, Chaplain, 416-813-4099
Michelle Voss Roberts, Principal

Toronto: **Woodsworth College**
119 Saint George St., Toronto, ON M5S 1A9, Canada
Tel: 416-978-4444; *Fax:* 416-978-6111
wdwregistrar@utoronto.ca
wdw.utoronto.ca

Full Time Equivalency: 6000

Toronto: **Wycliffe College**
5 Hoskin Ave., Toronto, ON M5S 1H7, Canada
Tel: 416-946-3535
www.wycliffecollege.ca
Note: Seminary at the University of Toronto affiliated with the Anglican Church of Canada

Toronto: **York University**
4700 Keele St., Toronto, ON M3J 1P3
Tel: 416-736-2100
www.yorku.ca
www.facebook.com/yorkuniversity
twitter.com/yorkuniversity
www.linkedin.com/school/york-university
www.instagram.com/yorkuniversity
Full Time Equivalency: 53000 *Number of Employees:* 7,000 administrative staff
Gregory Sorbara, Chancellor
Rhonda Lenton, President & Vice-Chancellor
president@yorku.ca
Lisa Philipps, Provost & Vice-President, Academic
Amir Asif, Vice-President, Research & Innovation
vpri@yorku.ca
Jeff O'Hagan, Vice-President, Advancement
vpadvmt@yorku.ca
Carol McAulay, Vice-President, Finance & Administration

Faculties
Faculty of Education
Winters College
4700 Keele St., Toronto, ON M3J 1P3
Tel: 416-736-5001
osp@edu.yorku.ca
edu.yorku.ca
www.facebook.com/YorkUeducation
twitter.com/yorkueducation
www.youtube.com/yorkueducation

Lyndon Martin, Dean

Faculty of Environmental Studies (FES)
Health, Nursing & Environmental Studies Bldg.
#137, 4700 Keele St., Toronto, ON M3J 1P3
Tel: 416-736-5252; *Fax:* 416-736-5679
fesinfo@yorku.ca
fes.yorku.ca
www.facebook.com/YorkUFES
twitter.com/environmentYork
www.linkedin.com/in/fesalum
www.youtube.com/user/environmentalstudies
Alice J. Hovorka, Dean
fesdean@yorku.ca

Glendon College
2275 Bayview Ave., Toronto, ON M4N 3M6
Tel: 416-487-6710
liaison@glendon.yorku.ca
www.glendon.yorku.ca
www.facebook.com/glendoncampus
twitter.com/glendoncampus

Enrollment: 2700
Ian Roberge, Interim Principal, 416-487-6727
principal@glendon.yorku.ca
Patrick Banville, Executive Officer, 416-487-6791
patrick.banville@glendon.yorku.ca

Faculty of Health
Tel: 416-736-5124; *Fax:* 416-736-5760
healthdn@yorku.ca
health.yorku.ca
www.facebook.com/yorkuhealth
twitter.com/YorkUHealth
www.youtube.com/user/FacultyofHealth
Enrollment: 9500
Paul W. McDonald, Dean

Faculty of Graduate Studies
4700 Keele St., Toronto, ON M3J 1P3
Tel: 416-736-5521; *Fax:* 416-736-5592
healthdn@yorku.ca
gradstudies.yorku.ca
www.facebook.com/YorkUGradStudies
twitter.com/YorkUFGS
www.instagram.com/yorkufgs
Enrollment: 6000
Thomas Loebel, Dean
fgsdean@yorku.ca

Faculty of Liberal Arts & Professional Studies (LA&PS)
Ross Bldg.
4700 Keele St., #S900, Toronto, ON M3J 1P3
Tel: 416-736-5220; *Fax:* 416-736-5750
laps@yorku.ca
laps.yorku.ca
www.facebook.com/yorkulaps
twitter.com/yorkULAPS
www.linkedin.com/groups/147130
www.instagram.com/yorkulaps
Enrollment: 24000 *Number of Employees:* 650
JJ McMurtry, Dean

Faculty of Science
Lumbers Bldg.
#355, 4700 Keele St., Toronto, ON M3J 1P3
Tel: 416-736-5085
science@yorku.ca
science.yorku.ca

Enrollment: 4250 *Number of Employees:* 229
Rui Wang, Dean, 416-736-2100, ext. 22316
scidean@yorku.ca

Schools

Osgoode Hall Law School
Ignat Kaneff Bldg.
4700 Keele St., Toronto, ON M3J 1P3
Tel: 416-736-5712
admissions@osgoode.yorku.ca
www.osgoode.yorku.ca
www.facebook.com/Osgoode
twitter.com/osgoodenews
www.linkedin.com/company/osgoode-hall-law-school
www.youtube.com/user/OsgoodeHallLawSchool
Number of Employees: 59 full-time faculty; 150 adjunct faculty
Mary G. Condon, Dean, 416-736-5199
lawdean@osgoode.yorku.ca

Schulich School of Business
111 Ian Macdonald Blvd., Toronto, ON M3J 1P3
Tel: 416-736-2100; *Fax:* 416-650-8174
concierge@schulich.yorku.ca
www.schulich.yorku.ca
Other Information: International Students: 416-736-5059
www.facebook.com/SchulichSchool
twitter.com/SchulichSchool
www.linkedin.com/company/schulichbusiness
www.instagram.com/schulichschool
Dezsö J. Horvath, Dean

School of the Arts, Media, Performance & Design
Joan & Martin Goldfarb Centre for Fine Arts
4700 Keele St., Toronto, ON M3J 1P3
Tel: 416-650-8176
ampd@yorku.ca
ampd.yorku.ca
Sarah Bay-Cheng, Dean

School of Public Policy & Administration (SPPA)
119 McLaughlin College
4700 Keele St., Toronto, ON M3J 1P3
Tel: 416-736-5384; *Fax:* 416-736-5382
lapssppa@yorku.ca
www.sppa.laps.yorku.ca
www.facebook.com/yorkusppa
twitter.com/YorkUSPPA
www.youtube.com/user/YorkUniverse
Alena Kimakova, Director
akimakov@yorku.ca

Lassonde School of Engineering
4700 Keele St., Toronto, ON M3J 1P3
Tel: 416-736-5484
ask@lassonde.yorku.ca
lassonde.yorku.ca
www.facebook.com/lassondeschool
twitter.com/lassondeschool
www.linkedin.com/company/lassonde-school-of-engineering
Enrollment: 3199 *Number of Employees:* 200
Jane Goodyer, Dean

Centres & Institutes

Canadian Centre for German & European Studies (CCGES)
Kaneff Tower, 7th Fl.
4700 Keele St., Toronto, ON M3J 1P3
Tel: 416-736-5695; *Fax:* 416-736-5696
ccges@yorku.ca

Dr. Christina Kraenzle, Contact
kraenzle@yorku.ca

Centre for Atmospheric Chemistry
Steacie Science and Engineering Bldg.
#006, 4700 Keele St., Toronto, ON M3J 1P3
Tel: 416-736-5410; *Fax:* 416-736-5411
cac@yorku.ca
cac.yorku.ca
Robert McLaren, Director
Carol V. Weldon, Coordinator, Research Centre

Israel & Golda Koschitzky Centre for Jewish Studies
Kaneff Tower, 7th Fl.
4700 Keele St., Toronto, ON M3J 1P3
Tel: 416-736-5823
cjs@yorku.ca
cjs.yorku.ca
www.facebook.com/CJSYorkU
Carl S. Ehrlich, Director, 416-736-5823
ehrlich@yorku.ca

Julia Feinberg, Centre Coordinator, 416-736-5823
cjs@yorku.ca

York Collegium for Practical Ethics (YCPE)
McLaughlin College
#119, 4700 Keele St., Toronto, ON M3J 1P3
Fax: 416-736-5436
ycpe.news.yorku.ca
Other Information: 416-736-2100, ext. 30446
twitter.com/YorkU_Ethics
Philip MacEwen, Co-Coordinator
Ian Stedman, Co-Coordinator

Centre for Refugee Studies (CRS)
Kaneff Tower, 8th Fl.
4700 Keele St., Toronto, ON M3J 1P3
Tel: 416-736-2100
crs@yorku.ca
crs.yorku.ca
www.facebook.com/centreforrefugeestudies
twitter.com/crsyorku
www.youtube.com/user/refugeeresearch
Michele Millard, Coordinator, 416-736-2100, ext. 30391
mmillard@yorku.ca

Centre for Research in Mass Spectrometry
Chemistry Bldg.
#240, 4700 Keele St., Toronto, ON M3J 1P3
Tel: 416-650-8426
mass-spectrometry.ca
Derek Wilson, Director, 416-650-8426
dkwilson@yorku.ca
Nicole Chevannes-McGregor, Centre Coordinator, 416-650-8426
nicolec@yorku.ca

Centre for Research on Latin America & the Caribbean
Kaneff Tower, 8th Fl.
4700 Keele St., Toronto, ON M3J 1P3
Tel: 416-736-5237; *Fax:* 416-736-5688
cerlac@yorku.ca
cerlac.info.yorku.ca
www.facebook.com/cerlac
twitter.com/CERLACYorkU
Alan Durston, Director
durston@yorku.ca
Camila Bonifaz, Coordinator, 416-736-2100, ext. 55237
cbonifaz@yorku.ca

Centre for Research on Work & Society (CRWS)
Kaneff Tower, 6th Fl.
4700 Keele St., Toronto, ON M3J 1P3
Tel: 416-736-5612; *Fax:* 416-736-5916
crws@yorku.ca
yorku.ca/crws
Stephanie Ross, Co-Director
stephr@yorku.ca
Mark Thomas, Co-Director
mpthomas@yorku.ca
Leah Vosko, Co-Director
lvosko@yorku.ca
Robin Smith, Administrator
robins@yorku.ca

The Centre for Vision Research (CVR)
#0009, Lassonde Bldg.
4700 Keele St., Toronto, ON M3J 1P3
Tel: 416-736-5659; *Fax:* 416-736-5857
cvr@yorku.ca
www.cvr.yorku.ca

Institute for Research on Digital Learning (IRDL)
Kaneff Tower, 7th Fl.
#715, 4700 Keele St., Toronto, ON M3J 1P3
irdl@yorku.ca
irdl.info.yorku.ca
www.facebook.com/irdlyork
twitter.com/YorkIRDL
Natalie Coulter, Director

Institute for Social Research (IRS)
Victor Phillip Dahdaleh Bldg.
#5075, 4700 Keele St., Toronto, ON M3J 1P3
Tel: 416-736-5061; *Fax:* 416-736-5749
Toll-Free: 888-847-0148
isrnews@yorku.ca
www.isryorku.ca
www.facebook.com/1467475560197399
twitter.com/isr_york
Lorne Foster, Director
lfoster@yorku.ca

Jack & Mae Nathanson Centre on Transnational Human Rights, Crime & Security
Also known as: Jack & Mae Nathanson Centre
Old Name: Jack & Mae Nathanson Centre for the Study of Organized Crime & Corruption
Osgoode Hall Law School, Ignat Kaneff Bldg.
#3067, 4700 Keele St., Toronto, ON M3J 1P3
Tel: 416-736-5586
nathansoncentre@osgoode.yorku.ca
nathanson.osgoode.yorku.ca
twitter.com/NathansonCentre
www.youtube.com/user/nathansoncentre
François Tanguay-Renaud, Co-Director
ftanguay-renaud@osgoode.yorku.ca
Heidi Matthews, Co-Director
hmatthews@osgoode.yorku.ca

LaMarsh Centre for Child & Youth Research
Also known as: LaMarsh
Victor Phillip Dahdaleh Bldg.
#5021, 4700 Keele St., Toronto, ON M3J 1P3
Tel: 416-736-5528; *Fax:* 416-736-5647
lamarsh@yorku.ca
lamarsh.info.yorku.ca
Gord Flett, Director
Irene N. Menard, Coordinator
backhous@yorku.ca

Robarts Centre for Canadian Studies
Kaneff Tower, 7th Fl.
4700 Keele St., Toronto, ON M3J 1P3
Tel: 416-736-5499; *Fax:* 416-650-8069
robarts.info.yorku.ca
www.facebook.com/RCCSYork
twitter.com/robartscentre
Gabrielle Slowey, Director
robdir@yorku.ca
Laura Taman, Coordinator, 416-736-5499
llt@yorku.ca

York Centre for Asian Research
Kaneff Tower, 8th Fl.
4700 Keele St., Toronto, ON M3J 1P3
Tel: 416-736-5821; *Fax:* 416-736-5688
ycar@yorku.ca
www.yorku.ca/ycar
www.facebook.com/146278765461794
twitter.com/asia_york
Abidin Kusno, Director
akusno15@yorku.ca

Centre for Feminist Research (CFR)
Kaneff Tower, 6th Fl.
4700 Keele St., Toronto, ON M3J 1P3
Tel: 416-736-5915
cfr@yorku.ca
cfr.info.yorku.ca
www.facebook.com/YorkCentreForFeministResearch
Enakshi Dua, Director, 416-736-2100, ext. 33691
edua@yorku.ca
Tiffany Pollock, Coordinator
cfr-coor@yorku.ca

York University English Language Institute (YUELI)
Founders College, Keele Campus, York University
#035, 4700 Keele St., Toronto, ON M3J 1P3
Tel: 416-736-5353; *Fax:* 416-736-5908
yueli@yorku.ca
yueli.yorku.ca
www.facebook.com/YorkUYUELI
twitter.com/YORKUYueli
Isaac Garcia-Sitton, Director

Waterloo: Conrad Grebel University College
140 Westmount Rd. North, Waterloo, ON N2L 3G6, Canada
Tel: 519-885-0220; *Fax:* 519-885-0014
congreb@uwaterloo.ca
uwaterloo.ca/grebel
www.facebook.com/ConradGrebel
twitter.com/Conrad_Grebel
www.youtube.com/user/ConradGrebelUC

Waterloo: University of Waterloo
200 University Ave. West, Waterloo, ON N2L 3G1, Canada
Tel: 519-888-4567
www.uwaterloo.ca
Other Information: 519-888-4911;
www.facebook.com/university.waterloo
twitter.com/uWaterloo
www.youtube.com/uwaterloo

Full Time Equivalency: 41000
Dominic Barton, Chancellor
Feridun Hamdullahpur, C.C., A.B., L.L.B., President & Vice-Chancellor

James Rush, Provost & Vice-President, Academic
Charmaine Dean, Vice-President, University Research
Joanne Shoveller, Vice-President, Advancement
Karen Jack, University Secretary
Cathy Newell Kelly, Registrar

Faculties
Faculty of Applied Health Sciences
200 University Ave., Waterloo, ON N2l 3G1
Tel: 519-888-4567; *Fax:* 519-746-6776
ahsrecep@uwaterloo.ca
uwaterloo.ca/applied-health-sciences
www.facebook.com/waterloo.appliedhealthsciences
twitter.com/ahswaterloo
www.linkedin.com/showcase/uwaterlooahs
www.instagram.com/uwaterlooahs
Lili Liu, Dean
lili.liu@uwaterloo.ca

Faculty of Arts
PAS Bldg.
#2401, 200 University Ave. West, Waterloo, ON N2L 3G1
Tel: 519-888-4567
arts@uwaterloo.ca
uwaterloo.ca/arts
www.facebook.com/waterlooarts
twitter.com/uwaterlooARTS
www.linkedin.com/showcase/faculty-of-arts
www.youtube.com/user/artsfaculty
Sheila Ager, Dean, 519-888-4567, ext. 32217
sager@uwaterloo.ca

Faculty of Engineering
Engineering 7
#7302, 200 University Ave. West, Waterloo, ON N2L 3G1
Tel: 519-888-4885
uwaterloo.ca/engineering
Other Information: 519-888-4567, ext. 44885
www.facebook.com/uWaterlooEngineering
twitter.com/waterlooENG
www.linkedin.com/showcase/faculty-of-engineering
www.instagram.com/uwaterlooeng
Enrollment: 10456 *Number of Employees:* 330
J. Richard Culham, Interim Dean, 519-888-4567, ext. 43347
engdean@uwaterloo.ca

Faculty of Environmental Studies
Environment 1
#347, 200 University Ave. West, Waterloo, ON N2L 3G1
uwaterloo.ca/environment
Other Information: 519-888-4567, ext.33463
www.facebook.com/envwaterloo
twitter.com/envwaterloo
www.linkedin.com/groups/3125591
www.instagram.com/envwaterloo
Enrollment: 2970
Jean Andrey, Dean, 519-888-4567, ext. 32884
jandrey@uwaterloo.ca

Graduate Studies & Postdoctoral Affairs
Needles Hall
#2201, 200 University Ave. West, Waterloo, ON N2L 3G1
uwaterloo.ca/graduate-studies-postdoctoral-affairs
Other Information: 519-888-4567, ext. 42268
www.facebook.com/uwaterloogspa
twitter.com/UWaterlooGSPA

Faculty of Mathematics
Mathematics & Computer Bldg.
#5203, 200 University Ave. West, Waterloo, ON N2L 3G1
dom.office@uwaterloo.ca
uwaterloo.ca/math
Other Information: 519-888-4567, ext. 33474
www.facebook.com/waterloo.math
twitter.com/WaterlooMath
www.linkedin.com/showcase/faculty-of-mathematics
www.instagram.com/waterloomath
Enrollment: 8600 *Number of Employees:* 260
Kevin Hare, Interim Dean, 519-888-4567, ext. 38636
deanmath@uwaterloo.ca

Faculty of Science
200 University Ave., Waterloo, ON N2L 3G1
science@uwaterloo.ca
uwaterloo.ca/science
www.facebook.com/WaterlooScience
twitter.com/waterloosci
www.instagram.com/waterloosci
Enrollment: 6329
Bob Lemieux, Dean, 519-888-4567, ext. 42353
rplemieux@uwaterloo.ca
Karen Trevors, Executive Officer, 519-888-4567, ext. 32101
karen.trevors@uwaterloo.ca

Katharine Tuerkes, Communications Officer, 519-888-4567, ext. 39173
katharine.tuerke@waterloo.ca

Affiliations
Conrad Grebel University College
140 Westmount Rd. North, Waterloo, ON N2L 3G6, Canada
Tel: 519-885-0220; *Fax:* 519-885-0014
congreb@uwaterloo.ca
uwaterloo.ca/grebel
twitter.com/Conrad_Grebel
www.linkedin.com/company/conrad-grebel-university-college
www.youtube.com/user/ConradGrebelUC
Full Time Equivalency: 4141
Marcus Shantz, President, 519-885-0220, ext. 24237
cgcpres@uwaterloo.ca
Troy Osborne, Dean, 519-885-0220, ext. 24260
t3osborn@uwaterloo.ca
Paul Penner, Director of Operations, 519-885-0220, ext. 24231
eppenner@uwaterloo.ca

Renison University College
240 Westmount Rd. North, Waterloo, ON N2L 3G4, Canada
Tel: 519-884-4404; *Fax:* 519-884-5135
uwaterloo.ca/renison
www.facebook.com/RenisonUniversityCollege
twitter.com/renisoncollege
www.youtube.com/user/renisonvideo
Note: College programs lead to a Bachelor of Arts or an Honours Bachelor of Social Work degree of the University of Waterloo.
Wendy Fletcher, President & Vice-Chancellor, 519-884-4404, ext. 28636
wendy.fletcher@uwaterloo.ca

St. Jerome's University
290 Westmount Rd. North, Waterloo, ON N2L 3G3
Tel: 519-884-8111
info@sju.ca
www.sju.ca
www.facebook.com/stjeromesuniversity
twitter.com/StJeromesUni
www.linkedin.com/groups/2548753
www.instagram.com/stjeromesuni
Note: Federated with the University of Waterloo, St. Jerome's University is a public Catholic university. Education in the Arts & Mathematics is provided.
James Beingessner, Chancellor
Katherine Bergman, President & Vice-Chancellor
Scott Kline, Dean & Vice-President, Academic
Scott Keys, Interim Vice-President, Administration

St. Paul's University College
University of Waterloo
190 Westmount Rd. North, Waterloo, ON N2L 3G5, Canada
Tel: 519-885-1460; *Fax:* 519-885-6364
stpauls@uwaterloo.ca
uwaterloo.ca/stpauls
www.facebook.com/StPaulsUniversityCollege
twitter.com/UWStPauls
www.linkedin.com/school/15093272
www.youtube.com/uwstpauls
Note: The residential teaching institution is affiliated with the University of Waterloo. It features the international development program.
Richard Myers, Principal, 519-885-1460, ext. 25200
stp.principal@uwaterloo.ca
Peter Frick, Academic Dean, 519-885-1460, ext. 25214
pfrick@uwaterloo.ca

Centres & Institutes
Centre for Extended Learning
Centre for Extended Learning
200 University Ave. West, Waterloo, ON N2L 3G1
Tel: 519-888-4002
extendedlearning@uwaterloo.ca
uwaterloo.ca/extended-learning
Aldo Caputo, Director, 519-888-4567, ext. 37065
acaputo@uwaterloo.ca

Centre for Teaching Excellence
EC3
195 Columbia St. West, 2nd Fl., Waterloo, ON N2L 3G1
Fax: 519-888-9806
cte@uwaterloo.ca
uwaterloo.ca/centre-for-teaching-excellence
Other Information: 519-888-4567, ext. 33353
www.facebook.com/Centre.for.Teaching.Excellence
twitter.com/uwcte
Donna Ellis, Director, 519-888-4567, ext. 35713
donnae@uwaterloo.ca

Waterloo Indigenous Student Centre
St. Paul's University College
190 Westmount Rd. North, Waterloo, ON N2L 3G5
Tel: 519-885-1460
uwaterloo.ca/stpauls/waterloo-indigenous-student-centre
twitter.com/UWIndig
Lori Campbell, Director, 519-885-1460, ext. 25220
lori.campbell@uwaterloo.ca

Women's Centre
Student Life Centre
#2101, 200 University Ave. West, Waterloo, ON N2L 3G1
womenscentre@wusa.ca
wusa.ca/services/womens-centre
Other Information: 519-888-4567, ext. 33457
www.facebook.com/uwwomenscentre
twitter.com/uwwomenscentre
www.instagram.com/uwwomenscentre

Waterloo: Wilfrid Laurier University
75 University Ave. West, Waterloo, ON N2L 3C5, Canada
Tel: 519-884-1970
chooselaurier@wlu.ca
www.wlu.ca
www.facebook.com/WilfridLaurierUniversity
twitter.com/Laurier
www.linkedin.com/school/wilfrid-laurier-university
www.youtube.com/lauriervideo
Full Time Equivalency: 18987
Deborah MacLatchy, President & Vice-Chancellor
Maureen Mancuso, Interim Provost & Vice-President, Academic
Tony Araujo, Vice-President, Finance & Administration
Jason Coolman, Interim Vice-President, Advancement & External Relations
David McMurray, Vice-President, Student Affairs
Jonathan Newman, Vice-President, Research

Faculties
Faculty of Arts
Dr. Alvin Woods Bldg.
#5-106, 75 University Ave. West, Waterloo, ON N2L 3C5
Tel: 519-884-0710
artsinfo@wlu.ca
twitter.com/LaurierArts
Richard Nemesvari, Dean
rnemesvari@wlu.ca

Faculty of Graduate & Postdoctoral Studies
DAWB 1-102
75 University Ave. West, Waterloo, ON N2L 3C5
Tel: 519-884-0710
fgps@wlu.ca
www.wlu.ca/gradstudies
www.facebook.com/LaurierGradStudies
twitter.com/Lauriergrad
www.youtube.com/lauriervideo
Douglas H. Deutschman, Dean

Faculty of Music
choosemusic@wlu.ca
www.wlu.ca/music
www.facebook.com/LaurierMusic
twitter.com/LaurierMusic
www.instagram.com/lauriermusic
Glen Carruthers, Dean
gcarruthers@wlu.ca

Faculty of Science
Science Bldg.
75 University Ave. West, #N1048, Waterloo, ON N2L 3C5
Tel: 519-884-0710; *Fax:* 519-884-0464
scienceinquiries@wlu.ca
www.wlu.ca/science
Kenneth Maly, Acting Dean
kmaly@wlu.ca

Lazaridis School of Business & Economics
Tel: 519-884-1970; *Fax:* 519-884-0201
www.wlu.ca/sbe
www.facebook.com/LazaridisSchool
twitter.com/LazaridisSchool
www.instagram.com/lazaridisschool
Enrollment: 5500
Micheál J. Kelly, Dean

Lyle S. Hallman Faculty of Social Work
120 Duke St. West, Kitchener, ON N2H 3W8, Canada
Tel: 519-884-0710; *Fax:* 519-888-9732
socialwork@wlu.ca
www.wlu.ca/socialwork
Dawn Buzza, Dean

Martin Luther University College
Tel: 519-884-0710; *Fax:* 519-725-2434
martin@luther.wlu.ca
luther.wlu.ca
www.facebook.com/LutherWaterloo
twitter.com/LutherWaterloo
www.instagram.com/lutherwaterloo
Mark Harris, Principal-Dean

<u>Campuses</u>
Brantford Campus
73 George St., Brantford, ON N2T 2Y3, Canada
Tel: 519-756-8228
servicelaurier@wlu.ca
Adam Lawrence, Dean of Students

Centre for Teaching Innovation & Excellence
75 University Ave. West, Waterloo, ON N2L 3C5
Tel: 519-884-0710
www.wlu.ca

Joseph Beer, Director
jbeer@wlu.ca

Windsor: Iona College
University of Windsor
401 Sunset Ave., Windsor, ON N9B 3P4, Canada
Tel: 519-253-3000
office@ionacollege.edu
www.uwindsor.ca/ionacollege
Note: Affiliate College to the University of Windsor, affiliated with the United Church of Canada, designed to promote theological education, social justice and Chaplaincy.
Norman King, Principal
Marilyn Farough, Chair & President

Windsor: University of Windsor
401 Sunset Ave., Windsor, ON N9B 3P4, Canada
Tel: 519-253-3000; *Fax:* 519-973-7050
www.uwindsor.ca
www.facebook.com/uwindsor
twitter.com/uwindsor
www.linkedin.com/groups/38761
www.youtube.com/uwindsor
Full Time Equivalency: 15587

Faculties
Faculty of Arts, Humanities & Social Sciences
Chrysler Hall Tower
#207, 401 Sunset Ave., Windsor, ON N9B 3P4
Tel: 519-253-3000
www.uwindsor.ca/fahss
twitter.com/UWinFAHSS
Marcello Guarini, Dean, 519-253-3000, ext. 2024
mguarini@uwindsor.ca

Faculty of Education
401 Sunset Ave., Windsor, ON N9B 3P4
Fax: 519-971-3694
educ@uwindsor.ca
www.uwindsor.ca/education
Other Information: 519-253-3000, ext. 3800
twitter.com/uwindsored
Ken Montgomery, Dean, 519-253-3000, ext. 3801
deanofed@uwindsor.ca

Faculty of Engineering
401 Sunset Ave., Windsor, ON N9B 3P4
www.uwindsor.ca/engineering
www.facebook.com/UWindsorEngineering
twitter.com/UWindsorENG
Enrollment: 3400 *Number of Employees:* 125
Mehrdad Saif, Dean, 519-253-3000, ext. 2566
deanengg@uwindsor.ca

Faculty of Graduate Studies
Chrysler Hall Tower
401 Sunset Ave., Windsor, ON N9B 3P4
gradst@uwindsor.ca
uwindsor.ca/graduate-studies
Other Information: 519-253-3000, ext.2109
Patricia Weir, Dean, 519-253-3000, ext. 2107
gradst@uwindsor.ca

Faculty of Human Kinetics
401 Sunset Ave., Windsor, ON N9B 3P4
Tel: 519-253-3000; *Fax:* 519-973-7056
hk@uwindsor.ca
www.uwindsor.ca/humankinetics
www.facebook.com/UWindsorHK
twitter.com/UWindsorKIN
www.instagram.com/uwindsorkinesiology
Michael Khan, Dean
makhan@uwindsor.ca

Faculty of Law
401 Sunset Ave., Windsor, ON N9B 3P4
uwlaw@uwindsor.ca
uwindsor.ca/law
Other Information: 519-253-3000, ext. 2989
Christopher Waters, Dean, 519-253-3000, ext. 2930
cwaters@uwindsor.ca

Faculty of Nursing
Toldo Health Education Centre
#336, 401 Sunset Ave., Windsor, ON N9B 3P4
Tel: 519-253-3000; *Fax:* 519-973-7084
nurse@uwindsor.ca
www.uwindsor.ca/nursing
twitter.com/UWinNursing
Linda J. Patrick, RN, BScN, MA, MSc, PhD, Dean

Faculty of Science
Essex Hall
#242, 401 Sunset Ave., Windsor, ON N9B 3P4
Fax: 519-973-7068
science@uwindsor.ca
uwindsor.ca/science
Other Information: 519-253-3000, ext. 3009
twitter.com/ScienceUWindsor
Chris Houser, Dean, 519-253-3000, ext. 3010
chouser@uwindsor.ca

Odette School of Business
Odette Bldg.
401 Sunset Ave., Windsor, ON N9B 3P4
Fax: 519-973-7073
business@uwindsor.ca
odette.uwindsor.ca
Other Information: 519-253-3000, ext. 3153
Mitchell Fields, Dean, 519-253-3000, ext. 3091
mfields@uwindsor.ca

Schools
School of Computer Science
Lambton Tower
401 Sunset Ave., 5th Fl., Windsor, ON N9B 3P4
Fax: 519-973-7093
csinfo@uwindsor.ca
uwindsor.ca/science/computerscience
Other Information: 519-253-3000, ext. 2991
twitter.com/wicyswindsor
Ziad Kobti, Director, 519-253-3000, ext. 2990
kobti@uwindsor.ca

School of Creative Arts
Armouries Bldg.
37 University Ave. East, Windsor, ON N9A 1E4
soca@uwindsor.ca
uwindsor.ca/soca
Other Information: 519-253-3000, ext. 2829
twitter.com/UWindsorSoca
Vincent Georgie, Director, 519-253-3000, ext. 2828
vgeorgie@uwindsor.ca

School of Dramatic Art
Jackman Dramatic Art Centre
401 Sunset Ave., Windsor, ON N9B 3P4
drama@uwindsor.ca
uwindsor.ca/drama
Other Information: 519-253-3000, ext. 2804 or 2805
Tina Pugliese, Director, 519-253-3000, ext. 2805
tinap@uwindsor.ca

School of Social Work
#201-E, 167 Ferry St., Windsor, ON N9A 0C5
Tel: 519-253-3000; *Fax:* 519-973-7036
socwork@uwindsor.ca
www.uwindsor.ca/socialwork
Robin Wright, Director, 518-253-3000, ext. 3060
rwright@uwindsor.ca

Schulich School of Medicine & Dentistry - Windsor Campus
Dr. Murray O'Neil Medical Education Centre
#1100, 401 Sunset Ave., Windsor, ON N9B 3P4
Tel: 519-561-1411
www.uwindsor.ca/medicine

Affiliations
Assumption University
Assumption Hall
400 Huron Church Rd., 2nd Fl., Windsor, ON N9C 2J9, Canada
Tel: 519-973-7033; *Fax:* 519-973-7089
info@assumption.ca
assumptionu.ca
www.facebook.com/WindsorCampusMin
twitter.com/assumptionu
Most Rev. Ronald P. Fabbro, C.S.B., D.D., Bishop of L, Chancellor
John Capucci, Principal & Chief Administrator

Canterbury College
2500 University Ave. West, Windsor, ON N9B 3Y2
Tel: 519-971-3646; *Fax:* 519-971-3645
canter@uwindsor.ca
www.uwindsor.ca/canterbury
twitter.com/cantercuryc
Note: Canterbury College offers the following courses: Doctor of Ministry Degree (in affiliation with Ashland Theological Seminary at Ashland University); certificate courses for the Anglican Community of Deacons & interested lay people; & professional courses for the community.
Dr. Gordon W.F. Drake, Principal
gdrake@uwindsor.ca
Shelley Bolger, General Manager
bolgers@uwindsor.ca
Brenda Smith, Coordinator, Residence Admissions
brsmith@uwindsor.ca

Iona College
University of Windsor
401 Sunset Ave., Windsor, ON N9B 3P4
Tel: 519-253-3000
office@ionacollege.edu
uwindsor.ca/ionacollege
Other Information: 519-253-3000, ext. 7039
www.facebook.com/ionacollegecanada
Norman King, Principal

Colleges

Barrie: Georgian College
1 Georgian Dr., Barrie, ON L4M 3X9
Tel: 705-728-1968; *Fax:* 705-722-5123
inquire@georgianc.on.ca
www.georgianc.on.ca
www.facebook.com/georgiancollege
twitter.com/georgiancollege
www.linkedin.com/school/georgiancollege
www.youtube.com/c/GeorgiancollegeCa
Full Time Equivalency: 9000
MaryLynn West-Moynes, President & CEO

Midland Campus
649 Prospect Blvd., Midland, ON L4R 4K6
Tel: 705-526-3666
midland@georgiancollege.ca

Muskoka Campus
111 Wellington St., Bracebridge, ON P1L 1E2
muskoka@georgiancollege.ca
Other Information: 705-646-7629, ext. 4850

Orangeville Campus
22 Centennial Rd., Orangeville, ON L9W 1P8
Tel: 519-940-0331
orangeville@georgiancollege.ca

Orillia Campus
825 Memorial Ave., Orillia, ON L3V 6S2
Tel: 705-325-2740

Owen Sound Campus
1450 - 8th St. East, Owen Sound, ON N4K 5R4
Tel: 519-376-0840

South Georgian Bay Campus
499 Raglan St., Collingwood, ON L9Y 3Z1
Tel: 705-445-2961
southgeorgianbay@georgiancollege.ca

Belleville: Loyalist College of Applied Arts & Technology
P.O. Box 4200
376 Wallbridge-Loyalist Rd., Belleville, ON K8N 5B9
Tel: 613-969-1913; *Fax:* 613-962-1376
Toll-Free: 888-569-2547
info@loyalistcollege.com
www.loyalistcollege.com
www.facebook.com/loyalistcollege
twitter.com/loyalistcollege
www.linkedin.com/company/loyalist-college
www.youtube.com/user/goloyalist
Ann Marie Vaughan, President & CEO, 613-969-1913, ext. 2201
avaughan@loyalistc.on.ca

Hamilton: Mohawk College
Fennell Campus
P.O. Box 2034
135 Fennell Ave. West, Hamilton, ON L8N 3T2
Tel: 905-575-1212; *Fax:* 905-575-2378
www.mohawkcollege.ca
www.facebook.com/mohawkcollege
twitter.com/mohawkcollege
www.linkedin.com/school/mohawkcollege
www.youtube.com/user/mohawkcollege
Full Time Equivalency: 30000

Ron McKerlie, President
president@mohawkcollege.ca
Angela Zehr, Chief Financial Officer
angela.zehr@mohawkcollege.ca
Alison Horton, Vice-President, Academic
alison.horton@mohawkcollege.ca

Campuses
Stoney Creek Campus for Skilled Trades
481 Barton St. East, Stoney Creek, ON L8E 2L7
Tel: 905-575-1212; *Fax:* 905-575-2549

Centres & Institutes
Centre for Aviation Technology
Hamilton International Airport
9500 Airport Rd., Hamilton, ON L0R 1W0
Tel: 905-575-1212

Nadine Ogborn, Manager
nadine.ogborn@mohawkcollege.ca

Mohawk - McMaster Institute for Applied Health Sciences
1400 Main St. West, Hamilton, ON L8S 1C7
Tel: 905-540-4247; *Fax:* 905-528-8242

Kingston: St. Lawrence College
Also known as: Collège Saint-Laurent
Kingston Campus
100 Portsmouth Ave., Kingston, ON K7L 5A6
Tel: 613-544-5400; *Fax:* 613-545-3923
Toll-Free: 800-463-0752
ask@sl.on.ca
www.stlawrencecollege.ca
www.facebook.com/stlawrencecollege
twitter.com/whatsinsideslc
www.linkedin.com/school/st—lawrence-college
www.youtube.com/user/aboutslc
Full Time Equivalency: 10000
Glenn Vollebregt, President & CEO

Campuses
Brockville Campus
2288 Parkedale Ave., Brockville, ON K6V 5X3
Tel: 613-345-0660

Beverlie Dietze, Campus Dean, ext. 3260
bdietze@sl.on.ca

Cornwall Campus
2 St Lawrence Dr., Cornwall, ON K6H 4Z1
Tel: 613-933-6080

Don Fairweather, Campus Dean, ext. 2223
dfairweather@sl.on.ca

Kitchener: Conestoga College Institute of Technology & Advanced Learning
299 Doon Valley Dr., Kitchener, ON N2G 4M4
Tel: 519-748-5220; *Fax:* 519-895-1097
www.conestogac.on.ca
www.facebook.com/ConestogaCollege
twitter.com/ConestogaC
www.youtube.com/c/ConestogaCollegeOfficial
Full Time Equivalency: 23000
John W. Tibbits, President
jtibbits@conestogac.on.ca

Campuses
Brantford Campus
274 Colborne St., Brantford, ON N3T 2H5
Tel: 226-250-1772
www.conestogac.on.ca/about/campuses/brantford
Note: School of Engineering Technology & Trades; Institute of
Food Processing Technology

Cambridge Campus
850 Fountain St. South, Cambridge, ON N3H 0A8
Tel: 519-748-5220
www.conestogac.on.ca/about/campuses/cambridge-fountain-stre
et
Note: School of Engineering Technology & Trades; Institute of
Food Processing Technology

Cambridge Downtown Campus
#402, 150 Main St., Cambridge, ON N1R 6P9
Tel: 519-623-4890
www.conestogac.on.ca/about/campuses/cambridge-downtown
Note: Language Instruction for Newcomers to Canada

Guelph Campus
460 Speedvale Ave. West, Guelph, ON N1H 6N6
Tel: 519-824-9390
www.conestogac.on.ca/about/campuses/guelph
Note: Business Foundations, General Business & Office
Administration

Kitchener Downtown Campus
49 Frederick St., Kitchener, ON N2H 6M7
Tel: 519-748-5220
www.conestogac.on.ca/about/campuses/kitchener-downtown

Note: Business Foundations, General Business & Office
Administration

Stratford Campus
130 Youngs St., Stratford, ON N5A 1J7
Tel: 519-271-5700
www.conestogac.on.ca/about/campuses/stratford
Note: Continuing education & acdemic upgrading

Waterloo Campus
108 University Ave. East, Waterloo, ON N2J 2W2
Tel: 519-885-0300
www.conestogac.on.ca/about/campuses/waterloo
Note: Skilled trades & culinary arts training; English studies;
Roofing Skills Training Centre & Heating, Refrigeration & Air
Conditioning Training Centre; Masonry Centre

Ingersoll Skills Training Centre
420 Thomas St., Ingersoll, ON N5C 3J7
Tel: 519-485-5666
www.conestogac.on.ca/about/campuses/ingersoll-skills-training-
centre

London: Fanshawe College
P.O. Box 7005
1001 Fanshawe College Blvd., London, ON N5Y 5R6
Tel: 519-452-4430; *Fax:* 519-452-4420
www.fanshawec.ca
www.facebook.com/fanshaweapplicants
twitter.com/fanshawecollege
www.linkedin.com/company/fanshawe-college
www.youtube.com/myfanshawe
Full Time Equivalency: 15000
Peter Devlin, President

Campuses
Downtown London Campus
Citi Plaza Mall
#114, 355 Wellington St., London, ON N6A 3N7, Canada
Tel: 519-667-2392

James N. Allan Campus (Simcoe)
P.O. Box 10
634 Ireland Rd., Simcoe, ON N3Y 4K8, Canada
Tel: 519-426-8260; *Fax:* 519-428-3112

St. Thomas/Elgin Campus
120 Bill Martyn Pkwy., St Thomas, ON N5R 6A7, Canada
Tel: 519-633-2030; *Fax:* 519-633-0043

Woodstock Campus
369 Finkle St., Woodstock, ON N4V 1A3, Canada
Tel: 519-421-0144; *Fax:* 519-539-3870

Centres & Institutes
Centre for Applied Transportation Technology
Z Bldg.
1764 Oxford St., London, ON N5V 5R6, Canada
Tel: 519-452-4430; *Fax:* 519-452-4420

Centre for Digital & Performance Arts
137 Dundas St., London, ON N6A 1E9
Tel: 519-452-4430

Centre for Sustainable Energy & Environments
1001 Fanshawe College Blvd., #T3010, London, ON N5Y 5R6
Tel: 519-452-4430

Dan Douglas, Dean
ddouglas@fanshawec.ca

North Bay: Canadore College of Applied Arts & Technology
P.O. Box 5001
100 College Dr., North Bay, ON P1B 8K9
Tel: 705-474-7600; *Toll-Free:* 855-495-7915
info@canadorecollege.ca
www.canadorecollege.ca
www.facebook.com/canadorecollege
twitter.com/canadorecollege
www.linkedin.com/school/canadore-college
www.youtube.com/c/CanadoreLiaison
Full Time Equivalency: 3500
George Burton, President & CEO
george.burton@canadorecollege.ca
Ahmed Obaide, Vice-President, Academic

Campuses
Commerce Court Campus
60 Commerce Cres., North Bay, ON
Tel: 705-474-7600

Aviation Campus
55 Aviation Ave., North Bay, ON
Tel: 705-474-7600

West Parry Sound Campus
1 College Dr., Parry Sound, ON P2A 0A9
Tel: 705-746-9222

Oakville: Sheridan College Institute of Technology & Advanced Learning
Also known as: Sheridan College
1430 Trafalgar Rd., Oakville, ON L6H 2L1
Tel: 905-845-9430
infosheridan@sheridancollege.ca
www.sheridancollege.ca
www.facebook.com/sheridaninstitute
twitter.com/sheridancollege
www.linkedin.com/school/sheridan
www.youtube.com/c/sheridancollege
Full Time Equivalency: 43000 *Note:* The polytechnic institute
offers pre-apprenticeship & apprenticeship training, one-year
certificate & graduate certificates, two & three-year diplomas &
Bachelor's degrees in applied areas of study. Collaborative
degree progrmas are provided through partnerships with the
following universities: Brock University, University of Toronto at
Mississauga, & York University.
Janet Morrison, President

Campuses
Davis Campus
7899 McLaughlin Rd., Brampton, ON L6Y 5H9
Tel: 905-459-7533

Enrollment: 11200

Hazel McCallum (Mississauga) Campus
4180 Duke of York Blvd., Mississauga, ON L5B 0G5
Tel: 905-845-9430

Oshawa: Durham College
P.O. Box 385
2000 Simcoe St. North, Oshawa, ON L1H 7K4, Canada
Tel: 905-721-2000; *Fax:* 905-721-3113
dccares@durhamcollege.ca
www.durhamcollege.ca
www.facebook.com/durhamcollege
twitter.com/durhamcollege
www.linkedin.com/company/durham-college
Full Time Equivalency: 11110 *Number of Employees:* 800
full-time; 1000 part-time
Don Lovisa, President
Meri Kim Oliver, Vice-President, Student Affairs
Elaine Popp, Vice-President, Academic
Scott Blakey, Chief Administrative Officer
Barbara MacCheyne, Chief Financial Officer

Schools
School of Continuing Education
Gordon Willey building A160
2000 Simcoe St. North, Oshawa, ON L1H 7K4, Canada
Tel: 905-721-3052
coned@durhamcollege.ca
Note: The Cannabis Industry Specialization Program prepares
students for a career in all aspects of the cannabis industry.
Offered part-time, in-class and online. Also available; Medical
Cannabis Fundamentals for Business Professionals as a
two-day workshop. Durham College is partnering with GrowWise
Health Limited.

Campuses
Whitby Campus
1610 Champlain Ave., Whitby, ON L1N 6A7, Canada
Tel: 905-721-2000
dccares@durhamcollege.ca

Ottawa: Algonquin College of Applied Arts & Technology
1385 Woodroffe Ave., Ottawa, ON K2G 1V8, Canada
Tel: 613-727-4723
www.algonquincollege.com
www.facebook.com/algonquincollege
twitter.com/AlgonquinColleg
www.linkedin.com/company/14808
www.youtube.com/user/algonquinvideos
Full Time Equivalency: 19000
Claude Brulé, President & Chief Executive Officer

Faculties
School of Advanced Technology (SAT)
www.algonquincollege.com/sat
Chris Janzen, Dean

School of Health & Community Studies
Tel: 613-727-4723
www.algonquincollege.com/healthandcommunity
twitter.com/AChealthstudies
Jane Trakalo, Acting Dean

School of Media & Design
www.algonquincollege.com/mediaanddesign
Robyn Heaton, Dean, 613-727-4723, ext. 5410
heatonr@algonquincollege.com

School of Business
www.algonquincollege.com/business

Dave Donaldson, Dean, 613-727-4723, ext. 5227
donaldd@algonquincollege.com

School of Hospitality & Tourism
www.algonquincollege.com/hospitalityandtourism
Jim Kyte, Dean
kytej@algonquincollege.com

Campuses
Pembroke Campus
1 College Way, Pembroke, ON K8A 0C8, Canada
Tel: 613-735-4700

Perth Campus
7 Craig St., Perth, ON K7H 1X7, Canada
Tel: 613-267-2859

Centres & Institutes
Algonquin Centre for Construction Excellence (ACCE)
Tel: 613-727-4723
ACCE@algonquincollege.com
www.algonquincollege.com/acce
Shaun Barr, Academic Chair
barrs@algonquincollege.com
Eric Marois, Academic Chair
maroise@algonquincollege.com
Amandah Selvey, Associate Chair
selveya@algonquincollege.com

Mamidosewin Centre
1385 Woodroffe Ave., #E122, Ottawa, ON K2G 1V8
Tel: 613-727-4723; Fax: 613-727-7829
www.algonquincollege.com/mamidosewin
André O'Bonsawin, Manager, Aboriginal Portf
obonsaa@algonquincollege.com

Peterborough: Sir Sandford Fleming College
Also known as: Fleming College
Sutherland Campus
599 Brealey Dr., Peterborough, ON K9J 7B1
Tel: 705-749-5530; Toll-Free: 866-353-6464
info@flemingcollege.ca
flemingcollege.ca
www.facebook.com/flemingcollege
twitter.com/flemingcollege
www.linkedin.com/company/323364
www.youtube.com/flemingcollege
Full Time Equivalency: 16000 Note: The College consists of the following schools: School of Business & Technology; School of Environmental & Natural Resource Sciences; School of Health & Wellness; School of Interdisciplinary Studies; School of Law, Justice & Community Services; School of Continuing Education & Skilled Trades; & the Haliburton School of The Arts.
Dan Marinigh, Chair
Maureen Adamson, President

Schools
School of Continuing Education
Toll-Free: 888-269-6929
coned@flemingcollege.ca
Other Information: 705-749-5530, ext. 1502
Note: The Legalization of Cannabis in Canada is an overview course that examines the history of cannabis within Canada to date. Offered online only.

Campuses
Cobourg Campus
1005 Elgin St. West, Cobourg, ON K9A 5J4
Tel: 905-372-6865; Fax: 905-372-8570
Toll-Free: 866-353-6464
Note: The Cobourg Campus offers academic upgrading & part time studies, as well as esthetician studies.

Frost Campus
P.O. Box 8000
200 Albert St. South, Lindsay, ON K9V 5E6, Canada
Tel: 705-324-9144; Fax: 705-878-9312
Toll-Free: 866-353-6464
Note: The Frost Campus features Fleming College's School of Environmental & Natural Resource Sciences, The Centre for Alternative Wastewater Treatment, The Centre for Heavy Equipment Technology, & The Geomatics Institute.

Haliburton Campus
P.O. Box 839
297 College Dr., Haliburton, ON K0M 1S0, Canada
Tel: 705-457-1680; Fax: 705-457-2255
Toll-Free: 866-353-6464
askus@hsad.ca
Note: The Haliburton Campus features the Haliburton School of Art & Design & offers Fleming's Sustainable Building Design & Construction program.

Sarnia: Lambton College of Applied Arts & Technology
Also known as: Lambton College
South Bldg., Main Campus
1457 London Rd., Sarnia, ON N7S 6K4
Tel: 519-542-7751
info@lambtoncollege.ca
www.lambton.on.ca
www.facebook.com/lambtoncollege
twitter.com/lambtoncollege
www.linkedin.com/school/lambton-college-sarnia
www.youtube.com/c/LambtonCollegeSarnia
Full Time Equivalency: 3500
Judy Morris, President & CEO, 519-542-7751, ext. 3320
judy.morris@lambtoncollege.ca

Campuses
Mississauga Campus
121 Brunel Rd., Mississauga, ON L4Z 3E9
Tel: 905-890-7833
lambton@queenscollege.ca
Note: Queen's College is licensed to administer the curriculum of the Lambton Mississauga campus. The campus focuses on interntional students.

Toronto Campus
#400, 265 Yorkland Blvd., Toronto, ON M2J 1S5
Tel: 416-485-2098
lambtonintoronto@lambtoncollege.ca
www.lambton.on.ca/Toronto

Sault Ste Marie: Algoma University
1520 Queen St. East, Sault Ste Marie, ON P6A 2G4
Tel: 705-949-2301; Fax: 705-949-6583
Toll-Free: 888-254-6628
info@algomau.ca
www.algomau.ca
www.facebook.com/algomau
twitter.com/algomau
www.linkedin.com/company/algoma-university
www.youtube.com/user/algomauniversity
Full Time Equivalency: 1300
Dr Richard Myers, President
Richard McCutcheon, Academic Dean
dean@algomau.ca
David Marasco, Registrar
registrar@algomau.ca

Campuses
Brampton Campus
#102/103, 24 Queen St. East, Brampton, ON L6V 1A3, Canada
Tel: 905-451-0100; Fax: 905-451-0102
brampton@algomau.ca

Timmins Campus
4715 Hwy. 101 East, South Porcupine, ON P0N 1H0, Canada
Tel: 705-235-2311
timmins@algomau.ca

St. Thomas Campus
50 Wellington St., St Thomas, ON N5R 2P8, Canada
Tel: 519-633-6501
info@algomau.ca

Sault Ste Marie: Sault College of Applied Arts & Technology
443 Northern Ave., Sault Ste Marie, ON P6A 5L3
Tel: 705-759-2554; Fax: 705-759-3273
Toll-Free: 1-800-461-2260
registrar@saultcollege.ca
www.saultcollege.ca
www.facebook.com/SaultCollege
twitter.com/SaultCollege
www.youtube.com/thesaultcollege
Full Time Equivalency: 4500 Note: The College offers education & training to full-time & part-time students in post-secondary, apprenticeship, adult retraining, continuing education, & contract training programs. Specializes in Environmental Studies, Nursing & Aviation.
Peter Berlingieri, Chair
Dr. Ron Common, President

Sudbury: Cambrian College of Applied Arts & Technology
1400 Barrydowne Rd., Sudbury, ON P3A 3V8
Tel: 705-566-8101; Fax: 705-524-7334
Toll-Free: 800-461-7145
info@cambriancollege.ca
cambriancollege.ca
www.facebook.com/cambriancollege
twitter.com/CambrianCollege
www.linkedin.com/school/cambrian-college
www.youtube.com/user/CambrianCollege

Full Time Equivalency: 4500
Bill Best, President

Campuses
Manitoulin Campus
7 Water St., Little Current, ON P0P 1K0
Tel: 705-368-3194; Fax: 705-368-3496

Espanola Campus
#101, 91 Tudhope St., Espanola, ON P5E 1S6
Tel: 705-869-4113; Fax: 705-869-3071

Sudbury: Collège Boréal
21, boul Lasalle, Sudbury, ON P3A 6B1
Tél: 705-560-6673; Ligne sans frais: 800-361-6673
info@collegeboreal.ca
www.collegeboreal.ca
www.facebook.com/CollegeBoreal
twitter.com/collegeboreal
www.youtube.com/collegeboreal
Note: Le Collège Boréal est un collège des arts et des technologies appliqués francophone. Son campus principal est à Sudbury, en Ontario, avec six autres campus situés à Toronto, Timmins, Nipissing Ouest, Hearst, Kapuskasing, et New Liskeard.
Daniel Giroux, Président
Michel Doucet, Vice-président

Schools
Formation Continue
fc@collegeboreal.ca
continue.collegeboreal.ca
Note: Offre trois cours sur la formation du cannabis, comprenant le marketing et les ventes, la production et les finances. Les cours sont offerts en français et en anglais. Les cours sont exclusivement offerts en ligne.

Thunder Bay: Confederation College
P.O. Box 398
1450 Nakina Dr., Thunder Bay, ON P7C 4W1, Canada
Tel: 807-475-6110; Fax: 807-473-3727
Toll-Free: 800-465-5493
www.confederationcollege.ca
www.facebook.com/confederation
twitter.com/confederation
www.youtube.com/confederationcollege
Full Time Equivalency: 3200
Kathleen Lynch, President, 807-473-3825
klynch@confederationc.on.ca

Campuses
Dryden Campus
100 Casimir Ave., Dryden, ON P8N 3L4, Canada
Tel: 807-223-3035; Fax: 807-223-5460
drydencampus@confederationcollege.ca
www.confederationcollege.ca/dryden
Angelina Anderson, Director
angelina@confederationcollege.ca

Greenstone Campus (Geraldton)
P.O. Box 368
500 - 2nd St. West, Geraldton, ON P0T 1M0, Canada
Tel: 807-854-0652; Fax: 807-854-0809
www.confederationcollege.ca/geraldton
Anne Renaud, Director
arenaud@confederationcollege.ca

Lake of the Woods Campus (Kenora)
P.O. Box 1370
900 Golf Course Rd., Kenora, ON P9N 3X7, Canada
Tel: 807-468-3121; Fax: 807-468-3601
kenoracampus@confederationcollege.ca
www.confederationcollege.ca/kenora
Laura Christie, Director
laura.christie@confederationcollege.ca

Northshore Campus (Marathon)
P.O. Box 520
14 Hemlo Dr., Marathon, ON P0T 2E0, Canada
Tel: 807-229-2464; Fax: 807-229-3393
northshorecampus@confederationcollege.ca
www.confederationcollege.ca/marathon
Anne Renaud, Director
arenaud@confederationcollege.ca

Rainy River District Campus (Fort Frances)
440 McIrvine Rd., Fort Frances, ON P9A 3T8, Canada
Tel: 807-274-5395; Fax: 807-274-2462
fortfrancescampus@confederationcollege.ca
www.confederationcollege.ca/fort-frances
Sandra Turner, Manager
sturner9@confederationcollege.ca

Red Lake Campus
P.O. Box 328
60B Hwy. 105, Red Lake, ON P0V 2M0, Canada
Tel: 807-727-2604; *Fax:* 807-727-2144
redlakecampus@confederationcollege.ca
www.confederationcollege.ca/red-lake
Laura Christie, Director
laura.christie@confederationcollege.ca

Sioux Lookout Campus
70 Wellington St., Sioux Lookout, ON P8T 1E1, Canada
Tel: 807-737-2851; *Fax:* 807-737-2436
siouxlookoutcampus@confederationcollege.ca
www.confederationcollege.ca/sioux-lookout
Angelina Anderson, Director
angelina@confederationcollege.ca

Wawa Campus
3 Boyer St., Wawa, ON P0S 1K0, Canada
Tel: 705-856-0713; *Fax:* 705-856-0443
wawacampus@confederationcollege.ca
www.confederationcollege.ca/wawa
Anne Renaud, Director
arenaud@confederationcollege.ca

Aviation Centre of Excellence
2003 Derek Burney Dr., Thunder Bay, ON P7K 1J4
Tel: 807-474-2013
www.confederationcollege.ca/aviation-centre-of-excellence

Confederation Natural Resources Centre (CNRC)
P.O. Box 398
Thunder Bay, ON P7C 4W1
Tel: 807-475-6110

Toronto: Centennial College of Applied Arts & Technology
P.O. Box 631 A
Toronto, ON M1K 5E9
Tel: 416-289-5000; *Toll-Free:* 800-268-4419
success@centennialcollege.ca
www.centennialcollege.ca
www.facebook.com/centennialcollege
twitter.com/CentennialEDU
www.linkedin.com/school/centennial-college
www.youtube.com/c/centennialcollege
Full Time Equivalency: 25000
Craig Stephenson, President

Campuses
Ashtonbee Campus
75 Ashtonbee Rd., Toronto, ON M1L 4N4

Downsview Campus
65 Carl Hall Rd., Toronto, ON M3K 2C1

Morningside Campus
755 Morningside Ave., Toronto, ON M1C 5J9
Note: School of Health Studies, Engineering Technology & Applied Science.

Progress Campus
941 Progress Ave., Toronto, ON M1G 3T8
Note: Houses Business & Hospitality, Tourism & Culture, Advanced Manufacturing & Automation Engineering Technology, as well as Child Studies & Community Service

Centennial Energy Institute (CEI)
P.O. Box 631 A
Toronto, ON M1K 5E9
Tel: 416-289-5000
cei@centennialcollege.ca

Centre for Global Citizenship Education & Inclusion (GCEI)
P.O. Box 631 A
941 Progress Ave., #B2-12, Toronto, ON M1K 5E9
Tel: 416-289-5000
www.facebook.com/CCGCEI
twitter.com/CentennialGCEI
Yasmin Razack, Director

Story Arts Centre
951 Carlaw Ave., Toronto, ON M4K 3M2
Note: Houses School of Communications, Media & Design

Toronto: George Brown College
St. James Campus
P.O. Box 1015 B
200 King St. East, Toronto, ON M5T 2T9
Tel: 416-415-2000; *Toll-Free:* 800-265-2002
ask.george@georgebrown.ca
www.georgebrown.ca
TTY: 877-515-5559
www.facebook.com/georgebrowncollege
twitter.com/GBCollege
www.linkedin.com/company/george-brown-college
www.youtube.com/user/georgebrowncollege

Full Time Equivalency: 31300
Anne Sado, President
asado@georgebrown.ca
Cory Ross, PhD, Vice-President, Academic

Faculties
Faculty of Business & Legal Studies
cebusiness@georgebrown.ca
coned.georgebrown.ca
Other Information: 416-415-5000, ext. 2163
Note: Offers a two-day certificate course, Cannabis Business Fundamentals.

Schools
School of Design
341 Richmond St. East, Toronto, ON M5A 1L1
www.georgebrown.ca/arts-design-information-technology/design

Campuses
Casa Loma Campus
160 Kendal Ave., Toronto, ON M5R 1M3
Tel: 416-415-2000

Ryerson Campus
Eric Palin Hall, Ryerson University
99 Gerrard St. East, Toronto, ON M5B 2K8
ece@georgebrown.ca
www.georgebrown.ca/about/campuses-locations/ryerson
Note: A number of George Brown early childhood education programs are taught at Ryerson University.

Waterfront Campus
Centre for Health Sciences
51 Dockside Dr., Toronto, ON M5A 0B6

Centres & Institutes
Centre for Arts, Design & Information Technology
Bldg. E
230 Richmond St. East, Toronto, ON M5A 1P4
Tel: 416-415-5000
www.georgebrown.ca/arts-design-information-technology

Centre for Business
290 Adelaide St. East, Toronto, ON M5A 1N1
Tel: 416-415-5000
business@georgebrown.ca
www.georgebrown.ca/business

Centre for Community Services & Early Childhood
160 Kendall Ave., Toronto, ON M5R 1M3
Tel: 416-415-5000
www.georgebrown.ca/community-services-early-childhood

Centre for Construction & Engineering Technologies
160 Kendall Ave., Toronto, ON M5R 1M3
Tel: 416-415-5000

Centre for Hospitality & Culinary Arts
300 Adelaide St. East, Toronto, ON M5A 1N1
www.georgebrown.ca/hospitality-culinary-arts

Centre for Health Sciences
51 Dockside Dr., Toronto, ON M5A 0B6
Tel: 416-415-5000
www.georgebrown.ca/health-sciences

Centre for Preparatory & Liberal Studies
160 Kendall Ave., Toronto, ON M5R 1M3
Tel: 416-415-5000
liberalarts@georgebrown.ca
www.georgebrown.ca/preparatory-liberal-studies

Young Centre for the Performing Arts
50 Tankhouse Lane, Toronto, ON M5A 3C4
performingarts@georgebrown.ca

Toronto: Humber Institute of Technology & Advanced Learning
Also known as: Humber College
North Campus
205 Humber College Blvd., Toronto, ON M9W 5L7
Tel: 416-675-3111; *Fax:* 416-675-2427
enquiry@humber.ca
humber.ca
www.facebook.com/humbercollege
twitter.com/humbercollege
www.linkedin.com/school/humber-college
www.youtube.com/c/humbercollege
Full Time Equivalency: 19000
Chris Whitaker, President & CEO
chris.whitaker@humber.ca

Campuses
Lakeshore Campus
2 Colonel Samuel Smith Park Dr., Toronto, ON M8V 4B6
Full Time Equivalency: 10600

Orangeville Campus
Alder Street Recreation Complex
275 Alder St., Orangeville, ON L9W 5A9
Full Time Equivalency: 200

Transportation Training Centre (TTC)
30 Carrier Dr., Toronto, ON M9W 5T7
Fax: 416-798-0307
truck.Info@humber.ca
humber.ca/trucking
Other Information: 416-675-6622, ext 5800

Toronto: Seneca College of Applied Arts & Technology
Newnham Campus
1750 Finch Ave. East, Toronto, ON M2J 2X5
Tel: 416-491-5050; *Fax:* 416-493-3958
admissions@senecacollege.ca
www.senecacollege.ca
Other Information: 416-493-4144
www.facebook.com/senecacollege
twitter.com/SenecaCollege
www.youtube.com/user/VideoSeneca
Note: The polytechnic educational institution consists of the following faculties & schools: Applied Arts & Health Sciences; Applied Science & Engineering Technology; Business; Communication, Art & Design; Continuing Education; & Liberal Arts.
Janet Beed, B.N., M.Sc.N., Chair
David Agnew, President
president@senecacollege.ca

Campuses
Jane Campus
21 Beverly Hills Dr., Toronto, ON M3L 1A2
Tel: 416-491-5050; *Fax:* 416-235-0462

King Campus
13990 Dufferin St., King City, ON L7B 1B3
Tel: 416-491-5050

Markham Campus
8 The Seneca Way, Markham, ON L3R 5Y1
Tel: 416-491-5050

Newmarket Campus
Weston Produce Plaza
#3, 16655 Yonge St., Newmarket, ON L3X 1V6
Tel: 905-898-6199
Note: The campus will close on March 31, 2019.

Peterborough Aviation Campus
#925, 580 Aiport Rd., Peterborough, ON K9J 0E7
Tel: 416-491-5050
Other Information: 705-775-2376

Scarborough Campus
3660 Midland Ave., 2nd Fl., Toronto, ON M1V 0B8
Tel: 416-293-3722

Seneca @ York Campus
70 The Pond Rd., Toronto, ON M3J 3M6
Tel: 416-491-5050

Vaughan Campus
1490 Major Mackenzie Dr. West, #D5, Vaughan, ON L6A 4H6
Tel: 905-417-1781
Note: The campus will close on March 31, 2020.

Yorkgate Campus
1 York Gate Blvd., Toronto, ON M3N 3A1
Tel: 416-491-5050

Centre for Advanced Technologies
21 Beverly Hills Dr., Toronto, ON M3L 1A2
Tel: 416-491-5050
www.senecacollege.ca

Centre for Financial Services
1750 Finch Ave. East, Toronto, ON M2J 2X5
Tel: 416-491-5050
www.senecacollege.ca/school/cfs

Centre for Human Resources
1750 Finch Ave. East, Toronto, ON M2J 2X5
Tel: 416-491-5050
www.senecacollege.ca

Centre for the Built Environment
1750 Finch Ave. East, Toronto, ON M2J 2X5
Tel: 416-491-5050
www.senecacollege.ca

Welland: Niagara College
Welland Campus
100 Niagara College Blvd., Welland, ON L3C 7L3
Tel: 905-735-2211
info@niagaracollege.ca
www.niagaracollege.ca
Other Information: Grimsby Phone: 905-563-3254
www.facebook.com/niagaracollege
twitter.com/NiagaraCollege
www.youtube.com/user/niagaracollegecanada
Full Time Equivalency: 10000 *Note:* Niagara College offers over
100 post-secondary diploma & graduate certificate programs,
skills & apprenticeship training programs, plus two bachelor
degree programs.
John Scott, Chair
Dan Patterson, President, 905-641-2252, ext. 4000
president@niagaracollege.ca

Schools
School of Environment & Horticulture
Niagara-on-the-Lake Campus
135 Taylor Rd., Niagara-on-the-Lake, ON L0S 1J0
myfuturenc@niagaracollege.ca
www.niagaracollege.ca/environment-horticulture-studies
Other Information: 905-735-2211, ext. 7559
Note: The Commercial Cannabis Production Program is a
one-year, post-grad certificate program offering training in
biology of cannabis production, including plant nutrition, climate
control, pest control, etc. Niagara College is partnering with
Canopy Growth.

Campuses
Niagara-on-the-Lake Campus
135 Taylor Rd., Niagara-on-the-Lake, ON L0S 1J0, Canada
Tel: 905-641-2252

Centres & Institutes
Centre for Students with Disabilities
100 Niagara College Blvd., Welland, ON L3C 7L3
Tel: 905-735-2211; *Fax:* 905-736-6008
www.niagaracollege.ca/cswd

Windsor: St. Clair College
South Campus
2000 Talbot Rd. West, Windsor, ON N9A 6S4
Tel: 519-966-1656; *Fax:* 519-972-3811
Toll-Free: 1-800-387-0524
info@stclaircollege.ca
www.stclaircollege.ca
www.facebook.com/StClairCollege
twitter.com/stclaircollege
www.youtube.com/stclairmarketing
Full Time Equivalency: 8300 *Note:* The College consists of the
following schools of specialization: School of Liberal Arts &
Sciences; School of Business & Information Technology; School
of Academic Studies; School of Community Studies; School of
Media, Art & Design; School of Engineering Technologies;
School of Health Sciences; & School of Skilled Trades.
Nancy Jammu-Taylor, Chair
Patricia France, President, 519-972-2701
pfrance@stclaircollege.ca
Michael Silvaggi, Registrar, 519-972-2727, ext. 4260
msilvaggi@stclaircollege.ca

Campuses
Chatham Campus
1001 Grand Ave. West, Chatham, ON N7M 5W4, Canada
Tel: 519-354-9100; *Fax:* 519-354-6941
Note: The campus provides programs in business, technology, &
health & community studies.

Centres & Institutes
Centre For Applied Health Sciences
2000 Talbot Rd. West, Windsor, ON N9A 6S4
www.stclaircollege.ca
Monica Tighe, Chair, School of Health Sciences
mtighe@stclaircollege.ca

Ford Centre for Excellence in Manufacturing
2000 Talbot Rd. West, Windsor, ON N9A 6S4
www.stclaircollege.ca/fcem

St. Clair Centre for the Arts
201 Riverside Dr. West, Windsor, ON N9A 5K4
Tel: 519-252-8311; *Fax:* 519-973-4976
Enrollment: 500 *Note:* The campus offers studies in media, art &
design.
Joe D'Angela, Director, 519-252-8311, ext. 4357
jdangela@stclaircollege.ca

Post Secondary/Technical

Ancaster: Redeemer University College
777 Garner Rd. East, Ancaster, ON L9K 1J4, Canada
Tel: 905-648-2131; *Fax:* 905-648-2134
Toll-Free: 877-779-0913
communications@redeemer.ca
www.redeemer.ca
www.facebook.com/redeemer
twitter.com/RedeemerUC
Enrollment: 725 *Number of Employees:* 75 full-time & part-time
faculty; 97 full-time, part-time & casual staff; 20 coaches
Robert J. Graham, President
rgraham@redeemer.ca
Ed Bosveld, Vice-President, Administration & Finance
ebosveld@redeemer.ca
Kyle Spyksma, Dean, Sciences
kspyksma@redeemer.ca
Susan J. Van Weelden, Dean, Social Sciences
svanweelden@redeemer.ca
Hendrika Schoon, Dean, Students
hschoon@redeemer.ca

Belleville: Quinte Ballet School of Canada (QBSC)
196 Palmer Rd., Belleville, ON K8P 4E1
Tel: 613-962-9274; *Fax:* 613-962-9275
Toll-Free: 866-962-9274
info@quinteballetschool.com
www.quinteballetschool.com
www.facebook.com/quinteballetschool
Note: Full-time professional ballet school.
Jane Gardner, General Manager
generalmanager@quinteballetschool.com
Catherine Taylor, Artistic Director
artisticdirector@quinteballetschool.com

Dundas: Dundas Valley School of Art (DVSA)
21 Ogilvie St., Dundas, ON L9H 2S1
Tel: 905-628-6357; *Fax:* 905-628-1087
info@dvsa.ca
dvsa.ca
www.facebook.com/MyDVSA
twitter.com/DVSA2010
www.youtube.com/c/DundasValleySchoolofArt
Claire Loughheed, Executive Director, 905-628-6357, ext. 205

Hamilton: Canadian Institute for Non-destructive
Evaluation (CINDE)
135 Fennell Ave. West, Hamilton, ON L9C 0E5
Tel: 905-387-1655; *Fax:* 905-574-6080
Toll-Free: 800-964-9488
info@cinde.ca
www.cinde.ca
Note: The institute is a private career college providing training &
certification testing to NDT personnnel.
Glenn Tubrett, Chief Executive Officer
g.tubrett@cinde.ca

Hamilton: Canadian Society for Medical Laboratory
Science (CSMLS)
Société canadienne de science de laboratoire
médical (SCSL
33 Wellington St. North, Hamilton, ON L8R 1M7
Tel: 905-528-8642; *Fax:* 905-528-4968
Toll-Free: 800-263-8277
info@csmls.org
www.csmls.org
Note: Certifications & Prior Learning Assessment programs for
medical laboratory technology, diagnostic cytology & clinical
genetics technology.
Denise Neutel, Director, Certification & Prior Learning
Assessment
Lorna Zilic, Manager, Certification & Prior Learning Assessment

Hamilton: Grand Health Academy
760 King St. East, Hamilton, ON L8M 1A6
Tel: 905-577-7707; *Fax:* 905-577-7738
contact@grandhealthacademy.com
www.grandhealthacademy.com
www.facebook.com/grandhealthacademy
Note: Established in 1992, Grand Health Academy offers
programs that prepare students to become personal support
workers, food service workers, pharmacy assistants, &
rehabilitation assistants.

Hamilton: Ontario Association of Medical Radiation
Sciences (OAMRS)
#415A, 175 Longwood Rd. South, Hamilton, ON L8P 0A1
Tel: 289-674-0034; *Fax:* 289-674-0037
Toll-Free: 800-387-4674
www.oamrs.org
Note: Offers online courses, face-to-face sessions & webinars.

Greg Toffner, President & CEO
toffnerg@oamrs.org

London: AlphaLogic Career College
#108, 920 Commissioners Rd. East, London, ON N5Z 3J1
Tel: 519-858-0010
info@alphalogic.ca
www.alphalogic.ca
www.facebook.com/alphalogiccareercollegeLondonOn
Note: Founded in 1995, the private career college offers diploma
programs, industry standard certifications & courses in the areas
of customer service, network administration, desktop support &
medical office & automotive specialties.

London: Elegance Schools Inc.
301 Oxford St. West, London, ON N6H 1S6
Tel: 519-434-1181; *Fax:* 519-434-1182
eleganceschools.on.ca
www.facebook.com/eleganceschools
Note: Esthetics & electrolysis.

London: St. Peter's Seminary
1040 Waterloo St. North, London, ON N6A 3Y1
Tel: 519-432-1824; *Fax:* 519-432-0964
Toll-Free: 888-548-9649
reception@spseminary.ca
www.stpetersseminary.ca
Rev. Dennis Grecco, Rector
dgrecco@uwo.ca

London: Westervelt College
303 Richmond St., London, ON N6B 2H8, Canada
Tel: 519-668-2000; *Fax:* 519-659-2516
info@westerveltcollege.com
www.westervelt.ca
Note: Westervelt College opened in 1885. The college has
faculties of healthcare, business, law, & technology. There are
three campuses located in southwestern Ontario - London,
Kitchener, & Brantford.

Mississauga: BITTS International Career College
(BITTS)
#230, 7895 Tranmere Dr., Mississauga, ON L5S 1V9
Tel: 905-790-3940; *Toll-Free:* 866-399-2055
info@bitts.ca
www.bitts.ca
www.facebook.com/bittscanada
twitter.com/bittscanada
www.linkedin.com/company/bitts-international-career-college

Campuses
Brampton Campus
#205, 5 Montpelier St., Brampton, ON L6Y 6H4

Mississauga: BizTech College
#205, 5170 Dixie Rd., Mississauga, ON L4W 1E3
Tel: 905-212-9039
info@biztechcollege.com
biztechcollege.com
www.facebook.com/BiztechCollege
twitter.com/Biztechcollege
www.linkedin.com/company/biztechcollege
www.youtube.com/user/BiztechCollege

Mississauga: Canadian Institute of Management &
Technology (CIMT) College
#100, 7200 Goreway Dr., Mississauga, ON L4T 2T7
Tel: 905-671-9999; *Fax:* 905-671-3332
info@cimtcollege.com
www.cimtcollege.com
www.facebook.com/CIMTCollege
twitter.com/cimtcollege
www.youtube.com/user/CIMTCOLLEGE
Note: Diploma & post-graduate diploma programs in the fields of
business & management, healthcare & technology.

Campuses
Brampton Campus
#1, 7900 Hurontario St., Brampton, ON L6Y 0P6
Tel: 905-671-9999; *Fax:* 905-874-1700

Hamilton - Concession Campus
574 Concession St., Hamilton, ON L8V 1B1
Tel: 905-385-7727; *Fax:* 905-385-7477

Hamilton - King Campus
760 King St. East, Hamilton, ON L8M 1A6
Tel: 905-577-7707; *Fax:* 905-577-7738

Mississauga Campus
#105, 250 Dundas St. East, Mississauga, ON L5B 1J2
Tel: 905-671-9999; *Fax:* 905-671-3332

Scarborough Campus
#202, 1711 McGowan Rd., Toronto, ON M1S 2Y3
Tel: 416-421-9999; *Fax:* 905-671-3332

Mississauga: triOS College
#103, 6755 Mississauga Rd., Mississauga, ON L5N 7Y2
Tel: 905-814-7212; *Fax:* 905-813-8250
Toll-Free: 800-898-7467
www.trios.com
twitter.com/trioscollegeBTH
www.linkedin.com/company/trios-college
www.youtube.com/user/triosTV
Note: triOS is a private career college offering numerous career-focused diploma programs.
Frank Gerencser, Chief Executive Officer
Stuart Bentley, President

Campuses
Windsor Campus
7610 Tecumseh Rd. East, Windsor, ON N8T 1E9
Tel: 519-945-0770; *Fax:* 519-945-3662

London Campus
520 First St., London, ON N5V 3C6
Tel: 519-455-0551; *Fax:* 519-455-0090

Kitchener Campus
110 King St. East, Kitchener, ON N2G 0A5
Tel: 519-578-0838; *Fax:* 519-578-8081

Hamilton Campus
4 Hughson St. South, Hamilton, ON L8N 3Z1
Tel: 905-528-8972; *Fax:* 905-528-9608

Mississauga Campus
55 City Centre Dr., 2nd Fl., Mississauga, ON L5B 1M3
Tel: 905-949-4955; *Fax:* 905-897-9755

Brampton Campus
252 Queen St. East, Brampton, ON L6V 1C1
Tel: 905-450-2230; *Fax:* 905-450-3041

Toronto Campus
#200, 425 Bloor St. East, Toronto, ON M4W 3R4
Tel: 416-922-4250; *Fax:* 416-413-0862

Scarborough Campus
#1, 1333 Kennedy Rd., Toronto, ON M1P 2L6
Tel: 416-646-1222; *Fax:* 416-755-3225

Oshawa Campus
200 John St. West, #C5, Oshawa, ON L1J 2B4
Tel: 905-435-9911; *Fax:* 905-435-9985

Niagara Falls: Niagara Parks School of Horticulture
P.O. Box 150
Niagara Falls, ON L2E 6T2
Tel: 905-356-8554
schoolofhorticulture@niagaraparks.com
www.niagaraparks.com/niagara-parks-school-of-horticulture

Norwood: Eastern Ontario Fire Academy
P.O. Box 460
36 Industrial Dr., Norwood, ON K0L 2V0
Tel: 705-639-2121; *Fax:* 905-426-3032
info@eofa.ca
www.eoeta.ca
www.facebook.com/eoeta

Ohsweken: Six Nations Polytechnic
P.O. Box 700
2160 Fourth Line, Ohsweken, ON N0A 1M0
Tel: 519-445-0023
reception@snpolytechnic.com
www.snpolytechnic.com
www.facebook.com/sixnationspolytechnic
twitter.com/snpolytechnic
www.linkedin.com/company/six-nations-polytechnic
www.youtube.com/c/SNPolytechnic
Note: Offers postsecondary education & training with focus on the history, culture, & philosophy of the region's Indigenous peoples.
Rebecca Jamieson, President & CEO
president@snpolytechnic.com

Campuses
Brantford Campus
411 Elgin St., Brantford, ON N3S 7P5
Tel: 226-493-1245

Ottawa: Algonquin Careers Academy
1830 Bank St., Ottawa, ON K1V 7Y6
Tel: 613-722-7811
missinfo@algonquinacademy.com
www.algonquinacademy.com
www.facebook.com/AlgonquinCareersAcademy
www.linkedin.com/company/algonquin
Note: Founded in 1981, the Algonquin Careers Academy offers programs in areas such as travel counselling, personal support work, medical lab assistance, medical office assistance, health & fitness promotion & accounting.

Campuses
Mississauga Campus
#600, 3025 Hurontario St., Mississauga, ON L5A 2H1
Tel: 905-361-2380

Ottawa: Canadian Police College (CPC)
Collège canadien de police
P.O. Box 8900
1 Sandridge Rd., Ottawa, ON K1G 3J2
Tel: 613-993-9501; *Fax:* 613-990-9738
cpcregistrar@rcmp-grc.gc.ca
www.cpc.gc.ca
www.linkedin.com/company/canadian-police-college
Note: Provides law enforcement training. National police service of the RCMP.

Campuses
Canadian Police College West
Collège canadien de police
Pacific Region Training Centre
#1100, 45337 Calais Cres., Chilliwack, BC V2R 0N6
Tel: 604-703-7500
Sue Gadsby, Course Administrator
susan.gadsby@rcmp-grc.gc.ca

Ottawa: La Cité collégiale
801 Aviation Pkwy., Ottawa, ON K1K 4R3
Tél: 613-742-2483; *Téléc:* 613-742-2481
Ligne sans frais: 800-267-2483
info@collegelacite.ca
www.collegelacite.ca
www.facebook.com/collegeLaCite
twitter.com/collegelacite
www.youtube.com/c/CollègeLaCité1
Lise Bourgeois, Présidente

Campuses
Campus Alphonse-Desjardins
Centre des métiers Minto
8700, boul Jeanne D'Arc nord, Orléans, ON K4A 0S9
Tél: 613-742-2483; *Ligne sans frais:* 800-267-2483

Campus de Hawkesbury
570, rue Kitchener, Hawkesbury, ON K6A 2P3

Campus de Toronto
#301, 555 Richmond St. West, Toronto, ON M5V 3B1
Tél: 416-964-9694
www.collegelacite.ca/toronto

Ottawa: International Academy Health Education Centre
380 Forest St., Ottawa, ON K2B 8E6, Canada
Tel: 613-820-0318; *Fax:* 613-820-7478
Toll-Free: 800-267-8732
info@intlacademy.com
www.intlacademy.com
www.facebook.com/internationalacademyhealtheducation
www.youtube.com/channel/UCCzjnU6PgSoZwvIKjIC1hhg
Note: Nutrition; herbs; iridology; reflexology; aromatherapy; homeopathy; shiatsu / accupressure; massage
Dorothy Marshall, Ph.D., N.D., C.H.H.P., N., Executive Director

Ottawa: International Academy of Health Education
380 Forest St., Ottawa, ON K2B 8E6, Canada
Tel: 613-820-0318; *Fax:* 613-820-7478
Toll-Free: 1-800-267-8732
info@intlacademy.com
www.intlacademy.com
www.facebook.com/internationalacademyhealtheducation
Note: Nutrition; herbs; iridology; reflexology
Ian R. Marshall, President & Dean
Dorothy Marshall, Executive Director

Ottawa: Ottawa School of Art
Byward Market
35 George St., Ottawa, ON K1N 8W5
Tel: 613-241-7471; *Fax:* 613-241-4391
info@artottawa.ca
artottawa.ca
www.facebook.com/artottawa
twitter.com/artottawa
Jeff Stellick, Executive Director
director@artottawa.ca

Campuses
Orléans Campus
Shenkman Arts Centre
245 Centrum Blvd., Orléans, ON K1E 0A1
Tel: 613-580-2765; *Fax:* 613-580-2771
osao.info@artottawa.ca

Ottawa: Versailles Academy of Make-Up Arts, Esthetics, Hair
#1, 1930 Bank St., Ottawa, ON K1V 7Z8
Tel: 613-521-4155; *Fax:* 613-521-6945
info@versaillesacademy.com
www.versaillesacademy.com
www.facebook.com/VersaillesAcademy
Note: Founded in 1981, the private career college offers training in the cosmetic, hairstyling & esthetic fields.

Ottawa: Willis College
Laurent Shopping Centre
#20, 1200 St Laurent Blvd., Ottawa, ON K1K 3B8
Tel: 613-233-1128; *Toll-Free:* 877-233-1128
info@ottawa.williscollege.com
williscollege.com
www.facebook.com/WillisCollege
twitter.com/williscollege
www.linkedin.com/school/willis-college
www.youtube.com/user/williscollege
Note: The college offers E-business, IT & health care training.
Henry Devlin, President & CEO

Campuses
Arnprior Campus
39 Winner's Circle Dr., Arnprior, ON K7S 3G9
Tel: 613-623-1114; *Toll-Free:* 855-853-2260

Winnipeg Campus
#200, 464 Hargrave St., Winnipeg, MB R3A 0X5
Tel: 204-956-4608; *Toll-Free:* 866-579-4154

Sudbury: Transport Training Centres of Canada
Sudbury Campus
2565 Kingsway Blvd., Sudbury, ON P3B 2G1
Tel: 705-521-1157; *Toll-Free:* 800-805-0662
ttcc@ttcc.ca
ttcc.ca
www.facebook.com/transporttraining

Campuses
Barrie Campus
40 Alliance Blvd., Barrie, ON L4M 5K3
Tel: 705-724-1172

Belleville Campus
#312, 100 Bell Blvd., 3rd Fl., Belleville, ON K8P 4Y7
Tel: 613-771-0973

Cambridge Campus
#5, 1111 Franklin Blvd., Cambridge, ON N1R 8B5
Tel: 519-653-9235

Chatham Campus
91 Heritage Rd., Chatham, ON N7M 5W7
Tel: 519-354-4951

Cornwall Campus
#109, 120 Tollgate Rd. West, Cornwall, ON K6J 5M3
Tel: 613-930-2446

Dartmouth Campus
#1, 9 Pettipas Dr., Dartmouth, NS B3B 1K1
Tel: 902-468-8999;

Fredericton Campus
Fredericton, NB
Toll-Free: 800-805-0662

Hamilton Campus
400 Grays Rd., Hamilton, ON L8E 3J6
Tel: 905-561-4575

Kingston Campus
1341 Midland Ave., Kingston, ON K7P 2W5

London Campus
1020 Adelaide St., London, ON N6E 1R6
Tel: 519-686-6229

Moncton Campus
154 Edinburgh Dr., Moncton, NB E1E 2K7
Tel: 506-854-4049

North Bay Campus
17 Willow Dr., North Bay, ON P1B 8Z4
Tel: 705-840-1176

Oshawa Campus
200 John St. West, #B4, Oshawa, ON L1J 2B4
Tel: 905-668-4211

Ottawa Campus
1540 Star Top Rd., Ottawa, ON K1B 3W6
Tel: 613-244-3444

Owen Sound Campus
#210A, 1717 - 2nd Ave. East, Owen Sound, ON N4K 6V4
Tel: 519-371-6512

Peterborough Campus
#6B, 724 Erskine Ave., Peterborough, ON K9J 5T9
Tel: 705-741-4518

Saint John Campus
Saint John, NB
Toll-Free: 800-805-0662

Sarnia Campus
#8A, 1030 Confederation St., Sarnia, ON N7S 3Y5
Toll-Free: 800-805-0662

Sault Ste Marie Campus
815 Great Northern Rd., 2nd Fl., Sault Ste Marie, ON P6A 5K7
Tel: 705-254-4383

St Catharines Campus
#8, 360 York Rd., Niagara on the Lake, ON L0S 1J0
Tel: 905-687-8462

Timmins Campus
#2, 3820 Hwy. 101 West, Timmins, ON P4N 0E4
Tel: 705-267-2199

Thunder Bay Campus
195 Gore St. East, Thunder Bay, ON P7E 3R2
Tel: 807-622-1152

Windsor Campus
6000 Rhodes Dr., Windsor, ON N8N 2M1
Tel: 519-251-8222;

Thunder Bay: Northern Ontario School of Medicine (NOSM)
West Campus, Lakehead University
955 Oliver Rd., Thunder Bay, ON P7B 5E1, Canada
Tel: 807-766-7300; *Fax:* 807-766-7370
Toll-Free: 800-461-8777
communications@nosm.ca
www.nosm.ca
www.facebook.com/thenosm
twitter.com/thenosm
www.youtube.com/user/NOSMtv
Note: 4-year MD program
Dr. Robert Haché, Chair
Dr. Sarita Verma, Dean & CEO

Campuses
East Campus
935 Ramsey Lake Rd., Sudbury, ON P3E 2C6, Canada
Tel: 705-675-4883; *Fax:* 705-675-4858
Note: Associated with Laurentian University.

West Campus
955 Oliver Rd., Thunder Bay, ON P7B 5E1, Canada
Tel: 807-766-7300; *Fax:* 807-766-7370
Note: Associated with Lakehead University.

Timmins: Northern College
P.O. Box 3211
Timmins, ON P4N 8R6
Tel: 705-235-3211; *Fax:* 705-235-7279
info@northern.on.ca
www.northernc.on.ca
www.facebook.com/northernc
twitter.com/mynorthernc
www.youtube.com/c/NorthernCollegeProud
Audrey J. Penner, President

Campuses
Haileybury Campus
P.O. Box 2060
640 Latchford St., Haileybury, ON P0J 1K0
Tel: 705-672-3376; *Fax:* 705-672-2014

Kirkland Lake Campus
140 Government Rd. East, Kirkland Lake, ON P2N 3L8
Tel: 705-567-9291; *Fax:* 705-568-8186

Timmins Campus
4715 Hwy. 101 East, South Porcupine, ON P0N 1H0
Tel: 705-235-3211; *Fax:* 705-235-7279

Moosonee Campus
P.O. Box 130
1st Ave., Moosonee, ON P0L 1Y0
Tel: 705-336-2913; *Fax:* 705-336-2393

Toronto: Academy of Applied Pharmaceutical Sciences (AAPS)
200 Consumers Rd., #200, Toronto, ON M2J 4R4
Tel: 416-502-2277; *Fax:* 416-502-2278
Toll-Free: 855-502-2288
info@aaps.ca
www.aaps.ca
Note: Pharmaceutical, Food, Clinical, and Cannabis Training School

Steven Tanner, Campus Mananger & Director of Student Affairs

Campuses
Mississauga Campus
Unit 140
2960 Drew Rd., Mississauga, ON L4T 0A5
Tel: 416-502-2277; *Toll-Free:* 855-502-2288
info@aaps.ca
www.aaps.ca

Toronto: Acupuncture & Integrative Academy Inc.
Also known as: AIM Academy
Old Name: Shiatsu School of Canada Inc.
#300, 455 Spadina Ave., Toronto, ON M5S 2G8, Canada
Tel: 416-323-1818; *Fax:* 416-323-1681
Toll-Free: 800-263-1703
info@aim-academy.ca
www.aim-academy.ca
Note: Offers acupuncture programs & courses.
Enza Ierullo, Executive Director, 416-323-1818, ext. 202
Sarah Calder, Office Manager, 416-323-1818, ext. 201
s.calder@aim-academy.ca

Toronto: APLUS Institute
Madison Centre
#15, 4950 Yonge St., Toronto, ON M2N 6K1
Tel: 416-222-0500
info@aplusinstitute.com
aplusinstitute.ca
Note: Dental Hygiene Programs.

Toronto: Automotive Training Centres (ATC)
Toronto Campus
152 Norseman St., Toronto, ON M8Z 2R4
Toll-Free: 800-458-7473
www.autotrainingcentre.com
Note: ATC is a private college specializing in automotive training.

Campuses
Cambridge Campus
25 Fleming Dr., Cambridge, ON N1T 2A9
Toll-Free: 866-994-2284

Montréal Campus
7555, boul Henri-Bourassa, Montréal, QC H1E 1N9
Toll-Free: 877-725-6026

Surrey Campus
12160 - 88th Ave., Surrey, BC V3W 3J2
Toll-Free: 888-546-2886

Toronto: Bryan College of Applied Health & Business Science
1200 Lawrence Ave. West, Toronto, ON M6A 1E3
Tel: 416-630-6300; *Fax:* 416-630-9066
Toll-Free: 888-641-6300
receptiondesk@bryancollege.ca
bryancollege.ca
www.facebook.com/bryancollege.ca
Adriana Costenaro, Campus President

Toronto: Business & Technical Training College
Also known as: BTT College
#411, 1280 Finch Ave. West, Toronto, ON M3J 3K6
Tel: 416-483-3567
iwantinfo@bttcollege.com
www.bttcollege.com
www.facebook.com/bttcollege

Toronto: Canadian Business College
Toronto Campus
2 Bloor St. West, 22nd Fl., Toronto, ON M4W 3E2
info@canadianbusinesscollege.com
www.canadianbusinesscollege.com
www.facebook.com/canadianbusinesscollege
twitter.com/canbizcollege
www.linkedin.com/school/canadian-business-college
Note: Courses are offered in the areas of business, information technology, digital media, law, health, community service & child care.

Campuses
Mississauga Campus
#600, 77 City Centre Dr., Mississauga, ON L5B 1M5

Scarborough Campus
#303, 55 Town Centre Ct., Toronto, ON M1P 4X4

Toronto: The Canadian College of Naturopathic Medicine
1255 Sheppard Ave. East, Toronto, ON M2K 1E2, Canada
Tel: 416-498-1255; *Toll-Free:* 1-866-241-2266
www.ccnm.edu
www.facebook.com/myccnm
twitter.com/myccnm
www.linkedin.com/school/myccnm
www.instagram.com/myccnm
Enrollment: 600 *Number of Employees:* 100 full time; 100 part time *Note:* Naturopathic medical education, research & clinical practice; 4,500+ hours of classroom & clinical training.
Bob Bernhardt, President & CEO
Nicholas De Groot, Dean

Toronto: Canadian Jewellers Association (CJA)
#600, 27 Queen St. East, Toronto, ON M5C 2M6
Tel: 416-368-7616; *Fax:* 416-368-1986
Toll-Free: 800-580-0942
info@canadianjewellers.com
www.canadianjewellers.com
Note: The CJA offers programs that include Jewellery Education Training System (JETS), Certified Jewellery Retail Professional Program (CJRP) & Accredited Appraiser Program.
Valentina Cova, Director, Membership & Education Services
valentina@canadianjewellers.com

Toronto: Canadian Memorial Chiropractic College (CMCC)
6100 Leslie St., Toronto, ON M2H 3J1
Tel: 416-482-2340; *Fax:* 416-646-1114
Toll-Free: 800-463-2923
communications@cmcc.ca
www.cmcc.ca
www.facebook.com/cmccnews
twitter.com/cmccnews
www.linkedin.com/school/canadian-memorial-chiropractic-college
Note: CMCC is an academic institution offering a second entry undergraduate professional degree (Doctor of Chiropractic) as well as post-graduate & continuing education programs.
David J. Wickes, President
president@cmcc.ca

Toronto: Canadian School of Private Investigation & Security Ltd.
2828 Dufferin St., Toronto, ON M6B 3S3
Tel: 416-785-5701; *Toll-Free:* 844-645-4468
info@cspis.com
cspis.com
www.facebook.com/CanadianSchoolOfPrivateInvestigation
Note: Founded in 1980, the college provides education in private investigation, paralegal, security, law enforcement & police foundations training.
Edward Franco, General Manager

Toronto: Canadian Securities Institute (CSI)
200 Wellington St. West, 15th Fl., Toronto, ON M5V 3C7
Tel: 416-364-9130; *Fax:* 866-866-2660
Toll-Free: 866-866-2601
customer_support@csi.ca
www.csi.ca
www.facebook.com/csiglobal
twitter.com/CSIGlobalEd
www.linkedin.com/school/canadian-securities-institute
Note: CSI provides career training & educational services for financial professionals.

Campuses
Montréal Office
#400, 625, boul René-Lévesque ouest, Montréal, QC H3B 1R2

Toronto: Chartered Professional Accountants of Ontario
Also known as: CPA Ontario
P.O. Box 358
#3400, 130 King St. West, Toronto, ON M5X 1E1
Toll-Free: 800-387-0735
www.cpaontario.ca
www.facebook.com/CPAOntario
twitter.com/CPA_Ontario
www.linkedin.com/company/cpa-ontario
Note: Works in partnership with post-secondary institutions to offer courses in accounting & finance.
Carol Wilding, President & CEO

Toronto: CJ Health Care College - Scarborough Campus
#401, 1371 Neilson Rd., Toronto, ON M1B 4Z8, Canada
Tel: 416-283-8252; *Fax:* 416-283-3796
admin.scar@cjcollege.com
www.cjcollege.com
Note: Health care related program.

Campuses
Toronto Campus
1123 Albion Rd., #L101, Toronto, ON M9V 1A9, Canada
Tel: 416-422-5900; *Fax:* 416-746-3330
admin.tor@cjcollege.com

Toronto: Complections College of Makeup Art & Design
110 Lombard St., Toronto, ON M5C 1M3
Tel: 416-968-6739; *Fax:* 416-968-7340
www.complectionsmake-up.com
www.facebook.com/ComplectionsMakeup
twitter.com/Complections
www.youtube.com/user/ComplectionsMakeup
Note: Complections, the International Academy of Make-up Artistry offers instruction that leads to a career in makeup artistry.
Pamela Earle, President, Complections International Academy

Toronto: Credit Institute of Canada (CIC)
#211, 3 Concorde Gate, Toronto, ON M3C 3N7
Tel: 416-572-2615; *Fax:* 416-572-2619
geninfo@creditedu.org
creditinstitute.org
www.facebook.com/creditedu
twitter.com/creditinstitute
www.linkedin.com/company/the-credit-institute-of-canada
Note: Offers courses in credit management.
Jay McKeown, President & Dean
Nawshad Khadaroo, General Manager
nkhadaroo@creditedu.org

Toronto: Forum for Intercultural Leadership & Learning
Toronto School of Theology
47 Queen's Park Cres. East, Toronto, ON M5S 2C3
Tel: 416-972-9494
www.interculturalleadership.ca
www.facebook.com/InterculturalLeadershipandLearning
Note: Cross cultural orientation programs for church related personnel & volunteers involved in global mission & ministry.

Toronto: Frontier College
35 Jackes Ave., Toronto, ON M4T 1E2
Tel: 416-923-3591; *Fax:* 416-323-3522
Toll-Free: 800-555-6523
information@frontiercollege.ca
www.frontiercollege.ca
www.facebook.com/FrontierCollege
twitter.com/FrontierCollege
www.linkedin.com/company/frontier-college
www.youtube.com/user/frontiercollege
Note: The college is a volunteer-based, charitable literacy organization.
Stephen Faul, President & CEO

Toronto: Herzing College
Toronto, ON
www.herzing.ca
Note: Information technology programs (programming, networking, database management & microprocessor technology), healthcare & legal.

Campuses
Montréal Campus
1616, boul René-Lévesque ouest, Montréal, QC H3H 1P8
Tél: 514-935-7494; *Téléc:* 514-933-6182
mtl-info@herzing.ca
www.herzing.ca/locations/montreal
www.facebook.com/herzingmontreal
Note: Founded in 1968, Herzing College Montreal prepares students for careers in business, technology & design.

Montréal-Est Campus
8350-8370, boul Lacordaire, Montréal, QC H1R 3Y6
Tél: 514-935-7494; *Téléc:* 514-933-6182
mtl-info@herzing.ca

Ottawa Campus
Laurent Shopping Center
P.O. Box 225
#408, 1200 St Laurent Blvd., Ottawa, ON K1K 3B8
Tel: 613-742-8099; *Fax:* 613-742-8336
otw-info@herzing.ca
www.herzing.ca/locations/ottawa
www.facebook.com/herzingottawa

Toronto Campus
11 Kodiak Cres., Toronto, ON M3J 3E5
Tel: 416-599-6996; *Fax:* 416-599-0192
tor-info@herzing.ca
www.herzing.ca/locations/toronto
www.facebook.com/herzingtoronto
George Hood, Campus President

Winnipeg Campus
1700 Portage Ave., Winnipeg, MB R3J 0E1
Tel: 204-775-8175; *Fax:* 204-783-8107
wpg-info@herzing.ca
www.herzing.ca/locations/winnipeg
Kerry Swanson, President

Toronto: ICT Schools
Toronto Campus - Kikkawa College, The Crossways M
2340 Dundas St. West, #G-04, Toronto, ON M6P 4A9
Tel: 416-762-4857; *Fax:* 416-762-5733
Toll-Free: 888-890-5888
kcadmin@ictschools.com
ictschools.com
Note: Massage therapy course instruction.

Campuses
Halifax Campus - Northumberland College
1888 Brunswick St., 5th Fl., Halifax, NS B3J 3J8
Tel: 902-425-2869; *Fax:* 902-425-2858
Toll-Free: 888-862-2230
ncregistrar@ictschools.com

Toronto: Institute of Technical Trades Ltd.
749 Warden Ave., Toronto, ON M1L 4A8
Tel: 416-750-1950; *Fax:* 416-750-4702
Toll-Free: 800-461-4981
info@instituteoftechnicaltrades.com
www.instituteoftechnicaltrades.com
www.facebook.com/instituteoftechnicaltrades
Note: Welding & CNC machine setup operation.

Toronto: International Institute of Travel & Business
#402, 120 Carlton St., Toronto, ON M5A 4K2
Tel: 416-924-2271; *Fax:* 416-924-9632
iit@iitravel.com
www.iitravel.com
www.facebook.com/iitcollege
www.linkedin.com/company/international-institute-of-travel
Note: Travel & tourism training.

Toronto: Medix College
Toronto Campus
#300, 700 Lawrence Ave. West, Toronto, ON M6A 3B4
Tel: 416-630-8021
www.medixcollege.ca
www.facebook.com/MedixCollege
twitter.com/medix_college
Note: Health care programs

Campuses
Brampton Campus
#60, 499 Main St. South, Brampton, ON L6Y 1N7
Tel: 905-487-1163

Scarborough Campus
#205, 2130 Lawrence Ave. East, Toronto, ON M1R 3A6
Tel: 416-701-1201

Toronto: Montessori Teachers College
12 Bannockburn Ave., Toronto, ON M5M 2M8
Tel: 416-640-1565
admin@mtcedu.com
www.montessoriteacherscollege.com
Paula Glasgow, Dean

Campuses
Calgary Campus
4963 Front St. SE, Calgary, AB T3M 2M3
Tel: 403-991-6359

Toronto: Mothercraft College of Early Childhood Education
Also known as: Mothercraft College
646 St Clair Ave. West, Toronto, ON M6C 1A9
Tel: 416-483-0511; *Fax:* 416-483-0119
college@mothercraft.org
www.mothercraft.ca
Note: The college provides training programs for child care providers & other professionals. It offers a diploma in Early Childhood Education.
Michele Lupa, Executive Director, 416-920-4054, ext. 102
michele.lupa@mothercraft.org

Toronto: New Skills College of Health, Business, & Technology
1500 Birchmount Rd., Toronto, ON M1P 2G5
Tel: 416-269-8878; *Fax:* 416-266-3898
info@newskillshealth.ca
www.newskillscollege.ca
Note: The New Skills College is a member of the Ontario Association of Career Colleges. The college provides training for health care personnel. Examples of programs include training for food handlers, personal attendants, & medical office assistants.

Toronto: North American College of Pharmaceutical Technology (NACPT)
Also known as: Pharma College
#9, 5310 Finch Ave. East, Toronto, ON M1S 5E8
Tel: 416-412-7374
info@nacptpharmacollege.com
www.nacptpharmacollege.com
Other Information: Text: 647-998-7374
www.facebook.com/nacptpharmacollege
twitter.com/NACPT_Pharma
Rathi Param, B.Sc., Post Grad Cert.,in, President & Dean
Sam Subramaniam, M.Sc., CA, Vice President
Sanjida Ahmed, Ph.D, Director, Strategy Planning & Program Development

Mississauga Campus
Suite #201
25 Watline Ave., Mississauga, ON L4Z 2Z1

Toronto: Outward Bound Canada
#910, 2200 Yonge St., Toronto, ON M4S 2C6
Toll-Free: 888-688-9273
info@outwardbound.ca
www.outwardbound.ca
www.facebook.com/outwardboundcanada
twitter.com/OutwardBoundCan
www.linkedin.com/school/outward-bound-canada
www.youtube.com/user/OutwardBoundCanada
Note: Not-for-profit educational organization offering urban & wilderness programs to high schools, universities, community & corporate groups, government agencies & learning institutes in Canada.
Andrew Young, Executive Director

Toronto: The Royal Conservatory of Music
McMaster Hall
273 Bloor St. West, Toronto, ON M5S 1W2
Tel: 416-408-2824; *Toll-Free:* 800-461-6058
www.rcmusic.ca
www.facebook.com/theroyalconservatory
twitter.com/the_rcm
www.linkedin.com/school/theroyalconservatory
www.youtube.com/c/TheRoyalConservatory
Note: The Royal Conservatory was founded in 1886. The Conservatory's core programs are as follows: The Royal Conservatory School; The Glenn Gould School; the Young Artists Performance Academy; Learning Through the Arts; The Frederick Harris Music Co., Limited; & Examinations. Every year, approximately 600,000 people from across Canada participate in music education programs offered by The Royal Conservatory.
Tim Price, Chair
Michael M. Koerner, President & CEO

Schools
The Glenn Gould School
#202, 273 Bloor St. West, Toronto, ON M5S 1W2
Tel: 416-408-2824; *Fax:* 416-408-5025
Toll-Free: 800-462-3815
glenngouldschool@rcmusic.ca
www.rcmusic.com/ggs/home
Enrollment: 130 *Note:* Professional training in music performance & pedagogy at the post-secondary & post-graduate levels.
James Anagnoson, Dean

The Royal Conservatory School
273 Bloor St. West, Toronto, ON M5S 1W2
Tel: 416-408-2825; *Fax:* 866-263-4447
conservatoryschool@rcmusic.ca
www.rcmusic.com/learning/royal-conservatory-school
Note: Community-based music school providing group classes & private lessons for people of all ages.
Jeremy Trupp, Dean

Toronto: St. Augustine's Seminary of Toronto
2661 Kingston Rd., Toronto, ON M1M 1M3
Tel: 416-261-7207; *Fax:* 416-261-2529
staugustines.on.ca
www.facebook.com/StAugustinesTO
twitter.com/StAugustinesTO
www.youtube.com/c/StAugustinesSeminary
Rev. Robert Barringer, President

Rev. Edwin Gonsalves, Rector

Toronto: Stafford House International
Toronto School
5 Park Home Ave., Toronto, ON M2N 6L4
Tel: 416-223-7855
info@staffordhouse.com
www.staffordhouse.com
www.facebook.com/StaffordHouseInternational
twitter.com/staffordhouse
www.linkedin.com/school/stafford-house-international

Campuses
Calgary School
#100, 840 - 6th Ave. SW, Calgary, AB T2P 3E5
Tel: 403-265-6936

Toronto: Sutherland Chan School & Teaching Clinic
15 Gervais Dr., Toronto, ON M3C 1Y8
Tel: 416-924-1107
admissions@sutherland-chan.com
sutherland-chan.com
www.facebook.com/SutherlandChan
Grace Chan, Co-Founder
grace@sutherland-chan.com
Debra Curties, Executive Director
debra@sutherland-chan.com

Toronto: Toronto Art Therapy Institute (TATI)
8 Prince Arthur Ave., 2nd Fl., Toronto, ON M5R 1A9
Tel: 416-924-6221
contact@tati.on.ca
tati.on.ca

Helene Burt, Executive Director

Toronto: Toronto Baptist Seminary & Bible College
130 Gerrard St. East, Toronto, ON M5A 3T4
Tel: 416-925-3263
inquiry@tbs.edu
tbs.edu
www.facebook.com/TorontoBaptistSeminary
twitter.com/tbsedu
www.youtube.com/c/TorontoBaptistSeminaryBibleCollege
Note: The school offers residential studies as well as an
extension program (correspondence courses, evening classes &
summer school).
Glendon G. Thompson, President

Toronto: Toronto Film School
415 Yonge St., 8th Fl., Toronto, ON M5B 2E7
Tel: 416-929-0121; *Fax:* 416-644-1903
Toll-Free: 866-467-0661
www.torontofilmschool.ca
www.facebook.com/TorontoFilmSchool
twitter.com/tofilmschool
www.linkedin.com/school/toronto-film-school
www.youtube.com/c/TorontoFilmSchoolChannel
Note: Toronto Film School is an associate of Yorkville University.

Campuses
Dundas Campus
#704, 10 Dundas St. East, Toronto, ON M5B 2G9

415 Yonge Campus
415 Yonge St., 8th Fl., Toronto, ON M5B 2E7

460 Yonge Campus
460 Yonge St., Toronto, ON M4Y 1W9

Toronto: Toronto Institute of Pharmaceutical
Technology (TIPT)
#800, 55 Town Centre Ct., Toronto, ON M1P 4X4
Tel: 416-296-8860; *Fax:* 416-296-7077
info@tipt.com
www.tipt.com
www.facebook.com/TIPTechnology
twitter.com/tiptechnology
www.linkedin.com/school/tiptechnology
Alexander MacGregor, President & Dean

Toronto: Travel College Canada
#428, 700 Lawrence Ave. West, Toronto, ON M6A 3B4
Tel: 416-481-2265
info@travelcollege.ca
www.travelcollege.ca
www.facebook.com/TravelCollegeCanada
twitter.com/Travel_College
Note: Travel & tourism industry courses, customer service.
Louise Blazik, Founder & Director

Waterloo: Shad Canada
419A Phillip St., Waterloo, ON N2L 3X2
Tel: 519-884-8844; *Fax:* 519-884-0665
info@shad.ca
www.shad.ca
www.facebook.com/ShadProgram
twitter.com/shadnetwork
www.linkedin.com/company/shadcanada
www.youtube.com/user/SHADVideoChannel
Note: Four week summer enrichment program for students in
grades 10, 11 or 12, secondaire V or CEGEP I for Quebec
students or the international equivalent. The program includes
the sciences, technology & entrepreneurship. Shad Canada is
held on campus at 19 universities across Canada. Students live
in residence at each university for the month of July.
Tim Jackson, President & CEO
tim@shad.ca

Prince Edward Island

Government Agencies

Summerside: Prince Edward Island Department of
Education & Lifelong Learning
Holman Centre
#101, 250 Water St., Summerside, PE C1N 1B6, Canada
Tel: 902-438-4130; *Fax:* 902-438-4062
DeptELL@gov.pe.ca
www.princeedwardisland.ca
Other Information: Charlottetown Phone: 902-368-4600
Hon. Natalie Jameson, Minister, 902-368-4610
MinisterELL@gov.pe.ca

School Boards/Districts/Divisions

Public

Stratford: Prince Edward Island Public Schools
Branch (PSB)
Stratford Office
#2, 234 Shakespeare Dr., Stratford, PE C1B 2V8
Tel: 902-368-6990; *Fax:* 902-368-6960
Toll-Free: 800-280-7965
elsb-web@edu.pe.ca
edu.princeedwardisland.ca/psb
www.facebook.com/publicschoolsbranch
twitter.com/psbpei
www.instagram.com/psbpei
Number of Schools: 56 *Grades:* K - 12 *Enrollment:* 19000
Number of Employees: 4,000
Bethany MacLeod, Chair, Board
Norbert Carpenter, Acting Director, Public Schools Branch,
902-368-6850
Kelly Drummond, Director, Human Resources, 902-368-6819
ktdrummond@gov.pe.ca
Becky Chiasson, Director, Corporate Services, 902-368-6845
blchiasson@edu.pe.ca
Terri MacAdam, Director, Student Services, 902-368-6854
temacadam@edu.pe.ca
Blake Crockett, Coordinator, Financial Services, 902-888-8428
bocrockett@edu.pe.ca

Campuses
Summerside Office
#201, 250 Water St., Summerside, PE C1N 1B6
Tel: 902-888-8400; *Fax:* 902-888-8449
Toll-Free: 800-280-7965

French

Abram Village: La Commission scolaire de langue
française de l'Île-du-Prince-Édouard (CSLF)
French Language School Board of Prince Edward
Island
1596 rte. 124, Abram Village, PE C0B 2E0, Canada
Tél: 902-854-2975; *Téléc:* 902-854-2981
cslf@edu.pe.ca
cslfipe.wordpress.com
www.facebook.com/158736104225285
Number of Schools: 6
Marise Chapman, Directrice générale Intérim
mbchapman@edu.pe.ca
Rachelle Arsenault, Secrétaire administrative
raarsenault@edu.pe.ca
Julie Gagnon, Directrice de l'instruction
jggagnon@edu.pe.ca
Brad Samson, Directeur des services administratifs et financiers
blsamson@edu.pe.ca
Nathalie Malo, Gestionnaire des ressources humaines et du
transport scolaire
nmalo@edu.pe.ca

Schools: Specialized

First Nations

Lennox Island: John J. Sark Memorial School
24 Eagle Feather Trl., Lennox Island, PE C0B 1P0, Canada
Tel: 902-831-2777; *Fax:* 902-831-3065
www.johnjsark.wordpress.com/contact/
www.facebook.com/johnj.sarkmemorial
Grades: K.-6 *Enrollment:* 50 *Number of Employees:* 10 *Note:*
Curriculum includes Mi'kmaq language & culture.
Neil Forbes, Education Director
neil.forbes@lennoxisland.com

Schools: Independent & Private

Protestant

Charlottetown: Grace Christian School
50 Kirkdale Rd., Charlottetown, PE C1E 1N6, Canada
Tel: 902-628-1668; *Fax:* 902-628-1668
office@gcspei.ca
www.gcspei.ca
www.facebook.com/GCSPEI
twitter.com/gcs_pei
www.instagram.com/gcspei
Grades: JK-12 *Note:* A ministry of Grace Baptist Church
Jason Biech, Principal
principal@gcspei.ca

Charlottetown: Immanuel Christian School
68 Allen St., Charlottetown, PE C1A 2V8, Canada
Tel: 902-628-6465; *Fax:* 902-628-1831
office@icspei.ca
www.icspei.ca
Grades: JK-9 *Enrollment:* 118
Rob MacDonald, Principal

Independent & Private Schools

Charlottetown: Fair Isle Adventist School
20 Lapthorne Ave., Charlottetown, PE C1A 2M2, Canada
Tel: 902-894-9301
Grades: 1-9; Seventh-day Adventist *Enrollment:* 7

Universities & Colleges

Universities

Charlottetown: University of Prince Edward Island
550 University Ave., Charlottetown, PE C1A 4P3, Canada
Tel: 902-628-4353
www.upei.ca
www.facebook.com/UniversityofPEI
twitter.com/upei
www.youtube.com/UofPEI
Full Time Equivalency: 4926
Hon. Catherine Callbeck, Chancellor
Alaa Abd-El-Aziz, President & Vice-Chancellor
presidentea@upei.ca
Dr. Kathy Gottschall-Pass, Interim Vice-President, Academic &
Research
research@upei.ca
Jackie Podger, Vice-President, Administration & Finance
Dana Sanderson, Chief Information Officer
Donna Sutton, Registrar
dsutton@upei.ca

Faculties
Faculty of Arts
Tel: 902-566-0307
arts@upei.ca
www.upei.ca/arts
Dr. Nebojsa Kujundzic, Dean

Faculty of Business
Tel: 902-566-0626; *Fax:* 902-628-4302
business@upei.ca
www.upei.ca/business
Other Information: 902-566-0564
Dr. Juergen Krause, Dean

Faculty of Education
Tel: 902-620-5154
education@upei.ca
www.upei.ca/education
Ronald J. MacDonald, Dean
rjmacdonald@upei.ca

Faculty of Nursing
Health Sciences Bldg.
#128, 550 University Ave., Charlottetown, PE C1A 4P3
Tel: 902-566-0768
nursing@upei.ca
www.upei.ca/nursing
Jo-Ann Mary MacDonald, Interim Dean
jammacdonald@upei.ca

Faculty of Science
Tel: 902-566-0382
science@upei.ca
www.upei.ca/science
Dr. Debbie MacLellan, Dean

Atlantic Veterinary College (AVC)
Tel: 902-566-0882
avc@upei.ca
www.upei.ca/avc
Dr. Greg Keefe, Dean

Schools
School of Professional Education and Career Development
cmiller@upei.ca
www.upei.ca/professionaldevelopment
Note: Offers a two-day in-class workshop, Cannabis Knowledge for Organizations: Health, Culture, and Policy. Workshop held in Charlottetown and Summerside.

Post Secondary/Technical

Charlottetown: **Holland College of Applied Arts & Technology**
140 Weymouth St., Charlottetown, PE C1A 4Z1
Tel: 902-629-4217; *Fax:* 902-629-4239
Toll-Free: 800-446-5265
info@hollandcollege.com
www.facebook.com/HollandCollege
twitter.com/hollandcollege
www.linkedin.com/school/hollandcollege
www.instagram.com/hollandcollege
Alexander MacDonald, President
gamacdonald@hollandcollege.com

Campuses
Atlantic Police Academy
P.O. Box 156
66 Argus Ave., Slemon Park, PE C0B 2A0
Tel: 902-888-6700; *Fax:* 902-888-6725

Summerside Waterfront Campus
98 Water St., Summerside, PE C1N 4N6
Tel: 902-888-6448

West Prince Campus
509 Church St., Alberton, PE C0B 1B0
Tel: 902-853-6040

Centres & Institutes
Belmont Centre
34 Belmont St., Charlottetown, PE C1A 5H1
Tel: 902-629-4235

Georgetown Centre
117 Kent St., Georgetown, PE C0A 1L0
Tel: 902-652-2055; *Fax:* 902-652-2424

Marine Training Centre
100 Water St., Summerside, PE C1N 1A9
Tel: 902-888-6485; *Fax:* 902-888-6404
marine@hollandcollege.com

Tourism & Culinary Centre
4 Sydney St., Charlottetown, PE C1A 1E9
Tel: 902-894-6805; *Fax:* 902-894-6801
Toll-Free: 877-475-2844
www.facebook.com/CulinaryInstituteofCanada

Summerside: **The College of Piping & Celtic Performing Arts of Canada**
619 Water St. East, Summerside, PE C1N 4H8, Canada
Tel: 902-436-5377; *Fax:* 902-436-4930
Toll-Free: 877-224-7473
info@collegeofpiping.com
www.collegeofpiping.com
www.facebook.com/collegeofpiping
twitter.com/CoP1989
www.youtube.com/user/TheCollegeofpiping1
James MacHattie, Director of Education
james.machattie@collegeofpiping.com
Jennifer Campbell, Executive Director
jennifer.campbell@collegeofpiping.com

Québec

Government Agencies

Québec: **Ministère de l'Éducation et de l'Enseignement supérieur**
Renseignement generaux
1035, rue De La Chevrotière, Québec, QC G1R 5A5, Canada
Tél: 418-643-7095; *Téléc:* 418-646-6561
Ligne sans frais: 866-747-6626
www.education.gouv.qc.ca
www.facebook.com/quebeceducation
twitter.com/educationQC
www.youtube.com/user/MELSQuebec
L'hon. Jean-François Roberge, Ministre de l'Éducation et de L'Enseignement supérieur, 418-644-0664
ministre@education.gouv.qc.ca
L'hon. Danielle McCann, Ministre de l'Enseignement supérieur, 418-781-6500
ministre_mes@mes.gouv.qc.ca
L'hon. Isabelle Charest, Ministre déléguée à l'Éducation, 418-266-3255
ministre.deleguee@education.gouv.qc.ca

School Boards/Districts/Divisions

Public

Châteauguay: **New Frontiers School Board**
Commission scolaire New Frontiers
219, rue McLeod, Châteauguay, QC J6J 2H4
Tel: 450-691-1440; *Toll-Free:* 800-461-1440
info@nfsb.qc.ca
www.nfsb.qc.ca
www.facebook.com/nfschoolboard
Number of Schools: 10 elementary; 2 secondary; 3 adult/vocational *Grades:* K - 12; Audlt Ed. *Enrollment:* 4000
Rob Buttars, Director General

Gatineau: **Western Québec School Board**
Commission scolaire Western Québec
15, rue Katimavik, Gatineau, QC J9J 0E9
Tel: 819-684-2336; *Fax:* 819-684-1328
Toll-Free: 800-363-9111
wqsb@wqsb.qc.ca
westernquebec.ca
www.facebook.com/westernquebec
twitter.com/westernquebec
www.linkedin.com/company/westernquebec
Number of Schools: 19 primary; 6 secondary *Grades:* Prim - Sec
Mike Dubeau, Director General & Director, School Org & Transport
mdubeau@wqsb.qc.ca
Ruth Ahern, Assistant Director General
rahern@wqsb.qc.ca
George Singfield, Secretary General & Director, Corporate Services
georgesingfield@wqsb.qc.ca
Terry Kharyati, Director, Human Resources & Secondary Education
tkharyati@wqsb.qc.ca
Martine Lupien, Director, Finance
mlupien@wqsb.qc.ca

Magog: **Eastern Townships School Board**
Commission scolaire Eastern Townships
340, rue Saint-Jean-Bosco, Magog, QC J1X 1K9
Tel: 819-868-3100; *Fax:* 819-868-2286
priests@etsb.qc.ca
www.etsb.qc.ca
www.facebook.com/ETSB2
Number of Schools: 20 primary; 4 secondary; 2 training centres
Grades: Prim - Sec
Michel Soucy, Director General, 819-868-3100, ext. 55005
dg@etsb.qc.ca
Kandy Mackey, Assistant Director General, 819-868-3100, ext. 55015
mackeyk@etsb.qc.ca

Montréal: **English Montreal School Board (EMSB)**
Commission scolaire English-Montréal
6000 Fielding Ave., Montréal, QC H3X 1T4
Tel: 514-483-7200
www.emsb.qc.ca
www.facebook.com/EnglishMTL
twitter.com/EnglishMTL
Number of Schools: 77 Schools *Grades:* Elem. - Sec.; Adult Ed.
Enrollment: 44000 *Number of Employees:* 4000
Angela Mancini, Chair, Board
amancini2@emsb.qc.ca

Evelyn Alfonsi, Interim Director General/ADG, Education Division, 514-483-7200, ext. 7228
ealfonsi@emsb.qc.ca
Anna Sanalitro, Director, 514-483-7200, ext. 7355
asanalitro@emsb.qc.ca
Benoît Duhême, Assistant Director General, Administration Division, 514-483-7200, ext. 7227
bduheme@emsb.qc.ca
Nathalie Lauzière, Secretary General, 514-483-7200, ext. 7264
nlauziere@emsb.qc.ca
Ann Watson, Director, Human Resources, 514-483-7200, ext. 7279
awatson@emsb.qc.ca
Livia Nassivera, Director, Financial Services, 514-483-7200, ext. 7485
lnassivera@emsb.qc.ca

Montréal: **Lester B. Pearson School Board**
Commission scolaire Lester-B.-Pearson
1925, av Brookdale, Montréal, QC H9P 2Y7
Tel: 514-422-3000
info@lbpsb.qc.ca
www.lbpsb.qc.ca
www.facebook.com/LBPSB
twitter.com/lbpsb
www.linkedin.com/company/lester-b.-pearson-school-board
Number of Schools: 37 primary; 12 secondary; 8 centres
Grades: Pre - Sec; Adult Ed. *Enrollment:* 22000
Cindy Finn, Director General

New Carlisle: **Eastern Shores School Board (ESSB)**
Commission scolaire Eastern Shores
40, rue Mount Sorrel, New Carlisle, QC G0C 1Z0
Tel: 418-752-2247; *Fax:* 418-752-6447
info@essb.qc.ca
www.essb.qc.ca
www.facebook.com/easternshores2016
Number of Schools: 16 schools; 5 adult education centers
Grades: Pre - Sec *Enrollment:* 1700
Hugh Wood, Director General, 419-752-2247, ext. 250
dgessb@essb.qc.ca
Jane Bradbury, Assistant Director General, 419-752-2247, ext. 261
jane.bradbury@essb.qc.ca
Dave Smith, Director, Human Resources, 419-752-2247, ext. 228
diane.smith@essb.qc.ca

Québec: **Central Québec School Board (CQSB)**
Commission scolaire Central Québec
2046, ch Saint-Louis, Québec, QC G1T 1P4
Tel: 418-688-8730; *Fax:* 418-682-5891
Toll-Free: 800-249-5573
cqsb@cqsb.qc.ca
www.cqsb.qc.ca
www.facebook.com/798517930189372
twitter.com/CQSB
www.linkedin.com/company/central-quebec-school-board
Number of Schools: 20 *Grades:* K - 12; Adult Ed. *Enrollment:* 4785 *Number of Employees:* 387
Stephen Pigeon, Director General, 418-688-8730, ext. 3010
dg@cqsb.qc.ca
Nancy L'Heureux, Assistant Director General & Director, Human Resources, 418-688-8730, ext. 3063
hrhiring@laliberte@cqsb.qc.ca
Sandra Griffin, Secretary General, 418-688-8730, ext. 3020
SecGen-Com@cqsb.qc.ca
Guylaine Allard, Director, Financial Services, 418-688-8730, ext. 3000
finance@cqsb.qc.ca
Jennifer Bignell, Buyer, 418-688-8730, ext. 3050
jennifer.bignell@cqsb.qc.ca
Stephen Burke, Chair, Board

Rosemère: **Sir Wilfrid Laurier School Board**
Commission scolaire Sir-Wilfrid-Laurier
235, montée Lesage, Rosemère, QC J7A 4Y6
Tel: 450-621-5600; *Toll-Free:* 866-621-5600
communications@swlauriersb.qc.ca
www.swlauriersb.qc.ca
www.facebook.com/SWLSB
www.linkedin.com/company/swlsb
Number of Schools: 26 elementary; 9 secondary *Grades:* Prim. - Sec. *Enrollment:* 14000
Gaëlle Absolonne, Director General
Anna Sollazzo, Secretary General
Michel Dufour, Director, Material Resources
Stephanie Krenn, Director, Human Resources

Saint-Hubert: Commission scolaire Riverside
Riverside School Board
7525, ch de Chambly, Saint-Hubert, QC J3Y 5K2
Tel: 450-672-4010; *Fax:* 450-465-8809
rsb@rsb.qc.ca
www.rsb.qc.ca
www.facebook.com/131360617030576
twitter.com/CSRiversideSB
Number of Schools: 19 écoles primaires; 6 écoles secondaires
Grades: Prim - Sec *Enrollment:* 9139 *Number of Employees:* 2 300
Sylvain Racette, Directeur général, 450-672-4010, ext. 5040
sracette@rsb.qc.ca
Kimberly Barnes, Directrice, Ressources humaines, 450-672-4010, ext. 5250
kbarnes@rsb.qc.ca
Michel Bergeron, Directeur, Ressources financières, 450-672-4010, ext. 5260
michel.bergeron@rsb.qc.ca
Pierre M. Gagnon, Directeur, Ressources matérielles, 450-672-4010, ext. 5275
pierrem.gagnon@rsb.qc.ca
Jessica Saada, Directrice, Services éducatifs et des écoles, 450-672-4010, ext. 5246
jsaada@rsb.qc.ca

French

Alma: Centre de services scolaire du Lac-Saint-Jean
350, boul Champlain sud, Alma, QC G8B 5W2
Tél: 418-669-6000; *Téléc:* 418-669-6351
php.cslsj.qc.ca
www.facebook.com/cslslsj
www.youtube.com/user/cslsjalma
Number of Schools: 20 écoles primaires; 4 écoles secondaires; 3 centres d'éducation des adultes *Grades:* Prim - Sec
Enrollment: 8000 *Number of Employees:* 1 000
Marc-Pascal Harvey, Directeur général, 418-669-6000, ext. 5100
direction@cslsj.qc.ca
Christine Flaherty, Directrice générale adjointe, 418-669-6000, ext. 5200
secgen@cslsj.qc.ca
Jérôme Carette, Directeur, Service des ressources humaines, 418-669-6000, ext. 5501
jerome.carette@cslsj.qc.ca
Dave Corneau, Directrice, Service des ressources matérielles, 418-669-6000, ext. 5701
dave.corneau@cslsj.qc.ca
Manon Lepage, Directrice, Services éducatifs (jeunes et adultes), 418-669-6000, ext. 5301
manon.lepage@cslsj.qc.ca
Maryse Pilote, Directrice, Ressources financières, 418-669-6000, ext. 5601
maryse.pilote@cslsj.qc.ca

Amos: Centre de services scolaire Harricana
341, rue Principale nord, Amos, QC J9T 2L8
Tél: 819-732-6561; *Téléc:* 819-732-1623
communications@csharricana.qc.ca
www.csharricana.qc.ca
www.facebook.com/CSHarricana
Number of Schools: 20 écoles primaires; 3 écoles secondaires
Grades: Prim - Sec; éducation des adultes
Yannick Roy, Directeur général
Francis Audet, Directeur, Ressources matérielles
Pascal Germain, Directeur, Ressources financières
Maxime Pellerin, Directeur, Ressources humaines

Amqui: Centre de services scolaire des Monts-et-Marées
93, rue du Parc, Amqui, QC G5J 2L8
Tél: 418-629-6200
www.csmm.qc.ca
www.facebook.com/commissionscolairedesmontsetmarees
Number of Schools: 20 primaires; 4 secondaires; 2 primaires et secondaires; 2 centres d'éducation des adultes *Grades:* Pre - Sec; d'éducation des adultes *Enrollment:* 6700 *Number of Employees:* 1 100 *Note:* Centre de services de Matane: 530, av Saint-Jérôme, 418-566-2500.

Baie-Comeau: Centre de services scolaire de l'Estuaire
620, rue Jalbert, Baie-Comeau, QC G5C 0B8
Tél: 418-589-0806; *Ligne sans frais:* 877-589-0806
www.csestuaire.qc.ca
Number of Schools: 20 écoles primaires; 1 école primaire et secondaire; 4 écoles secondaires *Grades:* Prim - Sec
Enrollment: 4300 *Number of Employees:* 1 000
Nadine Desrosiers, Directrice générale, 418-589-0806, ext. 4813
nadine.desrosiers@csestuaire.qc.ca
Lucie Bhérer, Directrice générale adjointe, 418-589-0806, ext. 4823

Beauharnois: Centre de services scolaire de la Vallée-des-Tisserands
630, rue Ellice, Beauharnois, QC J6N 3S1
Tél: 450-225-2788; *Téléc:* 450-225-0691
Ligne sans frais: 877-225-2788
info@csvt.qc.ca
www.csvt.qc.ca
www.facebook.com/centreservicesscolaireVT
Number of Schools: 27 écoles primaires; 5 écoles secondaires; 4 centres *Grades:* Pre - Sec *Enrollment:* 9000 *Number of Employees:* 1 700
Marc Girard, Directeur général, 450-225-2788, ext. 6319
dg@csvt.qc.ca
Michèle Couture, Directrice, Services des ressources financières, 450-225-2788, ext. 6325
finances@csvt.qc.ca
Christian Duval, Directeur, Services des ressources éducatives
Luc Langevin, Directeur, Secrétariat général et des communications, 450-225-2788, ext. 6314
Martin Laframboise, Directeur, Services des ressources matérielles, 450-225-2788, ext. 6359
materielles@csvt.qc.ca
François Robichaud, Directeur, Services des ressources humaines, 450-225-2788, ext. 6337
humaines@csvt.qc.ca

Blanc-Sablon: Centre de services scolaire du Littoral
1581, boul Docteur-Camille-Marcoux, Blanc-Sablon, QC G0G 1C0
Tél: 418-461-2810; *Téléc:* 418-461-2601
Ligne sans frais: 877-745-7226
dg@csdulittoral.qc.ca
csdulittoral.qc.ca
Number of Schools: 13 *Grades:* Pre - Sec *Enrollment:* 450
Number of Employees: 190
Philip Joycey, Administrateur
Marc-André Masse, Secrétaire général, 418-962-5558, ext. 5520
sg@csdulittoral.qc.ca
Marie-Pier Rioux, Directeur, Ressources financières, 418-962-5558, ext. 5564
srf@csdulittoral.qc.ca

Bonaventure: Centre de services scolaire René-Lévesque
145, av Louisbourg, Bonaventure, QC G0C 1E0
Tél: 418-534-3003; *Téléc:* 418-534-3220
www.csrl.qc.ca
www.facebook.com/CSSReneLevesque
Number of Schools: 20 écoles primaires; 5 écoles secondaires; 2 écoles primaires-secondaires; 4 centres *Grades:* Prim - Sec; éducation des adultes *Enrollment:* 7300 *Number of Employees:* 1 300
Louis Bujold, Directeur général, 418-534-3003, ext. 6007
dg@csrl.net
Josée Arseneau, Directrice générale adjointe, 418-534-3003, ext. 6007
Samuel Johnson, Directeur, Ressources financières, 418-534-3003, ext. 6011
samuel.johnson@csrl.net
Nicolas Tchernof, Directeur, Service des ressources humaines, 418-534-3003, ext. 6019
nicolas.tchernof@csrl.net

Chibougamau: Centre de services scolaire de la Baie-James
596, 4e rue, Chibougamau, QC G8P 1S3
Tél: 418-748-7621; *Téléc:* 418-748-7581
www.csbj.qc.ca
www.facebook.com/csbaiejames
Number of Schools: 8 écoles primaires; 5 écoles secondaires
Grades: Prim - Sec *Enrollment:* 1700
Michel Laplace, Directeur général, 418-748-7621, ext. 2223

Chicoutimi: Centre de services scolaire des Rives-du-Saguenay
36, rue Jacques-Cartier est, Chicoutimi, QC G7H 1W2
Tél: 418-698-5000; *Téléc:* 418-698-5262
info@csrsaguenay.qc.ca
www.csrsaguenay.qc.ca
www.facebook.com/CSSRSaguenay
www.youtube.com/user/csrsaguenay
Number of Schools: 31 écoles primaires; 4 écoles secondaires
Grades: Prim - Sec *Enrollment:* 10800 *Number of Employees:* 2 500
Chantale Cyr, Directrice générale
chantale.cyr@csrsaguenay.qc.ca
Martin Lapierre, Directeur général adjoint
martin.lapierre@csrsaguenay.qc.ca
Jean-François Delisle, Secrétaire générale, 418-698-5000, ext. 5204
jean-francois.delisle@csrsaguenay.qc.ca

Isabelle Boivin, Directrice, Services éducatifs jeunes, 418-698-5000, ext. 5405
isabelle.boivin@csrsaguenay.qc.ca

Donnacona: Centre de services scolaire de Portneuf
310, rue de l'Église, Donnacona, QC G3M 1Z8
Tél: 418-285-2600; *Téléc:* 418-285-2738
www.facebook.com/csportneuf
Number of Schools: 13 primaires; 3 secondaires; 2 centres
Grades: Pre - Sec
Marie-Claude Tardif, Directrice générale, 418-285-2600, ext. 5005
mctardif@csportneuf.qc.ca
Jean-François Lussier, Directeur, Service des ressources matérielles et financières, 418-285-2600, ext. 5052
jflussier@csportneuf.qc.ca
Karine Toupin, Directrice, Services du sécrétariat général, 418-285-2600, ext. 5005
ktoupin@csportneuf.qc.ca

Drummondville: Centre de services scolaire des Chênes
P.O. Box 846
457, rue des Écoles, Drummondville, QC J2B 6X1
Tél: 819-478-6700
commentaires@cssdeschenes.qc.ca
www.cssdeschenes.gouv.qc.ca
www.facebook.com/csdeschenes
Number of Schools: 34 écoles primaires; 9 écoles secondaires
Grades: Pre - Sec *Enrollment:* 14000 *Number of Employees:* 1 400
Lucien Maltais, Directeur général
lucien.maltais@csdeschenes.qc.ca
Bernard Gauthier, Secrétaire général
bernard.gauthier@csdeschenes.qc.ca
Daniel Dumaine, Directeur, Service des ressources humaines
daniel.dumaine@csdeschenes.qc.ca
Yves Gendron, Directeur, Service des ressources matérielles
yves.gendron@csdeschenes.qc.ca
Carmen Lemire, Directrice, Service des ressources financières
carmen.lemire@csdeschenes.qc.ca

East Angus: Centre de services scolaire des Hauts-Cantons
308, rue Palmer, East Angus, QC J0B 1R0
Tél: 819-832-4953; *Téléc:* 819-832-4863
info@cshc.qc.ca
www.cshc.qc.ca
www.facebook.com/CSHautsCantons
Number of Schools: 30 écoles primaires; 3 écoles secondaires
Grades: Pre - Sec
Martial Gaudreau, Directeur général, 819-832-4953
Grégoire Francoeur, Dir., Services des ressources financières et matérielles, 819-849-7051
Dany Grégoire, Dir., Service de l'enseignement et du transport scolaire
Julie Morin, Directrice du service des ressources humaines

Gaspé: Centre de services scolaire des Chic-Chocs
102, rue Jacques-Cartier, Gaspé, QC G4X 2S9
Tél: 418-368-3499; *Téléc:* 418-368-6531
info@cschic-chocs.qc.ca
www.cschic-chocs.qc.ca
www.facebook.com/CSSChicChocs
Number of Schools: 13 écoles primaires; 3 écoles secondaires; 4 écoles primaires et secondaires *Grades:* Pre - Sec *Enrollment:* 4430
Julie Pariseau, Présidente

Gatineau: Centre de services scolaire au Coeur-des-Vallées
582, rue MacLaren est, Gatineau, QC J8L 2W2
Tél: 819-986-8511; *Téléc:* 819-986-9283
Ligne sans frais: 800-958-9966
info@cscv.qc.ca
www.cscv.qc.ca
www.facebook.com/958921427624587
Number of Schools: 16 écoles primaires; 5 écoles secondaires; 4 centres d'éducation pour les adultes *Grades:* Pre. - Sec.
Enrollment: 6900 *Number of Employees:* 1000
Eric Antoine, Président
Daniel Bellemare, Directeur général
Daniel Bellemare, Directrice Générale Adjointe aux Affaires Éducatives
Yannick Lyrette, Directeur, Service des Ressources Financières
Odette Bernier, Directrice, Service des ressources humaines

Gatineau: Commission scolaire des Draveurs
200, boul Maloney est, Gatineau, QC J8P 1K3
Tél: 819-663-9221; *Téléc:* 819-663-6176
reception@csdraveurs.qc.ca
www.csdraveurs.qc.ca

Number of Schools: 25 écoles primaires; 4 écoles secondaires; 1 centre d'éducation des adultes *Grades:* Prim. - Sec.; Éducation des adultes *Enrollment:* 18000 *Number of Employees:* 3,000
Claude Beaulieu, Président
Manon Dufour, Directrice générale, 819-663-9221, ext. 11102
dg@csdraveurs.qc.ca
Christian Laforest, Secrétaire général, 819-663-9221, ext. 12102
ssgc@csdraveurs.qc.ca
Sara Duguay, Directrice, Service des ressources financières, 819-663-9221, ext. 14102
srf@csdraveurs.qc.ca
Julie Legault, Directeur, Service des ressources éducatives, 819-663-9221, ext. 13102
sre@csdraveurs.qc.ca
Lyne Normand, Directrice, Service des ressources informatiques, 819-663-9221, ext. 17802
srict@csdraveurs.qc.ca
Chantal Patrice, Directrice, Service des ressources matérielles, 819-663-9221, ext. 19102
srm@csdraveurs.qc.ca
Denis St-Onge, Directeur, Service des ressources humaines, 819-663-9221, ext. 15012
srh@csdraveurs.qc.ca

Gatineau: Commission scolaire des Portages-de-l'Outaouais (CSPO)
225, rue St-Rédempteur, Gatineau, QC J8X 2T3
Tél: 819-771-4548; *Téléc:* 819-771-6964
reception@cspo.qc.ca
www.cspo.qc.ca
www.facebook.com/506236389459645
Number of Schools: 25 écoles primaires; 4 écoles secondaires; 2 centres de formation; 1 centres des adultes *Grades:* Pre. - Sec.; Éducation des adultes *Enrollment:* 18500 *Number of Employees:* 1,819
Nadine Peterson, Directrice générale, 819-771-4548, ext. 851700
nadine.peterson@cspo.qc.ca
Caroline Sauvé, Secrétaire générale, 819-771-4548, ext. 850700
Touria Chraibi, Directrice, Service des ressources matérielles, 819-771-4548
Isabelle Lemay, Directrice, Service des ressources éducatives, 819-771-4548, ext. 854700
Rémi Lupien, Directeur, Service des ressources financières, 819-771-4548, ext. 856700

Granby: Centre de services scolaire du Val-des-Cerfs (CSSVDC)
P.O. Box 9000
55, rue Court, Granby, QC J2G 9H7
Tél: 450-372-0221; *Téléc:* 450-372-3150
descerfs@csvdc.qc.ca
www.csvdc.qc.ca
www.facebook.com/CSS.Val.des.Cerfs
www.youtube.com/user/csduvaldescerfs
Number of Schools: 35 écoles primaires; 7 écoles secondaires; 2 centres d'éducation des adultes *Grades:* Prim - Sec; éducatioin des adultes *Enrollment:* 17500 *Number of Employees:* 3 000
Eric Racine, Directeur général
Josée Lapointe, Directrice, Ressources humaines
Nathalie Paré, Directrice, Ressources financières

Havre-Saint-Pierre: Centre de services scolaire de la Moyenne-Côte-Nord
1235, rue de la Digue, Havre-Saint-Pierre, QC G0G 1P0
Tél: 418-538-3044; *Téléc:* 418-538-3268
info@csmcn.qc.ca
www.csmcn.qc.ca
Number of Schools: 7 écoles primaires; 2 écoles secondaires *Grades:* Pre - Sec *Enrollment:* 700 *Number of Employees:* 300
Mario Cyr, Directeur général
mario-cyr@csmcn.qc.ca
Annick Dupuis, Secrétaire générale et Directrice, Ressources humaines
annick-dupuis@csmcn.qc.ca
Fanny Cormier, Directrice, Ressources financières
fanny-cormier@csmcn.qc.ca

Jonquière: Centre de services scolaire De La Jonquière
P.O. Box 1600
3644, rue St-Jules, Jonquière, QC G7X 7X4
Tél: 418-542-7551; *Téléc:* 418-542-1505
info@csjonquiere.qc.ca
www.csjonquiere.qc.ca
www.facebook.com/cssdelajonquiere
Number of Schools: 17 écoles primaires; 3 écoles secondaires *Grades:* Prim - Sec *Enrollment:* 10000 *Number of Employees:* 2 633

Jacynthe Bond, Directrice générale, 418-542-7551, ext. 4270
dgenerale@csjonquiere.qc.ca
Alexandra Cormier, Directrice, Ressources humaines, 418-542-7551, ext. 4276
rhumaines@csjonquiere.qc.ca
Steeve Steeve, Directeur, Ressources financières, 418-542-7551, ext. 4234
steeve.neron01@csjonquiere.qc.ca
Caroline Tremblay, Directrice par intérim , Services éducatifs jeunes et adultes, 418-542-7551, ext. 4218
caroline.tremblay01@csjonquiere.qc.ca

L'Étang-du-Nord: Commission scolaire des Iles
1419, ch de l'Étang-du-Nord, L'Étang-du-Nord, QC G4T 3B9
Tél: 418-986-5511; *Téléc:* 418-986-3552
secdgrh@csdesiles.qc.ca
www.csdesiles.qc.ca
Number of Schools: 6 écoles; 1 centre de formation professionnelle et de formation générale aux adultes *Grades:* Pre - Sec *Enrollment:* 1300 *Number of Employees:* 285
Brigitte Aucoin, Directrice générale, 418-986-5511, ext. 1101
Donald Chiasson, Directeur, Service de secrétariat général, 418-986-5511, ext. 1201
Danielle Gallant, Directrice, Ressources financières, 418-986-5511, ext. 1301

La Malbaie: Centre de services scolaire de Charlevoix
100, rue Laure-Gaudreault, La Malbaie, QC G5A 0A8
Tél: 418-665-3765; *Téléc:* 418-665-6805
www.cscharlevoix.qc.ca
www.facebook.com/csscharlevoix
twitter.com/csscharlevoix
Number of Schools: 14 écoles primaires; 3 écoles secondaires *Grades:* Prim - Sec
Lucie Maltais, Présidente
Martine Vallée, Directrice générale, 418-665-3765, ext. 3000
dg@cscharlevoix.qc.ca

La Prairie: Centre de services scolaire des Grandes-Seigneuries (CSSDGS)
50, boul Taschereau, 2e étage, La Prairie, QC J5R 4V3
Tél: 514-380-8899
communications@csdgs.qc.ca
www.cssdgs.gouv.qc.ca
www.facebook.com/cssdgs.gouv.qc.ca
twitter.com/CSSDGS
Number of Schools: 38 primaires; 12 secondaires; 2 centres de formation générale aux adultes *Grades:* Prim - Sec *Enrollment:* 26000 *Number of Employees:* 3 355
Kathlyn Morel, Directrice générale, 514-380-8899, ext. 3903
directiongenerale@csdgs.qc.ca
Daniel Bouthillette, Directeur général adjoint, 514-380-8899, ext. 3949
Pascale Gingras, Directrice générale adjointe, 514-380-8899, ext. 3993
Marie-Claude Huberdeau, Directrice générale adjointe, 514-380-8899, ext. 3993

La Sarre: Centre de services scolaire du Lac-Abitibi
500, rue Principale, La Sarre, QC J9Z 2A2
Tél: 819-333-5411; *Téléc:* 819-333-3044
SiteWeb@csdla.qc.ca
www.csdla.qc.ca
Number of Schools: 6 écoles primaires; 4 écoles secondaires; 2 centres de formation
Mélanie Boulet, Présidente
Isabelle Godbout, Directrice générale, 819-333-5411, ext. 2224

Laval: Commission scolaire de Laval (CSDL)
955, boul Saint-Martin ouest, Laval, QC H7S 1M5
Tél: 450-662-7000
www2.cslaval.qc.ca
www.facebook.com/CommissionscolairedeLaval
www.linkedin.com/company/commission-scolaire-de-laval
Number of Schools: 56 écoles primaires; 14 écoles secondaires; 4 centres d'éducation des adultes *Grades:* Prim. - Sec.; Éducation des adultes *Enrollment:* 54000 *Number of Employees:* 9,000
Yves-Michel Volcy, Directeur général, 450-662-7000, ext. 1001
Stella Duval, Secrétaire générale, 450-662-7000, ext. 1201
secretariatgeneral@cslaval.qc.ca
Louise Lortie, Présidente, 450-662-7000, ext. 1050
llortie@cslaval.qc.ca
Catherine Roussel, Directrice, Service des ressources humaines, 450-662-7000, ext. 1160
rh-direction@cslaval.qc.ca
Dominique Sylvain, Directrice, Service des ressources financières, 450-662-7000, ext. 1878
finances@cslaval.qc.ca

Longueuil: Commission scolaire Marie-Victorin (CSMV)
13, rue St-Laurent est, Longueuil, QC J4H 4B7
Tél: 450-670-0730
info@csmv.qc.ca
www.csmv.qc.ca
www.facebook.com/csmarievictorin
www.linkedin.com/company/commission-scolaire-marie-victorin
www.youtube.com/csmarievictorin
Number of Schools: 72 établissements *Grades:* Pre. - Sec.; Éducation des adultes *Enrollment:* 41000 *Number of Employees:* 4500
Marie-Dominique Taillon, Directrice générale
France Blouin, Directrice générale adjointe
Hugo Clermont, Directeur générale adjointe
Marc-André Petit, Directeur général adjoint
Ghislain Plourde, Directeur général adjoint
Carole Lavallée, Présidente, 450-670-0730, ext. 2045
clavallee@csmv.qc.ca

Magog: Centre de services scolaire des Sommets
449, rue Percy, Magog, QC J1X 1B5
Tél: 819-847-1610; *Téléc:* 819-847-2065
Ligne sans frais: 888-847-1610
info@csdessommets.qc.ca
www.csdessommets.qc.ca
Number of Schools: 28 primaires; 4 secondaires *Grades:* Pre - Sec *Enrollment:* 9686 *Number of Employees:* 1 439
Édith Pelletier, Directrice générale, 819 847-1610, ext. 18800
dgenerale@csdessommets.qc.ca
Lyne Beauchamp, Directrice, Secrétariat général, 819-847-1610, ext. 18853
sgeneral@csdessommets.qc.ca
Daniel Blais, Directeur, Service des ressources financières, 819-847-1610, ext. 18831
rfinancieres@csdessommets.qc.ca
Martin Charron, Directeur, Ressources humaines, 819-847-1610, ext. 18842
rhumaines@csdessommets.qc.ca
Serge Dion, Directrice, Service des ressources éducatives, 819-847-1610, ext. 18820
reduc@csdessommets.qc.ca

Maniwaki: Commission scolaire des Hauts-Bois-de-l'Outaouais (CSHBO)
331, rue du Couvent, Maniwaki, QC J9E 1H5, Canada
Tél: 819-449-7866; *Téléc:* 819-449-2636
Ligne sans frais: 888-831-9606
info@cshbo.qc.ca
www.facebook.com/cshbo
Number of Schools: 19 écoles primaires; 3 écoles secondaires; 5 établissements des adultes *Grades:* Mat./Prim./Sec.; Adulte *Enrollment:* 3000 *Number of Employees:* 580
Denis Rossignol, Directeur général, 819-449-7866, ext. 16235
Denis.Rossignol@cshbo.qc.ca
Richard Leblanc, Secrétaire général, 819-449-7866, ext. 16228
richard.leblanc@cshbo.qc.ca
Charles Pétrin, Directeur, service des ressources matérielles, 819-449-7866, ext. 16224
charles.petrin@cshbo.qc.ca
Manon Riel, Directrice, service des ressources financières, 819-449-7866, ext. 16223
France Lagarde, Directrice, service des ressources éducatives, 819-449-7866, ext. 16237
France.Lagarde@cshbo.qc.ca
Monia Lirette, Régisseuse aux communications, 819-449-7866, ext. 16239
monia.lirette@cshbo.qc.ca
Stéphane Rondeau, Directeur général adjoint, 819-449-7866, ext. 16238
stephane.rondeau@cshbo.qc.ca

Mont-Laurier: Commission scolaire Pierre-Neveu (CSPN)
525, rue de la Madone, Mont-Laurier, QC J9L 1S4, Canada
Tél: 819-623-4310; *Téléc:* 819-623-7979
Ligne sans frais: 866-334-4114
cspn@cspn.qc.ca
www.cspn.qc.ca
Number of Schools: 22 écoles primaires; 3 écoles secondaires *Grades:* Prim - Sec; préscolaire; adultes *Enrollment:* 4234
Julie Bellavance, Directrice générale, 819-623-4114, ext. 5402
bellavance.julie@cspn.qc.ca
Manon Plouffe, Directrice, Ressources Humaines, 819-623-4114, ext. 5432
plouffe.manon@cspn.qc.ca
Annie Lamoureux, Directrice, Ressources financières et taxation, 819-623-4114, ext. 5412
lamoureux.annie@cspn.qc.ca

Hugo Charbonneau, Directeur, Ressources matérielles, 819-623-4114, ext. 5442
charbonneau.hugo@cspn.qc.ca
Jacinthe Fex, Secrétaire général, 819-623-4114, ext. 5452
fex.jacinthe@cspn.qc.ca

Montmagny: Centre de services scolaire de la Côte-du-Sud
157, rue Saint-Louis, Montmagny, QC G5V 4N3
Tél: 418-248-1001; *Téléc:* 418-248-9797
info@cscotesud.qc.ca
www.facebook.com/csscotedusud
Number of Schools: 39 écoles primaires; 9 écoles secondaires
Grades: Prim - Sec *Enrollment:* 8100
Jean-Marc Jean, Directeur général, 418-248-1001, ext. 8481
jeanmarc.jean@cscotesud.qc.ca
Pierre Côté, Directeur général adjoint et Secrétaire général, 418-248-1001, ext. 8483
pierre.cote@cscotesud.qc.ca
Annie Ménard, Directrice, Ressources financières, 418-248-1001, ext. 8411
annie.menard@cscotesud.qc.ca
Hugo Morin, Directeur, Ressources matérielles, 418-248-1001, ext. 8451
hugo.morin@cscotesud.qc.ca

Montréal: Centre de services scolaire Marguerite-Bourgeoys
1100, boul de la Côte-Vertu, Montréal, QC H4L 4V1
Tél: 514-855-4500; *Téléc:* 514-855-4749
www.csmb.qc.ca
www.facebook.com/csmbourgeoys
twitter.com/csmbourgeoys
www.linkedin.com/company/commission-scolaire-marguerite-bourgeoys
www.youtube.com/c/CommissionscolaireMargueriteBourgeoys
Number of Schools: 75 primaries; 14 secondaires; 3 spécialisées; 10 centres *Enrollment:* 72000 *Number of Employees:* 11 500
Dominic Bertrand, Directeur général
Marie-Josée Villeneuve, Secrétaire générale

Montréal: Commission scolaire de la Pointe-de-l'Île (CSPI)
550, 53e av, Montréal, QC H1A 2T7
Tél: 514-642-9520
info@cspi.qc.ca
www3.cspi.qc.ca
www.facebook.com/cspointedelile
Number of Schools: 41 écoles primaires; 7 écoles secondaires; 3 écoles spécialisées; 8 centres d'éducation des adultes *Grades:* Prim - Sec.; Adultes *Enrollment:* 43600 *Number of Employees:* 8,600
Miville Boudreault, Président
Antoine El-Khoury, Directeur général
Alain Bouchard, Directeur, Réseau - secteur des adultes
René Brodeur, Directeur, Ressources financières
Josée Dumouchel, Directrice, Ressources humaines
Martin Bergeron, Directeur, Ressources matérielles
Valérie Biron, Directrice, Services corporatifs & secrétariat général

Montréal: Commission scolaire de Montréal (CSDM)
3737, rue Sherbrooke est, Montréal, QC H1X 3B3
Tél: 514-596-6000
info@csdm.qc.ca
csdm.ca
www.facebook.com/commission.scolaire.de.montreal
twitter.com/csdemontreal
Number of Schools: 189 établissements *Grades:* Pré. - Sec.
Enrollment: 115018 *Number of Employees:* 16,405
Robert Gendron, Directeur général, 514-596-4245, ext. 6312
gendronr@csdm.qc.ca

Nicolet: Centre de services scolaire de la Riveraine
375, rue de Monseigneur-Brunault, Nicolet, QC J3T 1Y6
Tél: 819-293-5821; *Téléc:* 819-293-8691
information@csriveraine.qc.ca
www.csriveraine.qc.ca
www.facebook.com/567750354695183
Number of Schools: 37 *Grades:* Prim - Sec; éducation des adultes *Enrollment:* 9471
Pascal Blondin, Directeur général, 819-293-5821, ext. 4502
direction.generale@csriveraine.qc.ca
Isabelle Bourque, Secrétaire générale, 819-293-5821, ext. 4506
Sophie Dubord, Directrice, Service des ressources humaines, 819-293-5821, ext. 4550
service.rh@csriveraine.qc.ca
Myriam Noël, Directrice, Service des ressources financières, 819-293-5821, ext. 4511
service.rf@csriveraine.qc.ca

Québec: Centre de services scolaire de la Capitale
1900, rue Côté, Québec, QC G1N 3Y5
Tél: 418-686-4040; *Téléc:* 418-686-4032
adm2@cscapitale.qc.ca
www.cscapitale.qc.ca
www.facebook.com/784251858319961
www.linkedin.com/company/commission-scolaire-de-la-capitale
www.instagram.com/cscapitale
Number of Schools: 66 établissements scolaires *Grades:* K - 12; Adultes *Enrollment:* 28859 *Number of Employees:* 6,089
Manon Robitaille, Présidente, 418-686-4040, ext. 2003
Pierre Lapointe, Directeur général, 418-686-4040, ext. 2003
dgcapitale@cscapitale.qc.ca
Mireille Dion, Directrice générale adjointe, Affaires éducatives, 418-686-4040, ext. 2030
Richard Vallée, Directeur général adjoint, Affaires administratives, 418-686-4040, ext. 2010
Marc Drolet, Directeur, Services des ressources financières, 418-686-4040, ext. 2600
srf@cscapitale.qc.ca
Éric Fortin, Directeur, Services des ressources matérielles, 418-686-4040, ext. 2500
srm@cscapitale.qc.ca
André-Marc Goulet, Directeur, Services éducatifs des jeunes, 418-686-4040, ext. 2200
sej@cscapitale.qc.ca
Nancy Paquet, Directrice, Services des ressources humaines, 418-686-4040, ext. 2400
srh@cscapitale.qc.ca
Érick Parent, Directeur, Information & Secrétaire général, 418-686-4040, ext. 2100
sg@cscapitale.qc.ca
Maude Plourde, Directrice, Services de la formation professionnelle, 418-686-4040, ext. 2300
sfpea@cscapitale.qc.ca

Québec: Centre de services scolaire des Premières-Seigneuries
643, av du Cénacle, Québec, QC G1E 1B3
Tél: 418-666-4666; *Téléc:* 418-666-9783
sic@csdps.qc.ca
www.csdps.qc.ca
www.facebook.com/cssdespremieresseigneuries
Number of Schools: 36 écoles primaires; 7 écoles secondaires *Grades:* Prim.-Sec. *Enrollment:* 29460 *Number of Employees:* 6 000
Marie-Claude Asselin, Directrice générale
dg@csdps.qc.ca
Annie Fournier, Directrice générale adjointe
Nicolas Maheux, Directeur général adjointe
Martine Chouinard, Secrétaire général
secgen@csdps.qc.ca
Jean-Marc Drolet, Directeur, Ressources matérielles, 418-666-4666, ext. 8471
srm@csdps.qc.ca
Érick Gaboury, Directeur, Ressources humaines
srh@csdps.qc.ca
Bernard Rousseau, Directeur, Ressources financières, 418-666-4666, ext. 1217
srf@csdps.qc.ca

Québec: Commission scolaire des Découvreurs
#100, 945, av Wolfe, Québec, QC G1V 4E2
Tél: 418-652-2121; *Téléc:* 418-652-2146
www.csdecou.qc.ca
Number of Schools: 22 *Grades:* Prim. - Sec.; Adultes
Enrollment: 17595 *Number of Employees:* 2,000
Alain Fortier, Président, 418-652-2121, ext. 4242
alain.fortier@csdecou.qc
Christian Pleau, Directeur général, 418-652-2121
dgdecou@csdecou.qc.ca
Guillaume Métivier, Directeur, Ressources financière, 418-652-2121, ext. 4166
srf@csdecou.qc.ca
Julie Aubin, Directrice, Ressources matérielles, 418-652-2121, ext. 4117
srm@csdecou.qc.ca
Éric Beaupré, Directeur, Services éducatifs, 418-652-2121
seduc@csdecou.qc.ca
Marie-Pierre Lamarche, Directrice, Ressources humaines, 418-652-2121, ext. 4111
srhum@csdecou.qc.ca
Mélanie Charest, Directrice, Secrétariat général et communications, 418-652-2121, ext. 4241
secgen@csdecou.qc.ca

Repentigny: Centre de services scolaire des Affluents
80, rue Jean-Baptiste-Meilleur, Repentigny, QC J6A 6C5
Tél: 450-492-9400; *Téléc:* 450-492-3720
info@csda.ca
www.csda.ca
www.facebook.com/cssdesaffluents
Number of Schools: 48 écoles primaires; 14 écoles secondaires *Grades:* Prim - Sec *Enrollment:* 35000 *Number of Employees:* 5 500
Isabelle Gélinas, Directrice générale
direction.generale@csda.ca
Anne Turcotte, Directrice, Service des ressources financières, 450-492-9400
anne.turcotte@csda.ca

Rimouski: Centre de services scolaire des Phares
435, av Rouleau, Rimouski, QC G5L 8V4
Tél: 418-723-5927; *Téléc:* 418-724-3350
webmestre@csphares.qc.ca
www.csphares.qc.ca
www.facebook.com/csphares
Number of Schools: 34 *Grades:* Prim - Sec *Enrollment:* 10000
Number of Employees: 1 500
Madeleine Dugas, Directrice générale, 418-723-5927, ext. 1010
dgphares@csphares.qc.ca
Jocelyn Michaud, Directeur général adjoint
Cathy-Maude Croft, Secrétaire générale, 418-723-5927, ext. 1010
secretariatgeneral@csphares.qc.ca
Rock Bouffard, Directeur, Services des ressources humaines, 418-723-5927, ext. 1040
rock_bouffard@csphares.qc.ca
Marie-Hélène Ouellet, Directrice, Service des ressources financières, 418-723-5927, ext. 1060
sec.ress.fin@csphares.qc.ca

Rivière-du-Loup: Centre de services scolaire de Kamouraska—Rivière-du-Loup
P.O. Box 910
464, rue Lafontaine, Rivière-du-Loup, QC G5R 3C2
Tél: 418-868-8201; *Téléc:* 418-862-0964
webmestre@cskamloup.qc.ca
www.cskamloup.qc.ca
www.facebook.com/cskamloup.qc.ca
twitter.com/cskamloup
www.youtube.com/user/pavillondelavenir
Number of Schools: 15 écoles primaires; 2 écoles secondaires
Grades: Prim - Sec *Enrollment:* 7000 *Number of Employees:* 900
Antoine Déry, Directeur général
dirgen@cskamloup.qc.ca
Geneviève Soucy, Directrice, Secrétariat général et communications
secgen@cskamloup.qc.ca

Roberval: Centre de services scolaire du Pays-des-Bleuets
828, boul Saint-Joseph, Roberval, QC G8H 2L5
Tél: 418-275-4136; *Téléc:* 418-275-6217
communication@cspaysbleuets.qc.ca
www.cspaysbleuets.qc.ca
www.facebook.com/cspaysdesbleuets
twitter.com/CSPaysBleuets
Number of Schools: 35 écoles, centres et sous-centres *Grades:* Prim - Sec *Enrollment:* 7000 *Number of Employees:* 1 000 *Note:* Secteur Dolbeau-Mistassini: 1950, boul Sacré-Coeur, Dolbeau-Mistassini, QC G8L 2R3, 418-276-2012.
Patrice Boivin, Directeur général, 418-275-4136, ext. 1000
Carl Gauthier, Directeur, Ressources matérielles
Chantale Rivard, Directeur, Ressources financières
Nadia Tremblay, Directeur, Ressources humaines, 418-275-4136, ext. 1012

Rouyn-Noranda: Centre de services scolaire de Rouyn-Noranda
P.O. Box 908
70, rue des Oblats est, Rouyn-Noranda, QC J9X 5C9
Tél: 819-762-8161
webinfo@csrn.qc.ca
www.csrn.qc.ca
Number of Schools: 17 primaires; 2 secondaires; 2 centres
Grades: Prim - Sec
Yves Bédard, Directeur général, 819-762-8161, ext. 1210
dgcsrn@csrn.qc.ca
Stéphanie Dupont, Directeur, Ressources financières, 819-762-8161, ext. 1250
Édith-Martine Lapierre, Directrice, Ressources matérielles, 819-762-8161, ext. 1260
lapierreem@csrn.qc.ca

Mélanie Savard, Directrice, Ressources humaines, 819-762-8161, ext. 1240
resshum@csrn.qc.ca

Saint-Bruno-de-Montarville: Centre de services scolaire des Patriotes (CSSP)
1740, rue Roberval, Saint-Bruno-de-Montarville, QC J3V 3R3
Tél: 450-441-2919; *Téléc:* 450-441-0838
info@csp.ca
csp.ca
www.facebook.com/Commissionscolairedespatriotes
twitter.com/cspatriotes
Number of Schools: 69 *Grades:* Prim.-Sec. *Enrollment:* 36024
Number of Employees: 4 825
Luc Lapointe, Directeur général

Saint-Félix-de-Valois: Centre de services scolaire des Samares
4671, rue Principale, Saint-Félix-de-Valois, QC J0K 2M0
Tél: 450-758-3500; *Téléc:* 450-889-8604
sg@cssamares.qc.ca
cssamares.ca
www.facebook.com/CSSSamares
Number of Schools: 67 écoles primaires; 12 écoles secondaires
Grades: K - 12
Nancy Lapointe, Directrice générale
dg@cssamares.qc.ca

Saint-Georges: Centre de services scolaire de la Beauce-Etchemin
1925, 118e rue, Saint-Georges, QC G5Y 7R7
Tél: 418-228-5541; *Téléc:* 418-228-5549
secretariat.general@csbe.qc.ca
www.csbe.qc.ca
www.facebook.com/csbeauceetchemin
Number of Schools: 55 écoles primaires; 10 écoles secondaires; 9 centres d'éducation des adultes *Grades:* Prim - Sec; d'éducation des adultes *Enrollment:* 18420
Normand Lessard, Directeur général, 418-228-5541, ext. 2503
direction.generale@csbe.qc.ca
Patrick Beaudoin, Directeur, Service des finances, 418-228-5541, ext. 2520
patrick.beaudoin@csbe.qc.ca
Marie-ve Dutil, Directrice, Secrétariat général et services corporatifs
Marie-Josée Fecteau, Directrice, Service de la formation professionnelle
Pascal Lamontagne, Directeur, Service des ressources humaines

Saint-Hyacinthe: Centre de services scolaire de Saint-Hyacinthe (CSSSSH)
2255, av Sainte-Anne, Saint-Hyacinthe, QC J2S 5H7
Tél: 450-773-8401; *Téléc:* 450-773-6876
information@csssh.gouv.qc.ca
www.cssh.qc.ca
www.facebook.com/centredeservicesscolairedesthyacinthe
www.linkedin.com/company/csssh
Number of Schools: 30 elementales; 4 secondaires; 4 autres
Grades: Prim - Sec *Enrollment:* 17000 *Number of Employees:* 3 000
Jean-Pierre Bédard, Directeur général, 450-773-8401, ext. 6559
jean-pierre.bedard@cssh.qc.ca
Daniel Camirand, Directeur général adjoint et secrétaire général, 450-773-8401, ext. 6590
daniel.camirand@cssh.qc.ca
Sylvie Girard, Directrice, Service des ressources financières, 450-773-8401, ext. 6280
sylvie.girard@cssh.qc.ca
Chantal Langelier, Directrice, Service des ressources humaines, 450-773-8401, ext. 6586
chantal.langelier@cssh.qc.ca
Jean-François Soumis, Directeur, Service des ressources matérielles, 450-773-8401, ext. 6585
jean-francois.soumis@cssh.qc.ca
Karina St-Germain, Directrice, Services éducatifs, 450-773-8401, ext. 6247
karina.st-germain@cssh.qc.ca

Saint-Jean-sur-Richelieu: Centre de services scolaire des Hautes-Rivières
210, rue Notre-Dame, Saint-Jean-sur-Richelieu, QC J3B 6N3
Tél: 450-359-6411; *Téléc:* 450-359-1569
Ligne sans frais: 877-359-6411
cacommunications@csdhr.qc.ca
www.csdhr.qc.ca
www.facebook.com/CommissionScolaireDesHautesRivieres
Number of Schools: 43 écoles *Grades:* Pre-Sec; adultes
Enrollment: 17000 *Number of Employees:* 2 500
Dominique Lachapelle, Directrice générale, 450-359-6411, ext. 7240
cadg@csdhr.qc.ca

Katleen Loiselle, Directrice, Ressources humaines, 450-359-6411, ext. 7236
caressourceshumaines@csdhr.qc.ca
Élizabeth McDonough, Directeur, Ressources matérielles, 450-359-6411, ext. 7249
caressourcesmaterielles@csdhr.qc.ca
Chantal Noël, Directrice, Ressources financières, 450-359-6411, ext. 7207
caressourcesfinancieres@csdhr.qc.ca

Saint-Jérôme: Commission scolaire de la Rivière-du-Nord (CSRDN)
995, rue Labelle, Saint-Jérôme, QC J7Z 5N7, Canada
Tél: 450-438-3131
www2.csrdn.qc.ca
www.facebook.com/CommissionscolaireRDN
twitter.com/CSRDN
Number of Schools: 44 écoles primaires; 8 écoles secondaires; Centres de formation professionnelle *Grades:* Prim - Sec *Enrollment:* 30586 *Number of Employees:* 4875 *Note:* Centre administratif II: 795, rue Melançon, 450-438-3131.
Jean-Pierre Joubert, Président
Guylaine Desroches, Directrice générale
Sébastien Tardif, Directeur général adjoint à la réussite
René Brisson, Directeur général adjoint
Michael Charette, Directeur général adjoint

Saint-Romuald: Centre de services scolaire des Navigateurs
1860, 1e rue, Saint-Romuald, QC G6W 5M6
Tél: 418-839-0500
dg@csnavigateurs.qc.ca
web.csdn.qc.ca
www.linkedin.com/company/csdn
Number of Schools: 37 primaires; 4 primaires-secondaires; 8 secondaires; 5 centres de formation professionnelle *Grades:* Pre - Sec *Enrollment:* 26000 *Number of Employees:* 3 800
Esther Lemieux, Directrice générale, 418-839-0500, ext. 51000
Dany Deschênes, Directeur, Ressources matérielles, 418-839-0500, ext. 58000
Jean-François Houle, Dir., Services des ressources financières et du transport, 418-839-0500, ext. 57000
Manon Robitaille, Directrice, Ressources humaines, 418-839-0500, ext. 56000
Pascale Girard Toupin, Directrice, Services éducatifs, 418-839-0500, ext. 52000

Sainte-Agathe-des-Monts: Centre de services scolaire des Laurentides
13, rue Saint-Antoine, Sainte-Agathe-des-Monts, QC J8C 2C3
Tél: 819-326-0333; *Téléc:* 819-326-2121
info@cslaurentides.qc.ca
www.cslaurentides.qc.ca
Number of Schools: 16 écoles primaires; 5 écoles secondaires *Grades:* Prim - Sec *Enrollment:* 8500 *Number of Employees:* 1 500
Sébastien Tardif, Directeur général
direction.generale@cslaurentides.qc.ca
Marie-Josée Albert, Directrice, Service des ressources financières, 819-326-0333, ext. 2015
ressources.financieres@cslaurentides.qc.ca
Samuel Fortin, Directeur, Service des ressources matérielles, 819-326-0333, ext. 2017
ressources.materielles@cslaurentides.qc.ca
Nancy Perron, Directrice, Service des ressources humaines, 819-326-0333, ext. 2013
ressources.humaines@cslaurentides.qc.ca
Julie Richer, Directrice, Services éducatifs, 819-326-0333, ext. 2008
ressources.educatives.direction@cslaurentides.qc.ca

Sept-Iles: Centre de services scolaire du Fer
30, rue Comeau, Sept-Iles, QC G4R 4N2
Tél: 418-968-9901; *Téléc:* 418-962-7760
www.csdufer.qc.ca
www.facebook.com/760112104064270
Number of Schools: 13 écoles primaires; 4 écoles secondaires; 4 centres de formation des adultes *Grades:* Pre - Sec
Richard Poirier, Directeur général, 418-964-2741
Johanne Moreau, Directrice des ressources humaines et secrétaire général, 418-964-2735
Anna Blais, Directrice des ressources financières, 418-964-2727
Kathleen Boulianne, Directrice des services éducatifs, 418-964-2862

Shawinigan: Centre de services scolaire de l'Énergie
P.O. Box 580
2072, rue Gignac, Shawinigan, QC G9N 6V7
Tél: 819-539-6971; *Téléc:* 819-539-7797
Ligne sans frais: 888-711-0013
cse@csenergie.qc.ca
www.facebook.com/emapCSSE
Number of Schools: 25 écoles primaires; 7 écoles secondaires; 4 centres *Grades:* Pre - Sec *Enrollment:* 9200 *Number of Employees:* 2 200
Maxime Trudel, Président
Denis Lemaire, Directeur général, 819-539-6971, ext. 2225
dlemaire@csenergie.qc.ca
Louise Dauphinais, Dir. général adjoint et Dir., Services éducatifs (jeunes), 819-539-6971, ext. 2266
ldauphinais@csenergie.qc.ca

Sherbrooke: Commission scolaire de la Région-de-Sherbrooke (CSRS)
2955, boul de l'Université, Sherbrooke, QC J1K 2Y3
Tél: 819-822-5540; *Téléc:* 819-822-5530
www.csrs.qc.ca
www.facebook.com/CSSsherbrooke
twitter.com/cssherbrooke
www.youtube.com/user/CSSherbrooke
Number of Schools: 47 établissements *Grades:* Prim. - Sec.; Éducation des adultes *Enrollment:* 25000 *Number of Employees:* 3,750
Christian Provencher, Directeur général, 819-822-5540, ext. 20211
dg@csrs.qc.ca
Julie Boivin, Directrice, Service des ressources financières
RFTS@csrs.qc.ca
Donald Landry, Directeur, Service des communications, 819-822-5540, ext. 21710
comm@csrs.qc.ca
Paule Corriveau, Directrice, Service des ressources matérielles, 819-822-5540, ext. 20410
rmti@csrs.qc.ca
Daniel Samson, Directeur, Service des ressources humaines
711ressourceshumaines@csrs.qc.ca

Sorel-Tracy: Centre de services scolaire de Sorel-Tracy
41, av de l'Hôtel-Dieu, Sorel-Tracy, QC J3P 1L1
Tél: 450-746-3990; *Téléc:* 450-746-4474
www.cs-soreltracy.qc.ca
www.facebook.com/cssoreltracy
Number of Schools: 14 écoles primaires; 2 écoles secondaires; 2 centres de formation professionnelle *Grades:* Prim.-Sec. *Enrollment:* 5442
Christian Lacourse, Directeur général
Laurence Cournoyer, Secrétariat général
Ralph Beaulieu, Directeur, Services des ressources matérielles
Stéphanie Fréchette, Directrice, Services des ressources financières
Caroline Gendron, Directrice, Services des ressources humaines
Martine Rondeau, Directrice, Services éducatifs

Témiscouata-sur-le-Lac: Centre de services scolaire du Fleuve-et-des-Lacs
14, rue du Vieux-Chemin, Témiscouata-sur-le-Lac, QC G0L 1E0
Tél: 418-854-2370
csfl.qc.ca
Number of Schools: 34 écoles primaires; 6 écoles secondaires *Grades:* Pre - Sec
Bernard D'Amours, Directeur général, 418-854-2370, ext. 2114
dg@csfl.qc.ca
Catherine Boulay, Directrice, Secrétariat général et communications, 418-854-2370, ext. 2104
Emmanuelle Ouellet, Directrice, Ressources financières, 418-854-2370, ext. 2202
ouelletem@csfl.qc.ca

Thetford Mines: Centre de services scolaire des Appalaches (CSSa)
650, rue Lapierre, Thetford Mines, QC G6G 7P1
Tél: 418-338-7800; *Téléc:* 418-338-7845
communications@cssappalaches.qc.ca
www.cssappalaches.qc.ca
www.facebook.com/csappalaches
Number of Schools: 19 primaires; 4 secondaires; 2 centres de formation professionnelle *Grades:* Prim - Sec *Enrollment:* 5000
Number of Employees: 570
Jean Roberge, Directeur général
dgcsa@cssappalaches.qc.ca
André Dallaire, Directeur, Service des ressources matérielles
andre.dallaire@cssappalaches.qc.ca

Karine Guay, Directeur, Service des ressources financières
karine.guay@csappalaches.qc.ca
Martin Vallée, Directeur, Service des ressources humaines
martin.vallee@csappalaches.qc.ca

Trois-Rivières: **Centre de services scolaire du Chemin-du-Roy**
P.O. Box 100
1515, rue Sainte-Marguerite, Trois-Rivières, QC G9A 5E7
Tél: 819-379-6565; *Téléc:* 819-379-2068
info@csduroy.qc.ca
www.csduroy.qc.ca
www.facebook.com/csduroy
www.youtube.com/user/csduroy
Number of Schools: 73 établissements *Grades:* Pré.- Sec.; Éducation des adultes *Enrollment:* 20087 *Number of Employees:* 2,938
Luc Galvani, Directeur général, 819-379-5989, ext. 7272
dgduroy@csduroy.qc.ca
Ginette Masse, Directrice générale adjointe, Services éducatifs, 819-379-5989, ext. 7272
dga.gm@csduroy.qc.ca
Laurent Cabana, Directeur général adjoint, Services administratifs, 819-379-5989, ext. 7272
dga.lc@csduroy.qc.ca
Martin Samson, Directeur, Service des ressources humaines, 819-379-5989, ext. 7254
rh@csduroy.qc.ca
Patricia Hinse, Directrice par interim, Service des ressources financières, 819-379-5989, ext. 7371
rf.dir@csduroy.qc.ca
Claude Lessard, Président

Val-d'Or: **Centre de services scolaire de l'Or-et-des-Bois**
799, boul Forest, Val-d'Or, QC J9P 2L4
Tél: 819-825-4220; *Téléc:* 819-825-5305
info@csob.qc.ca
csob.qc.ca
www.facebook.com/profilcsob
Number of Schools: 13 écoles primaires; 4 écoles secondaires; 2 centres *Grades:* Prim - Sec *Enrollment:* 6000 *Number of Employees:* 1 100
Alain Guillemette, Directeur général, 819-825-4220, ext. 3010
guillemette.alain@csob.qc.ca
Nathalie Legault, Secrétaire générale, 819-825-4220, ext. 3011
legault.nathalie@csob.qc.ca
Isabelle Bergeron, Directrice, Service des ressources humaines, 819-825-4220, ext. 3030
bergeron.isabelle@csob.qc.ca
Claudie Brière, Directeur, Service des ressources financières, 819-825-4220, ext. 3050
briere.claudie@csob.qc.ca
Annik Imbeault, Directrice, Ressources éducatives, 819-825-4220, ext. 3020
imbeault.annik@csob.qc.ca
Patrick Lortie, Directeur, Ressources matérielles et approvisionnement, 819-825-4220, ext. 3040
lortie.patrick@csob.qc.ca

Vaudreuil-Dorion: **Centre de services scolaire des Trois-Lacs**
400, av St-Charles, Vaudreuil-Dorion, QC J7V 6B1
Tél: 514-477-7000; *Téléc:* 514-477-7022
www.cstrois-lacs.qc.ca
www.facebook.com/csdestroislacs
Number of Schools: 25 primaires; 3 écoles secondaires *Grades:* Prim - Sec *Enrollment:* 16000
Sophie Proulx, Directrice générale, 514-477-7022
dgenerale@cstrois-lacs.qc.ca
Francys Robidoux, Directeur, Service des ressources financières
resfin@cstrois-lacs.qc.ca
Sandra Sheehy, Directrice, Service des ressources matérielles, 514-477-7000, ext. 1920
sandra.sheehy@cstrois-lacs.qc.ca

Victoriaville: **Centre de services scolaire des Bois-Francs**
P.O. Box 40
40, boul Bois-Francs nord, Victoriaville, QC G6P 6S5
Tél: 819-758-6453; *Téléc:* 819-758-5827
info@csbf.qc.ca
www.csbf.qc.ca
www.facebook.com/csboisfrancs
Number of Schools: 54 écoles et centres de formation *Grades:* Prim - Sec *Enrollment:* 14000 *Number of Employees:* 2 200
Alain Desruisseaux, Directeur général
Michael Provencher, Secrétaire général
Frédéric Gagnon, Directeur, Service des ressources informatique & matérielles
Mélanie Garneau, Directrice, Service des ressources humaines

Sandra Houle, Directrice, Services éducatifs, secteurs jeunes, adultes
Josée Maheu, Directrice, Service des ressources financières

Ville-Marie: **Centre de services scolaire du Lac-Témiscamingue**
2, rue Maisonneuve, Ville-Marie, QC J9V 1V4
Tél: 819-629-2472; *Téléc:* 866-233-9122
courrier@cslt.qc.ca
www.cslt.qc.ca
www.facebook.com/css.lactemisamingue
www.linkedin.com/company/commission-scolaire-du-lac-t-misca mingue
Number of Schools: 14 écoles primaires; 4 écoles secondaires; 4 centres d'éducation des adultes *Grades:* Prim.-Sec.
Éric Larivière, Directeur général, 819-629-2472, ext. 1101
eric.lariviere@cslt.qc.ca
Josée Beaulé, Directrice, Services des ressources humaines et financières
josee.beaule@cslt.qc.ca
Joël Fleury, Directeur, Service des ressources matérielles
joel.fleury@cslt.qc.ca
Nicole Lavoie, Directrice, Services éducatifs du primaire et du secondaire
nicole.lavoie@cslt.qc.ca

First Nations

Mistissini: **Commission scolaire Crie**
Cree School Board
203, rue Principale, Mistissini, QC G0W 1C0
Tel: 418-923-2764; *Toll-Free:* 1-866-999-2764
info@cscree.qc.ca
eeyoueducation.ca
www.facebook.com/CreeSchoolBd
twitter.com/CreeSchoolBoard
www.linkedin.com/company/creeschoolboard
Number of Schools: 11 *Enrollment:* 5000
Caroline Mark, Director General, 418-923-2764, ext. 201
cmark@cscree.qc.ca
Doreen Blackned, Secretary General Director, 418-923-2764, ext. 218
doreen.blackned@cscree.qc.ca
Guylaine Houle, Director, Material Resources, 418-923-2764, ext. 1206
ghoule@cscree.qc.ca
Darren MacLeod, Director, Finance & Administrative Services, 418-923-2764, ext. 1262
darren.macleod@cscree.qc.ca
Natalie Petawabano, Director, Human Resources, 418-923-2764, ext. 1211
npetawabano@cscree.qc.ca

Montréal: **Kativik School Board**
Commission scolaire Kativik
Also known as: Kativik Ilisarniliriniq
#400, 9800, boul Cavendish, Montréal, QC H4M 2V9
Tel: 514-482-8220; *Fax:* 514-482-8278
www.kativik.qc.ca
www.facebook.com/ilisarniq
twitter.com/ilisarniq
Number of Schools: 17 primary & secondary; 6 adult education centres *Grades:* Prim - Sec
Sarah Aloupa, President
Harriet Keleutak, Director General

Schools: Cégep

Cégep

Alma: **Collège d'Alma**
675, boul Auger ouest, Alma, QC G8B 2B7
Tél: 418-668-2387; *Téléc:* 418-668-7336
college@calma.qc.ca
www.collegealma.ca
www.facebook.com/CollegedAlma
www.instagram.com/collegealma
Grades: Préuniv., Techniques, Form. cont.
Josée Ouellet, Directrice générale

Baie-Comeau: **Cégep de Baie-Comeau**
537, boul Blanche, Baie-Comeau, QC G5C 2B2
Tél: 418-589-5707; *Ligne sans frais:* 800-463-2030
communications@cegepbc.ca
cegepbc.ca
www.facebook.com/cegepbc
www.instagram.com/cegepbc
Grades: Préuniv., Techniques, Form. cont.
Manon Couturier, Directrice générale

Chicoutimi: **Cégep de Chicoutimi**
534, rue Jacques-Cartier est, Chicoutimi, QC G7H 1Z6
Tél: 418-549-9520; *Téléc:* 418-549-1315
info@cchic.ca
cchic.ca
www.facebook.com/CegepChicoutimi
twitter.com/CegepChicoutimi
www.linkedin.com/school/cegepdechicoutimi
www.instagram.com/cegepchicoutimi
Grades: Préuniv., Techniques, Form. cont. *Enrollment:* 3000
André Gobeil, Direction générale
direction.generale@cchic.ca

Drummondville: **Cégep de Drummondville**
960, rue St-Georges, Drummondville, QC J2C 6A2
Tél: 819-478-4671; *Téléc:* 819-474-6859
communications@cegepdrummond.ca
cegepdrummond.ca
www.facebook.com/cegepdrummond
www.linkedin.com/school/cegepdrummond
www.youtube.com/c/cegepdrummond
Grades: Préuniv., Techniques *Enrollment:* 2000
Pierre Leblanc, Directeur général

Gaspé: **Cégep de la Gaspésie et des Îles**
96, rue Jacques-Cartier, Gaspé, QC G4X 2S8
Tél: 418-368-2201; *Téléc:* 418-368-7003
Ligne sans frais: 1-888-368-2201
information@cegepgim.ca
www.cegepgim.ca
www.facebook.com/cegep.gaspesie.iles
twitter.com/cegepgim
www.youtube.com/user/cegepgim
Grades: Préuniv., Techniques, Form. cont. *Enrollment:* 1140
Yves Galipeau, Directeur général

Campuses
Campus de Carleton-sur-Mer
776, boul Perron, Carleton-sur-Mer, QC G0C 1J0
Tél: 418-364-3341; *Ligne sans frais:* 866-424-3341
www.cegepgim.ca

Campus des Iles-de-la-Madeleine
15, ch de la Piscine, L'Étang-du-Nord, QC G4T 3X4
Tél: 418-986-5187
www.cegepgim.ca

École des pêches et de l'aquaculture du Québec
167, Grande-Allée est, Grande-Rivière, QC G0C 1V0
Tél: 418-385-2241
epaqgr@gmail.com
www.epaq.qc.ca
www.facebook.com/epaqgr

Gatineau: **Cégep de l'Outaouais**
Campus Gabrielle-Roy
333, boul de la Cité-des-Jeunes, Gatineau, QC J8Y 6M4
Tél: 819-770-4012; *Téléc:* 819-770-8167
Ligne sans frais: 866-770-4012
communications@cegepoutaouais.qc.ca
cegepoutaouais.qc.ca
www.facebook.com/cegep.outaouais
twitter.com/CegepOutaouais
www.youtube.com/CegepOutaouais
Enrollment: 5000 *Number of Employees:* 600
Diana Dumitru, Directrice générale, 819-600-7665
diana.dumitru@videotron.ca

Campuses
Campus Félix-Leclerc
820, boul de la Gappe, Gatineau, QC J8T 7T7
Tél: 819-770-4012

Campus Louis-Reboul
125, boul Sacré-Coeur, Gatineau, QC J8X 1C5
Tél: 819-770-4012

Gatineau: **Cégep Heritage College**
325, boul de la Cité des Jeunes, Gatineau, QC J8Y 6T3
Tél: 819-778-2270
informationoffice@cegep-heritage.qc.ca
www.cegep-heritage.qc.ca
www.facebook.com/cegepheritagecollege
www.youtube.com/user/heritagecollegevideo
Enrollment: 1200 *Number of Employees:* 246 *Note:* Career Programs (Nursing; Early Childhood Ed.; New Media & Publication Design; Electronics; Computer Science); Pre-University Programs: Liberal Arts, Sciences, Commerce, Social Sciences, Visual Arts; Continuing Ed.: French as a Second Language; Distance Education; Corporate Training.
Gordon McIvor, Director General
dg@cegep-heritage.qc.ca

Campuses
Campus Pontiac
1259, Hwy. 148, Campbell's Bay, QC J0X 1K0
Tel: 819-648-2567
conted@cegep-heritage.qc.ca
www.cegep-heritage.qc.ca

Granby: **Cégep de Granby Haute-Yamaska**
P.O. Box 7000
235, rue St-Jacques, Granby, QC J2G 9H7
Tél: 450-372-6614; *Téléc:* 450-372-6565
info@cegepgranby.qc.ca
cegepgranby.qc.ca
www.facebook.com/CegepGranby
twitter.com/CegepGranby
www.linkedin.com/school/cegepdegranby
www.youtube.com/user/CegepdeGranby
Yvan O'Connor, Directeur général
yoconnor@cegepgranby.qc.ca

Jonquière: **Cégep de Jonquière**
2505, rue St-Hubert, Jonquière, QC G7X 7W2
Tél: 418-547-2191
cegep@cjonquiere.qc.ca
www.cegepjonquiere.ca
www.facebook.com/cegepjonq
twitter.com/CegepJonquiere
www.youtube.com/user/cegepdejonquiere
Enrollment: 3200
Raynald Thibeault, Directeur général
raynaldthibeault@cegepjonquiere.ca
Mario Julien, Directeur, Études
mariojulien@cegepjonquiere.ca

La Pocatière: **Cégep de La Pocatière**
140, 4e av, La Pocatière, QC G0R 1Z0
Tél: 418-856-1525; *Téléc:* 418-856-4589
information@cegeplapocatiere.qc.ca
www.cegeplapocatiere.qc.ca
www.facebook.com/cegeplapocatiere
www.youtube.com/user/cegeplapocatiere
Enrollment: 900
Marie-Claude Deschênes, Directrice générale

Lasalle: **Cégep André-Laurendeau**
1111, rue Lapierre, Lasalle, QC H8N 2J4
Tél: 514-364-3320; *Téléc:* 514-364-7130
www.claurendeau.qc.ca
www.facebook.com/CegepAndreLaurendeau
Grades: Préuniv., Tech., Form. continue *Enrollment:* 5000
Claude Roy, Directeur général

Laval: **Collège Montmorency**
475, boul de l'Avenir, Laval, QC H7N 5H9
Tél: 450-975-6100
communication@cmontmorency.qc.ca
www.cmontmorency.qc.ca
www.facebook.com/cmontmo
www.linkedin.com/company/c-gep-montmorency
Olivier Simard, Directeur général, 450-975-6100, ext. 6110
dg@cmontmorency.qc.ca

Lévis: **Cégep de Lévis-Lauzon**
205, rte Mgr-Bourget, Lévis, QC G6V 6Z9
Tél: 418-833-5110; *Téléc:* 418-833-8502
Ligne sans frais: 888-833-5110
communications@cegeplevis.ca
www.cegeplevis.ca
www.facebook.com/cegeplevis
www.youtube.com/user/larouchm
Enrollment: 2885
Martine Nollet, Directrice générale
martine.nollet@cegeplevis.ca

Longueuil: **Collège Édouard-Montpetit**
945, ch de Chambly, Longueuil, QC J4H 3M6
Tél: 450-679-2631; *Téléc:* 450-679-5570
communications@cegepmontpetit.ca
www.cegepmontpetit.ca
www.facebook.com/cegepmontpetit
www.linkedin.com/school/coll-ge-douard-montpetit
www.youtube.com/user/collegeemontpetit
Enrollment: 8000 *Number of Employees:* 1 000
Sylvain Lambert, Directeur général
dir.generale@cegepmontpetit.ca

Matane: **Cégep de Matane**
616, av St-Rédempteur, Matane, QC G4W 1L1
Tél: 418-562-1240; *Téléc:* 418-566-2115
Ligne sans frais: 800-463-4299
information@cegep-matane.qc.ca
www.cegep-matane.qc.ca
www.facebook.com/cegepdematane
twitter.com/cegepmatane
www.linkedin.com/school/cégep-de-matane
www.youtube.com/user/cegepdematane
Enrollment: 2500
Pierre Bédard, Directeur général
bedard.pierre@cegep-matane.qc.ca

Saint-Jérôme: **Cégep de Saint-Jérôme**
455, rue Fournier, Saint-Jérôme, QC J7Z 4V2
Tél: 450-436-1580; *Téléc:* 450-436-1756
Ligne sans frais: 877-450-2785
info@cstj.qc.ca
cstj.qc.ca
www.linkedin.com/school/cegep-saint-jerome
Enrollment: 7000 *Number of Employees:* 700
Nadine Le Gal, Directrice générale

Mont-Tremblant: **Centre Collégial de Mont-Tremblant**
619, boul du Dr Gervais, Mont-Tremblant, QC J8E 2T3
Tél: 819-429-6155; *Téléc:* 819-429-5939
Ligne sans frais: 877-450-2785
ccmt.cstj.qc.ca

Mont-Laurier: **Centre Collégial de Mont-Laurier**
700, rue Parent, Mont-Laurier, QC J9L 2K1
Tél: 819-623-1525; *Téléc:* 819-923-4749
Ligne sans frais: 877-450-2785
ccml.cstj.qc.ca

Montréal: **Cégep de Saint-Laurent**
625, av Ste-Croix, Montréal, QC H4L 3X7
Tél: 514-747-6521; *Téléc:* 514-748-1249
info@cegepsl.qu.ca
www.cegepsl.qu.ca
www.facebook.com/cegepsl
twitter.com/cegepsl
www.linkedin.com/school/c-gep-de-saint-laurent
Enrollment: 2500
Mathieu Cormier, Directeur général

Montréal: **Cégep du Vieux Montréal**
255, rue Ontario est, Montréal, QC H2X 1X6
Tél: 514-982-3437
infoprogrammes@cvm.qc.ca
www.cvm.qc.ca
www.facebook.com/cegepduvieuxmontreal
twitter.com/cegepduvieuxmtl
www.linkedin.com/school/cegep-du-vieux-montreal
Enrollment: 6100
Mylène Boisclair, Directrice générale
mboisclair@cvm.qc.ca

Montréal: **Cégep Gérald-Godin**
15615, boul Gouin ouest, Montréal, QC H9H 5K8
Tél: 514-626-2666; *Téléc:* 514-626-6866
information@cgodin.qc.ca
www.cgodin.qc.ca
www.facebook.com/cegepgeraldgodin
twitter.com/geraldgodin
www.linkedin.com/company/cegep-gerald-godin
www.youtube.com/user/CollegeGeraldGodin
Enrollment: 1200
Philippe Gribeauval, Directeur général, 514-626-2666, ext. 5250
p.gribeauval@cgodin.qc.ca

Montréal: **Cégep John Abbott College**
#21, 257, rue Lakeshore, Montréal, QC H9X 3L9
Tel: 514-457-6610
communications@johnabbott.qc.ca
www.johnabbott.qc.ca
www.facebook.com/johnabbottcollege
twitter.com/JAC_Montreal
www.linkedin.com/school/cegep-john-abbott-college
www.youtube.com/user/JACmontreal
Enrollment: 8700
John Halpin, Director General
john.halpin@johnabbott.qc.ca

Montréal: **Cégep Marie-Victorin**
7000, rue Marie-Victorin, Montréal, QC H1G 2J6
Tél: 514-325-0150; *Téléc:* 514-328-3830
promotion@collegemv.qc.ca
www.collegemv.qc.ca
www.facebook.com/cegepmarievictorin
twitter.com/cegepmarievic
www.linkedin.com/company/c-gep-marie-victorin
www.youtube.com/user/cegepmarievictorin
Enrollment: 4100
Sylvain Mandeville, Directeur général

Montréal: **Collège Ahuntsic**
9155, rue St-Hubert, Montréal, QC H2M 1Y8
Tél: 514-389-5921; *Ligne sans frais:* 866-389-5921
communications@collegeahuntsic.qc.ca
www.collegeahuntsic.qc.ca
www.facebook.com/collegeahuntsic
twitter.com/CollegeAhuntsic
www.youtube.com/user/CollegeAhuntsic
Enrollment: 10000
Nathalie Valleé, Directrice générale, 514-389-5921, ext. 2110
nathalie.vallee@collegeahuntsic.qc.ca

Montréal: **Collège de Bois-de-Boulogne**
10555, av de Bois-de-Boulogne, Montréal, QC H4N 1L4
Tél: 514-332-3000
info@bdeb.qc.ca
www.bdeb.qc.ca
www.facebook.com/college.de.bois.de.boulogne
www.linkedin.com/company/coll-ge-de-bois-de-boulogne
www.instagram.com/collegebdeb
Grades: Préuniv., Techniques, Form. cont. *Enrollment:* 2700
Guy Dumais, Directeur général

Montréal: **Collège de Maisonneuve**
Également connu sous le nom de: Cégep de
Maisonneuve
3800, rue Sherbrooke est, Montréal, QC H1X 2A2
Tél: 514-254-7131
communic@cmaisonneuve.qc.ca
www.cmaisonneuve.qc.ca
www.facebook.com/CollegeMaisonneuve
twitter.com/CdeMaisonneuve
www.linkedin.com/school/collegedemaisonneuve
www.youtube.com/user/communicmaisonneuve
Grades: Préuniv., Techniques *Enrollment:* 7000
Malika Habel, Directrice générale

Campuses
Campus 2030
#430, 2030, boul Pie-IX, Montréal, QC H1V 2C8
Tél: 514-254-7131
sfc@cmaisonneuve.qc.ca

Campus 6220
6220, rue Sherbrooke est, Montréal, QC H1N 1C1
Tél: 514-254-7131
fc6220@cmaisonneuve.qc.ca

Montréal: **Collège de Rosemont**
6400, 16e av, Montréal, QC H1X 2S9
Tél: 514-376-1620; *Téléc:* 514-376-1440
www.crosemont.qc.ca
www.facebook.com/collegederosemont
twitter.com/CollegeRosemont
www.linkedin.com/school/collegederosemont
www.youtube.com/c/collegerosemont
Caroline Roy, Directrice générale

Montréal: **Dawson College**
Collège Dawson
3040, rue Sherbrooke ouest, Montréal, QC H3Z 1A4
Tel: 514-931-8731; *Fax:* 514-931-5181
info@dawsoncollege.qc.ca
www.dawsoncollege.qc.ca
www.facebook.com/dawsoncollege
twitter.com/college_dawson
www.linkedin.com/school/dawson-college
www.instagram.com/dawsoncollege
Enrollment: 10000 *Number of Employees:* 1,000
Diane Gauvin, Director General
dgauvin@dawsoncollege.qc.ca
Carmela Gumelli, Interim Academic Dean
cgumelli@dawsoncollege.qc.ca

Québec: **Cégep de Sainte-Foy**
2410, ch Sainte-Foy, Québec, QC G1V 1T3
Tél: 418-659-6600; *Téléc:* 418-659-4563
info@csfoy.ca
www.csfoy.ca
www.facebook.com/cegepsaintefoy
twitter.com/cegepsaintefoy
www.youtube.com/user/cegepstefoy

Grades: Préuniv., Techniques, Form. cont. Enrollment: 9800
Number of Employees: 1 500
Monique Provencher. Directrice générale par interim,
418-659-6600, ext. 3604

Québec: Cégep François-Xavier-Garneau
1660, boul de l'Entente, Québec, QC G1S 4S3
Tél: 418-688-8310; Téléc: 418-688-1539
communications@cegepgarneau.ca
www.cegepgarneau.ca
www.facebook.com/CegepGarneau
twitter.com/cegepgarneau
www.linkedin.com/school/cégep-garneau
www.youtube.com/user/garneaucegep
Grades: Préuniv., Bacc. int'l, Tech. Enrollment: 8000 Number of
Employees: 600 professeurs; 200 personnel non enseignant
Patricia Poirier, Directrice générale
ppoirier@cegepgarneau.ca

Québec: Cégep Limoilou
1300, 8e av, Québec, QC G1J 5L5
Tél: 418-647-6600; Téléc: 418-647-6798
www.cegeplimoilou.ca
www.facebook.com/CegepLimoilou
twitter.com/cegeplimoilou
www.linkedin.com/company/cegeplimoilou
www.youtube.com/c/cegeplimoilou
Enrollment: 4000 Number of Employees: 750
Chantal Arbour, Directrice générale

Campuses
Campus de Charlesbourg
7600, av 3e est, Québec, QC G1H 7L4
Tél: 418-647-6600; Téléc: 418-647-5798

Repentigny: Cégep régional de Lanaudière
781, rue Notre-Dame, Repentigny, QC J5Y 1B4
Tél: 450-470-0911; Téléc: 450-581-1567
infocom@collanaud.qc.ca
www.collanaud.qc.ca
twitter.com/cegeplanaudiere
www.linkedin.com/groups/2996990
www.youtube.com/user/Collanaud
Enrollment: 6200 Number of Employees: 950
Hélène Bailleu, Directrice générale

Campuses
Collège constituant de L'Assomption
180, rue Dorval, L'Assomption, QC J5W 6C1
Tél: 450-470-0922; Téléc: 450-589-8926
direction-crla@cegep-lanaudiere.qc.ca
www.cegep-lanaudiere.qc.ca/lassomption
www.facebook.com/cegeplassomption

Collège constituant de Joliette
20, rue St-Charles sud, Joliette, QC J6E 4T1
Tél: 450-759-1661; Téléc: 450-759-7120
www.cegep-lanaudiere.qc.ca/joliette
www.facebook.com/cegepjoliette

Collège constituant de Terrebonne
2505, boul des Entreprises, Terrebonne, QC J6X 5S5
Tél: 450-470-0977; Téléc: 450-477-6933
terrebonne.registraire@cegep-lanaudiere.qc.ca
www.cegep-lanaudiere.qc.ca/terrebonne
www.facebook.com/cegepterrebonne

Rimouski: Cégep de Rimouski
60, rue de l'Évêché ouest, Rimouski, QC G5L 4H6
Tél: 418-723-1880; Téléc: 418-724-4961
Ligne sans frais: 800-463-0617
information.scolaire@cegep-rimouski.qc.ca
www.cegep-rimouski.qc.ca
www.facebook.com/CegepdeRimouski
twitter.com/cegeprimouski
www.linkedin.com/school/cegepderimouski
www.youtube.com/user/cegeprimouski
Enrollment: 2600
François Dornier, Directeur général
francois.dornier@cegep-rimouski.qc.ca

Rivière-du-Loup: Cégep de Rivière-du-Loup
80, rue Frontenac, Rivière-du-Loup, QC G5R 1R1
Tél: 418-862-6903; Téléc: 418-862-4959
communications@cegeprdl.ca
www.cegeprdl.ca
www.facebook.com/cegeprdl
twitter.com/cegeprdl
www.linkedin.com/school/c-gep-de-rivi-re-du-loup
www.youtube.com/user/cegeprdl
Grades: Préuniv., Techniques, Form. cont. Enrollment: 2200
René Gingras, Directeur général
rene.gingras@cegeprdl.ca

Rouyn-Noranda: Cégep de l'Abitibi-Témiscamingue
425, boul du Collège, Rouyn-Noranda, QC J9X 5E5
Tél: 819-762-0931; Téléc: 819-762-2071
Ligne sans frais: 866-234-3728
info.rn@cegepat.qc.ca
www.cegepat.qc.ca
www.facebook.com/CegepAbitibiTemiscamingue
Grades: Préuniv., Techniques, Form. cont. Enrollment: 2400
Sylvain Blais, Directeur général
sylvain.blais@cegepat.qc.ca

Saint-Hyacinthe: Cégep de Saint-Hyacinthe
3000, av Boullé, Saint-Hyacinthe, QC J2S 1H9
Tél: 450-773-6800; Téléc: 450-773-9971
info@cegepsth.qc.ca
www.cegepsth.qc.ca
www.facebook.com/cegepsaintefoy
twitter.com/cegepsaintefoy
www.youtube.com/user/cegepdesaintefoy
Grades: Préuniv., Techniques, Form. cont. Enrollment: 4500
Number of Employees: 1 000
Emmanuel Montini, Directeur général, 450-773-6800, ext. 2259
dirgenerale@cegepsth.qc.ca

Saint-Jean-sur-Richelieu: Cégep
Saint-Jean-sur-Richelieu
P.O. Box 1018
30, boul du Séminaire, Saint-Jean-sur-Richelieu, QC J3B
7B1
Tél: 450-347-5301
communications@cstjean.qu.ca
www.cstjean.qc.ca
www.facebook.com/278415881842
www.youtube.com/user/cegepstjean
Grades: Préuniv., Techniques, Form. cont. Enrollment: 5900
Number of Employees: 400
Nathalie Beaudoin, Directrice générale, 450-347-5301, ext. 2277
nathalie.beaudoin@cstjean.qc.ca

Campuses
Campus Brossard
#175, 7055, boul Taschereau, Brossard, QC J4Z 1A7
Tél: 450-676-1745
fcbrossard@cstjean.qc.ca
www.cstjean.qc.ca

Sainte-Thérèse: Collège Lionel-Groulx
100, rue Duquet, Sainte-Thérèse, QC J7E 3G6
Tél: 450-430-3120; Téléc: 450-971-7883
info@clg.qc.ca
www.clg.qc.ca
www.facebook.com/clionelgroulx
twitter.com/clionelgroulx
www.linkedin.com/school/collegelionelgroulx
www.youtube.com/c/CollègeLionelGroulx
Grades: Préuniv., Techniques, Form. cont. Enrollment: 4000
Number of Employees: 800
Michel Louis Beauchamp, Directeur général
direction_generale@clg.qc.ca

Salaberry-de-Valleyfield: Collège de Valleyfield
169, rue Champlain, Salaberry-de-Valleyfield, QC J6T 1X6
Tél: 450-373-9441; Téléc: 450-373-7719
communication@colval.qc.ca
www.colval.qc.ca
www.facebook.com/colval
www.linkedin.com/school/collège-de-valleyfield
Enrollment: 2000
Marc Rémillard, Directeur général
dgvalleyfield@colval.qc.ca

Sept-Îles: Cégep de Sept-Îles
175, rue De La Vérendrye, Sept-Îles, QC G4R 5B7
Tél: 418-962-9848; Téléc: 418-962-2458
communications@cegepsi.ca
cegepsi.ca
www.facebook.com/cegepdeseptiles
www.linkedin.com/school/c-gep-de-sept—les
www.youtube.com/user/7ilescegep
Donald Bherer, Directeur général
donald.bherer@cegepsi.ca

Shawinigan: Collège Shawinigan
P.O. Box 610
2263, av du Collège, Shawinigan, QC G9N 6V8
Tél: 819-539-6401; Téléc: 819-539-8819
information@cshawi.ca
www.cegepshawinigan.ca
www.facebook.com/cegepshawinigan
Enrollment: 1200
Éric Milette, Directeur général

Sherbrooke: Cégep de Sherbrooke
475, rue du Cégep, Sherbrooke, QC J1E 4K1
Tél: 819-564-6350
communications@cegepsherbrooke.qc.ca
www.cegepsherbrooke.qc.ca
www.facebook.com/cegepsherbrooke
www.linkedin.com/school/c-gep-de-sherbrooke
www.youtube.com/user/cegepsherbrooke
Grades: Préuniv., Techniques, Form. cont. Enrollment: 6000
Number of Employees: 750
Marie-France Bélanger, Directrice général, 819-564-6350, ext.
5114

Sherbrooke: Champlain Regional College
1301, boul de Portland, Sherbrooke, QC J1J 1S2
Tel: 819-564-3600
www.crc-sher.qc.ca
www.linkedin.com/school/champlain-college_2
Enrollment: 2700
Odette Côté, Director General, 819-564-3600, ext. 638
ocote@crcmail.net

Campuses
Champlain Lennoxville
2580 College St., Lennoxville, QC J1M 0C8
Tel: 819-564-3666; Fax: 819-564-5171
info@crc-lennox.qc.ca
www.crc-lennox.qc.ca
www.facebook.com/champlaincollegelennoxville

Champlain St. Lambert
900, rue Riverside, Saint-Lambert, QC J4P 3P2
Tel: 450-672-7360; Fax: 450-672-9299
admissions@crcmail.net
www.champlainonline.com
www.facebook.com/ChamplainCollegeSaintLambert

Champlain St. Lawrence
790, av Nérée-Tremblay, Québec, QC G1V 4K2
Tel: 418-656-6921; Fax: 418-656-6925
welcometoslc@slc.qc.ca
slc.qc.ca

Sorel-Tracy: Cégep de Sorel-Tracy
3000, boul Tracy, Sorel-Tracy, QC J3R 5B9
Tél: 450-742-6651; Téléc: 450-742-1878
info@cegepst.qc.ca
www.cegepst.qc.ca
www.facebook.com/cegepst
twitter.com/cegepsoreltracy
www.youtube.com/user/cegepsoreltracy
Grades: Préuniv., Techniques, Form. cont.
Stéphanie Desmarais, Directrice générale, 450-742-6651, ext.
2102
stephanie.desmarais@cegepst.qc.ca

Campuses
Campus de Varennes
1555, boul Lionel-Boulet, Varennes, QC J3X 1P7
Tél: 450-929-0852; Téléc: 450-929-0810
fcontinue@cegepst.qc.ca
www.cegepst.qc.ca

St-Félicien: Cégep de St-Félicien
P.O. Box 7300
1105, boul Hamel, St-Félicien, QC G8K 2R8
Tél: 418-679-5412; Téléc: 418-679-0238
info@cegepstfe.qc.ca
www.cstfelicien.qc.ca
www.facebook.com/cegepstfe
www.linkedin.com/school/cégep-de-saint-félicien
www.youtube.com/user/cegepstfe
Grades: Préuniv., Techniques Enrollment: 1000
Sylvie Prescott, Directrice générale

St-Georges: Cégep Beauce-Appalaches
1055, 116e rue, St-Georges, QC G5Y 3G1
Tél: 418-228-8896; Téléc: 418-228-0562
Ligne sans frais: 800-893-5111
info@cegepba.qc.ca
cegepba.qc.ca
www.facebook.com/cegepba
www.instagram.com/cegepba
Enrollment: 1878
Pierre Leblanc, Directeur général

Thetford Mines: Cégep de Thetford
671, boul Frontenac ouest, Thetford Mines, QC G6G 1N1
Tél: 418-338-8591; Téléc: 418-338-3498
communication@cegepthetford.ca
www.cegepthetford.ca
www.facebook.com/cegepthetford
www.linkedin.com/school/cegep-de-thetford
www.youtube.com/c/CégepdeThetford_T
Enrollment: 1000 Number of Employees: 200

Robert Rousseau, Directeur général
rrousseau@cegepthetford.ca

<u>Campuses</u>
Campus Collégial de Lotbinière
1080, av Bergeron, St-Agapit, QC G0S 1Z0
Tél: 418-338-8591; *Téléc:* 418-338-3498
info@ceclotbiniere.ca
www.ceclotbiniere.ca

Trois-Rivières: **Cégep de Trois-Rivières**
P.O. Box 97
3500, rue De Courval, Trois-Rivières, QC G9A 5E6
Tél: 819-376-1721; *Téléc:* 819-693-8023
infoprog@cegeptr.qc.ca
www.cegeptr.qc.ca
www.facebook.com/cegeptr
twitter.com/cegeptr
www.linkedin.com/school/cegeptr
www.youtube.com/user/cegeptroisrivieres
Grades: Préuniv., Techniques, Form. cont. *Enrollment:* 8700
Number of Employees: 700
Louis Gendron, Directeur général, 819-376-1721, ext. 2010
louis.gendron@cegeptr.qu.ca

Victoriaville: **Cégep de Victoriaville**
475, rue Notre-Dame est, Victoriaville, QC G6P 4B3
Tél: 819-758-6401
information@cgpvicto.qc.ca
www.cegepvicto.ca
www.facebook.com/cegepvicto
www.linkedin.com/school/cegep-de-victoriaville
www.youtube.com/c/CégepdeVictoriavilleCOMM
Number of Schools: 3
Denis Deschamps, Directeur général, 819-758-6401, ext. 2400
dg@cegepvictor.ca

Schools: Specialized

First Nations

Betsiamites: **École Nussim du conseil de bande de Betsiamites**
P.O. Box 70
4, rue Pulis, Betsiamites, QC G0H 1B0, Canada
Tél: 418-567-2215; *Téléc:* 418-567-8010
Grades: K-8

Côte-Nord-du-Golfe-du-Saint-Lau: **École Olamen du Conseil des Montagnais (La Romaine)**
P.O. Box 222
Côte-Nord-du-Golfe-du-Saint-Lau, QC G0G 1M0, Canada
Tél: 418-229-2450
webmestre@olamen.qc.ca
Grades: K-12

Kawawachikamach: **École Jimmy Sandy Memorial**
P.O. Box 5152
Kawawachikamach, QC G0G 2Z0, Canada
Tél: 418-585-3811; *Téléc:* 418-585-3347
Grades: K-4

Malioténam: **École Tshishteshinu du conseil des Montagnais de Sept-Iles et Maliotenam**
P.O. Box 430 Moise
Malioténam, QC G0G 2B0, Canada
Tél: 418-927-2956; *Téléc:* 418-927-3127
Grades: K-8

Manawan: **École Otapi**
470, rue Otapi, Manawan, QC J0K 1M0, Canada
Tél: 819-971-1379
www.otapi.ca
Grades: 9-12

Manawan: **École Simon P. Ottawa**
150, rue Wapoc, Manawan, QC J0K 1M0, Canada
Tél: 819-971-8817; *Téléc:* 819-871-8872
Grades: K-12

Mashteuiatsh: **École Amishk**
225, rue Uapileu, Mashteuiatsh, QC G0W 2H0, Canada
Tél: 418-275-2473; *Téléc:* 418-275-0002
ecole.amishk@mashteuiatsh.ca
Grades: K-8 *Enrollment:* 300

Mashteuiatsh: **École secondaire Kassinu Mamu**
507, rue Uapileu, Mashteuiatsh, QC G0W 2H0, Canada
Tél: 418-275-2473
kassinu.mamu@mashteuiatsh.ca
www.monecole-myschool.com/kassinumamu/
Grades: Sec.

Natashquan: **École Uauitshitun Natashquan**
132, rue Tettaut RR1, Natashquan, QC G0G 2E0, Canada
Tél: 418-726-3368
uauitshitun@monecole-myschool.com
www.monecole-myschool.com/uauitshitun
Grades: K-12

Obedjiwan: **École Mikisiw**
92, rue Tcikatnaw, Obedjiwan, QC G0W 3B0, Canada
Tél: 819-974-1221
Grades: 9-12

Obedjiwan: **École Niska**
70, rue Niska Obedjiwan, Obedjiwan, QC G0W 3B0, Canada
Tél: 819-974-8842
Grades: K-8
Francine Gagnon Awashish, Directrice

Pessamit: **École secondaire Uashkaikan du conseil de bande de Betsiamites**
63, rue Messek, Pessamit, QC G0H 1B0, Canada
Tél: 418-567-2271
Grades: 9-12

Pikogan: **École Mikwan**
P.O. Box 36
RR#4, Pikogan, QC J9T 3A3, Canada
Tél: 819-732-5213
Grades: K-8

Sept-Iles: **École Johnny-Pilot du conseil des Montagnais de Sept-Iles et Maliotenam**
P.O. Box 8000
100, rue Pashin, Sept-Iles, QC G4R 5V2, Canada
Tél: 418-962-5777; *Téléc:* 418-961-2666
ecolejonnypilot@globetrotter.net
Grades: K-8

Sept-Iles: **École Manikanetish du conseil des Montagnais de Sept-Iles et Maliotenam**
P.O. Box 8000
1, rue Ukuias, Sept-Iles, QC G4R 2N5, Canada
Tél: 418-968-1550; *Téléc:* 418-962-6509
Grades: 9-12

St-Augustin: **École Pakuashipi**
P.O. Box 68
52, rue Pakua, St-Augustin, QC G0G 2R0, Canada
Tél: 418-947-2729; *Téléc:* 418-947-2209
pakuashipi@yahoo.ca
www.monecole-myschool.com/pakuashipi/home.html
Grades: K-12

Wemotaci: **École primaire Seskitin**
P.O. Box 214
41, rue Kenosi, Wemotaci, QC G0X 3R0, Canada
Tél: 819-666-2226
ericniquay@hotmail.com
www.monecole-myschool.com/seskitin
Grades: Elem.
Viviane Chilton, Directrice

Wemotaci: **École secondaire Nikanik**
P.O. Box 222 B
20, rue Waratinak, Wemotaci, QC G0X 3R0, Canada
Tél: 819-666-2232
waratinak@monecole-myschool.com
www.monecole-myschool.com/waratinak
Nicole Potvin, Directrice

Hearing Impaired

Montréal: **Mackay Centre School**
6333, rue de Terrebonne, Montréal, QC H4B 1A8
Tel: 514-483-0550; *Fax:* 514-487-3676
www.mackay.emsb.qc.ca
Grades: Pre.-6 *Enrollment:* 170 *Number of Employees:* 29
teachers (3 for the deaf, 26 for the physically disabled) *Note:*
School for the deaf / hearing impaired & children with disabilities.
Anna Sanalitro, Principal, 514-483-0550, ext. 2253
asanalitro@emsb.qc.ca
Greg Watson, Vice-Principal, 514-483-0550, ext. 3253
gwatson@emsb.qc.ca
Sharon Wood, Secretary, 514-483-0550, ext. 1253
swood@emsb.qc.ca

Special Education

Westmount: **École orale de Montréal pour le sourds**
Montreal Oral School for the Deaf
4670, Ste. Catherine St. ouest, Westmount, QC H3Z 1S5
Tel: 514-488-4946; *Fax:* 514-488-0802
info@montrealoralschool.com
www.montrealoralschool.com
TTY: 514-488-4946
Note: School for the deaf with programs in both French and English.

Schools: Independent & Private

Protestant

Dollard-des-Ormeaux: **Emmanuel Christian School**
École chrétienne Emmanuel
4698 St-Jean Blvd., Dollard-des-Ormeaux, QC H9H 4S5, Canada
Tel: 514-696-6430; *Fax:* 514-696-3687
info@emmanuelcs.ca
www.emmanuelcs.ca
www.facebook.com/emmanuelcs.ca
Grades: K-11; Eng./Fr. *Enrollment:* 300 *Note:* A Christian
education, with instruction in English & French.
Jean-Daniel Lussier, Principal
jdlussier@emmanuelcs.ca

Catholic

Ayer's Cliff: **Collège Servite**
470, rue Main, Ayer's Cliff, QC J0B 1C0, Canada
Tél: 819-838-4221; *Téléc:* 819-838-4222
courrier@collegeservite.ca
www.collegeservite.ca
Grades: Sec. *Note:* Confessionnelle catholique.
François Leblanc, Directeur général
fleblanc@collegeservite.ca
France Gagnon, Secrétaire pédagogique

Coaticook: **Collège Rivier**
343, rue St-Jacques nord, Coaticook, QC J1A 2R2, Canada
Tél: 819-849-4833; *Téléc:* 819-849-3621
crivier@crivier.qc.ca
www.crivier.qc.ca
www.facebook.com/collegerivier1870
Grades: Sec.; Pens. & Ext. *Note:* École catholique, privée et mixte.
Benoit Hélie, Directeur général
dgrivier@crivier.qc.ca

Dolbeau-Mistassini: **Juvénat Saint-Jean**
200, boul Wallberg, Dolbeau-Mistassini, QC G8L 6A5, Canada
Tél: 418-276-3340; *Téléc:* 418-276-1757
juvenatstjean@hotmail.com
www.juvenatstjean.ca
Grades: Sec.; Pens. & Ext.
Marc Tremblay, Directeur général

Grenville-sur-la-Rouge: **Séminaire du Sacré-Coeur**
2738, rte 148, Grenville-sur-la-Rouge, QC J0V 1B0, Canada
Tél: 819-242-0957; *Téléc:* 819-242-4089
administration@ssc.quebec
www.seminairedusacrecoeur.qc.ca
Grades: Sec.; Pens. & Ext.
Christian Lavergne, Directeur général

Lévis: **École Sainte-Famille (Fraternité St-Pie X) inc.**
10425, boul Guillaume-Couture, Lévis, QC G6V 9R6, Canada
Tél: 418-837-3028; *Téléc:* 418-837-7070
www.sspx.ca/ecolesf
Grades: Prim./Sec. *Enrollment:* 85
Olivier Berteaux, Directeur

Métabetchouan-Lac-à-la-Croix: **Séminaire Marie-Reine-du-Clergé**
1569, rte 169, Métabetchouan-Lac-à-la-Croix, QC G8G 1A8, Canada
Tél: 418-349-2816; *Téléc:* 418-349-8055
secretariat@smrc.qc.ca
www.smrc.qc.ca
www.facebook.com/seminairemariereineduclerge
Grades: Sec.; Pens. & Ext.
Patrick Desmeules, Directeur général
direction@smrc.qc.ca

Montréal: **Collège de Montréal**
1931, rue Sherbrooke ouest, Montréal, QC H3H 1E3, Canada
Tél: 514-933-7397; *Téléc:* 514-933-3225
cdm@college-montreal.qc.ca
www.college-montreal.qc.ca

Grades: Sec. *Note:* École catholique privée.
Patricia Steben, Directrice générale

Montréal: **École Augustin Roscelli inc.**
11960, boul de l'Acadie, Montréal, QC H3M 2T7, Canada
Tél: 514-334-0057; *Téléc:* 514-334-4060
www.ecoleaugustinroscelli.com
Grades: Mat./Prim. *Note:* École Catholique, privée, mixte.

Montréal: **École Marie-Clarac**
École Marie-Clarac secondaire
3541, boul Gouin est, Montréal, QC H1H 5L8, Canada
Tél: 514-322-1161; *Téléc:* 514-322-6664
info@marie-clarac.qc.ca
www.ecolemarie-clarac.qc.ca
Grades: Mat./Prim./Sec.; mixte; filles *Note:* Garderie et préscolaire/primaire (mixte); secondaire (filles); dirigée par les Soeurs de Charité de Sainte-Marie. École Marie-Clarac primaire: 11273, av de Mère-Anselme, Montréal H1H 4Z2, 514-322-1161 poste 130.
Sr. Jacinthe Caron, Directrice générale

Montréal: **École Saint-Joseph (1985) inc.**
4080, av De Lorimier, Montréal, QC H2K 3X7, Canada
Tél: 514-526-8288; *Téléc:* 514-526-5498
secretariat@stjoseph.qc.ca
www.stjoseph.qc.ca
www.facebook.com/Estj1985
twitter.com/estj1985
Grades: Mat./Prim.
Frédéric Brazeau, Directeur général
fbrazeau@stjoseph.qc.ca

Montréal: **Externat Mont-Jésus-Marie**
2755, ch de la Côte-Ste-Catherine, Montréal, QC H3T 1B5, Canada
Tél: 514-272-1035
www.montjesusmarie.com
Grades: Mat./Prim.
Sylvie Gagné, Directrice générale
Sylvie Judy Quinn, Directrice de la pédagogie

Montréal: **Loyola High School**
7272, rue Sherbrooke ouest, Montréal, QC H4B 1R2, Canada
Tel: 514-486-1101; *Fax:* 514-486-7266
admin@loyola.ca
www.loyola.ca
www.facebook.com/LoyolaMontreal
twitter.com/loyolamontreal
www.youtube.com/user/LoyolaHSMontreal
Grades: Sec.; Boys; Eng.
Richard Meagher, Principal
meagherr@loyola.ca

Montréal: **Pensionnat du Saint-Nom-de-Marie**
628, ch de la Côte Ste-Catherine, Montréal, QC H2V 2C5
Tél: 514-735-5261; *Téléc:* 514-735-5266
admission@psnm.qc.ca
www.psnm.qc.ca
www.facebook.com/PSNMOutremont
www.linkedin.com/company/pensionnat-du-saint-nom-de-marie
www.youtube.com/user/PSNMtv
Grades: Sec.; filles; Pens. & Ext. *Enrollment:* 1000 *Number of Employees:* 55 enseignants
Yves Petit, Directeur général

Montréal: **The Sacred Heart School of Montréal**
3635, av Atwater, Montréal, QC H3H 1Y4, Canada
Tel: 514-937-2845; *Fax:* 514-937-8214
info@sacredheart.qc.ca
www.sacredheart.qc.ca
www.facebook.com/SacredHeartMontreal
twitter.com/TheSHSM
www.instagram.com/SacredHeartMontreal
Grades: Sec.; Girls; Eng.; Res & Day *Note:* One of Canada's oldest independent Catholic schools for girls.
Shawn O'Donnell, Head of School
sodonnell@sacredheart.qc.ca

Québec: **Collège Jésus-Marie de Sillery (CJMDS)**
2047, ch St-Louis, Québec, QC G1T 1P3, Canada
Tél: 418-687-9250; *Téléc:* 418-687-9847
admission@cjmds.qc.ca
www.collegejesusmarie.com
www.facebook.com/cjmds
twitter.com/cjmds
Grades: Mat.-Sec.; Pens. & Ext. *Note:* Dirigé par la Congrégation des Religieuses de Jésus-Marie; programme enrichi au primaire, programme d'éducation internationale au secondaire.
Maude Dubé, Directrice générale

Québec: **Collège Saint-Charles-Garnier**
1150, boul René-Lévesque ouest, Québec, QC G1S 1V7, Canada
Tél: 418-681-0107; *Téléc:* 418-681-9631
cscg@collegegarnier.qc.ca
www.collegesaint-charles.com
www.facebook.com/collegesaintcharles
Grades: Sec. *Note:* Propriétaire du Collège des Jésuites.
Marc-André Séguin, Directeur général

Québec: **Externat Saint-Coeur de Marie**
30, av des Cascades, Québec, QC G1E 2J8, Canada
Tél: 418-663-0605; *Téléc:* 418-663-9484
info@externat-scm.ca
www.externat-scm.ca
Grades: Prim.; Pens. & Ext.
Richard Morin, Directeur général
richard.morin@externat-scm.ca

Rosemère: **Externat Sacré-Coeur**
535, rue Lefrançois, Rosemère, QC J7A 4R5, Canada
Tél: 450-621-6720; *Téléc:* 450-621-1525
courrier@externat.qc.ca
www.externat.qc.ca
Grades: Sec. *Enrollment:* 1000
Denyse Hébert, Directrice générale
dhebert@externat.qc.ca

Saint-Augustin-de-Desmaures: **Séminaire Saint-François**
4900, rue Saint-Félix, Saint-Augustin-de-Desmaures, QC G3A 0L4, Canada
Tél: 418-872-0611; *Téléc:* 418-872-5845
info@ss-f.com
www.ss-f.com
www.facebook.com/seminairesaintfrancois
twitter.com/SSF1952
www.youtube.com/user/seminairestfrancois
Grades: Sec.; Pens. & Ext.
Simon Robitaille, Directeur général
s.robitaille@ss-f.com

Saint-Hyacinthe: **École secondaire Saint-Joseph de Saint-Hyacinthe**
2875, av Bourdages nord, Saint-Hyacinthe, QC J2S 5S3, Canada
Tél: 450-774-3775; *Téléc:* 450-774-6340
www.essj.qc.ca
Grades: Sec.; Pens. & Ext.
Simone Leblanc, Directrice général

Saint-Laurent: **École bilingue Notre-Dame de Sion**
1775, boul Décarie, Saint-Laurent, QC H4L 3N5, Canada
Tél: 514-747-3895; *Téléc:* 514-747-5492
cnicolet@ebnds.ca
www.ebnds.ca
Grades: Mat./Prim.; Fr./Angl.
Gisèle Séguin, Acting Principal
gseguin@ebnds.ca

Saint-Michel-de-Bellechasse: **Collège Dina-Bélanger**
P.O. Box 897
1, rue St-Georges, Saint-Michel-de-Bellechasse, QC G0R 3S0, Canada
Tél: 418-884-2360; *Téléc:* 418-884-3274
secretariat@collegedina-belanger.qc.ca
collegedina-belanger.qc.ca
www.facebook.com/collegedinabelanger
Grades: Sec.; Pens. & Ext. *Enrollment:* 300 *Note:* Dirigé par les Relgieuses de Jésus-Marie.
Sr Yvette Rioux, Directrice générale

Sherbrooke: **Collège du Sacré-Coeur**
155, rue Belvédère nord, Sherbrooke, QC J1H 4A7, Canada
Tél: 819-569-9457; *Téléc:* 819-820-0636
info@cscoeur.ca
www.cscoeur.ca
www.facebook.com/CSCoeur
twitter.com/cscoeur
www.instagram.com/college_du_sacre_coeur
Grades: Sec.; filles
Sonia Daoust, Directrice générale
sdaoust@cscoeur.ca

St-Bruno-de-Montarville: **Collège Trinité**
1475, ch des Vingt, St-Bruno-de-Montarville, QC J3V 4P6, Canada
Tél: 450-653-2409; *Téléc:* 450-441-4786
secretariat@ctrinite.ca
www.collegetrinite.ca
www.facebook.com/Ctrinite
twitter.com/collegetrinite
www.instagram.com/college_trinite

Grades: Sec.
Josée Beaulieu, Directrice générale

Trois-Rivières: **Séminaire Saint-Joseph**
858, rue Laviolette, Trois-Rivières, QC G9A 5S3, Canada
Tél: 819-376-4459; *Téléc:* 819-378-0607
info@ssj.qc.ca
www.facebook.com/SeminaireSaintJoseph
www.youtube.com/SeminaireSaintJoseph
Grades: Sec.; Pens. & Ext.
Martine Roy, Directrice générale
martine.roy@ssj.qc.ca

Hearing Impaired

Montréal: **École orale de Montréal pour les sourds inc.**
Montreal Oral School for the Deaf Inc.
4670, rue Sainte-Catherine ouest, Montréal, QC H3Z 1S5, Canada
Tél: 514-488-4946; *Téléc:* 514-488-0802
info@montrealoralschool.com
www.montrealoralschool.com
Grades: Mat./Prim.; Éd. spéc. *Note:* Mission: enseigner aux enfants sourds à parler & à communiquer verbalement. Programmes d'études et programmes d'intégration; services cliniques; counseling.
Martha Pérusse, Directrice

Special Education

Montréal: **L'École à Pas de Géant (Montréal)**
Giant Steps School (Montréal)
5460, av Connaught, Montréal, QC H4V 1X7, Canada
Tél: 514-935-1911; *Téléc:* 514-935-9768
info@giantstepsmontreal.com
giantstepsmontreal.com
www.facebook.com/185516821567574
Grades: Mat./Prim./Sec; Éd. spéc. *Note:* Favoriser l'éducation et l'insertion scolaire et sociale des jeunes autistes.
Nick Katalifos, Président, Conseil d'administration

Montréal: **École Peter Hall inc.**
Peter Hall School
Campus Côte-Vertu & Centre administratif
840, boul de la Côte-Vertu, Montréal, QC H4L 1Y4, Canada
Tél: 514-747-4075; *Téléc:* 514-747-0164
cote-vertu@peterhall.qc.ca
www.peterhall.qc.ca
Grades: Mat./Prim./Sec.; Fr./Angl.; Éd.Spec *Note:* Services éducatifs pour des élèves de 4 à 21 ans présentant une déficience intellectuelle.
Jean Laliberté, Directeur général
Maryvonne Robert, Principal
mrobert@peterhall.qc.ca
Campuses
École Peter Hall Ouimet
1455, rue Rochon, Québec, QC H4L 1W1, Canada
Tél: 514-748-1050; *Téléc:* 514-748-7544
ouimet@peterhall.qc.ca
Grades: Mat./Prim./Sec.; Fr./Angl.; Éd.Spec

Montréal: **Summit School**
École le Sommet
1750, rue Deguire, Montréal, QC H4L 1M7
Tel: 514-744-2867; *Fax:* 514-744-6410
admin@summit-school.com
www.summit-school.com
Grades: Spec. Ed.; Eng. *Enrollment:* 620 *Number of Employees:* 250 *Note:* Educational services for special needs students, from ages 4 to 21, with developmental disabilities such as autism, behavioural disturbances & other associated problems. Offers different programs depending on age & level. Does not offer a high school leaving certificate.
Herman Erdogmus, Director General & Principal, 514-744-2867, ext. 225
herdogmus@summit-school.com
Bena Finkelberg, Vice-Principal, 514-744-2867, ext. 236
bfinkelberg@summit-school.com
Lucy Orsini, Registrar, 514-744-2867, ext. 266
lucy@summit-school.com
Alexandra Schor, Director, Finance, 514-744-2867, ext. 256
aschor@summit-school.com

Independent & Private Schools

Anjou: **Le Collège d'Anjou**
11 000, Renaude Lapointe, Anjou, QC H1J 2V7, Canada
Tél: 514-322-8111; *Téléc:* 514-322-8112
info@collegedanjou.com
www.collegedanjou.qc.ca

Grades: Sec.
Luc Plante, Directeur général
Frédéric Desjardins, Directeur des services pédagogiques
Stéphanie Lajoie, Directrice de la vie scolaire

Baie-d'Urfé: École internationale allemande Alexander von Humboldt inc. (AvH)
Alexander von Humboldt German International School Inc.
216, rue Victoria, Baie-d'Urfé, QC H9X 2H9, Canada
Tél: 514-457-2886; Téléc: 514-457-2885
avh@avh.montreal.qc.ca
www.avh.montreal.qc.ca
www.facebook.com/avh.school
Grades: Mat./Prim./Sec.; Deutsche/Fr./Eng. Note:
Environnement multilingue: allemand, anglais, français; sciences naturelles & sociales; arts; Dipl. d'études sec. du Québec & bacc. allemand international; Deutsches Sprachdiplom der Kultusministerkonferenz.
Thomas Linse, Principal, 514-457-2886
linse@avh.montreal.qc.ca
Gitta Roes, Business Manager, 514-457-2886, ext. 223
roes@avh.montreal.qc.ca

Beauceville: École Jésus-Marie de Beauceville
670, 9e av, Beauceville, QC G5X 3P6, Canada
Tél: 418-774-3709; Téléc: 418-774-5749
secretariat@ejm.qc.ca
www.ejm.qc.com
www.facebook.com/ecolejesusmarie
www.flickr.com/photos/ejm_photos_web
Grades: Sec.; Pens. & Ext.
Luc Provençal, Directeur général
dir-gen@ejm.qc.ca

Blainville: Montessori International School Blainville
325, ch du Bas de Sainte Thérèse, Blainville, QC J7A 0A3
Tél: 450-965-7878; Téléc: 450-965-7878
montessoriinternationalblainville.com
Grades: Pre./K./Elem.

Boucherville: École Les Trois Saisons
570, boul de Mortagne, Boucherville, QC J4B 5E4, Canada
Tél: 450-641-2000; Téléc: 450-641-0927
info@3saisons.ca
www.ecoletroissaisons.com
Grades: Prim.
Katia Surprenant, Directrice générale

Brossard: Académie Marie-Laurier
Marie-Laurier Academy
1555, av Stravinski, Brossard, QC J4X 2H5, Canada
Tél: 450-923-2787; Téléc: 450-923-2291
academie@marielaurier.com
www.marielaurier.com
Grades: Mat./Prim./Sec.; Fr./Angl. Note: Enseignement bilingue.

Chicoutimi: École Apostolique de Chicoutimi
913, rue Jacques-Cartier est, Chicoutimi, QC G7H 2A3, Canada
Tél: 418-549-3302; Téléc: 418-615-2030
info@lecoleapostolique.com
www.lecoleapostolique.com
Grades: Prim.
Marie-Claude Bradette, Directrice générale

Chicoutimi: Séminaire de Chicoutimi
Services éducatifs
679, rue Chabanel, Chicoutimi, QC G7H 1Z7, Canada
Tél: 418-549-0190; Téléc: 418-549-1524
info@sdec.education
seminairedechicoutimi.ca
www.facebook.com/sdec.education
Grades: Sec. Number of Employees: 40
Louis Prévost, Directeur général, 418-549-0190, ext. 301
louis.prevost@sdec.education
Cathia Grosjean, Secrétaire, 418-549-0190, ext. 305

Côte Saint-Luc: L'Académie Hébraïque Inc.
Hebrew Academy
5700, av Kellert, Côte Saint-Luc, QC H4W 1T4, Canada
Tél: 514-489-5321; Téléc: 514-489-8607
www.ha-mtl.org
www.facebook.com/517747401648939
twitter.com/MyHA_updates
www.youtube.com/user/HebrewAcademyVideos
Grades: Mat.-12é années; Angl./Fr.
Linda Lehrer, Directrice générale
director@ha-mtl.org

Dollard-des-Ormeaux: Collège de l'Ouest de l'Île
West Island College
851, rue Tecumseh, Dollard-des-Ormeaux, QC H9B 2L2, Canada
Tél: 514-683-4660; Téléc: 514-683-1702
info@wicmtl.ca
www.wicmtl.ca
www.facebook.com/WICMontreal
twitter.com/WICMtli
www.youtube.com/user/westislandcollege
Grades: Sec.; Fr./Angl.
Michel Lafrance, Directeur général
mlafrance@wicmtl.ca
Rob Reid, Directeur des études
rreid@wicmtl.ca
Lise Lafontaine, Directrice des finances et opérations
llafontainte@wicmtl.ca

Dollard-des-Ormeaux: Hebrew Foundation School
École de formation hébraïque
2, rue Hope, Dollard-des-Ormeaux, QC H9A 2V5, Canada
Tel: 514-684-6270; Fax: 514-684-1998
hebrewfoundation@hfs.qc.ca
hfs.qc.ca
Grades: Pre./Elem.; Eng./Fr. Note: Programmes include M.E.L.S. French Immersion, traditional Jewish subjects, as well as the standard curriculum, dance & visual arts; instruction in English, French & Hebrew.
Brian Seltmann, Principal
seltmannb@hfs.qc.ca

Dollard-des-Ormeaux: The Learning Tree
L'Arbre de Connaissance
16, rue Séville, Dollard-des-Ormeaux, QC H9B 2V5
Tel: 514-683-8426
info@thelearningtree.ca
www.thelearningtree.ca
Grades: Preschool & Pre-Kindergarten Enrollment: 160 Number of Employees: 25
Linda McPherson, Director

Drummondville: Collège Saint-Bernard
25, av des Frères, Drummondville, QC J2B 6A2, Canada
Tél: 819-478-3330; Téléc: 819-478-2582
csb@csb.qc.ca
www.csb.qc.ca
www.facebook.com/lecollege
www.linkedin.com/company/coll-ge-saint-bernard
Grades: Mat.-Sec.; Pens. & Ext.
Dominic Guévin, Directeur général

Gatineau: Collège Saint-Alexandre
2425, rue Saint-Louis, Gatineau, QC J8V 1E7, Canada
Tél: 819-561-3812; Téléc: 819-561-5205
www.college-stalexandre.qc.ca
www.facebook.com/amicalecsa
twitter.com/collstalexandre
Grades: Sec. Enrollment: 970 Number of Employees: 90
Mario Vachon, Directeur général
mario.vachon@i-alex.qc.ca

Gatineau: Collège Saint-Joseph de Hull
174, rue Notre-Dame-de-l'Île, Gatineau, QC J8X 3T4, Canada
Tél: 819-776-3123; Téléc: 819-776-0992
direction@collegestjoseph.ca
www.collegestjoseph.ca
Grades: Sec.; filles
Georges Najm, Directeur général

Gatineau: École Montessori de l'Outaouais inc.
161, rue Principale, Gatineau, QC J9H 3M9, Canada
Tél: 819-682-3299; Téléc: 819-682-7484
info.montessori@videotron.ca
www.montessori-outaouais.qc.ca
www.facebook.com/454754347958701
Grades: Mat./Prim.
Michèle Cusson, Directrice générale
directionmontessori@videotron.ca

Granby: Collège Mont-Sacré-Coeur
210, rue Denison est, Granby, QC J2H 2R6, Canada
Tél: 450-372-6882; Téléc: 450-372-9219
info@college-msc.qc.ca
www.college-msc.qc.ca
www.facebook.com/134318786713143
twitter.com/CollegeMSC
Grades: Sec. Note: Programme Exploration; Programme sports instensifs; Programme anglais intensif.
Claude Lacroix, Directeur général
c.lacroix@college-msc.qc.ca

Granby: École secondaire du Verbe Divin
P.O. Box 786
1021, rue Cowie, Granby, QC J2G 8W8, Canada
Tél: 450-378-1074; Téléc: 450-378-4566
info@verbedivin.com
www.verbedivin.com
www.facebook.com/verbedivin
twitter.com/ESVDgranby
Grades: Sec. Note: Programmes - Immersion anglaise; Sports-Élite; Arts-Élite; Voyages; Programme Découverte.
Jean Striganuk, Directeur général
dirgen@verbedivin.com

Joliette: Académie Antoine Manseau
P.O. Box 410
20, rue St-Charles-Borromée sud, Joliette, QC J6E 3Z9, Canada
Tél: 450-753-4271; Téléc: 450-753-3661
courrier@amanseau.qc.ca
www.amanseau.qc.ca
www.facebook.com/167439409986600
Grades: Sec.
Robert Cyr, Directeur général
robert.cyr@amanseau.qc.ca

Joliette: École les Mélèzes
393, rue de Lanaudière, Joliette, QC J6E 3L9, Canada
Tél: 450-752-4433; Téléc: 450-752-4337
www.ecolelesmelezes.ca
Grades: Mat./Prim.; Pens. & Ext.
Renée Champagne, Directrice générale
renee.champagne@lesmelezes.qc.ca

Kirkland: Académie Marie-Claire
18190, boul Elkas, Kirkland, QC H9J 3Y4, Canada
Tél: 514-697-9995; Téléc: 514-697-5575
www.amcca.ca
Grades: Mat./Prim. Note: 1ère année à 6ème année.
Enseignement bilingue.
Marie-Claire Martin, Directrice
mmartin@amcca.ca

Kirkland: Kuper Academy
High School
2975, rue Edmond, Kirkland, QC H9H 5K5, Canada
Tel: 514-426-3007; Fax: 514-426-0377
admissions@kuperacademy.ca
www.kuperacademy.ca
www.flickr.com/photos/69326354@N04
Grades: K.-11; Eng. Note: Liberal arts, mathematics, sciences, social sciences, & creative & performing arts.
Joan Salette, Head of School

L'Assomption: Collège de l'Assomption
270, boul de l'Ange-Gardien, L'Assomption, QC J5W 1R7, Canada
Tél: 450-589-5621; Téléc: 450-589-2910
dirgen@classomption.qc.ca
www.classomption.qc.ca
www.facebook.com/classomption
www.instagram.com/collegedelassomption
Grades: Sec.
Annie Moreau, Directrice générale

La Pocatière: Collège de Sainte-Anne-de-la-Pocatière
100, 4e av, La Pocatière, QC G0R 1Z0, Canada
Tél: 418-856-3012; Téléc: 418-856-5611
Ligne sans frais: 877-783-2663
info@leadercsa.com
www.leadercsa.com
Grades: Sec.; Pens. & Ext. Note: Le programme Leader est offert.
Stéphane Lemelin, Directeur général, 418-856-3012, ext. 245

La Prairie: Collège Jean de la Mennais
870, ch de St-Jean, La Prairie, QC J5R 2L5, Canada
Tél: 450-659-7657; Téléc: 450-659-3717
administration@jdlm.qc.ca
www.jdlm.qc.ca
Grades: Prim./Sec.
Richard Myre, Directeur général

Laval: Académie Lavalloise
5290, boul des Laurentides Auteuil, Laval, QC H7K 2J8, Canada
Tél: 450-628-1430; Téléc: 866-550-2066
info@academielavalloise.com
www.academielavalloise.com
www.facebook.com/academielavalloise
Grades: Mat./Prim. Enrollment: 300
Tessa Zakaib, Directrice générale
tessa.zakaib@academielavalloise.com

Laval: Collège Citoyen
4001, boul Sainte-Rose, Laval, QC H7R 1W6, Canada
Tél: 450-254-2447
info@collegecitoyen.ca
www.collegecitoyen.ca
www.facebook.com/CollegeCitoyen
Grades: Sec. *Enrollment:* 400
Myriam Stephens, Directrice générale

Laval: Collège Laval
1275, av du Collège, Laval, QC H7C 1W8, Canada
Tél: 450-661-7714; *Téléc:* 450-661-7146
secretariat@collegelaval.ca
www.collegelaval.ca
www.facebook.com/collegelaval
www.youtube.com/user/CollegeLaval12
Grades: Sec. *Note:* Centre sportif, salle de théâtre, laboratoires informatiques, bibliothèque.
Michel Baillargeon, Directeur général
michel.baillargeon@collegelaval.ca
Amélie Lapierre, Directrice des communications
amelie.lapierre@collegelaval.ca

Laval: Collège Letendre
1000, boul de l'Avenir, Laval, QC H7N 6J6, Canada
Tél: 450-688-9933; *Téléc:* 450-688-3591
information@collegeletendre.qc.ca
www.collegeletendre.com
www.facebook.com/collegeletendre
www.youtube.com/user/CollegeLetendre
Grades: Sec.
Yves Legault, Directeur
yves.legault@collegeletendre.qc.ca

Laval: École Charles-Perrault (Laval)
1750, boul de la Concorde est, Laval, QC H7G 2E7, Canada
Tél: 450-975-2233
direction@charles-perrault-laval.com
www.ecolecharlesperrault.com
www.facebook.com/ECPLaval
Grades: Mat./Prim./Sec. *Enrollment:* 380

Laval: École Notre-Dame de Nareg
500, 67e av, Laval, QC H7V 2M2, Canada
Tél: 450-680-1168
Grades: Mat./Prim.

Laval: École Socrates-Démosthène Démosthène
1565, boul Saint-Martin ouest, Laval, QC H7S 1N1, Canada
Tél: 450-972-1800
demosthene@hcgm.org
www.socdem.org
Grades: Mat./Prim. *Note:* École privée de la communauté greque orthodoxe de Laval; formation générale; langues d'enseignement: française, greque et anglaise.
Chris Adamopoulos, Directeur général, 514-738-2421, ext. 113
socdem@hcgm.org

Campuses
Socrates II
5757, av Wilderton, Montréal, QC H3S 2K8, Canada
Tél: 514-738-2421
soc2@hcgm.org

Socrates III
11, 11e rue, Roxboro, QC H8Y 1K6, Canada
Tél: 514-685-1833
soc3@hcgm.org

Socrates IV
5220, Grande Allée, St-Hubert, QC J3Y 1A1, Canada
Tél: 450-656-4832
soc4@hcgm.org

Socrates V
931, rue Emerson, Laval, QC H7W 3Y5, Canada
Tél: 450-681-5142
soc5@hcgm.org

Lévis: Juvénat Notre-Dame du Saint-Laurent
30, rue du Juvénat, Lévis, QC G6V 6P5, Canada
Tél: 418-839-9592; *Téléc:* 418-839-5605
juvenat@jnd.qc.ca
www.jnd.qc.ca
www.facebook.com/juvenat222
www.youtube.com/user/jndsaintlaurent/videos
Grades: Sec.
Claude Gélinas, Directeur général, 418-839-9592, ext. 222
cgelinas@jnd.qc.ca

Longueuil: Collège Charles-Lemoyne inc.
Administration générale/Campus Longueuil
901, ch Tiffin, Longueuil, QC J4P 3G6, Canada
Tél: 514-875-0505; *Téléc:* 450-463-4494
college@cclemoyne.edu
monccl.com/college
www.facebook.com/collegecharleslemoyne
twitter.com/charleslemoyne
www.youtube.com/cclemoynetv
Grades: Sec. *Note:* Campus Longueuil: 901, ch Tiffin; Campus Ville de Sainte-Catherine: 125, place Charles-Lemoyne.
David Bowles, Directeur général

Longueuil: Collège Notre-Dame-de-Lourdes
845, ch Tiffin, Longueuil, QC J4P 3G5, Canada
Tél: 450-670-4740; *Téléc:* 450-670-2800
college@ndl.qc.ca
www.ndl.qc.ca
twitter.com/collegendl
www.instagram.com/collegenotredamedelourdes
Grades: Sec.
Isabelle Marcotte, Directrice générale

Mont-Royal: École première Mesifta du Canada
2355, av Ekers, Mont-Royal, QC H3S 1C6, Canada
Tél: 514-738-1738
Grades: Mat./Prim./Sec. *Note:* École juive.

Mont-Saint-Hilaire: Collège Saint-Hilaire inc.
800, rue Rouillard, Mont-Saint-Hilaire, QC J3G 4S6, Canada
Tél: 450-467-7001; *Téléc:* 450-467-9040
csh@csh.qc.ca
www.csh.qc.ca
www.facebook.com/723729260979541
Grades: Sec. *Enrollment:* 600
Diane Lavoie, Directrice générale

Montréal: Académie Beth Rivkah
5001, rue Vézina, Montréal, QC H3W 1C2, Canada
Tél: 514-731-3681
info@bethrivkah.com
www.bethrivkah.com
Grades: Mat./Prim./Sec.; filles *Enrollment:* 600 *Note:* Une école pour filles juives, fondée en 1956 par le Rebbe Menachem Schneerson de Loubavitch.
Rabbi Yosef Minkowitz, Principal
yminkowitz@bethrivkah.com

Montréal: Académie Louis-Pasteur
7220, rue Marie-Victorin, Montréal, QC H1G 2J5, Canada
Tél: 514-322-6123; *Téléc:* 514-322-6787
info@academielouispasteur.com
www.academielouispasteur.com
www.facebook.com/academieLP
Grades: Mat./Prim. *Note:* École primaire privée qui accueille des enfants de la maternelle à la 6e année.
Mark Passaretti, Directeur général
mpassaretti@academielouispasteur.com

Montréal: Académie Michèle-Provost inc.
1517, av des Pins ouest, Montréal, QC H3G 1B3, Canada
Tél: 514-934-0596; *Téléc:* 514-934-2390
info@academiemicheleprovost.qc.ca
www.academiemicheleprovost.qc.ca
www.facebook.com/AcademieMicheleProvost
Grades: Prim./Sec.; Pens. & Ext. *Number of Employees:* 45 enseignants; 10 surveillants; 5 techniciens
Franco Baschiera, Président et directeur général

Montréal: Académie Saint-Louis de France
5320, rue d'Amos, Montréal, QC H1G 2Y1, Canada
Tél: 514-725-0340
www.academiesldf.com
Grades: Mat./Prim. *Enrollment:* 150
Pascal Foucault, Directeur
pascal.foucault@academiesldf.ca

Montréal: The Akiva School
450 Kensington Ave., Montréal, QC H3Y 3A2, Canada
Tel: 514-939-2430; *Fax:* 514-939-2432
www.akivaschool.com
www.facebook.com/akivaschool
twitter.com/akivaschool
www.instagram.com/akiva_school
Grades: JK-6; *Eng./Fr./Hebrew Note:* Jewish community school; programmes include English Language Arts, Français, Judaic Studies, Music, Mathematics, Art, Media & Technology, Physical Education, & Ethics & Religious Cultures.
Cooki Levy, Interim Head of School
cooki@akivaschool.com

Montréal: Centennial Academy
L'Académie Centennale
Middle School Campus
3744, av Prud'homme, Montréal, QC H4A 3H6, Canada
Tel: 514-486-5533; *Fax:* 514-486-1401
info@centennial.qc.ca
www.centennial.qc.ca
www.facebook.com/220929721364999
Grades: Sec.; Eng.
Angéla Burgos, Head of School
aburgos@centennial.qc.ca

Campuses
Senior School Campus
5000, rue Côte St. Luc, Montréal, QC H3G 2W9, Canada
Tel: 514-486-5533; *Fax:* 514-486-1401

Montréal: Centre d'intégration scolaire inc.
6361, 6e av, Montréal, QC H1Y 2R7, Canada
Tél: 514-374-8490; *Téléc:* 514-374-3978
www.cisi.qc.ca
Grades: Prim./Sec.; Éd. spéc.
Patrice Allard, Directeur général, 514-374-8490, ext. 222
pallard@cisi.qc.ca

Montréal: Centre François-Michelle
10095, rue Meunier, Montréal, QC H3L 2Z1, Canada
Tél: 514-381-4418; *Fax:* 514-381-2895
dsormany@francois-michelle.qc.ca
www.francois-michelle.qc.ca
Grades: Mat./Prim./Sec.; Éd. spéc.
Marie-Claude Bénard, Directrice générale, 514-381-4418
mcbenard@francois-michelle.qc.ca

Montréal: Collège Beaubois
4901, rue du Collège Beaubois, Montréal, QC H8Y 3T4, Canada
Tél: 514-684-7642
info@collegebeaubois.qc.ca
www.collegebeaubois.qc.ca
www.facebook.com/271757196171526
twitter.com/collegebeaubois
www.linkedin.com/company/coll-ge-beaubois
www.youtube.com/user/Beaubois1967
Grades: Mat./Prim./Sec.
Isabelle Talon, Directrice générale
italon@collegebeaubois.qc.ca

Montréal: Collège Charlemagne inc.
5000, rue Pilon, Montréal, QC H9K 1G4, Canada
Tél: 514-626-7060; *Téléc:* 514-626-1654
info@collegecharlemagne.com
www.collegecharlemagne.com
Grades: Mat./Prim./Sec.
Julie Beaudet, Directrice générale
jbeaudet@collegecharlemagne.com

Montréal: Collège Français - Secondaire Montréal
185, av Fairmount ouest, Montréal, QC H2T 2M6, Canada
Tél: 514-495-2581; *Téléc:* 514-271-2823
info@collegefrancais.ca
www.collegefrancais.ca
Grades: Sec.; Pens. & Ext.
Claude Bigras, Directeur exécutif
Alexandre Bigras, Directeur administratif
Jean-Louis Portal, Directeur général
jlportal@collegefrancais.ca
Richard Campeau-Smith, Directeur de niveau
rcsmith@collegefrancais.ca
Suzanne Howison, Directrice de niveau
showison@collegefrancais.ca

Campuses
Collège Français - Primaire Longueuil
1391, rue Beauregard, Longueuil, QC J4K 2M3, Canada
Tél: 514-670-7391; *Téléc:* 514-279-5131
info@collegefrancais.ca
www.collegefrancais.ca
Grades: Mat./Prim.
Lélia Farout, Directrice générale
lfarout@collegefrancais.ca

Collège Français - Secondaire Longueuil
1340, boul Nobert, Longueuil, QC J4K 2P4, Canada
Tél: 450-679-0770; *Téléc:* 450-679-0921
info@collegefrancais.ca
www.collegefrancais.ca
Grades: Sec.
Marie-Pier Cournoyer, Directrice
mar_cournoyer@collegefrancais.ca

Montréal: Collège international Marie de France
4635, ch Queen Mary, Montréal, QC H3W 1W3
Tél: 514-737-1177; *Téléc:* 514-737-0789
college@mariedefrance.qc.ca
www.mariedefrance.qc.ca
www.facebook.com/123134007735961
www.youtube.com/user/videocimf
Grades: Mat./Prim./Sec. *Enrollment:* 1800
Brigitte Peytier, Directrice générale

Montréal: Collège Jean-Eudes
3535, boul Rosemont, Montréal, QC H1X 1K7, Canada
Tél: 514-376-5740; *Téléc:* 514-376-4325
info@cje.qc.ca
www.jeaneudes.qc.ca
www.facebook.com/collegejeaneudes
Grades: Sec. *Enrollment:* 1700
Nancy Desbiens, Directrice générale

Montréal: Collège Jeanne-Normandin
690, boul Crémazie est, Montréal, QC H2P 1E9
Tél: 514-381-3945; *Téléc:* 514-381-1695
info@jeanne-normandin.qc.ca
www.jeanne-normandin.qc.ca
www.facebook.com/143937785728317
Grades: Sec.; filles
Marie Robert, Directrice générale

Montréal: Collège Mont-Royal
2165, rue Baldwin, Montréal, QC H1L 5A7, Canada
Tél: 514-351-7851; *Téléc:* 514-351-3124
mradm@collegemont-royal.qc.ca
www.collegemont-royal.qc.ca
www.facebook.com/collegemontroyal
www.instagram.com/collegemontroyal
Grades: Sec.
Anne-Marie Blais, Directrice générale

Montréal: Collège Mont-Saint-Louis
1700, boul Henri-Bourassa est, Montréal, QC H2C 1J3, Canada
Tél: 514-382-1560; *Téléc:* 514-382-5886
info@msl.qc.ca
www.msl.qc.ca
www.facebook.com/CollegeMSL
Grades: Sec.
Sylvie Drolet, Directrice générale

Montréal: Collège Notre-Dame
3791, ch Queen Mary, Montréal, QC H3V 1A8, Canada
Tél: 514-739-3371; *Téléc:* 514-739-4833
info@collegenotredame.com
www.collegenotre-dame.qc.ca
www.facebook.com/collegenotredamepageofficielle
twitter.com/College_N_dame
www.youtube.com/user/CNDMontreal
Grades: Sec.
Lotfi Tazi, Directeur général

Montréal: College Prep International
7475, rue Sherbrooke ouest, Montréal, QC H4B 1S3, Canada
Tel: 514-489-7287; *Fax:* 514-489-7280
info@prepinternational.com
www.prepinternational.com
www.facebook.com/CollegePrepInternational
twitter.com/prepmontreal
Grades: Elem./Sec.; Eng. *Note:* A private, non-sectarian & co-educational school.
Ursulene T. Mora, CEO

Montréal: Collège Regina Assumpta
1750, rue Sauriol est, Montréal, QC H2C 1X4, Canada
Tél: 514-382-4121; *Téléc:* 514-387-7825
info@reginaassumpta.qc.ca
www.reginaassumpta.qc.ca
www.facebook.com/CRAofficielle
Grades: Sec. *Note:* Programme de musique; danse; centre culturel & sportif; chapelle.
Michel Laplante, Directeur général

Montréal: Collège Reine-Marie
9300, boul Saint-Michel, Montréal, QC H1Z 3H1, Canada
Tél: 514-382-0484; *Téléc:* 514-858-1401
info@reine-marie.qc.ca
www.reine-marie.qc.ca
www.facebook.com/college.reinemarie
twitter.com/creinemarie
Grades: Sec. *Enrollment:* 500
Marc Tremblay, Directeur général

Montréal: Collège Sainte-Anne de Lachine
1250, boul St-Joseph, Montréal, QC H8S 2M8, Canada
Tél: 514-637-3571; *Téléc:* 514-637-8906
www.sainteanne.ca
twitter.com/SainteAnne1861
www.linkedin.com/company/college-sainte-anne
www.youtube.com/user/collegeintsainteanne
Grades: Sec.
Ugo Cavenaghi, M.Éd., M.B.A., Directeur général

Montréal: Collège Sainte-Marcelline
9155, boul Gouin ouest, Montréal, QC H4K 1C3, Canada
Tél: 514-334-9651; *Téléc:* 514-334-0210
college.marcelline.qc.ca
www.facebook.com/188810277886895
Grades: Mat./Prim./Sec. *Note:* Enseignement préscolaire et primaire pour garçons et filles; et l'enseignement secondaire pour filles.
Sr. Teresa Belgiojoso, Directrice générale

Montréal: Collège St-Jean-Vianney
12630, boul Gouin est, Montréal, QC H1C 1B9, Canada
Tél: 514-648-3821; *Téléc:* 514-648-8401
college@st-jean-vianney.qc.ca
www.st-jean-vianney.qc.ca
www.facebook.com/collegestjeanvianney
twitter.com/collgestjeanvia
www.youtube.com/user/csjv2011
Grades: Sec.
Éric Deguire, Directeur général

Montréal: Collège Ville-Marie
2850, rue Sherbrooke est, Montréal, QC H2K 1H3, Canada
Tél: 514-525-2516; *Téléc:* 514-525-7675
college@cvmarie.qc.ca
www.cvmarie.qc.ca
www.facebook.com/collegevillemarie
Grades: Sec. *Note:* Programme d'Éducation internationale.
Marie-Claude Girard, Directrice générale

Montréal: École Alex Manoogian
755, rue Manoogian, Montréal, QC H4N 1Z5, Canada
Tél: 514-744-5636; *Téléc:* 514-744-2785
info@alexmanoogian.qc.ca
www.alexmanoogian.qc.ca
www.facebook.com/ecolealexmanoogian
twitter.com/ecolealexman
www.linkedin.com/company/-cole-alex-manoogian-de-f-u-g-a-b
www.youtube.com/user/ecolealexmanoogian
Grades: Mat./Prim./Sec.; Fr./Eng./Armenian *Note:* La première école arménienne au Canada; école privée.
Sébastien Stasse, Directeur général
sebastienstasse@alexmanoogian.qc.ca

Montréal: L'École Ali Ibn Abi Talib
1610, rue de Beauharnois ouest, Montréal, QC H4N 1J5, Canada
Tél: 514-744-0801; *Téléc:* 514-387-3457
info@ecoleali.com
www.ecoleali.com
Grades: Mat./Prim./Sec.
Bilal Jundi, Directeur

Montréal: L'École arménienne Sourp Hagop
3400, rue Nadon, Montréal, QC H4J 1P5, Canada
Tél: 514-332-1373; *Téléc:* 514-332-8303
secretariat@ecolesourphagop.com
www.ecolesourphagop.com
Grades: Mat./Prim./Sec. *Enrollment:* 700
Léna Kadian, Directrice générale

Montréal: École au Jardin Bleu inc.
1690, rue Sauvé est, Montréal, QC H2C 2A8, Canada
Tél: 514-388-4949
ecole@ecoleaujardinbleu.ca
www.ecoleaujardinbleu.ca
Grades: Mat./Prim. *Note:* École privée française d'allégeance catholique.

Montréal: École Charles-Perrault (Pierrefonds)
106, rue Cartier, Montréal, QC H8Y 1G8, Canada
Tél: 514-684-5043; *Téléc:* 514-684-5048
www.ecolecharles-perrault.ca
www.facebook.com/EcoleCharlesPerraultPierrefonds
Grades: Mat./Prim.
Martine Azzouz, Directrice
direction@ecolecharles-perrault.ca

Montréal: L'École des Premières Lettres
5210, rue Waverly, Montréal, QC H2T 2X7, Canada
Tél: 514-272-2229; *Téléc:* 514-272-3330
secretariat@premiereslettres.com
www.premiereslettres.com
Grades: Mat./Prim.

Anne Deguilhem, Directrice générale
adeguilhem@premiereslettres.com

Montréal: École Maïmonide
Campus Jacob Safra
1900, rue Bourdon, Montréal, QC H4M 2X7, Canada
Tél: 514-744-5300; *Téléc:* 514-744-4838
info@ecolemaimonide.org
www.ecolemaimonide.org
Grades: Mat./Prim./Sec. *Note:* École de la communauté Sépharade de Montréal. Campus Parkhaven: 5615, rue Parkhaven, Côte Saint-Luc, 514-488-9224.
Salomon Oziel, Président

Montréal: École Michelet
10550, av Pelletier, Montréal, QC H1H 3R5, Canada
Tél: 514-321-9551; *Téléc:* 514-321-9111
michelet@qc.aira.com
www.ecolemichelet.com
Grades: Prim.
Lucienne Mortier, Directrice générale

Montréal: École Montessori de Montréal
1505, rue Serre, Montréal, QC H8N 1N3
Tél: 514-363-6603; *Téléc:* 514-363-0942
direction@ecolemontessorimontreal.com
www.ecolemontessorimontreal.com
Grades: K.-6 *Enrollment:* 265
Anne Mansour, Directrice

Montréal: École Montessori International
10025, boul. de l'Acadie, Montréal, QC H4N 2S1
Tél: 514-331-1244
Grades: Pre.-6 *Enrollment:* 250

Campuses
Pavillon Blainville
325, ch du Bas-de-Ste-Thérèse, Blainville, QC J7A 0A3
Tel: 450-965-7878

Montréal: École Montessori Ville-Marie inc.
760, rue Saint-Germain, Montréal, QC H4L 3R5, Canada
Tél: 514-335-6688; *Téléc:* 514-333-8988
info@ecolemontessorivillemarie.com
www.ecolemontessorivillemarie.com
Grades: Mat./Prim. *Note:* Campus Laval-Duvernay: 755, rue Roland-Forget. Enseignement bilingue.

Montréal: École Pasteur
Pavillon Khalil Gibran
12345, av de la Miséricorde, Montréal, QC H4J 2E8, Canada
Tél: 514-331-0850; *Téléc:* 514-331-2312
information@ecolepasteur.net
www.ecolepasteur.qc.ca
Grades: Mat./Prim./Sec. *Enrollment:* 800 *Note:* Pavillon Victor-Hugo: 12525 rue Lachapelle, Montréal.
Volta Ramirez, Directeur général

Montréal: École Rudolf Steiner de Montréal
4855, av Kensington, Montréal, QC H3X 3S6, Canada
Tél: 514-481-5686; *Téléc:* 514-221-3677
info@ersm.org
www.ersm.org
Grades: Mat./Prim./Sec. *Note:* Pédagogie Waldorf.

Montréal: École secondaire Duval
260, boul Henri-Bourassa est, Montréal, QC H3L 1B8, Canada
Tél: 514-382-6070; *Téléc:* 514-382-7207
info@ecoleduval.com
www.ecoleduval.com
www.facebook.com/ecoleduval
Grades: Sec. *Note:* École sec. pour élèves qui ont abandonné leurs études régulières mais désirent obtenir leur diplôme dans les plus brefs délais, ou qui désirent satisfaire aux préalables d'un programme ou suivre un cours pour l'admission au collégial; cours individualisés ou cours de groupe.
Karl Duval, Directeur
karl.duval@ecoleduval.com

Montréal: École Vanguard Québec ltée (École primaire interculturelle)
Vanguard Québec School
5935, ch de la Côte-de-Liesse, Montréal, QC H4T 1C3
Tél: 514-747-5500; *Téléc:* 514-747-2831
cccaputo@vanguardquebec.qc.ca
www.vanguardquebec.qc.ca
www.facebook.com/250813081726346
Grades: Prim./Sec.; Fr./Angl.; Éd. spéc. *Note:* Services adaptés à des élèves présentant des difficultés graves d'apprentissage. École Vanguard Primaire Interculturelle: 1150, rue Deguire, (514) 747-3711 (Denise Bédard, directrice). École Vanguard Secondaire Francophone: 83, boul des Prairies, Laval, (450) 972-6268 (François Papineau, directeur). École Vanguard

Secondaire Interculturelle: 175, rue Metcalfe, (514) 932-9770 (Maryse Bessette, directrice).
Carolyn Coffin-Caputo, Directrice générale, 514-747-5500

Montréal: Écoles musulmanes de Montréal
Campus Secondaire
2255, boul Cavendish, Montréal, QC H4B 2L7, Canada
Tél: 514-484-5084
contact@emms.ca
www.emms.ca
Grades: Prim./Sec. *Note:* Campus Primaire: 7445, av Chester, Montréal, 514-484-8845.

Montréal: Greaves Adventist Academy
2330 West Hill Ave., Montréal, QC H4B 2S3, Canada
Tél: 514-486-5092; *Fax:* 514-486-0515
www.greavesadventistacademy.com
Grades: K - 11 *Note:* Greaves Adventist Academy is a private, non-subsidized English institution.
T. Z. Cousins, Principal

Montréal: Jewish People's Schools & Peretz Schools Inc.
Les Écoles juives populaires et Les Écoles Peretz inc.
Also known as: JPPS-Bialik
6500, ch Kildare, Montréal, QC H4W 3B8, Canada
Tél: 514-731-3841
admissions@jpps.ca
jppsbialik.ca
www.facebook.com/JPPSBialikSchool
twitter.com/JPPS_Bialik
Grades: Pre./Elem./Sec.; Eng./Fr. *Note:* One educational system retaining the names of both founding schools, united in 1971. JPPS-Bialik is a Jewish day school system in Montréal, comprising: Bialik High School, 6500, ch Kildare, 514-481-2736; JPPS Elementary School, 6500, ch Kildare, 514-731-6456; and JPPS Children's Centre, 5838 av Westminster, 514-488-1232. Instruction in English, French & Hebrew, with language programmes in French, Hebrew, Yiddish; mathematics, sciences & technology, Judaic Studies, Social Sciences, Arts; athletics; library.

Montréal: Kells Academy
6865, boul de Maisonneuve ouest, Montréal, QC H4B 1T1, Canada
Tél: 514-485-8565; *Fax:* 514-485-8505
kadmin@kells.ca
www.kells.ca
www.facebook.com/KellsAcademy
twitter.com/KellsAcademy
www.youtube.com/user/KellsAcademy1978
Grades: K-12; Eng. *Enrollment:* 450 *Number of Employees:* 65
Note: Offers a virtual Grade 12 program as of September 2017.
Irene Woods, Director
Lesley Farrell, Admissions Coordinator

<u>Campuses</u>
Elementary Campus
2290, boul Cavendish, Montréal, QC H4B 2M7, Canada
Tél: 514-487-2345
elementary@kells.ca
Grades: K-6; Eng.
Marla Perlman, Principal

Montréal: Lower Canada College
4090, av Royal, Montréal, QC H4A 2M5, Canada
Tél: 514-482-9916; *Fax:* 514-482-0195
admissions@lcc.ca
www.lcc.ca
www.facebook.com/lowercanadacollege
twitter.com/wearelcc
www.instagram.com/lower_canada_college
Grades: K-11; Eng./Fr.
Christopher J. Shannon, Headmaster
cshannon@lcc.ca

Montréal: Orchard House
Maison Orchard
4176, boul Grand, Montréal, QC H4B 2X4
Tél: 514-483-6556
admin@orchard-house.ca
www.orchard-house.ca
www.facebook.com/Orchard.House.Preschools
www.youtube.com/user/OrchardHouseMontreal
Yasmine Ghandour, Founder & General Director

<u>Campuses</u>
Pointe-Claire Campus
159, Place Frontenac, Montréal, QC H9R 4Z7
Tél: 514-630-3993

Montréal: Pensionnat Notre-Dame-des-Anges
5680, boul Rosemont, Montréal, QC H1T 2H2, Canada
Tél: 514-254-6447; *Téléc:* 514-254-6261
pnda@pnda.qc.ca
www.pnda.qc.ca
Grades: Prim.
Dominic Blanchette, Directeur général

Montréal: The Priory School inc.
3120 The Boulevard, Montréal, QC H3Y 1R9, Canada
Tel: 514-935-5966; *Fax:* 514-935-1428
info@priory.qc.ca
www.priory.qc.ca
Grades: K./Elem.; Eng.
Tim Peters, Headmaster

Montréal: St. George's School of Montreal
École St-Georges de Montréal
3100 The Boulevard, Montréal, QC H3Y 1R9, Canada
Tel: 514-937-9289; *Fax:* 514-933-3621
info@stgeorges.qc.ca
www.stgeorges.qc.ca
Other Information: Admissions: 514-904-0542
www.facebook.com/stgeorgesschoolofmontreal
twitter.com/StGeorgesMtl
www.youtube.com/user/StGeorgesSchoolMtl
Grades: K-11; Eng. *Note:* A co-educational, non-denominational school. Elementary School Campus: 3685 The Boulevard, Westmount.
Sharon Klein, Head of School
sharon.klein@stgeorges.qc.ca

Montréal: Solomon Schechter Academy
Académie Solomon Schechter
5555, ch de la Côte-St-Luc, Montréal, QC H3X 2C9, Canada
Tel: 514-485-0866; *Fax:* 514-485-2267
www.solomonschechter.ca
Grades: Pre.-6; Eng., Fr. & Hebrew *Enrollment:* 651 *Number of Employees:* 55 teachers; 9 administrators *Note:* Committed to the values of Conservative Judaism; affiliated with the Shaare Zion Synagogue. Pre-Kindergarten to Gr. 6. Instruction in English, French & Hebrew.
Steven Erdelyi, Head of School
serdelyi@solomonschechter.ca
Tina Roth, Dean of Students
troth@solomonschechter.ca
Jonathan Kuczer, Executive Director
jkuczer@solomonschechter.ca
Vienna Blum, Director, Communications
vblum@solomonschechter.ca
Naomi Blumer, Director, Development & Coordinator, Admissions
nblumer@solomonschechter.ca
Randy Mendel, Director, Early Childhood
rmendel@solomonschechter.ca

Montréal: Talmud Torahs Unis de Montréal/Herzliah
United Talmud Torahs of Montreal/Herzliah
École primaire Talmud Torah
4850, av Saint-Kevin, Montréal, QC H3W 1P2, Canada
Tél: 514-739-2297; *Téléc:* 514-739-5280
www.azrieli-tth.ca
www.facebook.com/TalmudTorahHerzliah
twitter.com/AzrieliTTH
www.youtube.com/user/talmudtorahherz
Grades: Pre./Elem./Sec.; Eng./Fr.
Kelly Castiel, Directrice générale
Michelle Toledano, Directrice

<u>Campuses</u>
École secondaire Herzliah
4840, av Saint-Kevin, Montréal, QC H3W 1P2, Canada
Tél: 514-739-2294; *Téléc:* 514-739-2296
Linda Leiberman, Directrice

Montréal: Trafalgar School for Girls
3495, rue Simpson, Montréal, QC H3G 2J7
Tel: 514-935-2644; *Fax:* 514-935-2359
admissions@trafalgar.qc.ca
www.trafalgar.qc.ca
www.facebook.com/TrafalgarSchoolforGirls
Grades: Sec.; Girls; Eng. *Enrollment:* 175 *Number of Employees:* 40
Geoffrey Dowd, Principal
gd@trafalgar.qc.ca

Montréal: Villa Maria
4245, boul Décarie, Montréal, QC H4A 3K4, Canada
Tél: 514-484-4950; *Fax:* 514-484-4492
info@villamaria.qc.ca
www.villamaria.qc.ca
www.facebook.com/VillaMariaMTL
www.youtube.com/user/EcoleSecondaireVilla

Grades: Sec.; Eng./Fr. *Note:* Committed to students' proficiency in French & English; programmes include languages; arts (visual arts, drama, music); mathematics & sciences; technology; social sciences; ethics & religious culture; physical education & health.
Marie Anna Bacchi, Director General

Montréal: Villa Sainte-Marcelline
815, av Upper Belmont, Montréal, QC H3Y 1K5, Canada
Tél: 514-488-2528
info@villa.marcelline.qc.ca
villa.marcelline.qc.ca
Grades: Mat./Prim./Sec.; filles
Mathilde Fantone, Directrice générale

Montréal: Yeshiva Gedola Merkaz Hatorah
6155, ch Deacon, Montréal, QC H3S 2P4, Canada
Tél: 514-735-6611; *Fax:* 514-343-0083
mainoffice@yeshivagedola.org
www.yeshivagedola.com
Grades: Pre./Elem./Sec.; Eng./Fr. *Enrollment:* 375
Rabbi Moshe Glustein, Director

Montréal-Nord: Centre Académique Fournier
10339, av du Parc-Georges, Montréal-Nord, QC H1H 4Y4, Canada
Tél: 514-321-2642; *Téléc:* 514-321-0278
www.academiefournier.qc.ca
Grades: Prim./Sec.; Éd. spéc.
Paola Gravino, Directrice générale
paola.gravino@academiefournier.qc.ca

Nicolet: Collège Notre-Dame-de-l'Assomption (CNDA)
225, rue St-Jean-Baptiste, Nicolet, QC J3T 0A2, Canada
Tél: 819-293-4500; *Téléc:* 819-293-2099
info@cnda.qc.ca
www.cnda.qc.ca
www.facebook.com/CNDA.page.officielle
Grades: Sec.; Pens. & Ext. *Note:* École secondaire privée mixte. Pensionnat pour filles et garçons 5 ou 7 jours.
Mylène Proulx, Directrice générale

Outremont: Belz Community School
École communautaire Belz
Also known as: Belz Girls School
1495, av Ducharme, Outremont, QC H2V 1E8, Canada
Tel: 514-271-0611; *Fax:* 514-271-9329
belz@belzschool.org
Grades: Pre./Elem./Sec.; Fr./Eng.; girls *Enrollment:* 382 *Note:* Belz Boys School: 6508, Durocher, Outremont, (514) 270-5086.
Helen Liberman, Principal

Outremont: Beth Jacob School Inc.
École Beth Jacob inc.
1750, av Glendale, Outremont, QC H2V 1B3, Canada
Tel: 514-739-3614
Grades: Pre./Elem./Sec.; Eng./Fr.; Girls

Outremont: Collège Stanislas - Montréal
780, boul Dollard, Outremont, QC H2V 3G5, Canada
Tél: 514-273-9521; *Téléc:* 514-273-3409
direction@stanislas.qc.ca
www.stanislas.qc.ca
www.facebook.com/collegestanislasmontreal
twitter.com/stanmontreal
www.youtube.com/stanislasMontreal
Grades: Mat./Prim./Sec./Coll. *Enrollment:* 2150
Philippe Warin, Proviseur/Directeur général

<u>Campuses</u>
Collège Stanislas - Québec
1605, ch Sainte-Foy, Québec, QC G1S 2P1, Canada
Tél: 418-527-9998; *Téléc:* 418-527-0399
dirquebec@stanislas.qc.ca
www.stanislas.qc.ca
www.facebook.com/collegestanislasquebec
twitter.com/stanquebec
www.youtube.com/StanislasQuebec
Grades: Mat./Prim./Sec./Coll.

Outremont: École Buissonnière, centre de formation artistique inc.
215, av de l'Épée, Outremont, QC H2V 3T3, Canada
Tél: 514-272-4739; *Téléc:* 514-907-5094
info@ecolebuissonniere.ca
www.ecolebuissonniere.ca
Grades: Mat./Prim. *Note:* Intégration des arts aux programmes du Min. de l'Éducation; arts plastiques, musique, danse, art dramatique.
Hélène Bourduas, Directrice générale
Martine Duff, Directrice financière

Québec: Académie Saint-Louis - préscolaire et primaire
2200, de la Rive Boisée Nord, Québec, QC G2C 0J1, Canada
Tél: 418-767-2200; *Téléc:* 418-767-2211
www.aslouis.qc.ca
Grades: Prim. *Note:* Programme d'éducation internationale.

Québec: Académie Saint-Louis (Québec)
1500, rue de La Rive-Boisée sud, Québec, QC G2C 2B3, Canada
Tél: 418-845-5121; *Téléc:* 418-845-5244
www.aslouis.qc.ca
Grades: Sec. *Note:* Programmes: Concentration Langues; Études-Sports: Hockey, Golf, Natation, Football, Cheerleading, et Soccer féminin.
Mireille Guay, Directrice générale

Campuses
Préscolaire et Primaire
2200, rue de la Rive Boisée Nord, Québec, QC G2C 0J1, Canada
Tél: 418-767-2200; *Téléc:* 418-767-2211
Grades: Mat./Prim.

Québec: Centre Psycho-Pédagogique de Québec inc. (École Saint-François)
1000, rue du Joli-Bois, Québec, QC G1V 3Z6, Canada
Tél: 418-650-1171; *Téléc:* 418-650-1145
adm@cppq.qc.ca
Grades: Prim./Sec./; Éd. spéc. *Enrollment:* 200 *Note:* Favoriser l'intégration sociale de filles et garçons présentant des difficultés d'adaptation scolaire.
Jean-Marie Guay, Directeur

Québec: Collège de Champigny
1400, rte de l'Aéroport, Québec, QC G2G 1G6, Canada
Tél: 418-872-0508; *Téléc:* 418-872-1002
www.collegedechampigny.com
www.facebook.com/collegedechampigny
twitter.com/ColldeChampigny
Grades: Sec.
Jean Garneau, Directeur général
jgarneau@collegedechampigny.com

Québec: Le Collège François-de-Laval
6, rue de la Vielle-Université, Québec, QC G1R 5X8, Canada
Tél: 418-694-1020; *Téléc:* 418-694-1072
admission@collegefdl.ca
www.psq.qc.ca
www.facebook.com/collegefdl
Grades: Sec.
Marc Dallaire, Directeur général
dg@collegefdl.ca

Québec: L'École des Ursulines de Québec et de Loretteville
4, rue du Parloir, Québec, QC G1R 4M5, Canada
Tél: 418-692-2612; *Téléc:* 418-692-1240
reception_euq@ursulinesquebec.com
www.euq.ca
www.facebook.com/ursulinesquebec
twitter.com/ursulinesquebec
Grades: Prim./Sec.; filles; Pens. & Ext. *Note:* Loretteville: 63, rue Racine, 418-692-2612, ext. 215.
Jacques Ménard, Directeur général
menardj@ursulinesquebec.com

Québec: École Montessori de Québec inc.
1265, av du Buisson, Québec, QC G1T 2C4, Canada
Tél: 418-688-7646; *Téléc:* 418-687-5282
info@montessori-qc.net
www.montessori-qc.net
www.facebook.com/EcoleMontessoriDeQuebec
Grades: Mat./Prim.

Québec: École secondaire François-Bourrin
50, av des Cascades, Québec, QC G1E 2J7, Canada
Tél: 418-661-6978; *Téléc:* 418-661-4778
efb@fbourrin.qc.ca
www.fbourrin.qc.ca
www.facebook.com/281347008560492
Grades: Sec.
Mario Tremblay, Directeur général

Québec: Externat Saint-Jean-Eudes
650, av du Bourg-Royal, Québec, QC G2L 1M8, Canada
Tél: 418-627-1550; *Téléc:* 418-627-0770
info@sje.ca
www.saint-jean-eudes.com
www.facebook.com/ecolesecondairesaintjeaneudes
Grades: Sec. *Enrollment:* 1000
Mélanie Lanouette, Directrice générale

Québec: Externat St-Jean-Berchmans
2303, ch Saint-Louis, Québec, QC G1T 1R5, Canada
Tél: 418-687-5871; *Téléc:* 418-687-5886
sec@externatsjb.com
www.externatsjb.com
www.facebook.com/externatsjb
twitter.com/ExternatSJB
Grades: Mat./Prim.
Alain Roy, Directeur général

Québec: Institut St-Joseph
Pavillon Saint-Vallier
900, av Joffre, Québec, QC G1S 4Z3, Canada
Tél: 418-688-0736; *Téléc:* 418-688-0737
www.st-joseph.qc.ca
www.facebook.com/institutstjoseph
Grades: Mat./Prim.
Guylaine Feuiltault, Directrice générale
gfeuiltault@istj.qc.ca

Québec: Réseau VISION
Également connu sous le nom de: Écoles VISION Schools
Siège social
#300, 1995, rue Frank-Carrel, Québec, QC G1N 4H9, Canada
Tél: 418-653-3547; *Téléc:* 418-653-6435
Ligne sans frais: 866-553-3547
info@visionschools.com
www.visionschools.com
Number of Schools: 21 *Grades:* Mat./Prim./Sec. *Enrollment:* 3000
Richard Dumais, Président

Québec: Séminaire des Pères Maristes
2315, ch Saint-Louis, Québec, QC G1T 1R5, Canada
Tél: 418-651-4944; *Téléc:* 418-651-6841
spmecole@spmaristes.qc.ca
www.spmaristes.qc.ca
Grades: Sec.
François Sylvain, Directeur général

Rawdon: Collège Champagneur
3713, rue Queen, Rawdon, QC J0K 1S0, Canada
Tél: 450-834-5401; *Téléc:* 450-834-6500
secretariat@champagneur.qc.ca
www.champagneur.qc.ca
Grades: Secondaire *Note:* Privée mixte.
Johanne Lamy, Directrice générale

Rawdon: École Marie-Anne
4567, rue du Mont-Pontbriand, Rawdon, QC J0K 1S0, Canada
Tél: 450-834-4668; *Téléc:* 855-266-4257
administration@ecolemarieanne.org
www.ecolemarieanne.org
fr-fr.facebook.com/1408332619430862
Grades: Mat./Prim. *Enrollment:* 175
Anne-Marie Breault, Directrice générale

Repentigny: Académie François-Labelle
1227, rue Notre-Dame, Repentigny, QC J5Y 3H2
Tél: 450-582-2020; *Téléc:* 450-582-9732
afl@academiefrancoislabelle.qc.ca
www.academiefrancoislabelle.qc.ca
www.facebook.com/173472472741596
Grades: Mat./Prim.
Michèle Beaudry, Directrice générale

Repentigny: Centre Académique de Lanaudière
930, boul L'Assomption, Repentigny, QC J6A 5H5, Canada
Tél: 450-654-5026
info@lecadl.com
www.lecadl.com
www.facebook.com/1481335528764835
Grades: Mat./Prim.
Roger Normandin, Directeur général

Rigaud: Collège Bourget
65, rue St-Pierre, Rigaud, QC J0P 1P0, Canada
Tél: 450-451-0815; *Téléc:* 450-451-4171
dg@collegebourget.qc.ca
www.collegebourget.qc.ca
Grades: Mat.-12è années
Jean-Marc St-Jacques, c.s.v., Directeur général

Rivière-du-Loup: Collège Notre-Dame
P.O. Box 786
56, rue Saint-Henri, Rivière-du-Loup, QC G5R 3Z5, Canada
Tél: 418-862-8257; *Téléc:* 418-862-8495
www.collegenotredame.ca
www.facebook.com/CollegeNotreDameRdLPageofficielle
Grades: Sec. *Enrollment:* 500

Guy April, Directeur général
dg@collegenotredame.ca

Saint-Augustin-de-Desmaures: Collège Saint-Augustin
4950, rue Lionel-Groulx, Saint-Augustin-de-Desmaures, QC G3A 1V2, Canada
Tél: 418-872-0954
Grades: Sec.; Pens. & Ext.

Saint-Bruno-de-Montarville: Académie des Sacrés-Coeurs
1575, ch des Vingt, Saint-Bruno-de-Montarville, QC J3V 4P6, Canada
Tél: 450-653-3681; *Téléc:* 450-653-0816
info@academiedsc.ca
www.academiedessacrescoeurs.ca
Grades: Mat./Prim.; Pens. & Ext.
Évelyne Gosselin, Directrice générale

Saint-Gabriel-de-Valcartier: École secondaire Mont-Saint-Sacrement
200, boul St-Sacrement, Saint-Gabriel-de-Valcartier, QC G0A 4S0, Canada
Tél: 418-844-3771; *Téléc:* 418-844-2926
secretariat@mss.qc.ca
www.mss.qc.ca
Grades: Sec. *Note:* Programme Baccalauréat international; Programme Magellan.
Pierre Lantier, Directeur général

Saint-Hyacinthe: Collège Saint-Maurice
630, rue Girouard ouest, Saint-Hyacinthe, QC J2S 2Y3, Canada
Tél: 450-773-7478; *Téléc:* 450-773-1413
info.college@csm.qc.ca
www.csm.qc.ca
www.facebook.com/CollegeSaintMaurice
www.instagram.com/collegesaintmaurice
Grades: Sec. *Note:* École secondaire mixte; Quatre programmes: programme d'éducation intermédiaire (PEI), Découverte+, Multimédia (IMT) et STIM
Marie-Claude Tardif, Directrice générale
Brigitte Gascon, Directrice des services pédagogiques
Guylaine Doyon, Directrice des élèves
Nathalie Lanoix, Directrice des services administratifs

Saint-Hyacinthe: La Petite Académie
1090, av Pratte, Saint-Hyacinthe, QC J2S 4B6, Canada
Tél: 450-771-0644; *Téléc:* 450-771-7242
info@lapetiteacademie.qc.ca
lapetiteacademie.qc.ca
www.facebook.com/lapetiteacademieduboise
Grades: Mat./Prim.
Lise Thiboutot, Directrice générale

Saint-Jacques: Collège Esther-Blondin
101, rue Ste-Anne, Saint-Jacques, QC J0K 2R0, Canada
Tél: 450-839-3672; *Téléc:* 450-839-3951
admin@collegeblondin.qc.ca
www.collegeblondin.qc.ca
Grades: Sec.; Pens. & Ext. *Note:* Membre, Soc. des établissements du bacc. international du Québec, et Org. du bacc. international; le collège est reconnu École Verte Brundtland.
Chantal Longpré, Directrice générale

Saint-Jean-sur-Richelieu: École secondaire Marcellin-Champagnat
14, ch des Patriotes est, Saint-Jean-sur-Richelieu, QC J2X 5P9, Canada
Tél: 450-347-5343; *Téléc:* 450-347-2423
webmaster@esmc.qc.ca
www.esmc.qc.ca
Grades: Sec.
Richard Custeau, Directeur général
richard.custeau@i-esmc.qc.ca

Saint-Jérôme: Académie Lafontaine
2171, boul Maurice, Saint-Jérôme, QC J7Y 4M7, Canada
Tél: 450-431-3733; *Téléc:* 450-431-7390
info@academielafontaine.qc.ca
www.academielafontaine.qc.ca
www.facebook.com/academielafontaineqcca
Grades: Mat.-Sec. *Note:* Camps du jour; piscine; cantine.
Hugues Lagarde, Directeur général

Saint-Lambert: Collège Durocher Saint-Lambert
Pavillon Durocher
857, rue Riverside, Saint-Lambert, QC J4P 1C2, Canada
Tél: 450-465-7213; *Téléc:* 450-465-0860
info@cdsl.qc.ca
www.facebook.com/collegedurochersaintlambert
Grades: Sec. *Note:* Pavillon Saint-Lambert: 375, rue Riverside, 450-671-5585.
Francis Roy, Directeur général

Saint-Laurent: École Jeunes musulmans canadiens
Également connu sous le nom de: École JMC
5919, boul Henri-Bourassa ouest, Saint-Laurent, QC H4R 1B7
Tél: 514-956-9559
admin@ecolejmc.ca
www.ecolejmc.ca
www.facebook.com/202175506482274
Grades: Prim. - Sec. *Enrollment:* 450
Layla Sawaf, Directrice générale

Saint-Laurent: Education Plus
1275, rue Hodge, Saint-Laurent, QC H4N 2B1, Canada
Tel: 514-733-9600; *Fax:* 514-733-3060
edplus@runbox.com
edplus.ca
Grades: 10 - 11 *Enrollment:* 40 *Note:* Relationship-based education, flexible structure, informal environment; Life Skills courses; drama; arts; English & French language skills.
James Watts, Director
j.watts@sympatico.ca

Sainte-Thérèse: Académie Ste-Thérèse
Campus Jacques-About
425, rue Blainville est, Sainte-Thérèse, QC J7E 1N7, Canada
Tél: 450-434-1130; *Téléc:* 450-434-0010
infostetherese@academie.ste-therese.com
www.academie.ste-therese.com
Grades: Mat./Prim./Sec.; Pens. & Ext. *Note:* Campus Rosemère: 1, ch des Écoliers, Rosemère, 450-434-1131.
Rose De Angelis, Directrice générale
rdeangelis@academie.ste-therese.com

Sept-Îles: Institut d'enseignement de Sept-Îles inc.
737, av Gamache, Sept-Îles, QC G4R 2J8, Canada
Tél: 418-968-9104; *Téléc:* 418-962-8561
www.iesi.in
www.facebook.com/iesi.in
www.youtube.com/user/IESIvids
Grades: Sec. *Enrollment:* 236
Jean-Sébastien Roy, Directeur général
jean-sebastien.roy@iesi.in

Shawinigan: Séminaire Sainte-Marie
5655, boul des Hêtres, Shawinigan, QC G9N 4V9, Canada
Tél: 819-539-5493; *Téléc:* 819-539-1749
www.seminairestemarie.com
www.facebook.com/seminairesaintemarie
twitter.com/SemSteMarie
Grades: Sec.
Stéphanie Plante, Directrice générale

Sherbrooke: Bishop's College School, Inc. (BCS)
P.O. Box 5001 Lennoxville
80, ch Moulton Hill, Sherbrooke, QC J1M 1Z8, Canada
Tel: 819-566-0227; *Fax:* 819-566-8182
Toll-Free: 877-570-7542
admissions@bishopscollegeschool.com
www.bishopscollegeschool.com
www.facebook.com/bishopscollegeschool
twitter.com/BCS_Today
www.instagram.com/bishopscollegeschool
Grades: 7-12 *Enrollment:* 260 *Number of Employees:* 30 teachers *Note:* Bishop's College School is an English language boarding & day school.
Tyler Lewis, Head of School, 819-566-0227, ext. 201
tlewis@bishopscollegeschool.com
Sandra Edwards, Director, Finance & Operations, 819-566-0227, ext. 205
sedwards@bishopscollegeschool.com

Sherbrooke: Collège du Mont-Sainte-Anne
2100, ch de Ste-Catherine, Sherbrooke, QC J1N 3V5, Canada
Tél: 819-823-3003; *Téléc:* 819-569-9636
secretariat@collegemsa.net
www.collegemsa.com
Grades: Sec.; garçons; Pens. & Ext.
Nathalie Marceau, Directrice

Sherbrooke: Collège Mont Notre-Dame de Sherbrooke inc.
114, rue de la Cathédrale, Sherbrooke, QC J1H 4M1, Canada
Tél: 819-563-4104; *Téléc:* 819-563-8689
www.mont-notre-dame.qc.ca
www.facebook.com/423552584428886
twitter.com/montnotredame
www.youtube.com/user/CollegeMontNotreDame
Grades: Mat./Prim./Sec.; filles *Enrollment:* 450 *Note:* Programme d'éducation international; école de musique; école de danse; Espagnol; sports.
Éric Faucher, Directeur général
efaucher@lemont.ca

Sherbrooke: École Plein Soleil (Association coopérative)
300-458, rue de Montréal, Sherbrooke, QC J1H 1E5, Canada
Tél: 819-569-8359; *Téléc:* 819-569-3979
info@pleinsoleil.qc.ca
www.pleinsoleil.qc.ca
Grades: Mat./Prim. *Note:* Programme d'éducation internationale.
Marie-Josée Mayrand, Directrice générale
mjmayrand@pleinsoleil.qc.ca

Sherbrooke: École secondaire de Bromptonville
125, rue du Frère-Théode, Sherbrooke, QC J1C 0S3, Canada
Tél: 819-846-2738; *Téléc:* 819-846-4808
esb@esb1954.com
www.ecolesecondairebromptonville.com
www.facebook.com/esbromptonville
Grades: Sec.; Pens. & Ext.
Simon Croteau, Directeur général
simon.croteau@esb1954.com

Sherbrooke: Séminaire de Sherbrooke
195, rue Marquette, Sherbrooke, QC J1H 1L6, Canada
Tél: 819-563-2050; *Téléc:* 819-562-8261
courrier@seminaire-sherbrooke.qc.ca
www.seminaire-sherbrooke.qc.ca
Grades: Sec. *Note:* Secondaire et collégial; formation continue.
Caroline Champeau, Rectrice-Directrice générale
cchampeau@seminaire-sherbrooke.qc.ca

Sherbrooke: Séminaire Salésien
135, rue Don Bosco nord, Sherbrooke, QC J1L 1E5, Canada
Tél: 819-566-2222; *Téléc:* 819-566-6969
www.lesalesien.com
www.facebook.com/lesalesien
twitter.com/salesien
www.youtube.com/leseminairesalesien
Grades: Sec. *Enrollment:* 720
Jean-Marc Poulin, Directeur général

Stanstead: Stanstead College
450 Dufferin St., Stanstead, QC J0B 3E0, Canada
Tel: 819-876-7891; *Fax:* 819-876-5891
admissions@stansteadcollege.com
www.stansteadcollege.com
www.facebook.com/78975058390
twitter.com/stansteadcolleg
www.youtube.com/user/StansteadSpartans
Grades: 7 - 12 *Enrollment:* 195 *Note:* Co-educational; curriculum/instruction in English, with programmes in French, arts, music, drama; athletics.
Michael T. Wolfe, Headmaster, 819-876-7891, ext. 230
michael.wolfe@stansteadcollege.com

Terrebonne: Collège Saint-Sacrement
901, rue St-Louis, Terrebonne, QC J6W 1K1, Canada
Tél: 450-471-6615; *Téléc:* 450-471-5904
www.collegesaintsacrement.qc.ca
www.facebook.com/CollegeSaintSacrement
twitter.com/SaintSacrement
Grades: Sec.
Stéphane Mayer, Directeur général

Trois-Rivières: Collège Marie-de-l'Incarnation
725, rue Hart, Trois-Rivières, QC G9A 4R9, Canada
Tél: 819-379-3223; *Téléc:* 819-379-3226
reception@cmitr.com
www.cmitr.qc.ca
www.facebook.com/cmitr
Grades: Mat./Prim./Sec.; Pens. & Ext.
Réjean Lemay, Directeur général
Martine Talbot, Directrice pédagogique

Trois-Rivières: École Val Marie
88, ch du Passage, Trois-Rivières, QC G8T 2M3, Canada
Tél: 819-379-8040; *Téléc:* 819-378-8559
secretariat@valmarie.net
www.valmarie.net
www.facebook.com/ecole.valmarie
Grades: Mat./Prim.; Pens. & Ext.

Carla Cholet, Directrice générale
carla.cholet@valmarie.net

Trois-Rivières: Institut secondaire Keranna (1992) inc.
6205, boul des Chenaux, Trois-Rivières, QC G8Y 6Z1, Canada
Tél: 819-378-4833; *Téléc:* 819-378-2417
keranna@keranna.qc.ca
keranna.qc.ca
www.facebook.com/Keranna
twitter.com/Keranna
Grades: Sec.
Julie L'Heureux, Directrice générale
julie.lheureux@keranna.qc.ca

Val-Morin: Collège Laurentien
1200, 14e av, Val-Morin, QC J0T 2R0, Canada
Tél: 819-322-2913; *Téléc:* 819-322-7086
www.collegelaurentien.ca
www.facebook.com/collegelaurentien
Grades: Prim./Sec.; Pens. & Ext.
Alain Houde, Directeur général
ahoude@collegelaurentien.ca

Varennes: Centre Éducatif Chante Plume
104, boul de la Marine, Varennes, QC J3X 1Z5, Canada
Tél: 450-652-6869; *Téléc:* 450-652-5773
varennes@visionschools.com
varennes.visionschools.com
Grades: Mat./Prim.
Colette Cardin, Directrice propriétaire

Varennes: Collège Saint-Paul
235, rue Sainte-Anne, Varennes, QC J3X 1P9, Canada
Tél: 450-652-2941; *Téléc:* 450-652-4461
reception@college-st-paul.qc.ca
www.college-st-paul.qc.ca
www.facebook.com/college.stpaul
Grades: Sec. *Note:* Programme de formation générale; Programme d'éducation internationale.
Cathie Bouchard, Directrice générale
cbouchard@college-st-paul.qc.ca

Vaudreuil-Dorion: Académie Vaudrin
1255, Émile-Bouchard, Vaudreuil-Dorion, QC J7V 0B7
Tél: 514-600-4415; *Téléc:* 450-510-0927
info@academievaudrin.ca
www.academievaudrin.ca
Grades: Pre.-6 *Enrollment:* 100
Michelle Vaudrin, Direction, fondatrice et directrice pédagogique

Victoriaville: Collège Clarétain
663, rue Gamache, Victoriaville, QC G6R 0W3, Canada
Tél: 819-752-4571; *Téléc:* 819-752-4572
administration@collegeclaretain.com
www.collegeclaretain.com
Grades: Sec.; Pens. & Ext. *Note:* École privée mixte.
Éric Gardner, Directeur des services pédagogiques
Martin Bélanger, Directeur des services aux élèves

Waterville: Collège François-Delaplace
365, rue Compton est, Waterville, QC J0B 3H0, Canada
Tél: 819-837-2882; *Téléc:* 819-837-0625
Ligne sans frais: 844-688-2882
secretariat@moncfd.com
www.college-francois-delaplace.qc.ca
www.facebook.com/collegefrancoisdelaplace
www.youtube.com/user/moncfd
Grades: Sec.; filles *Note:* École Verte Brundtland; école secondaire privée pour filles (pensionnaires & externes).
André Ricard, Directeur général
aricard@moncfd.com

Westmount: Miss Edgar's & Miss Cramp's School (ECS)
525 av Mount Pleasant, Westmount, QC H3Y 3H6, Canada
Tel: 514-935-6357; *Fax:* 514-935-1099
info@ecs.qc.ca
www.ecs.qc.ca
www.facebook.com/207534389310982
twitter.com/EdgarCramp
www.instagram.com/edgarcramp
Grades: K-11; Girls; Eng. & Fr. *Enrollment:* 344 *Note:* University preparatory programme, to Gr. 11; French Immersion junior school; arts, athletics, math, sciences, languages, citizenship education; extended day programme; library.
Lauren Aslin, Acting Head of School
aslinl@ecs.qc.ca

Westmount: Selwyn House
École Selwyn House
95, ch Côte-St-Antoine, Westmount, QC H3Y 2H8, Canada
Tel: 514-931-9481; *Fax:* 514-931-6118
www.selwyn.ca
Other Information: Admissions: 514-931-2775
www.facebook.com/SelwynHouseSchool
twitter.com/SelwynHouseMTL
Grades: K-11; Eng.; Boys *Enrollment:* 540 *Number of
Employees:* 56 full-time; 13 part-time
Hal Hannaford, Headmaster
hhannaford@selwyn.ca
Mike Downey, Head, Senior School
downeym@selwyn.ca
Kathy Funamoto, Head, Elementary School
funamoto@selwyn.ca
Carol Manning, Head, Middle School
manningc@selwyn.ca
Matilde Codina, Chief Financial Officer
codina@selwyn.ca
Nathalie Gervais, Director, Admissions
gervaisn@selwyn.ca
Mike Maurovich, Director, Athletics
maurovich@selwyn.ca
James McMillan, Director, Advancement
mcmillan@selwyn.ca
Brenda Montgomery, Director, Academic Innovation & Growth
montgomery@selwyn.ca
Jean-Pierre Trudeau, Director, Technology
trudeaujp@selwyn.ca

Westmount: The Study
3233, The Boulevard, Westmount, QC H3Y 1S4, Canada
Tel: 514-935-9352
info@thestudy.qc.ca
www.thestudy.qc.ca
www.facebook.com/TheStudyMontreal
twitter.com/thestudyschool
www.youtube.com/thestudyschool
Grades: K./Elem./Sec.; Eng.; Girls *Note:* Bilingual (English &
French) learning environment. The school is the first in Québec
to introduce a Mandarin language program at the primary level.
Nancy Sweer, Head of School, 514-935-9352, ext. 228
nsweer@thestudy.qc.ca

Universities & Colleges

Universities

Gatineau: Université du Québec en Outaouais
Pavillon Alexandre-Taché
P.O. Box 1250 Hull
283, boul Alexandre-Taché, Gatineau, QC J8X 3X7, Canada
Tél: 819-595-3900; *Télec:* 819-595-3924
Ligne sans frais: 1-800-567-1283
questions@uqo.ca
www.uqo.ca
www.facebook.com/Universite.Quebec.Outaouais
twitter.com/uqo
www.linkedin.com/groups/3000070
www.youtube.com/uqovideo
Full Time Equivalency: 7240
Armel Didier Tella, Président

Campuses
Campus Saint-Jérôme
5, rue Saint-Joseph, Saint-Jérôme, QC J7Z 0B7, Canada
Tél: 450-530-7616; *Télec:* 450-530-2916
Ligne sans frais: 800-567-1283
uqo.st-jerome@uqo.ca
uqo.ca/saint-jerome

Montréal: Concordia University
Université Concordia
Sir George Williams Campus
**1455, boul de Maisonneuve ouest, Montréal, QC H3G 1M8,
Canada**
Tel: 514-848-2424
www.concordia.ca
www.facebook.com/ConcordiaUniversity
twitter.com/Concordia
www.linkedin.com/company/concordia-university
www.youtube.com/ConcordiaUni
Full Time Equivalency: 45056
Alan Shepard, President & Vice-Chancellor
Graham Carr, Provost & Vice-President, Academic Affairs
Marcel Dupuis, Interim Vice-President, Advancement & External
Relations
Roger Côté, Vice-President, Services
Christophe Guy, Vice-President, Research & Graduate Studies
Philippe Beauregard, Chief Communications Officer
Denis Cossette, Chief Financial Officer

Faculties
Arts & Science
**1550, boul de Maisonneuve ouest, GM 1040-5, Montréal, QC
H3G 1M8**
Tel: 514-848-2424
www.concordia.ca/artsci
www.facebook.com/FASConcordia
twitter.com/FASConcordia
André Roy, Dean, 514-848-2424, ext. 2080
dean.artsci@concordia.ca

Engineering & Computer Science
1455, boul de Maisonneuve ouest, Montréal, QC H3G 1M8
Tel: 514-848-2424
www.concordia.ca/encs
Amir Asif, Dean
amir.asif@concordia.ca

Fine Arts
1455, boul de Maisonneuve ouest, Montréal, QC H3G 1M8
Tel: 514-848-2424
www.concordia.ca/finearts
www.facebook.com/studyfinearts.concordia
twitter.com/CU_FineArts
www.instagram.com/fineartsconcordia
Rebecca Duclos, Dean
dean.finearts@concordia.ca

John Molson School of Business (JMSB)
P.O. Box 2002 H
1450, rue Guy, Montréal, QC H3G 2V4
Fax: 514-848-2816
gradprograms.jmsb@concordia.ca
www.concordia.ca/jmsb
Other Information: Main Office: 514-848-2424, ext. 2727
Enrollment: 9222
Anne-Marie Croteau, Dean

Schools
Continuing Education
1250, rue Guy, FB-117, Montréal, QC H3G 1M8
Tel: 514-848-3600; *Fax:* 514-848-2806
cce@concordia.ca
www.concordia.ca/cce
www.facebook.com/concordiacontinuingeducation
www.linkedin.com/showcase/concordia-continuing-education

School of Graduate Studies
**1550, boul de Maisonneuve ouest, GM 930.01, Montréal, QC
H3G 1M8**
Tel: 514-848-2424; *Fax:* 514-848-2812
www.concordia.ca/sgs
www.facebook.com/ConcordiaGraduateStudies
twitter.com/ConcordiaGrad
Paula Wood-Adams, Dean

Campuses
Loyola Campus
7141, rue Sherbrooke ouest, Montréal, QC H4B 1R6

Centres & Institutes
Concordia Institute for Canadian Jewish Studies
1590, Docteur Penfield, SB-215, Montréal, QC H3G 1C5
Tel: 514-848-2424; *Fax:* 514-848-4541
www.concordia.ca/artsci/research/jewish-studies
Ira Robinson, Chair
ira.robinson@concordia.ca

Institute for Co-operative Education
**#430, 1550, boul de Maisonneuve ouest, Montréal, QC H3G
1M8**
Tel: 514-848-2424; *Fax:* 514-848-2811
coopinstitute@concordia.ca
www.concordia.ca/academics/co-op
www.facebook.com/ConcordiaCoop
twitter.com/concordiacoop
www.linkedin.com/groups/3214761
Claude Martel, Director, 514-848-2424, ext. 3951
claude.martel@concordia.ca

Simone de Beauvoir Institute
2170, rue Bishop, Montréal, QC H3G 1M8
Tel: 514-848-2424
www.concordia.ca/artsci/sdbi
www.facebook.com/SimonedeBeauvoirInstitute

Montréal: École de technologie supérieure
1100, rue Notre-Dame ouest, Montréal, QC H3C 1K3, Canada
Tél: 514-396-8800; *Télec:* 514-396-8950
Ligne sans frais: 1-888-394-7888
admission@etsmtl.ca
www.etsmtl.ca
www.facebook.com/etsmtl
twitter.com/etsmtl
www.youtube.com/user/etsmtl
Full Time Equivalency: 8980

Pierre Dumouchel, Directeur général

Montréal: HEC Montréal
Également connu sous le nom de: École des Hautes
Études Commerciales
Université de Montréal
**3000, ch de la Côte-Sainte-Catherine, Montréal, QC H3T 2A7,
Canada**
Tél: 514-340-6000; *Télec:* 514-340-6411
www.hec.ca
www.facebook.com/hecmontreal
twitter.com/HEC_Montreal
www.linkedin.com/company/hec-montreal
www.youtube.com/HECMontreal
Full Time Equivalency: 12000 *Note:* HEC Montréal est la
première école de gestion au Canada. Affaires internationales;
finance; gestion des opérations/logistique; gestion des
ressources humaines; management; marketing; méthodes
quantitatives de gestion; sciences comptables; technologies de
l'information; économie appliquée.
Michel Patry, Directeur

Montréal: McGill University
845, rue Sherbrooke ouest, Montréal, QC H3A 0G4
Tél: 514-398-4455
info.communications@mcgill.ca
www.mcgill.ca
www.facebook.com/McGillUniversity
twitter.com/mcgillu
www.linkedin.com/company/mcgill-university
www.instagram.com/mcgillu
Full Time Equivalency: 40153
Hon. Michael A. Meighen, Chancellor
Suzanne Fortier, Principal & Vice-Chancellor
suzanne.fortier@mcgill.ca
Christopher Manfredi, Provost & Vice-Principal, Academic
christopher.manfredi@mcgill.ca
Louis Arseneault, Vice-Principal, Communications & External
Relations
louis.arseneault@mcgill.ca
Yves Beauchamp, Vice-Principal, Administration & Finance
yves.beauchamp@mcgill.ca
Martha Crago, Vice-Principal, Research & Innovation
martha.crago@mcgill.ca
Marc Weinstein, Vice-Principal, University Advancement
marc.weinstein@mcgill.ca
Edyta Rogowska, Secretary-General
edyta.rogowska@mcgill.ca

Faculties
Agricultural & Environmental Sciences
Macdonald Stewart Bldg.
**21111, ch Lakeshore, #MS2-022A, Sainte-Anne-de-Bellevue,
QC H9X 3V9**
Tel: 514-398-7773
info.macdonald@mcgill.ca
www.mcgill.ca/macdonald
www.facebook.com/McGillMacCampus
tw·tter.com/McGillMacCampus
www.youtube.com/mcgilluniversity
Anja Geitmann, Dean
anja.geitmann@mcgill.ca

Faculty of Arts
Dawson Hall
853, rue Sherbrooke ouest, Montréal, QC H3A 0G5
Tel: 514-398-4212
www.mcgill.ca/arts
www.facebook.com/mcgillarts
twitter.com/mcgillarts
www.linkedin.com/school/mcgill-arts
www.instagram.com/mcgillarts
Enrollment: 9000 *Number of Employees:* 300 Faculty
Antonia Maioni, Dean, 514-398-4212

Faculty of Dentistry
#500, 2001, av McGill College, Montréal, QC H3A 1G1
Tel: 514-398-7203; *Fax:* 514-398-8900
undergrad.dentistry@mcgill.ca
www.mcgill.ca/dentistry
www.facebook.com/mcgilldentistry
twitter.com/DentistryMcGill
Elham Emami, Dean

Faculty of Education
3700, rue McTavish, Montréal, QC H3A 1Y2
Tel: 514-398-7042; *Fax:* 514-398-4679
isa.education@mcgill.ca
www.mcgill.ca/education
www.facebook.com/Mcgillfacultyofeducation
twitter.com/edumcgill
Dilson Rassier, Dean, 514-398-7037
dilson.rassier@mcgill.ca

Institut national de la recherche scientifique (INRS)
490, rue de la Couronne, Québec, QC G1K 9A9
Tél: 418-654-4677; Télec: 418-654-3876
Ligne sans frais: 877-326-5762
communications@inrs.ca
www.inrs.ca
www.facebook.com/UniversiteINRS
twitter.com/U_INRS
www.youtube.com/user/MyINRS
Full Time Equivalency: 600

Université TÉLUQ
455, rue du Parvis, Québec, QC G1K 9H6
Tél: 418-657-3695; Ligne sans frais: 888-843-4333
www.teluq.ca
www.facebook.com/universiteteluq
twitter.com/teluq
André G. Roy, Directeur général par intérim

Université TÉLUQ (Montréal)
#1105, 5800, rue Saint-Denis, Montréal, QC H2S 3L5
Tél: 514-843-2015

Québec: Université Laval
2325, rue de l'Université, Québec, QC G1V 0A6, Canada
Tél: 418-656-2131; Ligne sans frais: 1-877-785-2825
renseignements@ulaval.ca
www.ulaval.ca
www.facebook.com/ulaval
www.linkedin.com/company/universite-laval
twitter.com/universitelaval
www.youtube.com/ulavaltv
Full Time Equivalency: 44000 Note: Première université francophone d'Amérique, ouverte sur le monde et animée d'une culture de l'exigence, l'Université Laval contribue au développement de la société par la formation de personnes compétentes, responsables et promotrice de changement, par l'avancement et le partage des connaissances, dans un environnement dynamique de recherche et de création.

Campuses
Direction des Communications
Pavillon Maurice-Pollack
2305, rue de l'Université, Québec, QC G1V 0A6
Tel: 418-656-7266; Fax: 418-656-3087
dc@dc.ulaval.ca
www.dc.ulaval.ca

Jacques Villemure, Directeur
jacques.villemure@dc.ulaval.ca

Centre de recherche sur le cancer (CRC)
9, rue McMahon, Québec, QC G1R 3S3
Tél: 418-525-4444; Télec: 418-691-5439
secretaire@crc.ulaval.ca
www.crc.ulaval.ca

Luc Beaulieu, Directeur

Centre de recherche du CHU de Québec
2705, boul Laurier, Québec, QC G1V 4G2
Tél: 418-654-2296; Télec: 418-654-2298
sec_drs@crchudequebec.ulaval.ca
www.crchudequebec.ulaval.ca
www.facebook.com/crchuqc
twitter.com/crchuqc
www.linkedin.com/company/crchuq
www.youtube.com/user/chudequebec

Serge Rivest, Directeur

Rimouski: Université du Québec à Rimouski
P.O. Box 3300 A
300, allée des Ursulines, Rimouski, QC G5L 3A1, Canada
Tél: 418-723-1986; Télec: 418-724-1525
Ligne sans frais: 1-800-511-3382
uqar@uqar.ca
www.uqar.ca
www.facebook.com/accueil.uqar
twitter.com/UQAR
Full Time Equivalency: 7269
Jean-Pierre Ouellet, Recteur

Campuses
Campus de Lévis
1595, boul Alphonse-Desjardins, Lévis, QC G6V 0A6, Canada
Tél: 418-833-8800; Télec: 418-833-1113
Ligne sans frais: 1-800-463-4712

Rouyn-Noranda: Université du Québec en Abitibi-Témiscamingue (UQAT)
445, boul de l'Université, Rouyn-Noranda, QC J9X 5E4, Canada
Tél: 819-762-0971; Télec: 819-797-4727
information@uqat.ca
www.uqat.ca
www.facebook.com/uqat
twitter.com/UQAT
www.linkedin.com/company/uqat
www.youtube.com/uqatinformation
Denis Martel, Recteur

Sherbrooke: Université Bishop's
Bishop's University
2600, rue College, Sherbrooke, QC J1M 1Z7, Canada
Tel: 819-822-9600; Fax: 819-822-9661
admissions@ubishops.ca
www.ubishops.ca
www.facebook.com/ubishops
www.linkedin.com/school/bishop's-university
www.youtube.com/user/bishopsuniversity
Full Time Equivalency: 2400
Brian Levitt, Chancellor
Michael Goldbloom, Principal & Vice-Chancellor
Denise Lauzière, Chief of Staff

Faculties
Arts & Science
2600, rue College, Sherbrooke, QC J1M 1Z7
Tel: 819-822-9600; Fax: 819-822-9661
www.ubishops.ca/academic-programs/faculty-of-arts-and-science
Michele Murray, Dean
michele.murray@ubishops.ca

Continuing Education
2600, rue College, Sherbrooke, QC J1M 1Z7
Tel: 819-822-9670; Fax: 819-822-9700
Toll-Free: 877-822-8900
contedu@ubishops.ca
www.ubishops.ca/academic-programs/continuing-education
Kathryn Standish, Coordinator, 819-822-9600, ext. 2254
kathryn.standish@ubishops.ca

Schools
Williams School of Business
2600, rue College, Sherbrooke, QC J1M 1Z7
Tel: 819-822-9600; Fax: 819-822-9661
www.ubishops.ca/academic-programs/williams-school-of-business
www.facebook.com/yourwsb
Francine Turmel, Dean, 819-822-9600, ext. 2622
francine.turmel@ubishops.ca

School of Education
2600, rue College, Sherbrooke, QC J1M 1Z7
Tel: 819-822-9600; Fax: 819-822-9661
gse@ubishops.ca
www.ubishops.ca/academic-programs/school-of-education
Corinne Haigh, Dean, 819-822-9600, ext. 2401
corinne.haigh@ubishops.ca

Sherbrooke: Université de Sherbrooke
2500, boul de l'Université, Sherbrooke, QC J1K 2R1, Canada
Tél: 819-821-8000
www.usherbrooke.ca
www.facebook.com/USherbrooke
twitter.com/usherbrooke
www.youtube.com/USherbrookeTV
Full Time Equivalency: 24610
Pierre Cossette, Recteur
Vincent Aimez, Vice-recteur à la valorisation et aux partenariats
Jocelyne Faucher, Vice-rectrice à la vie étudiante et secrétaire générale
Jean Goulet, Vice-recteur aux ressources humaines
Christine Hudon, Vice-rectrice aux études
Jean-Pierre Perreault, Vice-recteur à la recherche et aux études supérieures
Denyse Rémillard, Vice-rectrice à l'administration et au développement durable

Centres & Institutes
Centre d'imagerie moléculaire de Sherbrooke (CIMS)
3001, 12e av nord, Sherbrooke, QC J1H 5N4
Tél: 819-346-1110; Télec: 819-829-3238
www.cims.med.usherbrooke.ca
Roger Lecomte, Directeur scientifique
Martin Lepage, Responsable scientifique de l'IRM CIMS

Centre de recherche interuniversitaire sur le français en usage au Québec (CRIFUQ)
2500, boul de l'Université, Sherbrooke, QC J1K 2R1
www.usherbrooke.ca/crifuq

Wim Remysen, Directeur, 819-821-8000, ext. 65520
wim.remysen@usherbrooke.ca

Centre de recherche sur l'enseignement et l'apprentissage des sciences (CREAS)
Faculté d'éducation
2500, boul de l'Université, #A7-350, Sherbrooke, QC J1K 2R1
Tél: 819-821-8000; Télec: 819-820-7009
www.usherbrooke.ca/creas
Mathieu Gagnon, Directeur
mathieu.gagnon3@usherbrooke.ca

Centre d'applications et de recherches en télédétection (CARTEL)
2500, boul de l'Université, Sherbrooke, QC J1K 2R1
Tél: 819-821-7180; Télec: 819-821-7944
Kalifa Goita, Directeur, 819-821-8000, ext. 62212
kalifa.goita@usherbrooke.ca

Centre de recherche en amélioration végétale
Également connu sous le nom de: Centre SEVE
Faculté des sciences, Département de biologie
2500, boul de l'Université, Sherbrooke, QC J1K 2R1
Tél: 819-821-8000; Télec: 819-821-8049
info@centreseve.org
www.centreseve.org
Anne-Marie Simao-Beaunin, Adjointe administrative, 819-821-8000, ext. 62001
a-m.simao@usherbrooke.ca

Trois-Rivières: Université du Québec à Trois-Rivières (UQTR)
P.O. Box 500
3351, boul des Forges, Trois-Rivières, QC G8Z 4M3, Canada
Tél: 819-376-5011; Télec: 819-376-5210
Ligne sans frais: 800-365-0922
communications@uqtr.ca
www.uqtr.ca
www.facebook.com/uqtr
twitter.com/UQTR
www.youtube.com/user/camerauqtr
Full Time Equivalency: 14500 Number of Employees: 1780
Daniel McMahon, Recteur
daniel.mcmahon@uqtr.ca

Colleges

La Pocatière: Institut de technologie agroalimentaire
Campus de La Pocatière
401, rue Poiré, La Pocatière, QC G0R 1Z0, Canada
Tél: 418-856-1110; Télec: 418-856-1719
ita@mapaq.gouv.qc.ca
www.ita.qc.ca
www.facebook.com/Institut.technologie.agroalimentaire.ITA
www.youtube.com/user/itamedias
Full Time Equivalency: 1000 Note: Spécialisé en agroalimentaire; Campus de Saint-Hyacinthe: 3230, rue Sicotte, (450) 778-6504; Collège Macdonald, Univ. McGill.
Carole Desrosiers, Directrice des services administratifs
Chantal Vallée, Directrice des études (intérim)

Campuses
Campus de Saint-Hyacinthe
3230, rue Sicotte, Saint-Hyacinthe, QC J2S 2M2, Canada
Tél: 450-778-6504; Fax: 450-778-6536
www.ita.qc.ca

Montréal: Institut de tourisme et d'hôtellerie du Québec (IHTQ)
3535, rue Saint-Denis, Montréal, QC H2X 3P1
Tél: 514-282-5111; Télec: 514-282-5126
Ligne sans frais: 800-361-5111
ecole@ithq.qc.ca
www.ithq.qc.ca
www.facebook.com/ITHQofficiel
twitter.com/ithqofficiel
www.linkedin.com/school/ithqofficiel
www.youtube.com/c/IthqQcCaecole
Grades: Sec., Préuniv., Univ., Form. cont.
Liza Frulla, Directrice générale

Montréal: The Montreal Diocesan Theological College
3475, rue University, Montréal, QC H3A 2A8
Tel: 514-849-3004; Fax: 514-849-4113
info@montrealdio.ca
montrealdio.ca
www.facebook.com/MontrealDio
twitter.com/montrealdio

Montréal: Polytechnique Montréal
Montreal Polytechnic
2500, ch de Polytechnique, Montréal, QC H3T 1J4
Tél: 514-340-4711
www.polymtl.ca
www.facebook.com/polymtl
twitter.com/polymtl
www.linkedin.com/school/polytechnique-montreal
www.youtube.com/user/polymtlvideos
Full Time Equivalency: 8600 *Note:* Fondée en 1873, le Polytechnique est une école d'ingénierie de classes internationale; programmes au baccalauréat, cycles supérieures, formation continue; recherche. Adresse postale: CP 6079, succ Centre-ville, Montréal, QC H3C 3A7.

Québec: Direction générale du Conservatoire de musique et d'art dramatique du Québec
225, Grande Allée est, Bloc C, 3e étage, Québec, QC G1R 5G5
Tél: 418-380-2327; *Téléc:* 418-380-2328
info@conservatoire.gouv.qc.ca
www.conservatoire.gouv.qc.ca
www.facebook.com/CMADQ
www.youtube.com/user/ConservatoireQc
Chantal Garon, Directrice générale, 418-380-2327, ext. 6327
Jean-François Latour, Directeur, Études, 418-380-2327, ext. 7276

Campuses
Conservatoire de musique de Saguenay
202, rue Jacques-Cartier est, Chicoutimi, QC G7H 6R8
Tél: 418-698-3505; *Fax:* 418-698-3521
cms@conservatoire.gouv.qc.ca
Louise Bouchard, Directrice
louise.bouchard@conservatoire.gouv.qc.ca

Conservatoire de musique de Gatineau
430, boul Alexandre-Taché, Gatineau, QC J9A 1M7
Tel: 819-772-3283; *Fax:* 819-772-3346
cmg@conservatoire.gouv.qc.ca
Marc Langis, Directeur
marc.langis@conservatoire.gouv.qc.ca

Conservatoire de musique de Montréal
4750, av Henri-Julien, 1e étage, Montréal, QC H2T 2C8
Tel: 514-873-4031; *Fax:* 514-873-4601
cmm@conservatoire.gouv.qc.ca
Manon Lafrance, Directrice
manon.lafrance@conservatoire.gouv.qc.ca

Conservatoire de musique de Québec
270, rue Jacques-Parizeau, Québec, QC G1R 5G1
Tel: 418-643-2190; *Fax:* 418-644-9658
cmq@conservatoire.gouv.qc.ca
Louis Dallaire, Directeur
louis.dallaire@conservatoire.gouv.qc.ca

Conservatoire de musique de Rimouski
22, rue Sainte-Marie, Rimouski, QC G5L 4E2
Tel: 418-727-3706; *Fax:* 418-727-3818
cmr@conservatoire.gouv.qc.ca
Annie Vanasse, Directrice
annie.vanasse@conservatoire.gouv.qc.ca

Conservatoire de musique de Trois-Rivières
587, rue Radisson, Trois-Rivières, QC G9A 2C8
Tel: 819-371-6748
cmtr@conservatoire.gouv.qc.ca
Eve Martin, Directrice
eve.martin@conservatoire.gouv.qc.ca

Conservatoire de musique de Val-d'Or
88, rue Allard, Val-d'Or, QC J9P 2Y1
Tel: 819-354-4585; *Fax:* 819-354-4297
cmvd@conservatoire.gouv.qc.ca
Isabelle Trottier, Directrice
isabelle.trottier@conservatoire.gouv.qc.ca

Conservatoire d'art dramatique de Montréal
4750, av Henri-Julien, 1e étage, Montréal, QC H2T 2C8
Tel: 514-873-4283; *Fax:* 514-864-2771
cadm@conservatoire.gouv.qc.ca
Benoît Dagenais, Directeur
benoit.dagenais@conservatoire.gouv.qc.ca

Conservatoire d'art dramatique de Québec
31, rue Mont-Carmel, Québec, QC G1R 4A6
Tel: 418-643-2139; *Fax:* 418-646-9255
cadq@conservatoire.gouv.qc.ca
Jacques Leblanc, Directeur
jacques.leblanc@conservatoire.gouv.qc.ca

Cégep

Lévis: Collège de Lévis
9, rue Monseigneur Gosselin, Lévis, QC G6V 5K1
Tél: 418-833-1249
info@collegedelevis.qc.ca
www.collegedelevis.qc.ca
www.facebook.com/collegedelevis
Grades: Sec.
David Lehoux, Directeur général
dlehoux@collegedelevis.qc.ca
Caroline Sirois, Directrice, Services éducatifs
csirois@collegedelevis.qc.ca

Montréal: Collège Jean-de-Brébeuf inc.
3200, ch Côte Ste-Catherine, Montréal, QC H3T 1C1
Tél: 514-342-9342
diradm@brebeuf.qc.ca
www.brebeuf.qc.ca
www.facebook.com/collegebrebeuf
www.linkedin.com/school/college-jean-de-brebeuf
www.youtube.com/user/collegejeandebrebeuf
Grades: Sec., Collégial
Luc Thifault, Directeur générale

Saint-Laurent: Vanier College
821, av Ste-Croix, Saint-Laurent, QC H4L 3X9
Tel: 514-744-7500; *Fax:* 514-744-7505
Toll-Free: 855-744-7500
info@vaniercollege.qc.ca
www.vaniercollege.qc.ca
www.facebook.com/vaniercollege
twitter.com/vaniercollege
www.linkedin.com/school/vanier-college
www.youtube.com/c/VanierCollegeTelevision
Full Time Equivalency: 6500 *Note:* The College is an English Cégep.
Normand W. Bernier, Director General
dg@vaniercollege.qc.ca
Danielle Lafille, Academic Dean
academicdean@vaniercollege.qc.ca

Faculties
Faculty of Arts, Business & Social Sciences
Alena Perout, Faculty Dean
perouta@vaniercollege.qc.ca

Faculty of General Education
www.vaniercollege.qc.ca/general-studies
Kelly Purdy, Faculty Dean
purdyk@vaniercollege.qc.ca

Faculty of Science & Technology
Haritos Kavallos, Faculty Dean
kavalloh@vaniercollege.qc.ca

Post Secondary/Technical

Drummondville: Collège Ellis
Campus de Drummondville
235, rue Moisan, Drummondville, QC J2C 1W9, Canada
Tél: 819-477-3113; *Téléc:* 819-477-4556
Ligne sans frais: 800-869-3113
www.ellis.qc.ca
www.facebook.com/lecollegeellis
www.youtube.com/user/collegeellis
Alain Scalzo, Directeur général

Campuses
Campus de Longueuil
#2060, 150, place Charles-Le Moyne, Longueuil, QC J4K 0A8, Canada
Tél: 450-463-1500
www.ellis.qc.ca

Campus de Trois-Rivières
90, rue Dorval, Trois-Rivières, QC G8T 5X7, Canada
Tél: 819-691-2600; *Téléc:* 819-691-3407
Ligne sans frais: 877-691-9800
www.ellis.qc.ca

Montréal: Collège André-Grasset
1001, boul Crémazie est, Montréal, QC H2M 1M3
Tél: 514-381-4293; *Téléc:* 514-381-7421
communications@grasset.qc.ca
www.grasset.qc.ca
www.facebook.com/CollegeAndreGrasset
www.linkedin.com/school/coll-ge-andr—grasset
Enrollment: 1000
Patrick Caron, Directeur général

Montréal: Collège d'enseignement en immobilier
Également connu sous le nom de: Collège CEI
#104, 405, av Ogilvy, Montréal, QC H3M 1M3
Tél: 514-905-1551; *Téléc:* 514-904-1453
Ligne sans frais: 866-905-1551
info@collegecei.com
www.college-cei.com
www.facebook.com/CollegeCEI
www.linkedin.com/company/collège-cei
Yves Tanguay, Directeur général

Montréal: Collège de photographie Marsan
Également connu sous le nom de: Collège Marsan / Marsan College
3536, boul St-Laurent, Montréal, QC H2X 2V1
Tél: 514-525-3030
info@collegemarsan.qc.ca
collegemarsan.qc.ca
www.facebook.com/CollegeMarsan
www.instagram.com/collegemarsan
Sophie Gilbert, Directrice

Montréal: Collège Jean-de-Brébeuf
3200, ch de la côte Ste-Catherine, Montréal, QC H3T 1C1
Tél: 514-342-9342
www.brebeuf.qc.ca
www.facebook.com/collegebrebeuf
www.youtube.com/user/collegejeandebrebeuf
Luc Thifault, Directeur général
dirgen@brebeuf.qc.ca
Nicole Gagné, Directrice, Ressources financières
dirfin@brebeuf.qc.ca
Huguette Maisonneuve, Directrice, Études
diretu.collegial@brebeuf.qc.ca

Montréal: Collège LaSalle
Lasalle College
2000, rue Sainte-Catherine ouest, Montréal, QC H3H 2T3
Tél: 514-939-2006; *Téléc:* 514-939-2015
Ligne sans frais: 800-363-3541
admission@collegelasalle.com
www.collegelasalle.com
www.facebook.com/collegelasalle
twitter.com/LaSalleCollege
www.youtube.com/c/LaSalleCollegeMontreal
Enrollment: 17000
Myrianne Collin, Directrice générale

Montréal: Collège Salette
3536, boul Saint-Laurent, Montréal, QC H2X 2V1
Tél: 514-388-5725; *Téléc:* 514-388-5957
info@collegesalette.com
collegesalette.com
www.facebook.com/CollegeSaletteMTL
Note: Design graphique, en design web et en illustration publicitaire.

Montréal: Collège Techniques de Montréal
#150, 8255, Mountain Sights, Montréal, QC H4P 2B5
Tél: 514-932-6444; *Téléc:* 514-932-6448
info@mtccollege.com
www.mtccollege.com

Montréal: École de Danse Contemporaine de Montréal
Édifice Wilder-Espace Danse
#600, 1435, rue De Bleury, Montréal, QC H3A 2H7
Tél: 514-866-9814; *Téléc:* 514-866-5887
info@edcm.ca
www.edcm.ca
www.facebook.com/EcoleDeDanseContemporaineDeMontreal
www.linkedin.com/company/école-de-danse-contemporaine-de-montréal
www.youtube.com/user/EcoledanseMTL
Yves Rocray, Directeur général

Montréal: École de Musique Vincent d'Indy
628, ch Côte-Sainte-Catherine, Montréal, QC H2V 2C5
Tél: 514-735-5261; *Téléc:* 514-735-5266
info@emvi.qc.ca
www.emvi.qc.ca
www.facebook.com/EcoleEMVI
www.linkedin.com/school/école-de-musique-vincent-d'indy
www.youtube.com/user/EMVImusique
Yves Petit, Directeur général

Montréal: École du Show-Business (ÉSB)
#300, 205, av Viger ouest, Montréal, QC H2Z 1G2
Tél: 514-316-0220
info@ecoledushowbusiness.com
www.ecoledushowbusiness.com
www.facebook.com/EcoleShowBusiness
Note: Formation aux différents métiers des arts de la scène.

Montréal: École nationale de cirque
National Circus School
8181, av du Cirque, Montréal, QC H1Z 4N9
Tél: 514-982-0859; *Téléc:* 514-982-6025
Ligne sans frais: 800-267-0859
info@enc.qc.ca
www.ecolenationaledecirque.ca
www.facebook.com/ecolenationaledecirque
twitter.com/enc_ecodecirque
www.linkedin.com/school/-cole-nationale-de-cirque
www.youtube.com/c/Écolenationaledecirque
Eric Langlois, Directeur général
directiongenerale@enc.qc.ca
Daniela Arendasova, Directrice, Études
darendasova@enc.qc.ca

Montréal: École nationale de l'humour
2120, rue Sherbrooke est, 7e étage, Montréal, QC H2K 1C3
Tél: 514-849-7876; *Téléc:* 514-849-3307
humour@enh.qc.ca
enh.qc.ca
www.facebook.com/ecolehumour
twitter.com/ecolehumour
www.youtube.com/c/Écolenationaledelhumour
Note: Formation professionnelle aux humoristes & aux auteurs.
Reconnue par le Min. de l'Éducation, du Loisir & du Sport du Québec.
Louise Richer, Directrice générale, 514-849-7876, ext. 222
lricher@enh.qc.ca

Montréal: École supérieure de ballet du Québec
4816, rue Rivard, Montréal, QC H2J 2N6
Tél: 514-849-4929
info@esbq.ca
www.esbq.ca
www.facebook.com/ecolesuperieuredeballetduquebec
Anik Bissonnette, Directrice artistique
Alix Laurent, Directeur général

Montréal: Institut supérieur d'informatique (ISI)
2100, boul de Maisonneuve est, Montréal, QC H2K 4S1
Tél: 514-842-2426
info@isi-mtl.com
isi-mtl.com
www.facebook.com/isimtl
Note: Propose des programmes spécialisés en informatique

Montréal: Institut Teccart
3030, rue Hochelaga, Montréal, QC H1W 1G2
Tél: 514-526-2501; *Téléc:* 514-526-9192
Ligne sans frais: 866-832-2278
teccart.qc.ca
Note: Collège privé subventionné qui offre des programmes en formation technique.

Campuses
Campus Brossard
7305, rue Marie-Victorin, Brossard, QC J4W 1A6
Tél: 514-875-9777; *Téléc:* 450-671-5928
Ligne sans frais: 800-268-9777

Campus Longueuil
4405, rue Leckie, Saint-Hubert, QC J3Y 9E6
Tél: 514-875-9777; *Téléc:* 450-671-5928
Ligne sans frais: 800-268-9777

Montréal: The International College of Spiritual & Psychic Sciences
P.O. Box 1387 H
Montréal, QC H3G 2N3
Tél: 514-937-8359; *Téléc:* 514-937-5380
info@iiihs.org
www.iiihs.org
Marilyn Zwaig Rossner, Ph.D., Dean
mrossner@iiihs.org

Montréal: National Theatre School of Canada (NTS)
École nationale de théâtre du Canada
5030, rue St-Denis, Montréal, QC H2J 2L8
Tel: 514-842-7954; *Fax:* 514-842-5661
Toll-Free: 866-547-7328
info@ent-nts.ca
ent-nts.qc.ca
www.facebook.com/entnts.montreal
twitter.com/ntsofcanada
www.youtube.com/user/ENTNTSMontreal
Enrollment: 160 *Number of Employees:* 25 *Note:* Offers training in acting, playwriting, directing, set & costume design & technical production in both English & French.
Gideon Arthurs, Chief Executive Officer
Michel Rafie, Director, Communications & Marketing
michelrafie@ent-nts.ca

Montréal: Trebas Institute
Institut Trebas
#600, 550, rue Sherbrooke ouest, Montréal, QC H3A 1B9
Tel: 514-845-4141; *Fax:* 514-845-2581
www.trebas.com
www.linkedin.com/company/trebas-institute
www.youtube.com/user/trebastube
Enrollment: 300
Luisa Tanzi, Président

Campuses
Toronto
#300, 543 Yonge St., Toronto, ON M4Y 1Y5
Tel: 416-966-3066; *Fax:* 416-966-0030
twitter.com/trebastoronto
Note: Audio Engineering & Production/DJ Arts, Entertainment Management, Film/Television Production
Sat Balraj, Director

Québec: Collège Mérici
755, Grande Allée ouest, Québec, QC G1S 1C1
Tél: 418-683-1591; *Téléc:* 418-682-8938
Ligne sans frais: 800-208-1463
information@merici.ca
www.merici.ca
www.facebook.com/Mericicollegialprive
www.youtube.com/user/LeCollegeMerici
Nicole Bilodeau, Directrice générale

Québec: Collège Radio Télévision de Québec Inc.
751, côte d'Abraham, Québec, QC G1R 1A2
Tél: 418-647-2095; *Téléc:* 418-522-5456
Ligne sans frais: 877-647-2095
info@crtq.net
www.crtq.net
www.facebook.com/115152496860

Québec: L'École de danse de Québec
Centre de production artistique et culturelle Aly
#214, 310, boul Langelier, Québec, QC G1K 5N3
Tél: 418-649-4715
info@ledq.qc.ca
ledq.qc.ca
www.facebook.com/ledq.qc.ca
www.youtube.com/c/LÉcolededansedeQuébec
Esther Carré, Directrice générale

Saint-Hubert: Académie de l'Entrepreneurship
#104, 4660, Montée St-Hubert, Saint-Hubert, QC J3Y 1V1
Tél: 450-676-5826; *Téléc:* 450-676-2261
Ligne sans frais: 888-676-5826
info@academie.ent.com
www.facebook.com/academieentrepreneurship
twitter.com/aeqinc
www.linkedin.com/company/académie-de-l'entrepreneurship

Campuses
2e Campus
#350, 1001, rue Sherbrooke est, Montréal, QC H2L 1L3
Tél: 514-360-7179

Trois-Rivières: Collège Laflèche
1687, boul du Carmel, Trois-Rivières, QC G8Z 3R8
Tél: 819-375-7346; *Téléc:* 819-375-7347
Ligne sans frais: 800-663-8105
college@clafleche.qc.ca
www.clafleche.qc.ca
www.facebook.com/CollegeLafleche
www.youtube.com/user/webmestrelafleche
Note: Le seul établissement collégial privé en Mauricie et au Centre-du-Québec à offrir à la fois des programmes préuniversitaires et techniques.
Luc Pellerin, Directeur général

Verdun: Collège de l'immobilier du Québec
600, ch du Golf, Verdun, QC H3E 1A8
Tél: 514-762-1862; *Téléc:* 514-762-4975
Ligne sans frais: 888-762-1862
info@collegeimmobilier.com
www.collegeimmobilier.com
www.facebook.com/collegeimmobilier
www.linkedin.com/company/coll-ge-de-l'immobilier-du-qu-bec
Sonia Béliveau, Directrice générale
sbeliveau@collegeimmobilier.com

Campuses
Campus de la Rive-Sud
#527, 6300, av Auteuil, Brossard, QC J4Z 3P2
Ligne sans frais: 888-762-1862

Campus Laval
#208, 3224 av Jean-Béraud, Laval, QC H7T 2S4
Ligne sans frais: 888-762-1862

Westmount: International Career School Canada
ICS Canada
#610, 245 Victoria Ave., Westmount, QC H3Z 2M6
Tel: 514-482-6951; *Fax:* 514-482-3868
Toll-Free: 888-427-2400
info@icslearn.ca
www.icslearn.ca
Note: At-home training in 50 career fields.
Frank Britt, Chief Executive Officer

Westmount: Marianopolis College
4873, av Westmount, Westmount, QC H3Y 1K9
Tel: 514-931-8792; *Fax:* 514-931-8790
info@marianopolis.edu
www.marianopolis.edu
www.facebook.com/marianopolis
twitter.com/MarianopolisEdu
www.youtube.com/user/bemarianopolis
Enrollment: 2000
Christian Corno, Director General
c.corno@marianopolis.edu

Saskatchewan

Government Agencies

Regina: Saskatchewan Ministry of Advanced Education
2010 12th Ave., Regina, SK S4P 0M3, Canada
Tel: 306-787-9478
inquiry4@gov.sk.ca
www.saskatchewan.ca
Hon. Gene Makowsky, Minister, 306-787-0341
minister.ae@gov.sk.ca

Regina: Saskatchewan Ministry of Education
2220 College Ave., 5th Fl., Regina, SK S4P 4V9, Canada
Tel: 306-787-9894; *Fax:* 306-798-2045
learning.inquiry@gov.sk.ca
www.saskatchewan.ca
Hon. Dustin Duncan, Minister, 306-787-7360
minister.edu@gov.sk.ca

School Boards/Districts/Divisions

Public

Creighton: Creighton School Division #111
325 Main St., Creighton, SK S0P 0A0
Tel: 306-688-5138; *Fax:* 306-688-3131
creightonschooldivision.com
Raymond Biberdorf, Chair
raybiberdorf@creightonschool.com
Vincent Cable, Director, Education
vcable@creightonschool.com

Humboldt: Horizon School Division No. 205
Also known as: Horizon School Division
P.O. Box 40
10366 - 8th Ave., Humboldt, SK S0K 2A0
Tel: 306-682-2558; *Fax:* 306-682-5154
Toll-Free: 866-963-2558
horizon@horizcnsd.ca
www.horizcnsd.ca
twitter.com/horizonsd205
www.instagram.com/horizonsd205
Number of Schools: 42 *Grades:* K.-12 *Enrollment:* 6343
Kevin C. Garinger, Director, Education & CEO, 306-682-8539
Randolph J. MacLean, Deputy Director, Education; Human Resources, 306-682-8638
Sarah Reding, Superintendent, Finance Services, 306-682-8631
Justin Arendt, Superintendent, Operational Services, 306-682-8611
Jim Hack, Chair, Board
Katherine Oviatt, Supervisor, Literacy & Early Learning Services, 306-682-8644
Darrell Paproski, Superintendent, Student Services, 306-682-8607

Ile-a-la-Crosse: Ile a la Crosse School Division #112
P.O. Box 89
Ile-a-la-Crosse, SK S0M 1C0
Tel: 306-833-2141; *Fax:* 306-833-2104
rossignolschools.com
twitter.com/ csd112
Number of Schools: 1 elementary school; 1 high school *Grades:* Pre - 12; adult education
Brenda Green, Director, Education
bgreen@icsd.ca
Jansen Corrigal, Secretary Treasurer
jcorrigal@icsd.ca

La Ronge: Northern Lights School Division #113
P.O. Box 6500
La Ronge, SK S0J 1L0
Tel: 306-425-3302; *Fax:* 306-425-3377
centraloffice@nlsd113.net
www.nlsd113.com
Other Information: Beauval Sub-Office: 306-288-2310;
suboffice@nlsd113.net
www.facebook.com/NLSD113
twitter.com/NLSD113

Number of Schools: 22 *Grades:* K-12
Richard Laliberte, Chair
Tom Harrington, Secretary-Treasurer
tomharrington@nlsd113.ca
Shahid Khawaja, Manager, Finance
shahidkhawaja@nlsd113.ca

Meadow Lake: Northwest School Division #203
525 - 5th St. West, Meadow Lake, SK S9X 1B4
Tel: 306-236-5614; *Fax:* 306-236-3922
office@nwsd.ca
www.nwsd.ca
www.facebook.com/NWSD203
twitter.com/northwestsd203
Number of Schools: 24 *Grades:* K - 12 *Enrollment:* 4600
Glen Winkler, Chair
glen.winkler@nwsd.ca

Melfort: North East School Division #200
P.O. Box 6000
402 Main St., Melfort, SK S0E 1A0
Tel: 306-752-5741; *Fax:* 306-752-1933
Toll-Free: 888-752-5741
divisionoffice@nesd.ca
www.nesd.ca
twitter.com/NESD200
Number of Schools: 21 *Grades:* Pre-K - 12 *Enrollment:* 5000
Marla Walton, Chair
Don Rempel, Director, Education
Eric Hufnagel, Superintendent, Student Services
Stacy Lair, Superintendent, School Services
Wanda McLeod, Superintendent, Business Administration
Heather Shwetz, Superintendent, Human Resources

Moose Jaw: Holy Trinity Roman Catholic Separate School Division #22
P.O. Box 1087
445 - 13th Ave. NE, Moose Jaw, SK S6H 6P9
Tel: 306-694-5333; *Fax:* 306-692-2238
contact@htcsd.ca
www.htcsd.ca
twitter.com/HolyTrinitySD
Number of Schools: 9 *Grades:* JK - 12 *Enrollment:* 2400
Sean Chase, Director, Education, 306-691-2400
sean.chase@htcsd.ca
Curt Van Parys, Chief Financial Officer, 306-691-2407
curt.vanparys@htcsd.ca
Dave DePape, Superintendent, Human Resources &
Operations, 306-691-2402
dave.depape@htcsd.ca
Ward Strueby, Superintendent, Learning, 306-691-2401
ward.strueby@htcsd.ca

Moose Jaw: Prairie South School Division #210
1075 - 9th Ave. NW, Moose Jaw, SK S6H 1V7
Tel: 306-694-1200; *Fax:* 306-694-4955
Toll-Free: 877-434-1200
www.prairiesouth.ca
www.facebook.com/prairiesouthschools210
twitter.com/PrairieSouth
Number of Schools: 38 *Enrollment:* 7100 *Number of Employees:* 1,400
Tony Baldwin, Director, Education, 306-694-1200, ext. 4008
baldwin.tony@prairiesouth.ca
Ryan Boughen, Superintendent, School Operations,
306-694-1200, ext. 4013
boughen.ryan@prairiesouth.ca
Derrick Huschi, Superintendent, School Operations,
306-694-1200, ext. 4010
huschi.derrick@prairiesouth.ca
Amy Johnson, Superintendent, Human Resources,
306-694-1200, ext. 4014
johnson.amy@prairiesouth.ca

North Battleford: Light of Christ Catholic School Division #16
10211 - 12th Ave., North Battleford, SK S9A 3X5
Tel: 306-445-6158; *Fax:* 306-445-3993
loccsd@loccsd.ca
www.loccsd.ca
www.facebook.com/loccsd
twitter.com/LightofChristCS
www.instagram.com/loccsd

Number of Schools: 7 *Grades:* Pre-K.-12 *Enrollment:* 2000 *Note:* This school division is an amalgamation of 4 boards: North Battleford RCSSD#16, Wilkie St. George RCSSD#85, Unity RCSSD#88 & Spiritwood RCSSD#82.
Glen Gantefoer, Chair
Cory Rideout, Director, Education, 306-445-6158
Jordan Kist, Chief Financial Officer, 306-445-6158
j.kist@loccsd.ca
Caralynn Gidych, Superintendent, Learning, 306-445-6158, ext. 104
c.gidych@loccsd.ca
Karen Hrabinsky, Superintendent, Learning, 306-445-6158, ext. 109
k.hrabinsky@loccsd.ca
Tyson Volk, Superintendent, Learning, 306-445-6158, ext. 119

North Battleford: Living Sky School Division #202
509 Pioneer Ave., North Battleford, SK S9A 4A5
Tel: 306-937-7702; *Fax:* 306-445-4332
office@lskysd.ca
www.livingskysd.ca
www.facebook.com/lskysd
twitter.com/LskySD
www.pinterest.com/lskysd
Number of Schools: 29 *Grades:* K - 12 *Enrollment:* 5700 *Number of Employees:* 900
Brenda Vickers, Director, Education, 306-937-7931
brenda.vickers@lskysd.ca
Lonny Darroch, Chief Financial Officer, 306-937-7924
lonny.darroch@lskysd.ca
Cathy Herrick, Superintendent, Learning, 306-937-7939
cathy.herrick@lskysd.ca
Tonya Lehman, Superintendent, Learning, 306-937-7925
tonya.lehman@lskysd.ca
Nancy Schultz, Superintendent, Learning, 306-937-7923
nancy.schultz@lskysd.ca
Jim Shevchuk, Superintendent, Learning, 306-937-7961
jim.shevchuk@lskysd.ca
Ruth Weber, Superintendent, Learning, 306-937-7904
ruth.weber@lskysd.ca

Prince Albert: Prince Albert Roman Catholic Separate School Division #6
Catholic Education Centre
118 - 11th St. East, Prince Albert, SK S6V 1A1
Tel: 306-953-7500; *Fax:* 306-763-1723
info@pacsd.ca
pacsd.ca
Number of Schools: 7 *Grades:* Pre - 12
Suzanne Stubbs, Chair
suzanne.stubbs@pacsd.ca
Lorel Trumier, Director, Education
lorel.trumier@pacsd.ca

Prince Albert: Saskatchewan Rivers School Division #119
545 - 11th St. East, Prince Albert, SK S6V 1B1
Tel: 306-764-1571; *Fax:* 306-763-4460
www.facebook.com/SRPSDPA
twitter.com/SRPSD119
Number of Schools: 32 *Grades:* Pre - 12 *Enrollment:* 9000
Barry Hollick, Chair
bhollick@srsd119.ca
Robert Bratvold, Director, Education
rbratvold@srsd119.ca

Regina: Prairie Valley School Division #208 (PVSD)
P.O. Box 1937
3080 Albert St. North, Regina, SK S4P 3E1
Tel: 306-949-3366; *Fax:* 306-543-1771
Toll-Free: 877-266-1666
reception@pvsd.ca
www.pvsd.ca
www.facebook.com/PrairieValleySchoolDivision
twitter.com/prairievalleysd
Number of Schools: 39 *Grades:* K - 12 *Enrollment:* 8590 *Number of Employees:* 1,300
Janet Kotylak, Chair, Board
janet.kotylak@pvsd.ca
Luc Lerminiaux, Director, Education & Chief Executive Officer
Dianne Ford, Deputy Director, Division Services & Chief Financial Officer
Mike Walter, Deputy Director, Instruction and School Operations
Mike Embury, Superintendent, Education - School Operations
Patty Brady, Superintendent, Education - School Operations
Lorrie Anne Harkness, Superintendent, Education - Learning Supports
Lyle Stecyk, Superintendent, Project Management

Regina: Regina Public Schools
Also known as: Regina School Division No.4
1600 - 4th Ave., Regina, SK S4R 8C8
Tel: 306-523-3000; *Fax:* 306-523-3031
info@rbe.sk.ca
reginapublicschools.ca/
Number of Schools: 44 elementary schools; 8 secondary schools; 3 faith-based associate schools *Grades:* Pre-K - 12 *Enrollment:* 24500 *Number of Employees:* 2,295
Greg Enion, Director, Education, 306-523-3017
greg.enion@rbe.sk.ca
Naomi Mellor, Deputy Director, Division Services & Secretary-Treasurer, 306-523-3018
naomi.mellor@rbe.sk.ca
Paula Hesselink, Superintendent, Human Resources & Workplace Diversity, 306-523-3059
paula.hesselink@rbe.sk.ca
Katherine Gagne, Chair, Board, 306-585-6601
gagne@accesscomm.ca

Rosetown: Sun West School Division #207
P.O. Box 700
501 - 1st St. West, Rosetown, SK S0L 2V0
Tel: 306-882-2677; *Toll-Free:* 866-375-2677
info@sunwestsd.ca
www.sunwestsd.ca
www.facebook.com/SunWestSD207
twitter.com/SunWestSD207
Number of Schools: 13 K - 12; 18 Hutterite; 6 elementary; 3 secondary; 1 middle *Grades:* K - 12 *Enrollment:* 5000 *Number of Employees:* 800
Randy Emmerson, Director, Education
guy.tetrault@sunwestsd.ca
Kelli Boklaschuk, Superintendent, Learning
Shari Martin, Superintendent, Operations
Ryan Smith, Superintendent, Business

Saskatoon: Greater Saskatoon Catholic Schools (GSCS)
420 - 22nd St. East, Saskatoon, SK S7K 1X3
Tel: 306-659-7000; *Fax:* 306-659-2007
info@gscs.ca
www.gscs.ca
www.facebook.com/GreaterSaskatoonCatholicSchools
twitter.com/GSCSNews
Number of Schools: 43 elementary schools; 7 secondary schools; *Grades:* Pre-K - 12 *Enrollment:* 19000 *Number of Employees:* 1,854 *Note:* Students have the opportunity to learn French, Cree or Ukrainian.
Diane Boyko, Chair, Board, 306-382-2832
DLBoyko@gscs.ca
Greg Chatlain, Director, Education, 306-659-7001
gchatlain@gscs.ca
Joel Lloyd, Chief Financial Officer, 306-659-7021
jlloyd@gscs.ca
Darryl Bazylak, Superintendent, Human Resource Services, 306-659-7040
dbazylak@gscs.ca
Tammy Schircliff, Superintendent, Education, 306-659-7056
tschircliff@gscs.ca
Gordon Martell, Superintendent, Education, 306-659-7056
gmartell@gscs.ca
Jenise Vangool, Superintendent, Education, 306-659-7041
jvangool@gscs.ca
Scott Gay, Superintendent, Education, 306-659-7114
sgay@gscs.ca
Terri Fradette, Superintendent, Education, 306-659-7059
tfradette@gscs.ca
Francois Rivard, Superintendent, Education, 306-659-7048
frivard@gscs.ca
Kent Gauthier, Superintendent, Education, 306-659-7048
kgauthier@gscs.ca

Saskatoon: Saskatoon Public Schools (SPSD)
310 - 21st St. East, Saskatoon, SK S7K 1M7
Tel: 306-683-8200; *Fax:* 306-657-3900
spsdinfo@spsd.sk.ca
www.spsd.sk.ca
www.facebook.com/SaskatoonPublicSchools
twitter.com/StoonPubSchools
www.instagram.com/saskatoonpublicschools
Number of Schools: 49 Elementary Schools; 10 Secondary Schools; 2 associate schools; 1 affiliate schools *Grades:* Pre-K - 12; Adult Ed. *Enrollment:* 25000 *Number of Employees:* 2,400
Colleen MacPherson, Chair, Board, 306-683-8465
macphersonc@spsd.sk.ca
Barry MacDougall, Director, Education, 306-683-8226
MacDougallB@spsd.skca
Shane Skjerven, Deputy Director, Education, 306-683-8215
SkjervenS@spsd
Garry Benning, Chief Financial Officer, 306-683-8231
BenningG@spsd.sk.ca

Jason Dunk, Chief Technology Officer, 306-683-8338
DunkJ@spsd.sk.ca
Stan Laba, Superintendent, Facilities, 306-683-8426
LabaS@spsd.sk.ca
Jaime Valentine, Superintendent, Human Resources,
306-683-8211
ValentineJ@spsd.sk.ca
Dave Derksen, Superintendent, Education, 306-683-8282
DerksenD@spsd.sk.ca
Brent Hills, Superintendent, Education, 306-683-8208
HillsB@spsd.sk.ca
Dean Newton, Superintendent, Education, 306-683-8208
NewtonD@spsd.sk.ca
Charlene Scrimshaw, Superintendent, Education, 306-683-8210
ScrimshawC@spsd.sk.ca
Donnalee Weinmaster, Superintendent, Education,
306-683-8210
WeinmasterD@spsd.sk.ca

Swift Current: Chinook School Division No. 211
P.O. Box 1809
2100 Gladstone St. East, Swift Current, SK S9H 4J8
Tel: 306-778-9200; *Fax:* 306-773-8011
Toll-Free: 877-321-9200
info@chinooksd.ca
www.chinooksd.ca
www.facebook.com/ChinookSD
twitter.com/ChinookSD
Number of Schools: 62 *Enrollment:* 6000 *Number of Employees:*
1,125
Kimberly Pridmore, Chair
kpridmore59@chinooksd.ca

Warman: Prairie Spirit School Division #206
P.O. Box 809
121 Collins St., Warman, SK S0K 4S0
Tel: 306-683-2800; *Fax:* 306-934-8221
contact@spiritsd.ca
www.spiritsd.ca
www.facebook.com/prairiespiritsd
twitter.com/prairiespiritsd
Number of Schools: 44 *Grades:* K - 12 *Enrollment:* 10868
Bernie Howe, Chair
bernie.howe@spiritsd.ca
Lori Jeschke, Director, Education
lori.jeschke@spiritsd.ca
Jim Shields, Deputy Director, Division Services & CFO
bob.bayles@spiritsd.ca

Weyburn: Holy Family Roman Catholic Separate School District #140
#103, 433 - 4th St. NE, Weyburn, SK S4H 0Y8
Tel: 306-842-7025; *Fax:* 306-842-7033
office.weyburn@holyfamilyrcssd.ca
holyfamilyrcssd.ca
twitter.com/Holyfamilyrcssd
Number of Schools: 5 *Grades:* K - 12 *Enrollment:* 1100
Bruno Tuchscherer, Chair
Gwen Keith, Director, Education
gwen.keith@holyfamilyrcssd.ca
Lisa Wonsiak, Chief Financial Officer & Manager, Human
Resources
lisa.wonsiak@holyfamilyrcssd.ca
Chad Fingler, Superintendent, School Operations
chad.fingler@holyfamilyrcssd.ca
Terry Jordens, Superintendent, Student Services & Assessment
terry.jordens@holyfamilyrcssd.ca

Weyburn: South East Cornerstone Public School Division #209 (SECPSD)
80A - 18th St., Weyburn, SK S4H 2W4
Tel: 306-848-0080; *Fax:* 306-848-4747
Toll-Free: 888-938-0080
contactus@secpsd.ca
www.secpsd.ca
twitter/com/secpsd
Number of Schools: 38 *Grades:* K - 12 *Enrollment:* 8200 *Number
of Employees:* 1030
Lynn Little, Director, Education & CEO
Keith Keating, Deputy Director, Education
Kevin Hengen, Superintendent of Schools, East Service Area
Aaron Hiske, Superintendent of Education
Gord Husband, Superintendent of Schools, West Service Area
Shelley Sargent, Superintendent of Schools, South Service Area
Shelley Toth, Superintendent of Division Services & CFO
Audrey Trombley, Chair, Board

Yorkton: Christ the Teacher Roman Catholic Separate School Division No. 212
45A Palliser Way, Yorkton, SK S3N 4C5
Tel: 306-783-8787; *Fax:* 306-783-4992
christtheteacher.ca
www.facebook.com/ChristtheTeacher
twitter.com/CTTCS_212
Number of Schools: 9 *Grades:* Pre-K - 12 *Enrollment:* 1800
Note: This division is an amalgamation of St. Henry's RCSSD
#5, Yorkton RCSSD #86, St. Theodore RCSSD #138, Melville
Rural RCSSD #217 and Yorkton Rural RCSSD #216.
Dwight Guy, Chair
Barb MacKesey, Director, Education
Chad Holinaty, Superintendent, Education
Delmar Zwirsky, Chief Financial Officer

Yorkton: Good Spirit School Division #204 (GSSD)
P.O. Box 5060
5B Schrader Dr., Yorkton, SK S3N 3Z4
Tel: 306-786-5500; *Fax:* 306-783-0355
Toll-Free: 866-390-0773
info@gssd.ca
www.gssd.ca
www.facebook.com/gssd204
twitter.com/gssd204
Number of Schools: 28 *Grades:* JK - 12 *Enrollment:* 6000
Bob Simpson, Chair
Quintin M. Robertson, Director, Education
Mark Forsythe, Superintendent, Education
Alisa Leidl, Superintendent, Education
Lisa Wotherspoon, Superintendent, Education

Protestant

Englefeld: Englefeld Protestant Separate School Division #132
Englefeld School
P.O. Box 100
Englefeld, SK S0K 1N0, Canada
Tel: 306-287-3568; *Fax:* 306-287-3569
admin.epssd@englefeld.ca
www.englefeld.ca/School/HomeSchool.html
twitter.com/englefeld
Marie Stockbrugger, Secretary

Catholic

Regina: Regina Catholic School Division (RCSD)
2160 Cameron St., Regina, SK S4T 2V6
Tel: 306-791-7200; *Fax:* 306-347-7699
rcs@rcsd.ca
www.rcsd.ca
twitter.com/RCSD_No81
Number of Schools: 24 elementary schools; 4 secondary
schools; 1 alternative school; 1 associate school *Grades:* K - 12
Enrollment: 12000 *Number of Employees:* 1,100
Domenic Scuglia, Director, Education
Heidi Hildebrand, Superintendent, Human Resource Services
Bob Kowalchuk, Chair, Board, 306-539-2195
b.kowalchuk@rcsd.ca
Kelley Ehman, Superintendent, Education Services
Stacey Gherasim, Superintendent, Education Services
Joanna Landry, Superintendent, Education Services
David Magnusson, Superintendent, Education Services

French

Regina: Conseil des écoles fransaskoises (CÉF)
#201, 1440 - 9e av nord, Regina, SK S4R 8B1
Tél: 306-757-7541; *Téléc:* 306-757-2040
Ligne sans frais: 877-273-6661
ecolefrancophone.ca
www.facebook.com/cefsk
twitter.com/cefsk
www.linkedin.com/company/conseil-des-coles-fransaskoises
Number of Schools: 15 *Grades:* Prémat. - Sec. *Enrollment:* 2000
Alpha Barry, Président, Conseil, 877-273-6661
abarry@cefsk.ca
Ronald Ajavon, Directeur général, Éducation, 306-719-7466
rajavon@cefsk.ca
André Messier, Directeur général adjoint, Éducation,
306-719-7484
amessier@cefsk.ca
Marcel Lizotte, Directeur, Ressources Humaines, 306-719-7470
mlizotte@cefsk.ca
Claude-Jean Harel, Coordonnateur, Communications,
306-527-4180
cjharel@cefsk.ca

Schools: Cégep

French

Gravelbourg: Collège Mathieu
P.O. Box 989
308 - 1st Ave. East, Gravelbourg, SK S0H 1X0
Tél: 306-648-3491; *Téléc:* 306-648-2295
Ligne sans frais: 800-663-5463
communications@collegemathieu.sk.ca
www.collegemathieu.sk.ca
www.facebook.com/CollegeMathieu
Francis Kasongo, Directeur général
direction@collegemathieu.sk.ca

Campuses
Campus de Saskatoon
#201, 308 - 4th Ave. North, Saskatoon, SK S7K 2L7
Tel: 306-384-2722; *Fax:* 306-384-2469
Toll-Free: 866-524-4404

Campus de Regina
3304 Dewdney Ave., Regina, SK S4T 7V1
Tel: 306-565-3525; *Fax:* 306-569-2609

Schools: Specialized

Special Education

Pilot Butte: Ranch Ehrlo Society
P.O. Box 570
Pilot Butte, SK S0G 3Z0
Tel: 306-781-1800; *Fax:* 306-757-0599
inquiries@ranchehrlo.ca
www.ehrlo.com
www.facebook.com/RanchEhrlo
twitter.com/RanchEhrlo
www.youtube.com/user/ranchehrlo1
Enrollment: 192 *Note:* Ranch Ehrlo Society is a residential
school for children, youth, & young adults who are experiencing
social, psychological, mental, psychiatric, &/or physical
difficulties. The Ranch offers holistic, psycho-social therapies, as
well as community & family programming.
Andrea Brittin, President

Campuses
Buckland Campus
P.O. Box 1892
Prince Albert, SK S6V 6J9
Tel: 306-764-4511; *Fax:* 306-764-0042
inquiries@ranchehrlo.ca

Corman Park Campus
P.O. Box 580
Martensville, SK S0K 2T0
Tel: 306-659-3100; *Fax:* 306-956-2570
inquiries@ranchehrlo.ca

Regina: Cornwall Alternative School
40 Dixon Cres., Regina, SK S4N 1V4, Canada
Tel: 306-522-0044; *Fax:* 306-359-0720
admin.cas@sasktel.net
www.cornwallalternativeschool.com
Grades: 7-10 *Enrollment:* 39
Gil Will, Acting Principal & CEO
David Halvorsen, Board Chairperson

Saskatoon: Radius Community Centre for Education & Employment
P.O. Box 1812
611 - 1st Ave. North, Bay 1, Saskatoon, SK S7K 1X7
Tel: 306-665-0362; *Fax:* 306-665-5579
info@radiuscentre.com
www.radiuscentre.com
twitter.com/RadCentre1970
Gail McKenzie-Wilcox, Principal

Schools: Independent & Private

Protestant

Battleford: Heritage Christian School
P.O. Box 490
11 - 20th St. West, Battleford, SK S0M 0E0, Canada
Tel: 306-446-3188; *Fax:* 306-446-3187
heritage@lskysd.ca
www.heritagechristianschool.lskysd.ca
Grades: Pre.-8 *Enrollment:* 42
Gerald Wiebe, Principal

Moose Jaw: **Cornerstone Christian School (CCS)**
43 Iroquois St. East, Moose Jaw, SK S6H 4S9
Tel: 306-693-2937; *Fax:* 306-694-1880
office@ccsmj.ca
www.ccsmj.ca
www.facebook.com/CornerstoneChristianSchoolMooseJaw
Grades: K.-12 *Note:* The school is recognized by the
Government of Saskatchewan as an Associate School. It is
responsible to the local public school board, the Prairie South
School Division #210.
Tanya Johnson, Vice-Principal

Outlook: **Lutheran Collegiate Bible Institute**
P.O. Box 459
Outlook, SK S0L 2N0, Canada
Tel: 306-867-8971; *Fax:* 306-867-9947
office@lcbi.sk.ca
www.lcbi.sk.ca
www.facebook.com/LCBIHighSchool
twitter.com/LCBINews
Grades: 10-12; Residential only
Leanne Engen, Principal
principal@lcbi.sk.ca

Regina: **Harvest City Christian Academy**
Harvest City Church
2202 - 8th Ave. North, Regina, SK S4R 7T9, Canada
Tel: 306-569-1935; *Fax:* 306-359-9047
www.harvestcitychristianacademy.com
Grades: K.-12; Day only
Todd Harrison, Principal
todd.harrison@hccmail.ca

Regina: **Regina Christian School (RCS)**
2505 - 23rd Ave., Regina, SK S4S 7K7, Canada
Tel: 306-775-0919; *Fax:* 306-775-3070
rcs.office@myaccess.ca
www.reginachristianschool.org
Other Information: rcs.development@myaccess.ca (E-mail,
Development)
www.facebook.com/RCSForTheGreaterGloryOfGod
twitter.com/RCS_ReginaSK
Grades: Pre.-12 *Enrollment:* 343 *Note:* The interdenominational
school's academic program is offered with an evangelical
Christian view.
Rod Rilling, B.Ed., B.A. (Hons), Principal

Rosthern: **Rosthern Junior College (RJC)**
P.O. Box 5020
410 - 6th Ave., Rosthern, SK S0K 3R0, Canada
Tel: 306-232-4222; *Fax:* 306-232-5250
office@rosthernjuniorcollege.ca
rosthernjuniorcollege.ca
www.facebook.com/rosthernjc
twitter.com/RosthernJC
www.youtube.com/RosthernJrCollege
Grades: 10-12 *Enrollment:* 75 *Note:* The Christian secondary
school operates within a Mennonite school community, for
students of any faith. Completion of enriched courses leads to a
Saskatchewan senior matriculation.
Ryan Wood, Principal
ryan.wood@rosthernjuniorcollege.ca

Saskatoon: **Legacy Christian Academy**
102 Pinehouse Dr., Saskatoon, SK S7K 5H7, Canada
Tel: 306-242-5086
www.legacychristianacademy.ca
www.facebook.com/321323657999012
Grades: K.-12

Saskatoon: **Saskatoon Christian School**
P.O. Box 8
Site 510, RR#5, Saskatoon, SK S7K 3J8, Canada
Tel: 306-343-1494; *Fax:* 306-343-0366
info@saskatoonchristianschool.ca
www.saskatoonchristianschool.ca
Grades: K.-12; Day only *Enrollment:* 375
Doug Wiebe, Principal
wiebedo@spsd.sk.ca

Catholic

Wilcox: **Athol Murray College of Notre Dame**
P.O. Box 100
49 Main St., Wilcox, SK S0G 5E0, Canada
Tel: 306-732-2080; *Fax:* 306-732-4409
info@notredame.ca
www.notredame.ca
www.facebook.com/notredamehounds
twitter.com/NotreDameHounds
www.linkedin.com/company/athol-murray-college-of-notre-dame
Grades: 9-12 *Enrollment:* 350 *Note:* Athol Murray College of
Notre Dame is an international coeducational & residential

college preparatory school. It is dedicated to Catholic Christian
education.
Robert Palmarin, B.Ed., M.Th., President, 306-732-1230
r.palmarin@notredame.ca
Trevor Novak, Executive Director, Business Operations
t.novak@notredame.ca
Dawn Froats, Director, Marketing & Communication
d.froats@notredame.ca
Marc Butikofer, Director, Development
m.butikofer@notredame.ca
Dave Pollon, Manager, Finance
d.pollon@notredame.ca

Independent & Private Schools

Caronport: **Caronport High School (CHS)**
c/o Briercrest College & Seminary
510 College Dr., Caronport, SK S0H 0S0, Canada
Tel: 306-756-3303; *Fax:* 306-756-5597
chs@briercrest.ca
www.caronporthighschool.ca
www.facebook.com/CaronportHighSchool
Grades: 9-12 *Number of Employees:* 22
Deborah Ike, Principal
deborahi@briercrest.ca

Regina: **Luther College High School**
1500 Royal St., Regina, SK S4T 5A5, Canada
Tel: 306-791-9150; *Fax:* 306-359-6962
www.luthercollege.edu/high-school
www.facebook.com/LCHSRegina
twitter.com/lchsregina
www.linkedin.com/company/luther-college-high-school
www.instagram.com/luther_college_hs
Grades: 9-12
Bryan Hillis, Principal
bryan.hillis@luthercollege.edu

Regina: **Regina Huda School**
40 Sheppard St., Regina, SK S4R 3M6, Canada
Tel: 306-565-1988; *Fax:* 306-565-2187
info@huda.ca
www.huda.ca
www.facebook.com/Regina.huda.school
twitter.com/newbuildingrhs
Grades: Pre.-12 *Note:* Regina Huda School strives to preserve
the Islamic identity by offering Islamic & Arabic studies for the
Muslim community.
Dr. Ayman Aboguddah, Board President
aboguddah@gmail.com
Starla Nistor, Principal
Pam Spock, Vice-Principal

Universities & Colleges

Universities

Caronport: **Briercrest College & Seminary**
510 College Dr., Caronport, SK S0H 0S0, Canada
Tel: 306-756-3200; *Fax:* 306-756-5500
Toll-Free: 800-667-5199
info@briercrest.ca
www.briercrest.ca
www.facebook.com/briercrest
twitter.com/briercrest
www.linkedin.com/school/briercrest-college-and-seminary
www.youtube.com/c/briercrest
Full Time Equivalency: 640 *Note:* The institution also operates
the Caronport High School.

Regina: **First Nations University of Canada**
1 First Nations Way, Regina, SK S4S 7K2, Canada
Tel: 306-790-5950; *Fax:* 306-790-5999
Toll-Free: 800-267-6303
www.fnuniv.ca
www.facebook.com/FNUNIV
twitter.com/FNUNIVCAN
pinterest.com/fnunivlibrary
Full Time Equivalency: 980

Campuses
Saskatoon Campus
229 - 4th Ave. South, Saskatoon, SK S7K 4K3, Canada
Tel: 306-931-1800; *Fax:* 306-931-1849
Toll-Free: 800-267-6303

Prince Albert Campus
1301 Central Ave., Prince Albert, SK S6V 4W1, Canada
Tel: 306-765-3333; *Fax:* 306-765-3330
Toll-Free: 800-267-6303

Regina: **University of Regina**
3737 Wascana Pkwy., Regina, SK S4S 0A2
Tel: 306-585-4111; *Fax:* 306-585-5203
registrar@uregina.ca
www.uregina.ca
www.facebook.com/UniversityofRegina
twitter.com/UofRegina
www.linkedin.com/company/university-of-regina
Full Time Equivalency: 14300 *Number of Employees:* 1250
Pam Klein, Chancellor
Dr. Thomas Chase, Interim President & Vice-Chancellor
Dr. David Gregory, Interim Provost & Vice-President, Academic
Dave Button, Vice-President, Administration
Dr. Kathleen McNutt, Interim Vice-President, Research
Glenys Sylvestre, University Secretary
glenys.sylvestre@uregina.ca
James D'Arcy, Registrar
james.darcy@uregina.ca

Faculties
Faculty of Arts
3737 Wascana Pkwy., #CL426, Regina, SK S4S 0A2
Tel: 306-585-5653
www.uregina.ca/arts
www.facebook.com/UofRArts
twitter.com/UofRArts

Richard Kleer, Dean

Faculty of Business Administration
3737 Wascana Pkwy., 5th Fl., Regina, SK S4S 0A2
Tel: 306-585-4724; *Fax:* 306-585-5361
www.uregina.ca/business
twitter.com/HillSchoolofBus
Andrew Gaudes, Dean
andrew.gaudes@uregina.ca

Faculty of Education
3737 Wascana Pkwy., Regina, SK S4S 0A2
Tel: 306-585-4537; *Fax:* 306-585-4880
education.counselling@uregina.ca
www.uregina.ca/education
www.facebook.com/uredspc
Jerome Cranston, Dean
jerome.cranston@uregina.ca

Faculty of Engineering & Applied Science
3737 Wascana Pkwy., Regina, SK S4S 0A2
Tel: 306-585-4734; *Fax:* 306-585-4855
engg@uregina.ca
wwww.uregina.ca/engineering
Esam Hussein, Dean
esam.hussein@uregina.ca

Faculty of Media, Art, & Performance
269 Riddell Centre, University of Regina
Regina, SK S4S 0A2
Tel: 306-585-5510; *Fax:* 306-585-5544
media.art.performance@uregina.ca
www.uregina.ca/mediaartperformance
Rae Staseson, Dean
map.dean@uregina.ca

Graduate Studies & Research
3737 Wascana Pkwy., Regina, SK S4S 0A2
Tel: 306-585-4161; *Fax:* 306-337-2444
grad.studies@uregina.ca
www.uregina.ca/gradstudies
Kathy McNutt, Dean
kathy.mcnutt@uregina.ca

Faculty of Kinesiology & Health Studies
3737 Wascana Pkwy., Regina, SK S4S 0A2
Tel: 306-585-4360; *Fax:* 306-585-4854
kinesiology@uregina.ca
www.uregina.ca/kinesiology
Dr. Harold Riemer, Dean
khs.dean@uregina.ca

Faculty of Science
3737 Wascana Pkwy., Regina, SK S4S 0A2
Tel: 306-585-4143
www.uregina.ca/science
Douglas Farenick, Dean

Faculty of Social Work
3737 Wascana Pkwy., Regina, SK S4S 0A2
Tel: 306-585-4554; *Fax:* 306-585-4872
sw.studentservices@uregina.ca
www.uregina.ca/socialwork
www.facebook.com/URsocialwork
www.youtube.com/user/URSocialWork
Judy White, Dean
sw.dean@uregina.ca

Schools

Conservatory of Performing Arts
3737 Wascana Pkwy., Regina, SK S4S 0A2
Tel: 306-585-5748
www.uregina.ca/cce/conservatory
www.facebook.com/uofrcce
Erika Folnovic, Program Coordinator
erika.folnovic@uregina.ca

Kenneth Levene Graduate School of Business
3737 Wascana Pkwy., Regina, SK S4S 0A2
Tel: 306-585-6294; *Fax:* 306-585-5361
www.uregina.ca/business/levene

Johnson-Shoyama Graduate School of Public Policy
2155 College Ave., 3rd Fl., Regina, SK S4S 0A2
Tel: 306-585-5460; *Fax:* 306-585-5461
jsgs@uregina.ca
www.schoolofpublicpolicy.sk.ca
www.facebook.com/JSGSPP
twitter.com/JSGSPP
www.youtube.com/user/jsgspp
Doug Moen, Interim Executive Director
doug.moen@uregina.ca

School of Journalism
3737 Wascana Pkwy., Regina, SK S4S 0A2
Tel: 306-585-4420; *Fax:* 306-585-4867
journalism@uregina.ca
www.uregina.ca/arts/journalism
www.facebook.com/URJSchool
twitter.com/URJschool
Gennadiy Chernov, Department Head
gennadiy.chernov@uregina.ca

Affiliations

Campion College
c/o University of Regina
3737 Wascana Pkwy., Regina, SK S4S 0A2, Canada
Tel: 306-586-4242; *Fax:* 306-359-1200
Toll-Free: 1-800-667-7282
campion.college@uregina.ca
www.campioncollege.ca
www.facebook.com/campioncollege
twitter.com/CampionUR
www.youtube.com/user/URCampion
Full Time Equivalency: 1000 *Number of Employees:* 31 faculty;
26 staff members; 1 campus minister
Dr. Sami Helewa, President, 306-359-1212
sami.helewa@uregina.ca
James Gustafson, Executive Director, Administration & Finance,
306-359-1231
james.gustafson@uregina.ca
SJ Kotylak, Director, Marketing & Communications,
306-359-1244
sj.kotylak@uregina.ca
Kenneth Yanko, Director, Facilities & Operations, 306-359-1249
ken.yanko@uregina.ca
Kelly Bourke, Campus Minister, 306-359-1235
kelly.bourke@uregina.ca
Allison Fizzard, Dean, 306-359-1237
allison.fizzard@uregina.ca
Heather Antonini, Registrar, 306-359-1225
heather.antonini@uregina.ca

First Nations University of Canada
1 First Nations Way, Regina, SK S4S 7K2
Tel: 306-790-5950; *Fax:* 306-790-5999
Toll-Free: 1-800-267-6303
www.fnuniv.ca
www.facebook.com/FNUNIV
www.pinterest.com/fnunivlibrary
Full Time Equivalency: 3000 *Note:* At the First Nations University
of Canada, students have the opportunity to learn in an
environment of First Nations languages, traditions, & values.
Mark S. Dockstator, President

Gabriel Dumont Institute (GDI)
917 - 22nd St. West, Saskatoon, SK S7M 0R9
Tel: 306-242-6070; *Fax:* 306-242-0002
Toll-Free: 877-488-6888
www.gdins.org
www.facebook.com/gabrieldumontinstitute
twitter.com/gdins_org
www.youtube.com/user/gabrieldumontins
Note: The Institute is designated as the official education arm of
the Métis Nation-Saskatchewan (MN-S).
Geordy McCaffrey, Executive Director

Luther College
c/o University of Regina
3737 Wascana Pkwy., Regina, SK S4S 0A2, Canada
Tel: 306-585-5333; *Fax:* 306-585-2949
Toll-Free: 800-588-4378
recruitment@luthercollege.edu
www.luthercollege.edu
www.facebook.com/LCUR1971
twitter.com/Lutheredu
Bryan Hillis, President, 306-585-5024
bryan.hillis@uregina.ca
Mark Duke, Director, Finance, 306-585-5023
mark.duke@luthercollege.edu
Yvonne Petry, Dean, 306-585-5039
yvonne.petry@uregina.ca
Tatum Cruise, Registrar, 306-585-5083
tatum.cruise@uregina.ca

Centres & Institutes

Centre on Aging & Health
Regina, SK S4S 0A2
Tel: 306-337-8477; *Fax:* 306-337-3204
cah@uregina.ca
www2.uregina.ca/cah
twitter.com/UofRAgingCentre
Thomas Hadjistavropoulos, Director
hadjistt@uregina.ca

Collaborative Centre for Justice & Safety
3737 Wascana Pkwy., Regina, SK S4S 0A2
Tel: 306-337-2570
www.justiceandsafety.ca
Steve Palmer, Executive Director
steve.palmer@uregina.ca

Indigenous Peoples' Health Research Centre (IPHRC)
1 First Nations Way, Regina, SK S4S 7K2
Tel: 306-337-2461; *Fax:* 306-585-5694
iphrc@uregina.ca
www.schoolofpublicpolicy.sk.ca/iphrc
www.facebook.com/IPHRC
twitter.com/iphrcsask
Cassandra Opikokew Wajuntah, Director
cassandra.wajuntah@uregina.ca

Saskatoon: College of Emmanuel & St. Chad
Also known as: University of Emmanuel College
114 Seminary Cres., Saskatoon, SK S7N 0X3, Canada
Tel: 306-975-3753; *Fax:* 306-934-2683
emmanuel.stchad@usask.ca
www.usask.ca/stu/emmanuel

Saskatoon: Lutheran Theological Seminary
114 Seminary Cres., Saskatoon, SK S7N 0X3, Canada
Tel: 306-966-7850; *Fax:* 306-966-7852
development.office@usask.ca
www.usask.ca/stu/luther
www.facebook.com/LTSSaskatoon
Full Time Equivalency: 142 *Note:* Theological college at the
University of Saskatchewan affiliated with the Evangelical
Lutheran Church in Canada

Saskatoon: University of Saskatchewan
Administration Bldg.
105 Administration Pl., Saskatoon, SK S7N 5A2
Tel: 306-966-4343
www.usask.ca
www.facebook.com/usask
twitter.com/usask
www.linkedin.com/company/university-of-saskatchewan
www.instagram.com/usask
Full Time Equivalency: 30000
Grit McCreath, Chancellor
Peter Stoicheff, President & Vice-Chancellor
Anthony Vannelli, Provost & Vice-President, Academic
Greg Fowler, Vice-President, Finance & Resources
Karen Chad, Vice-President, Research
Debra Pozega Osburn, Vice-President, University Relations
Chelsea Willness, University Secretary
university.secretary@usask.ca

Faculties

College of Agriculture & Bioresources
51 Campus Dr., Saskatoon, SK S7N 5A8
Tel: 306-966-4056; *Fax:* 306-966-8894
agbio.reception@usask.ca
agbio.usask.ca
Mary Buhr, Dean
mary.buhr@usask.ca

College of Arts & Science
9 Campus Dr., Saskatoon, SK S7N 5A5
Tel: 306-966-4232; *Fax:* 306-966-8839
officeofthedean@artsandscience.usask.ca
artsandscience.usask.ca
www.facebook.com/Arts.Science.UofS
twitter.com/usaskArtSci
www.youtube.com/user/artsandscienceUofS
Peta Bonham-Smith, Dean

Edwards School of Business
Nutrien Centre
25 Campus Dr., Saskatoon, SK S7N 5A7
Tel: 306-966-4785; *Fax:* 306-966-5408
undergrad@edwards.usask.ca
www.edwards.usask.ca
www.facebook.com/edwardsschoolofbusiness
twitter.com/edwards_school
www.youtube.com/ESBUofS
Keith A. Willoughby, Dean

College of Dentistry
Toll-Free: 877-363-7275
dentistry@usask.ca
www.usask.ca/centistry
Dr. Doug Brothwell, Dean, 306-966-5122
doug.brothwell@usask.ca

College of Education
28 Campus Dr., Saskatoon, SK S7N 0X1
Tel: 306-966-7647
edo.inquiries@usask.ca
www.usask.ca/education
Michelle Prytula, Dean
michelle.prytula@usask.ca

College of Engineering
57 Campus Dr., Saskatoon, SK S7N 5A9
Tel: 306-966-5273; *Fax:* 306-966-5205
coe.inquiries@usask.ca
engineering.usask.ca
www.facebook.com/engr.usask
twitter.com/usask_engr
Suzanne Kresta, Dean

School of Environment & Sustainability
Kirk Hall
#323, 117 Science Pl., Saskatoon, SK S7N 5C8
Tel: 306-966-1985
sens.info@usask.ca
sens.usask.ca
www.facebook.com/usasksenssa
twitter.com/usasksens
www.youtube.com/user/sensuofs
Irena Creed, Executive Director
sens.executivedirector@usask.ca

College of Graduate & Postdoctoral Studies
116 - 110 Science Pl., Saskatoon, SK S7N 5C9
Tel: 306-966-5751; *Fax:* 306-966-5756
grad.studies@usask.ca
www.usask.ca/cgps
Trever Crowe, Interim Dean
trever.crowe@usask.ca

College of Kinesiology
87 Campus Dr., Saskatoon, SK S7N 5B2
Tel: 306-966-1060; *Fax:* 306-966-6464
kinesiology.usask.ca
twitter.com/USaskKin
Dr. Chad London, Dean
chad.london@usask.ca

College of Law
15 Campus Dr., Saskatoon, SK S7N 5A6
Tel: 306-966-5869
law.usask.ca
www.facebook.com/UsaskLaw
twitter.com/UsaskLaw
www.youtube.com/user/CollegeOfLawUsask
Martin Phillipson, Dean
martin.phillipson@usask.ca

College of Medicine
Health Sciences Bldg.
107 Wiggins Rd., #5D40, Saskatoon, SK S7N 5E5
Tel: 306-966-2673
medicine.reception@usask.ca
www.medicine.usask.ca
www.facebook.com/uofscomalumniassoc
twitter.com/usaskmeddean
www.instagram.com/usaskmed
Dr. Preston Smith, M.D., Ph.D., FRCPC, Dean

College of Nursing
Health Sciences Bldg.
107 Wiggins Rd., #1A10, Saskatoon, SK S7N 5E5
Tel: 306-966-6221; *Fax:* 306-966-6621
Toll-Free: 844-966-6269
www.usask.ca/nursing
www.facebook.com/usaskNursing
twitter.com/uofsnursing
www.youtube.com/user/usasknursing
Cindy Peternelj-Taylor, Interim Dean
cindy.peternelj-taylor@usask.ca

College of Pharmacy & Nutrition
Health Sciences Bldg.
107 Wiggins Rd., #2A20.01, Saskatoon, SK S7N 5E5
Tel: 306-966-6327; *Fax:* 306-966-6377
pharmacy-nutrition@usask.ca
pharmacy-nutrition.usask.ca
www.facebook.com/usaskPharmNut
twitter.com/usaskPharmNut
www.instagram.com/usaskPharmNut
Jane Alcorn, Dean
jane.alcorn@usask.ca

School of Rehabilitation Science
Health Sciences Bldg.
#3400, 104 Clinic Pl., Saskatoon, SK S7N 2Z4
Tel: 306-966-6579; *Fax:* 306-966-6575
rehabscience.usask.ca
Dr. Cathy Arnold, Director
cathy.arnold@usask.ca

Western College of Veterinary Medicine
52 Campus Dr., Saskatoon, SK S7N 5B4
Tel: 306-966-7447; *Fax:* 306-966-8747
wcvm.usask.ca
Douglas Freeman, Dean
douglas.freeman@usask.ca

Affiliations
Briercrest College & Seminary
510 College Dr., Caronport, SK S0H 0S0
Tel: 306-756-3200; *Fax:* 306-756-5500
info@briercrest.ca
www.briercrest.ca
www.facebook.com/Briercrest
twitter.com/briercrest
www.youtube.com/user/BriercrestCollegeSem
Dr. Michael B. Pawelke, President

College of Emmanuel & St. Chad
114 Seminary Cres., Saskatoon, SK S7N 0X3
Tel: 306-975-3753; *Fax:* 306-934-2683
emmanuel.stchad@usask.ca
www.usask.ca/stu/emmanuel
Rev. Dr. Iain Luke, Principal
iain.luke@usask.ca
Lisa McInnis, Registrar
esc.registrar@usask.ca

Gabriel Dumont Institute
McLean Hall
#7, 106 Wiggins Rd., Saskatoon, SK S7N 5E6
Tel: 306-975-7095; *Fax:* 306-975-1108
gdins.org
Geordy McCaffrey, Executive Director

Lutheran Theological Seminary
114 Seminary Cres., Saskatoon, SK S7N 0X3
Tel: 306-966-7850; *Fax:* 306-966-7852
development.office@usask.ca
www.usask.ca/stu/luther
www.facebook.com/LTSSaskatoon
Rev. Dr. Gordon Jensen, Dean of Studies
gordon.jensen@usask.ca
Rev. Dr. William Harrison, President

St. Andrew's College
1121 College Dr., Saskatoon, SK S7N 0W3
Tel: 306-966-8970; *Fax:* 306-966-8981
Toll-Free: 1-877-644-8970
standrews.college@usask.ca
www.usask.ca/stu/standrews
www.facebook.com/StAndrewsCollegeSaskatoon
www.youtube.com/user/StAndrewsSaskatoon
Note: The College is a theological school of The United Church
of Canada.
Richard Manley-Tannis, Principal
richard.manley-tannis@usask.ca

St. Peter's College
P.O. Box 40
Muenster, SK S0K 2Y0
Tel: 306-682-7888; *Fax:* 306-682-4402
spc@stpeters.sk.ca
www.stpeterscollege.ca

Note: Affiliated with the University of Saskatchewan, the College
provides Arts & Science, Agriculture, & Commerce courses to
first and second year students.
Robert Harasymchuk, President

St. Thomas More College (STM)
1437 College Dr., Saskatoon, SK S7N 0W6
Tel: 306-966-8900; *Fax:* 306-966-8904
Toll-Free: 1-800-667-2019
www.stmcollege.ca
www.facebook.com/stmcollege
twitter.com/stm1936
www.youtube.com/stm1936
Note: St. Thomas More College is a Catholic, liberal arts college,
federated with the University of Saskatchewan.

<u>Centres & Institutes</u>
Canadian Centre for Health & Safety in Agriculture (CCHSA)
P.O. Box 23
104 Clinic Pl., Saskatoon, SK S7N 2Z4
Tel: 306-966-8286; *Fax:* 306-966-8799
cchsa.ccssma@usask.ca
cchsa-ccssma.usask.ca
Niels Koehncke, Director
niels.koehncke@usask.ca

Centre for Forensic Behavioural Science & Justice Studies
#110A, 9 Campus Dr., Saskatoon, SK S7N 5A5
Tel: 306-966-6818
www.usask.ca/cfbsjs
Stephen Wormith, Director
s.wormith@usask.ca

University Learning Centre
Murray Building
#106, 3 Campus Dr., Saskatoon, SK S7N 5A4
Tel: 306-966-2886
www.usask.ca

Centre for Integrative Medicine
HSC E-Wing, College of Medicine
107 Wiggins Rd., Saskatoon, SK S7N 5E5
Tel: 306-966-7935
integrative.medicine@usask.ca
Michael Epstein, Managing Director

Colleges

Saskatoon: **Gabriel Dumont Institute**
917 - 22nd St. West, Saskatoon, SK S7M 0R9
Tel: 306-242-6070; *Fax:* 306-242-0002
Toll-Free: 877-488-6888
info@gdins.org
gdins.org
www.facebook.com/gabrieldumontinstitute
twitter.com/gdins_org
www.youtube.com/user/gabrieldumontins
Note: The institute has partnerships with University of
Saskatchewan & University of Regina & the Educational arm of
the Métis Nation-Saskatchewan.

Saskatoon: **Horizon College & Seminary**
Also known as: Central Pentecostal College
604 Webster St., Saskatoon, SK S7N 3P9
Tel: 306-374-6655; *Fax:* 306-373-6968
Toll-Free: 877-374-6655
info@horizon.edu
www.horizon.edu
www.facebook.com/horizoncollegesk
twitter.com/HorizonCollege
www.youtube.com/user/HorizonCollegeSK
Note: Horizon is a Christian college founded in 1935.
Jeromey Martini, President

Post Secondary/Technical

Air Ronge: **Northlands College**
P.O. Box 1000
Hwy. 2 North, Air Ronge, SK S0J 3G0
Tel: 306-425-4480; *Fax:* 306-425-3002
Toll-Free: 888-311-1185
trainnorth.ca
www.facebook.com/northlandscollege
twitter.com/NorthlandsColg
www.youtube.com/c/NorthlandscollegeSkCa
Note: Program Centers are located in La Ronge (306-425-4353),
Buffalo Narrows (306-235-1765), & Creighton (306-688-8838).
Guy Penney, President & CEO

<u>Campuses</u>
Buffalo Narrows Campus
P.O. Box 190
Cummings Dr., Buffalo Narrows, SK S0M 0J0
Tel: 306-235-1765; *Fax:* 306-235-4346

Canoe Campus
P.O. Box 509
207 Boardman St., La Ronge, SK S0J 1L0
Tel: 306-425-4353; *Fax:* 306-425-2696

Creighton Campus
P.O. Box 400
120 King Cres., Creighton, SK S0P 0A0
Tel: 306-688-8838; *Fax:* 306-688-7710

Rock Campus
P.O. Box 658
1328 La Ronge Ave., La Ronge, SK S0J 1L0
Tel: 306-425-4354; *Fax:* 306-425-4372

Humboldt: **Carlton Trail Regional College**
P.O. Box 720
611 - 17th St., Humboldt, SK S0K 2A0
Tel: 306-682-2623; *Fax:* 306-682-3101
Toll-Free: 800-667-2623
information@carltontrailcollege.com
www.carltontrailcollege.com
Shelley Romanyszyn-Cross, President & CEO

Melville: **Parkland College**
Administration Office
P.O. Box 790
200 Block 9th Ave. East, Melville, SK S0A 2P0
Tel: 306-728-4471; *Fax:* 306-728-2576
info@parklandcollege.sk.ca
parklandcollege.sk.ca
www.facebook.com/CollegeofChoice
twitter.com/CollegeofChoice
www.youtube.com/user/CollegeofChoice
Mark Hoddenbagh, President & CEO

<u>Campuses</u>
Canora Campus
P.O. Box 776
418 Main St., Canora, SK S0A 0L0
Tel: 306-563-6808; *Fax:* 306-563-4307

Esterhazy Campus
P.O. Box 850
501 Kennedy Dr., Esterhazy, SK S0A 0X0
Tel: 306-745-2878; *Fax:* 306-745-2080

Fort Qu'Appelle Campus
P.O. Box 398
740 Sioux Ave., Fort Qu'Appelle, SK S0G 1S0
Tel: 306-332-5416; *Fax:* 306-332-5242

Yorkton Campus
200 Prystai Way, Yorkton, SK S3N 4G4
Tel: 306-783-6566; *Fax:* 306-786-7866

<u>Centres & Institutes</u>
Kamsack Training Centre
P.O. Box 1690
241 - 2nd St., Kamsack, SK S0A 1S0
Tel: 306-542-4268; *Fax:* 306-542-3941

Yorkton Trades & Technology Centre
273 Dracup Ave. North, Yorkton, SK S3N 4H8
Tel: 306-786-2760; *Fax:* 306-786-7866

Nipawin: **Cumberland College**
Nipawin Campus
P.O. Box 2225
503 - 2nd St. East, Nipawin, SK S0E 1E0
Tel: 306-862-9833; *Fax:* 306-862-4940
www.cumberlandcollege.sk.ca
www.facebook.com/CumberlandCollege
twitter.com/CumberlandCol
Mark Hoddenbagh, President & CEO
mhoddenbagh@cumberlandcollege.sk.ca

Melfort Campus
P.O. Box 2320
400 Burns Ave. East, Melfort, SK S0E 1A0
Tel: 306-752-2786; *Fax:* 306-752-3484
crc.melfort@cumberlandcollege.sk.ca

Tisdale Campus
P.O. Box 967
800 - 101st St., Tisdale, SK S0E 1T0
Tel: 306-873-2525; *Fax:* 306-873-4450
crc.tisdale@cumberlandcollege.sk.ca

North Battleford: **North West College**
10702 Diefenbaker Dr., North Battleford, SK S9A 4A8
Tel: 306-937-5100; *Fax:* 306-445-1575
inquiry@northwestcollege.ca
northwestcollege.ca
www.facebook.com/NWCollegeSK
Enrollment: 823
Jay Notay, President & CEO

Campuses
Meadow Lake Campus
720 - 5th St. West, Meadow Lake, SK S9X 1T9
Tel: 306-234-5100; Fax: 306-236-7630

Regina: Avant-Garde College
1033 - 8th Ave., Regina, SK S4R 1E1
Tel: 306-522-5900
info@avant-gardecollege.ca
www.avant-gardecollege.ca
www.facebook.com/Avantgardecollege
Note: Avant-Garde College operates as a full-service educational salon.

Regina: Globe Theatre Conservatory
1801 Scarth St., Regina, SK S4P 2G9
Tel: 306-525-6400; Fax: 306-352-4194
Toll-Free: 866-954-5623
theatreschool@globetheatrelive.com
globetheatrelive.com/globe-theatre-school/globe-theatre-school
www.facebook.com/GlobeTheatreSchool
twitter.com/GlobeRegina
Note: Actor training program.

Regina: INtouch Career College
3520 - 5th Ave., Regina, SK S4T 0M2
Tel: 306-781-0360
www.intouchcareercollege.com
May Thiessen, Contact
mthiessen@intouchcareercollege.com

Regina: Royal Canadian Mounted Police Training Academy
P.O. Box 6500
5600 - 11th Ave., Regina, SK S4P 3J7
Tel: 306-780-5900
www.rcmp-grc.gc.ca/depot
Note: All cadets of the RCMP undergo initial basic training at the RCMP Academy, Depot Division. The National Law Enforcement Training Program (NLET) is also offered.

Regina: The Style Academy
2455 Broad St., Regina, SK S4P 0C7
Tel: 306-522-0606; Fax: 306-522-3334
info@styleacademy.ca
styleacademy.ca
www.facebook.com/styleacademyyqr
Candyce Fiessel, Director, Operations

Regina: Western College of Remedial Massage Therapies
832 McCarthy Blvd., Regina, SK S4T 6S7
Tel: 306-757-2242
information@westerncollege.ca
westerncollege.ca
Wayne Baiton, Principal

Regina: Zoom Zoom Groom's Academy of Pet Grooming
1180 Winnipeg St., Regina, SK S4R 1J6
Tel: 306-533-9155
zzgroom@sasktel.net
zoomzoomgroom.com
www.facebook.com/zoomzoomgroom

Saskatoon: Academy of Fashion Design
218B Ave. B South, Saskatoon, SK S7M 1M4
Tel: 306-978-9088; Fax: 306-933-9362
Toll-Free: 877-978-9088
fashiondesign@sasktel.net
www.aofdesign.com
www.facebook.com/aoffashiondesign
Heather J. Brigidear, Program Coordinator

Saskatoon: McKay Career Training Inc.
133 - 3rd Ave. North, Saskatoon, SK S7K 2H4
Tel: 306-955-1616
admissions@mckaysk.ca
mckaysk.ca
www.facebook.com/McKaySK
www.linkedin.com/company/mckay-career-training-inc
Note: The organization offers courses & programs for positions that include medical & veterinary office assistant, graphic art / electronic prepress, multimedia, massage therapy.

Saskatoon: Practicum Training Institute Inc. (PTI)
P.O. Box 30029
1624 - 33rd St. West, Saskatoon, SK S7M 7M6
Tel: 306-955-0079; Fax: 306-955-0343
pti@sasktel.net
www.practicumtraininginstitute.ca
www.facebook.com/practicumtraininginstitute

Note: Practicum Training Institute provides practical training to those working or interested in the Heavy Equipment Operating Industry.
Darrell Johanson, Principal

Saskatoon: Professional Institute of Massage Therapy
#114, 701 Cynthia St., Saskatoon, SK S7L 6B7
Tel: 306-955-5833
saskatoon@pimtmassage.com
pimtmassage.com
www.facebook.com/PIMTMassage

Campuses
Calgary Campus
#103, 1422 Kensington Rd. NW, Calgary, AB T2N 3P9
Tel: 403-247-4319
admin@calgarymassageschool.com
calgarymassageschool.com
www.facebook.com/110655790675329

Saskatoon: The Recording Arts Institute of Saskatoon (RAIS)
1926 Alberta Ave., Saskatoon, SK S7K 1R9
Tel: 306-292-6744; Fax: 306-244-2116
info@rais.ca
rais.ca
www.facebook.com/TheRecordingArtsInstituteofSaskatoon
twitter.com/RAISSASK
Note: RAIS offers programs in Audio Engineering, Motion Picture Arts & 3D Animation.

Saskatoon: Saskatchewan Indian Institute of Technologies (SIIT)
Asimakaniseekan Askiy Reserve
#118, 335 Packham Ave., Saskatoon, SK S7N 4S1
Tel: 306-244-4444; Toll-Free: 877-282-5622
siit.ca
www.facebook.com/siitlive
twitter.com/SIITlive
www.linkedin.com/company/siit
www.instagram.com/siitlive
Riel Bellegarde, President & CEO

Saskatoon: Saskatchewan Polytechnic
Administrative Offices
#400, 119 4th Ave. South, Saskatoon, SK S7K 5X2, Canada
Tel: 306-933-7331; Toll-Free: 866-467-4278
askaquestion@saskpolytech.ca
saskpolytech.ca
www.facebook.com/saskpolytech
twitter.com/saskpolytech
www.youtube.com/user/saskpolytech

Campuses
Saskatchewan Polytechnic - Saskatoon Campus
P.O. Box 1520
1130 Idylwyld Dr., Saskatoon, SK S7K 3R5, Canada
Toll-Free: 866-467-4278

Saskatchewan Polytechnic - Moose Jaw Campus
P.O. Box 1420
600 Saskatchewan St., Moose Jaw, SK S6H 4R4, Canada
Toll-Free: 866-467-4278

Saskatchewan Polytechnic - Regina Campus
P.O. Box 556
4500 Wascana Pkwy., Regina, SK S4P 3A3, Canada
Toll-Free: 866-467-4278

Saskatchewan Polytechnic - Prince Albert Campus
1100 - 15 St. East, Prince Albert, SK S6V 7S4, Canada
Toll-Free: 866-467-4278

Saskatoon: Saskatoon Business College
221 - 3rd Ave. North, Saskatoon, SK S7K 2H7
Tel: 306-244-6333; Toll-Free: 800-679-7711
www.sbccollege.ca
www.facebook.com/saskatoonbusinesscollege
www.linkedin.com/company/saskatoon-business-college
Note: The college offers programs in law, business, health care, computers & more.
Marcia Whittaker, Principal

Saskatoon: Saskatoon Spa Academy Ltd.
511 - 33rd St. West, #J, Saskatoon, SK S7L 0V7
Tel: 306-477-0187
inquiries@spaacademy.ca
spaacademy.ca
www.facebook.com/SpaAcademy
twitter.com/SpaAcademySK
www.instagram.com/spaacademy
Veronica Lynne-Swirsky, Director, Education

Saskatoon: Western Academy Broadcasting College
1222 Alberta Ave., Saskatoon, SK S7K 1R4
Tel: 306-665-1771
wabc@shaw.ca
www.wabc-westernacademy.com
www.facebook.com/WesternAcademyBroadcastingCollege
Note: The academy specializes in radio & television broadcast education.

Swift Current: Great Plains College
Swift Current Campus
129 - 2nd Ave. NE, Swift Current, SK S9H 4G3
Tel: 306-773-1531; Fax: 306-773-2384
Toll-Free: 866-296-2472
info@greatplainscollege.ca
www.greatplainscollege.ca
www.facebook.com/greatplainscollege
twitter.com/GPCollege
www.linkedin.com/company/great-plains-college
www.youtube.com/c/greatplainscollege
David Keast, President & CEO

Campuses
Biggar Campus
P.O. Box 700
701 Dominion St., Biggar, SK S0K 0M0
Tel: 306-948-3363; Fax: 306-948-2094
biggar.office@greatplainscollege.ca

Kindersley Campus
P.O. Box 488
514 Main St., Kindersley, SK S0L 1S0
Tel: 306-463-6431; Fax: 306-463-1161
kindersley.office@greatplainscollege.ca

Maple Creek Campus
P.O. Box 1738
20 Pacific Ave., Maple Creek, SK S0N 1N0
Tel: 306-662-3829; Fax: 306-662-3849
maplecreek.office@greatplainscollege.ca

Martensville Campus
66 Main St., Martensville, SK S0K 2T0
Tel: 306-651-1510

Warman Campus
P.O. Box 1001
201 Central St., Warman, SK S0K 4S0
Tel: 306-242-5377; Fax: 306-242-8662
warman.office@greatplainscollege.ca

Tugaske: Timeless Instruments
P.O. Box 51
Tugaske, SK S0H 4B0
Tel: 306-759-2042; Toll-Free: 888-884-2753
www.timelessinstruments.com
www.facebook.com/115399595203630
Note: Timeless Instruments offers a 7 week apprenticeship designed to teach students the process of instrument Design, Construction, Assembly Finishing & Set-up.
David Freeman, Contact
david@timelessinstruments.com

Weyburn: Southeast College
Administrative Offices
P.O. Box 1565
633 King St., Weyburn, SK S4H 0T1
Tel: 306-848-2500; Fax: 306-848-2517
communications@southeastcollege.org
www.southeastcollege.org
www.facebook.com/southeastcollegesaskatchewan
twitter.com/SCSaskatchewan
www.youtube.com/user/SoutheastCollege
Patrick Stoddart, President & CEO

Campuses
Assiniboia Campus
Prince of Wales Bldg.
201 - 3rd Ave. West, Assiniboia, SK S0H 0B0
Tel: 306-642-4287; Fax: 306-642-3397

Estevan Campus
P.O. Box 1750
532 Bourquin Rd., Estevan, SK S4A 1C8
Tel: 306-634-4795; Fax: 306-637-5225

Moosomin Campus
610 Park Ave., Moosomin, SK S0G 3N0
Tel: 306-435-4631; Fax: 306-435-4639

Centres & Institutes
Indian Head Basic Education Centre
708 Otterloo St., Indian Head, SK S0G 2K0
Tel: 306-695-2228; Fax: 306-695-2226

Whitewood Learning Centre
708 - 5th Ave., Whitewood, SK S0G 5C0
Tel: 306-435-4631; *Fax:* 306-735-2999

Yukon Territory

Government Agencies

Whitehorse: **Yukon Department of Education**
Government of Yukon
P.O. Box 2703
1000 Lewes Blvd., Whitehorse, YT Y1A 2C6, Canada
Tel: 867-667-5141; *Fax:* 867-393-6254
Toll-Free: 800-661-0408
contact.education@gov.yk.ca
yukon.ca/en/education-and-schools
Hon. Jeanie McLean, Minister, 867-393-7494
Jeanie.McLean@yukon.ca

School Boards/Districts/Divisions

French

Whitehorse: **Commission scolaire francophone du Yukon (CSFY)**
478 rue Range, Whitehorse, YT Y1A 3A2
Tel: 867-667-8680; *Fax:* 867-393-6946
Toll-Free: 800-661-0408
info@csfy.ca
commissionscolaire.csfy.ca
Grades: Pre-K.-12 *Enrollment:* 165 *Note:* The board operates the Yukon's only French first language school, École Émilie-Tremblay.
Jean-Sébastien Blais, Président
presidence@csfy.ca
Marc Champagne, Directeur général
marc.champagne@yukon.ca

Schools: Independent & Private

Independent & Private Schools

Whitehorse: **Yukon Montessori School**
1191 First Ave., Whitehorse, YT Y1A 0K5
Tel: 867-334-7482
montessoriyukon@gmail.com
yukonmontessori.com
www.facebook.com/YukonMontessoriSchool
Grades: 1 - 6
Dominic Bradford, Head Teacher

Universities & Colleges

Colleges

Whitehorse: **Yukon University**
P.O. Box 2799
500 College Dr., Whitehorse, YT Y1A 5K4, Canada
Tel: 867-668-8800; *Toll-Free:* 800-661-0504
www.yukonu.ca
www.facebook.com/yukonuniversity
twitter.com/yukonu
www.linkedin.com/company/yukon-college
www.instagram.com/yukonuniversity
Maggie Matear, Interim President & Vice-Chancellor
Wally Rude, Registrar & Dean, Enrolment Services
wrude@yukonu.ca
Gayle Corry, Director, Finance & Administrative Services
gcorry@yukonu.ca
Giulia Lucchini, Director, Employee Relations & Organizational Development, 867-668-8787
glucchini@yukonu.ca

Post Secondary/Technical

Whitehorse: **Mile 918 Driver Development**
P.O. Box 322
Whitehorse, YT Y1A 1Y3
Tel: 867-667-6837; *Fax:* 867-668-2293
Note: Offers Class 1 & Class 3 Truck Driver Training, Air Brake Endorsement Courses & Upgrade Training.

International Schools

Overseas Schools/Programs

Bangladesh: **Dhaka: Canadian International School**
Block A, Banani
110 Rd. 27, Dhaka, Bangladesh
info@canadaeducationbd.com
www.canadaeducationbd.com
Grades: K - 12 *Enrollment:* 200 *Note:* Nova Scotia curriculum.

Bangladesh: **Gulshan-2, Dhaka: Canadian Trillinium School (CTS)**
7 Rd. 62, Gulshan-2, Dhaka, Bangladesh
contact@cts.edu.bd
www.cts.edu.bd
Other Information: Phone: +88-02-882-3958
Grades: K - 12 *Note:* New Brunswick curriculum.

Bermuda: **Hamilton: Mount Saint Agnes Academy**
19 Dundonald St. West, Hamilton, Bermuda
msaoffice@msa.bm
www.msa.bm
Other Information: Phone: +441-292-4134; Fax: +441-295-7265
www.facebook.com/MSAbermuda
Grades: K - 12 *Enrollment:* 362 *Note:* Alberta curriculum.

Brazil: **Boa Viagem, Recife, PE: Colégio Santa Maria**
Rua Pe. Bernardino, Pessoa, 512, Boa Viagem, PE, Brazil
www.stamaria.com.br/boa-viagem
Other Information: Phone: +55-51-020-210
Grades: K - 12 *Enrollment:* 25 *Note:* New Brunswick curriculum.

Cambodia: **Chamkarmorn, Phnom Penh: Canadian International School of Phnom Penh**
Bassac Garden City
41 Preah Norodom Blvd., Chamkarmorn, Phnom Penh, Cambodia
info@cisp.edu.kh
www.cisp.edu.kh
Other Information: Phone: +855-23-727-788; Fax: +855-23-727-766
www.facebook.com/CanadianInternationalSchoolOfPhnomPenh
Grades: K - 12 *Enrollment:* 600 *Note:* Alberta curriculum.

Canada: **Richmond Hill: Canadian College Italy - The Renaissance School**
Canadian Head Office
#301, 1595 - 16th Ave., Richmond Hill, ON L4B 3N9
Tel: 647-938-7244
admissions@canadiancollegeitaly.com
www.canadiancollegeitaly.com
Other Information: Int'l Phone: +39-0872-71-49-69; Fax: +39-0872-450-28
www.facebook.com/canadiancollegeitaly
Grades: 9 - 12 *Enrollment:* 100 *Note:* Ontario curriculum. It is located at Via Cavour 13, Lanciano (CH), Italy 66034.
Santino Bellisario, Head

Canada: **Vancouver: Maple Leaf Educational Systems**
Vancouver Office
#400, 601 West Broadway, Vancouver, BC V5Z 4C2
Tel: 604-675-6910; *Fax:* 604-675-6911
info@mapleleafschools.com
corporate.mapleleafschools.com
www.facebook.com/MLESIR
twitter.com/teachmapleleaf
www.linkedin.com/company/mles
Number of Schools: 32 pre; 32 elementary; 29 middle; 18 secondary; 3 foreign national *Grades:* Pre-K - 12 *Number of Employees:* 6,000 *Note:* Maple Leaf Educational Systems was founded in 1995, with the goal of blending Eastern & Western educational practices. Maple Leaf schools offer Canadian & Chinese accreditation & diplomas. The Chinese Office can be contacted at: Jinshitan National Holiday Resort, No. 9 Central St., Dalian, China 116650.
Sherman Jen, Chair & CEO

China: **Wuhu, Anhui: Anhui Concord College of Sino-Canada (ACCSC)**
Wanchunzhonglu, Chengdongxinqu, Wuhu, Anhui, China
Grades: K - 12 *Enrollment:* 1000 *Note:* The ACCSC is a joint Canadian-Chinese boarding senior-high school with New Brunswick curriculum.

China: **Beijing: Beijing Concord College of Sino-Canada (BCCSC)**
Tongzhou District
Conglin, Zhuangyuan, Beijing, China
www.ccsc.com.cn/index.php/Index/ccsc/e/e

Grades: 10 - 12 *Note:* New Brunswick curriculum.

China: **Beijing: Beijing No. 25 Middle School**
East District
55 Dengshikou Dajie, Beijing, China
Grades: 10 - 12 *Note:* Nova Scotia curriculum.

China: **Jiangmen City: Boren Sino - Canadian School**
65 Shuanglong Ave., Jiangmen City, China
academics@borenschool.com
borenschool.com
Other Information: Phone: +86-750-321-7848
Grades: 9 - 12 *Note:* Ontario curriculum.

China: **Changchun City, Jilin Province: Canada Changchun Secondary School**
2666 Jingyang Da Lu, Changchun City, Jilin Province, China
Tel: 604-760-7564
www.kezhi.ca/changchun-secondary-school
Grades: 10 - 12 *Enrollment:* 55 *Note:* British Columbia curriculum.

China: **Hefei, Anhui Province: Canada Hefei Secondary School**
2356 Xizang Rd., Hefei, Anhui Province, China
www.kezhi.ca/hefei-secondary-school
Grades: 10 - 12 *Enrollment:* 235 *Note:* British Columbia curriculum.

China: **Kunming, Yunnan Province: Canada Kunming Secondary School**
247 Baita Lu, Kunming, Yunnan Province, China
www.kezhi.ca/kunming-secondary-school
Grades: 10 - 12 *Enrollment:* 85 *Note:* British Columbia curriculum.

China: **Langfang, Hebei Province: Canada Langfang Secondary School**
350 Jianguo Road, Langfang, Hebei Province, China
www.kezhi.ca/langfang-secondary-school
Grades: 10 - 12 *Enrollment:* 135 *Note:* British Columbia curriculum.

China: **Qingdao, Shandong Province: Canada Qingdao Secondary School**
2 Yangxin Rd., Shibei District, Qingdao, Shandong Province, China
Tel: 778-893-8566
info@cess.ca
www.csee.ca/18201.html
Grades: 10 - 11 *Note:* British Columbia curriculum.

China: **Tai'an, Shandong Province: Canada Shandong Secondary School**
52 Wenhua Rd., Tai'an, Shandong Province, China
Tel: 778-893-8566
info@cess.ca
www.csee.ca/14422.html
Grades: 10 - 12 *Note:* British Columbia curriculum.

China: **Weifang, Shandong Province: Canada Weifang Secondary School**
High Tech Zone
East Baotong St., Weifang, Shandong Province, China
info@cess.ca
www.csee.ca/9273.html
Grades: 10 - 12 *Enrollment:* 60 *Note:* British Columbia curriculum.

China: **Zibo, Shandong Province: Canada Zibo Secondary School**
119 Liuquan Rd., Zhangdian District, Zibo, Shandong Province, China
www.kezhi.ca/zibo-no-11-secondary-school-czss
Grades: 10 - 12 *Enrollment:* 125 *Note:* British Columbia curriculum.

China: **Beijing: Canadian International School of Beijing**
38 Liangmaqiao, Lu Chaoyang District, Beijing, China
www.cisbeijing.com
Other Information: Phone: +86-10-6465-7788; Fax: +86-10-6465-7788
twitter.com/CISBeijing
Grades: K - 12 *Enrollment:* 1000 *Number of Employees:* 130 *Note:* New Brunswick curriculum.

China: Panyu District, Guangzhou: Canadian International School of Guangzhou (CIS)
122 Dongyi Rd., Panyu District, Guangzhou, China
info@cisgz.com
cisgz.com
Other Information: Phone: +86-20-3993-9920
www.facebook.com/CISGZ
www.linkedin.com/company/cisgz
Grades: K - 12 *Enrollment:* 500 *Note:* The school teaches Alberta curriculum.
Gary Rehman, Principal

China: Aberdeen, Hong Kong SAR: Canadian International School of Hong Kong (CDNIS)
36 Nam Long Shan Rd., Aberdeen, Hong Kong SAR, China
schoolinfo@cdnis.edu.hk
www.cdnis.edu.hk
Other Information: Phone: +852-2525-7088
Grades: Pre.-12 *Enrollment:* 1800 *Number of Employees:* 300
Note: International Baccalaureate and Ontario Secondary School Diploma
Melanie Hnetka, Senior Manager, Communications
melaniehnetka@cdnis.edu.hk

China: Zhejiang Province, Wenzhou: Canadian Secondary Wenzhou No. 22 School
East Xueyuan Rd., Zhejiang Province, Wenzhou, China
csw-english.cinec.ca
Grades: 10 - 12 *Enrollment:* 125 *Note:* British Columbia curriculum.
Kent Tamblyn, Principal
kenttamblyn@gmail.com

China: Changchun, Jilin Province: Changchun Experimental High School
Jingyue Development Zone
2002 Fuzhi Rd., Changchun, Jilin Province, China
Other Information: Phone: +86-431-86801086; Fax: +86-431-86801559
Grades: 10 - 12 *Enrollment:* 64 *Note:* Nova Scotia curriculum.

China: Chengdu, Sichuan Province: Chengdu Foreign Language School
High-tech West Zone
Yangxi Xian, Chengdu, Sichuan Province, China
www.cfls.net.cn
Other Information: Phone: +86-2887820291
Grades: 10 - 12 *Note:* Nova Scotia curriculum.

China: Kowloon, Hong Kong SAR: Christian Alliance International School (CAIS)
33 King Lam St., Lai Chi Kok, Kowloon, Hong Kong SAR, China
info@caisbv.edu.hk
www.caisbv.edu.hk
Other Information: Phone: 852-3699-3899; Fax: 852-3699-3900
www.facebook.com/CAIS.HK
Grades: Pre.-12 *Enrollment:* 1400 *Number of Employees:* 160
Note: Alberta curriculum; Advanced Placement (AP) courses
Dr. Cora Hui, Principal cum Interim Head of School
Dr. Richard Lee, Principal
Vinod Khiatani, Director, School Development
khiataniv@caisbv.edu.hk

China: Guangzhou, Guangdong Province: Clifford International School (CIS)
Clifford Estates
8 Shiguang Rd., Clifford Estates Panyu, Guangzhou, Guangdong Province, China
international@cliffordschool.org
www.cliffordschool.org
Other Information: Phones: +86-20-8471-8273
Grades: 1 - 12 *Note:* Manitoba curriculum.

China: Hong Kong: Delia School of Canada Elementary Section
Tai Fung Ave., Taikoo Shing, Hong Kong, China
e.office@delia.edu.hk
www.delia.edu.hk
Other Information: Tel.: 3658 0508; Fax: 2560 6184
Grades: Pre.-6 *Note:* Ontario curriculum.
Tammie McGee, Deputy Principal, Elementary Section

Campuses
Secondary Section
Tai Fung Ave., Taikoo Shing, Hong Kong, China
s.office@delia.edu.hk
Other Information: Tel.: 3658 0338; Fax: 2885 7824
Grades: 7-12
Allan Morrison, Deputy Principal, Secondary Section

China: Guangzhou, Guangzhou Province: English School attached Guangdong University of Foreign Studies
599, Guanghua One, Dalang, Baiyun District, Guangzhou, Guangzhou Province, China
Grades: 10 - 12 *Enrollment:* 150 *Note:* Nova Scotia curriculum.

China: Ganzhou, Jiangxi: Ganzhou No. 3 Middle School (China)
30 Youth Rd., Ganzhou, Jiangxi, China
Grades: 10 - 11 *Note:* Prince Edward Island curriculum.

China: Tongxiang, Zhejiang Province: Grand Canadian Academy (Jiaxing) (GCA)
c/o Maodun High School (Tongxiang)
288 Zhenxing Donglu, Tongxiang, Zhejiang Province, China
www.gcahighschool.ca/jiaxing
Other Information: Phone & Fax: 573-8810-7576; Alt. Phone: 573-8810-7658
Grades: 9 - 12 *Enrollment:* 100 *Note:* British Columbia curriculum.
Darren Larson, Principal
dlarson@gcahighschool.ca

China: Guiyang, Guizhou: Guiyang Concord College of Sino-Canada (GCCSC)
Jinzhu West Rd., New World Terrace, Guanshan lake D, Guiyang, Guizhou, China
Grades: 1 - 12 *Note:* New Brunswick curriculum.

China: Guiyang, Guizhou Province: Guiyang No. 1 High School
1 Xingzhu East Road, Jinyang New District, Guiyang, Guizhou Province, China
Grades: 10 - 12 *Enrollment:* 100 *Note:* Nova Scotia curriculum.

China: Harbin, Heilongjiang: Harbin Shenghengji Concord College of Sino-Canada (HSCCSC)
1357 Longzing Rd., Songbei District, Harbin, Heilongjiang, China
Other Information: Phone: +86-451-8588-8599
Note: New Brunswick curriculum.

China: Zhengzhou, Henan Province: Henan Experimental High School
60 Wenhua Rd., Zhengzhou, Henan Province, China
Grades: 10 - 12 *Note:* Nova Scotia curriculum.

China: Changsha, Hunan: Hunan Concord College of Sino-Canada (HCCSC)
99 jingyuan Rd., Yeulu District, Changsha, Hunan, China
www.hccsc.com.cn
Other Information: Phone: +86-731-8299-1111
Grades: K - 12 *Note:* New Brunswick curriculum.

China: Shenzhen, Guangdong: International School of Nanshan Shenzhen (ISNS)
11 Longyuan Rd., Nanshan District, Shenzhen, Guangdong, China
admissions@isnsz.com
www.isnsz.com
Other Information: Phone: +86-755-2666-1000; Fax: +86-755-2645-4090
Grades: K - 12 *Enrollment:* 300 *Note:* New Brunswick curriculum.

China: Jiaxing City, Zhejiang Province: Jiaxing Senior High School
365 Hongyin Rd., Jiaxing City, Zhejiang Province, China
jiaxing-english.cinec.ca
Grades: 10 - 12 *Enrollment:* 50 *Note:* British Columbia curriculum.

China: Jilin City, Jilin Province: Jilin No. 1 High School
155 Song Jiang West Rd., Jilin City, Jilin Province, China
sinocanadianprogram.com
Other Information: Phone: +86-432-64852111; Fax: +86-043-24826017
Grades: 10 - 12 *Enrollment:* 91 *Note:* Nova Scotia curriculum.

China: Karamay, Xin Jiang: Karamay Senior High School
58 Zhun Ge Er St., Karamay, Xin Jiang, China
Other Information: Phone: +86-990-6236538
Grades: 10 - 12 *Enrollment:* 72 *Note:* Nova Scotia curriculum.

China: Luoyang, Henan Province: Luoyang No. 1 High School (East Campus)
1 Shuanglang St., Chenhe District, Luoyang, Henan Province, China
Other Information: Phone: +86-186-2375-8712
Grades: 10 - 12 *Note:* Nova Scotia curriculum.

China: Shanghai, Huangpu District: Luwan Senior High School
885 Xietu Rd., Shanghai, Huangpu District, China
english.luwan.cinec.ca
Grades: 10 - 12 *Enrollment:* 62 *Note:* British Columbia curriculum.

China: Dalian, Liaoning Province: Maple Leaf Foreign Nationals School - Dalian
30 Gaoyan St., Zhongshan District, Dalian, Liaoning Province, China
china.mapleleafschools.com/schools/dalian
Other Information: Phone: +86-4080-6301
Grades: K - 9 *Enrollment:* 98 *Note:* British Columbia curriculum.

China: Wuhan, Hubei Province: Maple Leaf Foreign Nationals School - Wuhan
East Lake Hi-Tech Development Zone
1018 Minzu Ave., Wuhan, Hubei Province, China
info@mapleleafedu.com
china.mapleleafschools.com/schools/wuhan
Grades: K - 9 *Enrollment:* 66 *Note:* British Columbia curriculum.
Darrell Goss, Principal
dgoss@mapleleaf.net.ca
George Watson, Superintendent, BC Program, 604-675-6910
georgewatson.mapleleaf@gmail.com

China: Zhenjiang, Jiangsu Province: Maple Leaf International High School - Zhenjiang
Dagang High School, South Campus
Zhaosheng Rd., Dagang Count, Zhenjiang, Jiangsu Province, China
china.mapleleafschools.com/schools/zhenjiang
Grades: 11 - 12 *Enrollment:* 957 *Note:* British Columbia curriculum.

China: Chongqing, Jiangsu Province: Maple Leaf International School - Chongqing
#1 Maple Leaf Rd., Chongqing, Jiangsu Province, China
china.mapleleafschools.com/schools/chongqing
Other Information: Phone: +86-4080-6301
Grades: 10 - 12 *Enrollment:* 376 *Note:* British Columbia curriculum.

China: Haikou, Hainan Province: Maple Leaf International School - Hainan
Haikou, Hainan Province, China
info@mapleleafedu.com
china.mapleleafschools.com/schools/haikou
Grades: Secondary *Enrollment:* 44 *Note:* British Columbia curriculum.

China: Shijiazhuang City, Hebei Provin: Middle School attached to Hebei Normal University - Shijiazhuang
315 Zhongshan East Rd., Shijiazhuang City, Hebei Provin, China
Grades: 10 - 12 *Note:* Nova Scotia curriculum.

China: Nanchang, Jiangxi Province: Nanchang No. 2 High School
Honggutan, New District, Nanchang, Jiangxi Province, China
Grades: 10 - 12 *Note:* Nova Scotia curriculum.

China: Nanjing, Jiangsu Province: Nanjing Foreign Language School British Columbia Academy (NFLS BC)
30 East Beijing Rd., Nanjing, Jiangsu Province, China
bca.nfls.com.cn/moodle
www.linkedin.com/company/nanjing-foreign-language-school
Grades: 10 - 12 *Enrollment:* 302 *Note:* British Columbia curriculum.

China: Nanjing, Jiangsu Province: Nanjing-Bond International College
Nanjing No. 13 High School
#14, Xijia Datang, Xuanwu District, Nanjing, Jiangsu Province, China
bond13z@yahoo.com.cn
bond.nj13z.cn
Other Information: Phone: 011-86-25-8326-9911; Fax: 011-86-25-8326-9927
Grades: 9 - 12 *Note:* Ontario curriculum.

China: Xuhui District, Shanghai: Shanghai Nanyang Model High School
1118 Tianyaoqiao Rd., Xuhui District, Shanghai, China
nanmo-english.cinec.ca
Other Information: Phone: +86-21-628-25748
Grades: 10 - 12 *Enrollment:* 231 *Note:* British Columbia curriculum.

China: Minhang District, Shanghai: **Shanghai United International School (SUIS)**
55 Wan Yuan Rd., Minhang District, Shanghai, China
Grades: 10 - 12 *Enrollment:* 317 *Note:* British Columbia curriculum.

China: Shenyang, Liaoning Province: **Shenyang No. 2 High School (North Campus)**
198 Shenbei Rd., Shenbei New District, Shenyang, Liaoning Province, China
sy2zscc.webs.com
Other Information: Phone: +86-24-88043958
Grades: 10 - 12 *Enrollment:* 263 *Note:* Nova Scotia curriculum.

China: Nanshan District, Shenzhen, Gua: **Shenzhen (Nanshan) Concord College of Sino-Canada (SCCSC)**
166 Nanguang Rd., Nanshan District, Shenzhen, Gua, China
Grades: 10 - 12 *Enrollment:* 900 *Note:* New Brunswick curriculum.

China: Dongcheng District, Beijing, Fe: **Sino Bright School No. 8**
#1803, No. 5 Jianguomen North St., Dongcheng District, Beijing, Fe, China
www.sinobrightschool.net
Other Information: Phone: +86-10-6553-8727; Fax: +86-10-6553-7171
Grades: 12 *Enrollment:* 159 *Note:* British Columbia curriculum.

China: Wujiang City, Suzhou, Jiangsu P: **Sino-Canada High School**
1 Kangli Dadao, Lili zhen, Wujiang City, Suzhou, Jiangsu P, China
www.sinocanadahighschool.com
Other Information: Phone: +86-400-1888-366
www.linkedin.com/school/sino-canada
Grades: 1 - 12 *Enrollment:* 2100 *Note:* British Columbia curriculum.

China: Suzhou, Jiangsu Province: **Soochow University High School - Canadian Program**
Suzhou Industrial Park
29 Dongzhen Rd., Suzhou, Jiangsu Province, China
en.szcanada.com
Other Information: Phone: 0512-62519226
Grades: 10 - 12 *Enrollment:* 131 *Note:* Nova Scotia curriculum.

China: Lubei District, Tangshan, Hebei: **Tangshan No. 1 High School**
369 Xiangyun Rd., Lubei District, Tangshan, Hebei, China
Grades: 10 - 12 *Enrollment:* 224 *Note:* Nova Scotia curriculum.

China: Xingtai, Hebei Province: **Xingtai No. 1 High School**
118 Zhonghua dajie, Qiaoxi District, Xingtai, Hebei Province, China
Grades: 10 - 12 *Enrollment:* 57 *Note:* Nova Scotia curriculum.

China: Yizhuang, Beijing: **Yang Guang Qing International School of Beijing (YGQ)**
Beijing Economic & Development Zone
2 Tian Bao North St., Yizhuang, Beijing, China
ygqen.cnming.net
www.facebook.com/ygqbeijing
Grades: 10 - 12 *Note:* Manitoba curriculum.

China: WuQing District, Tianjin: **Yinghua-Bond International College**
Yong Yang West Rd., WuQing District, Tianjin, China
www.tjyh2003.com
Other Information: Phone: 011-86-22-5961-1023; Fax: 011-86-22-5961-1166
Grades: 9 - 12 *Note:* Ontario curriculum.

Colombia: La Estrella, Antioquia: **Colegio Canadiense**
Cra 51 #97 Sur 137, La Estrella, Antioquia, Colombia
comunicaciones@colegiocanadiense.edu.co
www.colegiocanadiense.edu.co
Other Information: Tel.: (+57) 300 530 5309
www.facebook.com/colecanadiense01
www.youtube.com/c/ComunicacionesColegioCanadiense
Grades: 10 - 12 *Enrollment:* 116 *Note:* British Columbia curriculum.

Egypt: El Sherouk City, Cairo: **British Columbia Canadian International School (BCCIS)**
P.O. Box 98
5th Settlement Section, 34 Suez Rd. Entrance, El Sherouk City, Cairo, Egypt
admin@bccis.ca
bccis.ca
Other Information: Phone: +20-1002128113
www.facebook.com/bcciscairo
Grades: K - 12 *Enrollment:* 1000 *Number of Employees:* 100
Note: British Columbia curriculum.

Egypt: Zone 4, New Greater Cairo: **Canadian International School of Egypt (CISE)**
El Tagamosa El Khames, Zone 4, New Greater Cairo, Egypt
admission@cise-eg.com
cise-egypt.com
Other Information: Phone: +202-25418277; Fax: +202-25418299
www.facebook.com/CISIANS
www.instagram.com/canadian_int_school_of_egypt
Grades: JK - 12 *Note:* The school teaches Ontario curriculum.
Charles Blanchard, Director

Egypt: 6th of October City, Giza: **Heritage International School**
Al-Yasmine Greenland, Second Touristic Village
P.O. Box 38
6th of October City, Giza, Egypt
info@heritageinternationalschool.com
heritageinternationalschool.com
www.facebook.com/218640688193402
twitter.com/heritageegypt
Grades: K - 12 *Note:* Manitoba curriculum.

Ghana: Accra: **Canadian Independent College Ghana (CIC)**
Airport Residential Area
#Z-26 Patrice Lumumba Rd., Accra, Ghana
ghana@cicbaden.ca
www.ghanacic.com
Other Information: Phone: 233-302-760-571; 233-240-301-303; 233-554-830-443
Grades: Pre.-Sec. *Enrollment:* 48 *Number of Employees:* 31
Note: Ontario curriculum.
Dr. Heather Bohez, B.Sc., N.D., Director
Agnes Attakora-Gyan, Principal, 233240301303
ghana@cicbaden.ca
Akosua Konadu Arhin, Office Manager, 233554830443
business@cicbaden.ca

Hong Kong: New Territories, Hong Kong SAR: **Renaissance College Hong Kong (RCHK)**
5 Hang Ming St., New Territories, Hong Kong SAR, Hong Kong
info@rchk.edu.hk
www.rchk.edu.hk
Other Information: Phone: 852-3556-5556; Fax: 852-3556-3446
www.facebook.com/RenaissanceCollegeHK
twitter.com/RCHKschool
Enrollment: 2000
Harry Brown, Principal

India: Bangalore: **Canadian International School**
4 & 20 Manchenahalli, Yelahanka, Bangalore, India
info@cisb.org.in
www.canadianinternationalschool.com
Other Information: Phone: +91-804249-4444
www.facebook.com/canadianinternationalschoolbangalore
twitter.com/cisblearns
www.linkedin.com/school/canadian-international-school
www.youtube.com/c/CanadianInternationalSchoolBangalore
Grades: K - 12 *Note:* Provides a learning experience to mainly expatriate & Indian students The school is accredited by the International Baccalaureate Organization & Ontario Ministry of Education, & is a member of the Council of International Schools.
Ramani Sastri, Chair
Ted Mockrish, Head, School
hos@cisb.org.in

Japan: Tokyo: **Canadian International School (Japan)**
5-8-20 Kitashinagawa, Shinagawa-ku, Tokyo, Japan
study@cisjapan.net
www.cisjapan.net
Other Information: Phone: 03-5793-1392; Fax: 03-5793-3559
Grades: 1 - 12 *Enrollment:* 273 *Note:* Prince Edward Island curriculum.

Japan: Saitama, Tokyo: **Columbia International School of Japan**
153 Matsugo, Tokorozawa, Saitama, Tokyo, Japan
admissions@columbia-ca.co.jp
columbia-ca.co.jp
Other Information: Phone: +81-4-2946-1911; Fax: +81-4-2946-1955
Grades: K - 12 *Enrollment:* 280 *Note:* Ontario curriculum.

Japan: Tosa City, Kochi Prefecture: **Meitoku Gijuku School**
Ryu Campus
564 Ryu Usa Cho, Tosa City, Kochi Prefecture, Japan
info@meitoku-gijuku.ed.jp
www.meitoku-gijuku.ed.jp/english
Other Information: Phone: 088-828-6688; Fax: 088-856-3060
Grades: 11 *Note:* Manitoba curriculum.

Macao: Taipa: **The International School of Macao (TIS)**
Block K, Macau University of Science & Technology
Avenida Wai Long, Taipa, Macao
info@tis.edu.mo
tis.edu.mo
Other Information: Phone: +853-2853-3700; Fax: +853-2853-3702
www.facebook.com/TISMacao
twitter.com/TISMacao
www.linkedin.com/company/the-international-school-of-macao
Grades: 7 - 12 *Note:* Alberta curriculum.

Malaysia: Petaling Jaya, Selangor: **Sunway College (Canadian International Matriculation Programme)**
#3 Jalan Universiti, Jalan Kolej, Bandar Sunway, Petaling Jaya, Selangor, Malaysia
infosis@sunway.edu.my
college.sunway.edu.my/programmes/pre-u/cimp
Other Information: Phone: 011-603-7491-8623, ext. 8124; Fax: 011-603-5635-8630
Grades: 9 - 12 *Note:* Ontario curriculum.

Malaysia: Selangor: **Taylor's College International Canadian Pre-University**
No. 1, Jalan SS15/8, 47500 Subang Jaya, Selangor, Malaysia
admission@taylors.edu.my
college.taylors.edu.my/en/study/pre-u-programme.html
Other Information: Phone: 603-5636-2641; Fax: 603-5634-5209
Grades: 9 - 12 *Enrollment:* 490 *Note:* Ontario curriculum.

Mexico: Acueducto Providencia, Guadalaj: **Canadian School Guadalajara**
Montevideo 3306, Acueducto Providencia, Guadalaj, Mexico
www.canadianschool.com.mx/en/guadalajara
Other Information: Phones: 3610-17-06; 3641-64-52
www.facebook.com/176388335730456
Grades: K - 9 *Enrollment:* 132 *Note:* Alberta curriculum.

Netherlands Antilles: St. Maarten: **Caribbean International Academy (CIA)**
P.O. Box 5454
Cupecoy, Tigris Rd., #4, Simpson Bay, St. Maarten, Netherlands Antilles
admissions@ciaschool.com
ciaschool.com
Other Information: Phone: +1-721-545-3871; Fax: +1-721-545-3872
www.facebook.com/CaribbeanIntlAcademy
Grades: JK - 12 *Enrollment:* 200 *Number of Employees:* 30
Note: The school teaches Ontario curriculum.

Qatar: Doha: **Blyth Academy Qatar**
P.O. Box 24359
Doha, Qatar
marketing@blythacademyqatar.com
blythacademyqatar.com
Other Information: Phone: +974-4421-7553
www.facebook.com/blythacademy
twitter.com/BlythQatar
www.linkedin.com/company/blyth-academy-
Grades: JK - 12 *Note:* Alberta curriculum.

Qatar: Doha, Muaither: **Hayat Universal School Qatar (HUBS)**
Muaither Bldg. 55, Area 53
P.O. Box 6124
Muaither St. North, Doha, Muaither, Qatar
info.qa@hayatschool.com
www.hayatschool.com/qatar/qatarmain.htm
Grades: 1 - 12 *Enrollment:* 828 *Note:* British Columbia curriculum.

Saint Lucia: **Rodney Bay: International School of St. Lucia (ISSL)**
P.O. Box 2701
Rodney Bay, Saint Lucia
reception@intschoolstlucia.org
intschoolstlucia.org
Other Information: Phone: +758-458-0989
www.facebook.com/107231472671756
Grades: 10 - 12 *Enrollment:* 50 *Note:* New Brunswick curriculum.

Singapore: **Singapore: Canadian International School (Singapore)**
7 Jurong West St. 41, Singapore, Singapore
www.cis.edu.sg
Other Information: Phone: 65-6467-1732; Fax: 65-6467-1729
www.facebook.com/CIS.edu.sg
twitter.com/cissingapore
Number of Schools: 2 *Grades:* Pre.-12 *Enrollment:* 2500 *Note:* Ontario curriculum.

Campuses
Tanjong Katong Campus
371 Tanjong Katong Rd., Singapore 437128, Singapore
Other Information: Phone: 65-6345-1573; Fax: 65-6345-4057
Grades: Pre.-6

South Korea: **Yeonsu-gu, Incheon: CMIS Canada**
IGC Support Center, Incheon Global Campus
SongdoMunhwa-ro 119, Yeonsu-gu, Incheon, South Korea
Tel: 032-715-8000; *Fax:* 032-715-8080
info@cmis.kr
www.cmis.kr
Other Information: Phone: +82-32-715-8000; Fax: +82-32-428-0579
www.facebook.com/271476482896372
Grades: K - 12 *Enrollment:* 142 *Note:* Manitoba curriculum.

Switzerland: **Neuchâtel: Neuchâtel Junior College**
Crêt-Taconnet, 4, Neuchâtel, Switzerland
admissions@neuchatel.org
www.njc.ch
Other Information: 032-722-1869
www.facebook.com/neuchateljuniorcollege
twitter.com/neuchjrcollege
www.linkedin.com/company/neuch-tel-junior-college
www.instagram.com/neuchateljuniorcollege
Grades: 12 & AP *Enrollment:* 90 *Note:* Ontario curriculum.

Andrew J. Keleher, Head of School
Affiliations
Canadian Office
#1310, 44 Victoria St., Toronto, ON M5C 1Y2
Tel: 416-368-8169; *Fax:* 416-368-0956
Toll-Free: 800-263-2923
Note: The Canadian Head Office is responsible for admissions, alumni publications, events & records, & fundraising.
Dayle Leishman, Director, Canadian Operations
dleishman@neuchatel.org
Brenda Neil, Director, Admission
admissions@neuchatel.org
Sarah Morison, Director, Advancement
advancement@neuchatel.org

Thailand: **Phasicharoen, Bangkok: British Columbia International School, Bangkok (BCISB)**
606 Kalaprapruek Rd., Bang Wa, Phasicharoen, Bangkok, Thailand
contact@bcisb.ac.th
bcisb.ac.th
Other Information: Phone: +662-802-1188
www.facebook.com/bcisb.thailand
Grades: 10 - 12 *Note:* British Columbia curriculum.

The Netherlands: **Brunssum: AFNORTH International School in the Netherlands**
Ferdinand Bolstraat 1, Brunssum, The Netherlands
directorate@afnorth-is.com
afnorth-is.com
Other Information: Phone: +31-455-278-221
twitter.com/AFNORTH_IS
Grades: 9 - 12 *Enrollment:* 900 *Note:* Institution offers programs following the curriculum of Ontario.

Trinidad & Tobago: **Petit Valley: Maple Leaf International School - Trinidad & Tobago**
Alyce Heights Dr., Alyce Glen, Petit Valley, Trinidad & Tobago
Tel: 868-632-9578; *Fax:* 868-633-3968
mlis@mapleleaf-school.com
www.mapleleaf-school.com
www.facebook.com/mapleleafschool
www.instagram.com/mapleleaf_tt
Grades: 9 - 12 *Enrollment:* 350 *Note:* The school offers Ontario curriculum.

Richard Rozario, Principal
rrozario@mapleleaf-school.com
Laila Mohammed Pantin, Manager, Finance & Operations
lpantin@mapleleaf-school.com

Trinidad & Tobago: **Chaguanas: Trillium International School**
Liberty Centre
Hakim Juman St., Chaguanas, Trinidad & Tobago
Tel: 868-665-2641; *Fax:* 868-665-6174
trillium@tstt.net.tt
www.trilliumtt.com
www.facebook.com/Trilliumintschool
Grades: K - 12 *Note:* Ontario curriculum.
Betty Craig, Principal

United Arab Emirates: **Abu Dhabi: Abu Dhabi Grammar School (Canada)**
Tourist Club Area
P.O. Box 27161
Abu Dhabi, United Arab Emirates
agsadmin@agsgrmmr.sch.ae
www.agsgrmmr.sch.ae
Other Information: Phone: +971-2-644-4703; Fax: +971-2-645-4703
Grades: K - 12 *Enrollment:* 1080 *Note:* Institution offers programs following the curriculum of Nova Scotia.

United Arab Emirates: **Abu Dhabi: Canadian International School (Abu Dhabi) (CIS)**
P.O. Box 3976
Khalifa A City, Abu Dhabi, United Arab Emirates
reception@cisabudhabi.com
cisabudhabi.com
Other Information: Phone: +971-2-556-4206
Grades: K - 12 *Enrollment:* 550 *Note:* Alberta curriculum.

SECTION 7

GOVERNMENT:
FEDERAL & PROVINCIAL

Listings in this section are as current as possible at the time of publication. For appointments made and results of elections held after publication, please refer to Canada's Information Resource Centre (CIRC), if your library subscribes to this online database.

Government Quick Reference Guide

ACTS & REGULATIONS

Justice Canada, 284 Wellington St., Ottawa, ON K1A 0H8
613-957-4222, Fax: 613-954-0811, webadmin@justice.gc.ca
Office of the Administrator of the Ship-source Oil Pollution Fund, #830, 180 Kent St., Ottawa, ON K1A 0N5
613-991-1726, Fax: 613-990-5423, info@sopf-cidphn.gc.ca
Office of the Senate Ethics Officer, Thomas D'Arcy McGee Bldg., #526, 90 Sparks St., Ottawa, ON K1P 5B4
613-947-3566, Fax: 613-947-3577, 800-267-7362, cse-seo@sen.parl.gc.ca
Policy Horizons Canada, 360 Albert St., 15th Fl., Ottawa, ON K1R 7X7
613-947-3800, Fax: 613-995-6006, questions@horizons.gc.ca
Public Prosecution Service of Canada, 160 Elgin St., 12th Fl., Ottawa, ON K1A 0H8
613-957-6489, 877-505-7772, info@ppsc.gc.ca

Alberta
Alberta Justice & Solicitor General, John E. Brownlee Bldg., 10365 - 97th St., 9th Fl., Edmonton, AB T5J 3W7
780-427-2745

British Columbia
British Columbia Ministry of Attorney General & Minister responsible for Housing, PO Box 9044 Prov Govt, Victoria, BC V8W 9E2

Manitoba
Manitoba Justice, Administration & Finance, #1110, 405 Broadway Ave., Winnipeg, MB R3C 3L6
204-945-2878

New Brunswick
New Brunswick Department of Justice & Public Safety, Marysville Place, 3rd Fl., PO Box 6000, Fredericton, NB E3B 5H1
506-453-3992, DPS-MSP.Information@gnb.ca

Newfoundland & Labrador
Newfoundland & Labrador Department of Justice & Public Safety, East Block, Confederation Bldg., 4th Fl., PO Box 8700, St. John's, NL A1B 4J6
709-729-2869, Fax: 709-729-0469, justice@gov.nl.ca
Newfoundland & Labrador Department of Transportation & Infrastructure, Confederation Bldg., Prince Philip Dr., PO Box 8700, St. John's, NL A1B 4J6
709-729-2300, ti@gov.nl.ca

Northwest Territories
Northwest Territories Department of Justice, 4903 - 49th St., PO Box 1320, Yellowknife, NT X1A 2L9
867-767-9256, justice_communications@gov.nt.ca

Nova Scotia
Nova Scotia Department of Justice, 1690 Hollis St., PO Box 7, Halifax, NS B3J 2L6
902-424-4030, justweb@gov.ns.ca

Nunavut
Nunavut Territory Department of Justice, PO Box 1000 500, Iqaluit, NU X0A 0H0
867-975-6170, Fax: 867-975-6195, justice@gov.nu.ca

Ontario
Ontario Ministry of the Attorney General, McMurtry-Scott Bldg., 720 Bay St., 11th Fl., Toronto, ON M7A 2S9
416-326-2220, Fax: 416-326-4016, 800-518-7901, attorneygeneral@ontario.ca

Prince Edward Island
Prince Edward Island Department of Justice & Public Safety, Shaw Bldg. South, 95 Rochford St., 4th Fl., PO Box 2000, Charlottetown, PE C1A 7N8
902-368-4589, Fax: 902-368-5283, DeptJPS@gov.pe.ca

Quebec
Les Publications du Québec, 1000, rte de l'Église, 5e étage, Québec, QC G1V 3V9
418-643-5150, Fax: 418-643-6177, 800-463-2100
Ministère de la Justice, Édifice Louis-Philippe-Pigeon, 1200, rte de l'Église, Québec, QC G1V 4M1
418-643-5140, 866-536-5140, informations@justice.gouv.qc.ca

Saskatchewan
Saskatchewan Justice & Attorney General, 1874 Scarth St., Regina, SK S4P 4B3

Yukon Territory
Yukon French Language Services Directorate, 305 Jarvis St., 3rd Fl., PO Box 2703, Whitehorse, YT Y1A 2C6
867-667-8260, Fax: 867-393-6226, info.dsf-flsd@yukon.ca
Yukon Justice, Andrew Philipsen Law Centre, 2134 - 2nd Ave., PO Box 2703, Whitehorse, YT Y1A 2C6
867-667-3033, Fax: 867-667-5200, justice@yukon.ca

ADOPTION
See Also: Child Welfare

Nunavut
Nunavut Territory Department of Family Services, PO Box 1000 1200, Iqaluit, NU X0A 0H0
867-975-5200, Fax: 867-975-5722

AGRICULTURE
See Also: Land Resources
Agriculture & Agri-Food Canada, 1341 Baseline Rd., Ottawa, ON K1A 0C5
613-773-1000, Fax: 613-773-1081, 855-773-0241, info@agr.gc.ca
Canadian Grain Commission, #600, 303 Main St., Winnipeg, MB R3C 3G8
204-984-0506, Fax: 204-983-2751, 800-853-6705, contact@grainscanada.gc.ca
Farm Products Council of Canada, Building 59, Central Experimental Farm, 960 Carling Ave., Ottawa, ON K1A 0C6
613-759-1555, Fax: 613-759-1566, 855-611-1165, aafc.fpcc-cpac.aac@canada.ca

Alberta
Agricultural Products Marketing Council, JG O'Donoghue Bldg., #305, 7000 - 113 St., Edmonton, AB T6H 5T6
780-427-2164
Agriculture Financial Services Corporation, 5718 - 56 Ave., Lacombe, AB T4L 1B1
877-899-2372, info@afsc.ca
Alberta Agriculture & Forestry, JG O'Donoghue Bldg., #100A, 7000 - 113th St., Edmonton, AB T6H 5T6
403-742-7901
Farmers' Advocate Office, JG O'Donoghue Bldg., #100, 7000 - 113 St., Edmonton, AB T6H 5T6
Fax: 780-427-3913, -310-3276, farmers.advocate@gov.ab.ca
Northern Alberta Development Council, Peace River Office, Provincial Building, #206, 9621 - 96 Ave., PO Box 900-14, Peace River, AB T8S 1T4
780-624-6274, Fax: 780-624-6184, -310-0000, nadc.council@gov.ab.ca

British Columbia
AgriStability, 200, 1690 Powick Rd., Kelowna, BC V1X 7G5
877-343-2767, Fax: 877-605-8467, agristability@gov.bc.ca
British Columbia Farm Industry Review Board, 780 Blanshard St., PO Box 9129 Prov Govt, Victoria, BC V8W 9B5
250-356-8945, Fax: 250-356-5131, firb@gov.bc.ca
British Columbia Ministry of Agriculture, Food & Fisheries, PO Box 9043 Prov Govt, Victoria, BC V8W 9E2
888-221-7141, agriservicebc@gov.bc.ca

Manitoba
Agricultural Societies, 1129 Queens Ave., Brandon, MB R7A 1L9
204-726-6195, Fax: 204-726-6260
Manitoba Agriculture, Legislative Bldg., #165, 450 Broadway, Winnipeg, MB R3C 0V8
204-945-3722, Fax: 204-945-3470, minagr@leg.gov.mb.ca

New Brunswick
New Brunswick Agricultural Insurance Commission, c/o Department of Agriculture, Aquaculture & Fisheries, PO Box 6000, Fredericton, NB E3B 5H1
506-453-2666, Fax: 506-453-7406, DAAF-MAAP@gnb.ca
New Brunswick Department of Agriculture, Aquaculture & Fisheries, Agricultural Research Station (Experimental Farm), PO Box 6000, Fredericton, NB E3B 5H1
506-453-3826, Fax: 506-453-7170, DAAF-MAAP@gnb.ca
New Brunswick Grain Commission, c/o Department of Agriculture, Aquaculture & Fisheries, PO Box 6000, Fredericton, NB E3B 5H1
506-859-3309, Fax: 506-856-2092, DAAF-MAAP@gnb.ca

Newfoundland & Labrador
Newfoundland & Labrador Crop Insurance Agency, PO Box 2006, Corner Brook, NL A2H 6J8
709-637-2077, Fax: 709-637-2591

Northwest Territories
Agricultural Products Marketing Council, PO Box 1320, Yellowknife, NT X1A 2L9
Fax: 867-873-0563
Northwest Territories Department of Environment & Natural Resources, PO Box 1320, Yellowknife, NT X1A 2L9
867-767-9055, enr_communications@gov.nt.ca
Northwest Territories Egg Producers Board, 7 Studney Dr., PO Box 4386, Hay River, NT X0E 1G3
867-874-0645, Fax: 867-874-6840, manager_nwteggproducers@yahoo.ca

Nova Scotia
Nova Scotia Crop & Livestock Insurance Commission, 74 Research Dr., Truro, NS B6L 2R2
902-893-6370, 800-565-6371, nsclic@novascotia.ca
Nova Scotia Department of Agriculture, 1800 Argyle St., 6th Fl., Halifax, NS B3J 3N8
902-424-4560, Fax: 902-424-4671, 800-279-0825
Nova Scotia Farm Loan Board, 74 Research Dr., Truro, NS B6L 2R2
902-893-6506, Fax: 902-895-7693, FLBNS@novascotia.ca

Ontario
Ontario Ministry of Agriculture, Food & Rural Affairs, Ontario Government Bldg., 1 Stone Rd. West, Guelph, ON N1G 4Y2
519-826-3100, Fax: 519-826-4335, 888-466-2372, about.omafra@ontario.ca

Prince Edward Island
Prince Edward Island Department of Agriculture & Land, Jones Bldg., 11 Kent St., 5th Fl., PO Box 2000, Charlottetown, PE C1A 7N8
902-368-4880, Fax: 902-368-4857

Quebec
La financière agricole de Québec, 1400, boul Guillaume-Couture, Lévis, QC G6W 8K7
418-838-5602, Fax: 418-833-3871, 800-749-3646
Ministère de l'Agriculture, des Pêcheries et de l'Alimentation du Québec, 200, ch Sainte-Foy, Québec, QC G1R 4X6
418-380-2110, 888-222-6272

Saskatchewan
Agricultural Implements Board, #302, 3085 Albert St., Regina, SK S4S 0B1
Fax: 306-787-8599
Farmland Security Board, #315, 3988 Albert St., Regina, SK S4S 3R1
306-787-5047, Fax: 306-787-8599,
Prairie Agricultural Machinery Institute, 2215 - 8th Ave., PO Box 1150, Humboldt, SK S0K 2A0
306-682-5033, Fax: 306-682-5080, 800-567-7264, pami@pami.ca
Saskatchewan Agriculture, Walter Scott Bldg., 3085 Albert St., Regina, SK S4S 0B1
866-457-2377
Saskatchewan Sheep Development Board, 2213C Hanselman Crt., Saskatoon, SK S7L 6A8
306-933-5200, Fax: 306-933-7182, sheepdb@sasktel.net

AGRICULTURE & FOOD
Agriculture & Agri-Food Canada, 1341 Baseline Rd., Ottawa, ON K1A 0C5
613-773-1000, Fax: 613-773-1081, 855-773-0241, info@agr.gc.ca
Market & Industry Services Branch, Tower 5, 1341 Baseline Rd., Ottawa, ON K1A 0C5
613-759-1000, Fax: 613-773-1711
Science & Technology Branch, Tower 5, 1341 Baseline Rd., Ottawa, ON K1A 0C5
Fax: 613-773-1711
Strategic Policy Branch, Tower 7, 1341 Baseline Rd., Ottawa, ON K1A 0C5
613-759-1000, Fax: 613-773-2121

Alberta
Agricultural Products Marketing Council, JG O'Donoghue Bldg., #305, 7000 - 113 St., Edmonton, AB T6H 5T6
780-427-2164
Agriculture Financial Services Corporation, 5718 - 56 Ave., Lacombe, AB T4L 1B1
877-899-2372, info@afsc.ca
Alberta Agriculture & Forestry, JG O'Donoghue Bldg., #100A, 7000 - 113th St., Edmonton, AB T6H 5T6
403-742-7901
Farmers' Advocate Office, JG O'Donoghue Bldg., #100, 7000 - 113 St., Edmonton, AB T6H 5T6
Fax: 780-427-3913, -310-3276, farmers.advocate@gov.ab.ca
Irrigation Council, Provincial Bldg., 200 - 5 Ave. South, 3rd Fl., Lethbridge, AB T1J 4L1
403-381-5176, Fax: 403-382-4406

British Columbia
Agricultural Land Commission, #133, 4940 Canada Way, Burnaby, BC V5G 4K6
604-660-7000, Fax: 604-660-7033, ALCBurnaby@Victoria1.gov.bc.ca
AgriStability, 200, 1690 Powick Rd., Kelowna, BC V1X 7G5
877-343-2767, Fax: 877-605-8467, agristability@gov.bc.ca
British Columbia Broiler Hatching Egg Commission, #180, 32160 South Fraser Way, Abbotsford, BC V2T 1W5
604-850-1854, Fax: 604-850-1683, info@bcbhec.com
British Columbia Chicken Marketing Board, #101, 32450 Simon Ave., Abbotsford, BC V2T 4J2
604-859-2868, Fax: 604-859-2811, info@bcchicken.ca
British Columbia Cranberry Marketing Commission, 36376 Stephen Leacock Dr., Abbotsford, BC V3G 0C2
604-557-8717, info@bccranberries.com
British Columbia Egg Marketing Board, #250, 32160 South Fraser Way, Abbotsford, BC V2T 1W5
604-556-3348, Fax: 604-556-3410, bcemb@bcegg.com
British Columbia Hog Marketing Commission, PO Box 8000-280, Abbotsford, BC V2S 6H1
604-287-4647, Fax: 604-820-6647, info@bcpork.ca
British Columbia Milk Marketing Board, #200, 32160 South Fraser Way, Abbotsford, BC V2T 1W5
604-556-3444, Fax: 604-556-7717, info@milk-bc.com

British Columbia Ministry of Agriculture, Food & Fisheries, PO Box 9043 Prov Govt, Victoria, BC V8W 9E2
888-221-7141, agriservicebc@gov.bc.ca
British Columbia Turkey Marketing Board, #106, 19329 Enterprise Way, Surrey, BC V3S 6J8
604-534-5644, Fax: 604-534-3651, info@bcturkey.com
British Columbia Vegetable Marketing Commission, #207, 15252 - 32nd Ave., Surrey, BC V3S 0R7
604-542-9734, Fax: 604-542-9735, info@bcveg.com

Manitoba
Agricultural Societies, 1129 Queens Ave., Brandon, MB R7A 1L9
204-726-6195, Fax: 204-726-6260
Manitoba Agricultural Services Corporation, #400, 50 - 24th St. NW, Portage la Prairie, MB R1N 3V9
204-239-3246, Fax: 204-239-3401, mailbox@masc.mb.ca
Manitoba Agriculture, Legislative Bldg., #165, 450 Broadway, Winnipeg, MB R3C 0V8
204-945-3722, Fax: 204-945-3470, minagr@leg.gov.mb.ca

New Brunswick
New Brunswick Agricultural Insurance Commission, c/o Department of Agriculture, Aquaculture & Fisheries, PO Box 6000, Fredericton, NB E3B 5H1
506-453-2666, Fax: 506-453-7406, DAAF-MAAP@gnb.ca
New Brunswick Farm Products Commission, c/o Department of Agriculture, Aquaculture & Fisheries, PO Box 6000, Fredericton, NB E3B 5H1
506-453-3647, Fax: 506-444-5969, DAAF-MAAP@gnb.ca
New Brunswick Grain Commission, c/o Department of Agriculture, Aquaculture & Fisheries, PO Box 6000, Fredericton, NB E3B 5H1
506-859-3309, Fax: 506-856-2092, DAAF-MAAP@gnb.ca

Newfoundland & Labrador
Chicken Farmers of Newfoundland & Labrador, PC Box 8098, St. John's, NL A1B 3M9
709-747-1493
Farm Industry Review Board, 192 Wheeler's Rd., PO Box 2006, Corner Brook, NL A2H 6J8
709-637-2672, Fax: 709-637-2365
Newfoundland & Labrador Crop Insurance Agency, PO Box 2006, Corner Brook, NL A2H 6J8
709-637-2077, Fax: 709-637-2591
Newfoundland & Labrador Department of Industry, Energy & Technology, Natural Resources Bldg., 50 Elizabeth Ave., PO Box 8700, St. John's, NL A1B 4J6
709-729-3017, Fax: 709-729-0059

Nova Scotia
Natural Products Marketing Council, 74 Research Dr., Bible Hill, NS B6L 2R2
902-893-6511, Fax: 902-893-7579
Nova Scotia Crop & Livestock Insurance Commission, 74 Research Dr., Truro, NS B6L 2R2
902-893-6370, 800-565-6371, nsclic@novascotia.ca
Nova Scotia Department of Agriculture, 1800 Argyle St., 6th Fl., Halifax, NS B3J 3N8
902-424-4560, Fax: 902-424-4671, 800-279-0825

Ontario
Agricorp, Ontario Government Bldg NW, 1 Stone Rd. West, 3rd Fl., PO Box 3660 Central, Guelph, ON N1H 8M4
Fax: 519-826-4118, 888-247-4999, contact@agricorp.com
Agricultural Research Institute of Ontario, Ontario Government Bldg NW, 1 Stone Rd. West, 2nd Fl., Guelph, ON N1G 4Y2
519-826-4197, Fax: 519-826-4211, research.omafra@ontario.ca
Agriculture, Food & Rural Affairs Tribunal & Board of Negotiation, Ontario Government Bldg NW, 1 Stone Rd. West, 2nd Fl., Guelph, ON N1G 4Y2
519-826-3433, Fax: 519-826-4232, appeals.tribunal.omafra@ontario.ca
Ontario Ministry of Agriculture, Food & Rural Affairs, Ontario Government Bldg., 1 Stone Rd. West, Guelph, ON N1G 4Y2
519-826-3100, Fax: 519-826-4335, 888-466-2372, about.omafra@ontario.ca
Policy Division, Ontario Government Bldg, 1 Stone Rd. West, 2nd Fl., Guelph, ON N1G 4Y2
519-826-4020, Fax: 519-826-3492

Prince Edward Island
Agricultural Insurance Corporation, 7 Gerald McCarville Drive, Kensington, PE C0B 1M0
BIO|FOOD|TECH, 101 Belvedere Ave., PO Box 2000, Charlottetown, PE C1A 7N8
902-368-5548, Fax: 902-368-5549, 877-368-5548, biofoodtech@biofoodtech.ca
Policy & Agriculture Resources, Jones Bldg., 11 Kent St., 5th Fl., Charlottetown, PE C1A 7N8
Prince Edward Island Department of Agriculture & Land, Jones Bldg., 11 Kent St., 5th Fl., PO Box 2000, Charlottetown, PE C1A 7N8
902-368-4880, Fax: 902-368-4857

Quebec
Commission de protection du territoire agricole du Québec, 200, ch Ste-Foy, 2e étage, Québec, QC G1R 4X6
418-643-3314, Fax: 418-643-2261, 800-667-5294, info@cptaq.gouv.qc.ca
Conseil des appellations réservées et des termes valorisant, #4.03, 201 boul Crémazie est, Montréal, QC H2M 1L2
514-864-8999, Fax: 514-873-2580, info@cartv.gouv.qc.ca
Ministère de l'Agriculture, des Pêcheries et de l'Alimentation du Québec, 200, ch Sainte-Foy, Québec, QC G1R 4X6
418-380-2110, 888-222-6272
Régie des marchés agricoles et alimentaires du Québec, 201, boul Crémazie est, 5e étage, Montréal, QC H2M 1L3
514-873-4024, Fax: 514-873-3984, rmaaqc@rmaaq.gouv.qc.ca

Saskatchewan
Agri-Food Council, #315, 3085 Albert St., Regina, SK S4S 0B1
Fax: 306-787-8599
Saskatchewan Agriculture, Walter Scott Bldg., 3085 Albert St., Regina, SK S4S 0B1
866-457-2377
Saskatchewan Crop Insurance Corporation, 484 Prince William Dr., PO Box 3000, Melville, SK S0A 2P0
306-728-7200, Fax: 306-728-7202, 888-935-0000, customer.service@scic.gov.sk.ca
Saskatchewan Egg Producers, #1, 123 Pinehouse Dr., Saskatoon, SK S7K 5W1
306-664-4131, Fax: 306-664-4140, info@saskegg.ca
Saskatchewan Milk Marketing Board, 470 Maxwell Cres., Regina, SK S4N 6L7
306-949-6999, Fax: 306-949-2605, info@saskmilk.ca

Yukon Territory
Yukon Environment, 10 Burns Rd., Whitehorse, YT Y1A 2C6
867-667-5652, Fax: 867-393-7197, environmentyukon@yukon.ca

AIR
Prince Edward Island
Prince Edward Island Department of Environment, Energy & Climate Action, Jones Bldg., 11 Kent St., 4th Fl., Charlottetown, PE C1A 7N8
902-368-5044, Fax: 902-368-5830, 866-368-5044, DeptEECA@gov.pe.ca

---

AIR POLLUTION
See Also: Environment
Environmental Protection Branch, 351, boul Saint-Joseph, Gatineau, QC K1A 0H3
819-953-1711, Fax: 819-953-9452
International Joint Commission, 234 Laurier Ave. West, 22nd Fl., Ottawa, ON K1P 6K6
613-995-2984, Fax: 613-993-5583, commission@ottawa.ijc.org
Meteorological Service of Canada, 351, boul Saint-Joseph, Gatineau, QC K1A 0H3
819-934-5395, Fax: 819-934-1255

Alberta
Alberta Environment & Parks, Forestry Bldg., 9920 - 108th St., Main Fl., Edmonton, AB T5K 2M4
780-944-0313
Emissions Reduction Alberta, #746, 10104 - 103rd Ave. NW, Edmonton, AB T5J 0H8
780-498-2068, info@eralberta.ca

British Columbia
British Columbia Ministry of Environment & Climate Change Strategy, PO Box 9047 Prov Govt, Victoria, BC V8W 9E2

Manitoba
Manitoba Conservation & Climate, 200 Saulteaux Cres., PO Box 22, Winnipeg, MB R3J 3W3
204-945-6784, Fax: 204-948-2656, 800-214-6497, cc@gov.mb.ca

New Brunswick
New Brunswick Department of Environment & Local Government, Marysville Place, 20 McGloin St., Fredericton, NB E3B 5H1
506-453-2690, Fax: 506-457-4994, elg/egl-info@gnb.ca
New Brunswick Department of Natural Resources & Energy Development, Hugh John Flemming Forestry Centre, PO Box 6000, Fredericton, NB E3B 5H1
506-453-3826, Fax: 506-444-4367, dnr_mrnweb@gnb.ca

Northwest Territories
Northwest Territories Department of Environment & Natural Resources, PO Box 1320, Yellowknife, NT X1A 2L9
867-767-9055, enr_communications@gov.nt.ca

Nova Scotia
Nova Scotia Department of Environment, #1800, 1894 Barrington St., PO Box 442, Halifax, NS B3J 2P8
902-424-3600, Fax: 902-424-0501, 877-936-8476

Nunavut
Nunavut Territory Department of Environment, PO Box 1000 1320, Iqaluit, NU X0A 0H0
867-975-7700, Fax: 867-975-7742, environment@gov.nu.ca

Ontario
Ontario Ministry of Environment, Conservation & Parks, Ferguson Block, 77 Wellesley St. West, 11th Fl., Toronto, ON M7A 2T5
416-325-4000, Fax: 416-314-6713, 800-565-4923

Prince Edward Island
Prince Edward Island Department of Environment, Energy & Climate Action, Jones Bldg., 11 Kent St., 4th Fl., Charlottetown, PE C1A 7N8
902-368-5044, Fax: 902-368-5830, 866-368-5044, DeptEECA@gov.pe.ca

Quebec
Ministère de l'Environnement et de la Lutte contre les changements climatiques, Édifice Marie-Guyart, 675, boul René-Lévesque est, 30e étage, Québec, QC G1R 5V7
418-521-3830, Fax: 418-646-5974, 800-561-1616, relations.medias@mddelcc.gouv.qc.ca

Saskatchewan
Saskatchewan Environment, 3211 Albert St., Regina, SK S4S 5W6
306-787-2584, Fax: 306-787-9544, 800-567-4224, centre.inquiry@gov.sk.ca

Yukon Territory
Yukon Environment, 10 Burns Rd., Whitehorse, YT Y1A 2C6
867-667-5652, Fax: 867-393-7197, environmentyukon@yukon.ca

AIRPORTS & AVIATION
See Also: Transportation
Canadian Air Transport Security Authority, 99 Bank St., 13th Fl., Ottawa, ON K1P 6B9
Fax: 613-990-1295, 888-294-2202, correspondence1@catsa-acsta.gc.ca
Transport Canada, Place de Ville, 330 Sparks St., Ottawa, ON K1A 0N5
613-990-2309, Fax: 613-954-4731, 866-995-9737
Transportation Appeal Tribunal of Canada, #1201, 333 Laurier Ave. West, 12th Fl., Ottawa, ON K1A 0N5
613-990-6906, Fax: 613-990-9153, info@tatc.gc.ca

Newfoundland & Labrador
Newfoundland & Labrador Department of Transportation & Infrastructure, Confederation Bldg., Prince Philip Dr., PO Box 8700, St. John's, NL A1B 4J6
709-729-2300, ti@gov.nl.ca

Northwest Territories
Northwest Territories Department of Infrastructure, Stuart M. Hodgson Bldg., 5009 - 49th St., 3rd Fl., PO Box 1320, Yellowknife, NT X1A 2L9
INF_Communications@gov.nt.ca

Nunavut
Nunavut Territory Department of Community & Government Services, W.G. Brown Bldg., 4th Fl., PO Box 1000 700, Iqaluit, NU X0A 0H0
867-975-5406, Fax: 867-975-5305, cgscomms@gov.nu.ca

Ontario
Ontario Ministry of Transportation, 777 Bay St., 5th Fl., Toronto, ON M7A 1Z8
416-235-4686, Fax: 416-327-9185, 800-268-4686

Saskatchewan
Saskatchewan Highways, Victoria Tower, 1855 Victoria Ave., Regina, SK S4P 3T2
306-933-5186, MHI.CustomerService@gov.sk.ca

Yukon Territory
Yukon Highways & Public Works, PO Box 2703, Whitehorse, YT Y1A 2C6
867-667-3732, Fax: 867-393-6218, hpw-info@yukon.ca

APPRENTICESHIP PROGRAMS
Canadian Council of Directors of Apprenticeship, 140 Promenade du Portage, 6th Fl., Phase IV, Gatineau, QC K1A 0J9
Fax: 819-994-0202, 877-599-6933, redseal-sceaurouge@hrsdc-rhdcc.gc.ca

Alberta
Alberta Advanced Education, Legislature Bldg., #403, 10800 - 97th Ave., Edmonton, AB T5K 2B6
780-422-5400
Apprenticeship & Student Aid Division, Commerce Place, 10155 - 102nd St., 6th Fl., Edmonton, AB T5J 4L5

New Brunswick
New Brunswick Department of Post-Secondary Education, Training & Labour, Chestnut Complex, PO Box 6000, Fredericton, NB E3B 5H1
506-453-2597, Fax: 506-453-3618, dpetlinfo@gnb.ca

Northwest Territories
Apprenticeship, Trade & Occupations Certification Board, PO Box 1320, Yellowknife, NT X1A 2L9
867-767-9351, apprenticeship@gov.nt.ca
Prince Edward Island
SkillsPEI, Atlantic Technology Centre, #212, 176 Great George St., Charlottetown, PE C1A 4K9
902-368-6290, Fax: 902-368-6340, 877-491-4766
Quebec
Conseil consultatif du travail et de la main d'oeuvre, #17.100, 500, boul René-Lévesque ouest, Montréal, QC H2Z 1W7
514-873-2880, Fax: 514-873-1129
Saskatchewan
Saskatchewan Advanced Education, #1120, 2010 - 12th Ave., Regina, SK S4P 0M3
aeeinquiry@gov.sk.ca
Saskatchewan Apprenticeship & Trade Certification Commission, 2140 Hamilton St., Regina, SK S4P 2E3
306-787-2444, Fax: 306-787-5105, 877-363-0536, apprenticeship@gov.sk.ca
Yukon Territory
Yukon Education, 1000 Lewes Blvd., Whitehorse, YT Y1A 3H9
867-667-5141, Fax: 867-393-6254, edu-communications@yukon.ca

AQUACULTURE
See Also: Fisheries
Aquatic & Crop Resource Development Industry Partnership Facility, 550 University Ave., Charlottetown, PE C1A 4P3
Centre for Aquaculture & Environmental Research, 4160 Marine Dr., West Vancouver, BC V7V 1N6

ARCTIC & NORTHERN AFFAIRS
Crown-Indigenous Relations & Northern Affairs, Public Enquiries Contact Centre, 10, rue Wellington, Gatineau, QC K1A 0H4
Fax: 866-817-3977, 800-567-9604, aadnc.infopubs.aandc@canada.ca
Polar Knowledge Canada, #200, 170 Laurier Ave. West, 2nd Fl., Ottawa, ON K1P 5V5
613-943-8605, info@polar.gc.ca
British Columbia
Northern Development Initiative Trust, #301, 1268 Fifth Ave., Prince George, BC V2L 3L2
250-561-2525, Fax: 250-561-2563, info@northerndevelopment.bc.ca
Manitoba
Manitoba Indigenous Reconciliation & Northern Relations, Legislative Bldg., #301, 450 Broadway, Winnipeg, MB R3C 0V8
204-945-3788, Fax: 204-945-1383, INRweb@gov.mb.ca
Northwest Territories
Northwest Territories Department of Environment & Natural Resources, PO Box 1320, Yellowknife, NT X1A 2L9
867-767-9055, enr_communications@gov.nt.ca
Nunavut
Nunavut Territory Department of Executive & Intergovernmental Affairs, 1084 Aeroplex bldg., PO Box 1000 200, Iqaluit, NU X0A 0H0
867-975-6000, Fax: 867-975-6099
Ontario
Northern Development Division, Roberta Bondar Place, #200, 70 Foster Dr., Sault Ste. Marie, ON P6A 6V8
705-945-5900, Fax: 705-945-5931, 800-461-2287
Ontario Ministry of Northern Development, Mines, Natural Resources & Forestry, Natural Resources Information & Support Centre, 300 Water St., Toronto, ON K9J 8M5
800-667-1940
Yukon Territory
Yukon Economic Development, 303 Alexander St., Whitehorse, YT Y1A 2L5
800-661-0408, ecdev@yukon.ca

ARTS & CULTURE
Canada Council for the Arts, 150 Elgin St., 2nd Fl., PO Box 1047, Ottawa, ON K1P 5V8
613-566-4414, Fax: 613-566-4390, 800-263-5588, info@canadacouncil.ca
Canada Place Corporation, 100 The Pointe, 999 Canada Pl., Vancouver, BC V6C 3T4
604-775-7063
Canada Science & Technology Museum Corporation, PO Box 9724 T, Ottawa, ON K1G 5A3
613-991-3044, Fax: 613-993-7923, 866-442-4416, cts@techno-science.ca
Canadian Broadcasting Corporation, 181 Queen St., PO Box 3220 C, Ottawa, ON K1Y 1E4
613-288-6000, liaison@cbc.ca

Canadian Heritage, 15, rue Eddy, Gatineau, QC K1A 0M5
819-997-0055, 866-811-0055, PCH.info-info.PCH@canada.ca
Canadian Museum for Human Rights, 85 Israel Asper Way, Winnipeg, MB R3C 0L5
204-289-2000, Fax: 204-289-2001, 877-877-6037, info@humanrights.ca
Canadian Museum of History, 100, rue Laurier, Gatineau, QC K1A 0M8
819-776-7000, 800-555-5621
Canadian Museum of Nature, 240 McLeod St., PO Box 3443 D, Ottawa, ON K1P 6P4
613-566-4700, Fax: 613-364-4021, 800-263-4433
Library of Parliament, Information Servicce, Parliament of Canada, Ottawa, ON K1A 0A9
613-992-4793, 866-599-4999, info@parl.gc.ca
National Arts Centre, 1 Elgin St., PO Box 1534 B, Ottawa, ON K1P 5W1
613-947-7000, Fax: 613-947-7112, 866-850-2787
National Film Board of Canada, Operational Headquarters, Norman McLaren Building, 3155, ch de la Côte-de-Liesse, PO Box 1600 Centre-ville, Montréal, QC H3C 3H5
514-283-9000, 800-267-7710
National Gallery of Canada, 380 Sussex Dr., PO Box 427 A, Ottawa, ON K1N 9N4
613-990-1985, Fax: 613-993-4385, 800-319-2787, info@gallery.ca
Parks Canada, National Office, 30, rue Victoria, Gatineau, QC J8X 0B3
819-420-9486, 888-773-8888, information@pc.gc.ca
Telefilm Canada, #500, 360, rue Saint-Jacques, Montréal, QC H2Y 1P5
514-283-6363, Fax: 514-283-8212, 800-567-0890, info@telefilm.gc.ca
Alberta
Alberta Culture & Status of Women, Communications Branch, Standard Life Centre, 10405 Jasper Ave., 7th Fl., Edmonton, AB T5J 4R7
780-427-6530, Fax: 780-427-1496, 800-232-7215, culture.communications@gov.ab.ca
British Columbia
Arts, Culture, & Sport Division, PO Box 9490 Prov Govt, Victoria, BC V8W 9N7
250-356-6914, Fax: 250-387-7973
B.C. Place, 777 Pacific Blvd., Vancouver, BC V6B 4Y8
604-669-2300, Fax: 604-661-3412, stadium@bcpavco.com
British Columbia Arts Council, 800 Johnson St., PO Box 9819 Prov Govt, Victoria, BC V8W 9W3
250-356-1718, Fax: 250-387-4099, BCArtsCouncil@gov.bc.ca
British Columbia Ministry of Social Development & Poverty Reduction, PO Box 9058 Prov Govt, Victoria, BC V8W 9E1
866-866-0800
British Columbia Pavilion Corporation, #200, 999 Canada Place, Vancouver, BC V6C 3C1
604-482-2200, Fax: 604-681-9017, info@bcpavco.com
Creative BC, 2225 West Broadway, Vancouver, BC V6K 2E4
604-736-7997, Fax: 604-736-7290
Islands Trust, #200, 1627 Fort St., Victoria, BC V8R 1H8
250-405-5151, Fax: 250-405-5155
Manitoba
Communications Services Manitoba, 155 Carlton St., 10th Fl., Winnipeg, MB R3C 3H8
204-945-3765
Heritage Grants Advisory Council, c/o Heritage Grants Program, #330, 213 Notre Dame Ave., Winnipeg, MB R3B 1N3
204-945-2213, Fax: 204-948-2086
Le Centre Culturel franco-manitobain/Franco-Manitoban Cultural Centre, 340, boul Provencher, Winnipeg, MB R2H 0G7
204-233-8972, Fax: 204-233-3324, communication@ccfm.mb.ca
Manitoba Arts Council, #525, 93 Lombard Ave., Winnipeg, MB R3B 3B1
204-945-2237, Fax: 204-945-5925, 866-994-2787, info@artscouncil.mb.ca
Manitoba Centennial Centre Corporation, #1000, 555 Main St., Winnipeg, MB R3B 1C3
204-956-1360, Fax: 204-944-1390, inquiries@mbccc.ca
Manitoba Film Classification Board, #216, 301 Weston St., Winnipeg, MB R3E 3H4
204-945-8962, Fax: 204-945-0890, 866-612-2399, mfcb@gov.mb.ca
Manitoba Heritage Council, c/o Historic Resources Branch, 213 Notre Dame Ave., Main Fl., Winnipeg, MB R3B 1N3
204-945-2118, Fax: 204-948-2384, hrb@gov.mb.ca
Manitoba Museum, 190 Rupert Ave., Winnipeg, MB R3B 0N2
204-956-2830, Fax: 204-942-3679, info@manitobamuseum.ca
Manitoba Sport, Culture & Heritage, Legislative Bldg., #118, 450 Broadway, Winnipeg, MB R3C 0V8

Multiculturalism Secretariat, 213 Notre Dame Ave., 6th Fl., Winnipeg, MB R3B 1N3
204-945-5632, multisec@gov.mb.ca
New Brunswick
Arts New Brunswick, #201, 225 King St., Fredericton, NB E3B 1E1
506-444-4444, Fax: 506-444-5543, 866-460-2787
New Brunswick Department of Social Development, Sartain MacDonald Bldg., PO Box 6000, Fredericton, NB E3B 5H1
506-453-2001, Fax: 506-453-2164, sd-ds@gnb.ca
Newfoundland & Labrador
Newfoundland & Labrador Arts Council/ArtsNL, The Newman Bldg., 1 Springdale St., PO Box 98, St. John's, NL A1C 5H5
709-726-2212, Fax: 709-726-0619, 866-726-2212, nlacmail@nlac.ca
Newfoundland & Labrador Department of Tourism, Culture, Arts & Recreation, PO Box 8700, St. John's, NL A1B 4J6
709-729-7000, tcar@gov.nl.ca
Provincial Information & Library Resources Board, 48 St. George's Ave., Stephenville, NL A2H 1K9
709-643-0900, Fax: 709-643-0925
Northwest Territories
Northwest Territories Arts Council, PO Box 1320, Yellowknife, NT X1A 2L9
867-767-9347, Fax: 867-873-0205, 877-445-2787
Northwest Territories Department of Education, Culture & Employment, PO Box 1320, Yellowknife, NT X1A 2L9
ecepublicaffairs@gov.nt.ca
Nova Scotia
Art Gallery of Nova Scotia, 1723 Hollis St., PO Box 2262, Halifax, NS B3J 3C8
902-424-5280, Fax: 902-424-7359, info.agns@novascotia.ca
Nova Scotia Business Inc., PO Box 2374, Halifax, NS B3J 3E4
902-424-6650, 800-260-6682, info@nsbi.ca
Nova Scotia Museum, 1747 Summer St., Halifax, NS B3H 3A6
Fax: 902-424-0560, museum@novascotia.ca
Nunavut
Nunavut Territory Department of Culture & Heritage, PO Box 1000 800, Iqaluit, NU X0A 0H0
867-975-5500, Fax: 867-975-5504, 866-934-2035
Ontario
Art Gallery of Ontario, 317 Dundas St. West, Toronto, ON M5T 1G4
416-977-0414, Fax: 416-979-6669, 877-225-4246
Corporate Services Division, Mowat Block, 900 Bay St., 5th Fl., Toronto, ON M7A 1L2
416-325-6866, Fax: 416-314-7014, 888-664-6008
Ontario Arts Council, 151 Bloor St. West, 5th Fl., Toronto, ON M5S 1T6
416-961-1660, Fax: 416-961-7796, 800-387-0058, info@arts.on.ca
Ontario Heritage Trust, 10 Adelaide St. East, Toronto, ON M5C 1J3
416-325-5000, Fax: 416-325-5071
Ontario Library Service, Head Office, 334 Regent St., Sudbury, ON P3C 4E2
800-387-5765, info@olservice.ca
Ontario Media Development Corporation, South Tower, #501, 175 Bloor St. East, Toronto, ON M4W 3R8
416-314-6858, Fax: 416-314-6876, reception@omdc.on.ca
Ontario Ministry of Heritage, Sport, Tourism & Culture Industries, 438 University Ave., 6th Fl., Toronto, ON M5G 2K8
416-326-9326, Fax: 416-314-7854, 888-997-9015
Ontario Place Corporation, 955 Lake Shore Blvd. West, Toronto, ON M6K 3B9
416-314-9900, Fax: 416-314-9989, 866-663-4386
Ottawa Convention Centre, 55 Colonel By Dr., Ottawa, ON K1N 9J2
613-563-1984, Fax: 613-563-7646, 800-450-0077
Royal Ontario Museum, 100 Queen's Park Cres., Toronto, ON M5S 2C6
416-586-5549, Fax: 416-586-5685, info@rom.on.ca
Prince Edward Island
Prince Edward Island Department of Social Development & Housing, Jones Bldg., 11 Kent St., 2nd Fl., PO Box 2000, Charlottetown, PE C1A 7N8
902-620-3777, Fax: 902-368-4740, 866-594-3777, DeptSDH@gov.pe.ca
Quebec
Bibliothèque et Archives nationales du Québec (BAnQ), 475, boul de Maisonneuve est, Montréal, QC H2L 5C4
514-873-1100, Fax: 514-873-9312, 800-363-9028
Conseil des arts et des lettres du Québec, 79, boul René-Lévesque est, 3e étage, Québec, QC G1R 5N5
418-643-1707, Fax: 418-643-4558, 800-608-3350, info@calq.gouv.qc.ca
Conseil du patrimoine culturel du Québec, 225, Grande Allée est, Québec, QC G1R 5G5
418-643-8378, Fax: 418-643-8591, 844-701-0912, info@cpcq.gouv.qc.ca

Ministère de la Culture et Communications, 225, Grande Allée est, Québec, QC G1R 5G5
888-380-8882

Musée d'art contemporain de Montréal, 185, rue Sainte-Catherine ouest, Montréal, QC H2X 3X5
514-847-6226, Fax: 514-847-6292, info@macm.org

Musée de la civilisation, 85, rue Dalhousie, CP 155 B, Québec, QC G1K 8R2
418-643-2158, 866-710-8031, renseignements@mcq.org

Musée national des beaux-arts du Québec, Parc des Champs-de-Bataille, 1, av Wolfe-Montcalm, Québec, QC G1R 5H3
418-643-2150, 866-220-2150, info@mnbaq.org

Régie du cinéma, #100, 390, rue Notre-Dame ouest, Montréal, QC H2Y 1T9
514-873-2371, Fax: 514-873-8874, 800-463-2463

Société de développement des entreprises culturelles, #800, 215, rue Saint-Jacques, Montréal, QC H2Y 1M6
514-841-2200, Fax: 514-841-8606, 800-363-0401, info@sodec.gouv.qc.ca

Société de la Place des Arts de Montréal, 260, boul de Maisonneuve ouest, Montréal, QC H2X 1Y9
514-285-4200, Fax: 514-285-1968, info@placedesarts.com

Société de télédiffusion du Québec (Télé-Québec), 1000, rue Fullum, Montréal, QC H2K 3L7
514-521-2424, Fax: 514-864-1970, info@telequebec.tv

Société du Grand Théâtre de Québec, 269, boul René-Lévesque est, Québec, QC G1R 2B3
418-643-8111, 877-643-8131, gtq@grandtheatre.qc.ca

Saskatchewan
Conexus Arts Centre, 200A Lakeshore Dr., Regina, SK S4S 7L3
306-565-4500, Fax: 306-565-3274, 800-667-8497, reception@conexusartscentre.ca

Provincial Archives of Saskatchewan, PO Box 1665, Regina, SK S4P 3C6
306-787-4068, Fax: 306-787-1975

Provincial Capital Commission, PO Box 7111, Regina, SK S4P 3S7
306-522-3661, Fax: 306-565-2742

Royal Saskatchewan Museum, 2445 Albert St., Regina, SK S4P 4W7
306-787-2815, Fax: 306-787-2820, info@royalsaskmuseum.ca

Saskatchewan Arts Board (SK Arts), 1355 Broad St., Regina, SK S4R 7V1
306-787-4056, 800-667-7526, info@sk-arts.ca

Yukon Territory
Yukon Tourism & Culture, PO Box 2703, Whitehorse, YT Y1A 2C6
867-393-7048

ASSESSMENT
Northwest Territories
Northwest Territories Department of Municipal & Community Affairs, PO Box 1320, Yellowknife, NT X1A 2L9

ASTRONOMY
See Also: Space & Astronomy
Canada-France-Hawaii Telescope, CFHT Corporation, #65, 1238 Mamalahoa Hwy., Kamuela, HI
808-885-7944, Fax: 808-885-7288, info@cfht.hawaii.edu

Canadian Astronomy Data Centre, NRC Herzberg Astronomy & Astrophysics, 5071 West Saanich Rd., Victoria, BC V9E 2E7
250-363-0001, Fax: 250-363-0045, cadc@nrc.gc.ca

Dominion Astrophysical Observatory, NRC Herzberg Astronomy & Astrophysics, 5071 West Saanich Rd., Victoria, BC V9E 2E7
250-363-0001, NRC.NSIHerzbergAstroInfoISN.CNRC@nrc-cnrc.gc.ca

Dominion Radio Astrophysical Observatory, 717 White Lake Rd., PO Box 248, Penticton, BC V2A 6J9
250-497-2300, NRC.DRAO-OFR.CNRC@nrc-cnrc.gc.ca

Gemini Observatory, 670 N. A'ohoku Place, Hilo, HI
808-974-2500, Fax: 808-974-2589

ATTORNEYS-GENERAL
See Also: Justice Departments
Public Prosecution Service of Canada, 160 Elgin St., 12th Fl., Ottawa, ON K1A 0H8
613-957-6489, 877-505-7772, info@ppsc.gc.ca

Manitoba
Manitoba Justice, Administration & Finance, #1110, 405 Broadway Ave., Winnipeg, MB R3C 3L6
204-945-2878

New Brunswick
New Brunswick Department of Justice & Public Safety, Marysville Place, 3rd Fl., PO Box 6000, Fredericton, NB E3B 5H1
506-453-3992, DPS-MSP.Information@gnb.ca

Office of the Attorney General, Chancery Place, PO Box 6000, Fredericton, NB E3B 5H1
506-453-3992, Fax: 506-453-3992

Ontario
Ontario Ministry of the Attorney General, McMurtry-Scott Bldg., 720 Bay St., 11th Fl., Toronto, ON M7A 2S9
416-326-2220, Fax: 416-326-4016, 800-518-7901, attorneygeneral@ontario.ca

Saskatchewan
Saskatchewan Justice & Attorney General, 1874 Scarth St., Regina, SK S4P 4B3

AUDITORS-GENERAL
Auditor General of Canada, 240 Sparks St., Ottawa, ON K1A 0G6
613-952-0213, Fax: 613-957-0474, 888-761-5953, infomedia@oag-bvg.gc.ca

Alberta
Alberta Office of the Auditor General, 9925 - 109th St., 8th Fl., Edmonton, AB T5K 2J8
780-427-4222, Fax: 780-422-9555, info@oag.ab.ca

British Columbia
Office of the Auditor General, 623 Fort St., PO Box 9036 Prov Govt, Victoria, BC V8W 9A2
250-419-6100, Fax: 250-387-1230

Office of the Auditor General for Local Government, #201, 10470 - 152nd St., Surrey, BC V3R 0Y3
604-930-7100, info@aglg.ca

Manitoba
Office of the Auditor General, #500, 330 Portage Ave., Winnipeg, MB R3C 0C4
204-945-3790, Fax: 204-945-2169, contact@oag.mb.ca

New Brunswick
Office of the Auditor General, HSBC Place, 520 King St., Fredericton, NB E3B 6G3
506-453-2243, Fax: 506-453-3067, agnb@gnb.ca

Newfoundland & Labrador
Office of the Auditor General, PO Box 8700, St. John's, NL A1B 4J6
709-729-2700, oagmail@oag.nl.ca

Nova Scotia
Office of the Auditor General, Royal Centre, #400, 5161 George St., Halifax, NS B3J 1M7
902-424-5907, Fax: 902-424-4350

Ontario
Office of the Auditor General, #1530, 20 Dundas St. West, 15th Fl., Toronto, ON M5G 2C2
416-327-2381, Fax: 416-327-9862, comments@auditor.on.ca

Prince Edward Island
Office of the Auditor General, Shaw Bldg., 105 Rochford St. North, 2nd Fl., PO Box 2000, Charlottetown, PE C1A 7N8
902-368-4520, Fax: 902-368-4598

Quebec
Vérificateur général du Québec, #300, 750, boul Charest est, Québec, QC G1K 9J6
418-691-5900, Fax: 418-644-4460, verificateur.general@vgq.qc.ca

Saskatchewan
Provincial Auditor Saskatchewan, Chateau Tower, #1500, 1920 Broad St., Regina, SK S4P 3V2
306-787-6398, Fax: 306-787-6383, info@auditor.sk.ca

AUTOMOBILE INSURANCE
See Also: Insurance (Life, Fire Property)
Alberta
Alberta Automobile Insurance Rate Board, Canadian Western Bank Place, #2440, 10303 Jasper Ave., Edmonton, AB T5J 3N6
780-427-5428, Fax: 780-638-4254, -310-0000, airb@gov.ab.ca

British Columbia
Insurance Corporation of British Columbia, 151 West Esplanade, North Vancouver, BC V7M 3H9
604-661-2800, 800-663-3051

Manitoba
Manitoba Public Insurance Corporation, 234 Donald St., #B100, PO Box 6300, Winnipeg, MB R3C 4A4
204-985-7000, Fax: 204-985-3525, 800-665-2410

Northwest Territories
Northwest Territories Department of Finance, PO Box 1320, Yellowknife, NT X1A 2L9

Ontario
Financial Services Commission of Ontario, North York City Ctr., 5160 Yonge St., 17th Fl., PO Box 85, Toronto, ON M2N 6L9
416-250-7250, Fax: 416-590-7070, 800-668-0128, contactcentre@fsco.gov.on.ca

Quebec
Société de l'assurance automobile du Québec, 333, boul Jean-Lesage, CP 19600 Terminus, Québec, QC G1K 8J6
418-643-7620, Fax: 418-644-0339, 800-361-7620

Saskatchewan
Automobile Injury Appeal Commission, #504, 2400 College Ave., Regina, SK S4P 1C8
306-798-5545, Fax: 306-798-5540, 866-798-5544, aiac@gov.sk.ca

Saskatchewan Government Insurance, 2260 - 11th Ave., Regina, SK S4P 0J9
306-751-1200, Fax: 306-787-7477, 844-855-2744, sgiinquiries@sgi.sk.ca

Yukon Territory
Yukon Justice, Andrew Philipsen Law Centre, 2134 - 2nd Ave., PO Box 2703, Whitehorse, YT Y1A 2C6
867-667-3033, Fax: 867-667-5200, justice@yukon.ca

BANKING & FINANCIAL INSTITUTIONS
Bank of Canada, 234 Wellington St., Ottawa, ON K1A 0G9
613-782-8111, Fax: 613-782-7713, 800-303-1282, info@bankofcanada.ca

Business Development Bank of Canada, #100, 5, Place Ville-Marie, Montréal, QC H3B 5E7
Fax: 877-329-9232, 877-232-2269

Canada Deposit Insurance Corporation, 50 O'Connor St., 17th Floor, Ottawa, ON K1P 6L2
Fax: 613-996-6095, 800-461-2342, info@cdic.ca

Finance Canada, 90 Elgin St., Ottawa, ON K1A 0G5
613-369-3710, Fax: 613-369-4065, fin.financepublic-financepublique.fin@canada.ca

Financial Consumer Agency of Canada, 427 Laurier Ave. West, 6th Fl., Ottawa, ON K1R 1B9
613-960-4666, Fax: 613-941-1436

Office of the Superintendent of Financial Institutions, Kent Square, 255 Albert St., 12th Fl., Ottawa, ON K1A 0H2
613-990-7788, Fax: 613-990-5591, 800-385-8647, information@osfi-bsif.gc.ca

Alberta
Alberta Treasury Board & Finance, 9820 - 107th St., 9th Fl., Edmonton, AB T5K 1E7
780-427-3035, Fax: 780-427-1147

ATB Financial, #2100, 10020 - 100 St. NW, Edmonton, AB T5J 0N3
403-245-8110, 800-332-8383

Credit Union Deposit Guarantee Corporation, #2000, 10104 - 103 St., Edmonton, AB T5J 0H8
780-428-6680, Fax: 780-428-7571, 800-661-0351, mail@cudgc.ab.ca

Treasury & Risk Management Division, Federal Bldg., 9820 - 107th St., 8th Fl., Edmonton, AB T5K 1E7

British Columbia
British Columbia Ministry of Finance, PO Box 9417 Prov Govt, Victoria, BC V8W 9V1

Financial Institutions Commission, #2800, 555 West Hastings, Vancouver, BC V6B 4N6
604-660-3555, Fax: 604-660-3365, 866-206-3030, FICOM@ficombc.ca

Manitoba
Deposit Guarantee Corporation of Manitoba, #390, 200 Graham Ave., Winnipeg, MB R3C 4L5
204-942-8480, Fax: 204-947-1723, 800-697-4447, mail@depositguarantee.mb.ca

Manitoba Finance, Legislative Bldg., #103, 450 Broadway, Winnipeg, MB R3C 0V8
204-945-3744

Manitoba Financial Services Agency, c/o Financial Institutions Regulation Branch, #207, 400 St. Mary Ave., Winnipeg, MB R3C 4K5
204-945-2542, Fax: 204-948-2268, 800-282-8069, insurance@gov.mb.ca

New Brunswick
New Brunswick Department of Finance, Chancery Place, 675 King St., 5th Fl., Fredericton, NB E3B 5H1
506-453-2264, Fax: 506-453-7195, TB-CT@gnb.ca

Newfoundland & Labrador
Credit Union Deposit Guarantee Corporation, PO Box 340, Marystown, NL A0E 2M0
709-279-0170, Fax: 709-279-0177, 877-279-0170, CUDGCNL@gov.nl.ca

Newfoundland & Labrador Department of Finance, Confederation Bldg., PO Box 8700, St. John's, NL A1B 4J6
709-729-3166, finance@gov.nl.ca

Northwest Territories
Northwest Territories Department of Finance, PO Box 1320, Yellowknife, NT X1A 2L9

Nunavut

Nunavut Business Credit Corporation, Parnaivak Bldg., #100, PO Box 2548, Iqaluit, NU X0A 0H0
867-975-7891, Fax: 867-975-7897, 800-758-0038, credit@nbcc.nu.ca

Nunavut Territory Department of Finance, PO Box 1000 430, Iqaluit, NU X0A 0H0
867-975-6222, Fax: 867-975-6220, 888-668-9993, gnhr@gov.nu.ca

Ontario

Deposit Insurance Corporation of Ontario, #700, 4711 Yonge St., Toronto, ON M2N 6K8
416-325-9444, Fax: 416-325-9722, 800-268-6653, info@dico.com

Financial Services Commission of Ontario, North York City Ctr., 5160 Yonge St., 17th Fl., PO Box 85, Toronto, ON M2N 6L9
416-250-7250, Fax: 416-590-7070, 800-668-0128, contactcentre@fsco.gov.on.ca

Ontario Ministry of Finance, 95 Grosvenor St., Toronto, ON M7A 1Y8
Fax: 866-888-3850, 866-668-8297

Prince Edward Island

Prince Edward Island Department of Finance, Shaw Bldg., 95 Rochford St. South, 2nd Fl., PO Box 2000, Charlottetown, PE C1A 7N8
902-368-4040, Fax: 902-368-6575, DeptFinance@gov.pe.ca

Quebec

Caisse de dépôt et placement du Québec, Édifice Jacques-Parizeau, 1000, place Jean-Paul-Riopelle, Montréal, QC H2Z 2B3
514-842-3261, Fax: 514-842-4833, 866-330-3936, info@cdpq.com

Ministère des Finances, 12, rue Saint-Louis, Québec, QC G1R 5L3
418-528-9323, Fax: 418-646-1631, info@finances.gouv.qc.ca

Saskatchewan

Financial & Consumer Affairs Authority, #601, 1919 Saskatchewan Dr., Regina, SK S4P 4H2
306-787-5645, Fax: 306-787-5899, 877-880-5550, consumerprotection@gov.sk.ca

Saskatchewan Finance, 2350 Albert St., Regina, SK S4P 4A6
ficommunications@gov.sk.ca

Yukon Territory

Yukon Finance, PO Box 2703, Whitehorse, YT Y1A 2C6
867-667-5343, Fax: 867-393-6217, fininfo@yukon.ca

BILINGUALISM

Canadian Heritage, 15, rue Eddy, Gatineau, QC K1A 0M5
819-997-0055, 866-811-0055, PCH.info-info.PCH@canada.ca

Office of the Commissioner of Official Languages, 30 Victoria St., 6th Fl., Gatineau, QC K1A 0T8
819-420-4877, Fax: 819-420-4873, 877-996-6368

Manitoba

Division du Bureau de l'éducation française, #509, 1181 Portage Ave., Winnipeg, MB R3C 0T3
204-945-6916, Fax: 204-948-2997

Le Centre Culturel franco-manitobain/Franco-Manitoban Cultural Centre, 340, boul Provencher, Winnipeg, MB R2H 0G7
204-233-8972, Fax: 204-233-3324, communication@ccfm.mb.ca

Northwest Territories

Office of the Languages Commissioner, 202 McDougall Rd., Fort Smith, NT X0E 0P0
867-872-3706, 800-661-0889, admin@olc-nt.ca

Nunavut

Nunavut Territory Department of Culture & Heritage, PO Box 1000 800, Iqaluit, NU X0A 0H0
867-975-5500, Fax: 867-975-5504, 866-934-2035

Ontario

Office of Francophone Affairs, #2501, 700 Bay St., 25th Fl., Toronto, ON M7A 0A2
416-325-4983, 800-268-7507

Ontario French-Language Education Communications Authority, #600, 21 College St., 6th Fl., Toronto, ON M5Y 2M5
416-968-3536, Fax: 416-968-8203

Quebec

Ministère des Relations internationales et Francophonie, Édifice Hector-Fabre, 525, boul Réne-Lévesque est, Québec, QC G1R 5R9
418-649-2300, Fax: 418-649-2656

Yukon Territory

Yukon French Language Services Directorate, 305 Jarvis St., 3rd Fl., PO Box 2703, Whitehorse, YT Y1A 2C6
867-667-8260, Fax: 867-393-6226, info.dsf-flsd@yukon.ca

BIOTECHNOLOGY

Industrial Partnership Facility: Montréal, c/o Montréal (av Royalmount) Research Facilities, 6100, av Royalmount, Montréal, QC H4P 2R2

Prince Edward Island

BIO|FOOD|TECH, 101 Belvedere Ave., PO Box 2000, Charlottetown, PE C1A 7N8
902-368-5548, Fax: 902-368-5549, 877-368-5548, biofoodtech@biofoodtech.ca

BOARDS OF REVIEW

Canada Industrial Relations Board, 240 Sparks St., 4th Fl. West, Ottawa, ON K1A 0X8
Fax: 613-995-9493, 800-575-9696

Canadian International Trade Tribunal, Standard Life Centre, 333 Laurier Ave. West, 15th Floor, Ottawa, ON K1A 0G7
613-990-2452, Fax: 613-990-2439, 855-307-2488, citt-tcce@tribunal.gc.ca

Canadian Nuclear Safety Commission, 280 Slater St., PO Box 1046 B, Ottawa, ON K1P 5S9
613-995-5894, Fax: 613-995-5086, 800-668-5284, cnsc.information.ccsn@canada.ca

Commission for Public Complaints Against the Royal Canadian Mounted Police, National Intake Office, PO Box 88689, Surrey, BC V3W 0X1
Fax: 604-501-4095, 800-665-6878

Committee on the Status of Endangered Wildlife in Canada, c/o Dept. of Biological Sciences, Simon Fraser University, 8888 University Dr., Burnaby, BC V5A 1S6

Federal Public Sector Labour Relations & Employment Board, C.D. Howe Bldg., West Tower, 240 Sparks St., 6th Fl., PO Box 1525 B, Ottawa, ON K1P 5V2
613-990-1800, Fax: 613-990-1849, 866-931-3454, mail.courrier@fpslreb-crtespf.gc.ca

Immigration & Refugee Board of Canada, Minto Place, Canada Bldg., 344 Slater St., 12th Fl., Ottawa, ON K1A 0K1
Fax: 613-943-1550

Mackenzie Valley Environmental Impact Review Board, 200 Scotia Centre, #5102, 50th Ave., PO Box 938, Yellowknife, NT X1A 2N7
867-766-7050, Fax: 867-766-7074, 866-912-3472

Nunavut Impact Review Board, 29 Mitik St., PO Box 1360, Cambridge Bay, NU X0B 0C0
Fax: 867-983-2594, 866-233-3033, info@nirb.ca

Nunavut Water Board, PO Box 119, Gjoa Haven, NU X0B 1J0
867-360-6338

Patented Medicine Prices Review Board, Standard Life Centre, #1400, 333 Laurier Ave. West, PO Box L40, Ottawa, ON K1P 1C1
613-288-9597, Fax: 613-288-9643, 877-861-2350, PMPRB.Information-Renseignements.CEPMB@pmprb-cepm b.gc.ca

Porcupine Caribou Management Board, PO Box 31723, Whitehorse, YT Y1A 6L3
867-633-4780, Fax: 867-393-3904

Royal Canadian Mounted Police External Review Committee, PO Box 1159 B, Ottawa, ON K1P 5R2
613-998-2134, Fax: 613-990-8969, org@erc-cee.gc.ca

Security Intelligence Review Committee, PO Box 2430 D, Ottawa, ON K1P 5W5
613-907-4404, Fax: 613-907-4445, info@sirc-csars.gc.ca

Veterans Review & Appeal Board, Daniel J. MacDonald Bldg., 161 Grafton St., PO Box 9900, Charlottetown, PE C1A 8V7
902-566-8751, Fax: 902-566-7850, 800-450-8006, vrab.vrab-tacra.tacra@vrab-tacra.gc.ca

Alberta

Alberta Review Board, #1120, 10235 - 101 St., Edmonton, AB T5J 3E9
780-422-5994, Fax: 780-427-1762

British Columbia

British Columbia Review Board, #1270, 605 Robson St., Vancouver, BC V6B 5J3
604-660-8789, Fax: 604-660-8809, 877-305-2277

Manitoba

Manitoba Criminal Code Review Board, #2, 408 York Ave., Winnipeg, MB R3C 0P9
204-945-4438

Northwest Territories

Northwest Territories Legal Aid Commission, 4915 - 48th St., PO Box 1320, Yellowknife, NT X1A 2L9
867-767-9361, Fax: 867-873-5320, 844-835-8050, lac@gov.nt.ca

Territorial Board of Revision, c/o Secretary, Board of Revision, #400, 5201 - 50th Ave., Yellowknife, NT X1A 2L9
867-767-9161, Fax: 867-873-0609

Ontario

Bail Verification & Supervision Program, Atrium on Bay, 595 Bay St., 8th Fl., Toronto, ON M5G 2M6
416-314-2507

Medical Eligibility Committee, 151 Bloor St. West, 9th Fl., Toronto, ON M5S 1S4
416-327-8512, Fax: 416-327-8524, 866-282-2179

Ontario Review Board, 151 Bloor St. West, 10th Fl., Toronto, ON M5S 2T5
416-327-8866, Fax: 416-327-8867, orb@ontario.ca

Public Accountants Council, #901, 1200 Bay St., Toronto, ON M5R 2A5
416-920-1444, 800-387-2154

Safety, Licensing Appeals & Standards Tribunals Ontario, #401, 20 Dundas St. West, 4th Fl., Toronto, ON M5T 2Z5
Fax: 416-327-6379, 844-242-0608, slastoinfo@ontario.ca

Quebec

Bureau d'audiences publiques sur l'environnement, Édifice Lomer-Gouin, #2.10, 575, rue Jacques-Parizeau, Québec, QC G1R 6A6
418-643-7447, Fax: 418-643-9474, 800-463-4732, communication@bape.gouv.qc.ca

Saskatchewan

Public & Private Rights Board, #23, 3085 Albert St., Regina, SK S4S 0B1
306-787-4071, Fax: 306-787-0088

Surface Rights Board of Arbitration, #102, 113 - 2nd Ave. East, PO Box 1597, Kindersley, SK S0L 1S0
306-463-5447, Fax: 306-463-5449, surfacerightsboard@gov.sk.ca

BROADCASTING

Canadian Broadcasting Corporation, 181 Queen St., PO Box 3220 C, Ottawa, ON K1Y 1E4
613-288-6000, liaison@cbc.ca

Canadian Radio-Television & Telecommunications Commission, Central Building, 1, promenade du Portage, Les Terrasses de la Chaudière, Gatineau, QC J8X 4B1
819-997-0313, Fax: 819-994-0218, 877-249-2782

Nova Scotia

Communications Nova Scotia, Provincial Bldg., 1723 Hollis St., 3rd Fl., PO Box 608, Halifax, NS B3J 2R7
902-424-7690, Fax: 902-424-0515, CNSClientSVC@novascotia.ca

Quebec

Société de télédiffusion du Québec (Télé-Québec), 1000, rue Fullum, Montréal, QC H2K 3L7
514-521-2424, Fax: 514-864-1970, info@telequebec.tv

BUDGET PLANNING

Finance Canada, 90 Elgin St., Ottawa, ON K1A 0G5
613-369-3710, Fax: 613-369-4065, fin.financepublic-financepublique.fin@canada.ca

Parliamentary Budget Officer, #919, 50 O'Connor St., Ottawa, ON K1A 0A9
613-992-8026, pbo-dpb@parl.gc.ca

Alberta

Alberta Treasury Board & Finance, 9820 - 107th St., 9th Fl., Edmonton, AB T5K 1E7
780-427-3035, Fax: 780-427-1147

British Columbia

British Columbia Ministry of Finance, PO Box 9417 Prov Govt, Victoria, BC V8W 9V1

Provincial Treasury, PO Box 9414 Prov Govt, Victoria, BC V8V 9V1
250-387-4541, Fax: 250-356-3041

Manitoba

Manitoba Finance, Legislative Bldg., #103, 450 Broadway, Winnipeg, MB R3C 0V8
204-945-3744

Treasury Division, #350, 363 Broadway, Winnipeg, MB R3C 3N9
204-945-3702, Fax: 204-948-2233

New Brunswick

New Brunswick Department of Finance, Chancery Place, 675 King St., 5th Fl., Fredericton, NB E3B 5H1
506-453-2264, Fax: 506-453-7195, TB-CT@gnb.ca

Newfoundland & Labrador

Newfoundland & Labrador Department of Finance, Confederation Bldg., PO Box 8700, St. John's, NL A1B 4J6
709-729-3166, finance@gov.nl.ca

Northwest Territories

Financial Management Board Secretariat, PO Box 1320, Yellowknife, NT X1A 2L9

Northwest Territories Department of Finance, PO Box 1320, Yellowknife, NT X1A 2L9

Nova Scotia

Nova Scotia Department of Finance & Treasury Board, Provincial Bldg., 1723 Hollis St., 7th Fl., PO Box 187, Halifax, NS B3J 2N3
902-424-5554, Fax: 902-424-0635, FinanceWeb@novascotia.ca

Nunavut

Nunavut Territory Department of Finance, PO Box 1000 430, Iqaluit, NU X0A 0H0
867-975-6222, Fax: 867-975-6220, 888-668-9993, gnhr@gov.nu.ca

Ontario

Office of the Budget, Frost Bldg. South, 7 Queen's Park Cres., 4th Fl., Toronto, ON M7A 1Y7

Ontario Ministry of Finance, 95 Grosvenor St., Toronto, ON M7A 1Y8
Fax: 866-888-3850, 866-668-8297

Prince Edward Island

Prince Edward Island Department of Finance, Shaw Bldg., 95 Rochford St. South, 2nd Fl., PO Box 2000, Charlottetown, PE C1A 7N8
902-368-4040, Fax: 902-368-6575, DeptFinance@gov.pe.ca

Quebec

Ministère des Finances, 12, rue Saint-Louis, Québec, QC G1R 5L3
418-528-9323, Fax: 418-646-1631, info@finances.gouv.qc.ca

Saskatchewan

Saskatchewan Finance, 2350 Albert St., Regina, SK S4P 4A6
ficommunications@gov.sk.ca

Yukon Territory

Yukon Finance, PO Box 2703, Whitehorse, YT Y1A 2C6
867-667-5343, Fax: 867-393-6217, fininfo@yukon.ca

BUSINESS & FINANCE

Atlantic Canada Opportunities Agency, Blue Cross Centre, 644 Main St., 3rd Fl., PO Box 6051, Moncton, NB E1C 9J8
506-851-2271, Fax: 506-851-7403, 800-561-7862, ACOA.information.APECA@canada.ca

Auditor General of Canada, 240 Sparks St., Ottawa, ON K1A 0G6
613-952-0213, Fax: 613-957-0474, 888-761-5953, infomedia@oag-bvg.gc.ca

Bank of Canada, 234 Wellington St., Ottawa, ON K1A 0G9
613-782-8111, Fax: 613-782-7713, 800-303-1282, info@bankofcanada.ca

Business Development Bank of Canada, #100, 5, Place Ville-Marie, Montréal, QC H3B 5E7
Fax: 877-329-9232, 877-232-2269

Canada Business Network, 235 Queen St., Ottawa, ON K1A 0H5
888-576-4444

Canada Deposit Insurance Corporation, 50 O'Connor St., 17th Floor, Ottawa, ON K1P 6L2
Fax: 613-996-6095, 800-461-2342, info@cdic.ca

Canada Economic Development for Québec Regions, #500, 800, boul René-Lévesque ouest, Montréal, QC H3B 1X9
514-283-6412, Fax: 514-283-3302, 866-385-6412

Canada Mortgage & Housing Corporation, 700 Montreal Rd., Ottawa, ON K1A 0P7
613-748-2000, Fax: 613-748-2098, 800-668-2642, chic@cmhc-schl.gc.ca

Canada Pension Plan Investment Board, #2500, 1 Queen St. East, Toronto, ON M5C 2W5
416-868-4075, Fax: 416-868-8689, 866-557-9510, contact@cppib.com

Canada Revenue Agency, 875 Heron Rd., Ottawa, ON K1A 1A2
800-267-6999,

Canada Savings Bonds, #201, 50 O'Connor St., PO Box 2770 D, Ottawa, ON K1P 1J7
905-754-2012, Fax: 613-782-8096, 800-575-5151

Canadian Commercial Corporation, #700, 350 Albert St., Ottawa, ON K1A 0S6
613-996-0034, Fax: 613-995-2121, 800-748-8191, info@ccc.ca

Competition Bureau Canada, Place du Portage, Phase I, 50 Victoria St., Ottawa, ON K1A 0C9
819-997-4282, Fax: 819-997-0324, 800-348-5358

Competition Tribunal, Thomas D'Arcy McGee Bldg., #600, 90 Sparks St., Ottawa, ON K1P 5B4
613-957-3172, Fax: 613-957-3170, tribunal@ct-tc.gc.ca

Export Development Canada, 150 Slater St., Ottawa, ON K1A 1K3
613-598-2500, Fax: 613-598-3811, 800-229-0575, support@edc.ca

Farm Credit Canada, 1800 Hamilton St., Regina, SK S4P 4L3
306-780-8100, Fax: 306-780-8919, 888-332-3301, csc@fcc-fac.ca

Finance Canada, 90 Elgin St., Ottawa, ON K1A 0G5
613-369-3710, Fax: 613-369-4065, fin.financepublic-financepublique.fin@canada.ca

Financial Transactions & Reports Analysis Centre of Canada, 234 Laurier Ave. West, 24th Fl., Ottawa, ON K1P 1H7
Fax: 613-943-7931, 866-346-8722, guidelines-lignesdirectrices@fintrac-canafe.gc.ca

Freshwater Fish Marketing Corporation, 1199 Plessis Rd., Winnipeg, MB R2C 3L4
204-983-6601, Fax: 204-983-6497, sandic@freshwaterfish.com

Global Affairs Canada, Enquiries Service, 125 Sussex Dr., Ottawa, ON K1A 0G2
Fax: 613-996-9709, 800-267-8376

Innovation, Science & Economic Development Canada, C.D. Howe Building, 235 Queen St., Ottawa, ON K1A 0H5
613-954-5031, Fax: 613-954-2340, 800-328-6189, info@ic.gc.ca

Office of the Superintendent of Financial Institutions, Kent Square, 255 Albert St., 12th Fl., Ottawa, ON K1A 0H2
613-990-7788, Fax: 613-990-5591, 800-385-8647, information@osfi-bsif.gc.ca

Public Sector Pension Investment Board, #200, 440 Laurier Ave. West, Ottawa, ON K1R 7X6
613-782-3095, Fax: 613-782-6864, info@investpsp.ca

Royal Canadian Mint, 320 Sussex Dr., Ottawa, ON K1A 0G8
613-954-2626, Fax: 613-998-4130, 800-267-1871

Statistics Canada, 150 Tunney's Pasture Driveway, Ottawa, ON K1A 0T6
514-283-8300, Fax: 514-283-9350, 800-263-1136, STATCAN.infostats-infostats.STATCAN@canada.ca

Treasury Board of Canada Secretariat, East Tower, 140 O'Connor St., 9th Fl., Ottawa, ON K1A 0R5
613-957-2400, Fax: 613-941-4000, 877-636-0656

Western Economic Diversification Canada, Canada Place, #1500, 9700 Jasper Ave. NW, Edmonton, AB T5J 4H7
780-495-4164, Fax: 780-495-4557, 888-338-9378, WD.contactus-contactez-nous.DEO@canada.ca

Alberta

Agricultural Products Marketing Council, JG O'Donoghue Bldg., #305, 7000 - 113 St., Edmonton, AB T6H 5T6
780-427-2164

Alberta Automobile Insurance Rate Board, Canadian Western Bank Place, #2440, 10303 Jasper Ave., Edmonton, AB T5J 3N6
780-427-5428, Fax: 780-638-4254, -310-0000, airb@gov.ab.ca

Alberta Capital Finance Authority, Sun Life Place, #2160, 10123 - 99 St. NW, Edmonton, AB T5J 3H1
780-427-9711, Fax: 780-422-2175, webacfa@gov.ab.ca

Alberta Enterprise Corporation Board, TD Tower, #1405, 10088 - 102 Ave., Edmonton, AB T5J 2Z2
587-402-6601, Fax: 587-402-6612, 877-336-3474, info@alberta-enterprise.ca

Alberta Investment Management Corporation, #1100, 10830 Jasper Ave., Edmonton, AB T5J 2B3
780-392-3600

Alberta Office of the Auditor General, 9925 - 109th St., 8th Fl., Edmonton, AB T5K 2J8
780-427-4222, Fax: 780-422-9555, info@oag.ab.ca

Alberta Securities Commission, #600, 250 - 5th St. SW, Calgary, AB T2P 0R4
403-297-6454, Fax: 403-297-6156, 877-355-0585, inquiries@asc.ca

Alberta Treasury Board & Finance, 9820 - 107th St., 9th Fl., Edmonton, AB T5K 1E7
780-427-3035, Fax: 780-427-1147

ATB Financial, #2100, 10020 - 100 St. NW, Edmonton, AB T5J 0N3
403-245-8110, 800-332-8383

Credit Union Deposit Guarantee Corporation, #2000, 10104 - 103 St., Edmonton, AB T5J 0H8
780-428-6680, Fax: 780-428-7571, 800-661-0351, mail@cudgc.ab.ca

Treasury & Risk Management Division, Federal Bldg., 9820 - 107th St., 8th Fl., Edmonton, AB T5K 1E7

British Columbia

Auditor Certification Board, PO Box 9431 Prov Govt, Victoria, BC V8W 9V3
250-356-8658, Fax: 250-356-9422, Ken.Worthy@gov.bc.ca

BC Immigrant Investment Fund Ltd. & BC Renaissance Capital Fund Ltd., #301, 865 Hornby St., Vancouver, BC V6Z 2G3
Fax: 250-952-0371

British Columbia Innovation Council, 1188 West Georgia St., 9th Fl., Vancouver, BC V6E 4A2
604-683-2724, Fax: 604-683-6567, 800-665-7222, info@bcic.ca

British Columbia Lottery Corporation, 74 West Seymour St., Kamloops, BC V2C 1E2
250-828-5500, Fax: 250-828-5631, 866-815-0222

British Columbia Ministry of Finance, PO Box 9417 Prov Govt, Victoria, BC V8W 9V1

British Columbia Ministry of Jobs, Economic Recovery & Innovation, PO Box 9071 Prov Govt, Victoria, BC V8W 9T2
250-356-2771, Fax: 250-953-0927

British Columbia Ministry of Social Development & Poverty Reduction, PO Box 9058 Prov Govt, Victoria, BC V8W 9E1
866-866-0800

British Columbia Pension Corporation, 2995 Jutland Rd., PO Box 9460, Victoria, BC V8W 9V8
250-387-1014, Fax: 250-953-0429, 800-663-8823, PensionCorp@pensionsbc.ca

British Columbia Securities Commission, Pacific Centre, 701 West Georgia St., 12th Fl., PO Box 10142, Vancouver, BC V7Y 1L2
604-899-6500, Fax: 604-899-6506, 800-373-6393, inquiries@bcsc.bc.ca

Financial Institutions Commission, #2800, 555 West Hastings, Vancouver, BC V6B 4N6
604-660-3555, Fax: 604-660-3365, 866-206-3030, FICOM@ficombc.ca

Insurance Corporation of British Columbia, 151 West Esplanade, North Vancouver, BC V7M 3H9
604-661-2800, 800-663-3051

Insurance Council of British Columbia, #300, 1040 West Georgia St., PO Box 7, Vancouver, BC V6E 4H1
604-688-0321, Fax: 604-662-7767, 877-688-0321, info@insurancecouncilofbc.com

Office of the Auditor General, 623 Fort St., PO Box 9036 Prov Govt, Victoria, BC V8W 9A2
250-419-6100, Fax: 250-387-1230

Office of the Auditor General for Local Government, #201, 10470 - 152nd St., Surrey, BC V3R 0Y3
604-930-7100, info@aglg.ca

Public Sector Employers' Council Secretariat, #210, 880 Douglas St., PO Box 9400 Prov Govt, Victoria, BC V8V 9V1
250-387-0842, Fax: 250-387-6258, PSEC@gov.bc.ca

Timber Export Advisory Committee, PO Box 9514 Prov Govt, Victoria, BC V8W 9C2
250-387-8916, Fax: 250-387-5050

Manitoba

Business Services Division, #250, 240 Graham Ave., Winnipeg, MB R3C 0J7
204-945-8200, EMBinfo@gov.mb.ca

Business Transformation & Technology, #1100, 215 Garry St., Winnipeg, MB R3C 3Z1
204-945-2342, Fax: 204-948-3385, btt@gov.mb.ca

Claimant Adviser Office, #200, 330 Portage Ave., Winnipeg, MB R3C 0C4
204-945-7413, Fax: 204-948-3157, cao@gov.mb.ca

Communities Economic Development Fund, 15 Moak Cres., Thompson, MB R8N 2B8
204-778-4138, Fax: 204-778-4313, 800-561-4315

Comptroller Division, #715, 401 York Ave., Winnipeg, MB R3C 0P8
204-945-4920, Fax: 204-948-3539

Crown Corporations Council, #1130, 444 St. Mary Ave., Winnipeg, MB R3C 3T1
204-949-5270, Fax: 204-949-5283, info@crowncc.mb.ca

Deposit Guarantee Corporation of Manitoba, #390, 200 Graham Ave., Winnipeg, MB R3C 4L5
204-942-8480, Fax: 204-947-1723, 800-697-4447, mail@depositguarantee.mb.ca

Entrepreneurship Manitoba, #1010, 405 Broadway, Winnipeg, MB R3C 3L6
204-945-8200, 855-836-7250, embinfo@gov.mb.ca

Finance Research Division, #910, 386 Broadway, Winnipeg, MB R3C 3R6
204-945-3757, Fax: 204-945-5051

Heritage Grants Advisory Council, c/o Heritage Grants Program, #330, 213 Notre Dame Ave., Winnipeg, MB R3B 1N3
204-945-2213, Fax: 204-948-2086

Manitoba Bureau of Statistics, #824, 155 Carlton St., Winnipeg, MB R3C 3H9
204-945-2406

Manitoba Economic Development & Jobs, Economic Development Office, #1010, 259 Portage Ave., Winnipeg, MB R3B 3P4
204-945-1055, Fax: 204-948-2964, 866-570-7577, edo@gov.mb.ca

Manitoba Finance, Legislative Bldg., #103, 450 Broadway, Winnipeg, MB R3C 0V8
204-945-3744

Manitoba Public Insurance Corporation, 234 Donald St., #B100, PO Box 6300, Winnipeg, MB R3C 4A4
204-985-7000, Fax: 204-985-3525, 800-665-2410

Manitoba Securities Commission, #500, 400 St. Mary Ave., Winnipeg, MB R3C 4K5
204-945-2548, Fax: 204-945-0330, securities@gov.mb.ca

Office of the Auditor General, #500, 330 Portage Ave., Winnipeg, MB R3C 0C4
204-945-3790, Fax: 204-945-2169, contact@oag.mb.ca

Pension Commission of Manitoba, #1004, 401 York Ave., Winnipeg, MB R3C 0P8
204-945-2740, Fax: 204-948-2375, pensions@gov.mb.ca

Treasury Board Secretariat, #200, 386 Broadway, Winnipeg, MB R3C 3R6
204-945-4150, Fax: 204-948-4878

New Brunswick

Atlantic Lottery Corporation, 922 Main St., PO Box 5500, Moncton, NB E1C 8W6
800-561-3942, info@alc.ca

Financial & Consumer Services Commission, #300, 85 Charlotte St., Saint John, NB E2L 2J2
506-658-3060, Fax: 506-658-3059, 866-933-2222, info@fcnb.ca

New Brunswick Department of Finance, Chancery Place, 675 King St., 5th Fl., Fredericton, NB E3B 5H1
506-453-2264, Fax: 506-453-7195, TB-CT@gnb.ca

New Brunswick Farm Products Commission, c/o Department of Agriculture, Aquaculture & Fisheries, PO Box 6000, Fredericton, NB E3B 5H1
506-453-3647, Fax: 506-444-5969, DAAF-MAAP@gnb.ca
New Brunswick Jobs Board, Chancery Place, PO Box 6000, Fredericton, NB E3B 5H1
New Brunswick Lotteries & Gaming Corporation, Chancery Place, 4th Fl., 675 King St., PO Box 6000, Fredericton, NB E3B 5H1
506-453-2451, Fax: 506-453-2053
Office of the Auditor General, HSBC Place, 520 King St., Fredericton, NB E3B 6G3
506-453-2243, Fax: 506-453-3067, agnb@gnb.ca
Regional Development Corporation, Chancery Place, 3rd Fl., PO Box 6000, Fredericton, NB E3B 5H1
506-453-2277, Fax: 506-453-7988, rdc-sdr@gnb.ca

Newfoundland & Labrador
Credit Union Deposit Guarantee Corporation, PO Box 340, Marystown, NL A0E 2M0
709-279-0170, Fax: 709-279-0177, 877-279-0170, CUDGCNL@gov.nl.ca
Newfoundland & Labrador Department of Finance, Confederation Bldg., PO Box 8700, St. John's, NL A1B 4J6
709-729-3166, finance@gov.nl.ca
Newfoundland & Labrador Department of Tourism, Culture, Arts & Recreation, PO Box 8700, St. John's, NL A1B 4J6
709-729-7000, tcar@gov.nl.ca
Office of the Auditor General, PO Box 8700, St. John's, NL A1B 4J6
709-729-2700, oagmail@oag.nl.ca

Northwest Territories
Financial Management Board Secretariat, PO Box 1320, Yellowknife, NT X1A 2L9
Northwest Territories Department of Finance, PO Box 1320, Yellowknife, NT X1A 2L9

Nova Scotia
Events East Group, 1800 Argyle St., PO Box 955, Halifax, NS B3J 2V9
902-421-8686, Fax: 902-422-2922
Nova Scotia Business Inc., PO Box 2374, Halifax, NS B3J 3E4
902-424-6650, 800-260-6682, info@nsbi.ca
Nova Scotia Department of Finance & Treasury Board, Provincial Bldg., 1723 Hollis St., 7th Fl., PO Box 187, Halifax, NS B3J 2N3
902-424-5554, Fax: 902-424-0635, FinanceWeb@novascotia.ca
Nova Scotia Department of Inclusive Economic Growth, CIBC Bldg., 1809 Barrington St., #M103, Halifax, NS B3J 3K8
902-424-0377, Fax: 902-424-0500
Nova Scotia Gaming Corporation, Summit Place, 1601 Lower Water St., 5th Fl., PO Box 1501, Halifax, NS B3J 2Y3
902-424-2203, Fax: 902-424-0724
Nova Scotia Securities Commission, PO Box 458, Halifax, NS B3J 2P8
902-424-7768, Fax: 902-424-4625, 855-424-2499, NSSCinquiries@novascotia.ca
Office of the Auditor General, Royal Centre, #400, 5161 George St., Halifax, NS B3J 1M7
902-424-5907, Fax: 902-424-4350

Nunavut
Legal Registries, PO Box 1000 570, Iqaluit, NU X0A 0H0
867-975-6590, Fax: 867-975-6594, Legal.Registries@gov.nu.ca
Nunavut Territory Department of Finance, PO Box 1000 430, Iqaluit, NU X0A 0H0
867-975-6222, Fax: 867-975-6220, 888-668-9993, gnhr@gov.nu.ca

Ontario
Advertising Review Board, Macdonald Block, #M2-56, 900 Bay St., 2nd Fl., Toronto, ON M7A 1N3
416-327-2183, Fax: 416-327-2179
Agriculture, Food & Rural Affairs Tribunal & Board of Negotiation, Ontario Government Bldg NW, 1 Stone Rd. West, 2nd Fl., Guelph, ON N1G 4Y2
519-826-3433, Fax: 519-826-4232, appeals.tribunal.omafra@ontario.ca
Corporate Management & Services Division, 400 University Ave., 14th Fl., Toronto, ON M7A 1T7
Deposit Insurance Corporation of Ontario, #700, 4711 Yonge St., Toronto, ON M2N 6K8
416-325-9444, Fax: 416-325-9722, 800-268-6653, info@dico.com
Financial Services Commission of Ontario, North York City Ctr., 5160 Yonge St., 17th Fl., PO Box 85, Toronto, ON M2N 6L9
416-250-7250, Fax: 416-590-7070, 800-668-0128, contactcentre@fsco.gov.on.ca
Grain Financial Protection Board, 1 Stone Rd. West, 1st Fl., PO Box 3660 Central, Guelph, ON N1H 8M4
519-826-3949, Fax: 519-826-3367

Liquor Control Board of Ontario, 55 Lake Shore Blvd. East, Toronto, ON M5E 1A4
416-365-5900, Fax: 416-864-2476, 800-668-5226, infoline@lcbo.com
Livestock Financial Protection Board, Ontario Government Bldg NW, 1 Stone Rd., West, 5th Fl., Guelph, ON N1G 4Y2
519-826-3886, Fax: 519-826-4375
Metro Toronto Convention Centre Corporation, 255 Front St. West, Toronto, ON M5V 2W6
416-585-8000, Fax: 416-585-8270, info@mtccc.com
Normal Farm Practices Protection Board, Ontario Government Bldg NW, 1 Stone Rd. West, 2nd Fl., Guelph, ON N1G 4Y2
519-826-3433, Fax: 519-826-4232
Office of the Auditor General, #1530, 20 Dundas St. West, 15th Fl., Toronto, ON M5G 2C2
416-327-2381, Fax: 416-327-9862, comments@auditor.on.ca
Ontario Electricity Financial Corporation, #1400, 1 Dundas St. West, Toronto, ON M7A 1Y7
416-325-8000, Fax: 416-325-8005
Ontario Farm Products Marketing Commission, Ontario Government Bldg SW, 1 Stone Rd. West, 5th Fl., Guelph, ON N1G 4Y2
519-826-4220, Fax: 519-826-3400, ontariofarm.productsmarketing@ontario.ca
Ontario Financing Authority, 1 Dundas St. West, 14th Fl., Toronto, ON M7A 1Y7
416-325-8000, Fax: 416-325-8005, investor@ofina.on.ca
Ontario Food Terminal Board, 165 The Queensway, Toronto, ON M8Y 1H8
416-259-5479, Fax: 416-259-4303, oftboard@interlog.com
Ontario Lottery & Gaming Corporation, Roberta Bondar Pl., #800, 70 Foster Dr., Sault Ste. Marie, ON P6A 6V2
705-946-6464, Fax: 705-946-6600, 800-387-0098
Ontario Ministry of Economic Development, Job Creation & Trade, 56 Wellesley St. West, 7th Fl., Toronto, ON M7A 2E7
416-325-6666, 800-268-7095
Ontario Ministry of Finance, 95 Grosvenor St., Toronto, ON M7A 1Y8
Fax: 866-888-3850, 866-668-8297
Ontario Ministry of Government & Consumer Services, Mowat Block, 900 Bay St., 6th Fl., Toronto, ON M7A 1L2
416-212-2665, Fax: 416-326-7445, 844-286-8404
Ontario Place Corporation, 955 Lake Shore Blvd. West, Toronto, ON M6K 3B9
416-314-9900, Fax: 416-314-9989, 866-663-4386
Ontario Securities Commission, 20 Queen St. West, 20th Fl., PO Box 55, Toronto, ON M5H 3S8
416-593-8314, Fax: 416-593-8122, 877-785-1555, inquiries@osc.gov.on.ca
Ottawa Convention Centre, 55 Colonel By Dr., Ottawa, ON K1N 9J2
613-563-1984, Fax: 613-563-7646, 800-450-0077
Pay Equity Office, #300, 180 Dundas St. West, Toronto, ON M7A 2S6
416-314-1896, Fax: 416-314-8741, 800-387-8813
Policy Division, Ontario Government Bldg, 1 Stone Rd. West, 2nd Fl., Guelph, ON N1G 4Y2
519-826-4020, Fax: 519-826-3492
Rural Economic Development Advisory Panel, 1 Stone Rd. West, 4th Fl., Guelph, ON N1G 4Y2
Fax: 519-826-4336, 888-588-4111, red.omafra@ontario.ca

Prince Edward Island
Agricultural Insurance Corporation, 7 Gerald McCarville Drive, Kensington, PE C0B 1M0
Charlottetown Area Development Corporation, 4 Pownal St., PO Box 786, Charlottetown, PE C1A 7L9
902-892-5341, Fax: 902-368-1935
Finance PEI, 94 Euston St., 2nd Fl., Charlottetown, PE C1A 1R7
902-368-6300, Fax: 902-368-6255, financepei@gov.pe.ca
Office of the Auditor General, Shaw Bldg., 105 Rochford St. North, 2nd Fl., PO Box 2000, Charlottetown, PE C1A 7N8
902-368-4520, Fax: 902-368-4598,
Prince Edward Island Department of Finance, Shaw Bldg., 95 Rochford St. South, 2nd Fl., PO Box 2000, Charlottetown, PE C1A 7N8
902-368-4040, Fax: 902-368-6575, DeptFinance@gov.pe.ca

Quebec
Autorité des marchés financiers, Tour de la Bourse, 800, rue du Square-Victoria, 22e étage, CP 246, Montréal, QC H4Z 1G3
514-395-0337, Fax: 514-873-3090, 877-525-0337
Caisse de dépôt et placement du Québec, Édifice Jacques-Parizeau, 1000, place Jean-Paul-Riopelle, Montréal, QC H2Z 2B3
514-842-3261, Fax: 514-842-4833, 866-330-3936, info@cdpq.com
Centre du services partagés du Québec, 875, Grande Allée est, 4e étage, section 4.550, Québec, QC G1R 5W5
418-644-2777, Fax: 418-644-0462, 855-644-2777, cspq@cspq.gouv.qc.ca

Financement-Québec, 12, rue Saint-Louis, 3e étage, Québec, QC G1R 5L3
418-691-2203, Fax: 418-644-6214, financement.regroupe@finances.gouv.qc.ca
Ministère de l'Économie et de l'Innovation, 710, Place D'Youville, 3e étage, Québec, QC G1R 4Y4
418-691-5950, Fax: 418-644-0118, 866-680-1884
Ministère des Finances, 12, rue Saint-Louis, Québec, QC G1R 5L3
418-528-9323, Fax: 418-646-1631, info@finances.gouv.qc.ca
Ministère des Relations internationales et Francophonie, Édifice Hector-Fabre, 525, boul Réne-Lévesque est, Québec, QC G1R 5R9
418-649-2300, Fax: 418-649-2656
Le Protecteur du Citoyen, 800, place D'Youville, 19e étage, Québec, QC G1R 3P4
418-643-2688, Fax: 418-643-8759, 800-463-5070, protecteur@protecteurducitoyen.qc.ca
Revenu Québec, 3800, rue de Marly, Québec, QC G1X 4A5
418-652-6831, Fax: 418-646-0167, cabinet@revenuquebec.ca
Secrétariat du Conseil du trésor, 875, Grande Allée est, 2e étage, secteur 800, Québec, QC G1R 5R8
418-643-1529, Fax: 418-643-9226, 866-552-5158, communication@sct.gouv.qc.ca
Société de financement des infrastructures locales, Ministère des Finances, 12, rue Saint-Louis, Québec, QC G1R 5L3
418-528-9323, Fax: 418-646-1631, info@finances.gouv.qc.ca
Société du Centre des congrès de Québec, 900, boul René-Lévesque est, 2e étage, Québec, QC G1R 2B5
418-644-4000, Fax: 418-644-6455, 888-679-4000
Société du Palais des congrès de Montréal, 159, rue Saint-Antoine ouest, 9é étage, Montréal, QC H2Z 1H2
514-871-8122, Fax: 514-871-9389, 800-268-8122, info@congresmtl.com
Tribunal administratif des marchés financiers, #16.40, 500, boul Réné-Lévesque ouest, Montréal, QC H2Z 1W7
514-873-2211, Fax: 514-873-2162, 877-873-2211, secretariattmf@tmf.gouv.qc.ca
Vérificateur général du Québec, #300, 750, boul Charest est, Québec, QC G1K 9J6
418-691-5900, Fax: 418-644-4460, verificateur.general@vgq.qc.ca

Saskatchewan
Board of Revenue Commissioners, #480, 2151 Scarth St., Regina, SK S4P 2H8
306-787-6221, Fax: 306-787-1610
Crown Investments Corporation of Saskatchewan, #400, 2400 College Ave., Regina, SK S4P 1C8
306-787-6851, Fax: 306-787-0294
Financial & Consumer Affairs Authority, #601, 1919 Saskatchewan Dr., Regina, SK S4P 4H2
306-787-5645, Fax: 306-787-5899, 877-880-5550, consumerprotection@gov.sk.ca
Municipal Financing Corporation of Saskatchewan, 2350 Albert St., 6th Fl., Regina, SK S4P 4A6
306-787-8150, Fax: 306-787-8493, mfc@gov.sk.ca
Provincial Auditor Saskatchewan, Chateau Tower, #1500, 1920 Broad St., Regina, SK S4P 3V2
306-787-6398, Fax: 306-787-6383, info@auditor.sk.ca
Saskatchewan Crop Insurance Corporation, 484 Prince William Dr., PO Box 3000, Melville, SK S0A 2P0
306-728-7200, Fax: 306-728-7202, 888-935-0000, customer.service@scic.gov.sk.ca
Saskatchewan Energy & Resources, #1000, 2103 - 11th Ave., Regina, SK S4P 3Z8
Saskatchewan Finance, 2350 Albert St., Regina, SK S4P 4A6
ficommunications@gov.sk.ca
Saskatchewan Government Insurance, 2260 - 11th Ave., Regina, SK S4P 0J9
306-751-1200, Fax: 306-787-7477, 844-855-2744, sgiinquiries@sgi.sk.ca

Yukon Territory
Assessement Appeal Board, PO Box 2703, Whitehorse, YT Y1A 2C6
867-667-5268, Fax: 867-667-8276
Yukon Finance, PO Box 2703, Whitehorse, YT Y1A 2C6
867-667-5343, Fax: 867-393-6217, fininfo@yukon.ca

BUSINESS ASSISTANCE PROGRAMS
Canada Business Network, 235 Queen St., Ottawa, ON K1A 0H5
888-576-4444

BUSINESS DEVELOPMENT
See Also: Industry; Science & Technology
Atlantic Canada Opportunities Agency, Blue Cross Centre, 644 Main St., 3rd Fl., PO Box 6051, Moncton, NB E1C 9J8
506-851-2271, Fax: 506-851-7403, 800-561-7862, ACOA.information.APECA@canada.ca

Business Development Bank of Canada, #100, 5, Place Ville-Marie, Montréal, QC H3B 5E7
Fax: 877-329-9232, 877-232-2269
Canada Business Network, 235 Queen St., Ottawa, ON K1A 0H5
888-576-4444
Canada Economic Development for Québec Regions, #500, 800, boul René-Lévesque ouest, Montréal, QC H3B 1X9
514-283-6412, Fax: 514-283-3302, 866-385-6412
Canadian Northern Economic Development Agency, Ottawa, ON K1A 0H4
855-897-2667,
CanNor.InfoNorth.InfoNord.CanNor@canada.ca
Export Development Canada, 150 Slater St., Ottawa, ON K1A 1K3
613-598-2500, Fax: 613-598-3811, 800-229-0575, support@edc.ca
Federal Economic Development Agency for Southern Ontario, #101, 139 Northfield Dr. West, Waterloo, ON N2L 5A6
Fax: 519-725-4976, 866-593-5505
FedNor (Federal Economic Development Initiative in Northern Ontario), 19 Lisgar St., Sudbury, ON P3E 3L4
Fax: 705-671-0717, 877-333-6673
Innovation, Science & Economic Development Canada, C.D. Howe Building, 235 Queen St., Ottawa, ON K1A 0H5
613-954-5031, Fax: 613-954-2340, 800-328-6189, info@ic.gc.ca
Market & Industry Services Branch, Tower 5, 1341 Baseline Rd., Ottawa, ON K1A 0C5
613-759-1000, Fax: 613-773-1711
Western Economic Diversification Canada, Canada Place, #1500, 9700 Jasper Ave. NW, Edmonton, AB T5J 4H7
780-495-4164, Fax: 780-495-4557, 888-338-9378, WD.contactus-contactez-nous.DEO@canada.ca

Alberta
Alberta Enterprise Corporation Board, TD Tower, #1405, 10088 - 102 Ave., Edmonton, AB T5J 2Z2
587-402-6601, Fax: 587-402-6612, 877-336-3474, info@alberta-enterprise.ca
Alberta Innovates, 250 Karl Clark Rd., Edmonton, AB T6N 1E4
877-423-5727, info@albertainnovates.ca
Northern Alberta Development Council, Peace River Office, Provincial Building, #206, 9621 - 96 Ave., PO Box 900-14, Peace River, AB T8S 1T4
780-624-6274, Fax: 780-624-6184, -310-0000, nadc.council@gov.ab.ca

British Columbia
British Columbia Innovation Council, 1188 West Georgia St., 9th Fl., Vancouver, BC V6E 4A2
604-683-2724, Fax: 604-683-6567, 800-665-7222, info@bcic.ca
British Columbia Ministry of Jobs, Economic Recovery & Innovation, PO Box 9071 Prov Govt, Victoria, BC V8W 9T2
250-356-2771, Fax: 250-953-0927
British Columbia Ministry of Social Development & Poverty Reduction, PO Box 9058 Prov Govt, Victoria, BC V8W 9E1
866-866-0800
Northern Development Initiative Trust, #301, 1268 Fifth Ave., Prince George, BC V2L 3L2
250-561-2525, Fax: 250-561-2563, info@northerndevelopment.bc.ca

Manitoba
Business Transformation & Technology, #1100, 215 Garry St., Winnipeg, MB R3C 3Z1
204-945-2342, Fax: 204-948-3385, btt@gov.mb.ca
Entrepreneurship Manitoba, #1010, 405 Broadway, Winnipeg, MB R3C 3L6
204-945-8200, 855-836-7250, embinfo@gov.mb.ca
Manitoba Economic Development & Jobs, Economic Development Office, #1010, 259 Portage Ave., Winnipeg, MB R3B 3P4
204-945-1055, Fax: 204-948-2964, 866-570-7577, edo@gov.mb.ca
Mineral Resources Division, The Paris Bldg., 259 Portage Ave., 9th Fl., Winnipeg, MB R3B 3P4
204-945-6569, 800-223-5215, minesinfo@gov.mb.ca
Workforce Development, #260, 800 Portage Ave., Winnipeg, MB R3G 0N4
204-945-5643

New Brunswick
New Brunswick Jobs Board, Chancery Place, PO Box 6000, Fredericton, NB E3B 5H1
Opportunities New Brunswick, Place 2000, 250 King St., PO Box 6000, Fredericton, NB E3B 5H1
506-453-5471, Fax: 506-444-5277, 855-746-4662, info@onbcanada.ca
Regional Development Corporation, Chancery Place, 3rd Fl., PO Box 6000, Fredericton, NB E3B 5H1
506-453-2277, Fax: 506-453-7988, rdc-sdr@gnb.ca

Newfoundland & Labrador
Newfoundland & Labrador Department of Tourism, Culture, Arts & Recreation, PO Box 8700, St. John's, NL A1B 4J6
709-729-7000, tcar@gov.nl.ca

Northwest Territories
Northwest Territories Business Development & Investment Corporation, 5009 - 50th Ave., PO Box 1320, Yellowknife, NT X1A 2L9
867-767-9075, Fax: 867-765-0652, 800-661-0599
Northwest Territories Department of Industry, Tourism & Investment, PO Box 1320, Yellowknife, NT X1A 2L9

Nova Scotia
Innovacorp, #400, 1871 Hollis St., Halifax, NS B3J 0C3
902-424-8670, Fax: 902-424-4679, 800-565-7051, info@innovacorp.ca
Nova Scotia Business Inc., PO Box 2374, Halifax, NS B3J 3E4
902-424-6650, 800-260-6682, info@nsbi.ca
Nova Scotia Department of Inclusive Economic Growth, CIBC Bldg., 1809 Barrington St., #M103, Halifax, NS B3J 3K8
902-424-0377, Fax: 902-424-0500

Nunavut
Nunavut Territory Department of Economic Development & Transportation, Inuksugait Plaza, Bldg. 1104A, PO Box 1000 1500, Iqaluit, NU X0A 0H0
867-975-7800, Fax: 867-975-7870, 888-975-5999, edt@gov.nu.ca

Ontario
Northern Development Division, Roberta Bondar Place, #200, 70 Foster Dr., Sault Ste. Marie, ON P6A 6V8
705-945-5900, Fax: 705-945-5931, 800-461-2287
Ontario Ministry of Economic Development, Job Creation & Trade, 56 Wellesley St. West, 7th Fl., Toronto, ON M7A 2E7
416-325-6666, 800-268-7095
Ontario Ministry of Government & Consumer Services, Mowat Block, 900 Bay St., 6th Fl., Toronto, ON M7A 1L2
416-212-2665, Fax: 416-326-7445, 844-286-8404

Prince Edward Island
Charlottetown Area Development Corporation, 4 Pownal St., PO Box 786, Charlottetown, PE C1A 7L9
902-892-5341, Fax: 902-368-1935
Innovation PEI, 94 Euston St., PO Box 910, Charlottetown, PE C1A 7L9
902-368-6300, Fax: 902-368-6301, 800-563-3734, innovation@gov.pe.ca

Quebec
Commission de la capitale nationale du Québec, Edifice Hector-Fabre, 525, boul René-Lévesque est, RC, Québec, QC G1R 5S9
418-528-0773, Fax: 418-528-0833, 800-442-0773, commission@capitale.gouv.qc.ca
Ministère des Finances, 12, rue Saint-Louis, Québec, QC G1R 5L3
418-528-9323, Fax: 418-646-1631, info@finances.gouv.qc.ca

Saskatchewan
Saskatchewan Energy & Resources, #1000, 2103 - 11th Ave., Regina, SK S4P 3Z8

Yukon Territory
Yukon Development Corporation, #234, 2180 - 2nd Ave., Whitehorse, YT Y1A 5N6
867-456-3995, ydc-admin@yukon.ca
Yukon Economic Development, 303 Alexander St., Whitehorse, YT Y1A 2L5
800-661-0408, ecdev@yukon.ca

BUSINESS REGULATIONS

Canada Revenue Agency, 875 Heron Rd., Ottawa, ON K1A 1A2
800-267-6999
Innovation, Science & Economic Development Canada, C.D. Howe Building, 235 Queen St., Ottawa, ON K1A 0H5
613-954-5031, Fax: 613-954-2340, 800-328-6189, info@ic.gc.ca

British Columbia
Corporate Services Division, PO Box 9415 Prov Govt, Victoria, BC V8W 9V1

Nova Scotia
Nova Scotia Business Inc., PO Box 2374, Halifax, NS B3J 3E4
902-424-6650, 800-260-6682, info@nsbi.ca
Service Nova Scotia & Internal Services, PO Box 2734, Halifax, NS B3J 3K5
902-424-5200, Fax: 902-424-0720, 800-670-4357, askus@novascotia.ca

Nunavut
Nunavut Territory Department of Finance, PO Box 1000 430, Iqaluit, NU X0A 0H0
867-975-6222, Fax: 867-975-6220, 888-668-9993, gnhr@gov.nu.ca

Ontario
Office of the Fairness Commissioner, #1201, 595 Bay St., Toronto, ON M7A 2B4
416-325-9380, Fax: 416-326-6081, 877-727-5365, ofc@ontario.ca
ServiceOntario, College Park, 777 Bay St., 15th Fl., Toronto, ON M7A 2J3
Fax: 416-326-1313, 800-267-8097

CABINETS & EXECUTIVE COUNCILS

See Also: Government (General Information); Parliament
The Canadian Ministry, Information Service, Parliament of Canada, Ottawa, ON K1A 0A9
613-992-4793, 866-599-4999, info@parl.gc.ca
Alberta
Executive Council, Legislature Bldg., 10800 - 97th Ave., Edmonton, AB T5K 2B6
British Columbia
Executive Council of the Government of British Columbia, PO Box 9487 Prov Govt, Victoria, BC V8W 9W6
Manitoba
Executive Council, Legislative Bldg., 450 Broadway, Winnipeg, MB R3C 0V8
New Brunswick
Executive Council, Centennial Bldg., PO Box 6000, Fredericton, NB E3B 5H1
506-444-4417, Fax: 506-453-2266, executivecounciloffice@gnb.ca
Newfoundland & Labrador
Executive Council, c/o Communications Branch, East Block, Confederation Building, 10th Fl., St. John's, NL A1B 4J6
info@gov.nl.ca
Northwest Territories
Executive Council, PO Box 1320, Yellowknife, NT X1A 2L9
executive_communications@gov.nt.ca
Nova Scotia
Executive Council Office, One Government Place, 1700 Granville St., 5th Fl., PO Box 2125, Halifax, NS B3J 3B7
902-424-8940, Fax: 902-424-0667, 866-206-6844, Executive.Council@novascotia.ca
Nunavut
Executive Council, PO Box 2410, Iqaluit, NU X0A 0H0
Ontario
Cabinet of Ontario, Legislative Bldg., Queen's Park, Toronto, ON M7A 1A1
Prince Edward Island
Executive Council, Shaw Bldg., 5th Fl., PO Box 2000, Charlottetown, PE C1A 7N8
902-368-4502, Fax: 902-368-6118
Quebec
Ministère du Conseil exécutif, 875, Grande Allée est, Québec, QC G1R 4Y8
418-644-7600, communic@mce.gouv.qc.ca
Saskatchewan
Executive Council, Communications Services, Executive Council, #130, 3085 Albert St., Regina, SK S4S 0B1
Yukon Territory
Executive Council, 2071 - 2nd Ave., PO Box 2703, Whitehorse, YT Y1A 2C6
eco@yukon.ca

CANADIANS & SOCIETY

Beverly & Qamanirjuaq Caribou Management Board, Secretariat, PO Box 629, Stonewall, MB R0C 2Z0
Canada Council for the Arts, 150 Elgin St., 2nd Fl., PO Box 1047, Ottawa, ON K1P 5V8
613-566-4414, Fax: 613-566-4390, 800-263-5588, info@canadacouncil.ca
Canada Lands Company Ltd., #1700, 1 University Ave., Toronto, ON M5J 2P1
416-214-1250, Fax: 416-214-1121
Canadian Heritage, 15, rue Eddy, Gatineau, QC K1A 0M5
819-997-0055, 866-811-0055, PCH.info-info.PCH@canada.ca
Canadian Human Rights Commission, 344 Slater St., 8th Fl., Ottawa, ON K1A 1E1
Fax: 613-996-9661, 888-214-1090, info.com@chrc-ccdp.gc.ca
Canadian Human Rights Tribunal, 160 Elgin St., 11th Fl., Ottawa, ON K1A 1J4
613-995-1707, Fax: 613-995-3484, registrar@chrt-tcdp.gc.ca
Canadian Race Relations Foundation, #225, 6 Garamond Ct., Toronto, ON M3C 1Z5
416-441-1900, Fax: 416-441-2752, 888-240-4936, info@crrf-fcrr.ca
Crown-Indigenous Relations & Northern Affairs, Public Enquiries Contact Centre, 10, rue Wellington, Gatineau, QC K1A 0H4
Fax: 866-817-3977, 800-567-9604, aadnc.infopubs.aandc@canada.ca

Employment & Social Development Canada, 140, promenade du Portage, Gatineau, QC K1A 0J9

First Nations Tax Commission, Head Office, #321, 345 Chief Alex Thomas Way, Kamloops, BC V2H 1H1
250-828-9857, Fax: 250-828-9858, 855-682-3682, mail@fntc.ca

Global Affairs Canada, Enquiries Service, 125 Sussex Dr., Ottawa, ON K1A 0G2
Fax: 613-996-9709, 800-267-8376

Government of Canada, c/o Canada Enquiry Centre, Service Canada, Ottawa, ON K1A 0J9
800-622-6232

Historic Sites & Monuments Board of Canada, 30 Victoria St., 3rd Fl., Gatineau, QC J8X 0B3
Fax: 819-420-9260, 855-283-8730, hsmbc-clmhc@pc.gc.ca

Immigration & Refugee Board of Canada, Minto Place, Canada Bldg., 344 Slater St., 12th Fl., Ottawa, ON K1A 0K1
Fax: 613-943-1550

Immigration, Refugees & Citizenship, Jean Edmonds, South Tower, 365 Laurier Ave. West, Ottawa, ON K1A 1L1
888-242-2100

Indian Oil & Gas Canada, #100, 9911 Chiila Blvd., Tsuu T'ina, AB T2W 6H6
403-292-5625, Fax: 403-292-5618, aadnc.contactiogc.aandc@canada.ca

Mental Health Commission of Canada, #1210, 350 Albert St., Ottawa, ON K1R 1A4
613-683-3755, Fax: 613-798-2989, mhccinfo@mentalhealthcommission.ca

National Battlefields Commission, 390, av de Bernières, Québec, QC G1R 2L7
418-648-3506, Fax: 418-648-3638, information@ccbn-nbc.gc.ca

National Capital Commission, #202, 40 Elgin St., Ottawa, ON K1P 1C7
613-239-5000, Fax: 613-239-5063, 800-465-1867, info@ncc-ccn.ca

National Seniors Council, Phase IV, 8th Floor, Mail Stop 802, 140, promenade du Portage, Gatineau, QC K1A 0J9
Fax: 819-953-9298, 800-622-6232

Networks of Centres of Excellence of Canada, 350 Albert Street, 16th Fl., Ottawa, ON K1A 1H5
613-995-6010, Fax: 613-992-7356, info@nce-rce.gc.ca

Nunavut Impact Review Board, 29 Mitik St., PO Box 1360, Cambridge Bay, NU X0B 0C0
Fax: 867-983-2594, 866-233-3033, info@nirb.ca

Nunavut Planning Commission, PO Box 2101, Cambridge Bay, NU X0B 0C0

Nunavut Water Board, PO Box 119, Gjoa Haven, NU X0B 1J0
867-360-6338

Office of the Commissioner of Official Languages, 30 Victoria St., 6th Fl., Gatineau, ON K1A 0T8
819-420-4877, Fax: 819-420-4873, 877-996-6368

Office of the Prime Minister, Liberal Party of Canada / Liberal Research Bureau, 80 Wellington St., Ottawa, ON K1A 0A2
Fax: 613-941-6900

Office of the Public Sector Integrity Commissioner of Canada, 60 Queen St., 7th Fl., Ottawa, ON K1P 5Y7
613-941-6400, Fax: 613-941-6535, 866-941-6400

Passport, c/o Passport Program, Gatineau, QC K1A 0G3
800-567-6868

Porcupine Caribou Management Board, PO Box 31723, Whitehorse, YT Y1A 6L3
867-633-4780, Fax: 867-393-3904

Public Health Agency of Canada, 130 Colonnade Rd., Ottawa, ON K1A 0K9
844-280-5020

Social Sciences & Humanities Research Council of Canada, Constitution Sq., 350 Albert St., PO Box 1610 B, Ottawa, ON K1P 6G4
613-992-0691

Specific Claims Tribunal Canada, #400, 427 Laurier Ave. West, 4th Fl., PO Box 31, Ottawa, ON K1R 7Y2
613-947-0751, Fax: 613-943-0586, claims.revendications@sct-trp.ca

Status of Women Canada, PO Box 8097 T CSC, Ottawa, ON K1G 3H6
613-995-7835, Fax: 819-420-6906, 855-969-9922, communications@swc-cfc.gc.ca

Veterans Affairs Canada, 161 Grafton St., PO Box 7700, Charlottetown, PE C1A 8M9
613-996-2242, 866-522-2122, information@vac-acc.gc.ca

Veterans Review & Appeal Board, Daniel J. MacDonald Bldg., 161 Grafton St., PO Box 9900, Charlottetown, PE C1A 8V7
902-566-8751, Fax: 902-566-7850, 800-450-8006, vrab.vrab-tacra.tacra@vrab-tacra.gc.ca

Alberta
Alberta Health, PO Box 1360 Main, Edmonton, AB T5J 2N3
780-427-7164

Appeals Secretariat, Agronomy Centre, #201, 6903 - 116 St., Edmonton, AB T6H 5Z2
780-427-2709, Fax: 780-422-1088, -310-0000, CSS.Appeals@gov.ab.ca

Labour Relations Board, Labour Building, #501, 10808 - 99 Ave., Edmonton, AB T5K 0G5
780-427-8547, Fax: 780-422-0970, 800-463-2572, alrbinfo@gov.ab.ca

Premier's Council on the Status of Persons with Disabilities, HSBC Building, #1110, 10555 - 106 St., Edmonton, AB T5J 2Y2
Fax: 780-415-0097, 800-272-8841, pcspd@gov.ab.ca

Seniors Advisory Council for Alberta, Standard Life Centre, #600, 10405 Jasper Ave., 6th Fl., Edmonton, AB T5J 4R7
780-422-2321, Fax: 780-422-8762, -310-0000, saca@gov.ab.ca

Status of Women, Oxbridge Place, 9820 - 106th St., 5th Fl., Edmonton, AB T5K 2J6
780-644-7559

British Columbia
British Columbia Ministry of Children & Family Development, Customer Service Centre, PO Box 9770 Prov Govt, Victoria, BC V8W 9S5
250-387-7027, 877-387-7027, mcf.info@gov.bc.ca

British Columbia Ministry of Tourism, Arts, Culture & Sport, PO Box 9082 Prov Govt, Victoria, BC V8W 9E2

British Columbia Treaty Commission, #700, 1111 Melville St., Vancouver, BC V6E 3V6
604-482-9200, Fax: 604-482-9222, 855-482-9200, info@bctreaty.net

Local Government, PO Box 9490 Prov Govt, Victoria, BC V8W 9N7
250-356-6575, Fax: 250-387-7973

Native Economic Development Advisory Board, PO Box 9100 Prov Govt, Victoria, BC V8W 9B1
250-387-2536

Manitoba
Communications Services Manitoba, 155 Carlton St., 10th Fl., Winnipeg, MB R3C 3H8
204-945-3765

Communities Economic Development Fund, 15 Moak Cres., Thompson, MB R8N 2B8
204-778-4138, Fax: 204-778-4313, 800-561-4315

Heritage Grants Advisory Council, c/o Heritage Grants Program, #330, 213 Notre Dame Ave., Winnipeg, MB R3B 1N3
204-945-2213, Fax: 204-948-2086

Le Centre Culturel franco-manitobain/Franco-Manitoban Cultural Centre, 340, boul Provencher, Winnipeg, MB R2H 0G7
204-233-8972, Fax: 204-233-3324, communication@ccfm.mb.ca

Manitoba Centennial Centre Corporation, #1000, 555 Main St., Winnipeg, MB R3B 1C3
204-956-1360, Fax: 204-944-1390, inquiries@mbccc.ca

Manitoba Education, Legislative Bldg., #162, 450 Broadway, Winnipeg, MB R3C 0V8
204-945-3720, Fax: 204-945-1291

Manitoba Families, Legislative Bldg., #357, 450 Broadway, Winnipeg, MB R3C 0V8
204-945-3744, 866-626-4862

Manitoba Film Classification Board, #216, 301 Weston St., Winnipeg, MB R3E 3H4
204-945-8962, Fax: 204-945-0890, 866-612-2399, mfcb@gov.mb.ca

Manitoba Heritage Council, c/o Historic Resources Branch, 213 Notre Dame Ave., Main Fl., Winnipeg, MB R3B 1N3
204-945-2118, Fax: 204-948-2384, hrb@gov.mb.ca

Manitoba Human Rights Commission, #700, 175 Hargrave St., Winnipeg, MB R3C 3R8
204-945-3007, Fax: 204-945-1292, 888-884-8681, hrc@gov.mb.ca

Manitoba Indigenous Reconciliation & Northern Relations, Legislative Bldg., #301, 450 Broadway, Winnipeg, MB R3C 0V8
204-945-3788, Fax: 204-945-1383, INRweb@gov.mb.ca

Manitoba Sport, Culture & Heritage, Legislative Bldg., #118, 450 Broadway, Winnipeg, MB R3C 0V8

Mental Health & Addictions, Primary Health Care & Seniors, 300 Carlton St., 4th Floor, Winnipeg, MB R3B 3M9
204-788-6666

Multiculturalism Secretariat, 213 Notre Dame Ave., 6th Fl., Winnipeg, MB R3B 1N3
204-945-5632, multisec@gov.mb.ca

Seniors & Healthy Aging Secretariat, #1610, 155 Carlton St., Winnipeg, MB R3C 3H8
204-945-6565, Fax: 204-948-2514, 800-665-6565, seniors@gov.mb.ca

Status of Women Secretariat, #409, 401 York Ave., Winnipeg, MB R3C 0P8
204-945-6281, Fax: 204-945-6511, 800-263-0234, msw@gov.mb.ca

New Brunswick
Intergovernmental Affairs Division, Chancery Place, 675 King St., 5th Fl., Fredericton, NB E3B 1E9
506-444-4948, Fax: 506-453-2995, iga@gnb.ca

New Brunswick Department of Health, HSBC Place, PO Box 5100, Fredericton, NB E3B 5G8
506-457-4800, Fax: 506-453-5243, Health.Sante@gnb.ca

New Brunswick Department of Social Development, Sartain MacDonald Bldg., PO Box 6000, Fredericton, NB E3B 5H1
506-453-2001, Fax: 506-453-2164, sd-ds@gnb.ca

New Brunswick Human Rights Commission, Barry House, 751 Brunswick St., PO Box 6000, Fredericton, NB E3B 5H1
506-453-2301, Fax: 506-453-2653, 888-471-2233, hrc.cdp@gnb.ca

Premier's Council on the Status of Disabled Persons, #140, Place 2000, 1st Fl., PO Box 6000, Fredericton, NB E3B 5H1
506-444-3000, Fax: 506-444-3001, 800-442-4412, pcd-cpmph@gnb.ca

Regional Development Corporation, Chancery Place, 3rd Fl., PO Box 6000, Fredericton, NB E3B 5H1
506-453-2277, Fax: 506-453-7988, rdc-sdr@gnb.ca

Newfoundland & Labrador
Newfoundland & Labrador Department of Immigration, Population Growth & Skills, West Block, Confederation Bldg., 3rd Fl., PO Box 8700, St. John's, NL A1B 4J6
709-729-1795, isl@gov.nl.ca

Newfoundland & Labrador Department of Tourism, Culture, Arts & Recreation, PO Box 8700, St. John's, NL A1B 4J6
709-729-7000, tcar@gov.nl.ca

Newfoundland & Labrador Human Rights Commission, The Beothuk Bldg., 21 Crosbie Pl., PO Box 8700, St. John's, NL A1B 4J6
709-729-2709, Fax: 709-729-0790, 800-563-5808, humanrights@gov.nl.ca

Provincial Advisory Council on the Status of Women, #103, 15 Hallett Cres., St. John's, NL A1B 4C4
709-753-7270, Fax: 709-753-2606, 877-753-7270, info@pacsw.ca

Northwest Territories
Northwest Territories Department of Municipal & Community Affairs, PO Box 1320, Yellowknife, NT X1A 2L9

Office of the Languages Commissioner, 202 McDougall Rd., Fort Smith, NT X0E 0P0
867-872-3706, 800-661-0889, admin@olc-nt.ca

Status of Women Council of the Northwest Territories, Northwest Tower, 4th Fl., PO Box 1320, Yellowknife, NT X1A 2L9
888-234-4485

Nova Scotia
Nova Scotia Advisory Commission on AIDS, Barrington Tower, 1894 Barrington St., Halifax, NS B3J 2L4
902-424-5730, AIDS@novascotia.ca

Nova Scotia Advisory Council on the Status of Women, PO Box 745, Halifax, NS B3J 2T3
902-424-8662, Fax: 902-424-0573, 800-565-8662, women@novascotia.ca

Nova Scotia Department of Community Services, Nelson Place, 5675 Spring Garden Rd., 8th Fl., PO Box 696, Halifax, NS B3J 2T7
877-424-1177

Nova Scotia Department of Seniors, 1741 Brunswick St., 2nd Fl., Halifax, NS B3J 3X8
902-424-0770, Fax: 902-424-0561, 844-277-0770, seniors@novascotia.ca

Nova Scotia Disabled Persons Commission, Nelson Place, 5675 Spring Garden Rd., 7th Fl., PO Box 222 CRO, Halifax, NS B3J 2M4
902-424-8280, Fax: 902-424-0592, 800-565-8280, disability@gov.ns.ca

Nova Scotia Human Rights Commission, Park Lane Terrace, #305, 5657 Spring Garden Rd., PO Box 2221, Halifax, NS B3J 3C4
902-424-4111, Fax: 902-424-0596, 877-269-7699, hrcinquiries@novascotia.ca

Service Nova Scotia & Internal Services, PO Box 2734, Halifax, NS B3J 3K5
902-424-5200, Fax: 902-424-0720, 800-670-4357, askus@novascotia.ca

Nunavut
Nunavut Territory Department of Family Services, PO Box 1000 1200, Iqaluit, NU X0A 0H0
867-975-5200, Fax: 867-975-5722

Ontario
Office of Francophone Affairs, #2501, 700 Bay St., 25th Fl., Toronto, ON M7A 0A2
416-325-4983, 800-268-7507

Ontario Heritage Trust, 10 Adelaide St. East, Toronto, ON M5C 1J3
416-325-5000, Fax: 416-325-5071

Ontario Human Rights Commission, 180 Dundas St. West, 9th Fl., Toronto, ON M7A 2G5
  416-326-9511, Fax: 416-314-4494, 800-387-9080, info@ohrc.on.ca
Ontario Ministry of Citizenship & Multiculturalism, 56 Wellesley St. West, 14th Fl., Toronto, ON M7A 2E7
  416-212-0036
Ontario Ministry of Government & Consumer Services, Mowat Block, 900 Bay St., 6th Fl., Toronto, ON M7A 1L2
  416-212-2665, Fax: 416-326-7445, 844-286-8404
Ontario Ministry of Indigenous Affairs, 160 Bloor St. East, 4th Fl., Toronto, ON M7A 2E6
  416-326-4740, 866-381-5337
Royal Ontario Museum, 100 Queen's Park Cres., Toronto, ON M5S 2C6
  416-586-5549, Fax: 416-586-5685, info@rom.on.ca
Women's Issues, #601D, 777 Bay St., 6th Fl., Toronto, ON M7A 2J4

Prince Edward Island
Prince Edward Island Department of Social Development & Housing, Jones Bldg., 11 Kent St., 2nd Fl., PO Box 2000, Charlottetown, PE C1A 7N8
  902-620-3777, Fax: 902-368-4740, 866-594-3777, DeptSDH@gov.pe.ca
Prince Edward Island Human Rights Commission, 53 Water St., PO Box 2000, Charlottetown, PE C1A 7N8
  902-368-4180, Fax: 902-368-4236, 800-237-5031, contact@peihumanrights.ca

Quebec
Conseil des arts et des lettres du Québec, 79, boul René-Lévesque est, 3e étage, Québec, QC G1R 5N5
  418-643-1707, Fax: 418-643-4558, 800-608-3350, info@calq.gouv.qc.ca
Conseil du patrimoine culturel du Québec, 225, Grande Allée est, Québec, QC G1R 5G5
  418-643-8378, Fax: 418-643-8591, 844-701-0912, info@cpcq.gouv.qc.ca
Conseil du statut de la femme, #300, 800, place D'Youville, 3e étage, Québec, QC G1R 6E2
  418-643-4326, Fax: 418-643-8926, 800-463-2851, csf@csf.gouv.qc.ca
Ministère de l'Immigration, de la Francisation et de l'Intégration, 285, rue Notre-Dame ouest, 4e étage, Montréal, QC H2Y 1T8
  877-864-9191
Ministère de la Culture et Communications, 225, Grande Allée est, Québec, QC G1R 5G5
  888-380-8882
Ministère de la Santé et des Services sociaux, Direction des communications, 1075, ch Sainte-Foy, 15e étage, Québec, QC G1S 2M1
  418-644-4545, 877-644-4545
Ministère des Relations internationales et Francophonie, Édifice Hector-Fabre, 525, boul Réne-Lévesque est, Québec, QC G1R 5R9
  418-649-2300, Fax: 418-649-2656
Ministère du Travail, de l'Emploi et de la Solidarité sociale, 150, rue Monseigneur-Ross, 5e étage, Québec, QC G4X 2S7
  514-873-4000, 877-767-8773
Office des personnes handicapées du Québec, 309, rue Brock, Drummondville, QC J2B 1C5
  Fax: 819-475-8753, 800-567-1465, info@ophq.gouv.qc.ca
Secrétariat aux affaires autochtones, 905, av Honoré-Mercier, 1e étage, Québec, QC G1R 5M6
  418-643-3166, Fax: 418-646-4918
Secrétariat du Québec aux relations canadiennes, 875, Grande Allée est, 3e étage, Québec, QC G1R 4Y8
  418-643-4011, Fax: 418-528-0052
Secrétariat à la politique linguistique, 225 Grande-Allée est, 4e étage, bloc A, Québec, QC G1R 5G5
  418-643-4248, Fax: 418-646-7832
Société de développement des entreprises culturelles, #800, 215, rue Saint-Jacques, Montréal, QC H2Y 1M6
  514-841-2200, Fax: 514-841-8606, 800-363-0401, info@sodec.gouv.qc.ca
Tribunal administratif du Québec, 575, rue Jacques-Parizeau, Québec, QC G1R 5R4
  418-643-3418, Fax: 418-643-5335, 800-567-0278, tribunal.administratif@taq.gouv.qc.ca

Saskatchewan
Saskatchewan Heritage Foundation, 3211 Albert St., 1st Fl., Regina, SK S4S 5W6
Saskatchewan Human Rights Commission, PO Box 6011, Saskatoon, SK S7K 4E4
  306-933-5952, Fax: 306-933-7863, 800-667-9249, shrc@gov.sk.ca
Saskatchewan Social Services, 1920 Broad St., Regina, SK S4P 3V6
  306-787-3800, socialservicesinquiry@gov.sk.ca

Yukon Territory
Yukon Community Services, PO Box 2703, Whitehorse, YT Y1A 2C6
  867-667-5811, Fax: 867-393-6295, 800-661-0408
Yukon Health & Social Services, PO Box 2703, Whitehorse, YT Y1A 2C6
  867-667-3673, Fax: 867-667-3096, 800-661-0408, hss@yukon.ca
Yukon Human Rights Commission, #215, 305 Main St., Whitehorse, YT Y1A 2B4
  867-667-6226, Fax: 867-667-2662, 800-661-0535, info@yukonhumanrights.ca
Yukon Women's Directorate, #1, 404 Hason St., PO Box 2703, Whitehorse, YT Y1A 2C6
  867-667-3030

CANNABIS CONTROL
Canadian Food Inspection Agency, 1400 Merivale Rd., Ottawa, ON K1A 0Y9
  613-225-2342, 800-442-2342

Alberta
Alberta Gaming, Liquor & Cannabis Commission, 50 Corriveau Ave., St Albert, AB T8N 3T5
  780-447-8600, Fax: 780-447-8989, 800-272-8876

British Columbia
Liquor & Cannabis Regulation Branch, PO Box 9292 Prov Govt, Victoria, BC V8W 9J8
  250-952-5787, Fax: 250-952-7066, 866-209-2111, lclb.lclb@gov.bc.ca
Liquor Distribution Branch, 3383 Gilmore Way, Burnaby, BC V5G 4S1
  604-252-7400, inquiries@bcliquorstores.com
Policing & Security Branch, PO Box 9285 Prov Govt, Victoria, BC V8W 9J7
  250-387-1100, Fax: 250-356-7747, sgpcsb@gov.bc.ca

Manitoba
Liquor, Gaming & Cannabis Authority of Manitoba, 1055 Milt Stegall Dr., Winnipeg, MB R3G 0Z6
  204-927-5300, Fax: 204-927-5385, 800-782-0363, information@lgcamb.ca

New Brunswick
Cannabis NB, Centennial Bldg., PO Box 6000, Fredericton, NB E3B 5H1

Newfoundland & Labrador
Cannabis NL, 90 Kenmount Rd., PO Box 8750 A, St. John's, NL A1B 3V1
  709-724-1200, 844-757-5986, info@shopcannabisnl.com

Northwest Territories
Northwest Territories Liquor & Cannabis Commission, #201, 31 Capital Dr., Hay River, NT X0E 1G2
  867-874-8700, Fax: 867-874-8720

Nova Scotia
Nova Scotia Liquor Corporation, Bayers Lake Business Park, 93 Chain Lake Dr., Halifax, NS B3S 1A3
  800-567-5874, contactus@myNSLC.com

Nunavut
Nunavut Liquor & Cannabis Commission, PO Box 9, Rankin Inlet, NU X0C 0G0
  867-645-8575, Fax: 867-645-3327, 855-844-5488, info@nulc.ca

Ontario
Ontario Cannabis Retail Corporation / Ontario Cannabis Store, c/o Liquor Control Board of Ontario, 55 Lake Shore Blvd. East, Toronto, ON M5E 1A4
  888-910-0627
Ontario Legalization of Cannabis Secretariat, McMurtry-Scott Bldg., 720 Bay St., 11th Fl., Toronto, ON M7A 2S9

Prince Edward Island
Prince Edward Island Cannabis Management Corporation / PEI Cannabis, 85 Belvedere Ave., Charlottetown, PE C1A 6B2
  902-368-5551, infopeicmc@peicannabiscorp.com
Prince Edward Island Liquor Control Commission, 3 Garfield St., PO Box 967, Charlottetown, PE C1A 7M4
  902-368-5710, Fax: 902-368-5735

Quebec
Société Québécoise du Cannabis, 7500, rue Tellier, Montréal, QC H1N 3W5
  514-504-7732, 888-551-2161

Saskatchewan
Saskatchewan Liquor & Gaming Authority, 2500 Victoria Ave., PO Box 5054, Regina, SK S4P 3M3
  306-787-5563, inquiry@slga.gov.sk.ca

Yukon Territory
Yukon Liquor Corporation, 9031 Quartz Rd., Whitehorse, YT Y1A 4P9
  867-667-5245, Fax: 867-393-6306, yukon.liquor@yukon.ca

CAREER PLANNING
Alberta
Alberta Labour & Immigration, Legislature Bldg., #107, 10800 - 97th Ave., Edmonton, AB T5K 2B6
  780-427-3731, 877-427-3731

Manitoba
Aboriginal Education Directorate, Murdo Scribe Centre, 510 Selkirk Ave., Winnipeg, MB R2W 2M7
  204-945-7886, Fax: 204-948-2010, aedinfo@gov.mb.ca

New Brunswick
New Brunswick Department of Post-Secondary Education, Training & Labour, Chestnut Complex, PO Box 6000, Fredericton, NB E3B 5H1
  506-453-2597, Fax: 506-453-3618, dpetlinfo@gnb.ca

Nova Scotia
Nova Scotia Department of Advanced Education, 1505 Barrington St., PO Box 697, Halifax, NS B3J 2T8
  902-424-5301, Fax: 902-424-2203, lae-correspondence@novascotia.ca

Ontario
Ontario Ministry of Colleges & Universities, 438 University Ave., 5th Fl., Toronto, ON M7A 2A5
  416-325-2929, Fax: 416-325-6348, 800-387-5514, information.met@ontario.ca
Ontario Ministry of Labour, Training & Skills Development, 400 University Ave., 14th Fl., Toronto, ON M7A 1T7
  416-326-7160, 800-531-5551

Saskatchewan
Saskatchewan Education, 2220 College Ave., Regina, SK S4P 4V9
  learning.inquiry@gov.sk.ca
Saskatchewan Labour Relations & Workplace Safety, #300, 1870 Albert St., Regina, SK S4P 4W1
  Fax: 306-787-7404

CENSORSHIP (MEDIA)
Canadian Broadcasting Corporation, 181 Queen St., PO Box 3220 C, Ottawa, ON K1Y 1E4
  613-288-6000, liaison@cbc.ca
Canadian Radio-Television & Telecommunications Commission, Central Building, 1, promenade du Portage, Les Terrasses de la Chaudière, Gatineau, QC J8X 4B1
  819-997-0313, Fax: 819-994-0218, 877-249-2782

Manitoba
Manitoba Film Classification Board, #216, 301 Weston St., Winnipeg, MB R3E 3H4
  204-945-8962, Fax: 204-945-0890, 866-612-2399, mfcb@gov.mb.ca

Nunavut
Nunavut Territory Department of Community & Government Services, W.G. Brown Bldg., 4th Fl., PO Box 1000 700, Iqaluit, NU X0A 0H0
  867-975-5406, Fax: 867-975-5305, cgscomms@gov.nu.ca

Quebec
Régie du cinéma, #100, 390, rue Notre-Dame ouest, Montréal, QC H2Y 1T9
  514-873-2371, Fax: 514-873-8874, 800-463-2463

CHILD WELFARE
See Also: Day Care Services
Alberta
Alberta Children's Services, Office of the Minister, Legislature Bldg., #204, 10800 - 97th Ave., Edmonton, AB T5K 2B6
Alberta Office of the Child & Youth Advocate, #600, 9925 - 109th St. NW, Edmonton, AB T5K 2J8
  780-422-6056, Fax: 780-422-3675, 800-661-3446, ca.information@ocya.alberta.ca
Premier's Council on Alberta's Promise, AMEC Place, #2520, 801 - 6 Ave. SW, Calgary, AB T2P 3W2
  403-297-7500, Fax: 403-297-6664, 866-313-7500, info@albertaspromise.org

British Columbia
Office of the Representative for Children & Youth, #400, 1019 Wharf St., Victoria, BC V8W 2Y9
  250-356-6710, Fax: 250-356-0837, 800-476-3933, rcy@rcybc.ca

Manitoba
Child & Family Services, 777 Portage Ave., Winnipeg, MB R3G 0N3
  204-945-6964, cfsd@gov.mb.ca
Manitoba Education, Legislative Bldg., #162, 450 Broadway, Winnipeg, MB R3C 0V8
  204-945-3720, Fax: 204-945-1291
Manitoba Healthy Child Office, 332 Bannatyne Ave., 3rd Fl., Winnipeg, MB R3A 0E2
  204-945-2266, 888-848-0140, healthychild@gov.mb.ca

Newfoundland & Labrador
Newfoundland & Labrador Department of Children, Seniors & Social Development, PO Box 8700, St. John's, NL A1B 4J6
709-729-0760, Fax: 709-729-0870, CSSDInfo@gov.nl.ca
Newfoundland & Labrador Department of Education, West Block, Confederation Bldg., 100 Prince Philip Dr., 3rd Fl., PO Box 8700, St. John's, NL A1B 4J6
709-729-5097, Fax: 709-729-1400, education@gov.nl.ca
Northwest Territories
Northwest Territories Department of Health & Social Services, PO Box 1320, Yellowknife, NT X1A 2L9
Nova Scotia
Nova Scotia Department of Education & Early Childhood Development, 2021 Brunswick St., PO Box 578, Halifax, NS B3J 2S9
902-424-5168, Fax: 902-424-0511, 888-825-7770
Nunavut
Nunavut Territory Department of Family Services, PO Box 1000 1200, Iqaluit, NU X0A 0H0
867-975-5200, Fax: 867-975-5722
Nunavut Territory Department of Health, PO Box 1000 1000, Iqaluit, NU X0A 0H0
867-975-5700, Fax: 867-975-5705, 800-661-0833
Ontario
Office of the Children's Lawyer, 393 University Ave., 14th Fl., Toronto, ON M5G 1W9
416-314-8000, Fax: 416-314-8050
Office of the Ombudsman, Bell Trinity Sq., South Tower, 483 Bay St., 10th Fl., Toronto, ON M5G 2C9
416-586-3300, Fax: 416-586-3485, 800-263-1830, info@ombudsman.on.ca
Ontario Ministry of Children, Community & Social Services, Hepburn Block, 80 Grosvenor St., 6th Fl., Toronto, ON M7A 1E9
416-325-5666, 888-789-4199
Prince Edward Island
Prince Edward Island Department of Education & Lifelong Learning, Holman Centre, #101, 250 Water St., Summerside, PE C1N 1B6
902-438-4130, Fax: 902-438-4062, DeptELL@gov.pe.ca
Yukon Territory
Yukon Child & Youth Advocate Office, #19, 2070 Second Ave., Whitehorse, YT Y1A 1B1
867-456-5575, Fax: 867-456-5574, 800-661-0408, info@ycao.ca

CITIZENSHIP
Immigration & Refugee Board of Canada, Minto Place, Canada Bldg., 344 Slater St., 12th Fl., Ottawa, ON K1A 0K1
Fax: 613-943-1550
Manitoba
Manitoba Education, Legislative Bldg., #162, 450 Broadway, Winnipeg, MB R3C 0V8
204-945-3720, Fax: 204-945-1291
Nova Scotia
Office of Immigration, 1469 Brenton St., 3rd Fl., PO Box 1535, Halifax, NS B3J 2Y3
902-424-5230, Fax: 902-424-7936, 877-292-9597, immigration@novascotia.ca
Ontario
Ontario Ministry of Citizenship & Multiculturalism, 56 Wellesley St. West, 14th Fl., Toronto, ON M7A 2E7
416-212-0036,
Quebec
Ministère de l'Immigration, de la Francisation et de l'Intégration, 285, rue Notre-Dame ouest, 4e étage, Montréal, QC H2Y 1T8
877-864-9191

CLIMATE & WEATHER
Atmospheric Science & Technology, 351, boul Saint-Joseph, Gatineau, QC K1A 0H3
Canadian Space Agency, John H. Chapman Space Centre, 6767, rte de l'Aéroport, Saint-Hubert, QC J3Y 8Y9
450-926-4800, Fax: 450-926-4352, asc.info.csa@canada.ca
Climatic Testing Facility, Ottawa Uplands Research Facilities, 2320 Lester Rd., Ottawa, ON K1V 1S2
613-998-9639
Environment & Climate Change Canada, 200, rue Sacré-Coeur, 12th Fl., Gatineau, QC K1A 0H3
819-938-3860, 800-668-6767, eec.enviroinfo.ec@canada.ca
Meteorological Service of Canada, 351, boul Saint-Joseph, Gatineau, QC K1A 0H3
819-934-5395, Fax: 819-934-1255

CLIMATE CHANGE
Alberta
Climate Change Division, Petroleum Plaza ST, 9915 - 108th St., 11th Fl., Edmonton, AB T5K 2G8

Safety & Policy Division, Twin Atria Bldg., 4999 - 98th Ave., Main Fl., Edmonton, AB T6B 2X3
780-427-8901, Fax: 780-415-0782, 800-666-5036
Prince Edward Island
Prince Edward Island Department of Environment, Energy & Climate Action, Jones Bldg., 11 Kent St., 4th Fl., Charlottetown, PE C1A 7N8
902-368-5044, Fax: 902-368-5830, 866-368-5044, DeptEECA@gov.pe.ca
Quebec
Ministère de l'Environnement et de la Lutte contre les changements climatiques, Édifice Marie-Guyart, 675, boul René-Lévesque est, 30e étage, Québec, QC G1R 5V7
418-521-3830, Fax: 418-646-5974, 800-561-1616, relations.medias@mddelcc.gouv.qc.ca

COAL
See Also: Energy
Alberta
Alberta Energy Regulator, #1000, 250 - 5 St. SW, Calgary, AB T2P 0R4
403-297-8311, Fax: 403-297-7336, 855-297-8311, inquiries@aer.ca
Ontario
Ontario Power Generation, 700 University Ave., Toronto, ON M5G 1X6
416-592-2555, 877-592-2555, webmaster@opg.com
Saskatchewan
Saskatchewan Power Corporation (SaskPower), 2025 Victoria Ave., Regina, SK S4P 0S1
888-757-6937

COMMUNICATIONS
See Also: Telecommunications
Canada Post Corporation, Corporate Secretariat, 2701 Riverside Dr., Ottawa, ON K1A 0B1
416-979-3033, 866-607-6301
Canadian Broadcasting Corporation, 181 Queen St., PO Box 3220 C, Ottawa, ON K1Y 1E4
613-288-6000, liaison@cbc.ca
Canadian Radio-Television & Telecommunications Commission, Central Building, 1, promenade du Portage, Les Terrasses de la Chaudière, Gatineau, QC J8X 4B1
819-997-0313, Fax: 819-994-0218, 877-249-2782
Communications Research Centre Canada, 3701 Carling Ave., PO Box 11490 H, Ottawa, ON K2H 8S2
613-991-3313, Fax: 613-998-5355, info@crc.gc.ca
Spectrum, Information Technologies & Telecommunications, Journal Tower North, 300 Slater St., 20th Fl., Ottawa, ON K1A 0C8
613-998-0368, Fax: 613-952-1203
Manitoba
Communications Services Manitoba, 155 Carlton St., 10th Fl., Winnipeg, MB R3C 3H8
204-945-3765
Ontario
Ontario Library Service, Head Office, 334 Regent St., Sudbury, ON P3C 4E2
800-387-5765, info@olservice.ca
Quebec
Ministère de la Culture et Communications, 225, Grande Allée est, Québec, QC G1R 5G5
888-380-8882
Saskatchewan
Saskatchewan Telecommunications (SaskTel), 2121 Saskatchewan Dr., Regina, SK S4P 3Y2
800-727-5835, corporate.comments@sasktel.sk.ca

COMMUNITY & MUNICIPAL DEVELOPMENT
Atlantic Canada Opportunities Agency, Blue Cross Centre, 644 Main St., 3rd Fl., PO Box 6051, Moncton, NB E1C 9J8
506-851-2271, Fax: 506-851-7403, 800-561-7862, ACOA.information.APECA@canada.ca
Canada Economic Development for Québec Regions, #500, 800, boul René-Lévesque ouest, Montréal, QC H3B 1X9
514-283-6412, Fax: 514-283-3302, 866-385-6412
Canadian Northern Economic Development Agency, Ottawa, ON K1A 0H4
855-897-2667,
CanNor.InfoNorth.InfoNord.CanNor@canada.ca
Destination Canada, #800, 1045 Howe St., Vancouver, BC V6Z 2A9
604-638-8300
Federal Economic Development Agency for Southern Ontario, #101, 139 Northfield Dr. West, Waterloo, ON N2L 5A6
Fax: 519-725-4976, 866-593-5505
FedNor (Federal Economic Development Initiative in Northern Ontario), 19 Lisgar St., Sudbury, ON P3E 3L4
Fax: 705-671-0717, 877-333-6673

Western Economic Diversification Canada, Canada Place, #1500, 9700 Jasper Ave. NW, Edmonton, AB T5J 4H7
780-495-4164, Fax: 780-495-4557, 888-338-9378, WD.contactus-contactez-nous.DEO@canada.ca
British Columbia
Local Government, PO Box 9490 Prov Govt, Victoria, BC V8W 9N7
250-356-6575, Fax: 250-387-7973
Manitoba
Manitoba Indigenous Reconciliation & Northern Relations, Legislative Bldg., #301, 450 Broadway, Winnipeg, MB R3C 0V8
204-945-3788, Fax: 204-945-1383, INRweb@gov.mb.ca
New Brunswick
Regional Development Corporation, Chancery Place, 3rd Fl., PO Box 6000, Fredericton, NB E3B 5H1
506-453-2277, Fax: 506-453-7988, rdc-sdr@gnb.ca
Newfoundland & Labrador
Newfoundland & Labrador Department of Health & Community Services, West Block, Confederation Bldg., 100 Prince Philip Dr., 1st Fl., PO Box 8700, St. John's, NL A1B 4J6
709-729-4984, healthinfo@gov.nl.ca
Newfoundland & Labrador Department of Municipal & Provincial Affairs, West Block, Confederation Bldg., PO Box 8700, St. John's, NL A1B 4J6
MAPAInfo@gov.nl.ca
Northwest Territories
Northwest Territories Department of Municipal & Community Affairs, PO Box 1320, Yellowknife, NT X1A 2L9
School of Community Government, #500, 5201 - 50th Ave., PO Box 1320, Yellowknife, NT X1A 3S9
867-767-9163, Fax: 867-873-0584, maca_scg@gov.nt.ca
Nova Scotia
Nova Scotia Department of Municipal Affairs, PO Box 216, Halifax, NS B3J 2M4
902-424-6642
Office of L'nu Affairs, 5251 Duke St., 5th Fl., PO Box 1617, Halifax, NS B3J 2Y3
902-424-7409, Fax: 902-424-4225, LnuAffairs@novascotia.ca
Nunavut
Nunavut Development Corporation, PO Box 249, Rankin Inlet, NU X0C 0G0
867-645-3170, Fax: 867-645-3755, 866-645-3170, opportunities@ndcorp.nu.ca
Nunavut Territory Department of Community & Government Services, W.G. Brown Bldg., 4th Fl., PO Box 1000 700, Iqaluit, NU X0A 0H0
867-975-5406, Fax: 867-975-5305, cgscomms@gov.nu.ca
Ontario
Ontario Ministry of Municipal Affairs & Housing, College Park, 777 Bay St., 17th Fl., Toronto, ON M7A 2J3
416-585-7041, Fax: 416-585-4230, mininfo@ontario.ca
Prince Edward Island
SkillsPEI, Atlantic Technology Centre, #212, 176 Great George St., Charlottetown, PE C1A 4K9
902-368-6290, Fax: 902-368-6340, 877-491-4766
Quebec
Ministère des affaires municipales et Habitation, Aile Chaveau, 10, rue Pierre-Olivier-Chauveau, Québec, QC G1R 4J3
418-691-2015, Fax: 418-643-7385, communications@mamrot.gouv.qc.ca
Ministère des Finances, 12, rue Saint-Louis, Québec, QC G1R 5L3
418-528-9323, Fax: 418-646-1631, info@finances.gouv.qc.ca
Saskatchewan
Saskatchewan Government Relations, 1855 Victoria Ave., Regina, SK S4P 3T2

COMMUNITY FINANCING
Atlantic Canada Opportunities Agency, Blue Cross Centre, 644 Main St., 3rd Fl., PO Box 6051, Moncton, NB E1C 9J8
506-851-2271, Fax: 506-851-7403, 800-561-7862, ACOA.information.APECA@canada.ca
Business Development Bank of Canada, #100, 5, Place Ville-Marie, Montréal, QC H3B 5E7
Fax: 877-329-9232, 877-232-2269
Canada Economic Development for Québec Regions, #500, 800, boul René-Lévesque ouest, Montréal, QC H3B 1X9
514-283-6412, Fax: 514-283-3302, 866-385-6412
Canada Savings Bonds, #201, 50 O'Connor St., PO Box 2770 D, Ottawa, ON K1P 1J7
905-754-2012, Fax: 613-782-8096, 800-575-5151
Finance Canada, 90 Elgin St., Ottawa, ON K1A 0G5
613-369-3710, Fax: 613-369-4065, fin.financepublic-financepublique.fin@canada.ca
Western Economic Diversification Canada, Canada Place, #1500, 9700 Jasper Ave. NW, Edmonton, AB T5J 4H7
780-495-4164, Fax: 780-495-4557, 888-338-9378, WD.contactus-contactez-nous.DEO@canada.ca

Alberta
Alberta Capital Finance Authority, Sun Life Place, #2160, 10123 - 99 St. NW, Edmonton, AB T5J 3H1
780-427-9711, Fax: 780-422-2175, webacfa@gov.ab.ca
Manitoba
Communities Economic Development Fund, 15 Moak Cres., Thompson, MB R8N 2B8
204-778-4138, Fax: 204-778-4313, 800-561-4315
Nova Scotia
Nova Scotia Municipal Finance Corporation, PO Box 850 M, Halifax, NS B3J 2V2
902-424-4590, Fax: 902-424-0525
Prince Edward Island
SkillsPEI, Atlantic Technology Centre, #212, 176 Great George St., Charlottetown, PE C1A 4K9
902-368-6290, Fax: 902-368-6340, 877-491-4766
Quebec
Ministère des affaires municipales et Habitation, Aile Chaveau, 10, rue Pierre-Olivier-Chauveau, Québec, QC G1R 4J3
418-691-2015, Fax: 418-643-7385, communications@mamrot.gouv.qc.ca
Yukon
Yukon Economic Development, 303 Alexander St., Whitehorse, YT Y1A 2L5
800-661-0408, ecdev@yukon.ca

COMMUNITY SERVICES

Alberta
Alberta Community & Social Services, Office of the Minister, Legislature Bldg., #224, 10800 - 97th Ave., Edmonton, AB T5K 2B6
780-644-9992, 877-644-9992
British Columbia
British Columbia Ministry of Tourism, Arts, Culture & Sport, PO Box 9082 Prov Govt, Victoria, BC V8W 9E2
Manitoba
Community Service Delivery, #119, 114 Garry St., Winnipeg, MB R3C 4V4
204-945-1634, csd@gov.mb.ca
New Brunswick
New Brunswick Department of Social Development, Sartain MacDonald Bldg., PO Box 6000, Fredericton, NB E3B 5H1
506-453-2001, Fax: 506-453-2164, sd-ds@gnb.ca
Newfoundland & Labrador
Newfoundland & Labrador Department of Health & Community Services, West Block, Confederation Bldg., 100 Prince Philip Dr., 1st Fl., PO Box 8700, St. John's, NL A1B 4J6
709-729-4984, healthinfo@gov.nl.ca
Northwest Territories
Northwest Territories Department of Municipal & Community Affairs, PO Box 1320, Yellowknife, NT X1A 2L9
Nova Scotia
Community Sector Council of Nova Scotia, Halifax Shopping Centre, PO Box 29028, Halifax, NS B3L 4T8
902-424-4585, info@csc-ns.ca
Nova Scotia Department of Community Services, Nelson Place, 5675 Spring Garden Rd., 8th Fl., PO Box 696, Halifax, NS B3J 2T7
877-424-1177
Nunavut
Nunavut Territory Department of Community & Government Services, W.G. Brown Bldg., 4th Fl., PO Box 1000 700, Iqaluit, NU X0A 0H0
867-975-5406, Fax: 867-975-5305, cgscomms@gov.nu.ca
Prince Edward Island
Prince Edward Island Department of Social Development & Housing, Jones Bldg., 11 Kent St., 2nd Fl., PO Box 2000, Charlottetown, PE C1A 7N8
902-620-3777, Fax: 902-368-4740, 866-594-3777, DeptSDH@gov.pe.ca
Saskatchewan
Saskatchewan Social Services, 1920 Broad St., Regina, SK S4P 3V6
306-787-3800, socialservicesinquiry@gov.sk.ca
Yukon Territory
Yukon Community Services, PO Box 2703, Whitehorse, YT Y1A 2C6
867-667-5811, Fax: 867-393-6295, 800-661-0408

CONFLICT OF INTEREST

Office of the Conflict of Interest & Ethics Commissioner, Commissioner's Office, 66 Slater St., 22nd Fl., PO Box 16, Ottawa, ON K1A 0A6
613-995-0721, Fax: 613-995-7308, ciec-ccie@parl.gc.ca
Office of the Senate Ethics Officer, Thomas D'Arcy McGee Bldg., #526, 90 Sparks St., Ottawa, ON K1P 5B4
613-947-3566, Fax: 613-947-3577, 800-267-7362, cse-seo@sen.parl.gc.ca

Alberta
Alberta Office of the Ethics Commissioner, #1250, 9925 - 109th St. NW, Edmonton, AB T5K 2J8
780-422-2273, Fax: 780-422-2261, generalinfo@ethicscommissioner.ab.ca
British Columbia
Office of the Conflict of Interest Commissioner, 421 Menzies St., 1st Fl., Victoria, BC V8V 1X4
250-356-0750, Fax: 250-356-6580, conflictofinterest@coibc.ca
Ontario
Conflict of Interest Commissioner, #1802, 2 Bloor St. East, Toronto, ON M4W 3J5
416-212-3606, Fax: 416-325-4330, 866-956-1191, coicommissioner@ontario.ca
Office of the Integrity Commissioner, #2100, 2 Bloor St. West, Toronto, ON M4W 3E2
416-314-8983, Fax: 416-314-8987, 866-884-4470, info@oico.on.ca
Prince Edward Island
Office of the Conflict of Interest Commissioner, 197 Richmond St., 1st Fl., PO Box 2000, Charlottetown, PE C1A 7N8
902-368-5970, Fax: 902-368-5175

CONSERVATION & ECOLOGY

See Also: Heritage Resources; Natural Resources
Canadian Heritage, 15, rue Eddy, Gatineau, QC K1A 0M5
819-997-0055, 866-811-0055, PCH.info-info.PCH@canada.ca
Commission for Environmental Cooperation, Secretariat, #200, 393, rue Saint-Jacques ouest, Montréal, QC H2Y 1N9
514-350-4300, Fax: 514-350-4314, info@cec.org
Environment & Climate Change Canada, 200, rue Sacré-Coeur, 12th Fl., Gatineau, QC K1A 0H3
819-938-3860, 800-668-6767, eec.enviroinfo.ec@canada.ca
Natural Resources Canada, 580 Booth St., Ottawa, ON K1A 0E4
343-292-6096, Fax: 613-992-7211
North American Bird Conservation Initiative, Canadian Wildlife Service, 351 St. Joseph Blvd., Gatineau, QC K1A 0H3
819-994-0512, Fax: 819-994-4445, ec.icoancanada-nabcicanada.ec@canada.ca
North American Waterfowl Management Plan, NAWCC (Canada) Secretariat, Place Vincent Massey, 351 St. Joseph Blvd., 14th Fl., Gatineau, QC K1A 0H3
819-938-4030, Fax: 819-934-6017, ec.pnags-nawmp.ec@canada.ca
Parks Canada, National Office, 30, rue Victoria, Gatineau, QC J8X 0B3
819-420-9486, 888-773-8888, information@pc.gc.ca
Polar Knowledge Canada, #200, 170 Laurier Ave. West, 2nd Fl., Ottawa, ON K1P 5V5
613-943-8605, info@polar.gc.ca
Alberta
Alberta Environment & Parks, Forestry Bldg., 9920 - 108th St., Main Fl., Edmonton, AB T5K 2M4
780-944-0313
Alberta Environmental Appeals Board, Peace Hills Trust Tower, #306, 10011 - 109 St., Edmonton, AB T5J 3S8
780-427-6207, Fax: 780-427-4693
Alberta Used Oil Management Association, Empire Building, #1008, 10080 Jasper Ave., Edmonton, AB T5J 1V9
780-414-1510, Fax: 780-414-1519, 866-414-1510, auoma@usedoilrecycling.ca
Beverage Container Management Board, #100, 8616 - 51 Ave., Edmonton, AB T6E 6E6
780-424-3193, Fax: 780-428-4620, 888-424-7671, info@bcmb.ab.ca
Forestry Division, Petroleum Plaza ST, 9915 - 108th St., 10th Fl., Edmonton, AB T5K 2G8
Land Use Secretariat, Centre West Bldg., 10035 - 108th St., 9th Fl., Edmonton, AB T5J 3E1
780-644-7972, Fax: 780-644-1034, luf@gov.ab.ca
Natural Resources Conservation Board, Sterling Place, 9940 - 106 St., 4th Fl., Edmonton, AB T5K 2N2
780-422-1977, Fax: 780-427-0607, 866-383-6722, info@nrcb.ca
Special Areas Board, Special Areas Board Administration, 212 - 2nd Ave. West, PO Box 820, Hanna, AB T0J 1P0
403-854-5600, Fax: 403-854-5527
British Columbia
British Columbia Assessment Authority, #400, 3450 Uptown Blvd., Victoria, BC V8Z 0B9
604-739-8588, Fax: 855-995-6209, 866-825-8322
British Columbia Ministry of Environment & Climate Change Strategy, PO Box 9047 Prov Govt, Victoria, BC V8W 9E2
Environmental Appeal Board, 747 Fort St., 4th Fl., PO Box 9425 Prov Govt, Victoria, BC V8W 3E9
250-387-3464, Fax: 250-356-9923, eabinfo@gov.bc.ca
Forest Appeals Commission, 747 Fort St., 4th Fl., PO Box 9425 Prov Govt, Victoria, BC V8W 9V1
250-387-3464, Fax: 250-356-9923, facinfo@gov.bc.ca

Forest Practices Board, 310, 1675 Douglas St., PO Box 9905 Prov Govt, Victoria, BC V8W 9R1
250-213-4700, Fax: 250-213-4725, 800-994-5899, fpboard@gov.bc.ca
Manitoba
Clean Environment Commission, #305, 155 Carlton St., Winnipeg, MB R3C 3H8
204-945-0594, Fax: 204-945-0090, 800-597-3556, cec@gov.mb.ca
Ecological Reserves Advisory Committee, c/o Manitoba Conservation, Parks & Natural Areas Branch, 200 Saulteaux Cres., PO Box 53, Winnipeg, MB R3J 3W3
204-945-4148, Fax: 204-945-0012
Manitoba Conservation & Climate, 200 Saulteaux Cres., PO Box 22, Winnipeg, MB R3J 3W3
204-945-6784, Fax: 204-948-2656, 800-214-6497, cc@gov.mb.ca
New Brunswick
New Brunswick Department of Environment & Local Government, Marysville Place, 20 McGloin St., Fredericton, NB E3B 5H1
506-453-2690, Fax: 506-457-4994, elg/egl-info@gnb.ca
Newfoundland & Labrador
Newfoundland & Labrador Department of Environment & Climate Change, PO Box 8700, St. John's, NL A1B 4J6
ECCInfo@gov.nl.ca
Northwest Territories
Northwest Territories Department of Environment & Natural Resources, PO Box 1320, Yellowknife, NT X1A 2L9
867-767-9055, enr_communications@gov.nt.ca
Nova Scotia
Nova Scotia Department of Lands & Forestry, PO Box 698, Halifax, NS B3J 2T9
902-424-5935, Fax: 902-424-7735, 800-565-2224
Ontario
Ontario Ministry of Environment, Conservation & Parks, Ferguson Block, 77 Wellesley St. West, 11th Fl., Toronto, ON M7A 2T5
416-325-4000, Fax: 416-314-6713, 800-565-4923
Ontario Ministry of Northern Development, Mines, Natural Resources & Forestry, Natural Resources Information & Support Centre, 300 Water St., Toronto, ON K9J 8M5
800-667-1940,
Prince Edward Island
Prince Edward Island Department of Economic Growth, Tourism & Culture, PO Box 2000, Charlottetown, PE C1A 7N8
902-368-5540, Fax: 902-368-5277, tpswitch@gov.pe.ca
Prince Edward Island Department of Justice & Public Safety, Shaw Bldg. South, 95 Rochford St., 4th Fl., PO Box 2000, Charlottetown, PE C1A 7N8
902-368-4589, Fax: 902-368-5283, DeptJPS@gov.pe.ca
Quebec
Comité consultatif de l'environnement Kativik, CP 930, Kuujjuaq, QC J0M 1C0
819-964-2961, Fax: 819-964-0694, keac-ccek@krg.ca
Fondation de la faune du Québec, #420, 1175, av Lavigerie, Québec, QC G1V 4P1
418-644-7926, Fax: 418-643-7655, 877-639-0742, ffq@fondationdelafaune.qc.ca
Ministère de l'Environnement et de la Lutte contre les changements climatiques, Édifice Marie-Guyart, 675, boul René-Lévesque est, 30e étage, Québec, QC G1R 5V7
418-521-3830, Fax: 418-646-5974, 800-561-1616, relations.medias@mddelcc.gouv.qc.ca
Société de développement de la Baie James, #10, 462, 3e rue, Chibougamau, QC G8P 1N7
418-748-7777, Fax: 418-748-6868, chi@sdbj.gouv.qc.ca
Société québécoise de récupération et recyclage, #411, 300, rue Saint-Paul, Québec, QC G1K 7R1
418-643-0394, Fax: 418-643-6507, 800-807-0678, info@recyc-quebec.gouv.qc.ca
Saskatchewan
Saskatchewan Assessment Management Agency, #200, 2201 - 11th Ave., Regina, SK S4P 0J8
306-924-8000, Fax: 306-924-8070, 800-667-7262, info.request@sama.sk.ca
Saskatchewan Conservation Data Centre, Fish & Wildlife Branch, Ministry of Environment, 3211 Albert St., Regina, SK S4S 5W6
306-787-7196, Fax: 306-787-9544
Saskatchewan Environment, 3211 Albert St., Regina, SK S4S 5W6
306-787-2584, Fax: 306-787-9544, 800-567-4224, centre.inquiry@gov.sk.ca
Saskatchewan Water Security Agency, #400, 111 Fairford St. East, Moose Jaw, SK S6H 7X9
306-694-3900, Fax: 306-694-3105, comm@wsask.ca
Yukon Territory
Alsek Renewable Resources Council, PO Box 2077, Haines Junction, YT Y0B 1L0
867-634-2524, Fax: 867-634-2527, admin@alsekrrc.ca

Carmacks Renewable Resource Council, PO Box 122, Carmacks, YT Y0B 1C0
867-863-6838, Fax: 867-863-6429, carmacksrrc@northwestel.net
Dawson District Renewable Resource Council, PO Box 1380, Dawson City, YT Y0B 1G0
867-993-6976, Fax: 867-993-6093, dawsonrrc@northwestel.net
Mayo District Renewable Resources Council, PO Box 249, Mayo, YT Y0B 1M0
867-996-2942, Fax: 867-996-2948, mayorrc@northwestel.net
Selkirk Renewable Resources Council, PO Box 32, Pelly Crossing, YT Y0B 1P0
867-537-3937, Fax: 867-537-3938, selkirkrrc@northwestel.net
Teslin Renewable Resource Council, PO Box 186, Teslin, YT Y0A 1B0
867-390-2323, Fax: 867-390-2919, teslinrrc@northwestel.net
Yukon Environment, 10 Burns Rd., Whitehorse, YT Y1A 2C6
867-667-5652, Fax: 867-393-7197, environmentyukon@yukon.ca

CONSTRUCTION
Canada Infrastructure Bank, 150 King St. West, PO Box 15, Toronto, ON M5H 1J9
833-551-5245
Canada Mortgage & Housing Corporation, 700 Montreal Rd., Ottawa, ON K1A 0P7
613-748-2000, Fax: 613-748-2098, 800-668-2642, chic@cmhc-schl.gc.ca
Defence Construction Canada, Constitution Square, 350 Albert St., 19th Fl., Ottawa, ON K1A 0K3
613-998-9548, Fax: 613-998-1061, 800-514-3555, info@dcc-cdc.gc.ca
Hygrothermal Performance of Buildings Research Facilities, c/o National Research Council, 1200 Montreal Rd., Ottawa, ON K1A 0R6
613-993-9101
Infrastructure Canada, #1100, 180 Kent St., Ottawa, ON K1P 0B6
613-948-1148, 877-250-7154, ifc.info@canada.ca

Alberta
Alberta Infrastructure, Infrastructure Bldg., 6950 - 113th St., Edmonton, AB T6H 5V7
780-415-0507, Fax: 780-427-2187, Infra.Contact.Us.m@gov.ab.ca
Alberta Transportation, Communications Branch, Twin Atria Bldg., 4999 - 98th Ave., 2nd Fl., Edmonton, AB T6B 2X3
780-427-7674, Fax: 780-466-3166, Trans.Contact.Us.m@gov.ab.ca
Corporate Strategies & Services Division, Infrastructure Bldg., 6950 - 113th St., 2nd Fl., Edmonton, AB T6H 5V7

British Columbia
British Columbia Ministry of Transportation & Infrastructure, PO Box 9850 Prov Govt, Victoria, BC V8W 9T5
250-387-3198, Fax: 250-356-7706, tran.webmaster@gov.bc.ca
Building Code Appeal Board, c/o Building & Safety Standards Branch, PO Box 9844 Prov Govt, Victoria, BC V8W 1A4
250-387-3133, Fax: 250-387-8164, Building.Safety@gov.bc.ca
Partnerships BC, 900 - 1285 West Pender St., PO Box 9478 Prov Govt, Vancouver, BC V6E 4B1
604-681-2443, Fax: 604-806-4190, partnershipsbc@partnershipsbc.ca

Manitoba
Manitoba Infrastructure, Legislative Bldg., #203, 450 Broadway, Winnipeg, MB R3C 0V8

New Brunswick
New Brunswick Department of Transportation & Infrastructure, Kings Place, PO Box 6000, Fredericton, NB E3B 5H1
506-453-3939, Fax: 506-453-7987, transportation.web@gnb.ca

Newfoundland & Labrador
Newfoundland & Labrador Department of Transportation & Infrastructure, Confederation Bldg., Prince Philip Dr., PO Box 8700, St. John's, NL A1B 4J6
709-729-2300, ti@gov.nl.ca

Nova Scotia
Nova Scotia Department of Transportation & Active Transit, PO Box 186, Halifax, NS B3J 2N2
902-424-2297, Fax: 902-424-0532, tpwpaff@novascotia.ca

Nunavut
Nunavut Territory Department of Community & Government Services, W.G. Brown Bldg., 4th Fl., PO Box 1000 700, Iqaluit, NU X0A 0H0
867-975-5406, Fax: 867-975-5305, cgscomms@gov.nu.ca

Ontario
Ontario Capital Growth Corporation, Ontario Investment & Trade Centre, 250 Yonge St., 35th Fl., Toronto, ON M5B 2L7
416-325-6874, Fax: 416-212-0794
Ontario Ministry of Economic Development, Job Creation & Trade, 56 Wellesley St. West, 7th Fl., Toronto, ON M7A 2E7
416-325-6666, 800-268-7095
Ontario Ministry of Infrastructure, 777 Bay St., 5th Fl., Toronto, ON M5G 2C8
416-327-4412

Prince Edward Island
Prince Edward Island Department of Transportation & Infrastructure, Jones Bldg., 11 Kent St., 3rd Fl., PO Box 2000, Charlottetown, PE C1A 7N8
902-368-5100, Fax: 902-368-5395, DeptTIE@gov.pe.ca

Quebec
Commission de la capitale nationale du Québec, Edifice Hector-Fabre, 525, boul René-Lévesque est, RC, Québec, QC G1R 5S9
418-528-0773, Fax: 418-528-0833, 800-442-0773, commission@capitale.gouv.qc.ca
Commission de la construction du Québec, 8485, av Christophe-Colomb, Montréal, QC H2M 0A7
Modernisation des centres hospitaliers universitaires de Montréal, CHUM, CUSM, CHU Sainte-Justine, #10.049, 2021, rue Union, Montréal, QC H3A 2S9
514-864-9883, Fax: 514-873-7362, info.construction3chu@msss.gouv.qc.ca
Régie du bâtiment du Québec, 545, boul Crémazie est, 4e étage, Montréal, QC H2M 2V2
514-873-0976, 800-361-0761
Société québécoise des infrastructures, Édifice Marie-Fitzbach, 1075, rue de l'Amérique-Française, Québec, QC G1R 5P8
418-646-1766, Fax: 418-646-6911, courrier@sqi.gouv.qc.ca

Saskatchewan
Saskatchewan Highways, Victoria Tower, 1855 Victoria Ave., Regina, SK S4P 3T2
306-933-5186, MHI.CustomerService@gov.sk.ca
SaskBuilds & Procurement, 1920 Rose St., Regina, SK S4P 0A9
306-787-6911, Fax: 306-787-1061, cs.receptioncenturyplaza@gov.sk.ca

CONSUMER PROTECTION
See Also: Public Safety
Financial Consumer Agency of Canada, 427 Laurier Ave. West, 6th Fl., Ottawa, ON K1R 1B9
613-960-4666, Fax: 613-941-1436

Alberta
Service Alberta, Government of Alberta, PO Box 1333, Edmonton, AB T5J 2N2
780-427-4088, -310-0000, service.alberta@gov.ab.ca

British Columbia
Consumer Protection B.C., #307, 3450 Uptown Blvd., PO Box 9244, Victoria, BC V8W 0B9
Fax: 250-920-7181, 888-564-9963, info@consumerprotectionbc.ca

Manitoba
Manitoba Sport, Culture & Heritage, Legislative Bldg., #118, 450 Broadway, Winnipeg, MB R3C 0V8
Seniors & Healthy Aging Secretariat, #1610, 155 Carlton St., Winnipeg, MB R3C 3H8
204-945-6565, Fax: 204-948-2514, 800-665-6565, seniors@gov.mb.ca

Nunavut
Nunavut Territory Department of Community & Government Services, W.G. Brown Bldg., 4th Fl., PO Box 1000 700, Iqaluit, NU X0A 0H0
867-975-5406, Fax: 867-975-5305, cgscomms@gov.nu.ca

Ontario
Ontario Ministry of Government & Consumer Services, Mowat Block, 900 Bay St., 6th Fl., Toronto, ON M7A 1L2
416-212-2665, Fax: 416-326-7445, 844-286-8404

Quebec
Office de la protection du consommateur, #450, 400, boul Jean-Lesage, Québec, QC G1K 8W4
418-643-1484, Fax: 418-528-0979, 888-672-2556

Yukon Territory
Corporate Policy & Consumer Affairs Division, Berska Bldg., 307 Black St., 2nd Fl., Whitehorse, YT Y1A 2N1

CONVENTION FACILITIES
See Also: Tourism & Tourist Information
British Columbia
British Columbia Pavilion Corporation, #200, 999 Canada Place, Vancouver, BC V6C 3C1
604-482-2200, Fax: 604-681-9017, info@bcpavco.com
Vancouver Convention Centre, 1055 Canada Pl., Vancouver, BC V6C 0C3
604-689-8232, Fax: 604-647-7232, 866-785-8232, info@vancouverconventioncentre.com

COPYRIGHT
See Also: Patents & Copyright
Canadian Intellectual Property Office, Place du Portage I, #C-229, 50, rue Victoria, Gatineau, QC K1A 0C9
819-997-1936, Fax: 819-953-2476, 866-997-1936, cipo.contact@ic.gc.ca

CORONERS
British Columbia
B.C. Coroners Service, Chief Coroner's Office, Metrotower II, #800, 4720 Kingsway, Burnaby, BC V5H 4N2
604-660-7745, Fax: 604-660-7766, CoronerRequest@gov.bc.ca

Manitoba
Office of the Chief Medical Examiner, #210, 1 Wesley Ave., Winnipeg, MB R3C 4C6
204-945-2088, 800-282-8069

Nova Scotia
Nova Scotia Medical Examiner Service, Dr. William D. Finn Centre for Forensic Medicine, 51 Garland Ave., Dartmouth, NS B3B 0J2
902-424-2722, Fax: 902-424-0607, 888-424-4336

Nunavut
Office of the Chief Coroner, PO Box 1000 590, Iqaluit, NU X0A 0H0
867-975-6562, Fax: 867-975-6367, 844-778-1022, coroner@gov.nu.ca

Ontario
Office of the Chief Coroner & Ontario Forensic Pathology Service, 25 Morton Shulman Ave., Toronto, ON M3M 0B1

Quebec
Bureau du coroner, Édifice le Delta 2, #390, 2875, boul Laurier, Québec, QC G1V 5B1
Fax: 418-643-6174, 888-267-6637, clientele.coroner@msp.gouv.qc.ca

Saskatchewan
Saskatchewan Coroners Service, #1050, 2010 - 12th Ave., Regina, SK S4P 0M3
306-787-5541, Fax: 306-787-5503, 866-592-7845, coroner@gov.sk.ca

CORRECTIONAL SERVICES
Correctional Service Canada, 340 Laurier Ave. West, Ottawa, ON K1A 0P9
613-992-5891, Fax: 613-943-1630
Office of the Correctional Investigator, PO Box 3421 D, Ottawa, ON K1P 6L4
Fax: 613-990-9091, 877-885-8848, org@oci-bec.gc.ca

British Columbia
Corrections Branch, PO Box 9278 Prov Govt, Victoria, BC V8W 9J7
250-387-6366, 888-952-7968

Manitoba
Community Safety Division, Manitoba Corrections Head Office, #810, 405 Broadway, Winnipeg, MB R3C 3L6
204-945-7804

Nunavut
Baffin Correctional Centre, PO Box 1000, Iqaluit, NU X0A 0H0
867-979-8100, Fax: 867-979-4646

Ontario
Correctional Services, George Drew Bldg, 25 Grosvenor St., 17th Fl., Toronto, ON M7A 1Y6

Saskatchewan
Saskatchewan Corrections, Policing & Public Safety, Legislative Bldg., #345, 2405 Legislative Dr., Regina, SK S4S 0B3

CRIMES COMPENSATION
Alberta
Criminal Injuries Review Board, #1502, 10025 - 102A Ave., Edmonton, AB T5J 2Z2
780-427-7330, Fax: 780-427-7347

Manitoba
Compensation for Victims of Crime, #1410, 405 Broadway, Winnipeg, MB R3C 3L6
204-945-0899, Fax: 204-948-3071, 800-262-9344

Northwest Territories
Victims Assistance Committee, c/o Community Justice Division, PO Box 1320, Yellowknife, NT X1A 2L9
867-920-6911, Fax: 867-873-0199

Ontario
Office for Victims of Crime, 700 Bay St., 3rd Fl., Toronto, ON M5G 1Z6
416-326-1682, Fax: 416-326-4497, 887-435-7661, ovc@ontario.ca

CROP MANAGEMENT
Aquatic & Crop Resource Development Industry Partnership Facility, 550 University Ave., Charlottetown, PE C1A 4P3

CULTURE & HERITAGE
See Also: Arts & Culture
Canadian Heritage, 15, rue Eddy, Gatineau, QC K1A 0M5
819-997-0055, 866-811-0055,
PCH.info-info.PCH@canada.ca
Crown-Indigenous Relations & Northern Affairs, Public Enquiries
Contact Centre, 10, rue Wellington, Gatineau, QC K1A 0H4
Fax: 866-817-3977, 800-567-9604,
aadnc.infopubs.aandc@canada.ca
Historic Sites & Monuments Board of Canada, 30 Victoria St.,
3rd Fl., Gatineau, QC J8X 0B3
Fax: 819-420-9260, 855-283-8730, hsmbc-clmhc@pc.gc.ca

Alberta
Alberta Culture & Status of Women, Communications Branch,
Standard Life Centre, 10405 Jasper Ave., 7th Fl., Edmonton,
AB T5J 4R7
780-427-6530, Fax: 780-427-1496, 800-232-7215,
culture.communications@gov.ab.ca

British Columbia
British Columbia Ministry of Tourism, Arts, Culture & Sport, PO
Box 9082 Prov Govt, Victoria, BC V8W 9E2

Manitoba
Manitoba Heritage Council, c/o Historic Resources Branch, 213
Notre Dame Ave., Main Fl., Winnipeg, MB R3B 1N3
204-945-2118, Fax: 204-948-2384, hrb@gov.mb.ca
Manitoba Sport, Culture & Heritage, Legislative Bldg., #118, 450
Broadway, Winnipeg, MB R3C 0V8

New Brunswick
New Brunswick Department of Tourism, Heritage & Culture,
Marysville Place, 4th Fl., PO Box 6000, Fredericton, NB E3B
5H1
506-453-3115, Fax: 506-444-5760, thctpcinfo@gnb.ca

Newfoundland & Labrador
Newfoundland & Labrador Department of Tourism, Culture, Arts
& Recreation, PO Box 8700, St. John's, NL A1B 4J6
709-729-7000, tcar@gov.nl.ca

Northwest Territories
Aboriginal Languages Revitalization Board, PO Box 1320,
Yellowknife, NT X1A 2L9
Northwest Territories Department of Education, Culture &
Employment, PO Box 1320, Yellowknife, NT X1A 2L9
ecepublicaffairs@gov.nt.ca
Northwest Territories Department of the Executive & Indigenous
Affairs, PO Box 1320, Yellowknife, NT X1A 2L9
Official Languages Board, PO Box 1320, Yellowknife, NT X1A
2L9

Nova Scotia
Office of African Nova Scotian Affairs, 1741 Brunswick St., 3rd
Fl., PO Box 2691 Central, Halifax, NS B3J 2R5
902-424-5555, Fax: 902-424-7189, 866-580-2672,
ANSA@novascotia.ca
Office of Gaelic Affairs, 1741 Brunswick St., 3rd Fl., PO Box 456
Central, Halifax, NS B3J 2R5
902-424-4298, Fax: 902-424-0171, 888-842-3542,
gaelicinfo@gov.ns.ca

Ontario
Ontario Ministry of Heritage, Sport, Tourism & Culture Industries,
438 University Ave., 6th Fl., Toronto, ON M5G 2K8
416-326-9326, Fax: 416-314-7854, 888-997-9015

Quebec
Commission de la capitale nationale du Québec, Edifice
Hector-Fabre, 525, boul René-Lévesque est, RC, Québec,
QC G1R 5S9
418-528-0773, Fax: 418-528-0833, 800-442-0773,
commission@capitale.gouv.qc.ca
Secrétariat à la Capitale-Nationale, 700, boul René-Lévesque
est, 31e étage, Québec, QC G1R 5H1
418-528-8549, Fax: 418-528-8558
Secrétariat à la politique linguistique, 225 Grande-Allée est, 4e
étage, bloc A, Québec, QC G1R 5G5
418-643-4248, Fax: 418-646-7832

Saskatchewan
Provincial Capital Commission, PO Box 7111, Regina, SK S4P
3S7
306-522-3661, Fax: 306-565-2742
Saskatchewan Parks, Culture & Sport, 3211 Albert St., 1st Fl.,
Regina, SK S4S 5W6
306-787-5729, Fax: 306-798-0033, pcs.info@gov.sk.ca

CURRENCY
Bank of Canada, 234 Wellington St., Ottawa, ON K1A 0G9
613-782-8111, Fax: 613-782-7713, 800-303-1282,
info@bankofcanada.ca
Royal Canadian Mint, 320 Sussex Dr., Ottawa, ON K1A 0G8
613-954-2626, Fax: 613-998-4130, 800-267-1871

CUSTOMS
Canada Border Services Agency, Headquarters, 191 Laurier
Ave. West, Ottawa, ON K1A 0L8
800-461-9999, contact@cbsa.gc.ca

DAIRY INDUSTRY
Agriculture & Agri-Food Canada, 1341 Baseline Rd., Ottawa, ON
K1A 0C5
613-773-1000, Fax: 613-773-1081, 855-773-0241,
info@agr.gc.ca
Canadian Dairy Commission, Central Experimental Farm, NCC
Driveway, Bldg. 55, 960 Carling Ave., Ottawa, ON K1A 0Z2
613-792-2000, Fax: 613-792-2009, cdc-ccl@cdc-ccl.gc.ca

Alberta
Alberta Agriculture & Forestry, JG O'Donoghue Bldg., #100A,
7000 - 113th St., Edmonton, AB T6H 5T6
403-742-7901

British Columbia
British Columbia Milk Marketing Board, #200, 32160 South
Fraser Way, Abbotsford, BC V2T 1W5
604-556-3444, Fax: 604-556-7717, info@milk-bc.com
British Columbia Ministry of Agriculture, Food & Fisheries, PO
Box 9043 Prov Govt, Victoria, BC V8W 9E2
888-221-7141, agriservicebc@gov.bc.ca

Manitoba
Manitoba Agriculture, Legislative Bldg., #165, 450 Broadway,
Winnipeg, MB R3C 0V8
204-945-3722, Fax: 204-945-3470, minagr@leg.gov.mb.ca

New Brunswick
New Brunswick Department of Agriculture, Aquaculture &
Fisheries, Agricultural Research Station (Experimental Farm),
PO Box 6000, Fredericton, NB E3B 5H1
506-453-3826, Fax: 506-453-7170, DAAF-MAAP@gnb.ca

Nova Scotia
Nova Scotia Department of Agriculture, 1800 Argyle St., 6th Fl.,
Halifax, NS B3J 3N8
902-424-4560, Fax: 902-424-4671, 800-279-0825

Ontario
Ontario Ministry of Agriculture, Food & Rural Affairs, Ontario
Government Bldg., 1 Stone Rd. West, Guelph, ON N1G 4Y2
519-826-3100, Fax: 519-826-4335, 888-466-2372,
about.omafra@ontario.ca

Prince Edward Island
Prince Edward Island Department of Agriculture & Land, Jones
Bldg., 11 Kent St., 5th Fl., PO Box 2000, Charlottetown, PE
C1A 7N8
902-368-4880, Fax: 902-368-4857

Quebec
Ministère de l'Agriculture, des Pêcheries et de l'Alimentation du
Québec, 200, ch Sainte-Foy, Québec, QC G1R 4X6
418-380-2110, 888-222-6272

Saskatchewan
Saskatchewan Agriculture, Walter Scott Bldg., 3085 Albert St.,
Regina, SK S4S 0B1
866-457-2377

DANGEROUS GOODS & HAZARDOUS MATERIALS
See Also: Occupational Safety; Waste Management
British Columbia
British Columbia Ministry of Transportation & Infrastructure, PO
Box 9850 Prov Govt, Victoria, BC V8W 9T5
250-387-3198, Fax: 250-356-7706,
tran.webmaster@gov.bc.ca

Nova Scotia
Nova Scotia Department of Transportation & Active Transit, PO
Box 186, Halifax, NS B3J 2N2
902-424-2297, Fax: 902-424-0532, tpwpaff@novascotia.ca

Ontario
Ontario Ministry of Transportation, 777 Bay St., 5th Fl., Toronto,
ON M7A 1Z8
416-235-4686, Fax: 416-327-9185, 800-268-4686

Prince Edward Island
Prince Edward Island Department of Transportation &
Infrastructure, Jones Bldg., 11 Kent St., 3rd Fl., PO Box 2000,
Charlottetown, PE C1A 7N8
902-368-5100, Fax: 902-368-5395, DeptTIE@gov.pe.ca

Quebec
Ministère de l'Environnement et de la Lutte contre les
changements climatiques, Édifice Marie-Guyart, 675, boul
René-Lévesque est, 30e étage, Québec, QC G1R 5V7
418-521-3830, Fax: 418-646-5974, 800-561-1616,
relations.medias@mddelcc.gouv.qc.ca

Saskatchewan
Saskatchewan Highways, Victoria Tower, 1855 Victoria Ave.,
Regina, SK S4P 3T2
306-933-5186, MHI.CustomerService@gov.sk.ca

Yukon Territory
Yukon Highways & Public Works, PO Box 2703, Whitehorse, YT
Y1A 2C6
867-667-3732, Fax: 867-393-6218, hpw-info@yukon.ca

DEBT MANAGEMENT
Finance Canada, 90 Elgin St., Ottawa, ON K1A 0G5
613-369-3710, Fax: 613-369-4065,
fin.financepublic-financepublique.fin@canada.ca
Manitoba
Treasury Division, #350, 363 Broadway, Winnipeg, MB R3C 3N9
204-945-3702, Fax: 204-948-2233
Prince Edward Island
Debt, Investment & Pension Management, Shaw Bldg. South, 95
Rochford St., 3rd Fl., PO Box 2000, Charlottetown, PE C1A
7N8
Saskatchewan
Provincial Mediation Board, #304, 1855 Victoria Ave., Regina,
SK S4P 3T2
306-787-5408, 877-787-5408, pmb@gov.sk.ca
Saskatchewan Finance, 2350 Albert St., Regina, SK S4P 4A6
ficommunications@gov.sk.ca

DEFENCE
See Also: Emergency Response; Public Safety
Canadian Joint Operations Command, National Defence
Headquarters, MGen George R. Pearkes Bldg., 101 Colonel
By Dr., Ottawa, ON K1A 0K2
866-377-0811
Canadian Special Operations Forces Command, CANSOFCOM
Public Affairs, 101 Colonel By Dr., Ottawa, ON K1A 0K2
866-377-0811
Defence Construction Canada, Constitution Square, 350 Albert
St., 19th Fl., Ottawa, ON K1A 0K3
613-998-9548, Fax: 613-998-1061, 800-514-3555,
info@dcc-cdc.gc.ca
Defence Research & Development Canada, 101 Colonel By Dr.,
Ottawa, ON K1A 0K2
613-995-2534, 888-995-2534, information@forces.gc.ca
Department of National Defence & the Canadian Armed Forces,
National Defence HQ, Major-General George R. Pearkes
Bldg., 101 Colonel By Dr., Ottawa, ON K1A 0K2
613-995-2534, Fax: 613-992-4739, 888-995-2534,
information@forces.gc.ca
Military Grievances External Review Committee, 60 Queen St.,
10th Fl., Ottawa, ON K1P 5Y7
613-996-8529, Fax: 613-996-6491, 877-276-4193,
mgerc-ceegm@mgerc-ceegm.gc.ca
Military Police Complaints Commission, 270 Albert St., 10th Fl.,
Ottawa, ON K1P 5G8
613-947-5625, Fax: 613-947-5713, 800-632-0566,
commission@mpcc-cppm.gc.ca
Royal Canadian Air Force, MGen George R. Pearkes Building,
101 Colonel By Dr., Ottawa, ON K1A 0K2
Royal Canadian Navy, National Defence HQ, MGen George R.
Pearkes Building, 101 Colonel By Dr., Ottawa, ON K1A 0K2
information@forces.gc.ca

DISABLED PERSONS SERVICES
Canadian Human Rights Commission, 344 Slater St., 8th Fl.,
Ottawa, ON K1A 1E1
Fax: 613-996-9661, 888-214-1090,
info.com@chrc-ccdp.gc.ca
Alberta
Alberta Community & Social Services, Office of the Minister,
Legislature Bldg., #224, 10800 - 97th Ave., Edmonton, AB
T5K 2B6
780-644-9992, 877-644-9992
Alberta Health, PO Box 1360 Main, Edmonton, AB T5J 2N3
780-427-7164
Appeals Secretariat, Agronomy Centre, #201, 6903 - 116 St.,
Edmonton, AB T6H 5Z2
780-427-2709, Fax: 780-422-1088, -310-0000,
CSS.Appeals@gov.ab.ca
Premier's Council on the Status of Persons with Disabilities,
HSBC Building, #1110, 10055 - 106 St., Edmonton, AB T5J
2Y2
Fax: 780-415-0097, 800-272-8841, pcspd@gov.ab.ca
Manitoba
Manitoba Developmental Centre, 840 - 3rd St. NE, Portage la
Prairie, MB R1N 3C6
204-856-4200, csd@gov.mb.ca
New Brunswick
Premier's Council on the Status of Disabled Persons, #140,
Place 2000, 1st Fl., PO Box 6000, Fredericton, NB E3B 5H1
506-444-3000, Fax: 506-444-3001, 800-442-4412,
pcd-cpmph@gnb.ca
Newfoundland & Labrador
Newfoundland & Labrador Department of Children, Seniors &
Social Development, PO Box 8700, St. John's, NL A1B 4J6
709-729-0760, Fax: 709-729-0870, CSSDInfo@gov.nl.ca
Provincial Advisory Council for the Inclusion of Persons with
Disabilities, c/o Department of Seniors, Wellness & Social
Development, PO Box 8700, St. John's, NL A1B 4J6

Nova Scotia
Nova Scotia Disabled Persons Commission, Nelson Place, 5675 Spring Garden Rd., 7th Fl., PO Box 222 CRO, Halifax, NS B3J 2M4
902-424-8280, Fax: 902-424-0592, 800-565-8280, disability@gov.ns.ca

Nunavut
Nunavut Territory Department of Culture & Heritage, PO Box 1000 800, Iqaluit, NU X0A 0H0
867-975-5500, Fax: 867-975-5504, 866-934-2035

Ontario
Health System Quality & Funding Division, Hepburn Block, 80 Grosvenor St., 5th Fl., Toronto, ON M7A 1R3

Quebec
Office des personnes handicapées du Québec, 309, rue Brock, Drummondville, QC J2B 1C5
Fax: 819-475-8753, 800-567-1465, info@ophq.gouv.qc.ca

DISCRIMINATION & EMPLOYMENT EQUITY
Canadian Human Rights Commission, 344 Slater St., 8th Fl., Ottawa, ON K1A 1E1
Fax: 613-996-9661, 888-214-1090, info.com@chrc-ccdp.gc.ca
Canadian Human Rights Tribunal, 160 Elgin St., 11th Fl., Ottawa, ON K1A 1J4
613-995-1707, Fax: 613-995-3484, registrar@chrt-tcdp.gc.ca
Office of the Public Sector Integrity Commissioner of Canada, 60 Queen St., 7th Fl., Ottawa, ON K1P 5Y7
613-941-6400, Fax: 613-941-6535, 866-941-6400

Alberta
Labour Relations Board, Labour Building, #501, 10808 - 99 Ave., Edmonton, AB T5K 0G5
780-427-8547, Fax: 780-422-0970, 800-463-2572, alrbinfo@gov.ab.ca

British Columbia
British Columbia Human Rights Tribunal, #1170, 605 Robson St., Vancouver, BC V6B 5J3
604-775-2000, Fax: 604-775-2020, 888-440-8844, BCHumanRightsTribunal@gov.bc.ca

Manitoba
Manitoba Human Rights Commission, #700, 175 Hargrave St., Winnipeg, MB R3C 3R8
204-945-3007, Fax: 204-945-1292, 888-884-8681, hrc@gov.mb.ca

New Brunswick
New Brunswick Human Rights Commission, Barry House, 751 Brunswick St., PO Box 6000, Fredericton, NB E3B 5H1
506-453-2301, Fax: 506-453-2653, 888-471-2233, hrc.cdp@gnb.ca

Newfoundland & Labrador
Newfoundland & Labrador Human Rights Commission, The Beothuk Bldg., 21 Crosbie Pl., PO Box 8700, St. John's, NL A1B 4J6
709-729-2709, Fax: 709-729-0790, 800-563-5808, humanrights@gov.nl.ca

Nova Scotia
Nova Scotia Human Rights Commission, Park Lane Terrace, #305, 5657 Spring Garden Rd., PO Box 2221, Halifax, NS B3J 3C4
902-424-4111, Fax: 902-424-0596, 877-269-7699, hrcinquiries@novascotia.ca

Ontario
Ontario Human Rights Commission, 180 Dundas St. West, 9th Fl., Toronto, ON M7A 2G5
416-326-9511, Fax: 416-314-4494, 800-387-9080, info@ohrc.on.ca

Prince Edward Island
Prince Edward Island Human Rights Commission, 53 Water St., PO Box 2000, Charlottetown, PE C1A 7N8
902-368-4180, Fax: 902-368-4236, 800-237-5031, contact@peihumanrights.ca

Saskatchewan
Saskatchewan Human Rights Commission, PO Box 6011, Saskatoon, SK S7K 4E4
306-933-5952, Fax: 306-933-7863, 800-667-9249, shrc@gov.sk.ca

Yukon Territory
Yukon Human Rights Commission, #215, 305 Main St., Whitehorse, YT Y1A 2B4
867-667-6226, Fax: 867-667-2662, 800-661-0535, info@yukonhumanrights.ca

DIVORCE
Justice Canada, 284 Wellington St., Ottawa, ON K1A 0H8
613-957-4222, Fax: 613-954-0811, webadmin@justice.gc.ca

DRIVERS' LICENCES
Alberta
Alberta Transportation, Communications Branch, Twin Atria Bldg., 4999 - 98th Ave., 2nd Fl., Edmonton, AB T6B 2X3
780-427-7674, Fax: 780-466-3166, Trans.Contact.Us.m@gov.ab.ca

British Columbia
British Columbia Ministry of Transportation & Infrastructure, PO Box 9850 Prov Govt, Victoria, BC V8W 9T5
250-387-3198, Fax: 250-356-7706, tran.webmaster@gov.bc.ca

Manitoba
Manitoba Infrastructure, Legislative Bldg., #203, 450 Broadway, Winnipeg, MB R3C 0V8

Northwest Territories
Northwest Territories Department of Infrastructure, Stuart M. Hodgson Bldg., 5009 - 49th St., 3rd Fl., PO Box 1320, Yellowknife, NT X1A 2L9
INF_Communications@gov.nt.ca

Nova Scotia
Service Nova Scotia & Internal Services, PO Box 2734, Halifax, NS B3J 3K5
902-424-5200, Fax: 902-424-0720, 800-670-4357, askus@novascotia.ca

Ontario
Ontario Ministry of Transportation, 777 Bay St., 5th Fl., Toronto, ON M7A 1Z8
416-235-4686, Fax: 416-327-9185, 800-268-4686

Prince Edward Island
Prince Edward Island Department of Transportation & Infrastructure, Jones Bldg., 11 Kent St., 3rd Fl., PO Box 2000, Charlottetown, PE C1A 7N8
902-368-5100, Fax: 902-368-5395, DeptTIE@gov.pe.ca

Quebec
Société de l'assurance automobile du Québec, 333, boul Jean-Lesage, CP 19600 Terminus, Québec, QC G1K 8J6
418-643-7620, Fax: 418-644-0339, 800-361-7620

Saskatchewan
Saskatchewan Government Insurance, 2260 - 11th Ave., Regina, SK S4P 0J9
306-751-1200, Fax: 306-787-7477, 844-855-2744, sgiinquiries@sgi.sk.ca

DRUGS & ALCOHOL
See Also: Liquor Control
Canadian Centre on Substance Abuse, #500, 75 Albert St., Ottawa, ON K1P 5E7
613-235-4048, Fax: 613-235-8101, info@ccsa.ca

Alberta
Alberta Health Services, Corporate Office, North Tower, Seventh Street Plaza, 10030 - 107th St. NW, 14th Fl., Edmonton, AB T5J 3E4
780-342-2000, Fax: 780-342-2060, 888-342-2471, ahs.corp@albertahealthservices.ca

British Columbia
British Columbia Ministry of Health, PO Box 9639 Prov Govt, Victoria, BC V8W 9P1
800-663-7867, HLTH.Health@gov.bc.ca
British Columbia Ministry of Mental Health & Addictions, PO Box 9644 Prov Govt, Victoria, BC V8W 9P1
604-660-2421, 800-663-7867, HLTH.Health@gov.bc.ca

Manitoba
Addictions Foundation of Manitoba, 1031 Portage Ave., Winnipeg, MB R3G 0R8
204-981-6691, Fax: 204-944-7082, 866-638-2561, execoff@afm.mb.ca

Quebec
Ministère de la Santé et des Services sociaux, Direction des communications, 1075, ch Sainte-Foy, 15e étage, Québec, QC G1S 2M1
418-644-4545, 877-644-4545
Modernisation des centres hospitaliers universitaires de Montréal, CHUM, CUSM, CHU Sainte-Justine, #10.049, 2021, rue Union, Montréal, QC H3A 2S9
514-864-9883, Fax: 514-873-7362, info.construction3chu@msss.gouv.qc.ca

ECONOMIC DEVELOPMENT
See Also: Business Development
Canada Economic Development for Québec Regions, #500, 800, boul René-Lévesque ouest, Montréal, QC H3B 1X9
514-283-6412, Fax: 514-283-3302, 866-385-6412
Canadian Northern Economic Development Agency, Ottawa, ON K1A 0H4
855-897-2667, CanNor.InfoNorth.InfoNord.CanNor@canada.ca
Federal Economic Development Agency for Southern Ontario, #101, 139 Northfield Dr. West, Waterloo, ON N2L 5A6
Fax: 519-725-4976, 866-593-5505

FedNor (Federal Economic Development Initiative in Northern Ontario), 19 Lisgar St., Sudbury, ON P3E 3L4
Fax: 705-671-0717, 877-333-6673

Alberta
Alberta Innovates, 250 Karl Clark Rd., Edmonton, AB T6N 1E4
877-423-5727, info@albertainnovates.ca
Alberta Jobs, Economy & Innovation, Commerce Place, 10155 - 102nd St., 12th Fl., Edmonton, AB T5J 4G8
InnoTech Alberta, 250 Karl Clark Rd., Edmonton, AB T6N 1H2
780-450-5111, Fax: 780-450-5333, info@innotechalberta.ca

British Columbia
Native Economic Development Advisory Board, PO Box 9100 Prov Govt, Victoria, BC V8W 9B1
250-387-2536

Manitoba
Manitoba Economic Development & Jobs, Economic Development Office, #1010, 259 Portage Ave., Winnipeg, MB R3B 3P4
204-945-1055, Fax: 204-948-2964, 866-570-7577, edo@gov.mb.ca

New Brunswick
Economic & Social Inclusion Corporation, Kings Place, #423, 440 King St., 4th Fl., PO Box 6000, Fredericton, NB E3B 5H1
506-444-2977, Fax: 506-444-2978, 888-295-4545, esic-sies@gnb.ca
New Brunswick Jobs Board, Chancery Place, PO Box 6000, Fredericton, NB E3B 5H1
Opportunities New Brunswick, Place 2000, 250 King St., PO Box 6000, Fredericton, NB E3B 5H1
506-453-5471, Fax: 506-444-5277, 855-746-4662, info@onbcanada.ca

Nunavut
Nunavut Development Corporation, PO Box 249, Rankin Inlet, NU X0C 0G0
867-645-3170, Fax: 867-645-3755, 866-645-3170, opportunities@ndcorp.nu.ca
Nunavut Territory Department of Economic Development & Transportation, Inuksugait Plaza, Bldg. 1104A, PO Box 1000 1500, Iqaluit, NU X0A 0H0
867-975-7800, Fax: 867-975-7870, 888-975-5999, edt@gov.nu.ca

Ontario
Ontario Ministry of Agriculture, Food & Rural Affairs, Ontario Government Bldg., 1 Stone Rd. West, Guelph, ON N1G 4Y2
519-826-3100, Fax: 519-826-4335, 888-466-2372, about.omafra@ontario.ca
Ontario Ministry of Economic Development, Job Creation & Trade, 56 Wellesley St. West, 7th Fl., Toronto, ON M7A 2E7
416-325-6666, 800-268-7095
Rural Economic Development Advisory Panel, 1 Stone Rd. West, 4th Fl., Guelph, ON N1G 4Y2
Fax: 519-826-4336, 888-588-4111, red.omafra@ontario.ca

Prince Edward Island
Innovation PEI, 94 Euston St., PO Box 910, Charlottetown, PE C1A 7L9
902-368-6300, Fax: 902-368-6301, 800-563-3734, innovation@gov.pe.ca

Quebec
Investissement Québec, #60, 1195, av Lavigerie, Québec, QC G1V 4N3
418-643-5172, Fax: 418-528-2063, 844-474-6367
Ministère de l'Économie et de l'Innovation, 710, Place D'Youville, 3e étage, Québec, QC G1R 4Y4
418-691-5950, Fax: 418-644-0118, 866-680-1884
Secrétariat à la Capitale-Nationale, 700, boul René-Lévesque est, 31e étage, Québec, QC G1R 5H1
418-528-8549, Fax: 418-528-8558,

Saskatchewan
Municipal Financing Corporation of Saskatchewan, 2350 Albert St., 6th Fl., Regina, SK S4P 4A6
306-787-8150, Fax: 306-787-8493, mfc@gov.sk.ca
Saskatchewan Trade & Export Development, #1000, 2103 - 11th Ave., Regina, SK S4P 3Z8

Yukon Territory
Yukon Economic Development, 303 Alexander St., Whitehorse, YT Y1A 2L5
800-661-0408, ecdev@yukon.ca

EDUCATION
Canada School of Public Service, 373 Sussex Dr., Ottawa, ON K1N 6Z2
819-953-5400, Fax: 866-944-0454, 866-703-9598, info@csps-efpc.gc.ca
Canadian Council of Directors of Apprenticeship, 140 Promenade du Portage, 6th Fl., Phase IV, Gatineau, QC K1A 0J9
Fax: 819-994-0202, 877-599-6933, redseal-sceaurouge@hrsdc-rhdcc.gc.ca

Alberta

Alberta Advanced Education, Legislature Bldg., #403, 10800 - 97th Ave., Edmonton, AB T5K 2B6
780-422-5400

Alberta Apprenticeship & Industry Training Board, Centre for Applied Technologies Bldg., #430, 11763 - 106 St., Edmonton, AB T5G 2R1
403-476-9757, Fax: 780-422-3734, -310-0000

Alberta Council on Admissions & Transfer, Commerce Place, 10155 - 102 St., 8th Fl., Edmonton, AB T5J 4L5
780-422-9021, Fax: 780-422-3688, -310-0000, acat@gov.ab.ca

Alberta Education, Commerce Place, 10155 - 102nd St., 8th Fl., Edmonton, AB T5J 4L5
780-427-7219, Fax: 780-427-0591

Alberta Teachers' Retirement Fund, Barnett House, #600, 11010 - 142 St. NW, Edmonton, AB T5N 2R1
780-451-4166, Fax: 780-452-3547, 800-661-9582, info@atrf.com

Apprenticeship & Student Aid Division, Commerce Place, 10155 - 102nd St., 6th Fl., Edmonton, AB T5J 4L5

Campus Alberta Quality Council, Commerce Place, 10155 - 102 St., 8th Fl., Edmonton, AB T5J 4L5
780-427-8921, Fax: 780-641-9783, caqc@gov.ab.ca

British Columbia

Auditor Certification Board, PO Box 9431 Prov Govt, Victoria, BC V8W 9V3
250-356-8658, Fax: 250-356-9422, Ken.Worthy@gov.bc.ca

British Columbia Council on Admissions & Transfer, #709, 555 Seymour St., Vancouver, BC V6B 3H6
604-412-7700, Fax: 604-683-0576, info@bccat.ca

British Columbia Ministry of Advanced Education & Skills Training, PO Box 9080 Prov Govt, Victoria, BC V8W 9E2
250-356-5170, AEST.GeneralInquiries@gov.bc.ca

British Columbia Ministry of Education, PO Box 9179 Prov Govt, Victoria, BC V8W 9E2
800-663-7867, servicebc@gov.bc.ca

Degree Quality Assessment Board, Degree Quality Assessment Board Secretariat, 835 Humboldt St., 3rd Fl., PO Box 9177 Prov Govt, Victoria, BC V8W 9H8
250-356-9734, DQABsecretariat@gov.bc.ca

Education Advisory Council, c/o Mike Roberts, Superintendent, Liaison, #1550, 555 West Hastings, PO Box 121110, Vancouver, BC V6B 4N6
604-660-1483, Fax: 604-660-2124

Justice Education Society, #260, 800 Hornby St., Vancouver, BC V6Z 2C3
604-660-9870, Fax: 604-775-3476, info@justiceeducation.ca

Premier's Technology Council, #1600, 800 Robson St., Vancouver, BC V6Z 3E7
604-827-4629, premiers.technologycouncil@gov.bc.ca

Private Career Training Institutions Agency, #203, 1155 West Pender St., Vancouver, BC V6E 2P4
604-569-0033, Fax: 778-945-0606, 800-661-7441, info@pctia.bc.ca

Teacher Regulation Branch, #400, 2025 West Broadway, Vancouver, BC V6J 1Z6
604-660-6060, Fax: 604-775-4859, 800-555-3684

Manitoba

Division du Bureau de l'éducation française, #509, 1181 Portage Ave., Winnipeg, MB R3C 0T3
204-945-6916, Fax: 204-948-2997

Manitoba Education, Legislative Bldg., #162, 450 Broadway, Winnipeg, MB R3C 0V8
204-945-3720, Fax: 204-945-1291

Manitoba Education, Research & Learning Information Networks, University of Manitoba, #100, 135 Innovation Dr., Winnipeg, MB R3T 6A8
204-474-7800, Fax: 204-474-7830, 800-430-6404

School Programs Division, #307, 1181 Portage Ave., Winnipeg, MB R3G 0T3
204-945-7934, Fax: 204-945-8303

New Brunswick

Atlantic Education International Inc., #500, 1133 Regent St., Fredericton, NB E3B 3Z2
506-453-8300, Fax: 506-453-5894

New Brunswick Department of Education & Early Childhood Development, Place 2000, PO Box 6000, Fredericton, NB E3B 5H1
506-453-3678, Fax: 506-453-4810, edcommunication@gnb.ca

New Brunswick Department of Post-Secondary Education, Training & Labour, Chestnut Complex, PO Box 6000, Fredericton, NB E3B 5H1
506-453-2597, Fax: 506-453-3618, dpetlinfo@gnb.ca

Newfoundland & Labrador

Newfoundland & Labrador Department of Education, West Block, Confederation Bldg., 100 Prince Philip Dr., 3rd Fl., PO Box 8700, St. John's, NL A1B 4J6
709-729-5097, Fax: 709-729-1400, education@gov.nl.ca

Newfoundland & Labrador Department of Immigration, Population Growth & Skills, West Block, Confederation Bldg., 3rd Fl., PO Box 8700, St. John's, NL A1B 4J6
709-729-1795, isl@gov.nl.ca

Northwest Territories

Aurora Research Institute, 191 MacKenzie Rd., PO Box 1450, Inuvik, NT X0E 0T0
867-777-3298, Fax: 867-777-4264

Northwest Territories Department of Education, Culture & Employment, PO Box 1320, Yellowknife, NT X1A 2L9
ecepublicaffairs@gov.nt.ca

Nova Scotia

Atlantic Provinces Special Education Authority, 5940 South St., Halifax, NS B3H 1S6
902-424-8500, Fax: 902-423-8700

Council of Atlantic Ministers of Education & Training, PO Box 2044, Halifax, NS B3J 2Z1
902-424-5352, Fax: 902-424-8976, camet-camef@cap-cpma.ca

Nova Scotia Apprenticeship Agency, Thompson Bldg., 1256 Barrington St., 3rd Fl., PO Box 578, Halifax, NS B3J 2S9
902-424-5651, Fax: 902-424-0717, 800-494-5651, apprenticeship@novascotia.ca

Nova Scotia Apprenticeship Board, 2021 Brunswick St., PO Box 578, Halifax, NS B3J 2S9

Nova Scotia Department of Advanced Education, 1505 Barrington St., PO Box 697, Halifax, NS B3J 2T8
902-424-5301, Fax: 902-424-2203, lae-correspondence@novascotia.ca

Nova Scotia Department of Education & Early Childhood Development, 2021 Brunswick St., PO Box 578, Halifax, NS B3J 2S9
902-424-5168, Fax: 902-424-0511, 888-825-7770

Nunavut

Nunavut Territory Department of Education, Bldg. 1107, 2nd Fl., PO Box 1000 900, Iqaluit, NU X0A 0H0
867-975-5600, Fax: 867-975-5605, info.edu@gov.nu.ca

Ontario

Academic & Experience Requirements Committee of the Association of Ontario Land Surveyors, 1043 McNicoll Ave., Toronto, ON M1W 3W6
416-491-9020, Fax: 416-491-2576

Board of Negotiation, Ontario Government Bldg NW, 1 Stone Rd. West, 2nd Fl., Guelph, ON N1G 4Y2

Capital & Business Support Division, Mowat Block, 900 Bay St., 20th fl., Toronto, ON M7A 1L2
416-325-6127, Fax: 416-325-9560

College of Trades Appointments Council, Mowat Block, 900 Bay St., 23rd Fl., Toronto, ON M7A 1L2
416-326-5629, Fax: 416-326-5653, appointments.council@ontario.ca

Higher Education Quality Council of Ontario, #2402, 1 Yonge St., Toronto, ON M5E 1E5
416-212-3893, Fax: 416-212-3899, info@heqco.ca

Ontario French-Language Education Communications Authority, #600, 21 College St., 6th Fl., Toronto, ON MRY 2M5
416-968-3536, Fax: 416-968-8203

Ontario Graduate Scholarship Program Selection Board, 189 Red River Rd., 4th Fl., PO Box 4500, Thunder Bay, ON P7B 6G9
807-343-7257, Fax: 807-343-7278, 800-465-3957

Ontario Ministry of Colleges & Universities, 438 University Ave., 5th Fl., Toronto, ON M7A 2A5
416-325-2929, Fax: 416-325-6348, 800-387-5514, information.met@ontario.ca

Ontario Ministry of Education, 315 Front Street, 14th Fl., Toronto, ON M7A 0B8
416-325-2929, 800-387-5514

Ontario Student Assistance Program Financial Eligibility Advisory Committee, Mowat Block, 900 Bay St., 9th Fl., Toronto, ON M7A 1L2
416-314-0714, Fax: 416-325-3096

Post-secondary Education Division, Mowat Block, 900 Bay St., 7th Fl., Toronto, ON M7A 1L2
416-325-2199, Fax: 416-326-3256

Post-secondary Education Quality Assessment Board, Mowat Block, 900 Bay St., 23rd Fl., Toronto, ON M7A 1L2
416-212-1230, Fax: 416-212-6620, peqab@ontario.ca

System Planning, Research & Innovation Division, Mowat Block, 900 Bay St., 10th fl., Toronto, ON M7A 1L2

Training Completion Assurance Fund Advisory Board, 77 Wellesley St. West, PO Box 977, Toronto, ON M7A 1N3
416-314-0500, Fax: 416-314-0499, 866-330-3395, tcaf-pcc@ontario.ca

Prince Edward Island

Prince Edward Island Department of Education & Lifelong Learning, Holman Centre, #101, 250 Water St., Summerside, PE C1N 1B6
902-438-4130, Fax: 902-438-4062, DeptELL@gov.pe.ca

Prince Edward Island School Athletic Association, #101, 250 Water St., Summerside, PE C1N 1B6
902-438-4846, info@peisaa.pe.ca

Quebec

Comité consultatif sur l'accessibilité financière aux études, 1035, rue de la Chevrotière, 20e étage, Québec, QC G1R 5A5
418-644-3468

Commission consultative de l'enseignement privé, 1035, rue de la Chevrotière, 26e étage, Québec, QC G1R 5A5
418-646-1249

Commission d'évaluation de l'enseignement collégial, #400, 888, rue St-Jean, 4e étage, Québec, QC G1R 5H6
418-643-9938, Fax: 418-643-9019, info@ceec.gouv.qc.ca

Commission de l'éducation en langue anglaise, 600, rue Fullum, 11e étage, Montréal, QC H2K 4L1
514-873-5656, Fax: 514-864-4181

Conseil supérieur de l'éducation, #180, 1175, av Lavigerie, Québec, QC G1V 5B2
418-643-3850, Fax: 418-644-2530, conseil@cse.gouv.qc.ca

Ministère de l'Éducation et de l'Enseignement supérieur, 1035, rue de la Chevrotière, 28e étage, Québec, QC G1R 5A5
418-643-7095, Fax: 418-646-6561, 866-747-6626

Saskatchewan

Saskatchewan Advanced Education, #1120, 2010 - 12th Ave., Regina, SK S4P 0M3
aeeinquiry@gov.sk.ca

Saskatchewan Education, 2220 College Ave., Regina, SK S4P 4V9
learning.inquiry@gov.sk.ca

Saskatchewan Research Council, #125, 15 Innovation Blvd., Saskatoon, SK S7N 2X8
306-933-5400, Fax: 306-933-7446

Teachers' Superannuation Commission, #129, 3085 Albert St., Regina, SK S4S 0B1
306-787-6440, Fax: 306-787-1939, 877-364-8202, mail@stsc.gov.sk.ca

Yukon Territory

Yukon Education, 1000 Lewes Blvd., Whitehorse, YT Y1A 3H9
867-667-5141, Fax: 867-393-6254, edu-communications@yukon.ca

EDUCATION & TRAINING

Employment & Social Development Canada, 140, promenade du Portage, Gatineau, QC K1A 0J9

Alberta

Alberta Labour & Immigration, Legislature Bldg., #107, 10800 - 97th Ave., Edmonton, AB T5K 2B6
780-427-3731, 877-427-3731

Northern Alberta Development Council, Peace River Office, Provincial Building, #206, 9621 - 96 Ave., PO Box 900-14, Peace River, AB T8S 1T4
780-624-6274, Fax: 780-624-6184, -310-0000, nadc.council@gov.ab.ca

British Columbia

Private Career Training Institutions Agency, #203, 1155 West Pender St., Vancouver, BC V6E 2P4
604-569-0033, Fax: 778-945-0606, 800-661-7441, info@pctia.bc.ca

Teacher Regulation Branch, #400, 2025 West Broadway, Vancouver, BC V6J 1Z6
604-660-6060, Fax: 604-775-4859, 800-555-3684

Manitoba

Manitoba Advanced Education, Skills & Immigration, Legislative Bldg., #352, 450 Broadway, Winnipeg, MB R3C 0V8

New Brunswick

New Brunswick Department of Post-Secondary Education, Training & Labour, Chestnut Complex, PO Box 6000, Fredericton, NB E3B 5H1
506-453-2597, Fax: 506-453-3618, dpetlinfo@gnb.ca

Northwest Territories

Northwest Territories Department of Education, Culture & Employment, PO Box 1320, Yellowknife, NT X1A 2L9
ecepublicaffairs@gov.nt.ca

School of Community Government, #500, 5201 - 50th Ave., PO Box 1320, Yellowknife, NT X1A 3S9
867-767-9163, Fax: 867-873-0584, maca_scg@gov.nt.ca

Nova Scotia

Nova Scotia Department of Advanced Education, 1505 Barrington St., PO Box 697, Halifax, NS B3J 2T8
902-424-5301, Fax: 902-424-2203, lae-correspondence@novascotia.ca

Nova Scotia Department of Labour, Skills & Immigration, 1469 Brenton St., 3rd Fl., PO Box 1535, Halifax, NS B3J 2Y3

Ontario

Ontario Ministry of Labour, Training & Skills Development, 400 University Ave., 14th Fl., Toronto, ON M7A 1T7
416-326-7160, 800-531-5551

Training Completion Assurance Fund Advisory Board, 77 Wellesley St. West, PO Box 977, Toronto, ON M7A 1N3
416-314-0500, Fax: 416-314-0499, 866-330-3395, tcaf-pcc@ontario.ca

Prince Edward Island
Council of the College of Physicians & Surgeons of PEI, 14 Paramount Dr., Charlottetown, PE C1E 0C7
902-566-3861, Fax: 902-566-3986
Council of the PEI College of Physiotherapists, PO Box 20078, Charlottetown, PE C1A 9E3
contact@peicpt.com

Saskatchewan
Saskatchewan Advanced Education, #1120, 2010 - 12th Ave., Regina, SK S4P 0M3
aeeinquiry@gov.sk.ca
Saskatchewan Police College, College West Bldg., University of Regina, #217, 3737 Wascana Pkwy., Regina, SK S4S 0A2
306-787-8870, Fax: 306-787-8876

ELECTED OFFICIALS & CONSTITUENCIES

Forty-Fourth Parliament - Canada, House of Commons, Parliament Buildings, Ottawa, BC K1A 0A6

Alberta
Thirtieth Legislature - Alberta, Legislature Bldg., 10800 - 97th Ave., Edmonton, AB T5K 2B6

British Columbia
Forty-second Legislature - British Columbia, Parliament Buildings, Victoria, BC V8V 1X4
250-387-3785, Fax: 250-387-0942, officeoftheclerk@leg.bc.ca

Manitoba
Forty-second Legislature - Manitoba, Legislative Bldg., 450 Broadway, Winnipeg, MB R3C 0V8
204-945-3636, Fax: 204-948-2507, clerkla@leg.gov.mb.ca

New Brunswick
Sixtieth Legislative Assembly - New Brunswick, Centre Block, Legislative Bldg., 706 Queen St., PO Box 6000, Fredericton, NB E3B 5H1
506-453-2506, Fax: 506-453-7154, wwwleg@gnb.ca

Newfoundland & Labrador
Fiftieth House of Assembly - Newfoundland & Labrador, Confederation Bldg., PO Box 8700, St. John's, NL A1B 4J6
709-729-3405, ClerkHOA@gov.nl.ca

Northwest Territories
Nineteenth Legislative Assembly - Northwest Territories, 4570 - 48th St., PO Box 1320, Yellowknife, NT X1A 2L9
867-669-2200, Fax: 867-920-4735, 800-661-0784

Nova Scotia
Sixty-fourth General Assembly - Nova Scotia, Province House, 1726 Hollis St., Halifax, NS B3J 2Y3
902-424-4661, Fax: 902-424-0574

Nunavut
Fifth Legislative Assembly - Nunavut, PO Box 1200, Iqaluit, NU X0A 0H0

Ontario
Forty-second Provincial Parliament - Ontario, Clerk's Office, #104, Legislative Bldg., Queen's Park, Toronto, ON M7A 1A2
416-325-7500, Fax: 416-325-7489, web@ola.org

Prince Edward Island
Sixty-sixth General Assembly - Prince Edward Island, Province House, 165 Richmond St., 1st Fl., PO Box 2000, Charlottetown, PE C1A 7N8
902-368-5970, Fax: 902-368-5175, 877-315-5518

Quebec
Quarante-deuxième assemblée nationale, Hôtel du Parlement, 1045, rue des Parlementaires, Québec, QC G1A 1A4
418-643-7239, Fax: 418-646-4271, 866-337-8837

Saskatchewan
Twenty-ninth Legislature - Saskatchewan, Legislative Bldg., 2405 Legislative Dr., Regina, SK S4S 0B3

Yukon Territory
Thirty-fifth Legislative Assembly - Yukon Territory, Yukon Legislative Assembly Office, 2071 - 2nd Ave., PO Box 2703, Whitehorse, YT Y1A 2C6

ELECTIONS

Elections Canada, 30 Victoria St., Gatineau, ON K1A 0M6
613-993-2975, Fax: 613-954-8584, 800-463-6868
Office of the Commissioner of Canada Elections, PO Box 8000 T, Ottawa, ON K1G 3Z1
Fax: 819-939-1801, 855-759-6740, info@cef-cce.gc.ca

Alberta
Alberta Office of the Chief Electoral Officer / Elections Alberta, #100, 11510 Kingsway Ave., Edmonton, AB T5G 2Y5
780-427-7191, Fax: 780-422-2900, -310-0000, info@elections.ab.ca

British Columbia
Elections British Columbia, PO Box 9275 Prov Govt, Victoria, BC V8W 9J6
250-387-5305, Fax: 250-387-3578, 800-661-8683, electionsbc@elections.bc.ca

Manitoba
Elections Manitoba, #120, 200 Vaughan St., Winnipeg, MB R3C 1T5
204-945-3225, Fax: 204-945-6011, 866-628-6837, election@elections.mb.ca

New Brunswick
Office of the Chief Electoral Officer, Sartain MacDonald Bldg., #102, 551 King St., PO Box 6000, Fredericton, NB E3B 5H1
506-453-2218, Fax: 506-457-4926, 800-308-2922, info@electionsnb.ca

Newfoundland & Labrador
Office of the Chief Electoral Officer, 39 Hallett Cr., St. John's, NL A1B 4C4
877-729-7987, enl@gov.nl.ca

Northwest Territories
Elections NWT/Plebiscite Office, YK Centre East, #7, 4915 - 48th St., 3rd Fl., Yellowknife, NT X1A 3S4
867-767-9100, Fax: 867-920-9100, 844-767-9100, info@electionsnwt.ca

Nova Scotia
Elections Nova Scotia, #505, 202 Brownlow Ave., Dartmouth, NS B3B 1T5
902-424-8584, Fax: 902-424-6622, 800-565-1504, elections@novascotia.ca

Nunavut
Nunavut Legislative Assembly, 926 Federal Rd., PO Box 1200, Iqaluit, NU X0A 0H0
867-975-5000, Fax: 867-975-5190, 877-334-7266, leginfo@assembly.nu.ca

Ontario
Elections Ontario, 51 Rolark Dr., Toronto, ON M1R 3B1
416-326-6300, Fax: 416-326-6200, 888-668-8683, info@elections.on.ca

Prince Edward Island
Elections Prince Edward Island, Atlantic Technology Centre, #160, 176 Great George St., Charlottetown, PE C1A 4K3
902-368-5895, Fax: 902-368-6500, 888-234-8783

Quebec
Directeur général des Élections du Québec, Édifice René-Lévesque, 3460, rue de la Pérade, Québec, QC G1X 3Y5
418-528-0422, Fax: 418-643-7291, 888-353-2846, info@electionsquebec.qc.ca

Saskatchewan
Elections Saskatchewan, #301, 3303 Hillsdale St., Regina, SK S4S 6W9
306-787-4000, Fax: 306-787-4052, 877-958-8683, info@elections.sk.ca

Yukon Territory
Elections Yukon, Yukon Government Bldg., PO Box 2703, Whitehorse, YT Y1A 2C6
867-667-8683, Fax: 867-393-6977, 866-668-8683, info@electionsyukon.ca

EMERGENCY MEASURES

Emergency Management & Programs Branch, 340 Laurier Ave. West, Ottawa, ON K1A 0P8
Environment & Climate Change Canada, 200, rue Sacré-Coeur, 12th Fl., Gatineau, QC K1A 0H3
819-938-3860, 800-668-6767, eec.enviroinfo.ec@canada.ca
National Search & Rescue Secretariat, 275 Slater St., 4th Fl., Ottawa, ON K1A 0K2
Fax: 613-996-3746, 800-727-9414
Public Safety Canada, 269 Laurier Ave. West, Ottawa, ON K1A 0P8
613-944-4875, Fax: 613-954-5186, 800-830-3118

Alberta
Alberta Emergency Management Agency, Terrace Bldg., 9515 - 107 St., 4th Fl., Edmonton, AB T5K 2C1
780-422-9000, Fax: 780-644-1044, -310-0000, aema@gov.ab.ca
Alberta Environment & Parks, Forestry Bldg., 9920 - 108th St., Main Fl., Edmonton, AB T5K 2M4
780-944-0313,

Manitoba
Emergency Measures Organization, #1525, 405 Broadway Ave., Winnipeg, MB R3C 3L6
204-945-4772, Fax: 204-945-4929, 888-267-8298, emo@gov.mb.ca

Nova Scotia
Emergency Management Office, PO Box 2581, Halifax, NS B3J 3N5
902-424-5620, Fax: 902-424-5376, 866-424-5620, emo@novascotia.ca

Nunavut
Nunavut Emergency Management, PO Box 1000 700, Iqaluit, NU X0A 0H0
Fax: 867-979-4221, 800-693-1666, NEM@gov.nu.ca

Ontario
Office of the Fire Marshal & Emergency Management, 25 Morton Shulman Ave., Toronto, ON M3M 0B1
647-329-1100, Fax: 647-329-1143

EMPLOYMENT

Public Service Commission, 22, rue Eddy, Gatineau, QC K1A 0M7
800-645-5605

Alberta
Alberta Labour & Immigration, Legislature Bldg., #107, 10800 - 97th Ave., Edmonton, AB T5K 2B6
780-427-3731, 877-427-3731
Public Service Commission, Peace Hills Trust Tower, 10011 - 109th St., 7th Fl., Edmonton, AB T5J 3S8
780-408-8450

British Columbia
British Columbia Ministry of Labour, PO Box 9064 Prov Govt, Victoria, BC V8W 9K4
250-953-0910, Fax: 250-953-0928
British Columbia Public Service Agency, PO Box 9404 Prov Govt, Victoria, BC V8W 9V1
250-387-0518, Fax: 250-356-7074
Employment & Assistance Appeal Tribunal, PO Box 9994 Prov Govt, Victoria, BC V8W 9R7
250-356-6374, Fax: 250-356-9687, 866-557-0035, eaat@gov.bc.ca
Office of the Merit Commissioner, #502, 947 Fort St., PO Box 9037 Prov Govt, Victoria, BC V8W 9A3
250-953-4208, Fax: 250-953-4160, merit@meritcomm.bc.ca

Manitoba
Manitoba Civil Service Commission, #935, 155 Carlton St., Winnipeg, MB R3C 3H8
204-945-2332, Fax: 204-945-1486, 800-282-8069, csc@gov.mb.ca

New Brunswick
New Brunswick Jobs Board, Chancery Place, PO Box 6000, Fredericton, NB E3B 5H1

Newfoundland & Labrador
Newfoundland & Labrador Department of Immigration, Population Growth & Skills, West Block, Confederation Bldg., 3rd Fl., PO Box 8700, St. John's, NL A1B 4J6
709-729-1795, isl@gov.nl.ca
Newfoundland & Labrador Public Service Commission, 261 Kenmount Rd., PO Box 8700, St. John's, NL A1B 4J6
709-729-5810, Fax: 709-729-6234, 855-330-5810, contactpsc@gov.nl.ca

Northwest Territories
Northwest Territories Department of Finance, PO Box 1320, Yellowknife, NT X1A 2L9

Nova Scotia
Nova Scotia Public Service Commission, PO Box 943, Halifax, NS B3J 2V9
902-424-7660, reception-psc@novascotia.ca

Ontario
Public Service Commission, Whitney Block, 99 Wellesley St. West, 5th Fl., Toronto, ON M7A 1W4
416-325-1750

Prince Edward Island
Prince Edward Island Department of Fisheries & Communities, 548 Main St., PO Box 1180, Montague, PE C0A 1R0
902-838-0983, Fax: 902-838-0972, DeptFC@gov.pe.ca
Public Service Commission, Shaw Bldg. North, 105 Rochford St., 1st Fl., PO Box 2000, Charlottetown, PE C1A 7N8
902-368-4080, Fax: 902-368-4383

Quebec
Commission de la fonction publique, 800, Place D'Youville, 7e étage, Québec, QC G1R 3P4
418-643-1425, Fax: 418-643-7264, 800-432-0432, cfp@cfp.gouv.qc.ca
Emploi-Québec, Direction du Centre de communication avec la clientèle, 150, rue Monseigneur-Ross, 5e étage, Gaspé, QC G4X 2S7
514-873-4000, 877-767-8773
Ministère du Travail, de l'Emploi et de la Solidarité sociale, 150, rue Monseigneur-Ross, 5e étage, Québec, QC G4X 2S7
514-873-4000, 877-767-8773

Saskatchewan
Saskatchewan Advanced Education, #1120, 2010 - 12th Ave., Regina, SK S4P 0M3
aeeinquiry@gov.sk.ca
Saskatchewan Immigration & Career Training, #1000, 2103 - 11th Ave., Regina, SK S4P 3Z8
Fax: 306-787-7977

Yukon Territory
Yukon Public Service Commission, 2071 - 2nd Ave., PO Box 2703, Whitehorse, YT Y1A 2C6
867-667-5653, Fax: 867-667-5755, pscwebsite@yukon.ca

EMPLOYMENT EQUITY

See Also: Discrimination & Employment Equity
Office of the Public Sector Integrity Commissioner of Canada, 60 Queen St., 7th Fl., Ottawa, ON K1P 5Y7
613-941-6400, Fax: 613-941-6535, 866-941-6400

British Columbia
Office of the Merit Commissioner, #502, 947 Fort St., PO Box 9037 Prov Govt, Victoria, BC V8W 9A3
250-953-4208, Fax: 250-953-4160, merit@meritcomm.bc.ca

EMPLOYMENT INSURANCE

Canada Employment Insurance Commission, 140, Promenade du Portage, Phase IV, Gatineau, QC K1A 0J9
800-206-7218
Service Canada, 140, promenade du Portage, Gatineau, QC K1A 0J9
800-622-6232

Saskatchewan
Saskatchewan Labour Relations & Workplace Safety, #300, 1870 Albert St., Regina, SK S4P 4W1
Fax: 306-787-7404

ENERGY

See Also: Natural Resources
Canada Energy Regulator, #210, 517 - 10th Ave. SW, Calgary, AB T2R 0A8
403-292-4800, Fax: 403-292-5503, 800-899-1265,
Canadian Nuclear Safety Commission, 280 Slater St., PO Box 1046 B, Ottawa, ON K1P 5S9
613-995-5894, Fax: 613-995-5086, 800-668-5284, cnsc.information.ccsn@canada.ca
Indian Oil & Gas Canada, #100, 9911 Chiila Blvd., Tsuu T'ina (Sarcee), AB T2W 6H6
403-292-5625, Fax: 403-292-5618, aadnc.contactiogc.aandc@canada.ca
Office of Energy Efficiency, CEF, Building 3, Observatory Cres., 930 Carling Ave., Ottawa, ON K1A 0Y3
Waste Biotreatability Facility, c/o Montréal (av Royalmount) Research Facilities, 6100, av Royalmount, Montréal, QC H4P 2R2

Alberta
Alberta Energy, North Petroleum Plaza, 9945 - 108th St., Edmonton, AB T5K 2G6
780-427-8050, Fax: 780-422-9522
Alberta Energy Regulator, #1000, 250 - 5 St. SW, Calgary, AB T2P 0R4
403-297-8311, Fax: 403-297-7336, 855-297-8311, inquiries@aer.ca
Alberta Utilities Commission, Eau Caire Tower, #1400, 600 - 3rd Ave. SW, Calgary, AB T2P 0G5
-310-4282, info@auc.ab.ca
Emissions Reduction Alberta, #746, 10104 - 103rd Ave. NW, Edmonton, AB T5J 0H8
780-498-2068, info@eralberta.ca
Surface Rights Board, 1229 - 91 St. SW, Edmonton, AB T6X 1E9
780-427-2444, Fax: 780-427-5798, -310-0000, srb.lcb@gov.ab.ca

British Columbia
British Columbia Hydro, 333 Dunsmuir St., PO Box 8910, Vancouver, BC V6B 4N1
604-224-9376, 800-224-9376
British Columbia Ministry of Energy, Mines & Low Carbon Innovation, PO Box 9060 Prov Govt, Victoria, BC V8W 9E3
250-952-0628
British Columbia Utilities Commission, #410, 900 Howe St., Vancouver, BC V6Z 2N3
604-660-4700, Fax: 604-660-1102, 800-663-1385, commission.secretary@bcuc.com
Oil & Gas Commission, 6534 Airport Rd., Fort St. John, BC V1J 4M6
250-794-5200, Fax: 250-794-5375
Powerex Corp., #1300, 666 Burrard St., Vancouver, BC V6C 2X8
604-891-5000, Fax: 604-891-6060, 800-220-4907
Powertech Labs Inc., 12388 - 88 Ave., Surrey, BC V8W 7R7
604-590-7500, Fax: 604-590-6611

Manitoba
Manitoba Hydro, 360 Portage Ave., PO Box 815 Main, Winnipeg, MB R3C 2P4
204-480-5900, Fax: 204-360-6155, 888-624-9376
Mineral Resources Division, The Paris Bldg., 259 Portage Ave., 9th Fl., Winnipeg, MB R3B 3P4
204-945-6569, 800-223-5215, minesinfo@gov.mb.ca

Power Engineers Advisory Board, Norquay Bldg., #500, 401 York Ave., Winnipeg, MB R3C 0P8
204-945-3373, Fax: 204-948-2309

New Brunswick
New Brunswick Department of Natural Resources & Energy Development, Hugh John Flemming Forestry Centre, PO Box 6000, Fredericton, NB E3B 5H1
506-453-3826, Fax: 506-444-4367, dnr_mrnweb@gnb.ca

Newfoundland & Labrador
Canada-Newfoundland & Labrador Offshore Petroleum Board, West Campus Hall, The Tower Corporate Campus, #7100, 240 Waterford Bridge Rd., St. John's, NL A1E 1E2
709-778-1400, information@cnlopb.ca
Nalcor Energy, 500 Columbus Dr., St. John's, NL A1E 2B2
709-737-1400, Fax: 709-737-1800, info@nalcorenergy.com
Newfoundland & Labrador Board of Commissioners of Public Utilities, PO Box 21040, St. John's, NL A1A 5B2
Fax: 709-726-9604, 866-782-0006, ito@pub.nl.ca
Newfoundland & Labrador Hydro, Hydro Place, 500 Columbus Dr., PO Box 12400, St. John's, NL A1B 4K7
709-737-1400, Fax: 709-737-1800, 888-737-1296, hydro@nlh.nl.ca

Northwest Territories
Northwest Territories Department of Environment & Natural Resources, PO Box 1320, Yellowknife, NT X1A 2L9
867-767-9055, enr_communications@gov.nt.ca
Northwest Territories Power Corporation, 4 Capital Dr., Hay River, NT X0E 1G2
867-874-5200, 800-661-0855, info@ntpc.com

Nova Scotia
Canada-Nova Scotia Offshore Petroleum Board, TD Centre, 1791 Barrington St., 8th Fl., Halifax, NS B3J 3K9
902-422-5588, Fax: 902-422-1799, info@cnsopb.ns.ca
Nova Scotia Department of Energy & Mines, Joseph Howe Bldg., 1690 Hollis St., PO Box 2664, Halifax, NS B3J 3J9
902-424-4575, Fax: 902-424-3265, enerinfo@novascotia.ca
Nova Scotia Utility & Review Board, Summit Place, 1601 Lower Water St., 3rd Fl., Halifax, NS B3J 3S3
902-424-4448, Fax: 902-424-3919, 855-442-4448, board@novascotia.ca

Nunavut
Nunavut Energy Secretariat, c/o Dept. of Economic Development & Transportation, Iqaluit, NU X0A 0H0
867-975-7704, nunavutenergy@gov.nu.ca

Ontario
Hydro One Inc., South Tower, 483 Bay St., 8th Fl., Toronto, ON M5G 2P5
416-345-5000, Fax: 905-944-3251, 877-955-1155, customercommunications@hydroone.com
Independent Electricity System Operator, #1600, 120 Adelaide St. West, Toronto, ON M5H 1T1
905-403-6900, Fax: 905-403-6921, 877-797-9473, customer.relations@ieso.ca
Ontario Energy Board, #2700, 2300 Yonge St., PO Box 2319, Toronto, ON M4P 1E4
416-481-1967, Fax: 416-440-7656, 888-632-6273
Ontario Ministry of Energy, 77 Grenville St., Toronto, ON M7A 2C1
416-327-6758, 888-668-4636, energy@ontario.ca
Ontario Ministry of Environment, Conservation & Parks, Ferguson Block, 77 Wellesley St. West, 11th Fl., Toronto, ON M7A 2T5
416-325-4000, Fax: 416-314-6713, 800-565-4923
Ontario Power Generation, 700 University Ave., Toronto, ON M5G 1X6
416-592-2555, 877-592-2555, webmaster@opg.com

Prince Edward Island
Prince Edward Island Department of Justice & Public Safety, Shaw Bldg. South, 95 Rochford St., 4th Fl., PO Box 2000, Charlottetown, PE C1A 7N8
902-368-4589, Fax: 902-368-5283, DeptJPS@gov.pe.ca
Prince Edward Island Energy Corporation, Sullivan Bldg., 16 Fitzroy St., PO Box 2000, Charlottetown, PE C1A 7N8

Quebec
Coopérative régionale d'électricité de Saint-Jean-Baptiste-de-Rouville, 3113, rue Principale, Saint-Jean-Baptiste, QC J0L 1B0
450-467-5583, Fax: 450-467-0092, 800-267-5583, info@coopsjb.ca
Énergie, #A301 - 5700, 4e av ouest, Québec, QC G1H 6R1
Hydro-Québec, Édifice Jean-Lesage, 75, boul René-Lévesque ouest, Montréal, QC H2Z 1A4
514-385-7252, 888-385-7252
Régie de l'énergie, Tour de la Bourse, #2.55, 800, Place Victoria, Montréal, QC H4Z 1A2
514-873-2452, Fax: 514-873-2070, 888-873-2452, secretariat@regie-energie.qc.ca
Société d'énergie de la Baie-James, #1100, 800, de Maisonneuve est, Montréal, QC H2L 4L8
514-286-2020

Transition énergetique Québec, 5700, 4e av ouest, #B406, Québec, QC G1H 6R1
418-627-6379, Fax: 418-643-5828, 877-727-6655, transitionenergetique@teq.gouv.qc.ca

Saskatchewan
NorthPoint Energy Solutions Inc., 2025 Victoria Ave., Regina, SK S4P 0S1
Saskatchewan Energy & Resources, #1000, 2103 - 11th Ave., Regina, SK S4P 3Z8
Saskatchewan Power Corporation (SaskPower), 2025 Victoria Ave., Regina, SK S4P 0S1
888-757-6937
SaskEnergy Incorporated, 1777 Victoria Ave., Regina, SK S4P 4K5
306-777-9225, 800-567-8899, webmaster@saskenergy.com

Yukon Territory
Yukon Energy Corporation, 2 Miles Canyon Rd., PO Box 5920, Whitehorse, YT Y1A 6S7
867-393-5300, 866-926-3749, communications@yec.yk.ca
Yukon Energy, Mines & Resources, PO Box 2703, Whitehorse, YT Y1A 2C6
867-667-3123, Fax: 867-393-7421, 800-661-0408, emr@yukon.ca

ENGINEERING & CONSULTING

Canada Infrastructure Bank, 150 King St. West, PO Box 15, Toronto, ON M5H 1J9
833-551-5245
Defence Construction Canada, Constitution Square, 350 Albert St., 19th Fl., Ottawa, ON K1A 0K3
613-998-9548, Fax: 613-998-1061, 800-514-3555, info@dcc-cdc.gc.ca
Impact Assessment Agency of Canada, Place Bell Canada, 160 Elgin St., 22nd Fl., Ottawa, ON K1A 0H3
613-957-0700, Fax: 613-957-0862, 866-582-1884
Infrastructure Canada, #1100, 180 Kent St., Ottawa, ON K1P 0B6
613-948-1148, 877-250-7154, ifc.info@canada.ca
Natural Sciences & Engineering Research Council of Canada, 350 Albert St., 16th Fl., Ottawa, ON K1A 1H5
613-995-4273, Fax: 613-992-5337, 855-275-2861

Alberta
Alberta Infrastructure, Infrastructure Bldg., 6950 - 113th St., Edmonton, AB T6H 5V7
780-415-0507, Fax: 780-427-2187, Infra.Contact.Us.m@gov.ab.ca
C-FER Technologies, 200 Karl Clark Rd., Edmonton, AB T6N 1H2
780-450-3300, Fax: 780-450-3700
Safety & Policy Division, Twin Atria Bldg., 4999 - 98th Ave., Main Fl., Edmonton, AB T6B 2X3
780-427-8901, Fax: 780-415-0782, 800-666-5036

British Columbia
British Columbia Ministry of Transportation & Infrastructure, PO Box 9850 Prov Govt, Victoria, BC V8W 9T5
250-387-3198, Fax: 250-356-7706, tran.webmaster@gov.bc.ca
Partnerships BC, 900 - 1285 West Pender St., PO Box 9478 Prov Govt, Vancouver, BC V6E 4B1
604-681-2443, Fax: 604-806-4190, partnershipsbc@partnershipsbc.ca
Transportation Policy & Programs Division, PO Box 9850 Prov Govt, Victoria, BC V8W 9T5
250-387-5062, Fax: 250-387-6431

Manitoba
Manitoba Infrastructure, Legislative Bldg., #203, 450 Broadway, Winnipeg, MB R3C 0V8
Power Engineers Advisory Board, Norquay Bldg., #500, 401 York Ave., Winnipeg, MB R3C 0P8
204-945-3373, Fax: 204-948-2309

New Brunswick
New Brunswick Department of Transportation & Infrastructure, Kings Place, PO Box 6000, Fredericton, NB E3B 5H1
506-453-3939, Fax: 506-453-7987, transportation.web@gnb.ca

Nova Scotia
Nova Scotia Department of Transportation & Active Transit, PO Box 186, Halifax, NS B3J 2N2
902-424-2297, Fax: 902-424-0532, tpwpaff@novascotia.ca

Ontario
Ontario Capital Growth Corporation, Ontario Investment & Trade Centre, 250 Yonge St., 35th Fl., Toronto, ON M5B 2L7
416-325-6874, Fax: 416-212-0794
Ontario Ministry of Economic Development, Job Creation & Trade, 56 Wellesley St. West, 7th Fl., Toronto, ON M7A 2E7
416-325-6666, 800-268-7095
Ontario Ministry of Infrastructure, 777 Bay St., 5th Fl., Toronto, ON M5G 2C8
416-327-4412

Prince Edward Island
Prince Edward Island Department of Transportation & Infrastructure, Jones Bldg., 11 Kent St., 3rd Fl., PO Box 2000, Charlottetown, PE C1A 7N8
902-368-5100, Fax: 902-368-5395, DeptTIE@gov.pe.ca
Saskatchewan
Saskatchewan Highways, Victoria Tower, 1855 Victoria Ave., Regina, SK S4P 3T2
306-933-5186, MHI.CustomerService@gov.sk.ca
SaskBuilds & Procurement, 1920 Rose St., Regina, SK S4P 0A9
306-787-6911, Fax: 306-787-1061, cs.receptioncenturyplaza@gov.sk.ca

ENVIRONMENT

Commissioner of the Environment & Sustainable Development, 240 Sparks St., Ottawa, ON K1A 0G6
613-952-0213, Fax: 613-957-0474
Environment & Climate Change Canada, 200, rue Sacré-Coeur, 12th Fl., Gatineau, QC K1A 0H3
819-938-3860, 800-668-6767, eec.enviroinfo.ec@canada.ca
Environmental Protection Review Canada, 240 Sparks St., 4th Fl. West, Ottawa, ON K1A 0X8
Fax: 613-907-1337, eprc-rpec@eprc-rpec.gc.ca
Alberta
Alberta Environment & Parks, Forestry Bldg., 9920 - 108th St., Main Fl., Edmonton, AB T5K 2M4
780-944-0313
British Columbia
British Columbia Ministry of Environment & Climate Change Strategy, PO Box 9047 Prov Govt, Victoria, BC V8W 9E2
Manitoba
Manitoba Conservation & Climate, 200 Saulteaux Cres., PO Box 22, Winnipeg, MB R3J 3W3
204-945-6784, Fax: 204-948-2656, 800-214-6497, cc@gov.mb.ca
Manitoba Round Table for Sustainable Development, #160, 123 Main St., PO Box 70, Winnipeg, MB R3C 1A5
204-945-4391, Fax: 204-948-4730, mrtsd@gov.mb.ca
New Brunswick
New Brunswick Department of Environment & Local Government, Marysville Place, 20 McGloin St., Fredericton, NB E3B 5H1
506-453-2690, Fax: 506-457-4994, elg/egl-info@gnb.ca
Northwest Territories
Northwest Territories Department of Environment & Natural Resources, PO Box 1320, Yellowknife, NT X1A 2L9
867-767-9055, enr_communications@gov.nt.ca
Nova Scotia
Divert NS, #400, 35 Commercial St., Truro, NS B2N 3H9
902-895-7732, Fax: 902-897-3256, 877-313-7732, info@divertns.ca
Nova Scotia Department of Environment, #1800, 1894 Barrington St., PO Box 442, Halifax, NS B3J 2P8
902-424-3600, Fax: 902-424-0501, 877-936-8476
Nova Scotia Lands Inc., PO Box 430 A, Sydney, NS B1P 6H2
Nunavut
Nunavut Territory Department of Environment, PO Box 1000 1320, Iqaluit, NU X0A 0H0
867-975-7700, Fax: 867-975-7742, environment@gov.nu.ca
Ontario
Environmental Commissioner of Ontario, #605, 1075 Bay St., Toronto, ON M5S 2B1
416-325-3377, Fax: 416-325-3370, 800-701-6454, commissioner@eco.on.ca
Ontario Ministry of Environment, Conservation & Parks, Ferguson Block, 77 Wellesley St. West, 11th Fl., Toronto, ON M7A 2T5
416-325-4000, Fax: 416-314-6713, 800-565-4923
Prince Edward Island
Climate Change & Environment, Jones Bldg., 11 Kent St., 4th Fl., PO Box 2000, Charlottetown, PE C1A 7N8
Prince Edward Island Department of Justice & Public Safety, Shaw Bldg. South, 95 Rochford St., 4th Fl., PO Box 2000, Charlottetown, PE C1A 7N8
902-368-4589, Fax: 902-368-5283, DeptJPS@gov.pe.ca
Quebec
Bureau d'audiences publiques sur l'environnement, Édifice Lomer-Gouin, #2.10, 575, rue Jacques-Parizeau, Québec, QC G1R 6A6
418-643-7447, Fax: 418-643-9474, 800-463-4732, communication@bape.gouv.qc.ca
Ministère de l'Environnement et de la Lutte contre les changements climatiques, Édifice Marie-Guyart, 675, boul René-Lévesque est, 30e étage, Québec, QC G1R 5V7
418-521-3830, Fax: 418-646-5974, 800-561-1616, relations.medias@mddelcc.gouv.qc.ca

Saskatchewan
Saskatchewan Environment, 3211 Albert St., Regina, SK S4S 5W6
306-787-2584, Fax: 306-787-9544, 800-567-4224, centre.inquiry@gov.sk.ca

ENVIRONMENT DEPARTMENTS/MINISTRIES

Environment & Climate Change Canada, 200, rue Sacré-Coeur, 12th Fl., Gatineau, QC K1A 0H3
819-938-3860, 800-668-6767, eec.enviroinfo.ec@canada.ca
Alberta
Alberta Environment & Parks, Forestry Bldg., 9920 - 108th St., Main Fl., Edmonton, AB T5K 2M4
780-944-0313
British Columbia
British Columbia Ministry of Environment & Climate Change Strategy, PO Box 9047 Prov Govt, Victoria, BC V8W 9E2
Manitoba
Manitoba Conservation & Climate, 200 Saulteaux Cres., PO Box 22, Winnipeg, MB R3J 3W3
204-945-6784, Fax: 204-948-2656, 800-214-6497, cc@gov.mb.ca
New Brunswick
New Brunswick Department of Environment & Local Government, Marysville Place, 20 McGloin St., Fredericton, NB E3B 5H1
506-453-2690, Fax: 506-457-4994, elg/egl-info@gnb.ca
Newfoundland & Labrador
Newfoundland & Labrador Department of Environment & Climate Change, PO Box 8700, St. John's, NL A1B 4J6
ECCInfo@gov.nl.ca
Northwest Territories
Northwest Territories Department of Environment & Natural Resources, PO Box 1320, Yellowknife, NT X1A 2L9
867-767-9055, enr_communications@gov.nt.ca
Nova Scotia
Nova Scotia Department of Environment, #1800, 1894 Barrington St., PO Box 442, Halifax, NS B3J 2P8
902-424-3600, Fax: 902-424-0501, 877-936-8476
Nunavut
Nunavut Territory Department of Environment, PO Box 1000 1320, Iqaluit, NU X0A 0H0
867-975-7700, Fax: 867-975-7742, environment@gov.nu.ca
Ontario
Ontario Ministry of Environment, Conservation & Parks, Ferguson Block, 77 Wellesley St. West, 11th Fl., Toronto, ON M7A 2T5
416-325-4000, Fax: 416-314-6713, 800-565-4923
Prince Edward Island
Prince Edward Island Department of Environment, Energy & Climate Action, Jones Bldg., 11 Kent St., 4th Fl., Charlottetown, PE C1A 7N8
902-368-5044, Fax: 902-368-5830, 866-368-5044, DeptEECA@gov.pe.ca
Prince Edward Island Department of Justice & Public Safety, Shaw Bldg. South, 95 Rochford St., 4th Fl., PO Box 2000, Charlottetown, PE C1A 7N8
902-368-4589, Fax: 902-368-5283, DeptJPS@gov.pe.ca
Quebec
Ministère de l'Environnement et de la Lutte contre les changements climatiques, Édifice Marie-Guyart, 675, boul René-Lévesque est, 30e étage, Québec, QC G1R 5V7
418-521-3830, Fax: 418-646-5974, 800-561-1616, relations.medias@mddelcc.gouv.qc.ca
Saskatchewan
Saskatchewan Environment, 3211 Albert St., Regina, SK S4S 5W6
306-787-2584, Fax: 306-787-9544, 800-567-4224, centre.inquiry@gov.sk.ca
Yukon Territory
Yukon Environment, 10 Burns Rd., Whitehorse, YT Y1A 2C6
867-667-5652, Fax: 867-393-7197, environmentyukon@yukon.ca

ENVIRONMENTAL ASSESSMENT

Impact Assessment Agency of Canada, Place Bell Canada, 160 Elgin St., 22nd Fl., Ottawa, ON K1A 0H3
613-957-0700, Fax: 613-957-0862, 866-582-1884
Alberta
InnoTech Alberta, 250 Karl Clark Rd., Edmonton, AB T6N 1H2
780-450-5111, Fax: 780-450-5333, info@innotechalberta.ca
Prince Edward Island
Climate Change & Environment, Jones Bldg., 11 Kent St., 4th Fl., PO Box 2000, Charlottetown, PE C1A 7N8
Land & Environment, Jones Bldg., 11 Kent St., 3rd Fl., PO Box 2000, Charlottetown, PE C1A 7N8

ENVIRONMENTAL HEALTH

Centre for Aquaculture & Environmental Research, 4160 Marine Dr., West Vancouver, BC V7V 1N6
Environmental Protection Review Canada, 240 Sparks St., 4th Fl. West, Ottawa, ON K1A 0X8
Fax: 613-907-1337, eprc-rpec@eprc-rpec.gc.ca
Alberta
C-FER Technologies, 200 Karl Clark Rd., Edmonton, AB T6N 1H2
780-450-3300, Fax: 780-450-3700
Emissions Reduction Alberta, #746, 10104 - 103rd Ave. NW, Edmonton, AB T5J 0H8
780-498-2068, info@eralberta.ca
InnoTech Alberta, 250 Karl Clark Rd., Edmonton, AB T6N 1H2
780-450-5111, Fax: 780-450-5333, info@innotechalberta.ca
Prince Edward Island
Climate Change & Environment, Jones Bldg., 11 Kent St., 4th Fl., PO Box 2000, Charlottetown, PE C1A 7N8

EROSION CONTROL

Science & Technology Branch, Tower 5, 1341 Baseline Rd., Ottawa, ON K1A 0C5
Fax: 613-773-1711,
Prince Edward Island
Policy & Agriculture Resources, Jones Bldg., 11 Kent St., 5th Fl., Charlottetown, PE C1A 7N8
Quebec
Commission de protection du territoire agricole du Québec, 200, ch Ste-Foy, 2e étage, Québec, QC G1R 4X6
418-643-3314, Fax: 418-643-2261, 800-667-5294, info@cptaq.gouv.qc.ca
Saskatchewan
Saskatchewan Agriculture, Walter Scott Bldg., 3085 Albert St., Regina, SK S4S 0B1
866-457-2377

EXPORT DEVELOPMENT

Business Development Bank of Canada, #100, 5, Place Ville-Marie, Montréal, QC H3B 5E7
Fax: 877-329-9232, 877-232-2269
Canadian Trade Commissioner Service, TCS Enquiries Service, c/o Global Affairs Canada, 125 Sussex Dr., Ottawa, ON K1A 0G2
613-944-9991, Fax: 613-996-9709, 888-306-9991, trade@international.gc.ca
Export Development Canada, 150 Slater St., Ottawa, ON K1A 1K3
613-598-2500, Fax: 613-598-3811, 800-229-0575, support@edc.ca
Innovation, Science & Economic Development Canada, C.D. Howe Building, 235 Queen St., Ottawa, ON K1A 0H5
613-954-5031, Fax: 613-954-2340, 800-328-6189, info@ic.gc.ca
Western Economic Diversification Canada, Canada Place, #1500, 9700 Jasper Ave. NW, Edmonton, AB T5J 4H7
780-495-4164, Fax: 780-495-4557, 888-338-9378, WD.contactus-contactez-nous.DEO@canada.ca
Ontario
Ontario Ministry of Economic Development, Job Creation & Trade, 56 Wellesley St. West, 7th Fl., Toronto, ON M7A 2E7
416-325-6666, 800-268-7095
Quebec
Ministère de l'Économie et de l'Innovation, 710, Place D'Youville, 3e étage, Québec, QC G1R 4Y4
418-691-5950, Fax: 418-644-0118, 866-680-1884
Saskatchewan
Saskatchewan Energy & Resources, #1000, 2103 - 11th Ave., Regina, SK S4P 3Z8

EXPROPRIATION

Canada Lands Company Ltd., #1700, 1 University Ave., Toronto, ON M5J 2P1
416-214-1250, Fax: 416-214-1121
Department of National Defence & the Canadian Armed Forces, National Defence HQ, Major-General George R. Pearkes Bldg., 101 Colonel By Dr., Ottawa, ON K1A 0K2
613-995-2534, Fax: 613-992-4739, 888-995-2534, information@forces.gc.ca
Justice Canada, 284 Wellington St., Ottawa, ON K1A 0H8
613-957-4222, Fax: 613-954-0811, webadmin@justice.gc.ca
Alberta
Land Compensation Board, 1229 - 91 St. SW, Edmonton, AB T6X 1E9
780-427-2444, Fax: 780-427-5798, -310-000, srb.lcb@gov.ab.ca
Manitoba
Manitoba Land Value Appraisal Commission, #1144, 363 Broadway, Winnipeg, MB R3C 3N9
204-945-5455, Fax: 204-948-2235

Quebec
Ministère des Transports, #4.010, 500, boul René-Lévesque est, Québec, QC H2Z 1W7
888-355-0511, communications@mtq.gouv.qc.ca
Saskatchewan
Public & Private Rights Board, #23, 3085 Albert St., Regina, SK S4S 0B1
306-787-4071, Fax: 306-787-0088

FAMILY BENEFITS
See Also: Income Security; Social Services
British Columbia
British Columbia Ministry of Children & Family Development, Customer Service Centre, PO Box 9770 Prov Govt, Victoria, BC V8W 9S5
250-387-7027, 877-387-7027, mcf.info@gov.bc.ca
Manitoba
Child & Family Services, 777 Portage Ave., Winnipeg, MB R3G 0N3
204-945-6964, cfsd@gov.mb.ca
Manitoba Families, Legislative Bldg., #357, 450 Broadway, Winnipeg, MB R3C 0V8
204-945-3744, 866-626-4862
New Brunswick
New Brunswick Department of Social Development, Sartain MacDonald Bldg., PO Box 6000, Fredericton, NB E3B 5H1
506-453-2001, Fax: 506-453-2164, sd-ds@gnb.ca
Newfoundland & Labrador
Newfoundland & Labrador Department of Immigration, Population Growth & Skills, West Block, Confederation Bldg., 3rd Fl., PO Box 8700, St. John's, NL A1B 4J6
709-729-1795, isl@gov.nl.ca
Northwest Territories
Northwest Territories Department of Education, Culture & Employment, PO Box 1320, Yellowknife, NT X1A 2L9
ecepublicaffairs@gov.nt.ca
Nunavut
Nunavut Territory Department of Family Services, PO Box 1000 1200, Iqaluit, NU X0A 0H0
867-975-5200, Fax: 867-975-5722
Quebec
Conseil de gestion de l'assurance parentale, #104, 1122, Grande Allée ouest, Québec, QC G1S 1E5
418-643-1009, Fax: 418-643-6738, 888-610-7727
Ministère de la Famille, Service des renseignements, 600, rue Fullum, 6e étage, Montréal, QC H2K 4S7
855-336-8568
Ministère du Travail, de l'Emploi et de la Solidarité sociale, 150, rue Monseigneur-Ross, 5e étage, Québec, QC G4X 2S7
514-873-4000, 877-767-8773
Régime québécois d'assurance parentale, 19, rue Perreault ouest, 1e étage, Rouyn-Noranda, QC J9X 0A1
418-643-7246, 888-610-7727

FEDERAL-PROVINCIAL AFFAIRS
Canadian Intergovernmental Conference Secretariat, 222 Queen St., 10th Fl., PO Box 488 A, Ottawa, ON K1N 8V5
613-995-2341, Fax: 613-996-6091, info@scics.gc.ca
British Columbia
Intergovernmental Relations Secretariat, PO Box 9433 Prov Govt, Victoria, BC V8W 9V3
250-387-0783, Fax: 250-387-1920, igrs@gov.bc.ca
New Brunswick
Intergovernmental Affairs Division, Chancery Place, 675 King St., 5th Fl., Fredericton, NB E3B 1E9
506-444-4948, Fax: 506-453-2995, iga@gnb.ca
Newfoundland & Labrador
Newfoundland & Labrador Department of Environment & Climate Change, PO Box 8700, St. John's, NL A1B 4J6
ECCInfo@gov.nl.ca
Northwest Territories
Northwest Territories Department of the Executive & Indigenous Affairs, PO Box 1320, Yellowknife, NT X1A 2L9
Nova Scotia
Nova Scotia Department of Intergovernmental Affairs, Duke Tower, 5251 Duke St., 5th Fl., PO Box 1617, Halifax, NS B3J 2Y3
902-424-5153, Fax: 902-424-0728
Nunavut
Nunavut Territory Department of Executive & Intergovernmental Affairs, 1084 Aeroplex bldg., PO Box 1000 200, Iqaluit, NU X0A 0H0
867-975-6000, Fax: 867-975-6099
Ontario
Ontario Ministry of Intergovernmental Affairs, Legislative Bldg., #223, 223 Queen's Park, Toronto, ON M7A 1A4
416-326-1234, 800-268-7095

Quebec
Secrétariat du Québec aux relations canadiennes, 875, Grande Allée est, 3e étage, Québec, QC G1R 4Y8
418-643-4011, Fax: 418-528-0052

FILM PRODUCTION & COLLECTIONS
Canadian Broadcasting Corporation, 181 Queen St., PO Box 3220 C, Ottawa, ON K1Y 1E4
613-288-6000, liaison@cbc.ca
National Film Board of Canada, Operational Headquarters, Norman McLaren Building, 3155, ch de la Côte-de-Liesse, PO Box 1600 Centre-ville, Montréal, QC H3C 3H5
514-283-9000, 800-267-7710
Telefilm Canada, #500, 360, rue Saint-Jacques, Montréal, QC H2Y 1P5
514-283-6363, Fax: 514-283-8212, 800-567-0890, info@telefilm.gc.ca
Alberta
Alberta Film, Whitemud Crossing, #140, 4211 - 106 St., Edmonton, AB T6J 6L7
780-422-8584, Fax: 780-422-8582, 888-813-1738, info@albertafilm.ca
British Columbia
Creative BC, 2225 West Broadway, Vancouver, BC V6K 2E4
604-736-7997, Fax: 604-736-7290
Manitoba
Manitoba Film & Music, #410, 93 Lombard Ave., Winnipeg, MB R3B 3B1
204-947-2040, Fax: 204-956-5261, info@mbfilmmusic.ca
Newfoundland & Labrador
Newfoundland & Labrador Film Development Corporation, 12 King's Bridge Rd., St. John's, NL A1C 3K3
709-738-3456, Fax: 709-739-1680, 877-738-3456, info@nlfdc.ca
Nova Scotia
Nova Scotia Business Inc., PO Box 2374, Halifax, NS B3J 3E4
902-424-6650, 800-260-6682, info@nsbi.ca
Ontario
Ontario Media Development Corporation, South Tower, #501, 175 Bloor St. East, Toronto, ON M4W 3R8
416-314-6858, Fax: 416-314-6876, reception@omdc.on.ca

FINANCE
See Also: Banking & Financial Institutions
Finance Canada, 90 Elgin St., Ottawa, ON K1A 0G5
613-369-3710, Fax: 613-369-4065, fin.financepublic-financepublique.fin@canada.ca
Alberta
Alberta Securities Commission, #600, 250 - 5th St. SW, Calgary, AB T2P 0R4
403-297-6454, Fax: 403-297-6156, 877-355-0585, inquiries@asc.ca
Alberta Treasury Board & Finance, 9820 - 107th St., 9th Fl., Edmonton, AB T5K 1E7
780-427-3035, Fax: 780-427-1147
British Columbia
British Columbia Ministry of Finance, PO Box 9417 Prov Govt, Victoria, BC V8W 9V1
British Columbia Securities Commission, Pacific Centre, 701 West Georgia St., 12th Fl., PO Box 10142, Vancouver, BC V7Y 1L2
604-899-6500, Fax: 604-899-6506, 800-373-6393, inquiries@bcsc.bc.ca
Manitoba
Manitoba Finance, Legislative Bldg., #103, 450 Broadway, Winnipeg, MB R3C 0V8
204-945-3744
Manitoba Securities Commission, #500, 400 St. Mary Ave., Winnipeg, MB R3C 4K5
204-945-2548, Fax: 204-945-0330, securities@gov.mb.ca
New Brunswick
Financial & Consumer Services Commission, #300, 85 Charlotte St., Saint John, NB E2L 2J2
506-658-3060, Fax: 506-658-3059, 866-933-2222, info@fcnb.ca
New Brunswick Department of Finance, Chancery Place, 675 King St., 5th Fl., Fredericton, NB E3B 5H1
506-453-2264, Fax: 506-453-7195, TB-CT@gnb.ca
Newfoundland & Labrador
Newfoundland & Labrador Department of Finance, Confederation Bldg., PO Box 8700, St. John's, NL A1B 4J6
709-729-3166, finance@gov.nl.ca
Northwest Territories
Northwest Territories Department of Finance, PO Box 1320, Yellowknife, NT X1A 2L9

Nova Scotia
Nova Scotia Department of Finance & Treasury Board, Provincial Bldg., 1723 Hollis St., 7th Fl., PO Box 187, Halifax, NS B3J 2N3
902-424-5554, Fax: 902-424-0635, FinanceWeb@novascotia.ca
Nova Scotia Securities Commission, PO Box 458, Halifax, NS B3J 2P8
902-424-7768, Fax: 902-424-4625, 855-424-2499, NSSCinquiries@novascotia.ca
Nunavut
Nunavut Territory Department of Finance, PO Box 1000 430, Iqaluit, NU X0A 0H0
867-975-6222, Fax: 867-975-6220, 888-668-9993, gnhr@gov.nu.ca
Ontario
Ontario Ministry of Finance, 95 Grosvenor St., Toronto, ON M7A 1Y8
Fax: 866-888-3850, 866-668-8297
Ontario Securities Commission, 20 Queen St. West, 20th Fl., PO Box 55, Toronto, ON M5H 3S8
416-593-8314, Fax: 416-593-8122, 877-785-1555, inquiries@osc.gov.on.ca
Prince Edward Island
Prince Edward Island Department of Finance, Shaw Bldg., 95 Rochford St. South, 2nd Fl., PO Box 2000, Charlottetown, PE C1A 7N8
902-368-4040, Fax: 902-368-6575, DeptFinance@gov.pe.ca
Quebec
Ministère des Finances, 12, rue Saint-Louis, Québec, QC G1R 5L3
418-528-9323, Fax: 418-646-1631, info@finances.gouv.qc.ca
Tribunal administratif des marchés financiers, #16.40, 500, boul Réné-Lévesque ouest, Montréal, QC H2Z 1W7
514-873-2211, Fax: 514-873-2162, 877-873-2211, secretariattmf@tmf.gouv.qc.ca
Saskatchewan
Saskatchewan Finance, 2350 Albert St., Regina, SK S4P 4A6
ficommunications@gov.sk.ca
Saskatchewan Trade & Export Development, #1000, 2103 - 11th Ave., Regina, SK S4P 3Z8
Yukon Territory
Yukon Finance, PO Box 2703, Whitehorse, YT Y1A 2C6
867-667-5343, Fax: 867-393-6217, fininfo@yukon.ca

FINANCING & LOANS
See Also: Investment
Business Development Bank of Canada, #100, 5, Place Ville-Marie, Montréal, QC H3B 5E7
Fax: 877-329-9232, 877-232-2269
Canada Mortgage & Housing Corporation, 700 Montreal Rd., Ottawa, ON K1A 0P7
613-748-2000, Fax: 613-748-2098, 800-668-2642, chic@cmhc-schl.gc.ca
Farm Credit Canada, 1800 Hamilton St., Regina, SK S4P 4L3
306-780-8100, Fax: 306-780-8919, 888-332-3301, csc@fcc-fac.ca
Alberta
Alberta Capital Finance Authority, Sun Life Place, #2160, 10123 - 99 St. NW, Edmonton, AB T5J 3H1
780-427-9711, Fax: 780-422-2175, webacfa@gov.ab.ca
Alberta Enterprise Corporation Board, TD Tower, #1405, 10088 - 102 Ave., Edmonton, AB T5J 2Z2
587-402-6601, Fax: 587-402-6612, 877-336-3474, info@alberta-enterprise.ca
ATB Financial, #2100, 10020 - 100 St. NW, Edmonton, AB T5J 0N3
403-245-8110, 800-332-8383
British Columbia
Provincial Treasury, PO Box 9414 Prov Govt, Victoria, BC V8V 9V1
250-387-4541, Fax: 250-356-3041
Manitoba
Business Services Division, #250, 240 Graham Ave., Winnipeg, MB R3C 0J7
204-945-8200, EMBinfo@gov.mb.ca
Newfoundland & Labrador
Newfoundland & Labrador Department of Finance, Confederation Bldg., PO Box 8700, St. John's, NL A1B 4J6
709-729-3166, finance@gov.nl.ca
Northwest Territories
Northwest Territories Department of Industry, Tourism & Investment, PO Box 1320, Yellowknife, NT X1A 2L9
Nova Scotia
Nova Scotia Farm Loan Board, 74 Research Dr., Truro, NS B6L 2R2
902-893-6506, Fax: 902-895-7693, FLBNS@novascotia.ca

Nunavut
Nunavut Business Credit Corporation, Parnaivak Bldg., #100,
PO Box 2548, Iqaluit, NU X0A 0H0
867-975-7891, Fax: 867-975-7897, 800-758-0038,
credit@nbcc.nu.ca

Ontario
Ontario Electricity Financial Corporation, #1400, 1 Dundas St.
West, Toronto, ON M7A 1Y7
416-325-8000, Fax: 416-325-8005
Ontario Financing Authority, 1 Dundas St. West, 14th Fl.,
Toronto, ON M7A 1Y7
416-325-8000, Fax: 416-325-8005, investor@ofina.on.ca
Ontario Ministry of Agriculture, Food & Rural Affairs, Ontario
Government Bldg., 1 Stone Rd. West, Guelph, ON N1G 4Y2
519-826-3100, Fax: 519-826-4335, 888-466-2372,
about.omafra@ontario.ca

Quebec
Caisse de dépôt et placement du Québec, Édifice
Jacques-Parizeau, 1000, place Jean-Paul-Riopelle, Montréal,
QC H2Z 2B3
514-842-3261, Fax: 514-842-4833, 866-330-3936,
info@cdpq.com
Financement-Québec, 12, rue Saint-Louis, 3e étage, Québec,
QC G1R 5L3
418-691-2203, Fax: 418-644-6214,
financement.regroupe@finances.gouv.qc.ca
La financière agricole de Québec, 1400, boul
Guillaume-Couture, Lévis, QC G6W 8K7
418-838-5602, Fax: 418-833-3871, 800-749-3646

Yukon Territory
Yukon Economic Development, 303 Alexander St., Whitehorse,
YT Y1A 2L5
800-661-0408, ecdev@yukon.ca

FIRE PREVENTION
Fire Safety Testing Facility, National Fire Laboratory, Bldg. U-96,
Concession 8, Mississippi Mills, ON K0A 1A0
613-993-9101

Alberta
Alberta Emergency Management Agency, Terrace Bldg., 9515 -
107 St., 4th Fl., Edmonton, AB T5K 2C1
780-422-9000, Fax: 780-644-1044, -310-0000,
aema@gov.ab.ca

Newfoundland & Labrador
Eastern Regional Service Board, #3, 255 Majors Path, St.
John's, NL A1A 0L5
709-579-7960, Fax: 709-579-5392, info@ersbnl.ca

Northwest Territories
Northwest Territories Department of Municipal & Community
Affairs, PO Box 1320, Yellowknife, NT X1A 2L9

Nova Scotia
Emergency Management Office, PO Box 2581, Halifax, NS B3J
3N5
902-424-5620, Fax: 902-424-5376, 866-424-5620,
emo@novascotia.ca
Office of the Fire Marshal, PO Box 231 Halifax Central, Halifax,
NS B3J 2M4
902-424-5721, Fax: 902-424-3239, 800-559-3473,
ofm@novascotia.ca

Nunavut
Nunavut Emergency Management, PO Box 1000 700, Iqaluit,
NU X0A 0H0
Fax: 867-979-4221, 800-693-1666, NEM@gov.nu.ca

Ontario
Fire Safety Commission, Place Nouveau Bldg., 5775 Yonge St.,
7th Fl., Toronto, ON M2M 4J1
416-325-3100, Fax: 416-314-1217,
info@firesafetycouncil.com
Office of the Fire Marshal & Emergency Management, 25 Morton
Shulman Ave., Toronto, ON M3M 0B1
647-329-1100, Fax: 647-329-1143
Safety, Licensing Appeals & Standards Tribunals Ontario, #401,
20 Dundas St. West, 4th Fl., Toronto, ON M5T 2Z5
Fax: 416-327-6379, 844-242-0608, slastoinfo@ontario.ca

Yukon Territory
Fire & Life Safety / Fire Marshal's Office, 91790 Alaska Hwy.,
PO Box 2703 C-20, Whitehorse, YT Y1A 2C6
867-456-6517, CS.FMO@yukon.ca

FISH & GAME REGULATIONS
Newfoundland & Labrador
Fish Processing Licensing Board, c/o Fish Processing Licensing
Board Secretariat, 30 Strawberry Marsh Rd., St. John's, NL
A1B 4J6
FPLBSecretariat@gov.nl.ca

FISHERIES
Fisheries & Oceans Canada, 200 Kent St., Ottawa, ON K1A 0E6
613-993-0999, Fax: 613-990-1866, info@dfo-mpo.gc.ca
Freshwater Fish Marketing Corporation, 1199 Plessis Rd.,
Winnipeg, MB R2C 3L4
204-983-6601, Fax: 204-983-6497,
sandic@freshwaterfish.com
Gulf Fisheries Centre, 343, av Université, CP 5030, Moncton,
NB E1C 9B6
506-851-6227, Fax: 506-851-2435, info@dfo-mpo.gc.ca

British Columbia
British Columbia Ministry of Agriculture, Food & Fisheries, PO
Box 9043 Prov Govt, Victoria, BC V8W 9E2
888-221-7141, agriservicebc@gov.bc.ca

New Brunswick
New Brunswick Department of Agriculture, Aquaculture &
Fisheries, Agricultural Research Station (Experimental Farm),
PO Box 6000, Fredericton, NB E3B 5H1
506-453-3826, Fax: 506-453-7170, DAAF-MAAP@gnb.ca

Newfoundland & Labrador
Newfoundland & Labrador Department of Fisheries, Forestry &
Agriculture, Petten Bldg., 30 Strawberry Marsh Rd., PO Box
8700, St. John's, NL A1B 4J6
709-729-3705, Fax: 709-729-0360

Northwest Territories
Northwest Territories Department of Environment & Natural
Resources, PO Box 1320, Yellowknife, NT X1A 2L9
867-767-9055, enr_communications@gov.nt.ca

Nova Scotia
Fisheries & Aquaculture Loan Board, 74 Research Dr., Bible Hill,
NS B6L 2R2
902-896-4800
Nova Scotia Department of Fisheries & Aquaculture, #607, 1800
Argyle St., Halifax, NS B3J 2R5
902-424-4560, Fax: 902-424-4671,
aquaculture@novascotia.ca

Ontario
Ontario Fish & Wildlife Heritage Commission, Robinson Pl., 300
Water St., 5th Fl., PO Box 7000, Peterborough, ON K9J 8M5
705-755-1905, Fax: 705-755-1900

Prince Edward Island
Prince Edward Island Department of Agriculture & Land, Jones
Bldg., 11 Kent St., 5th Fl., PO Box 2000, Charlottetown, PE
C1A 7N8
902-368-4880, Fax: 902-368-4857
Prince Edward Island Department of Fisheries & Communities,
548 Main St., PO Box 1180, Montague, PE C0A 1R0
902-838-0983, Fax: 902-838-0972, DeptFC@gov.pe.ca

FISHERIES & WILDLIFE
Beverly & Qamanirjuaq Caribou Management Board,
Secretariat, PO Box 629, Stonewall, MB R0C 2Z0
Committee on the Status of Endangered Wildlife in Canada, c/o
Dept. of Biological Sciences, Simon Fraser University, 8888
University Dr., Burnaby, BC V5A 1S6
Fisheries & Oceans Canada, 200 Kent St., Ottawa, ON K1A 0E6
613-993-0999, Fax: 613-990-1866, info@dfo-mpo.gc.ca
Natural Resources Canada, 580 Booth St., Ottawa, ON K1A 0E4
343-292-6096, Fax: 613-992-7210
North American Bird Conservation Initiative, Canadian Wildlife
Service, 351 St. Joseph Blvd., Gatineau, QC K1A 0H3
819-994-0512, Fax: 819-994-4445,
ec.icoancanada-nabcicanada.ec@canada.ca
North American Waterfowl Management Plan, NAWCC
(Canada) Secretariat, Place Vincent Massey, 351 St. Joseph
Blvd., 14th Fl., Gatineau, QC K1A 0H3
819-938-4030, Fax: 819-934-6017,
ec.pnags-nawmp.ec@canada.ca
Porcupine Caribou Management Board, PO Box 31723,
Whitehorse, YT Y1A 6L3
867-633-4780, Fax: 867-393-3904

Alberta
Alberta Environment & Parks, Forestry Bldg., 9920 - 108th St.,
Main Fl., Edmonton, AB T5K 2M4
780-944-0313

British Columbia
British Columbia Ministry of Environment & Climate Change
Strategy, PO Box 9047 Prov Govt, Victoria, BC V8W 9E2

Manitoba
Endangered Species Advisory Committee, 200 Saulteaux Cres.,
PO Box 24, Winnipeg, MB R3J 3W3
204-945-7775, Fax: 204-945-3077
Manitoba Habitat Heritage Corporation, #200, 1555 St. James
St., Winnipeg, MB R3H 1B5
204-784-4350, Fax: 204-784-7359

New Brunswick
New Brunswick Department of Agriculture, Aquaculture &
Fisheries, Agricultural Research Station (Experimental Farm),
PO Box 6000, Fredericton, NB E3B 5H1
506-453-3826, Fax: 506-453-7170, DAAF-MAAP@gnb.ca

Newfoundland & Labrador
Newfoundland & Labrador Department of Fisheries, Forestry &
Agriculture, Petten Bldg., 30 Strawberry Marsh Rd., PO Box
8700, St. John's, NL A1B 4J6
709-729-3705, Fax: 709-729-0360

Northwest Territories
Northwest Territories Department of Environment & Natural
Resources, PO Box 1320, Yellowknife, NT X1A 2L9
867-767-9055, enr_communications@gov.nt.ca

Nova Scotia
Nova Scotia Department of Lands & Forestry, PO Box 698,
Halifax, NS B3J 2T9
902-424-5935, Fax: 902-424-7735, 800-565-2224

Ontario
Ontario Ministry of Northern Development, Mines, Natural
Resources & Forestry, Natural Resources Information &
Support Centre, 300 Water St., Toronto, ON K9J 8M5
800-667-1940

Prince Edward Island
Prince Edward Island Department of Environment, Energy &
Climate Action, Jones Bldg., 11 Kent St., 4th Fl.,
Charlottetown, PE C1A 7N8
902-368-5044, Fax: 902-368-5830, 866-368-5044,
DeptEECA@gov.pe.ca
Prince Edward Island Department of Justice & Public Safety,
Shaw Bldg. South, 95 Rochford St., 4th Fl., PO Box 2000,
Charlottetown, PE C1A 7N8
902-368-4589, Fax: 902-368-5283, DeptJPS@gov.pe.ca

Quebec
Ministère de l'Agriculture, des Pêcheries et de l'Alimentation du
Québec, 200, ch Sainte-Foy, Québec, QC G1R 4X6
418-380-2110, 888-222-6272,
Ministère des Forêts, Faune et Parcs, Service à la clientèle,
#A409 - 5700, 4e av ouest, Québec, QC G1H 6R1
Fax: 418-644-6513, 844-523-6738,
services.clientele@mrnf.gouv.qc.ca
Société des établissements de plein air du Québec, Place de la
Cité, Tour Cominar, #1300, 2640, boul Laurier, Québec, QC
G1V 5C2
418-686-4875, Fax: 418-643-8177, 800-665-6527,
inforeservation@sepaq.com

Yukon Territory
Yukon Environment, 10 Burns Rd., Whitehorse, YT Y1A 2C6
867-667-5652, Fax: 867-393-7197,
environmentyukon@yukon.ca
Yukon Fish & Wildlife Management Board, 409 Black St., 2nd
Fl., PO Box 31104, Whitehorse, YT Y1A 5P7
867-667-3754, Fax: 867-393-6947, officemanager@yfwmb.ca

FOREST RESOURCES
Natural Resources Canada, 580 Booth St., Ottawa, ON K1A 0E4
343-292-6096, Fax: 613-992-7211

Alberta
Alberta Agriculture & Forestry, JG O'Donoghue Bldg., #100A,
7000 - 113th St., Edmonton, AB T6H 5T6
403-427-7901
Forestry Division, Petroleum Plaza ST, 9915 - 108th St., 10th
Fl., Edmonton, AB T5K 2G8

British Columbia
British Columbia Ministry of Forests, Lands, Natural Resource
Operations & Rural Development, PO Box 9049 Prov Govt,
Victoria, BC V8W 9E2
800-663-7867, FLNRO.MediaRequests@gov.bc.ca
Forestry Innovation Investment Ltd., #1200, 1130 West Pender
St., Vancouver, BC V6E 4A4
604-685-7507, Fax: 604-685-5373, info@bcfii.ca

New Brunswick
New Brunswick Forest Products Commission, Hugh John
Flemming Forestry Centre, PO Box 6000, Fredericton, NB
E3B 5H1
506-453-2196, Fax: 506-457-4966, dnr_mrnweb@gnb.ca

Nova Scotia
Nova Scotia Primary Forest Products Marketing Board, PO Box
698, Halifax, NS B3J 2T9
nspfpmb@gov.ns.ca

Nunavut

Nunavut Territory Department of Environment, PO Box 1000 1320, Iqaluit, NU X0A 0H0
  867-975-7700, Fax: 867-975-7742, environment@gov.nu.ca

Ontario

Algonquin Forestry Authority - Huntsville, 222 Main St. West, Huntsville, ON P1H 1Y1
  705-789-9647, Fax: 705-789-3353, info@algonquinforestry.on.ca

Algonquin Forestry Authority - Pembroke, Victoria Centre, 84 Isabella St., 2nd Fl., Pembroke, ON K8A 5S5
  613-735-0173, Fax: 613-735-4192, info@algonquinforestry.on.ca

Prince Edward Island

Prince Edward Island Department of Environment, Energy & Climate Action, Jones Bldg., 11 Kent St., 4th Fl., Charlottetown, PE C1A 7N8
  902-368-5044, Fax: 902-368-5830, 866-368-5044, DeptEECA@gov.pe.ca

Quebec

Forestier en chef, 845, boul Saint-Joseph, Roberval, QC G8H 2L4
  418-275-7770, Fax: 418-275-8884, bureau@forestierenchef.gouv.qc.ca

Ministère des Forêts, Faune et Parcs, Service à la clientèle, #A409 - 5700, 4e av ouest, Québec, QC G1H 6R1
  Fax: 418-644-6513, 844-523-6738, services.clientele@mrnf.gouv.qc.ca

Yukon Territory

Yukon Energy, Mines & Resources, PO Box 2703, Whitehorse, YT Y1A 2C6
  867-667-3123, Fax: 867-393-7421, 800-661-0408, emr@yukon.ca

Yukon Environment, 10 Burns Rd., Whitehorse, YT Y1A 2C6
  867-667-5652, Fax: 867-393-7197, environmentyukon@yukon.ca

FORESTRY & PAPER

Natural Resources Canada, 580 Booth St., Ottawa, ON K1A 0E4
  343-292-6096, Fax: 613-992-7211

Alberta

Forestry Division, Petroleum Plaza ST, 9915 - 108th St., 10th Fl., Edmonton, AB T5K 2G8

British Columbia

British Columbia Ministry of Forests, Lands, Natural Resource Operations & Rural Development, PO Box 9049 Prov Govt, Victoria, BC V8W 9E2
  800-663-7867, FLNRO.MediaRequests@gov.bc.ca

Forest Practices Board, 310, 1675 Douglas St., PO Box 9905 Prov Govt, Victoria, BC V8W 9R1
  250-213-4700, Fax: 250-213-4725, 800-994-5899, fpboard@gov.bc.ca

Timber Export Advisory Committee, PO Box 9514 Prov Govt, Victoria, BC V8W 9C2
  250-387-8916, Fax: 250-387-5050

Newfoundland & Labrador

Newfoundland & Labrador Department of Industry, Energy & Technology, Natural Resources Bldg., 50 Elizabeth Ave., PO Box 8700, St. John's, NL A1B 4J6
  709-729-3017, Fax: 709-729-0059

Nova Scotia

Nova Scotia Department of Lands & Forestry, PO Box 698, Halifax, NS B3J 2T9
  902-424-5935, Fax: 902-424-7735, 800-565-2224

Ontario

Algonquin Forestry Authority - Huntsville, 222 Main St. West, Huntsville, ON P1H 1Y1
  705-789-9647, Fax: 705-789-3353, info@algonquinforestry.on.ca

Algonquin Forestry Authority - Pembroke, Victoria Centre, 84 Isabella St., 2nd Fl., Pembroke, ON K8A 5S5
  613-735-0173, Fax: 613-735-4192, info@algonquinforestry.on.ca

Ontario Ministry of Northern Development, Mines, Natural Resources & Forestry, Natural Resources Information & Support Centre, 300 Water St., Toronto, ON K9J 8M5
  800-667-1940

Quebec

Ministère de l'Environnement et de la Lutte contre les changements climatiques, Édifice Marie-Guyart, 675, boul René-Lévesque est, 30e étage, Québec, QC G1R 5V7
  418-521-3830, Fax: 418-646-5974, 800-561-1616, relations.medias@mddelcc.gouv.qc.ca

Saskatchewan

Saskatchewan Environment, 3211 Albert St., Regina, SK S4S 5W6
  306-787-2584, Fax: 306-787-9544, 800-567-4224, centre.inquiry@gov.sk.ca

Yukon Territory

Yukon Environment, 10 Burns Rd., Whitehorse, YT Y1A 2C6
  867-667-5652, Fax: 867-393-7197, environmentyukon@yukon.ca

GAS

See Also: Oil & Natural Gas Resources

Gas Turbine Research Facility, c/o National Research Council, 1200 Montreal Rd., Ottawa, ON K1A 0R6
  613-993-9101,

GEOLOGICAL SERVICES

Earth Sciences Sector, 588 Booth St., Ottawa, ON K1A 0Y7

Geological Survey of Canada, 601 Booth St., Ottawa, ON K1A 0E8

Surveyor General Branch - Geomatics Canada, #605, 9700 Jasper Ave., Edmonton, AB T5J 4C3
  780-495-2519, Fax: 780-495-4052

Alberta

Alberta Energy Regulator, #1000, 250 - 5 St. SW, Calgary, AB T2P 0R4
  403-297-8311, Fax: 403-297-7336, 855-297-8311, inquiries@aer.ca

British Columbia

British Columbia Ministry of Energy, Mines & Low Carbon Innovation, PO Box 9060 Prov Govt, Victoria, BC V8W 9E3
  250-952-0628

Northwest Territories

Northwest Territories Geological Survey, 4601B - 52 Ave., PO Box 1320, Yellowknife, NT X1A 2L9
  867-767-9211, Fax: 867-873-2652, ntgs@gov.nt.ca

Nova Scotia

GeoNOVA, 160 Willow St., Amherst, NS B4H 3W5
  902-667-7231, 800-798-0706, geoinfo@novascotia.ca

GOVERNMENT

Auditor General of Canada, 240 Sparks St., Ottawa, ON K1A 0G6
  613-952-0213, Fax: 613-957-0474, 888-761-5953, infomedia@oag-bvg.gc.ca

Bank of Canada, 234 Wellington St., Ottawa, ON K1A 0G9
  613-782-8111, Fax: 613-782-7713, 800-303-1282, info@bankofcanada.ca

Business Development Bank of Canada, #100, 5, Place Ville-Marie, Montréal, QC H3B 5E7
  Fax: 877-329-9232, 877-232-2269

Canada Economic Development for Québec Regions, #500, 800, boul René-Lévesque ouest, Montréal, QC H3B 1X9
  514-283-6412, Fax: 514-283-3302, 866-385-6412

Canada Lands Company Ltd., #1700, 1 University Ave., Toronto, ON M5J 2P1
  416-214-1250, Fax: 416-214-1121

Canada Revenue Agency, 875 Heron Rd., Ottawa, ON K1A 1A2
  800-267-6999

Canadian Intergovernmental Conference Secretariat, 222 Queen St., 10th Fl., PO Box 488 A, Ottawa, ON K1N 8V5
  613-995-2341, Fax: 613-996-6091, info@scics.gc.ca

Canadian Nuclear Safety Commission, 280 Slater St., PO Box 1046 B, Ottawa, ON K1P 5S9
  613-995-5894, Fax: 613-995-5086, 800-668-5284, cnsc.information.ccsn@canada.ca

Committees of the House of Commons, Committees Directorate, House of Commons, 131 Queen St., 6th Fl., Ottawa, ON K1A 0A6
  613-992-3150, cmteweb@parl.gc.ca

Crown-Indigenous Relations & Northern Affairs, Public Enquiries Contact Centre, 10, rue Wellington, Gatineau, QC K1A 0H4
  Fax: 866-817-3977, 800-567-9604, aandc.infopubs.aandc@canada.ca

Defence Construction Canada, Constitution Square, 350 Albert St., 19th Fl., Ottawa, ON K1A 0K3
  613-998-9548, Fax: 613-998-1061, 800-514-3555, info@dcc-cdc.gc.ca

Department of National Defence & the Canadian Armed Forces, National Defence HQ, Major-General George R. Pearkes Bldg., 101 Colonel By Dr., Ottawa, ON K1A 0K2
  613-995-2534, Fax: 613-992-4739, 888-995-2534, information@forces.gc.ca

Elections Canada, 30 Victoria St., Gatineau, ON K1A 0M6
  613-993-2975, Fax: 613-954-8584, 800-463-6868

Federal Public Sector Labour Relations & Employment Board, C.D. Howe Bldg., West Tower, 240 Sparks St., 6th Fl., PO Box 1525 B, Ottawa, ON K1P 5V2
  613-990-1800, Fax: 613-990-1849, 866-931-3454, mail.courrier@fpslreb-crtespf.gc.ca

Finance Canada, 90 Elgin St., Ottawa, ON K1A 0G5
  613-369-3710, Fax: 613-369-4065, fin.financepublic-financepublique.fin@canada.ca

First Nations Tax Commission, Head Office, #321, 345 Chief Alex Thomas Way, Kamloops, BC V2H 1H1
  250-828-9857, Fax: 250-828-9858, 855-682-3682, mail@fntc.ca

Forty-Fourth Parliament - Canada, House of Commons, Parliament Buildings, Ottawa, BC K1A 0A6

Global Affairs Canada, Enquiries Service, 125 Sussex Dr., Ottawa, ON K1A 0G2
  Fax: 613-996-9709, 800-267-8376

Government of Canada, c/o Canada Enquiry Centre, Service Canada, Ottawa, ON K1A 0J9
  800-622-6232

Governor General & Commander-in-Chief of Canada, Rideau Hall, 1 Sussex Dr., Ottawa, ON K1A 0A1
  613-993-8200, Fax: 613-998-8760, 800-465-6890, info@gg.ca

House of Commons, Canada, House of Commons, Centre Block, Parliament Buildings, 111 Wellington St., Ottawa, ON K1A 0A6
  613-992-4793, 866-599-4999, info@parl.gc.ca

Indian Oil & Gas Canada, #100, 9911 Chiila Blvd., Tsuu T'ina, AB T2W 6H6
  403-292-5625, Fax: 403-292-5618, aandc.contactiogc.aandc@canada.ca

Innovation, Science & Economic Development Canada, C.D. Howe Building, 235 Queen St., Ottawa, ON K1A 0H5
  613-954-5031, Fax: 613-954-2340, 800-328-6189, info@ic.gc.ca

International Development Research Centre, 150 Kent St., PO Box 8500, Ottawa, ON K1G 3H9
  613-236-6163, Fax: 613-238-7230, info@idrc.ca

Justice Canada, 284 Wellington St., Ottawa, ON K1A 0H8
  613-957-4222, Fax: 613-954-0811, webadmin@justice.gc.ca

Nunavut Impact Review Board, 29 Mitik St., PO Box 1360, Cambridge Bay, NU X0B 0C0
  Fax: 867-983-2594, 866-233-3033, info@nirb.ca

Nunavut Planning Commission, PO Box 2101, Cambridge Bay, NU X0B 0C0

Office of the Commissioner of Official Languages, 30 Victoria St., 6th Fl., Gatineau, ON K1A 0T8
  819-420-4877, Fax: 819-420-4873, 877-996-6368

Office of the Conflict of Interest & Ethics Commissioner, Commissioner's Office, 66 Slater St., 22nd Fl., PO Box 16, Ottawa, ON K1A 0A6
  613-995-0721, Fax: 613-995-7308, ciec-ccie@parl.gc.ca

Office of the Leader, Bloc Québécois, Centre Block, 111 Wellington St., Ottawa, ON K1A 0A6

Office of the Leader, Green Party of Canada, Confederation Bldg., 229 Wellington St., Ottawa, ON K1A 0A6
  613-996-1119, Fax: 613-996-0850, 866-868-3447, info@greenparty.ca

Office of the Leader, Official Opposition, Conservative Party of Canada / Conservative Party Research Bureau, Centre Block, 111 Wellington St., Ottawa, ON K1A 0A6
  613-995-1333, Fax: 613-995-1337

Office of the Ombudsman, PO Box 90026, Ottawa, ON K1V 1J8
  Fax: 800-204-4193, 800-204-4198

Office of the Prime Minister, Liberal Party of Canada / Liberal Research Bureau, 80 Wellington St., Ottawa, ON K1A 0A2
  Fax: 613-941-6900

Office of the Senate Ethics Officer, Thomas D'Arcy McGee Bldg., #526, 90 Sparks St., Ottawa, ON K1P 5B4
  613-947-3566, Fax: 613-947-3577, 800-267-7362, cse-seo@sen.parl.gc.ca

Office of the Taxpayers' Ombudsman, #600, 150 Slater St., Ottawa, ON K1A 1K3
  613-946-2310, Fax: 613-941-6319, 866-586-3839

Policy Horizons Canada, 360 Albert St., 15th Fl., Ottawa, ON K1R 7X7
  613-947-3800, Fax: 613-995-6006, questions@horizons.gc.ca

Privy Council Office, #1000, 85 Sparks St., Ottawa, ON K1A 0A3
  613-957-5153, Fax: 613-997-5043, info@pco-bcp.gc.ca

Public Service Commission, 22, rue Eddy, Gatineau, QC K1A 0M7
  800-645-5605

Public Services & Procurement, Place du Portage, Phase III, 11, rue Laurier, Ottawa, ON K1A 0S5
  questions@tpsgc-pwgsc.gc.ca

Royal Canadian Mint, 320 Sussex Dr., Ottawa, ON K1A 0G8
  613-954-2626, Fax: 613-998-4130, 800-267-1871

Senate of Canada, Ottawa, ON K1A 0A4
  800-267-7362, sencom@sen.parl.gc.ca

Statistics Canada, 150 Tunney's Pasture Driveway, Ottawa, ON K1A 0T6
  514-283-8300, Fax: 514-283-9350, 800-263-1136, STATCAN.infostats-infostats.STATCAN@canada.ca

The Canadian Ministry, Information Service, Parliament of Canada, Ottawa, ON K1A 0A9
  613-992-4793, 866-599-4999, info@parl.gc.ca

Treasury Board of Canada Secretariat, East Tower, 140 O'Connor St., 9th Fl., Ottawa, ON K1A 0R5
613-957-2400, Fax: 613-941-4000, 877-636-0656,

Alberta

Alberta Apprenticeship & Industry Training Board, Centre for Applied Technologies Bldg., #430, 11763 - 106 St., Edmonton, AB T5G 2R1
403-476-9757, Fax: 780-422-3734, -310-0000

Alberta Infrastructure, Infrastructure Bldg., 6950 - 113th St., Edmonton, AB T6H 5V7
780-415-0507, Fax: 780-427-2187,
Infra.Contact.Us.m@gov.ab.ca

Alberta Municipal Affairs, Communications Branch, Commerce Place, 10155 - 102nd St., 18th Fl., Edmonton, AB T5J 4L4
780-427-2732, Fax: 780-422-1419

Alberta Office of the Auditor General, 9925 - 109th St., 8th Fl., Edmonton, AB T5K 2J8
780-427-4222, Fax: 780-422-9555, info@oag.ab.ca

Alberta Office of the Chief Electoral Officer / Elections Alberta, #100, 11510 Kingsway Ave., Edmonton, AB T5G 2Y5
780-427-7191, Fax: 780-422-2900, -310-0000,
info@elections.ab.ca

Alberta Office of the Ethics Commissioner, #1250, 9925 - 109th St. NW, Edmonton, AB T5K 2J8
780-422-2273, Fax: 780-422-2261,
generalinfo@ethicscommissioner.ab.ca

Alberta Office of the Ombudsman, Canadian Western Bank Bldg., #700, 9925 - 109th St., Edmonton, AB T5K 2J8
780-427-2756, Fax: 780-427-2759, 888-455-2756,
info@ombudsman.ab.ca

Alberta Review Board, #1120, 10235 - 101 St., Edmonton, AB T5J 3E9
780-422-5994, Fax: 780-427-1762

Alberta Treasury Board & Finance, 9820 - 107th St., 9th Fl., Edmonton, AB T5K 1E7
780-427-3035, Fax: 780-427-1147

Executive Council, Legislature Bldg., 10800 - 97th Ave., Edmonton, AB T5K 2B6

Government of Alberta, PO Box 1333, Edmonton, AB T5J 2N2
780-427-2711, service.alberta@gov.ab.ca

Legislative Assembly of Alberta, 9718 - 107th St., Edmonton, AB T5K 1E4
780-427-2826, laocommunications@assembly.ab.ca

Office of the Lieutenant Governor, Office of the Lieutenant Governor of AB, Legislature Bldg., 10800 - 97th Ave., 3rd Fl., Edmonton, AB T5K 2B6
780-427-7243, ltgov@gov.ab.ca

Office of the Premier, Office of the Premier, Legislature Bldg., #307, 10800 - 97th Ave., Edmonton, AB T5K 2B6

Public Service Commission, Peace Hills Trust Tower, 10011 - 109th St., 7th Fl., Edmonton, AB T5J 3S8
780-408-8450

Special Areas Board, Special Areas Board Administration, 212 - 2nd Ave. West, PO Box 820, Hanna, AB T0J 1P0
403-854-5600, Fax: 403-854-5527

Thirtieth Legislature - Alberta, Legislature Bldg., 10800 - 97th Ave., Edmonton, AB T5K 2B6

British Columbia

Agricultural Land Commission, #133, 4940 Canada Way, Burnaby, BC V5G 4K6
604-660-7000, Fax: 604-660-7033,
ALCBurnaby@Victoria1.gov.bc.ca

British Columbia Assessment Authority, #400, 3450 Uptown Blvd., Victoria, BC V8Z 0B9
604-739-8588, Fax: 855-995-6209, 866-825-8322

British Columbia Legislative Assembly & Independent Offices, Clerk's Office, Parliament Bldgs., Victoria, BC V8V 1X4
250-387-3785, Fax: 250-387-0942,
officeoftheclerk@leg.bc.ca

British Columbia Pavilion Corporation, #200, 999 Canada Place, Vancouver, BC V6C 3C1
604-482-2200, Fax: 604-681-9017, info@bcpavco.com

British Columbia Public Service Agency, PO Box 9404 Prov Govt, Victoria, BC V8W 9V1
250-387-0518, Fax: 250-356-7074

British Columbia Treaty Commission, #700, 1111 Melville St., Vancouver, BC V6E 3V6
604-482-9200, Fax: 604-482-9222, 855-482-9200,
info@bctreaty.net

British Columbia Utilities Commission, #410, 900 Howe St., Vancouver, BC V6Z 2N3
604-660-4700, Fax: 604-660-1102, 800-663-1385,
commission.secretary@bcuc.com

Court Services Branch, PO Box 9249 Prov Govt, Victoria, BC V8W 9J2
250-356-1550, Fax: 250-356-8152

Elections British Columbia, PO Box 9275 Prov Govt, Victoria, BC V8W 9J6
250-387-5305, Fax: 250-387-3578, 800-661-8683,
electionsbc@elections.bc.ca

Elections British Columbia, #100, 1112 Fort St., PO Box 9275 Stn Prov Govt, Victoria, BC v8W 9J6
250-387-5305, Fax: 250-387-3578, 800-661-8683,
electionsbc@elections.bc.ca

Executive Council of the Government of British Columbia, PO Box 9487 Prov Govt, Victoria, BC V8W 9W6

Forty-second Legislature - British Columbia, Parliament Buildings, Victoria, BC V8V 1X4
250-387-3785, Fax: 250-387-0942,
officeoftheclerk@leg.bc.ca

Government of British Columbia, Parliament Bldgs., Victoria, BC V8V 1X4
250-387-6121, 800-663-7867

Office of the Auditor General, 623 Fort St., PO Box 9036 Prov Govt, Victoria, BC V8W 9A2
250-419-6100, Fax: 250-387-1230

Office of the Auditor General for Local Government, #201, 10470 - 152nd St., Surrey, BC V3R 0Y3
604-930-7100, info@aglg.ca

Office of the Conflict of Interest Commissioner, 421 Menzies St., 1st Fl., Victoria, BC V8V 1X4
250-356-0750, Fax: 250-356-6580,
conflictofinterest@coibc.ca

Office of the Lieutenant Governor, Government House, 1401 Rockland Ave., Victoria, BC V8S 1V9
250-387-2080, Fax: 250-387-2078, ghinfo@gov.bc.ca

Office of the Ombudsperson, 947 Fort St., 2nd Fl., PO Box 9039 Prov Govt, Victoria, BC V8W 9A5
250-387-5855, Fax: 250-387-0198, 800-567-3247

Office of the Premier & Cabinet Office, PO Box 9041 Prov Govt, Victoria, BC V8W 9E1
250-387-1715, Fax: 250-387-0087, premier@gov.bc.ca

Manitoba

Board of Electrical Examiners, Norquay Bldg., #500, 401 York Ave., Winnipeg, MB R3C 0P8
204-945-3373, Fax: 204-948-2309

Civil Service Commission Board, #935, 155 Carlton St., Winnipeg, MB R3C 3H8
204-945-1435, Fax: 204-945-1486

Crown Corporations Council, #1130, 444 St. Mary Ave., Winnipeg, MB R3C 3T1
204-949-5270, Fax: 204-949-5283, info@crownec.mb.ca

Elections Manitoba, #120, 200 Vaughan St., Winnipeg, MB R3C 1T5
204-945-3225, Fax: 204-945-6011, 866-628-6837,
election@elections.mb.ca

Executive Council, Legislative Bldg., 450 Broadway, Winnipeg, MB R3C 0V8

Finance Research Division, #910, 386 Broadway, Winnipeg, MB R3C 3R6
204-945-3757, Fax: 204-945-5051

Forty-second Legislature - Manitoba, Legislative Bldg., 450 Broadway, Winnipeg, MB R3C 0V8
204-945-3636, Fax: 204-948-2507, clerkla@leg.gov.mb.ca

Government of Manitoba, Legislative Bldg., 450 Broadway, Winnipeg, MB R3C 0V8
204-945-3744, 866-626-4862, mgi@gov.mb.ca

Manitoba Civil Service Commission, #935, 155 Carlton St., Winnipeg, MB R3C 3H8
204-945-2332, Fax: 204-945-1486, 800-282-8069,
csc@gov.mb.ca

Manitoba Land Value Appraisal Commission, #1144, 363 Broadway, Winnipeg, MB R3C 3N9
204-945-5455, Fax: 204-948-2235

Manitoba Legislative Assembly, c/o Clerk's Office, Legislative Bldg., #237, 450 Broadway, Winnipeg, MB R3C 0V8
204-945-3636, Fax: 204-948-2507, clerkla@leg.gov.mb.ca

Manitoba Municipal Board, #1144, 363 Broadway, Winnipeg, MB R3C 3N9
204-945-2941, Fax: 204-948-2235

Manitoba Office of the Ombudsman, Colony Square, #750, 500 Portage Ave., Winnipeg, MB R3C 3X1
204-982-9130, Fax: 204-942-7803, 800-665-0531,
ombudsman@ombudsman.mb.ca

Office of the Auditor General, #500, 330 Portage Ave., Winnipeg, MB R3C 0C4
204-945-3790, Fax: 204-945-2169, contact@oag.mb.ca

Office of the Lieutenant Governor, Legislative Bldg., #235, 450 Broadway, Winnipeg, MB R3C 0V8
204-945-2753, Fax: 204-945-4329, ltgov@leg.gov.mb.ca

Office of the Premier, Legislative Bldg., #204, 450 Broadway, Winnipeg, MB R3C 0V8
204-945-3714, Fax: 204-949-1484, premier@leg.gov.mb.ca

Treasury Board Secretariat, #200, 386 Broadway, Winnipeg, MB R3C 3R6
204-945-4150, Fax: 204-948-4878

New Brunswick

Executive Council, Centennial Bldg., PO Box 6000, Fredericton, NB E3B 5H1
506-444-4417, Fax: 506-453-2266,
executivecounciloffice@gnb.ca

Government of New Brunswick, PO Box 6000, Fredericton, NB E3B 5H1

Intergovernmental Affairs Division, Chancery Place, 675 King St., 5th Fl., Fredericton, NB E3B 1E9
506-444-4948, Fax: 506-453-2995, iga@gnb.ca

Legislative Assembly of New Brunswick, Legislative Bldg., Centre Block, PO Box 6000, Fredericton, NB E3B 5H1
506-453-2506, Fax: 506-453-7154, wwwleg@gnb.ca

Office of the Auditor General, HSBC Place, 520 King St., Fredericton, NB E3B 6G3
506-453-2243, Fax: 506-453-3067, agnb@gnb.ca

Office of the Chief Electoral Officer, Sartain MacDonald Bldg., #102, 551 King St., PO Box 6000, Fredericton, NB E3B 5H1
506-453-2218, Fax: 506-457-4926, 800-308-2922,
info@electionsnb.ca

Office of the Lieutenant-Governor, Government House, PO Box 6000, Fredericton, NB E3B 5H1
506-453-2505, Fax: 506-444-5280, LTgov@gnb.ca

Office of the Ombudsman, 548 York St., PO Box 6000, Fredericton, NB E3B 5H1
506-453-2789, Fax: 506-453-5599, 888-465-1100

Office of the Premier, Centennial Bldg., PO Box 6000, Fredericton, NB E3B 5H1
506-453-2144, Fax: 506-453-7407, premier@gnb.ca

Sixtieth Legislative Assembly - New Brunswick, Centre Block, Legislative Bldg., 706 Queen St., PO Box 6000, Fredericton, NB E3B 5H1
506-453-2506, Fax: 506-453-7154, wwwleg@gnb.ca

Newfoundland & Labrador

Executive Council, c/o Communications Branch, East Block, Confederation Building, 10th Fl., St. John's, NL A1B 4J6
info@gov.nl.ca

Fiftieth House of Assembly - Newfoundland & Labrador, Confederation Bldg., PO Box 8700, St. John's, NL A1B 4J6
709-729-3405, ClerkHOA@gov.nl.ca

Government of Newfoundland & Labrador, Confederation Bldg., St. John's, NL A1B 4J6
info@gov.nl.ca

House of Assembly, c/o Clerk's Office, Confederation Bldg., PO Box 8700, St. John's, NL A1B 4J6
709-729-3405

Newfoundland & Labrador Department of Digital Government & Service NL, 100 Prince Phillip Dr., PO Box 8700, St. John's, NL A1B 4J6
709-729-4834, servicenlinfo@gov.nl.ca

Newfoundland & Labrador Department of Environment & Climate Change, PO Box 8700, St. John's, NL A1B 4J6
ECCInfo@gov.nl.ca

Newfoundland & Labrador Department of Municipal & Provincial Affairs, West Block, Confederation Bldg., PO Box 8700, St. John's, NL A1B 4J6
MAPAInfo@gov.nl.ca

Newfoundland & Labrador Public Service Commission, 261 Kenmount Rd., PO Box 8700, St. John's, NL A1B 4J6
709-729-5810, Fax: 709-729-6234, 855-330-5810,
contactpsc@gov.nl.ca

Office of the Auditor General, PO Box 8700, St. John's, NL A1B 4J6
709-729-2700, oagmail@oag.nl.ca

Office of the Chief Electoral Officer, 39 Hallett Cr., St. John's, NL A1B 4C4
877-729-7987, enl@gov.nl.ca

Office of the Lieutenant Governor, Government House, 50 Military Rd., PO Box 5517, St. John's, NL A1C 5W4
709-729-4494, Fax: 709-729-2234,
governmenthouse@gov.nl.ca

Office of the Premier, East Block, Confederation Bldg., PO Box 8700, St. John's, NL A1B 4J6
709-729-3570, Fax: 709-729-5875, premier@gov.nl.ca

Office of Women & Gender Equality, West Block, Confederation Bldg., 4th Fl., PO Box 8700, St. John's, NL A1B 4J6
709-729-5009, Fax: 709-729-1418

Northwest Territories

Executive Council, PO Box 1320, Yellowknife, NT X1A 2L9
executive_communications@gov.nt.ca

Financial Management Board Secretariat, PO Box 1320, Yellowknife, NT X1A 2L9

Government of the Northwest Territories, PO Box 1320, Yellowknife, NT X1A 2L9
867-767-9000

Nineteenth Legislative Assembly - Northwest Territories, 4570 - 48th St., PO Box 1320, Yellowknife, NT X1A 2L9
867-669-2200, Fax: 867-920-4735, 800-661-0784

Northwest Territories Department of the Executive & Indigenous Affairs, PO Box 1320, Yellowknife, NT X1A 2L9

Northwest Territories Legislative Assembly, 4570 - 48th St., PO Box 1320, Yellowknife, NT X1A 2L9
867-669-2200, 800-661-0784

Office of the Commissioner, 803 Northwest Tower, PO Box 1320, Yellowknife, NT X1A 2L9
867-873-7400, Fax: 867-873-0223, 888-270-3318,
commissioner@gov.nt.ca

Office of the Premier, Legislative Assembly Bldg., PO Box 1320, Yellowknife, NT X1A 2L9

Nova Scotia

Council of Atlantic Premiers, Council Secretariat, #1006, 5161 George St., PO Box 2044, Halifax, NS B3J 2Z1
902-424-7590, Fax: 902-424-8976, info@cap-cpma.ca

Crown Land Information Management Centre, 1701 Hollis St., PO Box 698, Halifax, NS B3J 2T9
902-424-3171, Fax: 902-424-7068, crownland@novascotia.ca

Elections Nova Scotia, #505, 202 Brownlow Ave., Dartmouth, NS B3B 1T5
902-424-8584, Fax: 902-424-6622, 800-565-1504, elections@novascotia.ca

Executive Council Office, One Government Place, 1700 Granville St., 5th Fl., PO Box 2125, Halifax, NS B3J 3B7
902-424-8940, Fax: 902-424-0667, 866-206-6844, Executive.Council@novascotia.ca

Government of Nova Scotia, Province House, 1726 Hollis St., Halifax, NS B3J 2Y3
800-670-4357

Legislative House of Assembly, Province House, 1726 Hollis St., Halifax, NS B3J 2Y3
902-424-5978, Fax: 902-424-0632, info@nslegislature.ca

Nova Scotia Department of Municipal Affairs, PO Box 216, Halifax, NS B3J 2M4
902-424-6642

Nova Scotia Public Service Commission, PO Box 943, Halifax, NS B3J 2V9
902-424-7660, reception-psc@novascotia.ca

Nova Scotia Utility & Review Board, Summit Place, 1601 Lower Water St., 3rd Fl., Halifax, NS B3J 3S3
902-424-4448, Fax: 902-424-3919, 855-442-4448, board@novascotia.ca

Office of Acadian Affairs, Dennis Bldg., 1741 Brunswick St., 3rd Fl., PO Box 682, Halifax, NS B3J 2T3
902-424-0497, Fax: 902-428-0124, 866-382-5811, bonjour@novascotia.ca

Office of the Auditor General, Royal Centre, #400, 5161 George St., Halifax, NS B3J 1M7
902-424-5907, Fax: 902-424-4350

Office of the Lieutenant Governor, Government House, 1451 Barrington St., Halifax, NS B3J 1Z2
902-424-7001, Fax: 902-424-1790, lgoffice@novascotia.ca

Office of the Ombudsman, PO Box 2152, Halifax, NS B3J 3B7
902-424-6780, Fax: 902-424-6675, 800-670-1111, ombudsman@novascotia.ca

Office of the Premier, One Government Place, 1700 Granville St., 7th Fl., PO Box 726, Halifax, NS B3J 2T3
902-424-6600, Fax: 902-424-7648, 800-267-1993, premier@novascotia.ca

Service Nova Scotia & Internal Services, PO Box 2734, Halifax, NS B3J 3K5
902-424-5200, Fax: 902-424-0720, 800-670-4357, askus@novascotia.ca

Sixty-fourth General Assembly - Nova Scotia, Province House, 1726 Hollis St., Halifax, NS B3J 2Y3
902-424-4661, Fax: 902-424-0574

Nunavut

Executive Council, PO Box 2410, Iqaluit, NU X0A 0H0

Fifth Legislative Assembly - Nunavut, PO Box 1200, Iqaluit, NU X0A 0H0

Government of Nunavut, PO Box 1000 200, Iqaluit, NU X0A 0H0
867-975-6000, Fax: 867-975-6099, 877-212-6438, info@gov.nu.ca

Nunavut Legislative Assembly, 926 Federal Rd., PO Box 1200, Iqaluit, NU X0A 0H0
867-975-5000, Fax: 867-975-5190, 877-334-7266, leginfo@assembly.nu.ca

Nunavut Territory Department of Community & Government Services, W.G. Brown Bldg., 4th Fl., PO Box 1000 700, Iqaluit, NU X0A 0H0
867-975-5406, Fax: 867-975-5305, cgscomms@gov.nu.ca

Nunavut Territory Department of Culture & Heritage, PO Box 1000 800, Iqaluit, NU X0A 0H0
867-975-5500, Fax: 867-975-5504, 866-934-2035

Nunavut Territory Department of Education, Bldg. 1107, 2nd Fl., PO Box 1000 900, Iqaluit, NU X0A 0H0
867-975-5600, Fax: 867-975-5605, info.edu@gov.nu.ca

Nunavut Territory Department of Environment, PO Box 1000 1320, Iqaluit, NU X0A 0H0
867-975-7700, Fax: 867-975-7742, environment@gov.nu.ca

Nunavut Territory Department of Executive & Intergovernmental Affairs, 1084 Aeroplex bldg., PO Box 1000 200, Iqaluit, NU X0A 0H0
867-975-6000, Fax: 867-975-6099

Nunavut Territory Department of Finance, PO Box 1000 430, Iqaluit, NU X0A 0H0
867-975-6222, Fax: 867-975-6220, 888-668-9993, gnhr@gov.nu.ca

Nunavut Territory Department of Health, PO Box 1000 1000, Iqaluit, NU X0A 0H0
867-975-5700, Fax: 867-975-5705, 800-661-0833

Office of the Commissioner, PO Box 2379, Iqaluit, NU X0A 0H0
867-975-5120, Fax: 867-975-5123, nunavutcommissioner@gov.nu.ca

Office of the Premier, PO Box 2410, Iqaluit, NU X0A 0H0
867-975-5050, Fax: 867-975-5051

Ontario

Cabinet of Ontario, Legislative Bldg., Queen's Park, Toronto, ON M7A 1A1

Cancer Care Ontario, 620 University Ave., 15th Fl., Toronto, ON M5G 2L7
416-971-9800, Fax: 416-971-6888,

Elections Ontario, 51 Rolark Dr., Toronto, ON M1R 3B1
416-326-6300, Fax: 416-326-6200, 888-668-8683, info@elections.on.ca

Forty-second Provincial Parliament - Ontario, Clerk's Office, #104, Legislative Bldg., Queen's Park, Toronto, ON M7A 1A2
416-325-7500, Fax: 416-325-7489, web@ola.org

Government of Ontario, Queen's Park, Toronto, ON M7A 1A2
416-326-1234, 800-267-8097

Municipal Services Division, 777 Bay St., 16th Fl., Toronto, ON M5G 2E5
Fax: 416-585-6445

Office of the Auditor General, #1530, 20 Dundas St. West, 15th Fl., Toronto, ON M5G 2C2
416-327-2381, Fax: 416-327-9862, comments@auditor.on.ca

Office of the Integrity Commissioner, #2100, 2 Bloor St. West, Toronto, ON M4W 3E2
416-314-8983, Fax: 416-314-8987, 866-884-4470, info@oico.on.ca

Office of the Lieutenant Governor, Legislative Bldg., Queen's Park, Toronto, ON M7A 1A1
416-325-7780, lt.gov@ontario.ca

Office of the Ombudsman, Bell Trinity Sq., South Tower, 483 Bay St., 10th Fl., Toronto, ON M5G 2C9
416-586-3300, Fax: 416-586-3485, 800-263-1830, info@ombudsman.on.ca

Office of the Premier, Legislative Bldg., Queen's Park, Toronto, ON M7A 1A1
416-325-1941

Ontario Legislative Assembly, c/o Clerk of the Legislative Assembly, #104, Legislative Bldg., Queen's Park, Toronto, ON M7A 1A2
416-325-7500, Fax: 416-325-7489, web@ola.org

Ontario Mental Health Foundation, 441 Jarvis St., 2nd Fl., Toronto, ON M4Y 2G8
416-920-7721, Fax: 416-920-0026

Ontario Ministry of Infrastructure, 777 Bay St., 5th Fl., Toronto, ON M5G 2C8
416-327-4412

Ontario Ministry of Intergovernmental Affairs, Legislative Bldg., #223, 223 Queen's Park, Toronto, ON M7A 1A4
416-326-1234, 800-268-7095

Ontario Ministry of Municipal Affairs & Housing, College Park, 777 Bay St., 17th Fl., Toronto, ON M7A 2J3
416-585-7041, Fax: 416-585-4230, mininfo@ontario.ca

Ontario Pension Board, Sun Life Bldg., #2200, 200 King St. West, Toronto, ON M5H 3X6
416-364-8558, Fax: 416-364-7578, 800-668-6203, office.services@opb.ca

Public Service Commission, Whitney Block, 99 Wellesley St. West, 5th Fl., Toronto, ON M7A 1W4
416-325-1750

Treasury Board Secretariat, 315 Front St. West, 7th Fl., Toronto, ON M7A 0B8

Prince Edward Island

Elections Prince Edward Island, Atlantic Technology Centre, #160, 176 Great George St., Charlottetown, PE C1A 4K3
902-368-5895, Fax: 902-368-6500, 888-234-8783

Executive Council, Shaw Bldg., 5th Fl., PO Box 2000, Charlottetown, PE C1A 7N8
902-368-4502, Fax: 902-368-6118

Government of Prince Edward Island, Island Information Service, PO Box 2000, Charlottetown, PE C1A 7N8
902-368-4000, 800-236-5196, island@gov.pe.ca

Office of the Conflict of Interest Commissioner, 197 Richmond St., 1st Fl., PO Box 2000, Charlottetown, PE C1A 7N8
902-368-5970, Fax: 902-368-5175

Office of the Premier, Shaw Bldg., 95 Rochford St. South, 5th Fl., PO Box 2000, Charlottetown, PE C1A 7N8
902-368-4400, Fax: 902-368-4416, premier@gov.pe.ca

Prince Edward Island Legislative Assembly, 197 Richmond St., PO Box 2000, Charlottetown, PE C1A 7N8
902-368-5970, Fax: 902-368-5175, assembly@assembly.pe.ca

Public Service Commission, Shaw Bldg. North, 105 Rochford St., 1st Fl., PO Box 2000, Charlottetown, PE C1A 7N8
902-368-4080, Fax: 902-368-4383

Sixty-sixth General Assembly - Prince Edward Island, Province House, 165 Richmond St., 1st Fl., PO Box 2000, Charlottetown, PE C1A 7N8
902-368-5970, Fax: 902-368-5175, 877-315-5518

Quebec

Bureau du coroner, Édifice le Delta 2, #390, 2875, boul Laurier, Québec, QC G1V 5B1
Fax: 418-643-6174, 888-267-6637, clientele.coroner@msp.gouv.qc.ca

Cabinet du Lieutenant-gouverneur, Édifice André-Laurendeau, 1050, rue des Parlementaires R.C., Québec, QC G1A 1A1
418-643-5385, Fax: 418-644-4677, 866-791-0766, infoCLG@mce.gouv.qc.ca

Cabinet du premier ministre, Édifice Honoré-Mercier, 835, boul René-Lévesque est, 3e étage, Québec, QC G1A 1B4
418-643-5321, Fax: 418-643-3924

Centre de recherche industrielle du Québec, 333, rue Franquet, Québec, QC G1P 4C7
418-659-1550, Fax: 418-652-2251, 800-667-2386, infocriq@criq.qc.ca

Centre du services partagés du Québec, 875, Grande Allée est, 4e étage, section 4.550, Québec, QC G1R 5W5
418-644-2777, Fax: 418-644-0462, 855-644-2777, cspq@cspq.gouv.qc.ca

Comité de déontologie policière, Tour du Saint-Laurent, #A-200, 2525, boul Laurier, 2e étage, Québec, QC G1V 4Z6
418-646-1936, Fax: 418-528-0987, comite.deontologie@msp.gouv.qc.ca

Commissaire à la déontologie policière, #1.06, 2535, boul Laurier, Québec, QC G1V 4M3
418-643-7897, Fax: 418-528-9473, 877-237-7897, deontologie-policiere.quebec@msp.gouv.qc.ca

Commission de la fonction publique, 800, Place D'Youville, 7e étage, Québec, QC G1R 3P4
418-643-1425, Fax: 418-643-7264, 800-432-0432, cfp@cfp.gouv.qc.ca

Commission de la fonction publique (Québec), 800, Place d'Youville, 7e étage, Québec, QC G1R 3P4
418-643-1425, Fax: 418-643-7264, 800-432-0432, cfp@cfp.gouv.qc.ca

Commission des droits de la personne et des droits de la jeunesse, 360, rue Saint-Jacques, 2e étage, Montréal, QC H2Y 1P5
514-873-5146, Fax: 514-873-6032, 800-361-6477, information@cdpdj.qc.ca

Commission québécoise des libérations conditionnelles, #1.32A, 300, boul Jean-Lesage, Québec, QC G1K 8K6
418-646-8300, Fax: 418-643-7217, cqlc@cqlc.gouv.qc.ca

Directeur général des Élections du Québec, Édifice René-Lévesque, 3460, rue de la Pérade, Québec, QC G1X 3Y5
418-528-0422, Fax: 418-643-7291, 888-353-2846, info@electionsquebec.qc.ca

École nationale de police du Québec, 350, rue Marguerite-d'Youville, Nicolet, QC J3T 1X4
819-293-8631, Fax: 819-293-8630, courriel@enpq.qc.ca

Financement-Québec, 12, rue Saint-Louis, 3e étage, Québec, QC G1R 5L3
418-691-2203, Fax: 418-644-6214, financement.regroupe@finances.gouv.qc.ca

Gouvernement du Québec, Hôtel du Parlement, 1045, rue des Parlementaires, Québec, QC G1A 1A3
418-644-4545, 877-644-4545

Institut de la statistique du Québec, 200, ch Ste-Foy, 3e étage, Québec, QC G1R 5T4
418-691-2401, Fax: 418-643-4129, 800-463-4090

L'Assemblée nationale, Hôtel du Parlement, 1045, rue des Parlementaires, Québec, QC G1A 1A3
418-643-7239, Fax: 418-646-4271, 866-337-8837, renseignements@assnat.qc.ca

Ministère de l'Immigration, de la Francisation et de l'Intégration, 285, rue Notre-Dame ouest, 4e étage, Montréal, QC H2Y 1T8
877-864-9191

Ministère des affaires municipales et Habitation, Aile Chaveau, 10, rue Pierre-Olivier-Chauveau, Québec, QC G1R 4J3
418-691-2015, Fax: 418-643-7385, communications@mamrot.gouv.qc.ca

Ministère des Finances, 12, rue Saint-Louis, Québec, QC G1R 5L3
418-528-9323, Fax: 418-646-1631, info@finances.gouv.qc.ca

Ministère des Relations internationales et Francophonie, Édifice Hector-Fabre, 525, boul Réne-Lévesque est, Québec, QC G1R 5R9
418-649-2300, Fax: 418-649-2656

Ministère de l'Énergie et des Ressources naturelles, Service à la clientèle, 5700, 4e av ouest, #A301, Québec, QC G1H 6R1
866-248-6936, services.clientele@mern.gouv.qc.ca

Ministère du Conseil exécutif, 875, Grande Allée est, Québec, QC G1R 4Y8
418-644-7600, communic@mce.gouv.qc.ca

Quarante-deuxième assemblée nationale, Hôtel du Parlement, 1045, rue des Parlementaires, Québec, QC G1A 1A4
418-643-7239, Fax: 418-646-4271, 866-337-8837

Régie des alcools, des courses et des jeux, 560, boul Charest est, Québec, QC G1K 3J3
418-643-7667, Fax: 418-643-5971, 800-363-0320

Secrétariat du Québec aux relations canadiennes, 875, Grande Allée est, 3e étage, Québec, QC G1R 4Y8
418-643-4011, Fax: 418-528-0052
Société des alcools du Québec, 7500, rue Tellier, Montréal, QC H1N 3W5
514-254-2020, 866-873-2020

Saskatchewan
Board of Revenue Commissioners, #480, 2151 Scarth St., Regina, SK S4P 2H8
306-787-6221, Fax: 306-787-1610
Elections Saskatchewan, #301, 3303 Hillsdale St., Regina, SK S4S 6W9
306-787-4000, Fax: 306-787-4052, 877-958-8683, info@elections.sk.ca
Executive Council, Communications Services, Executive Council, #130, 3085 Albert St., Regina, SK S4S 0B1
Government of Saskatchewan, 2405 Legislative Dr., Regina, SK S4S 0B3
Legislative Assembly of Saskatchewan, Office of the Clerk, Legislative Bldg., #239, 2405 Legislative Dr., Regina, SK S4S 0B3
info@legassembly.sk.ca
Office of the Lieutenant Governor, Government House, 4607 Dewdney Ave., Regina, SK S4T 1B7
306-787-4070, Fax: 306-787-7716, lgo@ltgov.sk.ca
Office of the Premier, Legislative Bldg., #226, 2405 Legislative Dr., Regina, SK S4S 0B3
306-787-9433, Fax: 306-787-0885,
Ombudsman Saskatchewan, #500, 2103 - 11th Ave., Regina, SK S4P 3Z8
306-787-6211, Fax: 306-787-9090, 800-667-9787, ombreg@ombudsman.sk.ca
Provincial Auditor Saskatchewan, Chateau Tower, #1500, 1920 Broad St., Regina, SK S4P 3V2
306-787-6398, Fax: 306-787-6383, info@auditor.sk.ca
Twenty-ninth Legislature - Saskatchewan, Legislative Bldg., 2405 Legislative Dr., Regina, SK S4S 0B3

Yukon Territory
Executive Council, 2071 - 2nd Ave., PO Box 2703, Whitehorse, YT Y1A 2C6
eco@yukon.ca
Government of the Yukon Territory, PO Box 2703, Whitehorse, YT Y1A 2C6
867-667-5811, 800-661-0408, inquiry.desk@yukon.ca
Office of the Commissioner of Yukon, Taylor House, 412 Main St., Whitehorse, YT Y1A 2B7
867-667-5121, commissioner@yukon.ca
Office of the Premier, 2071 - 2nd Ave., PO Box 2703, Whitehorse, YT Y1A 2C6
Thirty-fifth Legislative Assembly - Yukon Territory, Yukon Legislative Assembly Office, 2071 - 2nd Ave., PO Box 2703, Whitehorse, YT Y1A 2C6
Yukon Legislative Assembly, 2071 - 2nd Ave., PO Box 2703, Whitehorse, YT Y1A 2C6
867-667-5498, yla@yukon.ca
Yukon Public Service Commission, 2071 - 2nd Ave., PO Box 2703, Whitehorse, YT Y1A 2C6
867-667-5653, Fax: 867-667-5755, pscwebsite@yukon.ca

GOVERNMENT (GENERAL INFORMATION)
Auditor General of Canada, 240 Sparks St., Ottawa, ON K1A 0G6
613-952-0213, Fax: 613-957-0474, 888-761-5953, infomedia@oag-bvg.gc.ca
Correctional Service Canada, 340 Laurier Ave. West, Ottawa, ON K1A 0P9
613-992-5891, Fax: 613-943-1630
Crown-Indigenous Relations & Northern Affairs, Public Enquiries Contact Centre, 10, rue Wellington, Gatineau, QC K1A 0H4
Fax: 866-817-3977, 800-567-9604, aadnc.infopubs.aandc@canada.ca
Department of National Defence & the Canadian Armed Forces, National Defence HQ, Major-General George R. Pearkes Bldg., 101 Colonel By Dr., Ottawa, ON K1A 0K2
613-995-2534, Fax: 613-992-4739, 888-995-2534, information@forces.gc.ca
Employment & Social Development Canada, 140, promenade du Portage, Gatineau, QC K1A 0J9
Environment & Climate Change Canada, 200, rue Sacré-Coeur, 12th Fl., Gatineau, QC K1A 0H3
819-938-3860, 800-668-6767, eec.enviroinfo.ec@canada.ca
Fisheries & Oceans Canada, 200 Kent St., Ottawa, ON K1A 0E6
613-993-0999, Fax: 613-990-1866, info@dfo-mpo.gc.ca
Global Affairs Canada, Enquiries Service, 125 Sussex Dr., Ottawa, ON K1A 0G2
Fax: 613-996-9709, 800-267-8376
Health Canada, Address Locator 0900C2, Ottawa, ON K1A 0K9
613-957-2991, Fax: 613-941-5366, 866-225-0709, info@hc-sc.gc.ca

House of Commons, Canada, House of Commons, Centre Block, Parliament Buildings, 111 Wellington St., Ottawa, ON K1A 0A6
613-992-4793, 866-599-4999, info@parl.gc.ca
Immigration, Refugees & Citizenship, Jean Edmonds, South Tower, 365 Laurier Ave. West, Ottawa, ON K1A 1L1
888-242-2100
Innovation, Science & Economic Development Canada, C.D. Howe Building, 235 Queen St., Ottawa, ON K1A 0H5
613-954-5031, Fax: 613-954-2340, 800-328-6189, info@ic.gc.ca
Office of the Prime Minister, Liberal Party of Canada / Liberal Research Bureau, 80 Wellington St., Ottawa, ON K1A 0A2
Fax: 613-941-6900
Service Canada, 140, promenade du Portage, Gatineau, QC K1A 0J9
800-622-6232
Statistics Canada, 150 Tunney's Pasture Driveway, Ottawa, ON K1A 0T6
514-283-8300, Fax: 514-283-9350, 800-263-1136, STATCAN.infostats-infostats.STATCAN@canada.ca
Transport Canada, Place de Ville, 330 Sparks St., Ottawa, ON K1A 0N5
613-990-2309, Fax: 613-954-4731, 866-995-9737
Treasury Board of Canada Secretariat, East Tower, 140 O'Connor St., 9th Fl., Ottawa, ON K1A 0R5
613-957-2400, Fax: 613-941-4000, 877-636-0656
Veterans Affairs Canada, 161 Grafton St., PO Box 7700, Charlottetown, PE C1A 8M9
613-996-2242, 866-522-2122, information@vac-acc.gc.ca

Alberta
Service Alberta, Government of Alberta, PO Box 1333, Edmonton, AB T5J 2N2
780-427-4088, -310-0000, service.alberta@gov.ab.ca

British Columbia
Service B.C., PO Box 9804 Prov Govt, Victoria, BC V8W 9W1
250-387-6121, Fax: 250-387-5633, 800-663-7867

New Brunswick
Service New Brunswick, Lincoln Place, PO Box 1998, Fredericton, NB E3B 5G4
506-684-7901, 888-762-8600, snb@snb.ca

Newfoundland & Labrador
Newfoundland & Labrador Department of Digital Government & Service NL, 100 Prince Phillip Dr., PO Box 8700, St. John's, NL A1B 4J6
709-729-4834, servicenlinfo@gov.nl.ca

Nova Scotia
Nova Scotia Department of Municipal Affairs, PO Box 216, Halifax, NS B3J 2M4
902-424-6642
Service Nova Scotia & Internal Services, PO Box 2734, Halifax, NS B3J 3K5
902-424-5200, Fax: 902-424-0720, 800-670-4357, askus@novascotia.ca

Nunavut
Nunavut Territory Department of Executive & Intergovernmental Affairs, 1084 Aeroplex bldg., PO Box 1000 200, Iqaluit, NU X0A 0H0
867-975-6000, Fax: 867-975-6099

Ontario
ServiceOntario, College Park, 777 Bay St., 15th Fl., Toronto, ON M7A 2J3
Fax: 416-326-1313, 800-267-8097

Quebec
Services Québec, Bureau de la qualité, 800, Place D'Youville, 20e étage, Québec, QC G1R 3P4
418-644-4545, 877-644-4545

Yukon Territory
Government Inquiry Office, Government of Yukon Administration Bldg., 2071 - 2nd Ave., PO Box 2703, Whitehorse, YT Y1A 2C6
867-393-6930, 800-661-0408, inquiry.desk@yukon.ca

GOVERNMENT PURCHASING
See Also: Purchasing
Public Services & Procurement, Place du Portage, Phase III, 11, rue Laurier, Ottawa, ON K1A 0S5
questions@tpsgc-pwgsc.gc.ca
Saskatchewan
SaskBuilds & Procurement, 1920 Rose St., Regina, SK S4P 0A9
306-787-6911, Fax: 306-787-1061, cs.receptioncenturyplaza@gov.sk.ca

GRANTS & SUBSIDIES
See Also: Student Aid
Atlantic Canada Opportunities Agency, Blue Cross Centre, 644 Main St., 3rd Fl., PO Box 6051, Moncton, NB E1C 9J8
506-851-2271, Fax: 506-851-7403, 800-561-7862, ACOA.information.APECA@canada.ca

Business Development Bank of Canada, #100, 5, Place Ville-Marie, Montréal, QC H3B 5E7
Fax: 877-329-9232, 877-232-2269,
Canada Council for the Arts, 150 Elgin St., 2nd Fl., PO Box 1047, Ottawa, ON K1P 5V8
613-566-4414, Fax: 613-566-4390, 800-263-5588, info@canadacouncil.ca
Canada Economic Development for Québec Regions, #500, 800, boul René-Lévesque ouest, Montréal, QC H3B 1X9
514-283-6412, Fax: 514-283-3302, 866-385-6412
Canada Mortgage & Housing Corporation, 700 Montreal Rd., Ottawa, ON K1A 0P7
613-748-2000, Fax: 613-748-2098, 800-668-2642, chic@cmhc-schl.gc.ca
Canadian Institutes of Health Research, 160 Elgin St., 10th Fl., Ottawa, ON K1A 0W9
613-954-1968, Fax: 613-954-1800, 888-603-4178, support@cihr-irsc.gc.ca
International Development Research Centre, 150 Kent St., PO Box 8500, Ottawa, ON K1G 3H9
613-236-6163, Fax: 613-238-7230, info@idrc.ca
National Film Board of Canada, Operational Headquarters, Norman McLaren Building, 3155, ch de la Côte-de-Liesse, PO Box 1600 Centre-ville, Montréal, QC H3C 3H5
514-283-9000, 800-267-7710
Natural Sciences & Engineering Research Council of Canada, 350 Albert St., 16th Fl., Ottawa, ON K1A 1H5
613-995-4273, Fax: 613-992-5337, 855-275-2861
Networks of Centres of Excellence of Canada, 350 Albert Street, 16th Fl., Ottawa, ON K1A 1H5
613-995-6010, Fax: 613-992-7356, info@nce-rce.gc.ca
Western Economic Diversification Canada, Canada Place, #1500, 9700 Jasper Ave. NW, Edmonton, AB T5J 4H7
780-495-4164, Fax: 780-495-4557, 888-338-9378, WD.contactus-contactez-nous.DEO@canada.ca

Alberta
Municipal Assessment & Grants Division, Commerce Place, 10155 - 102nd St., 15th Fl., Edmonton, AB T5J 4L4

Nova Scotia
Nova Scotia Department of Finance & Treasury Board, Provincial Bldg., 1723 Hollis St., 7th Fl., PO Box 187, Halifax, NS B3J 2N3
902-424-5554, Fax: 902-424-0635, FinanceWeb@novascotia.ca

Ontario
Ontario Trillium Foundation, 800 Bay St., 5th Fl., Toronto, ON M5S 3A9
416-963-4927, Fax: 416-963-8781, 800-263-2887, otf@otf.ca

Saskatchewan
Saskatchewan Energy & Resources, #1000, 2103 - 11th Ave., Regina, SK S4P 3Z8

HAZARDOUS MATERIALS
Atomic Energy of Canada Limited, Head Office, Chalk River Laboratories, 286 Plant Rd., Chalk River, ON K0J 1J0
888-220-2465, communications@aecl.ca
Canadian Nuclear Laboratories, Head Office, Chalk River Laboratories, 286 Plant Rd., Chalk River, ON K0J 1J0
866-513-2325, communications@cnl.ca
Health Canada, Address Locator 0900C2, Ottawa, ON K1A 0K9
613-957-2991, Fax: 613-941-5366, 866-225-0709, info@hc-sc.gc.ca
Low-Level Radioactive Waste Management Office, 115 Toronto Rd., Port Hope, ON L1A 3S4
905-885-9488

Manitoba
Emergency Measures Organization, #1525, 405 Broadway Ave., Winnipeg, MB R3C 3L6
204-945-4772, Fax: 204-945-4929, 888-267-8298, emo@gov.mb.ca

Ontario
Ontario Ministry of Environment, Conservation & Parks, Ferguson Block, 77 Wellesley St. West, 11th Fl., Toronto, ON M7A 2T5
416-325-4000, Fax: 416-314-6713, 800-565-4923
Pesticides Advisory Committee, Foster Bldg, 40 St. Clair Ave. West, 7th Fl., Toronto, ON M4V 1M2
416-314-9230, Fax: 416-314-9237

HEALTH
Canadian Centre for Occupational Health & Safety, 135 Hunter St. East, Hamilton, ON L8N 1M5
905-572-2981, Fax: 905-572-4500, 800-668-4284
Canadian Centre on Substance Abuse, #500, 75 Albert St., Ottawa, ON K1P 5E7
613-235-4048, Fax: 613-235-8101, info@ccsa.ca
Canadian Food Inspection Agency, 1400 Merivale Rd., Ottawa, ON K1A 0Y9
613-225-2342, 800-442-2342

Health Canada, Address Locator 0900C2, Ottawa, ON K1A 0K9
613-957-2991, Fax: 613-941-5366, 866-225-0709,
info@hc-sc.gc.ca

Medical Device Facilities, Boucherville Research Facilities, 75,
boul de Mortagne, Boucherville, QC J4B 6Y4
450-641-5100

National Seniors Council, Phase IV, 8th Floor, Mail Stop 802,
140, promenade du Portage, Gatineau, QC K1A 0J9
Fax: 819-953-9298, 800-622-6232

Patented Medicine Prices Review Board, Standard Life Centre,
#1400, 333 Laurier Ave. West, PO Box L40, Ottawa, ON K1P
1C1
613-288-9597, Fax: 613-288-9643, 877-861-2350,
PMPRB.Information-Renseignements.CEPMB@pmprb-cepm
b.gc.ca

Public Health Agency of Canada, 130 Colonnade Rd., Ottawa,
ON K1A 0K9
844-280-5020

Veterans Affairs Canada, 161 Grafton St., PO Box 7700,
Charlottetown, PE C1A 8M9
613-996-2242, 866-522-2122, information@vac-acc.gc.ca

Zebrafish Screening Facility, 1411 Oxford St., Halifax, NS B3H
3Z1
902-426-8332

Alberta
Alberta Health, PO Box 1360 Main, Edmonton, AB T5J 2N3
780-427-7164

Alberta Health Advocates, 106th St. Tower, 10055 - 106th St.,
9th Fl., Edmonton, AB T5J 2Y2
780-422-1812, Fax: 780-422-0695, -310-0000,
info@albertahealthadvocates.ca

Alberta Health Services, Corporate Office, North Tower, Seventh
Street Plaza, 10030 - 107th St. NW, 14th Fl., Edmonton, AB
T5J 3E4
780-342-2000, Fax: 780-342-2060, 888-342-2471,
ahs.corp@albertahealthservices.ca

Alberta Innovates, 250 Karl Clark Rd., Edmonton, AB T6N 1E4
877-423-5727, info@albertainnovates.ca

Alberta Seniors & Housing, PO Box 3100, Edmonton, AB T5J
4W3
780-644-9992, Fax: 780-422-5954, 877-644-9992

Health Quality Council of Alberta, #210, 811 - 14 St. NW,
Calgary, AB T2N 2A4
403-297-8162, Fax: 403-297-8258, 855-508-8162,
info@hqca.ca

Occupational Health & Safety Council, Standard Life Centre,
10405 Jasper Ave., Edmonton, AB T5J 3N4
780-415-8690, 866-415-8690

Office of the Chief Medical Officer of Health, ATB Place, 10025
Jasper Ave., 24th Fl., Edmonton, AB T5J 1S6
780-427-5263, Fax: 780-427-7683

Premier's Council on the Status of Persons with Disabilities,
HSBC Building, #1110, 10055 - 106 St., Edmonton, AB T5J
2Y2
Fax: 780-415-0097, 800-272-8841, pcspd@gov.ab.ca

Seniors Advisory Council for Alberta, Standard Life Centre,
#600, 10405 Jasper Ave., 6th Fl., Edmonton, AB T5J 4R7
780-422-2321, Fax: 780-422-8762, -310-0000,
saca@gov.ab.ca

British Columbia
British Columbia Centre for Disease Control, 655 West 12th
Ave., Vancouver, BC V5Z 4R4
604-707-2400, Fax: 604-707-2401, admininfo@bccdc.ca

British Columbia Ministry of Health, PO Box 9639 Prov Govt,
Victoria, BC V8W 9P1
800-663-7867, HLTH.Health@gov.bc.ca

Manitoba
Manitoba Council on Aging, #1610, 155 Carlton St., Winnipeg,
MB R3C 3H8
204-945-6565, 800-665-6565, seniors@gov.mb.ca

Manitoba Drug Standards & Therapeutics Committee, #1014,
300 Carlton St., Winnipeg, MB R3B 3M9
204-786-7233

Manitoba Health & Seniors Care, #100, 300 Carlton St.,
Winnipeg, MB R3B 3M9
204-945-3744, 866-626-4862, mgi@gov.mb.ca

Mental Health & Addictions, Primary Health Care & Seniors, 300
Carlton St., 4th Floor, Winnipeg, MB R3B 3M9
204-788-6666

Office of the Chief Medical Examiner, #210, 1 Wesley Ave.,
Winnipeg, MB R3C 4C6
204-945-2088, 800-282-8069,

New Brunswick
New Brunswick Department of Health, HSBC Place, PO Box
5100, Fredericton, NB E3B 5G8
506-457-4800, Fax: 506-453-5243, Health.Sante@gnb.ca

New Brunswick Department of Tourism, Heritage & Culture,
Marysville Place, 4th Fl., PO Box 6000, Fredericton, NB E3B
5H1
506-453-3115, Fax: 506-444-5760, thctpcinfo@gnb.ca

Premier's Council on the Status of Disabled Persons, #140,
Place 2000, 1st Fl., PO Box 6000, Fredericton, NB E3B 5H1
506-444-3000, Fax: 506-444-3001, 800-442-4412,
pcd-cpmph@gnb.ca

WorkSafeNB, 1 Portland St., PO Box 160, Saint John, NB E2L
3X9
506-632-2200, 800-222-9775, communications@ws-ts.nb.ca

Newfoundland & Labrador
Central Regional Health Authority, 21 Carmelite Rd., Grand
Falls-Windsor, NL A2A 1Y4
709-292-2138, Fax: 709-292-2249, 888-799-2272,
communications@centralhealth.nl.ca

Eastern Regional Health Authority, Health Sciences Centre,
#1345, Prince Philip Dr., Level 1, St. John's, NL A1B 3V6
709-777-6500, 877-444-1399,
client.relations@easternhealth.ca

Health Research Ethics Authority, #200, 95 Bonaventure Ave.,
2nd Fl., St. John's, NL A1B 2X5
709-777-6974, Fax: 709-777-8776, info@hrea.ca

Labrador-Grenfell Regional Health Authority, Administration
Bldg., PO Box 7000 C, Happy Valley-Goose Bay, NL A0P
1C0
709-897-2267, Fax: 709-896-4032

Newfoundland & Labrador Centre for Health Information, 70
O'Leary Ave., St. John's, NL A1B 2C7
709-752-6000, Fax: 709-752-6011, 877-752-6006,
inforequests@nlchi.nl.ca

Newfoundland & Labrador Department of Children, Seniors &
Social Development, PO Box 8700, St. John's, NL A1B 4J6
709-729-0760, Fax: 709-729-0870, CSSDInfo@gov.nl.ca

Newfoundland & Labrador Department of Health & Community
Services, West Block, Confederation Bldg., 100 Prince Philip
Dr., 1st Fl., PO Box 8700, St. John's, NL A1B 4J6
709-729-4984, healthinfo@gov.nl.ca

Provincial Wellness Advisory Council, c/o Department of
Seniors, Wellness & Social Development, PO Box 8700, St.
John's, NL A1B 4J6

Western Regional Health Authority, Corporate Office, 1
Brookfield Ave., Corner Brook, NL A2H 6J7
709-637-5000

Northwest Territories
Northwest Territories Department of Health & Social Services,
PO Box 1320, Yellowknife, NT X1A 2L9

Northwest Territories Health & Social Services Authority, PO
Box 1320, Yellowknife, NT X1A 2L9
867-767-9090, hss_transformation@gov.nt.ca

Nova Scotia
Nova Scotia Advisory Commission on AIDS, Barrington Tower,
1894 Barrington St., Halifax, NS B3J 2L4
902-424-5730, AIDS@novascotia.ca

Nova Scotia Department of Health & Wellness, PO Box 488,
Halifax, NS B3J 2R8
902-424-5818, 800-387-6665

Nova Scotia Medical Examiner Service, Dr. William D. Finn
Centre for Forensic Medicine, 51 Garland Ave., Dartmouth,
NS B3B 0J2
902-424-2722, Fax: 902-424-0607, 888-424-4336

Nunavut
Nunavut Territory Department of Culture & Heritage, PO Box
1000 800, Iqaluit, NU X0A 0H0
867-975-5500, Fax: 867-975-5504, 866-934-2035

Nunavut Territory Department of Health, PO Box 1000 1000,
Iqaluit, NU X0A 0H0
867-975-5700, Fax: 867-975-5705, 800-661-0833

Ontario
Cancer Care Ontario, 620 University Ave., 15th Fl., Toronto, ON
M5G 2L7
416-971-9800, Fax: 416-971-6888

Chiropractic Review Committee, #900, 130 Bloor St. West,
Toronto, ON M5S 1N5
416-929-0409

Consent & Capacity Board, 151 Bloor St. West, 10th Fl.,
Toronto, ON M5S 2T5
416-327-4142, Fax: 416-327-4207, 866-777-7391,
ccb@ontario.ca

Health Quality Ontario, 130 Bloor St. West, 10th Fl., Toronto,
ON M5S 1N5
416-323-6868, Fax: 416-323-9261, 866-623-6868,
info@hqontario.ca

Health Services Information & Information Technology Cluster,
56 Wellesley St. West, 10th Fl., Toronto, ON M5S 2S3
416-314-0234, Fax: 416-314-4182

Health System Quality & Funding Division, Hepburn Block, 80
Grosvenor St., 5th Fl., Toronto, ON M7A 1R3

Medical Eligibility Committee, 151 Bloor St. West, 9th Fl.,
Toronto, ON M5S 1S4
416-327-8512, Fax: 416-327-8524, 866-282-2179

Ontario Mental Health Foundation, 441 Jarvis St., 2nd Fl.,
Toronto, ON M4Y 2G8
416-920-7721, Fax: 416-920-0026

Ontario Ministry of Health, Hepburn Block, 80 Grosvenor St.,
10th Fl, Toronto, ON M7A 2C4
416-327-4327, 800-268-1153

Ontario Ministry of Long-Term Care, 400 University Ave., 6th Fl.,
Toronto, ON M7A 1N3
416-327-4327, Fax: 416-327-8497, 800-268-1153

Ontario Review Board, 151 Bloor St. West, 10th Fl., Toronto, ON
M5S 2T5
416-327-8866, Fax: 416-327-8867, orb@ontario.ca

Pesticides Advisory Committee, Foster Bldg., 40 St. Clair Ave.
West, 7th Fl., Toronto, ON M4V 1M2
416-314-9363, Fax: 416-314-9237

Trillium Gift of Life Network, #900, 522 University Ave., Toronto,
ON M5G 1W7
416-363-4001, Fax: 416-363-4002, 800-263-2833

Prince Edward Island
BIO|FOOD|TECH, 101 Belvedere Ave., PO Box 2000,
Charlottetown, PE C1A 7N8
902-368-5548, Fax: 902-368-5549, 877-368-5548,
biofoodtech@biofoodtech.ca

Health PEI, 16 Garfield St., PO Box 2000, Charlottetown, PE
C1A 7N8
902-368-6130, Fax: 902-368-6136, healthinput@gov.pe.ca

Prince Edward Island Department of Health & Wellness, Shaw
Bldg., 105 Rochford St. North, 4th Fl., Charlottetown, PE C1A
7N8
902-368-6414, Fax: 902-368-4121, DeptHW@gov.pe.ca

Quebec
Bureau du coroner, Édifice le Delta 2, #390, 2875, boul Laurier,
Québec, QC G1V 5B1
Fax: 418-643-6174, 888-267-6637,
clientele.coroner@msp.gouv.qc.ca

Commissaire à la santé et au bien-être, Bureau de Québec,
1005, ch Ste-Fot, 1er étage, Québec, QC G1S 4N4
418-266-5990

Commission des normes, de l'équité, de la santé et de la
sécurité du travail, 524, rue Bourdages, Québec, QC G1M
1A1
Fax: 418-266-4015, 844-838-0808

Héma-Québec, 4045, boul Côte-Vertu, Montréal, QC H4R 2W7
514-832-5000, Fax: 514-832-1025, 888-666-4362

Institut national d'excellence en santé et en services sociaux,
2535, boul Laurier, 5e étage, Québec, QC G1V 4M3
418-643-1339, Fax: 418-646-8349, inesss@inesss.qc.ca

Institut national de santé publique du Québec, 945, av Wolfe,
Québec, QC G1V 5B3
418-650-5115, info@inspq.qc.ca

Ministère de la Santé et des Services sociaux, Direction des
communications, 1075, ch Sainte-Foy, 15e étage, Québec,
QC G1S 2M1
418-644-4545, 877-644-4545

Modernisation des centres hospitaliers universitaires de
Montréal, CHUM, CUSM, CHU Sainte-Justine, #10.049,
2021, rue Union, Montréal, QC H3A 2S9
514-864-9883, Fax: 514-873-7362,
info.construction3chu@mssss.gouv.qc.ca

Régie de l'assurance maladie du Québec, CP 6600, Québec,
QC G1K 7T3
418-646-4636, 800-561-9749

Secrétariat à l'accès aux services en langue anglaise et aux
communautés culturelles, 475, boul de Maisonneuve est,
Montréal, QC H2L 5C4
514-873-5163, Fax: 514-873-9876

Urgences-santé Québec, 6700, rue Jarry est, Montréal, QC H1P
0A4
514-723-5600, info@urgences-sante.qc.ca

Saskatchewan
eHealth Saskatchewan, 2130 - 11th Ave., Regina, SK S4P 0J5
306-337-5000, 855-347-5465

Health Quality Council, Atrium Bldg., Innovation Place, 241, 111
Research Dr., Saskatoon, SK S7N 3R2
306-668-8810, Fax: 306-668-8820, info@hqc.sk.ca

Saskatchewan Health, T.C. Douglas Bldg., 3475 Albert St.,
Regina, SK S4S 6X6
306-787-0146, 800-667-7766, info@health.gov.sk.ca

Saskatchewan Health Research Foundation, Atrium Bldg.,
Innovation Place, #204, 111 Research Dr., Saskatoon, SK
S7N 3R2
639-398-8400, 800-975-1699, info@shrf.ca

Yukon Territory
Yukon Health & Social Services, PO Box 2703, Whitehorse, YT
Y1A 2C6
867-667-3673, Fax: 867-667-3096, 800-661-0408,
hss@yukon.ca

HEALTH & SAFETY
Canadian Centre for Occupational Health & Safety, 135 Hunter
St. East, Hamilton, ON L8N 1M5
905-572-2981, Fax: 905-572-4500, 800-668-4284

Canadian Coast Guard, Centennial Towers, #6S018, 200 Kent St., Ottawa, ON K1A 0E6
613-993-0999, Fax: 613-990-1866, info@dfo-mpo.gc.ca
Canadian Food Inspection Agency, 1400 Merivale Rd., Ottawa, ON K1A 0Y9
613-225-2342, 800-442-2342
Department of National Defence & the Canadian Armed Forces, National Defence HQ, Major-General George R. Pearkes Bldg., 101 Colonel By Dr., Ottawa, ON K1A 0K2
613-995-2534, Fax: 613-992-4739, 888-995-2534, information@forces.gc.ca
Employment & Social Development Canada, 140, promenade du Portage, Gatineau, QC K1A 0J9
Health Canada, Address Locator 0900C2, Ottawa, ON K1A 0K9
613-957-2991, Fax: 613-941-5366, 866-225-0709, info@hc-sc.gc.ca
Impact Assessment Agency of Canada, Place Bell Canada, 160 Elgin St., 22nd Fl., Ottawa, ON K1A 0H3
613-957-0700, Fax: 613-957-0862, 866-582-1884
Public Health Agency of Canada, 130 Colonnade Rd., Ottawa, ON K1A 0K9
844-280-5020
Public Safety Canada, 269 Laurier Ave. West, Ottawa, ON K1A 0P8
613-944-4875, Fax: 613-954-5186, 800-830-3118
Transportation Safety Board of Canada, 200, promenade du Portage, 4e étage, Gatineau, QC K1A 1K8
819-994-3741, Fax: 819-997-2239, 800-387-3557, communications@bst-tsb.gc.ca

Alberta
Alberta Children's Services, Office of the Minister, Legislature Bldg., #204, 10800 - 97th Ave., Edmonton, AB T5K 2B6
Alberta Emergency Management Agency, Terrace Bldg., 9515 - 107 St., 4th Fl., Edmonton, AB T5K 2C1
780-422-9000, Fax: 780-644-1044, -310-0000, aema@gov.ab.ca
Alberta Health, PO Box 1360 Main, Edmonton, AB T5J 2N3
780-427-7164
Corporate Strategies & Services Division, Infrastructure Bldg., 6950 - 113th St., 2nd Fl., Edmonton, AB T6H 5V7
InnoTech Alberta, 250 Karl Clark Rd., Edmonton, AB T6N 1H2
780-450-5111, Fax: 780-450-5333, info@innotechalberta.ca
Occupational Health & Safety Council, Standard Life Centre, 10405 Jasper Ave., Edmonton, AB T5J 3N4
780-415-8690, 866-415-8690
Transportation Safety Board, North Office, Twin Atria Building, 4999 - 98 Ave., Main Fl., Edmonton, AB T6B 2X3
780-427-7178, Fax: 780-422-9739, -310-0000
Workers' Compensation Board, 9912 - 107 St., PO Box 2415, Edmonton, AB T5J 2S5
780-498-3999, Fax: 780-427-5863, 866-922-9221

British Columbia
British Columbia Centre for Disease Control, 655 West 12th Ave., Vancouver, BC V5Z 4R4
604-707-2400, Fax: 604-707-2401, admininfo@bccdc.ca
British Columbia Ministry of Health, PO Box 9639 Prov Govt, Victoria, BC V8W 9P1
800-663-7867, HLTH.Health@gov.bc.ca
Workers' Compensation Board of British Columbia, PO Box 5350 Terminal, Vancouver, BC V6B 5L5
604-276-3100, Fax: 604-276-3247, 888-621-7233

Manitoba
Advisory Council on Workplace Safety & Health, 401 York Ave., 2nd Fl., Winnipeg, MB R3C 0P8
204-945-3446, Fax: 204-948-2209, 866-888-8186, wshcompl@gov.mb.ca
Emergency Measures Organization, #1525, 405 Broadway Ave., Winnipeg, MB R3C 3L6
204-945-4772, Fax: 204-945-4929, 888-267-8298, emo@gov.mb.ca
Manitoba Health & Seniors Care, #100, 300 Carlton St., Winnipeg, MB R3B 3M9
204-945-3744, 866-626-4862, mgi@gov.mb.ca

New Brunswick
New Brunswick Department of Health, HSBC Place, PO Box 5100, Fredericton, NB E3B 5G8
506-457-4800, Fax: 506-453-5243, Health.Sante@gnb.ca
New Brunswick Department of Post-Secondary Education, Training & Labour, Chestnut Complex, PO Box 6000, Fredericton, NB E3B 5H1
506-453-2597, Fax: 506-453-3618, dpetlinfo@gnb.ca
WorkSafeNB, 1 Portland St., PO Box 160, Saint John, NB E2L 3X9
506-632-2200, 800-222-9775, communications@ws-ts.nb.ca

Newfoundland & Labrador
Newfoundland & Labrador Department of Health & Community Services, West Block, Confederation Bldg., 100 Prince Philip Dr., 1st Fl., PO Box 8700, St. John's, NL A1B 4J6
709-729-4984, healthinfo@gov.nl.ca

Newfoundland & Labrador Workplace Health, Safety & Compensation Commission (WorkplaceNL), 146 - 148 Forest Rd., PO Box 9000, St. John's, NL A1A 3B8
709-778-1000, Fax: 709-738-1714, 800-563-9000, info@workplacenl.ca

Northwest Territories
Northwest Territories & Nunavut Workers' Safety & Compensation Commission, Centre Square Tower, 5022 - 49th St., 5th Fl., PO Box 8888, Yellowknife, NT X1A 2R3
867-920-3888, Fax: 867-873-4596, 800-661-0792
Northwest Territories Department of Health & Social Services, PO Box 1320, Yellowknife, NT X1A 2L9

Nova Scotia
Emergency Management Office, PO Box 2581, Halifax, NS B3J 3N5
902-424-5620, Fax: 902-424-5376, 866-424-5620, emo@novascotia.ca
Nova Scotia Department of Advanced Education, 1505 Barrington St., PO Box 697, Halifax, NS B3J 2T8
902-424-5301, Fax: 902-424-2203, lae-correspondence@novascotia.ca
Nova Scotia Department of Health & Wellness, PO Box 488, Halifax, NS B3J 2R8
902-424-5818, 800-387-6665

Nunavut
Nunavut Emergency Management, PO Box 1000 700, Iqaluit, NU X0A 0H0
Fax: 867-979-4221, 800-693-1666, NEM@gov.nu.ca

Ontario
Ontario Ministry of Government & Consumer Services, Mowat Block, 900 Bay St., 6th Fl., Toronto, ON M7A 1L2
416-212-2665, Fax: 416-326-7445, 844-286-8404
Ontario Ministry of Health, Hepburn Block, 80 Grosvenor St., 10th Fl., Toronto, ON M7A 2C4
416-327-4327, 800-268-1153
Ontario Ministry of Labour, Training & Skills Development, 400 University Ave., 14th Fl., Toronto, ON M7A 1T7
416-326-7160, 800-531-5551
Road User Safety Division, Bldg A, 87 Sir William Hearst Ave., Toronto, ON M3M 0B4
416-235-2999, Fax: 416-235-4153

Prince Edward Island
Prince Edward Island Department of Health & Wellness, Shaw Bldg., 105 Rochford St. North, 4th Fl., Charlottetown, PE C1A 7N8
902-368-6414, Fax: 902-368-4121, DeptHW@gov.pe.ca
Prince Edward Island Workers' Compensation Board, 14 Weymouth St., PO Box 757, Charlottetown, PE C1A 7L7
902-368-5680, Fax: 902-368-5696, 800-237-5049

Quebec
Commission des normes, de l'équité, de la santé et de la sécurité du travail, 524, rue Bourdages, Québec, QC G1M 1A1
Fax: 418-266-4015, 844-838-0808
Ministère de la Santé et des Services sociaux, Direction des communications, 1075, ch Sainte-Foy, 15e étage, Québec, QC G1S 2M1
418-644-4545, 877-644-4545
Ministère de la Sécurité publique, Tour des Laurentides, 2525, boul Laurier, 5e étage, Québec, QC G1V 2L2
418-643-2112, Fax: 418-646-6168, 800-361-3795
Ministère du Travail, de l'Emploi et de la Solidarité sociale, 150, rue Monseigneur-Ross, 5e étage, Québec, QC G4X 2S7
514-873-4000, 877-767-8773

Saskatchewan
Saskatchewan Health, T.C. Douglas Bldg., 3475 Albert St., Regina, SK S4S 6X6
306-787-0146, 800-667-7766, info@health.gov.sk.ca
Saskatchewan Labour Relations & Workplace Safety, #300, 1870 Albert St., Regina, SK S4P 4W1
Fax: 306-787-7404,

Yukon Territory
Yukon Health & Social Services, PO Box 2703, Whitehorse, YT Y1A 2C6
867-667-3673, Fax: 867-667-3096, 800-661-0408, hss@yukon.ca
Yukon Workers' Compensation Health & Safety Board, 401 Strickland St., Whitehorse, YT Y1A 5N8
867-667-5645, Fax: 867-393-6279, 800-661-0443, worksafe@yukon.ca

HEALTH CARE INSURANCE

Health Canada, Address Locator 0900C2, Ottawa, ON K1A 0K9
613-957-2991, Fax: 613-941-5366, 866-225-0709, info@hc-sc.gc.ca
British Columbia
Medical Services Commission, PO Box 9652 Prov Govt, Victoria, BC V8W 9P4
250-952-3073, Fax: 250-952-3133

Newfoundland & Labrador
Newfoundland & Labrador Department of Health & Community Services, West Block, Confederation Bldg., 100 Prince Philip Dr., 1st Fl., PO Box 8700, St. John's, NL A1B 4J6
709-729-4984, healthinfo@gov.nl.ca
Northwest Territories
Northwest Territories Department of Health & Social Services, PO Box 1320, Yellowknife, NT X1A 2L9
Nunavut
Nunavut Territory Department of Health, PO Box 1000 1000, Iqaluit, NU X0A 0H0
867-975-5700, Fax: 867-975-5705, 800-661-0833
Ontario
Health Services Information & Information Technology Cluster, 56 Wellesley St. West, 10th Fl., Toronto, ON M5S 2S3
416-314-0234, Fax: 416-314-4182
Prince Edward Island
Prince Edward Island Department of Health & Wellness, Shaw Bldg., 105 Rochford St. North, 4th Fl., Charlottetown, PE C1A 7N8
902-368-6414, Fax: 902-368-4121, DeptHW@gov.pe.ca
Quebec
Régie de l'assurance maladie du Québec, CP 6600, Québec, QC G1K 7T3
418-646-4636, 800-561-9749

HEALTH SERVICES
See Also: Health Care Insurance; Occupational Safety
Canadian Centre for Occupational Health & Safety, 135 Hunter St. East, Hamilton, ON L8N 1M5
905-572-2981, Fax: 905-572-4500, 800-668-4284
Canadian Institutes of Health Research, 160 Elgin St., 10th Fl., Ottawa, ON K1A 0W9
613-954-1968, Fax: 613-954-1800, 888-603-4178, support@cihr-irsc.gc.ca
Health Canada, Address Locator 0900C2, Ottawa, ON K1A 0K9
613-957-2991, Fax: 613-941-5366, 866-225-0709, info@hc-sc.gc.ca
Networks of Centres of Excellence of Canada, 350 Albert Street, 16th Fl., Ottawa, ON K1A 1H5
613-995-6010, Fax: 613-992-7356, info@nce-rce.gc.ca
Public Health Agency of Canada, 130 Colonnade Rd., Ottawa, ON K1A 0K9
844-280-5020
Veterans Affairs Canada, 161 Grafton St., PO Box 7700, Charlottetown, PE C1A 8M9
613-996-2242, 866-522-2122, information@vac-acc.gc.ca
Alberta
Alberta Health, PO Box 1360 Main, Edmonton, AB T5J 2N3
780-427-7164
Alberta Health Advocates, 106th St. Tower, 10055 - 106th St., 9th Fl., Edmonton, AB T5J 2Y2
780-422-1812, Fax: 780-422-0695, -310-0000, info@albertahealthadvocates.ca
Alberta Seniors & Housing, PO Box 3100, Edmonton, AB T5J 4W3
780-644-9992, Fax: 780-422-5954, 877-644-9992
British Columbia
British Columbia Centre for Disease Control, 655 West 12th Ave., Vancouver, BC V5Z 4R4
604-707-2400, Fax: 604-707-2401, admininfo@bccdc.ca
British Columbia Ministry of Health, PO Box 9639 Prov Govt, Victoria, BC V8W 9P1
800-663-7867, HLTH.Health@gov.bc.ca
Medical Services Commission, PO Box 9652 Prov Govt, Victoria, BC V8W 9P4
250-952-3073, Fax: 250-952-3133
Manitoba
Manitoba Health & Seniors Care, #100, 300 Carlton St., Winnipeg, MB R3B 3M9
204-945-3744, 866-626-4862, mgi@gov.mb.ca
Manitoba Health Appeal Board, #102, 500 Portage Ave., Winnipeg, MB R3C 3X1
204-945-5408, Fax: 204-948-2024, 866-744-3257, appeals@gov.mb.ca
Manitoba Healthy Child Office, 332 Bannatyne Ave., 3rd Fl., Winnipeg, MB R3A 0E2
204-945-2266, 888-848-0140, healthychild@gov.mb.ca
New Brunswick
New Brunswick Department of Health, HSBC Place, PO Box 5100, Fredericton, NB E3B 5G8
506-457-4800, Fax: 506-453-5243, Health.Sante@gnb.ca
Newfoundland & Labrador
Central Regional Health Authority, 21 Carmelite Rd., Grand Falls-Windsor, NL A2A 1Y4
709-292-2138, Fax: 709-292-2249, 888-799-2272, communications@centralhealth.nl.ca

Eastern Regional Health Authority, Health Sciences Centre, #1345, Prince Philip Dr., Level 1, St. John's, NL A1B 3V6
709-777-6500, 877-444-1399,
client.relations@easternhealth.ca
Health Research Ethics Authority, #200, 95 Bonaventure Ave., 2nd Fl., St. John's, NL A1B 2X5
709-777-6974, Fax: 709-777-8776, info@hrea.ca
Labrador-Grenfell Regional Health Authority, Administration Bldg., PO Box 7000 C, Happy Valley-Goose Bay, NL A0P 1C0
709-897-2267, Fax: 709-896-4032
Newfoundland & Labrador Centre for Health Information, 70 O'Leary Ave., St. John's, NL A1B 2C7
709-752-6000, Fax: 709-752-6011, 877-752-6006, inforequests@nlchi.nl.ca
Newfoundland & Labrador Department of Children, Seniors & Social Development, PO Box 8700, St. John's, NL A1B 4J6
709-729-0760, Fax: 709-729-0870, CSSDInfo@gov.nl.ca
Newfoundland & Labrador Department of Health & Community Services, West Block, Confederation Bldg., 100 Prince Philip Dr., 1st Fl., PO Box 8700, St. John's, NL A1B 4J6
709-729-4984, healthinfo@gov.nl.ca
Western Regional Health Authority, Corporate Office, 1 Brookfield Ave., Corner Brook, NL A2H 6J7
709-637-5000

Northwest Territories
Northwest Territories Department of Health & Social Services, PO Box 1320, Yellowknife, NT X1A 2L9
Northwest Territories Health & Social Services Authority, PO Box 1320, Yellowknife, NT X1A 2L9
867-767-9090, hss_transformation@gov.nt.ca

Nova Scotia
Nova Scotia Department of Health & Wellness, PO Box 488, Halifax, NS B3J 2R8
902-424-5818, 800-387-6665

Nunavut
Nunavut Territory Department of Health, PO Box 1000 1000, Iqaluit, NU X0A 0H0
867-975-5700, Fax: 867-975-5705, 800-661-0833

Ontario
Health Services Information & Information Technology Cluster, 56 Wellesley St. West, 10th Fl., Toronto, ON M5S 2S3
416-314-0234, Fax: 416-314-4182,

Prince Edward Island
Council of the Association of Registered Nurses of PEI, #6, 161 Maypoint Rd., Charlottetown, PE C1E 1X6
902-368-3764, Fax: 902-368-1430, 844-843-3933, info@arnpei.ca
Council of the College of Physicians & Surgeons of PEI, 14 Paramount Dr., Charlottetown, PE C1E 0C7
902-566-3861, Fax: 902-566-3986
Council of the Denturist Society of PEI, c/o Accu-Bite Denture Clinic, 500 Main St., PO Box 1589, Montague, PE C0A 1R0
902-838-2350
Council of the PEI College of Physiotherapists, PO Box 20078, Charlottetown, PE C1A 9E3
contact@peicpt.com
Dental Council of PEI, 184 Belvedere Ave., Charlottetown, PE C1A 2Z1
902-628-8156, Fax: 902-892-0234, info@dcpei.ca
Dietitians Registration Board, PO Box 362, Charlottetown, PE C1A 7K7
info@peidietitians.ca
Health PEI, 16 Garfield St., PO Box 2000, Charlottetown, PE C1A 7N8
902-368-6130, Fax: 902-368-6136, healthinput@gov.pe.ca
Prince Edward Island College of Optometrists, 15 Ellis Rd., Charlottetown, PE C1A 9B3
902-368-3001, Fax: 902-628-6604, info@peico.ca
Prince Edward Island College of Pharmacists, 375 Trans Canada Hwy., PO Box 208, Cornwall, PE C0A 1H0
902-628-3561, Fax: 902-628-6946, info@pepharmacists.ca
Prince Edward Island Department of Health & Wellness, Shaw Bldg., 105 Rochford St. North, 4th Fl., Charlottetown, PE C1A 7N8
902-368-6414, Fax: 902-368-4121, DeptHW@gov.pe.ca
Prince Edward Island Licensed Practical Nurses Registration Board, #204, 155 Belvedere Ave., Charlottetown, PE C1A 2Y9
902-566-1512
Prince Edward Island Occupational Therapists Registration Board, PO Box 2248 Central, Charlottetown, PE C1A 8B9
Prince Edward Island Psychologists Registration Board, c/o Dept. of Psychology, UPEI, 550 University Ave., Charlottetown, PE C1A 4P3
902-566-0549

Quebec
Héma-Québec, 4045, boul Côte-Vertu, Montréal, QC H4R 2W7
514-832-5000, Fax: 514-832-1025, 888-666-4362

Institut national de santé publique du Québec, 945, av Wolfe, Québec, QC G1V 5B3
418-650-5115, info@inspq.qc.ca
Ministère de la Santé et des Services sociaux, Direction des communications, 1075, ch Sainte-Foy, 15e étage, Québec, QC G1S 2M1
418-644-4545, 877-644-4545

Saskatchewan
eHealth Saskatchewan, 2130 - 11th Ave., Regina, SK S4P 0J5
306-337-5000, 855-347-5465
Saskatchewan Health, T.C. Douglas Bldg., 3475 Albert St., Regina, SK S4S 6X6
306-787-0146, 800-667-7766, info@health.gov.sk.ca
Saskatchewan Health Research Foundation, Atrium Bldg., Innovation Place, #204, 111 Research Dr., Saskatoon, SK S7N 3R2
639-398-8400, 800-975-1699, info@shrf.ca

HERITAGE RESOURCES
See Also: Land Resources; Parks
Canadian Heritage, 15, rue Eddy, Gatineau, QC K1A 0M5
819-997-0055, 866-811-0055,
PCH.info-info.PCH@canada.ca
Parks Canada, National Office, 30, rue Victoria, Gatineau, QC J8X 0B3
819-420-9486, 888-773-8888, information@pc.gc.ca

Manitoba
Heritage Grants Advisory Council, c/o Heritage Grants Program, #330, 213 Notre Dame Ave., Winnipeg, MB R3B 1N3
204-945-2213, Fax: 204-948-2086
Manitoba Heritage Council, c/o Historic Resources Branch, 213 Notre Dame Ave., Main Fl., Winnipeg, MB R3B 1N3
204-945-2118, Fax: 204-948-2384, hrb@gov.mb.ca
Manitoba Sport, Culture & Heritage, Legislative Bldg., #118, 450 Broadway, Winnipeg, MB R3C 0V8

Newfoundland & Labrador
Heritage Foundation of Newfoundland & Labrador, The Newman Bldg., 1 Springdale St., PO Box 5171, St. John's, NL A1C 5V5
709-739-1892, Fax: 709-739-6592, 888-739-1892, info@heritagenl.ca

Nunavut
Nunavut Territory Department of Culture & Heritage, PO Box 1000 800, Iqaluit, NU X0A 0H0
867-975-5500, Fax: 867-975-5504, 866-934-2035

Ontario
Ontario Heritage Trust, 10 Adelaide St. East, Toronto, ON M5C 1J3
416-325-5000, Fax: 416-325-5071
Ontario Ministry of Heritage, Sport, Tourism & Culture Industries, 438 University Ave., 6th Fl., Toronto, ON M5G 2K8
416-326-9326, Fax: 416-314-7854, 888-997-9015

Quebec
Conseil du patrimoine culturel du Québec, 225, Grande Allée est, Québec, QC G1R 5G5
418-643-8378, Fax: 418-643-8591, 844-701-0912, info@cpcq.gouv.qc.ca

Saskatchewan
Provincial Archives of Saskatchewan, PO Box 1665, Regina, SK S4P 3C6
306-787-4068, Fax: 306-787-1975
Provincial Capital Commission, PO Box 7111, Regina, SK S4P 3S7
306-522-3661, Fax: 306-565-2742
Saskatchewan Heritage Foundation, 3211 Albert St., 1st Fl., Regina, SK S4S 5W6
Wanuskewin Heritage Park, RR#4 Penner Rd., Saskatoon, SK S7K 3J7
306-931-6767

Yukon Territory
Yukon Tourism & Culture, PO Box 2703, Whitehorse, YT Y1A 2C6
867-393-7048

HISTORY & ARCHIVES
Canada Council for the Arts, 150 Elgin St., 2nd Fl., PO Box 1047, Ottawa, ON K1P 5V8
613-566-4414, Fax: 613-566-4390, 800-263-5588, info@canadacouncil.ca
Library & Archives Canada, 395 Wellington St., Ottawa, ON K1A 0N4
613-996-5115, Fax: 613-995-6274, 866-578-7777
Library of Parliament, Information Servicce, Parliament of Canada, Ottawa, ON K1A 0A9
613-992-4793, 866-599-4999, info@parl.gc.ca

Ontario
Information, Privacy & Archives Division, 134 Ian Macdonald Blvd., Toronto, ON M7A 2C5
416-327-1600, Fax: 416-327-1999, 800-668-9933

Prince Edward Island
Prince Edward Island Sports Hall of Fame & Museum, Inc. Board, 40 Enman Cres., Charlottetown, PE C1E 1E6
902-393-5474, peisportshall@gmail.com

Quebec
Bibliothèque et Archives nationales du Québec (BAnQ), 475, boul de Maisonneuve est, Montréal, QC H2L 5C4
514-873-1100, Fax: 514-873-9312, 800-363-9028

Saskatchewan
Provincial Archives of Saskatchewan, PO Box 1665, Regina, SK S4P 3C6
306-787-4068, Fax: 306-787-1975,

HOSPITALS
See Also: Health Care Insurance
Alberta
Alberta Health, PO Box 1360 Main, Edmonton, AB T5J 2N3
780-427-7164
British Columbia
British Columbia Ministry of Health, PO Box 9639 Prov Govt, Victoria, BC V8W 9P1
800-663-7867, HLTH.Health@gov.bc.ca
Hospital Appeal Board, 747 Fort St., 4th Fl., PO Box 9425 Prov Govt, Victoria, BC V8W 9V1
250-387-3464, Fax: 250-356-9923, hab@gov.bc.ca
Northwest Territories
Northwest Territories Department of Health & Social Services, PO Box 1320, Yellowknife, NT X1A 2L9
Nunavut
Nunavut Territory Department of Health, PO Box 1000 1000, Iqaluit, NU X0A 0H0
867-975-5700, Fax: 867-975-5705, 800-661-0833
Prince Edward Island
Prince Edward Island Department of Health & Wellness, Shaw Bldg., 105 Rochford St. North, 4th Fl., Charlottetown, PE C1A 7N8
902-368-6414, Fax: 902-368-4121, DeptHW@gov.pe.ca
Quebec
Ministère de la Santé et des Services sociaux, Direction des communications, 1075, ch Sainte-Foy, 15e étage, Québec, QC G1S 2M1
418-644-4545, 877-644-4545

HOUSING
Canada Mortgage & Housing Corporation, 700 Montreal Rd., Ottawa, ON K1A 0P7
613-748-2000, Fax: 613-748-2098, 800-668-2642, chic@cmhc-schl.gc.ca
Canadian Centre for Housing Technology, c/o National Research Council Canada, Building M-20, 1200 Montreal Rd., Ottawa, ON K1A 0R6
British Columbia
British Columbia Housing Management Commission (BC Housing), #1701, 4555 Kingsway, Burnaby, BC V5H 4V8
604-433-1711, Fax: 604-439-4722, webeditor@bchousing.org
British Columbia Ministry of Municipal Affairs, PO Box 9056 Prov Govt, Victoria, BC V8W 9E2
250-387-2283, Fax: 250-387-4312
Building Code Appeal Board, c/o Building & Safety Standards Branch, PO Box 9844 Prov Govt, Victoria, BC V8W 1A4
250-387-3133, Fax: 250-387-8164,
Building.Safety@gov.bc.ca
Local Government, PO Box 9490 Prov Govt, Victoria, BC V8W 9N7
250-356-6575, Fax: 250-387-7973
Safety Standards Appeal Board, 614 Humboldt St., 4th Fl., PO Box 9844 Prov Govt, Victoria, BC V8W 9T2
250-387-4021, Fax: 250-356-6645
Manitoba
Manitoba Families, Legislative Bldg., #357, 450 Broadway, Winnipeg, MB R3C 0V8
204-945-3744, 866-626-4862
New Brunswick
New Brunswick Department of Social Development, Sartain MacDonald Bldg., PO Box 6000, Fredericton, NB E3B 5H1
506-453-2001, Fax: 506-453-2164, sd-ds@gnb.ca
Newfoundland & Labrador
Newfoundland & Labrador Housing Corporation, Sir Brian Dunfield Bldg., 2 Canada Dr., PO Box 220, St. John's, NL A1C 5J2
709-724-3000, Fax: 709-724-3250
Northwest Territories
Northwest Territories Housing Corporation, Scotia Centre, 5102 - 50th Ave., PO Box 2100, Yellowknife, NT X1A 2P6
867-767-9080, Fax: 867-873-9426, 844-698-4663
Nova Scotia
Cape Breton Island Housing Authority, 18 Dolbin St., PO Box 1372, Sydney, NS B1P 6K3
902-539-8520, Fax: 902-539-0330, 800-565-3135

Cobequid Housing Authority, 114 Victoria East, PO Box 753, Amherst, NS B4H 4B9
902-667-8757, Fax: 902-667-1686, 800-934-2445
Eastern Mainland Housing Authority, 7 Campbell's Lane, New Glasgow, NS B2H 2H9
902-752-1225, Fax: 902-752-1315, 800-933-2101
Housing Nova Scotia, Maritime Centre, 1505 Barrington St., 14th Fl., Halifax, NS B3J 3K5
844-424-5110, housingns@novascotia.ca
Nova Scotia Department of Municipal Affairs, PO Box 216, Halifax, NS B3J 2M4
902-424-6642

Nunavut
Nunavut Housing Corporation, Headquarters, PO Box 480, Arviat, NU X0C 0E0
867-857-3000, Fax: 867-857-3040
Nunavut Territory Department of Community & Government Services, W.G. Brown Bldg., 4th Fl., PO Box 1000 700, Iqaluit, NU X0A 0H0
867-975-5406, Fax: 867-975-5305, cgscomms@gov.nu.ca

Ontario
Housing Division, College Park, 777 Bay St., 14th Fl., Toronto, ON M5G 2E5
416-585-6738, Fax: 416-585-6800

Quebec
Société d'habitation du Québec, Aile St-Amable, 1054, rue Louis-Alexandre-Taschereau, 3e étage, Québec, QC G1R 5E7
Fax: 418-643-2533, 800-463-4315

Yukon Territory
Yukon Housing Corporation, 410G Jarvis St., PO Box 2703, Whitehorse, YT Y1A 2H5
867-667-5712, Fax: 867-393-7597, ykhouse@yukon.ca

HUMAN RIGHTS
See Also: Boards of Review
Canadian Human Rights Commission, 344 Slater St., 8th Fl., Ottawa, ON K1A 1E1
Fax: 613-996-9661, 888-214-1090, info.com@chrc-ccdp.gc.ca
Canadian Human Rights Tribunal, 160 Elgin St., 11th Fl., Ottawa, ON K1A 1J4
613-995-1707, Fax: 613-995-3484, registrar@chrt-tcdp.gc.ca
Canadian Museum for Human Rights, 85 Israel Asper Way, Winnipeg, MB R3C 0L5
204-289-2000, Fax: 204-289-2001, 877-877-6037, info@humanrights.ca
National Aboriginal Initiative, #750, 175 Hargrave St., Winnipeg, MA RC3 3R8
204-983-2189, Fax: 204-983-6132, 866-772-4880

Alberta
Alberta Human Rights Commission, Northern Regional Office, Standard Life Centre, #800, 10405 Jasper Ave., Edmonton, AB T5J 4R7
780-427-7661, Fax: 780-427-6013, humanrights@gov.ab.ca

British Columbia
British Columbia Human Rights Tribunal, #1170, 605 Robson St., Vancouver, BC V6B 5J3
604-775-2000, Fax: 604-775-2020, 888-440-8844, BCHumanRightsTribunal@gov.bc.ca

Manitoba
Manitoba Human Rights Commission, #700, 175 Hargrave St., Winnipeg, MB R3C 3R8
204-945-3007, Fax: 204-945-1292, 888-884-8681, hrc@gov.mb.ca

New Brunswick
New Brunswick Human Rights Commission, Barry House, 751 Brunswick St., PO Box 6000, Fredericton, NB E3B 5H1
506-453-2301, Fax: 506-453-2653, 888-471-2233, hrc.cdp@gnb.ca

Newfoundland & Labrador
Newfoundland & Labrador Human Rights Commission, The Beothuk Bldg., 21 Crosbie Pl., PO Box 8700, St. John's, NL A1B 4J6
709-729-2709, Fax: 709-729-0790, 800-563-5808, humanrights@gov.nl.ca

Nova Scotia
Nova Scotia Human Rights Commission, Park Lane Terrace, #305, 5657 Spring Garden Rd., PO Box 2221, Halifax, NS B3J 3C4
902-424-4111, Fax: 902-424-0596, 877-269-7699, hrcinquiries@novascotia.ca

Nunavut
Nunavut Human Rights Tribunal, PO Box 15, Coral Harbour, NU X0C 0C0
866-413-6478, nunavuthumanrights@gov.nu.ca

Ontario
Ontario Human Rights Commission, 180 Dundas St. West, 9th Fl., Toronto, ON M7A 2G5
416-326-9511, Fax: 416-314-4494, 800-387-9080, info@ohrc.on.ca

Prince Edward Island
Prince Edward Island Human Rights Commission, 53 Water St., PO Box 2000, Charlottetown, PE C1A 7N8
902-368-4180, Fax: 902-368-4236, 800-237-5031, contact@peihumanrights.ca

Quebec
Commission des droits de la personne et des droits de la jeunesse, 360, rue Saint-Jacques, 2e étage, Montréal, QC H2Y 1P5
514-873-5146, Fax: 514-873-6032, 800-361-6477, information@cdpdj.qc.ca

Saskatchewan
Saskatchewan Human Rights Commission, PO Box 6011, Saskatoon, SK S7K 4E4
306-933-5952, Fax: 306-933-7863, 800-667-9249, shrc@gov.sk.ca

Yukon Territory
Yukon Human Rights Commission, #215, 305 Main St., Whitehorse, YT Y1A 2B4
867-667-6226, Fax: 867-667-2662, 800-661-0535, info@yukonhumanrights.ca

HYDRO, ELECTRIC POWER
Canada Energy Regulator, #210, 517 - 10th Ave. SW, Calgary, AB T2R 0A8
403-292-4800, Fax: 403-292-5503, 800-899-1265

Alberta
Alberta Energy Regulator, #1000, 250 - 5 St. SW, Calgary, AB T2P 0R4
403-297-8311, Fax: 403-297-7336, 855-297-8311, inquiries@aer.ca
Alberta Utilities Commission, Eau Caire Tower, #1400, 600 - 3rd Ave. SW, Calgary, AB T2P 0G5
-310-4282, info@auc.ab.ca

British Columbia
British Columbia Hydro, 333 Dunsmuir St., PO Box 8910, Vancouver, BC V6B 4N1
604-224-9376, 800-224-9376
Powertech Labs Inc., 12388 - 88 Ave., Surrey, BC V8W 7R7
604-590-7500, Fax: 604-590-6611

Manitoba
Manitoba Hydro, 360 Portage Ave., PO Box 815 Main, Winnipeg, MB R3C 2P4
204-480-5900, Fax: 204-360-6155, 888-624-9376

Newfoundland & Labrador
Nalcor Energy, 500 Columbus Dr., St. John's, NL A1E 2B2
709-737-1400, Fax: 709-737-1800, info@nalcorenergy.com
Newfoundland & Labrador Hydro, Hydro Place, 500 Columbus Dr., PO Box 12400, St. John's, NL A1B 4K7
709-737-1400, Fax: 709-737-1800, 888-737-1296, hydro@nlh.nl.ca

Northwest Territories
Northwest Territories Power Corporation, 4 Capital Dr., Hay River, NT X0E 1G2
867-874-5200, 800-661-0855, info@ntpc.com

Nova Scotia
Nova Scotia Utility & Review Board, Summit Place, 1601 Lower Water St., 3rd Fl., Halifax, NS B3J 3S3
902-424-4448, Fax: 902-424-3919, 855-442-4448, board@novascotia.ca

Ontario
Hydro One Inc., South Tower, 483 Bay St., 8th Fl., Toronto, ON M5G 2P5
416-345-5000, Fax: 905-944-3251, 877-955-1155, customercommunications@hydroone.com
Independent Electricity System Operator, #1600, 120 Adelaide St. West, Toronto, ON M5H 1T1
905-403-6900, Fax: 905-403-6921, 877-797-9473, customer.relations@ieso.ca
Ontario Power Generation, 700 University Ave., Toronto, ON M5G 1X6
416-592-2555, 877-592-2555, webmaster@opg.com

Quebec
Coopérative régionale d'électricité de Saint-Jean-Baptiste-de-Rouville, 3113, rue Principale, Saint-Jean-Baptiste, QC J0L 1B0
450-467-5583, Fax: 450-467-0092, 800-267-5583, info@coopsjb.com
Hydro-Québec, Édifice Jean-Lesage, 75, boul René-Lévesque ouest, Montréal, QC H2Z 1A4
514-385-7252, 888-385-7252
Société d'énergie de la Baie-James, #1100, 800, de Maisonneuve est, Montréal, QC H2L 4L8
514-286-2020

Saskatchewan
Saskatchewan Power Corporation (SaskPower), 2025 Victoria Ave., Regina, SK S4P 0S1
888-757-6937

Yukon Territory
Yukon Energy Corporation, 2 Miles Canyon Rd., PO Box 5920, Whitehorse, YT Y1A 6S7
867-393-5300, 866-926-3749, communications@yec.yk.ca

IMMIGRATION
See Also: Citizenship
Immigration & Refugee Board of Canada, Minto Place, Canada Bldg., 344 Slater St., 12th Fl., Ottawa, ON K1A 0K1
Fax: 613-943-1550
Immigration, Refugees & Citizenship, Jean Edmonds, South Tower, 365 Laurier Ave. West, Ottawa, ON K1A 1L1
888-242-2100
Passport, c/o Passport Program, Gatineau, QC K1A 0G3
800-567-6868

Alberta
Alberta Labour & Immigration, Legislature Bldg., #107, 10800 - 97th Ave., Edmonton, AB T5K 2B6
780-427-3731, 877-427-3731

British Columbia
BC Immigrant Investment Fund Ltd. & BC Renaissance Capital Fund Ltd., #301, 865 Hornby St., Vancouver, BC V6Z 2G3
Fax: 250-952-0371,

Manitoba
Manitoba Advanced Education, Skills & Immigration, Legislative Bldg., #352, 450 Broadway, Winnipeg, MB R3C 0V8
Manitoba Education, Legislative Bldg., #162, 450 Broadway, Winnipeg, MB R3C 0V8
204-945-3720, Fax: 204-945-1291

Newfoundland & Labrador
Office of Immigration & Multiculturalism, c/o Department of Advanced Education, Skills & Labour, 100 Prince Phillip Dr., PO Box 8700, St. John's, NL A1B 4J6
170-972-9714, Fax: 709-729-7381, 888-632-4555, AESL@gov.nl.ca

Nova Scotia
Nova Scotia Department of Labour, Skills & Immigration, 1469 Brenton St., 3rd Fl., PO Box 1535, Halifax, NS B3J 2Y3
Office of Immigration, 1469 Brenton St., 3rd Fl., PO Box 1535, Halifax, NS B3J 2Y3
902-424-5230, Fax: 902-424-7936, 877-292-9597, immigration@novascotia.ca

Prince Edward Island
Island Investment Development Inc., 94 Euston St., 2nd Fl., PO Box 1176, Charlottetown, PE C1A 7M8
902-620-3628, Fax: 902-368-5886, opportunitiespei@gov.pe.ca

Quebec
Ministère de l'Immigration, de la Francisation et de l'Intégration, 285, rue Notre-Dame ouest, 4e étage, Montréal, QC H2Y 1T8
877-864-9191

Saskatchewan
Saskatchewan Immigration & Career Training, #1000, 2103 - 11th Ave., Regina, SK S4P 3Z8
Fax: 306-787-7977

IMPORTS
See Also: Trade
Canada Border Services Agency, Headquarters, 191 Laurier Ave. West, Ottawa, ON K1A 0L8
800-461-9999, contact@cbsa.gc.ca
Canadian International Trade Tribunal, Standard Life Centre, 333 Laurier Ave. West, 15th Floor, Ottawa, ON K1A 0G7
613-990-2452, Fax: 613-990-2439, 855-307-2488, citt-tcce@tribunal.gc.ca

Quebec
Revenu Québec, 3800, rue de Marly, Québec, QC G1X 4A5
418-652-6831, Fax: 418-646-0167, cabinet@revenuquebec.ca

INCOME SECURITY
See Also: Social Services
Yukon Territory
Yukon Health & Social Services, PO Box 2703, Whitehorse, YT Y1A 2C6
867-667-3673, Fax: 867-667-3096, 800-661-0408, hss@yukon.ca

INCORPORATION OF COMPANIES & ASSOCIATIONS
Northwest Territories
Northwest Territories Department of Justice, 4903 - 49th St., PO Box 1320, Yellowknife, NT X1A 2L9
867-767-9256, justice_communications@gov.nt.ca

Nova Scotia
Nova Scotia Department of Inclusive Economic Growth, CIBC
  Bldg., 1809 Barrington St., #M103, Halifax, NS B3J 3K8
  902-424-0377, Fax: 902-424-0500
Registry of Joint Stock Companies, PO Box 1529, Halifax, NS
  B3J 2Y4
  902-424-7770, Fax: 902-424-4633, 800-225-8227,
  rjsc@novascotia.ca

Nunavut
Legal Registries, PO Box 1000 570, Iqaluit, NU X0A 0H0
  867-975-6590, Fax: 867-975-6594,
  Legal.Registries@gov.nu.ca

Ontario
ServiceOntario, College Park, 777 Bay St., 15th Floor, Toronto, ON
  M7A 2J3
  Fax: 416-326-1313, 800-267-8097

Saskatchewan
Court Services Division, #1010, 1874 Scarth St., Regina, SK
  S4P 4B3
  306-787-5359, Fax: 306-787-8737

Yukon Territory
Yukon Community Services, PO Box 2703, Whitehorse, YT Y1A
  2C6
  867-667-5811, Fax: 867-393-6295, 800-661-0408

INDIGENOUS AFFAIRS
Canadian Heritage, 15, rue Eddy, Gatineau, QC K1A 0M5
  819-997-0055, 866-811-0055,
  PCH.info-info.PCH@canada.ca
Canadian Northern Economic Development Agency, Ottawa, ON
  K1A 0H4
  855-897-2667,
  CanNor.InfoNorth.InfoNord.CanNor@canada.ca
Crown-Indigenous Relations & Northern Affairs, Public Enquiries
  Contact Centre, 10, rue Wellington, Gatineau, QC K1A 0H4
  Fax: 866-817-3977, 800-567-9604,
  aadnc.infopubs.aandc@canada.ca
First Nations Tax Commission, Head Office, #321, 345 Chief
  Alex Thomas Way, Kamloops, BC V2H 1H1
  250-828-9857, Fax: 250-828-9858, 855-682-3682,
  mail@fntc.ca
Indian Oil & Gas Canada, #100, 9911 Chiila Blvd., Tsuu T'ina,
  AB T2W 6H6
  403-292-5625, Fax: 403-292-5618,
  aadnc.contactiogc.aandc@canada.ca
National Aboriginal Initiative, #750, 175 Hargrave St., Winnipeg,
  MA RC3 3R8
  204-983-2189, Fax: 204-983-6132, 866-772-4880
Specific Claims Tribunal Canada, #400, 427 Laurier Ave. West,
  4th Fl., PO Box 31, Ottawa, ON K1R 7Y2
  613-947-0751, Fax: 613-943-0586,
  claims.revendications@sct-trp.ca

Alberta
Alberta Indigenous Relations, Commerce Place, 10155 - 102nd
  St. NW, 19th Fl., Edmonton, AB T5J 4G8
  Fax: 780-427-4019

British Columbia
British Columbia Ministry of Indigenous Relations &
  Reconciliation, 2957 Jutland Rd., PO Box 9100 Prov Govt,
  Victoria, BC V8W 9B1
  250-387-6121, 800-663-7867
British Columbia Treaty Commission, #700, 1111 Melville St.,
  Vancouver, BC V6E 3V6
  604-482-9200, Fax: 604-482-9222, 855-482-9200,
  info@bctreaty.net
Native Economic Development Advisory Board, PO Box 9100
  Prov Govt, Victoria, BC V8W 9B1
  250-387-2536

Manitoba
Manitoba Indigenous Reconciliation & Northern Relations,
  Legislative Bldg., #301, 450 Broadway, Winnipeg, MB R3C
  OV8
  204-945-3788, Fax: 204-945-1383, INRweb@gov.mb.ca

New Brunswick
Aboriginal Affairs Secretariat, Chancery Place, PO Box 6000,
  Fredericton, NB E3B 5H8
  506-462-5846, Fax: 506-444-5142, AboriginalAffairs@gnb.ca

Newfoundland & Labrador
Labrador Affairs Secretariat, Labrador Affairs, #438, 440
  Hamilton River Rd., PO Box 3014 B, Happy Valley - Goose
  Bay, NL A0P 1E0
  709-896-1780, Fax: 709-896-0045, 888-435-8111
Office of Indigenous Affairs & Reconciliation, East Block,
  Confederation Bldg., 6th Fl., PO Box 8700, St. John's, NL
  A1B 4J6
  709-729-4776, Fax: 709-729-4900

Northwest Territories
Northwest Territories Department of Lands, Gallery Bldg., 4923 -
  52nd St., 1st & 2nd Fl., PO Box 1320, Yellowknife, NT X1A
  2L9
  867-767-9185, Fax: 867-669-0905, 855-698-5263,
  Lands@gov.nt.ca
Northwest Territories Department of the Executive & Indigenous
  Affairs, PO Box 1320, Yellowknife, NT X1A 2L9

Nova Scotia
Office of L'nu Affairs, 5251 Duke St., 5th Fl., PO Box 1617,
  Halifax, NS B3J 2Y3
  902-424-7409, Fax: 902-424-4225, LnuAffairs@novascotia.ca

Nunavut
Nunavut Territory Department of Culture & Heritage, PO Box
  1000 800, Iqaluit, NU X0A 0H0
  867-975-5500, Fax: 867-975-5504, 866-934-2035

Ontario
Ontario Ministry of Indigenous Affairs, 160 Bloor St. East, 4th Fl.,
  Toronto, ON M7A 2E6
  416-326-4740, 866-381-5337

Quebec
Secrétariat aux affaires autochtones, 905, av Honoré-Mercier,
  1e étage, Québec, QC G1R 5M6
  418-643-3166, Fax: 418-646-4918

Saskatchewan
Indigenous & Northern Relations, 1855 Victoria Ave., 2nd Fl.,
  Regina, SK S4P 3T2
  306-798-0183, Fax: 306-787-6014, fnmr@gov.sk.ca
Saskatchewan Government Relations, 1855 Victoria Ave.,
  Regina, SK S4P 3T2

INDIGENOUS PEOPLES & NORTHERN AFFAIRS
Canadian Northern Economic Development Agency, Ottawa, ON
  K1A 0H4
  855-897-2667,
  CanNor.InfoNorth.InfoNord.CanNor@canada.ca
Crown-Indigenous Relations & Northern Affairs, Public Enquiries
  Contact Centre, 10, rue Wellington, Gatineau, QC K1A 0H4
  Fax: 866-817-3977, 800-567-9604,
  aadnc.infopubs.aandc@canada.ca

Alberta
Alberta Indigenous Relations, Commerce Place, 10155 - 102nd
  St. NW, 19th Fl., Edmonton, AB T5J 4G8
  Fax: 780-427-4019

British Columbia
British Columbia Ministry of Indigenous Relations &
  Reconciliation, 2957 Jutland Rd., PO Box 9100 Prov Govt,
  Victoria, BC V8W 9B1
  250-387-6121, 800-663-7867

Manitoba
Manitoba Indigenous Reconciliation & Northern Relations,
  Legislative Bldg., #301, 450 Broadway, Winnipeg, MB R3C
  OV8
  204-945-3788, Fax: 204-945-1383, INRweb@gov.mb.ca

New Brunswick
Aboriginal Affairs Secretariat, Chancery Place, PO Box 6000,
  Fredericton, NB E3B 5H8
  506-462-5846, Fax: 506-444-5142, AboriginalAffairs@gnb.ca

Northwest Territories
Northwest Territories Department of the Executive & Indigenous
  Affairs, PO Box 1320, Yellowknife, NT X1A 2L9

Nova Scotia
Office of L'nu Affairs, 5251 Duke St., 5th Fl., PO Box 1617,
  Halifax, NS B3J 2Y3
  902-424-7409, Fax: 902-424-4225, LnuAffairs@novascotia.ca

Ontario
Ontario Ministry of Indigenous Affairs, 160 Bloor St. East, 4th Fl.,
  Toronto, ON M7A 2E6
  416-326-4740, 866-381-5337

Yukon Territory
Yukon Development Corporation, #234, 2180 - 2nd Ave.,
  Whitehorse, YT Y1A 5N6
  867-456-3995, ydc-admin@yukon.ca

INDUSTRIAL RELATIONS
See Also: Labour
Canada Industrial Relations Board, 240 Sparks St., 4th Fl. West,
  Ottawa, ON K1A 0X8
  Fax: 613-995-9493, 800-575-9696

INDUSTRY
See Also: Business Development
Agriculture & Agri-Food Canada, 1341 Baseline Rd., Ottawa, ON
  K1A 0C5
  613-773-1000, Fax: 613-773-1081, 855-773-0241,
  info@agr.gc.ca

Atlantic Canada Opportunities Agency, Blue Cross Centre, 644
  Main St., 3rd Fl., PO Box 6051, Moncton, NB E1C 9J8
  506-851-2271, Fax: 506-851-7403, 800-561-7862,
  ACOA.information.APECA@canada.ca
Canada Energy Regulator, #210, 517 - 10th Ave. SW, Calgary,
  AB T2R 0A8
  403-292-4800, Fax: 403-292-5503, 800-899-1265
Canada Mortgage & Housing Corporation, 700 Montreal Rd.,
  Ottawa, ON K1A 0P7
  613-748-2000, Fax: 613-748-2098, 800-668-2642,
  chic@cmhc-schl.gc.ca
Canadian Dairy Commission, Central Experimental Farm, NCC
  Driveway, Bldg. 55, 960 Carling Ave., Ottawa, ON K1A 0Z2
  613-792-2000, Fax: 613-792-2009, cdc-ccl@cdc-ccl.gc.ca
Canadian Food Inspection Agency, 1400 Merivale Rd., Ottawa,
  ON K1A 0Y9
  613-225-2342, 800-442-2342
Canadian Grain Commission, #600, 303 Main St., Winnipeg, MB
  R3C 3G8
  204-984-0506, Fax: 204-983-2751, 800-853-6705,
  contact@grainscanada.gc.ca
Canadian International Trade Tribunal, Standard Life Centre,
  333 Laurier Ave. West, 15th Floor, Ottawa, ON K1A 0G7
  613-990-2452, Fax: 613-990-2439, 855-307-2488,
  citt-tcce@tribunal.gc.ca
Canadian Nuclear Safety Commission, 280 Slater St., PO Box
  1046 B, Ottawa, ON K1P 5S9
  613-995-5894, Fax: 613-995-5086, 800-668-5284,
  cnsc.information.ccsn@canada.ca
Canadian Radio-Television & Telecommunications Commission,
  Central Building, 1, promenade du Portage, Les Terrasses de
  la Chaudière, Gatineau, QC J8X 4B1
  819-997-0313, Fax: 819-994-0218, 877-249-2782
Canadian Space Agency, John H. Chapman Space Centre,
  6767, rte de l'Aéroport, Saint-Hubert, QC J3Y 8Y9
  450-926-4800, Fax: 450-926-4352, asc.info.csa@canada.ca
Communications Research Centre Canada, 3701 Carling Ave.,
  PO Box 11490 H, Ottawa, ON K2H 8S2
  613-991-3313, Fax: 613-998-5355, info@crc.gc.ca
Competition Bureau Canada, Place du Portage, Phase I, 50
  Victoria St., Ottawa, ON K1A 0C9
  819-997-4282, Fax: 819-997-0324, 800-348-5358,
Competition Tribunal, Thomas D'Arcy McGee Bldg., #600, 90
  Sparks St., Ottawa, ON K1P 5B4
  613-957-3172, Fax: 613-957-3170, tribunal@ct-tc.gc.ca
Defence Construction Canada, Constitution Square, 350 Albert
  St., 19th Fl., Ottawa, ON K1A 0K3
  613-998-9548, Fax: 613-998-1061, 800-514-3555,
  info@dcc-cdc.gc.ca
Earth Sciences Sector, 588 Booth St., Ottawa, ON K1A 0Y7
Export Development Canada, 150 Slater St., Ottawa, ON K1A
  1K3
  613-598-2500, Fax: 613-598-3811, 800-229-0575,
  support@edc.ca
Farm Credit Canada, 1800 Hamilton St., Regina, SK S4P 4L3
  306-780-8100, Fax: 306-780-8919, 888-332-3301,
  csc@fcc-fac.ca
Farm Products Council of Canada, Building 59, Central
  Experimental Farm, 960 Carling Ave., Ottawa, ON K1A 0C6
  613-759-1555, Fax: 613-759-1566, 855-611-1165,
  aafc.fpcc-cpac.aac@canada.ca
Fisheries & Oceans Canada, 200 Kent St., Ottawa, ON K1A 0E6
  613-993-0999, Fax: 613-990-1866, info@dfo-mpo.gc.ca
Freshwater Fish Marketing Corporation, 1199 Plessis Rd.,
  Winnipeg, MB R2C 3L4
  204-983-6601, Fax: 204-983-6497,
  sandic@freshwaterfish.com
Global Affairs Canada, Enquiries Service, 125 Sussex Dr.,
  Ottawa, ON K1A 0G2
  Fax: 613-996-9709, 800-267-8376
Indian Oil & Gas Canada, #100, 9911 Chiila Blvd., Tsuu T'ina
  (Sarcee), AB T2W 6H6
  403-292-5625, Fax: 403-292-5618,
  aadnc.contactiogc.aandc@canada.ca
Innovation, Science & Economic Development Canada, C.D.
  Howe Building, 235 Queen St., Ottawa, ON K1A 0H5
  613-954-5031, Fax: 613-954-2340, 800-328-6189,
  info@ic.gc.ca
National Film Board of Canada, Operational Headquarters,
  Norman McLaren Building, 3155, ch de la Côte-de-Liesse, PO
  Box 1600 Centre-ville, Montréal, QC H3C 3H5
  514-283-9000, 800-267-7710
National Research Council Canada, Building M-58, 1200
  Montreal Rd., Ottawa, ON K1A 0R6
  613-993-9101, Fax: 613-991-9096, 877-672-2672,
  info@nrc-cnrc.ca
Natural Resources Canada, 580 Booth St., Ottawa, ON K1A 0E4
  343-292-6096, Fax: 613-992-7211
Natural Sciences & Engineering Research Council of Canada,
  350 Albert St., 16th Fl., Ottawa, ON K1A 1H5
  613-995-4273, Fax: 613-992-5337, 855-275-2861

Office of the Superintendent of Financial Institutions, Kent Square, 255 Albert St., 12th Fl., Ottawa, ON K1A 0H2
613-990-7788, Fax: 613-990-5591, 800-385-8647, information@osfi-bsif.gc.ca
Patented Medicine Prices Review Board, Standard Life Centre, #1400, 333 Laurier Ave. West, PO Box L40, Ottawa, ON K1P 1C1
613-288-9597, Fax: 613-288-9643, 877-861-2350, PMPRB.Information-Renseignements.CEPMB@pmprb-cepmb.gc.ca
Spectrum, Information Technologies & Telecommunications, Journal Tower North, 300 Slater St., 20th Fl., Ottawa, ON K1A 0C8
613-998-0368, Fax: 613-952-1203
Standards Council of Canada, #600, 55 Metcalfe St., Ottawa, ON K1P 6L5
613-238-3222, Fax: 613-569-7808, info@scc.ca
Telefilm Canada, #500, 360, rue Saint-Jacques, Montréal, QC H2Y 1P5
514-283-6363, Fax: 514-283-8212, 800-567-0890, info@telefilm.gc.ca
Western Economic Diversification Canada, Canada Place, #1500, 9700 Jasper Ave. NW, Edmonton, AB T5J 4H7
780-495-4164, Fax: 780-495-4557, 888-338-9378, WD.contactus-contactez-nous.DEO@canada.ca

Alberta
Alberta Agriculture & Forestry, JG O'Donoghue Bldg., #100A, 7000 - 113th St., Edmonton, AB T6H 5T6
403-742-7901
Alberta Energy, North Petroleum Plaza, 9945 - 108th St., Edmonton, AB T5K 2G6
780-427-8050, Fax: 780-422-9522
Alberta Energy Regulator, #1000, 250 - 5 St. SW, Calgary, AB T2P 0R4
403-297-8311, Fax: 403-297-7336, 855-297-8311, inquiries@aer.ca
Apprenticeship & Student Aid Division, Commerce Place, 10155 - 102nd St., 6th Fl., Edmonton, AB T5J 4L5
Land Compensation Board, 1229 - 91 St. SW, Edmonton, AB T6X 1E9
780-427-2444, Fax: 780-427-5798, -310-000, srb.lcb@gov.ab.ca

British Columbia
Agricultural Land Commission, #133, 4940 Canada Way, Burnaby, BC V5G 4K6
604-660-7000, Fax: 604-660-7033, ALCBurnaby@Victoria1.gov.bc.ca
British Columbia Farm Industry Review Board, 780 Blanshard St., PO Box 9129 Prov Govt, Victoria, BC V8W 9B5
250-356-8945, Fax: 250-356-5131, firb@gov.bc.ca
British Columbia Hydro, 333 Dunsmuir St., PO Box 8910, Vancouver, BC V6B 4N1
604-224-9376, 800-224-9376
British Columbia Ministry of Agriculture, Food & Fisheries, PO Box 9043 Prov Govt, Victoria, BC V8W 9E2
888-221-7141, agriservicebc@gov.bc.ca
British Columbia Ministry of Energy, Mines & Low Carbon Innovation, PO Box 9060 Prov Govt, Victoria, BC V8W 9E3
250-952-0628
British Columbia Ministry of Forests, Lands, Natural Resource Operations & Rural Development, PO Box 9049 Prov Govt, Victoria, BC V8W 9E2
800-663-7867, FLNRO.MediaRequests@gov.bc.ca
British Columbia Ministry of Jobs, Economic Recovery & Innovation, PO Box 9071 Prov Govt, Victoria, BC V8W 9T2
250-356-2771, Fax: 250-953-0927
British Columbia Utilities Commission, #410, 900 Howe St., Vancouver, BC V6Z 2N3
604-660-4700, Fax: 604-660-1102, 604-663-1385, commission.secretary@bcuc.com
Financial Institutions Commission, #2800, 555 West Hastings, Vancouver, BC V6B 4N6
604-660-3555, Fax: 604-660-3365, 866-206-3030, FICOM@ficombc.ca
Forest Practices Board, 310, 1675 Douglas St., PO Box 9905 Prov Govt, Victoria, BC V8W 9R1
250-213-4700, Fax: 250-213-4725, 800-994-5899, fpboard@gov.bc.ca
Insurance Council of British Columbia, #300, 1040 West Georgia St., PO Box 7, Vancouver, BC V6E 4H1
604-688-0321, Fax: 604-662-7767, 877-688-0321, info@insurancecouncilofbc.com
Oil & Gas Commission, 6534 Airport Rd., Fort St. John, BC V1J 4M6
250-794-5200, Fax: 250-794-5375
Real Estate Council of British Columbia, #900, 750 West Pender St., Vancouver, BC V6C 2T8
604-683-9664, Fax: 604-683-9017, 877-683-9664, info@recbc.ca

Manitoba
Advisory Council on Workplace Safety & Health, 401 York Ave., 2nd Fl., Winnipeg, MB R3C 0P8
204-945-3446, Fax: 204-948-2209, 866-888-8186, wshcompl@gov.mb.ca
Agricultural Societies, 1129 Queens Ave., Brandon, MB R7A 1L9
204-726-6195, Fax: 204-726-6260
Crown Corporations Council, #1130, 444 St. Mary Ave., Winnipeg, MB R3C 3T1
204-949-5270, Fax: 204-949-5283, info@crowncc.mb.ca
Entrepreneurship Manitoba, #1010, 405 Broadway, Winnipeg, MB R3C 3L6
204-945-8200, 855-836-7250, embinfo@gov.mb.ca
Manitoba Agricultural Services Corporation, #400, 50 - 24th St. NW, Portage la Prairie, MB R1N 3V9
204-239-3246, Fax: 204-239-3401, mailbox@masc.mb.ca
Manitoba Agriculture, Legislative Bldg., #165, 450 Broadway, Winnipeg, MB R3C 0V8
204-945-3722, Fax: 204-945-3470, minagr@leg.gov.mb.ca
Manitoba Bureau of Statistics, #824, 155 Carlton St., Winnipeg, MB R3C 3H9
204-945-2406
Manitoba Economic Development & Jobs, Economic Development Office, #1010, 259 Portage Ave., Winnipeg, MB R3B 3P4
204-945-1055, Fax: 204-948-2964, 866-570-5577, edo@gov.mb.ca
Manitoba Education, Legislative Bldg., #162, 450 Broadway, Winnipeg, MB R3C 0V8
204-945-3720, Fax: 204-945-1291
Manitoba Habitat Heritage Corporation, #200, 1555 St. James St., Winnipeg, MB R3H 1B5
204-784-4350, Fax: 204-784-7359
Manitoba Hydro, 360 Portage Ave., PO Box 815 Main, Winnipeg, MB R3C 2P4
204-480-5900, Fax: 204-360-6155, 888-624-9376
Manitoba Indigenous Reconciliation & Northern Relations, Legislative Bldg., #301, 450 Broadway, Winnipeg, MB R3C 0V8
204-945-3788, Fax: 204-945-1383, INRweb@gov.mb.ca
Taxicab Board, #200, 301 Weston St., Winnipeg, MB R3E 3H4
204-945-8919, Fax: 204-948-2315, taxicabboardoffice@gov.mb.ca
Tourism Secretariat, 213 Notre Dame Ave., 6th Fl., Winnipeg, MB R3B 1N3
204-945-0216, tourismsec@gov.mb.ca
Workers' Compensation Board of Manitoba, 333 Broadway Ave., Winnipeg, MB R3C 4W3
204-954-4321, Fax: 204-954-4999, 800-362-3340, wcb@wcb.mb.ca

New Brunswick
New Brunswick Department of Agriculture, Aquaculture & Fisheries, Agricultural Research Station (Experimental Farm), PO Box 6000, Fredericton, NB E3B 5H1
506-453-3826, Fax: 506-453-7170, DAAF-MAAP@gnb.ca
New Brunswick Department of Environment & Local Government, Marysville Place, 20 McGloin St., Fredericton, NB E3B 5H1
506-453-2690, Fax: 506-457-4994, elg/egl-info@gnb.ca
New Brunswick Department of Natural Resources & Energy Development, Hugh John Flemming Forestry Centre, PO Box 6000, Fredericton, NB E3B 5H1
506-453-3826, Fax: 506-444-4367, dnr_mrnweb@gnb.ca
New Brunswick Department of Social Development, Sartain MacDonald Bldg., PO Box 6000, Fredericton, NB E3B 5H1
506-453-2001, Fax: 506-453-2164, sd-ds@gnb.ca
New Brunswick Farm Products Commission, c/o Department of Agriculture, Aquaculture & Fisheries, PO Box 6000, Fredericton, NB E3B 5H1
506-453-3647, Fax: 506-444-5969, DAAF-MAAP@gnb.ca
New Brunswick Liquor Corporation, 170 Wilsey Rd., PO Box 20787, Fredericton, NB E3B 5B8
506-452-6826, Fax: 506-462-2024, receptionist@anbl.com
New Brunswick Research & Productivity Council, 921 College Hill Rd., Fredericton, NB E3B 6Z9
506-452-1212, Fax: 506-452-1395, 800-563-0844, info@rpc.ca
Regional Development Corporation, Chancery Place, 3rd Fl., PO Box 6000, Fredericton, NB E3B 5H1
506-453-2277, Fax: 506-453-7988, rdc-sdr@gnb.ca
WorkSafeNB, 1 Portland St., PO Box 160, Saint John, NB E2L 3X9
506-632-2200, 800-222-9775, communications@ws-ts.nb.ca

Newfoundland & Labrador
Labour Relations Board, Natural Resources Bldg., 50 Elizabeth Ave., 5th Fl., PO Box 8700, St. John's, NL A1B 4J6
709-729-2707, Fax: 709-729-5738, lrb@gov.nl.ca
Nalcor Energy, 500 Columbus Dr., St. John's, NL A1E 2B2
709-737-1400, Fax: 709-737-1800, info@nalcorenergy.com

Newfoundland & Labrador Board of Commissioners of Public Utilities, PO Box 21040, St. John's, NL A1A 5B2
Fax: 709-726-9604, 866-782-0006, ito@pub.nl.ca
Newfoundland & Labrador Department of Fisheries, Forestry & Agriculture, Petten Bldg., 30 Strawberry Marsh Rd., PO Box 8700, St. John's, NL A1B 4J6
709-729-3705, Fax: 709-729-0360
Newfoundland & Labrador Department of Industry, Energy & Technology, Natural Resources Bldg., 50 Elizabeth Ave., PO Box 8700, St. John's, NL A1B 4J6
709-729-3017, Fax: 709-729-0059
Newfoundland & Labrador Housing Corporation, Sir Brian Dunfield Bldg., 2 Canada Dr., PO Box 220, St. John's, NL A1C 5J2
709-724-3000, Fax: 709-724-3250
Newfoundland & Labrador Hydro, Hydro Place, 500 Columbus Dr., PO Box 12400, St. John's, NL A1B 4K7
709-737-1400, Fax: 709-737-1800, 888-737-1296, hydro@nlh.nl.ca
Newfoundland & Labrador Liquor Corporation, 90 Kenmount Rd., PO Box 8750 A, St. John's, NL A1B 3V1
709-724-1100, info@nfliquor.com
Professional Fish Harvesters Certification Board, 368 Hamilton Ave., PO Box 8541, St. John's, NL A1B 3P2
709-722-8170, Fax: 709-722-8201, pfh@pfhcb.com

Northwest Territories
Northwest Territories Department of Environment & Natural Resources, PO Box 1320, Yellowknife, NT X1A 2L9
867-767-9055, enr_communications@gov.nt.ca
Northwest Territories Department of Industry, Tourism & Investment, PO Box 1320, Yellowknife, NT X1A 2L9
Northwest Territories Housing Corporation, Scotia Centre, 5102 - 50th Ave., PO Box 2100, Yellowknife, NT X1A 2P6
867-767-9080, Fax: 867-873-9426, 844-698-4663
Northwest Territories Liquor & Cannabis Commission, #201, 31 Capital Dr., Hay River, NT X0E 1G2
867-874-8700, Fax: 867-874-8720
Northwest Territories Liquor Licensing Board, #204, 31 Capital Dr., Hay River, NT X0E 1G2
867-874-8715, Fax: 867-874-8722, 800-351-7770, LLBinfo@gov.nt.ca
Northwest Territories Power Corporation, 4 Capital Dr., Hay River, NT X0E 1G2
867-874-5200, 800-661-0855, info@ntpc.com

Nova Scotia
Crane Operators Appeal Board, 5151 Terminal Rd., 7th Fl., PO Box 697, Halifax, NS B3J 2T8
902-424-8595, Fax: 902-424-0217
Develop Nova Scotia, Old Red Store, Historic Properties, #301, 1875 Upper Water St., Halifax, NS B3J 1S9
902-422-6591, Fax: 902-377-4801, info@developns.ca
Innovacorp, #400, 1871 Hollis St., Halifax, NS B3J 0C3
902-424-8670, Fax: 902-424-4679, 800-565-7051, info@innovacorp.ca
Nova Scotia Business Inc., PO Box 2374, Halifax, NS B3J 3E4
902-424-6650, 800-260-6682, info@nsbi.ca
Nova Scotia Department of Agriculture, 1800 Argyle St., 6th Fl., Halifax, NS B3J 3N8
902-424-4560, Fax: 902-424-4671, 800-279-0825
Nova Scotia Department of Energy & Mines, Joseph Howe Bldg., 1690 Hollis St., PO Box 2664, Halifax, NS B3J 3J9
902-424-4575, Fax: 902-424-3265, enerinfo@novascotia.ca
Nova Scotia Department of Inclusive Economic Growth, CIBC Bldg., 1809 Barrington St., #M103, Halifax, NS B3J 3K8
902-424-0377, Fax: 902-424-0500
Nova Scotia Department of Lands & Forestry, PO Box 698, Halifax, NS B3J 2T9
902-424-5935, Fax: 902-424-7735, 800-565-2224
Nova Scotia Farm Loan Board, 74 Research Dr., Truro, NS B6L 2R2
902-893-6506, Fax: 902-895-7693, FLBNS@novascotia.ca
Nova Scotia Liquor Corporation, Bayers Lake Business Park, 93 Chain Lake Dr., Halifax, NS B3S 1A3
800-567-5874, contactus@myNSLC.com
Nova Scotia Utility & Review Board, Summit Place, 1601 Lower Water St., 3rd Fl., Halifax, NS B3J 3S3
902-424-4448, Fax: 902-424-3919, 855-442-4448, board@novascotia.ca

Nunavut
Liquor Licensing Board, PO Box 1000 330, Iqaluit, NU X0A 0H0
867-975-5875, Fax: 867-975-5805, nllb@gov.nu.ca
Nunavut Territory Department of Economic Development & Transportation, Inuksugait Plaza, Bldg. 1104A, PO Box 1000 1500, Iqaluit, NU X0A 0H0
867-975-7800, Fax: 867-975-7870, 888-975-5999, edt@gov.nu.ca

Ontario
Agricorp, Ontario Government Bldg NW, 1 Stone Rd. West, 3rd Fl., PO Box 3660 Central, Guelph, ON N1H 8M4
Fax: 519-826-4118, 888-247-4999, contact@agricorp.com

Agricultural Research Institute of Ontario, Ontario Government Bldg NW, 1 Stone Rd. West, 2nd Fl., Guelph, ON N1G 4Y2
519-826-4197, Fax: 519-826-4211, research.omafra@ontario.ca

Corporate Services Division, Mowat Block, 900 BaySt., 5th Fl., Toronto, ON M7A 1L2
416-325-6866, Fax: 416-314-7014

Environmental Commissioner of Ontario, #605, 1075 Bay St., Toronto, ON M5S 2B1
416-325-3377, Fax: 416-325-3370, 800-701-6454, commissioner@eco.on.ca

Environmental Sciences & Standards Division, 135 St Clair Ave. West, 14th Fl., Toronto, ON M4V 1P5

Health System Quality & Funding Division, Hepburn Block, 80 Grosvenor St., 5th Fl., Toronto, ON M7A 1R3

Hydro One Inc., South Tower, 483 Bay St., 8th Fl., Toronto, ON M5G 2P5
416-345-5000, Fax: 905-944-3251, 877-955-1155, customercommunications@hydroone.com

Independent Electricity System Operator, #1600, 120 Adelaide St. West, Toronto, ON M5H 1T1
905-403-6900, Fax: 905-403-6921, 877-797-9473, customer.relations@ieso.ca

Office of the Employer Advisor, 505 University Ave., 20th Fl., Toronto, ON M5G 2P1
416-327-0020, Fax: 416-327-0726, 800-387-0774

Office of the Fairness Commissioner, #1201, 595 Bay St., Toronto, ON M7A 2B4
416-325-9380, Fax: 416-326-6081, 877-727-5365, ofc@ontario.ca

Ontario Media Development Corporation, South Tower, #501, 175 Bloor St. East, Toronto, ON M4W 3R8
416-314-6858, Fax: 416-314-6876, reception@omdc.on.ca

Ontario Ministry of Agriculture, Food & Rural Affairs, Ontario Government Bldg., 1 Stone Rd. West, Guelph, ON N1G 4Y2
519-826-3100, Fax: 519-826-4335, 888-466-2372, about.omafra@ontario.ca

Ontario Ministry of Economic Development, Job Creation & Trade, 56 Wellesley St. West, 7th Fl., Toronto, ON M7A 2E7
416-325-6666, 800-268-7095

Ontario Ministry of Environment, Conservation & Parks, Ferguson Block, 77 Wellesley St. West, 11th Fl., Toronto, ON M7A 2T5
416-325-4000, Fax: 416-314-6713, 800-565-4923

Ontario Ministry of Government & Consumer Services, Mowat Block, 900 Bay St., 6th Fl., Toronto, ON M7A 1L2
416-212-2665, Fax: 416-326-7445, 844-286-8404

Ontario Ministry of Heritage, Sport, Tourism & Culture Industries, 438 University Ave., 6th Fl., Toronto, ON M5G 2K8
416-326-9326, Fax: 416-314-7854, 888-997-9015

Ontario Ministry of Labour, Training & Skills Development, 400 University Ave., 14th Fl., Toronto, ON M7A 1T7
416-326-7160, 800-531-5551

Ontario Ministry of Municipal Affairs & Housing, College Park, 777 Bay St., 17th Fl., Toronto, ON M7A 2J3
416-585-7041, Fax: 416-585-4230, mininfo@ontario.ca

Ontario Ministry of Northern Development, Mines, Natural Resources & Forestry, Natural Resources Information & Support Centre, 300 Water St., Toronto, ON K9J 8M5
800-667-1940

Ontario Power Generation, 700 University Ave., Toronto, ON M5G 1X6
416-592-2555, 877-592-2555, webmaster@opg.com

Policy Division, Ontario Government Bldg, 1 Stone Rd. West, 2nd Fl., Guelph, ON N1G 4Y2
519-826-4020, Fax: 519-826-3492

ServiceOntario, College Park, 777 Bay St., 15th Fl., Toronto, ON M7A 2J3
Fax: 416-326-1313, 800-267-8097

Workplace Safety & Insurance Board, 200 Front St. West, Ground Fl., Toronto, ON M5V 3J1
416-344-1000, Fax: 416-344-4684, 800-387-0750,

Prince Edward Island
Advisory Council on the Status of Women, Sherwood Business Centre, 161 St. Peter's Rd., Main Level, PO Box 2000, Charlottetown, PE C1A 7N8
902-368-4510, Fax: 902-368-3269, info@peistatusofwomen.ca

Agricultural Insurance Corporation, 7 Gerald McCarville Drive, Kensington, PE C0B 1M0

Anne of Green Gables Licensing Authority Inc., 94 Euston St., PO Box 910, Charlottetown, PE C1A 7L9
902-368-5961

BIO|FOOD|TECH, 101 Belvedere Ave., PO Box 2000, Charlottetown, PE C1A 7N8
902-368-5548, Fax: 902-368-5549, 877-368-5548, biofoodtech@biofoodtech.ca

Charlottetown Area Development Corporation, 4 Pownal St., PO Box 786, Charlottetown, PE C1A 7L9
902-892-5341, Fax: 902-368-1935

Grain Elevators Corporation, 62 Victoria St., PO Box 250, Kensington, PE C0B 1M0
902-836-8935, Fax: 902-836-8926

Innovation PEI, 94 Euston St., PO Box 910, Charlottetown, PE C1A 7L9
902-368-6300, Fax: 902-368-6301, 800-563-3734, innovation@gov.pe.ca

Prince Edward Island Department of Agriculture & Land, Jones Bldg., 11 Kent St., 5th Fl., PO Box 2000, Charlottetown, PE C1A 7N8
902-368-4880, Fax: 902-368-4857

Prince Edward Island Department of Economic Growth, Tourism & Culture, PO Box 2000, Charlottetown, PE C1A 7N8
902-368-5540, Fax: 902-368-5277, tpswitch@gov.pe.ca

Prince Edward Island Department of Transportation & Infrastructure, Jones Bldg., 11 Kent St., 3rd Fl., PO Box 2000, Charlottetown, PE C1A 7N8
902-368-5100, Fax: 902-368-5395, DeptTIE@gov.pe.ca

Prince Edward Island Liquor Control Commission, 3 Garfield St., PO Box 967, Charlottetown, PE C1A 7M4
902-368-5710, Fax: 902-368-5735

Prince Edward Island Workers' Compensation Board, 14 Weymouth St., PO Box 757, Charlottetown, PE C1A 7L7
902-368-5680, Fax: 902-368-5696, 800-237-5049

SkillsPEI, Atlantic Technology Centre, #212, 176 Great George St., Charlottetown, PE C1A 4K9
902-368-6290, Fax: 902-368-6340, 877-491-4766

Quebec
Centre de recherche industrielle du Québec, 333, rue Franquet, Québec, QC G1P 4C7
418-659-1550, Fax: 418-652-2251, 800-667-2386, infocriq@criq.qc.ca

Comité conjoint de chasse, de pêche et de piégeage, #1420, 1080, Côte du Beaver Hall, Montréal, QC H2Z 1N8
514-284-2151, Fax: 514-284-0039, infohftcc@cccpp-hftcc.com

Commission de protection du territoire agricole du Québec, 200, ch Ste-Foy, 2e étage, Québec, QC G1R 4X6
418-643-3314, Fax: 418-643-2261, 800-667-5294, info@cptaq.gouv.qc.ca

Conseil consultatif du travail et de la main d'oeuvre, #17.100, 500, boul René-Lévesque ouest, Montréal, QC H2Z 1W7
514-873-2880, Fax: 514-873-1129

Financement-Québec, 12, rue Saint-Louis, 3e étage, Québec, QC G1R 5L3
418-691-2203, Fax: 418-644-6214, financement.regroupe@finances.gouv.qc.ca

Hydro-Québec, Édifice Jean-Lesage, 75, boul René-Lévesque ouest, Montréal, QC H2Z 1A4
514-385-7252, 888-385-7252

La financière agricole de Québec, 1400, boul Guillaume-Couture, Lévis, QC G6W 8K7
418-838-5602, Fax: 418-833-3871, 800-749-3646

Ministère de l'Agriculture, des Pêcheries et de l'Alimentation du Québec, 200, ch Sainte-Foy, Québec, QC G1R 4X6
418-380-2110, 888-222-6272

Ministère de l'Environnement et de la Lutte contre les changements climatiques, Édifice Marie-Guyart, 675, boul René-Lévesque est, 30e étage, Québec, QC G1R 5V7
418-521-3830, Fax: 418-646-5974, 800-561-1616, relations.medias@mddelcc.gouv.qc.ca

Ministère de la Culture et Communications, 225, Grande Allée est, Québec, QC G1R 5G5
888-380-8882

Ministère des Finances, 12, rue Saint-Louis, Québec, QC G1R 5L3
418-528-9323, Fax: 418-646-1631, info@finances.gouv.qc.ca

Ministère du Tourisme, #400, 900, boul René-Lévesque est, Québec, QC G1R 2B5
418-643-5959, Fax: 418-646-8723, 800-482-2433, relations.publiques@tourisme.gouv.qc.ca

Office de la sécurité du revenu des chasseurs et piégeurs cris, Édifice Champlain, #1100, 2700, boul Laurier, Québec, QC G1V 4K5
418-643-7300, Fax: 418-643-6803, 800-363-1560, courrier@osrcpc.ca

Régie des marchés agricoles et alimentaires du Québec, 201, boul Crémazie est, 5e étage, Montréal, QC H2M 1L3
514-873-4024, Fax: 514-873-3984, rmaaqc@rmaaq.gouv.qc.ca

Régie du bâtiment du Québec, 545, boul Crémazie est, 4e étage, Montréal, QC H2M 2V2
514-873-0976, 800-361-0761

Société d'habitation du Québec, Aile St-Amable, 1054, rue Louis-Alexandre-Taschereau, 3e étage, Québec, QC G1R 5E7
Fax: 418-643-2533, 800-463-4315

Société de développement des entreprises culturelles, #800, 215, rue Saint-Jacques, Montréal, QC H2Y 1M6
514-841-2200, Fax: 514-841-8606, 800-363-0401, info@sodec.gouv.qc.ca

Société des alcools du Québec, 7500, rue Tellier, Montréal, QC H1N 3W5
514-254-2020, 866-873-2020

Société du parc industriel et portuaire de Bécancour, 1000, boul Arthur-Sicard, Bécancour, QC G9H 2Z8
819-294-6656, Fax: 819-294-9020, info@spipb.com

Société québécoise de récupération et de recyclage, #411, 300, rue Saint-Paul, Québec, QC G1K 7R1
418-643-0394, Fax: 418-643-6507, 800-807-0678, info@recyc-quebec.gouv.qc.ca

Transition énergetique Québec, 5700, 4e av ouest, #B406, Québec, QC G1H 6R1
418-627-6379, Fax: 418-643-5828, 877-727-6655, transitionenergetique@teq.gouv.qc.ca

Saskatchewan
Agri-Food Council, #315, 3085 Albert St., Regina, SK S4S 0B1
Fax: 306-787-8599

Crown Investments Corporation of Saskatchewan, #400, 2400 College Ave., Regina, SK S4P 1C8
306-787-6851, Fax: 306-787-0294

Farmland Security Board, #315, 3988 Albert St., Regina, SK S4S 3R1
306-787-5047, Fax: 306-787-8599

Labour Relations Board, #1600, 1920 Broad St., Regina, SK S4P 3V2
306-787-2406, Fax: 306-787-2664

Prairie Agricultural Machinery Institute, 2215 - 8th Ave., PO Box 1150, Humboldt, SK S0K 2A0
306-682-5033, Fax: 306-682-5080, 800-567-7264, pami@pami.ca

Saskatchewan Agriculture, Walter Scott Bldg., 3085 Albert St., Regina, SK S4S 0B1
866-457-2377

Saskatchewan Crop Insurance Corporation, 484 Prince William Dr., PO Box 3000, Melville, SK S0A 2P0
306-728-7200, Fax: 306-728-7202, 888-935-0000, customer.service@scic.gov.sk.ca

Saskatchewan Energy & Resources, #1000, 2103 - 11th Ave., Regina, SK S4P 3Z8

Saskatchewan Environment, 3211 Albert St., Regina, SK S4S 5W6
306-787-2584, Fax: 306-787-9544, 800-567-4224, centre.inquiry@gov.sk.ca

Saskatchewan Liquor & Gaming Authority, 2500 Victoria Ave., PO Box 5054, Regina, SK S4P 3M3
306-787-5563, inquiry@slga.gov.sk.ca

Saskatchewan Power Corporation (SaskPower), 2025 Victoria Ave., Regina, SK S4P 0S1
888-757-6937

Saskatchewan Water Corporation (SaskWater), #200, 111 Fairford St. East, Moose Jaw, SK S6H 1C8
Fax: 306-694-3207, 888-230-1111, communications@saskwater.com

Saskatchewan Workers' Compensation Board, #200, 1881 Scarth St., Regina, SK S4P 4L1
306-787-4370, Fax: 306-787-4311, 800-667-7590, webmaster@wcbsask.com

SaskEnergy Incorporated, 1777 Victoria Ave., Regina, SK S4P 4K5
306-777-9225, 800-567-8899, webmaster@saskenergy.com

Yukon Territory
Yukon Development Corporation, #234, 2180 - 2nd Ave., Whitehorse, YT Y1A 5N6
867-456-3995, ydc-admin@yukon.ca

Yukon Economic Development, 303 Alexander St., Whitehorse, YT Y1A 2L5
800-661-0408, ecdev@yukon.ca

Yukon Environment, 10 Burns Rd., Whitehorse, YT Y1A 2C6
867-667-5652, Fax: 867-393-7197, environmentyukon@yukon.ca

Yukon Housing Corporation, 410G Jarvis St., PO Box 2703, Whitehorse, YT Y1A 2H5
867-667-5712, Fax: 867-393-7597, ykhouse@yukon.ca

Yukon Liquor Corporation, 9031 Quartz Rd., Whitehorse, YT Y1A 4P9
867-667-5245, Fax: 867-393-6306, yukon.liquor@yukon.ca

Yukon Tourism & Culture, PO Box 2703, Whitehorse, YT Y1A 2C6
867-393-7048

INDUSTRY & TRADE
Atlantic Canada Opportunities Agency, Blue Cross Centre, 644 Main St., 3rd Fl., PO Box 6051, Moncton, NB E1C 9J8
506-851-2271, Fax: 506-851-7403, 800-561-7862, ACOA.information.APECA@canada.ca

Business Development Bank of Canada, #100, 5, Place Ville-Marie, Montréal, QC H3B 5E7
Fax: 877-329-9232, 877-232-2269

Defence Construction Canada, Constitution Square, 350 Albert St., 19th Fl., Ottawa, ON K1A 0K3
613-998-9548, Fax: 613-998-1061, 800-514-3555, info@dcc-cdc.gc.ca

Export Development Canada, 150 Slater St., Ottawa, ON K1A 1K3
613-598-2500, Fax: 613-598-3811, 800-229-0575, support@edc.ca

Global Affairs Canada, Enquiries Service, 125 Sussex Dr., Ottawa, ON K1A 0G2
Fax: 613-996-9709, 800-267-8376

Innovation, Science & Economic Development Canada, C.D. Howe Building, 235 Queen St., Ottawa, ON K1A 0H5
613-954-5031, Fax: 613-954-2340, 800-328-6189, info@ic.gc.ca

Market & Industry Services Branch, Tower 5, 1341 Baseline Rd., Ottawa, ON K1A 0C5
613-759-1000, Fax: 613-773-1711

Standards Council of Canada, #600, 55 Metcalfe St., Ottawa, ON K1P 6L5
613-238-3222, Fax: 613-569-7808, info@scc.ca

Western Economic Diversification Canada, Canada Place, #1500, 9700 Jasper Ave. NW, Edmonton, AB T5J 4H7
780-495-4164, Fax: 780-495-4557, 888-338-9378, WD.contactus-contactez-nous.DEO@canada.ca

British Columbia

British Columbia Ministry of Jobs, Economic Recovery & Innovation, PO Box 9071 Prov Govt, Victoria, BC V8W 9T2
250-356-2771, Fax: 250-953-0927

Timber Export Advisory Committee, PO Box 9514 Prov Govt, Victoria, BC V8W 9C2
250-387-8916, Fax: 250-387-5050

Manitoba

Manitoba Economic Development & Jobs, Economic Development Office, #1010, 259 Portage Ave., Winnipeg, MB R3B 3P4
204-945-1055, Fax: 204-948-2964, 866-570-7577, edo@gov.mb.ca

New Brunswick

Regional Development Corporation, Chancery Place, 3rd Fl., PO Box 6000, Fredericton, NB E3B 5H1
506-453-2277, Fax: 506-453-7988, rdc-sdr@gnb.ca

Northwest Territories

Northwest Territories Department of Environment & Natural Resources, PO Box 1320, Yellowknife, NT X1A 2L9
867-767-9055, enr_communications@gov.nt.ca

Nova Scotia

Nova Scotia Department of Agriculture, 1800 Argyle St., 6th Fl., Halifax, NS B3J 3N8
902-424-4560, Fax: 902-424-4671, 800-279-0825

Nova Scotia Department of Inclusive Economic Growth, CIBC Bldg., 1809 Barrington St., #M103, Halifax, NS B3J 3K8
902-424-0377, Fax: 902-424-0500

Workers' Compensation Board of Nova Scotia, 5668 South St., PO Box 1150, Halifax, NS B3J 2Y2
902-491-8999, 800-870-3331, info@wcb.ns.ca

Ontario

Ontario Ministry of Economic Development, Job Creation & Trade, 56 Wellesley St. West, 7th Fl., Toronto, ON M7A 2E7
416-325-6666, 800-268-7095

Prince Edward Island

Labour & Industrial Relations, 16 St. Peters Rd., Charlottetown, PE C1A 7N8

Saskatchewan

Saskatchewan Energy & Resources, #1000, 2103 - 11th Ave., Regina, SK S4P 3Z8

Yukon Territory

Yukon Development Corporation, #234, 2180 - 2nd Ave., Whitehorse, YT Y1A 5N6
867-456-3995, ydc-admin@yukon.ca

INFORMATION & PRIVACY COMMISSIONER

Office of the Information Commissioner of Canada, 30, rue Victoria, Gatineau, QC K1A 1H3
Fax: 819-994-1768, 800-267-0441, general@oic-ci.gc.ca

Privacy Commissioner of Canada, 30, rue Victoria, Gatineau, QC K1A 1H3
819-994-5444, Fax: 819-994-5424, 800-282-1376

Alberta

Alberta Office of the Information & Privacy Commissioner, Office of the Information & Privacy Commissioner (Edmonton), #410, 9925 - 109th St., Edmonton, AB T5K 2J8
780-422-6860, Fax: 780-422-5682, 888-878-4044, generalinfo@oipc.ab.ca

British Columbia

Office of the Information & Privacy Commissioner for British Columbia, 947 Fort St., 4th Fl., PO Box 9038 Prov Govt, Victoria, BC V8W 9A4
250-387-5629, Fax: 250-387-1696, 800-663-7867, info@oipc.bc.ca

Nova Scotia

Office of the Information & Privacy Commissioner, PO Box 181, Halifax, NS B3J 2M4
902-424-4684, Fax: 902-424-8303, 866-243-1564, oipcns@novascotia.ca

Ontario

Information & Privacy Commissioner of Ontario, #1400, 2 Bloor St. East, Toronto, ON M4W 1A8
416-326-3333, Fax: 416-325-9195, 800-387-0073, info@ipc.on.ca

Prince Edward Island

Office of the Information & Privacy Commissioner, J. Angus MacLean Bldg., 180 Richmond St., 2nd Fl., PO Box 2000, Charlottetown, PE C1A 7L3

Saskatchewan

Information & Privacy Commissioner of Saskatchewan, #503, 1801 Hamilton St., Regina, SK S4P 4B4
306-787-8350, Fax: 306-798-1603, 877-748-2298, webmaster@oipc.sk.ca

Yukon Territory

Yukon Ombudsman, Information & Privacy Commissioner, 3162 - 3rd Ave., Main Fl., Whitehorse, YT Y1A 1G3
867-667-8468, Fax: 867-667-8469, info@yukonombudsman.ca

INFORMATION RESOURCES

Innovation, Science & Economic Development Canada, C.D. Howe Building, 235 Queen St., Ottawa, ON K1A 0H5
613-954-5031, Fax: 613-954-2340, 800-328-6189, info@ic.gc.ca

National Research Council Canada - National Science Library, Bldg. M-55, 1200 Montreal Rd., Ottawa, ON K1A 0R6
613-993-9101, 800-668-1222

Public Services & Procurement, Place du Portage, Phase III, 11, rue Laurier, Ottawa, ON K1A 0S5
questions@tpsgc-pwgsc.gc.ca

Shared Services Canada, 434 Queen St., PO Box 9808 T CSC, Ottawa, ON K1G 4A8
613-947-6296, 855-215-3656, information@ssc-spc.gc.ca

Statistics Canada, 150 Tunney's Pasture Driveway, Ottawa, ON K1A 0T6
514-283-8300, Fax: 514-283-9350, 800-263-1136, STATCAN.infostats-infostats.STATCAN@canada.ca

Surveyor General Branch - Geomatics Canada, #605, 9700 Jasper Ave., Edmonton, AB T5J 4C3
780-495-2519, Fax: 780-495-4052

Newfoundland & Labrador

Office of the Chief Information Officer, 40 Higgins Line, PO Box 8700, St. John's, NL A1B 4J6
709-729-4000, Fax: 709-729-6767, ocio@gov.nl.ca

Nova Scotia

GeoNOVA, 160 Willow St., Amherst, NS B4H 3W5
902-667-7231, 800-798-0706, geoinfo@novascotia.ca

Ontario

Ontario Geographic Names Board, Robinson Place, 300 Water St., PO Box 7000, Peterborough, ON K9J 8M5
705-755-2134

Saskatchewan

Saskatchewan Conservation Data Centre, Fish & Wildlife Branch, Ministry of Environment, 3211 Albert St., Regina, SK S4S 5W6
306-787-7196, Fax: 306-787-9544

INSURANCE

Alberta

Agriculture Financial Services Corporation, 5718 - 56 Ave., Lacombe, AB T4L 1B1
877-899-2372, info@afsc.ca

Alberta Accreditation Committee, #500, 222 - 58th Ave. SW, Calgary, AB T2H 2S3
accreditation@abcouncil.ab.ca

Alberta Insurance Council, #500, 222 - 58th Ave. SW, Calgary, AB T2H 2S3
800-461-3367, info@abcouncil.ab.ca

New Brunswick

New Brunswick Agricultural Insurance Commission, c/o Department of Agriculture, Aquaculture & Fisheries, PO Box 6000, Fredericton, NB E3B 5H1
506-453-2666, Fax: 506-453-7406, DAAF-MAAP@gnb.ca

Newfoundland & Labrador

Newfoundland & Labrador Crop Insurance Agency, PO Box 2006, Corner Brook, NL A2H 6J8
709-637-2077, Fax: 709-637-2591

Quebec

Régime québécois d'assurance parentale, 19, rue Perreault ouest, 1e étage, Rouyn-Noranda, QC J9X 0A1
418-643-7246, 888-610-7727

INSURANCE (LIFE, FIRE, PROPERTY)

See Also: Automobile Insurance; Health Care Insurance

Canada Deposit Insurance Corporation, 50 O'Connor St., 17th Floor, Ottawa, ON K1P 6L2
Fax: 613-996-6095, 800-461-2342, info@cdic.ca

Office of the Superintendent of Financial Institutions, Kent Square, 255 Albert St., 12th Fl., Ottawa, ON K1A 0H2
613-990-7788, Fax: 613-990-5591, 800-385-8647, information@osfi-bsif.gc.ca

Alberta

Economics & Fiscal Policy Division, Federal Bldg., 9820 - 107th St., 8th Fl., Edmonton, AB T5K 1E7

British Columbia

Insurance Council of British Columbia, #300, 1040 West Georgia St., PO Box 7, Vancouver, BC V6E 4H1
604-688-0321, Fax: 604-662-7767, 877-688-0321, info@insurancecouncilofbc.com

Manitoba

Manitoba Financial Services Agency, c/o Financial Institutions Regulation Branch, #207, 400 St. Mary Ave., Winnipeg, MB R3C 4K5
204-945-2542, Fax: 204-948-2268, 800-282-8069, insurance@gov.mb.ca

Manitoba Public Insurance Corporation, 234 Donald St., #B100, PO Box 6300, Winnipeg, MB R3C 4A4
204-985-7000, Fax: 204-985-3525, 800-665-2410

Northwest Territories

Northwest Territories Department of Finance, PO Box 1320, Yellowknife, NT X1A 2L9

Nova Scotia

Nova Scotia Crop & Livestock Insurance Commission, 74 Research Dr., Truro, NS B6L 2R2
902-893-6370, 800-565-6371, nsclic@novascotia.ca

Ontario

Deposit Insurance Corporation of Ontario, #700, 4711 Yonge St., Toronto, ON M2N 6K8
416-325-9444, Fax: 416-325-9722, 800-268-6653, info@dico.com

Financial Services Commission of Ontario, North York City Ctr., 5160 Yonge St., 17th Fl., PO Box 85, Toronto, ON M2N 6L9
416-250-7250, Fax: 416-590-7070, 800-668-0128, contactcentre@fsco.gov.on.ca

Workplace Safety & Insurance Board, 200 Front St. West, Ground Fl., Toronto, ON M5V 3J1
416-344-1000, Fax: 416-344-4684, 800-387-0750

Prince Edward Island

Agricultural Insurance Corporation, 7 Gerald McCarville Drive, Kensington, PE C0B 1M0

Saskatchewan

Financial & Consumer Affairs Authority, #601, 1919 Saskatchewan Dr., Regina, SK S4P 4H2
306-787-5645, Fax: 306-787-5899, 877-880-5550, consumerprotection@gov.sk.ca

Saskatchewan Crop Insurance Corporation, 484 Prince William Dr., PO Box 3000, Melville, SK S0A 2P0
306-728-7200, Fax: 306-728-7202, 888-935-0000, customer.service@scic.gov.sk.ca

Saskatchewan Government Insurance, 2260 - 11th Ave., Regina, SK S4P 0J9
306-751-1200, Fax: 306-787-7477, 844-855-2744, sgiinquiries@sgi.sk.ca

INTERGOVERNMENTAL AFFAIRS

See Also: Federal-Provincial Affairs; International Affairs

Canadian Intergovernmental Conference Secretariat, 222 Queen St., 10th Fl., PO Box 488 A, Ottawa, ON K1N 8V5
613-995-2341, Fax: 613-996-6091, info@scics.gc.ca

Destination Canada, #800, 1045 Howe St., Vancouver, BC V6Z 2A9
604-638-8300

British Columbia

Intergovernmental Relations Secretariat, PO Box 9433 Prov Govt, Victoria, BC V8W 9V3
250-387-0783, Fax: 250-387-1920, igrs@gov.bc.ca

Manitoba

Finance Research Division, #910, 386 Broadway, Winnipeg, MB R3C 3R6
204-945-3757, Fax: 204-945-5051

New Brunswick

Intergovernmental Affairs Division, Chancery Place, 675 King St., 5th Fl., Fredericton, NB E3B 1E9
506-444-4948, Fax: 506-453-2995, iga@gnb.ca

Newfoundland & Labrador

Labrador Affairs Secretariat, Labrador Affairs, #438, 440 Hamilton River Rd., PO Box 3014 B, Happy Valley - Goose Bay, NL A0P 1E0
709-896-1780, Fax: 709-896-0045, 888-435-8111

Newfoundland & Labrador Department of Environment & Climate Change, PO Box 8700, St. John's, NL A1B 4J6
ECCInfo@gov.nl.ca

Northwest Territories
Northwest Territories Department of the Executive & Indigenous Affairs, PO Box 1320, Yellowknife, NT X1A 2L9

Nova Scotia
Nova Scotia Department of Intergovernmental Affairs, Duke Tower, 5251 Duke St., 5th Fl., PO Box 1617, Halifax, NS B3J 2Y3
902-424-5153, Fax: 902-424-0728
Office of Acadian Affairs, Dennis Bldg., 1741 Brunswick St., 3rd Fl., PO Box 682, Halifax, NS B3J 2T3
902-424-0497, Fax: 902-428-0124, 866-382-5811, bonjour@novascotia.ca

Nunavut
Nunavut Territory Department of Executive & Intergovernmental Affairs, 1084 Aeroplex bldg., PO Box 1000 200, Iqaluit, NU X0A 0H0
867-975-6000, Fax: 867-975-6099

Ontario
Ontario Ministry of Intergovernmental Affairs, Legislative Bldg., #223, 223 Queen's Park, Toronto, ON M7A 1A4
416-326-1234, 800-268-7095

Saskatchewan
Intergovernmental Affairs, Legislative Bldg., #135, 2405 Legislative Dr., Regina, SK S4S 0B3
306-787-4474

INTERNATIONAL AFFAIRS
See Also: Trade
Canadian International Trade Tribunal, Standard Life Centre, 333 Laurier Ave. West, 15th Floor, Ottawa, ON K1A 0G7
613-990-2452, Fax: 613-990-2439, 855-307-2488, citt-tcce@tribunal.gc.ca
Department of National Defence & the Canadian Armed Forces, National Defence HQ, Major-General George R. Pearkes Bldg., 101 Colonel By Dr., Ottawa, ON K1A 0K2
613-995-2534, Fax: 613-992-4739, 888-995-2534, information@forces.gc.ca
Destination Canada, #800, 1045 Howe St., Vancouver, BC V6Z 2A9
604-638-8300
Global Affairs Canada, Enquiries Service, 125 Sussex Dr., Ottawa, ON K1A 0G2
Fax: 613-996-9709, 800-267-8376
International Development Research Centre, 150 Kent St., PO Box 8500, Ottawa, ON K1G 3H9
613-236-6163, Fax: 613-238-7230, info@idrc.ca

British Columbia
Intergovernmental Relations Secretariat, PO Box 9433 Prov Govt, Victoria, BC V8W 9V3
250-387-0783, Fax: 250-387-1920, igrs@gov.bc.ca

New Brunswick
Intergovernmental Affairs Division, Chancery Place, 675 King St., 5th Fl., Fredericton, NB E3B 1E9
506-444-4948, Fax: 506-453-2995, iga@gnb.ca

Ontario
Ontario Ministry of Intergovernmental Affairs, Legislative Bldg., #223, 223 Queen's Park, Toronto, ON M7A 1A4
416-326-1234, 800-268-7095

Quebec
Ministère des Relations internationales et Francophonie, Édifice Hector-Fabre, 525, boul Réne-Lévesque est, Québec, QC G1R 5R9
418-649-2300, Fax: 418-649-2656

INTERNATIONAL AID
Global Affairs Canada, Enquiries Service, 125 Sussex Dr., Ottawa, ON K1A 0G2
Fax: 613-996-9709, 800-267-8376
International Development Research Centre, 150 Kent St., PO Box 8500, Ottawa, ON K1G 3H9
613-236-6163, Fax: 613-238-7230, info@idrc.ca

INTERNATIONAL TRADE
See Also: Trade
Canadian International Trade Tribunal, Standard Life Centre, 333 Laurier Ave. West, 15th Floor, Ottawa, ON K1A 0G7
613-990-2452, Fax: 613-990-2439, 855-307-2488, citt-tcce@tribunal.gc.ca
Global Affairs Canada, Enquiries Service, 125 Sussex Dr., Ottawa, ON K1A 0G2
Fax: 613-996-9709, 800-267-8376

British Columbia
British Columbia Ministry of Jobs, Economic Recovery & Innovation, PO Box 9071 Prov Govt, Victoria, BC V8W 9T2
250-356-2771, Fax: 250-953-0927

Ontario
Ontario Ministry of Citizenship & Multiculturalism, 56 Wellesley St. West, 14th Fl., Toronto, ON M7A 2E7
416-212-0036

INUIT
See Also: Indigenous Affairs
Canadian Northern Economic Development Agency, Ottawa, ON K1A 0H4
855-897-2667,
CanNor.InfoNorth.InfoNord.CanNor@canada.ca

INVESTMENT
See Also: Business Development; Industry
Canada Economic Development for Québec Regions, #500, 800, boul René-Lévesque ouest, Montréal, QC H3B 1X9
514-283-6412, Fax: 514-283-3302, 866-385-6412
Canada Infrastructure Bank, 150 King St. West, PO Box 15, Toronto, ON M5H 1J9
833-551-5245
Canada Pension Plan Investment Board, #2500, 1 Queen St. East, Toronto, ON M5C 2W5
416-868-4075, Fax: 416-868-8689, 866-557-9510, contact@cppib.com
Canada Savings Bonds, #201, 50 O'Connor St., PO Box 2770 D, Ottawa, ON K1P 1J7
905-754-2012, Fax: 613-782-8096, 800-575-5151
Canadian Northern Economic Development Agency, Ottawa, ON K1A 0H4
855-897-2667,
CanNor.InfoNorth.InfoNord.CanNor@canada.ca
Federal Economic Development Agency for Southern Ontario, #101, 139 Northfield Dr. West, Waterloo, ON N2L 5A6
Fax: 519-725-4976, 866-593-5505
FedNor (Federal Economic Development Initiative in Northern Ontario), 19 Lisgar St., Sudbury, ON P3E 3L4
Fax: 705-671-0717, 877-333-6673
Finance Canada, 90 Elgin St., Ottawa, ON K1A 0G5
613-369-3710, Fax: 613-369-4065, fin.financepublic-financepublique.fin@canada.ca
Innovation, Science & Economic Development Canada, C.D. Howe Building, 235 Queen St., Ottawa, ON K1A 0H5
613-954-5031, Fax: 613-954-2340, 800-328-6189, info@ic.gc.ca
Public Sector Pension Investment Board, #200, 440 Laurier Ave. West, Ottawa, ON K1R 7X6
613-782-3095, Fax: 613-782-6864, info@investpsp.ca

Alberta
Alberta Investment Management Corporation, #1100, 10830 Jasper Ave., Edmonton, AB T5J 2B3
780-392-3600
Alberta Securities Commission, #600, 250 - 5th St. SW, Calgary, AB T2P 0R4
403-297-6454, Fax: 403-297-6156, 877-355-0585, inquiries@asc.ca
Tax & Revenue Administration Division, Sir Frederick W. Haultain Bldg., 9811 - 109th St., 2nd Fl., Edmonton, AB T5K 2L5
780-427-3044, Fax: 780-427-0348, tra.revenue@gov.ab.ca

British Columbia
BC Immigrant Investment Fund Ltd. & BC Renaissance Capital Fund Ltd., #301, 865 Hornby St., Vancouver, BC V6Z 2G3
Fax: 250-952-0371
British Columbia Ministry of Jobs, Economic Recovery & Innovation, PO Box 9071 Prov Govt, Victoria, BC V8W 9T2
250-356-2771, Fax: 250-953-0927
British Columbia Securities Commission, Pacific Centre, 701 West Georgia St., 12th Fl., PO Box 10142, Vancouver, BC V7Y 1L2
604-899-6500, Fax: 604-899-6506, 800-373-6393, inquiries@bcsc.bc.ca
Forestry Innovation Investment Ltd., #1200, 1130 West Pender St., Vancouver, BC V6E 4A4
604-685-7507, Fax: 604-685-5373, info@bcfii.ca

Manitoba
Manitoba Securities Commission, #500, 400 St. Mary Ave., Winnipeg, MB R3C 4K5
204-945-2548, Fax: 204-945-0330, securities@gov.mb.ca
Treasury Division, #350, 363 Broadway, Winnipeg, MB R3C 3N9
204-945-3702, Fax: 204-948-2233

New Brunswick
Financial & Consumer Services Commission, #300, 85 Charlotte St., Saint John, NB E2L 2J2
506-658-3060, Fax: 506-658-3059, 866-933-2222, info@fcnb.ca
Opportunities New Brunswick, Place 2000, 250 King St., PO Box 6000, Fredericton, NB E3B 5H1
506-453-5471, Fax: 506-444-5277, 855-746-4662, info@onbcanada.ca

Northwest Territories
Northwest Territories Business Development & Investment Corporation, 5009 - 50th Ave., PO Box 1320, Yellowknife, NT X1A 2L9
867-767-9075, Fax: 867-765-0652, 800-661-0599
Northwest Territories Department of Industry, Tourism & Investment, PO Box 1320, Yellowknife, NT X1A 2L9

Nova Scotia
Innovacorp, #400, 1871 Hollis St., Halifax, NS B3J 0C3
902-424-8670, Fax: 902-424-4679, 800-565-7051, info@innovacorp.ca
Nova Scotia Securities Commission, PO Box 458, Halifax, NS B3J 2P8
902-424-7768, Fax: 902-424-4625, 855-424-2499, NSSCinquiries@novascotia.ca

Ontario
Ontario Securities Commission, 20 Queen St. West, 20th Fl., PO Box 55, Toronto, ON M5H 3S8
416-593-8314, Fax: 416-593-8122, 877-785-1555, inquiries@osc.gov.on.ca

Prince Edward Island
Charlottetown Area Development Corporation, 4 Pownal St., PO Box 786, Charlottetown, PE C1A 7L9
902-892-5341, Fax: 902-368-1935
Debt, Investment & Pension Management, Shaw Bldg. South, 95 Rochford St., 3rd Fl., PO Box 2000, Charlottetown, PE C1A 7N8

Quebec
Financement-Québec, 12, rue Saint-Louis, 3e étage, Québec, QC G1R 5L3
418-691-2203, Fax: 418-644-6214, financement.regroupe@finances.gouv.qc.ca
Investissement Québec, #60, 1195, av Lavigerie, Québec, QC G1V 4N3
418-643-5172, Fax: 418-528-2063, 844-474-6367

JUSTICE
Justice Canada, 284 Wellington St., Ottawa, ON K1A 0H8
613-957-4222, Fax: 613-954-0811, webadmin@justice.gc.ca
Public Prosecution Service of Canada, 160 Elgin St., 12th Fl., Ottawa, ON K1A 0H8
613-957-6489, 877-505-7772, info@ppsc.gc.ca

Alberta
Alberta Justice & Solicitor General, John E. Brownlee Bldg., 10365 - 97th St., 9th Fl., Edmonton, AB T5J 3W7
780-427-2745
Alberta Office of the Public Interest Commissioner, #700, 9925 - 109th St., Edmonton, AB T5K 2J8
780-641-8659, 855-641-8659, info@pic.alberta.ca

British Columbia
British Columbia Ministry of Attorney General & Minister responsible for Housing, PO Box 9044 Prov Govt, Victoria, BC V8W 9E2
British Columbia Ministry of Public Safety & Solicitor General, PO Box 9290 Prov Govt, Victoria, BC V8W 9J7
250-356-0149, Fax: 250-387-6224, 800-663-7867, PSSG.Correspondence@gov.bc.ca
Justice Education Society, #260, 800 Hornby St., Vancouver, BC V6Z 2C3
604-660-9870, Fax: 604-775-3476, info@justiceeducation.ca

Manitoba
Manitoba Justice, Administration & Finance, #1110, 405 Broadway Ave., Winnipeg, MB R3C 3L6
204-945-2878

New Brunswick
New Brunswick Department of Justice & Public Safety, Marysville Place, 3rd Fl., PO Box 6000, Fredericton, NB E3B 5H1
506-453-3992, DPS-MSP.Information@gnb.ca

Nova Scotia
Nova Scotia Department of Justice, 1690 Hollis St., PO Box 7, Halifax, NS B3J 2L6
902-424-4030, justweb@gov.ns.ca
Office of the Police Complaints Commissioner, 1690 Hollis St., 3rd Fl., PO Box 1573, Halifax, NS B3J 2Y3
902-424-3246, Fax: 902-424-1777, polcom@novascotia.ca

Nunavut
Nunavut Territory Department of Justice, PO Box 1000 500, Iqaluit, NU X0A 0H0
867-975-6170, Fax: 867-975-6195, justice@gov.nu.ca

Ontario
Ontario Ministry of the Attorney General, McMurtry-Scott Bldg., 720 Bay St., 11th Fl., Toronto, ON M7A 2S9
416-326-2220, Fax: 416-326-4016, 800-518-7901, attorneygeneral@ontario.ca
Special Investigations Unit, 5090 Commerce Blvd., Mississauga, ON L4W 5M4
416-622-0748, Fax: 416-622-2455, 800-787-8529

Quebec
Bureau des enquêtes indépandantes, #6.01, 201, Place Charles-Lemoyne, Longueuil, QC J4K 2T5
450-640-1350, Fax: 450-670-6386
Ministère de la Justice, Édifice Louis-Philippe-Pigeon, 1200, rte de l'Église, Québec, QC G1V 4M1
418-643-5140, 866-536-5140, informations@justice.gouv.qc.ca

Saskatchewan
Saskatchewan Justice & Attorney General, 1874 Scarth St., Regina, SK S4P 4B3
Yukon Territory
Yukon Justice, Andrew Philipsen Law Centre, 2134 - 2nd Ave., PO Box 2703, Whitehorse, YT Y1A 2C6
867-667-3033, Fax: 867-667-5200, justice@yukon.ca

JUSTICE DEPARTMENTS
Justice Canada, 284 Wellington St., Ottawa, ON K1A 0H8
613-957-4222, Fax: 613-954-0811, webadmin@justice.gc.ca
Alberta
Alberta Justice & Solicitor General, John E. Brownlee Bldg., 10365 - 97th St., 9th Fl., Edmonton, AB T5J 3W7
780-427-2745
British Columbia
British Columbia Ministry of Attorney General & Minister responsible for Housing, PO Box 9044 Prov Govt, Victoria, BC V8W 9E2
British Columbia Ministry of Public Safety & Solicitor General, PO Box 9290 Prov Govt, Victoria, BC V8W 9J7
250-356-0149, Fax: 250-387-6224, 800-663-7867, PSSG.Correspondence@gov.bc.ca
Manitoba
Manitoba Justice, Administration & Finance, #1110, 405 Broadway Ave., Winnipeg, MB R3C 3L6
204-945-2878,
New Brunswick
New Brunswick Department of Justice & Public Safety, Marysville Place, 3rd Fl., PO Box 6000, Fredericton, NB E3B 5H1
506-453-3992, DPS-MSP.Information@gnb.ca
Newfoundland & Labrador
Newfoundland & Labrador Department of Justice & Public Safety, East Block, Confederation Bldg., 4th Fl., PO Box 8700, St. John's, NL A1B 4J6
709-729-2869, Fax: 709-729-0469, justice@gov.nl.ca
Northwest Territories
Northwest Territories Department of Justice, 4903 - 49th St., PO Box 1320, Yellowknife, NT X1A 2L9
867-767-9256, justice_communications@gov.nt.ca
Nova Scotia
Nova Scotia Department of Justice, 1690 Hollis St., PO Box 7, Halifax, NS B3J 2L6
902-424-4030, justweb@gov.ns.ca
Nunavut
Nunavut Territory Department of Justice, PO Box 1000 500, Iqaluit, NU X0A 0H0
867-975-6170, Fax: 867-975-6195, justice@gov.nu.ca
Ontario
Ontario Ministry of the Attorney General, McMurtry-Scott Bldg., 720 Bay St., 11th Fl., Toronto, ON M7A 2S9
416-326-2220, Fax: 416-326-4016, 800-518-7901, attorneygeneral@ontario.ca
Prince Edward Island
Prince Edward Island Department of Justice & Public Safety, Shaw Bldg. South, 95 Rochford St., 4th Fl., PO Box 2000, Charlottetown, PE C1A 7N8
902-368-4589, Fax: 902-368-5283, DeptJPS@gov.pe.ca
Quebec
Ministère de la Justice, Édifice Louis-Philippe-Pigeon, 1200, rte de l'Église, Québec, QC G1V 4M1
418-643-5140, 866-536-5140, informations@justice.gouv.qc.ca
Saskatchewan
Saskatchewan Justice & Attorney General, 1874 Scarth St., Regina, SK S4P 4B3
Yukon Territory
Yukon Justice, Andrew Philipsen Law Centre, 2134 - 2nd Ave., PO Box 2703, Whitehorse, YT Y1A 2C6
867-667-3033, Fax: 867-667-5200, justice@yukon.ca

LABOUR
Canada Industrial Relations Board, 240 Sparks St., 4th Fl. West, Ottawa, ON K1A 0X8
Fax: 613-995-9493, 800-575-9696
Canadian Council of Directors of Apprenticeship, 140 Promenade du Portage, 6th Fl., Phase IV, Gatineau, QC K1A 0J9
Fax: 819-994-0202, 877-599-6933, redseal-sceaurouge@hrsdc-rhdcc.gc.ca
Employment & Social Development Canada, 140, promenade du Portage, Gatineau, QC K1A 0J9
Federal Public Sector Labour Relations & Employment Board, C.D. Howe Bldg., West Tower, 240 Sparks St., 6th Fl., PO Box 1525 B, Ottawa, ON K1P 5V2
613-990-1800, Fax: 613-990-1849, 866-931-3454, mail.courrier@fpslreb-crtespf.gc.ca

National Joint Council, C.D. Howe Building, 240 Sparks St. West, 7th Fl., PO Box 1525 B, Ottawa, ON K1P 5V2
613-990-1805, Fax: 613-990-7071, email.courrier@njc-cnm.gc.ca
Public Service Commission, 22, rue Eddy, Gatineau, QC K1A 0M7
800-645-5605
Public Service Labour Relations Board, CD Howe Building, 240 Sparks St., 6th Fl., PO Box 1525 B, Ottawa, ON K1P 5V2
613-990-1800, Fax: 613-990-1849, 866-931-3454, mail.courrier@pslrb-crtfp.gc.ca
Alberta
Alberta Apprenticeship & Industry Training Board, Centre for Applied Technologies Bldg., #430, 11763 - 106 St., Edmonton, AB T5G 2R1
403-476-9757, Fax: 780-422-3734, -310-0000
Alberta Labour & Immigration, Legislature Bldg., #107, 10800 - 97th Ave., Edmonton, AB T5K 2B6
780-427-3731, 877-427-3731
Apprenticeship & Student Aid Division, Commerce Place, 10155 - 102nd St., 6th Fl., Edmonton, AB T5J 4L5
Health Quality Council of Alberta, #210, 811 - 14 St. NW, Calgary, AB T2N 2A4
403-297-8162, Fax: 403-297-8258, 855-508-8162, info@hqca.ca
Labour Relations Board, Labour Building, #501, 10808 - 99 Ave., Edmonton, AB T5K 0G5
780-427-8547, Fax: 780-422-0970, 800-463-2572, alrbinfo@gov.ab.ca
Occupational Health & Safety Council, Standard Life Centre, 10405 Jasper Ave., Edmonton, AB T5J 3N4
780-415-8690, 866-415-8690
Public Service Commission, Peace Hills Trust Tower, 10011 - 109th St., 7th Fl., Edmonton, AB T5J 3S8
780-408-8450
British Columbia
British Columbia Labour Relations Board, Oceanic Plaza, #600, 1066 West Hastings St., Vancouver, BC V6E 3X1
604-660-1300, Fax: 604-660-1892, information@lrb.bc.ca
British Columbia Ministry of Labour, PO Box 9064 Prov Govt, Victoria, BC V8W 9K4
250-953-0910, Fax: 250-953-0928
British Columbia Public Service Agency, PO Box 9404 Prov Govt, Victoria, BC V8W 9V1
250-387-0518, Fax: 250-356-7074
Employment Standards Tribunal, Oceanic Plaza, #650, 1066 West Hastings St., Vancouver, BC V6E 3X1
604-775-3512, Fax: 604-775-3372, registrar@bcest.bc.ca
Workers' Compensation Appeal Tribunal, #150, 4600 Jacombs Rd., Richmond, BC V6V 3B1
604-664-7800, Fax: 604-664-7898, 800-663-2782
Workers' Compensation Board of British Columbia, PO Box 5350 Terminal, Vancouver, BC V6B 5L5
604-276-3100, Fax: 604-276-3247, 888-621-7233
Manitoba
Advisory Council on Workplace Safety & Health, 401 York Ave., 2nd Fl., Winnipeg, MB R3C 0P8
204-945-3446, Fax: 204-948-2209, 866-888-8186, wshcompl@gov.mb.ca
Board of Electrical Examiners, Norquay Bldg., #500, 401 York Ave, Winnipeg, MB R3C 0P8
204-945-3373, Fax: 204-948-2309
Civil Service Commission Board, #935, 155 Carlton St., Winnipeg, MB R3C 3H8
204-945-1435, Fax: 204-945-1486
Manitoba Advanced Education, Skills & Immigration, Legislative Bldg., #352, 450 Broadway, Winnipeg, MB R3C 0V8
Manitoba Civil Service Commission, #935, 155 Carlton St., Winnipeg, MB R3C 3H8
204-945-2332, Fax: 204-945-1486, 800-282-8069, csc@gov.mb.ca
Manitoba Education, Legislative Bldg., #162, 450 Broadway, Winnipeg, MB R3C 0V8
204-945-3720, Fax: 204-945-1291
Manitoba Families, Legislative Bldg., #357, 450 Broadway, Winnipeg, MB R3C 0V8
204-945-3744, 866-626-4862
Pension Commission of Manitoba, #1004, 401 York Ave., Winnipeg, MB R3C 0P8
204-945-2740, Fax: 204-948-2375, pensions@gov.mb.ca
Workers' Compensation Board of Manitoba, 333 Broadway Ave., Winnipeg, MB R3C 4W3
204-954-4321, Fax: 204-954-4999, 800-362-3340, wcb@wcb.mb.ca
New Brunswick
New Brunswick Department of Post-Secondary Education, Training & Labour, Chestnut Complex, PO Box 6000, Fredericton, NB E3B 5H1
506-453-2597, Fax: 506-453-3618, dpetlinfo@gnb.ca

WorkSafeNB, 1 Portland St., PO Box 160, Saint John, NB E2L 3X9
506-632-2200, 800-222-9775, communications@ws-ts.nb.ca
Newfoundland & Labrador
Labour Relations Board, Natural Resources Bldg., 50 Elizabeth Ave., 5th Fl., PO Box 8700, St. John's, NL A1B 4J6
709-729-2707, Fax: 709-729-5738, lrb@gov.nl.ca
Newfoundland & Labrador Department of Immigration, Population Growth & Skills, West Block, Confederation Bldg., 3rd Fl., PO Box 8700, St. John's, NL A1B 4J6
709-729-1795, isl@gov.nl.ca
Newfoundland & Labrador Public Service Commission, 261 Kenmount Rd., PO Box 8700, St. John's, NL A1B 4J6
709-729-5810, Fax: 709-729-6234, 855-330-5810, contactpsc@gov.nl.ca
Newfoundland & Labrador Workplace Health, Safety & Compensation Commission (WorkplaceNL), 146 - 148 Forest Rd., PO Box 9000, St. John's, NL A1A 3B8
709-778-1000, Fax: 709-738-1714, 800-563-9000, info@workplacenl.ca
Northwest Territories
Apprenticeship, Trade & Occupations Certification Board, PO Box 1320, Yellowknife, NT X1A 2L9
867-767-9351, apprenticeship@gov.nt.ca
Northwest Territories & Nunavut Workers' Safety & Compensation Commission, Centre Square Tower, 5022 - 49th St., 5th Fl., PO Box 8888, Yellowknife, NT X1A 2R3
867-920-3888, Fax: 867-873-4596, 800-661-0792
Northwest Territories Department of Education, Culture & Employment, PO Box 1320, Yellowknife, NT X1A 2L9
ecepublicaffairs@gov.nt.ca
Nova Scotia
Labour Board of Nova Scotia, PO Box 202, Halifax, NS B3J 2M4
902-424-6730, Fax: 902-424-1744, 877-424-6730, labourboard@novascotia.ca
Nova Scotia Department of Advanced Education, 1505 Barrington St., PO Box 697, Halifax, NS B3J 2T8
902-424-5301, Fax: 902-424-2203, lae-correspondence@novascotia.ca
Nova Scotia Department of Labour, Skills & Immigration, 1469 Brenton St., 3rd Fl., PO Box 1535, Halifax, NS B3J 2Y3
Nova Scotia Public Service Commission, PO Box 943, Halifax, NS B3J 2V9
902-424-7660, reception-psc@novascotia.ca
Pay Equity Commission, 5151 Terminal Rd., 6th Fl., PO Box 697, Halifax, NS B3J 2T8
902-424-8466, Fax: 902-424-0575
Workers' Advisers Program, #309, 5640 Spring Garden Rd., PO Box 1063, Halifax, NS B3J 3M7
902-424-5050, Fax: 902-424-0530, 800-774-4712
Workers' Compensation Appeals Tribunal, #201, 1465 Brenton St., Halifax, NS B3J 3T4
902-424-2250, Fax: 902-424-2321, 800-274-8281
Workers' Compensation Board of Nova Scotia, 5668 South St., PO Box 1150, Halifax, NS B3J 2Y2
902-491-8999, 800-870-3331, info@wcb.ns.ca
Nunavut
Labour Standards Board, PO Box 1269, Iqaluit, NU X0A 0H0
867-975-6159, Fax: 867-975-6376, nlsb@gov.nu.ca
Ontario
Corporate Management & Services Division, 400 University Ave., 14th Fl., Toronto, ON M7A 1T7
Office of the Employer Advisor, 505 University Ave., 20th Fl., Toronto, ON M5G 2P1
416-327-0020, Fax: 416-327-0726, 800-387-0774
Office of the Worker Advisor, #1300, 123 Edward St., Toronto, ON M5G 1E2
416-325-8570, Fax: 416-325-4830, 800-660-6769, owaweb@ontario.ca
Ontario Labour Relations Board, 505 University Ave., 2nd Fl., Toronto, ON M5G 2P1
416-326-7500, Fax: 416-326-7531, 877-339-3335
Ontario Ministry of Colleges & Universities, 438 University Ave., 5th Fl., Toronto, ON M7A 2A5
416-325-2929, Fax: 416-325-6348, 800-387-5514, information.met@ontario.ca
Ontario Ministry of Education, 315 Front Street, 14th Fl., Toronto, ON M7A 0B8
416-325-2929, 800-387-5514
Ontario Ministry of Labour, Training & Skills Development, 400 University Ave., 14th Fl., Toronto, ON M7A 1T7
416-326-7160, 800-531-5551
Operations Division, 400 University Ave., 14th Fl., Toronto, ON M7A 1T7
416-326-7606, Fax: 416-212-4455, 800-531-5551
Pay Equity Office, #300, 180 Dundas St. West, Toronto, ON M7A 2S6
416-314-1896, Fax: 416-314-8741, 800-387-8813
Public Service Appeal Boards, Dundas/Edward Ctr., #600, 180 Dundas St. West, Toronto, ON M5G 1Z8
416-326-1388, Fax: 416-326-1396

Public Service Commission, Whitney Block, 99 Wellesley St. West, 5th Fl., Toronto, ON M7A 1W4
416-325-1750
Treasury Board Secretariat, 315 Front St. West, 7th Fl., Toronto, ON M7A 0B8
Workplace Safety & Insurance Board, 200 Front St. West, Ground Fl., Toronto, ON M5V 3J1
416-344-1000, Fax: 416-344-4684, 800-387-0750

Prince Edward Island
Advisory Council on the Status of Women, Sherwood Business Centre, 161 St. Peter's Rd., Main Level, PO Box 2000, Charlottetown, PE C1A 7N8
902-368-4510, Fax: 902-368-3269, info@peistatusofwomen.ca
Prince Edward Island Department of Justice & Public Safety, Shaw Bldg. South, 95 Rochford St., 4th Fl., PO Box 2000, Charlottetown, PE C1A 7N8
902-368-4589, Fax: 902-368-5283, DeptJPS@gov.pe.ca
Prince Edward Island Workers' Compensation Board, 14 Weymouth St., PO Box 757, Charlottetown, PE C1A 7L7
902-368-5680, Fax: 902-368-5696, 800-237-5049
Public Service Commission, Shaw Bldg. North, 105 Rochford St., 1st Fl., PO Box 2000, Charlottetown, PE C1A 7N8
902-368-4080, Fax: 902-368-4383
Workers Compensation Appeal Tribunal, c/o Executive Council, 95 Rochford St., PO Box 2000, Charlottetown, PE C1A 7N8
902-569-0545

Quebec
Commission de la construction du Québec, 8485, av Christophe-Colomb, Montréal, QC H2M 0A7
Commission de la fonction publique, 800, Place D'Youville, 7e étage, Québec, QC G1R 3P4
418-643-1425, Fax: 418-643-7264, 800-432-0432, cfp@cfp.gouv.qc.ca
Commission des normes, de l'équité, de la santé et de la sécurité du travail, 524, rue Bourdages, Québec, QC G1M 1A1
Fax: 418-266-4015, 844-838-0808
Commission des partenaires du marché du travail, Tour de la Place-Victoria, 800, rue du Square-Victoria, 28e étage, CP 100, Montréal, QC H4Z 1B7
514-873-5252, 866-640-3059, partenaires@mess.gouv.qc.ca
Conseil consultatif du travail et de la main d'oeuvre, #17.100, 500, boul René-Lévesque ouest, Montréal, QC H2Z 1W7
514-873-2880, Fax: 514-873-1129
Ministère du Travail, de l'Emploi et de la Solidarité sociale, 150, rue Monseigneur-Ross, 5e étage, Québec, QC G4X 2S7
514-873-4000, 877-767-8773
Office des professions du Québec, 800, Place D'Youville, 10e étage, Québec, QC G1R 5Z3
418-643-6912, Fax: 418-643-0973, 800-643-6912
Régie du bâtiment du Québec, 545, boul Crémazie est, 4e étage, Montréal, QC H2M 2V2
514-873-0976, 800-361-0761
Tribunal administratif du travail, 900, boul René-Lévesque est, 5e étage, Québec, QC G1R 6C9
418-643-3208, Fax: 418-643-8946, 866-864-3646

Saskatchewan
Labour Relations Board, #1600, 1920 Broad St., Regina, SK S4P 3V2
306-787-2406, Fax: 306-787-2664
Office of the Workers' Advocate, #300, 1870 Albert St., Regina, SK S4P 4W1
Fax: 306-787-0249, 877-787-2456, workersadvocate@gov.sk.ca
Saskatchewan Education, 2220 College Ave., Regina, SK S4P 4V9
learning.inquiry@gov.sk.ca
Saskatchewan Labour Relations & Workplace Safety, #300, 1870 Albert St., Regina, SK S4P 4W1
Fax: 306-787-7404
Saskatchewan Workers' Compensation Board, #200, 1881 Scarth St., Regina, SK S4P 4L1
306-787-4370, Fax: 306-787-4311, 800-667-7590, webmaster@wcbsask.com

Yukon Territory
Yukon Public Service Commission, 2071 - 2nd Ave., PO Box 2703, Whitehorse, YT Y1A 2C6
867-667-5653, Fax: 867-667-5755, pscwebsite@yukon.ca
Yukon Workers' Compensation Health & Safety Board, 401 Strickland St., Whitehorse, YT Y1A 5N8
867-667-5645, Fax: 867-393-6279, 800-661-0443, worksafe@yukon.ca

LAND RESOURCES
See Also: Agriculture; Forest Resources; Parks
Canada Lands Company Ltd., #1700, 1 University Ave., Toronto, ON M5J 2P1
416-214-1250, Fax: 416-214-1121
Natural Resources Canada, 580 Booth St., Ottawa, ON K1A 0E4
343-292-6096, Fax: 613-992-7211

Parks Canada, National Office, 30, rue Victoria, Gatineau, QC J8X 0B3
819-420-9486, 888-773-8888, information@pc.gc.ca
Alberta
Land Use Secretariat, Centre West Bldg., 10035 - 108th St., 9th Fl., Edmonton, AB T5J 3E1
780-644-7972, Fax: 780-644-1034, luf@gov.ab.ca
Special Areas Board, Special Areas Board Administration, 212 - 2nd Ave. West, PO Box 820, Hanna, AB T0J 1P0
403-854-5600, Fax: 403-854-5527
British Columbia
Surface Rights Board of British Columbia, #10, 10551 Shellbridge Way, Richmond, BC V6X 2W9
604-775-1740, Fax: 604-775-1742, 888-775-1740, office@surfacerightsboard.bc.ca
Manitoba
Manitoba Land Value Appraisal Commission, #1144, 363 Broadway, Winnipeg, MB R3C 3N9
204-945-5455, Fax: 204-948-2235
Northwest Territories
Northwest Territories Department of Environment & Natural Resources, PO Box 1320, Yellowknife, NT X1A 2L9
867-767-9055, enr_communications@gov.nt.ca
Northwest Territories Department of Lands, Gallery Bldg., 4923 - 52nd St., 1st & 2nd Fl., PO Box 1320, Yellowknife, NT X1A 2L9
867-767-9185, Fax: 867-669-0905, 855-698-5263, Lands@gov.nt.ca
Northwest Territories Department of Municipal & Community Affairs, PO Box 1320, Yellowknife, NT X1A 2L9
Nova Scotia
Crown Land Information Management Centre, 1701 Hollis St., PO Box 698, Halifax, NS B3J 2T9
902-424-3171, Fax: 902-424-7068, crownland@novascotia.ca
Nova Scotia Lands Inc., PO Box 430 A, Sydney, NS B1P 6H2
Nunavut
Nunavut Territory Department of Environment, PO Box 1000 1320, Iqaluit, NU X0A 0H0
867-975-7700, Fax: 867-975-7742, environment@gov.nu.ca
Prince Edward Island
Prince Edward Island Department of Justice & Public Safety, Shaw Bldg. South, 95 Rochford St., 4th Fl., PO Box 2000, Charlottetown, PE C1A 7N8
902-368-4589, Fax: 902-368-5283, DeptJPS@gov.pe.ca
Quebec
Commission de protection du territoire agricole du Québec, 200, ch Ste-Foy, 2e étage, Québec, QC G1R 4X6
418-643-3314, Fax: 418-643-2261, 800-667-5294, info@cptaq.gouv.qc.ca
Territoire, #E330 - 5700, 4e av ouest, Québec, QC G1H 6R1
418-627-6297

LAND TITLES
See Also: Real Estate
Canada Lands Company Ltd., #1700, 1 University Ave., Toronto, ON M5J 2P1
416-214-1250, Fax: 416-214-1121
British Columbia
British Columbia Assessment Authority, #400, 3450 Uptown Blvd., Victoria, BC V8Z 0B9
604-739-8588, Fax: 855-995-6209, 866-825-8322
New Brunswick
Service New Brunswick, Lincoln Place, PO Box 1998, Fredericton, NB E3B 5G4
506-684-7901, 888-762-8600, snb@snb.ca
Nunavut
Legal Registries, PO Box 1000 570, Iqaluit, NU X0A 0H0
867-975-6590, Fax: 867-975-6594, Legal.Registries@gov.nu.ca
Saskatchewan
Court Services Division, #1010, 1874 Scarth St., Regina, SK S4P 4B3
306-787-5359, Fax: 306-787-8737

LANDLORD & TENANT REGULATIONS
Alberta
Alberta Justice & Solicitor General, John E. Brownlee Bldg., 10365 - 97th St., 9th Fl., Edmonton, AB T5J 3W7
780-427-2745
British Columbia
British Columbia Ministry of Municipal Affairs, PO Box 9056 Prov Govt, Victoria, BC V8W 9E2
250-387-2283, Fax: 250-387-4312
Surface Rights Board of British Columbia, #10, 10551 Shellbridge Way, Richmond, BC V6X 2W9
604-775-1740, Fax: 604-775-1742, 888-775-1740, office@surfacerightsboard.bc.ca

Northwest Territories
Northwest Territories Housing Corporation, Scotia Centre, 5102 - 50th Ave., PO Box 2100, Yellowknife, NT X1A 2P6
867-767-9080, Fax: 867-873-9426, 844-698-4663
Nunavut
Nunavut Housing Corporation, Headquarters, PO Box 480, Arviat, NU X0C 0E0
867-857-3000, Fax: 867-857-3040
Prince Edward Island
Prince Edward Island Regulatory & Appeals Commission, National Bank Tower, #501, 134 Kent St., PO Box 577, Charlottetown, PE C1A 7L1
902-892-3501, Fax: 902-566-4076, 800-501-6268, info@irac.pe.ca
Quebec
Régie du logement du Québec, Village Olympique, #2360, 5199, rue Sherbrooke est, Montréal, QC H1T 3X1
514-873-2245, Fax: 514-864-8077, 800-683-2245
Saskatchewan
Office of Residential Tenancies, #304, 1855 Victoria Ave., Regina, SK S4P 3T2
888-215-2222, ort@gov.sk.ca
Provincial Mediation Board, #304, 1855 Victoria Ave., Regina, SK S4P 3T2
306-787-5408, 877-787-5408, pmb@gov.sk.ca

LANDS & SOILS
Agriculture & Agri-Food Canada, 1341 Baseline Rd., Ottawa, ON K1A 0C5
613-773-1000, Fax: 613-773-1081, 855-773-0241, info@agr.gc.ca
Canada Centre for Mapping & Earth Observation, #212, 50, Place de la Cité, PO Box 162, Sherbrooke, QC J1H 4G9
Crown-Indigenous Relations & Northern Affairs, Public Enquiries Contact Centre, 10, rue Wellington, Gatineau, QC K1A 0H4
Fax: 866-817-3977, 800-567-9604, aadnc.infopubs.aandc@canada.ca
Earth Sciences Sector, 588 Booth St., Ottawa, ON K1A 0Y7
Natural Resources Canada, 580 Booth St., Ottawa, ON K1A 0E4
343-292-6096, Fax: 613-992-7211
Alberta
Irrigation Council, Provincial Bldg., 200 - 5 Ave. South, 3rd Fl., Lethbridge, AB T1J 4L1
403-381-5176, Fax: 403-382-4406,
Land Compensation Board, 1229 - 91 St. SW, Edmonton, AB T6X 1E9
780-427-2444, Fax: 780-427-5798, -310-000, srb.lcb@gov.ab.ca
British Columbia
British Columbia Ministry of Environment & Climate Change Strategy, PO Box 9047 Prov Govt, Victoria, BC V8W 9E2
Forest Practices Board, 310, 1675 Douglas St., PO Box 9905 Prov Govt, Victoria, BC V8W 9R1
250-213-4700, Fax: 250-213-4725, 800-994-5899, fpboard@gov.bc.ca
Timber Export Advisory Committee, PO Box 9514 Prov Govt, Victoria, BC V8W 9C2
250-387-8916, Fax: 250-387-5050
New Brunswick
New Brunswick Department of Environment & Local Government, Marysville Place, 20 McGloin St., Fredericton, NB E3B 5H1
506-453-2690, Fax: 506-457-4994, elg/egl-info@gnb.ca
New Brunswick Department of Natural Resources & Energy Development, Hugh John Flemming Forestry Centre, PO Box 6000, Fredericton, NB E3B 5H1
506-453-3826, Fax: 506-444-4367, dnr_mrnweb@gnb.ca
Newfoundland & Labrador
Newfoundland & Labrador Department of Digital Government & Service NL, 100 Prince Phillip Dr., PO Box 8700, St. John's, NL A1B 4J6
709-729-4834, servicenlinfo@gov.nl.ca
Northwest Territories
Northwest Territories Department of Environment & Natural Resources, PO Box 1320, Yellowknife, NT X1A 2L9
867-767-9055, enr_communications@gov.nt.ca
Northwest Territories Department of Lands, Gallery Bldg., 4923 - 52nd St., 1st & 2nd Fl., PO Box 1320, Yellowknife, NT X1A 2L9
867-767-9185, Fax: 867-669-0905, 855-698-5263, Lands@gov.nt.ca
Nova Scotia
Nova Scotia Department of Lands & Forestry, PO Box 698, Halifax, NS B3J 2T9
902-424-5935, Fax: 902-424-7735, 800-565-2224
Nova Scotia Lands Inc., PO Box 430 A, Sydney, NS B1P 6H2

Quebec

Ministère de l'Environnement et de la Lutte contre les changements climatiques, Édifice Marie-Guyart, 675, boul René-Lévesque est, 30e étage, Québec, QC G1R 5V7
418-521-3830, Fax: 418-646-5974, 800-561-1616, relations.medias@mddelcc.gouv.qc.ca
Territoire, #E330 - 5700, 4e av ouest, Québec, QC G1H 6R1
418-627-6297

Saskatchewan

Saskatchewan Assessment Management Agency, #200, 2201 - 11th Ave., Regina, SK S4P 0J8
306-924-8000, Fax: 306-924-8070, 800-667-7262, info.request@sama.sk.ca

Yukon Territory

Carmacks Renewable Resource Council, PO Box 122, Carmacks, YT Y0B 1C0
867-863-6838, Fax: 867-863-6429, carmacksrrc@northwestel.net
Selkirk Renewable Resources Council, PO Box 32, Pelly Crossing, YT Y0B 1P0
867-537-3937, Fax: 867-537-3938, selkirkrrc@northwestel.net
Yukon Environment, 10 Burns Rd., Whitehorse, YT Y1A 2C6
867-667-5652, Fax: 867-393-7197, environmentyukon@yukon.ca

LANGUAGE (OFFICIAL)

See Also: Bilingualism

Northwest Territories

Official Languages Board, PO Box 1320, Yellowknife, NT X1A 2L9

Quebec

Secrétariat à la politique linguistique, 225 Grande-Allée est, 4e étage, bloc A, Québec, QC G1R 5G5
418-643-4248, Fax: 418-646-7832

LAW & JUSTICE

Auditor General of Canada, 240 Sparks St., Ottawa, ON K1A 0G6
613-952-0213, Fax: 613-957-0474, 888-761-5953, infomedia@oag-bvg.gc.ca
Canadian Human Rights Commission, 344 Slater St., 8th Fl., Ottawa, ON K1A 1E1
Fax: 613-996-9661, 888-214-1090, info.com@chrc-ccdp.gc.ca
Canadian Human Rights Tribunal, 160 Elgin St., 11th Fl., Ottawa, ON K1A 1J4
613-995-1707, Fax: 613-995-3484, registrar@chrt-tcdp.gc.ca
Canadian International Trade Tribunal, Standard Life Centre, 333 Laurier Ave. West, 15th Floor, Ottawa, ON K1A 0G7
613-990-2452, Fax: 613-990-2439, 855-307-2488, citt-tcce@tribunal.gc.ca
Canadian Judicial Council, Ottawa, ON K1A 0W8
613-288-1566, Fax: 613-288-1575, info@cjc-ccm.gc.ca
Canadian Radio-Television & Telecommunications Commission, Central Building, 1, promenade du Portage, Les Terrasses de la Chaudière, Gatineau, QC J8X 4B1
819-997-0313, Fax: 819-994-0218, 877-249-2782
Canadian Security Intelligence Service, PO Box 9732 T, Ottawa, ON K1G 4G4
613-993-9620, Fax: 613-231-0612
Commission for Public Complaints Against the Royal Canadian Mounted Police, National Intake Office, PO Box 88689, Surrey, BC V3W 0X1
Fax: 604-501-4095, 800-665-6878
Copyright Board of Canada, #800, 56 Sparks St., Ottawa, ON K1A 0C9
613-952-8621, Fax: 613-952-8630, secretariat@cb-cda.gc.ca
Correctional Service Canada, 340 Laurier Ave. West, Ottawa, ON K1A 0P9
613-992-5891, Fax: 613-943-1630
Defence Research & Development Canada, 101 Colonel By Dr., Ottawa, ON K1A 0K2
613-995-2534, 888-995-2534, information@forces.gc.ca
Financial Transactions & Reports Analysis Centre of Canada, 234 Laurier Ave. West, 24th Fl., Ottawa, ON K1P 1H7
Fax: 613-943-7931, 866-346-8722, guidelines-lignesdirectrices@fintrac-canafe.gc.ca
Immigration & Refugee Board of Canada, Minto Place, Canada Bldg., 344 Slater St., 12th Fl., Ottawa, ON K1A 0K1
Fax: 613-943-1550
International Joint Commission, 234 Laurier Ave. West, 22nd Fl., Ottawa, ON K1P 6K6
613-995-2984, Fax: 613-993-5583, commission@ottawa.ijc.org
Justice Canada, 284 Wellington St., Ottawa, ON K1A 0H8
613-957-4222, Fax: 613-954-0811, webadmin@justice.gc.ca
Military Grievances External Review Committee, 60 Queen St., 10th Fl., Ottawa, ON K1P 5Y7
613-996-8529, Fax: 613-996-6491, 877-276-4193, mgerc-ceegm@mgerc-ceegm.gc.ca

Military Police Complaints Commission, 270 Albert St., 10th Fl., Ottawa, ON K1P 5G8
613-947-5625, Fax: 613-947-5713, 800-632-0566, commission@mpcc-cppm.gc.ca
Office of the Commissioner for Federal Judicial Affairs, 99 Metcalfe St., 8th Fl., Ottawa, ON K1A 1E3
613-995-5140, Fax: 613-995-5615, 877-583-4266
Office of the Conflict of Interest & Ethics Commissioner, Commissioner's Office, 66 Slater St., 22nd Fl., PO Box 16, Ottawa, ON K1A 0A6
613-995-0721, Fax: 613-995-7308, ciec-ccie@parl.gc.ca
Office of the Correctional Investigator, PO Box 3421 D, Ottawa, ON K1P 6L4
Fax: 613-990-9091, 877-885-8848, org@oci-bec.gc.ca
Office of the Ombudsman, PO Box 90026, Ottawa, ON K1V 1J8
Fax: 800-204-4193, 800-204-4198
Parole Board of Canada, Communications Division, National Office, 410 Laurier Ave. West, Ottawa, ON K1A 0R1
613-954-7474, Fax: 613-941-4981, info@pbc-clcc.gc.ca
Passport, c/o Passport Program, Gatineau, QC K1A 0G3
800-567-6868
Public Prosecution Service of Canada, 160 Elgin St., 12th Fl., Ottawa, ON K1A 0H8
613-957-6489, 877-505-7772, info@ppsc.gc.ca
Royal Canadian Mounted Police, 73 Leikin Dr., Ottawa, ON K1A 0R2
613-993-7267, Fax: 613-993-0260
Royal Canadian Mounted Police External Review Committee, PO Box 1159 B, Ottawa, ON K1P 5R2
613-998-2134, Fax: 613-990-8969, org@erc-cee.gc.ca
Security Intelligence Review Committee, PO Box 2430 D, Ottawa, ON K1P 5W5
613-907-4404, Fax: 613-907-4445, info@sirc-csars.gc.ca
Transportation Appeal Tribunal of Canada, #1201, 333 Laurier Ave. West, 12th Fl., Ottawa, ON K1A 0N5
613-990-6906, Fax: 613-990-9153, info@tatc.gc.ca
Transportation Safety Board of Canada, 200, promenade du Portage, 4e étage, Gatineau, QC K1A 1K8
819-994-3741, Fax: 819-997-2239, 800-387-3557, communications@bst-tsb.gc.ca
Veterans Review & Appeal Board, Daniel J. MacDonald Bldg., 161 Grafton St., PO Box 9900, Charlottetown, PE C1A 8V7
902-566-8751, Fax: 902-566-7850, 800-450-8006, vrab.vrab-tacra.tacra@vrab-tacra.gc.ca

Alberta

Alberta Justice & Solicitor General, John E. Brownlee Bldg., 10365 - 97th St., 9th Fl., Edmonton, AB T5J 3W7
780-427-2745
Alberta Office of the Ethics Commissioner, #1250, 9925 - 109th St. NW, Edmonton, AB T5K 2J8
780-422-2273, Fax: 780-422-2261, generalinfo@ethicscommissioner.ab.ca
Alberta Office of the Ombudsman, Canadian Western Bank Bldg., #700, 9925 - 109th St., Edmonton, AB T5K 2J8
780-427-2756, Fax: 780-427-2759, 888-455-2756, info@ombudsman.ab.ca
Alberta Review Board, #1120, 10235 - 101 St., Edmonton, AB T5J 3E9
780-422-5994, Fax: 780-427-1762
Criminal Injuries Review Board, #1502, 10025 - 102A Ave., Edmonton, AB T5J 2Z2
780-427-7330, Fax: 780-427-7347
Fatality Review Board, Office of the Chief Medical Examiner, 4070 Bowness Rd. NW, Calgary, AB T3B 3R7
403-297-8123, Fax: 403-297-3429
Land Compensation Board, 1229 - 91 St. SW, Edmonton, AB T6X 1E9
780-427-2444, Fax: 780-427-5798, -310-000, srb.lcb@gov.ab.ca
Law Enforcement Review Board, c/o Board Secretary, Oxford Tower, #1502, 10025 - 102A Ave., Edmonton, AB T5J 2Z2
780-422-9376, Fax: 780-422-9372, lerb@gov.ab.ca
Legal Services Division, Bowker Bldg., 9833 - 109th St., 2nd Fl., Edmonton, AB T5K 2E8
780-422-0500
Public Security Division, John E. Brownlee Bldg., 10365 - 97th St., 10th Fl., Edmonton, AB T5J 3W7

British Columbia

British Columbia Law Institute, University of British Columbia, 1822 East Mall, Vancouver, BC V6T 1Z1
604-822-0142, Fax: 604-822-0144, bcli@bcli.org
British Columbia Ministry of Attorney General & Minister responsible for Housing, PO Box 9044 Prov Govt, Victoria, BC V8W 9E2
British Columbia Ministry of Public Safety & Solicitor General, PO Box 9290 Prov Govt, Victoria, BC V8W 9J7
250-356-0149, Fax: 250-387-6224, 800-663-7867, PSSG.Correspondence@gov.bc.ca

British Columbia Office of the Police Complaint Commissioner, #501, 947 Fort St., PO Box 9895 Prov Govt, Victoria, BC V8W 9T8
250-356-7458, Fax: 250-356-6503, 877-999-8707, info@opcc.bc.ca
British Columbia Review Board, #1270, 605 Robson St., Vancouver, BC V6B 5J3
604-660-8789, Fax: 604-660-8809, 877-305-2277
Court Services Branch, PO Box 9249 Prov Govt, Victoria, BC V8W 9J2
250-356-1550, Fax: 250-356-8152
Judicial Council of British Columbia, Office of the Chief Judge, #337, 800 Hornby St., Vancouver, BC V6Z 2C5
604-660-2864, Fax: 604-660-1108, info@provincialcourt.bc.ca
Legal Services Society, #400, 510 Burrard St., Vancouver, BC V6C 3A8
604-601-6000
Office of the Conflict of Interest Commissioner, 421 Menzies St., 1st Fl., Victoria, BC V8V 1X4
250-356-0750, Fax: 250-356-6580, conflictofinterest@coibc.ca
Office of the Ombudsperson, 947 Fort St., 2nd Fl., PO Box 9039 Prov Govt, Victoria, BC V8W 9A5
250-387-5855, Fax: 250-387-0198, 800-567-3247
Office of the Representative for Children & Youth, #400, 1019 Wharf St., Victoria, BC V8W 2Y9
250-356-6710, Fax: 250-356-0837, 800-476-3933, rcy@rcybc.ca
Public Guardian & Trustee of British Columbia, #700, 808 West Hastings St., Vancouver, BC V6C 3L3
604-660-4444, Fax: 604-660-0374, 800-663-7867, clientservice@trustee.bc.ca

Manitoba

Advisory Council on Workplace Safety & Health, 401 York Ave., 2nd Fl., Winnipeg, MB R3C 0P8
204-945-3446, Fax: 204-948-2209, 866-888-8186, wshcompl@gov.mb.ca
Compensation for Victims of Crime, #1410, 405 Broadway, Winnipeg, MB R3C 3L6
204-945-0899, Fax: 204-948-3071, 800-262-9344
Comptroller Division, #715, 401 York Ave., Winnipeg, MB R3C 0P8
204-945-4920, Fax: 204-948-3539
Health Information Privacy Committee, #4043, 300 Carlton St., Winnipeg, MB R3B 3M9
Highway Traffic Board/Motor Transport Board, #200, 301 Weston St., Winnipeg, MB R3E 3H4
204-945-8912, Fax: 204-783-6529
Law Enforcement Review Agency, #420, 155 Carlton St., Winnipeg, MB R3C 3H8
204-945-8667, Fax: 204-948-1014, 800-282-8069, lera@gov.mb.ca
Legal Aid Manitoba, 287 Broadway, 4th Fl., Winnipeg, MB R3C 0R9
204-985-8500, Fax: 204-944-8582, 800-261-2960, info@legalaid.mb.ca
Manitoba Criminal Code Review Board, #2, 408 York Ave., Winnipeg, MB R3C 0P9
204-945-4438
Manitoba Film Classification Board, #216, 301 Weston St., Winnipeg, MB R3E 3H4
204-945-8962, Fax: 204-945-0890, 866-612-2399, mfcb@gov.mb.ca
Manitoba Human Rights Commission, #700, 175 Hargrave Ave., Winnipeg, MB R3C 3R8
204-945-3007, Fax: 204-945-1292, 888-884-8681, hrc@gov.mb.ca
Manitoba Justice, Administration & Finance, #1110, 405 Broadway Ave., Winnipeg, MB R3C 3L6
204-945-2878
Manitoba Land Value Appraisal Commission, #1144, 363 Broadway, Winnipeg, MB R3C 3N9
204-945-5455, Fax: 204-948-2235
Manitoba Law Reform Commission, #432, 405 Broadway, Winnipeg, MB R3C 3L6
204-945-2896, Fax: 204-948-2184, mail@manitobalawreform.ca
Manitoba Liquor & Lotteries, 830 Empress St., Winnipeg, MB R3G 3H3
204-957-2500, Fax: 204-284-3500, 800-265-3912
Manitoba Office of the Ombudsman, Colony Square, #750, 500 Portage Ave., Winnipeg, MB R3C 3X1
204-982-9130, Fax: 204-942-7803, 800-665-0531, ombudsman@ombudsman.mb.ca
Medical Review Committee, #200, 301 Weston St., Winnipeg, MB R3E 3H4
204-945-7350, Fax: 204-948-2682
Office of the Auditor General, #500, 330 Portage Ave., Winnipeg, MB R3C 0C4
204-945-3790, Fax: 204-945-2169, contact@oag.mb.ca

Office of the Chief Medical Examiner, #210, 1 Wesley Ave., Winnipeg, MB R3C 4C6
204-945-2088, 800-282-8069

Office of the Public Trustee, #500, 155 Carlton St., Winnipeg, MB R3C 5R9
204-945-2700, Fax: 204-948-2251, PGT@gov.mb.ca

Workers' Compensation Board of Manitoba, 333 Broadway Ave., Winnipeg, MB R3C 4W3
204-954-4321, Fax: 204-954-4999, 800-362-3340, wcb@wcb.mb.ca

New Brunswick

New Brunswick Department of Justice & Public Safety, Marysville Place, 3rd Fl., PO Box 6000, Fredericton, NB E3B 5H1
506-453-3992, DPS-MSP.information@gnb.ca

New Brunswick Human Rights Commission, Barry House, 751 Brunswick St., PO Box 6000, Fredericton, NB E3B 5H1
506-453-2301, Fax: 506-453-2653, 888-471-2233, hrc.cdp@gnb.ca

New Brunswick Liquor Corporation, 170 Wilsey Rd., PO Box 20787, Fredericton, NB E3B 5B8
506-452-6826, Fax: 506-462-2024, receptionist@anbl.com

New Brunswick Police Commission, Fredericton City Centre, #202, 435 King St., Fredericton, NB E3B 1E5
506-453-2069, Fax: 506-457-3542, nbpc@gnb.ca

Office of the Attorney General, Chancery Place, PO Box 6000, Fredericton, NB E3B 5H1
506-453-3992, Fax: 506-453-3992

Office of the Ombudsman, 548 York St., PO Box 6000, Fredericton, NB E3B 5H1
506-453-2789, Fax: 506-453-5599, 888-465-1100

WorkSafeNB, 1 Portland St., PO Box 160, Saint John, NB E2L 3X9
506-632-2200, 800-222-9775, communications@ws-ts.nb.ca

Newfoundland & Labrador

Newfoundland & Labrador Department of Justice & Public Safety, East Block, Confederation Bldg., 4th Fl., PO Box 8700, St. John's, NL A1B 4J6
709-729-2869, Fax: 709-729-0469, justice@gov.nl.ca

Newfoundland & Labrador Human Rights Commission, The Beothuk Bldg., 21 Crosbie Pl., PO Box 8700, St. John's, NL A1B 4J6
709-729-2709, Fax: 709-729-0790, 800-563-5808, humanrights@gov.nl.ca

Newfoundland & Labrador Legal Aid Commission, #300, 251 Empire Ave., St. John's, NL A1C 5J9
709-753-7860, Fax: 709-753-7851, 800-563-9911, nlac@legalaid.nl.ca

Royal Newfoundland Constabulary Public Complaints Commission, PO Box 8700, St. John's, NL A1B 4J6
709-834-6171, Fax: 709-834-6178, rnccomplaintscommission@gov.nl.ca

Northwest Territories

Assessment Appeal Tribunal, c/o Secretary, Board of Revision, #400, 5201 - 50th Ave., PO Box 1320, Yellowknife, NT X1A 2L9
867-767-9161, Fax: 867-873-0609

Northwest Territories & Nunavut Workers' Safety & Compensation Commission, Centre Square Tower, 5022 - 49th St., 5th Fl., PO Box 8888, Yellowknife, NT X1A 2R3
867-920-3888, Fax: 867-873-4596, 800-661-0792

Northwest Territories Department of Justice, 4903 - 49th St., PO Box 1320, Yellowknife, NT X1A 2L9
867-767-9256, justice_communications@gov.nt.ca

Northwest Territories Legal Aid Commission, 4915 - 48th St., PO Box 1320, Yellowknife, NT X1A 2L9
867-767-9361, Fax: 867-873-5320, 844-835-8050, lac@gov.nt.ca

Northwest Territories Liquor & Cannabis Commission, #201, 31 Capital Dr., Hay River, NT X0E 1G2
867-874-8700, Fax: 867-874-8720

Northwest Territories Liquor Licensing Board, #204, 31 Capital Dr., Hay River, NT X0E 1G2
867-874-8715, Fax: 867-874-8722, 800-351-7770, LLBinfo@gov.nt.ca

Territorial Board of Revision, c/o Secretary, Board of Revision, #400, 5201 - 50th Ave., Yellowknife, NT X1A 2L9
867-767-9161, Fax: 867-873-0609

Victims Assistance Committee, c/o Community Justice Division, PO Box 1320, Yellowknife, NT X1A 2L9
867-920-6911, Fax: 867-873-0199

Nova Scotia

Nova Scotia Department of Justice, 1690 Hollis St., PO Box 7, Halifax, NS B3J 2L6
902-424-4030, justweb@gov.ns.ca

Nova Scotia Human Rights Commission, Park Lane Terrace, #305, 5657 Spring Garden Rd., PO Box 2221, Halifax, NS B3J 3C4
902-424-4111, Fax: 902-424-0596, 877-269-7699, hrcinquiries@novascotia.ca

Nova Scotia Legal Aid Commission, Office of the Executive Director, #920, 1701 Hollis St., Halifax, NS B3J 3M8
902-420-6578, 877-420-6578

Nova Scotia Medical Examiner Service, Dr. William D. Finn Centre for Forensic Medicine, 51 Garland Ave., Dartmouth, NS B3B 0J2
902-424-2722, Fax: 902-424-0607, 888-424-4336

Office of the Ombudsman, PO Box 2152, Halifax, NS B3J 3B7
902-424-6780, Fax: 902-424-6675, 800-670-1111, ombudsman@novascotia.ca

Workers' Compensation Appeals Tribunal, #201, 1465 Brenton St., Halifax, NS B3J 3T4
902-424-2250, Fax: 902-424-2321, 800-274-8281

Workers' Compensation Board of Nova Scotia, 5668 South St., PO Box 1150, Halifax, NS B3J 2Y2
902-491-8999, 800-870-3331, info@wcb.ns.ca

Nunavut

Baffin Correctional Centre, PO Box 1000, Iqaluit, NU X0A 0H0
867-979-8100, Fax: 867-979-4646

Legal Registries, PO Box 1000 570, Iqaluit, NU X0A 0H0
867-975-6590, Fax: 867-975-6594, Legal.Registries@gov.nu.ca

Legal Services Board of Nunavut, 1104-B Inuksugait Plaza, PO Box 29, Iqaluit, NU X0A 0H0
867-975-6395

Liquor Licensing Board, PO Box 1000 330, Iqaluit, NU X0A 0H0
867-975-5875, Fax: 867-975-5805, nllb@gov.nu.ca

Nunavut Criminal Code Review Board, PO Box 1269, Iqaluit, NU X0A 0H0
867-975-6532, Fax: 867-975-6511, nccrb@gov.nu.ca

Nunavut Territory Department of Justice, PO Box 1000 500, Iqaluit, NU X0A 0H0
867-975-6170, Fax: 867-975-6195, justice@gov.nu.ca

Young Offenders Facility / Isumaqsunngittut Youth Centre, 1548 Federal Rd., PO Box 1439, Iqaluit, NU X0A 0H0
867-979-4452, Fax: 867-979-5506

Ontario

Alcohol & Gaming Commission of Ontario, 90 Sheppard Ave. East, Toronto, ON M2N 0A4
416-326-8700, 800-522-2876, customer.service@agco.ca

Chief Inquiry Officer - Expropriations Act, McMurtry-Scott Bldg., 720 Bay St., 8th Fl., Toronto, ON M7A 2S9
416-314-2226

Council of the Association of Ontario Land Surveyors, 1043 McNicoll Ave., Toronto, ON M1W 3W6
416-491-9020, Fax: 416-491-2576, 800-268-0718

Environmental Sciences & Standards Division, 135 St Clair Ave. West, 14th Fl., Toronto, ON M4V 1P5

Judicial Appointments Advisory Committee, McMurtry-Scott Bldg., 720 Bay St., 3rd Fl., Toronto, ON M7A 2S9
416-326-4060, Fax: 416-212-7316

Legal Aid Ontario, Atrium on Bay, #200, 40 Dundas St. West, Toronto, ON M5G 2H1
416-979-1446, Fax: 416-979-8669, 800-668-8258, info@lao.on.ca

Liquor Control Board of Ontario, 55 Lake Shore Blvd. East, Toronto, ON M5E 1A4
416-365-5900, Fax: 416-864-2476, 800-668-5226, infoline@lcbo.com

Office for Victims of Crime, 700 Bay St., 3rd Fl., Toronto, ON M5G 1Z6
416-326-1682, Fax: 416-326-4497, 887-435-7661, ovc@ontario.ca

Office of the Children's Lawyer, 393 University Ave., 14th Fl., Toronto, ON M5G 1W9
416-314-8000, Fax: 416-314-8050

Office of the Integrity Commissioner, #2100, 2 Bloor St. West, Toronto, ON M4W 3E2
416-314-8983, Fax: 416-314-8987, 866-884-4470, info@oico.on.ca

Office of the Ombudsman, Bell Trinity Sq., South Tower, 483 Bay St., 10th Fl., Toronto, ON M5G 2C9
416-586-3300, Fax: 416-586-3485, 800-263-1830, info@ombudsman.on.ca

Ontario Human Rights Commission, 180 Dundas St. West, 9th Fl., Toronto, ON M7A 2G5
416-326-9511, Fax: 416-314-4494, 800-387-9080, info@ohrc.on.ca

Ontario Labour Relations Board, 505 University Ave., 2nd Fl., Toronto, ON M5G 2P1
416-326-7500, Fax: 416-326-7531, 877-339-3335

Ontario Ministry of the Attorney General, McMurtry-Scott Bldg., 720 Bay St., 11th Fl., Toronto, ON M7A 2S9
416-326-2220, Fax: 416-326-4016, 800-518-7901, attorneygeneral@ontario.ca

Ontario Police Arbitration Commission, George Drew Bldg., 25 Grosvenor St., 15th Fl., Toronto, ON M7A 1Y6
416-314-3520, Fax: 416-314-3522, 866-517-0571

Ontario Review Board, 151 Bloor St. West, 10th Fl., Toronto, ON M5S 2T5
416-327-8866, Fax: 416-327-8867, orb@ontario.ca

Ontario Solicitor General, George Drew Bldg., 25 Grosvenor St., 18th Fl., Toronto, ON M7A 1Y6
416-326-5000, Fax: 416-325-6067, 866-517-0571, mcscs.feedback@ontario.ca

OPSEU Pension Trust, #1200, 1 Adelaide St. East, Toronto, ON M5C 3A7
416-681-6161, Fax: 416-681-6175, 800-637-0024

Public Accountants Council, #901, 1200 Bay St., Toronto, ON M5R 2A5
416-920-1444, 800-387-2154

Road User Safety Division, Bldg A, 87 Sir William Hearst Ave., Toronto, ON M3M 0B4
416-235-2999, Fax: 416-235-4153

Safety, Licensing Appeals & Standards Tribunals Ontario, #401, 20 Dundas St. West, 4th Fl., Toronto, ON M5T 2Z5
Fax: 416-327-6379, 844-242-0608, slastoinfo@ontario.ca

ServiceOntario, College Park, 777 Bay St., 15th Fl., Toronto, ON M7A 2J3
Fax: 416-326-1313, 800-267-8097

Workplace Safety & Insurance Board, 200 Front St. West, Ground Fl., Toronto, ON M5V 3J1
416-344-1000, Fax: 416-344-4684, 800-387-0750

Prince Edward Island

Advisory Council on the Status of Women, Sherwood Business Centre, 161 St. Peter's Rd., Main Level, PO Box 2000, Charlottetown, PE C1A 7N8
902-368-4510, Fax: 902-368-3269, info@peistatusofwomen.ca

Office of the Auditor General, Shaw Bldg., 105 Rochford St. North, 2nd Fl., PO Box 2000, Charlottetown, PE C1A 7N8
902-368-4520, Fax: 902-368-4598

Office of the Conflict of Interest Commissioner, 197 Richmond St., 1st Fl., PO Box 2000, Charlottetown, PE C1A 7N8
902-368-5970, Fax: 902-368-5175

Prince Edward Island Human Rights Commission, 53 Water St., PO Box 2000, Charlottetown, PE C1A 7N8
902-368-4180, Fax: 902-368-4236, 800-237-5031, contact@peihumanrights.ca

Prince Edward Island Liquor Control Commission, 3 Garfield St., PO Box 967, Charlottetown, PE C1A 7M4
902-368-5710, Fax: 902-368-5735

Prince Edward Island Regulatory & Appeals Commission, National Bank Tower, #501, 134 Kent St., PO Box 577, Charlottetown, PE C1A 7L1
902-892-3501, Fax: 902-566-4076, 800-501-6268, info@irac.pe.ca

Prince Edward Island Workers' Compensation Board, 14 Weymouth St., PO Box 757, Charlottetown, PE C1A 7L7
902-368-5680, Fax: 902-368-5696, 800-237-5049

Workers Compensation Appeal Tribunal, c/o Executive Council, 95 Rochford St., PO Box 2000, Charlottetown, PE C1A 7N8
902-569-0545

Quebec

Bureau du coroner, Édifice le Delta 2, #390, 2875, boul Laurier, Québec, QC G1V 5B1
Fax: 418-643-6174, 888-267-6637, clientele.coroner@msp.gouv.qc.ca

Comité de déontologie policière, Tour du Saint-Laurent, #A-200, 2525, boul Laurier, 2e étage, Québec, QC G1V 4Z6
418-646-1936, Fax: 418-528-0987, comite.deontologie@msp.gouv.qc.ca

Commissaire à la déontologie policière, #1.06, 2535, boul Laurier, Québec, QC G1V 4M3
418-643-7897, Fax: 418-528-9473, 877-237-7897, deontologie-policiere.quebec@msp.gouv.qc.ca

Commissaire à la lutte contre la corruption (Unité permanente anticorruption), #3010, 2100, av Pierre-Dupuy, Montréal, QC H3C 3R5
514-228-3098, Fax: 514-873-0177, 855-567-8722

Commission des droits de la personne et des droits de la jeunesse, 360, rue Saint-Jacques, 2e étage, Montréal, QC H2Y 1P5
514-873-5146, Fax: 514-873-6032, 800-361-6477, information@cdpdj.qc.ca

Commission des services juridiques, Tour de l'Est, #1404, 2, Complexe Desjardins, CP 123, Montréal, QC H5B 1B3
514-873-3562, Fax: 514-864-2351, info@csj.qc.ca

Commission québécoise des libérations conditionnelles, #1.32A, 300, boul Jean-Lesage, Québec, QC G1K 8K6
418-646-8300, Fax: 418-643-7217, cqlc@cqlc.gouv.qc.ca

Conseil de la justice administrative, #4.30, 575, rue Jacques-Parizeau, Québec, QC G1R 2G4
418-644-6279, Fax: 418-528-8471, 888-848-2581, plaintes@cja.gouv.qc.ca

Conseil de la magistrature, #RC.01, 300, boul Jean-Lesage, Québec, QC G1K 8K6
418-644-2196, Fax: 418-528-1581, information@cm.gouv.qc.ca

Directeur des poursuites criminelles et pénales, Tour 1, #500, 2828, boul Laurier, Québec, QC G1V 0B9
418-643-4085, Fax: 418-643-7462, info@dpcp.gouv.qc.ca

École nationale de police du Québec, 350, rue Marguerite-d'Youville, Nicolet, QC J3T 1X4
819-293-8631, Fax: 819-293-8630, courriel@enpq.qc.ca
Fonds d'aide aux actions collectifs, #10.30, 1, rue Notre-Dame est, Montréal, QC H2Y 1B6
514-393-2087, Fax: 514-864-2998, farc@justice.gouv.qc.ca
Ministère de la Justice, Édifice Louis-Philippe-Pigeon, 1200, rte de l'Église, Québec, QC G1V 4M1
418-643-5140, 866-536-5140,
informations@justice.gouv.qc.ca
Ministère de la Sécurité publique, Tour des Laurentides, 2525, boul Laurier, 5e étage, Québec, QC G1V 2L2
418-643-2112, Fax: 418-646-6168, 800-361-3795
Le Protecteur du Citoyen, 800, place D'Youville, 19e étage, Québec, QC G1R 3P4
418-643-2688, Fax: 418-643-8759, 800-463-5070,
protecteur@protecteurducitoyen.qc.ca
Régie des alcools, des courses et des jeux, 560, boul Charest est, Québec, QC G1K 3J3
418-643-7667, Fax: 418-643-5971, 800-363-0320
Société des alcools du Québec, 7500, rue Tellier, Montréal, QC H1N 3W5
514-254-2020, 866-873-2020
Société québécoise d'information juridique, #600, 715, rue du Square-Victoria, Montréal, QC H2Y 2H7
514-842-8745, 800-363-6718
Sûreté du Québec, Grand quartier général, 1701, rue Parthenais, Montréal, QC H2K 3S7
514-598-4141, Fax: 514-598-4242
Tribunal administratif du Québec, 575, rue Jacques-Parizeau, Québec, QC G1R 5R4
418-643-3418, Fax: 418-643-5335, 800-567-0278,
tribunal.administratif@taq.gouv.qc.ca
Vérificateur général du Québec, #300, 750, boul Charest est, Québec, QC G1K 9J6
418-691-5900, Fax: 418-644-4460,
verificateur.general@vgq.qc.ca

Saskatchewan
Financial & Consumer Affairs Authority, #601, 1919 Saskatchewan Dr., Regina, SK S4P 4H2
306-787-5645, Fax: 306-787-5899, 877-880-5550,
consumerprotection@gov.sk.ca
Law Reform Commission of Saskatchewan, c/o University of Saskatchewan, College of Law, #184, 15 Campus Dr., Saskatoon, SK S7N 5A6
306-966-1625, Fax: 306-966-5900
Legal Aid Saskatchewan, #502, 201 - 21st St. East, Saskatoon, SK S7K 0B8
306-933-5300, Fax: 306-933-6764, 800-667-3764,
headoffice@legalaid.sk.ca
Ombudsman Saskatchewan, #500, 2103 - 11th Ave., Regina, SK S4P 3Z8
306-787-6211, Fax: 306-787-9090, 800-667-9787,
ombreg@ombudsman.sk.ca
Public & Private Rights Board, #23, 3085 Albert St., Regina, SK S4S 0B1
306-787-4071, Fax: 306-787-0088
Saskatchewan Human Rights Commission, PO Box 6011, Saskatoon, SK S7K 4E4
306-933-5952, Fax: 306-933-7863, 800-667-9249,
shrc@gov.sk.ca
Saskatchewan Justice & Attorney General, 1874 Scarth St., Regina, SK S4P 4B3
Saskatchewan Liquor & Gaming Authority, 2500 Victoria Ave., PO Box 5054, Regina, SK S4P 3M3
306-787-5563, inquiry@slga.gov.sk.ca
Saskatchewan Public Complaints Commission, #300, 1919 Saskatchewan Dr., Regina, SK S4P 4H2
306-787-6519, Fax: 306-787-6528, 866-256-6194
Saskatchewan Review Board, 220 - 19th St. East, 3rd Fl., Saskatoon, SK S7K 0A2
306-933-7892
Saskatchewan Workers' Compensation Board, #200, 1881 Scarth St., Regina, SK S4P 4L1
306-787-4370, Fax: 306-787-4311, 800-667-7590,
webmaster@wcbsask.com
Surface Rights Board of Arbitration, #102, 113 - 2nd Ave. East, PO Box 1597, Kindersley, SK S0L 1S0
306-463-5447, Fax: 306-463-5449,
surfacerightsboard@gov.sk.ca

Yukon Territory
Judicial Council, PO Box 31222, Whitehorse, YT Y1A 5P7
867-667-5438, Fax: 867-393-6400
Law Society of Yukon - Discipline Committee, #304, 104 Elliott St., Whitehorse, YT Y1A 0M2
867-668-4231, Fax: 867-667-7556,
info@lawsocietyyukon.com
Law Society of Yukon - Executive, #304, 104 Elliott St., Whitehorse, YT Y1A 0M2
867-668-4231, Fax: 867-667-7556,
info@lawsocietyyukon.com

Yukon Human Rights Commission, #215, 305 Main St., Whitehorse, YT Y1A 2B4
867-667-6226, Fax: 867-667-2662, 800-661-0535,
info@yukonhumanrights.ca
Yukon Justice, Andrew Philipsen Law Centre, 2134 - 2nd Ave., PO Box 2703, Whitehorse, YT Y1A 2C6
867-667-3033, Fax: 867-667-5200, justice@yukon.ca
Yukon Law Foundation Board of Directors, PO Box 31789, Whitehorse, YT Y1A 6L3
867-667-7500, Fax: 867-393-3904,
execdir@yukonlawfoundation.com
Yukon Legal Services Society, #203, 2131 - 2nd Ave., Whitehorse, YT Y1A 1C3
867-667-5210, Fax: 867-667-8649, intake@legalaid.yk.ca
Yukon Liquor Corporation, 9031 Quartz Rd., Whitehorse, YT Y1A 4P9
867-667-5245, Fax: 867-393-6306, yukon.liquor@yukon.ca
Yukon Workers' Compensation Health & Safety Board, 401 Strickland St., Whitehorse, YT Y1A 5N8
867-667-5645, Fax: 867-393-6279, 800-661-0443,
worksafe@yukon.ca

LEGAL & REGULATORY
Canadian Coast Guard, Centennial Towers, #6S018, 200 Kent St., Ottawa, ON K1A 0E6
613-993-0999, Fax: 613-990-1866, info@dfo-mpo.gc.ca
Commission for Environmental Cooperation, Secretariat, #200, 393, rue Saint-Jacques ouest, Montréal, QC H2Y 1N9
514-350-4300, Fax: 514-350-4314, info@cec.org
Office of the Public Sector Integrity Commissioner of Canada, 60 Queen 7th Fl., Ottawa, ON K1P 5Y7
613-941-6400, Fax: 613-941-6535, 866-941-6400
Public Servants Disclosure Protection Tribunal, #600, 90 Sparks St., Ottawa, ON K1P 5B4
613-948-8460, Fax: 613-943-8325, tribunal@psdpt-tpfd.gc.ca
Standards Council of Canada, #600, 55 Metcalfe St., Ottawa, ON K1P 6L5
613-238-3222, Fax: 613-569-7808, info@scc.ca

Northwest Territories
Assessment Appeal Tribunal, c/o Secretary, Board of Revision, #400, 5201 - 50th Ave., PO Box 1320, Yellowknife, NT X1A 2L9
867-767-9161, Fax: 867-873-0609

Nova Scotia
Crane Operators Appeal Board, 5151 Terminal Rd., 7th Fl., PO Box 697, Halifax, NS B3J 2T8
902-424-8595, Fax: 902-424-0217
Workers' Advisers Program, #309, 5640 Spring Garden Rd., PO Box 1063, Halifax, NS B3J 3M7
902-424-5050, Fax: 902-424-0530, 800-774-4712
Workers' Compensation Board of Nova Scotia, 5668 South St., PO Box 1150, Halifax, NS B3J 2Y2
902-491-8999, 800-870-3331, info@wcb.ns.ca

Ontario
Environmental Commissioner of Ontario, #605, 1075 Bay St., Toronto, ON M5S 2B1
416-325-3377, Fax: 416-325-3370, 800-701-6454,
commissioner@eco.on.ca
Ontario Solicitor General, George Drew Bldg., 25 Grosvenor St., 18th Fl., Toronto, ON M7A 1Y6
416-326-5000, Fax: 416-325-6067, 866-517-0571,
mcscs.feedback@ontario.ca
Road User Safety Division, Bldg A, 87 Sir William Hearst Ave., Toronto, ON M3M 0B4
416-235-2999, Fax: 416-235-4153

Prince Edward Island
Prince Edward Island Regulatory & Appeals Commission, National Bank Tower, #501, 134 Kent St., PO Box 577, Charlottetown, PE C1A 7L1
902-892-3501, Fax: 902-566-4076, 800-501-6268,
info@irac.pe.ca

LEGAL AID SERVICES
British Columbia
Legal Services Society, #400, 510 Burrard St., Vancouver, BC V6C 3A8
604-601-6000
Manitoba
Legal Aid Manitoba, 287 Broadway, 4th Fl., Winnipeg, MB R3C 0R9
204-985-8500, Fax: 204-944-8582, 800-261-2960,
info@legalaid.mb.ca
New Brunswick
New Brunswick Legal Aid Services Commission, #501, 500 Beaverbrook Ct., Fredericton, NB E3B 5X4
506-444-2776, Fax: 506-444-2290, info@legalaid.nb.ca

Newfoundland & Labrador
Newfoundland & Labrador Legal Aid Commission, #300, 251 Empire Ave., St. John's, NL A1C 5J9
709-753-7860, Fax: 709-753-7851, 800-563-9911,
nlac@legalaid.nl.ca
Northwest Territories
Northwest Territories Legal Aid Commission, 4915 - 48th St., PO Box 1320, Yellowknife, NT X1A 2L9
867-767-9301, Fax: 867-873-5320, 844-835-8050,
lac@gov.nt.ca
Nova Scotia
Nova Scotia Legal Aid Commission, Office of the Executive Director, #920, 1701 Hollis St., Halifax, NS B3J 3M8
902-420-6578, 877-420-6578
Nunavut
Legal Services Board of Nunavut, 1104-B Inuksugait Plaza, PO Box 29, Iqaluit, NU X0A 0H0
867-975-6395
Ontario
Legal Aid Ontario, Atrium on Bay, #200, 40 Dundas St. West, Toronto, ON M5G 2H1
416-979-1446, Fax: 416-979-8669, 800-668-8258,
info@lao.on.ca
Prince Edward Island
Legal Aid, 40 Great George St., PO Box 2000, Charlottetown, PE C1A 7N8
Quebec
Fonds d'aide aux actions collectifs, #10.30, 1, rue Notre-Dame est, Montréal, QC H2Y 1B6
514-393-2087, Fax: 514-864-2998, farc@justice.gouv.qc.ca
Saskatchewan
Legal Aid Saskatchewan, #502, 201 - 21st St. East, Saskatoon, SK S7K 0B8
306-933-5300, Fax: 306-933-6764, 800-667-3764,
headoffice@legalaid.sk.ca
Yukon Territory
Yukon Legal Services Society, #203, 2131 - 2nd Ave., Whitehorse, YT Y1A 1C3
867-667-5210, Fax: 867-667-8649, intake@legalaid.yk.ca

LEGISLATIVE ASSEMBLIES/NATIONAL ASSEMBLIES/HOUSES
House of Commons, Canada, House of Commons, Centre Block, Parliament Buildings, 111 Wellington St., Ottawa, ON K1A 0A6
613-992-4793, 866-599-4999, info@parl.gc.ca
Alberta
Legislative Assembly of Alberta, 9718 - 107th St., Edmonton, AB T5K 1E4
780-427-2826, laocommunications@assembly.ab.ca
British Columbia
British Columbia Legislative Assembly & Independent Offices, Clerk's Office, Parliament Bldgs., Victoria, BC V8V 1X4
250-387-3785, Fax: 250-387-0942,
officeoftheclerk@leg.bc.ca
Manitoba
Manitoba Legislative Assembly, c/o Clerk's Office, Legislative Bldg., #237, 450 Broadway, Winnipeg, MB R3C 0V8
204-945-3636, Fax: 204-948-2507, clerkla@leg.gov.mb.ca
New Brunswick
Legislative Assembly of New Brunswick, Legislative Bldg., Centre Block, PO Box 6000, Fredericton, NB E3B 5H1
506-453-2506, Fax: 506-453-7154, wwwleg@gnb.ca
Newfoundland & Labrador
House of Assembly, c/o Clerk's Office, Confederation Bldg., PO Box 8700, St. John's, NL A1B 4J6
709-729-3405
Northwest Territories
Northwest Territories Legislative Assembly, 4570 - 48th St., PO Box 1320, Yellowknife, NT X1A 2L9
867-669-2200, 800-661-0784
Nova Scotia
Legislative House of Assembly, Province House, 1726 Hollis St., Halifax, NS B3J 2Y3
902-424-5978, Fax: 902-424-0632, info@nslegislature.ca
Nunavut
Nunavut Legislative Assembly, 926 Federal Rd., PO Box 1200, Iqaluit, NU X0A 0H0
867-975-5000, Fax: 867-975-5190, 877-334-7266,
leginfo@assembly.nu.ca
Ontario
Ontario Legislative Assembly, c/o Clerk of the Legislative Assembly, #104, Legislative Bldg., Queen's Park, Toronto, ON M7A 1A2
416-325-7500, Fax: 416-325-7489, web@ola.org

Prince Edward Island
Prince Edward Island Legislative Assembly, 197 Richmond St.,
PO Box 2000, Charlottetown, PE C1A 7N8
902-368-5970, Fax: 902-368-5175,
assembly@assembly.pe.ca

Quebec
L'Assemblée nationale, Hôtel du Parlement, 1045, rue des
Parlementaires, Québec, QC G1A 1A3
418-643-7239, Fax: 418-646-4271, 866-337-8837,
renseignements@assnat.qc.ca

Saskatchewan
Legislative Assembly of Saskatchewan, Office of the Clerk,
Legislative Bldg., #239, 2405 Legislative Dr., Regina, SK S4S
0B3
info@legassembly.sk.ca

Yukon Territory
Yukon Legislative Assembly, 2071 - 2nd Ave., PO Box 2703,
Whitehorse, YT Y1A 2C6
867-667-5498, yla@yukon.ca

LEISURE CRAFT & VEHICLE REGULATIONS
Nova Scotia
Nova Scotia Department of Transportation & Active Transit, PO
Box 186, Halifax, NS B3J 2N2
902-424-2297, Fax: 902-424-0532, tpwpaff@novascotia.ca
Service Nova Scotia & Internal Services, PO Box 2734, Halifax,
NS B3J 3K5
902-424-5200, Fax: 902-424-0720, 800-670-4357,
askus@novascotia.ca

Ontario
Ontario Ministry of Transportation, 777 Bay St., 5th Fl., Toronto,
ON M7A 1Z8
416-235-4686, Fax: 416-327-9185, 800-268-4686

Quebec
Ministère des Transports, #4.010, 500, boul René-Lévesque est,
Québec, QC H2Z 1W7
888-355-0511, communications@mtq.gouv.qc.ca

Saskatchewan
Saskatchewan Government Insurance, 2260 - 11th Ave.,
Regina, SK S4P 0J9
306-751-1200, Fax: 306-787-7477, 844-855-2744,
sgiinquiries@sgi.sk.ca

LIBRARIES
Library & Archives Canada, 395 Wellington St., Ottawa, ON K1A
0N4
613-996-5115, Fax: 613-995-6274, 866-578-7777
Library of Parliament, Information Servicce, Parliament of
Canada, Ottawa, ON K1A 0A9
613-992-4793, 866-599-4999, info@parl.gc.ca
National Research Council Canada - National Science Library,
Bldg. M-55, 1200 Montreal Rd., Ottawa, ON K1A 0R6
613-993-9101, 800-668-1222

New Brunswick
Legislative Assembly of New Brunswick, Legislative Bldg.,
Centre Block, PO Box 6000, Fredericton, NB E3B 5H1
506-453-2506, Fax: 506-453-7154, wwwleg@gnb.ca

Newfoundland & Labrador
Provincial Information & Library Resources Board, 48 St.
George's Ave., Stephenville, NL A2H 1K9
709-643-0900, Fax: 709-643-0925

Nova Scotia
Legislative House of Assembly, Province House, 1726 Hollis St.,
Halifax, NS B3J 2Y3
902-424-5978, Fax: 902-424-0632, info@nslegislature.ca

Nunavut
Nunavut Territory Department of Culture & Heritage, PO Box
1000 800, Iqaluit, NU X0A 0H0
867-975-5500, Fax: 867-975-5504, 866-934-2035

Ontario
Ontario Library Service, Head Office, 334 Regent St., Sudbury,
ON P3C 4E2
800-387-5765, info@olservice.ca

Quebec
Bibliothèque et Archives nationales du Québec (BAnQ), 475,
boul de Maisonneuve est, Montréal, QC H2L 5C4
514-873-1100, Fax: 514-873-9312, 800-363-9028

LIQUOR CONTROL
See Also: Drugs & Alcohol
Alberta
Alberta Gaming, Liquor & Cannabis Commission, 50 Corriveau
Ave., St Albert, AB T8N 3T5
780-447-8600, Fax: 780-447-8989, 800-272-8876

British Columbia
Liquor & Cannabis Regulation Branch, PO Box 9292 Prov Govt,
Victoria, BC V8W 9J8
250-952-5787, Fax: 250-952-7066, 866-209-2111,
lclb.lclb@gov.bc.ca

Liquor Distribution Branch, 3383 Gilmore Way, Burnaby, BC
V5G 4S1
604-252-7400, inquiries@bcliquorstores.com
Manitoba
Liquor, Gaming & Cannabis Authority of Manitoba, 1055 Milt
Stegall Dr., Winnipeg, MB R3G 0Z6
204-927-5300, Fax: 204-927-5385, 800-782-0363,
information@lgcamb.ca
Manitoba Liquor & Lotteries, 830 Empress St., Winnipeg, MB
R3G 3H3
204-957-2500, Fax: 204-284-3500, 800-265-3912
New Brunswick
New Brunswick Liquor Corporation, 170 Wilsey Rd., PO Box
20787, Fredericton, NB E3B 5B8
506-452-6826, Fax: 506-462-2024, receptionist@anbl.com
Newfoundland & Labrador
Newfoundland & Labrador Liquor Corporation, 90 Kenmount
Rd., PO Box 8750 A, St. John's, NL A1B 3V1
709-724-1100, info@nfliquor.com
Northwest Territories
Northwest Territories Liquor & Cannabis Commission, #201, 31
Capital Dr., Hay River, NT X0E 1G2
867-874-8700, Fax: 867-874-8720
Northwest Territories Liquor Licensing Board, #204, 31 Capital
Dr., Hay River, NT X0E 1G2
867-874-8715, Fax: 867-874-8722, 800-351-7770,
LLBinfo@gov.nt.ca
Nova Scotia
Nova Scotia Liquor Corporation, Bayers Lake Business Park, 93
Chain Lake Dr., Halifax, NS B3S 1A3
800-567-5874, contactus@myNSLC.com
Nunavut
Liquor Licensing Board, PO Box 1000 330, Iqaluit, NU X0A 0H0
867-975-5875, Fax: 867-975-5805, nllb@gov.nu.ca
Nunavut Liquor & Cannabis Commission, PO Box 9, Rankin
Inlet, NU X0C 0G0
867-645-8575, Fax: 867-645-3327, 855-844-5488,
info@nulc.ca
Ontario
Alcohol & Gaming Commission of Ontario, 90 Sheppard Ave.
East, Toronto, ON M2N 0A4
416-326-8700, 800-522-2876, customer.service@agco.ca
Liquor Control Board of Ontario, 55 Lake Shore Blvd. East,
Toronto, ON M5E 1A4
416-365-5900, Fax: 416-864-2476, 800-668-5226,
infoline@lcbo.com
Prince Edward Island
Prince Edward Island Liquor Control Commission, 3 Garfield St.,
PO Box 967, Charlottetown, PE C1A 7M4
902-368-5710, Fax: 902-368-5735
Quebec
Régie des alcools, des courses et des jeux, 560, boul Charest
est, Québec, QC G1K 3J3
418-643-7667, Fax: 418-643-5971, 800-363-0320
Société des alcools du Québec, 7500, rue Tellier, Montréal, QC
H1N 3W5
514-254-2020, 866-873-2020
Saskatchewan
Saskatchewan Liquor & Gaming Authority, 2500 Victoria Ave.,
PO Box 5054, Regina, SK S4P 3M3
306-787-5563, inquiry@slga.gov.sk.ca
Yukon Territory
Yukon Liquor Corporation, 9031 Quartz Rd., Whitehorse, YT
Y1A 4P9
867-667-5245, Fax: 867-393-6306, yukon.liquor@yukon.ca

LOTTERIES & GAMING
Alberta
Alberta Gaming, Liquor & Cannabis Commission, 50 Corriveau
Ave., St Albert, AB T8N 3T5
780-447-8600, Fax: 780-447-8989, 800-272-8876
British Columbia
Arts, Culture, & Sport Division, PO Box 9490 Prov Govt, Victoria,
BC V8W 9N7
250-356-6914, Fax: 250-387-7973
British Columbia Lottery Corporation, 74 West Seymour St.,
Kamloops, BC V2C 1E2
250-828-5500, Fax: 250-828-5631, 866-815-0222
Gaming Policy & Enforcement, PO Box 9311 Prov Govt,
Victoria, BC V8W 9N1
250-387-1301, Fax: 250-387-1818,
Gaming.branch@gov.bc.ca
Manitoba
Liquor, Gaming & Cannabis Authority of Manitoba, 1055 Milt
Stegall Dr., Winnipeg, MB R3G 0Z6
204-927-5300, Fax: 204-927-5385, 800-782-0363,
information@lgcamb.ca
Manitoba Liquor & Lotteries, 830 Empress St., Winnipeg, MB
R3G 3H3
204-957-2500, Fax: 204-284-3500, 800-265-3912

New Brunswick
Atlantic Lottery Corporation, 922 Main St., PO Box 5500,
Moncton, NB E1C 8W6
800-561-3942, info@alc.ca
New Brunswick Lotteries & Gaming Corporation, Chancery
Place, 4th Fl., 675 King St., PO Box 6000, Fredericton, NB
E3B 5H1
506-453-2451, Fax: 506-453-2053
Newfoundland & Labrador
Newfoundland & Labrador Department of Digital Government &
Service NL, 100 Prince Phillip Dr., PO Box 8700, St. John's,
NL A1B 4J6
709-729-4834, servicenlinfo@gov.nl.ca
Nova Scotia
Nova Scotia Gaming Corporation, Summit Place, 1601 Lower
Water St., 5th Fl., PO Box 1501, Halifax, NS B3J 2Y3
902-424-2203, Fax: 902-424-0724
Nunavut
Nunavut Territory Department of Community & Government
Services, W.G. Brown Bldg., 4th Fl., PO Box 1000 700,
Iqaluit, NU X0A 0H0
867-975-5406, Fax: 867-975-5305, cgscomms@gov.nu.ca
Ontario
Alcohol & Gaming Commission of Ontario, 90 Sheppard Ave.
East, Toronto, ON M2N 0A4
416-326-8700, 800-522-2876, customer.service@agco.ca
Ontario Lottery & Gaming Corporation, Roberta Bondar Pl.,
#800, 70 Foster Dr., Sault Ste. Marie, ON P6A 6V2
705-946-6464, Fax: 705-946-6600, 800-387-0098
Quebec
Régie des alcools, des courses et des jeux, 560, boul Charest
est, Québec, QC G1K 3J3
418-643-7667, Fax: 418-643-5971, 800-363-0320
Société de financement des infrastructures locales, Ministère
des Finances, 12, rue Saint-Louis, Québec, QC G1R 5L3
418-528-9323, Fax: 418-646-1631, info@finances.gouv.qc.ca
Société des loteries du Québec, 500, rue Sherbrooke ouest,
Montréal, QC H3A 3G6
514-282-8000, Fax: 514-873-8999,
service_clientele@loto-quebec.com
Saskatchewan
Saskatchewan Gaming Corporation (SaskGaming), 1880
Saskatchewan Dr., 3rd Fl., Regina, SK S4P 0B2
306-787-1590, 800-555-3189, contact@casinoregina.com
Saskatchewan Liquor & Gaming Authority, 2500 Victoria Ave.,
PO Box 5054, Regina, SK S4P 3M3
306-787-5563, inquiry@slga.gov.sk.ca
Yukon Territory
Assessement Appeal Board, PO Box 2703, Whitehorse, YT Y1A
2C6
867-667-5268, Fax: 867-667-8276

MAPS, CHARTS & AERIAL PHOTOGRAPHS
Canada Centre for Mapping & Earth Observation, #212, 50,
Place de la Cité, PO Box 162, Sherbrooke, QC J1H 4G9
Surveyor General Branch - Geomatics Canada, #605, 9700
Jasper Ave., Edmonton, AB T5J 4C3
780-495-2519, Fax: 780-495-4052
Nova Scotia
GeoNOVA, 160 Willow St., Amherst, NS B4H 3W5
902-667-7231, 800-798-0706, geoinfo@novascotia.ca
Ontario
Council of the Association of Ontario Land Surveyors, 1043
McNicoll Ave., Toronto, ON M1W 3W6
416-491-9020, Fax: 416-491-2576, 800-268-0718

MARINE NAVIGATION
Atlantic Pilotage Authority, TD Centre, #1801, 1791 Barrington
St., Halifax, NS B3J 3K9
902-426-2550, Fax: 902-426-4004, 877-272-3477,
dispatch@atlanticpilotage.com
Great Lakes Pilotage Authority, 202 Pitt St., 2nd fl., PO Box 95,
Cornwall, ON K6H 5R9
613-933-2991, Fax: 613-932-3793
Pacific Pilotage Authority Canada, #1000, 1130 West Pender
St., Vancouver, BC V6E 4A4
604-666-6771, Fax: 604-666-1647, info@ppa.gc.ca
St. Lawrence Seaway Management Corporation, 202 Pitt St.,
Cornwall, ON K6J 3P7
613-932-5170, Fax: 613-932-7286, marketing@seaway.ca

MARINE SCIENCES
Marine Performance Evaluation & Testing Facilities, c/o National
Research Council, 1200 Montreal Rd., Ottawa, ON K1A 0R6

MENTAL HEALTH
See Also: Health Services

Mental Health Commission of Canada, #1210, 350 Albert St., Ottawa, ON K1R 1A4
613-683-3755, Fax: 613-798-2989, mhccinfo@mentalhealthcommission.ca

Alberta
Alberta Health, PO Box 1360 Main, Edmonton, AB T5J 2N3
780-427-7164
Alberta Health Advocates, 106th St. Tower, 10055 - 106th St., 9th Fl., Edmonton, AB T5J 2Y2
780-422-1812, Fax: 780-422-0695, -310-0000, info@albertahealthadvocates.ca

British Columbia
British Columbia Ministry of Mental Health & Addictions, PO Box 9644 Prov Govt, Victoria, BC V8W 9P1
604-660-2421, 800-663-7867, HLTH.Health@gov.bc.ca
British Columbia Review Board, #1270, 605 Robson St., Vancouver, BC V6B 5J3
604-660-8789, Fax: 604-660-8809, 877-305-2277
Mental Health Review Board, #1270, 605 Robson St., Vancouver, BC V6B 5J3
604-660-2325, Fax: 604-660-2403, 833-660-2325, MHRBscheduling@gov.bc.ca

New Brunswick
Psychiatric Patient Advocate Services Review Board, c/o Dept. of Health, Psychiatric Patient Advocate Services, #505, 860 Main St., Moncton, NB E1C 1G2
506-869-6818, Fax: 506-869-6101, 888-350-4133
Psychiatric Patient Advocate Services Tribunal, c/o Dept. of Health, Psychiatric Patient Advocate Services, #505, 860 Main St., Moncton, NB E1C 1G2
506-869-6818, Fax: 506-869-6101, 888-350-4133

Ontario
Ontario Mental Health Foundation, 441 Jarvis St., 2nd Fl., Toronto, ON M4Y 2G8
416-920-7721, Fax: 416-920-0026
Ontario Ministry of Health, Hepburn Block, 80 Grosvenor St., 10th Fl, Toronto, ON M7A 2C4
416-327-4327, 800-268-1153

Saskatchewan
Saskatchewan Review Board, 220 - 19th St. East, 3rd Fl., Saskatoon, SK S7K 0A2
306-933-7892

MINERALS & MINING
CanmetMINING, 555 Booth St., Ottawa, ON K1A 0G1
Fax: 613-947-6606
Earth Sciences Sector, 588 Booth St., Ottawa, ON K1A 0Y7

Alberta
Resource Development Policy Division, Petroleum Plaza NT, 9945 - 108th St., 8th Fl., Edmonton, AB T5K 2G6

British Columbia
British Columbia Ministry of Energy, Mines & Low Carbon Innovation, PO Box 9060 Prov Govt, Victoria, BC V8W 9E3
250-952-0628
Mines & Mineral Resources Division, PO Box 9320 Prov Govt, Victoria, BC V8W 9N3
250-952-0470, Fax: 250-952-0491

Manitoba
Mineral Resources Division, The Paris Bldg., 259 Portage Ave., 9th Fl., Winnipeg, MB R3B 3P4
204-945-6569, 800-223-5215, minesinfo@gov.mb.ca

New Brunswick
New Brunswick Department of Natural Resources & Energy Development, Hugh John Flemming Forestry Centre, PO Box 6000, Fredericton, NB E3B 5H1
506-453-3826, Fax: 506-444-4367, dnr_mrnweb@gnb.ca

Northwest Territories
Northwest Territories Department of Industry, Tourism & Investment, PO Box 1320, Yellowknife, NT X1A 2L9

Nova Scotia
Nova Scotia Department of Energy & Mines, Joseph Howe Bldg., 1690 Hollis St., PO Box 2664, Halifax, NS B3J 3J9
902-424-4575, Fax: 902-424-3265, enerinfo@novascotia.ca

Nunavut
Nunavut Territory Department of Environment, PO Box 1000 1320, Iqaluit, NU X0A 0H0
867-975-7700, Fax: 867-975-7742, environment@gov.nu.ca

Ontario
Mines & Minerals Division, Willet Green Miller Centre, 933 Ramsey Lake Rd., Level B6, Sudbury, ON P3E 6B5
705-670-5755, Fax: 705-670-5818, 888-415-9845

Quebec
Énergie, #A301 - 5700, 4e av ouest, Québec, QC G1H 6R1

Saskatchewan
Saskatchewan Energy & Resources, #1000, 2103 - 11th Ave., Regina, SK S4P 3Z8

Yukon Territory
Yukon Energy, Mines & Resources, PO Box 2703, Whitehorse, YT Y1A 2C6
867-667-3123, Fax: 867-393-7421, 800-661-0408, emr@yukon.ca

MINES & MINERALS
CanmetMATERIALS, 183 Longwood Rd. South, Hamilton, ON L8P 0A5
CanmetMINING, 555 Booth St., Ottawa, ON K1A 0G1
Fax: 613-947-6606

Alberta
Resource Development Policy Division, Petroleum Plaza NT, 9945 - 108th St., 8th Fl., Edmonton, AB T5K 2G6

British Columbia
British Columbia Ministry of Energy, Mines & Low Carbon Innovation, PO Box 9060 Prov Govt, Victoria, BC V8W 9E3
250-952-0628

Manitoba
Mineral Resources Division, The Paris Bldg., 259 Portage Ave., 9th Fl., Winnipeg, MB R3B 3P4
204-945-6569, 800-223-5215, minesinfo@gov.mb.ca

New Brunswick
New Brunswick Department of Natural Resources & Energy Development, Hugh John Flemming Forestry Centre, PO Box 6000, Fredericton, NB E3B 5H1
506-453-3826, Fax: 506-444-4367, dnr_mrnweb@gnb.ca

Northwest Territories
Northwest Territories Department of Environment & Natural Resources, PO Box 1320, Yellowknife, NT X1A 2L9
867-767-9055, enr_communications@gov.nt.ca

Ontario
Mines & Minerals Division, Willet Green Miller Centre, 933 Ramsey Lake Rd., Level B6, Sudbury, ON P3E 6B5
705-670-5755, Fax: 705-670-5818, 888-415-9845
Ontario Ministry of Northern Development, Mines, Natural Resources & Forestry, Natural Resources Information & Support Centre, 300 Water St., Toronto, ON K9J 8M5
800-667-1940

Quebec
Institut national des mines du Québec, 125, rue Self, Val-d'Or, QC J9P 3N2
819-825-4667, Fax: 819-825-4660, secretariat@inmq.qc.ca

Saskatchewan
Saskatchewan Energy & Resources, #1000, 2103 - 11th Ave., Regina, SK S4P 3Z8

MOTOR VEHICLES
See Also: Drivers' Licences

Alberta
Alberta Motor Vehicle Industry Council, #303, 9945 - 50 St., Edmonton, AB T6A 0L4
780-466-1140, Fax: 780-462-0633, 877-979-8100

British Columbia
RoadSafetyBC, PO Box 9254 Prov Govt, Victoria, BC V8W 9J2
250-387-7747, Fax: 250-356-5577, 855-387-7747, RoadSafetyBC@gov.bc.ca
Vehicle Sales Authority of British Columbia, #208, 5455 - 152 St., Surrey, BC V3S 5A5
604-574-5050, Fax: 604-574-5883, consumer.services@mvsabc.com

Nova Scotia
Motor Vehicle Appeal Board, 1672 Granville St., PO Box 186, Halifax, NS B3J 2N2
902-424-4256, 855-424-4256

MULTICULTURALISM
Canadian Race Relations Foundation, #225, 6 Garamond Ct., Toronto, ON M3C 1Z5
416-441-1900, Fax: 416-441-2752, 888-240-4936, info@crrf-fcrr.ca
Immigration & Refugee Board of Canada, Minto Place, Canada Bldg., 344 Slater St., 12th Fl., Ottawa, ON K1A 0K1
Fax: 613-943-1550
Immigration, Refugees & Citizenship, Jean Edmonds, South Tower, 365 Laurier Ave. West, Ottawa, ON K1A 1L1
888-242-2100

British Columbia
British Columbia Ministry of Advanced Education & Skills Training, PO Box 9080 Prov Govt, Victoria, BC V8W 9E2
250-356-5170, AEST.GeneralInquiries@gov.bc.ca
Multicultural Advisory Council of BC, Multiculturalism & Inclusive Communities Office, 605 Robson St., 5th Fl., Vancouver, BC V6B 5J3
604-775-0643, Fax: 604-775-0670, multiculturalism@gov.bc.ca

Manitoba
Manitoba Education, Legislative Bldg., #162, 450 Broadway, Winnipeg, MB R3C 0V8
204-945-3720, Fax: 204-945-1291
Multiculturalism Secretariat, 213 Notre Dame Ave., 6th Fl., Winnipeg, MB R3B 1N3
204-945-5632, multisec@gov.mb.ca

Newfoundland & Labrador
Office of Immigration & Multiculturalism, c/o Department of Advanced Education, Skills & Labour, 100 Prince Phillip Dr., PO Box 8700, St. John's, NL A1B 4J6
170-972-9714, Fax: 709-729-7381, 888-632-4555, AESL@gov.nl.ca

Northwest Territories
Northwest Territories Department of Education, Culture & Employment, PO Box 1320, Yellowknife, NT X1A 2L9
ecepublicaffairs@gov.nt.ca

Nova Scotia
Nova Scotia Department of Communities, Culture & Heritage, 1741 Brunswick St., 3rd Fl., PO Box 456 Central, Halifax, NS B3J 2R5
902-424-2170, cch@novascotia.ca
Office of Immigration, 1469 Brenton St., 3rd Fl., PO Box 1535, Halifax, NS B3J 2Y3
902-424-5230, Fax: 902-424-7936, 877-292-9597, immigration@novascotia.ca

Prince Edward Island
Prince Edward Island Department of Education & Lifelong Learning, Holman Centre, #101, 250 Water St., Summerside, PE C1N 1B6
902-438-4130, Fax: 902-438-4062, DeptELL@gov.pe.ca

Quebec
Ministère de l'Immigration, de la Francisation et de l'Intégration, 285, rue Notre-Dame ouest, 4e étage, Montréal, QC H2Y 1T8
877-864-9191
Ministère de la Culture et Communications, 225, Grande Allée est, Québec, QC G1R 5G5
888-380-8882

MUNICIPAL & RURAL AFFAIRS
Canada Economic Development for Québec Regions, #500, 800, boul René-Lévesque ouest, Montréal, QC H3B 1X9
514-283-6412, Fax: 514-283-3302, 866-385-6412
Canada Mortgage & Housing Corporation, 700 Montreal Rd., Ottawa, ON K1A 0P7
613-748-2000, Fax: 613-748-2098, 800-668-2642, chic@cmhc-schl.gc.ca
Crown-Indigenous Relations & Northern Affairs, Public Enquiries Contact Centre, 10, rue Wellington, Gatineau, QC K1A 0H4
Fax: 866-817-3977, 800-567-9604, aadnc.infopubs.aandc@canada.ca
Mackenzie Valley Environmental Impact Review Board, 200 Scotia Centre, #5102, 50th Ave., PO Box 938, Yellowknife, NT X1A 2N7
867-766-7050, Fax: 867-766-7074, 866-912-3472
Nunavut Impact Review Board, 29 Mitik St., PO Box 1360, Cambridge Bay, NU X0B 0C0
Fax: 867-983-2594, 866-233-3033, info@nirb.ca
Nunavut Planning Commission, PO Box 2101, Cambridge Bay, NU X0B 0C0

Alberta
Alberta Agriculture & Forestry, JG O'Donoghue Bldg., #100A, 7000 - 113th St., Edmonton, AB T6H 5T6
403-742-7901
Alberta Municipal Affairs, Communications Branch, Commerce Place, 10155 - 102nd St., 18th Fl., Edmonton, AB T5J 4L4
780-427-2732, Fax: 780-422-1419
Municipal Government Board, 1229 - 91st St. SW, 2nd Fl., Edmonton, AB T6X 1E9
780-427-4864, Fax: 780-427-0986, -310-0000, mgbmail@gov.ab.ca

British Columbia
Local Government, PO Box 9490 Prov Govt, Victoria, BC V8W 9N7
250-356-6575, Fax: 250-387-7973

Manitoba
Manitoba Indigenous Reconciliation & Northern Relations, Legislative Bldg., #301, 450 Broadway, Winnipeg, MB R3C 0V8
204-945-3788, Fax: 204-945-1383, INRweb@gov.mb.ca
Manitoba Municipal Board, #1144, 363 Broadway, Winnipeg, MB R3C 3N9
204-945-2941, Fax: 204-948-2235

New Brunswick
New Brunswick Department of Health, HSBC Place, PO Box 5100, Fredericton, NB E3B 5G8
506-457-4800, Fax: 506-453-5243, Health.Sante@gnb.ca
Regional Development Corporation, Chancery Place, 3rd Fl., PO Box 6000, Fredericton, NB E3B 5H1
506-453-2277, Fax: 506-453-7988, rdc-sdr@gnb.ca

Newfoundland & Labrador
Municipal Assessment Agency Inc., 75 O'Leary Ave., St. John's, NL A1B 2C9
709-724-1532, 877-777-2807, info@maa.ca
Newfoundland & Labrador Department of Environment & Climate Change, PO Box 8700, St. John's, NL A1B 4J6
ECCInfo@gov.nl.ca
Newfoundland & Labrador Department of Health & Community Services, West Block, Confederation Bldg., 100 Prince Philip Dr., 1st Fl., PO Box 8700, St. John's, NL A1B 4J6
709-729-4984, healthinfo@gov.nl.ca

Northwest Territories
Northwest Territories Department of Municipal & Community Affairs, PO Box 1320, Yellowknife, NT X1A 2L9

Nova Scotia
Nova Scotia Department of Municipal Affairs, PO Box 216, Halifax, NS B3J 2M4
902-424-6642
Nova Scotia Department of Transportation & Active Transit, PO Box 186, Halifax, NS B3J 2N2
902-424-2297, Fax: 902-424-0532, tpwpaff@novascotia.ca

Ontario
Northern Development Division, Roberta Bondar Place, #200, 70 Foster Dr., Sault Ste. Marie, ON P6A 6V8
705-945-5900, Fax: 705-945-5931, 800-461-2287
Ontario Ministry of Agriculture, Food & Rural Affairs, Ontario Government Bldg., 1 Stone Rd. West, Guelph, ON N1G 4Y2
519-826-3100, Fax: 519-826-4335, 888-466-2372, about.omafra@ontario.ca
Ontario Ministry of Municipal Affairs & Housing, College Park, 777 Bay St., 17th Fl., Toronto, ON M7A 2J3
416-585-7041, Fax: 416-585-4230, mininfo@ontario.ca

Prince Edward Island
Prince Edward Island Department of Fisheries & Communities, 548 Main St., PO Box 1180, Montague, PE C0A 1R0
902-838-0983, Fax: 902-838-0972, DeptFC@gov.pe.ca
Prince Edward Island Department of Transportation & Infrastructure, Jones Bldg., 11 Kent St., 3rd Fl., PO Box 2000, Charlottetown, PE C1A 7N8
902-368-5100, Fax: 902-368-5395, DeptTIE@gov.pe.ca

Quebec
Comité consultatif de l'environnement Kativik, CP 930, Kuujjuaq, QC J0M 1C0
819-964-2961, Fax: 819-964-0694, keac-ccek@krg.ca
Commission municipale du Québec, Mezzanine, aile Chauveau, 10, rue Pierre-Olivier-Chauveau, Québec, QC G1R 4J3
418-691-2014, Fax: 418-644-4676, 866-353-6767
Ministère des affaires municipales et Habitation, Aile Chauveau, 10, rue Pierre-Olivier-Chauveau, Québec, QC G1R 4J3
418-691-2015, Fax: 418-643-7385, communications@mamrot.gouv.qc.ca
Ministère des Finances, 12, rue Saint-Louis, Québec, QC G1R 5L3
418-528-9323, Fax: 418-646-1631, info@finances.gouv.qc.ca

Saskatchewan
Municipal Financing Corporation of Saskatchewan, 2350 Albert St., 6th Fl., Regina, SK S4P 4A6
306-787-8150, Fax: 306-787-8493, mfc@gov.sk.ca
Saskatchewan Government Relations, 1855 Victoria Ave., Regina, SK S4P 3T2
Saskatchewan Municipal Board, #480, 2151 Scarth St., Regina, SK S4P 2H8
306-787-6221, Fax: 306-787-1610, info@smb.gov.sk.ca

Yukon Territory
Yukon Community Services, PO Box 2703, Whitehorse, YT Y1A 2C6
867-667-5811, Fax: 867-393-6295, 800-661-0408

MUNICIPAL AFFAIRS

Alberta
Alberta Municipal Affairs, Communications Branch, Commerce Place, 10155 - 102nd St., 18th Fl., Edmonton, AB T5J 4L4
780-427-2732, Fax: 780-422-1419

British Columbia
British Columbia Ministry of Municipal Affairs, PO Box 9056 Prov Govt, Victoria, BC V8W 9E2
250-387-2283, Fax: 250-387-4312
Local Government, PO Box 9490 Prov Govt, Victoria, BC V8W 9N7
250-356-6575, Fax: 250-387-7973
Office of the Auditor General for Local Government, #201, 10470 - 152nd St., Surrey, BC V3R 0Y3
604-930-7100, info@aglg.ca

Manitoba
Manitoba Indigenous Reconciliation & Northern Relations, Legislative Bldg., #301, 450 Broadway, Winnipeg, MB R3C OV8
204-945-3788, Fax: 204-945-1383, INRweb@gov.mb.ca

Manitoba Municipal Board, #1144, 363 Broadway, Winnipeg, MB R3C 3N9
204-945-2941, Fax: 204-948-2235

New Brunswick
New Brunswick Department of Environment & Local Government, Marysville Place, 20 McGloin St., Fredericton, NB E3B 5H1
506-453-2690, Fax: 506-457-4994, elg/egl-info@gnb.ca
Regional Development Corporation, Chancery Place, 3rd Fl., PO Box 6000, Fredericton, NB E3B 5H1
506-453-2277, Fax: 506-453-7988, rdc-sdr@gnb.ca

Newfoundland & Labrador
Municipal Assessment Agency Inc., 75 O'Leary Ave., St. John's, NL A1B 2C9
709-724-1532, 877-777-2807, info@maa.ca
Newfoundland & Labrador Department of Environment & Climate Change, PO Box 8700, St. John's, NL A1B 4J6
ECCInfo@gov.nl.ca
Newfoundland & Labrador Department of Municipal & Provincial Affairs, West Block, Confederation Bldg., PO Box 8700, St. John's, NL A1B 4J6
MAPAInfo@gov.nl.ca

Northwest Territories
Northwest Territories Department of Municipal & Community Affairs, PO Box 1320, Yellowknife, NT X1A 2L9

Nova Scotia
Nova Scotia Department of Municipal Affairs, PO Box 216, Halifax, NS B3J 2M4
902-424-6642
Nova Scotia Municipal Finance Corporation, PO Box 850 M, Halifax, NS B3J 2V2
902-424-4590, Fax: 902-424-0525

Nunavut
Nunavut Territory Department of Community & Government Services, W.G. Brown Bldg., 4th Fl., PO Box 1000 700, Iqaluit, NU X0A 0H0
867-975-5406, Fax: 867-975-5305, cgscomms@gov.nu.ca

Ontario
Ontario Ministry of Municipal Affairs & Housing, College Park, 777 Bay St., 17th Fl., Toronto, ON M7A 2J3
416-585-7041, Fax: 416-585-4230, mininfo@ontario.ca

Prince Edward Island
Prince Edward Island Department of Fisheries & Communities, 548 Main St., PO Box 1180, Montague, PE C0A 1R0
902-838-0983, Fax: 902-838-0972, DeptFC@gov.pe.ca
Prince Edward Island Department of Social Development & Housing, Jones Bldg., 11 Kent St., 2nd Fl., PO Box 2000, Charlottetown, PE C1A 7N8
902-620-3777, Fax: 902-368-4740, 866-594-3777, DeptSDH@gov.pe.ca

Quebec
Ministère des affaires municipales et Habitation, Aile Chauveau, 10, rue Pierre-Olivier-Chauveau, Québec, QC G1R 4J3
418-691-2015, Fax: 418-643-7385, communications@mamrot.gouv.qc.ca

Saskatchewan
Municipal Financing Corporation of Saskatchewan, 2350 Albert St., 6th Fl., Regina, SK S4P 4A6
306-787-8150, Fax: 306-787-8493, mfc@gov.sk.ca
Saskatchewan Municipal Board, #480, 2151 Scarth St., Regina, SK S4P 2H8
306-787-6221, Fax: 306-787-1610, info@smb.gov.sk.ca

MUSEUMS

Canada Science & Technology Museum Corporation, PO Box 9724 T, Ottawa, ON K1G 5A3
613-991-3044, Fax: 613-993-7923, 866-442-4416, cts@techno-science.ca
Canadian Heritage, 15, rue Eddy, Gatineau, QC K1A 0M5
819-997-0055, 866-811-0055, PCH.info-info.PCH@canada.ca
Canadian Museum for Human Rights, 85 Israel Asper Way, Winnipeg, MB R3C 0L5
204-289-2000, Fax: 204-289-2001, 877-877-6037, info@humanrights.ca
Canadian Museum of History, 100, rue Laurier, Gatineau, QC K1A 0M8
819-776-7000, 800-555-5621
Canadian Museum of Nature, 240 McLeod St., PO Box 3443 D, Ottawa, ON K1P 6P4
613-566-4700, Fax: 613-364-4021, 800-263-4433
Canadian War Museum, 1 Vimy Pl., Ottawa, ON K1A 0M8
819-776-7000, 800-555-5621
National Gallery of Canada, 380 Sussex Dr., PO Box 427 A, Ottawa, ON K1N 9N4
613-990-1985, Fax: 613-993-4385, 800-319-2787, info@gallery.ca

Manitoba
Manitoba Museum, 190 Rupert Ave., Winnipeg, MB R3B 0N2
204-956-2830, Fax: 204-942-3679, info@manitobamuseum.ca

New Brunswick
New Brunswick Museum, Exhibition Centre, Market Square, Saint John, NB E2L 4Z6
506-643-2300, Fax: 506-643-6081, 888-268-9595, nbmuseum@nbm-mnb.ca

Newfoundland & Labrador
The Rooms Corporation, 9 Bonaventure Ave., PO Box 1800 C, St. John's, NL A1C 5P9
709-757-8000, Fax: 709-757-8017, information@therooms.ca

Nova Scotia
Art Gallery of Nova Scotia, 1723 Hollis St., PO Box 2262, Halifax, NS B3J 3C8
902-424-5280, Fax: 902-424-7359, info.agns@novascotia.ca
Nova Scotia Museum, 1747 Summer St., Halifax, NS B3H 3A6
Fax: 902-424-0560, museum@novascotia.ca

Ontario
Corporate Services Division, Mowat Block, 900 Bay St., 5th Fl., Toronto, ON M7A 1L2
416-325-6866, Fax: 416-314-7014, 888-664-6008
Royal Ontario Museum, 100 Queen's Park Cres., Toronto, ON M5S 2C6
416-586-5549, Fax: 416-586-5685, info@rom.on.ca

Quebec
Ministère de la Culture et Communications, 225, Grande Allée est, Québec, QC G1R 5G5
888-380-8882
Musée d'art contemporain de Montréal, 185, rue Sainte-Catherine ouest, Montréal, QC H2X 3X5
514-847-6226, Fax: 514-847-6292, info@macm.org
Musée de la civilisation, 85, rue Dalhousie, CP 155 B, Québec, QC G1K 8R2
418-643-2158, 866-710-8031, renseignements@mcq.org
Musée national des beaux-arts du Québec, Parc des Champs-de-Bataille, 1, av Wolfe-Montcalm, Québec, QC G1R 5H3
418-643-2150, 866-220-2150, info@mnbaq.org

Saskatchewan
Royal Saskatchewan Museum, 2445 Albert St., Regina, SK S4P 4W7
306-787-2815, Fax: 306-787-2820, info@royalsaskmuseum.ca
Western Development Museum, Curatorial Centre, 2935 Lorne Ave., Saskatoon, SK S7J 5A6
306-934-1400, 800-363-6345, info@wdm.ca

Yukon Territory
Yukon Tourism & Culture, PO Box 2703, Whitehorse, YT Y1A 2C6
867-393-7048

NATURAL GAS
See Also: Oil & Natural Gas Resources

Alberta
Alberta Utilities Commission, Eau Caire Tower, #1400, 600 - 3rd Ave. SW, Calgary, AB T2P 0G5
-310-4282, info@auc.ab.ca
Surface Rights Board, 1229 - 91 St. SW, Edmonton, AB T6X 1E9
780-427-2444, Fax: 780-427-5798, -310-0000, srb.lcb@gov.ab.ca

NATURAL RESOURCES

Canadian Museum of Nature, 240 McLeod St., PO Box 3443 D, Ottawa, ON K1P 6P4
613-566-4700, Fax: 613-364-4021, 800-263-4433
Natural Resources Canada, 580 Booth St., Ottawa, ON K1A 0E4
343-292-6096, Fax: 613-992-7211

Alberta
Natural Resources Conservation Board, Sterling Place, 9940 - 106 St., 4th Fl., Edmonton, AB T5K 2N2
780-422-1977, Fax: 780-427-0607, 866-383-6722, info@nrcb.ca

British Columbia
British Columbia Ministry of Environment & Climate Change Strategy, PO Box 9047 Prov Govt, Victoria, BC V8W 9E2
British Columbia Ministry of Forests, Lands, Natural Resource Operations & Rural Development, PO Box 9049 Prov Govt, Victoria, BC V8W 9E2
800-663-7867, FLNRO.MediaRequests@gov.bc.ca

Manitoba
Manitoba Conservation & Climate, 200 Saulteaux Cres., PO Box 22, Winnipeg, MB R3J 3W3
204-945-6784, Fax: 204-948-2656, 800-214-6497, cc@gov.mb.ca

New Brunswick
New Brunswick Department of Natural Resources & Energy Development, Hugh John Flemming Forestry Centre, PO Box 6000, Fredericton, NB E3B 5H1
506-453-3826, Fax: 506-444-4367, dnr_mrnweb@gnb.ca

Newfoundland & Labrador
Newfoundland & Labrador Department of Industry, Energy & Technology, Natural Resources Bldg., 50 Elizabeth Ave., PO Box 8700, St. John's, NL A1B 4J6
709-729-3017, Fax: 709-729-0059

Northwest Territories
Northwest Territories Department of Environment & Natural Resources, PO Box 1320, Yellowknife, NT X1A 2L9
867-767-9055, enr_communications@gov.nt.ca

Nova Scotia
Nova Scotia Department of Lands & Forestry, PO Box 698, Halifax, NS B3J 2T9
902-424-5935, Fax: 902-424-7735, 800-565-2224

Nunavut
Nunavut Territory Department of Environment, PO Box 1000 1320, Iqaluit, NU X0A 0H0
867-975-7700, Fax: 867-975-7742, environment@gov.nu.ca

Ontario
Ontario Ministry of Northern Development, Mines, Natural Resources & Forestry, Natural Resources Information & Support Centre, 300 Water St., Toronto, ON K9J 8M5
800-667-1940

Prince Edward Island
Prince Edward Island Department of Agriculture & Land, Jones Bldg., 11 Kent St., 5th Fl., PO Box 2000, Charlottetown, PE C1A 7N8
902-368-4880, Fax: 902-368-4857
Prince Edward Island Department of Justice & Public Safety, Shaw Bldg. South, 95 Rochford St., 4th Fl., PO Box 2000, Charlottetown, PE C1A 7N8
902-368-4589, Fax: 902-368-5283, DeptJPS@gov.pe.ca

Quebec
Ministère de l'Environnement et de la Lutte contre les changements climatiques, Édifice Marie-Guyart, 675, boul René-Lévesque est, 30e étage, Québec, QC G1R 5V7
418-521-3830, Fax: 418-646-5974, 800-561-1616, relations.medias@mddelcc.gouv.qc.ca
Ministère des Énergie et des Ressources naturelles, Service à la clientèle, 5700, 4e av ouest, #A301, Québec, QC G1H 6R1
866-248-6936, services.clientele@mern.gouv.qc.ca

Saskatchewan
Saskatchewan Energy & Resources, #1000, 2103 - 11th Ave., Regina, SK S4P 3Z8
Saskatchewan Environment, 3211 Albert St., Regina, SK S4S 5W6
306-787-2584, Fax: 306-787-9544, 800-567-4224, centre.inquiry@gov.sk.ca

Yukon Territory
Yukon Energy, Mines & Resources, PO Box 2703, Whitehorse, YT Y1A 2C6
867-667-3123, Fax: 867-393-7421, 800-661-0408, emr@yukon.ca
Yukon Environment, 10 Burns Rd., Whitehorse, YT Y1A 2C6
867-667-5652, Fax: 867-393-7197, environmentyukon@yukon.ca

NUCLEAR ENERGY
Atomic Energy of Canada Limited, Head Office, Chalk River Laboratories, 286 Plant Rd., Chalk River, ON K0J 1J0
888-220-2465, communications@aecl.ca
Canadian Nuclear Laboratories, Head Office, Chalk River Laboratories, 286 Plant Rd., Chalk River, ON K0J 1J0
866-513-2325, communications@cnl.ca
Canadian Nuclear Safety Commission, 280 Slater St., PO Box 1046 B, Ottawa, ON K1P 5S9
613-995-5894, Fax: 613-995-5086, 800-668-5284, cnsc.information.ccsn@canada.ca

Alberta
Alberta Energy, North Petroleum Plaza, 9945 - 108th St., Edmonton, AB T5K 2G6
780-427-8050, Fax: 780-422-9522

Ontario
Ontario Power Generation, 700 University Ave., Toronto, ON M5G 1X6
416-592-2555, 877-592-2555, webmaster@opg.com

Quebec
Hydro-Québec, Édifice Jean-Lesage, 75, boul René-Lévesque ouest, Montréal, QC H2Z 1A4
514-385-7252, 888-385-7252

NUTRITION
Science & Technology Branch, Tower 5, 1341 Baseline Rd., Ottawa, ON K1A 0C5
Fax: 613-773-1711

Manitoba
Manitoba Healthy Child Office, 332 Bannatyne Ave., 3rd Fl., Winnipeg, MB R3A 0E2
204-945-2266, 888-848-0140, healthychild@gov.mb.ca
Mental Health & Addictions, Primary Health Care & Seniors, 300 Carlton St., 4th Floor, Winnipeg, MB R3B 3M9
204-788-6666

Newfoundland & Labrador
Newfoundland & Labrador Department of Health & Community Services, West Block, Confederation Bldg., 100 Prince Philip Dr., 1st Fl., PO Box 8700, St. John's, NL A1B 4J6
709-729-4984, healthinfo@gov.nl.ca

Northwest Territories
Northwest Territories Department of Health & Social Services, PO Box 1320, Yellowknife, NT X1A 2L9

Nunavut
Nunavut Territory Department of Health, PO Box 1000 1000, Iqaluit, NU X0A 0H0
867-975-5700, Fax: 867-975-5705, 800-661-0833

Ontario
Ontario Ministry of Health, Hepburn Block, 80 Grosvenor St., 10th Fl, Toronto, ON M7A 2C4
416-327-4327, 800-268-1153

Prince Edward Island
Prince Edward Island Department of Health & Wellness, Shaw Bldg., 105 Rochford St. North, 4th Fl., Charlottetown, PE C1A 7N8
902-368-6414, Fax: 902-368-4121, DeptHW@gov.pe.ca

Quebec
Ministère de la Santé et des Services sociaux, Direction des communications, 1075, ch Sainte-Foy, 15e étage, Québec, QC G1S 2M1
418-644-4545, 877-644-4545,

Saskatchewan
Saskatchewan Health, T.C. Douglas Bldg., 3475 Albert St., Regina, SK S4S 6X6
306-787-0146, 800-667-7766, info@health.gov.sk.ca

OCCUPATIONAL SAFETY
See Also: Dangerous Goods & Hazardous Materials
Canadian Centre for Occupational Health & Safety, 135 Hunter St. East, Hamilton, ON L8N 1M5
905-572-2981, Fax: 905-572-4500, 800-668-4284

Alberta
Alberta Labour & Immigration, Legislature Bldg., #107, 10800 - 97th Ave., Edmonton, AB T5K 2B6
780-427-3731, 877-427-3731
Occupational Health & Safety Council, Standard Life Centre, 10405 Jasper Ave., Edmonton, AB T5J 3N4
780-415-8690, 866-415-8690

British Columbia
Workers' Compensation Board of British Columbia, PO Box 5350 Terminal, Vancouver, BC V6B 5L5
604-276-3100, Fax: 604-276-3247, 888-621-7233

Manitoba
Advisory Council on Workplace Safety & Health, 401 York Ave., 2nd Fl., Winnipeg, MB R3C 0P8
204-945-3446, Fax: 204-948-2209, 866-888-8186, wshcompl@gov.mb.ca

New Brunswick
WorkSafeNB, 1 Portland St., PO Box 160, Saint John, NB E2L 3X9
506-632-2200, 800-222-9775, communications@ws-ts.nb.ca

Newfoundland & Labrador
Newfoundland & Labrador Workplace Health, Safety & Compensation Commission (WorkplaceNL), 146 - 148 Forest Rd., PO Box 9000, St. John's, NL A1A 3B8
709-778-1000, Fax: 709-738-1714, 800-563-9000, info@workplacenl.ca

Northwest Territories
Northwest Territories & Nunavut Workers' Safety & Compensation Commission, Centre Square Tower, 5022 - 49th St., 5th Fl., PO Box 8888, Yellowknife, NT X1A 2R3
867-920-3888, Fax: 867-873-4596, 800-661-0792

Nova Scotia
Workers' Compensation Board of Nova Scotia, 5668 South St., PO Box 1150, Halifax, NS B3J 2Y2
902-491-8999, 800-870-3331, info@wcb.ns.ca

Ontario
Workplace Safety & Insurance Board, 200 Front St. West, Ground Fl., Toronto, ON M5V 3J1
416-344-1000, Fax: 416-344-4684, 800-387-0750

Prince Edward Island
Prince Edward Island Workers' Compensation Board, 14 Weymouth St., PO Box 757, Charlottetown, PE C1A 7L7
902-368-5680, Fax: 902-368-5696, 800-237-5049

Quebec
Commission des normes, de l'équité, de la santé et de la sécurité du travail, 524, rue Bourdages, Québec, QC G1M 1A1
Fax: 418-266-4015, 844-838-0808
Tribunal administratif du travail, 900, boul René-Lévesque est, 5e étage, Québec, QC G1R 6C9
418-643-3208, Fax: 418-643-8946, 866-864-3646

Saskatchewan
Office of the Workers' Advocate, #300, 1870 Albert St., Regina, SK S4P 4W1
Fax: 306-787-0249, 877-787-2456, workersadvocate@gov.sk.ca
Saskatchewan Workers' Compensation Board, #200, 1881 Scarth St., Regina, SK S4P 4L1
306-787-4370, Fax: 306-787-4311, 800-667-7590, webmaster@wcbsask.com

Yukon Territory
Yukon Workers' Compensation Health & Safety Board, 401 Strickland St., Whitehorse, YT Y1A 5N8
867-667-5645, Fax: 867-393-6279, 800-661-0443, worksafe@yukon.ca

OCCUPATIONAL TRAINING
Canada School of Public Service, 373 Sussex Dr., Ottawa, ON K1N 6Z2
819-953-5400, Fax: 866-944-0454, 866-703-9598, info@csps-efpc.gc.ca

Alberta
Alberta Labour & Immigration, Legislature Bldg., #107, 10800 - 97th Ave., Edmonton, AB T5K 2B6
780-427-3731, 877-427-3731
Apprenticeship & Student Aid Division, Commerce Place, 10155 - 102nd St., 6th Fl., Edmonton, AB T5J 4L5

Manitoba
Aboriginal Education Directorate, Murdo Scribe Centre, 510 Selkirk Ave., Winnipeg, MB R2W 2M7
204-945-7886, Fax: 204-948-2010, aedinfo@gov.mb.ca
Manitoba Advanced Education, Skills & Immigration, Legislative Bldg., #352, 450 Broadway, Winnipeg, MB R3C 0V8

New Brunswick
New Brunswick Department of Post-Secondary Education, Training & Labour, Chestnut Complex, PO Box 6000, Fredericton, NB E3B 5H1
506-453-2597, Fax: 506-453-3618, dpetlinfo@gnb.ca

Ontario
Ontario Ministry of Colleges & Universities, 438 University Ave., 5th Fl., Toronto, ON M7A 2A5
416-325-2929, Fax: 416-325-6348, 800-387-5514, information.met@ontario.ca

Quebec
École nationale de police du Québec, 350, rue Marguerite-d'Youville, Nicolet, QC J3T 1X4
819-293-8631, Fax: 819-293-8630, courriel@enpq.qc.ca
École nationale des pompiers du Québec, Palais de justice de Laval, #3.08, 2800, boul Saint-Martin ouest, Laval, QC H7T 2S9
450-680-6800, Fax: 450-680-6818, 866-680-3677, enpq@enpq.gouv.qc.ca

OCEANOGRAPHY
Bayfield Institute, 867 Lakeshore Rd., PO Box 5050, Burlington, ON L7R 4A6
905-336-4999
Bedford Institute of Oceanography, PO Box 1006, Dartmouth, NS B2Y 4A2
902-426-2373, Fax: 902-426-8484, webmasterbio-iob@dfo-mpo.gc.ca
Fisheries & Oceans Canada, 200 Kent St., Ottawa, ON K1A 0E6
613-993-0999, Fax: 613-990-1866, info@dfo-mpo.gc.ca
Institut Maurice-Lamontagne, 850, rte de le Mer, CP 1000, Mont-Joli, QC G5H 3Z4
418-775-0500, Fax: 418-775-0730
Institute of Ocean Sciences, 9860 West Saanich Rd., PO Box 6000, Sidney, BC V8L 4B2
250-363-6517
Ocean Technology Enterprise Centre, PO Box 12093, St. John's, NL A1B 3T5
709-772-2469

OIL & NATURAL GAS RESOURCES
See Also: Energy; Natural Resources
Canada Energy Regulator, #210, 517 - 10th Ave. SW, Calgary, AB T2R 0A8
403-292-4800, Fax: 403-292-5503, 800-899-1265,
Indian Oil & Gas Canada, #100, 9911 Chiila Blvd., Tsuu T'ina (Sarcee), AB T2W 6H6
403-292-5625, Fax: 403-292-5618, aadnc.contactiogc.aandc@canada.ca

Northern Pipeline Agency Canada, #470, 588 Booth St., Ottawa, ON K1A 0Y7
613-995-1150, info@npa.gc.ca

Alberta

Alberta Energy, North Petroleum Plaza, 9945 - 108th St., Edmonton, AB T5K 2G6
780-427-8050, Fax: 780-422-9522

Alberta Energy Regulator, #1000, 250 - 5 St. SW, Calgary, AB T2P 0R4
403-297-8311, Fax: 403-297-7336, 855-297-8311, inquiries@aer.ca

Surface Rights Board, 1229 - 91 St. SW, Edmonton, AB T6X 1E9
780-427-2444, Fax: 780-427-5798, -310-0000, srb.lcb@gov.ab.ca

British Columbia

British Columbia Utilities Commission, #410, 900 Howe St., Vancouver, BC V6Z 2N3
604-660-4700, Fax: 604-660-1102, 800-663-1385, commission.secretary@bcuc.com

Oil & Gas Commission, 6534 Airport Rd., Fort St. John, BC V1J 4M6
250-794-5200, Fax: 250-794-5375

Surface Rights Board of British Columbia, #10, 10551 Shellbridge Way, Richmond, BC V6X 2W9
604-775-1740, Fax: 604-775-1742, 888-775-1740, office@surfacerightsboard.bc.ca

Manitoba

Surface Rights Board, #360, 1395 Ellice Ave., Winnipeg, MB R3G 3P2
204-945-0731, Fax: 204-948-2578, 800-223-5215

New Brunswick

New Brunswick Department of Natural Resources & Energy Development, Hugh John Flemming Forestry Centre, PO Box 6000, Fredericton, NB E3B 5H1
506-453-3826, Fax: 506-444-4367, dnr_mrnweb@gnb.ca

Newfoundland & Labrador

Canada-Newfoundland & Labrador Offshore Petroleum Board, West Campus Hall, The Tower Corporate Campus, #7100, 240 Waterford Bridge Rd., St. John's, NL A1E 1E2
709-778-1400, information@cnlopb.ca

Northwest Territories

Office of the Regulator of Oil & Gas Operations, Northwest Tower, 5201 - 50th Ave., 4th Fl., PO Box 1320, Yellowknife, NT X1A 2L9
867-767-9097

Nova Scotia

Canada-Nova Scotia Offshore Petroleum Board, TD Centre, 1791 Barrington St., 8th Fl., Halifax, NS B3J 3K9
902-422-5588, Fax: 902-422-1799, info@cnsopb.ns.ca

Nova Scotia Department of Energy & Mines, Joseph Howe Bldg., 1690 Hollis St., PO Box 2664, Halifax, NS B3J 3J9
902-424-4575, Fax: 902-424-3265, enerinfo@novascotia.ca

Nova Scotia Utility & Review Board, Summit Place, 1601 Lower Water St., 3rd Fl., Halifax, NS B3J 3S3
902-424-4448, Fax: 902-424-3919, 855-442-4448, board@novascotia.ca

Nunavut

Nunavut Territory Department of Environment, PO Box 1000 1320, Iqaluit, NU X0A 0H0
867-975-7700, Fax: 867-975-7742, environment@gov.nu.ca

Ontario

Ontario Ministry of Northern Development, Mines, Natural Resources & Forestry, Natural Resources Information & Support Centre, 300 Water St., Toronto, ON K9J 8M5
800-667-1940

Saskatchewan

NorthPoint Energy Solutions Inc., 2025 Victoria Ave., Regina, SK S4P 0S1

SaskEnergy Incorporated, 1777 Victoria Ave., Regina, SK S4P 4K5
306-777-9225, 800-567-8899, webmaster@saskenergy.com

OIL SPILLS

Canadian Coast Guard, Centennial Towers, #6S018, 200 Kent St., Ottawa, ON K1A 0E6
613-993-0999, Fax: 613-990-1866, info@dfo-mpo.gc.ca

Office of the Administrator of the Ship-source Oil Pollution Fund, #830, 180 Kent St., Ottawa, ON K1A 0N5
613-991-1726, Fax: 613-990-5423, info@sopf-cidphn.gc.ca

Newfoundland & Labrador

Canada-Newfoundland & Labrador Offshore Petroleum Board, West Campus Hall, The Tower Corporate Campus, #7100, 240 Waterford Bridge Rd., St. John's, NL A1E 1E2
709-778-1400, information@cnlopb.ca

OMBUDSMEN

Office of the Commissioner of Official Languages, 30 Victoria St., 6th Fl., Gatineau, ON K1A 0T8
819-420-4877, Fax: 819-420-4873, 877-996-6368

Office of the Correctional Investigator, PO Box 3421 D, Ottawa, ON K1P 6L4
Fax: 613-990-9091, 877-885-8848, org@oci-bec.gc.ca

Office of the Ombudsman, PO Box 90026, Ottawa, ON K1V 1J8
Fax: 800-204-4193, 800-204-4198

Office of the Procurement Ombudsman, Constitution Square Bldg., #1150, 340 Albert St., 11th Fl., PO Box 151, Ottawa, ON K1R 7Y6
Fax: 613-947-9800, 866-734-5169, boa-opo@boa-opo.gc.ca

Office of the Taxpayers' Ombudsman, #600, 150 Slater St., Ottawa, ON K1A 1K3
613-946-2310, Fax: 613-941-6319, 866-586-3839

Veterans Ombudsman (Charlottetown), 134 Kent St., PO Box 66, Charlottetown, PE C1A 7K2
902-626-2919, Fax: 888-566-7582, 877-330-4343, VAC.OVOInfo-InfoBOV.ACC@ombudsman-veterans.gc.ca

Veterans Ombudsman (Ottawa), #1560, 360 Albert St., Ottawa, ON K1R 7X7
Fax: 888-566-7582, 877-330-4343, VAC.OVOInfo-InfoBOV.ACC@ombudsman-veterans.gc.ca

Alberta

Alberta Office of the Ombudsman, Canadian Western Bank Bldg., #700, 9925 - 109th St., Edmonton, AB T5K 2J8
780-427-2756, Fax: 780-427-2759, 888-455-2756, info@ombudsman.ab.ca

British Columbia

Office of the Ombudsperson, 947 Fort St., 2nd Fl., PO Box 9039 Prov Govt, Victoria, BC V8W 9A5
250-387-5855, Fax: 250-387-0198, 800-567-3247

Manitoba

Manitoba Office of the Ombudsman, Colony Square, #750, 500 Portage Ave., Winnipeg, MB R3C 3X1
204-982-9130, Fax: 204-942-7803, 800-665-0531, ombudsman@ombudsman.mb.ca

New Brunswick

Office of the Ombudsman, 548 York St., PO Box 6000, Fredericton, NB E3B 5H1
506-453-2789, Fax: 506-453-5599, 888-465-1100

Nova Scotia

Office of the Ombudsman, PO Box 2152, Halifax, NS B3J 3B7
902-424-6780, Fax: 902-424-6675, 800-670-1111, ombudsman@novascotia.ca

Ontario

Office of the Ombudsman, Bell Trinity Sq., South Tower, 483 Bay St., 10th Fl., Toronto, ON M5G 2C9
416-586-3300, Fax: 416-586-3485, 800-263-1830, info@ombudsman.on.ca

Quebec

Le Protecteur du Citoyen, 800, place D'Youville, 19e étage, Québec, QC G1R 3P4
418-643-2688, Fax: 418-643-8759, 800-463-5070, protecteur@protecteurducitoyen.qc.ca

Saskatchewan

Ombudsman Saskatchewan, #500, 2103 - 11th Ave., Regina, SK S4P 3Z8
306-787-6211, Fax: 306-787-9090, 800-667-9787, ombreg@ombudsman.sk.ca

PARKS & RECREATION

Canadian Heritage, 15, rue Eddy, Gatineau, QC K1A 0M5
819-997-0055, 866-811-0055, PCH.info-info.PCH@canada.ca

Historic Sites & Monuments Board of Canada, 30 Victoria St., 3rd Fl., Gatineau, QC J8X 0B3
Fax: 819-420-9260, 855-283-8730, hsmbc-clmhc@pc.gc.ca

Parc Downsview Park Inc., 70 Canuck Ave., Toronto, ON M3K 2C5
416-954-0544, downsviewevents@clc.ca

Parks Canada, National Office, 30, rue Victoria, Gatineau, QC J8X 0B3
819-420-9486, 888-773-8888, information@pc.gc.ca

Alberta

Alberta Environment & Parks, Forestry Bldg., 9920 - 108th St., Main Fl., Edmonton, AB T5K 2M4
780-944-0313

Parks Division, Oxbridge Place, 9820 - 106th St., 2nd Fl., Edmonton, AB T5K 2J6
780-427-3582, Fax: 780-427-5980, 866-427-3582

Special Areas Board, Special Areas Board Administration, 212 - 2nd Ave. West, PO Box 820, Hanna, AB T0J 1P0
403-854-5600, Fax: 403-854-5527

British Columbia

British Columbia Ministry of Environment & Climate Change Strategy, PO Box 9047 Prov Govt, Victoria, BC V8W 9E2

Manitoba

Ecological Reserves Advisory Committee, c/o Manitoba Conservation, Parks & Natural Areas Branch, 200 Saulteaux Cres., PO Box 53, Winnipeg, MB R3J 3W3
204-945-4148, Fax: 204-945-0012

New Brunswick

New Brunswick Department of Tourism, Heritage & Culture, Marysville Place, 4th Fl., PO Box 6000, Fredericton, NB E3B 5H1
506-453-3115, Fax: 506-444-5760, thctpcinfo@gnb.ca

Newfoundland & Labrador

Newfoundland & Labrador Department of Tourism, Culture, Arts & Recreation, PO Box 8700, St. John's, NL A1B 4J6
709-729-7000, tcar@gov.nl.ca

Northwest Territories

Northwest Territories Department of Environment & Natural Resources, PO Box 1320, Yellowknife, NT X1A 2L9
867-767-9055, enr_communications@gov.nt.ca

Nunavut

Nunavut Territory Department of Environment, PO Box 1000 1320, Iqaluit, NU X0A 0H0
867-975-7700, Fax: 867-975-7742, environment@gov.nu.ca

Ontario

Ontario Ministry of Economic Development, Job Creation & Trade, 56 Wellesley St. West, 7th Fl., Toronto, ON M7A 2E7
416-325-6666, 800-268-7095

Prince Edward Island

Labour & Industrial Relations, 16 St. Peters Rd., Charlottetown, PE C1A 7N8

Prince Edward Island Department of Economic Growth, Tourism & Culture, PO Box 2000, Charlottetown, PE C1A 7N8
902-368-5540, Fax: 902-368-5277, tpswitch@gov.pe.ca

Quebec

Ministère de l'Environnement et de la Lutte contre les changements climatiques, Édifice Marie-Guyart, 675, boul René-Lévesque est, 30e étage, Québec, QC G1R 5V7
418-521-3830, Fax: 418-646-5974, 800-561-1616, relations.medias@mddelcc.gouv.qc.ca

Ministère des Forêts, Faune et Parcs, Service à la clientèle, #A409 - 5700, 4e av ouest, Québec, QC G1H 6R1
Fax: 418-644-6513, 844-523-6738, services.clientele@mrnf.gouv.qc.ca

Société des établissements de plein air du Québec, Place de la Cité, Tour Cominar, #1300, 2640, boul Laurier, Québec, QC G1V 5C2
418-686-4875, Fax: 418-643-8177, 800-665-6527, inforeservation@sepaq.com

Société des établissements en plein air du Québec, Place de la Cité, Tour Cominar, #250, 2640, boul Laurier, 2e étage, Québec, QC G1V 5C2
418-686-4875, Fax: 418-643-8177, 800-665-6527, inforeservation@sepaq.com

Saskatchewan

Saskatchewan Parks, Culture & Sport, 3211 Albert St., 1st Fl., Regina, SK S4S 5W6
306-787-5729, Fax: 306-798-0033, pcs.info@gov.sk.ca

Yukon Territory

Yukon Tourism & Culture, PO Box 2703, Whitehorse, YT Y1A 2C6
867-393-7048

PARLIAMENT

See Also: Government (General Information); Protocol (State)

Forty-Fourth Parliament - Canada, House of Commons, Parliament Buildings, Ottawa, BC K1A 0A6

Library of Parliament, Information Servicce, Parliament of Canada, Ottawa, ON K1A 0A9
613-992-4793, 866-599-4999, info@parl.gc.ca

Office of the Leader, Bloc Québécois, Centre Block, 111 Wellington St., Ottawa, ON K1A 0A6

Office of the Leader, Green Party of Canada, Confederation Bldg., 229 Wellington St., Ottawa, ON K1A 0A6
613-996-1119, Fax: 613-996-0850, 866-868-3447, info@greenparty.ca

Office of the Leader, Official Opposition, Conservative Party of Canada / Conservative Party Research Bureau, Centre Block, 111 Wellington St., Ottawa, ON K1A 0A6
613-995-1333, Fax: 613-995-1337

Office of the Prime Minister, Liberal Party of Canada / Liberal Research Bureau, 80 Wellington St., Ottawa, ON K1A 0A2
Fax: 613-941-6900

Parliamentary Budget Officer, #919, 50 O'Connor St., Ottawa, ON K1A 0A9
613-992-8026, pbo-dpb@parl.gc.ca

Privy Council Office, #1000, 85 Sparks St., Ottawa, ON K1A 0A3
613-957-5153, Fax: 613-997-5043, info@pco-bcp.gc.ca

The Canadian Ministry, Information Service, Parliament of Canada, Ottawa, ON K1A 0A9
613-992-4793, 866-599-4999, info@parl.gc.ca

Alberta

Legislative Assembly of Alberta, 9718 - 107th St., Edmonton, AB T5K 1E4
780-427-2826, laocommunications@assembly.ab.ca

British Columbia
British Columbia Legislative Assembly & Independent Offices, Clerk's Office, Parliament Bldgs., Victoria, BC V8V 1X4
250-387-3785, Fax: 250-387-0942,
officeoftheclerk@leg.bc.ca

Manitoba
Manitoba Legislative Assembly, c/o Clerk's Office, Legislative Bldg., #237, 450 Broadway, Winnipeg, MB R3C 0V8
204-945-3636, Fax: 204-948-2507, clerkla@leg.gov.mb.ca

New Brunswick
Legislative Assembly of New Brunswick, Legislative Bldg., Centre Block, PO Box 6000, Fredericton, NB E3B 5H1
506-453-2506, Fax: 506-453-7154, wwwleg@gnb.ca

Northwest Territories
Northwest Territories Legislative Assembly, 4570 - 48th St., PO Box 1320, Yellowknife, NT X1A 2L9
867-669-2200, 800-661-0784

Nova Scotia
Legislative House of Assembly, Province House, 1726 Hollis St., Halifax, NS B3J 2Y3
902-424-5978, Fax: 902-424-0632, info@nslegislature.ca

Nunavut
Nunavut Legislative Assembly, 926 Federal Rd., PO Box 1200, Iqaluit, NU X0A 0H0
867-975-5000, Fax: 867-975-5190, 877-334-7266, leginfo@assembly.nu.ca

Ontario
Ontario Legislative Assembly, c/o Clerk of the Legislative Assembly, #104, Legislative Bldg., Queen's Park, Toronto, ON M7A 1A2
416-325-7500, Fax: 416-325-7489, web@ola.org

Prince Edward Island
Prince Edward Island Legislative Assembly, 197 Richmond St., PO Box 2000, Charlottetown, PE C1A 7N8
902-368-5970, Fax: 902-368-5175, assembly@assembly.pe.ca

Quebec
L'Assemblée nationale, Hôtel du Parlement, 1045, rue des Parlementaires, Québec, QC G1A 1A3
418-643-7239, Fax: 418-646-4271, 866-337-8837, renseignements@assnat.qc.ca

Saskatchewan
Legislative Assembly of Saskatchewan, Office of the Clerk, Legislative Bldg., #239, 2405 Legislative Dr., Regina, SK S4S 0B3
info@legassembly.sk.ca

Yukon Territory
Yukon Legislative Assembly, 2071 - 2nd Ave., PO Box 2703, Whitehorse, YT Y1A 2C6
867-667-5498, yla@yukon.ca

PAROLE BOARDS
See Also: Correctional Services
Parole Board of Canada, Communications Division, National Office, 410 Laurier Ave. West, Ottawa, ON K1A 0R1
613-954-7474, Fax: 613-941-4981, info@pbc-clcc.gc.ca

Alberta
Crown Prosecution Service Division, Bowker Bldg., 9833 - 109th St., 2nd Fl., Edmonton, AB T5K 2E8

Manitoba
Community Safety Division, Manitoba Corrections Head Office, #810, 405 Broadway, Winnipeg, MB R3C 3L6
204-945-7804

New Brunswick
New Brunswick Department of Justice & Public Safety, Marysville Place, 3rd Fl., PO Box 6000, Fredericton, NB E3B 5H1
506-453-3992, DPS-MSP.Information@gnb.ca

Ontario
Correctional Services, George Drew Bldg, 25 Grosvenor St., 17th Fl., Toronto, ON M7A 1Y6
Safety, Licensing Appeals & Standards Tribunals Ontario, #401, 20 Dundas St. West, 4th Fl., Toronto, ON M5T 2Z5
Fax: 416-327-6379, 844-242-0608, slastoinfo@ontario.ca

Quebec
Commission québécoise des libérations conditionnelles, #1.32A, 300, boul Jean-Lesage, Québec, QC G1K 8K6
418-646-8300, Fax: 418-643-7217, cqlc@cqlc.gouv.qc.ca

Saskatchewan
Justice Services Division, #1000, 1874 Scarth St., Regina, SK S4P 4B3
Fax: 306-787-3874

PASSPORT INFORMATION
See Also: Citizenship; Immigration
Passport, c/o Passport Program, Gatineau, QC K1A 0G3
800-567-6868

PATENTS & COPYRIGHT
Canadian Intellectual Property Office, Place du Portage I, #C-229, 50, rue Victoria, Gatineau, QC K1A 0C9
819-997-1936, Fax: 819-953-2476, 866-997-1936, cipo.contact@ic.gc.ca
Copyright Board of Canada, #800, 56 Sparks St., Ottawa, ON K1A 0C9
613-952-8621, Fax: 613-952-8630, secretariat@cb-cda.gc.ca

PAY EQUITY
Employment & Social Development Canada, 140, promenade du Portage, Gatineau, QC K1A 0J9

British Columbia
Employment Standards Tribunal, Oceanic Plaza, #650, 1066 West Hastings St., Vancouver, BC V6E 3X1
604-775-3512, Fax: 604-775-3372, registrar@bcest.bc.ca

Nova Scotia
Pay Equity Commission, 5151 Terminal Rd., 6th Fl., PO Box 697, Halifax, NS B3J 2T8
902-424-8466, Fax: 902-424-0575

Ontario
Pay Equity Office, #300, 180 Dundas St. West, Toronto, ON M7A 2S6
416-314-1896, Fax: 416-314-8741, 800-387-8813

Prince Edward Island
Workers Compensation Appeal Tribunal, c/o Executive Council, 95 Rochford St., PO Box 2000, Charlottetown, PE C1A 7N8
902-569-0545

PENSIONS
Canada Pension Plan Investment Board, #2500, 1 Queen St. East, Toronto, ON M5C 2W5
416-868-4075, Fax: 416-868-8689, 866-557-9510, contact@cppib.com
Finance Canada, 90 Elgin St., Ottawa, ON K1A 0G5
613-369-3710, Fax: 613-369-4065, fin.financepublic-financepublique.fin@canada.ca
Office of the Superintendent of Financial Institutions, Kent Square, 255 Albert St., 12th Fl., Ottawa, ON K1A 0H2
613-990-7788, Fax: 613-990-5591, 800-385-8647, information@osfi-bsif.gc.ca
Public Sector Pension Investment Board, #200, 440 Laurier Ave. West, Ottawa, ON K1R 7X6
613-782-3095, Fax: 613-782-6864, info@investpsp.ca
Service Canada, 140, promenade du Portage, Gatineau, QC K1A 0J9
800-622-6232
Social Security Tribunal, PO Box 9812 T, Ottawa, ON K1G 6S3
613-952-8805, 877-227-8577, info.sst-tss@canada.gc.ca
Veterans Affairs Canada, 161 Grafton St., PO Box 7700, Charlottetown, PE C1A 8M9
613-996-2242, 866-522-2122, information@vac-acc.gc.ca
Veterans Review & Appeal Board, Daniel J. MacDonald Bldg., 161 Grafton St., PO Box 9900, Charlottetown, PE C1A 8V7
902-566-8751, Fax: 902-566-7850, 800-450-8006, vrab.vrab-tacra.tacra@vrab-tacra.gc.ca

Alberta
Alberta Local Authorities Pension Plan Corp., c/o Alberta Pensions Services Corp., 5103 Windermere Blvd. SW, Edmonton, AB T6W 0S9
Fax: 780-421-1652, 877-649-5277, memberservices@lapp.ca
Alberta Pensions Services Corporation, 5103 Windermere Blvd. SW, Edmonton, AB T6W 0S9
780-427-2782, 800-661-8198, memberservices@apsc.ca
Alberta Teachers' Retirement Fund, Barnett House, #600, 11010 - 142 St. NW, Edmonton, AB T5N 2R1
780-451-4166, Fax: 780-452-3547, 800-661-9582, info@atrf.com
Management Employees Pension Board, c/o Alberta Pensions Services Corp., 5103 Windermere Blvd. SW, Edmonton, AB T6W 0S9
780-391-3693, Fax: 780-421-1652, 877-889-6377, board@mepp.ca
Public Service Pension Board, c/o Alberta Pensions Services Corp., 5103 Windermere Blvd. SW, Edmonton, AB T6W 0S9
Fax: 780-421-1652, 877-453-1777, board@pspp.ca
Special Forces Pension Board, c/o Alberta Pensions Services Corp, 5103 Windermere Blvd. SW, Edmonton, AB T6W 0S9
Fax: 780-421-1652, 877-809-7377, board@sfpp.ca

British Columbia
British Columbia Pension Corporation, 2995 Jutland Rd., PO Box 9460, Victoria, BC V8W 9V8
250-387-1014, Fax: 250-953-0429, 800-663-8823, PensionCorp@pensionsbc.ca

Manitoba
Pension Commission of Manitoba, #1004, 401 York Ave., Winnipeg, MB R3C 0P8
204-945-2740, Fax: 204-948-2375, pensions@gov.mb.ca

Teachers' Retirement Allowances Fund Board, Johnston Terminal, #330, 25 Forks Market Rd., Winnipeg, MB R3C 4S8
204-949-0048, Fax: 204-944-0361, 800-782-0714, info@traf.mb.ca

Newfoundland & Labrador
Pension Investment Committee, Confederation Bldg., PO Box 8700, St. John's, NL A1B 4J6

Nova Scotia
Nova Scotia Pension Services Corporation, Purdy's Landing, #400, 1949 Upper Water St., PO Box 371, Halifax, NS B3J 2P8
902-424-5070, Fax: 902-424-0662, 800-774-5070, pensionsinfo@nspension.ca

Ontario
Financial Services Commission of Ontario, North York City Ctr., 5160 Yonge St., 17th Fl., PO Box 85, Toronto, ON M2N 6L9
416-250-7250, Fax: 416-590-7070, 800-668-0128, contactcentre@fsco.gov.on.ca
Ontario Pension Board, Sun Life Bldg., #2200, 200 King St. West, Toronto, ON M5H 3X6
416-364-8558, Fax: 416-364-7578, 800-668-6203, office.services@opb.ca
OPSEU Pension Trust, #1200, 1 Adelaide St. East, Toronto, ON M5C 3A7
416-681-6161, Fax: 416-681-6175, 800-637-0024
Provincial Judges Pension Board, c/o Ontario Pension Board, #2200, 200 King St. West, Toronto, ON M5H 3X6
416-364-8558, Fax: 416-364-7578, 800-668-6203

Prince Edward Island
Debt, Investment & Pension Management, Shaw Bldg. South, 95 Rochford St., 3rd Fl., PO Box 2000, Charlottetown, PE C1A 7N8

Quebec
Retraite Québec, Place de la Cité, entrée 6, #548, 2600, boul Laurier, Québec, QC G1V 4T3

Saskatchewan
Crown Investments Corporation of Saskatchewan, #400, 2400 College Ave., Regina, SK S4P 1C8
306-787-6851, Fax: 306-787-0294
Financial & Consumer Affairs Authority, #601, 1919 Saskatchewan Dr., Regina, SK S4P 4H2
306-787-5645, Fax: 306-787-5899, 877-880-5550, consumerprotection@gov.sk.ca
Municipal Employees' Pension Commission, #110, 1801 Hamilton St., Regina, SK S4P 4W3
306-787-2684, Fax: 306-787-8822, 877-506-6377, mepp@peba.gov.sk.ca
Saskatchewan Pension Plan, PO Box 5555, Kindersley, SK S0L 1S0
306-463-5410, Fax: 306-463-3500, 800-667-7153, info@saskpension.com

PESTICIDES, HERBICIDES
Pest Management Regulatory Agency, 2720 Riverside Dr., Ottawa, ON K1A 0K9
613-736-3799, Fax: 613-736-3798, 800-267-6315, hc.pmra.info-arla.sc@canada.ca

Ontario
Pesticides Advisory Committee, Foster Bldg, 40 St. Clair Ave. West, 7th Fl., Toronto, ON M4V 1M2
416-314-9230, Fax: 416-314-9237

PIPELINES
Canada Energy Regulator, #210, 517 - 10th Ave. SW, Calgary, AB T2R 0A8
403-292-4800, Fax: 403-292-5503, 800-899-1265
Northern Pipeline Agency Canada, #470, 588 Booth St., Ottawa, ON K1A 0Y7
613-995-1150, info@npa.gc.ca

Alberta
Alberta Energy, North Petroleum Plaza, 9945 - 108th St., Edmonton, AB T5K 2G6
780-427-8050, Fax: 780-422-9522
Alberta Energy Regulator, #1000, 250 - 5 St. SW, Calgary, AB T2P 0R4
403-297-8311, Fax: 403-297-7336, 855-297-8311, inquiries@aer.ca
Surface Rights Board, 1229 - 91 St. SW, Edmonton, AB T6X 1E9
780-427-2444, Fax: 780-427-5798, -310-0000, srb.lcb@gov.ab.ca

British Columbia
British Columbia Hydro, 333 Dunsmuir St., PO Box 8910, Vancouver, BC V6B 4N1
604-224-9376, 800-224-9376

Northwest Territories
Northwest Territories Department of Environment & Natural Resources, PO Box 1320, Yellowknife, NT X1A 2L9
867-767-9055, enr_communications@gov.nt.ca

Nova Scotia

Nova Scotia Department of Energy & Mines, Joseph Howe Bldg., 1690 Hollis St., PO Box 2664, Halifax, NS B3J 3J9
902-424-4575, Fax: 902-424-3265, enerinfo@novascotia.ca

Nova Scotia Utility & Review Board, Summit Place, 1601 Lower Water St., 3rd Fl., Halifax, NS B3J 3S3
902-424-4448, Fax: 902-424-3919, 855-442-4448, board@novascotia.ca

Saskatchewan

SaskEnergy Incorporated, 1777 Victoria Ave., Regina, SK S4P 4K5
306-777-9225, 800-567-8899, webmaster@saskenergy.com

POLICING SERVICES

Royal Canadian Mounted Police, 73 Leikin Dr., Ottawa, ON K1A 0R2
613-993-7267, Fax: 613-993-0260

Alberta

Alberta Justice & Solicitor General, John E. Brownlee Bldg., 10365 - 97th St., 9th Fl., Edmonton, AB T5J 3W7
780-427-2745

Public Security Division, John E. Brownlee Bldg., 10365 - 97th St., 10th Fl., Edmonton, AB T5J 3W7

British Columbia

British Columbia Ministry of Attorney General & Minister responsible for Housing, PO Box 9044 Prov Govt, Victoria, BC V8W 9E2

British Columbia Ministry of Public Safety & Solicitor General, PO Box 9290 Prov Govt, Victoria, BC V8W 9J7
250-356-0149, Fax: 250-387-6224, 800-663-7867, PSSG.Correspondence@gov.bc.ca

Manitoba

Health Information Privacy Committee, #4043, 300 Carlton St., Winnipeg, MB R3B 3M9

Law Enforcement Review Agency, #420, 155 Carlton St., Winnipeg, MB R3C 3H8
204-945-8667, Fax: 204-948-1014, 800-282-8069, lera@gov.mb.ca

Manitoba Justice, Administration & Finance, #1110, 405 Broadway Ave., Winnipeg, MB R3C 3L6
204-945-2878

New Brunswick

New Brunswick Department of Justice & Public Safety, Marysville Place, 3rd Fl., PO Box 6000, Fredericton, NB E3B 5H1
506-453-3992, DPS-MSP.Information@gnb.ca

New Brunswick Police Commission, Fredericton City Centre, #202, 435 King St., Fredericton, NB E3B 1E5
506-453-2069, Fax: 506-457-3542, nbpc@gnb.ca

Newfoundland & Labrador

Newfoundland & Labrador Department of Justice & Public Safety, East Block, Confederation Bldg., 4th Fl., PO Box 8700, St. John's, NL A1B 4J6
709-729-2869, Fax: 709-729-0469, justice@gov.nl.ca

Royal Newfoundland Constabulary Public Complaints Commission, PO Box 8700, St. John's, NL A1B 4J6
709-834-6171, Fax: 709-834-6178, rncomplaintscommission@gov.nl.ca

Northwest Territories

Northwest Territories Department of Justice, 4903 - 49th St., PO Box 1320, Yellowknife, NT X1A 2L9
867-767-9256, justice_communications@gov.nt.ca

Nova Scotia

Nova Scotia Department of Justice, 1690 Hollis St., PO Box 7, Halifax, NS B3J 2L6
902-424-4030, justweb@gov.ns.ca

Office of the Police Complaints Commissioner, 1690 Hollis St., 3rd Fl., PO Box 1573, Halifax, NS B3J 2Y3
902-424-3246, Fax: 902-424-1777, polcom@novascotia.ca

Serious Incident Response Team, #203, 1256 Barrington St., Halifax, NS B3J 1Y6
902-424-2010, 855-450-2010, sirt@gov.ns.ca

Nunavut

Nunavut Territory Department of Justice, PO Box 1000 500, Iqaluit, NU X0A 0H0
867-975-6170, Fax: 867-975-6195, justice@gov.nu.ca

Ontario

Ontario Ministry of the Attorney General, McMurtry-Scott Bldg., 720 Bay St., 11th Fl., Toronto, ON M7A 2S9
416-326-2220, Fax: 416-326-4016, 800-518-7901, attorneygeneral@ontario.ca

Ontario Provincial Police, Lincoln M Alexander Bldg, 777 Memorial Ave, Orillia, ON L3V 7V3
705-329-6111, 888-310-1122

Special Investigations Unit, 5090 Commerce Blvd., Mississauga, ON L4W 5M4
416-622-0748, Fax: 416-622-2455, 800-787-8529

Quebec

Bureau des enquêtes indépendantes, #6.01, 201, Place Charles-Lemoyne, Longueuil, QC J4K 2T5
450-640-1350, Fax: 450-670-6386

Ministère de la Justice, Édifice Louis-Philippe-Pigeon, 1200, rte de l'Église, Québec, QC G1V 4M1
418-643-5140, 866-536-5140, informations@justice.gouv.qc.ca

Sûreté du Québec, Grand quartier général, 1701, rue Parthenais, Montréal, QC H2K 3S7
514-598-4141, Fax: 514-598-4242

Saskatchewan

Saskatchewan Justice & Attorney General, 1874 Scarth St., Regina, SK S4P 4B3

Saskatchewan Police College, College West Bldg., University of Regina, #217, 3737 Wascana Pkwy., Regina, SK S4S 0A2
306-787-8870, Fax: 306-787-8876

Saskatchewan Police Commission, #1850, 1881 Scarth St., Regina, SK S4P 4K9
306-787-9292, Fax: 306-798-4908

Saskatchewan Public Complaints Commission, #300, 1919 Saskatchewan Dr., Regina, SK S4P 4H2
306-787-6519, Fax: 306-787-6528, 866-256-6194

Yukon Territory

Yukon Justice, Andrew Philipsen Law Centre, 2134 - 2nd Ave., PO Box 2703, Whitehorse, YT Y1A 2C6
867-667-3033, Fax: 867-667-5200, justice@yukon.ca

POLITICS & SOCIETY

Auditor General of Canada, 240 Sparks St., Ottawa, ON K1A 0G6
613-952-0213, Fax: 613-957-0474, 888-761-5953, infomedia@oag-bvg.gc.ca

Commission for Environmental Cooperation, Secretariat, #200, 393, rue Saint-Jacques ouest, Montréal, QC H2Y 1N9
514-350-4300, Fax: 514-350-4314, info@cec.org

Department of National Defence & the Canadian Armed Forces, National Defence HQ, Major-General George R. Pearkes Bldg., 101 Colonel By Dr., Ottawa, ON K1A 0K2
613-995-2534, Fax: 613-992-4739, 888-995-2534, information@forces.gc.ca

Finance Canada, 90 Elgin St., Ottawa, ON K1A 0G5
613-369-3710, Fax: 613-369-4065, fin.financepublic-financepublique.fin@canada.ca

Global Affairs Canada, Enquiries Service, 125 Sussex Dr., Ottawa, ON K1A 0G2
Fax: 613-996-9709, 800-267-8376

International Development Research Centre, 150 Kent St., PO Box 8500, Ottawa, ON K1G 3H9
613-236-6163, Fax: 613-238-7230, info@idrc.ca

International Joint Commission, 234 Laurier Ave. West, 22nd Fl., Ottawa, ON K1P 6K6
613-995-2984, Fax: 613-993-5583, commission@ottawa.ijc.org

National Capital Commission, #202, 40 Elgin St., Ottawa, ON K1P 1C7
613-239-5000, Fax: 613-239-5063, 800-465-1867, info@ncc-ccn.ca

Policy Horizons Canada, 360 Albert St., 15th Fl., Ottawa, ON K1R 7X7
613-947-3800, Fax: 613-995-6006, questions@horizons.gc.ca

Public Safety Canada, 269 Laurier Ave. West, Ottawa, ON K1A 0P8
613-944-4875, Fax: 613-954-5186, 800-830-3118

Public Services & Procurement, Place du Portage, Phase III, 11, rue Laurier, Ottawa, ON K1A 0S5
questions@tpsgc-pwgsc.gc.ca

Strategic Policy Branch, Tower 7, 1341 Baseline Rd., Ottawa, ON K1A 0C5
613-759-1000, Fax: 613-773-2121

British Columbia

British Columbia Ministry of Tourism, Arts, Culture & Sport, PO Box 9082 Prov Govt, Victoria, BC V8W 9E2

Newfoundland & Labrador

Newfoundland & Labrador Department of Digital Government & Service NL, 100 Prince Phillip Dr., PO Box 8700, St. John's, NL A1B 4J6
709-729-4834, servicenlinfo@gov.nl.ca

Newfoundland & Labrador Department of Transportation & Infrastructure, Confederation Bldg., Prince Philip Dr., PO Box 8700, St. John's, NL A1B 4J6
709-729-2300, ti@gov.nl.ca

Northwest Territories

Northwest Territories Department of the Executive & Indigenous Affairs, PO Box 1320, Yellowknife, NT X1A 2L9

Ontario

Environmental Commissioner of Ontario, #605, 1075 Bay St., Toronto, ON M5S 2B1
416-325-3377, Fax: 416-325-3370, 800-701-6454, commissioner@eco.on.ca

Prince Edward Island

Prince Edward Island Department of Health & Wellness, Shaw Bldg., 105 Rochford St. North, 4th Fl., Charlottetown, PE C1A 7N8
902-368-6414, Fax: 902-368-4121, DeptHW@gov.pe.ca

POPULATION

See Also: Statistics

Statistics Canada, 150 Tunney's Pasture Driveway, Ottawa, ON K1A 0T6
514-283-8300, Fax: 514-283-9350, 800-263-1136, STATCAN.infostats-infostats.STATCAN@canada.ca

Manitoba

Manitoba Bureau of Statistics, #824, 155 Carlton St., Winnipeg, MB R3C 3H9
204-945-2406

Nunavut

Nunavut Territory Department of Executive & Intergovernmental Affairs, 1084 Aeroplex bldg., PO Box 1000 200, Iqaluit, NU X0A 0H0
867-975-6000, Fax: 867-975-6099

Quebec

Institut de la statistique du Québec, 200, ch Ste-Foy, 3e étage, Québec, QC G1R 5T4
418-691-2401, Fax: 418-643-4129, 800-463-4090

POSTAL SERVICE

Canada Post Corporation, Corporate Secretariat, 2701 Riverside Dr., Ottawa, ON K1A 0B1
416-979-3033, 866-607-6301

PREMIERS & LEADERS

See Also: Cabinets & Executive Councils; Government (General Info)

Office of the Prime Minister, Liberal Party of Canada / Liberal Research Bureau, 80 Wellington St., Ottawa, ON K1A 0A2
Fax: 613-941-6900

Alberta

Office of the Premier, Office of the Premier, Legislature Bldg., #307, 10800 - 97th Ave., Edmonton, AB T5K 2B6

British Columbia

Office of the Premier & Cabinet Office, PO Box 9041 Prov Govt, Victoria, BC V8W 9E1
250-387-1715, Fax: 250-387-0087, premier@gov.bc.ca

Manitoba

Office of the Premier, Legislative Bldg., #204, 450 Broadway, Winnipeg, MB R3C 0V8
204-945-3714, Fax: 204-949-1484, premier@leg.gov.mb.ca

New Brunswick

Office of the Premier, Centennial Bldg., PO Box 6000, Fredericton, NB E3B 5H1
506-453-2144, Fax: 506-453-7407, premier@gnb.ca

Newfoundland & Labrador

Office of the Premier, East Block, Confederation Bldg., PO Box 8700, St. John's, NL A1B 4J6
709-729-3570, Fax: 709-729-5875, premier@gov.nl.ca

Northwest Territories

Office of the Premier, Legislative Assembly Bldg., PO Box 1320, Yellowknife, NT X1A 2L9

Nova Scotia

Council of Atlantic Premiers, Council Secretariat, #1006, 5161 George St., PO Box 2044, Halifax, NS B3J 2Z1
902-424-7590, Fax: 902-424-8976, info@cap-cpma.ca

Office of the Premier, One Government Place, 1700 Granville St., 7th Fl., PO Box 726, Halifax, NS B3J 2T3
902-424-6600, Fax: 902-424-7648, 800-267-1993, premier@novascotia.ca

Nunavut

Office of the Premier, PO Box 2410, Iqaluit, NU X0A 0H0
867-975-5050, Fax: 867-975-5051

Ontario

Office of the Premier, Legislative Bldg., Queen's Park, Toronto, ON M7A 1A1
416-325-1941

Prince Edward Island

Office of the Premier, Shaw Bldg., 95 Rochford St. South, 5th Fl., PO Box 2000, Charlottetown, PE C1A 7N8
902-368-4400, Fax: 902-368-4416, premier@gov.pe.ca

Quebec

Cabinet du premier ministre, Édifice Honoré-Mercier, 835, boul René-Lévesque est, 3e étage, Québec, QC G1A 1B4
418-643-5321, Fax: 418-643-3924

Saskatchewan

Office of the Premier, Legislative Bldg., #226, 2405 Legislative Dr., Regina, SK S4S 0B3
306-787-9433, Fax: 306-787-0885

Yukon Territory

Office of the Premier, 2071 - 2nd Ave., PO Box 2703, Whitehorse, YT Y1A 2C6

PROCUREMENT, GOODS & SERVICES
See Also: Purchasing
Public Services & Procurement, Place du Portage, Phase III, 11, rue Laurier, Ottawa, ON K1A 0S5
questions@tpsgc-pwgsc.gc.ca
Saskatchewan
SaskBuilds & Procurement, 1920 Rose St., Regina, SK S4P 0A9
306-787-6911, Fax: 306-787-1061,
cs.receptioncenturyplaza@gov.sk.ca

PROPERTY
See Also: Real Estate
New Brunswick
Service New Brunswick, Lincoln Place, PO Box 1998, Fredericton, NB E3B 5G4
506-684-7901, 888-762-8600, snb@snb.ca

PROPERTY ASSESSMENT
British Columbia
British Columbia Assessment Authority, #400, 3450 Uptown Blvd., Victoria, BC V8Z 0B9
604-739-8588, Fax: 855-995-6209, 866-825-8322,
New Brunswick
Assessment & Planning Appeal Board, City Centre, 435 King St., PO Box 6000, Fredericton, NB E3B 5H1
506-453-2126, Fax: 506-444-4881, apab-cameu@gnb.ca
Newfoundland & Labrador
Municipal Assessment Agency Inc., 75 O'Leary Ave., St. John's, NL A1B 2C9
709-724-1532, 877-777-2807, info@maa.ca
Newfoundland & Labrador Department of Environment & Climate Change, PO Box 8700, St. John's, NL A1B 4J6
ECCInfo@gov.nl.ca
Northwest Territories
Assessment Appeal Tribunal, c/o Secretary, Board of Revision, #400, 5201 - 50th Ave., PO Box 1320, Yellowknife, NT X1A 2L9
867-767-9161, Fax: 867-873-0609
Prince Edward Island
Prince Edward Island Regulatory & Appeals Commission, National Bank Tower, #501, 134 Kent St., PO Box 577, Charlottetown, PE C1A 7L1
902-892-3501, Fax: 902-566-4076, 800-501-6268, info@irac.pe.ca
Saskatchewan
Saskatchewan Assessment Management Agency, #200, 2201 - 11th Ave., Regina, SK S4P 0J8
306-924-8000, Fax: 306-924-8070, 800-667-7262, info.request@sama.sk.ca

PROTOCOL (STATE)
See Also: Parliament
Governor General & Commander-in-Chief of Canada, Rideau Hall, 1 Sussex Dr., Ottawa, ON K1A 0A1
613-993-8200, Fax: 613-998-8760, 800-465-6890, info@gg.ca

PUBLIC SAFETY
See Also: Occupational Safety
Canadian Coast Guard, Centennial Towers, #6S018, 200 Kent St., Ottawa, ON K1A 0E6
613-993-0999, Fax: 613-990-1866, info@dfo-mpo.gc.ca
Canadian Security Intelligence Service, PO Box 9732 T, Ottawa, ON K1G 4G4
613-993-9620, Fax: 613-231-0612
Canadian Transportation Agency, Les Terrasses de la Chaudière, 15, rue Eddy, Gatineau, QC J8X 4B3
Fax: 819-997-6727, 888-222-2592, info@otc-cta.gc.ca
Communications Security Establishment Canada, 1500 Bronson Ave., PO Box 9703 Terminal, Ottawa, ON K1A 0K2
613-991-7600, Fax: 613-991-8514
Department of National Defence & the Canadian Armed Forces, National Defence HQ, Major-General George R. Pearkes Bldg., 101 Colonel By Dr., Ottawa, ON K1A 0K2
613-995-2534, Fax: 613-992-4739, 888-995-2534, information@forces.gc.ca
Justice Canada, 284 Wellington St., Ottawa, ON K1A 0H8
613-957-4222, Fax: 613-954-0811, webadmin@justice.gc.ca
Office of the Communications Security Establishment Commissioner, PO Box 1984 B, Ottawa, ON K1P 5R5
613-992-3044
Public Safety Canada, 269 Laurier Ave. West, Ottawa, ON K1A 0P8
613-944-4875, Fax: 613-954-5186, 800-830-3118
Royal Canadian Mounted Police, 73 Leikin Dr., Ottawa, ON K1A 0R2
613-993-7267, Fax: 613-993-0260

Alberta
Alberta Justice & Solicitor General, John E. Brownlee Bldg., 10365 - 97th St., 9th Fl., Edmonton, AB T5J 3W7
780-427-2745
Public Security Division, John E. Brownlee Bldg., 10365 - 97th St., 10th Fl., Edmonton, AB T5J 3W7
British Columbia
British Columbia Ministry of Attorney General & Minister responsible for Housing, PO Box 9044 Prov Govt, Victoria, BC V8W 9E2
British Columbia Ministry of Public Safety & Solicitor General, PO Box 9290 Prov Govt, Victoria, BC V8W 9J7
250-356-0149, Fax: 250-387-6224, 800-663-7867, PSSG.Correspondence@gov.bc.ca
British Columbia Safety Authority, #200, 505 - 6th St., New Westminster, BC V3L 0E1
866-566-7233, info@safetyauthority.ca
Safety Standards Appeal Board, 614 Humboldt St., 4th Fl., PO Box 9844 Prov Govt, Victoria, BC V8W 9T2
250-387-4021, Fax: 250-356-6645
Manitoba
Manitoba Justice, Administration & Finance, #1110, 405 Broadway Ave., Winnipeg, MB R3C 3L6
204-945-2878
New Brunswick
New Brunswick Department of Justice & Public Safety, Marysville Place, 3rd Fl., PO Box 6000, Fredericton, NB E3B 5H1
506-453-3992, DPS-MSP.Information@gnb.ca
Newfoundland & Labrador
Newfoundland & Labrador Department of Justice & Public Safety, East Block, Confederation Bldg., 4th Fl., PO Box 8700, St. John's, NL A1B 4J6
709-729-2869, Fax: 709-729-0469, justice@gov.nl.ca
Northwest Territories
Northwest Territories Department of Justice, 4903 - 49th St., PO Box 1320, Yellowknife, NT X1A 2L9
867-767-9256, justice_communications@gov.nt.ca
Nova Scotia
Nova Scotia Department of Justice, 1690 Hollis St., PO Box 7, Halifax, NS B3J 2L6
902-424-4030, justweb@gov.ns.ca
Nunavut
Nunavut Territory Department of Justice, PO Box 1000 500, Iqaluit, NU X0A 0H0
867-975-6170, Fax: 867-975-6195, justice@gov.nu.ca
Quebec
Ministère de la Justice, Édifice Louis-Philippe-Pigeon, 1200, rte de l'Église, Québec, QC G1V 4M1
418-643-5140, 866-536-5140,
informations@justice.gouv.qc.ca
Ministère de la Sécurité publique, Tour des Laurentides, 2525, boul Laurier, 5e étage, Québec, QC G1V 2L2
418-643-2112, Fax: 418-646-6168, 800-361-3795
Saskatchewan
Saskatchewan Corrections, Policing & Public Safety, Legislative Bldg., #345, 2405 Legislative Dr., Regina, SK S4S 0B3
Yukon Territory
Yukon Justice, Andrew Philipsen Law Centre, 2134 - 2nd Ave., PO Box 2703, Whitehorse, YT Y1A 2C6
867-667-3033, Fax: 867-667-5200, justice@yukon.ca

PUBLIC SERVICES
Canada Deposit Insurance Corporation, 50 O'Connor St., 17th Floor, Ottawa, ON K1P 6L2
Fax: 613-996-6095, 800-461-2342, info@cdic.ca
Canada Post Corporation, Corporate Secretariat, 2701 Riverside Dr., Ottawa, ON K1A 0B1
416-979-3033, 866-607-6301
Canadian Broadcasting Corporation, 181 Queen St., PO Box 3220 C, Ottawa, ON K1Y 1E4
613-288-6000, liaison@cbc.ca
Canadian Centre for Occupational Health & Safety, 135 Hunter St. East, Hamilton, ON L8N 1M5
905-572-2981, Fax: 905-572-4500, 800-668-4284
Canadian Coast Guard, Centennial Towers, #6S018, 200 Kent St., Ottawa, ON K1A 0E6
613-993-0999, Fax: 613-990-1866, info@dfo-mpo.gc.ca
Canadian Security Intelligence Service, PO Box 9732 T, Ottawa, ON K1G 4G4
613-993-9620, Fax: 613-231-0612
Commission for Public Complaints Against the Royal Canadian Mounted Police, National Intake Office, PO Box 88689, Surrey, BC V3W 0X1
Fax: 604-501-4095, 800-665-6878
Correctional Service Canada, 340 Laurier Ave. West, Ottawa, ON K1A 0P9
613-992-5891, Fax: 613-943-1630

Department of National Defence & the Canadian Armed Forces, National Defence HQ, Major-General George R. Pearkes Bldg., 101 Colonel By Dr., Ottawa, ON K1A 0K2
613-995-2534, Fax: 613-992-4739, 888-995-2534, information@forces.gc.ca
Employment & Social Development Canada, 140, promenade du Portage, Gatineau, QC K1A 0J9
Federal Public Sector Labour Relations & Employment Board, C.D. Howe Bldg., West Tower, 240 Sparks St., 6th Fl., PO Box 1525 B, Ottawa, ON K1P 5V2
613-990-1800, Fax: 613-990-1849, 866-931-3454, mail.courrier@fpslreb-crtespf.gc.ca
Immigration & Refugee Board of Canada, Minto Place, Canada Bldg., 344 Slater St., 12th Fl., Ottawa, ON K1A 0K1
Fax: 613-943-1550
Immigration, Refugees & Citizenship, Jean Edmonds, South Tower, 365 Laurier Ave. West, Ottawa, ON K1A 1L1
888-242-2100
MERX, Phase II, #103, 6 Antares Dr., Ottawa, ON K2E 8A9
613-727-4900, Fax: 888-235-5800, 800-964-6379, merx@merx.com
Military Police Complaints Commission, 270 Albert St., 10th Fl., Ottawa, ON K1P 5G8
613-947-5625, Fax: 613-947-5713, 800-632-0566, commission@mpcc-cppm.gc.ca
National Capital Commission, #202, 40 Elgin St., Ottawa, ON K1P 1C7
613-239-5000, Fax: 613-239-5063, 800-465-1867, info@ncc-ccn.ca
National Search & Rescue Secretariat, 275 Slater St., 4th Fl., Ottawa, ON K1A 0K2
Fax: 613-996-3746, 800-727-9414
Parole Board of Canada, Communications Division, National Office, 410 Laurier Ave. West, Ottawa, ON K1A 0R1
613-954-7474, Fax: 613-941-4981, info@pbc-clcc.gc.ca
Public Service Commission, 22, rue Eddy, Gatineau, QC K1A 0M7
800-645-5605
Public Services & Procurement, Place du Portage, Phase III, 11, rue Laurier, Ottawa, ON K1A 0S5
questions@tpsgc-pwgsc.gc.ca
Royal Canadian Mounted Police, 73 Leikin Dr., Ottawa, ON K1A 0R2
613-993-7267, Fax: 613-993-0260
Royal Canadian Mounted Police External Review Committee, PO Box 1159 B, Ottawa, ON K1P 5R2
613-998-2134, Fax: 613-990-8969, org@erc-cee.gc.ca
Security Intelligence Review Committee, PO Box 2430 D, Ottawa, ON K1P 5W5
613-907-4404, Fax: 613-907-4445, info@sirc-csars.gc.ca
Service Canada, 140, promenade du Portage, Gatineau, QC K1A 0J9
800-622-6232
Veterans Affairs Canada, 161 Grafton St., PO Box 7700, Charlottetown, PE C1A 8M9
613-996-2242, 866-522-2122, information@vac-acc.gc.ca
Veterans Review & Appeal Board, Daniel J. MacDonald Bldg., 161 Grafton St., PO Box 9900, Charlottetown, PE C1A 8V7
902-566-8751, Fax: 902-566-7850, 800-450-8006, vrab.vrab-tacra.tacra@vrab-tacra.gc.ca
Alberta
Alberta Capital Finance Authority, Sun Life Place, #2160, 10123 - 99 St. NW, Edmonton, AB T5J 3H1
780-427-9711, Fax: 780-422-2175, webacfa@gov.ab.ca
Alberta Emergency Management Agency, Terrace Bldg., 9515 - 107 St., 4th Fl., Edmonton, AB T5K 2C1
780-422-9000, Fax: 780-644-1044, -310-0000, aema@gov.ab.ca
Alberta Energy Regulator, #1000, 250 - 5 St. SW, Calgary, AB T2P 0R4
403-297-8311, Fax: 403-297-7336, 855-297-8311, inquiries@aer.ca
Alberta Health Services, Corporate Office, North Tower, Seventh Street Plaza, 10030 - 107th St. NW, 14th Fl., Edmonton, AB T5J 3E4
780-342-2000, Fax: 780-342-2060, 888-342-2471, ahs.corp@albertahealthservices.ca
Alberta Infrastructure, Infrastructure Bldg., 6950 - 113th St., Edmonton, AB T6H 5V7
780-415-0507, Fax: 780-427-2187, Infra.Contact.Us.m@gov.ab.ca
Alberta Justice & Solicitor General, John E. Brownlee Bldg., 10365 - 97th St., 9th Fl., Edmonton, AB T5J 3W7
780-427-2745
Alberta Municipal Affairs, Communications Branch, Commerce Place, 10155 - 102nd St., 18th Fl., Edmonton, AB T5J 4L4
780-427-2732, Fax: 780-422-1419
Alberta Office of the Public Interest Commissioner, #700, 9925 - 109th St., Edmonton, AB T5K 2J8
780-641-8659, 855-641-8659, info@pic.alberta.ca

Labour Relations Board, Labour Building, #501, 10808 - 99 Ave., Edmonton, AB T5K 0G5
780-427-8547, Fax: 780-422-0970, 800-463-2572, alrbinfo@gov.ab.ca

Legal Services Division, Bowker Bldg., 9833 - 109th St., 2nd Fl., Edmonton, AB T5K 2E8
780-422-0500

Municipal Government Board, 1229 - 91st St. SW, 2nd Fl., Edmonton, AB T6X 1E9
780-427-4864, Fax: 780-427-0986, -310-0000, mgbmail@gov.ab.ca

Public Security Division, John E. Brownlee Bldg., 10365 - 97th St., 10th Fl., Edmonton, AB T5J 3W7

Public Service Commission, Peace Hills Trust Tower, 10011 - 109th St., 7th Fl., Edmonton, AB T5J 3S8
780-408-8450

British Columbia
British Columbia Assessment Authority, #400, 3450 Uptown Blvd., Victoria, BC V8Z 0B9
604-739-8588, Fax: 855-995-6209, 866-825-8322

British Columbia Ferry Services Inc., c/o BC Ferry Authority, #500, 1321 Blanshard St., Victoria, BC V8W 0B7
250-381-1401, 888-223-3779, customerservice@bcferries.com

British Columbia Housing Management Commission (BC Housing), #1701, 4555 Kingsway, Burnaby, BC V5H 4V8
604-433-1711, Fax: 604-439-4722, webeditor@bchousing.org

British Columbia Ministry of Attorney General & Minister responsible for Housing, PO Box 9044 Prov Govt, Victoria, BC V8W 9E2

British Columbia Ministry of Children & Family Development, Customer Service Centre, PO Box 9770 Prov Govt, Victoria, BC V8W 9S5
250-387-7027, 877-387-7027, mcf.info@gov.bc.ca

British Columbia Ministry of Citizens' Services, PO Box 9068 Prov Govt, Victoria, BC V8W 9E2
604-660-2421, 800-663-7867, servicebc@gov.bc.ca

British Columbia Ministry of Public Safety & Solicitor General, PO Box 9290 Prov Govt, Victoria, BC V8W 9J7
250-356-0149, Fax: 250-387-6224, 800-663-7867, PSSG.Correspondence@gov.bc.ca

British Columbia Public Service Agency, PO Box 9404 Prov Govt, Victoria, BC V8W 9V1
250-387-0518, Fax: 250-356-7074

British Columbia Transit, 520 Gorge Rd. East, Victoria, BC V8W 2P3
250-385-2551

Local Government, PO Box 9490 Prov Govt, Victoria, BC V8W 9N7
250-356-6575, Fax: 250-387-7973

Office of the Representative for Children & Youth, #400, 1019 Wharf St., Victoria, BC V8W 2Y9
250-356-6710, Fax: 250-356-0837, 800-476-3933, rcy@rcybc.ca

Manitoba
Advisory Council on Workplace Safety & Health, 401 York Ave., 2nd Fl., Winnipeg, MB R3C 0P8
204-945-3446, Fax: 204-948-2209, 866-888-8186, wshcompl@gov.mb.ca

Civil Service Commission Board, #935, 155 Carlton St., Winnipeg, MB R3C 3H8
204-945-1435, Fax: 204-945-1486

Deposit Guarantee Corporation of Manitoba, #390, 200 Graham Ave., Winnipeg, MB R3C 4L5
204-942-8480, Fax: 204-947-1723, 800-697-4447, mail@depositguarantee.mb.ca

Emergency Measures Organization, #1525, 405 Broadway Ave., Winnipeg, MB R3C 3L6
204-945-4772, Fax: 204-945-4929, 888-267-8298, emo@gov.mb.ca

Health Information Privacy Committee, #4043, 300 Carlton St., Winnipeg, MB R3B 3M9

Manitoba Bureau of Statistics, #824, 155 Carlton St., Winnipeg, MB R3C 3H9
204-945-2406

Manitoba Civil Service Commission, #935, 155 Carlton St., Winnipeg, MB R3C 3H8
204-945-2332, Fax: 204-945-1486, 800-282-8069, csc@gov.mb.ca

Manitoba Families, Legislative Bldg., #357, 450 Broadway, Winnipeg, MB R3C 0V8
204-945-3744, 866-626-4862

Manitoba Film Classification Board, #216, 301 Weston St., Winnipeg, MB R3E 3H4
204-945-8962, Fax: 204-945-0890, 866-612-2399, mfcb@gov.mb.ca

Manitoba Health & Seniors Care, #100, 300 Carlton St., Winnipeg, MB R3B 3M9
204-945-3744, 866-626-4862, mgi@gov.mb.ca

Manitoba Human Rights Commission, #700, 175 Hargrave St., Winnipeg, MB R3C 3R8
204-945-3007, Fax: 204-945-1292, 888-884-8681, hrc@gov.mb.ca

Manitoba Hydro, 360 Portage Ave., PO Box 815 Main, Winnipeg, MB R3C 2P4
204-480-5900, Fax: 204-360-6155, 888-624-9376

Manitoba Infrastructure, Legislative Bldg., #203, 450 Broadway, Winnipeg, MB R3C 0V8

Manitoba Justice, Administration & Finance, #1110, 405 Broadway Ave., Winnipeg, MB R3C 3L6
204-945-2878,

Manitoba Land Value Appraisal Commission, #1144, 363 Broadway, Winnipeg, MB R3C 3N9
204-945-5455, Fax: 204-948-2235

Manitoba Public Insurance Corporation, 234 Donald St., #B100, PO Box 6300, Winnipeg, MB R3C 4A4
204-985-7000, Fax: 204-985-3525, 800-665-2410

Manitoba Sport, Culture & Heritage, Legislative Bldg., #118, 450 Broadway, Winnipeg, MB R3C 0V8

Mental Health & Addictions, Primary Health Care & Seniors, 300 Carlton St., 4th Floor, Winnipeg, MB R3B 3M9
204-788-6666

Office of the Auditor General, #500, 330 Portage Ave., Winnipeg, MB R3C 0C4
204-945-3790, Fax: 204-945-2169, contact@oag.mb.ca

Seniors & Healthy Aging Secretariat, #1610, 155 Carlton St., Winnipeg, MB R3C 3H8
204-945-6565, Fax: 204-948-2514, 800-665-6565, seniors@gov.mb.ca

Workers' Compensation Board of Manitoba, 333 Broadway Ave., Winnipeg, MB R3C 4W3
204-954-4321, Fax: 204-954-4999, 800-362-3340, wcb@wcb.mb.ca

New Brunswick
New Brunswick Department of Health, HSBC Place, PO Box 5100, Fredericton, NB E3B 5G8
506-457-4800, Fax: 506-453-5243, Health.Sante@gnb.ca

New Brunswick Department of Justice & Public Safety, Marysville Place, 3rd Fl., PO Box 6000, Fredericton, NB E3B 5H1
506-453-3992, DPS-MSP.Information@gnb.ca

New Brunswick Department of Post-Secondary Education, Training & Labour, Chestnut Complex, PO Box 6000, Fredericton, NB E3B 5H1
506-453-2597, Fax: 506-453-3618, dpetlinfo@gnb.ca

New Brunswick Department of Social Development, Sartain MacDonald Bldg., PO Box 6000, Fredericton, NB E3B 5H1
506-453-2001, Fax: 506-453-2164, sd-ds@gnb.ca

New Brunswick Human Rights Commission, Barry House, 751 Brunswick St., PO Box 6000, Fredericton, NB E3B 5H1
506-453-2301, Fax: 506-453-2653, 888-471-2233, hrc.cdp@gnb.ca

Office of the Ombudsman, 548 York St., PO Box 6000, Fredericton, NB E3B 5H1
506-453-2789, Fax: 506-453-5599, 888-465-1100

Premier's Council on the Status of Disabled Persons, #140, Place 2000, 1st Fl., PO Box 6000, Fredericton, NB E3B 5H1
506-444-3000, Fax: 506-444-3001, 800-442-4412, pcd-cpmph@gnb.ca

Service New Brunswick, Lincoln Place, PO Box 1998, Fredericton, NB E3B 5G4
506-684-7901, 888-762-8600, snb@snb.ca

Newfoundland & Labrador
Eastern Regional Service Board, #3, 255 Majors Path, St. John's, NL A1A 0L5
709-579-7960, Fax: 709-579-5392, info@ersbnl.ca

Income & Employment Support Appeal Board, Confederation Bldg., PO Box 8700, St. John's, NL A1B 4J6
709-729-2479, Fax: 709-729-5139

Newfoundland & Labrador Department of Digital Government & Service NL, 100 Prince Phillip Dr., PO Box 8700, St. John's, NL A1B 4J6
709-729-4834, servicenlinfo@gov.nl.ca

Newfoundland & Labrador Department of Environment & Climate Change, PO Box 8700, St. John's, NL A1B 4J6
ECCInfo@gov.nl.ca

Newfoundland & Labrador Department of Immigration, Population Growth & Skills, West Block, Confederation Bldg., 3rd Fl., PO Box 8700, St. John's, NL A1B 4J6
709-729-1795, isl@gov.nl.ca

Newfoundland & Labrador Department of Justice & Public Safety, East Block, Confederation Bldg., 4th Fl., PO Box 8700, St. John's, NL A1B 4J6
709-729-2869, Fax: 709-729-0469, justice@gov.nl.ca

Newfoundland & Labrador Department of Transportation & Infrastructure, Confederation Bldg., Prince Philip Dr., PO Box 8700, St. John's, NL A1B 4J6
709-729-2300, ti@gov.nl.ca

Newfoundland & Labrador Legal Aid Commission, #300, 251 Empire Ave., St. John's, NL A1C 5J9
709-753-7860, Fax: 709-753-7851, 800-563-9911, nlac@legalaid.nl.ca

Newfoundland & Labrador Liquor Corporation, 90 Kenmount Rd., PO Box 8750 A, St. John's, NL A1B 3V1
709-724-1100, info@nfliquor.com

Newfoundland & Labrador Public Service Commission, 261 Kenmount Rd., PO Box 8700, St. John's, NL A1B 4J6
709-729-5810, Fax: 709-729-6234, 855-330-5810, contactpsc@gov.nl.ca

Royal Newfoundland Constabulary Public Complaints Commission, PO Box 8700, St. John's, NL A1B 4J6
709-834-6171, Fax: 709-834-6178, rnccomplaintscommission@gov.nl.ca

Northwest Territories
Inuvialuit Water Board, Mack Travel Bldg., 151 Mackenzie Rd., 2nd Fl., PO Box 2531, Yellowknife, NT X0E 0T0
867-678-2942, Fax: 867-678-2943, info@inuvwb.ca

Northwest Territories Department of Health & Social Services, PO Box 1320, Yellowknife, NT X1A 2L9

Northwest Territories Department of Infrastructure, Stuart M. Hodgson Bldg., 5009 - 49th St., 3rd Fl., PO Box 1320, Yellowknife, NT X1A 2L9
INF_Communications@gov.nt.ca

Northwest Territories Department of Justice, 4903 - 49th St., PO Box 1320, Yellowknife, NT X1A 2L9
867-767-9256, justice_communications@gov.nt.ca

Northwest Territories Department of Municipal & Community Affairs, PO Box 1320, Yellowknife, NT X1A 2L9

Northwest Territories Housing Corporation, Scotia Centre, 5102 - 50th Ave., PO Box 2100, Yellowknife, NT X1A 2P6
867-767-9080, Fax: 867-873-9426, 844-698-4663

Northwest Territories Power Corporation, 4 Capital Dr., Hay River, NT X0E 1G2
867-874-5200, 800-661-0855, info@ntpc.com

Victims Assistance Committee, c/o Community Justice Division, PO Box 1320, Yellowknife, NT X1A 2L9
867-920-6911, Fax: 867-873-0199

Nova Scotia
Emergency Management Office, PO Box 2581, Halifax, NS B3J 3N5
902-424-5620, Fax: 902-424-5376, 866-424-5620, emo@novascotia.ca

Nova Scotia Department of Community Services, Nelson Place, 5675 Spring Garden Rd., 8th Fl., PO Box 696, Halifax, NS B3J 2T7
877-424-1177

Nova Scotia Department of Health & Wellness, PO Box 488, Halifax, NS B3J 2R8
902-424-5818, 800-387-6665

Nova Scotia Department of Justice, 1690 Hollis St., PO Box 7, Halifax, NS B3J 2L6
902-424-4030, justweb@gov.ns.ca

Nova Scotia Department of Transportation & Active Transit, PO Box 186, Halifax, NS B3J 2N2
902-424-2297, Fax: 902-424-0532, tpwpaff@novascotia.ca

Nova Scotia Disabled Persons Commission, Nelson Place, 5675 Spring Garden Rd., 7th Fl., PO Box 222 CRO, Halifax, NS B3J 2M4
902-424-8280, Fax: 902-424-0592, 800-565-8280, disability@gov.ns.ca

Nova Scotia Legal Aid Commission, Office of the Executive Director, #920, 1701 Hollis St., Halifax, NS B3J 3M8
902-420-6578, 877-420-6578

Nova Scotia Public Service Commission, PO Box 943, Halifax, NS B3J 2V9
902-424-7660, reception-psc@novascotia.ca

Service Nova Scotia & Internal Services, PO Box 2734, Halifax, NS B3J 3K5
902-424-5200, Fax: 902-424-0720, 800-670-4357, askus@novascotia.ca

Workers' Advisers Program, #309, 5640 Spring Garden Rd., PO Box 1063, Halifax, NS B3J 3M7
902-424-5050, Fax: 902-424-0530, 800-774-4712

Nunavut
Nunavut Emergency Management, PO Box 1000 700, Iqaluit, NU X0A 0H0
Fax: 867-979-4221, 800-693-1666, NEM@gov.nu.ca

Nunavut Territory Department of Community & Government Services, W.G. Brown Bldg., 4th Fl., PO Box 1000 700, Iqaluit, NU X0A 0H0
867-975-5406, Fax: 867-975-5305, cgscomms@gov.nu.ca

Nunavut Territory Department of Family Services, PO Box 1000 1200, Iqaluit, NU X0A 0H0
867-975-5200, Fax: 867-975-5722

Nunavut Territory Department of Finance, PO Box 1000 430, Iqaluit, NU X0A 0H0
867-975-6222, Fax: 867-975-6220, 888-668-9993, gnhr@gov.nu.ca

Nunavut Territory Department of Health, PO Box 1000 1000, Iqaluit, NU X0A 0H0
867-975-5700, Fax: 867-975-5705, 800-661-0833
Nunavut Territory Department of Justice, PO Box 1000 500, Iqaluit, NU X0A 0H0
867-975-6170, Fax: 867-975-6195, justice@gov.nu.ca

Ontario
Advertising Review Board, Macdonald Block, #M2-56, 900 Bay St., 2nd Fl., Toronto, ON M7A 1N3
416-327-2183, Fax: 416-327-2179
Deposit Insurance Corporation of Ontario, #700, 4711 Yonge St., Toronto, ON M2N 6K8
416-325-9444, Fax: 416-325-9722, 800-268-6653, info@dico.com
Health Services Information & Information Technology Cluster, 56 Wellesley St. West, 10th Fl., Toronto, ON M5S 2S3
416-314-0234, Fax: 416-314-4182
Human Rights Legal Support Centre, 400 University Ave., 7th Fl., Toronto, ON M7A 1T7
416-597-4900, Fax: 416-597-4901, 866-625-5179
Hydro One Inc., South Tower, 483 Bay St., 8th Fl., Toronto, ON M5G 2P5
416-345-5000, Fax: 905-944-3251, 877-955-1155, customercommunications@hydroone.com
Independent Electricity System Operator, #1600, 120 Adelaide St. West, Toronto, ON M5H 1T1
905-403-6900, Fax: 905-403-6921, 877-797-9473, customer.relations@ieso.ca
Office of the Employer Advisor, 505 University Ave., 20th Fl., Toronto, ON M5G 2P1
416-327-0020, Fax: 416-327-0726, 800-387-0774
Office of the Worker Advisor, #1300, 123 Edward St., Toronto, ON M5G 1E2
416-325-8570, Fax: 416-325-4830, 800-660-6769, owaweb@ontario.ca
Ontario Ministry of Infrastructure, 777 Bay St., 5th Fl., Toronto, ON M5G 2C8
416-327-4412
Ontario Ministry of Municipal Affairs & Housing, College Park, 777 Bay St., 17th Fl., Toronto, ON M7A 2J3
416-585-7041, Fax: 416-585-4230, mininfo@ontario.ca
Ontario Ministry of the Attorney General, McMurtry-Scott Bldg., 720 Bay St., 11th Fl., Toronto, ON M7A 2S9
416-326-2220, Fax: 416-326-4016, 800-518-7901, attorneygeneral@ontario.ca
Ontario Ministry of Transportation, 777 Bay St., 5th Fl., Toronto, ON M7A 1Z8
416-235-4686, Fax: 416-327-9185, 800-268-4686
Ontario Pension Board, Sun Life Bldg., #2200, 200 King St. West, Toronto, ON M5H 3X6
416-364-8558, Fax: 416-364-7578, 800-668-6203, office.services@opb.ca
Ontario Power Generation, 700 University Ave., Toronto, ON M5G 1X6
416-592-2555, 877-592-2555, webmaster@opg.com
Ontario Solicitor General, George Drew Bldg., 25 Grosvenor St., 18th Fl., Toronto, ON M7A 1Y6
416-326-5000, Fax: 416-325-6067, 866-517-0571, mcscs.feedback@ontario.ca
Public Service Commission, Whitney Block, 99 Wellesley St. West, 5th Fl., Toronto, ON M7A 1W4
416-325-1750
Safety, Licensing Appeals & Standards Tribunals Ontario, #401, 20 Dundas St. West, 4th Fl., Toronto, ON M5T 2Z5
Fax: 416-327-6379, 844-242-0608, slastoinfo@ontario.ca

Prince Edward Island
Island Waste Management Corporation, 110 Watts Ave., Charlottetown, PE C1E 2C1
902-882-0525, Fax: 902-894-0331, 888-280-8111, info@iwmc.pe.ca
Prince Edward Island Department of Health & Wellness, Shaw Bldg., 105 Rochford St. North, 4th Fl., Charlottetown, PE C1A 7N8
902-368-6414, Fax: 902-368-4121, DeptHW@gov.pe.ca
Prince Edward Island Department of Social Development & Housing, Jones Bldg., 11 Kent St., 2nd Fl., PO Box 2000, Charlottetown, PE C1A 7N8
902-620-3777, Fax: 902-368-4740, 866-594-3777, DeptSDH@gov.pe.ca
Public Service Commission, Shaw Bldg. North, 105 Rochford St., 1st Fl., PO Box 2000, Charlottetown, PE C1A 7N8
902-368-4080, Fax: 902-368-4383
SkillsPEI, Atlantic Technology Centre, #212, 176 Great George St., Charlottetown, PE C1A 4K9
902-368-6290, Fax: 902-368-6340, 877-491-4766

Quebec
Centre du services partagés du Québec, 875, Grande Allée est, 4e étage, section 4.550, Québec, QC G1R 5W5
418-644-2777, Fax: 418-644-0462, 855-644-2777, cspq@cspq.gouv.qc.ca

Commission de la fonction publique, 800, Place D'Youville, 7e étage, Québec, QC G1R 3P4
418-643-1425, Fax: 418-643-7264, 800-432-0432, cfp@cfp.gouv.qc.ca
Commission de la fonction publique (Québec), 800, Place d'Youville, 7e étage, Québec, QC G1R 3P4
418-643-1425, Fax: 418-643-7264, 800-432-0432, cfp@cfp.gouv.qc.ca
Commission municipale du Québec, Mezzanine, aile Chauveau, 10, rue Pierre-Olivier-Chauveau, Québec, QC G1R 4J3
418-691-2014, Fax: 418-644-4676, 866-353-6767
École nationale des pompiers du Québec, Palais de justice de Laval, #3.08, 2800, boul Saint-Martin ouest, Laval, QC H7T 2S9
450-680-6800, Fax: 450-680-6818, 866-680-3677, enpq@enpq.gouv.qc.ca
Hydro-Québec, Édifice Jean-Lesage, 75, boul René-Lévesque ouest, Montréal, QC H2Z 1A4
514-385-7252, 888-385-7252
Institut de la statistique du Québec, 200, ch Ste-Foy, 3e étage, Québec, QC G1R 5T4
418-691-2401, Fax: 418-643-4129, 800-463-4090
Ministère de la Justice, Édifice Louis-Philippe-Pigeon, 1200, rte de l'Église, Québec, QC G1V 4M1
418-643-5140, 866-536-5140, informations@justice.gouv.qc.ca
Ministère de la Santé et des Services sociaux, Direction des communications, 1075, ch Sainte-Foy, 15e étage, Québec, QC G1S 2M1
418-644-4545, 877-644-4545
Ministère de la Sécurité publique, Tour des Laurentides, 2525, boul Laurier, 5e étage, Québec, QC G1V 2L2
418-643-2112, Fax: 418-646-6168, 800-361-3795
Ministère des affaires municipales et Habitation, Aile Chauveau, 10, rue Pierre-Olivier-Chauveau, Québec, QC G1R 4J3
418-691-2015, Fax: 418-643-7385, communications@mamrot.gouv.qc.ca
Ministère du Travail, de l'Emploi et de la Solidarité sociale, 150, rue Monseigneur-Ross, 5e étage, Québec, QC G4X 2S7
514-873-4000, 877-767-8773
Modernisation des centres hospitaliers universitaires de Montréal, CHUM, CUSM, CHU Sainte-Justine, #10.049, 2021, rue Union, Montréal, QC H3A 2S9
514-864-9883, Fax: 514-873-7362, info.construction3chu@msss.gouv.qc.ca
Office des personnes handicapées du Québec, 309, rue Brock, Drummondville, QC J2B 1C5
Fax: 819-475-8753, 800-567-1465, info@ophq.gouv.qc.ca
Régie de l'assurance maladie du Québec, CP 6600, Québec, QC G1K 7T3
418-646-4636, 800-561-9749
Régie du logement du Québec, Village Olympique, #2360, 5199, rue Sherbrooke est, Montréal, QC H1T 3X1
514-873-2245, Fax: 514-864-8077, 800-683-2245
Société d'habitation du Québec, Aile St-Amable, 1054, rue Louis-Alexandre-Taschereau, 3e étage, Québec, QC G1R 5E7
Fax: 418-643-2533, 800-463-4315
Société de l'assurance automobile du Québec, 333, boul Jean-Lesage, CP 19600 Terminus, Québec, QC G1K 8J6
418-643-7620, Fax: 418-644-0339, 800-361-7620
Urgences-santé Québec, 6700, rue Jarry est, Montréal, QC H1P 0A4
514-723-5600, info@urgences-sante.qc.ca
Vérificateur général du Québec, #300, 750, boul Charest est, Québec, QC G1K 9J6
418-691-5900, Fax: 418-644-4460, verificateur.general@vgq.qc.ca

Saskatchewan
Crown Investments Corporation of Saskatchewan, #400, 2400 College Ave., Regina, SK S4P 1C8
306-787-6851, Fax: 306-787-0294
Legal Aid Saskatchewan, #502, 201 - 21st St. East, Saskatoon, SK S7K 0B8
306-933-5300, Fax: 306-933-6764, 800-667-3764, headoffice@legalaid.sk.ca
Provincial Auditor Saskatchewan, Chateau Tower, #1500, 1920 Broad St., Regina, SK S4P 3V2
306-787-6398, Fax: 306-787-6383, info@auditor.sk.ca
Saskatchewan Assessment Management Agency, #200, 2201 - 11th Ave., Regina, SK S4P 0J8
306-924-8000, Fax: 306-924-8070, 800-667-7262, info.request@sama.sk.ca
Saskatchewan Government Insurance, 2260 - 11th Ave., Regina, SK S4P 0J9
306-751-1200, Fax: 306-787-7477, 844-855-2744, sgiinquiries@sgi.sk.ca
Saskatchewan Justice & Attorney General, 1874 Scarth St., Regina, SK S4P 4B3
Saskatchewan Power Corporation (SaskPower), 2025 Victoria Ave., Regina, SK S4P 0S1
888-757-6937

Saskatchewan Social Services, 1920 Broad St., Regina, SK S4P 3V6
306-787-3800, socialservicesinquiry@gov.sk.ca
Saskatchewan Water Corporation (SaskWater), #200, 111 Fairford St. East, Moose Jaw, SK S6H 1C8
Fax: 306-694-3207, 888-230-1111, communications@saskwater.com
SaskEnergy Incorporated, 1777 Victoria Ave., Regina, SK S4P 4K5
306-777-9225, 800-567-8899, webmaster@saskenergy.com

Yukon Territory
Yukon Community Services, PO Box 2703, Whitehorse, YT Y1A 2C6
867-667-5811, Fax: 867-393-6295, 800-661-0408
Yukon Health & Social Services, PO Box 2703, Whitehorse, YT Y1A 2C6
867-667-3673, Fax: 867-667-3096, 800-661-0408, hss@yukon.ca
Yukon Housing Corporation, 410G Jarvis St., PO Box 2703, Whitehorse, YT Y1A 2H5
867-667-5712, Fax: 867-393-7597, ykhouse@yukon.ca
Yukon Justice, Andrew Philipsen Law Centre, 2134 - 2nd Ave., PO Box 2703, Whitehorse, YT Y1A 2C6
867-667-3033, Fax: 867-667-5200, justice@yukon.ca
Yukon Public Service Commission, 2071 - 2nd Ave., PO Box 2703, Whitehorse, YT Y1A 2C6
867-667-5653, Fax: 867-667-5755, pscwebsite@yukon.ca
Yukon Utilities Board, PO Box 31728, Whitehorse, YT Y1A 6L3
867-667-5058, Fax: 867-667-5059, yub@utilitiesboard.yk.ca

PUBLIC TRUSTEE

Alberta
Office of the Public Guardian & Trustee, John E. Browning Bldg., 10365 - 97th St., 4th Fl., Edmonton, AB T5J 3Z8
780-422-1868, Fax: 780-422-6051,

British Columbia
Public Guardian & Trustee of British Columbia, #700, 808 West Hastings St., Vancouver, BC V6C 3L3
604-660-4444, Fax: 604-660-0374, 800-663-7867, clientservice@trustee.bc.ca

Manitoba
Office of the Public Trustee, #500, 155 Carlton St., Winnipeg, MB R3C 5R9
204-945-2700, Fax: 204-948-2251, PGT@gov.mb.ca

Newfoundland & Labrador
Newfoundland & Labrador Department of Justice & Public Safety, East Block, Confederation Bldg., 4th Fl., PO Box 8700, St. John's, NL A1B 4J6
709-729-2869, Fax: 709-729-0469, justice@gov.nl.ca
Office of the Public Trustee, The Viking Bldg., #401, 136 Crosbie Rd., St. John's, NL A1B 3K3
709-729-0850, Fax: 709-729-3063, general@publictrusteenl.com

Nova Scotia
Public Trustee Office, #501, 1465 Brenton St., PO Box 685, Halifax, NS B3J 2T3
902-424-7760, Fax: 902-424-0616, publictrustee@gov.ns.ca

Nunavut
Office of the Public Trustee, PO Box 1000 560, Iqaluit, NU X0A 0H0
867-975-6338, Fax: 867-975-6343, 866-294-2127, PublicTrustee@gov.nu.ca

Ontario
Office of the Public Guardian & Trustee, Atrium on Bay, 595 Bay St., 8th Fl., Toronto, ON M5G 2M6
416-314-2800, Fax: 416-326-1366, 800-366-0335

Quebec
Curateur public du Québec, 600, boul René-Lévesque ouest, Montréal, QC H3B 4W9
514-873-4074, 800-363-9020

PUBLIC UTILITIES

Alberta
Alberta Energy Regulator, #1000, 250 - 5 St. SW, Calgary, AB T2P 0R4
403-297-8311, Fax: 403-297-7336, 855-297-8311, inquiries@aer.ca
Alberta Utilities Commission, Eau Caire Tower, #1400, 600 - 3rd Ave. SW, Calgary, AB T2P 0G5
-310-4282, info@auc.ab.ca

British Columbia
British Columbia Hydro, 333 Dunsmuir St., PO Box 8910, Vancouver, BC V6B 4N1
604-224-9376, 800-224-9376
British Columbia Utilities Commission, #410, 900 Howe St., Vancouver, BC V6Z 2N3
604-660-4700, Fax: 604-660-1102, 800-663-1385, commission.secretary@bcuc.com

Manitoba
Manitoba Hydro, 360 Portage Ave., PO Box 815 Main,
 Winnipeg, MB R3C 2P4
 204-480-5900, Fax: 204-360-6155, 888-624-9376
Newfoundland & Labrador
Nalcor Energy, 500 Columbus Dr., St. John's, NL A1E 2B2
 709-737-1400, Fax: 709-737-1800, info@nalcorenergy.com
Newfoundland & Labrador Board of Commissioners of Public
 Utilities, PO Box 21040, St. John's, NL A1A 5B2
 Fax: 709-726-9604, 866-782-0006, ito@pub.nl.ca
Newfoundland & Labrador Hydro, Hydro Place, 500 Columbus
 Dr., PO Box 12400, St. John's, NL A1B 4K7
 709-737-1400, Fax: 709-737-1800, 888-737-1296,
 hydro@nlh.nl.ca
Northwest Territories
Inuvialuit Water Board, Mack Travel Bldg., 151 Mackenzie Rd.,
 2nd Fl., PO Box 2531, Yellowknife, NT X0E 0T0
 867-678-2942, Fax: 867-678-2943, info@inuvwb.ca
Northwest Territories Power Corporation, 4 Capital Dr., Hay
 River, NT X0E 1G2
 867-874-5200, 800-661-0855, info@ntpc.com
Public Utilities Board of the Northwest Territories, #203, 62
 Woodland Dr., PO Box 4211, Hay River, NT X0E 1G1
 867-874-3944, Fax: 867-874-3639
Nova Scotia
Nova Scotia Utility & Review Board, Summit Place, 1601 Lower
 Water St., 3rd Fl., Halifax, NS B3J 3S3
 902-424-4448, Fax: 902-424-3919, 855-442-4448,
 board@novascotia.ca
Ontario
Hydro One Inc., South Tower, 483 Bay St., 8th Fl., Toronto, ON
 M5G 2P5
 416-345-5000, Fax: 905-944-3251, 877-955-1155,
 customercommunications@hydroone.com
Independent Electricity System Operator, #1600, 120 Adelaide
 St. West, Toronto, ON M5H 1T1
 905-403-6900, Fax: 905-403-6921, 877-797-9473,
 customer.relations@ieso.ca
Ontario Power Generation, 700 University Ave., Toronto, ON
 M5G 1X6
 416-592-2555, 877-592-2555, webmaster@opg.com
Prince Edward Island
Prince Edward Island Regulatory & Appeals Commission,
 National Bank Tower, #501, 134 Kent St., PO Box 577,
 Charlottetown, PE C1A 7L1
 902-892-3501, Fax: 902-566-4076, 800-501-6268,
 info@irac.pe.ca
Quebec
Coopérative régionale d'électricité de
 Saint-Jean-Baptiste-de-Rouville, 3113, rue Principale,
 Saint-Jean-Baptiste, QC J0L 1B0
 450-467-5583, Fax: 450-467-0092, 800-267-5583,
 info@coopsjb.com
Hydro-Québec, Édifice Jean-Lesage, 75, boul René-Lévesque
 ouest, Montréal, QC H2Z 1A4
 514-385-7252, 888-385-7252
Régie de l'énergie, Tour de la Bourse, #2.55, 800, Place
 Victoria, Montréal, QC H4Z 1A2
 514-873-2452, Fax: 514-873-2070, 888-873-2452,
 secretariat@regie-energie.qc.ca
Saskatchewan
Saskatchewan Power Corporation (SaskPower), 2025 Victoria
 Ave., Regina, SK S4P 0S1
 888-757-6937
Saskatchewan Water Corporation (SaskWater), #200, 111
 Fairford St. East, Moose Jaw, SK S6H 1C8
 Fax: 306-694-3207, 888-230-1111,
 communications@saskwater.com
SaskEnergy Incorporated, 1777 Victoria Ave., Regina, SK S4P
 4K5
 306-777-9225, 800-567-8899, webmaster@saskenergy.com
Yukon Territory
Yukon Energy Corporation, 2 Miles Canyon Rd., PO Box 5920,
 Whitehorse, YT Y1A 6S7
 867-393-5300, 866-926-3749, communications@yec.yk.ca
Yukon Utilities Board, PO Box 31728, Whitehorse, YT Y1A 6L3
 867-667-5058, Fax: 867-667-5059, yub@utilitiesboard.yk.ca

PUBLIC WORKS
Canada Infrastructure Bank, 150 King St. West, PO Box 15,
 Toronto, ON M5H 1J9
 833-551-5245
Infrastructure Canada, #1100, 180 Kent St., Ottawa, ON K1P
 0B6
 613-948-1148, 877-250-7154, ifc.info@canada.ca
Public Services & Procurement, Place du Portage, Phase III, 11,
 rue Laurier, Ottawa, ON K1A 0S5
 questions@tpsgc-pwgsc.gc.ca

Alberta
Alberta Infrastructure, Infrastructure Bldg., 6950 - 113th St.,
 Edmonton, AB T6H 5V7
 780-415-0507, Fax: 780-427-2187,
 Infra.Contact.Us.m@gov.ab.ca
Alberta Transportation, Communications Branch, Twin Atria
 Bldg., 4999 - 98th Ave., 2nd Fl., Edmonton, AB T6B 2X3
 780-427-7674, Fax: 780-466-3166,
 Trans.Contact.Us.m@gov.ab.ca
British Columbia
British Columbia Ministry of Transportation & Infrastructure, PO
 Box 9850 Prov Govt, Victoria, BC V8W 9T5
 250-387-3198, Fax: 250-356-7706,
 tran.webmaster@gov.bc.ca
Partnerships BC, 900 - 1285 West Pender St., PO Box 9478
 Prov Govt, Vancouver, BC V6E 4B1
 604-681-2443, Fax: 604-806-4190,
 partnershipsbc@partnershipsbc.ca
Manitoba
Manitoba Infrastructure, Legislative Bldg., #203, 450 Broadway,
 Winnipeg, MB R3C 0V8
New Brunswick
New Brunswick Department of Transportation & Infrastructure,
 Kings Place, PO Box 6000, Fredericton, NB E3B 5H1
 506-453-3939, Fax: 506-453-7987,
 transportation.web@gnb.ca
Newfoundland & Labrador
Newfoundland & Labrador Department of Transportation &
 Infrastructure, Confederation Bldg., Prince Philip Dr., PO Box
 8700, St. John's, NL A1B 4J6
 709-729-2300, ti@gov.nl.ca
Northwest Territories
Northwest Territories Department of Infrastructure, Stuart M.
 Hodgson Bldg., 5009 - 49th St., 3rd Fl., PO Box 1320,
 Yellowknife, NT X1A 2L9
 INF_Communications@gov.nt.ca
Nova Scotia
Nova Scotia Department of Transportation & Active Transit, PO
 Box 186, Halifax, NS B3J 2N2
 902-424-2297, Fax: 902-424-0532, tpwpaff@novascotia.ca
Nunavut
Nunavut Territory Department of Community & Government
 Services, W.G. Brown Bldg., 4th Fl., PO Box 1000 700,
 Iqaluit, NU X0A 0H0
 867-975-5406, Fax: 867-975-5305, cgscomms@gov.nu.ca
Ontario
Ontario Capital Growth Corporation, Ontario Investment & Trade
 Centre, 250 Yonge St., 35th Fl., Toronto, ON M5B 2L7
 416-325-6874, Fax: 416-212-0794
Ontario Ministry of Economic Development, Job Creation &
 Trade, 56 Wellesley St. West, 7th Fl., Toronto, ON M7A 2E7
 416-325-6666, 800-268-7095
Ontario Ministry of Infrastructure, 777 Bay St., 5th Fl., Toronto,
 ON M5G 2C8
 416-327-4412
Prince Edward Island
Prince Edward Island Department of Transportation &
 Infrastructure, Jones Bldg., 11 Kent St., 3rd Fl., PO Box 2000,
 Charlottetown, PE C1A 7N8
 902-368-5100, Fax: 902-368-5395, DeptTIE@gov.pe.ca
Saskatchewan
Saskatchewan Highways, Victoria Tower, 1855 Victoria Ave.,
 Regina, SK S4P 3T2
 306-933-5186, MHI.CustomerService@gov.sk.ca
SaskBuilds & Procurement, 1920 Rose St., Regina, SK S4P 0A9
 306-787-6911, Fax: 306-787-1061,
 cs.receptioncenturyplaza@gov.sk.ca
Yukon Territory
Yukon Highways & Public Works, PO Box 2703, Whitehorse, YT
 Y1A 2C6
 867-667-3732, Fax: 867-393-6218, hpw-info@yukon.ca

PUBLICATIONS
Public Services & Procurement, Place du Portage, Phase III, 11,
 rue Laurier, Ottawa, ON K1A 0S5
 questions@tpsgc-pwgsc.gc.ca
Nova Scotia
Communications Nova Scotia, Provincial Bldg., 1723 Hollis St.,
 3rd Fl., PO Box 608, Halifax, NS B3J 2R7
 902-424-7690, Fax: 902-424-0515,
 CNSClientSVC@novascotia.ca
Nunavut
Nunavut Legislative Assembly, 926 Federal Rd., PO Box 1200,
 Iqaluit, NU X0A 0H0
 867-975-5000, Fax: 867-975-5190, 877-334-7266,
 leginfo@assembly.nu.ca
Quebec
Ministère de la Culture et Communications, 225, Grande Allée
 est, Québec, QC G1R 5G5
 888-380-8882

Yukon Territory
Yukon Highways & Public Works, PO Box 2703, Whitehorse, YT
 Y1A 2C6
 867-667-3732, Fax: 867-393-6218, hpw-info@yukon.ca

PURCHASING
MERX, Phase II, #103, 6 Antares Dr., Ottawa, ON K2E 8A9
 613-727-4900, Fax: 888-235-5800, 800-964-6379,
 merx@merx.com
Alberta
Alberta Infrastructure, Infrastructure Bldg., 6950 - 113th St.,
 Edmonton, AB T6H 5V7
 780-415-0507, Fax: 780-427-2187,
 Infra.Contact.Us.m@gov.ab.ca
Newfoundland & Labrador
Newfoundland & Labrador Department of Digital Government &
 Service NL, 100 Prince Phillip Dr., PO Box 8700, St. John's,
 NL A1B 4J6
 709-729-4834, servicenlinfo@gov.nl.ca
Public Procurement Agency, 30 Strawberry Marsh Rd., St.
 John's, NL A1B 4R4
 709-729-3348, tenders@gov.nl.ca
Northwest Territories
Northwest Territories Department of Infrastructure, Stuart M.
 Hodgson Bldg., 5009 - 49th St., 3rd Fl., PO Box 1320,
 Yellowknife, NT X1A 2L9
 INF_Communications@gov.nt.ca
Nunavut
Nunavut Territory Department of Community & Government
 Services, W.G. Brown Bldg., 4th Fl., PO Box 1000 700,
 Iqaluit, NU X0A 0H0
 867-975-5406, Fax: 867-975-5305, cgscomms@gov.nu.ca
Ontario
Ontario Ministry of Infrastructure, 777 Bay St., 5th Fl., Toronto,
 ON M5G 2C8
 416-327-4412
Prince Edward Island
Prince Edward Island Department of Transportation &
 Infrastructure, Jones Bldg., 11 Kent St., 3rd Fl., PO Box 2000,
 Charlottetown, PE C1A 7N8
 902-368-5100, Fax: 902-368-5395, DeptTIE@gov.pe.ca

RAIL TRANSPORTATION
See Also: Transportation
Transportation Safety Board of Canada, 200, promenade du
 Portage, 4e étage, Gatineau, QC K1A 1K8
 819-994-3741, Fax: 819-997-2239, 800-387-3557,
 communications@bst-tsb.gc.ca
VIA Rail Canada Inc., CP 8116 Centre-Ville, Montréal, QC H3C
 3N3
 514-871-6000, Fax: 514-871-6104, 888-842-7245,
 customer_relations@viarail.ca
Alberta
Alberta Transportation, Communications Branch, Twin Atria
 Bldg., 4999 - 98th Ave., 2nd Fl., Edmonton, AB T6B 2X3
 780-427-7674, Fax: 780-466-3166,
 Trans.Contact.Us.m@gov.ab.ca
Manitoba
Manitoba Infrastructure, Legislative Bldg., #203, 450 Broadway,
 Winnipeg, MB R3C 0V8
New Brunswick
New Brunswick Department of Transportation & Infrastructure,
 Kings Place, PO Box 6000, Fredericton, NB E3B 5H1
 506-453-3939, Fax: 506-453-7987,
 transportation.web@gnb.ca
Newfoundland & Labrador
Newfoundland & Labrador Department of Transportation &
 Infrastructure, Confederation Bldg., Prince Philip Dr., PO Box
 8700, St. John's, NL A1B 4J6
 709-729-2300, ti@gov.nl.ca
Nova Scotia
Nova Scotia Department of Transportation & Active Transit, PO
 Box 186, Halifax, NS B3J 2N2
 902-424-2297, Fax: 902-424-0532, tpwpaff@novascotia.ca
Ontario
Metrolinx, 97 Front St. West, Toronto, ON M5J 1E6
 416-874-5900, Fax: 416-869-1755
Quebec
Société du port ferroviaire Baie-Comeau-Haute-Rive, 18, rte
 Maritime, Baie-Comeau, QC G4Z 2L6
 418-296-6785
Saskatchewan
Saskatchewan Highways, Victoria Tower, 1855 Victoria Ave.,
 Regina, SK S4P 3T2
 306-933-5186, MHI.CustomerService@gov.sk.ca

REAL ESTATE
See Also: Land Titles

Canada Mortgage & Housing Corporation, 700 Montreal Rd., Ottawa, ON K1A 0P7
613-748-2000, Fax: 613-748-2098, 800-668-2642, chic@cmhc-schl.gc.ca

British Columbia
Real Estate Council of British Columbia, #900, 750 West Pender St., Vancouver, BC V6C 2T8
604-683-9664, Fax: 604-683-9017, 877-683-9664, info@recbc.ca

Nova Scotia
Nova Scotia Department of Municipal Affairs, PO Box 216, Halifax, NS B3J 2M4
902-424-6642
Service Nova Scotia & Internal Services, PO Box 2734, Halifax, NS B3J 3K5
902-424-5200, Fax: 902-424-0720, 800-670-4357, askus@novascotia.ca

Nunavut
Legal Registries, PO Box 1000 570, Iqaluit, NU X0A 0H0
867-975-6590, Fax: 867-975-6594, Legal.Registries@gov.nu.ca

RECREATION
See Also: Tourism & Tourist Information
Canada Place Corporation, 100 The Pointe, 999 Canada Pl., Vancouver, BC V6C 3T4
604-775-7063
Canadian Heritage, 15, rue Eddy, Gatineau, QC K1A 0M5
819-997-0055, 866-811-0055, PCH.info-info.PCH@canada.ca
National Battlefields Commission, 390, av de Bernières, Québec, QC G1R 2L7
418-648-3506, Fax: 418-648-3638, information@ccbn-nbc.gc.ca
Parks Canada, National Office, 30, rue Victoria, Gatineau, QC J8X 0B3
819-420-9486, 888-773-8888, information@pc.gc.ca

Alberta
Horse Racing Alberta, #720, 9707 - 110 St. NW, Edmonton, AB T5K 2L9
780-415-5432, 888-553-7223, reception@thehorses.com

British Columbia
British Columbia Lottery Corporation, 74 West Seymour St., Kamloops, BC V2C 1E2
250-828-5500, Fax: 250-828-5631, 866-815-0222
British Columbia Ministry of Social Development & Poverty Reduction, PO Box 9058 Prov Govt, Victoria, BC V8W 9E1
866-866-0800

Manitoba
Manitoba Horse Racing Commission, #812, 401 York Ave., PO Box 46086 Westdale, Winnipeg, MB R3R 3S3
204-885-7770, Fax: 204-831-0942
Tourism Secretariat, 213 Notre Dame Ave., 6th Fl., Winnipeg, MB R3B 1N3
204-945-0216, tourismsec@gov.mb.ca

New Brunswick
Atlantic Lottery Corporation, 922 Main St., PO Box 5500, Moncton, NB E1C 8W6
800-561-3942, info@alc.ca
New Brunswick Department of Tourism, Heritage & Culture, Marysville Place, 4th Fl., PO Box 6000, Fredericton, NB E3B 5H1
506-453-3115, Fax: 506-444-5760, thctpcinfo@gnb.ca
New Brunswick Lotteries & Gaming Corporation, Chancery Place, 4th Fl., 675 King St., PO Box 6000, Fredericton, NB E3B 5H1
506-453-2451, Fax: 506-453-2053

Newfoundland & Labrador
Newfoundland & Labrador Department of Tourism, Culture, Arts & Recreation, PO Box 8700, St. John's, NL A1B 4J6
709-729-7000, tcar@gov.nl.ca

Nova Scotia
Events East Group, 1800 Argyle St., PO Box 955, Halifax, NS B3J 2V9
902-421-8686, Fax: 902-422-2922
Nova Scotia Gaming Corporation, Summit Place, 1601 Lower Water St., 5th Fl., PO Box 1501, Halifax, NS B3J 2Y3
902-424-2203, Fax: 902-424-0724

Ontario
Alcohol & Gaming Commission of Ontario, 90 Sheppard Ave. East, Toronto, ON M2N 0A4
416-326-8700, 800-522-2876, customer.service@agco.ca
Metro Toronto Convention Centre Corporation, 255 Front St. West, Toronto, ON M5V 2W6
416-585-8000, Fax: 416-585-8270, info@mtccc.com
Niagara Parks Commission, Oak Hall Administration Bldg., 7400 Portage Rd. South, PO Box 150, Niagara Falls, ON L2E 6T2
905-356-2241, Fax: 905-354-6041, 877-642-7275

Ontario Lottery & Gaming Corporation, Roberta Bondar Pl., #800, 70 Foster Dr., Sault Ste. Marie, ON P6A 6V2
705-946-6464, Fax: 705-946-6600, 800-387-0098
Ontario Ministry of Heritage, Sport, Tourism & Culture Industries, 438 University Ave., 6th Fl., Toronto, ON M5G 2K8
416-326-9326, Fax: 416-314-7854, 888-997-9015
Ontario Place Corporation, 955 Lake Shore Blvd. West, Toronto, ON M6K 3B9
416-314-9900, Fax: 416-314-9989, 866-663-4386
Ottawa Convention Centre, 55 Colonel By Dr., Ottawa, ON K1N 9J2
613-563-1984, Fax: 613-563-7646, 800-450-0077
St. Lawrence Parks Commission, 13740 County Rd. 2, Morrisburg, ON K0C 1X0
613-543-3704, Fax: 613-543-2847, 800-437-2233, getaway@parks.on.ca

Prince Edward Island
Atlantic Provinces Harness Racing Commission, 5 Gerald McCarville Dr., PO Box 128, Kensington, PE C0B 1M0
902-836-5500, Fax: 902-836-5320
Prince Edward Island Department of Economic Growth, Tourism & Culture, PO Box 2000, Charlottetown, PE C1A 7N8
902-368-5540, Fax: 902-368-5277, tpswitch@gov.pe.ca
Prince Edward Island Department of Social Development & Housing, Jones Bldg., 11 Kent St., 2nd Fl., PO Box 2000, Charlottetown, PE C1A 7N8
902-620-3777, Fax: 902-368-4740, 866-594-3777, DeptSDH@gov.pe.ca

Quebec
Comité conjoint de chasse, de pêche et de piégeage, #1420, 1080, Côte du Beaver Hall, Montréal, QC H2Z 1N8
514-284-2151, Fax: 514-284-0039, infohftcc@cccpp-hftcc.com
Régie des alcools, des courses et des jeux, 560, boul Charest est, Québec, QC G1K 3J3
418-643-7667, Fax: 418-643-5971, 800-363-0320
Société de financement des infrastructures locales, Ministère des Finances, 12, rue Saint-Louis, Québec, QC G1R 5L3
418-528-9323, Fax: 418-646-1631, info@finances.gouv.qc.ca
Société des établissements en plein air du Québec, Place de la Cité, Tour Cominar, #250, 2640, boul Laurier, 2e étage, Québec, QC G1V 5C2
418-686-4875, Fax: 418-643-8177, 800-665-6527, inforeservation@sepaq.com

Saskatchewan
Saskatchewan Liquor & Gaming Authority, 2500 Victoria Ave., PO Box 5054, Regina, SK S4P 3M3
306-787-5563, inquiry@slga.gov.sk.ca

Yukon Territory
Assessement Appeal Board, PO Box 2703, Whitehorse, YT Y1A 2C6
867-667-5268, Fax: 867-667-8276
Yukon Tourism & Culture, PO Box 2703, Whitehorse, YT Y1A 2C6
867-393-7048

RECYCLING
Alberta
Alberta Recycling Management Authority, Scotia Tower 1, #1800, 10060 Jasper Ave., PO Box 189, Edmonton, AB T5J 2J1
780-990-1111, Fax: 780-990-1122, 888-999-8762, info@albertarecycling.ca

Nova Scotia
Divert NS, #400, 35 Commercial St., Truro, NS B2N 3H9
902-895-7732, Fax: 902-897-3256, 877-313-7732, info@divertns.ca

RESEARCH
Canada Foundation for Innovation, #1100, 55 Metcalfe St., Ottawa, ON K1P 6L5
613-947-6496, Fax: 613-943-0923, feedback@innovation.ca
Policy Horizons Canada, 360 Albert St., 15th Fl., Ottawa, ON K1R 7X7
613-947-3800, Fax: 613-995-6006, questions@horizons.gc.ca

Alberta
Alberta Advanced Education, Legislature Bldg., #403, 10800 - 97th Ave., Edmonton, AB T5K 2B6
780-422-5400
Alberta Innovates, 250 Karl Clark Rd., Edmonton, AB T6N 1E4
877-423-5727, info@albertainnovates.ca
InnoTech Alberta, 250 Karl Clark Rd., Edmonton, AB T6N 1H2
780-450-5111, Fax: 780-450-5333, info@innotechalberta.ca

British Columbia
British Columbia Law Institute, University of British Columbia, 1822 East Mall, Vancouver, BC V6T 1Z1
604-822-0142, Fax: 604-822-0144, bcli@bcli.org

Quebec
Fonds de recherche du Québec - Société et culture, #470, 140, Grande Allée est, Québec, QC G1R 5M8
418-643-7582, frq.sc@frq.gouv.qc.ca

RESEARCH & DEVELOPMENT
Aerospace Manufacturing Technologies Centre, Campus Université de Montréal, 5145, av Decelles, Montréal, QC H3T 2B2
Aquatic & Crop Resource Development Industry Partnership Facility, 550 University Ave., Charlottetown, PE C1A 4P3
Atomic Energy of Canada Limited, Head Office, Chalk River Laboratories, 286 Plant Rd., Chalk River, ON K0J 1J0
888-220-2465, communications@aecl.ca
Automotive & Surface Transportation Facilities, Ottawa Uplands Research Facilities, 2320 Lester Rd., Ottawa, ON K1V 1S2
613-998-9639
Bayfield Institute, 867 Lakeshore Rd., PO Box 5050, Burlington, ON L7R 4A6
905-336-4999
Bedford Institute of Oceanography, PO Box 1006, Dartmouth, NS B2Y 4A2
902-426-2373, Fax: 902-426-8484, webmasterbio-iob@dfo-mpo.gc.ca
Canada Centre for Mapping & Earth Observation, #212, 50, Place de la Cité, PO Box 162, Sherbrooke, QC J1H 4G9
Canada Foundation for Innovation, #1100, 55 Metcalfe St., Ottawa, ON K1P 6L5
613-947-6496, Fax: 613-943-0923, feedback@innovation.ca
Canada-France-Hawaii Telescope, CFHT Corporation, #65, 1238 Mamalahoa Hwy., Kamuela, HI
808-885-7944, Fax: 808-885-7288, info@cfht.hawaii.edu
Canadian Astronomy Data Centre, NRC Herzberg Astronomy & Astrophysics, 5071 West Saanich Rd., Victoria, BC V9E 2E7
250-363-0001, Fax: 250-363-0045, cadc@nrc.gc.ca
Canadian Centre for Housing Technology, c/o National Research Council Canada, Building M-20, 1200 Montreal Rd., Ottawa, ON K1A 0R6
Canadian Hydrographic Service, 200 Kent St., Ottawa, ON K1A 0E6
613-998-4921, 866-546-3613, chsinfo@dfo-mpo.gc.ca
Canadian Nuclear Laboratories, Head Office, Chalk River Laboratories, 286 Plant Rd., Chalk River, ON K0J 1J0
866-513-2325, communications@cnl.ca
Canadian Photonics Fabrication Centre, c/o National Research Council Canada, Building M-50, 1200 Montreal Rd., Ottawa, ON K1A 0R6
613-993-9101
Canadian Space Agency, John H. Chapman Space Centre, 6767, rte de l'Aéroport, Saint-Hubert, QC J3Y 8Y9
450-926-4800, Fax: 450-926-4352, asc.info.csa@canada.ca
Cell Culture Pilot Plant, c/o Montréal (av Royalmount) Research Facilities, 6100, av Royalmount, Montréal, QC H4P 2R2
514-496-6100
Centre for Aquaculture & Environmental Research, 4160 Marine Dr., West Vancouver, BC V7V 1N6
Civil Infrastructure & Related Structures Testing Facilities, c/o National Research Council, 1200 Montreal Rd., Ottawa, ON K1A 0R6
613-993-9101
Climatic Testing Facility, Ottawa Uplands Research Facilities, 2320 Lester Rd., Ottawa, ON K1V 1S2
613-998-9639
Cultus Lake Salmon Research Lab, 4222 Columbia Valley Hwy., Cultus Lake, BC V2R 5B6
Dominion Astrophysical Observatory, NRC Herzberg Astronomy & Astrophysics, 5071 West Saanich Rd., Victoria, BC V9E 2E7
250-363-0001, NRC.NSIHerzbergAstroInfoISN.CNRC@nrc-cnrc.gc.ca
Dominion Radio Astrophysical Observatory, 717 White Lake Rd., PO Box 248, Penticton, BC V2A 6J9
250-497-2300, NRC.DRAO-OFR.CNRC@nrc-cnrc.gc.ca
Fire Safety Testing Facility, National Fire Laboratory, Bldg. U-96, Concession 8, Mississippi Mills, ON K0A 1A0
613-993-9101
Freshwater Institute, 501 University Cres., Winnipeg, MB R3T 2N6
Gas Turbine Research Facility, c/o National Research Council, 1200 Montreal Rd., Ottawa, ON K1A 0R6
613-993-9101
Gemini Observatory, 670 N. A'ohoku Place, Hilo, HI
808-974-2500, Fax: 808-974-2589
Hydraulics Laboratories, c/o National Research Council, 1200 Montreal Rd., Ottawa, ON K1A 0R6
Hygrothermal Performance of Buildings Research Facilities, c/o National Research Council, 1200 Montreal Rd., Ottawa, ON K1A 0R6
613-993-9101
Indoor Environment Testing Facilities, c/o National Research Council, 1200 Montreal Rd., Ottawa, ON K1A 0R6

Industrial Partnership Facility: Montréal, c/o Montréal (av Royalmount) Research Facilities, 6100, av Royalmount, Montréal, QC H4P 2R2

Institut Maurice-Lamontagne, 850, rte de le Mer, CP 1000, Mont-Joli, QC G5H 3Z4
418-775-0500, Fax: 418-775-0730

Institute of Ocean Sciences, 9860 West Saanich Rd., PO Box 6000, Sidney, BC V8L 4B2
250-363-6517

Marine Performance Evaluation & Testing Facilities, c/o National Research Council, 1200 Montreal Rd., Ottawa, ON K1A 0R6

Material Emissions Testing Facilities, c/o National Research Council, 1200 Montreal Rd., Ottawa, ON K1A 0R6

Medical Device Facilities, Boucherville Research Facilities, 75, boul de Mortagne, Boucherville, QC J4B 6Y4
450-641-5100

Microbial Fermentation Pilot Plant, c/o Montréal (av Royalmount) Research Facilities, 6100, av Royalmount, Montréal, QC H4P 2R2
514-496-6100

National Research Council Canada, Building M-58, 1200 Montreal Rd., Ottawa, ON K1A 0R6
613-993-9101, Fax: 613-991-9096, 877-672-2672, info@nrc-cnrc.ca

National Research Council Canada - Industrial Research Assistance Program, 1200 Montreal Rd., Ottawa, ON K1A 0R6
Fax: 613-952-1086, 877-994-4727, NRC.IRAPInfo-InfoPARI.CNRC@nrc-cnrc.gc.ca

Natural Sciences & Engineering Research Council of Canada, 350 Albert St., 16th Fl., Ottawa, ON K1A 1H5
613-995-4273, Fax: 613-992-5337, 855-275-2861

Networks of Centres of Excellence of Canada, 350 Albert Street, 16th Fl., Ottawa, ON K1A 1H5
613-995-6010, Fax: 613-992-7356, info@nce-rce.gc.ca

Ocean Technology Enterprise Centre, PO Box 12093, St. John's, NL A1B 3T5
709-772-2469

Pacific Biological Station, 3190 Hammond Bay Rd., Nanaimo, BC V9T 6N7
250-756-7000, Fax: 250-756-7053

Printable Electronics Labs, c/o National Research Council, 1200 Montreal Rd., Ottawa, ON K1A 0R6

Science & Technology Branch, Tower 5, 1341 Baseline Rd., Ottawa, ON K1A 0C5
Fax: 613-773-1711

Sea Lamprey Control Centre, 1219 Queen St. East, Sault Ste Marie, ON P6A 2E5

St. Andrews Biological Station, 531 Brandy Cove Rd., St Andrews, NB E5B 2L9
506-529-8854, Fax: 506-529-5862, xmarsabs@mar.dfo-mpo.gc.ca

Waste Biotreatability Facility, c/o Montréal (av Royalmount) Research Facilities, 6100, av Royalmount, Montréal, QC H4P 2R2

Wind Tunnel Testing Facilities, c/o National Research Council, 1200 Montreal Rd., Ottawa, ON K1A 0R6

Zebrafish Screening Facility, 1411 Oxford St., Halifax, NS B3H 3Z1
902-426-8332

Alberta
Alberta Advanced Education, Legislature Bldg., #403, 10800 - 97th Ave., Edmonton, AB T5K 2B6
780-422-5400

Alberta Innovates, 250 Karl Clark Rd., Edmonton, AB T6N 1E4
877-423-5727, info@albertainnovates.ca

Alberta Jobs, Economy & Innovation, Commerce Place, 10155 - 102nd Ave., 12th Fl., Edmonton, AB T5J 4G8

InnoTech Alberta, 250 Karl Clark Rd., Edmonton, AB T6N 1H2
780-450-5111, Fax: 780-450-5333, info@innotechalberta.ca

British Columbia
Powertech Labs Inc., 12388 - 88 Ave., Surrey, BC V8W 7R7
604-590-7500, Fax: 604-590-6611

New Brunswick
New Brunswick Research & Productivity Council, 921 College Hill Rd., Fredericton, NB E3B 6Z9
506-452-1212, Fax: 506-452-1395, 800-563-0844, info@rpc.ca

Northwest Territories
Aurora Research Institute, 191 MacKenzie Rd., PO Box 1450, Inuvik, NT X0E 0T0
867-777-3298, Fax: 867-777-4264

Prince Edward Island
Agricultural Insurance Corporation, 7 Gerald McCarville Drive, Kensington, PE C0B 1M0

BIO|FOOD|TECH, 101 Belvedere Ave., PO Box 2000, Charlottetown, PE C1A 7N8
902-368-5548, Fax: 902-368-5549, 877-368-5548, biofoodtech@biofoodtech.ca

Quebec
Centre de recherche industrielle du Québec, 333, rue Franquet, Québec, QC G1P 4C7
418-659-1550, Fax: 418-652-2251, 800-667-2386, infocriq@criq.qc.ca

Fonds de recherche du Québec - Société et culture, #470, 140, Grande Allée est, Québec, QC G1R 5M8
418-643-7582, frq.sc@frq.gouv.qc.ca

Ministère de l'Économie et de l'Innovation, 710, Place D'Youville, 3e étage, Québec, QC G1R 4Y4
418-691-5950, Fax: 418-644-0118, 866-680-1884

Saskatchewan
Prairie Agricultural Machinery Institute, 2215 - 8th Ave., PO Box 1150, Humboldt, SK S0K 2A0
306-682-5033, Fax: 306-682-5080, 800-567-7264, pami@pami.ca

Saskatchewan Health Research Foundation, Atrium Bldg., Innovation Place, #204, 111 Research Dr., Saskatoon, SK S7N 3R2
639-398-8400, 800-975-1699, info@shrf.ca

Saskatchewan Opportunities Corporation, Innovation Place, #114, 15 Innovation Blvd., Saskatoon, SK S7N 2X8
306-933-6295, Fax: 306-933-8215, saskatoon@innovationplace.com

Saskatchewan Power Corporation (SaskPower), 2025 Victoria Ave., Regina, SK S4P 0S1
888-757-6937

Saskatchewan Research Council, #125, 15 Innovation Blvd., Saskatoon, SK S7N 2X8
306-933-5400, Fax: 306-933-7446

ROUND TABLES
Manitoba
Manitoba Round Table for Sustainable Development, #160, 123 Main St., PO Box 70, Winnipeg, MB R3C 1A5
204-945-4391, Fax: 204-948-4730, mrtsd@gov.mb.ca

SALES TAX
Alberta
Financial Sector Regulation & Policy Division, Terrace Bldg., 9515 - 107th St., 4th Fl., Edmonton, AB T5K 2C3
780-427-8322

British Columbia
Employment & Labour Market Services Division, PO Box 9762 Prov Govt, Victoria, BC V8W 1A4
250-953-3921, Fax: 250-953-3928

Manitoba
Taxation Division, #101, 401 York Ave., Winnipeg, MB R3C 0P8
204-945-5603, Fax: 204-945-0896, 800-782-0318

Northwest Territories
Northwest Territories Department of Finance, PO Box 1320, Yellowknife, NT X1A 2L9

Nova Scotia
Provincial Tax Commission, PO Box 1003, Halifax, NS B3J 2X1
902-424-6538, Fax: 902-424-7434, taxcommission@novascotia.ca

Service Nova Scotia & Internal Services, PO Box 2734, Halifax, NS B3J 3K5
902-424-5200, Fax: 902-424-0720, 800-670-4357, askus@novascotia.ca

Nunavut
Nunavut Territory Department of Finance, PO Box 1000 430, Iqaluit, NU X0A 0H0
867-975-6222, Fax: 867-975-6220, 888-668-9993, gnhr@gov.nu.ca

Saskatchewan
Revenue Division, PO Box 200, Regina, SK S4P 2Z6
306-787-6645, Fax: 306-787-0776, 800-667-6102

SCHOOL BOARDS
See Also: Education
Nova Scotia
Annapolis Valley Regional Centre for Education, 121 Orchard St., PO Box 340, Berwick, NS B0P 1E0
902-538-4600, Fax: 902-538-4630, 800-850-3887

Cape Breton-Victoria Regional Centre for Education, 275 George St., Sydney, NS BIP IJ7
902-564-8293, Fax: 902-564-0123

Chignecto-Central Regional Centre for Education, 60 Lorne St., Truro, NS B2N 3K3
902-897-8900, 800-770-0008

Conseil scolaire acadien provincial, CP 88, Saulnierville, NS B0W 2Z0
902-769-5460, 888-533-2727

Halifax Regional Centre for Education, 33 Spectacle Lake Dr., Dartmouth, NS B3B 1X7
902-464-2000

South Shore Regional Centre for Education, 69 Wentzell Dr., Bridgewater, NS B4V 0A2
902-543-2468, Fax: 902-541-3060, 888-252-2217, receptionist@ssrce.ca

Strait Regional Centre for Education, #2, 304 Pitt St., Port Hawkesbury, NS B9A 2T9
902-625-2191, Fax: 902-625-2281, 800-650-4448, srsb@srsb.ca

Tri-County Regional Centre for Education, 79 Water St., Yarmouth, NS B5A 1L4
902-749-5696, Fax: 902-749-5697, 800-915-0113

Prince Edward Island
French Language School Board, 1596, rte 124, Abram-Village, PE C0B 2E0
902-854-2975, Fax: 902-854-2981, cslf@edu.pe.ca

SCIENCE & NATURE
Agriculture & Agri-Food Canada, 1341 Baseline Rd., Ottawa, ON K1A 0C5
613-773-1000, Fax: 613-773-1081, 855-773-0241, info@agr.gc.ca

Beverly & Qamanirjuaq Caribou Management Board, Secretariat, PO Box 629, Stonewall, MB R0C 2Z0

Canada Centre for Mapping & Earth Observation, #212, 50, Place de la Cité, PO Box 162, Sherbrooke, QC J1H 4G9

Canada Energy Regulator, #210, 517 - 10th Ave. SW, Calgary, AB T2R 0A8
403-292-4800, Fax: 403-292-5503, 800-899-1265

Canadian Institutes of Health Research, 160 Elgin St., 10th Fl., Ottawa, ON K1A 0W9
613-954-1968, Fax: 613-954-1800, 888-603-4178, support@cihr-irsc.gc.ca

Canadian Nuclear Safety Commission, 280 Slater St., PO Box 1046 B, Ottawa, ON K1P 5S9
613-995-5894, Fax: 613-995-5086, 800-668-5284, cnsc.information.ccsn@canada.ca

Canadian Space Agency, John H. Chapman Space Centre, 6767, rte de l'Aéroport, Saint-Hubert, QC J3Y 8Y9
450-926-4800, Fax: 450-926-4352, asc.info.csa@canada.ca

CanmetMINING, 555 Booth St., Ottawa, ON K1A 0G1
Fax: 613-947-6606

Cell Culture Pilot Plant, c/o Montréal (av Royalmount) Research Facilities, 6100, av Royalmount, Montréal, QC H4P 2R2
514-496-6100

Commission for Environmental Cooperation, Secretariat, #200, 393, rue Saint-Jacques ouest, Montréal, QC H2Y 1N9
514-350-4300, Fax: 514-350-4314, info@cec.org

Committee on the Status of Endangered Wildlife in Canada, c/o Dept. of Biological Sciences, Simon Fraser University, 8888 University Dr., Burnaby, BC V5A 1S6

Cultus Lake Salmon Research Lab, 4222 Columbia Valley Hwy., Cultus Lake, BC V2R 5B6

Earth Sciences Sector, 588 Booth St., Ottawa, ON K1A 0Y7

Environment & Climate Change Canada, 200, rue Sacré-Coeur, 12th Fl., Gatineau, QC K1A 0H3
819-938-3860, 800-668-6767, eec.enviroinfo.ec@canada.ca

Fisheries & Oceans Canada, 200 Kent St., Ottawa, ON K1A 0E6
613-993-0999, Fax: 613-990-1866, info@dfo-mpo.gc.ca

Geological Survey of Canada, 601 Booth St., Ottawa, ON K1A 0E8

Indian Oil & Gas Canada, #100, 9911 Chiila Blvd., Tsuu T'ina (Sarcee), AB T2W 6H6
403-292-5625, Fax: 403-292-5618, aadnc.contactiogc.aandc@canada.ca

International Development Research Centre, 150 Kent St., PO Box 8500, Ottawa, ON K1G 3H9
613-236-6163, Fax: 613-238-7230, info@idrc.ca

Mackenzie Valley Environmental Impact Review Board, 200 Scotia Centre, #5102, 50th Ave., PO Box 938, Yellowknife, NT X1A 2N7
867-766-7050, Fax: 867-766-7074, 866-912-3472

National Research Council Canada, Building M-58, 1200 Montreal Rd., Ottawa, ON K1A 0R6
613-993-9101, Fax: 613-991-9096, 877-672-2672, info@nrc-cnrc.ca

Natural Resources Canada, 580 Booth St., Ottawa, ON K1A 0E4
343-292-6096, Fax: 613-992-7211

Natural Sciences & Engineering Research Council of Canada, 350 Albert St., 16th Fl., Ottawa, ON K1A 1H5
613-995-4273, Fax: 613-992-5337, 855-275-2861

Networks of Centres of Excellence of Canada, 350 Albert Street, 16th Fl., Ottawa, ON K1A 1H5
613-995-6010, Fax: 613-992-7356, info@nce-rce.gc.ca

North American Bird Conservation Initiative, Canadian Wildlife Service, 351 St. Joseph Blvd., Gatineau, QC K1A 0H3
819-994-0512, Fax: 819-994-4445, ec.icoancanada-nabcicanada.ec@canada.ca

North American Waterfowl Management Plan, NAWCC (Canada) Secretariat, Place Vincent Massey, 351 St. Joseph Blvd., 14th Fl., Gatineau, QC K1A 0H3
819-938-4030, Fax: 819-934-6017, ec.pnags-nawmp.ec@canada.ca

Nunavut Impact Review Board, 29 Mitik St., PO Box 1360, Cambridge Bay, NU X0B 0C0
Fax: 867-983-2594, 866-233-3033, info@nirb.ca

Nunavut Water Board, PO Box 119, Gjoa Haven, NU X0B 1J0
867-360-6338

Operations, 200 Kent St., Ottawa, ON K1A 0E6

Pest Management Regulatory Agency, 2720 Riverside Dr., Ottawa, ON K1A 0K9
613-736-3799, Fax: 613-736-3798, 800-267-6315, hc.pmra.info-arla.sc@canada.ca

Polar Knowledge Canada, #200, 170 Laurier Ave. West, 2nd Fl., Ottawa, ON K1P 5V5
613-943-8605, info@polar.gc.ca

Porcupine Caribou Management Board, PO Box 31723, Whitehorse, YT Y1A 6L3
867-633-4780, Fax: 867-393-3904

Sea Lamprey Control Centre, 1219 Queen St. East, Sault Ste Marie, ON P6A 2E5

Social Sciences & Humanities Research Council of Canada, Constitution Sq., 350 Albert St., PO Box 1610 B, Ottawa, ON K1P 6G4
613-992-0691

Alberta
Alberta Agriculture & Forestry, JG O'Donoghue Bldg., #100A, 7000 - 113th St., Edmonton, AB T6H 5T6
403-742-7901

Alberta Energy, North Petroleum Plaza, 9945 - 108th St., Edmonton, AB T5K 2G6
780-427-8050, Fax: 780-422-9522

Alberta Environmental Appeals Board, Peace Hills Trust Tower, #306, 10011 - 109 St., Edmonton, AB T5J 3S8
780-427-6207, Fax: 780-427-4693

Alberta Recycling Management Authority, Scotia Tower 1, #1800, 10060 Jasper Ave., PO Box 189, Edmonton, AB T5J 2J1
780-990-1111, Fax: 780-990-1122, 888-999-8762, info@albertarecycling.ca

Alberta Used Oil Management Association, Empire Building, #1008, 10080 Jasper Ave., Edmonton, AB T5J 1V9
780-414-1510, Fax: 780-414-1519, 866-414-1510, auoma@usedoilrecycling.ca

Beverage Container Management Board, #100, 8616 - 51 Ave., Edmonton, AB T6E 6E6
780-424-3193, Fax: 780-428-4620, 888-424-7671, info@bcmb.ab.ca

Irrigation Council, Provincial Bldg., 200 - 5 Ave. South, 3rd Fl., Lethbridge, AB T1J 4L1
403-381-5176, Fax: 403-382-4406

Land Compensation Board, 1229 - 91 St. SW, Edmonton, AB T6X 1E9
780-427-2444, Fax: 780-427-5798, -310-000, srb.lcb@gov.ab.ca

Natural Resources Conservation Board, Sterling Place, 9940 - 106 St., 4th Fl., Edmonton, AB T5K 2N2
780-422-1977, Fax: 780-427-0607, 866-383-6722, info@nrcb.ca

Special Areas Board, Special Areas Board Administration, 212 - 2nd Ave. West, PO Box 820, Hanna, AB T0J 1P0
403-854-5600, Fax: 403-854-5527

British Columbia
Agricultural Land Commission, #133, 4940 Canada Way, Burnaby, BC V5G 4K6
604-660-7000, Fax: 604-660-7033, ALCBurnaby@Victoria1.gov.bc.ca

British Columbia Farm Industry Review Board, 780 Blanshard St., PO Box 9129 Prov Govt, Victoria, BC V8W 9B5
250-356-8945, Fax: 250-356-5131, firb@gov.bc.ca

British Columbia Ministry of Agriculture, Food & Fisheries, PO Box 9043 Prov Govt, Victoria, BC V8W 9E2
888-221-7141, agriservicebc@gov.bc.ca

British Columbia Ministry of Energy, Mines & Low Carbon Innovation, PO Box 9060 Prov Govt, Victoria, BC V8W 9E3
250-952-0628

British Columbia Ministry of Environment & Climate Change Strategy, PO Box 9047 Prov Govt, Victoria, BC V8W 9E2

British Columbia Ministry of Forests, Lands, Natural Resource Operations & Rural Development, PO Box 9049 Prov Govt, Victoria, BC V8W 9E2
800-663-7867, FLNRO.MediaRequests@gov.bc.ca

Environmental Appeal Board, 747 Fort St., 4th Fl., PO Box 9425 Prov Govt, Victoria, BC V8W 3E9
250-387-3464, Fax: 250-356-9923, eabinfo@gov.bc.ca

Environmental Protection Division, PO Box 9339, Victoria, BC V8W 9M1
250-387-1288, Fax: 250-387-5669

Forest Appeals Commission, 747 Fort St., 4th Fl., PO Box 9425 Prov Govt, Victoria, BC V8W 9V1
250-387-3464, Fax: 250-356-9923, facinfo@gov.bc.ca

Forest Practices Board, 310, 1675 Douglas St., PO Box 9905 Prov Govt, Victoria, BC V8W 9R1
250-213-4700, Fax: 250-213-4725, 800-994-5899, fpboard@gov.bc.ca

Forestry Innovation Investment Ltd., #1200, 1130 West Pender St., Vancouver, BC V6E 4A4
604-685-7507, Fax: 604-685-5373, info@bcfii.ca

Islands Trust, #200, 1627 Fort St., Victoria, BC V8R 1H8
250-405-5151, Fax: 250-405-5155

Oil & Gas Commission, 6534 Airport Rd., Fort St. John, BC V1J 4M6
250-794-5200, Fax: 250-794-5375

Timber Export Advisory Committee, PO Box 9514 Prov Govt, Victoria, BC V8W 9C2
250-387-8916, Fax: 250-387-5050

Manitoba
Agricultural Societies, 1129 Queens Ave., Brandon, MB R7A 1L9
204-726-6195, Fax: 204-726-6260

Clean Environment Commission, #305, 155 Carlton St., Winnipeg, MB R3C 3H8
204-945-0594, Fax: 204-945-0090, 800-597-3556, cec@gov.mb.ca

Ecological Reserves Advisory Committee, c/o Manitoba Conservation, Parks & Natural Areas Branch, 200 Saulteaux Cres., PO Box 53, Winnipeg, MB R3J 3W3
204-945-4148, Fax: 204-945-0012

Endangered Species Advisory Committee, 200 Saulteaux Cres., PO Box 24, Winnipeg, MB R3J 3W3
204-945-7775, Fax: 204-945-3077

Manitoba Agricultural Services Corporation, #400, 50 - 24th St. NW, Portage la Prairie, MB R1N 3V9
204-239-3246, Fax: 204-239-3401, mailbox@masc.mb.ca

Manitoba Agriculture, Legislative Bldg., #165, 450 Broadway, Winnipeg, MB R3C 0V8
204-945-3722, Fax: 204-945-3470, minagr@leg.gov.mb.ca

Manitoba Conservation & Climate, 200 Saulteaux Cres., PO Box 22, Winnipeg, MB R3J 3W3
204-945-6784, Fax: 204-948-2656, 800-214-6497, cc@gov.mb.ca

Manitoba Habitat Heritage Corporation, #200, 1555 St. James St., Winnipeg, MB R3H 1B5
204-784-4350, Fax: 204-784-7359

Manitoba Hydro, 360 Portage Ave., PO Box 815 Main, Winnipeg, MB R3C 2P4
204-480-5900, Fax: 204-360-6155, 888-624-9376

Manitoba Indigenous Reconciliation & Northern Relations, Legislative Bldg., #301, 450 Broadway, Winnipeg, MB R3C 0V8
204-945-3788, Fax: 204-945-1383, INRweb@gov.mb.ca

Mineral Resources Division, The Paris Bldg., 259 Portage Ave., 9th Fl., Winnipeg, MB R3B 3P4
204-945-6569, 800-223-5215, minesinfo@gov.mb.ca

New Brunswick
New Brunswick Department of Agriculture, Aquaculture & Fisheries, Agricultural Research Station (Experimental Farm), PO Box 6000, Fredericton, NB E3B 5H1
506-453-3826, Fax: 506-453-7170, DAAF-MAAP@gnb.ca

New Brunswick Department of Environment & Local Government, Marysville Place, 20 McGloin St., Fredericton, NB E3B 5H1
506-453-2690, Fax: 506-457-4994, elg/egl-info@gnb.ca

New Brunswick Department of Natural Resources & Energy Development, Hugh John Flemming Forestry Centre, PO Box 6000, Fredericton, NB E3B 5H1
506-453-3826, Fax: 506-444-4367, dnr_mrnweb@gnb.ca

New Brunswick Farm Products Commission, c/o Department of Agriculture, Aquaculture & Fisheries, PO Box 6000, Fredericton, NB E3B 5H1
506-453-3647, Fax: 506-444-5969, DAAF-MAAP@gnb.ca

New Brunswick Research & Productivity Council, 921 College Hill Rd., Fredericton, NB E3B 6Z9
506-452-1212, Fax: 506-452-1395, 800-563-0844, info@rpc.ca

Newfoundland & Labrador
Newfoundland & Labrador Department of Fisheries, Forestry & Agriculture, Petten Bldg., 30 Strawberry Marsh Rd., PO Box 8700, St. John's, NL A1B 4J6
709-729-3705, Fax: 709-729-0360

Newfoundland & Labrador Department of Industry, Energy & Technology, Natural Resources Bldg., 50 Elizabeth Ave., PO Box 8700, St. John's, NL A1B 4J6
709-729-3017, Fax: 709-729-0059

Professional Fish Harvesters Certification Board, 368 Hamilton Ave., PO Box 8541, St. John's, NL A1B 3P2
709-722-8170, Fax: 709-722-8201, pfh@pfhcb.com

Northwest Territories
Aurora Research Institute, 191 MacKenzie Rd., PO Box 1450, Inuvik, NT X0E 0T0
867-777-3298, Fax: 867-777-4264

Northwest Territories Department of Environment & Natural Resources, PO Box 1320, Yellowknife, NT X1A 2L9
867-767-9055, enr_communications@gov.nt.ca

Nova Scotia
Crown Land Information Management Centre, 1701 Hollis St., PO Box 698, Halifax, NS B3J 2T9
902-424-3171, Fax: 902-424-7068, crownland@novascotia.ca

GeoNOVA, 160 Willow St., Amherst, NS B4H 3W5
902-667-7231, 800-798-0706, geoinfo@novascotia.ca

Natural Products Marketing Council, 74 Research Dr., Bible Hill, NS B6L 2R2
902-893-6511, Fax: 902-893-7579

Nova Scotia Department of Agriculture, 1800 Argyle St., 6th Fl., Halifax, NS B3J 3N8
902-424-4560, Fax: 902-424-4671, 800-279-0825

Nova Scotia Department of Lands & Forestry, PO Box 698, Halifax, NS B3J 2T9
902-424-5935, Fax: 902-424-7735, 800-565-2224

Nova Scotia Farm Loan Board, 74 Research Dr., Truro, NS B6L 2R2
902-893-6506, Fax: 902-895-7693, FLBNS@novascotia.ca

Nunavut
Nunavut Territory Department of Environment, PO Box 1000 1320, Iqaluit, NU X0A 0H0
867-975-7700, Fax: 867-975-7742, environment@gov.nu.ca

Ontario
Advisory Council on Drinking Water Quality & Testing Standards, 40 St. Clair Ave. West, 9th Fl., Toronto, ON M4V 1M2
416-212-7779, Fax: 416-212-7595

Algonquin Forestry Authority - Huntsville, 222 Main St. West, Huntsville, ON P1H 1Y1
705-789-9647, Fax: 705-789-3353, info@algonquinforestry.on.ca

Algonquin Forestry Authority - Pembroke, Victoria Centre, 84 Isabella St., 2nd Fl., Pembroke, ON K8A 5S5
613-735-0173, Fax: 613-735-4192, info@algonquinforestry.on.ca

Bail Verification & Supervision Program, Atrium on Bay, 595 Bay St., 8th Fl., Toronto, ON M5G 2M6
416-314-2507

Cancer Care Ontario, 620 University Ave., 15th Fl., Toronto, ON M5G 2L7
416-971-9800, Fax: 416-971-6888

Council of the Association of Ontario Land Surveyors, 1043 McNicoll Ave., Toronto, ON M1W 3W6
416-491-9020, Fax: 416-491-2576, 800-268-0718

Environmental Commissioner of Ontario, #605, 1075 Bay St., Toronto, ON M5S 2B1
416-325-3377, Fax: 416-325-3370, 800-701-6454, commissioner@eco.on.ca

Environmental Sciences & Standards Division, 135 St Clair Ave. West, 14th Fl., Toronto, ON M4V 1P5

Huronia Historical Parks, 16164 Hwy. 12, PO Box 160, Midland, ON L4R 4K8
705-526-7838, Fax: 705-526-9193

Lake of the Woods Control Board, c/o Executive Engineer, 373 Sussex Dr., Block E1, Ottawa, ON K1A 0H3
Fax: 888-702-9632, 800-661-5922, secretariat@lwcb.ca

Livestock Medicines Advisory Committee, Ontario Government Bldg NE, 1 Stone Rd. West, 3rd Fl., Guelph, ON N1G 4Y2
519-826-4110, Fax: 519-826-3254, ag.info.omafra@ontario.ca

Mines & Minerals Division, Willet Green Miller Centre, 933 Ramsey Lake Rd., Level B6, Sudbury, ON P3E 6B5
705-670-5755, Fax: 705-670-5818, 888-415-9845

Niagara Escarpment Commission, 232 Guelph St., Georgetown, ON L7G 4B1
905-877-5191, Fax: 905-873-7452

Niagara Parks Commission, Oak Hall Administration Bldg., 7400 Portage Rd. South, PO Box 150, Niagara Falls, ON L2E 6T2
905-356-2241, Fax: 905-354-6041, 877-642-7275

Ontario Clean Water Agency, 1 Yonge St., 17th Fl., Toronto, ON M5E 1E5
416-314-5600, Fax: 416-314-8300, 800-667-6292, ocwa@ocwa.com

Ontario Fish & Wildlife Heritage Commission, Robinson Pl., 300 Water St., 5th Fl., PO Box 7000, Peterborough, ON K9J 8M5
705-755-1905, Fax: 705-755-1900

Ontario Geographic Names Board, Robinson Place, 300 Water St., PO Box 7000, Peterborough, ON K9J 8M5
705-755-2134

Ontario Ministry of Agriculture, Food & Rural Affairs, Ontario Government Bldg., 1 Stone Rd. West, Guelph, ON N1G 4Y2
519-826-3100, Fax: 519-826-4335, 888-466-2372, about.omafra@ontario.ca

Ontario Ministry of Environment, Conservation & Parks, Ferguson Block, 77 Wellesley St. West, 11th Fl., Toronto, ON M7A 2T5
416-325-4000, Fax: 416-314-6713, 800-565-4923
Ontario Ministry of Northern Development, Mines, Natural Resources & Forestry, Natural Resources Information & Support Centre, 300 Water St., Toronto, ON K9J 8M5
800-667-1940
Ontario Science Centre, 770 Don Mills Rd., Toronto, ON M3C 1T3
416-696-1000, Fax: 416-696-3166, 888-696-1110
Pesticides Advisory Committee, Foster Bldg, 40 St. Clair Ave. West, 7th Fl., Toronto, ON M4V 1M2
416-314-9230, Fax: 416-314-9237
Policy Division, Ontario Government Bldg, 1 Stone Rd. West, 2nd Fl., Guelph, ON N1G 4Y2
519-826-4020, Fax: 519-826-3492
Rabies Advisory Committee, Trent University Science Complex, 2140 East Bank Dr., PO Box 4840, Peterborough, ON K9J 8N8
705-755-2270
Royal Botanical Gardens, 680 Plains Rd. West, Burlington, ON L7T 4H4
905-527-1158, Fax: 905-577-0375, 800-694-4769, info@rbg.ca
Safety, Licensing Appeals & Standards Tribunals Ontario, #401, 20 Dundas St. West, 4th Fl., Toronto, ON M5T 2Z5
Fax: 416-327-6379, 844-242-0608, slastoinfo@ontario.ca
Science North, 100 Ramsey Lake Rd., Sudbury, ON P3E 5S9
705-522-3701, Fax: 705-522-4954, 800-461-4898, contactus@sciencenorth.ca
Shibogama Interim Planning Board, PO Box 105, Wunnumin, ON P0V 2Z0
807-442-2559, Fax: 807-442-2627
St. Lawrence Parks Commission, 13740 County Rd. 2, Morrisburg, ON K0C 1X0
613-543-3704, Fax: 613-543-2847, 800-437-2233, getaway@parks.on.ca
Windigo Interim Planning Board, PO Box 299, Sioux Lookout, ON P8T 1A3
807-737-1585, Fax: 807-737-3133

Prince Edward Island
Agricultural Insurance Corporation, 7 Gerald McCarville Drive, Kensington, PE C0B 1M0
Grain Elevators Corporation, 62 Victoria St., PO Box 250, Kensington, PE C0B 1M0
902-836-8935, Fax: 902-836-8926
Prince Edward Island Department of Agriculture & Land, Jones Bldg., 11 Kent St., 5th Fl., PO Box 2000, Charlottetown, PE C1A 7N8
902-368-4880, Fax: 902-368-4857
Prince Edward Island Energy Corporation, Sullivan Bldg., 16 Fitzroy St., PO Box 2000, Charlottetown, PE C1A 7N8

Quebec
Bureau d'audiences publiques sur l'environnement, Édifice Lomer-Gouin, #2.10, 575, rue Jacques-Parizeau, Québec, QC G1R 6A6
418-643-7447, Fax: 418-643-9474, 800-463-4732, communication@bape.gouv.qc.ca
Comité consultatif de l'environnement Kativik, CP 930, Kuujjuaq, QC J0M 1C0
819-964-2961, Fax: 819-964-0694, keac-ccek@krg.ca
Fondation de la faune du Québec, #420, 1175, av Lavigerie, Québec, QC G1V 4P1
418-644-7926, Fax: 418-643-7655, 877-639-0742, ffq@fondationdelafaune.qc.ca
Ministère de l'Agriculture, des Pêcheries et de l'Alimentation du Québec, 200, ch Sainte-Foy, Québec, QC G1R 4X6
418-380-2110, 888-222-6272
Ministère des Énergie et des Ressources naturelles, Service à la clientèle, 5700, 4e av ouest, #A301, Québec, QC G1H 6R1
866-248-6936, services.clientele@mern.gouv.qc.ca
Ottawa River Regulation Planning Board, 351 St. Joseph Blvd, Hull, QC J8Y 3Z5
613-997-1735, 800-778-1246, secretariat@ottawariver.ca
Régie de l'énergie, Tour de la Bourse, #2.55, 800, Place Victoria, Montréal, QC H4Z 1A2
514-873-2452, Fax: 514-873-2070, 888-873-2452, secretariat@regie-energie.qc.ca
Société de développement de la Baie James, #10, 462, 3e rue, Chibougamau, QC G8P 1N7
418-748-7777, Fax: 418-748-6868, chi@sdbj.gouv.qc.ca

Saskatchewan
Agri-Food Council, #315, 3085 Albert St., Regina, SK S4S 0B1
Fax: 306-787-8599
Agricultural Implements Board, #302, 3085 Albert St., Regina, SK S4S 0B1
Fax: 306-787-8599
Health Quality Council, Atrium Bldg., Innovation Place, 241, 111 Research Dr., Saskatoon, SK S7N 3R2
306-668-8810, Fax: 306-668-8820, info@hqc.sk.ca

Prairie Agricultural Machinery Institute, 2215 - 8th Ave., PO Box 1150, Humboldt, SK S0K 2A0
306-682-5033, Fax: 306-682-5080, 800-567-7264, pami@pami.ca
Saskatchewan Agriculture, Walter Scott Bldg., 3085 Albert St., Regina, SK S4S 0B1
866-457-2377
Saskatchewan Conservation Data Centre, Fish & Wildlife Branch, Ministry of Environment, 3211 Albert St., Regina, SK S4S 5W6
306-787-7196, Fax: 306-787-9544
Saskatchewan Crop Insurance Corporation, 484 Prince William Dr., PO Box 3000, Melville, SK S0A 2P0
306-728-7200, Fax: 306-728-7202, 888-935-0000, customer.service@scic.gov.sk.ca
Saskatchewan Environment, 3211 Albert St., Regina, SK S4S 5W6
306-787-2584, Fax: 306-787-9544, 800-567-4224, centre.inquiry@gov.sk.ca
Saskatchewan Research Council, #125, 15 Innovation Blvd., Saskatoon, SK S7N 2X8
306-933-5400, Fax: 306-933-7446
Saskatchewan Science Centre, 2903 Powerhouse Dr., Regina, SK S4N 0A1
306-791-7914, 800-667-6300, info@sasksciencecentre.com
Saskatchewan Sheep Development Board, 2213C Hanselman Crt., Saskatoon, SK S7L 6A8
306-933-5200, Fax: 306-933-7182, sheepdb@sasktel.net
Surface Rights Board of Arbitration, #102, 113 - 2nd Ave. East, PO Box 1597, Kindersley, SK S0L 1S0
306-463-5447, Fax: 306-463-5449, surfacerightsboard@gov.sk.ca

Yukon Territory
Alsek Renewable Resources Council, PO Box 2077, Haines Junction, YT Y0B 1L0
867-634-2524, Fax: 867-634-2527, admin@alsekrrc.ca
Carmacks Renewable Resource Council, PO Box 122, Carmacks, YT Y0B 1C0
867-863-6838, Fax: 867-863-6429, carmacksrrc@northwestel.net
Dawson District Renewable Resource Council, PO Box 1380, Dawson City, YT Y0B 1G0
867-993-6976, Fax: 867-993-6093, dawsonrrc@northwestel.net
Mayo District Renewable Resources Council, PO Box 249, Mayo, YT Y0B 1M0
867-996-2942, Fax: 867-996-2948, mayorrc@northwestel.net
Selkirk Renewable Resources Council, PO Box 32, Pelly Crossing, YT Y0B 1P0
867-537-3937, Fax: 867-537-3938, selkirkrrc@northwestel.net
Teslin Renewable Resource Council, PO Box 186, Teslin, YT Y0A 1B0
867-390-2323, Fax: 867-390-2919, teslinrrc@northwestel.net
Yukon Development Corporation, #234, 2180 - 2nd Ave., Whitehorse, YT Y1A 5N6
867-456-3995, ydc-admin@yukon.ca
Yukon Environment, 10 Burns Rd., Whitehorse, YT Y1A 2C6
867-667-5652, Fax: 867-393-7197, environmentyukon@yukon.ca
Yukon Fish & Wildlife Management Board, 409 Black St., 2nd Fl., PO Box 31104, Whitehorse, YT Y1A 5P7
867-667-3754, Fax: 867-393-6947, officemanager@yfwmb.ca

SCIENCE & TECHNOLOGY
See Also: Business Development
Aerospace Manufacturing Technologies Centre, Campus Université de Montréal, 5145, av Decelles, Montréal, QC H3T 2B2
Atomic Energy of Canada Limited, Head Office, Chalk River Laboratories, 286 Plant Rd., Chalk River, ON K0J 1J0
888-220-2465, communications@aecl.ca
Bedford Institute of Oceanography, PO Box 1006, Dartmouth, NS B2Y 4A2
902-426-2373, Fax: 902-426-8484, webmasterbio-iob@dfo-mpo.gc.ca
Canada Centre for Mapping & Earth Observation, #212, 50, Place de la Cité, PO Box 162, Sherbrooke, QC J1H 4G9
Canada Foundation for Innovation, #1100, 55 Metcalfe St., Ottawa, ON K1P 6L5
613-947-6496, Fax: 613-943-0923, feedback@innovation.ca
Canada Science & Technology Museum Corporation, PO Box 9724 T, Ottawa, ON K1G 5A3
613-991-3044, Fax: 613-993-7923, 866-442-4416, cts@techno-science.ca
Canadian Centre for Housing Technology, c/o National Research Council Canada, Building M-20, 1200 Montreal Rd., Ottawa, ON K1A 0R6
Canadian Food Inspection Agency, 1400 Merivale Rd., Ottawa, ON K1A 0Y9
613-225-2342, 800-442-2342

Canadian Institutes of Health Research, 160 Elgin St., 10th Fl., Ottawa, ON K1A 0W9
613-954-1968, Fax: 613-954-1800, 888-603-4178, support@cihr-irsc.gc.ca
Canadian Nuclear Laboratories, Head Office, Chalk River Laboratories, 286 Plant Rd., Chalk River, ON K0J 1J0
866-513-2325, communications@cnl.ca
Canadian Photonics Fabrication Centre, c/o National Research Council Canada, Building M-50, 1200 Montreal Rd., Ottawa, ON K1A 0R6
613-993-9101
Canadian Space Agency, John H. Chapman Space Centre, 6767, rte de l'Aéroport, Saint-Hubert, QC J3Y 8Y9
450-926-4800, Fax: 450-926-4352, asc.info.csa@canada.ca
CanmetMINING, 555 Booth St., Ottawa, ON K1A 0G1
Fax: 613-947-6606
Cultus Lake Salmon Research Lab, 4222 Columbia Valley Hwy., Cultus Lake, BC V2R 5B6
Freshwater Institute, 501 University Cres., Winnipeg, MB R3T 2N6
Hydraulics Laboratories, c/o National Research Council, 1200 Montreal Rd., Ottawa, ON K1A 0R6
Institut Maurice-Lamontagne, 850, rte de le Mer, CP 1000, Mont-Joli, QC G5H 3Z4
418-775-0500, Fax: 418-775-0730
Institute of Ocean Sciences, 9860 West Saanich Rd., PO Box 6000, Sidney, BC V8L 4B2
250-363-6517
International Development Research Centre, 150 Kent St., PO Box 8500, Ottawa, ON K1G 3H9
613-236-6163, Fax: 613-238-7230, info@idrc.ca
National Research Council Canada, Building M-58, 1200 Montreal Rd., Ottawa, ON K1A 0R6
613-993-9101, Fax: 613-991-9096, 877-672-2672, info@nrc-cnrc.ca
National Research Council Canada - National Science Library, Bldg. M-55, 1200 Montreal Rd., Ottawa, ON K1A 0R6
613-993-9101, 800-668-1222
Natural Sciences & Engineering Research Council of Canada, 350 Albert St., 16th Fl., Ottawa, ON K1A 1H5
613-995-4273, Fax: 613-992-5337, 855-275-2861
Networks of Centres of Excellence of Canada, 350 Albert Street, 16th Fl., Ottawa, ON K1A 1H5
613-995-6010, Fax: 613-992-7356, info@nce-rce.gc.ca
Pacific Biological Station, 3190 Hammond Bay Rd., Nanaimo, BC V9T 6N7
250-756-7000, Fax: 250-756-7053
Science, Technology & Innovation Council, 235 Queen St., 9th Fl., Ottawa, ON K1A 0H5
343-291-2362, Fax: 613-952-0459, info@stic-csti.ca
Sea Lamprey Control Centre, 1219 Queen St. East, Sault Ste Marie, ON P6A 2E5
Spectrum, Information Technologies & Telecommunications, Journal Tower North, 300 Slater St., 20th Fl., Ottawa, ON K1A 0C8
613-998-0368, Fax: 613-952-1203
St. Andrews Biological Station, 531 Brandy Cove Rd., St Andrews, NB E5B 2L9
506-529-8854, Fax: 506-529-5862, xmarsabs@mar.dfo-mpo.gc.ca

Alberta
Alberta Innovates, 250 Karl Clark Rd., Edmonton, AB T6N 1E4
877-423-5727, info@albertainnovates.ca

British Columbia
British Columbia Innovation Council, 1188 West Georgia St., 9th Fl., Vancouver, BC V6E 4A2
604-683-2724, Fax: 604-683-6567, 800-665-7222, info@bcic.ca
Powertech Labs Inc., 12388 - 88 Ave., Surrey, BC V8W 7R7
604-590-7500, Fax: 604-590-6611
Premier's Technology Council, #1600, 800 Robson St., Vancouver, BC V6Z 3E7
604-827-4629, premiers.technologycouncil@gov.bc.ca

Manitoba
Industrial Technology Centre, #200, 78 Innovation Dr., Winnipeg, MB R3T 6C2
204-480-3333, Fax: 204-480-0345, 800-728-7933, tech@itc.mb.ca
Manitoba Education, Research & Learning Information Networks, University of Manitoba, #100, 135 Innovation Dr., Winnipeg, MB R3T 6A8
204-474-7800, Fax: 204-474-7830, 800-430-6404
Mineral Resources Division, The Paris Bldg., 259 Portage Ave., 9th Fl., Winnipeg, MB R3B 3P4
204-945-6569, 800-223-5215, minesinfo@gov.mb.ca

New Brunswick
New Brunswick Research & Productivity Council, 921 College Hill Rd., Fredericton, NB E3B 6Z9
506-452-1212, Fax: 506-452-1395, 800-563-0844, info@rpc.ca

Northwest Territories
Aurora Research Institute, 191 MacKenzie Rd., PO Box 1450, Inuvik, NT X0E 0T0
867-777-3298, Fax: 867-777-4264
Nova Scotia
Innovacorp, #400, 1871 Hollis St., Halifax, NS B3J 0C3
902-424-8670, Fax: 902-424-4679, 800-565-7051, info@innovacorp.ca
Ontario
Environmental Sciences & Standards Division, 135 St Clair Ave. West, 14th Fl., Toronto, ON M4V 1P5
Ontario Science Centre, 770 Don Mills Rd., Toronto, ON M3C 1T3
416-696-1000, Fax: 416-696-3166, 888-696-1110
Science North, 100 Ramsey Lake Rd., Sudbury, ON P3E 5S9
705-522-3701, Fax: 705-522-4954, 800-461-4898, contactus@sciencenorth.ca
Quebec
Centre de recherche industrielle du Québec, 333, rue Franquet, Québec, QC G1P 4C7
418-659-1550, Fax: 418-652-2251, 800-667-2386, infocriq@criq.qc.ca
Commission de l'éthique en science et en technologie, #555, 888, rue Saint-Jean, Québec, QC G1R 5H6
418-691-5989, Fax: 418-646-0920, ethique@ethique.gouv.qc.ca
Ministère de l'Économie et de l'Innovation, 710, Place D'Youville, 3e étage, Québec, QC G1R 4Y4
418-691-5950, Fax: 418-644-0118, 866-680-1884
Saskatchewan
Prairie Agricultural Machinery Institute, 2215 - 8th Ave., PO Box 1150, Humboldt, SK S0K 2A0
306-682-5033, Fax: 306-682-5080, 800-567-7264, pami@pami.ca
Saskatchewan Opportunities Corporation, Innovation Place, #114, 15 Innovation Blvd., Saskatoon, SK S7N 2X8
306-933-6295, Fax: 306-933-8215, saskatoon@innovationplace.com
Saskatchewan Research Council, #125, 15 Innovation Blvd., Saskatoon, SK S7N 2X8
306-933-5400, Fax: 306-933-7446
Saskatchewan Science Centre, 2903 Powerhouse Dr., Regina, SK S4N 0A1
306-791-7914, 800-667-6300, info@sasksciencecentre.com
Yukon Territory
Yukon Energy, Mines & Resources, PO Box 2703, Whitehorse, YT Y1A 2C6
867-667-3123, Fax: 867-393-7421, 800-661-0408, emr@yukon.ca

SECURITIES ADMINISTRATION
See Also: Finance
Alberta
Alberta Securities Commission, #600, 250 - 5th St. SW, Calgary, AB T2P 0R4
403-297-6454, Fax: 403-297-6156, 877-355-0585, inquiries@asc.ca
British Columbia
British Columbia Securities Commission, Pacific Centre, 701 West Georgia St., 12th Fl., PO Box 10142, Vancouver, BC V7Y 1L2
604-899-6500, Fax: 604-899-6506, 800-373-6393, inquiries@bcsc.bc.ca
Manitoba
Manitoba Securities Commission, #500, 400 St. Mary Ave., Winnipeg, MB R3C 4K5
204-945-2548, Fax: 204-945-0330, securities@gov.mb.ca
New Brunswick
Financial & Consumer Services Commission, #300, 85 Charlotte St., Saint John, NB E2L 2J2
506-658-3060, Fax: 506-658-3059, 866-933-2222, info@fcnb.ca
Northwest Territories
Northwest Territories Department of Justice, 4903 - 49th St., PO Box 1320, Yellowknife, NT X1A 2L9
867-767-9256, justice_communications@gov.nt.ca
Nova Scotia
Nova Scotia Securities Commission, PO Box 458, Halifax, NS B3J 2P8
902-424-7768, Fax: 902-424-4625, 855-424-2499, NSSCinquiries@novascotia.ca
Ontario
Ontario Securities Commission, 20 Queen St. West, 20th Fl., PO Box 55, Toronto, ON M5H 3S8
416-593-8314, Fax: 416-593-8122, 877-785-1555, inquiries@osc.on.ca
Quebec
Autorité des marchés financiers, Tour de la Bourse, 800, rue du Square-Victoria, 22e étage, CP 246, Montréal, QC H4Z 1G3
514-395-0337, Fax: 514-873-3090, 877-525-0337

Saskatchewan
Financial & Consumer Affairs Authority, #601, 1919 Saskatchewan Dr., Regina, SK S4P 4H2
306-787-5645, Fax: 306-787-5899, 877-880-5550, consumerprotection@gov.sk.ca

SENIOR CITIZENS SERVICES
National Seniors Council, Phase IV, 8th Floor, Mail Stop 802, 140, promenade du Portage, Gatineau, QC K1A 0J9
Fax: 819-953-9298, 800-622-6232
Social Security Tribunal, PO Box 9812 T, Ottawa, ON K1G 6S3
613-952-8805, 877-227-8577, info.sst-tss@canada.gc.ca
Veterans Affairs Canada, 161 Grafton St., PO Box 7700, Charlottetown, PE C1A 8M9
613-996-2242, 866-522-2122, information@vac-acc.gc.ca
Alberta
Alberta Health, PO Box 1360 Main, Edmonton, AB T5J 2N3
780-427-7164
Alberta Health Advocates, 106th St. Tower, 10055 - 106th St., 9th Fl., Edmonton, AB T5J 2Y2
780-422-1812, Fax: 780-422-0695, -310-0000, info@albertahealthadvocates.ca
Alberta Seniors & Housing, PO Box 3100, Edmonton, AB T5J 4W3
780-644-9992, Fax: 780-422-5954, 877-644-9992
Office of the Seniors Advocate, Centre West Bldg., 10155 - 102nd St., 6th Fl., Edmonton, AB T5J 4G8
780-644-0682, Fax: 780-644-9685, 844-644-0682, seniors.advocate@gov.ab.ca
Seniors Advisory Council for Alberta, Standard Life Centre, #600, 10405 Jasper Ave., 6th Fl., Edmonton, AB T5J 4R7
780-422-2321, Fax: 780-422-8762, -310-0000, saca@gov.ab.ca
British Columbia
Office of the Seniors Advocate, PO Box 9651 Prov Govt, Victoria, BC V8W 9P4
250-952-3034, 877-952-3181, info@seniorsadvocatebc.ca
Manitoba
Manitoba Health & Seniors Care, #100, 300 Carlton St., Winnipeg, MB R3B 3M9
204-945-3744, 866-626-4862, mgi@gov.mb.ca
Seniors & Healthy Aging Secretariat, #1610, 155 Carlton St., Winnipeg, MB R3C 3H8
204-945-6565, Fax: 204-948-2514, 800-665-6565, seniors@gov.mb.ca
Newfoundland & Labrador
Ministerial Council on Aging & Seniors, c/o Department of Seniors, Wellness & Social Development, PO Box 8700, St. John's, NL A1B 4J6
Newfoundland & Labrador Department of Children, Seniors & Social Development, PO Box 8700, St. John's, NL A1B 4J6
709-729-0760, Fax: 709-729-0870, CSSDInfo@gov.nl.ca
Nova Scotia
Nova Scotia Department of Seniors, 1741 Brunswick St., 2nd Fl., Halifax, NS B3J 3X8
902-424-0770, Fax: 902-424-0561, 844-277-0770, seniors@novascotia.ca
Nunavut
Nunavut Territory Department of Culture & Heritage, PO Box 1000 800, Iqaluit, NU X0A 0H0
867-975-5500, Fax: 867-975-5504, 866-934-2035
Ontario
Ontario Ministry of Long-Term Care, 400 University Ave., 6th Fl., Toronto, ON M7A 1N3
416-327-4327, Fax: 416-327-8497, 800-268-1153
Ontario Ministry of Seniors & Accessibility, College Park, 777 Bay St., Toronto, ON M7A 1S5
416-326-7076, Fax: 416-326-7078, 888-910-1999, infoseniors@ontario.ca
Quebec
Ministère de la Famille, Service des renseignements, 600, rue Fullum, 6e étage, Montréal, QC H2K 4S7
855-336-8568
Ministère de la Santé et des Services sociaux, Direction des communications, 1075, ch Sainte-Foy, 15e étage, Québec, QC G1S 2M1
418-644-4545, 877-644-4545
Yukon Territory
Yukon Health & Social Services, PO Box 2703, Whitehorse, YT Y1A 2C6
867-667-3673, Fax: 867-667-3096, 800-661-0408, hss@yukon.ca

SOCIAL AFFAIRS
Alberta
Social Care Facilities Review Committee, Sterling Place, 9940 - 106 St., 6th Fl., Edmonton, AB T5K 2N2
780-638-1249, Fax: 780-415-5841, -310-0000

Newfoundland & Labrador
Office of Indigenous Affairs & Reconciliation, East Block, Confederation Bldg., 6th Fl., PO Box 8700, St. John's, NL A1B 4J6
709-729-4776, Fax: 709-729-4900

SOCIAL SERVICES
See Also: Community Services
Service Canada, 140, promenade du Portage, Gatineau, QC K1A 0J9
800-622-6232
Alberta
Alberta Community & Social Services, Office of the Minister, Legislature Bldg., #224, 10800 - 97th Ave., Edmonton, AB T5K 2B6
780-644-9992, 877-644-9992
Appeals Secretariat, Agronomy Centre, #201, 6903 - 116 St., Edmonton, AB T6H 5Z2
780-427-2709, Fax: 780-422-1088, -310-0000, CSS.Appeals@gov.ab.ca
Social Care Facilities Review Committee, Sterling Place, 9940 - 106 St., 6th Fl., Edmonton, AB T5K 2N2
780-638-1249, Fax: 780-415-5841, -310-0000
British Columbia
British Columbia College of Social Workers, #1430, 1200 West 73 Ave., Vancouver, BC V6P 6G5
604-737-4916, Fax: 604-737-6809, 877-576-6740, info@bccsw.ca
British Columbia Ministry of Tourism, Arts, Culture & Sport, PO Box 9082 Prov Govt, Victoria, BC V8W 9E2
New Brunswick
Economic & Social Inclusion Corporation, Kings Place, #423, 440 King St., 4th Fl., PO Box 6000, Fredericton, NB E3B 5H1
506-444-2977, Fax: 506-444-2978, 888-295-4545, esic-sies@gnb.ca
New Brunswick Department of Social Development, Sartain MacDonald Bldg., PO Box 6000, Fredericton, NB E3B 5H1
506-453-2001, Fax: 506-453-2164, sd-ds@gnb.ca
Newfoundland & Labrador
Newfoundland & Labrador Department of Immigration, Population Growth & Skills, West Block, Confederation Bldg., 3rd Fl., PO Box 8700, St. John's, NL A1B 4J6
709-729-1795, isl@gov.nl.ca
Office of Indigenous Affairs & Reconciliation, East Block, Confederation Bldg., 6th Fl., PO Box 8700, St. John's, NL A1B 4J6
709-729-4776, Fax: 709-729-4900
Northwest Territories
Northwest Territories Department of Health & Social Services, PO Box 1320, Yellowknife, NT X1A 2L9
Nova Scotia
Housing Nova Scotia, Maritime Centre, 1505 Barrington St., 14th Fl., Halifax, NS B3J 3K5
844-424-5110, housingns@novascotia.ca
Nunavut
Nunavut Territory Department of Family Services, PO Box 1000 1200, Iqaluit, NU X0A 0H0
867-975-5200, Fax: 867-975-5722
Nunavut Territory Department of Health, PO Box 1000 1000, Iqaluit, NU X0A 0H0
867-975-5700, Fax: 867-975-5705, 800-661-0833
Ontario
Social Assistance Programs Division, 2 Bloor St. West, 25th Fl., Toronto, ON M7A 1E9
Quebec
Comité consultatif de lutte contre la pauvreté et l'exclusion sociale, 425, rue Jacques-Parizeau, RC 145, Québec, QC G1R 4Z1
418-528-9866, Fax: 418-643-6623, infocclp@mess.gouv.qc.ca
Conseil de gestion de l'assurance parentale, #104, 1122, Grande Allée ouest, Québec, QC G1S 1E5
418-643-1009, Fax: 418-643-6738, 888-610-7727
Ministère de la Santé et des Services sociaux, Direction des communications, 1075, ch Sainte-Foy, 15e étage, Québec, QC G1S 2M1
418-644-4545, 877-644-4545
Saskatchewan
Saskatchewan Social Services, 1920 Broad St., Regina, SK S4P 3V6
306-787-3800, socialservicesinquiry@gov.sk.ca

SOIL RESOURCES
St. John's Research & Development Centre, Bldg. 25, 308 Brookfield Rd., St. John's, NL A1E 0B2
709-793-3186, aafc.st-johnsrdc@agr.gc.ca
Nova Scotia
Nova Scotia Department of Agriculture, 1800 Argyle St., 6th Fl., Halifax, NS B3J 3N8
902-424-4560, Fax: 902-424-4671, 800-279-0825

Quebec
Commission de protection du territoire agricole du Québec, 200, ch Ste-Foy, 2e étage, Québec, QC G1R 4X6
418-643-3314, Fax: 418-643-2261, 800-667-5294, info@cptaq.gouv.qc.ca

SOLICITORS GENERAL

Alberta
Alberta Justice & Solicitor General, John E. Brownlee Bldg., 10365 - 97th St., 9th Fl., Edmonton, AB T5J 3W7
780-427-2745

Newfoundland & Labrador
Newfoundland & Labrador Department of Justice & Public Safety, East Block, Confederation Bldg., 4th Fl., PO Box 8700, St. John's, NL A1B 4J6
709-729-2869, Fax: 709-729-0469, justice@gov.nl.ca

Nova Scotia
Nova Scotia Department of Justice, 1690 Hollis St., PO Box 7, Halifax, NS B3J 2L6
902-424-4030, justweb@gov.ns.ca

Ontario
Ontario Solicitor General, George Drew Bldg., 25 Grosvenor St., 18th Fl., Toronto, ON M7A 1Y6
416-326-5000, Fax: 416-325-6067, 866-517-0571, mcscs.feedback@ontario.ca

Quebec
Ministère de la Sécurité publique, Tour des Laurentides, 2525, boul Laurier, 5e étage, Québec, QC G1V 2L2
418-643-2112, Fax: 418-646-6168, 800-361-3795

Yukon Territory
Yukon Justice, Andrew Philipsen Law Centre, 2134 - 2nd Ave., PO Box 2703, Whitehorse, YT Y1A 2C6
867-667-3033, Fax: 867-667-5200, justice@yukon.ca

SPACE & ASTRONOMY

Canada Science & Technology Museum Corporation, PO Box 9724 T, Ottawa, ON K1G 5A3
613-991-3044, Fax: 613-993-7923, 866-442-4416, cts@techno-science.ca
Canadian Space Agency, John H. Chapman Space Centre, 6767, rte de l'Aéroport, Saint-Hubert, QC J3Y 8Y9
450-926-4800, Fax: 450-926-4352, asc.info.csa@canada.ca

SPORTS

See Also: Recreation
Alberta
Alberta Sport Connection, HSBC Bldg., #500, 10055 - 106 St., Edmonton, AB T5J 1G3
780-415-1167, Fax: 780-415-0308, -310-0000

British Columbia
Arts, Culture, & Sport Division, PO Box 9490 Prov Govt, Victoria, BC V8W 9N7
250-356-6914, Fax: 250-387-7973
British Columbia Ministry of Tourism, Arts, Culture & Sport, PO Box 9082 Prov Govt, Victoria, BC V8W 9E2

Manitoba
Manitoba Sport, Culture & Heritage, Legislative Bldg., #118, 450 Broadway, Winnipeg, MB R3C 0V8

New Brunswick
New Brunswick Department of Tourism, Heritage & Culture, Marysville Place, 4th Fl., PO Box 6000, Fredericton, NB E3B 5H1
506-453-3115, Fax: 506-444-5760, thctpcinfo@gnb.ca

Newfoundland & Labrador
Marble Mountain Development Corporation, PO Box 947, Corner Brook, NL A2H 6J2
709-637-7601, Fax: 709-634-1702, 888-462-7253, admin@skimarble.com
Newfoundland & Labrador Department of Children, Seniors & Social Development, PO Box 8700, St. John's, NL A1B 4J6
709-729-0760, Fax: 709-729-0870, CSSDInfo@gov.nl.ca

Ontario
Ontario Ministry of Heritage, Sport, Tourism & Culture Industries, 438 University Ave., 6th Fl., Toronto, ON M5G 2K8
416-326-9326, Fax: 416-314-7854, 888-997-9015

Prince Edward Island
Prince Edward Island School Athletic Association, #101, 250 Water St., Summerside, PE C1N 1B6
902-438-4846, info@peisaa.pe.ca
Prince Edward Island Sports Hall of Fame & Museum, Inc. Board, 40 Enman Cres., Charlottetown, PE C1E 1E6
902-393-5474, peisportshall@gmail.com

Quebec
Ministère de l'Éducation et de l'Enseignement supérieur, 1035, rue de la Chevrotière, 28e étage, Québec, QC G1R 5A5
418-643-7095, Fax: 418-646-6561, 866-747-6626
Régie des installations olympiques/Parc olympique Québec, 4141, av Pierre-De Coubertin, Montréal, QC H1V 3N7
514-252-4141, 877-997-0919, rio@rio.gouv.qc.ca

Saskatchewan
Saskatchewan Parks, Culture & Sport, 3211 Albert St., 1st Fl., Regina, SK S4S 5W6
306-787-5729, Fax: 306-798-0033, pcs.info@gov.sk.ca

STANDARDS

Standards Council of Canada, #600, 55 Metcalfe St., Ottawa, ON K1P 6L5
613-238-3222, Fax: 613-569-7808, info@scc.ca

STATISTICS

See Also: Vital Statistics
Statistics Canada, 150 Tunney's Pasture Driveway, Ottawa, ON K1A 0T6
514-283-8300, Fax: 514-283-9350, 800-263-1136, STATCAN.infostats-infostats.STATCAN@canada.ca

Manitoba
Manitoba Bureau of Statistics, #824, 155 Carlton St., Winnipeg, MB R3C 3H9
204-945-2406

Nunavut
Nunavut Territory Department of Executive & Intergovernmental Affairs, 1084 Aeroplex bldg., PO Box 1000 200, Iqaluit, NU X0A 0H0
867-975-6000, Fax: 867-975-6099

Prince Edward Island
Prince Edward Island Department of Health & Wellness, Shaw Bldg., 105 Rochford St. North, 4th Fl., Charlottetown, PE C1A 7N8
902-368-6414, Fax: 902-368-4121, DeptHW@gov.pe.ca

Quebec
Institut de la statistique du Québec, 200, ch Ste-Foy, 3e étage, Québec, QC G1R 5T4
418-691-2401, Fax: 418-643-4129, 800-463-4090

STUDENT AID

Northwest Territories
Student Financial Assistance Appeal Board, PO Box 1320, Yellowknife, NT X1A 2L9

Nunavut
Nunavut Territory Department of Education, Bldg. 1107, 2nd Fl., PO Box 1000 900, Iqaluit, NU X0A 0H0
867-975-5600, Fax: 867-975-5605, info.edu@gov.nu.ca

Ontario
Post-secondary Education Division, Mowat Block, 900 Bay St., 7th Fl., Toronto, ON M7A 1L2
416-325-2199, Fax: 416-326-3256

Quebec
Comité consultatif sur l'accessibilité financière aux études, 1035, rue de la Chevrotière, 20e étage, Québec, QC G1R 5A5
418-644-3468

Saskatchewan
Saskatchewan Education, 2220 College Ave., Regina, SK S4P 4V9
learning.inquiry@gov.sk.ca

SUSTAINABLE DEVELOPMENT

Canada Energy Regulator, #210, 517 - 10th Ave. SW, Calgary, AB T2R 0A8
403-292-4800, Fax: 403-292-5503, 800-899-1265
Commissioner of the Environment & Sustainable Development, 240 Sparks St., Ottawa, ON K1A 0G6
613-952-0213, Fax: 613-957-0474

Alberta
Alberta Energy, North Petroleum Plaza, 9945 - 108th St., Edmonton, AB T5K 2G6
780-427-8050, Fax: 780-422-9522

Manitoba
Manitoba Round Table for Sustainable Development, #160, 123 Main St., PO Box 70, Winnipeg, MB R3C 1A5
204-945-4391, Fax: 204-948-4730, mrtsd@gov.mb.ca

Quebec
Ministère de l'Environnement et de la Lutte contre les changements climatiques, Édifice Marie-Guyart, 675, boul René-Lévesque est, 30e étage, Québec, QC G1R 5V7
418-521-3830, Fax: 418-646-5974, 800-561-1616, relations.medias@mddelcc.gouv.qc.ca

Yukon Territory
Yukon Energy, Mines & Resources, PO Box 2703, Whitehorse, YT Y1A 2C6
867-667-3123, Fax: 867-393-7421, 800-661-0408, emr@yukon.ca

TAXATION

See Also: Sales Tax
Canada Revenue Agency, 875 Heron Rd., Ottawa, ON K1A 1A2
800-267-6999

First Nations Tax Commission, Head Office, #321, 345 Chief Alex Thomas Way, Kamloops, BC V2H 1H1
250-828-9857, Fax: 250-828-9858, 855-682-3682, mail@fntc.ca
Office of the Taxpayers' Ombudsman, #600, 150 Slater St., Ottawa, ON K1A 1K3
613-946-2310, Fax: 613-941-6319, 866-586-3839

Alberta
Financial Sector Regulation & Policy Division, Terrace Bldg., 9515 - 107th St., 4th Fl., Edmonton, AB T5K 2C3
780-427-8322

Manitoba
Taxation Division, #101, 401 York Ave., Winnipeg, MB R3C 0P8
204-945-5603, Fax: 204-945-0896, 800-782-0318

Nova Scotia
Provincial Tax Commission, PO Box 1003, Halifax, NS B3J 2X1
902-424-6538, Fax: 902-424-7434, taxcommission@novascotia.ca
Service Nova Scotia & Internal Services, PO Box 2734, Halifax, NS B3J 3K5
902-424-5200, Fax: 902-424-0720, 800-670-4357, askus@novascotia.ca

Saskatchewan
Board of Revenue Commissioners, #480, 2151 Scarth St., Regina, SK S4P 2H8
306-787-6221, Fax: 306-787-1610
Revenue Division, PO Box 200, Regina, SK S4P 2Z6
306-787-6645, Fax: 306-787-0776, 800-667-6102

TELECOMMUNICATIONS

See Also: Broadcasting
Canadian Broadcasting Corporation, 181 Queen St., PO Box 3220 C, Ottawa, ON K1Y 1E4
613-288-6000, liaison@cbc.ca
Canadian Radio-Television & Telecommunications Commission, Central Building, 1, promenade du Portage, Les Terrasses de la Chaudière, Gatineau, QC J8X 4B1
819-997-0313, Fax: 819-994-0218, 877-249-2782
Communications Research Centre Canada, 3701 Carling Ave., PO Box 11490 H, Ottawa, ON K2H 8S2
613-991-3313, Fax: 613-998-5355, info@crc.gc.ca
Shared Services Canada, 434 Queen St., PO Box 9808 T CSC, Ottawa, ON K1G 4A8
613-947-6296, 855-215-3656, information@ssc-spc.gc.ca
Spectrum, Information Technologies & Telecommunications, Journal Tower North, 300 Slater St., 20th Fl., Ottawa, ON K1A 0C8
613-998-0368, Fax: 613-952-1203

Quebec
Ministère de la Culture et Communications, 225, Grande Allée est, Québec, QC G1R 5G5
888-380-8882
Société de télédiffusion du Québec (Télé-Québec), 1000, rue Fullum, Montréal, QC H2K 3L7
514-521-2424, Fax: 514-864-1970, info@telequebec.tv

Saskatchewan
Saskatchewan Telecommunications (SaskTel), 2121 Saskatchewan Dr., Regina, SK S4P 3Y2
800-727-5835, corporate.comments@sasktel.sk.ca

TOURISM & TOURIST INFORMATION

Destination Canada, #800, 1045 Howe St., Vancouver, BC V6Z 2A9
604-638-8300
Old Port of Montréal Corporation Inc., 333, rue de la Commune ouest, Montréal, QC H2Y 2E2
514-283-5256, 800-971-7678
Parks Canada, National Office, 30, rue Victoria, Gatineau, QC J8X 0B3
819-420-9486, 888-773-8888, information@pc.gc.ca

Alberta
Alberta Culture & Status of Women, Communications Branch, Standard Life Centre, 10405 Jasper Ave., 7th Fl., Edmonton, AB T5J 4R7
780-427-6530, Fax: 780-427-1496, 800-232-7215, culture.communications@gov.ab.ca
Northern Alberta Development Council, Peace River Office, Provincial Building, #206, 9621 - 96 Ave., PO Box 900-14, Peace River, AB T8S 1T4
780-624-6274, Fax: 780-624-6184, -310-0000, nadc.council@gov.ab.ca
Travel Alberta, #400, 1601 - 9 Ave. SE, Calgary, AB T2G 0H4
403-648-1000, Fax: 403-648-1111, 800-252-3782, info@travelalberta.com

British Columbia
British Columbia Pavilion Corporation, #200, 999 Canada Place, Vancouver, BC V6C 3C1
604-482-2200, Fax: 604-681-9017, info@bcpavco.com

Destination British Columbia, 510 Burrard St., 12th Fl., Vancouver, BC V6C 3A8
604-660-2861, Fax: 604-660-3383, ContactTourism@DestinationBC.ca

Manitoba

Manitoba Sport, Culture & Heritage, Legislative Bldg., #118, 450 Broadway, Winnipeg, MB R3C 0V8
Tourism Secretariat, 213 Notre Dame Ave., 6th Fl., Winnipeg, MB R3B 1N3
204-945-0216, tourismsec@gov.mb.ca
Travel Manitoba, 21 Forks Market Rd., Winnipeg, MB R3C RT7
204-927-7800, 800-665-0040, contactus@travelmanitoba.com

New Brunswick

New Brunswick Department of Tourism, Heritage & Culture, Marysville Place, 4th Fl., PO Box 6000, Fredericton, NB E3B 5H1
506-453-3115, Fax: 506-444-5760, thctpcinfo@gnb.ca

Newfoundland & Labrador

Newfoundland & Labrador Department of Tourism, Culture, Arts & Recreation, PO Box 8700, St. John's, NL A1B 4J6
709-729-7000, tcar@gov.nl.ca

Northwest Territories

Northwest Territories Department of Industry, Tourism & Investment, PO Box 1320, Yellowknife, NT X1A 2L9

Nova Scotia

Tourism Nova Scotia, 8 Water St., PO Box 667, Windsor, NS B0N 2T0
902-798-6700, 800-565-0000, tnscommunications@novascotia.ca

Ontario

Business Transformation & Project Management Division, Hearst Block, 900 Bay St., 10th Fl., Toronto, ON M7A 2E2
Huronia Historical Parks, 16164 Hwy. 12, PO Box 160, Midland, ON L4R 4K8
705-526-7838, Fax: 705-526-9193
Ontario Ministry of Heritage, Sport, Tourism & Culture Industries, 438 University Ave., 6th Fl., Toronto, ON M5G 2K8
416-326-9326, Fax: 416-314-7854, 888-997-9015
Ontario Tourism Marketing Partnership Corporation, #900, 10 Dundas St. East, Toronto, ON M7A 2A1
416-212-0757, Fax: 416-325-6004, 800-668-2746

Prince Edward Island

Eastlink Centre Charlottetown, 46 Kensington Rd., Charlottetown, PE C1A 5H7
902-629-6600, Fax: 902-629-6650
Prince Edward Island Department of Economic Growth, Tourism & Culture, PO Box 2000, Charlottetown, PE C1A 7N8
902-368-5540, Fax: 902-368-5277, tpswitch@gov.pe.ca

Quebec

Commission de la capitale nationale du Québec, Edifice Hector-Fabre, 525, boul René-Lévesque est, RC, Québec, QC G1R 5S9
418-528-0773, Fax: 418-528-0833, 800-442-0773, commission@capitale.gouv.qc.ca
Institut de tourisme et d'hôtellerie du Québec, 3535, rue Saint-Denis, Montréal, QC H2X 3P1
514-282-5111, 800-282-5111, info@ithq.qc.ca
Ministère du Tourisme, #400, 900, boul René-Lévesque est, Québec, QC G1R 2B5
418-643-5959, Fax: 418-646-8723, 800-482-2433, relations.publiques@tourisme.gouv.qc.ca
Régie des installations olympiques/Parc olympique Québec, 4141, av Pierre-De Coubertin, Montréal, QC H1V 3N7
514-252-4141, 877-997-0919, rio@rio.gouv.qc.ca
Secrétariat à la Capitale-Nationale, 700, boul René-Lévesque est, 31e étage, Québec, QC G1R 5H1
418-528-8549, Fax: 418-528-8558
Société des établissements de plein air du Québec, Place de la Cité, Tour Cominar, #1300, 2640, boul Laurier, Québec, QC G1V 5C2
418-686-4875, Fax: 418-643-8177, 800-665-6527, inforeservation@sepaq.com
Société des établissements en plein air du Québec, Place de la Cité, Tour Cominar, #250, 2640, boul Laurier, 2e étage, Québec, QC G1V 5C2
418-686-4875, Fax: 418-643-8177, 800-665-6527, inforeservation@sepaq.com
Société du Centre des congrès de Québec, 900, boul René-Lévesque est, 2e étage, Québec, QC G1R 2B5
418-644-4000, Fax: 418-644-6455, 888-679-4000
Société du Palais des congrès de Montréal, 159, rue Saint-Antoine ouest, 9é étage, Montréal, QC H2Z 1H2
514-871-8122, Fax: 514-871-9389, 800-268-8122, info@congresmtl.com

Saskatchewan

Tourism Saskatchewan, #189, 1621 Albert St., Regina, SK S4P 2S5
306-787-9600, Fax: 306-787-6293, 877-237-2273, travel.info@tourismsask.com

Yukon Territory

Yukon Tourism & Culture, PO Box 2703, Whitehorse, YT Y1A 2C6
867-393-7048

TRADE

See Also: Business Development; Imports
Business Development Bank of Canada, #100, 5, Place Ville-Marie, Montréal, QC H3B 5E7
Fax: 877-329-9232, 877-232-2269
Canadian Commercial Corporation, #700, 350 Albert St., Ottawa, ON K1A 0S6
613-996-0034, Fax: 613-995-2121, 800-748-8191, info@ccc.ca
Canadian International Trade Tribunal, Standard Life Centre, 333 Laurier Ave. West, 15th Floor, Ottawa, ON K1A 0G7
613-990-2452, Fax: 613-990-2439, 855-307-2488, citt-tcce@tribunal.gc.ca
Canadian Trade Commissioner Service, TCS Enquiries Service, c/o Global Affairs Canada, 125 Sussex Dr., Ottawa, ON K1A 0G2
613-944-9991, Fax: 613-996-9709, 888-306-9991, trade@international.gc.ca
Commission for Environmental Cooperation, Secretariat, #200, 393, rue Saint-Jacques ouest, Montréal, QC H2Y 1N9
514-350-4300, Fax: 514-350-4314, info@cec.org
Export Development Canada, 150 Slater St., Ottawa, ON K1A 1K3
613-598-2500, Fax: 613-598-3811, 800-229-0575, support@edc.ca
Market & Industry Services Branch, Tower 5, 1341 Baseline Rd., Ottawa, ON K1A 0C5
613-759-1000, Fax: 613-773-1711

Alberta

Alberta Jobs, Economy & Innovation, Commerce Place, 10155 - 102nd St., 12th Fl., Edmonton, AB T5J 4G8

British Columbia

British Columbia Ministry of Social Development & Poverty Reduction, PO Box 9058 Prov Govt, Victoria, BC V8W 9E1
866-866-0800

Nova Scotia

Nova Scotia Department of Inclusive Economic Growth, CIBC Bldg., 1809 Barrington St., #M103, Halifax, NS B3J 3K8
902-424-0377, Fax: 902-424-0500
Nova Scotia Department of Intergovernmental Affairs, Duke Tower, 5251 Duke St., 5th Fl., PO Box 1617, Halifax, NS B3J 2Y3
902-424-5153, Fax: 902-424-0728

Quebec

Ministère des Finances, 12, rue Saint-Louis, Québec, QC G1R 5L3
418-528-9323, Fax: 418-646-1631, info@finances.gouv.qc.ca
Ministère des Relations internationales et Francophonie, Édifice Hector-Fabre, 525, boul Réne-Lévesque est, Québec, QC G1R 5R9
418-649-2300, Fax: 418-649-2656

Yukon Territory

Yukon Economic Development, 303 Alexander St., Whitehorse, YT Y1A 2L5
800-661-0408, ecdev@yukon.ca

TRADE-MARKS

See Also: Patents & Copyright
Canadian Intellectual Property Office, Place du Portage I, #C-229, 50, rue Victoria, Gatineau, QC K1A 0C9
819-997-1936, Fax: 819-953-2476, 866-997-1936, cipo.contact@ic.gc.ca

Prince Edward Island

Anne of Green Gables Licensing Authority Inc., 94 Euston St., PO Box 910, Charlottetown, PE C1A 7L9
902-368-5961

TRAINING

See Also: Apprenticeship Programs; Occupational Training

Alberta

Alberta Advanced Education, Legislature Bldg., #403, 10800 - 97th Ave., Edmonton, AB T5K 2B6
780-422-5400

Manitoba

Manitoba Advanced Education, Skills & Immigration, Legislative Bldg., #352, 450 Broadway, Winnipeg, MB R3C 0V8

TRANSPORTATION

Atlantic Pilotage Authority, TD Centre, #1801, 1791 Barrington St., Halifax, NS B3J 3K9
902-426-2550, Fax: 902-426-4004, 877-272-3477, dispatch@atlanticpilotage.com

Automotive & Surface Transportation Facilities, Ottawa Uplands Research Facilities, 2320 Lester Rd., Ottawa, ON K1V 1S2
613-998-9639
Canadian Air Transport Security Authority, 99 Bank St., 13th Fl., Ottawa, ON K1P 6B9
Fax: 613-990-1295, 888-294-2202, correspondence1@catsa-acsta.gc.ca
Canadian Coast Guard, Centennial Towers, #6S018, 200 Kent St., Ottawa, ON K1A 0E6
613-993-0999, Fax: 613-990-1866, info@dfo-mpo.gc.ca
Canadian Transportation Agency, Les Terrasses de la Chaudière, 15, rue Eddy, Gatineau, QC J8X 4B3
Fax: 819-997-6727, 888-222-2592, info@otc-cta.gc.ca
Federal Bridge Corporation Limited, #1210, 55 Metcalfe St., Ottawa, ON K1P 6L5
613-998-8427, Fax: 613-993-6945, info@federalbridge.ca
Great Lakes Pilotage Authority, 202 Pitt St., 2nd fl., PO Box 95, Cornwall, ON K6H 5R9
613-933-2991, Fax: 613-932-3793
Laurentian Pilotage Authority, Head Office, #1401, 999, boul Maisonneuve ouest, Montréal, QC H3A 3L4
514-283-6320, Fax: 514-496-2409, administration@apl.gc.ca
Marine Atlantic Inc., Corporate Office, Baine Johnston Centre, #302, 10 Fort William Pl., St. John's, NL A1C 1K4
800-897-2797, customer_relations@marine-atlantic.ca
Old Port of Montréal Corporation Inc., 333, rue de la Commune ouest, Montréal, QC H2Y 2E2
514-283-5256, 800-971-7678,
Pacific Pilotage Authority Canada, #1000, 1130 West Pender St., Vancouver, BC V6E 4A4
604-666-6771, Fax: 604-666-1647, info@ppa.gc.ca
St. Lawrence Seaway Management Corporation, 202 Pitt St., Cornwall, ON K6J 3P7
613-932-5170, Fax: 613-932-7286, marketing@seaway.ca
Transport Canada, Place de Ville, 330 Sparks St., Ottawa, ON K1A 0N5
613-990-2309, Fax: 613-954-4731, 866-995-9737
Transportation Appeal Tribunal of Canada, #1201, 333 Laurier Ave. West, 12th Fl., Ottawa, ON K1A 0N5
613-990-6906, Fax: 613-990-9153, info@tatc.gc.ca
Transportation Safety Board of Canada, 200, promenade du Portage, 4e étage, Gatineau, QC K1A 1K8
819-994-3741, Fax: 819-997-2239, 800-387-3557, communications@bst-tsb.gc.ca
VIA Rail Canada Inc., CP 8116 Centre-Ville, Montréal, QC H3C 3N3
514-871-6000, Fax: 514-871-6104, 888-842-7245, customer_relations@viarail.ca

Alberta

Alberta Automobile Insurance Rate Board, Canadian Western Bank Place, #2440, 10303 Jasper Ave., Edmonton, AB T5J 3N6
780-427-5428, Fax: 780-638-4254, -310-0000, airb@gov.ab.ca
Alberta Infrastructure, Infrastructure Bldg., 6950 - 113th St., Edmonton, AB T6H 5V7
780-415-0507, Fax: 780-427-2187, Infra.Contact.Us.m@gov.ab.ca
Alberta Transportation, Communications Branch, Twin Atria Bldg., 4999 - 98th Ave., 2nd Fl., Edmonton, AB T6B 2X3
780-427-7674, Fax: 780-466-3166, Trans.Contact.Us.m@gov.ab.ca
Corporate Strategies & Services Division, Infrastructure Bldg., 6950 - 113th St., 2nd Fl., Edmonton, AB T6H 5V7
Safety & Policy Division, Twin Atria Bldg., 4999 - 98th Ave., Main Fl., Edmonton, AB T6B 2X3
780-427-8901, Fax: 780-415-0782, 800-666-5036
Transportation Safety Board, North Office, Twin Atria Building, 4999 - 98 Ave., Main Fl., Edmonton, AB T6B 2X3
780-427-7178, Fax: 780-422-9739, -310-0000

British Columbia

British Columbia Ferry Commission, PO Box 9279 Prov Govt, Victoria, BC V8W 9J7
250-952-0112, info@bcferrycommission.ca
British Columbia Ferry Services Inc., c/o BC Ferry Authority, #500, 1321 Blanshard St., Victoria, BC V8W 0B7
250-381-1401, 888-223-3779, customerservice@bcferries.com
British Columbia Ministry of Transportation & Infrastructure, PO Box 9850 Prov Govt, Victoria, BC V8W 9T5
250-387-3198, Fax: 250-356-7706, tran.webmaster@gov.bc.ca
British Columbia Transit, 520 Gorge Rd. East, Victoria, BC V8W 2P3
250-385-2551
Passenger Transportation Board, #202, 940 Blanshard St., PO Box 9850 Prov Govt, Victoria, BC V8W 9T5
250-953-3777, Fax: 250-953-3788, ptboard@gov.bc.ca
Transportation Policy & Programs Division, PO Box 9850 Prov Govt, Victoria, BC V8W 9T5
250-387-5062, Fax: 250-387-6431

Manitoba
Highway Traffic Board/Motor Transport Board, #200, 301 Weston St., Winnipeg, MB R3E 3H4
204-945-8912, Fax: 204-783-6529
Manitoba Infrastructure, Legislative Bldg., #203, 450 Broadway, Winnipeg, MB R3C 0V8
Medical Review Committee, #200, 301 Weston St., Winnipeg, MB R3E 3H4
204-945-7350, Fax: 204-948-2682
Taxicab Board, #200, 301 Weston St., Winnipeg, MB R3E 3H4
204-945-8919, Fax: 204-948-2315, taxicabboardoffice@gov.mb.ca

New Brunswick
New Brunswick Department of Transportation & Infrastructure, Kings Place, PO Box 6000, Fredericton, NB E3B 5H1
506-453-3939, Fax: 506-453-7987, transportation.web@gnb.ca
Vehicle Management Agency, Vehicle Management Centre, 1050 College Hill Rd., PO Box 6000, Fredericton, NB E3B 5H1
506-453-3939, Fax: 506-453-3628, transportation.web@gnb.ca

Newfoundland & Labrador
Newfoundland & Labrador Department of Transportation & Infrastructure, Confederation Bldg., Prince Philip Dr., PO Box 8700, St. John's, NL A1B 4J6
709-729-2300, ti@gov.nl.ca

Northwest Territories
Northwest Territories Department of Infrastructure, Stuart M. Hodgson Bldg., 5009 - 49th St., 3rd Fl., PO Box 1320, Yellowknife, NT X1A 2L9
INF_Communications@gov.nt.ca

Nova Scotia
Nova Scotia Department of Transportation & Active Transit, PO Box 186, Halifax, NS B3J 2N2
902-424-2297, Fax: 902-424-0532, tpwpaff@novascotia.ca

Nunavut
Nunavut Territory Department of Community & Government Services, W.G. Brown Bldg., 4th Fl., PO Box 1000 700, Iqaluit, NU X0A 0H0
867-975-5406, Fax: 867-975-5305, cgscomms@gov.nu.ca
Nunavut Territory Department of Economic Development & Transportation, Inuksugait Plaza, Bldg. 1104A, PO Box 1000 1500, Iqaluit, NU X0A 0H0
867-975-7800, Fax: 867-975-7870, 888-975-5999, edt@gov.nu.ca

Ontario
Metrolinx, 97 Front St. West, Toronto, ON M5J 1E6
416-874-5900, Fax: 416-869-1755
Ontario Highway Transport Board, 151 Bloor St. West, 10th Fl., Toronto, ON M5S 2T5
416-326-6732, Fax: 416-326-6738, ohtb@mto.gov.on.ca
Ontario Ministry of Infrastructure, 777 Bay St., 5th Fl., Toronto, ON M5G 2C8
416-327-4412
Ontario Ministry of Transportation, 777 Bay St., 5th Fl., Toronto, ON M7A 1Z8
416-235-4686, Fax: 416-327-9185, 800-268-4686
Owen Sound Transportation Company Ltd., 717875, Hwy. 6, Owen Sound, ON N4K 5N7
519-376-8740, 800-265-3163
Road User Safety Division, Bldg A, 87 Sir William Hearst Ave., Toronto, ON M3M 0B4
416-235-2999, Fax: 416-235-4153

Prince Edward Island
Prince Edward Island Department of Transportation & Infrastructure, Jones Bldg., 11 Kent St., 3rd Fl., PO Box 2000, Charlottetown, PE C1A 7N8
902-368-5100, Fax: 902-368-5395, DeptTIE@gov.pe.ca

Quebec
Commission des transports du Québec, 200, ch Sainte-Foy, 7e étage, Québec, QC G1R 5V5
514-873-6424, Fax: 418-644-8034, 888-461-2433, courrier@ctq.gouv.qc.ca
Ministère des Transports, #4.010, 500, boul René-Lévesque est, Québec, QC H2Z 1W7
888-355-0511, communications@mtq.gouv.qc.ca
Réseau de transport métropolitain (Exo), 700, rue de la Gauchetière ouest, 26e étage, Montréal, QC H3B 5M2
514-287-8726, 888-702-8726
Société de l'assurance automobile du Québec, 333, boul Jean-Lesage, CP 19600 Terminus, Québec, QC G1K 8J6
418-643-7620, Fax: 418-644-0339, 800-361-7620
Société des traversiers du Québec, 250, rue Saint-Paul, Québec, QC G1K 9K9
418-643-2019, Fax: 418-643-7308, 877-787-7483, stq@traversiers.gouv.qc.ca
Société du parc industriel et portuaire de Bécancour, 1000, boul Arthur-Sicard, Bécancour, QC G9H 2Z8
819-294-6656, Fax: 819-294-9020, info@spipb.com

Société du port ferroviaire Baie-Comeau-Haute-Rive, 18, rte Maritime, Baie-Comeau, QC G4Z 2L6
418-296-6785

Saskatchewan
Global Transportation Hub Authority, #700, 1855 Victoria Ave., Regina, SK S4P 3T2
306-787-4842, Fax: 306-798-4600, inquiry@thegth.com
Highway Traffic Board, 1621A McDonald St., Regina, SK S4N 5R2
Fax: 306-798-0162, 855-775-8336, contactus.htb@gov.sk.ca
Saskatchewan Highways, Victoria Tower, 1855 Victoria Ave., Regina, SK S4P 3T2
306-933-5186, MHI.CustomerService@gov.sk.ca

Yukon Territory
Yukon Community Services, PO Box 2703, Whitehorse, YT Y1A 2C6
867-667-5811, Fax: 867-393-6295, 800-661-0408
Yukon Highways & Public Works, PO Box 2703, Whitehorse, YT Y1A 2C6
867-667-3732, Fax: 867-393-6218, hpw-info@yukon.ca

TRANSPORTATION OF DANGEROUS GOODS
Nova Scotia
Nova Scotia Department of Transportation & Active Transit, PO Box 186, Halifax, NS B3J 2N2
902-424-2297, Fax: 902-424-0532, tpwpaff@novascotia.ca
Ontario
Road User Safety Division, Bldg A, 87 Sir William Hearst Ave., Toronto, ON M3M 0B4
416-235-2999, Fax: 416-235-4153
Prince Edward Island
Prince Edward Island Department of Transportation & Infrastructure, Jones Bldg., 11 Kent St., 3rd Fl., PO Box 2000, Charlottetown, PE C1A 7N8
902-368-5100, Fax: 902-368-5395, DeptTIE@gov.pe.ca
Saskatchewan
Saskatchewan Highways, Victoria Tower, 1855 Victoria Ave., Regina, SK S4P 3T2
306-933-5186, MHI.CustomerService@gov.sk.ca

TRAPPING & FUR INDUSTRY
Ontario
Niagara Escarpment Commission, 232 Guelph St., Georgetown, ON L7G 4B1
905-877-5191, Fax: 905-873-7452
Quebec
Comité conjoint de chasse, de pêche et de piégeage, #1420, 1080, Côte du Beaver Hall, Montréal, QC H2Z 1N8
514-284-2151, Fax: 514-284-0039, infohftcc@cccpp-hftcc.com
Office de la sécurité du revenu des chasseurs et piégeurs cris, Édifice Champlain, #1100, 2700, boul Laurier, Québec, QC G1V 4K5
418-643-7300, Fax: 418-643-6803, 800-363-1560, courrier@osrcpc.ca
Saskatchewan
Saskatchewan Environment, 3211 Albert St., Regina, SK S4S 5W6
306-787-2584, Fax: 306-787-9544, 800-567-4224, centre.inquiry@gov.sk.ca

TREASURY SERVICES
See Also: Finance
Treasury Board of Canada Secretariat, East Tower, 140 O'Connor St., 9th Fl., Ottawa, ON K1A 0R5
613-957-2400, Fax: 613-941-4000, 877-636-0656
Alberta
Alberta Treasury Board & Finance, 9820 - 107th St., 9th Fl., Edmonton, AB T5K 1E7
780-427-3035, Fax: 780-427-1147
Treasury & Risk Management Division, Federal Bldg., 9820 - 107th St., 8th Fl., Edmonton, AB T5K 1E7
British Columbia
Provincial Treasury, PO Box 9414 Prov Govt, Victoria, BC V8V 9V1
250-387-4541, Fax: 250-356-3041
Manitoba
Treasury Board Secretariat, #200, 386 Broadway, Winnipeg, MB R3C 3R6
204-945-4150, Fax: 204-948-4878
Treasury Division, #350, 363 Broadway, Winnipeg, MB R3C 3N9
204-945-3702, Fax: 204-948-2233
Nova Scotia
Nova Scotia Department of Finance & Treasury Board, Provincial Bldg., 1723 Hollis St., 7th Fl., PO Box 187, Halifax, NS B3J 2N3
902-424-5554, Fax: 902-424-0635, FinanceWeb@novascotia.ca

Nunavut
Nunavut Territory Department of Finance, PO Box 1000 430, Iqaluit, NU X0A 0H0
867-975-6222, Fax: 867-975-6220, 888-668-9993, gnhr@gov.nu.ca
Ontario
Treasury Board Secretariat, 315 Front St. West, 7th Fl., Toronto, ON M7A 0B8
Quebec
Secrétariat du Conseil du trésor, 875, Grande Allée est, 2e étage, secteur 800, Québec, QC G1R 5R8
418-643-1529, Fax: 418-643-9226, 866-552-5158, communication@sct.gouv.qc.ca

URBAN RENEWAL & DESIGN
See Also: Municipal Affairs
Newfoundland & Labrador
Newfoundland & Labrador Housing Corporation, Sir Brian Dunfield Bldg., 2 Canada Dr., PO Box 220, St. John's, NL A1C 5J2
709-724-3000, Fax: 709-724-3250
Northwest Territories
Northwest Territories Department of Municipal & Community Affairs, PO Box 1320, Yellowknife, NT X1A 2L9
Ontario
Ontario Ministry of Municipal Affairs & Housing, College Park, 777 Bay St., 17th Fl., Toronto, ON M7A 2J3
416-585-7041, Fax: 416-585-4230, mininfo@ontario.ca
Prince Edward Island
SkillsPEI, Atlantic Technology Centre, #212, 176 Great George St., Charlottetown, PE C1A 4K9
902-368-6290, Fax: 902-368-6340, 877-491-4766
Quebec
Société d'habitation du Québec, Aile St-Amable, 1054, rue Louis-Alexandre-Taschereau, 3e étage, Québec, QC G1R 5E7
Fax: 418-643-2533, 800-463-4315

VETERANS AFFAIRS
Veterans Affairs Canada, 161 Grafton St., PO Box 7700, Charlottetown, PE C1A 8M9
613-996-2242, 866-522-2122, information@vac-acc.gc.ca

VICE-REGAL REPRESENTATIVES
Canadian Secretary to The Queen, 427 Laurier St., Ottawa, ON K1A 0M5
Governor General & Commander-in-Chief of Canada, Rideau Hall, 1 Sussex Dr., Ottawa, ON K1A 0A1
613-993-8200, Fax: 613-998-8760, 800-465-6890, info@gg.ca
Alberta
Office of the Lieutenant Governor, Office of the Lieutenant Governor of AB, Legislature Bldg., 10800 - 97th Ave., 3rd Fl., Edmonton, AB T5K 2B6
780-427-7243, ltgov@gov.ab.ca
British Columbia
Office of the Lieutenant Governor, Government House, 1401 Rockland Ave., Victoria, BC V8S 1V9
250-387-2080, Fax: 250-387-2078, ghinfo@gov.bc.ca
Manitoba
Office of the Lieutenant Governor, Legislative Bldg., #235, 450 Broadway, Winnipeg, MB R3C 0V8
204-945-2753, Fax: 204-945-4329, ltgov@leg.gov.mb.ca
New Brunswick
Office of the Lieutenant-Governor, Government House, PO Box 6000, Fredericton, NB E3B 5H1
506-453-2505, Fax: 506-444-5280, LTgov@gnb.ca
Newfoundland & Labrador
Office of the Lieutenant Governor, Government House, 50 Military Rd., PO Box 5517, St. John's, NL A1C 5W4
709-729-4494, Fax: 709-729-2234, governmenthouse@gov.nl.ca
Northwest Territories
Office of the Commissioner, 803 Northwest Tower, PO Box 1320, Yellowknife, NT X1A 2L9
867-873-7400, Fax: 867-873-0223, 888-270-3318, commissioner@gov.nt.ca
Nova Scotia
Office of the Lieutenant Governor, Government House, 1451 Barrington St., Halifax, NS B3J 1Z2
902-424-7001, Fax: 902-424-1790, lgoffice@novascotia.ca
Nunavut
Office of the Commissioner, PO Box 2379, Iqaluit, NU X0A 0H0
867-975-5120, Fax: 867-975-5123, nunavutcommissioner@gov.nu.ca
Ontario
Office of the Lieutenant Governor, Legislative Bldg., Queen's Park, Toronto, ON M7A 1A1
416-325-7780, lt.gov@ontario.ca

Prince Edward Island
Office of the Lieutenant Governor, Government House, PO Box
846, Charlottetown, PE C1A 7L9
902-368-5480, Fax: 902-368-5481

Quebec
Cabinet du Lieutenant-gouverneur, Édifice André-Laurendeau,
1050, rue des Parlementaires R.C., Québec, QC G1A 1A1
418-643-5385, Fax: 418-644-4677, 866-791-0766,
infoCLG@mce.gouv.qc.ca

Saskatchewan
Office of the Lieutenant Governor, Government House, 4607
Dewdney Ave., Regina, SK S4T 1B7
306-787-4070, Fax: 306-787-7716, lgo@ltgov.sk.ca

Yukon Territory
Office of the Commissioner of Yukon, Taylor House, 412 Main
St., Whitehorse, YT Y1A 2B7
867-667-5121, commissioner@yukon.ca

VIOLENCE
See Also: Policing Services
New Brunswick
New Brunswick Department of Social Development, Sartain
MacDonald Bldg., PO Box 6000, Fredericton, NB E3B 5H1
506-453-2001, Fax: 506-453-2164, sd-ds@gnb.ca

Nova Scotia
Nova Scotia Department of Community Services, Nelson Place,
5675 Spring Garden Rd., 8th Fl., PO Box 696, Halifax, NS
B3J 2T7
877-424-1177

Nunavut
Nunavut Territory Department of Family Services, PO Box 1000
1200, Iqaluit, NU X0A 0H0
867-975-5200, Fax: 867-975-5722

VITAL STATISTICS
Alberta
Service Alberta, Government of Alberta, PO Box 1333,
Edmonton, AB T5J 2N2
780-427-4088, -310-0000, service.alberta@gov.ab.ca

British Columbia
British Columbia Vital Statistics Agency, PO Box 9657 Prov
Govt, Victoria, BC V8W 9P3
250-952-2681, Fax: 250-952-9097, vsoffceo@gov.bc.ca

Nova Scotia
Service Nova Scotia & Internal Services, PO Box 2734, Halifax,
NS B3J 3K5
902-424-5200, Fax: 902-424-0720, 800-670-4357,
askus@novascotia.ca
Vital Statistics, PO Box 157, Halifax, NS B3J 2M9
902-424-4381, Fax: 902-450-7313, 877-848-2578,
vstat@novascotia.ca

Prince Edward Island
Prince Edward Island Department of Health & Wellness, Shaw
Bldg., 105 Rochford St. North, 4th Fl., Charlottetown, PE C1A
7N8
902-368-6414, Fax: 902-368-4121, DeptHW@gov.pe.ca

Quebec
Directeur de l'état civil, 2535, boul Laurier, Québec, QC G1V
5C5
418-644-4545, 877-644-4545

Saskatchewan
eHealth Saskatchewan, 2130 - 11th Ave., Regina, SK S4P 0J5
306-337-5000, 855-347-5465

WASTE & GARBAGE
Atomic Energy of Canada Limited, Head Office, Chalk River
Laboratories, 286 Plant Rd., Chalk River, ON K0J 1J0
888-220-2465, communications@aecl.ca
Canadian Nuclear Laboratories, Head Office, Chalk River
Laboratories, 286 Plant Rd., Chalk River, ON K0J 1J0
866-513-2325, communications@cnl.ca
Low-Level Radioactive Waste Management Office, 115 Toronto
Rd., Port Hope, ON L1A 3S4
905-885-9488

Newfoundland & Labrador
Newfoundland & Labrador Department of Digital Government &
Service NL, 100 Prince Phillip Dr., PO Box 8700, St. John's,
NL A1B 4J6
709-729-4834, servicenlinfo@gov.nl.ca
Newfoundland & Labrador Department of Environment & Climate
Change, PO Box 8700, St. John's, NL A1B 4J6
ECCInfo@gov.nl.ca

Nova Scotia
Divert NS, #400, 35 Commercial St., Truro, NS B2N 3H9
902-895-7732, Fax: 902-897-3256, 877-313-7732,
info@divertns.ca

Ontario
Ontario Ministry of Environment, Conservation & Parks,
Ferguson Block, 77 Wellesley St. West, 11th Fl., Toronto, ON
M7A 2T5
416-325-4000, Fax: 416-314-6713, 800-565-4923

Quebec
Bureau d'audiences publiques sur l'environnement, Édifice
Lomer-Gouin, #2.10, 575, rue Jacques-Parizeau, Québec,
QC G1R 6A6
418-643-7447, Fax: 418-643-9474, 800-463-4732,
communication@bape.gouv.qc.ca
Société québécoise de récupération et de recyclage, #411, 300,
rue Saint-Paul, Québec, QC G1K 7R1
418-643-0394, Fax: 418-643-6507, 800-807-0678,
info@recyc-quebec.gouv.qc.ca

WASTE MANAGEMENT
See Also: Dangerous Goods & Hazardous Materials
Atomic Energy of Canada Limited, Head Office, Chalk River
Laboratories, 286 Plant Rd., Chalk River, ON K0J 1J0
888-220-2465, communications@aecl.ca
Canadian Nuclear Laboratories, Head Office, Chalk River
Laboratories, 286 Plant Rd., Chalk River, ON K0J 1J0
866-513-2325, communications@cnl.ca
Waste Biotreatability Facility, c/o Montréal (av Royalmount)
Research Facilities, 6100, av Royalmount, Montréal, QC H4P
2R2

Alberta
Alberta Environment & Parks, Forestry Bldg., 9920 - 108th St.,
Main Fl., Edmonton, AB T5K 2M4
780-944-0313
Alberta Recycling Management Authority, Scotia Tower 1,
#1800, 10060 Jasper Ave., PO Box 189, Edmonton, AB T5J
2J1
780-990-1111, Fax: 780-990-1122, 888-999-8762,
info@albertarecycling.ca
Alberta Used Oil Management Association, Empire Building,
#1008, 10080 Jasper Ave., Edmonton, AB T5J 1V9
780-414-1510, Fax: 780-414-1519, 866-414-1510,
auoma@usedoilrecycling.ca
Beverage Container Management Board, #100, 8616 - 51 Ave.,
Edmonton, AB T6E 6E6
780-424-3193, Fax: 780-428-4620, 888-424-7671,
info@bcmb.ab.ca

Northwest Territories
Northwest Territories Department of Municipal & Community
Affairs, PO Box 1320, Yellowknife, NT X1A 2L9

Prince Edward Island
Island Waste Management Corporation, 110 Watts Ave.,
Charlottetown, PE C1E 2C1
902-882-0525, Fax: 902-894-0331, 888-280-8111,
info@iwmc.pe.ca

Quebec
Société québécoise de récupération et de recyclage, #411, 300,
rue Saint-Paul, Québec, QC G1K 7R1
418-643-0394, Fax: 418-643-6507, 800-807-0678,
info@recyc-quebec.gouv.qc.ca

Saskatchewan
Saskatchewan Environment, 3211 Albert St., Regina, SK S4S
5W6
306-787-2584, Fax: 306-787-9544, 800-567-4224,
centre.inquiry@gov.sk.ca

Yukon Territory
Yukon Environment, 10 Burns Rd., Whitehorse, YT Y1A 2C6
867-667-5652, Fax: 867-393-7197,
environmentyukon@yukon.ca

WATER & WASTEWATER
Bedford Institute of Oceanography, PO Box 1006, Dartmouth,
NS B2Y 4A2
902-426-2373, Fax: 902-426-8484,
webmasterbio-iob@dfo-mpo.gc.ca
Canadian Hydrographic Service, 200 Kent St., Ottawa, ON K1A
0E6
613-998-4921, 866-546-3613, chsinfo@dfo-mpo.gc.ca
Civil Infrastructure & Related Structures Testing Facilities, c/o
National Research Council, 1200 Montreal Rd., Ottawa, ON
K1A 0R6
613-993-9101
Environment & Climate Change Canada, 200, rue Sacré-Coeur,
12th Fl., Gatineau, QC K1A 0H3
819-938-3860, 800-668-6767, eec.enviroinfo.ec@canada.ca
Fisheries & Oceans Canada, 200 Kent St., Ottawa, ON K1A 0E6
613-993-0999, Fax: 613-990-1866, info@dfo-mpo.gc.ca
Freshwater Institute, 501 University Cres., Winnipeg, MB R3T
2N6
Institut Maurice-Lamontagne, 850, rte de le Mer, CP 1000,
Mont-Joli, QC G5H 3Z4
418-775-0500, Fax: 418-775-0730

Institute of Ocean Sciences, 9860 West Saanich Rd., PO Box
6000, Sidney, BC V8L 4B2
250-363-6517
Nunavut Water Board, PO Box 119, Gjoa Haven, NU X0B 1J0
867-360-6338

Alberta
Alberta Environment & Parks, Forestry Bldg., 9920 - 108th St.,
Main Fl., Edmonton, AB T5K 2M4
780-944-0313
Alberta Transportation, Communications Branch, Twin Atria
Bldg., 4999 - 98th Ave., 2nd Fl., Edmonton, AB T6B 2X3
780-427-7674, Fax: 780-466-3166,
Trans.Contact.Us.m@gov.ab.ca
Alberta Utilities Commission, Eau Caire Tower, #1400, 600 - 3rd
Ave. SW, Calgary, AB T2P 0G5
-310-4282, info@auc.ab.ca
Irrigation Council, Provincial Bldg., 200 - 5 Ave. South, 3rd Fl.,
Lethbridge, AB T1J 4L1
403-381-5176, Fax: 403-382-4406

British Columbia
British Columbia Ministry of Environment & Climate Change
Strategy, PO Box 9047 Prov Govt, Victoria, BC V8W 9E2
British Columbia Utilities Commission, #410, 900 Howe St.,
Vancouver, BC V6Z 2N3
604-660-4700, Fax: 604-660-1102, 800-663-1385,
commission.secretary@bcuc.com

Manitoba
Manitoba Conservation & Climate, 200 Saulteaux Cres., PO Box
22, Winnipeg, MB R3J 3W3
204-945-6784, Fax: 204-948-2656, 800-214-6497,
cc@gov.mb.ca
Manitoba Water Council, 200 Saulteaux Cres., PO Box 38,
Winnipeg, MB R3J 3W3
info@manitobawatercouncil.ca

New Brunswick
New Brunswick Department of Environment & Local
Government, Marysville Place, 20 McGloin St., Fredericton,
NB E3B 5H1
506-453-2690, Fax: 506-457-4994, elg/egl-info@gnb.ca
New Brunswick Department of Natural Resources & Energy
Development, Hugh John Flemming Forestry Centre, PO Box
6000, Fredericton, NB E3B 5H1
506-453-3826, Fax: 506-444-4367, dnr_mrnweb@gnb.ca

Newfoundland & Labrador
Newfoundland & Labrador Board of Commissioners of Public
Utilities, PO Box 21040, St. John's, NL A1A 5B2
Fax: 709-726-9604, 866-782-0006, ito@pub.nl.ca

Northwest Territories
Inuvialuit Water Board, Mack Travel Bldg., 151 Mackenzie Rd.,
2nd Fl., PO Box 2531, Yellowknife, NT X0E 0T0
867-678-2942, Fax: 867-678-2943, info@inuvwb.ca
Northwest Territories Department of Environment & Natural
Resources, PO Box 1320, Yellowknife, NT X1A 2L9
867-767-9055, enr_communications@gov.nt.ca

Nova Scotia
Develop Nova Scotia, Old Red Store, Historic Properties, #301,
1875 Upper Water St., Halifax, NS B3J 1S9
902-422-6591, Fax: 902-377-4801, info@developns.ca
Nova Scotia Department of Lands & Forestry, PO Box 698,
Halifax, NS B3J 2T9
902-424-5935, Fax: 902-424-7735, 800-565-2224,
Nova Scotia Utility & Review Board, Summit Place, 1601 Lower
Water St., 3rd Fl., Halifax, NS B3J 3S3
902-424-4448, Fax: 902-424-3919, 855-442-4448,
board@novascotia.ca

Ontario
Lake of the Woods Control Board, c/o Executive Engineer, 373
Sussex Dr., Block E1, Ottawa, ON K1A 0H3
Fax: 888-702-9632, 800-661-5922, secretariat@lwcb.ca
Ontario Clean Water Agency, 1 Yonge St., 17th Fl., Toronto, ON
M5E 1E5
416-314-5600, Fax: 416-314-8300, 800-667-6292,
ocwa@ocwa.com
Ontario Ministry of Environment, Conservation & Parks,
Ferguson Block, 77 Wellesley St. West, 11th Fl., Toronto, ON
M7A 2T5
416-325-4000, Fax: 416-314-6713, 800-565-4923
Ontario Ministry of Northern Development, Mines, Natural
Resources & Forestry, Natural Resources Information &
Support Centre, 300 Water St., Toronto, ON K9J 8M5
800-667-1940
Walkerton Clean Water Centre, 20 Ontario Rd., PO Box 160,
Walkerton, ON N0G 2V0
519-881-2003, Fax: 519-881-4947, 866-515-0550,
inquiry@wcwc.ca

Prince Edward Island
Prince Edward Island Department of Justice & Public Safety,
Shaw Bldg. South, 95 Rochford St., 4th Fl., PO Box 2000,
Charlottetown, PE C1A 7N8
902-368-4589, Fax: 902-368-5283, DeptJPS@gov.pe.ca

Quebec
Ministère de l'Environnement et de la Lutte contre les
changements climatiques, Édifice Marie-Guyart, 675, boul
René-Lévesque est, 30e étage, Québec, QC G1R 5V7
418-521-3830, Fax: 418-646-5974, 800-561-1616,
relations.medias@mddelcc.gouv.qc.ca
Saskatchewan
Saskatchewan Environment, 3211 Albert St., Regina, SK S4S
5W6
306-787-2584, Fax: 306-787-9544, 800-567-4224,
centre.inquiry@gov.sk.ca
Saskatchewan Water Corporation (SaskWater), #200, 111
Fairford St. East, Moose Jaw, SK S6H 1C8
Fax: 306-694-3207, 888-230-1111,
communications@saskwater.com
Saskatchewan Water Security Agency, #400, 111 Fairford St.
East, Moose Jaw, SK S6H 7X9
306-694-3900, Fax: 306-694-3105, comm@wsask.ca
Yukon Territory
Yukon Environment, 10 Burns Rd., Whitehorse, YT Y1A 2C6
867-667-5652, Fax: 867-393-7197,
environmentyukon@yukon.ca

WATER POLLUTION

See Also: Environment; Water Resources
Office of the Administrator of the Ship-source Oil Pollution Fund,
#830, 180 Kent St., Ottawa, ON K1A 0N5
613-991-1726, Fax: 613-990-5423, info@sopf-cidphn.gc.ca

WATER RESOURCES

See Also: Oceanography
Environmental Protection Branch, 351, boul Saint-Joseph,
Gatineau, QC K1A 0H3
819-953-1711, Fax: 819-953-9452
Freshwater Institute, 501 University Cres., Winnipeg, MB R3T
2N6
International Joint Commission, 234 Laurier Ave. West, 22nd Fl.,
Ottawa, ON K1P 6K6
613-995-2984, Fax: 613-993-5583,
commission@ottawa.ijc.org
Nunavut Water Board, PO Box 119, Gjoa Haven, NU X0B 1J0
867-360-6338
Water Science & Technology, 200, boul Sacré-Coeur, Gatineau,
QC K1A 0H3
819-994-4533
Alberta
Alberta Environment & Parks, Forestry Bldg., 9920 - 108th St.,
Main Fl., Edmonton, AB T5K 2M4
780-944-0313
British Columbia
Environmental Protection Division, PO Box 9339, Victoria, BC
V8W 9M1
250-387-1288, Fax: 250-387-5669
Manitoba
Manitoba Water Council, 200 Saulteaux Cres., PO Box 38,
Winnipeg, MB R3J 3W3
info@manitobawatercouncil.ca
New Brunswick
New Brunswick Department of Environment & Local
Government, Marysville Place, 20 McGloin St., Fredericton,
NB E3B 5H1
506-453-2690, Fax: 506-457-4994, elg/egl-info@gnb.ca
Northwest Territories
Inuvialuit Water Board, Mack Travel Bldg., 151 Mackenzie Rd.,
2nd Fl., PO Box 2531, Yellowknife, NT X0E 0T0
867-678-2942, Fax: 867-678-2943, info@inuvwb.ca
Nova Scotia
Nova Scotia Department of Agriculture, 1800 Argyle St., 6th Fl.,
Halifax, NS B3J 3N8
902-424-4560, Fax: 902-424-4671, 800-279-0825
Nunavut
Nunavut Territory Department of Health, PO Box 1000 1000,
Iqaluit, NU X0A 0H0
867-975-5700, Fax: 867-975-5705, 800-661-0833
Ontario
Advisory Council on Drinking Water Quality & Testing
Standards, 40 St. Clair Ave. West, 9th Fl., Toronto, ON M4V
1M2
416-212-7779, Fax: 416-212-7595
Drinking Water Management Division, 135 St Clair Ave. West,
14th Fl., Toronto, ON M4V 1P5
416-314-4475, Fax: 416-314-6935
Ontario Clean Water Agency, 1 Yonge St., 17th Fl., Toronto, ON
M5E 1E5
416-314-5600, Fax: 416-314-8300, 800-667-6292,
ocwa@ocwa.com
Walkerton Clean Water Centre, 20 Ontario Rd., PO Box 160,
Walkerton, ON N0G 2V0
519-881-2003, Fax: 519-881-4947, 866-515-0550,
inquiry@wcwc.ca

Prince Edward Island
Energy & Minerals, Jones Bldg., 4th Fl., PO Box 2000,
Charlottetown, PE C1A 7N8
Quebec
Ministère de l'Environnement et de la Lutte contre les
changements climatiques, Édifice Marie-Guyart, 675, boul
René-Lévesque est, 30e étage, Québec, QC G1R 5V7
418-521-3830, Fax: 418-646-5974, 800-561-1616,
relations.medias@mddelcc.gouv.qc.ca
Saskatchewan
Environmental Protection Division, 3211 Albert St., 5th Fl.,
Regina, SK S4S 5W6
Fax: 306-787-2947
Saskatchewan Environment, 3211 Albert St., Regina, SK S4S
5W6
306-787-2584, Fax: 306-787-9544, 800-567-4224,
centre.inquiry@gov.sk.ca
Saskatchewan Water Corporation (SaskWater), #200, 111
Fairford St. East, Moose Jaw, SK S6H 1C8
Fax: 306-694-3207, 888-230-1111,
communications@saskwater.com
Saskatchewan Water Security Agency, #400, 111 Fairford St.
East, Moose Jaw, SK S6H 7X9
306-694-3900, Fax: 306-694-3105, comm@wsask.ca
Yukon Territory
Yukon Environment, 10 Burns Rd., Whitehorse, YT Y1A 2C6
867-667-5652, Fax: 867-393-7197,
environmentyukon@yukon.ca

WEATHER

Environment & Climate Change Canada, 200, rue Sacré-Coeur,
12th Fl., Gatineau, QC K1A 0H3
819-938-3860, 800-668-6767, eec.enviroinfo.ec@canada.ca
Wind Tunnel Testing Facilities, c/o National Research Council,
1200 Montreal Rd., Ottawa, ON K1A 0R6

WEIGHTS & MEASURES

Standards Council of Canada, #600, 55 Metcalfe St., Ottawa,
ON K1P 6L5
613-238-3222, Fax: 613-569-7808, info@scc.ca

WELFARE

See Also: Income Security; Social Services
Quebec
Commissaire à la santé et au bien-être, Bureau de Québec,
1005, ch Ste-Foy, 1er étage, Québec, QC G1S 4N4
418-266-5990

WILDLIFE RESOURCES

Committee on the Status of Endangered Wildlife in Canada, c/o
Dept. of Biological Sciences, Simon Fraser University, 8888
University Dr., Burnaby, BC V5A 1S6
North American Bird Conservation Initiative, Canadian Wildlife
Service, 351 St. Joseph Blvd., Gatineau, QC K1A 0H3
819-994-0512, Fax: 819-994-4445,
ec.icoancanada-nabcicanada.ec@canada.ca
North American Waterfowl Management Plan, NAWCC
(Canada) Secretariat, Place Vincent Massey, 351 St. Joseph
Blvd., 14th Fl., Gatineau, QC K1A 0H3
819-938-4030, Fax: 819-934-6017,
ec.pnags-nawmp.ec@canada.ca
Manitoba
Endangered Species Advisory Committee, 200 Saulteaux Cres.,
PO Box 24, Winnipeg, MB R3J 3W3
204-945-7775, Fax: 204-945-3077
Nunavut
Nunavut Territory Department of Environment, PO Box 1000
1320, Iqaluit, NU X0A 0H0
867-975-7700, Fax: 867-975-7742, environment@gov.nu.ca
Ontario
Ontario Fish & Wildlife Heritage Commission, Robinson Pl., 300
Water St., 5th Fl., PO Box 7000, Peterborough, ON K9J 8M5
705-755-1905, Fax: 705-755-1900
Ontario Ministry of Environment, Conservation & Parks,
Ferguson Block, 77 Wellesley St. West, 11th Fl., Toronto, ON
M7A 2T5
416-325-4000, Fax: 416-314-6713, 800-565-4923
Quebec
Fondation de la faune du Québec, #420, 1175, av Lavigerie,
Québec, QC G1V 4P1
418-644-7926, Fax: 418-643-7655, 877-639-0742,
ffq@fondationdelafaune.qc.ca
Ministère des Forêts, Faune et Parcs, Service à la clientèle,
#A409 - 5700, 4e av ouest, Québec, QC G1H 6R1
Fax: 418-644-6513, 844-523-6738,
services.clientele@mmf.gouv.qc.ca
Ministère des Énergie et des Ressources naturelles, Service à la
clientèle, 5700, 4e av ouest, #A301, Québec, QC G1H 6R1
866-248-6936, services.clientele@mern.gouv.qc.ca

Société des établissements de plein air du Québec, Place de la
Cité, Tour Cominar, #1300, 2640, boul Laurier, Québec, QC
G1V 5C2
418-686-4875, Fax: 418-643-8177, 800-665-6527,
inforeservation@sepaq.com

WOMEN'S ISSUES

See Also: Pay Equity
Status of Women Canada, PO Box 8097 T CSC, Ottawa, ON
K1G 3H6
613-995-7835, Fax: 819-420-6906, 855-969-9922,
communications@swc-cfc.gc.ca
Alberta
Alberta Funeral Services Regulatory Board, #180, 2755
Broadmoor Blvd., Sherwood Park, AB T8H 2W7
780-452-6130, Fax: 780-452-6085, 800-563-4652,
office@afsrb.ab.ca
Status of Women, Oxbridge Place, 9820 - 106th St., 5th Fl.,
Edmonton, AB T5K 2J6
780-644-7559
Manitoba
Manitoba Women's Advisory Council, #409, 401 York Ave.,
Winnipeg, MB R3C 0P8
204-945-6281, Fax: 204-945-6511, 800-263-0234,
msw@gov.mb.ca
Status of Women Secretariat, #409, 401 York Ave., Winnipeg,
MB R3C 0P8
204-945-6281, Fax: 204-945-6511, 800-263-0234,
msw@gov.mb.ca
New Brunswick
New Brunswick Department of Social Development, Sartain
MacDonald Bldg., PO Box 6000, Fredericton, NB E3B 5H1
506-453-2001, Fax: 506-453-2164, sd-ds@gnb.ca
Women's Equality Branch, Sartain MacDonald Bldg., PO Box
6000, Fredericton, NB E3B 5H1
506-453-8126, 877-253-0266, web-edf@gnb.ca
Newfoundland & Labrador
Office of Women & Gender Equality, West Block, Confederation
Bldg., 4th Fl., PO Box 8700, St. John's, NL A1B 4J6
709-729-5009, Fax: 709-729-1418
Provincial Advisory Council on the Status of Women, #103, 15
Hallett Cres., St. John's, NL A1B 4C4
709-753-7270, Fax: 709-753-2606, 877-753-7270,
info@pacsw.ca
Northwest Territories
Status of Women Council of the Northwest Territories, Northwest
Tower, 4th Fl., PO Box 1320, Yellowknife, NT X1A 2L9
888-234-4485
Nova Scotia
Nova Scotia Advisory Council on the Status of Women, PO Box
745, Halifax, NS B3J 2T3
902-424-8662, Fax: 902-424-0573, 800-565-8662,
women@novascotia.ca
Nunavut
Nunavut Territory Department of Culture & Heritage, PO Box
1000 800, Iqaluit, NU X0A 0H0
867-975-5500, Fax: 867-975-5504, 866-934-2035
Ontario
Women's Issues, #601D, 777 Bay St., 6th Fl., Toronto, ON M7A
2J4
Quebec
Conseil du statut de la femme, #300, 800, place D'Youville, 3e
étage, Québec, QC G1R 6E2
418-643-4326, Fax: 418-643-8926, 800-463-2851,
csf@csf.gouv.qc.ca
Ministère de la Famille, Service des renseignements, 600, rue
Fullum, 6e étage, Montréal, QC H2K 4S7
855-336-8568
Secrétariat à la condition féminine, 905, av Honoré-Mercier, 3e
étage, Québec, QC G1R 5M6
418-643-9052, Fax: 418-643-4991
Yukon Territory
Yukon Women's Directorate, #1, 404 Hason St., PO Box 2703,
Whitehorse, YT Y1A 2C6
867-667-3030,

WORKERS' COMPENSATION

Alberta
Appeals Commission for Alberta Workers' Compensation,
Standard Life Centre, #1100, 10405 Jasper Ave., Edmonton,
AB T5J 3N4
780-412-8700, Fax: 780-412-8701, -310-0000,
AC.AcesAdmin@gov.ab.ca
Workers' Compensation Board, 9912 - 107 St., PO Box 2415,
Edmonton, AB T5J 2S5
780-498-3999, Fax: 780-427-5863, 866-922-9221
British Columbia
Workers' Compensation Appeal Tribunal, #150, 4600 Jacombs
Rd., Richmond, BC V6V 3B1
604-664-7800, Fax: 604-664-7898, 800-663-2782

Workers' Compensation Board of British Columbia, PO Box 5350 Terminal, Vancouver, BC V6B 5L5
604-276-3100, Fax: 604-276-3247, 888-621-7233
Manitoba
Workers' Compensation Board of Manitoba, 333 Broadway Ave., Winnipeg, MB R3C 4W3
204-954-4321, Fax: 204-954-4999, 800-362-3340, wcb@wcb.mb.ca
New Brunswick
WorkSafeNB, 1 Portland St., PO Box 160, Saint John, NB E2L 3X9
506-632-2200, 800-222-9775, communications@ws-ts.nb.ca
Newfoundland & Labrador
Newfoundland & Labrador Workplace Health, Safety & Compensation Commission (WorkplaceNL), 146 - 148 Forest Rd., PO Box 9000, St. John's, NL A1A 3B8
709-778-1000, Fax: 709-738-1714, 800-563-9000, info@workplacenl.ca
Northwest Territories
Northwest Territories & Nunavut Workers' Safety & Compensation Commission, Centre Square Tower, 5022 - 49th St., 5th Fl., PO Box 8888, Yellowknife, NT X1A 2R3
867-920-3888, Fax: 867-873-4596, 800-661-0792
Nova Scotia
Workers' Compensation Board of Nova Scotia, 5668 South St., PO Box 1150, Halifax, NS B3J 2Y2
902-491-8999, 800-870-3331, info@wcb.ns.ca
Ontario
Workplace Safety & Insurance Board, 200 Front St. West, Ground Fl., Toronto, ON M5V 3J1
416-344-1000, Fax: 416-344-4684, 800-387-0750
Prince Edward Island
Prince Edward Island Workers' Compensation Board, 14 Weymouth St., PO Box 757, Charlottetown, PE C1A 7L7
902-368-5680, Fax: 902-368-5696, 800-237-5049
Quebec
Commission des normes, de l'équité, de la santé et de la sécurité du travail, 524, rue Bourdages, Québec, QC G1M 1A1
Fax: 418-266-4015, 844-838-0808
Saskatchewan
Saskatchewan Workers' Compensation Board, #200, 1881 Scarth St., Regina, SK S4P 4L1
306-787-4370, Fax: 306-787-4311, 800-667-7590, webmaster@wcbsask.com
Yukon Territory
Yukon Workers' Compensation Health & Safety Board, 401 Strickland St., Whitehorse, YT Y1A 5N8
867-667-5645, Fax: 867-393-6279, 800-661-0443, worksafe@yukon.ca

YOUNG OFFENDERS

Justice Canada, 284 Wellington St., Ottawa, ON K1A 0H8
613-957-4222, Fax: 613-954-0811, webadmin@justice.gc.ca
Alberta
Alberta Justice & Solicitor General, John E. Brownlee Bldg., 10365 - 97th St., 9th Fl., Edmonton, AB T5J 3W7
780-427-2745
British Columbia
British Columbia Ministry of Attorney General & Minister responsible for Housing, PO Box 9044 Prov Govt, Victoria, BC V8W 9E2
Office of the Representative for Children & Youth, #400, 1019 Wharf St., Victoria, BC V8W 2Y9
250-356-6710, Fax: 250-356-0837, 800-476-3933, rcy@rcybc.ca
Northwest Territories
Northwest Territories Department of Justice, 4903 - 49th St., PO Box 1320, Yellowknife, NT X1A 2L9
867-767-9256, justice_communications@gov.nt.ca
Nova Scotia
Nova Scotia Department of Justice, 1690 Hollis St., PO Box 7, Halifax, NS B3J 2L6
902-424-4030, justweb@gov.ns.ca
Nunavut
Young Offenders Facility / Isumaqsunngittut Youth Centre, 1548 Federal Rd., PO Box 1439, Iqaluit, NU X0A 0H0
867-979-4452, Fax: 867-979-5506

YOUTH SERVICES

Federal Economic Development Agency for Southern Ontario, #101, 139 Northfield Dr. West, Waterloo, ON N2L 5A6
Fax: 519-725-4976, 866-593-5505
Alberta
Alberta Office of the Child & Youth Advocate, #600, 9925 - 109th St. NW, Edmonton, AB T5K 2J8
780-422-6056, Fax: 780-422-3675, 800-661-3446, ca.information@ocya.alberta.ca
British Columbia
Provincial Services, PO Box 9717 Prov Govt, Victoria, BC V8W 9S1
250-387-0978, Fax: 250-356-2079
Nunavut
Nunavut Territory Department of Culture & Heritage, PO Box 1000 800, Iqaluit, NU X0A 0H0
867-975-5500, Fax: 867-975-5504, 866-934-2035

Ontario
Office of the Ombudsman, Bell Trinity Sq., South Tower, 483 Bay St., 10th Fl., Toronto, ON M5G 2C9
416-586-3300, Fax: 416-586-3485, 800-263-1830, info@ombudsman.on.ca
Ontario Ministry of Children, Community & Social Services, Hepburn Block, 80 Grosvenor St., 6th Fl., Toronto, ON M7A 1E9
416-325-5666, 888-789-4199
Quebec
Commission des droits de la personne et des droits de la jeunesse, 360, rue Saint-Jacques, 2e étage, Montréal, QC H2Y 1P5
514-873-5146, Fax: 514-873-6032, 800-361-6477, information@cdpdj.qc.ca
Ministère de la Santé et des Services sociaux, Direction des communications, 1075, ch Sainte-Foy, 15e étage, Québec, QC G1S 2M1
418-644-4545, 877-644-4545
Yukon Territory
Yukon Child & Youth Advocate Office, #19, 2070 Second Ave., Whitehorse, YT Y1A 1B1
867-456-5575, Fax: 867-456-5574, 800-661-0408, info@ycao.ca

ZONING

British Columbia
British Columbia Ministry of Tourism, Arts, Culture & Sport, PO Box 9082 Prov Govt, Victoria, BC V8W 9E2
Manitoba
Manitoba Municipal Board, #1144, 363 Broadway, Winnipeg, MB R3C 3N9
204-945-2941, Fax: 204-948-2235
Quebec
Commission municipale du Québec, Mezzanine, aile Chauveau, 10, rue Pierre-Olivier-Chauveau, Québec, QC G1R 4J3
418-691-2014, Fax: 418-644-4676, 866-353-6767,

Government of Canada

c/o Canada Enquiry Centre, Service Canada, Ottawa, ON
K1A 0J9

Toll-Free: 800-622-6232
TTY: 800-926-9105
www.canada.ca
twitter.com/canada
www.facebook.com/CanadaAndTheWorld

All political authority in Canada is divided between the federal &
provincial governments, according to the provisions of the
Constitution Act, 1867. Local municipalities are a concern of the
provinces, & derive their authority from Acts of provincial
legislation. The Parliament of Canada consists of Her Majesty
Queen Elizabeth II (represented in Canada by the Governor
General, Her Excellency the Right Honourable Mary May
Simon), an Upper House called the Senate, & an elected House
of Commons.

Governor General & Commander-in-Chief of Canada / Gouverneur général et Commandant en chef du Canada

Rideau Hall, 1 Sussex Dr., Ottawa, ON K1A 0A1

Tel: 613-993-8200; *Fax:* 613-998-8760
Toll-Free: 800-465-6890
info@gg.ca
www.gg.ca
twitter.com/GGCanada
www.facebook.com/GovernorGeneralCanada
www.youtube.com/c/CanadaGG

Canada is a constitutional monarchy. Under the terms of its
Constitution, Her Majesty Queen Elizabeth II is the Head of
State. The duties of the Head of State in Canada are undertaken
by the Governor General as the Crown's representative. They
are also Commander-in-Chief of the Canadian Forces,
Chancellor & Principal Companion of the Order of Canada,
Chancellor & Commander of the Order of Military Merit, & Head
of the Canadian Heraldic Authority. The Office of the Governor
General encompasses a number of responsibilities, both
constitutional & traditional in nature. The Governor General of
Canada exercises powers & responsibilities belonging to the
Sovereign, with the advice of members of the Privy Council.
They are involved in the promotion of Canadian sovereignty at
home & represent Canada abroad. Canadian values, diversity,
inclusion, culture, & heritage are promoted by the Governor
General. National honours, decorations, & awards to recognize
people who have demonstrated excellence, valour, bravery, or
exceptional dedication to service are presented by the Governor
General.

Governor General & Commander-in-Chief of Canada, Rt.
Hon. Mary May Simon, C.C., C.M.M., C.O.M., O.Q., C.D.

Secretary to the Governor General, Ian McCowan
Tel: 613-302-7728; *Fax:* 613-993-1967

The Chancellery of Honours / Chancellerie
1 Sussex Dr., Ottawa, ON K1A 0A1
Deputy Secretary, Honours; Deputy Herald Chancellor, Marc
Thériault
Tel: 613-998-8731
Director, Honours, Orders, Ian Burgess
Tel: 613-993-3524
Director, Honours, Decorations & Medals, Peter Mills
Tel: 613-991-5845
Chief Herald of Canada & Director, Canadian Heraldic Authority,
Samy Khalid
Tel: 613-991-2227
Deputy Chief Herald of Canada & Assistant Director, Canadian
Heraldic Authority, Bruce Patterson
Tel: 613-291-5062

**Corporate Services Branch / Direction générale des
Services ministériels**
1 Sussex Dr., Ottawa, ON K1A 0A1
Director General, Fady Abdul-Nour
Tel: 613-991-9091; *Fax:* 613-998-8762

**Policy, Program & Protocol Branch / Politique, programme
et protocole**
1 Sussex Dr., Ottawa, ON K1A 0A1
Deputy Secretary, Vacant
Executive Director, Events, Household & Visitor Services,
Christine MacIntyre
Tel: 613-993-1901; *Fax:* 613-991-5113

Privy Council Office (PCO) / Bureau du Conseil privé (BCP)

#1000, 85 Sparks St., Ottawa, ON K1A 0A3

Tel: 613-957-5153; *Fax:* 613-997-5043
info@pco-bcp.gc.ca
www.canada.ca/en/privy-council.html
Other Communication: Media Phone: 613-957-5420; Email:
mediacentre@pco-bcp.gc.ca

The Privy Council Office provides non-partisan advice &
information from across the Public Service to the Prime Minister,
the Cabinet, & its decision-making structures. The key roles of
the Privy Council are as follows: advising the Prime Minister &
supporting the Cabinet; managing the Cabinet's decision-making
system & facilitating its efficient & effective functioning on a daily
basis; & providing public service leadership, including the
management of the appointments process for Crown
corporations & agencies, & senior positions in federal
departments. The Privy Council is led by the Clerk of the Privy
Council. A member of the Privy Council is awarded the title,
"Honourable," for life. The Governor General, the Prime Minister,
& the Chief Justice of Canada are accorded the title, "The Right
Honourable," for life.

President, Queen's Privy Council for Canada, Hon. Bill
Blair, P.C.
Tel: 613-992-1020; *Fax:* 613-992-3053
Bill.Blair@parl.gc.ca

Leader of the Government in the House of Commons,
Hon. Mark Holand, P.C.
Tel: 613-995-0580; *Fax:* 613-992-1710
mark.holland@parl.gc.ca

Chief Government Whip, Vacant

**Interim Clerk of the Privy Council & Secretary to the
Cabinet,** Janice Charette
Tel: 613-957-5400
www.clerk.gc.ca
twitter.com/Clerk_GC

**National Security & Intelligence Advisor to the Prime
Minister,** Vacant

Deputy Minister, COVID-19 Response (Communications),
Thao Pham
Tel: 613-957-5017

Deputy Minister, Intergovernmental Affairs, Michael
Vandergrift
Tel: 613-990-4187

**Deputy Clerk of the Privy Council & Associate Secretary
to the Cabinet,** Nathalie G. Drouin
Tel: 613-957-5466

Deputy Secretary to the Cabinet, Plans & Consultations,
Philip Jennings
Tel: 613-957-5461

Deputy Secretary to the Cabinet, Governance, Paul
Mackinnon
Tel: 613-957-5778

Deputy Secretary to the Cabinet, Results & Delivery,
Vacant

**Deputy Secretary to the Cabinet, Senior Personnel &
Public Service Renewal,** Janine Sherman
Tel: 613-957-5465

Deputy Secretary to the Cabinet, Operations, Shawn
Tupper
Tel: 613-957-5418

**Chief of Staff, Office of the Clerk of the Privy Council &
Secretary to the Cabinet,** Claudie Perreault
Tel: 613-957-5346

Counsel to the Clerk of the Privy Council, Jodie van Dieen
Tel: 613-957-5726

Director General, Data Integrety, Kara Beckles

Director General, Operations, Jean Tessier
Tel: 613-948-6677

Director General, Strategic Communications, Fiona
Nelson
Tel: 613-957-5173
Privy Council Members & Date When Sworn In

Hon. Paul Theodore Hellyer, Apr. 26, 1957
Right Hon. Joseph Jacques Jean Chrétien, Apr. 4, 1967
Hon. Alexander Bradshaw Campbell, Jul. 5, 1967
Hon. Otto Emil Lang, Jul. 6, 1968
Hon. James Hugh Faulkner, Nov. 27, 1972
Hon. André Ouellet, Nov. 27, 1972
Hon. Marc Lalonde, Nov. 27, 1972
Hon. J. Judd Buchanan, Aug. 8, 1974
Hon. Marcel Lessard, Sep. 26, 1975
Hon. Monique Bégin, Sep. 15, 1976
Hon. Jean-Jacques Blais, Sep. 15, 1976
Hon. Francis Fox, Sep. 15, 1976
Hon. Anthony Chisholm Abbott, Sep. 15, 1976
Hon. Iona Campagnolo, Sep. 15, 1976
Hon. John M. Reid, Nov. 24, 1978
Right Hon. Charles Joseph Clark, Jun. 4, 1979
Hon. John Carnell Crosbie, Jun. 4, 1979
Hon. David Samuel Horne MacDonald, Jun. 4, 1979
Hon. Elmer MacIntosh MacKay, Jun. 4, 1979
Hon. Arthur Jacob Epp, Jun. 4, 1979
Hon. John Allen Fraser, Jun. 4, 1979
Hon. David Edward Crombie, Jun. 4, 1979
Hon. Henry Perrin Beatty, Jun. 4, 1979
Hon. Gerald Augustine Regan, Mar. 3, 1980
Hon. James Sydney Clark Fleming, Mar. 3, 1980
Hon. Charles Lapointe, Mar. 3, 1980
Hon. Edward C. Lumley, Mar. 3, 1980
Hon. Yvon Pinard, Mar. 3, 1980
Hon. Donald James Johnston, Mar. 3, 1980
Hon. Lloyd Axworthy, Mar. 3, 1980
Hon. Paul James Cosgrove, Mar. 3, 1980
Hon. Judith A. Erola, Mar. 3, 1980
Hon. Jacob Austin, Sep. 22, 1981
Hon. Serge Joyal, Sep. 22, 1981
Hon. John Edward Broadbent, Apr. 17, 1982
Hon. William Grenville Davis, Apr. 17, 1982
Hon. Alfred Brian Peckford, Apr. 17, 1982
Hon. James Matthew Lee, Apr. 17, 1982
Hon. David Michael Collenette, Aug. 12, 1983
Hon. Céline Hervieux-Payette, Aug. 12, 1983
Hon. Roger Simmons, Aug. 12, 1983
Hon. Roy MacLaren, Aug. 17, 1983
Right Hon. Martin Brian Mulroney, May 7, 1984
Right Hon. Edward Richard Schreyer, Jun. 3, 1984
Hon. Herb Breau, Jun. 30, 1984
Hon. Joseph Roger Rémi Bujold, Jun. 30, 1984
Hon. Jack Burnett Murta, Sep. 17, 1984
Hon. Otto John Jelinek, Sep. 17, 1984
Hon. Thomas Edward Siddon, Sep. 17, 1984
Hon. Charles James Mayer, Sep. 17, 1984
Hon. Rev. Walter Franklin McLean, Sep. 17, 1984
Hon. Thomas Michael McMillan, Sep. 17, 1984
Hon. Patricia Carney, Sep. 17, 1984
Hon. André Bissonnette, Sep. 17, 1984
Hon. Suzanne Blais-Grenier, Sep. 17, 1984
Hon. Benoît Bouchard, Sep. 17, 1984
Hon. Andrée Champagne, Sep. 17, 1984
Hon. Michel Côté, Sep. 17, 1984
Hon. Barbara Jean McDougall, Sep. 17, 1984
Hon. Monique Vézina, Sep. 17, 1984
Hon. Saul Mark Cherniack, Nov. 30, 1984
Hon. Paule Gauthier, Nov. 30, 1984
Hon. Frank Oberle, Nov. 20, 1985
Hon. Lowell Murray, Jun. 30, 1986
Hon. Pierre H. Cadieux, Jun. 30, 1986
Hon. Jean J. Charest, Jun. 30, 1986
Hon. Thomas Hockin, Jun. 30, 1986
Hon. Monique Landry, Jun. 30, 1986
Hon. Bernard Valcourt, Jun. 30, 1986
Hon. Gerry Weiner, Jun. 30, 1986
Hon. John William Bosley, Jun. 30, 1987
Hon. Douglas Grinslade Lewis, Aug. 27, 1987
Hon. Pierre Blais, Aug. 27, 1987
Hon. Gerry St. Germain, Mar. 31, 1988
Hon. Lucien Bouchard, Mar. 31, 1988
Hon. John Horton McDermid, Sep. 15, 1988
Hon. Shirley Martin, Sep. 15, 1988
Hon. Mary Collins, Jan. 30, 1989
Hon. Alan Redway, Jan. 30, 1989
Hon. William Charles Winegard, Jan. 30, 1989
Right Hon. A. Kim Campbell, Jan. 30, 1989
Hon. Gilles Loiselle, Jan. 30, 1989
Hon. Marcel Danis, Feb. 23, 1990
Hon. Audrey McLaughlin, Jan. 10, 1991
Hon. Pauline Browes, Apr. 21, 1991
Hon. J.J. Michel Robert, Dec. 5, 1991
Hon. Lorne Edmund Nystrom, Jul. 1, 1992
Hon. John Charles Polanyi, Jul. 1, 1992

Hon. Maurice F. Strong, Jul. 1, 1992
Hon. Antonine Maillet, Jul. 1, 1992
Hon. Richard Cashin, Jul. 1, 1992
Hon. Paul M. Tellier, Jul. 1, 1992
Hon. David Robert Peterson, Jul. 1, 1992
Hon. Charles Rosner Bronfman, Oct. 21, 1992
Hon. Pierre H. Vincent, Jan. 4, 1993
Hon. James Stewart Edwards, Jun. 25, 1993
Hon. Robert Douglas Nicholson, Jun. 25, 1993
Hon. Barbara Jane Sparrow, Jun. 25, 1993
Hon. Peter L. McCreath, Jun. 25, 1993
Hon. Ian Angus Ross Reid, Jun. 25, 1993
Hon. Larry Schneider, Jun. 25, 1993
Hon. Garth Turner, Jun. 25, 1993
Hon. David Anderson, Nov. 4, 1993
Hon. Ralph Edward Goodale, Nov. 4, 1993
Hon. David Charles Dingwall, Nov. 4, 1993
Hon. Ron Irwin, Nov. 4, 1993
Hon. Brian Tobin, Nov. 4, 1993
Hon. Joyce Fairbairn, Nov. 4, 1993
Hon. Sheila Maureen Copps, Nov. 4, 1993
Hon. Sergio Marchi, Nov. 4, 1993
Hon. John Manley, Nov. 4, 1993
Right Hon. Paul Martin, Nov. 4, 1993
Hon. Douglas Young, Nov. 4, 1993
Hon. Michel Dupuy, Nov. 4, 1993
Hon. Arthur C. Eggleton, Nov. 4, 1993
Hon. Marcel Massé, Nov. 4, 1993
Hon. Anne McLellan, Nov. 4, 1993
Hon. Allan Rock, Nov. 4, 1993
Hon. Fernand Robichaud, Nov. 4, 1993
Hon. Ethel Blondin-Andrew, Nov. 4, 1993
Hon. Lawrence MacAulay, Nov. 4, 1993
Hon. Raymond Chan, Nov. 4, 1993
Hon. Jon Gerrard, Nov. 4, 1993
Hon. Douglas Peters, Nov. 4, 1993
Hon. Lucienne Robillard, Feb. 22, 1995
Hon. Jane Stewart, Jan. 25, 1996
Hon. Stéphane Dion, Jan. 25, 1996
Hon. Pierre Pettigrew, Jan. 25, 1996
Hon. Martin Cauchon, Jan. 25, 1996
Hon. Hedy Fry, Jan. 25, 1996
Hon. James Andrew Grant, Sep. 30, 1996
Hon. Don Boudria, Oct. 4, 1996
Hon. Lyle Vanclief, Jun. 11, 1997
Hon. Herb Dhaliwal, Jun. 11, 1997
Hon. David Kilgour, Jun. 11, 1997
Hon. James Scott Peterson, Jun. 11, 1997
Hon. Andrew Mitchell, Jun. 11, 1997
Hon. Gilbert Normand, Jun. 18, 1997
Hon. Robert (Bob) Keith Rae, Apr. 30, 1998
Hon. Claudette Bradshaw, Nov. 23, 1998
Hon. Jocelyne Bourgon, Dec. 14, 1998
Hon. Raymond A. Speaker, Jun. 9, 1999
Hon. Frank Joseph McKenna, Jun. 9, 1999
Hon. George Baker, Aug. 3, 1999
Hon. Robert Daniel Nault, Aug. 3, 1999
Hon. Maria Minna, Aug. 3, 1999
Hon. Elinor Caplan, Aug. 3, 1999
Hon. Denis Coderre, Aug. 3, 1999
Hon. J. Bernard Boudreau, Oct. 4, 1999
Right Hon. Beverley M. McLachlin, Jan. 12, 2000
Hon. Sharon Carstairs, Jan. 9, 2001
Hon. Robert G. Thibault, Jan. 9, 2001
Hon. Rey Pagtakhan, Jan. 9, 2001
Hon. Gary Albert Filmon, Oct. 4, 2001
Hon. Susan Whelan, Jan. 15, 2002
Hon. Maurizio Bevilacqua, Jan. 15, 2002
Hon. Paul DeVillers, Jan. 15, 2002
Hon. Gar Knutson, Jan. 15, 2002
Hon. Denis Paradis, Jan. 15, 2002
Hon. Claude Drouin, Jan. 15, 2002
Hon. John McCallum, Jan. 15, 2002
Hon. Stephen Owen, Jan. 15, 2002
Hon. William Graham, Jan. 16, 2002
Hon. Gerry Byrne, Jan. 16, 2002
Hon. Jean Augustine, May 26, 2002
Hon. Arnold Wayne Easter, Oct. 22, 2002
Hon. Baljit Singh Chadha, Feb. 20, 2003
Hon. Steven W. Mahoney, Apr. 11, 2003
Hon. Roy J. Romanow, Nov. 13, 2003
Hon. Albina Guarnieri, Dec. 12, 2003
Hon. Stan Kazmierczak Keyes, Dec. 12, 2003
Hon. Robert Speller, Dec. 12, 2003
Hon. Geoff Regan, Dec. 12, 2003
Hon. Tony Valeri, Dec. 12, 2003
Hon. David Pratt, Dec. 12, 2003
Hon. Irwin Cotler, Dec. 12, 2003

Hon. Judy Sgro, Dec. 12, 2003
Hon. Hélène Chalifour Scherrer, Dec. 12, 2003
Hon. Ruben John Efford, Dec. 12, 2003
Hon. Liza Frulla, Dec. 12, 2003
Hon. Joseph Robert Comuzzi, Dec. 12, 2003
Hon. Giuseppe (Joseph) Volpe, Dec. 12, 2003
Hon. Joseph McGuire, Dec. 12, 2003
Hon. Dr. Carolyn Bennett, Dec. 12, 2003
Hon. Jacques Saada, Dec. 12, 2003
Hon. M. Aileen Carroll, Dec. 12, 2003
Hon. André Harvey, Dec. 12, 2003
Hon. Susan Barnes, Dec. 12, 2003
Hon. David Price, Dec. 12, 2003
Hon. Jim Karygiannis, Dec. 12, 2003
Hon. Shawn Murphy, Dec. 12, 2003
Hon. Joseph Louis Jordan, Dec. 12, 2003
Hon. Roger Gallaway, Dec. 12, 2003
Hon. Paul Bonwick, Dec. 12, 2003
Hon. Eleni Bakopanos, Dec. 12, 2003
Hon. Georges Farrah, Dec. 12, 2003
Hon. Mark Eyking, Dec. 12, 2003
Hon. Dan McTeague, Dec. 12, 2003
Hon. Walt Lastewka, Dec. 12, 2003
Hon. Brenda Kay Chamberlain, Dec. 12, 2003
Hon. Larry Bagnell, Dec. 12, 2003
Hon. Gurbax Singh Malhi, Dec. 12, 2003
Hon. Joseph Frank Fontana, Dec. 12, 2003
Hon. Jerry Pickard, Dec. 12, 2003
Hon. John McKay, Dec. 12, 2003
Hon. Scott Brison, Dec. 12, 2003
Hon. John Ferguson Godfrey, Dec. 12, 2003
Hon. Rev. William Alexander Blaikie, Feb. 19, 2004
Hon. Grant Hill, Feb. 19, 2004
Right Hon. Stephen Joseph Harper, May 4, 2004
Hon. Joseph Mario Jacques Olivier, May 5, 2004
Hon. Ujjal Dosanjh, Jul. 20, 2004
Hon. Ken Dryden, Jul. 20, 2004
Hon. David Emerson, Jul. 20, 2004
Hon. Tony Ianno, Jul. 20, 2004
Hon. Sarmite Bulte, Jul. 20, 2004
Hon. Roy Cullen, Jul. 20, 2004
Hon. Marlene Jennings, Jul. 20, 2004
Hon. Dominic LeBlanc, Jul. 20, 2004
Hon. Judi Longfield, Jul. 20, 2004
Hon. Paul Macklin, Jul. 20, 2004
Hon. Keith P. Martin, Jul. 20, 2004
Hon. Karen Redman, Jul. 20, 2004
Hon. Raymond Simard, Jul. 20, 2004
Hon. Patricia Ann Torsney, Jul. 20, 2004
Hon. Bryon Wilfert, Jul. 20, 2004
Hon. Belinda Stronach, May 17, 2005
Hon. Aldéa Landry, Q.C., Jun. 24, 2005
Right Hon. Adrienne Clarkson, Oct. 3, 2005
Hon. Navdeep Bains, Oct. 7, 2005
Hon. Anita Neville, Oct. 7, 2005
Hon. Charles Hubbard, Oct. 7, 2005
Hon. Jean-Pierre Blackburn, Feb. 6, 2006
Hon. Gregory Francis Thompson, Feb. 6, 2006
Hon. Marjory LeBreton, Feb. 6, 2006
Hon. Monte Solberg, Feb. 6, 2006
Hon. Charles (Chuck) Strahl, Feb. 6, 2006
Hon. Gary Lunn, Feb. 6, 2006
Hon. Peter Gordon MacKay, Feb. 6, 2006
Hon. Loyola Hearn, Feb. 6, 2006
Hon. Stockwell Burt Day, Feb. 6, 2006
Hon. Carol Skelton, Feb. 6, 2006
Hon. Vic Toews, Feb. 6, 2006
Hon. Rona Ambrose, Feb. 6, 2006
Hon. Michael D. Chong, Feb. 6, 2006
Hon. Diane Finley, Feb. 6, 2006
Hon. Gordon O'Connor, Feb. 6, 2006
Hon. Beverley J. (Bev) Oda, Feb. 6, 2006
Hon. John Baird, Feb. 6, 2006
Hon. Maxime Bernier, Feb. 6, 2006
Hon. Lawrence Cannon, Feb. 6, 2006
Hon. Tony Clement, Feb. 6, 2006
Hon. Josée Verner, Feb. 6, 2006
Hon. Michael Fortier, Feb. 6, 2006
Hon. John Reynolds, Feb. 6, 2006
Hon. Jay D. Hill, Feb. 16, 2006
Hon. Peter Van Loan, Nov. 27, 2006
Hon. Jason Kenney, Jan. 4, 2007
Hon. Gerry Ritz, Jan. 4, 2007
Hon. Helena Guergis, Jan. 4, 2007
Hon. Christian Paradis, Jan. 4, 2007
Hon. Daniel Philip Hays, Jan. 22, 2007
Hon. James Abbott, Oct. 15, 2007
Hon. Diane Ablonczy, Aug. 14, 2007

Hon. James Moore, Jun. 25, 2008
Hon. Denis Losier, Sep. 3, 2008
Hon. Leona Aglukkaq, Oct. 30, 2008
Hon. Steven John Fletcher, Oct. 30, 2008
Hon. Dr. Gary Goodyear, Oct. 30, 2008
Hon. Peter Kent, Oct. 30, 2008
Hon. Denis Lebel, Oct. 30, 2008
Hon. Rob Merrifield, Oct. 30, 2008
Hon. Lisa Raitt, Oct. 30, 2008
Hon. Gail Shea, Oct. 30, 2008
Hon. Lynne Yelich, Oct. 30, 2008
Hon. Leonard Joseph Gustafson, Jan. 8, 2009
Hon. Frances Lankin, Jan. 22, 2009
Hon. Kevin Lynch, May 11, 2009
Hon. Rob Moore, Jan. 19, 2010
Hon. Michael Grant Ignatieff, May 7, 2010
Hon. Philippe Couillard, Jun. 21, 2010
Hon. John Duncan, Aug. 6, 2010
Hon. Rick Casson, Oct. 1, 2010
Hon. Laurie Hawn, Oct. 1, 2010
Hon. Julian Fantino, Jan. 4, 2011
Hon. Ted Menzies, Jan. 4, 2011
Hon. Steven Blaney, May 18, 2011
Hon. Edward Fast, May 18, 2011
Hon. Joe Oliver, May 18, 2011
Hon. Peter Penashue, May 18, 2011
Hon. Tim Uppal, May 18, 2011
Hon. Alice Wong, May 18, 2011
Hon. Bal Gosal, May 18, 2011
Hon. Peter Andrew Stewart Milliken, May 8, 2012
Hon. Ronald Cannan, Sep. 13, 2012
Hon. Mike Lake, Sep. 13, 2012
Hon. Thomas J. Mulcair, Sep. 14, 2012
Right Hon. Michaëlle Jean, Sep. 26, 2012
Hon. Kerry-Lynne D. Findlay, Feb. 22, 2013
Hon. Ernest Preston Manning, Mar. 6, 2013
Hon. Deborah Grey, Apr. 22, 2013
Hon. Shelly Glover, Jul. 15, 2013
Hon. Chris Alexander, Jul. 15, 2013
Hon. Kellie Leitch, Jul. 15, 2013
Hon. Kevin Sorenson, Jul. 15, 2013
Hon. Pierre Poilievre, Jul. 15, 2013
Hon. Candice Bergen, Jul. 15, 2013
Hon. Greg Rickford, Jul. 15, 2013
Hon. Michelle Rempel Garner, Jul. 15, 2013
Hon. L. Yves Fortier, Aug. 8, 2013
Hon. Claude Carignan, Sep. 3, 2013
Hon. Gerald J. Comeau, Sep. 19, 2013
Hon. Cyril Eugene McLean, Mar. 6, 2014
Hon. Ed Holder, Mar. 19, 2014
H.R.H. Prince of Wales Charles Philip Arthur George, May 18, 2014
Hon. Wayne G. Wouters, Dec. 10, 2014
Hon. Erin O'Toole, Jan. 5, 2015
Hon. Ian Carl Holloway, Q.C., Jan. 30, 2015
Hon. Noël A. Kinsella, Feb. 23, 2015
Hon. Marie-Lucie Morin, Apr. 20, 2015
Right Hon. Justin Pierre James Trudeau, Nov. 4, 2015
Hon. William Francis Morneau, Nov. 4, 2015
Hon. Jody Wilson-Raybould, Nov. 4, 2015
Hon. Judy M. Foote, Nov. 4, 2015
Hon. Chrystia Freeland, Nov. 4, 2015
Hon. Jane Philpott, Nov. 4, 2015
Hon. Jean-Yves Duclos, Nov. 4, 2015
Hon. Marc Garneau, Nov. 4, 2015
Hon. Marie-Claude Bibeau, Nov. 4, 2015
Hon. James Gordon Carr, Nov. 4, 2015
Hon. Mélanie Joly, Nov. 4, 2015
Hon. Diane Lebouthillier, Nov. 4, 2015
Hon. Kent Hehr, Nov. 4, 2015
Hon. Catherine McKenna, Nov. 4, 2015
Hon. Harjit Singh Sajjan, Nov. 4, 2015
Hon. MaryAnn Mihychuk, Nov. 4, 2015
Hon. Amarjeet Sohi, Nov. 4, 2015
Hon. Maryam Monsef, Nov. 4, 2015
Hon. Carla Qualtrough, Nov. 4, 2015
Hon. Hunter Tootoo, Nov. 4, 2015
Hon. Kirsty Duncan, Nov. 4, 2015
Hon. Patricia A. Hajdu, Nov. 4, 2015
Hon. Bardish Chagger, Nov. 4, 2015
Hon. Andrew Brooke Leslie, Feb. 15, 2016
Hon. Ginette C. Petitpas Taylor, Feb. 15, 2016
Hon. V. Peter Harder, Apr. 6, 2016
Hon. François-Philippe Champagne, Jan. 10, 2017
Hon. Karina Gould, Jan. 10, 2017
Hon. Ahmed D. Hussen, Jan. 10, 2017
Hon. Pablo Rodriguez, Jan. 10, 2017
Hon. Seamus Thomas Harris O'Regan, Aug. 28, 2017

Hon. Andrew Scheer, Sep. 25, 2017
Hon. David J. McGuinty, Jan. 8, 2018
Rt. Hon. David Johnston, C.C., C.M.M., C.O.M., C.D., Mar. 26, 2018
Hon. William Sterling Blair, Jul. 18, 2018
Hon. Mary F.Y. Ng, Jul. 18, 2018
Hon. Filomena Tassi, Jul. 18, 2018
Hon. Jonathan Wilkinson, Jul. 18, 2018
Hon. Mark Holland, Sep. 14, 2018
Hon. Bernadette Jordan, Jan. 14, 2019
Hon. David Lametti, Jan. 14, 2019
Hon. Joyce Murray, Mar. 18, 2019
Hon. Anita Anand, Nov. 20, 2019
Hon. Mona Fortier, Nov. 20, 2019
Hon. Steven Guilbeault, Nov. 20, 2019
Hon. Bernadette Jordan, Nov. 20, 2019
Hon. Marco E.L. Mendicino, Nov. 20, 2019
Hon. Marc Miller, Nov. 20, 2019
Hon. Deborah Schulte, Nov. 20, 2019
Hon. Daniel Vandal, Nov. 20, 2019
Hon. Marc Gold, Jan. 27, 2020
Hon. Omar Alghabra, Feb. 6, 2020

Corporate Services / Services ministériels

Assistant Deputy Minister, Matthew Shea
Tel: 613-957-5151
Chief Information Officer; Director General, IT, Sreejit Nair
Tel: 613-295-5196
Director General, Human Resources Division, Joseph Silva
Tel: 613-952-4802
Executive Director, Finance & Corporate Planning Directorate, Michael Hammond
Tel: 613-952-6786
Executive Director, Access to Information & Privacy, David Neilson
Tel: 613-957-5228
Executive Director, Logistics & Special Services Directorate, Andrea Taylor
Tel: 613-957-5104
Senior Director, Information Technology Services Directorate, Ken MacDonald
Tel: 613-957-5380

Office of Intergovernmental Affairs (IGA) / Affaires intergouvernementales

Tel: 613-957-5153; *Fax:* 613-957-5043
pqpcc.minister-ministre.pcprc@pco-bcp.gc.ca
www.canada.ca/en/intergovernmental-affairs.html
The federal government office is responsible for the management of federal-provincial-territorial relations (FPTR). The office supports & advises the Prime Minister & the Minister of Intergovernmental Affairs about issues related to federal-provincial-territorial relations, such as communications, policies, & parliamentary affairs. Fiscal federalism, the evolution of the federation, & Canadian unity are key areas for the IGA.
Prime Minister; Minister, Intergovernmental Affairs, Right Hon. Justin Pierre James Trudeau, P.C., B.A., B.Ed.
Tel: 613-992-4211; *Fax:* 613-941-6900
justin.trudeau@parl.gc.ca
Deputy Minister, Intergovernmental Affairs, Michael Vandergrift
Tel: 613-960-4187
Assistant Deputy Minister, Louise Baird
Tel: 613-948-4223

Senate of Canada / Sénat du Canada

Ottawa, ON K1A 0A4

Toll-Free: 800-267-7362
sencom@sen.parl.gc.ca
sencanada.ca
twitter.com/SenateCA
www.facebook.com/SenCanada
www.linkedin.com/company/sencanada
www.instagram.com/sencanada

Senators are appointed by the Governor General, upon the recommendation of the Prime Minister of Canada. Senators hold their positions only until they attain the age of 75 years.
To be eligible for appointment, a senatorial candidate must be a Canadian citizen, & be at least 30 years of age. The person must own $4,000 of equity in land in their province or territory, & have a personal net worth of at least $4,000. A senator must also be a resident of the province or territory for which they are appointed.
The main tasks of the Senate are as follows: to examine bills; to approve, reject, or amend legislation; to investigate policy matters & to present recommendations; & to examine the government's spending proposals. No bill may become law unless it is passed by the Senate.
The main thrust of the Senate's work is carried out in committees, where bills are interpreted & reviewed clause by clause, & evidence is heard from groups & individuals who may be affected by the particular bill under review. Senators'

committees, or study groups, investigate key issues, such as poverty, terrorism, literacy, children's rights, Aboriginal peoples, constitutional affairs, & foreign affairs. The Senate reports produced from these legislations have proved to be valuable, & have often led to changes in government policy or legislation.
The Senate, as originally constituted at Confederation, consisted of 72 members. Through the addition of new provinces & territories, & the general growth of Canada, the Senate now has 105 regular members. On January 29, 2014, Liberal Leader Justin Trudeau removed all 32 Liberal senators from the national Liberal caucus, but they still technically sit as Liberals.
Following the 2015 general election, Prime Minister Trudeau announced the creation of an independent advisory body to recommend Senate nominees through a merit-based system.
By provinces & territories, representation in the Senate of Canada is as follows (Oct. 2021):
Alberta 5;
British Columbia 5;
Manitoba 5;
New Brunswick 8;
Newfoundland & Labrador 5;
Northwest Territories 1;
Nova Scotia 9;
Nunavut 1;
Ontario 22;
Prince Edward Island 3;
Québec 24;
Saskatchewan 5;
Yukon 1.
By party affiliation, representation is as follows (Oct. 2020):
Independent Senators Group (ISG) 40;
Conservative 18;
Canadian Senators Group (CSG) 13;
Progressive Senate Group (PSG) 13;
Non-affiliated 11;
Vacant 10;
Total 105.

Political Officers

Speaker of the Senate, Hon. George Furey, Non-affiliated
Tel: 613-992-4416; *Fax:* 613-992-9772
Speaker-President@sen.parl.gc.ca
twitter.com/georgefureynl
Speaker pro tempore, Hon. Pierrette Ringuette, ISG
Tel: 613-943-2248; *Fax:* 613-943-2245
pierrette.ringuette@sen.parl.gc.ca
Government Representative in the Senate; Leader of the Government in the Senate, Hon. Marc Gold, Non-affiliated
Tel: 613-995-0222; *Fax:* 613-995-0207
marc.gold@sen.parl.gc.ca
twitter.com/SenMarcGold
Legislative Deputy to the Government Representative in the Senate; Deputy Leader of the Government in the Senate, Hon. Raymonde Gagné, Non-affiliated
Tel: 613-943-4323
Raymonde.Gagne@sen.parl.gc.ca
Government Liaison in the Senate, Hon. Patti LaBoucane-Benson, Non-affiliated
Tel: 613-943-8282
Patti.LaBoucane-Benson@sen.parl.gc.ca
Leader of the Opposition in the Senate, Hon. Donald Neil Plett, Conservative Party
Tel: 613-947-6416; *Fax:* 613-947-6447
don.plett@sen.parl.gc.ca
twitter.com/DonPlett
Deputy Leader of the Opposition in the Senate, Hon. Yonah Martin, Conservative Party
Tel: 613-943-4078; *Fax:* 613-943-4082
martin@sen.parl.gc.ca
Whip of the Opposition in the Senate, Hon. Judith G. Seidman, Conservative Party
Tel: 613-992-0110; *Fax:* 613-992-0118
judith.seidman@sen.parl.gc.ca
twitter.com/judithseidman
Deputy Whip of the Opposition in the Senate, Hon. Leo Housakos, Conservative Party
Tel: 613-947-4237; *Fax:* 613-947-4239
Leo.Housakos@sen.parl.gc.ca
Chair of the Conservative Caucus, Hon. Rose-May Poirier, Conservative Party
Tel: 613-943-4027; *Fax:* 613-943-4026
rosemay.poirier@sen.parl.gc.ca
rosemaypoirier.sencanada.ca
Facilitator, Independent Senators Group (ISG), Hon. Yuen Pau Woo, ISG
Tel: 613-995-9244; *Fax:* 613-995-9246
YuenPau.Woo@sen.parl.gc.ca
Deputy Facilitator, Independent Senators Group (ISG), Hon. Raymonde Saint-Germain, ISG
Tel: 613-995-9204; *Fax:* 613-995-9210
raymonde.saint-germain@sen.parl.gc.ca
Liaison, Independent Senators Group (ISG), Hon. Ratna Omidvar, ISG
Tel: 613-943-4330

Ratna.Omidvar@sen.parl.gc.ca
twitter.com/ratnaomi
Chamber Coordinator, Independent Senators Group (ISG), Hon. Pat Duncan, ISG
Tel: 613-947-7557; *Fax:* 613-947-7554
Pat.Duncan@sen.parl.gc.ca
twitter.com/YukonSenator
Leader, Canadian Senators Group (CSG), Hon. Scott Tannas, CSG
Tel: 613-943-2240
scott.tannas@sen.parl.gc.ca
Deputy Leader, Canadian Senators Group (CSG), Hon. Diane F. Griffin, CSG
Tel: 613-996-2140; *Fax:* 613-996-2133
Diane.Griffin@sen.parl.gc.ca
Liaison, Canadian Senators Group (CSG), Hon. Percy E. Downe, CSG
Tel: 613-943-8107; *Fax:* 613-943-8109
Percy.Downe@sen.parl.gc.ca
Chair, Canadian Senators Group (CSG), Hon. Robert Black, CSG
Tel: 613-943-3416
robert.black@sen.parl.gc.ca
Leader, Progressive Senate Group (PSG), Hon. Jane Cordy, PSG
Tel: 613-995-8409; *Fax:* 613-995-8432
jane.cordy@sen.parl.gc.ca
Deputy Leader, Progressive Senate Group (PSG), Hon. Pierre J Dalphond, PSG
Tel: 613-943-3688; *Fax:* 613-943-3684
PierreJ.Dalphond@sen.parl.gc.ca
Liaison, Progressive Senate Group (PSG), Hon. Patricia Bovey, PSG
Tel: 613-995-9176; *Fax:* 613-995-9182
Patricia.Bovey@sen.parl.gc.ca
Caucus Chair, Progressive Senate Group (PSG), Hon. Brian Francis, PSG
Tel: 613-943-8296; *Fax:* 613-943-8302
Brian.Francis@sen.parl.gc.ca

Senators, with appointment year & political affiliation

Hon. Margaret Dawn Anderson, 2018, PSG
Tel: 613-947-7570; *Fax:* 613-947-7251
MargaretDawn.Anderson@sen.parl.gc.ca
Hon. David Arnot, 2021, Non-affiliated
Tel: 343-550-8142
David.Arnot@sen.parl.gc.ca
Hon. Salma Ataullahjan, 2010, Conservative Party
Tel: 613-947-5906; *Fax:* 613-947-5908
salma.ataullahjan@sen.parl.gc.ca
senatorsalma.ca
twitter.com/SenatorSalma, www.facebook.com/SenatorSalma
Hon. Michèle Audette, 2021, Non-affiliated
Tel: 343-550-8142
Michele.Audette@sen.parl.gc.ca
Hon. Denise Batters, 2013, Conservative Party
Tel: 613-996-8922; *Fax:* 613-996-8964
denise.batters@sen.parl.gc.ca
denisebatters.ca
twitter.com/denisebatters,
www.facebook.com/sendenisebatters
Hon. Diane Bellemare, 2012, ISG
Tel: 613-943-1555; *Fax:* 613-943-1565
diane.bellemare@sen.parl.gc.ca
dianebellemaresen.ca
twitter.com/sendbellemare,
www.facebook.com/DianeBellemareSen
Hon. Wanda Elaine Thomas Bernard, 2016, PSG
Tel: 613-996-2090; *Fax:* 613-996-2010
WandaThomas.Bernard@sen.parl.gc.ca
twitter.com/SenatorWanda
Hon. Douglas Black, 2013, CSG
Tel: 613-996-8757; *Fax:* 613-996-8862
doug.black@sen.parl.gc.ca
dougblack.ca
twitter.com/DougBlackAB,
www.facebook.com/senatordougblack
Hon. Robert Black, 2018, CSG
Tel: 613-943-3416
robert.black@sen.parl.gc.ca
robblack.ca
twitter.com/SenatorRobBlack,
www.facebook.com/SenatorRobBlack
Hon. Peter M. Boehm, 2018, ISG
Tel: 613-943-8226
Peter.Boehm@sen.parl.gc.ca
twitter.com/SenBoehm
Hon. Pierre-Hugues Boisvenu, 2010, Conservative Party
Tel: 613-943-4030
boisvp@sen.parl.gc.ca
twitter.com/senatboisvenu, www.facebook.com/PHBoisvenu
Note: Senator Boisvenu left the Conservative caucus on June 4, 2015, amid the growing Senate expense scandal, but rejoined the caucus in November 2016.

Hon. Gwen Boniface, 2016, ISG
Tel: 613-995-9193
Gwen.Boniface@sen.parl.gc.ca
Hon. Patricia Bovey, 2016, PSG
Tel: 613-995-9176; *Fax:* 613-995-9182
Patricia.Bovey@sen.parl.gc.ca
www.patriciabovey.com
Hon. Yvonne Boyer, 2018, ISG
Tel: 613-943-3500; *Fax:* 613-943-3502
Yvonne.Boyer@sen.parl.gc.ca
twitter.com/senatorboyer
Hon. Patrick Brazeau, 2008, Non-affiliated
Tel: 613-995-8625; *Fax:* 613-995-8647
Patrick.Brazeau@sen.parl.gc.ca
twitter.com/senatorbrazeau
Hon. Bev Busson, C.M., C.O.M., O.B.C., 2018, ISG
Tel: 613-943-7930
Beverley.Busson@sen.parl.gc.ca
bevbusson.sencanada.ca
Hon. Larry W. Campbell, 2005, CSG
Tel: 613-995-4050
larry.campbell@sen.parl.gc.ca
larrycampbell.ca
Hon. Claude Carignan, P.C., 2009, Conservative Party
Tel: 613-992-0240; *Fax:* 613-992-0246
claude.carignan@sen.parl.gc.ca
www.claudecarignan.net
twitter.com/senatcarignan,
www.facebook.com/senateurcarignan
Hon. Daniel Christmas, 2016, ISG
Tel: 613-996-2188
daniel.christmas@sen.parl.gc.ca
Hon. Bernadette Clement, 2021, Non-affiliated
Tel: 613-944-1046
Bernadette.Clement@sen.parl.gc.ca
Hon. Jane Marie Cordy, 2000, PSG
Tel: 613-995-8409; *Fax:* 613-995-8432
jane.cordy@sen.parl.gc.ca
twitter.com/senatorcordy
Hon. René Cormier, 2016, ISG
Tel: 613-996-2247
Rene.Cormier@sen.parl.gc.ca
twitter.com/SenCormier, www.facebook.com/sencormier
Hon. Brent Cotter, 2020, ISG
Tel: 613-943-8708
Brent.Cotter@sen.parl.gc.ca
Hon. Mary Coyle, 2017, ISG
Tel: 613-943-1338; *Fax:* 613-943-1341
Mary.Coyle@sen.parl.gc.ca
twitter.com/SenCoyle
Hon. Jean-Guy Dagenais, 2012, CSG
Tel: 613-996-7644; *Fax:* 613-996-7649
jean-guy.dagenais@sen.parl.gc.ca
senateurdagenais.ca
twitter.com/senatdagenais
Hon. Pierre J. Dalphond, 2018, PSG
Tel: 613-943-3688; *Fax:* 613-943-3684
PierreJ.Dalphond@sen.parl.gc.ca
twitter.com/DalphondPierre
Hon. Donna Dasko, 2018, ISG
Tel: 613-943-3711; *Fax:* 613-943-3715
Donna.Dasko@sen.parl.gc.ca
Hon. Dennis Dawson, 2005, PSG
Tel: 613-995-3978; *Fax:* 613-995-3998
dennis.dawson@sen.parl.gc.ca
twitter.com/dennis_dawson
Hon. Colin Deacon, 2018, ISG
Tel: 613-943-3735
colin.deacon@sen.parl.gc.ca
colindeacon.ca
twitter.com/colindeacon,
www.facebook.com/SenatorColinDeacon,
www.linkedin.com/in/senatorcolindeacon
Hon. Marty Deacon, 2018, ISG
Tel: 613-220-6886
Marty.Deacon@sen.parl.gc.ca
senatormartydeacon.sencanada.ca
Hon. Tony Dean, 2016, ISG
Tel: 613-996-2312; *Fax:* 613-996-2287
Tony.Dean@sen.parl.gc.ca
tonydean.sencanada.ca
twitter.com/TonyDean_TO
Hon. Percy E. Downe, 2003, CSG
Tel: 613-943-8107; *Fax:* 613-943-8109
percy.downe@sen.parl.gc.ca
twitter.com/PercyDowne
Hon. Pat Duncan, 2018, ISG
Tel: 613-947-7557; *Fax:* 613-947-7554
Pat.Duncan@sen.parl.gc.ca
twitter.com/YukonSenator
Hon. Renée Dupuis, 2016, ISG
Tel: 613-996-2063; *Fax:* 613-996-2047
Renee.Dupuis@sen.parl.gc.ca

Hon. Éric Forest, 2016, ISG
Tel: 613-996-2171; *Fax:* 613-996-2168
Eric.Forest@sen.parl.gc.ca
twitter.com/EricForestSen, www.facebook.com/ericforest.sen
Hon. Josée Forest-Niesing, 2018, ISG
Tel: 613-943-8313; *Fax:* 613-943-8316
Josee.Forest-Niesing@sen.parl.gc.ca
www.facebook.com/352764032206313
Hon. Brian Francis, 2018, PSG
Tel: 613-943-8296; *Fax:* 613-943-8302
Brian.Francis@sen.parl.gc.ca
twitter.com/BrianFrancisPEI,
www.facebook.com/BrianFrancisPEI
Hon. George J. Furey, 1999, Non-affiliated
Tel: 613-992-4416; *Fax:* 613-992-9772
george.furey@sen.parl.gc.ca
twitter.com/georgefureynl
Hon. Raymonde Gagné, 2016, Non-affiliated
Tel: 613-943-4323
Raymonde.Gagne@sen.parl.gc.ca
Hon. Rosa Galvez, 2016, ISG
Tel: 613-996-2210; *Fax:* 613-996-2208
rosa.galvez@sen.parl.gc.ca
rosagalvez.ca
twitter.com/SenRosaGalvez,
www.facebook.com/SenRosaGalvez,
www.linkedin.com/in/rosa-galvez-37489713
Hon. Amina Gerba, 2021, PSG
Tel: 343-550-8142
Amina.Gerba@sen.parl.gc.ca
Hon. Clément Gignac, 2021, PSG
Tel: 613-944-1113
Clement.Gignac@sen.parl.gc.ca
Hon. Marc Gold, 2016, Non-affiliated
Tel: 613-995-0222; *Fax:* 613-995-0207
marc.gold@sen.parl.gc.ca
senate-gro.ca
twitter.com/SenMarcGold
Hon. Stephen Greene, 2009, CSG
Tel: 613-947-4210; *Fax:* 613-947-4224
stephen.greene@sen.parl.gc.ca
stephengreene.sencanada.ca
Hon. Diane F. Griffin, 2016, CSG
Tel: 613-996-2140; *Fax:* 613-996-2133
Diane.Griffin@sen.parl.gc.ca
twitter.com/SenDianeGriffin,
www.facebook.com/SenatorGriffin
Hon. Peter Harder, P.C., 2016, PSG
Tel: 613-943-8039
peter.harder@sen.parl.gc.ca
peterharder.sencanada.ca
twitter.com/SenHarder
Hon. Nancy Hartling, 2016, ISG
Tel: 613-995-9191
Nancy.Hartling@sen.parl.gc.ca
senatorhartling.sencanada.ca
www.facebook.com/SenatorHartling
Hon. Leo Housakos, 2008, Conservative Party
Tel: 613-947-4237; *Fax:* 613-947-4239
Leo.Housakos@sen.parl.gc.ca
leohousakos.sencanada.ca
twitter.com/SenatorHousakos
Hon. Mobina S.B. Jaffer, 2001, ISG
Tel: 613-992-0189; *Fax:* 613-992-0673
mobina.jaffer@sen.parl.gc.ca
mobinajaffer.ca
twitter.com/SenJaffer, www.facebook.com/SenatorJaffer
Hon. Marty Klyne, 2018, PSG
Tel: 613-944-3453; *Fax:* 613-943-7940
Marty.Klyne@sen.parl.gc.ca
Hon. Stan Kutcher, 2018, ISG
Tel: 613-947-7277
Stanley.Kutcher@sen.parl.gc.ca
stankutcher.sencanada.ca
twitter.com/stankutcher,
www.facebook.com/senator.stan.kutcher
Hon. Patti LaBoucane-Benson, 2018, Non-affiliated
Tel: 613-943-8282
Patti.LaBoucane-Benson@sen.parl.gc.ca
senlaboucanebenson.sencanada.ca
Hon. Frances Lankin, P.C., 2016, ISG
Tel: 613-995-2795; *Fax:* 613-995-2789
Frances.Lankin@sen.parl.gc.ca
Hon. Tony Loffreda, 2019, ISG
Tel: 613-943-5694
Tony.Loffreda@sen.parl.gc.ca
twitter.com/tonyloffreda,
www.facebook.com/SenatorTonyLoffreda,
www.linkedin.com/in/senator-tony-loffreda-cpa-73abb112
Hon. Sandra M. Lovelace Nicholas, 2005, PSG
Tel: 613-943-3635; *Fax:* 613-943-3637
carole.smith@sen.parl.gc.ca

Hon. Michael L. MacDonald, 2009, Conservative Party
Tel: 613-995-1866; *Fax:* 613-995-1853
michael.macdonald@sen.parl.gc.ca
Hon. Fabian Manning, 2011, Conservative Party
Tel: 613-947-4203; *Fax:* 613-947-4170
fabian.manning@sen.parl.gc.ca
www.fabianmanning.ca
Hon. Elizabeth (Beth) Marshall, 2010, Conservative Party
Tel: 613-943-4011
elizabeth.marshall@sen.parl.gc.ca
elizabethmarshall.ca
Hon. Yonah Martin, 2009, Conservative Party
Tel: 613-943-4078; *Fax:* 613-943-4082
martin@sen.parl.gc.ca
yonahmartin.sencanada.ca
Hon. Sabi Marwah, 2016, ISG
Tel: 613-947-6809
sabi.marwah@sen.parl.gc.ca
sabimarwah.sencanada.ca
Hon. Paul J. Massicotte, 2003, ISG
Tel: 613-943-5793; *Fax:* 613-943-8129
paul.massicotte@sen.parl.gc.ca
pauljmassicotte.sencanada.ca
twitter.com/SenMassicotte,
www.facebook.com/senatormassicotte
Hon. Mary Jane McCallum, 2017, ISG
Tel: 613-943-1330
MaryJane.McCallum@sen.parl.gc.ca
maryjanemccallum.ca
Hon. Marilou McPhedran, 2016, ISG
Tel: 613-996-2106
Marilou.McPhedran@sen.parl.gc.ca
twitter.com/SenMarilou, www.facebook.com/SenMarilou
Hon. Marie-Françoise Mégie, 2016, ISG
Tel: 613-996-2357
marie-francoise.megie@sen.parl.gc.ca
www.facebook.com/SenMegie
Hon. Terry M. Mercer, 2003, PSG
Tel: 613-996-2657; *Fax:* 613-947-2345
terry.mercer@sen.parl.gc.ca
Hon. Julie Miville-Dechêne, 2018, ISG
Tel: 613-943-4780
julie.miville-dechene@sen.parl.gc.ca
twitter.com/mivillej, www.facebook.com/senmivilledechene
Hon. Percy Mockler, 2009, Conservative Party
Tel: 613-947-4225; *Fax:* 613-947-4227
percy.mockler@sen.parl.gc.ca
percymockler.sencanada.ca
twitter.com/SenMockler,
www.facebook.com/senaterpercy.mockler.9
Hon. Lucie Moncion, 2016, ISG
Tel: 613-996-2224
Lucie.Moncion@sen.parl.gc.ca
twitter.com/SenLucieMoncion
Hon. Rosemary Moodie, 2018, ISG
Tel: 613-947-7237; *Fax:* 613-947-7239
Rosemary.Moodie@sen.parl.gc.ca
senmoodie.sencanada.ca
Hon. Thanh Hai Ngo, 2012, Conservative Party
Tel: 613-943-1599; *Fax:* 613-943-1592
thanhhai.ngo@sen.parl.gc.ca
senatorngo.com
twitter.com/SenatorNgo
Hon. Victor Oh, 2013, Conservative Party
Tel: 613-943-1880; *Fax:* 613-943-1882
senator.oh@sen.parl.gc.ca
twitter.com/SenatorVictorOh,
www.facebook.com/SenatorVictorOh
Hon. Ratna Omidvar, C.M., O.Ont., 2016, ISG
Tel: 613-943-4330
Ratna.Omidvar@sen.parl.gc.ca
www.ratnaomidvar.ca
twitter.com/ratnaomi
Hon. Kim Pate, 2016, ISG
Tel: 613-995-9220; *Fax:* 613-995-9218
Kim.Pate@sen.parl.gc.ca
twitter.com/KPateontheHill,
www.facebook.com/kim.pate.3152
Hon. Dennis Glen Patterson, 2009, Conservative Party
Tel: 613-992-0480; *Fax:* 613-992-0495
dennis.patterson@sen.parl.gc.ca
dennispatterson.ca
www.facebook.com/DennisGlenPatterson
Hon. Chantal Petitclerc, 2016, ISG
Tel: 613-995-0298
Chantal.Petitclerc@sen.parl.gc.ca
twitter.com/CPetitclerc, www.facebook.com/chantalpetitclerc
Hon. Donald Neil Plett, 2009, Conservative Party
Tel: 613-947-6416; *Fax:* 613-947-6447
don.plett@sen.parl.gc.ca
www.donplett.ca
twitter.com/DonPlett, www.facebook.com/senatorplett

Hon. Rose-May Poirier, 2010, Conservative Party
Tel: 613-943-4027; *Fax:* 613-943-4026
rosemay.poirier@sen.parl.gc.ca
rosemaypoirier.sencanada.ca
Hon. Jim Quinn, 2021, CSG
Tel: 613-944-1050
jim.quinn@sen.parl.gc.ca
Hon. Mohamed-Iqbal Ravalia, 2016, ISG
Tel: 613-943-3676
Mohamed-iqbal.ravalia@sen.parl.gc.ca
Hon. David Adams Richards, 2017, CSG
Tel: 613-943-6263; *Fax:* 613-943-6265
David.Richards@sen.parl.gc.ca
Hon. Pierrette Ringuette, 2002, ISG
Tel: 613-943-2248; *Fax:* 613-943-2245
pierrette.ringuette@sen.parl.gc.ca
pringuette.sencanada.ca
Hon. Raymonde Saint-Germain, 2016, ISG
Tel: 613-995-9204; *Fax:* 613-995-9210
raymonde.saint-germain@sen.parl.gc.ca
twitter.com/SenSaintGermain
Hon. Judith Seidman, 2009, Conservative Party
Tel: 613-992-0110; *Fax:* 613-992-0118
judith.seidman@sen.parl.gc.ca
www.judithseidman.ca
twitter.com/judithseidman
Hon. Paula Simons, 2018, ISG
Tel: 613-943-8242; *Fax:* 613-943-8267
Paula.Simons@sen.parl.gc.ca
senatorpaulasimons.ca
twitter.com/Paulatics,
www.facebook.com/SenatorPaulaSimons
Hon. Larry W. Smith, 2011, Conservative Party
Tel: 343-549-2746
larry.smith@sen.parl.gc.ca
twitter.com/SenLWSmith
Hon. Karen Sorensen, 2021, Non-affiliated
Tel: 343-550-8142
Karen.Sorensen@sen.parl.gc.ca
twitter.com/Karen_Banff
Hon. Scott Tannas, 2013, CSG
Tel: 613-943-2240
scott.tannas@sen.parl.gc.ca
www.facebook.com/ScottTannas.ca
Hon. Josée Verner, P.C., 2011, CSG
Tel: 613-996-6999
josee.verner@sen.parl.gc.ca
Hon. Pamela Wallin, O.C., S.O.M., 2009, CSG
Tel: 613-996-2794; *Fax:* 613-995-0173
pamela.wallin@sen.parl.gc.ca
www.facebook.com/SenPamelaWallin
Hon. David M. Wells, 2013, Conservative Party
Tel: 613-943-1788; *Fax:* 613-943-1926
davidwells@sen.parl.gc.ca
twitter.com/wellsdavid
Hon. Howard Wetston, 2016, ISG
Tel: 613-995-9197
Howard.Wetston@sen.parl.gc.ca
Hon. Vernon White, 2012, CSG
Tel: 613-996-7602; *Fax:* 613-996-7654
senatorwhite@sen.parl.gc.ca
sen.parl.gc.ca/vwhite
www.facebook.com/107421413000121
Hon. Yuen Pau Woo, 2016, ISG
Tel: 613-995-9244; *Fax:* 613-995-9246
YuenPau.Woo@sen.parl.gc.ca
www.senatoryuenpauwoo.ca
twitter.com/yuenpauwoo,
www.facebook.com/senatoryuenpauwoo
Hon. Hassan Yussuff, 2021, Non-affiliated
Tel: 613-944-1108
H.Yussuff@sen.parl.gc.ca

Clerk of the Senate & Clerk of the Parliaments & Chief Legislative Services Officer
Parliament Hill, Centre Block, #185-S, Ottawa, ON K1A 0A4
Interim Clerk of the Senate & Clerk of the Parliaments, Gérald Lafrenière
Tel: 613-992-2493
Principal Clerk, Committees Directorate, Blair Armitage
Tel: 613-996-5588
Principal Clerk, Chamber Operations & Procedure Office, Heather Lank
Tel: 613-996-0397
Usher of the Black Rod, J. Greg Peters
Tel: 613-992-8483

Clerk of the Standing Committee on Internal Economy, Budgets and Administration & Chief Corporate Services Officer
Parliament Hill, Centre Block, #675-F, Ottawa, ON K1A 0A4
Clerk of the Standing Committee on Internal Economy, Budgets & Administration & Chief Corporate Services Officer, Pascale

Legault
Tel: 613-996-2740
Procedural Clerk & Recording Secretary, Daniel Charbonneau
Tel: 613-301-7565
Comptroller & DCFO, Finance & Procurement Directorate, Nathalie Charpentier
Tel: 613-996-7031

Law Clerk & Parliamentary Counsel
Chambers Bldg., 40 Elgin St., 13th Fl., Ottawa, ON K1A 0A4
Law Clerk & Parliamentary Counsel, Philippe Hallée
Tel: 613-996-7184; *Fax:* 613-992-2125
Deputy Law Clerk & Parliamentary Counsel, Catherine Beaudoin
Tel: 613-996-2627; *Fax:* 613-992-2125

House of Commons, Canada / Chambre des communes

House of Commons, Centre Block, Parliament Buildings, 111 Wellington St., Ottawa, ON K1A 0A6

Tel: 613-992-4793
Toll-Free: 866-599-4999
TTY: 613-995-2266
info@parl.gc.ca
www.ourcommons.ca
Other Communication: General Twitter:
twitter.com/OurCommons
Information Service, Parliament of Canada
Ottawa, ON K1A 0A9
twitter.com/HoCChamber
www.linkedin.com/company/houseofcommons-
www.instagram.com/ourcommonsca

The House of Commons is the major law-making unit in Canada. The 338 members of the House represent each constituency, or riding, across Canada.
Members are elected in general elections, held at least once every four years (although the Canadian Charter of Rights & Freedoms allows for a maximum term of five years). During general elections, one candidate per riding is elected, based on the largest number of votes, even if his or her vote is less than half the total. When a member resigns or dies between general elections, a by-election is held.
The party that wins the largest number of seats in the general election usually forms the government. The party with the second largest number of votes becomes the Official Opposition. A minority government is created when one particular party holds no clear majority of seats in the House. In this case, the government is usually led by the party with the most seats in Parliament, providing it can sustain the support from other minor parties that enable it to pass legislation.
Any bills within federal jurisdiction must be passed by a majority of House members to become law. Members usually vote on proposed legislation according to party affiliation. They may vote against their party. They may also leave their elected party to sit as an independent within the House.
The Speaker of the House of Commons is a Member of Parliament, who is selected by fellow Members of Parliament through a secret ballot process. The Speaker's roles are to ensure that all procedures & rules are followed in the House, & to oversee administration in the House.

Officers & Officials of the House of Commons
Speaker of the House of Commons, Hon. Anthony Rota
Tel: 613-996-3085; *Fax:* 613-996-6988
Deputy Speaker; Chair, Committees of the Whole, Hon. Bruce Stanton
Tel: 613-992-6582; *Fax:* 613-996-3128
bruce.stanton@parl.gc.ca
Leader of the Government in the House of Commons, Hon. Pablo Rodriguez, P.C., B.A.A.
Tel: 613-995-0580; *Fax:* 613-992-1710
Pablo.Rodriguez@parl.gc.ca
House Leader, Official Opposition; House Leader, Conservative Party, Gérard Deltell
House Leader, New Democratic Party, Peter Julian
Chief Government Whip; Whip, Liberal Party, Hon. Mark Holland
Chief Opposition Whip; Whip, Conservative Party, Blake Richards
Whip, New Democratic Party, Rachel Blaney
Caucus Chair, Liberal Party, Francis Scarpaleggia, B.A., M.A., M.B.A.
Tel: 613-995-8281; *Fax:* 613-996-0828
francis.scarpaleggia@parl.gc.ca
Caucus Chair, Conservative Party, Tom Kmiec
Tel: 613-992-0846; *Fax:* 613-992-0883
tom.kmiec@parl.gc.ca
Caucus Chair, New Democratic Party, Brian Masse
Tel: 613-996-1541; *Fax:* 613-992-5397
brian.masse@parl.gc.ca
Responsible, Liberal Party Research Office, Right Hon. Justin Pierre James Trudeau, P.C., B.A., B.Ed.
Tel: 613-995-0253; *Fax:* 613-947-0310
justin.trudeau@parl.gc.ca
www.pm.gc.ca

Responsible, Conservative Party Research Office, Hon. Erin O'Toole, P.C.
Tel: 613-992-2792; *Fax:* 613-992-2794
erin.otool@parl.gc.ca
Responsible, New Democratic Party Research Office, Jagmeet Singh
Tel: 613-947-0867; *Fax:* 613-947-0868
jagmeet.singh@parl.gc.ca
twitter.com/thejagmeetsingh, www.facebook.com/jagmeetndp
Clerk, House of Commons, Charles Robert
Tel: 613-992-2986
charles.robert@parl.gc.ca
Chief of Staff, Office of the Clerk & Secretariat, Guillaume LaPerrière-Marcoux
Tel: 613-992-5687

Committees of the House of Commons / Comités de la chambre des communes

Committees Directorate, House of Commons, 131 Queen St., 6th Fl., Ottawa, ON K1A 0A6

Tel: 613-992-3150
cmteweb@parl.gc.ca
www.ourcommons.ca/Committees/en/Home
twitter.com/HoCCommittees

A committee consists of parliamentarians from the House of Commons, the Senate, or both. Committee members are selected for study & consideration of matters, including bills. Items for consideration by committess are referred by the House of Commons or the Senate.
Types of committees include the following: Committees of the Whole; Joint Committees; Legislative Committees; Liaison Committee; Standing Committees; & Special Committees.
The following were the House of Commons Committees as of Oct. 2021:
Access to Information, Privacy, & Ethics;
Agriculture & Agri-Food;
Canada-China Relations (Special Committee);
Canadian Heritage;
Citizenship & Immigration;
Economic Relationship between Canada & the United States (Special Committee);
Environment & Sustainable Development;
Finance;
Fisheries & Oceans;
Foreign Affairs & International Development;
Government Operations & Estimates;
Health;
Human Resources, Skills & Social Development, & the Status of Persons with Disabilities;
Indigenous & Northern Affairs;
Industry, Science, & Technology;
International Trade;
Justice & Human Rights;
Liaison;
National Defence;
Natural Resources;
Official Languages;
Procedure & House Affairs;
Public Accounts;
Public Safety & National Security;
Status of Women;
Transport, Infrastructure, & Communities;
& Veterans Affairs.
Principal Clerk, Committees, Jeffrey LeBlanc
Tel: 613-995-0516
jeffrey.leblanc@parl.gc.ca
Principal Clerk, Committees, Ian McDonald
Tel: 613-943-9484; *Fax:* 613-947-0309
ian.mcdonald@parl.gc.ca
Clerk, Access to Information, Privacy & Ethics Committee, Miriam Burke
Tel: 613-992-1240
ethi@parl.gc.ca
ourcommons.ca/ETHI-e
Clerk, Agriculture & Agri-Food Committee, Alexie Labelle
Tel: 613-943-0291
agri@parl.gc.ca
ourcommons.ca/AGRI-e
Clerk, Canada-China Relations Special Committee, Marie-France Lafleur
Tel: 613-992-4111
cacn.cmt@parl.gc.ca
ourcommons.ca/CACN-e
Clerk, Canadian Heritage Committee, Aimée Belmore
Tel: 613-947-6729
chpc@parl.gc.ca
ourcommons.ca/CHPC-e
Clerk, Citizenship & Immigration Committee, Leif-Erik Aune
Tel: 613-995-8525
cimm@parl.gc.ca
ourcommons.ca/CIMM-e
Clerk, Economic Relationship between Canada & the United States Special Committee, Erica Pereira

Tel: 613-943-0200
caam@parl.gc.ca
ourcommons.ca/CIMM-e
Clerk, Environment & Sustainable Development Committee,
Angela Crandall
Tel: 613-992-5023
envi@parl.gc.ca
ourcommons.ca/ENVI-e
Clerk, Finance Committee, Alexandre Roger
Tel: 613-992-9753
fina@parl.gc.ca
ourcommons.ca/FINA-e
Clerk, Fisheries & Oceans Committee, Tina Miller
Tel: 613-996-3105
fopo@parl.gc.ca
ourcommons.ca/FOPO-e
Clerk, Foreign Affairs & International Development Committee,
Erica Pereira
Tel: 613-996-1540
faae@parl.gc.ca
ourcommons.ca/FAAE-e
Clerk, Government Operations & Estimates Committee, Paul
Cardegna
Tel: 613-995-9469
oggo@parl.gc.ca
ourcommons.ca/OGGO-e
Clerk, Health Committee, Jean-François Pagé
Tel: 613-995-4108
hesa@parl.gc.ca
ourcommons.ca/HESA-e
Clerk, Human Resources, Skills, & Social Development & the
Status of Persons with Disabilities Committee, Danielle
Widmer
Tel: 613-996-1542
huma@parl.gc.ca
ourcommons.ca/HUMA-e
Clerk, Indigenous & Northern Affairs Committee, Naaman
Sugrue
Tel: 613-992-9672
inan@parl.gc.ca
ourcommons.ca/INAN-e
Clerk, Industry, Science, & Technology Committee, Michael
MacPherson
Tel: 613-947-1971
indu@parl.gc.ca
ourcommons.ca/INDU-e
Clerk, International Trade Committee, Christine Lafrance
Tel: 613-944-4364
ciit@parl.gc.ca
ourcommons.ca/CIIT-e
Clerk, Justice & Human Rights Committee, Marc-Olivier Girard
Tel: 613-996-1553
just@parl.gc.ca
ourcommons.ca/JUST-e
Clerk, Liaison Committee, Robert Benoit
Tel: 613-944-5652
liai@parl.gc.ca
ourcommons.ca/LIAI-e
Clerk, National Defence Committee, Wassim Bouanani
Tel: 613-995-9461
nddn@parl.gc.ca
ourcommons.ca/NDDN-e
Clerk, Natural Resources Committee, Hilary Jane Powell
Tel: 613-995-0047
rnnr@parl.gc.ca
ourcommons.ca/RNNR-e
Clerk, Official Languages Committee, Nancy Vohl
Tel: 613-947-8891
lang@parl.gc.ca
ourcommons.ca/LANG-e
Clerk, Procedure & House Affairs Committee, Justin Vaive
Tel: 613-996-7092
proc@parl.gc.ca
ourcommons.ca/PROC-e
Clerk, Public Accounts Committee, Angela Crandall
Tel: 613-996-1664
pacp@parl.gc.ca
ourcommons.ca/PACP-e
Clerk, Public Safety & National Security Committee, Mark
D'Amore
Tel: 613-944-5635
secu@parl.gc.ca
ourcommons.ca/SECU-e
Clerk, Status of Women Committee, Stephanie Bond
Tel: 613-995-6119
fewo@parl.gc.ca
ourcommons.ca/FEWO-e
Clerk, Transport, Infrastructure, & Communities Committee,
Michael MacPherson
Tel: 613-996-4663
tran@parl.gc.ca
ourcommons.ca/TRAN-e

Clerk, Veterans Affairs Committee, Benoit Jolicoeur
Tel: 613-944-9354
acva@parl.gc.ca
ourcommons.ca/ACVA-e

Corporate Security Office / Bureau de la sécurité institutionnelle

Sergeant-at-Arms, Patrick McDonell
Tel: 613-995-3557
patrick.mcdonell@parl.gc.ca
Deputy Sergeant-at-Arms, Michel Denault
Tel: 613-996-3021
michel.denault@parl.gc.ca
Deputy Director, Security Project Management Office &
Technical Operations, Gregory Dack
Tel: 613-996-5715
gregory.dack@parl.gc.ca

Digital Services & Real Property / Services numériques et Biens immobiliers

Chief Information Officer, Stéphan Aubé
Tel: 613-995-8884; *Fax:* 613-947-3547
stephan.aube@parl.gc.ca
Chief Technology Officer, Soufiane Ben Moussa
Tel: 613-947-5599; *Fax:* 613-947-3547
soufiane.benmoussa@parl.gc.ca
Senior Director, IT Operations & Services, Benoit Dicaire
Tel: 613-947-0253
benoit.dicaire@parl.gc.ca

Finance Services / Services des Finances

Chief Financial Officer, Daniel Paquette
Tel: 613-996-0485; *Fax:* 613-995-4970
daniel.g.paquette@parl.gc.ca
Deputy Chief Financial Officer, José Fernandez
Tel: 613-947-2570
jose.fernandez@parl.gc.ca
Senior Director, Financial Planning & Resource Management,
Elaine Valiquette
Tel: 613-992-6169
elaine.valiquette@parl.gc.ca

Human Resources Services / Services en ressources humaines

Chief Human Resources Officer, Michelle Laframboise
Tel: 613-943-0444
michelle.laframboise@parl.gc.ca
Senior Director, Talent Services, Carolyne Evangelidis
Tel: 613-943-1742
carolyne.evangelidis@parl.gc.ca
Senior Director, Employee Relations, Development & Wellness,
Mélanie Leclair
Tel: 613-947-2413
melanie.leclair@parl.gc.ca
Director, Members HR & Business Partner Services, Robyn
Daigle
Tel: 613-996-9959
robyn.daigle@parl.gc.ca

Law Clerk & Parliamentary Counsel / Légiste et Conseiller parlementaire

Law Clerk & Parliamentary Counsel, Philippe Dufresne
Tel: 613-996-1057
philippe.dufresne@parl.gc.ca
Deputy Law Clerk & Parliamentary Counsel, Legal Services,
Richard Denis
Tel: 613-943-2601
richard.denis@parl.gc.ca
Deputy Law Clerk & Parliamentary Counsel, Legislative
Services, Nathalie Caron
Tel: 613-995-6507
nathalie.caron@parl.gc.ca

Office of the Clerk & Secretariat / Bureau de la greffière et secrétariat

Clerk, House of Commons, Charles Robert
Tel: 613-992-2986
charles.robert@parl.gc.ca
Head, Corporate Communications, Kori Ghergari
Tel: 613-947-4876
kori.ghergari@parl.gc.ca

Parliamentary Precinct Operations / Opérations de la Cité parlementaire

Tel: 613-995-7521; *Fax:* 613-995-1650
Chief Operations Officer, Rebekah Kletke
Tel: 613-995-1990
rebekah.kletke@parl.gc.ca

Procedural Services / Services de la procédure

Deputy Clerk, House of Commons, Procedure, Vacant
Senior Principal Clerk, Parliamentary Information & Publications,
Ian McDonald
Tel: 613-943-9484
ian.mcdonald@parl.gc.ca

Principal Clerk, Committees, Robert Benoit
Tel: 613-944-5652
robert.benoit@parl.gc.ca
Principal Clerk, Legislative Services, Jean-Philippe Brochu
Tel: 613-992-4989
jean-philippe.brochu@parl.gc.ca

Office of the Prime Minister, Liberal Party of Canada / Liberal Research Bureau

80 Wellington St., Ottawa, ON K1A 0A2
Fax: 613-941-6900
pm.gc.ca
The Prime Minister is the Head of Government in Canada &
usually the leader of the party in power in the House of
Commons.
The Prime Minister recommends the appointment of the
Governor General to the monarchy, & is responsible for selecting
a team of ministers, who are then appointed by the Governor
General to the Queen's Privy Council. In addition, he or she also
controls the appointment of senators, judges, & parliamentary
secretaries. It is customary that the Prime Minister is also
appointed to the Imperial Privy Council & is thus titled, "The
Right Honourable". The Prime Minister has the right to dissolve
parliament & can therefore control the timing of general
elections.
The Prime Minister's Office is a central agency that features the
executive staff of the Prime Minister, such as partisan political
advisors & administrators, who provide support to the Prime
Minister exclusively.
The Right Hon. Justin Trudeau was sworn in as Canada's 23rd
Prime Minister at a ceremony held Nov. 4, 2015, at Rideau Hall.
He was re-elected in the 43rd general election held Oct. 21,
2019, & the 44th general election held Sept. 20, 2021.

**Prime Minister; Responsible, Liberal Party Research
Office,** Right Hon. Justin Pierre James Trudeau, P.C., B.A.,
B.Ed.
Tel: 613-995-0253; *Fax:* 613-947-0310
justin.trudeau@parl.gc.ca

Deputy Prime Minister; Minister, Finance, Hon. Chrystia
Freeland, P.C.
Tel: 613-992-5234; *Fax:* 613-996-9607
chrystia.freeland@parl.gc.ca

**Leader of the Government in the House of Commons;
Liberal Party House Leader,** Hon. Mark Holland, P.C.
Tel: 613-995-8042; *Fax:* 613-996-1289
mark.holland@parl.gc.ca

Caucus Chair, Liberal Party, Francis Scarpaleggia, B.A.,
M.A., M.B.A.
Tel: 613-995-8281; *Fax:* 613-996-0828
francis.scarpaleggia@parl.gc.ca

Chief Government Whip, Vacant

Chief of Staff, Katie Telford
Tel: 613-992-4211

Office of the Leader, Official Opposition, Conservative Party of Canada / Conservative Party Research Bureau

Centre Block, 111 Wellington St., Ottawa, ON K1A 0A6
Tel: 613-995-1333; *Fax:* 613-995-1337
www.conservative.ca
twitter.com/cpc_hq
www.facebook.com/cpcpcc
The Conservative Party of Canada became the Official
Opposition after losing to the Liberals in the 2015 general
election. Former Prime Minister Stephen Harper resigned as
Leader following the party's defeat. Rona Ambrose was chosen
as the party's Interim Leader at a meeting held Nov. 5, 2015.
Andrew Scheer was elected to be the party's full-time Leader at
a leadership convention held May 27, 2017. The Conservative
Party of Canada became the Official Opposition again in the
2019 Federal election. Andrew Sheer resigned as Leader in Dec.
2019. Erin O'Toole was elected to be the party's full-time Leader
after the vote held on Aug 24, 2020.

**Leader, Official Opposition; Party Leader, Conservative
Party of Canada; Responsible, Conservative Party
Research Office,** Hon. Erin O'Toole, P.C.
Tel: 613-992-2792; *Fax:* 613-992-2794
erin.otoole@parl.gc.ca

Deputy Leader, Conservative Party of Canada, Hon.
Candice Bergen
Tel: 613-995-9511
Candice.Bergen@parl.gc.ca

House Leader, Official Opposition, Hon. Gérard Deltell, P.C.
Tel: 613-996-4151; *Fax:* 613-954-2269
gerard.deltell@parl.gc.ca

Caucus Chair, Conservative Party of Canada, Tom Kmiec
Tel: 613-992-0846; *Fax:* 613-992-0883
tom.kmiec@parl.gc.ca

Chief Opposition Whip, Blake Richards
Tel: 613-996-5152; *Fax:* 613-947-4601
blake.richards@parl.gc.ca

Deputy Opposition Whip, Alex Ruff
Tel: 613-996-5191

Executive Director, Conservative Party of Canada, Jaime Girard

Centre Block, 111 Wellington St., Ottawa, ON K1A 0A6
Tel: 613-995-7224; *Fax:* 613-995-4565
www.ndp.ca
twitter.com/ndp
www.facebook.com/NDP.NPD
www.youtube.com/c/NDPNPD

Thomas Mulcair was elected leader of the Official Opposition & Leader of the New Democratic Party of Canada on March 24, 2011. Mulcair's election followed the August 2011 death of Jack Layton, Former Leader of the Official Opposition & Leader of the New Democratic Party. From July 28, 2011 to March 23, 2012, Nycole Turmel was the Interim Leader. After the 2015 general election, the NDP fell to Third Party status; Thomas Mulcair stayed on as Leader. Jagmeet Singh was elected as the NDP's new Leader at a convention held Oct. 1, 2017.

Party Leader, New Democratic Party, Jagmeet Singh
twitter.com/thejagmeetsingh, www.facebook.com/jagmeetndp

Deputy Leader, New Democratic Party, Alexandre Boulerice
Tel: 613-992-0423; *Fax:* 613-992-0878
Alexandre.Boulerice@parl.gc.ca

House Leader, New Democratic Party, Peter Julian
Tel: 613-992-4214; *Fax:* 613-947-9500
peter.julian@parl.gc.ca

Deputy House Leader, New Democratic Party, Heather McPherson
Tel: 613-995-7325

Caucus Chair, New Democratic Party, Brian Masse
Tel: 613-996-1541

Whip, New Democratic Party, Rachel Blaney
Tel: 613-992-2503; *Fax:* 613-996-3306
Rachel.Blaney@parl.gc.ca

President, New Democratic Party of Canada, Dhananjai Kohli

National Director, New Democratic Party of Canada, Jesse Calvert

Centre Block, 111 Wellington St., Ottawa, ON K1A 0A6
www.blocquebecois.org
twitter.com/blocquebecois
www.facebook.com/blocquebecois
www.youtube.com/user/blocquebecois

Following the May 2011 general election, Gilles Duceppe resigned as Leader of the Bloc Québécois party. On December 11, 2011, Daniel Paillé became the Leader & President of the Bloc Québécois. Paillé resigned on December 16, 2013, for health-related reasons. Mario Beaulieu was chosen to be the Bloc's new Leader on June 14, 2014. Former Leader Gilles Duceppe returned to the position on June 10, 2015, with Beaulieu staying on as Party President. Following the 2015 general election, Duceppe resigned again, & Rhéal Fortin took over as Interim Leader. Québec MNA Martine Ouellet became the full-time Leader on March 19, 2017, after no other candidates opposed her. She was defeated in a leadership review held June 2018, and was replaced on an interim basis by Mario Beaulieu. In Jan. 2019, Yves-François Blanchet was nominated without opposition to be the party's new leader on a permanent basis.

Leader, Bloc Québécois, Yves-François Blanchet
twitter.com/yfblanchet, www.facebook.com/yfblanchet

Caucus Chair, Bloc Québécois, Louis Plamondon
Tel: 613-995-9241; *Fax:* 613-995-6784
Louis.Plamondon@parl.gc.ca

House Leader, Bloc Québécois, Alain Therrien
Tel: 613-992-1084

Whip, Bloc Québécois, Claude DeBellefeuille
Tel: 613-995-2532

President, Bloc Québécois, Johanne Deschamps

Confederation Bldg., 229 Wellington St., Ottawa, ON K1A 0A6
Tel: 613-996-1119; *Fax:* 613-996-0850
Toll-Free: 866-868-3447
info@greenparty.ca
www.greenparty.ca
Other Communication: Media Requests, Email:
media@greenparty.ca
twitter.com/canadiangreens
www.facebook.com/GreenPartyofCanada
www.youtube.com/c/canadiangreenparty

Elizabeth May was elected the Leader of the Green Party of Canada in 2006. In the May 2011 election, May became the first Green Party candidate to be elected to the House of Commons. She was re-elected in the 2015 & 2019 general elections. On Nov. 5 2019, after 14 years of leadership, Elizabeth May stepped down as Party Leader. On Oct. 4 2020, Annamie Paul was elected as the new Leader of the Green Party of Canada. On Sept. 27, 2021 Annamie Paul resigned as Party Leader following the 2021 general election.

Leader, Green Party of Canada, Vacant

Deputy Leader, Green Party of Canada, Daniel Green

Deputy Leader, Green Party of Canada, Jo-Ann Roberts
brucehyer.ca
twitter.com/joannrobertsyyj

Information Service, Parliament of Canada, Ottawa, ON K1A 0A9
Tel: 613-992-4793
Toll-Free: 866-599-4999
TTY: 613-995-2266
info@parl.gc.ca
www.parl.gc.ca

The Canadian Ministry, or Cabinet, is the most significant of all federal government committees or councils. Cabinet members are selected & led by the Prime Minister. They must also be or become members of the Queen's Privy Council.
Cabinet ministers determine specific policies & are responsible for them in the House of Commons. The Cabinet is responsible for initiating all public bills in the House of Commons, & in some instances can create regulations that have the strength of law, termed decisions of the Governor-in-Council.
Cabinet meetings are usually closed to the public, allowing members to discuss their opinions on particular policy in secret. Once decided, members usually support all policy uniformly. If a minister is unable to support the Ministry, he or she is obligated to resign. Ministers are responsible to Parliament for their actions & the actions of their department.
The mailing address for all Cabinet members on Parliament Hill in Ottawa is as follows: House of Commons, Parliament Buildings, Ottawa, Ontario, K1A 0A6.
Members of the The Canadian Ministry are presented in order of precedence. A new cabinet was sworn in on Oct. 26, 2021, following the 2021 general election, and preliminary updates are as follows. Please refer to Canada's Information Resource Centre (CIRC) online for further updates as more information becomes available.

Members of The Canadian Ministry (Cabinet)
Prime Minister, Right Hon. Justin Pierre James Trudeau, P.C., B.A., B.Ed.
Tel: 613-995-0253; *Fax:* 613-947-0310
justin.trudeau@parl.gc.ca
Note: Web Sites: www.pm.gc.ca (Prime Minister of Canada); www.liberal.ca (Party)
Right Hon. Justin Pierre James Trudeau, Prime Minister, Office of the Prime Minister, Langevin Block
80 Wellington St.
Ottawa, ON K1A 0A2
Deputy Prime Minister; Minister, Finance, Hon. Chrystia Freeland, P.C.
Tel: 613-992-5234; *Fax:* 613-996-9607
chrystia.freeland@parl.gc.ca
Minister, Veterans Affairs, Hon. Lawrence MacAulay, P.C.
Tel: 613-995-9325; *Fax:* 613-995-2754
lawrence.macaulay@parl.gc.ca
Minister, Mental Health & Addictions; Association Minister, Health, Hon. Dr. Carolyn Bennett, P.C., M.D.
Tel: 613-995-9666; *Fax:* 613-947-4622
carolyn.bennett@parl.gc.ca
Minister, Intergovernmental Affairs; Minister, Infrastructure & Communities, Hon. Dominic LeBlanc, P.C., B.A., LL.B., LL.M.
Tel: 613-992-1020; *Fax:* 613-992-3053
dominic.leblanc@parl.gc.ca
President, Treasury Board, Hon. Mona Fortier, P.C.
Mona.Fortier@parl.gc.ca
Minister, Health, Hon. Jean-Yves Duclos, P.C.
Tel: 613-992-8865; *Fax:* 613-995-2805
Jean-Yves.Duclos@parl.gc.ca
Minister, Foreign Affairs, Hon. Mélanie Joly, P.C.
Tel: 613-992-0983; *Fax:* 613-992-1932
Melanie.Joly@parl.gc.ca
Minister, Agriculture & Agri-Food, Hon. Marie-Claude Bibeau, P.C.
Tel: 613-995-2024; *Fax:* 613-992-1696
Marie-Claude.Bibeau@parl.gc.ca
Minister, International Trade, Export Promotion, Small Business and Economic Development, Hon. Mary Ng, P.C.
Tel: 613-996-3374; *Fax:* 613-992-3921
Mary.Ng@parl.gc.ca
Minister, National Revenue, Hon. Diane Lebouthillier, P.C.
Tel: 613-992-6188; *Fax:* 613-992-6194
Diane.Lebouthillier@parl.gc.ca
Minister, National Defence, Hon. Anita Anand, P.C.
Anita.Anand@parl.gc.ca
Minister, Employment, Workforce Development & Disability Inclusion, Hon. Carla Qualtrough, P.C.
Tel: 613-992-2957; *Fax:* 613-992-3589
Carla.Qualtrough@parl.gc.ca
Minister, Indigenous Services; Minister responsible, Federal Economic Development Agency for Northern Ontario, Hon. Patricia Hajdu, P.C.
Tel: 613-996-4792; *Fax:* 613-996-9785
Patty.Hajdu@parl.gc.ca
Minister, Housing; Minister, Diversity & Inclusion, Hon. Ahmed Hussen, P.C.
Ahmed.Hussen@parl.gc.ca
Minister, Innovation, Science & Industry, Hon. François-Philippe Champagne, P.C.
Tel: 613-995-4895; *Fax:* 613-996-6883
Francois-Philippe.Champagne@parl.gc.ca
Minister, Families, Children & Social Development, Hon. Karina Gould, P.C.
Tel: 613-995-0881; *Fax:* 613-995-1091
Karina.Gould@parl.gc.ca
Minister, Labour, Hon. Seamus O'Regan, P.C.
Tel: 613-992-0927; *Fax:* 613-995-7858
Seamus.ORegan@parl.gc.ca
Leader of the Government in the House of Commons, Hon. Mark Holland, P.C.
Tel: 613-995-8042; *Fax:* 613-996-1289
mark.holland@parl.gc.ca
President of the Queen's Privy Council; Minister, Emergency Preparedness, Hon. Bill Blair, P.C.
Tel: 613-995-0284; *Fax:* 613-996-6309
Bill.Blair@parl.gc.ca
Minister, Public Services & Procurement, Hon. Filomena Tassi, P.C.
Tel: 613-992-1034; *Fax:* 613-995-1050
Filomena.Tassi@parl.gc.ca
Minister, Natural Resources, Hon. Jonathan Wilkinson, P.C.
Tel: 613-995-1225; *Fax:* 613-992-7319
Jonathan.Wilkinson@parl.gc.ca
Minister, Justice & Attorney General, Hon. David Lametti, P.C., B.A., LL.B., B.C.L., LL.M., D.Phil.
Tel: 613-943-6636; *Fax:* 613-943-6637
David.Lametti@parl.gc.ca
Minister, Fisheries, Oceans & the Canadian Coast Guard, Hon. Joyce Murray, P.C., M.B.A.
Tel: 613-992-2430; *Fax:* 613-995-0770
joyce.murray@parl.gc.ca
Minister, Tourism; Associate Minister, Finance, Hon. Randy Boissonnault, P.C.
randy.boissonnault@parl.gc.ca
Minister, Environment & Climate Change, Hon. Steven Guilbeault, P.C.
Steven.Guilbeault@parl.gc.ca
Minister, Public Safety, Hon. Marco Mendicino, P.C., B.A., LL.B.
Tel: 613-992-6361; *Fax:* 613-992-9791
Marco.Mendicino@parl.gc.ca
Minister, Crown-Indigenous Relations, Hon. Marc Miller, P.C.
Tel: 613-995-6403; *Fax:* 613-995-6404
Marc.Miller@parl.gc.ca

Minister, Northern Affairs; Minister responsible, Prairies Economic Development Canada & the Canadian Northern Economic Development Agency, Hon. Dan Vandal, P.C.
Tel: 613-995-0579; *Fax:* 613-996-7571
Dan.Vandal@parl.gc.ca

Minister, Transport, Hon. Omar Alghabra, P.C.
Tel: 613-992-1301; *Fax:* 613-992-1321
Omar.Alghabra@parl.gc.ca

Minister of Immigration, Refugees, and Citizenship, Sean Fraser, P.C.
Sean.Fraser@parl.gc.ca

Minister of Rural Economic Development, Gudie Hutchings, P.C.
Gudie.Hutchings@parl.gc.ca

Minister for Women, Gender Equality, & Youth, Marci Ien, P.C.
marci.ien@parl.gc.ca

Minister responsible for the Federal Economic Development Agency for Southern Ontario, Helena Jaczek, P.C.
helena.jaczek@parl.gc.ca

Minister of Seniors, Kamal Khera, P.C.
Kamal.Khera@parl.gc.ca

Minister of Official Languages; Minister responsible for the Atlantic Canada Opportunities Agency, Ginette Petitpas Taylor, P.C.
Ginette.PetitpasTaylor@parl.gc.ca

Minister of Sport; Minister responsible for the Economic Development Agency of Canada for the Regions of Quebec, Pascale St-Onge, P.C.
pascale.st-onge@parl.gc.ca

Forty-Fourth Parliament - Canada / Quarante-quatrième parlement du Canada

House of Commons, Parliament Buildings, Ottawa, BC K1A 0A6

www.parl.ca

Members of the House of Commons are elected by the people. The Speaker is elected by the House.
Last General Election: Sept. 20, 2021.
Political Party Leaders (Oct. 2021):
Liberal Party of Canada - The Right Hon. Justin Trudeau;
Conservative Party of Canada - Hon. Erin O'Toole;
New Democratic Party - Jagmeet Singh;
Green Party of Canada - Vacant;
Bloc Québécois - Yves-François Blanchet;
Representation in the House of Commons by province is as follows (Oct. 2021):
Alberta - Conservative Party of Canada 30, New Democratic Party 2, Liberal Part of Canada 2, Total 34;
British Columbia - Conservative Party of Canada 13, Liberal Party of Canada 15, New Democratic Party 13, Green Party of Canada 1, Total 42;
Manitoba - Conservative Party of Canada 7, Liberal Party of Canada 4, New Democratic Party 3, Total 14;
New Brunswick - Liberal Party of Canada 6, Conservative Party of Canada 4, Total 10;
Newfoundland & Labrador - Liberal Party of Canada 6, Conservative Party of Canada 1, Total 7;
Northwest Territories - Liberal Party of Canada 1, Total 1;
Nova Scotia - Liberal Party of Canada 8, Conservative Party of Canada 3, Total 11;
Nunavut - New Democratic Party 1, Total 1;
Ontario - Liberal Party of Canada 77, Conservative Party of Canada 37, New Democratic Party 5, Green Party of Canada 1, Independant 1, Total 121;
Prince Edward Island - Liberal Party of Canada 4, Total 4;
Québec - Liberal Party of Canada 35, Bloc Québécois 32, Conservative Party of Canada 10, New Democratic Party 1, Total 78;
Saskatchewan - Conservative Party of Canada 14, Total 14;
Yukon - Liberal Party of Canada 1, Total 1.
Representation in the House of Commons by party affiliation is as follows (Oct. 2021):
Liberal Party of Canada 159;
Conservative Party of Canada 119;
Bloc Québécois 32;
New Democratic Party 25;
Green Party of Canada 2;
Independent 1;
Total 336.
Indemnities, Salaries, & Allowances (2019):
The basic sessional indemnity for each member of the House of Commons is $185,800. In addition to the indemnity, members who occupy certain positions in the House of Commons receive additional remuneration.
Prime Minister: $185,800, plus a car allowance of $2,000;
Minister $88,700, plus a car allowance of $2,000;
Minister of State: $88,700, plus a car allowance of $2,000;
Secretary of State: $66,300;
Parliamentary Secretary: $18,100;
Speaker of the House of Commons: $88,700, plus a car allowance of $1,000;
Deputy Speaker, House of Commons: $45,900;
Leader of the Opposition in the House of Commons: $88,700,

plus a car allowance of $2,000;
Leaders of Other Parties: $62,900;
Opposition House Leader: $45,900;
House Leader of Other Parties: $18,100;
Deputy House Leaders of Government & Official Opposition: $18,100;
Deputy House Leaders of Other Parties: $6,400;
Chief Government Whip: $33,000;
Chief Opposition Whip: $33,000;
Whip of Other Parties: $12,800;
Chief Government Whip's Assistant: $12,800;
Deputy Whip of the Official Opposition: $12,800;
Deputy Whip of Other Parties: $6,400;
Caucus Chair of the Government & the Official Opposition: $12,800;
Caucus Chair of Other Parties: $6,400;
Deputy Chair, Committees of the Whole: $17,500;
Assistant Deputy Chair, Committees of the Whole: $18,100;
Chairs of Standing, Special, Standing Joint & Special Joint Committees (excluding the Liaison Committee & the Standing Joint Committee on the Library of Parliament): $12,800;
Vice-Chairs of Standing, Special, Standing Joint & Special Joint Committees (excluding the Liaison Committee & the Standing Joint Committee on the Library of Parliament): $6,400.
Mail may be sent postage-free to any Member of Parliament at the following address: House of Commons, Parliament Buildings, Ottawa, Ontario, K1A 0A6.
The following is a list of Members of Parliament, as of Oct. 2019, with their constituency, number of electors on lists for the 2019 election, party affiliation, & contact information:

Members of the Parliament of Canada

Ziad Aboultaif
Constituency: Edmonton — Manning, Alberta *No. of Constituents:* 89,075, Conservative Party
Tel: 613-992-0946; *Fax:* 613-992-0973
Ziad.Aboultaif@parl.gc.ca
mpziad.ca
Other Communications: Constituency Phone: 780-822-1540; Fax: 780-822-1544
twitter.com/ziad_aboultaif, www.facebook.com/ziad4manning
Constituency Office
#204A, 8119 - 160th Ave.
Edmonton, AB T5Z 0G3

Scott Aitchison
Constituency: Parry Sound — Muskoka, Ontario *No. of Constituents:* 82,930, Conservative Party
Tel: 613-944-7740; *Fax:* 613-992-5092
Scott.Aitchison@parl.gc.ca
www.conservative.ca/team-member/scott-aitchison
Other Communications: Constituency Phone: 705-789-4640
twitter.com/ScottAAitchison, www.facebook.com/scotttheMP
Constituency Office
#2, 94 Hanes Rd.
Huntsville, ON P1H 1M4

Dan Albas
Constituency: Central Okanagan — Similkameen — Nicola, British Columbia *No. of Constituents:* 94,331, Conservative Party
Tel: 613-995-1702
Toll-free: 800-665-8711; *Fax:* 613-995-1154
dan.albas@parl.gc.ca
danalbas.ca
Other Communications: Constituency Fax: 250-707-2153
twitter.com/DanAlbas, www.facebook.com/DanAlbas4COSN
Constituency Office
2562B Main St.
West Kelowna, BC V4T 2N5

John Aldag
Constituency: Cloverdale — Langley City *No. of Constituents:* 86,045, Liberal
john.aldag@parl.gc.ca
johnaldag.ca
twitter.com/jwaldag, www.facebook.com/JohnAldagLPC, www.linkedin.com/in/johnaldag

Hon. Omar Alghabra, P.C., P.Eng, M.B.A.
Constituency: Mississauga Centre, Ontario *No. of Constituents:* 87,047, Liberal
Tel: 613-992-1301; *Fax:* 613-992-1321
Omar.Alghabra@parl.gc.ca
www.omaralghabra.ca
Other Communications: Constituency Phone: 905-848-8595; Fax: 905-848-2712
twitter.com/OmarAlghabra, www.facebook.com/oalghabra, www.linkedin.com/in/omaralghabra
Constituency Office
#506, 10 Kingsbridge Garden Circle
Mississauga, ON L5R 3K6

Shafqat Ali
Constituency: Brampton Centre, Ontario *No. of Constituents:* 67,334, Liberal
shafqat.ali@parl.gc.ca
shafqatali.liberal.ca
Other Communications: Constituency Phone: 905-790-9211; Fax: 905-790-9507

twitter.com/Shafqat_Ali_1
Constituency Office
100 Kennedy Rd. South
Brampton, ON L6W 3E7

Dean Allison, B.A.
Constituency: Niagara West, Ontario *No. of Constituents:* 74,760, Conservative Party
Tel: 613-995-2772; *Fax:* 613-992-2727
dean.allison@parl.gc.ca
www.deanallison.ca
Other Communications: Constituency Phone: 905-563-7900; Fax: 905-563-7500
twitter.com/DeanAllisonMP, www.facebook.com/deanallison.mp
Constituency Office
4994 King St.
Beamsville, ON L0R 1B0

Hon. Anita Anand, P.C.
Constituency: Oakville, Ontario *No. of Constituents:* 90,144, Liberal
Tel: 613-995-4014; *Fax:* 613-992-0520
Anita.Anand@parl.gc.ca
anitaanand.liberal.ca
Other Communications: Constituency Phone: 905-338-2008; Fax: 905-338-5432
twitter.com/AnitaOakville, www.facebook.com/AnitaOakville, www.linkedin.com/in/anita-indira-anand-9857b229
Constituency Office
301 Robinson St.
Oakville, ON L6J 1G7

Gary Anandasangaree
Constituency: Scarborough — Rouge Park, Ontario *No. of Constituents:* 76,408, Liberal
Tel: 613-992-1351; *Fax:* 613-992-1373
Gary.Anandasangaree@parl.gc.ca
garyanandasangaree.libparl.ca
Other Communications: Constituency Phone: 416-283-1414; Fax: 416-283-5012
twitter.com/gary_srp, www.facebook.com/garyforsrp
Constituency Office
#3, 3600 Ellesmere Rd.
Toronto, ON M1C 4Y8

Charlie Angus
Constituency: Timmins — James Bay, Ontario *No. of Constituents:* 63,282, New Democratic Party
Tel: 613-992-2919; *Fax:* 613-995-0747
charlie.angus@parl.gc.ca
www.charlieangus.ca
Other Communications: Timmins: 705-268-6464; Kirkland Lake: 705-567-2747
twitter.com/CharlieAngusNDP, www.facebook.com/charlie.angus.58
Constituency Office
#202, 60 Wilson Ave.
Timmins, ON P4N 2S7

Mel Arnold
Constituency: North Okanagan — Shuswap, British Columbia *No. of Constituents:* 106,601, Conservative Party
Tel: 613-995-9095; *Fax:* 613-992-3195
Mel.Arnold@parl.gc.ca
melarnold.ca
Other Communications: Constituency Phone: 250-260-5020; Fax: 250-260-5025
twitter.com/melarnoldmp, www.facebook.com/MelArnoldMP, www.linkedin.com/in/mel-arnold-11372561
Constituency Office
3105 - 29th St.
Vernon, BC V1T 5A8

René Arseneault
Constituency: Madawaska — Restigouche, New Brunswick *No. of Constituents:* 50,631, Liberal
Tel: 613-995-0581; *Fax:* 613-996-9736
Rene.Arseneault@parl.gc.ca
renearseneault.liberal.ca
Other Communications: Dalhousie: 506-684-6267; Edmunston: 506-739-0285
Constituency Office
374 Adelaide St.
Dalhousie, NB E8C 1A5

Chandra Arya
Constituency: Nepean, Ontario *No. of Constituents:* 93,119, Liberal
Tel: 613-992-1325; *Fax:* 613-992-1336
Chandra.Arya@parl.gc.ca
chandraarya.libparl.ca
Other Communications: Constituency Phone: 613-825-5505; Fax: 613-825-2055
twitter.com/AryaCanada
Constituency Office
#201, 240 Kennevale Dr.
Nepean, ON K2J 6B6

Niki Ashton, B.A., M.A.
Constituency: Churchill — Keewatinook Aski, Manitoba *No. of Constituents:* 48,949, New Democratic Party

Tel: 613-992-3018; *Fax:* 613-996-5817
niki.ashton@parl.gc.ca
nikiashton.ndp.ca
Other Communications: Thompson: 204-677-1333; The Pas:
204-627-8716
twitter.com/nikiashton, www.facebook.com/MPNikiAshton
Constituency Office
#305, 83 Churchill Dr.
Thompson, MB R8N 0L6

Jenica Atwin
Constituency: Fredericton, New Brunswick *No. of
Constituents:* 65,825, Liberal
Tel: 613-992-1067; *Fax:* 613-996-9955
jenica.atwin@parl.gc.ca
jenicafredericton.ca
www.facebook.com/JenicaAtwinFredericton
Note: In June 2021, Jenica Atwin crossed the floor from the
Green Party to the Liberal Party.

Taylor Bachrach
Constituency: Skeena — Bulkley Valley, British Columbia *No.
of Constituents:* 66,421, New Democratic Party
Tel: 613-992-7688; *Fax:* 613-993-9007
taylore.bachrach@parl.gc.ca
taylorbachrach.ndp.ca
Other Communications: Smithers: 250-877-4140; Prince
Rupert: 250-622-2413
twitter.com/taylorbachrach,
www.facebook.com/taylorbachrach1
Constituency Office
1226 Main St.
Smithers, BC V0J 2N0

Vance Badawey
Constituency: Niagara Centre, Ontario *No. of Constituents:*
90,131, Liberal
Tel: 613-995-0988; *Fax:* 613-995-5245
Vance.Badawey@parl.gc.ca
vancebadawey.libparl.ca
Other Communications: Constituency Phone: 905-788-2204;
Fax: 905-788-0011
twitter.com/VBadawey, www.facebook.com/vbadawey,
www.linkedin.com/in/vance-badawey-78a66619
Constituency Office
#103, 136 East Main St.
Welland, ON L3B 3W6

Paramvir Bains
Constituency: Steveston — Richmond East, British Columbia
No. of Constituents: 73,840, Conservative Party
parm.bains@parl.gc.ca
Other Communications: Constituency Phone: 604-257-2900;
Fax: 604-257-2904
Constituency Office
3251 Chatham St.
Richmond, BC V7E 6B8

Yvan Baker
Constituency: Etobicoke Centre, Ontario *No. of Constituents:*
91,889, Liberal
Tel: 613-947-5000; *Fax:* 613-947-4276
yvan.baker@parl.gc.ca
www.yvanbaker.ca
Other Communications: Constituency Phone: 416-249-7322;
Fax: 416-249-6117
twitter.com/Yvan_Baker, www.facebook.com/yvanbaker
Constituency Office
#2, 577 Burnhamthorpe Rd.
Toronto, ON M9C 2Y3

Tony Baldinelli
Constituency: Niagara Falls, Ontario *No. of Constituents:*
112,870, Conservative Party
Tel: 613-995-1547; *Fax:* 613-992-7910
tony.baldinelli@parl.gc.ca
www.tonybaldinellimp.ca
Other Communications: Constituency Phone: 905-353-9590;
Fax: 905-353-9588
twitter.com/tony_baldinelli
Constituency Office
#107, 4056 Dorchester Rd.
Niagara Falls, ON L2E 6M9

John Barlow
Constituency: Foothills, Alberta *No. of Constituents:* 86,027,
Conservative Party
Tel: 613-995-8471; *Fax:* 613-996-9770
John.Barlow@parl.gc.ca
johnbarlowmp.ca
Other Communications: Constituency Phone: 403-603-3665;
Fax: 403-603-3669
twitter.com/johnbarlowmp, www.facebook.com/johnbarlowmp,
www.linkedin.com/in/john-barlow-14003743
Constituency Office
109 - 4th Ave. SW
High River, AB T1V 1M5

Michael Barrett
Constituency: Leeds — Grenville — Thousand Islands &
Rideau Lakes, Ontario *No. of Constituents:* 84,442,
Conservative Party

Tel: 613-992-8756
Toll-free: 866-498-3096; *Fax:* 613-996-9171
michael.barrett@parl.gc.ca
www.michaelbarrettmp.ca
Other Communications: Constituency Fax: 613-498-3100
twitter.com/MikeBarrettON,
www.facebook.com/MikeBarrettON
Note: Michael Barrett first won the riding in a by-election held
Nov. 3, 2018. He was re-elected in the 2019 general election.
Constituency Office
#205, 68 William St.
Brockville, ON K6V 4V5

Lisa Marie Barron
Constituency: Nanaimo — Ladysmith, British Columbia *No. of
Constituents:* 103,762, New Democratic Party
lisamarie.barron@parl.gc.ca
lisamariebarron.ndp.ca
Other Communications: Constituency Phone: 250-734-6400;
Fax: 250-734-6404
twitter.com/LisaMarieBarron,
www.facebook.com/ElectLisaMarieBarron,
www.linkedin.com/in/lisa-marie-barron-40827469
Constituency Office
#103, 495 Dunsmuir St.
Nanaimo, BC V9R 6B9

Xavier Barsalou-Duval
Circonscription électorale: Pierre-Boucher — Les Patriotes —
Verchères, Québec *Nombre de constituants:* 78,738, Bloc
Québécois
Tél: 613-996-2998
Téléc: 613-995-1062
Xavier.Barsalou-Duval@parl.gc.ca
Autres numéros: Constituency Phone: 450-652-4442; Fax:
450-652-4447
twitter.com/XBarsalouDuval,
www.facebook.com/xavierbarsalouduval,
www.linkedin.com/in/xavierbarsalouduval
Bureau de circonscription
#202, 1625, boul Lionel-Boulet
Varennes, QC J3X 1P7

Jaime Battiste
Constituency: Sydney — Victoria, Nova Scotia *No. of
Constituents:* 60,042, Liberal
Tel: 613-995-6459; *Fax:* 613-995-2963
jaime.battiste@parl.gc.ca
jaimebattiste.ca
Other Communications: Constituency Phone: 902-567-6275;
Fax: 902-564-2479
twitter.com/JaimeBattiste
Constituency Office
#207A, 201 Churchill Dr.
Sydney, NS B1S 2N9

Mario Beaulieu
Circonscription électorale: La Pointe-de-l'Île, Québec *Nombre
de constituants:* 85,589, Bloc Québécois
Tél: 613-995-6327
Téléc: 613-996-5173
Mario.Beaulieu@parl.gc.ca
Autres numéros: Constituency Phone: 514-645-0101; Fax:
514-645-0032
twitter.com/mario_beaulieu,
www.facebook.com/mariobeaulieu101
Bureau de circonscription
#100, 12500, boul Industriel
Montréal, QC H1B 5P5

Terry Beech
Constituency: Burnaby North — Seymour, British Columbia
No. of Constituents: 77,301, Liberal
Tel: 613-992-0802; *Fax:* 613-992-0824
Terry.Beech@parl.gc.ca
terrybeechmp.ca
Other Communications: Constituency Phone: 604-718-8870;
Fax: 604-718-8874
twitter.com/terrybeech, www.facebook.com/terryjamesbeech,
www.linkedin.com/in/terrybeech
Constituency Office
3906 Hastings St.
Burnaby, BC V5C 6C1

Rachel Bendayan
Circonscription électorale: Outremont, Québec *Nombre de
constituants:* 67,384, Liberal
rachel.bendayan@parl.gc.ca
rachelbendayan.libparl.ca
Autres numéros: Constituency Phone: 514-736-2727; Fax:
514-736-2726
twitter.com/RachelBendayan,
www.facebook.com/bendayan.rachel
Bureau de circonscription
#302, 154, av Laurier ouest
Montréal, QC H2T 2N7

Hon. Dr. Carolyn Bennett, P.C., M.D.
Constituency: Toronto—St. Paul's, Ontario *No. of
Constituents:* 84,110, Liberal
Tel: 613-995-9666; *Fax:* 613-947-4622

carolyn.bennett@parl.gc.ca
carolynbennett.libparl.ca
Other Communications: Constituency Phone: 416-952-3990;
Fax: 416-952-3995
twitter.com/Carolyn_Bennett,
www.facebook.com/carolyn.bennett.stpauls,
www.linkedin.com/in/carolyn-bennett-8110a313
Constituency Office
#103, 40 Holly St.
Toronto, ON M4S 3C3

Bob Benzen
Constituency: Calgary Heritage, Alberta *No. of Constituents:*
81,270, Conservative Party
Tel: 613-992-0250; *Fax:* 613-992-0251
Bob.Benzen@parl.gc.ca
bobbenzenmp.ca
Other Communications: Constituency Phone: 403-253-7990;
Fax: 403-253-8203
twitter.com/bobbenzen, www.facebook.com/BobBenzen
Note: Bob Benzen was first elected to the House of
Commons in a by-election held April 3, 2017. He was
re-elected in the 2019 general election.
Constituency Office
#1010, 10201 Southport Rd. SW
Calgary, AB T2W 4X9

Hon. Candice Bergen, P.C.
Constituency: Portage — Lisgar, Manitoba *No. of
Constituents:* 65,546, Conservative Party
Tel: 613-995-9511; *Fax:* 613-947-0313
candice.bergen@parl.gc.ca
candicebergen.ca
Other Communications: Morden: 204-822-7440; Portage
LaPrairie: 204-857-6184
twitter.com/CandiceBergenMP,
www.facebook.com/CandiceBergenMp
Constituency Office
886 Thornhill St., #E
Morden, MB R6M 2E1

Stéphane Bergeron
Circonscription électorale: Montarville, Québec *Nombre de
constituants:* 77,097, Bloc Québécois
Tél: 613-996-2416
Ligne sans frais: 833-615-0376
Téléc: 613-995-6973
stephane.bergeron@parl.gc.ca
Autres numéros: Circ. Tél: 450-922-2562; Téléc:
450-922-1223
twitter.com/sbergeron
Bureau de circonscription
#201, 1990, rue Léonard-de-Vinci
Sainte-Julie, QC J3E 1Y8

Luc Berthold
Circonscription électorale: Mégantic — L'Érable, Québec
Nombre de constituants: 70,683, Conservative Party
Tél: 613-995-1377
Téléc: 613-943-1562
Luc.Berthold@parl.gc.ca
lucberthold.ca
Autres numéros: Circ. Tél: 418-338-2903; Téléc:
418-338-3631
twitter.com/LucBerthold,
www.facebook.com/lucbertholdmeganticlerable,
www.linkedin.com/in/lucberthold
Bureau de circonscription
105A, rue Notre-Dame est
Thetford Mines, QC G6G 2J9

Sylvie Bérubé
Circonscription électorale: Abitibi — Baie-James — Nunavik
— Eeyou *Nombre de constituants:* 34,518, Bloc Québécois
Tél: 613-992-3030
Téléc: 613-996-0828
Sylvie.Berube@parl.gc.ca
Autres numéros: Circ. Tél: 819-824-2942; Téléc:
819-824-2958
Bureau de circonscription
#204, 888 - 3e av
Val-d'Or, QC J9P 5E6

James Bezan
Constituency: Selkirk — Interlake —Eastman, Manitoba *No.
of Constituents:* 72,707, Conservative Party
Tel: 613-992-2032; *Fax:* 613-992-6224
james.bezan@parl.gc.ca
jamesbezan.com
Other Communications: Constituency Phone: 204-785-6151;
Fax: 204-785-6153
twitter.com/jamesbezan, www.facebook.com/jamesbezan
Constituency Office
228 Manitoba Ave.
Selkirk, MB R1A 0Y5

Hon. Marie-Claude Bibeau, P.C.
Circonscription électorale: Compton — Stanstead, Québec
Nombre de constituants: 84,383, Liberal
Tél: 613-995-2024
Téléc: 613-992-1696

Marie-Claude.Bibeau@parl.gc.ca
marieclaudebibeau.libparl.ca
Autres numéros: Constituency Phone: 819-347-2598; Fax:
819-347-3583
twitter.com/mclaudebibeau,
www.facebook.com/mclaudebibeau,
www.linkedin.com/in/marie-claude-bibeau-b0b72518
Bureau de circonscription
#204, 175, rue Queen
Sherbrooke, QC J1M 1K1

Chris Bittle
Constituency: St. Catharines, Ontario *No. of Constituents:*
84,474, Liberal
Tel: 613-992-3352; *Fax:* 613-947-4402
Chris.Bittle@parl.gc.ca
chrisbittle.libparl.ca
Other Communications: Constituency Phone: 905-934-6767;
Fax: 905-934-1577
twitter.com/Chris_Bittle, www.facebook.com/ChrisBittleMP,
www.linkedin.com/in/chris-bittle-6085989
Constituency Office
#1, 61 Geneva St.
St Catharines, ON L2M 4M6

Daniel Blaikie
Constituency: Elmwood — Transcona, Manitoba *No. of
Constituents:* 69,498, New Democratic Party
Tel: 613-995-6339; *Fax:* 613-995-6688
Daniel.Blaikie@parl.gc.ca
www.danielblaikie.ca
Other Communications: Constituency Phone: 204-984-2499;
Fax: 204-984-2502
twitter.com/daniel_blaikie, www.facebook.com/BlaikieDaniel
Constituency Office
#207, 1111 Munroe Ave.
Winnipeg, MB R2K 3Z5

Hon. Bill Blair, P.C.
Constituency: Scarborough Southwest, Ontario *No. of
Constituents:* 78,246, Liberal
Tel: 613-995-0284; *Fax:* 613-996-6309
Bill.Blair@parl.gc.ca
billblair.libparl.ca
Other Communications: Constituency Phone: 416-261-8613;
Fax: 416-261-5268
twitter.com/BillBlair, www.facebook.com/williamsterlingblair
Constituency Office
2263 Kingston Rd.
Scarborough, ON M1N 1T8

Yves-François Blanchet
Circonscription électorale: Beloeil — Chambly, Québec
Nombre de constituants: 95,723, Bloc Québécois
Tél: 613-992-6035
Téléc: 613-947-5096
Yves-Francois.Blanchet@parl.gc.ca
Autres numéros: Circ. Tél: 450-658-0088; Téléc:
450-658-0885
twitter.com/yfblanchet, www.facebook.com/yfblanchet
Bureau de circonscription
270, boul Fréchette
Chambly, QC J3L 2Z5

Maxime Blanchette-Joncas
Circonscription électorale: Rimouski-Neigette — Témiscouata
— Les Basques, Québec *Nombre de constituants:* 69,939,
Bloc Québécois
Tél: 613-992-5302
Ligne sans frais: 866-720-2562
Téléc: 613-996-8298
maxime.blanchette-joncas@parl.gc.ca
Autres numéros: Circ. Tél: 418-725-2562; Téléc:
418-725-3993
twitter.com/BlanchetteMax,
www.facebook.com/MaximeBlanchetteJoncas.bq
Bureau de circonscription
#701, 320, rue Saint-Germain est
Rimouski, QC G5L 1C2

Rachel Blaney
Constituency: North Island — Powell River, British Columbia
No. of Constituents: 89,561, New Democratic Party
Tel: 613-992-2503; *Fax:* 613-996-3306
Rachel.Blaney@parl.gc.ca
rachelblaney.ndp.ca
Other Communications: Constituency Phone: 604-489-2286
twitter.com/RABlaney, www.facebook.com/Rachel.a.blaney,
www.linkedin.com/in/rachelablaney
Constituency Office
4697 Marine Ave.
Powell River, BC V8A 2L2

Kelly Block
Constituency: Carlton Trail — Eagle Creek, Saskatchewan
No. of Constituents: 57,601, Conservative Party
Tel: 613-995-1551; *Fax:* 613-943-2010
kelly.block@parl.gc.ca
www.kellyblockmp.ca
Other Communications: Martensville: 306-975-4004;
Humboldt: 306-682-1611

twitter.com/kellyblockmp, www.facebook.com/kellyblockmp
Constituency Office
#2B, 725 Centennial Dr. South
Martensville, SK S0K 2T0

Kody Blois
Constituency: Kings — Hants, Nova Scotia *No. of
Constituents:* 69,566, Liberal
Tel: 613-995-8231; *Fax:* 613-996-9349
kody.blois@parl.gc.ca
kodyblois.libparl.ca
Other Communications: Constituency Phone: 902-542-4010;
Fax: 902-542-4184
twitter.com/KodyBloisNS, www.facebook.com/KodyBloisNS,
www.linkedin.com/in/kodyblois
Constituency Office
#101, 24 Harbourside Dr.
Wolfville, NS B4P 2C1

Hon. Randy Boissonnault, P.C.
Constituency: Edmonton Centre, Alberta *No. of Constituents:*
81,766, Liberal
randy.boissonnault@parl.gc.ca
randyboissonnault.liberal.ca
Other Communications: Constituency Phone: 780-442-1888;
Fax: 780-442-1891
twitter.com/R_Boissonnault,
www.facebook.com/R.Boissonnault,
www.linkedin.com/in/randy-boissonnault-541079b4
Constituency Office
11156 - 142th St. NW
Edmonton, AB T5M 4G5

Alexandre Boulerice, B.A.
Circonscription électorale: Rosemont — La Petite-Patrie,
Québec *Nombre de constituants:* 85,290, New Democratic
Party
Tél: 613-992-0423
Téléc: 613-992-0878
Alexandre.Boulerice@parl.gc.ca
www.boulerice.org
Autres numéros: Circ. Tél: 514-729-5342; Téléc:
514-729-5875
twitter.com/alexboulerice,
www.facebook.com/alexandreboulerice
Bureau de circonscription
#208, 1453, rue Beaubien est
Montréal, QC H2G 3C6

Valerie Bradford
Constituency: Kitchener South — Hespeler, Ontario *No. of
Constituents:* 79,757, Liberal
valerie.bradford@parl.gc.ca
valeriebradford.liberal.ca
Other Communications: Constituency Phone: 519-571-5509;
Fax: 519-571-5515
twitter.com/ValBradford_,
www.facebook.com/ValerieBradfordKSH,
www.linkedin.com/in/valerie-bradford-4184776
Constituency Office
#2A, 153 Country Hill Dr.
Kitchener, ON N2E 2G7

Richard Bragdon
Constituency: Tobique — Mactaquac, New Brunswick *No. of
Constituents:* 55,104, Conservative Party
Tel: 613-947-4431
Toll-free: 800-671-6160; *Fax:* 613-947-4434
richard.bragdon@parl.gc.ca
www.richardbragdon.ca
twitter.com/RichardBragdon,
www.facebook.com/1499436196999231
Constituency Office
157 Otis Dr.
Nackawic, NB E6G 1G9

John Brassard
Constituency: Barrie — Innisfil, Ontario *No. of Constituents:*
86,772, Conservative Party
Tel: 613-992-3394; *Fax:* 613-996-7923
John.Brassard@parl.gc.ca
johnbrassard.com
Other Communications: Constituency Phone: 705-726-5959;
Fax: 705-726-3340
twitter.com/johnbrassardcpc,
www.facebook.com/JohnBrassardCPC
Constituency Office
#204B, 480 Huronia Rd.
Barrie, ON L4N 6M2

Élisabeth Brière
Circonscription électorale: Sherbrooke, Québec *Nombre de
constituants:* 88,936, Liberal
Tél: 613-943-7896
Téléc: 613-942-7902
elisabeth.briere@parl.gc.ca
elisabethbriere.libparl.ca
Autres numéros: Circ. Tél: 819-564-4200; Téléc:
819-564-3745
www.facebook.com/ElisabethBrierePLC
Bureau de circonscription

1640, rue King ouest, #M10
Sherbrooke, QC J1J 2C3

Larry Brock
Constituency: Brantford — Brant, Ontario *No. of Constituents:*
107,939, Conservative Party
larry.brock@parl.gc.ca
larrybrock.ca
Other Communications: Constituency Phone: 519-754-4300;
Fax: 519-751-8177
www.facebook.com/LarryBrock.BrantfordBrant,
www.linkedin.com/in/larry-brock-81a9a170
Constituency Office
#3, 108 St George St.
Brantford, ON N3R 1V6

Alexis Brunelle-Duceppe
Circonscription électorale: Lac-Saint-Jean, Québec *Nombre
de constituants:* 84,456, Bloc Québécois
Tél: 613-996-6236
Téléc: 613-996-6252
alexis.brunelle-duceppe@parl.gc.ca
Autres numéros: Circ. Tél: 418-669-0013; Téléc:
418-669-0048
twitter.com/Alduceppe, www.facebook.com/alduceppe
Bureau de circonscription
#7, 100, rue St-Joseph sud
Alma, QC G8B 7A6

Blaine Calkins, B.Sc.
Constituency: Red Deer — Lacombe, Alberta *No. of
Constituents:* 93,050, Conservative Party
Tel: 613-995-8886; *Fax:* 613-996-9860
blaine.calkins@parl.gc.ca
Other Communications: Constituency Phone: 587-621-0020;
Fax: 587-621-0029
twitter.com/blainefcalkins
Constituency Office
#201, 5025 Parkwood Rd.
PO Box 59
Blackfalds, AB T0M 0J0

Richard Cannings
Constituency: South Okanagan — West Kootenay, British
Columbia *No. of Constituents:* 98,589, New Democratic Party
Tel: 613-996-8036; *Fax:* 613-943-0922
Richard.Cannings@parl.gc.ca
richardcannings.ndp.ca
Other Communications: Penticton: 250-770-4480; Castlegar:
250-365-2792
twitter.com/CanningsNDP,
www.facebook.com/richardjcannings,
www.linkedin.com/in/richard-cannings-0160a536
Constituency Office
#202, 301 Main St.
Penticton, BC V2A 5B7

Frank Caputo
Constituency: Kamloops — Thompson — Cariboo, British
Columbia *No. of Constituents:* 102,759, Conservative Party
frank.caputo@parl.gc.ca
frankcaputo.ca
Other Communications: Constituency Phone: 250-851-4991;
Fax: 250-851-4994
twitter.com/frankcaputoktc,
www.facebook.com/frankcaputoktc
Constituency Office
#6, 275 Seymour St.
Kamloops, BC V2C 2E7

Hon. Jim Carr, O.M., P.C., B.A.
Constituency: Winnipeg South Centre, Manitoba *No. of
Constituents:* 71,156, Liberal
Tel: 613-992-9475; *Fax:* 613-992-9586
Jim.Carr@parl.gc.ca
jimcarr.libparl.ca
Other Communications: Constituency Phone: 204-983-1355;
Fax: 204-984-3979
twitter.com/jimcarr_wpg, www.facebook.com/JimCarrWSC
Constituency Office
#102, 611 Corydon Ave.
Winnipeg, MB R3L 0P3

Colin Carrie, B.Sc. (Hons.), D.C.
Constituency: Oshawa, Ontario *No. of Constituents:* 101,419,
Conservative Party
Tel: 613-996-4756; *Fax:* 613-992-1357
colin.carrie@parl.gc.ca
www.colincarriemp.ca
Other Communications: Constituency Phone: 905-440-4868;
Fax: 905-440-4872
twitter.com/ColinCarrieCPC
Constituency Office
#2B, 57 Simcoe St. South
Oshawa, O L1H 4G4

Sean Casey, Q.C., B.B.A., LL.B.
Constituency: Charlottetown, Prince Edward Island *No. of
Constituents:* 27,480, Liberal
Tel: 613-996-4714; *Fax:* 613-995-7685
sean.casey@parl.gc.ca
seancasey.libparl.ca

Other Communications: Constituency Phone: 902-566-7770; Fax: 902-566-7780
twitter.com/seancaseylpc,
www.facebook.com/SeanCaseyCharlottetown,
www.linkedin.com/in/seancaseycharlottetown
Constituency Office
#201, 75 Fitzroy Rd.
Charlottetown, PE C1A 1R6

Louise Chabot
Circonscription électorale: Thérèse — De Blainville, Quebec *Nombre de constituants:* 24,364, Bloc Québécois
Tél: 613-992-2617
Téléc: 613-992-6069
louise.chabot@parl.gc.ca
www.louisechabot.quebec
Autres numéros: Circ. Tél: 450-965-1188; Téléc: 450-965-3221
www.facebook.com/LouiseChabot.TDB
Bureau de circonscription
8, rue Saint-Charles
Sainte-Thérèse, QC J7E 2A2

Hon. Bardish Chagger, P.C.
Constituency: Waterloo, Ontario *No. of Constituents:* 78,527, Liberal
Tel: 613-996-5928; *Fax:* 613-992-6251
Bardish.Chagger@parl.gc.ca
bardishchaggermp.ca
Other Communications: Constituency Phone: 519-746-1573; Fax: 519-746-6436
twitter.com/BardishKW, www.facebook.com/bardish.chagger
Constituency Office
#360, 100 Regina St. South
Waterloo, ON N2J 4A8

Harnirjodh Chahal
Constituency: Calgary Skyview, Alberta *No. of Constituents:* 84,116, Liberal
george.chahal@parl.gc.ca
Other Communications: Constituency Phone: 403-291-0018; Fax: 403-291-9516
Constituency Office
#101, 2635 - 37th Ave. NE
Calgary, AB T1Y 5Z6

Adam Chambers
Constituency: Simcoe North, Ontario *No. of Constituents:* 97,148, Conservative Party
adam.chambers@parl.gc.ca
adamchambers.ca
Other Communications: Midland: 705-527-7654; Orillia: 705-327-0513
twitter.com/adamchamb,
www.facebook.com/adamchambers.ca
Constituency Office
504 Dominion Ave.
Midland, ON L4R 1P8

Hon. François-Philippe Champagne, P.C.
Circonscription électorale: Saint-Maurice — Champlain, Québec *Nombre de constituants:* 91,594, Liberal
Tél: 613-995-4895
Téléc: 613-996-6883
Francois-Philippe.Champagne@parl.gc.ca
Autres numéros: Shawinigan: 819-538-5291; La Tuque: 819-523-2696
twitter.com/FP_Champagne,
www.linkedin.com/in/francoisphilippechampagne
Bureau de circonscription
#1, 632, av Grand-Mère
Shawinigan, QC G9T 2H5

Martin Champoux
Circonscription électorale: Drummond, Québec *Nombre de constituants:* 83,916, Bloc Québécois
Tél: 613-947-4550
Téléc: 613-947-4551
martin.champoux@parl.gc.ca
Autres numéros: Circ. Tél: 819-477-3611; Téléc: 819-477-7116
twitter.com/martchampoux,
www.facebook.com/DeputeBQDrummond
Bureau de circonscription
#100, rue Marchand
Drummondville, QC J2C 4N1

Sophie Chatel
Circonscription électorale: Pontiac, Quebec *Nombre de constituants:* 91,656, Liberal
sophie.chatel@parl.gc.ca
sophiechatel.liberal.ca
Autres numéros: Gracefield: 819-463-0112; Campbells Bay: 819-648-2138
twitter.com/sophiechatel1,
www.linkedin.com/in/sophie-chatel-79401787
Bureau de circonscription
87B, rue St-Joseoph
Gracefield, QC J0X 1W0

Shaun Chen
Constituency: Scarborough North, Ontario *No. of*

Constituents: 66,018, Liberal
Tel: 613-996-9681; *Fax:* 613-996-6643
Shaun.Chen@parl.gc.ca
shaunchen.libparl.ca
Other Communications: Constituency Phone: 416-321-2436; Fax: 416-298-6035
twitter.com/shaun_chen, www.facebook.com/ShaunChenMP
Constituency Office
4386 Sheppard Ave. East, #C
Toronto, ON M1S 1T8

Paul Chiang
Constituency: Markham — Unionville, Ontario *No. of Constituents:* 88,538, Liberal
paul.chiang@parl.gc.ca
paulchiang.liberal.ca
Other Communications: Constituency Phone: 905-470-2024; Fax: 905-470-1366
twitter.com/paulchiangmu
Constituency Office
#201, 8300 Woodbine Ave.
Markham, ON L3R 9Y7

Hon. Michael D. Chong, P.C.
Constituency: Wellington — Halton Hills, Ontario *No. of Constituents:* 98,901, Conservative Party
Tel: 613-992-4179; *Fax:* 613-996-4907
michael.chong@parl.gc.ca
michaelchong.ca
Other Communications: Fergus: 519-843-7344; Georgetown: 905-702-2597
twitter.com/michaelchongmp,
www.linkedin.com/in/michael-chong-35363215
Constituency Office
190 St David St. South, #A
Fergus, ON N1M 2L3

Chad Collins
Constituency: Hamilton East — Stoney Creek, Ontario *No. of Constituents:* 84,643, Liberal
chad.collins@parl.gc.ca
Other Communications: Constituency Phone: 905-662-4763; Fax: 905-662-2285
www.linkedin.com/in/chad-collins-48bb5929
Constituency Office
#2, 42 King St. East
Stoney Creek, ON L8G 1K1

Laurel Collins
Constituency: Victoria, British Columbia *No. of Constituents:* 97,997, New Democratic Party
laurel.collins@parl.gc.ca
laurelcollins.ndp.ca
Other Communications: Constituency Phone: 250-363-3600; Fax: 250-363-8422
twitter.com/laurel_bc, www.facebook.com/CollinsLaurel, www.linkedin.com/in/laurel-collins
Constituency Office
1057 Fort St.
Victoria, BC V8V 3K5

Michael Cooper
Constituency: St. Albert — Edmonton, Albert *No. of Constituents:* 92,579, Conservative Party
Tel: 613-996-4722; *Fax:* 613-995-8880
Michael.Cooper@parl.gc.ca
michaelcoopermp.ca
Other Communications: Constituency Phone: 780-459-0809; Fax: 780-460-1246
twitter.com/Cooper4SAE,
facebook.com/michaelcooper4stalbertedmonton
Constituency Office
#220, 20 Perron St.
St Albert, AB T8N 1E4

Serge Cormier
Constituency: Acadie — Bathurst, New Brunswick *No. of Constituents:* 66,718, Liberal
Tel: 613-992-2165
Toll-free: 800-992-5699; *Fax:* 613-992-4558
Serge.Cormier@parl.gc.ca
sergecormier.libparl.ca
Other Communications: Constituency Phone: 506-726-5398; Fax: 506-726-5394
twitter.com/sergecormierlib,
www.facebook.com/sergecormier.acadiebathurst
Constituency Office
#314, 220 St-Pierre Blvd. West
Caraquet, NB E1W 1B5

Michael Coteau
Constituency: Don Valley East, Ontario *No. of Constituents:* 65,793, Liberal
michael.coteau@parl.gc.ca
michaelcoteau.liberal.ca
Other Communications: Constituency Phone: 416-443-0343; Fax: 416-443-1393
twitter.com/coteau, www.facebook.com/coteaumichael, www.linkedin.com/in/mcoteau
Constituency Office

#309, 220 Duncan Mill Rd.
Toronto, ON M3B 3J5

Chris d'Entremont
Constituency: West Nova, Nova Scotia *No. of Constituents:* 69,889, Conservative Party
Tel: 613-995-5711
Toll-free: 866-280-5302; *Fax:* 613-996-9857
chris.dentremont@parl.gc.ca
chrisdentremont.ca
Other Communications: Yarmouth: 902-742-6808; Kingston: 902-242-3605
twitter.com/cdentremontmp
www.facebook.com/chris.dentremont
Constituency Office
#223, 368 Main St.
Yarmouth, NS B5A 1E9

Julie Dabrusin
Constituency: Toronto — Danforth, Ontario *No. of Constituents:* 81,283, Liberal
Tel: 613-992-9381; *Fax:* 613-992-9389
Julie.Dabrusin@parl.gc.ca
juliedabrusin.libparl.ca
Other Communications: Constituency Phone: 416-405-8914; Fax: 416-405-8916
twitter.com/juliedabrusin,
www.facebook.com/JulieDabrusinTorontoDanforth
Constituency Office
1028 Queen St. East
Toronto, ON M4M 1K4

Marc Dalton
Circonscription électorale: Pitt Meadows — Maple Ridge, British Columbia *Nombre de constituants:* 79,960, Conservative Party
Tél: 613-947-4613
Téléc: 613-947-4615
marc.dalton@parl.gc.ca
www.marcdaltonmp.com
Autres numéros: Constituency Phone: 604-466-2761; Fax: 604-466-7593
twitter.com/MarcDalton
Constituency Office
22369 Lougheed Hwy.
Maple Ridge, BC V2X 2T3

Pam Damoff
Constituency: Oakville North — Burlington, Ontario *No. of Constituents:* 97,439, Liberal
Tel: 613-992-1338; *Fax:* 613-992-1344
Pam.Damoff@parl.gc.ca
pamdamoff.libparl.ca
Other Communications: Constituency Phone: 905-847-4043; Fax: 905-847-3037
twitter.com/PamDamoff, www.facebook.com/PamDamoff
Constituency Office
#590, 2525 Old Brunte Rd.
Oakville, ON L6M 4J2

Raquel Dancho
Constituency: Kildonan — St. Paul, Manitoba *No. of Constituents:* 65,719, Conservative Party
raquel.dancho@parl.gc.ca
www.raqueldancho.com
Other Communications: Constituency Phone: 204-984-6322; Fax: 204-984-6415
twitter.com/raqueldancho,
www.facebook.com/RaquelDancho,
www.linkedin.com/in/raquel-dancho-05ab2a126
Constituency Office
27 Red River Blvd. West, #B
Winnipeg, MB R2V 4E2

Scot Davidson
Constituency: York — Simcoe, Ontario *No. of Constituents:* 83,179, Conservative Party
Tel: 613-996-7752; *Fax:* 613-992-8351
scott.davidson@parl.gc.ca
www.scotdavidson.ca
Other Communications: Cosntituency Phone: 905-898-1600; Fax: 905-898-4600
twitter.com/ScotDavidsonMP,
www.facebook.com/ScotDavidsonMP
Note: Scot Davidson first won the riding in a by-election held Feb. 25, 2019. He was re-elected in the Oct. 21, 2019 general election.
Constituency Office
#10, 45 Grist Mill Rd.
Holland Landing, ON L9N 1M7

Don Davies, B.A., LL.B.
Constituency: Vancouver Kingsway, British Columbia *No. of Constituents:* 75,050, New Democratic Party
Tel: 613-943-0267; *Fax:* 613-943-0219
don.davies@parl.gc.ca
www.dondavies.ca
Other Communications: Constituency Phone: 604-775-6263; Fax: 604-775-6284
twitter.com/dondavies, www.facebook.com/DonDaviesNDP, www.linkedin.com/in/don-davies-9343ab30

Constituency Office
2951 Kingsway
Vancouver, BC V5R 5J4

Claude Debellefeuille
Circonscription électorale: Salaberry — Suroît, Québec
Nombre de constituants: 95,776, Bloc Québécois
Tél: 613-995-2532
Téléc: 913-941-3300
claude.debellefeuille@parl.gc.ca
Autres numéros: Circ. Tél: 450-371-0644; Téléc:
450-371-3330
twitter.com/claudedbf_bq,
www.facebook.com/claudedebellefeuilleBQ
Bureau de circonscription
106, rue Saint-Jean-Baptiste
Salaberry-de-Valleyfield, QC J6T 1Z8

Gérard Deltell
Circonscription électorale: Louis-Saint-Laurent, Québec
Nombre de constituants: 94,734, Conservative Party
Tél: 613-996-4151
Téléc: 613-954-2269
Gerard.Deltell@parl.gc.ca
Autres numéros: Circ. Tél: 418-842-5552; Téléc:
418-842-7333
twitter.com/gerarddeltell, www.facebook.com/deltell.gerard
Bureau de circonscription
#200, 9195, boul L'Ormière
Québec, QC G2B 3K2

Caroline Desbiens
Circonscription électorale: Beauport — Côte-de-Beaupré —
Ile d'Orléans — Chlevoix, Québec *Nombre de constituants:*
76,515, Bloc Québécois
Tél: 613-995-9732
Téléc: 613-996-2656
caroline.desbiens@parl.gc.ca
Autres numéros: Circ. Tél: 418-827-6776; Téléc:
418-827-7077
www.facebook.com/carolinedesbiensbq
Bureau de circonscription
#160, 9749, boul Sainte-Anne
Ste-Anne-de-Beaupré, QC G0A 3C0

Luc Desilets
Circonscription électorale: Rivière-des-Mille-Iles, Québec
Nombre de constituants: 82,203, Bloc Québécois
Tél: 613-992-7330
Téléc: 613-992-2602
luc.desilets@parl.gc.ca
lucdesilets.quebec
Autres numéros: Circ. Tél: 450-623-3335; Téléc:
450-623-3103
twitter.com/lucdesiletsbq, www.facebook.com/LucDesiletsBQ
Bureau de circonscription
45, rue Grignon
Saint-Eustache, QC J7P 4X2

Blake Desjarlais
Constituency: Edmonton Griesbach, Alberta *No. of
Constituents:* 82,242, New Democratic Party
blake.desjarlais@parl.gc.ca
blakedesjarlais.ndp.ca
Other Communications: Constituency Phone: 780-495-3261;
Fax: 780-495-5142
twitter.com/DesjarlaisBlake,
www.facebook.com/BlakeDesjarlaisNDP,
www.linkedin.com/in/blake-desjarlais-1a510612a
Constituency Office
#102, 10212 - 127th Ave. NW
Edmonton, AB T5E 0B8

Sukh Dhaliwal, P.Eng.
Constituency: Surrey — Newton, British Columbia *No. of
Constituents:* 67,247, Liberal
Tel: 613-992-0666; *Fax:* 613-992-1965
Sukh.Dhaliwal@parl.gc.ca
sukhdhaliwal.libparl.ca
Other Communications: Constituency Phone: 604-598-2200;
Fax: 604-598-2212
twitter.com/sukhdhaliwal,
www.facebook.com/sukhsinghdhaliwal
Constituency Office
#202, 12992 - 76th Ave.
Surrey, BC V2W 2V6

Anju Dhillon
Circonscription électorale: Dorval — Lachine — LaSalle,
Québec *Nombre de constituants:* 85,344, Liberal
Tél: 613-995-2251
Téléc: 613-996-1481
Anju.Dhillon@parl.gc.ca
anjudhillon.libparl.ca
Autres numéros: Circ. Tél: 514-639-4497; Téléc:
514-639-7407
twitter.com/adhillonDLL, www.facebook.com/anjudhillonDLL
Bureau de circonscription
735, rue Notre-Dame
Lachine, QC H8S 2B5

Lena Metlege Diab
Constituency: Halifax West, Nova Scotia *No. of Constituents:*
77,083, Liberal
lenametlege.diab@parl.gc.ca
lenametlegediab.liberal.ca
Other Communications: Constituency Phone: 902-426-2217;
Fax: 902-426-8339
www.facebook.com/LenaMetlegeDiabNS
Constituency Office
#222, 1496 Bedford Hwy.
Bedford, NS B4A 1E5

Todd Doherty
Constituency: Cariboo — Prince George, British Columbia
No. of Constituents: 84,116, Conservative Party
Tel: 613-995-6704; *Fax:* 613-996-9850
Todd.Doherty@parl.gc.ca
www.todddoherty.ca
Other Communications: Constituency Phone: 250-564-7771;
Fax: 250-564-6224
twitter.com/ToddDohertyMP,
www.facebook.com/ToddDohertyMP,
www.linkedin.com/in/todddohertyformp
Constituency Office
1520 - 3rd Ave.
Prince George, BC V2L 3G4

Han Dong
Constituency: Don Valley North, Ontario *No. of Constituents:*
75,566, Liberal
Tel: 613-995-4988; *Fax:* 613-995-1686
han.dong@parl.gc.ca
handong.libparl.ca
Other Communications: Constituency Phone: 416-443-0623;
Fax: 416-443-9819
twitter.com/handongontario,
www.facebook.com/HanDongOntario
Constituency Office
#100, 250 Consumers Rd.
Toronto, ON M2J 4R4

Terry Dowdall
Constituency: Simcoe — Grey, Ontario *No. of Constituents:*
115,193, Conservative Party
Tel: 613-992-4224; *Fax:* 613-992-2164
terry.dowdall@parl.gc.ca
terrydowdallmp.ca
Other Communications: Constituency Phone: 705-435-1809;
Fax: 705-435-6448
twitter.com/terrydowdall,
www.facebook.com/TerryDowdall.2019
Constituency Office
452 Victoria St. East
Alliston, ON L9R 1J8

Earl Dreeshen, B.Ed.
Constituency: Red Deer — Mountainview, Alberta *No. of
Constituents:* 89,098, Conservative Party
Tel: 613-995-0590; *Fax:* 613-995-6831
earl.dreeshen@parl.gc.ca
www.earldreeshen.ca
Other Communications: Constituency Phone: 403-347-7426;
Fax: 403-347-7423
twitter.com/earl_dreeshen,
www.facebook.com/EarlDreeshenMP,
www.linkedin.com/in/earl-dreeshen-a7aa878a
Constituency Office
4315 - 55th Ave.
Red Deer, AB T4N 4N7

Francis Drouin
Constituency: Glengarry — Prescott — Russell *No. of
Constituents:* 92,007, Liberal
Tel: 613-992-0490; *Fax:* 613-996-9123
Francis.Drouin@parl.gc.ca
francisdrouin.libparl.ca
Other Communications: Constituency Phone: 613-446-6310;
Fax: 613-446-5666
twitter.com/Francis_Drouin,
www.facebook.com/FrancisDrouinGPR
Constituency Office
#201, 1468 Laurier St.
Rockland, ON K4K 1C8

Emmanuel Dubourg, C.P.A., M.B.A.
Circonscription électorale: Bourassa, Québec *Nombre de
constituants:* 69,996, Liberal
Tél: 613-995-6108
Téléc: 613-995-9755
Emmanuel.Dubourg@parl.gc.ca
emmanueldubourg.libparl.ca
Autres numéros: Circ. Tél: 514-323-1212; Téléc:
514-323-2875
twitter.com/EmmanuelDubourg,
www.facebook.com/dubourgemmanuel
Bureau de circonscription
#203, 5835, boul Léger
Montréal, QC H1G 6E1

Hon. Jean-Yves Duclos, P.C.
Circonscription électorale: Québec, Québec *Nombre de

constituants:* 78,950, Liberal
Tél: 613-992-8865
Téléc: 613-995-2805
Jean-Yves.Duclos@parl.gc.ca
jeanyvesduclos.libparl.ca
Autres numéros: Circ. Tél: 418-523-6666; Téléc:
418-523-6672
twitter.com/jyduclos, www.facebook.com/jyduclosliberal,
www.linkedin.com/in/jean-yves-duclos-6405a344
Bureau de circonscription
#201, 600, boul Charest est
PO Box 30014 Main Sta.
Québec, QC G1K 3J4

Terry Duguid
Constituency: Winnipeg South, Manitoba *No. of Constituents:*
68,922, Liberal
Tel: 613-995-7517; *Fax:* 613-943-1466
Terry.Duguid@parl.gc.ca
terryduguid.libparl.ca
Other Communications: Constituency Phone: 204-984-6787;
Fax: 204-984-6792
twitter.com/TerryDuguid, www.facebook.com/terryduguidmp
Constituency Office
#103, 2800 Pembina Hwy.
Winnipeg, MB R3T 5P3

Eric Duncan
Constituency: Stormont — Dundas — South Glengarry,
Ontario *No. of Constituents:* 84,723, Conservative Party
Tel: 613-992-2521; *Fax:* 613-996-2119
eric.duncan@parl.gc.ca
ericduncanmp.ca
Other Communications: Constituency Phone: 613-937-3331;
Fax: 613-937-3251
twitter.com/ericduncanSDSG,
www.facebook.com/EricDuncanSDSG
Constituency Office
691 Brookdale Ave., #C
Cornwall, ON K6J 5C6

Hon. Kirsty Duncan, P.C., B.A., Ph.D.
Constituency: Etobicoke North, Ontario *No. of Constituents:*
73,970, Liberal
Tel: 613-995-4702; *Fax:* 613-995-8359
kirsty.duncan@parl.gc.ca
kirstyduncan.libparl.ca
Other Communications: Constituency Phone: 416-747-6003;
Fax: 416-747-8295
Constituency Office
815 Albion Rd.
Toronto, ON M9V 1A3

Julie Dzerowicz
Constituency: Davenport, Ontario *No. of Constituents:*
79,822, Liberal
Tel: 613-992-2576; *Fax:* 613-995-8202
Julie.Dzerowicz@parl.gc.ca
juliedzerowicz.libparl.ca
Other Communications: Constituency Phone: 416-654-8048;
Fax: 416-654-5083
twitter.com/JulieDzerowicz,
www.facebook.com/juliedzerowicz,
www.linkedin.com/in/julie-dzerowicz-59333aa
Constituency Office
1202 Bloor St. West
Toronto, ON M6H 1N2

Ali Ehsassi
Constituency: Willowdale, Ontario *No. of Constituents:*
78,809, Liberal
Tel: 613-992-4964; *Fax:* 613-992-1158
Ali.Ehsassi@parl.gc.ca
aliehsassi.libparl.ca
Other Communications: Constituency Phone: 416-223-2858;
Fax: 416-223-9715
twitter.com/AliEhsassi, www.facebook.com/ali.ehsassi
Constituency Office
115 Sheppard Ave. West
Toronto, ON M2N 1M7

Fayçal El-Khoury, B.Eng.
Circonscription électorale: Laval — Les Iles, Québec *Nombre
de constituants:* 83,233, Liberal
Tél: 613-992-2659
Téléc: 613-992-9469
Faycal.El-Khoury@parl.gc.ca
faycalelkhoury.libparl.ca
Autres numéros: Circ. Tél: 450-689-4594; Téléc:
450-689-5092
twitter.com/F_ElKhoury,
www.facebook.com/faycalelkhourymp
Bureau de circonscription
#200, 674, Place Publique
Laval, QC H7X 1G1

Stephen Ellis
Constituency: Cumberland — Colchester, Nova Scotia *No. of
Constituents:* 66,616, Conservative Party
stephen.ellis@parl.gc.ca
Other Communications: Constituency Phone: 902-667-8679;

Fax: 902-667-0742
www.facebook.com/DrSDEllis
Constituency Office
35 Church St.
Amherst, NS B4H 3A5
Dave Epp
Constituency: Chatham-Kent — Leamington, Ontario *No. of Constituents:* 86,165, Conservative Party
Tel: 613-992-2612; *Fax:* 613-992-1852
dave.ep@parl.gc.ca
daveepp.ca
Other Communications: Leamington: 519-326-9655;
Chatham: 519-358-7555
twitter.com/DaveEppCKL, www.facebook.com/DaveEppCKL
Constituency Office
#100, 75 Erie St. South
Leamington, ON N8H 3B2
Nathaniel Erskine-Smith
Constituency: Beaches — East York, Ontario *No. of Constituents:* 80,981, Liberal
Tel: 613-992-2115; *Fax:* 613-996-7942
Nathaniel.Erskine-Smith@parl.gc.ca
beynate.ca
Other Communications: Constituency Phone: 416-467-0860;
Fax: 416-467-0905
twitter.com/beynate, www.facebook.com/beynate,
www.linkedin.com/in/nerskinesmith
Constituency Office
1902 Danforth Ave.
Toronto, ON M4C 1J4
Rosemarie Ashley Falk
Constituency: Battlefords — Lloydminster, Saskatchewan *No. of Constituents:* 51,033, Conservative Party
Tel: 613-995-7080; *Fax:* 613-996-8472
Rosemarie.Falk@parl.gc.ca
www.rosemariefalk.ca
Other Communications: Constituency Phone: 306-825-5005
twitter.com/rosemarie_falk,
www.facebook.com/RosemarieFalkMP
Constituency Office
#3, 4304 - 40th Ave.
Lloydminster, SK S9V 2H1
Ted Falk
Constituency: Provencher, Manitoba *No. of Constituents:* 68,979, Conservative Party
Tel: 613-992-3128; *Fax:* 613-995-1049
ted.falk@parl.gc.ca
tedfalk.ca
Other Communications: Constituency Phone: 204-326-9889;
Fax: 204-346-9874
twitter.com/mptedfalk, www.facebook.com/TedFalkMP,
www.linkedin.com/in/ted-falk-7508b53a
Constituency Office
#9A, 90 Brandt St.
Steinbach, MB R5G 0T3
Hon. Edward Fast, P.C., LL.B.
Constituency: Abbotsford, British Columbia *No. of Constituents:* 74,814, Conservative Party
Tel: 613-995-0183; *Fax:* 613-996-9795
ed.fast@parl.gc.ca
edfast.ca
Other Communications: Constituency Phone: 604-557-7888;
Fax: 604-557-9918
twitter.com/HonEdFast
Constituency Office
#205, 2825 Clearbrook Rd.
Abbotsford, BC V2T 6S3
Greg Fergus
Circonscription électorale: Hull — Aylmer, Quebec *Nombre de constituants:* 79,072, Liberal
Tél: 613-992-7550
Téléc: 613-992-7599
Greg.Fergus@parl.gc.ca
gregfergus.libparl.ca
Autres numéros: Circ. Tél: 819-994-8844; Téléc:
819-994-8557
twitter.com/GregFergus,
www.facebook.com/GregFergusLiberal
Bureau de circonscription
#301, 179, promenade du Portage
Gatineau, QC J8X 2K5
Michelle Ferreri
Constituency: Peterborough — Kawartha, Ontario *No. of Constituents:* 99,635, Conservative Party
michelle.ferreri@parl.gc.ca
michelleferreri.ca
Other Communications: Constituency Phone: 705-745-2108;
Fax: 705-741-4123
twitter.com/mferreriptbokaw,
www.linkedin.com/in/michelle-ferreri-09027ba8
Constituency Office
#4, 417 Bethune St.
Peterborough, ON K9H 3Z1

Andy Fillmore
Constituency: Halifax, Nova Scotia *No. of Constituents:* 74,778, Liberal
Tel: 613-995-7614; *Fax:* 613-992-8569
Andy.Fillmore@parl.gc.ca
andyfillmore.liberal.ca
Other Communications: Constituency Phone: 902-426-8691;
Fax: 902-426-8693
twitter.com/AndyFillmoreHFX,
www.facebook.com/AndyFillmoreHFX,
www.linkedin.com/in/andyfillmore
Constituency Office
#808, 1888 Brunswick St.
Halifax, NS B3J 3J8
Hon. Kerry-Lynne Findlay, P.C.
Constituency: South Surrey — White Rock, British Columbia *No. of Constituents:* 84,138, Conservative Party
Tel: 613-947-4497; *Fax:* 613-947-4500
kerry-lynne.findlay@parl.gc.ca
klfindlay.com
Other Communications: Constituency Phone: 604-542-9495;
Fax: 604-542-9496
twitter.com/KerryLynneFindl,
www.facebook.com/kerrylynnefindlay,
www.linkedin.com/in/kerrylynnefindlay
Constituency Office
#135, 1959 - 152nd St.
Surrey, BC V4A 9E3
Darren Fisher
Constituency: Dartmouth — Cole Harbour, Nova Scotia *No. of Constituents:* 76,985, Liberal
Tel: 613-995-9378; *Fax:* 613-995-9379
Darren.Fisher@parl.gc.ca
darrenfisher.ca
Other Communications: Constituency Phone: 902-462-6453;
Fax: 902-462-6493
twitter.com/DarrenFisherNS,
www.facebook.com/DarrenFisherNS
Constituency Office
#200, 82 Tacoma Dr.
Darmouth, NS B2W 3E5
Peter Fonseca, B.A., B.Ed.
Constituency: Mississauga East — Cooksville, Ontario *No. of Constituents:* 85,584, Liberal
Tel: 613-996-0420; *Fax:* 613-996-0279
Peter.Fonseca@parl.gc.ca
www.peterfonseca.ca
Other Communications: Constituency Phone: 905-566-0009;
Fax: 905-566-0017
twitter.com/PeterFonsecaMP,
www.facebook.com/PeterFonsecaMP
Constituency Office
#3, 980 Burnhamthorpe Rd.
Mississauga, O L4Y 2X6
Hon. Mona Fortier, P.C.
Constituency: Ottawa — Vanier, Ontario *No. of Constituents:* 91,015, Liberal
Tel: 613-992-4766; *Fax:* 613-992-6448
Mona.Fortier@parl.gc.ca
monafortier.libparl.ca
Other Communications: Constituency Phone: 613-998-1860;
Fax: 613-947-7963
twitter.com/monafortier,
www.facebook.com/EquipeTeamMona
Constituency Office
233 Montreal Rd.
Vanier, ON K1L 6C7
Rhéal Fortin
Circonscription électorale: Rivière-du-Nord, Québec *Nombre de constituants:* 95,813, Bloc Québécois
Tél: 613-992-3257
Téléc: 613-992-2156
Rheal.Fortin@parl.gc.ca
Autres numéros: Constituency Phone: 450-565-0061; Fax:
450-565-0118
twitter.com/rhealfortin, www.facebook.com/566791310126350
Bureau de circonscription
#203, 72, rue de la Gare
Saint-Jérôme, QC J7Z 2B8
Peter Fragiskatos
Constituency: London North Centre, Ontario *No. of Constituents:* 95,472, Liberal
Tel: 613-992-0805; *Fax:* 613-992-9613
Peter.Fragiskatos@parl.gc.ca
peterfragiskatos.libparl.ca
Other Communications: Constituency Phone: 519-663-9777;
Fax: 519-663-2238
twitter.com/pfragiskatos, www.facebook.com/pfragiskatos
Constituency Office
231 Hyman St.
London, ON N6A 1N6
Hon. Sean Fraser, P.C.
Constituency: Central Nova, Nova Scotia *No. of Constituents:* 60,251, Liberal

Tel: 613-992-6022
Toll-free: 844-641-5886; *Fax:* 613-992-2337
Sean.Fraser@parl.gc.ca
www.seanfrasermp.ca
Other Communications: Constituency Phone: 902-867-2919;
Fax: 902-735-7103
twitter.com/seanfrasermp,
www.facebook.com/SeanFraserMP,
www.linkedin.com/in/sean-fraser-79509054
Constituency Office
#2A, 115 MacLean St.
New Glasgow, NS B2H 4M5
Hon. Chrystia Freeland, P.C.
Constituency: University — Rosedale, Ontario *No. of Constituents:* 80,567, Liberal
Tel: 613-992-5234; *Fax:* 613-996-9607
chrystia.freeland@parl.gc.ca
www.chrystiafreelandmp.com
Other Communications: Constituency Phone: 416-928-1451;
Fax: 416-928-2377
twitter.com/cafreeland, www.facebook.com/freelandchrystia
Constituency Office
#510, 344 Bloor St. West
Toronto, ON M5S 3A7
Hon. Hedy Fry, P.C., M.D., L.R.C.P.S.I., L.M.
Constituency: Vancouver Centre, British Columbia *No. of Constituents:* 91,545, Liberal
Tel: 613-992-3213; *Fax:* 613-995-0056
hedy.fry@parl.gc.ca
hedyfry.liberal.ca
Other Communications: Constituency Phone: 604-666-0135;
Fax: 604-666-0114
twitter.com/hedyfry, www.facebook.com/drhedyfry,
www.linkedin.com/in/hon-hedy-fry-6710b868
Constituency Office
#112, 1030 Denman St.
Vancouver, BC V6G 2M6
Iqwinder Gaheer
Constituency: Mississauga — Malton, Ontario *No. of Constituents:* 79,034, Liberal
iqwinder.gaheer@parl.gc.ca
iqwindergaheer.liberal.ca
Other Communications: Constituency Phone: 905-564-0228;
Fax: 905-564-1147
twitter.com/iqwindersgaheer,
www.facebook.com/IqwinderSGaheer,
www.linkedin.com/in/iqwinder-singh-gaheer-12105a167
Constituency Office
#210, 6660 Kennedy Rd.
Mississauga, ON L5T 2M9
Cheryl Gallant, B.Sc.
Constituency: Renfrew — Nipissing — Pembroke, Ontario *No. of Constituents:* 86,010, Conservative Party
Tel: 613-992-7712; *Fax:* 613-995-2561
cheryl.gallant@parl.gc.ca
cherylgallant.com
Other Communications: Constituency Phone: 613-732-4404;
Fax: 613-732-4697
twitter.com/cherylgallant, www.facebook.com/CherylGallant
Constituency Office
84 Isabella St., 1st Fl.
Pembroke, ON K8A 5S5
Hon. Marc Garneau, P.C., C.C., C.D., B.Sc., Ph.D., F.C.A.S.I.
Circonscription électorale: Notre-Dame-de-Grâce — Westmount, Québec *Nombre de constituants:* 76,499, Liberal
Tél: 613-996-7267
Téléc: 613-995-8632
marc.garneau@parl.gc.ca
marcgarneau.libparl.ca
Autres numéros: Circ. Tél: 514-283-2013; Téléc:
514-283-9790
twitter.com/MarcGarneau,
www.facebook.com/marcgarneaump
Bureau de circonscription
#340, 4060, rue Sainte-Catherine ouest
Montréal, QC H3Z 2Z3
Jean-Denis Garon
Circonscription électorale: Mirabel, Québec *Nombre de constituants:* 96,468, Bloc Québécois
jean-denis.garon@parl.gc.ca
Autres numéros: Circ. Tél: 450-430-5535; Téléc:
450-430-5155
twitter.com/JeanDenisGaron1,
www.facebook.com/jeandenisgaronbq
Bureau de circonscription
#102, 13479, boul Curé-Labelle
Mirabel, QC J7J 1H1
Randall Garrison, M.A.
Constituency: Esquimalt — Saanich — Sooke, British Columbia *No. of Constituents:* 99,285, New Democratic Party
Tel: 613-996-2625; *Fax:* 613-996-9779
randall.garrison@parl.gc.ca
randallgarrison.ndp.ca
Other Communications: Constituency Phone: 250-405-6550;

Fax: 250-405-6554
twitter.com/r_garrison,
www.facebook.com/RandallGarrisonPage
Constituency Office
#2, 50 Burnside Rd. West
Victoria, BC V9A 1B5

Marie-Hélène Gaudreau
Circonscription électorale: Laurentides — Labelle, Québec
Nombre de constituants: 100,315, Bloc Québécois
Tél: 613-992-2289
Téléc: 613-992-6864
mh.gaudreau@parl.gc.ca
mhgaudreau.quebec
Autres numéros: Circ. Tél: 819-326-4724; Téléc:
819-326-2008
twitter.com/mhgaudreaubq,
www.facebook.com/MHGaudreauBQ,
www.linkedin.com/in/MHGaudreauBQ
Bureau de circonscription
124, rue Principale est
Sainte-Agathe-des-Monts, QC J8C 1K1

Leah Gazan
Constituency: Winnipeg Centre, Manitoba *No. of
Constituents:* 59,012, New Democratic Party
Tel: 613-992-5308; *Fax:* 613-992-2890
leah.gazan@parl.gc.ca
www.leahgazan.ca
Other Communications: Constituency Phone: 204-984-6322;
Fax: 204-984-6415
twitter.com/LeahGazan
Constituency Office
892 Sargent Ave.
Winnipeg, MB R3E 0C7

Bernard Généreux
Circonscription électorale: Montmagny — L'Islet —
Kamouraska — Rivière-du-Loup, Québec *Nombre de
constituants:* 78,232, Conservative Party
Tél: 613-995-0265
Téléc: 613-943-1229
Bernard.Genereux@parl.gc.ca
www.bernardgenereux.ca
Autres numéros: Montmagny: 418-248-1211 Riviere-du-Loup:
418-868-1280
twitter.com/genereuxbernard,
www.facebook.com/genereuxbernard
Bureau de circonscription
#101, 6, rue St-Jean Baptiste est
Montmagny, QC G5V 1J7

Garnett Genuis
Constituency: Sherwood Park — Fort Saskatchewan, Alberta
No. of Constituents: 95,317, Conservative Party
Tel: 613-995-3611; *Fax:* 613-995-3612
Garnett.Genuis@parl.gc.ca
www.garnettgenuismp.ca
Other Communications: Constituency Phone: 780-467-4944;
Fax: 780-449-1471
twitter.com/GarnettGenuis, www.facebook.com/MPGenuis
Constituency Office
#214, 2018 Sherwood Dr.
Sherwood Park, AB T8A 5V3

Mark Gerretsen
Constituency: Kingston and the Islands, Ontario *No. of
Constituents:* 97,364, Liberal
Tel: 613-996-1955; *Fax:* 613-996-1958
Mark.Gerretsen@parl.gc.ca
markgerretsen.libparl.ca
Other Communications: Constituency Phone: 613-542-3243;
Fax: 613-542-5461
twitter.com/MarkGerretsen,
www.facebook.com/markgerretsen,
www.linkedin.com/in/markgerretsen
Constituency Office
841 Princess St.
Kingston, ON K7L 1G7

Marilène Gill
Circonscription électorale: Manicouagan, Québec *Nombre de
constituants:* 72,256, Bloc Québécois
Tél: 613-992-2363
Téléc: 613-996-7954
Marilene.Gill@parl.gc.ca
Autres numéros: Baie-Comeau: 418-589-0573; Sept-Iles:
418-960-1411
twitter.com/gillmarilene,
www.facebook.com/marilenegill.blocquebecois
Bureau de circonscription
#201, 1001, boul Laflèche
Baie-Comeau, QC G5C 1C8

Marilyn Gladu
Constituency: Sarnia — Lambton, Ontario *No. of
Constituents:* 84,875, Conservative Party
Tel: 613-957-2649; *Fax:* 613-957-2655
Marilyn.Gladu@parl.gc.ca
www.mpmarilyngladu.ca
Other Communications: Constituency Phone: 519-383-6600;

Fax: 519-383-0609
twitter.com/MarilynGladuSL,
www.linkedin.com/in/marilyn-gladu-05574713
Constituency Office
#2, 1000 Finch Dr.
Sarnia, ON N7S 6G5

Joël Godin
Circonscription électorale: Portneuf — Jacques-Cartier,
Québec *Nombre de constituants:* 92,931, Conservative Party
Tél: 613-992-2798
Téléc: 613-995-1637
Joel.Godin@parl.gc.ca
Autres numéros: Circ. Tél: 418-870-1571; Téléc:
418-870-1577
www.facebook.com/JoelGodinPJC
Bureau de circonscription
#230, 334, rte 138
Saint-Augustin-de-Desmaures, QC G3A 1G8

Laila Goodridge
Constituency: Fort McMurray — Cold Lake, Alberta *No. of
Constituents:* 78,157, Conservative Party
laila.goodridge@parl.gc.ca
lailagoodridge.ca
Other Communications: Constituency Phone: 780-743-2201;
Fax: 780-743-2287
twitter.com/LailaGoodridge, www.facebook.com/VoteLaila
Constituency Office
#112, 10021 Biggs Ave.
Fort McMurray, AB T9H 1S4

Hon. Karina Gould, P.C.
Constituency: Burlington, Ontario *No. of Constituents:* 99,927,
Liberal
Tel: 613-995-0881; *Fax:* 613-995-1091
Karina.Gould@parl.gc.ca
karinagould.libparl.ca
Other Communications: Constituency Phone: 905-639-5757;
Fax: 905-639-6031
twitter.com/karinagould, www.facebook.com/karina.gould,
www.linkedin.com/in/karinagould
Constituency Office
#209, 777 Guelph Line
Burlington, ON L7R 3N2

Jacques Gourde
Circonscription électorale: Lévis — Lotbinière, Québec
Nombre de constituants: 89,405, Conservative Party
Tél: 613-992-2639
Téléc: 613-992-1018
jacques.gourde@parl.gc.ca
Autres numéros: Circ. Tél: 418-836-0970; Téléc:
418-836-6177
Bureau de circonscription
2677, rue Lagueux
Lévis, QC G6J 1B7

Tracy Gray
Constituency: Kelowna — Lake Country, British Columbia *No.
of Constituents:* 99,992, Conservative Party
Tel: 613-992-7006; *Fax:* 613-992-7636
tracy.gray@parl.gc.ca
www.tracygraymp.ca
Other Communications: Constituency Phone: 250-470-5075;
Fax: 250-470-5077
twitter.com/tracygrayklc, www.facebook.com/VoteTracyGray
Constituency Office
#102, 1420 St Paul St.
Kelowna, BC V1Y 2E6

Matthew Green
Constituency: Hamilton Centre, Ontario *No. of Constituents:*
73,885, New Democratic Party
Tel: 613-995-1757; *Fax:* 613-992-8356
matthew.green@parl.gc.ca
Other Communications: Constituency Phone: 905-526-0770;
Fax: 905-526-9943
twitter.com/MatthewGreenNDP,
www.facebook.com/MatthewGreenNDP
Constituency Office
#1, 630 Main St. East
Hamilton, ON L8M 1J7

Hon. Steven Guilbeault, P.C.
Circonscription électorale: Laurier — Sainte-Marie, Québec
Nombre de constituants: 82,524, Liberal
Tél: 613-992-6779
Téléc: 613-995-8461
Steven.Guilbeault@parl.gc.ca
Autres numéros: Circ. Tél: 514-522-1339; Téléc:
514-522-9899
twitter.com/s_guilbeault,
www.facebook.com/steven.guilbeault,
www.linkedin.com/in/steven-guilbeault-7307a345
Bureau de circonscription
#604, 800, boul Maisonneuve est
Montréal, QC H2L 4L8

Hon. Patricia Hajdu, P.C.
Constituency: Thunder Bay — Superior North, Ontario *No. of
Constituents:* 65,928, Liberal

Tel: 613-996-4792; *Fax:* 613-996-9785
Patty.Hajdu@parl.gc.ca
pattyhajdu.libparl.ca
Other Communications: Constituency Phone: 807-766-2090;
Fax: 807-766-2094
twitter.com/PattyHajdu, www.facebook.com/PattyHajdu,
www.linkedin.com/in/patty-hajdu-825326a
Constituency Office
#3, 705 Red River Rd.
Thunder Bay, ON P7B 1J3

Jasraj Singh Hallan
Constituency: Calgary Forest Lawn, Alberta *No. of
Constituents:* 75,376, Conservative Party
Tel: 613-947-4566; *Fax:* 613-947-4569
jasrajsingh.hallan@parl.gc.ca
jasrajmp.ca
twitter.com/jasrajshallan, www.facebook.com/jasrajshallan
Constituency Office
#225, 525 - 28th St. SE
Calgary, AB T2A 6W9

Brendan Hanley
Constituency: Yukon, Yukon *No. of Constituents:* 28,897,
Liberal
brendan.hanley@parl.gc.ca
brendanhanley.liberal.ca
Other Communications: Constituency Phone: 867-668-6565;
Fax: 867-668-6570
Constituency Office
#204, 204 Black St.
Whitehorse, YT Y1A 2M9

Rachael Harder
Constituency: Lethbridge, Ontario *No. of Constituents:*
88,226, Conservative Party
Tel: 613-992-4516; *Fax:* 613-992-6181
Rachael.Harder@parl.gc.ca
www.rachaelharder.ca
Other Communications: Constituency Phone: 403-320-0070;
Fax: 403-380-4026
twitter.com/rachaelhardermp,
www.facebook.com/RachaelHarderMP
Constituency Office
255 - 8th St. South
Lethbridge, AB T1J 4Y1

Ken Hardie
Constituency: Fleetwood — Port Kells, British Columbia *No.
of Constituents:* 80,593, Liberal
Tel: 613-996-2205; *Fax:* 613-995-7139
Ken.Hardie@parl.gc.ca
kenhardie.libparl.ca
Other Communications: Constituency Phone: 604-501-5900;
Fax: 604-501-5901
twitter.com/KenHardie,
www.linkedin.com/in/ken-hardie-0b726b11
Constituency Office
#301, 16088 - 84th Ave.
Surrey, BC V4N 0V9

Lisa Hepfner
Constituency: Hamilton Mountain, Ontario *No. of
Constituents:* 80,992, Liberal
lisa.hepfner@parl.gc.ca
lisahepfner.liberal.ca
Other Communications: Constituency Phone: 905-574-3331;
Fax: 905-574-4980
twitter.com/lisahepfner2021,
www.facebook.com/lisahepfner2021,
www.linkedin.com/in/lisa-hepfner-mcm-97878b39
Constituency Office
#2, 555 Concession St., 2nd Fl.
Hamilton, ON L8V 1A8

Randy Hoback
Constituency: Prince Albert, Saskatchewan *No. of
Constituents:* 57,200, Conservative Party
Tel: 613-995-3295; *Fax:* 613-995-6819
randy.hoback@parl.gc.ca
randyhoback.com
Other Communications: Constituency Phone: 306-953-8622;
Fax: 306-953-8625
www.linkedin.com/in/mprandyhoback
Constituency Office
79 - 11th St. West
Prince Albert, SK S6V 3E8

Hon. Mark Holland, P.C., B.A.
Constituency: Ajax, Ontario *No. of Constituents:* 92,761,
Liberal
Tel: 613-995-8042; *Fax:* 613-996-1289
Mark.Holland@parl.gc.ca
markholland.libparl.ca
Other Communications: Constituency Phone: 905-426-6808;
Fax: 905-426-9564
twitter.com/markhollandlib,
www.facebook.com/mark.hollandlib
Constituency Office
#1, 100 Old Kingston Rd.
Ajax, ON L1T 2Z9

Anthony Housefather
Circonscription électorale: Mont-Royal, Québec *Nombre de constituants:* 73,163, Liberal
Tél: 613-995-0121
Téléc: 613-992-6762
Anthony.Housefather@parl.gc.ca
anthonyhousefather.libparl.ca
Autres numéros: Circ. Tél: 514-283-0171; Téléc: 514-283-2407
twitter.com/AHousefather,
www.facebook.com/anthonyhousefather,
www.linkedin.com/in/anthony-housefather-5984791
Bureau de circonscription
#316, 4770, av Kent
Montréal, QC H3W 1H2

Carol Hughes
Constituency: Algoma — Manitoulin — Kapuskasing, Ontario *No. of Constituents:* 65,420, New Democratic Party
Tel: 613-996-5376; *Fax:* 613-995-6661
carol.hughes@parl.gc.ca
carolhughes.ndp.ca
Other Communications: Elliot Lake: 705-848-8080;
Kapuskasing: 705-335-5533
twitter.com/CarolHughesMP,
www.facebook.com/38326584416
Constituency Office
289A Hillside Dr. South
Elliot Lake, ON P5A 1N7

Hon. Ahmed Hussen, P.C.
Constituency: York South — Weston, Ontario *No. of Constituents:* 77,931, Liberal
Tel: 613-995-0777; *Fax:* 613-992-2949
Ahmed.Hussen@parl.gc.ca
ahmedhussen.libparl.ca
Other Communications: Constituency Phone: 416-656-2526;
Fax: 416-656-9908
twitter.com/honahmedhussen,
www.facebook.com/HonAhmedHussen
Constituency Office
48 Rosemount Ave., #B
Toronto, ON M9N 3B3

Hon. Gudie Hutchings, P.C.
Constituency: Long Range Mountains, Newfoundland & Labrador *No. of Constituents:* 69,385, Liberal
Tel: 613-996-5511; *Fax:* 613-996-9632
Gudie.Hutchings@parl.gc.ca
gudiehutchings.libparl.ca
Other Communications: Constituency Phone: 709-637-4540;
Fax: 709-637-4537
twitter.com/Gudie, www.facebook.com/gudiehutchings
Constituency Office
#49, 51 Park St.
Corner Brook, NL A2H 2X1

Angelo Iacono
Circonscription électorale: Alfred-Pellan, Québec *Nombre de constituants:* 79,083, Liberal
Tél: 613-992-0611
Téléc: 613-992-8556
Angelo.Iacono@parl.gc.ca
angeloiacono.libparl.ca
Autres numéros: Circ. Tél: 450-661-4117; Téléc: 450-661-5623
twitter.com/iaconomp, www.facebook.com/AIaconoMP,
www.linkedin.com/in/angelo-iacono-86690427
Bureau de circonscription
#300, 3131, boul de la Concorde est
Laval, QC H7E 4W4

Lori Idlout
Constituency: Nunavut, Nunavut *No. of Constituents:* 18,665,
New Democratic Party
lori.idlout@parl.gc.ca
loriidlout.ndp.ca
twitter.com/loriidlout, www.facebook.com/Idlout4NDP,
www.linkedin.com/in/lori-idlout-0b730628

Hon. Marci Ien, P.C.
Circonscription électorale: Toronto Centre, Ontario *Nombre de constituants:* 10,579, Liberal
Tél: 613-992-1377
Téléc: 613-992-1383
marci.ien@parl.gc.ca
marci.liberal.ca
Autres numéros: Constituency Phone: 416-972-9749; Fax: 416-972-9891
twitter.com/MarciIen, www.facebook.com/MarciIenTO
Constituency Office
430 Parliament St.
Toronto, ON M5A 3A2

Hon. Helena Jaczek, P.C.
Circonscription électorale: Markham—Stouffville, Ontario
Nombre de constituants: 95,073, Liberal
Tél: 613-992-3640
Téléc: 613-992-3642
helena.jaczek@parl.gc.ca
helenajaczek.libparl.ca

Autres numéros: Constituency Phone: 905-471-8963; Fax: 905-471-7653
twitter.com/HelenaJaczek,
www.facebook.com/DrHelenaJaczek
Constituency Office
#204, 137 Main St. North
Markham, ON L3P 1Y2

Matt Jeneroux, B.A.
Constituency: Edmonton Riverbend, Alberta *No. of Constituents:* 86,609, Conservative Party
Tel: 613-992-3594; *Fax:* 613-992-3616
Matt.Jeneroux@parl.gc.ca
Other Communications: Constituency Phone: 780-495-4351;
Fax: 780-495-4485
twitter.com/jeneroux, www.facebook.com/mattjeneroux,
www.linkedin.com/in/matt-jeneroux-49a78713
Constituency Office
#204, 596 Riverbend Sq.
Edmonton, AB T6R 2E3

Gord Johns
Constituency: Courtenay — Alberni, British Columbia *No. of Constituents:* 100,510, New Democratic Party
Tel: 613-992-0903; *Fax:* 613-992-0913
Gord.Johns@parl.gc.ca
Other Communications: Constituency Phone: 250-947-2140;
Fax: 250-947-2144
twitter.com/GordJohns, www.facebook.com/GordJohnsNDP
Constituency Office
#12, 1209 East Island
Parksville, BC V9P 1R5

Hon. Mélanie Joly, P.C.
Circonscription électorale: Ahuntsic-Cartierville, Québec
Nombre de constituants: 83,176, Liberal
Tél: 613-992-0983
Téléc: 613-992-1932
Melanie.Joly@parl.gc.ca
Autres numéros: Circ. Tél: 514-383-3709; Téléc: 514-383-3589
twitter.com/melaniejoly, www.facebook.com/melanie.joly.965,
www.linkedin.com/in/mjoly
Bureau de circonscription
#1109, 225, rue Chabanel ouest
Montréal, QC H2N 2C9

Yvonne Jones
Constituency: Labrador, Newfoundland & Labrador *No. of Constituents:* 20,016, Liberal
Tel: 613-996-4630; *Fax:* 613-996-7132
yvonne.jones@parl.gc.ca
yvonnejones.libparl.ca
Other Communications: Constituency Phone: 709-896-2483;
Fax: 709-896-9425
twitter.com/YvonneJJones,
www.facebook.com/yvonnejonesliberal
Constituency Office
217 Hamilton River Rd.
PO Box 119 B Sta.
Happy Valley-Goose Bay, NL A0P 1E0

Majid Jowhari
Constituency: Richmond Hill, Ontario *No. of Constituents:* 84,660, Liberal
Tel: 613-992-3802; *Fax:* 613-996-1954
Majid.Jowhari@parl.gc.ca
majidjowhari.libparl.ca
Other Communications: Constituency Phone: 905-707-9701;
Fax: 905-707-9705
twitter.com/MajidJowhari, www.linkedin.com/in/majidjowhari
Constituency Office
#101, 100 Mural St.
Richmond Hill, ON L4B 1J3

Peter Julian, B.A.
Constituency: New Westminster — Burnaby, British Columbia
No. of Constituents: 85,807, New Democratic Party
Tel: 613-992-4214; *Fax:* 613-947-9500
peter.julian@parl.gc.ca
www.peterjulian.ca
Other Communications: Constituency Phone: 604-775-5707;
Fax: 604-775-5743
twitter.com/MPJulian, www.facebook.com/MPPeterJulian
Constituency Office
#110, 888 Carnarvon St.
New Westminster, BC V3M 0C6

Arielle Kayabaga
Constituency: London West, Ontario *No. of Constituents:* 99,677, Liberal
arielle.kayabaga@parl.gc.ca
ariellekayabaga.liberal.ca
Other Communications: Constituency Phone: 519-473-5955;
Fax: 519-473-7333
twitter.com/KayabagaArielle,
www.linkedin.com/in/ariellekayabaga
Constituency Office
#200, 390 Commissioners Rd. West
London, ON N6J 1Y3

Mike Kelloway
Constituency: Cape Breton — Canso, Nova Scotia *No. of Constituents:* 60,412, Liberal
Tel: 613-992-6756; *Fax:* 613-992-4053
mike.kelloway@parl.gc.ca
mikekelloway.libparl.ca
Other Communications: Constituency Phone: 902-842-9763
twitter.com/mikekelloway,
www.facebook.com/mike.kelloway.1
Constituency Office
78 Commercial St.
Dominion, NS B1G 1B4

Pat Kelly
Constituency: Calgary Rocky Ridge, Alberta *No. of Constituents:* 98,092, Conservative Party
Tel: 613-992-0826; *Fax:* 613-992-0845
Pat.Kelly@parl.gc.ca
patkellymp.ca
Other Communications: Constituency Phone: 403-282-7980;
Fax: 403-282-3587
twitter.com/PatKelly_MP, www.facebook.com/PatKellyMP,
www.linkedin.com/in/pat-kelly-15605742
Constituency Office
#202, 400 Crowfoot Cres.
Calgary, AB T3G 5H6

Iqra Khalid
Constituency: Mississauga — Erin Mills, Ontario *No. of Constituents:* 88,380, Liberal
Tel: 613-995-7321; *Fax:* 613-992-6708
Iqra.Khalid@parl.gc.ca
iqrakhalid.libparl.ca
Other Communications: Constituency Phone: 905-820-8814;
Fax: 905-820-4068
twitter.com/iamIqraKhalid
Constituency Office
#41, 3184 Ridgeway Dr.
Mississauga, ON L5L 5S7

Hon. Kamal Khera, P.C.
Constituency: Brampton West, Ontario *No. of Constituents:* 86,912, Liberal
Tel: 613-992-0778; *Fax:* 613-992-0800
Kamal.Khera@parl.gc.ca
kamalkhera.libparl.ca
Other Communications: Constituency Phone: 905-454-4758;
Fax: 905-454-3192
twitter.com/KamalKheraLib,
www.facebook.com/KamalKheraLiberal
Constituency Office
#10/10A, 35 Van Kirk Dr.
Brampton, ON L7A 1A5

Robert Gordon Kitchen
Constituency: Souris — Moose Mountain, Saskatchewan *No. of Constituents:* 51,957, Conservative Party
Tel: 613-992-7685; *Fax:* 613-995-8908
Robert.Kitchen@parl.gc.ca
www.drrobertkitchen.ca
Other Communications: Constituency Phone: 306-634-3000;
Fax: 306-634-4835
www.facebook.com/drrobertkitchen
Constituency Office
#308, 1133 - 4th St.
Estevan, SK S4A 0W6

Tom Kmiec, B.A., M.A.
Constituency: Calgary Shepard, Alberta *No. of Constituents:* 111,936, Conservative Party
Tel: 613-992-0846
Toll-free: 855-852-5710; *Fax:* 613-992-0883
Tom.Kmiec@parl.gc.ca
www.tomkmiecmp.ca
Other Communications: Constituency Phone: 403-974-1285
twitter.com/tomkmiec, www.facebook.com/TomKmiec,
www.linkedin.com/in/tomkmiec
Constituency Office
#40A, 12221 - 44th St. SE
Calgary, AB T2Z 4H3

Annie Koutrakis
Circonscription électorale: Vimy, Québec *Nombre de constituants:* 88,077, Liberal
Tél: 613-995-7298
Téléc: 613-996-1195
annie.koutrakis@parl.gc.ca
anniekoutrakis.libparl.ca
Autres numéros: Circ. Tél: 450-973-5660; Téléc: 450-973-5661
twitter.com/AnnieKoutrakis,
www.facebook.com/AnnieKoutrakisVimy
Bureau de circonscription
#405, 2500, boul Daniel-Johnson
Laval, QC H7T 2P6

Michael Kram
Constituency: Regina — Wascana, Saskatchewan *No. of Constituents:* 59,907, Conservative Party
Tel: 613-947-1153; *Fax:* 613-996-9790
michael.kram@parl.gc.ca

michaelkrammp.ca
Other Communications: Constituency Phone: 306-585-2202
twitter.com/MichaelKramSK
www.facebook.com/MichaelKramSK
Constituency Office
2723 East Quance St.
Regina, SK S4N 7M3

Shelby Kramp-Neuman
Constituency: Hastings — Lennox & Addington, Ontario *No. of Constituents:* 80,079, Conservative Party
Toll-free: 866-471-3800
shelby.kramp-neuman@parl.gc.ca
Constituency Office
81C Millennium Pkwy.
Belleville, ON K8N 4Z5

Damien Kurek
Constituency: Battle River — Crowfoot, Alberta *No. of Constituents:* 81,123, Conservative Party
Tel: 613-947-4608; *Fax:* 613-947-4611
damien.kurek@parl.gc.ca
www.damienkurek.ca
Other Communications: Constituency Phone: 780-608-4600;
Fax: 780-608-4603
twitter.com/dckurek, www.facebook.com/dckurek,
www.linkedin.com/in/dckurek
Constituency Office
4945 - 50th St.
Camrose, AB T4V 1P9

Stephanie Kusie
Constituency: Calgary Midnapore, Alberta *No. of Constituents:* 93,458, Conservative Party
Tel: 613-992-2235; *Fax:* 613-992-1920
Stephanie.Kusie@parl.gc.ca
stephaniekusiemp.ca
Other Communications: Constituency Phone: 403-225-3480;
Fax: 403-225-3504
twitter.com/StephanieKusie,
www.facebook.com/stephaniekusiepolitician,
www.linkedin.com/in/stephanie-kusie-03964a1b
Constituency Office
#204, 279 Midpark Way SE
Calgary, AB T2X 1M2

Irek Kusmierczyk
Constituency: Windsor — Tecumseh, Ontario *No. of Constituents:* 95,004, Liberal
Tel: 613-947-3445; *Fax:* 613-947-3448
irek.kusimierczyk@parl.gc.ca
irekkusmierczyk.libparl.ca
Other Communications: Constituency Phone: 519-979-2707;
Fax: 519-979-7747
twitter.com/Irek_K, www.facebook.com/TeamIrek
Constituency Office
#2, 9733 Tecumseh Rd. East
Windsor, ON N8R 1A5

Jenny Kwan, B.A.
Constituency: Vancouver East, British Columbia *No. of Constituents:* 91,951, New Democratic Party
Tel: 613-992-6030; *Fax:* 613-995-7412
Jenny.Kwan@parl.gc.ca
jennykwan.ndp.ca
Other Communications: Constituency Phone: 604-775-5800;
Fax: 604-775-5811
twitter.com/JennyKwanBC,
www.facebook.com/JennyKwanVanEast
Constituency Office
2572 East Hastings St.
Vancouver, BC V5K 1Z3

Hon. Mike Lake, P.C., B.Comm.
Constituency: Edmonton — Wetaskiwin, Alberta *No. of Constituents:* 122,984, Conservative Party
Tel: 613-995-8695; *Fax:* 613-995-6465
mike.lake@parl.gc.ca
mikelake.ca
Other Communications: Constituency Phone: 780-495-2149;
Fax: 780-495-2147
twitter.com/MikeLakeMP, www.facebook.com/MikeLakeMP
Constituency Office
1230 - 91st St. SW
Edmonton, AB T6X 0P2

Marie-France Lalonde
Constituency: Orléans, Ontario *No. of Constituents:* 106,021, Liberal
Tel: 613-995-1800; *Fax:* 613-995-6298
marie-france.lalonde@parl.gc.ca
mariefrancelalonde.libparl.ca
Other Communications: Constituency Phone: 613-834-1800;
Fax: 613-590-1201
twitter.com/mflalonde, www.facebook.com/LalondeMF
Constituency Office
255 Centrum Blvd., 2nd Fl.
Orléans, O K1E 3W3

Emmanuella Lambropoulos
Circonscription électorale: Saint-Laurent, Québec *Nombre de constituants:* 67,991, Liberal

Tél: 613-996-5789
Téléc: 613-996-6562
Emmanuella.Lambropoulos@parl.gc.ca
emmanuellalambropoulos.libparl.ca
Autres numéros: Circ. Tél: 514-335-6655; Téléc:
514-335-2712
twitter.com/emlambropoulos,
www.facebook.com/emlambropoulos
Bureau de circonscription
#440, 750, boul Marcel Laurin
Montréal, QC H4M 2M4

Hon. David Lametti, P.C., B.A., LL.B., B.C.L., LL.M., D.Phil.
Circonscription électorale: LaSalle — Émard — Verdun,
Québec *Nombre de constituants:* 82,321, Liberal
Tél: 613-943-6636
Téléc: 613-943-6637
David.Lametti@parl.gc.ca
davidlametti.liberal.ca
Autres numéros: Circ. Tél: 514-363-0954; Téléc:
514-367-5533
twitter.com/DavidLametti
Bureau de circonscription
6415, boul Monk
Montréal, QC H4E 3H8

Kevin Lamoureux
Constituency: Winnipeg North, Manitoba *No. of Constituents:* 62,958, Liberal
Tel: 613-996-6417; *Fax:* 613-996-9713
kevin.lamoureux@parl.gc.ca
kevinlamoureux.liberal.ca
Other Communications: Constituency Phone: 204-984-1767;
Fax: 204-984-1766
twitter.com/kevin_lamoureux,
www.facebook.com/mpkevin.ca,
www.linkedin.com/in/kevin-lamoureux-16541a5a
Constituency Office
98 Mandalay Dr.
Winnipeg, MB R2P 1V8

Melissa Lantsman
Constituency: Thornhill, Ontario *No. of Constituents:* 84,808,
Conservative Party
melissa.lantsman@parl.gc.ca
melissalantsman.ca
Other Communications: Constituency Phone: 905-886-9911;
Fax: 905-886-5267
twitter.com/MelissaLantsman,
www.facebook.com/melissalantsmanforthornhill,
www.linkedin.com/in/melissalantsman
Constituency Office
#23, 1118 Centre St.
Thornhill, ON L4J 7R9

Viviane LaPointe
Constituency: Sudbury, Ontario *No. of Constituents:* 74,030,
Liberal
viviane.lapointe@parl.gc.ca
vivianelapointe.liberal.ca
Other Communications: Constituency Phone: 705-673-7107;
Fax: 705-673-0944
twitter.com/vivianelapointe, www.facebook.com/vivforsudbury
Cosntituency Office
#302, 93 Cedar St.
Sudbury, ON P3E 1A7

Andréanne Larouche
Circonscription électorale: Shefford, Québec *Nombre de constituants:* 90,921, Bloc Québécois
Tél: 613-992-5279
Téléc: 613-992-7871
adreanne.larouche@parl.gc.ca
andreannelarouche.ca
Autres numéros: Circ. Tél: 450-378-3221; Téléc:
450-378-3380
twitter.com/A_Larouche_Shef,
www.facebook.com/votredeputeedeShefford
Bureau de circonscription
#101, 400, rue Principale
Granby, QC J2G 2W6

Patricia Lattanzio
Circonscription électorale: Saint-Léonard — Saint-Michel,
Québec *Nombre de constituants:* 76,885, Liberal
Tél: 613-995-9414
Téléc: 613-992-8523
patricia.lattanzio@parl.gc.ca
patricialattanzio.libparl.ca
Autres numéros: Circ. Tél: 514-256-4548; Téléc:
514-256-8828
twitter.com/PatriciaLattan3,
www.facebook.com/patricialattanzioplc
Bureau de circonscription
8370, boul Lacordaire
Montréal, QC H1R 3Y6

Stéphane Lauzon
Circonscription électorale: Argenteuil — La Petite-Nation,
Québec *Nombre de constituants:* 80,202, Liberal
Tél: 613-992-0902

Téléc: 613-992-2935
Stephane.Lauzon@parl.gc.ca
stephanelauzon.libparl.ca
Autres numéros: Lachute: 450-562-0737; Gatineau:
819-281-2626
twitter.com/stephanelauzon5,
www.facebook.com/stephane.lauzon.988
Bureau de circonscription
#204, 505, av Bethany
Lachute, QC J8H 4A6

Philip Lawrence
Constituency: Northumberland — Peterborough South,
Ontario *No. of Constituents:* 96,841, Conservative Party
Tel: 613-992-8585; *Fax:* 613-995-7536
philip.lawrence@parl.gc.ca
philiplawrencemp.ca
Other Communications: Constituency Phone: 905-372-8757;
Fax: 905-372-1500
twitter.com/PLawrenceMP,
www.facebook.com/philiplawrenceMP
Constituency Office
#4, 12 Elgin St. East
Cobourg, ON K9A 0C5

Hon. Dominic LeBlanc, P.C., B.A., LL.B., LL.M.
Constituency: Beauséjour, New Brunswick *No. of Constituents:* 69,444, Liberal
Tel: 613-992-1020; *Fax:* 613-992-3053
dominic.leblanc@parl.gc.ca
dominicleblanc.libparl.ca
Other Communications: Constituency Phone: 506-533-5700;
Fax: 506-533-5888
twitter.com/DLeBlancNB, www.facebook.com/leblancdominic
Constituency Office
328 Main St., #I
Shediac, NB E4P 2E3

Hon. Diane Lebouthillier, P.C.
Circonscription électorale: Gaspésie — Les
Iles-de-la-Madeleine, Québec *Nombre de constituants:*
64,748, Liberal
Tél: 613-992-6188
Téléc: 613-992-6194
Diane.Lebouthillier@parl.gc.ca
dianelebouthillier.libparl.ca
Autres numéros: Circ. Tél: 418-385-4264; Téléc:
418-385-4276
twitter.com/dilebouthillier, www.facebook.com/DiLebouthillier
Bureau de circonscription
#104, 153, Grande Allée est
Grande-Rivière, QC G0C 1V0

Richard Lehoux
Circonscription électorale: Beauce, Québec *Nombre de constituants:* 86,333, Conservative Party
Tél: 613-992-8053
Téléc: 613-995-0687
richard.lehoux@parl.gc.ca
Autres numéros: Circ. Tél: 418-387-4224; Téléc:
418-387-8124
www.facebook.com/richardlehouxpcc
Bureau de circonscription
#201, 250, boul Vachon nord
Sainte-Marie, QC G6E 4G3

Sébastien Lemire
Circonscription électorale: Abitibi — Témiscamingue, Quebec
Nombre de constituants: 82,341, Bloc Québécois
Tél: 613-996-3250
Ligne sans frais: 800-567-6433
Téléc: 613-992-3672
sebastien.lemire@parl.gc.ca
Autres numéros: Circ. Téléc: 819-762-8732
twitter.com/seblemire, www.facebook.com/seblemireAT
Bureau de circonscription
#15, 33A, rue Gamble ouest
Rouyn-Noranda, QC J9X 2R3

Chris Lewis
Constituency: Essex, Ontario *No. of Constituents:* 102,153,
Conservative Party
Tel: 613-992-1812; *Fax:* 613-995-0033
chris.lewis@parl.gc.ca
chrislewismp.ca
Other Communications: Constituency Phone: 519-776-4700;
Fax: 519-776-1383
twitter.com/ChrisLewisEssex,
www.facebook.com/ChrisLewisEssex
Constituency Office
#7B, 35 Victoria Ave.
Essex, ON N8M 1M4

Leslyn Lewis, B.A., M.E.S., J.D., PhD
Constituency: Haldimand — Norfolk, Ontario, Conservative
Party
Toll-free: 866-496-3400
leslyn.lewis@parl.gc.ca
leslynlewis.ca
Other Communications: Constituency Fax: 519-426-0003
twitter.com/LeslynLewis,

www.facebook.com/LeslynLewisCPC
Constituency Office
76 Kent St. South
Simcoe, ON N3Y 2Y1

Ron Liepert
Constituency: Calgary Signal Hill, Alberta *No. of Constituents:*
88,317, Conservative Party
Tel: 613-992-3066; *Fax:* 613-992-3256
Ron.Liepert@parl.gc.ca
ronliepertmp.ca
Other Communications: Constituency Phone: 403-292-6666;
Fax: 403-292-6670
twitter.com/ronliepert, www.facebook.com/ronliepert,
www.linkedin.com/in/ron-liepert-6a32a128
Constituency Office
#2216, 8561 - 8A Ave. SW
Calgary, AB T3H 0V5

Joël Lightbound
Circonscription électorale: Louis-Hébert, Québec *Nombre de
constituants:* 82,131, Liberal
Tél: 613-995-4995
Téléc: 613-996-8292
Joel.Lightbound@parl.gc.ca
joellightbound.libparl.ca
Autres numéros: Circ. Tél: 418-648-3244; Téléc:
418-648-3260
twitter.com/JoelLightbound,
www.facebook.com/joellightbound,
www.linkedin.com/in/joellightbound
Bureau de circonscription
#110, 3700, rue du Campanile
Québec, QC G1X 4G6

Dane Lloyd
Constituency: Sturgeon River — Parkland, Alberta *No. of
Constituents:* 92,965, Conservative Party
Tel: 613-996-9778; *Fax:* 613-996-0785
Dane.Lloyd@parl.gc.ca
danelloyd.com
Other Communications: Constituency Phone: 780-823-2050;
Fax: 780-823-2055
twitter.com/DaneLloydMP,
www.facebook.com/DaneLloydCPC
Constituency Office
#102, 4807 - 44th Ave.
Stony Plain, AB T7Z 1V5

Ben Lobb, B.Sc. Admin.
Constituency: Huron — Bruce, Ontario *No. of Constituents:*
86,147, Conservative Party
Tel: 613-992-8234; *Fax:* 613-995-6350
ben.lobb@parl.gc.ca
www.benlobb.com
Other Communications: Goderich: 519-524-6560; Port Elgin:
519-832-2999
twitter.com/benlobbmp, www.facebook.com/BenLobbMP
Constituency Office
30 Victoria St. North
Goderich, ON N7A 2R6

Wayne Long
Constituency: Saint John — Rothesay, New Brunswick *No. of
Constituents:* 63,371, Liberal
Tel: 613-947-2700; *Fax:* 613-947-4574
Wayne.Long@parl.gc.ca
waynelong.liberal.ca
Other Communications: Constituency Phone: 506-657-2500;
Fax: 506-657-2504
twitter.com/WayneLongSJ,
www.facebook.com/WayneLongMP,
www.linkedin.com/in/wayne-long-74839982
Constituency Office
1 Market Sq., #N306
Saint John, NB E2L 4Z6

Lloyd Longfield
Constituency: Guelph, Ontario *No. of Constituents:* 105,106,
Liberal
Tel: 613-996-4758; *Fax:* 613-996-9922
Lloyd.Longfield@parl.gc.ca
www.mplongfield.ca
Other Communications: Constituency Phone: 519-837-8276;
Fax: 519-837-8443
twitter.com/lloydlongfield, www.facebook.com/lloyd.longfield
Constituency Office
#103, 111 Farquhar St.
Guelph, ON N1H 3N4

Tim Louis
Constituency: Kitchener — Conestoga, Ontario *No. of
Constituents:* 74,562, Liberal
Tel: 613-992-4633; *Fax:* 613-992-9932
tim.louis@parl.gc.ca
timlouis.libparl.ca
Other Communications: Constituency Phone: 519-578-3777;
Fax: 519-578-0138
twitter.com/TimLouisKitCon,
www.facebook.com/TimLouisKitCon
Constituency Office

1187 Fischer-Hallman Rd.
Kitchener, ON N2E 4H9

Hon. Lawrence MacAulay, P.C.
Constituency: Cardigan, Prince Edward Island *No. of
Constituents:* 29,665, Liberal
Tel: 613-995-9325; *Fax:* 613-995-2754
lawrence.macaulay@parl.gc.ca
lawrencemacaulay.libparl.ca
Other Communications: Constituency Phone: 902-838-4139;
Fax: 902-838-3790
twitter.com/L_MacAulay,
www.facebook.com/LawrenceMacAulayCardigan
Constituency Office
551 Main St.
PO Box 1150
Montague, PE C0A 1R0

Heath MacDonald
Constituency: Malpeque, Prince Edward Island *No. of
Constituents:* 30,275, Liberal
Toll-free: 800-442-4050
heath.macdonald@parl.gc.ca
heathmacdonald.liberal.ca
Other Communications: Constituency Fax: 902-964-3242
twitter.com/CornwallHeath,
www.facebook.com/CornwallHeath,
www.linkedin.com/in/heath-macdonald-6148b932
Constituency Office
#1, 4283 Rte. 13
Hunter River, PE C0A 1N0

Alistair MacGregor
Constituency: Cowichan — Malahat — Langford, British
Columbia *No. of Constituents:* 92,637, New Democratic Party
Tel: 613-943-2180; *Fax:* 613-993-5577
Alistair.MacGregor@parl.gc.ca
alistairmacgregor.ndp.ca
Other Communications: Constituency Phone: 250-746-4896;
Fax: 250-746-2354
twitter.com/AMacGregor4CML,
www.facebook.com/alistair4ndp,
www.linkedin.com/in/alistair-macgregor-239552
Constituency Office
#101, 126 Ingram St.
Duncan, BC V9L 1P1

Dave MacKenzie
Constituency: Oxford, Ontario *No. of Constituents:* 92,758,
Conservative Party
Tel: 613-995-4432; *Fax:* 613-995-4433
dave.mackenzie@parl.gc.ca
davemackenzie.ca
Other Communications: Constituency Phone: 519-421-7214;
Fax: 519-421-9704
twitter.com/davemackenziemp,
www.facebook.com/DaveMacKenzieMP
Constituency Office
#4, 208 Huron St.
Woodstock, ON N4S 7A1

Steven MacKinnon
Circonscription électorale: Gatineau, Québec *Nombre de
constituants:* 84,463, Liberal
Tél: 613-992-4351
Téléc: 613-992-1037
Steven.MacKinnon@parl.gc.ca
stevenmackinnon.libparl.ca
Autres numéros: Circ. Tél: 819-561-5555; Téléc:
819-561-0005
twitter.com/stevenmackinnon,
www.facebook.com/stevenmackinnon,
www.linkedin.com/in/mackinnonsteven
Bureau de circonscription
#401, 160, boul de l'Hôpital
Gatineau, QC J8T 8J1

Larry Maguire
Constituency: Brandon — Souris, Manitoba *No. of
Constituents:* 62,415, Conservative Party
Tel: 613-995-9372; *Fax:* 613-992-1265
Larry.Maguire@parl.gc.ca
www.larrymaguire.com
Other Communications: Constituency Phone: 204-726-7600;
Fax: 204-726-7699
twitter.com/larrymaguiremp
www.facebook.com/larrymaguiremp
Constituency Office
658 - 10th St., #B
Brandon, MB R7A 4G5

James Maloney
Constituency: Etobicoke — Lakeshore, Ontario *No. of
Constituents:* 102,987, Liberal
Tel: 613-995-9364; *Fax:* 613-992-5880
James.Maloney@parl.gc.ca
jamesmaloney.libparl.ca
Other Communications: Constituency Phone: 416-251-5510;
Fax: 416-251-2845
twitter.com/j_maloney,
www.facebook.com/jamesmaloney.etobicoke

Constituency Office
#203, 1092 Islington Ave.
Toronto, ON M8Z 4R9

Richard Martel
Circonscription électorale: Chicoutimi — Le Fjord, Québec
Nombre de constituants: 66,152, Conservative Party
Tél: 613-992-7207
Téléc: 613-992-0431
Richard.Martel@parl.gc.ca
Autres numéros: Circ. Tél: 418-698-5648; Téléc:
418-698-5611
twitter.com/richardmartelpc,
www.facebook.com/richardmartelpcc
Bureau de circonscription
#101, 320, rue Ste-Anne
Chicoutimi, QC G7J 2M4

Soraya Martinez Ferrada
Circonscription électorale: Hochelaga, Québec *Nombre de
constituants:* 82,504, Liberal
Tél: 613-947-4576
Téléc: 613-947-4579
soraya.martinezferrada@parl.gc.ca
sorayamartinezferrada.ca
Autres numéros: Circ. Tél: 514-283-2655; Téléc:
514-283-6485
twitter.com/sorayamartinezf,
www.facebook.com/SorayaMartinezFerrada
Bureau de circonscription
#225, 2030, boul Pie-IX
Montréal, QC H1V 2C8

Brian Masse, B.A. (Hons.)
Constituency: Windsor West, Ontario *No. of Constituents:*
93,826, New Democratic Party
Tel: 613-996-1541; *Fax:* 613-992-5397
brian.masse@parl.gc.ca
brianmasse.ndp.ca
Other Communications: Constituency Phone: 519-255-1631;
Fax: 519-255-7913
twitter.com/BrianMasseMP,
www.facebook.com/brianmasse4ww
Constituency Office
#2, 1398 Ouellette Ave.
Windsor, ON N8X 1J8

Lindsay Mathyssen
Constituency: London — Fanshawe, Ontario *No. of
Constituents:* 92,880, New Democratic Party
Tel: 613-995-2901; *Fax:* 613-943-8717
lindsay.mathyssen@parl.gc.ca
lindsaymathyssen.ndp.ca
Other Communications: Constituency Phone: 519-685-4745;
Fax: 519-685-1462
twitter.com/LMathys,
www.facebook.com/LindsayMathyssenNDP
Constituency Office
1700 Dundas St., #D
London, ON N5W 3C9

Bryan May
Constituency: Cambridge, Ontario *No. of Constituents:*
89,914, Liberal
Tel: 613-996-1307; *Fax:* 613-996-8340
Bryan.May@parl.gc.ca
bryanmay.libparl.ca
Other Communications: Constituency Phone: 519-624-7440;
Fax: 519-624-3517
twitter.com/_BryanMay,
www.facebook.com/bryanmaycambridge,
www.linkedin.com/in/bryan-may-19605050
Constituency Office
534 Hespeler Rd., #A4
Cambridge, ON N1R 6J7

Elizabeth May, O.C., LL.B.
Constituency: Saanich — Gulf Islands, British Columbia *No.
of Constituents:* 90,685, Green Party of Canada
Tel: 613-996-1119; *Fax:* 613-996-0850
elizabeth.may@parl.gc.ca
elizabethmaymp.ca
Other Communications: Constituency Phone: 250-657-2000;
Fax: 250-657-2004
twitter.com/elizabethmay
Constituency Office
#1, 9711 - 4th St.
Sidney, BC V8L 2Y8

Dan Mazier
Constituency: Dauphin — Swan River — Marquette, Manitoba
No. of Constituents: 61,722, Conservative Party
Tel: 613-992-3176
Toll-free: 877-405-8946; *Fax:* 613-992-0930
dan.mazier@parl.gc.ca
www.dsrn.ca
twitter.com/MBDan7, www.facebook.com/DanMazierMB
Constituency Office
#22C, 1450 Main St. South
Dauphin, MB R7N 3H4

Kelly McCauley
Constituency: Edmonton West, Alberta *No. of Constituents:* 88,508, Conservative Party
Tel: 780-392-2515; *Fax:* 780-392-2519
Kelly.McCauley@parl.gc.ca
kellymccauley.ca
Other Communications: Constituency Phone: 780-392-2515; Fax: 780-392-2519
twitter.com/KellyMcCauleyMP,
www.linkedin.com/in/kjmccauley
Constituency Office
#104-105, 10471 - 178th St.
Edmonton, AB T5S 1R5

Ken McDonald
Constituency: Avalon, Newfoundland & Labrador *No. of Constituents:* 69,131, Liberal
Tel: 613-992-4133; *Fax:* 613-992-7277
Ken.McDonald@parl.gc.ca
kenmcdonald.libparl.ca
Other Communications: Constituency Phone: 709-834-3424; Fax: 709-834-3628
twitter.com/McDonald4Avalon,
www.facebook.com/McDonald4Avalon
Constituency Office
#105, 120 Conception Bay Hwy.
Conception Bay South, N A1W 3A6

Hon. David J. McGuinty, P.C., Dip. Agr., B.A., LL.B, LL.M.
Constituency: Ottawa South, Ontario *No. of Constituents:* 91,543, Liberal
Tel: 613-992-3269; *Fax:* 613-995-1534
david.mcguinty@parl.gc.ca
davidmcguinty.libparl.ca
Other Communications: Constituency Phone: 613-990-8640; Fax: 613-990-2592
www.linkedin.com/in/davidmcguinty
Constituency Office
1883 Bank St., #A
Ottawa, ON K1V 7Z9

Hon. John McKay, P.C., B.A., LL.B.
Constituency: Scarborough — Guildwood, Ontario *No. of Constituents:* 67,754, Liberal
Tel: 613-992-1447; *Fax:* 613-992-8968
john.mckay@parl.gc.ca
johnmckay.libparl.ca
Other Communications: Constituency Phone: 416-283-1226; Fax: 416-283-7935
twitter.com/JohnMcKayLib, www.facebook.com/johnmckaymp
Constituency Office
#10, 3785 Kingston Rd.
Toronto, ON M1J 3H4

Ron McKinnon
Constituency: Coquitlam — Port Coquitlam, British Columbia *No. of Constituents:* 91,889, Liberal
Tel: 613-992-9650; *Fax:* 613-992-9868
Ron.McKinnon@parl.gc.ca
ronmckinnon.libparl.ca
Other Communications: Constituency Phone: 604-927-1080; Fax: 604-927-1084
twitter.com/RonMcKinnonLib,
www.facebook.com/RonMcKinnonLib
Constituency Office
#101, 3278 Westwood St.
Port Coquitlam, BC V3C 3L8

Greg McLean
Constituency: Calgary Centre, Alberta *No. of Constituents:* 95,408, Conservative Party
Tel: 613-995-1561; *Fax:* 613-995-1862
greg.mclean@parl.gc.ca
www.gregmcleanmp.ca
Other Communications: Constituency Phone: 403-244-1880; Fax: 403-245-3468
twitter.com/gregmcleanyyc,
www.facebook.com/GregMcLeanYYC,
www.linkedin.com/in/greg-mclean-90b3737
Constituency Office
#445, 1414 - 8th St. SW
Calgary, AB T2R 1J6

Michael V. McLeod
Constituency: Northwest Territories, Northwest Territories *No. of Constituents:* 30,235, Liberal
Tel: 613-992-4587; *Fax:* 613-992-1586
Michael.McLeod@parl.gc.ca
michaelmcleod.libparl.ca
Other Communications: Constituency Phone: 867-873-6995; Fax: 867-920-4233
twitter.com/MMcLeodNWT, www.facebook.com/mmcleodnwt
Constituency Office
#114, 5109 - 48th St.
Yellowknife, NT X1A 1N5

Heather McPherson
Constituency: Edmonton — Strathcona, Alberta *No. of Constituents:* 77,285, New Democratic Party
Tel: 613-995-7325; *Fax:* 613-995-5342
heather.mcpherson@parl.gc.ca

heathermcpherson.ndp.ca
Other Communications: Constituency Phone: 780-495-8404; Fax: 780-495-8403
twitter.com/HMcPhersonMP
Constituency Office
10045 - 81st Ave.
Edmonton, AB T6E 1W7

Eric Melillo
Constituency: Kenora, Ontario *No. of Constituents:* 45,692, Conservative Party
Tel: 613-996-1161; *Fax:* 613-996-1759
eric.melillo@parl.gc.ca
ericmelillo.ca
Other Communications: Constituency Phone: 807-468-2170; Fax: 807-468-4896
twitter.com/eric_melillo, www.facebook.com/ericmelilloCPC
Constituency Office
#19, 308 - 2nd St. South
Kenora, ON P9N 1G4

Alexandra Mendes
Circonscription électorale: Brossard — Saint-Lambert, Québec *Nombre de constituants:* 83,447, Liberal
Tél: 613-995-9301
Téléc: 613-992-7273
Alexandra.Mendes@parl.gc.ca
alexandramendes.libparl.ca
Autres numéros: Circ. Tél: 450-466-6872; Téléc: 450-466-9822
twitter.com/alexandrabrstl,
www.facebook.com/AlexandraMendesLiberal2015,
www.linkedin.com/in/amendes
Bureau de circonscription
#225, 6955, boul Taschereau
Brossard, QC J4Z 1A7

Hon. Marco Mendicino, P.C., B.A., LL.B.
Constituency: Eglinton — Lawrence, Ontario *No. of Constituents:* 82,811, Liberal
Tel: 613-992-6361; *Fax:* 613-992-9791
Marco.Mendicino@parl.gc.ca
marcomendicinomp.ca
Other Communications: Constituency Phone: 416-781-5583; Fax: 416-781-5586
twitter.com/marcomendicino,
www.facebook.com/marcoelmendicino,
www.linkedin.com/in/marco-mendicino-070b5370
Constituency Office
511 Lawrence Ave. West
Toronto, ON M6A 1A3

Chung An Wilson Miao
Constituency: Richmond Centre, British Columbia *No. of Constituents:* 73,450, Liberal
wilson.miao@parl.gc.ca
wilsonmiao.liberal.ca
Other Communications: Constituency Phone: 604-775-5790; Fax: 604-775-6291
www.facebook.com/wilsonmiao.rc
Constituency Office
#360, 5951 Number 3 Rd.
Richmond, BC V6X 2E3

Kristina Michaud
Circonscription électorale: Avignon — La Mitis — Matane — Matapédia *Nombre de constituants:* 18,500, Bloc Québécois
Tél: 613-995-1013
Téléc: 613-995-5184
kristina.michaid@parl.gc.ca
www.kristinamichaud.quebec
Autres numéros: Circ. Tél: 418-629-6456; Téléc: 418-629-1204
twitter.com/krimichaudbq,
www.facebook.com/kristinamichaud.bq
Bureau de circonscription
35, boul Saint-Benoit est
Amqui, QC G5J 2B8

Hon. Marc Miller, P.C.
Circonscription électorale: Ville-Marie — Le Sud-Ouest — Ile-des-Soeurs, Québec *Nombre de constituants:* 88,117, Liberal
Tél: 613-995-6403
Téléc: 613-995-6404
Marc.Miller@parl.gc.ca
marcmiller.liberal.ca
Autres numéros: Circ. Tél: 514-496-4885; Téléc: 514-496-8097
twitter.com/MarcMillerVM,
www.facebook.com/MarcMillerVilleMarie
Bureau de circonscription
3175, rue Saint-Jacques
Montréal, QC H4C 1G7

Hon. Rob Moore, P.C.
Constituency: Fundy Royal, New Brunswick *No. of Constituents:* 64,992, Conservative Party
Tel: 613-996-2332; *Fax:* 613-995-4286
www.robmoore.ca
Other Communications: Constituency Phone: 506-832-4200;

Fax: 506-832-4235
twitter.com/robmoore_cpc,
www.facebook.com/RobMooreFundyRoyal
Constituency Office
#104, 599 Main St.
Hampton, NB E5N 6C2

Marty Morantz
Constituency: Charleswood — St. James — Assiniboia — Headingley, Manitoba *No. of Constituents:* 65,375, Conservative Party
Tel: 613-995-5609; *Fax:* 613-992-3199
marty.morantz@parl.gc.ca
Other Communications: Constituency Phone: 204-984-6432; Fax: 204-984-6451
twitter.com/marty_morantz
Constituency Office
3092 Portage Ave., #D
Winnipeg, MB R3K 0Y2

Michael Morrice
Constituency: Kitchener Centre, Ontario *No. of Constituents:* 83,177, Green Party of Canada
mike.morrice@parl.gc.ca
mikemorrice.ca
Other Communications: Constituency Phone: 519-741-2001; Fax: 519-579-2404
twitter.com/morricemike, www.facebook.com/morricemike,
www.linkedin.com/in/mikemorrice
Constituency Office
#202, 209 Frederick St.
Kitchener, ON N2H 2M7

Rob Morrison
Constituency: Kootenay—Columbia, British Columbia *No. of Constituents:* 91,652, Conservative Party
Tel: 613-995-7246; *Fax:* 613-996-9923
rob.morrison@parl.gc.ca
robmorrisonmp.ca
Other Communications: Constituency Phone: 250-417-2250; Fax: 250-417-2253
twitter.com/robmorrisonmp,
www.facebook.com/robmorrisonmp
Constituency Office
800C Baker St.
Cranbrook, BC V1C 1A2

Robert J. Morrissey
Constituency: Egmont, Prince Edward Island *No. of Constituents:* 28,400, Liberal
Tel: 613-992-9223
Toll-free: 800-224-0018; *Fax:* 613-992-1974
Robert.Morrissey@parl.gc.ca
robertmorrissey.libparl.ca
Other Communications: Constituency Fax: 902-432-6853
www.facebook.com/MorrisseyEgmont
Constituency Office
263 Heather Moyse Dr.
Summerside, PE C1N 5P1

Glen Motz
Constituency: Medicine Hat — Cardston — Warner, Alberta *No. of Constituents:* 78,384, Conservative Party
Tel: 613-996-0633
Toll-free: 844-781-9061; *Fax:* 613-995-5752
glen.motz@parl.gc.ca
glenmotzmp.com
Other Communications: Constituency Fax: 403-528-4365
twitter.com/GlenMotz, www.facebook.com/GlenMotz
Constituency Office
#306, 2810 - 13th Ave. SE
Medicine Hat, AB T1A 3P9

Hon. Joyce Murray, P.C., M.B.A.
Constituency: Vancouver Quadra, British Columbia *No. of Constituents:* 74,984, Liberal
Tel: 613-992-2430; *Fax:* 613-995-0770
joyce.murray@parl.gc.ca
joycemurray.libparl.ca
Other Communications: Constituency Phone: 604-664-9220; Fax: 604-664-9221
twitter.com/joycemurray, www.facebook.com/mpjoycemurray
Constituency Office
#206, 2112 West Broadway
Vancouver, BC V6K 2C8

Dan Muys
Constituency: Flamborough — Glanbrook, Ontario *No. of Constituents:* 89,282, Conservative Party
dan.muys@parl.gc.ca
danmuys.ca
Other Communications: Constituency Phone: 905-648-3850; Fax: 905-648-3898
www.facebook.com/danmuysforfg
Constituency Office
#3, 1654 Wilson St. West
Jerseyville, ON L0R 1R0

Yasir Naqvi
Constituency: Ottawa Centre, Ontario *No. of Constituents:* 99,049, Liberal
yasir.naqvi@parl.gc.ca

Arif Virani, B.A., LL.B.
Constituency: Parkdale — High Park, Ontario *No. of Constituents:* 82,797, Liberal
Tel: 613-992-2936; *Fax:* 613-995-1629
Arif.Virani@parl.gc.ca
arifvirani.libparl.ca
Other Communications: Constituency Phone: 416-769-5072;
Fax: 416-769-8343
twitter.com/ArifViraniMP, www.facebook.com/ArifViraniMP,
www.linkedin.com/in/arifvirani
Constituency Office
1596 Bloor St. West
Toronto, ON M6P 1A7

Brad Vis
Constituency: Mission — Matsqui — Fraser Canyon, British Columbia *No. of Constituents:* 69,190, Conservative Party
Tel: 613-992-1248; *Fax:* 613-992-1298
brad.vis@parl.gc.ca
bradvis.ca
Other Communications: Constituency Phone: 604-814-5710;
Fax: 604-814-5714
twitter.com/bradleyvis, www.facebook.com/BradVisMP
Constituency Office
#7, 32650 Logan Ave.
Mission, BC V2V 6C7

Kevin Vuong
Constituency: Spadina — Fort York, Ontario *No. of Constituents:* 90,022, Independent
kevin.vuong@parl.gc.ca
Other Communications: Constituency Phone: 416-533-2710;
Fax: 416-533-2236
twitter.com/KevinVuongTO,
www.linkedin.com/in/kevinvuongto
Note: Kevin Vuong was balloted as a Liberal in the 2021 general election, but he was expelled from the Liberal party days before the election.
Constituency Office
#307, 280 Spadina Ave.
Toronto, ON M5T 2C7

Cathay Wagantall
Constituency: Yorkton — Melville, Saskatoon *No. of Constituents:* 52,768, Conservative Party
Tel: 613-992-4394; *Fax:* 613-992-8676
Cathay.Wagantall@parl.gc.ca
www.cathaywagantall.ca
Other Communications: Constituency Phone: 306-782-3309;
Fax: 306-786-7207
twitter.com/cathayw, www.facebook.com/CathayWagantallYM
Constituency Office
43 Betts Ave.
Yorkton, SK S3N 1M1

Chris Warkentin
Constituency: Grande Prairie — Mackenzie, Alberta *No. of Constituents:* 84,688, Conservative Party
Tel: 613-992-5685; *Fax:* 613-947-4782
chris.warkentin@parl.gc.ca
Other Communications: Constituency Phone: 780-538-1677;
Fax: 780-538-9257
twitter.com/chriswarkentin, www.facebook.com/chriswarkentin
Constituency Office
#201, 10625 West Side Dr.
Grande Prairie, AB T8V 8E6

Kevin Waugh
Constituency: Saskatoon — Grasswood, Saskatchewan *No. of Constituents:* 64,150, Conservative Party
Tel: 613-995-5653; *Fax:* 613-995-0126
Kevin.Waugh@parl.gc.ca
kevinwaugh.ca
Other Communications: Constituency Phone: 306-975-6472;
Fax: 306-975-6492
twitter.com/kevinwaugh_cpc,
www.facebook.com/kevinwaughmp
Constituency Office
#5, 2720 - 8th St. East
Saskatoon, SK S7H 0V8

Len Webber
Constituency: Calgary Confederation, Alberta *No. of Constituents:* 91,789, Conservative Party
Tel: 613-996-2756; *Fax:* 613-992-2537
Len.Webber@parl.gc.ca
www.lenwebbermp.ca
Other Communications: Constituency Phone: 403-220-0888;
Fax: 403-299-8024
twitter.com/Webber4Confed,
www.facebook.com/lenwebberyyc
Constituency Office
2020 - 10th St. NW
Calgary, AB T2M 3M2

Patrick Weiler
Constituency: West Vancouver — Sunshine Coast — Sea to Sky Country, British Columbia *No. of Constituents:* 94,491, Liberal
Tel: 613-947-4617; *Fax:* 613-947-4620
patrick.weiler@parl.gc.ca

patrickweiler.libparl.ca
Other Communications: Constituency Phone: 604-913-2660;
Fax: 604-913-2664
twitter.com/PatrickBWeiler,
www.facebook.com/PatrickBWeiler,
www.linkedin.com/in/patrickbweiler
Constituency Office
6367 Bruce St.
West Vancouver, BC V7W 2G5

Hon. Jonathan Wilkinson, P.C.
Constituency: North Vancouver, British Columbia *No. of Constituents:* 88,254, Liberal
Tel: 613-995-1225; *Fax:* 613-992-7319
Jonathan.Wilkinson@parl.gc.ca
jonathanwilkinson.libparl.ca
Other Communications: Constituency Phone: 604-775-6333;
Fax: 604-775-6332
twitter.com/JonathanWNV,
www.facebook.com/JonathanWilkinsonNorthVancouver,
www.linkedin.com/in/jwilkinson495
Constituency Office
#210, 310 Esplanade East
North Vancouver, BC V7L 1A4

Ryan Williams
Constituency: Bay of Quinte, Ontario *No. of Constituents:* 93,859, Conservative Party
ryan.williams@parl.gc.ca
Other Communications: Constituency Phone: 613-969-3300;
Fax: 613-969-3313
twitter.com/Ryan_r_Williams,
www.facebook.com/VoteRyanWilliams,
www.linkedin.com/in/ryan-williams-428a2527
Constituency Office
250 Sidney St.
Belleville, ON K8P 3Z3

John Williamson
Constituency: New Brunswick Southwest, New Brunswick *No. of Constituents:* 53,556, Conservative Party
Tel: 613-995-5550
Toll-free: 888-350-4734; *Fax:* 613-995-5226
John.Williamson@parl.gc.ca
www.johnwilliamsonmp.ca
Other Communications: Constituency Fax: 506-466-2813
twitter.com/johnwilliamson_,
www.facebook.com/johnwilliamsonNB
Constituency Office
69 Milltown Blvd.
St Stephen, NB E3L 1G5

Jean Yip
Constituency: Scarborough — Agincourt, Ontario *No. of Constituents:* 71,325, Liberal
Tel: 613-992-4501; *Fax:* 613-995-1612
Jean.Yip@parl.gc.ca
jeanyip.libparl.ca
Other Communications: Constituency Phone: 416-321-5454;
Fax: 416-321-5456
twitter.com/jeanyip3,
www.facebook.com/JeanYip.Scarborough
Constituency Office
#201, 3195 Sheppard Ave. East
Toronto, ON M1T 3K1

Salma Zahid
Constituency: Scarborough Centre, Ontario *No. of Constituents:* 75,662, Liberal
Tel: 613-992-6823; *Fax:* 613-943-1045
Salma.Zahid@parl.gc.ca
salmazahid.libparl.ca
Other Communications: Constituency Phone: 416-752-2358;
Fax: 416-752-4624
twitter.com/SalmaZahid15, www.facebook.com/salmazahid15
Constituency Office
#5, 2155 Lawrence Ave. East
Toronto, ON M1R 5G9

Bonita Zarrillo
Constituency: Port Moody — Coquitlam, British Columbia *No. of Constituents:* 82,048, New Democratic Party
bonita.zarrillo@parl.gc.ca
bonitazarrillo.ndp.ca
Other Communications: Constituency Phone: 604-664-9229;
Fax: 604-664-9231
twitter.com/BonitaZarrillo,
www.facebook.com/BonitaZarrilloNDP
Constituency Office
1116 Austin Ave.
Coquitlam, BC V3K 3P5

Bob Zimmer, B.A.
Constituency: Prince George — Peace River — Northern Rockies, British Columbia *No. of Constituents:* 79,397, Conservative Party
Tel: 613-947-4524
Toll-free: 855-767-4567; *Fax:* 613-947-4527
Bob.Zimmer@parl.gc.ca
www.bobzimmer.ca
Other Communications: Constituency Phones: 250-787-1192;

250-719-6848
twitter.com/bobzimmermp,
www.facebook.com/bobzimmercpc
Constituency Office
9916 - 100th Ave.
Fort St. John, BC V1J 1Y5

Sameer Zuberi
Circonscription électorale: Pierrefonds—Dollard, Québec *Nombre de constituants:* 83,369, Liberal
Tél: 613-992-2689
Téléc: 613-996-8478
sameer.zuberi@parl.gc.ca
sameerzuberi.libparl.ca
Autres numéros: Circ. Tél: 514-624-5725; Téléc: 514-624-5728
twitter.com/SameerZuberi, www.linkedin.com/in/sameerzuberi
Bureau de circonscription
#501, 3883, boul St-Jean
Dollard-des-Ormeaux, QC H9G 3B9

Federal Government Departments & Agencies / Agences et départements du gouvernement fédéral

Office of the Administrator of the Ship-source Oil Pollution Fund (SOPF) / Administrateur de la caisse d'indemnisation des dommages dus à la pollution par les hydrocarbures causée par les navires

#830, 180 Kent St., Ottawa, ON K1A 0N5
Tel: 613-991-1726; *Fax:* 613-990-5423
info@sopf-cidphn.gc.ca
sopf.gc.ca

The Administrator oversees the Ship-source Oil Pollution Fund, which provides compensation for oil spills from ships, & handles all claims filed against it.

Executive Assistant, Rollande Bureau
Tel: 613-991-1726

Director, Corporate Services, Monique Pronovost
Tel: 613-993-5439; *Fax:* 613-990-5423

Payroll & Finance Officer, Dianne Richer
Tel: 613-990-6852

Agriculture & Agri-Food Canada / Agriculture et agro-alimentaire Canada

1341 Baseline Rd., Ottawa, ON K1A 0C5
Tel: 613-773-1000; *Fax:* 613-773-1081
Toll-Free: 855-773-0241
TTY: 613-773-2600
info@agr.gc.ca
www.agr.gc.ca
Other Communication: Toll-Free Phone: AgriInvest & AgriStability, 866-367-8506; Agricultural Innovation Program, 877-246-4682; Prairie Shelterbelt Program, 866-766-2284
twitter.com/aafc_canada
www.facebook.com/canadianagriculture

Agriculture & Agri-Food Canada is responsible for all matters related to agriculture. Examples of services provided by Agriculture & Agri-Food Canada include the following: research, development, & technology; policies & programs; the inspection & regulation of animals & plant-life forms; the coordination of rural development; the support of agricultural productivity & trade; the stabilization of farm incomes; & the provision of information. The goals of Agriculture & Agri-Food Canada are as follows: to achieve security of the food system; to ensure health of the environment; & to provide innovation for growth. Agriculture & Agri-Food Canada reports to Parliament & Canadians through the Minister of Agriculture & Agri-Food. The department was responsible for the Canadian Wheat Board prior to its privatization. On April 15, 2015, the sale of the Canadian Wheat Board to the G3 Global Grain Group was announced, creating G3 Canada Limited. The G3 Global Grain Group owns 50.1%, while the rest is kept in trust for farmers delivering grain to the company.

Minister, Agriculture & Agri-Food, Hon. Marie-Claude Bibeau, P.C.
Tel: 613-995-2024; *Fax:* 613-992-1696
Marie-Claude.Bibeau@parl.gc.ca

Parliamentary Secretary, Neil Ellis
Tel: 613-773-1059
neil.ellis@parl.gc.ca

Associated Agencies, Boards & Commissions:

• Canada Agricultural Review Tribunal (CART) / Commission de révision agricole du Canada (CRAC)
333 Laurier Ave. West, 15th Fl.
Ottawa, ON K1A 0G7
Tel: 613-943-6405; *Fax:* 613-943-6429
infotribunal@cart-crac.gc.ca
www.cart-crac.gc.ca
The Tribunal provides independent oversight of the use of Administrative Monetary Penalties by federal agencies, with regards to agriculture & agri-food.

• Canadian Dairy Commission (CDC) / Commission canadienne du lait
See Entry Name Index for detailed listing.

• Canadian Food Inspection Agency (CFIA) / Agence canadienne d'inspection des aliments
See Entry Name Index for detailed listing.

• Canadian Grain Commission (CGC) / Commission canadienne des grains
See Entry Name Index for detailed listing.

• Canadian International Grains Institute / Institut international du Canada pour le grain
#1000, 303 Main St.
Winnipeg, MB R3C 3G7
Tel: 204-983-5344; *Fax:* 204-983-2642
cigi@cigi.ca
cigi.ca

• Canadian Pari-Mutuel Agency (CPMA) / Agence canadienne du pari mutuel (ACPM)
PO Box 5904 Merivale
Ottawa, ON K2C 3X7
Tel: 613-759-6100; *Fax:* 613-759-6230
Toll-free: 800-268-8835
cpmawebacpm@agr.gc.ca
agr.gc.ca/eng/about-us/partners-and-agencies/?id=1360701203481

• Farm Credit Canada (FCC) / Financement agricole Canada
See Entry Name Index for detailed listing.

• Farm Products Council of Canada (FPCC) / Conseil des produits agricoles du Canada (CPAC)
See Entry Name Index for detailed listing.

Agri-Food Trade Services for Exporters / Service d'exportation agroalimentaire
aafc.mas-sam.aac@canada.ca
Other Communication: URL:
www.agr.gc.ca/eng/industry-markets-and-trade/agri-food-trade-services-for-exporters
Online resources for helping agricultural exporters reach global markets, including current opportunities, marketing tools, trade show service, AgriMarketing Program for small & medium-sized enterprises, & trade contacts (including the Trade Commissioner Service).

Agriculture & Food Inspection Legal Services / Services juridiques - Agriculture et inspection des aliments
Tower 7, 1341 Baseline Rd., Ottawa, ON K1A 0C5
Tel: 613-759-1000; *Fax:* 613-773-2929
Executive Director & Senior General Counsel, Allen Kristine
Tel: 613-773-5772
allen.kristine@agr.gc.ca
General Counsel & Deputy Executive Director, Ann Snow
Tel: 613-773-2901
General Counsel & Deputy Executive Director, Paula Wilson
Tel: 613-773-2901; *Fax:* 613-773-2929
paula.wilson@canada.ca

Deputy Minister's Office / Bureau du sous-ministre
Tower 7, 1341 Baseline Rd., Ottawa, ON K1A 0C5
Tel: 613-759-1011; *Fax:* 613-759-1040
The Deputy Minister's Office oversees the following organizations: Corporate Secretariat; Food Safety Review Secretariat; & Portfolio Coordination Secretariat.
Deputy Minister, Chris Forbes
Tel: 613-773-1011; *Fax:* 613-773-1040
chris.forbes@canada.ca
Executive Assistant to the Associate Deputy Minister, Louise Laroche
Tel: 613-773-1046

Information Systems Branch / Direction générale des systèmes d'information
Tower 4, 1341 Baseline Rd., Ottawa, ON K1A 0C5
Tel: 613-759-1000; *Fax:* 613-773-0666
The Information Systems Branch of Agriculture & Agri-Food Canada is reponsible for the following organizations: Applications Development Directorate; Information Management Services; IT Operations; & the Strategic Management Directorate.
Chief Information Officer, Vidya Shankarnarayan
Tel: 613-773-1395

Director General, Application & Knowledge Services, Gaea Guruprasad
Tel: 613-773-0684; *Fax:* 613-773-0666
gaea.guruprasad@canada.ca
Acting Director General, Transformation & Modernization Services, Jacint Boucher
Tel: 613-868-6059
Project Leader & Supervisor, Shared Services Canada (SSC at AAFC), Dave Bartlett
Tel: 506-260-6990; *Fax:* 506-460-4333
dave.bartlett@canada.ca
Information Coordinator, Strategic Management, Lorna Smith
Tel: 613-773-0616; *Fax:* 613-773-0666
lorna.smith@canada.ca

Market & Industry Services Branch (MISB) / Direction générale des services à l'industrie et aux marchés
Tower 5, 1341 Baseline Rd., Ottawa, ON K1A 0C5
Tel: 613-759-1000; *Fax:* 613-773-1711
The Market & Industry Services Branch of Agriculture & Agri-Food Canada oversees the following organizations: Bilateral Relations & Technical Trade Policy Directorate; Food Value Chain Bureau; International Markets Bureau; Market Access Secretariat; Negotiations & Multilateral Trade Policy Directorate; & the Operations Directorate. The Operations Directorate operates regional offices throughout Canada, which provide access to market & trade programs & services. Marketing & trade officers offer the following information: statistics by country & product; market access advice; investment opportunities; regulatory issues; export counselling; & news about promotional events.
Assistant Deputy Minister, Frédéric Seppey
Tel: 613-773-0985; *Fax:* 613-773-1711
frederic.seppey@canada.ca
Chief Agriculture Negotiator & Director General, Trade Agreements & Negotiations, Aaron Fowler
Tel: 613-773-1371; *Fax:* 613-773-1855
aaron.fowler@canada.ca
Director General, Sector Development & Analysis Directorate, Marco Valicenti
Tel: 613-773-1808; *Fax:* 613-773-0300
marco.valicenti@canada.ca
Acting Director General, Regional Operations Directorate, Glenda Taylor
Tel: 613-773-3412
Director, Policy Planning & Emergency Management, Lucie Dubois
Tel: 613-773-0246

Office of Audit & Evaluation
Tower 4, 1341 Baseline Rd., Ottawa, ON K1A 0C5
Tel: 613-759-1000; *Fax:* 613-773-2727
Agriculture & Agri-Food Canada's Office of Audit & Evaluation is responsible for the following services: evaluation; governance & review; & internal audit & assurance.
Director General, Kimberly Saunders
Tel: 613-773-0322; *Fax:* 613-773-0666
kimberly.saunders@canada.ca
Director, Evaluation Services, Kathleen McGuire
Tel: 613-773-0190; *Fax:* 613-773-0666
kathleen.mcguire@agr.gc.ca
Director, Internal Audit, Abdihalli Roble
Tel: 613-773-0669; *Fax:* 613-773-0666
abdillahi.roble@canada.ca

Programs Branch / Direction générale des programmes
Tower 7, 1341 Baseline Rd., Ottawa, ON K1A 0C5
Tel: 613-759-1000; *Fax:* 613-773-2121
The Programs Branch of Agriculture & Agri-Food Canada oversees the following organizations: Agriculture Transformation Programs Directorate; Business Risk Management Program Development; Centre of Program Excellence (COPE); Farm Income Programs Directorate; Finance & Renewal Programs Directorate; & Service Policy & Transformation Directorate.
Director, Management Services Unit, Julie Desroches
Tel: 613-773-3511; *Fax:* 613-773-2098
julie.desroches@canada.ca
Director, Innovation Programs Directorate, John Fox
Tel: 613-773-3017; *Fax:* 613-773-1928
john.fox@canada.ca
Director, Business Risk Management Programs Directorate, Francesco Del Bianco
Tel: 613-773-1665; *Fax:* 613-773-2020
francesco.delbianco@canada.ca
Director, Farm Income Programs Directorate, France Guimond
Tel: 204-259-5800; *Fax:* 204-259-5888
france.guimond@canada.ca

Science & Technology Branch / Direction générale des sciences et de la technologie
Tower 5, 1341 Baseline Rd., Ottawa, ON K1A 0C5
Fax: 613-773-1711

Scientists from Agriculture & Agri-Food Canada work on projects to benefit the agricultural & agri-food sector at research centres located across Canada.
Assistant Deputy Minister, Brian T. Gray
Tel: 613-773-1860; *Fax:* 613-773-1717
brian.gray@agr.ca
Associate Assistant Deputy Minister, Gilles Saindon
Tel: 613-773-1840; *Fax:* 613-773-1844
gilles.saindon@agr.ca
Director General, Partnerships & Planning Directorate, Michael Whittaker
Tel: 613-773-2308; *Fax:* 613-773-1855
michael.j.whittaker@agr.gc.ca

Research Centres

Agassiz Research & Development Centre
6947 Hwy. 7, Stn. 1000, Agassiz, BC V0M 1A0
Tel: 604-796-6100
aafc.agassizrdc@agr.gc.ca

Brandon Research Centre
2701 Grand Valley Rd., PO Box 1000A Brandon, MB R7A 5Y3
Tel: 204-578-6500
aafc.brandonrdc@agr.gc.ca

Charlottetown Research & Development Centre
440 University Ave., Charlottetown, PE C1A 4N6
Tel: 902-370-1400
aafc.charlottetownrdc@agr.gc.ca

Fredericton Research & Development Centre
850 Lincoln Rd., Stn. 20280, Fredericton, NB E3B 4Z7
Tel: 506-460-4300
aafc.frederictonrdc@agr.gc.ca

Guelph Research & Development Centre
93 Stone Rd. West, Guelph, ON N1G 5C9
Tel: 519-829-2400
aafc.guelphrdc@agr.gc.ca

Harrow Research & Development Centre
2585 County Rd. 20, Harrow, ON N0R 1G0
Tel: 519-738-2251
aafc.harrowrdc@agr.gc.ca
The Crops & Livestock Research Centre (CLRC) in Charlottetown, Prince Edward Island is one of Agriculture and Agri-Food Canada's network of 19 research centres. The Centre's mandate is to develop scientific knowledge & new technologies in agriculture with the prime focus on Prince Edward Island & Atlantic Canada.

Kentville Research & Development Centre
32 Main St., Kentville, NS B4N 1J5
Tél: 902-365-8555
aafc.kentvillerdc@agr.gc.ca
The Dairy & Swine Research & Development Centre oversees the operations of the Beef Research Farm in Kapuskasing, Ontario, as well as the Office of Intellectual Property & Commercialization in Sherbrooke, Québec.

Lacombe Research & Development Centre
6000 C & E Trail, Lacombe, AB T4L 1W1
Tel: 403-782-8100
aafc.lacomberdc@agr.gc.ca

Lethbridge Research & Development Centre
5403 - 1 Ave. South, Lethbridge, AB T1J 4B1
Tel: 403-327-4561
aafc.lethbridgerdc@agr.gc.ca

London Research & Development Centre
1391 Sandford St., London, ON N5V 4T3
Tel: 519-457-1470
aafc.londonrdc@agr.gc.ca

Morden Research & Development Centre
#100, 101 Rte. 100, Morden, MB R6M 1Y5
Tel: 204-822-7556
aafc.mordenrdc@agr.gc.ca

Ottawa Research & Development Centre
960 Carling Ave., Ottawa, ON K1A 0C6
Tel: 613-759-1858
aafc.ottawardc@agr.gc.ca

Québec Research & Development Centre
2560 Hochelaga Blvd., Québec, QC G1V 2J3
Tel: 418-657-7980
The Lacombe Research Centre is responsible for the operations of research farms in Beaverlodge & Fort Vermilion in Alberta.

Saint-Hyacinthe Research & Development Centre
3600, boul Casavant ouest, Saint-Hyacinthe, QC J2S 8E3
Tel: 450-768-7999
aafc.saint-hyacintherdc@agr.gc.ca
The Lethbridge Research Centre oversees the operations of the Onefour Research Substation, the Stavely Research Substation, & the Vauxhall Research Substation in Alberta.

Saint-Jean-sur-Richelieu Research & Development Centre
430, boul Gouin, Saint-Jean-sur-Richelieu, QC J3B 3E6
Tel: 579-224-3100
aafc.saint-jean-sur-richelieurdc@agr.gc.ca
The Pacific Agri-Food Research Centre oversees the following organizations: the Agassiz Site, the Kamloops Range Research Unit, & the Summerland Site.

Saskatoon Research Centre
107 Science Pl., Saskatoon, SK S7N 0X2
Tel: 306-385-9301; *Fax:* 306-385-9482

Sherbrooke Research & Development Centre
2000 College St., Sherbrooke, QC J1M 0C8
Tel: 819-565-9171
The Semiarid Prairie Agricultural Research Centre is responsible for the operations of research farms in Indian Head & Regina, Saskatchewan.

St. John's Research & Development Centre
Bldg. 25, 308 Brookfield Rd., St. John's, NL A1E 0B2
Tel: 709-793-3186
aafc.st-johnsrdc@agr.gc.ca
The Soils & Crops Research & Development Centre is also responsible for a research farm in Normandin, Québec.

Summerland Research & Development Centre
4200 Hwy. 97 South, Summerland, BC V0H 1Z0
Tel: 250-494-7711
aafc.summerlandrdc@agr.gc.ca
The Southern Crop Protection & Food Research Centre oversees the operations of research farms in Delhi & Vineland, Ontario, as well as an Office of Intellectual Property & Commercialization in London, Ontario.

Swift Current Research & Development Centre
Stn. 1030, Swift Current, SK S9H 3X2
Tel: 306-770-4400
aafc.swift.currentrdc@agr.gc.ca
The Southern Crop Protection & Food Research Centre oversees the operations of research farms in Delhi & Vineland, Ontario, as well as an Office of Intellectual Property & Commercialization in London, Ontario.

Strategic Policy Branch / Direction générale des politiques stratégiques
Tower 7, 1341 Baseline Rd., Ottawa, ON K1A 0C5
Tel: 613-759-1000; *Fax:* 613-773-2121
The Strategic Policy Branch of Agriculture & Agri-Food Canada includes the following organizations: Policy Development & Analysis Directorate; Policy, Planning, & Integration Directorate; Branch Planning & Resource Management; & the Research & Analysis Directorate.
Assistant Deputy Minister, Tom Rosser
Tel: 613-773-0508
tom.rosser@canada.ca
Director General, Research & Analysis Directorate, Kara Beckles
Tel: 613-773-3159; *Fax:* 613-773-2444
kara.beckles@canada.ca
Director General, Policy, Planning & Integration Directorate, Rosser Lloyd
Tel: 613-773-2116; *Fax:* 613-773-2332
rosser.lloyd@canada.ca
Director General, Policy Development & Analysis Directorate, Matt Parry
Tel: 613-773-0894; *Fax:* 613-773-2111
matt.parry@canada.ca
Executive Director, Cross-Sectoral Issues, Nicole Howe
Tel: 613-773-2755; *Fax:* 613-773-2111
nicole.howe@canada.ca
Executive Director, Policy, Planning & Integration Directorate, Jody Proctor
Tel: 613-773-2494; *Fax:* 613-773-2332
jody.proctor2@canada.ca

Atlantic Canada Opportunities Agency (ACOA) / Agence de promotion économique du Canada atlantique (APECA)

Blue Cross Centre, 644 Main St., 3rd Fl., PO Box 6051 Moncton, NB E1C 9J8
Tel: 506-851-2271; *Fax:* 506-851-7403
Toll-Free: 800-561-7862
TTY: 877-456-6500
ACOA.information.APECA@canada.ca
www.acoa-apeca.gc.ca
Other Communication: Secure Fax: 506-857-1301
twitter.com/acoacanada
www.linkedin.com/company/acoa-apeca
www.youtube.com/ACOACanada
The role of the Atlantic Canada Opportunities Agency is the development of opportunities for economic growth in Atlantic Canada. The agency achieves its mission in the following ways: assisting businesses to become more innovative, productive, & competitive; promoting the strengths of Atlantic Canada; & helping communities to develop more diversified local economies. In March 2014, the ACOA assumed responsibility for economic development in Cape Breton, after the closing of Enterprise Cape Breton Corporation.

Minister Responsible; Minister, Economic Development & Official Languages, Hon. Ginette Petitpas Taylor, P.C.

President, Francis P. McGuire
Tel: 506-851-6128
ACOA.president-president.APECA@canada.ca

Vice-President, Finance & Corporate Services, Stephane Lagace
Tel: 506-851-6438

Vice-President, Policy, Programs & Communications, Daryell Nowlan
Tel: 506-851-3805

Director General, Policy, Wade Aucoin
Tel: 506-381-0324

Director General, Communications, Kevin Dubé
Tel: 506-851-7632
Other Communications: Alt. Phone: 506-851-7632

Director General, Chief Information Officer Directorate, Marc Gagnon
Tel: 506-851-6511

Director General, Trade, Investment & Growth, Kalie Hatt-Kilburn
Tel: 506-851-6496

Director General, Human Resources, Nancy Pike
Tel: 506-851-2141

Atlantic Pilotage Authority (APA) / Administration de pilotage de l'Atlantique

TD Centre, #1801, 1791 Barrington St., Halifax, NS B3J 3K9
Tel: 902-426-2550; *Fax:* 902-426-4004
Toll-Free: 877-272-3477
dispatch@atlanticpilotage.com
www.atlanticpilotage.com
Other Communication: Toll-Free Fax: 877-745-3477; Fax to Email Direct: 866-774-2477
The Atlantic Pilotage Authority is a Federal Crown Corporation responsible for the safe & efficient operation, maintenance & administration of marine pilotage service to Atlantic Canada.

Chair, Anne Galbraith

Chief Executive Officer, Sean Griffiths
Tel: 902-426-2553

Chief Financial Officer, Peter L. MacArthur
Tel: 902-426-8657

Atomic Energy of Canada Limited (AECL) / Énergie atomique du Canada Ltée (EACL)

Head Office, Chalk River Laboratories, 286 Plant Rd., Chalk River, ON K0J 1J0
Toll-Free: 888-220-2465
communications@aecl.ca
www.aecl.ca
Atomic Energy of Canada develops peaceful applications from nuclear technology. Services include research, design, engineering, waste management, & decommissioning.
It was announced on February 28, 2013, that the Government of

Canada is seeking to shift management & operation of AECL's Nuclear Laboratories to a Government-owned, Contractor-operated (GoCo) model, similar to models in the US & UK. Canadian Nuclear Laboratories was created in 2014 in the first phase of this shift. In June 2015 it was announced that the Canadian National Energy Alliance won the contract to operate Canadian Nuclear Laboratories, leaving AECL as a small Crown corporation dedicated to managing the contract.

Chair, Claude Lajeunesse

President & Chief Executive Officer, Richard Sexton

Vice-President; General Counsel; Corporate Secretary, Grant Gardiner

Vice-President, Site Operations & Infrastructure Oversight, Frank Gibbs

Vice-President, Science, Technology & Commercial Oversight, Shannon Quinn

Vice-President, Business Operations & Chief Financial Officer, David Smith

Lead Contracting Officer, David Hess

Canadian Nuclear Laboratories (CNL) / Laboratoires Nucléaires Canadiens (LNC)
Head Office, Chalk River Laboratories, 286 Plant Rd., Stn. 508A, Chalk River, ON K0J 1J0
Toll-Free: 866-513-2325
communications@cnl.ca
www.cnl.ca
Other Communication: Community Enquiries: 800-364-6989; Media Enquiries: 866-886-2325; Library Requests: 613-584-3311, ext. 43900
twitter.com/CNL_LNC
www.linkedin.com/company/9191967
www.youtube.com/c/CNLCanada
Canadian Nuclear Laboratories was created as a subsidiary of Atomic Energy of Canada during the organization's restructuring. As of November 2014, CNL is responsible for all day-to-day operations of AECL sites. It is also responsible for managing Canada's nuclear legacy liabilities through decommissioning & site remediation, & management of the legacy waste.
The following offices & laboratories are part of Atomic Energy of Canada/Canadian Nuclear Laboratories: Whiteshell Laboratories in Pinawa, Manitoba (204-753-2311); Low-Level Radioactive Waste Management in Port Hope, Ontario (905-885-9488); Port Hope Area Initiative (905-885-0291); Centre for Nuclear Energy Research at the University of New Brunswick in Fredericton (506-453-5111).
Chair, Mark Morant
President & CEO, Mark Lesinski
Vice-President, Operations & Chief Nuclear Officer, David Cox
Vice-President, Health, Safety, Security, Environment & Quality, Kevin Daniels
Vice-President, Research & Development, Kathryn McCarthy
Vice-President, Business Development & Commercial Ventures, Corey McDaniel
Vice-President, Legal, Doug McIntyre
Vice-President, Decommissioning & Waste Management, Kurt Kehler
Vice-President, Capital Projects, Ted Preisig
Vice-President, Corporate Affairs, Lou Riccoboni
Vice-President, Finance & Chief Financial Officer, Monica Steedman
Vice-President, Human Resources, Esther Zdolec

Low-Level Radioactive Waste Management Office (LLRWMO) / Bureau de gestion des déchets radioactifs de faible activité (BGDRFA)
115 Toronto Rd., Port Hope, ON L1A 3S4
Tel: 905-885-9488
www.cnl.ca/en/home/environmental-stewardship/llrwmo.aspx
Other Communication: Inquiries, Phone: 905-885-0291; Fax: 905-885-9344; Email: nationalprograms@cnl.ca
Carries out the responsibilities of the federal government for low-level radioactive waste (LLRW) management in Canada.

Auditor General of Canada / Vérificateur général du Canada

240 Sparks St., Ottawa, ON K1A 0G6
Tel: 613-952-0213; *Fax:* 613-957-0474
Toll-Free: 888-761-5953
TTY: 613-954-8042
infomedia@oag-bvg.gc.ca
www.oag-bvg.gc.ca
Other Communication: Media Relations Phone: 888-761-5953;
Work Opportunities, Email: emplo@oag-bvg.gc.ca
twitter.com/oag_bvg
www.facebook.com/oagcanada
www.linkedin.com/company/office-of-the-auditor-general-of-cana
da

The Office of the Auditor General of Canada was established in 1878. Today, the head office in Ottawa & regional offices in Halifax, Montréal, Edmonton, & Vancouver employ approximately 575 employees. The Office of the Auditor General of Canada provides objective, fact-based information required by Parliament to hold the federal government accountable for its stewardship of public funds. An Officer of Parliament, the Auditor General of Canada is responsible for auditing the following organizations: federal government departments; federal government agencies; most Crown corporations; many federal organizations; the government of the Yukon; the government of the Northwest Territories; & the government of Nunavut. The Auditor General, Michael Ferguson, reports publicly to the House of Commons about matters he believes should be brought to the attention of the House of Commons. The report can include chapters on audits & studies, sustainable development strategies, & environmental petitions.

Auditor General, Karen Hogan

Assistant Auditor General, Stuart Barr
Tel: 613-952-0213 ext: 5450

Assistant Auditor General, Jerome Berthelette
Tel: 613-952-0213 ext: 4505

Assistant Auditor General, Nancy Cheng
Tel: 613-952-0213 ext: 6262

Assistant Auditor General, Terrance DeJong
Tel: 613-952-0213 ext: 2488

Assistant Auditor General, Sylvain Ricard
Tel: 613-952-0213 ext: 5358

Senior General Counsel, Anne Marie Smith
Tel: 613-952-0213 ext: 6302

Principal, Practice Review & Internal Audit, Louise Bertrand
Tel: 613-952-0213 ext: 2904

Principal, Strategic Planning, Ronald Bergin
Tel: 613-952-0213 ext: 6241

Principal Parliamentary Liaison, Michelle Salvail
Tel: 613-952-0213 ext: 5234

Commissioner of the Environment & Sustainable Development / Commissaire à l'environnement et au développement durable
240 Sparks St., Ottawa, ON K1A 0G6
Tel: 613-952-0213; *Fax:* 613-957-0474
www.oag-bvg.gc.ca/internet/English/au_fs_e_370.html#Commis
sioner
Commissioner, Environment & Sustainable Development, Julie Gelfand
Tel: 613-952-0213 ext: 6400
Principal, Sustainable Development Strategies, Audits, & Studies, Sharon Clark
Tel: 613-952-0213 ext: 6426
Principal, Sustainable Development Strategies, Audits, & Studies, Kimberly Leach
Tel: 613-952-0213 ext: 6242

Bank of Canada / Banque du Canada

234 Wellington St., Ottawa, ON K1A 0G9
Tel: 613-782-8111; *Fax:* 613-782-7713
Toll-Free: 800-303-1282
TTY: 888-418-1461
info@bankofcanada.ca
www.bankofcanada.ca
Other Communication: Access to information & privacy issues, Email: ATIP-AIPRP@bankofcanada.ca; Media, Email: communications@bankofcanada.ca
twitter.com/bankofcanada
www.linkedin.com/company/12682
www.youtube.com/user/bankofcanadaofficial

Founded in 1934, the Bank of Canada was originally a privately owned corporation. It became a Crown corporation, belonging to the federal government, in 1938. As Canada's central bank, the role of the Bank of Canada is the promotion of the economic & financial welfare of the nation. The following are the main responsibilities of the Bank of Canada: Canada's financial system; monetary policy; funds management; & bank notes. The Governor & Senior Deputy of the Bank of Canada are appointed by the Bank's Board of Directors, with the approval of the Cabinet. Regional offices of the Bank of Canada are located in the following cities: Halifax; Montréal; Toronto; Calgary; Vancouver; & New York.

Governor, Tiff Macklem

Senior Deputy Governor, Carolyn Wilkins

Deputy Governor, Timothy Lane

Deputy Governor, Lynn Patterson

Deputy Governor, Lawrence Schembri

Chief Operating Officer, Filipe Dinis

Audit / Vérification
Managing Director & Chief Internal Auditor, Michael O'Bryan

Canadian Economic Analysis / Analyses de l'économie canadienne
Managing Director, Eric Santor

Communications / Services de communications
Managing Director, Jeremy Harrison

Corporate Services / Services de gestion
Managing Director, Julie Champagne

Currency / Monnaie
Managing Director, Maureen Carroll

Executive & Legal Services / Services à la Haute Direction et Services juridiques
General Counsel & Corporate Secretary, Jeremy S.T. Farr

Financial Markets / Marchés financiers
Managing Director, Toni Gravelle

Financial Services / Services financiers
Chief Financial Officer, Carmen Vierula

Financial Stability / Stabilité financière
Managing Director, Grahame Johnson

Funds Management & Banking / Gestion financière et bancaire
Managing Director, Carol Brigham

Human Resources / Services des ressources humaines
Managing Director & Chief Human Resources Officer, Alexis Corbett

Information Technology Services / Services des technologies de l'information
Managing Director & Chief Information Officer, Sylvian Chalut

International Economic Analysis / Analyses de l'économie internationale
Managing Director, Rhys R. Mendes

Business Development Bank of Canada (BDC) / Banque de développement du Canada (BDC)

#100, 5, Place Ville-Marie, Montréal, QC H3B 5E7
Fax: 877-329-9232
Toll-Free: 877-232-2269
www.bdc.ca
twitter.com/bdc_ca
www.facebook.com/bdc.ca
www.linkedin.com/company/bdc
instagram.com/bdc_ca

The Business Development Bank of Canada is a financial institution which is wholly owned by the Government of Canada.

It was created by an Act of Parliament in 1944. The Bank is governed by an independent Board of Directors, & reports to the Minister of Industry. The mission of the Business Development Bank of Canada is to assist in the establishment & development of Canadian businesses in all industries. The Bank focuses its efforts on small & medium-sized enterprises. The following services are carried out by the Business Development Bank of Canada: consulting services; flexible financing, such as long term business financing & subordinate financing; & venture capital. 123 branches of the Business Development Bank of Canada are located throughout Canada. Smaller communities are served by satellite branches, consultants & travelling account managers.

Chair, Mike Pedersen

President & Chief Executive Officer, Michael Denham

Chief Strategy Officer, Michel Bergeron

Chief Marketing Officer, Annie Marsolais

Executive Vice-President, Financing, Pierre Dubreuil

Executive Vice-President, BDC Advisory Services, Peter Lawler

Executive Vice-President & Chief Financial Officer, Stefano Lucarelli

Executive Vice-President, BDC Capital, Jérôme Nycz

Executive Vice-President & Chief Risk Officer, Christopher Rankin

Senior Vice President & Chief Information Officer, Stéphane Bilodeau

Senior Vice President, Human Resources, Mary Karamanos

Senior Vice President, Legal Affairs; Corporate Secretary, Louise Paradis

Canada Border Services Agency (CBSA) / Agence des services frontaliers du Canada (ASFC)

Headquarters, 191 Laurier Ave. West, Ottawa, ON K1A 0L8
Toll-Free: 800-461-9999
TTY: 866-335-3237
contact@cbsa.gc.ca
www.cbsa-asfc.gc.ca
Other Communication: Border Information Service, Service in French, Toll-Free Phone: 800-959-2036; Public Safety Canada, Phone: 613-944-4875, Toll-Free: 800-830-3118
twitter.com/CanBorder
www.facebook.com/CanBorder
www.youtube.com/CanBorder

Established in 2003, as a response to the need for increased border services, the Canada Border Services Agency ensures the security & prosperity of Canada. The agency is responsible for managing the access of people & goods to & from Canada. To carry out its mission, Canada Border Services Agency administers more than ninety pieces of legislation. Some of the agencies duties include the following: managing 117 border crossings; offering services at points throughout Canada & internationally; operating detention centres across the nation; conducting marine operations at the ports of Prince Rupert, Vancouver, Montréal, & Halifax; managing postal services at major mail centres in Montréal, Toronto, & Vancouver; & forming part of more than twenty Integrated Border Enforcement Teams across Canada.

Minister, Public Safety & Emergency Preparedness, Hon. Marco Mendicino, P.C.

President, John Ossowski
Tel: 613-952-3200; *Fax:* 613-948-3177

Executive Vice-President, Paul MacKinnon

Chief of Staff, Stephen Scott
Tel: 613-957-2779; *Fax:* 613-952-1851

Regional Director General, Southern Ontario, Richard Comerford
Tel: 905-354-5353

Regional Director General, Northern Ontario, Shawn Hoags
Tel: 613-991-0566

Regional Director General, Québec, Annie Beauséjour
Tel: 514-283-8700 ext: 8353

Regional Director General, Prairie, Kim R. Scoville
Tel: 587-475-2117

Executive Director, Operations, Pacific, John Dyck
Tel: 604-666-1132

Comptrollership Branch
219 Laurier Ave. West, 9th Fl., Ottawa, ON K1A 0L8
Vice-President, Jonathan Moor
Tel: 613-948-8604
Deputy Chief Financial Officer, Gibby Armstrong
Tel: 613-948-9287
Director General, National Real Property & Accommodations Directorate, Chenard Charles
Tel: 343-291-5646
Director General, Agency Comptroller Directorate, Jimmy Fecteau
Tel: 343-291-5684
Director General, Security & Professional Standards Directorate, Pierre Lessard
Tel: 343-291-7726
Director General, Transformation & Oversight Directorate, Scott Taymun
Tel: 343-291-5825
Director, Corporate Accounting Division, Gaetan Gervais
Tel: 343-291-5760
Director General, Security & Professional Standards Directorate, Pierre Giguère
Tel: 343-291-7726
Director, Revenue Accounting & Reporting Division, Marc Séguin
Tel: 343-291-5740

Human Resources Branch
99 Metcalfe St., 3rd Fl., Ottawa, ON K1A 0L8
Vice-President, Jacqueline Rigg
Tel: 613-948-3180; *Fax:* 613-952-1783
Director General, Training & Development Directorate, Keren Hawkins
Tel: 613-948-3328
Director General, Labour Relations & Compensation Directorate, Marc Thibodeau
Tel: 613-948-9861; *Fax:* 613-948-9838
Director General, Management Cadre Programs and Services, France Guèvremont
Tel: 613-948-9828
Director, Occupational Health & Safety & Wellness Division, Tammy Edwards
Tel: 613-941-1032
Acting Director, Branch Planning & Integration Management Division, Nathalie Gervais
Tel: 343-291-6571
Director, Labour Relations Program & Compensation Division, Josée Lefebvre
Tel: 613-948-9856

Information, Science & Technology Branch
191 Laurier Ave. West, 7th Fl., Ottawa, ON K1A 0L8
Vice-President & Chief Information Officer, Minh Doan
Tel: 613-948-9694
Director General, Travellers Project Portfolio Directorate, Kelly Belanger
Tel: 343-291-6859
Acting Director General, Business, Corporate Projects & Portfolio Management Directorate, Geneviève Binet
Tel: 343-291-7733
Acting Director General, Commercial Portfolio Directorate, Franco Germano
Tel: 343-291-6147
Director General, Enterprise Architecture, Information Management & Common Services Directorate, Gino Lechasseur
Tel: 343-291-7415
Director General, Business Application Services Directorate, Cameron MacDonald
Tel: 343-291-6018
Director General, Enterprise Services Directorate, Daniel Tremblay
Tel: 343-291-6655

Operations Branch
191 Laurier Ave. West, 18th Fl., Ottawa, ON K1A 0L8
Vice-President, Jacques Cloutier
Tel: 613-948-4111
Associate Vice-President, Denis R. Vinette
Tel: 613-952-5269; *Fax:* 613-948-7130
Director General, Enforcement & Intelligence Operations Directorate, Andrew LeFrank
Tel: 613-948-0215

Executive Director, Commercial Operations, Catherine Parker
Tel: 343-291-5809
Director, Border Operations Directorate, Paulette Lefebvre
Tel: 613-948-9379
Acting Director, Inland Enforcement Operations & Case Management Division, Sharon Spicer
Tel: 613-952-2549

Programs Branch
191 Laurier Ave. West, 15th Fl., Ottawa, ON K1A 0L8
Vice-President, Martin Bolduc
Tel: 613-948-4445; *Fax:* 613-952-2622
Associate Vice-President, Peter Hill
Tel: 613-952-2531; *Fax:* 613-952-2622
Director General, Traveller Program Directorate, Sébastien Aubertin-Giguère
Tel: 613-952-3266
Director General, Trade & Anti-dumping Programs Directorate, Doug Band
Tel: 613-954-7338
Director General, Enforcement & Intelligence Programs Directorate, Jennifer Lutfalah
Tel: 613-948-9041
Director General, Beyond the Border Governance & Coordination Directorate, Kristine Stolarik
Tel: 613-954-7282
Director, Inland Enforcement Program Management Division, Stephen Bolton
Tel: 613-954-7251
Acting Director, Traveller Transformation - Air Mode Division, Dale Brown
Tel: 343-291-7790
Director, Program & Policy Management Division, Michael Junek
Tel: 613-954-7507
Director, Global Border Management Division, Charlene Larose
Tel: 613-954-6356
Director, Trade Policy Division, Yannick Mondy
Tel: 613-941-4459
Director, Traveller Transformation - Land, Marine & Rail Modes Division, Maria Romeo
Tel: 343-291-5609
Deputy Director, Indigenous Affairs Secretariat, Nicole Elmy
Tel: 343-291-7346

Canada Business Network / Réseau Entreprises Canada

235 Queen St., Ottawa, ON K1A 0H5
Toll-Free: 888-576-4444
TTY: 800-457-8466
www.canadabusiness.ca
twitter.com/CanadaBusiness
www.facebook.com/CanadaBusiness
www.youtube.com/CanadaBusinessCBN

Canada Business provides a wide range of information on government services, programs & regulations to Canadian business people. The base framework is an organized network of centres across Canada, one in each province & territory. The network of Canada Business is expanding to include regional access partners in many other communities across Canada. The centres offer various products & services aimed at helping clients obtain quick, accurate & comprehensive business information. Each centre exists as a result of cooperative arrangements between federal & provincial governments, & in some cases, the private sector. Administration & management of the CBSC varies depending on location between the following federal agencies: Innovation, Science & Economic Development; Atlantic Canada Opportunities Agency; Canada Economic Development for Quebec Regions; Canadian Northern Economic Development Agency; Federal Economic Development Agency for Southern Ontario; & Western Economic Diversification Canada.

Regional Offices
Business InfoCentre at the World Trade Centre Winnipeg (BIC)
#300, 219 Provencher Blvd., Winnipeg, MB R2H 0G4
Tel: 204-253-4888; *Fax:* 204-289-4092
Toll-Free: 800-665-2019
TTY: 800-457-8466
info@wtcwinnipeg.com
www.wtcwinnipeg.com/bic
twitter.com/WTCWinnipeg
www.facebook.com/WorldTradeCentreWinnipeg
www.linkedin.com/company/world-trade-centre-winnipeg

Business Link - Alberta's Business Information Service
#500, 10150 - 100 St. NW, Edmonton, AB T5J 0P6
Tel: 780-422-7722; *Fax:* 780-422-0055
Toll-Free: 800-272-9675
TTY: 800-457-8466
askus@businesslink.ca
businesslink.ca
twitter.com/BusinessLinkAB
www.facebook.com/BusinessLinkAB
www.linkedin.com/company/business-link-ab

Canada Business New Brunswick
PO Box 5002 Campbellton, NB E3N 3L3
Fax: 506-789-4737
Toll-Free: 888-576-4444
TTY: 800-457-8466
info.cb.nb@acoa-apeca.gc.ca

Canada Business Newfoundland & Labrador
John Cabot Bldg., 10 Barter's Hill, 11th Fl., St. John's, NL A1C 5M5
Tel: 709-722-2751; *Fax:* 709-772-2712
Toll-Free: 888-576-4444
TTY: 800-457-8466
info.cb@acoa-apeca.gc.ca

Canada Business Nova Scotia
#700, 1801 Hollis St., Halifax, NS B3J 3C8
Toll-Free: 888-576-4444
TTY: 800-457-8466
info.cb.ns@acoa-apeca.gc.ca

Canada Business NWT (CBNWT) / Entreprises Canada TNO
#701, 5201 - 50 Ave., Yellowknife, NT X1A 3S9
Tel: 876-873-7958
Toll-Free: 888-576-4444
TTY: 800-457-8466
brad_poulter@gov.nt.ca
Other Communication: Alt. Phone: 867-873-7960

Canada Business Ontario
151 Yonge St., 4th Fl., Toronto, ON M5C 2W7
Tel: 416-775-3456
Toll-Free: 888-576-4444
TTY: 800-457-8466
cbo@feddevontario.gc.ca
www.cbo-eco.ca

Canada Business Prince Edward Island
PO Box 40 Charlottetown, PE C1A 7K2
Toll-Free: 888-576-4444
TTY: 800-457-8466
info.cb.pei@acoa-apeca.gc.ca

Canada Business Yukon
2180 - 2nd Ave., Whitehorse, YT Y1A 5N6
Tel: 867-457-0150
Toll-Free: 888-576-4444
TTY: 800-457-8466
info@yukonstruct.com

Info entrepreneurs
#W204, 380, rue St-Antoine ouest, Montréal, QC H2Y 3X7
Tel: 514-496-4636
Téléc: 514-496-5934
Ligne sans frais: 888-576-4444
TTY: 800-457-8466
www.infoentrepreneurs.org
Autres nombres: Toll-Free Fax: 888-417-0442; Québec, Phone: 418-649-6116; Fax: 418-682-1144
twitter.com/acclr_ccmm
www.facebook.com/AcclrCCMM
www.linkedin.com/showcase/acclr—services-aux-entreprises

Nunavut Service Centre
Inuksugait Plaza, PO Box 1480 Iqaluit, NU X0A 0H0
Tel: 867-975-7860; *Fax:* 867-975-7885
Toll-Free: 888-576-4444
TTY: 800-457-8466
val.kosmenko@baffinbdc.ca
Other Communication: Rankin Inlet, Phone: 867-645-8450, Fax: 867-645-8455; Cambridge Bay, Phone: 867-983-7383, Fax: 967-983-7380

Small Business B.C.
#54, 601 West Cordova St., Vancouver, BC V6B 1G1
Tel: 604-775-5525; *Fax:* 604-775-5520
Toll-Free: 800-667-2272
TTY: 800-457-8466
askus@smallbusinessbc.ca
www.smallbusinessbc.ca
Other Communication: Feedback, Email: feedback@smallbusinessbc.ca
twitter.com/smallbusinessbc
www.facebook.com/smallbusinessbc
www.linkedin.com/company/small-business-bc
www.youtube.com/user/SmallBusinessBC

Square One: Saskatchewan's Business Resource Centre
250 - 3rd Ave. South, Saskatoon, SK S7K 1L9
Tel: 306-242-4101
Toll-Free: 888-576-4444
TTY: 800-457-8466
info@squareonesask.ca
squareonesask.ca
Other Communication: Toll-Free Fax: 888-417-0442
twitter.com/squareonesask
www.facebook.com/SquareOneSask
www.linkedin.com/company/squareonesask
www.instagram.com/squareonesask

Canada Council for the Arts / Conseil des Arts du Canada

150 Elgin St., 2nd Fl., PO Box 1047 Ottawa, ON K1P 5V8
Tel: 613-566-4414; *Fax:* 613-566-4390
Toll-Free: 800-263-5588
TTY: 866-585-5559
info@canadacouncil.ca
www.canadacouncil.ca
twitter.com/canadacouncil
www.facebook.com/canadacouncil
www.youtube.com/canadacouncil

The Canada Council for the Arts is a national arm's-length agency created by an Act of Parliament in 1957. According to the Canada Council Act, the role of the Council is to foster & promote the study & enjoyment of, & the production of works in the arts. To fulfill this mandate, the Council offers a broad range of grants & services to professional Canadian artists & arts organizations in dance, interdisciplinary work & performance art, media arts, music, interdisciplinary work, theatre, visual arts, & writing & publishing. The Council awards more than 100 prizes every year. It administers the Killam Program of scholarly awards, the Governor General's Literary Awards & the Governor General's Awards in Visual & Media Arts. The Canadian Commission for UNESCO & the Public Lending Right Commission operate under its aegis.

Chair, Pierre Lassonde, C.M., O.Q.

Vice-Chair, Nathalie Bondil

Director & Chief Executive Officer, Simon Brault
Tel: 613-566-4414 ext: 4201
director@canadacouncil.ca

Chief Financial Officer & Chief Security Officer, Carole Boileau
Tel: 613-566-4414 ext: 4045

Director, Marketing Communications, Nichole McGill
Tel: 613-566-4414 ext: 5145

Canada Deposit Insurance Corporation (CDIC) / Société d'assurance-dépôts du Canada (SADC)

50 O'Connor St., 17th Floor, Ottawa, ON K1P 6L2
Fax: 613-996-6095
Toll-Free: 800-461-2342
TTY: 613-943-6456
info@cdic.ca
www.cdic.ca
Other Communication: Toll Free: 800-461-7232 (French); Email (French): info@sadc.ca; URL (French): www.sadc.ca
twitter.com/CDIC_SADC
www.youtube.com/user/cdicchannel

CDIC, a Crown corporation established in 1967, ensures eligible deposits in member institutions (banks, trust companies, loan companies & cooperative credit associations) in case a member becomes insolvent. Funding is provided by its member institutions through premiums paid on insured deposits. Reports to government through the Minister of Finance. CDIC responsibilities include: providing deposit insurance in case of member failure; contributing to the stability of the Canadian financial system.

Chair, Robert Sanderson

President & Chief Executive Officer, Peter Routledge

Senior Vice-President, Insurance & Risk Assessment, Dean A. Cosman

Senior Vice-President, Resolution Division, Michael Mercer

Vice-President, Finance & Administration & Chief Financial Officer, Anthony Carty

Vice-President, Corporate Affairs & General Counsel, Chantal Richer

Canada Economic Development for Québec Regions / Développement économique Canada pour les régions du Québec

#500, 800, boul René-Lévesque ouest, Montréal, QC H3B 1X9
Tel: 514-283-6412; *Fax:* 514-283-3302
Toll-Free: 866-385-6412
TTY: 844-805-8727
www.dec-ced.gc.ca
twitter.com/CanEconDev
www.facebook.com/DefiPropulsionFastForwardChallenge
www.linkedin.com/company/dec-ced

Defines federal objectives relating to development opportunities & delivers business assistance programs for small- & medium-sized businesses in Québec for innovation, entrepreneurial & market development purposes. Supports a series of programs for appropriate environmental initiatives in various regions of Québec. The agency fosters alliances among the various environmental industry stakeholders including small- & medium-sized enterprises & industrial associations. Goals include a strengthening of existing & new partnerships, & an improvement of access to government programs. The agency also provides a significant amount of support for research & development in areas of environmental technology, demonstration, marketing & transfer projects. Supports initiatives that contribute to making Montréal an industrial centre of excellence in the environment. Aids small- & medium-sized firms in gaining access to federal procurement process, & encourages training & education focusing on business management. Helps business develop export markets through cooperative efforts with Innovation, Science & Economic Development & Foreign Affairs & International Trade Canada

Minister Responsible, Hon. Pascale St-Onge, P.C.

Deputy Minister & President, Manon Brassard

Chief of Staff, Simon Labrecque
Tel: 514-283-8119; *Fax:* 514-283-7778

Officer, Ministerial Correspondence, Michele Bouchard
Tel: 514-283-7459; *Fax:* 514-283-7778

Corporate Services Sector / Secteur Services Corporatifs
Vice-President, Guy Lepage
Chief of Staff, Brigitte Flamand
Tel: 514-283-0161; *Fax:* 514-496-5449

Legal Services
Tel: 514-283-2997; *Fax:* 514-283-1549
Executive Director & Senior General Counsel, Christine Calvé
Tel: 514-283-2997; *Fax:* 514-283-1549

Operations / Opérations
Vice-President, Mark Quinlan
Director General, Regional Operations, Georges Arseneau
Director General, Strategic Partnerships, Jean-Philippe Brassard

Branch & Regional Operations
Director General, Regional Operations, Georges Arseneau
Tel: 418-648-3019

Policy & Communications
Vice-President, Jean-Frédéric Lafaille
Acting Chief of Staff, Nathalie Jutras
Tel: 514-496-2941; *Fax:* 514-283-5940
Director General, Policy, Research & Programs, Marie-Eve Harvey

Canada Energy Regulator (CER) / Régie de l'énergie du Canada (REC)

#210, 517 - 10th Ave. SW, Calgary, AB T2R 0A8
Tel: 403-292-4800; *Fax:* 403-292-5503
Toll-Free: 800-899-1265
TTY: 877-288-8803
www.cer-rec.gc.ca
twitter.com/CER_REC
www.facebook.com/CER.REC
www.linkedin.com/company/cer-rec
www.youtube.com/c/CanadaEnergyRegulator

The CER is responsible for monitoring companies operating oil & gas pipelines & electrical powerlines that cross a national, provincial or territorial border.

Chief Executive Officer, Gitane De Silva

Secretary of the Commission, Jean-Denis Charlebois
Tel: 403-299-3632
jean-denis.charlebois@cer-rec.gc.ca

Acting Executive Vice-President, Regulatory, Chris Loewen

Tel: 403-299-3186
chris.loewen@cer-rec.gc.ca

Acting Executive Vice-President, Law & General Counsel, Laurel Sherret
Tel: 403-471-1421
Laurel.Sherret@neb-one.gc.ca

Executive Vice-President, Transparency & Strategic Management, Tracy Sletto
Tel: 403-299-3698
tracy.sletto@cer-rec.gc.ca

Vice-President & Chief of Staff, Katherine Murphy
Tel: 403-299-3937
katherine.murphy@cer-rec.gc.ca

Vice-President, Performance & Results, Mark Power
Tel: 403-299-3666
mark.power@cer-rec.gc.ca

Vice-President, Projects, Jonathan Timlin
Tel: 403-221-3268
jonathan.timlin@cer-rec.gc.ca

Vice-President, People & Workforce Supports, Alexis Williamson
Tel: 403-970-4354
alexis.williamson@cer-rec.gc.ca

Canada Foundation for Innovation (CFI) / Fondation canadienne pour l'innovation (FCI)

#1100, 55 Metcalfe St., Ottawa, ON K1P 6L5
Tel: 613-947-6496; *Fax:* 613-943-0923
feedback@innovation.ca
www.innovation.ca
twitter.com/innovationca
www.facebook.com/innovationincanada
www.youtube.com/user/InnovationCanada

Established by the Canadian government in 1997, the Foundation's mission is to strengthen the nation's ability to undertake research & technological initiatives. The CFI helps fund research facilities in universities, colleges, hospitals, & non-profit institutions across the country.

Co-Chair, Ronald Morrison

Co-Chair, Emoke Szathmáry

President & CEO, Roseann O'Reilly
Tel: 613-947-7260
roseann.runte@innovation.ca

External Relations & Communications
Vice-President, Pierre Normand
Tel: 613-943-0211
pierre.normand@innovation.ca
Director, Communications, Elizabeth Shilts
Tel: 613-996-4421
elizabeth.shilts@innovation.ca

Finance & Corporate Services
Vice-President, Manon Harvey
Tel: 613-947-6497
manon.harvey@innovation.ca
Director, Corporate Services, John Fryer
Tel: 613-947-3208
john.fryer@innovation.ca

Programs & Performance
Interim Vice-President, Mohamad Nasser-Eddine
Tel: 613-996-3110
mohamad.nasser-eddine@innovation.ca
Director, Performance, Analytics & Evaluation, Laura Hillier
Tel: 613-996-5936
laura.hillier@innovation.ca

Canada Industrial Relations Board (CIRB) / Conseil canadien des relations industrielles (CCRI)

240 Sparks St., 4th Fl. West, Ottawa, ON K1A 0X8
Fax: 613-995-9493
Toll-Free: 800-575-9696
TTY: 800-855-0511
www.cirb-ccri.gc.ca
twitter.com/CIRBCCRI

The Board is an independent, administrative, quasi-judicial tribunal that administers Part I & certain provisions of Part II of the Canada Labour Code. Its responsibilities include the granting or revoking of collective bargaining rights; the mediation & adjudication of unfair labour practice complaints; the determination of unlawful strikes & lockouts & other matters. As of April 2013, the Board became responsible for the duties formerly carried out by the Canadian Artists & Producers Professional Relations Tribunal.

Chair, Ginette Brazeau
Tel: 613-995-7046; *Fax:* 613-947-3894

Vice-Chair, Annie Berthiaume
Toll-free: 800-575-9696

Vice-Chair, Allison Smith
Toll-free: 800-575-9696

Case Management Secretariat Directorate
Director, Communications Case Management Services, Justine Abel
Tel: 613-947-5432
Operational Policy & Procedures Officer, Caroline Cadieux
Tel: 613-947-5387

Legal Services
Senior Counsel, Susan Nicholas
Tel: 613-947-5456; *Fax:* 613-947-5460

Canada Infrastructure Bank / Banque de l'infrastructure du Canada

150 King St. West, PO Box 15 Toronto, ON M5H 1J9
Toll-Free: 833-551-5245
canadainfrastructurebank.ca
A Crown corporation that uses federal support to attract private sector & institutional investment to new revenue-generating infrastructure projects. Provincial, territorial, municipal & Indigenous governments can access financing.

Chair, Janice Fukakusa

President & CEO, Pierre Lavallée

Chief Financial Officer & Chief Administrative Officer, Annie Ropar

Canada Lands Company Ltd. (CLCL) / Société immobilière du Canada limitée (SICL)

#1700, 1 University Ave., Toronto, ON M5J 2P1
Tel: 416-214-1250; *Fax:* 416-214-1121
clc.ca
CLCL is a Crown corporation with a mandate to enhance the quality of life of the communities in which it conducts business, to generate best value for the taxpayer through the orderly disposal of strategic real estate properties no longer required by the federal government, as well as the management of certain other select properties. The agency reports to government through the Minister of Transport, Infrastructure & Communities.

President & Chief Executive Officer, John McBain

Executive Vice President, Real Estate & Old Port of Montréal, Robert A. Howald

Executive Vice President, Attractions, Neil Jones

Chief Financial Officer & Vice-President, Finance, Matthew Tapscott

Chief Legal Officer & Corporate Secretary, Greg Barker

Vice-President, Real Estate (West), Chris Elkey

Vice-President, Real Estate (National Capital Region/Atlantic & Acquisitions), Tara Dinsmore

Vice-President, Corporate Communications, Marcelo Gomez-Wiuckstern

Vice-President, Real Estate (British Columbia & Ontario), Deanna Grinnell

Vice-President, Human Resources, Teresa Law

Vice-President, Real Estate (Québec) & Old Port of Montréal, Pierre-Marc Mongeau

Director, Corporate Communications, Manon Lapensée
mlapensee@clc.ca

Old Port of Montréal Corporation Inc. / Société du Vieux port de Montréal
333, rue de la Commune ouest, Montréal, QC H2Y 2E2
Tél: 514-283-5256
Ligne sans frais: 800-971-7678
www.oldportcorporation.com

Parc Downsview Park Inc.
70 Canuck Ave., Toronto, ON M3K 2C5
Tel: 416-954-0544
downsviewevents@clc.ca
www.downsviewpark.ca
Other Communication: Media Phone: 416-952-6112
twitter.com/downsviewpark
www.facebook.com/DownsviewParkOfficialPage
www.youtube.com/user/DownsviewPark

Canada Mortgage & Housing Corporation (CMHC) / Société canadienne d'hypothèques et de logement (SCHL)

700 Montreal Rd., Ottawa, ON K1A 0P7
Tel: 613-748-2000; *Fax:* 613-748-2098
Toll-Free: 800-668-2642
TTY: 613-748-2447
chic@cmhc-schl.gc.ca
www.cmhc-schl.gc.ca
Other Communication: Canadian Housing Information Centre:
613-748-2367
twitter.com/CMHC_ca
www.facebook.com/cmhc.schl
www.youtube.com/CMHCca
CMHC works closely with a network of professional associations, groups & institutions concerned with regional planning & the residential sector. It prepares various research projects for the examination of relationships between urban areas, housing & sustainable development issues. Involved in numerous technical research projects addressing interrelationships between housing, energy & resource use. Through its research & information transfer function, CMHC will undertake initiatives such as identifying approaches & solutions that lead to more sustainable & healthy communities, examining barriers to potential development of brownfield sites. CMHC will focus on ways to reduce residential energy consumption in multiple-unit housing, educate consumers on energy-saving changes to homes. The Healthy Housing Initiative combines passive solar, energy-efficient design, construction & appliances, integrated with renewable energy systems, to achieve net zero energy consumption on an annual basis, significantly reducing environmental impacts & GHG emissions. Twenty demonstration projects across Canada are underway.

Minister Responsible; Minister, Families, Children & Social Development, Hon. Ahmed Hussen
Ahmed.Hussen@parl.gc.ca

Chair, Robert Kelly
Tel: 613-748-2787

President & Chief Executive Officer; Board Member, Evan Siddall
Tel: 613-748-2186

Senior Vice-President, Policy & Innovation, Michel Tremblay
Tel: 613-748-2994

Senior Vice-President, General Counsel & Corporate Secretary, Deborah Greenberg
Tel: 613-748-2892

Senior Vice-President, Regional Operations & Assisted Housing, Charles MacArthur
Tel: 613-748-2251

Senior Vice-President, Insurance, Steven Mennill
Tel: 613-748-2772

Chief Financial Officer & Senior Vice-President, Capital Markets, Wojo Zielonka
Tel: 613-748-2012

Chief Risk Officer, Nadine Leblanc
Tel: 613-748-2198

Senior Vice-President, Human Resources, Marie-Claude Tremblay
Tel: 613-748-2082

Chief Information Officer, Paul Mason

Vice President, Insurance Operations, Glen Trevisani
Tel: 613-748-4049

Canada Pension Plan Investment Board / Office d'investissement du Régime de pensions du Canada

#2500, 1 Queen St. East, Toronto, ON M5C 2W5
Tel: 416-868-4075; *Fax:* 416-868-8689
Toll-Free: 866-557-9510
contact@cppib.com
www.cppib.ca
twitter.com/cppib
www.linkedin.com/company/23230
www.youtube.com/user/CPPIB
The CPP Investment Board is a Crown corporation created as part of the 1997 reforms designed to ensure the soundness & sustainability of the CPP. The Board operates under similar investment rules as other pension plans in Canada, which require the prudent management of pension plan assets in the interests of plan contributors & beneficiaries.

Chair, Board of Directors, Heather Munroe-Blum

President & Chief Executive Officer, Mark Machin

Senior Managing Director & Chief Financial & Risk Officer, Neil Beaumont

Senior Managing Director & Head of International, Head of Europe (London Office), Alain Carrier

Senior Managing Director & Global Head, Real Assets, Edwin D. Cass

Senior Managing Director, Graeme Eadie

Senior Managing Director & Global Head, Private Investments, Shane Feeney

Senior Managing Director & Global Head, Investment Partnerships, Pierre Lavallée

Senior Managing Director & Global Head, Public Affairs & Communications, Michel Leduc

Senior Managing Director & Chief Investment Strategist, Geoffrey Rubin

Senior Managing Director & Chief Talent Officer, Mary Sullivan

Senior Managing Director, General Counsel & Corporate Secretary, Patrice Walch-Watson

Senior Managing Director & Global Head, Public Market Investments, Eric M. Wetlaufer

Senior Managing Director & Chief Operations Officer, Nicholas Zelenczuk

Canada Place Corporation / Corporation Place du Canada

100 The Pointe, 999 Canada Pl., Vancouver, BC V6C 3T4
Tel: 604-775-7063
www.canadaplace.ca
Other Communication: Media Phone: 604-665-9267
twitter.com/canadaplace
www.facebook.com/CanadaPlace
www.youtube.com/user/CanadaPlaceCorp
The Corporation, which merged with Port Metro Vancouver, is in charge of property management at Canada Place in Vancouver, which includes a cruise ship facility, a trade & convention centre, a hotel, an IMAX theatre, & a parking structure

Canada Post Corporation / Société canadienne des postes

Corporate Secretariat, 2701 Riverside Dr., Ottawa, ON K1A 0B1
Tel: 416-979-3033
Toll-Free: 866-607-6301
TTY: 800-267-2797
www.canadapost.ca
Other Communication: Postal Security, Phone: 800-267-1177
twitter.com/canadapostcorp
www.facebook.com/canadapost
www.linkedin.com/company/canada-post
Canada Post is a federal commercial Crown corporation responsible for Canada's postal system. For postal rates, codes, abbreviations & other general information, see Canada Post online, or Postal Information in the main Index of the Canadian Almanac & Directory.

Minister Responsible; Minister, Public Services & Procurement, Hon. Filomena Tassi, P.C.

President & CEO, Doug Ettinger

Chief Financial Officer, Wayne Cheeseman

Senior Vice-President, Strategy & Corporate Marketing, Leonard Diplock

Chief Information Technology Officer, Anik Dubreuil

Chief Human Resources Officer, Ann Therese MacEachern

Senior Vice-President, Corporate Affairs, Susan Margles

Chief Operating Officer, Mary Traversy

Vice-President, Engineering, Jay Davis

Vice-President, Operations Integration, Manon Fortin

Vice-President, Pension Fund & Chief Investment Officer, Douglas Greaves

Vice-President, Parcels & International Business, Rod Hart

Vice-President, Finance & Comptroller, Barbara MacKenzie

Vice-President, Sales, Serge Pitre

Vice-President, Communications & Public Affairs, Jo-Anne Polak

Vice-President, Operations, Brian Wilson

ePost / Postel
#1300, 393 University Ave., Toronto, ON M5G 1E6
Toll-Free: 877-376-1212
epoinfo@canadapost.ca

Office of the Ombudsman / Bureau de l'ombudsman
PO Box 90026 Ottawa, ON K1V 1J8
Fax: 800-204-4193
Toll-Free: 800-204-4198
www.ombudsman.postescanadapost.ca
Ombudsman, Nabil R. Allaf

Canada Revenue Agency (CRA) / Agence du revenu du Canada

875 Heron Rd., Ottawa, ON K1A 1A2
Toll-Free: 800-267-6999
TTY: 800-665-0354
www.canada.ca/en/revenue-agency.html
Other Communication: Individual Income Tax Enquiries:
800-959-8281; Telerefund: 800-959-1956; Business & Self-Employed Individuals: 800-959-5525
twitter.com/canrevagency
www.facebook.com/canrevagency
www.linkedin.conm/company/cra-arc
www.youtube.com/user/CanRevAgency
The Canada Revenue Agency administers tax laws for the Canadian federal government & for most provincial & territorial governments. The Agency is also responsible for various social & economic benefit & incentive programs, which are delivered through the tax system.

Minister, National Revenue, Hon. Diane Lebouthillier, P.C.
Tel: 613-992-6188; *Fax:* 613-992-6194
Diane.Lebouthillier@parl.gc.ca

Commissioner & Chief Executive Officer, Bob Hamilton
Tel: 613-957-3688; *Fax:* 613-952-1547

Deputy Commissioner, Christine Donoghue
Tel: 613-957-3688; *Fax:* 613-952-1547

Appeals Branch / Direction générale des appels
Assistant Commissioner, Cathy Hawara
Tel: 613-960-2388; *Fax:* 613-952-5965
Director General, Tax & Charities Appeals Directorate, Catherine Letellier de St-Just
Tel: 613-960-2308
Director General, Relief, Redress & Branch Services Directorate, Catherine Massé
Tel: 613-960-2232
Director General, Objections & Litigation Management Directorate, Trevor Saxton
Tel: 613-960-2374

Director, Branch Planning & Management Services Division, Petra Bolduc
Tel: 613-960-2205
Director, International, Financial & GST Division, Isabelle Brault
Tel: 613-960-2307
Director, CPP/EI Appeals & Service Feedback Division, Éric Giguère
Tel: 613-954-4273
Director, Litigation Program Management Division, Christine Kinglsey
Tel: 613-948-0290
Director, Business Intelligence & Technology Division, Tamara Kluke
Tel: 613-960-2372
Director, Taxpayer Relief Policy & Program Division, David Moffat
Tel: 613-960-2236
Acting Director, Risk & Law Management Division, Nicole Mondou
Tel: 613-960-2297
Acting Director, Income Tax, Charities & Policy Division, Isaac Piotrkowski
Tel: 613-960-2294
Director, Objections Program Management Division, Mo Tait
Tel: 613-960-2364

Assessment, Benefit & Services Branch / Direction générale de cotisation, de prestation et de service
Assistant Commissioner, Frank Vermaeten
Tel: 613-941-5007; *Fax:* 613-954-4434
Deputy Assistant Commissioner, Cynthia Leblanc
Tel: 613-954-6614
Deputy Assistant Commissioner, Gillian Pranke
Tel: 613-954-6143
Director General, Individual Returns Directorate, Clément Bouchard
Tel: 613-957-7497; *Fax:* 613-941-2090
Director General, Benefit Programs Directorate, Nathalie Dumais
Tel: 613-957-9338; *Fax:* 613-946-6719
Director General, Call Centre Services Directorate, Michael Honcoop
Tel: 613-957-9362

Audit, Evaluation & Risk Branch / Direction générale de la vérification, de l'évaluation et des risques
Assistant Commissioner & Chief Audit Executive, Brian Philbin
Tel: 613-670-9375; *Fax:* 613-952-0512
Director, Enterprise Risk Management Division, Valérie Bournival
Tel: 613-954-7819
Director, Program Evaluation Division, Myles Kennedy
Tel: 613-954-7881
Acting Director, Internal Audit Division, Jovalyn Tuitt
Tel: 613-670-9107

Collections & Verifications Branch / Direction Générale des Recouvrements et de la Vérification
Assistant Commissioner, Michael Snaauw
Tel: 613-954-1269; *Fax:* 613-952-6395
Deputy Assistant Commissioner, Josée Dussault
Tel: 613-957-8174; *Fax:* 613-952-6395
Director General, Technology & Business Intelligence Directorate, Enikö Vermes
Tel: 613-957-1863; *Fax:* 613-960-0340
Director, Initial Intervention & Resolution Division, Terry Brown
Tel: 613-954-8291
Director, Employer Compliance Division, Lyne Levac
Tel: 613-954-1307
Director, Tax Programs Division, Guy Lafrance
Tel: 613-954-1502
Director, Sector Programs Division, Jane Mah
Tel: 613-954-8291
Director, Program Analysis & Resource Allocation Division, Pat O'Connor
Tel: 613-952-6656

Domestic Compliance Programs Branch / Direction general des programmes d'observation nationaux
Fax: 613-952-6772
Assistant Commissioner, Anne-Marie Lévesque
Tel: 613-960-2388; *Fax:* 613-952-5695
Director General, Small & Medium Enterprises Directorate, Susan Betts
Tel: 613-946-3447
Director General, Scientific Research & Experimental Development Directorate, Jason Charron
Tel: 613-952-7472
Director General, GST/HST Directorate, Mark Richer
Tel: 613-970-7875
Acting Director, Leads & Voluntary Disclosures Division, Sahil Behal
Tel: 613-670-7872

Director, Specialty Audit Division, Deanne Field
Tel: 613-941-5128
Acting Director, Small & Medium Business Audit Division, Harry Gill
Tel: 613-670-7600
Director, Financial SR&ED & Film Division, Elizabeth Koopman
Tel: 613-957-7633
Director, Aggressive GST/HST Planning & Refund Integrity Division, Sylvain Lessard
Tel: 613-670-7870
Director, Stakeholder Relations Division, Frank Milito
Tel: 613-957-9390
Director, Program Management Division, Jean-François Normand
Tel: 613-948-3640
Director, Small & Medium Audit Division, Donna O'Connor
Tel: 613-670-1375
Director, Business Intelligence Division, Shawn O'Toole
Tel: 613-670-7689
Director, Business Management Division, Jody Unrau
Tel: 613-941-0156
Acting Director, Business Audit Division, Mike Warren
Tel: 613-957-3622

Finance & Administration Branch / Direction générale des finances et de l'administration
Assistant Commissioner & Chief Financial Officer, Kami Ramcharan
Tel: 613-946-1763; *Fax:* 613-948-5776
Deputy Assistant Commissioner & Agency Comptroller, Janique Caron
Tel: 613-948-5240; *Fax:* 613-948-5776
Deputy Assistant Commissioner & Agency Comptroller, Hugo Pagé
Tel: 613-948-5240; *Fax:* 613-948-5776
Director General, Financial Administration Directorate, Sylvie Godin
Tel: 613-957-7343
Director General, Security & Internal Affairs Directorate, Dana-Lynne Hills
Tel: 613-948-2449
Director General, Administration Directorate, Roger Houde
Tel: 613-947-3262
Director General, Financial Management Advisory Services Directorate, Nathalie Meilleur
Tel: 613-698-2213
Acting Director General, Resource Management Directorate, Rachelle Reilly
Tel: 613-957-7339
Director General, Real Property & Service Integration Directorate, Nandini Srikantiah
Tel: 613-670-8889
Director, Internal Controls Division, Brenda Abramson
Tel: 613-946-2820
Director, Contracting Division, Jean-Claude Azar
Tel: 613-995-4794
Director, Revenue Accounting, Reporting & Analysis Division, Brenda Brulotte
Tel: 613-954-6226
Director, Internal Affairs & Fraud Control Division, Maura Butko
Tel: 613-948-2438
Director, Resource Strategies, Costing & Analysis Division, Malcolm Churches
Tel: 613-941-3810
Director, Revenue Accounting, Reporting & Analysis Division, Robert Denis
Tel: 613-954-6393
Director, Information Security Division, Chris Docherty
Tel: 613-943-9101
Director, National Real Property Stewardship Division, Mark Featherstone
Tel: 613-670-8886
Director, Strategic Investment Planning & Oversight Division, Michael Fowler
Tel: 613-954-6257
Director, National Real Property Solutions Division, Jeremy Hebert
Tel: 613-296-1477
Director, Emeregency Management & Security Operations Division, Debby Honcoop
Tel: 613-943-8925
Acting Director, Policy & Strategic Management Division, Omar Saeed
Tel: 613-947-3960
Director, Agency Logistics & Administrative Services Division, Deborah Turner
Tel: 613-947-3029

Human Resources Branch / Direction générale des ressources humaines
Fax: 613-957-2306

Assistant Commissioner & Chief Human Resources Officer, Dan Couture
Tel: 613-954-8200

Deputy Assistant Commissioner, Ann Marie Hume
Tel: 613-946-4527; Fax: 613-952-8557

Director General, Learning & Development Directorate, Karen Butcher
Tel: 613-670-9164

Director General, Employment Programs Directorate, David Conabree
Tel: 613-954-1623

Director General, Employment Programs Directorate, Nathalie Kachulis
Tel: 613-954-8166

Director General, Workplace Relations & Compensation Directorate, Maggie Trudel-Maagiore
Tel: 613-954-8150

Information Technology Branch / Direction générale de l'informatique
Fax: 613-957-9058

Assistant Commissioner & Chief Information Officer, Annette Butikofer
Tel: 613-946-6494; Fax: 613-960-5683

Director General, Corporate Enterprise Solutions Directorate, Lynne Sincennes
Tel: 613-954-9039

Director, Business Technologies & Innovation Division, Mary Beckett
Tel: 613-948-5553

Director, Corporate Administrative Systems Business Enterprise Solutions, Mario Kalabric
Tel: 613-948-5704

Director, Management Systems Division, Sonia Murray
Tel: 613-948-5291

Director, Branch Business Management Division, Snow Susan
Tel: 613-946-4977

Legal Services Branch / Direction générale des services juridiques
Fax: 613-954-6282

Executive Director & Senior General Counsel, Jade Boucher
Tel: 613-957-2358; Fax: 613-957-2371

Legislative Policy & Regulatory Affairs Branch / Politiques législatives et affaires réglementaires

Assistant Commissioner, Geoff Trueman
Tel: 613-957-3708; Fax: 613-957-2067

Deputy Assistant Commissioner, Cathy Hawara
Tel: 613-670-9556

Director General, Income Tax Rulings Directorate, Costa Dimitrakopoulos
Tel: 613-670-9560

Director General, Registered Plans Directorate, Michael Godwin
Tel: 613-954-0933

Director General, Legislative Policy Directorate, Randy Hewlett
Tel: 613-670-9058

Director General, Excise & GST/HST Rulings Directorate, Danielle Laflèche
Tel: 613-670-1441

Director General, Charities Directorate, Tony Manconi
Tel: 613-670-9570

Director, International Division, Milled Azzi
Tel: 613-670-1363

Director, Financial Institutions & Real Property Division, Marcel Boivin
Tel: 613-670-7949

Director, Financial Industries & Trusts Division, Stéphane Charette
Tel: 613-670-9012

Director, Planning & Management Services Division, Linda Desrochers
Tel: 613-957-8682

Director, Legislative Amendments Division, Robert Greene
Tel: 613-670-9568

Director, Excise Duties & Taxes Division, Ron Hagmann
Tel: 613-670-7360

Director, CPP/EI Rulings Division, Danielle Héroux
Tel: 613-670-7380

Director, Dedicated Telephone Serivce, Publication & Operations Division, Adrianna McGilivray
Tel: 613-670-0608

Director, General Operations & Border Issues Division, Patrick McKinnon
Tel: 613-954-7959

Director, Director, Public Service Bodies & Governments Division, Philippe Nault
Tel: 613-670-7939

Director, Business Integration & Program Operations Division, Luisa Rizzo
Tel: 613-670-1462

Director, International Relations & Treatiess Division, Guylaine Robert
Tel: 613-670-9558

Public Affairs Branch / Direction générale des affaires publiques

Assistant Commissioner & Chief Privacy Officer, Maxime Guenette
Tel: 613-957-3508; Fax: 613-954-7955

Director General, Communications Directorate, Jane Hazel
Tel: 613-948-4847

Director General, Ministerial Services & Operations Directorate, Lorraine Redekop
Tel: 613-957-8438

Director, Strategic Regional Communications Division, Jacqueline Couture
Tel: 613-957-8540

Director, Electronic & Print Media Directorate, Steve Enright
Tel: 613-960-5523

Director, Parliamentary Affairs Division, Tara Hall
Tel: 613-957-9710

Director, Access to Information & Privacy Directorate, Marie-Claude Juneau
Tel: 613-960-5378

Strategy & Integration Branch / Direction generale de la strategie et de l'integration

Assistant Commissioner, Mireille Éthier
Tel: 613-952-3660; Fax: 613-941-3438

Director General, Agency Strategy & Reporting Directorate, France Bilodeau
Tel: 613-954-6082

Director General, Information & Relationship Management Directorate, Wayne Lepine
Tel: 613-670-7658

Director General, Agency Analytics & Data Directorate, Chantal Quinn
Tel: 613-670-7168

Director, Provincial & Territorial Affairs Division, Curtis Bell
Tel: 613-670-7657

Director, Planning & Reporting Division, Ryan Boudreau
Tel: 613-954-6065

Director, Business Statistics Division, Nicole Crutcher
Tel: 613-670-9347

Director, Information Management Division, Shannon Drew
Tel: 613-670-8959

Director, Federal, Aboriginal & Québec Affairs Division, Isabelle Gervais
Tel: 613-670-0804

Director, Change Management Division, Cary O'Brien
Tel: 613-946-8650

Director, Accelerated Business Solutions Lab, André Patry
Tel: 613-941-2668

Director, Individual Statistics Division, Jack Pearson
Tel: 613-670-0953

Director, Agency Data Program Division, Jean-Francois Ruel
Tel: 613-670-7303

Canada School of Public Service (CCMD) / École de la fonction publique du Canada (EEPC)

373 Sussex Dr., Ottawa, ON K1N 6Z2
Tel: 819-953-5400; Fax: 866-944-0454
Toll-Free: 866-703-9598
info@csps-efpc.gc.ca
www.csps-efpc.gc.ca
Other Communication: Media, Phone: 613-996-2744; Email: media@csps-efpc.gc.ca
twitter.com/School_GC
www.linkedin.com/company/canada-school-of-public-service

The CSPS is a learning provider for the Public Service of Canada. The School brings together three well-established federal public service learning organizations: the Canadian Centre for Management Development, Training & Development Canada (Public Service Commission) & Language Training Canada. It contributes to building & maintaining a modern, high-quality, professional public service that is at the leading-edge of knowledge in modern public administration & public sector management. Through up-to-date adult learning techniques, it provides public servants across the country with access to the common learning opportunities they require to effectively serve Canada & Canadians

Minister Responsible; President, Treasury Board, Hon. Mona Fortier, P.C.

Deputy Minister & President, Taki Sarantakis
Tel: 613-992-8165; Fax: 613-943-1038

Vice-President, Learning Programs, Margaret Meroni
Tel: 613-992-8346; Fax: 613-992-3663

Canada Science & Technology Museum Corporation (CSTM) / Musée des sciences et de la technologie du Canada (MSTC)

PO Box 9724 Stn. T, Ottawa, ON K1G 5A3
Tel: 613-991-3044; Fax: 613-993-7923
Toll-Free: 866-442-4416
cts@techno-science.ca
techno-science.ca
twitter.com/IngeniumCa
www.facebook.com/IngeniumCa

The Corporation, comprising the Ingenium brand, is the only comprehensive science & technology collecting institution in Canada, & focuses on the major subject areas of: aviation, communications, manufacturing, natural resources, & renewable resources including agriculture, scientific instrumentation, & transportation. The Corporation operates three Museums: the Canada Agriculture Museum, the Canada Aviation Museum & the Canada Science & Technology Museum.

Chair, Dr. Gary Polonsky

Vice-Chair, Jim Silye

President & Chief Operating Officer, Christina Tessier

Vice-President, Collection, Research & Corporate Governance, Monique Horth
Tel: 613-991-9508

Canadian Broadcasting Corporation (CBC) / Société Radio-Canada (SRC)

181 Queen St., PO Box 3220 Stn. C, Ottawa, ON K1Y 1E4
Tel: 613-288-6000
TTY: 613-288-6455
liaison@cbc.ca
www.cbc.radio-canada.ca
Other Communication: Toll Free: 866-306-4636
twitter.com/CBCRadioCanada
www.facebook.com/CBCRadioCanada

The Canadian Broadcasting Corporation (CBC) is a Crown corporation governed by the 1991 Broadcasting Act & subject to regulations of the Canadian Radio-television & Telecommunications Commission (CRTC). The CBC operates four national radio networks, CBC Radio One & CBC Radio Two in English, & ICI Radio-Canada Première & Espace musique in French, featuring information & general interest programs as well as classical music & cultural programs; two self-supporting specialty cable television services, CBC News Network in English & Ici RDI in French, which feature news & information programs 24 hours a day, seven days a week; & radio & television services for Canada's North in English, French & eight aboriginal languages. CBC also provides, on behalf of the Government of Canada, an online multilingual service called Radio Canada International (formerly a shortwave radio service), which publishes content in five languages.

Chair, Board of Directors, Michael Goldbloom

President & Chief Executive Officer, Catherine Tait

Executive Vice-President, Radio-Canada, Michel Bissonnette

Executive Vice-President, Media Technology & Infrastructure Services, Daniel Boudreau

Executive Vice-President & CFO, Judith Purves

Executive Vice-President, CBC, Barbara Williams

Vice-President, Legal Services, General Counsel & Corporate Secretary, Sylvie Gadoury

Vice-President, People & Culture, Mario Dubé

CBC/Radio-Canada - English Services
PO Box 500 Stn. A, Toronto, ON M5W 1E6
Toll-Free: 866-306-4636
TTY: 866-220-6045
www.cbc.radio-canada.ca

CBC/Radio-Canada - French Services / ICI Radio-Canada
1400, boul René-Lévesque est, CP 6000 Succ Centre-ville, Montréal, QC H3C 3A8

Tél: 514-597-6000
Ligne sans frais: 866-306-4636
TTY: 514-597-6013
www.radio-canada.ca
twitter.com/CBCRadioCanada
www.facebook.com/CBCRadioCanada
www.linkedin.com/grp/home?gid=2280703
instagram.com/cbcradiocanada

CBC/Radio-Canada - Ombudsmen
www.ombudsman.cbc.radio-canada.ca
Ombudsman, CBC, English Services, Esther Enkin
Tel: 416-205-2978; *Fax:* 416-205-2825
ombudsman@cbc.ca
twitter.com/CBCOmbudsman
PO Box 500 A Sta.
Toronto, ON M5W 1E6
Ombudsman, Radio-Canada, French Services, Guy Gendron
Tél: 514-597-4757
Ligne sans frais: 877-846-4737
Téléc: 514-597-5253
ombudsman@radio-canada.ca
twitter.com/ombudsmanrc
PO Box 6000
Montreal, QC H3C 3A8

Radio Canada International
1400, boul René-Lévesque est, CP 6000 Montréal, QC H2L 2M2

Tél: 514-597-7461
info@rcinet.ca
www.rcinet.ca
twitter.com/RCInet
www.facebook.com/rcinet

Radio Canada International was transitioned to an online-only service in 2012. It now produces online content in five languages: English, French, Spanish, Arabic & Chinese. The aim of RCInet.ca is to produce programs for people who know little or nothing about Canada, & to accomplish this the service publishes a variety of interviews, feature reports, columns, news, a current affairs blog & a multimedia section.

CBC Regional Offices

Alberta (English & French)
Edmonton City Centre, #123, 10062 - 102nd Ave., PO Box 555 Edmonton, AB T5J 2P4
Tel: 780-468-7500
www.cbc.ca/edmonton/contact
Atlantic Provinces (French Services) / Radio-Canada Acadie
#15, 165, rue Main, Moncton, NB E1C 1B8
Tel: 506-853-6666
www.cbc.ca/nb/contact
British Columbia (English & French)
700 Hamilton St., PO Box 4600 Vancouver, BC V6B 4A2
Tel: 604-662-6000
Toll-Free: 866-306-4636
www.cbc.ca/bc/contact

CBC North
PO Box 160 Yellowknife, NT X1A 2N2
Tel: 867-920-5400
www.cbc.ca/north/contact
CBC North also operates offices in the Yukon (867-668-8400), Nunavut (867-979-6100), & Québec (1-877-597-4369).
Canadian Broadcasting Centre
PO Box 500 Stn. A, Toronto, ON M5W 1E6
Tel: 416-205-3311
www.cbc.ca/toronto/contact
Manitoba (English & French)
541 Portage Ave., Winnipeg, MB R3B 2G1
Tel: 204-788-3222
TTY: 866-220-6045
www.cbc.ca/manitoba/contact
Maritimes (English)
PO Box 3000 Halifax, NS B3J 3E9
Tel: 902-420-8311
www.cbc.ca/ns/contact
Newfoundland (English)
PO Box 12010 Stn. A, St. John's, NL A1B 3T8
Tel: 709-576-5000
www.cbc.ca/nl/contact
Ottawa Production Centre
181 Queen St., PO Box 3220 Stn. C, Ottawa, ON K1Y 1E4
Tel: 613-288-6000
www.cbc.ca/ottawa/contact

Prince Edward Island (English & French)
430 University Ave., PO Box 2230 Charlottetown, PE C1A 8B9
Tel: 902-629-6400
www.cbc.ca/pei/contact
Québec (English) / Maison de Radio-Canada
CP 6000 Montréal, QC H3C 3A8
Tél: 514-597-6000
www.cbc.ca/montreal/contact
Québec (French) / Société Radio-Canada
CP 18800 Québec, QC G1K 9L4
Saskatchewan (English & French)
2440 Broad St., Regina, SK S4P 4A1
Tel: 306-347-9540
www.cbc.ca/sask/contact

Canadian Centre for Occupational Health & Safety (CCOHS) / Centre canadien d'hygiène et de sécurité au travail (CCHST)

135 Hunter St. East, Hamilton, ON L8N 1M5
Tel: 905-572-2981; *Fax:* 905-572-4500
Toll-Free: 800-668-4284
www.ccohs.ca
twitter.com/ccohs
www.facebook.com/CCOHS
www.youtube.com/ccohs
The CCOHS provides occupational health & safety & environmental information in the form of publications, responses to inquiries & a computerized information service available in various formats. Topics include: environmental acts & regulations; occupational & environmental health data; toxic effects of chemical substances; transport of dangerous goods; chemical evaluation; hazardous substances; & domestic substances listed under the Canadian Environmental Protection Act; biological hazards; & ergonomics

Chair, Council of Governors, Gary Robertson

President & CEO, Anne Tennier
Tel: 905-572-2981 ext: 4432

Vice-President, Operations, Gareth Jones
Tel: 905-572-2981 ext: 4537

Chief Financial Officer & Vice-President, Finance, Kimberly Pirhonen
Tel: 905-572-2981 ext: 4402

Director, Marketing & Communications, Lynda Brown
Tel: 905-572-2981 ext: 4472

Canadian Centre on Substance Abuse (CCSA) / Centre canadien de lutte contre l'alcoolisme et les toxicomanies (CCLAT)

#500, 75 Albert St., Ottawa, ON K1P 5E7
Tel: 613-235-4048; *Fax:* 613-235-8101
info@ccsa.ca
www.ccsa.ca
Other Communication: Publications: publications@ccsa.ca; Media: media@ccsa.ca
twitter.com/CCSAcanada
www.facebook.com/CCSA.CCDUS
www.youtube.com/user/CCSACCLAT
The CCSA is a non-profit organization working to minimize the harm associated with the use of alcohol, tobacco & other drugs.

Chair, Vaughan Dowie
Tel: 613-235-4048 ext: 232

Chief Executive Officer, Rita Notarandrea
Tel: 613-235-4048 ext: 227

Vice-President, Operations & Strategies, Rhowena Martin
Tel: 613-235-4048 ext: 239

Director, Public Affairs & Communications, Scott Hannant

Canadian Commercial Corporation (CCC) / Corporation commerciale canadienne

#700, 350 Albert St., Ottawa, ON K1A 0S6
Tel: 613-996-0034; *Fax:* 613-995-2121
Toll-Free: 800-748-8191
info@ccc.ca
www.ccc.ca
The CCC is a Crown corporation mandated to facilitate international trade, particularly in government markets. The Corporation specializes in international procurement markets for Canadian companies & provides services to help them win,

negotiate & manage export contracts. As prime contractor, CCC offers a government-to-government agreement that simplifies customer access to Canadian technology & expertise. CCC contracts have a government guarantee for performance.

Interim President & CEO; Vice-President, Corporate Services; Chief Financial Officer, Ernie Briard
Tel: 613-995-4658; *Fax:* 613-995-2121

Vice-President, Business Development & Sales, Kim Douglas
Tel: 613-992-3506

Vice-President, Legal Services, Michelle Taylor
Tel: 613-995-0110

Canadian Dairy Commission (CDC) / Commission canadienne du lait (CCL)

Central Experimental Farm, NCC Driveway, Bldg. 55, 960 Carling Ave., Ottawa, ON K1A 0Z2
Tel: 613-792-2000; *Fax:* 613-792-2009
TTY: 613-792-2082
cdc-ccl@cdc-ccl.gc.ca
www.cdc-ccl.gc.ca
Other Communication: Special Milk Class Permits, Phone: 613-792-2057; Dairy Imports & Exports, Phone: 613-792-2010
The CDC is a federal Crown corporation that serves the interests of all dairy stakeholders, including producers, processors, further processors, exporters, consumers & governments. The key objectives of the CDC are to provide efficient milk & cream producers with the opportunity to obtain a fair return for their labour & investment & to ensure an adequate supply of high quality dairy products for consumers.

Chair, Robert Ingratta

Chief Executive Officer, Serge Riendeau
Tel: 613-792-2060

Commissioner, Jennifer Hayes
Tel: 418-355-8758; *Fax:* 613-792-2064
jennifer.hayes@canada.ca

Chief Operating Officer, Vacant

Director, Policy & Economics, Benoît Basillais
Tel: 613-792-2044; *Fax:* 613-792-2009
benoit.basillais@cdc-ccl.gc.ca

Director, Audit & Evaluation, Hossein Behzadi
Tel: 613-222-2468; *Fax:* 613-792-2009
hossein.behzadi@cdc-ccl.gc.ca

Director, Finance & Administration, Chantal Laframbois
Tel: 613-792-2056; *Fax:* 613-792-2009
chantal.laframboise@cdc-ccl.gc.ca

Impact Assessment Agency of Canada / Agence d'évaluation d'impact du Canada

Place Bell Canada, 160 Elgin St., 22nd Fl., Ottawa, ON K1A 0H3
Tel: 613-957-0700; *Fax:* 613-957-0862
Toll-Free: 866-582-1884
www.canada.ca/en/impact-assessment-agency.html
The Impact Assessment Agency of Canada was established in August 2019, & replaced the former Canadian Environmental Assessment Agency. It administers the Impact Assessment Act. The environmental assessment process identifies the environmental effects of proposed projects & measures to address those effects, in support of sustainable development. The agency promotes environmental assessment as a tool to protect & sustain a healthy environment in harmony with a growing economy. It advocates high-quality environmental assessments by assisting federal departments & agencies with training & guidance & by investing in the research & development of best practices. It provides administrative support to mediators & review panels & ensures that the public has opportunities to participate effectively in the environmental assessment process. Public participation strengthens the quality & credibility of environmental assessments by providing local & traditional knowledge, & insight into possible environmental effects. Three funding programs are also available. Accountable to the Minister of the Environment.

Interim President, David McGovern

Vice-President, Operations, Terence Hubbard
Tel: 613-948-2665
terence.hubbard@canada.ca

Vice-President, Corporate Services, Alan Kerr

Tel: 613-960-0897
Alan.Kerr@ceaa-acee.gc.ca

Vice-President, Policy Development, Christine Loth-Bown
Tel: 613-948-2662; Fax: 613-957-0897

Canadian Food Inspection Agency (CFIA) / Agence canadienne d'inspection des aliments (ACIA)

1400 Merivale Rd., Ottawa, ON K1A 0Y9
Tel: 613-225-2342
Toll-Free: 800-442-2342
TTY: 800-465-7735
www.inspection.gc.ca
Other Communication: Atlantic Area, Phone: 506-777-3939;
Ontario Area: 226-217-8555; Québec Area: 514-283-8888;
Western Area: 587-230-2200
twitter.com/CFIA_food
www.facebook.com/CFIACanada
www.linkedin.com/company/canadian-food-inspection-agency
The agency is responsible for all inspection services related to
food safety, economic fraud, trade-related requirements, &
animal & plant health programs.

Minister Responsible; Minister, Health, Hon. Jean-Yves
Duclos, P.C.

President, Siddika Mithani
Tel: 613-773-6000
siddika.mithani@canada.ca

Executive Vice-President, France Pégeot
Tel: 613-773-6500; Fax: 613-773-6060
france.pegeot@canada.ca

Chief Food Safety Officer & Vice-President, Science,
Vacant

Chief Veterinary Officer, Vacant

**Chief Financial Officer & Vice-President, Corporate
Management,** Dominique Osterrath
Tel: 613-773-5705; Fax: 613-773-5792
dominique.osterrath@canada.ca

Chief Redress Officer, Integrity & Redress Secretariat,
Merril Bawden
Tel: 613-773-5359
merril.bawden@canada.ca

Vice-President, Human Resources, Darlene de Gravina
Tel: 613-773-5720; Fax: 613-773-6060
darlene.degravina@canada.ca

Vice-President, Operations, Theresa Iuliano
Tel: 613-773-6127; Fax: 613-773-7388
theresa.iuliano@canada.ca

Vice-President, Science, Jaspinder Komal
Tel: 613-773-5747
jaspinder.komal@canada.ca

Acting Vice-President, Communications & Public Affairs,
Jonathan Massey-Smith
Tel: 613-773-5776; Fax: 613-773-5559
jonathan.massey-smith@canada.ca

**Vice-President, Innovation, Business & Service
Development,** Amanda Jane Preece
Tel: 613-773-5137
AmandaJane.Preece@canada.ca

Associate Vice-President, Policy & Programs, Colleen
Barnes
Tel: 613-773-5310; Fax: 613-228-6653
Colleen.Barnes@inspection.gc.ca

**Executive Director & Senior General Counsel, Agriculture
& Food Inspection Legal Services,** Carole Bidal
Tel: 613-773-5772; Fax: 613-773-5670
carole.bidal@canada.ca

Canadian Grain Commission (CGC) / Commission canadienne des grains (CCG)

#600, 303 Main St., Winnipeg, MB R3C 3G8
Tel: 204-984-0506; Fax: 204-983-2751
Toll-Free: 800-853-6705
TTY: 866-317-4289
contact@grainscanada.gc.ca
www.grainscanada.gc.ca
Other Communication: Grain Sanitation & Infestation Control
Industry Services, Fax: 204-984-7550; Licensing & Security Unit,
Fax: 204-983-4654; Statistics Unit, Phone: 204-983-2739
twitter.com/Grain_Canada
www.youtube.com/user/GrainCommission
The CGC is Canada's official grain quality assurance agency.
The CGC offers a wide range of programs & services. It
regulates grain handling in Canada & establishes & maintains
quality standards for Canadian grains. Responsibilities are as
follows: officially inspecting & grading grain; weighing grain at
terminal & transfer elevators; licensing grain elevators & dealers;
conducting & publishing statistical & economic studies; &
performing basic & applied research on Canadian grain.

Chief Commissioner, Vacant

Assistant Chief Commissioner, Doug Chorney
Tel: 204-983-2730

Commissioner, Lonny McKague
Tel: 204-983-2732

Chief Operating Officer, Jocelyn Beaudette
Tel: 204-983-2731

Chief Financial Officer, Cheryl Blahey
Tel: 204-984-7042; Fax: 204-984-7213

Chief Grain Inspector, Gino Castonguay
Tel: 204-983-2780

Chief Informatics Officer, Karl Daher
Tel: 204-984-6948; Fax: 204-983-0248

Chief Statistician, Anh Phan
Tel: 204-983-2739

Canadian Heritage / Patrimoine canadien

15, rue Eddy, Gatineau, QC K1A 0M5
Tel: 819-997-0055
Toll-Free: 866-811-0055
TTY: 888-997-3123
PCH.info-info.PCH@canada.ca
www.pch.gc.ca
twitter.com/CdnHeritage
www.facebook.com/CdnHeritage
www.youtube.com/CdnHeritage
Canadian Heritage works to achieve a more cohesive & creative
nation. Goals of the department are for Canadians to express &
share their cultural experiences with others in their own country
& globally & for Canadians to live in an inclusive society with
intercultural understanding & citizen participation.
Responsibilities are carried out by the following sectors:
Citizenship & Heritage; Cultural Affairs; Sport, Major Events &
Regions; & Strategic Policy, Planning & Corporate Affairs.

Minister, Canadian Heritage, Hon. Steven Guilbeault, P.C.
Steven.Guilbeault@parl.gc.ca

**Minister, Women & Gender Equality; Minister, Rural
Economic Development,** Vacant

Minister, Diversity & Inclusion & Youth, Bardish Chagger
Tel: 819-934-1122

Associated Agencies, Boards & Commissions:

• **Canada Council for the Arts / Conseil des Arts du Canada**
See Entry Name Index for detailed listing.
• **Canada Science & Technology Museum Corporation /
Musée des sciences et de la technologie du Canada**
See Entry Name Index for detailed listing.
• **Canadian Broadcasting Corporation (CBC) / Société
Radio-Canada (SRC)**
See Entry Name Index for detailed listing.
• **Canadian Museum of History / Musée canadien de
l'histoire**
See Entry Name Index for detailed listing.
• **Canadian Museum of Nature (CMN) / Musée canadien de la
nature (MCN)**
See Entry Name Index for detailed listing.
• **Canadian Radio-television & Telecommunications
Commission (CRTC) / Conseil de la radiodiffusion et des
télécommunications canadiennes**
See Entry Name Index for detailed listing.
• **Library & Archives Canada**
See Entry Name Index for detailed listing.
• **National Arts Centre (NAC) / Centre national des Arts
(CNA)**
See Entry Name Index for detailed listing.
• **National Battlefields Commission / Commission des
champs de bataille nationaux**
See Entry Name Index for detailed listing.
• **National Film Board of Canada / Office national du film du
Canada**
See Entry Name Index for detailed listing.
• **National Gallery of Canada / Musée des Beaux-Arts du
Canada**
See Entry Name Index for detailed listing.
• **Public Service Commission of Canada / Commission de la
fonction publique du Canada**
See Entry Name Index for detailed listing.
• **Status of Women Canada / Condition féminine Canada**
See Entry Name Index for detailed listing.
• **Telefilm Canada / Téléfilm Canada**
See Entry Name Index for detailed listing.

**Canadian Secretary to The Queen / Secrétaire canadien de
la Reine**
427 Laurier St., Ottawa, ON K1A 0M5
The Canadian Secretary to The Queen acts as the primary
means of communication between the monarch & the Canadian
Government, provincial governments, & the governments of
other Commonwealth realms. The Canadian Secretary also
drafts speeches the Queen will deliver, chairs (ex-officio) the
Advisory Committee on Vice-Regal Appointments, & is
responsible for tours of Canada conducted by members of the
Royal Family.
Canadian Secretary to The Queen, Kevin MacLeod, CVO, CD
Tel: 613-947-7035

Citizenship & Heritage Sector / Citoyenneté et patrimoine
Assistant Deputy Minister, Hubert Lussier
Tel: 819-997-2832; Fax: 819-994-5032
Hubert.Lussier@pch.gc.ca
Director General, Citizen Participation, William Fizet
Tel: 819-953-5999; Fax: 819-953-3515
William.Fizet@pch.gc.ca
Director General, Canadian Conservation Institute, Patricia Kell
Tel: 613-998-3721 ext: 115; Fax: 613-952-1431
Patricia.Kell@pch.gc.ca
Director, Policy, Research Planning & Regional Affairs, Paul
Turcotte
Tel: 819-934-6260
paul.turcotte@canada.ca
Director General, Citizen Participation, Michel Lemay
Tel: 819-953-5999; Fax: 819-953-3515
Michel.Lemay@pch.gc.ca
Director, Canadian Heritage Information Network (CHIN), Charlie
Costain
Tel: 613-998-3721 ext: 162; Fax: 613-998-4721
charlie.costain@canada.ca
Senior Director, Policy & Research, Yvan M. Déry
Tel: 819-994-2224; Fax: 819-994-3697
yvan.dery@pch.gc.ca

Canadian Human Rights Commission / Commission canadienne des droits de la personne

344 Slater St., 8th Fl., Ottawa, ON K1A 1E1
Fax: 613-996-9661
Toll-Free: 888-214-1090
TTY: 888-643-3304
info.com@chrc-ccdp.gc.ca
www.chrc-ccdp.gc.ca
Other Communication: Library, Email: library@chrc-ccdp.ca;
Media Relations, Email: communications@chrc-ccdp.gc.ca
twitter.com/cdnhumanrights
www.facebook.com/CanadianHumanRightsCommission
The Commission administers the Canadian Human Rights Act, which applies to federal government departments & agencies, & businesses under federal jurisdiction. The Commission accepts complaints of discrimination based on race, national or ethnic origin, colour, religion, age, sex, marital & family status, pardoned offence, disability & sexual orientation. It also administers the Employment Equity Act to remove barriers for four designated groups: women, Aboriginal peoples, persons with disabilities & members of visible minorities. Collect calls accepted throughout Canada.

Chief Commissioner, Marie-Claude Landry, Ad.E.
Tel: 613-943-9135

Deputy Chief Commissioner, Geneviève Chabot

Executive Director, Ian Fine
Tel: 613-943-9090

Deputy Executive Director & Senior General Counsel,
Monette Maillet
Tel: 613-943-9166; *Fax:* 613-941-6808

Director General, Complaints Serices Branch, Piero
Narducci
Tel: 613-943-9028

Director General, Policy & Communications Branch, Keith
Smith
Tel: 613-943-9126

Director, Administrative Services Division, Sarah
Stapenhurst
Tel: 613-943-9415

Director, Financial Services Division, André Pelchat
Tel: 613-943-9002

Director General, Corporate Management Branch, Natalie
Dagenais
Tel: 613-943-9133

Director, Human Resources Division, Mélanie Godin
Tel: 613-943-9024

Director, Compliance Promotion Division, Johanne
Lelièvre
Tel: 613-943-9009

General Counsel & Director, Legal Services, Valerie
Phillips
Tel: 613-943-9357

Director, Housing Division, Sacha Senécal
Tel: 613-943-9003

National Aboriginal Initiative (NAI) / Initiative Nationale Autochtone
#750, 175 Hargrave St., Winnipeg, MA RC3 3R8
Tel: 204-983-2189; *Fax:* 204-983-6132
Toll-Free: 866-772-4880
TTY: 866-772-4840
www.chrc-ccdp.gc.ca/eng/content/indigenous-peoples
twitter.com/cdnhumanrights
www.facebook.com/CanadianHumanRightsCommission
The National Aboriginal Initiative offers human rights expertise to First Nations governments & other Aboriginal organizations.
Director, Sherri Helgason
Tel: 204-983-4648

Canadian Human Rights Tribunal (CHRT) / Tribunal canadien des droits de la personne (TCDP)

160 Elgin St., 11th Fl., Ottawa, ON K1A 1J4
Tel: 613-995-1707; *Fax:* 613-995-3484
TTY: 613-947-1070
registrar@chrt-tcdp.gc.ca
www.chrt-tcdp.gc.ca
The CHRT is a quasi-judicial body that adjudicates complaints of discrimination referred to it by the Canadian Human Rights

Commission & determines whether the activities violate the Canadian Human Rights Act.

Chair, David Thomas
Tel: 613-995-1707

Vice-Chair, Jennifer Khurana
Tel: 613-995-1707

Canadian Institutes of Health Research (CIHR) / Instituts de recherche en santé du Canada (IRSC)

160 Elgin St., 10th Fl., Ottawa, ON K1A 0W9
Tel: 613-954-1968; *Fax:* 613-954-1800
Toll-Free: 888-603-4178
support@cihr-irsc.gc.ca
www.cihr-irsc.gc.ca
Other Communication: Reception: 613-941-2672
twitter.com/cihr_irsc
www.facebook.com/HealthResearchInCanada
linkedin.com/company/canadian-institutes-of-health-research
www.youtube.com/user/HealthResearchCanada
Promotes health research excellence in Canada through training & funding programs in basic, clinical, health systems & services, & population health research. Research is carried out in universities, in the health sciences faculties, affiliated hospitals & institutions & other faculties where research projects are highly relevant to human health. University-Industry programs create the opportunity for collaboration between Canadian companies & researchers conducting research in Canadian universities or affiliated institutions. Also manages the health-related Networks of Centres of Excellence & operates 13 "virtual" institutes, which link & support researchers pursuing common goals in specific areas of focus.

Chair & President, Michael Strong
Tel: 613-954-1808

Executive Vice-President, Michel Perron
Tel: 613-957-6134
michel.perron@cihr-irsc.gc.ca

Vice-President, Research Programs, Tammy Clifford
Tel: 613-954-1805
VPResearch@cihr-irsc.gc.ca

Chief Financial Officer & Vice-President, Resource Planning & Management, Thérèse Roy, CPA, CA
Tel: 613-954-1946
therese.roy@cihr-irsc.gc.ca

Acting Associate Vice-President, Research, Knowledge Translation & Ethics, Adrian Mota
Tel: 613-218-9347
adrian.mota@cihr-irsc.gc.ca

Acting Director General, Science Policy, Alison Bourgon
Tel: 613-941-4439

Director General, Strategic Partnerships & International Relations, David Clements
Tel: 613-948-2803

Acting Director General, Operations Support, Pierre Côté
Tel: 613-941-1090

Acting Director General, Communications, Nemesvary
Jacqueline
Tel: 613-954-2223

Director General, Initiative Management & Institute Support, Jeff Latimer
Tel: 613-960-6218

Director General & Chief Information Officer, Information Management, Technology & Security, Jason Reid
Tel: 613-957-6140

Director General, Human Resources, Liane Swanlund
Tel: 613-957-8762

Director General, Governance & Government Affairs,
Christian Sylvain
Tel: 613-948-2317

Director General, Program Design & Delivery, Kelly Taylor
Tel: 613-954-2028

Executive Director, Secretariat on Responsible Conduct of Research, Susan Zimmerman
Tel: 613-947-7148

Canadian Intergovernmental Conference Secretariat (CICS) / Secrétariat des conférences intergouvernementales canadiennes

222 Queen St., 10th Fl., PO Box 488 Stn. A, Ottawa, ON K1N 8V5
Tel: 613-995-2341; *Fax:* 613-996-6091
info@scics.gc.ca
www.scics.gc.ca
twitter.com/cics_info
CICS is a conference support body that provides the administrative services required for the planning & the conduct of federal-provincial-territorial & provincial-territorial conferences at the First Ministers, ministers & deputy ministers level. The agency is at the disposal of individual federal, provincial & territorial government departments, which may be called upon to organize & chair such meetings.

Secretary, André M. McArdle
Tel: 613-995-2345

Assistant Secretary, Brian J. Berry
Tel: 613-995-2344

Director, Corporate Services, Véronique Beaumier-Robert
Tel: 613-995-9943

Director, Information Services, Mario Giasson
Tel: 613-995-4203

Director, Conference Services, Rodrigue Hurtubise
Tel: 613-222-6411

Canadian International Trade Tribunal (CITT) / Tribunal canadien du commerce extérieur (TCCE)

Standard Life Centre, 333 Laurier Ave. West, 15th Floor, Ottawa, ON K1A 0G7
Tel: 613-990-2452; *Fax:* 613-990-2439
Toll-Free: 855-307-2488
citt-tcce@tribunal.gc.ca
www.citt-tcce.gc.ca
Other Communication: Media, Phone: 613-949-2309
The Tribunal is an independent, quasi-judicial body, which carries out both judicial & advisory functions relating to trade remedies for the North American Free Trade Agreement. In this capacity, the Tribunal succeeds the Procurement Review Board of Canada. Reports to government through the Minister of Finance.

Chair, Jean Bédard, LL.L., LL.M., M.B.A.
Tel: 613-993-7015

Member, Peter Burn

Member, Serge Fréchette

Member, Ann Penner

Canadian Judicial Council / Conseil canadien de la magistrature

Ottawa, ON K1A 0W8
Tel: 613-288-1566; *Fax:* 613-288-1575
info@cjc-ccm.gc.ca
www.cjc-ccm.gc.ca
The members of the Council include the Chief Justice of Canada (who acts as Chair), the Chief Justices & Associate Chief Justices of each Superior Court or Branch or Division thereof, the senior judges of the Supreme Court of the Yukon Territory, the Supreme Court of the Northwest Territories & the Nunavut Court of Justice, the Chief Judge & Associate Chief Judge of the Tax Court of Canada, & the Chief Justice of the Court Martial Court of Canada.

Executive Director & General Counsel, Norman Sabourin
Tel: 613-288-1566 ext: 301

Senior Counsel, Odette Lalumiere
Tel: 613-288-1566 ext: 312

Director, Committees Management, Josée Desjardins
Tel: 613-288-1566 ext: 309

Director, Communications & Registry Services, Johanna
Laporte
Tel: 613-288-1566

Canadian Museum for Human Rights (CMHR) / Musée canadien des droits de la personne (MCDP)

85 Israel Asper Way, Winnipeg, MB R3C 0L5
Tel: 204-289-2000; *Fax:* 204-289-2001
Toll-Free: 877-877-6037
TTY: 204-289-2050
info@humanrights.ca
humanrights.ca
twitter.com/cmhr_news
www.facebook.com/canadianmuseumforhumanrights
www.youtube.com/user/HumanRightsMuseum

The Canadian Museum for Human Rights was established in 2008 to explore the topic of human rights with particular attention to Canada, to encourage reflection & discussion & promote respect for others. The museum officially opened in September 2014.

President & Chief Executive Officer, Isha Khan

Chief Financial Officer, Susanne Robertson
Tel: 204-289-2102
susanne.robertson@humanrights.ca

Vice-President, Visitor Experience & Engagement,
Jacques Lavergne
Tel: 204-289-2230
jacques.lavergne@humanrights.ca

Director, Exhibitions, Helen Delacretaz
Tel: 204-289-2078

Chief Human Resources Officer, Lorraine Farmer
Tel: 204-289-2022

Director, Information Systems & Project Management,
Myriam Matwiy
Tel: 204-289-2180

Corporate Secretary, Lisanne Lambert
lisanne.lambert@humanrights.ca

Canadian Museum of History (CMH) / Musée canadien de l'histoire

100, rue Laurier, Gatineau, QC K1A 0M8
Tel: 819-776-7000
Toll-Free: 800-555-5621
TTY: 819-776-7003
www.civilization.ca
twitter.com/civilization
www.facebook.com/museumofcivilization
www.youtube.com/user/CanMusCiv

The Canadian Museum of History (formerly the Museum of Civilization Corporation) was established by the Museums Act. The Crown corporation manages the Canadian Museum of History, the Canadian War Museum & the Virtual Museum of New France in its efforts to promote increased awareness & understanding of Canadian history, culture & identity.

President & Chief Executive Officer, Mark O'Neill
Tel: 819-776-7116

Chief Operating Officer & Senior Vice-President, Heather Paszkowski
Tel: 819-776-8258

Vice-President, Human Resources, Julie Sylvestre
Tel: 819-776-8268

Vice-President, Public Affairs & Marketing, Lisa Walli
Tel: 819-776-8506

Vice-President, Development, Sylvie Madely
Tel: 819-776-8363

Director, Marketing & Business Operation, Michele Canto
Tel: 819-776-7144

Director, Corporate Affairs, Patricia Lynch
Tel: 819-776-7167

Director, Research, Dean Oliver, Ph.D.
Tel: 819-776-7172

Canadian War Museum (CWM) / Musée canadien de la guerre

1 Vimy Pl., Ottawa, ON K1A 0M8
Tel: 819-776-7000
Toll-Free: 800-555-5621
TTY: 819-776-7003
www.warmuseum.ca
twitter.com/CanWarMuseum
www.facebook.com/warmuseum
www.youtube.com/user/CanWarMus

The Canadian War Museum presents Canada's military heritage from earliest times to the present.

Director General, Canadian War Museum; Vice-President, Canadian History Museum, Stephen Quick
Tel: 819-776-8523
stephen.quick@warmuseum.ca

Director, Research, Vacant
Tel: 819-776-8619

Director, Exhibitions, Creative Development & Learning, Tony Glen
Tel: 819-776-8649
tony.glen@warmuseum.ca

Director, Collections, James Whitham
Tel: 819-776-8646
james.whitham@warmuseum.ca

Canadian Museum of Nature (CMN) / Musée Canadien de la Nature (MCN)

240 McLeod St., PO Box 3443 Stn. D, Ottawa, ON K1P 6P4
Tel: 613-566-4700; *Fax:* 613-364-4021
Toll-Free: 800-263-4433
TTY: 613-566-4770
www.nature.ca
Other Communication: Toll-Free TTY: 866-600-8801
twitter.com/MuseumofNature
www.facebook.com/canadianmuseumofnature
www.youtube.com/user/canadanaturemuseum

A diverse natural history collection encompassing some 10 million specimens, & thousands of species. Provides access to specimens & data for research & access to knowledge on biodiversity, biosystematics & the environment. Carries out research on management & care of collections & employs a staff of researchers working on national & international projects. Through public programs, CMN communicates knowledge & promotes understanding of science & nature to diverse audiences. It includes permanent, special & travelling exhibits, curriculum-based & interpretive programs, & print, electronic, audiovisual & multimedia publications.

President & Chief Executive Officer, Meg Beckel
Tel: 613-566-4733; *Fax:* 613-364-4020

Chief Information Officer & Vice-President, Corporate Services, Charles Bloom
Tel: 613-566-4214

Vice-President, Experience & Engagement, Ailsa Barry
Tel: 613-566-4744; *Fax:* 613-566-4759
Other Communications: Alt. Phone: 613-566-4286

Vice-President, Research & Collections, Jeffrey Saarela
Tel: 613-364-4080

Canadian Northern Economic Development Agency (CanNor) / Agence canadienne de développement économique du Nord

Ottawa, ON K1A 0H4
Toll-Free: 855-897-2667
CanNor.InfoNorth.InfoNord.CanNor@canada.ca
www.cannor.gc.ca

CanNor was established in 2009 to promote growth & development in Northern Canada through economic development programs & collaboration between northern & southern partnerships. The agency also coordinates the activities of other federal departments in relation to northern project development through the Northern Projects Management Office (NPMO). Programs offered by the agency include: Strategic Investments in Northern Economic Development (SINED); Aboriginal Economic Development (AED); Northern Adult Basic Education Program (NABEP); Community Infrastructure Improvement Fund (CIIF); & promotion of official language minority communities.

Minister Responsible; Minister, Economic Development, Hon. Dan Vandal, P.C.

President, Paula Isaak
Tel: 613-947-0221; *Fax:* 613-947-0242

Northern Projects Management Office (NPMO) / Bureau de gestion des projets nordiques

Nova Plaza, 5019 - 52nd St., 3rd Fl., PO Box 1500 Yellowknife, NT X1A 2R3
Tel: 867-920-6766

The NMPO provides the following services: issues management & advice for industry & communities; coordinating the participation of federal departments in the regulatory review process; providing transparency through publicly tracking the progress of projects.

Director General, Lisa Dyer
Tel: 867-669-2593; *Fax:* 867-766-8401

Canadian Nuclear Safety Commission (CNSC) / Commission canadienne de sûreté nucléaire (CCSN)

280 Slater St., PO Box 1046 Stn. B, Ottawa, ON K1P 5S9
Tel: 613-995-5894; *Fax:* 613-995-5086
Toll-Free: 800-668-5284
cnsc.information.ccsn@canada.ca
www.nuclearsafety.gc.ca
Other Communication: Alt. Emails:
cnsc.interventions.ccsn@cnsc-ccsn.gc.ca (Hearings & Meetings); cnsc.pfp.ccsn@cnsc-ccsn.gc.ca (Participant Funding Program)
www.facebook.com/CanadianNuclearSafetyCommission
www.youtube.com/user/cnscccsn

Federal agency which regulates activities involving nuclear energy & prescribed substances in the interests of health & safety for workers & the public. Areas covered under the AECB's licensing process include the nuclear fuel cycle (from mining to waste disposal), heavy water plants, research reactors & accelerators, & radioisotopes. Operations ensure that the use of nuclear energy in Canada does not pose undue risk to health, safety, security & the environment. The Research & Support Program (RSP) augments & extends the AECB's regulatory program beyond the capability of in-house resources. It produces pertinent & independent information that will assist the Board & its staff in making sound, timely & credible decisions on regulating nuclear facilities & materials. The nine sectors of the program include: safety of nuclear facilities; radioactive waste management; health physics; physical security; development of regulatory processes; & social services

President & CEO, Rumina Velshi
Tel: 613-992-8828

Executive Vice-President & Chief Regulatory Operations Officer, Ramzi Jammal
Tel: 613-947-8899
Other Communications: Executive Assistant, Phone: 613-947-8896

Chief Financial Officer & Vice-President, Corporate Services Branch, Stéphane Cyr
Tel: 613-995-0104

Vice-President, Regulatory Affairs & Chief Communications Officer, Jason K. Cameron
Tel: 613-947-3773

Vice-President, Technical Support Branch & Chief Science Officer, Peter H. Elder
Tel: 613-947-8931

Director General, Security & Safeguards, Kathleen Heppell-Masys
Tel: 613-992-2943

Director General, Environmental & Radiation Protection & Assessment, Haidy Tadros
Tel: 613-943-3352

Director General, Assessment & Analysis, David Newland
Tel: 613-995-2031

Director General, Safety Management, Greg Lamarre
Tel: 613-991-3220

Canadian Race Relations Foundation (CRRF) / Fondation canadienne des relations raciales (TCRR)

#225, 6 Garamond Ct., Toronto, ON M3C 1Z5
Tel: 416-441-1900; *Fax:* 416-441-2752
Toll-Free: 888-240-4936
info@crrf-fcrr.ca
www.crr.ca
Other Communication: Toll-Free Fax: 888-399-0333
twitter.com/CRRF
www.facebook.com/FCRRCRRF
www.linkedin.com/company/the-canadian-race-relations-foundati on

Crown corporation operating at arms length from the federal government from which it receives no funding. The Foundation is committed to building a national framework for the fight against racism in Canadian society.

Minister Responsible; Minister, Canadian Heritage, Vacant

Chair, Albert C. Lo

Executive Director, Lilian Ma
Tel: 416-441-1900 ext: 202

Director, Finance & Administration, Arsalan Tavassoli
Tel: 416-441-1900 ext: 203

Canadian Radio-Television & Telecommunications Commission (CRTC) / Conseil de la radiodiffusion et des télécommunications Canadiennes

Central Building, 1, promenade du Portage, Les Terrasses de la Chaudière, Gatineau, QC J8X 4B1
Tel: 819-997-0313; *Fax:* 819-994-0218
Toll-Free: 877-249-2782
TTY: 819-994-0423
www.crtc.gc.ca
Other Communication: Toll-Free TTY: 877-909-2782
Mailing Address: CRTC
Ottawa, ON K1A ON2
twitter.com/CRTCeng
www.youtube.com/user/CRTCgcca

The CRTC is vested with the authority to regulate & supervise all aspects of the Canadian broadcasting system, as well as to regulate telecommunications common carriers & service providers that fall under federal jurisdiction. Reports to Parliament through the Minister of Canadian Heritage.

Chair & CEO, Ian Scott
Tel: 819-997-3430

Vice-Chair, Telecommunications, Christianne Laizner
Tel: 819-997-4645

Vice-Chair, Broadcasting, Caroline J. Simard
Tel: 819-994-0870

Commissioner, Quebec, Alicia Barin
Tel: 817-664-6859

Commissioner, Atlantic/Nunavut Regions, Ellen Desmond
Tel: 819-000-0000

Commissioner, Manitoba/Saskatchewan Regions, Joanne Levy
Tel: 306-780-3423

Commissioner, Ontario Region, Monique Lafontaine

Commissioner, British Columbia/Yukon Regions, Stephen B. Simpson
Tel: 604-666-2914

Commissioner, Alberta/Northwest Territories Regions, Nirmala Naidoo
Tel: 819-000-0000

Secretary General, Claude Doucet
Tel: 819-953-5889

Executive Director, Broadcasting, Scott Shortliffe
Tel: 819-997-4534

Executive Director, Telecommunications, Chris Seidl
Tel: 819-956-4480; *Fax:* 819-997-4550

Chief Compliance & Enforcement Officer, Steven Harroun
Tel: 819-953-4719

Canadian Security Intelligence Service (CSIS) / Service canadien du renseignement de sécurité

PO Box 9732 Stn. T, Ottawa, ON K1G 4G4
Tel: 613-993-9620; *Fax:* 613-231-0612
TTY: 613-991-9228
www.csis.gc.ca
twitter.com/csiscanada

CSIS is part of Canada's national security establishment. It investigates threats, analyzes information & produces intelligence in order to advise the government on protecting the country & its citizens.

Director, David Vigneault

Canadian Space Agency (CSA) / Agence spatiale canadienne (ASC)

John H. Chapman Space Centre, 6767, rte de l'Aéroport, Saint-Hubert, QC J3Y 8Y9
Tel: 450-926-4800; *Fax:* 450-926-4352
asc.info.csa@canada.ca
www.asc-csa.gc.ca
twitter.com/csa_asc
www.facebook.com/CanadianSpaceAgency
www.youtube.com/user/Canadianspaceagency

Established in 1989, & responsible for coordinating all civil, space-related policies & programs on behalf of the Government of Canada. Scientific research & industrial development in earth observation, space science & exploration, satellite communications, & space awareness & learning. RADARSAT International (RSI) develops products & services demanded by world markets. RADARSAT-1, the first Canadian commercial Earth Observation (EO) satellite, is uniquely capable of responding to disasters around the world. The system can support the operational mapping & monitoring of natural disasters in four critical ways: prevention, preparedness, emergency response & recovery. Moreover, the development of the high performance RADARSAT-2, launched in 2007, further enhances Canada's competitive position. RADARSAT-2 offers improved quality of data images to meet the growing world demand of Earth observation information. The SCISAT satellite is used in ozone depletion research. The RADARSAT Constellation launched in June 2019, with a mission to provide total coverage of Canada's land & oceans via a three-satellite configuration.

Minister, Innovation, Science & Industry, Hon. François-Philippe Champagne, P.C.
Tel: 613-995-4895; *Fax:* 613-996-6883
Francois-Philippe.Champagne@parl.gc.ca

President & CEO, Lisa Campbell

Vice-President, Science & Technology, Luc Brûlé
Tel: 450-926-4750; *Fax:* 450-926-4315

Vice-President, Space Program Policy, Sonia David
Tel: 819-420-9725

Chief of Staff, Nathalie Verville
Tel: 450-926-6501

Executive Director & General Counsel, Legal Services, Christine Calve
Tel: 450-926-4335

Executive Director, Corporate Services & Human Resources, Yves Saulnier
Tel: 450-926-4667; *Fax:* 450-926-4612

Canadian Transportation Agency (CTA) / Office des transports du Canada (OTC)

Les Terrasses de la Chaudière, 15, rue Eddy, Gatineau, QC J8X 4B3
Fax: 819-997-6727
Toll-Free: 888-222-2592
TTY: 800-669-5575
info@otc-cta.gc.ca
www.cta-otc.gc.ca
twitter.com/CTA_gc

Responsible for the economic regulation of transportation in Canada. The agency requires that all applications for new railway lines, modifications to existing railway lines, disputed railway crossings at grade, grade separation, utility crossings & private crossings be accompanied by an environment impact assessment

Chair & Chief Executive Officer, Scott Streiner
Tel: 819-953-7600; *Fax:* 819-953-9979

Vice-Chair, Liz Barker
Tel: 819-997-9233

Director General, Ghislain Blanchard
Tel: 613-301-9261; *Fax:* 819-953-5564
ghislain.blanchard@otc-cta.gc.ca

Chief Dispute Resolution Officer, Douglas Smith
Tel: 819-953-5074; *Fax:* 819-953-5562
Douglas.Smith@otc-cta.gc.ca

Director, Workplace & Workforce, Nadine Brisson
Tel: 613-793-4751
Nadine.Brisson@otc-cta.gc.ca

Senior Director, Air Determinations, Carole Girard

Tel: 819-997-8761; *Fax:* 819-953-8957
carole.girard@otc-cta.gc.ca

Chief Corporate Officer, Internal Services Branch, Mireille Drouin
Tel: 873-353-4988

Director, Communications, Alexandre Robertson
Tel: 819-953-8926; *Fax:* 819-953-8353
Alexandre.Robertson@otc-cta.gc.ca

Chief Strategy Officer, Analysis & Outreach Branch, Marcia Jones
Tel: 613-864-9918

Office of the Conflict of Interest & Ethics Commissioner / Commissariat aux conflits d'intérêts et à l'éthique

Commissioner's Office, 66 Slater St., 22nd Fl., PO Box 16 Ottawa, ON K1A 0A6
Tel: 613-995-0721; *Fax:* 613-995-7308
ciec-ccie@parl.gc.ca
www.ciec-ccie.gc.ca
twitter.com/CIEC_CCIE

The Conflict of Interest & Ethics Commissioner is an independent Officer of Parliament. Responsibilities include assisting elected & appointed officials to avoid conflicts between their private interests & public duties.

Conflict of Interest & Ethics Commissioner, Mario Dion
Tel: 613-995-0721; *Fax:* 613-995-7308

Acting Director, Communications, Outreach & Planning, Margot Booth
Tel: 613-996-4880; *Fax:* 613-995-7308

Senior General Counsel, Investigations & Legal Services, Matine Richard
Tel: 613-996-6028; *Fax:* 613-995-7308

Copyright Board of Canada / Commission du droit d'auteur du Canada

#800, 56 Sparks St., Ottawa, ON K1A 0C9
Tel: 613-952-8621; *Fax:* 613-952-8630
secretariat@cb-cda.gc.ca
www.cb-cda.gc.ca

The Board is an economic regulatory body empowered to establish, either mandatorily or at the request of an interested party, the royalties to be paid for the use of copyrighted works, when the administration of such copyright is entrusted to a collective-administration society. The Board also has the right to supervise agreements between users & licensing bodies & issues licences when the copyright owner cannot be located.

Chair, Justice Robert A. Blair

Vice-Chair & Chief Executive Officer, Nathalie Théberge

Secretary General, Gilles McDougall
Tel: 613-952-8624
gilles.mcdougall@cb-cda.gc.ca

General Counsel, Sylvain Audet
Tel: 613-960-8356
sylvain.audet@cb-cda.gc.ca

Director, Research & Analysis, Raphael Solomon
Tel: 613-946-4456
raphael.solomon@cb-cda.gc.ca

Office of the Correctional Investigator / L'Enquêteur correctionnel Canada

PO Box 3421 Stn. D, Ottawa, ON K1P 6L4
Fax: 613-990-9091
Toll-Free: 877-885-8848
org@oci-bec.gc.ca
www.oci-bec.gc.ca

Investigates complaints from inmates in Canadian institutions. Reports on problems inmates have that fall within the responsibility of the Department of Public Safety & Emergency Preparedness & meet certain conditions.

Correctional Investigator of Canada; Executive Director & General Counsel, Ivan Zinger
Tel: 613-990-2690

Chief Financial Officer; Director, Corporate Services & Planning, Nahie Bassett
Tel: 343-550-4480

Director, Policy & Research, David Hooey
Tel: 613-990-2693; *Fax:* 613-990-0563

Director of Investigations, Frédéric Héran
Tel: 613-716-2884

Director, Investigations, Derek Janhevich
Tel: 613-550-2572

Correctional Service Canada (CSC) / Service correctionnel Canada

340 Laurier Ave. West, Ottawa, ON K1A 0P9
Tel: 613-992-5891; *Fax:* 613-943-1630
www.csc-scc.gc.ca
twitter.com/csc_scc_en
www.youtube.com/user/CSCsccEN
An agency within Public Safety & Emergency Preparedness Canada responsible for the administration of sentences with respect to convicted offenders sentenced to two or more years as decided by the federal courts, & certain provincial inmates who have been transferred to a federal institution. CSC is also responsible for the supervision of inmates who have been granted conditional release by the authority of the National Parole Board.

Minister, Public Safety & Emergency Preparedness, Hon. Marco Mendicino, P.C.

Commissioner, Anne Kelly
Tel: 613-995-5781; *Fax:* 613-943-1630

Senior Deputy Commissioner, Alain Tousignant
Tel: 613-947-0643

Director General, Aboriginal Initiatives Directorate, Lisa Allgaier
Tel: 613-995-5465; *Fax:* 613-943-0493

Acting Director General, Executive Secretariat, Linda T. Roy
Tel: 613-947-1379; *Fax:* 613-943-1630

Director General & Chief Information Officer, Information Management Services, Dung-Chi Tran
Tel: 613-995-3912; *Fax:* 613-995-7647

Chief Audit Executive, Internal Audit, Sylvie Soucy
Tel: 613-943-0330; *Fax:* 613-995-0026

Executive Director & General Counsel, Legal Services, Barbara Massey
Tel: 613-992-9009; *Fax:* 613-995-9971

Communications & Engagement / Communications et Engagement
Assistant Commissioner, Scott Harris
Tel: 613-545-8211
Associate Assistant Commissioner, Public Affairs, Amy Jarrette
Tel: 613-996-5476

Corporate Services / Services corporatifs
Assistant Commissioner, Corporate Services & Chief Financial Officer, Liette Dumas-Sluyter
Tel: 613-995-4242; *Fax:* 613-992-8443
Director General & Deputy Chief Financial Officer, Resource Management Branch, Denis Bombardier
Tel: 613-992-8432
Director General, Technical Services, Ghislain Sauvé
Tel: 613-943-0976; *Fax:* 613-996-9421
Senior Director, Facilities, Philippe Poirier
Tel: 613-995-2015; *Fax:* 613-996-9421

Correctional Operations & Programs / Opérations et programmes correctionnels
Assistant Commissioner, Fraser Macaulay
Tel: 613-943-0499; *Fax:* 613-996-6174
Chief Executive Officer, CORCAN, Lynn Garrow
Tel: 613-996-4530; *Fax:* 613-996-9864
www.csc-scc.gc.ca/corcan
Director General, Offender Programs & Reintegration, Michael Bettmann
Tel: 613-995-6547; *Fax:* 613-996-0428
Director General, Community Reintegration Branch, Carmen Long
Tel: 613-943-9256
Associate Director General, Chaplaincy, Bill Rasmus
Tel: 613-943-3145; *Fax:* 613-952-8464

Health Services / Services de santé
Assistant Commissioner, Jenifer Wheatley
Tel: 613-995-8023; *Fax:* 613-992-9995

Director General, Clinical Services & Public Health, Henry de Souza
Tel: 613-947-1013; *Fax:* 613-995-6277
Director General, Mental Health, Dr. Manjeet Sethi
Tel: 613-992-8788; *Fax:* 613-995-6277
National Coordinator, Institutional Mental Health Initiatives, Natalie Gabora-Roth
Tel: 613-316-7285; *Fax:* 613-995-6277

Human Resource Management / Gestion des ressources humaines
Assistant Commissioner, Nick Fabiano
Tel: 613-995-8899
Director General, Learning & Development, Bev Arseneault
Tel: 613-995-7807
Senior Director, Classification, Resourcing & Operations, Marie-Pierre Jackson
Tel: 613-996-1371

Policy / Politiques
Assistant Commissioner, Larry Motiuk
Tel: 613-996-2180; *Fax:* 613-995-3606
Director General, Rights, Redress & Resolution, Julie Keravel
Tel: 613-992-9281; *Fax:* 613-943-4391
Acting Director General, Values, Integrity & Conflict Management, Jacques Vanasse
Tel: 613-943-0511; *Fax:* 613-996-8397
Director, Evaluation, Brigitte de Blois
Tel: 613-2827; *Fax:* 613-996-3287
Senior Director, Research NHQ, Kelly Taylor
Tel: 613-900-0000; *Fax:* 613-941-8477

Women Offender Sector / Secteur des délinquantes
Deputy Commissioner for Women, Jennifer Wheatley
Tel: 613-992-6067; *Fax:* 613-992-4692
Director General, Interventions, Kelly Hartle
Tel: 613-947-0238; *Fax:* 613-992-4692

Crown-Indigenous Relations & Northern Affairs (CIRNAC) / Relations Couronne-Autochtones et affaires du Nord (RCAANC)

Public Enquiries Contact Centre, 10, rue Wellington, Gatineau, QC K1A 0H4
Fax: 866-817-3977
Toll-Free: 800-567-9604
TTY: 866-553-0554
aadnc.infopubs.aandc@canada.ca
www.canada.ca/en/crown-indigenous-relations-northern-affairs.html
Other Communication: Media relations, Email:
rcaanc.media.cirnac@canada.ca
twitter.com/gcindigenous
www.facebook.com/gcindigenous
instagram.com/gcindigenous
Prime Minister Trudeau announced the dissolution of Indigenous & Northern Affairs Canada in August 2017, & the creation of two new departments: Indigenous Services Canada & Crown-Indigenous Relations & Northern Affairs Canada. Crown-Indigenous Relations & Northern Affairs Canada's mandate involves the renewal of the nation-to-nation, Inuit-Crown, & government-to-government relationship between Canada and Indigenous Peoples. The Ministry will accelerate progress towards self-determinization & develop a Recognition & Implementation of Indigenous Rights Framework. Its priorities include modernizing institutional structures & governance for Indigenous peoples & unlocking social, economic & community potential in Canada's North.

Minister, Crown-Indigenous Relations, Hon. Marc Miller, P.C.

Minister, Northern Affairs, Hon. Dan Vandal, P.C.
Tel: 613-995-0579; *Fax:* 613-996-7571
Dan.Vandal@parl.gc.ca

Director, Communications & Issues Management, James Fitzmorris
Tel: 819-997-0002

Director, Parliamentary Affairs, Vincent Haraldsen
Tel: 819-997-0002

Chief of Staff, Sarah Welch
Tel: 819-997-0002

Associated Agencies, Boards & Commissions:
• Beverly & Qamanirjuaq Caribou Management Board
Secretariat
PO Box 629
Stonewall, MB R0C 2Z0
www.arctic-caribou.com

Group of hunters, biologists & wildlife managers working together to conserve Canada's vast Beverly & Qamanirjuaq caribou herds for the welfare of traditional caribou-using communities in northern Manitoba, Saskatchewan, Northwest Territories & Nunavut.

• First Nations Tax Commission (FNTC) / Commission de la fiscalité des premières nations (CFPN)
Head Office
#321, 345 Chief Alex Thomas Way
Kamloops, BC V2H 1H1
Tel: 250-828-9857; *Fax:* 250-828-9858
Toll-free: 855-682-3682
mail@fntc.ca
www.fntc.ca
The FNTC operates in the larger context of First Nation issues which goes beyond property tax. The FNTC is concerned with reducing the barriers to economic development on First Nation lands, increasing investor certainty, and enabling First Nations to be part of their regional economies. The FNTC is working to fill the institutional vacuum that has prevented First Nations from participating in the market economy and creating a national regulatory framework for First Nation tax systems that meets or beats the standards of provinces.

• Indian Oil & Gas Canada (IOGC) / Pétrole et gaz des Indiens du Canada
#100, 9911 Chiila Blvd.
Tsuu T'ina (Sarcee), AB T2W 6H6
Tel: 403-292-5625; *Fax:* 403-292-5618
aandc.contactiogc.aandc@canada.ca
www.pgic-iogc.gc.ca
Indian Oil & Gas Canada (IOGC) is an organization committed to managing and regulating oil and gas resources on First Nation reserve lands. It is a special operating agency within Indigenous & Northern Affairs.

• Mackenzie Valley Environmental Impact Review Board
200 Scotia Centre
#5102, 50th Ave.
PO Box 938
Yellowknife, NT X1A 2N7
Tel: 867-766-7050; *Fax:* 867-766-7074
Toll-free: 866-912-3472
www.reviewboard.ca
In 1998, the Mackenzie Valley Environmental Impact Review Board was established under the Mackenzie Valley Resources Management Act. The co-management Review Board is made up of members nominated by First Nations & federal & territorial governments. Board members represent the interests of all residents of the Mackenzie Valley.

• Nunavut Impact Review Board
29 Mitik St.
PO Box 1360
Cambridge Bay, NU X0B 0C0
Fax: 867-983-2594
Toll-free: 866-233-3033
info@nirb.ca
www.nirb.ca
Other Communication: Alt. Fax: 867-983-2574
An institution of the government established under the Nunavut Land Claims Agreement to conduct environmental & socio-economic assessments. The NIRB process involves participation by members of the community, Inuit organizations, the Government of Nunavut & the Government of Canada through the entire environmental assessment. Under the Canadian Environmental Assessment Act, the federal departments with specific responsibilities for the project must ensure that the requirements of the Act are met throughout the assessment process. This open process facilitates sound environmental stewardship & promotes economic & sustainable development.

• Nunavut Planning Commission
PO Box 2101
Cambridge Bay, NU X0B 0C0
www.nunavut.ca
Other Communication: Iqaluit, Phone: 867-979-3444; Arviat, Phone: 867-857-2242; Cambridge Bay, Phone: 867-983-4625
Responsible for land use planning & environmental reporting & management in Nunavut.

• Nunavut Water Board
PO Box 119
Gjoa Haven, NU X0B 1J0
Tel: 867-360-6338
www.nwb-oen.org
Responsible for the regulation, use & management of water in the Nunavut Settlement Area.

• **Polar Knowledge Canada (POLAR) / Savoir polaire Canada (POLAIRE)**
See Entry Name Index for detailed listing.

• **Porcupine Caribou Management Board**
PO Box 31723
Whitehorse, YT Y1A 6L3
Tel: 867-633-4780; *Fax:* 867-393-3904
www.pcmb.ca
Works to manage the Porcupine Caribou herd, one of the largest herds of migratory caribou in North America, & to protect & maintain its habitat.

• **Truth & Reconciliation Commission of Canada**
c/o National Centre for Truth & Reconciliation
Chancellor's Hall, 177 Dysart Rd.
Winnipeg, MB R3T 2N2
Tel: 204-474-6069
Toll-free: 855-415-4534
nctr@umanitoba.ca
nctr.ca
The Commission was established as part of the Indian Residential Schools Settlement Agreement, to learn the truth about what happened in Canada's residential schools & report those findings to the Canadian public.
As of December 18, 2015, the Commission completed its mandate, & its work transferred to the National Centre for Truth & Reconciliation at the University of Manitoba.

Deputy Minister's Office / Bureau de sous-ministre
Deputy Minister, Hélène Laurendeau
Tel: 819-997-0133
Associate Deputy Minister, Diane Lafleur
Tel: 819-934-0583

Audit & Evaluation Sector / Secteur de la vérification et de l'évaluation
Chief Audit & Evaluation Executive, David Peckham
Tel: 819-953-2614
Senior Director, Evaluation, Peformance Measurement & Review Branch, Stephanie Barozzi
Tel: 819-994-1571
Senior Director, Audit & Assurance Services, Audrey Furey
Tel: 819-994-1259
Director, Risk Management, Phil Dupuis
Tel: 819-997-8147
Director, People, Jean-Marc Lafreniere
Tel: 819-994-4837

Communications Branch / Direction général des communications
Director General, Peter Edwards
Tel: 819-997-9595
Senior Director, Strategic Communications, Robert Makichuk
Tel: 819-997-0025
Director, Digital Communications, Guy Levac
Tel: 819-994-3248
Director, Corporate Communications, Pamela Monfils
Tel: 613-325-3907

Human Resources & Workplace Services / Services des ressources humaines et du milieu de travail
Director General, Line Lamothe
Tel: 819-994-7398
Senior Director, HR Services Delivery & Data, Daniel Archambault
Tel: 819-994-7402
Senior Director, Strategic HR Management & Executive Group, Geoff Zerr
Tel: 819-997-9646
Director, Learning & Well-Being, Christine Duong
Tel: 819-997-8159
Director, Security & Accomodation, Rémy Payette
Tel: 819-997-3036
Director, Policy & Human Resources Programs, Karine Renoux
Tel: 819-953-0805
Director, Centre for Integrity, Values & Conflict Resolution, John Tremble
Tel: 819-994-7641

Indian Residential School Adjudication Secretariat / Secrétariat de l'arbitrade des pensionnats indiens
Executive Director, Shelley Trevethan
Tel: 819-934-0318
Chief Adjudicator, Daniel Shapiro
Director, Strategic Planning & Performance Management, Martine Gravelle
Tel: 819-934-0106
Acting Director, Client Services Management, Catherine Henderson
Tel: 819-934-1749
Acting Director, Operations, Shelley McAmmond
Tel: 306-209-1418
Acting Manager, Hearing Management, Suzanne Huggins
Tel: 306-501-0648

Acting Manager, Post Hearing Resolution, Dan Marchment
Tel: 306-790-4799
Head, Case Management Operations - Notice Program, Darcy Brierley
Tel: 306-501-6981

Legal Services / Service juridiques
Senior General Counsel, Marie Bourry
Tel: 819-994-6558
Director & General Counsel, Negotiations & Northern Affairs, Ronald Burnett
Tel: 819-953-0170
Director & General Counsel, Specific Claims, Duaine Simms
Tel: 819-934-9118
Director & General Counsel, Operations & Programs, Michelle Smith
Tel: 819-953-2291
Senior Counsel, First Nations Inuit Health, Bernard M. Hanssens
Tel: 613-952-4160

Indian Oil & Gas Canada (IOGC) / Pétrolières et gazières des Premières Nations (PGIC)
#100, 9911 Chiila Blvd., Tsuu T'ina, AB T2W 6H6
Tel: 403-292-5625; *Fax:* 403-292-5618
aandc.contactiogc.aandc@canada.ca
www.pgic-iogc.gc.ca/eng/1100110010002/1100110010005
Indian Oil & Gas Canada (IOGC) is an organization that manages & regulates oil & gas resources on First Nations reserve lands. It is an operating agency within Crown-Indigenous Relations & Northern Affairs Canada (CIRNAC). IOGC operates pursuant to the Indian Oil and Gas Act & Indian Oil and Gas Regulations, 1995.
Executive Director & Chief Financial Officer, Strater Crowfoot
Tel: 403-292-5628
Director, Strategic Projects, Bill Currie
Tel: 403-813-0467
Acting Manager, Communications, Shirley Conrad
Tel: 403-292-5872

Defence Construction Canada (DCC) / Construction de Défense Canada (CDC)

Constitution Square, 350 Albert St., 19th Fl., Ottawa, ON K1A 0K3
Tel: 613-998-9548; *Fax:* 613-998-1061
Toll-Free: 800-514-3555
info@dcc-cdc.gc.ca
www.dcc-cdc.gc.ca
twitter.com/dcc_cdc
www.facebook.com/dcc.cdc
www.linkedin.com/company/693781
www.youtube.com/user/DCCCommunications
Federal government crown corporation responsible for the contracting & supervising of major military construction & maintenance projects required by National Defence. Services include construction, project management, environmental services & operational support services. DCC provides environmental science & environmental engineering services to help fulfill the Department of National Defence's sustainable development strategy, including: environmental impact & site assessment; environmental site remediation; environmental support for project & program management; sustainable development strategy support services; policy, compliance & advisory services; site decommissioning services; facility deconstruction & demolition; firing range decommissioning; waste management auditing & planning; waste reduction planning; landfill inventories & investigations; hazardous waste management; UST removals; training & education; ISO 14000 environmental management systems; environmental CIS applications; environmental checklists for property transactions & decommissioning; environmental monitoring & compliance auditing; designated substances inventories; environmental disclosures reporting; treatment & disposal facilities conceptual designs; environmental contrac ting & contract management; energy conservation. Projects include: the DEW (Distant Early Warning) Line cleanup; Hanger 1 at 8 Wing Trenton; P3 development of the new Communications Security Establishment Canada facility; creation of the Building Information Modelling tool; removal of unexploded ordinance; overhaul of the Fleet Maintenance Facility (FMF) Cape Breton Shop at CFB Esquimalt; & Goose Bay Remediation Project.

President & Chief Executive Officer, Derrick Cheung
Tel: 613-998-9541; *Fax:* 613-998-1218

Chief Financial Officer & Vice-President, Finance & Human Resources, Juliet Woodfield
Tel: 613-998-0052

Vice-President, Operations - Sevice Delivery & Corporate Planning, Karl McQuillan
Tel: 613-949-7721

Vice-President, Operations - Procurement, Mélinda

Nycholat
Tel: 613-991-9313; *Fax:* 613-991-9953

Vice-President, Operations - Business Management, Ross Welsman
Tel: 613-990-2869; *Fax:* 613-998-9547

Director, Ontario Region, John Graham, P.Eng., PMP
Tel: 613-384-1256 ext: 230; *Fax:* 613-384-7747
Howard Maitland Building
#205, 780 Midpark Dr.
Kingston, ON K7M 7P6

Director, Western Region, Grant Sayers
Tel: 514-283-8071 ext: 2729; *Fax:* 780-495-5959
#210, 13220 St. Albert Trail
Edmonton, AB T5L 4W1

Director, Québec Region, Nicolas Forget
Tel: 514-283-8071 ext: 8165
#224, 2030, boul Pie-IX
Montréal, QC H1V 2C8

Director, Atlantic Region, George Theoharopoulos, P.Eng.
Tel: 902-426-4040; *Fax:* 902-426-9655
#202, 1597 Bedford Hwy.
Bedford, NS B4A 1E7

Regional Director, National Capital Region, Elizabeth Mah
Tel: 613-949-7718; *Fax:* 613-998-9547
#202, 1597 Bedford Hwy.
Bedford, NS B4A 1E7

Defence Research & Development Canada / Recherche et développement pour la défense Canada

101 Colonel By Dr., Ottawa, ON K1A 0K2
Tel: 613-995-2534
Toll-Free: 888-995-2534
TTY: 800-467-9877
information@forces.gc.ca
www.drdc-rddc.gc.ca
Other Communication: mlo-blm@forces.gc.ca
Provides research & development both nationally & internationally by providing the Canadian Forces with relevant & timely technologies, while at the same time offering attractive collaborative opportunities to other government departments, the private sector, academia & international allies.

Chief Executive Officer, Isabelle Desmartis

Chief of Staff, Sophie Brisebois
Tel: 613-901-1845

Director General, Science & Technology Centre Operations, Jocelyn Tremblay
Tel: 613-992-0737

Director General, Military Personnel Research & Analysis, Susan Truscott
Tel: 613-992-6162

Destination Canada (DC)

#800, 1045 Howe St., Vancouver, BC V6Z 2A9
Tel: 604-638-8300
en.destinationcanada.com
twitter.com/DestinationCAN
www.facebook.com/ExploreCanada
www.linkedin.com/company/destination-canada
www.youtube.com/user/CTCNewsNouvellesCCT
Formerly known as the Canadian Tourism Commission, Destination Canada is a unique partnership between tourism business & associations, provincial & territorial governments, & the Government of Canada. Destination Canada's mission is to sustain a vibrant & profitable Canadian tourism industry. The agency maintains offices in the following countries: Australia, Brazil, China, France, Germany, India, Japan, Mexico, South Korean, the United Kingdom & the United States.

Chair, Ben Cowan-Dewar

President & Chief Executive Officer, Marsha Walden

Chief Financial Officer, Anwar Chaudhry

Chief Marketing Officer, Gloria Loree

Vice-President, International, Maureen Riley

Vice-President, Strategy & Stakeholder Relations, David Robinson

General Counsel & Corporate Secretary, Sarah Sidhu

Elections Canada / Élections Canada

30 Victoria St., Gatineau, ON K1A 0M6
Tel: 613-993-2975; *Fax:* 613-954-8584
Toll-Free: 800-463-6868
TTY: 800-361-8935
www.elections.ca
Other Communication: Toll-Free Fax: 888-524-1444; Toll-Free
Phone (Mexico): 001-800-514-6868
twitter.com/electionscan_e
www.facebook.com/electionscane
instagram.com/electioncan_e
The Chief Electoral Officer of Canada is responsible for the
conduct of federal elections & referendums in Canada & for
ensuring that all provisions of the Canada Elections Act are
complied with & enforced. Major activities include the
maintenance of the National Register of Electors, the production
of lists of electors, the training of returning officers, the revisions
of polling division boundaries & the acquisition of election
materials & supplies. Elections Canada is also responsible for
the compilation & publishing of statutory & statistical reports, &
the provision of advice & assistance to Parliament, as required.
The agency also implements public education & information
programs. As well, its mandate includes the registration of
political parties & third parties engaged in election advertising, &
the certification of statutory payments to be made to auditors,
political parties, & candidates under the election expenses
provisions of the Act. Following each decennial census, the
Chief Electoral Officer must calculate the number of electoral
districts to be assigned to each province according to rules
contained in s. 51 of the Constitution Act, prepare population
distribution maps for use by the ten electoral boundaires
commissions (one per province) that are directly responsible for
readjusting federal electoral boundaries & publishing their
reports.

Chief Electoral Officer & Deputy Chief Electoral Officer,
Stéphane Perrault
Tel: 819-939-2080

Chief of Staff, Office of the CEO, Karine Morin
Tel: 819-939-2127; *Fax:* 819-939-1811

Electoral Events & Innovation / Scrutins et innovation

Deputy Chief Electoral Officer, Michel Roussel
Tel: 819-939-1755
Executive Director, Voting Services Modernization (VSM),
Jacques Mailloux
Tel: 819-939-1630
Senior Director, Electoral Data Management and Readiness,
Maurice Bastarache
Tel: 819-939-1731
Senior Director, Operations & Field Governance, Dani Srour
Tel: 819-939-2208
Senior Director, Electoral Operations Planning & Administration,
Denis Bazinet
Tel: 819-939-1400
Director, National Register of Electors, Céline Desbiens
Tel: 819-939-1686
Director, Electoral Geography, Pierre Desjardins
Tel: 819-939-1734
Director, Operational Support Services, Olivier Girouard
Tel: 819-939-1600
Director, Alternative Voting Method & Operational Outreach,
Sylvie Jacmain
Tel: 819-939-1631
Director, Analysis & Quality, Daniel Larrivée
Tel: 819-939-1729
Director, Field Personnel Governance & Readiness, Paul
Legault
Tel: 819-939-1643

Internal Services / Services internes

Deputy Chief Electoral Officer, France Labine
Tel: 819-939-1466
Chief Information Officer & Chief Security Officer, Serge Caron
Tel: 819-939-1230
Chief Human Resources Officer, Vivian Cousineau
Tel: 819-939-2012
Chief, Financial Planning Advisor, Serge Gallant
Tel: 819-939-1502
Chief, Corporate Accounting & Policies, Francine Lafrance
Tel: 819-939-1498
Chief, Corporate Financial Planning & Costing, Luiz Perri
Tel: 819-939-1505
Chief, Financial Reporting & Systems, Serge Sabourin
Tel: 819-939-1482
Director, IT Infrastructure Operations, Craig Becker
Tel: 819-934-1518

Director, Project Portfolio Management, Salil Dhingra
Tel: 819-939-2399
Director, Policy & Research, Alain Pelletier
Tel: 819-939-1912

Regulatory & Public Affairs / Affaires régulatoires et publiques

Executive Director, Policy & Public Affairs, Susan Torosian
Tel: 819-939-1856
Senior Director & General Counsel, Legal Services, Anne
Lawson
Tel: 819-939-2088
Senior Director, Electoral Integrity, Josée Villeneuve
Tel: 819-939-2699
Director, Political Financing & Audit, François LeBlanc
Tel: 819-939-1943
Director, Regulatory Affairs & Systems, Jeff Merrett
Tel: 819-939-2044

Employment & Social Development Canada / Emploi et Développement social Canada

140, promenade du Portage, Gatineau, QC K1A 0J9
www.canada.ca/en/employment-social-development.html
Other Communication: Media enquiries: 819-994-5559
twitter.com/socdevsoc
www.facebook.com/socialdevelopmentcanada
www.linkedin.com/company/247896
instagram.com/esdc.edsc
In Nov. 2015, Prime Minister Trudeau created two new portfolios
to fall under Employment & Social Development Canada:
Families, Children & Social Development, & Employment,
Workforce Development & Labour.
The department works to build a competitive country & to
support Canadians in making choices to live productively. The
following are key responsibilities of the federal department:
developing policies to assist Canadians to use their talents, skills
& resources to participate in learning, work, & their community;
creating programs to support initiative to help citizens in life
transitions; improving outcomes for people through services
offered by Service Canada & other partners; & establishing a
healthy work environment.

**Minister, Employment, Workforce Development &
Disability Inclusion,** Hon. Carla Qualtrough, P.C.
Tel: 613-992-2957; *Fax:* 613-992-3589
Carla.Qualtrough@parl.gc.ca

Minister, Families, Children & Social Development, Hon.
Karina Gould, P.C

Minister, Labour, Hon. Seamus O'Regan, P.C.

Minister, Seniors, Hon. Kamal Khera, P.C.

Associated Agencies, Boards & Commissions:

**• Canada Employment Insurance Commission (CEIC) /
Commission de l'assurance-emploi du Canada (CAEC)**
140, Promenade du Portage, Phase IV
Gatineau, QC K1A 0J9
Toll-free: 800-206-7218
www.esdc.gc.ca/en/ei/commission.page
Manages the Employment Insurance Program.

**• Canada Industrial Relations Board / Conseil canadien des
relations industrielles**
See Entry Name Index for detailed listing.

**• Canadian Centre for Occupational Health & Safety / Centre
canadien d'hygiène et de sécurité au travail**
See Entry Name Index for detailed listing.

**• Canadian Council of Directors of Apprenticeship (CCDA) /
Conseil canadien des directeurs de l'apprentissage**
140 Promenade du Portage, 6th Fl., Phase IV
Gatineau, QC K1A 0J9
Fax: 819-994-0202
Toll-free: 877-599-6933
TTY: 800-926-9105
redseal-sceaurouge@hrsdc-rhdcc.gc.ca
www.red-seal.ca
A national body responsible for the certification of skilled
workers, in the regulated trade, under the Interprovincial
Standards (Red Seal) Program. This program is designed to
facilitate the mobility of workers employed in the appreticeable
occupations in Canada through the establishment of common
standards for certification. The apprenticeship program is
generally administered by provincial & territorial departments
responsible for education, labour & training (under the direction
of the provincial & territorial Director of Apprenticeship) with
authority delegated from the legislation in each province &
territory. Through the program, apprentices who have completed
their training & certified journeymen are able to obtain a Red
Seal endorsement on their Certificate of Qualification by
successfully completing an Interprovincial Standards

Examination. The program encourages standardization of
provincial & territorial apprenticeship training & certification
programs. The Red Seal allows qualified trade persons to
practice the trade in any province or territory in Canada where
the trade is designated without having to write further
examinations.

**• Social Security Tribunal (SST) / Tribunal de la sécurité
sociale (TSS)**
PO Box 9812 T
Ottawa, ON K1G 6S3
Tel: 613-952-8805
Toll-free: 877-227-8577
TTY: 800-465-7735
info.sst-tss@canada.gc.ca
www1.canada.ca/en/sst/index.html
Other Communication: Toll-Free Fax: 855-814-4117
The Social Security Tribunal was created April 1, 2013 to
function as an independent administrative tribunal & provide
appeal processes for Employment Insurance (EI), Canada
Pension Plan (CPP) & Old Age Security (OAS) decisions.

Corporate Secretariat / Secrétariat du Ministère

Corporate Secretary, Cheryl Fischer
Tel: 819-994-1122
cheryl.fischer@hrsdc-rhdcc.gc.ca

Chief Financial Officer's Office / Bureau de l'agent principal des finances

Chief Financial Officer, Mark Perlman
Tel: 819-654-6634
mark.perlman@hrsdc-rhdcc.gc.ca
Senior Director General, Corporate Accounting & Reporting,
Patrick Amyot
Tel: 819-654-6437; *Fax:* 819-997-6149
patrick.amyot@hrsdc-rhdcc.gc.ca
Senior Director General, Investment, Asset & Procurement
Management, Alain R. Gélinas
Tel: 819-654-5847; *Fax:* 819-994-1114
alain.r.gelinas@hrsdc-rhdcc.gc.ca
Senior Director, Enabling Services, Sara Lantz
Tel: 819-654-6546
sara.lantz@hrsdc-rhdcc.gc.ca
Senior Director, Financial Management Services, Brian Leonard
Tel: 819-654-6645
brian.leonard@hrsdc-rhdcc.gc.ca
Senior Director, Corporate Resource Management, Jennifer
McMurtry
Tel: 819-654-6580
jennifer.mcmurtry@hrsdc-rhdcc.gc.ca
Senior Director, Planning & Expenditure Management, Michel
Racine
Tel: 819-654-6561; *Fax:* 819-994-6411
michel.racine@hrsdc-rhdcc.gc.ca
Senior Director, Strategic Financial Analysis & Costing, Frédéric
Souligny
Tel: 819-654-6531
frederic.souligny@hrsdc-rhdcc.gc.ca

Internal Audit Services Branch / Direction générale des services de vérification interne

Chief Audit Executive, Vincent DaLuz
Tel: 819-654-5767
vincent.daluz@hrsdc-rhdcc.gc.ca
Senior Director, Audit Operations, Brigitte Marois
Tel: 819-654-5779
brigitte.marois@hrsdc-rhdcc.gc.ca
Director, OAG & Central Agencies Liaison, Karla Dufour
Tel: 819-654-5772
karla.dufour@hrsdc-rhdcc.gc.ca

Innovation, Information & Technology Branch / Direction générale d'innovation, information et technologie

Innovation, Information & Technology provides information &
technology services to the ministry, including business
applications that support & streamline work processes, access
data, & process millions of benefit-related transactions to
address Canadians' needs. It is also responsible for the
provision & management of telephony & data networks,
applications & data stores, & new processes & technologies.
Chief Information Officer, Peter Littlefield
Tel: 819-654-1400; *Fax:* 819-654-1306
peter.littlefield@hrsdc-rhdcc.gc.ca
Executive Director, Enterprise Services, Barbara Cretzman
Tel: 819-654-0468
barbara.cretzman@hrsdc-rhdcc.gc.ca
Executive Director, Client Service Operations & Solutions
Development, Mario Tanguay
Tel: 819-654-0758
mario.tanguay@hrsdc-rhdcc.gc.ca
Director General, Business Relationship Management, Linda
Stutchbury
Tel: 587-756-0688
linda.stutchbury@hrsdc-rhdcc.gc.ca

Director General, Strategy, Planning, Architecture &
Management, Lorne Sundby
Tel: 587-756-0700; *Fax:* 780-495-6431
lorne.sundby@hrsdc-rhdsc.gc.ca

Learning Branch / Direction générale de l'apprentissage
Innovation, Information & Technology provides information &
technology services to the ministry, including business
applications that support & streamline work processes, access
data, & process millions of benefit-related transactions to
address Canadians' needs. It is also responsible for the
provision & management of telephony & data networks,
applications & data stores, & new processes & technologies.
Assistant Deputy Minister, Alexis Jonathan Conrad
Tel: 819-654-8448
alexis.conrad@hrsdc-rhdcc.gc.ca
Director General, Program Policy Planning, Danièle Besner
Tel: 819-654-8739
daniele.besner@hrsdc-rhdcc.gc.ca
Director General, Canada Education Savings Program, Glennie
Graham
Tel: 819-654-8427
glennie.graham@hrsdc-rhdcc.gc.ca
Director General, Canada Education Savings Program, David
Swol
Tel: 819-654-8605
david.swol@hrsdc-rhdcc.gc.ca

**Office of the Deputy Minister of Labour / Cabinet de
Sous-ministre du travail**
Deputy Minister of Labour, Chantal Maheu
Tel: 819-654-5344
chantal.maheu@labour-travail.gc.ca
Senior Advisor to the Deputy Minister of Labour, Kim Bellem
Tel: 819-654-4143
kim.oliver@labour-travail.gc.ca

Program Operations Branch / Opérations des programmes
Program Operations handles the operation & coordination of the
Grant & Contributions programs across the Department.
Assistant Deputy Minister, Stephanie A. Hebert
Tel: 819-654-2447
stephanie.a.hebert@hrsdc-rhdcc.gc.ca
Director General, Strategic Directions, Katie Alexander
Tel: 819-654-2625
katie.alexander@hrsdc-rhdcc.gc.ca
Director General, Program & Services Oversight, Lorri
Biesenthal
Tel: 819-654-2609
lorri.biesenthal@servicecanada.gc.ca
Director General, Centre of Expertise (Gs & Cs Delivery),
Shelley Dooher
Tel: 819-654-2641
shelley.dooher@hrsdc-rhdcc.gc.ca

**Public Affairs & Stakeholder Relations Branch / Affaires
publiques et Relations avec les intervenants**
Public Affairs & Stakeholder Relations informs Canadians about
HRSDC's mandate, policies & programs. It also supports
departmental activities in engaging & communicating with
stakeholders & citizens.
Assistant Deputy Minister, James Gilbert
Tel: 819-654-1741; *Fax:* 819-934-5751
james.gilbert@hrsdc-rhdcc.gc.ca
Director General, Employment Communications Directorate,
Debora Brown
Tel: 819-654-4540
deborah.brown@hrsdc-rhdcc.gc.ca
Director General, Labour, Seniors & Social Development
Communications Directorate, Barry Frewer
Tel: 819-654-1883
barry.frewer@hrsdc-rhdcc.gc.ca
Director General, Strategic Communications & Stakeholder
Relations Directorate, Benoit Trottier
Tel: 819-654-1744
benoit.trottier@hrsdc-rhdcc.gc.ca
Director, Branch Management Services, Aline Michaud
Tel: 819-654-1729
aline.michaud@hrsdc-rhdcc.gc.ca

Service Canada
140, promenade du Portage, Gatineau, QC K1A 0J9
Toll-Free: 800-622-6232
TTY: 800-926-9105
www.servicecanada.gc.ca
Other Communication: Media enquiries, Phone: 819-994-5559;
Twitter (Français): twitter.com/servicecanada_f
twitter.com/servicecanada_e
www.linkedin.com/company/service-canada
www.youtube.com/user/ServiceCanadaE
Service Canada provides convenient access to a great range of
Government of Canada programs & services. Service Canada
Centres, as well as scheduled outreach sites, are located
throughout Canada. The Service Canada web site & call centres
are also available to assist Canadian citizens.
The following contact information is for frequently used
programs:
Apprenticeship Grants: Toll-Free Phone 1-866-742-3644, TTY
1-800-255-4786;
Canada Pension Plan (CPP): Toll-Free Phone 1-800-277-9914,
TTY 1-800-255-4786;
Employer Contact Centre: Toll-Free Phone 1-800-367-5693, TTY
1-855-881-9874;
Employment Insurance (EI): Toll-Free Phone 1-800-206-7218,
TTY 1-800-529-3742;
Old Age Security (OAS): Toll-Free Phone 1-800-277-9914, TTY
1-800-255-4786;
Passports: Toll-Free Phone: 1-800-567-6868, TTY
1-866-255-7655;
Social Insurance Number (SIN): Toll-Free Phone:
1-800-206-7218;
Wage Earner Protection Program (WEPP): Toll-Free Phone
1-866-683-6516, TTY 1-800-926-9105.
Senior Associate Deputy Minister, Employment & Social
Development Canada; Chief Operating Officer, Service
Canada, Leslie MacLean
Tel: 819-654-5754; *Fax:* 819-934-5770
leslie.maclean@hrsdc-rhdcc.gc.ca
Senior Assistant Deputy Minister, Processing & Payment
Services, Benoit Long
Tel: 819-654-6949
benoit.long@hrsdc-rhdcc.gc.ca
Assistant Deputy Minister, Western Canada & Territories, Sylvie
Bérubé
Tel: 604-974-6341
sylvie.berube@servicecanada.gc.ca
Assistant Deputy Minister, Integrity Services, Elise Boisjoly
Tel: 819-654-4826; *Fax:* 819-934-9312
elise.boisjoly@hrsdc-rhdcc.gc.ca
Assistant Deputy Minister, Québec Region, Claire Caloren
Tel: 438-892-1480
Assistant Deputy Minister, Atlantic Region, Sara Filbee
Tel: 902-356-4546
sara.filbee@servicecanada.gc.ca
Assistant Deputy Minister, Citizen Services, Peter Simeoni
Tel: 819-654-5079; *Fax:* 819-997-5433
peter.simeoni@servicecanada.gc.ca
Assistant Deputy Minister, Ontario Region, Mary Ann Triggs
Tel: 647-790-9507
maryann.triggs@servicecanada.gc.ca
Senior Director General, Service Policy, Partnerships &
Performance, Cheryl Fisher
Tel: 819-654-6139
cheryl.fisher@servicecanada.gc.ca

Alberta Service Canada Centres
Brooks
Cassils Plaza, 608 - 2 St. West, Brooks, AB T1R 1A8
Calgary - 4th Ave. SE
**Calgary Centre Service Canada Centre, Harry Hays Building,
#270, 220 - 4 Ave. SE, Calgary, AB T2G 4X3**
Calgary - Crowchild Trail NW
**Calgary North Service Canada Centre, One Executive Place,
1816 Crowchild Trail NW, Main Fl., Calgary, AB T2M 3Y7**
Calgary - Fisher St. SE
**Calgary South Service Canada Centre, Fisher Park Place II,
#100, 6712 Fisher St. SE, Calgary, AB T2H 2A7**
Calgary - Marlborough Way NE
**Calgary East Service Canada Centre, #1502, 515
Marlborough Way NE, Calgary, AB T2A 7E7**
Camrose
**Federal Building, 4901 - 50 Ave., 2nd Fl., Camrose, AB T4V
0S2**
Canmore
**Building C, #113, 802 Bow Valley Trail, Canmore, AB T1W
1N6**
Edmonton - 87th Ave. NW
**Edmonton Meadowlark Service Canada, Meadowlark
Shopping Ctr, #120, 15710 - 87th Ave. NW, Edmonton, AB
T5R 5W9**
Edmonton - 137th Ave. NW
**Edmonton North Service Canada Centre, Northgate Centre,
#2000, 9499 - 137th Ave. NW, Edmonton, AB T5E 5R8**
Tel: 780-495-3904
Toll-Free: 800-622-6232
Edmonton - Jasper Ave.
**Edmonton Canada Place Service Canada Centre, Canada
Place, 9700 Jasper Ave., Main Fl., Edmonton, AB T5J 4C3**
Edmonton - Millbourne Shopping Centre NW
**Edmonton Millbourne Service Canada Centre, #148,
Millbourne Shopping Centre NW, Edmonton, AB T6K 3L6**

Edson
4905 - 4 Ave., Edson, AB T7E 1T5
Fort McMurray
**#107, 8530 Manning Ave., Main Fl., Fort McMurray, AB T9H
5G2**
Grande Prairie
**Towne Centre Mall, #100, 9845 - 99 Ave., Grande Prairie, AB
T8V 0R3**
Lethbridge
**Crowsnest Trail Plaza, 101, 920 - 2A Ave. North, Lethbridge,
AB T1H 0E3**
Lloydminster
4114 - 70th Ave., Lloydminster, AB T9V 2X3
Medicine Hat
Northside Centre, 78 - 8 St. NW, Medicine Hat, AB T1A 6P1
Red Deer
#101, 4901 - 46th St., Red Deer, AB T4N 1N2
St Paul
4807 - 50 Ave., St Paul, AB T0A 3A0
Slave Lake
**Sawridge Plaza, 100 Main St. South, Slave Lake, AB T0G
2A3**

Service Canada Outreach Sites - Alberta

Toll-Free: 800-622-6232
TTY: 800-926-9105
The following places in Alberta are scheduled outreach sites for
Service Canada:
Athabasca (Duniece Centre, 4810 - 50th St., 3rd Fl.);
Barrhead (6203 - 49 St.);
Blairmore (Provincial Building, 12501 - 20th Ave.);
Cold Lake (Cold Lake Public Library, 5513B - 48th Ave.);
Drayton Valley (5136 - 1 Ave., 2nd Fl.);
Drumheller (90 - 3rd Ave., 4th Fl.);
Falher (308 Main St.);
Grande Cache (4500 Pine Plaza);
High Level (Provincial Building, 10106 - 100 Ave.);
High Prairie (5226 - 53 Ave., 2nd Fl.);
Hinton (568 Carmichael Lane);
Hobbema (Maskwacis Health Centre);
Jasper (Château Jasper, 96 Geikie St.);
Lac La Biche (Provincial Building, 503 Beaver Hill Rd.);
Peace River (Valley Chrysler Building, 9603 - 90 Ave.);
Rocky Mountain House (4919 - 51st St.);
Stettler (4835 - 50 St.);
Taber (5324 - 48th Ave.);
Vegreville (5121 - 49 St.);
Wabasca-Desmarais (891 Mistassiniy Rd.);
Westlock (11304 - 99 St.);
Whitecourt (Midtown Mall, 5115 - 49th St.).

British Columbia Service Canada Centres
Abbotsford
100, 32525 Simon Ave., Abbotsford, BC V2T 6T6
Burnaby
#100, 3480 Gilmore Way, Burnaby, BC V5G 4Y1
Campbell River
#101, 950 Alder St., Campbell River, BC V9W 2P8
Chilliwack
#100, 9345 Main St., Chilliwack, BC V2P 4M3
Coquitlam
#100, 2963 Glen Dr., Coquitlam, BC V3B 2P7
Courtenay
**Comox Valley Service Canada Centre, 130 - 19 St.,
Courtenay, BC V9N 8S1**
Cranbrook
1113 Baker St., Cranbrook, BC V1C 1A7
Dawson Creek
#103, 1508 - 102 Ave., Dawson Creek, BC V1G 2E2
Duncan
**Cowichan Service Canada Centre, 211 Jubilee St., Duncan,
BC V9L 1W8**
Kamloops
317 Seymour St., 1st Fl., Kamloops, BC V2C 2E8
Kelowna
#106, 471 Queensway, Kelowna, BC V1Y 6S5
Langley
#102, 8747 - 204 St., Langley, BC V1M 2Y5
Maple Ridge
**Ridge Meadows Service Canada Centre, 22325 Lougheed
Hwy., Maple Ridge, BC V2X 2T3**
Nanaimo
#201, 60 Front St., Nanaimo, BC V9R 5H7

Nelson
Chahko Mika Mall, 1125 Lakeside Dr., Main Fl., Nelson, BC V1L 5Z3

New Westminster
#201, 620 Royal Ave., New Westminster, BC V3M 1J2

North Vancouver
North Shore Service Canada Centre, #100, 221 West Esplanade, North Vancouver, BC V7M 3N7

Penticton
#101, 386 Ellis St., Penticton, BC V2A 8C9

Port Alberni
4805 Mar St., #A, Port Alberni, BC V9Y 8J5

Powell River
7061 Duncan St., #A, Powell River, BC V8A 1W1

Prince George
1363 - 4 Ave., Prince George, BC V2L 3J6

Prince Rupert
#100, 215 - 3 St., Prince Rupert, BC V8J 3J9

Quesnel
283 Reid St. East, Quesnel, BC V2J 2M1

Richmond
#350, 5611 Cooney Rd., Richmond, BC V6X 3J6

Salmon Arm
191 Shuswap St. NW, 1st Fl., Salmon Arm, BC V1E 4P6

Smithers
1020 Murray St., Smithers, BC V0J 2N0

Squamish
1440 Winnipeg St., Squamish, BC V8B 0C3

Surrey - 104th Ave.
Surrey North Service Canada Centre, 13889 - 104 Ave., Surrey, BC V3T 1W8

Surrey - Hwy. 10
Surrey South Service Canada Centre, #103, 15295 Hwy. 10, Surrey, BC V3S 0X9

Terrace
4630 Lazelle Ave., Terrace, BC V8G 1S6

Trail
#101, 1101 Dewdney Ave., Trail, BC V1R 4T1

Vancouver - Broadway
Vancouver (West Broadway) Service Centre, 1263 West Broadway, Vancouver, BC V6H 1G7

Vancouver - Hastings St. West
Sinclair Centre Service Canada Centre, #125, 757 Hastings St. West, Vancouver, BC V6C 1A1

Vancouver - Kingsway
Vancouver East Service Canada Centre, 1420 Kingsway, Vancouver, BC V5N 2R5

Vanderhoof
189 Stewart St. East, RR#2, Vanderhoof, BC V0J 3A2

Vernon
3202 - 31st St., Vernon, BC V1T 2H3

Victoria - Douglas St.
1401 Douglas St., Victoria, BC V8W 2G2

Victoria - Jacklin Rd.
Victoria West Shore Service Canada Centre, 3179 Jacklin Rd., Victoria, BC V9B 3Y7

Williams Lake
79 - Fourth Ave. South, Williams Lake, BC V2G 1J6

Service Canada Outreach Sites - British Columbia

Toll-Free: 800-622-6232
TTY: 800-926-9105

The following places in British Columbia are scheduled outreach sites for Service Canada:
Alert Bay (Namgis Health Centre, 48 School Rd.);
Bella Bella (Heiltsuk Social Development Office);
Cache Creek (Village of Cache Creek Offices, 1389 Quartz Rd.);
Clearwater (Community Resource Centre for the North Thompson, 751 Clearwater Village Rd.);
Fort St John (10600 - 100th St.);
Hope (895 - 3rd Ave.);
Lytton (Village of Lytton Office, 380 Main St.);
Mackenzie (64 Centennial Dr.);
Masset (1666 Orr St.);
Merritt (Rail Yard Mall, 2194 Coutlee Ave.);
Port Hardy (8785 Gray St.);
Richmond - Multi-Language Extension Services in Cantonese & Mandarin (Immigrant Services Society, #150, 8400 Alexandra Rd.);
Sechelt (#102, 5710 Teredo St.);
Surrey - Multi-Language Extension Services in Punjabi (#205, 12725 - 80th Ave.);

Surrey - Multi-Language Extension Services in Punjabi (DiverseCity, #1107, 7330 - 137th St.);
Vancouver - Multi-Language Extension Services in Cantonese & Mandarin (MOSAIC, 1720 Grant St., Fl. 2);
Vancouver - Multi-Language Extension Services in Cantonese & Mandarin (SUCCESS, 28 West Pender St.);
Vancouver - Multi-Language Extension Services in Punjabi (Progressive Intercultural Community Services Society, 8153 Main St.);
Whistler (Whistler Chamber of Commerce, #201, 4230 Gateway Dr.).

Manitoba Service Canada Centres

Brandon
Government of Canada Building, #100, 1039 Princess Ave., Brandon, MB R7A 4J5

Churchill
1 Mantayo Seepee Meskanow, Churchill, MB R0B 0E0

Dauphin
181 - 1st Ave. NE, Dauphin, MB R7N 1A6
Tel: 800-622-6232; *Fax:* 204-622-4045

Flin Flon
Government of Canada Building, 111 Main St., Flin Flon, MB R8A 1J9

Morden
Government of Canada Building, 158 Stephen St., Morden, MB R6M 1T3

Notre Dame de Lourdes
51 Rodgers St., Notre Dame de Lourdes, MB R0G 1M0

Portage la Prairie
Government of Canada Building, 1016 Saskatchewan Ave. East, Portage La Prairie, MB R1N 3V2

Saint Pierre Jolys
427 Sabourin St., Saint Pierre Jolys, MB R0A 1V0

Selkirk
51 Main St., Selkirk, MB R1A 1P9
Fax: 204-785-6222

Steinbach
Steinbach Place, 321 Main St., Main Fl., Steinbach, MB R5G 1Z2

Swan River
#1, 355 Kelsey Trail, Swan River, MB R0L 1Z0

The Pas
Uptown Mall, 333 Edwards Ave., PO Box 660 The Pas, MB R9A 1K7

Thompson
60 Moak Cres., Thompson, MB R8N 2B7

Winnipeg - Henderson Hwy.
Winnipeg NE Service Canada Ctr., Kildonan Village Mall, 1122 Henderson Hwy., Winnipeg, MB R2G 1L1

Winnipeg - Portage Ave.
Winnipeg South-West Service Canada Centre, Westwood Centre, 3338 Portage Ave., Winnipeg, MB R3K 0Z1

Winnipeg - St. Mary's Rd.
Winnipeg St-Vital Service Canada Centre, 1001 St. Mary's Rd., Winnipeg, MB R2M 3S4

Winnipeg - York Ave.
Winnipeg Centre Service Canada Ctr., Stanley Knowles Bldg., 391 York Ave., Winnipeg, MB R3C 0P4

Service Canada Outreach Sites - Manitoba
Toll-Free: 800-622-6232
TTY: 800-926-9105
The following places in Manitoba are scheduled outreach sites for Service Canada:
Arborg (317 River Rd.);
Ashern (Fieldstone Ventures Education & Training Centre, 61 Main St.);
Beausejour (20 - 1st St. South);
Carberry (112 Main St.);
Carman (15 - 1st Ave. SW);
Deloraine (220 South Railway Ave. West);
Fisher Branch (23 Main St.);
Gillam (323 Railway Ave.);
Gimli (62 - 2nd Ave., 2nd Fl.);
Gladstone (MAFRI Gladstone GO Centre, 37 Morris Ave. North);
Killarney (318 Williams Ave.);
Lac du Bonnet (4 Park Ave.);
McCreary (436 - 2nd Ave.);
Minnedosa (Yellowhead Regional Employment Skills & Services, 133 Main St. South);
Morris (220 Main St. North);
Neepawa (290 Davidson St.);
Russell (IGA Mall, Main St. & Lawrence Ave.);
Saint-Georges (Allard Library, 104086 Hwy. #11);
Saint Laurent (Saint Laurent Recreation Cente, Lot 825, Hwy. #6);

Shoal Lake (438 Station St.);
Snow Lake (Snow Lake Family Resource Centre, 131 Balsam St.);
Sprague (East Borderland Primary Health Care Centre, Hwy. #12 & Rte. 308);
Stonewall (South Interlake Regional Library, 419 Main St.);
Teulon (19 Beach Rd.);
Virden (227 Wellington St. West);
Winnipeg (#100, 614 des Meurons St.);
Winnipegosis (Village of Winnipegosis Office, 130 - 2 nd St.)

New Brunswick Service Canada Centres

Bathurst
Nicolas Denys Building, 120 Harbourview Blvd., 1st Fl., Bathurst, NB E2A 7R2

Campbellton
Campbellton City Center Mall, #111, 157 Water St., Campbellton, NB E3N 3L4

Caraquet
Bellevue Place, 20E St. Pierre Blvd. West, Caraquet, NB E1W 1B6

Dalhousie
Darlington Mall, 110 Plaza Blvd., Dalhousie, NB E8C 2E2

Edmundston
Federal Building, 22 Emmerson St., Edmundston, NB E3V 1R8

Fredericton
Federal Building, 633 Queen St., Fredericton, NB E3B 1C3

Grand Falls / Grand-Sault
#100, 441 Madawaska Rd., Grand Falls, NB E3Y 1C6

Miramichi
Roach Building, 150 Pleasant St., Miramichi, NB E1V 1Y1

Moncton
Heritage Court, #310, 95 Foundry St., Moncton, NB E1C 5H7

Richibucto
Cartier Place, 25 Cartier Blvd., Richibucto, NB E4W 3W7

Sackville
East Main Plaza, 170 Main St., Sackville, NB E4L 4B4

Saint John
1 Agar Pl., 1st Fl., Saint John, NB E2L 5G4

Saint Quentin
193 Canada St., Saint-Quentin, NB E8A 1J8

St. Stephen
Post Office Building, 93 Milltown Blvd., St Stephen, NB E3L 1G5

Shediac
Centre-Ville Mall, 342 Main St., Shediac, NB E4P 2E7

Shippagan
196A J.D. Gauthier Blvd., 1st Fl., Shippagan, NB E8S 1P2

Sussex
Mapleton Place, 10 Gateway St., Sussex, NB E4E 1T1

Tracadie-Sheila
Le Rond Point Shopping Center, #17, 3409 Principale St., Tracadie-Sheila, NB E1X 1C7

Woodstock
Post Office Building, 680 Main St., Woodstock, NB E7M 5Z9

Service Canada Outreach Sites - New Brunswick
Toll-Free: 800-622-6232
TTY: 800-926-9105
The following places in New Brunswick are scheduled outreach sites for Service Canada:
Baie-Sainte-Anne (5383 Rte. 117);
Doaktown (328 Main St.);
Florenceville-Bristol (#1, 8768 Main St.);
Grand Manan (North Head Grand Manan Business Center, 130 Rte. 776);
Minto (420 Pleasant Dr.);
Neguac (430 Principale St.);
Perth-Andover (588E East Riverside Dr.);
Rogersville (11117 Main St.);
Fredericton (Kchikhusis Complex, 150 Cliffe St., Fl. 3);
Tobique Narrows (Tobique Employment & Training Centre, 278 Main St.).

Newfoundland & Labrador Service Canada Centres

Channel-Port-aux-Basques
#4, 10 High St., Channel-Port-aux-Basques, NL A0M 1C0

Clarenville
Park Place, 50 Manitoba Dr., Clarenville, NL A5A 1K5

Corner Brook
Joseph R. Smallwood Building, 1 Regent Sq., Corner Brook, NL A2H 7K6

Gander
McCurdy Complex, 1 Markham Place, 3rd Fl., Gander, NL A1V 0A8

Grand Falls-Windsor
Bayley Building, #100, 4A Bayley St., Grand Falls, NL A2A 2T5

Happy Valley-Goose Bay
23 Broomfield St., Happy Valley-Goose Bay, NL A0P 1E0

Harbour Grace
Babb Building, 33-35 Harvey St., Harbour Grace, NL A0A 2M0

Labrador City
Labrador Mall, 500 Vanier Ave., Labrador City, NL A2V 2W7

Marystown
Jerrett Building, #130, 140 Ville Marie Dr., Marystown, NL A0E 2M0

Placentia
Dalfens Mall, 61 Blockhouse Rd., Placentia, NL A0B 2Y0

Rocky Harbour
Budgeon Building, 118 Pond Rd., Rocky Harbour, NL A0K 4N0

St. Anthony
Viking Mall, 1 Goose Cove Rd., St. Anthony, NL A0K 4S0

St. John's
Building 223, Pleasantville, 223 Churchill Ave., St. John's, NL A1A 1N3

Springdale
Wells Building, 130 Main St., RR#2, Springdale, NL A0J 1T0

Stephenville
133 Carolina Ave., Stephenville, NL A2N 2S5

Service Canada Outreach Sites - Newfoundland & Labrador
Toll-Free: 800-622-6232
TTY: 800-926-9105
The following places in Newfoundland & Labrador are scheduled outreach sites for Service Canada:
Baie Verte (Barker Building, 325 Hwy. #410);
Bonavista (Bonavista Campus, College of the North Atlantic, #A118, 301 Confederation Dr.);
Burgeo (142 Reach Rd.);
Forteau (32 Main St.);
Harbour Breton (Halfyard Building, #30, 42 Canada Dr.);
Mainland (School & Community Centre of Sainte-Anne, Rte. 463);
Newville (Development Association Building, Rte. 340);
Old Perlican (John Hoskins Community Centre, 575A Main St.);
Pollards Point (Main St.);
Port Saunders (Dobbin Building, 90 Main St.);
Ramea (21 Main St.);
Saint Alban's (St. Alban's Resource Centre, 3 Cormier Ave.);
Sheshatshiu (Innu Nation Building, Main Fl.);
Trepassey (Opportunities Complex, Main Hwy.);
Wesleyville (Employment Assistance Office, Cape Freels Development Association, 344 Main St.)

Northwest Territories Service Canada Centres

Fort Simpson
Federal Building, 9606 - 100th St., Fort Simpson, NT X0E 0N0

Fort Smith
Federal Building, 149 McDougal Rd., Fort Smith, NT X0E 0P0

Hay River
Federal Building, #204, 41 Capital Dr., Hay River, NT X0E 1G2

Inuvik
85 Kingmingya Rd., Inuvik, NT X0E 0T0

Yellowknife
Greenstone Building, 5101 - 50 Ave., Main Fl., Yellowknife, NT X1A 3Z4

Service Canada Outreach Sites - Northwest Territories
Toll-Free: 800-622-6232
TTY: 800-926-9105
The following places in the Northwest Territories are scheduled outreach sites for Service Canada:
Behchoko (Tli Cho Government Building);
Deline (Deline Charter Community Office);
Fort Liard (Deh Cho Health & Social Services);
Fort Providence (Zhati Koe Friendship Centre);
Fort Resolution (Deninu Ku'e First Nation Office);
Tuktoyaktuk (Tuktoyaktuk Community Corporation Office).

Nova Scotia Service Canada Centres

Amherst
#202, 26-28 Prince Arthur St., Amherst, NS B4H 1V6

Antigonish
Federal Building, 325 Main St., 2nd Fl., Antigonish, NS B2G 2C3

Bedford
Royal Bank Building, 1597 Bedford Hwy., 2nd Fl., Bedford, NS B4A 1E7

Bridgewater
Dawson B. Dauphinee Building, 77 Dufferin St., Bridgewater, NS B4V 9A2

Dartmouth
Belmont House, 33 Alderney Dr., 3rd Fl., Dartmouth, NS B2Y 2N4

Digby
98 Sydney St., Digby, NS B0V 1A0

Glace Bay
Senator's Place, #101, 633 Main St., Glace Bay, NS B1A 6J3

Guysborough
Chedabucto Centre, 9996 Hwy. #16, Guysborough, NS B0H 1N0

Halifax
Tower 2, Mumford Towers, 7001 Mumford Rd., Halifax, NS B3L 4R3

Inverness
15926 Central Ave., Inverness, NS B0E 1N0

Kentville
Federal Building, 495 Main St., 2nd Fl., Kentville, NS B4N 3W5

New Glasgow
340 East River Rd., New Glasgow, NS B2H 3P7

North Sydney
105 King St., Main Fl., North Sydney, NS B2A 3S1

Port Hawkesbury
Shediac Shopping Centre, #8, 811 Reeves St., Port Hawkesbury, NS B9A 2S4

Shelburne
Loyalist Plaza, 218 Water St., Shelburne, NS B0T 1W0

Sydney
Commerce Tower, 15 Dorchester St., 1st Fl., Sydney, NS B1P 5Y9

Truro
181 Willow St., Truro, NS B2N 4Z9

Windsor
80 Water St., Windsor, NS B0N 2T0

Yarmouth
Canada Post Office Building, 13 Willow St., 2nd Fl., Yarmouth, NS B5A 1T8

Service Canada Outreach Sites - Nova Scotia
Toll-Free: 800-622-6232
TTY: 800-926-910
The following places in Nova Scotia are scheduled outreach sites for Service Canada:
Church Point (Sainte-Anne University Campus, 1649 Rte. 1);
Sheet Harbour (Bluewater Building, 22756 Hwy. 7, 2nd Fl.).

Nunavut Service Canada Centres

Cambridge Bay
16 Mitik St., 1st Fl., PO Box 2010 Cambridge Bay, NU X0B 0C0

Iqaluit
#306, Iqaluit House, Building 622, Main Fl., Queen Elizabeth Way, PO Box 639 Iqaluit, NU X0A 0H0
Tel: 867-975-4700

Rankin Inlet
Rockland Building, PO Box 97 Rankin Inlet, NU X0C 0G0

Ontario Service Canada Centres

Ajax
#200, 274 Mackenzie Ave., Ajax, ON L1S 2E9

Arnprior
Heritage Square, #1 & 2, 75 Elgin St. West, Arnprior, ON K7S 3T9

Bancroft
Fairway Plaza, 5 Fairway Blvd., Bancroft, ON K0L 1C0

Barrie
48 Owen St., 1st Fl., Barrie, ON L4M 3H1

Belleville
Business Building, 1 North Front St., 2nd Fl., Belleville, ON K8P 5G9

Bracebridge
Federal Bldg., 98 Manitoba St., 2nd Fl., Bracebridge, ON P1L 2B5

Brampton
Human Resources Development Canada, 18 Corporation Dr., Brampton, ON L6S 6B2

Brantford
58 Dalhousie St., 2nd Fl., Brantford, ON N3T 2J2

Brockville
Thomas Fuller Building, 14 Court House Ave., 1st Fl., Brockville, ON K6V 4T1

Burlington
#108E, 676 Appleby Line, Burlington, ON L7L 5Y1

Cambridge
#2C, 350 Conestoga Blvd., Cambridge, ON N1R 7L7

Carleton Place
46 Lansdowne Ave., Carleton Place, ON K7C 2T8

Chatham
Chatham-Kent Service Canada Centre, Federal Building, 120 Wellington St. West, Chatham, ON N7M 3P3

Cobourg
1005 Elgin St. West, Cobourg, ON K9A 5J4

Collingwood
44 Huronontario St., Collingwood, ON L9Y 2L6

Cornwall
#100, 111 Water St. East, Cornwall, ON K6H 6S2

Dryden
119 King St., Dryden, ON P8N 1C1

East Gwillimbury
Newmarket Service Canada Centre, #1, 18183 Yonge St. East, East Gwillimbury, ON L9N 0H9

Elliot Lake
Ministry, Training, Colleges & Universities, Employment Ctr, 50 Hillside Dr. North, Elliot Lake, ON P5A 1X4

Espanola
#2, 721 Centre St., Espanola, ON P5E 1T3

Fort Frances
301 Scott St., Fort Frances, ON P9A 1H1

Gananoque
5 Charles St. South, Gananoque, ON K7G 1V9

Georgetown
232 Guelph St., 1st Fl., Georgetown, ON L7G 4B1

Geraldton
208 Beamish Ave. West, Geraldton, ON P0T 1M0

Goderich
52 East St., Goderich, ON N7A 1N3

Guelph
259 Woodlawn Rd. West, #C, Guelph, ON N1H 8J1

Hamilton - Barton St. East
Hamilton East Service Canada Centre, Red Hill Creek Centre, 2255 Barton St. East, Hamilton, ON L8H 7T4

Hamilton - Upper James St.
Hamilton Main Service Canada Centre, 1550 Upper James St., 1st Fl., Hamilton, ON L9B 2L6

Hawkesbury
521 Main St. East, Hawkesbury, ON K6A 1B3

Kapuskasing
8 Queen St., Kapuskasing, ON P5N 1G7

Kenora
Kenora Market Square, #201, 308 - 2nd St. South, Kenora, ON P9N 1G4

Kingston
Frontenac Mall, 1300 Bath Rd., 1st Fl., Kingston, ON K7M 4X4

Kirkland Lake
Ontario Northlands Telecommunications Building, 10 Government Rd. East, Kirkland Lake, ON P2N 1A2

Kitchener
409 Weber St. West, Kitchener, ON N2H 4B1

Leamington
Leamington Mall, 215 Talbot St. East, Leamington, ON N8H 3X5

Lindsay
65 Kent St. West, Lindsay, ON K9V 2Y3

Listowel
210 Main St. East, Listowel, ON N4W 2B7

London
Dominion Public Building, 457 Richmond St., London, ON N6A 3E3

Malton
#5, 6877 Goreway Dr., Malton, ON L4V 1L9

Marathon
#105, 52 Peninsula Rd., Marathon, ON P0T 2E0

Markham
#14, 5051 Hwy. #7 East, Markham, ON L3R 1N3

Midland
Huronia Mall, 9225 Hwy. #93, RR#2, Midland, ON L4R 4K4

Milton
Trafalgar Square, 310 Main St. East, Milton, ON L9T 1P4

Mississauga - Dixie Rd.
Mississauga East Service Canada Centre, 2525 Dixie Rd., Mississauga, ON L4Y 2A1

Mississauga - Glen Erin Dr.
Mississauga West Service Canada Centre, 3085A Glen Erin Dr., Mississauga, ON L5L 1J3

Napanee
Murphy's Plaza, 2 Dairy Ave., Napanee, ON K7R 3T1

New Liskeard
280 Armstrong St. North, RR#3, New Liskeard, ON P0J 1P0

Niagara Falls
Customs Building, 5853 Peer St., Niagara Falls, ON L2G 1X4

North Bay
Canada Place, #102, 107 Shirreff Ave., North Bay, ON P1B 7K8

Oakville
#5B, 117 Cross Ave., Oakville, ON L6J 2W7

Orangeville
#102, 210 Broadway Ave., Orangeville, ON L9W 5G4

Orillia
#101, 50 Andrew St. South, Orillia, ON L3V 7T5

Oshawa
Midtown Mall, #6C, 200 John St. West, Oshawa, ON L1J 2B4

Ottawa - Carling Ave.
Ottawa West Service Canada Centre, Lincoln Fields Galleria, 2525 Carling Ave., 1st Fl., Ottawa, ON K2B 7Z2

Ottawa - Laurier Ave. West
Ottawa Government Service Centre, 110 Laurier Ave. West, Ottawa, ON K1P 1J1

Ottawa - Laurier Ave. West
Ottawa Centre Service Canada Centre, L'Esplanade Laurier, 300 Laurier Ave. West, 2nd Fl., Ottawa, ON K1A 0R3

Ottawa - Ogilvie Rd.
Ottawa East Service Canada Centre, Beacon Hill Shopping Ctr, 2339 Ogilvie Rd., Ottawa, ON K1J 8M6

Owen Sound
Heritage Place Shopping Centre, 1350 - 16 St. East, Owen Sound, ON N4K 6N7

Parry Sound
74 James St., 2nd Fl., Parry Sound, ON P2A 1T8

Pembroke
141 Lake St., Pembroke, ON K8A 5L8

Perth
The Factory, 40 Sunset Blvd., Perth, ON K7H 2Y4

Peterborough
219 George St. North, Peterborough, ON K9J 3G7

Picton
229 Main St., Picton, ON K0K 2T0

Prescott
292 Centre St., Prescott, ON K0E 1T0
Tel: 613-925-2808; *Fax:* 613-925-3846
ontario.inquiry@hrsdc-rhdcc.gc.ca

Renfrew
350 Raglan St. South, Renfrew, ON K7V 1R7

Richmond Hill
35 Beresford Dr., Richmond Hill, ON L4B 4M3

St Catharines
Henley Square Plaza, 395 Ontario St., #E & F, St Catharines, ON L2N 7N6

St Thomas
#34, 1010 Talbot St., St Thomas, ON N5P 4N2

Sarnia
529 Exmouth St., Sarnia, ON N7T 5P6

Sault Ste. Marie
22 Bay St., 1st Fl., Sault Ste. Marie, ON P6A 5S2

Simcoe
5 Queensway East, Simcoe, ON N3Y 5K2

Smiths Falls
#115, 91 Cornelia St. West, Smiths Falls, ON K7A 5L3

Stratford
#2, 61 Lorne Ave. East, Ground Fl., Stratford, ON N5A 6S4

Sudbury
Federal Building, 19 Lisgar St., Main Fl., Sudbury, ON P3E 3L4

Thunder Bay
975 Alloy Dr., Thunder Bay, ON P7B 5Z8

Tillsonburg
Livingston Centre, 96 Tillson Ave., Tillsonburg, ON N4G 3A1

Timmins
120 Cedar St. South, 1st Fl., Timmins, ON P4N 2G8

Toronto - Chesswood Dr.
Toronto North Service Canada Centre, 3737 Chesswood Dr., Toronto, ON M3J 2P6

Toronto - College St.
#100, 559 College St., Toronto, ON M6G 1A9

Toronto - Dundas St. West
Toronto Etobicoke Service Canada Centre, 5343 Dundas St. West, Toronto, ON M9B 6K6

Toronto - Gerrard St. East
Gerrard Square Mall, 1000 Gerrard St. East, #DD10/11, 2nd Fl., Toronto, ON M4M 1Z3

Toronto - Lawrence Ave. West
Lawrence Square, #103-105, 700 Lawrence Ave. West, Toronto, ON M6A 3B3

Toronto - Queen St. West
Toronto City Hall Service Canada Centre, City Hall, 100 Queen St. West, 1st Fl., Toronto, ON M5H 2N2

Toronto - St. Clair Ave. East
Toronto Centre Service Canada Ctr., Arthur Meighen Building, 25 St. Clair Ave. East, 1st Fl., Toronto, ON M4T 3A4

Toronto - Tapscott Rd.
Toronto Malvern Service Canada Ctr., Malvern Town Ctr. Mall, 31 Tapscott Rd., Toronto, ON M1B 4Y7

Toronto - Town Centre Ct.
Toronto Scarborough Service Canada Centre, Canada Centre, 200 Town Centre Ct., 1st Fl., Toronto, ON M1P 4X9

Toronto - Yonge St.
Toronto Willowdale Service Canada Ctr., Joseph Shepard Bldg, 4900 Yonge St., 1st Fl., Toronto, ON M2N 6B1

Trenton
50 Dundas St. West, Trenton, ON K8V 6R5

Walkerton
200 McNab St., Walkerton, ON N0G 2V0

Wallaceburg
Municipal Service Centre, 786 Dufferin Ave., 2nd Fl., Wallaceburg, ON N8A 2V3

Welland
250 Thorold Rd. West, Welland, ON L3C 3W2
Tel: 905-988-2700; *Fax:* 905-735-7036

Windsor
#103, 400 City Hall Sq. East, Windsor, ON N9A 7K6

Woodstock
#101, 959 Dundas St., Woodstock, ON N4S 1H2

Service Canada Outreach Sites - Ontario
Toll-Free: 800-622-6232
TTY: 800-926-9105
The following places in Ontario are scheduled outreach sites for Service Canada:
Alliston (49 Wellington St. West);
Amherstburg (179 Victoria St. South);
Ancaster (Ancaster Square, 300 Wilson St. East);
Atikokan (Atikokan Employment Centre, #206, 214 Main St. West);
Attawapiskat (Attawapiskat Development Corporation, 1001 Riverside Rd. West);
Aylmer (Aylmer Community Services, 25 Centre St.);
Bearskin Lake (Bearskin Lake Band Office);
Belle River (499 Notre Dame St.);
Big Trout Lake (Big Trout Lake Band Council Office);
Blind River (62 Queen Ave.);
Bolton (Caledon Community Services, 18 King St. East, Upper Fl.);
Bowmanville (132 Church St.);
Brampton (Community Door, 7700 Hurontario St.);
Cat Lake (Cat Lake First Nation Band Office;
Chapleau (Sudbury Manitoulin District Social Services Administration Board Office, 12 Birch St.);
Cochrane (143 Fourth Ave.);
Cornwall Island (CIA 111 Building);
Deer Lake (Deer Lake First Nation Band Office);
Dundas (Old Town Hall, 60 Main St., Main Fl.);
Dunnville (Dunnville Employment Centre, St. Leonard's

Community Services, 208 Broad St. East);
Embrun (La Cité Collégiale, 993 Notre Dame St.);
Exeter (349 Main St. South);
Fenelon Falls (Fenelon Falls Branch, Kawartha Lakes Public Library, 19 Market St.);
Fergus (552 Wellington County Rd. 18 West);
Flamborough (#117, 7 Innovation Dr.);
Flinton (3641 Flinton Rd.);
Forest (6247 Indian Lane, RR#2);
Fort Albany (Peetabeck Health Services);
Fort Erie (469 Central Ave.);
Fort Hope (Fort Hope Band Council Office);
Fort Severn (Fort Severn Band Council Office);
Gore Bay (35 Merideth St.);
Grimsby (63 Main St. West);
Haliburton (49 Maple Ave.);
Hamilton (71 Main St. West, 1st Fl.);
Havelock (13 Quebec St.);
Hearst (523 Hwy. 11 East);
Hudson (Lac Seul First Nation Band Office);
Huntsville (207 Main St. West);
Iroquois Falls (33 Ambridge Dr.);
Kasabonika (Kasabonika First Nations Band Council);
Kashechewan (13B Riverside Rd. West);
Keewaydin (Keewaywin First Nation Band Office);
Kemptville (#3 & 4, 125 Prescott St.);
Kenora (Dalles First Nation Band Office);
Keswick (90 Wexford Dr.);
Kincardine (727 Queen St.);
Kingfisher Lake (Kingfisher Lake Band Council Office);
Lansdowne House (Lansdowne House First Nation Band Office);
Madoc (20 Davidson St.);
Mindemoya (6020 Hwy. #542);
Monetville (Dokis Reserve Rd.);
Moose Factory (22 Jonathan Cheechoo Dr.);
Moosonee (34 Revillion Rd. North);
Muncey (300 East River Rd.);
Muskrat Dam (Muskrat Dam Band Council Office);
New Osnaburgh (Mishkeegogamang First Nation Band Office);
Nipigon (5 Wadsworth Dr., 1st Fl.);
North Spirit Lake (North Spirit Lake First Nation Band Office);
Petrolia (4200 Petrolia Line);
Pikangikum (Pikangikum Band Council Office);
Poplar Hill (Poplar Hill Band Council Office);
Port Colborne (92 Charlotte St.);
Port Perry (#3, 119 Perry St.);
Red Lake (227 Howey St.);
Sachigo Lake (Sachigo Band Council Office);
Sandy Lake (Sandy Lake Band Council Office);
Seaforth (138 Main St. South);
Shelburne (167 Centre St.);
Shoal Lake (Shoal Lake First Nation Band Office);
Sioux Lookout (80 Front St.);
Sioux Narrows (Northwest Angle First Nation Band Office);
Slate Falls (48 Lakeview Dr.);
Southwold (Oneida First Nation Administrative Building;
Strathroy (34 Frank St.);
Sturgeon Falls (109 Third St.)
Summer Beaver (Summer Beaver First Nation Band Office);
Terrace Bay (Hwy, #17 & Selkirk Ave.);
Tilbury (20 Queen St. North);
Thessalon (214 Main St.);
Toronto (220 Attwell Dr.);
Toronto (58 Cecil St.);
Toronto (55 John St.);
Toronto (779 The Queensway);
Toronto (605 Rogers Rd.);
Toronto (29 St. Dennis Dr.);
Toronto (2900 Warden Ave.);
Uxbridge (#201, 2 Campbell Dr.);
Vaughan (9100 Jane St.);
Wasaga Beach (30 Lewis St.);
Wawa (48 Mission Rd.);
Webequie (Webequie First Nation Band Council);
West Lorne (160 Main St.);
Wiarton (542 Berford St.);
Wikwemikong (19A Complex Dr.);
Wingham (152 Josephine St.);
Woodbridge (8401 Weston Rd.);
Wunnumin Lake (Wunnumin Lake First Nation Band Council Office)

Prince Edward Island Service Canada Centres

Charlottetown
Jean Canfield Government of Canada Building, 191 University Ave., 1st Fl., Charlottetown, PE C1A 4L2

Montague
491 Main St., Montague, PE C0A 1R0

O'Leary
371 Main St., O'Leary, PE C0B 1V0

Souris
Save Easy Mall, 173 Main St., 2nd Fl., Souris, PE C0A 2B0

Summerside
Government of Canada Building, 294 Church St., Summerside, PE C1N 0C1

Service Canada Outreach Sites - Prince Edward Island
Toll-Free: 800-622-6232
TTY: 800-926-9105
The following place in Prince Edward Island is a scheduled outreach site for Service Canada: 48 Mill Rd., Wellington, PE, C0B 2E0.

Québec Service Canada Centres

Alma
Complexe Jacques-Gagnon, #105, 100, rue Saint-Joseph sud, Alma, QC G8B 7A6

Amos
502, 4e rue est, Amos, QC J9T 2R9

Asbestos
#204, 309, rue Chassé, Asbestos, QC J1T 2B4

Baie-Comeau
Centre d'achats Laflèche, #204, 625, boul Laflèche ouest, Baie-Comeau, QC G5C 1C4

Bécancour
#200, 1580, boul de Port-Royal, 1e étage, Bécancour, QC G9H 1X6

Brossard
Centre de ressources humaines Canada, 2501, boul Lapinière, 1e étage, Brossard, QC J4Z 3P1

Campbell's Bay
2, rue John, Campbell's Bay, QC J0X 1K0

Cap-aux-Meules
Centre de ressources humaines Canada, #200, 380, ch Principal, Cap-aux-Meules, QC G4T 1S2

Causapscal
8, rue Saint-Jacques nord, Causapscal, QC G0J 1J0

Chandler
#201, 75, boul René-Lévesque est, Chandler, QC G0C 1K0

Châteauguay
#101, 245, boul Saint-Jean Baptiste, Châteauguay, QC J6K 3C3

Chibougamau
623, 3e rue, Chibougamau, QC G8P 3A2

Chicoutimi
98, rue Racine est, Chicoutimi, QC G7H 1R1

Chisasibi
453, rue Wolverine, Chisasibi, QC J0M 1E0

Coaticook
#300, 14, rue Adams, Coaticook, QC J1A 1K3

Cote Saint-Luc
Côte-des-Neiges Service Canada Centre, Carré Décarie, #3015, 6900, boul Décarie, 3e étage, Cote-St-Luc, QC H3X 2T8

Cowansville
224, rue du Sud, 2e étage, Cowansville, QC J2K 2X4

Dolbeau -Mistassini
1400, rue des Érables, Dolbeau-Mistassini, QC G8L 2W7

Donnacona
#110, 100, rte 138, Donnacona, QC G3M 1B5

Drummondville
Édifice Surprenant, 1525, boul Saint-Joseph, Drummondville, QC J2C 2E9

Forestville
Centre Forestville, #800, 25, rte 138 est, Forestville, QC G0T 1E0

Gaspé
Édifice Frédérica-Giroux, 98, rue de la Reine, 1e étage, Gaspé, QC G4X 2V4

Gatineau - Bellehumeur
L'Atrium, #150, 85, rue Bellehumeur, Gatineau, QC J8T 8B7

Gatineau - MacLaren est
Buckingham (Gatineau) Service Canada Center, 101, rue MacLaren est, 2e étage, Gatineau, QC J8L 1J9

Gatineau - Saint-Joseph
Hull-Aylmer (Gatineau) Service Canada Centre, 920, boul Saint-Joseph, Gatineau, QC J8Z 1S9

Granby
82, rue Robinson sud, Granby, QC J2G 7L4

Joliette
Comlexe Joliette, #100, 46, rue Gauthier sud, Joliette, QC J6E 4J4

Jonquière
#102, 3750, boul du Royaume, Jonquière, QC G7X 0A4

Kuujjuaq
Nunavik Service Canada Center, 5207, ch de l'Aéroport, Kuujjuaq, QC J0M 1C0

La Malbaie
541, rue Saint-Étienne, La Malbaie, QC G5A 1J3

La Pocatière
Les Cours Painchaud, #103, 708 - 4e av, La Pocatière, QC G0R 1Z0

La Sarre
Carrefour La Sarre Marketplace, #30, 255 - 3e rue est, La Sarre, QC J9Z 3N7

La Tuque
Carrefour La Tuque Inc., 290, rue Saint-Joseph, La Tuque, QC G9X 3Z8

Lac Mégantic
#201, 5200, rue Frontenac, 2e étage, Lac-Mégantic, QC G6B 1H3

Laval
1041, boul des Laurentides, Laval, QC H7G 2W2

Lévis
Place Lévis, #175, 50, rte du Président-Kennedy, Lévis, QC G6V 6W8

Longueuil
#100, 1195, ch du Tremblay, Longueuil, QC J4N 1R4

Louiseville
507, rue Marcel, Louiseville, QC J5V 1N1

Magog
#100A, 1700, rue Sherbrooke, Magog, QC J1X 5B4

Maniwaki
Galeries Maniwaki, #220, 100, rue Principale sud, Maniwaki, QC J9E 3L4

Matane
Les Galeries du Vieux-Port, #220, 750, av du Phare ouest, Matane, QC G4W 3W8

Mont-Laurier
431, rue de la Madone, 1e étage, Mont-Laurier, QC J9L 1S1

Montmagny
37, av Sainte-Brigitte sud, Montmagny, QC G5V 2Y3

Montréal - Chauveau
Mercier (Montréal) Service Canada Centre, 5455, rue Chauveau, 1e étage, Montréal, QC H1N 1G8
Téléc: 514-255-0624

Montréal - Jarry est
Villeray (Montréal) Service Canada Centre, #300, 1415, rue Jarry est, 3e étage, Montréal, QC H2E 3B2

Montréal - Jean-Talon est
Saint-Léonard (Montréal) Service Canada Centre, #500, 6020, rue Jean-Talon est, Montréal, QC H1S 3B1

Montréal - Newman
Lasalle (Montréal) Service Canada Centre, 7655, boul Newman, Montréal, QC H8N 1X7

Montréal - René-Lévesque ouest
Montréal Downtown Service Canada Centre, Place Guy-Favreau, #034, 200, boul René-Lévesque ouest, Montréal, QC H2Z 1X4

Montréal - Sherbrooke est
Pointe-aux-Trembles (Montréal) Service Canada Centre, 13313, rue Sherbrooke est, Montréal, QC H1A 1C2

Montréal - Transcanadienne
Pointe-Claire (Montréal) Service Canada Centre, #100, 6500, aut Transcanadienne, 1e étage, Montréal, QC H9R 0A5

Montréal - Wellington
Verdun Service Canada Centre, 4110, rue Wellington, 2e étage, Montréal, QC H4G 1V7

New Richmond
Carrefour Baie-des-Chaleurs, 122, boul Perron ouest, 2e étage, New Richmond, QC G0C 2B0

Québec - Gare-du-Palais
Québec (Centre-Ville) Service Canada Centre, 330, rue de la Gare-du-Palais, Québec, QC G1K 3X2

Québec - Montmorency
La Cité-Limoilou Service Canada Centre, #101, 2500, boul Montmorency, Québec, QC G1J 5C7

Québec - Quatre-Bourgeois
Sainte-Foy (Québec) Service Canada Centre, #200, 3229, ch des Quatre-Bourgeois, 3e étage, Québec, QC G1W 0C1

Repentigny
Place Repentigny, #54, 155, rue Notre-Dame, Repentigny, QC J6A 7G5

Rimouski
Édifice Boisé Langevin, #102, 287, rue Pierre-Saindon, Rimouski, QC G5L 9A7

Rivière-du-Loup
298, boul Armand-Thériault, 2e étage, Rivière-du-Loup, QC G5R 4C2

Roberval
Plaza Roberval, #202, 755, boul Saint-Joseph, Roberval, QC G8H 2L4

Rouyn-Noranda
Édifice Réal-Caouette, #300, 151, av du Lac, Rouyn-Noranda, QC J9X 6C3

Saint-Eustache
250, boul Arthur-Sauvé, Saint-Eustache, QC J7R 2H9

Saint-Georges
Centre de ressources humaines Canada, 11400, 1e av est, 2e étage, Saint-Georges, QC G5Y 7H2

Saint-Hyacinthe
Galeries St-Hyacinthe Shopping Mall, #2500, 3225, av Cusson, 2e étage, Saint-Hyacinthe, QC J2S 0H7

Saint-Jean-sur-Richelieu
#106, 320, boul du Séminaire nord, Saint-Jean-sur-Richelieu, QC J3B 5K9

Saint-Jérôme
#100, 339, boul Jean-Paul-Hogue, Saint-Jérôme, QC J7Z 7A5

Sainte-Agathe-des-Monts
118, rue Principale est, 2e étage, Sainte-Agathe-des-Monts, QC J8C 1L8

Sainte-Anne-des-Monts
230, 1e av ouest, Sainte-Anne-des-Monts, QC G4V 1E2

Sainte-Thérèse
#110, 100, boul Ducharme, Sainte-Thérèse, QC J7E 1X2

Salaberry-de-Valleyfield
Valleyfield Service Canada Centre, #100, 73, rue Maden, Salaberry-de-Valleyfield, QC J6S 3V4

Senneterre
761, 10e av, Senneterre, QC J0Y 2M0

Sept-îles
701, boul Laure, 3e étage, Sept-îles, QC G4R 1X8

Shawinigan
444, 5e rue, Shawinigan, QC G9N 1E6

Sherbrooke
124, rue Wellington nord, Sherbrooke, QC J1H 5X8

Sorel-Tracy
101, rue Augusta, Sorel-Tracy, QC J3P 1A8

Terrebonne
835, montée Masson, Terrebonne, QC J6W 2C7

Thetford Mines
#500, 350, boul Frontenac ouest, Thetford Mines, QC G6G 6N7

Trois-Rivières
#100, 1660, rue Royale, Trois-Rivières, QC G9A 4K3

Val-d'Or
400, av Centrale, Val-d'Or, QC J9P 1P3

Vaudreuil-Dorion
2555, rue Dutrisac, Vaudreuil-Dorion, QC J7V 7E6

Victoriaville
84, boul Labbé sud, Victoriaville, QC G6S 1K4

Ville-Marie
69B, rue Sainte-Anne, Ville-Marie, QC J9V 2B6

Service Canada Outreach Sites - Québec
Ligne sans frais: 800-622-6232
TTY: 800-926-9105
The following places in Québec are scheduled outreach sites for Service Canada:
L'Anse-Saint-Jean (La Petite École Community Centre, 239, rue St-Jean-Baptiste);
Baie-Saint-Paul (René-Richard Library, 9, rue Forget);
Belleterre (Saint-Andre School, 255, 3e av);
Cadillac (2, rue Dumont est);
Chapeau (120, rue King);
Chénéville (90A, rue Albert Ferland);
Dégelis (663, 6e rue ouest);
Fortierville (Fortierville Municipal Library, 198A, rue de la Fabrique);
Grande-Entrée (Auberge La Salicorne, 355, rte 199);
Grande-Vallée (1, rue du Vieux Pont);
Lac-Sainte-Marie (Lac-Ste-Marie City Hall, 106, ch Lac-Ste-Marie);
Lachute (Maison populaire d'Argenteuil, 335, rue Principale);
Lamarche (100, rue Principale);
Lebel-sur-Quévillon (107, rue Principal sud);

Les Escoumins (459, rte 138);
Lyster (2375, rue Bécancour);
Matagami (180, place du Commerce);
Matapédia (City Hall, 1, rue de l'Hôtel-de-ville);
Mont-Joli (1572, boul Jacque Cartier);
Mont-Louis (40, 7e rue est);
New Carlisle (208, rue Gerard D. Levesque);
Normandin (Town Hall, 1048, rue Saint-Cyrille);
Notre-Dame-de-Montauban (421, rue Principal);
Notre-Dame-du-Laus (Municipal Library, 4, rue de l'Église);
Pohénégamook (1309, rue Principale);
Potton (The Re illy House, 302, rue Principale);
Port-Cartier (4C, boul des îles);
Rivière-Rouge (Municipal Library, 230, rue de L'Annonciation sud);
Sacré-Coeur (88, rue Principale nord);
Saint-Fabien-de-Panet (195, rue Bilodeau);
Saint-Michel-des-Saints (521, rue Brassard);
Saint-Pamphile (164, rue de l'Église ouest);
Taschereau (52, rue Morin);
Témiscaming (Le Centre, 20, rue Humphrey);
Weedon (Weedon Community Centre, #314, 209 rue des Érables).

Saskatchewan Service Canada Centres

Estevan
#10, 419 Kensington Ave., Estevan, SK S4A 2A1

La Ronge
1016 La Ronge Ave., La Ronge, SK S0J 1L0

Melfort
McKendry Plaza, 104 McKendry Ave. West, Melfort, SK S0E 1A0

Moose Jaw
Victoria Place, #501, 111 Fairford St. East, Moose Jaw, SK S6H 7X5

North Battleford
Territorial Place, #15, 9800 Territorial Dr., North Battleford, SK S9A 3N6

Prince Albert
1288 Central Ave., Prince Albert, SK S6V 4V8

Regina
Alvin Hamilton Building, 1783 Hamilton St., Regina, SK S4P 2B6

Saskatoon
Federal Building, 101 - 22 St. East, Saskatoon, SK S7K 0E1

Swift Current
Chinook Building, 250 Central Ave. North, Swift Current, SK S9H 0L2

Weyburn
City Centre Mall, 110 Souris Ave., Main Fl., Weyburn, SK S4H 2Z8

Yorkton
Imperial Plaza, 214 Smith St. East, Yorkton, SK S3N 3S6

Service Canada Outreach Sites - Saskatchewan
Toll-Free: 800-622-6232
TTY: 800-926-9105
The following places in Saskatchewan are scheduled outreach sites for Service Canada:
Assiniboia (313 Centre St.);
Beauval (Lavoie St.);
Black Lake (Black Lake First Nation Band Office);
Buffalo Narrows (#4, 1491 Pederson Ave.);
Carlyle (100 Main St.);
Clearwater River (Clearwater Dene Nation Band Office);
Davidson (204 Washington St.);
Debden (204 - 2nd Ave. East);
Domremy (Domremy Fransaskois Community Centre, 109 - 1st St. North);
Fond-du-Lac (Fond-du-Lac First Nation Band Office;
Gravelbourg (133 - 5th Ave. East);
Hudson Bay (501 Prince St.);
Humboldt (623 - 7th St.);
Ile-à-la-Crosse (Lajeunesse Ave.);
Kindersley (207 Main St.);
La Loche (La Loche Recreation Centre (Montgrand St.);
Maple Creek (114 Jasper St.);
Meadow Lake (Meadow Lake Tribal Council Main Office, 8155 Flying Dust First Nation);
Nipawin (233 Centre St.);
North Battleford (1371 - 103rd St.);
Ponteix (Royer Cultural Centre, 110 Railway Ave.);
Preeceville (27 Main St. North);
Regina (3115 - 5th Ave.);
St. Isidore-de-Bellevue (Bellevue Cultural Association, 716 Hwy. #225);
Shaunavon (23 - 4th Ave. West);
Stony Rapids (Transwest Air Terminal, 2nd Fl.);
Uranium City (Northern Settlement of Uranium City Office, 205 Fredette Rd.);

Wollaston Lake (Economic Development Office);
Wynyard (400A Ave. D West);
Zenon Park (Zenon Park Fransaskoise Association, 755 Main St.).

Yukon Service Canada Centres

Whitehorse
Elijah Smith Building, #125, 300 Main St., Whitehorse, YT Y1A 2B5

Service Canada Outreach Sites - Yukon
The following places in the Yukon are scheduled outreach sites for Service Canada:
Dawson City (Oak Hall, 1017 - 2nd Ave.);
Watson Lake (Yukon College Campus, Robert Campbell Hwy.).

Skills & Employment Branch / Direction générale des compétences et de l'emploi

Skills & Employment provides programs & initiatives that promote skills development, labour market participation & inclusiveness, as well as ensuring labour market efficiency. Specifically, these programs seek to address the employment & skills needs of those facing employment barriers, & contribute to life long learning & building a skilled inclusive labour force. Other programs that support an efficient labour market include the labour market integration of recent immigrants, the entry of temporary foreign workers, the mobility of workers across Canada & the dissemination of labour market information. This branch is also responsible for programs that provide temporary income support to eligible unemployed workers.
Senior Assistant Deputy Minister, Rachel Wernick
Tel: 819-654-5991
rachel.wernick@hrsdc-rhdcc.gc.ca
Associate Assistant Deputy Minister, Elisha Ram
Tel: 819-654-5212
Elisha.ram@hrsdc-rhdcc.gc.ca
Director General, Employment Programs & Partnerships Directorate, John Atherton
Tel: 819-654-3289
john.atherton@hrsdc-rhdcc.gc.ca
Director General, Horizontal Management & Integration Directorate, Michel C. Caron
Tel: 819-654-2814
michel.caron@hrsdc-rhdcc.gc.ca
Director General, Workplace Partnerships Directorate, Stephen Johnson
Tel: 819-654-3801
stephen.johnson@hrsdc-rhdcc.gc.ca
Director General, Employment Insurance Policy, Annette Ryan
Tel: 819-654-3056
annette.ryan@hrsdc-rhdcc.gc.ca
Director General, Strategic Partnership & Business Development, Candice St-Aubin
Tel: 819-654-5166
candice.staubin@hrsdc-rhdcc.gc.ca
Director General, Aboriginal Affairs Directorate, James Sutherland
Tel: 819-654-3109
james.sutherland@hrsdc-rhdcc.gc.ca
Director General, Youth & Skills Innovation, Jocelyne Voisin
Tel: 819-654-6732
jocelyne.voisin@hrsdc-rhdcc.gc.ca
Director of Operations, Labour Market Integration, Jonathan Wells
Tel: 819-654-2899
jonathan.wells@hrsdc-rhdcc.gc.ca

Strategic & Service Policy Branch / Direction générale des politiques stratégiques et de service

Strategic Policy & Research leads on integrating human resources & social development issues in strategic policy, evaluation, & knowledge & research dissemination. It also leads on emerging & long-term policy development, corporate planning, & central agency, intergovernmental & international relations.
Chief Data Officer, Sandy Kyriakatos
Tel: 819-654-3746
sandy.kyriakatos@hrsdc-rhdcc.gc.ca
Director General, Service Policy & Strategy, Catherine Bennett
catherine.bennett@hrsdc-rhdcc.gc.ca

Environment & Climate Change Canada / Environnement et du Changement climatique

200, rue Sacré-Coeur, 12th Fl., Gatineau, QC K1A 0H3
Tel: 819-938-3860
Toll-Free: 800-668-6767
eec.enviroinfo.ec@canada.ca
www.canada.ca/en/environment-climate-change.html
Other Communication: Media Relations, Toll-Free Phone: 844-836-7799; Email: ec.media.ec@canada.ca
twitter.com/environmentca
www.facebook.com/environmentandclimatechange
instagram.com/canenvironment

Environment became Environment & Climate Change in Nov. 2015, under Prime Minister Justin Trudeau. The department fosters a national capacity for sustainable development in cooperation with other governments, departments of government & the private sector that will result in a safe & healthy environment & a sound & prosperous economy by: undertaking & promoting programs to augment understanding of the environment; supporting environmentally responsible public & private decision-making; warning Canadians of risks to & from the environment; engaging Canadians as partners in measurably beneficial action to conserve, protect & restore the integrity of Canada's environment for the benefit of present & future generations.

Minister, Environment & Climate Change, Hon. Steven Guilbeault, P.C.

Deputy Minister, Stephen Lucas
Tel: 819-994-5020

Director General, Audit & Evaluation, Robert D'Aoust
Tel: 819-938-5017; *Fax:* 819-938-5453
robert.daoust@canada.ca

Associated Agencies, Boards & Commissions:

• Committee on the Status of Endangered Wildlife in Canada (COSEWIC) / Comité sur la situation des espèces en péril au Canada
c/o Dept. of Biological Sciences, Simon Fraser University
8888 University Dr.
Burnaby, BC V5A 1S6
canada.ca/en/services/environment/wildlife-plants-species.html
Other Communication: Species at Risk Act Public Registry:
www.sararegistry.gc.ca
Committee of experts that assesses & designates which wild species are in some danger of disappearing from Canada. COSEWIC determines the national status of wild Canadian species, subspecies & separate populations suspected of being at risk. COSEWIC bases its decisions on the best up-to-date scientific information & Aboriginal traditional knowledge available. All native mammals, birds, reptiles, amphibians, fish, mollusks, lepidopterans (butterflies & moths), vascular plants, mosses & lichens are included in its current mandate. In its 2010 Annual report, COSEWIC's assessment results indicate there are 602 species in the risk category (extirpated, endangered, threatened or of special concern) & 13 species found to be extinct.

• North American Waterfowl Management Plan (NAWMP) / Le plan nord-américain de gestion de la sauvagine
NAWCC (Canada) Secretariat, Place Vincent Massey
351 St. Joseph Blvd., 14th Fl.
Gatineau, QC K1A 0H3
Tel: 819-938-4030; *Fax:* 819-934-6017
ec.pnags-nawmp.ec@canada.ca
nawmp.wetlandnetwork.ca
The North American Waterfowl Management Plan is an international action plan to conserve migratory birds throughout the continent. The Plan's goal is to return waterfowl populations to their 1970's levels by conserving wetland & upland habitat. Canada & the United States signed the Plan in 1986 in reaction to critically low numbers of waterfowl. Mexico joined in 1994 making it a truly continental effort. The Plan is a partnership of federal, provincial/state & municipal governments, non-governmental organizations, private companies & many individuals, all working towards achieving better wetland habitat for the benefit of migratory birds, other wetland-associated species & people. The Plan's unique combination of biology, landscape conservation & partnerships comprise its exemplary conservation legacy. Plan projects are international in scope, but implemented at regional levels. These projects contribute to the protection of habitat & wildlife species across the North American landscape.

• North American Bird Conservation Initiative (NABCI)
Canadian Wildlife Service
351 St. Joseph Blvd.
Gatineau, QC K1A 0H3
Tel: 819-994-0512; *Fax:* 819-994-4445
ec.icoancanada-nabcicanada.ec@canada.ca
www.nabci.net
The NABCI is a coordinated effort among Canada, the United States & Mexico to maintain the diversity & abundance of all North American birds. National coordination of this effort in Canada occurs through the NABCI Canada Council, chaired by the Asst. Deputy Minister of Environment Canada's Environmental Conservation Service. Council members include representatives from provincial governments, non-government organizations, four bird plans (waterfowl, landbirds, shorebirds, waterbirds), & habitat joint ventures. In Canada, there are four habitat joint ventures (Pacific Birds Habitat, Canadian Intermountain, Prairie Habitat, Eastern Habitat) & three species (Arctic Goose, Black Duck, Sea Duck).

Environmental Protection Branch / Direction générale de la protection de l'environnement
351, boul Saint-Joseph, Gatineau, QC K1A 0H3
Tel: 819-953-1711; *Fax:* 819-953-9452
Assessment & management of risk associated with domestic & international sources of pollution. The range of activity is broad, assessment of substances & practices that pose a risk to the environment, development & implementation of environmental protection measures including pollution prevention, regulations, permits & technology advancement & ensuring compliance with federal pollution & wildlife laws. These activities lead to improvements in environmental quality which helps to support the health of Canadians & their economic security.
Assistant Deputy Minister, Mike Beale
Tel: 819-420-7871
mike.beale@canada.ca
Director General, Industrial Sectors, Chemicals, & Waste Directorate, Marc D'Iorio
Tel: 819-420-7600
Acting Director General, Legislative & Regulatory Affairs, Stéphanie Johnson
Tel: 819-938-5507
Director General, Carbon Pricing Bureau, Judy Meltzer
Tel: 819-240-7751
Director General, Energy & Transportation, Helen Ryan
Tel: 819-420-8055
Executive Director, Oil, Gas & Alternative Energy, Cam Carruthers
Tel: 819-938-5711
Executive Director, Environmental Assessment, Mary J. Taylor
Tel: 819-938-4021
Director, Transportation, Stéphane Couroux
Tel: 819-420-8020
Director, Electricity & Combustion Division, Paola Mellow
Tel: 819-420-7761
Acting Director, Environmental Emergencies Division, Tanya Bryant
Tel: 819-938-4072
Acting Program Manager, Contaminated Sites, Nicole Cote
Tel: 819-938-5603

Human Resources Branch / Direction générale des ressources humaines
Director General, Workforce Development & Wellness Services, Nathalie Clément
Tel: 819-938-4670
Director General, Integrated Classification and Staffing Solutions, Gaveen Cadotte
Tel: 819-938-4690
Director General, Human Resources Business Transformation Directorate, Jocelyne Kharyati
Tel: 819-938-4583
jocelyne.kharyati@canada.ca
Acting Director, Executive Group Services and Programs, Amélie LaPenna
Tel: 819-420-7248

International Affairs Branch / Direction générale des affaires internationales
200, boul Sacré-Coeur, Gatineau, QC K1A 0H3
Tel: 819-934-6020; *Fax:* 819-953-9412
Assistant Deputy Minister, Isabelle Berard
Tel: 819-938-3722
Director General, Bilateral Affairs & Trade Directorate, Lucie Desforges
Tel: 819-938-3475
Director General, G7 Task Team, Nancy Hamzawi
Tel: 819-938-3569
Director General, Climate Change International, Catherine Stewart
Tel: 819-938-3784
Director, Bilateral Affairs Division (Europe, Asia, Africa, Oceania), Jennie Chen
Tel: 819-938-3495
Director, Trade & Clean Technology, Xin Gao
Tel: 819-938-9456
Director, Americas Division, Daniel Hallman
Tel: 819-938-3763

Legal Services / Services juridiques
351, boul Saint-Joseph, Gatineau, QC K1A 0H3
Senior Counsel, Yves Leboeuf
Tel: 819-938-5035
Legal Counsel, Vincent Fréchette
Tel: 819-938-4927
Legal Counsel, Dawn Pritchard
Tel: 819-938-5916

Meteorological Service of Canada (MSC) / Le service météorologique du Canada (SMC)
351, boul Saint-Joseph, Gatineau, QC K1A 0H3
Tel: 819-934-5395; *Fax:* 819-934-1255

The Meteorological Service of Canada monitors water quantities, provides information & conducts research on climate, atmospheric science, air quality, ice & other environmental issues.
Assistant Deputy Minister, David Grimes
Tel: 819-938-4385; *Fax:* 819-934-1255
Director General, Policy, Planning & Partnerships Directorate, Dilhari Fernando
Tel: 819-938-4373
Director General, Monitoring & Data Services Directorate, David Harper
Tel: 819-938-4564
Director General, Canadian Centre for Meteorological & Environmental Prediction, Michel Jean
Tel: 514-421-4601
Executive Director, National Programs and Business Development, Ken MacDonald
Tel: 819-938-4446
Director, Prediction Services, Bill Appleby
Tel: 902-426-4053
Director, Aviation & Defence Services, Mario Ouellet
Tel: 819-938-4432
Director, Marine & Ice Services, John Parker
Tel: 902-426-3836

Science & Technology Branch / Direction générale des sciences et de la technologie
351, boul Saint-Joseph, Gatineau, QC K1A 0H3
Tel: 819-994-4751; *Fax:* 819-997-1541
Assistant Deputy Minister, Nancy Hamzawi
Tel: 819-938-5629; *Fax:* 819-953-5371
nancy.hamzawi@canada.ca

Atmospheric Science & Technology / Sciences et technologie atmosphériques
351, boul Saint-Joseph, Gatineau, QC K1A 0H3
Director General, Laird J. Shutt
Tel: 613-949-8306
laird.shutt@canada.ca
Executive Director, Air Quality Research Division, Bernard Vigneault
Tel: 613-949-7571
bernard.vigneault@canada.ca

Science & Risk Assessment Directorate / Direction générale de Science et évaluation des risques
351, boul Saint-Joseph, Gatineau, QC K1A 0H3
Tel: 819-953-3091; *Fax:* 819-953-5371
Director General, Jacqueline Gonçalves
Tel: 819-938-5200; *Fax:* 819-938-5212
jacqueline.goncalves@canada.ca

Science & Technology Strategies / Science et technologies, statégies
200, boul Sacré-Coeur, 11e étage, Gatineau, QC K1A 0H3
Tel: 905-336-4503

Water Science & Technology / Science et technologie de l'eau
200, boul Sacré-Coeur, Gatineau, QC K1A 0H3
Tel: 819-994-4533
Director General, Kevin J. Cash
Tel: 613-949-8312
kevin.cash@canada.ca

Strategic Policy Branch / Direction générale de la politique stratégique
Assistant Deputy Minister, Hilary Geller
Tel: 819-938-3782
hilary.geller@canada.ca
Acting Executive Director, Policy Development, Laniel Bateman
Tel: 873-469-1516
laniel.bateman@canada.ca
Director General, Economic Analysis Directorate, Derek Hermanutz
Tel: 873-469-1471
derek.hermanutz@canada.ca
Deputy Director, Intergovernmental Affairs, Tony Kourie
Tel: 819-938-9322
tony.kourie@canada.ca

Commission for Environmental Cooperation (CEC) / Commission coopération environnementale

Secretariat, #200, 393, rue Saint-Jacques ouest, Montréal, QC H2Y 1N9
Tel: 514-350-4300; *Fax:* 514-350-4314
info@cec.org
www.cec.org
twitter.com/cecweb
www.facebook.com/cecconnect
The Commission for Environmental Cooperation (CEC) is an international organization created by Canada, Mexico & the United States under the North American Agreement on Environmental Cooperation (NAAEC). The CEC was established to address regional environmental concerns, help prevent potential trade & environmental conflicts & to promote the effective enforcement of environmental law. The Agreement complements the environmental provisions of the North American Free Trade Agreement (NAFTA).

Executive Director, César Rafael Chávez
Tel: 514-350-4317
crchavez@cec.org

Acting Unit Head, Communications, Megan Ainscow
Tel: 514-350-4372
mainscow@cec.org

Unit Head, Environmental Quality, Orlando Cabrera-Rivera
Tel: 514-350-4323
ocabrera@cec.org

Unit Head, Green Growth, David Donaldson
Tel: 514-350-4337
ddonaldson@cec.org

Unit Head, Administration, Riccardo Embriaco
Tel: 514-350-4356
rembriaco@cec.org

Unit Head, SEM & Legal, Robert Moyer
Tel: 514-350-4340
rmoyer@cec.org

Unit Head, Ecosystems, Lucie Robidoux
Tel: 514-350-4311
lrobidoux@cec.org

Environmental Protection Review Canada / Révision de la protection de l'environnement Canada

240 Sparks St., 4th Fl. West, Ottawa, ON K1A 0X8
Fax: 613-907-1337
eprc-rpec@eprc-rpec.gc.ca
www.eprc-rpec.gc.ca

Environmental Protection Review Canada is a group of expert adjudicators, entirely separate from Environment & Climate Change, that conducts reviews of Environmental Protection Compliance Orders (EPCOs). Under the Canadian Environmental Protection Act, 1999 (CEPA, 1999), enforcement officers have the power to issue EPCOs to prevent a violation, to stop an on-going violation or to require that violations be corrected. Any person who has been issued an EPCO may ask for an independent review conducted by a Review Officer. Review Officers have the authority to confirm or cancel an EPCO. They may also amend, suspend, add or delete a term or condition of the Order. The decisions of Review Officers may be appealed to the Federal Court, Trial Division.

Chief Review Officer, Jerry V. DeMarco, B.A., LL.B., M.E.S., M.M., M.Sc., MCIP.

Export Development Canada (EDC) / Exportation et développement Canada (SEE)

150 Slater St., Ottawa, ON K1A 1K3
Tel: 613-598-2500; *Fax:* 613-598-3811
Toll-Free: 800-229-0575
TTY: 866-574-0451
support@edc.ca
www.edc.ca
Other Communication: Trade Advisors, Toll-Free Phone:
888-220-0047; Customer Care: 866-716-7201
twitter.com/ExportDevCanada
www.facebook.com/ExportDevCanada
www.linkedin.com/company/export-development-canada
www.youtube.com/ExportDevCanada
A financial services corporation assisting Canadian business to succeed in foreign markets. EDC provides a wide range of financial solutions to exporters across Canada & their customers around the world. The corporation's risk management services include: export-credit insurance protecting exporters against losses due to non-payment relating to commercial & political risks; & flexible medium- or long-term financing & guarantees. As a financially self-sustaining Crown corporation, EDC operates on commercial principles, charging fees & premiums for its products & interest on its loans. EDC is governed by a board of directors composed of representatives from both the private & public sectors, & reports to Parliament through the minister for international trade. An Environmental Review Directive is used to assess the environmental impacts of projects EDC is asked to support. EDC pursues an international multilateral consensus on environmental review practices so that all exporters are subject to the same rules. EDC has adopted & implemented the OECD Recommendation on Common Approaches on Environment & Officially Supported Export Credits. EDC has signed the UNEP Statement of Financial Institutions. Through the EnviroExport

initiative, EDC helps Canadia n environmental exporters succeed internationally through financing products. Where EDC is considering providing financing support, political risk insurance or equity to the sponsor of a Category A project under the Environmental Review Directive, EDC will seek consent to inform the public on its website that it is considering support to such a project.

Chair, Martine Irman

President & CEO, Mairead Lavery

Senior Vice-President & Global Head, Financing & Investments, Carl Burlock

Senior Vice-President, Human Resources, Stephanie Butt Thibodeau

Senior Vice-President, Corporate Affairs & Secretary, Catherine Decarie

Senior Vice-President & Chief Risk Officer, Enterprise Risk Management, Al Hamdani

Chief Financial Officer & Senior Vice-President, Finance & Technology, Ken Kember

Senior Vice-President, Strategy & Innovation, Derek Layne

Acting Senior Vice-President, Mike Neals

Senior Vice-President, Insurance & Working Capital Solutions, Clive Witter

Farm Credit Canada / Financement agricole Canada

1800 Hamilton St., Regina, SK S4P 4L3
Tel: 306-780-8100; Fax: 306-780-8919
Toll-Free: 888-332-3301
TTY: 306-780-6974
csc@fcc-fac.ca
www.fcc-fac.com
twitter.com/FCCagriculture
www.facebook.com/fccagriculture
www.linkedin.com/company/farm-credit-canada
www.youtube.com/fcctvonline

Federal Crown corporation reporting to Parliament through the Minister of Agriculture & Agri-Food. Under the Farm Credit Canada Act FCC offers financing to primary producers & agribusiness through 100 offices in rural communities across Canada.

President & Chief Executive Officer, Michael Hoffort, P.Ag.

Executive Vice-President & Chief Financial Officer, Rick Hoffman, CPA, CMA, MBA, ICD.D

Executive Vice-President & Chief Risk Officer, Corinna Mitchell-Beaudin

Executive Vice-President & Chief Operating Officer, Sophie Perreault

Executive Vice-President & Chief Information Officer, Travis Asmundson

Executive Vice-President & Chief Marketing Officer, Todd Klink

Executive Vice-President & Chief Human Resource Officer, Greg Honey

Executive Vice-President, Law & Corporate Secretary, Greg Willner, B.Admin., LL.B.

Farm Products Council of Canada (FPCC) / Conseil des produits agricoles du Canada (CPAC)

Building 59, Central Experimental Farm, 960 Carling Ave., Ottawa, ON K1A 0C6
Tel: 613-759-1555; Fax: 613-759-1566
Toll-Free: 855-611-1165
TTY: 613-759-1737
aafc.fpcc-cpac.aac@canada.ca
www.fpcc-cpac.gc.ca

In 1972, the Natioanl Farm Products Council was established by Parliament. The National Farm Products Council became known as the Farm Products Council of Canada in 2009.
The mission of the council is as follows: to oversee the national supply management agencies for poultry & eggs & the national promotion research agencies; to liaise with provincial governments interested in the work of the national agencies; to

review operations of the national agencies to ensure they act in accordance with the Farm Products Agencies Act; to investigate complaints in relation to national agency decisions & to hold public hearings if necessary; to administer the Agricultural Products Marketing Act & to encourage effective marketing of farm products; & to advise the Minister on matters related to the national agencies.
The Council consists of at least three members & up to seven. Members of the Council are appointed by Cabinet.

Chair, Brian Douglas
Tel: 613-759-1560

Federal Economic Development Agency for Southern Ontario (FedDev Ontario) / Agence fédérale de développement économique pour le Sud de l'Ontario

#101, 139 Northfield Dr. West, Waterloo, ON N2L 5A6
Fax: 519-725-4976
Toll-Free: 866-593-5505
www.feddevontario.gc.ca
twitter.com/FedDevOntario
www.youtube.com/user/FedDevOntario

FedDev Ontario was launched in 2009, & has the mandate to strengthen the economy in Southern Ontario. It accomplishes this through investment, job creation & programs. Examples of programs & initiatives are as follows: Applied Research & Commercialization Initiative; Building Canada Fund-Communities Component; Canada-Ontario Infrastructure Program; Canada-Ontario Municipal Rural Infrastructure Fund; Canada Strategic Infrastructure Fund; Community Adjustment Fund; Community Infrastructure Improvement Fund; Community Futures Program; Eastern Ontario Development Program; Economic Development Initiative; Graduate Enterprise Internship; Investing in Business Innovation; Municipal Rural Infrastructure Fund Top-Up; Ontario Potable Water Program; Prosperity Initiative; Recreational Infrastructure Canada Program in Ontario; Scientists & Engineers in Business; Southern Ontario Development Program; Technology Development Program; & Youth STEM.

Minister Responsible; Minister, Economic Development, Hon. Helena Jaczek, P.C.

President, James Meddings
Tel: 613-960-7093; Fax: 613-952-9384

Director General, Human Resources, Raquel Fragoso
Tel: 613-799-5824

Acting Director General, Communications, Kerri Dunning
Tel: 416-954-6652; Fax: 416-973-6400

Business, Innovation & Community Development / Innovation, commerciale et développement communautaire
Vice-President, Colette Downie
Tel: 613-698-5158
Director General, Innovation & Community Development, Linda Cousineau
Tel: 519-590-9255
Acting Director General, Innovation & Business Development, Diana Lakoseljac
Tel: 647-286-2170

Policy, Partnerships & Performance Management / Politiques, partenariats et gestion de rendement
Vice-President, Vacant
Director General, Partnerships & External Relations Directorate, Bohdana Dutka
Tel: 613-960-6154
Director General, Strategic Policy, Anoop Kapoor
Tel: 613-960-8944

Office of the Commissioner for Federal Judicial Affairs / Commissariat à la magistrature fédérale Canada

99 Metcalfe St., 8th Fl., Ottawa, ON K1A 1E3
Tel: 613-995-5140; Fax: 613-995-5615
Toll-Free: 877-583-4266
www.fja-cmf.gc.ca

Established in 1978, the Office of the Commissioner for Federal Judicial Affairs is responsible for the administration of Part I of the Judges Act. Federally appointed judges are provided with administrative services independent of the Department of Justice. Approximately 1,100 active judges & 800 retired judges are served by the Commissioners' Office.
The Office is also engaged in the following duties: management of the Judicial Appointments Secretariat & the Federal Courts Reports Section; coordination of initiatives related to the judiciary's role in international cooperation; preparation of a

budget; administration of a judical intranet & a virtual library; & the provision of language training to judges.

Commissioner for Federal Judicial Affairs Canada, Marc A. Giroux

Executive Director, Judicial Appointments; Senior Legal Counsel, Véronique Joly
Tel: 613-992-9400; Fax: 613-941-0607

Executive Editor, Federal Courts Reports, François Boivin
Tel: 613-947-8491; Fax: 613-995-5615

Director, Compensation, Pension, Benefits, & Human Resources, Nikki Clemenhagen
Tel: 613-947-9899; Fax: 613-995-5615

Director, Finance & Administration, Errolyn Humphreys
Tel: 613-947-8492; Fax: 613-995-5615

Director, Judges' Language Training, Dominique Allard
Tel: 613-992-2950; Fax: 613-947-8503

Director, International Programs, Oleg Shakov
Tel: 613-992-2990; Fax: 613-995-5615

Federal Public Sector Labour Relations & Employment Board (FPSLREB) / Commission des relations de travail et de l'emploi dans le secteur public fédéral (CRTESPF)

C.D. Howe Bldg., West Tower, 240 Sparks St., 6th Fl., PO Box 1525 Stn. B, Ottawa, ON K1P 5V2
Tel: 613-990-1800; Fax: 613-990-1849
Toll-Free: 866-931-3454
TTY: 866-389-6901
mail.courrier@fpslreb-crtespf.gc.ca
pslreb-crtefp.gc.ca
Other Communication: Staffing Complaints: director.directeur@fpslreb-crtespf.gc.ca; Jacob Finkelman Library: library-bibliotheque@tribunal.gc.ca

The FPSLREB was created in 2014 when the Public Service Labour Relations Board & the Public Service Staffing Tribunal merged. It is an independent quasi-judicial statutory tribunal operating under the Federal Public Sector Labour Relations & Employment Board Act, & is responsible for administering collective bargaining & grievance adjudication systems for the federal public service & Parliament.

Chair, Catherine Ebbs

Finance Canada / Finances Canada

90 Elgin St., Ottawa, ON K1A 0G5
Tel: 613-369-3710; Fax: 613-369-4065
TTY: 613-369-3230
fin.financepublic-financepublique.fin@canada.ca
www.fin.gc.ca
Other Communication: Media Enquiries, Phone: 613-369-4000; Email: fin.media-media.fin@canada.ca
twitter.com/financecanada
www.linkedin.com/company/finance-canada

The Department of Finance Canada is responsible for providing the federal government with analysis & advice on financial & economic issues. It also monitors & researches the performance of the Canadian economy's major factors (output, growth, employment, income, price stability, monetary policy, & long-term change). Interacting with various other federal departments & agencies, the Department encourages coordination in all federal initiatives with an impact on the economy. Emphasis is placed on consulting with the public regarding policy directions & options.

Deputy Minister, Paul Rochon
Tel: 613-369-4434

Associate Deputy Minister, Ava Yaskiel
Tel: 613-369-4431

Associate Deputy Minister & G7/G20 & FSB Deputy for Canada, Rob Stewart
Tel: 613-369-3878

Associated Agencies, Boards & Commissions:

• **Auditor General of Canada / Vérificateur Général du Canada**
See Entry Name Index for detailed listing.

• **Bank of Canada / Banque du Canada**
See Entry Name Index for detailed listing.

• **Canada Deposit Insurance Corporation / Société d'assurance-dépôts du Canada**
See Entry Name Index for detailed listing.

• **Canada Savings Bonds (CSB) / Obligations d'épargne du Canada (OEC)**
#201, 50 O'Connor St.
PO Box 2770 D
Ottawa, ON K1P 1J7
Tel: 905-754-2012; *Fax:* 613-782-8096
Toll-free: 800-575-5151
TTY: 800-354-2222
www.csb.gc.ca
Other Communication: Payroll Savings, Employees:
877-899-3599; Employers: 888-467-5999; Payroll Savings,
Email, Employers: employerhelpdesk@csb.gc.ca

• **Canada Revenue Agency / Agence du revenu du Canada**
See Entry Name Index for detailed listing.

• **Financial Consumer Agency of Canada / Agence de la consommation en matière financière du Canada**
See Entry Name Index for detailed listing.

• **Financial Transactions & Reports Analysis Centre of Canada (FINTRAC) / Centre d'analyse des opérations et déclarations financières du Canada (CANAFE)**
234 Laurier Ave. West, 24th Fl.
Ottawa, ON K1P 1H7
Fax: 613-943-7931
Toll-free: 866-346-8722
guidelines-lignesdirectrices@fintrac-canafe.gc.ca
www.fintrac.gc.ca
Other Communication: Electronic Reporting:
F2R@fintrac-canafe.gc.ca; Law Enforcement & Partner
Agencies: partner-partenaire@fintrac-canafe.gc.ca
Created in 2000, FINTRAC is Canada's financial intelligence
unit, a specialized agency created to collect, analyze & disclose
financial information & intelligence on suspected money
laundering & terrorist activities financing.

• **Office of the Superintendent of Financial Institutions / Bureau du surintendant des institutions financières Canada**
See Entry Name Index for detailed listing.

Consultations & Communications Branch / Direction des consultations et des communications
Assistant Deputy Minister, Sarah Lawley
Director General, Marie-Elise Rancourt
Tel: 613-369-9426

Corporate Services Branch / Direction des services ministériels
Provides joint services for the federal Treasury Board Secretariat
& Finance Canada.
Assistant Deputy Minister, Edward Poznanski
Tel: 613-369-3595
Director General, Information Management & Technology
Directorate, Philippe Lajeunesse
Tel: 613-369-3509
Director General, Financial Management Directorate, Adelle
Laniel
Tel: 613-369-3900
Director General, Human Resources & Security, Janelle Wright
Tel: 613-369-3499
Senior Director & Deputy CIO, Strategic Planning & IM, Marc
Robillard
Tel: 613-369-3431

Economic & Fiscal Policy Branch / Direction de la politique économique et fiscale
Assistant Deputy Minister, Nick Leswick
Tel: 613-369-3346
Director General, Fiscal Policy, Bradley Recker
Tel: 613-369-5667
Director General, Economic Analysis & Forecasting Division,
Julie Turcotte
Tel: 613-369-5648
Senior Director, Forecast & Model Development, Matthew Emde
Tel: 613-369-4103
Senior Director, Economic Studies & Policy Analysis Division,
Michael Garrard
Tel: 613-369-4183
Senior Director, Expenditure Analysis & Forecasting, Rod
Greenough
Tel: 613-369-5663

Economic Development & Corporate Finance / Développement économique et finances intégrées
Assistant Deputy Minister, Richard Botham
Tel: 613-369-3623

Associate Assistant Deputy Minister, Soren Halverson
Tel: 613-369-3628
Director General, Sectoral Policy Analysis, Evelyn Dancey
Tel: 613-369-3642
Director General, Corporate Finance, Natural Resources &
Environment, Samuel Millar
Tel: 613-369-4122
Director General, Microeconomic Policy Analysis, Greg Reade
Tel: 613-369-3613
Director, Defence, Edward Malota
Tel: 613-369-9267

Federal-Provincial Relations & Social Policy Branch / Direction des relations fédérales-provinciales et de la politique sociale
Assistant Deputy Minister, Michelle Kovacevic
Tel: 613-369-9572
Director General, Social Policy, Roger Charland
Tel: 613-369-3887
Director General, Federal-Provincial Relations, Galen
Countryman
Tel: 613-369-5662
Senior Director, Indigenous Policy, Alexandrea Howard
Tel: 613-369-3554
Senior Director, Equalization & TFF Policy, Suzanne Kennedy
Tel: 613-369-5640
Senior Director, Health, Culture, Housing, Omar Rajabali
Tel: 613-369-4112

Financial Sector Policy Branch / Direction de la politique du secteur financier
Assistant Deputy Minister, Leah Anderson
Tel: 613-369-3620
Associate Assistant Deputy Minister, Annette Ryan
Tel: 613-369-4457
Director General, Financial System Division, Lisa Pezzack
Tel: 613-369-3864
Director General, Financial Institutions Division, Eleanor Ryan
Tel: 613-369-3904
Senior Director, Strategy & Coordination, Julien Brazeau
Tel: 613-369-6698
Senior Director, Framework Policy, Manuel Dussault
Tel: 613-369-3912
Senior Director, Pensions Policy, Lynn Hemmings
Tel: 613-369-3865
Senior Director, Market Policy, Robert Sample
Tel: 613-369-3899

International Trade & Finance Branch / Finances et échanges internationaux
Assistant Deputy Minister, Stewart Rick
Tel: 613-369-5691
Associate Assistant Deputy Minister, Paul Samson
Tel: 613-369-3603
Director General, International Policy & Analysis Division,
Antoine Brunelle-Côté
Tel: 613-369-3221
Director General, International Trade Policy Division, Patrick
Halley
Tel: 613-369-4036
Senior Director, Trade Rules, Michèle Govier
Tel: 613-369-4028

Law Branch / Direction juridique
Assistant Deputy Minister, Isabelle Jacques
Tel: 613-369-3305
Executive Director & Senior General Counsel, Finance Legal
Services, Jenifer Aitken
Tel: 613-369-3271
Executive Director & Senior General Counsel, Finance Legal
Services, Cindy Shipton-Mitchell
Tel: 613-369-3316
Executive Director & General Counsel, Finance Legal Services,
Robert Wong
Tel: 613-369-3335
Deputy Executive Director & Senior Counsel, Tax Counsel
Division, Thomas Boucher
Tel: 613-369-3342
Senior Counsel, General Legal Services Division, Yvonne
Milosevic
Tel: 613-369-3313
Director, Office of Values and Ethics, Gregory Gauthier
Tel: 613-369-3426

Tax Policy Branch / Direction de la politique de l'impôt
Senior Assistant Deputy Minister, Andrew Marsland
Tel: 613-369-3739
Assistant Deputy Minister, Tax Legislation, Brian Ernewein
Tel: 613-369-3743
Associate Assistant Deputy Minister, Miodrag Jovanovic
Tel: 613-369-3738

Director General, Intergovernmental Tax Policy, Evaluation &
Research Division, Isabella Chan
Tel: 613-369-9483
Director General, Tax Legislation, Ted Cook
Tel: 613-369-3685
Director General, Sales Tax Division, Phil King
Tel: 613-369-5609
Director General, Business Income Tax, Maude Lavoie
Tel: 613-369-3805
Director General, Personal Income Tax, Pierre Leblanc
Tel: 613-369-5721
Director General, GST Legislation, Pierre Mercille
Tel: 613-369-3792
Senior Director, Economic Analysis & Revenue Allocation, Bill
Chandler
Tel: 613-369-3756
Senior Director, Corporate & International Tax, Marc Darmo
Tel: 613-369-3683
Senior Director, Federal-Provincial Taxation Section, Claudine
Gagnon
Tel: 613-369-3818
Senior Director, Tax Legislation Division, Trevor McGowan
Tel: 613-369-3677
Senior Director, International Tax, Peter Repetto
Tel: 613-369-3686
Senior Director, International Taxation & Special Projects, Oliver
Rogerson
Tel: 613-369-4197
Senior Director, Quantitative Analysis Section, Marc Séguin
Tel: 613-369-3704
Senior Director, Tax Treaties, Stephanie Smith
Tel: 613-369-3659

Financial Consumer Agency of Canada (FCAC) / Agence de la consommation en matière financière du Canada (ACFC)

427 Laurier Ave. West, 6th Fl., Ottawa, ON K1R 1B9
Tel: 613-960-4666; *Fax:* 613-941-1436
TTY: 866-914-6097
www.canada.ca/en/financial-consumer-agency.html
Other Communication: Toll-Free Phone (English): 866-461-3222;
866-461-2232 (French)
twitter.com/fcacan
www.facebook.com/fcacan
www.linkedin.com/company/financial-consumer-agency-of-canad
a
Created by Parliament in 2001, the Financial Consumer Agency
of Canada (FCAC) exists to protect Canada's financial
consumers; to make them aware of their rights & responsibilities;
& to inform Canadians about the financial products & services
available to them. The FCAC ensures that the nearly 500
federally regulated financial institutions respect the consumer
provisions in the laws that govern them & monitors the voluntary
codes of conduct financial institutions have adopted. As well as
informing people about their rights as financial consumers, the
FCAC provides information & tools to help consumers shop
around for the best financial product/service for their situation.
As of July 2010, the FCAC oversees payment card network
operators & their commerical practices.

Commissioner, Lucie Tedesco
Tel: 613-941-4335

Deputy Commissioner, Brigitte Goulard
Tel: 613-641-4300; *Fax:* 613-941-1436

Financial Literacy Leader, Jane Rooney
Tel: 613-941-1528

Senior Counsel, Legal Services, Ekaterina Ohandjanian
Tel: 613-941-1425

Managing Director, Compliance Supervision & Promotion, Richard Bilodeau
Tel: 613-960-3382

Managing Director, Corporate Services Branch, Lesley
Ryan
Tel: 613-941-4239

Director, Marketing & Communications Branch,
André-Marc Allain
Tel: 613-941-4770

Director, Information Management/Information Technology Division, André Gilbert
Tel: 613-960-4622

Director, Education, Policy & Research, Bruno Levesque
Tel: 613-954-0274

Director, Finance & Administrative Services, Paul Potvin

Director, Financial Literacy/Coordination & Collaboration,
Jeremie Ryan
Tel: 613-957-7864

Office of the Superintendent of Financial Institutions (OSFI) / Bureau du surintendant des institutions financières Canada (BSIF)

Kent Square, 255 Albert St., 12th Fl., Ottawa, ON K1A 0H2
Tel: 613-990-7788; *Fax:* 613-990-5591
Toll-Free: 800-385-8647
TTY: 613-943-3980
information@osfi-bsif.gc.ca
www.osfi-bsif.gc.ca
Other Communication: Information (Ottawa-Gatineau), Phone:
613-943-3950

Responsible for regulating & supervising financial institutions & pension plans under federal jurisdiction. Included under federal jurisdiction are: banks, some insurance companies, trust companies, loan companies, cooperative credit associations, & fraternal benefit societies. OSFI monitors & examines these institutions & pension plans for solvency, liquidity, & compliance with legislation, regulations & Office guidelines. Provides actuarial services & advice to the Government of Canada. Reports to government through the Minister of Finance.

Superintendent, Jeremy Rudin
Tel: 613-990-3667; *Fax:* 613-993-6782
jeremy.rudin@osfi-bsif.gc.ca

Chief Actuary, Jean-Claude Ménard
Tel: 613-990-7577

Chief Audit Executive, Kent Trainor
Tel: 416-952-6688

Assistant Superintendent, Corporate Services Sector,
Michelle Doucet
Tel: 613-990-8761

Assistant Superintendent, Risk Support Sector, Ben R. Gully
Tel: 416-973-5469

Assistant Superintendent, Insurance Supervision Sector,
Neville S. Henderson
Tel: 416-954-0489

Assistant Superintendent, Deposit-Taking Supervision Sector, James Hubbs
Tel: 416-973-2598

Assistant Superintendent, Regulation Sector, Carolyn Rogers
Tel: 613-949-7643

Fisheries & Oceans Canada (DFO) / Pêches et Océans Canada (MPO)

200 Kent St., Ottawa, ON K1A 0E6
Tel: 613-993-0999; *Fax:* 613-990-1866
TTY: 800-465-7735
info@dfo-mpo.gc.ca
www.dfo-mpo.gc.ca
twitter.com/fishoceanscan
www.facebook.com/fisheriesoceanscanada

The Department of Fisheries & Oceans (DFO), on behalf of the Government of Canada, is responsible for policies & programs in support of Canada's economic, ecological & scientific interests in the oceans & freshwater fish habitat; for the conservation & sustainable utilization of Canada's fisheries resources in marine & inland waters; & for safe, effective & environmentally sound marine services responsive to the needs of Canadians in a global economy. The Department's mandate is extremely broad & covers management & protection of the marine & fisheries resources inside the 200-mile exclusive economic zone; management & protection of freshwater fisheries resources; marine safety along the world's longest coastline; facilitation of marine transportation; protection of the marine environment; support to other federal government institutions & objectives, as the government's civilian marine service; & research to support government priorities such as climate change & biodiversity. Because of its broad mandate, DFO does not operate alone. Federal & provincial governments share jurisdiction in a number of areas related to the Department's mandate.

Minister, Fisheries, Oceans & the Canadian Coast Guard,
Hon. Joyce Murray, P.C.

Deputy Minister, Catherine Blewett
Tel: 613-993-2200

Director & Senior General Counsel, Legal Services Unit,
Stephen Sharzer
Tel: 613-993-0966

Associated Agencies, Boards & Commissions:
• **Freshwater Fish Marketing Corporation / Office de commercialisation du poisson d'eau douce**
See Entry Name Index for detailed listing.

Canadian Coast Guard (CCG) / Garde côtière canadienne
Centennial Towers, #6S018, 200 Kent St., Ottawa, ON K1A 0E6
Tel: 613-993-0999; *Fax:* 613-990-1866
TTY: 800-465-7735
info@dfo-mpo.gc.ca
www.ccg-gcc.gc.ca
Other Communication: Coast Guard College, Toll-Free:
888-582-9090; Email: CCGCregistrar@dfo-mpo.gc.ca
twitter.com/CCG_GCC
www.youtube.com/user/CCGrecruitmentGCC

The Canadian Coast Guard provides the following maritime programs & services: search & rescue; marine communications & traffic services, including radio communications & radio navigational aids services; marine navigation services, a program which establishes & maintains navigational aids to assist vessels in safe navigation; enrivonmental response program, which works to minimize impacts of marine pollution incidents & to provide humanitarian aid in disasters; aids to navigation, such as the Differential Global Positioning System (DGPS) & Notices to Mariners (NOTMAR); icebreaking services; & client relations & international affairs.
Commissioner, Jeffery Hutchinson
Tel: 613-990-5813; *Fax:* 613-990-2780
Assistant Commissioner, Roger Girouard
Tel: 250-480-2766
Assistant Commissioner, Central & Arctic Region, Johnny Leclair
Tel: 514-283-0054
Deputy Commissioner, Operations, Mario Pelletier
Tel: 613-998-1575; *Fax:* 613-990-2780
Deputy Commissioner, Strategy & Shipbuilding, Andy Smith
Tel: 613-993-7728

Ecosystems & Ocean Science / Sciences des écosystèmes et des océans
200 Kent St., Ottawa, ON K1A 0E6
Responsible for the management & development of all federal fisheries & habitat in Canada. The division conserves, protects, develops & enhances fishery resources & habitats, encompassing the Atlantic & Pacific sectors, adjacent provinces, & the 200-mile offshore zone. Also manages Canadian parts of trans-boundary rivers.
Assistant Deputy Minister, Arran McPherson
Tel: 613-990-0271
Director General, Canadian Hydrographic Service, Geneviève Béchard
Tel: 613-990-6234
Acting Director General, Ecosystem Science Directorate, Louise Laverdure
Tel: 613-990-7075
Director General, Strategic & Regulatory Science Directorate, Wayne Moore
Tel: 613-990-0001
Director, Ocean Protection Plan, Una Blumberga
Tel: 613-898-9463

Canadian Hydrographic Service (CHS) / Service hydrographique du Canada
200 Kent St., Ottawa, ON K1A 0E6
Tel: 613-998-4921
Toll-Free: 866-546-3613
chsinfo@dfo-mpo.gc.ca
www.charts.gc.ca/help-aide/about-apropos/index-eng.asp
Federal program which offers the following: conducts field studies & gathers hydrographic information on tides, water levels & currents; compiles & publishes navigational charts & manuals for Canadian & adjacent international waters; works with Natural Resources Canada to cooperatively map boundary waters.
Director General, Denis Hains
Tel: 613-990-6234
Executive Director, Canada Meteorological & Oceanographic Society, Vacant
Executive Director Emeritus, Canada Meteorological & Oceanographic Society, Uri Schwarz
Tel: 613-991-0151

Fisheries & Harbour Management / Gestion des pêches et des ports
200 Kent St., Ottawa, ON K1A 0E6
Assistant Deputy Minister, Sylvie Lapointe
Tel: 613-990-9864

Director General, Fisheries Resource Management, Adam Burns
Tel: 613-993-6853
Director General, Small Craft Harbours, Denise Frenette
Tel: 506-381-3003
Director General, Conservation & Protection, Darren Goetze
Tel: 613-993-1414
Director General, Fisheries & Licence Policy, Mark Waddell
Tel: 613-949-4922
Director, International Fisheries Management & Bilateral Relations Bureau, Robert Day
Tel: 613-991-6135
Director, National Fisheries Intelligence Services, Yves Goulet
Tel: 613-991-9436
Director, Integrated Resource Management - National Programs, Randy Jenkins
Tel: 613-990-0018

Human Resources & Corporate Services / Services généraux
200 Kent St., Ottawa, ON K1A 0E6
Assistant Deputy Minister, Dominic Laporte
Tel: 613-993-8726; *Fax:* 613-993-3246
Chief Information Officer & Director General, Information Management & Technology Services, Hachem Ben Essalah
Tel: 613-993-2051
Director General, Human Resources, Tom Balfour
Tel: 613-990-0013
Director General, Real Property & Environmental Management, Bill Varvaris
Tel: 613-993-9291; *Fax:* 613-991-0061
Director, Program Planning & Coordination Unit, Sylvie Buendia Riva
Tel: 613-990-0110; *Fax:* 613-991-0061
Director, Strategic Business Management Branch, Glen Condran
Tel: 613-991-4313; *Fax:* 613-991-0061
Director, HRCS Enablers Readiness Team (HERO), Sharon Ford
Tel: 613-853-8364; *Fax:* 613-991-0061
Director, Centre for Values, Integrity & Conflict Resolution, Shauna M. Guillemin
Tel: 613-990-0048; *Fax:* 613-991-0061

National Strategies / Stratégies nationales
200 Kent St., Ottawa, ON K1A 0E6
Director General, Marc Sanderson
Tel: 613-991-3007
Director, Economic Industry Intelligence, Robert Brooks
Tel: 613-852-6307
Acting Director, Horizontal Priorities, Nadia Gilbert
Tel: 613-998-1411
Acting Regional Director, Oceans Protection Plan, Katie Jollez
Tel: 613-863-5793
Acting Director, Preparedness & Response, Kathy Nghiem
Tel: 613-462-4667
Director, Cost Recovery, Andrea Raper
Tel: 613-990-3115
Director, Safe Shipping, Lisa Vandehei
Tel: 613-998-1408

Operations / Opérations
200 Kent St., Ottawa, ON K1A 0E6
Responsible for the management & development of all federal fisheries & habitat in Canada. The division conserves, protects, develops & enhances fishery resources & habitats, encompassing the Atlantic & Pacific sectors, adjacent provinces, & the 200-mile offshore zone. Also manages Canadian parts of trans-boundary rivers.
Director General, Julie Gascon
Tel: 613-990-9172
Director, Maritime Security & Intelligence, Tanya Alvaro
Tel: 613-991-4503
Acting Director, Workforce Development & Information Strategies, Roch Barrette
Tel: 613-619-4076
Director, Pay Operations Support, Sonja Dannenberg
Tel: 613-282-4829
Director, Operational Business, Michele Le Blanc
Tel: 613-949-9125
Director, Maritime Security, Simon Melanson
Tel: 613-993-6943
Acting Director, Operational Personnel, Denise Veber
Tel: 613-991-0262

Strategic Policy / Politiques stratégiques
200 Kent St., Ottawa, ON K1A 0E6
Provides leadership in recommending, developing & monitoring policy frameworks that advance DFO's initiatives, support DFO programs, & are responsive to the changing needs of DFO clients. Provides strategic advice on departmental programs, develops long-term planning priorities for the department & coordinates cross-sectoral activities in support of government goals & departmental objectives.

Senior Assistant Deputy Minister, Anne Lamar
Tel: 613-993-1808; *Fax:* 613-993-6958
Director General, Economic Analysis & Statistics, Robert Elliott
Tel: 613-993-8597
Director General, Strategic Policy Directorate, Paul Gillis
Tel: 613-990-0287
Director General, Communications Branch, Marian Hubley
Tel: 613-990-0219
Director General, Aboriginal Affairs, Robert Lamirande
Tel: 613-991-6979
Acting Senior Director, Intergovernmental Affairs, Todd Williams
Tel: 613-991-4842
Acting Director, Global & Northern Affairs, Andrew McMaster
Tel: 613-993-0982
Acting Director, Trade & International Market Access, Ingrid Schenk
Tel: 613-949-7507

Research Facilities

www.dfo-mpo.gc.ca/science/regions/index-eng.htm

Bayfield Institute
867 Lakeshore Rd., PO Box 5050 Burlington, ON L7R 4A6
Tel: 905-336-4999
Comprises fisheries research, habitat management, hydrographic surveys & chart production & ships support. Together with the Freshwater Institute in Winnipeg, it provides the federal Fisheries & Oceans science programs for the Central & Arctic Region. Multiple partnerships with a variety of external stakeholders allow the Institute to be recognized internationally as a site of leading research in freshwater science.

Bedford Institute of Oceanography (BIO) / L'institut océanographique de Bedford
PO Box 1006 Dartmouth, NS B2Y 4A2
Tel: 902-426-2373; *Fax:* 902-426-8484
webmasterbio-iob@dfo-mpo.gc.ca
Administered by Fisheries & Oceans, Bedford Institute of Oceanography (BIO) is Canada's largest centre for ocean research. Scientists, engineers & technicians primarily from Fisheries & Oceans, & Natural Resources Canada, (smaller components are from National Defense & Environment & Climate Change) perform targeted research & provide advice on Atlantic marine environments. Programs include: fisheries research, ocean sciences & management, habitat ecology, marine chemistry, Canadian Hydrographic Service (producing navigation charts for the Atlantic & Arctic areas), marine environmental regional & resources geoscience, & seabird research & management. BIO based staff also conduct joint projects, such as sea floor mapping & exploration, & provide scientific response to marine environmental emergencies. Also located at Bedford is the Canadian Shark Research Laboratory & the Otolith Research Laboratory.

Centre for Aquaculture & Environmental Research / Centre de recherche sur l'aquaculture et l'environnement
4160 Marine Dr., West Vancouver, BC V7V 1N6
The Center for Aquaculture & Environmental Research (CAER) is a specialized centre for aquaculture & coastal research co-founded by Fisheries & Oceans Canada & the University of British Columbia.

Coldbrook Biodiversity Facility / Centre de biodiversité de Coldbrook
1420 Fish Hatchery Rd., Coldbrook, NS B4R 1B6
Tel: 902-679-5572
The Center for Aquaculture & Environmental Research (CAER) is a specialized centre for aquaculture & coastal research co-founded by Fisheries & Oceans Canada & the University of British Columbia.

Cultus Lake Salmon Research Lab / Laboratoire de recherche sur le saumon du lac Cultus
4222 Columbia Valley Hwy., Cultus Lake, BC V2R 5B6
The facility houses several laboratories, including an inorganic chemistry laboratory & a radioisotope laboratory. Artificial streams, ponds & an experimental hatchery are located on-site.

Freshwater Institute / Institut des eaux douces
501 University Cres., Winnipeg, MB R3T 2N6
Main areas of research are: fish habitats; limnology emphasizing mechanisms & processes of biological production & decomposition in lakes; studies related to energy development use, acidification, radionuclide & heavy metal pollution. Arctic research emphasizes commercially important fish & marine mammals & associated ecosystems, & the effects of hydroelectric developments & toxic chemical pollution on aquatic ecosystems. The Institute supports a major field camp at the Experimental Lakes Area. Activities include freshwater & arctic science, science oceans initiative, fish habitat management, fisheries management, small craft harbours, corporate services, communications & regional senior management. The federal fish inspection program, recently transferred to the new Canadian Food Inspection Agency (CFIA), continues to operate out of the FWI.

Gulf Fisheries Centre (GFC) / Centre de poissonerie du gulfe
343, av Université, CP 5030 Moncton, NB E1C 9B6
Tél: 506-851-6227
Téléc: 506-851-2435
info@dfo-mpo.gc.ca
The Gulf Fisheries Centre is home to one of two laboratories in Canada that specialize in shellfish health. Also contains the Mère Juliette Library, which is open to the general public. The library's collection contains 20,000 books & reports, 100 scientific journals, 10,000 microfiches & over a hundred videos.

Institut Maurice-Lamontagne (IML) / Maurice Lamontagne Institute (MLI)
850, rte de le Mer, CP 1000 Mont-Joli, QC G5H 3Z4
Tél: 418-775-0500
Téléc: 418-775-0730
Provides extensive research on: fisheries, fish habitat, oceanography, hydrography; development of marine renewable resources in the fields of fisheries, ocean industry development, commercial shipping & recreational boating. Main area of focus centres on the Gulf of St. Lawrence & estuary, Saguenay Fjord, Canadian Arctic, & the James, Hudson & Ungava Bays. Also performs the following research: environmental chemistry research on the distribution, transport & fate of contaminants in sediments, water & the food chain; ecotoxicology research & field assessments for biomarkers, fish pathology & embryotoxicity; molecular toxicology research for biomarkers, fish reproduction & steroid hormones; bioremediation study on the microbial degradation of petroleum oil hydrocarbons & microbial bioassays. Projects include the temporal & spatial monitoring of organic & inorganic contaminants in fish, shellfish & sediments of the St. Lawrence gulf & estuary. Also studying the effects of pulp & paper effluents & mercury & municipal effluents on the reproduction of fish.

Institute of Ocean Sciences (IOS) / Institut des sciences de la mer (ISM)
9860 West Saanich Rd., PO Box 6000 Sidney, BC V8L 4B2
Tel: 250-363-6517
Science divisions at IOS include: Canadian Hydrographic Service, Marine Environment & Habitat Science, Ocean Science & Productivity. Other departments & organizations at the IOS facility include: GSC Pacific - Sidney Pacific Geoscience Centre, Canadian Wildlife Service, Canadian Coast Guard, North Pacific Marine Science Organization (PICES).

Mactaquac Biodiversity Facility / Centre de biodiversité de Mactaquac
114 Fish Hatchery Lane, French Village, NB E3E 2C6
Tel: 506-363-3021
Science divisions at IOS include: Canadian Hydrographic Service, Marine Environment & Habitat Science, Ocean Science & Productivity. Other departments & organizations at the IOS facility include: GSC Pacific - Sidney Pacific Geoscience Centre, Canadian Wildlife Service, Canadian Coast Guard, North Pacific Marine Science Organization (PICES).

Northwest Atlantic Fisheries Centre / Centre des pêches de l'Atlantique Nord-ouest
80 East White Hills Rd., St. John's, NL A1A 5J7
Tel: 709-772-4423; *Fax:* 709-772-4880
The Eastern Arctic field camp at Resolute Bay has been inactive for several years due to deteriorating conditions. However, with increasing interest in how global warming is affecting arctic marine conditions, the site, which includes a laboratory, warehouse & living quarters may be re-opened in the future.

Pacific Biological Station (PBS) / La station de biologie du Pacifique
3190 Hammond Bay Rd., Nanaimo, BC V9T 6N7
Tel: 250-756-7000; *Fax:* 250-756-7053
Research at PBS responds to stock assessment, aquaculture, marine environment & habitat science, & ocean science & productivity priorities.

St. Andrews Biological Station (SABS) / La Station biologique de St. Andrews
531 Brandy Cove Rd., St Andrews, NB E5B 2L9
Tel: 506-529-8854; *Fax:* 506-529-5862
xmarsabs@mar.dfo-mpo.gc.ca
Chemical & ecological studies on the interaction between oceanography & fisheries/aquaculture & the aquatic environment. Stock assessments & associated research on commercially important groundfish, pelagic finfish, invertebrate species in the Bay of Fundy & other areas of Atlantic Canada. Research in support of the existing salmon aquaculture industry & research on other species with potential for aquaculture in Atlantic Canada. Major environmental research projects include: risk assessment of organic chemicals to fisheries; biochemical indicators of health of aquatic animals; aquatic toxicity of marine phytotoxins; molluscan toxins, techniques & improvements; phytotoxin research; aquaculture ecology research; effectiveness of acid rain control programs; effects of aquaculture in the coastal environment.

Sea Lamprey Control Centre / Centre de contôle de la lamproie de mer
1219 Queen St. East, Sault Ste Marie, ON P6A 2E5
The Centre is a combined office, lab, warehouse, aquarium, & maintenance & chemical storage facility that houses Canada's Sea Lamprey Control program & the research lab of the Great Lakes Laboratory for Fisheries & Aquatic Sciences (GLLFAS). It is located on the grounds of the Sault Ste. Marie Canal National Historic Site.

Freshwater Fish Marketing Corporation / Office de commercialisation du poisson d'eau douce

1199 Plessis Rd., Winnipeg, MB R2C 3L4
Tel: 204-983-6601; *Fax:* 204-983-6497
sandic@freshwaterfish.com
www.freshwaterfish.com
The Corporation is a buyer, processor & marketer of freshwater fish, harvested from over 400 lakes in Manitoba, Saskatchewan, Alberta, the Northwest Territories & Northwestern Ontario. Reports to the government through the Minister of Fisheries & Oceans.

President & Chief Executive Officer, Stan Lazar

Vice-President, Field Operations, Dave Bergunder
dave.bergunder@freshwaterfish.com

Vice-President, Sales & Marketing, Eddie Campbell

Vice-President, Human Resources & Government Services, Wendy Matheson
wendy.matheson@freshwaterfish.com

Director, Plant Operations, Dawn Kjarsgaard
dawn.kjarsgaard@freshwaterfish.com

Manager, Business Development, Rob Black
rob.black@freshwaterfish.com

Global Affairs Canada (GAC) / Affaires mondiales Canada (AMC)

Enquiries Service, 125 Sussex Dr., Ottawa, ON K1A 0G2
Fax: 613-996-9709
Toll-Free: 800-267-8376
TTY: 613-944-1310
www.international.gc.ca
Other Communication: Emergency Assistance While Abroad, Email: sos@international.gc.ca; Jules Léger Library, Phone: 343-203-6150
twitter.com/canadatrade
www.facebook.com/canadaandtheworld
www.linkedin.com/groups/1808582
www.instagram.com/gacanada.amcanada
In 1909, the Canada Department of External Affairs was established. Prior to the 2015 general election, the department was known as Foreign Affairs, Trade & Development Canada. After the election, Prime Minister Trudeau renamed the department Global Affairs Canada.
The department's mandate includes the following responsibilities: to manage the nation's diplomatic & consular relations; to ensure that foreign policy advances national interests; to promote international trade; to strengthen trading arrangements; to increase free & fair market access at bilateral, regional, & global levels; & to work with partners to attain improved economic opportunity & enhanced security for Canadians at home & abroad.
The department funds the following programs in Canada & throughout the world: Anti-Crime Capacity Building Program; Canada in La Francophonie; Canadian International Arctic Fund; Counter-Terrorism Capacity Building Program; Global Commerce Support Program (Invest Canada-Community Initiatives, Going Global Innovation, & Global Opportunities for Associations); Global Partnership Program; Global Peace and Security Fund (Global Peace & Security Program, Global Peace Operations Program, & Glyn Berry Program); International Education & Youth; International Science & Technology Partnerships Program; Investment Cooperation Program; Permanent Secretariat of the UN Convention on Biological Diversity; United Nations Trust Fund on Indigenous Issues; & United Nations Voluntary Fund for Victims of Torture.
The department also offers travel reports & warnings, such as information about security, entry requirements, health conditions, & local customs & laws (travel.gc.ca/travelling/advisories).
In March 2013, the Canadian International Development Agency (CIDA) merged with the former Department of Foreign Affairs & International Trade (DFAIT).

Minister, Foreign Affairs, Hon. Mélanie Joly, P.C.

Minister, International Development, Hon. Harjit Sajjan, P.C.

Tel: 613-995-0881; *Fax:* 613-995-1091
Karina.Gould@parl.gc.ca

Minister, Small Business & Export Promotion; Minister, International Trade, Hon. Mary Ng, P.C.
Tel: 613-996-3374; *Fax:* 613-992-3921
Mary.Ng@parl.gc.ca

Associated Agencies, Boards & Commissions:
• **Canadian Commercial Corporation**
See Entry Name Index for detailed listing.
• **Export Development Canada**
See Entry Name Index for detailed listing.
• **International Development Research Centre**
See Entry Name Index for detailed listing.
• **International Joint Commission**
See Entry Name Index for detailed listing.
• **National Capital Commission**
See Entry Name Index for detailed listing.
• **North American Free Trade Agreement (NAFTA) Canadian Secretariat**
See Entry Name Index for detailed listing.

Office of the Minister, Foreign Affairs
The Minister of Foreign Affairs is responsible for Canada's foreign policy & issues related to external affairs. The Minister oversees the International Centre for Human Rights & Democratic Development, the International Development Research Centre, the International Joint Commission, & the National Capital Commission.
Minister, Foreign Affairs, Hon. Marc Garneau, P.C.
Tel: 613-996-7267; *Fax:* 613-995-8632
marc.garneau@parl.gc.ca
Director, Parliamentary Affairs, Vincent Garneau
Tel: 343-203-1851
Director, Operations, Dahlia Dtein
Tel: 343-203-1851
Director, Policy, Laurence Deschamps-Laporte
Tel: 343-203-1851
Director, Communications, Laurence Deschamps-Laporte
Tel: 343-203-1851
Parliamentary Secretary, Matt DeCourcey
Tel: 343-203-1851

Office of the Minister, International Development
www.international.gc.ca/development-developpement/index.aspx
twitter.com/dfatd_dev
www.facebook.com/DFATDDevelopment
The Minister of International Development is responsible for Canada's international development & humanitarian objectives through managing support & resources, & engaging in policy development in Canada & internationally.
Minister, International Development, Hon. Karina Gould, P.C.
Tel: 613-995-0881; *Fax:* 613-995-1091
Karina.Gould@parl.gc.ca
Director, Communications, Louis Bélanger
Tel: 343-203-6238
Director, Parliamentary Affairs, Russell Milon
Tel: 343-203-5975
Director, Policy, Suzanne Taylor
Tel: 343-203-6238
Parliamentary Secretary, Celina Caesar-Chavannes
Tel: 343-203-6238

Office of the Minister, International Trade Diversification
Responsibilities of the Minister of Foreign Affairs include international trade & commerce. The Minister oversee the Canadian Commercial Corporation, Export Development Canada, & NAFTA - Canadian Secretariat.
Minister, International Trade; Minister, Small Business & Export Promotion, Hon. Mary Ng, P.C.
Tel: 613-996-3374; *Fax:* 613-992-3921
Mary.Ng@parl.gc.ca
Director, Policy, Christopher A. Berzins
Tel: 343-203-7332
Director, Parliamentary Affairs, Jamie Innes
Tel: 343-203-7332
Director, Communications, Jamie Innes
Tel: 343-203-7332

Office of the Deputy Minister, Foreign Affairs
Deputy Minister, Foreign Affairs, Ian Shugart
Tel: 343-203-4911
Executive Director, Sara Cohen
Tel: 343-203-5986

Office of the Associate Deputy Minister, Foreign Affairs
Associate Deputy Minister, David Morrison
Tel: 343-203-1680
Director, Office of the Associate Deputy Minister, Victoria Fuller
Tel: 343-203-5983

Office of the Deputy Minister, International Development
Deputy Minister, International Development, Diane Jacovella
Tel: 343-203-6089
Executive Advisor, Nicole Martel
Tel: 343-203-6622

Office of the Deputy Minister, International Trade
Deputy Minister, International Trade, John Hannaford
Tel: 343-203-5000
Executive Director, Shendra Melia
Tel: 343-203-5961

Americas / Amériques
Assistant Deputy Minister, Michael Grant
Tel: 343-203-3555
Director General, Central America & Caribbean Bureau, Julia Cyrenne
Tel: 343-203-4648
Director General, Geographic Coordination & Mission Support Bureau, Stuart P. Savage
Tel: 343-203-3645
Director General, Latin America & Caribbean Bureau, Cheryl Urban
Tel: 343-203-2707
Director General, North America Strategy Bureau, Eric Walsh
Tel: 343-203-3548
Director General, North America Advocacy & Commercial Programs, Sara Wilshaw
Tel: 343-203-3585

Asia Pacific / Asie-Pacifique
Assistant Deputy Minister, Donald Bobiash
Tel: 343-203-2197
Director General, Southeast Asia, Ian Burchett
Tel: 343-203-3406
Director General, South Asia, David B. Hartman
Tel: 343-203-4492
Director General, North Asia & Oceania, Sarah J. Taylor
Tel: 343-203-3463
Director, Business Management Office for Asia & the Americas, Mark Burger
Tel: 343-203-1840
Director, Strategic Planning Operations & TRIGR, Andrew (Drew) Smith
Tel: 343-203-4509

Chief Audit Executive / Dirigeant principal de la vérification
Chief Audit Executive, Brahim Achtoutal
Tel: 343-203-5354
Director, Management Audits, John Corbeil
Tel: 343-203-5353
Director, Program Audit, Jacques Côté
Tel: 343-203-5355

Consular, Security, & Emergency Management (CSO) / Services consulaire, sécurité et gestion d'urgence (DPS)
Assistant Deputy Minister, Heather L. Jeffrey
Tel: 343-203-2556
Director General, Consular Policy Bureau, Mark Berman
Tel: 343-203-2758
Director General, Consular Operations, Lisa Helfand
Tel: 343-203-2756
Director, Emergency Operations, Brent Robson
Tel: 343-203-2656

Corporate Planning, Finance & Information Technology / Planification ministérielle, finance et technologie de l'information
Assistant Deputy Minister & Chief Financial Officer, Arun Thangaraj
Tel: 343-203-1433
Director General, Financial Resource Planning & Management, Shirley Carruthers
Tel: 343-203-5385
Director General, Information Management & Technology, Kristina Casey
Tel: 343-203-1196
Director General, Corporate Planning & Reporting, Laura Gorrie
Tel: 343-203-6363
Director General, Corporate Procurement & Asset Management, Bob L. Lawson
Tel: 343-203-1462
Director General, Grants & Contributions Management, Mark Lusignan
Tel: 343-203-5583

Corporate Secretary / Secrétaire des services intégrés
Corporate Secretary & Director General, Jennifer MacIntyre
Tel: 343-203-3506
Executive Director, Owen Teo
Tel: 343-203-0000
Executive Director, Cabinet & Parliamentary Affairs Division, Colleen Calvert
Tel: 343-203-3511

Director, ATIP, Patrick Picard
Tel: 343-203-2147

Europe, Arctic, Middle East, & Maghreb / Europe, Arctique, Moyen-Orient et Maghreb
Assistant Deputy Minister, Stefanie Beck
Tel: 343-203-3445
Director General, Bureau of European Affairs, Tina-Louise Csontos
Tel: 343-203-3663
Director General, Middle East Bureau, Mark Glauser
Tel: 343-203-3304
Director General & Senior Arctic Official, Circumpolar & Eastern Europe, Alison LeClaire
Tel: 343-203-2320
Director General, North Africa, Israel, West Bank/Gaza, Troy Lulashnyk
Tel: 343-203-4513
Director, Business Management Office - Europe, Middle East, Maghreb & Africa, Guillaume Bernard
Tel: 343-203-3630

Global Issues & Development / Enjeux mondiaux et du développement
Assistant Deputy Minister, Christopher MacLennan
Tel: 343-203-2437
Director General, Health & Nutrition, Amy Baker
Tel: 343-203-6241
Director General, Economic Development, Wendy Drukier
Tel: 343-203-4782
Director General, International Organizations, Michael Gort
Tel: 343-203-2697
Director General, International Humanitarian Assistance, Stephen Salewicz
Tel: 343-203-6094
Director General, Social Development, Nancy Smyth
Tel: 343-203-1571
Director General, Food Security & Environment, Sue Szabo
Tel: 343-203-6098

Human Resources / Ressources humaines
Assistant Deputy Minister, Francis Trudel
Tel: 343-203-2009; *Fax:* 613-944-2411
Executive Director, Colin Gascon
Tel: 343-203-1969
Director General & Dean, Canadian Foreign Service Institute, Roxanne Dubé
Tel: 343-203-8155
Director General, Workplace Relations & Corporate Health Bureau, Claude Houde
Tel: 343-203-3779
Director General, Assignments & Executive Management, Heidi Kutz
Tel: 343-203-2008
Director General, Corporate & Operational Human Resources, Sheila Tenasco-Banerjee
Tel: 343-203-5587

Inspection, Integrity & Values & Ethics Bureau / Direction générale de l'inspection, de l'intégrité, des valeurs et de l'éthique
Director General, Tamara Guttman
Tel: 343-203-1507
Deputy Inspector General & Director, Inspections, Pierre Giroux
Tel: 343-203-1506
Director, Special Investigations Division, Jérôme Bernier
Tel: 343-203-1538

International Business Development, Investment & Innovation (Chief Trade Commissioner) / Développement du commerce international, investissement et innovation (Délégué commercial en chef)
Assistant Deputy Minister & Chief Trade Commissioner, Ailish Campbell
Tel: 343-203-1875
Director General, Investment & Innovation, Emmanuel Kamarianakis
Tel: 343-203-4113
Director General, Trade Portfolio Strategy & Coordination, Chris Moran
Tel: 343-203-1882
Director General, Regional Trade Operations & Intergovernmental Relations, Christopher J. Thornley
Tel: 343-203-2112
Director General, Trade Sectors, Christopher Wilkie
Tel: 343-203-3828
Chief Operating Officer, Invest Canada Hub Transition Team, Kim Butler
Tel: 343-203-3828

Canadian Trade Commissioner Service (TCS) / Service des délégués commerciaux du Canada (SDC)
TCS Enquiries Service, c/o Global Affairs Canada, 125 Sussex Dr., Ottawa, ON K1A 0G2
Tel: 613-944-9991; *Fax:* 613-996-9709
Toll-Free: 888-306-9991
trade@international.gc.ca
www.tradecommissioner.gc.ca
twitter.com/tcs_sdc
www.facebook.com/canadatrade
www.linkedin.com/company/the-canadian-trade-commissioner-service

The Canadian Trade Commissioner Service was founded in 1894, & now has offices across Canada & in 160 countries worldwide. With a mandate to help Canadian businesses succeed in the global marketplace, the TCS offers intelligence, qualified contacts, partnership opportunities & practical advice on foreign markets. Note that the Virtual Trade Commissioner has closed, & information on trade commissioners' coordinates, market information & events by region, sector & country can be found on the TCS website.
Director General, Trade Commissioner Service - Operations, Duane McMullen
Tel: 343-203-1879

Trade Offices in Canada
tradecommissioner.gc.ca/office-bureau/canada.aspx
Atlantic Region - Halifax Regional Office
#415, 1791 Barrington St., Halifax, NS B3J 3L1
Fax: 902-426-5218
Toll-Free: 888-306-9991
roatl-atlantic@international.gc.ca
tradecommissioner.gc.ca/nova-scotia-nouvelle-ecosse
Senior Trade Commissioner & Director, Christine Smith
christine.smith@international.gc.ca
Deputy Director, Carolyn Wood
carolyn.wood2@international.gc.ca

Ontario Region - Toronto Regional Office
180 Queen St. West, 9th Fl., Toronto, ON M5V 3X3
Fax: 416-973-8161
Toll-Free: 888-306-9991
ontario.tcs-sdc@international.gc.ca
tradecommissioner.gc.ca/ontario
Director & Senior Trade Commissioner, Patricia Langan-Torell

Pacific Region - Vancouver Regional Office
#2000, 300 West Georgia St., Vancouver, BC V6B 6E1
Fax: 604-666-0954
Toll-Free: 888-306-9991
pacific-pacifique.tcs-sdc@international.gc.ca
tradecommissioner.gc.ca/british-columbia-colombie-britannique
Director & Senior Trade Commissioner, Christian Hansen
Tel: 604-666-8888

Prairies & Northwest Territories Region - Calgary Regional Office
East Tower, #418, 220 - 4th Ave. SE, Calgary, AB T2G 4X3
Fax: 403-292-4578
Toll-Free: 888-306-9991
prairies.tcs-sdc@international.gc.ca
tradecommissioner.gc.ca/alberta
Senior Trade Commissioner & Regional Director, Darryl Davies
darryl.davies@international.gc.ca

Quebec Region & Nunavut - Montréal Regional Office
Place Bonaventure, Portail Sud-Ouest, #8750, 800, rue de la Gauchetiere ouest, Montréal, QC H5A 1K6
Fax: 514-283-8794
Toll-Free: 888-306-9991
quebec.tcs-sdc@international.gc.ca
tradecommissioner.gc.ca/quebec
Senior Trade Commissioner, Joanne Lemay

International Platform / Plateforme internationale
Assistant Deputy Minister, Dan Danagher
Tel: 343-203-1484
Acting Director General, IPB Corporate Services Bureau, Dominique Bélanger
Tel: 343-203-1487
Director General, Project Delivery, Professional & Technical Services, Eugene Chown
Tel: 343-203-8263
Director General, Client Relations & Mission Operations, Peter Lundy
Tel: 343-203-1354
Director General, Planning & Stewardship, Karl Shepherd
Tel: 343-203-8355
Executive Director, International Platform Branch Transformation, Andrew Stirling
Tel: 343-203-5789

International Security / Sécurité internationale
Assistant Deputy Minister, Mark Gwozdecky
Tel: 343-203-5966

Director General, Counter-Terrorism, Crime & Intelligence Bureau, Martin Benajmin
Tel: 343-203-3176
Director General, Peace & Stabilization Operations, Larisa Galadza
Tel: 343-203-2825
Director General, International Security Policy Bureau, Cindy Termorshuizen
Tel: 343-203-3935
Executive Director, Office of Human Rights, Freedom & Inclusion - Human Rights, Mark Allen
Tel: 343-203-2907
Director, Office of Human Rights, Freedom & Inclusion - Democracy, Tara J. Denham
Tel: 343-203-2322
Director, Office of Human Rights, Freedom & Inclusion - Religious Freedom, Giuliana Natale
Tel: 343-203-3351

Office of Protocol / Bureau du Protocole
Chief of Protocol, Roy B. Norton
Tel: 343-203-3005
Deputy Chief of Protocol & Director, Diplomatic Corps Services, Mary Anne Dehler
Tel: 343-203-3015
Deputy Chief of Protocol & Director, Official Events, Isabelle Savard
Tel: 343-203-2877
Deputy Director, Privileges, Immunities & Accreditation, Stéphane Henry
Tel: 343-203-3021
Deputy Director, Heads of Mission & Outreach Programs, Jane Rooney
Tel: 343-203-3007
Deputy Director, Management Services, Tracie Royal
Tel: 343-203-3029

Partnerships for Development Innovation / Partenariats pour l'innovation dans le développement
Assistant Deputy Minister, Caroline Leclerc
Tel: 343-203-4725
Director General, Canadian Partnership for Health & Social Development, Louise Holt
Tel: 343-203-0580
Director General, Inclusive Growth, Governance & Innovation, Joshua Tabah
Tel: 343-203-6507
Director General, Engaging Canadians, Marianick Tremblay
Tel: 343-203-6485

Public Affairs / Affaires publiques
Assistant Deputy Minister, Stéphane Levesque
Tel: 343-203-1650
Director General, Public Affairs, Charles Mojsej
Tel: 343-203-1711
Executive Director, Development, Latifa Belmahdi
Tel: 343-203-1660
Acting Executive Director, Trade, Vikas Sharma
Tel: 343-203-8456
Deputy Director, Public Affairs & Public Diplomacy, Evan Potter
Tel: 343-203-1683

Strategic Policy / Politique stratégique
Assistant Deputy Minister, Elissa A. Golberg
Tel: 343-203-6494
Director General, Evaluation & Results Bureau, Ralph Jansen
Tel: 343-203-4731
Director General, International Assistance Policy, Deirdre Kent
Tel: 343-203-4729
Director General, International Economic Policy, Marie-Josée Langlois
Tel: 343-203-5147
Director General, Foreign Policy, Alexandre Lévêque
Tel: 343-203-2110

Sub-Saharan Africa / Afrique subsaharienne
Assistant Deputy Minister, Leslie Norton
Tel: 343-203-4945
Director General, Pan-Africa Bureau, Paula Caldwell
Tel: 343-203-3339
Director General, Southern & Eastern Africa Bureau, Marc-Andre Fredette
Tel: 343-203-4928
Director, Benin, Burkina Faso, DRC & Nigeria Development Division, Paul Amrita
Tel: 343-203-5024
Director, West & Central Africa Bureau, Jean-Bernard Parenteau
Tel: 343-203-5028
Deputy Director, Mali Development Division, Amélie Bordeleau
Tel: 343-203-4849
Deputy Director, Benin & Burkina Faso Division, Jan Jakobiec
Tel: 343-203-5018

Deputy Director, Senegal Development Division, Pascale Turcotte
Tel: 343-203-4851

Trade Policy & Negotiations Branch / Politique & négociations commerciales
Assistant Deputy Minister, Steve Verheul
Tel: 343-203-4455
Associate Assistant Deputy Minister, Bruce Christie
Tel: 343-203-4120
Chief Air Negotiator/Director General, Intellectual Property & Services Trade, Louis Marcotte
Tel: 343-203-4453
Director General & Special Advisor, Trade Policy & Negotiations, André Downs
Tel: 343-203-4082
Director General, Market Access, Doug Forsyth
Tel: 343-203-4414
Director General, Trade Negotiations, Kendal Hembroff
Tel: 343-203-4226
Director General, Trade & Export Controls, Rouben Khatchadourian
Tel: 343-203-4337
Director General, North American Trade Policy & Negotiations Bureau, Martin Moen
Tel: 343-203-4190
Director, Canada-European Union Comprehensive Economic & Trade Agreement (CETA) Secretariat, Mary-Catherine Speirs
Tel: 343-203-4097

Great Lakes Pilotage Authority (GLPA) / Administration de pilotage des Grands Lacs (APGL)

202 Pitt St., 2nd fl., PO Box 95 Cornwall, ON K6H 5R9
Tel: 613-933-2991; *Fax:* 613-932-3793
www.glpa-apgl.com
The Authority provides pilotage services in the waters of the St. Lawrence River commencing at the northern entrance of St. Lambert Lock, the Great Lakes area & the Port of Churchill, Manitoba. Reports to government through the Minister of Transport.

Chair, Danièle Dion

Chief Executive Officer, Robert Lemire, C.A.
rlemire@glpa-apgl.com

Chief Financial Officer, Stéphane Bissonnette
sbissonnette@glpa-apgl.com

Director, Operations, Diane Couture
dcouture@glpa-apgl.com

Health Canada / Santé Canada

Address Locator 0900C2, Ottawa, ON K1A 0K9
Tel: 613-957-2991; *Fax:* 613-941-5366
Toll-Free: 866-225-0709
TTY: 800-465-7735
info@hc-sc.gc.ca
www.canada.ca/en/health-canada.html
Other Communication: Information on Medical Marijuana: 866-337-7705; omc-bcm@hc-sc.gc.ca
twitter.com/healthcanada
www.facebook.com/HealthyCdns
www.youtube.com/user/healthcanada

In partnership with provincial & territorial governments, Health Canada (HC) develops health policy, enforces health regulations, promotes disease prevention, & enhances healthy living for all Canadians. HC ensures that health services are available & accessible to First Nations & Inuit communities. It works closely with other federal departments, agencies & health stakeholders to reduce health & safety risks to Canadians. Through its Health Intelligence Network, HC works with other levels of government & the health care system in the surveillance, prevention, control & research of disease outbreaks across Canada & around the world. It also monitors health & safety risks related to the sale & use of drugs, food, chemicals, pesticides, medical devices & certain consumer products. HC negotiates agreements regarding hazardous materials in the workplace, performs medical assessments for pilots & air traffic controllers, & conducts environmental health assessments. As of April 1, 2013, Health Canada assumed the responsibilities & functions under the Hazardous Materials Information Review Act, formerly carried out by the Hazardous Materials Information Review Commission.

Minister, Health, Hon. Jean-Yves Duclos, P.C.

Deputy Minister, Stephen Lucas
Tel: 613-957-7519

Ombudsman, Ombudsman, Integrigrity & Resolution

Office (OIRO), Karen Shepherd
Tel: 613-948-8259

Director, Parliamentary Affairs, Adam Exton
Tel: 613-957-0200

Director, Policy, Kathryn Nowers
Tel: 613-957-0200

Associated Agencies, Boards & Commissions:

• **Canadian Institutes of Health Research / Instituts de recherche en santé du Canada**
See Entry Name Index for detailed listing.

• **Mental Health Commission of Canada (MHCC) / Commission de la santé mentale du Canada**
#1210, 350 Albert St.
Ottawa, ON K1R 1A4
Tel: 613-683-3755; *Fax:* 613-798-2989
mhccinfo@mentalhealthcommission.ca
www.mentalhealthcommission.ca
The Mental Health Commission of Canada is mandated to improve the mental health system & help change Canadians' attitudes & behaviours around mental health issues.

• **Pest Management Regulatory Agency (PMRA) / Agence de réglementation de la lutte antiparasitaire (ARLA)**
See Entry Name Index for detailed listing.

• **Public Health Agency of Canada / Agence de santé publique du Canada**
130 Colonnade Rd.
Ottawa, ON K1A 0K9
Toll-free: 844-280-5020
www.phac-aspc.gc.ca
Promotes & protects the health & safety of all Canadians. Its activities focus on preventing chronic diseases, including cancer & heart disease, preventing injuries, & responding to public health emergencies & infectious disease outbreaks.

Health Canada Regulations Section / Section de la réglementation
General Counsel & Director, Claude Lesage
Tel: 613-952-9645

Legal Services / Services juridiques
www.hc-sc.gc.ca/ahc-asc/branch-dirgen/ls-sj/index-eng.php
Executive Director & Senior General Counsel, Samantha Dickson
Tel: 613-957-3766

Chief Financial Officer Branch (CFOB) / Direction générale du contrôleur ministériel (DGCM)
hc-sc.gc.ca/ahc-asc/branch-dirgen/cfob-dgcm/index-eng.php
Other Communication: Management Accountability Division,
Email: mcs-sfcm@hc-sc.gc.ca
The CFOB is the departmental focal point of accountability to ensure rigorous stewardship of resources & managing for results. The CFO provides the Minister, Deputy Minister, Associate Deputy Minister & the Departmental Executive with strategic advice on efficiency of expenditures & value-for-money, as well as anticipating & promoting future trends. The CFO reports directly to the Deputy Minister & is a key member of Health Canada's Senior Management Board. The CFO is also the lead executive with Central Agencies for overall financial management, with a functional reporting relationship to the Comptroller General of Canada.
Assistant Deputy Minister & Chief Financial Officer, Randy Larkin
Tel: 613-952-3985

Financial Operations Directorate
Director General, Todd Mitton
Tel: 613-957-7762
Executive Director, Policy, Internal Controls & Corp Accounting, Stanley Xu
Tel: 613-957-7324

Planning & Corporate Management Practices Directorate
Director General, Marc Desjardins
Tel: 613-948-6357

Resource Management Directorate
Director General, Edward de Sousa
Tel: 613-946-6358
Executive Director, Financial Management Office, Serena Francis
Tel: 613-957-1048

Communications & Public Affairs Branch / Direction générale des affaires publiques et des communications
The Communications & Public Affairs Branch integrates national & regional perspectives into all of its policies & strategies, communications & consultation functions. The Branch plays a key role in delivering Health Canada's commitment to transparency. Through the branch, Health Canada aims to continue improving communications & the flow of information to & from stakeholders, clients, partners, media & the Canadian public.
Assistant Deputy Minister, Jennifer Hollington
Tel: 613-960-2176
Director General, Public Affairs, Renee Couturier
Tel: 613-957-0215
Director General, Ministerial Communications, Jaimie Early
Tel: 613-948-8916
Director General, Strategic Communications Directorate, Sara MacKenzie
Tel: 613-960-6040

Controlled Substances & Cannabis Branch / Direction générale des substances contrôlées et du cannabis
Other Communication: URL:
www.canada.ca/en/health-canada/services/drugs-medication/cannabis/laws-regulations.html
Assistant Deputy Minister, Jacqueline Bogden
Tel: 613-957-2715
Associate Assistant Deputy Minister, Eric Costen
Tel: 613-948-8825
Director General, Licensing & medical Access, Cannabis, Todd Cain
Tel: 613-948-8302
Director General, Strategic Policy, Cannabis, John Clare
Tel: 613-941-2045
Acting Director General & Executive Director, Opioid Response Team, Jennifer Novak
Tel: 613-946-8099
Director General, Compliance, David Pellman
Tel: 613-948-6030
Director General, Tobacco Control, James Van Loon
Tel: 613-941-1977

Corporate Services Branch (CSB) / Direction générale aux services de gestion
The CSB provides corporate support & services across the Department in the following areas: human resources management; official languages; real property & facilities management; occupational health, safety emergency & security management; information technology & information management; executive correspondence; & access to information & privacy requests/issues.
Assistant Deputy Minister, Debbie Beresford-Green
Tel: 613-946-3200
Chief Information Officer, Information Management, Scott McKenna
Tel: 902-426-4600
Director General, Real Property & Security Directorate, Mark Featherstone
Tel: 613-952-6190
Director General, Human Resources, Daryl Gauthier
Tel: 613-957-3236
Director General, Planning, Integration & Management Services Directorate, Jean-Francois Luc
Tel: 613-946-8132
Director General, Specialized Health Services Directorate, Nancy Porteous
Tel: 613-957-7669
Executive Director, Real Property & Security Directorate, Paul Bortolotti
Tel: 613-952-0936
Executive Director, Security & Departmental Security Officer, Sandra Entwistle
Tel: 613-952-9550
Executive Director, Executive Group Services Division, Peter Hooey
Tel: 613-668-7893
Executive Director, Strategic Human Resources Management & Executive Group Services Division, Joanne Lirette
Tel: 613-957-3253
Acting Executive Director, Labour Relations, Michel Nasrallah
Tel: 613-954-2899
Executive Director, National Capital Real Property Division, Muhammad Nuraddeen
Tel: 613-946-3208
Executive Director, National Centralized HR Services, Cathy Peters
Tel: 613-957-2997
Executive Director, Information Management Services Directorate, Jason Reid
Tel: 613-595-0890
Executive Director, Business Renewal & Enterprise Architecture Directorate, Ian Skinner
Tel: 613-954-2647

Deputy Minister's Office / Bureau de la Sous-Ministre
Deputy Minister, Stephen Lucas
Tel: 613-957-7519
Associate Deputy Minister, Harpreet Kochlar
Tel: 613-954-5904
Associate Deputy Minister, Stephanie Poliquin
Tel: 613-957-7519

Health Products & Food Branch (HPFB) / Direction générale des produits de santé et des aliments (DGPSA)
HPFB's mandate is to take an integrated approach to the management of risks & benefits related to health products & food by minimizing health factors to Canadians while maximizing the safety provided by the regulatory system for health products & food; & to promote conditions that enable Canadians to make healthy choices & provide information so that they can make informed decisions about their health. The Environmental Impact Initiative develops strategy & policy in response to the Canadian Environmental Protection Act requirement that all new substances for use in Canada must be assessed for direct & indirect impact on human health & the environment.
Assistant Deputy Minister, Pierre Sabourin
Tel: 613-957-1804
Director General, Natural & Non-Prescription Health Products Directorate, Manon Bombardier
Tel: 613-952-2558
Director General, Office of Nutrition Policy & Promotion, Alfred Aziz, PhD
Tel: 613-948-2541
Director General, Veterinary Drugs Directorate, Mary-Jane Ireland
Tel: 613-954-1873
Director General, Biologics & Genetic Therapies Directorate, Celia Lourenco, PhD
Tel: 613-946-0099
Director General, Food Directorate, Karen McIntyre
Tel: 613-957-1820
Director General, Marketed Health Products Directorate, Marc Mes
Tel: 613-941-8889
Director General, Policy, Planning & International Affairs Directorate, Ed Morgan
Tel: 613-952-8149
Director General, Resource Management & Operations Directorate, Etienne Ouimette
Tel: 613-957-6690
Director General, Therapeutic Products Directorate, Dr. John Patrick Stewart
Tel: 613-957-6466
Senior Executive Director, Therapeutic Products Directorate, Marilena Bassi
Tel: 613-952-4619
Senior Medical Officer & Manager, Clinical Trials Division, Centre for Evaluation of Radiopharmaceuticals & Biotherapeutics, Daniel Keene
Tel: 613-960-0827

Healthy Environments & Consumer Safety (HECSB) / Direction générale, santé environnementale et sécurité des consommateurs (DGSESC)
The HECSB mission is to help Canadians to maintain & improve their health by promoting healthy & safe living, working & recreational environments & by reducing the harm caused by tobacco, alcohol, controlled substances, environmental contaminants, & unsafe consumer & industrial products.
Acting Assistant Deputy Minister, David Morin
Tel: 613-946-6701
Director General, Environmental & Radiation Health Sciences, Tim Singer
Tel: 613-954-3859

Consumer & Hazardous Products Safety Directorate / Direction de la sécurité des produits de consommation et des produits dangereux
hc.cps-spc.sc@canada.ca
Director General, Roger Charland
Tel: 613-957-1422

Safe Environments Programme (SEP) / Programme de la sécurité des milieux (PSM)
Investigates, monitors & assesses health risks in the work, home & natural environments. Areas investigated & regulated include: medical devices, chemicals & biotechnology products in the environment, drinking water, air quality, tobacco, hazardous products & toxic waste, as well as anything that emits radiation from natural & human sources. Aims to protect Canadians from health hazards associated with natural & man-made environments through assessment & investigation of the health effects of environmental pollutants & health hazards associated with radiation sources & hazardous products.
Acting Director General, Safe Environments Directorate, Greg Carreau
Tel: 613-954-0291

Pest Management Regulatory Agency (PMRA) / Agence de réglementation de la lutte antiparasitaire (ARLA)
2720 Riverside Dr., Ottawa, ON K1A 0K9

Tel: 613-736-3799; *Fax:* 613-736-3798
Toll-Free: 800-267-6315
TTY: 800-465-7735
hc.pmra.info-arla.sc@canada.ca
www.hc-sc.gc.ca/cps-spc/pest/index-eng.php
Other Communication: Agency URL:
www.hc-sc.gc.ca/ahc-asc/branch-dirgen/pmra-arla/index-eng.ph
p

Created in 1995, The PMRA determines if proposed pesticides can be used safely when label directions are followed & will be effective for their intended use. If there is reasonable certainty from scientific evaluation that no harm to human health, future generations or the environment will result from exposure to or use of a pesticide, its registration for use in Canada will be approved. Once the pesticides are on the market, the PMRA monitors their use through a series of education, compliance & enforcement programs. Pesticides are also reviewed every fifteen years or sooner as new information is discovered & as science evolves. Companies are also required to report any incident they receive about their products,just as the public is encouraged to report any incidents to these companies or through the Incident Reporting Program. The PMRA administers the Pest Control Products Act on behalf of the Minister of Health.

Regulatory, Operations & Enforcement Branch / Direction générale des opérations réglementaires et de l'application de la loi
Assistant Deputy Minister, Stefania Trombetti
Tel: 613-954-0690
Director General, Laboratories, Marie-France Blain
Tel: 450-928-4100
Director General, Medical Devices & Clinical Compliance, Ruth Rancy
Tel: 613-941-3344
Director General, Planning & Operations Directorate, Debbie Holbrook
Tel: 613-957-3152
Director General, Consumer Product Safety, Tobacco, Pesticides, Krista Locke
Tel: 902-407-7810
Other Communications: Secure Phone: 902-426-8248
Director General, Policy & Regulatory Strategies, Greg Loyst
Tel: 613-948-4274
National Director, Clinical Compliance, Border, & Vigilance, Alex Basiji
Tel: 416-973-1452

Cannabis Directorate / La direction du cannabis
Director General, Sara O'Connor
Tel: 613-960-1840
Director, Cannabis Inspections Operations, Gladis Lemus
Tel: 604-658-2809

Strategic Policy Branch (SPB) / Direction générale de la politique stratégique (DGPS)
The SPB plays a lead role in health policy, communications & consultations. The SPB's objective is to promote national coordination & development of a strong, shared knowledge base to address health & health care priorities for all Canadians. They also aim to facilitate successful health system adaptation to changes in technology, society, industry & the environment, such that Canadians will continue to be protected from health risks, have access to quality health care, & gain positive health benefits from information & innovation.
Assistant Deputy Minister, Abby Hoffman
Tel: 613-946-1791
Director General, Health Care Programs & Policy Directorate, Vacant
Acting Executive Director, Health Care Strategies Directorate, Peggy Ainslie
Tel: 613-957-9945
Executive Director, Canada Health Act Division, Gigi Mandy
Tel: 613-954-8685
Executive Director, Health Programs & Strategic Initiatives, Cindy Moriarty
Tel: 613-946-9375
Executive Director, Office of Pharmaceuticals Management Strategies, Karen Reynolds
Tel: 613-957-1692

Immigration & Refugee Board of Canada (IRB) / Commission de l'immigration et du statut de réfugié du Canada (CISR)

Minto Place, Canada Bldg., 344 Slater St., 12th Fl., Ottawa, ON K1A 0K1
Fax: 613-943-1550
www.irb-cisr.gc.ca
Other Communication: Legacy Office (Claims before December 2012): 833-534-2292
twitter.com/irb_canada
www.facebook.com/irbcanada
www.linkedin.com/company/immigration-and-refugee-board

The IRB is an independent administrative tribunal that reports to Parliament through the Minister of Immigration, Refugees & Citizenship. The Board's mission, on behalf of Canadians, is to make well-reasoned decisions on immigration & refugee matters efficiently, fairly, & in accordance with the law. As Canada's largest federal tribunal, the IRB consists of three divisions. The Refugee Protection Division decides claims for refugee protection made by persons in Canada. The Immigration Division conducts detention reviews & immigration inquiries for certain categories of people believed to be inadmissable, or removable from, Canada. The Immigration Appeal Division hears appeals of sponsorship applications refused by officials of Immigration, Refugees & Citizenship; appeals from certain removal orders made against permanent residents, refugees & other protected persons, & holders of permanent resident visas; appeals by permanent residents who have been found outside Canada not to have fulfilled their residency obligation; & appeals by Immigration, Refugees & Citizenship from decisions of the Immigration Division at admissability hearings.

Chair, Richard Wex
Tel: 613-670-6862

Deputy Chair, Immigration Appeal Division, Paul Aterman
Tel: 613-943-8630; *Fax:* 613-947-4860

Deputy Chair, Refugee Protection Division, Shereen Benzvy Miller
Tel: 613-670-6993

Deputy Chair, Immigration Division, Roula Eatrides
Tel: 613-670-7004

Deputy Chair, Refugee Appeal Division, Paula Thompson
Tel: 613-670-6907

Director General, Policy, Planning & Corporate Affairs Branch, Greg Kipling
Tel: 613-670-6958

Director General, Integrated Resource Management Branch, Barbara Wyant
Tel: 613-670-6985

Senior Director, Registry & Regional Support Services, Anab Ahmed
Tel: 613-670-6905

Chief Information Officer & Director, Information Management & Information Technology, Jean Côté
Tel: 613-670-6926

Director, Research Directorate, Danielle Blab
Tel: 613-291-5209

Director, Communications, Stephen Bolton
Tel: 613-670-6886

Director, Case Management Transformation, Cielle Laveaux
Tel: 514-449-2997

Acting Director, Linguistic Services Directorate, Sandra Morin
Tel: 613-220-3701

Director, Finance Directorate, Marcel Poirier
Tel: 613-670-6968

Director, Administration Directorate, Michel Thériault
Tel: 613-790-2448

Director, Access to Information & Privacy, Eric Villemaire
Tel: 613-716-9986

Senior General Counsel, Holly Holtman
Tel: 613-670-6910

Immigration, Refugees & Citizenship / Immigration, des Réfugiés et de la Citoyenneté

Jean Edmonds, South Tower, 365 Laurier Ave. West, Ottawa, ON K1A 1L1
Toll-Free: 888-242-2100
TTY: 888-576-8502
www.cic.gc.ca
twitter.com/citimmcanada
www.facebook.com/citcanada
instagram.com/citimmcanada

The Department of Immigration, Refugees & Citizenship (formerly Citizenship & Immigration (CIC), renamed Nov. 2015 by Prime Minister Trudeau) administers Canada's citizenship & immigration policies, procedures & service. The department is responsible for the following: examining immigrants, visitors & people claiming refugee status at land borders, seaports & airports; processing applications for permanent residence, extensions of visitor status requests & sponsorships for relatives & refugees overseas; admitting students, temporary workers & qualified business immigrants; investigating & removing people who are in Canada illegally; working with & helping fund a network of settlement agencies & services to help immigrants adapt to & participate in day-to-day Canadian life; promoting the acceptance of immigrants by Canadians; cooperating with various levels of government on enforcement, program development & the delivery of services; accepting applications & verifying the eligibility & documentation of applicants; granting citizenship & administration of the Oath of numerous community facilities across Canada; confirming Canadian citizenship status &; issuing proofs of citizenship to Canadians. The Immigration & Refugee Board reports to Parliament through the minister.

Minister, Immigration, Refugees & Citizenship, Hon. Sean Fraser, P.C.

Chief of Staff to the Minister, Ali Salam
Tel: 613-954-1064

Director, Policy, Kyle Nicholson
Tel: 613-954-1064

Director, Operations & Outreach, Zubair Patel
Tel: 613-954-1064

Director, Parliamentary Affairs, Olga Radchenko
Tel: 613-954-1064

Office of the Deputy Minister / Cabinet du sous-ministre
Fax: 613-954-3509
Other Communication: Secure Fax: 613-954-5448
Deputy Minister, Marta Morgan
Tel: 613-437-7830
Executive Director & Senior General Counsel, Legal Services, Caroline Fobes
Tel: 613-437-6722

Communications Branch / Direction générale des communications
Tel: 613-954-9019; *Fax:* 613-941-7099
Director General, David Hickey
Tel: 613-437-7634; *Fax:* 613-941-7099

Office of Internal Audit & Accountability / Bureau de vérification interne et responsabilisation
Fax: 613-952-6556
Director General & Chief Audit Executive, Raymond Kunze
Tel: 613-437-7226

Office of the Assistant Deputy Minister, Chief Financial Officer / Bureau de la sous-ministre adjointe, administrateur principal des finances
Fax: 613-957-2772
Assistant Deputy Minister & Chief Financial Officer, Daniel Mills
Tel: 613-437-6396
Director General, Financial Management, Christopher Meyers
Tel: 613-437-8537; *Fax:* 613-952-9772
Director General, Financial Operations, Nathalie Proulx
Tel: 873-408-0403

Office of the Assistant Deputy Minister, Corporate Services / Bureau de la sous-ministre adjointe, Services ministériels
Fax: 613-954-7360
Assistant Deputy Minister & Chief Information Officer, Zaina Sovani
Tel: 613-437-9190
Director General, Major Projects Branch, Ralph Bishop
Tel: 613-437-6643
Director General, Administration, Security & Accommodation, Bob Lanouette
Tel: 613-437-9206
Director General, Corporate Affairs, Michael Olsen
Tel: 613-437-7103; *Fax:* 613-957-5946

Director General, Solutions & Information Management Branch, Rachel Porteous
Tel: 613-437-7409

Office of the Assistant Deputy Minister, Operations / Bureau de la sous-ministre adjointe, Opérations
Fax: 613-957-8887
Associate Assistant Deputy Minister, Dawn Edlund
Tel: 613-952-1770

Centralized Network Branch / Réseau centralisé
Other Communication: Secure Fax: 613-941-6970
Director General, Heather Primeau
Tel: 613-437-6563

Citizenship & Passport Program Guidance Branch / Guidance des programmes de citoyenneté et de passeport
Fax: 613-941-7020
Director General, Lu Fernandes
Tel: 613-437-6763
Director, Service Management, Rouba Dabboussy
Tel: 613-437-9740
Director, Business Strategy & Innovation, Patrick Laflamme
Tel: 613-437-9722
Director, Passport Program Guidance, Allison Little Fortin
Tel: 613-437-9771
Director, Passport Foreign Operations, Mélanie Pronovost
Tel: 873-408-0532
Director, Corporate Support Services, Natasha Rysanek
Tel: 873-408-0193

Domestic Network Branch / Réseau national
Fax: 613-954-4621

International Network Branch / Réseau international
Fax: 613-941-2179
Director General, Mark Giralt
Tel: 613-437-7266
Acting Senior Director, Resettlement Operations, Jean-Marc Gionet
Tel: 613-437-7356
Acting Senior Director, Geographic Operations, Olivier Jacques
Tel: 613-437-7081
Director, NHQ - International Network, René Côté
Tel: 873-408-0210
Director, Workforce Management, Taitu Deguefé
Tel: 613-437-7310
Director, International Support, Jacquelyn Facette
Tel: 613-437-6390
Director, Strategic Planning & Delivery, Oscar Jacobs
Tel: 613-437-7330

Office of the Assistant Deputy Minister, Strategic & Program Policy / Cabinet du sous-ministre adjoint, Politiques stratégiques et de programmes
Fax: 613-946-6048
Assistant Deputy Minister, Paul McKinnon
Tel: 613-437-8297
Associate Assistant Deputy Minister, Mike MacDonald
Tel: 613-437-7132
Director General, Citizenship Branch, Alec Attfield
Tel: 613-437-6672
Director General, Admissibility Branch, Mieke Bos
Tel: 613-437-5937
Director General, Strategic Policy & Planning, Matt de Vlieger
Tel: 613-437-7499
Director General, Immigration Branch, Natasha Kim
Tel: 613-437-9683
Director General, International & Intergovernmental Relations, Glen Linder
Tel: 613-437-7492
Director General, Refugee Affairs, Fraser Valentine
Tel: 613-437-9196

Office of the Assistant Deputy Minister, Settlement & Immigration / Cabinet du sous-ministre adjoint, l'établissement et de l'intégration
Fax: 613-954-5896
Assistant Deputy Minister, David Manicom
Tel: 613-437-9152

Passport / Passeport
c/o Passport Program, Gatineau, QC K1A 0G3
Toll-Free: 800-567-6868
TTY: 866-255-7655
canada.ca/en/immigration-refugees-citizenship/services/canadians
twitter.com/passportcan
www.facebook.com/passportcan
Passport Canada became defunct in 2013, after the amended Canadian Passport Order. Immigration, Refugees & Citizenship Canada is the issuing authority. Passports include regular passports, diplomatic passports, special passports, emergency travel documents, & temporary passports. Examples of Canadian travel documents are refugee travel documents &

certificates of identity.
Passport Canada service locations include Passport Canada regional offices, selected Canada Post counters, Service Canada Centres, & Government of Canada offices abroad. Only these locations are authorized to collect passport processing fees.
Non-Canadians may use Passport Canada's central office in Gatineau, Québec. It is responsible for certificates of identity & travel documents.
Persons who are sixteen years of age or older must apply for a passport using general adult application forms, which are available free of charge. An application must include the completed application form, proof of Canadian citizenship, two photographs, a document to support identity, plus the required fee.
Child applications must be complete for all Canadians who are under sixteen years of age. As of October 1, 2012, all applications for a child's passport require a detailed proof of parent age document to demonstrate a child & parent relationship.
Since 2009, everyone who travels to the United States by land, sea, or air, including Canadian & U.S. citizens, must present a valid passport or another secure document.
As of July 1, 2013, all new Canadian passports are issued as ePassports, which contain enhanced security features & embedded electronic chips.
Director General, Passport Modernization Project Office, Pemi Gill
Tel: 613-437-6950
Director, Investigation Division, Peter Bulatovic
Tel: 819-934-8525
Director, Strategic Management Division, Hubert Laferrière
Tel: 819-934-3841

Passport Offices
Persons who plan to travel within the next twenty business days should apply in person at a Passport Canada office.
Passport Canada offices are also able to deal with complex cases, such as lost, stolen, damaged, or inaccessible passports, absence of a guarantor, & applications for children when only one parent is participating.

Brampton
#401, 40 Gillingham Dr., Brampton, ON L6X 4X7
Urgent service is unavailable at the Brampton office. Clients who require express or pick-up service may use the Mississauga Passport Canada office.

Calgary - 4th Ave.
Harry Hays Building, #150, 220 - 4th Ave. SE, Calgary, AB T2G 4X3

Calgary - Sunpark Dr. SE
#120, 23 Sunpark Dr. SE, Calgary, AB T2X 3V1
Urgent service is unavailable at this office. Persons who need express or pick-up service are encouraged to apply at the 4th Avenue South East office in Calgary.

Chicoutimi
98, rue Racine est, Chicoutimi, QC G7H 1R1

Edmonton
Canada Place Building NW, #126, 9700 Jasper Ave., Edmonton, AB T5J 4C3

Fredericton
Frederick Square, #430, 77 Westmorland St., Fredericton, NB E3B 6Z3

Gatineau
Place du Centre, 200, promenade du Portage, 2e étage, Gatineau, QC K1A 0G4

Halifax
Maritime Centre, #1508, 1505 Barrington St.. 15th Fl., Halifax, NS B3J 3K5

Hamilton
Standard Life Building, 120 King St. West, Plaza Level, Hamilton, ON L8P 4V2

Kelowna
Capri Centre, #110, 1835 Gordon Dr., Kelowna, BC V1Y 3H4
In-person service & express service are available. Urgent service is unavailable at the Kelowna office.

Kitchener
40 Weber St. East, Mezzanine Level, Kitchener, ON N2H 6R3

Laval
Place Laval, #500, 3, Place Laval, Laval, QC H7N 1A2

London
Cherryhill Village Mall, #76, 301 Oxford St. West, London, ON N6H 1S6

Mississauga
Central Parkway Mall, #22, 377 Burnhamthorpe Rd. East, Main Fl., Mississauga, ON L5A 3Y1

Montréal - Marcel-Laurin
#100, 2089, boul Marcel-Laurin, Montréal, QC H4R 1K4

Montréal - René-Levesque ouest
Tour Ouest, Complexe Guy Favreau, #103, 200, boul René-Lévesque ouest, Montréal, QC H2Z 1X4

Montréal - Transcanadienne
Le Centre Commercial Fairview Pointe-Claire, #C-022A, 6815, rte Transcanadienne, Montréal, QC H9R 1C4

Ottawa
#115, 885 Meadowlands Dr. East, Ottawa, ON K2C 3N2
Secondary Address: 1430 Prince of Wales Dr.
Ottawa, ON K2C 1N6

Québec
Tour Cominar, Place de la Cité, #200, 2640, boul Laurier, 2e étage, Québec, QC G1V 5C2

Regina
#500, 1870 Albert St., Regina, SK S4P 4B7

Richmond
#310, 5611 Cooney Rd., Richmond, BC V6X 3J6
Urgent service is not available at the Richmond location. In-person & express service are available, however. Passports must be picked up at the the Vancouver Passport Canada office.

St. Catharines
Pen Centre Shopping Plaza, #604, 221 Glendale Ave., St Catharines, ON L2T 2K9

St. John's
TD Place, #802, 140 Water St., St. John's, NL A1C 6H6

Saskatoon
Federal Building, #405, 101 - 22 St. East, Saskatoon, SK S7K 0E1

Surrey
Central City Shopping Centre, #1109, 10153 King George Blvd., Surrey, BC V3T 2W1

Thunder Bay
979 Alloy Dr., 2nd Fl., Thunder Bay, ON P7B 5Z8

Toronto - Town Centre Crt.
#210, 200 Town Centre Crt., Toronto, ON M1P 4Y7

Toronto - Victoria St.
#300, 74 Victoria St., Toronto, ON M5C 2A5

Toronto - Yonge St.
Joseph Sheppard Building, 4900 Yonge St., 3rd Fl., Toronto, ON M2N 6A4

Vancouver
Sinclair Centre, #200, 757 Hastings St. West, Vancouver, BC V6C 1A1

Victoria
Bay Centre, 1150 Douglas St., Level 4, Victoria, BC V8W 3M9

Whitby
Whitby Mall, #6, 1615 Dundas St. East, Whitby, ON L1N 2L1
Urgent service is not available at the Whitby location. In-person & express service are available, however. Passports must be picked up at the the Scarborough Passport Canada office.

Windsor
CIBC Building, #503, 100 Ouellette Ave., Windsor, ON N9A 6T3

Winnipeg
#400, 433 Main St., Winnipeg, MB R3B 1B3

Canada Post Receiving Agents
To facilitate access to passport services throughout Canada, Canada Post acts as a passport receiving agent on behalf of Passport Canada.
General passport applications for adults & children & simplified renewal passport applications are collected, along with citizenship documents & application fees. Application packages are sent to Passport Canada to be processed.
A $20 non-refundable convenience fee, plus applicable taxes, is payable to Canada Post for each general adult & child's passport application.

Acton
Acton Stn. Main, 53 Bower St., Acton, ON L7J 1E0
Toll-Free: 800-267-1177

Ancaster
Meadowlands Post Office, 27 Legend Crt., Ancaster, ON L9K 1J0
Toll-Free: 800-267-1177

Belleville
Belleville Stn. Main, 21 College St. West, #D, Belleville, ON K8N 3B0
Toll-Free: 800-267-1177

Boucherville
BP Boucherville, 131, rue Jacques-Ménard, Boucherville, QC J4B 5B0
Toll-Free: 800-267-1177

Bracebridge
Bracebridge Stn. Main, 98 Manitoba St., Bracebridge, ON P1L 1A0
Toll-Free: 800-267-1177

Brantford
Brantford Stn. Main, 58 Dalhousie St., PO Box 1962 Brantford, ON N3T 2J0
Toll-Free: 800-267-1177

Brossard
BP Brossard, 10, de la Place-du-Commerce, Brossard, QC J4W 4T0
Toll-Free: 800-267-1177

Cambridge
Cambridge CSC, 33 Water St. North, Cambridge, ON N1R 3B0
Toll-Free: 800-267-1177

Charlottetown
Charlottetown Stn. Central, 101 Kent St., Charlottetown, PE C1A 1M0
Toll-Free: 800-267-1177

Chatham
Chatham Post Office, 120 Wellington St. West, Chatham, ON N7M 4V0
Toll-Free: 800-267-1177

Guelph
Guelph Stn. Main, 88 Wyndham St. North, Guelph, ON N1H 4E0
Toll-Free: 800-267-1177

Kingston
Kingston Post Office, 120 Clarence St., Kingston, ON K7L 1X0
Toll-Free: 800-267-1177

Lévis
Succ. Lévis, 4870, boul de la Rive sud, Lévis, QC G6V 3P0
Toll-Free: 800-267-1177

Midland
Midland Post Office, 525 Dominion Ave., Midland, ON L4R 1P0
Toll-Free: 800-267-1177

Moncton
Moncton Main Post Office, 281 St. George St., Moncton, NB E1C 1H0
Toll-Free: 800-267-1177

Montréal - Donegani
BP Pointe-Claire, 15, av Donegani, Montréal, QC H9R 2V0
Toll-Free: 800-267-1177

Montréal - Joseph-Renaud
Succ. Anjou, 7200, boul Joseph-Renaud, Montréal, QC H1K 3X0
Toll-Free: 800-267-1177

Newmarket
Newmarket Stn. Main, 190 Mulock Dr., Newmarket, ON L3Y 3N0
Toll-Free: 800-267-1177

North Bay
North Bay Main Post Office, 101 Worthington St. East, North Bay, ON P1B 1H0
Toll-Free: 800-267-1177

Oakville
146 Lakeshore West, Oakville, ON L6K 1E0
Toll-Free: 800-267-1177

Orillia
Orillia Stn. Main, 25 Peter St. North, Orillia, ON L3V 4Y0
Toll-Free: 800-267-1177

Ottawa - Riverside Dr.
Canada Post Place Post Office, 2701 Riverside Dr., Ottawa, ON K1A 0B1
Toll-Free: 800-267-1177

Ottawa - Sandford Fleming Ave.
Ottawa Post Office, 1424 Sanford Fleming Ave., Ottawa, ON K1A 0C1
Toll-Free: 800-267-1177

Owen Sound
Owen Sound Stn. Main, 901 - 3rd Ave. East, Owen Sound, ON N4K 2K0
Toll-Free: 800-267-1177

Peterborough
Peterborough Post Office, 150 King St., Peterborough, ON K9J 2R0
Toll-Free: 800-267-1177

Pickering
Pickering Main Post Office, 1740 Kingston Rd., Pickering, ON L1V 1C0
Toll-Free: 800-267-1177

Prince George
Prince George Stn. A, 1323 - 5th Ave., Prince George, BC V2L 3L0
Toll-Free: 800-267-1177

Québec - Bouvier
Succ. Québec Centre, #145, 710, rue Bouvier, Québec, QC G2J 1C0
Toll-Free: 800-267-1177

Québec - Chaudière
Succ. Cap-Rouge, #122, 1100, boul de la Chaudière, Québec, QC G1Y 1C0
Toll-Free: 800-267-1177

Québec - Fort
BP Québec Haute-Ville, 5, rue du Fort, Québec, QC G1R 2J0
Toll-Free: 800-267-1177

Rimouski
Rimouski Succ. A, 136, rue Saint-Germain ouest, Rimouski, QC G5L 4B0
Toll-Free: 800-267-1177

Saint Bruno
Saint-Bruno Succ. Bureau-Chef, 50, rue de la Rabastalière ouest, Saint-Bruno, QC J3V 1Y0
Toll-Free: 800-267-1177

Saint John
Saint John Area Stn. Main, 125 Rothesay Ave., Saint John, NB E2L 2B0
Toll-Free: 800-267-1177

Sarnia
Sarnia Stn. Main, 105 Christina St. South, Sarnia, ON N7T 2M0
Toll-Free: 800-267-1177

Sault Ste Marie
Sault Ste Marie Main Post Office, 451 Queen St. East, Sault Ste Marie, ON P6A 1Z0
Toll-Free: 800-267-1177

Stratford
Stratford Stn. Main, 75 Waterloo St. South, Stratford, ON N5A 4A0
Toll-Free: 800-267-1177

Sudbury - Lasalle Blvd.
Sudbury Stn. A, 1776 Lasalle Blvd., Sudbury, ON P3A 2A0
Toll-Free: 800-267-1177

Sudbury - Lisgar St.
Sudbury Stn. B, 1 Lisgar St., Sudbury, ON P3E 3L0
Toll-Free: 800-267-1177

Summerside
Summerside Main Post Office, 454 Granville St., Summerside, PE C1N 3K0
Toll-Free: 800-267-1177

Sydney
Sydney Stn. A, 269 Charlotte St., Sydney, NS B1P 1T0
Toll-Free: 800-267-1177

Toronto
Toronto Stn. K, 2384 Yonge St., Toronto, ON M4P 2E0
Toll-Free: 800-267-1177

Trois-Rivières
BP Trois-Rivières, 1285, rue Notre-Dame, Trois-Rivières, QC G9A 4X0
Toll-Free: 800-267-1177

Uxbridge
Uxbridge Stn. Main, 67 Brock St. West, Uxbridge, ON L9P 1A0
Toll-Free: 800-267-1177

Woodstock
Woodstock Stn. Main, 433 Norwich Ave., Woodstock, ON N4S 3W0
Toll-Free: 800-267-1177

Yarmouth
Yarmouth Main Post Office, 15 Willow St., Yarmouth, NS B5A 1T0
Toll-Free: 800-267-1177

Service Canada Receiving Agents

As a receiving agent, a Service Canada Centre accepts general passport applications for both adults & children, as well as simplified renewal passport applications. Application packages are then sent to Passport Canada for processing. When Passport Canada has approved & issued passports, they are delivered to the mailing addresses on the applications.
The service provided by Service Canada is free of charge.

Abbotsford
#100, 32525 Simon Ave., Abbotsford, BC V2T 6T6

Ajax
#200, 274 Mackenzie Ave., Ajax, ON L1S 2E9

Amherst
#202, 26-28 Prince Arthur St., Amherst, NS B4H 1V6

Asbestos
#204, 309, rue Chassé, Asbestos, QC J1T 2B4

Baie Comeau
Centre d'achats Laflèche, #204, 625, boul Laflèche ouest, Baie-Comeau, QC G5C 1C4

Barrie
48 Owen St., 1st Fl., Barrie, ON L4M 3H1

Bedford
Royal Bank Building, 1597 Bedford Hwy., 2nd Fl., Bedford, NS B4A 1E7

Bracebridge
Federal Building, 98 Manitoba St., 2nd Fl., Bracebridge, ON P1L 2B5

Brandon
Government of Canada Building, #100, 1039 Princess Ave., Brandon, MB R7A 4J5

Bridgewater
Dawson B. Dauphinee Building, 77 Dufferin St., Bridgewater, NS B4V 9A2

Brockville
The Fuller Building, 14 Court House Ave., 1st Fl., Brockville, ON K6V 4T1

Brooks
Cassils Shopping Plaza, 608 - 2 St. West, Brooks, AB T1R 1A8

Brossard
2501, boul Lapiniere, 1e étage, Brossard, QC J4Z 3P1

Burnaby
#100, 3480 Gilmore Way, Burnaby, BC V5G 4Y1

Calgary - Crowchild Trail NW
Calgary North Service Canada Centre, One Executive Place, 1816 Crowchild Trail NW, Main Fl., Calgary, AB T2M 3Y7

Calgary - Fisher St. SE
Calgary South Service Canada Centre, Fisher Park Place II, #100, 6712 Fisher St. SE, Calgary, AB T2H 2A7

Calgary - Marlborough Way NE
Calgary East Service Canada Centre, Marlborough Mall, #1502, 515 Marlborough Way NE, Calgary, AB T2A 7E7

Campbellton
Campbellton City Center Mall, #111, 157 Water St., Campbellton, NB E3N 3L4

Cambridge Bay
16 Mitik St., 1st Fl., PO Box 2010 Cambridge Bay, NU X0B 0C0

Canmore
Building C, Canmore Gateway Shops, #113, 802 Bow Valley Trail, Canmore, AB T1W 1N6

Charlottetown
Jean Canfield Government of Canada Building, 191 University Ave., 1st Fl., Charlottetown, PE C1A 4L2

Chibougamau
623, 3e rue, Chibougamau, QC G8P 3A2

Chilliwack
#100, 9345 Main St., Chilliwack, BC V2P 4M3

Coaticook
289, rue Baldwin, Coaticook, QC J1A 2A2

Collingwood
44 Hurontario St., Collingwood, ON L9Y 2L6

Coquitlam
#100, 2963 Glen Dr., Coquitlam, BC V3B 2P7

Corner Brook
Joseph R. Smallwood Building, 1 Regent Sq., Corner Brook, NL A2H 7K6

Cornwall
#100, 111 Water St. East, Cornwall, ON K6H 6S2

Courtenay
Comox Valley Service Canada Centre, 130 - 19th St., Courtenay, BC V9N 8S1

Cowansville
224, rue du Sud, 2e étage, Cowansville, QC J2K 2X4

Cranbrook
1113 Baker St., Cranbrook, BC V1C 1A7

Drummondville
Édifice Surprenant, 1525, boul Saint-Joseph, Drummondville, QC J2C 2E9

East Gwillimbury
Newmarket Service Canada Centre, #1, 18183 Yonge St., East Gwillimbury, ON L9N 0H9

Edmonton - 87th Ave. NW
Edmonton Meadowlark Service Canada, Meadowlark Shopping Ctr, #120, 15710 - 87th Ave. NW, Edmonton, AB T5R 5W9

Edmonton - 50th St. NW
Hermitage Square, 12735 - 50th St. NW, Edmonton, AB T5A 4L8

Edmonton - Millbourne Market Mall
Edmonton Millbourne Service Canada Centre, #148, Millbourne Market Mall, Edmonton, AB T6K 3L6

Edmundston
Federal Building, 22 Emmerson St., Edmundston, NB E3V 1R8

Edson
4905 - 4th Ave., Edson, AB T7E 1C6

Elliot Lake
White Mountain Academy Of The Arts, #2, 99 Spine Rd., Elliot Lake, ON P5A 3S9

Espanola
#2, 721 Centre St., Espanola, ON P5E 1T3

Estevan
#10, 419 Kensington Ave., Estevan, SK S4A 2A1

Flin Flon
Government of Canada Building, 111 Main St., Flin Flon, MB R8A 1J9

Fort Frances
301 Scott St., Fort Frances, ON P9A 1H1

Fort McMurray
#107, 8530 Manning Ave., Main Fl., Fort McMurray, AB T9H 5G2

Fort Simpson
Federal Building, 9606 - 100th St., Fort Simpson, NT X0E 0N0

Fort Smith
Federal Building, 136 McDougal Rd., Fort Smith, NT X0E 0P0

Gander
McCurdy Complex, 1 Markham Pl., 3rd Fl., Gander, NL A1V 0A8

Gaspé
Édifice Frederica-Giroux, 98, rue de la Reine, 1e étage, Gaspé, QC G4X 2V4

Georgetown
232 Guelph St., 1st Fl., Georgetown, ON L7G 4B1

Glace Bay
Senator's Place, #101, 633 Main St., Glace Bay, NS B1A 6J3

Grand Falls / Grand-Sault
#100, 441 Madawaska Rd., Grand Falls, NB E3Y 1C6

Grande Prairie
Towne Centre Mall, #100, 9845 - 99th Ave., Grande Prairie, AB T8V 0R3

Happy Valley-Goose Bay
23 Broomfield St., Happy Valley-Goose Bay, NL A0P 1E0

Hawkesbury
521 Main St. East, Hawkesbury, ON K6A 1B3

Hay River
Federal Building, #204, 41 Capital Dr., Hay River, NT X0E 1G2

Inuvik
85 Kingmingya Rd., Inuvik, NT X0E 0T0

Iqaluit
#306, 933 Mivvik St., Iqaluit, NU X0A 0H0

Kamloops
520 Seymour St., 1st Fl., Kamloops, BC V2C 2G9

Kapuskasing
8 Queen St., Kapuskasing, ON P5N 1G7

Kelowna
#106, 471 Queensway, Kelowna, BC V1Y 6S5

Kenora
Kenora Market Square, #201, 308 - 2nd St., Kenora, ON P9N 1G4

Kentville
Federal Building, 495 Main St., 2nd Fl., Kentville, NS B4N 3W5

La Tuque
Carrefour La Tuque Inc., #14, 290, rue Saint-Joseph, La Tuque, QC G9X 3Z8

Labrador City
Labrador Mall, 500 Vanier Ave., Labrador City, NL A2V 2W7

Langley
#202, 8747 - 204th St., Langley, BC V1M 2Y5

Lethbridge
Crowsnest Trail Plaza, #101, 920 - 2A Ave. North, Lethbridge, AB T1H 0E3

Lévis
Place Lévis, #175, 50, rte du Président-Kennedy, Lévis, QC G6V 6W8

Lloydminster
4114 - 70th Ave., Lloydminster, AB T9V 2X3

Longueuil
#100, 1195, ch du Tremblay, Longueuil, QC J4N 1R4

Magog
#100A, 1700, rue Sherbrooke, Magog, QC J1X 5B4

Maple Ridge
Ridge Meadows Service Canada Centre, 22325 Lougheed Hwy., Maple Ridge, BC V2X 2T3

Marystown
Jerrett Building, #130, 140 Ville-Marie Dr., Marystown, NL A0E 2M0

Medicine Hat
Northside Centre, 78 - 8th St. NW, Medicine Hat, AB T1A 6P1

Melfort
McKendry Plaza, 104 McKendry Ave. West, Melfort, SK S0E 1A0

Miramichi
139 Douglastown Blvd., Miramichi, NB E1V 0A4

Moncton
Heritage Court, #110, 95 Foundry St., Moncton, NB E1C 5H7

Montague
491 Main St., Montague, PE C0A 1R0

Montréal - Newman
Lasalle (Montréal) Service Canada Centre, 7655, boul Newman, Montréal, QC H8N 1X7

Montréal - Wellington
Verdun Service Canada Centre, 4110, rue Wellington, 2e étage, Montréal, QC H4G 1V7

Moose Jaw
Victoria Place, #501, 111 Fairford St. East, Moose Jaw, SK S6H 7X5

Morden
Government of Canada Building, 158 Stephen St., Morden, MB R6M 1T3

Nanaimo
#201, 60 Front St., Nanaimo, BC V9R 5H7

Nelson
Chahko Mika Mall, 1125 Lakeside Dr., Main Fl., Nelson, BC V1L 5Z3

New Glasgow
340 East River Rd., New Glasgow, NS B2H 3P7

New Liskeard
280 Armstrong St. North,, New Liskeard, ON P0J 1P0

New Westminster
#201, 620 Royal Ave., New Westminster, BC V3M 1J2

North Battleford
1401 - 101st St., North Battleford, SK S9A 1A1

North Bay
Canada Place, #102, 107 Shirreff Ave., North Bay, ON P1B 7K8

North Vancouver
North Shore Service Canada Centre, #100, 221 West Esplanade, North Vancouver, BC V7M 3N7

Notre Dame de Lourdes
51 Rodgers St., Notre Dame de Lourdes, MB R0G 1M0

O'Leary
371 Main St., O'Leary, PE C0B 1V0

Oakville
#5B, 117 Cross Ave., Oakville, ON L6J 2W7

Orangeville
#102, 210 Broadway Ave., Orangeville, ON L9W 5G4

Oshawa
Midtown Mall, #6C, 200 John St. West, Oshawa, ON L1J 2B4

Ottawa - Carling Ave.
Ottawa West Service Canada Centre, Lincoln Fields Galleria, 2525 Carling Ave., 1st Fl., Ottawa, ON K2B 7Z2

Ottawa - Ogilvie Rd.
Ottawa East Service Canada Centre, Beacon Hill Shopping Ctr, 2339 Ogilvie Rd., Ottawa, ON K1J 8M6

Owen Sound
Heritage Place Shopping Centre, 1350 - 16th St. East, Owen Sound, ON N4K 6N7

Parry Sound
74 James St., 2nd Fl., Parry Sound, ON P2A 1T8

Pembroke
141 Lake St., Pembroke, ON K8A 5L8

Penticton
#101, 386 Ellis St., Penticton, BC V2A 8C9

Peterborough
219 George St. North, Peterborough, ON K9J 3G7

Placentia
Dalfens Mall, 61 Blockhouse Rd., Placentia, NL A0B 2Y0

Powell River
7061 Duncan St., #A, Powell River, BC V8A 1W1

Prince Albert
South Hill Mall, 2995 - 2nd Ave. West, Prince Albert, SK S6V 5V5

Prince George
1363 - 4th Ave., Prince George, BC V2L 3J6

Rankin Inlet
#164, 1 Mivvik Ave., PO Box 97 Rankin Inlet, NU X0C 0G0

Red Deer
#101, 4901 - 46th St., Red Deer, AB T4N 1N2

Regina
Alvin Hamilton Building, 1783 Hamilton St., Regina, SK S4P 2B6

Repentigny
#200, 667, rue Notre-Dame, Repentigny, QC J6A 2W5

Richmond Hill
35 Beresford Dr., Richmond Hill, ON L4B 4M3

Rouyn-Noranda
Édifice Réal Caouette, #300, 151, av du Lac, Rouyn-Noranda, QC J9X 6C3

St. Anthony
Viking Mall, 1 Goose Cove Rd., St. Anthony, NL A0K 4S0

Saint-Hyacinthe
Galeries St-Hyacinthe Shopping Mall, #2550, 3225, av Cusson, 2e étage, Saint-Hyacinthe, QC J2S 0H7

Saint John
1 Agar Pl., 1st Fl., Saint John, NB E2L 5G4

Saint-Quentin
193 Canada St., Saint-Quentin, NB E8A 1J8

St Stephen
Canada Post Building, 93 Milltown Blvd., St Stephen, NB E3L 1G5

Salaberry-de-Valleyfield
Valleyfield Service Canada Centre, #100, 73, rue Maden, Salaberry-de-Valleyfield, QC J6S 3V4

Salmon Arm
191 Shuswap St. NW, 1st Fl., Salmon Arm, BC V1E 4P6

Sault Ste. Marie
22 Bay St., 1st Fl., Sault Ste. Marie, ON P6A 5S2

Sept-Îles
701, boul Laure, 3e étage, Sept-Îles, QC G4R 1X8

Shediac
Centre-Ville Mall, 342 Main St., Shediac, NB E4P 2E7

Sherbrooke
124, rue Wellington nord, Sherbrooke, QC J1H 5X8

Souris
IGA Mall, 173 Main St., 2nd Fl., Souris, PE C0A 2B0

Steinbach
Steinbach Place, 321 Main St., Main Fl., Steinbach, MB R5G 1Z2

Summerside
Government of Canada Building, 294 Church St., Summerside, PE C1N 0C1

Terrace
4630 Lazelle Ave., Terrace, BC V8G 1S6

The Pas
Uptown Mall, 333 Edwards Ave., The Pas, MB R9A 1K7

Thetford Mines
#500, 350, boul Frontenac ouest, Thetford Mines, QC G6G 6N7

Thompson
40-B Moak Cres., Thompson, MB R8N 2B7

Timmins
120 Cedar St. South, 1st Fl., Timmins, ON P4N 2G8

Toronto - College St.
#100, 559 College St., Toronto, ON M6G 1A9

Toronto - Lawrence Ave. West
Lawrence Square, #103-105, 700 Lawrence Ave. West, Toronto, ON M6A 3B3

Toronto - St. Clair Ave. East
Toronto Centre Service Canada Ctr., Arthur Meighen Building, 25 St. Clair Ave. East, 1st Fl., Toronto, ON M4T 3A4

Trois-Rivières
#100, 1660, rue Royale, Trois-Rivières, QC G9A 4K3

Val d'Or
400, av Centrale, Val-d'Or, QC J9P 1P3

Vancouver
1263 West Broadway, Vancouver, BC V6H 1G7

Victoria
Victoria West Shore Service Canada Centre, 3179 Jacklin Rd., Victoria, BC V9B 3Y7

Weyburn
City Centre Mall, 110 Souris Ave., Main Fl., Weyburn, SK S4H 2Z8

Whitehorse
Elijah Smith Building, #125, 300 Main St., Whitehorse, YT Y1A 2B5

Woodstock
Canada Post Building, 680 Main St., Woodstock, NB E7M 5Z9

Yellowknife
Greenstone Building, 5101 - 50th Ave., Main Fl., Yellowknife, NT X1A 3Z4

Yorkton
Imperial Plaza, 214 Smith St. East, Yorkton, SK S3N 3S6

Office of the Information Commissioner of Canada / Commissariat à l'information du Canada

30, rue Victoria, Gatineau, QC K1A 1H3
Fax: 819-994-1768
Toll-Free: 800-267-0441
general@oic-ci.gc.ca
www.oic-ci.gc.ca
twitter.com/oic_ci_Canada
www.facebook.com/oiccanada

The Office of the Information Commissioner of Canada was established in 1983. It investigates complaints from people & organizations who believe they have been denied rights under the Access of Information Act, Canada's freedom of information legislation.
An independent ombudsperson appointed by Parliament, the Information Commissioner has strong investigative powers. The Information Commissioner mediates between government institutions & dissatisfied applicants, & may refer cases to the Federal Court for resolution.

Information Commissioner, Caroline Maynard
Tel: 819-994-0001; *Fax:* 819-994-1768

Deputy Commissioner, Legal Services & Public Affairs, Gino Grondin
Tel: 819-994-0008

Deputy Commissioner, Investigations & Governance, Layla Michaud
Tel: 819-994-0004

Director, Financial Management, Procurement, & Audit, Stephen Campbell
Tel: 819-994-1783

Director, Public Affairs, James Ellard
Tel: 819-994-1931

Director, Information Management & Technology Division, Serge Galipeau
Tel: 819-360-4625

Director, Investigations, Christian Picard
Tel: 819-994-0537

Indigenous Services Canada (ISC) / Services aux Autochtones Canada (SAC)

Public Enquiries Contact Centre, 10, rue Wellington, Gatineau, QC K1A 0H4
Fax: 819-994-1768
Toll-Free: 800-267-0441
general@oic-ci.gc.ca
www.canada.ca/en/indigenous-services-canada.html
twitter.com/gcindigenous
www.facebook.com/gcindigenous
instagram.com/gcindigenous
Prime Minister Trudeau announced the dissolution of Indigenous & Northern Affairs Canada in August 2017, & the creation of two new departments: Indigenous Services Canada & Crown-Indigenous Relations & Northern Affairs Canada. Indigenous Services Canada's mandate is to work collaboratively with partners to improve access to high quality servies for First Nations, Inuit & Métis. The department's vision is to support & empower Indigenous peoples, address socio-economic community conditions & improve service delivery.

Minister, Indigenous Services, Hon. Patricia Hajdu, P.C.

Deputy Minister, Jean-Francois Tremblay
Tel: 819-956-5527
jean-francois.tremblay@canada.ca

Director, Policy, Jessica Hayden
Tel: 819-956-5388

Director, Parliamentary Affairs, Jeff Valois
Tel: 819-956-5521

Chief of Staff, Rachel Doran
Tel: 819-956-5388

Office of the Deputy Minister / Bureau de sous-ministre
Deputy Minister, Jean-Francois Tremblay
Tel: 819-956-5527
Associate Deputy Minister, Sony Perron
Tel: 819-997-8127
Director General, Communications, Aruna Sadana
Tel: 819-994-1813
Executive Director, Innovation & Services, Hillary Thatcher
Tel: 819-934-2639
Chief of Staff, Kenza El Bied
Tel: 819-956-5520

Chief Finances, Results & Delivery Officer Sector / Secteur du dirigeant principal des finances, des résultats et de l'éxecution
Chief Finances, Results & Delivery Officer, Paul Thoppil
Tel: 819-956-8188
Director General, Planning & Resource Management, Marc Geoffrion
Tel: 819-994-6649
Senior Policy Advisor, Aurora Zhang
Tel: 819-956-8192

Education & Social Development Programs & Partnerships Sector / Secteur des programmes et des partnerariats en matière d'éducation et de développement social
Director General, Social Programs & Policy Branch, David Peckham
david.peckham2@canada.ca
Senior Director, Income Support & Urban Aboriginal Strategy, Annie Comtois
annie.comtois@canada.ca
Senior Director, Education Branch, Program Directorate, Shelie Laforest
shelie.laforest@canada.ca

First Nations & Inuit Health Branch (FNIHB) / Direction générale de la santé des Premières nations et des Inuits (DGSPNI)
Assists First Nations & Inuit communities & people to address health inequalities & diseases threats through health surveillance & population health interventions. Ensures the availability of, or access to, health services for First Nations & Inuit people. Devolves control & management of community-based health services to First Nations & Inuit communities & organizations. The Environmental Health Division addresses conditions in the environment that could affect the health of community members, such as drinking water quality, mould, food safety, facilities inspections, transportation of dangerous goods. The Environmental Research Division conducts, coordinates & funds contaminants-related research, coordinates the replacement or upgrading of diesel-fuel tanks & remediation of fuel oil-contaminated sites, lab services for testing of PCBs & mercury, drinking water-related research & testing.
Senior Assistant Deputy Minister, Sony Perron
Tel: 613-957-7701

Assistant Deputy Minister, Regional Operations, Valerie Gideon
Tel: 613-946-1722
Chief Medical Officer of Health & Executive Director, Population & Public Health, Tom Wong
Tel: 613-952-9616
Director General, Non-Insured Health Benefits Directorate, Scott Doidge
Tel: 613-954-8825
Director General, Strategic Policy, Planning & Information, Mary-Luisa Kapelus
Tel: 613-954-2445
Director General, Delivery, Active Response & Coordination, Aruna Sadana
Tel: 613-954-0765
Director General, Branch, Anthony Sangster
Tel: 613-818-1243
Executive Director, Primary Health Care, Robin Buckland
Tel: 613-957-6359
Executive Director, Operational Services & Systems Division, Jean Pruneau
Tel: 613-960-3656
Executive Director, Internal Client Services Directorate, Susan Russell
Tel: 613-952-3151
Acting Executive Director, Policy & Partnerships, Tasha Stefanis
Tel: 613-941-1606

Capacity, Infrastructure & Accountability Division / Division de la capacité, de l'infrastructure et de l'imputabilité
National Manager, FNIHB eHealth Canada, Jeff Niles
Tel: 613-697-1479
Manager, Health Facilities & Capital Program, Gordon Roston
Tel: 613-793-5364

Health Programs & Governance Division / Programmes de santé et gouvernance
Manager, Alana Vadneau
Tel: 613-797-7813

Internal Client Services Directorate / Direction des services aux clients internes
Executive Director, Lana Thomas
Tel: 613-952-3151
Senior Manager, Information Management & Information Technology, Stéphane Romain
Tel: 613-218-0407
Manager, Information & Records Management, Norma Mahon
Tel: 613-854-5923
Manager, Information Management, Nathan Nash
Tel: 613-406-9306
Manager, Funding Arrangements, Terence Roy
Tel: 613-220-8082
Manager, Workforce Development, HR Projects & Planning, Edward Suma
Tel: 613-266-3530
Lead Project Officer, Aboriginal Programming, Michèle Elliott
Tel: 613-404-2405
Medical Officer, Internal Client Services Directorate, Barbara Young
Tel: 613-948-9420

Non-Insured Health Benefits Directorate / Direction des services de santé non assurés
Director General, Scott Doidge
Tel: 613-954-8825
Director, NIHB Operational Review, Douglas Booker
Tel: 613-957-3294
Director, Program Policy & Planning, Heather Hudson
Tel: 613-948-6379
Acting Director, Business Support, Audit & Negotiations, Kendra MacLean
Tel: 613-952-8580
Director, Benefits Management & Review Services Division, Vacant
Manager, Pharmacy Policy Development, Susan Pierce
Tel: 613-957-7674
National Dental Advisor, Terry Hupman
Tel: 613-960-3652

Population Health & Primary Care Directorate / Direction de la santé de la population et des soins primaires
Chief Medical Officer of Public Health & Executive Director, Tom Wong
Tel: 613-952-9616
Executive Director, Office of Primary Health Care, Robin Buckland
Tel: 613-957-6359
Director, Jordan's Principle, Bonnie Beach
Tel: 613-960-4480
Manager, Quality Improvement & Accreditation Program, Jennifer Greene
Tel: 613-944-4356

Strategic Policy, Planning & Information / Politique stratégique, planification et information

Executive Director, Policy & Partnerships, Chantal Marin-Comeau
Tel: 613-941-1606

Assistant Executive Director, Reconciliation & Relationships, Nadjat Belakroum
Tel: 613-948-8861

Deputy Director, Surveillance Health Information Policy & Coordination Unit, Marie-Pierre Wallace
Tel: 819-994-0607

Manager, British Columbia Tripartite Relations, Helen Leung
Tel: 613-957-3774

Regional Operations Sector

Senior Assistant Deputy Minister, Lynda Clairmont
Tel: 819-953-5574

Director General, Regional Infrastructure Delivery Branch, Claudia Ferland
Tel: 819-953-4632

Director General, Sector Operations Branch, Dianne Galus
Tel: 819-934-1828

Director General, Community Infrastructure Branch, Lyse Langevin
Tel: 819-934-0615

Senior Director, Infrastructure Service Reform Directorate, Ntalka Cmoc
Tel: 819-953-6043

Senior Director, Housing Team Directorate, Lillian Hopkins
Tel: 819-934-2628

Senior Director, Strategic Water Management Team Directorate, Chad Westmacott
Tel: 819-956-5543

Director, Regional Support Services, Lysane Bolduc
Tel: 819-953-2369

Director, Major Infrastructure Project Delivery, Marie-Josee Goulet
Tel: 819-953-2456

Director, Strategic Portfolio Management & Reporting, Sylvie Gravel
Tel: 819-934-2528

Director, Emergency Management, Todd Kuiack
Tel: 819-953-5438

Director, Planning & Business Integration Directorate, Tammy Lacroix
Tel: 819-934-2513

Director, Sustainable Operations, Lori Macadam
Tel: 819-956-3545

Director, Outreach & Change Management Directorate, Sean Somers
Tel: 819-953-4966

Infrastructure Canada

#1100, 180 Kent St., Ottawa, ON K1P 0B6
Tel: 613-948-1148
Toll-Free: 877-250-7154
TTY: 800-465-7735
ifc.info@canada.ca
www.infrastructure.gc.ca
Other Communication: Media Relations, Phone: 613-960-9251,
Email: infc.media.infc@canada.ca
twitter.com/infc_eng
www.facebook.com/infrastructurecanadaeng
instagram.com/infragram_can

Infrastructure Canada is engaged in the following tasks to ensure modern public infrastructure for the benefit of Canadians: developing policies; establishing partnerships; fostering knowledge; making investments; & delivering programs.
To address local, regional, & national priorities, Infrastructure Canada works with municipalities, provinces & territories, other federal departments & agencies, as well as private companies & the non-profit sector to build & revitalize the infrastructure required by Canadians.

Minister, Infrastructure & Communities, Hon. Dominic LeBlanc, P.C.

Deputy Minister, Kelly Gillis
Tel: 613-960-5661

Associate Deputy Minister & Chief Financial Officer, Darlene Boileau
Tel: 613-948-9161

Director General, Communications, Peter Wallace
Tel: 613-948-2940

Audit & Evaluation Branch

Independent audits are conducted to ensure proper processes of Infrastructure Canada. Evaluation programs are also carried out to assess the value of the department's programs & initiatives.

The work of the Audit & Evaluation Branch supports decision making within Infrastructure Canada.

Chief Audit & Evaluation Executive, Isabelle Trépanier
Tel: 613-954-4879; *Fax:* 613-941-5050
isabelle.trepanier@infc.gc.ca

Director, Internal Audit, Michèle Serano
Tel: 613-946-8751; *Fax:* 613-941-5050

Corporate Services Branch

The Corporate Services Branch supports corporate functions & provides information management & technology services.
Specific duties include administration, human resources services, procurement, financial services, & maintenance of the Shared Information Management System for Infrastructure.

Assistant Deputy Minister & Chief Financial Officer, Corporate Services, Nathalie Bertrand
Tel: 613-948-9161; *Fax:* 613-960-6348

Chief Information Officer & Director General, Angus Howieson
Tel: 613-946-0509; *Fax:* 613-948-2963

Director General, Human Resources, Laurie Pratt-Tremblay
Tel: 613-948-3773

Director, Financial Operations & Administration, Eric Gagnon
Tel: 613-948-4424

Director, Operations Support, Security & Information Management Services, Derek Dawson
Tel: 613-948-8002

Director, Applications Services, Sherry Shaaked
Tel: 613-948-9719

Director, Financial Management Advisory Services, Nicole Thomas
Tel: 613-948-3781

Investment, Partnerships & Innovation Branch

The Corporate Services Branch supports corporate functions & provides information management & technology services.
Specific duties include administration, human resources services, procurement, financial services, & maintenance of the Shared Information Management System for Infrastructure.

Assistant Deputy Minister, Glenn Campbell
Tel: 613-941-0722

Senior Director, Lisa Mitchell
Tel: 613-948-6111

Principal Advisor, Vania Karam
Tel: 613-408-3808

Policy & Results Branch

The following responsibilities are handled by the Policy & Communications Branch: identifying infrastructure priorities; conducting research that contributes to policy development; assessing investments; providing correspondence services; & coordinating communications on infrastructure & sharing knowledge.

Assistant Deputy Minister, Gerard Peets
Tel: 613-948-6328

Director General, Policy & Results, Economic Analysis and Results, Sean Keenan
Tel: 613-954-7786

Director General, Strategic & Sectoral Policy, Tushara Williams
Tel: 613-957-4337

Director, Sectoral Policy, Robert Judge
Tel: 613-948-9160

Director, Horizontal Results & Reporting, Tahanee McKnight
Tel: 613-960-9634

Director, Strategic Policy, Helen Smiley
Tel: 613-946-9922

Program Operations Branch

The Program Operations Branch is responsible for the following activities: implementing programs; administering funding agreements; managing the federal Gas Tax transfer to Canadian municipalities to support environmentally sustainable infrastructure; & conducting environment assessments & program evaluations.

Assistant Deputy Minister, Marc Fortin
Tel: 613-948-8003; *Fax:* 613-960-9423

Director General, Major Bridges, Natalie Bossé
Tel: 613-998-1900

Director General, Program Operations, North/Atlantic/Ontario, Éric Landry
Tel: 613-960-6774

Director General, Program Operations, Québec/West, Nathalie Lechasseur
Tel: 613-960-9500

Director, Governance & Reporting, Makuc Bogdan
Tel: 613-960-9247

Transport & Infrastructure Legal Services

The Program Operations Branch is responsible for the following activities: implementing programs; administering funding agreements; managing the federal Gas Tax transfer to Canadian municipalities to support environmentally sustainable infrastructure; & conducting environment assessments & program evaluations.

Senior General Counsel & Executive Director, Henry Schultz
Tel: 613-990-5768

General Counsel & Deputy Executive Director, Alain Langlois
Tel: 613-991-2518

Manager, Legal Support Services Division, Deborah Quaicoe
Tel: 613-949-4160

Innovation, Science & Economic Development Canada / Innovation, des science et du développement économique

C.D. Howe Building, 235 Queen St., Ottawa, ON K1A 0H5
Tel: 613-954-5031; *Fax:* 613-954-2340
Toll-Free: 800-328-6189
TTY: 866-694-8389
info@ic.gc.ca
www.ic.gc.ca
twitter.com/ISED_CA
www.linkedin.com/company/industry-canada
www.youtube.com/user/IndustryCanadaGC

The mission of Innovation, Science & Economic Development (formerly Industry Canada, renamed by Prime Minister Trudeau after the 2015 general election) is to help make Canadians more productive & competitive in a global, knowledge-based economy. The department's policies, programs & services assist in the creation of an economy that provides more & better-paying jobs for Canadians; supports stronger business growth through sustained improvements in productivity; & gives consumers, businesses & investors confidence that the marketplace is fair, efficient & competitive. To reach its clients, the department collaborates extensively with partners at all levels of government & the private sector.

Minister, Innovation, Science & Industry, Hon. François-Philippe Champagne, P.C.
Tel: 613-995-4895; *Fax:* 613-996-6883
Francois-Philippe.Champagne@parl.gc.ca

Minister, Economic Development & Official Languages, Hon. Mary Ng, P.C.

Deputy Minister, Innovation, Science & Economic Development, John Knubley
Tel: 343-291-2804; *Fax:* 613-954-3272

Deputy Minister, Tourism, Official Languages & La Francophonie, Guylaine Roy
Tel: 343-291-3680

Chief Science Advisor, Mona Nemer
Tel: 343-291-0457

Associate Deputy Minister, Vacant

Associate Deputy Minister, Paul Thompson
Tel: 343-291-2051

Associated Agencies, Boards & Commissions:

• Communications Research Centre Canada (CRC) / Centre de recherches sur les communications
3701 Carling Ave.
PO Box 11490 H
Ottawa, ON K2H 8S2
Tel: 613-991-3313; *Fax:* 613-998-5355
info@crc.gc.ca
www.crc.gc.ca

Dedicated to advanced communications research & development for over 50 years. Key research areas include radio science, terrestrial wireless systems, satellite communications broadcasting & broadband network technologies. CRC has a long history of technology transfer. CRC operates an Innovation Centre, a technology incubator for small & medium-sized high-tech start-ups, which provides increased access to CRC's technologies, research expertise & unique laboratories & facilities.

• Competition Tribunal (CT) / Tribunal de la concurrence (TC)
Thomas D'Arcy McGee Bldg.
#600, 90 Sparks St.
Ottawa, ON K1P 5B4
Tel: 613-957-3172; *Fax:* 613-957-3170
tribunal@ct-tc.gc.ca
www.ct-tc.gc.ca
Hears & decides all applications made under Parts V11.1 & VIII of the Competition Act.

• Destination Canada (DC)
See Entry Name Index for detailed listing.

• Patent Appeal Board (PAB) / Commission d'appel des brevets (CAB)
The Patent Appeal Board reviews rejected applications, chairs re-examination boards, reviews rejections of re-issue applications & provides other functions.

• **Science, Technology & Innovation Council (STIC) / Conseil des sciences, de la technologie et de l'innovation (CSTI)**
235 Queen St., 9th Fl.
Ottawa, ON K1A 0H5
Tel: 343-291-2362; *Fax:* 613-952-0459
info@stic-csti.ca
www.stic-csti.ca
Provides the Minister of Industry with policy advice on science & technology & measures Canada's science & technology performance against international standards.

• **Standards Council of Canada (SCC) / Conseil canadien des normes (CCN)**
See Entry Name Index for detailed listing.

Audit & Evaluation Branch / Direction générale de la vérification et de l'évaluation
Tel: 343-291-2356; *Fax:* 343-291-2485
Chief Audit Executive & Director General, Audit & Evaluation, Brian Gear, CAE
Tel: 343-291-2355; *Fax:* 343-291-2485

Canadian Intellectual Property Office (CIPO) / Office de la propriété intellectuelle du Canada (OPIC)
Place du Portage I, #C-229, 50, rue Victoria, Gatineau, QC K1A 0C9
Tel: 819-997-1936; *Fax:* 819-953-2476
Toll-Free: 866-997-1936
TTY: 866-442-2476
cipo.contact@ic.gc.ca
www.cipo.ic.gc.ca
Other Communication: International Calls: 819-934-0544; OPIC Fax: 819-953-6742
twitter.com/CIPO_Canada
www.linkedin.com/company/canadian-intellectual-property-office
Chief Executive Officer; Commissioner of Patents, Registrar of Trade-marks, Johanne Bélisle
Tel: 819-997-1057; *Fax:* 819-997-1890
Director General, Business Services & Programs Branch, Martin Cloutier
Tel: 819-997-2469; *Fax:* 819-953-5400
Director General, Patent Branch, Virginie Ethier
Tel: 819-997-2949; *Fax:* 819-994-1989
Director General, Corporate Strategies & Services Branch, Konstantinos Georgaras
Tel: 819-994-2828; *Fax:* 819-953-8638
Director General, Trade-Marks Branch, Mesmin Pierre
Tel: 819-994-4600; *Fax:* 819-997-6357
Senior Director, Policy, International Affairs & Research Office, Anne-Marie Monteith
Tel: 819-994-2757; *Fax:* 819-953-8638

Chief Information Office Sector / Secteur du bureau principal de l'information
Tel: 613-954-3570; *Fax:* 613-941-1938
Chief Information Officer, Rick Rinholm
Tel: 343-291-1444; *Fax:* 613-941-1938
Director General, Strategy & Information Services Branch, Kelly Acton
Tel: 343-291-1573; *Fax:* 343-291-1606
Director General, Enterprise & Corporate Services Branch, Daniel Boulet
Tel: 343-291-1576; *Fax:* 343-291-1607
Director General, Workplace Technology Services Branch, Pierre Gravel
Tel: 343-291-1404
Director General, Business Services Branch, Patti Pomeroy
Tel: 343-291-1292
Acting Director, CIO Business Management Directorate, Julie Correia
Tel: 343-291-1407; *Fax:* 343-291-1604

Communications & Marketing Branch / Direction générale des communications et du marketing
Director General, Kelly Acton
Tel: 343-291-1652
Executive Director, Ministerial & Media Services, Jason Bett
Tel: 343-291-3722

Competition Bureau Canada / Bureau de la concurrence Canada
Place du Portage, Phase I, 50 Victoria St., Ottawa, ON K1A 0C9
Tel: 819-997-4282; *Fax:* 819-997-0324
Toll-Free: 800-348-5358
TTY: 800-642-3844
www.competitionbureau.gc.ca
twitter.com/CompBureau
www.facebook.com/competitionbureaucanada
www.linkedin.com/company/canadian-competition-bureau
www.youtube.com/user/competitionbureau
The Competition Bureau is the organization responsible for the enforcement of the Competition Act, the Consumer Packaging & Labelling Act except as it relates to food, the Precious Metals Marking Act & the Textile Labelling Act. The Competition Bureau

ensures compliance by the business community with legislation administered by the Bureau, & oversees the development of policy & dissemination of information aimed at ensuring optimal compliance levels.
Commissioner of Competition, Matthew Boswell
Tel: 819-997-3304

Corporate Management Sector / Secteur de la gestion intégrée
Tel: 613-941-9578; *Fax:* 613-998-6950
Chief Financial Officer, David Enns
Tel: 343-291-2970; *Fax:* 613-998-6950
Director General, Resource Planning & Investments Branch, Michelle Baron
Tel: 343-291-2715; *Fax:* 343-291-3296
Director General, Corporate Finance, Systems & Procurement Branch, Simon Brault
Tel: 343-291-2967; *Fax:* 613-941-0319
Director General, Corporate Planning & Governance, Barbara Gibbon
Tel: 613-960-8800; *Fax:* 613-957-4788
Director General, Human Resources Branch, Caroline Dunn
Tel: 343-291-3251; *Fax:* 613-952-0239
Director General, Corporate Facilities & Security Branch, Garima Dwivedi
Tel: 613-954-5074

Industry Sector / Secteur de l'industrie
Tel: 613-954-3395; *Fax:* 613-941-1134
Industry Sector (IS) assists Canadian industry & businesses compete, expand & create jobs in the knowledge-based economy. IS contributes to Innovation, Science & Economic Development's strategic objectives, trade, investment, innovation, connectedness & marketplace. It facilitates delivery of industrial, related policy analyses & strategies to promote global competitiveness of Canadian industry. IS provides a broad range of services, information resources, sector policies & strategies to support business growth. IS provides Canadian businesses with timely information products, business tools, research, strategic analyses, data & information resources.
Senior Assistant Deputy Minister, Mitch Davies
Tel: 343-291-2116; *Fax:* 613-941-1134
Assistant Deputy Minister, Eric Dagenais
Tel: 343-291-3940

Aerospace, Defence & Marine Branch / Aérospatiale, defense et la marine
Tel: 343-291-2105; *Fax:* 613-998-6703
Director General, Mary Gregory
Tel: 343-291-2128; *Fax:* 613-998-6703
Deputy Director, Space & Marine Directorate, Guillaume Cote
Tel: 613-618-2117; *Fax:* 866-694-8389
Senior Director, Aerospace, André Bernier
Tel: 343-291-2097; *Fax:* 613-952-5822

Automotive & Transportation Industries Branch / Direction générale des industries de l'automobile et des transports
Tel: 613-952-0441; *Fax:* 613-952-8088
Director General, Colette Downie
Tel: 343-291-2114; *Fax:* 613-952-8088

Investment Review Branch / Direction générale de l'examen des investissements
Tel: 343-291-1887; *Fax:* 343-291-2469
Director General, Patricia Brady
Tel: 343-291-2706; *Fax:* 343-291-2469

Manufacturing & Life Sciences Branch / Industries de la fabrication et des sciences de la vie
Tel: 343-291-2892; *Fax:* 613-954-3107
Director General, Sheryl Groeneweg
Tel: 343-291-2674
Corporate Secretary, Shelley Dooher
Tel: 343-291-2811; *Fax:* 343-291-2506

Science & Research Sector / Secteur des sciences et de la recherche
Assistant Deputy Minister, Nipun Vats
Tel: 343-291-2366
Director General, Science Programs & Partnerships, Michelle Gravelle
Tel: 343-291-2355
Director General, Clean Technology & Clean Growth Branch, Elaine Hood
Tel: 343-291-1587
Director General, Science Policy Branch, Marie-Hélène Légaré
Tel: 343-291-2376
Senior Director, Science, Technology & Innovation Council Secretariat, Dianne Caldbick
Tel: 343-291-2365
Senior Director, External Relations, Daniel Dufour
Tel: 343-291-2369
Senior Director, Digital Research Infrastructure Strategy, Sinead Tuite
Tel: 343-291-3414

Senior Director, Infrastructure Fund & Corporate Services, Melanie Vanstone
Tel: 343-291-3445

Small Business & Marketplace Services / Services axés sur le marché et la petite entreprise
Assistant Deputy Minister, Frances McRae
Tel: 343-291-1800

Corporations Canada
365 Laurier Ave. West, Ottawa, ON K1A 0C8
Tel: 613-941-4550; *Fax:* 613-941-0601
corporationscanada.ic.gc.ca
Director General, Corporations Canada, Ray Edwards
Tel: 343-291-4143

Measurement Canada / Mesures Canada
151 Tunney's Pasture Driveway, Ottawa, ON K1A 0C9
Tel: 613-952-0652; *Fax:* 613-957-1265
mc.ic.gc.ca
Provides services for companies selling measured products
President, Diane Allan
Tel: 613-952-0655
Vice-President, Program Development Directorate, Carl Cotton
Tel: 613-941-8918
Vice-President, Engineering & Laboratory Services, Benoit Desforges
Tel: 613-952-0610
Vice-President, Innovative Services Directorate, Sonia Roussy
Tel: 613-952-4285
Vice-President, David Spicer
Tel: 613-941-8919
Director, Ontario Region, John McCarty
Tel: 905-943-8729; *Fax:* 905-943-8738
232 Yorktech Dr.
Markham, ON L6G 1A6
Director, Prairie & Northern Region, John Pheifer
Tel: 204-983-8919; *Fax:* 204-983-5511
232 Yorktech Dr.
Markham, ON L6G 1A6
Director, Eastern Region, Jeffrey Watters
Tel: 514-496-7511; *Fax:* 514-283-7230
232 Yorktech Dr.
Markham, ON L6G 1A6

Office of the Superintendent of Bankruptcy / Bureau du surintendant des faillites
155 Queen St., Ottawa, ON K1A 0H5
Tel: 613-941-1000; *Fax:* 613-941-2862
osb-bsf.ic.gc.ca
Superintendent of Bankruptcy, Elisabeth Lang
Deputy Superintendent, Roula Eatrides
Tel: 613-946-2157; *Fax:* 613-948-6367
Director General, Outreach Services, Harvey Wong
Tel: 613-941-2854; *Fax:* 613-941-2862
Director, Eastern Region, Samra Rabie
Tel: 514-283-3422; *Fax:* 514-283-5130
1155, rue Metcalfe
Montréal, QC H3B 2V6
Director, Central Region, Jack Steinman
Tel: 416-954-6310; *Fax:* 416-973-6964
25 St. Clair Ave. East
Toronto, ON M4T 1M2

Small Business Branch / Direction générale de la petite entreprise
Tel: 343-291-1790; *Fax:* 343-291-2474
Director General, Etienne-Rene Massie
Tel: 343-291-1882

Tourism Branch / Direction générale du tourisme
Tel: 613-948-8009; *Fax:* 613-952-0290
Director General, Ilona Rehberg
Tel: 343-291-1779; *Fax:* 613-960-5770

Spectrum, Information Technologies & Telecommunications / Spectre, technologies de l'information et télécommunications
Journal Tower North, 300 Slater St., 20th Fl., Ottawa, ON K1A 0C8
Tel: 613-998-0368; *Fax:* 613-952-1203
www.ic.gc.ca/eic/site/020.nsf/eng/h_00593.html
Contributes to the Innovation, Science & Economic Development mandate by fostering the early development & use of information & communications technologies, infrastructures & services. The sector uses its policy & regulatory rule-making powers, & marketplace & industry sectoral development services to ensure Canada has a world-class telecommunications & information infrastructure; promote the international competitiveness of Canadian information technologies by all sectors of the Canadian economy; & ensure effective & efficient use of the radio frequency spectrum.
Senior Assistant Deputy Minister, Corinne Charette
Tel: 343-291-3939; *Fax:* 613-952-1203

Assistant Deputy Minister, Éric Dagenais
Tel: 343-291-3940; *Fax:* 343-291-3874
Director General, Information & Communications Technologies Branch, Krista Campbell
Tel: 613-954-5598; *Fax:* 613-957-4076
Acting Director General, Engineering, Planning & Standards Branch, Martin Proulx
Tel: 343-291-1500; *Fax:* 343-291-1906
Director General, Spectrum Licensing Policy Branch, Fiona Gilfillan
Tel: 343-291-1270; *Fax:* 343-291-1269
Director General, Governance, Policy Coordination & Planning, Shirley Anne Scharf
Tel: 343-291-3827
Director General, Connecting Canadians Branch, Susan Hart
Tel: 343-291-3803
Director General, Spectrum Management Operations Branch, Peter Hill
Tel: 343-291-3462; *Fax:* 343-291-3526
Director General, Digital Policy Branch, Krista Campbell
Tel: 613-954-5598; *Fax:* 613-957-4076
Senior Director, Spectrum Management Operations, Lynne Fancy
Tel: 343-291-3488; *Fax:* 343-291-3526
Director, Spectrum - Central and Western Ontario District, Lou Battiston
Tel: 905-639-6508; *Fax:* 905-639-6551
Director, Spectrum - Western Region Spectrum Operations, Morris Bodnar
Tel: 250-470-5040; *Fax:* 250-470-5045

Digital Policy Branch / Direction générale des politiques numériques
Tel: 613-991-1177; *Fax:* 613-957-1201
Formerly known as the Electronic Commerce Branch. Coordinates the development & implementation of a national electronic commerce strategy. It is responsible for both domestic & international aspects of electronic commerce. The Canadian Electronic Commerce Strategy was announced in September 1998. The Strategy, which was developed in collaboration with provincial & territorial governments, industry & consumer groups, among others, establishes a framework, goals, timetable, & implementation plan for electronic commerce domestically. The Strategy involves coordinating strategic elements that fall within the federal government's responsibilities, including the policy development areas of encryption & privacy. The branch develops policies, legislation & regulations that promote business innovation, competition, & growth in the online marketplace.
Director General, Krista Campbell
Tel: 613-954-5598; *Fax:* 613-957-4076

Strategy & Innovation Policy Sector / Secteur des stratégies et politiques d'innovation
Tel: 613-943-7152; *Fax:* 613-947-2959
Senior Assistant Deputy Minister, Lisa Setlakwe
Tel: 343-291-2294
Director General, Strategy, Research & Results Branch, Erin Lynch
Tel: 343-291-1931
Director General, Telecommunications & Internet Policy Branch, Pamela Miller
Tel: 343-291-2634
Director General, Marketplace Framework Policy Branch, Mark Schaan
Tel: 343-291-3700
Director General, External & Trade Policy Branch, Jordan Zed
Tel: 343-291-2649

FedNor (Federal Economic Development Initiative in Northern Ontario) / FedNor (Initiative fédérale du développement économique dans le Nord de l'Ontario)
19 Lisgar St., Sudbury, ON P3E 3L4
Fax: 705-671-0717
Toll-Free: 877-333-6673
TTY: 866-694-8389
fednor.gc.ca
twitter.com/FedNor
Director General, Aime Dimatteo
Tel: 705-671-0723; *Fax:* 705-670-6103

International Development Research Centre (IDRC) / Centre de recherches pour le développement international (CRDI)

150 Kent St., PO Box 8500 Ottawa, ON K1G 3H9
Tel: 613-236-6163; *Fax:* 613-238-7230
info@idrc.ca
www.idrc.ca
Other Communication: Library Reference Desk: library@idrc.ca;
Careers: careers@idrc.ca; Fellowships & Awards: awards@idrc.ca
twitter.com/Idrc_crdi
www.facebook.com/IDRC.CRDI
www.youtube.com/idrccrdi

Helps scientists in developing countries identify long-term, practical solutions to pressing development problems. Support is given directly to scientists working in universities, private enterprise, government & non-profit-making organizations. Priority is given to research aimed at achieving equitable & sustainable development. One of the three program areas of focus is Environmental & Natural Resource Management. Initiatives in this area include a rural poverty & environment program initiative, an urban poverty & environment program, ecosystem approaches to human health, an international model forest network, biodiversity & regional water demand initiative. Reports to Parliament through the Minister of Foreign Affairs.

Chair, Margaret Biggs

President, Jean Lebel
Tel: 613-696-2539; *Fax:* 613-238-7230
jlebel@idrc.ca

Vice-President, Resources Branch & Chief Financial Officer, Genevieve Leguerrier
Tel: 613-696-2432

Vice-President, Program & Partnership Branch, Dominique Charron
Tel: 613-696-2079

Vice-President, Strategy, Regions & Policy, Federico Burone
Tel: 613-696-2432

Director, Grants Administration Division, Katrina Millard
Tel: 613-696-2246

Director, Agriculture & Environment, Corral Alba
Tel: 613-696-2327

Director, Finance & Administration Division, Richard Cavanagh
Tel: 613-696-2167

Director, Human Resources, Nicole Leclerc
Tel: 613-696-2199

Director, Corporate Communications, Christel Binnie
Tel: 613-236-6163 ext: 2059; *Fax:* 613-563-2476
cbinnie@idrc.ca

Director, Information Management & Technology Division, Denis Trudeau
Tel: 613-696-2606

International Joint Commission (IJC) / Commission mixte internationale (CMI)

234 Laurier Ave. West, 22nd Fl., Ottawa, ON K1P 6K6
Tel: 613-995-2984; *Fax:* 613-993-5583
commission@ottawa.ijc.org
www.ijc.org
twitter.com/IJCsharedwaters
www.facebook.com/internationaljointcommission
www.flickr.com/photos/internationaljointcommission
Established by the Boundary Waters Treaty of 1909 & is responsible for approving (by Order of Approval) certain works in boundary waters which affect levels & flows on both sides of the Canada-US border. The commission provides recommendations on matters along the common boundary which have been referred to the Commission by the governments. Also monitors & assesses the Great Lakes Water Quality Agreement (GLWQA) & is responsible for reviewing & commenting on Remedial Action Plans (RAPs) in coordination with eight US states & the province of Ontario.

Canadian Commissioner & Chair, Pierre Béland

Commissioner, Henry Lickers

Secretary of the Canadian Section, Camille Mageau
Tel: 613-943-6366
mageauc@ottawa.ijc.org

Director, Sciences & Engineering, Pierre Yves Caux
Tel: 613-992-5727
cauxpy@ottawa.ijc.org

Great Lakes Regional Office / Bureau régional des Grands Lacs
100 Ouellette Ave., 8th fl., Windsor, ON N9A 6T3
Tel: 519-257-6700; *Fax:* 519-257-6740
Director, Great Lakes Regional Office, David Burden
Tel: 519-257-6715
burdend@windsor.ijc.org

United States Section / Section des États-Unis
#615, 2000 L St., NW, Washington, DC 20440 USA
Tel: 202-736-9009; *Fax:* 202-632-2006
commission@washington.ijc.org
Chair & Commissioner, Lana Pollack
Tel: 202-632-2007
Commissioner, Rich Moy
Secretary, Charles A. Lawson
Tel: 202-736-9008
lawsonc@washington.ijc.org
Public Information Officer, Frank Bevacqua
Tel: 202-736-9024
bevacquaf@washington.ijc.org

Invest in Canada / Investir au Canada

info@invcanada.ca
www.investcanada.ca
twitter.com/Invest_Canada
www.linkedin.com/company/invest-in-canada-investir-au-canada
www.instagram.com/invcanada
A federal investment promotion agency mandated to spur job growth in Canada by fascilitating global business investment.

Chair, Mitch Garber

Chief Executive Officer, Ian Mckay

Justice Canada

284 Wellington St., Ottawa, ON K1A 0H8
Tel: 613-957-4222; *Fax:* 613-954-0811
TTY: 613-992-4556
webadmin@justice.gc.ca
www.justice.gc.ca
Other Communication: Media Relations, Phone: 613-957-4207;
Access to Information and Privacy Phone: 613-952-8361
twitter.com/justicecanadaen
www.facebook.com/justicecanadaen
The Department ensures that the Canadian justice system is fair, accessible & efficient. Responsibilities are as follows: provision of policy & program advice & direction by the development of the legal content of bills, regulations, & guidelines; proscecution of federal offences throughout Canada; litigation of civil cases by or on behalf of the federal Crown; & provision of legal advice to federal law enforcement agencies & other government departments.

Minister, Justice & Attorney General of Canada, Hon. David Lametti, P.C., B.A., LL.B., B.C.L., LL.M., D.Phil.
Tel: 613-943-6636; *Fax:* 613-943-6637
David.Lametti@parl.gc.ca

Deputy Minister & Deputy Attorney General, Nathalie G. Drouin
Tel: 613-957-4998

Associate Deputy Minister, Francois A. Daigle
Tel: 613-941-4073; *Fax:* 613-941-4074

Federal Ombudsman for Victims of Crime, Heidi Illingworth
Tel: 613-957-6554; *Fax:* 613-941-3498
www.victimsfirst.gc.ca

Senior Counsel & Manager, Deputy Minister & Deputy Attorney General's Office, Marie-Claude Filion
Tel: 613-952-0627
www.victimsfirst.gc.ca

Aboriginal Affairs Portfolio / Portefeuille des affaires autochtones

Fax: 613-954-4737

Assistant Deputy Minister, Laurie Sargent
Tel: 613-907-3648
Senior General Counsel & Senior Advisor to the ADM, Ronald S. Stevenson
Tel: 613-907-3621; Fax: 613-954-4737
Director General & Senior General Counsel, Aboriginal Law Centre, Ana Stuhec
Tel: 613-907-3630
Senior General Counsel, CIRNAC/ISC Legal Services, Marie Bourry
Tel: 819-994-6558
Chief, Cost Recovery Operations, Colleen McElroy
Tel: 613-907-3643

Business & Regulatory Law Portfolio / Portefeuille du droit des affaires et du droit réglementaire

Fax: 613-946-9988

Assistant Deputy Minister, Andrew Saranchuk
Tel: 613-957-4944
Deputy Assistant Deputy Minister, Caroline Clark
Tel: 613-957-4638
Executive Director & Senior General Counsel, Agriculture & Agri-Food Canada Legal Services (AFI), Mark Belliveau
Tel: 506-777-3727
Acting Executive Director & Senior General Counsel, Environment and Climate Change Canada Legal Services (ECCC), Edith Bostwick
Tel: 819-938-4915
Executive Director & Senior General Counsel, Health Canada Legal Services (HC), Shalene Curtis-Micallef
Tel: 613-957-3766
Executive Director & Senior General Counsel, Employment & Social Development / Veterans Affairs (LSU), Catherine Drew
Tel: 819-654-2072
Executive Director & Senior General Counsel, Competition Bureau Legal Services (CB), David Dunbar
Tel: 819-994-7714
Executive Director & Senior General Counsel, Natural Resources Canada Legal Services (NRCan), Stéphane Lamoureux
Tel: 343-292-7223
Executive Director & Senior General Counsel, Global Affairs Canada Legal Services (GAC), Daniel Roussy
Tel: 343-203-2274
Executive Director & Senior General Counsel, Canadian Heritage Legal Services (PCH), Louise Senechal
Tel: 819-997-2729
Executive Director & Senior General Counsel, Innovation, Science & Economic Development Legal Services (ISEDC), Alain Vauclair
Tel: 343-291-2267
Executive Director & General Counsel, Commercial Law Section (CLS), Matthew Zadro
Tel: 613-941-8381

Central Agencies Portfolio / Groupes centraux

Fax: 613-995-7223

Assistant Deputy Minister, Isabelle Jacques
Tel: 613-369-3377
Executive Director & Senior General Counsel, Treasury Board Secretariat - Legal Services, Dora Benbaruk
Tel: 613-952-3379
Executive Director & General Counsel, Office of the Superintendent of Financial Institutions - Legal Services, Gino Richer
Tel: 613-949-8933

Communications Branch

Fax: 613-941-2329

Director General, Shirley Anne Off
Tel: 613-957-9596
Deputy Director General, Strategic Operations Division, Kirstan Gagnon
Tel: 613-954-6327

Management Sector / Secteur de la gestion

Fax: 613-952-2178

Assistant Deputy Minister & Chief Financial Officer, Johanne Bernard
Tel: 613-907-3724
Corporate Counsel, Vacant
Chief Information Officer, Dugald Topshee
Tel: 613-941-3444
Acting Director General, Human Resources Branch, Martine Dagenais
Tel: 613-941-1867; Fax: 613-954-5740
Director General, Corporate Services Branch, Ivan Sicard
Tel: 613-907-3709

Acting Senior Director, HR Operations & Client Services Division, Bruno Thériault
Tel: 613-946-7475
Chief, Financial Controls, Ellen Li
Tel: 613-946-7493
Director, Corporate HR Planning, Programs & Systems Division, Robert Beeraj
Tel: 613-948-3009
Director, Labour Relations & Compensation Divison, Virginie Emiel-Wildhaber
Tel: 613-946-0211
Director, Access to Information & Privacy Office, Francine Farley
Tel: 613-907-3678

National Litigation Sector / Secteur national du contentieux

Assistant Deputy Attorney General, Geoffrey M. Bickert
Tel: 613-670-6357; Fax: 613-941-1972
Deputy Assistant Deputy Attorney General, Jodie van Dieen
Tel: 613-670-6367
Chief General Counsel, Robert Frater
Tel: 613-670-6289
Director General & Senior General Counsel, International Assistance Group, Janet Henchey
Tel: 613-948-3003
Director General & Senior General Counsel, Civil Litigation Section, Catherine Lawrence
Tel: 613-670-6258
Director & General Counsel, National Security Group, Catheryne Beaudette
Tel: 613-952-6783
Director & General Counsel, National eDiscovery & Litigation Support Services, James Stringham
Tel: 613-948-3477
Director General, Business Integration & Strategies Branch, Yves Marion
Tel: 613-670-8506

Policy Sector / Secteur des politiques

Fax: 613-957-9949

Senior Assistant Deputy Minister, Laurie Wright
Tel: 613-957-4730
Senior Counsel & Special Advisor to the Senior Assistant Deputy Minister, Nathalie Hébert
Tel: 613-957-3548
Director General, Programs Branch, Elizabeth Hendy
Tel: 613-957-4344
Director General, International Development Section, Serge Lortie
Tel: 613-957-3184
Director General & General Counsel, Youth Justice & Strategic Initiatives Section, Danièle Ménard
Tel: 613-954-2730
Director General, Policy Integration & Coordination Section, Stephen Mihorean
Tel: 613-941-2267
Director General & Senior General Counsel, Criminal Law Policy Section, Carole Morency
Tel: 613-941-4044
Deputy Director General, Intergovernmental & External Relations Division, Janet McIntyre
Tel: 613-957-4924
Director, Indigenous Justice Program, Karolyn Lui
Tel: 613-946-6903

Public Law & Legislative Services Sector / Secteur du droit public et des services législatifs

Fax: 613-952-4137

Assistant Deputy Minister, Nancy Othmer
Tel: 613-941-7890
Acting Deputy Assistant Deputy Minister, Edward Livingstone
Tel: 613-952-5619
Acting Director General & Senior General Counsel, Human Rights Law Section, Raymond MacCallum
Tel: 613-957-4939
Acting Director General & Senior General Counsel, Constitutional, Administrative & International Law Section, Julie Wellington
Tel: 613-941-2326
Acting Director & General Counsel, Transport Canada Regulations Section, Isabelle Parrot
Tel: 613-993-6458
Director & General Counsel, Bijuralism Group, Luc Gagné
Tel: 613-952-1119
Senior Counsel & Assistant Director, Legislation Section, Louise Faille
Tel: 613-957-0018
Senior Counsel, Advisory & Development Services Section, Daniel C. Blasioli
Tel: 613-957-4937
Senior Counsel, Health Canada Regulations Section, Rob Billingsley
Tel: 613-952-9633

Public Safety, Defence & Immigration Portfolio / Sécurité Publique, défense & immigration

Assistant Deputy Minister, Elisabeth Eid
Tel: 613-952-4774; Fax: 613-952-7370
Deputy Assistant Deputy Minister, Leigh Taylor
Tel: 613-948-1463
Executive Director & Senior General Counsel, Legal Services: Immigration, Refugees and Citizenship Canada, Caroline Fobes
Tel: 613-437-6722
Executive Director & General Counsel, Legal Services: Correctional Service Canada, Laurel Johnson
Tel: 613-992-9009
Executive Director & Senior General Counsel, Legal Services: Public Safety Canada, Christian Roy
Tel: 613-991-9375
Executive Director & Senior General Counsel, Legal Services: Canada Border Services Agency, Julie Watkinson
Tel: 613-946-2406
Deputy Executive Director & General Counsel, Legal Services: Royal Canadian Mounted Police, Barbara Massey
Tel: 613-843-6394
Legal Advisor & Senior General Counsel, Department of National Defence & the Canadian Forces, Michel Sousa
Tel: 613-995-0828
Director & General Counsel, Legal Issues Coordination Group, Kristine Allen
Tel: 613-948-1461
Director & General Counsel, Crimes Against Humanity & War Crimes Section, Terry Beitner
Tel: 613-954-2351
Director & General Counsel, Communications Security Establishment, Manon Lefebvre
Tel: 613-991-5592
Senior General Counsel, National Security Litigation & Advisory Group, Mylène Bouzigon
Tel: 613-842-1197
Acting Senior Counsel, Parole Board of Canada, Agnès Levesque
Tel: 613-954-2331

Tax Law Services Portfolio / Services du droit fiscal

Fax: 613-941-1221

Assistant Deputy Minister, Lynn Lovett
Tel: 613-670-6416
Deputy Assistant Deputy Minister, Anick Pelletier
Tel: 613-670-8270
Executive Director & Senior General Counsel, Tax Law Services, Canada Revenue Agency, Jade Boucher
Tel: 613-957-2358
Deputy Executive Director & Senior General Counsel, Tax Law Services, Canada Revenue Agency, Duaine Simms
Tel: 613-952-6648
Deputy Director & Senior Counsel, Tax Law Services, Julian Malone
Tel: 613-670-6477
Director, Business Management Section, Nicolas Wojcik
Tel: 613-670-6405

Laurentian Pilotage Authority (LPA) / Administration de pilotage des Laurentides (APL)

Head Office, #1401, 999, boul Maisonneuve ouest, Montréal, QC H3A 3L4

Tél: 514-283-6320
Téléc: 514-496-2409
administration@apl.gc.ca
www.pilotagestlaurent.gc.ca
Autres nombres: Dispatch Center, Toll-Free Phone: 800-361-0747; Email: pilote-mtl@apl.gc.ca; Billing Department, Phone: 514-283-6320; Email: facturation-billing@apl.gc.ca
In 1972, the Laurentian Pilotage Authority was created under the Pilotage Act.
The Crown corporation has the following objectives: to operate a pilotage service in Canadian waters in & around the province of Québec, except the waters of Cap d'Espoir & Chaleur Bay; to maintain a service in the interest of navigational safety; & to charge pilotage tariffs in order to finance operations.

Chair, Vacant

Chief Executive Officer, Fulvio Fracassi
Tel: 514-283-6320 ext: 204

Director, Administrative Services, Claude Lambert
Tel: 514-283-6320 ext: 212

Director, Dispatch Services, Steve Lapointe
Tel: 514-283-6320 ext: 300

Senior Director, Operations, Sylvia Masson
Tel: 514-283-6320

Advisor, Human Resources, Isabelle Roy
Tel: 514-283-6320 ext: 213

Secretary; Legal Advisor, Mario St-Pierre
Tel: 514-283-6320 ext: 209

Library & Archives Canada (LAC) / Bibliothèque et archives Canada

395 Wellington St., Ottawa, ON K1A 0N4
Tel: 613-996-5115; *Fax:* 613-995-6274
Toll-Free: 866-578-7777
TTY: 866-299-1699
www.bac-lac.gc.ca
Other Communication: Media Relations, Phone: 613-293-4298;
Interlibrary Loans: 613-996-7527; Theses Canada:
819-994-6882; Copyright Bureau: 613-992-2567
twitter.com/@LibraryArchives
www.facebook.com/LibraryArchives
www.youtube.com/user/LibraryArchiveCanada
The mission of Library & Archives Canada is to collect &
preserve the documentary heritage of Canada. Library &
Archives Canada ensures that publications, archival records,
photographs, sound & audio-visual materials, & electronic
documents are accessible to all Canadians. The organization
also works to facilitate cooperation among communities involved
in the acquisition, preservation, & diffusion of knowledge. Library
& Archives Canada provides services the the public,
government, plus libraries, archives, & publishers.

Librarian & Archivist of Canada, Leslie Weir
Tel: 819-934-5800
leslie.weir@canada.ca

Chief of Staff, Jill Scott
Tel: 819-934-5799

Director General, Communications, Cécile Lemaire
Tel: 613-790-0584

Corporate Services / Services Corporatifs
Assistant Deputy Minister & Chief Financial Officer, Hervé Déry
Tel: 819-934-4618; *Fax:* 819-934-5264
herve.dery@canada.ca
Senior Director General & Chief Financial Officer, Mark C.
Melanson
Tel: 819-934-4627; *Fax:* 819-934-4428
mark.melanson@canada.ca
Senior Director General & Chief Information Officer, Paul
Wagner
Tel: 819-997-4111; *Fax:* 819-994-6835
paul.wagner@canada.ca
Director General, Strategic Planning & Infrastructure
Management, Serge Corbeil
Tel: 819-934-5876; *Fax:* 819-934-5267
serge.corbeil@canada.ca
Director General, Innovation & Digital Transformation, Michael
Corbett
Tel: 613-818-7471
michael.corbett@canada.ca

Corporate Secretary / Secrétaire général
Corporate Secretary, Fabien Lengellé
Tel: 819-994-6982; *Fax:* 819-934-4422
fabien.lengelle@canada.ca

Operations Sector / Secteur des opérations
Chief Operating Officer, Normand Charbonneau
Tel: 819-934-5790
normand.charbonneau@canada.ca
Director General, Evaluation & Acquisitions Branch, Chantal
Marin-Comeau
Tel: 819-934-5860; *Fax:* 819-934-7534
chantal.marin-comeau@canada.ca
Director General, Government Records Branch, Robert
McIntosh
Tel: 613-762-9354; *Fax:* 819-934-5393
robert.mcintosh@canada.ca
Director General, Public Services Branch, Johanna Smith
Tel: 613-897-4742
johanna.smith@canada.ca

Library of Parliament / Bibliothèque du Parlement

Information Servicce, Parliament of Canada, Ottawa, ON K1A 0A9
Tel: 613-992-4793
Toll-Free: 866-599-4999
TTY: 613-995-2266
info@parl.gc.ca
lop.parl.ca/sites/PublicWebsite/default/en_CA
Other Communication: Visitor Information, Phone: 613-996-0896
twitter.com/LoPResearch
www.facebook.com/PARLyouth
www.linkedin.com/company/library-of-parliament
twitter.com/LoPInformation
The Library of Parliament provides services to parliamentarians
& the public. Services to parliamentarians include reference,
research, & analysis, internaitonal news and access to the
library's extensive collection of resources. Services to the public
include information about Parliament, classroom resources, &
guided tours of the Parliament buildings.

Parliamentary Librarian, Heather Lank
Tel: 613-992-3122

**Director General, Information & Document Resource
Service,** Sonia Bebbington
Tel: 613-996-8558

Director General, Business Support Services, Lynn Potter
Tel: 613-286-6571

Director General, Business Support Services, Manon
Robert
Tel: 613-992-6826

Senior Director, Legal & Social Affairs, Kristen Douglas
Tel: 613-995-3476

**Senior Director, Reference, Current Awareness & User
Services,** Joseph Jackson
Tel: 613-851-4672

Senior Director, Public Education Programs, Benoit Morin
Tel: 613-943-6401

**Senior Director, Economics, Resources & International
Affairs,** Marcus Pistor
Tel: 613-947-6330

Marine Atlantic Inc. / Marine Atlantique

**Corporate Office, Baine Johnston Centre, #302, 10 Fort
William Pl., St. John's, NL A1C 1K4**
Toll-Free: 800-897-2797
customer_relations@marine-atlantic.ca
www.marineatlantic.ca
twitter.com/MAferries
www.facebook.com/marineatlanticferries
www.linkedin.com/company/marineatlantic
www.youtube.com/user/maferries
Marine Atlantic is a Crown corporation that strives to provide
safe & environmentally responsible ferry service between the
island of Newfoundland & the province of Nova Scotia.
Two routes are available. A year round service is provided
between Port aux Basques, Newfoundland & Labrador & North
Sydney, Nova Scotia. The second route is available between
mid-June & late September between Argentia, Newfoundland &
Labrador & North Sydney, Nova Scotia.

Acting Chair, Sharon Duggan

President & CEO, Paul Griffin

Director, Passenger Services, Neil Paterson

Manager, Marketing, Vicki Rose

Military Grievances External Review Committee / Comité externe d'examen des griefs militaires

60 Queen St., 10th Fl., Ottawa, ON K1P 5Y7
Tel: 613-996-8529; *Fax:* 613-996-6491
Toll-Free: 877-276-4193
TTY: 877-986-1666
mgerc-ceegm@mgerc-ceegm.gc.ca
mgerc-ceegm.gc.ca
Other Communication: Toll-Free Fax: 866-716-6601
Formerly known as the Canadian Forces Grievance Board, the
Committee is an administrative tribunal with quasi-judicial
powers, independent from the Department of National Defence
(DND) & the Canadian Forces (CF). The former Board was
created on March 1, 2000, in accordance with legislation
enacted in December 1998 that contained amendments to the

National Defence Act. The Committee was renamed on June 19,
2013, with the enactment of Bill C-15.
The Committee conducts objective & transparent reviews of
grievances with due respect to fairness & equity for each
individual member of the CF, regardless of rank or position. It
plays a unique role within the military grievance review process
because it ensures that the rights of CF personnel are
considered fairly & impartially in the best interests of both parties
concerned, thus balancing the rights of the grievor against the
legal & operational requirements of the CF.

Chair, Christine Guérette
Tel: 613-220-9735

Vice-Chair, Dominic McAlea
Tel: 613-996-8628

Director General, Operations & General Counsel, Vihar
Joshi
Tel: 613-293-7298

Acting Registrar, Narom Sing
Tel: 613-299-7585

Senior Legal Counsel, Operations Directorate, Tasha
Emmerton
Tel: 613-299-8934

National Arts Centre (NAC) / Centre national des Arts (CNA)

1 Elgin St., PO Box 1534 Stn. B, Ottawa, ON K1P 5W1
Tel: 613-947-7000; *Fax:* 613-947-7112
Toll-Free: 866-850-2787
www.nac-cna.ca
twitter.com/canadasnac
www.facebook.com/CanadasNAC
www.youtube.com/user/NACvideosCNA
The National Arts Centre is a multidisciplinary, bilingual
performing arts centre that was created by an Act of the
Parliament of Canada & opened to the public in 1969. It is home
to the National Arts Centre Orchestra. The National Arts Centre
works to develop performing arts in the National Capital Region
& to help the Canada Council develop performing arts
throughout Canada.
The Centre raises approximately half of its revenues from ticket,
food, & parking sales, & well as hall rental fees & fundraising
through the National Arts Centre Foundation. Other revenues
are derived from the federal government.

Chair, National Arts Centre Board of Trustees, Adrian
Burns

President & CEO, Christopher Deacon
president@nac-cna.ca

Chief Executive Officer, National Arts Centre Foundation,
Jayne Watson
Jayne.Watson@nac-cna.ca

Chief Financial Officer & Director, Finance, Daniel Senyk
Daniel.Senyk@nac-cna.ca

Managing Director, NAC Orchestra, Arna Kristin
Einarsdottir

Managing Director, English Theatre, David Abel

Director, Music Education & Community Engagement,
Geneviève Cimon
Genevieve.Cimon@nac-cna.ca

Director, Production Operations, Mike Damato
production@nac-cna.ca

Artistic Director, French Theatre, Brigitte Haentjens
Brigitte.Haentjens@nac-cna.ca

Director, Marketing, Diane Landry
Diane.Landry@nac-cna.ca

Director, Operations, David McCuaig
David.McCuaig@nac-cna.ca

National Battlefields Commission (NBC) / Commission des champs de bataille nationaux

390, av de Bernières, Québec, QC G1R 2L7
Tel: 418-648-3506; *Fax:* 418-648-3638
information@ccbn-nbc.gc.ca
www.ccbn-nbc.gc.ca
Other Communication: Communications, Phone: 418-648-4801;
Archives: 418-648-2589; Finances: 418-648-4666
twitter.com/plainsabraham
www.facebook.com/plainsofabraham

In 1908, an Act was passed to create the National Battlefields Commission. The purpose of the Commission is to acquire & preserve historical battlefields & to create national parks from these battlefields for the benefit of the public. The federal government agency, with its nine-member board of directors, operates under the portfolio of the Minister of Canadian Heritage.
The Commission has a sustainable development policy for the conservation of the Plains of Abraham park.

Chair, Jean Pierre Robert

Secretary - Director General, Michèle Gagné
Tel: 418-648-3553

Director, Institutional Affairs, Anne Chouinard
Tel: 418-648-2540; *Fax:* 418-648-3638

Director, Administration, Bernard Laquerre
Tel: 418-648-4666; *Fax:* 418-649-6345

National Capital Commission (NCC) / Commission de la capitale nationale (CCN)

#202, 40 Elgin St., Ottawa, ON K1P 1C7
Tel: 613-239-5000; *Fax:* 613-239-5063
Toll-Free: 800-465-1867
TTY: 866-661-3530
info@ncc-ccn.gc.ca
www.ncc-ccn.gc.ca
Other Communication: Emergency Service, Phone:
613-239-5353; Gatineau Park Visitor Centre: 819-827-2020;
Volunteer Centre: 613-239-5373; Skateway: 613-239-5234;
Sponsorship: 613-239-5625
www.youtube.com/user/nccvidccn

The National Capital Commission is a Crown corporation. It was established by Parliament in 1959 to act as a steward for federal buildings & lands in Canada's National Capital Region.
The Commission works to ensure that the region is a place of national significance & pride. It consists of the following corporate, advisory, & special committees: Executive; Audit; Governance; Advisory Committee on Planning, Design, & Realty; Advisory Committee on Communications, Marketing, & Programming; Advisory Committee on the Official Residences of Canada; & Canadiana Fund.
In accordance with the National Capital Act, the Commission's board of directors is appointed by the Minister of Foreign Affairs, with the approval of the Governor-in-Council. The National Capital Commission is accountable to Parliament & reports through the Minister of Foreign Affairs.

Minister Responsible; Minister, Canadian Heritage,
Vacant

Chair, Marc Seaman

Chief Executive Officer, Tobi Nussbaum

Chief Financial Officer & Vice-President, Customer Service Branch, Michel Houle
Tel: 613-239-5678 ext: 5086

Vice-President, Capital Stewardship Branch, Anne Ménard
Tel: 613-239-5678 ext: 5782

Acting Vice-President, Capital Planning, Pierre Vaillancourt
Tel: 613-239-5678 ext: 5871

Vice-President, Public, Legal & Corporate Affairs, Nicolas Ruszkowski
Tel: 613-239-5678 ext: 5670

Vice-President, Official Residences, Greg J. Kenney
Tel: 613-239-5678 ext: 5723

Vice-President, Human Resources, Céline Larabie
Tel: 613-239-5678 ext: 5656

Director, Audit, Research, Evaluation & Ethics; Chief Audit Executive, Jayne Hinchliff-Milne
Tel: 613-239-5678 ext: 5629; *Fax:* 613-239-5695

Department of National Defence & the Canadian Armed Forces / Le Ministère de la Défense nationale et les Forces armées canadiennes

National Defence HQ, Major-General George R. Pearkes Bldg., 101 Colonel By Dr., Ottawa, ON K1A 0K2
Tel: 613-995-2534; *Fax:* 613-992-4739
Toll-Free: 888-995-2534
TTY: 800-467-9877
information@forces.gc.ca
www.forces.gc.ca
Other Communication: CF Recruiting, Phone: 800-856-8488;
Access to Information, Phone: 613-992-0996; Media Inquiries,
Phone: 613-996-2353 or 866-377-0811
twitter.com/CanadianForces
www.facebook.com/CanadianForces
www.linkedin.com/company/1564
www.youtube.com/user/CanadianForcesVideos

The Department of National Defence, the Canadian Armed Forces, & related organizations provide services to defend Canada & Canadian interests.
The Defence Portfolio comprises the following organizations, which are the responsibility of the Minister of National Defence: The Office of the Legal Advisor to the Department of National Defence & the Canadian Forces; National Search & Rescue Secretariat; Defence Research & Development Canada; Communications Security Establishment; Cadets & Junior Canadian Rangers; Canadian Forces Housing Agency; Judge Advocate General; Military Police Complaints Commission; Canadian Forces Grievance Board; Office of the Chief Miltary Judge; The Office of the National Defence & Canadian Forces Ombudsman; & the Canadian Forces Personnel Support Agency.
Some of the Canadian Forces' current operations include: Operation Impact, against the Islamic State of Iraq & the Levant (ISIL), also known as Daesh, in the Republic of Iraq; Operation Caribbe in the Caribbean Sea; Operation Artemis at sea; Operation Calumet in the Sinai Peninsula; & Operation Nunalivut in Nunavut.

Governor General, Rt. Hon. Mary May Simon
Rideau Hall
1 Sussex Dr.
Ottawa, ON K1A 0A1

Minister, National Defence, Hon. Anita Anand, P.C.

Associate Minister, National Defence, Hon. Lawrence MacAulay, P.C.
Tel: 613-995-9325; *Fax:* 613-995-2754
lawrence.macaulay@parl.gc.ca

Chief of Defence Staff for the Canadian Forces, Gen Jonathan Vance
Tel: 613-992-7405

Vice-Chief of Defence Staff, Vacant

Chair, Defence Science Advisory Board, Wayne Williams
Tel: 613-992-4070; *Fax:* 613-996-9168

Interim Ombudsman, Gregory Lick

Chief of Staff to the Minister, Brian Bohunicky
Tel: 613-996-3100

Chief of Staff to the Associate Minister, Vacant

Director, Parliamentary Affairs, Louis Landry
Tel: 613-996-3100

Director, General Operations, Robyn Hynes
Tel: 613-992-0787; *Fax:* 613-992-3167

Director, Strategic Planning & Research, Mary Kirby
Tel: 613-992-0787; *Fax:* 613-992-3167

Director, Communications, Renée Filiatrault
Tel: 613-996-3100

Associated Agencies, Boards & Commissions:

• Communications Security Establishment Canada / Centre de la sécurité des telecommunications Canada
1500 Bronson Ave.
PO Box 9703 Terminal
Ottawa, ON K1A 0K2
Tel: 613-991-7600; *Fax:* 613-991-8514
www.cse-cst.gc.ca
The Communications Security Establishment is Canada's national cryptologic agency, providing the Government of Canada with two key services: foreign signals intelligence in support of defence & foreign policy, & the protection of electronic information & communication.

• Office of the Communications Security Establishment Commissioner / Bureau du Commissaire du Centre de la sécurité des télécommunications
PO Box 1984 B
Ottawa, ON K1P 5R5
Tel: 613-992-3044
www.ocsec-bccst.gc.ca
The Commissioner reviews the activities of the Communications Security Establishment for compliance with the law; advises the Minister of National Defence & the Attorney General of Canada of any CSE activity not in compliance with the law; receives complaints about CSE activities; carries out specific duties under the public interest provisions of the Security of Information Act.

• Military Police Complaints Commission / Commission d'examen des plaintes concernant la police militaire
270 Albert St., 10th Fl.
Ottawa, ON K1P 5G8
Tel: 613-947-5625; *Fax:* 613-947-5713
Toll-free: 800-632-0566
commission@mpcc-cppm.gc.ca
www.mpcc-cppm.gc.ca
Other Communication: Toll-Free Fax: 877-947-5713
Quasi-judicial, independent civilian agency examines complaints arising from either the conduct of military police members in the exercise of policing duties or functions or from interference in or obstruction of their police investigations.

Deputy Minister of National Defence / Sous-ministre de la Défense nationale

The following positions report to the Deputy Minister of National Defence: Associate Deputy Minister of National Defence; Assistant Deputy Minister, Finance & Corporate Services; Assistant Deputy Minister, Human Resources - Civilian; Assistant Deputy Minister, Infrastructure & Environment; Assistant Deputy Minister, Policy; & Assistant Deputy Minister, Materiel.
The following positions report to both the Deputy Minister of National Defence & the Chief of the Defence Staff: Vice Chief of the Defence Staff; Assistant Deputy Minister, Information Management; Assistant Deputy Minister, Public Affairs; Assistant Deputy Minister, Science & Technology; Chief Review, Services; & the Department of National Defence & Canadian Forces Legal Advisor.
The Judge Advocate General is responsible to the Minister of National Defence & accountable for legal advice given to the Deputy Minister of National Defence & the Chief of the Defence Staff.

Deputy Minister, National Defence, Jody Thomas
Tel: 613-992-4258; *Fax:* 613-995-2028
Senior Associate Deputy Minister, National Defence, W. (Bill) Davern Jones
Tel: 613-992-0275; *Fax:* 613-995-2028
Assistant Deputy Minister, Review Services, Amipal Manchanda
Tel: 613-992-7975; *Fax:* 613-947-5843
Corporate Secretary, Larry Surtees
Tel: 613-996-6402; *Fax:* 613-992-0313
Director General, Audit, Jean-Francois Riel
Tel: 613-992-4936; *Fax:* 613-992-0528
Executive Director, Evaluation Operations, Vacant
Tel: 613-992-0345; *Fax:* 613-992-0528

Chief Military Personnel (CMP) / Chef - Personnel militaire (CPM)

www.cmp-cpm.forces.gc.ca
Other Communication: Media Liaison Office, Phone:
866-377-0811; CF Member Assistance Program: 800-268-7708;
CF Pension Program: 800-267-0325; Honours & Recognition:
877-741-8332

The Chief Military Personnel has the following responsibilities: providing guidance to the Canadian Forces about military personnel management issues; establishing policies & programs to maintain the profession of arms; monitoring compliance with Canadian Forces personnel management policies; & overseeing the management of the Canadian Forces Personnel System.
The Chief Military Personnel manages programs & services such as compensation & benefits, careers & training, work environment, human resources intiatives, & health services.

Chief of Military Personnel, LGen C.T. Whitecross, CMM, MSM, CD
Surgeon General / Commander, Canadian Forces Health Services Group, BGen H.C. MacKay, OMM, CD, QHP
Director General, Military Personnel Research & Analysis, Susan Truscott
Tel: 613-992-6162; *Fax:* 613-995-5785

Finance & Corporate Services / Finances et serices du ministère

Assistant Deputy Minister, Claude C.R. Rochette
Tel: 613-992-5669; *Fax:* 613-992-9693
Director General, Financial Management, Werner Liedtke
Tel: 613-992-6907; *Fax:* 613-992-4639
Director General, Financial Operations, Dale MacMillan
Tel: 613-971-6506; *Fax:* 613-971-6507

Director General, Strategic Finance & Financial Arrangements, Ian Poulter
 Tel: 613-943-5279; *Fax:* 613-992-8712

Human Resources - Civilian / Ressources humaines - Civils
Assistant Deputy Minister, Kin Choi
 Tel: 613-971-0245; *Fax:* 613-971-0247
Director General, Workplace Management, Susan Harrison
 Tel: 613-971-0202; *Fax:* 613-971-0103
Director General, Human Resources Strategic Directions, Vacant
 Tel: 613-971-0248; *Fax:* 613-971-0236
Director General, Civilian Human Resources Management Operations, Vacant
 Tel: 613-971-0524; *Fax:* 613-971-0103

Information Management / Gestion de l'information
Assistant Deputy Minister, Len Bastien
 Tel: 613-995-2017; *Fax:* 613-995-2189
Chief of Staff, MGen Gregory Loos
 Tel: 613-992-5420; *Fax:* 613-995-2189
Director General, Information Management Technology & Strategic Planning, Guy Charron
 Tel: 613-992-1674; *Fax:* 613-992-4223
Director General, Information Management Project Delivery, Tony Hoe
 Tel: 613-992-9119
Director General, Enterprise Application Services, Claude Lareau
 Tel: 613-960-9915; *Fax:* 613-960-9920

Infrastructure & Environment / Infrastructure et environnement
Assistant Deputy Minister, Jaime Pitfield
 Tel: 613-947-4061
Chief of Staff, Vacant
Chief Executive Officer, Canadian Forces Housing Agency, Dominique Francoeur
 Tel: 613-998-5904; *Fax:* 613-991-1988
Director General, Portfolio Requirements, Susan Chambers
 Tel: 613-995-0923; *Fax:* 613-995-1031
Director General, Environment, Rose Kattackal
 Tel: 613-995-5586; *Fax:* 613-995-1031

Judge Advocate General's Office / Juge-avocat général
101 Colonel By Dr., Ottawa, ON K1A 0K2
 Tel: 613-992-5678; *Fax:* 613-992-1211
Judge Advocate General, MGen Blaise Cathcart
 Tel: 613-992-3019; *Fax:* 613-992-5678
Acting Deputy Judge Advocate General, Operations, Cdr. Geneviève Bernachez
 Tel: 613-996-6456; *Fax:* 613-945-0242
Deputy Judge Advocate General, Regional Services - Ottawa, Vacant
 Tel: 613-996-6456
Deputy Judge Advocate General, Military Justice & Administrative Law, Vacant

Materiel / Matériels
Assistant Deputy Minister, Patrick Finn
 Tel: 613-992-6622; *Fax:* 613-945-0949
Chief of Staff, André Fillion
 Tel: 613-992-6622; *Fax:* 613-995-0028
Director General, Major Project Services (Air), Troy Crosby
 Tel: 819-997-6306; *Fax:* 819-997-9699
Director, Major Project Services, Vacant
 Tel: 819-997-6134; *Fax:* 819-997-6072
Director, Major Project Delivery (Land & Sea), Ian Mack
 Tel: 819-939-6963; *Fax:* 819-997-7252

Aerospace Equipment Program Management / Gestion du programme d'équipement aérospatial
Director General, Vacant
 Tel: 613-939-3354; *Fax:* 819-990-5236

International & Industry Programs / Programmes Internationaux et industriels
Director General, Vacant
 Tel: 613-992-3730; *Fax:* 613-995-0028

Land Equipment Program Management / Gestion du programme d'équipement terrestre
Director General, Vacant
 Tel: 819-997-9474; *Fax:* 819-994-3143

Maritime Equipment Program Management / Gestion du programme d'équipement maritime
Director General, Vacant
 Tel: 819-939-3500; *Fax:* 819-997-7058

Materiel Systems & Supply Chain / Systèmes de matériel et chaîne d'approvisionnement
Director General, Vacant
 Tel: 819-994-9461; *Fax:* 819-994-1627

Procurement Services / Services d'acquisition
Director General, Vacant
 Tel: 613-997-3356; *Fax:* 613-997-3211

Policy / Politiques
Assistant Deputy Minister, Gordon Venner
 Tel: 613-992-3458; *Fax:* 613-995-6631
Director General, International Security Policy, Vacant
 Tel: 613-992-2769; *Fax:* 613-992-3990
Director General, Policy Planning, Vacant
 Tel: 613-992-0799; *Fax:* 613-995-0446
Director General, Policy Coordination, Nada Vrany
 Tel: 613-995-8332; *Fax:* 613-995-2876

Public Affairs / Affaires publiques
Assistant Deputy Minister, Edison Stewart
 Tel: 613-996-0562; *Fax:* 613-995-2610
Chief of Staff & Director, Vacant
 Tel: 613-995-1497
Director General, Marketing, Janice Keenan
 Tel: 819-997-1846; *Fax:* 819-997-1880
Director General, Public Affairs Strategic Planning, Sophie Galarneau
 Tel: 613-943-5353; *Fax:* 613-995-2610

Science & Technology / Science et technologie
Assistant Deputy Minister, Dr. Marc Fortin
 Tel: 613-996-2020; *Fax:* 613-995-3402
Chief of Staff, Camille Boulet
 Tel: 613-996-7215; *Fax:* 613-995-3402
Director General, Defence Research & Development Canada - Centre for Security Science, Mark Williamson
 Tel: 613-944-8195; *Fax:* 613-995-0002
Director General, Research & Development Corporate Services, Mylène Ouellet
 Tel: 613-992-6105; *Fax:* 613-996-0038

Office of the Chief of the Defence Staff / Chef d'état-major de la défense
The following organizations report to the Chief of the Defence Staff: Canadian Army; Royal Canadian Air Force; Royal Canadian Navy; Canadian Joint Operations Command; Canadian Special Operations Forces Command; & Chief of Military Personnel.
The following positions report to both the Chief of the Defence Staff & the Deputy Minister of National Defence: Vice Chief of the Defence Staff; Chief, Review Services; Department of National Defence & Canadian Forces Legal Advisor; Assistant Deputy Minister, Information Management; Assistant Deputy Minister, Public Affairs; & Assistant Deputy Minister, Science & Technology.
Chief of Defence Staff for the Canadian Forces, Gen Jonathan Vance
 Tel: 613-992-7405
Vice-Chief of Defence Staff, Vacant

Canadian Army / Armée canadienne
National Defence HQ, MGen George R. Pearkes Building, 110 Colonel By Dr., Ottawa, K1A 0K2
 Tel: 613-995-2534
 Toll-Free: 888-995-2534
 TTY: 800-467-9877
 information@forces.gc.ca
 www.army.forces.gc.ca
 twitter.com/canadianarmy
 www.facebook.com/CANArmy
 www.youtube.com/CanadianArmyNews
The land component of the combined Canadian Forces is the Canadian Army. To provide trained, combat-ready troops in order to meet the nation's defense objectives around the globe is the mission of the Canadian Army. The Army has more than 186 regular & reserve units located in over 400 communities throughout Canada, with over 40,000 soldiers.
The following are the types of units that make up the Canadian Army: infantry, armour, artillery, engineers, signals, & combat support.
In addition to several training facilities, the Army operates the following major support bases: Gagetown, New Brunswick; Valcartier, Québec; Montréal, Québec; Petawawa, Ontario; Kingston, Ontario; Shilo, Manitoba; & Edmonton, Alberta.
Commander, Canadian Army, LGen Wayne Eyre
 twitter.com/Army_Comd
Deputy Commander, Canadian Army, MGen J.C.G. Juneau, OMM, MSM, CD
Army Sergeant Major, CWO A. Guimond, MMM, CD
Chief of Staff, Army Strategy, BGen S.M. Cadden, CD
Chief of Staff, Army Operations, BGen J.P.H.H. Gosselin, OMM, MSM, CD
Chief of Staff, Army Reserve, BGen R.R.E. MacKenzie, OMM, CD
Commander, Canadian Army Doctrine & Training Centre Headquarters, MGen J.M. Lanthier, OMM, MSC, MSM, CD

Land Force Doctrine & Training System (LFDTS) / Système de la doctrine et de l'instruction de la Force terrestre (SDIFT)
Canadian Forces Base Kingston, PO Box 17000 Stn. Forces, Kingston, ON K7K 7B4
 www.army-armee.forces.gc.ca/en/doctrine-training/index.page
 Other Communication: Public Affairs, Phone: 613-541-5010, ext. 4538, Fax: 613-540-8028
The Land Force Doctrine & Training System is responsible for leading land warfare intellectual development & land operations training for the Canadian Army. Land Force training & doctrine development includes simulation & digitization.
The following are units of the Land Force Doctrine & Training System: Headquarters; Canadian Land Force Command & Staff College; Peace Support Training Centre; 2 Electronic Warfare Squadron; Combat Training Centre, located at CFB Gagetown, New Brunswick & 8 Wing Trenton, Ontario; & the Canadian Manoeuvre Training Centre in Wainwright, Alberta.
Commander, Land Force Doctrine & Training System, MGen J.M. Lanthier, OMM, MSC, MSM, CD
Chief Warrant Officer, CWO D.C. Tofts

2nd Canadian Division / 2e Division du Canada
Pierre Le Moyne d'Iberville Building, CP 600 Succ K, Montréal, QC H1N 3R2
 Tel: 514-252-2777
 www.army-armee.forces.gc.ca/en/quebec/index.page
 Autres nombres: Media, Phone: 514-252-2777, ext. 4211, Fax: 514-252-2029
 www.facebook.com/2DivCA
Established in 1992, the 2nd Canadian Division (formerly Land Force Québec Area) comprises Regular & Reserve Land Force units in the province of Québec. The mission of the 2nd Canadian Division is the provision of combat-ready, versatile land forces.
Commander, 2nd Canadian Division & Joint Task Force East, BGen Stéphane Lafaut, OMM, MSC, CD

3rd Canadian Division / 3e Division du Canada
700 Vimy Ave., PO Box 10500 Stn. Forces, Edmonton, AB T5J 4J5
 Tel: 780-973-4011
 Toll-Free: 877-973-1944
 www.army-armee.forces.gc.ca/en/western/index.page
 Other Communication: Public Affairs, Phone: 780-973-1942, Fax: 780-973-1939
 twitter.com/3CdnDiv
 www.facebook.com/3CdnDiv
 www.youtube.com/c/ThirdCanadianDivision
The 3rd Canadian Division (formerly Land Force Western Area) was established in 1991. The role of the 3rd Canadian Division is to oversee all regular & reserve army units from Thunder Bay, Ontario to Vancouver Island, British Columbia.
The following organizations are part of Land Force Western Area: One Regular Mechanized Brigade Group, One Area Support Group, three Reserve Brigade Groups, & the Western Area Training Centre.
Commander, 3rd Canadian Division & Joint Task Force West, BGen W.D. Eyre, MSC, CD

4th Canadian Division / 4e Division du Canada
The LCol George Taylor Denison III Armoury, 1 Yukon Lane, Toronto, ON M3K 0A1
 Tel: 416-633-6200
 www.army-armee.forces.gc.ca/en/central/index.page
 Other Communication: Media, Phone: 416-633-6200, ext. 5500
 twitter.com/4CdnDiv4DivCA
 www.facebook.com/4CdnDiv4DivCA
 www.flickr.com/photos/lfca_multimedia
The 4th Canadian Division (formerly Land Force Central Area) is the Canadian Army in Ontario. The mandate of Land Force Central Area is the generation & maintenance of combat capable, multi-purpose land forces to handle the defence objectives of the nation. The 4th Canadian Division consists of over 21,000 personnel in 35 communities throughout Ontario. The Area's largest regular force units are Canadian Forces Base Kingston & Canadian Forces Base Petawawa.
Commander, 4th Canadian Division & Joint Task Force Central, BGen Lowell Thomas, OMM, CD
Sergeant Major, CWO Stuart Hartnell, MMM, MSM, CD

5th Canadian Division / 5e Division du Canada
PO Box 99000 Stn. Forces, Halifax, NS B3K 5X5
 Tel: 902-427-7576
 www.army-armee.forces.gc.ca/en/atlantic/index.page
 twitter.com/5CdnDiv
 www.facebook.com/CANArmyAtlantic
 www.youtube.com/user/CANArmyAtlantic
All Army Regular & Reserve Force elements in New Brunswick, Nova Scotia, Prince Edward Island & Newfoundland & Labrador are the responsibility of the 5th Canadian Division (formerly Land Force Atlantic Area). Exceptions are the 2nd Battalion, The Royal Canadian Regiment & the Combat Training Centre in Gagetown, New Brunswick. The Area comprises approximately 7,000 personnel.

The Land Force Atlantic Areas is involved in recruiting, training, & forging units ready for peacekeeping, peace support, & peace enforcement operations throughout the world.
Commander, BGen Carl Turenne, OMM, MSC, CD
Division Chief Warrant Officer, CWO S.E. Croucher, MMM, CD

Canadian Forces Base Edmonton (CFB Edmonton) / Base des Forces canadiennes Edmonton (BFC Edmonton)
PO Box 10500 Stn. Forces, Edmonton, AB T5J 4J5
www.army-armee.forces.gc.ca/en/cfb-edmonton/index.page
CFB Edmonton provides infrastructure & support to units located in & near Edmonton as well as to elements situated in the Northwest Territories & Yukon.
Commander, Col S.M. Lacroix
Sergeant Major, CWO J.M. Doppler
Officer, Public Affairs, Capt Donna Riguidel
Tel: 780-973-4011 ext: 8023
donna.riguidel@forces.gc.ca

Canadian Forces Base Gagetown (CFB Gagetown) / Base des Forces canadiennes Gagetown (BFC Gagetown)
PO Box 17000 Stn. Forces, Oromocto, NB E2V 4J5
Tel: 506-422-2000
www.army-armee.forces.gc.ca/en/5-cdsb-gagetown/index.page
www.facebook.com/CanadianForcesBaseGagetown
Opened in 1958, CFB Gagetown is the largest military facility in eastern Canada.
Operational units situated at CFB Gagetown include the 2nd Battalion of the Royal Canadian Regiment, 4 Engineer Support Regiment, 4 Air Defence Regiment, 403 Operational (Helicopter) Training Squadron, & C Squadron of the Royal Canadian Dragoons. The base also features the Joint Meteorological Centre, the Land Force Atlantic Area Training Centre, the Land Force Trials & Evaluation Unit, & the Argonaut Army Cadet Summer Training Centre.
Commanding Officer, CFB Gagetown, Col D.A. MacIsaac

Canadian Forces Base Kingston (CFB Kingston) / Base des Forces canadiennes Kingston (BFC Kingston)
PO Box 17000 Stn. Forces, Kingston, ON K7K 7B4
Tel: 613-541-5010
www.army-armee.forces.gc.ca/en/cfb-kingston/index.page
Other Communication: Base Duty Centre: 613-541-5330; Military Police: 613-541-5648
The following units are located at CFB Kingston: 1st Canadian Division; Canadian Forces Recruiting Centre Detachment Kingston; CF Joint Signal Regiment; 2 Area Support Group Signal Squadron Detachment Kingston; CF Joint Support Group; 21 Electronic Warfare Regiment; 1 Wing Kingston; Canadian Forces National Counter-Intelligence Unit Detachment Kingston; 2 MP Regiment Detachment Kingston; Kingston Garrison Learning & Career Centre; Canadian Forces School of Military Intelligence; Canadian Forces National Counter-Intelligence Unit Detachment Kingston; Canadian Forces Crypto Maintenance Unit; Land Force Doctrine & Training System; Canadian Forces School of Communications & Electronics; Canadian Defence Academy; 1 Dental Unit - Detachment Kingston; 33 CF Health Services Centre; Civilian Human Resources Office; Dispute Resolution Centre; Canadian Forces Housing Unit; MPO 305 Vimy Post Office, & the Military Communications & Electronics Museum. The base also serves base & cadet units.
Commander, Col S.R. Kelsey, CD
Sergeant Major, CWO Terry Garand, MMM, CD

Canadian Forces Base Montréal (CFB Montréal) / Base des Forces canadiennes Montréal (BFC Montréal)
Richelain, QC J0J 1R0
www.army-armee.forces.gc.ca/en/cfb-montreal/index.page
The Montréal base supports lodger & integral units in the area as well as reserves & cadets
Commander, Col Sébastien Bouchard
Sergeant Major, CWO Mario Tremblay

Canadian Forces Base Petawawa (CFB Petawawa) / Base des Forces candiennes Petawawa (BFC Petawawa)
CFB/ASU Petawawa Base HQ, Building S-111, 101 Menin Rd., PO Box 9999 Stn. Main, Petawawa, ON K8H 2X3
Tel: 613-687-5511
petawawapublicaffairs@forces.gc.ca
www.army-armee.forces.gc.ca/en/cfb-petawawa/index.page
twitter.com/GarrisonPet
www.facebook.com/100533039582
Garrison support services are provided for 2 Canadian Mechanized Brigade Group & lodger units at CFB Petawawa. There are approximately 5,400 military members at the base.
Commander, Col J.R.M. Gagné, MSM, CD
Sergeant Major, CWO W.A. Richards, MMM, MSM, CD

Canadian Forces Base Shilo (CFB Shilo) / Base des Forces canadiennes Shilo (BFC Shilo)
CFB Shilo, PO Box 5000 Stn. Main, Shilo, MB R0K 2A0
Tel: 204-765-3000
www.army-armee.forces.gc.ca/en/cfb-shilo/index.page
Canadian Forces Base / Area Support Unit Shilo, located in southwestern Manitoba, is home to the Second Battalion

---

Princess Patricia's Canadian Light Infantry & the First Regiment Royal Canadian Horse Artillery, which are both part of 1 Canadian Mechanized Brigade Group. The base also features part of the Western Area Training Centre, 11 CF Health Services Centre, 742 Signals Squadron Detachment Shilo, & RCA Brandon's Reserve Unit.
Commander, LCol John Cochrane

Canadian Forces Base Suffield (CFB Suffield) / Base des Forces canadiennes Suffield (BFC Suffield)
CFB Suffield Headquarters, Building 393, Falaise St., PO Box 6000 Stn. Main, Medicine Hat, AB T1A 8K8
Tel: 403-544-4405
www.army-armee.forces.gc.ca/en/cfb-suffield/index.page
Under the Canadian Army command of the Land Forces Western Area, CFB Suffield hosts the largest military training area in Canada. The range & training area is used by organizations such as Defence Research & Development Canada - Suffield & the British Army Training Unit Suffield.
Commander, LCol John C. Scott
Base Regimental Sergeant Major, CWO Richard Stacey, MMM, SMV, CD

Canadian Forces Base Valcartier (CFB Valcartier) / Base des forces canadiennes Valcartier (BFC Valcartier)
CP 100 Succ Forces, Courcelette, QC G0A 4Z0
www.army-armee.forces.gc.ca/en/cfb-valcartier/index.page
CFB Valcartier is home to the 5th Canadian Mechanized Brigade Group.
Commander, Col Sébastien Bouchard
Sergeant Major, CWO Mario Tremblay

Canadian Forces Base Wainwright (CFB Wainwright) / Base des forces canadiennes Wainwright (BFC Wainwright)
Wainwright Garrison, General Delivery, Stn. Main, Denwood, AB T0B 1B0
www.army-armee.forces.gc.ca/en/cfb-wainwright/index.page
CFB Wainwright features the Canadian Manoeuvre Training Centre.
Public Affairs Officer, Capt. Denny Brown
Tel: 780-842-1363 ext: 1201
denny.brown@forces.gc.ca

Royal Canadian Air Force (RCAF) / Aviation royale canadienne (ARC)
MGen George R. Pearkes Building, 101 Colonel By Dr., Ottawa, ON K1A 0K2
www.rcaf-arc.forces.gc.ca
Other Communication: Media Liaison: 613-996-2353; Toll-Free:
866-377-0811
twitter.com/RCAF_ARC
www.facebook.com/rcaf1924
www.youtube.com/user/RCAFIMAGERY
The Commander of Air Command & Chief of the Air Forces Staff is responsible for training, generating, & maintaining multi-purpose, combat capable air forces to serve the nation. The Commander of 1 Canadian Air Division oversees operational & tactical control of the air force. There are wings in the following locations throughout Canada: Bagotville, Québec; Borden, Ontario; Cold Lake, Alberta; Comox, British Columbia; Gander, Newfoundland & Labrador; Goose Bay, Newfoundland & Labrador; Greenwood, Nova Scotia; Kingston, Ontario; Moose Jaw, Saskatchewan; North Bay, Ontario; Shearwater, Nova Scotia; Trenton, Ontario; & Winnipeg, Manitoba.
Operations include missions in areas of conflict, support operations for troops, & support for humanitarian aid & diplomatic missions. Locations of recent operations include Haiti, Libya, Afghanistan & Mali.
Commander of the Royal Canadian Air Force, L.Gen Al Meinzinger
Commander, 1 Canadian Air Division, MGen D.L.R. Wheeler
Chief Warrant Officer of the Royal Canadian Air Force, CWO Gérard Poitras

Canadian Forces Station Alert (CFS Alert)
c/o 8 Wing / CFB Trenton, PO Box 1000 Stn. Forces, Astra, ON K0K 3W0
Tel: 613-392-2811
www.rcaf-arc.forces.gc.ca/en/8-wing/alert.page
The Air Force commands CFS Alert. The station is a unit of 8 Wing Trenton, Ontario.

Canadian Forces Base Bagotville: 3 Wing (CFB Bagotville) / Base des forces canadiennes Bagotville: 3e escadre (BFC Bagotville)
CP 5000 Succ Bureau-chef, Alouette, QC G0V 1A0
3escbagotville@forces.gc.ca
www.rcaf-arc.forces.gc.ca/en/3-wing/index.page
Autres nombres: Public Affairs, Fax: 418-677-4073
The following are 3 Wing Squadrons: 414 Electronic Warfare Squadron; 425 Tactical Fighter Squadron; 439 Combat Support Squadron; 3 Air Maintenance Squadron; & 12 Radar Squadron.
Wing Commander, Col Darcy Molstad, CD

Canadian Forces Base Borden: 16 Wing (CFB Borden) / Base des Forces canadiennes Borden: 16 escadre (BFC Borden)
16 Wing Headquarters, PO Box 1000 Stn. Main, Borden, ON L0M 1C0
Tel: 705-424-1200
www.rcaf-arc.forces.gc.ca/en/16-wing/index.page
Other Communication: Public Affairs, Phone: 705-424-1200, ext. 3162
www.facebook.com/CanadianForcesBaseBorden
The following schools at Borden provide air force technical training & professional development: Air Command Academy; Canadian Forces School of Aerospace Technology & Engineering; & Canadian Forces School of Aerospace Control Operations.
Wing Commander, Col Yve Thomson, CD

Canadian Forces Base Cold Lake: 4 Wing (CFB Cold Lake) / Base des Forces canadiennes Cold Lake: 4 escadre (BFC Cold Lake)
PO Box 6550 Stn. Forces, Cold Lake, AB T9M 2C6
4wingcoldlake@forces.gc.ca
www.rcaf-arc.forces.gc.ca/en/4-wing/index.page
Other Communication: Public Affairs, Phone: 780-840-8000, ext 8121, Fax: 780-840-7300
Fighter pilot training for the Canadian Forces takes place at Cold Lake. The base deploys & supports fighter aircraft to meet the domestic & international commitments of the Royal Canadian Air Force.
4 Wing is home to the following squadrons: 409 Tactical Fighter Squadron; 410 Tactical Fighter Squadron; 417 Combat Support Squadron; 419 Tactical Fighter Training Squadron; 1 Air Maintenance Squadron; CF-18 Weapon System Manager Detachment Cold Lake; 42 Radar Squadron; 10 Field Technical Training Squadron; & 4 Airfield Defence Detachment.
Wing Commander, Col E.J. Kenny, MSM, CD

Canadian Forces Base Comox: 19 Wing (CFB Comox) / Base des Forces canadiennes Commox: 19e escadre (BFC Comox)
PO Box 1000 Stn. Main, Lazo, BC V0R 2K0
Tel: 250-339-8211
19WingPublicAffairs@forces.gc.ca
www.rcaf-arc.forces.gc.ca/en/19-wing/index.page
Other Communication: Public Affairs, Phone: 250-339-8201; Fax: 250-339-8120; Joint Rescue Coordination Ctr., Phone: 250-413-8937; Wing Operations (Noise Complaints), Phone: 250-339-8231
Based on Vancouver Island, British Columbia, 19 Wing is known for its CP-140 Aurora Long Range Patrol Aircraft crews that embark on surveillance missions over the Pacific Ocean.
Search & rescue teams, which are part of the 442 Transport & Rescue Squadron based at 19 Wing, fly the CC-115 Buffalo Search & Rescue Aircraft & CH-149 Cormorant Helicopters on operations from the Arctic to the border between British Columbia & Washington, & from the Pacific Ocean to the Rocky Mountains. The Wing is also home to the Canadian Forces School of Search & Rescue & the Regional Cadet Gliding School (Pacific).
Wing Commander, Col Tom Dunne, CD

Canadian Forces Base Gander: 9 Wing (CFB Gander) / Base des Forces canadiennes Gander: 9e escadre (BFC Gander)
PO Box 6000 Gander, NL A1V 1X1
Tel: 709-256-1703; *Fax:* 709-256-1735
www.rcaf-arc.forces.gc.ca/en/9-wing/index.page
Other Communication: Public Affairs, Phone: 709-256-1703, ext. 1126
The Gander base is a major military establishment in Newfoundland & Labrador. It supports the Canadian Forces Recruiting Centre Detachment Corner Brook, plus several Cadet Corps. Armouries are maintained in Corner Brook, Stepheville, & Grand Falls-Windsor.
9 Wing Gander is responsible for search & rescue services in Newfoundland & Labrador & northeastern Québec.
The base is also home to CFS Lietrim Detachment Gander. Its role is the operation & maintenance of signals intelligence.
The Wing also features Canadian Coastal Radar, which it operates & maintains on behalf of Fighter Group Canadian NORAD Region Headquarters.
Wing Commander, LCol Pierre Haché

Canadian Forces Base Goose Bay: 5 Wing (CFB Goose Bay) / Base des Forces canadiennes Goose Bay: 5e escadre (BFC Goose Bay)
PO Box 7002 Stn. A, Happy Valley-Goose Bay, NL A0P 1S0
www.rcaf-arc.forces.gc.ca/en/5-wing/index.page
Other Communication: Public Affairs, Phone: 709-896-6928, Fax: 709-896-6997; SERCO Customer Service Help Desk: 709-896-6900, ext. 6946, csc.bmx@serco-na.com
5 Wing Goose Bay supports Canadian Forces, North American Aerospace Defense Command (NORAD), & Allied training & operations.
Wing Commander, LCol Luc Sabourin

Canadian Forces Base Greenwood: 14 Wing (CFB Greenwood) / Base des Forces canadiennes Greenwood: 14e escadre (BFC Greenwood)
PO Box 5000 Stn. Main, Greenwood, NS B0P 1N0
Tel: 902-765-1494
www.rcaf-arc.forces.gc.ca/en/14-wing/index.page
Other Communication: Public Affairs, Phone: 902-765-1494, ext. 5101, Fax: 902-765-1757

The roles of 14 Wing Greenwood include sovereignty & surveillance missions over the Atlantic Ocean by CP-140 Aurora Long Range Patrol Aircraft crews, as well as search & rescue services throughout Atlantic Canada & eastern Québec. 413 Transport & Rescue Squadron members use CC-130 Hercules Aircraft & CH-149 Cormorant Helicopters during their operations.

Wing Commander, Col Patrick Thauberger, CD

Canadian Forces Base Kingston: 1 Wing (CFB Kingston) / Base des Forces canadiennes Kingston: 1re escadre (BFC Kingston)
Sergeant KS Smith CD Building, PO Box 17000 Stn. Forces, Kingston, ON K7K 7B4
Tel: 613-541-5010
1wingpublicaffairs@forces.gc.ca
www.rcaf-arc.forces.gc.ca/en/1-wing/index.page
Other Communication: Public Affairs, Phone: 613-541-5010, ext. 8251

Equipped with a fleet of CH-146 Griffons, 1 Wing supports the Canadian Army by airlifting troops & equipment around the world. The headquarters for 1 Wing is situated in Kingston, with seven tactical helicopter & training squadrons throughout Canada.
The following squadrons are part of 1 Wing: 403 Helicopter Operational Training Squadron at Gagetown, New Brunswick; 430 Escadron tactique d'helicoptères at Valcartier, Québec; 438 Escadron tactique d'helicoptères at St-Hubert, Québec; 427 Special Operations Aviation Squadron & 450 Tactical Helicopter Squadron at Petawawa, Ontario; 400 Tactical Helicopter Squadron; & 408 Tactical Helicopter Squadron at Edmonton, Alberta.

Wing Commander, Col Scott Clancy, OMM, MSM, CD

Canadian Forces Base Moose Jaw: 15 Wing (CFB Moose Jaw) / Base des Forces canadiennes Moose Jaw: 15e escadre (BFC Moose Jaw)
PO Box 5000 Moose Jaw, SK S6H 7Z8
15wingpao@forces.gc.ca
www.rcaf-arc.forces.gc.ca/en/15-wing/index.page
Other Communication: Public Affairs, Phone: 306-694-2823, Fax: 306-694-2880

The Moose Jaw Saskatchewan base is home to the military air demonstration team, the Canadian Forces Snowbirds, 2 Canadian Forces Flying Training School, 3 Canadian Forces Flying Training School, & the North Atlantic Treaty Organization (NATO) Flying Training in Canada program.

Wing Commander, Col A.R. Day

Canadian Forces Base North Bay: 22 Wing (CFB North Bay) / Base des Forces canadiennes North Bay: 22e escadre (BFC North Bay)
General Delivery, Hornell Heights, ON POH 1PO
Tel: 705-494-2011; *Fax:* 705-494-6261
22WgPublicAffairsOff@forces.gc.ca
www.rcaf-arc.forces.gc.ca/en/22-wing/index.page

The role of 22 Wing North Bay is the provision of surveillance, identification, control, & warning for the aerospace defence of Canada & North Americ. Radar information is received via satellite from the North Warning System across the Canadian Arctic, coastal radars on the east & west coasts of Canada, & Airborne Warning & Control System Aircraft. Members of 21 Aerospace Control & Warning Squadron are on guard every hour of every day. 51 Aerospace Control & Warning Operational Training Squadron is also located at North Bay.

Wing Commander, Col Henrik N. Smith, CD

Canadian Forces Base Shearwater: 12 Wing (CFB Shearwater) / Base des Forces canadiennes Shearwater: 12e escadre (BFC Shearwater)
PO Box 5000 Stn. Main, Shearwater, NS B0J 3A0
www.rcaf-arc.forces.gc.ca/en/12-wing/index.page
Other Communication: Public Affairs, Phone: 902-720-1996

12 Wing Shearwater supports the Navy with helicopter air detachments for both domestic & international operations. Helicopter air detachments deploy with Navy ships. Operations in recent years have included Operation LAMA to help Newfoundland communities affected by Hurricane Igor, Operation HESTIA to assist persons affected by the earthquake in Haiti, & Operation SAIPH to counter piracy activity off the Horn of Africa.

Wing Commander, Col P.C. Allan, CD

Canadian Forces Base Trenton: 8 Wing (CFB Trenton) / Base des Forces canadiennes Trenton: 8e escadre (BFC Trenton)
PO Box 1000 Stn. Forces, Astra, ON K0K 3W0
Tel: 613-392-2811
www.rcaf-arc.forces.gc.ca/en/8-wing/index.page
Other Communication: Public Affairs, Phone: 613-392-2811, ext. 4565

8 Wing at CFB Trenton conducts search & rescue operations for a region under the jurisdiction of the Joint Rescue Coordination Centre Trenton. The Wing is also engaged in airlifting troops, equipment, supplies, & humanitarian aid throughout the world. CFB Trenton also hosts the parachute demonstration team known as the Skyhawks.

Wing Commander, Col C. Keiver, MSM, CD

Canadian Forces Base Winnipeg: 17 Wing (CFB Winnnipeg) / Base des Forces canadiennes Winnipeg: 17e escadre (BFC Winnipeg)
PO Box 17000 Stn. Forces, Winnipeg, MB R3J 3Y5
PubAffairs@forces.gc.ca
www.rcaf-arc.forces.gc.ca/en/17-wing/index.page
Other Communication: Public Affairs, Phone: 204-833-2500, ext. 6499, Fax: 204-833-2594

17 Wing Winnipeg supports units from the border between Alberta & Saskatchewan to Thunder Bay Ontario, & from the high Arctic to the 49th Parallel.
Command elements include 1 Canadian Air Division / Canadian North American Aerospace Defense Command (NORAD) Region Headquarters, 2 Canadian Air Division / Air Force Training & Doctrine, & 38 Canadian Brigade Group Headquarters.
The Wing also comprises the following training schools: 1 Canadian Forces Flying Training School; The Canadian Forces School of Aerospace Studies; THe Canadian Forces School of Meteorology; & The Canadian Forces School of Survival & Aeromedical Training.

Wing Commander, Col Andy Cook

Royal Canadian Navy (RCN) / Marine royale canadienne (MRC)
National Defence HQ, MGen George R. Pearkes Building, 101 Colonel By Dr., Ottawa, ON K1A 0K2
information@forces.gc.ca
www.navy-marine.forces.gc.ca
Other Communication: Public Affairs, Phone: 613-995-2534, Toll-Free: 888-995-2534
twitter.com/rcn_mrc
www.youtube.com/user/RoyalCanadianNavy

The Royal Canadian Navy carries out the following mission: to provide a multipurpose, combat-capable force; to exercise sovereignty over Canadian waters; to monitor & safeguard Canada's maritime approaches; to protect offshore natural resources; & to contribute to global security.
The following are some of the Royal Canadian Navy's recent operations: participation in counter-narcotic operations in the Caribbean Basin; joint North Atlantic Treaty Organization training exercises in the Black Sea; & participation in Operation Artimis, counterterrorism & maritime security operations in the Red Sea, the Gulf of Aden, the Gulf of Oman & the Indian Ocean.

Commander, Canadian Army; Interim Commander of the Royal Canadian Navy, LGen Wayne Eyre
Command Chief of the Royal Canadian Navy, CPO1 David Steeves

Maritime Forces Atlantic (MARLANT) / Forces maritimes de l'Atlantique (FMARA)
Maritime Forces Atlantic Headquarters, PO Box 99000 Stn. Forces, Halifax, NS B3K 5X5
www.navy-marine.forces.gc.ca/en/about/structure-marlant-home.page
Other Communication: Public Affairs, Fax: 902-452-5280; Media Inquiries, Phone: 902-427-3766

Maritime Forces Atlantic consists of the Her Majesty's Canadian (HMC) Dockyard, CFB Stadacona, the CF Station at St. John's, & the Atlantic Fleet of ships.
The Commander of Maritime Forces Atlantic carries out the following responsibitlities: generation of ships & sailors that can respond to events that affect Canadian interests; command of the Royal Canadian Navy's Atlantic Fleet & the Halifax Search & Rescue Region; support to government departments & agencies in areas such as fisheries protection & environmental monitoring; & support for members of the sea, air, & army cadets in the Atlantic provinces.

Commander, Maritime Forces Atlantic; Commander, Joint Task Force Atlantic, RAdm John Newton, OMM, MSM, CD
Formation Chief Petty Officer, CPO1 Pierre Auger

Maritime Forces Pacific (MARPAC) / Forces maritimes du Pacifique (FMARP)
Maritime Forces Pacific Headquarters, PO Box 17000 Stn. Forces, Victoria, BC V9A 7N2
www.navy-marine.forces.gc.ca/en/about/structure-marpac-home.page
Other Communication: Public Affairs, Phone: 250-363-5789, Fax: 250-363-5202
twitter.com/marpac
www.facebook.com/maritime.forces.pacific
www.youtube.com/navywebmaster

Maritime Forces Pacific consists of the following organizations: Joint Task Force (Pacific); 443 Maritime Helicopter Squadron; Joint Rescue Co-ordination Centre Victoria; Regional Joint Operations Centre (Pacific); VENTURE, The Naval Officers Training Centre; Canadian Forces Fleet School Equimalt; Regional Cadet Support Unit (Pacific); RAVEN Aboriginal Youth Initiative; Canadian Forces Ammunition Depot Rocky Point; & the Victoria In-Service Support Contract On-Site Management Team, in support of Canadian Submarine Extended Docking Work Periods.

Commander, Maritime Forces Pacific, RAdm Gilles Couturier, OMM, CD
Maritime Forces Pacific Chief Petty Officer, CPO1 M. Feltham, MMM, CD

The Naval Reserve / La Réserve navale
Naval Reserve Headquarters, PO Box 1000 Stn. Forces, Courcelette, QC G0A 4Z0
www.navy-marine.forces.gc.ca/en/about/structure-navres-home.page
Other Communication: Public Affairs, Phone: 418-694-5560, ext. 5303, Fax: 418-694-5377

Naval Reservists serve on a part time basis to augment the Regular Force. They do not have to participate in missions overseas. Roles for The Naval Reserve include the operation of Maritime Coastal Defence Vessels, port security, diving, & public relations.

Commander, Naval Reserve, Cmdre M.B. Mulkins, OMM, CD
Formation Chief, CPO1 David R. Arsenault, MMM, CD

Canadian Forces Base Esquimalt (CFB Equimalt) / Base des Forces canadiennes Esquimalt (BFC Esquimalt)
PO Box 17000 Stn. Forces, Victoria, BC V9A 7N2
cfbesquimalt@outlook.com
Other Communication: Public Affairs, Phone: 250-363-4006, Fax: 250-363-5527

CFB Esquimalt is home to the Canadian Pacific Naval Fleet. The base provides support services to ships & personnel of the Martime Forces Pacific & the Joint Task Force Pacific. CFB Esquimalt also features organizations such as the the Naval Officers Training Centre, the Canadian Forces Fleet School, the Port Operations & Emergency Services Branch, & Canadian Forces Health Services Centre (Pacific).

Canadian Forces Base Halifax (CFB Halifax) / Base des Forces canadiennes Halifax (BFC Halifax)
PO Box 99000 Stn. Forces, Halifax, NS B3K 5X5
Other Communication: Public Affairs, Fax: 902-427-2218; Media Request Line: 902-427-3766

CFB Halifax is the home port of the Atlantic Fleet. The base provides harbour support, emergency response services, logistics, environmental management, & construction engineering to Maritime Forces Atlantic.

Canadian Forces Station St. John's (CFS St. John's) / Station des Forces canadiennes St. John's (SFC St. John's)
115 The Boulevard, St. John's, NL A1A 0P5
Tel: 709-773-3900
www.cg.cfpsa.ca

Canadian Forces Station St. John's supports Royal Canadian Navy personnel as they work to protect Canada's Atlantic waters. The station also hosts training for sea, air & army cadets.

Canadian Joint Operations Command (CJOC) / Commandement des opérations interarmées du Canada (COIC)
National Defence Headquarters, MGen George R. Pearkes Bldg., 101 Colonel By Dr., Ottawa, ON K1A 0K2
Toll-Free: 866-377-0811
www.forces.gc.ca/en/operations.page
Other Communication: Public Affairs, Phone: 613-996-2353, Fax: 613-996-8330
twitter.com/CFOperations
www.flickr.com/photos/cfoperations

Canadian Joint Operations Command of the Canadian Forces uses an integrated command structure to develop, generate, & integrate joint force capabilities in order to conduct operations in North America & throughout the world.
Canadian Joint Operations Command consists of the following: headquarters in Ottawa, Ontario; regional Joint Task Force headquarters throughout Canada; units that make up the Canadian Forces Joint Operational Support Group across Canada; task forces deployed on continental operations in

Canada & North America; & task forces deployed on expeditionary operations throughout the world.
Commander, Canadian Joint Operations Command, Vacant

Canadian Special Operations Forces Command (CANSOFCOM) / Commandement des Forces d'opérations spéciales du Canada (COMFOSCAN)

CANSOFCOM Public Affairs, 101 Colonel By Dr., Ottawa, ON K1A 0K2
Toll-Free: 866-377-0811
www.forces.gc.ca/en/operations-special-forces/index.page
Other Communication: Public Affairs, Phone: 613-996-2353,
Fax: 613-996-8330

Canadian Special Operations Forces Command is engaged in the following strategic tasks: generating deployable Special Operations Forces; developing the capabilities of Special Operation Forces; commanding Special Operations Forces; giving advice on special operations to the Chief of the Defence Staff & other Canadian Forces commanders; & maintaining relationships with allied special operations forces & security partners.
Canadian Special Operations Forces Command is comprised of the following organizations: Joint Task Force 2; 427 Special Operations Aviation Squadron; Canadian Joint Incident Response Unit; & Canadian Special Operations Regiment. Examples of operational tasks performed by personnel of the Canadian Special Operations Forces Command include the following: maritime counter-terrorism; hostage rescue; support for non-combatant evacuation operations; & protection of Government of Canada personnel.
Commander, Canadian Special Operations Forces, Command Headquarters, Maj-Gen Peter Dawe

National Film Board of Canada (NFB) / Office national du film du Canada (ONF)

Operational Headquarters, Norman McLaren Building, 3155, ch de la Côte-de-Liesse, PO Box 1600 Stn. Centre-ville, Montréal, QC H3C 3H5
Tel: 514-283-9000
Toll-Free: 800-267-7710
www.onf-nfb.gc.ca
Other Communication: Alt. URL: www.nfb.ca
twitter.com/thenfb
www.facebook.com/nfb.ca
www.youtube.com/nfb

Created by an act of Parliament in 1939, the National Film Board is Canada's public producer & distributor of audiovisual works that feature distinctive & innovative Canadian content. The federal cultural agency works to achieve its mandate to produce, distribute, & promote Canadian films, in accordance with the National Film Act. The National Film Board specializes in documentaries about social issues, animated films, & alternative drama that offer a unique Canadian perpective for Canadians & other countries.
Canadians can access National Film Board productions in both English & French in each region of the country through public libraries that hold collections of National Film Board films & an online "Screening Room". Works can also be viewed on television, in theatres, & on mobile devices.
The National Film Board carries out its mission within the Department of Canadian Heritage.

Government Film Commissioner; Chair, National Film Board of Canada, Claude Joli-Coeur
Tel: 514-283-9245

Director General, Creation & Innovation, André Picard
Tel: 514-242-0376

Director General, Finance, Operations, & Technology, Luisa Frate
Tel: 514-283-9051

Director General, French Program, Michèle Bélanger
Tel: 514-283-9285

Director General, Legal & Human Resources Services, François Tremblay
Tel: 438-938-3670

Director General, English Program, Michelle van Beusekom
Tel: 514-242-0376

National Film Board of Canada Studios

Edmonton - North West Centre (English)
#100, 10815 - 104 Ave., Edmonton, AB T5J 4N6
Tel: 780-495-3013; *Fax:* 780-495-6412
northwest@nfb.ca
Executive Producer, David Christensen
Tel: 780-495-3015

Halifax - Atlantic Centre (English)
Cornwallis House, #201, 5475 Spring Garden Rd., Halifax, NS B3J 3T2
Tel: 902-426-6000; *Fax:* 902-426-8901
atlantic@nfb.ca
Executive Producer, Kent Martin
Tel: 902-426-7351
Moncton - Canadian Francophonie Studio - Acadie (French)
#100, rue 95 Foundry, Moncton, NB E1C 5H7
Tel: 506-851-6104; *Fax:* 506-851-2246
Toll-Free: 866-663-8331
infofrancophonieacadie@nfb.ca
Executive Producer, Jacques Turgeon
Tel: 506-851-6105
Montréal - Digital Studio (French)
3155, ch de la Côte-de-Liesse, Montréal, QC H4N 2N4
Tel: 514-283-0733; *Fax:* 514-283-6403
Executive Producer, Hugues Sweeney
h.sweeney@onf.ca
Montréal - English Animation Studio
3155, ch de la Côte-de-Liesse, Montréal, QC H4N 2N4
Tel: 514-261-1650; *Fax:* 514-283-3211
animation@nfb.ca
Executive Producer, Michael Fukushima
Montréal - French Animation & Youth Studio (French)
3155, ch de la Côte-de-Liesse, Montréal, QC H4N 2N4
Tel: 514-283-9332; *Fax:* 514-283-4443
animation@nfb.ca
Executive Producer & Producer, Julie Roy
Montréal - Québec Centre (English)
3155, ch de la Côte-de-Liesse, Montréal, QC H4N 2N4
Tel: 514-827-5048
quebeccentre@nfb.ca
Montréal - Québec Studio (French)
3155, ch de la Côte-de-Liesse, Montréal, QC H4N 2N4
Tel: 514-496-1171; *Fax:* 514-283-7914
studioquebec@onf.ca
Executive Producer & Producer, Coletter Loumède
St. John's - Atlantic Centre (English)
#102, 28 Cochrane St., St. John's, NL A1C 3L3
Tel: 709-763-0425
atlantic@nfb.ca
Executive Producer, Annette Clarke
Toronto - Canadian Francophonie Studio (French)
150 John St., 3rd Fl., Toronto, ON M5V 3C3
Tel: 416-973-5382; *Fax:* 416-973-2594
Toll-Free: 866-663-7668
infofrancophonie@nfb.ca
Executive Producer, Dominic Desjardins
Toronto - Ontario Centre (English)
150 John St., 3rd Fl., Toronto, ON M5V 3C3
Tel: 416-973-6856; *Fax:* 416-973-9640
ontarioinfo@nfb.ca
Executive Producer, Anita Lee
Vancouver - Digital Studio (English)
#250, 351 Abbott St., Vancouver, BC V6B 0G6
Tel: 604-666-3838
interactiveproposals@nfb.ca
Executive Producer, Loc Dao
Vancouver - Pacific & Yukon Centre (English)
#250, 351 Abbott St., Vancouver, BC V6B 0G6
Executive Producer, Shirley Vercruysse
s.vercruysse@nfb.ca
Winnipeg - North West Centre (English)
145 McDermot Ave., Winnipeg, MB R3B 0R9
Tel: 204-983-5852; *Fax:* 204-983-0742
northwest@nfb.ca

National Gallery of Canada (NGC) / Musée des Beaux-Arts du Canada (MBAC)

380 Sussex Dr., PO Box 427 Stn. A, Ottawa, ON K1N 9N4
Tel: 613-990-1985; *Fax:* 613-993-4385
Toll-Free: 800-319-2787
TTY: 613-990-0777
info@gallery.ca
www.gallery.ca
Other Communication: Box Office, Phone: 888-541-8888; Group Tours, Phone: 613-990-4888; Library, Phone: 613-998-8949, Email: erefel@gallery.ca; Archives, Phone: 613-990-0597
twitter.com/gallerydotca
www.facebook.com/nationalgallerycanada
www.youtube.com/user/ngcmedia

The National Gallery of Canada contains the most comprehensive collection of contemporary & historic Canadian art. The collection is accessible to the public for appreciation, advancement of knowledge, & research.
The Board of Trustees of the National Gallery of Canada serves as the gallery's governing body & acts in accordance with the Museums Act. The Board, which consists of eleven members, is assisted by the following committees: the Executive Committee; the Acquisitions Committee; the Audit & Finance Committee; the Governance & Nominating Committee; the Human Resources Committee; & the Porgrammes & Advancement Committee. The Board of Trustees reports to Parliament through the Minister of Canadian Heritage & Official Languages.

Chair, Françoise E. Lyon

Vice-Chair, Anne-Marie H. Applin

Chief Executive Officer & Director, Marc Mayer

Chief Curator; Deputy Director, Collections, Research & Education, Vacant

Chief Financial Officer & Deputy Director, Administration, Julie Peckham

Deputy Director, Advancement & Public Engagement, Jean-François Bilodeau

Director, Conservation & Technical Research, Stephen Gritt
Tel: 613-990-1941

Director, Human Resources, Sylvie Sarault

Director, Facilities Planning Management, Edmond Richard
Tel: 613-993-9355

Chief, Bookstore, Patrick Aubin
Tel: 613-990-8566

Chief, Technical Services, Jean-François Castonguay
Tel: 613-990-4998

Chief, Finance, M.J. Lacombe

Chief, Design Services, Gordon Filewych
Tel: 613-990-8908

Chief, Information Technology Systems, Nigel Holmes
Tel: 613-990-2453

Chief, Restoration & Conservation, John McElhone
Tel: 613-991-0011

Chief, Publications & Copyright, Ivan Parisien
Tel: 613-990-0532

Chief, Education & Public Programs, Megan Richardson
Tel: 613-990-0574

Chief, Protection Services, Gary Rousseau
Tel: 613-990-6432

Chief, Collections Management & Outreach, Stacey Wakeford

Chief, Strategic Management, Christine Sadler
Tel: 613-990-7549

Chief, Strategic Planning & Risk Management, Margaret Skulskau
Tel: 613-990-3483

Chief, Visitor Services, Léo Tousignant
Tel: 613-990-5572

Chief, Membership & Annual Giving, Taylor van Blokland

Curator, Contemporary Art, Josée Drouin-Brisebois
Tel: 613-990-7645

Curator, Canadian Art, Katerina Atanassova

Curator, Indigenous Art, Greg Hill
Tel: 613-949-0327

Curator, Photographs Collection, Ann Thomas
Tel: 613-990-1961

National Joint Council (NJC) / Conseil national mixte (CNM)

C.D. Howe Building, 240 Sparks St. West, 7th Fl., PO Box 1525 Stn. B, Ottawa, ON K1P 5V2
Tel: 613-990-1805; *Fax:* 613-990-7071
email.courrier@njc-cnm.gc.ca
www.njc-cnm.gc.ca
The National Joint Council was established in 1944. As part of the Public Service of Canada, the Council provides a forum for consultation on workplace policies & information sharing between public service bargaining agents & the government as employer.
The parties work together to resolve workplace problems & to establish terms of employment. The National Joint Council's working committess consist of representatives from both sides of the Council. The following committees address labour relations issues: Executive; Foreign Service Directives; Government Travel; Isolated Posts & Government Housing; Joint Employment Equity; Occupational Health & Safety; Official Languages; Relocation; Service-Wide Committee on Occupational Health & Safety; Union Management Relations; & Work Force Adjustment.

General Secretary, Sean Ross
Sean.Ross@njc-cnm.gc.ca

Secretary to the NJC & Manager, NJC Operations, Elizabeth Shum
Elizabeth.Shum@njc-cnm.gc.ca

National Research Council Canada (NRC) / Conseil national de recherches Canada (CNRC)

Building M-58, 1200 Montreal Rd., Ottawa, ON K1A 0R6
Tel: 613-993-9101; *Fax:* 613-991-9096
Toll-Free: 877-672-2672
TTY: 613-949-3042
info@nrc-cnrc.ca
www.nrc-cnrc.gc.ca
Other Communication: Media Relations, Toll-free Phone: 855-282-1637; Email: media@nrc-cnrc.gc.ca
twitter.com/nrc_cnrc
www.linkedin.com/company/8417
www.instagram.com/nrc_cnrc
The National Research Council is the Government of Canada's agency for research & development. Reporting to Parliament is through the Minister of Industry. The Council works with partners & clients to meet industrial & societal needs, in accordance with the National Research Council Act.
Technical & advisory services are available to assist enterprises solve technical problems. The following are some examples of the specialized services available: analytical chemistry services, calibration services, cold regions techologies & services, molecular biology services, environmental hydraulics services, marine performance & evaluation services, flight test & evaluation services, surface transportation services, medical diagnostics, nuclear magnetic resonance services, & protein purification services.
The National Research Council encourages & engages in research & business partnerships. Licensing opportunities are available for research & development solutions.

President, Iain Stewart
Tel: 613-993-2024

Chief Financial Officer & Vice-President, Corporate Services, Dale MacMillan
Tel: 613-991-5457

Vice-President, Engineering, Michel Dumoulin
Tel: 613-949-5956

Vice-President, Human Resources, Emily Harrison
Tel: 613-993-9136

Vice-President, Emerging Technologies, Geneviève Tanguay

Executive Director, National Office, Bradley Goodyear
Tel: 613-998-2626
Bradley.Goodyear@nrc-cnrc.gc.ca

Executive Director, Security Branch, Timothy Grubb
timothy.grubb@canada.ca

National Research Council Canada - National Science Library / Bibliothèque scientifique nationale

Bldg. M-55, 1200 Montreal Rd., Ottawa, ON K1A 0R6
Tel: 613-993-9101
Toll-Free: 800-668-1222
science-libraries.canada.ca/eng/national-science-library
Formerly known as the Canada Institute for Scientific & Technical Information (l'Institut canadien de l'information scientifique et technique), the National Science Library was founded in 1924. Under the National Research Council Act, the NRC is mandated to operate & maintain a national library. The Library supports Canada's research, innovation, & health communities by supplying resources & services to aid in discoveries & commercialization.
The main library, located in Ottawa, is open to the public (all branch libraries across Canada were closed by the end of 2012). Library users have online access to the NRC-CISTI Public Catalogue in order to search for & order print & electronic holdings in the areas of science, technology, engineering, & medicine. Interlibrary Loan services are handled by Infotrieve. The Library features the following online services: DataCite Canada; DOCLINE in Canada; PubMed Central Canada; & the NRC Archives. The Archives service offers information about the development of scientific research at the Council & the history of science in Canada.
The National Science Library is governed by a Director General & an Advisory Board that comprises national & international stakeholders from the library, publishing, academic, & business sectors. Board members are appointed by the Council of the National Research Council Canada.
In 2017, the National Science Library joined the Federal Science Library online portal.
Chief, Federal Science Library, Lynne McAvoy
Tel: 613-998-7184

National Research Council Canada - Industrial Research Assistance Program (NRC-IRAP) / Programme d'aide à la recherche industrielle (PARI)

1200 Montreal Rd., Ottawa, ON K1A 0R6
Fax: 613-952-1086
Toll-Free: 877-994-4727
NRC.IRAPInfo-InfoPARI.CNRC@nrc-cnrc.gc.ca
www.nrc-cnrc.gc.ca/eng/irap/index.html
The Industrial Research Assistance Program offers advisory & funding services to help businesses with their research & development projects. Firms are assisted in both the development & commercialization of technologies.
For information about the Industrial Research Assistance Program or to consult an Industrial Technology Advisor, contact one of the regional offices located across Canada. Industrial Technology Advisors are available to support clients through each stage of their projects, by connecting firms with national & international industry experts & possible business partners.
Vice-President, David Lisk
Tel: 613-993-0695
Executive Director, National Office, Bradley Goodyear
Tel: 613-998-2626
Director, National Programs & Partnerships, Byron (Drew) Chassin de Kergommeaux
Tel: 613-991-6974

National Research Council Canada - Research Facilities

nrc-cnrc.gc.ca/eng/solutions/facilities/index.html
The National Research Council provides Canadian businesses access to research facilities & research experts. The research infrastructure enables businesses to pursue research & development opportunities & to accelerate product development.

Advanced, Non-Linear Optical Imaging & Microscopy Facility (CARSLab) / Imagerie et microscopie optiques non linéaires de pointe (CARSLab)

100 Sussex Dr., Ottawa, ON K1N 5A2
CARSLab stands for Coherent Anti-Stokes Raman Scattering Laboratory. Clients are offered state-of-the-art multimodal imaging capability. Workshops & hands on training is available for person to learn more about the CARS technique. The CARSLab facility can be available to Centres of Research Excellence & other research groupings.
Contact, Aaron Rodericks
Tel: 613-998-5663
Aaron.Rodericks@nrc-cnrc.gc.ca

Aerospace Manufacturing Technologies Centre (AMTC) / Le centre de technologies de fabrication en aérospatiale

Campus Université de Montréal, 5145, av Decelles, Montréal, QC H3T 2B2
www.nrc-cnrc.gc.ca/eng/solutions/facilities/amtc_index.html
Industries are assisted in the implementation of advanced manufacturing methods for aerospace. Examples of technologies investigated include automation & robotics, metal forming & joining, fabrication of composite structures, & material removal.
Contact, Matthew Tobin
Tel: 613-990-0765
Matthew.Tobin@nrc-cnrc.gc.ca

Cell Culture Pilot Plant / Usine pilote, culture cellulaire

c/o Montréal (av Royalmount) Research Facilities, 6100, av Royalmount, Montréal, QC H4P 2R2
Tél: 514-496-6100
The pilot plant offers expertise in viral infection processes, virus recovery & purification, cell culture in bioreactors, & HPLC assays.
Team Leader, Cell Culture Scale-Up, Sven Ansorge
Tel: 514-283-3915
Sven.Ansorge@cnrc-nrc.gc.ca

Aquatic & Crop Resource Development Industry Partnership Facility / Installation de partenariat de développment des cultures et des ressources aquatiques

550 University Ave., Charlottetown, PE C1A 4P3
www.nrc-cnrc.gc.ca/eng/rd/aquatic/index.html
The Industry Partnership Facility in Charlottetown serves scientists from industries with commercial potential for products connected to aquatic & crop resource development.
Director General, Denise LeBlanc
#232, 550 University Ave.
Charlottetown, PE C1A 4P3
Contact, Laurel O'Connor
Tel: 306-975-4573
Laurel.oconnor@nrc-cnrc.gc.ca
#232, 550 University Ave.
Charlottetown, PE C1A 4P3

Atacama Large Millimetre/submillimetre Array (ALMA) / Observatoire ALMA (Atacama Large Millimetre/submillimetre Array)

Santiago Central Office, Alonso de Córdova 3107, Vitacura - Santiago
www.almaobservatory.org
Other Communication: International Phone: 56-2-2467-6100
Secondary Address: Kilómetro 121, Carretera CH 23
Operations Support Facility
San Pedro de Atacama, Chile
twitter.com/ALMAObs
www.facebook.com/ALMA.Radiotelescope
www.youtube.com/user/almaobservatory
Located in Chile, the ALMA Observatory studies the millimetre & sub-millimetre universe at high angular resolution & with great sensitivity. It is funded & operated by an international partnership involving North America, Europe & East Asia. The NRC is partnered with the US National Radio Astronomy Observatory as part of the North American component of the project.
Contact, Gerald Schieven
Tel: 250-363-6919
gerald.schieven@nrc-cnrc.gc.ca

Automotive & Surface Transportation Facilities / Installations d'Automobile et transport de surface

Ottawa Uplands Research Facilities, 2320 Lester Rd., Ottawa, ON K1V 1S2
Tel: 613-998-9639
The Ottawa location of the National Research Council's Surface Transportation research facilities feature areas to test road, military, & rail vehicles & components. Examples of facilities include environmental chambers, the compression & tension facility, the heavy vehicle tilt facility, the rail vehicle impact facility, vibration testing facilities, as well as the railway, wheel, bearing, & brake facility.
Portfolio Business Advisor, Craig A. Ceppetelli, BSc., MBA
Tel: 613-998-9388
Craig.Ceppetelli@nrc-cnrc.gc.ca
Contact, Aluminium Technology Centre, Stéphan Simard
Tel: 418-545-5544
Stephan.Simard@cnrc-nrc.gc.ca
501, boul Université est
Saguenay, QC G7H 8C3
Contact, Wind Tunnel Testing Facilities, Matthew Tobin
Tel: 613-990-0765
Matthew.Tobin@nrc-cnrc.gc.ca
1200 Monteal Rd.
Ottawa, ON K1A 0R6

Canada-France-Hawaii Telescope (CFHT) / Télescope Canada-France-Hawaï (TCFH)
CFHT Corporation, #65, 1238 Mamalahoa Hwy., Kamuela, HI 96743 USA
Tel: 808-885-7944; Fax: 808-885-7288
info@cfht.hawaii.edu
www.cfht.hawaii.edu
twitter.com/CFHTelescope
www.facebook.com/cfhtelescope
Located in Hawaii, the CFHT is a joint facility of the NRC, the Centre National de la Recherche Scientifique, France, & the University of Hawaii.
Contact, J.J. Kavelaars
Tel: 250-363-8694
JJ.Kavelaars@nrc-cnrc.gc.ca

Canadian Astronomy Data Centre (CADC) / Centre canadien de données astronomiques (CCDA)
NRC Herzberg Astronomy & Astrophysics, 5071 West Saanich Rd., Victoria, BC V9E 2E7
Tel: 250-363-0001; Fax: 250-363-0045
cadc@nrc.gc.ca
www.cadc-ccda.hia-iha.nrc-cnrc.gc.ca
Established in 1986 by the NRC, through a grant from the Canadian Space Agency (CSA). Operates as one of three world-wide distribution centres for astronomical data obtained with the Hubble Space Telescope (HST).
General Manager, NRC Herzberg, Gregory Fahlman
Tel: 250-363-0040; Fax: 250-363-8483

Canadian Centre for Housing Technology (CCHT) / Centre canadien des technologies résidentielles
c/o National Research Council Canada, Building M-20, 1200 Montreal Rd., Ottawa, ON K1A 0R6
www.ccht-cctr.gc.ca
Operated jointly by the National Research Council, Natural Resources Canada, & the Canada Mortgage & Housing Corporation, the Canadian Centre for Housing Technology offers research & demonstrations related to innovative technology in housing. The present focus is upon energy efficiency & energy conversion systems.
Facilities on the six acre site include two research houses, the InfoCentre, & four serviced lots to develop & build new concepts. The testing facilities are available to the construction industry on a fee-for-service basis.
Contact, General & Project Inquiries, Mike Swinton
Tel: 613-993-9708
Mike.Swinton@nrc-cnrc.gc.ca

Canadian Photonics Fabrication Centre (CPFC) / Centre canadien de fabrication de dispositifs photoniques
c/o National Research Council Canada, Building M-50, 1200 Montreal Rd., Ottawa, ON K1A 0R6
Tel: 613-993-9101
The Canadian Photonics Fabrication Centre has test & measurement capabilities for experts to assist companies in the diagnosis of material & fabrication related problems.
Contact, George Ross
Tel: 613-949-3717
George.Ross@nrc-cnrc.gc.ca

Civil Infrastructure & Related Structures Testing Facilities / Installation d'essai des infrastructures civiles et des structures annexes
c/o National Research Council, 1200 Montreal Rd., Ottawa, ON K1A 0R6
Tel: 613-993-9101
Testing facilities are available to evaluate the design, performance, rehabilitation, & management of concrete structures & buried utilities.
Contact, Dino Zuppa
Tel: 613-949-0073
Dino.Zuppa@nrc-cnrc.gc.ca

Climatic Testing Facility / Installation d'essais climatiques
Ottawa Uplands Research Facilities, 2320 Lester Rd., Ottawa, ON K1V 1S2
Tel: 613-998-9639
Evaluates the performance of commercial & military equipment, vehicles, & components under severe climatic conditions.
Portfolio Business Advisor, Craig A. Ceppetelli, BSc., MBA
Tel: 613-998-9388
Craig.Ceppetelli@nrc-cnrc.gc.ca

Dominion Astrophysical Observatory (DAO) / Observatoire fédéral d'astrophysique
NRC Herzberg Astronomy & Astrophysics, 5071 West Saanich Rd., Victoria, BC V9E 2E7
Tel: 250-363-0001
NRC.NSIHerzbergAstroInfoISN.CNRC@nrc-cnrc.gc.ca
Operating since 1916, the DAO operates the 1.8-metre Plaskett Telescope & the 1.2-metre telescope, featuring the high-resolution McKellar spectrograph.

General Manager, NRC Herzberg, Gregory Fahlman
Tel: 250-363-0040; Fax: 250-363-8483

Dominion Radio Astrophysical Observatory (DRAO) / Observatoire fédéral de radioastrophysique
717 White Lake Rd., PO Box 248 Penticton, BC V2A 6J9
Tel: 250-497-2300
NRC.DRAO-OFR.CNRC@nrc-cnrc.gc.ca
The DRAO operates three telescopes: a 26-metre fully steerable dish, a seven-antenna aperture synthesis array & a solar radio flux monitor.

Fire Safety Testing Facility / Installations d'essais en sécurité incendie
National Fire Laboratory, Bldg. U-96, Concession 8, Mississippi Mills, ON K0A 1A0
Tel: 613-993-9101
Secondary Address: 1200 Montreal Rd.
c/o National Research Council
Ottawa, ON K1A 0R6
The Mississippi Mills location offers a Burn Hall & 10-storey Smoke Tower complex with full-sized stair, elevator & service shafts.
The Ottawa location offers column, floor & wall test furnaces & an intermediate-scale furnace.
Contact, Dino Zuppa
Tel: 613-949-0073
Dino.Zuppa@nrc-cnrc.gc.ca

Gas Turbine Research Facility / Installation de recherche sur les turbines à gaz
c/o National Research Council, 1200 Montreal Rd., Ottawa, ON K1A 0R6
Tel: 613-993-9101
The National Research Council helps industries develop & evaluate gas turbine engines & components to meet operational, safety, & environmental requirements.
Contact, Matthew Tobin
Tel: 613-990-0765
Matthew.Tobin@nrc-cnrc.gc.ca

Gemini Observatory / Observatoire Gemini
670 N. A'ohoku Place, Hilo, HI 96720 USA
Tel: 808-974-2500; Fax: 808-974-2589
Secondary Address: Casilla 603
c/o AURA
La Serena, Chile
www.facebook.com/GeminiObservatory
Twin 8.1-metre diameter optical/infrared telescopes located in Hawaii & Chile, operated by a partnership of five countries: Canada, the US, Australia, Brazil & Argentina.
Contact, Dr. Stéphanie Côté
Stephanie.Cote@nrc-cnrc.gc.ca

Hydraulics Laboratories / Laboratoires hydrauliques
c/o National Research Council, 1200 Montreal Rd., Ottawa, ON K1A 0R6
The National Research Council operates hydraulics laboratories for applied research & commercial studies. Studies focus upon civil engineering hydraulics, port & harbour developments, coastal science & engineering, & offshore energy projects.

Hygrothermal Performance of Buildings Research Facilities / Les installations de recherche en performance hygrothermique
c/o National Research Council, 1200 Montreal Rd., Ottawa, ON K1A 0R6
Tel: 613-993-9101
The Envelope Environmental Exposure Facility has an automated environmental chamber, so that interior & exterior climatic conditions can be simulated. This testing can lead to improved design, construction, & operation of energy-efficient building systems.
The Guarded Hot Box Environmental Test Facility helps builders of wall systems & manufacturers of insulation determine the thermal resistance of products.
The Dynamic Roofing Facility is used to evaluate the dynamic wind uplift performance of roofing assemblies. The facility is important to manufacturers that want to sell their products in areas that experience high wind conditions, such as the southern & eastern coasts of North America.
Contact, Dino Zuppa
Tel: 613-949-0073
Dino.Zuppa@nrc-cnrc.gc.ca

Indoor Environment Testing Facilities / Installations d'essai sur l'environnement intérieur
c/o National Research Council, 1200 Montreal Rd., Ottawa, ON K1A 0R6
The National Research Council's indoor envrionment testing facilities include an indoor air testing facility, an indoor environment facility, a floor sound transmission testing facility, & a wall sound transmission testing facility. Through testing,

industries can develop technologies for the design & operation of energy-efficient, cost-effective, & healthy indoor environments.
Contact, Chris Pezoulas
Tel: 613-993-9502
Christopher.Pezoulas@nrc-cnrc.gc.ca

Industrial Partnership Facility: Montréal (IPF) / Installation de partenariat industriel à Montréal
c/o Montréal (av Royalmount) Research Facilities, 6100, av Royalmount, Montréal, QC H4P 2R2
The scientific complex offers services to companies engaged in biotechnology research & development. Both large & small businesses have access to these advanced facilities & experts to create & test new technologies.
Property Officer, Québec, Leasing & Property, Louise Demers-Thorne
Tel: 514-496-1733
Louise.Demers-Thorne@cnrc-nrc.gc.ca

Marine Performance Evaluation & Testing Facilities / Installation d'essais et évaluation en performance marine
c/o National Research Council, 1200 Montreal Rd., Ottawa, ON K1A 0R6
St. John's Research FacilitiesPO Box 12093 Sta. St. John's, NL A1B 3T5
Marine performance evaluation & testing facilities in Ottawa, Ontario include the following: an ice tank, a large scale wave flume, a large area basin, a coastal wave basin, & a multidirectional wave basin.
The following facilities are located in St. John's Newfoundland & Labrador: cold room laboratories, a towing tank, an ice tank, & an offshore energy basin.
Research is conducted into problems involving marine environments, vessels, & structures.
Contact, Ottawa, Enzo Gardin
Tel: 613-991-2987
Enzo.Gardin@nrc-cnrc.gc.ca
Contact, St. John's, Mark Murphy
Tel: 709-772-2105
Mark.Murphy@nrc-cnrc.gc.ca

Material Emissions Testing Facilities / Laboratoire des émissions émanant des matériaux
c/o National Research Council, 1200 Montreal Rd., Ottawa, ON K1A 0R6
The materiel emissions testing facilities are able to measure the emission of volatile organic compounds from building materials & consumer products. Equipment is also capable of determining the efficiency of air cleaning devices.
Contact, Dino Zuppa
Tel: 613-949-0073
Dino.Zuppa@nrc-cnrc.gc.ca

Medical Device Facilities / Installations de dispositifs médicaux
Boucherville Research Facilities, 75, boul de Mortagne, Boucherville, QC J4B 6Y4
Tel: 450-641-5100
Secondary Address: 435 Ellice Ave.
Winnipeg Research Facilities
Winnipeg, MB R3B 1Y6
The National Research Council's medical device facilities offer assistance to healthcare organizations with research & development needs. Facilities are located in Boucherville Québec, Winnipeg Manitoba, & Halifax Nova Scotia.
The Boucherville site provides expertise in functional nanomaterials & virtual reality surgical planning for surgical oncology.
The Winnipeg facility's areas of interest include early stage disease diagnoses that are minially invasive & techology that reduces or eliminates hospital stays.
The Halifax locations focus upon translational neuroscience. Halifax's Neuroimaging Research Laboratory is situated at the QEII's Health Sciences Centre's Halifax Infirmary (#3900, 1796 Summer St, Halifax, NS B3H 3A7). The city's Clinicial Laboratory for Magnetoencephalography / Biomedical MRI Research is located at the IWK Health Centre (Goldbloom Pavillion, 5850 University Ave, Halifax, NS B3K 6R8).
Contact, Eileen Raymond
Tel: 514-496-6349
Eileen.Raymond@nrc-cnrc.gc.ca

Microbial Fermentation Pilot Plant / Usine pilote spécialisée en fermentation microbienne
c/o Montréal (av Royalmount) Research Facilities, 6100, av Royalmount, Montréal, QC H4P 2R2
Tel: 514-496-6100
Secondary Address: 100 Sussex Dr.
Sussex Drive Research Facilities
Ottawa, ON K1N 5A2
The following are some of the services in the areas of molecular biology, microbial physiology, & microbial fermentation technology offered by the pilot plant: training & scientific & technical guidance; testing new control & monitoring equipment;

screening activities; analytical services to support bioprocessing operations; product purification; handling methanol-oxidizing microorganisms; & selection of recombinant strains such as E.coli.
Team Leader, Microbial Fermentation, Luke Masson
Tel: 514-496-3123
Luke.Masson@cnrc-nrc.gc.ca

Ocean Technology Enterprise Centre (OTEC) / Centre des entreprises de technologies océaniques
PO Box 12093 St. John's, NL A1B 3T5
Tel: 709-772-2469
Opened in 2003, the Ocean Technology Enterprise Centre conducts ocean engineering research to benefit the Canadian marine industry. The Centre, which is housed within the National Research Council's Industry Partnership Facility on the campus of Memorial University, provides facilities & expertise to assist ocean technology companies in the development of technologies.
Contact, Noel Murphy
Tel: 709-772-4939
Noel.Murphy@nrc-cnrc.gc.ca

Printable Electronics Labs / Le laboratoire du programme-phare Électronique imprimable
c/o National Research Council, 1200 Montreal Rd., Ottawa, ON K1A 0R6
Secondary Address: 75, boul de Mortagne
Boucherville Research Facilities
Boucherville, QC J4B 6Y4
Focuses on applications of state-of-the-art, multi-functional printing tools.
The Ottawa facility provides the following: large-scale inkjet printing; sheet-to-sheet gravure; flexographic & screen printing; organic & inorganic solution processing.
The Boucherville facility offers automated nano imprinting & nano embossing.
Contact, Michael Davison
Tel: 613-998-9414
Michael.Davison@nrc-cnrc.gc.ca

Waste Biotreatability Facility / Services d'évaluation de la biotraitabilité
c/o Montréal (av Royalmount) Research Facilities, 6100, av Royalmount, Montréal, QC H4P 2R2
The Waste Biotreatability Facility is engaged in the evaluation of organic waste for its biotreatability & its potential to produce energy such as hydrogen & methane. The facility is part of the Industrial Partnership Facility: Montréal.
Property Officer, Québec, Leasing & Property, Louise Demers-Thorne
Tel: 514-496-1733
Louise.Demers-Thorne@cnrc-nrc.gc.ca

Wind Tunnel Testing Facilities / Installations d'essais en souffleries
c/o National Research Council, 1200 Montreal Rd., Ottawa, ON K1A 0R6
To support the research of government, industries, & universities, the National Research Council provides six wind tunnels, plus experties in aerodynamic noise measurement, pressure sensitive paint technology, & flow mapping. Part of the Automotive & Surface Transportation Facilities.
Contact, Matthew Tobin
Tel: 613-990-0765
Matthew.Tobin@nrc-cnrc.gc.ca

Zebrafish Screening Facility
1411 Oxford St., Halifax, NS B3H 3Z1
Tel: 902-426-8332
Testing services are available for pharmacological & toxicology activity. The National Research Council's Zebrafish Screening Facility can be accessed by companies & research organizations by entering into a technical service agreement or research collaboration.
Contact, James De Pater
Tel: 613-614-9547
James.DePater@nrc-cnrc.gc.ca

National Seniors Council (NSC) / Conseil national des aînés (CNA)

Phase IV, 8th Floor, Mail Stop 802, 140, promenade du Portage, Gatineau, QC K1A 0J9
Fax: 819-953-9298
Toll-Free: 800-622-6232
TTY: 800-926-9105
www.canada.ca/en/national-seniors-council.html
The Council, formerly known as the National Advisory Council on Aging, advises the Minister of Employment & Social Development, the Minister of Health, & the Minister of State (Seniors) on issues related to the aging of the Canadian population & the quality of life of seniors. It reviews the needs & problems of seniors & recommends remedial action, liaises with

other groups interested in aging, encourages public discussion & publishes & disseminates information on aging.

Chair, Dr. Suzanne Dupuis-Blanchard

Natural Resources Canada (NRCan) / Ressources naturelles Canada (RNCan)

580 Booth St., Ottawa, ON K1A 0E4
Tel: 343-292-6096; *Fax:* 613-992-7211
TTY: 613-996-4397
www.nrcan.gc.ca
Other Communication: Media, Phone: 343-292-6100; Email: NRCan.media_relations-media_relations.RNCan@canada.ca
twitter.com/NRCan
www.facebook.com/EnvironmentandNaturalResourcesinCanada
www.linkedin.com/company/natural-resources-canada
www.youtube.com/user/NaturalResourcesCa
Advances development of Canada's economy by contributing to the development & use of Canada's mineral & energy resources in a manner consistent with federal environmental & social objectives; advances knowledge of the Canadian landmass through scientific & science-related activities.

Minister, Natural Resources, Hon. Jonathan Wilkinson, P.C.

Deputy Minister, Christyne Tremblay
Tel: 343-292-6799; *Fax:* 613-992-3828
christyne.tremblay@canada.ca

Associate Deputy Minister, Shawn Tupper
Tel: 343-292-6799; *Fax:* 613-992-3828
shawn.tupper@canada.ca

Chief of Staff, Janet Annesley
Tel: 343-292-6837
janet.annesley@canada.ca

Chief Audit Executive, Christian Asselin
Tel: 343-292-8752; *Fax:* 613-992-8799
Christian.Asselin@NRCan-RNCan.gc.ca

Chief Scientist, Donna Kirkwood
Tel: 343-292-8154
donna.kirkwood@canada.ca

Executive Director, Task Force on Energy Security, Prosperity & Sustainability, Gregory Jack
Tel: 613-943-5764; *Fax:* 613-992-1392
Gregory.Jack@NRCan-RNCan.gc.ca
#244, 155 Queen St., 2nd Fl.
Ottawa, ON K1A 0E4

Director, Operations, Northern Pipeline Agency, Vacant

Canadian Forest Service (CFS) / Service canadien des forêts
Tel: 613-995-0947; *Fax:* 613-947-7395
TTY: 613-996-4397
www.nrcan.gc.ca/forests
Promotes the sustainable development of Canada's forests & competitiveness of the Canadian forest sector for the well-being of present & future generations of Canadians. It focuses on forest science & technology, & related national policy coordination. The CFS maintains five research centres across the country that share responsibility for research in the areas of biodiversity; biotechnology; climate change; ecology & ecosystems; entomology; forest conditions, monitoring & reporting; forest fires; forest & landscape management; pathology; silviculture & regeneration; & socioeconomics.
Assistant Deputy Minister, Glenn Mason
Tel: 343-292-8555; *Fax:* 613-947-7395
glenn.mason@canada.ca

Planning, Operations & Information Branch / Direction de la planification, des opérations et de l'information
Director General, Joanne Frappier
Tel: 343-292-8558; *Fax:* 613-947-9100
joanne.frappier@canada.ca

Policy, Economics & Industry Branch / Direction de la politique, de l'économie et de l'industrie
Acting Director General, Darcy Booth
Tel: 613-947-9051; *Fax:* 613-947-9020
Darcie.Booth@NRCan-RNCan.gc.ca

Science & Programs Branch / Direction des sciences et des programmes
Acting Director General, Mike Fullerton
Tel: 343-292-8588; *Fax:* 613-947-9035
mike.fullerton@canada.ca

CFS Regional Offices
Atlantic Forestry Centre (AFC) / Centre de foresterie de l'Atlantique (CFA)
1350 Regent St. South, PO Box 4000 Fredericton, NB E3B 5P7
Tel: 506-452-3500; *Fax:* 506-452-3525
www.nrcan.gc.ca/forests/research-centres/afc/13447
Responsible for the overall Canadian Forest Service operations & programs in the Atlantic region. Liaises & negotiates with provincial government, industry officials, & other sector-related senior management on behalf of the CFS in the region.
Regional Director General, Derek MacFarlane
Tel: 506-452-3508
Derek.MacFarlane@NRCan-RNCan.gc.ca

Canadian Wood Fibre Centre (CWFC) / Centre canadien sur la fibre de bois (CCFB)
580 Booth St., 7th Floor, Ottawa, ON K1A 0E4
Tel: 613-947-9001; *Fax:* 613-947-9033
www.nrcan.gc.ca/forests/research-centres/cwfc/13457
The Canadian Wood Fibre Centre (CWFC) brings together forest sector researchers to develop solutions for the Canadian forest sector's wood fibre related industries in an environmentally responsible manner. Its mission is to create innovative knowledge to expand the economic opportunities for the forest sector to benefit from Canadian wood fibre.
Executive Director, George Alexande Bruemmer
Tel: 613-947-7331; *Fax:* 613-947-8863
GeorgeAlexande.Bruemmer@NRCan-RNCan.gc.ca

Great Lakes Forestry Centre (GLFC) / Centre de foresterie des Grands Lacs (CFGL)
1219 Queen St. East, PO Box 490 Sault Ste Marie, ON P6A 2E5
Tel: 705-949-9461; *Fax:* 705-541-5700
www.nrcan.gc.ca/forests/research-centres/glfc/13459
Responsibilities include: forest research & regional forestry activities in Ontario; provides the primary federal focus for forestry in Ontario; emphasis on boreal mixed wood forest management & environmental impacts of pollutants & forestry practices; efforts also directed at the reduction of losses from insects, disease & fire; ecosystem dynamics & classification; nutrient problems & impacts from forestry practices; acid rain impacts (carbon dioxide/nitrogen oxide interactions).
Director General, David Nanang
Tel: 705-541-5555
David.Nanang@NRCan-RNCan.gc.ca

Laurentian Forestry Centre (LFC) / Centre de foresterie des Laurentides (CFL)
1055, rue du PEPS, CP 10380 Succ Sainte-Foy, Québec, QC G1V 4C7
www.nrcan.gc.ca/forests/research-centres/lfc/13473
Responsibilities include: increasing scientific & technical knowledge in the area of forest biology which includes biodiversity, tree biotechnology & advanced genetics, pest management methods, & in the area of forest ecosystem which cover forest ecosystem processes, effects of forestry practices, landscape management & climate change.
Director General, Jacinthe Leclerc
Tel: 418-648-5847
Jacinthe.Leclerc@RNCan-NRCan.gc.ca

Northern Forestry Centre (NFC) / Centre de foresterie du Nord (CFN)
5320 - 122 St., Edmonton, AB T6H 3S5
Tel: 780-435-7210; *Fax:* 780-435-7359
www.nrcan.gc.ca/forests/research-centres/nofc/13485
Responsibilities include: socio-economics & forest sociology; fire ecology, environment, & advanced fire management & prediction systems; climate change & forest interactions; carbon budget modeling; forest health, insect, & disease monitoring & management systems; remote sensing applications & landscape level classification systems; ecosystems productivity; biodiversity. Regional coordination of national programs relating to Model Forests & First Nation Forestry. Responsible for the direction of forestry programs in the provinces of Alberta, Saskatchewan, Manitoba & the NWT, including R&D, & four federal-provincial partnership agreements in forestry.
Director General, Michael Norton
Tel: 780-435-7202; *Fax:* 780-435-7396
michael.norton@canada.ca

Pacific Forestry Centre (PFC) / Centre de foresterie du Pacifique (CFP)
506 West Burnside Rd., Victoria, BC V8Z 1M5
Tel: 250-363-0600; *Fax:* 250-363-6004
www.nrcan.gc.ca/forests/research-centres/pfc/13489
Responsibilities include: forest management of federal lands; first nations programs; first nations land claims resource analysis; economic analysis of the regional forest sector (value-added, labour costs, & industrial sustainability); national strategic planning for the forestry practices & landscape management networks; science & technology programs in both

forest biology (ecosystems processes, climate change, pest management, & tree biotechnology). Advises the CFS ADM on all forestry matters relating to the Pacific & Yukon region. The Mountain Pine Beetle Action Plan 2005-2010 set out strategies for confronting the infestation.
Director General, Judi Beck
Tel: 250-298-2300
judi.beck@nrcan-rncan.gc.ca

Communications & Portfolio Sector / Secteur des communications et du portefeuille
Assistant Deputy Minister, Mollie Johnson
Tel: 343-292-8922
mollie.johnson@canada.ca
Acting Director General, Portfolio Management & Corporate Secretariat Branch, Jean-Clement Chenier
Tel: 343-292-6110; Fax: 613-947-1208
jean-clement.chenier@canada.ca
Director General, Engagement & Digital Communications, Jon Ward
Tel: 343-543-3255
jon.ward@canada.ca

Corporate Management & Services Sector / Secteur de la gestion et des services intégrés
Fax: 613-922-8922
Assistant Deputy Minister, CMSS & Chief Financial Officer, Kami Ramcharan
Tel: 343-292-8168; Fax: 613-992-8922
kami.ramcharan@canada.ca
Director General, Finance & Procurement Branch, Marc Bélisle
Tel: 613-943-8763; Fax: 613-996-2151
Marc.Belisle@NRCan-RNCan.gc.ca
Director General & Chief Human Resources Officer, Cheri Crosby
Tel: 613-995-1261; Fax: 613-995-4289
Cheri.Crosby@NRCan-RNCan.gc.ca
Director General & Chief Information Officer, Chief Information Office & Security Branch, Pierre Ferland
Tel: 613-943-0469
Pierre.Ferland@NRCan-RNCan.gc.ca
Executive Director, Planning & Operations Branch, Kelly Morrison
Tel: 613-947-2758; Fax: 613-992-8922
Kelly.Morrison@NRCan-RNCan.gc.ca
Senior Director, Executive Services & Talent Management Division, Michel Brazeau
Tel: 613-947-8243; Fax: 613-947-2034
Michel.Brazeau@NRCan-RNCan.gc.ca
Senior Director, Workplace Services, Tambrae Knapp
Tel: 613-947-2039; Fax: 613-995-3800
Tambrae.Knapp@NRCan-RNCan.gc.ca

Earth Sciences Sector / Secteur des sciences de la Terre
588 Booth St., Ottawa, ON K1A 0Y7
www.nrcan.gc.ca/earth-sciences
Provides Canadians with timely & reliable geomatics & geoscience knowledge, products & services of the highest standards & in the most cost-effective manner possible. The Earth Sciences Sector is a predominantly science- & technology-based sector & includes the Geological Survey of Canada, Geomatics Canada, & the Polar Continental Shelf Project. These groups are major contributors to the comprehensive geoscience knowledge base of Canada & provide surveying, mapping, remote sensing, & digital information services describing the Canadian landmass.
Chief Scientist & Assistant Deputy Minister, Judith Bossé
Tel: 343-292-6605; Fax: 613-995-1509
judith.bosse@canada.ca

Canada Centre for Mapping & Earth Observation / Centre canadien de cartographie et d'observation de la Terre
#212, 50, Place de la Cité, PO Box 162 Sherbrooke, QC J1H 4G9
Remote sensing data for Canada; development of remote sensing technology & applications in conjunction with the private sector, & in support of environmental monitoring; development of the Canadian geospatial data infrastructure for distribution of remote sensing & other geographical databases, in partnership with other departments; development of GIS applications.
Director General, Prashant Shukle
Tel: 613-759-1196; Fax: 613-759-1204
prashant.shukle@canada.ca

Geological Survey of Canada (GSC) / Commission géologique du Canada
601 Booth St., Ottawa, ON K1A 0E8
www.nrcan.gc.ca/earth-sciences
Geoscientific information & research, geoscience surveys, sustainable development of Canada's resources, environmental protection, technology innovation.
Director General, Central & Northern Canada Branch, Vacant
Director General, Atlantic & Western Canada Branch, Daniel Lebel

Tel: 613-992-1400; Fax: 613-995-6575
daniel.lebel@canada.ca
Science-Business Programs Advisor, Dan Richardson
Tel: 613-996-9151; Fax: 613-996-6575
dan.richardson@canada.ca

Surveyor General Branch - Geomatics Canada (SGB) / Direction de l'arpenteur général - Géomatique Canada (DAG)
#605, 9700 Jasper Ave., Edmonton, AB T5J 4C3
Tel: 780-495-2519; Fax: 780-495-4052
nrcan.gc.ca/earth-sciences/geomatics/canada-lands-surveys/10 780
Surveys Canadian lands & waters; prepares & distributes topographic, geographic, electoral & aeronautical maps & digital products, surveys federal-provincial boundaries; manages a national program for acquiring & using remote sensing data. Associated offices include the Canada Map Office, Geogrpahical Names Board of Canada & National Air Photo Library.
Surveyor General/International Boundary Commissioner, Peter Sullivan
Tel: 780-495-7347; Fax: 780-495-4052
Peter.Sullivan@NRCan-RNCan.gc.ca

Strategic Policy & Operations Branch / Direction de la politique stratégique et des opérations
588 Booth St., Ottawa, ON K1A 0Y7
Director General, Mary Preville
Tel: 343-292-6515; Fax: 613-996-9670
mary.preville@canada.ca

Energy Sector / Secteur de la politique énergétique
Fax: 613-992-1405
www.nrcan.gc.ca/energy
Develops & promotes economic, regulatory & voluntary approaches to encourage sustainable development of energy resources to meet domestic needs & export markets. Advises the government on federal energy policies, strategies, emergency plans & activities; promotes efficient energy use.
Assistant Deputy Minister, Jay Khosla
Tel: 343-292-6265; Fax: 613-992-1405
jay.khosla@canada.ca

Electricity Resources Branch / Direction des ressources en électricité
Legislative, policy & regulatory responsibilities for renewable energies, electricity, oil & gas, frontier lands activities. Provides leadership on policy on nuclear energy, uranium, radioactive waste & related environmental issues.
Director General, Niall O'Dea
Tel: 343-292-6200; Fax: 613-947-4205
niall.odea@canada.ca

Energy Policy Branch / Direction de la politique énergétique
Developing, planning & coordinating policy matters relating to the energy sector, including management of petroleum exploration & development, electricity markets & alternative energy, & the design or delivery of specific energy efficiency programs & services.
Director General, Drew Leyburne
Tel: 343-292-6448; Fax: 613-996-5943
drew.leyburne@canada.ca

Energy Safety & Security / Sûreté énergétique et sécurité
Director General, Jeff Labonté
Tel: 343-292-6258; Fax: 613-992-8738
jeff.labonte@canada.ca

Office of Energy Efficiency (OEE) / Office de l'éfficacité énergétique
CEF, Building 3, Observatory Cres., 930 Carling Ave., Ottawa, ON K1A 0Y3
www.nrcan.gc.ca/energy/offices-labs/office-energy-efficiency
Policy & programs in support of efficient use of energy, use of alternative energy & transportation fuels. Grants & incentives, workshops, statistics & analysis & free publications are offered.
Director General, Patricia Fuller
Tel: 343-292-6310
patricia.fuller@canada.ca

Petroleum Resources Branch / Direction des ressources pétrolières
Legislative, policy & regulatory responsibilities for all sources of energy supplies, such as renewable energies, electricity, oil & gas, frontier lands activities.
Director General, Terence Hubbard
Tel: 343-292-6165; Fax: 613-992-8738
terence.hubbard@canada.ca

Innovation & Energy Technology Sector / Secteur de l'innovation et de la technologie énergétique
Assistant Deputy Minister, Frank Des Rosiers
Tel: 343-292-8817; Fax: 613-944-4747
frank.desrosiers@canada.ca

Office of Energy Research & Development (OERD) / Bureau de recherche et développement énergétique (BRDE)
Fax: 613-995-6146
Coordinates the following federal funding programs: Clean Energy Fund; ecoENERGY Innovation Initiative; ecoENERGY Technology Initiative; & Energy Research & Development (PERD). PERD is intended for research & development in energy efficiency & climate change, transportation & renewable energy. The OERD coordinates & represents Canada in international collaboration energy R&D through international mechanisms such as the International Energy Agency & the MOU with US DOE International Energy Agency.
Director General, Yiota Kokkinos
Tel: 343-292-8951
yiota.kokkinos@canada.ca

Major Projects Management Office / Bureau de gestion des grands projets
580 Booth St., Ottawa, ON K1A 0E4
Assistant Deputy Minister, Erin O'Gorman
Tel: 343-292-8830; Fax: 613-995-7555
erin.ogorman@canada.ca
Director General, Jim Clarke
Tel: 343-292-8825; Fax: 613-995-7555
jim.clarke@canada.ca
Director General, Policies, Mollie Johnson
Tel: 343-292-8824
mollie.johnson2@canada.ca
Director General, Strategic Projects Secretariat, Timothy Gardiner
Tel: 343-292-8805
timothy.gardiner@canada.ca

Minerals & Metals Sector / Secteur des minéraux et des métaux
www.nrcan.gc.ca/mining-materials/mining
MMS is the federal government's primary source of scientific & technological knowledge, & policy advice, on Canada's mineral & metal resources & on explosives regulation & technology. In addition to housing three scientific research institutions, MMS has the government lead in promoting sustainable development & responsible use of Canada's mineral & metal resources. The Sector is a leader in the generation & dissemination of knowledge on the Canadian minerals & metals industry, & collaborates with & provides research services to governmental, institutional & industrial clients for the development of new technology with economic, environmental & social benefits to Canadians.
Assistant Deputy Minister, Marian Campbell Jarvis
Tel: 343-292-8722; Fax: 613-996-7425
marian.campbelljarvis@canada.ca

CanmetMATERIALS / CanmetMATÉRIAUX
183 Longwood Rd. South, Hamilton, ON L8P 0A5
CanmetMATERIALS focuses on the fabrication, processing & evaluation of metals & materials. It operates facilities in Hamilton & Calgary, & is the largest research centre of its kind in Canada.
Director General, Philippe Dauphin
Tel: 905-645-0698; Fax: 905-645-0831
philippe.dauphin@canada.ca

CanmetMINING / CanmetMINES
555 Booth St., Ottawa, ON K1A 0G1
Fax: 613-947-6606
CanmetMINING leads & participates in mining & innovative national collaborations to develop green mining science & technologies.
Director General, Magdi Habib
Tel: 613-995-4776; Fax: 613-992-8928
magdi.habib@canada.ca

Explosives Safety & Security Branch / Direction de la sécurité et de ls sûreté des explosifs
Director General, Patrick O'Neill
Tel: 343-292-8748; Fax: 613-948-5195
patrick.oneill@canada.ca

Industry & Economic Analysis Branch / Direction de l'analyse industrielle et économique
Acting Director General, David McNabb
Tel: 343-292-6083
david.mcnabb@canada.ca

Minerals, Metals & Materials Policy Branch / Direction de la politique des minéraux, métaux et matériaux
Director General, Stefania Trombetti
Tel: 343-292-8704; Fax: 613-952-7501
stefania.trombetti@canada.ca

Natural Sciences & Engineering Research Council of Canada (NSERC) / Conseil des recherches en sciences naturelles et en génie du Canada (CRSNG)

350 Albert St., 16th Fl., Ottawa, ON K1A 1H5
Tel: 613-995-4273; *Fax:* 613-992-5337
Toll-Free: 855-275-2861
www.nserc-crsng.gc.ca
twitter.com/nserc_crsng
www.facebook.com/nserccanada
www.linkedin.com/company/nserc-crsng
www.youtube.com/user/NSERCTube

Science & Engineering Research Canada (NSERC) is a federal agency whose role is to make investments in people, discovery & innovation for the benefit of all Canadians. With an annual budget of more than $860 million, it supports more than 20,000 university students & postdoctoral fellows in their advanced studies. NSERC promotes discovery by funding more than 10,000 university professors every year & helps make innovation happen by encouraging more than 500 Canadian companies to participate & invest in university research projects.

Interim President, Digvir S. Jayas
pres@nserc-crsng.gc.ca

Chief Financial Officer & Vice-President, Common Administrative Services, Patricia Sauvé-McCuan
Tel: 613-995-3914; *Fax:* 613-944-1760
Patricia.Sauve-McCuan@nserc-crsng.gc.ca

Chief Operating Officer & Vice-President, Research Partnerships, Marc Fortin
Tel: 613-992-1585
Marc.Fortin@nserc-crsng.gc.ca

Vice-President, Research Grants & Scholarships, Danika Goosney
Tel: 613-995-5833
Danika.Goosney@nserc-crsng.gc.ca

Vice-President, Communications, Corporate & International Affairs Directorate, Alfred LeBlanc
Tel: 613-943-5317
Alfred.Leblanc@nserc-crsng.gc.ca

Associate Vice-President, Networks of Centres of Excellence, Jean Saint-Vil
Tel: 613-995-6010
Jean.Saint-Vil@nserc-crsng.gc.ca

Executive Director, Corporate Planning & Policy, Kevin Fitzgibbons
Tel: 613-995-6449
Kevin.Fitzgibbons@nserc-crsng.gc.ca

Director General, Human Resources, Jennifer Gualtieri
Tel: 613-944-9264
Jennifer.Gualtieri@nserc-crsng.gc.ca

Director General & Chief Information Officer, Information & Innovation Solutions, Philippe Johnston
Tel: 613-996-8820
Philippe.Johnston@nserc-crsng.gc.ca

Director General & Deputy Chief Financial Officer, Finance & Awards Administration Division, Nathalie Manseau
Tel: 613-996-8269
Nathalie.Manseau@nserc-crsng.gc.ca

Networks of Centres of Excellence of Canada (NCE) / Réseaux de centres d'excellence (RCE)

350 Albert Street, 16th Fl., Ottawa, ON K1A 1H5
Tel: 613-995-6010; *Fax:* 613-992-7356
info@nce-rce.gc.ca
www.nce-rce.gc.ca
twitter.com/nce_rce
www.facebook.com/networksofcentresofexcellence
www.linkedin.com/company/networks-of-centres-of-excellence

The Networks of Centres of Excellence (NCE) is mandated to persue discoveries in the fields of natural sciences, engineering, social sciences & health sciences, in order to transform them into products, services & processes that improve the lives of Canadians. In partnership with Innovation, Science & Economic Development & Health Canada, NCE is jointly administered by The Canadian Institutes of Health Research (CIHR), the Natural Sciences & Engineering Research Council (NSERC) & the Social Sciences & Humanities Research Council (SSHRC).

Chair, Management Committee, Marc Fortin

Associate Vice-President, NCE Secretariat, Jean Saint-Vil

Tel: 613-992-5512
Jean.Saint-Vil@nce-rce.gc.ca

Deputy Director, Centres of Excellence for Commercialization & Research (CECR) & Business-Led Networks of Centres of Excellence (BL-NCE), Denis Godin
Tel: 613-947-8894
Denis.Godin@nce-rce.gc.ca

Deputy Director, Networks of Centres of Excellence (NCE) Program, Brigit Viens
Tel: 613-947-4538
Brigit.Viens@nce-rce.gc.ca

Northern Pipeline Agency Canada (NPAC) / Administration du pipe-line du Nord Canada (APNC)

#470, 588 Booth St., Ottawa, ON K1A 0Y7
Tel: 613-995-1150
info@npa.gc.ca
npa.gc.ca

Established to carry out federal responsibilities in relation to the planning & construction of the Canadian portion of the Alaska Highway Gas Pipeline.

Commissioner, Bob Hamilton
Tel: 343-292-6799; *Fax:* 613-992-3828

Office of the Commissioner of Official Languages / Commissariat aux langues officielles

30 Victoria St., 6th Fl., Gatineau, ON K1A 0T8
Tel: 819-420-4877; *Fax:* 819-420-4873
Toll-Free: 877-996-6368
TTY: 800-880-1990
www.ocol-clo.gc.ca
twitter.com/OCOLCanada
www.facebook.com/officiallanguages

Responsible for ensuring the equality of English & French in Parliament, within the Government of Canada, the federal administration, & the institutions subject to the Official Languages Act; the preservation & development of official language communities in Canada; & the equality of English & French in Canadian society.

Commissioner of Official Languages, Madeleine Meilleur

Assistant Commissioner, Policy & Communications Branch, Mary Donaghy
Tel: 819-420-4832; *Fax:* 819-420-4828

Assistant Commissioner, Corporate Management Branch, Eric Trépanier
Tel: 819-420-4850; *Fax:* 819-420-4873

Assistant Commissioner, Compliance Assurance Branch, Ghislaine Saikaley
Tel: 819-420-4853; *Fax:* 819-420-4854

Pacific Pilotage Authority Canada / Administration de pilotage du Pacifique Canada

#1000, 1130 West Pender St., Vancouver, BC V6E 4A4
Tel: 604-666-6771; *Fax:* 604-666-1647
info@ppa.gc.ca
www.ppa.gc.ca
Other Communication: Vancouver Dispatch: 604-666-6776, Fax: 604-666-6093; Victoria Dispatch: 250-363-3878, Fax: 250-363-3293

Operates pilotage services in Canadian waters in & around British Columbia. Reports to government through the Minister of Transportation.

Chair, Lorraine Cunningham
lcunningham@ppa.gc.ca

Chief Executive Officer, Kevin Obermeyer
oberkev@ppa.gc.ca

Director, Finance & Administration, Stefan Woloszyn
swoloszyn@ppa.gc.ca

Director, Marine Operations, Capt. Brian Young
youngb@ppa.gc.ca

Parks Canada / Parcs Canada

National Office, 30, rue Victoria, Gatineau, QC J8X 0B3
Tel: 819-420-9486
Toll-Free: 888-773-8888
TTY: 866-787-6221
information@pc.gc.ca
www.pc.gc.ca
twitter.com/ParksCanada
www.facebook.com/ParksCanada
www.youtube.com/user/ParksCanadaAgency

Responsible for the protection, management, operation & maintenance of national parks, historic sites, canals & other significant examples of Canada's natural & cultural heritage, for the benefit, understanding & enjoyment of Canadians. Administers one of the largest park systems in the world. There are 46 national parks & national park reserves in total. In addition to the national parks, national historic sites & national marine conservation areas, Parks Canada coordinates other heritage programs, including federal heritage buildings, heritage railway stations, grave sites of Canadian Prime Ministers, heritage rivers, archaeology programs, international programs.

Minister, Environment & Climate Change; Minister Responsible, Parks Canada, Hon. Steven Guilbeault, P.C.

President & CEO, Ron Hallman

Vice-President of External Relations & Visitor Experience, Michael Nadler
Tel: 819-420-9409

Chief Audit & Evaluation Executive, Office of Internal Audit & Evaluation, Brian Evans
Tel: 819-420-5132; *Fax:* 819-420-5133
Other Communications: Alt. Phone: 613-889-1675

Ombudsman & Director, Centre for Values & Ethics, Judith Brunet
Tel: 819-420-5033

Chief of Staff & Corporate Secretary, Jesse Fleming
Tel: 819-420-5145; *Fax:* 819-420-5144

Director, Indigenous Affairs Branch, Susan Russell
Tel: 819-420-9792

Associated Agencies, Boards & Commissions:
• **Historic Sites & Monuments Board of Canada / Commission des lieux et monuments historiques du Canada**
30 Victoria St., 3rd Fl.
Gatineau, QC J8X 0B3
Fax: 819-420-9260
Toll-free: 855-283-8730
hsmbc-clmhc@pc.gc.ca
www.pc.gc.ca/eng/clmhc-hsmbc/index.aspx
A seventeen-member advisory board which reports to the Minister of Environment & recommends whether persons, places or events are of national historic &/or architectural significance, & therefore warrant commemoration. The board also makes recommendations concerning the designation of heritage railway stations.

Chief Financial Officer Directorate / Dirigeante principale des finances
Chief Financial Officer, Sylvain Michaud
Tel: 819-420-9518

External Relations & Visitor Experience Directorate / Direction générale des relations externes et expériences des visiteurs
On Oct. 17, 2018, cannabis was legalized for recreational use. It may be used on Parks Canada property, but is restricted to visitors' campsites. Specific regulations per province can be found here:
www.pc.gc.ca/en/voyage-travel/securite-safety/cannabis.
Acting CEO & Vice-President, External Relations & Visitor Experience, Michael Nadler
Tel: 819-420-9409
National Director, Corporate Communications, Jason Bouzanis
Tel: 819-420-9390
Other Communications: Alternate Phone: 613-808-4793
Director, Visitor Experience, Ed Jager
Tel: 819-420-9397
Other Communications: Alternate Phone: 613-853-7447
Director, Outreach & Marketing, Élisabeth Lacoursiere
Tel: 819-420-9516
Other Communications: Alternate Phone: 613-898-4629
Director, Strategic Partnering, Dean L. Marchand
Tel: 819-420-9398
Other Communications: Alternate Phone: 819-639-5044

Director, National Celebrations, John L. Thomson
Tel: 819-420-9400
Other Communications: Alternate Phone: 819-210-5729

Human Resources Directorate / Direction générale des ressources humaines
Chief Human Resources Officer, Pierre Richer de La Flèche
Tel: 819-420-9133; *Fax:* 819-420-9135

Indigenous Affairs, Heritage Conservation & Commemoration Directorate / Direction générale des affaires authochtones, de la conservation et de la commémoration du patrimoine
Vice-President, George Green
Tel: 819-420-9256
Director, Cultural Heritage Policies, Genevieve Charrois
Tel: 819-420-9255; *Fax:* 819-953-4909

Protected Areas Establishment & Conservation Directorate / Direction générale de l'Établissement et conservation des aires protégées
Vice-President, Rob Prosper
Tel: 819-420-9267; *Fax:* 819-420-9273
Other Communications: Alternate Phone: 613-889-6900
Chief Ecosystem Scientist, Gilles Seutin
Tel: 819-420-9269; *Fax:* 819-420-9273
Other Communications: Alternate Phone: 613-277-8447
Executive Director, World Conservation Congress Lead, Natural Resource Conservation Branch, Mike P. Wong
Tel: 819-420-9271; *Fax:* 819-420-9273
Executive Director, Natural Resource Conservation Branch, Nadine Crookes
Tel: 250-726-7165; *Fax:* 250-726-3520

Strategic Policy & Investment Directorate / Direction générale des Politiques stratégiques et investissement
Vice-President, Strategic Policy & Investment, Jane Pearse
Tel: 819-420-9114
Other Communications: Alternate Phone: 613-614-0644
Chief Information Officer, Greg Thompson
Tel: 403-762-1528; *Fax:* 403-762-1555

Atlantic National Parks/National Historic Sites

Alexander Graham Bell Historic Site of Canada
PO Box 159 Baddeck, NS B0E 1B0
Tel: 902-295-2069; *Fax:* 902-295-3496
information@pc.gc.ca
www.pc.gc.ca/eng/lhn-nhs/ns/grahambell/index.aspx
twitter.com/ParksCanada_NS
www.facebook.com/AGBNHS

Ardgowan National Historic Site of Canada
2 Palmer's Lane, Charlottetown, PE C1A 5V8
Tel: 902-566-7050; *Fax:* 902-566-7226
www.pc.gc.ca/eng/lhn-nhs/pe/ardgowan/index.aspx
twitter.com/ParksCanadaPEI

Bank Fishery National Heritage Exhibit
PO Box 9080 Stn. A, Halifax, NS B3K 5M7
Tel: 902-426-5080; *Fax:* 902-426-4228
information@pc.gc.ca
www.pc.gc.ca/lhn-nhs/ns/bank/index.aspx
twitter.com/ParksCanada_NS

Boishébert & Beaubears Shipbuilding National Historic Sites of Canada
186, route 117, Kouchibouguac National Park, NB E4X 2P1
Tel: 506-876-2443; *Fax:* 506-876-4802
TTY: 506-876-4205
kouch.info@pc.gc.ca
www.pc.gc.ca/lhn-nhs/nb/boishebert/index.aspx
twitter.com/nhsnb

Canso Islands National Historic Site of Canada
1465 Union St., PO Box 159 Baddeck, NS B0E 1B0
Tel: 902-295-2069; *Fax:* 902-295-3496
information@pc.gc.ca
www.pc.gc.ca/lhn-nhs/ns/canso/index.aspx
Other Communication: Summer Phone: 902-366-3136
twitter.com/ParksCanada_NS
www.facebook.com/cansoislands

Cape Breton Highlands National Park of Canada
Ingonish Beach, NS B0C 1L0
Tel: 902-224-2306; *Fax:* 902-285-2866
cbhnp.info@pc.gc.ca
www.pc.gc.ca/pn-np/ns/cbreton/index.aspx
twitter.com/ParksCanada_NS
www.facebook.com/CBHNP

Cape Spear National Historic Site of Canada
PO Box 1268 St. John's, NL A1C 5M9
Tel: 709-772-5367; *Fax:* 709-772-6302
cape.spear@pc.gc.ca
www.pc.gc.ca/lhn-nhs/nl/spear/index.aspx
twitter.com/ParksCanadaNL

Carleton Martello Tower National Historic Site of Canada
454 Whipple St., Saint John, NB E2M 2R3
Tel: 506-636-4011; *Fax:* 506-636-4574
TTY: 506-887-6015
info.martello@pc.gc.ca
www.pc.gc.ca/lhn-nhs/nb/carleton/index.aspx

Castle Hill National Historic Site of Canada
PO Box 10 Stn. Jerseyside, Placentia Bay, NL A0B 2G0
Tel: 709-227-2401; *Fax:* 709-227-2452
castle.hill@pc.gc.ca
www.pc.gc.ca/lhn-nhs/nl/castlehill/index.aspx
Other Communication: Off-season: 709-772-6709, Fax: 709-772-6388
Off-season AddressPO Box 1268 Sta. St. John's, NL A1C 5M9
twitter.com/ParksCanadaNL

Fort Amherst/Port-La-Joye National Historic Site of Canada
2 Palmers Lane, Charlottetown, PE C1A 5V8
Tel: 902-566-7050; *Fax:* 902-566-7226
pljfa.info@pc.gc.ca
www.pc.gc.ca/lhn-nhs/pe/amherst/index.aspx
twitter.com/ParksCanadaPEI

Fort Anne National Historic Site of Canada
PO Box 9 Annapolis Royal, NS B0S 1A0
Tel: 902-532-2397; *Fax:* 902-532-2232
information@pc.gc.ca
www.pc.gc.ca/lhn-nhs/ns/fortanne/index.aspx
Other Communication: Off-season: 902-532-2321
twitter.com/ParksCanada_NS

Fort Beauséjour National Historic Site of Canada
111 Fort Beauséjour Rd., Aulac, NB E4L 2W5
Tel: 506-364-5080; *Fax:* 506-536-4399
fort.beausejour@pc.gc.ca
www.pc.gc.ca/lhn-nhs/nb/beausejour/index.aspx

Fort Edward National Historic Site of Canada
PO Box 9 Annapolis Royal, NS B0S 1A0
Tel: 902-532-2321; *Fax:* 902-532-2232
information@pc.gc.ca
www.pc.gc.ca/lhn-nhs/ns/edward/index.aspx
Other Communication: June - Sept.: 902-798-2639; West Hants Historical Society: 902-798-4706
twitter.com/ParksCanada_NS

Fort McNab National Historic Site of Canada
c/o Halifax Citadel National Historic Site, PO Box 9080 Stn. A, Halifax, NS B3K 5M7
Tel: 902-426-5080; *Fax:* 902-426-4228
halifax.citadel@pc.gc.ca
www.pc.gc.ca/lhn-nhs/ns/mcnab/index.aspx
twitter.com/ParksCanada_NS

Fortress of Louisbourg National Historic Site
259 Park Service Rd., Louisbourg, NS B1C 2L2
Tel: 902-733-3552; *Fax:* 902-733-2362
louisbourg.info@pc.gc.ca
www.pc.gc.ca/lhn-nhs/ns/louisbourg/index.aspx
twitter.com/ParksCanada_NS
www.facebook.com/FortressOfLouisbourgNHS

Fundy National Park of Canada
PO Box 1001 Alma, NB E4H 1B4
Tel: 506-887-6000; *Fax:* 506-887-6008
TTY: 506-887-6015
fundy.info@pc.gc.ca
www.pc.gc.ca/pn-np/nb/fundy/index.aspx

Grand Pré National Historic Site of Canada
PO Box 150 Grand Pré, NS B0P 1M0
Tel: 902-542-3631; *Fax:* 902-542-1691
Toll-Free: 866-542-3631
grandpre.info@pc.gc.ca
www.pc.gc.ca/lhn-nhs/ns/grandpre/index.aspx
twitter.com/ParksCanada_NS
www.facebook.com/GrandPreNHS

Georges Island National Historic Site of Canada
c/o Halifax Citadel National Historic Site of Canada, PO Box 9080 Stn. A, Halifax, NS B3K 5M7
Tel: 902-426-5080; *Fax:* 902-426-4228
halifax.citadel@pc.gc.ca
www.pc.gc.ca/lhn-nhs/ns/georges/index.aspx
twitter.com/ParksCanada_NS

Green Gables Heritage Place
2 Palmer's Lane, Charlottetown, PE C1A 5V6
Tel: 902-963-7874; *Fax:* 902-963-7869
greengables.info@pc.gc.ca
www.pc.gc.ca/lhn-nhs/pe/greengables/index.aspx
twitter.com/ParksCanadaPEI

Gros Morne National Park of Canada
PO Box 130 Rocky Harbour, NL A0K 4N0
Tel: 709-458-2417; *Fax:* 709-458-2059
TTY: 709-772-4564
grosmorne.info@pc.gc.ca
www.pc.gc.ca/pn-np/nl/grosmorne/index.aspx
Other Communication: Emergency: 877-852-3100
twitter.com/ParksCanadaNL

Halifax Citadel National Historic Site of Canada
PO Box 9080 Stn. A, Halifax, NS B3K 5M7
Tel: 902-426-5080; *Fax:* 902-426-4228
halifax.citadel@pc.gc.ca
www.pc.gc.ca/lhn-nhs/ns/halifax/index.aspx
twitter.com/ParksCanada_NS

Hawthorne Cottage National Historic Site of Canada
PO Box 5542 St. John's, NL A1C 5W4
Tel: 709-753-9262; *Fax:* 709-753-0879
info@historicsites.ca
www.pc.gc.ca/lhn-nhs/nl/hawthorne/index.aspx
Other Communication: Off-season: 709-528-4004
twitter.com/ParksCanadaNL

Kejimkujik National Park of Canada
PO Box 236 Maitland Bridge, NS B0T 1B0
Tel: 902-682-2772
Toll-Free: 888-773-8888
kejimkujik.info@pc.gc.ca
www.pc.gc.ca/pn-np/ns/kejimkujik/index_e.asp
twitter.com/ParksCanada_NS
www.facebook.com/Kejimkujik

Kouchibouguac National Park of Canada
186, Route 117, Kouchibouguac National Park, NB E4X 2P1
Tel: 506-876-2443; *Fax:* 506-876-4802
Toll-Free: 888-773-8888
TTY: 506-876-4205
kouch.info@pc.gc.ca
www.pc.gc.ca/pn-np/nb/kouchibouguac/index.aspx

L'Anse aux Meadows National Historic Site of Canada
PO Box 70 St-Lunaire-Griquet, NL A0K 2X0
Tel: 709-623-2608; *Fax:* 709-623-2028
viking.lam@pc.gc.ca
www.pc.gc.ca/lhn-nhs/nl/meadows/index.aspx
twitter.com/ParksCanadaNL

Marconi National Historic Site of Canada
PO Box 159 Baddeck, NS B0E 1B0
Tel: 902-295-2069; *Fax:* 902-295-3496
information@pc.gc.ca
www.pc.gc.ca/lhn-nhs/ns/marconi/index.aspx
Other Communication: Summer Phone: 902-842-2530
twitter.com/ParksCanada_NS
www.facebook.com/MarconiNHS

Monument Lefebvre National Historic Site of Canada
480 Centrale Rd., Memramcook, NB E4K 3S6
Tel: 506-758-9808; *Fax:* 506-758-9813
monument@nbnet.nb.ca
www.pc.gc.ca/lhn-nhs/nb/lefebvre/index.aspx

Port-au-Choix National Historic Site of Canada
PO Box 140 Port au Choix, NL A0K 4C0
Tel: 709-458-2417; *Fax:* 709-861-3827
pac-historic-site@pc.gc.ca
www.pc.gc.ca/lhn-nhs/nl/portauchoix/index.aspx
Other Communication: Seasonal: 709-861-3522
twitter.com/ParksCanadaNL

Port Royal National Historic Site of Canada
PO Box 9 Annapolis Royal, NS B0S 1A0
Tel: 902-532-2898; *Fax:* 902-532-2232
information@pc.gc.ca
www.pc.gc.ca/lhn-nhs/ns/portroyal/index.aspx
Other Communication: Off-season: 902-532-2321
twitter.com/ParksCanada_NS

Prince Edward Island National Park of Canada
2 Palmers Lane, Charlottetown, PE C1A 5V8
Tel: 902-672-6350; *Fax:* 902-672-6370
pnipe.peinp@pc.gc.ca
www.pc.gc.ca/pn-np/pe/pei-ipe/index.aspx
twitter.com/ParksCanadaPEI
www.facebook.com/PEInationalpark

Prince of Wales Tower National Historic Site
c/o Halifax Citadel National Historic Site, PO Box 9080 Stn. A, Halifax, NS B3K 5M7
Tel: 902-426-5080; *Fax:* 902-426-4228
halifax.citadel@pc.gc.ca
www.pc.gc.ca/lhn-nhs/ns/prince/index.aspx
twitter.com/ParksCanada_NS

Province House National Historic Site of Canada
2 Palmer's Lane, Charlottetown, PE C1A 5V8
Tel: 902-566-7050; *Fax:* 902-566-7226
www.pc.gc.ca/lhn-nhs/pe/provincehouse/index.aspx
twitter.com/ParksCanadaPEI

Red Bay National Historic Site of Canada
PO Box 103 Red Bay, NL A0K 4K0
Tel: 709-920-2142; *Fax:* 709-458-2144
redbay.info@pc.gc.ca
www.pc.gc.ca/lhn-nhs/nl/redbay/index.aspx
Other Communication: Summer: 709-458-2417; Fax: 709-458-2059
twitter.com/ParksCanadaNL

Ryan Premises National Historic Site
PO Box 1451 Bonavista, NL A0C 1B0
Tel: 709-468-1600; *Fax:* 709-468-1604
ryan.premises@pc.gc.ca
www.pc.gc.ca/lhn-nhs/nl/ryan/index.aspx
twitter.com/ParksCanadaNL

Sable Island National Park Reserve
c/o Halifax Citadel National Historic Site, PO Box 9080 Stn. A, Halifax, NS B3K 5M7
Tel: 902-426-1993; *Fax:* 902-426-4228
sable@pc.gc.ca
www.pc.gc.ca/eng/pn-np/ns/sable/index.aspx
twitter.com/ParksCanada_NS

St. Andrews Blockhouse National Historic Site of Canada
454 Whipple St., Saint John, NB E2M 2R3
Tel: 506-636-4011; *Fax:* 506-636-4574
TTY: 506-887-6015
fundy.info@pc.gc.ca
www.pc.gc.ca/lhn-nhs/nb/standrews/index.aspx
Other Communication: Summer: 506-529-4270

St. Peters Canada National Historic Site of Canada
160 Toulouse St., PO Box 8 St Peter's, NS B0E 3B0
Tel: 902-295-2069; *Fax:* 902-295-3496
information@pc.gc.ca
www.pc.gc.ca/lhn-nhs/ns/stpeters/index.aspx
Other Communication: Summer Phone: 902-535-2118
twitter.com/ParksCanada_NS
www.facebook.com/StPetersCanal

Signal Hill National Historic Site of Canada
PO Box 1268 St. John's, NL A1C 5M9
Tel: 709-772-5367; *Fax:* 709-772-6302
signal.hill@pc.gc.ca
www.pc.gc.ca/lhn-nhs/nl/signalhill/index.aspx
twitter.com/ParksCanadaNL
www.facebook.com/SignalHillNHS

Terra Nova National Park of Canada
General Delivery, Glovertown, NL A0G 2L0
Tel: 709-533-2801; *Fax:* 709-533-2706
info.tnnp@pc.gc.ca
www.pc.gc.ca/pn-np/nl/terranova/index.aspx
twitter.com/ParksCanadaNL
www.facebook.com/TerraNovaNP

York Redoubt National Historic Site of Canada
c/o Halifax Citadel National Historic Site, PO Box 9080 Stn. A, Halifax, NS B3K 5M7
Tel: 902-426-5080; *Fax:* 902-426-4228
halifax.citadel@pc.gc.ca
www.pc.gc.ca/lhn-nhs/ns/york/index.aspx
twitter.com/ParksCanada_NS

Ontario National Parks/National Historic Sites

Battle of the Windmill National Historic Site of Canada
370 Vankoughnet St., PO Box 479 Prescott, ON K0E 1T0
Tel: 613-925-2896; *Fax:* 613-925-1536
ont.wellington@pc.gc.ca
www.pc.gc.ca/lhn-nhs/on/windmill/index.aspx

Bellevue House National Historic Site of Canada
35 Centre St., Kingston, ON K7L 4E5
Tel: 613-545-8666; *Fax:* 613-545-8721
bellevue.house@pc.gc.ca
www.pc.gc.ca/lhn-nhs/on/bellevue/index.aspx

Bethune Memorial House National Historic Site of Canada
235 John St. North, Gravenhurst, ON P1P 1G4
Tel: 705-687-4261; *Fax:* 705-687-4935
ont-bethune@pc.gc.ca
www.pc.gc.ca/lhn-nhs/on/bethune/index.aspx

Bois Blanc Island Lighthouse National Historic Site of Canada
c/o Fort Malden N.H.S., 100 Laird Ave., PO Box 38 Amherstburg, ON N9V 2Z2
Tel: 519-736-5416; *Fax:* 519-736-6603
ont.fort-malden@pc.gc.ca
www.pc.gc.ca/lhn-nhs/on/boisblanc/index.aspx
www.facebook.com/FortMaldenNHS

Bruce Peninsula National Park
PO Box 189 Tobermory, ON N0H 2R0
Tel: 519-596-2233; *Fax:* 519-596-2298
bruce-fathomfive@pc.gc.ca
www.pc.gc.ca/pn-np/on/bruce/index.aspx
twitter.com/BrucePNP
www.facebook.com/BrucePeninsulaNP

Butler's Barracks c/o Fort George National Historic Site
c/o Niagara National Historic Sites, 26 Queen St., PO Box 787 Niagara-on-the-Lake, ON L0S 1J0
Tel: 905-468-6614; *Fax:* 905-468-8523
ont-niagara@pc.gc.ca
www.pc.gc.ca/lhn-nhs/on/fortgeorge/index.aspx
twitter.com/FortGeorgeNHS
www.facebook.com/FortGeorgeNHS

Fort George National Historic Site of Canada
c/o Niagara National Historic Sites, 26 Queen St., PO Box 787 Niagara-on-the-Lake, ON L0S 1J0
Tel: 905-468-6614; *Fax:* 905-468-8523
ont-niagara@pc.gc.ca
www.pc.gc.ca/lhn-nhs/on/fortgeorge/index.aspx
twitter.com/FortGeorgeNHS
www.facebook.com/FortGeorgeNHS

Fathom Five National Marine Park of Canada
PO Box 189 Tobermory, ON N0H 2R0
Tel: 519-596-2233; *Fax:* 519-596-2298
bruce-fathomfive@pc.gc.ca
www.pc.gc.ca/eng/amnc-nmca/on/fathomfive/index.aspx
twitter.com/BrucePNP
www.facebook.com/BrucePeninsulaNP

Fort Malden National Historic Site
100 Laird Ave., PO Box 38 Amherstburg, ON N9V 2Z2
Tel: 519-736-5416; *Fax:* 519-736-6603
ont.fort-malden@pc.gc.ca
www.pc.gc.ca/eng/lhn-nhs/on/malden/index.aspx
www.facebook.com/FortMaldenNHS

Fort Mississauga c/o Fort George National Historic Site
c/o Niagara National Historic Sites, 26 Queen St., PO Box 787 Niagara on the Lake, ON L0S 1J0
Tel: 905-468-6614; *Fax:* 905-468-8523
ont-niagara@pc.gc.ca
www.pc.gc.ca/lhn-nhs/on/fortgeorge/natcul/natcul2b.aspx

Fort St. Joseph National Historic Site of Canada
PO Box 220 Richards Landing, ON P0R 1J0
Tel: 705-246-2664; *Fax:* 705-246-1796
fortstjoseph-info@pc.gc.ca
www.pc.gc.ca/lhn-nhs/on/stjoseph.aspx
twitter.com/FortStJosephNHS
www.facebook.com/FortStJosephNHS

Fort Wellington National Historic Site of Canada
PO Box 479 Prescott, ON K0E 1T0
Tel: 613-925-2896; *Fax:* 613-925-1536
TTY: 613-925-2896
ont-wellington@pc.gc.ca
www.pc.gc.ca/lhn-nhs/on/wellington.aspx

Georgian Bay Islands National Park of Canada
901 Wye Valley Rd., PO Box 9 Midland, ON L4R 4K6
Tel: 705-527-7200; *Fax:* 705-526-5939
info.gbi@pc.gc.ca
www.pc.gc.ca/eng/pn-np/on/georg/index.aspx
twitter.com/GBINP

Inverarden House National Historic Site of Canada
370 Vankoughnet St., PO Box 479 Prescott, ON K0E 1T0
Tel: 613-925-2896; *Fax:* 613-925-1536
ont-wellington@pc.gc.ca
www.pc.gc.ca/lhn-nhs/on/inverarden/index.aspx

Kingston Martello Towers
c/o Bellevue House N.H.S., 35 Centre St., Kingston, ON K7L 4E5
Tel: 613-545-8666; *Fax:* 613-545-8721
Bellevue.House@pc.gc.ca
www.pc.gc.ca/lhn-nhs/on/bellevue/index.aspx

Laurier House National Historic Site of Canada
335 Laurier Ave. East, Ottawa, ON K1A 6R4
Tel: 613-992-8142; *Fax:* 613-947-4851
laurier-house@pc.gc.ca
www.pc.gc.ca/lhn-nhs/on/laurier.aspx

Point Clark Lighthouse National Historic Site of Canada
c/o Georgian Bay Islands National Park of Canada, 901 Wye Valley Rd., PO Box 9 Midland, ON L4R 4K6
Tel: 705-526-9804; *Fax:* 705-526-5939
www.pc.gc.ca/lhn-nhs/on/clark.aspx

Point Pelee National Park of Canada
407 Monarch Lane, RR#1, Leamington, ON N8H 3V4
Tel: 519-322-2365; *Fax:* 519-322-1277
Toll-Free: 888-773-8888
TTY: 866-787-6221
pelee.info@pc.gc.ca
www.pc.gc.ca/fra/pn-np/on/pelee.aspx
twitter.com/PointPeleeNP
www.facebook.com/PointPeleeNP

Pukaskwa National Park of Canada
PO Box 212 Heron Bay, ON P0T 1R0
Tel: 807-229-0801; *Fax:* 807-229-2097
ont-pukaskwa@pc.gc.ca
www.pc.gc.ca/pn-np/on/pukaskwa.aspx
twitter.com/PukaskwaNP
www.facebook.com/PukaskwaNP

Queenston Heights & Brock's Monument
14184 Niagara River Pky., Niagara-on-the-Lake, ON L0S 1J0
Tel: 905-262-4759
ont-niagara@pc.gc.ca
www.pc.gc.ca/lhn-nhs/on/queenston/index.aspx
twitter.com/FortGeorgeNHS
www.facebook.com/FortGeorgeNHS

Rouge National Urban Park
105 Guildwood Parkway, PO Box 11024 Toronto, ON M1E 1N0
Tel: 416-264-2020; *Fax:* 416-264-2167
rouge@pc.gc.ca
www.pc.gc.ca/en/pn-np/on/rouge
twitter.com/rougepark
www.facebook.com/rougeNUP

St. Lawrence Islands National Park of Canada
2 County Rd. 5, RR#3, Mallorytown, ON K0E 1R0
Tel: 613-923-5261; *Fax:* 613-923-1021
ont-sli@pc.gc.ca
www.pc.gc.ca/pn-np/on/lawren/index.aspx
twitter.com/TINationalPark
www.facebook.com/TINationalPark

Sir John Johnson National Historic Site of Canada
c/o Fort Wellington National Historic Site, 370 Vanhoughnet St., PO Box 479 Prescott, ON K0E 1T0
Tel: 613-925-2896; *Fax:* 613-925-1536
ont.wellington@pc.gc.ca
www.pc.gc.ca/lhn-nhs/on/johnjohnson/index.aspx
Other Communication: Sir John Johnson Manor House Committee, Phone: 613-347-2356; Email: sirjohnjohnson@sympatico.ca

Woodside National Historic Site of Canada
528 Wellington St. North, Kitchener, ON N2H 5L5
Tel: 519-571-5684; *Fax:* 519-571-5686
Toll-Free: 888-773-8888
ont-woodside@pc.gc.ca
www.pc.gc.ca/lhn-nhs/on/woodside/index.aspx
twitter.com/ParksCanada
www.facebook.com/WoodsideNHS

Québec National Parks/National Historic Sites

Artillery Park c/o Fortifications of Québec National Historic Site of Canada
2, rue d'Auteuil, Québec, QC G1R 5C2
Tél: 418-648-7016
Ligne sans frais: 888-773-8888
TTY: 866-787-6221
information@pc.gc.ca
www.pc.gc.ca/lhn-nhs/qc/fortifications/index.aspx

Battle of the Châteauguay National Historic Site of Canada
2371, rue Rivière Châteauguay, Howick, QC J0S 1G0
Tél: 450-829-2003
Téléc: 450-829-3325
bataille.chateauguay@pc.gc.ca
www.pc.gc.ca/lhn-nhs/qc/chateauguay/index.aspx
Autres nombres: Hors saison: 819-423-6965

Battle of the Restigouche National Historic Site of Canada
Rte 132, CP 359 Pointe-à-la-Croix, QC G0C 1L0
Tél: 418-788-5676
Téléc: 418-788-5895
Ligne sans frais: 888-773-8888
TTY: 866-787-6221
information@pc.gc.ca
www.pc.gc.ca/lhn-nhs/qc/ristigouche.aspx

Carillon Barracks National Historic Site of Canada
308A, ch du Fleuve, Coteau-du-Lac, QC J0P 1B0
Tél: 450-763-5631
Téléc: 450-763-1654
Ligne sans frais: 888-773-8888
TTY: 866-787-6221
information@pc.gc.ca
www.pc.gc.ca/lhn-nhs/qc/carillon/index.aspx
Autres nombres: Hors saison: 819-423-6965

Cartier-Brébeuf National Historic Site of Canada
2, rue D'Auteuil, Québec, QC G1R 5C2
Tél: 418-648-7016
Ligne sans frais: 888-773-8888
TTY: 866-787-6221
information@pc.gc.ca
www.pc.gc.ca/lhn-nhs/qc/cartierbrebeuf.aspx

Coteau-du-Lac National Historic Site of Canada
308A, ch du Fleuve, Coteau-du-Lac, QC J0P 1B0
Tél: 450-763-5631
Ligne sans frais: 888-773-8888
TTY: 866-787-6221
reservations.coteau@pc.gc.ca
www.pc.gc.ca/lhn-nhs/qc/coteaudulac.aspx

Forges du Saint-Maurice National Historic Site of Canada
10000, boul des Forges, Trois-Rivières, QC G9C 1B1
Tél: 819-378-5116
Ligne sans frais: 888-773-8888
information@pc.gc.ca
www.pc.gc.ca/lhn-nhs/qc/saintmaurice.aspx
Autres nombres: Hors saison: 514-283-2282

Forillon National Park of Canada
122, boul Gaspé, Gaspé, QC G4X 1A9
Tél: 418-368-5505
Téléc: 418-368-6837
Ligne sans frais: 888-773-8888
TTY: 866-787-6221
information@pc.gc.ca
www.pc.gc.ca/pn-np/qc/forillon.aspx
twitter.com/ForillonNP
www.facebook.com/ForillonNP

Fort Chambly National Historic Site of Canada
2, rue de Richelieu, Chambly, QC J3L 2B9
Tél: 450-658-1585
Téléc: 450-658-7216
Ligne sans frais: 888-773-8888
TTY: 866-787-6221
information@pc.gc.ca
www.pc.gc.ca/lhn-nhs/qc/fortchambly/index.aspx

Fort Lennox National Historic Site of Canada
1, 61e av, St-Paul-de-l'Ile-aux-Noix, QC J0J 1G0
Tél: 450-291-5700
Téléc: 450-291-4389
Ligne sans frais: 888-773-8888
information@pc.gc.ca
www.pc.gc.ca/lhn-nhs/qc/lennox.aspx
Autres nombres: Hors saison: 450-658-1585

Fort Témiscamingue National Historic Site of Canada
834, ch du Vieux-Fort, Duhamel ouest, QC J9V 1N7
Tél: 819-629-3222
Téléc: 819-629-2977
Ligne sans frais: 888-773-8888
TTY: 866-787-6221
information@pc.gc.ca
www.pc.gc.ca/fra/lhn-nhs/qc/temiscamingue.aspx
Autres nombres: Hors saison: 514-283-2282

Fortifications of Québec National Historic Site of Canada
2, rue d'Auteuil, Québec, QC G1R 5C2
Tél: 418-648-7016
Ligne sans frais: 888-773-8888
TTY: 866-787-6221
information@pc.gc.ca
www.pc.gc.ca/lhn-nhs/qc/fortifications/index.aspx

Grosse île & the Irish Memorial National Historic Site of Canada
2, rue D'Auteuil, Québec, QC G1R 5C2
Tél: 418-234-8841
Téléc: 866-790-8991
Ligne sans frais: 888-773-8888
TTY: 866-787-6221
information@pc.gc.ca
www.pc.gc.ca/lhn-nhs/qc/grosseile/index.aspx

La Mauricie National Park of Canada
702, 5e rue, Shawinigan, QC G9N 1E9
Tél: 819-538-3232
Téléc: 819-536-3661
Ligne sans frais: 888-773-8888
information@pc.gc.ca
www.pc.gc.ca/fra/pn-np/qc/mauricie.aspx
www.facebook.com/MauricieNP

Lévis Forts National Historic Site of Canada
41, ch du Gouvernement, Québec, QC G1R 5C2
Tél: 418-835-5182
Téléc: 418-948-9119
Ligne sans frais: 888-773-8888
information@pc.gc.ca
www.pc.gc.ca/lhn-nhs/qc/levis/index.aspx

Louis S. St-Laurent National Historic Site of Canada
6790, rte Louis-St-Laurent, Compton, QC J0B 1L0
Tél: 819-835-5448
Téléc: 819-835-9101
Ligne sans frais: 888-773-8888
TTY: 866-787-6221
information@pc.gc.ca
www.pc.gc.ca/fra/lhn-nhs/qc/stlaurent.aspx
Autres nombres: Hors saison: 450-658-1585

Manoir Papineau National Historic Site of Canada
500, rue Notre-Dame, Montebello, QC J0V 1L0
Tél: 819-423-6965
Téléc: 819-423-6455
Ligne sans frais: 888-773-8888
TTY: 866-787-6221
manoir.papineau@pc.gc.ca
www.pc.gc.ca/fra/lhn-nhs/qc/manoirpapineau/index.aspx

Mingan Archipelago National Park Reserve of Canada
1340, rue de la Digue, Havre-Saint-Pierre, QC G0G 1P0
Tél: 418-538-3331
Téléc: 418-538-3595
information@pc.gc.ca
www.pc.gc.ca/pn-np/qc/mingan.aspx
Autres nombres: Information et / ou réservations: 418-538-3285;
418-949-2126
twitter.com/MinganNPR
www.facebook.com/MinganNPR

Pointe-au-Père Lighthouse National Historic Site of Canada
1034, rue du Phare, Pointe-au-Père, QC G5M 1L8
Tél: 418-368-5505
Ligne sans frais: 888-773-8888
TTY: 866-787-6221
information@pc.gc.ca
www.pc.gc.ca/lhn-nhs/qc/pointaupere/index.aspx

Saguenay St. Lawrence Marine Park of Canada
182, rte de l'Église, Tadoussac, QC G0T 2A0
Tél: 418-235-4703
Téléc: 418-235-4686
info.marinepark@pc.gc.ca
www.pc.gc.ca/amnc-nmca/qc/saguenay/default.aspx

Sir George-Étienne Cartier National Historic Site of Canada
458, rue Notre-Dame est, Montréal, QC H2Y 1C8
Tél: 514-283-2282
Téléc: 514-283-5560
Ligne sans frais: 888-773-8888
TTY: 866-558-2950
information@pc.gc.ca
www.pc.gc.ca/lhn-nhs/qc/etiennecartier.aspx

Sir Wilfrid Laurier National Historic Site of Canada
945, 12e av, St-Lin-Laurentides, QC J5M 2W4
Tél: 450-439-3702
Téléc: 450-439-5721
Ligne sans frais: 888-773-8888
TTY: 866-787-6221
reservations.wilfridlaurier@pc.gc.ca
www.pc.gc.ca/fra/lhn-nhs/qc/wilfridlaurier.aspx
Autres nombres: Hors saison: 819-423-6965

The Fur Trade at Lachine National Historic Site of Canada
1255, boul Saint-Joseph, Lachine, QC H8S 2M2
Tél: 514-637-7433
Téléc: 514-637-5325
information@pc.gc.ca
www.pc.gc.ca/lhn-nhs/qc/lachine/index.aspx
Autres nombres: Hors saison: 514-283-2282

Western & Northern Canada National Parks/National Historic Sites

Aulavik National Park of Canada
PO Box 29 Sachs Harbour, NT X0E 0Z0
Tel: 867-777-8800; *Fax:* 867-777-8820
www.pc.gc.ca/pn-np/nt/aulavik/index_e.asp

Auyuittuq National Park of Canada
PO Box 353 Pangnirtung, NU X0A 0R0
Tel: 867-473-2500; *Fax:* 867-473-8612
nunavut.info@pc.gc.ca
www.pc.gc.ca/pn-np/nu/auyuittuq/index_e.asp
twitter.com/ParksCanNunavut
www.facebook.com/ParksCanadaNunavut

Banff National Park of Canada
PO Box 900 Banff, AB T1L 1K2
Tel: 403-762-1550; *Fax:* 403-762-1551
banff.vrc@pc.gc.ca
www.pc.gc.ca/pn-np/ab/banff/index_e.asp
twitter.com/banffnp
www.facebook.com/BanffNP
www.youtube.com/view_play_list?p=7ABD4B2249F753EB

Banff Park Museum National Historic Site of Canada
PO Box 900 Banff, AB T1L 1K2
Tel: 403-762-1558; *Fax:* 403-762-1565
banff.vrc@pc.gc.ca
www.pc.gc.ca/eng/lhn-nhs/ab/banff/index.aspx

Bar U Ranch National Historic Site of Canada
PO Box 168 Longview, AB T0L 1H0
Tel: 403-395-2212; *Fax:* 403-395-2331
BarU.Info@pc.gc.ca
www.pc.gc.ca/lhn-nhs/ab/baru/index_e.asp

Batoche National Historic Site of Canada
RR#1 Box 1040, Wakaw, SK S0K 4P0
Tel: 306-423-6227; *Fax:* 306-423-5400
TTY: 306-423-5540
batoche.info@pc.gc.ca
www.pc.gc.ca/eng/lhn-nhs/sk/batoche/index.aspx
twitter.com/parkscanada_sk
www.facebook.com/saskNHS

Cave & Basin National Historic Site of Canada
PO Box 900 Banff, AB T1L 1K2
Tel: 403-762-1566; *Fax:* 403-762-1565
caveandbasin@pc.gc.ca
pc.gc.ca/eng/lhn-nhs/ab/caveandbasin/index.aspx

Chilkoot Trail National Historic Site of Canada
#205, 300 Main St., Whitehorse, YT Y1A 2B5
Tel: 867-667-3910; *Fax:* 867-393-6701
Toll-Free: 800-661-0486
whitehorse.info@pc.gc.ca
www.pc.gc.ca/lhn-nhs/yt/chilkoot/index_e.asp
twitter.com/ParksCanYukon
www.facebook.com/ParksCanadaYukon

Dawson Historical Complex National Historic Site of Canada
PO Box 390 Dawson City, YT Y0B 1G0
Tel: 867-993-7200; *Fax:* 867-993-7203
dawson.info@pc.gc.ca
www.pc.gc.ca/lhn-nhs/yt/klondike.aspx
twitter.com/ParksCanYukon
www.facebook.com/ParksCanadaYukon

Dredge No. 4 National Historic Site of Canada
PO Box 390 Dawson City, YT Y0B 1G0
Tel: 867-993-7200; *Fax:* 867-993-7203
dawson.info@pc.gc.ca
www.pc.gc.ca/lhn-nhs/yt/klondike.aspx
twitter.com/ParksCanYukon
www.facebook.com/ParksCanadaYukon

Elk Island National Park of Canada
#1, 54401 Range Road 203, Fort Saskatchewan, AB T8L 0V3
Tel: 780-992-5790; *Fax:* 780-992-2951
elk.island@pc.gc.ca
www.pc.gc.ca/pn-np/ab/elkisland/index_e.asp
twitter.com/ElkIslandNP
www.facebook.com/ParksCanada

Fisgard Lighthouse National Historic Site of Canada
603 Fort Rodd Hill Rd., Victoria, BC V9C 2W8
Tel: 250-478-5849; *Fax:* 250-478-2816
fort.rodd@pc.gc.ca
www.pc.gc.ca/lhn-nhs/bc/fisgard/index_e.asp
twitter.com/FortRoddFisgard
www.facebook.com/FortRoddFisgardNHS

Fort Battleford National Historic Site of Canada
PO Box 70 Battleford, SK S0M 0E0
Tel: 306-937-2621; *Fax:* 306-937-3370
TTY: 306-937-3199
battleford.info@pc.gc.ca
www.pc.gc.ca/lhn-nhs/sk/battleford/index_e.asp
twitter.com/parkscanada_sk
www.facebook.com/saskNHS

Fort Langley National Historic Site of Canada
23433 Mavis Ave., PO Box 129 Fort Langley, BC V1M 2R5
Tel: 604-513-4777; *Fax:* 604-513-4798
fort.langley@pc.gc.ca
www.pc.gc.ca/lhn-nhs/bc/langley/index_e.asp
twitter.com/FortLangleyNHS
www.facebook.com/FortLangleyNHS

Fort Rodd Hill National Historic Site of Canada
603 Fort Rodd Hill Rd., Victoria, BC V9C 2W8
Tel: 250-478-5849; *Fax:* 250-478-2816
fort.rodd@pc.gc.ca
www.pc.gc.ca/lhn-nhs/bc/fortroddhill/index_e.asp
twitter.com/FortRoddFisgard
www.facebook.com/FortRoddFisgardNHS

Fort St. James National Historic Site of Canada
PO Box 1148 Fort St James, BC V0J 1P0
Tel: 250-996-7191; *Fax:* 250-996-8566
stjames@pc.gc.ca
www.pc.gc.ca/lhn-nhs/bc/stjames/index_e.asp

Fort Walsh National Historic Site of Canada
PO Box 278 Maple Creek, SK S0N 1N0
Tel: 306-662-3590; *Fax:* 306-662-2711
TTY: 306-662-3124
fort.walsh@pc.gc.ca
www.pc.gc.ca/eng/lhn-nhs/sk/walsh/index.aspx
Other Communication: Administration: 306-662-2645
twitter.com/parkscanada_sk
www.facebook.com/saskNHS

Gitwangak Battle Hill National Historic Site of Canada
PO Box 37 Queen Charlotte, BC V0T 1S0
Tel: 250-559-8818; *Fax:* 250-559-8366
TTY: 250-559-8139
gwaii.haanas@pc.gc.ca
www.pc.gc.ca/lhn-nhs/bc/kitwanga/index_E.asp

Glacier National Park of Canada
PO Box 350 Revelstoke, BC V0E 2S0
Tel: 250-837-7500; *Fax:* 250-837-7536
TTY: 866-787-6221
www.pc.gc.ca/pn-np/bc/glacier/index_e.asp
www.facebook.com/MRGnationalparks

Grasslands National Park of Canada
PO Box 150 Val Marie, SK S0N 2T0
Tel: 306-476-2018; *Fax:* 306-298-2042
Toll-Free: 877-345-2257
grasslands.info@pc.gc.ca
www.pc.gc.ca/eng/pn-np/sk/grasslands/index.aspx
twitter.com/parkscanada_sk
www.facebook.com/grasslandsNP

Gulf Islands National Park Reserve of Canada
2220 Harbour Rd., Sidney, BC V8L 2P6
Tel: 250-654-4000; *Fax:* 250-654-4014
Toll-Free: 866-944-1744
gulf.islands@pc.gc.ca
www.pc.gc.ca/pn-np/bc/gulf/index_E.asp
twitter.com/GulfIslandsNPR
www.facebook.com/GulfIslandsNPR

Gulf of Georgia Cannery National Historic Site of Canada
12138 - 4 Ave., Richmond, BC V7E 3J1
Tel: 604-664-9009; *Fax:* 604-664-9008
gog.info@pc.gc.ca
www.pc.gc.ca/lhn-nhs/bc/georgia/index_e.asp

Gwaii Haanas National Park Reserve & Haida Heritage Site of Canada
Haida Heritage Centre, 60 Second Beach Rd., PO Box 37
Queen Charlotte, BC V0T 1S0
Tel: 250-559-8818; *Fax:* 250-559-8366
Toll-Free: 877-559-8818
gwaii.haanas@pc.gc.ca
www.pc.gc.ca/gwaiihaanas
www.facebook.com/GwaiiHaanas

Ivvavik National Park of Canada
PO Box 1840 Inuvik, NT X0E 0T0
Tel: 867-777-8800; *Fax:* 867-777-8820
inuvik.info@pc.gc.ca
www.pc.gc.ca/pn-np/yt/ivvavik/index_e.asp

Jasper National Park of Canada
PO Box 10 Jasper, AB T0E 1E0
Tel: 780-852-6176; *Fax:* 780-852-1865
pnj.jnp@pc.gc.ca
www.pc.gc.ca/pn-np/ab/jasper/index_e.asp
twitter.com/JasperNP
www.facebook.com/JasperNP

Kluane National Park & Reserve of Canada
PO Box 5495 Haines Junction, YT Y0B 1L0
Tel: 867-634-7207; *Fax:* 867-634-7208
kluane.info@pc.gc.ca
www.pc.gc.ca/pn-np/yt/kluane/index_e.asp
twitter.com/ParksCanYukon
www.facebook.com/ParksCanadaYukon

Kootenay National Park of Canada
PO Box 220 Radium Hot Springs, BC V0A 1M0
Tel: 250-347-9505
Toll-Free: 888-773-8888
kootenay.info@pc.gc.ca
www.pc.gc.ca/pn-np/bc/kootenay/index_e.asp
twitter.com/KootenayNP
www.facebook.com/KootenayNP

Lower Fort Garry National Historic Site of Canada
5925 Highway 9, St. Andrews, MB R1A 4A8
Tel: 204-785-6050; *Fax:* 204-482-5887
Toll-Free: 888-773-8888
TTY: 866-787-6221
lfg.info@pc.gc.ca
www.pc.gc.ca/lhn-nhs/mb/fortgarry/index_e.asp
twitter.com/ParksCanadaWPG
www.facebook.com/ParksCanadaWPG

Motherwell Homestead National Historic Site of Canada
PO Box 70 Abernethy, SK S0A 0A0
Tel: 306-333-2116; *Fax:* 306-333-2210
Motherwell.Homestead@pc.gc.ca
www.pc.gc.ca/eng/lhn-nhs/sk/motherwell/index.aspx
twitter.com/parkscanada_sk
www.facebook.com/saskNHS

Mount Revelstoke National Park of Canada
PO Box 350 Revelstoke, BC V0E 2S0
Tel: 250-837-7500; *Fax:* 250-837-7536
TTY: 866-787-6221
www.pc.gc.ca/pn-np/bc/revelstoke/index_e.asp
www.facebook.com/MRGnationalparks

Nahanni National Park Reserve of Canada
10002 - 100 St., PO Box 348 Fort Simpson, NT X0E 0N0
Tel: 867-695-7750; *Fax:* 867-695-2446
nahanni.info@pc.gc.ca
www.pc.gc.ca/pn-np/nt/nahanni/index_e.asp

Pacific Rim National Park Reserve of Canada
2040 Pacific Rim Hwy., PO Box 280 Ucluelet, BC V0R 3A0
Tel: 250-726-3500; *Fax:* 250-726-3520
pacrim.info@pc.gc.ca
www.pc.gc.ca/pn-np/bc/pacificrim/index_e.asp
twitter.com/pacificrimNPR
www.facebook.com/PacificRimNPR

Prince Albert National Park of Canada
PO Box 100 Waskesiu Lake, SK S0J 2Y0
Tel: 306-663-4522
panp.info@pc.gc.ca
www.pc.gc.ca/eng/pn-np/sk/princealbert/index.aspx
twitter.com/parkscanada_sk

Prince of Wales Fort National Historic Site of Canada
PO Box 127 Churchill, MB R0B 0E0
Tel: 204-675-8863; *Fax:* 204-675-2026
TTY: 866-787-6221
mannorth.nhs@pc.gc.ca
www.pc.gc.ca/lhn-nhs/mb/prince/index_e.asp

Qausuittuq National Park of Canada
nunavut.info@pc.gc.ca
twitter.com/ParksCanNunavut
www.facebook.com/ParksCanadaNunavut

Quttinirpaaq National Park of Canada
PO Box 278 Iqaluit, NU X0A 0H0
Tel: 867-975-4673; *Fax:* 867-975-4674
nunavut.info@pc.gc.ca
www.pc.gc.ca/pn-np/nu/quttinirpaaq/index_e.asp
twitter.com/ParksCanNunavut
www.facebook.com/ParksCanadaNunavut

Riding Mountain National Park of Canada
PO Box 299 Onanole, MB R0J 2H0
Tel: 204-848-7275; *Fax:* 204-848-2596
rmnp.info@pc.gc.ca
www.pc.gc.ca/pn-np/mb/riding/index_e.asp
twitter.com/@RidingNP
www.facebook.com/RidingNP

Riel House National Historic Site of Canada
330 River Rd. (St. Vidal), Winnipeg, MB R1A 3Y3
Tel: 204-983-6757; *Fax:* 204-984-0679
TTY: 866-787-6221
riel.info@pc.gc.ca
www.pc.gc.ca/lhn-nhs/mb/riel/index_E.asp
twitter.com/ParksCanadaWPG
www.facebook.com/ParksCanadaWPG

Rocky Mountain House National Historic Site of Canada
Site 127, Comp 6, RR#4, Rocky Mountain House, AB T4T 2A4
Tel: 403-845-2412; *Fax:* 403-845-5320
rocky.info@pc.gc.ca
www.pc.gc.ca/lhn-nhs/ab/rockymountain/index_E.asp

Sirmilik National Park of Canada
PO Box 300 Pond Inlet, NU X0A 0S0
Tel: 867-899-8092; *Fax:* 867-899-8104
sirmilik.info@pc.gc.ca
www.pc.gc.ca/pn-np/nu/sirmilik/index_e.asp
twitter.com/ParksCanNunavut
www.facebook.com/ParksCanadaNunavut

SS Keno National Historic Site of Canada
PO Box 390 Dawson City, YT Y0B 1G0
Tel: 867-993-7200; *Fax:* 867-993-7203
dawson.info@pc.gc.ca
www.pc.gc.ca/lhn-nhs/yt/sskeno/index_e.asp
twitter.com/ParksCanYukon
www.facebook.com/ParksCanadaYukon

SS Klondike National Historic Site of Canada
#205, 300 Main St., Whitehorse, YT Y1A 2B5
Tel: 867-667-3910; *Fax:* 867-393-6701
Toll-Free: 800-661-0486
whitehorse.info@pc.gc.ca
www.pc.gc.ca/lhn-nhs/yt/ssklondike/index_E.asp
Other Communication: Summer: 867-667-4511
twitter.com/ParksCanYukon
www.facebook.com/ParksCanadaYukon

St. Andrews Rectory National Historic Site of Canada
374, chemin River, St. Andrews, MB R1A 2Y1
Tel: 204-785-6050; *Fax:* 204-482-5887
Toll-Free: 888-773-8888
TTY: 866-787-6221
lfg.info@pc.gc.ca
www.pc.gc.ca/lhn-nhs/mb/standrews/contact_e.asp

The Forks National Historic Site of Canada
Manitoba Field Unit, 145 McDermot Ave., Winnipeg, MB R3B 0R9
Tel: 204-983-6757; *Fax:* 204-984-0679
Toll-Free: 888-773-8888
TTY: 866-787-6221
forks.fourche@pc.gc.ca
www.pc.gc.ca/lhn-nhs/mb/forks/index_e.asp
twitter.com/ParksCanadaWPG
www.facebook.com/ParksCanadaWPG

Tuktut Nogait National Park of Canada
PO Box 91 Paulatuk, NT X0E 1N0
Tel: 867-580-3233; *Fax:* 867-580-3234
inuvik.info@pc.gc.ca
www.pc.gc.ca/pn-np/nt/tuktutnogait/index_e.asp

Ukkusiksalik National Park of Canada
PO Box 220 Repulse Bay, NU X0C 0H0
Tel: 867-462-4500; *Fax:* 867-462-4095
ukkusiksalik.info@pc.gc.ca
www.pc.gc.ca/pn-np/nu/ukkusiksalik/index_E.asp
twitter.com/ParksCanNunavut
www.facebook.com/ParksCanadaNunavut

Vuntut National Park of Canada
PO Box 19 Old Crow, YT Y0B 1N0
Tel: 867-667-3910; *Fax:* 867-393-6701
vuntut.info@pc.gc.ca
www.pc.gc.ca/pn-np/yt/vuntut/index_E.asp
twitter.com/ParksCanYukon
www.facebook.com/ParksCanadaYukon

Wapusk National Park of Canada
Churchill Office, PO Box 127 Churchill, MB R0B 0E0
Tel: 204-675-8863; *Fax:* 204-675-2026
Toll-Free: 888-773-8888
TTY: 866-787-6221
wapusk.np@pc.gc.ca
www.pc.gc.ca/pn-np/mb/wapusk/index_e.asp

Waterton Lakes National Park of Canada
PO Box 200 Waterton Park, AB T0K 2M0
Tel: 403-859-5133; *Fax:* 403-859-5152
waterton.info@pc.gc.ca
www.pc.gc.ca/pn-np/ab/waterton/index_E.asp
twitter.com/watertonlakesnp
www.facebook.com/WatertonLakesNP

Wood Buffalo National Park of Canada
PO Box 750 Fort Smith, NT X0E 0P0
Tel: 867-872-7900; *Fax:* 867-872-3910
TTY: 867-872-7961
wbnp.info@pc.gc.ca
www.pc.gc.ca/pn-np/nt/woodbuffalo/index_e.asp
Other Communication: 24 Hour Hotline: 867-872-7962

Yoho National Park of Canada
PO Box 99 Field, BC V0A 1G0
Tel: 250-343-6783
yoho.info@pc.gc.ca
www.pc.gc.ca/pn-np/bc/yoho/index_E.asp

York Factory National Historic Site of Canada
PO Box 127 Churchill, MB R0B 0E0
Tel: 204-675-8863; *Fax:* 204-675-2026
mannorth.nhs@pc.gc.ca
www.pc.gc.ca/lhn-nhs/mb/yorkfactory/index_E.asp

Parliamentary Budget Officer (PBO)

#919, 50 O'Connor St., Ottawa, ON K1A 0A9
Tel: 613-992-8026
pbo-dpb@parl.gc.ca
www.pbo-dpb.gc.ca
twitter.com/pbo_dpb
The PBO provides independent analysis to Parliament on the budget, estimates & other documents, as well as significant matters relating to the nation's finances or economy. The PBO will also estimate the financial cost of any parliamentary proposal, at the request of a committee or parliamentarian. Prior to an election, the PBO may also be asked to estimate the financial cost of a proposed election campaign.

Parliamentary Budget Officer, Yves Giroux

Deputy Parliamentary Budget Officer, Mostafa Askari
Mostafa.Askari@parl.gc.ca

Chief Financial Officer & Senior Director, Costing & Budgetary Analysis, Jason Jacques
Jason.Jacques@parl.gc.ca

Senior Director, Economic & Fiscal Analysis & Forecasting, Chris Matier
Chris.Matier@parl.gc.ca

Senior Director, Costing & Program Analysis, Peter Weltman

Parole Board of Canada (PBC) / Commission des libérations conditionnelles du Canada (CLCC)

Communications Division, National Office, 410 Laurier Ave. West, Ottawa, ON K1A 0R1
Tel: 613-954-7474; *Fax:* 613-941-4981
info@pbc-clcc.gc.ca
www.pbc-clcc.gc.ca
Other Communication: Record Suspension Information: 800-874-2652, suspension@pbc-clcc.gc.ca; Victim Information: 866-789-4636; Media Relations: 613-960-1856, media@pbc-clcc.gc.ca
www.youtube.com/user/PBCclcc
The Parole Board of Canada is an agency within the portfolio of Public Safety Canada. The chairperson of the Board reports to Parliament through Public Safety Canada.
The role of the Parole Board of Canada is to make independent, conditional release & record suspension decisions. The independent administrative tribunal is also responsible for making clemency recommendations. The Parole Board of Canada acts under the authority of the Corrections & Conditional Release Act & regulations, the Criminal Code of Canada, the Criminal Records Act & regulations, the Letters Patent, & the Privacy & Access to Information Acts.
The national office in Ottawa contains the Appeal Division of the Board. Regional offices are located throughout the country.

Chair, Jennifer Oades
Tel: 613-954-1154

Executive Director General, Daryl Churney
Tel: 613-954-1153

Chief Financial Officer, Chantal Lemyre
Tel: 613-954-7476

Director General, Policy & Operations Division, Suzanne Brisebois
Tel: 613-941-3380

Director, Public Affairs, Jennifer McNaughton
Tel: 613-954-6547

Acting Director, Record Suspension Program, Amélie Brisebois
Tel: 613-954-5973; *Fax:* 613-941-4981

Director, Clemency & Record Suspension, Denis Ladouceur
Tel: 613-954-5913; *Fax:* 613-941-4981

Director, Corporate Services, Eric McMullen
Tel: 613-954-7771; *Fax:* 613-957-7729

Director, Board Members Training & Development, Céline St-Onge
Tel: 613-954-5944; *Fax:* 613-941-6444
Other Communications: Alternate Phone: 613-608-7334

Patented Medicine Prices Review Board / Conseil d'examen du prix des médicaments brevetés

Standard Life Centre, #1400, 333 Laurier Ave. West, PO Box L40 Ottawa, ON K1P 1C1
Tel: 613-288-9597; *Fax:* 613-288-9643
Toll-Free: 877-861-2350
TTY: 613-288-9654
PMPRB.Information-Renseignements.CEPMB@pmprb-cepmb.g c.ca
www.pmprb-cepmb.gc.ca
twitter.com/PMPRB_CEPMB
The Patented Medicine Prices Review Board (PMPRB) is an independent quasi-judicial body established by Parliament in 1987 under the Patent Act (Act). The PMPRB is responsible for regulating the prices that patentees charge, the "factory-gate" price, for prescription & non-prescription patented drugs sold in Canada, to wholesalers, hospitals or pharmacies, for human and veterinary use to ensure that they are not excessive. The PMPRB regulates the price of each patented drug product, including each strength of each dosage form of each patented medicine sold in Canada.

Chair, Dr. Mitchell Levine
Tel: 613-288-9665

Executive Director, Douglas Clark
Tel: 613-288-9633

Director, Regulatory Affairs & Outreach, Guillaume Couillard
Tel: 613-288-9635; *Fax:* 613-288-9643

Polar Knowledge Canada (POLAR) / Savoir polaire Canada (POLAIRE)

#200, 170 Laurier Ave. West, 2nd Fl., Ottawa, ON K1P 5V5
Tel: 613-943-8605
info@polar.gc.ca
www.canada.ca/en/polar-knowledge
Other Communication: Archived Canadian Polar Commission, URL: www.polarcom.gc.ca; Communications, Phone: 613-292-1759; Email: communications@polar.gc.ca
Secondary Address: 1 Uvajuq Rd.
Canadian High Arctic Research Station CampusPO Box 2150 Sta.
Cambridge Bay, NU X0B 0C0
twitter.com/POLARCanada
www.facebook.com/PolarKnowledge
Polar Knowledge Canada was created in 2015, merging the mandate of the Canadian Polar Commission with the Canadian High Arctic Research Station (CHARS) initiative at Indigenous & Northern Affairs.
The former Canadian Polar Commission was mandated to enhance the public's awareness of polar regions & to foster both international & domestic liaison & cooperation in circumpolar research & technology development. One of the Commission's main objectives in the short term is focus on climate change & energy. Maintains the Canadian Polar Information System (CPIS) which, in addition to polar data & information, includes

services such as the Polar Science Forum, Researcher's Directory, Researcher's Toolbox, & links to International Partners. Research funding initiatives include the Scientific Committee on Antarctic Research (SCAR) Fellowship, Northern Scientific Training Program, & Canadian Northern Studies Trust.

Minister Responsible; Minister, Crown-Indigenous Relations, Hon. Marc Miller, P.C

President, David J. Scott, Ph.D
Tel: 613-943-8605

Policy Horizons Canada / Horizons de politiques Canada

360 Albert St., 15th Fl., Ottawa, ON K1R 7X7
Tel: 613-947-3800; *Fax:* 613-995-6006
questions@horizons.gc.ca
www.horizons.gc.ca
Other Communication: Media, Email: media@hrsdc-rhdcc.gc.ca
twitter.com/PolicyHorizons
www.linkedin.com/company/policy-horizons-canada
www.instagram.com/horizonscanada
Formerly known as the Policy Research Initiative, Policy Horizons Canada serves the deputy minister & federal policy communities within the government by providing insight & research to help policymakers create new policies at a faster, more productive rate.

Assistant Deputy Minister, Alexis Conrad

Executive Head, Kristel Van der Elst
Tel: 613-992-8059
kristel.vanderelst@horizons.gc.ca

Senior Director, Eric Ward
Tel: 343-550-4997
eric.ward@horizons.gc.ca

Chief Futurist, Peter Padbury
Tel: 613-943-8412
peter.padbury@horizons.gc.ca

Privacy Commissioner of Canada / Commissariat à la protection de la vie privée du Canada

30, rue Victoria, Gatineau, QC K1A 1H3
Tel: 819-994-5444; *Fax:* 819-994-5424
Toll-Free: 800-282-1376
TTY: 819-994-6591
www.priv.gc.ca
twitter.com/PrivacyPrivee
The Privacy Commissioner of Canada is an Officer of Parliament mandated to protect & promote privacy rights, working independently from Government, reporting directly to the House of Commons & the Senate. The Privacy Commissioner oversees two federal privacy laws: the Privacy Act, which covers the federal government, & the new Personal Information Protection & Electronic Documents (PIPEDA) Act, which covers the collection use & disclosure of personal information in the course of commercial activities, except in provinces which have not, by then, enacted legislation that is deemed to be substantially similar to the federal law. The Privacy Commissioner's powers include: investigating complaints & conducting audits under both federal privacy laws; publishing information about personal information handling practices in the public & private sectors; conducting research into privacy issues; & promoting awareness & understanding of privacy issues in Canada.

Privacy Commissioner, Daniel Therrien
Tel: 819-994-5841; *Fax:* 819-994-5424
Other Communications: Executive Assistant, Phone: 819-994-5835

Chief Financial Officer & Director General, Corporate Services Branch, Daniel Nadeau
Tel: 819-994-6503; *Fax:* 819-994-5424

Chief Privacy Officer & Director, Access to Information & Privacy, Johane Lessard
Tel: 819-994-5970; *Fax:* 819-994-5424

Director General, Communications Branch, Anne-Marie Hayden
Tel: 819-994-5581; *Fax:* 819-994-5424
Anne-Marie.Hayden@priv.gc.ca

Director General, PIPEDA Investigations Branch, Brent Homan
Tel: 819-994-6261; *Fax:* 819-994-5424

Director General & Senior General Counsel, Legal

- **Defence Construction Canada / Construction de Défense Canada**

See Entry Name Index for detailed listing.

- **Public Service Labour Relations Board (PSLREB) / Commission des relations de travail et de l'emploi dans la fonction publique (CRTEFP)**

CD Howe Building
240 Sparks St., 6th Fl.
PO Box 1525 B
Ottawa, ON K1P 5V2
Tel: 613-990-1800; *Fax:* 613-990-1849
Toll-free: 866-931-3454
TTY: 866-389-6901
mail.courrier@pslrb-crtfp.gc.ca
www.pslreb-crtefp.gc.ca
Other Communication: Jacob Finkelman Library: 613-990-1800; library-bibliotheque@pslrb-crtfp.gc.ca; Staffing Complaints: 613-949-6516; Fax: 613-949-6551; 866-637-4491

Independent, quasi-judicial statutory tribunal responsible for administering the collective bargaining & grievance adjudication systems in the federal Public & Parliamentary Service. Also provides mediation & conflict resolution services, compensation analysis & research services. The PSLREB was created with the merger of the Public Service Labour Relations Board (PSLRB) & the Public Service Staffing Tribunal (PSST) in November 2014.

Accounting, Banking & Compensation Branch / Direction générale de la comptabilité, gestion bancaire et rémunération

Responsible for managing the operations of the federal treasury, including issuing Receiver General payments for major government programs as well as maintaining the Accounts of Canada & producing the Government's financial statements. Responsible for providing government-wide accounting & reporting services. Directs the management & delivery of the administration of the public service pension & group insurance plans & maintains accounts for the various pension funds. Focuses in the financial management & control framework for the Department.

Assistant Deputy Minister, Accounting, Banking & Compensation, Brigitte Fortin
Tel: 819-420-5286; *Fax:* 819-934-0932
brigitte.fortin@tpsgc-pwgsc.gc.ca
Acting Director General, Central Accounting & Reporting Sector, Jean-René Drapeau
Tel: 819-420-5281; *Fax:* 819-956-8400
jean-rene.drapeau@tpsgc-pwgsc.gc.ca
Director General, Transformation of Pay Administration, Kristine Renic
Tel: 819-954-8394
kristine.renic@tpsgc-pwgsc.gc.ca
Acting Director General, Pension Modernization Project Directorate, Jeff Marcantonio
Tel: 613-948-6218; *Fax:* 613-952-7989
jeff.marcantonio@tpsgc-pwgsc.gc.ca
Director General, Compensation, Carrie Roussin
Tel: 819-956-0481; *Fax:* 819-956-3000
carrie.roussin@tpsgc-pwgsc.gc.ca
Director General, Government of Canada Pension Centre, David Stevens
Tel: 506-533-5555; *Fax:* 506-533-5607
david.stevens@pwgsc-tpsgc.gc.ca

Acquisitions Branch / Direction générale des approvisionnements

Provides departments & agencies with expert assistance at each stage of the supply cycle & offers tools that simplify & accelerate the acquisition of goods & services. It ensures that the government exercises due diligence & maintains the integrity of the procurement process. It is a primary service provider offering client departments a broad base of procurement solutions aimed at securing best value for their procurement dollar.

Assistant Deputy Minister, Vacant
Director General, Office of Small & Medium Enterprises & Strategic Engagement, Desmond Gray
Tel: 819-956-8416; *Fax:* 819-956-6859
desmond.gray@tpsgc-pwgsc.gc.ca
Director, Traffic Management Directorate, Jacques Amyot
Tel: 819-956-7301; *Fax:* 819-956-4644
jacques.amyot@tpsgc-pwgsc.gc.ca
Director General, Business Management Sector, Robin Dubeau
Tel: 819-420-1518
robin.dubeau@tpsgc-pwgsc.gc.ca
Director General, Policy, Risk, Integrity & Strategic Management Sector, Gail Bradshaw
Tel: 819-956-0299; *Fax:* 819-956-0355
gail.bradshaw@tpsgc-pwgsc.gc.ca
Director General, Marine Sector, Scott Leslie
Tel: 613-943-3338; *Fax:* 613-944-7870
scott.leslie@tpsgc-pwgsc.gc.ca
Director General, Defence Procurement, Washington Region, Lorna Prosper

Tel: 202-682-7604; *Fax:* 202-682-7613
Lorna.Prosper@tpsgc-pwgsc.gc.ca
Director General, Services & Technology Acquisition Management Sector, Normand Masse
Tel: 819-956-3937; *Fax:* 819-956-2675
normand.masse@tpsgc-pwgsc.gc.ca
Director General, Defence & Major Projects Sector, Cathy A. Sabiston
Tel: 819-956-0010; *Fax:* 819-956-9110
cathy.sabiston@tpsgc-pwgsc.gc.ca
Senior Director, Risk, Quality & Integrity Management Directorate, Matthew Sreter
Tel: 819-956-0920; *Fax:* 819-956-0400
matthew.sreter@tpsgc-pwgsc.gc.ca
Director General, Land & Aerospace Equipment Procurement & Support Sector, Sylvain Cyr
Tel: 819-956-7113; *Fax:* 819-956-5650
sylvain.cyr@tpsgc-pwgsc.gc.ca

Chief Information Officer Branch / Direction générale du dirigeant principal de l'information

Acting Chief Information Officer, Luc Lafrance
Tel: 819-420-5991
Luc.Lafrance@tpsgc-pwgsc.gc.ca
Senior Director, Enterprise Case & Information Management Solutions, Shannon Archibald
Tel: 819-420-5841
shannon.archibald@tpsgc-pwgsc.gc.ca
Director, Support Services Competency Centre, Mark Armstrong
Tel: 819-956-3508
Mark.Armstrong@tpsgc-pwgsc.gc.ca
Director General, Chief Technology Officer, Rachel Porteous
Tel: 819-956-4745
rachel.porteous@tpsgc-pwgsc.gc.ca
Director, IT Project Portfolio Management, Michael Bennett
Tel: 819-420-5847
michael.bennett@tpsgc-pwgsc.gc.ca
Senior Director, Enterprise Architecture & Innovation, Mark Steski
Tel: 819-956-3101
Mark.Steski@tpsgc-pwgsc.gc.ca
Director, Strategic Planning & Management Services, Philip Quinlan
Tel: 819-934-5125
Philip.Quinlan@tpsgc-pwgsc.gc.ca
Director General, Solution Design, John MacKenzie
Tel: 819-420-5740; *Fax:* 819-956-2960
john.mackenzie@tpsgc-pwgsc.gc.ca
Director, Shared Case Management System, Justin Blanchette
Tel: 613-513-5996
justin.blanchette@tpsgc-pwgsc.gc.ca
Director General, In-Service Support, Robert Templeton
Tel: 819-420-0386
robert.templeton@tpsgc-pwgsc.gc.ca

Departmental Oversight Branch / Direction générale de la surveillance

Assistant Deputy Minister, Barbara Glover
Tel: 819-997-1094; *Fax:* 819-956-9949
barbara.glover@tpsgc-pwgsc.gc.ca
Chief Audit & Evaluation Executive, Linda Anglin
Tel: 819-420-5909; *Fax:* 819-956-9721
linda.anglin@tpsgc-pwgsc.gc.ca
Director General, Forensic Accounting Management Group, Micheline Nehmé
Tel: 819-956-3360; *Fax:* 819-956-7860
Director General, Operational Integrity Sector, Simona Wambera
Tel: 819-956-9978; *Fax:* 819-956-6402
simona.wambera@tpsgc-pwgsc.gc.ca
Director General, Industrial Security Sector, Jennifer E. Stewart
Tel: 819-948-1777; *Fax:* 819-948-4144
jennifer.stewart@pwgsc-tpsgc.gc.ca
Director, Continuous Audit & Advisory Services, Renaud Génier
Tel: 819-956-5853; *Fax:* 819-956-9721
renaud.genier@tpsgc-pwgsc.gc.ca
Senior Director, Canadian Industrial Security Directorate, Pascal Girard
Tel: 613-952-7907
pascal.girard@tpsgc-pwgsc.gc.ca

Finance & Administration Branch / Direction générale des finances et de l'administration

Acting Chief Financial Officer, Julie Charron
Tel: 819-420-5660; *Fax:* 819-956-0162
julie.charron@tpsgc-pwgsc.gc.ca
Director General, SIGMA, André-Guy Chéchippe
Tel: 819-934-1057; *Fax:* 819-934-6955
andre-guy.chechippe@tpsgc-pwgsc.gc.ca
Acting Head, Financial Operations, Monique Arnold
Tel: 873-469-4244
monique.arnold@tpsgc-pwgsc.gc.ca

Director General, Financial Management, Jacques Cormier
Tel: 819-420-6163; *Fax:* 819-956-7956
jacques.cormier@tpsgc-pwgsc.gc.ca
Director General, Corporate Accommodation & Materiel Management, Helen Bélanger
Tel: 819-420-2155
helen.belanger@tpsgc-pwgsc.gc.ca
Director, Financial Services for Finance & Administration Branch & ISB, Michel Brunette
Tel: 819-420-6164; *Fax:* 819-956-7956
michel.brunette@tpsgc-pwgsc.gc.ca
Senior Director, Budget Management, Mohammad Rahman
Tel: 819-420-5221; *Fax:* 819-956-0162
mohammad.rahman@tpsgc-pwgsc.gc.ca

Human Resources Branch / Direction générale des ressources humaines

Fax: 819-956-7724

Acting Assistant Deputy Minister, André Latreille
Tel: 819-420-1579; *Fax:* 819-934-2523
andre.v.latreille@tpsgc-pwgsc.gc.ca
Director General, Labour Relations & Ethics, OHS, Compensation & Well-being, Marielle Doyon
Tel: 819-420-1575
marielle.doyon@tpsgc-pwgsc.gc.ca
Director General, Corporate Human Resources Policies & Programs, Danielle Jean-Venne
Tel: 819-956-9716; *Fax:* 819-956-9955
danielle.jean-venne@tpsgc-pwgsc.gc.ca
Director General, Human Resources Operations, Karl Shepherd
Tel: 819-956-8365; *Fax:* 819-956-4760
Karl.shepherd@tpsgc-pwgsc.gc.ca

Integrated Services Branch / Direction generale des services intégrés

Assistant Deputy Minister, Sarah Paquet
Tel: 613-992-0679
sarah.paquet@tpsgc-pwgsc.gc.ca
Acting Director General, Business Planning & Management Services, Debbie Roberts
Tel: 613-943-6434
debbie.roberts@tpsgc-pwgsc.gc.ca
Director General, Service Integration Sector, Réa McKay
Tel: 613-992-2999 ext: 9
rea.mckay@tpsgc-pwgsc.gc.ca
Director General, Government Information Services Sector, Marc Saint-Pierre
Tel: 613-992-9218; *Fax:* 613-947-6949
marc.saint-pierre@tpsgc-pwgsc.gc.ca
Acting Director General, Shared Services Integration Sector, Stéphane J. Guèvremont
Tel: 613-282-4273; *Fax:* 613-943-6435
stephane.guevremont@tpsgc-pwgsc.gc.ca
Acting Director Director, Shared Services Integration Sector, Jacqueline Jodoin
Tel: 613-387-3414; *Fax:* 613-992-5980
jacqeline.jodoin@tpsgc-pwgsc.gc.ca
Director, GCDOCS Enterprise Program Management Office, Jennifer Woods
Tel: 613-513-9683
jennifer.woods@tpsgc-pwgsc.gc.ca

MERX

Phase II, #103, 6 Antares Dr., Ottawa, ON K2E 8A9
Tel: 613-727-4900; *Fax:* 888-235-5800
Toll-Free: 800-964-6379
merx@merx.com
www.merx.com
Other Communication: Agencies, Crown & Private Corporations, Email: priv@merx.com

The federal government's Government Electronic Tendering Service (GETS) contracts MERX to advertise government procurement opportunities online. Architectural & engineering consulting services, or services related to real property above $84,000 are advertised on MERX; below $84,000, they are handled through SELECT. Construction opportunities above $100,000 are advertised through MERX; below are handled through SELECT. MERX is used for printing services valued at $10,000 or above, & most goods & services valued at $25,000 or above. Below this level Public Services & Procurement uses a variety of bid solicitation methods: T-buys (purchasing by telephone when the product or service is required quickly & can easily be identified over the phone); RFQ (Request for Quotation); an Invitation to Tender (ITT) is used for straightforward requirements above $25,000 & where the lowest price will determine the awarding of the contract; RFP (Request for Proposal) for more complex requirements above $25,000; RFSO (Request for Standing Offer); RFSA (Request for Supply Arrangement); Sole-sourcing, subject to trade agreements & government contracting regulations. For products, individual departments have authority to buy up to $5,000 directly from suppliers; above $5,000, the department must go to Public Services & Procurement. Departments have authority to purchase nearly all their services; for program delivery services, departments may buy directly from suppliers up to $400,000 competitively or up to $100,000 without competition; they may also buy competitively up to $2 million when they advertise their requirements through MERX. Subscribers to MERX have access to an opportunity matching service, may view historical opportunities, review contract awards & international opportunities

Office of the Procurement Ombudsman / Bureau de l'ombudsman de l'approvisionnement
Constitution Square Bldg., #1150, 340 Albert St., 11th Fl., PO Box 151 Ottawa, ON K1R 7Y6
Fax: 613-947-9800
Toll-Free: 866-734-5169
TTY: 800-926-9105
boa-opo@boa-opo.gc.ca
opo-boa.gc.ca
twitter.com/OPO_Canada

The Procurement Ombudsman reviews complaints with respect to awarded contracts for the acquisition of goods below $25,000 & services below $100,000; reviews complaints with respect to the administration of contracts, no matter the value; reviews departmental practices for acquiring goods & services; & helps provide an alternative dispute resolution process if agreeable to both parties.

Procurement Ombudsman, Alexander Jeglic
Tel: 613-947-9664
alexander.jeglic@opo-boa.gc.ca
Acting Director, Procurement Inquiries & Reviews, Margherita Finn
Tel: 613-947-9676
margherita.finn@opo-boa.gc.ca
Director, Quality Assurance & Risk Management, Eimer Sim
Tel: 613-947-9697
Director, Communications & Corporate Management, Anik Trépanier
Tel: 613-947-9731
anik.trepanier@opo-boa.gc.ca

Parliamentary Precinct Branch / Direction générale de la cité parlementaire
Assistant Deputy Minister, Rob Wright
Tel: 819-775-7325; Fax: 819-775-7479
rob.wright@tpsgc-pwgsc.gc.ca
Acting General, Owner-Investor, Program, Portfolio & Client Relationship Management, William Harris
Tel: 819-775-7415; Fax: 819-775-7313
william.harris@tpsgc-pwgsc.gc.ca
Director General, LTVP Project Management & Delivery, Ezio DiMillo
Tel: 819-775-7412; Fax: 819-775-7321
ezio.dimillo@tpsgc-pwgsc.gc.ca
Senior Director, Wellington & Senate Accommodations, Thierry Montpetit
Tel: 819-775-5731; Fax: 819-775-7179
thierry.montpetit@tpsgc-pwgsc.gc.ca

Policy, Planning & Communications Branch / Direction générale des politiques, de la planification et des communications
Assistant Deputy Minister, Alfred MacLeod
Tel: 819-420-5341; Fax: 819-956-5145
alfred.macleod@tpsgc-pwgsc.gc.ca
Director General, Ministerial Services & Access to Information, Anne-Marie Pelletier
Tel: 819-956-5132; Fax: 819-956-9538
anne-marie.pelletier@tpsgc-pwgsc.gc.ca
Director General, Office of Greening Government Operation, Vacant
Tel: 613-948-2430

Real Property Branch / Biens immobiliers
Fax: 613-736-2789
Manages office space & other general-purpose property; acts as custodian for $7.6 billion of real property holdings; administers 2,000 lease contracts; provides working space for 241,000 public servants in 1,810 locations across Canada; provides professional & technical services to government departments & agencies. Government buildings are 34 per cent more energy efficient & 24 per cent more greenhouse gas efficient than in 1990. Green Leases address key environmental standards such as proper management of wastewater, indoor air quality, recycling, energy efficient lighting fixtures, greenhouse gas reduction. Works with other departments on the remediation of contaminated sites & is the federal lead in the cleanup of the Sydney Tar Ponds in Nova Scotia.
Assistant Deputy Minister, Kevin Radford
Tel: 819-956-3189
Kevin.Radford@tpsgc-pwgsc.gc.ca
Director General, AFD Sector, Mark Campbell
Tel: 819-775-7217; Fax: 819-775-7279
mark.campbell@tpsgc-pwgsc.gc.ca
Director General, Accommodation, Portfolio Management & Real Estate Services, Terry Homma

Tel: 819-420-2640; Fax: 819-956-1600
terry.homma@tpsgc-pwgsc.gc.ca
Director General, Special Initiatives Sector, Ralph Collins
Tel: 613-736-3298; Fax: 613-947-9300
ralph.collins@tpsgc-pwgsc.gc.ca
Director General, Professional & Technical Service Management, Veronica Silva
Tel: 873-469-3571; Fax: 819-956-2021
veronica.silva@tpsgc-pwgsc.gc.ca
Director, Program Management Sector, Suzanne Bastien
Tel: 613-816-1575
suzanne.bastien@tpsgc-pwgsc.gc.ca
Director, Project Management Directorate, Carole Beauchamp
Tel: 819-775-7216
carole.beauchamp@tpsgc-pwgsc.gc.ca
Director General, Client Consultancy & Real Property Solutions, Toby Greenbaum
Tel: 613-960-6713; Fax: 613-960-6399
toby.greenbaum@tpsgc-pwgsc.gc.ca
Director General, Engineering Assets Strategy, Marilea Pirie
Tel: 604-666-5191; Fax: 604-775-6806
marilea.pirie@pwgsc-tpsgc.gc.ca
Acting Director General, CRA Portfolio, Lisa Lafosse
Tel: 613-670-8889
lisa.lafosse@tpsgc-pwgsc.gc.ca
Senior Director, Real Property Branch Transformation, Guylaine Boucher
Tel: 613-944-5403
Guylaine.Boucher@tpsgc-pwgsc.gc.ca
Director General, Program Management Sector, Stephen Twiss
Tel: 819-420-2693; Fax: 819-934-0980
stephen.twiss@tpsgc-pwgsc.gc.ca
Director General, Major Crown Projects, Jean Vézina
Tel: 819-956-4935; Fax: 819-956-7384
jean.vezina@tpsgc-pwgsc.gc.ca
Director, Energy Services Acquisition Program, Tomasz Smetny-Sowa
Tel: 613-736-2644
tomasz.smetny-sowa@tpsgc-pwgsc.gc.ca
Director, Special Initiatives Sector, John Paul Lamberti
Tel: 613-808-4279
johnpaul.lamberti@tpsgc-pwgsc.gc.ca

Translation Bureau / Bureau de traduction
Cremazie Bldg., 70, rue Cremazie, Gatineau, QC K1A 0S5
Fax: 819-997-9227
Chief Executive Officer, Donna Achimov
Tel: 819-997-8825; Fax: 819-934-1008
donna.achimov@tpsgc-pwgsc.gc.ca
Other Communications: Alternate Phone: 613-240-2552
Vice-President, Corporate Services, Lucie Séguin
Tel: 819-994-5221
Lucie.Seguin@tpsgc-pwgsc.gc.ca
Vice-President, Linguistic Services, Adam Gibson
Tel: 819-994-1391; Fax: 819-953-3827
adam.gibson@tpsgc-pwgsc.gc.ca
Acting Vice-President, Service Strategies & Partnership, Nancy Gauthier
Tel: 819-997-7620; Fax: 819-997-8197
Nancy.Gauthier@tpsgc-pwgsc.gc.ca

Royal Canadian Mint / Monnaie royale canadienne
320 Sussex Dr., Ottawa, ON K1A 0G8
Tel: 613-954-2626; Fax: 613-998-4130
Toll-Free: 800-267-1871
TTY: 613-949-7731
www.mint.ca
twitter.com/CanadianMint
www.facebook.com/RoyalCanadianMint
www.youtube.com/user/canadianmint
The RCM has two plants located in Ottawa & Winnipeg. Foreign & domestic circulating coinage is manufactured in Winnipeg. The Ottawa facility is responsible for the production of foreign & domestic numismatic products, precious metals & the refining of gold. The RCM also operates boutiques in Ottawa, Winnipeg & Vancouver. Reports to government through Public Services & Procurement.

Chair, Phyllis Clark

President & CEO, Marie Lemay

Vice-President, Corporate & Legal Affairs & Corporate Secretary, Simon Kamel
Tel: 613-993-1732; Fax: 613-990-4465

Chief Financial Officer & Vice-President, Finance & Administration, Jennifer Camelon
Tel: 613-998-9835

Royal Canadian Mounted Police (RCMP) / Gendarmerie royale du Canada (GRC)

73 Leikin Dr., Ottawa, ON K1A 0R2
Tel: 613-993-7267; Fax: 613-993-0260
TTY: 613-825-1391
www.rcmp-grc.gc.ca
twitter.com/rcmpgrcpolice
www.facebook.com/rcmpgrc
www.youtube.com/rcmpgrcpolice
In 1873 the North West Mounted Police was constituted to provide Police protection in the unsettled portions of the North West. In 1904 the title Royal was given to the Force. In 1920 The Dominion Police was amalgamated with this Force & the name changed to Royal Canadian Mounted Police. The headquarters was moved from Regina to Ottawa & the Force may be called upon to perform duties in any portion of the Dominion. In 1928 the RCMP absorbed the Saskatchewan Provincial Police & in 1932 the Provincial Police Forces of Alberta, Manitoba, New Brunswick, Nova Scotia & PEI were absorbed in like manner.

Commissioner, Brenda Lucki

Deputy Commissioner, Specialized Policing Services, Jennifer Strachan
Tel: 613-843-4631

Deputy Commissioner, Federal Policing, Gilles Michaud

Assistant Commissioner, Technical Operations Directorate, Jeff Adam
Tel: 613-993-2986

Assistant Commissioner, Criminal Intelligence Directorate, John Maclaughlan
Tel: 613-990-0876

Assistant Commissioner, Forensic Science & Identification Services, Philipe Thibodeau
Tel: 613-998-6303

Chief Financial & Administrative Officer, Corporate Management & Comptrollership, Dennis Watters
Tel: 613-823-1784
Other Communications: Alt. Phone: 613-823-1784

Chief Strategic Policy & Planning Officer, Strategic Policy & Planning Directorate, Rennie Marcoux
Tel: 613-843-4525; Fax: 613-825-1949

Senior General Counsel, Legal Services, Liliana Longo
Tel: 613-843-4451; Fax: 613-825-7489

Director General, Occupational Health & Safety Branch, Sylvie Châteauvert
Tel: 613-843-5319

Director General, Canadian Criminal Real Time Identification Services, Serge Côté
Tel: 613-998-6140

Director General, Criminal Intelligence Directorate, Robert Fahlman
Tel: 613-993-4256

Director General, Corporate Accounting, Policy & Control, Hélène Filion
Tel: 613-843-3704

Director General, International Policing, C/Supt. Barbara A.S. Fleury
Tel: 613-993-5168; Fax: 613-991-4876

Director General, Real Property Management, Sheila Jamieson
Tel: 613-843-3808

Director General, Assets Management & Programs Branch, Milton Jardine
Tel: 613-843-3769; Fax: 613-825-7518

Director General, Intelligence Analysis & Communications, Criminal Analysis Branch, Agnes Jelking
Tel: 613-993-6466

Director General, National Security Program, C/Supt. Dan Killam
Tel: 613-993-0297

Director General, Procurement & Contracting Branch,

Heather MacDonald
Tel: 613-843-6942; *Fax:* 613-825-0082

Director General, Financial Management, Denise Nesrallah
Tel: 613-843-5453

Director General, Corporate Management Systems, Alain Séguin
Tel: 613-843-5054

Director General, Financial Crime, C/Supt. Stephen White
Tel: 613-990-1670

Acting Executive Director, Public Affairs, Sharon Tessier
Tel: 613-843-3151

St. Lawrence Seaway Management Corporation (SLSMC) / Corporation de Gestion de la Voie Maritime du Saint-Laurent (CGVMSL)

202 Pitt St., Cornwall, ON K6J 3P7
Tel: 613-932-5170; *Fax:* 613-932-7286
marketing@seaway.ca
www.greatlakes-seaway.com
Other Communication: Statistics/Research: billing@seaway.ca;
Publications: publications@seaway.ca
A not-for-profit corporation responsible for the safe & efficient movement of marine traffic through Canadian Seaway facilities. It shares operations with its American counterpart, the Saint Lawrence Seaway Development Corporation, in operating & maintaining 15 locks between Montréal & Lake Erie.

Chair, Tim Dool

President & CEO, Terence F. Bowles

Security Intelligence Review Committee (SIRC) / Comité de Surveillance des activités de renseignement de sécurité (CSARS)

PO Box 2430 Stn. D, Ottawa, ON K1P 5W5
Tel: 613-907-4404; *Fax:* 613-907-4445
info@sirc-csars.gc.ca
www.sirc-csars.gc.ca
Other Communication: Media Liaison:
Communications@sirc-csars.gc.ca
Has as its mandate, under the Canadian Security Intelligence Service Act, to carry out the independent & external review of the Canadian Security Intelligence Service (CSIS) & to investigate complaints about CSIS activities. It is also required to investigate complaints from individuals who have had their employment prospects affected by the denial of a security clearance, & complaints referred to it by the Human Rights Commission. It is required to investigate reports made to it by the Minister of Immigration, Refugees & Citizenship, & the Solicitor General of Canada, which relate to national security or to an individual's involvement in organized crime. The Committee is required to report annually to Parliament through the Minister of Public Safety & Emergency Preparedness on these matters.

Chair, Hon. Pierre Blais, P.C.
Tel: 613-907-4401

Acting Executive Director, Chantelle Bowers
Tel: 613-907-4400

Office of the Senate Ethics Officer (SEO) / Bureau du conseiller sénatorial en éthique (CSE)

Thomas D'Arcy McGee Bldg., #526, 90 Sparks St., Ottawa, ON K1P 5B4
Tel: 613-947-3566; *Fax:* 613-947-3577
Toll-Free: 800-267-7362
cse-seo@sen.parl.gc.ca
sen.parl.gc.ca/seo-cse
The Senate Ethics Officer is responsible for administering, interpreting & applying the Conflict of Interest Code for Senators, which seeks to enhance public trust in senators & the Senate, provide guidance to senators on conflict of interest matters & to establish standards & a transparent system for proper conduct.

Senate Ethics Officer, Pierre Legault, LL.L., LL.B.
Tel: 613-947-3566

Assistant Senate Ethics Officer & General Counsel,
Deborah Palumbo
Tel: 613-943-3652

Shared Services Canada (SSC) / Services Partagés Canada (SPC)

434 Queen St., PO Box 9808 Stn. T CSC, Ottawa, ON K1G 4A8
Tel: 613-947-6296
Toll-Free: 855-215-3656
information@ssc-spc.gc.ca
www.ssc-spc.gc.ca
Other Communication: Media, Phone: 613-947-6276; Email:
media@ssc-spc.gc.ca; ATIP, Phone: 613-996-0756; Email:
ATIP-AIPRP@ssc-spc.gc.ca
twitter.com/ssc_ca
www.flickr.com/photos/ssc_spc
Created in 2011, Shared Services Canada is responsible for delivering email, data centre & telecommunication services to 43 federal departments & agencies (known as Partner Organizations). It reports to Parliament through the Minister of Public Services & Procurement.

Minister Responsible; Minister, Public Services & Procurement, Hon. Filomena Tassi, P.C.

President, Ron Parker
Tel: 613-670-1777
ron.parker@canada.ca

Chief Operating Officer, John A. Glowacki Jr.
Tel: 613-943-7558
john.glowacki@ssc-spc.gc.ca

Chief of Staff, James van Raalte
Tel: 613-992-5547
James.vanRaalte@ssc-spc.gc.ca

Chief Audit & Evaluation Executive, Yves Genest
Tel: 613-941-1576; *Fax:* 613-941-1611
yves.genest@canada.ca

Director General, Strategic Policy Integration, Graham Barr
Tel: 613-943-7559
graham.barr@ssc-spc.gc.ca

Chief Financial Officer's Office & Corporate Services / Bureau du Chef des services financiers et services ministériels
Acting Senior Assistant Deputy Minister, Elizabeth Tromp
Tel: 613-995-5622; *Fax:* 613-995-0930
Elizabeth.Tromp@ssc-spc.gc.ca
Associate Assistant Deputy Minister, Corporate Services, Camille Therriault-Power
Tel: 613-996-0024
Camille.Therriault-Power@ssc-spc.gc.ca
Senior Director General, Organizational Effectiveness, Frances McRae
Tel: 613-996-0627
Frances.McRae@ssc-spc.gc.ca
Director General, Procurement & Vendor Relationships, Pat Breton
Tel: 613-960-7028; *Fax:* 613-292-5029
pat.breton@canada.ca
Director General, Finance & DCFO Services, Manon N. Fillion
Tel: 613-608-3507; *Fax:* 613-608-3507
manon.fillion@canada.ca
Director General, Human Resources & Workplace, Rose Kattackal
rose.kattackal@canada.ca
Director General, Corporate Secretariat's Office, Violaine Sauvé
violaine.sauve@canada.ca
Director General, Chief Information & Security Office, Pankaj Sehgal
Tel: 613-996-0195
pankaj.sehgal@canada.ca
Director General, Communications, Organizational Effectiveness, Michelle Shipman
Tel: 613-410-3890
michelle.shipman@canada.ca

Operations / Opérations
Senior Assistant Deputy Minister, Kevin Radford
Tel: 613-996-0002
kevin.radford@ssc-spc.gc.ca
Director General, EDC Delivery Management, Nasser Alsukayri
Tel: 613-818-1799
nasser.alsukayri@canada.ca
Director General, Cyber Protection & IT Security Operations, Eric Belzile
Tel: 613-290-8682
Eric.Belzile@ssc-spc.gc.ca
Director General, Resource Planning & Change Readiness, Sylvie Bussière

Tel: 613-943-8322; *Fax:* 613-996-0930
sylvie.bussiere@canada.ca
Acting Director General, Finance Portfolio, Ken Canam
Tel: 613-948-0976
Ken.Canam@ssc-spc.gc.ca
Director General, Data Centre Horizontal, Guy Charron
Tel: 613-954-9562
guy.charron@ssc-spc.gc.ca
Director General, Economic & International Portfolio Lead (ATD), Jocelyn Côté
Tel: 343-203-1174; *Fax:* 613-944-0044
Jocelyn.Cote@ssc-spc.gc.ca
Director General, Enterprise IT Service Management, Brendan Dunne
Tel: 613-748-2646
brendan.dunne@canada.ca
Director General, National Security Portfolio, José Gendron
Tel: 613-960-4360; *Fax:* 613-301-4485
jose.gendron@canada.ca
Director General, Science Portfolio, Surinder S. Komal
Tel: 613-952-1210; *Fax:* 613-993-8930
surinder.komal@canada.ca
Director General, Enterprise Network & Telecom Services, Patrice Nadeau
Tel: 613-952-1202
patrice.nadeau@canada.ca
Director General, Enterprise Data Centres, Patrice Rondeau
patrice.rondeau@canada.ca

Projects & Client Relationships / Projets et Relations clients
Senior Assistant Deputy Minister, Peter Bruce
Tel: 613-996-0970
Peter.Bruce@ssc-spc.gc.ca
Director General, Telecom & Cyber Security Projects, Afif Chaaban
Tel: 613-952-3687
afif.chaaban@canada.ca
Director General, Client Relations & Business Intake, Jean-François Lymburner
Tel: 613-868-5049
jean-francois.lymburner@canada.ca
Acting Director General, Enterprise Data Centre Projects, Ken MacDonald
Tel: 613-222-6018
ken.macdonald@canada.ca
Director General, Project Management Centre of Excellence, Rama Rai
Tel: 819-997-8909
rama.rai@canada.ca

Transformation, Service Strategy & Design / Transformation, stratégie de services et conception
Director General, Transformation Program Office, Gilles Dufour
Tel: 613-302-6514
gilles.dufour@canada.ca
Director General, Distributed Computing Transformation Program, Gail Eagen
Tel: 613-952-1399; *Fax:* 613-941-2784
gail.eagen@canada.ca
Other Communications: Alt. Phone: 613-286-7563
Director General, Telecommunications Transformation Program, Michel Fortin
Tel: 613-948-7670
michel.fortin@canada.ca
Director General, Enterprise Architecture, Shirley Ivan
Tel: 613-793-9143
shirley.ivan@canada.ca
Acting Director General, Cyber & IT Security Transformation Program, Simon Levesque
Tel: 613-668-0060
simon.levesque@canada.ca
Director General, Data Centre Consolidation, Peter Littlefield
Tel: 613-954-0255
peter.littlefield@canada.ca
Director General, Cyber & IT Security Transformation Program, Raj Thuppal
Tel: 613-960-3600
Raj.thuppal@ssc-spc.gc.ca
Manager, Executive Office, Sylvie Labelle
Tel: 613-995-5715

Social Sciences & Humanities Research Council of Canada (SSHRC) / Conseil de recherches en sciences humaines du Canada (CRSH)

Constitution Sq., 350 Albert St., PO Box 1610 Stn. B, Ottawa, ON K1P 6G4
Tel: 613-992-0691
www.sshrc-crsh.gc.ca
twitter.com/SSHRC_CRSH
www.facebook.com/researchfunding
www.youtube.com/user/SSHRC1

The key national research agency investing in the knowledge & skills Canada needs to build the quality of its social, cultural & economic life. SSHRC supports university-based research & training in the human sciences. It funds basic, applied & collaborative research, student training, research partnerships, knowledge transfer & the communication of research findings in all disciplines of the social sciences & humanities. Grants & fellowships are awarded through national competitions adjudicated by eminent researchers & scholars.

President, Ted Hewitt
Tel: 613-995-5488
ted.hewitt@sshrc-crsh.gc.ca

Executive Vice-President, Brent Herbert-Copley
Tel: 613-995-5457
Brent.Herbert-Copley@sshrc-crsh.gc.ca

CFO & Vice-President, Common Administrative Services, Patricia Sauvé-McCuan
Tel: 613-995-3914; *Fax:* 613-944-1760
Patricia.Sauve-McCuan@sshrc-crsh.gc.ca

Vice-President, Research Programs, Dominique Bérubé
Tel: 613-995-5495
Dominique.Berube@sshrc-crsh.gc.ca

Specific Claims Tribunal Canada (SCT) / Tribunal des revendications particulières Canada (TRP)

#400, 427 Laurier Ave. West, 4th Fl., PO Box 31 Ottawa, ON K1R 7Y2
Tel: 613-947-0751; *Fax:* 613-943-0586
claims.revendications@sct-trp.ca
www.sct-trp.ca

Created in 2008 as part of the federal government's Justice at Last policy. The Tribunal is an independent group of six federal judges who can make binding rulings on monetary damage claims filed by First Nations groups against the Crown.

Chair, Hon. Harry Slade

Standards Council of Canada (SCC) / Conseil canadien des normes (CCN)

#600, 55 Metcalfe St., Ottawa, ON K1P 6L5
Tel: 613-238-3222; *Fax:* 613-569-7808
info@scc.ca
www.scc.ca
Other Communication: Standards Purchasing, Email: global@ihs.com
twitter.com/StandardsCanada
www.facebook.com/standardscanada
www.linkedin.com/company/standards-council-of-canada
www.youtube.com/user/StandardsCanada

Federal Crown corporation with the mandate to promote efficient & effective standardization. The organization reports to Parliament through the Minister of Industry & oversees Canada's National Standards System. The National Standards System comprises organizations & individuals involved in voluntary standards development, promotion & implementation. In addition, more than 400 organizations have been accredited by the Standards Council, including environmental management systems (EMS) registration organizations that perform registrations to ISO 14000 series standards. The Council offers accreditation to registration bodies for specialized environmental management systems in industry-specific areas, including sustainable forestry management (CAN/CSZ809-02). Manages the Program for the Accreditation of Laboratories - Canada (PALCAN) which seeks to identify & accredit competent testing laboratories. Initial assessment is made & regular follow-up audits are performed; accredited organizations are included in the Standards Council directory of accredited testing organizations. Users of testing services can eliminate or reduce their need to establish the competence of a prospective lab. In cooperation with the Canadian Association of Environmental Analytical Laboratories (CAEAL), SCC operates an accreditation program for environmental analytical laboratories. SCC's website provides free access to a wide variety of standards information, including searchable databases containing information on Canadian, foreign & international standards, regulations & SCC-accredited organizations. More specealized information is available through SCC's information & Research Service. Other accreditation programs include ones for registrars of ISO 14000 environmental management systems; environmental auditor certifiers & auditor training course providers.

Chair, Kathy Milsom, P.Eng., ICD.D

Chief Executive Officer, Chantal Guay, ind., P.Eng.

Chief Financial Officer & Vice-President, Corporate Services, Greg Fyfe

Vice-President, Accreditation Services, Elias Rafoul
Tel: 613-238-3222 ext: 329

Vice-President, Strategy & Stakeholder Engagement, Richard Tremblay

Vice-President, Standards & International Relations, Mkabi Walcott
Tel: 613-238-3222 ext: 434

Corporate Secretary & Vice-President, Communications & Corporate Planning, Sandra E. Watson
Tel: 613-238-3222 ext: 403

Statistics Canada / Statistique Canada

150 Tunney's Pasture Driveway, Ottawa, ON K1A 0T6
Tel: 514-283-8300; *Fax:* 514-283-9350
Toll-Free: 800-263-1136
TTY: 800-363-7629
STATCAN.infostats-infostats.STATCAN@canada.ca
www.statcan.ca
Other Communication: Media, Phone: 613-951-4636; Email: STATCAN.mediahotline-ligneinfomedias.STATCAN@canada.ca
twitter.com/statcan_eng
www.facebook.com/statisticscanada
www.youtube.com/statisticscanada

Agency of the federal government, headed by the Chief Statistician of Canada which reports to Parliament through the Minister of Industry. As Canada's central statistical agency, it has a mandate to collect, compile, analyse, abstract & publish statistical information relating to the commercial, industrial, financial, social, economic & general activities & condition of the people of Canada; coordinates activities with its federal & provincial partners in the national statistical system to avoid duplication of effort & to ensure the consistency & usefulness of statistics. The agency profiles & measures both social & economic changes in Canada. It presents a comprehensive picture of the national economy through statistics on manufacturing, agriculture, retail sales, services, prices, productivity changes, trade, transportation, employment & unemployment, & aggregate measures such as gross domestic product. It also presents a comprehensive picture of social conditions through statistics on demography, health, areas. In Nov. 2015, Prime Minister Trudeau reintroduced the long-form census, which had been replaced by the Conservatives in 2010 with the National Household Survey.

Chief Statistician of Canada, Anil Arora
Tel: 613-951-9757
Anil.Arora@canada.ca

Chief Audit & Evaluation Executive, Audit & Evaluation Branch, Steven McRoberts
Tel: 613-951-9717; *Fax:* 613-952-9099
steven.mcroberts@canada.ca

Analytical Studies, Methodology & Statistical Infrastructure
Director General, Analytical Studies Branch, Isabelle Amano
Tel: 613-951-3807
isabelle.amano@canada.ca

Census, Operations & Communications
Assistant Chief Statistician, Stéphane Dufour
Tel: 613-951-9866
stephane.dufour@canada.ca
Chief Information Officer & Director General, Martin St-Yves
Tel: 613-951-9466
martin.st-yves@canada.ca
Director General, Operations, Yves Béland
Tel: 613-951-1494
yves.beland@canada.ca
Other Communications: Alternate Phone: 613-293-3048
Director General, IT Operations Branch, Martin Carbonneau
Tel: 613-951-1735
martin.carbonneau@canada.ca

Corporate Services
Assistant Chief Statistician & Chief Financial Officer, Stéphane Dufour
Tel: 613-951-9866; *Fax:* 613-951-5290
stephane.dufour@canada.ca
Other Communications: Alternate Phone: 613-371-1491
Director General, Human Resources, Deirdre Keane
Tel: 613-951-9955; *Fax:* 613-951-0967
deirdre.keane@canada.ca
Director General, Finance Branch, Monia Lahaie
Tel: 613-951-1376
monia.lahaie@canada.ca

Director General & Chief Information Officer, Informatics Branch, Martin St-Yves
Tel: 613-951-9466; *Fax:* 613-951-4674
martin.st-yves@canada.ca
Other Communications: Alternate Phone: 613-850-4100

Economic Statistics
Director General, Industry Statistics, Richard Evans
Tel: 613-951-5249
richard.evans@canada.ca
Director General, Economy-wide Statistics, Daniela Ravindra
Tel: 613-951-3514; *Fax:* 613-951-0411
daniela.ravindra@canada.ca
Other Communications: Alternate Phone: 613-851-4745

Social, Health & Labour Statistics
Chief, David Ogden
Tel: 613-720-6945
david.ogden@canada.ca
Director General, Census Subject Matter, Social & Demographic Statistics, Heather Druburgh
Tel: 613-951-0501
heather.dryburgh@canada.ca
Director General, Education, Labour & Income Statistics, Karen Mihorean
Tel: 613-951-9869
karen.mihorean@canada.ca

Status of Women Canada (SWC) / Condition féminine Canada (CFC)

PO Box 8097 Stn. T CSC, Ottawa, ON K1G 3H6
Tel: 613-995-7835; *Fax:* 819-420-6906
Toll-Free: 855-969-9922
TTY: 819-420-6905
communications@swc-cfc.gc.ca
www.swc-cfc.gc.ca
Other Communication: Women's Program: wpppf@swc-cfc.gc.ca
Secondary Address: 22 Eddy St., 10th Fl. Gatineau, QC J8X 2V6
twitter.com/Women_Canada
www.facebook.com/womencanada
www.linkedin.com/company/status-of-women-canada
www.youtube.com/user/CanadaSWC

The federal government agency promotes gender equality, & the participation of women in the economic, social, cultural, & political life in Canada. Status of Women Canada focuses its work in the following areas: improvement of women's economic autonomy & well-being; elimination of systemic violence against women & children; & the advancement of women's human rights. To achieve results, SWC works with & supports research organizations, equality-seeking organizations, the non-governmental, voluntary & private sectors, & international organizations.

Minister, Women, Gender Equality & Youth, Hon. Marci Ien, P.C.

Deputy Minister, Gina Wilson
Tel: 819-420-6801; *Fax:* 819-420-6805
Gina.Wilson@cfc-swc.gc.ca

Senior Director General, Women's Program & Regional Operations Directorate, Nancy Gardiner
Tel: 819-420-6850; *Fax:* 819-420-6907
Nancy.Gardiner@cfc-swc.gc.ca

Director General, Policy & External Relations, Justine Akman
Tel: 819-420-6871; *Fax:* 819-420-6908
justine.akman@cfc-swc.gc.ca
TTY: 819-420-6905

Director General, Communications & Public Affairs, Nanci-Jean Waugh
Tel: 819-420-6810; *Fax:* 819-420-6906
nanci-jean.waugh@cfc-swc.gc.ca

Office of the Taxpayers' Ombudsman (OTO) / Bureau de l'ombudsman des contribuables (BOC)

#600, 150 Slater St., Ottawa, ON K1A 1K3
Tel: 613-946-2310; *Fax:* 613-941-6319
Toll-Free: 866-586-3839
www.oto-boc.gc.ca
Other Communication: Toll-Free Fax: 866-586-3855
twitter.com/OTO_Canada

The Office of the Taxpayers' Ombudsman seeks to hold the Canada Revenue Agency accountable to taxpayers & benefit recipients. The Office is organized into five operating units: Intake, Complaint Investigation, Systemic Investigation, Communications & Corporate Services.

Taxpayers' Ombudsman, Sherra Profit

Director, Josée M. Labelle
Tel: 613-946-2975

Manager, Intake & Complaint Investigations, Joan Alain
Tel: 613-946-2520

Manager, Systemic Examinations, Lorna Riopelle
Tel: 613-941-6225

Telefilm Canada / Téléfilm Canada

#500, 360, rue Saint-Jacques, Montréal, QC H2Y 1P5
Tél: 514-283-6363
Téléc: 514-283-8212
Ligne sans frais: 800-567-0890
info@telefilm.gc.ca
www.telefilm.ca
Autres nombres: Alt. Phone: 514-283-0838
twitter.com/Telefilm_Canada
www.facebook.com/telefilmcanada
www.linkedin.com/groups/Telefilm-Canada-1988416
www.instagram.com/Telefilm_Canada

Telefilm Canada is a Crown corporation reporting to Parliament through the Department of Canadian Heritage. Headquartered in Montréal, Telefilm provides services to the Canadian audiovisual industry by means of four regional offices located in Vancouver, Toronto, Montréal & Halifax. Dedicated to the development & promotion of the Canadian audiovisual industry.

Acting Chair, G. Grant Machum

Executive Director, Christa Dickenson

Director, National Promotion & Communications, Francesca Accinelli

Director, Business Affairs & Coproduction, Roxanne Girard

Director, Legal Services & Access to Information; Corporate Secretary, Stéphane Odesse, LL.B., D.Fisc.

Director, Administration & Corporate Services, Denis Pion

Director, International Promotion, Marielle Poupelin

Director, Project Financing, Michel Pradier

Transport Canada (TC) / Transports Canada

Place de Ville, 330 Sparks St., Ottawa, ON K1A 0N5
Tel: 613-990-2309; *Fax:* 613-954-4731
Toll-Free: 866-995-9737
TTY: 888-675-6863
www.tc.gc.ca
Other Communication: Air Cargo: aircargo-fretaerien@tc.gc.ca;
Civil Aviation: services@tc.gc.ca; ecoTECHNOLOGY:
etv@tc.gc.ca: Marine: marinesafety-securitemaritime@tc.gc.ca
twitter.com/transport_gc
www.facebook.com/401846167974
www.youtube.com/TransportCanada

Responsible for transportation policies & programs at a federal level; promoting safe, secure, efficient & environmentally responsible transporation. Transport Canada is also responsible for dealing with fitness for duty considerations for federally-regulated employers in the air, marine, rail & motor vehicle modes of transportation, as related to medical state & impairment.

Minister, Transport, Hon. Omar Alghabra, P.C.
Tel: 613-992-1301; *Fax:* 613-992-1321
Omar.Alghabra@parl.gc.ca

Deputy Minister, Michael Keenan
Tel: 613-990-4507; *Fax:* 613-991-0851
michael.keenan@tc.gc.ca

Chief of Staff, Jean-Philippe Arseneau
Tel: 613-991-0700; *Fax:* 613-995-0327
jean-philippe.arseneau@tc.gc.ca

Chief, Audit & Evaluation Executive & Integrity Officer, Martin Rubenstein
Tel: 613-990-5462; *Fax:* 613-990-6455
martin.rubenstein@tc.gc.ca

Director General, Corporate Secretariat, Simon Dubé
Tel: 613-952-4315; *Fax:* 613-990-1878
simon.dube@tc.gc.ca

Executive Director to the Deputy Minister, Ana Renart
Tel: 613-990-9002; *Fax:* 613-991-0851
ana.renart@tc.gc.ca

Executive Director, Legal Services, Henry K. Schultz
Tel: 613-990-5768; *Fax:* 613-990-5777
henry.schultz@tc.gc.ca

Associated Agencies, Boards & Commissions:

• Atlantic Pilotage Authority Canada / Administration de pilotage de l'Atlantique Canada
See Entry Name Index for detailed listing.

• Canada Lands Company / Société Immobilière du Canada
See Entry Name Index for detailed listing.

• Canada Mortgage & Housing Corporation / Société canadienne d'hypothèques et de logement
See Entry Name Index for detailed listing.

• Canada Post Corporation / Société canadienne des postes
See Entry Name Index for detailed listing.

• Canadian Air Transport Security Authority (CATSA) / Administration canadienne de la sûreté du transport aérien (ACSTA)
99 Bank St., 13th Fl.
Ottawa, ON K1P 6B9
Fax: 613-990-1295
Toll-free: 888-294-2202
TTY: 613-949-5534
correspondence1@catsa-acsta.gc.ca
www.catsa-acsta.gc.ca
CATSA secures critical elements of the air transportation system - from passenger screening to baggage screening - & encourages Canadians to Pack Smart for the benefit of all air travellers.

• Canadian Transportation Agency / Office des transports du Canada
See Entry Name Index for detailed listing.

• Federal Bridge Corporation Limited (FBCL) / Société des ponts fédéraux Limitée
#1210, 55 Metcalfe St.
Ottawa, ON K1P 6L5
Tel: 613-998-8427; *Fax:* 613-993-6945
info@federalbridge.ca
www.federalbridge.ca
Other Communication: Cornwall Phone: 613-932-3629; Sault Ste. Marie Phone: 705-256-8208
The FBCL was incorporated in 1998 to assume the non-navigational management responsibilities of the St. Lawrence Seaway Authority, including the Jacques Cartier & Champlain Bridges Incorporated, & in a joint venture with its U.S. partner, the Seaway International Bridge Corporation, Ltd. At the same time, the FBCL assumed responsibility for the management of the Canadian portion of the Thousand Islands International Bridge. In 2000, the FBCL acquired the Canadian half of the Sault Ste. Marie International Bridge.

• Great Lakes Pilotage Authority / Administration de pilotage des Grands Lacs
See Entry Name Index for detailed listing.

• Laurentian Pilotage Authority / Administration de pilotage des Laurentides Canada
See Entry Name Index for detailed listing.

• Marine Atlantic Inc. / Marine Atlantique
See Entry Name Index for detailed listing.

• Pacific Pilotage Authority / Administration de Pilotage du Pacifique Canada
See Entry Name Index for detailed listing.

• Royal Canadian Mint / Monnaie royale canadienne
See Entry Name Index for detailed listing.

• Transportation Appeal Tribunal of Canada / Anciennement le Tribunal de l'aviation civile
#1201, 333 Laurier Ave. West, 12th Fl.
Ottawa, ON K1A 0N5
Tel: 613-990-6906; *Fax:* 613-990-9153
info@tatc.gc.ca
www.tatc.gc.ca
The Tribunal provides an independent review process for anyone who has been given notice of an administrative or enforcement action taken by the Minister of Transport, railway safety inspectors or the Canadian Transportation Agency under various federal transportation Acts.

• Transportation Safety Board of Canada / Bureau de la sécurité des transports du Canada
See Entry Name Index for detailed listing.

• VIA Rail Canada Inc.
See Entry Name Index for detailed listing.

Communications Group / Groupe Communications
Tel: 613-993-0055; *Fax:* 613-991-6719

Director General, Dan Dugas
Tel: 613-990-6138; *Fax:* 613-991-6719
dan.dugas@tc.gc.ca
Executive Director, Operations, Jacqueline Roy
Tel: 613-993-7649
jacqueline.roy@tc.gc.ca
Acting Director, Web, Outreach & Creative Services, Anick Rainville
Tel: 613-949-6588; *Fax:* 613-990-0680
anick.rainville@tc.gc.ca

Corporate Services / Services généraux
Tel: 613-991-6567; *Fax:* 613-991-0426
Corporate Services is part of the Department's administration business line & is responsible for providing services & functional expertise in the areas of finance & administration, technology & information management, human resources & access to information, Crown corporation portfolio coordination, internal audit & evaluation services.
Assistant Deputy Minister & Chief Financial Officer, Corporate Services, Ryan Pilgrim
Tel: 613-991-6565; *Fax:* 613-991-4410
ryan.pilgrim@tc.gc.ca
Executive Director, Corporate Planning & Reporting, Kurt Chin Quee
Tel: 613-993-5769
kurt.chinquee@tc.gc.ca

Finance & Administration / Finances et administration
Chief Procurement Officer & Director General, Deloranda Munro
Tel: 613-993-4307; *Fax:* 613-991-4410
deloranda.munro@tc.gc.ca

Human Resources Directorate / Direction générale des ressources humaines
Director General, Tracey Sametz
Tel: 613-991-6317
tracey.sametz@tc.gc.ca
Executive Director, HR Policies & Operations, Erika Henley
Tel: 613-991-6485
erika.henley@tc.gc.ca

Technology & Information Management Services Directorate / Direction générale des services de gestion de la technologie et de l'information
Chief Information Officer & Director General, Chris Molinski
Tel: 613-998-6465; *Fax:* 613-990-2469
chris.molinski@tc.gc.ca
Director, Application Services, Tracey Boicey
Tel: 613-998-0739; *Fax:* 613-954-4493
tracey.boicey@tc.gc.ca
Director, Production Operations & Service Management, Louise Séguin
Tel: 613-991-6599
louise.seguin@tc.gc.ca

Policy Group / Groupe de politiques
Responsible for setting policies relating to rail, marine, highways & borders, motor carrier, air, airports & accessible transportation, as well as setting departmental strategic policy & coordinating intergovernmental relations; assessing the performance of the overall transportation systems & its components, & developing supporting databases, forecasts & economic analysis; administering the management agreement with the St. Lawrence Seaway Management Corporation; & supporting rail passenger services through payments to VIA Rail & three regional railways, & ferry services through payments to Marine Atlantic & to provincial & private operators & border infrastructure improvements.
Assistant Deputy Minister, Lawrence Hanson
Tel: 613-998-1880; *Fax:* 613-991-1440
lawrence.hanson@tc.gc.ca
Director General, Pilotage Act Review, Colin Stacey
Tel: 613-991-2998
colin.stacey@tc.gc.ca

Air Policy / Politique du transport aérien
Fax: 613-991-6445
Director General, Sara Wiebe
Tel: 613-993-0054; *Fax:* 613-991-6445
sara.wiebe@tc.gc.ca
Executive Director, International Air Policy, Marc Rioux
Tel: 613-993-1718; *Fax:* 613-991-6445
marc.rioux@tc.gc.ca

Crown Corporation Governance / Gouvernance de société d'État
Executive Director, Crown Corporations & Portfolio Governance, April Nakatsu
Tel: 613-991-2998; *Fax:* 613-991-4277
april.nakatsu@tc.gc.ca

Economic Analysis / Analyse économiques
Tel: 613-877-8066; *Fax:* 613-957-3280
Director General, Transportation & Economic Analysis & Chief Economist, Christian Dea

Tel: 613-949-7217
christian.dea@tc.gc.ca

Environmental Policy / Politiques environnementales
Director General, Ellen Burack
Tel: 613-949-2677; *Fax:* 613-949-9415
ellen.burack@tc.gc.ca

International & Intergovernmental Relations / Relations internationales et intergouvernementales
Director General, Sandra LaFortune
Tel: 613-991-6500; *Fax:* 613-990-6422
sandra.lafortune@tc.gc.ca

Marine Policy / Politique maritime
Fax: 613-998-1845

Director General, Marc-Yves Bertin
Tel: 613-991-3536
marc-yves.bertin@tc.gc.ca

Strategic Policy & Innovation / Politiques stratégiques
Tel: 613-949-9596; *Fax:* 613-990-1719
Director General, Craig Hutton
Tel: 613-949-7277; *Fax:* 613-990-1719
craig.hutton@tc.gc.ca
Senior Director, Policy Integration & Research, Jacques Rochon
Tel: 613-991-2967; *Fax:* 613-990-1719
jacques.rochon@tc.gc.ca

Surface Transportation Policy / Politiques sur le transport terrestre des marchandises
Fax: 613-998-2686

Director General, David McNabb
Tel: 613-998-2689; *Fax:* 613-998-2686
david.mcnabb@tc.gc.ca

Programs Group / Groupe des programmes
www.tc.gc.ca/en/programs-policies/programs.html
Responsible for the transfer of ports, harbours & airports to communities & other interests; the oversight & lease management of divested facilities; the operation of facilities not yet divested; & real property management. Responsible for environmental programs & policies, including environmental management system, sustainable development strategies, environmental assessment & national environmental issues in transportation, such as climate change.
Assistant Deputy Minister, Programs, Anuradha Marisetti
Tel: 613-990-3001
anuradha.marisetti@tc.gc.ca
Senior Director, Detroit River International Crossing, Windsor Gateway Project, Marie-Hélène Lévesque
Tel: 613-991-4702; *Fax:* 613-990-9639
marie-helene.levesque@tc.gc.ca

Air & Marine Programs / Programmes aériens et maritimes
Tel: 613-949-4904; *Fax:* 613-990-8889
Director General, Ross Ezzeddin
Tel: 613-990-1340
ross.ezzeddin@tc.gc.ca

Environmental Affairs / Affaires environnementales
Fax: 613-957-4260
Director General, Sustainable Transportation Stewardship, Jim Lothrop
Tel: 613-991-5995; *Fax:* 613-993-8674
jim.lothrop@tc.gc.ca
Acting Director, Multimodal Investment Strategies, Dominic Cliche
Tel: 613-990-5891; *Fax:* 613-993-8674
dominic.cliche@tc.gc.ca
Senior Director, Environmental Management, Alec Simpson
Tel: 613-990-0512
alec.simpson@tc.gc.ca

Transportation Infrasturcture Programs / Programmes d'infrastructure de transport
Fax: 613-990-9639
Director General, Jane Weldon
Tel: 613-998-8137
jane.weldon@tc.gc.ca

Safety & Security Group / Groupe de sécurité et sûreté
Tel: 613-990-9262; *Fax:* 613-990-2947
The ADM, Safety & Security, directs the development of transportation safety & security legislation, regulations & national standards; is responsible for the uniform implementation of monitoring, testing, inspection, research & development, & subsidy programs in the aviation, marine, rail & road modes of transport; oversees the delivery of aircraft services to government & other transportation bodies; & is responsible for development & enforcement of regulations & standards under federal jurisdiction, to protect public safety in the transportation of dangerous goods, & to prevent unlawful interference in the aviation, marine & railways modes of transport, as well as ensuring that the department is prepared to respond to transportation & transportation-related emergencies.

Assistant Deputy Minister, Kevin Brosseau
Tel: 613-990-3842
kevin.brosseau@tc.gc.ca
Associate Assistant Deputy Minister, Aaaron J. McCorie
Tel: 613-990-8636
aaron.mccrorie@tc.gc.ca

Aircraft Services / Services des aéronefs
Tel: 613-998-7991; *Fax:* 613-991-0365
Director General, John Madower
Tel: 613-998-3316
john.madower@tc.gc.ca
Executive Director, Technical Services, Francois Laniel
Tel: 613-998-3403
francois.laniel@tc.gc.ca

Aviation Security Directorate / Direction générale de la sûreté aérienne
Executive Director, Aviation Security Operations, Mario Saucier
Tel: 613-990-1076; *Fax:* 613-998-9010
mario.saucier@tc.gc.ca

Civil Aviation / Aviation civile
Tel: 613-773-8383; *Fax:* 613-996-9178
Director General, Nicholas Robinson
Tel: 613-990-1322
nicholas.robinson@tc.gc.ca

Marine Safety & Security / Sécurité et sûreté maritimes
www.tc.gc.ca/eng/marine-menu.htm
Responsible for the administration of national & international laws designed to ensure the safe operation, navigation, design & maintenance of ships, protection of life & property, & prevention of ship-source pollution. Transport Canada has assumed responsibility for environmental response from Fisheries & Oceans Canada. Strictly enforces pollution prevention regulations through the inspection of ships for compliance with pollution prevention regulations & through investigation of pollution incidents.
Executive Director, Navigation Safety & Environmental Programs, Naim Nazha
Tel: 613-991-3131; *Fax:* 613-949-9444
naim.nazha@tc.gc.ca
Director, Strategic Planning & Technical Training Services, Johanne Lafleur
Tel: 613-991-0758
johanne.lafleur@tc.gc.ca
Director, Marine Security Operations, Malick Sidibé
Tel: 613-990-1450; *Fax:* 613-949-3909
malick.sidibe@tc.gc.ca

Rail Safety / Sécurité ferroviaire
www.tc.gc.ca/eng/rail-menu.htm
Administers the Railway Safety Act & associated regulations; provides funding for improvements to railway grade crossings; administers Part II of the Canada Labour Code, relating to the safety & health of employees; & ensures, for specific railway works, that environmental impacts are assessed in compliance with the Canadian Environmental Assessment Act.
Director General, Brigitte Diogo
Tel: 613-998-8697; *Fax:* 613-990-7767
brigitte.diogo@tc.gc.ca

Road Safety & Motor Vehicle Registration / Direction de la sécurité routière et de la réglementation automobile
Fax: 613-990-2914
Toll-Free: 800-333-0371
www.tc.gc.ca/eng/road-menu.htm
Administers the Motor Vehicle Safety Act by developing vehicle & motor vehicle equipment safety standards, emission standards & testing procedures; responds to public enquiries & complaints of alleged vehicle safety defects, emission defects & fuel consumption deficiencies; &, in conjunction with Natural Resources Canada, provides fuel consumption information through vehicle labels & the Fuel Consumption Guide. Also administers the Motor Vehicle Transport Act, which governs the safety fitness of extra-provincial trucks & buses. The enforcement of this act is largely delegated to the provinces.

Security Program Support / Soutien au programme de sûreté
Responsible for the development & enforcement of regulations & standards to prevent unlawful interference with air, rail & marine transportation; management of departmental security.
Executive Director, Emergency Preparedness, Julie L. Spallin
Tel: 613-947-5076
julie.spallin@tc.gc.ca

Transportation of Dangerous Goods / Transport des marchandises dangereuses
Regulatory development, information & guidance on dangerous goods transport for the public, industry & government. Represents Canada on international organizations responsible for establishing uniform international requirements, such as the United Nations Committee of Experts on the Transport of Dangerous Goods, Association of American Railroads (AAR) Tankcar Committee & International Civil Aviation Organization

(ICAO) Dangerous Goods Panel. Branches are responsible for regulatory affairs, research, evaluation, compliance & response, review of remedial measures, development of training programs.
Director General, Vacant

Transportation Safety Board of Canada (TSB) / Bureau de la sécurité des transports du Canada (BST)

200, promenade du Portage, 4e étage, Gatineau, QC K1A 1K8
Tel: 819-994-3741; *Fax:* 819-997-2239
Toll-Free: 800-387-3557
TTY: 819-953-7287
communications@bst-tsb.gc.ca
www.tsb.gc.ca
twitter.com/TSBCanada
www.youtube.com/tsbcanada
The Board is an independent agency reporting to Parliament through the President of the Queen's Privy Council. The formal name for the Board is the Canadian Transportation Accident Investigation & Safety Board. Its sole aim is the advancement of transportation safety in the marine, rail, pipeline & air modes of transport. The TSB conducts independent investigations into selected transportation occurences in order to make findings as to their causes & contributing factors; identifies safety deficiences, & makes recommendations designed to prevent further occurences. Because the Board is independent, its transportation accident investigations are completely separate from the regulatory agencies responsible for transportation. In making findings & recommendations it is not the function of the Board to assign fault or determine civil liability.

Chair, Kathy Fox
Tel: 819-994-8000; *Fax:* 819-994-9759
kathy.fox@bst-tsb.gc.ca

Chief Operating Officer, Jean L. Laporte
Tel: 819-994-8004; *Fax:* 819-994-9759
Jean.Laporte@bst-tsb.gc.ca

Director, Communications, Rox-Anne D'Aoust
Tel: 819-994-8032; *Fax:* 819-953-1733
roxanne.daoust@bst-tsb.gc.ca

Director, Investigations, Rail/Pipeline, Kirby Jang
Tel: 819-953-6470; *Fax:* 819-953-7876
Kirby.jang@bst-tsb.gc.ca
Other Communications: Administrative Assistant, Phone: 819-953-1646

Director, Operational Services Branch, Breton Martin
Tel: 613-291-3026
martin.breton@bst-tsb.gc.ca

Director, Investigations, Marine, Marc-André Poisson
Tel: 819-953-1398
Marc-Andre.Poisson@bst-tsb.gc.ca

Director, Investigations, Air, Natacha Van Themsche
Tel: 819-994-3813; *Fax:* 819-953-9586
natacha.vanthemsche@bst-tsb.gc.ca

Corporate Services Directorate / Direction générale des services intégrés
Director General, Chantal Lemyre
Tel: 819-994-8003; *Fax:* 819-953-9648
chantal.lemyre@bst-tsb.gc.ca

Operations Services Branch / Services à l'appui des opérations
Director, Leo Donati
Tel: 819-994-4135; *Fax:* 819-953-2160
leo.donati@bst-tsb.gc.ca
Other Communications: Alternate Phone: 613-990-0999\

Treasury Board of Canada Secretariat / Secrétariat du Conseil du Trésor du Canada

East Tower, 140 O'Connor St., 9th Fl., Ottawa, ON K1A 0R5
Tel: 613-957-2400; *Fax:* 613-941-4000
Toll-Free: 877-636-0656
TTY: 613-957-9090
www.tbs-sct.gc.ca
twitter.com/tbs_Canada
www.youtube.com/channel/UCV7uvs-FoatgAuyzjpJTS3g

The Treasury Board is a Cabinet Committee of government headed by the President of the Treasury Board. The committee constituting the Treasury Board includes, in addition to the President, the Minister of Finance & four other ministers appointed by the Governor-in-Council. The main role of the Treasury Board is the management of the government's financial, personnel & administrative responsibilities. The Treasury Board derives its authority primarily from the Financial Administration Act & is supported by the Treasury Board Secretariat.

President, Treasury Board, Hon. Mona Fortier, P.C.

Secretary, Peter Wallace

Associate Secretary, Iain Stewart
Tel: 613-369-3184

Chief of Staff, President's Office, Sabina Saini
Tel: 613-369-3170

Executive Director & Senior General Counsel, Treasury Board Secretariat Legal Services, Dora Benbaruk
Tel: 613-952-3379; *Fax:* 613-954-5806

Director General, Internal Audit & Evaluation Bureau, Mike Milito
Tel: 613-369-9674

Director, Parliamentary Affairs, President's Office, Edward Rawlinson
Tel: 613-369-3170

Director, Evaluation, Internal Audit & Evaluation Bureau, Elena Petrus
Tel: 613-404-9960

Director, Policy, President's Office, Tisha Ashton
Tel: 613-369-3170

Press Secretary, Jean-Luc Ferland
Tel: 613-369-3170

Associated Agencies, Boards & Commissions:

• Public Sector Pension Investment Board / Office d'investissement des régimes de pensions du secteur public
#200, 440 Laurier Ave. West
Ottawa, ON K1R 7X6
Tel: 613-782-3095; *Fax:* 613-782-6864
info@investpsp.ca
www.investpsp.ca
Crown corporation established by Parliament by the Public Sector Pension Investment Board Act (September 1999). The mandate of PSP Investments is to manage employer & employee contributions made after April 1, 2000 to the federal Public Service, the Canadian Forces & the Royal Canadian Mounted Police pension funds.

Canadian Digital Service (CDS) / Service numérique canadien (SNC)

cds-snc@tbs-sct.gc.ca
digital.canada.ca
twitter.com/CDS_GC
www.linkedin.com/company/cds-snc
The Canadian Digital Service works with federal departments to create efficient digital services.
Chief Executive Officer, Aaron Snow
Tel: 613-790-3126
aaron.snow@tbs-sct.gc.ca
Executive Director, Anatole Papadopoulos
Tel: 613-240-6759
Anatole.Papadopoulos@tbs-sct.gc.ca
Senior Director, Pascale Elvas
Tel: 613-854-1587
Pascale.Elvas@tbs-sct.gc.ca

Chief Information Officer Branch / Direction du dirigeant principal de l'information

Chief Information Officer of the Government of Canada, John Messina
Tel: 613-369-9633

Deputy Chief Information Officer, Dave Adamson
Tel: 613-369-9637; *Fax:* 613-818-0431
Chief Technology Officer of the Government of Canada, Wade Daley
Tel: 613-369-9652; *Fax:* 613-946-4334
Executive Director, IT Project Review & Oversight, Leslie Crone
Tel: 613-369-9671
Executive Director, Information Management & Open Government, Stephen B. Walker
Tel: 613-369-9699
Executive Director, Security & Identity Management, Rita Whittle
Tel: 613-369-9683
Executive Director, Service Policy, Service & GC 2.0 Policy & Community Enablement Division, Nicholas Wise
Tel: 613-369-9655; *Fax:* 613-266-6204
Senior Director, IT Architecture, Information Technology, Serge Caron
Tel: 613-369-9650
Senior Director, Cyber Security, Security & Identity Management, Daniel Couillard
Tel: 613-369-9679; *Fax:* 613-790-2435
Senior Director, IT Policy Development & Oversight, Information Technology, Catherine Droessler
Tel: 613-369-9649
Senior Director, Corporate Engagement, Governance & Renewal, Web Standard Office, Michel Laviolette
Tel: 613-716-5816; *Fax:* 613-954-5811
Director, IT-Enabled Project Review, Claire Pereira
Tel: 613-946-5055; *Fax:* 613-946-4334

Corporate Services Sector / Secteur des services ministériels

Assistant Secretary, Corporate Services & CFO, Renée Lafontaine
Tel: 613-369-9440
Executive Director, Financial Management Directorate, Grace Chennette
Tel: 613-369-9441
Executive Director & Chief Information Officer, Paul Girard
Tel: 613-992-4306; *Fax:* 613-943-2077
Executive Director & Chief Information Officer, Marc Brouillard
Tel: 613-369-9599; *Fax:* 613-816-3365
Director, Corporate Administration & Security, Jodi C. Doyle
Tel: 613-369-3059; *Fax:* 613-898-6765

Economic Sector / Secteur des programmes économiques

Assistant Secretary, Taki Sarantakis
Tel: 613-369-9500
Executive Director, Industrial Division, Gibby Armstrong
Tel: 613-369-9497
Executive Director, Resource Division, Samantha Tattersall
Tel: 613-369-9503; *Fax:* 613-948-6062

Expenditure Management Sector / Secteur de la gestion des dépenses

Assistant Secretary, Brian Pagan
Tel: 613-369-9581
Deputy Assistant Secretary, Vacant
Executive Director, Program Performance & Evaluation Division, Kiran Hanspal
Tel: 613-369-9568
Executive Director, Expenditure Strategies & Estimates, Marcia Santiago
Tel: 613-369-9589
Executive Director, Expenditure Analysis & Compensation Planning, Richard Stuart
Tel: 613-369-9573
Director, Strategic Review, Spending Review Coordination, Erik De Vries
Tel: 613-369-9582
Senior Director, Spending Reviews & Expenditure Policy, Tom Roberts
Tel: 613-369-9495
Senior Director, Centre of Excellence for Evaluation, Anne Routhier
Tel: 613-369-9622
Senior Director, Expend Operations & Estimates, Strategies, Darryl Sprecher
Tel: 613-369-9590

Federal Contaminated Sites Inventory / Inventaire des sites contaminés fédéraux

www.tbs-sct.gc.ca/fcsi-rscf
Includes all known federal contaminated sites for which federal departments & agencies (excluding Crown corporations) are accountable. Also includes some non-federal sites for which the government has accepted some or all responsibility. Sites are classified at the time of assessment for contaminants, in a system developed by the Canadian Council of Ministers of Environment.

Government Operations Sector / Secteur des opérations gouvernementales

Assistant Secretary, Nancy Chahwan
Tel: 613-369-9538
Executive Director, Government Operations & Services Directorate, Alexis Conrad
Tel: 613-868-7004; *Fax:* 613-995-2873

Human Resources Division / Division des ressources humaines

Executive Director, Caroline Curran
Tel: 613-369-9468

International Affairs, Security & Justice Sector / Secteur des affaires internationales, de la sécurité et de la justice

Assistant Secretary, Michael Vandergrift
Tel: 613-369-9530
Executive Director, International Affairs, Immigration & Defense, Mieke Bos
Tel: 613-369-9527
Executive Director, Security & Justice Division, Rob Chambers
Tel: 613-369-9526
Executive Director, International Affairs & Development Division, Mélanie Robert
Tel: 613-369-9557

Office of the Comptroller General (OCG) / Bureau du contrôleur général (BCG)

www.tbs-sct.gc.ca/ocg-bcg
Comptroller General of Canada, Bill Matthews
Tel: 613-369-3081
Assistant Comptroller General, Internal Audit, Anthea English
Tel: 613-369-3093
Assistant Comptroller General, Financial Management, Patricia Sauvé-McCuan
Tel: 613-369-3126; *Fax:* 613-952-2399
Assistant Comptroller General, Acquired Services & Assets, Elisa Mayhew
Tel: 613-369-3148
Assistant Comptroller General, Acquired Services & Assets, Marc O'Sullivan
Tel: 613-369-3079
Assistant Comptroller General, Financial Management, Roger Ermuth
Tel: 613-369-3119; *Fax:* 613-952-9613
Executive Director, Policy & Liaison, Terry Hunt
Tel: 613-369-3095; *Fax:* 613-952-3698
Executive Director, Costing Centre of Expertise, Michael Lionais
Tel: 613-369-3118
Executive Director, Government Accounting Policy & Reporting, Diane Peressini
Tel: 613-369-3107
Senior Director, Corporate Financial Systems, Daniel Banville
Tel: 613-808-9947; *Fax:* 613-943-3166
Senior Director, Real Property & Materiel Policy Division, Kevin Colenutt
Tel: 613-369-3141
Senior Director, Cost Assessment Operations, Donna Dériger
Tel: 613-369-3116
Senior Executive Director, Strategic Planning & Information Management, Dorene Hartling
Tel: 613-218-2568; *Fax:* 613-369-3115
Executive Director, Audit Operations, Hugo Pagé
Tel: 613-369-3091
Manager, Procurement Policy, Danielle Aubin
Tel: 613-415-6014
Senior Director, Investment Planning & Project Management, Lisa Reynolds
Tel: 613-369-3142
Director, Financial Management Community Development, Sylvie Séguin
Tel: 613-369-3102
Senior Director, Public Accounts Policy & Reporting, Darlene Bess
Tel: 613-369-3105

Office of the Chief Human Resources Officer (OCHRO) / Bureau du dirigeant principal des ressources humaines (BDPRH)

www.tbs-sct.gc.ca/chro-dprh
Formerly known as Canada Public Service Agency, the Office of the Chief Human Resources Officer is responsible for matters relating to human resources, pensions & benefits, labour relations & compensation.
Chief Human Resources Officer, Anne Marie Smart
Tel: 613-952-1225
Chief of Staff, Christiane Allard
Tel: 613-960-6915
Assistant Deputy Minister, Compensation & Labour Relations Sector, Manon Brassard
Tel: 613-952-3000
Assistant Deputy Minister, Pensions & Benefits, Bayla Kolk
Tel: 613-957-6410; *Fax:* 613-946-6200

Visitng Assistant Deputy Minister, ADM Collective Management, Susan MacGowan
Tel: 613-992-9160; *Fax:* 613-992-5412
Assistant Deputy Minister, Governance, Planning & Policy Sector, Sally Thornton
Tel: 613-952-1173
Associate Assistant Deputy Minister, Compensation & Labour Relations Sector, Carl Trottier
Tel: 613-960-3845; *Fax:* 613-952-8100
Executive Director, Executive Policies, Luna Bengio
Tel: 613-943-7925
Executive Director, Labour Relations, Don Graham
Tel: 613-952-2962; *Fax:* 613-952-9421
Executive Director, Pension Policy & Program, Dominique Laporte
Tel: 613-952-3262
Executive Director, Business Intelligence & Modernization, Myriam Boudreault
Tel: 613-948-9476
Executive Director, Official Languages Centre of Excellence, Marc Tremblay
Tel: 613-948-2932
Executive Director, People Management & Community Engagement, Margaret Van Amelsvoort-Thoms
Tel: 613-957-9684; *Fax:* 613-941-9450
Executive Director, Strategic Compensation Management, Baxter Williams
Tel: 613-946-3069
Senior Director, Non-Core Public Administration, David Belovich
Tel: 613-952-2952; *Fax:* 613-952-3002
Senior Director, Workplace Wellness & Productivity Strategy, Ashique Biswas
Tel: 613-952-3261; *Fax:* 613-946-6200
Senior Director, Equitable Compensation, Renée Caron
Tel: 613-948-5097; *Fax:* 613-952-9421
Senior Director, Pension Policy & Stakeholder Relations, Kim Gowing
Tel: 613-952-3121; *Fax:* 613-954-0013
Executive Director, Labour Relations, Drew Heavens
Tel: 613-952-2962; *Fax:* 613-952-0701
Senior Director, Workforce Organization & Classification, Laurie Pratt-Tremblay
Tel: 613-952-3278
Senior Director, Strategic CPA Compensation Management, Kevin R. Marchand
Tel: 613-952-3295; *Fax:* 613-952-3295
Senior Director, ADM Collective Management, Elaine Coldwell
Tel: 613-943-3088
Executive Director, HR Project Management & Implementation, Debra Tattrie
Tel: 613-960-9441
Senior Director, Union Engagement & NJC Support, Claudia Zovatto
Tel: 613-957-9678; *Fax:* 613-952-3002

Office of the Commissioner of Lobbying (OCL) / Commissariat au lobbying du Canada (CAL)
410 Laurier Ave. West, 8th Fl., Ottawa, ON K1R 1B7
Tel: 613-957-2760
info@lobbycanada.gc.ca
lobbycanada.gc.ca
Commissioner of Lobbying, Nancy Bélanger
Tel: 613-941-3782; *Fax:* 613-957-3078
nancy.belanger@lobbycanada.gc.ca

Priorities & Planning / Priorités et planification
Assistant Secretary, Roger Scott-Douglas
Tel: 613-369-9433
Executive Director, MAF & Risk Management Directorate, Paule Labbé
Tel: 613-369-9427; *Fax:* 613-952-1782
Executive Director, Strategic Policy, Kathleen Owens
Tel: 613-369-9423

Regulatory Affairs / Affaires réglementaires
Assistant Secretary, Francis Bilodeau
Tel: 613-369-9542
Executive Director, Regulatory Affairs Directorate, Doug Band
Tel: 613-369-9515

Social & Cultural Sector / Secteur des programmes sociaux et culturels
Assistant Secretary, Annette Gibbons
Tel: 613-369-9487
Executive Director, ESDC & Canadian Heritage, Jennifer Aitken
Tel: 613-369-9486
Executive Director, Heritage, Cultural & Veterans Affairs, Vacant
Executive Director, INAC, Health & Veterans, Isabella Chan
Tel: 613-369-9483

Strategic Communications & Ministerial Affairs / Communications stratégiques et affaires ministérielles
Assistant Secretary, Jayne Huntley
Tel: 613-369-9369

Executive Director, Strategic Communications & Parliamentary Relations, Louise Baird
Tel: 613-369-3199
Senior Director, Ministerial Services, Janice Young
Tel: 613-369-3195; *Fax:* 613-952-6596

Veterans Affairs Canada / Anciens combattants Canada
161 Grafton St., PO Box 7700 Charlottetown, PE C1A 8M9
Tel: 613-996-2242
Toll-Free: 866-522-2122
information@vac-acc.gc.ca
www.veterans.gc.ca
Other Communication: Toll-Free French: 866-522-2022; Media Relations: 613-992-7468
twitter.com/veteransENG_ca
www.facebook.com/VeteransAffairsCanada
www.youtube.com/user/VeteransAffairsCa
Provides pensions for disability or death, economic support in the form of allowances, & health care benefits & services to veterans & members of the Canadian Armed Forces, members & ex-members of the RCMP, & their dependents.

Minister, Veterans Affairs; Associate Minister of National Defence, Hon. Lawrence MacAulay, P.C.
Tel: 613-995-9325; *Fax:* 613-995-2754
lawrence.macaulay@parl.gc.ca

Chief of Staff, Christine Tabbert
Tel: 613-996-4649

Director, Communications, John Embury
Tel: 613-996-4649; *Fax:* 613-954-1054

Associated Agencies, Boards & Commissions:
• **Veterans Review & Appeal Board (VRAB) / Tribunal des anciens combattants (révision et appel) (TACRA)**
Daniel J. MacDonald Bldg.
161 Grafton St.
PO Box 9900
Charlottetown, PE C1A 8V7
Tel: 902-566-8751; *Fax:* 902-566-7850
Toll-free: 800-450-8006
vrab.vrab-tacra.tacra@vrab-tacra.gc.ca
www.vrab-tacra.gc.ca
Other Communication: Ligne sans frais: 877-368-0859
The Board is an independent Board with full and exclusive jurisdiction to hear appeals from the decisions of the Minister of Veterans Affairs. The Board may affirm, vary or reverse the Minister's decisions, or refer decisions back to the Minister for reconsideration. The Board is completely independent from the Department of Veterans Affairs.

Deputy Minister's Office
Deputy Minister, Gen (Ret) Walter Natynczyk, CMM, MSC, CD
Associate Deputy Minister, Vacant

Audit & Evaluation Division / Direction générale de la vérification et de l'évaluation
Director General, Sheri Ostridge
Tel: 902-566-8018; *Fax:* 902-566-8343

Bureau of Pensions Advocates (BPA) / Bureau de services juridiques des pensions (BSJP)
Toll-Free: 877-228-2250
Other Communication: URL:
www.veterans.gc.ca/eng/about-us/organization/bureau-pensions-advocates
The Bureau provides free legal help for people who are not satisfied with decisions about their claims for disability benefits. The BPA operates 14 offices across the country, as well as an Appeal Unit in Charlottetown.
Executive Director & Chief Pensions Advocate, Anthony Saez
Tel: 902-566-8916; *Fax:* 902-566-7804
Other Communications: Alt. Phone: 604-666-3627

Chief Financial Officer & Corporate Services Branch / Secteur de la dirigeante principale des finances et services ministériels
Assistant Deputy Minister, Elizabeth Stuart
Tel: 902-566-8047; *Fax:* 902-566-8521
Director General, Information Technology & Information Management Division, Mitch Freeman
Tel: 902-566-8236
Director General, Human Resources Division, Kiran Hanspal
Tel: 902-566-8408; *Fax:* 902-566-8425
Director General, Finance Division, Maureen Sinnott
Tel: 902-566-8320; *Fax:* 902-368-0411
Executive Director, HR Transformation, Louise Wallis
Tel: 902-566-8375; *Fax:* 902-566-8425
Senior Director, Corporate Finance, Christina Hutchins
Tel: 902-566-8531; *Fax:* 902-368-0411

Acting Senior Director, Workplace Management, Heather Jarmyn
Tel: 902-368-0957

Service Delivery Branch / Prestation des services
Director General, Centralized Operations Division, Rick Christopher
Tel: 902-566-8644; *Fax:* 902-566-8337
Director General, Service Delivery & Program Management, Elizabeth Douglas
Tel: 902-566-8808; *Fax:* 902-314-8897

Strategic Oversight & Communications / Supervision stratégique et des communications
Acting Assistant Deputy Minister, Charlotte Bastien
Tel: 613-995-5204
Director General, Strategic Coordination & Liaison & Transformation Division, Lorri Biesenthal
Tel: 613-992-4903
Director General, Strategic Planning, Results & Cabinet Business, Jay Wakelin
Tel: 902-992-4235

Strategic Policy & Commemoration / Politiques stratégiques et Commémoration
Assistant Deputy Minister, Bernard Butler
Tel: 902-566-8100
Director General, Team 20/20, Janice Burke
Tel: 902-370-0931
Director General, European Operations Division, Greg Kennedy
Other Communications: Phone: 011-333-2150-6867; Fax: 011-333-2158-5834
Vimy, Nord-Pas-de-Calais
Director General, Policy & Research Division, Faith McIntyre
Tel: 902-566-7438; *Fax:* 902-370-4533
Director General, Commemoration Division, Hélène Robichaud
Tel: 902-566-8026; *Fax:* 902-566-7056
Senior Director, Special Projects, Vimy 100 Task Force, Sylvie Thibodeau-Sealy
Tel: 902-314-0153

Veterans Ombudsman (Charlottetown) / Ombudsman des vétérans (Charlottetown)
134 Kent St., PO Box 66 Charlottetown, PE C1A 7K2
Tel: 902-626-2919; *Fax:* 888-566-7582
Toll-Free: 877-330-4343
VAC.OVOInfo-InfoBOV.ACC@ombudsman-veterans.gc.ca
www.ombudsman-veterans.gc.ca
twitter.com/VetsOmbudsman
www.facebook.com/VeteransOmbudsman
www.youtube.com/user/ovoview
Director, Corporate Services & Charlottetown Operations, Michel Guay
Tel: 902-626-2663; *Fax:* 902-566-7582

Veterans Ombudsman (Ottawa) / Ombudsman des vétérans (Ottawa)
#1560, 360 Albert St., Ottawa, ON K1R 7X7
Fax: 888-566-7582
Toll-Free: 877-330-4343
VAC.OVOInfo-InfoBOV.ACC@ombudsman-veterans.gc.ca
www.ombudsman-veterans.gc.ca
twitter.com/VetsOmbudsman
www.facebook.com/VeteransOmbudsman
www.youtube.com/user/ovoview
Veterans Ombudsman, Vacant
Deputy Ombudsman & Executive Director, Operations, Sharon Squire
Tel: 613-944-2943; *Fax:* 613-944-2939

VIA Rail Canada Inc.
CP 8116 Succ Centre-Ville, Montréal, QC H3C 3N3
Tél: 514-871-6000
Téléc: 514-871-6104
Ligne sans frais: 888-842-7245
TTY: 800-268-9503
customer_relations@viarail.ca
www.viarail.ca
Autres nombres: Customer Relations, Toll-Free Phone: 800-681-2561
twitter.com/VIA_Rail
www.facebook.com/viarailcanada
www.youtube.com/user/VIARailCanadaInc
Established in 1977, VIA Rail Canada is a Crown corporation that manages the national passenger rail network. The corporation serves 450 communities throughout Canada. VIA works to offer safe, efficient, & environmentally responsible public transportation.
Environmental intiatives include a reduction in emissions & a reduce, re-use & recycle program. Under the capital investment plan, older locomotives & passenger cars are being rebuilt. The corporation also offers a Green Procurement Guide to promote the use of environmentally responsible products in all its activities.

President & CEO, Yves Desjardins-Siciliano

Chief Transportation & Safety Officer, Marc Beaulieu

Chief Human Resources Officer, Linda Bergeron

Chief Mechnical & Maintenance Officer, Mario Bergeron

Chief Communications Officer, Ann Bouthillier

Chief Business Transformation Officer, Sonia Corriveau

Chief Financial Officer, Patricia Jasmin, CPA, CA

Chief Commercial Officer, Martin Landry

Chief Legal & Risk Officer; Corporate Secretary,
Jean-François Legault

Chief Asset Management Officer, Robert St-Jean, CPA, CA

Western Economic Diversification Canada (WD) / Diversification de l'économie de l'Ouest Canada (DEO)

Canada Place, #1500, 9700 Jasper Ave. NW, Edmonton, AB T5J 4H7
Tel: 780-495-4164; *Fax:* 780-495-4557
Toll-Free: 888-338-9378
TTY: 877-303-3388
WD.contactus-contactez-nous.DEO@canada.ca
www.wd-deo.gc.ca
twitter.com/wd_canada
inkedin.com/company/westerneconomicdiversificationcanada
Responsible for promoting economic growth & diversification in the West. By investing in innovation, fostering entrepreneurship & using partnerships to enhance community sustainability, WD is helping to create a more prosperous future for western Canadians.Invests in R&D & commercialization in environmental technologies as a focus area for innovation strategies.

Minister Responsible; Minister, Economic Development, Hon. Mary Ng., P.C.

Deputy Minister, Dylan Jones
Tel: 780-495-5772; *Fax:* 780-495-4434
TTY: 877-303-3388

Chief of Staff to the Minister, Jerra Kosick
Tel: 613-952-7418; *Fax:* 613-957-1155

Headquarters / Administration centrale
Fax: 780-495-5808
Executive Director, Finance & Corporate Management, Cathy McLean
Tel: 780-495-4301; *Fax:* 780-495-7618
Director General, Finance & Management Accountability, Kathryn Mattern
Tel: 780-495-4407; *Fax:* 780-495-4434
Director, Human Resources, Patrick Faulkner
Tel: 780-495-2992; *Fax:* 780-495-6874
Director, Centre of Expertise, Andre Gareau
Tel: 780-495-4166
Director, Information Management & Information Technology, Grant Gaudin
Tel: 780-495-6734; *Fax:* 780-495-5808
Manager, Consultations, Marketing & Communications, Jaime Burke
Tel: 604-666-1318; *Fax:* 604-666-2353

Government of Alberta

Seat of Government: PO Box 1333 Edmonton, AB T5J 2N2
Tel: 780-427-2711
TTY: 800-232-7125
service.alberta@gov.ab.ca
www.alberta.ca
Other Communication: TTY: 780-427-9999 (in Edmonton)
twitter.com/YourAlberta
www.facebook.com/youralberta.ca
www.linkedin.com/company/government-of-alberta
www.youtube.com/user/YourAlberta
Alberta was proclaimed as a province on September 1, 1905.
The population as of the 2016 StatsCan census was 4,067,175.
Alberta has a land area of 640,330.56 sq km.

Office of the Lieutenant Governor

Office of the Lieutenant Governor of AB, Legislature Bldg., 10800 - 97th Ave., 3rd Fl., Edmonton, AB T5K 2B6
Tel: 780-427-7243
ltgov@gov.ab.ca
lieutenantgovernor.ab.ca
twitter.com/ltgovab
www.flickr.com/photos/lieutenantgovernorofalberta
The representative of the Crown in Alberta is the Lieutenant Governor, who is appointed by the Governor General, with the advice of the Prime Minister of Canada.

Lieutenant Governor, Hon. Salma Lakhani, AOE, B.Sc.

Private Secretary to the Lieutenant Governor, Brian Roach
Tel: 780-427-8308; *Fax:* 780-422-5134
brian.roach@gov.ab.ca

Communications Officer, Janet Resta
Tel: 780-427-9222
janet.resta@gov.ab.ca

Office of the Premier

Office of the Premier, Legislature Bldg., #307, 10800 - 97th Ave., Edmonton, AB T5K 2B6
www.alberta.ca/premier.aspx
The head of government in Alberta is the Premier. The Premier of the province is the leader of the political party that has the most seats in the Legislative Assembly. The Premier is head of the Executive Council, which works to put government policy into practice.
UCP Leader Jason Kenney was elected as Alberta's eighteenth Premier in a general election held April 16, 2019.
The following services are provided by the Office of the Premier: the provision of support to the Premier; issues management; the provision of strategic advice; correspondence; & scheduling.

Premier; President, Executive Council, Hon. Jason Kenney, P.C.
Tel: 780-427-2251; *Fax:* 780-427-1349
premier@gov.ab.ca

Chief of Staff, Pam Livingston
pam.livingston@gov.ab.ca

Principal Secretary, Lawrence Kaumeyer
lawrence.kaumeyer@gov.ab.ca

Director, Operations, John Whittaker
john.whittaker@gov.ab.ca

Executive Council

Legislature Bldg., 10800 - 97th Ave., Edmonton, AB T5K 2B6
www.alberta.ca/premier-cabinet.aspx
The Executive Council consists of the Premier & cabinet ministers. Cabinet ministers are selected by the Premier from elected members of the Premier's party.
The Cabinet carries out the following functions: approving Orders in Council; ratifying policy matters; & acting as the final authority on issues related to the operation of the government.
The following is a list of members of the Executive Council, presented in order of precedence:

Premier; President, Executive Council; Minister, Intergovernmental Relations, Hon. Jason Kenney, P.C.
Tel: 780-427-2251; *Fax:* 780-427-1349
premier@gov.ab.ca
www.alberta.ca/premier.aspx

President, Treasury Board & Minister, Finance, Hon. Travis Toews
Tel: 780-415-4855
tbf.minister@gov.ab.ca
www.alberta.ca/travis-toews-bio.aspx

Minister, Environment & Parks; House Leader, Hon. Jason Nixon
Tel: 780-427-2391; *Fax:* 780-422-6259
aep.minister@gov.ab.ca
www.alberta.ca/minister-of-environment-and-parks.aspx

Minister, Energy, Hon. Sonya Savage
Tel: 780-427-3740; *Fax:* 780-644-1222
minister.energy@gov.ab.ca
www.alberta.ca/sonya-savage-bio.aspx

Minister, Culture, Hon. Ron Orr
Tel: 780-422-3559; *Fax:* 780-427-0188
cmsw.minister@gov.ab.ca
www.alberta.ca/minister-of-culture.aspx

Minister, Labour & Immigration, Hon. Tyler Shandro
Tel: 780-638-9400; *Fax:* 780-638-9401
labour.minister@gov.ab.ca

Minister, Agriculture & Forestry, Hon. Devin Dreeshen
Tel: 780-427-2137; *Fax:* 780-422-6035
AF.minister@gov.ab.ca
www.alberta.ca/devin-dreeshen-bio.aspx

Minister, Jobs, Economy & Innovation, Hon. Doug Schweitzer
Tel: 780-427-2339; *Fax:* 780-422-6621
ministryofjustice@gov.ab.ca
www.alberta.ca/doug-schweitzer-bio.aspx

Minister, Service Alberta, Hon. Nate Glubish
Tel: 780-422-6880; *Fax:* 780-422-2496
ministersa@gov.ab.ca
www.alberta.ca/nate-glubish-bio.aspx

Minister, Education, Hon. Adriana LaGrange
Tel: 780-427-5010; *Fax:* 780-427-5018
education.minister@gov.ab.ca
www.alberta.ca/adriana-lagrange-bio.aspx

Minister, Transportation, Hon. Rajan Sawhney
Tel: 780-642-7208; *Fax:* 780-422-2002
transportation.minister@gov.ab.ca
www.alberta.ca/rajan-sawhney-bio.aspx

Minister, Municipal Affairs, Hon. Ric McIver
Tel: 780-427-3744; *Fax:* 780-422-9550
minister.municipalaffairs@gov.ab.ca
www.alberta.ca/ric-mciver-bio.aspx

Minister, Advanced Education, Hon. Demetrios Nicolaides
Tel: 780-427-5777; *Fax:* 780-422-8733
ae.minister@gov.ab.ca
www.alberta.ca/demetrios-nicolaides-bio.aspx

Minister, Infrastructure, Hon. Prasad Panda
Tel: 780-427-5041; *Fax:* 780-644-1204
infrastructure.minister@gov.ab.ca
www.alberta.ca/prasad-panda-bio.aspx

Minister, Seniors & Housing, Hon. Josephine Pon
Tel: 780-415-9550; *Fax:* 780-415-9411
sh.minister@gov.ab.ca
www.alberta.ca/minister-of-seniors-and-housing.aspx

Minister, Community & Social Services, Hon. Jason Luan
Tel: 780-643-6210; *Fax:* 780-643-6214
css.minister@gov.ab.ca
www.alberta.ca/jason-luan-bio.aspx

Minister, Children's Services, Hon. Rebecca Schulz
Tel: 780-644-5255; *Fax:* 780-644-6817
cs.minister@gov.ab.ca
www.alberta.ca/rebecca-schulz-bio.aspx

Minister, Justice & Solicitor General, Hon. Kaycee Madu
Tel: 780-427-3744
minister.municipalaffairs@gov.ab.ca
www.alberta.ca/kaycee-madu-bio.aspx

Minister, Health, Hon. Jason Copping
Tel: 780-427-3665; *Fax:* 780-415-0961
health.minister@gov.ab.ca

Minister, Indigenous Relations, Hon. Rick Wilson
Tel: 780-422-4144; *Fax:* 780-638-4052
ir.ministeroffice@gov.ab.ca
www.alberta.ca/minister-of-indigenous-relations.aspx

Associate Minister, Immigration & Multiculturalism, Hon. Muhammad Yaseen
Tel: 780-638-9400; *Fax:* 780-638-9401
www.alberta.ca/muhammad-yaseen-bio.aspx

Associate Minister, Status of Women, Hon. Whitney Issik
Tel: 780-422-3559; *Fax:* 780-427-0188
www.alberta.ca/whitney-issik-biography.aspx

Associate Minister, Rural Economic Development, Hon. Nate Horner
Tel: 780-644-8554; *Fax:* 780-644-8572
www.alberta.ca/nate-horner-bio.aspx

Associate Minister, Red Tape Reduction, Hon. Tanya Fir
Tel: 780-427-0240
associateminister-rtr@gov.ab.ca
www.alberta.ca/tanya-fir-bio.aspx

Associate Minister, Mental Health & Addictions, Hon. Mike Ellis
Tel: 780-427-0165
associateminister-mha@gov.ab.ca

Associate Minister, Natural Gas & Electricity, Hon. Dale Nally
Tel: 780-427-0265; Fax: 780-644-1222
aminister.natgas@gov.ab.ca
www.alberta.ca/dale-nally-bio.aspx

Deputy Minister's Office
Tel: 780-422-4910
www.alberta.ca/executive-council.aspx
The Executive Council Office is led by the Deputy Minister of the Executive Council.
Deputy Minister, Executive Council, Ray Gilmour
ray.gilmour@gov.ab.ca
Associate Deputy Minister & Deputy Minister, Operations, Coleen Volk
coleen.volk@gov.ab.ca
Chief of Staff, Jenn Anderson
Tel: 780-975-4593
jenn.anderson@gov.ab.ca

Cabinet Coordination Office & Ministry Services
Deputy Clerk, Executive Council & Deputy Secretary to Cabinet, Christopher McPherson
Tel: 780-292-0568
christopher.mcpherson@gov.ab.ca
Chief of Protocol, Shannon Haggarty
Tel: 780-422-2236
shannon.haggarty@gov.ab.ca
Executive Director, Cabinet Coordination Office, Meghann Eagle
Tel: 780-554-3996
meghann.eagle@gov.ab.ca

Intergovernmental Relations
Deputy Minister, Coleen Volk
coleen.volk@gov.ab.ca

Policy Coordination Office
Deputy Minister, Mark T. Cameron
Tel: 780-638-4702
mark.t.cameron@gov.ab.ca
Assistant Deputy Minister, Economic Policy, Zoe Addington
Tel: 780-422-5933
zoe.addington@gov.ab.ca
Assistant Deputy Minister, Legislative Review, Suzanne Harbottie
Tel: 780-721-0300
Assistant Deputy Minister, Social Policy, Shaun Peddie
Tel: 587-984-6293

Cabinet Policy Committees
www.alberta.ca/government-committees.aspx
The following are Alberta's cabinet policy committees:
Community & Families; Jobs & Economy; Resource & Sustainable Development.

Legislative Assembly of Alberta

9718 - 107th St., Edmonton, AB T5K 1E4
Tel: 780-427-2826
laocommunications@assembly.ab.ca
www.assembly.ab.ca
Other Communication: Reference information:
library.requests@assembly.ab.ca; Visitor Services Office:
visitorinfo@assembly.ab.ca
twitter.com/LegAssemblyofAB
www.facebook.com/LegAssemblyofAB
www.linkedin.com/company/legislative-assembly-of-alberta
www.youtube.com/user/AlbertaLegislature
The Legislative Assembly of Alberta is elected by voters. It consists of government members & opposition members.
The Legislative Assembly Office carries out the following main responsibilities: supporting the Speaker of the Legislative Assembly; supporting members; recording proceedings & maintaining records of the Legislative Assembly; educating the public; & providing services to external clients.
The Legislative Assembly Office is organized by services such as the following: management & communication services; house & committee services; legal services; human resource services; financial management & administrative services; visitor, ceremonial, & security services; library services; public information & reporting services; & information technology services.

Clerk, Shannon Dean
shannon.dean@assembly.ab.ca
Note: The Clerk acts as the Chief Executive Officer of the Legislative Assembly Office. In the Chamber, the Clerk

advises the Speaker about procedure. He also calls out the daily order of business.

Executive Director, Corporate Services, Ruth McHugh
Tel: 780-643-2989
ruth.mchugh@assembly.ab.ca
Note: Financial Management & Administrative Services is responsible for financial processing, reporting, & control.

Sergeant-at-Arms, Chris Caughell
Tel: 780-427-2326
Note: The following duties are performed: management of visitors' services for the Legislative Assembly; provision of security services; & the execution of ceremonial functions for the Legislative Assembly.

Legislature Librarian, Valerie Footz
Tel: 780-427-0202; Fax: 780-427-6016
val.footz@assembly.ab.ca
Note: The Legislature Library provides services to Members of the Legislative Assembly of Alberta, Members' staff, Legislative Assembly Office staff, & the general public.

Office of the Speaker
Legislature Bldg., #325, 10800 - 97th Ave., Edmonton, AB T5K 2B6
The Speaker of the Alberta Legislative Assembly maintains orderly debate in the Chamber. He cannot engage in debate in the Assembly. As head of the Legislative Assembly Office, the Speaker also plays a role in the maintenance of records of the Assembly & the provision of services to members.
Speaker, Hon. Nathan Cooper
Constituency: Medicine Hat, New Democratic Party
Tel: 780-427-2464; Fax: 780-422-9553
nathan.cooper@assembly.ab.ca
Deputy Speaker, Angela Pitt
Constituency: Peace River, New Democratic Party
Tel: 780-644-7121; Fax: 780-638-3506
Airdrie.East@assembly.ab.ca

Government Members' Caucus Office
Federal Bldg., 9820 - 107th St., 6th Fl., Edmonton, AB T5K 1E7
Tel: 780-644-2297; Fax: 780-638-3506
info@unitedconservative.ca
www.unitedconservative.ca
twitter.com/Alberta_UCP
www.facebook.com/UnitedConservativePartyAlberta
www.linkedin.com/company/united-conservative-party-of-alberta
www.instagram.com/Alberta_UCP
The United Conservative Party was created with the merger of the Wildrose Alliance Party of Alberta & the Progressive Conservative Party of Alberta on July 22, 2017. The party won the 2019 general election.
Premier; Leader, United Conservative Party, Hon. Jason Kenney, P.C.
Tel: 780-427-2251; Fax: 780-427-1349
premier@gov.ab.ca
Government House Leader, Hon. Jason Nixon
Tel: 780-427-2391
aep.minister@gov.ab.ca
Chief Government Whip, Hon. Whitney Issik
Tel: 780-427-0165
Calgary.West@assembly.ab.ca
Deputy Government Whip, Brad Rutherford
Tel: 780-638-3171; Fax: 780-638-3506
Deputy Government House Leader, Joseph Schow
Tel: 780-638-1158; Fax: 780-638-3506
Cardston.Siksika@assembly.ab.ca
Executive Director, Caucus, Brittany Baltimore
Tel: 780-644-2297
brittany.baltimore@assembly.ab.ca

New Democratic Party Office (Official Opposition)
Federal Bldg., 9820 - 107th St., 5th Fl., Edmonton, AB T5K 1E7
Tel: 780-427-1800; Fax: 780-415-0701
info@albertandp.ca
www.albertandp.ca
twitter.com/AlbertaNDP
www.facebook.com/AlbertaNDP
www.youtube.com/user/AlbertaNDP
Leader, Official Opposition; Leader, New Democratic Party of Alberta, Hon. Rachel Notley
Edmonton.Strathcona@assembly.ab.ca
Official Opposition Deputy Leader, Sarah Hoffman
Edmonton.Glenora@assembly.ab.ca
Official Opposition House Leader, Christina Gray
Edmonton.Millwoods@assembly.ab.ca
Official Opposition Whip, David Eggen
Edmonton.Northwest@assembly.ab.ca
Official Opposition Deputy House Leader, Thomas Dang
Edmonton.South@assembly.ab.ca

Official Opposition Deputy Whip, Lorne Dach
Edmonton.McClung@assembly.ab.ca
Executive Director, Government Caucus, Sandra Houston
sandra.houston@assembly.ab.ca

Committees of the Legislative Assembly of Alberta
Legislative Branch, Legislature Annex, #801, 9718 - 107th St., Edmonton, AB T5K 1E4
Tel: 780-427-1350; Fax: 780-427-5688
committees@assembly.ab.ca
www.assembly.ab.ca/assembly-business/committees
Committees of the Legislative Assembly of Alberta include select special committees, special standing committees, legislative policy committees, & standing committees.
There is currently one special standing committee, Members' Services.
Legislative policy committees include the following: Alberta's Economic Future; Families & Communities; & Resource Stewardship.
Current standing committees are as follows: Alberta Heritage Savings Trust Fund; Legislative Offices; Private Bills & Private Members' Public Bills; Privileges & Elections, Standing Orders & Printing; & Public Accounts.
Chair, Special Standing Committee on Members' Services, Hon. Nathan Cooper
Constituency: Olds-Didsbury-Three Hills, United Conservative Party of Alberta
Chair, Standing Committee on Alberta's Economic Future, Nathan Neudorf
Constituency: Athabasca-Barrhead-Westlock, United Conservative Party of Alberta
Chair, Standing Committee on Families & Communities, Lori Sigurdson
Constituency: Fort McMurray-Lac La Biche, United Conservative Party of Alberta
Chair, Standing Committee on Resource Stewardship, David B. Hanson
Constituency: Bonnyville-Cold Lake-St. Paul, United Conservative Party of Alberta
Chair, Standing Committee on the Alberta Heritage Savings Trust Fund, Ronald Orr
Constituency: Calgary-Fish Creek, United Conservative Party of Alberta
Chair, Standing Committee on Legislative Offices, Joseph Schow
Constituency: Calgary-West, United Conservative Party of Alberta
Chair, Standing Committee on Private Bills & Private Members' Public Bills, Mike Ellis
Constituency: Calgary-West, United Conservative Party of Alberta
Chair, Standing Committee on Privileges & Elections, Standing Orders & Printing, Mark Smith
Constituency: Drayton Valley-Devon, United Conservative Party of Alberta
Chair, Standing Committee on Public Accounts, Shannon Phillips
Constituency: Lethbridge-West, New Democratic Party

Thirtieth Legislature - Alberta

Legislature Bldg., 10800 - 97th Ave., Edmonton, AB T5K 2B6
www.assembly.ab.ca

Last General Election, April 16, 2019.
Next General Election: March 1-May 31, 2023.
Party Standings (Oct. 2021):
United Conservative Party 60;
New Democratic Party 24;
Independent 2;
Vacant 1;
Total 87.
Indemnities, Salaries, & Allowances (2020):
MLA indemnity $120,936, with no MLA tax free allowance.
In addition to this are the following indemnities & allowances:
Premier $65,244;
Speaker $60,468;
Ministers with portfolio $60,468;
Ministers without portfolio $27,216;
Leader of the Official Opposition $60,468;
Deputy Speaker & Chair of Committees $30,240;
Deputy Chair of Committees $15,120;
Leader of a recognized opposition party $27,216.
The following are special members' allowances:
Official Opposition House Leader: $15,120;
Third Party House Leader (recognized opposition party): $12,096;
Chief Government Whip: $12,096;
Assistant Government Whip: $9,072;
Chief Opposition Whip: $9,072;
Assistant Opposition Whip: $7,260;
Third Party Whip: $7,260.
The following is a list of members, with their constituency, the

number of electors in their electoral division, their party affiliation, & contact information:

Members of the Legislative Assembly of Alberta

Leela Sharon Aheer
Constituency: Chestermere-Strathmore, United Conservative Party of Alberta
Tel: 587-689-5071; *Fax:* 780-638-3506
Chestermere.Strathmore@assembly.ab.ca
Other Communications: Constituency Phone: 403-962-0126
twitter.com/leelaaheer,
www.facebook.com/LeelaSharonAheer
Constituency Office
129 - 2nd Ave.
Strathmore, AB T1P 1K1

Tracy Allard
Constituency: Grande Prairie, United Conservative Party of Alberta
Tel: 587-404-9528; *Fax:* 780-638-3506
GrandePrairie@assembly.ab.ca
Other Communications: Constituency Phone: 780-538-1800;
Fax: 780-538-1802
www.facebook.com/tracyallardGP
Constituency Office
#207, 10605 West Side Dr.
Grande Prairie, AB T8V 8E6

Mickey Amery
Constituency: Calgary-Cross, United Conservative Party of Alberta
Tel: 780-638-1371; *Fax:* 780-638-3506
Calgary.Cross@assembly.ab.ca
Other Communications: Constituency Phone: 403-248-4487;
Fax: 403-273-2898
Constituency Office
#766, 2220 - 68th St. NE
Calgary, AB T1Y 6Y7

Jackie Armstrong-Homeniuk
Constituency: Fort Saskatchewan-Vegreville, United Conservative Party of Alberta
Tel: 780-638-3157; *Fax:* 780-638-3506
FortSaskatchewan.Vegreville@assembly.ab.ca
Other Communications: Constituency Phone: 780-632-6840;
Fax: 780-632-2708
www.facebook.com/JackieArmstrongHomeniuk
Constituency Office
4927 - 51st Ave.
PO Box 451
Vegreville, AB T9C 1M1

Drew Barnes
Constituency: Cypress-Medicine Hat, Independent
Tel: 780-427-6662
cypress.medicinehat@assembly.ab.ca
Other Communications: Constituency Phone: 403-528-2191
twitter.com/drew__barnes,
www.facebook.com/barnesdrewcypmedhat,
www.linkedin.com/in/drew-barnes-5606a917
Note: On May 13, 2021 Drew Barnes was expelled from the United Conservative Party.
Constituency Office, Trans Canada Place
#5, 1299 Trans Canada Way
Medicine Hat, AB T1B 1H9

Deron Bilous
Constituency: Edmonton-Beverly-Clareview, New Democratic Party
Tel: 780-415-1800; *Fax:* 780-415-0701
edmonton.beverlyclareview@assembly.ab.ca
deronbilous.albertandp.ca
Other Communications: Constituency Phone: 780-476-6467;
Fax: 780-476-6473
twitter.com/DeronBilous, www.facebook.com/deronbilousAB
Constituency Office, Hermitage Mall
#552, 40 St. & Hermitage Rd.
Edmonton, AB T5A 4N2

Jon Carson
Constituency: Edmonton-West Henday, New Democratic Party
Tel: 780-415-1800; *Fax:* 780-415-0701
Edmonton.WestHenday@assembly.ab.ca
joncarson.albertandp.ca
Other Communications: Constituency Phone: 780-414-0711;
Fax: 780-414-0713
twitter.com/joncarsonndp, www.facebook.com/JonCNDP
Constituency Office
#103, 14020 - 128th Ave.
Edmonton, AB T5L 4M8

Joe Ceci
Constituency: Calgary-Buffalo, New Democratic Party
Tel: 780-415-1800; *Fax:* 780-415-0701
Calgary.Buffalo@assembly.ab.ca
joececi.albertandp.ca
Other Communications: Constituency Phone: 403-244-7737;
Fax: 403-541-9106
twitter.com/joececiyyc, www.facebook.com/joe.ceci.ndp
Constituency Office

1173 - 11th Ave. SW
Calgary, AB T2R 0G4

Speaker, Hon. Nathan M. Cooper
Constituency: Olds-Didsbury-Three Hills, United Conservative Party of Alberta
Tel: 780-427-2464; *Fax:* 780-422-9553
OldsDidsbury.ThreeHills@assembly.ab.ca
Other Communications: Constituency Phone: 403-556-3132
twitter.com/NathanCooperAB,
www.facebook.com/nathancooperODT
Constituency Office
4905B - 50th Ave.
PO Box 3909
Olds, AB T4H 1P6

Minister, Health, Hon. Jason Copping
Constituency: Calgary-Varsity, United Conservative Party of Alberta
Tel: 780-638-9400; *Fax:* 780-638-9401
Calgary.Varsity@assembly.ab.ca
Other Communications: Constituency Phone: 403-216-5436
twitter.com/JasonCoppingAB,
www.facebook.com/jasoncoppingAB
Constituency Office
#201, 1055 - 20th Ave. NW
Calgary, AB T2M 1E7

Deputy Whip, Official Opposition, Lorne Dach
Constituency: Edmonton-McClung, New Democratic Party
Tel: 780-415-1800; *Fax:* 780-415-0701
Edmonton.McClung@assembly.ab.ca
lornedach.albertandp.ca
Other Communications: Constituency Phone: 780-408-1860;
Fax: 780-408-1864
twitter.com/lornedach, www.facebook.com/dachndp
Constituency Office
#301, 6650 - 177th St.
Edmonton, AB T5T 4J5

Deputy House Leader, Official Opposition, Thomas Dang
Constituency: Edmonton-South, New Democratic Party
Tel: 780-415-1800; *Fax:* 780-415-0701
Edmonton.South@assembly.ab.ca
thomasdang.albertandp.ca
Other Communications: Constituency Phone: 780-643-9153;
Fax: 780-540-8441
twitter.com/thomasdangab,
www.facebook.com/ThomasDangAB
Constituency Office
#202, 856 - 119th St. SW
Edmonton, AB T6W 0J1

Jasvir Deol
Constituency: Edmonton-Meadows, New Democratic Party
Tel: 780-415-1800; *Fax:* 780-415-0701
Edmonton.Meadows@assembly.ab.ca
jasvirdeol.albertandp.ca
Other Communications: Constituency Phone: 780-466-3737;
Fax: 780-468-3359
Constituency Office
#204B, 3323 - 34th St. NW
Edmonton, AB T6T 2K6

Minister, Agriculture & Forestry, Hon. Devin Dreeshen
Constituency: Innisfail-Sylvan Lake, United Conservative Party of Alberta
Tel: 780-427-2137
Toll-free: 88- 65- 253; *Fax:* 780-422-6035
Innisfail.SylvanLake@assembly.ab.ca
Other Communications: Constituency Phone: 403-865-7580;
Fax: 403-865-7585
twitter.com/devindvote,
www.facebook.com/DevinDreeshen4AB
Constituency Office
5027 - 49th St.
Innisfail, AB T4G 1M1

Whip, Official Opposition, David Eggen
Constituency: Edmonton-North West, New Democratic Party
Tel: 780-415-1800; *Fax:* 780-415-0701
Edmonton.Northwest@assembly.ab.ca
davideggen.albertandp.ca
Other Communications: Constituency Phone: 780-451-2345;
Fax: 780-451-2344
twitter.com/davideggenAB,
www.facebook.com/DavidEggenAB
Constituency Office
10212 - 127th Ave., #A
Edmonton, AB T5E 0B8

Associate Minister, Mental Health & Addictions, Hon. Mike Ellis
Constituency: Calgary-West, United Conservative Party of Alberta
Tel: 780-427-0165; *Fax:* 780-638-3506
Calgary.West@assembly.ab.ca
Other Communications: Constituency Phone: 403-216-5439;
Fax: 403-216-5441
twitter.com/mikeellisucp
Constituency Office
#234, 333 Aspen Glen Landing SW
Calgary, AB T3H 0N6

Richard Feehan
Constituency: Edmonton-Rutherford *No. of Constituents:* 26,885, New Democratic Party
Tel: 780-415-1800; *Fax:* 780-415-0701
Edmonton.Rutherford@assembly.ab.ca
richardfeehan.albertandp.ca
Other Communications: Constituency Phone: 780-414-1311;
Fax: 780-414-1314
twitter.com/feehanrichard
Constituency Office
308 Saddleback Rd.
Edmonton, AB T6J 4R7

Associate Minister, Red Tape Reduction, Hon. Tanya Fir
Constituency: Calgary-Peigan, United Conservative Party of Alberta
Tel: 780-427-0240; *Fax:* 780-638-3506
Calgary.Peigan@assembly.ab.ca
Other Communications: Constituency Phone: 587-392-8850
twitter.com/tanya_fir, www.facebook.com/tanyafirMLA
Constituency Office
#255, 11488 - 24th St. SE
Calgary, AB T2Z 4C9

Kathleen Ganley
Constituency: Calgary-Mountain View, New Democratic Party
Tel: 780-415-1800; *Fax:* 780-415-0701
Calgary.MountainView@assembly.ab.ca
kathleenganley.albertandp.ca
Other Communications: Constituency Phone: 403-216-5445;
Fax: 403-216-5447
twitter.com/kathleenganley,
www.facebook.com/KathleenGanley
Constituency Office
#102, 723 - 14th St. NW
Calgary, AB T2N 2A4

Shane Getson
Constituency: Lac Ste. Anne-Parkland, United Conservative Party of Alberta
Tel: 780-638-3021; *Fax:* 780-638-3506
LacSteAnne.Parkland@assembly.ab.ca
Other Communications: Constituency Phone: 780-967-0760;
Fax: 780-967-4338
Constituency Office
#18, 4708 Lac Ste. Anne Trail North
PO Box 248 Onoway Sta.
Onoway, AB T0E 1V0

Michaela Glasgo
Constituency: Brooks-Medicine Hat, United Conservative Party of Alberta
Tel: 780-638-3022; *Fax:* 780-638-3506
Brooks.MedicineHat@assembly.ab.ca
Other Communications: Constituency Phone: 587-270-5110;
Fax: 587-270-5113
twitter.com/michaelaglasgo,
www.facebook.com/glasgomichaela
Constituency Office
#4, 650 Cassils Rd. East
Brooks, AB T1R 1M6

Minister, Service Alberta, Hon. Nate Glubish
Constituency: Strathcona-Sherwood Park, United Conservative Party of Alberta
Tel: 780-422-6880; *Fax:* 780-422-2496
Strathcona.Sherwoodpark@assembly.ab.ca
Other Communications: Constituency Phone: 780-416-2492;
Fax: 780-416-7093
twitter.com/nateglubish, www.facebook.com/nateglubish,
www.linkedin.com/in/nateglubish
Constituency Office, Athabasca Professional Bldg.
#105, 80 Chippewa Rd.
Sherwood Park, AB T8A 4W6

Nicole Goehring
Constituency: Edmonton-Castle Downs, New Democratic Party
Tel: 780-415-1800; *Fax:* 780-415-0701
Edmonton.Castledowns@assembly.ab.ca
nicolegoehring.albertandp.ca
Other Communications: Constituency Phone: 780-414-0705;
Fax: 780-414-0707
twitter.com/nicolergoehring,
www.facebook.com/nicolegoehringndp
Constituency Office
12120 - 161st Ave.
Edmonton, AB T5X 5M8

Richard Gotfried
Constituency: Calgary-Fish Creek *No. of Constituents:* 29,254, United Conservative Party of Alberta
Tel: 780-643-6541; *Fax:* 780-638-3506
Calgary.FishCreek@assembly.ab.ca
Other Communications: Constituency Phone: 403-278-4444
twitter.com/RichardGotfried,
www.facebook.com/RichardGotfriedAB,
www.linkedin.com/in/richardgotfried
Constituency Office
#7, 1215 Lake Sylvan Dr. SE
Calgary, AB T2J 3Z5

House Leader, Official Opposition, Christina Gray
Constituency: Edmonton-Mill Woods, New Democratic Party
Tel: 780-415-1800; *Fax:* 780-415-0701
Edmonton.Millwoods@assembly.ab.ca
christinagray.albertandp.ca
Other Communications: Constituency Phone: 780-414-1000;
Fax: 780-414-1278
twitter.com/christinandp, www.facebook.com/ChristinaNDP
Constituency Office
3448 - 93rd St.
Edmonton, AB T6E 6A4

Pete Guthrie
Constituency: Airdrie-Cochrane, United Conservative Party of
Alberta
Tel: 780-638-3018; *Fax:* 780-638-3506
Airdrie.Cochrane@assembly.ab.ca
Other Communications: Constituency Phone: 587-493-2050;
Fax: 587-493-9562
Constituency Office
#1B, 60 Railway St. East
Cochrane, AB T4C 1B5

David B. Hanson
Constituency: Bonnyville-Cold Lake-St. Paul, United
Conservative Party of Alberta
Tel: 587-404-8096; *Fax:* 780-638-3506
Bonnyville.ColdLake.StPaul@assembly.ab.ca
Other Communications: Constituency Phone: 780-826-5658;
Fax: 780-826-2165
www.facebook.com/davidhansonmla
Constituency Office
#2, 4428 - 50th Ave.
PO Box 5160
Bonnyville, AB T9N 2G4

Sarah Hoffman
Constituency: Edmonton-Glenora, New Democratic Party
Tel: 780-415-1800; *Fax:* 780-415-0701
Edmonton.Glenora@assembly.ab.ca
sarahhoffman.albertandp.ca
Other Communications: Constituency Phone: 780-455-7979;
Fax: 780-455-2197
twitter.com/shoffmanab, www.facebook.com/shoffmanAB
Constituency Office
#201, 12408 - 108th Ave.
Edmonton, AB T5M 0H3

Associate Minister, Rural Economic Development, Hon. Nate
Horner
Constituency: Drumheller-Stettler, United Conservative Party
of Alberta
Tel: 780-644-8554; *Fax:* 780-644-8554
Drumheller.Stettler@assembly.ab.ca
Other Communications: Constituency Phone: 587-774-0306
www.facebook.com/natehorner.alberta
Constituency Office
#400, 300 South Railway Ave. East
PO Box 1929
Drumheller, AB T0J 0Y0

Grant Hunter
Constituency: Taber-Warner, United Conservative Party of
Alberta
Tel: 587-689-5072; *Fax:* 780-638-3506
Taber.Warner@assembly.ab.ca
Other Communications: Constituency Phone: 403-223-0001
twitter.com/granthunterucp,
www.facebook.com/GrantHunterAB,
www.linkedin.com/in/grant-hunter-a37a77105
Constituency Office
5402 - 50 Ave.
Taber, AB T1G 1T9

Janis Irwin
Constituency: Edmonton-Highlands-Norwood, New
Democratic Party
Tel: 780-415-1800; *Fax:* 780-415-0701
Edmonton.HighlandsNorwood@assembly.ab.ca
janisirwin.albertandp.ca
Other Communications: Constituency Phone: 780-414-0682
twitter.com/JanisIrwin, www.facebook.com/JanisIrwin,
www.linkedin.com/in/janisirwin
Constituency Office
6519 - 112th Ave.
Edmonton, AB T5W 0P1

Associate Minister, Status of Women; Chief Government Whip,
Hon. Whitney Issik
Constituency: Calgary-Glenmore, United Conservative Party
of Alberta
Tel: 780-422-3559; *Fax:* 780-427-0188
Calgary.Glenmore@assembly.ab.ca
Other Communications: Constituency Phone: 403-216-5421
www.facebook.com/WhitneyIssik
Constituency Office
#311A, 2525 Woodview Dr. SW
Calgary, AB T2W 4N4

Matt Jones
Constituency: Calgary-South East, United Conservative Party
of Alberta

Tel: 780-638-3020; *Fax:* 780-638-3506
Calgary.SouthEast@assembly.ab.ca
Other Communications: Constituency Phone: 403-215-8930
twitter.com/MattJonesYYC,
www.facebook.com/MattJonesYYC,
www.linkedin.com/in/matt-jones-cfa-a8111421
Constituency Office
#202, 5126 - 126th Ave. SE
Calgary, AB T2Z 0H2

Premier; President, Executive Council; Minister,
Intergovernmental Relations, Hon. Jason Kenney, P.C.
Constituency: Calgary-Lougheed, United Conservative Party
of Alberta
Tel: 780-427-2251; *Fax:* 780-427-1349
Calgary.Lougheed@assembly.ab.ca
Other Communications: Constituency Phone: 403-238-1212;
Fax: 403-251-5453
twitter.com/jkenney, www.facebook.com/kenneyjasont
Constituency Office
#2105, 230 Eversyde Blvd. SW
Calgary, AB T2Y 0J4

Minister, Education, Hon. Adriana LaGrange
Constituency: Red Deer-North, United Conservative Party of
Alberta
Tel: 780-427-5010; *Fax:* 780-427-5018
RedDeer.North@assembly.ab.ca
Other Communications: Constituency Phone: 403-342-2263
twitter.com/adrianalagrange,
www.facebook.com/AdrianaLaGrangeRD
Constituency Office
#202, 5913 - 50th Ave.
Red Deer, AB T4N 4C4

Todd Loewen
Constituency: Central Peace-Notley, Independent
Tel: 780-427-5967
Toll-free: 866-835-4988
CentralPeace.Notley@assembly.ab.ca
Other Communications: Constituency Phone: 780-835-7211;
Fax: 780-835-7212
www.facebook.com/ToddLoewenAB
Note: On May 13, 2021 Todd Loewen was expelled from the
United Conservative Party.
Constituency Office
10410 - 110th St.
PO Box 9
Fairview, AB T0H 1L0

Martin Long
Constituency: West Yellowhead, United Conservative Party of
Alberta
Tel: 780-638-3015; *Fax:* 780-638-3506
West.Yellowhead@assembly.ab.ca
Other Communications: Constituency Phone: 780-712-7790;
Fax: 587-466-0463
Constituency Office
524B - 50th St.
Edson, AB T7E 1V1

Jackie Lovely
Constituency: Camrose, United Conservative Party of Alberta
Tel: 780-638-1258; *Fax:* 780-638-3506
Camrose@assembly.ab.ca
Other Communications: Constituency Phone: 780-672-0000;
Fax: 780-672-6945
twitter.com/jackielovelymla
Constituency Office
4870 - 51st St.
Camrose, AB T4V 1S1

Rod Loyola
Constituency: Edmonton-Ellerslie, New Democratic Party
Tel: 780-415-1800; *Fax:* 780-415-0701
Edmonton.Ellerslie@assembly.ab.ca
rodloyola.albertandp.ca
Other Communications: Constituency Phone: 780-414-2000;
Fax: 780-414-6383
twitter.com/rod_loyola, www.facebook.com/rodloyolandp
Constituency Office
5732 - 19A Ave.
Edmonton, AB T6L 1L8

Minister, Community & Social Services, Hon. Jason Luan
Constituency: Calgary-Foothills, United Conservative Party of
Alberta
Tel: 780-643-6210; *Fax:* 780-643-6214
Calgary.Foothills@assembly.ab.ca
Other Communications: Constituency Phone: 403-216-5444
twitter.com/jasonluan88, www.facebook.com/jason.luan.1,
www.linkedin.com/in/jason-luan-33268b48
Constituency Office
#29, 735 Ranchlands Blvd. NW
Calgary, AB T3G 3A9

Minister, Justice & Solicitor General, Hon. Kaycee Madu, Q.C.
Constituency: Edmonton-South West, United Conservative
Party of Alberta
Tel: 780-427-2339; *Fax:* 780-422-6621
Edmonton.SouthWest@assembly.ab.ca
Other Communications: Constituency Phone: 780-415-8692;

Fax: 780-415-8693
twitter.com/kayceemaduyeg
Constituency Office
5160 Windermere Blvd.
Edmonton, AB T6W 0L9

Minister, Municipal Affairs, Hon. Ric McIver
Constituency: Calgary-Hays, United Conservative Party of
Alberta
Tel: 780-427-3744; *Fax:* 780-422-9550
Calgary.Hays@assembly.ab.ca
Other Communications: Constituency Phone: 403-215-4380;
Fax: 403-215-4383
twitter.com/RicMcIver, www.facebook.com/RicMcIver,
www.linkedin.com/in/ric-mciver-34a49810
Constituency Office
#222, 5126 - 126th Ave. SE
Calgary, AB T2Z 0H2

Nicholas Milliken
Constituency: Calgary-Currie, United Conservative Party of
Alberta
Tel: 780-643-1040; *Fax:* 780-638-3506
Calgary.Currie@assembly.ab.ca
nicholasmilliken.nationbuilder.com
Other Communications: Constituency Phone: 403-246-4794
twitter.com/nickmilliken, www.facebook.com/nicholasmilliken,
www.linkedin.com/in/nicholas-milliken-61a61532
Constituency Office
#211, 1608 - 17th Ave. SW
Calgary, AB T2T 0E3

Associate Minister, Natural Gas & Electricity, Hon. Dale Nally
Constituency: Morinville-St. Albert, United Conservative Party
of Alberta
Tel: 780-427-0265; *Fax:* 780-638-3506
Morinville.StAlbert@assembly.ab.ca
Other Communications: Constituency Phone: 780-572-6161;
Fax: 780-572-6162
Constituency Office
9805 - 100th St.
Morinville, AB T8R 1R3

Nathan Neudorf
Constituency: Lethbridge-East, United Conservative Party of
Alberta
Tel: 780-643-1034; *Fax:* 780-638-3506
Lethbridge.East@assembly.ab.ca
Other Communications: Constituency Phone: 403-320-1011;
Fax: 403-328-6613
www.facebook.com/nathanneudorf,
www.linkedin.com/in/nathan-neudorf-75b67a5b
Constituency Office
#10, 550 WT Hill Blvd. South
Lethbridge, AB T1J 4Z9

Minister, Advanced Education, Hon. Demetrios Nicolaides
Constituency: Calgary-Bow, United Conservative Party of
Alberta
Tel: 780-427-5777; *Fax:* 780-422-8733
Calgary.Bow@assembly.ab.ca
Other Communications: Constituency Phone: 403-216-5400;
Fax: 403-216-5402
Constituency Office
8561 - 8A Ave. SW
Calgary, AB T3H 0V5

Chris Nielsen
Constituency: Edmonton-Decore, New Democratic Party
Tel: 780-415-1800; *Fax:* 780-415-0701
Edmonton.Decore@assembly.ab.ca
chrisnielsen.albertandp.ca
Other Communications: Constituency Phone: 780-414-1328;
Fax: 780-414-1330
twitter.com/chrisnielsenndp,
www.facebook.com/ChrisNielsenNDP
Constituency Office
#203, 8119 - 160th Ave.
Edmonton, AB T5Z 0G3

Minister, Environment & Parks; Government House Leader,
Hon. Jason Nixon
Constituency: Rimbey-Rocky Mountain House-Sundre, United
Conservative Party of Alberta
Tel: 780-427-2391; *Fax:* 780-422-6259
Rimbey.RockyMountainhouse.Sundre@assembly.ab.ca
Other Communications: Constituency Phone: 403-638-5029;
403-638-2685
twitter.com/JasonNixonAB, www.facebook.com/jason.j.nixon,
www.linkedin.com/in/jasonjnixon
Constituency Office
101 - 6th St. SW
PO Box 1547
Sundre, AB T0M 1X0

Jeremy Nixon
Constituency: Calgary-Klein, United Conservative Party of
Alberta
Tel: 780-643-1039; *Fax:* 780-638-3506
Calgary.Klein@assembly.ab.ca
Other Communications: Constituency Phone: 403-216-5430;
Fax: 403-216-5432

Constituency Office
#201, 1055 - 20th Ave. NW
Calgary, AB T2M 1E7
Leader, Official Opposition, Rachel Notley
Constituency: Edmonton-Strathcona, New Democratic Party
Tel: 780-415-1800; *Fax:* 780-415-0701
Edmonton.Strathcona@assembly.ab.ca
Other Communications: Constituency Phone: 780-414-0702
twitter.com/RachelNotley, www.facebook.com/rachelnotley
Constituency Office, Strathcona Professional Centre
#101, 10328 - 81st Ave. NW
Edmonton, AB T6E 1X2
Minister, Culture, Hon. Ronald Orr
Constituency: Lacombe-Ponoka, United Conservative Party of Alberta
Tel: 780-422-3559; *Fax:* 780-427-0188
Lacombe.Ponoka@assembly.ab.ca
Other Communications: Constituency Phone: 403-782-7725
www.facebook.com/RonOrrAB
Constituency Office
#101, 4892 - 46th St.
Lacombe, A T4L 2B4
Rakhi Pancholi
Constituency: Edmonton-Whitemud, New Democratic Party
Tel: 780-415-1800; *Fax:* 780-415-0701
Edmonton.Whitemud@assembly.ab.ca
rakhipancholi.albertandp.ca
Other Communications: Constituency Phone: 780-413-5970;
Fax: 780-413-5971
twitter.com/pancholi_rakhi
Constituency Office
#203, 596 Riverbend Sq.
Edmonton, AB T6R 2E3
Minister, Infrastructure, Hon. Prasad Panda
Constituency: Calgary-Edgemont, United Conservative Party of Alberta
Tel: 780-427-5041; *Fax:* 780-644-1204
Calgary.Edgemont@assembly.ab.ca
www.prasadpanda.ca
Other Communications: Constituency Phone: 403-288-4453;
Fax: 587-393-8055
twitter.com/prasadpandayyc,
www.facebook.com/PrasadPandaYYC,
www.linkedin.com/in/prasadpanda
Constituency Office
#222, 5149 Country Hills Blvd. NW
Calgary, AB T3A 5K8
Shannon Phillips
Constituency: Lethbridge-West, New Democratic Party
Tel: 780-415-1801; *Fax:* 780-415-0701
Lethbridge.West@assembly.ab.ca
shannonphillips.albertandp.ca
Other Communications: Constituency Phone: 403-329-4644;
Fax: 587-425-5869
twitter.com/sphillipsab,
www.facebook.com/ShannonPhillipsLethbridge
Constituency Office
#110, 410 Stafford Dr. South
Lethbridge, AB T1J 2L2
Deputy Speaker; Chair of Committees, Angela Pitt
Constituency: Airdrie, United Conservative Party of Alberta
Tel: 780-644-7121; *Fax:* 780-638-3506
Airdrie.East@assembly.ab.ca
angelapitt.ca
Other Communications: Constituency Phone: 403-948-8741;
Fax: 403-948-8744
www.facebook.com/AngelaPittAirdrie
Constituency Office
209 Bowers St.
Airdrie, AB T4B 0R6
Minister, Seniors & Housing, Hon. Josephine Pon
Constituency: Calgary-Beddington, United Conservative Party of Alberta
Tel: 780-415-9550; *Fax:* 780-415-9411
Calgary.Beddington@assembly.ab.ca
Other Communications: Constituency Phone: 403-215-7710
twitter.com/ponjosephine, www.facebook.com/PonJosephine,
www.linkedin.com/in/josephine-pon-6007ba30
Constituency Office
#106, 8220 Centre St. NE
Calgary, AB T3K 1J7
Pat Rehn
Constituency: Lesser Slave Lake, United Conservative Party of Alberta
Tel: 780-638-2818; *Fax:* 780-638-3506
Lesser.SlaveLake@assembly.ab.ca
Other Communications: Constituency Phone: 825-219-1000;
Fax: 780-849-4132
Constituency Office, Visitor Information Centre
12 Poplar Dr.
Slave Lake, AB T0G 2A0
Roger Reid
Constituency: Livingstone-Macleod, United Conservative Party of Alberta

Tel: 780-638-1241; *Fax:* 780-638-3506
Livingstone.Macleod@assembly.ab.ca
Other Communications: Constituency Phone: 825-212-2000;
Fax: 403-652-3486
www.facebook.com/RogerReidAB,
www.linkedin.com/in/rogerreid
Constituency Office
618 Center St. East
High River, AB T1V 1E9
Marie Renaud
Constituency: St. Albert, New Democratic Party
Tel: 780-415-1800; *Fax:* 780-415-0701
St.Albert@assembly.ab.ca
marierenaud.albertandp.ca
Other Communications: Constituency Phone: 780-459-9113;
Fax: 780-460-9815
twitter.com/mariefrrenaud,
www.facebook.com/MarieRenaudNDP
Constituency Office
#109B, 50 St Thomas St.
St Albert, AB T8N 6Z8
Miranda Rosin
Constituency: Banff-Kananaskis, United Conservative Party of Alberta
Tel: 780-643-1027; *Fax:* 780-638-3506
Banff.Kananaskis@assembly.ab.ca
www.mirandarosin.com
Other Communications: Constituency Phone: 403-609-4509;
Fax: 403-609-4513
www.facebook.com/mirandarosin,
www.linkedin.com/in/mirandarosin
Constituency Office
#206, 1080 Railway Ave.
Canmore, AB T1W 1P4
Garth Rowswell
Constituency: Vermilion-Lloydminster-Wainwright, United Conservative Party of Alberta
Tel: 780-638-1398; *Fax:* 780-638-3506
Vermilion.Lloydminster.Wainwright@assembly.ab.ca
Other Communications: Constituency Phone: 780-842-6177
www.facebook.com/GarthRowswellMLA
Constituency Office
123 - 10th St.
Wainwright, AB T9W 1N6
Deputy Government Whip, Brad Rutherford
Constituency: Leduc-Beaumont, United Conservative Party of Alberta
Tel: 780-638-3171; *Fax:* 780-638-3506
Leduc.Beaumont@assembly.ab.ca
Other Communications: Constituency Phone: 780-929-3290;
Fax: 780-929-7881
www.facebook.com/bradrutherforducp,
www.linkedin.com/in/brad-rutherford-b73b3898
Constituency Office
#106, 6202 - 29th Ave.
Beaumont, AB T4X 0H5
Irfan Sabir
Constituency: Calgary-McCall, New Democratic Party
Tel: 780-415-1800; *Fax:* 780-415-0701
Calgary.McCall@assembly.ab.ca
irfansabir.albertandp.ca
Other Communications: Constituency Phone: 403-216-5424;
Fax: 403-216-5426
Constituency Office
#223, 4850 Westwinds Dr. NE
Calgary, AB T3J 3Z5
Minister, Energy, Hon. Sonya Savage
Constituency: Calgary-North West, United Conservative Party of Alberta
Tel: 780-427-3740; *Fax:* 780-644-1222
Calgary.Northwest@assembly.ab.ca
Other Communications: Constituency Phone: 403-297-7104
Constituency Office
#7223, 8650 - 112th Ave. NW
Calgary, AB T3R 0R5
Minister, Transportation, Hon. Rajan Sawhney
Constituency: Calgary-North East, United Conservative Party of Alberta
Tel: 780-427-2080; *Fax:* 780-422-2002
Calgary.NorthEast@assembly.ab.ca
Other Communications: Constituency Phone: 587-318-2946
twitter.com/rajanjsaw, www.facebook.com/rajanjsawhney,
www.linkedin.com/in/rajansaw
Constituency Office
#1080, 11124 - 36th St. NE
Calgary, AB T3N 1L3
Marlin Schmidt
Constituency: Edmonton-Gold Bar, New Democratic Party
Tel: 780-415-1800; *Fax:* 780-415-0701
Edmonton.Goldbar@assembly.ab.ca
marlinschmidt.albertandp.ca
Other Communications: Constituency Phone: 780-414-1015;
Fax: 780-414-1017
www.facebook.com/marlinschmidtAB

Constituency Office
#100, 8925 - 82nd Ave.
Edmonton, AB T6C 0Z2
Deputy Government House Leader, Joseph Schow
Constituency: Cardston-Siksika, United Conservative Party of Alberta
Tel: 780-638-1158; *Fax:* 780-638-3506
Cardston.Siksika@assembly.ab.ca
Other Communications: Constituency Phone: 403-653-5070
www.facebook.com/josephschowucp
Constituency Office, Carriage Lane Mall
#1, 555 Main St.
Cardston, AB T0K 0K0
Minister, Children's Services, Hon. Rebecca Schulz
Constituency: Calgary-Shaw, United Conservative Party of Alberta
Tel: 780-644-5255; *Fax:* 780-644-6817
Calgary.Shaw@assembly.ab.ca
www.rebeccaschulz.ca
Other Communications: Constituency Phone: 403-256-8969;
Fax: 403-256-8970
twitter.com/rebeccakschulz,
www.facebook.com/rebeccaschulzyyc
Constituency Office
#230, 251 Midpark Blvd. SE
Calgary, AB T2X 1S3
Minister, Jobs, Economy & Innovation, Hon. Doug Schweitzer, Q.C.
Constituency: Calgary-Elbow, United Conservative Party of Alberta
Tel: 780-427-2339; *Fax:* 780-422-6621
Calgary.Elbow@assembly.ab.ca
www.dougschweitzer.com
Other Communications: Constituency Phone: 403-252-0346;
Fax: 403-252-0520
twitter.com/doug_schweitzer,
www.linkedin.com/in/doug-schweitzer-573a443b
Constituency Office
#205, 5005 Elbow Dr. SW
Calgary, AB T2S 2T6
Minister, Labour & Immigration, Hon. Tyler Shandro, Q.C.
Constituency: Calgary-Acadia, United Conservative Party of Alberta
Tel: 780-427-3665; *Fax:* 780-415-0961
Calgary.Acadia@assembly.ab.ca
www.tylershandro.com
Other Communications: Constituency Phone: 403-640-1363
twitter.com/shandro, www.facebook.com/TylerSShandro
Constituency Office
#105, 10333 Southport Rd. SW
Calgary, AB T2W 3X6
David Shepherd
Constituency: Edmonton-City Centre, New Democratic Party
Edmonton.CityCentre@assembly.ab.ca
davidshepherd.albertandp.ca
Other Communications: Constituency Phone: 780-414-0743
twitter.com/dshepyeg, www.facebook.com/dmshepYEG
Constituency Office
10208 - 112th St.
Edmonton, AB T5K 1M4
Lori Sigurdson
Constituency: Edmonton-Riverview, New Democratic Party
Tel: 780-415-1800; *Fax:* 780-415-0701
Edmonton.Riverview@assembly.ab.ca
lorisigurdson.albertandp.ca
Other Communications: Constituency Phone: 780-414-0719
twitter.com/lorisigurdson,
www.facebook.com/lorisigurdson.ndp
Constituency Office
9202B - 149th St.
Edmonton, AB T5R 1C3
R.J. Sigurdson
Constituency: Highwood, United Conservative Party of Alberta
Tel: 780-638-3156; *Fax:* 780-638-3506
Highwood@assembly.ab.ca
Other Communications: Constituency Phone: 403-995-5488;
Fax: 403-995-5490
www.linkedin.com/in/rj-sigurdson-660b6935
Constituency Office
#5, 49 Elizabeth St.
PO Box 568
Okotoks, AB T1S 1A7
Peter Singh
Constituency: Calgary-East, United Conservative Party of Alberta
Tel: 780-638-1399; *Fax:* 780-638-3506
Calgary.East@assembly.ab.ca
Other Communications: Constituency Phone: 587-496-2052;
Fax: 403-235-4772
Constituency Office
#202, 3505 - 52nd St. SE
Calgary, A T2B 3R3

Mark Smith
Constituency: Drayton Valley-Devon, United Conservative Party of Alberta
Tel: 780-644-7146; *Fax:* 780-638-3506
draytonvalley.devon@assembly.ab.ca
Other Communications: Constituency Phone: 780-542-3355; Fax: 780-542-3331
www.facebook.com/MarkSmithAlberta
Constituency Office
5136B - 52nd Ave.
PO Box 7272
Drayton Valley, AB T7A 1S5
Jason Stephan
Constituency: Red Deer-South, United Conservative Party of Alberta
Tel: 780-638-3176; *Fax:* 780-638-3506
RedDeer.South@assembly.ab.ca
Other Communications: Constituency Phone: 403-340-3565; Fax: 403-340-5977
Constituency Office
#201, 4327 - 54th Ave.
Red Deer, AB T4N 4L9
Heather Sweet
Constituency: Edmonton-Manning, New Democratic Party
Tel: 780-415-1800; *Fax:* 780-415-0701
Edmonton.Manning@assembly.ab.ca
heathersweet.albertandp.ca
Other Communications: Constituency Phone: 780-414-0714
twitter.com/heathersweetab,
www.facebook.com/heathersweetab
Constituency Office
14904 - 50th St.
Edmonton, AB T5A 5H7
Minister, Finance; President, Treasury Board, Hon. Travis Toews
Constituency: Grande Prairie-Wapiti, United Conservative Party of Alberta
Tel: 780-415-4855; *Fax:* 780-638-3506
GrandePrairie.Wapiti@assembly.ab.ca
Other Communications: Constituency Phone: 825-412-2050; Fax: 780-539-0628
www.facebook.com/TravisToewsAB
Constituency Office
15602C - 102nd St.
Grande Prairie, AB T8X 0K7
Devinder Toor
Constituency: Calgary-Falconridge, United Conservative Party of Alberta
Tel: 780-638-3016; *Fax:* 780-638-3506
Calgary.Falconridge@assembly.ab.ca
Other Communications: Constituency Phone: 403-280-4022; Fax: 403-280-3877
Constituency Office
#215, 5401 Temple Dr. NE
PO Box 45
Calgary, AB T1Y 3R7
Searle Turton
Constituency: Spruce Grove-Stony Plain, United Conservative Party of Alberta
Tel: 780-638-3144; *Fax:* 780-638-3506
SpruceGrove.StonyPlain@assembly.ab.ca
Other Communications: Constituency Phone: 780-962-6606; Fax: 780-962-1568
twitter.com/searleturton, www.facebook.com/searleturton
Constituency Office
#60, 210 McLeod Ave.
Spruce Grove, AB T7X 2K5
Glenn van Dijken
Constituency: Athabasca-Barrhead-Westlock, United Conservative Party of Alberta
Tel: 780-644-7152; *Fax:* 780-638-3506
Athabasca.Barrhead.Westlock@assembly.ab.ca
Other Communications: Constituency Phone: 780-674-3225; Fax: 780-674-6183
twitter.com/glennvandijken,
www.facebook.com/glenn.van.dijken
Constituency Office
5106 - 50th St.
Barrhead, AB T7N 1A3
Jordan Walker
Constituency: Sherwood Park, United Conservative Party of Alberta
Tel: 780-638-3017; *Fax:* 780-638-3506
Sherwood.Park@assembly.ab.ca
Other Communications: Constituency Phone: 780-417-4747; Fax: 780-417-4748
twitter.com/jordanwalkerab,
www.facebook.com/jwalkeralberta
Constituency Office, Athabasca Professional Bldg.
#105, 80 Chippewa Rd.
Sherwood Park, AB T8A 4W6
Dan Williams
Constituency: Peace River, United Conservative Party of Alberta

Tel: 780-638-3019; *Fax:* 780-638-3506
Peace.River@assembly.ab.ca
Other Communications: Constituency Phone: 780-928-5100
Constituency Office
10013 - 101st Ave.
PO Box 2793
La Crete, AB T0H 2H0
Minister, Indigenous Relations, Hon. Rick Wilson
Constituency: Maskwacis-Wetaskiwin, United Conservative Party of Alberta
Tel: 780-422-4144; *Fax:* 780-638-4052
Maskwacis.Wetaskiwin@assembly.ab.ca
Other Communications: Constituency Phone: 780-360-8003; Fax: 780-312-1882
twitter.com/Richard4Alberta,
www.facebook.com/RickWilsonforAlberta
Constituency Office
5019 - 50th St.
Wetaskiwin, AB T9A 1K1
Tany Yao
Constituency: Fort McMurray-Wood Buffalo, United Conservative Party of Alberta
Tel: 780-644-7129; *Fax:* 780-638-3506
fortmcmurray.woodbuffalo@assembly.ab.ca
Other Communications: Constituency Phone: 780-790-6014
twitter.com/tanyyao, www.facebook.com/TanyYaoAB
Constituency Office
#102, 9912 Franklin Ave.
Fort McMurray, AB T9H 2K4
Associate Minister, Immigration & Multiculturalism, Hon. Muhammad Yaseen
Constituency: Calgary-North, United Conservative Party of Alberta
Tel: 780-638-9400; *Fax:* 780-638-9401
Calgary.North@assembly.ab.ca
Other Communications: Constituency Phone: 403-274-1931
www.facebook.com/MuhammadYaseenYYC
Constituency Office
#104, 200 Country Hills Landing NW
Calgary, AB T3K 5P3
Vacant
Constituency: Fort McMurray-Lac La Biche
Note: In August, 2021 Laila Goodridge risgned as Fort McMurray-Lac La Biche MLA to run in the 2021 federal election.

Alberta Government Departments & Agencies

Alberta Advanced Education

Legislature Bldg., #403, 10800 - 97th Ave., Edmonton, AB T5K 2B6
Tel: 780-422-5400
www.alberta.ca/advanced-education.aspx
On Oct. 22, 2015, Premier Notley created Alberta Economic Development & Trade, drawing from parts of Innovation & Advanced Education, & leaving Advanced Education as its own portfolio. The key responsibilities of Advanced Education include post-secondary matters, apprenticeship & industry training & adult learning.
The following are some specific activities: funding public post-secondary institutions in Alberta; developing program standards with industry; counselling apprentices & employers; certifying apprentices & occupational trainees; providing student financial assistance; funding education providers; & funding apprentices.

Minister, Advanced Education, Hon. Demetrios Nicolaides
Tel: 780-427-5777; *Fax:* 780-422-8733
ae.minister@gov.ab.ca

Deputy Minister, Curtis Clarke
Tel: 780-415-4744
curtis.clarke@gov.ab.ca

Executive Director, Human Resources, Rodney Yaremchuk
Tel: 780-415-9109
rodney.yaremchuk@gov.ab.ca

Director, Communications, Jo-Anne Nugent
Tel: 780-427-3807
jo-anne.nugent@gov.ab.ca

Associated Agencies, Boards & Commissions:

• **Alberta Apprenticeship & Industry Training Board**
Centre for Applied Technologies Bldg.
#430, 11763 - 106 St.
Edmonton, AB T5G 2R1
Tel: 403-476-9757; *Fax:* 780-422-3734
Toll-free: -310-0000
TTY: 780-427-9999
tradesecrets.gov.ab.ca
Other Communication: General Inquiries, Phone: 780-427-8765; TTY Toll-Free: 800-232-7215
Board members are appointed by the Lieutenant Governor in Council, upon recommendation of the Minister of Advanced Education. The mission of the board is to maintain high quality training & certification standards in the apprenticeship & industry training system. The board offers recommendations to the Minister about the needs of the labour market in Alberta & the training & certification of persons in designated trades & occupations.

• **Alberta Council on Admissions & Transfer (ACAT)**
Commerce Place
10155 - 102 St., 8th Fl.
Edmonton, AB T5J 4L5
Tel: 780-422-9021; *Fax:* 780-422-3688
Toll-free: -310-0000
TTY: 780-427-9999
acat@gov.ab.ca
www.acat.gov.ab.ca
Other Communication: TTY Toll-Free: 800-232-7215
Established in 1974, the independent body advocates for learners by working to ensure transferability of educational courses & programs to benefit students. The role of the council is to develop policies & procedures to facilitate transfer agreements among post-secondary institutions.

• **Campus Alberta Quality Council (CAQC)**
Commerce Place
10155 - 102 St., 8th Fl.
Edmonton, AB T5J 4L5
Tel: 780-427-8921; *Fax:* 780-641-9783
caqc@gov.ab.ca
caqc.alberta.ca
The arms-length quality assurance agency makes recommendations to the Minister of Advanced Education & Technology on applications from post-secondary institutions that want to offer new degree programs. All degree programs, except for degrees in divinity, offered by resident institutions & non-resident institutions in Alberta must be approved by the Minister.

Advanced Learning & Community Partnerships Division
Commerce Place, 10155 - 102nd St., 7th Fl., Edmonton, AB T5J 4L5
Assistant Deputy Minister, Peter Leclaire
Tel: 780-641-9349
peter.leclaire@gov.ab.ca
Executive Director, External Relations Sector, Erin Gregg
Tel: 780-644-1856
erin.gregg@gov.ab.ca
Executive Director, Operations, Gilbert Perras
Tel: 780-638-3588
gilbert.perras@gov.ab.ca
Executive Director, Campus Alberta Sector, David E. Williams
Tel: 780-415-9668
david.e.williams@gov.ab.ca

Apprenticeship & Student Aid Division
Commerce Place, 10155 - 102nd St., 6th Fl., Edmonton, AB T5J 4L5
Assistant Deputy Minister, Andy Weiler
Tel: 780-644-7732
andy.weiler@gov.ab.ca
Executive Director, Policy & Standards, Carla Corbett
Tel: 780-422-1193
carla.corbett@gov.ab.ca
Executive Director, Student Aid, Maggie DesLauriers
Tel: 780-422-4498; *Fax:* 780-422-4517
maggie.deslauriers@gov.ab.ca
Executive Director, Foundational Learning Supports, David Schneider
Tel: 780-415-9106
david.schneider@gov.ab.ca

Strategic & Corporate Services Division
Commerce Pl., 10155 - 102nd St., 12th Fl., Edmonton, AB T5J 4G8
Assistant Deputy Minister, Dan Rizzoli
Tel: 780-415-2966
dan.rizzoli@gov.ab.ca
Senior Financial Officer, Corporate Services, Richard Isaak
Tel: 780-415-9149
richard.isaak@gov.ab.ca
Executive Director, Strategic Policy & Planning, Carmen Baldwin-Dery

Tel: 780-427-3630
carmen.baldwin-dery@gov.ab.ca
Senior Director, Strategic Policy, Sandra Duxbury
Tel: 780-427-4498
sandra.duxbury@gov.ab.ca
Senior Director, Cross Ministry & Intergovernmental Strategies,
Carolyn Fewkes
Tel: 780-422-4062
carolyn.fewkes@gov.ab.ca

Alberta Agriculture & Forestry

JG O'Donoghue Bldg., #100A, 7000 - 113th St., Edmonton, AB T6H 5T6

Tel: 403-742-7901
www.alberta.ca/agriculture-and-forestry.aspx
twitter.com/AlbertaAg
www.facebook.com/AgricultureAlberta
www.youtube.com/user/AlbertaAgriculture
The department changed from Agriculture & Rural Development
to Agriculture & Forestry following the May 2015 general
election, when it absorbed the Forestry Division from
Environment & Sustainable Resource Development (renamed
Environment & Parks after the election).

Minister, Agriculture & Forestry, Hon. Devin Dreeshen
Tel: 780-427-2137; *Fax:* 780-422-6035
af.minister.m@gov.ab.ca

Deputy Minister, Andre Tremblay
Tel: 780-427-2145; *Fax:* 780-415-6002
andre.tremblay@gov.ab.ca

Associated Agencies, Boards & Commissions:
• **Agriculture Financial Services Corporation (AFSC)**
5718 - 56 Ave.
Lacombe, AB T4L 1B1
Toll-free: 877-899-2372
info@afsc.ca
www.afsc.ca
Other Communication: Toll-Free Fax: 855-700-2372
The Agriculture Financial Services Corporation provides loans,
crop insurance & farm income disaster assistance to farmers,
agricultural & small businesses. Although the AFSC is a
provincial crown corporation, it has a public sector board of
directors, & works closely with private sector companies through
business alliances.

• **Agricultural Products Marketing Council**
JG O'Donoghue Bldg.
#305, 7000 - 113 St.
Edmonton, AB T6H 5T6
Tel: 780-427-2164
www.agriculture.alberta.ca/marketingcouncil
The Alberta Agricultural Products Marketing Council supports
legislation & regulations & offers policy advice to the Minister of
Agriculture & Rural Development & industry organizations.

• **Irrigation Council**
Provincial Bldg.
200 - 5 Ave. South, 3rd Fl.
Lethbridge, AB T1J 4L1
Tel: 403-381-5176; *Fax:* 403-382-4406
www1.agric.gov.ab.ca/$department/deptdocs.nsf/all/irc9432
The Irrigation Council was established under Section 50 of the
Irrigation Districts Act. The provincial agency reports to the
Minister of Agriculture & Rural Development.

• **Farmers' Advocate Office (FAO)**
JG O'Donoghue Bldg.
#100, 7000 - 113 St.
Edmonton, AB T6H 5T6
Fax: 780-427-3913
Toll-free: -310-3276
farmers.advocate@gov.ab.ca
www.farmersadvocate.gov.ab.ca
The Farmers' Advocate Office offers rural consumer protection,
rural opportunities, & fair process for rural Albertans. The Office
supports programs to settle disputes or offer appeals privately.

Food & Value Added Processing Division
JG O'Donoghue Bldg., 7000 - 113th St., 3rd Fl., Edmonton, AB T6H 5T6

Tel: 780-427-6159
Assistant Deputy Minister, Lisa Sadownik
Tel: 780-644-2909; *Fax:* 780-422-6317
lisa.sadownik@gov.ab.ca
Executive Director, Food & Bio-Processing Branch, Ken Gossen
Tel: 780-980-4860
ken.gossen@gov.ab.ca
Acting Executive Director, Rural Development Branch, Murray
Greer
Tel: 780-980-4722
murray.greer@gov.ab.ca

Executive Director, Food Safety Branch, Jeff Stewart
Tel: 780-641-9084
jeff.stewart@gov.ab.ca

Forestry Division
Petroleum Plaza ST, 9915 - 108th St., 10th Fl., Edmonton, AB T5K 2G8
Assistant Deputy Minister, Bruce Mayer
Tel: 780-427-3542; *Fax:* 780-427-0923
bruce.mayer@gov.ab.ca
Executive Director, Wildfire Management Branch, Wally Born
Tel: 780-638-3948
wally.born@gov.ab.ca
Executive Director, Forest Tenure, Trade & Policy Branch,
Daniel Lux
Tel: 780-644-2246; *Fax:* 780-644-5728
daniel.lux@gov.ab.ca
Executive Director, Forest Management Branch, Darren Tapp
Tel: 780-427-5324; *Fax:* 780-427-0085
darren.tapp@gov.ab.ca

Intergovernmental Relations, Trade & Environment Division
JG O'Donoghue Bldg., 7000 - 113th St., 3rd Fl., Edmonton, AB T6H 5T6
Assistant Deputy Minister, Dave Burdek
Tel: 780-427-1957; *Fax:* 780-422-6317
dave.burdek@gov.ab.ca
Executive Director, Economics & Competitiveness Branch, Don
Brown
Tel: 780-644-5634
don.brown@gov.ab.ca
Executive Director, Policy, Strategy & Intergovernmental Affairs
Branch, Darren Chase
Tel: 780-427-3338
darren.chase@gov.ab.ca
Executive Director, Environmental Stewardship Branch, Sean
Royer
Tel: 780-427-0674
sean.royer@gov.ab.ca
Executive Director, Irrigation & Farm Water Branch, Jamie Wuite
Tel: 780-427-3747
jamie.wuite@gov.ab.ca

Livestock & Crops Division
JG O'Donoghue Bldg., 7000 - 113th St., 3rd Fl., Edmonton, AB T6H 5T6
Assistant Deputy Minister, Jamie Curran
Tel: 780-427-2439
jamie.curran@gov.ab.ca
Executive Director, Crop Research & Extension Branch, Dr.
James Calpas
Tel: 780-782-8614
james.calpas@gov.ab.ca
Executive Director & Assistant Chief Provincial Veterinarian,
Animal Health & Assurance Branch, Dr. Gerald Hauer
Tel: 780-427-3448
gerald.hauer@gov.ab.ca
Executive Director, Crop Health & Assurance Branch, Jake
Kotowich
Tel: 780-422-1236
jake.kotowich@gov.ab.ca

Strategy, Planning & Governance Division
JG O'Donoghue Bldg., 7000 - 113th St., 3rd Fl., Edmonton, AB T6H 5T6
Assistant Deputy Minister, Freda Molenkamp-Oudman
Tel: 780-644-4128
freda.molenkamp-oudman@gov.ab.ca
Executive Director, Strategy, Policy & Extension Services
Branch, Katrina Bluetchen
Tel: 780-427-4532
katrina.bluetchen@gov.ab.ca
Executive Director, Rural Development Branch, Greg Rudolf
Tel: 780-644-3029
greg.rudolf@gov.ab.ca
Executive Director / Senior Financial Officer, Financial Services
Branch, Christine Yaremko
Tel: 780-427-3216
christine.yaremko@gov.ab.ca

Alberta Office of the Auditor General

9925 - 109th St., 8th Fl., Edmonton, AB T5K 2J8
Tel: 780-427-4222; *Fax:* 780-422-9555
info@oag.ab.ca
www.oag.ab.ca
Secondary Address: #820, 600 - 6th Ave. SW
Calgary, AB T2P 0S5
Alt. Fax: 403-297-5195
twitter.com/AuditorGenAB
www.facebook.com/AuditorGenAB
www.linkedin.com/company/office-of-the-auditor-general-of-alberta

The Auditor General of Alberta is the independent auditor of all
Government of Alberta ministries, departments, regulated funds,
& agencies. Audits identify areas where improvement is required
for the use of public resources & provide recommendations to
improve practices.

Auditor General, W. Doug Wylie
Tel: 780-422-8372
dwylie@oag.ab.ca

Assistant Auditor General, Robert Driesen
Tel: 780-422-8445
rdriesen@oag.ab.ca

Assistant Auditor General, Brad Ireland
Tel: 780-422-6447
bireland@oag.ab.ca

Assistant Auditor General, Eric Leonty
Tel: 780-422-8448
eleonty@oag.ab.ca

Chief Operating Officer, Corporate Services, Ruth McHugh
Tel: 780-422-6517
rmchugh@oag.ab.ca

Senior Financial Officer, Loulou Eng, CMA
Tel: 780-422-6355
leng@oag.ab.ca

Executive Director, People & Culture, Steve Fedorchuk
Tel: 780-422-6788
sfedorchuk@oag.ab.ca

Executive Director, Stakeholder Engagement, Val
Mellesmoen
Tel: 780-644-4806
vmellesmoen@oag.ab.ca

Alberta Office of the Child & Youth Advocate (OCYA)

#600, 9925 - 109th St. NW, Edmonton, AB T5K 2J8
Tel: 780-422-6056; *Fax:* 780-422-3675
Toll-Free: 800-661-3446
ca.information@ocya.alberta.ca
www.ocya.alberta.ca
Secondary Address: #2420, 801 - 6 Ave. SW
South Office
Calgary, AB T2P 3W3
Alt. Fax: 403-297-4456
twitter.com/AlbertaCYA
www.facebook.com/AlbertaOCYA
www.youtube.com/user/AlbertaAdvocate
As of April 1, 2012, the Child & Youth Advocate is an
independent officer reporting to the Legislature under the Child &
Youth Advocate Act.

Child & Youth Advocate, Del Graff
Tel: 780-422-6056; *Fax:* 780-422-3675
del.graff@ocya.alberta.ca

Executive Director, Child & Youth Advocacy, Jackie
Stewart
Tel: 780-644-2363
jackie.stewart@ocya.alberta.ca

Alberta Children's Services

Office of the Minister, Legislature Bldg., #204, 10800 - 97th Ave., Edmonton, AB T5K 2B6
www.alberta.ca/childrens-services.aspx
The Ministry of Children's Services was created in January 2017,
formed from the previous Ministry of Human Services. Its
responsibilities include child care & intervention, early childhood
development, foster care, adoption, & improvements for children
& youth.

Minister, Hon. Rebecca Schulz
Tel: 780-644-5255; *Fax:* 780-644-6817
cs.minister@gov.ab.ca

Deputy Minister, Darlene Bouwsema
Tel: 780-644-1500
darlene.bouwsema@gov.ab.ca

Child Intervention Division
Sterling Pl., 9940 - 106th St., Edmonton, AB T5K 2N2
Tel: 780-422-0305; *Fax:* 780-422-5415
Assistant Deputy Minister, Rae-Ann Lajeunesse
Tel: 780-644-3010
rae-ann.lajeunesse@gov.ab.ca
Executive Director, Child, Youth & Family Enhancement Act,
Elden Block

Tel: 780-638-1229
elden.block@gov.ab.ca

Corporate Services Division
Standard Life Centre, 10405 Jasper Ave., 4th Fl., Edmonton, AB T5J 4R7
Tel: 780-638-3560; *Fax:* 780-644-2524
Assistant Deputy Minister, Chi Loo
Tel: 780-422-3179
chi.loo@gov.ab.ca
Acting Executive Director, Corporate Finance & Senior Financial Officer & Director, Mahmud Dhala
Tel: 780-427-2190
mahmud.dhala@gov.ab.ca
Executive Director, Business Services, Kevin Molcak
Tel: 780-644-1125; *Fax:* 780-427-9376
kevin.molcak@gov.ab.ca
Provincial Director, Emergency Management & Business Continuity Services, Sonya Perkins
Tel: 780-644-1782; *Fax:* 780-427-9376
sonya.perkins@gov.ab.ca

Family & Community Resiliency Division
Sterling Pl., 9940 - 106th St., 12th Fl., Edmonton, AB T5K 2N2
Assistant Deputy Minister, Mark Hattori
Tel: 780-415-1548
mark.hattori@gov.ab.ca
Executive Director, Regional & Community Program Delivery, Russ Pickford
Tel: 780-638-1273
russ.pickford@gov.ab.ca
Executive Director, Prevention, Early Intervention & Youth Branch, Silvia Vajushi
Tel: 780-638-1266
silvia.vajushi@gov.ab.ca

Policy Integration & Indigenous Connections Division
Sterling Place, 9940 - 106th St., 5th Fl., Edmonton, AB T5K 2N2
Assistant Deputy Minister, Gloria Iatridis
Tel: 780-415-2209; *Fax:* 780-422-0562
gloria.iatridis@gov.ab.ca
Executive Director, Indigenous & Community Connections Branch, Peter Crossen
Tel: 780-644-7782
peter.crossen@gov.ab.ca
Executive Director, Policy Branch, Sheryl Fricke
Tel: 780-415-2221
sheryl.fricke@gov.ab.ca
Executive Director, Social Innovation, Sandra Klashinsky
Tel: 780-427-7242; *Fax:* 780-422-0562
sandra.klashinsky@gov.ab.ca

Alberta Community & Social Services

Office of the Minister, Legislature Bldg., #224, 10800 - 97th Ave., Edmonton, AB T5K 2B6
Tel: 780-644-9992
Toll-Free: 877-644-9992
www.alberta.ca/community-and-social-services.aspx
twitter.com/AlbertaCSS
The Ministry of Community & Social Services was created in January 2017, drawing from the former Ministry of Human Services. Its responsibilities include income, employment, disabilities & community-based support, family violence prevention, & family & community support services.

Minister, Hon. Jason Luan
Tel: 780-643-6210; *Fax:* 780-643-6214
css.minister@gov.ab.ca

Deputy Minister, Cynthia Farmer
Tel: 780-427-6448

Executive Lead, PDD Review Secretariat, Kindy Joseph
Tel: 780-644-8613
kindy.joseph@gov.ab.ca

Director, Communications, Tamara Magnan
Tel: 780-415-6490
tamara.magnan@gov.ab.ca

Associated Agencies, Boards & Commissions:
• Appeals Secretariat
Agronomy Centre
#201, 6903 - 116 St.
Edmonton, AB T6H 5Z2
Tel: 780-427-2709; *Fax:* 780-422-1088
Toll-free: -310-0000
CSS.Appeals@gov.ab.ca
humanservices.alberta.ca/department/appeals-secretariat.html
Other Communication: Regional Phones: 403-297-5636 (Calgary); 403-340-5531 (Red Deer); Lethbridge (403-381-5681)

Provides appeal options for people in Alberta whose benefits through Assured Income for the Severely Handicapped Act (AISH) or Alberta Works Income Supports (IESA) have been denied, changed or cancelled.

• McCullough Centre
PO Box 130
Gunn, AB T0E 1A0
Tel: 780-967-2221; *Fax:* 780-967-3494
Since 1941, the McCullough Centre (formerly the Gunn Centre) has offered services to disadvantaged men. The Centre provides temporary accommodation & support services to help men reestablish their lives.

• Premier's Council on Alberta's Promise
AMEC Place
#2520, 801 - 6 Ave. SW
Calgary, AB T2P 3W2
Tel: 403-297-7500; *Fax:* 403-297-6664
Toll-free: 866-313-7500
info@albertaspromise.org
www.albertaspromise.org
Founded in 2003, Alberta's Promise supports the following Five Promises made to the province's children & youth: A Healthy Start, Caring Adults, Child & Youth Friendly Communities, Lifelong Learning, & Opportunities to Contribute.

• Premier's Council on the Status of Persons with Disabilities
HSBC Building
#1110, 10055 - 106 St.
Edmonton, AB T5J 2Y2
Fax: 780-415-0097
Toll-free: 800-272-8841
pcspd@gov.ab.ca
www.alberta.ca/premiers-council-persons-with-disabilities.aspx
Established in 1988, the mandate for the Premier's Council on the Status of Persons with Disabilities is outlined in the Premier's Council on the Status of Persons with Disabilities Act. The Premier's Council consists of up to fifteen volunteer members who communicate the concerns of Alberta's disability community to the provincial government.

• Social Care Facilities Review Committee (SCFRC)
Sterling Place
9940 - 106 St., 6th Fl.
Edmonton, AB T5K 2N2
Tel: 780-638-1249; *Fax:* 780-415-5841
Toll-free: -310-0000
humanservices.alberta.ca/department/15042.html
The committee is a citizens' panel that visits a sampling of social care facilities throughout Alberta every year to review services provided & to determine recipients' satisfaction with those services.

Community Services & Supports Division
Capital Boul., #44, 10044 - 108th St., 3rd Fl., Edmonton, AB T5J 5E6
Assistant Deputy Minister, Chris Wells
Tel: 780-644-1911
chris.wells@gov.ab.ca
Executive Director, Cross Ministry & Community Partnership Initiatives, Brian Bechtel
Tel: 780-638-1135
brian.bechtel@gov.ab.ca
Executive Director, Housing & Homeless Supports, Sharon Blackwell
Tel: 403-297-3196
sharon.blackwell@gov.ab.ca
Executive Director, Family & Community Services Branch, Ken Dropko
Tel: 780-644-2485; *Fax:* 780-644-2671
ken.dropko@gov.ab.ca

Corporate Services Division
Standard Life Centre, 10405 Jasper Ave., 4th Fl., Edmonton, AB T5J 4R7
Tel: 780-638-3560; *Fax:* 780-644-2524

Delivery Services Portfolio
Petwin Tower Bldg., 10707 - 100th Ave., 8th Fl., Edmonton, AB T5J 3M1
Assistant Deputy Minister, Jason Chance
Tel: 780-644-5570
jason.chance@gov.ab.ca
Director & Executive Advisor, Robin J. Anderson
Tel: 780-644-2912
robin.j.anderson@gov.ab.ca

Disabilities, Inclusion & Accessibility Division
Milner Bldg., 10040 - 104th St., 12th Fl., Edmonton, AB T5J 0Z2
Assistant Deputy Minister, John Stinson
Tel: 780-641-9749
john.stinson@gov.ab.ca

Executive Director, Income Supports Branch, Stephen Gauk
Tel: 780-422-7960
stephen.gauk@gov.ab.ca
Executive Director, Disability Services Branch, Roxanne Gerbrandt
Tel: 780-408-8369
roxanne.gerbrandt@gov.ab.ca

Strategic Planning, Policy & Quality Assurance Division
Sterling Place, 9940 - 106th St., 6th Fl., Edmonton, AB T5K 2N2
Assistant Deputy Minister, Jason Chance
Tel: 780-644-5570
jason.chance@gov.ab.ca
Executive Director, Strategic Policy, Crista Carmichael
Tel: 780-408-8414; *Fax:* 780-644-2953
crista.carmichael@gov.ab.ca
Executive Director, Performance Management & Analytics, Dale Sobkovich
Tel: 780-415-4503; *Fax:* 780-415-5841
dale.sobkovich@gov.ab.ca

Alberta Culture & Status of Women

Communications Branch, Standard Life Centre, 10405 Jasper Ave., 7th Fl., Edmonton, AB T5J 4R7
Tel: 780-427-6530; *Fax:* 780-427-1496
Toll-Free: 800-232-7215
TTY: 780-427-9999
culture.communications@gov.ab.ca
www.alberta.ca/culture-and-status-of-women.aspx
Other Communication: Toll-Free TTY: 800-232-7215; Privacy Email: ccs.communications@gov.ab.ca
twitter.com/AlbertaCulture
www.youtube.com/user/AlbertaCulture

Formerly known as Culture & Tourism, Culture, Culture & Community Services, & before that Culture & Community Spirit, the ministry was renamed following the 2019 general election. Alberta's Culture continues to support arts & cultural industries throughout Alberta. Financial assistance is provided to the non-profit sector, film, the arts, & heritage.
The ministry also oversees areas such as anti-racism, prevention of violence against women & girls, community grants for women, & the Francophone Secretariat.

Minister, Culture, Hon. Ron Orr
Tel: 780-422-3559; *Fax:* 780-427-0188
cmsw.minister@gov.ab.ca

Associate Minister, Status of Women, Hon. Whitney Issik
Tel: 780-422-3559; *Fax:* 780-427-0188

Deputy Minister, Lora Pillipow
Tel: 780-427-2921
lora.pillipow@gov.ab.ca

Executive Director, Francophone Secretariat, Cindie LeBlanc
Tel: 780-415-3232; *Fax:* 780-422-7533
cindie.leblanc@gov.ab.ca
www.alberta.ca/francophone-secretariat.aspx
Other Communications: Main Secretariat Number: 780-415-3348

Associated Agencies, Boards & Commissions:
• Alberta Film
Whitemud Crossing
#140, 4211 - 106 St.
Edmonton, AB T6J 6L7
Tel: 780-422-8584; *Fax:* 780-422-8582
Toll-free: 888-813-1738
info@albertafilm.ca
www.albertafilm.ca
Alberta Film is mandated to support the screen-based production industry in Alberta, through areas such as marketing, location scouting & industry development. The Alberta Production Grant provides funding for screen-based production.

• Alberta Foundation for the Arts (AFA)
10708 - 105 Ave.
Edmonton, AB T5H 0A1
Tel: 780-427-9968
Toll-free: -310-0000
www.affta.ab.ca
The Foundation supports the development of arts throughout Alberta. It works to maintain & expand the AFA art collection for Albertans.

• Alberta Historical Resources Foundation (AHRF)
Old St. Stephen's College
8820 - 112 St.
Edmonton, AB T6G 2P8
Tel: 780-431-2300; *Fax:* 780-427-5598
Toll-free: -310-0000
www.culture.alberta.ca/ahrf

authority for confined feeding operations in Alberta. Its work in this area inclues administering policies, fulfilling applications, & conducting board reviews.

• Surface Rights Board (SRB)
1229 - 91 St. SW
Edmonton, AB T6X 1E9
Tel: 780-427-2444; *Fax:* 780-427-5798
Toll-free: -310-0000
srb.lcb@gov.ab.ca
www.surfacerights.gov.ab.ca
The Surface Rights Board holds hearings on disputes related to energy activities & land access. The hearing usually involves a panel of three members of the Surface Rights Board. Members of the Board are appointed by an Order in Counsel, according to the Surface Rights Act. Affected parties may also participate in the hearings, which are open to the public.
The Board delivers decisions, within its legislated mandate, about compensation to landowners, surrounding issues such as oil & gas & power line activity. In determining compensation, the Board considers factors such as the value of the land, loss of use, inconvenience, nuisance, & noise, & adverse effects on remaining land.

• Wildlife Predator & Shot Livestock Compensation Committee
9920 - 108 St.
Edmonton, AB T5K 2M4
The reimbursement paid to a livestock producer, when an animal has been injured by a wildlife predator, or shot, is determined by the Predator & Shot Livestock Compensation Committee of Alberta. Compensation provided to the livestock owner is based upon a schedule for losses or injury to specified livestock.

Land Use Secretariat
Centre West Bldg., 10035 - 108th St., 9th Fl., Edmonton, AB T5J 3E1
Tel: 780-644-7972; *Fax:* 780-644-1034
luf@gov.ab.ca
www.landuse.alberta.ca
The Land Use Secretariat is a leader in the implementation of Alberta's Land-use Framework. The Secretariat assists regional advisory councils in offering advice to government about developing regional plans.
Stewardship Commissioner, Rick Blackwood
Tel: 780-427-1139; *Fax:* 780-415-9669
rick.blackwood@gov.ab.ca

Climate Change Division
Petroleum Plaza ST, 9915 - 108th St., 11th Fl., Edmonton, AB T5K 2G8
The Alberta Climate Change Office was created in 2016 to help implement the province's climate change strategy. It later became the Climate Change Division after the 2019 general election.
Assistant Deputy Minister, Robert Savage
Tel: 780-644-4918
robert.savage@gov.ab.ca
Executive Director, Implementation, Legislation & Evaluation Branch, Krista Berezowski
Tel: 780-644-1831
krista.berezowski@gov.ab.ca
Executive Director, Policy, Robert Hamaliuk
Tel: 780-644-8364
robert.hamaliuk@gov.ab.ca
Executive Director, Regulatory & Compliance, Justin Wheler
Tel: 780-644-5715
justin.wheler@gov.ab.ca

Corporate Services Division
Petroleum Plaza ST, 9915 - 108th St., 10th Fl, Edmonton, AB T5K 2G8
Tel: 780-643-0890
Assistant Deputy Minister, Tom Davis
Tel: 780-644-3205
tom.davis@gov.ab.ca
Chief Information Officer & Executive Director, Informatics Branch, Mark Diner
Tel: 780-415-2463
mark.diner@gov.ab.ca
Oxbridge Place
9820 - 106 St.
Edmonton, AB T5K 2J6
Executive Director, Corporate Performance Branch, Susan Campbell
Tel: 780-644-1006
susan.campbell@gov.ab.ca

Environmental Monitoring & Science Division
9888 Jasper Ave., 10th Fl., Edmonton, AB T5J 5C6
Chief Scientist & Assistant Deputy Minister, Frederick Wrona
Tel: 780-229-7270
fred.wrona@gov.ab.ca

Executive Director, Science Branch, Bill Donahue
Tel: 780-229-7320
bill.donahue@gov.ab.ca
Executive Director, Integrated Environmental Analytics & Prediction Branch, Monique Dube
Tel: 403-297-5917
monique.dube@gov.ab.ca
Executive Director, Oil Sands Monitoring Program Secretariat, Sandra Honour
Tel: 780-229-7314
sandra.honour@gov.ab.ca
Executive Director, Indigenous Knowledge, Community Monitoring & Citizen Science Branch, Gleb Raygorodetsky
Tel: 780-229-7234
gleb.raygorodetsky@gov.ab.ca
Executive Director, Environmental Monitoring & Observations Branch, Garry Scrimgeour
Tel: 780-229-7299
garry.scrimgeour@gov.ab.ca

Operations Division
Petroleum Plaza ST, 9915 - 108th St., 10th Fl., Edmonton, AB T5K 2G8
Tel: 780-427-1335
Assistant Deputy Minister, John Conrad
Tel: 780-422-7669; *Fax:* 780-422-5141
john.conrad@gov.ab.ca
Executive Director, Operations Infrastructure Branch, David Ardell
Tel: 403-297-5892
dave.ardell@gov.ab.ca
Executive Director, Alberta Environmental Support & Emergency Response Team (ASERT), Nick Grimshaw
Tel: 780-427-8536; *Fax:* 780-427-2278
nick.grimshaw@gov.ab.ca
Director, Surveys / Alberta Boundary Commissioner, Ravi Shrivastava
Tel: 780-422-0020
ravi.shrivastava@gov.ab.ca

Parks Division
Oxbridge Place, 9820 - 106th St., 2nd Fl., Edmonton, AB T5K 2J6
Tel: 780-427-3582; *Fax:* 780-427-5980
Toll-Free: 866-427-3582
Assistant Deputy Minister, Mike Fernandez
Tel: 780-868-5659
mike.fernandez@gov.ab.ca
Executive Director, Parks Program Coordination, Scott Jones
Tel: 780-427-8783; *Fax:* 780-427-5980
scott.jones@gov.ab.ca
Executive Director, Parks Regional Operations, Robert Hugill
Tel: 403-362-1203
rob.hugill@gov.ab.ca

Policy & Planning Division
Petroleum Plaza ST, 9915 - 108th St., 11th Fl., Edmonton, AB T5K 2G8
Tel: 780-422-8183
Assistant Deputy Minister, Ronda Goulden
Tel: 780-638-4728
ronda.goulden@gov.ab.ca
Executive Director, Wildlife Management Branch, Ron Bjorge
Tel: 780-427-9503
ron.bjorge@gov.ab.ca
Executive Director, Planning Branch, Brian Makowecki
Tel: 780-422-4569
brian.makowecki@gov.ab.ca
Executive Director, Water Policy Branch, Mary Metz
Tel: 780-644-8856
mary.metz@gov.ab.ca
Executive Director, Fish & Wildlife Policy Branch, Travis Ripley
Tel: 780-427-7763
travis.ripley@gov.ab.ca
Executive Director, Land Policy Branch, Karen Wronko
Tel: 780-422-8420
karen.wronko@gov.ab.ca

Strategy Division
Petroleum Plaza ST, 9915 - 108th St., 11th Fl., Edmonton, AB T5K 2G8
Tel: 780-644-5545
Assistant Deputy Minister, Rick Blackwood
Tel: 780-427-1139; *Fax:* 780-415-9669
rick.blackwood@gov.ab.ca
Executive Director, Innovation & Intergovernmental Services Branch, Cam Lane
Tel: 780-427-9451
cam.lane@gov.ab.ca
Executive Director, Community Engagement Branch, Robert Stokes
Tel: 780-422-2690; *Fax:* 780-421-0028
robert.stokes@gov.ab.ca

#1250, 9925 - 109th St. NW, Edmonton, AB T5K 2J8
Tel: 780-422-2273; *Fax:* 780-422-2261
generalinfo@ethicscommissioner.ab.ca
www.ethicscommissioner.ab.ca
Other Communication: Alt. Email: info@ethicscommissioner.ab.ca
Established in 1992, the Office of the Ethics Commissioner for the Province of Alberta is engaged in the promotion of public confidence in the ethics of each Member of the Legislative Assembly. The Hon. Marguerite Trussler, Q.C., is Alberta's fourth Ethics Commissioner & was officially sworn in on June 4, 2014.

Alberta Ethics Commissioner, Marguerite Trussler, Q.C.

Chief Administrative Officer, Kent Ziegler
Tel: 780-422-4974; *Fax:* 780-422-2261
kziegler@ethicscommissioner.ab.ca

Registrar, Lobbyists Act, & General Counsel, Lara Draper
Tel: 780-644-3879; *Fax:* 780-422-2261
ldraper@ethicscommissioner.ab.ca

Alberta Health
PO Box 1360 Stn. Main, Edmonton, AB T5J 2N3
Tel: 780-427-7164
TTY: 800-232-7215
www.alberta.ca/health.aspx
twitter.com/goahealth
Formerly Alberta Health & Wellness, Alberta Health is involved in the following activities: establishing legislation, policy, & standards; supporting the health system; allocating resources; & administering provincial programs.
In 2012, Alberta Health absorbed elements of the former Alberta Seniors. In 2014, Premier Jim Prentice made Seniors a separate department again.

Minister, Hon. Jason Copping
Tel: 780-427-3665; *Fax:* 780-415-0961
health.minister@gov.ab.ca

Associate Minister, Mental Health & Addictions, Hon. Mike Ellis
Tel: 780-427-0165
associateminister-mha@gov.ab.ca

Deputy Minister, Paul Wynnyk
Tel: 780-422-0747

Health Advocate & Mental Health Patient Advocate, Office of the Alberta Health Advocates, Janice L. Harrington
janice.harrington@albertahealthadvocates.ca

Associated Agencies, Boards & Commissions:
• Alberta Health Advocates (AHA)
106th St. Tower
10055 - 106th St., 9th Fl.
Edmonton, AB T5J 2Y2
Tel: 780-422-1812; *Fax:* 780-422-0695
Toll-free: -310-0000
info@albertahealthadvocates.ca
www.albertahealthadvocates.ca
The Office of the Health Advocate opened April 1, 2014, & is divided into three divisions: Health, Mental Health (created in 1990) & Seniors.

• Alberta Health Services (AHS)
Corporate Office, North Tower, Seventh Street Plaza
10030 - 107th St. NW, 14th Fl.
Edmonton, AB T5J 3E4
Tel: 780-342-2000; *Fax:* 780-342-2060
Toll-free: 888-342-2471
ahs.corp@albertahealthservices.ca
www.albertahealthservices.ca
Other Communication: Board Office, Phone: 866-943-1120; Fax: 403-943-1124, Email: ahs.board@ahs.ca
Alberta Health Services was established in 2008, & became operational in 2009. The provincial health authority plans & delivers health services throughout Alberta. In December 2013, plans were finalized to privatize all diagnostic lab services in Edmonton.

• Health Quality Council of Alberta (HQCA)
#210, 811 - 14 St. NW
Calgary, AB T2N 2A4
Tel: 403-297-8162; *Fax:* 403-297-8258
Toll-free: 855-508-8162
info@hqca.ca
www.hqca.ca
Other Communication: Edmonton Office, Phone: 780-429-3008
The Health Quality Council of Alberta is legislated under the Regional Health Authorities Act. The Council's responsibilities

are set forth in the Health Quality Council of Alberta Regulation. The independent organization strives to improve the health service quality, patient safety, & performance of the health system in Alberta.

Office of the Chief Medical Officer of Health (OCMOH)
ATB Place, 10025 Jasper Ave., 24th Fl., Edmonton, AB T5J 1S6

Tel: 780-427-5263; *Fax:* 780-427-7683
www.alberta.ca/office-of-the-chief-medical-officer-of-health.aspx
The Office of the Chief Medical Officer of Health offers guidelines to Alberta Health Services about public health policy. The Office also provides information to the public about communicable diseases & public health programs.
The Chief Medical Officer of Health works under the authority of the Public Health Act to promote & protect the health of the people of Alberta.
Chief Medical Officer of Health, Dr. Deena Hinshaw
  deena.hinshaw@gov.ab.ca
Deputy Chief Medical Officer of Health, Dr. Marcia Johnson

Financial & Corporate Services Division
ATB Place, 10025 Jasper Ave., 16th Fl., Edmonton, AB T5J 1S6

Assistant Deputy Minister, Aaron Neumeyer
  Tel: 780-644-6820
  aaron.neumeyer@gov.ab.ca
Executive Director, Corporate Services, Stephen Arthur
  Tel: 780-415-0201
  stephen.arthur@gov.ab.ca
Executive Director, Financial Planning Branch, Dan Hemming
  Tel: 780-427-7100
  dan.hemming@gov.ab.ca
Acting Executive Director, Health Facilities Planning, Michael J. Mah
  Tel: 780-638-3546; *Fax:* 780-422-3672
  michael.j.mah@gov.ab.ca
Executive Director & Senior Financial Officer, Financial Reporting Branch, Scott McIntyre
  Tel: 780-427-6011
  scott.mcintyre@gov.ab.ca

Health Information Systems Division
ATB Place, 10025 Jasper Ave., 21st Fl., Edmonton, AB T5J 1S6

Assistant Deputy Minister, Kim Wieringa
  Tel: 780-415-2492; *Fax:* 780-422-5176
  kim.wieringa@gov.ab.ca
Executive Director, Information Technology & Operations, Ranjit Sandhu
  Tel: 780-415-1562
  ranjit.sandhu@gov.ab.ca
Executive Director, Information Management Branch, Quinn Mah
  Tel: 780-422-1251
  quinn.mah@gov.ab.ca
Executive Director, Strategic IMT Services Branch, Vacant

Health Workforce Planning & Accountability Division
ATB Place, 10025 Jasper Ave., 10th Fl., Edmonton, AB T5J 1S6

Assistant Deputy Minister, Leann Wagner
  Tel: 780-427-1572
  leann.wagner@gov.ab.ca
Executive Director, Health Professional Regulation & Physician Workforce Branch, Ali Abdelrahman
  Tel: 780-415-1720
  ali.abdelrahman@gov.ab.ca
Executive Director, Provider Compensation & Strategic Partnerships Branch, Camille Bailer
  camille.bailer@gov.ab.ca
Executive Director, Health Workforce Partnerships Branch, Martin Tailleur
  Tel: 780-415-1427
  martin.tailleur@gov.ab.ca

Health Service Delivery Division
ATB Place, 10025 Jasper Ave., 18th Fl., Edmonton, AB T5J 1S6

Assistant Deputy Minister, John Cabral
  Tel: 780-422-7270
  john.cabral@gov.ab.ca
Provincial MES Medical Director, Dr. Sunil Sookram
  Tel: 780-422-2061
  sunil.sookram@gov.ab.ca
Executive Director, Primary & Community Health Branch, Shannon Berg
  Tel: 780-641-9067; *Fax:* 780-427-8055
  shannon.berg@gov.ab.ca
Executive Director, Addiction & Mental Health Branch, Michelle Craig
  Tel: 780-641-8644
  michelle.craig@gov.ab.ca

Executive Director, Continuing Care Branch, Corinne Schalm
  Tel: 780-644-3621; *Fax:* 780-422-1515
  corinne.schalm@gov.ab.ca

Health Standards, Quality & Performance
ATB Place, North Tower, 10025 Jasper Ave., 22nd Fl., Edmonton, AB T5J 1S6

Assistant Deputy Minister, Dr. Dean Screpnek
  Tel: 780-422-8989; *Fax:* 780-638-3811
  dean.screpnek@gov.ab.ca
Executive Director & Provincial Health Analytics Officer, Analytics & Performance Reporting Branch, Larry Svenson
  Tel: 780-422-4767
  larry.svenson@gov.ab.ca

Pharmaceutical & Supplementary Benefits Division
ATB Place, 10025 Jasper Ave., 11th Fl., Edmonton, AB T5J 1S6

Assistant Deputy Minister, Graham Statt
  Tel: 780-644-4948; *Fax:* 780-422-3646
  graham.statt@gov.ab.ca
Executive Director, Health Insurance Programs, Donna Manuel
  Tel: 780-644-3149; *Fax:* 780-644-1445
  donna.manuel@gov.ab.ca
Executive Director, Pharmaceutical & Health Benefits Branch, Chad Mitchell
  Tel: 780-422-9632
  chad.mitchell@gov.ab.ca

Public Health & Compliance Division
ATB Place, North Tower, 10025 Jasper Ave., 24th Fl., Edmonton, AB T5J 1S6

Executive Secretary, Samantha Sterling
  Tel: 780-427-7140
  samantha.sterling@gov.ab.ca
Executive Director, Health & Wellness Promotion Branch, Jessica Carlson
  Tel: 780-422-4222
  jessica.carlson@gov.ab.ca
Executive Director, Health Protection Branch, Scott F. Harris
  Tel: 780-638-4315
  scott.f.harris@gov.ab.ca
Executive Director, Compliance & Monitoring Branch, David Wheeler
  Tel: 780-415-2803
  david.wheeler@gov.ab.ca

Alberta Indigenous Relations

Commerce Place, 10155 - 102nd St. NW, 19th Fl., Edmonton, AB T5J 4G8

Fax: 780-427-4019
www.alberta.ca/indigenous-relations.aspx
twitter.com/youralberta
www.youtube.com/user/aralberta
Indigenous Relations works with Aboriginal communities & other partners to enhance social & economic opportunities for Alberta's Aboriginal people.

Minister, Indigenous Relations, Hon. Rick Wilson
  Tel: 780-422-4144; *Fax:* 780-638-4052
  ir.ministeroffice@gov.ab.ca

Deputy Minister, Donavon Young
  Tel: 780-643-9081; *Fax:* 780-422-2745
  donavon.young@gov.ab.ca

Director, Communications, Olga Michailides
  Tel: 780-427-4210
  olga.michailides@gov.ab.ca

Associated Agencies, Boards & Commissions:
• **Métis Settlements Appeal Tribunal (MSAT)**
#200, 10335 - 172 St.
Edmonton, AB T5S 1K9
Tel: 780-422-1541; *Fax:* 780-422-0019
Toll-free: 800-661-8864
msat.info@gov.ab.ca
www.msat.gov.ab.ca

• **Northern Alberta Development Council (NADC)**
Peace River Office, Provincial Building
#206, 9621 - 96 Ave.
PO Box 900-14
Peace River, AB T8S 1T4
Tel: 780-624-6274; *Fax:* 780-624-6184
Toll-free: -310-0000
nadc.council@gov.ab.ca
www.nadc.ca
Other Communication: Bursary Information, Email:
nadc.bursary@gov.ab.ca
The Northern Alberta Development Council focuses on the advancement of the northern economy. The Council is engaged

in projects involving tourism, transportation, educational initiatives, value-added agriculture, & inter-jurisdictional projects.

Consultation & Land Claims
Commerce Place, 10155 - 102nd St., 20th Fl., Edmonton, AB T5J 4G8

Tel: 780-427-0417; *Fax:* 780-427-0401
Assistant Deputy Minister, Lisa Tchir, Q.C.
  Tel: 780-641-9968
  lisa.tchir@gov.ab.ca
Acting Executive Director, Aboriginal Consultation, Trish Merrithew-Mercredi
  Tel: 780-643-6215
  trish.merrithew-mercredi@gov.ab.ca
Acting Executive Director, Stewardship & Policy Integration, Lance Wilson
  Tel: 780-638-4375; *Fax:* 780-643-6595
  lance.wilson@gov.ab.ca
Director, Land Claims, Steven Andres
  Tel: 780-427-6084; *Fax:* 780-427-0401
  steven.andres@gov.ab.ca

First Nations Relations
Commerce Place, 10155 - 102nd St., 19th Fl., Edmonton, AB T5J 4G8

Assistant Deputy Minister, Clay Buchanan
  Tel: 780-422-5925; *Fax:* 780-427-4019
  clay.buchanan@gov.ab.ca
Executive Director, Métis Relations, Cynthia Dunnigan
  Tel: 780-415-6141
  cynthia.dunnigan@gov.ab.ca
Executive Director, Aboriginal Initiatives, Sheila Harrison
  Tel: 780-427-5071
  sheila.harrison@gov.ab.ca
Executive Director, First Nations Relations, Trish Merrithew-Mercredi
  Tel: 780-643-6215
  trish.merrithew-mercredi@gov.ab.ca

Indigenous Climate Leadership & Corporate Services
Commerce Place, 10155 - 102nd St., 20th Fl., Edmonton, AB T5J 4G8

Assistant Deputy Minister, John Donner
  Tel: 780-643-3880; *Fax:* 780-427-0401
  john.donner@gov.ab.ca
Executive Director & Senior Financial Officer, Finance, Lorne Harvey
  Tel: 780-422-2429
  lorne.harvey@gov.ab.ca
Executive Director, Strategic Initiatives, Karen Young
  Tel: 780-644-5708
  karen.young@gov.ab.ca

Alberta Office of the Information & Privacy Commissioner

Office of the Information & Privacy Commissioner (Edmonton), #410, 9925 - 109th St., Edmonton, AB T5K 2J8
Tel: 780-422-6860; *Fax:* 780-422-5682
Toll-Free: 888-878-4044
generalinfo@oipc.ab.ca
www.oipc.ab.ca
Secondary Address: #2460, 801 - 6th Ave. SW
Calgary, AB T2P 3W2
Alt. Fax: 403-297-2711
twitter.com/ABoipc
The Information & Privacy Commissioner has offices in Calgary & Edmonton. In Calgary, issues related to the Personal Information Protection Act are addressed. The Edmonton office handles issues under the Freedom of Information & Protection of Privacy Act & the Health Information Act.

Information & Privacy Commissioner, Jill Clayton
  Tel: 780-422-6860; *Fax:* 780-422-5682
  jclayton@oipc.ab.ca

Assistant Commissioner, LeRoy Brower
  Tel: 780-422-6860; *Fax:* 780-422-5682
  lbrower@oipc.ab.ca

Alberta Infrastructure

Infrastructure Bldg., 6950 - 113th St., Edmonton, AB T6H 5V7
Tel: 780-415-0507; *Fax:* 780-427-2187
Infra.Contact.Us.m@gov.ab.ca
www.alberta.ca/infrastructure.aspx
The Ministry supports the provision of well-designed, high-quality public infrastructure for the people of Alberta.

Minister, Hon. Prasad Panda
  Tel: 780-427-5041; *Fax:* 780-644-1204
  infrastructure.minister@gov.ab.ca

Deputy Minister, Shannon Flint
Tel: 780-427-3835; *Fax:* 780-422-6565
shannon.flint@gov.ab.ca

Capital Projects Delivery Division
Infrastructure Bldg., 6950 - 113th St., 2nd Fl., Edmonton, AB T6H 5V7
Assistant Deputy Minister, Tracy Allen
Tel: 780-427-0289
tracy.allen@gov.ab.ca
Executive Director, Technical Services Branch, Vince Farmer
Tel: 780-644-2739
vince.farmer@gov.ab.ca
Executive Director, Health Facilities Branch, Neil Kjelland
Tel: 780-415-1028
neil.kjelland@gov.ab.ca
Executive Director, Government Facilities, Trevor Peter
Tel: 780-422-7389
trevor.peter@gov.ab.ca

Corporate Strategies & Services Division
Infrastructure Bldg., 6950 - 113th St., 2nd Fl., Edmonton, AB T6H 5V7
Assistant Deputy Minister, Jennifer Flaman
Tel: 780-953-1736
jennifer.flaman@gov.ab.ca
Executive Director, Procurement & Cost Management Branch, Lara Check
Tel: 780-638-1846
lara.check@gov.ab.ca
Executive Director, Operations & Administration, Cynthia Evans
Tel: 780-221-6301
cynthia.evans@gov.ab.ca
Executive Director, Capital Planning Branch, Jennifer Hibbert
Tel: 780-644-5114
jennifer.hibbert@gov.ab.ca
Executive Director, Policy & Strategic Intitiatives Branch, Jennifer Flaman
Tel: 780-953-1736
jennifer.flaman@gov.ab.ca
Executive Director & Senior Financial Officer, Finance Branch, Faye McCann
Tel: 780-644-8774; *Fax:* 780-643-0803
faye.mccann@gov.ab.ca
Executive Director, Technical Services Branch, Jason Nault
Tel: 780-446-0518
jason.nault@gov.ab.ca

Properties Division
Infrastructure Bldg., 6950 - 113th St., 3rd Fl., Edmonton, AB T6H 5V7
Tel: 780-427-3881
Assistant Deputy Minister, Andy Ridge
Tel: 780-915-4236
andy.ridge@gov.ab.ca
Executive Director, Reality Services Branch, Tracy Hayden
Tel: 780-913-9189
tracy.hayden@gov.ab.ca
Executive Director, Asset Management Branch, Julie Houtstra
Tel: 780-819-5105
julie.houtstra@gov.ab.ca
Executive Director, Property Management Branch, Leonid Oukrainski
Tel: 780-422-4606
leonid.oukrainski@gov.ab.ca

Alberta Innovates

250 Karl Clark Rd., Edmonton, AB T6N 1E4
Toll-Free: 877-423-5727
info@albertainnovates.ca
albertainnovates.ca
twitter.com/abinnovates
www.facebook.com/AlbertaInnovates
www.linkedin.com/company/alberta-innovates
Alberta Innovates became a single Crown corporation in Nov. 2016, with two applied research subsidiaries, InnoTech Alberta & C-FER Technologies, serving public & private sector interests. The original system was created in 2010 with four corporations working together: Bio Solutions, Energy & Environment Solutions, Health Solutions, & Technology Futures. These general areas are still overseen by the consolidated Alberta Innovates, including Bio Sector, Health Innovations, Clean Energy, & Cross Sectoral Investments.

Chair, Brenda Kenny

Vice-Chair, Anne Snowdon

Chief Executive Officer, Laura J. Kilcrease

Executive Vice-President, Operations, Steve McMahon

Vice-President, Marketing & Communications, Lyn Brown

Vice-President, Investments, Rollie Dykstra
Tel: 780-450-5111

Vice-President, Finance & Corporate Secretary, Maureen Fromhart

Vice-President, Health, Tim Murphy
Tel: 780-423-5727
Toll-free: 877-423-5727
Health Innovations
#1500, 10104 - 103 Ave.
Edmonton, AB T5J 0H8

Vice-President, Clean Energy, John Zhou
Tel: 403-297-7089
#2540, 801 - 6 Ave. SW
Calgary, AB T2P 3W2

Executive Director, Bio-Industrial Services, Steve Price
Tel: 780-450-5111

Executive Director, Human Resources, Katherine Salucop

C-FER Technologies
200 Karl Clark Rd., Edmonton, AB T6N 1H2
Tel: 780-450-3300; *Fax:* 780-450-3700
www.cfertech.com
This not-for-profit, fee-for-service subsidiary of Alberta Innovates specializes in full-scale testing & engineering consulting to the global energy industry, to advance safety, environmental performance & efficiency.
The head office on Karl Clark Rd. focuses on Upstream Oil & Gas/Other Industries.
Managing Director, Francisco Alhanati
Chief Engineer & C-FER Fellow, Maher Nessim
C-FER Fellow, Cam Matthews

InnoTech Alberta
250 Karl Clark Rd., Edmonton, AB T6N 1H2
Tel: 780-450-5111; *Fax:* 780-450-5333
info@innotechalberta.ca
innotechalberta.ca
Other Communication: Shipping & Receiving, Phone: 780-450-5010
InnoTech Alberta focuses on converting applied research to economic, social & environmental benefits for the province. It operates laboratories, performs applied research & development, & delivers laboratory services in key areas for government & industry clients.
Managing Director, Ross Chow
Tel: 780-450-5078
Ross.Chow@innotechalberta.ca
Manager, Media Relations, Dwayne Brunner
dwayne.brunner@albertainnovates.ca
Other Communications: 1-877-423-5727, ext. 224
Manager, Business Relations, Michelle Hiltz
Tel: 780-450-5518
Michelle.Hiltz@innotechalberta.ca

Alberta Jobs, Economy & Innovation

Commerce Place, 10155 - 102nd St., 12th Fl., Edmonton, AB T5J 4G8
www.alberta.ca/jobs-economy-and-innovation.aspx
twitter.com/AlbertaEconomy
www.linkedin.com/company/invest-alberta
Formerly known as Economic Development, Trade & Tourism, & before that Economic Development & Trade, the ministry (created in 2020) focuses on the following priorities: Economic Development & Small & Medium-Sized Enterprises; Science & Innovation (including the Alberta Innovated programs); Tourism; & Trade & Investment Attraction (including Alberta's international offices).
The following international offices work to promote trade & to attract investment & other interests such as culture & education: Alberta Beijing Office; Alberta Hong Kong Office; Alberta New Delhi Office; Alberta Japan Office; Alberta South Korea Office; Alberta Guangzhou Office; Alberta Mexico Office; Alberta Shanghai Office; Alberta Singapore Office; Alberta Taiwan Office; Alberta United Kingdom Office; & Alberta Washington, D.C. Office.

Minister, Hon. Doug Schweitzer
Tel: 780-644-8554; *Fax:* 780-644-8572
jei.ministeroffice@gov.ab.ca

Associate Minister, Rural Economic Development, Hon. Nate Horner
Tel: 780-644-8554; *Fax:* 780-644-8572

Parliamentary Secretary, Small Business & Tourism, Hon. Martin Long
Tel: 780-638-3015; *Fax:* 780-638-3506

Deputy Minister, Kate White
Tel: 780-415-0900
kate.white@gov.ab.ca

Director, Communications, Iris Dias
Tel: 780-644-5601

Associated Agencies, Boards & Commissions:
· Alberta Enterprise Corporation Board
TD Tower
#1405, 10088 - 102 Ave.
Edmonton, AB T5J 2Z2
Tel: 587-402-6601; *Fax:* 587-402-6612
Toll-free: 877-336-3474
info@alberta-enterprise.ca
www.alberta-enterprise.ca
The Alberta Enterprise Corporation Board was established in 2008 through the Alberta Enterprise Corporation Act. The Alberta Enterprise Fund is the corporation's fund that targets technology venture capital funds.
· Alberta Innovates
See Entry Name Index for detailed listing.

Investment Attraction & Trade Division
Commerce Pl., 10155 - 102nd St., 4th Fl., Edmonton, AB T5J 4L6
Acting Assistant Deputy Minister & Executive Director, International Services, Tristan Sanregret
Tel: 780-427-6024
tristan.sanregret@gov.ab.ca
Executive Director, Investment Services, Tom Mansfield
Tel: 780-427-6483
tom.mansfield@gov.ab.ca
Executive Director, Trade Services, Nancy Wu
Tel: 780-643-1660
nancy.wu@gov.ab.ca

Policy & Strategy Division
Commerce Pl., 10155 - 102nd St., 13th Fl., Edmonton, AB T5J 4G8
Tel: 780-427-6543; *Fax:* 780-422-2635
Assistant Deputy Minister, Sonya Johnston
Tel: 780-415-9260
sonya.johnston@gov.ab.ca
Executive Director, Finance & Corporate Services, Jeanette Stead
Tel: 780-638-3959
jeanette.stead@gov.ab.ca
Executive Director, Policy & Strategic, Alisa Neuman
Tel: 780-643-2969
alisa.neuman@gov.ab.ca

Tourism & Economic Development Division
Commerce Place, 10155 - 102nd St., 6th Fl., Edmonton, AB T5J 4L6
Assistant Deputy Minister, Michele Evans
Tel: 780-644-7175
michele.evans@gov.ab.ca
Executive Director, Tourism & Economic Capacity, Roger Kramers
Tel: 780-643-1368
roger.kramers@gov.ab.ca
Executive Director, Economic Development, Brent Lakeman
Tel: 780-643-6511
brent.lakeman@gov.ab.ca

Alberta Justice & Solicitor General

John E. Brownlee Bldg., 10365 - 97th St., 9th Fl., Edmonton, AB T5J 3W7
Tel: 780-427-2745
TTY: 800-232-7215
www.alberta.ca/justice-and-solicitor-general.aspx
twitter.com/AlbertaJSG
www.facebook.com/AlbertaCorrections
www.youtube.com/user/absolgen
In 2012, then-Premier Alison Redford announced the creation of the Ministry of Justice & Solicitor General, through the merger of Alberta Solicitor General & Public Security with Alberta Justice. The mission of Alberta Justice & Solicitor General is to provide a fiar & safe province. Its core businesses are as follows: promoting safe communities for the people of Alberta; facilitating access to justice; & providing legal & strategic services to government.

Minister, Justice; Solicitor General, Hon. Kaycee Madu
Tel: 780-427-2339; *Fax:* 780-422-6621
ministryofjustice@gov.ab.ca

Deputy Minister, Justice; Deputy Attorney General, Frank Bosscha, Q.C.
Tel: 780-427-5032
frank.bosscha@gov.ab.ca

Associate Deputy Minister, Dennis Cooley
Tel: 780-427-5032
dennis.cooley@gov.ab.ca

Associated Agencies, Boards & Commissions:

• Alberta Human Rights Commission
Northern Regional Office, Standard Life Centre
#800, 10405 Jasper Ave.
Edmonton, AB T5J 4R7
Tel: 780-427-7661; *Fax:* 780-427-6013
TTY: 800-232-7215
humanrights@gov.ab.ca
www.albertahumanrights.ab.ca
Other Communication: Education & Community Services,
Phone: 403-297-8407, Email:
educationcommunityservices@gov.ab.ca
The Alberta Human Rights Act established the Alberta Human Rights Commission. In accordance with the Alberta Human Rights Act, the Commission works to foster equality & to reduce discrimination.

• Alberta Review Board
#1120, 10235 - 101 St.
Edmonton, AB T5J 3E9
Tel: 780-422-5994; *Fax:* 780-427-1762
The Alberta Review Board is composed of nine members who are appointed by the Lieutenant Governor in Council.
The Board is responsible for making or reviewing dispositions about any accused person for whom one of the following verdicts is rendered: unfit to stand trial, or not criminally responsible because of mental disorder. The Alberta Review Board also determines whether a person is subject to a detention order, a conditional discharge, or an absolute discharge.

• Criminal Injuries Review Board (CIRB)
#1502, 10025 - 102A Ave.
Edmonton, AB T5J 2Z2
Tel: 780-427-7330; *Fax:* 780-427-7347
Established in 1997, the Criminal Injuries Review Board operates as an autonomous body, in accordance with the Victims of Crime Act. Members of the Board are appointed by the Lieutenant Governor in Council, as recommended by the Minister. They review the decisions of the Director of Victims of Crime Financial Benefits Program, or his or her designate.

• Fatality Review Board
Office of the Chief Medical Examiner
4070 Bowness Rd. NW
Calgary, AB T3B 3R7
Tel: 403-297-8123; *Fax:* 403-297-3429
The Lieutenant Governor in Council appoints the members of the Fatality Review Board. The board consists of the chief medical examiner, a physician, a lawyer, & a layperson.
The Fatality Review Board reviews deaths investigated by the Office of the Chief Medical Examiner & makes recommendations to the Minister of Justice & Solicitor General about whether or not a public fatality inquiry should take place in order to prevent similar deaths in the future.

• Law Enforcement Review Board (LERB)
c/o Board Secretary, Oxford Tower
#1502, 10025 - 102A Ave.
Edmonton, AB T5J 2Z2
Tel: 780-422-9376; *Fax:* 780-422-4782
lerb@gov.ab.ca
Established under Alberta's Police Act, the Law Enforcement Review Board conducts its business as an independent, quasi-judicial organization. Members of the Board are appointed by the Lieutenant Governor in Council as recommended by the Minister. They are charged with the responsibility of reviewing public complaints about the conduct of police officers & appeals by police officers.

Corporate Services Division
Bowker Bldg., 9833 - 109th St., 2nd Fl., Edmonton, AB T5K 2E8
Assistant Deputy Minister, Gerald Lamoureux
Tel: 780-427-3301
gerald.lamoureux@gov.ab.ca
Executive Director, Training Academy, Carol Arnold-Schutta
Tel: 780-644-1778; *Fax:* 780-422-2854
carol.arnold-schutta@gov.ab.ca
Executive Director, Policy & Planning Services Branch, Fiona Lavoy
Tel: 780-644-2092
fiona.lavoy@gov.ab.ca

Executive Director, Engagement Services Branch, Gail Thomsen
Tel: 780-644-8417
gail.thomsen@gov.ab.ca
Executive Director & Senior Financial Officer, Financial Services Branch, Brad Wells
Tel: 780-415-1946
brad.wells@gov.ab.ca

Correctional Services Division
John E. Brownlee Bldg., 10365 - 97th St., 10th Fl., Edmonton, AB T5J 3W7
The following branches make up the Correctional Services Division: adult centre operations; community corrections & release program; strategic services; & young offenders.
Assistant Deputy Minister, Kim Sanderson
Tel: 780-427-3440; *Fax:* 780-427-5905
kim.sanderson@gov.ab.ca
Executive Director, Strategic Services Branch, Carol Moerth
Tel: 780-643-6845
carol.moerth@gov.ab.ca
Executive Director, Young Offender Branch, Joanne Panasiuk
Tel: 780-422-5019; *Fax:* 780-422-0732
joanne.panasiuk@gov.ab.ca
Executive Director, Business Analysis, Innovation & Strategy Branch, Jamie Reynar
Tel: 780-638-3486
jamie.reynar@gov.ab.ca
Executive Director, Adult Centre Operations Branch, Wayne Reddon
Tel: 780-427-4703
wayne.reddon@gov.ab.ca

Crown Prosecution Service Division
Bowker Bldg., 9833 - 109th St., 2nd Fl., Edmonton, AB T5K 2E8
Assistant Deputy Minister, Eric Tolppanen
Tel: 780-427-5046
eric.tolppanen@gov.ab.ca
Executive Director, Specialized Prosecutions (Edmonton), Sheila Brown, Q.C.
Tel: 780-422-0640; *Fax:* 780-422-1217
sheila.brown@gov.ab.ca
John E. Brownlee Building
10365 - 97 St., 5th Fl.
Edmonton, AB T5J 3W7
Executive Director, Appeals, Education, & Prosecution Policy Branch, Sarah Langley
Tel: 780-422-5402
sarah.langley@gov.ab.ca
Centrium Place
#300, 332 - 6th Ave. SW
Calgary, AB T2P 0B2
Executive Director / Crown Prosecutor, Specialized Prosecutions (Calgary), Peter MacKenzie
Tel: 403-297-3410
peter.mackenzie@gov.ab.ca
Centrium Place
#300, 332 - 6th Ave. SW
Calgary, AB T2P 0B2

Justice Services Division
Bowker Bldg., 9833 - 109th St., 2nd Fl., Edmonton, AB T5K 2E8
The Justice Services Division oversees claims & recoveries, the maintenance enforcement program, & the Medical Examiner's Office.
Assistant Deputy Minister, David Peace
Tel: 780-638-4616
david.peace@gov.ab.ca
Executive Director, Family Support Order Services Branch, Lori Marshall
Tel: 780-401-7501
lori.marshall@gov.ab.ca
Sun Life Building
10123 - 99 St., 6th Fl.
Edmonton, AB T5J 3H1
Executive Director, Strategic Program Services, Leslie Noel
Tel: 780-638-4569
leslie.noel@gov.ab.ca
Sun Life Building
10123 - 99 St., 6th Fl.
Edmonton, AB T5J 3H1
Executive Director, Claims & Recoveries, Don Smallwood
Tel: 780-427-8255
don.smallwood@gov.ab.ca
Sun Life Building
10123 - 99 St., 6th Fl.
Edmonton, AB T5J 3H1
Acting Property Rights Advocate, Karen Johnson
Tel: 780-422-1401; *Fax:* 780-440-8724
karen.johnson@gov.ab.ca
Provincial Bldg.

200 - 5th Ave. South
Lethbridge, AB T1J 4L1
Sheriff, Civil Enforcement, Patricia Wilson
Tel: 780-427-4270
patricia.wilson@gov.ab.ca
Provincial Bldg.
200 - 5th Ave. South
Lethbridge, AB T1J 4L1

Office of the Chief Medical Examiner
Northern Regional Office, 7007 - 116th St., Edmonton, AB T6H 5R8
Tel: 780-427-0373; *Fax:* 780-422-1265
ocme_admin@gov.ab.ca
www.alberta.ca/office-of-chief-medical-examiner.aspx
Secondary Address: 4070 Bowness Rd. NW
Southern Regional Office
Calgary, AB T3B 3R7
Alt. Fax: 403-297-3429
Chief Medical Examiner, Vacant
Chief Toxicologist, Craig Chatterton
Tel: 780-427-4987
craig.chatterton@gov.ab.ca

Office of the Public Guardian & Trustee
John E. Browning Bldg., 10365 - 97th St., 4th Fl., Edmonton, AB T5J 3Z8
Tel: 780-422-1868; *Fax:* 780-422-6051
www.alberta.ca/office-public-guardian-trustee.aspx
Executive Director, Barb Martini
Tel: 780-422-2029
barb.martini@gov.ab.ca
Associate Public Guardian & Trustee, Tim Lowe
Tel: 403-340-5502
tim.lowe@gov.ab.ca
Public Guardian, Calgary, Graham Badry
Tel: 403-592-4099
graham.badry@gov.ab.ca
Public Guardian, Southern Region, Connie MacDonald
Tel: 403-381-5653
connie.macdonald@gov.ab.ca
Public Guardian, Edmonton, Shirley Peleshytyk
Tel: 780-427-9950
shirley.peleshytyk@gov.ab.ca

Legal Services Division
Bowker Bldg., 9833 - 109th St., 2nd Fl., Edmonton, AB T5K 2E8
Tel: 780-422-0500
The following branches are part of the Legal Services Division: divisional planning & management; government client services; & legal policy & ministerial services.
Assistant Deputy Minister, Vacant
Executive Director, Government Client Services Branch, Barbara Mason
Tel: 780-427-9618; *Fax:* 780-425-0310
barb.mason@gov.ab.ca
Executive Director, Legal Policy & Ministerial Services Branch, Susanne Stushnoff
Tel: 780-644-3426
susanne.stushnoff@gov.ab.ca
Chief Legislative Counsel, Legislative Counsel Office, Peter Pagano, Q.C.
Tel: 780-427-0303; *Fax:* 780-422-7366
peter.pagano@gov.ab.ca

Public Security Division
John E. Brownlee Bldg., 10365 - 97th St., 10th Fl., Edmonton, AB T5J 3W7
The following branches are part of the Public Security Division: commercial vehicle enforcement; fish & wildlife enforcement; law enforcement & oversight; parks enforcement; policy & program development; & sheriffs branch. The division is also responsible for the Alberta Serious Incident Response Team.
Senior Assistant Deputy Minister, Bill Sweeney
Tel: 780-427-3457; *Fax:* 780-427-1194
bill.sweeney@gov.ab.ca
Chief Fish & Wildlife Officer, Fish & Wildlife Enforcement Branch, Daniel Boyco
Tel: 780-427-2372; *Fax:* 780-422-9560
daniel.boyco@gov.ab.ca
Great West Life Building
9920 - 108 St., 3rd Fl.
Edmonton, AB T5K 2M4
Executive Director, Policy & Program Development Branch, Kathy Collins
Tel: 780-427-7051; *Fax:* 780-422-4213
kathy.collins@gov.ab.ca
Executive Director, Law Enforcement & Oversight Branch, Marlin Degrand
Tel: 780-427-6887; *Fax:* 780-427-5916
marlin.degrand@gov.ab.ca
Chief Sheriff / Executive Director, Sheriffs Branch, Lee Newton
Tel: 780-422-3500; *Fax:* 780-422-3365

lee.newton@gov.ab.ca
Oxford Tower
#702, 10025 - 102A Ave.
Edmonton, AB T5J 2Z2
Executive Director, Alberta Serious Incident Response Team
(ASIRT), Susan Hughson
Tel: 780-644-1483; *Fax:* 780-644-1497
sue.hughson@gov.ab.ca
Petroleum Plaza
9915 - 108 St., 14th Fl.
Edmonton, AB T5K 2G8

Resolution & Court Administration Services Division (RCAS)

John E. Brownlee Bldg., 10365 - 97th St., Edmonton, AB T5J 3W7

Tel: 780-638-4747
Toll-Free: 855-738-4747

The Resolution & Court Administration Services Division oversees the Court of Appeal, the Court of Queen's Bench, the Provincial Court, Law Information Centres, & Alberta Law Libraries.
Assistant Deputy Minister, Mary MacDonald
Tel: 780-427-9620
mary.macdonald@gov.ab.ca
Registrar, Court of Appeal, Heidi Schubert
Tel: 780-422-2416; *Fax:* 780-422-5507
heidi.schubert@gov.ab.ca
Law Courts Building South
1A Sir Winston Churchill Sq., 5th Fl.
Edmonton, AB T5J 0R2
Executive Director, Strategic & Business Support, Trevor Bergen
Tel: 780-644-1399
trevor.bergen@gov.ab.ca
Calgary Courts Centre
601 - 5th St. SW
Calgary, AB T2P 5P7
Executive Director, Court of Queen's Bench - Judicial, Corinne Jamieson
Tel: 403-297-2877; *Fax:* 403-297-8625
corinne.jamieson@gov.ab.ca
Calgary Courts Centre
601 - 5th St. SW
Calgary, AB T2P 5P7
Executive Director, Provincial Court Administration, Sharon Lepetich
Tel: 403-297-2313; *Fax:* 403-297-7152
sharon.lepetich@gov.ab.ca
Calgary Courts Centre
601 - 5th St, SW
Calgary, AB T2P 5P7
Executive Director, Resolution Services, Faye Morrison
Tel: 780-968-3463
faye.morrison@gov.ab.ca

Alberta Labour & Immigration

Legislature Bldg., #107, 10800 - 97th Ave., Edmonton, AB T5K 2B6

Tel: 780-427-3731
Toll-Free: 877-427-3731
www.alberta.ca/labour-and-immigration.aspx
Other Communication: Temporary Foreign Workers, Phone:
780-644-9955; Toll-Free Phone: 877-944-9955; Occupational
Health & Safety, Phone: 780-415-8690; Toll-Free Phone:
866-415-8690

The Ministry of Labour & Immigration (formerly the Ministry of Labour prior to the 2019 general election) is mandated to provide support to both employees & employers, with an emphasis on maintaining safe, fair & healthy workplaces. It also provides resources for immigrants & refugees.

Minister, Hon. Tyler Shandro
Tel: 780-638-9400; *Fax:* 780-638-9401
labour.minister@gov.ab.ca

Associate Minister, Immigration & Multiculturalism, Hon.
Muhammad Yaseen
Tel: 780-638-9400; *Fax:* 780-638-9401

Deputy Minister, Shawn McLeod
Tel: 780-643-1725; *Fax:* 780-641-9351
shawn.mcleod@gov.ab.ca

Private Sector Union Liaison, Searle Turton
Tel: 780-638-3144; *Fax:* 780-638-3506

Associated Agencies, Boards & Commissions:

• **Appeals Commission for Alberta Workers' Compensation**
Standard Life Centre
#1100, 10405 Jasper Ave.
Edmonton, AB T5J 3N4
Tel: 780-412-8700; *Fax:* 780-412-8701
Toll-free: -310-0000
AC.AcesAdmin@gov.ab.ca
www.appealscommission.ab.ca
Other Communication: Toll-Free Phone Outside Alberta:
866-222-4109
The Appeals Commission for Alberta Workers' Compensation strives to offer an independent, fair, & timely appeals process. The Commission works to operate consistently with legislation & policy.

• **Labour Relations Board (ALRB)**
Labour Building
#501, 10808 - 99 Ave.
Edmonton, AB T5K 0G5
Tel: 780-427-8547; *Fax:* 780-422-0970
Toll-free: 800-463-2572
alrbinfo@gov.ab.ca
www.alrb.gov.ab.ca
Other Communication: Calgary Phone: 403-297-4334; Fax:
403-297-5884
The independent & impartial tribunal is involved in the application & interpretation of labour lawa in Alberta. The Alberta Labour Relations Board administers the Labour Relations Code to handle disputes between trade unions & employers.

• **Occupational Health & Safety Council (OHSC)**
Standard Life Centre
10405 Jasper Ave.
Edmonton, AB T5J 3N4
Tel: 780-415-8690
Toll-free: 866-415-8690
TTY: 800-232-7215
work.alberta.ca/occupational-health-safety/6446.html
Under the Occupational Health & Safety Act, the Occupational Health & Safety Council advises the Minister about matters related to the health & safety of Alberta's workers. Nine members serve on the Council, including the chair & representatives from employers, employees, & the public.

• **Workers' Compensation Board (WCB)**
9912 - 107 St.
PO Box 2415
Edmonton, AB T5J 2S5
Tel: 780-498-3999; *Fax:* 780-427-5863
Toll-free: 866-922-9221
TTY: 780-498-7895
www.wcb.ab.ca
Other Communication: Calgary, Phone: 403-517-6000; Toll-Free Phone, outside Alberta: 800-661-9608; Claims, Toll-Free Fax:
800-661-1993
The independent organization manages workers' compensation insurance, based on legislation. The Alberta Workers' Compensation Board compensates injured workers for costs such as lost income & health care.

Safe, Fair & Healthy Workplaces Division

Labour Bldg., 10808 - 99th Ave., 10th Fl., Edmonton, AB T5K 0G5
Assistant Deputy Minister, Jody Young
Tel: 780-643-1391; *Fax:* 780-643-1392
jody.young@gov.ab.ca
Executive Director, Employment Standards Program Delivery,
Darren Caul
Tel: 780-422-5932; *Fax:* 780-644-5424
darren.caul@gov.ab.ca
Executive Director, Occupational Health & Safety Program
Delivery, Rob Feagan
Tel: 780-415-0603; *Fax:* 780-644-1508
rob.feagan@gov.ab.ca

Strategy & Policy Division

Labour Bldg., 10808 - 99th Ave., 9th Fl., Edmonton, AB T5K 0G5
Assistant Deputy Minister, Lenore Neudorf
Tel: 780-643-1348
lenore.neudorf@gov.ab.ca

Workforce Strategies Division

Labour Bldg., 10808 - 99th Ave., 10th Fl., Edmonton, AB T5K 0G5

Tel: 780-638-3531; *Fax:* 780-422-2889
Assistant Deputy Minister, Maryann Everett
Tel: 780-422-9493; *Fax:* 780-422-2889
maryann.everett@gov.ab.ca
Executive Director, Training & Employment Services, Noelle
Becker
Tel: 403-529-3692
noelle.becker@gov.ab.ca

Executive Director, Newcomer Support, Gosia Cichy-Weclaw
Tel: 780-422-1851; *Fax:* 780-422-6400
gosia.cichy-weclaw@gov.ab.ca
Executive Director, Program Effectiveness, Deb Kaweski
Tel: 780-415-0530
deb.kaweski@gov.ab.ca
Executive Director, Employer Services, Sue Welke
Tel: 780-427-7462
sue.welke@gov.ab.ca

Alberta Municipal Affairs

Communications Branch, Commerce Place, 10155 - 102nd St., 18th Fl., Edmonton, AB T5J 4L4

Tel: 780-427-2732; *Fax:* 780-422-1419
www.alberta.ca/municipal-affairs.aspx

In 2011, under then-Premier Redford, the Ministry of Municipal Affairs took on the responsibilities of the former Ministry of Housing & Urban Affairs.
Alberta's Ministry of Municipal Affairs is engaged in the following activities: assisting Alberta's municipalities in the provision of well-managed, accountable local government; managing municipal & library system boards; administering a safety system for the construction & maintenance of equipment & buildings; ensuring safe, affordable, & sustainable housing for Albertans; & assisting urban communities.

Minister, Hon. Ric McIver
Tel: 780-427-3744; *Fax:* 780-422-9550
minister.municipalaffairs@gov.ab.ca

Deputy Minister, Brandy Cox
Tel: 780-415-1599

Associated Agencies, Boards & Commissions:
• **Alberta Emergency Management Agency (AEMA)**
Terrace Bldg.
9515 - 107 St., 4th Fl.
Edmonton, AB T5K 2C1
Tel: 780-422-9000; *Fax:* 780-644-1044
Toll-free: -310-0000
aema@gov.ab.ca
www.aema.alberta.ca
Other Communication: Alberta Emergency Management Agency
Response Readiness Centre, Phone: 866-618-2362
The Alberta Emergency Management Agency coordinates organizations, such as government, municipalities, & first responders, which are involved in the prevention, preparedness, & response to emergencies.

• **Capital Region Board**
Bell Tower
#1100, 10104 - 103 Ave.
Edmonton, AB T5J 0H8
Tel: 780-638-6000; *Fax:* 780-638-6009
www.capitalregionboard.ab.ca
The Government of Alberta established the Capital Region Board in 2008. The Board consists of members from twenty-four participating municipalities. They serve on the following committees: land use; transit; Geographic Information Services; housing; & governance.
The following are the municipalities of the Capital Region Board: Town of Beaumont; Town of Bon Accord; Town of Bruderheim; Town of Calmar; Town of Devon; City of Edmonton; City of Fort Saskatchewan; Town of Gibbons; Lamont County; Town of Lamont; City of Leduc; Leduc County; Town of Legal; Town of Morinville; Parkland County; Town of Redwater; City of St. Albert; City of Spruce Grove; Town of Stony Plain; Strathcona County; Sturgeon County; Village of Thorsby; Village of Wabamun; & the Village of Warburg.

• **Municipal Government Board (MGB)**
1229 - 91st St. SW, 2nd Fl.
Edmonton, AB T6X 1E9
Tel: 780-427-4864; *Fax:* 780-427-0986
Toll-free: -310-0000
mgbmail@gov.ab.ca
www.municipalaffairs.alberta.ca
Operating as an independent & impartial body, the Municipal Government Board decides upon certain appeals & disputes from the Municipal Government Act. Examples of issues dealt with by the Municipal Government Board are as follows: disputes between municipalities; annexation matters; linear property assessment complaints; & appeals about equalized assessment & subdivisions.

• Safety Codes Council (SCC)
#500, 10405 Jasper Ave.
Edmonton, AB T5J 3N4
Tel: 780-413-0099; *Fax:* 780-424-5134
Toll-free: 888-413-0099
sccinfo@safetycodes.ab.ca
www.safetycodes.ab.ca
Other Communication: Alt. Emails: training@safetycodes.ab.ca;
certification@safetycodes.ab.ca;
masterelectricians@safetycodes.ab.ca;
askasca@safetycodes.ab.ca
The Safety Codes Council is a corporation that supports the
Ministry of Municipal Affairs' administration of the Safety Codes
Act. The Council has the following business units: Accreditation
& Appeals; Administration; Certification & Policy; Electronic
Business Solutions; & Training.

• Special Areas Board
Special Areas Board Administration
212 - 2nd Ave. West
PO Box 820
Hanna, AB T0J 1P0
Tel: 403-854-5600; *Fax:* 403-854-5527
www.specialareas.ab.ca
Other Communication: Hanna, Phone: 403-854-5625; Oyen,
Phone: 403-664-3618, Fax: 403-664-3320; Consort, Phone:
403-577-3523, Fax: 403-577-2446; Youngstown, Phone:
403-779-3733
The Special Areas Board is responsible for the management of
public land in Alberta's three Special Areas. The Board also
provides municipal services to eastern Alberta's dryland region.
The following are examples of programs & services offered by
the Special Areas Board: protective & emergency services;
construction & maintenance of local roads; provision of water
services; management of public land; operation & maintenance
of Special Areas recreational parks & community pastures;
conservation programming; agricultural development; &
economic development programs.

Corporate Strategic Services Division
Assistant Deputy Minister, Anthony Lemphers
Tel: 780-415-9099; *Fax:* 780-422-4923
anthony.lemphers@gov.ab.ca
Executive Director & Senior Financial Officer, Financial Services,
Dan Balderston
Tel: 780-644-8098; *Fax:* 780-422-5840
dan.balderston@gov.ab.ca
Executive Director, Corporate Planning & Policy, Indira
Breitkreuz
Tel: 780-422-7317; *Fax:* 780-422-4923
indira.breitkreuz@gov.ab.ca
Director, Public Library Services, Diana Davidson
Tel: 780-415-0284; *Fax:* 780-415-8594
diana.davidson@gov.ab.ca

Municipal Assessment & Grants Division
Commerce Place, 10155 - 102nd St., 15th Fl., Edmonton, AB
T5J 4L4
Assistant Deputy Minister, Ethan Bayne
Tel: 780-427-9660; *Fax:* 780-427-0453
ethan.bayne@gov.ab.ca
Executive Director, Grants & Education Property Tax Branch,
Janice Romanyshyn
Tel: 780-415-0833; *Fax:* 780-644-2114
janice.romanyshyn@gov.ab.ca
Executive Director, Assessment Services Branch, Steve White
Tel: 780-422-1377; *Fax:* 780-422-3110
steve.white@gov.ab.ca

Municipal Services & Legislation Division
Commerce Place, 10155 - 102nd St., 17th Fl., Edmonton, AB
T5J 4L4
Assistant Deputy Minister, Gary Sandberg
Tel: 780-422-8034; *Fax:* 780-420-1016
gary.sandberg@gov.ab.ca
Executive Director, Municipal Capacity & Sustainability Branch,
Cathy Maniego
Tel: 780-641-9245; *Fax:* 780-420-1016
cathy.maniego@gov.ab.ca
Executive Director, Strategic Policy & Planning, Alexander
Nnamonu
Tel: 780-644-2905; *Fax:* 780-422-4923
alexander.nnamonu@gov.ab.ca

Public Safety Division
Commerce Place, 10155 - 102nd St., 16th Fl., Edmonton, AB
T5J 4L4
Toll-Free: 866-421-6929
safety.services@gov.ab.ca
Assistant Deputy Minister, Dale Beesley
Tel: 780-644-5624; *Fax:* 780-427-2538
dale.beesley@gov.ab.ca
Executive Director, Community & Technical Support Branch,
Thomas Djurfors

Tel: 780-644-5682
thomas.djurfors@gov.ab.ca
Executive Director, Strategic & System Support Branch, Monte
Krueger
Tel: 780-427-6133; *Fax:* 780-427-2538
monte.krueger@gov.ab.ca
Fire Commissioner, Kevan Jess
Tel: 780-644-1010
kevan.jess@gov.ab.ca

Alberta Office of the Ombudsman

**Canadian Western Bank Bldg., #700, 9925 - 109th St.,
Edmonton, AB T5K 2J8**
Tel: 780-427-2756; *Fax:* 780-427-2759
Toll-Free: 888-455-2756
info@ombudsman.ab.ca
www.ombudsman.ab.ca
Secondary Address: #2560, 801 - 6 Ave. SW
Calgary Regional Office
Calgary, AB T2P 3W2
Alt. Fax: 403-297-5121
twitter.com/AB_Ombudsman
www.linkedin.com/company/office-of-the-alberta-ombudsman
As an Officer of the Legislative Assembly of Alberta, the Alberta
Ombudsman reports directly to the Legislative Assembly. The
Ombudsman carries out his role under the authority of Alberta's
Ombudsman Act.
The Alberta Ombudsman operates independently from the
Alberta government to investigate & respond to written
complaints about unfair treatment from Alberta government
authorities, designated professional organizations. The
Ombudsman also handles the patient concerns resolution
process of Alberta Health Services.

Ombudsman & Public Interest Commissioner, Marianne
Ryan

Deputy Ombudsman, Peter Sherstan

General Counsel, Rodney Fong
rodney.fong@ombudsman.ab.ca

**Alberta Office of the Public Interest Commissioner
(PIC)**

#700, 9925 - 109th St., Edmonton, AB T5K 2J8
Tel: 780-641-8659
Toll-Free: 855-641-8659
info@pic.alberta.ca
yourvoiceprotected.ca
The Office of the Public Interest Commissioner investigates
disclosures of wrongdoing & complaints of reprisals for
employees of government ministries, agencies, boards &
commissions, & other public entities.

Public Interest Commissioner & Alberta Ombudsman,
Marianne Ryan
Note: Alberta Ombudsman Peter Hourihan was appointed as
the province's first Public Interest Commissioner in April 2013.

Deputy Commissioner, Marianne Ryan
Tel: 780-641-8659
info@pic.alberta.ca

Alberta Seniors & Housing

PO Box 3100 Edmonton, AB T5J 4W3
Tel: 780-644-9992; *Fax:* 780-422-5954
Toll-Free: 877-644-9992
TTY: 800-232-7215
www.alberta.ca/seniors-and-housing.aspx
Other Communication: Housing Programs: 780-422-0122
Alberta Seniors & Housing is responsible for programming for
seniors, as well as housing & community services.

Minister, Hon. Josephine Pon
Tel: 780-415-9550; *Fax:* 780-422-8733
sh.minister@gov.ab.ca

Deputy Minister, Susan Taylor
susan.taylor@gov.ab.ca

Associated Agencies, Boards & Commissions:
• Seniors Advisory Council for Alberta (SACA)
Standard Life Centre
#600, 10405 Jasper Ave., 6th Fl.
Edmonton, AB T5J 4R7
Tel: 780-422-2321; *Fax:* 780-422-8762
Toll-free: -310-0000
saca@gov.ab.ca
The Seniors Advisory Council for Alberta consults with senior
citizens & seniors' organizations in communities throughout

Alberta. The Council then informs the Government of Alberta,
through the Minister of Seniors & Community Supports, about
the issues that affect Alberta's seniors.
The Seniors Advisory Council for Alberta is also engaged in
planning the Seniors' Week celebration each years, supporting
workshops for frontline workers & seniors, & participating in
research projects.

Office of the Seniors Advocate
**Centre West Bldg., 10155 - 102nd St., 6th Fl., Edmonton, AB
T5J 4G8**
Tel: 780-644-0682; *Fax:* 780-644-9685
Toll-Free: 844-644-0682
TTY: 844-392-9025
seniors.advocate@gov.ab.ca
seniorsadvocateab.ca
The Seniors Advocate provides links to government &
community programs & services for seniors, as well as
identifying systemic issues & providing policy advice to the
Government of Alberta.
Alberta Seniors Advocate, Sheree Kwong See
Tel: 780-644-0678
sheree.kwongsee@gov.ab.ca

Housing Division
**44 Capital Blvd., 10044 - 108th St., 3rd Fl., Edmonton, AB
T5J 5E6**
Tel: 780-422-0122
Other Communication: Rural & Native Mortgage Portfolio,
Phone: 780-427-6897
Assistant Deputy Minister, John Thomson
Tel: 780-643-1020; *Fax:* 780-422-5124
john.thomson@gov.ab.ca
Executive Director, Capital Initiatives, Lynda Cuppens
Tel: 780-422-8474
lynda.cuppens@gov.ab.ca
Executive Director, Provincial Affordable Housing Strategy,
Shawn Ewasiuk
Tel: 780-644-9674
shawn.ewasiuk@gov.ab.ca
Executive Director, Housing Operations, Dean Lussier
Tel: 780-427-1751
dean.lussier@gov.ab.ca

Seniors Services Division
**Standard Life Centre, 10405 Jasper Ave., 6th Fl., Edmonton,
AB T5J 4R7**
Assistant Deputy Minister, Evan Romanow
Tel: 780-644-7666
evan.romanow@gov.ab.ca
Executive Director, Seniors Strategic Planning Branch, Kesa
Shikaze
Tel: 825-468-4355
kesa.shikaze@gov.ab.ca

Strategic Services Division
**44 Capital Blvd., 10044 - 108th St., 12th Fl., Edmonton, AB
T5J 5E6**
Assistant Deputy Minister, Suzanne Anselmo
Tel: 780-641-9865; *Fax:* 780-644-5586
suzanne.anselmo@gov.ab.ca
Executive Director & Senior Financial Officer, Financial Services
Branch, Darren Baptista
Tel: 780-422-0927; *Fax:* 780-644-5586
darren.baptista@gov.ab.ca
Executive Director, Policy, Planning & Legislative Services
Branch, Matt Barker
Tel: 780-638-4115
matt.barker@gov.ab.ca

Service Alberta

**Government of Alberta, PO Box 1333 Edmonton, AB T5J
2N2**
Tel: 780-427-4088
Toll-Free: -310-0000
service.alberta@gov.ab.ca
www.alberta.ca/service-alberta.aspx
Other Communication: Consumer Information, Email:
cs@gov.ab.ca; Corporate Registry, Email: cr@gov.ab.ca; Land
Titles, Email: lto@gov.ab.ca; Landlords & Tenants, Email:
rta@gov.ab.ca
twitter.com/ServiceAlberta
www.facebook.com/ConsumerProtectionAlberta
The Ministry of Service Alberta offers information, services &
products to Albertans. The following are examples of the
ministry's services: delivery of shared services to ministries,
such as printing documents & technical support; management of
the government's vehicle fleet; administration of the Freedom of
Information & Protection of Privacy legislation; provision of
licensing & registry services; & enforcement of high standards of
consumer protection.

Minister, Hon. Nate Glubish

Tel: 780-422-6880; *Fax:* 780-422-2496
ministersa@gov.ab.ca

Deputy Minister, Cynthia Farmer
Tel: 780-427-1990
cynthia.farmer@gov.ab.ca

Associated Agencies, Boards & Commissions:

• **Alberta Funeral Services Regulatory Board (AFSRB)**
#180, 2755 Broadmoor Blvd.
Sherwood Park, AB T8H 2W7
Tel: 780-452-6130; *Fax:* 780-452-6085
Toll-free: 800-563-4652
office@afsrb.ab.ca
www.afsrb.ab.ca
In 1992, the Alberta Funeral Services Regulatory Board was established under the Licensing of Trades & Businesses Act & the Funeral Services Business Licensing Regulation.
The Board provides the following services: establishing educational standards; licensing pre-need salespeople, funeral directors, embalmers, funeral businesses, & crematories; monitoring performance standards; & investigating consumer complaints.

• **Alberta Motor Vehicle Industry Council (AMVIC)**
#303, 9945 - 50 St.
Edmonton, AB T6A 0L4
Tel: 780-466-1140; *Fax:* 780-462-0633
Toll-free: 877-979-8100
www.amvic.org
The Alberta Motor Vehicle Industry Council is responsible for the administration & enforcement of automotive industry regulations, under Alberta's Fair Trading Act.

• **Real Estate Council of Alberta (RECA)**
#202, 1506 - 11 Ave. SW
Calgary, AB T3C 0M9
Tel: 403-228-2954; *Fax:* 403-228-3065
Toll-free: 888-425-2754
info@reca.ca
www.reca.ca
Operating under the Real Estate Act of Alberta, the Real Estate Council of Alberta is responsible for the regulation of professionals in the real estate, real estate appraisal, & mortgage broker industries. The Council is made up of the following committees: Audit, Finance, Governance, Hearings, & the Education Ad Hoc Committee.

FOIP Review & Transformation Division
Telus House at ATB Place, 10020 - 100th St., 29th Fl., Edmonton, AB T5J 0N3
Assistant Deputy Minister, Manon Plante
Tel: 780-422-2340
manon.plante@gov.ab.ca
Executive Director, Information Access & Privacy, Veronica Chodak
Tel: 780-644-4964
veronica.chodak@gov.ab.ca

Office of the Corporate Chief Information Officer Division
ATB Place South, 10020 - 100th St., 29th Fl., Edmonton, AB T5J 0N3
Senior Assistant Deputy Minister & Corporate CIO, Stephen Bull
Tel: 780-644-8414
stephen.bull@gov.ab.ca
Sector CIO, Community Services & Safety Sector, Sheri Binges
Tel: 780-644-7790
sheri.binges@gov.ab.ca
Sector CIO, People, Families & Communities Sector, Sabina Posadziejewski
Tel: 825-468-4090
sabina.posadziejewski@gov.ab.ca
Sector CIO, Workforce Development Sector, Stacey Reynhoudt
Tel: 780-427-7384
stacey.reynhoudt@gov.ab.ca
Sector CIO, Government Services Sector, Stacy Shenfield
Tel: 780-415-8934
stacy.shenfield@gov.ab.ca
Sector CIO, Environment & Resources Sector, Susan Wilson-Ferguson
Tel: 780-217-5497
susan.wilson-ferguson@gov.ab.ca
Acting Executive Director, Corporate Information Security Office, Michael Alguire
Tel: 780-644-0910
michael.alguire@gov.ab.ca
Executive Director, Strategy & Governance Sector, Barry Chatwin
Tel: 780-644-4523
barry.chatwin@gov.ab.ca
Executive Director, Business Support Services, Dana Thompson
Tel: 780-422-4623
dana.thompson@gov.ab.ca

Executive Director, IMT Sector Integration, Paul Thorsteinson
Tel: 780-991-4965
paul.thorsteinson@gov.ab.ca
Executive Director & CIO, Economy & Growth Sector, Geoffrey Wacowich
Tel: 780-644-3043
geoffrey.wacowich@gov.ab.ca
Executive Lead, Enterprise IMT Services Sector, Martin Dinel
Tel: 780-427-2429
martin.dinel@gov.ab.ca

Shared Services Division
Telus House at ATB Place, 10020 - 100th St., 29th Fl., Edmonton, AB T5J 0N3
Acting Assistant Deputy Minister, Brandy Cox
Tel: 780-415-1599
brandy.cox@gov.ab.ca
Executive Director, Service Delivery, Anoushka Fernandes
Tel: 780-427-0254
anoushka.fernandes@gov.ab.ca
Executive Director, Client Services Operations, Liane Stangenberg
Tel: 780-644-8344
liane.stangenberg@gov.ab.ca
Acting Executive Director, Procurement Services; Director, Corporate Purchasing Section, Danis Lee
Tel: 780-643-1800; *Fax:* 780-422-9672
danis.lee@gov.ab.ca
Executive Director, Service Development & Quality (SDQ), Andre Cyr
Tel: 780-422-5619
andre.cyr@gov.ab.ca

Strategic & Consumer Services Division
ATB Place South, 10020 - 100th St., 29th Fl., Edmonton, AB T5J 0N3
Assistant Deputy Minister, Brandy Cox
Tel: 780-415-1599
brandy.cox@gov.ab.ca
Utilities Consumer Advocate, Chris Hunt
Tel: 403-592-2600
Toll-free: -10 -822; *Fax:* 403-592-2604
chris.hunt@gov.ab.ca
www.ucahelps.alberta.ca
Other Communications: General Email: ucahelps@gov.ab.ca
Terrace Bldg.
9515 - 107 St., 5th Fl.
Edmonton, AB T5K 2C1
Executive Director, Policy, Governance & Legislative Services, Andrew Dore
Tel: 780-427-1466
andrew.dore@gov.ab.ca
Executive Director, Consumer Services Programs, Lois Flynn
Tel: 780-422-8177; *Fax:* 780-427-3033
lois.flynn@gov.ab.ca
Executive Director, Land Titles & Surveys, Richard Schlachter
Tel: 780-427-0108
richard.schlachter@gov.ab.ca

Strategic Planning & Financial Services
Commerce Place, 10155 - 102nd St., 13th Fl., Edmonton, AB T5J 4G8
Executive Director & Senior Financial Officer, Strategic Planning & Financial Services, Darrell Dancause
Tel: 780-415-8975
darrell.dancause@gov.ab.ca

Alberta Transportation

Communications Branch, Twin Atria Bldg., 4999 - 98th Ave., 2nd Fl., Edmonton, AB T6B 2X3
Tel: 780-427-7674; *Fax:* 780-466-3166
Trans.Contact.Us.m@gov.ab.ca
www.alberta.ca/transportation.aspx
Alberta's Ministry of Transportation consists of the Department of Transportation & the Transportation Safety Board. The Ministry strives to provide a safe & sustainable transportation system & water management infrastructure throughout the province.
Key activities of the Department are as follows: leading the planning, construction & preservation of highways across Alberta; offering information & education about transportation safety services & enforcement programs; designing, building, & maintaining the water management infrastructure in the province; managing grant programs to assist municipalities; & representing Alberta at all levels of government to ensure regulatory harmonization.

Associated Agencies, Boards & Commissions:

• **Transportation Safety Board**
North Office, Twin Atria Building
4999 - 98 Ave., Main Fl.
Edmonton, AB T6B 2X3
Tel: 780-427-7178; *Fax:* 780-422-9739
Toll-free: -310-0000
www.atsb.alberta.ca
The Alberta Transportation Safety Board reports to the Minister of Transportation, through the Chair. The Board's members are chosen through a public recruitment process.
The Board hears appeals about licence suspensions & vehicle seizures. Its decisions are made in accordance with the Traffic Safety Act & the Railway (Alberta) Act.

Planning, Finance & Technical Standards Division
Twin Atria Bldg., 4999 - 98th Ave., 3rd Fl., Edmonton, AB T6B 2X3
Assistant Deputy Minister, Ranjit Tharmalingam
Tel: 780-422-7672; *Fax:* 780-644-7220
ranjit.tharmalingam@gov.ab.ca
Senior Financial Officer, Finance Branch, Dale Fung
Tel: 780-427-2030
dale.fung@gov.ab.ca
Executive Director, Planning & Program Management Branch, Scott Beeby
Tel: 780-415-0775
scott.beeby@gov.ab.ca
Executive Director, Enterprise Resource Planning & Change Management Branch, Ross Danyluk
Tel: 780-644-2663
ross.danyluk@gov.ab.ca

Construction & Maintenance Division
Twin Atria Bldg., 4999 - 98th Ave., 2nd Fl., Edmonton, AB T6B 2X3
Assistant Deputy Minister, Tom Loo
Tel: 780-415-4876
tom.loo@gov.ab.ca
Executive Director, Major Capital Projects, Landon Reppert
Tel: 780-644-1199
landon.reppert@gov.ab.ca

Safety & Policy Division
Twin Atria Bldg., 4999 - 98th Ave., Main Fl., Edmonton, AB T6B 2X3
Tel: 780-427-8901; *Fax:* 780-415-0782
Toll-Free: 800-666-5036
The division supports initiatives such as barrier-free transportation, climate change initiatives & border crossing issues, as well as leading reviews & changes to statutes & regulations.
Assistant Deputy Minister, Crystal Damer
Tel: 780-415-1281
crystal.damer@gov.ab.ca
Executive Director, Transportation Policy Branch, Wendy Doyle
Tel: 780-427-6588
wendy.doyle@gov.ab.ca
Executive Director, Commercial & Vehicle Safety Branch, Trudy Nastiuk
Tel: 780-422-3759; *Fax:* 780-422-9193
trudy.nastiuk@gov.ab.ca
Executive Director, Driver Programs, Terry Wallace
Tel: 780-427-7508; *Fax:* 780-422-6612
terry.wallace@gov.ab.ca

Alberta Treasury Board & Finance

9820 - 107th St., 9th Fl., Edmonton, AB T5K 1E7
Tel: 780-427-3035; *Fax:* 780-427-1147
www.alberta.ca/treasury-board-and-finance.aspx
twitter.com/Alberta_Finance
Alberta's Treasury Board manages government spending by carrying out the following responsibilities: leading the provincial government's capital planning process; providing advice & analysis on costs & capital spending; identifying alternatives for financing capital projects; & ensuring accounting standards & financial reporting. The ministry also oversees economic development & corporate human resources.
Alberta Finance offers financial, economic, & fiscal policy advice to government. The Ministry also provides tax & regulatory administration to support strong government finances & to ensure that Alberta has a productive & competitive economy. The two ministries were combined in 2012 by then-Premier Redford.

Minister, Finance; President, Treasury Board, Hon. Travis Toews
Tel: 780-415-4855
tbf.minister@gov.ab.ca
Legislature Building
#323, 10800 - 97 Ave.
Edmonton, AB T5K 2B6

Associate Minister, Red Tape Reduction, Hon. Tanya Fir
Tel: 780-427-0240
associateminister-rtr@gov.ab.ca
Legislature Building
#323, 10800 - 97 Ave.
Edmonton, AB T5K 2B6

Deputy Minister, Athana Mentzelopoulos
Tel: 780-415-4515
athana.mentzelopoulos@gov.ab.ca

Assistant Deputy Minister, Corporate Planning & Red Tape Reduction, David Stanford
Tel: 780-203-5372

Associated Agencies, Boards & Commissions:

• **Alberta Accreditation Committee (AAC)**
#500, 222 - 58th Ave. SW
Calgary, AB T2H 2S3
accreditation@abcouncil.ab.ca
www.albertaaac.ca
The Accreditation Committee is responsible for reviewing & approving continuing education providers, continuing education courses, & the hours for each course or seminar that can be used towards the 15-hour requirement that licensed agents & adjusters must complete each licensing year.

• **Alberta Automobile Insurance Rate Board (AIRB)**
Canadian Western Bank Place
#2440, 10303 Jasper Ave.
Edmonton, AB T5J 3N6
Tel: 780-427-5428; *Fax:* 780-638-4254
Toll-free: -310-0000
airb@gov.ab.ca
www.airb.alberta.ca
The Automobile Insurance Rate Board is engaged in the following activities: setting premiums for basic coverage; monitoring premiums for optional coverage; & reviewing & approving rating programs for new insurers.

• **Alberta Capital Finance Authority (ACFA)**
Sun Life Place
#2160, 10123 - 99 St. NW
Edmonton, AB T5J 3H1
Tel: 780-427-9711; *Fax:* 780-422-2175
webacfa@gov.ab.ca
www.acfa.gov.ab.ca
Other Communication: Rate Information Line: 780-422-2632
Established in 1956, the Alberta Capital Finance Authority is a non-profit corporation that acts under the authority of the Alberta Capital Finance Authority Act (Alberta). Flexible funding for capital projects is provided by the provincial authority to Alberta's municipalities, school boards, & other local entities, at interest rates based on the cost of its borrowings.

• **Alberta Gaming, Liquor & Cannabis Commission (AGLCC)**
50 Corriveau Ave.
St Albert, AB T8N 3T5
Tel: 780-447-8600; *Fax:* 780-447-8989
Toll-free: 800-272-8876
www.aglc.ca
Other Communication: Illegal Tobacco Hotline: 800-577-2522; Smart Training: 877-436-6336; Alberta Cannabis Call Centre: 855-436-5677
The AGLC is a crown commercial enterprise consisting of a Board responsible for the Gaming & Liquor Act, & a Corporation that controls day-to-day operations. Offices are located in Calgary, Red Deer, Grande Prairie & Lethbridge. As of 2018, the AGLC is also responsible for the oversight of private retailers & distribution of cannabis in the province.
Calgary: 403-292-7300; Red Deer: 403-314-2656; Grande Prairie: 780-832-3000; Lethbridge: 403-331-6500.

• **Alberta Insurance Council (AIC)**
#500, 222 - 58th Ave. SW
Calgary, AB T2H 2S3
Toll-free: 800-461-3367
info@abcouncil.ab.ca
www.abcouncil.ab.ca
Other Communication: Licensing: licensing@abcouncil.ab.ca; Exams: exams@abcouncil.ab.ca
The AIC is an industry-funded regulator responsible for administering the province's insurance laws surrounding insurance agents & adjusters.

• **Alberta Investment Management Corporation (AIMCo)**
#1100, 10830 Jasper Ave.
Edmonton, AB T5J 2B3
Tel: 780-392-3600
www.aimco.alberta.ca
Other Communication: Toronto Office, Phone: 647-789-5700
Established as a Crown corporation in 2008, the Alberta Investment Management Corporation provides investment management services for a group of Alberta public sector funds.

• **Alberta Local Authorities Pension Plan Corp. (ALAPP)**
c/o Alberta Pensions Services Corp.
5103 Windermere Blvd. SW
Edmonton, AB T6W 0S9
Fax: 780-421-1652
Toll-free: 877-649-5277
memberservices@lapp.ca
www.lapp.ca
LAPP is the 7th largest pension plan in Canada, with the backing of a $35-billion pension fund. ALAPP Corp. sets the strategic direction for the Plan on funding, investments & design, as well as coordinating the activities of the Alberta Investment Management Corp. (AIMCo) & Alberta Pensions Services (APS).

• **Alberta Pensions Services Corporation (APS)**
5103 Windermere Blvd. SW
Edmonton, AB T6W 0S9
Tel: 780-427-2782
Toll-free: 800-661-8198
memberservices@apsc.ca
www.apsc.ca
Other Communication: Alt. Emails: employerservices@apsc.ca; pay@apsc.ca; privacy@apsc.ca; mediacontact@apsc.ca
Alberta Pensions Services Corporation was incorporated in 1995, under the Business Corporations Act of Alberta. The Crown Corporation administers seven statutory pension plans & two supplementary retirement plans.

• **Alberta Securities Commission (ASC)**
#600, 250 - 5th St. SW
Calgary, AB T2P 0R4
Tel: 403-297-6454; *Fax:* 403-297-6156
Toll-free: 877-355-0585
inquiries@asc.ca
www.albertasecurities.com
Other Communication: Alt. -mails: complaints@asc.ca; checkfirst@asc.ca; sedar.sedi@asc.ca; records.requests@asc.ca; registration@asc.ca; media@asc.ca; registrar@asc.ca; webmaster@asc.ca
The Alberta Securities Commission is a regulatory agency that is responsible for the administration of the Alberta Securities Act. The capital market in Alberta is regulated by the Alberta Securities Commission to protect investors.
The Alberta Securities Commission also works as a member of the Canadian Securities Administrators to coordinate & improve the regulation of Canada's capital markets.

• **Alberta Teachers' Retirement Fund (ATRF)**
Barnett House
#600, 11010 - 142 St. NW
Edmonton, AB T5N 2R1
Tel: 780-451-4166; *Fax:* 780-452-3547
Toll-free: 800-661-9582
info@atrf.com
www.atrf.com
Other Communication: Alt. Emails: member@atrf.com (Member Plan Inquiries); retiredmember@atrf.com (Retired Members); helpdesk@atrf.com (Employer Inquiries)
Established under the Teachers' Pension Plans Act, the Alberta Teachers' Retirement Fund has administered a pension plan for teachers employed in Alberta's school jurisdictions & charter schools since 1939.
The independent corporation also administers the Private School Teachers' Pension Plan for teachers at Alberta's private schools that have joined the plan.

• **ATB Financial**
#2100, 10020 - 100 St. NW
Edmonton, AB T5J 0N3
Tel: 403-245-8110
Toll-free: 800-332-8383
www.atb.com
Other Communication: Privacy, Phone: 866-858-4175; Online Banking, Phone: 866-282-4932; Business Online Banking, Phone: 888-655-5152; MasterCard, Phone: 800-661-2266
Established in 1938, ATB Financial has been a provincial Crown corporation since 1997. As the largest Alberta-based financial institution, ATB Financial serves more than 725,000 customers in 244 communities.

• **Credit Union Deposit Guarantee Corporation (CUDGC)**
#2000, 10104 - 103 St.
Edmonton, AB T5J 0H8
Tel: 780-428-6680; *Fax:* 780-428-7571
Toll-free: 800-661-0351
mail@cudgc.ab.ca
www.cudgc.ab.ca
Established untder the Alberta Credit Union Act, the Credit Union Deposit Guarantee Corporation is a provincial corporation. The Corporation is administered by a Board of Directors, who are appointed by the Lieutenant Governor in Council of Alberta. The Credit Union Deposit Guarantee Corporation guarantees deposits held with Alberta's credit unions & works to ensure that credit unions employ sound business practices.

• **Horse Racing Alberta (HRA)**
#720, 9707 - 110 St. NW
Edmonton, AB T5K 2L9
Tel: 780-415-5432
Toll-free: 888-553-7223
reception@thehorses.com
www.thehorses.com
A private not-for-profit corporation established in 1996 with the proclamation of the Racing Corporation Act.

• **Management Employees Pension Board**
c/o Alberta Pensions Services Corp.
5103 Windermere Blvd. SW
Edmonton, AB T6W 0S9
Tel: 780-391-3693; *Fax:* 780-421-1652
Toll-free: 877-889-6377
board@mepp.ca
www.mepp.ca
Other Communication: Member Services: memberservices@mepp.ca; Employers: employerservices@apsc.ca; Pensioners: pay@mepp.ca
The Board oversees the Management Employees Pension Plan (MEPP), which was established in 1972 as the Public Service Management Pension Plan. In 1993, the plan was split in two: active members on or after Aug. 1, 1992 became members of MEPP, while members who left the Plan or retired before Aug. 1, 1992, and those who had 35 years of pensionable service by Aug. 1, 1992, became members of the Public Service Management (Closed Membership) Pension Plan.

• **Public Service Pension Board**
c/o Alberta Pensions Services Corp.
5103 Windermere Blvd. SW
Edmonton, AB T6W 0S9
Fax: 780-421-1652
Toll-free: 877-453-1777
board@pspp.ca
www.pspp.ca
Other Communication: Members: memberservices@pspp.ca; Employers: employerservices@apsc.ca; Pensioners: pay@pspp.ca
The Board oversees the Public Service Pension Plan (PSPP), which is a defined benefit pension plan for full-time public service employees.

• **Special Forces Pension Board**
c/o Alberta Pensions Services Corp
5103 Windermere Blvd. SW
Edmonton, AB T6W 0S9
Fax: 780-421-1652
Toll-free: 877-809-7377
board@sfpp.ca
www.sfpp.ca
Other Communication: Members: memberservices@sfpp.ca; Employers: employerservices@apsc.ca; Pensioners: pay@sfpp.ca
The Board oversees the Special Forces Pension Plan (SFPP), which is a defined benefit pension plan for full-time police officers.

Provincial Bargaining Coordination Office
Petwin Tower, 10707 - 100th Ave., Edmonton, AB T5J 2W3
Tel: 780-638-9550
Chief Advisor on Negotiations, Kevin Davediuk
Tel: 780-638-9562
kevin.davediuk@gov.ab.ca
Executive Director, Labour Relations, Research, Analysis & Compensation Branch, Tim Thompson
Tel: 780-415-0527
tim.thompson@gov.ab.ca

Budget Development & Reporting Division
Federal Bldg., 9820 - 107th St., 9th Fl., Edmonton, AB T5K 1E7
The Budget Development & Reporting Division is responsible for preparing the annual Budget, as well as annual reports & consolidated financial statements.
Assistant Deputy Minister, Mary Persson
Tel: 780-644-8078
mary.persson@gov.ab.ca
Executive Director, Budget Development & Planning 1, Ryan Fernandez
Tel: 780-427-7635
ryan.fernandez@gov.ab.ca
Executive Director, Revenue, Reporting & Information Systems, James Forrest
Tel: 780-427-8752
james.forrest@gov.ab.ca
Executive Director, Budget Development & Planning 2, Greg Findlay
Tel: 780-415-9258
greg.findlay@gov.ab.ca
Executive Director, Budget Development & Planning, Charlene Wong

Tel: 780-427-8781
charlene.wong@gov.ab.ca

Communications & Public Engagement
Federal Bldg., 9820 - 107th St., 7th Fl., Edmonton, AB T5K 1E7

Formerly known as the Public Affairs Bureau, the Communications & Public Engagement branch was moved from the Executive Council to Treasury Board & Finance in July 2017.
Managing Director, Corey Hogan
Tel: 780-644-3024
corey.hogan@gov.ab.ca
Assistant Deputy Minister, Communications - Economic, Kim Capstick
Tel: 780-643-9341
kim.capstick@gov.ab.ca
Assistant Deputy Minister, Communications - Social, Carol Chawrun
Tel: 780-427-9274
carol.chawrun@gov.ab.ca
Executive Director, Insights, Joanne Rosnau
Tel: 780-643-2933
joanne.rosnau@gov.ab.ca
Executive Director, Outreach, Gene Smith
Tel: 780-644-8813
gene.smith@gov.ab.ca

Office of the Controller
Terrace Bldg., 9515 - 107th St., 3rd Fl., Edmonton, AB T5K 2C3
Tel: 780-427-3076; *Fax:* 780-422-2164
The Office of the Controller handles the following responsibilities: overseeing financial management & control policies; ensuring government accounting standards; reporting financial information; & planning.
Controller, Dan Stadlwieser
Tel: 780-644-4736
dan.stadlwieser@gov.ab.ca
Executive Director, Financial Accounting & Standards, Diem Fernandez
Tel: 780-427-7333
diem.fernandez@gov.ab.ca
Executive Director, Corporate Consolidations & Reporting, Hardeep Minhas
Tel: 780-644-4582
hardeep.minhas@gov.ab.ca

Corporate Internal Audit Services
Terrace Bldg., 9515 - 107th St., 3rd Fl., Edmonton, AB T5K 2C3
Tel: 780-644-7185
Corporate Internal Audit Services works with Alberta's government ministries to identify areas for improvement. Following the performance of internal audits, recommendations are provided to better operations & fiscal management.
Acting Chief Internal Auditor, Kathleen Gora
Tel: 780-644-5271
kathleen.gora@gov.ab.ca
Executive Director, Enterprise Audits & Professional Practice, Kathleen Gora
Tel: 780-644-5271
kathleen.gora@gov.ab.ca

Economics & Fiscal Policy Division
Federal Bldg., 9820 - 107th St., 8th Fl., Edmonton, AB T5K 1E7

Assistant Deputy Minister, Mark Parsons
Tel: 780-427-8790; *Fax:* 780-426-3951
mark.parsons@gov.ab.ca
Chief Economist & Executive Director, Economics & Revenue Forecasting, Catherine Rothrock
Tel: 780-427-2758; *Fax:* 780-426-3951
catherine.rothrock@gov.ab.ca
Executive Director, Tax Policy, Joffre Hotz
Tel: 780-427-8727
joffre.hotz@gov.ab.ca
Executive Director, Fiscal Planning & Analysis, Stephen Tkachyk
Tel: 780-427-8804; *Fax:* 780-427-1296
stephen.tkachyk@gov.ab.ca
Chief Statistician/Director, Office of Statistics & Information (OSI), Ryan Mazan
Tel: 780-643-1074; *Fax:* 780-426-3951
ryan.mazan@gov.ab.ca

Financial Sector Regulation & Policy Division (FSRP)
Terrace Bldg., 9515 - 107th St., 4th Fl., Edmonton, AB T5K 2C3
Tel: 780-427-8322
Assistant Deputy Minister & Superintendent of Financial Institutions, Insurance & Pensions; Deputy Superintendent, Pensions, Darren Hedley
Tel: 780-427-9722
darren.hedley@gov.ab.ca

Deputy Superintendent, Financial Institutions Regulation, Peter Baba
Tel: 780-415-2450; *Fax:* 780-420-0752
peter.baba@gov.ab.ca
Deputy Superintendent, Insurance Regulations & Market Conduct, David Sorensen
Tel: 780-427-8896; *Fax:* 780-420-0752
david.sorensen@gov.ab.ca
Executive Director, Project Management Office, Christina Dentzien
Tel: 780-415-9233
christina.dentzien@gov.ab.ca

Public Service Commission
Peace Hills Trust Tower, 10011 - 109th St., 7th Fl., Edmonton, AB T5J 3S8
Tel: 780-408-8450
www.alberta.ca/public-service-commission.aspx
Formerly known as Corporate Human Resources, the Public Service Commission is responsible for the following: administering Alberta's Public Service Act and the Code of Conduct and Ethics for the Public Service of Alberta; representing the Government of Alberta as the Employer in collective bargaining and other labour relations matters; & advising the President of the Treasury Board/Minister of Finance, the Deputy Minister of the Executive Council, & other Deputy Ministers and Senior Officials on human resource issues.
Deputy Minister, Tim Grant
Tel: 780-408-8450; *Fax:* 780-422-5428
tim.grant@gov.ab.ca
Assistant Deputy Minister, Strategic Services & Public Agency Secretariat, Ross Nairne
Tel: 780-427-8866
ross.nairne@gov.ab.ca
Assistant Deputy Minister, Labour Relations Policy & Programs Division, Michelle Dorval
Tel: 780-427-1294
michelle.dorval@gov.ab.ca
Assistant Deputy Minister, HR Service Delivery Division, Cindy McKinley
Tel: 780-408-8412
cindy.mckinley@gov.ab.ca
Executive Director, HR Portfolio 2 (Children's Services; Community & Social Services; Health, Seniors & Housing), Judi Carmichael
Tel: 780-644-5420
judi.carmichael@gov.ab.ca
Executive Director, HR Portfolio 1 (Justice; Solicitor General; Treasury Board & Finance), Cheryl Leske
Tel: 780-644-2355
cheryl.leske@gov.ab.ca
Executive Director, HR Portfolio 4 (Municipal Affairs; Infrastructure; Transportation; Culture, Multiculturalism and Status of Women; Education & Labour), Rick Nisbet
Tel: 780-913-7468
rick.nisbet@gov.ab.ca
Executive Director, HR Portfolio 3 (Economic Development, Trade & Tourism; Advanced Education; Environment & Parks; Energy & Indigenous Relations; Agriculture), Armin Pyde
Tel: 587-986-4231
armin.pyde@gov.ab.ca
Executive Director, Talent Acquisition Services, Renee Redinger
Tel: 780-293-2397
renee.redinger@gov.ab.ca

Strategic & Business Services Division
Terrace Bldg., 9515 - 107th St., 4th Fl., Edmonton, AB T5K 2C3
Tel: 780-427-3052
Other Communication: Air Charter Services Dispatch, Phone: 780-427-5251
Assistant Deputy Minister, LeighAnne Lumbard
Tel: 780-422-3027
leighanne.lumbard@gov.ab.ca
Executive Director, Corporate Planning, Policy & Administration, Tanya Bowerman
Tel: 780-422-2640
tanya.bowerman@gov.ab.ca
Acting Executive Director, Financial Services; Director, Financial Planning & Budgets, Craig K. Johnson
Tel: 780-644-7041
craig.k.johnson@gov.ab.ca
Executive Director, Pension Policy, David Mulyk
Tel: 780-415-0514
david.mulyk@gov.ab.ca

Tax & Revenue Administration Division (TRA)
Sir Frederick W. Haultain Bldg., 9811 - 109th St., 2nd Fl., Edmonton, AB T5K 2L5
Tel: 780-427-3044; *Fax:* 780-427-0348
tra.revenue@gov.ab.ca
www.finance.alberta.ca/publications/tax_rebates

Assistant Deputy Minister, Michael Hocken
Tel: 780-644-4075
michael.hocken@gov.ab.ca
Executive Director, Strategic & Client Services (SCS), Irene Chan
Tel: 780-644-4171
irene.chan@gov.ab.ca
Executive Director, Revenue Operations, Kent Heine
Tel: 780-644-4257; *Fax:* 780-644-4921
kent.heine@gov.ab.ca
Executive Director, Tax Services, Angelina Leung
Tel: 780-644-4064; *Fax:* 780-427-5074
angelina.leung@gov.ab.ca
Executive Director, Audit, Zoya Kingston
Tel: 780-644-4245
zoya.kingston@gov.ab.ca

Treasury & Risk Management Division
Federal Bldg., 9820 - 107th St., 8th Fl., Edmonton, AB T5K 1E7
Assistant Deputy Minister, Lowell Epp
Tel: 780-422-4052; *Fax:* 780-427-0780
lowell.epp@gov.ab.ca
Executive Director, Risk Management & Insurance, Mark Day
Tel: 780-644-4045; *Fax:* 780-422-5271
mark.day@gov.ab.ca
Executive Director, Banking & Debt Operations, Laura Spencer
Tel: 780-415-9184
laura.spencer@gov.ab.ca
Executive Director, Capital Markets, Stephen J. Thompson
Tel: 780-644-5011
stephen.j.thompson@gov.ab.ca

Government of British Columbia

Seat of Government: Parliament Bldgs., Victoria, BC V8V 1X4
Tel: 250-387-6121
Toll-Free: 800-663-7867
TTY: 800-661-8773
www2.gov.bc.ca
Other Communication: Vancouver, Phone: 604-660-2421; Vancouver, TTY: 604-775-0303; Outside BC, Phone: 604-660-2421
twitter.com/BCGovNews
www.facebook.com/BCProvincialGovernment
www.youtube.com/user/ProvinceofBC
The Province of British Columbia entered Confederation on July 20, 1871. According to the 2016 StatsCan census, the population of the province is 4,648,055. British Columbia's land area is 922,503.01 sq km.

Office of the Lieutenant Governor

Government House, 1401 Rockland Ave., Victoria, BC V8S 1V9
Tel: 250-387-2080; *Fax:* 250-387-2078
ghinfo@gov.bc.ca
ltgov.bc.ca
twitter.com/LGJanetAustin
www.facebook.com/BCLieutenantGovernor
The Hon. Janet Austin was sworn in as the 30th Lieutenant Governor of British Columbia on April 24, 2018.

Lieutenant Governor, Hon. Janet Austin, OBC

Private Secretary to the Lieutenant Governor & Executive Director, Government House, Jerymy Brownridge
Tel: 250-387-2083; *Fax:* 250-387-2078

Director, Operations & Management Services, Thandi Williams
Tel: 778-974-5542

Office of the Premier & Cabinet Office

PO Box 9041 Stn. Prov Govt, Victoria, BC V8W 9E1
Tel: 250-387-1715; *Fax:* 250-387-0087
premier@gov.bc.ca
www.gov.bc.ca/premier
Other Communication: Premier's Vancouver Office, Phone: 604-775-1600, Fax: 604-775-1688
John Horgan was sworn in as British Columbia's 36th Premier on July 18, 2017, following the defeat of former Premier Christy Clark's newly elected government in a non-confidence vote held June 29, 2017.

Premier; President, Executive Council, Hon. John Horgan
Tel: 250-387-1715

Deputy Minister to the Premier, Lori Wanamaker
Tel: 250-356-2206

douglas.routley.mla@leg.bc.ca
dougroutley.ca
Other Communications: Constituency Phone: 250-245-9375;
Fax: 250-245-8164
twitter.com/dougroutley17
Constituency Office
#1, 16 High St.
PO Box 269
Ladysmith, BC V9G 1A2

Roly Russel
Constituency: Boundary-Similkameen *No. of Constituents:*
7,529, New Democratic Party
Tel: 250-387-3655; *Fax:* 250-387-4860
roly.russell.MLA@leg.bc.ca
Other Communications: Constituency Phone: 250-498-5122
Constituency Office
PO Box 1592
Grand Forks, BC V0H 1H0

John Rustad
Constituency: Nechako Lakes *No. of Constituents:* 4,120,
Liberal
Tel: 250-356-6171
Toll-free: 877-964-5650; *Fax:* 250-387-9066
john.rustad.mla@leg.bc.ca
Other Communications: Constituency Phone: 250-567-6820;
Fax: 250-567-6822
twitter.com/johnrustad4bc, www.facebook.com/johnrustadbc
Constituency Office
183 - 1st St.
PO Box 421
Vanderhoof, BC V0J 3A0

Harwinder Sandhu
Constituency: Vernon-Monashee *No. of Constituents:* 10,222,
New Democratic Party
Tel: 250-387-3655
Toll-free: 866-870-4189; *Fax:* 250-387-4860
harwinder.sandhu.MLA@leg.bc.ca
Other Communications: Constituency Phone: 250-503-3600
Constituency Office
2920 - 28th Ave., #B
Vernon, BC V1T 1V9

Government Caucus Deputy Chair, Niki Sharma
Constituency: Vancouver-Hastings *No. of Constituents:*
7,253, New Democratic Party
Tel: 250-387-3655; *Fax:* 250-387-4860
niki.sharma.MLA@leg.bc.ca
Other Communications: Constituency Phone: 604-775-2277
Constituency Office
2365 East Hastings St.
Vancouver, BC V5L 1V6

Tom Shypitka
Constituency: Kootenay East *No. of Constituents:* 8,270,
Liberal
Tel: 250-356-6171; *Fax:* 250-387-9066
tom.shypitka.mla@leg.bc.ca
tomshypitka.ca
Other Communications: Constituency Phone: 250-417-6022
twitter.com/tomshypitka, www.facebook.com/tomshypitka,
www.linkedin.com/in/tom-shypitka-209841155
Constituency Office
#302, 535 Victoria Ave. North
Cranbrook, BC V1C 6S3

**Minister, Social Development & Poverty Reduction, Hon.
Nicholas Simons**
Constituency: Powell River-Sunshine Coast *No. of
Constituents:* 7,719, New Democratic Party
Tel: 250-356-7750
Toll-free: 866-373-0792; *Fax:* 250-356-7292
nicholas.simons.mla@leg.bc.ca
nicholassimonsmla.ca
Other Communications: Constituency Phone: 604-485-1249;
Fax: 604-485-2533
twitter.com/NicholasSimons,
www.facebook.com/NicholasSimonsSunshineCoast
Constituency Office
#109, 4675 Marine Ave.
Powell River, BC V8A 2L2

Jinny Sims
Constituency: Surrey-Panorama *No. of Constituents:* 7,967,
New Democratic Party
Tel: 250-387-9699; *Fax:* 250-952-7628
jinny.sims.mla@leg.bc.ca
jinnysimsmla.ca
Other Communications: Constituency Phone: 778-593-2262
twitter.com/jinnysims, www.facebook.com/jinnysims
Constituency Office
#204, 14360 - 64th Ave.
Surrey, BC V3W 1Z1

Aman Singh
Constituency: Richmond-Queensborough *No. of Constituents:*
6,275, New Democratic Party
Tel: 250-387-3655; *Fax:* 250-387-4860
aman.singh.MLA@leg.bc.ca
Other Communications: Constituency Phone: 604-664-0700

Constituency Office
12560 Bridgeport Rd.
Richmond, BC V6V 2N5

Rachna Singh
Constituency: Surrey-Green Timbers *No. of Constituents:*
5,589, New Democratic Party
Tel: 250-387-3655; *Fax:* 250-387-4680
rachna.singh.mla@leg.bc.ca
rachnasingh.ca
Other Communications: Constituency Phone: 604-501-8325;
Fax: 604-590-5873
twitter.com/rachnasinghndp,
www.facebook.com/RachnaSinghSGT
Constituency Office
#100, 9030 King George Blvd.
Surery, BC V3V 7Y3

Mike Starchuk
Constituency: Surrey-Cloverdale *No. of Constituents:* 7,915,
New Democratic Party
Tel: 250-387-3655; *Fax:* 250-387-4860
mike.starchuk.MLA@leg.bc.ca
Other Communications: Constituency Phone: 778-571-5503

Ben Stewart
Constituency: Kelowna West *No. of Constituents:* 9,033
Tel: 250-356-6171; *Fax:* 250-387-9066
Ben.Stewart.MLA@leg.bc.ca
Other Communications: Constituency Phone: 250-768-8426;
Fax: 250-768-8436
twitter.com/benstewartbc, www.facebook.com/benstewartBC
Constituency Office
#3, 2429 Dobbin Rd.
West Kelowna, BC V4T 2L4

Todd Stone
Constituency: Kamloops-South Thompson *No. of
Constituents:* 9,574, Liberal
Tel: 250-356-6171; *Fax:* 250-387-9066
todd.stone.mla@leg.bc.ca
Other Communications: Constituency Phone: 250-374-2880;
Fax: 250-377-3448
twitter.com/toddstonebc, www.facebook.com/ToddGStone
Constituency Office
446 Victoria St.
Kamloops, BC V2C 2A7

Jordan Sturdy
Constituency: West Vancouver-Sea to Sky *No. of
Constituents:* 7,019, Green Party of Canada
Tel: 250-356-6171; *Fax:* 250-387-9066
jordan.sturdy.MLA@leg.bc.ca
Other Communications: Constituency Phone: 604-922-1153;
Fax: 604-922-1167
Constituency Office
6650 Royal Ave.
West Vancouver, BC V7W 2B8

Jackie Tegart
Constituency: Fraser-Nicola *No. of Constituents:* 4,703,
Liberal
Tel: 250-356-6171
Toll-free: 877-378-4802; *Fax:* 250-387-9066
jackie.tegart.mla@leg.bc.ca
Other Communications: Constituency Phone: 250-453-9726;
Fax: 250-453-9765
twitter.com/tegart_jackie, www.facebook.com/tegartjackie
Constituency Office
405 Railway Ave.
PO Box 279
Ashcroft, BC V0K 1A0

Adam Walker
Constituency: Parksville-Qualicum *No. of Constituents:* 7,308,
New Democratic Party
Tel: 250-387-3655; *Fax:* 250-387-4860
adam.walker.MLA@leg.bc.ca
Other Communications: Constituency Phone: 250-248-2625
Constituency Office
184 - 2nd Ave. West, #A
Qualicum Beach, BC V9K 2T5

Teresa Wat
Constituency: Richmond North Centre *No. of Constituents:*
4,523, Liberal
Tel: 250-356-6171; *Fax:* 250-387-9066
teresa.wat.mla@leg.bc.ca
Other Communications: Constituency Phone: 604-775-0754;
Fax: 604-775-0898
twitter.com/Teresa_Wat,
www.facebook.com/TeresaWatForRichmond
Constituency Office
#300, 8120 Granville Ave.
Richmond, BC V6Y 1P3

Minister, Education, Hon. Jennifer Whiteside
Constituency: New Westminster *No. of Constituents:* 9,176,
New Democratic Party
Tel: 250-356-8247; *Fax:* 250-356-0948
jennifer.whiteside.MLA@leg.bc.ca
Other Communications: Constituency Phone: 604-775-2101
Constituency Office

335 - 6th St.
New Westminster, BC V3L 3A9

**Leader of the Opposition; Leader, Liberal Party of BC, Andrew
Wilkinson, Q.C.**
Constituency: Vancouver-Quilchena *No. of Constituents:*
6,549, Liberal
Tel: 250-356-6171; *Fax:* 250-387-9066
andrew.wilkinson.mla@leg.bc.ca
Other Communications: Constituency Phone: 604-664-0748;
Fax: 604-664-0750
twitter.com/Wilkinson4BC,
www.facebook.com/AndrewWilkinsonForBC,
www.linkedin.com/in/andrew-wilkinson-41bb848
Constituency Office
5640 Dunbar St.
Vancouver, BC V6N 1W7

Henry Yao
Constituency: Richmond South Centre *No. of Constituents:*
4,187, New Democratic Party
Tel: 250-387-3655; *Fax:* 250-387-4860
henry.yao.MLA@leg.bc.ca
Other Communications: Constituency Phone: 604-775-0891
Constituency Office
#130, 8040 Garden City Rd.
Richmond, BC V6Y 2N9

British Columbia Government Departments & Agencies

British Columbia Ministry of Advanced Education & Skills Training

PO Box 9080 Stn. Prov Govt, Victoria, BC V8W 9E2
Tel: 250-356-5170
AEST.GeneralInquiries@gov.bc.ca
www.gov.bc.ca/aeit

The Ministry of Advanced Education & Skills Training is
responsible for post-secondary education & skills training
systems in British Columbia as well as labour market information
& programs. The ministry was formerly known as Advanced
Education, but was renamed in 2017 by Premier John Horgan.

Minister, Hon. Anne Kang
Tel: 250-356-0179; *Fax:* 250-952-0260
AEST.Minister@gov.bc.ca

Deputy Minister, Shannon Baskerville
Tel: 250-356-5173; *Fax:* 250-356-5468
AEST.DeputyMinister@gov.bc.ca
PO Box 9884 Prov Govt Sta.
Victoria, BC V8W 9T6

Associated Agencies, Boards & Commissions:
**• British Columbia Council on Admissions & Transfer
(BCCAT)**
#709, 555 Seymour St.
Vancouver, BC V6B 3H6
Tel: 604-412-7700; *Fax:* 604-683-0576
info@bccat.ca
www.bccat.ca

• Degree Quality Assessment Board (DQAB)
Degree Quality Assessment Board Secretariat
835 Humboldt St., 3rd Fl.
PO Box 9177 Prov Govt
Victoria, BC V8W 9H8
Tel: 250-356-9734
DQABsecretariat@gov.bc.ca

The Degree Quality Assessment Board reviews applications
from British Columbia public post-secondary institutions, &
private & out-of-province public post-secondary institutions.
Applications concern new degree programs & exempt status, &
the use of the word university. Recommendations are then made
to the Minister of Advanced Education & Labour Market
Development.

• Private Career Training Institutions Agency (PCTIA)
#203, 1155 West Pender St.
Vancouver, BC V6E 2P4
Tel: 604-569-0033; *Fax:* 778-945-0606
Toll-free: 800-661-7441
info@pctia.bc.ca
www.pctia.bc.ca
Other Communication: Student Support Inquiries:
PTI.StudentSupport@gov.bc.ca

The Private Career Training Institutions Agency is the regulatory
agency for private training institutions in British Columbia. The
Agency works in accordance with the Private Career Training
Institutions Act, Regulations & Bylaws.

Financial & Management Services Division
PO Box 9134 Stn. Prov Govt, Victoria, BC V8W 9B5
Tel: 250-356-2496; *Fax:* 250-356-5468

Assistant Deputy Minister & EFO, Kevin Brewster
Tel: 250-356-2496; *Fax:* 250-356-5468
Chief Financial Officer, Donna Porter
Tel: 250-356-6819; *Fax:* 250-356-8851
Donna.Porter@gov.bc.ca
Chief Information Officer & Executive Director, Technology &
Business Transformation Branch, Trevor Hurst
Tel: 250-415-5899; *Fax:* 250-952-0739
Trevor.Hurst@gov.bc.ca
Executive Director, Sector Business Innovation, Jeanne M.
Sedun
Tel: 250-952-7412
Jeanne.Sedun@gov.bc.ca
Executive Director, Post-Secondary Finance, James Postans
Tel: 250-356-7896
AVED.PostSecondaryFinanceBranch@gov.bc.ca
Director, Capital Asset Management, Deborah Gogela
Tel: 250-387-0890
Deborah.Gogela@gov.bc.ca
Director, Capital Asset Management, Alison Prince
Tel: 250-356-9097
Alison.Prince@gov.bc.ca
Director, Sector Business Innovation, Nancy Singh
Tel: 250-356-8042
Nancy.Singh@gov.bc.ca
Director, Business Solutions, Marlowe Stone
Tel: 250-514-4192
Marlowe.Stone@gov.bc.ca

Governance, Legislation & Strategic Policy
PO Box 9157 Stn. Prov Govt, Victoria, BC V8W 9H2
Tel: 250-356-0826; *Fax:* 250-356-5468
Assistant Deputy Minister, Tony Loughran
Tel: 250-356-0826; *Fax:* 250-356-5468
Acting Assistant Deputy Minister, Governance & Quality
Assurance Branch, Tony Loughran
Tel: 250-356-5406
Executive Director & Registrar, Private Training Institutions,
Monica Lust
Tel: 604-569-0031
Executive Director, Planning, International & Intergovernmental,
Kelly McConnan
Tel: 250-387-3435
Kelly.McConnan@gov.bc.ca
Acting Executive Director, Post-Secondary Audit &
Accountability Branch, Cathy Stock
Tel: 250-387-1105; *Fax:* 250-387-1377
Cathy.Stock@gov.bc.ca
Senior Economist, Research & Analysis, Leila Hazemi
Tel: 250-356-9563
Leila.Hazemi@gov.bc.ca
Director, International Education, Laurie Brucker
Tel: 250-356-5432
Laurie.Brucker@gov.bc.ca
Director, Strategic Planning & Business Solutions, Sharlane
Callow
Tel: 250-356-7210
Sharlane.Callow@gov.bc.ca
Director, Statkeholder Engagement & Policy, Serena Chandi
Tel: 604-569-0036
Serena.Chandi@gov.bc.ca
Director, Strategic Policy & Initiatives, Kate Cotie
Tel: 250-387-6197
Kate.Cotie@gov.bc.ca
Director, Legislation & Board Appointment, Rachel Franklin
Tel: 250-507-7128
Director, Intergovernmental Relations, Randall Gerlach
Tel: 250-356-2217
Randall.Gerlach@gov.bc.ca
Director, Quality Assurance, Dorothy Rogers
Tel: 250-387-6298
Director, Regulation, Marianne Schwan
Tel: 250-569-0019
Marianne.Schwan@gov.bc.ca

Institutions & Programs Division
PO Box 9877 Stn. Prov Govt, Victoria, BC V8W 9T6
Tel: 250-952-0697; *Fax:* 250-356-5468
Assistant Deputy Minister, Jeff Vasey
Tel: 250-952-0697; *Fax:* 250-356-5468
AVED.ADMInstitutionsandPrgms@gov.bc.ca
Executive Director, Teaching Universities, Institutes & Aboriginal
Programs Branch, Deborah Hull
Tel: 250-387-1446; *Fax:* 250-952-6110
Deborah.Hull@gov.bc.ca
Executive Director, Colleges & Skills Development Branch,
Acting Executive Director, Research Universities & Health
Programs Branch, Nicola Lemmer
Tel: 250-387-1950; *Fax:* 250-952-6110
Nicola.Lemmer@gov.bc.ca
Executive Director, Student Services Branch, Daryn Martinuk
Tel: 250-356-5277

Director, Research Universities, Susan Burns
Tel: 250-356-6114; *Fax:* 250-387-2360
Director, Policy & Communications, Teresa Butler
Tel: 250-387-6191
Director, Adult Education, Bryan Dreilich
Tel: 250-387-3395
Bryan.Dreilich@gov.bc.ca
Acting Director, Aboriginal Programs, Carrie Dusterhoft
Tel: 250-952-0705
AVED.TeachUniversInstandAboriginalPrgms@gov.bc.ca
Director, Teaching Universities, Institutes, Nell Hodges
Tel: 250-387-6182; *Fax:* 250-952-6110
Nell.Hodges@gov.bc.ca
Director, Tuition Fee Waiver, Tony Nelson
Tel: 250-387-6616
Director, Colleges, Melanie Nielsen
Tel: 250-387-6156; *Fax:* 250-952-6110
Melanie.Nielsen@gov.bc.ca
Director, Health Programs, Kevin Perrault
Tel: 250-356-8257
Director, Service Delivery, Alys Pivetta
Director, Skills Development, Vincent Portal
Tel: 250-516-8439; *Fax:* 250-952-6110
Vincent.Portal@gov.bc.ca
Director, Finance & Program Planning, Rosilyn Soo
Tel: 250-356-1409
Director, Planning Board, Darryl Soper
Tel: 250-387-6138

British Columbia Ministry of Agriculture, Food & Fisheries

PO Box 9043 Stn. Prov Govt, Victoria, BC V8W 9E2
Toll-Free: 888-221-7141
agriservicebc@gov.bc.ca
www.gov.bc.ca/agri
Other Communication: Agriculture Communications Office,
Phone: 250-356-1674
The mission of the Ministry is to stabilize & expand agrifoods
production & incomes, to safeguard animal, plant, & human
health, & to encourage environmental stewardship.
Responsibilities include agriculture, acquacultures & food
industry development, fish processing, meat processing policy,
food safety & quality, & crop insurance. Following the 2020
general election, it was renamed from the Ministry of Agriculture
to the Ministry of Agriculture Agriculture, Food & Fisheries.

Minister, Hon. Lana Popham
Tel: 250-387-1023; *Fax:* 250-387-1522
AGR.Minister@gov.bc.ca

Deputy Minister, Tom Ethier
Tel: 778-974-3844; *Fax:* 250-356-7279
PO Box 9120 Prov Govt Sta.
Victoria, BC V8W 9B4

Associated Agencies, Boards & Commissions:

• Agricultural Land Commission (ALC)
#133, 4940 Canada Way
Burnaby, BC V5G 4K6
Tel: 604-660-7000; *Fax:* 604-660-7033
ALCBurnaby@Victoria1.gov.bc.ca
www.alc.gov.bc.ca
The independent Crown agency strives to preserve agricultural
land in British Columbia. The Provincial Agricultural Land
Commission also works to encourage & enable farm businesses
throughout the province. The Commission's chief responsibility is
the administration of the Agricultural Land Commission Act.

• AgriStability
200, 1690 Powick Rd.
Kelowna, BC V1X 7G5
Tel: 877-343-2767; *Fax:* 877-605-8467
agristability@gov.bc.ca
www.agf.gov.bc.ca/agristability
Responsibility for AgriStability was transferred to the British
Columbia Ministry of Agriculture from Agriculture & Agri-Food
Canada in January 2010. AgriStability offices are as follows:
1767 Angus Campbell Rd., Abbotsford, BC V3G 2M3; #201, 583
Fairview Rd., Oliver, BC V0H 1T0; #200, 1500 Hardy St.,
Kelowna, BC V1Y 8H2; 10043 - 100th St., Fort St. John, BC V1J
3Y5.

**• British Columbia Broiler Hatching Egg Commission
(BCBHEC)**
#180, 32160 South Fraser Way
Abbotsford, BC V2T 1W5
Tel: 604-850-1854; *Fax:* 604-850-1683
info@bcbhec.com
www.bcbhec.com
The British Columbia Broiler Hatching Egg Commission was
formed in 1988 under the British Columbia Natural Products
Marketing Act, & seeks to promote a better understanding of the
broiler hatching egg industry.

• British Columbia Chicken Marketing Board (BCCMB)
#101, 32450 Simon Ave.
Abbotsford, BC V2T 4J2
Tel: 604-859-2868; *Fax:* 604-859-2811
info@bcchicken.ca
www.bcchicken.ca
The purpose of the BC Chicken Marketing Board is to monitor &
regulate the production of chicken in British Columbia. The
Board works closely with hatcheries, growers, truckers &
processors, & carries out field inspections, to accomplish this.

**• British Columbia Cranberry Marketing Commission
(BCCMC)**
36376 Stephen Leacock Dr.
Abbotsford, BC V3G 0C2
Tel: 604-557-8717
info@bccranberries.com
www.bccranberries.com
Since 1968 the BCCMC has administered the British Columbia
Cranberry Marketing Scheme, established under the Natural
Products Marketing (BC) Act. The Commission reports to the
British Columbia Farm Industry Review Board.

• British Columbia Egg Marketing Board (BCEMB)
#250, 32160 South Fraser Way
Abbotsford, BC V2T 1W5
Tel: 604-556-3348; *Fax:* 604-556-3410
bcemb@bcegg.com
www.bcegg.com
The BCEMB was established in 1967 in order to better regulate
the price of eggs.

• British Columbia Farm Industry Review Board (BCFIRB)
780 Blanshard St.
PO Box 9129 Prov Govt
Victoria, BC V8W 9B5
Tel: 250-356-8945; *Fax:* 250-356-5131
firb@gov.bc.ca
www.firb.gov.bc.ca
The British Columbia Farm Industry Review Board is a statutory
appeal body. It is engaged in the general supervision of
marketing boards & commodity boards which operate in the
agricultural & aquaculture sectors.

• British Columbia Hog Marketing Commission (BCHMC)
PO Box 8000-280
Abbotsford, BC V2S 6H1
Tel: 604-287-4647; *Fax:* 604-820-6647
info@bcpork.ca
www.bcpork.ca
The Commission seeks to promote BC-grown pork through the
use of its logo on all BC pork products.

• British Columbia Milk Marketing Board (BCMMB)
#200, 32160 South Fraser Way
Abbotsford, BC V2T 1W5
Tel: 604-556-3444; *Fax:* 604-556-7717
info@milk-bc.com
bcmilkmarketing.worldsecuresystems.com
The Board is responsible for promoting, controlling & regulating
the production, transportation, packing, storing & marketing of all
BC milk products.

• British Columbia Turkey Marketing Board (BCTMB)
#106, 19329 Enterprise Way
Surrey, BC V3S 6J8
Tel: 604-534-5644; *Fax:* 604-534-3651
info@bcturkey.com
www.bcturkey.com
Established in 1966, the Board oversees the licensing of turkey
farmers and processors; prices for live turkeys; maintaining of a
quota system; & promoting turkey products, under the authority
of the Natural Products Marketing (BC) Act.

**• British Columbia Vegetable Marketing Commission
(BCVMC)**
#207, 15252 - 32nd Ave.
Surrey, BC V3S 0R7
Tel: 604-542-9734; *Fax:* 604-542-9735
info@bcveg.com
bcveg.com
The Commission is responsible for promoting controlled
marketing for BC vegetable producers, under the authority of the
Natural Products Marketing (BC) Act.

Agriculture Science & Policy
PO Box 9120 Stn. Prov Govt, Victoria, BC V8W 9B4
Tel: 250-356-1816; *Fax:* 250-356-7279
Assistant Deputy Minister, James Mack
Tel: 778-698-3290
James.Mack@gov.bc.ca
Executive Director, Corporate Governance, Policy & Legislation
Branch, Lorie Hrycuik
Tel: 778-974-3766
Lorie.Hrycuik@gov.bc.ca

Executive Director, Food Safety & Inspection Branch, Gavin Last
Tel: 778-974-3819
Gavin.Last@gov.bc.ca
Compliance & Enforcement Officer, Seafood Safety & Quality, Stella Lukman
Tel: 778-866-5287
Stella.Lukman@gov.bc.ca
Operations Manager, Seafood Safety & Quality, Wayne A. Sparanese
Tel: 250-897-7526
Wayne.Sparanese@gov.bc.ca
Finance & Admin Coordinator, Corporate Governance, Policy & Legislation Branch, Julene Warwick
Tel: 250-356-2944
Julene.Warwick@gov.bc.ca

Business Development Division
PO Box 9120 Stn. Prov Govt, Victoria, BC V8W 9B4
Tel: 250-356-1122; *Fax:* 250-356-7279
Assistant Deputy Minister, Arif Lalani
Tel: 778-698-2618
Executive Director, Sector Development Branch, Mark Raymond
Tel: 604-556-3107
Mark.Raymond@gov.bc.ca
780 Blanshard St.
PO Box 9308 Prov Govt Sta.
Victoria, BC V8W 9N1
Executive Director, Business Risk Management Branch, Byron Jonson
Tel: 250-861-7200; *Fax:* 250-861-7490
Byron.Jonson@gov.bc.ca

British Columbia Ministry of Attorney General & Minister responsible for Housing

PO Box 9044 Stn. Prov Govt, Victoria, BC V8W 9E2
www.gov.bc.ca/justice
The Ministry of Attorney General works to ensure safety for the people of British Columbia by seeing that public affairs are administered according to the law & by leading law reform. In 2020, Housing was added as a responsibility of the Attorney General.
The following are examples of general responsibilities of the ministry: legal services to government; consumer services; crime prevention programs; emergency social services; provincial emergency management; criminal justice; legal aid; court administration; police & correctional services; victim assistance; & the protection order registry.

Attorney General; Minister responsible, Housing, Hon. David Eby
Tel: 250-387-1866; *Fax:* 250-387-6411
ag.minister@gov.bc.ca

Deputy Attorney General, Richard Fyfe, Q.C.
Tel: 250-356-0149; *Fax:* 250-387-6224
PO Box 9290 Prov Govt Sta.
Victoria, BC V8W 9J7

Associated Agencies, Boards & Commissions:
• **British Columbia Ferry Commission**
PO Box 9279 Prov Govt
Victoria, BC V8W 9J7
Tel: 250-952-0112
info@bcferrycommission.com
www.bcferrycommission.com
The British Columbia Ferry Commission was established under the Coastal Ferry Act, 2003. The fares & service levels of the province's ferry operator, British Columbia Ferry Services Inc., are regulated by the Commission. The Commission is a quasi-judicial regulatory agency independent of both the provincial government and of BC Ferries.

• **British Columbia Human Rights Tribunal**
#1170, 605 Robson St.
Vancouver, BC V6B 5J3
Tel: 604-775-2000; *Fax:* 604-775-2020
Toll-free: 888-440-8844
TTY: 604-775-2021
BCHumanRightsTribunal@gov.bc.ca
www.bchrt.bc.ca
The independent, quasi-judicial body was established by the British Columbia Human Rights Code. The British Columbia Human Rights Tribunal is engaged in accepting, screening, mediating, & adjudicating human rights complaints.

• **British Columbia Law Institute (BCLI)**
University of British Columbia
1822 East Mall
Vancouver, BC V6T 1Z1
Tel: 604-822-0142; *Fax:* 604-822-0144
bcli@bcli.org
www.bcli.org

The Institute was created in 1997 under the Provincial Society Act, & is tasked with promoting clarity in modern law; improvement in the administration of justice; & scholarly legal research. Formerly known as the British Columbia Law Reform Commission.

• **British Columbia Office of the Police Complaint Commissioner**
#501, 947 Fort St.
PO Box 9895 Prov Govt
Victoria, BC V8W 9T8
Tel: 250-356-7458; *Fax:* 250-356-6503
Toll-free: 877-999-8707
info@opcc.bc.ca
www.opcc.bc.ca
Provides impartial civilian oversight of complaints by the public involving municipal police.

• **Liquor Distribution Branch**
3383 Gilmore Way
Burnaby, BC V5G 4S1
Tel: 604-252-7400
inquiries@bcliquorstores.com
www.bcliquorstores.com
Other Communication: B.C. Cannabis Stores: bccannabisstores.com; CustomerCareCentre@bcldb.com
Sole buyer and re-seller of liquor in the province; responsible for operating B.C. Liquor Stores & B.C. Cannabis Stores across the province.

• **British Columbia Review Board**
#1270, 605 Robson St.
Vancouver, BC V6B 5J3
Tel: 604-660-8789; *Fax:* 604-660-8809
Toll-free: 877-305-2277
www.bcrb.bc.ca
The British Columbia Review Board was created in accordance with the Criminal Code of Canada. The Board is an independent tribunal, with responsibility for holding hearings to establish & review dispositions. The dispositions involve persons who have been charged with criminal offenses & received verdicts of not criminally responsible on account of mental disorder, or unfit to stand trial on account of mental disorder.

• **Elections British Columbia**
See Entry Name Index for detailed listing.
#100, 1112 Fort St.
PO Box 9275 Stn Prov Govt
Victoria, BC v8W 9J6
Tel: 250-387-5305; *Fax:* 250-387-3578
Toll-free: 800-661-8683
TTY: 888-456-5448
electionsbc@elections.bc.ca
elections.bc.ca

• **Environmental Appeal Board (EAB)**
747 Fort St., 4th Fl.
PO Box 9425 Prov Govt
Victoria, BC V8W 3E9
Tel: 250-387-3464; *Fax:* 250-356-9923
eabinfo@gov.bc.ca
www.eab.gov.bc.ca
Hears appeals from decisions made by government officials related to environmental issues, under the following acts: Environmental Management Act, Greenhouse Gas Industrial Reporting & Control Act, Greenhouse Gas Reduction (Renewable and Low Carbon Fuels) Act, Integrated Pest Management Act, Water Stewardship Act, Water Users' Communities Act, & Wildlife Act.

• **Forest Appeals Commission (FAC)**
747 Fort St., 4th Fl.
PO Box 9425 Prov Govt
Victoria, BC V8W 9V1
Tel: 250-387-3464; *Fax:* 250-356-9923
facinfo@gov.bc.ca
www.fac.gov.bc.ca
The independent agency hears appeals under the following statutes: Forest Practices Code of British Columbia Act; Forest & Range Practices Act; Private Managed Forest Land Act; Wildfire Act; Forest Act; Range Act.

• **Judicial Council of British Columbia**
Office of the Chief Judge
#337, 800 Hornby St.
Vancouver, BC V6Z 2C5
Tel: 604-660-2864; *Fax:* 604-660-1108
info@provincialcourt.bc.ca
www.provincialcourt.bc.ca/judicial-council
As designated by the Provincial Court Act, the Judicial Council of British Columbia consists of nine members. The process of the Judicial Council is governed by a Procedure Bylaw. The overall goal of the Council is the improvement of the quality of judicial service in the province.

• **Justice Education Society (JES)**
#260, 800 Hornby St.
Vancouver, BC V6Z 2C3
Tel: 604-660-9870; *Fax:* 604-775-3476
info@justiceeducation.ca
www.justiceeducation.ca
Formerly the Law Courts Education Society, renamed in 2009, the Justice Education Society seeks to promote the understanding of, and access to, Canada's justice system for all groups of people, but especially youth, Aboriginals, ethnic & immigrant communities, deaf people, those with learning disabilities, & other groups as required.

• **Legal Services Society (LSS)**
#400, 510 Burrard St.
Vancouver, BC V6C 3A8
Tel: 604-601-6000
www.lss.bc.ca
Other Communication: Call Centre: 866-577-2525; 604-408-2172 (Greater Vancouver)
The Legal Services Society was established by the Legal Services Society Act. The non-profit Society provides legal information, advice, & representation services to assist British Columbians in the resolution of their legal issues. Regional centres & local agents' offices are located throughout the province.

• **Office of the Representative for Children & Youth (RCY)**
#400, 1019 Wharf St.
Victoria, BC V8W 2Y9
Tel: 250-356-6710; *Fax:* 250-356-0837
Toll-free: 800-476-3933
rcy@rcybc.ca
www.rcybc.ca
Other Communication: Northern Office - Prince George: 250-561-4626; Lower Mainland Office - Burnaby: 604-775-3213
Acting in accordance with British Columbia's Representative for Children and Youth Act, the Representative for Children & Youth is responsible for advocacy, monitoring, & investigation.

• **Public Guardian & Trustee of British Columbia (PGT)**
#700, 808 West Hastings St.
Vancouver, BC V6C 3L3
Tel: 604-660-4444; *Fax:* 604-660-0374
Toll-free: 800-663-7867
clientservice@trustee.bc.ca
www.trustee.bc.ca
Other Communication: Communications & Media Relations: 604-660-4474; Child & Youth Svs.: 604-775-3480; Estate & Personal Trust Svs.: 604-660-4444; Email: estates@trustee.bc.ca
The Public Guardian & Trustee of British Columbia was established under the Public Guardian & Trustee Act. The corporation offers the following programs: Child & Youth Services; Services to Adults; & Estate & Personal Trust Services.

Liquor & Cannabis Regulation Branch (LCRB)
PO Box 9292 Stn. Prov Govt, Victoria, BC V8W 9J8
Tel: 250-952-5787; *Fax:* 250-952-7066
Toll-Free: 866-209-2111
lclb.lclb@gov.bc.ca
Other Communication: URL: www2.gov.bc.ca/gov/content/employment-business/business/liquor-regulation-licensing
Secondary Address: #400, 645 Tyee Rd.
Victoria, BC V9A 6X5
Formerly known as the Liquor Control & Licensing Branch, the LCRB regulates the province's liquor & recreational cannabis industries, including establishments, manufacturers, & special events.
Cannabis Retail Licence: cannabisregs@gov.bc.ca
Liquor Policy Questions: LCLBLiquorPolicy@gov.bc.ca
Liquor Licence Renewal Helpdesk: LCLBOneStopHelp@gov.bc.ca
Liquor Special Event Permit Helpdesk: lclb.sep@gov.bc.ca.

Corporate Management Services Branch
Assistant Deputy Minister, Shauna Brouwer
Tel: 250-387-5258
Chief Financial Officer & Executive Director, Finance & Administration Division, David Hoadley
Tel: 250-356-5393; *Fax:* 250-356-3739
Executive Director, Facilities Services Division, Betty Chen-Mack
Tel: 250-356-7159; *Fax:* 250-356-9528
Betty.ChenMack@gov.bc.ca
Executive Director, Organizational Development Team Office, Cheryl Hall
Tel: 250-360-7740; *Fax:* 250-356-6323
Cheryl.Hall@gov.bc.ca

Court Services Branch
PO Box 9249 Stn. Prov Govt, Victoria, BC V8W 9J2
Tel: 250-356-1550; *Fax:* 250-356-8152
Assistant Deputy Minister, Court Services, Vacant

Chief Sheriff & Executive Director, Sheriff Services Corporate Programs, Paul Corrado
Tel: 250-660-8089
Executive Director, Service Reform, Bernard Achampong
Tel: 250-387-7847; *Fax:* 250-356-8152
Bernard.Achampong@gov.bc.ca
Executive Director, Corporate Support, Jenny Manton
Tel: 250-356-1525; *Fax:* 250-387-4743
Jenny.Manton@gov.bc.ca
Director, Court Innovation, Kevin Conn
Tel: 604-660-0226
Kevin.Conn@gov.bc.ca

Criminal Justice Branch

PO Box 9276 Stn. Prov Govt, Victoria, BC V8W 9J7
Tel: 250-387-3840; *Fax:* 250-387-0090
www.ag.gov.bc.ca/prosecution-service
Assistant Deputy Attorney General, Peter Juk, Q.C.
Tel: 250-387-5174

Information Systems Branch

PO Box 9262 Stn. Prov Govt, Victoria, BC V8W 9J4
Tel: 250-356-8787; *Fax:* 250-356-7699
Acting ADM & Chief Information Officer, Robert O'Neill
Tel: 778-698-5783
Team Lead, IM/IT Governance & Strategy, Enterprise Architecture, Patricia Campbell
Tel: 250-953-3186
Patricia.Campbell@gov.bc.ca

Justice Services Branch

agjuserv@gov.bc.ca
Assistant Deputy Minister, Kurt Sandstrom
Tel: 778-974-3689; *Fax:* 250-356-2721
Kurt.Sandstrom@gov.bc.ca
Executive Director, Maintenance Enforcement & Locate Services, Christopher Beresford
Tel: 604-660-2528; *Fax:* 604-660-1346
Chris.Beresford@gov.bc.ca
Executive Director, Civil Policy & Legislation Office, Nancy Carter
Tel: 250-356-6182; *Fax:* 250-387-4525
Nancy.Carter@gov.bc.ca
Executive Director, Criminal Justice & Legal Access Policy Division, James Deitch
Tel: 250-387-2109
James.Deitch@gov.bc.ca
Executive Director, Family Justice Services Division, Stephanie Melvin
Tel: 250-387-5903; *Fax:* 250-356-1279
www.ag.gov.bc.ca/family-justice
Executive Director, Dispute Resolution Office, David Merner
Tel: 250-514-5507; *Fax:* 250-387-1189
David.Merner@gov.bc.ca
Executive Director, Policy & Legislation Division, Julie Williams
Julie.Williams@gov.bc.ca

Legal Services Branch

PO Box 9280 Stn. Prov Govt, Victoria, BC V8W 9J7
Tel: 250-356-9260; *Fax:* 250-356-5111
Assistant Deputy Attorney General, James Harvey; *Fax:* 250-356-5111
James.Harvey@gov.bc.ca
Acting Chief Legislative Counsel, Kevin Kohan
Kevin.Kohan@gov.bc.ca
Senior Legislative Counsel & Registrar of Regulations, Rodney Fehr
Rodney.Fehr@gov.bc.ca
Executive Director, Business Operations & Strategic Initiatives, Aaron Plater
Tel: 778-698-3550
Aaron.Plater@gov.bc.ca

623 Fort St., PO Box 9036 Stn. Prov Govt, Victoria, BC V8W 9A2
Tel: 250-419-6100; *Fax:* 250-387-1230
www.bcauditor.com
twitter.com/BCAuditorGen
www.facebook.com/OAGBC
www.linkedin.com/company/1318180
www.youtube.com/user/BCAuditorGeneral
The chief responsibility of the Office of the Auditor General is auditing most of the British Columbia provincial government, with its ministries, Crown corporations, & other organizations.

Auditor General, Michael Pickup, FCPA, FCA
Tel: 250-419-6100
bcauditor@bcauditor.com

Deputy Auditor General, Russ Jones, FCPA, FCA
Tel: 250-419-6103

Assistant Auditor General, IT Audit & Corporate Services, Cornell Dover, CPA, CA, CISA
Tel: 250-419-6139

Executive Director, Professional Practices Group, Bridget Parrish, CPA, CA
Tel: 250-419-6104

Financial Audit

Assistant Auditor General, Stuart Newton, CA, CIA
Tel: 250-419-6230
snewton@bcauditor.com
Executive Director, Peter Bourne, CPA, CA, CIA
Tel: 250-419-6141
pbourne@bcauditor.com
Executive Director, Lisa Moore, CPA, CA
Tel: 250-419-6188
lmoore@bcauditor.com

Performance Audit

Assistant Auditor General, Sheila Dodds, CPA, CA, CIA
Tel: 250-419-6149
sdodds@bcauditor.com
Assistant Auditor General, Malcolm Gaston, CPA, CMA, CPFA
Tel: 250-419-6105
mgaston@bcauditor.com
Assistant Auditor General, Morris Sydor, MBA, CPA, CA
Tel: 250-419-6106
msydor@bcauditor.com
Executive Director, Compliance, Controls & Research Group, Ed Ryan
Tel: 250-419-6225
eryan@bcauditor.com

#201, 10470 - 152nd St., Surrey, BC V3R 0Y3
Tel: 604-930-7100
info@aglg.ca
www.aglg.ca
twitter.com/BC_AGLG
The Office was created through the Auditor General for Local Government Act in 2012, & is mandated to assist local governments in improving their operations.

Chair, Audit Council, Anthony Ariganello

Auditor General for Local Government, Vacant

Deputy Auditor General for Local Government, Terri Van Sleuwen, CPA, CGA
Tel: 604-930-7108
Terri.VanSleuwen@aglg.ca

655 West 12th Ave., Vancouver, BC V5Z 4R4
Tel: 604-707-2400; *Fax:* 604-707-2401
admininfo@bccdc.ca
www.bccdc.ca
Other Communication: Media/Communications, Phone: 604-707-2412
twitter.com/cdcofbc
The BCCDC is both a provincial & national leader in public health as it detects, treats, & prevents diseases in its patients. Not only does it offer direct services for people with diseases & health concerns, but it also provides analytical & policy support to health authorities at all levels of government.

Executive Medical Director, Dr. Mark Tyndall

Medical Director, Communicable Disease Prevention & Control Service, Dr. Eleni Galanis

Medical Director, Environmental Health Services, Dr. Tom Kosatsky

Medical Director, Immunization Programs & Vaccine Preventable Diseases, Dr. Monika Naus

Customer Service Centre, PO Box 9770 Stn. Prov Govt, Victoria, BC V8W 9S5
Tel: 250-387-7027
Toll-Free: 877-387-7027
TTY: 800-667-4770
mcf.info@gov.bc.ca
www.gov.bc.ca/mcf
Other Communication: Helpline for Children: 310-1234; Emergencies outside office hours: 800-663-9122
The Ministry of Children & Family Development works to support healthy child development, to maximize the potential of children & youth, & to achieve meaningful outcomes for children, youth, & families. A client-centered approach is used to deliver services. The following services are available to families throughout British Columbia: adoption services; early childhood development & child care services; child safety, family support, & children in care services; services for children & youth with special needs; mental health services for children & youth; & youth justice services.

Minister, Hon. Mitzi Dean
Tel: 250-387-1977; *Fax:* 250-356-0948
mcf.minister@gov.bc.ca

Minister of State, Child Care, Hon. Katrina Chen
Tel: 250-356-5781; *Fax:* 250-356-0201
cc.minister@gov.bc.ca

Deputy Minister, Allison Bond
Tel: 778-698-7038
mcf.deputyminister@gov.bc.ca
PO Box 9721 Prov Govt Sta.
Victoria, BC V8W 9S2

Director, Social Policy, Secure Tomorrow Policy Secretariat, Lori MacKenzie
Tel: 250-882-5067
Lori.MacKenzie@gov.bc.ca
PO Box 9721 Prov Govt Sta.
Victoria, BC V8W 9S2

Associated Agencies, Boards & Commissions:
• **British Columbia College of Social Workers (BCCSW)**
#1430, 1200 West 73 Ave.
Vancouver, BC V6P 6G5
Tel: 604-737-4916; *Fax:* 604-737-6809
Toll-free: 877-576-6740
info@bccsw.ca
www.bccollegeofsocialworkers.ca
The regulatory body for the practice of social work in British Columbia is the Board of Registration for Social Workers in BC. The Board's responsibility is establishing & supporting high standards for Registered Social Workers in the province.

Aboriginal Services

PO Box 9777 Stn. Prov Govt, Victoria, BC V8W 9S5
Tel: 250-356-9791; *Fax:* 250-387-1732
Executive Director, Divisional Operations, Shane DeMeyer
Tel: 250-387-7081

Provincial Services

PO Box 9717 Stn. Prov Govt, Victoria, BC V8W 9S1
Tel: 250-387-0978; *Fax:* 250-356-2079
Executive Director, Youth Custody Services, Lenora Angel
Tel: 250-889-4970
PO Box 9719 Prov Govt Sta.
Victoria, BC V8W 9S5
Provincial Director, Youth Forensic Psychiatric Services, Andre Picard
Tel: 778-452-2202; *Fax:* 778-452-2201
Provincial Clinical Director, Youth Forensic Psychiatric Services, Dr. Kulwant Riar
Tel: 778-452-2205; *Fax:* 778-452-2201

Finance & Corporate Services

PO Box 9721 Stn. Prov Govt, Victoria, BC V8W 9S2
Tel: 250-387-5275; *Fax:* 250-356-6534
Assistant Deputy Minister, Vacant
Chief Financial Officer, Anne Minnings
Tel: 778-698-7373; *Fax:* 250-356-2899
Anne.Minnings@gov.bc.ca
Executive Director, Procurement & Contract Management Branch, Vacant
Executive Director, Strategic Human Resources, Tim Osborne
Tel: 778-698-5066
Executive Director, Modelling, Analysis & Information Management Branch, Martin P. Wright
Tel: 778-698-5109; *Fax:* 250-387-7618

Policy & Provincial Services
PO Box 9738 Stn. Prov Govt, Victoria, BC V8W 9S2
Tel: 250-387-5954; *Fax:* 250-387-2481
Assistant Deputy Minister, Christine Massey
Tel: 778-698-7121; *Fax:* 250-387-2481
Executive Director, Child Care Programs & Services Branch, Jonathan Barry
Tel: 250-387-7762
Toll-free: 888-338-6622; *Fax:* 250-387-2997
Executive Director, Child & Youth Mental Health Policy, Robert Lampard
Tel: 778-698-7125; *Fax:* 250-356-0580
MCF.ChildYouthMentalHealth@gov.bc.ca
Executive Director, CW, Permanency, QA & Aboriginal Policy, Cheryl May
Tel: 250-356-5581
Executive Director, Children & Youth with Special Needs Policy, Aleksandra Stevanovic
Tel: 778-698-7361
Aleksandra.Stevanovic@gov.bc.ca
Executive Director, MSD & MCFD Legislation & Litigation, Michael Turanski
Tel: 778-698-7724; *Fax:* 250-356-8182

Provincial Office for the Early Years
PO Box 9721 Stn. Prov Govt, Victoria, BC V8W 9S2
Tel: 250-387-5942; *Fax:* 250-356-0311
Executive Director, Emily Horton
Tel: 778-698-5140
Director, Danielle Smith
Tel: 778-698-7368
Director, Stakeholder Engagement & Coordination, Jan White
Tel: 779-698-5141

Office of the Provincial Director of Child Welfare
PO Box 9721 Stn. Prov Govt, Victoria, BC V8W 9S2
Tel: 250-356-9791; *Fax:* 250-356-6534
Assistant Deputy Minister & Provincial Director, Child Welfare, Cory Heavener
Tel: 778-698-5126
Deputy Director, Child Welfare, Alex Scheiber
Tel: 778-698-4966
Regional Assistant Deputy Minister, Child Welfare, Teresa Dobmeier
Tel: 250-819-4999
Executive Director, Guardianship, Adoption & Permanency Planning, Renaa Bacy
Tel: 250-387-2281
MCF.AdoptionsBranch@gov.bc.ca

Strategic Priorities Division
PO Box 9768 Stn. Prov Govt, Victoria, BC V8W 9S5
Tel: 250-356-9808; *Fax:* 250-387-8000
Assistant Deputy Minister, Carolyn Kamper
Tel: 778-698-8835
Acting Executive Director, Project & Support Services, Andy Davidson
Tel: 250-818-2731
Executive Director, Provincial Office of Domestic Violence, Vacant
Acting Executive Director, Procurement & Contract Management Branch, Catherine Talbott
Tel: 778-698-8821

British Columbia Ministry of Citizens' Services

PO Box 9068 Stn. Prov Govt, Victoria, BC V8W 9E2
Tel: 604-660-2421
Toll-Free: 800-663-7867
servicebc@gov.bc.ca
www.gov.bc.ca/lctz
The Ministry of Citizens' Services was created in 2017 by Premier John Horgan.

Minister, Hon. Lisa Beare
Tel: 250-387-9699; *Fax:* 250-952-7628
citz.minister@gov.bc.ca

Deputy Minister, Shauna Brouwer
Tel: 250-387-8852; *Fax:* 250-387-8561

Associated Agencies, Boards & Commissions:
• **British Columbia Innovation Council (BCIC)**
1188 West Georgia St., 9th Fl.
Vancouver, BC V6E 4A2
Tel: 604-683-2724; *Fax:* 604-683-6567
Toll-free: 800-665-7222
info@bcic.ca
www.bcic.ca
Other Communication: Program Inquiries, Email:
programs@bcic.ca
The British Columbia Innovation Council strives to advance innovation & commercialization by focusing on the following

strategies: developing, recruiting & retaining science & technology professionals; fostering innovation & entrepreneurship; & bringing innovation to commercial success by establishing partnerships.
• **Premier's Technology Council (PTC)**
#1600, 800 Robson St.
Vancouver, BC V6Z 3E7
Tel: 604-827-4629
premiers.technologycouncil@gov.bc.ca
www.gov.bc.ca/premier/technology_council
The 23 member Premier's Technology Council advises the Premier on all technology related issues that affect British Columbia & its residents.

Corporate Information & Records Management Office
PO Box 9417 Stn. Prov Govt, Victoria, BC V8W 9V1
Tel: 250-387-1655
Acting Assistant Deputy Minister & Chief Records Officer, Joel Fairbairn
Tel: 778-698-2896
Joel.Fairbairn@gov.bc.ca
Executive Director, Information Access Operations, Chad Hoskins
Tel: 250-356-7343; *Fax:* 250-387-9843
Chad.Hoskins@gov.bc.ca
Executive Director, Government Records Service, Susan Laidlaw
Tel: 778-698-2900
Susan.Laidlaw@gov.bc.ca
Acting Executive Director, Strategic Policy & Legislation, Melissa Sexsmith
Tel: 250-952-0045
Melissa.M.Sexsmith@gov.bc.ca
Executive Director, Information Transformation, David Sherwood
Tel: 250-480-8771
David.Sherwood@gov.bc.ca
Executive Director, Privacy, Compliance & Training, Matt Reid
Matt.Reed@gov.bc.ca
Director, Infrastructure & Strategy, Terrell Les Strange
Tel: 778-698-3883
Terrell.LesStrange@gov.bc.ca
Director, Information Solutions & Transformation, Elizabeth Vander Beesen
Tel: 250-387-1430

Office of the Associate Deputy Minister - Citizens' Services
PO Box 9440 Stn. Prov Govt, Victoria, BC V8W 9V3
Tel: 250-387-8842; *Fax:* 250-387-8561
Associate Deputy Minister, Sarf Ahmed
Tel: 250-387-0315; *Fax:* 250-387-8561
Sarf.Ahmed@gov.bc.ca

Corporate Services Division
Tel: 250-952-7635; *Fax:* 250-387-5693
Assistant Deputy Minister & Executive Financial Officer, Colin McEwan
Tel: 250-952-7635
Chief Financial Officer & Executive Director, Financial & Administrative Services Branch, Philip Twyford
Tel: 250-516-0268
Philip.Twyford@gov.bc.ca
Acting Ministry Chief Information Officer & Executive Director, Information Management Branch, Shane Hoag
Tel: 250-216-5381
Shane.Hoag@gov.bc.ca
Executive Director, Planning, Performance & Communications, Jody Elson
Tel: 250-507-0239
Jody.Elson@gov.bc.ca
Executive Director, Corporate Projects, Vacant
Acting Director, Corporate Communications, Joy Bissonnette
Tel: 250-216-2290
Joy.Bissonnette@gov.bc.ca
Director, Corporate Planning & Reporting, Marion Brulot
Tel: 778-698-2422
Marion.Brulot@gov.bc.ca
Director, Budgets & Corporate Reporting, Tony Dierick
Tel: 250-507-7321
Tony.Dierick@gov.bc.ca
Director, Financial Policy, Reporting & Operations, Sandra Hall
Tel: 778-698-2458
Sandra.Hall@gov.bc.ca
Acting Director, Strategic Human Resources, Anne McKinnon
Tel: 250-588-9241
Anne.McKinnon@gov.bc.ca
Director, Facilities Management & Ministry Security Officer, Jeff Treloar
Tel: 250-812-3448
Jeff.Treloar@gov.bc.ca
Assistant Deputy Minister, Bobbi Sadler
Tel: 778-698-2332

Executive Director, Strategic Partnership Office, Pelle Agerup
Tel: 250-882-0455
Pelle.Agerup@gov.bc.ca
Executive Director, Supply Services, Dawson Brenner
Tel: 250-356-0600
Dawson.Brenner@gov.bc.ca
Executive Director, Procurement Transformation, Brooke Hayes
Tel: 778-698-2243
Brooke.Hayes@gov.bc.ca
Executive Director, Procurement Services, Mark T. Ross
Tel: 778-698-2370
Procurement@gov.bc.ca

Real Property Division
4000 Seymour Pl., PO Box 9412 Victoria, BC V8W 9V1
Tel: 250-387-8280; *Fax:* 250-952-8289
Assistant Deputy Minister, Sunny Dhaliwal
Sunny.Dhaliwal@gov.bc.ca
Executive Director, Asset Management Branch, Jon Burbee
Tel: 250-213-7439; *Fax:* 250-952-8289
Jon.Burbee@gov.bc.ca
Executive Director, Accommodation Management, Lorne DeLarge
Tel: 778-698-3993; *Fax:* 250-952-8293
Lorne.DeLarge@gov.bc.ca
Executive Director, Client Services, Rebecca Guthrie
Tel: 250-889-3993
Rebecca.Guthrie@gov.bc.ca
Executive Director, Strategic Real Estate Services, Robin Levesque
Tel: 778-698-4778
Robin.Levesque@gov.bc.ca
Executive Director, Real Estate Release Business Services, Stephen Marquet
Tel: 250-889-7876
Stephen.Marguet@gov.bc.ca
Executive Director, Facilities Management Services, Graham Taylor
Tel: 778-698-2289; *Fax:* 250-952-8407
Graham.Taylor@gov.bc.ca
Executive Director, Workplace Development Services, Vacant
Director, Asset Management, Asset Portfolio, Matthew Andrews
Tel: 250-213-6821
Matthew.Andrews@gov.bc.ca
Director, Real Estate & First Nation Engagement, Yvonne Diebert
Tel: 250-387-6348
Yvonne.Deibert@gov.bc.ca
Director, Asset Management, Corporate Sustainability, Bernie Gaudet
Tel: 250-920-8435; *Fax:* 250-952-8407
Bernie.Gaudet@gov.bc.ca
Director, Accomodation Projects, John Hammond
Tel: 778-698-2552
John.Hammond@gov.bc.ca
Director, Facilities Management Services, Operations, Jennifer Hoffman
Tel: 250-361-8185
Jennifer.Hoffman@gov.bc.ca
Director, Facilities Management Procurement Project, Karen Liversedge
Tel: 778-698-2660
Karen.Liversedge@gov.bc.ca
Director, Accomodations Management, Workplace Strategies & Planning, Rob Macdonald
Tel: 250-952-8315; *Fax:* 250-952-8293
Robert.Macdonald@gov.bc.ca
Director, Stakeholder & Community Engagement, Jason Macnaughton
Tel: 250-387-6318
Jason.Macnaughton@gov.bc.ca
Director, Accommodation Management, Leasing Services, John Marsh
Tel: 250-952-8412; *Fax:* 250-952-8288
John.Marsh@gov.bc.ca
Director, Real Estate Business, Lorraine McMillan
Tel: 250-952-8321; *Fax:* 250-952-8285
Lorraine.McMillan@gov.bc.ca
Director, Client Services Integration, Kwabena Owusu-Nyamekye
Tel: 778-677-6430
Kwabena.OwusuNyamekye@gov.bc.ca
Director, Facilities Management Services, Governance, Claire Steel
Tel: 250-818-9988
Director, Financial Planning & Reporting, May Yu
Tel: 778-698-2147
May.Yu@gov.bc.ca

Office of the Chief Information Officer (OCIO)
PO Box 9412 Stn. Prov Govt, Victoria, BC V8W 9V1
Tel: 250-356-7970; *Fax:* 250-387-1940
Toll-Free: 800-663-7867
LCTZ.ChiefInformationOfficer@gov.bc.ca
www.cio.gov.bc.ca
Other Communication: To report an information incident, such as a privacy breach, phone: 866-660-0811, option 3; BC Privacy Helpline, Phone: 250-356-1851, Tel: 250-953-0455
The Office of the Chief Information Officer guides & promotes the management of government information as an asset to business.
Examples of responsibilities include records management, legislation that governs the protection of privacy & personal information, freedom of information requests, & governance for corporate IM/IT policy, such as technology architecture & standards, data access, & information security.
Associate Deputy Minister & Government Chief Information Officer, C.J. Ritchie
CJ.Ritchie@gov.bc.ca
Executive Director, IM/IT Capital Investment, Corinne Timmermann
Tel: 250-952-9528
Corinne.Timmermann@gov.bc.ca
Executive Director, Network BC, Howard Randell
Tel: 250-953-3978
Director, Financial Advisory & Decision Support Services, Belinda Lucoe
Tel: 250-415-3783

Service B.C.
PO Box 9804 Stn. Prov Govt, Victoria, BC V8W 9W1
Tel: 250-387-6121; *Fax:* 250-387-5633
Toll-Free: 800-663-7867
TTY: 800-661-8773
www.servicebc.gov.bc.ca
Other Communication: Vancouver & outside B.C., Phone: 604-660-2421; Southeast Service BC Centre, Phone: 250-354-6109; Vancouver Island / South Coast Service BC Centre: 250-356-7302
Service BC provides frontline government services & information to businesses, residents, & visitors in British Columbia. Areas of service include education, training, employment & labour standards, doing business in the province, licensing & registration, taxation, health services, legal services, family support services, property, transportation, tourism, recreation, & publications. Service is available by phone, online, or in person at Service BC Centres throughout the province.
Assistant Deputy Minister, Beverly Dicks
Tel: 778-698-2377; *Fax:* 250-387-5633
Beverly.Dicks@gov.bc.ca
Research Director, BC Stats, Christina Campbell
Tel: 778-698-5195
Cristina.Campbell@gov.bc.ca
Acting Executive Director, Strategic Support Services, Adriana Poveda
Tel: 778-698-2090
Adriana.Poveda@gov.bc.ca
Executive Director, Service Delivery, Ron Hinshaw
Tel: 250-356-2031
Ron.Hinshaw@gov.bc.ca
Executive Director, Registries & Online Services, Carol Prest
Tel: 778-698-1401
Carol.Prest@gov.bc.ca
Executive Director, Transformation/Service Delivery & Integration, Vacant
Director, Registries & Online Services, Business & Project Services, Ian Armstrong
Tel: 250-356-2024
Ian.Armstrong@gov.bc.ca
Director, Application Management, Ian Bott
Tel: 250-356-9407
Director, Service Delivery, Contact Centres, Jeannette Eason
Tel: 778-698-2045
Jeannette.Eason@gov.bc.ca
Director, LeanBC, Shelley McNelis
Tel: 250-508-5116
Director, Service Delivery, Strategic Initiatives, Adriana Poveda
Tel: 778-698-2090
Adriana.Poveda@gov.bc.ca
Director, BC Stats, Research & Reporting, James Prouten
Tel: 250-580-4823
Director, BC Stats, Demographic Analysis, Jackie Storen
Tel: 250-216-2291
Jackie.Storen@gov.bc.ca

Strategic Planning & Policy
PO Box 9412 Stn. Prov Govt, Victoria, BC V8W 9V1
Tel: 250-216-7511

Executive Director, Niki Sedmak
Tel: 250-744-9193
Niki.Sedmak@gov.bc.ca

Senior Director, Business Relationship Management, Lisa Koorbatoff
Tel: 250-952-9453
Lisa.Koorbatoff@gov.bc.ca
Director, Business Relationship Communications, Sharon Koot
Tel: 250-952-9562
Sharon.Koot@gov.bc.ca
Acting Director, Susan E. Simmons
Tel: 250-508-3683
Susan.E.Simmons@gov.bc.ca
Director, Policy & Legislation, Ceri Sanderson
Tel: 250-516-7382
Ceri.Sanderson@gov.bc.ca

Technology Solutions
PO Box 9412 Stn. Prov Govt, Victoria, BC V8W 9V1
Tel: 250-387-4779; *Fax:* 250-387-5693
Acting Assistant Deputy Minister, Ian Donaldson
Tel: 250-387-4779; *Fax:* 250-387-5693
Executive Director, Device Services - Administrators Office, Nadine Criddle
Tel: 250-356-1328
Nadine.Criddle@gov.bc.ca
Executive Director, Hosting, Ian Donaldson
Tel: 250-213-7394
Ian.Donaldson@gov.bc.ca
Executive Director, Device Services, Dan Ehle
Tel: 250-387-4828
Dan.Ehle@gov.bc.ca
Executive Director, Corporate Software Branch, Stephen Gordon
Tel: 250-634-8448
Stephen.Gordon@gov.bc.ca
Executive Director, Network, Communications & Collaboration Services, Chris Hauff
Tel: 250-953-6285
Chris.Hauff@gov.bc.ca
Executive Director, Provincial Identity Management Program, Sophia Howse
Tel: 250-213-7855
Sophia.Howse@gov.bc.ca
Chief Information Security Officer & Executive Director, Information Security, Gary Perkins
Tel: 250-387-7590
Gary.Perkins@gov.bc.ca
Executive Director, Architecture, Standards & Planning, Derek Rutherford
Tel: 250-356-7915
Derek.Rutherford@gov.bc.ca
Executive Director, BC Developmers' Exchange & DevOps Branch, Peter Watkins
Tel: 250-514-2739
Peter.Watkins@gov.bc.ca
Executive Director, Service Management, Terry Whitney
Tel: 250-704-6209
Terry.Whitney@gov.bc.ca

Office of the Conflict of Interest Commissioner

421 Menzies St., 1st Fl., Victoria, BC V8V 1X4
Tel: 250-356-0750; *Fax:* 250-356-6580
conflictofinterest@coibc.ca
www.coibc.ca
The Conflict of Interest Commissioner is an independent Officer of the Legislative Assembly. The following roles are carried out by the Commissioner: advising Members of the Legislative Assembly; meeting with Members of the Legislative Assembly for review of disclosure of Members' interests, & obligations imposed by the Members' Conflict of Interest Act; & undertaking investigations into alleged contraventions of the Act or the Constitution Act, section 25.

Interim Conflict of Interest Commissioner, Lynn Smith, Q.C.

Executive Coordinator, Linda Pink
Tel: 250-356-0750
Linda.Pink@coibc.ca

Destination B.C. Corp.

#12, 510 Burrard St., Victoria, BC V6C 3A8
Tel: 604-660-2861; *Fax:* 604-660-3383
Toll-Free: 800-822-7899
ContactTourism@DestinationBC.ca
www.destinationbc.ca
Other Communication: Tourism URL: www.hellobc.com; Tourism Business Customer Service, Email: ProductServices@gov.bc.ca; Marketing: consumermarketing@destinationbc.ca
Secondary Address: #700, 1483 Douglas St. Victoria, BC V8W 3K4
Alt. Fax: 604-660-3383
twitter.com/Destination_BC
www.facebook.com/HelloBC
www.youtube.com/user/TourismBC

Operating as Destination British Columbia, the corporation was founded in 2012 under the British Columbia Business Corporations Act, & operates as a crown corporation under the Destination BC Corp. Act. Its mandate is to work with tourism stakeholders across BC to market the province as a tourism destination at the international, national & provincial levels.

Chair, Andrea Shaw

President & CEO, Marsha Walden
Tel: 604-953-6724
Marsha.Walden@DestinationBC.ca

Chief Financial Officer & Executive Director, Corporate Services, Dean Skinner
Tel: 250-356-5648
Dean.Skinner@DestinationBC.ca

Vice-President, Global Marketing, Maya Lange
Tel: 604-953-6712
Maya.Lange@DestinationBC.ca

Vice-President, Destination & Industry Development, Grant Mackay
Tel: 604-953-6740
Grant.Mackay@DestinationBC.ca

Vice-President, Corporate Development, Richard Porges
Tel: 250-356-9936
Richard.Porges@DestinationBC.ca

British Columbia Ministry of Education

PO Box 9179 Stn. Prov Govt, Victoria, BC V8W 9E2
Toll-Free: 800-663-7867
servicebc@gov.bc.ca
www.gov.bc.ca/bced
Other Communication: Media Inquiries, Phone: 250-356-5963
The Ministry of Education works with stakeholders in all stages of the education system, from early learning programs & kindergarten to grade 12 to life-long literacy. Early learning programs include the ministry initiative, StrongStart. Life-long literacy initiatives include programs at community learning centres & public libraries.

Minister, Hon. Jennifer Whiteside
Tel: 250-356-8247; *Fax:* 250-356-0948
educ.minister@gov.bc.ca

Deputy Minister, Scott MacDonald; *Fax:* 205-953-4985
dm.education@gov.bc.ca

Director, Executive Operations, Sheila Purdy
Tel: 250-216-3648; *Fax:* 250-953-4985
Sheila.Purdy@gov.bc.ca

Associated Agencies, Boards & Commissions:
• Education Advisory Council
c/o Mike Roberts, Superintendent, Liaison
#1550, 555 West Hastings
PO Box 121110
Vancouver, BC V6B 4N6
Tel: 604-660-1483; *Fax:* 604-660-2124

The purpose of the Education Advisory Council is to advise the Minister of Education on all areas of the education system, including: curriculum & assessment; the teaching profession; system governance; & finance.
• Teacher Regulation Branch
#400, 2025 West Broadway
Vancouver, BC V6J 1Z6
Tel: 604-660-6060; *Fax:* 604-775-4859
Toll-free: 800-555-3684
www.bcteacherregulation.ca
The Teacher Regulation Branch ensures that standards for education at met and maintained by the teachers in the province.

Governance & Analytics
Tel: 604-660-1415; *Fax:* 604-660-2124
www.bced.gov.bc.ca/departments/liaison
Assistant Deputy Minister, Keith Godin
Tel: 250-356-6760
EDUC.GAD@gov.bc.ca
Executive Director, Strategic Project Branch, Sohee Ahn
Tel: 250-507-7932
Executive Director, Legislation, Policy & Governance, Dave Duerksen
Tel: 250-387-8037
EDUC.Governance.Legislation@gov.bc.ca
Executive Director, Education Analytics Branch, Darlene Therrien
Tel: 250-387-8037
Darlene.Therrien@gov.bc.ca

International Education, Independent Schools & Partner Relations
PO Box 9161 Stn. Prov Govt, Victoria, BC V8W 9H3
Tel: 250-356-0891
EDUCADMO@Victoria1.gov.bc.ca
Acting Assistant Deputy Minister, Paul Squires
Tel: 250-886-1582
Paul.Squires@gov.bc.ca
Executive Director, Teacher Regulation Branch, Wilma Clarke
Tel: 604-775-4817; *Fax:* 604-775-4860
Wilma.Clarke@gov.bc.ca
Executive Director, Independent Schools, Brian Jonker
Tel: 250-217-3991
EDUC.IndependentSchoolsOffice@gov.bc.ca

Learning Division
PO Box 9887 Stn. Prov Govt, Victoria, BC V8W 9T6
Tel: 250-216-6038; *Fax:* 250-387-6315
EDUC.learningdivision@gov.bc.ca
Assistant Deputy Minister, Jennifer McCrea
Tel: 250-896-3735; *Fax:* 250-387-6315
EDUC.learningdivision@gov.bc.ca
Executive Director, Shelaina Postings
Tel: 778-679-8531
Shelaina.Postings@gov.bc.ca
Executive Director, Custom Programs & Projects, Tim Winkelmans
Tel: 250-217-6643; *Fax:* 250-356-8334
Tim.Winkelmans@gov.bc.ca

Learning Modernization Project
PO Box 9146 Stn. Prov Govt, Victoria, BC V8W 9H1
Tel: 250-356-6760; *Fax:* 250-953-3225
EDUC.GovernanceDepartment@gov.bc.ca
Superintendent, Learning Transformation, Suzanne Hoffman
Tel: 604-418-5287
Suzanne.Hoffman@gov.bc.ca
Executive Director, Education Transformation, Kim Lacharite
Tel: 250-588-1700
Kim.Lacharite@gov.bc.ca
Executive Director, Curriculum & Assessment, Nancy Walt
Tel: 250-217-4978
Nancy.Walt@gov.bc.ca

Resource Management & Executive Financial Office
PO Box 9151 Stn. Prov Govt, Victoria, BC V8W 9H1
Tel: 250-356-2588; *Fax:* 250-953-4985
www.bced.gov.bc.ca/departments/resource_man/
Assistant Deputy Minister, Reg Bawa
Tel: 250-356-1883
Education.ResourceManagementAndCorporateServices@gov.bc.ca
Executive Director, People & Workplace Initiatives Branch, Heather Beaton
Tel: 250-216-4244
PWI@gov.bc.ca
Executive Director, Sector Resourcing & Service Delivery Branch, Kim Horn
Tel: 250-896-3680
Kim.Horn@gov.bc.ca
Chief Financial Officer & Executive Director, Financial Services Branch, Tiffany Ma
Tel: 250-387-6282; *Fax:* 250-953-4985
Financial.Services@gov.bc.ca
Executive Director, Capital Delivery Unit, Ryan Spillett
Tel: 250-885-3699; *Fax:* 250-953-4985
Ryan.Spillett@gov.bc.ca
Director, School District Financial Reporting, Ian Aaron
Tel: 250-415-1073; *Fax:* 250-953-4985
Director, People & Workplace Initatives Branch, Jennifer Farrow
Tel: 250-888-5878
PWI@gov.bc.ca
Director, Funding & Allocation, Jonathan Foweraker
Tel: 250-896-2673
Jonathan.Foweraker@gov.bc.ca
Director, Financial Operations Unit, Trevor Miller
Tel: 250-812-5326
Director, Capital Standards Unit, Michael Nyikes
Tel: 250-893-6268
Michael.Nyikes@gov.bc.ca
Director, Sector Resourcing & Service Delivery Branch, Service Delivery Unit, Caroline Ponsford
Tel: 250-216-6347
Caroline.Ponsford@gov.bc.ca
Director, Financial Planning & Analysis Unit, Hayley Rissley
Tel: 250-213-2640
Director, Policy, Procurement & Governance Unit, Amanda Thompson
Tel: 250-896-8588
Director, Corporate Services & Initiatives, Julie Turner
Tel: 250-889-4643
Julie.Turner@gov.bc.ca

Services & Technology Division
PO Box 9132 Stn. Prov Govt, Victoria, BC V8W 9B5
Tel: 250-356-8363
Assistant Deputy Minister, Sally Barton
ADM.ServicesTechnology@gov.bc.ca
Ministry Information Security Officer, Vicki Baleshta
Tel: 250-356-6716
Executive Director, Student Information Services, Eleanor Liddy
Tel: 250-508-1119
Eleanor.Liddy@gov.bc.ca
Chief Information Officer & Executive Director, Information Technology, HB Teo
Tel: 250-217-9756
HB.Teo@gov.bc.ca

Elections British Columbia

PO Box 9275 Stn. Prov Govt, Victoria, BC V8W 9J6
Tel: 250-387-5305; *Fax:* 250-387-3578
Toll-Free: 800-661-8683
TTY: 888-456-5448
electionsbc@elections.bc.ca
www.elections.bc.ca
Other Communication: Toll-free Fax: 866-466-0665
twitter.com/ElectionsBC
www.facebook.com/ElectionsBC
www.youtube.com/ElectionsBConline
Elections British Columbia is a non-partisan, independent Office of the Legislature. Its responsibility is the administration of the electoral process in the province, including provincial general elections, by-elections, provincial referendums, & recall & initiative petitions & votes.

Chief Electoral Officer, Anton Boegman

Deputy Chief Electoral Officer, Electoral Operations, Anton Boegman
Tel: 250-356-2713
Anton.Boegman@elections.bc.ca

Deputy Chief Electoral Officer, Funding & Disclosure, Nola Western
Tel: 250-387-4141
Nola.Western@elections.bc.ca

Director, Information Technology, Yvonne Koehn
Tel: 250-387-1945
Yvonne.Koehn@elections.bc.ca

Director, Corporate Planning & Event Leader, Jill Lawrance
Tel: 250-387-7258
Jill.Lawrance@elections.bc.ca

British Columbia Ministry of Energy, Mines & Low Carbon Innovation

PO Box 9060 Stn. Prov Govt, Victoria, BC V8W 9E3
Tel: 250-952-0628
The Ministry of Energy, Mines & Petroleum Resources was created in 2017 by Premier John Horgan. The development of sustainable & competitive energy & mineral resource sectors in British Columbia is the focus of the Ministry. To develop legislation & guidelines, the ministry consults with other ministries & levels of government, as well as communities, First Nations, the public, energy & mining companies & environmental organizations.
In 2020, the ministry was renmaed from the Ministry of Energy, Mines & Petroleum Resources to the Ministry of Energy, Mines & Low Carbon Innovation.

Minister, Hon. Bruce Ralston
Tel: 250-953-0900; *Fax:* 250-356-2965
empr.minister@gov.bc.ca

Deputy Minister, Fazil Mihlar
Tel: 250-952-0504
Fazil.Mihlar@gov.bc.ca
PO Box 9319 Prov Govt Sta.
Victoria, BC V8W 9N3

Executive Director, LNG Canada Implementation Secretariat, Rachel Shaw
Tel: 778-974-2149
Rachel.Shaw@gov.bc.ca
PO Box 9319 Prov Govt Sta.
Victoria, BC V8W 9N3

Director, Executive Operations & Planning, Monica Jang
Tel: 604-660-3346; *Fax:* 250-952-0269
Monica.Jang@gov.bc.ca
PO Box 9319 Prov Govt Sta.
Victoria, BC V8W 9N3

Associated Agencies, Boards & Commissions:
• Oil & Gas Commission (OGC)
6534 Airport Rd.
Fort St. John, BC V1J 4M6
Tel: 250-794-5200; *Fax:* 250-794-5375
www.bcogc.ca
Other Communication: Incident Reporting: 800-663-3456;
Victoria: 250-419-4400
The Oil & Gas Commission was enacted under the Oil & Gas Commission Act, The Commission regulates British Columbia's oil & gas activities & pipelines.

• Surface Rights Board of British Columbia (SRB)
#10, 10551 Shellbridge Way
Richmond, BC V6X 2W9
Tel: 604-775-1740; *Fax:* 604-775-1742
Toll-free: 888-775-1740
office@surfacerightsboard.bc.ca
www.surfacerightsboard.bc.ca
Other Communication: Toll-Free Fax: 888-775-1742
The Board is mandated to help solve disputes between landowners & companies requiring access to private land for the purpose of exploring, developing or producing Crown-owned resources such as oil, gas, coal, minerals & geothermal.

Corporate Initiatives Branch
PO Box 9315 Stn. Prov Govt, Victoria, BC V8W 9N1
Fax: 250-952-0258
Executive Director, Fraser Marshall
Tel: 778-698-7191
Fraser.Marshall@gov.bc.ca
Director, Organizational Effectiveness, Ryan Forman
Tel: 778-698-7248
Ryan.Forman@gov.bc.ca
Director, Energy & Industry Decarbonization, Guy Gensey
Tel: 778-698-7144
Guy.Gensey@gov.bc.ca
Director, Corporate Initiatives, Daymon Trachsel
Tel: 778-698-7283
Daymon.Trachsel@gov.bc.ca

Electricity & Alternative Energy Division
PO Box 9314 Stn. Prov Govt, Victoria, BC V8W 9N1
Tel: 250-952-0673; *Fax:* 250-952-0258
Assistant Deputy Minister, Les MacLaren
Tel: 778-698-7183; *Fax:* 250-952-0258
Les.MacLaren@gov.bc.ca
Executive Director, Electricity Transmission/Inter-jurisdictional Branch, Regional Operations, Julie Chace
Tel: 778-698-7289
Executive Director, Columbia River Treaty (CRT) Review Team, Kathy Eichenberger
Tel: 250-952-3368
Kathy.Eichenberger@gov.bc.ca
Executive Director, Alternative Energy & Innovative Clean Energy (ICE) Fund, Dan Green
Tel: 250-952-0279; *Fax:* 250-952-0351
Dan.Green@gov.bc.ca
Executive Director, Electricity Transmission/Inter-jurisdictional Branch, Paul Wieringa
Tel: 778-698-7251

Mines & Mineral Resources Division
PO Box 9320 Stn. Prov Govt, Victoria, BC V8W 9N3
Tel: 250-952-0470; *Fax:* 250-952-0491
Assistant Deputy Minister, Peter Robb
Tel: 778-698-7233; *Fax:* 250-952-0491
Peter.Robb@gov.bc.ca
Chief Inspector & Executive Director, Health & Safety, Health & Safety & Permitting Branch, Al Hoffman
Tel: 250-952-0494; *Fax:* 250-952-0491
Al.Hoffman@gov.bc.ca
Deputy Chief Inspector, Mines, Compliance & Enforcement, Tania Demchuk
Tel: 778-698-7222; *Fax:* 250-952-0491
Tania.Demchuk@gov.bc.ca
Deputy Chief Inspector, Mines, Permitting, Health & Safety & Permitting Branch, Diane Howe
Tel: 250-952-0183
Diane.Howe@gov.bc.ca
Deputy Chief Inspector, Mines, Health & Safety, Health & Safety & Permitting Branch, Rolly Thorpe
Tel: 778-698-7234
Rolly.Thorpe@gov.bc.ca
Chief Gold Commissioner & Executive Director, Mineral Titles, Mark Messmer
Tel: 604-660-2814
Mark.Messmer@gov.bc.ca
Chief Geologist & Executive Director, British Columbia Geological Survey, Stephen Rowins
Tel: 250-952-0454; *Fax:* 250-952-0381
Stephen.Rowins@gov.bc.ca

Acting Executive Director, Major Mine Permitting Office, Amy Avila
Tel: 778-698-7296; *Fax:* 250-952-0491
Amy.Avila@gov.bc.ca
Executive Director, Policy, Legislation & Issues Resolution Branch, Chris Trumpy
Tel: 778-698-7295; *Fax:* 250-952-0271
Chris.Trumpy@gov.bc.ca

Upstream Development Division
Fax: 250-952-0926
Assistant Deputy Minister, Ines Piccinino
Tel: 778-698-3679
Ines.Piccinino@gov.bc.ca
Executive Director, Policy & Royalty Branch, Richard Grieve
Tel: 778-698-3703; *Fax:* 250-953-3770
Richard.Grieve@gov.bc.ca
Executive Director, Tenure & Geoscience Branch, Garth Thoroughgood
Tel: 250-952-6382; *Fax:* 250-952-0331
Garth.Thoroughgood@gov.bc.ca

British Columbia Ministry of Environment & Climate Change Strategy

PO Box 9047 Stn. Prov Govt, Victoria, BC V8W 9E2
www.gov.bc.ca/env
The following responsibilities are handled by the Ministry of the Environment & Climate Change Strategy: establishment of standards; administration of legislation; promotion of stewardship & sustainability, through environmental protection; development of partnerships, by engaging stakeholders, First Nations, & citizens in policy & program development; & conservation, maintenance, & enhancement of ecosystems & native species. The ministry seeks to protect, manage & conserve BC's water, land, air & living resources.

Minister, Hon. George Heyman
Tel: 250-387-1187; *Fax:* 250-387-1356
env.minister@gov.bc.ca

Deputy Minister, Kevin Jardine
Tel: 250-387-5429; *Fax:* 250-387-6003
dm.env@gov.bc.ca

Director, Executive Operations, Jennifer Meadows
Tel: 778-698-1669
Jennifer.Meadows@gov.bc.ca

Associated Agencies, Boards & Commissions:
• **British Columbia Environmental Assessment Office**
See Entry Name Index for detailed listing.

B.C. Parks & Conservation Officer Service
PO Box 9376 Stn. Prov Govt, Victoria, BC V8W 9M1
Tel: 250-356-9234; *Fax:* 250-356-9197
conservation.officer.service@gov.bc.ca
www.env.gov.bc.ca/cos
Other Communication: Wildlife conflict: 877-952-7277
Assistant Deputy Minister, Jim Standen
Tel: 250-387-1228; *Fax:* 250-953-3414
Jim.Standen@gov.bc.ca
Chief Conservation Officer, Enforcement Program/Conservation Officer Service, Doug Forsdick
Tel: 250-614-9904; *Fax:* 250-356-9197
Deputy Chief Conservation Officer, David Airey
Tel: 778-698-4262
David.Airey@gov.bc.ca
Deputy Chief, Program Support, Aaron Canuel; *Fax:* 250-356-9197
Aaron.Canuel@gov.bc.ca
Executive Director, Regional Operations, Bob C. Austad
Tel: 778-698-4281; *Fax:* 250-387-5757
Bob.Austad@gov.bc.ca
Executive Director, BC Parks - Provincial Services Branch, David Ranson
Tel: 778-698-4286; *Fax:* 250-387-5757
David.Ranson@gov.bc.ca

Climate Action Secretariat
PO Box 9486 Stn. Prov Govt, Victoria, BC V8W 9W6
Fax: 250-356-7286
climateactionsecretariat@gov.bc.ca
www.env.gov.bc.ca/cas//index.html
Assistant Deputy Minister, Jeremy Hewitt
Tel: 778-698-4833
Jeremy.Hewitt@gov.bc.ca
Acting Executive Director, Clean Growth Branch, Neil Dobson
Tel: 778-698-4064
Executive Director, Climate Risk & Investment Branch, Suzanne Spence
Tel: 778-698-4000

Director, Economics & Analysis, Neil Dobson
Tel: 778-698-4064
Director, Industrial Reporting & Control, Adria Fradley
Tel: 778-698-4012
Director, Carbon Neutral Government, Orest Maslany
Tel: 778-698-4069
Director, Climate Risk Management, Thomas White
Tel: 778-698-4075
Manager, Secretariat Operations, Beverley Stainton
Tel: 778-698-4034
Assistant Deputy Minister, Scott Bailey
Tel: 250-387-2307; *Fax:* 250-356-6448
Scott.Bailey@gov.bc.ca
Associate Deputy Minister, Kevin Jardine
Tel: 250-356-7478; *Fax:* 250-356-6448
eaoinfo@gov.bc.ca
Executive Director, Strategic Services & Compliance, Paul Craven
Tel: 778-698-9333; *Fax:* 250-356-6448
Paul.Craven@gov.bc.ca
Executive Director, First Nations Relations, Cory Waters
Tel: 250-387-0236; *Fax:* 250-356-6448
Cory.Waters@gov.bc.ca

Environmental Protection Division
PO Box 9339 Victoria, BC V8W 9M1
Tel: 250-387-1288; *Fax:* 250-387-5669
www.env.gov.bc.ca/epd/
Assistant Deputy Minister, David P. Morel
Tel: 778-698-5461; *Fax:* 250-387-5669
David.Morel@gov.bc.ca
Executive Director, Environmental Emergencies & Land Remediation Branch, Cameron Lewis
Tel: 778-698-4897; *Fax:* 250-387-8897
Cameron.Lewis@gov.bc.ca
Executive Director, Environmental Standards Branch, Kris Ord
Tel: 778-698-5628; *Fax:* 250-356-7197

Environmental Sustainability & Strategic Policy Division
PO Box 9335 Stn. Prov Govt, Victoria, BC V8W 9M1
Tel: 250-387-9666; *Fax:* 250-387-8894
Assistant Deputy Minister, Jennifer McGuire
Tel: 778-698-8521; *Fax:* 250-953-3414
Executive Director, Ecosystems Branch, Alec Dale
Tel: 778-698-4384; *Fax:* 250-387-9750
Executive Director, Strategic Policy Branch, Anthony J. Danks
Tel: 778-698-4409; *Fax:* 250-387-8894
Anthony.Danks@gov.bc.ca
Executive Director, Knowledge Management Branch, R. David Tesch
Tel: 778-698-4406; *Fax:* 250-356-9836

British Columbia Ferry Services Inc.

c/o BC Ferry Authority, #500, 1321 Blanshard St., Victoria, BC V8W 0B7
Tel: 250-381-1401
Toll-Free: 888-223-3779
customerservice@bcferries.com
www.bcferries.com
Other Communication: Outside North America Phone: 250-386-3431; BC Ferry Authority, URL: www.bcferryauthority.com
twitter.com/BCFerries
www.facebook.com/BCFerries
www.instagram.com/bcferries
BC Ferries operates as the primary provider of coastal ferry service in British Columbia. The fleet covers 24 routes with 35 vessels. BC Ferry Authority holds the single issued voting share of BC Ferries.

Chair, Donald P. Hayes

Vice Chair, P. Geoffrey Plant, Q.C.

President & Chief Executive Officer, Mark Collins

Executive Vice-President, Human Resources & Corporate Development, Glen N. Schwartz

British Columbia Ministry of Finance

PO Box 9417 Stn. Prov Govt, Victoria, BC V8W 9V1
www.gov.bc.ca/fin
Other Communication: Media Inquiries, Phone: 250-387-5710
The Ministry of Finance establishes, implements, & reviews the government's financial management, fiscal, economic, & taxation policies. Responsibilities are as follows: economic planning, budgeting, & reporting; policy development for the financial, corporate, & real estate sectors; overseeing financial & administrative governance for the public service; banking & risk management services for government; tax & non-tax administration; loan administration & collection; administering a

governance framework for Crown agencies; & regulating the financial services & real estate sectors.

Minister, Hon. Selina Robinson
Tel: 250-387-3751; *Fax:* 250-387-5594
fin.minister@gov.bc.ca

Deputy Minister, Heather Wood
Tel: 250-387-3184; *Fax:* 250-387-1655
Heather.Wood@gov.bc.ca
PO Box 9417 Prov Govt Sta.
Victoria, BC V8W 9V1

Assistant Deputy Minister, Strategic Initiatives, Doug Foster
Tel: 250-387-9022
Doug.Foster@gov.bc.ca

Associated Agencies, Boards & Commissions:
• **Auditor Certification Board**
PO Box 9431 Prov Govt
Victoria, BC V8W 9V3
Tel: 250-356-8658; *Fax:* 250-356-9422
Ken.Worthy@gov.bc.ca
The Auditor Certification Board is authorized under the Business Corporations Act. The Board receives applications from individuals who apply to becertified as auditors. Persons with the necessary qualifications are then certified.

• **British Columbia Securities Commission (BCSC)**
Pacific Centre
701 West Georgia St., 12th Fl.
PO Box 10142
Vancouver, BC V7Y 1L2
Tel: 604-899-6500; *Fax:* 604-899-6506
Toll-free: 800-373-6393
inquiries@bcsc.bc.ca
www.bcsc.bc.ca
The British Columbia Securities Commission is an independent provincial government agency. Through administration of the Securities Act, the Commission regulates securities trading in British Columbia.

• **British Columbia Lottery Corporation (BCLC)**
74 West Seymour St.
Kamloops, BC V2C 1E2
Tel: 250-828-5500; *Fax:* 250-828-5631
Toll-free: 866-815-0222
www.bclc.com
Other Communication: Vancouver Phone: 604-215-0649

• **Financial Institutions Commission (FICOM)**
#2800, 555 West Hastings
Vancouver, BC V6B 4N6
Tel: 604-660-3555; *Fax:* 604-660-3365
Toll-free: 866-206-3030
FICOM@ficombc.ca
www.fic.gov.bc.ca
Other Communication: HR@ficombc.ca; CUandTrusts@ficombc.ca; DepositInsurance@ficombc.ca; Insurance@ficombc.ca; Pensions@ficombc.ca; RealEstate@ficombc.ca; MortgageBrokers@ficombc.ca
The Financial Institutions Commission is a regulatory agency of British Columbia's Ministry of Finance. The Commission's responsibility is the administration of statutes that regulate the financial services, pension, & real estate sectors in the province.

• **Insurance Council of British Columbia**
#300, 1040 West Georgia St.
PO Box 7
Vancouver, BC V6E 4H1
Tel: 604-688-0321; *Fax:* 604-662-7767
Toll-free: 877-688-0321
info@insurancecouncilofbc.com
www.insurancecouncilofbc.com
The Insurance Council of British Columbia reports to the province's Minister of Finance. The Council has the following responsibilities: Licensing insurance agents, salespersons, & adjusters; Regulating insurance licensees; & Investigating & disciplining licensees.

• **Partnerships BC**
900 - 1285 West Pender St.
PO Box 9478 Prov Govt
Vancouver, BC V6E 4B1
Tel: 604-681-2443; *Fax:* 604-806-4190
partnershipsbc@partnershipsbc.ca
www.partnershipsbc.ca
Partnerships BC is mandated to plan, deliver & provide oversight of major infrastructure projects in the province.

• Public Sector Employers' Council Secretariat (PSEC)
#210, 880 Douglas St.
PO Box 9400 Prov Govt
Victoria, BC V8V 9V1
Tel: 250-387-0842; *Fax:* 250-387-6258
PSEC@gov.bc.ca
The coordination of the management of labour relations policies & practices in the public sector is the principal responsibility of the Public Sector Employers' Council. The Council consists of the following members: eight Ministers or Deputy Ministers; Commissioner of the BC Public Service Agency; & representatives from six public sector employers' associations. The Public Sector Employers' Council Secretariat carries out the work of the Council.

• Real Estate Council of British Columbia (RECBC)
#900, 750 West Pender St.
Vancouver, BC V6C 2T8
Tel: 604-683-9664; *Fax:* 604-683-9017
Toll-free: 877-683-9664
info@recbc.ca
www.recbc.ca
The Real Estate Council of British Columbia is a regulatory agency with the following responsibilities under the requirements of the Real Estate Services Act: Licensing individuals & brokerages involved in real estate sales, rental & strata property management; Enforcing licensing qualifications & licensee conduct; & Investigating complaints against licensees & imposing discipline.

Crown Agencies Resource Office
PO Box 9416 Stn. Prov Govt, Victoria, BC V8W 9V1
Tel: 250-387-8499; *Fax:* 250-356-2001
CARO@gov.bc.ca
www.gov.bc.ca/caro
Executive Lead, Lynne Holt
Tel: 778-698-8523; *Fax:* 250-387-8540
Lynne.Holt@gov.bc.ca
Executive Director, Angela Swan
Tel: 250-893-1333; *Fax:* 250-387-8540

Gaming Policy & Enforcement
PO Box 9311 Stn. Prov Govt, Victoria, BC V8W 9N1
Tel: 250-387-1301; *Fax:* 250-387-1818
Gaming.branch@gov.bc.ca
www.gaming.gov.bc.ca
Assistant Deputy Minister, John Mazure
Tel: 250-387-1301; *Fax:* 250-387-1818
Gaming.branch@gov.bc.ca
Executive Director, Licensing, Registration & Certification Division, Kim Bruce
Tel: 250-356-2980; *Fax:* 250-356-0782
Kim.M.Bruce@gov.bc.ca
Executive Director, Compliance Division, Anna Fitzgerald
Tel: 604-660-0459; *Fax:* 250-356-0794
Anna.Fitzgerald@gov.bc.ca
Executive Director, Community Supports Division, David Horricks
Tel: 250-387-3211; *Fax:* 250-387-1818
David.Horricks@gov.bc.ca
Other Communications: Cell Phone: 250-516-4362
Executive Director, Strategic Policy & Projects Division, Michele Jaggi-Smith
Tel: 250-356-1109; *Fax:* 250-356-1910
Michele.JaggiSmith@gov.bc.ca

Internal Audit & Advisory Services
PO Box 9413 Stn. Prov Govt, Victoria, BC V8W 9V1
Tel: 250-387-6303; *Fax:* 250-356-2001
www.fin.bc.ca/ocg/ias/ias.htm
Executive Director, Alexsandro Amaral
Tel: 250-387-9235; *Fax:* 250-387-8545
Alexsandro.Amaral@gov.bc.ca
Executive Director, Stephen Ward
Tel: 250-387-0283; *Fax:* 250-387-8545
Stephen.Ward@gov.bc.ca
Director, Serena DeCiantis
Tel: 250-356-9490
Serena.DeCiantis@gov.bc.ca
Director, IM/IT Audit, Denise Ho
Tel: 250-387-8177
Denise.Ho@gov.bc.ca
Director, Michael McStravick
Tel: 250-387-8177
Michael.McStravick@gov.bc.ca
Financial Officer, Jeanie Mow
Tel: 250-387-8196
Jeanie.Mow@gov.bc.ca

Corporate Services Division
PO Box 9415 Stn. Prov Govt, Victoria, BC V8W 9V1
Assistant Deputy Minister & Executive Financial Officer, Tara Richards
Tel: 778-698-8711
Tara.Richards@gov.bc.ca

Chief Information Officer & Executive Director, Information Management, Michael Carpenter
Tel: 778-698-3027; *Fax:* 250-356-1494
Michael.Carpenter@gov.bc.ca
PO Box 9424 Prov Govt Sta.
Victoria, BC V8W 9V1
Chief Financial Officer & Executive Director, Corporate Financial & Facilities Services, Steve Klak
Tel: 778-698-8556
Steve.Klak@gov.bc.ca
Executive Director, Strategic Human Resources, Raeleen Siu
Tel: 778-698-8559; *Fax:* 250-356-7326
Raeleen.Siu@gov.bc.ca
PO Box 9420 Prov Govt Sta.
Victoria, BC V8W 9V1
Executive Director, Performance Management & Corporate Priorities Branch, Kashi Tanaka
Tel: 778-698-8562; *Fax:* 250-356-7326
Kashi.Tanaka@gov.bc.ca

Secretary to Treasury Board
PO Box 9417 Stn. Prov Govt, Victoria, BC V8W 9V8
Tel: 250-387-8675; *Fax:* 250-356-9054
Associate Deputy Minister & Secretary to Treasury Board, Heather Wood
Tel: 778-698-1549
Chief Economist & Executive Director, Economic Forecasting & Policy Analysis, Sadaf Mirza
Tel: 778-698-1534
Sadaf.Mirza@gov.bc.ca
Executive Director, Economic Development, Alex Chandler
Tel: 250-387-3943; *Fax:* 250-387-9054
Alex.Chandler@gov.bc.ca
Executive Director, Social Policy, Jonathan Dube
Tel: 250-356-5900
Jonathan.Dube@gov.bc.ca
Executive Director, SUCH Ministries, Gord Enemark
Tel: 250-356-5032; *Fax:* 250-387-9054
Gord.Enemark@gov.bc.ca
Executive Director, Capital, Heather Hill
Tel: 250-387-9007
Heather.Hill@gov.bc.ca
Executive Director, Fiscal Planning, Dave Riley
Tel: 250-387-9030; *Fax:* 250-387-0300
Dave.Riley@gov.bc.ca
Executive Director, Financial Planning & Estimates, Chris Skiliings
Tel: 250-356-5300; *Fax:* 250-387-0300
Chris.Skillings@gov.bc.ca

Government Communications & Public Engagement
PO Box 9409 Stn. Prov Govt, Victoria, BC V8W 9V1
Tel: 250-387-1337; *Fax:* 250-387-3534
Deputy Minister, Evan Lloyd
Tel: 778-698-4798
Evan.Lloyd@gov.bc.ca
Assistant Deputy Minister, Strategic Communications Division, Robb Gibbs
Tel: 778-584-1242
Robb.Gibbs@gov.bc.ca
Assistant Deputy Minister, Strategic Issues Division, Eric Kristianson
Tel: 778-698-8511
Eric.Kristianson@gov.bc.ca
Assistant Deputy Minister, Communications Operations Division, Mike Lowe
Tel: 778-698-7411
Mike.Lowe@gov.bc.ca
Acting Assistant Deputy Minister, Government Digital Experience Division, David Hume
Tel: 250-589-9043
David.Hume@gov.bc.ca
Acting Executive Director, Finance & Corporate Services, Ramen Dale
Tel: 250-952-8810
Raman.Dale@gov.bc.ca
Executive Director, Strategic Issues Division, Matt Hannah
Tel: 778-698-1249
Matt.Hannah@gov.bc.ca
Executive Director, Digital Communications, Karl Hardin
Tel: 778-584-1251
Karl.Hardin@gov.bc.ca
Executive Director, Communications (Social Ministries), Marq LeGuilloux
Tel: 778-698-8926
Marg.LeGuilloux@gov.bc.ca
Executive Director, Cabinet Priorities, Cara McGregor
Tel: 250-213-9574
Cara.McGregor@gov.bc.ca
Executive Director, Government Communications & Public Engagement, Walter Moser
Tel: 250-217-6017
Walter.Moser@gov.bc.ca

Executive Director, Confidence & Supply Agreement Secretariat, Donna Sanford
Tel: 250-893-4771
Donna.Sanford@gov.bc.ca
Executive Director, Ministry Support - Resource Sector, Don Zadravec
Tel: 778-584-1252
Don.Zadravec@gov.bc.ca
Executive Director, Ministry Support - Economy Sector, Sarah Zaharia
Tel: 778-584-1258
Sarah.Zaharia@gov.bc.ca
Director, Events Services, Rick Devereaux
Tel: 250-812-1207
Rick.Devereux@gov.bc.ca
Director, Cultural Transformation, Brooke Finnigan
Tel: 250-361-6549
Brooke.Finnigan@gov.bc.ca
Director, Strategic Deisgn & Transformation, Irene Guglielmi
Tel: 250-216-7038
Irene.Guglielmi@gov.bc.ca
Director, Writing & Editorial Services, Grant Kerr
Tel: 778-698-3636
Grant.Kerr@gov.bc.ca
Director, Advertising & Marketing Services, Kathryn LeSueur
Tel: 778-698-8674
Kathryn.LeSueur@gov.bc.ca
Director, Program Design, Savannah Murphy
Tel: 250-588-4488
Savannah.Murphy@gov.bc.ca
Director, Graphic Communications, Andrew Pratt
Tel: 250-356-8120
Andrew.Pratt@gov.bc.ca
Director, Media Monitoring Services, Scott Ryckman
Tel: 250-356-5735
Scott.Ryckman@gov.bc.ca
Director, Media Relations/BC Newsroom, Stephanie Sherlock
Tel: 778-584-1254
Stephanie.Sherlock@gov.bc.ca
Director, Citizen Engagement, Tanya Twynstra
Tel: 250-507-2163
Tanya.Twynstra@gov.bc.ca
Director, Design Policy, David Wrate
Tel: 250-588-9231
David.Wrate@gov.bc.ca

Office of the Comptroller General
PO Box 9413 Stn. Prov Govt, Victoria, BC V8W 9V1
Fax: 250-356-2001
Comptroller.General@gov.bc.ca
www.fin.gov.bc.ca/ocg.htm
Other Communication: Legal Encumbrance Inquiries, Phone: 250-387-3364
The Office of the Comptroller General oversees the quality & integrity of the government's financial management & control systems.
Acting Comptroller General, Carl Fishcher
Tel: 250-387-6692; *Fax:* 250-356-2001
Comptroller.General@gov.bc.ca
Executive Director, Corporate Compliance & Controls Monitoring Branch & Executive Director, Investigations, Alex Kortum
Tel: 250-216-5145
Alex.Kortum@gov.bc.ca
Acting Executive Director, Financial Reporting & Advisory Services, Diane Lianga
Tel: 778-698-5428; *Fax:* 250-356-8388
Diane.Lianga@gov.bc.ca
Executive Director, Financial Management Branch, Tamara McLeod
Tel: 250-216-6057; *Fax:* 250-356-6164
Tamara.McLeod@gov.bc.ca
Executive Director, Corporate Accounting Services, Steve Rossander
Tel: 250-415-7673; *Fax:* 250-356-6164
Steve.Rossander@gov.bc.ca

Policy & Legislation Division
Tel: 250-356-9911; *Fax:* 250-952-0137
Acting Assistant Deputy Minister, Christina Dawkins
Tel: 778-974-4347; *Fax:* 250-952-0137
Christina.Dawkins@gov.bc.ca
Executive Director, Tax Policy Branch, Richard Purnell
Tel: 778-698-5864; *Fax:* 250-387-9061
Richard.Purnell@gov.bc.ca
Acting Executive Director, Financial & Corporate Sector Policy Branch, Joseph Primeau
Tel: 778-698-5265; *Fax:* 250-387-9093
Joseph.Primeau@gov.bc.ca
Acting Executive Director, Legislative Policy Projects, Strategic Projects, Kari Toovey
Tel: 778-698-5262
Kari.Toovey@gov.bc.ca

Senior Director, Income Tax, Paul Flanagan
Tel: 250-387-9014; *Fax:* 250-387-9061
Paul.Flanagan@gov.bc.ca

Provincial Treasury
PO Box 9414 Stn. Prov Govt, Victoria, BC V8V 9V1
Tel: 250-387-4541; *Fax:* 250-356-3041
www.fin.gov.bc.ca/pt.htm
Assistant Deputy Minister, Jim Hopkins
Tel: 250-387-5729; *Fax:* 250-356-3041
Jim.Hopkins@gov.bc.ca
Chief Security Officer, Risk Mitigation & Government Security,
Paul N. Stanley
Tel: 778-698-5722; *Fax:* 250-356-6222
Paul.Stanley@gov.bc.ca
Executive Director, Risk Management, Linda Irvine
Tel: 778-698-5721; *Fax:* 250-356-6222
Executive Director, Debt Management, Sam Myers
Tel: 250-387-8815; *Fax:* 250-387-3024
Sam.Myers@gov.bc.ca
Executive Director, Financial Management, Vacant; *Fax:*
250-387-3024

Revenue Division
Fax: 250-387-3000
Assistant Deputy Minister, Jordan Goss
Tel: 250-387-0665; *Fax:* 250-387-3000
Executive Director, Public Information & Corporate Services
Branch, Ann Davies
Tel: 778-698-4800
Ann.Davies@gov.bc.ca
Executive Director, Property Taxation Branch, Steven B. Emery
Tel: 778-698-3892; *Fax:* 250-387-2210
Executive Director, Receivables Management Office, Dennis
Forbes
Tel: 250-356-8031; *Fax:* 250-356-5604
Dennis.Forbes@gov.bc.ca
Executive Director, Consumer Taxation Programs Branch,
Michelle Lee
Tel: 778-698-9609
Michelle.Lee@gov.bc.ca
Executive Director, Income Taxation Branch, Paula Harper
Tel: 250-387-3968; *Fax:* 250-356-9243
Executive Director, Revenue Solutions Branch, Steve Pleva
Tel: 778-698-7410; *Fax:* 250-356-1706
Steve.Pleva@gov.bc.ca
Executive Director, Mineral, Oil & Gas Revenue Branch, Andrew
Ritonja
Tel: 778-698-5024; *Fax:* 250-952-0191
Andrew.Ritonja@gov.bc.ca
Executive Director, Tax Appeals & Litigation Branch, Hilary
Vance
Tel: 778-698-5377; *Fax:* 250-387-5883
Hilary.Vance@gov.bc.ca

British Columbia Ministry of Forests, Lands, Natural Resource Operations & Rural Development

PO Box 9049 Stn. Prov Govt, Victoria, BC V8W 9E2
Toll-Free: 800-663-7867
TTY: 800-661-8773
FLNRO.MediaRequests@gov.bc.ca
www.gov.bc.ca/for
Other Communication: Media Phone: 250-356-5261
The Ministry of Forests, Lands, Natural Resource Operations &
Rural Development establishes policies for access to & use of
British Columbia's forests, land, & natural resources. Services
provided enable stewardship & sustainable management of the
province's resources. Responsibilities of the ministry include
Aboriginal consultation; Crown land administration policy;
resource roads & bridges policy; forest, range, & grazing
stewardship policy; pest & disease management policy; water
use planning; timber supply & sales; fish, wildlife, & habitat
management; licensing for hunting, trapping, & angling;
recreation sites & trails; & wildfire management. The ministry
was renamed in 2017 by Premier John Horgan, adding Rural
Development as a priority.

Minister, Hon. Katrine Conroy
Tel: 250-387-6240; *Fax:* 250-387-1040
flnr.minister@gov.bc.ca

Minister of State, Lands & Natural Resource Operations,
Hon. Nathan Cullen
Tel: 250-387-3655; *Fax:* 250-356-4680

Deputy Minister, Richard Manwaring
Tel: 250-952-6500
FLNR.DMO@gov.bc.ca
PO Box 9352 Prov Govt Sta.
Victoria, BC V8W 9M1

Associated Agencies, Boards & Commissions:

• **Forest Practices Board (FPB)**
310, 1675 Douglas St.
PO Box 9905 Prov Govt
Victoria, BC V8W 9R1
Tel: 250-213-4700; *Fax:* 250-213-4725
Toll-free: 800-994-5899
fpboard@gov.bc.ca
www.bcfpb.ca
British Columbia's Forest Practices Board is responsible for
reporting to the government & public about compliance with the
Forest & Range Practices Act. The Board engages in the
following activities: Investigation of public complaints;
undertaking special investigations; auditing forest practices of
government, government enforcement of the Forest & Range
Practices Act, & licence holders on public lands; participation in
appeals; & provision of reports & recommendations.

• **Muskwa-Kechika Advisory Board (M-KAB)**
MKMASupport@shaw.ca
www.muskwa-kechika.com
The Board oversees the preservation of the Muskwa-Kechika
Management Area, & ensures that activities carried out within
the area meet the standards set by the Muskwa-Kechika
Management Plan.

• **Timber Export Advisory Committee**
PO Box 9514 Prov Govt
Victoria, BC V8W 9C2
Tel: 250-387-8916; *Fax:* 250-387-5050

Associate Deputy Minister's Office, Forest Sector
PO Box 9352 Stn. Prov Govt, Victoria, BC V8W 9M1
Executive Director, Corporate Initiatives, Rose Ellis
Tel: 778-974-5875
Rose.Ellis@gov.bc.ca

Rural Development, Lands & Innovation Division
PO Box 9352 Stn. Prov Govt, Victoria, BC V8W 9M1
Tel: 250-387-1057; *Fax:* 250-953-3603
Ensures that forestry laws are being followed in BC's public
forests, & takes action where there is non-compliance. C&E staff
enforce forest management laws & combat forest crimes such
as theft, arson & mischief. Officials conduct more than 16,000
inspections a year to assess compliance with forest laws. Where
there is evidence of a contravention, an investigation is
conducted, which may lead to the issuance of a violation ticket,
penalty or other enforcement action. The most serious forest
crimes are prosecuted through the court system.
Assistant Deputy Minister, Dave Peterson
Tel: 778-974-5838; *Fax:* 250-953-3603
Dave.Peterson@gov.bc.ca
Acting Executive Director, Community Wildfire Recovery Branch,
David Borth
Tel: 250-371-3905
David.Borth@gov.bc.ca
Acting Executive Director, Provincial Disaster Recovery Branch,
Ron Burleson
Tel: 250-280-3981
Ron.Burleson@gov.bc.ca
Executive Director, Regional Economic Operations Branch,
Sarah Fraser
Tel: 778-698-7253
Sarah.Fraser@gov.bc.ca
Executive Director, Crown Land Opportunities, Bonnie
Ruscheinski
Tel: 778-974-5870
Bonnie.Ruscheinski@gov.bc.ca
Director, Lands Branch, Michelle Porter
Tel: 778-974-5845
Michelle.Porter@gov.bc.ca
Director, Innovation, Bioeconomy & Indigenous Opportunities
Branch, James Sandland
Tel: 778-974-2490; *Fax:* 250-953-3603
James.Sandland@gov.bc.ca
Director, Rural Policy & Programs Branch, Claudia Trudeau
Tel: 250-387-8372
Claudia.Trudeau@gov.bc.ca

Timber Operations, Pricing & First Nations Division
PO Box 9352 Stn. Prov Govt, Victoria, BC V8W 9M1
Fax: 250-387-3291
Assistant Deputy Minister, Chris Stagg
Tel: 250-565-4112; *Fax:* 250-387-3291
Chris.Stagg@gov.bc.ca
Executive Director, BC Timber Sales, Mike Falkiner
Tel: 250-387-1236; *Fax:* 250-387-3291
Mike.Falkiner@gov.bc.ca
Executive Director, Timber Operations, Pricing & First Nations
Division, Paul S. Knowles
Tel: 250-387-3162; *Fax:* 250-387-3291
Paul.S.Knowles@gov.bc.ca
Executive Director, Timber Pricing Branch, Steve Kozuki
Tel: 778-765-0938
Steve.Kozuki@gov.bc.ca

Executive Director, Timber Pricing & Softwood Lumber, Vera Sit
Tel: 250-356-1019; *Fax:* 250-387-3291
Vera.Sit@gov.bc.ca

Corporate Services for the Natural Resouces Sector
Assistant Deputy Minister, CSNR & Executive Financial Officer,
Forests, Lands & Natural Resource Operations, Trish Dohan
Tel: 250-953-4745
Trish.Dohan@gov.bc.ca
Assistant Deputy Minister & Executive Financial Officer, MARR,
AGRI, ENV, MEM & NGD, Wes Boyd
Tel: 250-508-5791
Wes.Boyd@gov.bc.ca
Executive Director, People & Workplace Strategies, Suzanne
Spence
Tel: 778-698-4002
Suzanne.Spence@gov.bc.ca

Client Services Branch
Executive Director, Wendy Byrnes
Tel: 250-371-6232
Wendy.Byrnes@gov.bc.ca

Financial Services Branch
Chief Financial Officer & Executive Director, Murray Jacobs
Tel: 778-698-3726
Murray.Jacobs@gov.bc.ca

Information Management
PO Box 9364 Stn. Prov Govt, Victoria, BC V8W 9M3
Chief Information Officer & Executive Director, Denise
Rossander
Tel: 250-952-0944

Integrated Resource Operations Division
PO Box 9352 Stn. Prov Govt, Victoria, BC V8W 9M1
Tel: 250-356-1874; *Fax:* 250-387-3291
Assistant Deputy Minister, Mary Sue Maloughney
Tel: 250-356-1874
MarySue.Maloughney@gov.bc.ca
Executive Director, Integrated Resource Operations Division,
Andrew Calarco
Tel: 778-698-8399
Andrew.Calarco@gov.bc.ca
Acting Executive Director, Mountain Resorts, Jennifer Goad
Tel: 250-356-5411
Jennifer.Goad@gov.bc.ca
Executive Director, BC Wildfire Services, Madeline Maley
Tel: 250-312-3032; *Fax:* 250-387-5685
Madeline.Maley@gov.bc.ca

Office of the Chief Forester
PO Box 9352 Stn. Prov Govt, Victoria, BC V8W 9M1
Fax: 250-387-3291
Assistant Deputy Minister & Chief Forester, Diane Nicholls
Tel: 778-974-5840
Executive Director, Deputy Chief Forester, Shane Berg
Tel: 250-851-6333
Shane.Berg@gov.bc.ca
Executive Director, Strategic Initiatives, Meggin Messenger
Tel: 778-974-5850
Meggin.Messenger@gov.bc.ca
Director, Climate Change & Integrated Planning Branch,
Thomas White
Tel: 778-698-4075
Thomas.White@gov.bc.ca
Director, Forest Improvement & Research Management Branch,
Patrick Martin
Tel: 778-974-2952
Pat.Martin@gov.bc.ca
Director, Forest Analysis & Inventory Branch, Albert Nussbaum
Tel: 778-974-5490
Albert.Nussbaum@gov.bc.ca
Director, Operations, Forest Improvement & Research
Management Branch, Keith Thomas
Tel: 250-387-4895
Keith.Thomas@gov.bc.ca

NRS Transformation Secretariat
PO Box 9352 Stn. Prov Govt, Victoria, BC V8W 9M1
Tel: 250-356-0972; *Fax:* 250-356-2150
Assistant Deputy Minister, Wilf Bangert
Tel: 250-387-6096
Wilf.R.Bangert@gov.bc.ca
Executive Director, Sector Innovation & Integration, Rumon
Carter
Tel: 778-698-5459
Rumon.Carter@gov.bc.ca
Executive Director, Business Transformation, Mike Hykaway
Tel: 778-698-8553
Mike.Hykaway@gov.bc.ca
Executive Director, Transformation Portfolio Office, Adam Taylor
Tel: 250-580-1208
Adam.Taylor@gov.bc.ca

Director, Communications & Engagement, Bonnie Bates Gibbs
Tel: 250-580-6453
Bonnie.BatesGibbs@gov.bc.ca
Director, Change Management Office, Tracy Houser
Tel: 778-698-2363
Tracy.Houser@gov.bc.ca
Director, AMO & Finance, Pete Provan
Tel: 250-516-4115
Pete.Provan@gov.bc.ca

Resource Stewardship Division
PO Box 9352 Stn. Prov Govt, Victoria, BC V8W 9M1
Tel: 250-356-0972; *Fax:* 250-356-2150
Assistant Deputy Minister, Tom Ethier
Tel: 778-974-5804; *Fax:* 250-356-2150
Acting Executive Director, Resource Planning & Assessment
Branch, Brian Bawtinheimer
Tel: 778-974-2497
Brian.Bawtinheimer@gov.bc.ca
Executive Director, Provincial Caribou Recovery Program, Paul
Rasmussen
Tel: 250-608-1077; *Fax:* 250-356-2150
Paul.Rasmussen@gov.bc.ca
Executive Director, Natural Resources, Ward Trotter
Tel: 250-387-3787; *Fax:* 250-356-2150
Ward.Trotter@gov.bc.ca

British Columbia Ministry of Health

PO Box 9639 Stn. Prov Govt, Victoria, BC V8W 9P1
Toll-Free: 800-663-7867
HLTH.Health@gov.bc.ca
www.gov.bc.ca/health
Other Communication: Media Inquiries, Phone: 250-888-0263
The Ministry of Health is responsible for ensuring quality, timely,
& cost effective health services for all citizens of British
Columbia. To guide & enhance British Columbia's health
services, the ministry works with health authorities, agencies,
care providers, & other groups.

Minister, Hon. Adrian Dix
Tel: 250-953-3547; *Fax:* 250-356-9587
hlth.minister@gov.bc.ca

Deputy Minister, Stephen Brown
Tel: 250-952-1590; *Fax:* 250-952-1909
hlth.dmoffice@gov.bc.ca

Associated Agencies, Boards & Commissions:
• **Hospital Appeal Board (HAB)**
747 Fort St., 4th Fl.
PO Box 9425 Prov Govt
Victoria, BC V8W 9V1
Tel: 250-387-3464; *Fax:* 250-356-9923
hab@gov.bc.ca
www.hab.gov.bc.ca
The Hospital Appeal Board of British Columbia is an
independent, quasi-judicial administrative appeal tribunal, which
was created by the Hospital Act. The Board provides an appeal
process for medical practitioners. The role of the Board is to
review hospital board of management decisions concerning
hospital privileges. Board members are appointed by British
Columbia's Minister of Health.

• **Medical Services Commission (MSC)**
PO Box 9652 Prov Govt
Victoria, BC V8W 9P4
Tel: 250-952-3073; *Fax:* 250-952-3133
The Medical Services Commission is a statutory body made up
of nine members. In accordance with the Medicare Protection
Act & Regulations, the Commission acts on behalf of the
Government of British Columbia to manage the Medical Services
Plan. The Commission works to ensure British Columbia
residents have access to medical care, & to manage the
provision & payment of medical services.

• **Mental Health Review Board (MHRB)**
#1270, 605 Robson St.
Vancouver, BC V6B 5J3
Tel: 604-660-2325; *Fax:* 604-660-2403
Toll-free: 833-660-2325
MHRBscheduling@gov.bc.ca
www.mentalhealthreviewboard.gov.bc.ca

Clinical Leadership
Fax: 250-952-1909
Associate Deputy Minister, David Byres
Tel: 250-952-1615
David.Byres@gov.bc.ca
Assistant Deputy Minister, Specialized Services Division, Teri
Collins
Tel: 250-952-2569
Assistant Deputy Minister, Primary Care Division, Ted Patterson
Tel: 250-952-3465

Assistant Deputy Minister, Provincial, Hospital & Laboratory
Health Services Division, Ian Rongve
Tel: 250-953-4504
Executive Director, Corporate Issues & Client Relations, Thomas
Guerrero
Tel: 250-952-2419
Executive Lead, Population & Public Health, Lorie Hrycuik
Tel: 250-952-1731
Senior Analyst, Cannabis Policy, Kathleen Perkin
Tel: 778-974-4141

Pharmaceutical Services Division
Fax: 250-952-1909
Assistant Deputy Minister, Mitch Moneo
Tel: 250-952-1464
Executive Director, PharmaCare Information, Policy &
Evaluation, John Capelli
Tel: 250-952-2951
Executive Director, Business Management, Supplier Relations &
Systems, Kelly Uyeno
Tel: 778-572-2122

Corporate Services
Fax: 250-952-1909
Associate Deputy Minister, Peter Pokorny
Tel: 778-698-8046
Executive Director, Nursing Policy Secretariat, Joanne Maclaran
Tel: 778-698-5063
Joanne.Maclaren@gov.bc.ca
Chief Nurse & Professional Practice Officer, Nursing Policy
Secretariat, Natasha Prodan-Bhalla
Tel: 250-413-7507

Health Sector IM/IT
Fax: 250-952-1909
Assistant Deputy Minister, Corrie Barclay
Tel: 250-419-8747
Chief Medical Information Officer, Provincial Digital Health
Initiative, Dr. Douglas Kingsford
Tel: 250-718-5285
Chief Information Officer, Health IT Strategy, Paul Shrimpton
Tel: 778-974-2675
Executive Director, IT Services Branch, Jeff Aitken
Tel: 250-952-1170
Jeff.Aitken@gov.bc.ca
Executive Director, Vendor Management Office, Guy Cookson
Tel: 778-698-9143
Executive Director, Business Services & Strategic Priorities,
Brad Glazer
Tel: 778-698-9484
Executive Director, Health Benefits Digital Office, Daisy Jassar
Tel: 778-698-4753
Executive Director, Health Information Privacy, Security &
Legislation Branch, Alison Pearce
Tel: 250-415-1061
Executive Director, HSIMIT, Leanne Thain
Tel: 778-835-8993
Executive Director, Digital Health Strategic Initiatives, Zen
Tharani
Tel: 250-882-0739

Health Sector Information, Analysis & Reporting
Fax: 250-952-1909
Assistant Deputy Minister, Martin Wright
Tel: 778-698-5109
Chief Data Steward & Executive Director, Data Manadement &
Stewardship, Andrew Elderfield
Tel: 250-952-2306
Executive Director, Integrated Analytics, Primary & Acute Care &
Sector Workforce, Eric Larson
Tel: 250-952-1242
Executive Director, Performance, Partnerships & Methodologies
Branch, Heather Richards
Tel: 250-952-2014
Executive Director, Business Services & Transformation,
Michelle Perren
Tel: 778-698-5075
Acting Executive Director, British Columbia Vital Statistics
Agency, Jack Shewchuk
Tel: 250-952-9039
Executive Director, Integrated Analytics - Community & Cross
Sector, Christine Voggenreiter
Tel: 250-952-1450

Finance & Corporate Services
Tel: 250-952-2067; *Fax:* 250-952-1573
Assistant Deputy Minister & EFO, Philip Twyford
Tel: 250-952-2067
Chief Financial Officer & Executive Director, Finance & Decision
Support, Dave Boychuk
Tel: 778-698-3136
Executive Director, Regional Grants - Decision Support, Gordon
Cross
Tel: 250-952-1120

Executive Director, Capital Services, Kirk Eaton
Tel: 778-698-0411
Executive Director, Business Financial Transformation, Kerri
Harrison
Tel: 250-952-2687
Executive Director, Audit & Investigations Branch, Marie
Thelisma
Tel: 250-952-1665

Office of the Provincial Health Officer
PO Box 9648 Stn. Prov Govt, Victoria, BC V8W 9P4
Tel: 250-952-1330; *Fax:* 250-952-1570
Provincial Health Officer, Dr. Bonnie Henry
Tel: 250-952-1330
Acting Deputy Provincial Health Officer, Dr. Brian Emerson
Tel: 250-952-1701
Provincial Drinking Water Officer, Joanne Edwards
Tel: 250-952-1572

Office of the Seniors Advocate
PO Box 9651 Stn. Prov Govt, Victoria, BC V8W 9P4
Tel: 250-952-3034
Toll-Free: 877-952-3181
info@seniorsadvocatebc.ca
www.seniorsadvocatebc.ca
Seniors Advocate, Isobel Mackenzie
Tel: 778-698-8143
Executive Director, Bruce Ronayne
Tel: 250-952-2998
Chief Operating Officer, Doreh Mohsenzadeh
Tel: 236-478-2597

British Columbia Hydro

333 Dunsmuir St., PO Box 8910 Vancouver, BC V6B 4N1
Tel: 604-224-9376
Toll-Free: 800-224-9376
www.bchydro.com
twitter.com/bchydro
www.facebook.com/bchydro
www.youtube.com/bchydro
The Clean Energy Act consolidated BC Hydro & the BC
Transmission Corporation in 2010. BC Hydro is a crown
corporation that reports to the British Columbia Ministry of
Energy & Mines. The mission of the corporation is the delivery of
energy, in an envrionmentally & socially responsible manner, to
meet the province's demand for electricity. Four million
customers are provided with power via a network of over 78,000
km of transmission & distribution lines, as well as 31
hydroelectric facilities & two thermal generating plants. In 2015,
the corporation reported that 98% of the electricity generated
came from clean & renewable sources.
BC Hydro also has offices in Burnaby, Vernon & Prince George.

Chair, Kenneth G. Peterson
Tel: 604-623-4234

President, Chris O'Riley
Tel: 604-623-4577

President & CEO, Powerex, Teresa Conway
Tel: 604-891-5065

**Executive Vice-President, Finance & Business Services &
Chief Financial Officer,** Cheryl Yaremko
Tel: 604-623-4110

General Counsel, Ray Aldeguer

**Senior Vice-President, Corporate Affairs & Chief Human
Resources Officer,** Janet Fraser

**Senior Vice-President, Training, Development &
Generation,** Vacant

**Senior Vice-President, Safety, Security & Emergency
Management,** Hugo Shaw

Associated Agencies, Boards & Commissions:
• **Powerex Corp.**
#1300, 666 Burrard St.
Vancouver, BC V6C 2X8
Tel: 604-891-5000; *Fax:* 604-891-6060
Toll-free: 800-220-4907
www2.powerex.com
A wholly-owned subsidiary of BC Hydro, Powerex Corp. markets
wholesale energy products & services to utilities, power pools,
industrials, & power marketers in North America, particularly
western Canada, the western United States.

• Powertech Labs Inc.
12388 - 88 Ave.
Surrey, BC V8W 7R7
Tel: 604-590-7500; *Fax:* 604-590-6611
www.powertechlabs.com
A wholly owned subsidiary of BC Hydro, Powertech Labs offers environmental, mechanical, electrical, metallurgical, civil, chemical, gas technologies, & structural engineering to deal with technical problems with power equipment & systems.

British Columbia Ministry of Indigenous Relations & Reconciliation

2957 Jutland Rd., PO Box 9100 Stn. Prov Govt, Victoria, BC V8W 9B1

Tel: 250-387-6121
Toll-Free: 800-663-7867
www.gov.bc.ca/irr
Other Communication: Vancouver Phone: 604-660-2421
The Ministry of Indigenous Relations & Reconciliation (formerly Aboriginal Relations & Reconciliation) works to achieve the following goals: reconciliation with Indigenous peoples; negotiation of lasting agreements; strengthening relationships with the Métis Nation; development of partnerships with Indigenous people, organizations, & communities; support of capacity building in Indigenous communities; provision of advice on policy related to Indigenous peoples; & revitalization of Indigenous language & culture.

Minister, Hon. Murray Rankin
Tel: 250-953-4844; *Fax:* 250-953-4896
IRR.Minister@gov.bc.ca

Deputy Minister, Doug Caul
Tel: 778-974-2080; *Fax:* 250-387-6073
Doug.Caul@gov.bc.ca
PO Box 9100 Prov Govt Sta.
Victoria, BC V8W 9B1

Assistant Deputy Minister, Reconciliation Transformation & Strategies Division, Jessica Wood
Tel: 250-356-0226
Jessica.D.Wood@gov.bc.ca
PO Box 9100 Prov Govt Sta.
Victoria, BC V8W 9B1

Associated Agencies, Boards & Commissions:
• British Columbia Treaty Commission (BCTC)
#700, 1111 Melville St.
Vancouver, BC V6E 3V6
Tel: 604-482-9200; *Fax:* 604-482-9222
Toll-free: 855-482-9200
info@bctreaty.net
www.bctreaty.net
The independent & neutral body facilitates treaty negotiations among the governments of Canada, British Columbia, & First Nations in BC.

• Native Economic Development Advisory Board
PO Box 9100 Prov Govt
Victoria, BC V8W 9B1
Tel: 250-387-2536
www.gov.bc.ca/arr/economic/fcf/nedab.html
Supporting sustainable Aboriginal economic development throughout British Columbia is the role of the Native Economic Development Advisory Board.

Fiscal Negotiations Team
Fax: 250-387-5213
Chief Negotiator, Rob Draeseke
Tel: 778-974-2105
Rob.Draeseke@gov.bc.ca
Director, Cost Sharing Arrangements, Greg Brunette
Tel: 778-974-2109; *Fax:* 250-387-6594
Greg.Brunette@gov.bc.ca
Director, Cost-sharing & Financial Mandates, Elisabeth Ellis
Tel: 778-974-2109; *Fax:* 250-387-6594
Elisabeth.Ellis@gov.bc.ca
Director, Fiscal Arrangements & Climate Change, Michael Matsubuchi
Tel: 250-415-8863; *Fax:* 250-387-6594
Michael.Matsubuchi@gov.bc.ca

Negotiations & Regional Operations Division
Fax: 250-387-6073
Assistant Deputy Minister, Douglas S. Scott
Tel: 250-356-1086
Douglas.S.Scott@gov.bc.ca
Chief Negotiator, Trish Balcaen
Tel: 250-356-1645; *Fax:* 250-387-6073
Trish.Balcaen@gov.bc.ca
Chief Negotiator, South Area, Alexandra Banford
Tel: 250-387-7796; *Fax:* 250-387-6073
Alexandra.Banford@gov.bc.ca

Chief Negotiator, Heinz Dyck
Tel: 250-356-7971; *Fax:* 250-387-6073
Heinz.Dyck@gov.bc.ca
Chief Negotiator, Mark Lofthouse
Tel: 250-387-0024; *Fax:* 250-387-0887
Mark.Lofthouse@gov.bc.ca
Other Communications: Cell Phone: 250-480-8899
Chief Negotiator, Tom McCarthy
Tel: 250-847-1032; *Fax:* 250-387-6073
Tom.McCarthy@gov.bc.ca

Strategic Partnerships & Initiatives Division
Fax: 250-387-6073
Assistant Deputy Minister, Laurel Nash
Tel: 250-953-4004
Laurel.Nash@gov.bc.ca
Negotiator & Director, Critical Incidents & Emergency Management, Tena Gilmore
Tel: 250-356-9693
Tena.Gilmore@gov.bc.ca
Executive Director, Implementation & Land Services Branch, Brendan McCombs
Tel: 778-698-8382
Brendan.McCombs@gov.bc.ca
Executive Director, LNG & Major Projects, Major Projects & Cross-Gov't Initiatives Branch, Giovanni Puggioni
Tel: 778-974-2143
Giovanni.Puggioni@gov.bc.ca

Office of the Information & Privacy Commissioner for British Columbia (OIPC)

947 Fort St., 4th Fl., PO Box 9038 Stn. Prov Govt, Victoria, BC V8W 9A4

Tel: 250-387-5629; *Fax:* 250-387-1696
Toll-Free: 800-663-7867
info@oipc.bc.ca
www.oipc.bc.ca
Other Communication: Vancouver Phone: 604-660-2421
twitter.com/BCInfoPrivacy
Operating independently from the government, the Office of the Information & Privacy Commissioner is responsible for monitoring & enforcing the following acts in British Columbia: Freedom of Information & Protection of Privacy Act; & Personal Information Protection Act.

Commissioner, Michael McEvoy
Note: On March 22, 2016, Elizabeth Denham announced she would be stepping down as Information & Privacy Commissioner once her term ended on July 6, 2016.

Deputy Commissioner, Jay Fedorak

Registrar of Inquiries, Cindy Hamilton
Tel: 250-387-5629

Insurance Corporation of British Columbia (ICBC)

151 West Esplanade, North Vancouver, BC V7M 3H9
Tel: 604-661-2800
Toll-Free: 800-663-3051
www.icbc.com
Other Communication: New Claims, Lower Mainland Phone: 604-520-8222; Elsewhere in BC, Toll Free: 800-910-4222; TIPS Lower Mainland, Phone: 604-661-6844; TIPS BC Line: 800-661-6844
twitter.com/icbc
www.facebook.com/theICBC
www.linkedin.com/company/icbc
www.youtube.com/icbc
A provincial Crown corporation, The Insurance Corporation of British Columbia was established in 1973. The main responsibilities of the Insurance Corporation of British Columbia are as follows: Provision of universal auto insurance to motorists in British Columbia; Registration & licensing of vehicles; & Driver licensing.

Chair, Joy MacPhail

President & Chief Executive Officer, Mark Blucher

Chief Actuary & Chief Financial Officer, Bill Carpenter

Chief Information & Technology Officer, Gary Eastwood

Chief Investment Officer, Alison Gould

British Columbia Ministry of Jobs, Economic Recovery & Innovation

PO Box 9071 Stn. Prov Govt, Victoria, BC V8W 9T2
Tel: 250-356-2771; *Fax:* 250-953-0927
www.gov.bc.ca/jti
Other Communication: Media Relations, Phone: 250-952-1889
The former Ministry of Jobs, Tourism, & Skills Training was reorganized into the Ministry of Jobs, Trade & Technology in 2017, after John Horgan became Premier. In 2020, it was renamed to the Ministry of Jobs, Economic Recovery & Innovation.

Minister, Hon. Ravi Kahlon
Tel: 250-356-2771; *Fax:* 250-356-3000
JEDC.Minister@gov.bc.ca

Minister of State, Trade, Hon. George Chow
Tel: 250-356-9139
TRD.Minister@gov.bc.ca

Deputy Minister, Bobbi Plecas
Tel: 250-952-0102; *Fax:* 250-356-1195
Bobbi.Plecas@gov.bc.ca

Director, Executive Operations, Tara Cameron
Tel: 778-698-4842
Tara.Cameron@gov.bc.ca

Associated Agencies, Boards & Commissions:
• BC Immigrant Investment Fund Ltd. & BC Renaissance Capital Fund Ltd. (BCIIF)
#301, 865 Hornby St.
Vancouver, BC V6Z 2G3
Fax: 250-952-0371
bciif.ca
BCIIF is wholly owned by the Province of British Columbia & was incorporated in 2000 under the Company Act of British Columbia. It utilizes funds provided under the federal Immigrant Investor Program (IIP) & has an investment portfolio structured into the following three asset classes: Money Market & Central Depository Investments; Infrastructure Investments; & Venture Capital Investments.

• Forestry Innovation Investment Ltd. (FII)
#1200, 1130 West Pender St.
Vancouver, BC V6E 4A4
Tel: 604-685-7507; *Fax:* 604-685-5373
info@bcfii.ca
www.bcfii.ca
British Columbia's Forestry Innovation Investment strives to support a prosperous & environmentally sustainable forest economy in the province. The role of the organization includes the following activities: Promotion of British Columbia's forest practices & wood products to international markets; Working in partnership with the forestry sector, the Government of British Columbia, & the Government of Canada; & Assisting the forestry sector with issues such as Mountain Pine Beetle outbreak.

• Multicultural Advisory Council of BC (MAC)
Multiculturalism & Inclusive Communities Office
605 Robson St., 5th Fl.
Vancouver, BC V6B 5J3
Tel: 604-775-0643; *Fax:* 604-775-0670
multiculturalism@gov.bc.ca
Other Communication: Alternate Phone: 604-660-5140
Members of the Multicultural Advisory Council advise the minister responsible for multiculturalism about issues related to multiculturalism & anti-racism. The Multiculturalism Act of British Columbia guides the council.

• British Columbia Labour Relations Board
Oceanic Plaza
#600, 1066 West Hastings St.
Vancouver, BC V6E 3X1
Tel: 604-660-1300; *Fax:* 604-660-1892
information@lrb.bc.ca
www.lrb.bc.ca
The British Columbia Labour Relations Board is an independent, administrative tribunal. The Board is responsible for mediating & adjudicating employment & labour relations matters related to unionized workplaces.

• Employment Standards Tribunal
Oceanic Plaza
#650, 1066 West Hastings St.
Vancouver, BC V6E 3X1
Tel: 604-775-3512; *Fax:* 604-775-3372
registrar@bcest.bc.ca
www.bcest.bc.ca
Established under the Employment Standards Act, the Employment Standards Tribunal operates as an administrative tribunal. The responsibility of the Tribunal is to provide an independent appeal of Determinations made by the Director of Employment Standards.

• **Industry Training Authority (ITA)**
8100 Granville Ave., 8th Fl.
Richmond, BC V6Y 3T6
Tel: 778-328-8700; *Fax:* 778-328-8701
Toll-free: 866-660-6011
customerservice@itabc.ca
www.itabc.ca
British Columbia's Industry Training Authority is a provincial
government agency which oversees the province's training &
apprenticeship system. The ITA works with industry, employers,
training providers, trainees, & apprentices.

• **Northern Development Initiative Trust**
#301, 1268 Fifth Ave.
Prince George, BC V2L 3L2
Tel: 250-561-2525; *Fax:* 250-561-2563
info@northerndevelopment.bc.ca
northerndevelopment.bc.ca
The Northern Trust consists of a Board of Directors which makes
funding decisions for programs of the Trust. According to
provincial legislation, investments can be made in the following
areas: agriculture, economic development, energy, forestry,
mining, Olympic opportunities; pine beetle recovery, small
business, tourism, & transportation.

• **Southern Interior Development Initiative Trust**
#103, 2802 - 30th St.
Vernon, BC V1T 8G7
Tel: 250-545-6829; *Fax:* 250-545-6896
admin@sidit-bc.ca
www.sidit-bc.ca
The government of British Columbia enacted legislation in 2006
to establish the Southern Interior Development Initiative Trust.
The mission of the Trust is to grow & diversify the economy of
the Southern Interior of British Columbia through investments in
economic development projects that will benefit the area.

• **Workers' Compensation Appeal Tribunal (WCAT)**
#150, 4600 Jacombs Rd.
Richmond, BC V6V 3B1
Tel: 604-664-7800; *Fax:* 604-664-7898
Toll-free: 800-663-2782
www.wcat.bc.ca
The Workers' Compensation Appeal Tribunal of British Columbia
is an independent appeal tribunal, which was established by the
Workers Compensation Amendment Act (No. 2), 2002. The
Tribunal decides appeals from workers & employers from
decisions of the Workers' Compensation Board (WorkSafeBC).

International Trade Division
Assistant Deputy Minister, Tracy Campbell
Tel: 778-698-7606
Tracy.Campbell@gov.bc.ca
Executive Director, Trade Policy & Negotiations, Steve Anderson
Tel: 778-698-8769
Executive Director, International Strategy & Research Branch,
David Collier
Tel: 604-218-9036
David.Collier@gov.bc.ca
Executive Director, Trade Readiness & Services, John
McDonald
Tel: 604-775-2202
John.McDonald@gov.bc.ca
Executive Director, Investor Services, Leslie Teramoto
Tel: 604-775-2201
Leslie.Teramoto@gov.bc.ca
Executive Director, Strategy, Business Intelligence & Marketing,
Nichola Wade
Tel: 778-698-8781
Nichola.Wade@gov.bc.ca

International Markets
Fax: 604-775-2197
Executive Director, Henry Han
Tel: 604-660-5888
Henry.Han@gov.bc.ca

International Markets - East Asia
Fax: 604-775-2197
Executive Director, Paul Irwin
Tel: 604-660-5906
Paul.Irwin@gov.bc.ca

Investment, Innovation & Technology Division
Assistant Deputy Minister, Silas Brownsey
Tel: 778-974-6148
Silas.Brownsey@gov.bc.ca
Innovation Commissioner, Alan Winter
Tel: 778-698-1503
Alan.Winter@gov.bc.ca
Executive Director, Strategic Initiatives, Jane Burnes
Tel: 250-889-1054
Jane.Burnes@gov.bc.ca
Acting Executive Director, Technology & Innovation, Christine
Fast

Tel: 778-698-9900
Christine.Fast@gov.bc.ca
Executive Director, Design, Coordination & Outreach, Greg
Goodwin
Tel: 778-698-1619
Greg.Goodwin@gov.bc.ca

Management Services Division
PO Box 9842 Stn. Prov Govt, Victoria, BC V8W 9T2
Tel: 250-387-8705; *Fax:* 250-387-7973
Assistant Deputy Minister, Tracy Campbell
Tel: 250-387-8705
Tracy.Campbell@gov.bc.ca
Acting Chief Information Officer & Executive Director,
Information Systems Branch, Nainesh Agarwal
Tel: 250-387-8034
Nainesh.Agarwal@gov.bc.ca
Executive Director, Corporate Planning & Priorities Branch,
Danine Leduc
Tel: 778-698-3563
Danine.Leduc@gov.bc.ca
Executive Director, Financial Initiatives, Karyn Scott
Tel: 250-387-4056
Karyn.Scott@gov.bc.ca
Executive Director, Strategic Human Resources Branch,
Roberta Turton
Tel: 778-698-4955
Roberta.Turton@gov.bc.ca

Small Business, Jobs & Workforce Division
PO Box 9854 Stn. Prov Govt, Victoria, BC V8W 9T5
Tel: 250-387-0661; *Fax:* 250-952-0113
Assistant Deputy Minister, Christine Little
Tel: 778-698-1708
Christine.Little@gov.bc.ca
Executive Director, Sector & Regulatory Competitiveness,
Francois Bertrand
Tel: 778-698-1627
Francois.Bertrand@gov.bc.ca
Executive Director, Economic Policy & Strategic Initiatives,
Angelo Cocco
Tel: 250-952-0612
Angelo.Cocco@gov.bc.ca
Executive Director, Small Business, Jaclyn Hunter
Tel: 778-698-1662
Jaclynn.Hunter@gov.bc.ca
Executive Director, BC Stats, Elizabeth Vickery
Tel: 250-217-5055
Elizabeth.Vickery@gov.bc.ca

British Columbia Ministry of Labour

PO Box 9064 Stn. Prov Govt, Victoria, BC V8W 9K4
Tel: 250-953-0910; *Fax:* 250-953-0928
www.gov.bc.ca/LBR
The Ministry of Labour was created in 2017, after John Horgan
became Premier.

Minister, Hon. Harry Bains
Tel: 250-953-0910; *Fax:* 250-387-4680
LBR.Minister@gov.bc.ca

Deputy Minister, Trevor Hughes
Tel: 778-698-1614; *Fax:* 250-356-5186
LBR.Deputy@gov.bc.ca

Executive Director, Labour Policy & Legislation, John
Blakely
Tel: 778-974-2173
John.Blakely@gov.bc.ca

Executive Director, Employers' Advisers Office, Dave
Haralds
Tel: 604-713-0301
Dave.Haralds@eao-bc.org
www.gov.bc.ca/employersadvisers

Office of the Merit Commissioner

**#502, 947 Fort St., PO Box 9037 Stn. Prov Govt, Victoria, BC
V8W 9A3**
Tel: 250-953-4208; *Fax:* 250-953-4160
merit@meritcomm.bc.ca
www.meritcomm.bc.ca
The Merit Commissioner is an independent officer reporting
directly to the Legislative Assembly of British Columbia. The
Commissioner is reponsible for upholding the principle of merit
as outlined in The Public Service Act, which governs the hiring of
public servants based on their qualifications, rather than their
political beliefs.

Merit Commissioner, Maureen Baird, Q.C.

Director, Audit & Review, Catherine Arber
Tel: 250-953-4113
carber@meritcomm.bc.ca

British Columbia Ministry of Mental Health & Addictions

PO Box 9644 Stn. Prov Govt, Victoria, BC V8W 9P1
Tel: 604-660-2421
Toll-Free: 800-663-7867
HLTH.Health@gov.bc.ca
Other Communication: Victoria, Phone: 250-387-6121
The Ministry of Mental Health & Addictions was created in 2017
by Premier John Horgan.

Minister, Hon. Sheila Malcolmson
Tel: 250-952-7623; *Fax:* 250-387-4680
mh.minister@gov.bc.ca

Deputy Minister, Christine Massey
Tel: 250-880-5114; *Fax:* 250-952-1052

**Executive Lead, Corporate Services & Financial
Accountability,** Dara Landry
Tel: 778-698-8566
Dara.Landry@gov.bc.ca

Strategic Policy & Planning
Fax: 250-952-1052
Associate Deputy Minister, Nick Grant
Tel: 250-952-1876
Executive Director, Strategic Planning, Lori MacKenzie
Tel: 778-698-7593
Lori.MacKenzie@gov.bc.ca
Senior Director, Indigenous Partnerships & Wellness, Matthew
Kinch
Tel: 778-974-4869
Matthew.Kinch@gov.bc.ca

Strategic Priorities & Initiatives
Tel: 250-882-9765; *Fax:* 250-952-1052
The Ministry of Mental Health & Addictions was created in 2017
by Premier John Horgan.
Assistant Deputy Minister, Taryn Walsh
Tel: 778-698-3096
Executive Director, Substance Use & Strategic Initiatives, Ally
Butler
Tel: 778-366-5962
Ally.Butler@gov.bc.ca
Executive Director, OERC, Justine Patterson
Tel: 778-572-2315
Justine.Patterson@gov.bc.ca
Senior Director, Partnerships & Engagement, Regan Hansen
Tel: 250-952-2781
Regan.Hansen@gov.bc.ca

British Columbia Ministry of Municipal Affairs

PO Box 9056 Stn. Prov Govt, Victoria, BC V8W 9E2
Tel: 250-387-2283; *Fax:* 250-387-4312
www.gov.bc.ca/cscd
The Ministry of Municipal Affairs was created in 2017 by Premier
John Horgan.

Minister, Hon. Josie Osborne
Tel: 250-387-2283; *Fax:* 250-387-4312
mah.minister@gov.bc.ca

Deputy Minister, Okenge Yuma Morisho
Tel: 250-387-0752; *Fax:* 250-387-7973
Okenge.YumaMorisho@gov.bc.ca
PO Box 9490 Prov Govt Sta.
Victoria, BC V8W 9N7

Associated Agencies, Boards & Commissions:
• **British Columbia Assessment Authority (BCAA)**
#400, 3450 Uptown Blvd.
Victoria, BC V8Z 0B9
Tel: 604-739-8588; *Fax:* 855-995-6209
Toll-free: 866-825-8322
www.bcassessment.ca
The British Columbia Assessment Authority is an independent,
provincial Crown corporation. Governed by a Board of Directors,
the role of BC Assessment is the production of annual property
assessments for each property owner in British Columbia. Area
offices are located across the province.

• British Columbia Housing Management Commission (BC Housing)
#1701, 4555 Kingsway
Burnaby, BC V5H 4V8
Tel: 604-433-1711; Fax: 604-439-4722
webeditor@bchousing.org
bchousing.org
Other Communication: tenantinquiries@bchousing.org;
media@bchousing.org; FOIPP@bchousing.org;
purchasing@bchousing.org; imt@bchousing.org;
hpo@hpo.bc.ca
BC Housing develops, manages & administers subsidized
housing across British Columbia.

• British Columbia Safety Authority
#200, 505 - 6th St.
New Westminster, BC V3L 0E1
Toll-free: 866-566-7233
info@safetyauthority.ca
safetyauthority.ca
Other Communication: Toll-Free Fax: 888-660-3508; Media
Contact, Phone: 778-396-2164; Email:
media@safetyauthority.ca
Oversees the safe installation & operation of technical systems
& equipment.

• Building Code Appeal Board (BCAB)
c/o Building & Safety Standards Branch
PO Box 9844 Prov Govt
Victoria, BC V8W 1A4
Tel: 250-387-3133; Fax: 250-387-8164
Building.Safety@gov.bc.ca
www.housing.gov.bc.ca/bcab

• Property Assessment Appeal Board (PAAB)
#10, 10551 Shellbridge Way
Richmond, BC V6X 2W9
Tel: 604-775-1740; Fax: 604-775-1742
Toll-free: 888-775-1740
office@paab.bc.ca
www.assessmentappeal.bc.ca
Other Communication: Toll-Free Fax: 888-775-1742
The Board assists with assessment appeals for all types of
properties, dealing with issues such as market value,
classification, and qualification for tax exemption.

• Safety Standards Appeal Board
614 Humboldt St., 4th Fl.
PO Box 9844 Prov Govt
Victoria, BC V8W 9T2
Tel: 250-387-4021; Fax: 250-356-6645
www.housing.gov.bc.ca/SSAB
Resolves appeals from decisions made under the Safety
Standards Act & the Homeowner Protection Act.

Community & Legislative Services Division
PO Box 9490 Stn. Prov Govt, Victoria, BC V8W 9N7
Fax: 250-387-7973
Assistant Deputy Minister, David Curtis
Tel: 778-698-5845
David.Curtis@gov.bc.ca
Executive Director, Community Policy & Legislation, Jodi Dong
Tel: 778-698-3399
Jodi.Dong@gov.bc.ca
Executive Director, Property Assessment Services, Rob Fraser
Tel: 778-698-3560
Rob.Fraser@gov.bc.ca
Acting Executive Director, Community Gaming Grants, David E.
Pyatt
Tel: 778-698-3345
David.Pyatt@gov.bc.ca

Office of Housing & Construction Standards
PO Box 9844 Stn. Prov Govt, Victoria, BC V8W 9T2
Assistant Deputy Minister, Gregory Steves
Tel: 250-356-2115
Executive Director, Building & Safety Standards Branch, Andrew
Pape-Salmon
Tel: 250-812-1933; Fax: 250-356-9377
Andrew.PapeSalmon@gov.bc.ca

Local Government
PO Box 9490 Stn. Prov Govt, Victoria, BC V8W 9N7
Tel: 250-356-6575; Fax: 250-387-7973
www.cd.gov.bc.ca/lgd
Working with a great range of partners, the Local Government
Department develops communities that can manage change &
offer affordable services to residents of British Columbia. The
Department's programs include the following: developing local
government legislation; facilitating partnerships with local
governments & First Nations; fostering positive
inter-governmental relations to facilitate community & regional
planning; offering financial support; & providing information &
advice.

Assistant Deputy Minister, Tara Faganello
Tel: 250-356-6575; Fax: 250-387-7973
Tara.Faganello@gov.bc.ca
Executive Director, Planning & Land Use Management, Jessica
Brooks
Tel: 778-698-3483
Jessica.Brooks@gov.bc.ca
800 Johnson St., 6th Fl.
PO Box 9847 Prov Govt Sta.
Victoria, BC V8W 9T2
Executive Director, Local Government Infrastructure & Finance,
Liam Edwards
Tel: 778-698-3230; Fax: 250-387-7972
Liam.Edwards@gov.bc.ca
800 Johnson St., 4th Fl.
PO Box 9838 Prov Govt Sta.
Victoria, BC V8W 9T1
Executive Director, Governance & Structure, Nicola Marotz
Tel: 778-698-3221; Fax: 250-387-7972
Nicola.Marotz@gov.bc.ca
800 Johnson St., 6th Fl.
PO Box 9847 Prov Govt Sta.
Victoria, BC V8W 9T2

Office of the Ombudsperson

947 Fort St., 2nd Fl., PO Box 9039 Stn. Prov Govt, Victoria,
BC V8W 9A5
Tel: 250-387-5855; Fax: 250-387-0198
Toll-Free: 800-567-3247
www.ombudsman.bc.ca
www.youtube.com/user/bcombudsperson
Complaints about the services of public agencies are submitted
to the Office of the Ombudsperson. The responsibility of the
Office of the Ombudsperson is to investigate impartially these
inquiries about the practices of public agencies within its
jurisdiction. The Office determines if public agencies acted fairly
in accordance with relevant legislation & policies.

Ombudsperson, Jay Chalke
Tel: 250-356-1559

Deputy Ombudsperson, David Paradiso
Tel: 250-387-0189

Chief Financial Officer, Leoni Gingras
Tel: 250-356-0568

Executive Director, Investigations, Bruce Clarke
Tel: 250-356-5723

Executive Director, Corporate Services, Dave Van Swieten
Tel: 250-387-4896

British Columbia Pavilion Corporation (PavCo)

#200, 999 Canada Place, Vancouver, BC V6C 3C1
Tel: 604-482-2200; Fax: 604-681-9017
info@bcpavco.com
www.bcpavco.com
The BC Pavilion Corporation is a provincial crown corporation of
British Columbia's Ministry of Transportation & Infrastructure.
The corporation's divisions include Corporate Office, BC Place,
& the Vancouver Convention Centre.

Chair, Stuart McLaughlin

President & Chief Executive Officer, Ken Cretney
Tel: 604-647-7201

Chief Finance Officer, Rehana Din
Tel: 604-484-5226

B.C. Place
777 Pacific Blvd., Vancouver, BC V6B 4Y8
Tel: 604-669-2300; Fax: 604-661-3412
stadium@bcpavco.com
bcplace.com
Other Communication: Sales & Partnerships, Phone:
604-661-3634
twitter.com/bcplace
www.facebook.com/BCPlaceStadium
instagram.com/bcplacestadium
Director, Business Management Division, Graham Ramsay
Tel: 604-661-3403

Vancouver Convention Centre
1055 Canada Pl., Vancouver, BC V6C 0C3
Tel: 604-689-8232; Fax: 604-647-7232
Toll-Free: 866-785-8232
info@vancouverconventioncentre.com
www.vancouverconventioncentre.com
Secondary Address: 999 Canada Pl.
Vancouver Convention Centre East
Vancouver, BC V6C 3C1
President & Chief Executive Officer, Vacant
General Manager, Craig Lehto
Tel: 604-647-7204
Vice-President, Sales & Marketing, Claire Smith
Tel: 604-647-7354

British Columbia Pension Corporation

2995 Jutland Rd., PO Box 9460 Victoria, BC V8W 9V8
Tel: 250-387-1014; Fax: 250-953-0429
Toll-Free: 800-663-8823
PensionCorp@pensionsbc.ca
www.pensionsbc.ca
Other Communication: College Pension Plan: 888-440-0111;
Municipal Pension Plan: 800-668-6335; Public Service Pension
Plan: 800-665-3554; Teachers' Pension Plan: 800-665-6770
Established under the Public Sector Pension Plans Act, the
Pension Corporation administers the College, Municipal, Public
Service, Teachers' & WorkSafeBC pension plans.

Chair, Weldon Cowan

Chief Executive Officer, Laura Nashman
Tel: 778-698-6456

**Chief Financial Officer & Vice-President, Corporate
Services,** Trevor Fedyna

Vice-President, Transformation & Information Services,
Dave Marecek

Vice-President, Member Experience, Kevin Olinek

Vice-President, Pension Operations, Lanny Smith

Vice-President, Board Services, Aaron Walker-Duncan

British Columbia Ministry of Public Safety & Solicitor General

PO Box 9290 Stn. Prov Govt, Victoria, BC V8W 9J7
Tel: 250-356-0149; Fax: 250-387-6224
Toll-Free: 800-663-7867
PSSG.Correspondence@gov.bc.ca
Other Communication: URL:
www2.gov.bc.ca/gov/content/governments/organizational-structu
re/ministries-organizations/ministries/public-safety-solicitor-gener
al

The Ministry of Public Safety & Solicitor General was
re-established by Premier Christy Clark in December 2015, &
works jointly with the Ministry of Justice to oversee the
administration of justice, protection of rights & public safety in
the province.

Minister & Solicitor General, Hon. Mike Farnworth
Tel: 250-356-2178; Fax: 250-356-2965
PSSG.Minister@gov.bc.ca

Deputy Solicitor General, Mark Sieben
Tel: 250-356-0149; Fax: 250-387-6224

Deputy Minister, Emergency Management B.C., Tara
Richards
Tel: 778-974-5190
Emergency.Management.Deputy.Minister@gov.bc.ca

Associated Agencies, Boards & Commissions:
• Consumer Protection B.C.
#307, 3450 Uptown Blvd.
PO Box 9244
Victoria, BC V8W 0B9
Fax: 250-920-7181
Toll-free: 888-564-9963
info@consumerprotectionbc.ca
www.consumerprotectionbc.ca
Established in 2004 under the Business Practices & Consumer
Protection Authority Act, Consumer Protection B.C. administers
the following consumer protection laws: Business Practices &
Consumer Protection Act, the Cremation, Interment & Funeral
Services Act, & the Motion Picture Act.

• Vehicle Sales Authority of British Columbia (VSA)
#208, 5455 - 152 St.
Surrey, BC V3S 5A5
Tel: 604-574-5050; *Fax:* 604-574-5883
consumer.services@mvsabc.com
mvsabc.com
Other Communication: Alt. Emails: licensing@mvsabc.com;
compensationfund@mvsabc.com; training@mvsabc.com;
communications@mvsabc.com
The VSA licenses motor vehicle dealerships & salespeople;
certifies & provides continuing education for salespeople; assists
consumers; investigates consumer complaints & provides
dispute resolution; & carries out compliance action.

Corporate Policy & Planning Office
PO Box 9283 Stn. Prov Govt, Victoria, BC V8W 9J7
Tel: 250-387-0306
Executive Director, Toby Louie
Tel: 250-356-6389
Toby.Louie@gov.bc.ca

B.C. Coroners Service
Chief Coroner's Office, Metrotower II, #800, 4720 Kingsway,
Burnaby, BC V5H 4N2
Tel: 604-660-7745; *Fax:* 604-660-7766
CoronerRequest@gov.bc.ca
www.pssg.gov.bc.ca/coroners
BC Coroners Service investigates all unexpected, unnatural,
unexplained, & unattended deaths in the province.
Improvements to public safety & recommendations to prevent
similar deaths are made by the Coroners Service.
Chief Coroner, Lisa Lapointe
Tel: 250-356-9326
Deputy Chief Coroner, Operations, Vacant
Deputy Chief Coroner, Investigations, Vincent Stancato
Tel: 604-660-7745; *Fax:* 604-660-7766
Vincent.Stancato@gov.bc.ca
Executive Director, Legal Services & Inquests, John McNamee
Tel: 604-660-6945

Community Safety & Crime Prevention Branch
Fax: 604-660-5340
VictimServicesandCrimePrevention@gov.bc.ca
www.pssg.gov.bc.ca/victimservices
Other Communication: Civil Forfeiture Office, Email:
CivilFO@gov.bc.ca
Assistant Deputy Minister, Lisa Anderson
Executive Director, Service Delivery, Stephen Ford
Tel: 604-660-3834
Stephen.Ford@gov.bc.ca
Executive Director, Community Programs & Strategic Policy,
Marcie Mezzarobba
Tel: 604-660-3868
Marcie.Mezzarobba@gov.bc.ca

Corporate Management Services Branch
Assistant Deputy Minister, Shauna Brouwer
Tel: 250-387-5258; *Fax:* 250-387-0081
Chief Financial Officer & Executive Director, Finance &
Administration Division, David Hoadley
Tel: 250-356-5393; *Fax:* 250-356-3739
David.Hoadley@gov.bc.ca
Financial Officer, Community Safety & Crime Prevention, Lisa
Chong
Tel: 604-660-1901
Lisa.Chong@gov.bc.ca
Acting Executive Director, Crown Agencies, Holly Cairns
Tel: 250-356-5760
Holly.Cairns@gov.bc.ca
Executive Director, Facilities Services Division, Betty Chen-Mack
Tel: 250-356-7159
Betty.ChenMack@gov.bc.ca
Executive Director, Organizational Development Team Office,
Cheryl Hall
Tel: 250-360-7740; *Fax:* 250-356-6323
Cheryl.Hall@gov.bc.ca

Corrections Branch
PO Box 9278 Stn. Prov Govt, Victoria, BC V8W 9J7
Tel: 250-387-6366
Toll-Free: 888-952-7968
www.pssg.gov.bc.ca/corrections
Other Communication: Adult Custody Phone: 250-387-5098;
Community Corrections & Corporate Programs Phone:
250-356-7930
The Corrections Branch consists of the Adult Custody Division &
the Community Corrections & Corporate Programs Division. The
Adult Custody Division operates correctional centres for persons
awaiting trial or serving a provincial custody sentence. The
Community Corrections & Corporate Programs Division operates
over fifty community corrections offices throughout British
Columbia.
Assistant Deputy Minister, Corrections, Vacant
Tel: 250-387-5363; *Fax:* 250-387-5698

Assistant Deputy Minister, Strategic Operations, Elenore Arend
Tel: 778-974-3009
Elenore.Arend@gov.bc.ca
Provincial Director, Adult Custody Division, Stephanie
Macpherson
Tel: 778-974-3013
Provincial Director, Community Corrections & Corporate
Programs Division, Bill Small
Tel: 778-974-3011; *Fax:* 250-952-6883
Bill.Small@gov.bc.ca
Deputy Provincial Director, Adult Custody Division, Dana Tadla
Tel: 250-387-5098; *Fax:* 250-952-6883
Deputy Provincial Director, Community Corrections & Corproate
Programs Headquarters, Dina Green
Tel: 250-387-6040; *Fax:* 250-952-6883
Deputy Provincial Director, Adult Custody Division, David
Friesen
Tel: 250-387-5098; *Fax:* 250-952-6883

Information Systems Branch
PO Box 9262 Stn. Prov Govt, Victoria, BC V8W 9J4
Tel: 250-356-8787; *Fax:* 250-356-7699
Acting Assistant Deputy Minister, Chief Information Officer &
Executive Director, Client Services, Robert O'Neill
Tel: 778-698-5783
Chief Security Architect, Security Division, John Zimmerman
Tel: 250-356-7121; *Fax:* 250-356-7699
John.Zimmermann@gov.bc.ca
Chief Technology Officer & Executive Director, Business
Services Division, Craig Randle
Craig.Randle@gov.bc.ca
Business Operations Officer, Hiliary Girard
Tel: 250-356-9160; *Fax:* 250-356-7699
Executive Director, Strategic Initiatives, Chris Mah
Tel: 778-698-2921
Chris.Mah@gov.bc.ca
Executive Director, Strategic Projects, Tracee Schmidt
Tel: 250-217-7279
Tracee.Schmidt@gov.bc.ca

Policing & Security Branch
PO Box 9285 Stn. Prov Govt, Victoria, BC V8W 9J7
Tel: 250-387-1100; *Fax:* 250-356-7747
sgpcsb@gov.bc.ca
Assistant Deputy Minister & Director, Police Services, Brenda
Butterworth-Carr
Tel: 250-387-1100
Brenda.ButterworthCarr@gov.bc.ca
Executive Director, Policing, Security & Law Enforcement
Infrastructure & Finance, Jim MacAulay
Tel: 778-698-8324
sgpcsb@gov.bc.ca
Executive Director, Police Services, Sandra Sajko
Tel: 778-974-4302
sgpcsb@gov.bc.ca
Executive Director, Security Programs Division, Robyn White
Tel: 778-974-4196
sgspdsec@gov.bc.ca

Cannabis Legalization & Regulation Secretariat
PO Box 9237 Stn. Prov Govt, Victoria, BC V8W 9J1
Tel: 778-698-9859
Cannabis.Secretariat@gov.bc.ca
Executive Director, Cannabis Legislation & Regulation, Mary
Shaw
Tel: 778-698-9859

RoadSafetyBC
PO Box 9254 Stn. Prov Govt, Victoria, BC V8W 9J2
Tel: 250-387-7747; *Fax:* 250-356-5577
Toll-Free: 855-387-7747
RoadSafetyBC@gov.bc.ca
www.gov.bc.ca/roadsafetybc
twitter.com/RoadSafetyBC
The Office of the Superintendent of Motor Vehicles is
responsible for regulating drivers in British Columbia. The
following services are provided: establishment & maintenance of
standards for driving behaviour & medical fitness; provision of an
independent method of appeal of certain Insurance Corporation
of British Columbia decisions; scheduling & hearing evidence
related to proposals by the Insurance Corporation of British
Columbia concerning licences, driving training schools, &
AirCare Certified repair facilities; & reviewing driving prohibitions
& vehicle impoundments imposed by police.
Superintendent of Motor Vehicles, Patricia Boyle
Executive Director, Strategic Initiatives, Steven Roberts
Steven.Roberts@gov.bc.ca

British Columbia Public Service Agency

PO Box 9404 Stn. Prov Govt, Victoria, BC V8W 9V1
Tel: 250-387-0518; *Fax:* 250-356-7074
search.employment.gov.bc.ca
Other Communication: Careers & MyHR, URL:
www2.gov.bc.ca/myhr
The provision of human resource management services is the
responsibility of the BC Public Service Agency. The services are
provided to persons & organizations working in the province's
public sector. It is overseen by the Ministry of Finance.

Deputy Minister, Bobbi Sadler
Tel: 250-356-7074

Assistant Deputy Minister, Alyson Blackstock
Tel: 778-698-7912; *Fax:* 250-387-0527
Alyson.Blackstock@gov.bc.ca

Assistant Deputy Minister, People & Organizational
Development, Debbie Godfrey
Tel: 250-952-1026; *Fax:* 250-356-7074
Debbie.Godfrey@gov.bc.ca

Assistant Deputy Minister, Corporate Services, Bruce
Richmond
Tel: 778-698-7972; *Fax:* 250-356-7074
Bruce.Richmond@gov.bc.ca

**British Columbia Ministry of Social Development &
Poverty Reduction**

PO Box 9058 Stn. Prov Govt, Victoria, BC V8W 9E1
Toll-Free: 866-866-0800
TTY: 800-661-8773
www.gov.bc.ca/sdpr
Formerly known as Social Development & Social Innovation, the
Ministry of Social Development & Poverty Reduction was crated
in 2017 by Premier John Horgan. The main responsibilities of the
ministry include supporting community living services that assist
persons with developmental disabilities; providing employment
programs & services to unemployed & underemployed persons;
& delivering income assistance to persons in need.

Minister, Hon. Nicholas Simons
Tel: 250-356-7750; *Fax:* 250-356-7292
SDPR.Minister@gov.bc.ca

Deputy Minister, David Galbraith
Tel: 250-387-2325
PO Box 9934 Prov Govt Sta.
Victoria, BC V8W 9R2

Advocate for Service Quality, Leanne Dospital
Tel: 604-398-3722; *Fax:* 604-660-1821
Leanne.Dospital@gov.bc.ca

Director, Executive Operations, Karen Milne
Tel: 778-698-7601; *Fax:* 250-698-7601

Associated Agencies, Boards & Commissions:
• Employment & Assistance Appeal Tribunal
PO Box 9994 Prov Govt
Victoria, BC V8W 9R7
Tel: 250-356-6374; *Fax:* 250-356-9687
Toll-free: 866-557-0035
eaat@gov.bc.ca
www.gov.bc.ca/eaat
Other Communication: Toll-Free Fax: 877-356-9687

Corporate Services Division
PO Box 9940 Stn. Prov Govt, Victoria, BC V8W 9R2
Tel: 250-387-3159; *Fax:* 250-387-2418
Assistant Deputy Minister & Executive Financial Officer, Michel
Lord
Tel: 778-698-7775; *Fax:* 250-387-2418
Michael.Lord@gov.bc.ca
Chief Financial Officer & Executive Director, Financial &
Administrative Services Branch, Nicole Wright
Tel: 250-415-6421; *Fax:* 250-356-5994
Nicole.Wright@gov.bc.ca
Executive Director, Corporate Planning & Strategic Initiatives,
Mark S. Medgyesi
Tel: 778-698-7773
Mark.Medgyesi@gov.bc.ca
Director, Facilities & Workplace Solutions, Joel Crocker
Tel: 250-217-4971; *Fax:* 250-356-5994
Joel.Crocker@gov.bc.ca
Acting Director, Corporate Communications, Kimberlee Johns
Tel: 778-690-2082; *Fax:* 250-387-4264
Kimberlee.Johns@gov.bc.ca

Employment & Labour Market Services Division
PO Box 9762 Stn. Prov Govt, Victoria, BC V8W 1A4
Tel: 250-953-3921; *Fax:* 250-953-3928
Assistant Deputy Minister, Chris Brown
Tel: 778-698-7584; *Fax:* 250-953-3928
Executive Director, Program Policy & Development, Ian Ross
Tel: 778-698-7733
Executive Director, Services to Adults with Developmental
Disabilities (STADD), Kelly McQuillen
Tel: 778-698-4774

Information Services Division
PO Box 9436 Stn. Prov Govt, Victoria, BC V8W 9W3
Tel: 778-698-3802
Assistant Deputy Minister, Rob Byers
Tel: 778-698-3813
Executive Director, Business Performance Branch, Mary
LaBoucane
Tel: 250-812-2083
Executive Director, Business Operations Branch, Alison Looysen
Tel: 250-508-0417
Executive Director & Chief Technology Officer, Daisy Jassar
Tel: 778-698-4753

Research, Innovation & Policy Division
PO Box 9934 Stn. Prov Gov, Victoria, BC V8W 9R2
Tel: 778-698-7689; *Fax:* 250-387-5775
Assistant Deputy Minister, Molly Harrington
Tel: 778-698-7689; *Fax:* 250-387-2418
Acting Executive Director, Ministry of Social
Development-Ministry of Children & Family Development
Legislation, Litigation & Appeals Branch, Cary Chiu
Tel: 778-698-7686
Executive Director, Research Branch, Robert Bruce
Tel: 778-698-7694; *Fax:* 250-387-8164
Robert.Bruce@gov.bc.ca
Executive Director, Accessibility Secretariat, Guillaume Dufresne
Tel: 778-698-7727
Guillaume.Dufresne@gov.bc.ca
Executive Director, Strategic Policy, Michael Turanski
Tel: 778-698-7724; *Fax:* 250-387-8164
Michael.Turanski@gov.bc.ca
Director, Acessibility Secretariat, Tim Cottrell
Tel: 778-698-7685; *Fax:* 250-387-8164
Director, Analytics & Forecasting, Linda DeBenedictis
Tel: 778-698-7719; *Fax:* 250-387-8164
Linda.DeBenedictis@gov.bc.ca

Service Delivery Division
Assistant Deputy Minister, Debi Upton
Tel: 778-698-7636
Executive Director, Operations Support, Heather Brazier
Tel: 250-974-2292
Acting Executive Director, Strategic Services Branch, Dana
Jansen
Tel: 778-698-7656
Executive Director, Virtual Services, Inderjit Randhawa
Executive Director, Prevention & Loss Management Services,
Kim Saastad
Tel: 778-362-7102

British Columbia Ministry of Tourism, Arts, Culture & Sport

PO Box 9082 Stn. Prov Govt, Victoria, BC V8W 9E2
www.gov.bc.ca/tacs
The Ministry of Tourism, Arts, Culture & Sport was created in
2017 by Premier John Horgan. The ministry's goal is to integrate
the tourism sector with the arts, culture & sport sector to
promote British Columbia for citizens, visitors & investors.

Minister, Hon. Melanie Mark
Tel: 250-953-0905; *Fax:* 250-387-4680
TAC.Minister@gov.bc.ca

Deputy Minister, Neilane Mayhew
Tel: 778-698-0450; *Fax:* 250-356-1195
TAC.DeputyMinister@gov.bc.ca

Acting Director, Executive Operations, Andrea Berkes
Tel: 778-405-1897; *Fax:* 250-356-1195
Andrea.Berkes@gov.bc.ca

Associated Agencies, Boards & Commissions:
• **British Columbia Arts Council (BCAC)**
800 Johnson St.
PO Box 9819 Prov Govt
Victoria, BC V8W 9W3
Tel: 250-356-1718; *Fax:* 250-387-4099
BCArtsCouncil@gov.bc.ca
www.bcartscouncil.ca

The BC Arts Council supports arts & cultural activities across the
province, including professional dance companies, art galleries,
local museums & music festivals.
• **British Columbia Games Society**
#200, 990 Fort St.
Victoria, BC V8V 3K2
Tel: 250-387-1375; *Fax:* 250-387-4489
www.bcgames.org
The BC Games Society is incorporated under the Societies Act.
With responsibility to British Columbia's Minister of Healthy
Living & Sport, the Crown Agency works with its partners to
provide event management leadership. The Society strives to
create development opportunities for athletes, coaches, &
officials, sport organizations, & host communities.

• **Creative BC**
2225 West Broadway
Vancouver, BC V6K 2E4
Tel: 604-736-7997; *Fax:* 604-736-7290
www.creativebc.com
Creative BC's mission is to ensure that film & television
production thrives for Canadian & international clients. As one of
the largest production centres in North America, the province
offers film producers & production companies a great range of
services.

• **Destination British Columbia**
510 Burrard St., 12th Fl.
Vancouver, BC V6C 3A8
Tel: 604-660-2861; *Fax:* 604-660-3383
ContactTourism@DestinationBC.ca
www.destinationbc.ca
Destination British Columbia is a Crown corporation which
provides information for industry & the media. Its goals are
increases in revenue, economic benefits, & employment in
British Columbia, through the promotion of development &
growth in the tourism industry. The organization is accountable
to the Minister of Tourism, Culture & The Arts.

• **Islands Trust**
#200, 1627 Fort St.
Victoria, BC V8R 1H8
Tel: 250-405-5151; *Fax:* 250-405-5155
www.islandstrust.bc.ca
Other Communication: Northern Office: 250-247-2063; Salt
Spring Office: 250-537-9144
The Islands Trust area covers the following islands & waters
between the British Columbia mainland & southern Vancouver
Island: Bowen, Denman, Gabriola, Galiano, Gambier, Hornby,
Lasqueti, Mayne, North Pender, Salt Spring, Saturna, South
Pender, & Thetis. The Trust is a federation of independent local
governments. The federation plans land use & regulates
development to preserve & protect the area and its environment.

Arts, Culture, & Sport Division
PO Box 9490 Stn. Prov Govt, Victoria, BC V8W 9N7
Tel: 250-356-6914; *Fax:* 250-387-7973
In March 2014, this branch assumed responsibility for outreach
programs, such as Capital for Kids, formerly administered by the
BC Provincial Capital Commission.
Assistant Deputy Minister, Vacant
BC Athletic Commissioner, Wayne Willows
Tel: 778-698-3375
Athletic.Commissioner@gov.bc.ca
Executive Director, Sport Branch, Margo Ross
Tel: 778-698-3371; *Fax:* 250-356-2842
Margo.Ross@gov.bc.ca
Executive Director, Arts, Culture & BC Arts Council, Gillian
Wood
Tel: 778-698-3523; *Fax:* 250-387-4099
Gillian.Wood@gov.bc.ca

Corporate Initiatives & Multiculturalism Division
PO Box 9855 Stn. Prov Govt, Victoria, BC V8W 9T5
In March 2014, this branch assumed responsibility for outreach
programs, such as Capital for Kids, formerly administered by the
BC Provincial Capital Commission.
Executive Lead, Dean Sekyer
Tel: 778-698-8777
Dean.Sekyer@gov.bc.ca
Executive Director, Multiculturalism, Sasha Hobbs
Sasha.Hobbs@gov.bc.ca
Senior Director, Corporate Planning & Strategic Initiatives, Gail
Greenwood
Tel: 778-698-8770
Gail.Greenwood@gov.bc.ca

Tourism, Arts & Culture Division
PO Box 9812 Stn. Prov Gov, Victoria, BC V8W 9W1
Fax: 250-387-7973
Assistant Deputy Minister, Claire Avison
Tel: 778-698-0455
Claire.Avison@gov.bc.ca

Executive Director, Tourism, Suzanne Ferguson
Tel: 778-698-9355; *Fax:* 250-952-0351
Suzanne.Ferguson@gov.bc.ca
Executive Director, Corporate Initiatives & Strategic Policy, Brian
Jonker
Tel: 250-214-3991
Brian.Jonker@gov.bc.ca

British Columbia Ministry of Transportation & Infrastructure

PO Box 9850 Stn. Prov Govt, Victoria, BC V8W 9T5
Tel: 250-387-3198; *Fax:* 250-356-7706
tran.webmaster@gov.bc.ca
www.gov.bc.ca/tran
The mission of the Ministry of Transportation & Infrastructure is
to plan tranportation networks, to establish policies, to provide
transportation services & infrastructure, & to administer acts &
regulations related to transportation & infrastructure.
Specific responsibilities include the following: working with
partners to fund cost-effective public transit, ferry services, &
cycling networks; managing funding for public infrastructure;
maintaining highways; setting commercial vehicle operating
standards & overseeing vehicle safety inspections; & licensing
commercial passenger transporation.

Minister, Hon. Rob Fleming
Tel: 250-387-1978; *Fax:* 250-356-2290
Minister.Transportation@gov.bc.ca

Minister of State, Infrastructure, Hon. Bowinn Ma
Tel: 250-704-3020

Deputy Minister, Kaye Krishna
Tel: 250-387-3280; *Fax:* 250-387-6431
DeputyMinister.Transportation@gov.bc.ca
PO Box 9850 Prov Govt Sta.
Victoria, BC V8W 9T5

Associated Agencies, Boards & Commissions:
• **British Columbia Ferry Services Inc.**
See Entry Name Index for detailed listing.
• **British Columbia Pavilion Corporation (PavCo)**
See Entry Name Index for detailed listing.
• **British Columbia Railway Company**
#600, 221 West Esplanade
North Vancouver, BC V7M 3J3
Tel: 604-678-4735; *Fax:* 604-678-4736
www.bcrco.com
• **British Columbia Transit**
520 Gorge Rd. East
Victoria, BC V8W 2P3
Tel: 250-385-2551
www.bctransit.com
Other Communication: Community transit information:
transitinfo@bctransit.com

A provincial crown agency, BC Transit coordinates the delivery of
public transportation in British Columbia, outside the Greater
Vancouver Regional District. The corporation's specific role, in
accordance with the BC Transit Act, is the planning, acquisition,
construction, operation, & maintenance of public passenger
transportation systems & rail systems.

• **Passenger Transportation Board**
#202, 940 Blanshard St.
PO Box 9850 Prov Govt
Victoria, BC V8W 9T5
Tel: 250-953-3777; *Fax:* 250-953-3788
ptboard@gov.bc.ca
www.ptboard.bc.ca
The Passenger Transportation Board carries out its
responsibilities in accordance with the Passenger Transportation
Act. The independent tribunal makes decisions regarding the
operation of passenger directed vehicles and inter-city buses in
British Columbia.

Finance & Management Services Department
PO Box 9850 Victoria, BC V8W 9T5
Tel: 250-387-3100; *Fax:* 250-387-6431
Assistant Deputy Minister & Executive Financial Officer, Nancy
Bain
Tel: 250-387-3100; *Fax:* 250-387-6431
Nancy.Bain@gov.bc.ca
Chief Financial Officer & Executive Director, Financial
Management, Patricia Marsh
Tel: 250-387-7505; *Fax:* 250-387-7505
Patricia.A.Marsh@gov.bc.ca
Chief Information Officer & Executive Director, Information
Management Branch, Debbie Fritz
Tel: 778-698-3008; *Fax:* 250-356-7184
Debbie.Fritz@gov.bc.ca
Executive Director, Crown Agencies, Carol Bishop
Tel: 250-387-1936; *Fax:* 250-356-7706

Carol.Bishop@gov.bc.ca
Other Communications: Cell Phone: 250-888-1251
Executive Director, Finance Major Projects, Dave Stewart
Tel: 250-387-5708; *Fax:* 250-387-7645
Dave.Stewart@gov.bc.ca
Executive Director, Strategic Human Resources, Melissa Thickens
Tel: 250-356-9783; *Fax:* 250-387-5334
Melissa.Thickens@gov.bc.ca

Highway Operations Department
PO Box 9850 Victoria, BC V8W 9T5
Tel: 250-387-3260; *Fax:* 250-387-6431
Assistant Deputy Minister, Vacant
Tel: 250-387-7671; *Fax:* 250-387-6431
Chief Engineer, Dirk Nyland
Tel: 778-974-5412; *Fax:* 250-387-7735
Dirk.Nyland@gov.bc.ca
Other Communications: Cell Phone: 250-812-6645
Executive Director, Engineering Services, Ed Miska
Tel: 778-974-5327; *Fax:* 250-387-7735
Ed.Miska@gov.bc.ca

Infrastructure & Major Projects Division
PO Box 9850 Stn. Prov Govt, Victoria, BC V8W 9T5
Tel: 250-387-6742; *Fax:* 250-387-6431
Assistant Deputy Minister, Patrick Livolsi
Tel: 250-387-6742; *Fax:* 250-387-6431
Patrick.Livolsi@gov.bc.ca
Executive Director, Major Projects & Alternate Procurement, Lisa Gow
Tel: 250-356-0514; *Fax:* 250-356-2112
Lisa.Gow@gov.bc.ca
Executive Director, Planning & Programming Branch, David Marr
Tel: 250-356-2100; *Fax:* 250-356-0897
David.Marr@gov.bc.ca
Executive Director, Infrastructure Development Branch, Renee Mounteney
Tel: 250-208-8876; *Fax:* 250-356-0897

Partnerships Division
PO Box 9850 Stn. Prov Govt, Victoria, BC V8W 9T5
Tel: 250-356-1403; *Fax:* 250-387-6431
Assistant Deputy Minister, Silas Brownsey
Tel: 250-387-5062; *Fax:* 250-387-6431
Silas.Brownsey@gov.bc.ca
Senior Finance Officer, Project Governance & Corporate Initiative Branch, Laurie Watkins
Tel: 250-356-1571; *Fax:* 250-356-2112
Laurie.Watkins@gov.bc.ca
Executive Director, Properties & Land Management Branch & Executive Director, Pacific Gateway Branch, David Greer
Tel: 250-356-7904
David.Greer@gov.bc.ca
Acting Executive Director, Transit Branch, Andrea Mercer
Tel: 250-387-4851; *Fax:* 250-387-5012
Andrea.Mercer@gov.bc.ca

Transportation Policy & Programs Division
PO Box 9850 Stn. Prov Govt, Victoria, BC V8W 9T5
Tel: 250-387-5062; *Fax:* 250-387-6431
Assistant Deputy Minister, Deborah Bowman
Tel: 250-356-6225; *Fax:* 250-387-6431
Deborah.Bowman@gov.bc.ca
Executive Director, Marine Branch, Kirk Handrahan
Tel: 778-974-5301; *Fax:* 250-356-0897
Kirk.Handrahan@gov.bc.ca
Registrar & Director, Passenger Transportation Branch, Michele Jaggi-Smith
Tel: 778-698-2640; *Fax:* 604-527-2205
Michele.JaggiSmith@gov.bc.ca
www.th.gov.bc.ca/rpt
Other Communications:
passengertransportationbr@gov.bc.ca

British Columbia Utilities Commission (BCUC)

#410, 900 Howe St., Vancouver, BC V6Z 2N3
Tel: 604-660-4700; *Fax:* 604-660-1102
Toll-Free: 800-663-1385
commission.secretary@bcuc.com
www.bcuc.com
twitter.com/BCutilitiescom
www.linkedin.com/company/bc-utilities-commission
The British Columbia Utilities Commission is an independent regulatory agency of the Provincial Government of British Columbia. The Commission's regulates the province's natural gas & electricity utilities. Other activities of the Utilities Commission include the regulation of universal compulsory automobile insurance & intra-provincial pipelines.

Chair & Chief Executive Officer, David Morton
Tel: 604-660-4700; *Fax:* 604-660-2700
david.morton@bcuc.com

British Columbia Vital Statistics Agency

PO Box 9657 Stn. Prov Govt, Victoria, BC V8W 9P3
Tel: 250-952-2681; *Fax:* 250-952-9097
vsoffceo@gov.bc.ca
www2.gov.bc.ca/gov/content/life-events
The Vital Statistics Agency operates under the Ministry of Health, & offers the following services: Birth registration; marriage certificates; death certificates; wills; name changes; & geneaology.

Registrar General, Jack Shewchuk
Tel: 250-952-9039; *Fax:* 250-952-9097
Jack.Shewchuk@gov.bc.ca

Director, Information Technology Services, Suzanne Jennings
Tel: 250-952-9084
Suzanne.Jennings@gov.bc.ca

Workers' Compensation Board of British Columbia

PO Box 5350 Stn. Terminal, Vancouver, BC V6B 5L5
Tel: 604-276-3100; *Fax:* 604-276-3247
Toll-Free: 888-621-7233
www.worksafe.com
Other Communication: Claims: 604-231-8888, Fax: 604-233-9777; Employer services/Assessments: 604-244-6181, Fax: 604-244-6490
Secondary Address: 6951 Westminster Hwy.
Head Office Street Address
Richmond, BC
twitter.com/WorkSafeBC
www.facebook.com/worksafebc
www.linkedin.com/company/worksafebc
www.youtube.com/user/WorkSafeBC
The Workers' Compensation Board of British Columbia, or WorkSafeBC, assists workers & employers in British Columbia by promoting health & safety in workplaces. WorkSafeBC's key responsiblities are as follows: consultation with & education of employers & workers; monitoring compliance with the Occupational Health & Safety Regulation; & provision of return-to-work compensation, rehabilitation, health care benefits, & other services for parties affected by work-related injuries or diseases.

Chair, Ralph McGinn

Interim President & Chief Executive Officer; Senior Vice-President, Finance & IT; Chief Financial Officer, Brian Erickson

Senior Vice-President, Operations, Worker & Employer Services Division, Trevor Alexander

Chief Information Officer, Information Technology Division, Clare Murray

Government of Manitoba

Seat of Government: Legislative Bldg., 450 Broadway, Winnipeg, MB R3C 0V8
Tel: 204-945-3744
Toll-Free: 866-626-4862
mgi@gov.mb.ca
www.gov.mb.ca
twitter.com/MBGov
www.facebook.com/ManitobaGovernment
www.linkedin.com/company/government-of-manitoba
www.youtube.com/user/ManitobaGovernment
The Province of Manitoba entered Confederation July 15, 1870. It has a land area of 552,370.99 sq km, & the StatsCan census population in 2016 was 1,278,365.

Office of the Lieutenant Governor

Legislative Bldg., #235, 450 Broadway, Winnipeg, MB R3C 0V8
Tel: 204-945-2753; *Fax:* 204-945-4329
ltgov@leg.gov.mb.ca
www.manitobalg.ca

Lieutenant Governor, Hon. Janice Filmon, CM, OM

Executive Director/Private Secretary, Kate Gameiro
Tel: 204-945-2752
kate.gameiro@leg.gov.mb.ca

Government House Event Coordinator, Lisa Vermette
Tel: 204-945-2753
lisa.vermette@leg.gov.mb.ca

Office of the Premier

Legislative Bldg., #204, 450 Broadway, Winnipeg, MB R3C 0V8
Tel: 204-945-3714; *Fax:* 204-949-1484
premier@leg.gov.mb.ca
www.gov.mb.ca/minister/premier

Premier; President, Executive Council; Minister, Intergovernmental Affairs & International Relations, Hon. Kelvin Goertzen
Tel: 204-945-3714; *Fax:* 204-945-1484
premier@leg.gov.mb.ca

Deputy Premier; Minister, Families; Minister Responsible, Francophone Affairs, Hon. Rochelle Squires
Tel: 204-945-4173; *Fax:* 204-945-5149
minfs@leg.gov.mb.ca

Executive Council

Legislative Bldg., 450 Broadway, Winnipeg, MB R3C 0V8
www.gov.mb.ca/minister
The following is a list of Cabinet Ministers of the Government of Manitoba in order of precedence:

Premier; President, Executive Council; Minister, Intergovernmental Affairs & International Relations, Hon. Kelvin Goertzen
Tel: 204-945-3714; *Fax:* 204-945-1484
premier@leg.gov.mb.ca

Deputy Premier; Minister, Families; Minister Responsible, Francophone Affairs, Hon. Rochelle Squires
Tel: 204-945-4173; *Fax:* 204-945-5149
minfs@leg.gov.mb.ca

Minister, Infrastructure, Hon. Ron Schuler
Tel: 204-945-3723; *Fax:* 204-945-7610
minmi@leg.gov.mb.ca

Minister, Agriculture & Resource Development, Hon. Ralph Eichler
Tel: 204-945-3722; *Fax:* 204-945-3470
minagr@leg.gov.mb.ca

Minister, Education, Hon. Cliff Cullen
Tel: 204-945-3720; *Fax:* 204-945-1291
minedu@leg.gov.mb.ca

Minister, Justice; Attorney General; Keeper of the Great Seal, Hon. Cameron Friesen
Tel: 204-945-3728; *Fax:* 204-945-2517
minjus@leg.gov.mb.ca

Minister, Sport, Culture & Heritage; Minister Responsible, Status of Women, Hon. Cathy Cox
Tel: 204-945-3729; *Fax:* 204-945-5223
minsch@leg.gov.mb.ca

Minister, Finance, Hon. Scott Fielding
Tel: 204-945-3952; *Fax:* 204-945-6057
minfin@leg.gov.mb.ca

Minister, Crown Services, Hon. Jeff Wharton
Tel: 204-945-8020; *Fax:* 204-948-7700
mincrown@leg.gov.mb.ca

Minister, Central Services; Minister Responsible, Civil Service, Hon. Reg Helwer
Tel: 204-945-6215
mincentral@leg.gov.mb.ca

Minister, Conservtion & Climate, Hon. Sarah Guillemard
Tel: 204-945-3730; *Fax:* 204-945-3586
mincc@leg.gov.mb.ca

Minister, Advanced Education, Skills & Immigration, Hon. Wayne Ewasko
Tel: 204-945-8480
minaesi@leg.gov.mb.ca

Minister, Municipal Relations, Hon. Derek Johnson
Tel: 204-945-5854; *Fax:* 204-948-4783
minmr@leg.gov.mb.ca

Minister, Health & Seniors Care; Minister, Mental Health, Wellness & Recovery, Hon. Audrey Gordon
Tel: 204-945-1211
minmhwr@leg.gov.mb.ca

Minister, Indigenous Reconciliation & Northern Relations, Hon. Alan Lagimodiere

Tel: 204-945-3788; *Fax:* 204-945-1383
minindnr@leg.gov.mb.ca

Minister, Economic Development & Jobs, Hon. Jon Reyes
Tel: 204-945-0067; *Fax:* 204-945-4882
minedj@leg.gov.mb.ca

Manitoba Legislative Assembly

c/o Clerk's Office, Legislative Bldg., #237, 450 Broadway, Winnipeg, MB R3C 0V8
Tel: 204-945-3636; *Fax:* 204-948-2507
clerkla@leg.gov.mb.ca
www.gov.mb.ca/legislature

Clerk of the Legislative Assembly, Patricia Chaychuk
Tel: 204-945-3636
clerk@leg.gov.mb.ca

Deputy Clerk of the Legislative Assembly, Rick Yarish
Tel: 204-945-0245

Speaker of the House, Hon. Myrna Driedger
Tel: 204-945-3706; *Fax:* 204-945-1443
speaker@leg.gov.mb.ca

Chief Electoral Officer, Shipra Verma, CPA, CA
Tel: 204-945-3225
Toll-free: 866-628-6837; *Fax:* 204-945-6011
election@elections.mb.ca
www.electionsmanitoba.ca

Ombudsman, Jill Perron
Tel: 204-982-9130; *Fax:* 204-942-7803
ombudsman@ombudsman.mb.ca
www.ombudsman.mb.ca

Lobbyist Registrar, Information & Privacy Adjudicator & Conflict of Interest Commissioner, Jeffrey Schnoor, Q.C.
Tel: 204-948-3466
mbcoic@legassembly.mb.ca
www.mbcoic.ca/commissioner.html

Children's & Youth Advocate, Daphne Penrose, MSW, RSW
Tel: 204-988-7440
Toll-free: 800-263-7146; *Fax:* 204-988-7472
www.childrensadvocate.mb.ca

Auditor General, Tyson Shtykalo
Tel: 204-945-3790
tyson.shtykalo@oag.mb.ca
www.oag.mb.ca

Journals Clerk/Clerk Assistant, Monique Grenier
Tel: 204-945-6331
monique.grenier@leg.gov.mb.ca

Government Caucus Office (Progressive Conservative Party)
Legislative Bldg., #227, 450 Broadway, Winnipeg, MB R3C 0V8
Tel: 204-945-3709; *Fax:* 204-945-1284
info@pcmbcaucus.com
pcmbcaucus.com
twitter.com/PCcaucus
www.facebook.com/ManitobaPCcaucus
www.youtube.com/c/ManitobaPCCaucus
Premier; Government House Leader, Hon. Kelvin Goertzen
Tel: 204-945-3714; *Fax:* 204-945-1484
premier@leg.gov.mb.ca
Leader, Progressive Conservative Part of Manitoba, Vacant
Caucus Chair, Greg Nesbitt
greg.nesbitt@leg.gov.mb.ca
Government House Leader, Vacant

Official Opposition Office (New Democratic Party)
Legislative Bldg., #234, 450 Broadway, Winnipeg, MB R3C 0V8
Tel: 204-945-3710; *Fax:* 204-948-2005
Toll-Free: 855-494-7371
information@yourmanitoba.ca
www.yourmanitoba.ca
twitter.com/mbndp
www.facebook.com/manitobandpcaucus
www.youtube.com/user/yourmanitoba
Leader, Manitoba New Democratic Party, Wab Kinew
Tel: 204-945-3284
wab.kinew@leg.gov.mb.ca
Caucus Whip, Matt Wiebe
matt.wiebe@leg.gov.mb.ca
Opposition House Leader, Nahanni Fontaine
nahanni.fontaine@leg.gov.mb.ca

Deputy Whip, Amanda Lathlin
amanda.lathlin@leg.gov.mb.ca
Caucus Chair, Bernadette Smith
Deputy Caucus Chair, Tom Lindsey
tom.lindsey@leg.gov.mb.ca

Legislative Committees
Legislative Bldg., #251, 450 Broadway, Winnipeg, MB R3C 0V8
Fax: 204-945-0038
gov.mb.ca/legislature/committees/index.html
At the beginning of the first session of each Legislature, a Special Committee consisting of seven members recommends a list of members to serve on the various committees. Once the Special Committee's report is adopted, the standing committees are created. The following standing committees have been established: Agriculture & Food; Crown Corporations; Human Resources; Intergovernmental Affairs; Justice; Legislative Affairs; Private Bills; Public Accounts; Rules of the House; Social & Economic Development; & Statutory Regulations & Orders.
Committee Clerk, Tim Abbott
Tel: 204-945-0796
Tim.Abbott@leg.gov.mb.ca
Committee Clerk, Katerina Tefft
Tel: 204-945-4729
katerina.tefft@leg.gov.mb.ca

Forty-second Legislature - Manitoba

Legislative Bldg., 450 Broadway, Winnipeg, MB R3C 0V8
Tel: 204-945-3636; *Fax:* 204-948-2507
clerkla@leg.gov.mb.ca
www.gov.mb.ca/legislature
Last General Election: Sept. 10, 2019.
Next General Election: 2023.
Party Standings (Oct. 2021):
Progressive Conservative 35;
New Democratic Party 18;
Independent Liberal 3;
Vacant 1;
Total 57.
MLA Remuneration (effective April 1, 2021):
MLA basic annual salary $97,753;
Additional Annual Salaries:
Premier $81,917;
Cabinet Ministers $53,519;
Cabinet Ministers without portfolio $45,109
Speaker $53,519;
Deputy Speaker $11,043;
Leader of the Official Opposition $53,519;
Leader of a Recognized Opposition Party $45,109;
Deputy Chairperson of the Committee of the Whole House $7,887;
Government House Leader $11,043;
Government Whip $7,887;
Official Opposition House Leader $7,887;
Official Opposition Whip $6,312;
House Leader of a Recognized Opposition Party $6,312;
Whip of a Recognized Opposition Party $4,735;
Caucus Chair $6,799;
Caucus Chair of the Official Opposition $6,799;
Legislative Assistant $4,735;
Permanent Chairperson, Standing or Special Committees $204 per meeting to an annual maximum of $4,735.
All members of the Legislative Assembly of Manitoba may be reached at the following address: 450 Broadway Ave., Winnipeg, MB R3C 0V8.
The following is a list of Members of the Legislative Assembly of Manitoba, with their constituency, number of registered voters in the constituency, party affiliation, & contact information:
Members of the Legislative Assembly of Manitoba
Danielle Adams
Constituency: Thompson *No. of Constituents:* 13,267, New Democratic Party
Tel: 204-945-3710; *Fax:* 204-945-2005
Danielle.Adams@mbleg.ca
www.mbndp.ca/danielleadams
Other Communications: Constituency Phone: 204-677-2744; Fax: 204-677-2803
Constituency Office
#402, 79 Selkirk Ave.
Thompson, MB R8N 0M5
Nello Altomare
Constituency: Transcona *No. of Constituents:* 16,701, New Democratic Party
Tel: 204-945-3710; *Fax:* 204-948-2005
Nello.Altomare@mbleg.ca
www.mbndp.ca/nelloaltomare
Other Communications: Constituency Phone: 204-594-2025
Constituency Office
127 Regent Ave. West
Winnipeg, MB R2C 1R1
Uzoma Asagwara
Constituency: Union Station *No. of Constituents:* 12,699, New

Democratic Party
Tel: 204-945-3710; *Fax:* 204-945-2005
Uzoma.Asagwara@mbleg.ca
www.mbndp.ca/uzomaasagwara
Other Communications: Constituency Phone: 204-306-8581
Constituency Office
#1, 331 Smith St.
Winnipeg, MB R3C 0V8
Diljeet Brar
Constituency: Burrows *No. of Constituents:* 14,124, New Democratic Party
Tel: 204-945-3710; *Fax:* 204-945-2005
Diljeet.Brar@mbleg.ca
www.mbndp.ca/diljeetbrar
Other Communications: Constituency Phone: 204-415-7621
Constituency Office
#3, 350 Keewatin St.
Winnipeg, MB R2X 2R9
Ian Bushie
Constituency: Keewatinook *No. of Constituents:* 13,422, New Democratic Party
Tel: 204-945-3710; *Fax:* 204-945-2005
Ian.Bushie@leg.gov.mb.ca
www.mbndp.ca/ianbushie
Other Communications: Constituency Phone: 204-363-7810
Constituency Office
PO Box 2565
Wanipigow, MB R0E 2E0
Eileen Clarke
Constituency: Agassiz *No. of Constituents:* 13,514, Progressive Conservative
Tel: 204-945-3709; *Fax:* 204-945-1284
Eileen.Clarke@leg.gov.mb.ca
eileenclarke.ca
Other Communications: Constituency Phone: 204-385-2469; Fax: 204-385-2477
www.facebook.com/eileen.clarke.351
Constituency Office
17B Dennis St. West
PO Box 25
Gladstone, MB R0J 0T0
Minister, Sport, Culture & Heritage; Minister Responsible, Status of Women, Hon. Cathy Cox
Constituency: Kildonan-River East *No. of Constituents:* 17,661, Progressive Conservative
Tel: 204-945-3729; *Fax:* 204-945-5223
minsch@leg.gov.mb.ca
Other Communications: Constituency Phone: 204-334-7866; Fax: 204-338-7697
Constituency Office
#13E, 1795 Henderson Hwy.
Winnipeg, MB R2G 1P3
Minister, Education, Hon. Cliff Cullen
Constituency: Spruce Woods *No. of Constituents:* 14,746, Progressive Conservative
Tel: 204-945-3720; *Fax:* 204-945-1291
minedu@leg.gov.mb.ca
cliffcullen.ca
Other Communications: Constituency Phone: 204-827-3956; Fax: 204-827-3957
Constituency Office
101 Broadway St.
PO Box 129
Glenboro, MB R0K 0X0
Speaker of the House, Hon. Myrna Driedger
Constituency: Roblin *No. of Constituents:* 18,257, Progressive Conservative
Tel: 204-945-3706; *Fax:* 204-945-1443
myrna.driedger@leg.gov.mb.ca
www.myrnadriedger.com
Other Communications: Constituency Phone: 204-885-0594; Fax: 204-885-5525
twitter.com/MyrnaBDriedger
Constituency Office
5120B Roblin Blvd.
Winnipeg, MB R3R 0G9
Minister, Agriculture & Resource Development, Hon. Ralph Eichler
Constituency: Lakeside *No. of Constituents:* 16,039, Progressive Conservative
Tel: 204-945-3722; *Fax:* 204-945-3470
minagr@leg.gov.mb.ca
ralpheichler.com
Other Communications: Constituency Phone: 204-467-9482; Fax: 204-467-7580
Constituency Office
319 Main St.
PO Box 1845
Stonewall, MB R0C 2Z0
Minister, Advanced Education, Skills & Immigration, Hon. Wayne Ewasko
Constituency: Lac du Bonnet *No. of Constituents:* 15,477, Progressive Conservative
Tel: 204-945-8480

minaesi@leg.gov.mb.ca
Other Communications: Constituency Phone: 204-268-3282;
Fax: 204-268-3976
Constituency Office
638 Park Ave.
PO Box 1299
Beausejour, MB R0E 0C0
Minister, Finance, Hon. Scott Fielding
Constituency: Kirkfield Park *No. of Constituents:* 17,789,
Progressive Conservative
Tel: 204-945-3952; *Fax:* 204-945-6057
minfin@leg.gov.mb.ca
scottfielding.ca
Other Communications: Constituency Phone: 204-889-0540;
Fax: 204-895-4260
www.facebook.com/scott.fielding.1029
Constituency Office
3129 Portage Ave.
Winnipeg, MB R3K 0W4
Opposition House Leader, Nahanni Fontaine
Constituency: St. Johns *No. of Constituents:* 14,600, New
Democratic Party
Tel: 204-945-3710; *Fax:* 204-945-2005
nahanni.fontaine@leg.gov.mb.ca
www.mbndp.ca/nahannifontaine
Other Communications: Constituency Phone: 204-582-1550;
Fax: 204-586-3736
twitter.com/NahanniFontaine
Constituency Office
1763 Main St.
Winnipeg, MB R2V 1Z8
Minister, Justice; Attorney General; Keeper of the Great Seal,
Hon. Cameron Friesen
Constituency: Morden-Winkler *No. of Constituents:* 14,813,
Progressive Conservative
Tel: 204-945-3728; *Fax:* 204-945-2517
minjus@leg.gov.mb.ca
cameronfriesen.ca
Other Communications: Constituency Phone: 204-822-1088;
Fax: 204-822-1086
www.facebook.com/CameronFriesen.MordenWinkler
Constituency Office
108A - 8th St.
Morden, MB R6M 1Y7
Hon. Jon Gerrard, P.C.
Constituency: River Heights *No. of Constituents:* 16,757,
Liberal
Tel: 204-945-5194; *Fax:* 204-948-3220
jon.gerrard@leg.gov.mb.ca
www.jongerrardmla.ca
Other Communications: Constituency Phone: 204-289-1560;
Fax: 204-289-1561
twitter.com/drjongerrard,
www.facebook.com/manitobaliberaljongerrard,
www.linkedin.com/in/jon-gerrard-0362b819
Note: Jon Gerrard currently sits as an Independent Liberal, as
the Manitoba Liberal Party did not achieve party status in the
2019 general election.
Constituency Office
877 Corydon Ave.
Winnipeg, MB R3M 0W7
Premier; President, Executive Council; Minister,
Intergovernmental Affairs & International Relations, Hon.
Kelvin Goertzen
Constituency: Steinbach *No. of Constituents:* 14,623,
Progressive Conservative
Tel: 204-945-3714; *Fax:* 204-949-1484
premier@leg.gov.mb.ca
kelvingoertzen.ca
Other Communications: Constituency Phone: 204-326-5763;
Fax: 204-346-9913
Constituency Office
227 Main St., #C2
Steinbach, MB R5G 1Y9
Minister, Health & Seniors Care; Minister, Minister, Mental
Health, Wellness & Recovery, Hon. Audrey Gordon
Constituency: Southdale *No. of Constituents:* 17,301,
Progressive Conservative
Tel: 204-945-3731; *Fax:* 204-945-5149
minhsc@leg.gov.mb.ca
Other Communications: Constituency Phone: 204-415-7397
twitter.com/audreygordonmb,
www.linkedin.com/in/audrey-gordon-3467a15b
Constituency Office
#175, 115 Vermillion
Winnipeg, MB R2J 4A9
Josh Guenter
Constituency: Borderland *No. of Constituents:* 11,996,
Progressive Conservative
Tel: 204-945-3709; *Fax:* 204-945-1284
Josh.Guenter@leg.gov.mb.ca
Other Communications: Constituency Phone: 204-324-8957
Constituency Office

104 - 2nd St. NE
Altona, MB R0G 0B0
Minister, Conservation & Climate, Hon. Sarah Guillemard
Constituency: Fort Richmond *No. of Constituents:* 13,474,
Progressive Conservative
Tel: 204-945-3730; *Fax:* 204-945-3586
mincc@leg.gov.mb.ca
www.sarahguillemard.com
Other Communications: Constituency Phone: 204-221-8881
twitter.com/MinSGuillemard,
www.facebook.com/fortrichmondvoices
Constituency Office
#27, 2285 Pembina Hwy.
Winnipeg, MB R3T 2H5
Minister, Central Services; Minister Responsible for Civil
Service, Hon. Reg Helwer
Constituency: Brandon West *No. of Constituents:* 14,522,
Progressive Conservative
Tel: 204-945-6215
mincentral@leg.gov.mb.ca
reghelwer.com
Other Communications: Constituency Phone: 204-728-2410;
Fax: 204-726-4740
twitter.com/reghelwer
Constituency Office
#30, 3300 Victoria Ave.
Brandon, MB R7B 0N2
Len Isleifson
Constituency: Brandon East *No. of Constituents:* 14,292,
Progressive Conservative
Tel: 204-945-3709; *Fax:* 204-945-1284
len.isleifson@leg.gov.mb.ca
www.pcmanitoba.com/len_isleifson
Other Communications: Constituency Phone: 204-717-0977
twitter.com/LenIsleifson, www.facebook.com/LenIsleifsonMLA
Constituency Office
217 - 10th St., #A
Brandon, MB R7A 4E9
Minister, Municipal Relations, Hon. Derek Johnson
Constituency: Interlake-Gimli *No. of Constituents:* 16,100,
Progressive Conservative
Tel: 204-945-5854
minmr@leg.gov.mb.ca
www.pcmanitoba.com/derek_johnson
Other Communications: Constituency Phone: 204-376-3401;
Fax: 204-376-3401
twitter.com/interlakepc, www.facebook.com/InterlakePC
Constituency Office
#1, 356 River Rd.
PO Box 662
Arborg, MB R0C 0A0
Scott Johnston
Constituency: Assiniboia *No. of Constituents:* 17,080,
Progressive Conservative
Tel: 204-945-3709; *Fax:* 204-945-1284
scott.johnston@leg.gov.mb.ca
www.pcmanitoba.com/scott_johnston
Other Communications: Constituency Phone: 204-615-6044
Constituency Office
#9, 3421 Portage Ave.
Winnipeg, MB R3K 2C9
Leader, Manitoba New Democratic Party, Wab Kinew
Constituency: Fort Rouge *No. of Constituents:* 16,870, New
Democratic Party
Tel: 204-945-3284; *Fax:* 204-945-3583
wab.kinew@mbleg.ca
www.mbndp.ca/wab
Other Communications: Constituency Phone: 204-613-1922
twitter.com/WabKinew, www.facebook.com/WabKinew
Constituency Office
565 1/2 Osborne St.
Winnipeg, MB R3L 2B3
Bob Lagassé
Constituency: Dawson Trail *No. of Constituents:* 14,386,
Progressive Conservative
Tel: 204-945-3709; *Fax:* 204-945-1284
bob.lagasse@leg.gov.mb.ca
boblagasse.ca
Other Communications: Constituency Phone: 204-807-4663
www.facebook.com/BoblagasseMla
Constituency Office
#8B, 555 Traverse Rd.
Ste Anne, MB R5H 1B2
Minister, Indigenous Reconciliation & Northern Relations, Hon.
Alan Lagimodiere
Constituency: Selkirk *No. of Constituents:* 15,964,
Progressive Conservative
Tel: 204-945-3788; *Fax:* 204-945-1383
alan.lagimodiere@leg.gov.mb.ca
alanlagimodiere.ca
Other Communications: Constituency Phone: 204-482-4955
twitter.com/AlanLagimodiere,
www.facebook.com/Alanlagimodiereselkirk
Constituency Office

232A Manitoba Ave.
Selkirk, MB R1A 0Y5
Leader, Manitoba Liberal Party, Dougald Lamont
Constituency: St. Boniface *No. of Constituents:* 16,824,
Liberal
Tel: 204-945-6276; *Fax:* 204-948-3220
Dougald.Lamont@leg.gov.mb.ca
www.manitobaliberals.ca/leader
Other Communications: Constituency Phone: 204-792-8806
twitter.com/dougaldlamont
www.facebook.com/DougaldOurNewWay,
www.linkedin.com/in/dougaldlamont
Note: Dougald Lamont currently sits as an Independent
Liberal, as the Manitoba Liberal Party did not achieve party
status in the 2019 general election.
Constituency Office
118 Main St.
Winnipeg, MB R2H 0T1
Cindy Lamoureux
Constituency: Tyndall Park *No. of Constituents:* 14,068,
Liberal
Tel: 204-945-6276; *Fax:* 204-948-3220
cindy.lamoureux@leg.gov.mb.ca
www.gocindy.ca
Other Communications: Constituency Phone: 204-615-9961
www.facebook.com/CindyLamoureuxTyndallPark
Note: Cindy Lamoureux currently sits as an Independent
Liberal, as the Manitoba Liberal Party did not achieve party
status in the 2019 general election.
Constituency Office
80 Mandalay Dr.
Winnipeg, MB R2P 1P5
Amanda Lathlin
Constituency: The Pas-Kameesak *No. of Constituents:*
12,766, New Democratic Party
Tel: 204-945-3710; *Fax:* 204-948-2005
Amanda.Lathlin@leg.gov.mb.ca
www.mbndp.ca/amandalathlin
Other Communications: Constituency Phone: 204-623-2034;
Fax: 204-623-2068
www.facebook.com/AmandaLathlinMLA
Constituency Office
1416 Gordon Ave.
PO Box 2160
The Pas, MB R9A 1L8
Tom Lindsey
Constituency: Flin Flon *No. of Constituents:* 14,896, New
Democratic Party
Tel: 204-945-3710; *Fax:* 204-945-2005
tom.lindsey@leg.gov.mb.ca
www.mbndp.ca/tomlindsey
Other Communications: Constituency Phone: 204-687-3246;
Fax: 204-687-5649
twitter.com/tomlindseyndp,
www.facebook.com/TomLindseyForFlinFlon
Constituency Office
93 Main St.
Flin Flon, MB R8A 1J9
Jim Maloway
Constituency: Elmwood *No. of Constituents:* 15,990, New
Democratic Party
Tel: 204-945-3710; *Fax:* 204-948-2005
jim.maloway@mbleg.ca
www.mbndp.ca/jimmaloway
Other Communications: Constituency Phone: 204-415-1122;
Fax: 204-414-9414
www.facebook.com/JimMalowayMB
Constituency Office
46 Stadacona St.
Winnipeg, MB R2L 2C8
Malaya Marcelino
Constituency: Notre Dame *No. of Constituents:* 13,044, New
Democratic Party
Tel: 204-945-3710; *Fax:* 204-945-2005
Malaya.Marcelino@mbleg.ca
www.mbndp.ca/malayamarcelino
Other Communications: Constituency Phone: 204-788-0800;
Fax: 204-788-4444
Constituency Office
849 Notre Dame Ave.
Winnipeg, MB R3E OM4
Shannon Martin
Constituency: Morris *No. of Constituents:* 15,643, Progressive
Conservative
Tel: 204-945-3709; *Fax:* 204-945-1284
shannon.martin@leg.gov.mb.ca
Other Communications: Constituency Phone: 204-336-2068
Constituency Office, Northgate Plaza
#210, 1375 McPhillips St.
Winnipeg, MB R2V 3V1
Brad Michaleski
Constituency: Dauphin *No. of Constituents:* 16,315,
Progressive Conservative
Tel: 204-945-3709; *Fax:* 204-945-1284

brad.michaleski@leg.gov.mb.ca
Other Communications: Constituency Phone: 204-701-0238;
Fax: 204-701-0181
twitter.com/bradmichaleski,
www.facebook.com/bradmichaleskimladauphin
Constituency Office
#16, 1450 Main St. South
Dauphin, MB R7N 3H4

Andrew Micklefield
Constituency: Rossmere *No. of Constituents:* 15,734,
Progressive Conservative
Tel: 204-945-3709; *Fax:* 204-945-1284
andrew.micklefield@leg.gov.mb.ca
www.pcmanitoba.com/andrew_micklefield
Other Communications: Constituency Phone: 204-289-4545
twitter.com/a_micklefield, www.facebook.com/amicklefield
Constituency Office
#3, 935 Macleod Ave.
Winnipeg, MB R2G 0Y4

Janice Morley-Lecomte
Constituency: Seine River *No. of Constituents:* 15,712,
Progressive Conservative
Tel: 204-945-3709; *Fax:* 204-945-1284
janice.morley-lecomte@leg.gov.mb.ca
www.pcmanitoba.com/janice_morley_lecomte
Other Communications: Constituency Phone: 204-253-4509
twitter.com/janicemlpcseine,
www.facebook.com/janice.seinerivermla
Constituency Office
#240, 600 St Anne's Rd.
Winnipeg, MB R2M 2S2

Jamie Moses
Constituency: St. Vital, New Democratic Party
Tel: 204-945-3710; *Fax:* 204-945-2005
Jamie.Moses@leg.gov.mb.ca
www.mbndp.ca/jamiemoses
Other Communications: Constituency Phone: 204-219-5407
twitter.com/jmoses6, www.facebook.com/jamiemosesstvital
Constituency Office
838 St Mary's Rd.
Winnipeg, MB R2M 3P4

Lisa Naylor
Constituency: Wolseley *No. of Constituents:* 16,418, New
Democratic Party
Tel: 204-945-3710; *Fax:* 204-945-2005
Lisa.Naylor@leg.gov.mb.ca
www.mbndp.ca/lisanaylor
Other Communications: Constituency Phone: 204-792-2773
twitter.com/lisa_naylor,
www.facebook.com/LisaNaylorWolseley
Constituency Office
#101, 686 Portage Ave.
Winnipeg, MB R3G 0M6

Government Caucus Chair, Greg Nesbitt
Constituency: Riding Mountain *No. of Constituents:* 16,761,
Progressive Conservative
Tel: 204-945-3709
Toll-free: 844-877-7767; *Fax:* 204-945-1284
greg.nesbitt@leg.gov.mb.ca
gregnesbitt.ca
Other Communications: Constituency Phone: 204-759-3313;
Fax: 204-759-3254
twitter.com/gregnesbittpc,
www.facebook.com/greg.nesbitt.pcridingmountain,
www.linkedin.com/in/greg-nesbitt-a2731b33
Constituency Office
#7, 515 - 4th Ave.
PO Box 100
Shoal Lake, MB R0J 1Z0

Blaine Pedersen
Constituency: Midland *No. of Constituents:* 15,259,
Progressive Conservative
Tel: 204-945-3709; *Fax:* 204-945-1284
Blaine.Pedersen@leg.gov.mb.ca
Other Communications: Constituency Phone: 204-745-2203;
Fax: 204-745-2205
twitter.com/blainepedersen,
www.facebook.com/blainepedersenmla
Constituency Office
PO Box 1944
Carman, MB R0G 0J0

Doyle Piwniuk
Constituency: Turtle Mountain *No. of Constituents:* 16,206,
Progressive Conservative
Tel: 204-945-3709; *Fax:* 204-945-1284
doyle.piwniuk@leg.gov.mb.ca
doylepiwniuk.ca
Other Communications: Constituency Phone: 204-552-0130;
Fax: 204-748-6492
www.facebook.com/dpiwniuk
Constituency Office
#610-620, 336 South Railway
Boissevain, MB R0M 2C0

Minister, Economic Development & Jobs, Hon. Jon Reyes
Constituency: Waverley *No. of Constituents:* 12,634,
Progressive Conservative
Tel: 209-450-0679; *Fax:* 204-945-4882
minedj@leg.gov.mb.ca
Other Communications: Constituency Phone: 204-261-7272
twitter.com/jonreyes204,
www.facebook.com/jonreyesinthecommunity,
www.linkedin.com/in/jon-reyes-2094962a
Constituency Office
#60, 2855 Pembina Hwy.
Winnipeg, MB R3T 2H5

Adrien Sala
Constituency: St. James *No. of Constituents:* 15,288, New
Democratic Party
Tel: 204-945-3710; *Fax:* 204-945-2005
Adrien.Sala@mbleg.ca
www.mbndp.ca/adriensala
Other Communications: Constituency Phone: 204-792-8779
twitter.com/AdrienLouisSala,
www.facebook.com/adriensalaforstjames,
www.linkedin.com/in/adriensala
Constituency Office
1885 Portage Ave., #E
Winnipeg, MB R3J 0H3

Mintu Sandhu
Constituency: The Maples *No. of Constituents:* 13,470, New
Democratic Party
Tel: 204-945-3710; *Fax:* 204-945-2005
Mintu.Sandhu@mbleg.ca
www.mbndp.ca/mintusandhu
Other Communications: Constituency Phone: 204-417-3486;
Fax: 204-417-3476
twitter.com/MlaSandhu,
www.facebook.com/MintuSandhuMLA
Constituency Office
#103, 1730 Leila Ave.
Winnipeg, MB R2P 1Z1

Minister, Infrastructure, Hon. Ron Schuler
Constituency: Springfield-Ritchot *No. of Constituents:* 15,822,
Progressive Conservative
Tel: 204-945-3723; *Fax:* 204-945-7610
minmi@leg.gov.mb.ca
www.pcmanitoba.com/ron_schuler
Other Communications: Constituency Phone: 204-330-3353
twitter.com/min_schuler
Constituency Office
#3, 777 Cedar Pl.
PO Box 150
Oakbank, MB R0E 1J0

Andrew Smith
Constituency: Lagimodière *No. of Constituents:* 16,172,
Progressive Conservative
Tel: 204-945-3709; *Fax:* 204-945-1284
andrew.smith@leg.gov.mb.ca
andrewsmithmla.ca
Other Communications: Constituency Phone: 204-416-7337
twitter.com/smith4lag,
www.linkedin.com/in/andrew-smith-79563a42
Constituency Office
#310, 119 Vermillion
Winnipeg, MB R2J 4A9

Caucus Chair, Official Opposition, Bernadette Smith
Constituency: Point Douglas *No. of Constituents:* 14,186,
New Democratic Party
Tel: 204-945-3710; *Fax:* 204-945-2005
bernadette.smith@mbleg.ca
www.mbndp.ca/bernadettesmith
Other Communications: Constituency Phone: 204-414-1477;
Fax: 204-615-5549
twitter.com/BSmithMB,
www.facebook.com/BernadetteSmithMB
Constituency Office
804 Selkirk Ave.
Winnipeg, MB R2W 2N6

Dennis Smook
Constituency: La Vérendrye *No. of Constituents:* 13,279,
Progressive Conservative
Tel: 204-945-3709; *Fax:* 204-945-1284
dennis.smook@leg.gov.mb.ca
dennissmook.ca
Other Communications: Constituency Phone: 204-424-5406;
Fax: 204-424-5458
twitter.com/smookdennis,
www.facebook.com/dennis4laverendrye
Constituency Office
205 Principale St.
PO Box 889
La Broquerie, MB R0A 0W0

Deputy Premier; Minister, Families; Minister Responsible,
Francophone Affairs, Hon. Rochelle Squires
Constituency: Riel *No. of Constituents:* 16,875, Progressive
Conservative
Tel: 204-945-4173; *Fax:* 204-945-5149

minfs@leg.gov.mb.ca
www.pcmanitoba.com/rochelle_squires
Other Communications: Constituency Phone: 204-615-5241;
Fax: 204-615-5242
twitter.com/MLASquires,
www.facebook.com/Rochellesquires.ca
Constituency Office
#5, 140 Meadowood Dr.
Winnipeg, MB R2M 5L8

Heather Stefanson
Constituency: Tuxedo *No. of Constituents:* 16,903,
Progressive Conservative
Tel: 204-945-3709; *Fax:* 204-945-1284
Heather.Stefanson@leg.gov.mb.ca
heatherstefanson.ca
Other Communications: Constituency Phone: 204-487-0013;
Fax: 204-487-0078
Constituency Office
1840 Grant Ave.
Winnipeg, MB R3N 0N4

James Teitsma
Constituency: Radisson *No. of Constituents:* 17,150,
Progressive Conservative
Tel: 204-945-3709; *Fax:* 204-945-1284
james.teitsma@leg.gov.mb.ca
jamesteitsma.ca
Other Communications: Constituency Phone: 204-691-7976
twitter.com/JamesTeitsma
Constituency Office
#220, 1615 Regent Ave. West
Winnipeg, MB R2C 5C6

Mark Wasyliw
Constituency: Fort Garry *No. of Constituents:* 15,399, New
Democratic Party
Tel: 204-945-3710; *Fax:* 204-945-2005
Mark.Wasyliw@mbleg.ca
www.mbndp.ca/mark_wasyliw
Other Communications: Constituency Phone: 204-421-4241
Constituency Office
#202, 1383 Pembina Hwy.
Winnipeg, MB R3T 2BN

Minister, Crown Services, Hon. Jeff Wharton
Constituency: Red River North *No. of Constituents:* 15,077,
Progressive Conservative
Tel: 204-945-8020; *Fax:* 204-948-7700
mincrown@leg.gov.mb.ca
jeffwharton.ca
Other Communications: Constituency Phone: 204-641-2107
twitter.com/jeffwharton4mla
Constituency Office
#12, 1014 Manitoba Ave.
Selkirk, MB R1A 4M2

Caucus Whip, Official Opposition, Matt Wiebe
Constituency: Concordia *No. of Constituents:* 15,021, New
Democratic Party
Tel: 204-945-3710; *Fax:* 204-948-2005
matt.wiebe@mbleg.ca
www.mbndp.ca/mattwiebe
Other Communications: Constituency Phone: 204-654-1857;
Fax: 204-663-1943
twitter.com/mattwiebemb
Constituency Office
#106, 1111 Munroe Ave.
Winnipeg, MB R2K 3Z5

Ian Wishart
Constituency: Portage la Prairie *No. of Constituents:* 14,279,
Progressive Conservative
Tel: 204-945-3709; *Fax:* 204-945-1284
Ian.Wishart@leg.gov.mb.ca
ianwishart.ca
Other Communications: Constituency Phone: 204-857-9267;
Fax: 204-857-9841
www.facebook.com/IanWishartforPortage
Constituency Office
46 Saskatchewan Ave. East
Portage la Prairie, MB R1N 0L2

Rick Wowchuk
Constituency: Swan River *No. of Constituents:* 14,790,
Progressive Conservative
Tel: 204-945-3709; *Fax:* 204-945-1284
rick.wowchuk@leg.gov.mb.ca
Other Communications: Constituency Phone: 204-614-7425;
Fax: 204-614-0152
Constituency Office
#3, 900 Main St.
PO Box 1688
Swan River, MB R0L 1Z0

Vacant
Constituency: Fort Whyte
Note: In August 2021, Brian Pallister stepped down as
Premier, Leader of the PC Party & announced his intention
not to run for re-election. In October 2021, he resigned his
legislature seat.

Manitoba Government Departments & Agencies

Manitoba Advanced Education, Skills & Immigration

Legislative Bldg., #352, 450 Broadway, Winnipeg, MB R3C 0V8

The department was created in 2021, previously having existed until 2016 as the Department of Advanced Education & Literacy when it was dissolved.

Minister, Wayne Ewasko
Tel: 204-945-8480
minaesi@leg.gov.mb.ca

Acting Deputy Minister, Tracey Maconachie
Tel: 204-945-5600
dmaesi@leg.gov.mb.ca

Manitoba Agriculture

Legislative Bldg., #165, 450 Broadway, Winnipeg, MB R3C 0V8

Tel: 204-945-3722; *Fax:* 204-945-3470
minagr@leg.gov.mb.ca
www.gov.mb.ca/agriculture
twitter.com/mbgovag
www.youtube.com/user/ManitobaAgriculture
Manitoba Agriculture, Food & Rural Development was renamed to Manitoba Agriculture following the 2016 general election.

Minister, Hon. Ralph Eichler
Tel: 204-945-3722; *Fax:* 204-945-3470
minagr@leg.gov.mb.ca

Deputy Minister, Dori Gingera-Beauchemin
Tel: 204-945-3734; *Fax:* 204-948-2095
dmagr@leg.gov.mb.ca

Chief Veterinary Officer, Dr. Scott Zaari

Acting Director, Financial & Administrative Services, Diane Dempster
Tel: 204-945-7347

Associated Agencies, Boards & Commissions:

• Agricultural Societies
1129 Queens Ave.
Brandon, MB R7A 1L9
Tel: 204-726-6195; *Fax:* 204-726-6260
Promotes improvement in agriculture & development of Manitoba agricultural products. Provide organizational assistance to rural & urban people.

• Agri-Food Research & Development Initiative Program Council (ARDI)
c/o Manitoba Agriculture
810 Phillips St.
PO Box 1240
Portage la Prairie, MB R1N 3J9

• Animal Care Appeal Board

• Farm Products Marketing Council
www.gov.mb.ca/agriculture/about/boards-and-commissions.html

• Manitoba Agricultural Services Corporation (MASC)
#400, 50 - 24th St. NW
Portage la Prairie, MB R1N 3V9
Tel: 204-239-3246; *Fax:* 204-239-3401
mailbox@masc.mb.ca
www.masc.mb.ca

• Manitoba Horse Racing Commission
#812, 401 York Ave.
PO Box 46086 Westdale
Winnipeg, MB R3R 3S3
Tel: 204-885-7770; *Fax:* 204-831-0942
www.manitobahorsecomm.org
Governs, directs, controls, & regulates horse racing & the operation of all race tracks in Manitoba.

• Manitoba Milk Prices Review Commission

• Manitoba Women's Institute Provincial Board
c/o Manitoba Women's Institute
1129 Queens Ave.
Brandon, MB R7A 1L9
Tel: 204-726-7135; *Fax:* 204-726-6260
www.mbwi.ca

• Veterinary Services Commission
www.gov.mb.ca/agriculture/about/boards-and-commissions.html

Agri-Food & Technology Transfer Division
Assistant Deputy Minister, Leloni Scott
Tel: 204-945-3735
Chief Operating Officer & General Manager, Food Development Centre, Vacant

Acting Executive Director, Planning & Service Innovation Directorate, Kim Beilby
Tel: 204-726-7023
Director, GO Teams, Gerald Huebner
Tel: 204-797-4522
Director, Economic Development Initiatives, Leo Prince
Tel: 204-945-2427

Policy & Transformation Division
Assistant Deputy Minister, David Hunt
Tel: 204-945-3910
Manager, Research Intelligence, Patti Rothenburger
Tel: 204-822-2856

Food Development Centre
Acting Chief Operating Officer, Robin Young
Tel: 204-239-3624
Manager, Pilot Plant & Commercial Activities, Javier Planinich
Tel: 204-871-5808
Manager, Product & Process Development, Alphonsus Utioh
Tel: 204-239-3179

Production & Economic Development Division
Assistant Deputy Minister, Maurice Bouvier
Tel: 204-945-3736
Director, Primary Agriculture, Miles Beaudin
Tel: 204-945-6773
Director, Food & Agri-Product Processing Branch, Leo Prince
Tel: 204-945-2427
Manager, Program Implementation, Michael Yacentiuk
Tel: 204-750-1474
Leader, Sector Planning, Scott Stothers
Tel: 204-945-3496

Office of the Auditor General

#500, 330 Portage Ave., Winnipeg, MB R3C 0C4
Tel: 204-945-3790; *Fax:* 204-945-2169
contact@oag.mb.ca
www.oag.mb.ca
twitter.com/AuditorGenMB
www.facebook.com/AuditorGenMB
www.linkedin.com/company/manitoba-auditor-general
Established under The Auditor General Act, the Office of the Auditor General is an independent office of the Legislative Assembly. Through audit of management practices & accountability reports, the Office contributes to effective governance & public trust.

Auditor General, Tyson Shtykalo, CPA, CA

Assistant Auditor General, Financial Statements, Natalie Bessette-Asumadu, CPA, CA

Assistant Auditor General, Performance Audit Services, Stacy Wowchuk, CPA, CA

Director, Corporate Services, Jay Shyiak

Manitoba Civil Service Commission

#935, 155 Carlton St., Winnipeg, MB R3C 3H8
Tel: 204-945-2332; *Fax:* 204-945-1486
Toll-Free: 800-282-8069
TTY: 204-945-1437
csc@gov.mb.ca
www.manitoba.ca/csc
Other Communication: Recruitment Support Services, Phone: 204-945-1334; Fax: 204-948-2193; Email: govjobs@gov.mb.ca

Minister Responsible; Minister, Central Services, Hon. Reg Helwer
Tel: 204-945-6215
mincentral@leg.gov.mb.ca

Commissioner, Charlene Paquin

Executive Director, Information Communication Technology Shared Services, Michael Antonio
Tel: 204-232-3560

Acting Executive Director, Human Resource Operations, Jane Morgan
Tel: 204-948-1266

Associated Agencies, Boards & Commissions:
• Civil Service Commission Board
#935, 155 Carlton St.
Winnipeg, MB R3C 3H8
Tel: 204-945-1435; *Fax:* 204-945-1486
www.gov.mb.ca/csc/aboutcsc/cscboard.html

• Civil Service Superannuation Board
#1200, 444 St. Mary Ave.
Winnipeg, MB R3C 3T1
Tel: 204-946-3200; *Fax:* 204-945-0237
Toll-free: 800-432-5134
askus@cssb.mb.ca
www.cssb.mb.ca

Manitoba Conservation & Climate

200 Saulteaux Cres., PO Box 22 Winnipeg, MB R3J 3W3
Tel: 204-945-6784; *Fax:* 204-948-2656
Toll-Free: 800-214-6497
cc@gov.mb.ca
www.manitoba.ca/sd

Manitoba Conservation & Climate was created in 2019. The department protects, conserves, manages & sustains development of forest, fisheries, wildlife, water, energy & Crown & Park land resources. It also protects environmental integrity, & ensures a high level of environmental quality.
The department is the lead agency for providing outdoor recreational opportunities for Manitobans & visitors.
It is a contributor to the economic development & well-being of the province, through resource-based harvesting operations, & in cooperation with other departments responsible for agriculture & tourism. Protecting people & property from floods, wildfires, & adverse effects of other natural occurrences, are also major roles.
The department administers legislation & regulations protecting the environment & public health, participates in approval, licensing & appeals for industrial development activities, administers waste reduction & pollution prevention activities, & monitors environmental quality.

Minister, Hon. Sarah Guillemard
Tel: 204-945-3730; *Fax:* 204-945-3586
mincc@leg.gov.mb.ca

Deputy Minister, Jan Forster
Tel: 204-945-3785; *Fax:* 204-948-2403
dmcc@leg.gov.mb.ca

Director, Indigenous Relations, Ron Missyabit
Tel: 204-945-7088

Associated Agencies, Boards & Commissions:

• Clean Environment Commission
#305, 155 Carlton St.
Winnipeg, MB R3C 3H8
Tel: 204-945-0594; *Fax:* 204-945-0090
Toll-free: 800-597-3556
cec@gov.mb.ca
www.cecmanitoba.ca
Arm's-length provincial agency that holds public hearings on the subject of the regulation of a broad range of private industry, municipal or provincial government operations. Investigates environmental matters or considers proposed abatement projects with public hearings. Reports to the Minister with advice & recommendations & acts as a mediator between two or more parties to an environmental dispute.

• Conservation Agreements Board
c/o Manitoba Habitat Heritage Corporation
#200, 1555 St James St.
Winnipeg, MB R3H 1B5
Tel: 204-784-4350
mhhc@mhhc.mb.ca
www.gov.mb.ca/conservation/wildlife/habcons/consagree.html

• Ecological Reserves Advisory Committee
c/o Manitoba Conservation, Parks & Natural Areas Branch
200 Saulteaux Cres.
PO Box 53
Winnipeg, MB R3J 3W3
Tel: 204-945-4148; *Fax:* 204-945-0012
www.gov.mb.ca/conservation/parks/ec_reserves/reserves.html

• Endangered Species Advisory Committee
200 Saulteaux Cres.
PO Box 24
Winnipeg, MB R3J 3W3
Tel: 204-945-7775; *Fax:* 204-945-3077

• Manitoba Habitat Heritage Corporation
#200, 1555 St. James St.
Winnipeg, MB R3H 1B5
Tel: 204-784-4350; *Fax:* 204-784-7359
www.mhhc.mb.ca

Act & The Election Financing Act.
#5, 165 Kennedy St.
Winnipeg, MB R3C 1S6

Director, Strategic Initiatives, Mark Robertson
Tel: 204-945-3900

Manitoba Families

Legislative Bldg., #357, 450 Broadway, Winnipeg, MB R3C 0V8

Tel: 204-945-3744
Toll-Free: 866-626-4862
TTY: 204-945-4796
www.gov.mb.ca/fs

Manitoba Family Services was renamed to Manitoba Families following the 2016 general election. The department supports citizens in need to achieve fuller participation in society & greater self-suffiency & independence. Helps keep children, families & communities safe & secure & promotes healthy citizen development & well-being. Mission is accomplished through: provision of financial support; provision of supports & services for adults & children with disabilities; provision of child protection & related services; assistance to people facing family violence or family disruption; provision of services & supports to promote the healthy development & well-being of children & families; assistance to Manitobans to access safe, appropriate & affordable housing; fostering community capacity & engaging the broader community to participate in & contribute to decision-making; & respectful & appropriate delivery of programs & services.

Minister, Hon. Rochelle Squires
Tel: 204-945-4173; *Fax:* 204-945-5149
minfs@leg.gov.mb.ca

Deputy Minister, Kathryn Gerrard
Tel: 204-945-6704; *Fax:* 204-945-1896
dmfs@leg.gov.mb.ca

Associated Agencies, Boards & Commissions:

• All Aboard Committee
Tel: 204-945-3380
allaboard@gov.mb.ca
www.gov.mb.ca/allaboard

• Cooperative Loans & Loans Guarantee Board
#400, 352 Donald St.
Winnipeg, MB R3B 2H8
Tel: 204-945-3379; *Fax:* 204-948-1065
Toll-free: 866-479-6155
co-ops@gov.mb.ca
www.entrepreneurshipmanitoba.ca/financial-programs

• Cooperative Promotion Board
c/o Business Development Specialist Cooperatives
#B11, 340 - 9th St.
Brandon, MB R7A 6C2
Tel: 204-726-7003; *Fax:* 204-724-2616
www.gov.mb.ca/jec/coop/Mobile/building/coop_promoboard.html

• Disabilities Issues Office
#630, 240 Graham Ave.
Winnipeg, MB R3C 0J7
Tel: 204-945-7613; *Fax:* 204-948-2896
dio@gov.mb.ca
www.gov.mb.ca/dio
Other Communication: Toll-Free Phone: 800-282-8069, ext. 7613; AccessibilityMB URL: www.accessibilitymb.ca

• Manitoba Community Services Council, Inc. (MCSC)
#102, 90 Garry St.
Winnipeg, MB R3C 4H1
Tel: 204-940-4450; *Fax:* 204-453-2692
applications@mbcsc.ca
www.mbcsc.ca

• Manitoba Housing & Renewal Corporation (Manitoba Housing & Community Development)
See Entry Name Index for detailed listing.

Administration & Finance
777 Portage Ave., 3rd Fl., Winnipeg, MB R3G 0N3

Tel: 204-945-3242
fadmin@gov.mb.ca

Acting Assistant Deputy Minister, Brian Brown
Tel: 204-945-5943
Executive Director, Project Management & Information & Technology, Sherry Zajac
Tel: 204-945-0032
Director, Financial & Administrative Services, Wayne Pestun
Tel: 204-945-4005
Project Manager, Agency Accountability & Support Unit, Rick Dykes
Tel: 204-945-1109

Non-Profit Organization Manager, Agency Accountability & Support Unit, Dennis Ceicko
Tel: 204-945-4869

Child & Family Services
777 Portage Ave., Winnipeg, MB R3G 0N3

Tel: 204-945-6964
cfsd@gov.mb.ca
www.gov.mb.ca/fs/childfam/index.html
Assistant Deputy Minister, Diane Kelly
Tel: 204-945-4575
Chief Executive Officer, General Child & Family Services Authority, Debbie Besant
Director, Bringing Families Together Project, Christy Holnbeck
Tel: 204-801-0964
Acting Manager of Administration, Child Protection, Sharon Field
Tel: 204-945-0840
Specialist, Community Development, Sharon Krysko
Tel: 204-945-2152
Provincial Adoption Clerk, Stephanie Turmaine
Tel: 204-945-6958

Community Programs & Corporate Services

cfsd@gov.mb.ca
Assistant Deputy Minister, Jennifer Rattray
Tel: 204-945-6374
Acting Executive Director, Children's disABILITY Services, Tracy Moore
Tel: 204-945-3255
Acting Executive Director, Corporate Services & Administration, Michelle Stephen-Wiens
Tel: 204-945-5810
Director, Early Learning & Child Care Program, Margaret Ferniuk
Tel: 204-945-2668
Vulnerable Persons' Commissioner, JoAnne Reinsch
Tel: 204-945-0564

Community Service Delivery
#119, 114 Garry St., Winnipeg, MB R3C 4V4

Tel: 204-945-1634
csd@gov.mb.ca
Assistant Deputy Minister, Michelle Dubik
Tel: 204-945-2204
Acting Executive Director, Rural & Northern Services, Dan Knight
Tel: 204-945-4998
Acting Director, Strategic Planning & Program Support, Cees deVries
Tel: 204-945-0454
Acting Director, Provincial Services, Esther Kiernan
Tel: 204-945-6854
Acting Assistant Director, Adult Disability Programs, Andrea Thibault-McNeill
Tel: 204-945-6131
Program Specialist, Community Living disABILITY Services, Craig Wynands
Tel: 204-945-5599

Manitoba Developmental Centre
840 - 3rd St. NE, Portage la Prairie, MB R1N 3C6

Tel: 204-856-4200
csd@gov.mb.ca
www.gov.mb.ca/fs/pwd/mdc
Chief Executive Officer, Tom Sidebottom
Tel: 204-856-4237
Director, Habilitation/Specialty Program, Melanie Ferg
Tel: 204-856-4223
Director, Operations, Michele Roteliuk
Tel: 204-856-4219
Acting Manager, Environmental Services, Shelly Strong
Tel: 204-856-4333

Manitoba Housing

www.gov.mb.ca/housing
Executive Director, Asset Management, Meghan O'Laughlin
Tel: 204-806-4514
Executive Director, Housing Delivery & Land Development, Dwayne Rewniak
Tel: 204-945-4703
Director, Security & IPMG, David Grayston
Tel: 204-945-5880
Director, Agency Services, Lisa May
Tel: 204-945-8129

Manitoba Finance

Legislative Bldg., #103, 450 Broadway, Winnipeg, MB R3C 0V8

Tel: 204-945-3744
www.gov.mb.ca/finance
Established in 1969 under authority of the Financial Administration Act. Responsible for central accounting, payroll & financial reporting services for the government, consumer &

corporate affairs & central financial control of cost-shared agreements. The ministry manages government borrowing programs & is responsible for federal-provincial relations.

Minister, Hon. Scott Fielding
Tel: 204-945-3952; *Fax:* 204-948-6057
minfin@leg.gov.mb.ca

Deputy Minister, Richard Groen
Tel: 204-945-5343; *Fax:* 204-945-1640
dmfin@leg.gov.mb.ca

Tax Appeals Commissioner, Dale Ammeter

Director, Insurance & Risk Management, Jim Swanson
Tel: 204-945-1919

Associated Agencies, Boards & Commissions:

• Crown Corporations Council / Conseil des corporations de la Couronne
#1130, 444 St. Mary Ave.
Winnipeg, MB R3C 3T1
Tel: 204-949-5270; *Fax:* 204-949-5283
info@crownnc.mb.ca
www.crownnc.mb.ca

• Deposit Guarantee Corporation of Manitoba
#390, 200 Graham Ave.
Winnipeg, MB R3C 4L5
Tel: 204-942-8480; *Fax:* 204-947-1723
Toll-free: 800-697-4447
mail@depositguarantee.mb.ca
depositguarantee.mb.ca

• Manitoba Securities Commission
#500, 400 St. Mary Ave.
Winnipeg, MB R3C 4K5
Tel: 204-945-2548; *Fax:* 204-945-0330
securities@gov.mb.ca
www.mbsecurities.ca
Other Communication: Real Estate Division, Phone: 204-945-2562; Fax: 204-948-4627; Email: realestate@gov.mb.ca
The Manitoba Securities Commission is an independent agency of the Government of Manitoba that protects investors & promotes fair & efficient capital markets throughout the province.

• Public Utilities Board
#400, 330 Portage Ave.
Winnipeg, MB R3C 0C4
Tel: 204-945-2638; *Fax:* 204-945-2643
Toll-free: 866-854-3698
publicutilities@gov.mb.ca
www.pub.gov.mb.ca

Comptroller Division
#715, 401 York Ave., Winnipeg, MB R3C 0P8

Tel: 204-945-4920; *Fax:* 204-948-3539
Provides central accounting, payroll & financial reporting services, & central financial control of cost-shared agreements for the government. The division develops government-wide financial systems, policies & procedures, & provides policy advice for financial & management systems. The division coordinates, develops & maintains departmental data processing systems, & provides direction to the government on the effective use of information systems technology
Provincial Comptroller, Aurel Tess
Tel: 204-945-4919
Executive Director, Internal Audit & Consulting Services, Dina Long
Tel: 204-945-8110
Director, All Charities Campaign, Debra Laturnus
Tel: 204-945-5621
Director, Disbursements & Accounting, Terry Patrick
Tel: 204-945-1343

Corporate Services Division
Assistant Deputy Minister, Ilana Dadds
Tel: 204-945-1469
Executive Director, Information Communication Technology Shared Services Branch, Michael Antonio
Tel: 204-232-3560
Director, Information Support Services for CSC, Phong Duong
Tel: 204-391-1535

Finance Research Division
#910, 386 Broadway, Winnipeg, MB R3C 3R6

Tel: 204-945-3757; *Fax:* 204-945-5051
www.gov.mb.ca/finance/fedprov
Provides research & analytical support for national/provincial fiscal & economic matters & inter-governmental financial relations. Also administers fiscal arrangements & tax collection agreements with the federal government & tax credit programs with federal & municipal governments

Assistant Deputy Minister, Silvester Komlodi
 Tel: 204-794-1282
Director, Economic & Fiscal Analysis, Narendra Budhia
 Tel: 204-945-5078

Manitoba Bureau of Statistics (MBS)
#824, 155 Carlton St., Winnipeg, MB R3C 3H9
 Tel: 204-945-2406
 www.gov.mb.ca/mbs

Acting Director, Michael Wisener
 Tel: 204-293-3183
Labour Market & Survey Statistician, Melissa Luff
 Tel: 204-945-2985
Demographics & Census Statistician, Tara Newton
 Tel: 204-945-2406
 tnewton@mbs.gov.mb.ca

Manitoba Financial Services Agency (MFSA)
c/o Financial Institutions Regulation Branch, #207, 400 St. Mary Ave., Winnipeg, MB R3C 4K5
 Tel: 204-945-2542; *Fax:* 204-948-2268
 Toll-Free: 800-282-8069
 insurance@gov.mb.ca
 www.mbfinancialinstitutions.ca
As part of the MFSA, the Financial Institutions Regulation Branch (FIRB) is responsible for administering The Insurance Act, The Credit Unions & Caisses Populaires Act, The Cooperatives Act & Part XXIV of The Corporations Act. The Manitoba Securities Commission is also part of the MFSA.
Chief Administrative Officer, David Cheop
 Tel: 204-945-2551
Superintendent, Financial Institutions, Scott Moore
 Tel: 204-945-1150

Priorities & Planning Secretariat
Director, Jaqueline Maxted
 Tel: 204-945-1931
Principal Secretary, Jonathan Scarth
 Tel: 204-945-0346
Senior Project Manager, Philip Goodman
 Tel: 204-945-1855
Senior Project Manager, David Mclaughlin
 Tel: 204-945-0460

Taxation Division
#101, 401 York Ave., Winnipeg, MB R3C 0P8
 Tel: 204-945-5603; *Fax:* 204-945-0896
 Toll-Free: 800-782-0318
 www.gov.mb.ca/finance/taxation
Tax Compliance Officer, Taxation Management & Research, Nadine Dupuis
 Tel: 204-470-8583

Treasury Board Secretariat
#200, 386 Broadway, Winnipeg, MB R3C 3R6
 Tel: 204-945-4150; *Fax:* 204-948-4878
 www.gov.mb.ca/finance/tb
The Treasury Board Secretariat provides financial and analytical support and advice to the Minister of Finance and Treasury Board.
Secretary, Paul Beauregard
 Tel: 204-945-1102
Assistant Deputy Minister, Strategic Initiatives, Mohammed Bhabha
 Tel: 204-792-9181
Assistant Deputy Minister, Fiscal Management & Capital Planning, Richard Groen
 Tel: 204-945-1096
Assistant Deputy Minister, Real Estate Services Division, Michal Kubasiewicz
 Tel: 204-799-0339
Acting Assistant Deputy Minister, Analysis & Strategic Management, Sarah Thiele
 Tel: 204-945-2788

Treasury Division
#350, 363 Broadway, Winnipeg, MB R3C 3N9
 Tel: 204-945-3702; *Fax:* 204-948-2233
 www.gov.mb.ca/finance/treasury
Created as a separate entity in 1976, to address the need for placing greater emphasis on the management of substantial amounts of money, debt & investments. Currency & interest rate risk management programs have been developed due to the increase in volumes & dollar values. The division assists with the arrangement of financing for municipalities, schools & hospitals
Assistant Deputy Minister, Garry Steski
 Tel: 204-945-6637
Director, Risk Management & Banking Branch, Bob Block
 Tel: 204-945-0363
Director, Capital Markets, Don Delisle
 Tel: 204-945-5404
Director, Treasury Operations, Scott Wiebe
 Tel: 204-945-6677

Manitoba Health & Seniors Care
#100, 300 Carlton St., Winnipeg, MB R3B 3M9
 Tel: 204-945-3744
 Toll-Free: 866-626-4862
 mgi@gov.mb.ca
 www.gov.mb.ca/health
The department is responsible for the overall quality of the health system in the province, for maintaining the health system, & for ensuring that the health needs of Manitobans are met. Services are provided through regional delivery systems, hospitals & other health care facilities. The Department also makes insured benefits claims payments for residents of Manitoba related to the cost of medical, hospital, personal care, pharmacare & other health services. To lead the way to quality health care, built with creativity, compassion, confidence, trust & respect; empower Manitobans through knowledge, choices & access to the best possible health resources; & build partnerships & alliances for healthy & supportive communities. To foster innovation in the health care system. This is accomplished through: developing mechanisms to assess & monitor quality of care, utilization & cost effectiveness; fostering behaviours & environments which promote health; & promoting responsiveness & flexibility of delivery systems, & alternative & less expensive services.

Minister; Minster, Mental Health, Wellness & Recovery,
Hon. Audrey Gordon
 Tel: 204-945-1211
 minmhwr@leg.gov.mb.ca

Deputy Minister, Karen Herd
 Tel: 204-945-3771; *Fax:* 204-948-2703
 dmhsal@leg.gov.mb.ca

Associated Agencies, Boards & Commissions:

• Addictions Foundation of Manitoba (AFM) / Fondation manitobaine de lutte contre les dépendances
1031 Portage Ave.
Winnipeg, MB R3G 0R8
 Tel: 204-981-6691; *Fax:* 204-944-7082
 Toll-free: 866-638-2561
 execoff@afm.mb.ca
 www.afm.mb.ca
 Other Communication: General Inquiries, Phone: 204-944-6200; Library, Email: library@afm.mb.ca

• Appeal Panel for Home Care
c/o Manitoba Health Appeal Board
#102, 500 Portage Ave.
Winnipeg, MB R3X 3X1
 Tel: 204-945-5408; *Fax:* 204-948-2024
 Toll-free: 866-744-3257
 appeals@gov.mb.ca
 www.gov.mb.ca/health/appealboard/appeals.html

• CancerCare Manitoba (CCMB)
 Tel: 204-787-2197
 Toll-free: 866-561-1026
 www.cancercare.mb.ca

• Funeral Board of Manitoba
254 Portage Ave.
Winnipeg, MB R3C 0B6
 Tel: 204-947-1098; *Fax:* 204-945-0424
 funeralboard@gov.mb.ca
 www.gov.mb.ca/funeraldirectorsboard

• Health Information Privacy Committee (HIPC)
#4043, 300 Carlton St.
Winnipeg, MB R3B 3M9
 www.gov.mb.ca/health/hipc

• Hearing Aid Board
#302, 258 Portage Ave.
Winnipeg, MB R3C 0B6
 Tel: 204-945-3800; *Fax:* 204-945-0728
 Toll-free: 800-782-0067

• Manitoba Council on Aging
#1610, 155 Carlton St.
Winnipeg, MB R3C 3H8
 Tel: 204-945-6565
 Toll-free: 800-665-6565
 seniors@gov.mb.ca
 www.gov.mb.ca/shas/manitobacouncil

• Manitoba Drug Standards & Therapeutics Committee (MDSTC)
#1014, 300 Carlton St.
Winnipeg, MB R3B 3M9
 Tel: 204-786-7233
 www.gov.mb.ca/health/mdbif/review.html
 Other Communication: Toll-Free Phone: 800-297-8099, ext. 7233

• Manitoba Health Appeal Board
#102, 500 Portage Ave.
Winnipeg, MB R3C 3X1
 Tel: 204-945-5408; *Fax:* 204-948-2024
 Toll-free: 866-744-3257
 appeals@gov.mb.ca
 www.gov.mb.ca/health/appealboard
Quasi-judicial body responsible for making decisions on appeals under The Health Services Insurance Act, The Ambulance Services Act & The Mental Health Act.

Administration & Finance
Assistant Deputy Minister & Chief Financial Officer, Dan Skwarchuk
 Tel: 204-788-2525
Comptroller, Tony Messner
 Tel: 204-786-7135
Executive Director, Finance, Rhonda Hogg
 Tel: 204-788-7138
Executive Director, Health Information Management, Deborah Malazdrewicz
 Tel: 204-786-7149
Executive Director, Management Services, Scott Murray
 Tel: 204-786-7230
Acting Director, Regional Finance, Charlyene Cosens
 Tel: 204-786-7260

Health Workforce Secretariat
Assistant Deputy Minister, Beth Beaupre
 Tel: 204-786-6674
Executive Director, Health Human Resource Planning, Sean Brygidyr
 Tel: 204-788-6767
Executive Director, Contracts & Negotiations, Pearl Reimer
 Tel: 204-788-6374
Acting Director, Fee for Service/Insured Benefits, Curtis Peters
 Tel: 204-786-7331

Mental Health & Addictions, Primary Health Care & Seniors
300 Carlton St., 4th Floor, Winnipeg, MB R3B 3M9
 Tel: 204-788-6666
 www.gov.mb.ca/health/publichealth
 Other Communication: Primary Care, Phone: 204-788-6732; Fax: 204-943-5305; Email: phc@gov.mb.ca; URL: www.gov.mb.ca/health/primarycare
Mission is to encourage the prevention of illness & injury, coordinate access to health care, & strengthen existing primary health care services with new initiatives
Assistant Deputy Minister, Marcia Thomson
 Tel: 204-784-3908
Chief Provincial Psychiatrist, Richard Zloty
 Tel: 204-788-6677
Executive Director, Continuing Care, Lorraine Dacombe Dewar
 Tel: 204-788-6649
Executive Director, Mental Health & Addictions, Carly Johnston
 Tel: 204-786-7281
Executive Director, Primary Health Care Branch, Barbara Wasilewski
 Tel: 204-788-7176

Seniors & Healthy Aging Secretariat
#1610, 155 Carlton St., Winnipeg, MB R3C 3H8
 Tel: 204-945-6565; *Fax:* 204-948-2514
 Toll-Free: 800-665-6565
 seniors@gov.mb.ca
 www.gov.mb.ca/healthyliving
Assistant Deputy Minister, Marcia Thomson
 Tel: 204-784-3908
Executive Director, Mental Health & Spiritual Health Care, Carly Johnston
 Tel: 204-786-7281
Executive Director, Addictions Policy & Support Branch, Tina Leclair
 Tel: 204-784-3913
Executive Director, Healthy Living & Healthy Populations, Debbie Nelson
 Tel: 204-788-6654

Provincial Policy & Programs
Executive Director, Provincial Drug Programs, Patricia Caetano
 Tel: 204-786-7333
Executive Director, Health Infrastructure, Bryan Payne
 Tel: 204-786-7232
Director, Corporate Services, Jeff Gunter
 Tel: 204-788-6749
Acting Director, Drug Management Policy, Jeff Onyskiw
 Tel: 204-788-6436
Manager, Protection for Persons in Care, Chris Campbell
 Tel: 204-786-7264
Coordinator, French Language Services, Richard Loiselle
 Tel: 204-788-6698; *Fax:* 204-772-2943

Regional Policy & Programs

Executive Director, Acute, Tertiary & Specialty Care, Brie DeMonte
Tel: 204-788-6331

Executive Director, Health Emergency Management, Corene Debreuil
Tel: 204-945-0711

Provincial Medical Director, Emergency Medical Services, Anthony Herd
Tel: 204-945-6501

Director, Medical Transportation Coordination Centre, John Jones
Tel: 204-571-8863

Director, Diagnostic Services, Provincial Cancer & Diagnostic Services Branch, Michele Mathae-Hunter
Tel: 204-788-6628

Director, Office of Provincial Transplant & Transfusion Services, Wendy Peppel
Tel: 204-786-7374

Disaster Management Specialist, Office of Disaster Management, Jennifer Chiarotto
Tel: 204-945-7434

Associated Agencies, Boards & Commissions:

• Interlake-Eastern Regional Health Authority
233A Main St.
Selkirk, MB R1A 1S1
Tel: 204-785-4700; *Fax:* 204-482-4300
Toll-free: 855-347-8500
info@ierha.ca
www.ierha.ca

• Northern Health Region
84 Church St.
Flin Flon, MB R8A 1L8
Tel: 204-687-1300; *Fax:* 204-687-6405
Toll-free: 888-340-6742

• Prairie Mountain Health
192 - 1st Ave. West
PO Box 579
Souris, MB R0K 2C0
Tel: 204-483-5000; *Fax:* 204-483-5005
Toll-free: 888-682-2253
prairiemountainhealth.ca

• Southern Health / Santé Sud
94 Principale St.
PO Box 470
La Broquerie, MB R0A 0W0
Tel: 204-424-5880; *Fax:* 204-424-5888
Toll-free: 800-742-6509
info@southernhealth.ca
www.southernhealth.ca

• Winnipeg Regional Health Authority
650 Main St., 4th Fl.
Winnipeg, MB R3B 1E2
Tel: 204-926-7000; *Fax:* 204-926-7007
www.wrha.mb.ca

Manitoba Human Rights Commission (MHRC)

#700, 175 Hargrave St., Winnipeg, MB R3C 3R8
Tel: 204-945-3007; *Fax:* 204-945-1292
Toll-Free: 888-884-8681
TTY: 888-897-2811
hrc@gov.mb.ca
www.manitobahumanrights.ca
Secondary Address: #341, 340 - 9th St.
Brandon Office
Brandon, MB R7A 6C2
twitter.com/MBHumanRights
www.facebook.com/ManitobaHumanRightsCommission

Acting Chair, John Burchill

Manitoba Hydro

360 Portage Ave., PO Box 815 Stn. Main, Winnipeg, MB R3C 2P4
Tel: 204-480-5900; *Fax:* 204-360-6155
Toll-Free: 888-624-9376
TTY: 855-287-6809
www.hydro.mb.ca
twitter.com/manitobahydro
www.facebook.com/ManitobaHydro
www.linkedin.com/company/manitoba-hydro
www.youtube.com/user/ManitobaHydro

Manitoba Hydro (MH) is a major energy utility. One of the largest electricity & natural gas utilities in Canada, it serves 580,262 electric customers throughout Manitoba & 281,990 gas customers in various communities throughout southern Manitoba. Virtually all electricity generated by the provincial Crown Corporation is from self-renewing water power. MH is the major distributor of natural gas in the province. Developing &

implementing an environmental management system consistent with ISO standards. Actively pursuing a vairety or projects & programs aimed at reducing GHG & vehicle emissions, recycling, conserving energy, digging out contaminated soils, partnering with NGOs.

President & CEO, Jay Grewal

Acting Chief Finance & Strategy Officer, Shawna C. Pachal

Vice-President, Indigenous Relations, Jeffrey Betker

Vice-President, Human Resources & Corporate Services, Bryan Luce

Vice-President, Transmission, Shane Mailey

Vice-President, Generation & Wholesale, Lorne Midford

Vice-President, Marketing & Customer Service, Siobhan Vinish

General Counsel & Corporate Secretary, Ken Tennenhouse

Manitoba Indigenous Reconciliation & Northern Relations

Legislative Bldg., #301, 450 Broadway, Winnipeg, MB R3C OV8
Tel: 204-945-3788; *Fax:* 204-945-1383
INRweb@gov.mb.ca
www.gov.mb.ca/inr

Aboriginal & Northern Affairs was renamed Indigenous & Municipal Relations following the 2016 general election. It was further divided by Premier Pallister in an August 2017 cabinet shuffle, into two new departments: Indigenous & Northern Relations, & Municipal Relations.
The department's goals are as follows: to improve the quality of life & opportunities for Indigenous peoples & northern communities; to facilitate better services, opportunities & results for Manitoba's Indigenous & northern people; to support the mental, emotional, physical & spiritual health of northern communities & Indigenous people; to resolve outstanding provincial obligations to Indigenous & northern communities; to foster self-determination, accountability & sustainable growth; & to strengthen the participation of Indigenous & northern people in Manitoba's economy.

Minister, Hon. Alan Lagimodiere
Tel: 204-945-3788; *Fax:* 204-945-1383
minindnr@leg.gov.mb.ca

Deputy Minister, Michelle Dubik
Tel: 204-945-0565; *Fax:* 204-945-5255
dmir@leg.gov.mb.ca

Executive Director, Northern Affairs Branch, Freda Albert
Tel: 204-677-6795

Director, Policy & Strategic Initiatives, Scott DeJaegher
Tel: 204-945-0572

Director, Community Engagement, Paul Doolan
Tel: 204-945-2161

Associated Agencies, Boards & Commissions:
• Northern Affairs Capital Approval Board
PO Box 2532
The Pas, MB R9A 1M3

Manitoba Infrastructure

Legislative Bldg., #203, 450 Broadway, Winnipeg, MB R3C OV8
www.gov.mb.ca/mit

Manitoba Infrastructure & Transportation was renamed Manitoba Infrastructure after the 2016 general election. The department is responsible for the development of transportation policy & legislation & for managing the province's infrastructure network. The department's transportation responsibilities include corporate policy & provincial legislation development, motor carrier safety regulation enforcement & the development of sustainable transportation initiatives. Manitoba Infrastructure is also responsible for the delivery of air ambulance flights, property management, procurement, fleet vehicles, Crown Lands stewardship, mail management & government building security.

Minister, Hon. Ron Schuler
Tel: 204-945-3723; *Fax:* 204-945-7610
minmi@leg.gov.mb.ca

Deputy Minister, Sarah Thiele
Tel: 204-945-3768; *Fax:* 204-945-4766
dmmi@leg.gov.mb.ca

Associated Agencies, Boards & Commissions:
• Crown Lands & Property Agency
#308, 25 Tupper St. North
Portage la Prairie, MB R1N 3K1
Tel: 204-239-3510; *Fax:* 204-239-3560
Toll-free: 888-210-9589
clpainfo@gov.mb.ca
www.clpamb.ca
• Disaster Financial Assistance Appeal Board
#1525, 405 Broadway
Winnipeg, MB R3C 3L6
Tel: 204-945-4772; *Fax:* 204-945-4929
Toll-free: 888-267-8298
dfa@gov.mb.ca
www.gov.mb.ca/emo/recover/home/appeal.html
Other Communication: Emergency Measures Organization,
Email: emo@gov.mb.ca
• Highway Traffic Board/Motor Transport Board
#200, 301 Weston St.
Winnipeg, MB R3E 3H4
Tel: 204-945-8912; *Fax:* 204-783-6529
www.gov.mb.ca/mit/boards/traffic.html
• Lake of the Woods Control Board (LWCB)
c/o Executive Engineer
373 Sussex Dr., Block E1
Ottawa, ON K1A 0H3
Fax: 888-702-9632
Toll-free: 800-661-5922
secretariat@lwcb.ca
www.lwcb.ca
• License Suspension Appeal Board
#200, 301 Weston St.
Winnipeg, MB R3E 3H4
Tel: 204-945-7350; *Fax:* 204-948-2682
www.gov.mb.ca/mit/boards/suspension.html
• Manitoba East Side Road Authority (ESRA)
#200, 155 Carlton St.
Winnipeg, MB R3C 3H8
Tel: 204-945-4900; *Fax:* 204-948-2462
Toll-free: 866-356-6355
eastside@gov.mb.ca
www.eastsideroadauthority.mb.ca
The Authority oversees the safety, reliability & improvement of transportation services between communities on the east side of Lake Winnipeg & the the rest of the province.
• Manitoba Floodway Authority (MFA)
#200, 155 Carlton St.
Winnipeg, MB R3C 3H8
Tel: 204-945-4900; *Fax:* 204-948-2462
Toll-free: 866-356-6355
floodway@gov.mb.ca
www.floodwayauthority.mb.ca
Separate, independent, publicly accountable provincial agency that will manage the expansion & maintenance of the Red River Floodway on behalf of Manitobans.
• Manitoba Land Value Appraisal Commission
#1144, 363 Broadway
Winnipeg, MB R3C 3N9
Tel: 204-945-5455; *Fax:* 204-948-2235
www.gov.mb.ca/mit/boards/land.html
• Medical Review Committee
#200, 301 Weston St.
Winnipeg, MB R3E 3H4
Tel: 204-945-7350; *Fax:* 204-948-2682
www.gov.mb.ca/mit/boards/medical.html

Corporate Services Division
Assistant Deputy Minister, Leigh Anne Solmundson Lumbard
Tel: 204-945-2964
Director, Comptrollership & Review, Rhonda Bistyak
Tel: 204-781-7372
Director, Financial Services, Lynn Cowley
Tel: 204-805-3883
Director, Occupational Safety, Health & Risk Management, Heather Newbiggin
Tel: 204-945-3809
Director, Information Technology Services, John Teillet
Tel: 204-792-7071
Director, Corporate Information Branch, Larisa Wydra
Tel: 204-805-2739

Emergency Measures Organization (EMO)
#1525, 405 Broadway Ave., Winnipeg, MB R3C 3L6
Tel: 204-945-4772; *Fax:* 204-945-4929
Toll-Free: 888-267-8298
emo@gov.mb.ca
www.gov.mb.ca/emo
Other Communication: Disaster Financial Assistance, Email:
dfa@gov.mb.ca
Coordinates emergency response, municipal emergency
planning & training, & disaster recovery programs
Assistant Deputy Minister, Lee Spencer
Tel: 204-945-3922
Director, Recovery, Jeremy Angus
Tel: 204-945-3050
Director, Operations, Michael Gagne
Tel: 204-945-4772
Director, Planning, Don Mackinnon
Tel: 204-945-4772

Engineering & Operations Division
Assistant Deputy Minister, Ron Weatherburn
Tel: 204-945-3775
Executive Director, Highway Engineering, Walter T. Burdz
Tel: 204-945-3772
Executive Director, Construction & Maintenance, Larry Halayko
Tel: 204-945-7035
Executive Director, Highway Regional Operations, Don McKibbin
Tel: 204-726-6807

Motor Carrier Division
Assistant Deputy Minister, Esther Nagtegaal
Tel: 204-945-5199
Director, Motor Carrier Strategic Initiatives, Lawrence Mercer
Tel: 204-945-1894
Manager, Commercial Vehicle Safety & Permits, Tracy Proctor
Tel: 204-945-3892

Transportation Policy Division
Assistant Deputy Minister, Esther Nagtegaal
Tel: 204-945-5199
Director, Transportation Policy & Service Development, Richard
Danis
Tel: 204-945-0800
Director, Transportation Systems Planning & Development,
Erica Vido
Tel: 204-945-2631
Director, Legislative & Regulatory Services, Vacant

Water Management & Structures Division
Assistant Deputy Minister, Doug McMahon
Tel: 204-945-3113
Chief Design Engineer, Al Nelson
Tel: 204-771-1507
Regional Operations Manager, Operations & Management, Scott
Jackson
Tel: 204-479-6480

Manitoba Justice

**Administration & Finance, #1110, 405 Broadway Ave.,
Winnipeg, MB R3C 3L6**
Tel: 204-945-2878
www.gov.mb.ca/justice
Promotes a safe, just & peaceful society supported by a justice
system that is fair, effective, trusted & understood by: providing a
fair & effective prosecution service; managing offenders in an
environment that promotes public safety & rehabilitation;
providing mechanisms for timely & peaceful resolution of civil &
criminal matters; providing legal advice & services to
government; providing programs which assist in protecting &
enforcing individual & collective rights; providing support &
assistance to victims of crime; & promoting effective policing &
crime prevention initiatives. Manitoba Justice employees may be
reached by contacting Manitoba Government Inquiry, Phone:
204-945-3744; Toll-Free Phone: 1-866-626-4862; TTY:
204-945-4796; E-mail: mgi@gov.mb.ca; URL:
www.gov.mb.ca/contact.

**Minister, Justice & Attorney General; Keeper of the Great
Seal,** Hon. Cameron Friesen
Tel: 204-945-3728; *Fax:* 204-945-2517
minjus@leg.gov.mb.ca

Deputy Minister & Deputy Attorney General, Dave Wright
Tel: 204-945-3739; *Fax:* 204-945-4133
dmjus@leg.gov.mb.ca

Associated Agencies, Boards & Commissions:

• **Automobile Injury Compensation Appeal Commission**
#301, 428 Portage Ave.
Winnipeg, MB R3C 0E2
Tel: 204-945-4155; *Fax:* 204-948-2402
Toll-free: 800-282-8069
autoinjury@gov.mb.ca
www.gov.mb.ca/cca/auto
Other Communication: Toll-Free Phone: 800-282-8069, ext.
4155

• **Claimant Adviser Office (CAO)**
#200, 330 Portage Ave.
Winnipeg, MB R3C 0C4
Tel: 204-945-7413; *Fax:* 204-948-3157
TTY: 800-855-0511
cao@gov.mb.ca
www.gov.mb.ca/cca/claimant
Other Communication: Toll-Free Phone: 800-282-8069, ext.
7413

• **Compensation for Victims of Crime**
#1410, 405 Broadway
Winnipeg, MB R3C 3L6
Tel: 204-945-0899; *Fax:* 204-948-3071
Toll-free: 800-262-9344
www.gov.mb.ca/justice/victims/compensation.html
The Compensation for Victims of Crime Program provides
compensation for personal injury or death resulting from certain
crimes occurring within Manitoba.

• **Law Enforcement Review Agency (LERA)**
#420, 155 Carlton St.
Winnipeg, MB R3C 3H8
Tel: 204-945-8667; *Fax:* 204-948-1014
Toll-free: 800-282-8069
lera@gov.mb.ca
www.gov.mb.ca/justice/lera
The mission of the Law Enforcement Review Agency (LERA) is
to deliver a judicious, timely, impartial, client-oriented service to
the public and to the police services and police officers within its
jurisdiction.

• **Legal Aid Manitoba**
287 Broadway, 4th Fl.
Winnipeg, MB R3C 0R9
Tel: 204-985-8500; *Fax:* 204-944-8582
Toll-free: 800-261-2960
info@legalaid.mb.ca
www.legalaidmb.ca
Legal Aid Manitoba works to ensure people with low incomes
have the protections guaranteed in Canada by the The Charter
of Rights & Freedoms, enacted as part of The Constitution Act in
1982.

• **Manitoba Criminal Code Review Board**
#2, 408 York Ave.
Winnipeg, MB R3C 0P9
Tel: 204-945-4438

• **Manitoba Human Rights Commission**
See Entry Name Index for detailed listing.

• **Manitoba Law Reform Commission**
#432, 405 Broadway
Winnipeg, MB R3C 3L6
Tel: 204-945-2896; *Fax:* 204-948-2184
mail@manitobalawreform.ca
www.manitobalawreform.ca
The Manitoba Law Reform Commission is an independent
agency of the Government of Manitoba established by The Law
Reform Commission Act, C.C.S.M. c. L95. The Commission's
duties are to inquire into & consider any matter relating to law in
Manitoba with a view to making recommendations for the
improvement, modernization & reform of law.

• **Office of the Chief Medical Examiner**
#210, 1 Wesley Ave.
Winnipeg, MB R3C 4C6
Tel: 204-945-2088
Toll-free: 800-282-8069
www.gov.mb.ca/justice/family/chief.html
Other Communication: After-Hours, Phone: 204-945-2088
The Chief Medical Examiner's Office investigates deaths where
the cause is not readily known or when the death is a result of
violence.

• **Office of the Public Trustee**
#500, 155 Carlton St.
Winnipeg, MB R3C 5R9
Tel: 204-945-2700; *Fax:* 204-948-2251
PGT@gov.mb.ca
www.gov.mb.ca/publictrustee
The Public Trustee of Manitoba is a provincial government
Special Operating Agency that manages & protects the affairs of
Manitobans who are unable to do so themselves & have no one
else willing or able to act. This includes mentally incompetent &
vulnerable adults, deceased estates, & children.

• **Residential Tenancies Commission**
#1650, 155 Carlton St.
Winnipeg, MB R3C 3H8
Tel: 204-945-2028; *Fax:* 204-945-5453
Toll-free: 800-782-8403
rtc@gov.mb.ca
www.gov.mb.ca/cca/residtc

Community Safety Division
**Manitoba Corrections Head Office, #810, 405 Broadway,
Winnipeg, MB R3C 3L6**
Tel: 204-945-7804
Acting Associate Deputy Minister, Greg Skelly
Tel: 204-945-6047
Executive Director, Probation, Todd Clarke
Tel: 204-945-6884
Acting Executive Director, Policing Services & Public Safety,
Owen Fergusson
Tel: 204-945-5557
Executive Director, Block by Block, Heather Leeman
Tel: 204-582-1657
Executive Director, Manitoba Police Commission, Andrew Minor
Tel: 204-948-1391
Executive Director, Independent Investigation Unit, Zane Tessler
Tel: 204-948-7007

Consumer Protection Division
Tel: 204-945-3744
Toll-Free: 866-626-4862
www.gov.mb.ca/cca
Assistant Deputy Minister, Gail Anderson
Tel: 204-945-3742
Registrar General, Barry C. Effler
Tel: 204-945-0446
Director, Residential Tenancies Branch, Kathryn Durkin-Chudd
Tel: 204-945-7594
Director, Consumer Protection Office, Beatrice Dyce
Tel: 204-945-4529
Acting Director, Claimant Adviser Office, Janelle Pariseau
Tel: 204-945-8171

Crown Law Division
Chief Medical Examiner, John Younes
Tel: 204-945-0571

Legislative Counsel Division
#410, 405 Broadway Ave., Winnipeg, MB R3C 3L6
Acting Legislative Counsel & Assistant Deputy Minister,
Christina Wasyliw
Tel: 204-945-1737

Liquor, Gaming & Cannabis Authority of Manitoba (LGCA)

1055 Milt Stegall Dr., Winnipeg, MB R3G 0Z6
Tel: 204-927-5300; *Fax:* 204-927-5385
Toll-Free: 800-782-0363
information@lgcamb.ca
lgcamb.ca
Other Communication: Toll-Free Fax: 866-999-6688
www.facebook.com/1391594234280994
The Liquor, Gaming & Cannabis Authority of Manitoba (formerly
the Liquor & Gaming Authority of Manitoba) was initially created
in 2014 with the merger of the Manitoba Gaming Control
Commission & the Regulatory Services Division of the Manitoba
Liquor Control Commission. The authority licenses liquor sales,
service & manufacturing, & licenses gaming employees,
products & operations.
As of 2018, the authority was renamed to reflect its expanded
mandate to also oversee the licensing of cannabis stores &
cannabis distributors.

Acting Chair, Stéphane D. Dorge

Vice-Chair, Vacant

Executive Director & CEO, Kristianne Dechant

Manitoba Liquor & Lotteries (MBLL)

830 Empress St., Winnipeg, MB R3G 3H3
Tel: 204-957-2500; *Fax:* 204-284-3500
Toll-Free: 800-265-3912
www.mbll.ca
Other Communication: Casinos Twitter:
twitter.com/Casinosofwpg
twitter.com/LiquorMarts
www.linkedin.com/company/manitoba-lotteries
The Crown Corporation was formed with the merger of the
Manitoba Liquor Control Commission & Manitoba Lotteries
Corporation in 2014. This coincided with the creation of the
Liquor & Gaming Authority of Manitoba.
Manitoba Liquor & Lotteries operates the following: Liquor Marts
& Liquor Mart Express stores; Club Regent Casino; McPhillips

Station Casino; Video Lotto & PlayNow.com; & distributes & sells Western Canada Lottery products through a network of lottery ticket retailers.

Minister responsible, Hon. Jeff Wharton
Tel: 204-945-8020; *Fax:* 204-948-7700
mincrown@leg.gov.mb.ca

Chair, Randy Williams

President & CEO, Manny Atwal

Chief Financial Officer, Heather Mitchell

Executive Vice-President, Liquor & Cannabis Operations, Robert Holmberg

Manitoba Municipal Relations

Legislative Bldg., #317, 450 Broadway, Winnipeg, MB R3C 0V8
Tel: 204-945-3744
Toll-Free: 866-626-4862
www.gov.mb.ca/mr
The department seeks to build & maintain strong, well-managed communities across the province by working with municipalities, planning districts, & non-governmental organizations.

Minister, Hon. Derek Johnson
Tel: 204-945-5854; *Fax:* 204-948-4783
minmr@leg.gov.mb.ca

Deputy Minister, Bruce Gray
Tel: 204-945-5568; *Fax:* 204-948-3121
dmmr@leg.gov.mb.ca

Director, Finance & Administrative Services, Shelly Ferens
Tel: 204-945-2199

Associated Agencies, Boards & Commissions:
• **Communities Economic Development Fund (CEDF)**
15 Moak Cres.
Thompson, MB R8N 2B8
Tel: 204-778-4138; *Fax:* 204-778-4313
Toll-free: 800-561-0145
www.cedf.mb.ca
• **Manitoba Municipal Board**
#1144, 363 Broadway
Winnipeg, MB R3C 3N9
Tel: 204-945-2941; *Fax:* 204-948-2235
www.gov.mb.ca/municipalboard
• **Manitoba Water Services Board (MWSB)**
#1A, 2010 Currie Blvd.
Brandon, MB R7B 4E7
Tel: 204-726-6076; *Fax:* 204-726-7196
mwsb@gov.mb.ca
www.mbwaterservicesboard.ca
A Crown Corporation that develops safe, affordable & sustainable water & wastewater infrastructure for rural Manitobans.
• **Taxicab Board**
#200, 301 Weston St.
Winnipeg, MB R3E 3H4
Tel: 204-945-8919; *Fax:* 204-948-2315
taxicabboardoffice@gov.mb.ca
www.gov.mb.ca/ia/taxicab/taxicab.html

Community Planning & Development
Assistant Deputy Minister, David Neufeld
Tel: 204-228-1338
Acting Director, Community & Regional Planning, Grant Melnychuk
Tel: 204-806-4578

Provincial-Municipal Support Services
Assistant Deputy Minister, Lesley McFarlane
Tel: 204-945-2565
Director, Rural Development, Mona Cornock
Tel: 204-726-6410
Director, Provincial Municipal Assessor, Lloyd Funk
Tel: 204-945-2604
Acting Director, Municipal Finance & Advisory Services, Nick Kulyk
Tel: 204-945-1944

Recreation & Regional Services
Executive Director, Annette Willborn
Tel: 204-945-0371

Manitoba Office of the Ombudsman

Colony Square, #750, 500 Portage Ave., Winnipeg, MB R3C 3X1
Tel: 204-982-9130; *Fax:* 204-942-7803
Toll-Free: 800-665-0531
ombudsman@ombudsman.mb.ca
www.ombudsman.mb.ca
Secondary Address: #202, 1011 Rosser Ave.
Scotia Towers
Brandon, MB R7A 0L5
Alt. Fax: 204-571-5157
www.facebook.com/manitobaombudsman
www.youtube.com/user/manitobaombudsman
The Ombudsman, an independent & non-partisan Officer of the Legislative Assembly, investigates complaints from persons who feel they have been unfairly dealt with by government departments or agencies.

Manitoba Ombudsman, Jill Perron
Tel: 204-982-9130

Manitoba Public Insurance Corporation

234 Donald St., #B100, PO Box 6300 Winnipeg, MB R3C 4A4
Tel: 204-985-7000; *Fax:* 204-985-3525
Toll-Free: 800-665-2410
TTY: 204-985-8832
www.mpi.mb.ca
Other Communication: Out-of-Province Claims, Toll-Free Phone:
800-661-6051
Administers Manitoba's Public Automobile Insurance Program & sells extension auto coverage on a competitive basis.

Minister Responsible, Jeff Wharton
Tel: 204-945-8020; *Fax:* 204-948-7700
mincrown@leg.gov.mb.ca

Chair, Mike Sullivan

President & CEO, Eric Herbelin

Chief Financial Officer & Vice-President, Finance, Mark Giesbrecht

Chief Operating Officer & Vice-President, Customer Service, Curtis Wennberg

Chief Information Officer & Vice-President, Information Technology & Business Transformation, Brad Bunko

Chief Actuary & Vice-President, Risk Management, Luke Johnston

Chief Human Resources Officer & Vice-President, Human Resources, Satvir Tkachuk

Manitoba Sport, Culture & Heritage

Legislative Bldg., #118, 450 Broadway, Winnipeg, MB R3C 0V8
www.gov.mb.ca/chc
Manitoba Tourism, Culture, Heritage, Sport & Consumer Protection was renamed to Sport, Culture & Heritage following the 2016 general election. The department is committed to the development & implementation of programs & services which promote & enhance the well-being, identity & creativity of Manitobans & which contribute to Manitoba's continued economic growth & steadily rising quality of life. Working with its partners in the community & with government, the department raises the national & international profile of the talents & abilities of Manitobans, encourages healthy active living, promotes pride of place, creates jobs & attracts & maintains investment in the province.

Minister, Hon. Cathy Cox
Tel: 204-945-3729; *Fax:* 204-945-5223
minsch@leg.gov.mb.ca

Deputy Minister, Jeff Hnatiuk
Tel: 204-945-3794; *Fax:* 204-948-3102
dmsch@leg.gov.mb.ca

Director, Sport Secretariat, Michael Benson
Tel: 204-945-8834

Associated Agencies, Boards & Commissions:

• **Le Centre Culturel franco-manitobain/Franco-Manitoban Cultural Centre (CCFM)**
340, boul Provencher
Winnipeg, MB R2H 0G7
Tel: 204-233-8972; *Fax:* 204-233-3324
communication@ccfm.mb.ca
www.ccfm.mb.ca
• **Heritage Grants Advisory Council**
c/o Heritage Grants Program
#330, 213 Notre Dame Ave.
Winnipeg, MB R3B 1N3
Tel: 204-945-2213; *Fax:* 204-948-2086
www.gov.mb.ca/chc/grants/hgp.html
• **Manitoba Arts Council (MAC)**
#525, 93 Lombard Ave.
Winnipeg, MB R3B 3B1
Tel: 204-945-2237; *Fax:* 204-945-5925
Toll-free: 866-994-2787
info@artscouncil.mb.ca
www.artscouncil.mb.ca
An arms-length agency of the provincial government dedicated to artistic excellence. It offers a broad-based granting program for professional artists & arts organizations. It promotes, preserves, supports & advocates for the arts as essential to the quality of life of all the people of Manitoba.
• **Manitoba Centennial Centre Corporation**
#1000, 555 Main St.
Winnipeg, MB R3B 1C3
Tel: 204-956-1360; *Fax:* 204-944-1390
inquiries@mbccc.ca
www.mbccc.ca
• **Manitoba Combative Sports Commission (MCSC)**
#628, 213 Notre Dame Ave.
Winnipeg, MB R3B 1N3
Tel: 204-945-1788; *Fax:* 204-948-3649
www.mbcombativesports.com
The Manitoba Combative Sports Commission regulates all professional contests or exhibitions of boxing, kick boxing & mixed martial arts, including the licensing & supervision of officials, athletes & promoters.
• **Manitoba Film Classification Board**
#216, 301 Weston St.
Winnipeg, MB R3E 3H4
Tel: 204-945-8962; *Fax:* 204-945-0890
Toll-free: 866-612-2399
mfcb@gov.mb.ca
www.gov.mb.ca/chc/mfcb
• **Manitoba Film & Music (MFM)**
#410, 93 Lombard Ave.
Winnipeg, MB R3B 3B1
Tel: 204-947-2040; *Fax:* 204-956-5261
info@mbfilmmusic.ca
mbfilmmusic.ca
Promotes the province's film & sound recording artists & industries.
• **Manitoba Heritage Council**
c/o Historic Resources Branch
213 Notre Dame Ave., Main Fl.
Winnipeg, MB R3B 1N3
Tel: 204-945-2118; *Fax:* 204-948-2384
hrb@gov.mb.ca
www.gov.mb.ca/chc/hrb
Protects, interprets & promotes the heritage resources of the province; offers advice & recommendations on places & events which should be protected by the department; protection of significant buildings & sites.
• **Manitoba Museum / Musée du Manitoba**
190 Rupert Ave.
Winnipeg, MB R3B 0N2
Tel: 204-956-2830; *Fax:* 204-942-3679
info@manitobamuseum.ca
www.manitobamuseum.ca
• **Manitoba Women's Advisory Council**
#409, 401 York Ave.
Winnipeg, MB R3C 0P8
Tel: 204-945-6281; *Fax:* 204-945-6511
Toll-free: 800-263-0234
msw@gov.mb.ca
www.gov.mb.ca/msw/mwac
• **Public Library Advisory Board**
#300, 1011 Rosser Ave.
Brandon, MB R7A 0L5
Tel: 204-726-6590; *Fax:* 204-726-6868
Toll-free: 800-252-9998
pls@gov.mb.ca

• **Sport Manitoba**
145 Pacific Ave.
Winnipeg, MB R3B 2Z6
Tel: 204-925-5600; *Fax:* 204-925-5916
info@sportmanitoba.ca
www.sportmanitoba.ca

• **Venture Manitoba Tours Ltd.**
PO Box 1000
Riverton, MB R0C 2R0
Tel: 204-378-2769; *Fax:* 204-378-2734
vmt@mts.net

Administration & Finance Division
Executive Financial Officer, David Paton
  Tel: 204-945-2233
Acting Director, Financial Services, Jeffrey Conquergood
  Tel: 204-945-5088
IT Director, Information Systems, Lori Contant
  Tel: 204-330-2895

Communications Services Manitoba
155 Carlton St., 10th Fl., Winnipeg, MB R3C 3H8
  Tel: 204-945-3765
Assistant Deputy Minister, Vacant
Director, Media, Production & Business Services, Michelle
  Gange
  Tel: 204-945-7121
Director, Public Affairs, Angela Jamieson
  Tel: 204-945-4971
Director of Creative Services; Acting Director, Advertising &
  Program Promotion, Cam McCullough
  Tel: 204-945-8830
Director, News Media Services, Eileen O'Donnell
  Tel: 204-945-4097

Culture & Heritage Programs
Assistant Deputy Minister, Veronica Dyck
  Tel: 204-945-4078
Director, Arts Branch, Sandy Baardman
  Tel: 204-945-4579
Director, Public Library Services, Trevor Surgenor
  Tel: 204-726-6864
  #200, 1595 - 1 St.
  Brandon, MB R7A 7A1

Historic Resources
213 Notre Dame Ave., Winnipeg, MB R3B 1N3
  Tel: 204-945-2118; *Fax:* 204-948-2384
  hrb@gov.mb.ca
  www.gov.mb.ca/chc/hrb
Director, Donna Dul
  Tel: 204-945-4389

Provincial Services
#100, 200 Vaughan St., Winnipeg, MB R3C 1T5
Archivist of Manitoba/Manitoba Legislative Librarian, Scott
  Goodine
  Tel: 204-945-6140
Director, Information & Privacy Policy Secretariat, Michael
  Baudic
  Tel: 204-945-2523

Francophone Affairs Secretariat
Legislative Bldg., #46, 450 Broadway, Winnipeg, MB R3C
0V8
  Tel: 204-945-4915; *Fax:* 204-948-2015
  FLS-SLF@leg.gov.mb.ca
Executive Director & Director of Translation Services, Teresa
  Collins
  Tel: 204-803-4704
FLS Coordinator, Bou Conde
  Tel: 204-945-0455
FLS Coordinator & Acting Planning/Programme Coordinatpr,
  Stephanie Holfeld
  Tel: 204-795-6265

Status of Women Secretariat
#409, 401 York Ave., Winnipeg, MB R3C 0P8
  Tel: 204-945-6281; *Fax:* 204-945-6511
  Toll-Free: 800-263-0234
  msw@gov.mb.ca
  www.gov.mb.ca/msw
Executive Director, Beth Ulrich
  Tel: 204-945-6281

Sport Secretariat
213 Notre Dame Ave., 6th Fl., Winnipeg, MB R3B 1N3
  Tel: 204-945-0216; *Fax:* 204-945-1675
  www.gov.mb.ca/chc/sport
Director, Michael Benson
  Tel: 204-945-8834
Sport Consultant & Executive Director, Manitoba Combative
  Sports Commission, Joel Fingard
  Tel: 204-945-1788
  joel.fingard@gov.mb.ca

Administrative Coordinator, Roxanne Catellier
  Tel: 204-945-0216

Travel Manitoba

21 Forks Market Rd., Winnipeg, MB R3C RT7
  Tel: 204-927-7800
  Toll-Free: 800-665-0040
  contactus@travelmanitoba.com
  www.travelmanitoba.com
  twitter.com/travelmanitoba
  www.facebook.com/TravelManitoba
  www.youtube.com/user/TravelManitoba

President & CEO, Colin Ferguson
coferguson@travelmanitoba.com

Senior Vice-President, Strategy & Market Development,
Brigitte Sandron
bsandron@travelmanitoba.com

Vice-President, Marketing & Communications, Linda
Whitfield
lwhitfield@travelmanitoba.com

Workers' Compensation Board of Manitoba (WCB)

333 Broadway Ave., Winnipeg, MB R3C 4W3
  Tel: 204-954-4321; *Fax:* 204-954-4999
  Toll-Free: 800-362-3340
  wcb@wcb.mb.ca
  www.wcb.mb.ca
  twitter.com/WCBManitoba
  www.facebook.com/WCBManitoba
  www.linkedin.com/company/wcb-manitoba

Chair, Michael Werier

President & CEO, Richard Deacon

Chief Operating Officer, SAFE Work Manitoba, Jamie Hall

**Chief Financial Officer, Finance & Administrative
Services,** Andria McCaughan

Vice-President, Assessments, Innovation & Technology,
Renzo Borgesa

Vice-President, Human Resources & Strategy Division,
Shannon Earle

**General Counsel & Vice-President, Compliance &
Corporate Services,** Lori Ferguson Sain

Vice-President, Compensation Services, Dan Holland

Government of New Brunswick

Seat of Government: PO Box 6000 Fredericton, NB E3B 5H1
  www.gnb.ca
  twitter.com/Gov_NB
  www.facebook.com/GovNB
  www.youtube.com/c/gnbca
The Province of New Brunswick entered Confederation July 1,
1867. It has a land area of 71,388.81 sq km. The StatsCan
census population in 2016 was 747,101.

Office of the Lieutenant-Governor / Bureau du lieutenant-gouverneur du Nouveau-Brunswick

Government House, PO Box 6000 Fredericton, NB E3B 5H1
  Tel: 506-453-2505; *Fax:* 506-444-5280
  LTgov@gnb.ca
  www2.gnb.ca/content/gnb/en/lgnb.html
The Lieutenant-Governor represents The Queen of Canada, Her
Majesty Queen Elizabeth II in New Brunswick. The
Lieutenant-Governor is appointed by the Governor
General-in-Council on the recommendation of the Prime Minister
of Canada.
The following are some responsibilities of the
Lieutenant-Governor: opening, proroguing & dissolving the
Legislative Assembly of New Brunswick; swearing in the Premier
& cabinet ministers; delivering the Speech from the Throne;
giving royal assents to bills passed by the legislature; presenting
awards; lending patronage to non-for-profit organizations; &
participating in dedications & investitures.

**Lieutenant-Governor of New Brunswick /
Lieutenante-gouverneure du Nouveau-Brunswick,** Hon.
Brenda Murphy

Chief of Staff, Judy Wagner
Judy.Wagner@gnb.ca

Office of the Premier / Cabinet du premier ministre

Centennial Bldg., PO Box 6000 Fredericton, NB E3B 5H1
  Tel: 506-453-2144; *Fax:* 506-453-7407
  premier@gnb.ca
  www.gnb.ca/premier

Premier; President, Executive Council, Hon. Blaine Higgs
premier@gnb.ca

Deputy Premier, Vacant

Executive Council / Conseil exécutif

Centennial Bldg., PO Box 6000 Fredericton, NB E3B 5H1
  Tel: 506-444-4417; *Fax:* 506-453-2266
  executivecounciloffice@gnb.ca
  www2.gnb.ca/content/gnb/en/departments/executive_council.ht
  ml
The following members of The Cabinet of the Government of
New Brunswick are listed in the order of precedence:

**Premier; President, Executive Council; Minister
responsible, Intergovernmental Affairs,** Hon. Blaine Higgs
premier@gnb.ca
Office of the Premier, Centennial Bldg.
670 King St.
PO Box 6000
Fredericton, NB E3B 5H1

Deputy Premier, Vacant

Minister, Agriculture, Aquaculture & Fisheries, Hon.
Margaret Johnson

**Minister, Aboriginal Affairs; Minister responsible,
Economic Development & Small Business, Opportunities
New Brunswick & Immigration,** Hon. Arlene Dunn

Minister, Education & Early Childhood Development,
Hon. Dominic Cardy
Dominic.Cardy@gnb.ca

**Minister, Environment & Climate Change; Minister
responsible, Regional Development Corporation,** Hon.
Gary Crossman

Minister, Local Government & Local Government Reform,
Hon. Daniel Allain

Minister, Finance; President, Treasury Board, Hon. Ernie
Steeves
ernie.steeves@gnb.ca

Minister, Health, Hon. Dorothy Shephard

Minister, Justice & Public Safety; Attorney General, Hon.
Hugh J.A. (Ted) Flemming, Q.C.

Minister, Post-Secondary Education, Training & Labour,
Hon. Trevor Holder
trevor.holder@gnb.ca

**Minister, Service New Brunswick; Minister responsible,
Military Affairs,** Hon. Mary Wilson

Minister, Social Development, Hon. Bruce Fitch

**Minister, Tourism, Heritage & Culture; Minister
responsible, Women's Equality,** Hon. Tammy
Scott-Wallace

Minister, Transportation & Infrastructure, Hon. Jill Green

Minister responsible, Francophonie, Hon. Glen Savoie

Minister, Natural Resources & Energy Development, Hon.
Mike Holland
Mike.Holland@gnb.ca

Executive Council Office / Bureau du Conseil exécutif

**Chancery Place, 6th Fl., PO Box 6000 Fredericton, NB E3B
5H1**
  Tel: 506-444-4417; *Fax:* 506-453-2266
  executivecounciloffice@gnb.ca
  www2.gnb.ca/content/gnb/en/departments/executive_council.ht
  ml
The Executive Council Office is responsible for the provision of
secretariat & administrative services to the following: the
Executive Council; ministers with policy coordination
responsibilities; & the Policy & Priorities Committee.

Premier; President, Executive Council, Hon. Blaine Higgs
premier@gnb.ca

Clerk of the Executive Council & Secretary to Cabinet; Chief Operating Officer, Cheryl Hansen
Tel: 506-444-4417
cheryl.hansen@gnb.ca

Deputy Secretary to Cabinet, Policy Board, Patricia Mackenzie
Tel: 506-453-2314
patricia.mackenzie@gnb.ca

Director, Operations, Sabrina Moffitt
Tel: 506-444-4417
Sabrina.Moffitt@gnb.ca

Associated Agencies, Boards & Commissions:
• **New Brunswick Jobs Board**
Chancery Place
PO Box 6000
Fredericton, NB E3B 5H1
The NB Jobs Board was announced in February 2015, with a mandate to focus on job creation & economic growth.

Intergovernmental Affairs Division
Chancery Place, 675 King St., 5th Fl., Fredericton, NB E3B 1E9
Tel: 506-444-4948; *Fax:* 506-453-2995
iga@gnb.ca
The Intergovernmental Affairs Division manages relations with other governments, communities & organizations.
Minister Responsible, Hon. Blaine Higgs
Assistant Deputy Minister, Charles Ayles
Tel: 506-453-5686
charles.ayles@gnb.ca
Chief of Protocol, Lana Tingley-Lacroix
Tel: 506-453-2671
lana.tingleylacroix@gnb.ca
Executive Director, Trade Policy Division, Serge Breau
Tel: 506-444-5137
serge.breau@gnb.ca
Director, International & Multilateral Francophonie, Isabelle Doucet
Tel: 506-444-5364
isabelle.doucet2@gnb.ca
Director, Canadian Intergovernmental Relations, Don Richardson
Tel: 506-444-5917
don.richardson@gnb.ca

Women's Equality Branch
Sartain MacDonald Bldg., PO Box 6000 Fredericton, NB E3B 5H1
Tel: 506-453-8126
Toll-Free: 877-253-0266
web-edf@gnb.ca
www.gnb.ca/women
twitter.com/WomenNB
www.facebook.com/WomenNBs
Women's Equality, a branch of the Executive Council Office, consists of the following units: Violence Prevention Initiatives; Wage Gap Reduction Initiatives; & Policy Assessment & Advice. The branch provides support on women's issues to the Minister Responsible for Women's Issues & to departments of the provincial government.
Minister Responsible, Hon. Tammy Scott-Wallace
Acting Assistant Deputy Minister, Nicole McCarty
Tel: 503-453-8126; *Fax:* 503-453-7977
Nicole.McCarty@gnb.ca
Director, Policy & Strategic Initiatives, A.J. Ripley
Tel: 506-230-3319; *Fax:* 506-453-7977
AJ.Ripley@gnb.ca
Director, Violence Prevention & Community Partnerships, Martine Stewart
Tel: 506-453-8126
martine.stewart@gnb.ca

Legislative Assembly of New Brunswick / Assemblée législative

Legislative Bldg., Centre Block, PO Box 6000 Fredericton, NB E3B 5H1
Tel: 506-453-2506; *Fax:* 506-453-7154
wwwleg@gnb.ca
www.gnb.ca/legis
The Office of the Legislative Assembly is responsible for the following services: assisting Members of the Legislative Assembly, their staff & the public; recording the proceedings of the Legislative Assembly; maintaining the records of the Legislative Assembly; & providing information services on behalf of the Legislative Assembly.

Speaker of the Legislative Assembly, Hon. Bill Oliver
Note: Premier Gallant & the government caucus announced on Oct. 7, 2014, that they would support Chris Collins as Speaker. He was officially named on Oct. 24, 2014.

Deputy Speaker, Andrea Anderson-Mason, Q.C.

Deputy Speaker, Sherry Wilson

Clerk of the Legislative Assembly, Shayne Davies
Tel: 506-453-2506; *Fax:* 506-453-7154
Shayne.Davies@gnb.ca

Official Reporter, Hansard Office, Linda Fahey
Tel: 506-453-8352; *Fax:* 506-453-3199
linda.fahey@gnb.ca
West Block
96 Saint John St.
PO Box 6000
Fredericton, NB E3B 5H1

Legislative Librarian, Kenda Clark-Gorey
Tel: 506-453-8346; *Fax:* 506-444-5889
kenda.clark.gorey@gnb.ca

Government Members Office (Progressive Conservative Party) / Bureau des députés du gouvernement
West Block, Departmental Bldg., PO Box 6000 Fredericton, NB E3B 5H1
Tel: 506-453-7494; *Fax:* 506-453-3461
Premier; President, Executive Council, Hon. Blaine Higgs
premier@gnb.ca
Note: Former Opposition Leader Blaine Higgs became Premier after Brian Gallant lost a confidence vote in the legislaute on Nov. 2, 2018.
Office of the Premier, Centennial Building
670 King St.
PO Box 6000
Fredericton, NB E3B 5H1
Government House Leader, Hon. Glen Savoie
Glen.Savoie@gnb.ca
Office of the Premier, Centennial Building
670 King St.
PO Box 6000
Fredericton, NB E3B 5H1
Government Whip, Jeff Carr
Jeff.Carr@gnb.ca
Office of the Premier, Centennial Building
670 King St.
PO Box 6000
Fredericton, NB E3B 5H1
Government Caucus Chair, Bill Hogan
Bill.Hogan@gnb.ca
Office of the Premier, Centennial Building
670 King St.
PO Box 6000
Fredericton, NB E3B 5H1

Office of the Official Opposition (Liberal Party) / Bureau de l'opposition officielle
East Block, Old Education Bldg., PO Box 6000 Fredericton, NB E3B 5H1
Tel: 506-453-2548; *Fax:* 506-453-3956
Interim Leader, Official Opposition, Roger Melanson
Roger.L.Melanson@gnb.ca
Opposition House Leader, Vacant
Acting Opposition Whip, Denis Landry
Denis.Landry2@gnb.ca
Opposition Caucus Chair, Francine Landry
Francine.Landry@gnb.ca

Office of the Third Party (Green Party) / Bureau du chef du tiers parti
West Block, Departmental Bldg., PO Box 6000 Fredericton, NB E3B 5H1
Tel: 506-457-6842; *Fax:* 506-453-7154
www.greenpartynb.ca
twitter.com/greenpartynb
www.facebook.com/GPNB.PVNB
www.youtube.com/user/GPVNB
On October 3, 2014, Premier Gallant announced that the Green Party would be given official Third Party status in the legislature, a first in New Brunswick history.
Leader, Green Party, David Coon
Tel: 506-455-0936
David.Coon@gnb.ca
Acting Chief of Staff, Josh O'Donnell
Josh.O'Donnell@gnb.ca

Standing Committees of the Legislative Assembly of New Brunswick
www1.gnb.ca/legis/committees/comm-index-e.asp

The following are the Standing Committees of the Legislative Assembly of New Brunswick: Climate Change & Environmental Stewardship; Economic Policy; Estimates & Fiscal Policy; Law Amendments; Legislative Administration; Private Bills; Procedure, Privileges & Legislative Officers; Public Accounts; & Social Policy.

Select Committees of the Legislative Assembly of New Brunswick
The House may appoint a Select Committee to consider & report on a particular subject or to undertake a specific task or inquiry. The current Select Committees are the Select Committee on Public Universities & the Select Committee on Accessbility in New Brunswick.

Sixtieth Legislative Assembly - New Brunswick / 60ème législature du Nouveau-Brunswick

Centre Block, Legislative Bldg., 706 Queen St., PO Box 6000 Fredericton, NB E3B 5H1
Tel: 506-453-2506; *Fax:* 506-453-7154
wwwleg@gnb.ca
www.gnb.ca/legis
Last General Election: September 14, 2020.
Next General Election: 2024.
Party Standings (Oct. 2021):
Progressive Conservative 26;
Liberal 16;
Green 3;
People's Alliance 2;
Vacant 2;
Total 49.
Members' Salaries, Indemnities, & Allowances (2008):
Members' annual indemnity $85,000.
Additional Members' Salaries, Indemnities, & Allowances:
Premier $79,000;
Cabinet Ministers $47,253;
Leader of the Opposition $55,300;
Leader of a Registered Political Party: $19,750;
Speaker $52,614;
Deputy Speaker $26,307;
Government Whip $26,307;
Official Opposition Whip $19,730;
Government House Leader $26,307;
Opposition House Leader $19,730.
Members of the Legislative Assembly may be reached at the following address: Members of the Legislative Assembly, Province of New Brunswick, PO Box 6000, Fredericton, NB E3B 5H1.
The following is a list of Members of the Legislative Assembly with preliminary information after the 2020 election, including their riding, the number of electors, party affiliation, & contact information:

Members of the Legislative Assembly of New Brunswick
Minister, Local Government & Local Governance Reform, Hon. Daniel Allain
Constituency: Moncton East, Electoral District 18 *No. of Constituents:* 3,525, Progressive Conservative
daniel.j.allain@gnb.ca
Other Communications: Constituency Phone: 506-856-3228
www.facebook.com/DanielAllainNB,
www.linkedin.com/in/daniel-allain-mba-7102b7aa
Constituency Office
75 Shediac Rd.
Moncton, NB E1A 2R6
Richard Ames
Constituency: Carleton-York, Electoral District 44 *No. of Constituents:* 12,117, Progressive Conservative
richard.ames@gnb.ca
Other Communications: Constituency Phone: 506-575-6088
www.facebook.com/MLAforCarletonYork
Constituency Office
PO Box 1123
Nackawic, NB E6G 2N1
Deputy Speaker, Hon. Andrea Anderson-Mason, Q.C.
Constituency: Fundy-The Isles-Saint John West, Electoral District 35 *No. of Constituents:* 11,538, Progressive Conservative
Andrea.AndersonMason@gnb.ca
Other Communications: Constituency Phone: 506-755-2810; Fax: 506-755-2806
twitter.com/onemainstreet,
www.facebook.com/AndreaAndersonMasonPC2018
Constituency Office
250 Main St.
Upper Letang, NB E5C 3V1
Kevin Arseneau
Constituency: Kent North, Electoral District 12 *No. of Constituents:* 12,459, Green Party of Canada
kevin.a.arseneau@gnb.ca
Other Communications: Constituency Phone: 506-521-5793
twitter.com/kevinarseneaunb,
www.facebook.com/KevinArseneauNB
Constituency Office

#1117, 3 Main St.
Rogersville, NB E4Y 2N3

Guy Arseneault
Constituency: Campbellton-Dalhousie, Electoral District 2,
Liberal
guy.arseneault@gnb.ca
Other Communications: Constituency Phone: 506-684-2600
twitter.com/GuyA_Liberal,
www.facebook.com/GuyArseneaultMLA
Constituency Office
#110, 113 Roseberry St.
Campbellton, NB E3N 2G6

Kris Austin
Constituency: Fredericton-Grand Lake, Electoral District 38
No. of Constituents: 11,835, PA
kris.austin@gnb.ca
Other Communications: Constituency Phone: 506-327-7014
twitter.com/krisaustinpa, www.facebook.com/KrisAustinPANB
Constituency Office
112 Main St.
Minto, NB E4B 3M2

Kathy Bockus
Constituency: Saint Croix, Electoral District 36 *No. of
Constituents:* 3,570, Progressive Conservative
kathy.bockus@gnb.ca
Other Communications: Constituency Phone: 506-466-1449;
Fax: 506-466-3196
www.facebook.com/KathyBockusPCcandidate
Constituency Office
#8, 78 Milltown Blvd.
St Stephen, NB E3L 1G6

Benoît Bourque
Constituency: Kent South, Electoral District 13 *No. of
Constituents:* 12,424, Liberal
Benoit.Bourque@gnb.ca
Other Communications: Constituency Phone: 506-743-0335;
Fax: 506-743-1273
www.facebook.com/benoitbourqueliberal
Constituency Office, J.K. Irving Center
30 Évangéline St.
Bouctouche, NB E4S 3E4

Minister, Education & Early Childhood Development, Hon.
Dominic Cardy
Constituency: Fredericton West-Hanwell, Electoral District 43
No. of Constituents: 12,146, Progressive Conservative
Dominic.Cardy@gnb.ca
Other Communications: Constituency Phone: 506-453-8461
twitter.com/DominicCardy,
www.linkedin.com/in/dominic-cardy-a927612
Constituency Office
1757 Hanwell Rd.
Hanwell, NB E3C 2B9

Government Whip, Jeff Carr
Constituency: New Maryland-Sunbury, Electoral District 39
No. of Constituents: 12,380, Progressive Conservative
Jeff.Carr@gnb.ca
Other Communications: Constituency Phone: 506-368-2938;
Fax: 506-368-2939
twitter.com/jeffcarr4nms, www.facebook.com/jeffcarr4nms
Constituency Office
189A Sunbury Dr.
Fredericton, NB E5L 1R5

Chuck Chiasson
Constituency: Victoria-La Vallée, Electoral District 47 *No. of
Constituents:* 11,685, Liberal
Tel: 506-475-1124
Chuck.Chiasson@gnb.ca
Other Communications: Constituency Phone: 506-475-1124
twitter.com/ChuckChiasson,
www.facebook.com/chuck.chiasson
Constituency Office
385 Broadway Blvd.
Grand Falls, NB E3Y 2K5

Keith Chiasson
Constituency: Tracadie-Sheila, Electoral District 8 *No. of
Constituents:* 11,943, Liberal
keith.chiasson@gnb.ca
Other Communications: Constituency Phone: 506-394-4038
twitter.com/chiassonkeith
Constituency Office
#4104, 3, rue Principale
Tracadie, NB E1X 1B8

Michelle Conroy
Constituency: Miramichi, Electoral District 10 *No. of
Constituents:* 11,248, PA
michelle.conroy@gnb.ca
Other Communications: Constituency Phone: 506-627-1684
www.facebook.com/michelleconroymla
Constituency Office
#3, 635 Water St.
Miramichi, NB E1N 1B2

Leader, Third Party (Green Party), David Coon
Constituency: Fredericton South, Electoral District 40 *No. of
Constituents:* 10,417, Green Party of Canada

Tel: 506-455-0936
David.Coon@gnb.ca
twitter.com/DavidCCoon,
www.facebook.com/david.coon.fredsouth,
www.linkedin.com/in/david-coon-49362471
Note: David Coon is the first Green Party member ever to be
elected to the New Brunswick Legislative Assembly.
Constituency Office
#102, 346 Queen St.
Fredericton, NB E3B 1B2

Minister, Environment & Climate Change; Minister responsible,
Regional Development Corporation, Hon. Gary Crossman
Constituency: Hampton, Electoral District 27 *No. of
Constituents:* 11,767, Progressive Conservative
Tel: 506-453-7494; *Fax:* 506-453-3461
Gary.Crossman@gnb.ca
Other Communications: Constituency Phone: 506-832-5700
twitter.com/GaryCrossman1,
www.facebook.com/GaryCrossmanNB,
www.linkedin.com/in/gary-crossman-a9016459
Constituency Office
PO Box 1212
Hampton, NB E5N 5L2

Ryan P. Cullins
Constituency: Fredericton-York, Electoral District 42 *No. of
Constituents:* 3,730, Progressive Conservative
ryan.cullins@gnb.ca
ryancullins.ca
Other Communications: Constituency Phone: 506-444-3952
www.facebook.com/RyanCullinsMLA
Constituency Office
#32, 435 Brookside Dr.
Fredericton, NB E3A 8V4

Jean-Claude (J.C.) D'Amours
Constituency: Edmundston-Madawaska Centre, Electoral
District 48, Liberal
jean-claude.d'amours@gnb.ca
Other Communications: Constituency Phone: 506-838-1031
www.facebook.com/jcdamoursliberal
Constituency Office
#30, 180 Hébert Blvd.
Edmundston, NB E3V 2S7

Minister, Aboriginal Affairs; Minister responsible, Economic
Development & Small Business, Opportunities New
Brunswick & Immigration, Hon. Arlene Dunn
Constituency: Saint John Harbour, Electoral District 32 *No. of
Constituents:* 2,181, Progressive Conservative
arlene.dunn@gnb.ca
Other Communications: Constituency Phone: 506-643-6138
Constituency Office
#140, 55 Union St.
Saint John, NB E2L 5B7

Minister, Social Development, Hon. R. Bruce Fitch
Constituency: Riverview, Electoral District 23 *No. of
Constituents:* 11,547, Progressive Conservative
Tel: 506-453-7494; *Fax:* 506-453-3461
bruce.fitch@gnb.ca
Other Communications: Constituency Phone: 506-869-6117;
Fax: 506-869-6114
twitter.com/brucefitchmla, www.facebook.com/BruceFitchMLA
Constituency Office
#18A, 567 Coverdale Rd.
Riverview, NB E1B 3K7

Minister, Justice & Public Safety & Attorney General, Hon. Hugh
J.A. (Ted) Flemming, Q.C.
Constituency: Rothesay, Electoral District 29 *No. of
Constituents:* 10,956, Progressive Conservative
hugh.flemming@gnb.ca
Other Communications: Constituency Phone: 506-848-5440
twitter.com/tedflemming,
www.facebook.com/flemmingforrothesay
Constituency Office
70 Hampton Rd.
Rothesay, NB

Hon. Robert Gauvin
Constituency: Shediac Bay-Dieppe, Electoral District 14 *No.
of Constituents:* 5,839, Liberal
robert.gauvin@gnb.ca
Other Communications: Constituency Phone: 506-869-7000;
Fax: 506-869-7007
Note: Hon. Robert Gauvin became an independant candidate
after leaving the Progressive Conservative Party over
health-care reforms in Feb. 2020. In Aug. 2020, he ran in the
Shediacl Bay-Dieppe riding as a member of the Liberal Party.
Constituency Office
#203, 650 Champlain St.
Dieppe, NB E1A 1P5

Minister, Transportation & Infrastructure, Hon. Jill Green
Constituency: Fredericton North, Electoral District 41 *No. of
Constituents:* 3,227, Progressive Conservative
jill.green@gnb.ca
Other Communications: Constituency Phone: 506-444-4401
twitter.com/jillgreenfton, www.facebook.com/jill.green.fton,
www.linkedin.com/in/jillegreen

Constituency Office
#4, 215 Main St.
Fredericton, NB E3A 1E1

Hon. Daniel Guitard
Constituency: Restigouche-Chaleur, Electoral District 3 *No. of
Constituents:* 11,397, Liberal
Tel: 506-453-2548; *Fax:* 506-453-3956
Daniel.Guitard@gnb.ca
Other Communications: Constituency Phone: 506-542-2424;
Fax: 506-542-2425
www.facebook.com/danielguitard.liberal
Constituency Office
691 Principale St.
Petit-Rocher, NB E8J 1G1

Premier; President, Executive Council; Minister responsible,
Intergovernmental Affairs, Hon. Blaine Higgs
Constituency: Quispamsis, Electoral District 28 *No. of
Constituents:* 11,710, Progressive Conservative
blaine.higgs@gnb.ca
Other Communications: Constituency Phone: 506-848-5422;
Fax: 506-848-5429
twitter.com/premierbhiggs,
www.facebook.com/PremierBlaineHiggs
Constituency Office
25 William Ct.
Quispamsis, NB E2E 4B1

Government Caucus Chair, Bill Hogan
Constituency: Carleton, Electoral District 45 *No. of
Constituents:* 3,536, Progressive Conservative
bill.hogan@gnb.ca
Other Communications: Constituency Phone: 506-277-6020
twitter.com/bhogan1961
Constituency Office
639 Main St.
Woodstock, NB E7M 2C7

Minister, Post-Secondary Education, Training & Labour, Hon.
Trevor Holder
Constituency: Portland-Simonds, Electoral District 31 *No. of
Constituents:* 11,093, Progressive Conservative
trevor.holder@gnb.ca
Other Communications: Constituency Phone: 506-657-2335;
Fax: 506-642-2588
www.facebook.com/TrevorHolderSJ
Constituency Office
#2, 229 Churchill Blvd.
Saint John, NB E2K 3E2

Minister, Natural Resources & Energy Development, Hon. Mike
Holland
Constituency: Albert, Electoral District 24 *No. of Constituents:*
12,320, Progressive Conservative
Mike.Holland@gnb.ca
Other Communications: Constituency Phone: 506-856-4961;
Fax: 506-856-2676
Constituency Office
1037 Route 114
Lower Coverdale, NB E1J 1A1

Minister, Agricultue, Aquaculture & Fisheries, Hon. Margaret
Johnson
Constituency: Carleton-Victoria, Electoral District 46 *No. of
Constituents:* 3,330, Progressive Conservative
margaret.johnson@gnb.ca
Other Communications: Constituency Phone: 506-324-4061
www.facebook.com/104502174795968
Constituency Office
836 Central St.
Centreville, NB E7K 2E7

Acting Opposition Whip, Denis Landry
Constituency: Bathurst East-Nepisiguit-Saint-Isidore, Electoral
District 5 *No. of Constituents:* 11,298, Liberal
denis.landry2@gnb.ca
Other Communications: Constituency Phone: 506-358-2530
Constituency Office
4024, bouls Fondateurs
Saint-Isidore, NB E8M 1G2

Opposition Caucus Chair, Francine Landry
Constituency: Madawaska Les Lacs-Edmundston, Electoral
District 49 *No. of Constituents:* 11,677, Liberal
Francine.Landry@gnb.ca
Other Communications: Constituency Phone: 506-735-7222
twitter.com/FrancineLandry,
www.facebook.com/francinelandryMLA
Constituency Office
174, rue de L'Église
Edmundston, NB E3V 1K2

Jacques Leblanc
Constituency: Shediac-Beaubassin-Cap-Pelé, Electoral
District 15 *No. of Constituents:* 12,554, Liberal
jacques.j.leblanc@gnb.ca
Other Communications: Constituency Phone: 506-533-3450
www.facebook.com/jacques.leblanc.5,
www.linkedin.com/in/jacques-leblanc-367672ba
Constituency Office
328 Main St., #H
Shediac, NB E4P 2E3

René Legacy
Constituency: Bathurst West-Beresford, Electoral District 4
No. of Constituents: 11,079, Liberal
rene.legacy@gnb.ca
Other Communications: Constituency Phone: 506-549-5329
www.facebook.com/renelegacy.liberal
Constituency Office
#103A, 1935 St Peter Ave.
Bathurst, NB E2A 7J5

Gilles LePage
Constituency: Restigouche West, Electoral District 1 *No. of Constituents:* 11,761, Liberal
Tel: 506-826-6120; *Fax:* 506-826-6122
Gilles.LePage@gnb.ca
Other Communications: Constituency Phone: 506-826-6120;
Fax: 506-826-6122
www.facebook.com/gilleslepageCandidat
Constituency Office
#4, 647, av des Pionniers
Balmoral, NB E8E 1B3

Eric Mallet
Constituency: Shippagan-Lamèque-Miscou, Electoral District 7, Liberal
eric.mallet@gnb.ca
Other Communications: Constituency Phone: 506-340-2901
www.facebook.com/eric.mallet.37
Constituency Office
234A, boul J.-D. Gauthier
Shippagan, NB E8S 1P8

Rob Mckee
Constituency: Moncton Centre, Electoral District 19 *No. of Constituents:* 10,841, Liberal
robert.mckee@gnb.ca
Other Communications: Constituency Phone: 506-856-6040;
Fax: 506-857-8747
twitter.com/robmckeemla,
www.facebook.com/monctonrobmckee
Constituency Office
234 Church St.
Moncton, NB E1C 5A5

Acting Leader of the Official Opposition, Roger Melanson
Constituency: Dieppe, Electoral District 17 *No. of Constituents:* 11,175, Liberal
roger.l.melanson@gnb.ca
Other Communications: Constituency Phone: 506-869-7000;
Fax: 506-869-7007
twitter.com/RogerMelanson,
www.facebook.com/rogerlmelanson,
www.linkedin.com/in/roger-melanson-0960934a
Constituency Office
#203, 650 Champlain St.
Dieppe, NB E1A 1P5

Megan Mitton
Constituency: Memramcook-Tantramar, Electoral District 16 *No. of Constituents:* 11,626, Green Party of Canada
megan.mitton@gnb.ca
Other Communications: Constituency Phone: 506-378-1565
twitter.com/meganmitton,
www.facebook.com/MeganMittonNB,
www.linkedin.com/in/meganamitton
Constituency Office
#1, 13 Lorne St.
Sackville, NB E4L 3Z6

Speaker, Hon. Bill Oliver
Constituency: Kings Centre, Electoral District 34 *No. of Constituents:* 11,357, Progressive Conservative
Bill.Oliver@gnb.ca
Other Communications: Constituency Phone: 506-839-3048;
Fax: 506-738-6461
www.facebook.com/BillOliverNB
Constituency Office
227 River Valley Dr.
Grand Bay-Westfield, NB E5K 1A5

Minister responsible, Francophonie; Government House Leader, Hon. Glen Savoie
Constituency: Saint John East, Electoral District 30 *No. of Constituents:* 11,526, Progressive Conservative
Tel: 506-453-7494; *Fax:* 506-453-3461
glen.savoie@gnb.ca
glensavoie.ca
Other Communications: Constituency Phone: 506-658-6333
www.facebook.com/GlenSavoieNB
Constituency Office
#2, 1210 Loch Lomond Rd.
Saint John, NB E2J 1Z6

Minister, Tourism, Heritage & Culture; Minister responsible, Women's Equality, Hon. Tammy Scott-Wallace
Constituency: Sussex-Fundy-St. Martins, Electoral District 26 *No. of Constituents:* 12,022, Progressive Conservative
tammy.scott-wallace@gnb.ca
Other Communications: Constituency Phone: 506-567-4689;
Fax: 506-433-2619
www.facebook.com/TammyScottWallaceMLA
Constituency Office

77 Wheeler Rd.
Four Corners, NB E4G 2W5

Minister, Health, Hon. Dorothy Shephard
Constituency: Saint John Lancaster, Electoral District 33 *No. of Constituents:* 10,696, Progressive Conservative
dorothy.shephard@gnb.ca
Other Communications: Constituency Phone: 506-643-2900;
Fax: 506-643-2999
twitter.com/ShephardDorothy
Constituency Office
649 Manawagonish Rd., #A
Saint John, NB E2M 3W5

Minister, Finance; President, Treasury Board, Hon. Ernie Steeves
Constituency: Moncton Northwest, Electoral District 21 *No. of Constituents:* 12,038, Progressive Conservative
Ernie.Steeves@gnb.ca
Other Communications: Constituency Phone: 506-383-2164
Constituency Office
1966 Mountain Rd.
Moncton, N E1G 1A9

Isabelle Thériault
Constituency: Caraquet, Electoral District 6 *No. of Constituents:* 11,137, Liberal
isabelle.theriault@gnb.ca
Other Communications: Constituency Phone: 506-724-1041
twitter.com/isatheriault_nb,
www.facebook.com/isabelle.liberale
Constituency Office
253, boul St.-Pierre ouest
Caraquet, NB E1W 1A4

Greg Turner
Constituency: Moncton South, Electoral District 20 *No. of Constituents:* 2,734, Progressive Conservative
greg.turner@gnb.ca
Other Communications: Constituency Phone: 506-856-3808
www.facebook.com/GregTurnerMoncton
Constituency Office
PO Box 1394
Moncton, NB E1C 8T6

Hon. Ross Wetmore
Constituency: Gagetown-Petitcodiac, Electoral District 25 *No. of Constituents:* 11,879, Progressive Conservative
ross.wetmore@gnb.ca
Other Communications: Constituency Phone: 506-488-3577;
Fax: 506-488-3511
www.facebook.com/voterosswetmore
Constituency Office
52B Babbit St.
Gagetown, NB E5M 1C7

Minister, Service New Brunswick; Minister responsible, Military Affairs, Hon. Mary Wilson
Constituency: Oromocto-Lincoln-Fredericton, Electoral District 37 *No. of Constituents:* 11,144, Progressive Conservative
mary.wilson@gnb.ca
Other Communications: Constituency Phone: 506-357-1177
Constituency Office, Pioneer Plaza
261 Restigouche Rd.
Oromocto, NB E2V 2H1

Hon. Sherry Wilson
Constituency: Moncton Southwest, Electoral District 22 *No. of Constituents:* 11,919, Progressive Conservative
sherry.wilson@gnb.ca
Other Communications: Constituency Phone: 506-382-6567;
Fax: 506-382-7232
www.facebook.com/sherrywilsonHQ,
www.linkedin.com/in/sherry-wilson-0a20a77a
Constituency Office
#9, 555 Edinburgh Dr.
Moncton, NB E1E 4E3

Vacant
Constituency: Miramichi Bay-Neguac, Electoral District 9
Note: In August 2021, Lisa Harris resigned as the District 9 MLA to run in the federal election.

Vacant
Constituency: Southwest Miramichi-Bay du Vin, Electoral District 11
Note: In August 2021, Jake Stewart resigned as the Distrct 11 MLA to run in the federal election.

New Brunswick Government Departments & Agencies / Ministères et organismes du gouvernement du Nouveau-Brunswick

Aboriginal Affairs Secretariat / Secrétariat des affaires autochtones

Chancery Place, PO Box 6000 Fredericton, NB E3B 5H8
Tel: 506-462-5846; *Fax:* 506-444-5142
AboriginalAffairs@gnb.ca
www.gnb.ca/aboriginal

The Aboriginal Affairs Secretariat strives to enhance the Government of New Brunswick's relationship with Mi'kmaq &

Maliseet (or Wolastoqiyik) communities & Aboriginal organizations. The Secretariat acts as a gateway for contact between First Nations & the province. It works with all provincial departments to address issues such as health, housing, education, family & community services, economic development, & natural resource management.

Minister Responsible, Hon. Arlene Dunn
Arlene.Dunn@gnb.ca

Acting Deputy Minister, Cade Libby
Tel: 506-453-5897
Cade.Libby@gnb.ca

Executive Director, Consultation & Negotiation, Andrew Foster
Tel: 506-470-1618
Andrew.Foster@gnb.ca

Acting Executive Director, Policy & Initiative Management, Danielle King
Tel: 506-453-3851
Danielle.King@gnb.ca

New Brunswick Department of Agriculture, Aquaculture & Fisheries / Agriculture, Aquaculture et Pêches

Agricultural Research Station (Experimental Farm), PO Box 6000 Fredericton, NB E3B 5H1
Tel: 506-453-3826; *Fax:* 506-453-7170
DAAF-MAAP@gnb.ca
www.gnb.ca/AgricultureAquacultureFisheries

Minister, Hon. Margaret Johnson
Margaret.Johnson@gnb.ca

Deputy Minister, Cathy Larochelle
Tel: 506-453-6417
cathy.larochelle@gnb.ca

Acting Director, Communications, Kelly Cormier
Tel: 506-453-5949; *Fax:* 506-453-8450
Kelly.Cormier@gnb.ca

Associated Agencies, Boards & Commissions:

• **New Brunswick Agricultural Insurance Commission / Commission de L'assurance Agricole du Nouveau-Brunswick**
c/o Department of Agriculture, Aquaculture & Fisheries
PO Box 6000
Fredericton, NB E3B 5H1
Tel: 506-453-2666; *Fax:* 506-453-7406
DAAF-MAAP@gnb.ca
The Agricultural Insurance Commission is responsible for administering the delivery of an agricultural insurance plan that provides producers with insurance protection against losses of production. This plan is funded through producer premiums & through contributions from the Province of New Brunswick & the Government of Canada.

• **New Brunswick Farm Products Commission / Commission des produits de ferme du Nouveau-Brunswick**
c/o Department of Agriculture, Aquaculture & Fisheries
PO Box 6000
Fredericton, NB E3B 5H1
Tel: 506-453-3647; *Fax:* 506-444-5969
DAAF-MAAP@gnb.ca
The Commission provides management & administrative support in the monitoring of commodity boards under the provisions of the Natural Products Act.

• **New Brunswick Grain Commission / Commission des grains du Nouveau-Brunswick**
c/o Department of Agriculture, Aquaculture & Fisheries
PO Box 6000
Fredericton, NB E3B 5H1
Tel: 506-859-3309; *Fax:* 506-856-2092
DAAF-MAAP@gnb.ca
Under the New Brunswick Grain Act, the NB Grain Commission promotes production & marketing of grain & maintains standards of quality for grain & grain handling.

Agriculture, Aquaculture & Fisheries Division / Agriculture, Aquaculture et Pêches
Provincial Director, Business Growth, Marc King
Tel: 506-743-7330
Marc.King@gnb.ca
Provincial Director, Agriculture, Kevin McCully
Tel: 506-453-2108
Kevin.McCully@gnb.ca
Provincial Director, Marketing & Trade - Food, Kimberly Watson
Tel: 506-444-2656
Kimberly.Watson@gnb.ca

Director, Crop Sector Development, Claude Berthéléme
Tel: 506-453-2108
claude.bertheleme@gnb.ca

Organizational Development & Services / Services et développement organisationnels
Assistant Deputy Minister, Kim Embleton
Tel: 506-453-2366
Kimberly.Embleton@gnb.ca
Director, Industry Financial Programs, Ryan Bourgeois
Tel: 506-453-2108
ryan.bourgeois@gnb.ca
Director, Crown Lands/Leasing & Licensing, Andrew Sullivan
Tel: 506-453-2252
daaf-maap@gnb.ca

Office of the Attorney General / Cabinet du procureur général

Chancery Place, PO Box 6000 Fredericton, NB E3B 5H1
Tel: 506-453-3992; *Fax:* 506-453-3992
www.gnb.ca/PublicSafety
The Office is mandated to promote the impartial administration of justice & to ensure protection of the public interest.

Attorney General, Hon. Hugh J.A. (Ted) Flemming, Q.C.
Hugh.Flemming@gnb.ca

Deputy Attorney General, Mike Comeau
Tel: 506-453-2208; *Fax:* 506-453-3870
Mike.Comeau@gnb.ca

Director, Corporate Communications, Shawn Berry
Tel: 506-462-5874
Shawn.Berry@gnb.ca

Administrative Services Division / Services administratifs
Tel: 506-453-2719; *Fax:* 506-453-8718
Director, Financial Services, Gayle Howard
Tel: 506-444-4015
gayle.howard@gnb.ca

Legal Services Branch / Services juridiques
Tel: 506-453-2222; *Fax:* 506-453-3275
Executive Director, Legal Advice Services Group, Diane Audet Leger
diane.audet-leger@gnb.ca
Acting Director, Litigation Group, David Eidt
Tel: 506-453-3964
david.eidt@gnb.ca
Director, Administration & Employment Law Group, Andrea Folster
Tel: 506-444-5595
andrea.folster@gnb.ca
Director, Corporate, Commercial & Property Law Group, Stephen Leavitt
Tel: 506-453-2222
Stephen.Leavitt@gnb.ca

Legislative Services Branch / Services législatifs
Tel: 506-453-2855; *Fax:* 506-457-7342
Registrar of Regulations & Director, Legislative Drafting (Anglophone), Susan Burns
susan.burns@gnb.ca
Director, Legislative Development, Elizabeth Strange
elizabeth.strange@gnb.ca
Director, Legislative Drafting (Francophone), Elena Bosi
Tel: 506-453-2544
elena.bosi@gnb.ca

Public Legal Education & Information Service of New Brunswick (PLEIS-NB) / Service public d'éducation et d'information juridiques du Nouveau-Brunswick (SPEIJ-NB)
Tel: 506-453-5369; *Fax:* 506-462-5193
pleisnb@web.ca
www.legal-info-legale.nb.ca
twitter.com/PLEIS_NB
www.facebook.com/PLEISNB
The mission of the Public Legal Education & Information Service is to assist the public by developing bilingual educational projects & services about the law. The service promotes access to the legal system & improves citizens' abilities to handle legal issues.
Executive Director, Deborah Doherty
Tel: 506-453-5369

Public Prosecution Services Branch / Poursuites publiques
Tel: 506-453-2784; *Fax:* 506-453-5364
Under the Public Prosecutions Branch, family & youth justice crown services are located in the following places:
Bathurst (506-547-2160);
Campbellton (506-789-2308);
Edmundston (506-735-2027);
Fredericton (506-453-2819);

Miramichi (506-627-4015);
Moncton (506-869-6211);
Saint John (506-658-2580).
Also operating under the Public Prosecutions Branch are the following offices that offer crown prosecutor services:
Bathurst (506-547-2160);
Campbellton (506-789-2308);
Caraquet (506-726-2794);
Edmundston (506-735-2027);
Fredericton (506-453-2819);
Miramichi (506-627-4015);
Moncton (506-856-2310);
Oromocto / Burton (506-357-4033);
Richibucto (506-523-7990);
Saint John (506-658-2580);
Tracadie-Sheila (506-394-3727);
Woodstock (506-325-4416).
Sheriff services are available at the following locations:
Bathurst (506-547-2163);
Campbellton (506-789-2100);
Edmundston (506-735-2032);
Fredericton (506-453-2801);
Miramichi (506-627-4026);
Moncton (506-856-2315);
Saint John (506-658-2569);
Woodstock (506-325-4426).
Director, Specialized Prosecutions, Cameron Gunn
Tel: 506-453-2784
cameron.gunn@gnb.ca

Office of the Auditor General / Bureau du Vérificateur général

HSBC Place, 520 King St., Fredericton, NB E3B 6G3
Tel: 506-453-2243; *Fax:* 506-453-3067
www.agnb-vgnb.ca
The role of the Office of the Auditor General is the promotion of accountability. On behalf of the Legislative Assembly, the Office of the Auditor General audits the accounts of the province & certain Crown agencies. Objective information is provided to the citizens of New Brunswick through the Legislative Assembly.

Acting Auditor General, Janice Leahy
Tel: 506-453-2465
Janice.Leahy@gnb.ca

Deputy Auditor General, Vacant

Director, Performance Audit, Abdalla Hamid
Tel: 506-453-6741; *Fax:* 506-453-3067
abdalla.hamid@gnb.ca

Director, Information Technology Audit, Peggy Isnor
Tel: 506-453-2243
peggy.isnor@gnb.ca

Director, Financial Audit, Julie Weeks
Tel: 506-453-4102
julie.weeks2@gnb.ca

Premier's Council on the Status of Disabled Persons / Conseil du Premier ministre sur la condition des personnes handicapées

#140, Place 2000, 1st Fl., PO Box 6000 Fredericton, NB E3B 5H1
Tel: 506-444-3000; *Fax:* 506-444-3001
Toll-Free: 800-442-4412
pcd-cpmph@gnb.ca
www2.gnb.ca/content/gnb/en/departments/pcsdp.html
twitter.com/nb_pcd
www.facebook.com/nbpcd
The role of the Premier's Council on the Status of Disabled Persons is to provide advice to the provincial government of New Brunswick & the public about issues of interest & concern that affect the status of persons with disabilities.

Premier; Minister Responsible, Hon. Blaine Higgs
premier@gnb.ca

Chair, Neil Pierce

Executive Director, Christyne Allain

Economic & Social Inclusion Corporation / Société d'inclusion économique et sociale

Kings Place, #423, 440 King St., 4th Fl., PO Box 6000 Fredericton, NB E3B 5H1
Tel: 506-444-2977; *Fax:* 506-444-2978
Toll-Free: 888-295-4545
esic-sies@gnb.ca
www.gnb.ca/poverty
Develops, oversees, coordinates & implements initiatives to reduce poverty & assist New Brunswickers in need.

Minister responsible, Hon. Bruce Fitch
Bruce.Fitch@gnb.ca

President, Eric Beaulieu
esic-sies@gnb.ca

Executive Director, Stéphane Leclair
stephane.leclair@gnb.ca

New Brunswick Department of Education & Early Childhood Development / Éducation et Développement de la petite enfance

Place 2000, PO Box 6000 Fredericton, NB E3B 5H1
Tel: 506-453-3678; *Fax:* 506-453-4810
edcommunication@gnb.ca
www.gnb.ca/education
The Department of Education & Early Childhood Development consists of an Early Learning & Child Care Sector, an Anglophone Sector & a Francophone Sector.
The Early Learning & Child Care Sector oversees the following programs & services: Prenatal Benefit Program; the Postnatal Benefit Program; the Infant Parent Attachment Program; Excellence in Parenting; the Pay Equity Program for Child Care Staff; early intervention standards; child day care; Early Childhood Development Centers; the Early Childhood Strategy; the Early Learning & Child Care Trust Fund; the curriculum for early learning & child care; & services for preschool children with autism.
The English Educational Services Division is responsible for curriculum development, student services, e-learning, & student evaluation & assessment.
The Francophone Educational Services Division oversees curriculum development & implementation, special education, psychology, guidance counselling, professional development, & assessment & evaluation.

Minister, Hon. Dominic Cardy
Dominic.Cardy@gnb.ca

Deputy Minister, George Daley
Tel: 506-453-2529
george.daley@gnb.ca

Sous-ministre, Marcel Lavoie
Tél: 506-453-2409
marcel.lavoie@gnb.ca

Acting Director, Communications, Danielle Elliott
Tel: 506-444-5395
danielle.elliott@gnb.ca

Associated Agencies, Boards & Commissions:
• Atlantic Education International Inc. (AEI)
#500, 1133 Regent St.
Fredericton, NB E3B 3Z2
Tel: 506-453-8300; *Fax:* 506-453-5894
www.aei-inc.ca
Created in 1997 to deliver international education opportunities

Corporate Services Division / Services généraux
Tel: 506-453-2085; *Fax:* 506-457-4810
Acting Assistant Deputy Minister, Julie Mason
Tel: 506-453-2085
julie.mason@gnb.ca
Director, Accountability & Quality Assurance, Lee Burry
Tel: 506-470-1278
lee.burry@gnb.ca
Director, Finance & Services, Audra McKnight
Tel: 506-453-6533
audra.mcknight@gnb.ca

Early Childhood Development Division / Développement de la petite enfance
Tel: 506-453-2950; *Fax:* 506-453-5629
Executive Director, Nicole Gervais
Tel: 506-457-7893
nicole.gervais@gnb.ca
Director, Anglophone Central Office, Diane Lutes
Tel: 506-453-6964
diane.lutes@gnb.ca

Director, Francophone Central Office, Josée Nadeau
  Tel: 506-453-5293
  josee.nadeau@gnb.ca

Educational Services (Anglophone) Division
Tel: 506-453-3326; *Fax:* 506-457-4810
Assistant Deputy Minister, Chris Treadwell
  Tel: 506-453-3326
  chris.treadwll@gnb.ca
Director, Learning & Achievement, Kimberly Bauer
  Tel: 506-453-2812
  kimberly.bauer@gnb.ca
Director, Analysis & Design Services, Inga Boehler
  Tel: 506-453-2040
  inga.boehler@gnb.ca
Director, Integrated Services, Bob Eckstein
  Tel: 506-444-2618
  bob.eckstein@gnb.ca
Director, Office of First Nation Education, Sacha Dewolfe
  Tel: 506-462-5013
  sacha.dewolfe@gnb.ca
Director, Confucius Institute, Teng Jing
  Tel: 506-871-4855
  teng.jing@gnb.ca
Acting Director, Assessment, Innovation & Technologies, Cathy Martin
  Tel: 506-453-2744
  sandra.mackinnon@gnb.ca

Policy & Planning Division / Politiques et planification
Tel: 506-453-3090; *Fax:* 506-453-3111
Executive Director, Policy & Planning, Christine Gilbert Estabrooks
  Tel: 506-453-3090
  christine.gilbertestabrooks@gnb.ca
Director, Policy & Legislative Affairs, Rachel Dion
  Tel: 506-444-5250
  rachel.dion@gnb.ca
Director, Corporate Data Management & Analysis, Monica LeBlanc
  Tel: 506-453-6124
  monica.leblanc@gnb.ca

Secteur des services éducatifs francophones
Tél: 506-453-2409
Téléc: 506-457-4810

Sous-ministre adjoint, Marcel Lavoie
  Tél: 506-453-2409
  Marcel.Lavoie@gnb.ca
Directeur, Services intégrées, Bob Eckstein
  Tél: 506-444-2618
  bob.eckstein@gnb.ca
Directrice, Mesure et l'évaluation, Lynn Marotte
  Tél: 506-453-2157
  lynn.marotte@gnb.ca
Directrice, Services d'appui à l'éducation, Tanya Roy
  Tél: 506-453-2750
  tanya.roy@gnb.ca

Office of the Chief Electoral Officer / Bureau de la directrice générale des élections

Sartain MacDonald Bldg., #102, 551 King St., PO Box 6000 Fredericton, NB E3B 5H1
Tel: 506-453-2218; *Fax:* 506-457-4926
Toll-Free: 800-308-2922
TTY: 888-718-0544
info@electionsnb.ca
www.electionsnb.ca
twitter.com/ElectionsNB
www.facebook.com/110758452300716

Chief Electoral Officer, Kim Poffenroth
Tel: 506-453-2218
kim.poffenroth@gnb.ca

Assistant Chief Electoral Officer, David Owens
david.owens@electionsnb.ca

Director, Operations, Craig Astle
craig.astle@electionsnb.ca

Director, Communications, Paul Harpelle
paul.harpelle@gnb.ca

Manager, Voter Information Systems, Ronald Armitage
ron.armitage@electionsnb.ca

New Brunswick Department of Environment & Local Government / Environnement et Gouvernements locaux

Marysville Place, 20 McGloin St., Fredericton, NB E3B 5H1
Tel: 506-453-2690; *Fax:* 506-457-4994
elg/egl-info@gnb.ca
www.gnb.ca/environment
Other Communication: Toll-free phone to report pesticide, oil, chemical spills, & other environmental emergencies:
800-565-1633

The Departemnt of Environment & Local Government is responsible for environmental stewardship & consultation with municipal governments & Local Service Districts concerning governance issues.

Minister, Local Government &nd Local Governance Reform, Hon. Gary Crossman
Daniel.J.Allain@gnb.ca

Minister, Environment & Climate Change, Hon. Gary Crossman
Gary.Crossman@gnb.ca

Deputy Minister, Environment & Climate Change, Libby Cade
Tel: 506-453-5897
cade.libby@gnb.ca

Deputy Minister, Environment & Local Government, Ryan Donaghy
Tel: 506-453-3256
ryan.donaghy@gnb.ca

Associated Agencies, Boards & Commissions:
· Assessment & Planning Appeal Board
City Centre
435 King St.
PO Box 6000
Fredericton, NB E3B 5H1
Tel: 506-453-2126; *Fax:* 506-444-4881
apab-cameu@gnb.ca
The Assessment & Planning Appeal Board hears property assessment appeals, appeals of land use & planning decisions, & appeals of local heritage review board decisions. The board consists of 11 regional panels from across New Brunswick.

Authorizations & Compliance Division / Division d'autorisations et de la conformité
The division oversees human resources, administrative services, information management, corporate finance & community funding.
Assistant Deputy Minister, Perry Haines
  Tel: 506-444-5119
  perry.haines@gnb.ca
Executive Director, Regional Operations & Compliance, David Schellenberg
  Tel: 506-453-2690
  dave.schellenberg@gnb.ca
Director, Authorizations, Mike Cormier
  Tel: 506-453-7945
  mike.cormier@gnb.ca
Acting Director, Source & Surface Water Management, Christie Ward
  Tel: 506-457-4850
  christie.ward@gnb.ca

Regional Operations & Compliance Branch Offices
Bathurst Regional Office
#202, 159 Main St., PO Box 5001 Bathurst, NB E2A 3Z9
Tel: 506-547-2092; *Fax:* 506-547-7655
elg/egl-region1@gnb.ca
Regional Director, Paul Fournier
  Tel: 506-547-2092
  paul.fournier@gnb.ca
Engineer, Gaétan Landry
  Tel: 506-547-2092
  gaetan.landry@gnb.ca
Fredericton Regional Office
12 McGloin St., Fredericton, NB E3A 5T8
Tel: 506-444-5149; *Fax:* 506-453-2893
elg/egl-region5@gnb.ca
Regional Director, Peter McLaughlin
  Tel: 506-444-5149
  peter.mclaughlin@gnb.ca
Grand Falls Regional Office
65 Broadway Blvd., PO Box 5001 Grand Falls, NB E3Z 1G1
Tel: 506-473-7744; *Fax:* 506-475-2510
elg/egl-region6@gnb.ca
Regional Director, Richard Keeley
  Tel: 506-473-7744
  richard.keeley@gnb.ca

Engineer, Roger Bélanger
  Tel: 506-473-7744
  roger.belanger@gnb.ca
Miramichi Regional Office
Industrial Park, 316 Dalton Ave., Miramichi, NB E1V 3N9
Tel: 506-778-6032; *Fax:* 506-778-6796
elg.egl-region2@gnb.ca
Acting Director, Ian Donald
  Tel: 506-777-8603
  ian.donald@gnb.ca
Moncton Regional Office
355 Dieppe Blvd., PO Box 5001 Moncton, NB E1C 8R3
Tel: 506-856-2374; *Fax:* 506-856-2370
elg.egl-region3@gnb.ca
Regional Director, Laurie Collette
  Tel: 506-856-2374
  laurie.collette@gnb.ca
Saint John Regional Office
8 Castle St., PO Box 5001 Saint John, NB E2L 4Y9
Tel: 506-658-2558; *Fax:* 506-658-3046
elg.egl-region4@gnb.ca
Regional Director, Patrick Stull
  Tel: 506-658-2558
  patrick.stull@gnb.ca

Corporate Services & Community Funding Division / Divison des services généraux et du financement communautaire
The division oversees human resources, administrative services, information management, corporate finance & community funding.
Assistant Deputy Minister, Sara Degrace
  Tel: 506-453-6285
  sara.degrace@gnb.ca
Director, Performance Excellence Process, Natalie Holder
  Tel: 506-478-4304
  natalie.holder@gnb.ca
Acting Director, Community Funding, Scott Lloy
  Tel: 506-457-4947
  scott.lloy@gnb.ca
Director, Corporate Finance & Administration, Melanie MacLean
  Tel: 506-453-2690
  melanie.maclean@gnb.ca

Environmental Science & Protection Division / Division de science et de la protection de l'environnement
Tel: 506-444-5119; *Fax:* 506-457-7333
elg/egl-info@gnb.ca
Assistant Deputy Minister, Katie Pettie
  Tel: 506-444-5382
  katie.pettie@gnb.ca
Director, Air & Water Sciences, Darryl Pupek
  Tel: 506-457-4844
  darryl.pupek@gnb.ca
Director, Environmental Impact Assessment, Paul Vanderlaan
  Tel: 506-444-5382
  paul.vanderlaan@gnb.ca
Director, Healthy Environments, Karen White-Masry
  Tel: 506-457-4844
  karen.white-masry@gnb.ca

Policy, Climate Change, First Nations & Public Engagement Division / Politiques des changements climatiques et de la participation des Premières Nations et du public
Tel: 506-444-3635; *Fax:* 506-453-3688
Assistant Deputy Minister, Lesley Rogers
  Tel: 506-453-3700
  lesley.rogers@gnb.ca
Executive Director, Climate Change Secretariat, Jeff Hoyt
  Tel: 506-447-0832
  jeff.hoyt@gnb.ca
Acting Director, Policy, Katherine Lefeuvre
  Tel: 506-453-3700
  katherine.lefeuvre@gnb.ca

Local Government Division / Gouvernnement locaux
Tel: 506-453-6285; *Fax:* 506-457-4994
The Local Government Division provides liaison services, financial support & assistance with municipal functions. Examples of activities include: overseeing the restructuring of municipalities & rural communities, & assisting Business Improvement Areas to improve downtown cores.
Acting Assistant Deputy Minister, Ryan Donaghy
  Tel: 506-453-6285
  ryan.donaghy@gnb.ca
Acting Director, Local Government Support Services, Martin Corbett
  Tel: 506-444-4423
  martin.corbett@gnb.ca
Acting Director, Provincial & Community Planning, Paul Jordan
  Tel: 506-453-6285
  Paul.Jordan@gnb.ca

Director, Community Finances, Grace Lee Cutler
Tel: 506-444-4423
Grace.leecutler@gnb.ca

New Brunswick Department of Finance / Finances

Chancery Place, 675 King St., 5th Fl., Fredericton, NB E3B 5H1
Tel: 506-453-2264; *Fax:* 506-453-7195
TB-CT@gnb.ca
www.gnb.ca/finance
The Department of Finance manages the public finances of New Brunswick.

Minister, Hon. Ernie Steeves
ernie.steeves@gnb.ca

Deputy Minister, Cheryl Hansen
Tel: 506-453-3036
Cheryl.Hansen@gnb.ca

Senior Director, Communications, Sivert Mélanie
Tel: 506-444-5026
Melanie.Sivret@gnb.ca

Associated Agencies, Boards & Commissions:
• **New Brunswick Lotteries & Gaming Corporation**
Chancery Place, 4th Fl.
675 King St.
PO Box 6000
Fredericton, NB E3B 5H1
Tel: 506-453-2451; *Fax:* 506-453-2053
The Lotteries Commission of New Brunswick, which was established as a Crown corporation under the Lotteries Act, is now named the New Brunswick Lotteries & Gaming Corporation.

Agency Relations & Gaming Policy / Relations avec les organismes et politique sur le jeu
Tel: 506-453-2451; *Fax:* 506-444-5056
Director, Agency Relations & Gaming Policy, Ian Hollohan
Tel: 506-453-5432
ian.hollohan@gnb.ca

Fiscal Policy Division / Politiques fiscales
Tel: 503-453-2451; *Fax:* 506-457-6456
The Fiscal Policy Division provides the following services: advice & analysis in the areas of fiscal & budget policy, federal-provincial fiscal relations, & the economy; statistical services for the government; & forecasting & monitoring of government revenues & the economy.
Assistant Deputy Minister, Fiscal Policy, Peter Kieley
Tel: 506-453-6921; *Fax:* 506-453-2281
peter.kieley@gnb.ca
Executive Director, Tax Policy, George McAllister
Tel: 506-453-6920
george.mcallister@gnb.ca
Director, Economic & Statistical Analysis, Todd Selby
Tel: 506-453-2451
todd.selby@gnb.ca

Fiscal Policy & Revenue Branch / Direction des Politique fiscale et revenus
Tel: 506-453-2451; *Fax:* 506-457-6456
Director, Vacant

Revenue Administration Division / Division de l'administration du revenu
Tel: 506-453-2451; *Fax:* 506-444-4920
The Revenue Administation Division provides effective, efficient & fair administration of assigned revenue acts. In addition, it provides policy & administration support to the Lotteries Commission.
Assistant Deputy Minister, Dany Couillard
Tel: 506-453-2451
dany.couillard@gnb.ca
Director, Account Management, John Maclean
Tel: 506-457-7659
john.maclean2@gnb.ca
Director, Research & Tax Administration Policy, Michelle Smith
Tel: 506-453-2451
michelle.smith@gnb.ca

Treasury Division / Trésorerie
Tel: 506-453-2451; *Fax:* 506-453-2053
The Treasury Division is responsible for financing the Province's cash requirements, cash management, administration of outstanding debt, investment management & administration of pension, sinking & special purpose trust funds, financial policy analysis & advice & Crown corporation & municipal financing.
Assistant Deputy Minister, Leonard Lee-White
Tel: 506-444-5141
leonard.lee-white@gnb.ca

New Brunswick Department of Health / Santé

HSBC Place, PO Box 5100 Fredericton, NB E3B 5G8
Tel: 506-457-4800; *Fax:* 506-453-5243
Health.Sante@gnb.ca
www.gnb.ca/health
twitter.com/NBHealth
The mission of New Brunswick's Department of Health is to work with New Brunswickers in achieving well-being, by promoting self-sufficiency & personal responsibility, & providing approved services as required.
The development & delivery of health programs & services to New Brunswick residents is supported by a range of internal department functions, such as administration, planning & evaluation, & program support. The department provides services to prevent illness & disability. Education & awareness-raising initiatives promote the health & well-being of New Brunswickers of all ages, so that they can achieve their best potential, while enjoying an independent & healthy lifestyle for as long as possible.
Public Health services are delivered through the province's seven health regions, under the management of Regional Directors. A Chief Medical Officer of Health & a Deputy Chief Medical Officer of Health oversee the development of policy & regulations, & provide medical operational support to the regional Medical Officers of Health. Public Health Services support healthy growth & development, foster healthy lifestyles, control communicable diseases, & protect the public from adverse health consequences of exposure to chemical, physical & biological agents.

Minister, Hon. Dorothy Shephard
Dorothy.Shephard@gnb.ca

Acting Deputy Minister, Heidi Liston
Tel: 506-453-2542; *Fax:* 506-453-5523
heidi.liston@gnb.ca

Director, Communications, Bruce Macfarlane
Tel: 506-444-4583
bruce.macfarlane@gnb.ca

Associated Agencies, Boards & Commissions:
• **Psychiatric Patient Advocate Services Review Board**
c/o Dept. of Health, Psychiatric Patient Advocate Services
#505, 860 Main St.
Moncton, NB E1C 1G2
Tel: 506-869-6818; *Fax:* 506-869-6101
Toll-free: 888-350-4133
www.gnb.ca/0055/advocate-e.asp
A senior lawyer, a psychiatrist (or a physician, if a psychiatrist is unavailable), & a lay person serve on the Psychiatric Patient Advocate Services Review Board, as required under section 30(2) of the Mental Health Act.
The Review Board is engaged in the following activities: granting certificates of detention; delivering an order to administer a treatment; reviewing a treatment; reviewing the status of an involuntary patient; reviewing a patient's competence to give consent; reviewing the patient's access to information regarding his treatment; reviewing a transfer to another jurisdiction; & reviewing the ability of an involuntary patient to manage her estate

• **Psychiatric Patient Advocate Services Tribunal**
c/o Dept. of Health, Psychiatric Patient Advocate Services
#505, 860 Main St.
Moncton, NB E1C 1G2
Tel: 506-869-6818; *Fax:* 506-869-6101
Toll-free: 888-350-4133
www.gnb.ca/0055/advocate-e.asp
The Psychiatric Patient Advocate Services Tribunal is made up of a lawyer & two members of the public. The tribunal authorizes involuntary admission according to the Mental Health Act. It also authorize the treatment of involuntary patients.

Office of the Chief Medical Officer of Health Division / Bureau du médecin-hygiéniste en chef
Tel: 506-444-2112; *Fax:* 506-453-5243
Chief Medical Officer, Jennifer Russell
Tel: 506-453-2280
jennifer.russell@gnb.ca
Deputy Chief Medical Officer of Health, Cristin Muecke
Tel: 506-453-2427
cristin.muecke@gnb.ca
Executive Director, Planning & Operations, Janique Robichaud-Savoie
Tel: 506-453-6962
janique.robichaud-savoie@gnb.ca

Corporate Services & Francophone Affairs Division / Services ministériels et Affaires francophones
Tel: 506-453-2745; *Fax:* 506-444-4698

Associate Deputy Minister, René Boudreau
Tel: 506-453-2536
rene.boudreau@gnb.ca
Executive Director, Financial Services, Janet Flowers
Tel: 506-444-2974
Janet.Flowers@gnb.ca
Executive Director, Medicare & Physician Services, Michel Léger
Tel: 506-453-2793
Michel.Leger@gnb.ca
Executive Director, Corporate Support & Infrastructure, Mark Thompson
Tel: 506-453-2745
mark.thompson@gnb.ca

Health Services & Programs Division / Services et programmes de santé
Assistant Deputy Minister, Mark Wies
Tel: 506-457-4800
Mark.Wies@gnb.ca
Executive Director, Innovation & e-Health, Travis Quigley
Tel: 506-471-9416
Travis.Quigley@gnb.ca
Director, Health Workforce Planning, Jake Arbuckle
Tel: 506-429-3419
jake.arbuckle@gnb.ca
Director, eHealthNB, Jerome Foster
Tel: 506-471-6522
Jerome.Foster@gnb.ca
Director, Psychiatric Patient Advocate Services, Ginette Vautour-Kerwin
Tel: 506-869-6818
ginette.vautour-kerwin@gnb.ca

Acute Care / Soins aigus
Tel: 506-444-4128; *Fax:* 506-453-2958
Other Communication: New Brunswick Cancer Network:
www.gnb.ca/0051/cancer/index-e.asp
Executive Director, Daniel Coulombe
Tel: 506-453-8161
dan.coulombe@gnb.ca
Coordinator, New Brunswick Cancer Network, Nichola Downey
Tel: 506-453-5521
nichola.downey@gnb.ca

Addiction & Mental Health Services / Services de traitement des dépendances et de santé mentale
Tel: 506-444-4442; *Fax:* 506-453-8711
Executive Director, Gisèle Maillet
Tel: 506-381-0854
gisele.maillet@gnb.ca

Pharmaceutical Services / Services pharmaceutiques
Executive Director, Leanne Jardine
Tel: 506-453-3884
leanne.jardine@gnb.ca
Director, Drug Formulary Management, Tina Leclerc
Tel: 506-457-3564
Tina.LeClerc@gnb.ca
Director, Drug Utilization, Vesna Nguyen
Tel: 506-457-7687
Vesna.Nguyen@gnb.ca
Director, Business Management, Kevin Pothier
Tel: 506-444-5961
Kevin.Pothier@gnb.ca

Primary Health Care / Soins de santé primaires
Tel: 506-457-4800; *Fax:* 506-453-8711
Executive Director, Heidi Liston
Tel: 506-292-8295
heidi.liston@gnb.ca
Director, Aging Population Services, Heather Bursey
Tel: 506-453-8416
heather.bursey2@gnb.ca
Director, Home Care, Jennifer Elliott
Tel: 506-444-5360
Jennifer.Elliott@gnb.ca
Director, Emergency Health Services, John Estey
Tel: 506-453-6349
john.estey@gnb.ca
Director, Primary Health Care, Noortje Kunnen
Tel: 506-453-6349
Noortje.Kunnen@gnb.ca

New Brunswick Human Rights Commission / Commission des droits de la personne

Barry House, 751 Brunswick St., PO Box 6000 Fredericton, NB E3B 5H1
Tel: 506-453-2301; *Fax:* 506-453-2653
Toll-Free: 888-471-2233
TTY: 506-453-2911
hrc.cdp@gnb.ca
www.gnb.ca/hrc-cdp/index-e.asp
The Human Rights Commission is a provincial government agency that promotes equality & investigates & tries to settle

complaints of discrimination & harassment. The Commission also works to prevent discrimination by promoting human rights & offering educational opportunities to employers, service providers & the general public.

Chair, Nathalie Chiasson
Tel: 406-453-2301
hrc.cdp@gnb.ca

Director, Marc-Alain Mallet
Tel: 506-453-2301
marc-alain.mallet@gnb.ca

Legal Counsel & Head of Mediation Unit, Sarina Mckinnon
Tel: 506-453-2301
sarina.mckinnon@gnb.ca

New Brunswick Department of Justice & Public Safety / Justice et Cabinet du Sécurité publique

Marysville Place, 3rd Fl., PO Box 6000 Fredericton, NB E3B 5H1

Tel: 506-453-3992
DPS-MSP.Information@gnb.ca
www.gnb.ca/PublicSafety

The department works to promote the impartial administration of justice & ensure protection of the public interest.

Minister, Hon. Hugh J.A. (Ted) Flemming, Q.C.
Hugh.Flemming@gnb.ca

Deputy Minister, Mike Comeau
Tel: 506-453-2208
Mike.Comeau@gnb.ca

Executive Director, Policy & Operations Support, Joanne Higgins
Tel: 506-453-7981
joanne.higgins@gnb.ca

Director, Communications, Robert Duguay
Tel: 506-453-8607
robert.duguay@gnb.ca

Associated Agencies, Boards & Commissions:
**• New Brunswick Legal Aid Services Commission /
Commission des services d'aide juridique**
#501, 500 Beaverbrook Ct.
Fredericton, NB E3B 5X4
Tel: 506-444-2776; *Fax:* 506-444-2290
info@legalaid.nb.ca
www.legalaid.nb.ca
Local legal aid offices are located in the following places:
Baththurst (506-546-5010);
Campbellton (506-753-6453);
Edmundston (506-735-4213);
Fredericton (506-444-2777);
Miramichi (506-622-1061);
Moncton (506-853-7300);
Saint John (506-633-6030);
Tracadie-Sheila (506-395-1507);
Woodstock (506-328-8127).

**• Financial & Consumer Services Commission (FCNB) /
Commission des services financiers et des services aux
consommateurs**
#300, 85 Charlotte St.
Saint John, NB E2L 2J2
Tel: 506-658-3060; *Fax:* 506-658-3059
Toll-free: 866-933-2222
info@fcnb.ca
www.fcnb.ca
The New Brunswick Securities Commission adminsters the province's Securities Statute. Staff of the commission are responsible for the following services: review of prospectuses; registration of companies & persons operating in the province's securities industry; consideration of exemption applications; & enforcement of securities laws.

Justice Services / Services à la justice
Tel: 506-453-3992; *Fax:* 506-453-3870
Assistant Deputy Minister, Charbel Awad
Tel: 506-453-6728
charbel.awad@gnb.ca
Chief Hearing Officer, Donald Boudreau
Tel: 506-547-2150
Director, Support Enforcement, Nancy Grant
Tel: 844-673-4499

Public Prosecution Services / Service des poursuites publiques
Tel: 506-453-2784; *Fax:* 506-453-5364

Assistant Deputy Attorney General, Luc Labonté
Tel: 506-453-2784
Luc.Labonte@gnb.ca

New Brunswick Liquor Corporation (Alcool NB Liquor) / Société des alcools du Nouveau-Brunswick

170 Wilsey Rd., PO Box 20787 Fredericton, NB E3B 5B8
Tel: 506-452-6826; *Fax:* 506-462-2024
receptionist@anbl.com
www.anbl.com
twitter.com/anbl_eng
www.facebook.com/anbl
www.linkedin.com/company/alcool-nb-liquor
www.instagram.com/anbl

The Crown corporation manufactures, buys, imports & sells liquor in the province of New Brunswick.

Chairperson, John Correia
Tel: 506-452-6826

Acting President & CEO, Lori Stickles
Tel: 506-452-6826
Lori.Stickles@anbl.com

Vice-President, Operations & Property Management, Brad Cameron
Tel: 506-452-6511
Brad.Cameron@anbl.com

Acting Vice-President, People & Culture, Reid Estey
Tel: 506-452-6826
Reid.Estey@anbl.com

Vice-President, Customer Strategy & Engagement, Paul Henderson
Tel: 506-452-6826
Paul.Henderson@anbl.com

Cannabis NB
Centennial Bldg., PO Box 6000 Fredericton, NB E3B 5H1
www.cannabis-nb.com
Other Communication: Store Locator:
www.cannabis-nb.com/stores
www.facebook.com/cannabisnb
www.instagram.com/cannabis_nb
Cannabis NB is a subsidiary of the New Brunswick Liquor Corporation, & is the only legal retailer of cannabis in the province. It manages sales of cannabis for the Cannabis Management Corporation. The agency operates 20 stores in 15 communities.
Senior Communications Officer, Marie-Andrée Bolduc
Tel: 506-462-2024
marie-andree.bolduc@cannabis-nb.com

New Brunswick Department of Natural Resources & Energy Development / Ressources naturelles et du Développement de l'énergie

Hugh John Flemming Forestry Centre, PO Box 6000 Fredericton, NB E3B 5H1
Tel: 506-453-3826; *Fax:* 506-444-4367
dnr_mrnweb@gnb.ca
www.gnb.ca/energy
The department was created in 2016 after the combination of the department of Natural Resources & the department of Energy & Mines.

Minister, Hon. Mike Holland
Mike.Holland@gnb.ca

Deputy Minister, Tom Macfarlane
Tel: 506-453-2501
Tom.Macfarlane@gnb.ca

Director, Energy, Heather Quinn
Tel: 506-977-2329
heather.quinn@gnb.ca

Associated Agencies, Boards & Commissions:
**• New Brunswick Forest Products Commission /
Commission des produits forestiers**
Hugh John Flemming Forestry Centre
PO Box 6000
Fredericton, NB E3B 5H1
Tel: 506-453-2196; *Fax:* 506-457-4966
dnr_mrnweb@gnb.ca

Corporate Communications Division / Services Généraux
Hugh John Flemming Forestry Centre, Fredericton, E3B 5H1
Director, Communications, Shawn Berry
Tel: 506-444-2915
shawn.berry@gnb.ca

Energy & Mines Division / Énergie et Mines
Tel: 506-453-3826; *Fax:* 506-444-4367
dem@gnb.ca

**Minerals & Resource Development Division /
Développement des minéraux et des ressources**
geoscience@gnb.ca
Director, Minerals & Resource Development, Craig Parks
Tel: 506-453-2364
craig.parks@gnb.ca

**Regional Operations & Support Services Division /
Ressources renouvelables et des Opérations**
Executive Director, Regional Operations & Support Services, Kristian J. Moore
Tel: 506-453-6171
kristian.moore@gnb.ca

Fish & Wildlife Branch / Direction du poisson et de la faune
fw_pfweb@gnb.ca
The Branch develops environmental protection plans to ensure the province's fisheries & wildlife resources are protected & maintained.
Director, Vacant

Forest Fire Management Branch / Gestion des forêts
The Branch manages Crown timber resources in accordance with Government Policy.

Office of the Ombudsman / Bureau de l'ombudsman

548 York St., PO Box 6000 Fredericton, NB E3B 5H1
Tel: 506-453-2789; *Fax:* 506-453-5599
Toll-Free: 888-465-1100
www.ombudnb.ca

The Ombudsman, independent of government, is an officer of the Legislative Assembly, with responsibilities under the Ombudsman Act, the Civil Service Act & the Archives Act. In 1994, the Civil Service Commission was amalgamated with the Office of the Ombudsman, which hears appeals & investigates complaints regarding selections for appointment in the Civil Service.

Ombudsman, Charles Murray
Tel: 506-453-2789; *Fax:* 506-453-5599
nbombud@gnb.ca

Director, Legal Affairs & Administration, Anne Furey
Tel: 506-453-2789
anne.furey@gnb.ca

Opportunities New Brunswick / Opportunités Nouveau-Brunswick

Place 2000, 250 King St., PO Box 6000 Fredericton, NB E3B 5H1
Tel: 506-453-5471; *Fax:* 506-444-5277
Toll-Free: 855-746-4662
info@onbcanada.ca
onbcanada.ca
twitter.com/onbcanada
www.facebook.com/opportunitiesns
www.linkedin.com/company/onbcanada

Opportunities NB was created in 2015 to replace Invest NB & the Department of Economic Development. Its mandate is to support business development inside New Brunswick; pursue growth opportunities outside the province; & work with economic departments, other public sector partners & stakeholders to construct a portfolio of growth opportunities both inside & outside the province.

Minister responsible, Hon. Arlene Dunn
Arlene.Dunn@gnb.ca

Chief Executive Officer, Sadie Perron
Tel: 506-453-2794
Sadie.Perron@onbcanada.ca

New Brunswick Police Commission (NBPC) / Commission de police du Nouveau-Brunswick

Fredericton City Centre, #202, 435 King St., Fredericton, NB E3B 1E5
Tel: 506-453-2069; *Fax:* 506-457-3542
nbpc@gnb.ca
www.nbpolicecommission.ca
twitter.com/nbpolicecommisn
The New Brunswick Police Commission is engaged in the following activities: investigating & determining complaints alleging misconduct by municipal & regional police officers; investigating any matter relating to any aspect of policing in any area of the province; determining the adequacy of municipal, regional & RCMP police forces within the province.

Chair, Lynn Chaplin

Executive Director, Jennifer Smith
Tel: 506-453-2069
Jennifer.Smith3@gnb.ca

New Brunswick Department of Post-Secondary Education, Training & Labour / Éducation postsecondaire, formation et travail

Chestnut Complex, PO Box 6000 Fredericton, NB E3B 5H1
Tel: 506-453-2597; *Fax:* 506-453-3618
dpetlinfo@gnb.ca
www.gnb.ca/petl

New Brunswick's Department of Post-Secondary Education, Training & Labour currently consists of the following divisions: Adult Learning & Employment; Communications; Corporate Services; Labour & Planning; Population Growth; & Post-Secondary Education.

Minister, Hon. Trevor Holder
trevor.holder@gnb.ca

Deputy Minister, Daniel Mills
Tel: 506-453-2597
daniel.mills@gnb.ca

Director, Communications, Dave MacLean
Tel: 506-457-4967
Dave.Maclean@gnb.ca

Adult Learning & Employment Division / Apprentissage pour adultes et emploi

Tel: 506-453-2587; *Fax:* 506-453-3038
Assistant Deputy Minister, Daniel Mills
Tel: 506-476-2556
daniel.mills@gnb.ca
Executive Director, Employment & Continuous Learning Services, Guy Lamarche
Tel: 506-462-5935
guy.lamarche@gnb.ca
Executive Director, Provincial Office, Sylvie Nadeau
Tel: 506-453-2354
sylvie.nadeau@gnb.ca
www.gnb.ca/publiclibraries
Director, Apprenticeship & Occupational Certification, Michael Barnett
Tel: 506-444-3657
michael.barnett@gnb.ca

Labour & Policy Division / Travail et Politique

Tel: 506-453-2592; *Fax:* 506-453-3038
Director, Policy, Research & Labour Market Analysis, Patricia Noble
Tel: 506-478-3680
patricia.noble@gnb.ca

Population Growth Division / Croissance démographique

#500, Beaverbrook Bldg., PO Box 6000 Fredericton, NB E3B 5H1
Tel: 506-453-3981; *Fax:* 506-444-6729
Issues such as immigration, attraction & repatriation, settlement & multiculturalism, & retention are handled by the Population Growth Division.
Assistant Deputy Minister, Charles Ayles
Tel: 506-444-5663
charles.ayles@gnb.ca
Director, Immigration, Settlement & Multiculturalism, Ashraf Ghanem
Tel: 506-457-7644
ashraf.ghanem@gnb.ca

Post-Secondary Education Division / Éducation Postsecondaire

Tel: 506-444-5732; *Fax:* 506-453-3038
Assistant Deputy Minister, France Haché
Tel: 506-457-4891
france.hache@gnb.ca
Acting Director, College Admissions Service, Debbie Cormier
Tel: 506-789-2016
debbie.cormier@gnb.ca
Director, Student Financial Services, Chris Ferguson
Tel: 506-453-3399
chris.ferguson@gnb.ca
Director, Research & Strategic Initiatives, Peter French
Tel: 506-457-6782
peter.french@gnb.ca
Director, Post-Secondary Relations, Giselle Goguen
Tel: 506-462-5135
giselle.goguen@gnb.ca

Regional Development Corporation (RDC) / Société d'aménagement régional (SAR)

Chancery Place, 3rd Fl., PO Box 6000 Fredericton, NB E3B 5H1
Tel: 506-453-2277; *Fax:* 506-453-7988
rdc-sdr@gnb.ca
www.gnb.ca/rdc

The Regional Development Corporation is a Crown corporation that carries out its mandate in accordance with the Regional Development Corporation Act. The following are responsibilities of the Corporation: administration & management of development agreements between the Province of New Brunswick & the federal government; assistance in the establishment & development of enterprises & institutions; assistance to municipalities in the planning & development of projects to benefit the public; assistance in the development of tourism & recreational facilities; planning, coordinating & guiding regional development; & performing duties assigned by the Lieutenant-Governor-in-Council.

Minister responsible, Hon. Gary Crossman
gary.crossman@gnb.ca

President, Cade Libby
Tel: 506-453-5897
Cade.Libby@gnb.ca

Vice-President, Regional Development, Rob Kelly
Tel: 506-453-2277
Rob.Kelly@gnb.ca

Vice-President, Corporate Services & Programs, Ann Marie Wood-Seems
Tel: 506-453-8526
annmarie.wood-seems@gnb.ca

New Brunswick Research & Productivity Council (RPC) / Conseil de la recherche et de la productivité du Nouveau-Brunswick (RPC)

921 College Hill Rd., Fredericton, NB E3B 6Z9
Tel: 506-452-1212; *Fax:* 506-452-1395
Toll-Free: 800-563-0844
info@rpc.ca
rpc.ca
Other Communication: Alt. Emails: accounting@rpc.ca; careers@rpc.ca
twitter.com/nb_rpc
www.linkedin.com/company/research-&-productivity-council

The New Brunswick Research & Productivity Council's vision is to excel in technological innovation, enabling its partners in business & industry to create wealth & high quality employment opportunities in New Brunswick.
The council works to steadily improve its capacity to develop & apply new technology, in partnership with firms in the private sector. It provides an expanding range of high quality technical services to clients in the global marketplace.
The Research & Productivity Council is registered to the ISO 9001:2000 International Standard.

Executive Director, Eric Cook
Tel: 506-452-1212
eric.cook@rpc.ca

Department Head, Physical Metallurgy, John Aikens
Tel: 506-452-1212
john.aikens@rpc.ca

Department Head, Air Quality Services, Diane Bothelho
Tel: 506-460-5659
diane.bothelho@rpc.ca

Department Head, Mining & Industrial Services, Leo Cheung
Tel: 506-452-1212
leo.cheung@rpc.ca

Department Head, Food, Fisheries & Aquaculture, Ben Forward
Tel: 506-452-1212
ben.forward@rpc.ca

Department Head, Inorganic Analytical Services, Ross Kean
Tel: 506-452-1212
ross.kean@rpc.ca

Department Head, Organic Analytical Services, Bruce Phillips
Tel: 506-452-1212
bruce.phillips@rpc.ca

Service New Brunswick / Service Nouveau Brunswick

Lincoln Place, PO Box 1998 Fredericton, NB E3B 5G4
Tel: 506-684-7901
Toll-Free: 888-762-8600
snb@snb.ca
www.snb.ca

Service New Brunswick provides the following services to the public: Service New Brunswick TeleServices (Call Centre); delivery of federal, provincial & municipal government services; Land Registry; Personal Property Registry; Corporate Registry; Property Assessment & Taxation System; & maintaining land information infrastructure.
On Oct. 1, 2015, the new Service New Brunswick was launched, bringing together the former Service New Brunswick, Department of Government Services, FacilicorpNB & New Brunswick Internal Services Agency under one organization.

Minister, Hon. Mary Wilson
Mary.Wilson@gnb.ca

Chief Executive Officer, Alan Roy
Tel: 506-444-2897
alan.roy@snb.ca

Executive Secretary, Becky Holland
Tel: 506-444-2897
becky.holland@snb.ca

Enterprise Services / Services organisationnels

Tel: 506-444-4600; *Fax:* 506-453-5384
Vice-President, Judy Ross
Tel: 506-457-3582
judy.ross@snb.ca
Director, Translation Bureau, Pascale Bergeron
Tel: 506-453-2920
pascale.bergeron@gnb.ca
Director, Corporate Operations, Craig Chouinard
Tel: 506-461-6797
craig.chouinard@snb.ca
Director, Corporate Marketing Services & Managed Print & Distribution, Rob MacLeod
Tel: 506-474-3452
rob.macleod@snb.ca
Director, Payroll & Benefits, Monica Ward
Tel: 506-444-3279
monica.ward@gnb.ca

Finance & Strategic Procurement / Finances et Approvisionnement stratégique

Tel: 506-453-3391; *Fax:* 506-453-7462
Vice-President, Renée Laforest
Tel: 506-999-0438
Renee.Laforest@snb.ca
Executive Director, Strategic Procurement, Ann Dolan
Tel: 506-663-2538
ann.dolan@snb.ca
Executive Director, Strategic Procurement, Joanne Lynch
Tel: 506-444-3280
joanne.lynch@snb.ca

Human Resources & Strategy / Ressources humaines et Stratégie

Tel: 506-457-3581; *Fax:* 506-444-5239
Vice-President, Dan Rae
Tel: 506-457-4805
dan.rae@snb.ca
Executive Director, Human Resources Client Services, Barbara Lapointe
Tel: 506-476-3278
barbara.lapointe@snb.ca
Managing Director, Environment & Local Government/Tourism, Heritage & Culture, Carrie Miles
Tel: 506-453-3115
carrie.miles@snb.ca
Managing Director, Transportation & Infrastructure, Julie Smith
Tel: 506-457-7523
julie.p.smith@snb.ca

Health Services / Services de santé

Tel: 506-457-3581; *Fax:* 506-444-2850
Vice-President, David Dumont
Tel: 506-663-2510
david.dumont@snb.ca
Executive Director, Supply Chain, Michel Levesque
Tel: 506-869-6140
michel.levesque@snb.ca

Public Services Division / Services publics

Tel: 506-457-7838; *Fax:* 506-453-5384
Vice-President, Customer Care, Rob Horwood
Tel: 506-457-7838
rob.horwood@snb.ca

Executive Director, Registries, Charles Boulay
 Tel: 506-453-2658
 charles.boulay@snb.ca
Executive Director, Valuation, Stephen Ward
 Tel: 506-453-2658
 stephen.ward@snb.ca
Director, Land Registry, Eric Nadeau
 Tel: 888-621-9789
 eric.nadeau@snb.ca

Technology Services / Services technologiques
 Tel: 506-444-4600; *Fax:* 506-444-3784
 Toll-Free: 888-487-5050
 NBISA-ASINB@gnb.ca
Executive Director, Strategy, Planning & Solutions Services,
 Robert Arsenault
 Tel: 506-444-4600
 robert.arsenault2@snb.ca
Executive Director, Health Application Services, Tania Davies
 Tel: 506-444-4600
 tania.davies@snb.ca
Executive Director, Client Services, Karen Harper
 Tel: 506-457-3581
 karen.harper@snb.ca
Executive Director, Infrastructure Operations, Michel Sanscartier
 Tel: 506-444-4600
 michel.sanscartier@snb.ca
Executive Director, Business Application Services, Carole
 Sharpe
 Tel: 506-444-4600
 carole.sharpe@snb.ca

New Brunswick Department of Social Development / Développement social

Sartain MacDonald Bldg., PO Box 6000 Fredericton, NB E3B 5H1
 Tel: 506-453-2001; *Fax:* 506-453-2164
 sd-ds@gnb.ca
 www.gnb.ca/socialdevelopment
The Department of Social Development oversees services to the following citizens of New Brunswick: seniors & persons with disabilities who need long-term care & nursing home services; children who require assistance to prepare for school; abused & neglected children & adults; families in need of affordable day care; & persons in need of affordable housing & social assistance.

 Minister, Hon. Bruce Fitch
 Bruce.Fitch@gnb.ca

 Deputy Minister, Eric Beaulieu
 Tel: 506-453-2590
 eric.beaulieu@gnb.ca

Corporate Services / Services ministériels
 Tel: 506-453-2379; *Fax:* 506-453-2164
Assistant Deputy Minister, Robert Penney
 Tel: 506-453-2379
 robert.penney@gnb.ca

Families & Children / Familles et des enfants
 Tel: 506-453-2181; *Fax:* 506-453-2164
Assistant Deputy Minister, Lisa Doucette
 Tel: 506-453-2181
 lisa.doucette@gnb.ca

Program Delivery / Prestation des programmes
 Tel: 506-453-2379; *Fax:* 506-453-2164
Assistant Deputy Minister, Jean Rioux
 Tel: 506-453-2379
 jean.rioux@gnb.ca

Seniors & Long Term Care / Aînés et Soins de longue durée
 Tel: 506-453-2940; *Fax:* 506-453-2164
 seniors@gnb.ca
 www.gnb.ca/seniors
Assistant Deputy Minister, Thomas MacFarlane
 Tel: 506-453-2001
 tom.macfarlane@gnb.ca

New Brunswick Department of Tourism, Heritage & Culture / Tourisme, Patrimoine et Culture

Marysville Place, 4th Fl., PO Box 6000 Fredericton, NB E3B 5H1
 Tel: 506-453-3115; *Fax:* 506-444-5760
 thctpcinfo@gnb.ca
 www.gnb.ca/tourism
 twitter.com/DestinationNB
 www.facebook.com/destinationnb
 www.instagram.com/destinationnb
The Department of Tourism, Heritage & Culture is engaged in facilitating community cultural development throughout New

Brunswick & maximizing the profile of the province's tourism industry.

 Minister, Hon. Tammy Scott-Wallace
 Tammy.Scott-Wallace@gnb.ca

 Deputy Minister, Yennah Hurley
 Tel: 506-453-3261
 yennah.hurley@gnb.ca

 Acting Director, Communications, Erika Jutras
 Tel: 506-444-3606
 Erika.Jutras@gnb.ca

Associated Agencies, Boards & Commissions:
• **Kings Landing Historical Settlement / Village historique de Kings Landing**
5804 Rte 102
Prince William, NB E6K 0A5
 Tel: 506-363-4999; *Fax:* 506-363-4989
kingslanding.nb.ca
• **Arts New Brunswick**
#201, 225 King St.
Fredericton, NB E3B 1E1
 Tel: 506-444-4444; *Fax:* 506-444-5543
 Toll-free: 866-460-2787
www.artsnb.ca
The New Brunswick Arts Board promotes the creation of art. The arts funding agency also administers funding programs for professional artists throughout New Brunswick.

• **New Brunswick Museum / Musée du Nouveau-Brunswick**
Exhibition Centre, Market Square
Saint John, NB E2L 4Z6
 Tel: 506-643-2300; *Fax:* 506-643-6081
 Toll-free: 888-268-9595
nbmuseum@nbm-mnb.ca
www.nbm-mnb.ca

Culture, Heritage & Archaeology / Culture, Patrimoine et Archéologie
 Tel: 506-453-3115; *Fax:* 506-453-6548
Cultural responsibilities include development of the arts, heritage, cultural industries, & the New Brunswick Museum.
Executive Director, Thierry Arseneau
 Tel: 506-440-8497
 thierry.arseneau@gnb.ca
Director, Heritage, Gilles Bourque
 Tel: 506-470-2837
 gilles.bourque@gnb.ca
Director, Archaeological Services, Brent Suttie
 Tel: 506-453-3014
 brent.suttie@gnb.ca

Parks, Recreation & Corporate Services / Parcs, loisirs et services ministériels
 Tel: 506-453-3115; *Fax:* 506-444-5760
Assistant Deputy Minister, Alain Basqué
 Tel: 506-476-0169
 alain.basque@gnb.ca
Director, Parks & Attractions, Allen Bard
 Tel: 506-238-4051
 allen.bard@gnb.ca
Director, Finance & Administration, Jo-Anne Bradley
 Tel: 506-292-1715
 jo-anne.bradley@gnb.ca
Director, Sport & Recreation, Jeffrey LeBlanc
 Tel: 506-447-0988
 jeffrey.leblank@gnb.ca
Director, Policy, Planning & Process Improvement, Bruce
 Matson
 Tel: 506-440-5544
 bruce.matson@gnb.ca

Tourism / Tourisme
 Tel: 506-453-3115; *Fax:* 506-444-5760
Assistant Deputy Minister, Carol Sharpe
 Tel: 506-440-6507
 carol.sharpe@gnb.ca

New Brunswick Department of Transportation & Infrastructure / Transports et Infrastructure

Kings Place, PO Box 6000 Fredericton, NB E3B 5H1
 Tel: 506-453-3939; *Fax:* 506-453-7987
 transportation.web@gnb.ca
 www.gnb.ca/transportation
The Department of Transportation & Infrastructure aims to maintain a safe transportation system & infrastructure within the province of New Brunswick. The department also monitors & advises on transportation & infrastructure issues of federal jurisdiction.

 Minister, Hon. Jill Green
 Jill.Green@gnb.ca

 Deputy Minister, John Logan
 Tel: 506-453-2549
 John.Logan2@gnb.ca

Associated Agencies, Boards & Commissions:
• **Vehicle Management Agency**
Vehicle Management Centre
1050 College Hill Rd.
PO Box 6000
Fredericton, NB E3B 5H1
 Tel: 506-453-3939; *Fax:* 506-453-3628
transportation.web@gnb.ca
The Vehicle Management Agency provides vehicle maintenance & fleet management services to the Government of New Brunswick.

Buildings Division / Édifices
 Tel: 506-453-3939; *Fax:* 506-462-2072
Assistant Deputy Minister, Robert Martin
 Tel: 506-453-2228
 bob.martin@gnb.ca
Executive Director, Facilities Management, Gary Lynch
 Tel: 506-453-2228
 gary.lynch@gnb.ca
Director, Planning & Project Development, Pam Barteaux
 Tel: 506-453-2362
 pam.barteaux@gnb.ca
Director, Design Services, Joel Bragdon
 Tel: 506-444-5519
 joel.bragdon@gnb.ca
Director, Construction Services, Wayne Larochelle
 Tel: 506-453-2239
 wayne.larochelle@gnb.ca

Strategic Services Division / Services stratégiques
 Tel: 506-453-3939; *Fax:* 506-453-7987
Assistant Deputy Minister, Mark Gaudet
 Tel: 506-453-3939
 mark.gaudet@gnb.ca
Director, Property Services, Colleen Brown
 Tel: 506-453-3939
 colleen.brown@gnb.ca
Director, Policy & Legislative Affairs, Shannon Sanford
 Tel: 506-453-3939
 shannon.sanford@gnb.ca
Director, Supply Chain Management, Mark Scott
 Tel: 506-453-3939
 mark.scott@gnb.ca

Transportation Agency / Transport
 Tel: 506-453-3939; *Fax:* 506-453-7987
Executive Director, Engineering Services, Serge Gagnon
 Tel: 506-457-7881
 serge.gagnon@gnb.ca
Executive Director, Operations, Jules Michaud
 Tel: 506-735-2050
 jules.michaud@gnb.ca
Director, Construction, Duane Clowater
 Tel: 506-453-3939
 duane.clowater@gnb.ca
Director, Operations, Ahmed Dassouki
 Tel: 506-453-3939
 ahmed.dassouki@gnb.ca
Director, Design, James Hoyt
 Tel: 506-453-3939
 james.hoyt@gnb.ca

Treasury Board / Conseil du trésor

Chancery Place, 5th Fl., PO Box 6000 Fredericton, NB E3B 5H1
 Tel: 506-453-2264; *Fax:* 506-453-7195
 tb-ct@gnb.ca

 President, Hon. Ernie Steeves
 ernie.steeves@gnb.ca

 Deputy Minister, Cheryl Hansen
 Tel: 506-453-3036
 cheryl.hansen@gnb.ca

Budget & Financial Management / Affaires budgétaires et financières
 Tel: 506-453-2808; *Fax:* 506-457-6456
Assistant Secretary to Treasury Board, Keith MacNevin
 Tel: 506-453-2808
 keith.macnevin@gnb.ca
Director, Budgets & Expenditure Monitoring, Nick McCann
 Tel: 506-453-8019
 nick.mccann@gnb.ca

Director, Treasury Board Secretariat, Jennifer Sherwood
Tel: 506-453-2808
jennifer.sherwood@gnb.ca

Office of the Chief Human Resources Officer (OCHRO) / Bureau du dirigeant principal des ressources humaines
Tel: 506-453-2264; *Fax:* 506-453-7195
This department has been merged with the Treasury Board as of June 6, 2016 as a part of a cabinet shuffle. The Department of Human Resources has responsibility for the policies that govern the recruitment, compensation & staff development for the provision of quality public services.
Assistant Deputy Minister, Frédéric Finn
Tel: 506-453-2264
frederic.finn@gnb.ca
Executive Director, Total Compensation & Benefits, Amy Beswarick
Tel: 506-444-4187
amy.beswarick@gnb.ca
Executive Director, Talent, Organizational Development & Wellness, Shannon Ferris
Tel: 506-444-4912
shannon.ferris@gnb.ca
Executive Director, Employee Relations, Luc Sirois
Tel: 506-453-2115
luc.sirois@gnb.ca
Director, Employee Safety & Wellness, Myrna Belyea-Tracy
Tel: 506-453-3789
myrna.belyea-tracy@gnb.ca
Director, Official Languages, Lori Anne McCracken
Tel: 506-453-8574
lorianne.mccracken@gnb.ca

Office of the Comptroller / Bureau du Contrôleur
Tel: 506-453-2565; *Fax:* 506-457-6878
The Office of the Comptroller, a division of the Treasury Board, provides leadership in accounting & internal auditing services to clients & encourages the effective management of the resources of the province.
Comptroller, Paul Martin
Tel: 506-453-2565
paul.martin@gnb.ca
Assistant Comptroller, David Nowland
Tel: 506-478-2739
david.nowland@gnb.ca
Acting Assistant Comptroller, Susan McIssac
Tel: 506-453-2565
susan.mcissac@gnb.ca
Director, Financial Business Systems, Leann Collings
Tel: 506-453-2565
leann.collings@gnb.ca
Acting Director, Accounting, Reporting & Financial Systems, Rebecca Stanley
Tel: 506-457-8097
rebecca.stanley@gnb.ca
Director, Audit & Consulting Services, Jennifer Urquhart
Tel: 506-453-2565
jennifer.urquhart@gnb.ca

WorkSafeNB / Travail sécuritaire NB

1 Portland St., PO Box 160 Saint John, NB E2L 3X9
Tel: 506-632-2200
Toll-Free: 800-222-9775
communications@ws-ts.nb.ca
www.worksafenb.ca
Other Communication: Toll-Free Fax: 888-629-4722
twitter.com/worksafenb
www.linkedin.com/company/worksafenb
WorkSafeNB is a Crown corporation, responsible for the application of the acts it administers on behalf of the workers & employers of New Brunswick. WorkSafeNB provides insurance for the workers it represents.

Chair, Mel Norton

President & CEO, Douglas Jones
douglas.jones@ws-ts.nb.ca

Chief Financial Officer, Perry Cheeks
perry.cheeks@ws-ts.nb.ca

Executive Director, Corporate Communications, Laragh Dooley
laragh.dooley@ws-ts.nb.ca

Executive Director, Human Resources, Josée Pelletier
josee.pelletier@ws-ts.nb.ca

Corporate Secretary & General Counsel, Susan Layton

Government of Newfoundland & Labrador
Seat of Government: Confederation Bldg., St. John's, NL A1B 4J6
info@gov.nl.ca
www.gov.nl.ca
twitter.com/GovNl
www.facebook.com/GovNL
www.linkedin.com/company/government-of-newfoundland-and-la brador
www.youtube.com/user/GovNL
The Province of Newfoundland & Labrador entered Confederation March 31, 1949. It has a land area of 370,514.08 sq km, & the StatsCan census population in 2016 was 519,716.

Office of the Lieutenant Governor

Government House, 50 Military Rd., PO Box 5517 St. John's, NL A1C 5W4
Tel: 709-729-4494; *Fax:* 709-729-2234
governmenthouse@gov.nl.ca
www.govhouse.nl.ca

Lieutenant Governor, The Hon. Judy May Foote, P.C., O.N.L.

Private Secretary, Peter Fitzgerald
Tel: 709-729-2669
peterfitzgerald@gov.nl.ca

Office of the Premier

East Block, Confederation Bldg., PO Box 8700 St. John's, NL A1B 4J6
Tel: 709-729-3570; *Fax:* 709-729-5875
premier@gov.nl.ca
www.gov.nl.ca/premier
Kathy Dunderdale, the province's first female Premier & tenth Premier overall, resigned on January 22, 2014. She had been Premier since December 3, 2010, having been re-elected in the general election of October 11, 2011. After her resignation, she retained her seat in the district of Virginia Waters until February 2014. Thomas W. Marshall became Acting Premier on January 24, 2014. Paul Davis won the PC leadership on Sept. 13, 2014, becoming the Premier-designate. He was sworn-in on Sept. 26, 2014. Davis lost in the 2015 general election to Liberal Leader Dwight Ball, who became the province's new Premier. In Feb. 2020, he announced his resignation & continued as Premier until Aug. 3 2020, when his successor, Andrew Furey, won the provincial Liberal leadership race & succeeded him.

Premier; President, Executive Council; Minister, Intergovernmental Affairs, Hon. Andrew Furey
Tel: 709-729-3565
andrewfurey@gov.nl.ca

Chief of Staff, Peter Miles
Tel: 709-729-3966
petermiles@gov.nl.ca

Executive Council

c/o Communications Branch, East Block, Confederation Building, 10th Fl., St. John's, NL A1B 4J6
info@gov.nl.ca
www.gov.nl.ca/exec
The mailing address for all Ministers of the Government of Newfoundland & Labrador is as follows: Confederation Building, PO Box 8700, St. John's NL A1B 4J6.
The following is the list of Cabinet Ministers:

Premier; President, Executive Council; Minister, Intergovernmental Affairs, Hon. Andrew Furey
andrewfurey@gov.nl.ca
www.gov.nl.ca/premier

Deputy Premier; Minister, Finance; Minister responsible, Public Service Commission; Newfoundland & Labrador Liquor Corporation, Hon. Siobhan Coady
Tel: 709-729-2920; *Fax:* 709-729-0059
siobhancoady@gov.nl.ca

Minister, Children, Seniors & Social Development; Minister responsible, Status of Persons with Disabilities; Community Sector; Newfoundland & Labrador Housing Corporation, Hon. John Abbott

Minister, Fisheries, Forestry & Agriculture, Hon. Derrick Bragg

Minister, Immigration, Population Growth & Skills, Hon. Gerry Byrne

Minister, Culture, Arts & Recreation; Government House Leader, Hon. Steve Crocker

Minister, Environment & Climate Change; Minister responsible, Labour; Workplace NL, Hon. Bernard Davis

Minister responsible, Indigenous Affairs & Reconciliation; Labrador Affairs; Deputy Government House Leader, Hon. Lisa Dempster

Minister, Health & Community Services, Hon. Dr. John Haggie
Tel: 709-729-3124; *Fax:* 709-729-0121
johnhaggie@gov.nl.ca

Minister, Justice & Public Safety; Attorney General, Hon. John Hogan, Q.C.

Minister, Municipal & Provincial Affairs; Registrar General, Hon. Krista Lynn Howell

Minister, Transportation & Infrastructure; Minister responsible, Public Procurement Agency, Hon. Elvis Loveless
elvisloveless@gov.nl.ca

Minister, Education, Hon. Tom Osborne

Minister, Industry, Energy & Technology, Hon. Andrew Parsons

Minister responsible, Women & Gender Equality, Hon. Pam Parsons

Minister, Digital Government & Service NL; Minister responsible, Office of the Chief Information Officer; Francophone Affairs, Hon. Sarah Stoodley

Associated Agencies, Boards & Commissions:
• **Muskrat Falls Oversight Committee**
www.gov.nl.ca/MFoversight
The Oversight Committee was established to strengthen & formalize pre-existing oversight for the Muskrat Falls project.

Cabinet Secretariat
East Block, Confederation Building, 4th Fl., PO Box 8700 St. John's, NL A1B 4J6
Tel: 709-729-3490; *Fax:* 709-729-5218
clerkofexecutivecoun@gov.nl.ca
www.gov.nl.ca/exec/cabinet
Clerk, Executive Council & Secretary to the Cabinet, Krista Quinlan
kristaquinlan@gov.nl.ca
Assistant Deputy Clerk, Nadine Devereaux
Tel: 709-729-1118
Assistant Secretary to Cabinet, Social Policy, Chad Blundon
Tel: 709-729-2244
ChadBlundon@gov.nl.ca

Communications & Public Engagements Branch
Assistant Deputy Minister, Carla Foote
Tel: 709-729-2233
carlafoote@gov.nl.ca
Associate Secretary to Cabinet, Scott Barfoot
ScottBarfoot@gov.nl.ca
Director, Strategic Communications (Operations), Luke Joyce
Tel: 709-729-0084
LukeJoyce@gov.nl.ca

Public Engagement & Planning Division
West Block, Confederation Bldg., 4th Fl., PO Box 8700 St. John's, NL A1B 4J6
Tel: 709-729-5790; *Fax:* 709-729-1673
ope@gov.nl.ca
www.gov.nl.ca/pep
Acting Director, Melanie Stokes
Tel: 709-729-3126
melaniestokes@gov.nl.ca

Intergovernmental Affairs Secretariat
East Block, Confederation Bldg., 7th Fl., PO Box 8700 St. John's, NL A1B 4J6
Tel: 709-729-2134; *Fax:* 709-729-5038
www.gov.nl.ca/exec/ias
The Secretariat was formed following the reorganization of the Executive Council, having been a part of the Intergovernmental & Indigenous Affairs Secretariat, which in turn was formed in 2017. It has the mandate to improve relationships with other governments & international organizations to support the province's policies.
Minister, Hon. Andrew Furey

Deputy Minister, Patricia A. Hearn
Tel: 709-729-2134
patriciaahearn@gov.nl.ca
Assistant Deputy Minister, Dan Mackenzie
Tel: 709-729-6267
danm@gov.nl.ca

Labrador Affairs Secretariat
Labrador Affairs, #438, 440 Hamilton River Rd., PO Box 3014 Stn. B, Happy Valley - Goose Bay, NL A0P 1E0
Tel: 709-896-1780; *Fax:* 709-896-0045
Toll-Free: 888-435-8111
www.gov.nl.ca/exec/las
Secondary Address: 6th Fl.
East Block, Confederation Bldg.PO Box 8700 B Sta.
St. John's, NL A1B 4J6
Minister responsible, Labrador Affairs, Hon. Lisa Dempster
Deputy Minister, Michelle Watkins
Tel: 709-896-4449
michellewatkins@gov.nl.ca
Director, Franca Smith
Tel: 709-944-1780
FrancaSmith@gov.nl.ca

Office of Indigenous Affairs & Reconciliation
East Block, Confederation Bldg., 6th Fl., PO Box 8700 St. John's, NL A1B 4J6
Tel: 709-729-4776; *Fax:* 709-729-4900
www.gov.nl.ca/exec/iar
The office was formed following the reorganization of the Executive Council, having been a part of the Intergovernmental & Indigenous Affairs Secretariat, which in turn was formed in 2017. The office aims to have a principle-based relationship with Indigenous people to support Indigenous communities.
Minister, Hon. Lisa Dempster
Deputy Minister, Aubrey Gover
Tel: 709-729-4665
aubreygover@gov.nl.ca
Assistant Deputy Minister, Judy White
Tel: 709-729-1495
judywhite@gov.nl.ca

Office of the Chief Information Officer (OCIO)
40 Higgins Line, PO Box 8700 St. John's, NL A1B 4J6
Tel: 709-729-4000; *Fax:* 709-729-6767
ocio@gov.nl.ca
www.gov.nl.ca/exec/ocio
The OCIO provides a professional Information Technology & Information Management capability aligned to support the business of government & the citizens of Newfoundland & Labrador.
Minister Responsible, Hon. Sarah Stoodley
Chief Information Officer, David Heffernan
Tel: 709-729-2617
daveheffernan@gov.nl.ca
Executive Director, Corporate Services & Projects Branch, Craig Harding
Tel: 709-729-1981
CraigHarding@gov.nl.ca
Executive Director, AIMS Branch, Julie Moore
Tel: 709-729-4329
JulieMoore@gov.nl.ca
Executive Director, Operations & Security, Randy Mouland
Tel: 709-729-5227
randymouland@gov.nl.ca

Office of Women & Gender Equality
West Block, Confederation Bldg., 4th Fl., PO Box 8700 St. John's, NL A1B 4J6
Tel: 709-729-5009; *Fax:* 709-729-1418
www.gov.nl.ca/exec/wge
Minister Responsible, Hon. Pam Parsons
Deputy Minister, Linda Ross
Tel: 709-729-5098
LindaRoss@gov.nl.ca

Treasury Board Secretariat (TBS)
East Block, Confederation Bldg., Main Fl., PO Box 8700 St. John's, NL A1B 4J6
Tel: 709-729-2476
www.gov.nl.ca/exec/tbs
Minister Responsible, Hon. Siobhan Coady
Secretary of Treasury Board, Michelle Jewer
Tel: 709-729-2476
michellejewer@gov.nl.ca
Assistant Deputy Minister & Deputy Secretary to Treasury Board, Justin Garrett
Tel: 709-729-4050
justingarrett@gov.nl.ca
Assistant Deputy Minister, Collective Bargaining, Elizabeth Lane
Tel: 709-729-1585
elizabethlane@gov.nl.ca

Office of the Comptroller General
Comptroller General, Michelle Jewer
Tel: 709-729-4866
michellejewer@gov.nl.ca

House of Assembly

c/o Clerk's Office, Confederation Bldg., PO Box 8700 St. John's, NL A1B 4J6
Tel: 709-729-3405
www.assembly.nl.ca
Other Communication: Legislative Library, Phone: 709-729-3604, Email: legislativelibrary@gov.nl.ca
twitter.com/NL_HOA

Clerk, Sandra Barnes
Tel: 709-729-3405
sbarnes@gov.nl.ca
Other Communications: Alternate Email: clerkhoa@gov.nl.ca

Speaker, Hon. Derek Bennett
Tel: 709-535-2131
derekbennett@gov.nl.ca

Deputy Speaker; Chair, Committees, Brian Warr
Tel: 709-673-3654
brianwarr@gov.nl.ca

Deputy Chair, Committees, Vacant

Sergeant-at-Arms, Wayne Harnum
wayneharnum@gov.nl.ca

Auditor General, Denise Hanrahan
Tel: 709-753-2700
denisehanrahan@oag.nl.ca
www.ag.gov.nl.ca/ag

Chief Electoral Officer; Commissioner for Legislative Standards, Bruce Chaulk
Tel: 709-729-0712
brucechaulk@gov.nl.ca
www.elections.gov.nl.ca
Note: Legislative Standards URL:
www.legislativestandardscomm.gov.nl.ca

Child & Youth Advocate, Jacqueline Lake Kavanagh
Tel: 709-753-3888
Toll-free: 877-753-3888; *Fax:* 709-753-3988
office@ocya.nl.ca
www.childandyouthadvocate.nl.ca
TTY: 709-753-4366

Citizens' Representative, Bradley Moss
Tel: 709-729-7647; *Fax:* 709-729-7696
citrep@gov.nl.ca
www.citizensrep.nl.ca
www.facebook.com/171628062894528

Information & Privacy Commissioner, Michael Harvey
Tel: 709-729-6309
Toll-free: 877-729-6309; *Fax:* 709-729-6500
commissioner@oipc.nl.ca
www.oipc.nl.ca
twitter.com/OIPCNL

Government Caucus Office (Liberal Party)
#102, 1 Crosbie Pl., St. John's, NL A1V 3Y8
Tel: 709-754-1813
Toll-Free: 888-971-6991
info@nlliberals.ca
nlliberals.ca
twitter.com/nlliberals
www.facebook.com/nlliberals
Premier; President, Executive Council; Minister, Intergovernmental Affairs, Hon. Andrew Furey
Government House Leader, Hon. Steve Crocker
Caucus Chair, Vacant
Caucus Whip, Vacant
Deputy Government House Leader, Hon. Lisa Dempster

Caucus Office of the Official Opposition (Progressive Conservative Party)
Confederation Bldg., PO Box 8700 St. John's, NL A1B 4J6
Tel: 709-753-6043
info@pcnl.ca
www.pcnl.ca
twitter.com/PCpartyNL
www.facebook.com/pcpartynl
Leader, PC Party; Leader, Official Opposition, David Brazil
Tel: 709-729-0334
davidbrazil@gov.nl.ca

Opposition House Leader & Caucus Chair, Official Opposition, Barry Petten
Tel: 709-834-6180
barrypetten@gov.nl.ca
Caucus Whip, Official Opposition, Chris Tibbs

Caucus Office of the Third Party (New Democratic Party)
Confederation Bldg., PO Box 8700 St. John's, NL A1B 4J6
Tel: 709-729-0270; *Fax:* 709-576-1443
Toll-Free: 855-729-0270
info@nl.ndp.ca
www.nl.ndp.ca
twitter.com/NLNDP
www.facebook.com/NLNDP
www.youtube.com/user/NLNDPCaucus
In the 2011 general election, five members of the New Democratic Party were elected to the House of Assembly. This was the largest Newfoundland & Labrador New Democratic Party Caucus in history. As of the 2021 general election, there were two members left in the House.
Leader, New Democratic Party, Alison Coffin
twitter.com/AlisonCoffin, www.facebook.com/AlisonCoffinNL
Third Party House Leader, James Dinn
JamesDinn@gov.nl.ca

Standing Committees of the House of Assembly
www.assembly.nl.ca/Committees
A five-member committee known as the Striking Committee prepares lists of Members to compose the Standing Committees of the House. The current Standing Committees are as follows: Government Services; Miscellaneous & Private Bills; Privileges & Elections; Public Accounts; Resource; Social Services; & Standing Orders.

Fiftieth House of Assembly - Newfoundland & Labrador

Confederation Bldg., PO Box 8700 St. John's, NL A1B 4J6
Tel: 709-729-3405
ClerkHOA@gov.nl.ca
www.assembly.nl.ca
Other Communication: Speaker's Office, Phone: 709-729-3404; Legislative Library, Phone: 709-729-3604; Tours, Phone: 709-729-3670

Last General Election: March 25, 2021.
Next General Election: 2023.
Party Standings (Oct. 2021):
Liberal 22;
Progressive Conservative 13;
New Democratic Party 2;
Independent 3;
Total 40.
Authorized Salaries & Committee Allowance for Members of the House of Assembly (April 2017): Member, Base Salary $95,357. In addition to this base salary are the following salaries for office holders:
Premier $65,168;
Minister $48,664;
Speaker $48,665;
Leader of the Opposition $48,665;
Deputy Speaker & Chair of Committees $12,166;
Opposition House Leader $24,330;
Leader of a Third Party $24,330;
Third Party House Leader $12,166;
Chair, Public Accounts Committee $12,166;
Vice-Chair, Public Accounts Committee $9,300;
Positions omitted receive no office-holder salary;
All members of the House of Assembly may be reached by including the member's name, the member's district, plus the following address: Confederation Building, PO Box 8700, St. John's NL, A1B 4J6.
The following is an alphabetical list of the members of the House of Assembly, with their electoral district, the total number of registered electors in their district for the 2021 election, plus the members' contact information:
Members of the House of Assembly of Newfoundland & Labrador
Premier; Leader, Liberal Party of Newfoundland & Labrador; Minister, Intergovernmental Affairs, Hon. Andrew Furey
Constituency: Humber — Gros Morne, Liberal
Tel: 709-635-0132; *Fax:* 709-635-0133
andrewfurey@gov.nl.ca
nlliberals.ca/leadership/premier
Constituency Office
#1, 20 Wellon Dr.
Deer Lake, NL A8A 2G5
Minister, Seniors & Social Development; Minister responsible, Status of Persons with Disabilities; Community Sector; Newfoundland & Labrador Housing Corporation, Hon. John Abbott
Constituency: St. John's East — Quidi Vidi, Liberal
Tel: 709-697-1057
JohnAbbott@gov.nl.ca

Other Communications: Constituency Phone: 709-729-3709
twitter.com/JohnAbbottnl, www.facebook.com/JohnAbbottnl
Speaker, Hon. Derek Bennett
Constituency: Lewisporte — Twillingate, Liberal
Toll-free: 877-585-0515
derekbennett@gov.nl.ca
Other Communications: Constituency Phone: 709-535-3780;
Fax: 709-535-2138
Constituency Office, Old Ferry Terminal Bldg.
122 Main St.
PO Box 248
Lewisporte, NL A0G 3A0
Minister, Fisheries, Forestry & Agriculture, Hon. Derrick Bragg
Constituency: Fogo Island — Cape Freels, Liberal
derrickbragg@gov.nl.ca
twitter.com/derrickbragg
Constituency Office
347-349 Main St.
PO Box 119
Wesleyville, NL A0G 4R0
Leader, Official Opposition; Leader, PC Party of Newfoundland
& Labrador, David Brazil
Constituency: Conception Bay East — Bell Island,
Progressive Conservative
davidbrazil@gov.nl.ca
Jordan Brown
Constituency: Labrador West, New Democratic Party
Tel: 709-729-0126
jordanbrown@gov.nl.ca
Other Communications: Constituency Phone: 709-944-4881;
Fax: 709-944-4880
twitter.com/JordanLabCity,
www.facebook.com/JordanLabWest
Constituency Office
PO Box 89
Wabush, NL A0R 1B0
Minister, Immigration, Population Growth & Skills, Hon. Gerry
Byrne, P.C.
Constituency: Corner Brook, Liberal
Tel: 709-729-3580
gerrybyrne@gov.nl.ca
twitter.com/gerry_byrne,
www.facebook.com/gerry.byrne.5209
Deputy Premier; President, Treasury Board; Minister, Finance;
Minister responsible, Newfoundland & Labrador Liquor
Corporation; Public Service Commission, Hon. Siobhan
Coady
Constituency: St. John's West, Liberal
siobhancoady@gov.nl.ca
Other Communications: Constituency Phone: 709-729-2449;
Fax: 709-729-0059
twitter.com/SiobhanCoadyNL,
www.facebook.com/SiobhanCoadyMHA
East Block, Confederation Bldg., Main Fl.
PO Box 8700
St. John's, NL A1B 4J6
Helen Conway Ottenheimer
Constituency: Harbour Main, Progressive Conservative
Toll-free: 877-787-0707
helenconwayottenheimer@gov.nl.ca
Other Communications: Constituency Phone: 709-229-0160
twitter.com/HelenConwayNL,
www.facebook.com/HelenConwayNL
Constituency Office
402 Conception Bay Hwy.
Holyrood, N A0A 2R0
Minister, Tourism, Culture, Arts & Recreation; Government
House Leader, Hon. Steve Crocker
Constituency: Carbonear — Trinity — Bay de Verde, Liberal
Toll-free: 844-583-0698
stevecrocker@gov.nl.ca
Other Communications: Constituency Phone: 709-596-8194;
Fax: 709-596-8196
twitter.com/stevecrockerlib,
www.facebook.com/SteveCrockerLib
Constituency Office
#3, 27 Goff Ave.
Carbonear, NL A1Y 1A6
Minister, Environment & Climate Change; Minister responsible,
Labour, Workplace NL, Hon. Bernard Davis
Constituency: Virginia Waters — Pleasantville, Liberal
bernarddavis@gov.nl.ca
twitter.com/bernardjdavis
Deputy Government House Leader; Minister responsible,
Indigenous Affairs & Reconciliation; Labrador Affairs, Hon.
Lisa Dempster
Constituency: Cartwright — L'Anse au Clair, Liberal
lisadempster@gov.nl.ca
Other Communications: Constituency Phone: 709-931-2118
twitter.com/LisaVDempster,
www.facebook.com/lisa.powelldempster
Third Party House Leader, James Dinn
Constituency: St. John's Centre, New Democratic Party

JamesDinn@gov.nl.ca
twitter.com/JimDinn
Paul Dinn
Constituency: Topsail — Paradise, Progressive Conservative
Tel: 709-729-6670; *Fax:* 709-729-0500
pauldinn@gov.nl.ca
twitter.com/DinnPaul
Constituency Office
1187 Kenmount Rd. Ext.
Paradise, NL A1L 0V8
Jeff Dwyer
Constituency: Placentia West — Bellevue, Progressive
Conservative
Toll-free: 800-423-3301; *Fax:* 709-729-5774
JeffDwyer@gov.nl.ca
Lela Evans
Constituency: Torngat Mountains, Progressive Conservative
LelaEvans@gov.nl.ca
www.facebook.com/LelaEvansNL
Pleaman Forsey
Constituency: Exploits, Progressive Conservative
Toll-free: 888-554-7799
pleamanforsey@gov.nl.ca
Other Communications: Constituency Phone: 709-258-2519;
Fax: 709-258-2518
Constituency Office
6 Dominic St.
Bishop's Falls, NL A0H 1C0
Hon. Sherry Gambin-Walsh
Constituency: Plantia - St. Mary's, Liberal
Toll-free: 877-898-0898
sherrygambinwalsh@gov.nl.ca
Other Communications: Constituency Phone: 709-227-1304;
Fax: 709-227-1307
Constituency Office
1 O'Reilly St.
PO Box 515
Placentia, NL A0B 2Y0
Minister, Health & Community Services, Hon. Dr. John Haggie
Constituency: Gander, Liberal
johnhaggie@gov.nl.ca
johnhaggie.ca
twitter.com/johnrockdoc, www.facebook.com/DrJohnHaggie
Minister, Justice & Public Safety; Attorney General, Hon. John
Hogan, Q.C.
Constituency: Windsor Lake, Liberal
JohnHogan@gov.nl.ca
Other Communications: Constituency Phone: 709-729-3529;
Fax: 709-729-0469
twitter.com/johnjhogan, facebook.com/johnhoganMHA
East Block, Confederation Bldg., 4th Fl.
PO Box 8700
St. John's, NL A1B 4J6
Krista Lynn Howell
Constituency: St. Barbe — L'Anse Aux Meadows, Liberal
Tel: 709-729-4729
kristalynnhowell@gov.nl.ca
Other Communications: Constituency Phone: 709-454-2633
Eddie Joyce
Constituency: Humber — Bay of Islands, Independent
ejoyce@gov.nl.ca
Other Communications: Constituency Phone: 709-634-7883;
Fax: 709-634-7885
Constituency Office, Sir Richard Squires Bldg., 4th Fl.
PO Box 2006
Corner Brook, NL A2H 6J8
Paul Lane
Constituency: Mount Pearl — Southlands, Independent
paullane@gov.nl.ca
Other Communications: Constituency Phone: 709-729-2231;
Fax: 709-729-2281
twitter.com/PaulLaneMHA, www.facebook.com/paullanemha
Minister, Transportation & Infrastructure; Minister responsible,
Public Procurement Agency, Elvis Loveless
Constituency: Fortune Bay — Cape La Hune, Liberal
ElvisLoveless@gov.nl.ca
twitter.com/elvisloveless
Hon. Loyola O'Driscoll
Constituency: Ferryland, Progressive Conservative
Toll-free: 800-634-5504
loyolaodriscoll@gov.nl.ca
Other Communications: Constituency Phone: 709-729-1390;
Fax: 709-729-5774
twitter.com/LoyolaOD,
www.facebook.com/LoyolaODriscollMHA
Minister, Education, Hon. Tom Osborne
Constituency: Waterford Valley, Liberal
Tel: 709-729-4882; *Fax:* 709-729-1746
tosborne@gov.nl.ca
Craig Pardy
Constituency: Bonavista, Progressive Conservative
CraigPardy@gov.nl.ca
twitter.com/craigpardy

Lloyd Parrott
Constituency: Terra Nova, Progressive Conservative
LloydParrott@gov.nl.ca
Other Communications: Constituency Phone: 709-466-4165;
Fax: 709-466-4178
twitter.com/lloyd_parrott, www.facebook.com/lloyd.parrott
Constituency Office
#204, 8 Myers Ave.
Clarenville, NL A5A 1T5
Minister, Industry, Energy & Technology, Hon. Andrew Parsons,
Q.C.
Constituency: Burgeo — La Poile, Liberal
Toll-free: 800-518-9479
andrewparsons@gov.nl.ca
Other Communications: Constituency Phone: 709-695-3585;
Fax: 709-695-5800
twitter.com/Andrew_Parsons1,
www.facebook.com/AndrewParsonsMHA
Constituency Office
PO Box 2263
Port aux Basques, NL A0M 1C0
Minister, Women & Gender Equality, Hon. Pam Parsons
Constituency: Harbour Grace — Port de Grave, Liberal
pamparsons@gov.nl.ca
Other Communications: Constituency Phone: 709-786-1372
twitter.com/PamNParsons,
www.facebook.com/pamforthepeople
Barry Petten
Constituency: Conception Bay South, Progressive
Conservative
Tel: 709-729-3391
barrypetten@gov.nl.ca
Other Communications: Constituency Phone: 709-834-6180;
Fax: 709-834-6182
twitter.com/BarryPetten, www.facebook.com/BarryPettenCBS
Constituency Office, Villa Nova Plaza
#118, 120 Conception Bay Hwy.
Conception Bay South, NL A1W 3A6
Hon. Paul Pike
Constituency: Burin — Grand Bank, Liberal
PaulPike@gov.nl.ca
Scott Reid
Constituency: St. George's — Humber, Liberal
ScottReid@gov.nl.ca
Other Communications: Constituency Phone: 709-646-3110
www.facebook.com/ScottReidLibNL
Minister, Digital Government & Service NL; Minister responsible,
Office of the Chief Information Officer; Francophone Affairs,
Hon. Sarah Stoodley
Constituency: Mount Scio, Liberal
Tel: 709-729-3083
sarahstoodley@gov.nl.ca
twitter.com/sarahlstoodley,
www.facebook.com/SarahStoodleyMountScio
Lucy Stolyes
Constituency: Mount Pearl North, Liberal
LucyStoyles@gov.nl.ca
Other Communications: Constituency Phone: 709-729-1526;
Fax: 709-729-5202
Caucus Whip, Official Opposition, Chris Tibbs
Constituency: Grand Falls-Windsor — Buchans, Progressive
Conservative
Toll-free: 866-610-4440
ChrisTibbs@gov.nl.ca
Other Communications: Constituency Phone: 709-489-3409;
Fax: 709-489-5480
www.facebook.com/chris.tibbs.96
Constituency Office, Provincial Bldg.
3 Cromer Ave.
Grand Falls-Windsor, NL A2A 1W9
Hon. Perry Trimper
Constituency: Lake Melville, Independent
Tel: 709-729-3404
Toll-free: 866-996-5670
perrytrimper@gov.nl.ca
Other Communications: Constituency Phone: 709-869-7975;
Fax: 709-869-7977
twitter.com/PerryTrimper, www.facebook.com/perry.trimper
Constituency Office
440 Hamilton River Rd.
PO Box 2582 B Sta.
Happy Valley-Goose Bay, NL A0P 1E0
Tony Wakeham
Constituency: Stephenville — Port au Port, Progressive
Conservative
TonyWakeham@gov.nl.ca
Other Communications: Constituency Phone: 709-643-0813;
Fax: 709-643-0814
twitter.com/TonyWakehamNL,
www.facebook.com/TonyWakehamNL
Joedy Wall
Constituency: Cape St. Francis, Progressive Conservative
JoedyWall@gov.nl.ca

Other Communications: Constituency Phone: 709-729-6979
twitter.com/wall_joedy, www.facebook.com/JoedyRWall
Deputy Speaker; Chair, Committees, Brian Warr
Constituency: Baie Verte — Green Bay, Liberal
brianwarr@gov.nl.ca
Other Communications: Constituency Phone: 709-673-3654

Newfoundland & Labrador Government Departments & Agencies

Office of the Auditor General

PO Box 8700 St. John's, NL A1B 4J6
Tel: 709-729-2700
oagmail@oag.nl.ca
www.ag.gov.nl.ca

The Auditor General's fundamental role is to bring an independent audit & reporting process to bear upon the manner in which Government & its various entities discharge their responsibilities, report on their planned programs and their use of public resources.

Auditor General, Denise Hanrahan
denisehanrahan@oag.nl.ca

Deputy Auditor General, Sandra Russell
srussell@oag.nl.ca

Secretary to the Executive, Nancy King
Tel: 709-729-5263
nking@oag.nl.ca

Newfoundland & Labrador Department of Children, Seniors & Social Development (CSSD)

PO Box 8700 St. John's, NL A1B 4J6
Tel: 709-729-0760; *Fax:* 709-729-0870
TTY: 888-729-5440
CSSDInfo@gov.nl.ca
www.gov.nl.ca/cssd

In August 2016, the Department of Child, Youth & Family Services & the Department of Seniors, Wellness & Social Development combined to create the Department of Children, Seniors & Social Development. The Department focuses on child protection, youth services, aging, seniors, health promotion, sport & general wellness. The Department is also responsible for the Poverty Reduction Strategy & the Disability Policy Office.

Minister, Hon. John Abbott

Deputy Minister, Susan Walsh
Tel: 709-729-0958
SWalsh@gov.nl.ca

Assistant Deputy Minister, Services Delivery & Regional Operations, Linda Clemens-Spurrell
Tel: 709-729-3473
lindaclemensspurrell@gov.nl.ca

Assistant Deputy Minister, Corporate Services & Performance Improvement, Brian Evans
Tel: 709-729-5108
brianevans@gov.nl.ca

Assistant Deputy Minister, Prevention & Early Intervention, Aisling Gogan
Tel: 709-729-0088
aislinggogan@gov.nl.ca

Assistant Deputy Minister, Policies & Programs, Sharlene Jones
Tel: 709-729-0656
sharlenejones@gov.nl.ca

Director, Communications, Michelle Hunt-Grouchy
Tel: 709-729-5148
michellehuntgrouchy@gov.nl.ca

Associated Agencies, Boards & Commissions:
• Newfoundland & Labrador Housing Corporation
See Entry Name Index for detailed listing.

• Newfoundland & Labrador Sports Centre Inc. (NLSC)
c/o Sport NL
1296A Kenmount Rd.
PO Box 8700
St. John's, NL A1B 4J6
Tel: 709-576-4932; *Fax:* 709-576-7493
sportnl@sportnl.ca
www.nlsportscentre.ca

A venue for athlete training, & a host to provincial, national & international competitions for members of Sport Newfoundland & Labrador (SNL).

• Ministerial Council on Aging & Seniors
c/o Department of Seniors, Wellness & Social Development
PO Box 8700
St. John's, NL A1B 4J6
www.cssd.gov.nl.ca/seniors/focus/ministerialcouncil.html
Develops legislation, policies & programs that affect an aging population, & oversees the implementation of the Provincial Healthy Aging Policy Framework.

• Provincial Advisory Council for the Inclusion of Persons with Disabilities
c/o Department of Seniors, Wellness & Social Development
PO Box 8700
St. John's, NL A1B 4J6
www.cssd.gov.nl.ca/disabilities/advisory_council.html
Advises the Minister Responsible for the Status of Persons with Disabilities on current issues & ways to make improvements.

• Provincial Wellness Advisory Council
c/o Department of Seniors, Wellness & Social Development
PO Box 8700
St. John's, NL A1B 4J6
cssd.gov.nl.ca/healthyliving/provincialwellness_advcouncil.html
Provides strategic advice on wellness issues, & implements & evaluates the Provincial Wellness Plan.

Child Protection & In Care Division
Tel: 709-729-2094

Director, Michelle Shallow
mshallow@gov.nl.ca
Director, Youth Corrections, Paul Ludlow
pludlow@gov.nl.ca

Healthy Living Division
Tel: 709-729-6243

Coordinator, Eat Great & Participate, Stephanie O'Brien
Tel: 709-729-4432
StephanieOBrien@psnl.ca

Poverty Reduction Strategy
Fax: 709-729-5139
Toll-Free: 866-883-6600
povertyreduction@gov.nl.ca
Director, Poverty Reduction & Well-Being, Dean Gambin
Tel: 709-729-1287
DeanGambin@gov.nl.ca
Program & Policy Development Specialist, Stacey Cheater
staceycheater@gov.nl.ca
Program & Policy Development Specialist, Emily Timmins
Tel: 709-729-5261
EmilyTimmins@gov.nl.ca

Seniors & Aging Division
Toll-Free: 888-494-2266
Other Communication: Seniors of Distinction Awards: Email:
seniorsofdistinction@gov.nl.ca
Consultant, Henry Kielley
HenryKielley@gov.nl.ca

Newfoundland & Labrador Department of Digital Government & Service NL

100 Prince Phillip Dr., PO Box 8700 St. John's, NL A1B 4J6
Tel: 709-729-4834
servicenlinfo@gov.nl.ca
www.gov.nl.ca/dgsnl

The department rovides a range of services to the people of Newfoundland & Labrador. Areas of attention include public health, public safety, environmental protection, vital statistics, motor vehicles, printing services, provincially regulated financial institutions, the operation of Government Service Centres, consumer & commercial affairs, & occupational health & safety. The department works in accordance with more than 150 pieces of legislation, regulations, standards, & codes of practice.
Service NL operates as a single access point for the public to common government services, such as licencing, permitting, & inspecting. The department handles the following responsibilities: issuing birth, marriage, & death certificates; testing & issuing driver licenses; issuing vehicle registrations; mediating landlord & tenant issues; registering companies, deeds, & lobbyists; investigating workplace incidents; issuing charitable gaming licences; & protecting the interests of consumers.
Service NL strives to provide services with a staff of more than 500 people at over 30 locations throughout Newfoundland & Labrador.

Minister, Hon. Sarah Stoodley

Deputy Minister, Sean Dutton

Tel: 709-729-4751
sdutton@gov.nl.ca

Director, Communications, Melony O'Neill
Tel: 709-729-4860; *Fax:* 709-729-4754
melonyoneill@gov.nl.ca

Associated Agencies, Boards & Commissions:
• Credit Union Deposit Guarantee Corporation
PO Box 340
Marystown, NL A0E 2M0
Tel: 709-279-0170; *Fax:* 709-279-0177
Toll-free: 877-279-0170
CUDGCNL@gov.nl.ca
www.cudgcnl.com
The Credit Union Deposit Guarantee Corporation is a provincial Crown corporation. The corporation administers the Credit Union Act & Regulations. The Credit Union Deposit Guarantee Corporation is responsible for ensuring compliance with the Credit Union Act & Regulations by credit unions, & insuring deposits of credit union members & associate members in Newfoundland & Labrador.

• Public Procurement Agency
30 Strawberry Marsh Rd.
St. John's, NL A1B 4R4
Tel: 709-729-3348
tenders@gov.nl.ca
www.gov.nl.ca/ppa
The Public Procurement Agency (formerly the Government Purchasing Agency) is the Government of Newfoundland & Labrador's central procurement unit. The agency manages the procurement process for goods & services for all government departments. It administers the the Agreement on Internal Trade & the Atlantic Procurement Agreement.

Digital Government & Services Branch
The Digital Government & Services Branch oversees the following: Government Service Centres; motor vehicle registration; occupational health & safety division; engineering & inspections; & program & support services. Government services staff handle matters related to vital statistics, public health & safety, environmental issues, accessibility, highway safety, as well as the processing of permits, licences, approvals & inspections.
Chief Information Officer; Associate Deputy Minister, Dave Heffernan
DaveHeffernan@gov.nl.ca
Assistant Deputy Minister, Gail Boland
Tel: 709-729-3056
gailboland@gov.nl.ca
Acting Director, Engineering & Inspections, David Brockerville
Tel: 709-729-2749; *Fax:* 709-729-2071
DavidBrockerville@gov.nl.ca
Director, Program & Support Services, Rick Curran
Tel: 709-729-3767
rjcurran@gov.nl.ca

Regulatory Affairs Branch
Regulatory Affairs Branch of Service NL carries out its functions through the Commercial Registrations Division, the Financial Services Regulation Division, & the Consumer Affairs Division. The Commercial Registrations Division is involved in administering the registries of deeds, personal property, condominiums, mechanics liens, co-operatives, limited partnerships, companies & lobbyists.
In the area of financial services, responsibilities include the regulation of industries such as the following: insurance, securities, real estate, mortgage broker, & pension. The Financial Services Regulation Division also administers the Consumer Protection Fund for Prepaid Funerals.
The Consumer Affairs Division strives to safeguard the consumer interests of Newfoundlanders & Labradorians. In the area of consumer protection, the division operates under the authority of the following acts: Architects Act; Business Electronic Filing Act; Certified General Accountants Act; Certified Management Accountants Act; Chartered Accountants Act; Collections Act; Consumer Protection & Business Practices Act; Electronic Commerce Act; Embalmers & Funeral Directors Act; Engineers & Geoscientists Act; Public Accountancy Act; & Sale of Goods Act. Associated regulations include the following: Collections Regulations; Embalmers & Funeral Directors Regulations; Engineers & Geoscientists Regulations; & Lottery Licensing Regulations. The Consumer Affairs Division also handles mediation of disputes between landlords & tenants.
Other services include regulation of the licencing of the following: charitable & non-profit oranganizations' lottery fundraising activities; corporations & individuals who provide private investigation & security services; direct sales contracts between business entities & consumers; & corporations & individuals who facilitate the collection of outstanding debts.
Assistant Deputy Minister, Scott Jones
Tel: 709-729-2570
ScottJones@gov.nl.ca

Director, Consumer Affairs, Jean Bishop
Tel: 709-729-2660; *Fax:* 709-729-6998
jeanebishop@rnc.gov.nl.ca
Director, Pension Benefit Standards, Michael Delaney
Tel: 709-729-6014
MichaelPDelaney@gov.nl.ca
Director, Commercial Registrations, Dean Doyle
doyled@gov.nl.ca
Director, Financial Services Regulation, Renee Dyer
Tel: 709-729-4909; *Fax:* 709-729-3205
ReneeDyer@gov.nl.ca
Director, Printing & Micrographic Services, Office of the Queen's
Printer, John Over
Tel: 709-729-5343
JohnOver@gov.nl.ca
Acting Registrar, Vital Statistics, Christine Martin
Tel: 709-729-6340
camartin@gov.nl.ca

Newfoundland & Labrador Department of Education

**West Block, Confederation Bldg., 100 Prince Philip Dr., 3rd
Fl., PO Box 8700 St. John's, NL A1B 4J6**
Tel: 709-729-5097; *Fax:* 709-729-1400
education@gov.nl.ca
www.gov.nl.ca/education
twitter.com/edu_govnl

Responsible for the K-12 & post-secondary school system,
literacy & library services; comprises four executive branches:
K-12 Education & Early Childhood Development; Corporate
Services; Post-Secondary Education; & Communications;
reporting to the department through their various boards are the
Provincial Information & Library Resources Board, the Literacy
Development Council, 4 geographical school boards & a
Francophone school board.
In October 2011, a separate Department called Advanced
Education & Skills was created by then-Premier Kathy
Dunderdale, until being folded back into the Department of
Education.
In September 2014, Premier Paul Davis expanded the ministry
to include Early Childhood Development, which included
educational functions previously administered by the Department
of Child, Youth & Family Services.

Minister, Hon. Tom Osborne

Deputy Minister, Greg O'Leary
Tel: 709-729-5086
GregOLeary@gov.nl.ca

Director, Communications, Christopher Pickard
Tel: 709-729-0048
ChristopherPickard@gov.nl.ca

Associated Agencies, Boards & Commissions:
• **Provincial Information & Library Resources Board**
48 St. George's Ave.
Stephenville, NL A2H 1K9
Tel: 709-643-0900; *Fax:* 709-643-0925
www.nlpl.ca
To establish & operate those public libraries in the province that
it considers necessary & provide support to ensure that library
materials, information & programs are available to meet the
needs of the public.

Corporate Services Branch
Assistant Deputy Minister, Brian Evans
Tel: 709-729-3041
brianevans@gov.nl.ca
Director, Financial Services, Tracy Stamp
Tel: 709-729-5168; *Fax:* 709-729-1400
tracystamp@gov.nl.ca

K-12 Education & Early Childhood Development
Assistant Deputy Minister, Brian Evans
Tel: 709-729-5720
brianevans@gov.nl.ca
Director, Program Development, Bradley Clarke
Tel: 709-729-3004
bradclarke@gov.nl.ca
Director, Early Childhood Learning, Mary Goss-Prowse
Tel: 709-729-4055
marygossprowse@gov.nl.ca
Director, Evaluation & Research, Joanne Hogan
Tel: 709-729-3000
JHogan@gov.nl.ca

Post-Secondary Education
Assistant Deputy Minister, Candice Ennis Williams
Tel: 709-729-3026; *Fax:* 709-729-2828
Director, Student Financial Services Division, Robert Feaver
Tel: 709-729-1553
robertfeaver@gov.nl.ca

Director, Literacy & Institutional Services Division, Regan Power
Tel: 709-729-2087
reganpower@gov.nl.ca

Office of the Chief Electoral Officer

39 Hallett Cr., St. John's, NL A1B 4C4
Toll-Free: 877-729-7987
enl@gov.nl.ca
www.elections.gov.nl.ca/elections
twitter.com/NLElections

**Chief Electoral Officer; Commissioner for Legislative
Standards,** Bruce Chaulk
Tel: 709-729-0712
brucechaulk@gov.nl.ca

**Assistant Chief Electoral Officer; Director, Election
Finance,** Travis Wooley
Tel: 709-729-4116
traviswooley@gov.nl.ca

**Director, Elections Operations & Special Ballot
Administrator,** Vacant

Newfoundland & Labrador Department of Environment & Climate Change

PO Box 8700 St. John's, NL A1B 4J6
ECCInfo@gov.nl.ca
www.gov.nl.ca/ecc
Works with municipalities to ensure communities are properly
managed & planned to ensure residents have a high standard of
living in a clean, healthy & safe environment. The department
was renamed in 2020.

Minister, Hon. Bernard Davis
Tel: 709-729-3046
ecc-minister@gov.nl.ca

Deputy Minister, Sean Dutton
Tel: 709-729-3049
sdutton@gov.nl.ca

Director, Communications, Jacquelyn Howard
Tel: 709-729-2575
jacquelynhoward@gov.nl.ca

Associated Agencies, Boards & Commissions:
• **Burin Peninsula Waste Management Corporation**
PO Box 510
Burin Bay Arm, NL A0E 1G0
Tel: 709-891-1717; *Fax:* 709-891-1727
admin@burinpenwaste.com
www.burinpenwaste.com
• **Central Newfoundland Waste Management Authority
(CNMW)**
Route 3-1-09
PO Box 254
Norris Arm, NL A0G 3M0
Tel: 709-653-2900; *Fax:* 709-653-2920
info@cnwmc.com
www.cnwmc.com
• **Eastern Regional Service Board**
#3, 255 Majors Path
St. John's, NL A1A 0L5
Tel: 709-579-7960; *Fax:* 709-579-5392
info@ersbnl.ca
easternregionalserviceboard.com
• **Green Bay Waste Authority Inc.**
160 Robert's Arm Rd.
South Brook, NL A0J 1S0
Tel: 709-657-2233
info@greenbaywaste.com
• **NL 911 Bureau Inc.**
57 Old Pennywell Rd.
St. John's, NL A1E 6A8
Tel: 709-758-0051; *Fax:* 709-758-1092
Toll-free: 844-659-1122
info@nl911.ca
nl911.ca
Created with the proclamation of the Emergency 911 Act in
February 2015, the board is responsible for the operation of the
province-wide basic 911 service as well as the future
development of Next Generation 911.
• **Northern Peninsula Regional Service Board**
#171, 173 West St.
PO Box 130
St. Anthony, NL A0K 4S0
Tel: 709-454-3110; *Fax:* 709-454-3818
www.norpenservices.ca

Environment Branch
Assistant Deputy Minister, Dan Michielsen
Tel: 709-729-3016
MichielsenD@gov.nl.ca
Director, Water Resources Management, Haseen Khan
Tel: 709-729-2563
hkhan@gov.nl.ca
Director, Environmental Assessment, Joanne Sweeney
Tel: 709-729-0673
joannesweeney@gov.nl.ca

Municipal Infrastructure Branch

Office of Climate Change (OCC)
PO Box 8700 St. John's, NL A1B 4J6
Tel: 709-729-1210
climatechange@gov.nl.ca
www.gov.nl.ca/ecc/occ
The OCC has lead responsibility for strategy & policy
development regarding climate change adaptation & energy
efficiency.
Assistant Deputy Minister, Susan Squires
Tel: 709-729-3016
susansquires@gov.nl.ca
Director, Government Relations, Research & Analysis, Gerald
Crane
Tel: 709-729-6909
geraldcrane@gov.nl.ca

Newfoundland & Labrador Department of Finance

Confederation Bldg., PO Box 8700 St. John's, NL A1B 4J6
Tel: 709-729-3166
finance@gov.nl.ca
www.fin.gov.nl.ca

Minister, Hon. Siobhan Coady
Tel: 709-729-3775; *Fax:* 709-729-1746
financeminister@gov.nl.ca

Deputy Minister, Paul Smith
Tel: 709-729-4039
smithp@gov.nl.ca

Director, Communications, Diana Quinton
Tel: 709-729-2477
dianaquinton@gov.nl.ca

Associated Agencies, Boards & Commissions:
• **Atlantic Lottery Corporation (ALC)**
922 Main St.
PO Box 5500
Moncton, NB E1C 8W6
Toll-free: 800-561-3942
info@alc.ca
www.alc.ca
The ALC manages the gaming businesses of the four Atlantic
provinces. The board of directors is made up of an independent,
non-voting chair & two representatives from each Atlantic
Province. The Newfoundland & Labrador office can be contacted
as follows: 30 Hallett Cres., St. John's, NL A1B 4C5. The Nova
Scotia office can be contacted as follows: 7 Mellor Ave.,
Dartmouth, NS B3B 0E8.

• **Cannabis NL**
90 Kenmount Rd.
PO Box 8750 A
St. John's, NL A1B 3V1
Tel: 709-724-1200
Toll-free: 844-757-5986
info@shopcannabisnl.com
shopcannabisnl.com
Cannabis NL is a division of the Newfoundland & Labrador
Liquor Corporation, & is responsible for regulating the
possession, sale & delivery of recreational cannabis in the
province. As well as online sales, it licenses a network of 25+
retail outlets.

• **Newfoundland & Labrador Government Sinking Fund -
Board of Trustees**
www.fin.gov.nl.ca/fin/department/agencies.html#3
The Board of Trustees consolidates & administers sinking funds
established by the Financial Administration Act for the
repayment of the Province's debenture debt.
• **Newfoundland & Labrador Industrial Development
Corporation (NIDC)**
Confederation Bldg.
PO Box 8700
St. John's, NL A1B 4J6
www.fin.gov.nl.ca/fin/department/agencies.html#4
The NIDC provides long-term financing to industrial &
resource-based projects, but has been largely inactive in recent
years as investments have been undertaken by the Province or
through other Crown Corporations.

• **Newfoundland & Labrador Liquor Corporation (NLC)**
90 Kenmount Rd.
PO Box 8750 A
St. John's, NL A1B 3V1
Tel: 709-724-1100
info@nfliquor.com
nlliquor.com

The Newfoundland Labrador Liquor Corporation (NLC) is a provincial crown corporation responsible for managing the importation, sale & distribution of beverage alcohol within the province.

• **Pension Investment Committee (PIC)**
Confederation Bldg.
PO Box 8700
St. John's, NL A1B 4J6

The PIC provides the Minister of Finance with advice regarding the operation & investment of the Province of Newfoundland & Labrador Pooled Pension Fund.

Economic, Fiscal & Statistics Branch
Assistant Deputy Minister, Doug Trask
Tel: 709-729-0864
dougtrask@gov.nl.ca
Director, Newfoundland & Labrador Statistics Agency, Robert Reid
Tel: 709-729-0158
robertr@gov.nl.ca

Tax & Fiscal Policy Branch
Assistant Deputy Minister, Doug Trask
Tel: 709-729-0864
dougtrask@gov.nl.ca
Director, Tax Policy Division, Jay Griffin
jgriffin@gov.nl.ca
Acting Director, Fiscal Policy Division, Amanda Hannaford
Tel: 709-729-2907
amandahannaford@gov.nl.ca
Director, Tax Administration Division, Cathy M. Whalen
Tel: 709-729-6307
cathywhalen@gov.nl.ca

Treasury Management & Budgeting Branch
Assistant Deputy Minister, Theresa Heffernan
Tel: 709-729-4039
theresah@gov.nl.ca
Acting Director, Economics Division, Ken Hicks
Tel: 709-729-2146
khicks@gov.nl.ca
Director, Newfoundland & Labrador Statistics Agency, Robert Reid
Tel: 709-729-0158
robertr@gov.nl.ca

Newfoundland & Labrador Department of Fisheries, Forestry & Agriculture

Petten Bldg., 30 Strawberry Marsh Rd., PO Box 8700 St. John's, NL A1B 4J6
Tel: 709-729-3705; *Fax:* 709-729-0360
www.gov.nl.ca/ffa
twitter.com/ffa_govnl

Contributes to economic & community growth in the province by encouraging sustainable growth & development of the harvesting, processing, & distribution sectors; includes providing support for the marketing of fish & aquaculture products produced in Newfoundland & Labrador for domestic & export markets. Responsible for: setting & enforcing standards for the processing & sale of fish products in the province; licensing fish processing establishments; undertaking developmental initiatives in the harvesting, processing, & marketing sectors of the fishing industry; developing, promoting & licensing of aquaculture facilities; developing & maintaining strategic fisheries infrastructure; articulating policies & providing advice for the management & development of fisheries & aquaculture; providing statistical information.
In August 2016, the Forestry & Agrifoods Agency & the Department of Fisheries & Aquaculture combined to create the Department of Fisheries, Forestry & Agrifoods, which became the Department of Fisheries & Land Resources, & most recently the Department of Fisheries, Forestry & Agriculture.

Minister, Hon. Derrick Bragg
ffaminister@gov.nl.ca

Deputy Minister, Tracy King
Tel: 709-729-3707
TracyKing@gov.nl.ca

Associated Agencies, Boards & Commissions:
• **Agricultural Land Consolidation Review Committee**
The Committee administers the Agricultural Land Consolidation Program, which allows retiring farmers & non-farmer landowners to sell their granted land to the provincial government.

• **Chicken Farmers of Newfoundland & Labrador (CFNL)**
PO Box 8098
St. John's, NL A1B 3M9
Tel: 709-747-1493
www.nlchicken.com

• **Farm Industry Review Board (FIRB)**
192 Wheeler's Rd.
PO Box 2006
Corner Brook, NL A2H 6J8
Tel: 709-637-2672; *Fax:* 709-637-2365
www.gov.nl.ca/ffa/agencies-boards-and-commissions
FIRB is responsible for controlling & directing the operations of the province's commodity boards, as well as providing farmers with protection against nuisance suits (as long as the farm in question is operating according to acceptable farm practices).

• **Fish Processing Licensing Board (FPLB)**
c/o Fish Processing Licensing Board Secretariat
30 Strawberry Marsh Rd.
St. John's, NL A1B 4J6
FPLBSecretariat@gov.nl.ca
www.gov.nl.ca/ffa/agencies-boards-and-commissions

• **Newfoundland & Labrador Crop Insurance Agency**
PO Box 2006
Corner Brook, NL A2H 6J8
Tel: 709-637-2077; *Fax:* 709-637-2591
www.gov.nl.ca/ffa/programs-and-funding/programs/prodinsur

• **Newfoundland & Labrador Livestock Owners Compensation Board**
www.gov.nl.ca/ffa/programs-and-funding/programs/animals/livestock

• **Professional Fish Harvesters Certification Board (PFHCB)**
368 Hamilton Ave.
PO Box 8541
St. John's, NL A1B 3P2
Tel: 709-722-8170; *Fax:* 709-722-8201
pfh@pfhcb.com
www.pfhcb.com

• **St. John's Land Development Advisory Authority**
• **St. John's Urban Region Agricultural Appeal Board**
• **Timber Scalers Board**
The Timber Scalers Board is currently inactive, with its mandate being fulfilled internally within the Department of Natural Resources. Its members remain on standby in the event the Minister required the board re-activated.

• **Wooddale Land Development Advisory Authority**
The Authority considers applications for development in the Wooddale Agriculture Development Area.

Agriculture & Lands
Assistant Deputy Minister, Keith Deering
Tel: 709-637-2339
keithdeering@gov.nl.ca
Director, Agriculture Business Development, Cynthia MacDonald
Tel: 709-637-2097
cindymacdonald@gov.nl.ca
Acting Director, Crown Lands Administration, Tara Morgan
taramorgan@gov.nl.ca

Enforcement & Resource Services
Assistant Deputy Minister, Chantelle MacDonald Newhook
Tel: 709-729-5029
cnewhook@gov.nl.ca
Director, Policy & Strategic Planning, Krista Connolly
Tel: 709-729-1364
kristaconnolly@gov.nl.ca
Director, GIS & Mapping, Peter Hearns
Tel: 709-637-2483
peterhearns@gov.nl.ca
Departmental Program Coordinator, Compliance & Enforcement Division, Rhonda Allen
Tel: 709-637-2039
rallen@gov.nl.ca

Fisheries & Aquaculture Division
Assistant Deputy Minister, Lorelei Roberts-Loder
Tel: 709-729-1725; *Fax:* 709-729-1884
lrobertsloder@gov.nl.ca
Director, Sustainable Fisheries & Oceans Policy, Tom Dooley
Tel: 709-729-0335
Director, Aquaculture Development, Stephanie Synard-McInnis
Tel: 709-292-4111
StephanieSynard@gov.nl.ca
Director/Provincial Aquaculture Veterinarian, Daryl Whelan
Tel: 709-729-6872
darylswhelan@gov.nl.ca
Manager, Aquaculture Licensing, Todd Budgell
Tel: 709-292-4106
tbudgell@gov.nl.ca

Aquaculture Development Officer, Melissa Burke
Tel: 709-538-3705
MelissaBurke@gov.nl.ca

Forestry & Wildlife Division
Assistant Deputy Minister, Stephen Balsom
Tel: 709-637-2339; *Fax:* 709-637-2461
stephenbalsom@gov.nl.ca
Director, Regional Services, Colin Carroll
Tel: 709-637-2410
Director, Forest Ecosystem Management, Bryan Oke
Tel: 709-637-2296

Newfoundland & Labrador Department of Health & Community Services (HCS)

West Block, Confederation Bldg., 100 Prince Philip Dr., 1st Fl., PO Box 8700 St. John's, NL A1B 4J6
Tel: 709-729-4984
healthinfo@gov.nl.ca
www.gov.nl.ca/hcs
Other Communication: Immunization Records, Phone: 709-729-0724; Cannabis Information: www.gov.nl.ca/cannabis; cannabis@gov.nl.ca

Provides a leadership role in health & community service programs & policy development for the province. This involves working in partnership with a number of key stakeholders including regional boards, community organizations, professional associations, post-secondary educational institutions, unions, consumer & other government departments.

Minister, Hon. Dr. John Haggie
Tel: 709-729-3124
hcsminister@gov.nl.ca

Deputy Minister, Karen Stone
Tel: 709-729-3125
karens@gov.nl.ca

Director, Communications, Tina Newhook
Tel: 709-729-1377; *Fax:* 709-728-2837
tinanewhook@gov.nl.ca

Associated Agencies, Boards & Commissions:
• **Central Regional Health Authority**
21 Carmelite Rd.
Grand Falls-Windsor, NL A2A 1Y4
Tel: 709-292-2138; *Fax:* 709-292-2249
Toll-free: 888-799-2272
communications@centralhealth.nl.ca
www.centralhealth.nl.ca

• **Eastern Regional Health Authority**
Health Sciences Centre
#1345, Prince Philip Dr., Level 1
St. John's, NL A1B 3V6
Tel: 709-777-6500
Toll-free: 877-444-1399
client.relations@easternhealth.ca
www.easternhealth.ca
Other Communication: Toll-Free Healthline: 888-709-2929

• **Health Research Ethics Authority (HREA)**
#200, 95 Bonaventure Ave., 2nd Fl.
St. John's, NL A1B 2X5
Tel: 709-777-6974; *Fax:* 709-777-8776
info@hrea.ca
www.hrea.ca
The HREA is responsible for supervising all health research involving human subjects conducted in Newfoundland & Labrador.

• **Labrador-Grenfell Regional Health Authority**
Administration Bldg.
PO Box 7000 C
Happy Valley-Goose Bay, NL A0P 1C0
Tel: 709-897-2267; *Fax:* 709-896-4032
www.lghealth.ca

• **Newfoundland & Labrador Centre for Health Information (NLCHI)**
70 O'Leary Ave.
St. John's, NL A1B 2C7
Tel: 709-752-6000; *Fax:* 709-752-6011
Toll-free: 877-752-6006
inforequests@nlchi.nl.ca
www.nlchi.nl.ca
Other Communication: Information Requests, Phone: 709-752-6513

• **Western Regional Health Authority**
Corporate Office
1 Brookfield Ave.
Corner Brook, NL A2H 6J7
Tel: 709-637-5000
www.westernhealth.nl.ca

Corporate Services Branch
Acting Assistant Deputy Minister, John McGrath
Tel: 709-729-5887
johnmcgrath@gov.nl.ca
Executive Director, Audit & Claims Integrity, Sheree Snow
ShereeSnow@gov.nl.ca

Policy, Planning & Performance Monitoring Branch
Assistant Deputy Minister, Tina Follett
Tel: 709-729-3659
tfollett@gov.nl.ca

Population Health Branch
Assistant Deputy Minister, Heather Hanrahan
Tel: 709-864-2887
HeatherHanrahan@gov.nl.ca
Chief Medical Officer of Health, Janice Fitzgerald
Acting Director, Mental Health & Addictions, Niki Legge
Tel: 709-729-2507
NikiLegge@gov.nl.ca

Professional Services Branch
Director, Drug Programs & Services, Jamie O'Dea
Tel: 709-729-7977
JamieODea@gov.nl.ca
Assistant Medical Director, Medical Services, Colleen Crowther
Tel: 709-758-1501
ColleenCrowther@gov.nl.ca

Regional Services Branch
Assistant Deputy Minister, Alan Doody
Tel: 709-729-0620
AlanDoody@gov.nl.ca
Chief Nurse; Manager, Office of Adverse Health Events, Jeannine Herritt
Tel: 709-729-4912
JeannineHerritt@gov.nl.ca

Newfoundland & Labrador Housing Corporation (NLHC)

Sir Brian Dunfield Bldg., 2 Canada Dr., PO Box 220 St. John's, NL A1C 5J2
Tel: 709-724-3000; *Fax:* 709-724-3250
www.nlhc.nf.ca
twitter.com/nlhousing
www.facebook.com/NewfoundlandLabradorHousing
www.linkedin.com/company/newfoundland-&-labrador-housing
Mandated to develop & administer housing assistance policy & programs for low to moderate income households.

Minister Responsible, Hon. John Abbott
Tel: 709-729-0659
JohnAbbott@gov.nl.ca

Chair & Chief Executive Officer, Julia Mullaley
Tel: 709-724-3054
jmmullaley@nlhc.nl.ca

Executive Director, Regional Operations & Program Delivery, Paul Abbott
Tel: 709-724-3187
pabbott@nlhc.nl.ca

Executive Director, Finance & Corporate Services, Mike Tizzard
Tel: 709-724-3053
mwtizzard@nlhc.nl.ca

Newfoundland & Labrador Human Rights Commission

The Beothuk Bldg., 21 Crosbie Pl., PO Box 8700 St. John's, NL A1B 4J6
Tel: 709-729-2709; *Fax:* 709-729-0790
Toll-Free: 800-563-5808
humanrights@gov.nl.ca
thinkhumanrights.ca
twitter.com/nlhumanrights

Chair, Judy White, Q.C.

Chief Adjudicator, Kim Horwood

Executive Director, Carey Majid
careymajid@gov.nl.ca

Newfoundland & Labrador Hydro

Hydro Place, 500 Columbus Dr., PO Box 12400 St. John's, NL A1B 4K7
Tel: 709-737-1400; *Fax:* 709-737-1800
Toll-Free: 888-737-1296
hydro@nlh.nl.ca
www.nlh.nl.ca
Other Communication: Vendor Information, Phone: 709-737-1335; Fax: 709-737-1795; Email: tenders@nlh.nl.ca; Customer Service, Email: customerservices@nlh.nl.ca
twitter.com/NLHydro
www.facebook.com/NLHydro
www.youtube.com/user/NLHydro
Crown corporation, owned by the Province of Newfoundland & Labrador, & a subsidiary of Nalcor Energy. Hydro generates, transmits & distributes electrical power & energy to utility, residential & industrial customers throughout the province. Hydro is the parent company of the Hydro Group of Companies (Hydro Group), comprising Newfoundland & Labrador Hydro, Churchill Falls (Labrador) Corporation Limited (CF(L)Co), Lower Churchill Development Corporation Limited (LCDC), Gull Island Power Company Limited (GIPCo), & Twin Falls Power Corporation Limited (TwinCo).
The Hydro Group's installed generating capacity is the fourth largest of all utility companies in Canada, consisting of nine hydroelectric plants, including the Churchill Falls hydraulic plant, which is the largest underground powerhouse in the world with a rated capacity of 5,428 megawatts (MW) of power, one oil-fired plant, four gas turbines & 25 diesel plants.

Chair, John Green, Q.C.

President, Jennifer Williams

Vice-President, Regulatory Affairs & Customer Service, Kevin Fagan

Vice-President, Engineering Services, Terry Gardiner

Newfoundland & Labrador Department of Immigration, Population Growth & Skills

West Block, Confederation Bldg., 3rd Fl., PO Box 8700 St. John's, NL A1B 4J6
Tel: 709-729-1795
isl@gov.nl.ca
www.gov.nl.ca/ipgs
Other Communication: Employment Supports & Services, Toll-Free: 800-563-6600
The department focuses upon the following tasks: protecting basic labour rights; assisting youth in the development of leadership skills; helping employers by providing access to needed workers; assisting people to find employment; improving the inclusion of persons with disabilities in society; supporting communities to attract & welcome immigrants; supporting persons during disasters; providing financial support for people with little or no income; & reducing poverty.
Income & financial services are available at the following locations: Avalon Region (877-729-7888); Central Region (888-632-4555); Labrador Region (888-773-9311); & Western Region (866-417-4753). In August 2016, the Labour Relations Agency was combined with the Department of Advanced Education & Skills to create the Department of Advanced Education, Skills & Labour. It was renamed Immigration, Skills & Labour in 2020, & Immigration, Population Growth & Skills in 2021.

Minister, Hon. Gerry Byrne
Tel: 709-729-3580; *Fax:* 709-729-6996

Deputy Minister, Vacant

Director, Communications, Tansy Mundon
TansyMundon@gov.nl.ca

Associated Agencies, Boards & Commissions:
• Income & Employment Support Appeal Board
Confederation Bldg.
PO Box 8700
St. John's, NL A1B 4J6
Tel: 709-729-2479; *Fax:* 709-729-5139

• Labour Relations Board
Natural Resources Bldg.
50 Elizabeth Ave., 5th Fl.
PO Box 8700
St. John's, NL A1B 4J6
Tel: 709-729-2707; *Fax:* 709-729-5738
lrb@gov.nl.ca
www.gov.nl.ca/lrb

• Standing Fish Price Setting Panel
Beothuck Bldg.
20 Crosbie Pl., 3rd Fl.
PO Box 8700
St. John's, NL A1B 4J6
Tel: 709-729-2711; *Fax:* 709-729-3528
www.gov.nl.ca/fishpanel

Corporate Services & Policy Branch
The Corporate Services & Policy Branch handles policy planning & evaluation, human resources, information technology services, & financial operations for the provincial office & regions.
Assistant Deputy Minister, Debbie Dunphy
Tel: 709-729-3594
DDunphy@gov.nl.ca
Director, Policy, Strategic Planning, & Quality Assurance Division, Stephen Dale
Tel: 709-729-5054
StephenDale@gov.nl.ca
Director, Information Management Division, Dave Moore
Tel: 709-729-5152
davemoore@gov.nl.ca

Immigration & Population Growth Branch
The Workforce Development & Immigration Branch consists of the following divisions: Employment & Training Programs; Immigration & Multiculturalism; Skills & Labour Market Research; & Workforce Development Secretariat.
Assistant Deputy Minister, Katie Norman
Tel: 709-729-0217
KatieNorman@gov.nl.ca
Director, Workforce Development Secretariat, Jennifer Meadus
Tel: 709-729-0541
jennifermeadus@gov.nl.ca

Office of Immigration & Multiculturalism (OIM)
c/o Department of Advanced Education, Skills & Labour, 100 Prince Phillip Dr., PO Box 8700 St. John's, NL A1B 4J6
Tel: 170-972-9714; *Fax:* 709-729-7381
Toll-Free: 888-632-4555
TTY: 877-292-4205
AESL@gov.nl.ca
www.gov.nl.ca/immigration
www.facebook.com/nlimmigration
The Office of Immigration & Multiculturalism is engaged in the implementation of the Provincial Immigration Strategy, which involves attracting & retaining immigrants to Newfoundland & Labrador.
Director, Remzi Cej
RemziCej@gov.nl.ca

Regional Service Delivery Branch
The Regional Service Delivery Branch is responsible for eligibility assessment for programs, issuing & monitoring benefits to clients, & providing other services such as career counseling, social work & community/business partnership development. Income & Social Supports is the policy division.
Regional contacts are as follows: Avalon: 1-877-729-7888, TTY: 1-888-380-2299; Central: 1-888-632-4555, TTY: 1-877-292-4205; Western: 1-866-417-4753, TTY: 1-888-445-8585; Labrador: 1-888-773-9311; TTY: 1-866-443-4046.
Assistant Deputy Minister, Walt Mavin
Tel: 709-729-2320
waltmavin@gov.nl.ca
Director, Apprenticeship & Trade Certification, Sandra E. Bishop
Tel: 709-729-6196; *Fax:* 709-729-5560
SandraEBishop@gov.nl.ca
Director, Employment & Training Programs Division, Heather Craniford
Tel: 709-729-0939; *Fax:* 709-729-1129
heathercraniford@gov.nl.ca
Director, Income Support, Cynthia King
Tel: 709-729-1334; *Fax:* 709-729-5560
CynthiaKing@gov.nl.ca

Newfoundland & Labrador Department of Industry, Energy & Technology

Natural Resources Bldg., 50 Elizabeth Ave., PO Box 8700 St. John's, NL A1B 4J6
Tel: 709-729-3017; *Fax:* 709-729-0059
www.gov.nl.ca/iet
Responsible for the management of the province's mineral, energy, land, forest & wildlife resources in a manner that will ensure optimum benefits for the people of the province. The department was renamed in 2020.

Minister, Hon. Andrew Parsons
IETMinister@gov.nl.ca

Deputy Minister, John Cowan
jcowan@gov.nl.ca

Assistant Deputy Minister, Business & Innovation, Fiona Langor
Tel: 709-729-5160
FLangor@gov.nl.ca

Assistant Deputy Minister, Corporate & Strategic Services, Megan Nesbitt
Tel: 709-729-1466
MeganNesbitt@gov.nl.ca

Assistant Deputy Minister, Industry & Economic Development, Gillian Skinner
Tel: 709-729-7451
gskinner@gov.nl.ca

Director, Communications, Tansy Mundon
Tel: 709-729-5282
tansymundon@gov.nl.ca

Acting Director, Information Management, Kirk Rogers
Tel: 709-729-1651
KirkRogers@gov.nl.ca

Associated Agencies, Boards & Commissions:

• Canada-Newfoundland & Labrador Offshore Petroleum Board (C-NLOPB)
West Campus Hall, The Tower Corporate Campus
#7100, 240 Waterford Bridge Rd.
St. John's, NL A1E 1E2
Tel: 709-778-1400
information@cnlopb.ca
www.cnlopb.ca
Other Communication: Core Storage & Research Centre,
Phone: 709-778-1500, Email: csrc@cnlopb.nl.na
Established in 1985, the Canada - Newfoundland & Labrador Offshore Petroleum Board applies the provisions of the *Atlantic Accord* & the *Atlantic Accord Implementation Acts.*
The Board regulates the oil & gas industrr for the Newfoundland & Labrador Offshore Area. Operator activity is overseen for legislative & regulatory compliance in the areas of environmental protection, resource management, offshore safety, & industrial benefits.
The role of the Canada - Newfoundland & Labrador Offshore Petroleum Board facilitates the exploration for & development of hydrocarbon resources.

• Mineral Rights Adjudication Board
Natural Resources Bldg.
PO Box 8700
St. John's, NL A1C 5X4
The Board is responsible for hearing & determining the outcome of questions, disputes & matters arising out of the application of the Minieral Act & the Mining Act & associated regulations.

• Nalcor Energy
See Entry Name Index for detailed listing.

Energy Branch
Assistant Deputy Minister, Energy Development, Craig Martin
Tel: 709-729-1644
CMartin@gov.nl.ca
Assistant Deputy Minister, Energy, Pierre Tobin
Tel: 709-729-2691
pierretobin@gov.nl.ca
Acting Director, Regulatory Affairs, Chris Carter
Tel: 709-729-1509
chriscarter@gov.nl.ca
Director, Petroleum Engineering, David Corkey
Tel: 709-729-7188
DavidCorkey@gov.nl.ca
Director, Petroleum Geoscience, Jovan Petrovic
Tel: 709-729-1821
jovanpetrovic@gov.nl.ca
Director, Royalties Administration & Monitoring, Kristopher Slaney
Tel: 709-729-4205
kristopherslaney@gov.nl.ca
Director, Electricity & Alternative Energy, Corey Snook
Tel: 709-729-3131
coreysnook@gov.nl.ca

Mines Branch
Promotes & facilitates the sustainable development of the province's mineral & energy resources through its resource assessment, management & development activities for the overall benefit of the citizens of Newfoundland & Labrador.
Assistant Deputy Minister, Mines & Mineral Development, Alex Smith
Tel: 709-729-2768
asmith@gov.nl.ca
Director, Geochemical Laboratory, Chris Finch
Tel: 709-729-3312
chrisfinch@gov.nl.ca

Director, Geological Survey, Dorothea Hanchar
Tel: 709-729-3419
dorotheahanchar@gov.nl.ca
Director, Mineral Lands Division, Kevin Sheppard
Tel: 709-729-6425
kevinsheppard@gov.nl.ca
Senior Geologist & Section Manager, Regional Geology, Alana Hinchey
Tel: 709-729-7725
alanahinchey@gov.nl.ca
Senior Geologist & Section Manager, Terrain Sciences & Geoscience Data Management, Sara Jenkins
Tel: 709-729-1161
sarajenkins@gov.nl.ca
Section Manager, Mineral Deposits, John Hinchey
Tel: 709-729-7976
johnhinchey@gov.nl.ca

Newfoundland & Labrador Department of Justice & Public Safety

East Block, Confederation Bldg., 4th Fl., PO Box 8700 St. John's, NL A1B 4J6
Tel: 709-729-2869; *Fax:* 709-729-0469
justice@gov.nl.ca
www.gov.nl.ca/jps

In September 2014, Premier Paul Davis created the new Department of Public Safety, which assumed the duties of the former Justice department — to ensure the impartial administration of justice & the protection of the public interest — & included Fire & Emergency Services - Newfoundland & Labrador. However, the name was changed again in October 2014 to Justice & Public Safety, in order to avoid confusion about the department's purpose.

Minister, Justice & Public Safety; Attorney General, Hon. John Hogan

Deputy Minister & Deputy Attorney General, Jennifer Mercer, Q.C.
jennifermercer@gov.nl.ca

Director, Communications, Danielle Barron
Tel: 709-729-5188
daniellebarron@gov.nl.ca

Associated Agencies, Boards & Commissions:

• Child Death Review Committee
Established by amendments to the Fatalities Investigations Act in 2012, the Committee reviews cases involving the deaths of children under 19 years, which have been provided by the Chief Medical Examiner.

• Commissioner of Lobbyists
689 Topsail Rd.
PO Box 8700
St. John's, NL A1B 4J6
Tel: 709-729-2918; *Fax:* 709-729-1302
www.gov.nl.ca/jps/department/branches/division/division-col

• Consumer Advocate
www.gov.nl.ca/jps/department/consumeradvocate

• Criminal Code Mental Disorder Review Board
www.gov.nl.ca/jps/department/criminalcode
The Board's mandate is to issue dispositions related to the management of persons accused of committing a crime who have been found not criminally responsible or unfit to stand trial due to a mental disorder. Three dispositions are at the Board's disposal: absolute discharge, conditionl discharge, or detention with or without conditions.

• Electoral Districts Boundaries Commission
83 Thorburn Rd.
PO Box 8700 C
St. John's, NL A1B 4J6
Mandated by the Electoral Boundaries Act, the Commission was responsible for dividing the province into 48 proposed one-member districts in 2006. The Commission was tasked with dividing the province into 40 proposed one-member districts in 2015.

• Fire & Emergency Services - Newfoundland & Labrador (FES-NL)
45 Majors Path, 2nd Fl.
PO Box 8700
St. John's, NL A1B 4J6
Tel: 709-729-1608; *Fax:* 709-729-2524
www.gov.nl.ca/jps/fes

• Human Rights Commission
See Entry Name Index for detailed listing.

• Newfoundland & Labrador Board of Commissioners of Public Utilities
See Entry Name Index for detailed listing.

• Newfoundland & Labrador Legal Aid Commission
#300, 251 Empire Ave.
St. John's, NL A1C 5J9
Tel: 709-753-7860; *Fax:* 709-753-7851
Toll-free: 800-563-9911
nlac@legalaid.nl.ca
www.legalaid.nl.ca
The Legal Aid Commission ensures that persons with limited financial means have access to legal counsel.

• Office of the Chief Medical Examiner
#1562, Health Sciences Centre, Level 1
St. John's, NL A1B 3V6
Tel: 709-737-6402
ocme@gov.nl.ca
www.gov.nl.ca/jps/department/branches/division/division-ocme

• Office of the Public Trustee
The Viking Bldg.
#401, 136 Crosbie Rd.
St. John's, NL A1B 3K3
Tel: 709-729-0850; *Fax:* 709-729-3063
general@publictrusteenl.ca
www.gov.nl.ca/jps/department/branches/division/trustee

• Royal Newfoundland Constabulary Public Complaints Commission
PO Box 8700
St. John's, NL A1B 4J6
Tel: 709-834-6171; *Fax:* 709-834-6178
rnccomplaintscommission@gov.nl.ca
www.rncpcc.ca
The Royal Newfoundland Constabulary Public Complaints Commission is an independent review authority established under Statute to hear & investigate complaints against members of the Royal Newfoundland Constabulary &, when appropriate, to conduct public hearings in respect of particular complaints.

Courts & Corporate Services
Assistant Deputy Minister, Donna Ballard
Tel: 709-729-6735
DBallard@gov.nl.ca
Director, Provincial Court Services, Joanne Turner
Tel: 709-729-2081
joanneturner@provincial.court.nl.ca
Acting Director, Policy & Strategic Planning, Pegah Memarpour
Tel: 709-729-7062
PegahMemarpour@gov.nl.ca

Office of the Legislative Counsel & Legal Services
Chief Legislative Counsel, Susan King
Tel: 709-729-4559; *Fax:* 709-729-2129
SusanKing@gov.nl.ca
Legislative Counsel, Angela Whitehead
Tel: 709-729-2877

Public Prosecutions Division
Assistant Deputy Minister & Director, Lloyd Strickland
Tel: 709-729-2868
lstrickland@gov.nl.ca

Public Safety & Enforcement
Assistant Deputy Minister, Tara Kelly
Tel: 709-729-7357
tarakelly@gov.nl.ca
www.rnc.gov.nl.ca
Chief, Royal Newfoundland Constabulary, Patrick Roche
www.rnc.gov.nl.ca
High Sheriff, Dean Whelan
Tel: 709-729-0944
deanwhelan@gov.nl.ca
Superintendent, Prisons, Graham Rogerson
Tel: 709-729-2978; *Fax:* 709-729-4312
grahamrogerson@gov.nl.ca

Municipal Assessment Agency Inc.

75 O'Leary Ave., St. John's, NL A1B 2C9
Tel: 709-724-1532
Toll-Free: 877-777-2807
info@maa.ca
maa.ca

The agency provides property assessment & valuation services. The head office location is also the Eastern Regional Office.

Chair, Dean Ball

CEO, Sean Martin

Newfoundland & Labrador Department of Municipal & Provincial Affairs

West Block, Confederation Bldg., PO Box 8700 St. John's, NL A1B 4J6

MAPAInfo@gov.nl.ca
www.gov.nl.ca/mpa

The department supports municipalities, communities & regions in economic, social & environmental sustainability goals through a range of services & supports.

Minister, Hon. Krista Lynn Howell

Deputy Minister, Ted Lomond
Tel: 709-729-3049
Tedlomond@gov.nl.ca

Municipalities Branch
Assistant Deputy Minister, Bren Hanlon
Tel: 709-729-5326
brenhanlon@gov.nl.ca
Director, Local Governance & Planning, Sandy Hounsell
Tel: 709-729-7390
sandyhounsell@gov.nl.ca
Director, Local Governance, Mary Oley
Tel: 709-729-1953
MaryOley@gov.nl.ca
Director, Policy & Strategic Planning, Emily Thompson
Tel: 709-729-1090
EmilyThompson@gov.nl.ca

Nalcor Energy

500 Columbus Dr., St. John's, NL A1E 2B2
Tel: 709-737-1400; *Fax:* 709-737-1800
info@nalcorenergy.com
www.nalcorenergy.com
twitter.com/NalcorEnergy
www.facebook.com/NalcorEnergy
www.youtube.com/user/NalcorEnergy

Crown corporation, founded in 2008 & owned by the Province of Newfoundland & Labrador. Nalcor is the parent company of Newfoundland & Labrador Hydro, which in turn is the parent of the Hydro Group of Companies. Nalcor's subsidiaries include: Newfoundland & Labrador Hydro, The Churchill Falls Generating Station, Lower Churchill Project, Oil & Gas & Bull Arm Fabrication.

Acting Chair, John Green

President & CEO, Jennifer Williams

Chief Financial Officer & Executive Vice-President, Finance, Carla Russel

Chief Human Resources Officer & Executive Vice-President, Corporate Services, Mike Roberts

Executive Vice-President, Power Development & Muskrat Falls Project, Gilbert Bennett

Executive Vice-President, Power Supply, Jim Haynes

Newfoundland & Labrador Public Service Commission (PSC)

261 Kenmount Rd., PO Box 8700 St. John's, NL A1B 4J6
Tel: 709-729-5810; *Fax:* 709-729-6234
Toll-Free: 855-330-5810
contactpsc@gov.nl.ca
www.psc.gov.nl.ca

Minister Responsible, Hon. Siobhan Coady
Tel: 709-729-3775; *Fax:* 709-729-2232
financeminister@gov.nl.ca

Chair & Chief Executive Officer, George Joyce
Tel: 709-729-2650
georgejoyce@gov.nl.ca

Commissioner, Ann Chafe
Tel: 709-729-2659
annchafe@gov.nl.ca

Director, Employee Assistance & Respectful Workplace, Ian Shortall
Tel: 709-729-5804
nshortall@gov.nl.ca

Newfoundland & Labrador Board of Commissioners of Public Utilities

PO Box 21040 St. John's, NL A1A 5B2
Fax: 709-726-9604
Toll-Free: 866-782-0006
ito@pub.nl.ca
www.pub.nf.ca

Regulates electrical utilities in Newfoundland & Labrador.

Chair, Darlene Whalen
dwhalen@pub.nl.ca

Vice-Chair, Dwanda Newman

Commissioner, John O'Brien

Provincial Advisory Council on the Status of Women (PACSW)

#103, 15 Hallett Cres., St. John's, NL A1B 4C4
Tel: 709-753-7270; *Fax:* 709-753-2606
Toll-Free: 877-753-7270
info@pacsw.ca
pacsw.ca
twitter.com/PACSWNL
www.facebook.com/PACSWNL

Minister Responsible, Hon. Pam Parsons

President & CEO, Paula Sheppard
Tel: 709-753-6124; *Fax:* 709-753-2606
paulasheppard@pacsw.ca

Newfoundland & Labrador Department of Tourism, Culture, Arts & Recreation

PO Box 8700 St. John's, NL A1B 4J6
Tel: 709-729-7000
tcar@gov.nl.ca
www.gov.nl.ca/tcar

The Department was created in 2004 to reflect the enhanced empasis placed on the innovation aspect of the provincial economic agenda. It is the lead agency for economic development in the province & in each of its regions. In September 2014, Premier Paul Davis created a new department called Business, Tourism, Culture & Rural Development. It absorbed responsibilities formerly held by Tourism, Culture & Recreation, including: conserving, preserving & protecting natural & cultural resources & promoting the resources for economic benefit, sport & recreation in the province. Programs assist in transforming the province's natural & cultural attractions into opportunities for employment & revenue generation. In February 2017, the department was renamed Tourism, Culture, Industry & Innovation & streamlined to better reflect its goals. Most recently, it was renamed Tourism, Culture, Arts & Recreation.

Minister, Hon. Steve Crocker
TCARMinister@gov.nl.ca

Deputy Minister, Jamie Chippett
Tel: 709-729-4732

Director, Communications, Debbie Marnell
Tel: 709-729-4570
debbiemarnell@gov.nl.ca

Associated Agencies, Boards & Commissions:
• Heritage Foundation of Newfoundland & Labrador (HFNL)
The Newman Bldg.
1 Springdale St.
PO Box 5171
St. John's, NL A1C 5V5
Tel: 709-739-1892; *Fax:* 709-739-6592
Toll-free: 888-739-1892
info@heritagenl.ca
heritagenl.ca

• Marble Mountain Development Corporation
PO Box 947
Corner Brook, NL A2H 6J2
Tel: 709-637-7601; *Fax:* 709-634-1702
Toll-free: 888-462-7253
admin@skimarble.com
skimarble.com

• Newfoundland & Labrador Arts Council/ArtsNL (NLAC)
The Newman Bldg.
1 Springdale St.
PO Box 98
St. John's, NL A1C 5H5
Tel: 709-726-2212; *Fax:* 709-726-0619
Toll-free: 866-726-2212
nlacmail@nlac.ca
www.nlac.ca

• Newfoundland & Labrador Film Development Corporation (NLFDC)
12 King's Bridge Rd.
St. John's, NL A1C 3K3
Tel: 709-738-3456; *Fax:* 709-739-1680
Toll-free: 877-738-3456
info@nlfdc.ca
nlfdc.ca

• The Rooms Corporation
9 Bonaventure Ave.
PO Box 1800 C
St. John's, NL A1C 5P9
Tel: 709-757-8000; *Fax:* 709-757-8017
information@therooms.ca
www.therooms.ca
Other Communication: Archives, Email: archives@therooms.ca

Tourism, Culture & Parks Branch
Markets the province as a travel destination & develops products, facilities & services in partnership with the tourism industry.
Assistant Deputy Minister, Judith Hearn
Tel: 709-729-2821
JudithHearn@gov.nl.ca
Director, Arts & Culture Centres, Aiden Flynn
Tel: 709-729-3904; *Fax:* 709-729-5952
aflynn@artsandculturecentre.com
artsandculturecentre.com
Director, Provincial Parks, Sian French
Tel: 709-637-2275
sianfrench@gov.nl.ca
artsandculturecentre.com
Director, Arts & Heritage Division, Gerry Osmond
Tel: 709-729-7397
GerryOsmond@gov.nl.ca
artsandculturecentre.com
Director, Tourism, Marketing & Visitors Services Division, Andrea Peddle
Tel: 709-729-2831
apeddle@gov.nl.ca
artsandculturecentre.com
Provincial Archaeologist, Jamie Brake
Tel: 709-729-2462
JamieBrake@gov.nl.ca
artsandculturecentre.com

Newfoundland & Labrador Department of Transportation & Infrastructure

Confederation Bldg., Prince Philip Dr., PO Box 8700 St. John's, NL A1B 4J6
Tel: 709-729-2300
ti@gov.nl.ca
www.gov.nl.ca/ti

To provide a safe, efficient & sustainable transportation system & to provide landlord services & support services such as leasing & mail services for all government departments. The department liaises with other agencies & the federal government to ensure the overall public works & transportation needs & interest of the province are fully provided & protected.

Minister, Hon. Elvis Loveless
Tel: 709-729-3679; *Fax:* 709-729-4285
timinister@gov.nl.ca

Deputy Minister, Cory Grandy
Tel: 709-729-3676
corygrandy@gov.nl.ca

Director, Communications, Brian Scott
Tel: 709-729-3015
Brianscott@gov.nl.ca

Air & Marine Services Branch
440 Main St., PO Box 97 Lewisporte, NL A0G 3A0
Toll-Free: 888-638-5454
TWMarine@gov.nl.ca

Assistant Deputy Minister, John Baker
Tel: 709-729-3796
jbaker@gov.nl.ca
Director, Marine Services, Steve Burbridge
Tel: 709-729-2758
StephenBurbridge@gov.nl.ca

Director, Air Services, Dion Geange
Tel: 709-256-1037
DionGeange@gov.nl.ca

Infrastructure Branch

Assistant Deputy Minister, Greg Clarke
Tel: 709-729-3796
GregClarke@gov.nl.ca

Director, Infrastructure Planning & Procurement, Steven Forward
Tel: 709-729-2632
StevenForward@gov.nl.ca

Director, Highway Design & Construction, Bill Hillier
Tel: 709-729-6610
williamhillier@gov.nl.ca

Director, Municipal Infrastructure, Kim Kieley
Tel: 709-729-7482
KimKieley@gov.nl.ca

Director, Building Design & Construction, Lisa Reid
Tel: 709-637-2258
LisaReid@gov.nl.ca

Operations Branch

Assistant Deputy Minister, Vacant

Director, Building Operations, Natalie Hallett
Tel: 709-729-4988
NatalieHallett@gov.nl.ca

Director, Equipment Maintenance, Shawn Marshall
Tel: 709-256-1047
ShawnMarshall@gov.nl.ca

Director, Highway Operations, Dion Tee
Tel: 709-898-7840
teedion@gov.nl.ca

Strategic & Corporate Services Branch

Assistant Deputy Minister, Tracy English
Tel: 709-729-6882
tenglish@gov.nl.ca

Director, Planning & Accommodations, Robyn Bursey
Tel: 709-729-4422
rbursey@gov.nl.ca

Director, Strategic & Support Services, Jennifer Crummey
Tel: 709-729-5399
JenniferCrummey@gov.nl.ca

Departmental Comptroller & Director, Financial & General Operations, Patrick Morrissey
Tel: 709-729-5356
PatrickMorrissey@gov.nl.ca

Newfoundland & Labrador Workplace Health, Safety & Compensation Commission (WorkplaceNL)

146 - 148 Forest Rd., PO Box 9000 St. John's, NL A1A 3B8
Tel: 709-778-1000; *Fax:* 709-738-1714
Toll-Free: 800-563-9000
info@workplacenl.ca
workplacenl.ca
www.facebook.com/WorkplaceNL
www.linkedin.com/company/workplacenl
www.youtube.com/user/safeworknl

Utilizing skilled, professional employees, in partnership with workplace parties, the commission facilitates safe & healthy workplaces by assisting employers & workers to prevent accidents, & manage workplace injuries / illnesses & return-to-work processes. Operating as the administrator of the workers' compensation insurance program, the commission provides a reasonable level of benefits to injured workers & their dependents based on reasonable assessment rates for employers, while maintaining or exceeding service level performance when compared to other jurisdictions in Canada.

Minister Responsible, Hon. Bernard Davis

Chair, John Peddle

Chief Executive Officer, Dennis Hogan

Chief Financial & Information Officer, Andrew Vavasour

General Counsel & Corporate Secretary, Ann Martin

Director, Communications, Carla Riggs

Director, Human Resources, Sonya Stanford

Government of the Northwest Territories

Seat of Government: PO Box 1320 Yellowknife, NT X1A 2L9
Tel: 867-767-9000
www.gov.nt.ca
The Northwest Territories was reconstituted September 1, 1905. It has a land area of 1,143,793.86 sq km, & the StatsCan census in 2016 showed the population was 41,786.
On April 1, 1999, the Northwest Territories was divided into two

new territories: Nunavut Territories & the as yet unnamed territory (known as the Northwest Territories). The Northwest Territories is governed by a fully elected Legislative Assembly of 19 members elected for a four-year term. Government is by consensus rather than party politics. The Legislature elects the Premier & a seven-member Executive Council, which is charged with the operation of government & the establishment of program & spending priorities. The Commissioner of the Northwest Territories is appointed by the Federal Government, & serves a role similar to that of a Lieutenant Governor in provincial jurisdictions.
With the implementation of the Northwest Territories Devolution Act on April 1, 2014, the government of the Northwest Territories gained power over its land & resources from the federal government.

Office of the Commissioner

803 Northwest Tower, PO Box 1320 Yellowknife, NT X1A 2L9
Tel: 867-873-7400; *Fax:* 867-873-0223
Toll-Free: 888-270-3318
commissioner@gov.nt.ca
www.commissioner.gov.nt.ca

Commissioner of the Northwest Territories, Margaret M. Thom
Note: On June 14, 2017, Prime Minister Trudeau named Margaret M. Thom as the new Commissioner of the Northwest Territories. She was officially sworn in on September 18, 2017.

Deputy Commissioner, Leonard Kenny

Office of the Premier

Legislative Assembly Bldg., PO Box 1320 Yellowknife, NT X1A 2L9
www.gov.nt.ca/en/premier

Premier, Hon. Caroline Cochrane
caroline_cochrane@gov.nt.ca

Executive Council

PO Box 1320 Yellowknife, NT X1A 2L9
executive_communications@gov.nt.ca
www.gov.nt.ca/premier/cabinet
Other Communication: Protocol: executive_protocol@gov.nt.ca;
Corporate Services: executive_services@gov.nt.ca
Coordination & advisory functions are performed for the Government of the Northwest Territories.

Premier; Minister, Executive & Indigenous Affairs; Minister responsible, COVID-19 Coordinating Secretariat, Hon. Caroline Cochrane
caroline_cochrane@gov.nt.ca

Deputy Premier; Minister, Infrastructure; Minister responsible, Northwest Territories Power Corporation, Hon. Diane Archie
diane_archie@gov.nt.ca

Minister responsible, Northwest Territories Housing Corporation; Homelessness; Public Utilities Board; Workers' Safety & Compensation Commission, Hon. Paulie Chinna
paulie_chinna@gov.nt.ca

Minister, Health & Social Services; Minister responsible, Persons with Disabilities & Seniors, Hon. Julie Green
julie_green@gov.nt.ca

Minister, Education, Culture & Employment; Minister, Justice; Government House Leader, Hon. R.J. Simpson
rj_simpson@gov.nt.ca

Minister, Environment & Natural Resources; Minister, Lands; Minister, Municipal & Community Affairs; Minister responsible, Youth, Hon. Shane Thompson
shane_thompson@gov.nt.ca

Minister, Finance; Minister, Industry, Tourism & Investment; Minister responsible, Business Development & Investment Corporation; Status of Women, Hon. Caroline Wawzonek
caroline_wawzonek@gov.nt.ca

Northwest Territories Department of the Executive & Indigenous Affairs

PO Box 1320 Yellowknife, NT X1A 2L9
www.eia.gov.nt.ca/en
Other Communication: Protocol, Email: executive_protocol@gov.nt.ca; Cannabis Information: www.eia.gov.nt.ca/en/cannabis

Premier, Hon. Caroline Cochrane

Secretary to Cabinet & Deputy Minister, Executive, Martin Goldney
Tel: 867-767-9145 ext: 11021

Principal Secretary, Shaleen Woodward
Tel: 867-767-9025 ext: 11082

Chief of Protocol, Carmen Moore
Tel: 867-767-9140 ext: 18072

Northwest Territories Legislative Assembly

4570 - 48th St., PO Box 1320 Yellowknife, NT X1A 2L9
Tel: 867-669-2200
Toll-Free: 800-661-0784
www.assembly.gov.nt.ca
Other Communication: Officer on Duty, Phone: 867-669-2226
twitter.com/AssemblyNWT
www.facebook.com/LegislativeAssemblyNWT

Clerk, Tim Mercer
Tel: 867-767-9130 ext: 12010
Tim_Mercer@gov.nt.ca

Speaker, Hon. Frederick Blake, Jr.

Sergeant-At-Arms, Brian Thagard
Tel: 867-767-9131 ext: 12036

Committee Clerk, Michael Ball
Tel: 867-767-9130 ext: 12016

Deputy Sergeant-At-Arms, Derek Edjericon
Tel: 867-767-9131 ext: 12037

Legislative Librarian, Gerald Burla
Tel: 867-767-9132 ext: 12056

Elections NWT/Plebiscite Office
YK Centre East, #7, 4915 - 48th St., 3rd Fl., Yellowknife, NT X1A 3S4
Tel: 867-767-9100; *Fax:* 867-920-9100
Toll-Free: 844-767-9100
info@electionsnwt.ca
www.electionsnwt.com
Other Communication: Toll-Free Fax: 844-973-9100
twitter.com/ElectionsNWT
www.facebook.com/ElectionsNWT
Chief Electoral Officer, Nicole Latour
Tel: 867-767-9100 ext: 16030
Nicole_Latour@gov.nt.ca
Deputy Chief Electoral Officer, Vacant

Office of the Integrity Commissioner
PO Box 1320 Yellowknife, NT X1A 2L9
Formerly named the Office of the Conflict of Interest Commissioner.
Integrity Commissioner, David Phillip Jones
Tel: 780-433-9000
dpjones@sagecounsel.com

Office of the Languages Commissioner
202 McDougall Rd., Fort Smith, NT X0E 0P0
Tel: 867-872-3706
Toll-Free: 800-661-0889
admin@olc-nt.ca
olc-nt.ca
Other Communication: Alt. Fax: 867-920-2511
Languages Commissioner, Brenda Gauthier

Standing Committees of the Legislature

www.assembly.gov.nt.ca/documents-proceedings/committees
The following are the Standing Committees of the 19th Legislative Assembly of the Northwest Territories: Priorities & Planning; Economic Development & Environment; Social Development; Government Operations; & Rules & Procedures.

Nineteenth Legislative Assembly - Northwest Territories

4570 - 48th St., PO Box 1320 Yellowknife, NT X1A 2L9
Tel: 867-669-2200; *Fax:* 867-920-4735
Toll-Free: 800-661-0784
www.ntassembly.ca
twitter.com/AssemblyNWT
www.facebook.com/LegislativeAssemblyNWT

Last General Election: Oct. 1, 2019.
Maximum Duration: Four years.
Salaries, Indemnities & Allowances (2021):
Members of the Legislative Assembly are entitled to an annual salary of $110,761. Members are entitled to a non-taxable annual expense allowance of $7,982 for a Minister or for Members living within commuting distance of the capital. Members, who are not Ministers, & who do not live within commuting distance of the capital, are entitled to an additional non-taxable non-accountable allowance of $7,982 for expenses incurred while in the capital while on constituency business or business as a Member. Up to $31,000 annually is paid to Members for capital accommodation, when their residence is not within 80 km of Yellowknife, & when they are attending sittings of the Legislature, committee meetings & performing constituency duties in Yellowknife. Members are provided with a set constituency-operating budget to defray the expenses of working on behalf of their constituents. In addition are the following remunerations:
Premier $84,241;
Minister $59,281;
Speaker $48,210;
Deputy Speaker $7,800;
Deputy Chair of Committee of the Whole $4,682; Chair of Caucus $3,456.
The address for all contacts is as follows: PO Box 1320, Yellowknife, NT, X1A 2L9. The following is a list of Members of the Legislative Assembly, with their constituency, the number of electors on the voting list for the the most recent election, plus contact information:

Members of the Legislative Assembly of the Northwest Territories

Deputy Premier; Minister, Infrastructure; Minister responsible, Northwest Territories Power Corporation, Hon. Diane Archie
Constituency: Inuvik Boot Lake
Tel: 867-767-9141 ext: 11124
diane_archie@ntassembly.ca
Constituency Office
#124, 198 Mackenzie Rd.
PO Box 1998
Inuvik, NT X0E 0T0
Speaker, Hon. Frederick Blake Jr.
Constituency: Mackenzie Delta
Tel: 867-767-9133 ext: 12005
frederick_blake@ntassembly.ca
Other Communications: Constituency Phone: 867-952-2652
Ronald Bonnetrouge
Constituency: Deh Cho
Tel: 867-767-9143 ext: 12105
ron_bonnetrouge@ntassembly.ca
Other Communications: Constituency Phone: 867-699-4003
Constituency Office
General Delivery
Fort Providence, NT
Minister responsible, Northwest Territories Housing Corporation; Homelessness; Public Utilities Board; Workers' Safety & Compensation Commission, Hon. Paulie Chinna
Constituency: Sahtu
Tel: 867-767-9141 ext: 11135
paulie_chinna@ntassembly.ca
Caitlin Cleveland
Constituency: Kam Lake
Tel: 867-767-9143 ext: 12135
caitlin_cleveland@ntassembly.ca
mla-kamlake.ca
Other Communications: Constituency Phone: 867-767-9143, ext. 12137
Premier; Minister, Executive & Indigenous Affairs, Hon. Caroline Cochrane
Constituency: Range Lake
caroline_cochrane@ntassembly.ca
Minister, Health & Social Services; Minister responsible, Persons with Disabilities & Seniors, Hon. Julie Green
Constituency: Yellowknife Centre
Tel: 867-767-9143 ext: 12180
julie_green@ntassembly.ca
Other Communications: Constituency Phone: 867-767-9143, ext. 12113
Jackie Jacobson
Constituency: Nunakput
Tel: 867-767-9143 ext: 12145
jackie_jacobson@ntassembly.ca
Other Communications: Constituency Phone: 867-977-2197
Constituency Office

General Delivery
Tuktoyaktuk, NT X0E 1C0
Rylund Johnson
Constituency: Yellowknife North
Tel: 867-767-9143 ext: 12170
rylund_johnson@ntassembly.ca
Other Communications: Constituency Phone: 867-767-9143, ext. 12173
Frieda Martselos
Constituency: Thebacha
Tel: 867-767-9143 ext: 12165
frieda_martselos@ntassembly.ca
Other Communications: Constituency Phone: 867-872-5511
Constituency Office
202 McDougal Rd.
Fort Smith, NT X0E 0P0
Hon. Katrina Nokleby
Constituency: Great Slave
Tel: 867-767-9141
katrina_nokleby@ntassembly.ca
Steve Norn
Constituency: Tu Nedhé - Wiilideh
Tel: 867-767-9143 ext: 12185
steve_norn@ntassembly.ca
Other Communications: Constituency Phone: 867-767-9143, ext. 12188
Kevin O'Reilly
Constituency: Frame Lake
Tel: 867-767-9143 ext: 12110
kevin_oreilly@ntassembly.ca
Lesa Semmler
Constituency: Inuvik Twin Lakes
Tel: 867-767-9143 ext: 12195
lesa_semmler@ntassembly.ca
Other Communications: Constituency Phone: 867-678-2429
Constituency Office
#123, 198 Mackenzie Rd.
PO Box 3130
Inuvik, NT X0E 0T0
Minister, Education, Culture & Employment; Minister, Justice; Government House Leader, Hon. R.J. Simpson
Constituency: Hay River North
Tel: 867-767-9141 ext: 11120
rj_simpson@ntassembly.ca
Other Communications: Constituency Phone: 867-874-6301
Constituency Office, Wright Centre
#104, 62 Woodland Dr.
Hay River, NT X0E 1G1
Rocky Simpson
Constituency: Hay River South
Tel: 867-767-9143 ext: 12120
rocky_simpson@ntassembly.ca
Other Communications: Constituency Phone: 867-874-6141
Constituency Office, Godwin Mall
#3, 66 Woodland Dr.
Hay River, NT X0E 1G1
Minister, Environment & Natural Resources; Minister, Lands; Minister Municipal & Community Affairs; Minister responsible, Youth, Hon. Shane Thompson
Constituency: Nahendeh
Tel: 867-767-9141 ext: 11128
shane_thompson@ntassembly.ca
Other Communications: Constituency Phone: 867-695-3780
Constituency Office
9706 - 100th St.
Fort Simpson, NT X0E 0N0
Minister, Finance; Minister, Industry, Tourism & Investment; Minister responsible, Business Development & Investment Corporation; Status of Women, Hon. Caroline Wawzonek
Constituency: Yellowknife South
Tel: 867-767-9143 ext: 12177
caroline_wawzonek@ntassembly.ca
Jane Weyallon Armstrong
Constituency: Monfwi
Tel: 867-767-9143 ext: 12190
Jane_WeyallonArmstrong@ntassembly.ca
Note: Jane Weyallon Armstrong was elected in a by-election held July 27, 2021.

Northwest Territories Government Departments & Agencies

Aurora Research Institute (ARI)

191 MacKenzie Rd., PO Box 1450 Inuvik, NT X0E 0T0
Tel: 867-777-3298; *Fax:* 867-777-4264
www.nwtresearch.com
twitter.com/nwtresearch
www.facebook.com/Aurora-Research-Institute-12456775429009
3

A division of Aurora College that is dedicated to excellence, leadership & innovations in Northern education & research. Administers the research licencing provisions of the Northwest

Territories Scientists Act & provides year round logistical assistance for researchers.

Vice-President, Research, Pippa Seccombe-Hett
pseccombe-hett@auroracollege.nt.ca

Northwest Territories Business Development & Investment Corporation (BDIC)

5009 - 50th Ave., PO Box 1320 Yellowknife, NT X1A 2L9
Tel: 867-767-9075; *Fax:* 867-765-0652
Toll-Free: 800-661-0599
www.bdic.ca

The BDIC provides access to business financing, support & development assistance to communities throughout the Northwest Territories. Their focus is the small & mid-sized business sector.
Subsidiaries include: Acho Dene Native Crafts; Arctic Canada Trading Company; Dene Fur Clouds; Mort McPherson Tent & Canvas; & Ulukhaktok Arts Centre.

Chair, Darrell Beaulieu

Chief Executive Officer, Pawan Chugh
Tel: 867-767-9075 ext: 86000

Director, Finance & Programs, Leonard Kwong
Tel: 867-767-9075 ext: 86030

Northwest Territories Department of Education, Culture & Employment (ECE)

PO Box 1320 Yellowknife, NT X1A 2L9
ecepublicaffairs@gov.nt.ca
www.ece.gov.nt.ca
Other Communication: Immigration: immigration@gov.nt.ca; Student Financial Assistance: nwtsfa@gov.nt.ca
The Ministry's responsibilities cover the following areas: Early Childhood; Kindergarten to Grade 12; Adult & Post-Secondary Education; Career Development & Employment; Apprenticeship & Occupational Certification; Culture, Heritage & Languages; Income Security; & Labour Services.

Minister, Hon. R.J. Simpson

Deputy Minister, John MacDonald
John_MacDonald@gov.nt.ca

Assistant Deputy Minister, Labour & Income Security,
Andy Bevan
Tel: 867-767-9065 ext: 71482
Andy_Bevan@gov.nt.ca

Assistant Deputy Minister, Corporate Services, Vacant
Tel: 867-767-9065 ext: 71464

Assistant Deputy Minister, Education & Culture, Vacant

Executive Director, Secretariat aux affaires francophones / Francophone affairs secreatariat, Benoit Boutin
Tel: 867-767-9343 ext: 71047

Director, Indigenous Languages & Education Secretariat,
Angela James
Tel: 867-767-9346 ext: 71035

Director, Health, Wellness & Student Support, Jessica Schmidt
Tel: 867-867-9346 ext: 71036

Director, Instructional & School Services, John Stewart
Tel: 867-767-9342 ext: 71289

Associated Agencies, Boards & Commissions:
• **Aboriginal Languages Revitalization Board**
PO Box 1320
Yellowknife, NT X1A 2L9
• **Apprenticeship, Trade & Occupations Certification Board (ATOCB)**
PO Box 1320
Yellowknife, NT X1A 2L9
Tel: 867-767-9351
apprenticeship@gov.nt.ca
The board provides advice & is the link between the Department & industry, aiming to fascilitate qualified apprentices & a skilled workforce.

• **Northwest Territories Arts Council**
PO Box 1320
Yellowknife, NT X1A 2L9
Tel: 867-767-9347; *Fax:* 867-873-0205
Toll-free: 877-445-2787
www.nwtartscouncil.ca

• **Northwest Territories Social Assistance Appeal Board**
PO Box 1320
Yellowknife, NT X1A 2L9

• **Official Languages Board**
PO Box 1320
Yellowknife, NT X1A 2L9

• **Student Financial Assistance Appeal Board**
PO Box 1320
Yellowknife, NT X1A 2L9

Culture & Heritage
Director, Culture & Heritage, Sarah Carr-Locke
Tel: 867-767-9347 ext: 71193

Early Childhood & School Services
Director, Early Childhood Development & Learning, Shelly
Kapraelian
Tel: 867-767-9354 ext: 71275

Education Operations & Development
Director, Education Operations & Development, Andrea
Giesbrecht
Tel: 867-767-9353 ext: 71260

Finance & Capital Planning
Director, Finance & Capital Planning, Marissa Martin
Tel: 867-767-9350 ext: 71126

Income Security Programs Division
Director, Income Security Programs, Nicole Beauchamp
Tel: 867-767-9355 ext: 71303

Labour Development & Standards
Director, Labour Development & Standards, & Apprenticeship,
Trade & Occupation Certification, Michael Saturnino
Tel: 867-767-9351 ext: 71152
Director, Adult & Postsecondary Education, Deana Twissell
Tel: 867-767-9345 ext: 71026

Planning, Research & Evaluation
Director, Planning, Research & Evaluation, Jennifer Young
Tel: 867-767-9349 ext: 71087

Policy, Legislation & Communications
Director, Policy, Legislation & Communications, Sam Shannon
Tel: 867-767-9352 ext: 71070

Northwest Territories Department of Environment & Natural Resources (ENR)

PO Box 1320 Yellowknife, NT X1A 2L9

Tel: 867-767-9055
enr_communications@gov.nt.ca
www.enr.gov.nt.ca

Operations cover a broad spectrum of activities directed at
promoting a healthy environment that supports traditional
lifestyles within a modern economy. The wise use & protection of
natural resources are encouraged. The Department's activities
are carried out through the following divisions: Environmental
Protection, Forest Management, Policy, Legislation &
Communications, Protected Areas Strategy, Informatics, &
Wildlife.

Minister, Hon. Shane Thompson

Deputy Minister, Erin Kelly

**Acting Assistant Deputy Minister, Environment & Climate
Change,** Nathen Richea
Tel: 867-767-9055 ext: 53000

Acting Assistant Deputy Minister, Operations, Brett Elkin
Tel: 867-767-9055 ext: 53000

Director, Conservation, Assessment & Monitoring, Julian
Kanigan
Tel: 867-767-9233 ext: 53065

Associated Agencies, Boards & Commissions:
• **Natural Resources Conservation Trust Fund Board of
Trustees**
PO Box 1320
Yellowknife, NT X1A 2L9
Tel: 867-873-7401; Fax: 867-873-0638

• **Waste Reduction & Recovery Advisory Committee**
PO Box 1320
Yellowknife, NT X1A 2L9
Tel: 867-873-7654; Fax: 867-873-0221
nwtrecycle@gov.nt.ca
icarenwt.ca

• **Deh Cho Land Use Planning Committee**
PO Box 199
Fort Providence, NT X0E 0L0
Tel: 867-699-3162; Fax: 867-699-3166
www.dehcholands.org

Environment
To protect & enhance the environmental quality in the North.
Departmental programs are designed to control the discharge of
contaminants & reduce their impacts on the natural environment.
This is a shared responsibility with federal, territorial, Aboriginal
& municipal agencies, as well as every resident of the Northwest
Territories. To promote energy conservation & the use of energy
efficient technology in the Northwest Territories, identify &
facilitate the development of alternative, local energy sources
which strengthen community economies, & promote & facilitate
energy planning.
Acting Director, Environment, Diep Duong
Tel: 867-767-9236 ext: 53175

Forest Management
Tel: 867-872-7700; Fax: 867-874-6236
Provides the policy, planning & regulatory framework for the
stewardship, protection & sustainable management of forest
resources on 33 million hectares of land in the Northwest
Territories, eight per cent of Canada's entire forested area.
Working with First Nations governments, communities, other
governments & non-governmental agencies on such a vast land
mass presents unique & complex challenges for forest
managers. The FMD coordinates & facilitates the
implementation of forest management programs & services
among the five administrative regions of ENR. The regional
offices have the primary responsibility for delivery of programs.
Regional staff implement forest resource & fire management
programs for the Department. Regional personnel receive
applications for approval to harvest, supervise harvesting
activities, ensure compliance with standards, support community
protection planning efforts & carry out fire management activities
under the direction of the Forest Management Division.
Acting Director, Forest Management, Michael Gravel
Tel: 867-872-7713

Water Resources
Fax: 867-873-4229
Acting Director, Water Resources, Nathen Richea
Tel: 867-767-9234 ext: 53110

Wildlife
Fax: 867-873-0293
Other Communication: Wildlife General Inquiries: 873-767-9237,
ext. 53468
Activities are directed towards maintaining productive
populations of all native wildlife in their natural habitats,
encouraging the wise use of wildlife populations within the limits
of sustainable yield & encouraging the active participation of
northern residents in the management of wildlife resources. In
addition to assistance programs that are designed to support the
hunting & trapping economy, the division provides support to
organizations of resource users to allow them to become more
involved in wildlife management.
Director, Wildlife, Brett Elkin
Tel: 873-767-9237 ext: 53222

Northwest Territories Department of Finance

PO Box 1320 Yellowknife, NT X1A 2L9
www.fin.gov.nt.ca
The Department of Finance obtains the financial resources to
carry on the functions of government & for intergovernmental
fiscal negotiations & arrangements.

Minister, Hon. Caroline Wawzonek

Deputy Minister, William Mackay

Chief Information Officer, Rick Wind
Tel: 867-767-9170 ext: 15457

Territorial Statistician, Bureau of Statistics, Vishni Peeris
Tel: 867-767-9169 ext: 15035
Vishni_Peeris@gov.nt.ca

Associated Agencies, Boards & Commissions:
• **Northwest Territories Liquor & Cannabis Commission
(NTLCC)**
#201, 31 Capital Dr.
Hay River, NT X0E 1G2
Tel: 867-874-8700; Fax: 867-874-8720
www.ntlcc.ca
Other Communication: Alt. URL:
www.fin.gov.nt.ca/services/liquor/liquor-commission
The Liquor Commission purchases, sells, classifies & distributes
liquor & cannabis in the Northwest Territories.

• **Northwest Territories Liquor Licensing Board**
#204, 31 Capital Dr.
Hay River, NT X0E 1G2
Tel: 867-874-8715; Fax: 867-874-8722
Toll-free: 800-351-7770
LLBinfo@gov.nt.ca
www.fin.gov.nt.ca/en/services/nwt-liquor-licensing-board
Independent from government, the Board administers several
parts of the NWT Liquor Act & the NWT Liquor Regulations, & is
responsible for licenses & permits.

Budget, Treasury & Debt Management
Fax: 867-873-0414
Treasury is responsible for managing the government's cash
position; conducting banking, borrowing & investment activities;
protecting the government's activities & assets from risk of loss
by means of appropriate insurance coverage & risk management
activities; & regulating insurance companies, agents, brokers &
adjusters operating in the NWT.
Deputy Secretary of the Financial Management Board, William
Mackay

Financial & Employee Shared Services
Tel: 867-767-9174; Fax: 867-873-0110
Financial_SharedServices@gov.nt.ca
www.fin.gov.nt.ca/services/financial-shared-services
Other Communication: Payroll & Benefits, Toll-Free Phone:
866-475-8162; Fax: 867-873-0167; Medical Travel Emergencies,
Toll-Free Phone: 844-367-9279
Executive Director, Tara Clowes
Tel: 867-767-9173 ext: 15135
Assistant Director, Paulette Doucet
Tel: 867-767-9173 ext: 15138

Fiscal Policy
Responsible for developing policies & providing research,
analysis & recommendations on the fiscal policies of
government. The Division also administers the Formula
Financing Agreement with Canada & is responsible for
intergovernmental fiscal relations.
Director, Fiscal Policy, Kelly Bluck
Tel: 867-767-9158 ext: 15050
Director, Management Board Secretariat, Terence Courtoreille
Tel: 867-767-9176 ext: 15235

Informatics Shared Services
Fax: 867-873-0296
Executive Director, Peter Brunette
Tel: 867-767-9172 ext: 15101

Labour Relations
Director, Nicole MacNeil
Tel: 867-767-9153 ext: 14085

Management & Recruitment Services
Director, Tara McRae
Tel: 867-767-9154 ext: 14141

Office of the Comptroller General
Comptroller General, Julie Mujcin
Tel: 867-767-9015 ext: 14000
Assistant Comptroller General, Accounting Services
Management, Louise Lavoie
Tel: 867-767-9171 ext: 15080
Director, Treasury & Superintendent of Insurance, Louise Lavoie
Tel: 867-767-9177 ext: 15250

Office of the Deputy Secretary of Human Resources
Deputy Secretary, Human Resources, Tara Hunter
Tel: 867-767-9015 ext: 14000
Tara_Hunter@gov.nt.ca
Director, Strategic Human Resources, Kim Wickens
Tel: 867-767-9152 ext: 14015

Shared Corporate Services
Fax: 867-920-7342
Director, Chervahun Emilien
Tel: 867-767-9168 ext: 15020

Financial Management Board Secretariat (FMBS)

PO Box 1320 Yellowknife, NT X1A 2L9
www.fin.gov.nt.ca/en/management-board-secretariat
Other Communication: Phone: 867-767-9168, ext. 15015
Coordinating & promoting the efficient use of the Government's
financial & information resources are the chief responsibilities of
the Financial Management Board Secretariat. The central
agency, that supports the Minister of Finance, provides
leadership in functions related to governmental business
planning, information management, & program & service
evaluation. The FMBS also supports sustainable resource
development, self-government development, & the improvement
of programs & services.

Minister, Finance, Hon. Caroline Wawzonek

Secretary, William Mackay

Comptroller General, Julie Mujcin
Tel: 867-767-9015 ext: 14000

Northwest Territories Department of Health & Social Services (HSS)

PO Box 1320 Yellowknife, NT X1A 2L9
www.hss.gov.nt.ca
Other Communication: Media Relations, Phone: 867-920-8927;
Health Care Coverage/Vital Statistics: 800-661-0830
www.youtube.com/user/HSSCommunications

The Department of Health & Social Services is mandated to provide a broad range of health & social programs & services to the residents of the NWT. Seven regional Health & Social Services Authorities plan, manage & deliver a full spectrum of community & facility-based services for health care & social services. Community health programs include daily sick clinics, public health clinics, home care, school health programs & educational programs. Visiting physicians & specialists routinely visit the communities.

Minister, Hon. Julie Green

Deputy Minister, Bruce Cooper
Tel: 867-767-9050 ext: 49005
Bruce_Cooper@gov.nt.ca

Assistant Deputy Minister, Corporate Services, Derek Elkin
Tel: 867-767-9050 ext: 49001
Derek_Elkin@gov.nt.ca

Assistant Deputy Minister, Health Programs, Jo-Anne Hubert
Tel: 867-767-9050 ext: 49002
Jo-Anne_Hubert@gov.nt.ca

Chief Public Health Officer, Kami Kandola
Tel: 867-767-9063 ext: 49215
Kami_Kandola@gov.nt.ca

Associated Agencies, Boards & Commissions:
• **Dental Registration Committee**
PO Box 1320
Yellowknife, NT X1A 2L9

• **Medical Registration Committee**
PO Box 1320
Yellowknife, NT X1A 2L9

Finance

Director, Finance, Jeannie Mathison
Tel: 867-767-9056 ext: 49100

Information Services

Fax: 867-873-0280

Chief Information Officer, Michele Herriot
Tel: 867-767-9054 ext: 49065
Brad_Herriot@gov.nt.ca
Chief Health Privacy Officer, Jannet Leggett
Tel: 867-767-9052 ext: 49040
Jannet_Ann_Leggett@gov.nt.ca

Health Services Administration

Toll-Free: 800-661-0830

Director, Health Services Administration, Nick Saturnino
Tel: 867-777-7400
Registrar General, Vital Statistics, Janetta Day
Tel: 867-777-7422
Jannet_Ann_Leggett@gov.nt.ca

Policy, Legislation & Communications

Fax: 867-873-0204

Director, Policy, Legislation & Communications, Gary Toft
Tel: 867-767-9052 ext: 49018

Population Health

Fax: 867-873-0442

Director, Population Health, Laura Seddon
Tel: 867-767-9066 ext: 49253
Chief Environmental Health Officer, Peter Workman
Tel: 867-767-9066 ext: 49260
Territorial Epidemiologist, Epidemiology & Disease Registries, Heather Hannah
Tel: 867-767-9066 ext: 49285

Seniors & Continuing Care Services

Fax: 867-920-3088

Director, Victorine Lafferty
Tel: 867-767-9030 ext: 49205
Public Guardian, Beatrice Raddi
Tel: 867-767-9155 ext: 49460

Territorial Health Services

Fax: 867-873-0196

Director, Territorial Health Services, Carol Amirault
Tel: 867-767-9062 ext: 49190

Territorial Social Programs

Assistant Deputy Minister, Patricia Kyle
Tel: 867-767-9050 ext: 49009
Patricia_Kyle@gov.nt.ca
Director, Carolyn Wilkes
Tel: 867-767-9061 ext: 49159

Northwest Territories Health & Social Services Authority (NTHSSA)

PO Box 1320 Yellowknife, NT X1A 2L9
Tel: 867-767-9090
hss_transformation@gov.nt.ca
www.nthssa.ca

The NTHSSA was formed in Aug. 2016 as a result of the amalgamation of six regional health authorities: Beaufort-Delta Health & Social Services Authority, Dehcho Health & Social Services Authority, Fort Smith Health & Social Services Authority, Sahtu Health & Social Services Authority, Stanton Territorial Health Authority, & Yellowknife Health & Social Services Authority. The authority maintains regional operations in those areas.

Minister responsible, Hon. Julie Green

Chief Executive Officer, Sue Cullen
Tel: 867-767-9090 ext: 40000
Sue_Cullen@gov.nt.ca

Territorial Medical Director, Dr. AnneMarie Pegg

Territorial Director of Finance, Tamara Spong
Tel: 867-765-4002
Tamara_Spong@gov.nt.ca

Executive Director, Stanton Renewal, Gloria Badari
Tel: 867-767-9127 ext: 35002

Executive Director, Corporate & Support Services, Tim VanOverliw
Tel: 867-767-9107 ext: 40020

Executive Director, Clinical Integration & Leadership Mentor, Georgina Veldhorst
Tel: 867-767-9106 ext: 40000

Northwest Territories Housing Corporation

Scotia Centre, 5102 - 50th Ave., PO Box 2100 Yellowknife, NT X1A 2P6
Tel: 867-767-9080; *Fax:* 867-873-9426
Toll-Free: 844-698-4663
www.nwthc.gov.nt.ca
www.facebook.com/NWTHC

The mandate of the Northwest Territories Housing Corporation is to ensure, where necessary, a sufficient supply of affordable, adequate & suitable housing to meet the needs of residents. To accomplish this mandate, the corporation works with citizens, communities, Local Housing Organizations, aboriginal organizations, the business community, non-government organizations, & other governments.

Minister responsible, Hon. Paulie Chinna

President & CEO, Eleanor Young
Tel: 867-767-9080 ext: 85000

Associate Deputy Minister, James Fulford

Vice-President, Finance & Infrastructure Services, Jim Martin
Tel: 867-767-9080 ext: 85035
Jim_Martin@gov.nt.ca

Vice-President, Programs & District Operations, Franklin Carpenter
Tel: 867-767-9080 ext: 85100
Franklin_Carpenter@gov.nt.ca

Northwest Territories Department of Industry, Tourism & Investment (ITI)

PO Box 1320 Yellowknife, NT X1A 2L9
www.iti.gov.nt.ca
twitter.com/GNWT_ITI

The Department of Industry, Tourism & Investment promotes & supports economic prosperity & community self-reliance in the Northwest Territories by providing programs & services.

Minister, Hon. Caroline Wawzonek

Deputy Minister, Pamela Strand
Tel: 867-767-9060 ext: 63000

Assistant Deputy Minister, Economic Development, Tracy St. Denis
Tel: 867-767-9060 ext: 63002
Tracy_St-Denis@gov.nt.ca

Assistant Deputy Minister, Mineral & Petroleum Resources, John Ketchum
Tel: 867-767-9060 ext: 63004

Associated Agencies, Boards & Commissions:
• **Agricultural Products Marketing Council**
PO Box 1320
Yellowknife, NT X1A 2L9
Fax: 867-873-0563
Other Communication: Phone: 867-767-9060, ext. 63002
• **Northwest Territories Egg Producers Board**
7 Studney Dr.
PO Box 4386
Hay River, NT X0E 1G3
Tel: 867-874-0645; *Fax:* 867-874-6840
manager_nwteggproducers@yahoo.ca

Business Support, Trade & Economic Analysis

Director, David Nightingale
Tel: 867-767-9205 ext: 63080

Diamonds, Royalties & Financial Analysis

Fax: 867-873-0254

Director, Rhona Stanislaus
Tel: 867-767-9207 ext: 63135

Economic Diversification

Director, Joel Holder
Tel: 867-767-9219 ext: 63099
Film Commissioner & Acting Manager, Arts & Fine Crafts Programming, Camilla MacEachern
Tel: 867-767-9219 ext: 63095

Mineral Resources

The Minerals Resources division develops & implements strategies to encourage & attract non-renewable resource investment in the Northwest Territories. It also provides advice on the geological potential, industrial activity & potential opportunities associated with mineral exploration in the Territory.
Director, Menzie McEachern
Tel: 867-767-9209 ext: 63160

Northwest Territories Geological Survey (NTGS)

4601B - 52 Ave., PO Box 1320 Yellowknife, NT X1A 2L9
Tel: 867-767-9211; *Fax:* 867-873-2652
ntgs@gov.nt.ca
www.nwtgeoscience.ca

Northwest Territories Geological Survey (NTGS) advances the geoscience knowledge of the Northwest Territories for the benefit of northerners through: delivery of geoscience research; analysis of mineral & petroleum resources; excellence in data management. In collaboration with its partners, NTGS provides analysis, information & advice to individuals, communities, governments, & the mining & petroleum industry.
Director, Northwest Territories Geological Survey, John Ketchum
Tel: 867-767-9211 ext: 63200
John_Ketchum@gov.nt.ca

Petroleum Resources

Director, Menzie McEachern
Tel: 867-777-7475

Policy, Legislation & Communications

Other Communication: General Inquiries, Phone: 867-767-9202, ext. 63455

Director, Natasha Brotherston
Tel: 867-767-9202 ext: 63035

Tourism & Parks

Tel: 867-767-9206; *Fax:* 867-873-0163

Develops, operates & maintains facilities that include parks, visitor centres & interpretive displays. The division is also responsible for implementing the Protected Areas Strategy for the Northwest Territories, in conjunction with Canada's Federal Government & other stakeholders. The division also provides support for tourism marketing, research & product development.
Director, Tourism & Parks, Evan Walz
Tel: 867-767-9206 ext: 63116

Northwest Territories Department of Infrastructure

Stuart M. Hodgson Bldg., 5009 - 49th St., 3rd Fl., PO Box 1320 Yellowknife, NT X1A 2L9
INF_Communications@gov.nt.ca
www.inf.gov.nt.ca
Other Communication: Media Inquiries, Phone: 867-767-9082, ext. 31046

The Department is responsible for the following priorities throughout the territory: planning, design, construction, acquisition, operation & maintenance of public buildings & transportation infrastructure & systems; environmental assessment & remediation of public infrastructure; property management; procurement shared services; information management and technology; disposal of surplus property & goods; & motor vehicle & mechanical / electrical regulatory services.

Minister, Hon. Diane Archie

Deputy Minister, Joe Dragon

Assistant Deputy Minister, Regional Operations, Jayleen Robertson
Tel: 867-767-9040 ext: 31000
Jayleen_Robertson@gov.nt.ca

Air, Marine & Safety
Fax: 867-873-0297
Director, Delia Chesworth
Tel: 867-767-9084 ext: 31060

Compliance & Licensing
Director, Steve Loutitt
Tel: 867-767-9088 ext: 31165

Corporate Information Management
Director, Patrick Bisaillon
Tel: 867-767-9046 ext: 32128

Design & Technical Services
Fax: 867-873-0226
Estimates the cost of building construction & renovation; consults in the plan of buildings so they meet program needs; reviews consultant designs of buildings & works; implements the Safe Drinking Water Initiatives.
Director, Mark Cronk
Tel: 867-767-9048 ext: 32060

Energy
Fax: 867-873-0100
Director, Andrew Stewart
Tel: 867-767-9021 ext: 32021

Facilities & Properties
Director, Jackie Hall
Tel: 867-767-9048 ext: 32042

Fuel Services
Fax: 867-777-7373
Director, Curt Snook
Tel: 867-767-9084 ext: 31100
Director, Marine Transportation Services, Derrick Briggs
Tel: 867-767-9021 ext: 32017

IT Operations
Fax: 867-873-0135
Director, Laurie Gault
Tel: 867-767-9024 ext: 32206

Policy, Legislation & Communications
Director, Catherine Boyd
Tel: 867-767-9082 ext: 31042
Director, Strategic Infrastructure, Sonya Saunders
Tel: 867-767-9082 ext: 31035

Procurement & Shared Services
Director, Bill Kaip
Tel: 867-767-9044 ext: 32100

Programs & Services
Assistant Deputy Minister, John Vandenberg
Tel: 867-767-9021 ext: 32004
Director, Marine Informatics, Steve Hagerman
Tel: 867-444-7446
Director, Infrastructure & Business Solutions, Brian Nagel
Tel: 867-767-9048 ext: 32040

Transportation
Director, Binay Yadav
Tel: 867-767-9086 ext: 31105
Senior Program Manager, Major Projects, Dean Ahmet
Tel: 867-777-2716

Inuvialuit Water Board (IWB)

Mack Travel Bldg., 151 Mackenzie Rd., 2nd Fl., PO Box 2531 Yellowknife, NT X0E 0T0
Tel: 867-678-2942; *Fax:* 867-678-2943
info@inuvwb.ca
www.inuvwb.ca

Formerly known as the Northwest Territories Water Board, the board is responsible for licensing water use & waste disposal in the Inuvialuit Settlement Region located within the Northwest Territories, under the Waters Act.

Chair, Roger Connelly

Executive Director, Mardy Semmler
Tel: 867-678-8609
semmlerm@inuvwb.ca

Northwest Territories Department of Justice

4903 - 49th St., PO Box 1320 Yellowknife, NT X1A 2L9
Tel: 867-767-9256
justice_communications@gov.nt.ca
www.justice.gov.nt.ca
The following are some of the services offered by the Department of Justice: Aboriginal Rights Court Challenges Program; Access to Information & Protection of Privacy; Commissioner for Oaths / Notary Public; Coroner; Corporate Registries; Land Titles Office; Legal Aid; Maintenance Enforcement; Mental Disorder Review Board; Personal Property Registry; Public Trustee; Rental Office; Securities Registry; Victim Services; Witness Expense Assistance Program; & Youth Justice.

Minister, Hon. R.J. Simpson

Deputy Minister, Charlene Doolittle

Assistant Deputy Minister & Attorney General, Mark Aitken
Tel: 867-767-9070 ext: 82000
Mark_Aitken@gov.nt.ca

Assistant Deputy Minister & Solicitor General, Kim Schofield
Tel: 867-767-9070 ext: 82000
Kim_Schofield@gov.nt.ca

Chief Coroner, Coroner's Office, Cathy Menard
Tel: 867-767-9251 ext: 82035
Toll-free: 866-443-5553
Cathy_Menard@gov.nt.ca

Public Trustee, Public Trustee's Office, Brian Asmundson
Tel: 867-767-9252 ext: 82447
Brian_Asmundson@gov.nt.ca

Children's Lawyer, Ken Kinnear
Tel: 867-767-9253 ext: 82055; *Fax:* 867-873-0184
Ken_Kinnear@gov.nt.ca

Deputy Chief Coroner, Adriana Zibolenova
Tel: 867-767-9251 ext: 82036; *Fax:* 867-873-0426

Associated Agencies, Boards & Commissions:
• **Northwest Territories Judicial Renumeration Commission**
5204 Lundquist Rd.
Yellowknife, NT X1A 3G2
Tel: 867-873-6024

• **Northwest Territories Legal Aid Commission**
4915 - 48th St.
PO Box 1320
Yellowknife, NT X1A 2L9
Tel: 867-767-9361; *Fax:* 867-873-5320
Toll-free: 844-835-8050
lac@gov.nt.ca
www.justice.gov.nt.ca/en/boards-agencies/legal-aid-commission

• **Northwest Territories Maintenance Enforcement Program (MEP)**
YK Centre East
#17, 4915 - 48th St.
Yellowknife, NT X1A 3S4
Tel: 867-767-9258
Toll-free: 800-661-0798
mep@gov.nt.ca

• **Victims Assistance Committee**
c/o Community Justice Division
PO Box 1320
Yellowknife, NT X1A 2L9
Tel: 867-920-6911; *Fax:* 867-873-0199

Office of the Regulator of Oil & Gas Operations (OROGO)

Northwest Tower, 5201 - 50th Ave., 4th Fl., PO Box 1320 Yellowknife, NT X1A 2L9
Tel: 867-767-9097
www.orogo.gov.nt.ca
Other Communication: Incident Reporting: 867-445-8551
twitter.com/OROGO_NWT
OROGO is responsible for ensuring safety, environmental protection & conservation of oil & gas resources, by regulating oil & gas operations in the territory outside federal areas & the Inuvialuit Settlement Region.
Executive Director, Vacant
Tel: 867-767-9097 ext: 78001

Community Justice & Community Policing
Fax: 867-873-0199
Other Communication: URL: www.justice.gov.nt.ca/en/divisions/community-justice-and-policing-division
Director, Community Justice & Community Policing, Leanne Gardiner
Tel: 867-767-9261 ext: 82210

Corrections Service
www.justice.gov.nt.ca/en/divisions/corrections-division
Director, Corrections Service, Robert Riches
Tel: 867-767-9263 ext: 82478
Assistant Director, Community Corrections, Adrien Barrieau
Tel: 867-767-9263 ext: 82240
Assistant Director, Facility Operations, Blair Van Metre
Tel: 867-767-9263 ext: 92241

Court Services
Fax: 867-873-0307
www.justice.gov.nt.ca/en/divisions/court-services-division
Other Communication: Family Law Mediation Program, Toll Free Phone: 866-217-8923
Director, Court Services, Jeff Round
Tel: 867-767-9285 ext: 82335
Chief Court Reporter, Lois Hewitt
Tel: 867-767-9285 ext: 82345

NWT Courts
4903 - 49th St., PO Box 550 Yellowknife, NT X1A 2N4
Fax: 867-873-0291
Toll-Free: 866-822-5864
www.nwtcourts.ca
Other Communication: Territorial Court: 867-767-9289; Supreme Court: 867-767-9288
Court Administrator, Northwest Territories Courts Registry, Denise Bertolini
Tel: 867-767-9287 ext: 82350

Corporate Services
Director, Mandi Bolstad
Tel: 867-767-9250 ext: 82021

Legal Division
Fax: 867-873-0234
www.justice.gov.nt.ca/en/divisions/legal-division
Director, Brad Patzer
Tel: 867-767-9257 ext: 82110

Legal Registries
Fax: 867-873-0243
www.justice.gov.nt.ca/en/divisions/legal-registries-division
Director; Registrar, Corporate Registries; Superintendent, Securities Office, Tom Hall
Tel: 867-767-9260 ext: 82180

Legislation Division
Fax: 867-920-8898
www.justice.gov.nt.ca/en/divisions/legislation-division
Director, Mike C. Reddy
Tel: 867-767-9259 ext: 82155

Policy & Planning
Fax: 867-873-0659
www.justice.gov.nt.ca/en/divisions/policy-and-planning-division
Director, Policy & Planning, Richard Robertson
Tel: 867-767-9256 ext: 82081

Northwest Territories Department of Lands

Gallery Bldg., 4923 - 52nd St., 1st & 2nd Fl., PO Box 1320 Yellowknife, NT X1A 2L9
Tel: 867-767-9185; *Fax:* 867-669-0905
Toll-Free: 855-698-5263
Lands@gov.nt.ca
www.lands.gov.nt.ca
The Department of Lands manages, administers & plans for the sustainable use of public land in the Northwest Territories.

Minister, Hon. Shane Thompson

Deputy Minister, Jamie Koe

Assistant Deputy Minister, Operations, Conrad Baetz
Tel: 867-767-9035 ext: 24000
Conrad_Baetz@gov.nt.ca

Executive Director, SSC - Informatics, Rohan Sooklal
Tel: 867-767-9186 ext: 24125

Director, Land Use & Sustainability, Terry Hall
Tel: 867-767-9183 ext: 24065

Director, Policy, Legislation & Communication, Shauna Hamilton
Tel: 867-767-9182 ext: 24045

Director, Finance & Administration, Brenda Hilderman
Tel: 867-767-9181 ext: 24030

Director, Securities & Project Assessment, Lorraine Seale
Tel: 867-767-9180 ext: 24020

Lands Administration
Director, Blair Chapman
Tel: 867-767-9184 ext: 24090

Northwest Territories Department of Municipal & Community Affairs

PO Box 1320 Yellowknife, NT X1A 2L9
www.maca.gov.nt.ca
Supports capable, accountable & self-directed community governments providing a safe, sustainable & healthy environment for community residents. Works with community governments & other partners in supporting community residents as they organize & manage democratic, responsible & accountable community governments. The Department assists municipalities with administrative services & infrastructure project management, provides expertise in engineering to communities & arranges for debentures on behalf of communities which are undertaking public works programs. Advisory services are supplied to community councils for the planning, development & administration of public lands within municipal boundaries. Technical expertise is provided for mapping, surveying & air photography & zoning by-law administration.

Minister, Hon. Shane Thompson

Deputy Minister, Laura Gareau
Tel: 867-767-9160 ext: 21000

Assistant Deputy Minister, Disaster Assistance, Lorie Fyfe
Tel: 867-767-9160 ext: 21013

Associated Agencies, Boards & Commissions:
• **Assessment Appeal Tribunal**
c/o Secretary, Board of Revision
#400, 5201 - 50th Ave.
PO Box 1320
Yellowknife, NT X1A 2L9
Tel: 867-767-9161; *Fax:* 867-873-0609
• **Territorial Board of Revision**
c/o Secretary, Board of Revision
#400, 5201 - 50th Ave.
Yellowknife, NT X1A 2L9
Tel: 867-767-9161; *Fax:* 867-873-0609

Community Governance
Fax: 867-873-0584
Director, Lorie Fyfe
Tel: 867-767-9165 ext: 21085

Community Operations
Fax: 867-873-0584
Director, Community Operations, Grace Lau-a
Tel: 867-767-9164 ext: 21068

Corporate Affairs
Fax: 867-873-0309
Director, Gary Schauerte
Tel: 867-767-9162 ext: 21035

Public Safety
Tel: 867-767-9161; *Fax:* 867-873-0206
Other Communication: 24/7 Emergency Measures Office, Phone: 867-920-2303
Director, Kevin Brezinski
Tel: 867-767-9161 ext: 21020
Fire Marshal, Chucker Dewar
Tel: 867-767-9161 ext: 21026; *Fax:* 867-873-0206

School of Community Government
#500, 5201 - 50th Ave., PO Box 1320 Yellowknife, NT X1A 3S9
Tel: 867-767-9163; *Fax:* 867-873-0584
maca_scg@gov.nt.ca
www.maca.gov.nt.ca/en/school-community-government
Director, Dan Schofield
Tel: 867-767-9163 ext: 21055

Sport, Recreation & Youth
Fax: 867-920-6467
Director, Ian Legaree
Tel: 867-767-9166 ext: 21000

Northwest Territories Power Corporation

4 Capital Dr., Hay River, NT X0E 1G2
Tel: 867-874-5200
Toll-Free: 800-661-0855
info@ntpc.com
www.ntpc.com
Other Communication: Billing inquiries: customercare@ntpc.com
twitter.com/NTPC_News
www.facebook.com/591764887576712
The NWT Power Corporation serves approximately 43,000 people in 33 communities across the Northwest Territories. Facilities include hydro-electric, diesel & natural gas generation plants, transmission systems, & several isolated electrical distribution systems. The Corporation works to provide environmentally sound, safe, reliable, cost-effective energy & related services in the territories.

Minister responsible, Hon. Diane Archie

Chair, Steve Loutitt

Acting President & CEO; Chief Financial Officer, Cory Strang

Chief Projects & Engineering Officer, Kumar Balachandran

Chief Operating Officer, Belinda Whitford

Public Utilities Board of the Northwest Territories (PUB)

#203, 62 Woodland Dr., PO Box 4211 Hay River, NT X0E 1G1
Tel: 867-874-3944; *Fax:* 867-874-3639
www.nwtpublicutilitiesboard.ca
The independent, quasi-judicial agency of the Government of the Northwest Territories is responsible for the regulation of public utilities in the territory. Its authority is from the Public Utilities Act. Issues are handled by an application & decision process.

Minister responsible, Hon. Paulie Chinna

Chair, Gordon Van Tighem

Vice-Chair, Tina Gargan

Board Secretary, Louise-Ann Beaulieu
louise-ann_beaulieu@gov.nt.ca

Status of Women Council of the Northwest Territories

Northwest Tower, 4th Fl., PO Box 1320 Yellowknife, NT X1A 2L9
Toll-Free: 888-234-4485
www.statusofwomen.nt.ca
twitter.com/StatusofWomenNT
www.facebook.com/113623588652526
www.youtube.com/user/statusofwomennwt
To work towards the equality of women through advice to the government; research; public education; advocacy on behalf of women; & workshops & other support for the development of women's groups, & other groups working on issues of concern to women.

Minister responsible, Hon. Caroline Wawzonek

President, Violet Camsell-Blondin

Executive Director, Louise Elder
Tel: 867-920-6177

Manager, Programs & Research, Annemieke Mulders
Tel: 867-920-8994

Northwest Territories & Nunavut Workers' Safety & Compensation Commission (WSCC)

Centre Square Tower, 5022 - 49th St., 5th Fl., PO Box 8888 Yellowknife, NT X1A 2R3
Tel: 867-920-3888; *Fax:* 867-873-4596
Toll-Free: 800-661-0792
www.wscc.nt.ca
Other Communication: Toll-Free Fax: 866-277-3677
Secondary Address: 630 Queen Elizabeth II Way
Oamutiq Bldg., 2nd Fl.PO Box 669 Sta.
Iqaluit, NU X0A 0H0
Alt. Fax: 867-979-8501
twitter.com/WSCCNTNU
www.facebook.com/WSCCNTNU
The Workers' Safety & Compensation Commission is engaged in the following activities: ensuring compensation & pensions are awarded to injured workers or their dependents; assessing sufficiently & fairly to meet obligations; maintaining balance in providing benefits to injured workers, while keeping costs to employers as low as possible; & promoting safe workplaces through education & enforcement.

Minister responsible (Northwest Territories), Hon. Paulie Chinna

Minister responsible (Nunavut), Hon. George Hickes
Tel: 867-975-5074; *Fax:* 867-975-2034
ghickes@gov.nu.ca

Chair, Jenni Bruce

President & CEO, Debbie Molloy
Tel: 867-669-4442

Vice-President, Corporate Services, Harmeet Jagpal
Tel: 867-669-4446

Vice-President, Financial Services, Len MacDonald
Tel: 867-920-3824

Chief Inspector of Mines, Fred Bailey
Tel: 867-669-4430

Chief Safety Officer, Bert Hausauer
Tel: 867-920-3876

Communications Officer, Ashley Makohoniuk
Tel: 867-446-4416

Government of Nova Scotia

Seat of Government: Province House, 1726 Hollis St., Halifax, NS B3J 2Y3
Toll-Free: 800-670-4357
TTY: 877-404-0867
novascotia.ca
twitter.com/nsgov
www.facebook.com/nsgov
www.linkedin.com/company/government-of-nova-scotia
www.youtube.com/user/nsgov
The Province of Nova Scotia entered Confederation July 1, 1867. It has a land area of 52,942.27 sq km, & the StatsCan census population in 2016 was 923,598.

Office of the Lieutenant Governor

Government House, 1451 Barrington St., Halifax, NS B3J 1Z2
Tel: 902-424-7001; *Fax:* 902-424-1790
lgoffice@novascotia.ca
lt.gov.ns.ca
Other Communication: Invitation to the Lieutenant Governor, Email: invite-lg@novascotia.ca
twitter.com/LtGovNS
www.facebook.com/LtGovNS
www.flickr.com/photos/lieutenantgovernor

Lieutenant Governor of Nova Scotia, Hon. Arthur Joseph LeBlanc, ONS, QC
Note: On June 14, 2017, Prime Minister Trudeau named Arthur Joseph LeBlanc as Nova Scotia's 33rd Lieutenant Governor. He was officially sworn in on June 28, 2017.

Executive Director, Government House; Private Secretary to the Lieutenant Governor, Christopher McCreery, MVO

Chief Commissionaire, Brian Graves, CWO

Chief Aide-de-Camp, Donald R. Moser, AdeC

Coordinator, In-house Events, Kelly Clelland

Office of the Premier

One Government Place, 1700 Granville St., 7th Fl., PO Box 726 Halifax, NS B3J 2T3
Tel: 902-424-6600; *Fax:* 902-424-7648
Toll-Free: 800-267-1993
premier@novascotia.ca
premier.novascotia.ca
The Honorable Tim Houston became Premier of Nova Scotia in the General Election of Aug. 17, 2021.

Premier & President, Executive Council, Hon. Tim Houston
Tel: 902-424-6600; *Fax:* 902-424-7648
premier@novascotia.ca

Deputy Premier & Deputy President, Executive Council, Hon. Allan MacMaster
Tel: 902-258-2216; *Fax:* 902-258-3231
mlamacmaster@bellaliant.com

Chief of Staff, Joanne MacRae

Chief Regulatory Officer, Office of Regulatory Affairs & Service Effectiveness, Fred Crooks
Fred.Crooks@NovaScotia.ca

Executive Council Office (ECO)

One Government Place, 1700 Granville St., 5th Fl., PO Box 2125 Halifax, NS B3J 3B7
Tel: 902-424-8940; *Fax:* 902-424-0667
Toll-Free: 866-206-6844
Executive.Council@novascotia.ca
www.novascotia.ca/exec_council
Other Communication: ABC Inquiries: 902-424-4877
The Executive Branch of government consists of ministers / Members of the Executive Council, who collectively form the Cabinet. Under the Executive Council Act, ministers are chosen by the Premier & appointed by the Lieutenant Governor. Led by the Premier / President of the Executive Council, The Executive Council Office (ECO) serves the Cabinet & its committees. In January 2016, the Office of Planning & Priorities was merged into the ECO.

Premier; President, Executive Council; Leader, Progressive Conservative Party of Nova Scotia; Minister, Intergovernmental Affairs; Minister, Trade; Minister, Regulatory Affairs & Service Effectiveness, Hon. Tim Houston, ECNS
Tel: 90- 42- 660; *Fax:* 902-424-7648
premier@novascotia.ca

Deputy Premier; Deputy President, Executive Council; Minister, Finance & Treasury Board; Minister, Labour Relations; Minister, Gaelic Affairs; Minister responsible, Credit Union Act; Insurance Act / Insurance Premiums Tax Act; Liquor Control Act; & others, Hon. Allan MacMaster
Tel: 902-424-5720; *Fax:* 902-424-0635
FinanceMinister@novascotia.ca
Note: Also Minister responsible for: Nova Scotia Liquor Corporation; Gaming Control Act, Part I; Securities Act; Utility & Review Board Act; Chartered Professional Accountants Act

Minister, Seniors & Long-term Care, Hon. Barbara Adams
Tel: 902-424-0770; *Fax:* 902-424-0561
seniorsmin@novascotia.ca

Minister, Labour Skills & Immigration; Minister responsible, Apprenticeship & Trades Qualifications Act; Workers' Compensation Act (except Part II), Hon. Jill S. Balser
Tel: 902-424-5230; *Fax:* 902-424-7936
ImmigrationMinister@novascotia.ca

Minister, Communications Nova Scotia; Minister responsible, Office of Mental Health & Addictions; Youth, Hon. Brian Comer
Tel: 902-424-3839; *Fax:* 902-424-3458
cnsminister@novascotia.ca

Minister, Economic Development; Minister responsible, Nova Scotia Business Incorporated; Innovation Corporation Act, Hon. Susan Corkum-Greek
Tel: 902-424-0377
IEGMinister@novascotia.ca

Minister, Fisheries & Aquaculture, Hon. Steve Craig
Tel: 902-424-8953; *Fax:* 902-428-3145
mindfa@novascotia.ca

Minister, Education & Early Childhood Development, Hon. Becky Druhan

Tel: 902-424-4236; *Fax:* 902-424-0680
educmin@novascotia.ca

Minister, Communities, Culture, Tourism & Heritage; Minister, African Nova Scotian Affairs; Minister responsible, Office of Equity & Anti-Racism Initiatives; Heritage Property Act; Voluntary Sector, Hon. Pat Dunn
Tel: 902-424-4889
min_cch@novascotia.ca

Minister, Environment & Climate Change; Chair, Treasury & Policy Board, Hon. Tim Halman
Tel: 902-424-3736; *Fax:* 902-424-1599
Minister.Environment@novascotia.ca

Attorney General & Minister, Justice; Provincial Secretary; Minister responsible, Elections Act; Human Rights Act; Regulations Act; Workers' Compensation Act, Part II; Accessibility Act; & others, Hon. Brad Johns
Tel: 902-424-4030
justmin@novascotia.ca
Note: Also Minister responsible for: Retail Business Uniform Closing Act; Nova Scotia Police Complaints Commissioner; Nova Scotia Police Review Board

Minister, Public Service Commission; Minister, Service Nova Scotia & Internal Services; Minister, Acadian Affairs & Francophonie; Minister responsible, Gaming Control Act, Part II; Residential Tenancies Act, Hon. Colton LeBlanc
Tel: 902-424-5465; *Fax:* 902-424-0555
min_psc@novascotia.ca

Minister, Municipal Affairs and Housing; Minister responsible, Office of Emergency Management; Military Relations, Hon. John Lohr
Tel: 902-424-4889; *Fax:* 902-424-4872
dmamin@novascotia.ca
Other Communications: Emergency Management Office:
emo@novascotia.ca

Minister, Community Services; Minister, L'nu Affairs; Minister responsible, Advisory Council on the Status of Women Act, Hon. Karla MacFarlane
Toll-free: 87- 42- 117; *Fax:* 902-424-3287
dcsmin@novascotia.ca
Other Communications: Status of Women:
women@novascotia.ca

Minister, Public Works; Minister responsible, Sydney Tar Ponds Agency (NS); Sydney Steel Corporation Act, Hon. Kim Masland
Tel: 902-424-2297; *Fax:* 902-424-0532
tirmin@novascotia.ca

Minister, Agriculture; Minister responsible, Maritime Provinces Harness Racing Commission Act, Hon. Greg Morrow
Tel: 902-424-4388; *Fax:* 902-424-0699
min_dag@novascotia.ca

Minister, Natural Resources & Renewables, Hon. Tory Rushton
Tel: 902-424-5935; *Fax:* 902-424-7735
mindnr@novascotia.ca

Minister, Health & Wellness; Minister responsible, Office of Healthcare Professionals Recruitment, Hon. Michelle Thompson
Tel: 902-424-5818; *Fax:* 902-424-0559
Health.Minister@novascotia.ca

Minister, Advanced Education, Hon. Brian Wong
Tel: 902-424-7628; *Fax:* 902-424-0651

Legislative House of Assembly

Province House, 1726 Hollis St., Halifax, NS B3J 2Y3
Tel: 902-424-5978; *Fax:* 902-424-0632
info@nslegislature.ca
nslegislature.ca
twitter.com/nsleg
www.facebook.com/NSLeg
www.youtube.com/c/NovaScotiaLegislature

Chief Clerk of the House, James Charlton

Speaker, House of Assembly, Hon. Keith Bain
Tel: 902-424-5707; *Fax:* 902-424-0632
speaker@novascotia.ca
Office of the Speaker, Province House, 1st Fl.
PO Box 1617
Halifax, NS B3J 1X5

Deputy Speaker, Lisa Lachance

Deputy Speaker, Angela Simmonds

Sergeant-at-Arms, David Fraser
Tel: 902-424-4603
David.Fraser@novascotia.ca

Chief Legislative Counsel, Gordon D. Hebb
Tel: 902-424-8941; *Fax:* 902-424-0547
Legc.office@novascotia.ca
Office of the Legislative Counsel, CIBC Bldg.
#802, 1809 Barrington St.
PO Box 1116
Halifax, NS B3J 2X1

Commissioner, Conflict of Interest, Hon. Joseph P. Kennedy
conflict.commissioner@novascotia.ca
PO Box 1617
Halifax, NS B3J 1X5

Legislative Librarian, David McDonald
Tel: 902-424-5932
leglib@novascotia.ca
Legislative Library, Province House, 2nd Fl.
1726, Hollis St.
Halifax, NS B3J 2P8

Editor, Hansard, Mike Chandler
Tel: 902-424-5706; *Fax:* 902-424-0593
publications@novascotia.ca
Note:
nslegislature.ca/about/supporting-offices/hansard-reporting-services
#600, 1800 Argyle St.
Halifax, NS B3J 2V9

Government Caucus Office (Progressive Conservative Party)
PC Caucus Office, #1001, 1660 Hollis St., Halifax, NS B3J 1V7
Fax: 902-424-7484
Toll-Free: 800-363-1998
pcmlas@gov.ns.ca
www.pcparty.ns.ca
twitter.com/nspc
Premier; Leader, Progressive Conservative Party of Nova Scotia, Hon. Tim Houston
Tel: 902-424-2731; *Fax:* 902-424-7484
premier@novascotia.ca
Government Caucus Chair, Hon. Karla MacFarlane
pictouwestmla@bellaliant.com
Government Whip, Vacant
President, Progressive Conservative Party of Nova Scotia, David Bond

Office of the Official Opposition (Liberal Party)
Nova Scotia Liberal Caucus Office, #1400, 5151 George St., PO Box 723 Halifax, NS B3J 2T3
Tel: 902-429-1993; *Fax:* 902-423-1624
office@liberal.ns.ca
liberal.ns.ca
twitter.com/NSLiberal
www.facebook.com/LiberalPartyNS
www.youtube.com/c/LiberalPartyNS
Leader, Official Opposition; Leader, Nova Scotia Liberal Party, Hon. Iain Rankin, ECNS
Tel: 902-404-7036; *Fax:* 902-404-7056
info@iainrankin.ca
Opposition Caucus Chair & Whip, Rafah DiCostanzo
Tel: 902-443-8318; *Fax:* 902-445-9287
rafah@rafahdicostanzo.com
Opposition House Leader, Vacant
President, Nova Scotia Liberal Party, Joseph Khoury

Office of the New Democratic Party
New Democratic Party Caucus Office, Centennial Bldg., #603, 5151 George St., Halifax, NS B3J 1M5
Tel: 902-423-9217
Toll-Free: 800-753-7696
nsndp.ca
twitter.com/nsndp
www.facebook.com/nsndp
Leader, New Democratic Party of Nova Scotia, Gary Burrill
Tel: 902-424-4134; *Fax:* 902-424-0504
gary@nsndp.ca
Note: Gary Burrill became the new Leader of the Nova Scotia NDP on Feb. 27, 2016. He was unelected at the time, but won the riding of Halifax Chebucto in the 2017 general election.

Caucus Chair, New Democratic Party of Nova Scotia, Susan Leblanc
susanleblancMLA@bellaliant.com
House Leader, New Democratic Party of Nova Scotia, Claudia Chender
ClaudiaChenderMLA@gmail.com
Caucus Whip, New Democratic Party of Nova Scotia, Kendra Coombes
kendracoombesmla@gmail.com
President, New Democratic Party of Nova Scotia, Jodi McDavid

Standing Committees of the House

Committee Room, One Government Place, 1700 Granville St., 2nd Fl., PO Box 2630 Stn. M, Halifax, NS B3J 3P7
Tel: 902-424-4432; *Fax:* 902-424-0513
legcomm@novascotia.ca
nslegislature.ca/legislative-business/committees
Legislative committees are appointed by the Nova Scotia House of Assembly & are comprised of Members of the House. The committee system allows for detailed examination of matters in a manner which would not be possible in the larger House & also allows members of the public to have direct input into the parliamentary process by making submissions & attending public hearings.
The following are the Standing Committees of the Legislative House of Assembly of Nova Scotia: Assembly Matters; Community Services; Health; Human Resources; Internal Affairs; Law Amendments; Natural Resources & Economic Development; Private & Local Bills; Public Accounts; & Veterans Affairs.

Clerk of Committees, David Hastings
Tel: 902-424-7481
David.Hastings@novascotia.ca
Committee Clerk, Heather Hoddinott
Tel: 902-424-5248
Heather.Hoddinott@novascotia.ca
Committee Clerk, Judy Kavanagh
Tel: 902-424-4494
Judy.Kavanagh@novascotia.ca
Committee Clerk, Kim Langille
Tel: 902-424-5247
Kim.Langille@novascotia.ca
Chief Legislative Counsel, Gordon Hebb, Q.C.
Tel: 902-424-8941; *Fax:* 902-424-0547
Legc.office@novascotia

Sixty-fourth General Assembly - Nova Scotia

Province House, 1726 Hollis St., Halifax, NS B3J 2Y3
Tel: 902-424-4661; *Fax:* 902-424-0574
nslegislature.ca

Last General Election, Aug. 17, 2021.
Maximum Duration, 5 years.
Party Standings (Oct. 2021):
Progressive Conservative 31;
Liberal 17;
New Democratic Party 6;
Independent 1;
Total: 55.
MLA Remuneration (January 2013):
MLA Indemnity $89,234.90;
Additional Indemnity:
Premier $112,791.20;
Speaker $49,046.51;
Deputy Speaker $24,523.25;
Minister with portfolio $49,046.51;
Minister without portfolio $49,046.51;
Leader of the Opposition $49,046.51;
Leader of a Recognized Opposition Party $24,523.25.
The following list features members, with their constituency, the number of electors on the official list for the 2021 provincial general election, party affiliation, & contact information:

Members of the Legislative Assembly of Nova Scotia
Minister, Seniors & Long-term Care, Hon. Barbara Adams
Constituency: Eastern Passage *No. of Constituents:* 10,512, Progressive Conservative
Tel: 902-424-0770; *Fax:* 902-424-0561
seniorsmin@novascotia.ca
Other Communications: Constituency Phone: 902-406-0656; Fax: 902-406-0070
www.facebook.com/BarbaraAdamsFORColeHarbourEastern Passage
Constituency Office
1488 Main Rd.
PO Box 116
Eastern Passage, NS B3G 1M5
Patricia Arab
Constituency: Fairview-Clayton Park *No. of Constituents:* 15,854, Liberal
Tel: 902-424-8637; *Fax:* 902-424-0539
info@patriciaarab.ca
www.patriciaarab.ca
Other Communications: Constituency Phone: 902-329-8683;

Fax: 902-444-7530
twitter.com/patriciaarab, www.facebook.com/PatriciaArab
Constituency Office
#203, 3845 Joseph Howe Dr.
Halifax, NS B3I 4H9
Speaker, House of Assembly, Hon. Keith Bain
Constituency: Victoria-The Lakes *No. of Constituents:* 12,690, Progressive Conservative
Tel: 902-424-2731; *Fax:* 902-424-7484
keithbainmla@bellaliant.com
Other Communications: Constituency Phone: 902-736-0301; Fax: 902-736-0411
www.facebook.com/keith.bain.334
Constituency Office
1415 Hwy. 105
Bras d'Or, NS B1Y 2N5
Minister, Labour Skills & Immigration; Minister responsible, Apprenticeship & Trades Qualifications Act; Workers' Compensation Act (except Part II), Hon. Jill S. Balser
Constituency: Digby-Annapolis *No. of Constituents:* 10,075, Progressive Conservative
Tel: 90- 42- 523; *Fax:* 902-424-7936
ImmigrationMinister@novascotia.ca
twitter.com/jillbalser
Danielle Barkhouse
Constituency: Chester-St. Margaret's *No. of Constituents:* 15,191, Progressive Conservative
Tel: 902-424-2731; *Fax:* 902-424-7484
pcbarkhouse@gmail.com
twitter.com/barkhouse4mla,
www.facebook.com/Barkhouse4MLA
Trevor Boudreau
Constituency: Richmond *No. of Constituents:* 7,658, Progressive Conservative
Tel: 902-424-2731; *Fax:* 902-424-7484
trevorboudreaupc@gmail.com
twitter.com/boudreaudr,
www.facebook.com/TrevorBoudreauNS
Leader, New Democratic Party of Nova Scotia, Gary Burrill
Constituency: Halifax Chebucto *No. of Constituents:* 12,481, New Democratic Party
Tel: 902-424-4134; *Fax:* 902-424-0504
garyburrillmla@gmail.com
Other Communications: Constituency Phone: 902-454-8365
twitter.com/garyburrill, www.facebook.com/GaryBurrillNDP
Constituency Office
#102, 6208 Quinpool Rd.
Halifax, NS B3L 1A3
House Leader, New Democratic Party of Nova Scotia, Claudia Chender
Constituency: Dartmouth South *No. of Constituents:* 13,721, New Democratic Party
Tel: 902-424-4134; *Fax:* 902-424-0504
claudiachendermla@gmail.com
Other Communications: Constituency Phone: 902-406-2301; Fax: 902-406-2275
www.linkedin.com/in/claudia-chender-02533412
Constituency Office
#120, 33 Ochterloney St.
Dartmouth, NS B2Y 4P5
Zach Churchill
Constituency: Yarmouth *No. of Constituents:* 14,041, Liberal
Tel: 902-424-8637; *Fax:* 902-424-0539
ca@zachchurchill.com
Other Communications: Constituency Phone: 902-742-4444; Fax: 902-742-7391
twitter.com/zachchurchill,
www.facebook.com/ZachChurchillNS
Constituency Office
#100, 396 Main St.
Yarmouth, NS B5A 1E9
Braedon Clark
Constituency: Bedford South *No. of Constituents:* 14,085, Liberal
Tel: 902-424-8637; *Fax:* 902-424-0539
braedon.bedfordsouth@gmail.com
twitter.com/Braedon_Clark,
www.facebook.com/BraedonClarkforBedfordSouth
Minister, Communications Nova Scotia; Minister responsible, Office of Mental Health & Addictions; Youth, Hon. Brian Comer
Constituency: Cape Breton East *No. of Constituents:* 13,801, Progressive Conservative
Tel: 902-424-3839; *Fax:* 902-424-3458
CNSMinister@novascotia.ca
Caucus Whip, New Democratic Party, Kendra Coombes
Constituency: Cape Breton Centre-Whitney Pier *No. of Constituents:* 14,705, New Democratic Party
Tel: 902-424-4134; *Fax:* 902-424-0504
kendracoombesmla@gmail.com
Other Communications: Constituency Phone: 902-862-6337
Constituency Office
3365 Plummer Ave.
New Waterford, NS B1H 1Y8

Minister, Economic Development; Minister responsible, Nova Scotia Business Incorporated; Innovation Corporation Act, Hon. Susan Corkum-Greek
Constituency: Lunenburg *No. of Constituents:* 14,555, Progressive Conservative
Tel: 902-424-0377
IEGMinister@novascotia.ca
www.facebook.com/susan.corkumgreek
Minister, Fisheries & Aquaculture, Hon. Steve Craig
Constituency: Sackville-Cobequid *No. of Constituents:* 15,318, Progressive Conservative
Tel: 902-424-8953; *Fax:* 902-428-3145
mindfa@novascotia.ca
Other Communications: Constituency Phone: 902-864-6271; Fax: 902-864-0483
Note: Steve Craig was first elected in a by-election held June 18, 2019.
Constituency Office
#104, 445 Sackville Dr.
Lower Sackville, NS B4C 2S1
Opposition Caucus Chair & Whip, Rafah DiCostanzo
Constituency: Clayton Park West *No. of Constituents:* 14,422, Liberal
Tel: 902-424-8637; *Fax:* 902-424-0539
Rafah@Rafahdicostanzo.com
Other Communications: Constituency Phone: 902-443-8318; Fax: 902-445-9287
twitter.com/rafahdicostanzo,
www.facebook.com/RafahDiCostanzoNS,
www.linkedin.com/in/rafah-dicostanzo-b2495315
Constituency Office
#201, 397 Bedford Hwy.
Halifax, NS B3M 2L3
Minister, Education & Early Childhood Development, Hon. Becky Druhan
Constituency: Lunenburg West *No. of Constituents:* 16,484, Progressive Conservative
Tel: 902-424-4236; *Fax:* 902-424-0680
educmin@novascotia.ca
twitter.com/beckydruhan,
www.facebook.com/BeckyDruhanNS
Ali Duale
Constituency: Halifax Armdale *No. of Constituents:* 14,131, Liberal
Tel: 902-424-8637; *Fax:* 902-424-0539
twitter.com/Aliduale1
Minister, Communities, Culture, Tourism & Heritage; Minister, African Nova Scotian Affairs; Minister responsible, Office of Equity & Anti-Racism Initiatives; Heritage Property Act; Voluntary Sector, Hon. Pat Dunn
Constituency: Pictou Centre *No. of Constituents:* 12,916, Progressive Conservative
Tel: 902-424-4889
min_cch@novascotia.ca
Other Communications: Constituency Phone: 902-752-3646; Fax: 902-752-6571
Constituency Office
#3, 342 Stewart St.
New Glasgow, NS B2H 2R7
Minister, Environment & Climate Change; Chair, Treasury & Policy Board, Hon. Tim Halman
Constituency: Dartmouth East *No. of Constituents:* 14,607, Progressive Conservative
Tel: 902-424-3736; *Fax:* 902-424-1599
Minister.Environment@novascotia.ca
Other Communications: Constituency Phone: 902-469-7353; Fax: 902-469-7351
www.facebook.com/timhalmanpc
Constituency Office
73 Tacoma Dr., 2nd Fl.
Dartmouth, NS B2W 3Y6
Suzy Hansen
Constituency: Halifax Needham *No. of Constituents:* 16,957, New Democratic Party
Tel: 902-424-4134; *Fax:* 902-424-0504
suzyhalifaxneedham@gmail.com
Other Communications: Constituency Phone: 902-455-7300; Fax: 902-455-7668
twitter.com/suzyhfx,
www.facebook.com/SuzyHalifaxNeedham
Constituency Office
#1000, 6080 Young St.
Halifax, NS B3K 5L2
Larry Harrison
Constituency: Colchester-Musquodoboit Valley *No. of Constituents:* 14,321, Progressive Conservative
Tel: 902-424-2731; *Fax:* 902-424-7484
larryharrisonmla@gmail.com
Other Communications: Constituency Phone: 902-639-1010; Fax: 902-639-2598
www.linkedin.com/in/larry-harrison-476b3713b
Constituency Office
87 Main St. West

PO Box 219
Stewiacke, NS B0N 2J0
Premier; President, Executive Council; Leader, Progressive Conservative Party of Nova Scotia; Minister, Intergovernmental Affairs; Minister, Trade; Minister, Regulatory Affairs & Service Effectiveness, Hon. Tim Houston
Constituency: Pictou East *No. of Constituents:* 11,532, Progressive Conservative
Tel: 902-424-5153; *Fax:* 902-424-0728
premier@novascotia.ca
Other Communications: Constituency Phone: 902-695-3582; Fax: 902-695-3581
twitter.com/TimHoustonNS, www.facebook.com/TimHoustonNS
Constituency Office, Site 40, Mod 7, Comp 7, RR#2
2042 Queen St.
Westville, NS B0K 2A0

Tony Ince
Constituency: Cole Harbour *No. of Constituents:* 10,051, Liberal
Tel: 902-424-8637; *Fax:* 902-424-0539
twitter.com/tonyincens

Keith Irving
Constituency: Kings South *No. of Constituents:* 16,531, Liberal
Tel: 902-424-8637; *Fax:* 902-424-0539
keith@irvingmla.ca
Other Communications: Constituency Phone: 902-542-0050; Fax: 902-542-3423
twitter.com/keithirvingns, www.facebook.com/KeithIrvingNS
Constituency Office
#3, 24 Harbourside Dr.
PO Box 2455
Wolfville, N B4P 2C1

Ben Jessome
Constituency: Hammonds Plains-Lucasville *No. of Constituents:* 13,995, Liberal
Tel: 902-424-8637; *Fax:* 902-424-0539
jessomeben@gmail.com
Other Communications: Constituency Phone: 902-404-9900; Fax: 902-404-8415
twitter.com/BenJessome, www.facebook.com/BenJessomeNS
Constituency Office
#3, 2120 Hammonds Plains Rd.
Hammonds Plains, NS B4B 1P3

Attorney General; Minister, Justice; Provincial Secretary; Minister responsible, Elections Act; Human Rights Act; Regulations Act; Workers' Compensation Act, Part II; Retail Business Uniform Closing Act; Accessibility Act, Hon. Brad Johns
Constituency: Sackville-Uniacke *No. of Constituents:* 13,809, Progressive Conservative
Tel: 902-424-4030
justmin@novascotia.ca
Other Communications: Constituency Phone: 902-865-6467
www.facebook.com/bradjohns.ca
Note: Also Minister responsible for the Nova Scotia Police Review Board
Constituency Office
#103, 1710 Sackville Dr.
Middle Sackville, NS B4E 3A9

Carman Kerr
Constituency: Annapolis *No. of Constituents:* 14,821, Liberal
Tel: 902-424-8637
Toll-free: 800-317-8533; *Fax:* 902-424-0539
Other Communications: Constituency Phone: 902-825-2093; Fax: 902-825-6306
Constituency Office
#2, 291 Marshall St.
PO Box 1420
Middleton, NS B0S 1P0

Lisa Lachance
Constituency: Halifax Citadel-Sable Island *No. of Constituents:* 16,444, New Democratic Party
Tel: 902-424-4134; *Fax:* 902-424-0504
lisalachancendp@gmail.com
twitter.com/lisalachancendp,
www.facebook.com/LisaLachanceNDP,
www.linkedin.com/in/lisa-lachance-41828731

Minister, Public Service Commission; Minister, Service Nova Scotia & Internal Services; Minister, Acadian Affairs & Francophonie; Minister responsible, Gaming Control Act, Part II; Residential Tenancies Act, Hon. Colton F. LeBlanc
Constituency: Argyle *No. of Constituents:* 6,583, Progressive Conservative
Tel: 902-424-5465; *Fax:* 902-424-0555
min_psc@novascotia.ca
www.facebook.com/ColtonLeBlancNS
Note: Colton LeBlanc was first elected in a by-election held Sept. 3, 2019.

Ronnie LeBlanc
Constituency: Clare *No. of Constituents:* 6,919, Liberal
Tel: 902-424-8637; *Fax:* 902-424-0539

Caucus Chair, New Democratic Party of Nova Scotia, Susan Leblanc
Constituency: Dartmouth North *No. of Constituents:* 16,392, New Democratic Party
Tel: 902-424-4134; *Fax:* 902-424-0504
susanleblancMLA@bellaliant.com
www.susanleblanc.ca
Other Communications: Constituency Phone: 902-463-6670; Fax: 902-463-6676
twitter.com/dartmouthsue, www.facebook.com/DANONSNDP
Constituency Office
#102, 260 Wyse Rd.
Dartmouth, NS B3A 1N3

Minister, Municipal Affairs & Housing; Minister responsible, Office of Emergency Management; Military Relations, Hon. John A. Lohr
Constituency: Kings North *No. of Constituents:* 16,115, Progressive Conservative
Tel: 902-424-6642
dmamin@novascotia.ca
www.johnlohr.ca
Other Communications: Constituency Phone: 902-365-3420; Fax: 902-365-3422
www.facebook.com/JohnLohrKingsNorth
Constituency Office
347 Main St.
Kentville, NS B4N 1K7

John A. MacDonald
Constituency: Hants East *No. of Constituents:* 17,464, Progressive Conservative
Tel: 902-424-2731; *Fax:* 902-424-7484
johna@johnamacdonald.ca
www.facebook.com/ElectJohnA,
www.linkedin.com/in/john-a-macdonald-133a832

Government Caucus Chair; Minister, Community Services; Minister, L'nu Affairs; Minister responsible, Advisory Council on the Status of Women Act, Hon. Karla MacFarlane
Constituency: Pictou West *No. of Constituents:* 11,398, Progressive Conservative
Toll-free: 877-424-1177; *Fax:* 90- 42- 328
dcsmin@novascotia.ca
Other Communications: Constituency Phone: 902-485-8958; Fax: 902-485-5135
twitter.com/karla_macf_pc,
www.facebook.com/KarlaMacFarlaneNS
Constituency Office
25B Front St.
PO Box 310
Pictou, NS B0K 1H0

Deputy Premier; Deputy President, Executive Council; Minister, Finance & Treasury Board; Minister, Labour Relations; Minister, Gaelic Affairs; Minister responsible, Credit Union Act; Insurance Act / Insurance Premiums Tax Act; Liquor Control Act; & others, Hon. Allan MacMaster
Constituency: Inverness *No. of Constituents:* 14,140, Progressive Conservative
Tel: 902-424-5720; *Fax:* 902-424-0635
FinanceMinister@novascotia.ca
Other Communications: Constituency Phone: 902-258-2216; Fax: 902-258-3231
www.facebook.com/AllanMacMasterInverness
Note: Also Minister responsible for: Nova Scotia Liquor Corporation; Gaming Control Act, Part I; Securities Act; Utility & Review Board Act; Chartered Professional Accountants Act
Constituency Office
15759 Central Ave.
Inverness, NS B0E 1N0

Brendan Maguire
Constituency: Halifax Atlantic *No. of Constituents:* 16,188, Liberal
Tel: 902-424-8637; *Fax:* 902-424-0539
brendan@brendanmaguire.ca
brendanmaguire.ca
Other Communications: Constituency Phone: 902-444-0147; Fax: 902-444-8941
twitter.com/bmaguirens,
www.facebook.com/BrendanMaguireNS
Constituency Office
349 Herring Cove Rd., #C
Halifax, NS B3V 1R9

Minister, Public Works; Minister responsible, Sydney Tar Ponds Agency (NS); Sydney Steel Corporation Act, Hon. Kim Masland
Constituency: Queens *No. of Constituents:* 8,868, Progressive Conservative
Tel: 902-424-2297; *Fax:* 902-424-0532
TIRMIN@novascotia.ca
Other Communications: Constituency Phone: 902-354-5470; Fax: 902-354-5472
www.facebook.com/KimMasland
Constituency Office
279 Main St.
PO Box 1206
Liverpool, NS B0T 1K0

Derek Mombourquette
Constituency: Sydney-Membertou *No. of Constituents:* 16,049, Liberal
Tel: 902-424-8637; *Fax:* 902-424-0539
info@mombourquette.ca
Other Communications: Constituency Phone: 902-562-8870; Fax: 902-562-5220
twitter.com/homematterscb,
www.facebook.com/HomeMattersCB
Constituency Office
500 Kings Rd.
Sydney, NS B1S 1B1

Minister, Agriculture; Minister responsible, Maritime Provinces Harness Racing Commission Act, Hon. Greg Morrow
Constituency: Guysborough-Tracadie *No. of Constituents:* 7,767, Progressive Conservative
Tel: 902-424-4388; *Fax:* 902-424-0699
min_dag@novascotia.ca

Lorelei Nicoll
Constituency: Cole Harbour-Dartmouth *No. of Constituents:* 16,040, Liberal
Tel: 902-424-8637; *Fax:* 902-424-0539
twitter.com/loreleinicoll, www.facebook.com/loreleinicoll

Chris Palmer
Constituency: Kings West *No. of Constituents:* 16,439, Progressive Conservative
Tel: 902-424-2731; *Fax:* 902-424-7484

Leader, Official Opposition; Leader, Nova Scotia Liberal Party, Hon. Iain Rankin
Constituency: Timberlea-Prospect *No. of Constituents:* 17,165, Liberal
Tel: 902-424-8637; *Fax:* 902-424-0539
info@iainrankin.ca
www.iainrankin.ca
Other Communications: Constituency Phone: 902-404-7036; Fax: 902-404-7056
twitter.com/IainTRankin, www.facebook.com/IainTRankin
Constituency Office
#100, 1268 St. Margaret's Bay Rd.
Beechville, NS B3T 1A7

Kelly Regan
Constituency: Bedford Basin *No. of Constituents:* 13,121, Liberal
Tel: 902-424-8637
Toll-free: 877-424-1177; *Fax:* 902-424-0539
kelly@kellyregan.ca
www.kellyregan.ca
Other Communications: Constituency Phone: 902-407-3777; Fax: 902-407-3779
www.facebook.com/kellyreganns,
www.linkedin.com/in/kelly-regan-a8693546
Constituency Office
#306, 1597 Bedford Hwy.
Bedford, NS B4A 1E7

Dave Ritcey
Constituency: Truro-Bible Hill-Millbrook-Salmon River *No. of Constituents:* 16,510, Progressive Conservative
Tel: 902-424-2731; *Fax:* 902-424-7484
mlaritcey@bellaliant.com
Other Communications: Constituency Phone: 902-897-0884
twitter.com/daveritcey, www.facebook.com/ritceydave,
www.linkedin.com/in/daveritcey
Constituency Office
141 Victoria St.
Truro, NS B2N 1Z3

Minister, Natural Resources & Renewables, Hon. Tory Rushton
Constituency: Cumberland South *No. of Constituents:* 10,989
Tel: 902-424-5935
Toll-free: 833-597-8679; *Fax:* 902-424-7735
mindnr@novascotia.ca
toryrushton.ca
Other Communications: Constituency Phone: 902-597-4039; Fax: 902-597-3310
twitter.com/toryrushton,
www.facebook.com/ToryRushtonCSPC
Note: Tory Rushton was first elected in a by-election held on June 19, 2018.
Constituency Office
6 McFarlane St.
PO Box 250
Springhill, NS B0M 1X0

Melissa Sheehy-Richard
Constituency: Hants West *No. of Constituents:* 16,485, Progressive Conservative
Tel: 902-424-2731; *Fax:* 902-424-7484
melissa@hantswestpc.com
twitter.com/melissasheehyr1,
www.facebook.com/melissaformla,
www.linkedin.com/in/melissa-sheehy-richard-318979149

Angela Simmonds
Constituency: Preston *No. of Constituents:* 11,055, Liberal
Tel: 902-424-8637; *Fax:* 902-424-0539

Kent Smith
Constituency: Eastern Shore *No. of Constituents:* 16,438,

Progressive Conservative
Tel: 902-424-2731; *Fax:* 902-424-7484
www.facebook.com/kentsmitheasternshore,
www.linkedin.com/in/kent-smith-783ba79
Elizabeth Smith-McCrossin
Constituency: Cumberland North *No. of Constituents:* 13,494,
Independent
elizabeth@working4you.ca
Other Communications: Constituency Phone: 902-661-2288;
Fax: 902-661-0114
www.facebook.com/NovaScotiaElizabeth
Constituency Office
5 Ratchford St., 2nd Fl.
Amherst, NS B4H 1X2
Tom Taggart
Constituency: Colchester North *No. of Constituents:* 14,906,
Progressive Conservative
Tel: 902-424-2731; *Fax:* 902-424-7484
Minister, Health & Wellness; Minister responsible, Office of
Healthcare Professionals Recruitment, Hon. Michelle
Thompson
Constituency: Antigonish *No. of Constituents:* 14,599,
Progressive Conservative
Tel: 902-424-5818; *Fax:* 902-424-0559
Health.Minister@novascotia.ca
Fred Tilley
Constituency: Northside-Westmount *No. of Constituents:*
16,251, Liberal
Tel: 902-424-8637; *Fax:* 902-424-0539
twitter.com/fredtilley2
John White
Constituency: Glace Bay-Dominion *No. of Constituents:*
13,478, Progressive Conservative
Tel: 902-424-2731; *Fax:* 902-424-7484
Minister, Advanced Education, Hon. Brian Wong
Constituency: Waverley-Fall River-Beaverbank *No. of
Constituents:* 17,272, Progressive Conservative
Tel: 902-424-7628; *Fax:* 902-424-0651
Nolan Young
Constituency: Shelburne *No. of Constituents:* 11,505,
Progressive Conservative
Tel: 902-424-2731; *Fax:* 902-424-7484

Nova Scotia Government Departments & Agencies

Office of Acadian Affairs / Affaires acadiennes

**Dennis Bldg., 1741 Brunswick St., 3rd Fl., PO Box 682
Halifax, NS B3J 2T3**
Tel: 902-424-0497; *Fax:* 902-428-0124
Toll-Free: 866-382-5811
bonjour@novascotia.ca
acadien.novascotia.ca
twitter.com/GouvNE
www.facebook.com/Affairesacadiennes
The mission of the Office of Acadian Affairs is to offer advice &
support to departments, offices, agencies, & Crown corporations
so they can develop & adapt policies, programs, & services that
reflect the needs of the Acadian & francophone community of
Nova Scotia.

Minister, Hon. Colton LeBlanc
min-oaa@gov.ns.ca

Executive Director, Mark Bannerman
mark.bannerman@novascotia.ca

Nova Scotia Department of Advanced Education

1505 Barrington St., PO Box 697 Halifax, NS B3J 2T8
Tel: 902-424-5301; *Fax:* 902-424-2203
lae-correspondence@novascotia.ca
beta.novascotia.ca/government/labour-and-advanced-education
twitter.com/NSLAE
Focuses on labour issues, employment rights & responsibilities,
adult learning, apprenticeship training & trade qualification, skill
development, public & workplace safety, industry regulation,
licensing & pensions. In April 2015, the Department gained
responsibility for the following programs after the dissolution of
Economic & Rural Development & Tourism: Strategic
Cooperative Education Incentive; Workplace Innovation
Productivity Skills Incentive; Student Career Development
Program; & Graduate to Opportunity.
In 2021, the department was renamed to Departemtn of
Advanced Education from the Department of Labour &
Advanced Education. A new Department of Labour, Skills &
Immigration was created, which will take on some of the former
department's responsibilities.

Minister, Hon. Brian Wong
Tel: 902-424-7628; *Fax:* 902-424-0651

Deputy Minister, Nancy MacLellan

Executive Director, Frederick Jeffers
Tel: 902-424-8477

Director, Strategy & Business Innovation, Brian Watson
Tel: 902-424-2106

Associated Agencies, Boards & Commissions:

• Community Sector Council of Nova Scotia
Halifax Shopping Centre
PO Box 29028
Halifax, NS B3L 4T8
Tel: 902-424-4585
info@csc-ns.ca
www.csc-ns.ca
The Council was established in December 2012 & seeks to to
develop organizational capacity within the non-profit sector, with
funds from the Department of Labour & Advanced Education.

• Crane Operators Appeal Board
5151 Terminal Rd., 7th Fl.
PO Box 697
Halifax, NS B3J 2T8
Tel: 902-424-8595; *Fax:* 902-424-0217
novascotia.ca/lae/coab
The Crane Operators Appeal Board was created pursuant to the
Crane Operators & Power Engineers Act, which came into force
on September 1, 2001. It is an independent adjudicative tribunal
charged with considering appeals filed under Part I of the Act.

• Elevators & Lifts Appeal Board
novascotia.ca/lae/elab

• Labour Board of Nova Scotia
PO Box 202
Halifax, NS B3J 2M4
Tel: 902-424-6730; *Fax:* 902-424-1744
Toll-free: 877-424-6730
labourboard@novascotia.ca
novascotia.ca/lae/labourboard
Other Communication: Alt. Email: labourboard@novascotia.ca

• Nova Scotia Apprenticeship Agency (NSAA)
Thompson Bldg.
1256 Barrington St., 3rd Fl.
PO Box 578
Halifax, NS B3J 2S9
Tel: 902-424-5651; *Fax:* 902-424-0717
Toll-free: 800-494-5651
apprenticeship@novascotia.ca
nsapprenticeship.ca
Established on July 1, 2014, to manage the trades training &
certification system in Nova Scotia. Operates under the authority
of the Apprenticeship & Trades Qualifications Act.

• Nova Scotia Apprenticeship Board
2021 Brunswick St.
PO Box 578
Halifax, NS B3J 2S9
www.nsapprenticeship.ca/agency/apprenticeship-board
The Nova Scotia Apprenticeship Board, which is linked with the
Nova Scotia Apprenticeship Agency as of 2014, is the voice of
industry to the Minister of Labour & Advanced Education. The
primary role of the board is to consult with industry on
apprenticeship matters & to make recommendations to the
Minister. In particular, the Board reviews current trade
regulations & recommends proposed trades for designation &
compulsory certification.

• Occupational Health & Safety Advisory Council
ohsac.gov.ns.ca

• Pay Equity Commission
5151 Terminal Rd., 6th Fl.
PO Box 697
Halifax, NS B3J 2T8
Tel: 902-424-8466; *Fax:* 902-424-0575
novascotia.ca/lae/payequity
The Pay Equity Commission is responsible for administrating the
Pay Equity Act. In addition to monitoring the pay equity process,
the Commission has the power to resolve disputes when
employers & employees cannot agree, conducts research,
maintains statistics, & advises the Minister of Labour on matters
relating to pay equity.

• Workers' Advisers Program
#309, 5640 Spring Garden Rd.
PO Box 1063
Halifax, NS B3J 3M7
Tel: 902-424-5050; *Fax:* 902-424-0530
Toll-free: 800-774-4712
TTY: 902-424-5050
novascotia.ca/lae/wap
The program is a legal clinic funded by the provincial
government offering services to injured workers. It aims to
provide legal assistance to injured workers denied Workers'
Compensation Board benefits.

Corporate Policy & Services Branch
Consists of Planning, Research & Accountability, Policy &
Planning & Professional Services.
Executive Director, Jeannine Jessome
Tel: 902-233-1558

Higher Education Branch
PO Box 697 Halifax, NS B3J 2T8
Consists of Post-Secondary Disability Services, Private Career
Colleges, Student Assistance & Universities & Colleges.
Executive Director, Universities & Colleges, Cheryl To
Tel: 902-424-3758

Safety Branch
Tel: 902-424-5400; *Fax:* 902-424-5640
Toll-Free: 800-952-2687
ohsdivision@novascotia.ca
Consists of Technical Safety & Occupational Health & Safety.
Executive Director, Technical Safety, Jeffrey Dolan
Tel: 902-424-5434
Director, Inspections & Compliance, Technical Safety, Gail
Keeping
Tel: 902-223-9350

Skills & Learning Branch
Consists of Adult Education, Employment Nova Scotia & Skill
Development. Apprenticeship functions are now handled by the
Nova Scotia Apprenticeship Agency, created on July 1, 2014.

Office of African Nova Scotian Affairs (ANSA)

**1741 Brunswick St., 3rd Fl., PO Box 2691 Stn. Central,
Halifax, NS B3J 2R5**
Tel: 902-424-5555; *Fax:* 902-424-7189
Toll-Free: 866-580-2672
ANSA@novascotia.ca
ansa.novascotia.ca
twitter.com/officeofansa
www.facebook.com/AfricanNSAffairs
The mission of the Office of African Nova Scotian Affairs is to
serve as a broker between community members & government,
& to advocate for cross-cultural understanding.

Minister, Hon. Pat Dunn
ansaminister@novascotia.ca

Chief Executive Officer, Wayn Hamilton
Tel: 902-424-6643
wayn.hamilton@novascotia.ca

Nova Scotia Department of Agriculture

1800 Argyle St., 6th Fl., Halifax, NS B3J 3N8
Tel: 902-424-4560; *Fax:* 902-424-4671
Toll-Free: 800-279-0825
novascotia.ca/agri
The Department of Agriculture has a legislated mandate to
support & develop the agriculture & food industries, recognizing
that these sectors are economic engines of Nova Scotia's rural
communities. Fosters prosperous & sustainable agriculture &
food industries through the delivery of quality public services for
the betterment of rural communities in Nova Scotia.

Minister, Hon. Greg Morrow
Tel: 902-424-4388; *Fax:* 902-424-0699
min_dag@gov.ns.ca

**Deputy Minister; Deputy Minister, Fisheries &
Aquaculture,** Loretta Robichaud

Director, Communications, Tina Thibeau
Tel: 902-424-0192
tina.thibeau@novascotia.ca

Associated Agencies, Boards & Commissions:

• Agricultural Marshland Conservation Commission
The Commission advises the Minister of Agriculture on the
conservation & protection of marshland, its development & use
in agriculture.

• Atlantic Provinces Harness Racing Commission
5 Gerald McCarville Dr.
PO Box 128
Kensington, PE C0B 1M0
Tel: 902-836-5500; *Fax:* 902-836-5320
atlanticphrc.ca
The Commission governs, regulates, & supervises harness
racing in all of its forms relevant & related to pari-mutuel betting.

• Crop & Livestock Arbitration Board
The Board deals with loss disputes between the Nova Scotia
Crop & Livestock Insurance Commission & insured persons.

• Farm Practices Board
The Board makes decisions on normal farm practices, as well as conducting studies & preparing reports on the matter.

• Farm Registration Appeal Committee
The Committee hears appeals under the Farm Registration Act & decides whether an organization meets the criteria for a general farm organization.

• Livestock Health Services Board
The Board advises the minister on livestock health policies.

• Natural Products Marketing Council (NPMC)
74 Research Dr.
Bible Hill, NS B6L 2R2
Tel: 902-893-6511; *Fax:* 902-893-7579
The Council, an agency of the NS Government, is responsible for the administration of the Natural Products Act & the Dairy Industry Act. Ten marketing boards are established under the Natural Products Act & the Dairy Farmers of Nova Scotia is established under the Dairy Industry Act. These boards are producer elected & the Council delegates or regulates authority to them specific to their farm product. The Council is a regulatory & supervisory body, a major role of which is to balance industry interests with the broader public interest.

• Nova Scotia Crop & Livestock Insurance Commission
74 Research Dr.
Truro, NS B6L 2R2
Tel: 902-893-6370
Toll-free: 800-565-6371
nsclic@novascotia.ca
Under the Crop & Livestock Insurance Act, the Commission is responsible for administering the program under the direction, supervision, & control of the Minister of Agriculture.

• Nova Scotia Farm Loan Board
74 Research Dr.
Truro, NS B6L 2R2
Tel: 902-893-6506; *Fax:* 902-895-7693
FLBNS@novascotia.ca
novascotia.ca/farmloan
Other Communication: Kentville location: Phone: 902-679-6009; Fax: 902-679-4997
The Nova Scotia Farm Loan Board operates as a Corporation of the Crown & supports the development of sustainable agriculture & agri-rural business in Nova Scotia through responsible lending.

• Weed Control Advisory Committee
Provides advice on the control of noxious or threatening weeds in the province.

Agriculture & Food Operations Branch
PO Box 890 Stn. Harlow Bldg., Truro, NS B2N 5G6
The Agriculture & Food Operations branch is responsible for advisory services & outreach, regional services, provincial programming & protection services.
Director, Resources Sustainability, Kevin Bekkers
Tel: 902-893-6363
Director, Regional Services, Rachael Cheverie
Tel: 902-896-2329
rachael.cheverie@novascotia.ca
Director, Sector Development & Innovation, Amy Melmock
Tel: 902-893-5966
Manager, Land Protection & Field Services, Carl Esau
Tel: 902-893-6568

Policy & Corporate Services Branch
74 Research Dr., Bible Hill, NS B6L 2R2
Responsible for procurement, leasing, building management & occupational health & safety; planning, policy & legislative development; research & analytics; Crown agencies; & programs & business risk management.
Program Administration Officer, Ernest Walker
Tel: 902-896-2468
Ernest.Walker@novascotia.ca
Director, Programs & Business Risk Management, Lori Kittilsen
Tel: 902-893-4518
lori.kittilsen@novascotia.ca
Director, Crown Lending Agencies, Jennifer Thompson
Tel: 902-893-6500

Office of the Auditor General

Royal Centre, #400, 5161 George St., Halifax, NS B3J 1M7
Tel: 902-424-5907; *Fax:* 902-424-4350
oag-ns.ca
twitter.com/OAG_NS
www.facebook.com/OAGNS
www.linkedin.com/company/oag-ns
The mission of the Auditor General is to make a significant contribution to enhanced accountability & performance in the provincial sector. The Auditor General serves the public interest as the House of Assembly's primary source of assurance on government performance.

Auditor General, Kim Adair-MacPherson
Tel: 902-424-4046
Kimberly.Adair-MacPherson@novascotia.ca

Deputy Auditor General, Mike MacPhee, CPA, CA
Tel: 902-424-4215
Mike.Macphee@novascotia.ca

Communications Nova Scotia

Provincial Bldg., 1723 Hollis St., 3rd Fl., PO Box 608 Halifax, NS B3J 2R7
Tel: 902-424-7690; *Fax:* 902-424-0515
CNSClientSVC@novascotia.ca
beta.novascotia.ca/government/communications-nova-scotia
Communications Nova Scotia strives to help Nova Scotians understand what their government is doing & why. They provide a complete range of professional communications services to provincial government departments, agencies, boards & commissions. A list of media contacts for provincial departments & agencies can be found on the CNS website.

Minister, Hon. Brian Comer
Tel: 902-424-3839; *Fax:* 902-424-3458
cnsminister@novascotia.ca

Deputy Minister; Chief Executive Officer, Laura Lee Langley
Tel: 902-424-4886
LauraLee.Langley@novascotia.ca

Associate Deputy Minister, Donna MacDonald
Donna.MacDonald@novascotia.ca

Nova Scotia Department of Communities, Culture & Heritage

1741 Brunswick St., 3rd Fl., PO Box 456 Stn. Central, Halifax, NS B3J 2R5
Tel: 902-424-2170
cch@novascotia.ca
cch.novascotia.ca
The Department of Communities, Culture & Heritage is responsible for contributing to the well-being & prosperity of Nova Scotia's diverse & creative communities through the promotion, development, preservation & celebration of culture, heritage, identity & languages, & by providing leadership, expertise, & innovation to stakeholders. As of April 2015, the Department oversees the Community Access Program.

Minister, Hon. Pat Dunn
Tel: 902-424-4889
min_cch@novascotia.ca

Deputy Minister, Justin Huston

Associate Deputy Minister, Melissa MacKinnon

Director, Communications, Brett Loney
Tel: 902-424-1593
Bretton.Loney@novascotia.ca

Associated Agencies, Boards & Commissions:
• Art Gallery of Nova Scotia (AGNS)
1723 Hollis St.
PO Box 2262
Halifax, NS B3J 3C8
Tel: 902-424-5280; *Fax:* 902-424-7359
info.agns@novascotia.ca
www.artgalleryofnovascotia.ca
• Nova Scotia Gaming Corporation (NSGC)
Summit Place
1601 Lower Water St., 5th Fl.
PO Box 1501
Halifax, NS B3J 2Y3
Tel: 902-424-2203; *Fax:* 902-424-0724
gamingns.ca
The Corporation monitors the gaming industry in Nova Scotia along with Atlantic Lottery Corporation & Great Canadian Gaming Corporation, ensuring that it is economically & socially responsible.
• Nova Scotia Museum (NSM)
1747 Summer St.
Halifax, NS B3H 3A6
Fax: 902-424-0560
museum@novascotia.ca
museum.novascotia.ca
Operates a family of 28 museums throughout the province.

Non-Profit Sector Unit
1741 Brunswick St., 3rd Fl., PO Box 456 Stn. Central, Halifax, NS B3J 2R5
novascotia.ca/NonProfitSector

Nova Scotia Archives
6016 University Ave., Halifax, NS B3H 1W4
Tel: 902-424-6060
archives@novascotia.ca
archives.novascotia.ca
twitter.com/NS_Archives
www.facebook.com/novascotiaarchives
www.youtube.com/c/nsarchives
As a documentary heritage institution for the province, the Nova Scotia Archives serves as the permanent repository for the archival records of the government of Nova Scotia; acquires & preserves provincially significant archival records from the private sector; delivers a range of professional, client-centred reference services; & provides strategic support & financial assistance to strengthen the provincial archival community. Their holdings include 12,500 metres of textual records, 535,000 photographs, 200,000 maps & plans, 16,000 sound recordings & 9,000 film reels.

Heritage Division
The mission of Heritage Division is to protect, enhance, & celebrate heritage for all Nova Scotians & for future generations.
Executive Director, Culture & Heritage Development, Christopher Shore
Tel: 902-424-8443
christopher.shore@novascotia.ca

Nova Scotia Department of Community Services

Nelson Place, 5675 Spring Garden Rd., 8th Fl., PO Box 696 Halifax, NS B3J 2T7
Toll-Free: 877-424-1177
beta.novascotia.ca/government/community-services
twitter.com/NS_DCS
The Department of Community Services is committed to a sustainable social service system that promotes the independence, self-reliance & security of the people it serves.

Minister, Hon. Karla MacFarlane; *Fax:* 902-424-3287
dcsmin@novascotia.ca

Deputy Minister, Tracey Taweel

Acting Associate Deputy Minister, Sandy Graves

Associated Agencies, Boards & Commissions:
• Cape Breton Island Housing Authority
18 Dolbin St.
PO Box 1372
Sydney, NS B1P 6K3
Tel: 902-539-8520; *Fax:* 902-539-0330
Toll-free: 800-565-3135
The Authority oversees Cape Breton, Richmond, Inverness & Victoria Counties.
• Cobequid Housing Authority
114 Victoria East
PO Box 753
Amherst, NS B4H 4B9
Tel: 902-667-8757; *Fax:* 902-667-1686
Toll-free: 800-934-2445
Other Communication: Truro Office Phone: 902-893-7235; Fax: 902-897-1149; Toll-Free Phone: 877-846-0440
The Authority oversees Cumberland & Colchester Counties.
• Eastern Mainland Housing Authority
7 Campbell's Lane
New Glasgow, NS B2H 2H9
Tel: 902-752-1225; *Fax:* 902-752-1315
Toll-free: 800-933-2101
The Authority oversees Antigonish, Guysborough & Pictou Counties.
• Metropolitan Regional Housing Authority
MacDonald Bldg.
2131 Gottingen St., 5th Fl.
Halifax, NS B3K 5Z7
Tel: 902-420-6000; *Fax:* 902-420-6020
Toll-free: 800-565-8859
Other Communication: Applications Phone: 902-420-6017
The Authority oversees all of Halifax Regional Municipality.

• Nova Scotia Disabled Persons Commission (NSDPC)
Nelson Place
5675 Spring Garden Rd., 7th Fl.
PO Box 222 CRO
Halifax, NS B3J 2M4
Tel: 902-424-8280; *Fax:* 902-424-0592
Toll-free: 800-565-8280
TTY: 877-996-9954
disability@gov.ns.ca
disability.novascotia.ca
The NSDPC gives people with disabilities a way to participate in the provincial government policy-making process. Its mission is to champion the social & economic inclusion of citizens with disabilities.

• Western Regional Housing Authority
25 Kentucky Ct.
New Minas, NS B4N 4N1
Tel: 902-681-3179; *Fax:* 902-681-0806
Toll-free: 800-441-0447
Other Communication: Middleton Phone: 902-825-3481; Bridgewater Phone: 902-543-8200; Yarmouth Phone: 902-742-4369
The Authority oversees the Counties of Annapolis, Kings, part of Hants, Lunenburg & Queens Regional Municipality, as well as the Counties of Digby, Yarmouth & Shelburne. It is responsible for the areas previously covered by the South Shore Housing Authority, the Annapolis Valley Housing Authority & the Tri-County Housing Authority.

Children, Youth & Families
novascotia.ca/coms/families
Director, Child Protection & Children in Care, Kelly Besler
Tel: 902-424-5662

Disability Support Program (DSP)
novascotia.ca/coms/disabilities
The DSP serves children, youth & adults with intellectual disabilities, long-term mental illness, & physical disabilities in a range of community-based, residential & vocational/day programs.
Director, Vicki Black
Tel: 902-424-6296
Director, Lisa Fullerton
Tel: 902-424-5522

Employment Support & Income Assistance
www.novascotia.ca/coms/employment
The Employment Support & Income Assistance (ESIA) program helps by giving money for living costs, or providing other kinds of help, when individuals are unable to support themselves or their family.
Director, Income Assistance, Patricia AuCoin
Tel: 902-424-6104

Council of Atlantic Premiers (CAP)

Council Secretariat, #1006, 5161 George St., PO Box 2044 Halifax, NS B3J 2Z1
Tel: 902-424-7590; *Fax:* 902-424-8976
info@cap-cpma.ca
cap-cpma.ca
The Premiers of New Brunswick, Newfoundland & Labrador, Nova Scotia & Prince Edward Island constitute the Council. It was established by memorandum of understanding to: promote unity of purpose among their respective Governments; ensure maximum coordination of the activities of the Governments & their agencies; & establish a framework for joint action & undertakings. The Council meets up to four times annually to discuss matters of mutual interest or concern to the four Atlantic governments. A Secretariat acts as the focal point for coordinating the efforts of the four Governments in identifying potential benefits that could result from a regional approach to policy formulation & program development.

Secretary to Council, Mary Moszynski
Tel: 902-424-7600
mary@cap-cpma.ca

Accounting & Pension Officer, Scott Desrochers
Tel: 902-424-8974
jruggles@cap-cpma.ca

Associated Agencies, Boards & Commissions:
• Council of Atlantic Ministers of Education & Training
PO Box 2044
Halifax, NS B3J 2Z1
Tel: 902-424-5352; *Fax:* 902-424-8976
camet-camef@cap-cpma.ca
camet-camef.ca

• Maritime Provinces Higher Education Commission (MPHEC) / Commission de l'engseignement supérieur des Provinces Maritimes (CESPM)
#401, 82 Westmorland
PO Box 6000
Fredericton, PE E3B 5H1
Tel: 506-453-2844
mphec@mphec.ca
www.mphec.ca
As an Agency of the Council of Atlantic Premiers that provides advice to Ministers responsible for Post-Secondary Education in the Maritimes, the Commission assists institutions & governments in enhancing a post-secondary learning environment that reflects quality, accessibility, mobility, relevance, accountability, scholarship & research.

Nova Scotia Department of Education & Early Childhood Development

2021 Brunswick St., PO Box 578 Halifax, NS B3J 2S9
Tel: 902-424-5168; *Fax:* 902-424-0511
Toll-Free: 888-825-7770
novascotia.ca/education
twitter.com/nseducation
www.facebook.com/NovaScotiaEducation
The mission of the Department of Education & Early Childhood Development is to provide children, students & families with a strong foundation for success by transforming the early years & public education system through an innovative curriculum, excellence in teaching & learning, equity throughout the system & collaborative partnerships.

Minister, Hon. Becky Druhan
Tel: 902-424-4236; *Fax:* 902-424-0680
educmin@novascotia.ca

Deputy Minister, Cathy Montreuil

Director, Patrick Kakembo
Tel: 902-424-7659

Associated Agencies, Boards & Commissions:
• Annapolis Valley Regional Centre for Education (AVRCE)
121 Orchard St.
PO Box 340
Berwick, NS B0P 1E0
Tel: 902-538-4600; *Fax:* 902-538-4630
Toll-free: 800-850-3887
avrce.ca

• Cape Breton-Victoria Regional Centre for Education (CB-VRCE)
275 George St.
Sydney, NS B1P IJ7
Tel: 902-564-8293; *Fax:* 902-564-0123
cbvrce.ca

• Chignecto-Central Regional Centre for Education (CCRCE)
60 Lorne St.
Truro, NS B2N 3K3
Tel: 902-897-8900
Toll-free: 800-770-0008
ccrce.ca

• Conseil scolaire acadien provincial (CSAP)
CP 88
Saulnierville, NS B0W 2Z0
Tél: 902-769-5460
Ligne sans frais: 888-533-2727
csap.ca

• Halifax Regional Centre for Education (HRCE)
33 Spectacle Lake Dr.
Dartmouth, NS B3B 1X7
Tel: 902-464-2000
www.hrce.ca

• South Shore Regional Centre for Education (SSRCE)
69 Wentzell Dr.
Bridgewater, NS B4V 0A2
Tel: 902-543-2468; *Fax:* 902-541-3060
Toll-free: 888-252-2217
receptionist@ssrce.ca
ssrce.ca

• Strait Regional Centre for Education (SRCE)
#2, 304 Pitt St.
Port Hawkesbury, NS B9A 2T9
Tel: 902-625-2191; *Fax:* 902-625-2281
Toll-free: 800-650-4448
srsb@srsb.ca
srce.ca

• Tri-County Regional Centre for Education (TCRCE)
79 Water St.
Yarmouth, NS B5A 1L4
Tel: 902-749-5696; *Fax:* 902-749-5697
Toll-free: 800-915-0113
www.tcrce.ca

Early Learning & Child Care (ELCC)
The mandate of this branch is to provide improved support to families with young children.
Director, Rola AbiHanna
Tel: 902-424-2611
Director, Early Childhood Development & PrePrimary, Sarah Melanson

Education Action Plan (EAP)
The EAP branch is responsible for creating courses & programs, as well as evaluting their effectiveness & impact on students.
Director, Curriculum Development, Jennifer Burke
Tel: 902-424-7143
Director, Personal Development & Wellness, Steve Machat
Tel: 902-424-7123

Educators
This branch is responsible for student assessment & evaluation, student achievement, educational research & partnerships, & teacher education & certification.
Director, Student Assessment & Evaluation, Shannon LeBlanc
Tel: 902-424-5458

Finance & Operations
The division is responsible for the financial management of the department as well as the facilities management.

French Programs & Services
The French Programs & Services Branch monitors & approves curriculum development for French first language education, collaborates with other branches of the department to ensure common services are available in French for first language schools, coordinates activities related to federal-provincial funding agreements for French minority language education and French language instruction, & coordinates & manages implementation of national official language programs in Nova Scotia.
Director, Brian Marchand
Tel: 902-424-8073

Inclusive Education Supports
The Inclusive Education Supports branch is responsible for designing the student support programs & services implemented in all public schools, including African Canadian & Mi'kmaq services.
Director, Mi'kmaw Services Branch, Roderick Francis
Tel: 902-424-8181

Strategic Policy & Research
This branch comprises policy, planning, legislation, research coordination, & statistics & data management services to all areas of the department.
Director, Policy & Planning, Karen McNeil Noel
Tel: 902-424-2668

Elections Nova Scotia

#505, 202 Brownlow Ave., Dartmouth, NS B3B 1T5
Tel: 902-424-8584; *Fax:* 902-424-6622
Toll-Free: 800-565-1504
TTY: 866-774-7074
elections@novascotia.ca
www.electionsnovascotia.ca
twitter.com/electionsns
www.facebook.com/electionsnovascotia
www.youtube.com/user/electionsNS
Elections Nova Scotia is independent of any political affiliation, including the government in power. It ensures that every election, by-election, & liquor plebiscite is held in a fair & impartial manner (according to the Elections Act & other relevant laws) & that all political parties & candidates act within the rules.

Chief Electoral Officer, Richard P. Temporale

Director, Operations, Naomi Ruth Shelton
Tel: 902-424-3275

Nova Scotia Department of Energy & Mines

Joseph Howe Bldg., 1690 Hollis St., PO Box 2664 Halifax, NS B3J 3J9
Tel: 902-424-4575; *Fax:* 902-424-3265
enerinfo@novascotia.ca
beta.novascotia.ca/government/energy-and-mines
twitter.com/NS_Energy_Mines
To serve as the government's focal point in the development of the province's energy & mineral resources. Responsible for a wide range of initiatives in the following areas: renewables;

energy efficiency; oil & gas; geoscience & mines; electricity; & industry development.

Minister, Natural Resources & Renewables, Hon. Tory Rushton
Tel: 902-424-5935; *Fax:* 902-424-7735
mindnr@novascotia.ca

Deputy Minister, Karen Gatien

Associated Agencies, Boards & Commissions:
• **Canada-Nova Scotia Offshore Petroleum Board (CNSOPB)**
TD Centre
1791 Barrington St., 8th Fl.
Halifax, NS B3J 3K9
Tel: 902-422-5588; *Fax:* 902-422-1799
info@cnsopb.ns.ca
www.cnsopb.ns.ca
Created in 1990, the Canada-Nova Scotia Offshore Petroleum Board regulates petroleum activities in the Nova Scotia Offshore Area.
The following are some of the responsibilities of the Board: protecting the environment; overseeing the health & safety of offshore workers; managing the conservation of offshore petroleum resources; issuing licences for offshore exploration & development; collecting & distributing data; & complying with provisions of the *Accord Acts* that deal with employment & industrial benefits.

Business Development & Corporate Services
Executive Director, Business Development & Corporate Services, Chris Spencer
Tel: 902-424-6773
Director, Business & Technology, Toby Balch
Tel: 902-225-3512
Director, Fiscal & Economic Affairs, Andrew Childs
Tel: 902-424-8159

Petroleum Resources
Director, Kimberly Ann Doane
Tel: 902-424-7146

Sustainable & Renewable Energy
Executive Director, Keith Collins
Tel: 902-424-2288
Director, Clean Growth, Sandra Farwell
Tel: 902-424-1700
Director, Electricity Policy & Programs, David Miller
Tel: 902-476-8441

Nova Scotia Department of Environment

#1800, 1894 Barrington St., PO Box 442 Halifax, NS B3J 2P8
Tel: 902-424-3600; *Fax:* 902-424-0501
Toll-Free: 877-936-8476
novascotia.ca/nse
Other Communication: Climate Change Unit:
climatechange.novascotia.ca; Email:
climatechange@novascotia.ca
Secondary Address: #2085, 1903 Barrington St.
Halifax, NS B3J 2P8
twitter.com/ns_environment
www.facebook.com/NovaScotiaEnvironment
Major program responsibilities for Nova Scotia Environment are environmental & natural areas management, environmental monitoring & compliance, & climate change. Pollution prevention, solid waste reduction & recycling, & environmental trade & innovation are all part of the department.

Minister, Hon. Tim Halman
Tel: 902-424-3736; *Fax:* 902-424-1599
Minister.Environment@novascotia.ca

Deputy Minister, Scott Farmer

Director, Elizabeth Kennedy
Tel: 902-225-4707

Director, Integration of Compliance & Operations, Janet MacKinnon
Tel: 902-266-5506

Director, Quality, Safety & Training, Sharon Munroe
Tel: 902-565-8096

Associated Agencies, Boards & Commissions:
• **Divert NS**
#400, 35 Commercial St.
Truro, NS B2N 3H9
Tel: 902-895-7732; *Fax:* 902-897-3256
Toll-free: 877-313-7732
info@divertns.ca
divertns.ca

Formerly known as Resource Recovery Fund Board (or RRFB Nova Scotia), Divert NS promotes recycling through environmental stewardship, education & programming. Its two core programs are the Beverage Container Deposit-Refund Program & the Used Tire Management Program. The corporation also operates a network of 75 Enviro-Depots across the province.

• **Environmental Trust Advisory Board**
• **On-Site Services Advisory Board**
• **Round Table on the Environment & Sustainable Prosperity**
novascotia.ca/nse/dept/minister.roundtable.asp

Conservation Enforcement
Director, Conservation Enforcement, Orlando Fraser
Tel: 902-798-7914

Environmental Health & Food Safety Division
The Environmental Health & Food Safety Division has responsibility for operations relating to environmental protection natural resource management. It also responds to requests for environmental assistance, approvals & investigations. Branches include: Conservation Enforcement, Environmental Health, Fisheries and Aquaculture & Food Protection.

Policy Division
novascotia.ca/nse/dept/division.pcs.asp
Founded in 2009, this division combines former divisions (Competitiveness & Compliance, Environmental Assessment, Information & Business Services, & Policy).
Executive Director, Policy, Lorrie Ann Roberts
Tel: 902-225-9528
Director, Lynn Bowen
Tel: 902-221-0104

Sustainability & Applied Science
The Division aims to provide leadership & coordination of community engagement activities in Environment (& more broadly) is responsible for delivery of major environmental service contracts with the private sector.
Executive Director, Andrew Murphy
Tel: 902-478-8358
Director, Protected Areas & Ecosystems, Peter Labor
Tel: 902-424-5071

Nova Scotia Department of Finance & Treasury Board

Provincial Bldg., 1723 Hollis St., 7th Fl., PO Box 187 Halifax, NS B3J 2N3
Tel: 902-424-5554; *Fax:* 902-424-0635
FinanceWeb@novascotia.ca
beta.novascotia.ca/government/finance-and-treasury-board
twitter.com/NSFinance
The Department of Finance & Treasury Board's vision is to provide financial leadership that strengthens Nova Scotia; & their mission is to provide corporate financial services & manage the province's financial affairs & policies in the interests of Nova Scotians.

Minister; Chair, Treasury & Policy Board, Hon. Allan MacMaster
Tel: 902-424-5720; *Fax:* 902-424-0635
FinanceMinister@novascotia.ca

Deputy Minister, Kelliann Dean

Associated Agencies, Boards & Commissions:
• **Nova Scotia Pension Services Corporation**
Purdy's Landing
#400, 1949 Upper Water St.
PO Box 371
Halifax, NS B3J 2P8
Tel: 902-424-5070; *Fax:* 902-424-0662
Toll-free: 800-774-5070
pensionsinfo@nspension.ca
www.novascotiapension.ca
Formerly known as the Nova Scotia Pension Agency, the Nova Scotia Pension Services Corporation (Pension Services Corp.) administers the pension benefits & investment assets of the Teachers' Pension Plan (TPP), the Public Service Superannuation Plan, the Members' Retiring Allowance (MLA Plan) & the three former Sydney Steel pension plans.

• **Nova Scotia Utility & Review Board**
See Entry Name Index for detailed listing.

Capital Markets Administration & Compliance
The Capital Markets Administration division provides all post-trade settlement & accounting functions for the Nova Scotia Pension Agency investment & the Province's debt portfolio activities.
Director, Capital Markets & Compliance, Jennifer Sanford
Tel: 902-424-3456

Corporate Strategic Initiatives
Executive Director, Strategic Financial Operations, William Varner
Tel: 902-229-8872

Financial Institutions
The Financial Institutions Division regulates the operations of credit unions, trust & loan companies & insurance companies, agents, brokers & adjusters in the Province. The Division also provides a complaint & enquiry service to the public relating to financial institutions & the insurance industry & collects & verifies the insurance premiums tax.

Fiscal & Economic Policy
Two main branches of this division are Taxation & Fiscal Policy & Economics & Statistics.
Director, Policy & Fiscal Planning, Michael Ingram
Tel: 902-424-7195
Michael.Ingram@novascotia.ca
Director, Economics & Statistics, Thomas Storring
Tel: 902-424-2410
Thomas.Storring@novascotia.ca

Government Accounting
Provides financial accounting services to all government departments & agencies.
Executive Director, Robert Bourgeois
Tel: 902-424-2079
Robert.Bourgeois@novascotia.ca
Director, Financial Accounting, Dana Jasper
Tel: 902-424-2222

Liability Management & Treasury Services
Responsible for ensuring effective money management, maximizing return on investments & minimizing debt servicing costs within risk tolerances acceptable to government.
Executive Director, Charles Allain
Tel: 902-424-2435
Charles.Allain@novascotia.ca
Director, Liability Management, Roy Spence
Tel: 902-424-8634
Roy.Spence@novascotia.ca

Treasury Board
The Treasury Board Division assists the Treasury & Policy Board in carrying out its duties under the Public Service Act.

Nova Scotia Department of Fisheries & Aquaculture

#607, 1800 Argyle St., Halifax, NS B3J 2R5
Tel: 902-424-4560; *Fax:* 902-424-4671
aquaculture@novascotia.ca
novascotia.ca/fish
Other Communication: Fish Buyers or Fish Processors
enquiries: fishstat@novascotia.ca
twitter.com/NSFisheries
The Department of Fisheries & Aquaculture's mission is to foster prosperous & sustainable fisheries, aquaculture & food industries through the delivery of quality public services for the betterment of coastal communities & of all Nova Scotians.

Minister, Hon. Steve Craig
Tel: 902-424-8953; *Fax:* 902-428-3145
mindfa@novascotia.ca

Deputy Minister, April Howe

Associated Agencies, Boards & Commissions:
• **Fisheries & Aquaculture Loan Board**
74 Research Dr.
Bible Hill, NS B6L 2R2
Tel: 902-896-4800
fishloan.novascotia.ca

Aquaculture Division
aquaculture@novascotia.ca
Executive Director, Bruce Hancock
Tel: 902-875-7842
Bruce.Hancock@novascotia.ca
Director, Carla Buchan
Tel: 902-266-9962

Inland Fisheries Division
91 Beeches Rd., PO Box 700 Pictou, NS B0K 1H0
Executive Director, Alan McNeill
Tel: 902-485-7024

Marine Division
Director, Geordie MacLachlan
Tel: 902-478-6147

Office of Gaelic Affairs (OGA)

1741 Brunswick St., 3rd Fl., PO Box 456 Stn. Central, Halifax, NS B3J 2R5

Tel: 902-424-4298; *Fax:* 902-424-0171
Toll-Free: 888-842-3542
gaelicinfo@gov.ns.ca
gaelic.novascotia.ca
Other Communication: Alt. Email: fiosgaidhlig@gov.ns.ca
twitter.com/ns_gaelic
www.facebook.com/gaelicaffairs

The OGA's mission is to renew the Gaelic language through its work with Nova Scotians across the province.

Minister, Hon. Allan MacMaster

Executive Director, Lewis MacKinnon
Tel: 902-424-4298
lewis.mackinnon@novascotia.ca

Nova Scotia Department of Health & Wellness

PO Box 488 Halifax, NS B3J 2R8

Tel: 902-424-5818
Toll-Free: 800-387-6665
TTY: 800-670-8888
novascotia.ca/dhw
Other Communication: TeleHealth Network: 800-889-5949
twitter.com/nshealth
www.facebook.com/NovaScotiaHealthAndWellness

Mission: Working together to empower individuals, families, partners, & communities to promote, improve, & maintain the health of Nova Scotians through a proactive & sustainable health care system.

Minister, Hon. Michelle Thompson
Tel: 902-424-5818; *Fax:* 902-424-0559
Health.Minister@novascotia.ca

Deputy Minister, Vacant

Senior Executive Director, Kimberlee Barro
Tel: 902-240-5232

Senior Executive Director, Public Health, Vanessa Chouinard
Tel: 902-722-1465

Senior Executive Director, Continuing Care, Vicki Elliott-Lopez
Tel: 902-424-5627

Senior Executive Director, Quality & Patient Safety, Ruby Knowles
Tel: 902-424-3221

Senior Executive Director, Clinical, Tanya Penney
Tel: 902-476-0978

Associated Agencies, Boards & Commissions:

• Nova Scotia Advisory Commission on AIDS
Barrington Tower
1894 Barrington St.
Halifax, NS B3J 2L4
Tel: 902-424-5730
AIDS@novascotia.ca
novascotia.ca/aids

Office of the Chief Public Health Officer
PO Box 488 Halifax, NS B3J 2R8
novascotia.ca/dhw/publichealth/cpho.asp
The Office of the Chief Public Health Officer is responsible for the Department of Health's legislated responsibility to protect & promote the public's health in the following areas: communicable disease control, environmental health, emergency preparedness & response. In addition, staff in the Office of the Chief Public Health Officer, in collaboration with academic expertise at Dalhousie University, function as an expert resource in community health science & an epidemiological resource for the department, the health districts, & other relevant government & community groups.
Chief Medical Officer of Health, Dr. Robert Strang
Tel: 902-424-2358; *Fax:* 902-424-0550

Nova Scotia Human Rights Commission

Park Lane Terrace, #305, 5657 Spring Garden Rd., PO Box 2221 Halifax, NS B3J 3C4

Tel: 902-424-4111; *Fax:* 902-424-0596
Toll-Free: 877-269-7699
hrcinquiries@novascotia.ca
humanrights.novascotia.ca
Other Communication: Education Inquiries:
hrceducation@novascotia.ca
twitter.com/NSHumanRights
www.facebook.com/NSHumanRights

Minister Responsible, Hon. Brad Johns
Tel: 902-424-4030
justmin@novascotia.ca

Chair, Cheryl Knockwood

Director & CEO, Joseph Fraser

Office of Immigration

1469 Brenton St., 3rd Fl., PO Box 1535 Halifax, NS B3J 2Y3
Tel: 902-424-5230; *Fax:* 902-424-7936
Toll-Free: 877-292-9597
immigration@novascotia.ca
novascotiaimmigration.com
twitter.com/nsimmigration
www.facebook.com/NSimmigration

Minister, Hon. Lena M. Diab
Tel: 902-424-5230; *Fax:* 902-424-7936
ImmigrationMinister@novascotia.ca

Executive Director, Shelley Bent James
Tel: 902-424-4993

Director, Communications, Elizabeth MacDonald
Tel: 902-424-4312
Elizabeth.MacDonald@novascotia.ca

Nova Scotia Department of Inclusive Economic Growth

CIBC Bldg., 1809 Barrington St., #M103, Halifax, NS B3J 3K8
Tel: 902-424-0377; *Fax:* 902-424-0500
beta.novascotia.ca/government/inclusive-economic-growth
twitter.com/NS_InclGrowth
The department was created with the 2015-2016 Budget, absorbing responsibilities formerly held by the Department of Economic & Rural Development & Tourism. Aligned with the Office of Regulatory & Service Effectiveness, the Department has three main focus areas: business strategy & planning; strategic projects & investments; & operational leadership, coordination & alignment. Its main objective is economic growth. In 2021, the Department of Business was renamed to the Department of Inclusive Economic Growth.

Minister, Hon. Susan Corkum-Greek
Tel: 902-424-0377
IEGMinister@novascotia.ca

Deputy Minister, Scott Farmer

Executive Director, Crown & Major Projects, Robert McMurray
Tel: 902-424-4165

Director, Crown Relations, Jeannie Chow
Tel: 902-424-2904

Director, Crown Relations, Melanie Fewer
Tel: 902-424-5122

Associated Agencies, Boards & Commissions:
• Develop Nova Scotia
Old Red Store, Historic Properties
#301, 1875 Upper Water St.
Halifax, NS B3J 1S9
Tel: 902-422-6591; *Fax:* 902-377-4801
info@developns.ca
developns.ca
In 2018, Waterfront Development Corporation Ltd. was renamed Develop Nova Scotia. Previously, it developed waterfronts as cultural & artistic hubs. Now, as a Crown corporation, its mandate encompasses investing in infrastructure, properties & programs to build on the province's natural assets. Its initial project is improving rural internet infrastructure.

• Events East Group
1800 Argyle St.
PO Box 955
Halifax, NS B3J 2V9
Tel: 902-421-8686; *Fax:* 902-422-2922
www.eventseast.com
Other Communication: Halifax Convention Centre:
www.halifaxconventioncentre.com
Events East Group (formerly known as Halifax Convention Centre Corporation) was created in 2017. It manages & operates the Halifax Convention Centre, Scotiabank Centre & Ticket Atlantic. Events East is a joint partnership between the Province of Nova Scotia & Halifax Regional Municipality.

• Innovacorp
#400, 1871 Hollis St.
Halifax, NS B3J 0C3
Tel: 902-424-8670; *Fax:* 902-424-4679
Toll-free: 800-565-7051
info@innovacorp.ca
www.innovacorp.ns.ca
A network of business resources for the early stage technology entrepreneur. Key services include research & development support, business advice, investment & partnership advice. Focuses on two main growth sectors: life sciences & information technology. In April 2015, Innovacorp assumed responsibility for the following programs after the dissolution of Economic & Rural Development & Tourism: Innovation & Business Competitiveness Fund; Production & Innovation Voucher; & Early Stage Commercialization.

• Nova Scotia Business Inc. (NSBI)
PO Box 2374
Halifax, NS B3J 3E4
Tel: 902-424-6650
Toll-free: 800-260-6682
info@nsbi.ca
www.novascotiabusiness.com
NSBI is the first point of contact for local companies that want to grow in Nova Scotia, & for international companies that have heard about the province & want to know more. As of April 2015, NSBI is responsible for International Commerce Programs & the Small Business Program Development Program, formerly overseen by Economic & Rural Development & Tourism. It also absorbed the mandate of Film & Creative Industries Nova Scotia (formerly Film Nova Scotia).

• Tourism Nova Scotia (TNS)
See Entry Name Index for detailed listing.

Office of the Information & Privacy Commissioner (OIPC)

PO Box 181 Halifax, NS B3J 2M4
Tel: 902-424-4684; *Fax:* 902-424-8303
Toll-Free: 866-243-1564
oipcns@novascotia.ca
oipc.novascotia.ca
twitter.com/NSInfoPrivacy
Nova Scotia was the first province in Canada to enact Freedom of Information legislation, in 1977. The Freedom of Information & Protection of Privacy Review of Privacy Office, now the Office of the Information & Privacy Commissioner, was established in 1994.

Information & Privacy Commissioner, Tricia Ralph

Nova Scotia Department of Infrastructure & Housing

Tel: 902-424-8445
beta.novascotia.ca/government/infrastructure-and-housing
twitter.com/NovaScotia_IAH

Minister, Hon. John Lohr

Deputy Minister, Paul LaFleche

Executive Director, Finance & Strategic Capital Planning, Diane Saurette
Tel: 902-722-1411

Associated Agencies, Boards & Commissions:
• Nova Scotia Affordable Housing Commission
nsaffordablehousingcommission.ca

Housing Nova Scotia
Maritime Centre, 1505 Barrington St., 14th Fl., Halifax, NS B3J 3K5

Toll-Free: 844-424-5110
housingns@novascotia.ca
housing.novascotia.ca
twitter.com/HousingNS
www.facebook.com/housingns
A provincial corporation that oversees the five Housing Authorities within the province. The corporation's mandate is to

ensure all residents of Nova Scotia have access to affordable housing in communities that offer needed services, supports & opportunities.
Chief Executive Officer, Eiryn Devereaux
Regional Administrator, Cyril Leblanc
   Tel: 902-563-2125

Nova Scotia Department of Intergovernmental Affairs

Duke Tower, 5251 Duke St., 5th Fl., PO Box 1617 Halifax, NS B3J 2Y3
   Tel: 902-424-5153; *Fax:* 902-424-0728
   novascotia.ca/iga

Provides leadership in the development of corporate strategies for Nova Scotia's relations with governments & organizations. Assumed responsibility for Trade Policy & Negotiations after Economic & Rural Development & Tourism was dissolved in 2015.

Minister, Hon. Tim Houston, ECNS
Tel: 902-424-5153; *Fax:* 902-424-0728
premier@novascotia.ca

Deputy Minister, Kelliann Dean
Tel: 902-424-7128; *Fax:* 902-424-4225
Kelliann.Dean@novascotia.ca

Executive Director, Albert Walzak
Tel: 902-424-1289

Director, Canada-United States Relations, Darryl Eisan
Tel: 902-722-5099

Director, Strategic Trade Policy, Angela Houston
Tel: 902-424-2827

Director, Regional Relations, Andrea Moe
Tel: 902-424-2384

Nova Scotia Department of Justice

1690 Hollis St., PO Box 7 Halifax, NS B3J 2L6
   Tel: 902-424-4030
   justweb@gov.ns.ca
   novascotia.ca/just

Minister & Attorney General, Hon. Brad Johns
Tel: 902-424-4030
justmin@novascotia.ca

Deputy Minister, Candace L. Thomas

Associate Deputy Minister, Lora MacEachern
Tel: 902-449-5765
Lora.MacEachern@novascotia.ca

Director, Communications, Jennifer Stairs
Tel: 902-424-6018

Associated Agencies, Boards & Commissions:
• **Criminal Code Review Board (CCRB)**
novascotia.ca/just/ccrb/ccrb_overview.asp
• **Human Rights Commission**
See Entry Name Index for detailed listing.
• **Nova Scotia Legal Aid Commission (NSLA)**
Office of the Executive Director
#920, 1701 Hollis St.
Halifax, NS B3J 3M8
Tel: 902-420-6578
Toll-free: 877-420-6578
www.nslegalaid.ca

• **Nova Scotia Medical Examiner Service**
Dr. William D. Finn Centre for Forensic Medicine
51 Garland Ave.
Dartmouth, NS B3B 0J2
Tel: 902-424-2722; *Fax:* 902-424-0607
Toll-free: 888-424-4336
novascotia.ca/just/cme
Other Communication: Toll-Free Fax: 866-603-4074
• **Office of the Police Complaints Commissioner (OPCC)**
1690 Hollis St., 3rd Fl.
PO Box 1573
Halifax, NS B3J 2Y3
Tel: 902-424-3246; *Fax:* 902-424-1777
polcom@novascotia.ca
novascotia.ca/opcc

• **Public Trustee Office**
#501, 1465 Brenton St.
PO Box 685
Halifax, NS B3J 2T3
Tel: 902-424-7760; *Fax:* 902-424-0616
publictrustee@gov.ns.ca
novascotia.ca/just/pto
Other Communication: Health Care Decisions Division, Phone: 902-424-4454; Fax: 902-428-2159; Email: publictrusteehcd@gov.ns.ca
• **Serious Incident Response Team (SiRT)**
#203, 1256 Barrington St.
Halifax, NS B3J 1Y6
Tel: 902-424-2010
Toll-free: 855-450-2010
sirt@gov.ns.ca
sirt.novascotia.ca
SiRT investigates matters involving death, serious injury, sexual assault & domestic violence, or other matters of significant public interest, arising from the actions of any police officer in Nova Scotia.
• **Workers' Compensation Appeals Tribunal**
#201, 1465 Brenton St.
Halifax, NS B3J 3T4
Tel: 902-424-2250; *Fax:* 902-424-2321
Toll-free: 800-274-8281
wcat.novascotia.ca

Correctional Services
   Tel: 902-424-7640; *Fax:* 902-424-0693
   novascotia.ca/just/Corrections
Executive Director, Chris Collett
   Tel: 902-424-7640
Director, John Scoville
   Tel: 902-717-0014
Director, Brenda Young
   Tel: 902-424-7641

Court Services
   novascotia.ca/just/Court_Services
Director, Allan Coley
   Tel: 902-424-0259
Director, Peter James
   Tel: 902-424-5172
Director, Claudia Mann
   Tel: 902-424-6414
Executive Director, Lauren Scaravelli
   Tel: 902-223-1616

Public Safety
   novascotia.ca/just/public_safety
Director, Public Safety & Investigations, Hayley Crichton
   Tel: 902-424-3315

Nova Scotia Department of Labour, Skills & Immigration

1469 Brenton St., 3rd Fl., PO Box 1535 Halifax, NS B3J 2Y3
The department was created following the 2021 general election, taking on responsibilities of the former Department of Labour & Advanced Education (now Department of Advanced Education). Its full scope & responsibilities are still forthcoming.

Minister, Hon. Jill S. Balser
Tel: 902-424-5230; *Fax:* 902-424-7936
ImmigrationMinister@novascotia.ca

Contact, Media, Monica MacLean
Tel: 902-220-0358
Monica.MacLean@novascotia.ca

Nova Scotia Department of Lands & Forestry

PO Box 698 Halifax, NS B3J 2T9
   Tel: 902-424-5935; *Fax:* 902-424-7735
   Toll-Free: 800-565-2224
   novascotia.ca/natr
Lands & Forestry (formerly Natural Resources) is responsible for the administration & management of provincial Crown lands, protection & sustainable development of forest resources & operation & maintenance of parks system, & promoting the conservation & sustainable use of wildlife populations, habitat & ecosystems. Initiatives include: a State of the Forest report; working with other departments on State of the Environment report; leading the development of a provincial climate change strategy; implementing recovery plans for endangered & threatened wildlife species; & developing strategic land use plans for Crown lands using an integrated resource management planning process.

Minister, Hon. Tory Rushton
mindnr@novascotia.ca

Deputy Minister, Vacant

Director, Petrie Robert
Tel: 902-680-5217

Associated Agencies, Boards & Commissions:
• **Crown Land Information Management Centre (CLIMC)**
1701 Hollis St.
PO Box 698
Halifax, NS B3J 2T9
Tel: 902-424-3171; *Fax:* 902-424-7068
crownland@novascotia.ca
novascotia.ca/natr/land/grantmap.asp
• **Nova Scotia Primary Forest Products Marketing Board**
PO Box 698
Halifax, NS B3J 2T9
nspfpmb@gov.ns.ca
novascotia.ca/pfpmb
The board oversees registration of bargaining agents & the supervision of collective bargaining between groups of pulpwood producers & large pulpwood mills within Nova Scotia.

Geoscience & Mines Branch
   Tel: 902-424-2035; *Fax:* 902-424-7735
   novascotia.ca/natr/meb
Implements policies & programs dealing with the exploration, development, management & efficient use of energy & mineral resources, promotes scientific studies of the geology of the province for use by government, industry & the public, provides a mineral rights tenure system to establish legal rights to minerals for exploration & development. Promotes concepts of environmental responsibility & sustainability.
Executive Director, Don James
   Tel: 902-424-2523
   Donald.James@novascotia.ca
Director, Mineral Management, George MacPherson
   Tel: 902-424-5618
   George.MacPherson@novascotia.ca
Director, Geological Survey, Diane Webber
   Tel: 902-456-4349
   Diane.Webber@novascotia.ca

Land Services Branch
   landweb@gov.ns.ca
   novascotia.ca/natr/thedepartment/landservices.asp
The Land Services Branch management oversees, coordinates & approves all activities within the Branch relating to the administration of Crown land. The Branch provides advice on legislative revisions & advises & drafts policies relating to the administration of Crown land.
Executive Director, Land Administration, Leslie Hickman
   Tel: 902-424-4006
   Leslie.Hickman@novascotia.ca
Director, Land Administration, Melanie Cameron
   Tel: 902-424-4006
Director, Land Service Program Renewal, Victoria Ross
   Tel: 902-220-1297

Policy, Planning & Support Services
   novascotia.ca/natr/thedepartment/planning.asp
Provides planning & policy coordination support to the Department, ensures that policies & plans developed in the Department are coordinated, supports the integrated management of natural resources. Also provides a range of administrative, planning, research, information management, information distribution, graphics, cartographic, & communication-related services.
Executive Director, Peter Geddes
   Tel: 902-424-4988
   Peter.Geddes@novascotia.ca

Regional Services Branch
   novascotia.ca/natr/thedepartment/regional.asp
   Other Communication: Field Offices:
   novascotia.ca/natr/staffdir/offices_map.asp
Delivers departmental programs & services through a field office network, responsible for forest management, Crown lands surveys, regional geological services, public outreach & education, Integrated Resource Management (IRM), hunter safety, forest fire prevention, detection & suppression, monitoring of forest insects & diseases, operation & maintenance of Provincial Parks, & resource conservation.
Executive Director, Walter Fanning
   Tel: 902-424-4445
   walter.fanning@novascotia.ca
Director, Occupational Health & Safety, Linda Redmond
   Tel: 902-476-2946

Renewable Resources
   novascotia.ca/natr/thedepartment/renewable.asp
The branch handles policy, planning & program development, including industry development, resource promotion, marketing,

resource inventories & research. The branch also prepares strategies & plans for the development, management & conservation of the province's forests, parks & wildlife resources.
Executive Director, Jonathan Porter
Tel: 902-424-4103
Jon.Porter@novascotia.ca
Director, Resource Management, Christopher Bailey
Tel: 902-424-0844

Nova Scotia Lands Inc.

PO Box 430 Stn. A, Sydney, NS B1P 6H2
www.nslands.ca
Crown corporation responsible for remediating & redeveloping crown-owned property in Nova Scotia, including land located in Sydney Mines, Sydney River, Grand Lake area, Catalone, Pictou, New Glasgow & Grand Narrows. The former Sydney Steel Plant property is currently undergoing remediation. NS Lands also manages the Harbourside Commercial Park in Sydney.

President & CEO, Stephen MacIsaac
Tel: 902-543-0681
stephen.macisaac@novascotia.ca

Executive Director, Environmental Assessment & Remediation, Donnie Burke
Tel: 902-567-2715
donnie.burke@novascotia.ca

Executive Director, Boat Harbour, Ken Swain
Tel: 902-424-3568
ken.swain@novascotia.ca

Nova Scotia Liquor Corporation (NSLC)

Bayers Lake Business Park, 93 Chain Lake Dr., Halifax, NS B3S 1A3
Toll-Free: 800-567-5874
contactus@myNSLC.com
www.mynslc.com
Other Communication: Cannabis, URL: cannabis.mynslc.com;
Toll-Free Phone: 800-380-7449
twitter.com/theNSLC
www.facebook.com/theNSLC
www.youtube.com/user/MyNSLC
The NSLC is mandated to manage the safe & responsible distribution & sale of beverage alcohol. As of 2018, its mandate expanded to include the sale of recreational cannabis.

Minister Responsible, Hon. Allan MacMaster
Tel: 902-424-5720; *Fax:* 902-424-0635
FinanceMinister@novascotia.ca

Chair, George McLellan

Senior Vice-President, Corporate Services, Dave DiPersio

Senior Vice-President, Finance, Caroline Duchesne

Senior Vice-President, Human Resources, Ryan Embrett

Senior Vice-President, Customer Operations, Paul Rapp

Office of L'nu Affairs (OLA)

5251 Duke St., 5th Fl., PO Box 1617 Halifax, NS B3J 2Y3
Tel: 902-424-7409; *Fax:* 902-424-4225
LnuAffairs@novascotia.ca
novascotia.ca/abor
twitter.com/nslnuaffairs
The Office undertakes activities that increase the level of public awareness of L'nu, Mi'kmaq, people & the issues they face. It also works collaboratively with the L'nu communities & organizations & other levels of government to coordinate L'nu & tri-partite initiatives, develop strategies, & build & maintain a sustainable foundation for L'nu-Government relations. As of April 2015, the Office oversees the Aboriginal Community Development Fund. In 2021, it was renamed from the Office of Aboriginal Affairs to the Office of L'nu Affairs.

Minister, Hon. Karla MacFarlane
OAA@novascotia.ca

Deputy Minister; Chief Executive Officer, Justin Huston
Tel: 902-424-7662

Nova Scotia Department of Municipal Affairs

PO Box 216 Halifax, NS B3J 2M4
Tel: 902-424-6642
beta.novascotia.ca/government/municipal-affairs

Provides programs, grants & funding opportunities for municipalities & community groups, as well as services & guidance to municipalities in areas such as budget planning & finance, land use planning & infrastructure development, & policy & program development. In April 2015, the Department gained responsibility for the Regional Enterprise Networks formerly overseen by Economic & Rural Development & Tourism.

Minister, Hon. John Lohr
Tel: 902-424-6642
dmamin@novascotia.ca

Deputy Minister, Paul LaFleche

Associate Deputy Minister, Mark Peck

Director, Workforce Development, Major Initiatives & Projects, Jacques Pelletier
Tel: 902-424-8448

Associated Agencies, Boards & Commissions:
• Nova Scotia Municipal Finance Corporation (NSMFC)
PO Box 850 M
Halifax, NS B3J 2V2
Tel: 902-424-4590; *Fax:* 902-424-0525
www.nsmfc.ca
NSMFC issues pooled debentures that provide low-cost, long-term capital financing for municipal capital projects. The NSMFC issues in capital markets twice a year, generally in the spring & fall. On occasion the NSMFC will do a single issue, provided the size is large enough.

Emergency Management Office (EMO)
PO Box 2581 Halifax, NS B3J 3N5
Tel: 902-424-5620; *Fax:* 902-424-5376
Toll-Free: 866-424-5620
emo@novascotia.ca
beta.novascotia.ca/government/emergency-management-office
Secondary Address: 33 Acadia St.
Dartmouth, NS B2Y 2N1
twitter.com/nsemo
www.facebook.com/EmergencyManagementOfficeNovaScotia
The EMO has the responsibility of assisting municipalities in planning & preparing for emergencies; is also responsible for the implementation of the province-wide 911 service. Coordinates emergency efforts of provincial & federal departments & agencies, as well as private health & social services, to provide assistance to disaster areas; sponsors the Ground Search & Rescue Program; maintains a professional planner at all offices. Coordinates all emergency preparedness training for municipal staff at the Emergency Preparedness College (Arnprior, ON) & through the Joint Emergency Preparedness Program (JEPP), which provides a federal government cost-sharing formula for emergency equipment for first-response agencies.
Executive Director, Paul Mason
Tel: 902-424-6206

Office of the Fire Marshal
PO Box 231 Stn. Halifax Central, Halifax, NS B3J 2M4
Tel: 902-424-5721; *Fax:* 902-424-3239
Toll-Free: 800-559-3473
ofm@novascotia.ca
beta.novascotia.ca/government/office-fire-marshal
Acting Fire Marshal, Douglas MacKenzie
Tel: 902-424-5721

Corporate Policy, Planning & Strategic Initiatives

Grants, Programs & Operations
Director, Finance, Grants, Programs & Operations, Hardy Stuckless
Tel: 902-424-2770

Municipal Planning & Advisory Services
Director, Governance & Advisory Services, Nicolas Barr
Tel: 902-424-4656

Office of the Ombudsman

PO Box 2152 Halifax, NS B3J 3B7
Tel: 902-424-6780; *Fax:* 902-424-6675
Toll-Free: 800-670-1111
ombudsman@novascotia.ca
ombudsman.novascotia.ca
twitter.com/NS_Ombudsman
www.facebook.com/107686089866

Ombudsman, William (Bill) Smith

Nova Scotia Public Service Commission (NSPSC)

PO Box 943 Halifax, NS B3J 2V9
Tel: 902-424-7660
reception-psc@novascotia.ca
beta.novascotia.ca/government/public-service-commission
twitter.com/NSPublicService

Minister, Hon. Colton LeBlanc
Tel: 902-424-5465; *Fax:* 902-424-0555
min_psc@novascotia.ca

Public Service Commissioner, Andrea Anderson
Andrea.Anderson@novascotia.ca

Executive Director, Sarah Bradfield
Tel: 902-430-0823

Director, Internal Communications & Strategic Relations, Angela Johnson
Tel: 902-476-7312

Nova Scotia Securities Commission (NSSC)

PO Box 458 Halifax, NS B3J 2P8
Tel: 902-424-7768; *Fax:* 902-424-4625
Toll-Free: 855-424-2499
NSSCinquiries@novascotia.ca
nssc.novascotia.ca
twitter.com/NSSCommission
www.linkedin.com/company/nova-scotia-securities-commission
Established to provide investors with protection in accordance with Nova Scotia's securities laws from practices & activities that tend to undermine investor confidence in the fairness & efficiency of capital markets.

Chair, Paul E. Radford, Q.C.

Executive Director, Helen Anderson
Tel: 902-424-0179

Director, Corporate Finance, Abel Lazarus
Tel: 902-424-6859

Nova Scotia Department of Seniors

1741 Brunswick St., 2nd Fl., Halifax, NS B3J 3X8
Tel: 902-424-0770; *Fax:* 902-424-0561
Toll-Free: 844-277-0770
seniors@novascotia.ca
novascotia.ca/seniors
twitter.com/NSSeniors
Committed to ensuring the inclusion, well-being, & independence of seniors in Nova Scotia by facilitating the development of policies on aging & programs for seniors across government & through the provision & coordination of strategic planning, support, services, programs & information.

Minister, Hon. Barbara Adams
seniorsmin@novascotia.ca

Deputy Minister, Paul LaFleche

Executive Director, Faizal Nanji
Tel: 902-424-7921

Service Nova Scotia & Internal Services (SNS-IS)

PO Box 2734 Halifax, NS B3J 3K5
Tel: 902-424-5200; *Fax:* 902-424-0720
Toll-Free: 800-670-4357
TTY: 877-404-0867
askus@novascotia.ca
Other Communication:
beta.novascotia.ca/government/service-nova-scotia-and-internal-services
twitter.com/ns_servicens
Provides assessment services, business licensing & registration, vehicle registration & driver licensing, taxation & revenue collection & vital statistics. As of April 1, 2015, a new structure was implemented in order to focus on improving service & modernizing programs & reducing red tape. In 2019, Service NS & the Department of Internal Services merged.

Minister, Hon. Colton LeBlanc
Tel: 902-424-3302; *Fax:* 902-424-6266
min_snsis@novascotia.ca

Deputy Minister, Joanne Munro
Tel: 902-424-4089; *Fax:* 902-424-5510
Joanne.Munro@novascotia.ca

Associate Deputy Minister; Chief Digital Officer, Nathasha Clarke

Associate Deputy Minister, Valerie Pottie Bunge

Executive Director, Alcohol & Gaming, John MacDonald
Tel: 902-424-0009

Director, Licensing & Registration, Jonpaul Landry
Tel: 902-424-6022

Associated Agencies, Boards & Commissions:
• **Motor Vehicle Appeal Board**
1672 Granville St.
PO Box 186
Halifax, NS B3J 2N2
Tel: 902-424-4256
Toll-free: 855-424-4256
novascotia.ca/sns/access/drivers/motor-vehicle-appeal-board.asp

• **Nova Scotia Lands Inc.**
See Entry Name Index for detailed listing.

Access Nova Scotia
PO Box 2734 Halifax, NS B3J 3K5
novascotia.ca/access-locations

Provincial Tax Commission
PO Box 1003 Halifax, NS B3J 2X1
Tel: 902-424-6538; *Fax:* 902-424-7434
taxcommission@novascotia.ca
Provincial Tax Commissioner, Sharon Johnson-Legere
Tel: 902-424-2572
Director, Audit & Enforcement, Bernard Meagher
Tel: 902-424-3192
bernard.meagher@novascotia.ca

Client Experience
Executive Director, Citizen Services, Gillian Latham
Tel: 902-424-6592
Executive Director, Digital Platforms, Arlene Williams
Tel: 902-240-7213

Registry of Motor Vehicles
novascotia.ca/driving-and-road-safety
Executive Director, Registries, Hayley Clarke
Tel: 902-424-7742
Director, Service Delivery, David McCarthy
Tel: 902-424-3091

Program Modernization
Executive Director, Business & Consumer Services, Michelle MacFarlane
Tel: 902-722-1443

Co-operatives
PO Box 1529 Truro Heights, NS B3J 2Y4
Tel: 902-424-7770; *Fax:* 902-424-4633
rjsc.coop@novascotia.ca

Land Programs
RegistrySupport@novascotia.ca
www.novascotia.ca/sns/access/land/land-registry.asp
Registrar General; Director, Theresa Graham
Tel: 902-424-5725

Property Online (POL)
RGLandTitles@gov.ns.ca
novascotia.ca/sns/access/land/property-online.asp
Property Online is maintained by the Land Programs section.

Registry of Joint Stock Companies
PO Box 1529 Halifax, NS B3J 2Y4
Tel: 902-424-7770; *Fax:* 902-424-4633
Toll-Free: 800-225-8227
rjsc@novascotia.ca
Other Communication: URL:
beta.novascotia.ca/programs-and-services/registry-joint-stock-companies
Executive Director, Registries, Hayley Clarke
Tel: 902-424-7742

Vital Statistics
PO Box 157 Halifax, NS B3J 2M9
Tel: 902-424-4381; *Fax:* 902-450-7313
Toll-Free: 877-848-2578
vstat@novascotia.ca

GeoNOVA
160 Willow St., Amherst, NS B4H 3W5
Tel: 902-667-7231
Toll-Free: 800-798-0706
geoinfo@novascotia.ca
geonova.novascotia.ca
twitter.com/NSGeoNOVA

Director, Geographic Information Services, Colin Wade MacDonald
Tel: 902-424-5281

Information Access & Privacy
PO Box 72 Halifax, NS B3J 2L4
Tel: 902-424-2985
Toll-Free: 844-424-2985
iapservices@novascotia.ca
Assists with Freedom of Information Protection of Privacy (FOIPOP) requests

Internal Audit
Provides assurance & advisory services to government.
Director, Internal Audit, Karl Villanueva
Tel: 902-424-3997

Procurement Services
#600, 5161 George St., Halifax, NS B3J 1M7
Tel: 902-424-3333
Toll-Free: 866-399-3377
procure@novascotia.ca
procurement.novascotia.ca
twitter.com/ns_procure
Manages major purchases for departments, agencies, boards & commissions. Also includes the Queen's Printer, which supplies, produces & distributes both regular & confidential documents.
Chief Procurement Officer & Executive Director, Procurement, Chris Mitchell
Chris.Mitchell@novascotia.ca
Director, Procurement Operations & Contract Management (Buildings, Highways & Fleet), Gen Sharkey
Tel: 902-424-4969
Genevieve.Sharkey@novascotia.ca
Director, Procurement Operations & Contract Management (General Goods, Services & IT), David Stevenson
David.Stevenson@novascotia.ca

Nova Scotia Advisory Council on the Status of Women

PO Box 745 Halifax, NS B3J 2T3
Tel: 902-424-8662; *Fax:* 902-424-0573
Toll-Free: 800-565-8662
women@novascotia.ca
women.novascotia.ca
twitter.com/StatusofWomenNS
www.facebook.com/StatusofWomenNS
The agency advocates for improved legislation, policies & programs for women, & provides research & policy advice to government on ways in which public policies & programs could better serve women.

Minister Responsible, Hon. Karla MacFarlane

Executive Director, Stephanie MacInnis-Langley

Tourism Nova Scotia (TNS)

8 Water St., PO Box 667 Windsor, NS B0N 2T0
Tel: 902-798-6700
Toll-Free: 800-565-0000
tnscommunications@novascotia.ca
tourismns.ca
Other Communication: Alt. Fax: 902-798-6600; Travel Information: explore@novascotia.ca
twitter.com/tourismns
www.linkedin.com/company/tourismnovascotia
Formerly known as the Nova Scotia Tourism Agency (NSTA), Tourism Nova Scotia is reponsible for designing a tourism strategy for Nova Scotia & creates sustainable growth in the industry.

Minister Responsible, Hon. Pat Dunn

Chair, R. Irene d'Entremont

Acting Chief Executive Officer, Darlene MacDonald

Chief Operating Officer, Jeff Shute

Chief Marketing Officer, Joann Fitzgerald

Nova Scotia Department of Transportation & Active Transit

PO Box 186 Halifax, NS B3J 2N2
Tel: 902-424-2297; *Fax:* 902-424-0532
tpwpaff@novascotia.ca
novascotia.ca/tran
Provides a transportation network for the safe & efficient movement of people & goods; serves the building, property & accommodation needs of government departments & agencies;

employs professional, dedicated people & offers a high level of customer service.

Minister, Hon. Kim Masland
tirmin@novascotia.ca

Deputy Minister, Paul T. LaFleche
Paul.LaFleche@novascotia.ca

Senior Executive Director, Royden Trainor

Executive Director, Strategic Infrastructure & Priority Policy, Bonnie Rankin
Tel: 902-220-6004

Director, Road Safety; Registrar, Kevin Mitchell
Tel: 902-424-7801

Highway Operations
This division provides for provincial highway & bridge maintenance, as well as the operation of the Department's fleet management & a strategic planning section. District Services provides general services on primary & secondary roads & works with private sector contractors to provide the public with enhanced road systems.
Executive Director, Highway Engineering & Construction, Donald Maillet
Tel: 902-424-0565
Executive Director, Maintenance & Operations, Mark Peachey
Tel: 902-424-7518

Public Works
novascotia.ca/tran/works
This division provides technical expertise & services required by the Department's highway, building & property divisions. The Design Services section (Building Design Group) provides architectural & engineering services throughout design, construction & inspection phases of building projects. The Construction Services section (Project Management Services Group) coordinates with other TIR & government groups to provide project management services through all phases of building projects. Building Services manages, operates, maintaines & renovates government buildings, infrastructure & properties, as well as providing trade & contract services at government-owned locations. Environmental Services provides services such as environmental site assessments, environmental protection planning, development and promotion of environmentally-sound construction and maintenance practices, cleanup of contaminated sites & more. The Real Property Services section provides real estate services to other government bodies, including boards, agencies & commissions.
Executive Director, Building Project Services, Gerard Jessome
Tel: 902-424-8831

Nova Scotia Utility & Review Board (NSUARB)

Summit Place, 1601 Lower Water St., 3rd Fl., Halifax, NS B3J 3S3
Tel: 902-424-4448; *Fax:* 902-424-3919
Toll-Free: 855-442-4448
board@novascotia.ca
nsuarb.novascotia.ca
The Board has a very broad mandate encompassing a number of Acts. Operations fall into two categories, regulatory & adjudicative. The regulatory category includes the regulation of public utilities, licensing of public passenger carriers, monitoring of automobile insurance rates, the approval of Halifax-Dartmouth bridge fares, & the regulation of natural gas distribution & pipelines. The Board conducts hearings relating to gaming control, liquor control & film classification. The adjudicative category includes appeals or applications relating to property assessments, expropriation compensation claims, planning & subdivisions, heritage properties, criminal injury compensation claims, municipal boundaries, municipal & school board electoral boundaries, as well as gasoline, diesel oil & tobacco taxes. The Board receives its authority from the Public Inquiries Act & the Utility & Review Board Act.

Minister Responsible, Hon. Allan MacMaster

Chair, Peter W. Gurnham, Q.C.

Chief Clerk, Bruce Kiley
Tel: 902-424-4448 ext: 9287

Workers' Compensation Board of Nova Scotia

5668 South St., PO Box 1150 Halifax, NS B3J 2Y2
Tel: 902-491-8999
Toll-Free: 800-870-3331
info@wcb.ns.ca
www.wcb.ns.ca
Other Communication: Claims & Injury Reporting, Fax:
902-491-8001
twitter.com/worksafeforlife
Coordinates the workers' compensation system to assist injured
workers & their employers by providing timely medical &
rehabilitative support to help injured workers return to work.
Also, to provide appropriate compensation for work-related
injuries & illnesses.

Acting Chair, Robert Patzelt

Chief Executive Officer, Stuart MacLean

Chief Financial Officer, Maureen Boyd

Government of Nunavut

Seat of Government: PO Box 1000 Stn. 200, Iqaluit, NU X0A
0H0
Tel: 867-975-6000; *Fax:* 867-975-6099
Toll-Free: 877-212-6438
info@gov.nu.ca
www.gov.nu.ca
twitter.com/GovofNunavut
www.facebook.com/GovofNunavut
www.youtube.com/c/GovofNunavut
On April 1, 1999, Nunavut Territory was created as part of the
Nunavut Land Claims Agreement signed in 1993. It has a land
area of 1,877,778.53 sq km, & the StatsCan census in 2016
showed the population was 35,944.
Nunavut Territory is governed by a fully elected Legislative
Assembly of 22 members who typically hold a four-year term.
Government is by consensus rather than party politics. The
Legislature elects the Premier & a seven-member Executive
Council, which is charged with the operation of government &
the establishment of program & spending priorities. The
Commissioner of Nunavut Territory is appointed by the Federal
Government, & serves a role similar to that of the Lieutenant
Governor in provincial jurisdictions.

Office of the Commissioner

PO Box 2379 Iqaluit, NU X0A 0H0
Tel: 867-975-5120; *Fax:* 867-975-5123
nunavutcommissioner@gov.nu.ca
www.commissioner.gov.nu.ca
Secondary Address: House 2554
Commissioner's Residence
Iqaluit, NU

Commissioner, Hon. Eva Qamaniq Aariak, C.M., O.Nu

Deputy Commissioner, Hon. Rebecca Williams

Office of the Premier

PO Box 2410 Iqaluit, NU X0A 0H0
Tel: 867-975-5050; *Fax:* 867-975-5051
www.premier.gov.nu.ca
The Honorable Joe Savikataaq became the fifth Premier of
Nunavut on June 14, 2018, after former Premier Paul Quassa
lost a non-confidence vote.

**Premier; Minister, Executive & Intergovernmental Affairs;
Minister, Indigenous Affairs; Minister responsible,
Immigration & Utility Rates Review Council; Minister,
Environment; Minister, Energy,** Hon. Joe Savikataaq
jsavikataaq@gov.nu.ca

Press Secretary, Catriona Macleod

Executive Council

PO Box 2410 Iqaluit, NU X0A 0H0
www.gov.nu.ca/cabinet
The following is a list of members of the Executive Council,
presented in order of appearance:

**Premier; Minister, Executive & Intergovernmental Affairs;
Minister, Indigenous Affairs; Minister responsible,
Immigration & Utility Rates Review Council; Minister,
Environment; Minister, Energy,** Hon. Joe Savikataaq
jsavikataaq@gov.nu.ca

**Deputy Premier; Minister, Economic Development &
Transportation; Minister responsible, Mines, Trade,**

**Nunavut Business Credit Corporation & Nunavut
Development Corporation,** Hon. David Akeeagok
dakeeagok@gov.nu.ca

**Government House Leader; Minister, Family Services;
Minister responsible, Status of Women, Homelessness, &
Poverty Reduction,** Hon. Elisapee Sheutiapik
esheutiapik@gov.nu.ca

**Minister, Finance; Chair, Financial Management Board;
Minister, Justice; Minister responsible, Human Rights
Tribunal, Labour, Liquor Commission, Liquor Licensing
Board, & Workers' Safety & Compensation Commission,**
Hon. George Hickes
ghickes@gov.nu.ca

**Minister, Community & Government Services; Minister
responsible, Qulliq Energy Corporation,** Hon. Jeannie
Ehaloak
jehaloak@gov.nu.ca

**Minister, Education; Minister responsible, Nunavut Arctic
College,** Hon. David Joanasie
djoanasie@gov.nu.ca

**Minister, Health; Minister responsible, Suicide Prevention
& Seniors,** Hon. Lorne Kusugak
lkusugak@gov.nu.ca

**Minister, Culture & Heritage; Minister, Languages;
Minister responsible, Nunavut Housing Corporation,** Hon.
Margaret Nakashuk
minnakashuk@gov.nu.ca

Nunavut Legislative Assembly

926 Federal Rd., PO Box 1200 Iqaluit, NU X0A 0H0
Tel: 867-975-5000; *Fax:* 867-975-5190
Toll-Free: 877-334-7266
leginfo@assembly.nu.ca
assembly.nu.ca

Speaker, Hon. Allan Rumbolt

Clerk of the Assembly, John Quirke
Tel: 867-975-5100

Law Clerk & Parliamentary Counsel, Michael Chandler
Tel: 867-975-5106

Clerk Assistant, Stephen Innuksuk
Tel: 867-975-5163
sinnuksuk@assembly.nu.ca

Legislative Librarian, Riel Gallant
Tel: 867-975-5134
PO Box 1200
Iqaluit, NU X0A 0H0 Canada

Standing & Special Committees
assembly.nu.ca/standing-and-special-committees
Standing Committees provide an opportunity to study legislation,
examine policy issues & review government spending proposals.
Special Committees investigate specific issues & policy areas.
The current Standing Committees are: Legislation; Oversight of
Government Operations & Public Accounts; Social Wellness;
Community & Economic Development; & Rules, Procedures &
Privileges.
Chair, Standing Committee on Legislation, John Main
Constituency: Arviat North-Whale Cove
Chair, Standing Committee on Oversight of Government
Operations & Public Accounts, John Main
Constituency: Arviat North-Whale Cove
Chair, Standing Committee on Social Wellness, Margaret
Nakashuk
Constituency: Pangnirtung
Chair, Standing Committee on Community & Economic
Development, Allan Rumbolt
Constituency: Hudson Bay
Chair, Standing Committee on Rules, Procedures & Privilages,
Cathy Towtongie
Constituency: Rankin Inlet North-Chesterfield Inlet

Fifth Legislative Assembly - Nunavut

PO Box 1200 Iqaluit, NU X0A 0H0
assembly.nu.ca
Last General Election: Oct. 30, 2017.
Next General Election: October 25, 2021.
Salaries, Indemnities & Allowances (2019):
MLAs $103,323 including a $1,000 tax free allowance.
In addition to this are the following indemnities & allowances:
Premier $95,198 total;

Deputy Premier $87,665 total;
Ministers & Speaker $80,134 total;
Deputy Speaker $20,665 total.
A taxable Northern allowance is paid to all Members & is
dependent upon the community & residence of the Member.
The address for all members of the Legislative Assembly is as
follows: Legislative Assembly of Nunavut, PO Box 1200, Iqaluit
NU X0A 0H0.
The following is a list of members, their constituency, the number
of persons on the official voters list for the most recent election,
& contact information (where available). Please see Canada's
Information Resource Centre (CIRC) for updated information
following the 2021 election.
Members of the Legislative Assembly of Nunavut
Deputy Premier; Minister, Economic Development &
Transportation; Minister responsible, Mines, Trade, Nunavut
Business Credit Corporation & Nunavut Development
Corporation, Hon. David Akeeagok
Constituency: Quttiktuq *No. of Constituents:* 550
Tel: 867-975-5026; *Fax:* 867-975-5016
dakeeagok@gov.nu.ca
Other Communications: Constituency Phone: 867-439-8050;
Fax: 867-439-8051
Constituency Office
PO Box 24
Arctic Bay, NU X0A 0A0
Tony Akoak
Constituency: Gjoa Haven *No. of Constituents:* 961
Tel: 867-975-5014; *Fax:* 867-975-5117
takoak@assembly.nu.ca
Other Communications: Constituency Phone: 867-360-6337;
Fax: 867-360-6819
Constituency Office
PO Box 8
Gjoa Haven, NU X0B 1J0
Adam Arreak Lightstone
Constituency: Iqaluit-Manirajak *No. of Constituents:* 1,070
Tel: 867-975-5135; *Fax:* 867-975-5037
alightstone@assembly.nu.ca
Other Communications: Constituency Phone: 867-979-4754;
Fax: 867-979-4753
Constituency Office
PO Box 2529
Iqaluit, NU X0A 0H0
Minister, Community & Government Services; Minister
responsible, Qulliq Energy Corporation, Hon. Jeannie
Ehaloak
Constituency: Cambridge Bay *No. of Constituents:* 911
Tel: 876-975-5028; *Fax:* 876-975-5128
jehaloak@gov.nu.ca
Other Communications: Constituency Phone: 867-983-3777;
Fax: 867-983-3778
Constituency Office
PO Box 2450
Cambridge Bay, NU X0B 0C0
Minister, Finance; Chair, Financial Management Board; Minister,
Justice; Minister responsible, Human Rights Tribunal, Labour,
Liquor Commission, Liquor Licensing Board & Workers'
Safety & Compensation Commission, Hon. George Hickes
Constituency: Iqaluit-Tasiluk *No. of Constituents:* 1,163
Tel: 867-975-5041; *Fax:* 867-975-5042
ghickes@gov.nu.ca
Other Communications: Constituency Phone: 867-979-6923;
Fax: 867-979-4604
Constituency Office
PO Box 2049
Iqaluit, NU X0A 0H0
Minister, Education; Minister responsible, Nunavut Arctic
College, Hon. David Joanasie
Constituency: South Baffin *No. of Constituents:* 932
Tel: 867-975-5023; *Fax:* 867-975-5103
djoanasie@gov.nu.ca
Other Communications: Constituency Phone: 867-897-8753;
Fax: 867-897-8645
Constituency Office
PO Box 156
Cape Dorset, NU X0A 0C0
Joelie Kaernerk
Constituency: Amittuq *No. of Constituents:* 648
Tel: 867-975-5017; *Fax:* 867-975-5109
jkaernerk@assembly.nu.ca
Other Communications: Constituency Phone: 867-928-8260;
Fax: 867-928-8261
Constituency Office, General Delivery
Hall Beach, NU X0A 0K0
Pauloosie Keyootak
Constituency: Uqqummiut *No. of Constituents:* 837
Tel: 867-975-5027; *Fax:* 867-975-5121
pkeyootak@assembly.nu.ca
Other Communications: Constituency Phone: 867-927-8004;
Fax: 867-927-8005
Constituency Office
PO Box 219
Qikiqtarjuaq, NU X0A 0B0

Minister, Health; Minister responsible, Suicide Prevention & Seniors, Hon. Lorne Kusugak
Constituency: Rankin Inlet South *No. of Constituents:* 736
Tel: 867-975-5074; *Fax:* 867-975-2034
lkusugak@gov.nu.ca
Other Communications: Constituency Phone: 867-645-4866;
Fax: 867-645-4865
Constituency Office
PO Box 887
Rankin Inlet, NU X0C 0G0

John Main
Constituency: Arviat North-Whale Cove *No. of Constituents:* 670
Tel: 867-975-5127; *Fax:* 867-975-5108
jmain@assembly.nu.ca
Other Communications: Constituency Phone: 867-857-4201,
Fax: 867-857-4205
Constituency Office
PO Box 242
Arviat, NU X0C 0E0

Minister, Culture & Heritage; Minister, Languages; Minister responsible, Nunavut Housing Corporation, Hon. Margaret Nakashuk
Constituency: Pangnirtung *No. of Constituents:* 677
Tel: 867-975-5070; *Fax:* 867-975-5073
minnakashuk@gov.nu.ca
Other Communications: Constituency Phone: 867-473-8220;
Fax: 867-473-8227
Constituency Office
PO Box 36
Pangnirtung, NU X0A 0R0

Patterk Netser
Constituency: Aivilik *No. of Constituents:* 831
Tel: 867-975-5139; *Fax:* 867-975-5061
pnetser@assembly.nu.ca
Other Communications: Constituency Phone: 867-925-9890;
Fax: 867-925-9891
Constituency Office, General Delivery
Coral Harbour, NU X0C 0C0

Calvin Pedersen
Constituency: Kugluktuk
Tel: 867-975-5141; *Fax:* 867-975-5049
cpedersen@assembly.nu.ca
Other Communications: Constituency Phone: 867-982-4232;
Fax: 867-982-5733
Constituency Office
PO Box 39
Kugluktuk, NU X0B 0E0

David Qamaniq
Constituency: Tununiq
Tel: 867-975-5035; *Fax:* 867-975-5112
dqamaniq@assembly.nu.ca
Other Communications: Constituency Phone: 867-899-8999;
Fax: 867-899-8713
Note: David Qamaniq was elected in a by-election held Sept. 16, 2019.
Constituency Office
PO Box 30
Pond Inlet, NU X0A 0S0

Emiliano Qirngnuq
Constituency: Netsilik *No. of Constituents:* 830
Tel: 867-975-5015; *Fax:* 867-975-5107
eqirngnuq@assembly.nu.ca
Other Communications: Constituency Phone: 867-769-6183;
Fax: 867-769-6184
Note: Emiliano Qirngnuq first won the riding in a by-election held Feb. 8, 2016.
Constituency Office, General Delivery
Kugaaruk, NU X0B 1K0

Speaker, Allan Rumbolt
Constituency: Hudson Bay *No. of Constituents:* 465
Tel: 867-975-5032; *Fax:* 867-975-5113
arumbolt@assembly.nu.ca
Other Communications: Constituency Phone: 867-266-8518;
Fax: 867-266-8315
Constituency Office
PO Box 228
Sanikiluaq, NU X0A 0W0

Premier; Minister, Executive & Intergovernmental Affairs; Minister, Indigenous Affairs; Minister responsible, Immigration & Utility Rates Review Council; Minister, Environment; Minister, Energy, Hon. Joe Savikataaq
Constituency: Arviat South *No. of Constituents:* 650
Tel: 867-975-5050; *Fax:* 867-975-5051
jsavikataaq@gov.nu.ca
Other Communications: Constituency Phone: 867-857-4485;
Fax: 867-857-4486
Constituency Office, General Delivery
Arviat, NU X0C 0E0

Government House Leader; Minister, Family Services; Minister responsible, Status of Women, Homelessness, & Poverty Reduction, Hon. Elisapee Sheutiapik
Constituency: Iqaluit-Sinaa *No. of Constituents:* 1,100
Tel: 867-975-5024; *Fax:* 867-975-5044

esheutiapik@gov.nu.ca
Other Communications: Constituency Phone: 867-979-4750;
Fax: 867-979-4751
Constituency Office
PO Box 2440
Iqaluit, NU X0A 0H0

Craig Simailak
Constituency: Bear Lake
Tel: 867-975-5148; *Fax:* 867-975-5116
csimailak@assembly.nu.ca
Other Communications: Constituency Phone: 867-793-4949;
Fax: 867-793-4950
Constituency Office
PO Box 376
Baker Lake, NU X0C 0A0

Cathy Q. Towtongie
Constituency: Rankin Inlet North-Chesterfield Inlet *No. of Constituents:* 822
Tel: 867-975-5045; *Fax:* 867-975-5046
ctowtongie@assembly.nu.ca
Other Communications: Constituency Phone: 867-645-4900;
Fax: 867-645-4981
Constituency Office
PO Box 874
Rankin Inlet, NU X0C 0G0

Vacant
Constituency: Aggu
Note: On Aug. 13, 2021 Paul Quassa resigned as the Aggu MLA.

Vacant
Constituency: Iqaluit-Niaqunnguu
Note: In August 2021, Pat Angnakak resigned as the Iqaluit-Niaqunnguu MLA to run in the federal election.

Nunavut Territory Government Departments & Agencies

Nunavut Territory Department of Community & Government Services

W.G. Brown Bldg., 4th Fl., PO Box 1000 Stn. 700, Iqaluit, NU X0A 0H0
Tel: 867-975-5406; *Fax:* 867-975-5305
cgscomms@gov.nu.ca
www.gov.nu.ca/community-and-government-services
To support the development, provision & maintenance of programs & services which affect the communities in all areas of municipal responsibility & transportation.

Minister, Hon. Jeannie Ehaloak
jehaloak@gov.nu.ca

Deputy Minister, Constance Hourie
Tel: 867-975-5306
CHourie@gov.nu.ca

Assistant Deputy Minister, Infrastructure, Eiryn Devereaux
Tel: 867-975-5374
edevereaux@gov.nu.ca

Corporate Chief Information Officer, Dean Wells
Tel: 867-975-6439
Dean.Wells@gov.nu.ca

Executive Director, Municipal Training Organization (MTO), Rachel Kunz
Tel: 867-975-5346
RKunz@nmto.ca

Nunavut Emergency Management
PO Box 1000 Stn. 700, Iqaluit, NU X0A 0H0
Fax: 867-979-4221
Toll-Free: 800-693-1666
NEM@gov.nu.ca
Other Communication: Emergency Services Response 24 Hours: 867-979-6262

Nunavut Emergency Management develops territorial emergency response plans, coordinates emergency operations at the territorial & regional levels, & supports community emergency response operations.
Director, Ed Zebedee
Tel: 867-975-5448
EZebedee@gov.nu.ca
Director, Safety Services, Richard Kelly
Tel: 867-975-5419
rkelly@gov.nu.ca
Director, Emergency Management, Jimmy Noble
Tel: 867-975-5477
JNoble@gov.nu.ca
Assistant Fire Marshall, Joanasie Adla
Tel: 867-975-5365
JAdla@gov.nu.ca

Nunavut Territory Department of Culture & Heritage

PO Box 1000 Stn. 800, Iqaluit, NU X0A 0H0
Tel: 867-975-5500; *Fax:* 867-975-5504
Toll-Free: 866-934-2035
www.gov.nu.ca/culture-and-heritage
Responsible for the protection, preservation & promotion of Inuit languages. Cultural initiatives & departmental goals are reached in coordination with & in support of elder & youth groups. Acts in respect to issues concerning women & people with disabilities. The government is dedicated to preserving & promoting elements that make up the Inuit identity.

Minister, Hon. Margaret Nakashuk
minnakashuk@gov.nu.ca

Deputy Minister, Teresa Hughes
Tel: 867-975-5501

Assistant Deputy Minister, Culture & Heritage, Gideonie Joamie
Tel: 867-975-5505
GJoamie@gov.nu.ca

Languages Commissioner, Inuit Uqausinginnik Taiguusiliuqtitit, Sandra Inutiq
Tel: 867-975-5080
langcom@langcom.nu.ca

Executive Director, Jeela Palluq-Cloutier
JPalluq-Cloutier@gov.nu.ca

Nunavut Territory Department of Economic Development & Transportation

Inuksugait Plaza, Bldg. 1104A, PO Box 1000 Stn. 1500, Iqaluit, NU X0A 0H0
Tel: 867-975-7800; *Fax:* 867-975-7870
Toll-Free: 888-975-5999
edt@gov.nu.ca
www.gov.nu.ca/edt

Minister; Deputy Premier, Hon. David Akeeagok
dakeeagok@gov.nu.ca

Deputy Minister, Jimi Onalik
Tel: 867-975-7829; *Fax:* 867-975-7880
jonalik@gov.nu.ca

Director, Finance & Administration, Jonathan Ferraby
Tel: 867-975-7816
jferraby@gov.nu.ca

Acting Director, Policy, Planning & Communications, Jimi Onalik
Tel: 867-975-7873
JOnalik@gov.nu.ca

Associated Agencies, Boards & Commissions:
• Nunavut Business Credit Corporation (NBCC)
Parnaivak Bldg.
#100
PO Box 2548
Iqaluit, NU X0A 0H0
Tel: 867-975-7891; *Fax:* 867-975-7897
Toll-free: 800-758-0038
credit@nbcc.nu.ca
www.nbcc.nu.ca

• Nunavut Development Corporation
PO Box 249
Rankin Inlet, NU X0C 0G0
Tel: 867-645-3170; *Fax:* 867-645-3755
Toll-free: 866-645-3170
opportunities@ndcorp.nu.ca
www.ndcorp.nu.ca
The corporation makes equity investments in economic sectors within Nunavut, in order to help create employment opportunities for residents. It is also mandated to grow Nunavut business, with an emphasis on investment in Nunavut's smaller communities.

• Nunavut Energy Secretariat
c/o Dept. of Economic Development & Transportation
Iqaluit, NU X0A 0H0
Tel: 867-975-7704
nunavutenergy@gov.nu.ca
The secretariat develops, coordinates & delivers Nunavut's energy strategy.

Economic Development
Director, Tourism & Cultural Industries, Nancy Guyon
Tel: 867-975-7856
NGuyon@gov.nu.ca

Director, Minerals & Petroleum Resources, David Kunuk
Tel: 867-975-7892
DKunuk@gov.nu.ca

Transportation

Director, Motor Vehicles, Lorna Gee
Tel: 867-360-4614
lgee@gov.nu.ca
Director, Nunavut Airports, Jamie Makpah
Tel: 867-645-8203
jmakpah@gov.nu.ca
Director, Transportation Policy & Planning, Art Stewart
Tel: 867-975-7826
artstewart@gov.nu.ca

Nunavut Territory Department of Education

Bldg. 1107, 2nd Fl., PO Box 1000 Stn. 900, Iqaluit, NU X0A 0H0
Tel: 867-975-5600; *Fax:* 867-975-5605
info.edu@gov.nu.ca
www.gov.nu.ca/education

Minister, Hon. David Joanasie
djoanasie@gov.nu.ca

Deputy Minister, Kathy Okpik
Tel: 867-975-5600

Executive Director, Trudy Pettigrew
Tel: 867-899-7335
TPettigrew@gov.nu.ca

Director, Resource Services, Melanie Abbott
Tel: 867-975-5657
MAbbott@gov.nu.ca

Director, Policy & Planning, Kuthula Matshazi
Tel: 867-975-5606
kmatshazi@gov.nu.ca

Director, Corporate Services, Heather Moffett
Tel: 867-975-5616; *Fax:* 867-975-5605
hmoffett@gov.nu.ca

Curriculum & School Services

Director, Student Achievement, Charlotte Borg
Tel: 867-975-5679
CBorg@gov.nu.ca
Director, Educator Development, Cully Robinson
Tel: 867-975-5672
CRobinson@gov.nu.ca
Director, French Education & Services, Martine St-Louis
Tel: 867-975-5627
MStlouis@gov.nu.ca
Director, Curriculum Services, Leigh Anne Willard
Tel: 867-857-3051
LWillard@gov.nu.ca

Nunavut Territory Department of Environment

PO Box 1000 Stn. 1320, Iqaluit, NU X0A 0H0
Tel: 867-975-7700; *Fax:* 867-975-7742
environment@gov.nu.ca
gov.nu.ca/environment

Minister, Hon. Joe Savikataaq
jsavikataaq@gov.nu.ca

Deputy Minister, Jimmy Noble, Jr.

Assistant Deputy Minister, Steve Pinksen
Tel: 867-975-7718
spinksen@gov.nu.ca

Chief Federal Negotiator for Nunavut Devolution, Fred Caron

Director, Policy, Planning & Legislation, Leanne Babstock
Tel: 867-975-7749
LBabstock@gov.nu.ca

Director, Policy & Planning, Jo-Anne Falkiner
Tel: 867-975-7719
JFalkiner@gov.nu.ca

Director, Corporate Services, Nikki Nweze
Tel: 867-975-7708
nnweze@gov.nu.ca

Environmental Protection

www.climatechangenunavut.ca

The division is divided into the following program areas: Pollution Control; Environmental Assessment and Land-Use Planning; & Climate Change.
Director & Acting Deputy Chief Environmental Protection Officer, Kristi Lowe
Tel: 867-975-7748
KLowe@gov.nu.ca

Parks & Heritage

www.nunavutparks.com
Other Communication: Alt. URL:
gov.nu.ca/environment/information/parks-and-heritage
Responsible for the planning, establishment, operations & the promotion of a system of territorial parks & conservation areas throughout Nunavut. In cooperation with Nunavummiut, Parks & Conservation Areas showcases Nunavut's protected areas locally, regionally, nationally, & internationally to ensure protected areas continue to reflect the Nunavut Territory's unique heritage & the spirit, principles & special relationships established through the Nunavut Land Claims Agreement & the Inuit Impact Benefit Agreements (IIBAs) for Territorial Parks.
Director, Parks & Special Places, Linda Vaillancourt
Tel: 867-975-7703
LVaillancourt@gov.nu.ca

Wildlife Management

gov.nu.ca/environment/information/wildlife-management
Responsible for the management of terrestrial wildlife species in Nunavut. In addition to the Nunavut Wildlife Act, Wildlife Management is responsible for fulfilling responsibilities under a wide range of federal legislation & both national & international agreements & conventions.
Wildlife Director, Drikus Gissing
Tel: 867-975-7790
dgissing@gov.nu.ca

Nunavut Territory Department of Executive & Intergovernmental Affairs (EIA)

1084 Aeroplex bldg., PO Box 1000 Stn. 200, Iqaluit, NU X0A 0H0
Tel: 867-975-6000; *Fax:* 867-975-6099
www.gov.nu.ca/eia
The department provides advice & administrative support to Cabinet & the government, works to ensure that the Nunavut Land Claims Agreement & Nunavut's relationships with other governments in Canada & the circumpolar world are used to support common goals. The department compiles & communicates information & evaluates government programs & data. The Intergovernmental Affairs Division is responsible for the management & development of government strategies, policies & initiatives relating to federal, provincial, territorial, circumpolar & aboriginal affairs. This office participates in preparations for Intergovernmental activities such as the Western & Annual Premiers Conferences, First Ministers meetings & the Social Union Framework Agreement, the Arctic Council, the Nunavut Implementation Panel & the Clyde River Protocol.

Premier; Minister, Hon. Joe Savikataaq
jsavikataaq@gov.nu.ca

Deputy Minister, William MacKay
Tel: 867-975-6010

Executive Director to URRC, Laurie-Anne White
Tel: 867-975-6054
laurieanne.white@gov.nu.ca

Director, Government Liaison Office, David Akoak
Tel: 867-975-6050
DAkoak@gov.nu.ca

Director, Intergovernmental Affairs, Anna Fowler
Tel: 867-975-6014
AFowler@gov.nu.ca

Director, Corporate Services, Les Hickey
Tel: 867-975-6026
LHickey@gov.nu.ca

Director, Policy, Planning & Evaluation, Rachel Mark
Tel: 867-975-6029; *Fax:* 867-975-6029
rmark@gov.nu.ca

Director, Aboriginal & Circumpolar Affairs, Letia Obed
Tel: 867-975-6036; *Fax:* 867-975-6091
lobed@gov.nu.ca

Director, Devolution Division, Mark Thompson
Tel: 867-975-6070
mthompson1@gov.nu.ca

Director, Public Service Training, Hanna Wolff

Tel: 867-975-6047
HWolff@gov.nu.ca

Nunavut Bureau of Statistics

www.stats.gov.nu.ca
The Bureau collects, records, analyzes & distributes statistical data on Nunavut to Nunavummiut & the rest of Canada.
Director/Territorial Statistician, Ryan Mazan
Tel: 867-473-2693
rmazan@gov.nu.ca

Nunavut Territory Department of Family Services

PO Box 1000 Stn. 1200, Iqaluit, NU X0A 0H0
Tel: 867-975-5200; *Fax:* 867-975-5722
www.gov.nu.ca/familyservices
Other Communication: Regional Contacts: Qikiqtani, Toll-Free Phone: 800-567-1514; Kivalliq: 800-953-8516; Kitikmeot: 800-661-0845
The department began operations in 2013-14 & was created by uniting resources from the Departments of Education, Health & Social Services, Executive & Intergovernmental Affairs, Economic Development & Transportation, Human Resources & the Nunavut Housing Corporation. Its goal is to provide access to social safety services, protect vulnerable members of the community, to improve standards of living & assist the Territory with becoming more self-reliant. Matters of concern to the department include child welfare, adoptions, social advocacy, poverty reduction initiatives, family violence prevention, income assistance, career development & financial assistance for post-secondary students.

Minister, Hon. Elisapee Sheutiapik
esheutiapik@gov.nu.ca

Deputy Minister, Yvonne Niego
Tel: 867-975-5220
yniego@gov.nu.ca

Assistant Deputy Minister, Sol Vardy
Tel: 867-975-5268
svardy@gov.nu.ca

Acting Director, Career Development, Robert Clift
Tel: 867-857-3079
RClift@gov.nu.ca

Director, Income Assistance, Larry Journal
Tel: 867-975-5242
LJournal@gov.nu.ca

Director, Poverty Reduction, Ed McKenna
Tel: 867-975-5213
emckenna@gov.nu.ca

Acting Director, Corporate Services, Ester Usman
Tel: 867-975-5276
EUsman@gov.nu.ca

Nunavut Territory Department of Finance

PO Box 1000 Stn. 430, Iqaluit, NU X0A 0H0
Tel: 867-975-6222; *Fax:* 867-975-6220
Toll-Free: 888-668-9993
gnhr@gov.nu.ca
gov.nu.ca/finance
The Department of Finance is committed to provide direction & leadership to ensure fiscal responsibility & to create a secure base for Nunavut's economic growth, while promoting & maintaining public confidence in the prudence, propriety & integrity of government financial operations & respecting the principles of Inuit Qaujimajatuqangit (IQ).

Minister; Chair, Financial Management Board, Hon. George Hickes
ghickes@gov.nu.ca

Deputy Minister; Secretary to the Financial Management Board, Dan Carlson
dcarlson@gov.nu.ca

Assistant Deputy Minister, Dan Carlson
Tel: 867-975-6813

Director, Financial Systems Management, Joey Bennett
Tel: 867-975-5817
JBennett@gov.nu.ca

Director, Expenditure Management, Camilius Egeni
Tel: 867-975-5835; *Fax:* 867-975-6825
cegeni@gov.nu.ca

Director, Corporate Services, Christine Ellsworth

Tel: 867-975-6812
cellsworth@gov.nu.ca

Director, Corporate Policy, Jo-Anne Falkiner
Tel: 867-975-5831
jfalkiner@gov.nu.ca

Director, Staffing, Janet Hodder
Tel: 867-975-6223
JHodder@gov.nu.ca

Director, Liquor Management, Marion Love
Tel: 867-645-8478
mlove@gov.nu.ca

Director, Compensation & Benefits, Tracey Moyles
Tel: 867-975-6870
tmoyles@gov.nu.ca

Director, Financial Reporting & Controls, Susan Nichols
Tel: 867-975-5840
SNichols@gov.nu.ca

Director, Financial Operations, Michael Pringle
Tel: 867-975-5829
mpringle@gov.nu.ca

Director, Corporate Services, Tanya Winmill
Tel: 867-975-6812
TWinmill@gov.nu.ca

Associated Agencies, Boards & Commissions:
• **Nunavut Liquor & Cannabis Commission (NULC)**
PO Box 9
Rankin Inlet, NU X0C 0G0
Tel: 867-645-8575; *Fax:* 867-645-3327
Toll-free: 855-844-5488
info@nulc.ca
www.nulc.ca
Other Communication: Alt. URL:
www.gov.nu.ca/finance/information/nunavut-liquor-commission
The Commission oversees the operation of liquor stores, as well as the purchasing, selling, classifying, & distributing of liquor in Nunavut. As of 2018, it also sells cannabis remotely (online & by phone), in physical stores, & through an Agent (Canopy Growth Corporation/Tweed).

Nunavut Territory Department of Health

PO Box 1000 Stn. 1000, Iqaluit, NU X0A 0H0
Tel: 867-975-5700; *Fax:* 867-975-5705
Toll-Free: 800-661-0833
www.gov.nu.ca/health
The Department provides health services & social programming, addressing the differing needs of every community through culturally appropriate programs.

Minister; Minister responsible, Suicide Prevention, Hon. Lorne Kusugak
lkusugak@gov.nu.ca

Deputy Minister, Ruby Brown
Tel: 867-975-5702
RBrown@gov.nu.ca

Assistant Deputy Minister, Jacquie Pepper-Journal
Tel: 867-975-5956
jpepper-journal@gov.nu.ca

Chief Medical Officer of Health, Dr. Michael Patterson
Tel: 867-975-5992
mpatterson@gov.nu.ca

Deputy Chief Medical Officer of Health, Jasmine Pawa
Tel: 867-975-5992
JPawa@gov.nu.ca

Territorial Director, Medical Affairs, Kevin Compton
Tel: 867-975-7146
kcompton@gov.nu.ca

Territorial Director, Home, Community & Continuing Care, Stephen Jackson
Tel: 867-975-5925
SJackson@gov.nu.ca

Territorial Director, Population Health, Allison MacRury
Tel: 867-975-5790
AMacRury@gov.nu.ca

Territorial Director, Pharmacy, Donna Mulvey
Tel: 867-975-8600 ext: 6302
DMulvey@gov.nu.ca

Executive Director, Corporate Services, Greg Babstock
Tel: 867-975-5736
GBabstock@gov.nu.ca

Acting Executive Director, Corporate, Robert Berniquez
Tel: 867-975-5762
RBerniquez@gov.nu.ca

Executive Director, Health Operations, Nancy Laframboise
Tel: 867-473-2638
NLaframboise@gov.nu.ca

Executive Director, Lynn Ryan MacKenzie
Tel: 867-975-5992
lmackenzie1@gov.nu.ca

Physician & Director, Medical Education, Dr. Madeleine Cole
Tel: 867-979-7300
mcole@gov.nu.ca

Director, Mental Health, Victoria Madsen
Tel: 867-975-5290
vmadsen@gov.nu.ca

Acting Director, Travel Programs, Andrea McFaul
Tel: 867-975-7142
AMcFaul@gov.nu.ca

Nunavut Housing Corporation

Headquarters, PO Box 480 Arviat, NU X0C 0E0
Tel: 867-857-3000; *Fax:* 867-857-3040
www.nunavuthousing.ca
DirectoratePO Box 1000 1400 Sta.
Iqaluit, NU X0A 0H0
Alt. Fax: 867-979-4194

Minister responsible, Hon. Margaret Nakashuk
minnakashuk@gov.nu.ca

President & CEO, Terry Audla
Tel: 867-975-7201
TAudla@gov.nu.ca

Chief Operating Officer, Stephen Hooey
Tel: 867-975-7251
SHooey@gov.nu.ca

Chief Financial Officer & Vice-President, Gershom Moyo
Tel: 867-975-7202
GMoyo@gov.nu.ca

Executive Director, Programs, Patsy Kuksuk
Tel: 867-857-3001
PKuksuk@gov.nu.ca

Nunavut Territory Department of Justice

PO Box 1000 Stn. 500, Iqaluit, NU X0A 0H0
Tel: 867-975-6170; *Fax:* 867-975-6195
justice@gov.nu.ca
www.gov.nu.ca/justice

Minister, Hon. George Hickes
ghickes@gov.nu.ca

Deputy Minister, Simon Awa
Tel: 867-975-6180

Assistant Deputy Minister, Riita Strickland
Tel: 867-975-6071
rstrickland@gov.nu.ca

Associated Agencies, Boards & Commissions:
• **Baffin Correctional Centre**
PO Box 1000
Iqaluit, NU X0A 0H0
Tel: 867-979-8100; *Fax:* 867-979-4646
• **Labour Standards Board**
PO Box 1269
Iqaluit, NU X0A 0H0
Tel: 867-975-6159; *Fax:* 867-975-6376
nlsb@gov.nu.ca
www.nu-nlsb.ca

• **Legal Services Board of Nunavut**
1104-B Inuksugait Plaza
PO Box 29
Iqaluit, NU X0A 0H0
Tel: 867-975-6395
nulas.ca
Other Communication: Kitikmeot Law Centre: 867-983-2906; Kivalliq Legal Services: 867-645-2536
• **Liquor Licensing Board**
PO Box 1000 330
Iqaluit, NU X0A 0H0
Tel: 867-975-5875; *Fax:* 867-975-5805
nllb@gov.nu.ca
Other Communication: URL:
gov.nu.ca/finance/information/about-nunavut-liquor-licensing-board
The Board issues all liquor licences & ensures that licence holders maintain their properties in accordance with the law.
• **Nunavut Criminal Code Review Board**
PO Box 1269
Iqaluit, NU X0A 0H0
Tel: 867-975-6532; *Fax:* 867-975-6511
nccrb@gov.nu.ca
www.nu-nrb.ca
• **Nunavut Human Rights Tribunal**
PO Box 15
Coral Harbour, NU X0C 0C0
Toll-free: 866-413-6478
nunavuthumanrights@gov.nu.ca
www.nhrt.ca
Other Communication: Toll-Free Fax: 888-220-1011
• **Office of the Chief Coroner**
PO Box 1000 590
Iqaluit, NU X0A 0H0
Tel: 867-975-6562; *Fax:* 867-975-6367
Toll-free: 844-778-1022
coroner@gov.nu.ca
nunavutcoroner.ca
• **Office of the Public Trustee**
PO Box 1000 560
Iqaluit, NU X0A 0H0
Tel: 867-975-6338; *Fax:* 867-975-6343
Toll-free: 866-294-2127
PublicTrustee@gov.nu.ca
www.gov.nu.ca/justice/programs-services/public-trustee-office
• **Young Offenders Facility / Isumaqsunngittut Youth Centre**
1548 Federal Rd.
PO Box 1439
Iqaluit, NU X0A 0H0
Tel: 867-979-4452; *Fax:* 867-979-5506

Community Justice
PO Box 1000 Stn. 510, Iqaluit, NU X0A 0H0
Tel: 867-975-6363; *Fax:* 867-975-6160
communityjustice@gov.nu.ca
Promotes community justice, family abuse intervention, & victim services development, as well as crime prevention programs.
Director, Matthew Parent
Tel: 867-975-6176
MParent@gov.nu.ca

Corporate Services
PO Box 1000 Stn. 520, Iqaluit, NU X0A 0H0
Tel: 867-975-6170; *Fax:* 867-975-6188
justice.corporate@gov.nu.ca
Provides financial support services to the department, including the negotiation of financial agreements between Nunavut & the federal government.
Director, Mubashir Mahmood
Tel: 867-975-6504
MMahmoodjus@gov.nu.ca

Corrections
PO Box 1000 Stn. 580, Iqaluit, NU X0A 0H0
Tel: 867-975-6500; *Fax:* 867-975-6515
corrections@gov.nu.ca
Provides security & management services, & promotes healing through the rehabilitation of inmates & young offenders.
Director, J.P. Deroy
Tel: 867-975-6501
jpderoy@gov.nu.ca

Court Services
PO Box 297 Iquluit, NU X0A 0H0
Tel: 867-975-6100; *Fax:* 867-975-6168
ncj.criminal@gov.nu.ca
www.nunavutcourts.ca
Other Communication: Alt. Emails: NCJ.Civil@gov.nu.ca;
courtlibrary@gov.nu.ca; NCJ.Sheriff@gov.nu.ca;
NCJ.Judgeschambers@gov.nu.ca; labourservices@gov.nu.ca;
rentaloffice@gov.nu.ca;

Responsibilities include: support services for the Nunavut Court of Justice; assistance for the public, judiciary, counsel, RCMP, & other officials; Sheriff's office; Justice of the Peace Program; Coroner's Program; Family Support Program; Commissioners for Oaths & Notaries Public Program; Labour Standards Administration; support for the Labour Standards Board & Nunavut Criminal Code Review Board; administration of the Residential Tenancies Act; & access to legal research through the courthouse law library.
Sheriff of Nunavut, Michael Hatch
Tel: 867-975-6119
MHatchJUS@gov.nu.ca
Other Communications: Alt. Email: NCJ.sheriff@gov.nu.ca
Chief Justice, Vacant
NCJ.JP@gov.nu.ca

Legal & Constitutional Law
PO Box 1000 Stn. 540, Iqaluit, NU X0A 0H0
Tel: 867-975-6320; *Fax:* 867-975-6349
justice.legal@gov.nu.ca
Provides legal services & advice to Cabinet, government departments, & certain boards & public agencies; also responsible for constitutional matters, such as the Nunavut Land Claims Agreement, Devolution, & the Canadian Charter of Rights & Freedoms.
Director, Adrienne Silk
Tel: 867-975-6172
ASilk@gov.nu.ca

Legal Registries
PO Box 1000 Stn. 570, Iqaluit, NU X0A 0H0
Tel: 867-975-6590; *Fax:* 867-975-6594
Legal.Registries@gov.nu.ca
nunavutlegalregistries.ca
Other Communication: Alt. Emails:
LandTitleSearches@gov.nu.ca;
LandTitleRegistrations@gov.nu.ca;
CorporateSearches@gov.nu.ca;
CorporateRegistrations@gov.nu.ca; Securities@gov.nu.ca
Contains the following registries & offices: Corporate Registries; Personal Property Registry; Land Titles Office; Office of the Superintendent of Securities; & Commissioner for Oaths & Notary Public.
Director, Jeff Mason
Tel: 867-975-6591
jmason@gov.nu.ca

Legislation
PO Box 1000 Stn. 550, Iqaluit, NU X0A 0H0
Tel: 867-975-6305; *Fax:* 867-975-6189
territorial.printer@gov.nu.ca
Responsible for drafting all bills, regulations & appointments; prints the Nunavut Gazette, & provides annual volumes of statutes.
Director, Norman Tarnow
Tel: 867-975-6332
NTarnow@gov.nu.ca
Nunavut Official Editor & Territorial Printer, Danielle Lepage
Tel: 867-975-6305
dlepage@gov.nu.ca

Policy & Planning
PO Box 1000 Stn. 500, Iqaluit, NU X0A 0H0
Tel: 867-975-6170; *Fax:* 867-975-6151
justice.policy@gov.nu.ca
Responsible for policies & briefings, consultations with other governments, access to information & protection of privacy, negotiating & managing grants & contribution funds, & responses to justice issues.
Director, Constance Merkosak
Tel: 867-975-6158
CMerkosak@gov.nu.ca

Northwest Territories & Nunavut Workers' Safety & Compensation Commission (WSCC)

For a detailed listing please see Northwest Territories.

Government of Ontario

Seat of Government: Queen's Park, Toronto, ON M7A 1A2
Tel: 416-326-1234
Toll-Free: 800-267-8097
TTY: 800-268-7095
www.ontario.ca
twitter.com/ongov
www.facebook.com/ONgov
www.linkedin.com/company/government-of-ontario
www.youtube.com/user/ONgov
The Province of Ontario entered Confederation July 1, 1867. It has a land area of 908,699.33 sq km, & the StatsCan census population in 2016 was 13,448,494.

Office of the Lieutenant Governor

Legislative Bldg., Queen's Park, Toronto, ON M7A 1A1
Tel: 416-325-7780
TTY: 416-325-5003
lt.gov@ontario.ca
www.lgontario.ca
twitter.com/LGLizDowdeswell
www.facebook.com/LGLizDowdeswell
www.youtube.com/c/OntarioLG
Represents Her Majesty The Queen in Ontario. The Office coordinates, supports & promotes the activities of the Lieutenant Governor. In her constitutional role, the Lieutenant Governor swears-in the Executive Council, outlines the Government's plans in the Speech from the Throne, provides the Royal Assent needed for bills to become laws, approves orders-in-council & appointments recommended by Cabinet, & prorogues or dissolves each session of Parliament. In her community role, she represents the people of Ontario & acts as the Province's official host, welcoming world leaders & diplomats. She hosts or attends hundreds of community events throughout Ontario & presents honours & awards to outstanding Ontarians. Elizabeth Dowdeswell was appointed as the 29th Lieutenant-Governor on June 26, 2014. She replaced David Onley, who held the position for seven years - the longest term for a Lieutenant Governor of Ontario since WWII.

Lieutenant Governor of Ontario, Hon. Elizabeth Dowdeswell, OC, OOnt
Tel: 416-325-7780

Chief of Staff/Private Secretary to the Lieutenant Governor, Anthony Hylton
Tel: 416-325-7781
anthony.hylton@ontario.ca

Chief Steward, Robert Adams
Tel: 416-325-7794
robert.adams@ontario.ca

Office of the Premier

Legislative Bldg., Queen's Park, Toronto, ON M7A 1A1
Tel: 416-325-1941
TTY: 800-387-5559
www.ontario.ca/page/premier
www.youtube.com/user/premierofontario

Premier; Minister, Intergovernmental Affairs, Hon. Doug Ford
doug.ford@pc.ola.org

Deputy Premier; Minister, Health, Hon. Christine Elliott
christine.elliott@pc.ola.org

Acting Chief of Staff, James Wallace
Tel: 416-325-7635
James.Wallace@ontario.ca

Deputy Chief of Staff, HR Administration & Tour, Simone Daniels
Tel: 416-325-7635
Simone.Daniels@ontario.ca

Deputy Chief of Staff, Policy, Vacant

Deputy Chief of Staff, Strategic Communications, Vacant

Deputy Chief of Staff, Issues Management, Media Relations & Legislative Affairs, Cody Welton
cody.welton@ontario.ca

Cabinet of Ontario

Legislative Bldg., Queen's Park, Toronto, ON M7A 1A1
www.ontario.ca/page/meet-premiers-team

Premier; Minister, Intergovernmental Affairs, Hon. Doug Ford
doug.ford@pc.ola.org

Deputy Premier; Minister, Health, Hon. Christine Elliott; *Fax:* 416-326-1571
christine.elliott@pc.ola.org

Minister, Finance, Hon. Peter Bethlenfalvy
Tel: 416-327-2333
peter.bethlenfalvy@pc.ola.org

Minister Without Portfolio; Government House Leader, Hon. Paul Calandra
Tel: 416-325-7754; *Fax:* 416-325-7755
paul.calandra@pc.ola.org

Minister, Seniors & Accessibility, Hon. Raymond Sung Joon Cho
Tel: 416-314-0797
raymond.cho@pc.ola.org

Minister, Municipal Affairs & Housing, Hon. Steve Clark
Tel: 416-585-7000; *Fax:* 416-585-6470
steve.clark@pc.ola.org

Attorney General, Hon. Doug Downey
Tel: 416-326-2220; *Fax:* 416-325-1219
doug.downey@pc.ola.org

Minister, Colleges & Universities, Hon. Jill Dunlop
Tel: 416-326-1600
jill.dunlop@pc.ola.org

Minister, Economic Development, Job Creation & Trade; Chair, Cabinet, Hon. Victor Fedeli
Tel: 416-326-8475
vic.fedeli@pc.ola.org

Minister, Children, Community & Social Services, Hon. Merrilee Fullerton
Tel: 416-325-5225
merrilee.fullerton@pc.ola.org

Minister, Citizenship & Multiculturalism, Hon. Parm Gill
Tel: 416-212-0036
parm.gill@pc.ola.org

Solicitor General, Hon. Sylvia Jones
Tel: 416-325-0408; *Fax:* 416-326-0498
sylvia.jones@pc.ola.org

Minister, Education, Hon. Stephen Lecce
Tel: 416-325-2600
stephen.lecce@pc.ola.org

Minister, Heritage, Sport, Tourism & Culture Industries, Hon. Lisa MacLeod
Tel: 416-314-1400
Lisa.macleodco@pc.ola.org

Minister, Labour, Training & Skills Development, Hon. Monte McNaughton
Tel: 416-326-7600
monte.mcnaughton@pc.ola.org

Minister, Transportation; Minister, Francophone Affairs, Hon. Caroline Mulroney
Tel: 416-327-9200
caroline.mulroney@pc.ola.org

Minister, Long-Term Care, Hon. Rod Phillips
Tel: 416-325-0145
rod.phillips@pc.ola.org

Minister, Environment, Conservation & Parks, Hon. David Piccini
Tel: 416-314-6790
david.piccini@pc.ola.org

Minister, Indigenous Affairs; Minister, Northern Development, Mines, Natural Resources & Forestry, Hon. Greg Rickford
Tel: 416-326-4740
greg.rickford@pc.ola.org

Minister, Government & Consumer Services, Hon. Ross Romano
Tel: 416-212-2665
ross.romano@pc.ola.org

President, Treasury Board, Hon. Prabmeet Singh Sarkaria
Tel: 416-327-2333
prabmeet.sarkaria@pc.ola.org

Minister, Energy, Hon. Todd Smith
Tel: 416-327-6758
todd.smithco@pc.ola.org

Minister, Infrastructure, Hon. Kinga Surma
Tel: 416-327-4412
kinga.surma@pc.ola.org

Minister, Agriculture, Food & Rural Affairs, Hon. Lisa Thompson
Tel: 416-326-3074
lisa.thompson@pc.ola.org

Associate Minister, Transportation (Transit-Oriented

Communities), Hon. Stan Cho
Tel: 416-327-9200
stan.cho@pc.ola.org

Associate Minister, Children & Women's Issues, Hon.
Jane McKenna
Tel: 416-325-5225
jane.mckenna@pc.ola.org

Associate Minister, Digital Government, Hon. Kaleed
Rasheed
Tel: 416-325-0400
kaleed.rasheedco@pc.ola.org

**Associate Minister, Small Business & Red Tape
Reduction,** Hon. Nina Tangri
Tel: 416-326-8475
nina.tangri@pc.ola.org

Associate Minister, Mental Health & Addictions, Hon.
Michael A. Tibollo
michael.tibolloCO@pc.ola.org

Cabinet Office

**Whitney Block, Queen's Park, 99 Wellesley St. West, 6th Fl.,
Toronto, ON M7A 1A1**
Tel: 416-325-7635; *Fax:* 416-325-3004
TTY: 416-314-5721

**Secretary of the Cabinet, Clerk of the Executive Council
& Head of the Ontario Public Service,** Michelle DiEmanuele
M.DiEmanuele@ontario.ca

Deputy Minister, Communications, Nina Chiarelli
nina.chiarelli@ontario.ca

**Deputy Minister, Policy & Delivery & Associate Secretary
of the Cabinet,** Martha Greenberg
Tel: 416-325-3759
martha.greenberg@ontario.ca

**Assistant Deputy Minister & Chief Administrative Officer,
Corporate Planning & Services,** Blair Dunker
Tel: 416-314-0817; *Fax:* 416-325-2388
blair.e.dunker@ontario.ca

**Acting Assistant Deputy Minister, Economic,
Environment, Justice & Intergovernmental Policy,**
Shannon Fuller
Tel: 416-276-7038
Shannon.Fuller@ontario.ca

**Acting Assistant Deputy Minister, Health, Social,
Education & Children's Policy,** David Wai
Tel: 416-505-4458
david.wai@ontario.ca

Associated Agencies, Boards & Commissions:

• Executive Development Committee
Queen's Park
Toronto, ON M5G 2K1
Tel: 416-325-1750

Ontario Legislative Assembly

**c/o Clerk of the Legislative Assembly, #104, Legislative
Bldg., Queen's Park, Toronto, ON M7A 1A2**
Tel: 416-325-7500; *Fax:* 416-325-7489
TTY: 416-325-9426
web@ola.org
www.ola.org
twitter.com/ONPARLeducation
www.facebook.com/LegislativeAssemblyofOntario
www.linkedin.com/company/legislative-assembly-of-ontario
www.youtube.com/user/OntarioLegislature
The Legislative Assembly, consisting of 124 elected Members of
Provincial Parliament (MPPs), represent the people in their
constituencies.

Speaker, Hon. Ted Arnott
Tel: 416-325-3880; *Fax:* 416-325-6649
ted.arnott@pc.ola.org

Deputy Speaker & Chair, Committee of the Whole House,
Bill Walker

Clerk, Todd Decker
Tel: 416-325-7341; *Fax:* 416-325-7344
tdecker@ola.org

**Sergeant-at-Arms & Executive Director, Precinct
Properties Division,** Jacquelyn Gordon

Tel: 416-325-7446; *Fax:* 416-325-7154
jgordon@ola.ca
#411, North Wing, Legislative Bldg., Queen's Park
Toronto, ON M7A 1A2 Canada

Deputy Clerk & Executive Director, Legislative Services,
Trevor Day
Tel: 416-325-3502; *Fax:* 416-325-5848
tday@ola.org
#1640, Whitney Block, Queen's Park
99 Wellesley St. W
Toronto, ON M7A 1A2 Canada

Executive Director, Administrative Services, Nancy
Marling
Tel: 416-325-3557
nmarling@ola.org
#2501, Whitney Block, Queen's Park
Toronto, ON M7A 1A2 Canada

**Legislative Librarian & Executive Director, Information &
Technology Services,** Vicki Whitmell
Tel: 416-325-3939; *Fax:* 416-325-3909
vwhitmell@ola.org
Other Communications: Reference Inquiries: 416-325-3900
#1413, Whitney Block
Toronto, ON M7A 1A9 Canada

Government Caucus Office (PC)

#251, Legislative Bldg., Queen's Park, Toronto, ON M7A 1A4
Tel: 416-325-7255; *Fax:* 416-325-7739
ontariopc.com
twitter.com/ontariopcparty
www.facebook.com/ontariopc
www.linkedin.com/company/ontario-pc-party
www.instagram.com/ontariopc
Chief Government Whip, Lorne Coe
lorne.coe@pc.ola.org
Chair, Government Caucus, Daryl Kramp
Tel: 416-326-7005
daryl.kramp@pc.ola.org
Government House Leader, Hon. Paul Calandra
Deputy Government House Leader, Andrea Khanjin
andrea.khanjin@pc.ola.org
Deputy Government Whip, Hon. Kaleed Rasheed
Tel: 416-326-7028
Kaleed.Rasheed@ontario.ca

Office of the Opposition (NDP)

#381, Legislative Bldg., Queen's Park, Toronto, ON M7A 1A5
Tel: 416-325-7116; *Fax:* 416-325-8222
TTY: 416-325-6564
ndpmail@ndp.on.ca
www.ondpcaucus.com
Other Communication: Ontario NDP URL: www.ontariondp.com
twitter.com/OntarioNDP
www.facebook.com/OntarioNDP
Leader, Official Opposition, Andrea Horwath
Tel: 416-325-8300
horwatha-qp@ndp.on.ca
Deputy Leader, Official Opposition, Sara Singh
Tel: 416-326-7610; *Fax:* 416-326-7615
SSingh-CO@ndp.on.ca
Chief Opposition Whip; Deputy Leader, Official Opposition, John
Vanthof
Tel: 416-325-2000; *Fax:* 416-325-1999
jvanthof-qp@ndp.on.ca
Caucus Chair, Official Opposition, Catherine Fife
Tel: 416-325-6913; *Fax:* 416-325-6942
cfife-qp@ndp.on.ca
Opposition House Leader, Peggy Sattler
Tel: 416-325-6908; *Fax:* 416-325-7030
Psattler-qp@ndp.on.ca

Standing Committees of the Legislative Assembly
www.ola.org/en/node/96451

Standing Committee on Estimates
Chair, Peter Tabuns
Constituency: Toronto-Danforth, New Democratic Party
Clerk, Thushitha Kobikrishna
comm-estimates@ola.org

Standing Committee on Finance & Economic Affairs
Chair, Amarjot Sandhu
Constituency: Oakville, Progressive Conservative
Clerk, Julia Douglas
Tel: 416-325-3515
comm-financeaffairs@ola.org

Standing Committee on General Government
Chair, Goldie Ghamari
Constituency: Peterborough-Kawartha, Progressive
Conservative

Clerk, Isaiah Thorning
Tel: 416-325-7352
comm-generalgov@ola.org

Standing Committee on Government Agencies
Chair, Gilles Bisson
Constituency: Timiskaming-Cochrane, New Democratic Party
Clerk, Julia Douglas
comm-govagencies@ola.org

Standing Committee on Justice Policy
Chair, Daryl Kramp
Clerk, Thushitha Kobikkrishna
comm-justicepolicy@ola.org

Standing Committee on the Legislative Assembly
Chair, Hon. Kaleed Rasheed
Constituency: Burlington, Progressive Conservative
Clerk, Tonia Grannum
comm-legisassembly@ola.org

Standing Committee on Public Accounts
Chair, Taras Natyshak
Constituency: Waterloo, New Democratic Party
Clerk, Christopher Tyrell
Tel: 416-325-3883
comm-publicaccounts@ola.org

Standing Committee on Regulations & Private Bills
Chair, Logan Kanapathi
Constituency: Mississauga East-Cooksville, Progressive
Conservative
Clerk, Isaiah Thorning
Tel: 416-325-3526
comm-regsprbills@ola.org

Standing Committee on Social Policy
Chair, Deepak Anand
Constituency: Mississauga-Streetsville, Progressive
Conservative
Clerk, Tanzima Khan
Tel: 416-325-3506
comm-socialpolicy@ola.org

Forty-second Provincial Parliament - Ontario

**Clerk's Office, #104, Legislative Bldg., Queen's Park,
Toronto, ON M7A 1A2**
Tel: 416-325-7500; *Fax:* 416-325-7489
TTY: 416-325-9426
web@ola.org
www.ola.org

Last General Election, June 7, 2018.
Maximum Duration, 5 years.
Party Standings (Oct. 2021):
Progressive Conservative Party 70;
New Democratic Party 40;
Liberal Party 7;
Green Party 1;
New Blue 1;
Independent 4;
Vacant 1;
Total Seats 124.
Salary Disclosure for 2016:
Member Base Pay: $116,550.00;
Premier $208,974.00;
Leader, Official Opposition $180,885.96;
Leader, Third Party $158,157.96;
Minister, Finance $165,851.04;
Speaker $152,913.96;
Chief Government Whip $134,758.09;
Chief Whip, Official Opposition $132,867.00;
Chief Whip, Third Party $131,235.00;
House Leader, Official Opposition $168,103.34;
House Leader, Third Party $134,732.04.
The following list features information about members after the
2018 election, with their constituency, party affiliation, & contact
information:

Members of Provincial Parliament
Deepak Anand
Constituency: Mississauga-Malton, Progressive Conservative
Tel: 416-326-7528; *Fax:* 416-326-7504
deepak.anand@pc.ola.org
deepakanand.nationbuilder.com
Other Communications: Constituency Phone: 905-696-0367;
Fax: 905-696-7545
twitter.com/DeepakAnandMPP,
www.facebook.com/DeepakAnandMPP
Constituency Office
#11, 7895 Tranmere Dr.
Mississauga, ON L5S 1V9
Jill Andrew
Constituency: Toronto-St. Paul's, New Democratic Party
Tel: 416-325-0071; *Fax:* 416-325-4728
JAndrew-QP@ndp.on.ca
www.jillandrewmpp.ca
Other Communications: Constituency Phone: 416-656-0943;

Fax: 416-656-0875
twitter.com/jillslastword, www.facebook.com/JillAndrewTO
Constituency Office
803 St Clair Ave. West
Toronto, ON M6C 1B9

Teresa J. Armstrong
Constituency: London-Fanshawe, New Democratic Party
Tel: 416-325-1872; *Fax:* 416-325-1912
tarmstrong-qp@ndp.on.ca
www.teresaarmstrong.com
Other Communications: Constituency Phone: 519-668-1104;
Fax: 519-668-1941
twitter.com/TArmstrongNDP,
www.facebook.com/TArmstrongNDP
Constituency Office
155 Clarke Rd.
London, ON N5W 5C9

Speaker, Hon. Ted Arnott
Constituency: Wellington-Halton Hills, Progressive
Conservative
Tel: 416-325-3880
Toll-free: 800-265-2366; *Fax:* 416-325-6649
ted.arnott@pc.ola.org
tedarnottmpp.com
Other Communications: Constituency Phone: 519-787-5247;
Fax: 519-787-5249
twitter.com/mpparnottwhh, www.facebook.com/ted.arnott.ont
Constituency Office
181 St Andrew St. East, 2nd Fl.
Fergus, ON N1M 1P9

Ian Arthur
Constituency: Kingston and the Islands, New Democratic
Party
Tel: 416-325-0168; *Fax:* 416-325-0088
IArthur-QP@ndp.on.ca
www.ianarthurmpp.ca
Other Communications: Constituency Phone: 613-547-2385;
Fax: 613-547-5001
twitter.com/IanArthurMPP, www.facebook.com/YGKIanArthur,
www.linkedin.com/in/ygkianarthur
Constituency Office, The LaSalle Mews
#2, 303 Bagot St.
Kingston, ON K7K 5W7

Roman Baber
Constituency: York Centre, Independent
Tel: 416-326-7114; *Fax:* 416-326-7113
rbaber@ola.org
romanbabermpp.ca
Other Communications: Constituency Phone: 416-630-0080;
Fax: 416-630-8828
twitter.com/roman_baber, www.facebook.com/yorkcentrepc
Note: Roman Baber was removed from the P.C. Caucus in
January 2021.
Constituency Office
830 Sheppard Ave. West
Toronto, ON M3H 2T1

Aris Babikian
Constituency: Scarborough-Agincourt, Progressive
Conservative
Tel: 416-326-7111; *Fax:* 416-326-7099
aris.babikian@pc.ola.org
www.arisbabikianmpp.ca
Other Communications: Constituency Phone: 416-297-6568;
Fax: 416-297-4962
twitter.com/Aris_Babikian, www.facebook.com/BabikianPC
Constituency Office
#207, 4002 Sheppard Ave. East
Toronto, ON M1S 4R5

Robert (Bob) Bailey
Constituency: Sarnia-Lambton, Progressive Conservative
Tel: 416-212-2665
bob.bailey@pc.ola.org
bobbaileympp.com
Other Communications: Constituency Phone: 519-337-0051;
Fax: 519-337-3246
twitter.com/BobBaileyPC,
www.facebook.com/BobBaileySarniaLambton
Constituency Office
#102, 805 Christina St. North
Point Edward, ON N7V 1X6

Toby Barrett
Constituency: Haldimand-Norfolk, Progressive Conservative
Tel: 416-325-8404
toby.barrett@pc.ola.org
tobybarrett.com
Other Communications: Constituency Phone: 519-428-0446;
Fax: 519-428-0835
twitter.com/TobyBarrettHN,
www.facebook.com/tobybarrett.mpp
Constituency Office
50B Gilbertson Dr.
Simcoe, ON N3Y 4L8

Doly Begum
Constituency: Scarborough Southwest, New Democratic

Party
Tel: 416-325-0908; *Fax:* 416-325-0685
DBegum-QP@ndp.on.ca
www.dolybegum.ca
Other Communications: Constituency Phone: 416-261-9525;
Fax: 416-261-0381
twitter.com/dolybegum,
www.facebook.com/DolyforScarborough
Constituency Office
#5A, 3110 Kingston Rd.
Toronto, ON M1M 1P2

Jessica Bell
Constituency: University-Rosedale, New Democratic Party
Tel: 416-325-1620; *Fax:* 416-325-1424
JBell-QP@ndp.on.ca
www.jessicabellmpp.ca
Other Communications: Constituency Phone: 416-535-7206
twitter.com/jessicabellto,
www.facebook.com/UniRoseJessicaBell
Constituency Office
#103, 719 Bloor St. West
Toronto, ON M6G 1L5

Rima Berns-McGown
Constituency: Beaches-East York, New Democratic Party
Tel: 416-325-2881; *Fax:* 416-325-2780
RBerns-McGown-QP@ndp.on.ca
www.beyrima.ca
Other Communications: Constituency Office: 416-690-1032;
Fax: 416-690-8420
twitter.com/beyrima,
www.facebook.com/mpprimabernsmcgown
Constituency Office
1821 Danforth Ave.
Toronto, ON M4C 1J2

Minister, Finance, Hon. Peter Bethlenfalvy
Constituency: Pickering-Uxbridge, Progressive Conservative
Tel: 416-325-0400
peter.bethlenfalvy@pc.ola.org
peterbethlenfalvympp.ca
Other Communications: Constituency Office: 905-509-0336;
Fax: 905-509-0334
twitter.com/pbethlenfalvy,
www.facebook.com/PeterBethlenfalvyMPP,
www.linkedin.com/in/peterbethlenfalvy
Constituency Office
#213, 1550 Kingston Rd.
Pickering, ON L1V 1C3

Gilles Bisson
Constituency: Timmins, New Democratic Party
Tel: 416-325-7122
Toll-free: 800-461-9878; *Fax:* 416-325-7181
gbisson@ndp.on.ca
www.gillesbisson.com
Other Communications: Constituency Office: 705-268-6400;
Fax: 705-266-9125
twitter.com/bissongilles,
www.facebook.com/GillesBissonONDP
Constituency Office
#202, 60 Wilson Ave.
Timmins, ON P4N 2S7

Stephen Blais
Constituency: Orleans, Liberal
sblais.mpp.co@liberal.ola.org
stephenblais.ca
Other Communications: Constituency Office: 613-834-8679;
Fax: 613-834-7647
twitter.com/StephenBlais, www.facebook.com/StephenBlais,
www.linkedin.com/in/stephenblais
Constituency Office
#204, 4473 Innes Rd.
Orleans, ON K4A 1A7

Will Bouma
Constituency: Brantford-Brant, Progressive Conservative
Tel: 416-326-7092
willem.bouma@pc.ola.org
willbouma.ca
Other Communications: Constituency Phone: 519-759-0361;
Fax: 519-759-6439
twitter.com/willboumabrant,
www.facebook.com/WillBoumaBrant,
www.linkedin.com/in/will-bouma-90059a40
Constituency Office
#101, 96 Nelson St.
Brantford, ON N3T 2X1

Guy Bourgouin
Constituency: Mushkegowuk-James Bay, New Democratic
Party
Tel: 416-326-7351; *Fax:* 416-326-6972
GBourgouin-QP@ndp.on.ca
www.guybourgouin.com
Other Communications: Constituency Phone: 705-335-6400
twitter.com/bourgouinguy,
www.facebook.com/guybourgouinmjb
Constituency Office

1-2 Ash St.
Kapuskasing, ON P5N 3H4

Jeff Burch
Constituency: Niagara Centre, New Democratic Party
Tel: 416-325-3990; *Fax:* 416-325-3415
JBurch-QP@ndp.on.ca
www.jeffburchmpp.ca
Other Communications: Constituency Phone: 905-732-6884;
Fax: 905-732-9782
twitter.com/jeffburch_, www.facebook.com/BurchJeff
Constituency Office
#102, 60 King St.
Welland, ON L3B 6A4

**Minister Without Portfolio; Government House Leader, Hon. Paul
Calandra**
Constituency: Markham-Stouffville, Progressive Conservative
Tel: 416-325-7754
Toll-free: 866-531-9551; *Fax:* 416-325-7755
paul.calandra@pc.ola.org
www.paulcalandra.com
Other Communications: Constituency Phone: 905-642-2588;
Fax: 905-642-1618
twitter.com/paulcalandra, www.facebook.com/Paul.Calandra
Constituency Office
#400, 37 Sandiford Dr.
Stouffville, ON L4A 3Z2

Minister, Seniors & Accessibility, Hon. Raymond Sung Joon Cho
Constituency: Scarborough-North, Progressive Conservative
Tel: 416-314-0797
raymond.cho@pc.ola.org
Other Communications: Constituency Phone: 416-297-5040;
Fax: 416-297-6767
twitter.com/raymondchopc
Constituency Office
4559 Sheppard Ave. East, #B
Toronto, ON M1S 1V3

**Associate Minister, Transportation (Transit-Oriented
Communities), Hon. Stan Cho**
Constituency: Willowdale, Progressive Conservative
Tel: 416-327-9200
stan.cho@pc.ola.org
www.stanchompp.ca
Other Communications: Constituency Phone: 416-733-7878;
Fax: 416-733-7709
twitter.com/stanchompp, www.facebook.com/StanChoMPP
Constituency Office, Newtonbrook Plaza
111 Sheppard Ave. West
Toronto, ON M2N 1M7

Minister, Municipal Affairs & Housing, Hon. Steve Clark
Constituency: Leeds-Grenville-Thousand Islands & Rideau
Lakes, Progressive Conservative
Tel: 416-585-7000
Toll-free: 800-267-4408; *Fax:* 416-585-6470
steve.clark@pc.ola.org
www.steveclarkmpp.com
Other Communications: Constituency Phone: 613-342-9522;
Fax: 613-342-2501
twitter.com/SteveClarkpc, www.facebook.com/steveclarkmpp,
www.linkedin.com/in/steve-clark-04aa0b44
Constituency Office
#101, 100 Strowger Blvd.
Brockville, ON K6V 5J9

Government Whip, Lorne Coe
Constituency: Whitby, Progressive Conservative
Tel: 416-325-1331; *Fax:* 416-325-1423
lorne.coe@pc.ola.org
www.lornecoempp.ca
Other Communications: Constituency Phone: 905-430-1141;
Fax: 905-430-1840
twitter.com/lornecoe, www.facebook.com/lornecoempp
Constituency Office
#101, 114 Dundas St. East
Whitby, ON L1N 2H7

Lucille Collard
Constituency: Ottawa-Vanier, Liberal
Tel: 416-325-0007; *Fax:* 416-325-0172
LCollard.mpp.co@liberal.ola.org
lucillecollard.ca
Other Communications: Constituency Phone: 613-744-4484;
Fax: 613-744-0889
twitter.com/LucilleCollard,
www.facebook.com/LucilleCollardMPP,
www.linkedin.com/in/lucille-collard-14942853
Note: Lucille Collard was elected in a by-election held Feb.
27, 2020.
Constituency Office
237 Montreal Rd.
Vanier, ON K1L 6C7

Stephen Crawford
Constituency: Oakville, Progressive Conservative
Tel: 416-326-7591
stephen.crawford@pc.ola.org
www.stephencrawfordmpp.ca
Other Communications: Constituency Phone: 905-827-5141;

Fax: 905-827-3786
twitter.com/stcrawford2,
www.facebook.com/SCrawfordforOakville,
www.linkedin.com/in/stephen-crawford-aa048232
Constituency Office
#1, 74 Rebecca St.
Oakville, ON L6K 1J2

Rudy Cuzzetto
Constituency: Mississauga-Lakeshore, Progressive
Conservative
Tel: 416-326-7239
rudy.cuzzetto@pc.ola.org
www.cuzzetto.com
Other Communications: Constituency Phone: 905-274-8228;
Fax: 905-274-8552
twitter.com/RudyCuzzetto,
www.facebook.com/RudyCuzzettoPC,
www.linkedin.com/in/rudy-cuzzetto-63691b90
Constituency Office
#1 & 2, 120 Lakeshore Rd. West
Mississauga, ON L5H 1E8

Attorney General, Hon. Doug Downey
Constituency: Barrie-Springwater-Oro-Medonte, Progressive
Conservative
Tel: 416-326-2220
Toll-free: 800-518-7901; *Fax:* 416-325-1219
doug.downey@pc.ola.org
www.dougdowney.ca
Other Communications: Constituency Phone: 705-726-5538;
Fax: 705-726-2880
twitter.com/douglasdowney,
www.facebook.com/DougDowneyMPP,
www.linkedin.com/in/doug-downey-aa311429
Constituency Office
#14, 20 Bell Farm Rd.
Barrie, ON L4M 6E4

Minister, Colleges & Universities, Hon. Jill Dunlop
Constituency: Simcoe North, Progressive Conservative
Tel: 416-326-1600
jill.dunlop@pc.ola.org
www.jilldunlopmpp.ca
Other Communications: Orillia: 705-326-3246; Midland:
705-526-8671
twitter.com/jilldunlop1, www.facebook.com/jilldunlopmpp,
www.linkedin.com/in/jill-dunlop
Constituency Office
14 Coldwater Rd. West
Orillia, ON L3V 3L1

Deputy Premier; Minister, Health, Hon. Christine Elliott
Constituency: Newmarket-Aurora, Progressive Conservative
Tel: 416-327-4300
Toll-free: 800-211-1881; *Fax:* 416-326-1571
christine.elliott@pc.ola.org
www.christineelliottmpp.ca
Other Communications: Constituency Phone: 905-853-9889;
Fax: 905-853-6115
twitter.com/celliottability,
www.facebook.com/ChristineElliottON
Constituency Office
#22, 16635 Yonge St.
Newmarket, ON L3X 1V6

Chair, Cabinet; Minister, Economic Development, Job Creation
& Trade, Hon. Victor Fedeli
Constituency: Nipissing, Progressive Conservative
Tel: 416-326-8475
vic.fedeli@pc.ola.org
fedeli.com
Other Communications: Constituency Phone: 705-474-8340;
Fax: 705-474-9747
twitter.com/VictorFedeli, www.facebook.com/vicfedeli,
www.linkedin.com/in/victorfedeli
Constituency Office
219 Main St. East
North Bay, ON P1B 1B2

Amy Fee
Constituency: Kitchener South-Hespeler, Progressive
Conservative
Tel: 416-325-7754; *Fax:* 416-325-7755
amy.fee@pc.ola.org
Other Communications: Constituency Phone: 519-650-9413;
Fax: 519-650-7006
Constituency Office
#4, 4281 King St. East
Kitchener, ON N2P 2E9

Caucus Chair, Official Opposition, Catherine Fife
Constituency: Waterloo, New Democratic Party
Tel: 416-325-6913; *Fax:* 416-325-6942
cfife-qp@ndp.on.ca
www.catherinefife.com
Other Communications: Constituency Phone: 519-725-3477;
Fax: 519-725-3667
twitter.com/CfifeKW, www.facebook.com/catherinefifeKW
Constituency Office

#220, 100 Regina St. South
Waterloo, ON N2J 4P9

Premier; Minister, Intergovernmental Affairs, Hon. Doug Ford
Constituency: Etobicoke North, Progressive Conservative
Tel: 416-325-1941; *Fax:* 416-325-3745
doug.ford@pc.ola.org
www.fordmpp.ca
Other Communications: Constituency Phone: 416-745-2859;
Fax: 416-745-4601
twitter.com/fordnation,
www.facebook.com/FordNationDougFord
Constituency Office
823 Albion Rd.
Etobicoke, ON M9V 1A3

House Leader, Ontario Liberal Caucus, John Fraser
Constituency: Ottawa South, Liberal
Tel: 416-325-4670; *Fax:* 416-325-4671
Jfraser.mpp.co@liberal.ola.org
johnfraser.onmpp.ca
Other Communications: Constituency Phone: 613-736-9573;
Fax: 613-736-7374
twitter.com/JohnFraserOS,
www.facebook.com/JohnFraserOttawaSouth
Constituency Office
1828 Bank St.
Ottawa, ON K1V 7Y6

Jennifer K. French
Constituency: Oshawa, New Democratic Party
Tel: 416-325-0117; *Fax:* 416-325-0084
JFrench-QP@ndp.on.ca
www.jenniferfrench.ca
Other Communications: Constituency Phone: 905-723-2411;
Fax: 905-723-1054
twitter.com/jennkfrench,
www.facebook.com/jenniferfrenchNDP
Constituency Office
#2, 78 Centre St. North
Oshawa, ON L1G 4B6

Minister, Children, Community & Social Services, Hon. Merrilee
Fullerton
Constituency: Kanata-Carleton, Progressive Conservative
Tel: 416-325-5225
merrilee.fullerton@pc.ola.org
www.merrileefullerton.ca
Other Communications: Constituency Phone: 613-599-3000;
Fax: 613-599-8183
twitter.com/DrFullertonMPP,
www.facebook.com/DrMerrileeFullerton,
www.linkedin.com/in/dr-merrilee-fullerton-71724620
Constituency Office
#100, 240 Michael Cowpland Dr.
Kanata, ON K2M 1P6

Wayne Gates
Constituency: Niagara Falls, New Democratic Party
Tel: 416-212-6102; *Fax:* 416-212-6106
wgates-qp@ndp.on.ca
www.waynegates.com
Other Communications: Niagara Falls: 905-357-0681; Fort
Erie: 905-871-8868
twitter.com/Wayne_Gates,
www.facebook.com/waynegatesniagara
Constituency Office
#1, 6746 Morrison St.
Niagara Falls, ON L2E 6Z8

France Gélinas
Constituency: Nickel Belt, New Democratic Party
Tel: 416-325-9203; *Fax:* 416-325-9185
fgelinas-qp@ndp.on.ca
francegelinas.ca
Other Communications: Constituency Phone: 705-969-3621;
Fax: 705-969-3538
twitter.com/NickelBelt, www.facebook.com/france.gelinas.92
Constituency Office, Hanmer Valley Shopping Plaza
#15, 5085 Hwy. 69 North
Hanmer, ON P3P 1P7

Goldie Ghamari
Constituency: Carleton, Progressive Conservative
Tel: 416-325-4890
goldie.ghamari@pc.ola.org
goldiempp.ca
Other Communications: Constituency Phone: 613-838-4425;
Fax: 613-838-6045
twitter.com/gghamari, www.facebook.com/gghamari,
www.linkedin.com/in/gghamari
Constituency Office
#30, 6179 Perth St.
Richmond, ON K0A 2Z0

Minister, Citizenship & Multiculturalism, Hon. Parm Gill
Constituency: Milton, Progressive Conservative
Tel: 416-212-0036
parm.gill@pc.ola.org
parmgill.nationbuilder.com
Other Communications: Constituency Phone: 905-878-1729;
Fax: 905-878-5144

twitter.com/parmgill, www.facebook.com/MPParmGill
Constituency Office
#206, 400 Main St. East
Milton, ON L9T 4X5

Chris Glover
Constituency: Spadina-Fort York, New Democratic Party
Tel: 416-326-7196; *Fax:* 416-326-7172
CGlover-CO@ndp.on.ca
www.chrisglovermpp.ca
Other Communications: Constituency Phone: 416-603-9664;
Fax: 416-603-1241
twitter.com/ChrisGloverMPP
Constituency Office
226 Bathurst St., #A
Toronto, ON M5T 2R9

Michael Gravelle
Constituency: Thunder Bay-Superior North, Liberal
Tel: 416-325-4757; *Fax:* 416-325-4752
mgravelle.mpp.co@liberal.ola.org
michaelgravelle.onmpp.ca
Other Communications: Constituency Phone: 807-345-3647;
Fax: 807-345-2922
twitter.com/MichaelGravelle
Constituency Office
179 Algoma St. South
Thunder Bay, ON P7B 3C1

Lisa Gretzky
Constituency: Windsor West, New Democratic Party
Tel: 416-325-0235; *Fax:* 416-325-0873
LGretzky-QP@ndp.on.ca
www.lisagretzkympp.ca
Other Communications: Constituency Phone: 519-977-7191;
Fax: 519-977-7029
twitter.com/LGretzky, www.facebook.com/LisaGretzky
Constituency Office
2443 Dougall Ave.
Windsor, ON N8X 1T3

Ernie Hardeman
Constituency: Oxford, Progressive Conservative
Toll-free: 800-265-4046
ernie.hardeman@pc.ola.org
erniehardemanmpp.com
Other Communications: Constituency Phone: 519-537-5222;
Fax: 519-537-3577
twitter.com/erniehardeman,
www.facebook.com/ErnieHardemanMPP,
www.linkedin.com/in/ernie-hardeman-37a18a2b
Constituency Office
12 Perry St., 2nd Fl.
Woodstock, ON N4S 3C2

Joel Harden
Constituency: Ottawa Centre, New Democratic Party
Tel: 416-326-7648; *Fax:* 416-326-7639
JHarden-QP@ndp.on.ca
www.joelharden.ca
Other Communications: Constituency Phone: 613-722-6414;
Fax: 613-722-6703
twitter.com/JoelHardenONDP,
www.facebook.com/JoelhardenONDP
Constituency Office
109 Catherine St.
Ottawa, ON K2P 0P4

Mike Harris
Constituency: Kitchener-Conestoga, Progressive
Conservative
mike.harris@pc.ola.org
Other Communications: Constituency Phone: 519-669-2090;
Fax: 519-669-0476
twitter.com/mikeharrisjrpc,
www.facebook.com/mikeharriskitcon
Constituency Office
#3 & 4, 63 Arthur St. South
Elmira, ON N3B 2M6

Faisal Hassan
Constituency: York South-Weston, New Democratic Party
Tel: 416-326-6961; *Fax:* 416-326-6957
FHassan-QP@ndp.on.ca
www.faisalhassan.ca
Other Communications: Constituency Phone: 416-243-7984;
Fax: 416-243-0327
twitter.com/FaisalHassanNDP,
www.facebook.com/FaisalHassanNDP,
www.linkedin.com/in/faisal-hassan-30591020
Constituency Office
1965 Weston Rd.
Toronto, ON M9N 1W8

Percy Hatfield
Constituency: Windsor-Tecumseh, New Democratic Party
Tel: 416-325-6773; *Fax:* 416-325-6795
PHatfield-QP@ndp.on.ca
www.percyhatfield.com
Other Communications: Constituency Phone: 519-251-5199;
Fax: 519-251-5299
twitter.com/PercyHatfield

Constituency Office
#1, 5452 Tecumseh Rd. East
Windsor, ON N8T 1C7
Randy Hillier
Constituency: Lanark-Frontenac-Kingston, Independent
Tel: 416-325-2244
RHillier-CO@ola.org
www.randyhilliermpp.com
Other Communications: Constituency Phone: 613-267-8239;
Fax: 613-267-7398
twitter.com/randyhillier, www.facebook.com/randy.hillier
Constituency Office
#1, 105 Dufferin St.
Perth, ON K7H 3A5
Christine Hogarth
Constituency: Etobicoke-Lakeshore, Progressive
Conservative
Tel: 437-288-7903
christine.hogarth@pc.ola.org
www.christinehogarthmpp.ca
Other Communications: Constituency Phone: 416-259-2249
twitter.com/chogarthpc
www.facebook.com/ChristineHogarthEL,
www.linkedin.com/in/christine-hogarth-70673a1b
Constituency Office
#21, 195 Norseman St.
Toronto, ON M8Z 0E9
Leader, New Democratic Party of Ontario; Leader, Official
Opposition, Andrea Horwath
Constituency: Hamilton Centre, New Democratic Party
Tel: 416-325-7116; *Fax:* 416-325-8222
horwatha-qp@ndp.on.ca
www.andreahorwath.ca
Other Communications: Constituency Phone: 905-544-9644;
Fax: 905-544-5152
twitter.com/andreahorwath,
www.facebook.com/AndreaHorwathONDP
Constituency Office
#200, 20 Hughson St. South
Hamilton, ON L8N 2A1
Mitzie Hunter
Constituency: Scarborough-Guildwood, Liberal
Tel: 416-325-4800; *Fax:* 416-325-4785
mhunter.mpp.co@liberal.ola.org
mitziehunter.onmpp.ca
Other Communications: Constituency Phone: 416-281-2787;
Fax: 416-281-2360
twitter.com/MitzieHunter,
www.facebook.com/MPPMitzieHunter,
www.linkedin.com/in/mitziehunter
Constituency Office
3785 Kingston Rd., #B1
Toronto, ON M1J 3M4
Solicitor General, Hon. Sylvia Jones
Constituency: Dufferin-Caledon, Progressive Conservative
Tel: 416-325-0408; *Fax:* 416-326-0498
sylvia.jones@pc.ola.org
sylviajonesmpp.ca
Other Communications: Constituency Phone: 519-941-7751;
Fax: 519-941-3246
twitter.com/SylviaJonesMPP,
www.facebook.com/Sylvia.JonesMPP,
www.linkedin.com/in/sylvia-jones-922b8247
Constituency Office
180 Broadway Ave., #A, 3rd Fl.
Orangeville, ON L9W 1K3
Logan Kanapathi
Constituency: Markham-Thornhill, Progressive Conservative
Tel: 416-325-4850; *Fax:* 416-325-4884
logan.kanapathi@pc.ola.org
logankanapathi.ca
Other Communications: Constituency Phone: 905-305-1935;
Fax: 905-305-1938
twitter.com/LoganKanapathi,
www.facebook.com/LoganKanapathi,
www.linkedin.com/in/logan-kanapathi-a2145833
Constituency Office
#3, 7380 McCowan Rd.
Markham, ON L3S 3H8
Belinda Karahalios
Constituency: Cambridge, NB
Tel: 416-325-0079
bkarahalios@ola.org
www.belindakarahaliosmpp.ca
Other Communications: Constituency Phone: 519-650-2770
twitter.com/BKarahalios
Note: Belinda Karahalios was removed from the P.C. Caucus
in July 2020. Karahalios then joined the New Blue Party of
Ontario, which was founded that month, as its only sitting
member.
Constituency Office
#409, 73 Water St. North
Cambridge, ON N1R 7L6

Bhutila Karpoche
Constituency: Parkdale-High Park, New Democratic Party
Tel: 416-325-3017; *Fax:* 416-325-2937
BKarpoche-QP@ndp.on.ca
www.bhutilakarpoche.ca
Other Communications: Constituency Phone: 416-763-5630;
Fax: 416-763-5640
twitter.com/bhutilakarpoche,
www.facebook.com/BhutilaKarpoche
Constituency Office
2849 Dundas St. West
Toronto, ON M6P 1Y6
Vincent Ke
Constituency: Don Valley North, Progressive Conservative
Tel: 416-325-6009
vincent.ke@pc.ola.org
vincentkempp.com
Other Communications: Constituency Phone: 416-494-8778;
Fax: 416-494-0110
twitter.com/vincentkempp, www.facebook.com/vincentkempp
Constituency Office
#103, 2175 Sheppard Ave. East
Toronto, ON M2J 1W8
Terence Kernaghan
Constituency: London North Centre, New Democratic Party
Tel: 416-326-7568; *Fax:* 416-326-7580
TKernaghan-QP@ndp.on.ca
www.terencekernaghan.ca
Other Communications: Constituency Phone: 519-432-7339;
Fax: 519-432-0613
twitter.com/kernaghant,
www.facebook.com/TerenceKernaghanLNC
Constituency Office
#105, 400 York St.
London, ON N6B 3N2
Deputy Government House Leader, Andrea Khanjin
Constituency: Barrie-Innisfil, Progressive Conservative
Tel: 416-314-6790
andrea.khanjin@pc.ola.org
www.andreampp.com
Other Communications: Constituency Phone: 705-722-0575;
Fax: 705-722-8835
twitter.com/andrea_khanjin,
www.facebook.com/AndreaKhanjinMPP,
www.linkedin.com/in/andrea-khanjin-203ab8a1
Constituency Office
#1, 237 Mapleview Dr. East
Barrie, ON L4N 0W5
Chair, Government Caucus, Daryl Kramp
Constituency: Hastings-Lennox & Addington, Progressive
Conservative
Tel: 416-326-7005
Toll-free: 855-229-6676; *Fax:* 416-326-6999
daryl.kramp@pc.ola.org
www.darylkrampmpp.ca
Other Communications: Madoc: 343-600-3310; Napanee:
613-308-9625
twitter.com/darylkramp
Constituency Office
26A St. Lawrence St. West
PO Box 70
Madoc, ON K0K 2K0
Natalia Kusendova
Constituency: Mississauga Centre, Progressive Conservative
Tel: 416-326-7102
natalia.kusendova@pc.ola.org
www.nataliakusendovampp.com
Other Communications: Constituency Phone: 905-890-1901
twitter.com/natkusendova,
www.facebook.com/NataliaKusendovaPC,
www.linkedin.com/in/natalia-kusendova-39301950
Constituency Office
10 Kingsbridge Garden Circle
Mississauga, ON L5R 3K7
Minister, Education, Hon. Stephen Lecce
Constituency: King-Vaughan, Progressive Conservative
Tel: 416-325-2600
stephen.lecce@pc.ola.org
www.stephenleccempp.ca
Other Communications: Constituency Phone: 647-560-9700;
Fax: 647-560-9701
twitter.com/sflecce, www.facebook.com/StephenLecceMPP,
www.linkedin.com/in/stephenlecce
Constituency Office
#1, 2220 King Rd.
King City, ON L7B 1L3
Laura Mae Lindo
Constituency: Kitchener Centre, New Democratic Party
Tel: 416-326-7221; *Fax:* 416-326-7217
LLindo-QP@ndp.on.ca
www.lauramaelindompp.ca
Other Communications: Constituency Phone: 519-579-5460;
Fax: 519-579-2121
twitter.com/lauramaelindo,

www.facebook.com/LauraMaeLindo
Constituency Office
#212, 25 Frederick St.
Kitchener, ON N2H 6M8
Minister, Heritage, Sport, Tourism & Culture Industries, Hon.
Lisa MacLeod
Constituency: Nepean, Progressive Conservative
Tel: 416-314-1400
Lisa.macleodco@pc.ola.org
www.lisamacleod.com
Other Communications: Constituency Phone: 613-823-2116;
Fax: 613-823-8284
twitter.com/MacLeodLisa,
www.facebook.com/LisaMacLeodNepean,
www.linkedin.com/in/lisa-macleod-16367513
Constituency Office
#222 & 223, 250B Greenbank Rd.
Nepean, ON K2H 8X4
Sol Mamakwa
Constituency: Kiiwetinoong, New Democratic Party
Tel: 416-326-7692; *Fax:* 416-326-7690
SMamakwa-QP@ndp.on.ca
www.solmamakwa.ca
Other Communications: Constituency Phone: 807-737-2210;
Fax: 807-737-1592
twitter.com/solmamakwa,
www.facebook.com/solmamakwampp,
www.linkedin.com/in/sol-mamakwa-3a854643
Constituency Office
#104, 73 King St.
PO Box 176
Sioux Lookout, ON P8T 1A1
Deputy Opposition Whip, Michael Mantha
Constituency: Algoma-Manitoulin, New Democratic Party
Tel: 416-325-1938
Toll-free: 800-831-1899; *Fax:* 416-325-1976
mmantha-qp@ndp.on.ca
www.michaelmantha.com
Other Communications: Constituency Phone: 705-461-9710,
Fax: 705-461-9720
twitter.com/m_mantha, www.facebook.com/MichaelMantha
Constituency Office
14 George Walk
Elliot Lake, ON P5A 2A4
Robin Martin
Constituency: Eglinton-Lawrence, Progressive Conservative
Tel: 416-327-4300
robin.martin@pc.ola.org
www.robinmartinmpp.ca
Other Communications: Constituency Phone: 416-781-2395;
Fax: 416-781-4116
twitter.com/robinmartinpc,
www.facebook.com/RobinMartinPC,
www.linkedin.com/in/robin-martin-37965221
Constituency Office
2882 Dufferin St.
Toronto, ON M6B 3S6
Gila Martow
Constituency: Thornhill, Progressive Conservative
Tel: 416-325-0100; *Fax:* 416-325-0092
gila.martow@pc.ola.org
gilamartow.nationbuilder.com
Other Communications: Constituency Phone: 905-731-8462;
Fax: 905-731-2984
twitter.com/GilaMartow, www.facebook.com/gila.martow
Constituency Office, Centre Street Square
#4, 1136 Centre St.
Thornhill, ON L4J 3M8
Jim McDonell
Constituency: Stormont-Dundas-South Glengarry,
Progressive Conservative
Tel: 416-585-7000
jim.mcdonell@pc.ola.org
jimmcdonellmpp.ca
Other Communications: Constituency Phone: 613-933-6513;
Fax: 613-933-6449
twitter.com/JimMcDonell,
www.facebook.com/jimmcdonellSDSG
Constituency Office, Time Square
120 - 2nd St. West
Cornwall, ON K6J 1G5
Associate Minister, Children & Women's Issues, Hon. Jane
McKenna
Constituency: Burlington, Progressive Conservative
Tel: 416-325-5225
jane.mckenna@pc.ola.org
www.janemckennampp.ca
Other Communications: Constituency Phone: 905-639-7924;
Fax: 905-639-3284
www.facebook.com/janemckennampp,
www.linkedin.com/in/jane-mckenna-8323a91a
Constituency Office
#104, 472 Brock Ave.
Burlington, ON L7S 1N1

Minister, Labour, Training & Skills Development, Hon. Monte McNaughton
Constituency: Lambton-Kent-Middlesex, Progressive Conservative
Tel: 416-326-7600
monte.mcnaughtonco@pc.ola.org
montemcnaughtonmpp.ca
Other Communications: Strathroy: 519-245-8696; Wallaceburg: 519-627-1015
twitter.com/MonteMcNaughton,
www.facebook.com/MonteMcNaughtonMPP,
www.linkedin.com/in/ monte-mcnaughton-877b20178
Constituency Office
81 Front St. West
Strathroy, ON N7G 1X6

Norm Miller
Constituency: Parry Sound-Muskoka, Progressive Conservative
Tel: 416-325-1012
Toll-free: 888-267-4826
norm.miller@pc.ola.org
normmillermpp.ca
Other Communications: Bracebridge: 705-645-8538; Parry Sound: 705-746-4266
twitter.com/normmillerpc
Constituency Office
#1, 165 Manitoba St.
Bracebridge, ON P1L 1S3

Paul Miller
Constituency: Hamilton East-Stoney Creek, New Democratic Party
Tel: 416-325-0707; *Fax:* 416-325-0853
pmiller-qp@ndp.on.ca
www.paulmiller.ca
Other Communications: Constituency Phone: 905-545-0114; Fax: 905-545-9024
twitter.com/mpppaulmiller,
www.facebook.com/PaulMillerHamilton
Constituency Office
289 Queenston Rd.
Hamilton, ON L8K 1H2

Christina Maria Mitas
Constituency: Scarborough Centre, Progressive Conservative
Tel: 416-326-7374; *Fax:* 416-326-7377
christina.mitas@pc.ola.org
www.mppmitas.ca
Other Communications: Constituency Phone: 416-615-2183; Fax: 416-615-2011
twitter.com/christina_mitas,
www.facebook.com/christinamitaspc,
www.linkedin.com/in/christinamitasmpp
Constituency Office
2063 Lawrence Ave. East
Scarborough, ON M1R 2Z4

Judith Monteith-Farrell
Constituency: Thunder Bay-Atikokan, New Democratic Party
Tel: 416-325-9820; *Fax:* 416-325-9800
JMonteith-Farrell-QP@ndp.on.ca
www.judithmonteithfarrell.ca
Other Communications: Atikokan: 807-597-2629; Thunder Bay: 807-622-1920
twitter.com/judith_ndp, www.facebook.com/JudithNDP
Constituency Office
#105, 105 Main St. East
PO Box 1886
Atikokan, ON P0T 1C0

Suze Morrison
Constituency: Toronto Centre, New Democratic Party
Tel: 416-326-7171
SMorrison-QP@ndp.on.ca
www.suzemorrison.ca
Other Communications: Constituency Phone: 416-972-7683; Fax: 416-972-7686
twitter.com/SuzeMorrison,
www.facebook.com/SuzeMorrisonMPP
Constituency Office
329 Parliament St.
Toronto, ON M5A 2Z3

Minister, Transportation; Minister, Francophone Affairs, Hon. Caroline Mulroney
Constituency: York-Simcoe, Progressive Conservative
Tel: 416-327-9200
caroline.mulroney@pc.ola.org
carolinemulroneympp.ca
Other Communications: Constituency Phone: 905-895-1555; Fax: 905-895-0337
twitter.com/c_mulroney,
www.facebook.com/carolinemulroneyPC,
www.linkedin.com/in/carolinemulroney
Constituency Office
#8, 45 Grist Mill Rd.
Holland Landing, ON L9N 1M7

Taras Natyshak
Constituency: Essex, New Democratic Party

Tel: 416-325-0714
Toll-free: 800-265-3909; *Fax:* 416-325-0980
tnatyshak-qp@ndp.on.ca
www.tarasnatyshak.com
Other Communications: Constituency Phone: 519-776-6420; Fax: 519-776-6980
twitter.com/TarasNatyshak,
www.facebook.com/TarasNatyshakNDP
Constituency Office
316 Talbot St. North
Essex, ON N8M 2E1

Rick Nicholls
Constituency: Chatham-Kent-Leamington, Independent
Tel: 416-325-9099; *Fax:* 416-325-9000
RNicholls@ola.org
ricknichollsmpp.ca
Other Communications: Chatham: 519-351-0510; Leamington: 519-326-3367
twitter.com/ricknichollsckl,
www.linkedin.com/in/rick-nicholls-b0528010
Note: Rick Nicholls was removed from the P.C. caucus in Aug. 2021, after refusing to receive the COVID-19 vaccine.
Constituency Office
#100, 111 Heritage Rd.
Chatham, ON N7M 5W7

Sam Oosterhoff
Constituency: Niagara West, Progressive Conservative
Tel: 416-326-1697
sam.oosterhoff@pc.ola.org
www.samoosterhoffmpp.ca
Other Communications: Constituency Phone: 905-563-1755; Fax: 905-563-1317
twitter.com/samoosterhoff,
www.facebook.com/samueloosterhoff
Note: Sam Oosterhoff won the riding in a by-election held Nov. 17, 2016. He was only 19 years old at the time of his election. He was re-elected in the June 2018 general election.
Constituency Office
4961 King St. East, #M1
Beamsville, ON L0R 1B0

Billy Pang
Constituency: Markham-Unionville, Progressive Conservative
Tel: 416-325-4960
billy.pang@pc.ola.org
www.billypangmpp.ca
Other Communications: Constituency Phone: 905-474-3288; Fax: 905-474-2878
twitter.com/billy__pang,
www.facebook.com/BillyPangMarkham
Constituency Office
#602, 3601 Hwy. 7 East
Markham, ON L3R 0M3

Lindsey Park
Constituency: Durham, Progressive Conservative
Tel: 416-326-2220
lindsey.park@pc.ola.org
lindseyparkmpp.ca
Other Communications: Constituency Phone: 905-697-1501; Fax: 905-697-1506
twitter.com/lparkpc, www.facebook.com/lparkpc
Constituency Office
23 King St. West
Bowmanville, ON L1C 1R2

Michael Parsa
Constituency: Aurora-Oak Ridges-Richmond Hill, Progressive Conservative
Toll-free: 888-486-5352
michael.parsaco@pc.ola.org
www.michaelparsampp.ca
Other Communications: Constituency Phone: 905-773-6250; 905-773-8158
twitter.com/michaelparsa
Constituency Office
#201, 13085 Yonge St.
Richmond Hill, ON L4E 3S8

Randy Pettapiece
Constituency: Perth-Wellington, Progressive Conservative
Tel: 416-326-3073
randy.pettapiece@pc.ola.org
pettapiece.ca
Other Communications: Constituency Phone: 519-272-0660; Fax: 519-272-1064
twitter.com/randypettapiece,
www.facebook.com/randypettapiece
Constituency Office
#2, 55 Lorne Ave. East
Stratford, ON N5A 6S4

Minister, Long-Term Care, Hon. Rod Phillips
Constituency: Ajax, Progressive Conservative
Tel: 416-325-0145
rod.phillips@pc.ola.org
www.rodphillips.ca
Other Communications: Constituency Phone: 905-427-2060; Fax: 905-427-6976

twitter.com/rodphillips01,
www.facebook.com/RodPhillipsMPP,
www.linkedin.com/in/rodphillips01
Constituency Office
#209, 1 Rossland Rd. West
Ajax, ON L1Z 1Z2

Minister, Environment, Conservation & Parks, Hon. David Piccini
Constituency: Northumberland-Peterborough South, Progressive Conservative
Tel: 416-314-6790
david.piccini@pc.ola.org
www.davidpiccinimpp.ca
Other Communications: Constituency Phone: 905-372-4000; Fax: 905-885-0050
twitter.com/DavidPiccini, www.facebook.com/MPPPiccini,
www.linkedin.com/in/david-piccini-b059221b8
Constituency Office
117 Peter St.
Port Hope, ON L1A 1C5

Tom Rakocevic
Constituency: Humber River-Black Creek, New Democratic Party
Tel: 416-326-7585; *Fax:* 416-326-7634
TRakocevic-QP@ndp.on.ca
www.tomrakocevicmpp.ca
Other Communications: Constituency Phone: 416-743-7272; Fax: 416-743-3292
twitter.com/rakocevict, www.facebook.com/TomRakocevic
Constituency Office
#38, 2300 Finch Ave. West
Toronto, ON M9M 2Y3

Associate Minister, Digital Government; Deputy Government Whip, Hon. Kaleed Rasheed
Constituency: Mississauga East-Cooksville, Progressive Conservative
Tel: 416-325-0400
kaleed.rasheed@pc.ola.org
www.kaleedrasheed.com
Other Communications: Constituency Phone: 905-238-1751; Fax: 905-238-4918
twitter.com/krasheedmpp, www.facebook.com/krasheedmpp,
www.linkedin.com/in/krasheedmpp
Constituency Office
#315, 1420 Burnhamthorpe Rd. East
Mississauga, ON L4X 2Z9

Minister, Indigenous Affairs; Minister, Northern Development, Mines, Natural Resources & Forestry, Hon. Greg Rickford
Constituency: Kenora-Rainy River, Progressive Conservative
Tel: 416-327-0633; *Fax:* 416-327-0665
greg.rickford@pc.ola.org
www.gregrickfordmpp.ca
Other Communications: Fort Frances: 807-274-7619; Dryden: 807-223-6456
twitter.com/gregrickford,
www.facebook.com/GregRickfordPC,
www.linkedin.com/in/greg-rickford-07a973117
Constituency Office
#1, 279 Scott St.
Fort Frances, ON P9A 1G8

Jeremy Roberts
Constituency: Ottawa West-Nepean, Progressive Conservative
Tel: 647-309-4348
jeremy.roberts@pc.ola.org
jeremyroberts.ca
Other Communications: Constituency Phone: 613-721-8075; Fax: 613-721-5756
twitter.com/jr_ottawa, www.facebook.com/electjeremy
Constituency Office
#500, 1580 Merivale Rd.
Nepean, ON K2G 4B5

Minister, Government & Consumer Services, Hon. Ross Romano
Constituency: Sault Ste. Marie, Progressive Conservative
Tel: 416-212-2665
ross.romano@pc.ola.org
rossromano.ca
Other Communications: Constituency Phone: 705-949-6959; Fax: 705-946-6269
twitter.com/RossRomanoSSM,
www.facebook.com/RossRomanoSSM,
www.linkedin.com/in/ross-romano-546242191
Constituency Office
#102, 390 Bay St.
Sault Ste Marie, ON P6A 1X2

Sheref Sabawy
Constituency: Mississauga-Erin Mills, Progressive Conservative
Tel: 416-326-7253; *Fax:* 416-326-7244
sheref.sabawy@pc.ola.org
www.sabawy.ca
Other Communications: Constituency Phone: 905-820-8851; Fax: 905-820-4307
twitter.com/SherefSabawyPC,

www.facebook.com/SherefSabawyPC,
www.linkedin.com/in/sheref-sabawy-3178754
Constituency Office
#40, 4181 Sladeview Cres.
Mississauga, ON L5L 5R2

Amarjot Sandhu
Constituency: Brampton West, Progressive Conservative
Tel: 416-326-7591
amarjot.sandhu@pc.ola.org
www.amarjotsandhu.com
Other Communications: Constituency Phone: 905-595-1532;
Fax: 905-457-8496
twitter.com/sandhuamarjot1,
www.facebook.com/bramptonwestpc,
www.linkedin.com/in/amarjot-sandhu-682b66b1
Constituency Office
#309, 10 Gillingham Dr.
Brampton, ON L6X 0G6

President, Treasury Board, Hon. Prabmeet Singh Sarkaria
Constituency: Brampton South, Progressive Conservative
Tel: 416-327-2333
prabmeet.sarkaria@pc.ola.org
www.prabmeetsarkariampp.ca
Other Communications: Constituency Phone: 905-796-8669;
Fax: 905-796-8069
twitter.com/PrabSarkaria,
www.facebook.com/prabmeetsinghsarkaria,
www.linkedin.com/in/prabmeet-sarkaria-9527b140
Constituency Office
#412A, 7700 Hurontario St.
Brampton, ON L6Y 4M3

Opposition House Leader, Peggy Sattler
Constituency: London West, New Democratic Party
Tel: 416-325-6908; *Fax:* 416-325-7030
Psattler-qp@ndp.on.ca
www.peggysattler.ca
Other Communications: Constituency Phone: 519-657-3120;
Fax: 519-657-0368
twitter.com/PeggySattlerNDP,
www.facebook.com/PeggySattlerMPP
Constituency Office
#101, 240 Commissioners Rd. West
London, ON N6J 1Y1

Leader, Green Party of Ontario, Mike Schreiner
Constituency: Guelph, Green Party of Canada
Tel: 416-325-4664; *Fax:* 416-325-4666
Mschreiner@ola.org
mikeschreinermpp.ca
Other Communications: Constituency Phone: 519-836-4190;
Fax: 519-836-4191
twitter.com/MikeSchreiner,
www.facebook.com/mike.schreiner
Note: In the 2018 general election, Mike Schreiner became
the first elected Green Party candidate in Ontario history.
Constituency Office
173 Woolwich St.
Guelph, ON N1H 3V4

Laurie Scott
Constituency: Haliburton-Kawartha Lakes-Brock, Progressive
Conservative
Toll-free: 800-424-2490
laurie.scott@pc.ola.org
www.lauriescottmpp.com
Other Communications: Constituency Phone: 705-324-6654
twitter.com/lauriescottpc, www.facebook.com/laurie.scott.794
Constituency Office
14 Lindsay St. North
Lindsay, ON K9V 1T4

Sandy Shaw
Constituency: Hamilton West-Ancaster-Dundas, New
Democratic Party
Tel: 416-326-6890; *Fax:* 416-326-6885
SShaw-QP@ndp.on.ca
www.sandyshawmpp.ca
Other Communications: Constituency Phone: 905-628-2755;
Fax: 905-628-1280
twitter.com/shaw_sandy,
www.facebook.com/SandyShawONDP
Constituency Office
177 King St. West
Hamilton, ON L9H 1V3

Amanda Simard
Constituency: Glengarry-Prescott-Russell, Liberal
Tel: 416-325-6206
Toll-free: 800-294-8250; *Fax:* 416-325-6182
asimard.mpp@liberal.ola.org
Other Communications: Constituency Phone: 613-632-2706;
Fax: 613-632-1554
twitter.com/asimardl, www.facebook.com/amanda.simard1,
www.linkedin.com/in/amanda-simard
Note: Amanda Simard left the P.C. caucus on Nov. 29, 2018,
after disagreements with the party's policies. On Jan. 16,
2020 Simard joined the Ontario Liberal caucus.
Constituency Office

290A McGill St.
Hawkesbury, ON K6A 1P8

Deputy Opposition House Leader, Gurratan Singh
Constituency: Brampton East, New Democratic Party
Tel: 416-326-7178; *Fax:* 416-326-7166
GSingh-QP@ndp.on.ca
bre.ontariondp.ca
Other Communications: Constituency Phone: 905-799-3939;
Fax: 905-799-9505
twitter.com/gurratansingh, www.facebook.com/gurratan.singh,
www.linkedin.com/in/gurratansingh
Constituency Office
#307, 1 Gateway Blvd.
Brampton, ON L6T 0G3

Deputy Leader, Official Opposition, Sara Singh
Constituency: Brampton Centre, New Democratic Party
Tel: 416-326-7610; *Fax:* 416-326-7615
SSingh-QP@ndp.on.ca
www.sarasinghmpp.ca
Other Communications: Constituency Phone: 905-454-1233;
Fax: 905-454-8292
twitter.com/SaraSinghMPP,
www.facebook.com/sarasinghMPP
Constituency Office, Lakeridge Plaza
#12, 456 Vodden St. East
Brampton, ON L6S 5Y7

Donna Skelly
Constituency: Flamborough-Glanbrook, Progressive
Conservative
donna.skelly@pc.ola.org
www.donnaskellympp.ca
Other Communications: Constituency Phone: 905-679-3770;
Fax: 905-679-0288
twitter.com/skellyhamilton,
www.facebook.com/DonnaSkellyMPP,
www.linkedin.com/in/donna-skelly-2b429264
Constituency Office
#104, 2000 Garth St.
Hamilton, ON L9B 0C1

David Smith
Constituency: Peterborough-Kawartha, Progressive
Conservative
Tel: 416-326-7406
dave.smith@pc.ola.org
www.davesmithptbo.com
Other Communications: Constituency Phone: 705-742-3777;
Fax: 705-742-1822
twitter.com/davesmithptbo,
www.facebook.com/DaveSmithPTBO,
www.linkedin.com/in/davesmithptbo
Constituency Office
#4, 1123 Water St.
Peterborough, ON K9H 3P7

Minister, Energy, Hon. Todd Smith
Constituency: Bay of Quinte, Progressive Conservative
Tel: 416-327-6758
todd.smithco@pc.ola.org
www.toddsmithmpp.ca
Other Communications: Constituency Phone: 613-962-1144;
Fax: 613-969-6381
twitter.com/toddsmithpc, www.facebook.com/toddsmithmpp,
www.linkedin.com/in/todd-smith-b76225a3
Constituency Office
5503 Hwy. 62 South, #D
PO Box 6-2
Belleville, ON K8N 0L5

Jennifer (Jennie) Stevens
Constituency: St. Catharines, New Democratic Party
Tel: 416-326-7127; *Fax:* 416-326-7126
JStevens-QP@ndp.on.ca
www.jenniestevens.ca
Other Communications: Constituency Phone: 905-935-0018;
Fax: 905-935-0191
twitter.com/JennieStevens_,
www.facebook.com/jenniestevensmpp
Constituency Office
209 Carlton St., #B
St Catharines, ON L2R 1S1

Marit Stiles
Constituency: Davenport, New Democratic Party
Tel: 416-326-7202; *Fax:* 416-326-7200
MStiles-QP@ndp.on.ca
www.maritstilesmpp.ca
Other Communications: Constituency Phone: 416-535-3158;
Fax: 416-535-6587
twitter.com/maritstiles, www.facebook.com/maritstilesNDP,
www.linkedin.com/in/marit-stiles-a197874
Constituency Office
1199 Bloor St. West
Toronto, ON M6H 1N4

Minister, Infrastructure, Hon. Kinga Surma
Constituency: Etobicoke Centre, Progressive Conservative
Tel: 416-327-4412
kinga.surmaco@pc.ola.org

www.kingasurmampp.ca
Other Communications: Constituency Phone: 416-234-2800;
Fax: 416-234-2276
twitter.com/KingaSurmaMPP,
www.facebook.com/surmakinga,
www.linkedin.com/in/kingasurmampp
Constituency Office, Lloydmanor Shopping Centre
#201, 201 Lloyd Manor Rd.
Toronto, ON M9B 6H6

Peter Tabuns
Constituency: Toronto-Danforth, New Democratic Party
Tel: 416-325-3250; *Fax:* 416-325-3252
tabunsp-qp@ndp.on.ca
www.petertabuns.ca
Other Communications: Constituency Phone: 416-461-0223;
Fax: 416-461-9542
twitter.com/Peter_Tabuns, www.facebook.com/peter.tabuns
Constituency Office
923 Danforth Ave.
Toronto, ON M4J 1L8

Associate Minister, Small Business & Red Tape Reduction, Hon.
Nina Tangri
Constituency: Mississauga-Streetsville, Progressive
Conservative
Tel: 416-326-8475
nina.tangri@pc.ola.org
www.ninatangri.ca
Other Communications: Constituency Phone: 905-569-1643;
Fax: 905-569-6416
twitter.com/ninatangri, www.facebook.com/ninatangriMPP,
www.linkedin.com/in/nina-tangri-a4691a27
Constituency Office
#110, 154 Queen St. South
Mississauga, ON L5M 2P4

Deputy Opposition Whip, Monique Taylor
Constituency: Hamilton Mountain, New Democratic Party
Tel: 416-325-1796; *Fax:* 416-325-1863
mtaylor-qp@ndp.on.ca
www.moniquetaylormpp.ca
Other Communications: Constituency Phone: 905-388-9734;
Fax: 905-388-7862
twitter.com/mtaylorndp, www.facebook.com/MPPTaylor
Constituency Office
#202, 555 Concession St.
Hamilton, ON L8V 1A8

Vijay Thanigasalam
Constituency: Scarborough-Rouge Park, Progressive
Conservative
Tel: 416-327-9200
vijay.thanigasalam@pc.ola.org
www.vijaythanigasalam.ca
Other Communications: Constituency Phone: 416-283-8448;
Fax: 416-283-1597
twitter.com/VijayThaniMPP,
www.facebook.com/vijaythaniofficial
Constituency Office
#105, 8130 Sheppard Ave. East
Toronto, ON M1B 3W3

Minister, Agriculture, Food & Rural Affairs, Hon. Lisa Thompson
Constituency: Huron-Bruce, Progressive Conservative
Tel: 416-326-3074
Toll-free: 866-396-3007
lisa.thompson@pc.ola.org
www.lisathompsonmpp.ca
Other Communications: Blyth: 519-523-4251; Kincardine:
519-396-3007
twitter.com/LisaThompsonMPP,
www.facebook.com/lisathompsonpc
Constituency Office
408 Queen St.
PO Box 426
Blyth, ON N0M 1H0

Associate Minister, Mental Health & Addictions, Hon. Michael A.
Tibollo
Constituency: Vaughan-Woodbridge, Progressive
Conservative
michael.tibolloCO@pc.ola.org
www.michaeltibollompp.ca
Other Communications: Constituency Office: 905-893-4428;
Fax: 905-893-4537
twitter.com/michaeltibollo, www.facebook.com/michaeltibollo,
www.linkedin.com/in/michaeltibollo
Constituency Office
#3, 5100 Rutherford Rd.
Woodbridge, ON L4H 2J2

Effie J. Triantafilopoulos
Constituency: Oakville North-Burlington, Progressive
Conservative
Tel: 416-325-6200
effie.triantafilopoulos@pc.ola.org
effiempp.ca
Other Communications: Constituency Office: 905-825-2455;
Fax: 905-825-0663
twitter.com/effie_onb, www.facebook.com/EffieONB,

www.linkedin.com/in/effie-triantafilopoulos
Constituency Office
#570, 2525 Old Bronte Rd.
Oakville, ON L6M 4J2
Chief Opposition Whip; Deputy Leader, Official Opposition, John Vanthof
Constituency: Timiskaming-Cochrane, New Democratic Party
Tel: 416-325-2000; *Fax:* 416-325-1999
jvanthof-qp@ndp.on.ca
johnvanthof.com
Other Communications: New Lisk.: 705-647-5995; Kirkland Lake: 705-567-4650
twitter.com/john_vanthof, www.facebook.com/JohnVanthof
Constituency Office, Pinewoods Centre
#5, 247 Whitewood Ave.
PO Box 398
New Liskeard, ON P0J 1P0
Daisy Wai
Constituency: Richmond Hill, Progressive Conservative
Tel: 416-314-0797
daisy.wai@pc.ola.org
www.daisywai.com
Other Communications: Constituency Phone: 905-884-8080;
Fax: 905-884-1040
twitter.com/DaisyWai_MPP,
www.facebook.com/DaisyWaiMPP
Constituency Office
#409, 9555 Yonge St.
Richmond Hill, ON L4C 9M5
Deputy Speaker & Chair, Committee of the Whole House, Bill Walker
Constituency: Bruce-Grey-Owen Sound, Progressive Conservative
Tel: 416-325-6242
Toll-free: 800-461-2664
bill.walker@pc.ola.org
www.billwalkermpp.com
Other Communications: Constituency Phone: 519-371-2421;
Fax: 519-371-0953
twitter.com/billwalkermpp,
www.facebook.com/BillWalkerMPP,
www.linkedin.com/in/bill-walker-01959454
Constituency Office
#100, 920 - 1st Ave. West
Owen Sound, ON N4K 4K5
Jamie West
Constituency: Sudbury, New Democratic Party
Tel: 416-326-7144; *Fax:* 416-326-7280
JWest-QP@ndp.on.ca
www.jamiewestmpp.ca
Other Communications: Constituency Phone: 705-675-1914;
Fax: 705-675-1456
twitter.com/jamiewestndp,
www.facebook.com/JamieWestNDP,
www.linkedin.com/in/jamie-west-05518bb3
Constituency Office
#4B, 555 Barrydowne Rd.
Sudbury, ON P3A 3T4
Jim Wilson
Constituency: Simcoe-Grey, Independent
Tel: 416-325-2069; *Fax:* 416-325-2079
jwilson@ola.org
www.jimwilsonmpp.com
Other Communications: Alliston: 705-435-4087; Collingwood: 705-446-1090
twitter.com/mppjimwilson, www.facebook.com/jimwilsonmpp
Constituency Office
50 Hume St.
Collingwood, ON L9Y 1V2
Kathleen O. Wynne
Constituency: Don Valley West, Liberal
Tel: 416-325-4705; *Fax:* 416-325-4726
kwynne.mpp.co@liberal.ola.org
kathleenwynne.onmpp.ca
Other Communications: Constituency Phone: 416-425-6777;
Fax: 416-425-0350
twitter.com/Kathleen_Wynne
Constituency Office
#101, 795 Eglinton Ave. East
Toronto, ON M4G 4E4
John Yakabuski
Constituency: Renfrew-Nipissing-Pembroke, Progressive Conservative
Tel: 416-314-2301
john.yakabuski@pc.ola.org
www.johnyakabuski.com
Other Communications: Constituency Phone: 613-735-6627;
Fax: 613-735-6692
twitter.com/jyakabuskimpp,
www.facebook.com/JohnYakabuskiMPP
Constituency Office, The Victoria Centre
#6, 84 Isabella St.
Pembroke, ON K8A 5S5

Kevin Yarde
Constituency: Brampton North, New Democratic Party
Tel: 416-326-6727; *Fax:* 416-326-6726
KYarde-QP@ndp.on.ca
www.kevinyarde.ca
Other Communications: Constituency Phone: 905-495-8030;
Fax: 905-495-1041
twitter.com/KevinYardeMPP,
www.facebook.com/KevinYardeBN
Constituency Office
#7, 10215 Kennedy Rd. North
Brampton, ON L6Z 0C5
Jeff Yurek
Constituency: Elgin-Middlesex-London, Progressive Conservative
Tel: 416-325-0112
Toll-free: 800-265-7638; *Fax:* 416-325-0149
jeff.yurek@pc.ola.org
www.jeffyurekmpp.com
Other Communications: Constituency Phone: 519-631-0666;
Fax: 519-631-9478
twitter.com/JeffYurekMPP, www.facebook.com/jeffyurekpc,
www.linkedin.com/in/jeff-yurek-rph-5b596212
Constituency Office
#201, 750 Talbot St.
St Thomas, ON N5P 1E2
Vacant
Constituency: Don Valley East
Note: In August 2021, Michael Coteau resigned as the Don Valley East MPP to run in the federal election.

Ontario Government Departments & Agencies

Ontario Ministry of Agriculture, Food & Rural Affairs

Ontario Government Bldg., 1 Stone Rd. West, Guelph, ON N1G 4Y2

Tel: 519-826-3100; *Fax:* 519-826-4335
Toll-Free: 888-466-2372
about.omafra@ontario.ca
www.omafra.gov.on.ca
Secondary Address: 77 Grenville St., 11th Fl.
Toronto, ON M5S 1B3
twitter.com/atomafra
www.youtube.com/user/atomafra
The Ministry works in partnership with an industry that employs over 640,000 people & contributes over $25 billion annually to the provincial economy. The Ministry plays a key role in bringing a strong agricultural & rural perspective to provincial policies. The Ministry works with other Ministries to resolve local economic issues & assists rural communities in retaining & attracting business. Staff at the Ministry's Guelph headquarters & across the province provide a wide range of agri-food & rural economic development programs & services to clients. The Rural Affairs section seeks to strengthen Ontario's rural communities through funding programs, economic development programs, infrastructure & broadband internet access. Serviced by the Office of the Chief Information Officer, Land & Resources I&IT Cluster.

Minister, Hon. Lisa Thompson
Tel: 416-326-3074
minister.omafra@ontario.ca

Deputy Minister, John Kelly
Tel: 519-826-4009
john.m.kelly@ontario.ca

Parliamentary Assistant, Randy Pettapiece
Tel: 416-326-3072
randy.pettapiece@ontario.ca

Director, Communications, Avi Yufest
avi.yufest@ontario.ca

Associated Agencies, Boards & Commissions:
• **Agricorp**
Ontario Government Bldg NW
1 Stone Rd. West, 3rd Fl.
PO Box 3660 Central
Guelph, ON N1H 8M4
Fax: 519-826-4118
Toll-free: 888-247-4999
TTY: 877-275-1380
contact@agricorp.com
www.agricorp.com
Other Communication: AgriStability Fax: 519-826-4334
Responsible for delivering government & non-government priority products & services that assist Ontario's agri-food industry in managing risks.

• **Agricultural Research Institute of Ontario (ARIO)**
Ontario Government Bldg NW
1 Stone Rd. West, 2nd Fl.
Guelph, ON N1G 4Y2
Tel: 519-826-4197; *Fax:* 519-826-4211
research.omafra@ontario.ca
www.omafra.gov.on.ca/english/research/ario/institute.htm
The role of ARIO is to enquire into programs of research with respect to agriculture, veterinary medicine & consumer studies; select & recommend areas of research for the betterment of agriculture, veterinary medicine & consumer studies; & stimulate interest in research as a means of developing a high degree of efficiency in the production & marketing of agricultural products in Ontario.

• **Agriculture, Food & Rural Affairs Tribunal & Board of Negotiation**
Ontario Government Bldg NW
1 Stone Rd. West, 2nd Fl.
Guelph, ON N1G 4Y2
Tel: 519-826-3433; *Fax:* 519-826-4232
appeals.tribunal.omafra@ontario.ca
www.omafra.gov.on.ca/english/tribunal/index.html
The Tribunal holds hearings & makes decisions on matters involving land drainage, marketing boards, crop insurance, farm property classification, the treatment of agricultural employees, licensing issues & many other topics.

• **Board of Negotiation**
Ontario Government Bldg NW
1 Stone Rd. West, 2nd Fl.
Guelph, ON N1G 4Y2
The Board negotiates claims concerning contaminant damage to property.

• **Grain Financial Protection Board**
1 Stone Rd. West, 1st Fl.
PO Box 3660 Central
Guelph, ON N1H 8M4
Tel: 519-826-3949; *Fax:* 519-826-3367
The Protection Board collects fees & administers funds for producers of grain, corn, soybeans, wheat & canola.

• **Livestock Financial Protection Board**
Ontario Government Bldg NW
1 Stone Rd. West, 5th Fl.
Guelph, ON N1G 4Y2
Tel: 519-826-3886; *Fax:* 519-826-4375
The Protection Board collects fees, administers the Fund for Livestock Producers & reviews claims made against the Fund.

• **Livestock Medicines Advisory Committee**
Ontario Government Bldg NE
1 Stone Rd. West, 3rd Fl.
Guelph, ON N1G 4Y2
Tel: 519-826-4110; *Fax:* 519-826-3254
ag.info.omafra@ontario.ca
The Committee provides advice to the minister on the sale, control, regulation & description of livestock medicines.

• **Normal Farm Practices Protection Board**
Ontario Government Bldg NW
1 Stone Rd. West, 2nd Fl.
Guelph, ON N1G 4Y2
Tel: 519-826-3433; *Fax:* 519-826-4232
The Board resolves disputes regarding agricultural operations & determins what constitutes a normal farm practice.

• **Ontario Farm Products Marketing Commission**
Ontario Government Bldg SW
1 Stone Rd. West, 5th Fl.
Guelph, ON N1G 4Y2
Tel: 519-826-4220; *Fax:* 519-826-3400
ontariofarm.productsmarketing.omafra@ontario.ca
www.omafra.gov.on.ca/english/farmproducts
The Commission administers the Farm Products Marketing Act & the Milk Act.

• **Ontario Food Terminal Board**
165 The Queensway
Toronto, ON M8Y 1H8
Tel: 416-259-5479; *Fax:* 416-259-4303
oftboard@interlog.com
www.oftb.com
The Board assists in the orderly marketing of fruit & vegetables in Ontario.

• **Rural Economic Development Advisory Panel (REDAP)**
1 Stone Rd. West, 4th Fl.
Guelph, ON N1G 4Y2
Fax: 519-826-4336
Toll-free: 888-588-4111
red.omafra@ontario.ca
www.ontario.ca/rural

Economic Development Division

Ontario Government Bldg, 1 Stone Rd. West, 3rd Fl., Guelph, N1G 4Y2

Fax: 519-826-3567
Toll-Free: 877-424-1300
Other Communication: Northern Ontario, Toll-Free Phone: 800-461-6132

Assistant Deputy Minister, Randy Jackiw
Tel: 519-826-3528
randy.jackiw@ontario.ca
Director, Agriculture Development, Annette Anderson
Tel: 519-826-6588; *Fax:* 519-826-3254
annette.anderson@ontario.ca
Director, Regional Economic Development, George Borovilos
george.borovilos@ontario.ca
Director, Rural Programs, Carolyn Hamilton
Tel: 519-826-3419; *Fax:* 519-826-4336
carolyn.hamilton3@ontario.ca
Director, Business Development, Doug Reddick
douglas.reddick@ontario.ca
omafra.gov.on.ca/english/food
Regional Administrative Coordinator, Wanda Martin-Koch
Tel: 519-846-3387
wanda.martin-koch@ontario.ca

Food Safety & Environment Division

Ontario Government Bldg, 1 Stone Rd. West, 5th Fl., Guelph, ON N1G 4Y2

Fax: 519-826-4416

Assistant Deputy Minister, Debra Sikora
Tel: 519-826-4301
debra.sikora@ontario.ca
Director, Food Inspection Branch, Gavin Downing
Tel: 519-826-4366; *Fax:* 519-826-4375
gavin.downing@ontario.ca
Director, Environmental Management, Colleen Fitzgerald-Hubble
Tel: 519-826-4975; *Fax:* 519-826-3259
colleen.fitzgerald-hubble@ontario.ca
Acting Director, Food Safety & Traceability Programs, Jason McLean
Tel: 519-826-3112
jason.mclean@ontario.ca
Director, Animal Health & Welfare/Office of the Chief Veterinarian for Ontario, Dr. Leslie Woodcock
Tel: 519-826-3577; *Fax:* 519-826-4375
leslie.woodcock@ontario.ca

Policy Division

Ontario Government Bldg, 1 Stone Rd. West, 2nd Fl., Guelph, ON N1G 4Y2

Tel: 519-826-4020; *Fax:* 519-826-3492

Responsible for the ministry's policy processes, the administration & delivery of several farm business risk management programs & the management of the ministry's strategic partnership with Agricorp.
Assistant Deputy Minister, Phil Malcolmson
Tel: 519-326-6463; *Fax:* 519-826-3492
phil.malcolmson@ontario.ca
Director, Food Safety & Environmental Policy Branch, Sharon Bailey
Tel: 519-826-6800; *Fax:* 519-826-3492
sharon.bailey@ontario.ca
Director, Farm Finance, Heather Cassidy
Tel: 519-826-3244; *Fax:* 519-826-3170
heather.cassidy@ontario.ca
Director, Rural & Agri-Food Corporate Policy Branch, Scott Duff
Tel: 519-826-4154
scott.duff@ontario.ca
Director, Economic Development Policy, Thom Hagerty
Tel: 519-826-3918; *Fax:* 519-826-4328
thom.hagerty@ontario.ca

Research & Corporate Services Division

Ontario Government Bldg, 1 Stone Rd. West, 2nd Fl., Guelph, ON N1G 4Y2

Tel: 519-826-4152; *Fax:* 519-826-3390

Assistant Deputy Minister & Chief Administrative Officer, Christine Primeau
Tel: 519-826-6599
christine.primeau@ontario.ca
Director, Business Services Branch, Heather Harrison
Tel: 519-826-4698
heather.harrison@ontario.ca
Director, French Language Services, Louise Gagnon
Tel: 416-212-4274
louise.gagnon@ontario.ca
Director, Strategic Human Resources, Alan Hogan
Tel: 519-826-3739
alan.hogan@ontario.ca
Director, Research & Innovation, Jen Liptrot
Tel: 519-826-4172; *Fax:* 519-826-4211
jen.liptrot@ontario.ca

Director, Business Planning & Financial Management, Lee-Ann Walker
Tel: 519-826-3336
leeann.walker@ontario.ca

Ontario Ministry of the Attorney General

McMurtry-Scott Bldg., 720 Bay St., 11th Fl., Toronto, ON M7A 2S9

Tel: 416-326-2220; *Fax:* 416-326-4016
Toll-Free: 800-518-7901
TTY: 416-326-4012
attorneygeneral@ontario.ca
www.attorneygeneral.jus.gov.on.ca
twitter.com/ontmag
www.flickr.com/photos/ontmag

Justice services are delivered to Ontarians by the Ministry of the Attorney General. The Ministry is engaged in the following activities: supporting victims of crime; providing justice support services to vulnerable people in the province; ensuring the availability of effective & efficient criminal, civil & family courts, plus related justice services; prosecuting crime; & giving legal advice & services to government.

Attorney General, Hon. Doug Downey
Tel: 416-326-2220
doug.downey@pc.ola.org

Deputy Attorney General, David Corbett
Tel: 416-326-2640
David.Corbett2@ontario.ca

Director, Communications, Jesse Robichaud
Tel: 416-326-2220
jesse.robichaud@ontario.ca

Associated Agencies, Boards & Commissions:

• Alcohol & Gaming Commission of Ontario (AGCO)
90 Sheppard Ave. East
Toronto, ON M2N 0A4
Tel: 416-326-8700
Toll-free: 800-522-2876
customer.service@agco.ca
www.agco.on.ca
Responsible for regulating alcohol, gaming & horse-racing, & cannabis retail stores in Ontario

• Bail Verification & Supervision Program
Atrium on Bay
595 Bay St., 8th Fl.
Toronto, ON M5G 2M6
Tel: 416-314-2507

• Chief Inquiry Officer - Expropriations Act
McMurtry-Scott Bldg.
720 Bay St., 8th Fl.
Toronto, ON M7A 2S9
Tel: 416-314-2226

• Environment & Land Tribunals Ontario (ELTO)
#1500, 655 Bay St.
Toronto, ON M5G 1E5
Tel: 416-212-6349; *Fax:* 416-314-3717
Toll-free: 866-448-2248
www.elto.gov.on.ca
Other Communication: Toll-Free Fax: 877-849-2066
The ELTO cluster contains the following tribunals: Assessment Review Board; Board of Negotiation; Conservation Review Board; Environmental Review Tribunal; & Ontario Municipal Board.

• Human Rights Legal Support Centre
400 University Ave., 7th Fl.
Toronto, ON M7A 1T7
Tel: 416-597-4900; *Fax:* 416-597-4901
Toll-free: 866-625-5179
hrlsc.on.ca
Other Communication: Toll-Free Fax: 866-355-6099

• Judicial Appointments Advisory Committee (JAAC)
McMurtry-Scott Bldg
720 Bay St., 3rd Fl.
Toronto, ON M7A 2S9
Tel: 416-326-4060; *Fax:* 416-212-7316
www.ontariocourts.ca/ocj/jaac

• Legal Aid Ontario (LAO)
Atrium on Bay
#200, 40 Dundas St. West
Toronto, ON M5G 2H1
Tel: 416-979-1446; *Fax:* 416-979-8669
Toll-free: 800-668-8258
TTY: 866-641-8867
info@lao.on.ca
www.legalaid.on.ca
Other Communication: Toll-Free TTY: 866-641-8867; Media, Email: media@lao.on.ca

• Office for Victims of Crime (OVC)
700 Bay St., 3rd Fl.
Toronto, ON M5G 1Z6
Tel: 416-326-1682; *Fax:* 416-326-4497
Toll-free: 887-435-7661
TTY: 416-325-9341
ovc@ontario.ca
www.ovc.gov.on.ca

• Ontario Human Rights Commission (OHRC)
See Entry Name Index for detailed listing.

• Public Accountants Council
#901, 1200 Bay St.
Toronto, ON M5R 2A5
Tel: 416-920-1444
Toll-free: 800-387-2154
pacont.org

• Safety, Licensing Appeals & Standards Tribunals Ontario (SLASTO)
#401, 20 Dundas St. West, 4th Fl.
Toronto, ON M5T 2Z5
Fax: 416-327-6379
Toll-free: 844-242-0608
TTY: 416-916-0162
slastoinfo@ontario.ca
www.slasto.gov.on.ca
Other Communication: Toll-Free TTY: 844-650-2819
Safety, Licensing Appeals & Standards Tribunals Ontario was created in 2013, clustering the following tribunals: Animal Care Review Board (ACRB); Fire Safety Commission (FSC); Licence Appeal Tribunal (LAT); Ontario Civilian Police Commission (OCPC); & Ontario Parole Board (OPB).

• Social Justice Tribunals Ontario (SJTO)
25 Grosvenor St., 4th Fl.
Toronto, ON M7A 1R1
Tel: 416-212-8000; *Fax:* 416-212-8024
Toll-free: 855-558-2514
sjtoinfo@ontario.ca
www.sjto.gov.on.ca
The SJTO cluster includes the following tribunals: Child & Family Services Review Board; Criminal Injuries Compensation Board; Human Rights Tribunal of Ontario; Landlord & Tenant Board; Ontario Special Education Tribunal (English/French); Social Benefits Tribunal; & Strategic Business Services.

• Special Investigations Unit (SIU) / Unité des Enquêtes Spéciales (UTS)
5090 Commerce Blvd.
Mississauga, ON L4W 5M4
Tel: 416-622-0748; *Fax:* 416-622-2455
Toll-free: 800-787-8529
www.siu.on.ca
Other Communication: Shift Supervisor Phone: 416-641-1879

Ontario Legalization of Cannabis Secretariat

McMurtry-Scott Bldg., 720 Bay St., 11th Fl., Toronto, ON M7A 2S9

The Secretariat leads & coordinates the province's efforts to respond to the legalization of cannabis in Canada.
Executive Director, Renu Kulendran
Tel: 416-326-5242
renu.kulendran@ontario.ca

Agency & Tribunal Relations Division

McMurtry-Scott Bldg., 120 Bay St., 3rd Fl., Toronto, ON M7A 2S9

Assistant Deputy Attorney General, Ali Arlani
Tel: 416-212-9721
ali.arlani@ontario.ca
Acting Legal Counsel, Elaine Penalagan
Tel: 416-314-1234
elaine.penalagan@ontario.ca

Civil Law Division

McMurtry-Scott Bldg., 720 Bay St., 6th Fl., Toronto, ON M7A 2S9

Assistant Deputy Attorney General, Michel Y. Hélie
Tel: 416-326-0190
michel.helie@ontario.ca
Director, Crown Law Office - Civil, Sean Kearney
Tel: 416-326-4100; *Fax:* 416-326-4181
sean.kearney@ontario.ca
Director, Education & Development Branch, Jane Price
Tel: 416-326-2153
jane.price@ontario.ca
Director, Strategic Business Management Branch, Kate Johnstone
Tel: 416-326-4173; *Fax:* 416-326-6996
kate.johnstone@ontario.ca
Director, Constitutional Law, Sarah Wright
Tel: 416-326-4454; *Fax:* 416-326-4015
sarah.wright@ontario.ca

Corporate Services Management Division
McMurtry-Scott Bldg., 720 Bay St., 7th Fl., Toronto, ON M7A 2S9
Tel: 416-326-4431; Fax: 416-326-4441
Assistant Deputy Attorney General & Chief Administrative Officer, Dante Pontone
Tel: 416-326-9844
dante.pontone@ontario.ca
Director, Human Resources Strategic Business Unit, Deen Ajasa
Tel: 416-326-3283; Fax: 416-326-2298
deen.ajasa@ontario.ca
Acting Director, Program Review, Renewal & Transformation Task Force, Sandy Henderson
Tel: 416-212-9834
sandy.henderson1@ontario.ca
Director, Facilities Management Branch, Susan Patterson
Tel: 416-212-7949; Fax: 416-326-4029
susan.patterson@ontario.ca
Director, Business & Fiscal Planning, Jatinder Singh
Tel: 416-326-4020; Fax: 416-326-6955
jatinder.singh@ontario.ca
Director, Justice Sector Security Office, Frank Skubic
Tel: 416-327-4155
frank.skubic@ontario.ca

Court Services Division
McMurtry-Scott Bldg., #204, 720 Bay St., 2nd Fl., Toronto, ON M7A 2S9
Tel: 416-326-4263; Fax: 416-326-2652
Assistant Deputy Attorney General, Sheila Bristo
Tel: 416-326-2609; Fax: 416-326-2652
sheila.bristo@ontario.ca
Acting Director, Corporate Support, Babi Banerjee
Tel: 416-326-0887
babi.banerjee@ontario.ca
Director, Program Management, Jill Hughes
Tel: 416-326-8851
jill.hughes@ontario.ca
Acting Director, Operational Support, Vaia Pappas
Tel: 416-326-2514
vaia.pappas@ontario.ca

Courts of Justice
McMurtry-Scott Bldg., 720 Bay St., Toronto, ON M7A 2S9
Tel: 416-327-5020
Other Communication: Fax: 416-327-6256 (Appeal Scheduling), 416-327-5032 (Intake Office)
Executive Legal Officer, Supior Court of Justice, Roslyn Levine
Tel: 416-327-5719
roselyn.levine@ontario.ca
Other Communications: Judges' Reception: 416-327-5101

Criminal Law Division
McMurtry-Scott Bldg, 720 Bay St., 6th Fl., Toronto, ON M7A 2S9
Tel: 416-326-2615; Fax: 416-326-2063
Assistant Deputy Attorney General, Susan Kyle
Tel: 416-326-2615
susan.kyle@ontario.ca
Director, Strategic Operations & Management Centre, Tammy Browes-Bugden
Tel: 416-326-2099; Fax: 416-326-2423
tammy.browes-bugden@ontario.ca
Director, Crown Law Office - Criminal, Howard Leibovich
Tel: 416-326-4600; Fax: 416-326-4619
howard.leibovich@ontario.ca
Director, The Office of Crown Strategic Initiatives, Mark Saltmarsh
Tel: 416-326-2419; Fax: 416-326-2063
mark.saltmarsh@ontario.ca

Indigenous Justice Division
McMurtry-Scott Bldg., 720 Bay St., 4th Fl., Toronto, ON M7A 2S9
Tel: 416-212-9347
Assistant Deputy Attorney General, Kimberly Murray
Tel: 416-212-9345
kimberly.murray@ontario.ca
Director, Indigenous Justice Branch, Jennifer Abbott
Tel: 416-326-0815
jennifer.abbott@ontario.ca
Director, Indigenous Legal Branch, Kirsten Manley-Casimir
Kirsten.Manley-Casimir@Ontario.ca

Legislative Counsel
Whitney Block, #3600, 99 Wellesley St. West, Toronto, ON M7A 1A2
Tel: 416-326-2841; Fax: 416-326-2806
Chief Legislative Counsel, Mark Spakowski
Tel: 416-326-2740
mark.spakowski@ontario.ca
Associate Chief Legislative Counsel, Legislative Council Services, Vacant

Director, French Legislative Services, Gerard Hernando
Tel: 416-326-2793
gerard.hernando@ontario.ca

Policy Division
McMurtry-Scott Bldg, 720 Bay St., 7th Fl., Toronto, ON M7A 2S9
Tel: 416-326-2500; Fax: 416-326-2699
Assistant Deputy Attorney General, Irwin Glasberg
irwin.glasberg@ontario.ca
Director, Agency & Tribunal Relations Branch, Mariela Orellana
mariela.orellana@ontario.ca
Director, Justice Policy Branch, Juliet Robin
juliet.robin@ontario.ca

Victims & Vulnerable Persons Division
18 King St. East, 7th Fl., Toronto, ON M5C 1C4
Tel: 416-325-3265; Fax: 416-212-1091
Assistant Deputy Attorney General, Juanita Dobson
Tel: 416-212-5059
juanita.dobson@ontario.ca
Director, Programs & Community Development, Linda D. Haldenby
Tel: 416-326-2428; Fax: 416-212-1091
linda.d.haldenby@ontario.ca

Office of the Children's Lawyer
393 University Ave., 14th Fl., Toronto, ON M5G 1W9
Tel: 416-314-8000; Fax: 416-314-8050
www.attorneygeneral.jus.gov.on.ca/english/family/ocl
Children's Lawyer for Ontario, Marian Jacko
Tel: 416-314-8011
marian.jacko@ontario.ca
Chief Administrative Officer, Margaret-Jean Morandin
Tel: 416-314-8038
margaretjean.morandin@ontario.ca

Office of the Public Guardian & Trustee (OPGT)
Atrium on Bay, 595 Bay St., 8th Fl., Toronto, ON M5G 2M6
Tel: 416-314-2800; Fax: 416-326-1366
Toll-Free: 800-366-0335
TTY: 416-314-2687
www.attorneygeneral.jus.gov.on.ca/english/family/pgt
Public Guardian & Trustee, Kenneth R. Goodman
Tel: 416-314-2960
ken.goodman@ontario.ca
Deputy Public Guardian & Trustee, Legal Director, Legal Services, Bruce Arnott
Tel: 416-314-2766
bruce.arnott@ontario.ca
Deputy Public Guardian & Trustee, Program Policy, Trudy Spinks
Tel: 416-314-3957
trudy.spinks@ontario.ca

Office of the Auditor General

#1530, 20 Dundas St. West, 15th Fl., Toronto, ON M5G 2C2
Tel: 416-327-2381; Fax: 416-327-9862
TTY: 416-327-6123
comments@auditor.on.ca
www.auditor.on.ca
twitter.com/OntarioAuditor

Auditor General, Bonnie Lysyk, MBA, FCPA, FCA, LPA
Tel: 416-327-1326
bonnie.lysyk@auditor.on.ca

Director, Attest (1), Laura Bell

Director, Health, Sandy Chan

Director, Infrastructure, Environment & Economic Development Portfolio, Kim Cho

Director, Education, Vanna Gotsis

Director, Justice, Regulatory & IT, Vince Mazzone

Director, Attest (2), John McDowell

Director, Public Accounts, Bill Pelow

Director, Social Services & Tax Revenue, Nick Stavropoulos

Director, Health & Energy, Gigi Yip

Hepburn Block, 80 Grosvenor St., 6th Fl., Toronto, ON M7A 1E9
Tel: 416-325-5666
Toll-Free: 888-789-4199
mcss.gov.on.ca
twitter.com/onsocialservice
www.facebook.com/ontariosocialservices
The Ministry of Children, Community & Social Services (formerly Children & Youth Services prior to the 2018 general election) provides social assistance, community & developmental services, & oversees the Family Responsibility Office & Ontario's Strategy to End Human Trafficking, as well as immigration matters.

Minister, Hon. Merrilee Fullerton
MinisterMCCSS@ontario.ca

Associate Minister, Children & Women's Issues, Hon. Jane McKenna
Tel: 416-325-5225
jane.mckenna@pc.ola.org

Deputy Minister, Denise Allyson Cole
Tel: 416-325-5225
denise.a.cole@ontario.ca

Parliamentary Assistant (Children & Autism), Amy Fee
amy.fee@pc.ola.org

Parliamentary Assistant (Community & Social Services), Jeremy Roberts
jeremy.roberts@pc.ola.org

Business Planning & Corporate Services Division
Hepburn Block, 80 Grosvenor St., 6th Fl., Toronto, ON M7A 1E9
Tel: 416-325-5595; Fax: 416-325-5615
Assistant Deputy Minister & Chief Administrative Officer, Nadia Cornacchia
Tel: 416-325-5588
nadia.cornacchia@ontario.ca
Acting Director, Corporate Services, Maxine Daley
Tel: 416-327-3950
maxine.daley@ontario.ca
Director, Financial Planning & Business Management, Sean Keelor
Tel: 416-219-3414
sean.keelor@ontario.ca
Director, Human Resources Strategic Business Unit, Patricia Kwasnik
Tel: 416-327-4766
patricia.kwasnik2@ontario.ca

Community & Developmental Services Division
315 Front St. West, Toronto, ON M7A 0B8
Assistant Deputy Minister, Rupert Gordon
rupert.gordon@ontario.ca
Director, Program Policy Implementation Branch, Chrstine Kuepfer
christine.kuepfer@ontario.ca

Family Responsibility Office
Bldg. B, 125 Sir William Hearst Ave., Toronto, ON M3M 0B5
Fax: 416-240-2401
Toll-Free: 800-463-3533
TTY: 416-240-2414
Acting Assistant Deputy Minister, Trevor Sparrow
Tel: 416-240-2477
trevor.sparrow@ontario.ca
Director, Strategic & Operational Effectiveness Branch, Trevor Sparrow
Tel: 416-240-2456
trevor.sparrow@ontario.ca
Acting Director, Client Services, Mena Zaffino
Tel: 416-240-4622
mena.zaffino@ontario.ca
Deputy Director, Legal Services, Helena Birt
Tel: 416-240-2482
helena.birt@ontario.ca

Policy Development & Program Design Division
56 Wellesley St. West, 14th Fl., Toronto, ON M5S 2S3
Tel: 416-212-1961; Fax: 416-314-1862
Acting Assistant Deputy Minister, Jennifer Morris
Tel: 416-212-1961
jennifer.morris@ontario.ca
Director, Specialized Services & Supports, Jane Cleve
Tel: 416-325-5331; Fax: 416-212-2021
jane.cleve@ontario.ca

Director, Ontario Autism Program Project Team, Sarah Hardy
Tel: 416-325-8409
sarah.hardy@ontario.ca
Director, Children & Youth at Risk, Marian Mlakar
Tel: 416-212-5205; *Fax:* 416-212-2021
marian.mlakar@ontario.ca
Acting Director, Child Welfare Secretariat, Peter Kiatipis
Tel: 416-325-3560; *Fax:* 416-326-8098
peter.kiatipis@ontario.ca

Service Delivery Division
56 Wellesley St. West, 14th Fl., Toronto, ON M5S 2S3
Tel: 416-212-5663; *Fax:* 416-314-1862
Assistant Deputy Minister, Rachel Kampus
Tel: 416-212-3141
rachel.kampus@ontario.ca
Acting Director, Children's Facilities, Shannon Bain
Tel: 416-858-2774 ext: 2140
shannon.bain@ontario.ca
Director, Resource Management, Harrison Moon
Tel: 416-212-8480
harrison.moon@ontario.ca
Director, Child Welfare Operations, Sandy Palinski
Tel: 416-327-2531
sandy.palinski@ontario.ca
Director, Client Services, Judy Switson
Tel: 416-326-3170; *Fax:* 416-325-9631
judy.switson@ontario.ca

Social Assistance Programs Division
2 Bloor St. West, 25th Fl., Toronto, ON M7A 1E9
Assistant Deputy Minister, Aklilu Tefera
Tel: 647-408-4184
aklilu.tefera@ontario.ca
Director, Social Assistance & Municipal Operations, Jeffrey Bowen
Tel: 416-212-1246; *Fax:* 416-212-1257
jeffrey.bowen@ontario.ca
Director, Social Assistance Services Modernization, Nelson Loureiro
Tel: 416-881-5006
nelson.loureiro@ontario.ca
Director, Social Assistance Services Delivery, Patti Redmond
Tel: 416-314-1122
patti.redmond@ontario.ca

Transformation & Implementation Division
56 Wellesley St., 15th Fl., Toronto, ON M5S 2S3
Assistant Deputy Minister, Melissa Thomson
Tel: 416-325-7887
melissa.thomson@ontario.ca
Director, Child Welfare Reform Project Team, Vacant
Team Lead, Service Systems Transformation, Mike G. Brooks
Tel: 416-212-9883
mike.g.brooks@ontario.ca
Acting Project Manager, System Transition Team, Rachel Robins
Tel: 416-326-9888
rachel.robins@ontario.ca

Youth Justice Services
56 Wellesley St. West, 14th fl., Toronto, ON M5S 2S3
Tel: 416-314-3502; *Fax:* 416-327-0478
Assistant Deputy Minister, David Mitchell
Tel: 416-327-9910
david.mitchell3@ontario.ca
Acting Director, Divisional Services, Jim Faulkner
Tel: 416-325-5464; *Fax:* 416-327-2418
jim.faulkner@ontario.ca
Director, Collaborative Initiatives, Angela James
Tel: 416-325-2174
angela.james@ontario.ca
Director, Operational Support & Program Effectiveness, Trish Moloughney
Tel: 416-212-7609; *Fax:* 416-327-0944
trish.moloughney@ontario.ca
Director, Direct Operated Facilities, John Scarfo
Tel: 905-826-1505
Toll-free: 844-805-3805; *Fax:* 905-826-1707
john.scarfo@ontario.ca
Acting Director, Planning & Program Development, Tamara Stone
Tel: 416-212-7610; *Fax:* 416-327-0944
tamara.stone@ontario.ca

Ontario Ministry of Citizenship & Multiculturalism

56 Wellesley St. West, 14th Fl., Toronto, ON M7A 2E7
Tel: 416-212-0036
www.ontario.ca/page/immigrate-to-ontario
The Ministry seeks to help newcomers successfully integrate into life in Ontario, both economically & socially, as well as securing future investment, trade & immigration in Ontario. In June 2016, the Ministry was divided into two portfolios:

Citizenship & Immigration, & International Trade. Serviced by the Culture & Innovation Audit Service Team & the Office of the Chief Information Officer, Community Services I&IT Cluster. After the 2018 general election, the Ministry of Citizenship & Immigration was folded into the Ministry of Children, Community & Social Services. In 2021, the Ministry was reestablished as the Ministry of Citizenship & Multiculturalism.

Minister, Hon. Parm Gill
minister.gill@ontario.ca

Deputy Minister, Greg Meredith
Tel: 416-326-7600
greg.meredith@ontario.ca

Associated Agencies, Boards & Commissions:
• Office of the Fairness Commissioner
#1201, 595 Bay St.
Toronto, ON M7A 2B4
Tel: 416-325-9380; *Fax:* 416-326-6081
Toll-free: 877-727-5365
ofc@ontario.ca
www.fairnesscommissioner.ca

Citizenship & Immigration Division

Immigration Selection Division

Ontario Refugee Resettlement Secretariat

Regional & Corporate Services Division

Ontario Ministry of Colleges & Universities

438 University Ave., 5th Fl., Toronto, ON M7A 2A5
Tel: 416-325-2929; *Fax:* 416-325-6348
Toll-Free: 800-387-5514
TTY: 416-325-3408
information.met@ontario.ca
www.ontario.ca/page/ministry-colleges-universities
twitter.com/ONtrainandstudy
www.facebook.com/ONtrainandstudy
www.instagram.com/ONtrainandstudy
Together with the Ministry of Education, the Ministry of Colleges & Universities (formerly Training, Colleges & Universities, & Advanced Education & Skills Development) is responsible for the administration of laws relating to education & skills training. It operates Employment Ontario & is responsible for postsecondary education in the province. Serviced by the Office of the Chief Information Officer, Community Services I&IT Cluster.

Minister, Hon. Jill Dunlop
Tel: 416-326-1600
jill.dunlop@ontario.ca

Deputy Minister, Shelley Tapp
Tel: 416-314-9244
shelley.tapp@ontario.ca

Parliamentary Assistant, Goldie Ghamari
Goldie.Gharmari@ontario.ca

Director, Communications, Nemone Smith
nemone.smith@ontario.ca

Associated Agencies, Boards & Commissions:
• College of Trades Appointments Council
Mowat Block
900 Bay St., 23rd Fl.
Toronto, ON M7A 1L2
Tel: 416-326-5629; *Fax:* 416-326-5653
appointments.council@ontario.ca
www.cot-appointments.ca
Other Communication: Alt. Phones: 416-326-5638;
416-212-9521
• Higher Education Quality Council of Ontario (HEQCO)
#2402, 1 Yonge St.
Toronto, ON M5E 1E5
Tel: 416-212-3893; *Fax:* 416-212-3899
info@heqco.ca
www.heqco.ca
• Ontario Graduate Scholarship Program Selection Board
189 Red River Rd., 4th Fl.
PO Box 4500
Thunder Bay, ON P7B 6G9
Tel: 807-343-7257; *Fax:* 807-343-7278
Toll-free: 800-465-3957
osap.gov.on.ca
Provides advice & recommendations to the minister concerning the policies & administration of the Ontario Graduate Scholarship program & selects successful candidates for funding under the program.

• Ontario Student Assistance Program Financial Eligibility Advisory Committee
Mowat Block
900 Bay St., 9th Fl.
Toronto, ON M7A 1L2
Tel: 416-314-0714; *Fax:* 416-325-3096
osap.gov.on.ca
• Post-secondary Education Quality Assessment Board
Mowat Block
900 Bay St., 23rd Fl.
Toronto, ON M7A 1L2
Tel: 416-212-1230; *Fax:* 416-212-6620
peqab@ontario.ca
peqab.ca
• Training Completion Assurance Fund Advisory Board
77 Wellesley St. West
PO Box 977
Toronto, ON M7A 1N3
Tel: 416-314-0500; *Fax:* 416-314-0499
Toll-free: 866-330-3395
tcaf-pcc@ontario.ca
www.tcu.gov.on.ca/pepg/audiences/pcc/tcaf.html

Corporate Management & Services Division
Mowat Block, 900 Bay St., 18th Fl., Toronto, ON M7A 1L2
Tel: 416-325-2772; *Fax:* 416-325-2778
Assistant Deputy Minister & Chief Administrative Officer, Bohodar Rubashewsky
Tel: 416-325-2773; *Fax:* 416-325-2778
bohodar.i.rubashewsky@ontario.ca
Director, Strategic Human Resources, Lisa Brisebois
Tel: 416-327-2731; *Fax:* 416-327-9043
lisa.brisebois@ontario.ca
Director, Legal Services, Shannon Chace
Tel: 416-326-5045
shannon.chace@ontario.ca
Director, Corporate Coordination Branch, Sarah Truscott
Tel: 416-326-6662; *Fax:* 416-314-0558
sarah.truscott@ontario.ca
Acting Director, Corporate Finance & Service, Sandra Yee
Tel: 416-325-7677; *Fax:* 416-325-1835
sandra.yee@ontario.ca

Employment & Training Division
Mowat Block, 900 Bay St., 3rd Fl., Toronto, ON M7A 1L2
Fax: 416-325-2995
Toll-Free: 888-562-4769
Assistant Deputy Minister, David Carter-Whitney
Tel: 416-325-2989
david.carter-whitney@ontario.ca
Director, Program Delivery Support Branch, Jacqueline Cureton
Tel: 416-327-1127
jacqueline.cureton@ontario.ca
Director, Organizational & Business Excellence Branch, John Michel
Tel: 416-325-4511; *Fax:* 416-325-6162
john.michel@ontario.ca
Director, Finance, Analysis & Systems Support Branch, Kirsten Cutler
kirsten.cutler@ontario.ca
Acting Project Lead, ETD Regional Review Project, Greg MacNeil
Tel: 416-326-3420
greg.macneil@ontario.ca

French-Language, Teaching, Learning & Achievement Division
Mowat Block, 900 Bay St., 22nd Fl., Toronto, ON M7A 1L2
Tel: 416-325-2132; *Fax:* 416-327-1182
Assistant Deputy Minister, Denys Giguere
Tel: 416-325-2132
denys.giguere@ontario.ca
Acting Director, French Language Education, Policies & Programs, Luc Davet
Tel: 416-327-9072
luc.davet@ontario.ca

Post-secondary Education Division
Mowat Block, 900 Bay St., 7th Fl., Toronto, ON M7A 1L2
Tel: 416-325-2199; *Fax:* 416-326-3256
Assistant Deputy Minister, David Carter-Whitney
Tel: 416-325-2199
david.carter-whitney@ontario.ca
Lead Director, Post-secondary Financial Information System Project, Barry McCartan
Tel: 416-325-9231
barry.mccartan@ontario.ca
Director, Post-secondary Accountability, Linda Hawke
Tel: 416-325-1815
linda.hawke@ontario.ca
Acting Director, Student Financial Assistance, Maria Mellas
Tel: 807-343-7251
maria.mellas@ontario.ca

Acting Director, OSAP Transformation, Noah Morris
noah.morris@ontario.ca
Director, Post-secondary Finance & Information Management
Branch, Kelly Shields
Tel: 416-325-1952
kelly.shields@ontario.ca
Director & Superintendent, Private Career Colleges, Carol
Strachan
Tel: 416-325-5859; *Fax:* 416-314-0499
carol.strachan@ontario.ca

Strategic Policy & Programs Division
#1747, 900 Bay St., 17th Fl., Toronto, ON M7A 1L2
Assistant Deputy Minister, Glenn Craney
Tel: 416-212-5420
glenn.craney@ontario.ca
Director, Indigenous Education Branch, Arnold Blackstar
Tel: 416-314-6165
arnold.blackstar@ontario.ca
Chief Executive Officer & Director, Postsecondary Education
Quality Assessment Board, James Brown
Tel: 416-325-2422; *Fax:* 416-212-6620
james.brown@ontario.ca
Acting Director, Research & Planning, Helen Cranley
Tel: 416-212-0419
helen.cranley@ontario.ca
Acting Director, Programs, Karen Garrett
Tel: 416-326-5849
karen.garrett@ontario.ca
Director, Strategic Policy, Zoe Kroeker
Tel: 416-212-6597
zoe.kroeker@ontario.ca
Director, Information Management & Strategy, Kristie Pratt
Tel: 416-327-6613
kristie.pratt2@ontario.ca

Workforce Policy & Innovation Division
Mowat Block, 900 Bay St., 17th Fl., Toronto, ON M7A 1L2
Assistant Deputy Minister, Erin McGinn
Tel: 416-314-5329
erin.mcginn@ontario.ca
Director, Partnerships & Implementation, David Bartucci
Tel: 416-314-5551
david.bartucci2@ontario.ca
Acting Director, Lifelong Learning & Essential Skills, Monica
Neitzert
Tel: 416-314-1062
monica.neitzert@ontario.ca
Acting Director, Strategic Workforce Policy & Programs Branch,
Suzanne Skinner
suzanne.skinner@ontario.ca

Ontario Ministry of Economic Development, Job Creation & Trade

56 Wellesley St. West, 7th Fl., Toronto, ON M7A 2E7
Tel: 416-325-6666
Toll-Free: 800-268-7095
TTY: 416-325-3408
www.ontario.ca/economy
www.youtube.com/user/OntarioEconomy
The Ministry (formerly known as Economic Development &
Growth prior to the 2018 general election) promotes economic
development & job creation in Ontario by creating a climate for
business to prosper, working to eliminate red tape, & stimulating
trade. The Ministry markets the province as a desirable place to
live, work, invest & raise a family. It works with its private sector
partners to ensure that its core responsibilities of employment &
business development, investment & trade continue to help
Ontario businesses compete globally; contribute to a
highly-skilled, well-educated workforce; & generate prosperity for
all Ontarians. In Northern Ontario, the Ministry is represented by
the Northern Development Division of the Ministry of Northern
Development & Mines.

Minister, Hon. Victor Fedeli
Tel: 416-326-8475
MEDJCT.Minister@ontario.ca

**Associate Minister, Small Business & Red Tape
Reduction,** Hon. Nina Tangri

Deputy Minister, Giles Gherson
giles.gherson@ontario.ca

Parliamentary Assistant, Job Creation & Trade, Donna
Skelly
Donna.Skelly@ontario.ca

Acting Director, Legal Services, Donna Glassman
donna.glassman3@ontario.ca

Acting Director, Communications, Jonathan Leigh
Jonathan.Leigh@ontario.ca

Associated Agencies, Boards & Commissions:
• Ontario Capital Growth Corporation
Ontario Investment & Trade Centre
250 Yonge St., 35th Fl.
Toronto, ON M5B 2L7
Tel: 416-325-6874; *Fax:* 416-212-0794
The OCGC was established by the Ontario Capital Growth
Corporation Act, 2008 and began operations in early 2009.

Business Partnerships & Programs Division
Assistant Deputy Minister, Nadia Cornacchia
nadia.cornacchia@ontario.ca
Director, Business Services Branch, Joanne Anderson
joanne.anderson2@ontario.ca
Acting Director, Funding Administration Branch, Clara Chan
Clara.Chan@ontario.ca
Director, Training Programs Branch, Trish Dyl
trish.dyl@ontario.ca
Director, Program Transformation Branch, Kathryn Royal
kathryn.royal@ontario.ca

Corporate Services Division
Mowat Block, 900 Bay St., 5th Fl., Toronto, ON M7A 1L2
Tel: 416-325-6866; *Fax:* 416-314-7014
TTY: 416-325-6707
Other Communication: Toll-Free TTY: 888-664-6008
Assistant Deputy Minister & Chief Administrative Officer, Robert
Burns
Tel: 416-327-3682
robert.burns@ontario.ca
Director, Strategic Human Resources Business, Christina Critelli
Tel: 416-325-6599
christina.critelli@ontario.ca
Director, Service Management & Facilities, Nelson Janicas
Tel: 416-314-3309
nelson.janicas@ontario.ca
Acting Director, Business Planning & Finance, Kate Johnstone
Tel: 416-327-1137; *Fax:* 416-327-4239
kate.johnstone@ontario.ca
Acting Project Director, Accessibility Innovation Showcase,
Kathy Tangorra
Tel: 416-212-0268
kathy.tangorra@ontario.ca

Economic Development Policy Division
56 Wellesley St. West, 11th Fl., Toronto, ON M5A 2S3
Assistant Deputy Minister, Jennifer Block
Tel: 647-228-6102
jennifer.block@ontario.ca
Director, Economic Data Analytics Branch, Richard Kikuta
richard.kikuta@ontario.ca
Director, Strategic & Corporate Policy Branch, Melinda Gibson
melinda.gibson@ontario.ca

Industry & Sector Strategy Division
Assistant Deputy Minister, Trevor Dauphinee
Tel: 416-212-7002
trevor.dauphinee@ontario.ca
Director, Sector Strategy Branch, Stephanie Appave
stephanie.appave@ontario.ca
Director, Advanced Technologies Branch, Andrew Guy
andrew.guy@ontario.ca
Director, Advanced Manufacturing Industries Branch, Brian Love
brian.love@ontario.ca

Research, Science & Commercialization Division
Assistant Deputy Minister, John W. Marshall
Tel: 416-327-2889
john.w.marshall@ontario.ca
Director, Scale-up Services Branch, George Cadete
george.cadete@ontario.ca
Acting Director, Commercialization & Scale-up Networks Branch,
Dolly Goyette
dolly.goyette@ontario.ca
Director, Science & Research Branch, Katherine Kelly Gatton
Tel: 416-327-2801
katherine.kellygatton@ontario.ca

Trade & Investment Division
Assistant Deputy Minister, David Barnes
Tel: 416-326-8886
david.barnes@ontario.ca

Ontario Ministry of Education

315 Front Street, 14th Fl., Toronto, ON M7A 0B8
Tel: 416-325-2929
Toll-Free: 800-387-5514
TTY: 800-268-7095
www.ontario.ca/page/ministry-education
twitter.com/ONEducation
www.facebook.com/OntarioEducation
The Ministry focuses on three priority areas: Attaining high levels
of student achievement; reducing gaps in student achievement;
& increasing public confidence in publicly funded education.

Minister, Hon. Stephen Lecce
Tel: 416-325-2600
minister.edu@ontario.ca

Deputy Minister, Nancy Naylor
Tel: 416-325-2600
EDU.DMO@ontario.ca

Parliamentary Assistant, Sam Oosterhoff
sam.oosterhoff@ontario.ca

Assistant Deputy Minister, Education Equity Secretariat,
Patrick Case
Tel: 416-326-8481
patrick.case@ontario.ca

Director, Communications, Nicholas Insley
Nicholas.Insley@ontario.ca

Associated Agencies, Boards & Commissions:
• Education Quality & Accountability Office (EQAO)
#1200, 2 Carlton St.
Toronto, ON M5B 2M9
Tel: 416-314-0146; *Fax:* 416-325-2956
Toll-free: 888-327-7377
www.eqao.com

• Languages of Instruction Commission of Ontario
Mowat Block
900 Bay St., 8th Fl.
Toronto, ON M7A 1L2
Tel: 416-314-3500; *Fax:* 416-325-2979

**• Minister's Advisory Council on Special Education
(MACSE)**
900 Bay St., 18th Fl.
Toronto, ON M7A 1L2
Tel: 416-314-2333; *Fax:* 416-314-0637
Toll-free: 877-699-5431
macse@ontario.ca

• Ontario Educational Communications Authority (TVO)
2180 Yonge St.
PO Box 200 Q
Toronto, ON M4T 2T1
Tel: 416-484-2600
Toll-free: 800-613-0513
ww3.tvo.org

**• Ontario French-Language Education Communications
Authority**
#600, 21 College St., 6th Fl.
Toronto, ON MRY 2M5
Tel: 416-968-3536; *Fax:* 416-968-8203
TTY: 800-387-8435
www3.tfo.org

• Provincial Schools Authority (PSA)
255 Ontario St. South
Milton, ON L9T 2M5
Tel: 905-878-2851; *Fax:* 905-878-8405

Capital & Business Support Division
Mowat Block, 900 Bay St., 20th fl., Toronto, ON M7A 1L2
Tel: 416-325-6127; *Fax:* 416-325-9560
Assistant Deputy Minister, Joshua Paul
Tel: 416-325-6127
joshua.paul@ontario.ca
Executive Director, Andrew Davis
Tel: 416-327-9356
andrew.davis@ontario.ca
Acting Director, Capital Programs Branch, Marilyn Lingbaoan
Tel: 416-326-5737
marilyn.lingbaoan@ontario.ca
Director, School Board Business Support Branch, Cheri
Hayward
Tel: 416-327-7503; *Fax:* 416-212-3990
cheri.hayward@ontario.ca
Director, Capital Policy Branch, Colleen Hogan
Tel: 416-325-1705; *Fax:* 416-326-9959
colleen.hogan@ontario.ca

Corporate Management & Services Division
Mowat Block, 900 Bay St., 18th Fl., Toronto, ON M7A 1L2
Tel: 416-325-2772; *Fax:* 416-325-2778
Assistant Deputy Minister & Chief Administrative Officer,
Bohodar Rubashewsky
Tel: 416-325-2773
bohodar.i.rubashewsky@ontario.ca
Director, Strategic Human Resources Branch, Lisa Brisebois
Tel: 416-327-2731; *Fax:* 416-327-9043
lisa.brisebois@ontario.ca
Director, Legal Services, Shannon Chase
Tel: 416-326-5045; *Fax:* 416-325-2410
shannon.chase@ontario.ca
Director, Education Audit Service Team, Warren McCay
Tel: 416-212-4814; *Fax:* 416-325-1120
warren.mccay@ontario.ca
Director, Corporate Coordination Branch, Sarah Truscott
Tel: 416-326-6662; *Fax:* 416-314-0558
sarah.truscott@ontario.ca
Acting Director, Corporate Finance & Services Branch, Sandra
Yee
Tel: 416-325-7677; *Fax:* 416-325-1835
sandra.yee@ontario.ca

Early Years & Child Care Division
Mowat Block, 900 Bay St., 24th Fl., Toronto, ON M7A 1L2
Tel: 416-314-8277; *Fax:* 416-314-7836
Associate Minister of Education, Early Years & Child Care, Indira
Naidoo-Harris
Tel: 416-325-0400
Assistant Deputy Minister, Shannon Fuller
Tel: 416-314-9433
shannon.fuller@ontario.ca
Director, Early Years & Child Care Policy, Jeff Butler
Tel: 416-318-8241
jeff.butler@ontario.ca
Director, Programs & Service Integration, Julia Danos
Tel: 416-314-8192
julia.danos@ontario.ca
Acting Director, Finance Accountability & Data Analysis,
Maxx-Phillippe Hollott
Tel: 416-314-0903
maxx-phillippe.hollot@ontario.ca
Acting Director, Child Care Quality Assurance & Licensing
Branch, Holly Moran
Tel: 416-314-2190
holly.moran@ontario.ca

Education Labour & Finance Division
Mowat Block, 900 Bay St., 12th Fl., Toronto, ON M7A 1L2
Assistant Deputy Minister, Andrew Davis
Tel: 416-326-6939
andrew.davis@ontario.ca
Acting Executive Director, Education Labour Relations Office,
Brian Blakeley
brian.blakeley@ontario.ca
Acting Director, Education Finance Office, Doreen Lamarche
Tel: 416-326-0999
doreen.lamarche@ontario.ca

**French-Language, Teaching, Learning & Achievement
Division**
Mowat Block, 900 Bay St., 22nd Fl., Toronto, ON M7A 1L2
Tel: 416-325-2132; *Fax:* 416-327-1182
Assistant Deputy Minister, Denys Giguere
Tel: 416-325-2132
denys.giguere@ontario.ca
Acting Director (Bilingual), French-Language Education Policies
& Programs, Luc Davet
Tel: 416-327-9072; *Fax:* 416-325-2156
luc.davet@ontario.ca
Acting Director, French-Language Teaching & Learning, Lillian
Patry
Tel: 613-733-6058
lillian.patry@ontario.ca

Indigenous Education & Well Being Division
Mowat Block, 900 Bay St., 13th Fl., Toronto, ON M7A 1L2
Assistant Deputy Minister, Denise R Dwyer
Tel: 416-326-4108
denise.dwyer@ontario.ca

**Office of the Chief Information Officer, Community Services
I&IT Cluster**
Mowat Block, 900 Bay St., 3rd Fl., Toronto, ON M7A 1L2
Tel: 416-325-4598; *Fax:* 416-325-8371
This office works in conjunction with the Ministry of Advanced
Education & Skills Development.
Chief Information Officer & Assistant Deputy Minister, Soussan
Tabari
Tel: 416-326-8216
soussan.tabari@ontario.ca

Director, Case & Grants Management Solutions, Sanaul Haque
Tel: 416-314-4954
sanaul.haque@ontario.ca
Director, iAccess Solutions, Sanjay Madan
Tel: 416-325-2264
sanjay.madan@ontario.ca
Director, Strategic Planning & Business Relationship
Management, Lolita Singh
Tel: 416-326-7942
lolita.singh@ontario.ca

Student Achievement Division
Mowat Block, 900 Bay St., 10th Fl., Toronto, ON M7A 1L2
Fax: 416-325-8565
Assistant Deputy Minister, Cathy Montreuil
Tel: 416-325-9964
cathy.montreuil@ontario.ca
Financial Officer, Inna Chedrina
Tel: 416-327-9991
inna.chedrina@ontario.ca
Director, Program Implementation, Marg Connor
Tel: 416-325-2564
marg.connor@ontario.ca
Director, Leadership Collaboration & Governance, Bruce Drewett
Tel: 416-325-1079
bruce.drewett@ontario.ca
Director, Curriculum, Assessment & Student Success, Shirley
Kendrick
Tel: 416-325-2576
shirley.kendrick@ontario.ca
Director, Student Achievement Supports, Bruce Shaw
Tel: 416-325-9979
bruce.shaw@ontario.ca
Director, Professionalism, Teaching Policy & Standards,
Demetra Saldaris
Tel: 416-325-7744
demetra.saldaris@ontario.ca

Student Support & Field Services Division
Mowat Block, 900 Bay St., 22nd Fl., Toronto, ON M7A 1L2
Tel: 416-325-2135; *Fax:* 416-327-1182
Assistant Deputy Minister, Martyn Beckett
Tel: 416-314-5788
martyn.beckett@ontario.ca
Executive Director, Provincial & Demonstration Schools, June
Rogers
Tel: 905-878-2851
june.rogers@ontario.ca
Director, Field Services, Dr. Steven Reid
Tel: 416-325-2588
steven.reid@ontario.ca
Director, Special Education / Success for All, Louise Sirisko
Tel: 416-325-2889
louise.sirisko@ontario.ca

System Planning, Research & Innovation Division
Mowat Block, 900 Bay St., 10th fl., Toronto, ON M7A 1L2
Acting Assistant Deputy Minister, Richard Franz
Tel: 416-314-0884
richard.franz@ontario.ca
Director, Strategic Planning & Transformation, Russell Riddell
Tel: 416-325-4835
russell.riddell@ontario.ca
Acting Director, Incubation & Design, Andrew Sally
Tel: 416-325-9963
andrew.sally@ontario.ca
Director, Education Research & Evaluation Strategy, Erica van
Roosmalen
Tel: 416-314-3819
erica.vanroosmalen@ontario.ca
Director, Education Statistics & Analysis Strategy, Eric Ward
Tel: 416-325-8159
eric.ward@ontario.ca

Elections Ontario

51 Rolark Dr., Toronto, ON M1R 3B1
Tel: 416-326-6300; *Fax:* 416-326-6200
Toll-Free: 888-668-8683
TTY: 888-292-2312
info@elections.on.ca
www.elections.on.ca
Other Communication: Election Finances Phone: 416-325-9401;
Fax: 416-325-9466; Toll-Free Phone: 866-566-9066
twitter.com/ElectionsON
www.facebook.com/ElectionsON
www.linkedin.com/company/433448
www.youtube.com/ElectionsON
The Office of the Chief Electoral Officer, known as Elections
Ontario, conducts general elections & by-elections to elect
members of the Legislative Assembly.

Chief Electoral Officer, Greg Essensa

Tel: 416-326-6383; *Fax:* 416-326-6201
ceo@elections.on.ca

Chief Operating Officer, Lalitha Flach
Tel: 416-326-5688
lalitha.flach@elections.on.ca

Chief Administrative Officer, Deborah Danis
Tel: 416-212-1662
deborah.danis@elections.on.ca

Ontario Ministry of Energy

77 Grenville St., Toronto, ON M7A 2C1
Tel: 416-327-6758
Toll-Free: 888-668-4636
TTY: 800-387-5559
energy@ontario.ca
www.ontario.ca/page/ministry-energy
twitter.com/onenergy
www.facebook.com/energyontario
The Ministry of Energy is responsible for ensuring that Ontario's
electricity system functions at a high level of reliability, security &
productivity. From 2018-2021, it was Minstry of Energy, Northern
Development & Mines before the latter responsibilities were
transferred to the Ministry of Natural Resources & Forestry
(which has since been succeeded).
The Ministry also focuses on promoting ingenuity & innovation in
the energy sector, by encouraging the development of new ideas
& technologies. Protecting the environment is also a top priority
for the Ministry, as it strives to develop renewable sources of
energy, cleaner forms of fuel, & foster a conservation culture.

Minister, Hon. Todd A. Smith
MinisterEnergy@ontario.ca

Deputy Minister, Stephen Rhodes
Tel: 416-327-6734
stephen.rhodes@ontario.ca

Parliamentary Assistant, Vacant

Director, Communications, Palmer Lockridge
Palmer.Lockridge@ontario.ca

Director, Operations & Caucus Relations, Manish
Sawhney
Tel: 437-248-3451
manish.sawhney@ontario.ca

Associated Agencies, Boards & Commissions:
• **Hydro One Inc.**
See Entry Name Index for detailed listing.

• **Independent Electricity System Operator**
See Entry Name Index for detailed listing.

• **Ontario Energy Board (OEB)**
#2700, 2300 Yonge St.
PO Box 2319
Toronto, ON M4P 1E4
Tel: 416-481-1967; *Fax:* 416-440-7656
Toll-free: 888-632-6273
www.ontarioenergyboard.ca
Other Communication: Consumer Relations Phone:
416-314-2455; Toll-Free: 877-632-2727

• **Ontario Power Generation**
See Entry Name Index for detailed listing.

Conservation & Renewable Energy Division
77 Grenville St., 5th Fl., Toronto, ON M7A 2C1
Tel: 416-314-6216; *Fax:* 416-325-3438
Provides analysis, advice & policy development on issues
relating to energy efficiency, demand management &
conservation, as well as administering the Energy Efficiency Act.
Assistant Deputy Minister, Kaili Sermat-Harding
Tel: 416-327-5555
kaili.sermat-harding@ontario.ca
Acting Director, Renewables & Energy Facilitation, Sam Colalillo
Tel: 416-326-3775
sam.colalillo@ontario.ca
Acting Director, Conservation Programs & Partnerships, Paul
Johnson
Tel: 416-212-9267
paul.johnson3@ontario.ca
Director, Conservation & Energy Efficiency, Usman Syed
Tel: 416-325-6651
usman.syed@ontario.ca

Corporate Services Division
Mowat Block, 900 Bay St., 5th Fl., Toronto, ON M7A 1L2
Tel: 416-325-6866; *Fax:* 416-314-7014
TTY: 416-325-6707

Provides a structure to identify strategic issues, to coordinate policy & program development; & to coordinate & integrate action by the Ministry & other governments.

Assistant Deputy Minister & Chief Administrative Officer, Robert Burns
Tel: 416-327-3682
robert.burns@ontario.ca

Director, Strategic Human Resources Business, Christina Critelli
Tel: 416-325-6599
christina.critelli@ontario.ca

Director, Service Management & Facilities, Nelson Janicas
Tel: 416-314-3309
nelson.janicas@ontario.ca

Acting Director, Business Planning & Finance, Kate Johnstone
Tel: 416-327-1137
kate.johnstone@ontario.ca

Energy Supply Policy Division
77 Grenville St., 7th Fl., Toronto, ON M7A 2C1
Tel: 416-327-7353; *Fax:* 416-314-6224

Assistant Deputy Minister, Steen Hume
Tel: 416-314-6190
steen.hume@ontario.ca

Director, Electricity Policy, Economics & System Planning, Tim Christie
Tel: 416-325-6708; *Fax:* 416-314-6224
tim.christie@ontario.ca

Director, Fuels Policy & Liaison, Doug MacCallum
Tel: 416-327-0116
doug.maccallum@ontario.ca

Director, Nuclear Supply, Adrian Nalasco
Tel: 416-325-8627
adrian.nalascao@ontario.ca

Strategic, Network & Agency Policy Division
77 Grenville St., 6th Fl., Toronto, ON M7A 2C1
Tel: 416-325-6559

Provides strategic policy coordination & development for the ministry as well as policy analysis & advice related to energy conservation & efficiency, demand management & conservation.

Acting Assistant Deputy Minister, Carolyn Calwell
Tel: 416-325-6544
carolyn.calwell@ontario.ca

Acting Director, Distribution & Agency Policy, Sunita Chander
Tel: 416-325-6594
sunita.chander@ontario.ca

Director, Energy Networks & Indigenous Policy, Ken Nakahara
Tel: 416-325-6729
ken.nakahara@ontario.ca

Director, Strategic Policy & Analytics, Shruti Talwar
Tel: 416-325-8698
shruti.talwar@ontario.ca

Ontario Ministry of Environment, Conservation & Parks

Ferguson Block, 77 Wellesley St. West, 11th Fl., Toronto, ON M7A 2T5
Tel: 416-325-4000; *Fax:* 416-314-6713
Toll-Free: 800-565-4923
TTY: 800-515-2759
www.ontario.ca/environment
Other Communication: Pollution Hotline: 866-663-8477; Spills or Emergencies: 800-268-6060

The Ministry (formerly Environment & Climate Change, prior to the 2018 general election) is responsible for protecting clean & safe air, land & water to ensure healthy communities, ecological protection & sustainable development for present & future generations of Ontarians. Using stringent regulations, targeted enforcement & a variety of other programs & initiatives, the Ministry continues to address environmental issues that have local, regional & global effects. The Ministry has built a strong foundation of clear laws, regulations, standards & permits & approvals. The Ministry monitors pollution & restoration trends in an effort to determine the effectiveness of its activities & to assess risks to human health & the environment. This information is used to develop & implement environmental legislation, regulations, standards, policies, guidelines & programs to enhance environmental protection. Serviced by the Office of the Chief Information Officer, Land & Resources I&IT Cluster.

Minister, Hon. David Piccini
Tel: 416-314-6790
minister.mecp@ontario.ca

Deputy Minister, Serge Imbrogno
Tel: 416-314-6753
serge.imbrogno@ontario.ca

Parliamentary Assistant, Andrea Khanjin
andrea.khanjin@ontario.ca

Director, Communications, Charlotte Beckett
charlotte.beckett@ontario.ca

Acting Director, Legal Services, Tom McKinlay
Tel: 416-327-2125
tom.mckinlay@ontario.ca

Associated Agencies, Boards & Commissions:

• Advisory Council on Drinking Water Quality & Testing Standards
40 St. Clair Ave. West, 9th Fl.
Toronto, ON M4V 1M2
Tel: 416-212-7779; *Fax:* 416-212-7595
www.odwac.gov.on.ca
The Council's mandate is to advise on drinking water standards, legislation, regulations & issues.

• Ontario Clean Water Agency (OCWA)
1 Yonge St., 17th Fl.
Toronto, ON M5E 1E5
Tel: 416-314-5600; *Fax:* 416-314-8300
Toll-free: 800-667-6292
ocwa@ocwa.com
www.ocwa.com
The Ontario Clean Water Agency (OCWA) was established as a Provincial Crown Agency in November 1993 & has since been committed to providing safe & reliable clean water services in Ontario.

• Pesticides Advisory Committee
Foster Bldg
40 St. Clair Ave. West, 7th Fl.
Toronto, ON M4V 1M2
Tel: 416-314-9230; *Fax:* 416-314-9237
www.opac.gov.on.ca
The committee advises the Minister of the Environment on matters pertaining to pesticides. It annually reviews the Pesticides Act & regulations, & government publications respecting pesticides & control of pests. The committee also recommends classifications for all new pesticide products prior to their marketing & use in Ontario, & publishes an annual report.

• Walkerton Clean Water Centre
20 Ontario Rd.
PO Box 160
Walkerton, ON N0G 2V0
Tel: 519-881-2003; *Fax:* 519-881-4947
Toll-free: 866-515-0550
inquiry@wcwc.ca
www.wcwc.ca
The Walkerton Clean Water Centre aims to create a world-class intitute dedicated to safe & secure drinking water for the people of Ontario. The Centre's work will complement & support that of the Ministry's with a focus on ensuring that training, education & information is available & accessible to owners, operators & operating authorities of Ontario's drinking water systems, particularly in rural & remote communities.

Climate Change & Resiliency Division
77 Wellesley St. West, 10th Fl., Toronto, ON M7A 2T5
Assistant Deputy Minister, Alex Wood
Tel: 416-325-8569
alex.wood@ontario.ca

Director, Climate Change Policy, Karen Moore
karen.moore4@ontario.ca

Director, Climate Change Programs, Heather E. Pearson
heather.e.pearson@ontario.ca

Director, Land & Water Policy, Ling Mark
Tel: 416-314-7020
ling.mark@ontario.ca

Director, Resource Recovery Policy, Wendy Ren
Tel: 416-327-9743
wendy.ren@ontario.ca

Director, Environmental Intergovernmental Affairs, Michael Stickings
Tel: 416-212-1340
michael.stickings@ontario.ca

Corporate Management Division
135 St Clair Ave. West, 14th Fl., Toronto, ON M4V 1P5
Tel: 416-314-6426; *Fax:* 416-314-6425

Director, Information Management & Access Branch, Geoffrey Gladdy
Tel: 416-327-1100
geoffrey.gladdy@ontario.ca

Director, Business & Fiscal Planning, Lucia Lau
Tel: 416-314-7370; *Fax:* 416-314-7858
lucia.lau@ontario.ca

Director, Strategic Human Resources, Jacques LeGris
Tel: 416-314-9305; *Fax:* 416-314-9313
jacques.legris@ontario.ca

Director, Transition Office, Becky Taylor
Tel: 416-314-5606; *Fax:* 416-325-7962
becky.taylor@ontario.ca

Drinking Water Management Division
135 St Clair Ave. West, 14th Fl., Toronto, ON M4V 1P5
Tel: 416-314-4475; *Fax:* 416-314-6935

The Drinking Water Management Division, led by the Chief Drinking Water Inspector, has lead responsibility for program & operational activities related to the protection & provision of safe drinking water in Ontario.

Acting Assistant Deputy Minister & Chief Drinking Water Inspector, Orna Salamon
Tel: 416-314-4463
orna.salamon@ontario.ca

Deputy Chief Drinking Water Inspector, Director, Safe Drinking Water, Cammy Mack
Tel: 416-314-1977
cammy.mack@ontario.ca

Acting Director, Source Protection Programs, Heather Malcolmson
Tel: 416-212-6459; *Fax:* 416-212-2757
heather.malcolmson@ontario.ca

Director, Indigenous Drinking Water Projects, Indra Prashad
Tel: 416-314-6437
indra.prashad@ontario.ca

Director, Drinking Water Programs, Ann Marie Weselan
Tel: 416-212-7456
annmarie.weselan@ontario.ca

Environmental Assessment Division
135 St Clair Ave. West, 14th Fl., Toronto, ON M4V 1P5
Assistant Deputy Minister, Sarah Paul
Tel: 416-314-9530
sarah.paul@ontario.ca

Director, Environmental Assessment & Permissions Branch, Heather Malcolmson
heather.malcolmson@ontario.ca

Environmental Sciences & Standards Division
135 St Clair Ave. West, 14th Fl., Toronto, ON M4V 1P5
The Environmental Sciences & Standards Division (ESSD) provides the best available science & technology to support decisions about the natural environment, & implements those decisions by developing & managing programs & partnerships, setting scientifically credible standards, monitoring the environment & providing valuable analytical & scientific expertise. Programs such as Drive Clean, that improve the environment & increase public awareness, are central to the ministry's efforts to strengthen environmental protection.

Assistant Deputy Minister, Orna Salamon
Tel: 416-314-4463
orna.salamon@ontario.ca

Director, Laboratory Services, Joseph Odumeru
joseph.odumeru@ontario.ca

Director, Environmental Monitoring & Reporting, Kathy McKague
kathy.mckague@ontario.ca

Director, Technical Assessment & Standards, Julie Schroeder
julie.schroeder@ontario.ca

Environmental Monitoring & Reporting Branch
Tel: 416-235-6300; *Fax:* 416-235-6235

Director, Kathy McKague
Tel: 416-235-6160
kathy.mckague@ontario.ca

Assistant Director, Cynthia Carr
Tel: 416-235-6262
cynthia.carr@ontario.ca

Laboratory Services Branch
Tel: 416-235-5743; *Fax:* 416-235-5744

Director, Joseph Odumeru
Tel: 416-235-5747
joseph.odumeru@ontario.ca

Standards Development Branch
Tel: 416-327-5519; *Fax:* 416-327-2936

Director, Sarah Paul
Tel: 416-327-5543
sarah.paul@ontario.ca

Operations Division
135 St Clair Ave. West, 8th Fl., Toronto, ON M4V 1P5
Tel: 416-314-6378; *Fax:* 416-314-6396

This division is the operations & program delivery arm of the ministry. It is responsible for delivering programs to protect air quality & surface & ground water quality & quantity; to ensure appropriate management of wastes; to ensure an adequate quality of drinking water; & to control the use of pesticides. In addition, the division is responsible for administering the ministry's approvals & licensing programs as well as an investigative & enforcement program to ensure compliance with environmental laws. The division has a province-wide network of regional, district & area offices.

Assistant Deputy Minister, Paul Nieweglowski
Tel: 416-314-6366
paul.nieweglowski@ontario.ca
Director, Environmental Approvals Access & Service Integration, Dolly Goyette
Tel: 416-314-8171; *Fax:* 416-314-8452
dolly.goyette@ontario.ca
Director, Northern Environmental Initiatives, Mary Hennessy
Tel: 416-314-7141
mary.hennessy@ontario.ca
Director, Environmental Approvals, Kathleen O'Neill
Tel: 416-314-0934
kathleen.oneill@ontario.ca
Director, Operations Integration - Spills Action Centre, Richard Raeburn-Gibson
Tel: 416-314-3994
richard.raeburngibson@ontario.ca
Director, Environmental Enforcement & Compliance Office, Greg Sones
Tel: 416-314-4241
greg.sones@ontario.ca

Environmental Commissioner of Ontario (ECO)

#605, 1075 Bay St., Toronto, ON M5S 2B1
Tel: 416-325-3377; *Fax:* 416-325-3370
Toll-Free: 800-701-6454
commissioner@eco.on.ca
www.eco.on.ca
twitter.com/Ont_ECO
facebook.com/OntarioEnvironmentalCommissioner
www.linkedin.com/company/2922304
www.youtube.com/user/EcoComms
An independent officer of the Legislative Assembly of Ontario, the Environmental Commissioner of Ontario promotes the values, goals & purposes of the Environmental Bill of Rights (EBR) to improve the quality of Ontario's natural environment. The ECO monitors & reports on the application of the EBR, provides public education to facilitate Ontario residents' participation in the EBR & reviews government accountability for environmental decision-making.

Commissioner, Dianne Saxe, Ph.D.
Tel: 416-325-3333
dianne.saxe@eco.on.ca

Deputy Commissioner, Tyler Schulz

Ontario Ministry of Finance

95 Grosvenor St., Toronto, ON M7A 1Y8
Fax: 866-888-3850
Toll-Free: 866-668-8297
TTY: 800-263-7776
www.ontario.ca/page/ministry-finance
twitter.com/onfinance
The Ministry of Finance recommends taxation, fiscal & economic policies. Other responsibilities include: the management of provincial finances & the development & allocation of Ontario's budget.

Minister, Hon. Peter Bethlenfalvy
Tel: 416-325-0400
Minister.fin@ontario.ca

Deputy Minister, Greg Orencsak
Tel: 416-325-1590
greg.orencsak@ontario.ca

Parliamentary Assistant, Will Bouma
Will.Bouma@ontario.ca

Parliamentary Assistant, Michael Parsa
Michael.Parsa@ontario.ca

Director, Communications Services, Kirsten Evans
Tel: 437-241-2589
kirsten.evans@ontario.ca

Associated Agencies, Boards & Commissions:
• **Deposit Insurance Corporation of Ontario (DICO)**
#700, 4711 Yonge St.
Toronto, ON M2N 6K8
Tel: 416-325-9444; *Fax:* 416-325-9722
Toll-free: 800-268-6653
info@dico.com
www.dico.com
The Deposit Insurance Corporation of Ontario provides deposit insurance, to the extent provided under the Credit Unions & Caisses Populaires Act, on deposits of members of credit unions & caisses populaires.

• **Financial Services Commission of Ontario (FSCO)**
North York City Ctr.
5160 Yonge St., 17th Fl.
PO Box 85
Toronto, ON M2N 6L9
Tel: 416-250-7250; *Fax:* 416-590-7070
Toll-free: 800-668-0128
TTY: 416-590-7108
contactcentre@fsco.gov.on.ca
www.fsco.gov.on.ca
Other Communication: Contact Centre Fax: 416-590-2040
The commission regulates insurance, pensions plans, credit unions, caisses populaires, mortgage brokers, cooperative corporations, & loan & trust companies in Ontario. FSCO provides regulatory services that protect financial services consumers & pension plan beneficiaries & support a healthy & competitive financial services industry.

• **Liquor Control Board of Ontario (LCBO)**
55 Lake Shore Blvd. East
Toronto, ON M5E 1A4
Tel: 416-365-5900; *Fax:* 416-864-2476
Toll-free: 800-668-5226
infoline@lcbo.com
www.lcbo.com
The Liquor Control Board of Ontario (LCBO) is a provincial Crown corporation that was established in 1927 by Lieutenant Governor William Donald Ross, on the advice of his Premier, Howard Ferguson, to sell liquor, wine, & beer through a chain of retail stores. In July 2016, the LCBO launched an online shopping platform.
In September 2017, Ontario announced that the LCBO would be in charge of establishing a subsidiary responsible for sales of recreational cannabis in the province, once legalized by the federal government. Subsequent to legalization on Oct. 17, 2018, the Ontario Cannabis Store commenced online sales. As of April 2019, cannabis can also be purchased in Ontario at physical, private retail locations that are licensed by the government.

• **Ontario Cannabis Retail Corporation / Ontario Cannabis Store (OCS)**
c/o Liquor Control Board of Ontario
55 Lake Shore Blvd. East
Toronto, ON M5E 1A4
Toll-free: 888-910-0627
ocs.ca
Other Communication: Alt. URLs: hellooocs.ca; www.doingbusinesswithocs.ca
The Ontario Cannabis Store has provided recreational cannabis since Oct. 17, 2019. At first the sole legal option for cannabis consumers post-legalization, the OCS will also become the provincial wholesaler of cannabis for private retail stores.

• **Ontario Electricity Financial Corporation (OEFC)**
#1400, 1 Dundas St. West
Toronto, ON M7A 1Y7
Tel: 416-325-8000; *Fax:* 416-325-8005
www.oefc.on.ca
The OEFC was established under the Electricity Act, 1998 as the legal continuation of the former Ontario Hydro.

• **Ontario Financing Authority (OFA)**
1 Dundas St. West, 14th Fl.
Toronto, ON M7A 1Y7
Tel: 416-325-8000; *Fax:* 416-325-8005
investor@ofina.on.ca
www.ofina.on.ca
Other Communication: Meetings, Email: irmanager@ofina.on.ca
The Ontario Financing Authority (OFA) is an agency of the Province of Ontario that manages the Province's debt and borrowing program. The OFA is governed by a Board of Directors that reports to the Minister of Finance.

• **Ontario Lottery & Gaming Corporation (OLG)**
Roberta Bondar Pl.
#800, 70 Foster Dr.
Sault Ste. Marie, ON P6A 6V2
Tel: 705-946-6464; *Fax:* 705-946-6600
Toll-free: 800-387-0098
www.olg.ca
Other Communication: Toronto Office Phone: 416-224-1772; Fax: 416-224-7000
Created on April 1, 2000 under the Ontario Lottery and Gaming Corporation Act, 1999, the Ontario Lottery & Gaming Corporation (OLG) is a provincial agency operating & managing province-wide lotteries, casinos & slots facilities at horse racing tracks.

• **Ontario Securities Commission (OSC)**
20 Queen St. West, 20th Fl.
PO Box 55
Toronto, ON M5H 3S8
Tel: 416-593-8314; *Fax:* 416-593-8122
Toll-free: 877-785-1555
TTY: 866-827-1295
inquiries@osc.gov.on.ca
www.osc.gov.on.ca
Other Communication: Public Records Phone: 416-593-3735; TTY: 866-827-1295; Email: record@osc.gov.on.ca
The mandate of the Ontario Securities Commission (OSC) is to protect investors while fostering capital formation & the efficiency & integrity of Ontario's & Canada's capital markets.
The Office of the Whistleblower was created in July 2016, making it the first paid whistleblower program by a securities regulator in Canada. Toll-Free Phone: 1-888-672-5553; URL: www.osc.gov.on.ca/en/whistleblower.htm.

Corporate & Quality Service Division
Michael Starr Bldg., 33 King St. West, 6th Fl., Toronto, ON L1H 8H5
Fax: 905-433-6688
Assistant Deputy Minister & Chief Administrative Officer, Helmut Zisser
Tel: 416-314-5158
helmut.zisser@ontario.ca
Director, Strategic Human Resources Services, Stephen Boyd
Tel: 905-433-6646
steve.boyd@ontario.ca
Director, Corporate Planning & Finance, Linda Gibney
Tel: 905-433-5637
linda.gibney@ontario.ca
Director, Business Services, Mimi Wong
Tel: 416-212-1435
mimi.wong@ontario.ca

Office of the Budget
Frost Bldg. South, 7 Queen's Park Cres., 4th Fl., Toronto, ON M7A 1Y7
Assistant Deputy Minister, Tim Schuurman
Tel: 416-327-0173
tim.schuurman@ontario.ca
Director, Fiscal Policy, Selena Esmail
Tel: 416-325-5621
selena.esmail@ontario.ca
Manager, Document Development & Support Unit, Thomas Sullivan
thomas.sullivan@ontario.ca

Office of Economic Policy
Frost Bldg. North, 95 Grosvenor St., 5th Fl., Toronto, ON M7A 1Z1
Assistant Deputy Minister & Chief Economist, Brian Lewis
Tel: 416-325-0850
brian.lewis@ontario.ca
Director, Industrial Economics, Rob Gray
Tel: 416-325-0801
rob.gray@ontario.ca
Director, Statistics & Integration, Melissa Kittmer
Tel: 416-325-4713
melissa.kittmer@ontario.ca
Director, Macroeconomics & Revenue, Paul D. Lewis
Tel: 416-325-0754
paul.d.lewis@ontario.ca

Office of Regulatory Policy & Agency Relations
Forst Bldg, 7 Queen's Park Cres., 2nd Fl., Toronto, ON M7A 1Y7
Associate Deputy Minister, Vacant
Assistant Deputy Minister, Government Business Enterprise, Scott Nelms
Tel: 416-212-6469
scott.nelms@ontario.ca
Director, Alcohol Policy; Project Director, Cannabis Retail Implementation Project, Jake Gregory
jake.gregory@ontario.ca
Acting Director, Gaming Policy, Tanya Watkins
tanya.watkins@ontario.ca

Financial Services Policy Division
Frost Bldg. North, 95 Grosvenor St., 4th Fl., Toronto, ON M7A 1Z1
Fax: 416-325-1187
Assistant Deputy Minister, David Wai
Tel: 416-326-9086
david.wai@ontario.ca
Director, Financial Institutions Policy, Joel Gorlick
Tel: 416-325-0928
joel.gorlick@ontario.ca
Acting Director, Securities Reform Policy, Colin Nickerson
Tel: 416-327-0940; *Fax:* 416-325-1187
colin.nickerson@ontario.ca

Income Security & Pension Policy Division
Frost Bldg. South, 7 Queen's Park Cres., 5th Fl., Toronto,
ON M7A 1Y7
Tel: 416-327-0133; *Fax:* 416-327-0160
Assistant Deputy Minister, Leah Myers
Tel: 416-212-5983
leah.myers@ontario.ca
Director, Income Security Policy, Norman Helfand
Tel: 416-325-5722
norman.helfand@ontario.ca
Director, BPS Pensions, Alex Killoch
Tel: 416-325-5724
alex.killoch@ontario.ca
Financial & Administrative Coordinator, Pension Policy, Lena
Roda
Tel: 416-327-0141
lena.roda@ontario.ca

Office of Tax, Benefits & Local Finance
Michael Starr Bldg., 33 King St. West, PO Box 623 Oshawa,
ON L1H 8H5
Toll-Free: 866-668-8297
Associate Deputy Minister, Agatha Garcia-Wright
Tel: 905-433-2292
agatha.garcia-wright@ontario.ca

Provincial-Local Finance Division
Tel: 416-327-0264; *Fax:* 416-325-7644
Assistant Deputy Minister, Allan Doheny
Tel: 416-327-9592
allan.doheny@ontario.ca
Director, Property Tax Policy, Chris Broughton
Tel: 416-314-3801; *Fax:* 416-314-3853
chris.broughton@ontario.ca
Director, Municipal Funding Policy, Robert Lowry
Tel: 416-325-4056
robert.lowry@ontario.ca
Director, Assessment Policy & Legislation, Diane Ross
Tel: 416-327-0266; *Fax:* 416-212-8406
diane.ross@ontario.ca

Strategy, Stewardship & Program Policy Division
Fax: 905-433-6686
Acting Assistant Deputy Minister, Alison Drummond
alison.drummond@ontario.ca
Director, Benefits Transformation, Mashood Mirza
Tel: 905-436-4519
mashood.mirza@ontario.ca
Director, Program Policy & Analytics, Mark Sharrett
Marc.Sharrett@ontario.ca
Director, Strategy, Stewardship & Risk Management, Jason
Stanley
jason.stanley@ontario.ca

Tax Compliance & Benefits Division
Toll-Free: 866-668-8297
Assistant Deputy Minister, Victoria Chiodi
victoria.chiodi@ontario.ca
Director, Compliance, Heather Bowie
Tel: 905-440-2442
heather.bowie@ontario.ca
Director, Advisory, Objections, Appeals & Services, Victoria
Chiodi
Tel: 905-435-2040; *Fax:* 905-435-2000
victoria.chiodi@ontario.ca
Director, Account Management & Collections, Maureen E. Kelly
Tel: 905-433-5640
maureen.e.kelly@ontario.ca

Taxation Policy Division
Tel: 416-314-0700
Assistant Deputy Minister, Sriram Subrahmanyan
Tel: 416-327-7294
sriram.subrahmanyan@ontario.ca
Financial & Administrative Officer, Ena Samaroo
Tel: 416-327-0220
ena.samaroo@ontario.ca
Director, Corporate & Commodity Taxation, Ann Langleben
Tel: 416-327-0222
ann.langleben@ontario.ca
Director, Personal Tax Policy & Design, Kostas Plainos
Tel: 416-327-0246
kostas.plainos@ontario.ca

Office of Francophone Affairs

#2501, 700 Bay St., 25th Fl., Toronto, ON M7A 0A2
Tel: 416-325-4983
Toll-Free: 800-268-7507
TTY: 416-325-0017
www.ontario.ca/page/ministry-francophone-affairs
A central agency that assists the Government of Ontario in its
delivery of services in French, & in the development of policies &
programs that meet the needs of the province's francophones.

Minister, Hon. Caroline Mulroney
Tel: 416-325-4947
caroline.mulroney@ontario.ca

Deputy Minister, Marie-Lison Fougère
Tel: 416-315-5210
marie-lison.fougere@ontario.ca

Parliamentary Assistant, Natalia Kusendova
Tel: 416-326-7102

Assistant Deputy Minister, Jean-Claude Camus
Tel: 416-325-2853
jean-claude.camus@ontario.ca

Ontario Ministry of Government & Consumer Services

Mowat Block, 900 Bay St., 6th Fl., Toronto, ON M7A 1L2
Tel: 416-212-2665; *Fax:* 416-326-7445
Toll-Free: 844-286-8404
TTY: 416-915-0001
www.ontario.ca/page/ministry-government-and-consumer-servic
es
Other Communication: Consumer Protection Branch Phone:
416-326-8800; Fax: 416-326-8665; TTY: 416-229-6086; Email:
consumer@ontario.ca
The Ministry seeks to educate, protect & serve consumers in
Ontario by maintaining a fair, safe & informed marketplace;
providing modern information services; & regulating practices
that serve the interests of Ontarians. In 2014 the existing
Ministry of Consumer Services was combined with Government
Services, bringing the two mandates together. The Ministry is
now responsible for the following main activities: providing
government information to individuals & businesses, including
distribution through Publications Ontario; protecting consumers
through information about frauds & scams & mediating
complaints about businesses; issuing birth, death & marriage
certificates; & managing Land Registry Offices throughout the
province.

Minister, Hon. Ross Romano
Tel: 416-212-2665
Ross.Romano@ontario.ca

Deputy Minister, Renu Kulendran
Tel: 416-557-9592
renu.kulendran@ontario.ca

Parliamentary Assistant, Robert (Bob) Bailey

Director, Communications, Sebastian Skamski
Tel: 416-327-2333
Sebastian.Skamski2@ontario.ca

Director, Legal Services, Fateh Salim
Tel: 416-314-7022
fateh.salim@ontario.ca

Associated Agencies, Boards & Commissions:
• Advertising Review Board
Macdonald Block
#M2-56, 900 Bay St., 2nd Fl.
Toronto, ON M7A 1N3
Tel: 416-327-2183; *Fax:* 416-327-2179

Consumer Services Operations Division
56 Wellesley St. West, 16th Fl., Toronto, ON M7A 1C1
Tel: 416-326-8800; *Fax:* 416-327-8461
Assistant Deputy Minister, Vacant

Corporate Services Division
College Park, 777 Bay St., 15th Fl., Toronto, ON M7A 2J3
Assistant Deputy Minister & Chief Administrative Officer, Clare
McMillan
Tel: 416-326-1895
clare.mcmillan@ontario.ca
Director, Organizational Development, Yvonne Defoe
Tel: 416-326-7156
yvonne.defore@ontario.ca

Government Services Integration Cluster
222 Jarvis St., 5th Fl., Toronto, ON M7A 0B6
Tel: 416-246-7171; *Fax:* 416-326-9424
Chief Information Officer, Renee Laforet
renee.laforet@ontario.ca
Director, Integrated Business Services, Susan McIntosh
Tel: 416-327-7867
susan.mcintosh@ontario.ca
Manager, Strategy, Planning & Architecture - Enterprise
Architecture, Moira Forbes
Tel: 416-326-5077
moira.forbes@ontario.ca

Information, Privacy & Archives Division
134 Ian Macdonald Blvd., Toronto, ON M7A 2C5
Tel: 416-327-1600; *Fax:* 416-327-1999
Toll-Free: 800-668-9933
www.archives.gov.on.ca
Other Communication: Circulation Desk: 416-327-1016; Main
Reading Room: 416-327-1582
twitter.com/ArchivesOntario
www.youtube.com/ArchivesOfOntario
Chief Privacy Officer & Archivist of Ontario, John Roberts
Tel: 416-327-1603; *Fax:* 416-327-1992
john.roberts@ontario.ca
Director, Archives Management & Information Storage, Janice
Orlando-Sottile
Tel: 416-327-1577; *Fax:* 416-327-1999
janice.orlando-sottile@ontario.ca
Director, Policy & Planning, Violeta Quintanilla-Webb
Tel: 416-327-1467; *Fax:* 416-327-1999
violeta.quintanilla-webb@ontario.ca

Ontario Shared Services
222 Jarvis St., 7th Fl., Toronto, ON M7A 0B6
Tel: 416-326-9300
Toll-Free: 866-979-9300
Acting Associate Deputy Minister, Heidi Francis
Tel: 416-325-5065
heidi.francis@ontario.ca
Director, OSS Blueprint Development Secretariat, Bernadette De
Souza
Tel: 416-326-9399
bernadette.desouza@ontario.ca
Acting Director, Strategy & Resource Management, David
Staszkiel
david.staszkiel@ontario.ca

Enterprise Business Services Division
Tel: 416-326-9300
Assistant Deputy Minister, Bev Hawton
Tel: 416-212-6569
bev.hawton@ontario.ca
Acting Director, Customer Relationship Management, Jim
Barclay
Tel: 416-314-2229
jim.barclay@ontario.ca
Director, Risk Management & Insurance Services, Daryl Carre
Tel: 416-314-3439
daryl.carre@ontario.ca
Director, Business Development & Services, Ana Matos-Clark
Tel: 416-212-6852
ana.matos-clark@ontario.ca
Acting Director, Document Solutions & Logistics, Nella Puntillo
Tel: 416-314-3656
nella.puntillo@ontario.ca

Enterprise Financial Services & Systems
Other Communication: OSS Contact Centre (GTA), Phone:
416-326-9300
Assistant Deputy Minister, Noah Morris
Tel: 416-327-2022
noah.morris@ontario.ca
Director, Business & Divisional Support Services, Lillian Duda
Tel: 416-326-0124
lillian.duda@ontario.ca
Director, Operations & Transformation Support, Alex
Goncharenko
Tel: 416-326-6424
alex.goncharenko@ontario.ca
Director, Business Application Solutions Support, Robert Tee
robert.tee@ontario.ca
Director, Client Services Management, Mano Sharma
Tel: 416-325-5782
mano.sharma@ontario.ca
Director, Financial Processing Operations, Ken Sheldon
Tel: 705-494-3104
ken.sheldon@ontario.ca

HR Service Delivery Division
Tel: 416-325-4789
Assistant Deputy Minister, Donna Holmes
Tel: 416-325-7612
donna.holmes@ontario.ca
Director, Centre for Employee Health, Safety & Wellness,
Margaret Cernigoj
Tel: 416-327-0164
margaret.carnigoj@ontario.ca
Acting Director, Talent Acquisition, Laila Kreig
Tel: 705-494-3379
laila.kreig@ontario.ca
Director, Job Evaluation Initiatives, Angela Sullivan
Tel: 416-327-8308
angela.sullivan@ontario.ca

Pay & Benefits Services Division
Tel: 416-326-9300; *Fax:* 416-325-1165

Assistant Deputy Minister, Kristen Delorme
Tel: 416-212-6731; *Fax:* 416-327-4246
kristen.delorme@ontario.ca
Director, Pay & Benefits Support, Hatem Belhi
Tel: 416-212-2402; *Fax:* 416-212-2916
hatem.belhi@ontario.ca
Director, Pay & Benefits Operations, Rob Gagne
Tel: 705-494-3176; *Fax:* 705-494-3141
rob.gagne@ontario.ca
Director, Pay & Benefits Business Solutions, George Karlos
Tel: 416-212-2933
george.karlos@ontario.ca

Supply Chain Ontario
Fax: 416-327-3573
www.ontario.ca/supplychain
Assistant Deputy Minister, Doug Kent
Tel: 416-327-7508
Doug.Kent@ontario.ca
Director, Supply Chain Program, Christopher Gonsalves
Tel: 416-314-1919
christopher.gonsalves@ontario.ca
Director, Strategic Procurement Services, Jim Hadjiyianni
Tel: 416-212-1055
jim.hadjiyianni@ontario.ca
Director, Program & Policy Enablement, Jackie Korecki
Tel: 416-327-8765
jackie.korecki@ontario.ca
Acting Director, Continuous Improvement & Strategic Planning,
Angela Lam
Tel: 416-325-7553
angela.lam@ontario.ca
Director, Enterprise Procurement, Wes Lapish
Tel: 416-327-3518
wes.lapish@ontario.ca

Policy, Planning & Oversight Division
56 Wellesley St. West, 6th Fl., Toronto, ON M7A 1C1
Acting Assistant Deputy Minister, Glen Padassery
Tel: 416-326-2826
glen.padassery@ontario.ca
Acting Director, Public Safety, Hussein Lalani
Tel: 416-326-8929
hussein.lalani@ontario.ca
Acting Director, Consumer Policy & Liaison, Nicholas Robins
Tel: 416-326-8868
nicholas.robins@ontario.ca

ServiceOntario
College Park, 777 Bay St., 15th Fl., Toronto, ON M7A 2J3
Fax: 416-326-1313
Toll-Free: 800-267-8097
TTY: 800-268-7095
www.serviceontario.ca
twitter.com/serviceontario
www.facebook.com/ServiceOntario
www.youtube.com/user/serviceontario
Associate Deputy Minister, Jim Cassimatis
Tel: 416-314-3709
jim.cassimatis@ontario.ca

Business Improvement Division
Assistant Deputy Minister, Bev Hawton
Tel: 416-326-6062
bev.hawton@ontario.ca
Director, Digital Services Transformation, Asim Hussain
Tel: 416-326-4897
asim.hussain@ontario.ca
Director, Business Effectiveness, Chris McAlpine
Tel: 416-326-1717; *Fax:* 416-326-3392
chris.mcalpine@ontario.ca
Other Communications: Thunder Bay, Fax: 807-343-7360
Acting Director, Retail & Enterprise Services Transformation,
Gabe Talarico
Tel: 416-326-5367
gabe.talarico@ontario.ca
Director, Business Services Transformation, Mario Tarsitano
Tel: 416-326-8573
mario.tarsitano@ontario.ca

Central Services Division
Fax: 416-326-5550
Assistant Deputy Minister, Robert Mathew
Tel: 416-325-2857
robert.mathew@ontario.ca
Director, Central Production & Verification Services, Denis Blais
Tel: 416-314-4879
denis.blais@ontario.ca
Director, Kingston Production & Verification Services, Karen
Harry
Tel: 613-545-4631
karen.harry@ontario.ca
Director, Regulatory Services, Bill Snell
Tel: 416-314-4886
bill.snell@ontario.ca

Director, Thunder Bay Production & Verification Services,
Alexandra Schmidt
Tel: 807-343-7408
alexandra.schmidt@ontario.ca

Customer Care Division
Assistant Deputy Minister, Cameron Sinclair
Tel: 416-326-2784; *Fax:* 416-326-1313
cameron.sinclair@ontario.ca
Director, Central Region Contact Centre Services, Mary Ben
Hamoud
Tel: 416-212-5377
mary.benhamoud@ontario.ca
Acting Director, East Retail Offices, Ann Gendron
Tel: 613-724-0922
ann.gendron@ontario.ca
Director, North Retail Offices, Louise R. Larocque
Tel: 705-564-4485; *Fax:* 705-564-7372
louise.larocque@ontario.ca
Director, Channel Strategy, Christine Levin
Tel: 613-548-6767 ext: 355
christine.levin@ontario.ca
Director, West Retail Offices, Tara Meagher
Tel: 519-826-4531; *Fax:* 519-826-6363
tara.meagher@ontario.ca
Director, Eastern Contact Centre Services, Rico Medeiros
Tel: 905-433-1792
rico.medeiros@ontario.ca
Acting Director, Central Retail Offices, Nadine Rhodd
Tel: 416-294-4424
nadine.rhodd@ontario.ca
Director, Private Service Providers, Jacqueline Spencer
Tel: 905-319-0959
jacqueline.spencer@ontario.ca

Strategic Planning, Partnerships & Policy Division
Assistant Deputy Minister, David Ward
Tel: 416-325-8804
david.ward@ontario.ca
Director, Partnerships & Business Development, Anne Matthews
anne.matthews@ontario.ca

Ontario Ministry of Health

**Hepburn Block, 80 Grosvenor St., 10th Fl, Toronto, ON M7A
2C4**
Tel: 416-327-4327
Toll-Free: 800-268-1153
TTY: 800-387-5559
www.health.gov.on.ca
twitter.com/ONThealth
www.facebook.com/ONThealth
The Ministry is responsible for administering the health care
system & providing services to the Ontario public through such
programs as health insurance, drug benefits, assistive devices,
care for the mentally ill, long-term care, home care, community &
public health, & health promotion & disease prevention. It also
regulates hospitals & nursing homes, operates psychiatric
hospitals & medical laboratories, & co-ordinates emergency
health services.
In Feb. 2019, the provincial government announced the creation
of a new agency called Ontario Health, that would consolidate 14
local health integration networks, including Cancer Care Ontario
& eHealth Ontario. In June 2019, the Ministry of Health &
Long-Term Care was split into two separate ministries.

Minister, Hon. Christine Elliott
christine.elliott@ontario.ca

Associate Minister, Mental Health & Addictions, Hon.
Michael Tibollo
michael.tibollo@ontario.ca

Deputy Minister, Dr. Catherine Zahn
Tel: 416-327-4496
Catherine.Zahn@ontario.ca

Parliamentary Assistant, Robin Martin
robin.martin@ontario.ca

Associate Deputy Minister, Health Services, Melanie
Fraser
Tel: 416-728-7849
Melanie.Fraser@ontario.ca

Associated Agencies, Boards & Commissions:
• **Cancer Care Ontario (CCO)**
620 University Ave., 15th Fl.
Toronto, ON M5G 2L7
Tel: 416-971-9800; *Fax:* 416-971-6888
TTY: 416-217-1815
www.cancercare.on.ca
An Ontario government agency, Cancer Care Ontario, aims to
improve the quality in disease prevention & screening, as well as

the delivery of care & the overall patient experience in relation to
cancer & chronic kidney disease.
• **Chiropody Review Committee**
3 Jackson Ave.
Toronto, ON M8X 2W2
Tel: 416-542-1333; *Fax:* 416-542-1666
Toll-free: 877-232-7653
The Chiropody Review Committee allows the General Manager
of OHIP to determine whether claims should be refused, reduced
or repaid.
• **Chiropractic Review Committee**
#900, 130 Bloor St. West
Toronto, ON M5S 1N5
Tel: 416-929-0409
The Chiropractic Review Committee allows the General
Manager of OHIP to determine whether claims should be
refused, reduced or repaid.
• **Consent & Capacity Board (CCB)**
151 Bloor St. West, 10th Fl.
Toronto, ON M5S 2T5
Tel: 416-327-4142; *Fax:* 416-327-4207
Toll-free: 866-777-7391
TTY: 877-301-0889
ccb@ontario.ca
www.ccboard.on.ca
Other Communication: Toll-Free Fax: 866-777-7273
The Board hears appeals relating to involuntary placement in a
psychiatric facility, capacity to make personal care & financial
decisions & access to personal records from a psychiatric
facility.
• **Dental Review Committee**
c/o Royal College of Dental Surgeons of Ontario
350 Rumsey Rd.
Toronto, ON M4G 1R8
Tel: 416-961-6555
A committee of the Royal College of Dental Surgeons that
reviews accounts of dentists referred to it by the General
Manager of the Ontario Health Insurance Plan.
• **eHealth Ontario**
College Park
#701, 777 Bay St.
PO Box 148
Toronto, ON M5G 2C8
Tel: 416-586-6500; *Fax:* 416-586-4363
Toll-free: 888-411-7742
TTY: 855-645-3390
info@ehealthontario.on.ca
www.ehealthontario.on.ca
Other Communication: Privacy Office, Phone: 416-946-4767;
Email: privacy@ehealthontario.on.ca
• **HealthForceOntario Marketing & Recruitment Agency
(HFO MRA)**
163 Queen St. East
Toronto, ON M5A 1S1
Tel: 416-862-2200; *Fax:* 416-862-4818
Toll-free: 800-596-4046
TTY: 416-862-4817
info@healthforceontario.ca
www.healthforceontario.ca
Other Communication: International Toll-Free: 800-596-4046,
ext. 4
HealthForceOntario seeks to identify & address the province's
health human resource needs on behalf of the Ministry of Health
& Long-Term Care, & the Ministry of Training, Colleges &
Universities.
• **Health Professionals Appeal & Review Board (HPARB)**
151 Bloor St. West, 9th Fl.
Toronto, ON M5S 1S4
Tel: 416-327-8512; *Fax:* 416-327-8524
Toll-free: 866-282-2179
The Review Board provides oversight to the regulated health
professions & veterinarians of Ontario.
• **Health Quality Ontario (HQO)**
130 Bloor St. West, 10th Fl.
Toronto, ON M5S 1N5
Tel: 416-323-6868; *Fax:* 416-323-9261
Toll-free: 866-623-6868
info@hqontario.ca
www.hqontario.ca
• **Health Services Appeal & Review Board (HSARB)**
151 Bloor St. West, 9th Fl.
Toronto, ON M5S 1S4
Tel: 416-327-8512; *Fax:* 416-327-8524
Toll-free: 866-282-2179
The Review Board conducts appeals and reviews under twelve
different health care statutes.

• Medical Eligibility Committee (MEC)
151 Bloor St. West, 9th Fl.
Toronto, ON M5S 1S4
Tel: 416-327-8512; *Fax:* 416-327-8524
Toll-free: 866-282-2179
Deals with the eligibility of insured services as well as other matters assigned to it by the act or the regulation or by the minister; makes recommendations to the general manager with respect to these decisions.

• Ontario Hepatitis C Assistance Plan Review Committee (OHCAP)
151 Bloor St. West, 9th Fl.
Toronto, ON M5S 1S4
Tel: 416-327-8512; *Fax:* 416-327-8524
At the request of applicants to the OHCAP who have been denied a benefit by the Program Office, the Review Committee conducts reviews of the Program Office's decisions and determines the applicant's entitlement to the specified program benefit.

• Ontario Mental Health Foundation (OMHF)
441 Jarvis St., 2nd Fl.
Toronto, ON M4Y 2G8
Tel: 416-920-7721; *Fax:* 416-920-0026
www.omhf.on.ca
The Ontario Mental Health Foundation (OMHF) provides grants and fellowships for mental health research.

• Ontario Review Board (ORB)
151 Bloor St. West, 10th Fl.
Toronto, ON M5S 2T5
Tel: 416-327-8866; *Fax:* 416-327-8867
TTY: 877-301-0889
orb@ontario.ca
www.orb.on.ca
The Ontario Review Board reviews the status of accused individuals who have not been found criminally responsible or unfit to stand trial for criminal offences on account of a mental disorde.r

• Optometry Review Committee
6 Crescent Rd., 3rd Fl.
Toronto, ON M4W 1T1
Tel: 416-962-4071
A committee of the College of Optometrists of Ontario that reviews accounts of optometrists referred to it by the General Manager of the Ontario Health Insurance Plan.

• Physician Payment Committee (PPRB)
151 Bloor St. West, 9th Fl.
Toronto, ON M5S 1S4
Tel: 416-327-8512
The Physician Payment Review Board (PPRB) conducts hearings regarding payment disputes between physicians and the General Manager of OHIP.

• Public Health Ontario (PHO)
#300, 480 University Ave.
Toronto, ON M5G 1V2
Tel: 647-260-7100; *Fax:* 647-260-7600
Toll-free: 877-543-8931
communications@oahpp.ca
www.publichealthontario.ca

• Transitional Physican Audit Panel
151 Bloor St. West, 9th Fl.
Toronto, ON M5S 2T5

• Trillium Gift of Life Network
#900, 522 University Ave.
Toronto, ON M5G 1W7
Tel: 416-363-4001; *Fax:* 416-363-4002
Toll-free: 800-263-2833
www.giftoflife.on.ca
Other Communication: Healthcare Professionals Organ & Tissue Referral: 416-363-4438; Toll-Free: 877-363-8456
The Trillium Gift of Life Network plans, promotes, coordinates & supports organ & tissue donation & transplantation across Ontario.

Chief Medical Officer of Health (CMOH)
393 University Ave., 21st Fl., Toronto, ON M5G 2M2
Tel: 416-212-3831; *Fax:* 416-325-8412
health.gov.on.ca/en/common/ministry/cmoh.aspx
Chief Medical Officer of Health, Dr. Kieran Moore
Tel: 416-212-3831
Kieran.Moore@ontario.ca

Community, Mental Health & Addictions & French Language Services Division
Hepburn Block, 1075 Bay St., Toronto, ON M5S 2B1
Fax: 416-212-1859
Assistant Deputy Minister, Tim G. Hadwen
Tel: 416-212-1134
tim.hadwen@ontario.ca

Acting Director, LHIN Renewal Branch & LHIN Liaison, Phil Graham
Phil.Graham@ontario.ca
Director, Mental Health & Addictions Policy, Accountability & Provincial Partnership, Patrick Mitchell
patrick.mitchell@ontario.ca
Director, Home & Community Care, Amy Olmstead
Tel: 416-327-7056
amy.olmstead@ontario.ca
Director, Primary Health Care Branch, Nadia Surani
Tel: 416-212-0832
nadia.surani@ontario.ca

Corporate Services Division
Hepburn Block, 80 Grosvenor St., 11th Fl., Toronto, ON M7A 1R3
Tel: 416-327-4266; *Fax:* 416-314-5915
Assistant Deputy Minister & Chief Administrative Officer, Justine Jackson
Tel: 416-327-4387
Justine.Jackson@ontario.ca
Acting Director, Accounting Policy & Financial Reporting, Mark Donaldson
Tel: 416-314-6162; *Fax:* 416-327-7364
mark.donaldson@ontario.ca
Director, Supply Chain & Facilities Branch, Shelley Gibson
Tel: 416-327-0782; *Fax:* 416-327-7312
shelley.gibson@ontario.ca
Director, HR Strategic Business Unit, Rhonda Lindo
Tel: 416-327-8747; *Fax:* 416-327-7580
rhonda.lindo@ontario.ca
Director, Business Innovation Office, Simon Trevarthen
Tel: 416-327-2299
simon.trevarthen@ontario.ca
Other Communications: Alt. Email: bio.mohltc@ontario.ca

Direct Services Division
56 Wellesley St. West, 2nd Fl., Toronto, ON M5S 2S3
Fax: 416-212-9710
Assistant Deputy Minister, Patricia Li
Tel: 416-327-4845
patricia.li@ontario.ca
Director, Psychiatric Patient Advocate Office & Acting Director, Assistive Devices Program, Nancy Dickson
Tel: 613-545-4366; *Fax:* 416-327-7008
nancy.dickson@ontario.ca
www.ppao.gov.on.ca
Other Communications: Alt. Email: ppao.moh@ontario.ca
Director, Claims Services, Josephine Fuller
Tel: 613-548-6333
Toll-free: 800-268-1154; *Fax:* 416-548-6320
josephine.fuller@ontario.ca
Acting Director, Emergency Health Services (Land & Air), Donna Piasentini
Tel: 416-327-7909
Toll-free: 800-461-6431; *Fax:* 416-327-7879
donna.piasentini@ontario.ca

www.health.gov.on.ca/english/public/program/ehs/ehs_mn.html

Drugs & Devices Division
Hepburn Block, 80 Grosvenor St., 9th Fl., Toronto, ON M7A 1R3
Tel: 416-212-4724; *Fax:* 416-325-6647
www.health.gov.on.ca/en/public/programs/drugs
Assistant Deputy Minister & Executive Officer, Suzanne McGurn
Tel: 416-327-0902
suzanne.mcgurn@ontario.ca
Director, Strategy Execution Branch, Joel Montesanti
joel.montesanti@ontario.ca
Director, Assistive Devices Program, Eva Roszuk
eva.roszuk@ontario.ca
Director, Drug Programs Delivery Branch, David Schachow
Tel: 416-327-8118; *Fax:* 416-327-8912
david.schachow@ontario.ca
Director, Drug Programs Policy & Strategy Branch, Angie Wong
Tel: 416-327-8315
angie.wong@ontario.ca

Health Capital Division
#601, 1075 Bay St., 6th Fl., Toronto, ON M5S 2B1
Tel: 416-326-2943
Assistant Deputy Minister, Peter Kaftarian
Tel: 416-314-0402
peter.kaftarian@ontario.ca
Director, Long-Term Care Home Renewal Branch, Brenda Blackstock
Tel: 416-212-1374
brenda.blackstock@ontario.ca
Director, Health Capital Investment Branch, James Stewart
Tel: 416-326-1088
james.stewart@ontario.ca

Health Services Information & Information Technology Cluster
56 Wellesley St. West, 10th Fl., Toronto, ON M5S 2S3
Tel: 416-314-0234; *Fax:* 416-314-4182
Associate Deputy Minister & Chief Information Officer, Lorelle Taylor
Tel: 416-314-1279; *Fax:* 416-314-0234
lorelle.taylor@ontario.ca
Executive Lead, Health Services Cluster, Elizabeth Hyland
liz.hyland@ontario.ca

Health System Quality & Funding Division
Hepburn Block, 80 Grosvenor St., 5th Fl., Toronto, ON M7A 1R3
Assistant Deputy Minister, Melissa Farrell
Tel: 416-327-8533
Melissa.Farrell@ontario.ca
Director, Health Sector Models Branch, Sherif Kaldas
Tel: 416-327-2396
sherif.kaldas@ontario.ca
Director, Hospitals Branch, Melanie Kohn
Tel: 416-326-6026
Melanie.Kohn@ontario.ca
Director, Policy & Innovation Branch, Jillian Paul
Tel: 416-325-5600
jillian.paul@ontario.ca
Director, HQO Liaison & Program Development Branch, Fredrika Scarth
Tel: 416-327-3932
fredrika.scarth@ontario.ca

Health Workforce Planning & Regulatory Affairs Division
56 Wellesley St. West, 12th Fl., Toronto, ON M5S 2S3
Tel: 416-212-6115; *Fax:* 416-327-1878
Assistant Deputy Minister, Denise Cole
Tel: 416-212-7688
denise.cole@ontario.ca

Negotiations & Accountability Management Division
Hepburn Block, 80 Grosvenor St., 5th Fl., Toronto, ON M7A 1R3
Tel: 416-212-7012
Assistant Deputy Minister, Lynn Guerriero
Tel: 416-212-7012
Lynn.Guerriero@ontario.ca
Senior Medical Advisor, Medical Advisory Unit, Dr. Garry Salisbury
Tel: 613-536-3078
garry.salisbury@ontario.ca
Director, Negotiations, David W. Clarke
Tel: 613-212-4904; *Fax:* 416-327-7519
david.w.clarke@ontario.ca
Director, Laboratories & Genetics Branch, Bonnie Reib
Tel: 416-212-1777; *Fax:* 416-327-7519
Bonnie.Reib@ontario.ca
Director, Health Services, Pauline Ryan
Tel: 613-536-3015
Toll-free: 866-684-8620; *Fax:* 613-536-3188
pauline.ryan@ontario.ca
Acting Director, Provincial Programs, Neeta Sarta
Tel: 416-326-3834
Neeta.Sarta@ontario.ca

Population & Public Health Division
College Park, #1903, 777 Bay St., 19th Fl., Toronto, M7A 1S5
Fax: 416-212-2200
Assistant Deputy Minister, Roselle Martino
Tel: 416-327-9555
roselle.martino@ontario.ca
Acting Director, Healthy Living Policy & Programs Branch, Dianne Alexander
Tel: 416-212-7637
dianne.alexander@ontario.ca
Director, Disease Prevention Policy & Programs Branch, Nina Arron
Tel: 416-212-4873
nina.arron@ontario.ca
Director, Health Protection Policy & Programs Branch, Laura Pisko
Tel: 416-327-7445
laura.pisko@ontario.ca
Director, Emergency Management Branch, Clint Shingler
Tel: 416-327-8865
clint.shingler@ontario.ca
Director, Accountability & Liaison Branch, Elizabeth Walker
Tel: 416-212-6359
elizabeth.walker@ontario.ca
Director, Planning & Performance Branch, Jackie Wood
Tel: 416-212-7785
jackie.wood@ontario.ca

Strategic Policy & Planning Division
Hepburn Block, 80 Grosvenor St., Toronto, M7A 1R3
Tel: 416-327-8295

Assistant Deputy Minister, Patrick Dicerni
Tel: 416-327-7261
patrick.dicerni@ontario.ca
Director, Mental Health & Addictions Branch, Marg Connor
Tel: 416-327-8996
marg.connor@ontario.ca
Director, Strategic Policy Branch, Sean Court
Tel: 416-327-7531
Sean.Court@ontario.ca
Director, Policy Coordination & Intergovernmental Relations
Branch, Louis Dimitracopoulos
Tel: 416-327-3314
anne.hayes@ontario.ca
Acting Director, Research, Analysis & Evaluation Branch, Anne
Hayes
Tel: 416-327-3314
anne.hayes@ontario.ca
Director, Health Equity Branch, Joanne Plaxton
Tel: 416-212-5218
joanne.plaxton@ontario.ca
Director, Capacity Planning & Priorities Branch, Michael
Robertson
Tel: 416-327-7615
michael.robertson@ontario.ca

Ontario Ministry of Heritage, Sport, Tourism & Culture Industries

438 University Ave., 6th Fl., Toronto, ON M5G 2K8
Tel: 416-326-9326; Fax: 416-314-7854
Toll-Free: 888-997-9015
TTY: 416-325-5807
www.mtc.gov.on.ca
Other Communication: Ontario Travel Information:
800-668-2746; Toll-Free TTY: 866-700-0040
twitter.com/ExploreON
www.facebook.com/ExploreON

Renamed in 2019, the Ministry's mandate includes promoting a
sustainable tourism industry in Ontario as a means of improving
quality of life, increasing community pride, & increasing
economic growth; encouraging & supporting the arts & culture
industries; protecting Ontario's heritage & furthering the public
library system; promoting sport & recreation activities; & working
with Ministry agencies, attractions, boards & commissions, the
tourism industry, other Ministries, other levels of government &
the private sector to achieve these goals.

Minister, Hon. Lisa MacLeod
Tel: 416-314-1400
Minister.MacLeod@ontario.ca

Deputy Minister, Kevin Finnerty
Tel: 416-450-3616
kevin.finnerty@ontario.ca

Parliamentary Assistant, Culture & Sport, Vincent Ke
Tel: 416-325-6009
vincent.ke@pc.ola.org

Parliamentary Assistant, Sheref Sabawy
sheref.sabawy@ontario.ca

Director, Communications, Derek Rowland
Tel: 647-272-6248
Derek.Rowland@ontario.ca

Associated Agencies, Boards & Commissions:

• **Art Gallery of Ontario (AGO)**
317 Dundas St. West
Toronto, ON M5T 1G4
Tel: 416-977-0414; Fax: 416-979-6669
Toll-free: 877-225-4246
www.ago.net
Other Communication: Art Rental & Sales: 416-977-4654;
Donations: 416-979-6619; membership Information:
416-979-6620; Resource Centres: 416-979-6642; Image
Resources: 416-979-6674

• **McMichael Canadian Art Collection**
10365 Islington Ave.
Kelinburg, ON L0J 1C0
Tel: 905-893-1121; Fax: 905-893-0692
Toll-free: 888-213-1121
info@mcmichael.com
www.mcmichael.com

• **Metro Toronto Convention Centre Corporation (MTCC)**
255 Front St. West
Toronto, ON M5V 2W6
Tel: 416-585-8000; Fax: 416-585-8270
info@mtccc.com
www.mtccc.com
Other Communication: Sales, Email: sales@mtccc.com

• **Niagara Parks Commission**
Oak Hall Administration Bldg.
7400 Portage Rd. South
PO Box 150
Niagara Falls, ON L2E 6T2
Tel: 905-356-2241; Fax: 905-354-6041
Toll-free: 877-642-7275
www.niagaraparks.com

• **Ontario Arts Council**
151 Bloor St. West, 5th Fl.
Toronto, ON M5S 1T6
Tel: 416-961-1660; Fax: 416-961-7796
Toll-free: 800-387-0058
info@arts.on.ca
www.arts.on.ca

• **Ontario Heritage Trust (OHT)**
10 Adelaide St. East
Toronto, ON M5C 1J3
Tel: 416-325-5000; Fax: 416-325-5071
www.heritagetrust.on.ca
Other Communication: TTY: 711-416-325-5000

• **Ontario Library Service (OLS) / Service des bibliothèques
de l'Ontario**
Head Office
334 Regent St.
Sudbury, ON P3C 4E2
Toll-free: 800-387-5765
info@olservice.ca
www.olservice.ca
Other Communication: Board, Email: board@olservice.ca; ILL
Inquiries: helpdesk@olservice.ca; Finance Inquiries:
finance@olservice.ca
In 2021, Ontario Library Servce - North (OLSN) & Southern
Ontario Library Service (SOLS) merged to form Ontario Library
Service.

• **Ontario Media Development Corporation (OMDC)**
South Tower
#501, 175 Bloor St. East
Toronto, ON M4W 3R8
Tel: 416-314-6858; Fax: 416-314-6876
reception@omdc.on.ca
www.omdc.on.ca
Formerly the Ontario Film Development Corporation (OFDC).

• **Ontario Place Corporation**
955 Lake Shore Blvd. West
Toronto, ON M6K 3B9
Tel: 416-314-9900; Fax: 416-314-9989
Toll-free: 866-663-4386
www.ontarioplace.com

• **Ontario Science Centre**
770 Don Mills Rd.
Toronto, ON M3C 1T3
Tel: 416-696-1000; Fax: 416-696-3166
Toll-free: 888-696-1110
TTY: 416-696-3202
www.ontariosciencecentre.ca

• **Ontario Tourism Marketing Partnership Corporation**
#900, 10 Dundas St. East
Toronto, ON M7A 2A1
Tel: 416-212-0757; Fax: 416-325-6004
Toll-free: 800-668-2746
www.ontariotravel.net

• **Ontario Trillium Foundation (OTF)**
800 Bay St., 5th Fl.
Toronto, ON M5S 3A9
Tel: 416-963-4927; Fax: 416-963-8781
Toll-free: 800-263-2887
TTY: 416-963-7905
otf@otf.ca
www.otf.ca
The Ontario Trillium Foundation provides grants to eligible
not-for-profit & charitable organizations in the areas of arts &
culture; sports & recreation; human & social services; & the
environment.

• **Ottawa Convention Centre**
55 Colonel By Dr.
Ottawa, ON K1N 9J2
Tel: 613-563-1984; Fax: 613-563-7646
Toll-free: 800-450-0077
www.shaw-centre.com

• **Royal Botanical Gardens (RBG)**
680 Plains Rd. West
Burlington, ON L7T 4H4
Tel: 905-527-1158; Fax: 905-577-0375
Toll-free: 800-694-4769
info@rbg.ca
www.rbg.ca
Other Communication: GTA Toll-Free: 905-825-5040

• **Royal Ontario Museum (ROM)**
100 Queen's Park Cres.
Toronto, ON M5S 2C6
Tel: 416-586-5549; Fax: 416-586-5685
TTY: 416-586-5550
info@rom.on.ca
www.rom.on.ca

• **Science North**
100 Ramsey Lake Rd.
Sudbury, ON P3E 5S9
Tel: 705-522-3701; Fax: 705-522-4954
Toll-free: 800-461-4898
contactus@sciencenorth.ca
www.sciencenorth.ca
Other Communication: Exhibit Fax: 705-522-1283

• **St. Lawrence Parks Commission**
13740 County Rd. 2
Morrisburg, ON K0C 1X0
Tel: 613-543-3704; Fax: 613-543-2847
Toll-free: 800-437-2233
TTY: 613-543-4181
getaway@parks.on.ca
www.parks.on.ca

Business Transformation & Project Management Division
Hearst Block, 900 Bay St., 10th Fl., Toronto, ON M7A 2E2
Assistant Deputy Minister, Ken Chan
Tel: 416-325-2861
ken.chan@ontario.ca
Director, Tourism Agencies, Jennifer Lang
Tel: 416-327-7414
jennifer.lang@ontario.ca

Culture Division
#1800, 401 Bay St., Toronto, ON M7A 0A7
Tel: 416-314-7265; Fax: 416-212-1802
Assistant Deputy Minister, Kevin Finnerty
Tel: 416-314-7262
kevin.finnerty@ontario.ca
Director, Programs & Services, Sean Fraser
Tel: 416-314-7342; Fax: 416-212-1802
sean.fraser@ontario.ca
Director, Culture Policy, Dawn Landry
dawn.landry@ontario.ca
Financial Officer, Jessie Oger
jessie.oger@ontario.ca
Director, Culture Policy, Dawn Landry
Tel: 416-212-7646; Fax: 416-314-7635
dawn.landry@ontario.ca

Sport, Recreation & Community Programs
College Park, 777 Bay St., 18th Fl., Toronto, ON M7A 1S5
Tel: 416-326-4371; Fax: 416-314-7458
Assistant Deputy Minister, Steve Harlow
Tel: 416-212-7397
steve.harlow@ontario.ca
Acting Director, Sport, Recreation & Community Programs,
Patricia Vena
patricia.vena@ontario.ca
Acting Director, Policy Branch, Susan Golets
Tel: 416-314-7696
susan.golets@ontario.ca

Tourism Division
Hearst Block, 900 Bay St., 10th Fl., Toronto, ON M7A 2E2
Tel: 416-325-6961
Assistant Deputy Minister, Richard McKinnell
Tel: 416-325-6961
richard.mckinnell@ontario.ca
Director, Investment & Development Office, Debbie Jewell
Tel: 416-314-7553
debbie.jewell@ontario.ca
Director, Tourism Policy & Research, Tony Marzotto
Tel: 416-325-6055
tony.marzotto@ontario.ca

Fort William Historical Park
1350 King Rd., Thunder Bay, ON P7K 1L7
Tel: 807-473-2344; Fax: 807-473-2327
info@fwhp.ca
www.fwhp.ca
twitter.com/FWHPtweets
www.facebook.com/fortwilliamhistoricalpark

General Manager, Sergio Buonocore
Tel: 807-473-2341; *Fax:* 807-473-2336
sergio.buonocore@ontario.ca

Huronia Historical Parks
16164 Hwy. 12, PO Box 160 Midland, ON L4R 4K8
Tel: 705-526-7838; *Fax:* 705-526-9193
TTY: 705-528-7697
www.hhp.on.ca

General Manager, Will Baird
Tel: 705-528-7690
will.baird@ontario.ca

Ontario Human Rights Commission (OHRC)

180 Dundas St. West, 9th Fl., Toronto, ON M7A 2G5
Tel: 416-326-9511; *Fax:* 416-314-4494
Toll-Free: 800-387-9080
TTY: 416-314-0503
info@ohrc.on.ca
www.ohrc.on.ca
twitter.com/OntHumanRights
www.facebook.com/the.ohrc

Chief Commissioner, Patricia DeGuire
cco@ohrc.on.ca

Chief Administrative Officer, Karen Pereira
Tel: 416-314-4480; *Fax:* 416-314-4494
karen.pereira@ohrc.on.ca

Executive Director & Chief Legal Council, Dianne Carter
Tel: 416-314-4562; *Fax:* 416-325-2004
dianne.carter@ohrc.on.ca

Director, Policy, Education, Monitoring & Outreach,
Shaheen Azmi
Tel: 416-314-4532; *Fax:* 416-314-4533
shaheen.azmi@ohrc.on.ca

Hydro One Inc.

South Tower, 483 Bay St., 8th Fl., Toronto, ON M5G 2P5
Tel: 416-345-5000; *Fax:* 905-944-3251
Toll-Free: 877-955-1155
customercommunications@hydroone.com
www.hydroone.com
Hydro One Networks Inc.PO Box 5700 Sta.
Markham, ON L3R 1C8
twitter.com/HydroOne
www.facebook.com/HydroOneOfficial
Subsidiaries are: Hydro One Networks Inc.; Hydro One Remote
Communities Inc.; Hydro One Telecom Inc.; Hydro One
Brampton Networks Inc.; Hydro One Sault Ste. Marie; Avista
Corp.
The Ontario government privatized Hydro One in Nov. 2015 with
an initial public offering of 13.6 percent of the company. The
government remains the single largest shareholder.

Chair, Tim Hodgson

President & CEO, Mark Poweska

Chief Financial Officer, Chris Lopez

Acting Chief Operating Officer, Darlene Bradley

Chief Information Officer, Brad Bowness

Chief Legal Officer, Paul Harricks

Chief Human Resources Officer, Saylor Millitz-Lee

Chief Corporate Affairs & Customer Care Officer, Jason
Fitzsimmons

Independent Electricity System Operator (IESO)

#1600, 120 Adelaide St. West, Toronto, ON M5H 1T1
Tel: 905-403-6900; *Fax:* 905-403-6921
Toll-Free: 877-797-9473
customer.relations@ieso.ca
www.ieso.ca
Other Communication: Reception: 905-855-6100; Conservation
Programs, Toll-Free Phone: 877-797-9473
twitter.com/ieso_tweets
www.facebook.com/OntarioIESO
www.linkedin.com/company/ieso
The IESO was established in 1998 by the Electricity Act of
Ontario. It is a not-for-profit organization engaged in the
following activities: balancing energy supply & demand &
directing energy flow; planning Ontario's medium- & long-term
energy needs & finding clean sources of energy; overseeing the
electricity wholesale market; & encouraging energy conservation

through programs such as saveONenergy.
On Jan. 1, 2015, the IESO absorbed the activites of the Ontario
Power Authority (OPA).

President & CEO, Peter Gregg

Interim Chief Financial Officer & Vice-President,
Corporate Services, Barb Anderson

Chief Operating Officer & Vice-President, Planning,
Acquisition & Operations, Leonard Kula

Chief Information Officer & Vice-President, Information &
Technology Serivces, Alex Foord

Vice-President, Legal Resources & Corporate
Governance, Michael Lyle

Vice-President, Human Resources, Marcia
Mendes-d'Abreu

Vice-President, Policy, Engagement & Innovation, Terry
Young

Ontario Ministry of Indigenous Affairs

160 Bloor St. East, 4th Fl., Toronto, ON M7A 2E6
Tel: 416-326-4740
Toll-Free: 866-381-5337
TTY: 866-686-6072
www.ontario.ca/page/ministry-indigenous-affairs
twitter.com/IndigenousON
www.facebook.com/IndigenousON
The Ministry of Indigenous Affairs (formely Indigenous Relations
& Reconciliation, & before that Aboriginal Affairs) was created in
2007 to replace the Ontario Secretariat of Aboriginal Affairs. It
provides corporate Indigenous policy development, management
support, & negotiates & settles land claims, while also managing
the Province's relationships with First Nations, Indigenous
organizations (including Métis, Native women, Inuit &
off-reserve) & the federal government. Serviced by the Office of
the Chief Information Officer, Land & Resources I&IT Cluster.

Minister, Hon. Greg Rickford
Tel: 416-326-4740
greg.rickfordco@pc.ola.org

Deputy Minister, Shawn Batise
Tel: 416-314-1141
shawn.batise@ontario.ca

Parliamentary Assistant, Dave Smith
david.g.smith@ontario.ca

Acting Director, Legal Services, Candice Telfer
candice.telfer@ontario.ca

Acting Director, Communications Services, Tom Zach
Tel: 416-553-9946
tom.zach@ontario.ca

Indigenous Relations & Programs Division
160 Bloor St. East, 4th Fl., Toronto, ON M7A 2E6
Tel: 416-326-4740; *Fax:* 416-325-1066
Assistant Deputy Minister, Michael Reid
Tel: 416-325-0301
michael.reid@ontario.ca
Director, Indigenous Relations, Heather Levecque
Tel: 416-325-7032
heather.levecque@ontario.ca
Director, Programs & Services, Nadia Temple
Tel: 416-314-6133
nadia.temple@ontario.ca

Negotiations & Reconciliation Division
160 Bloor St. East, 9th Fl., Toronto, ON M7A 2E6
Tel: 416-326-4740; *Fax:* 416-326-4710
The branch carries out the following responsibilities: researching
& conducting land claim negotiations; managing & coordinating
negotiations; representing the province for federally-led
governance negotiations; & implementing settlements.
Assistant Deputy Minister, Grant Wedge
Tel: 416-326-4741
grant.wedge@ontario.ca
Acting Director, Negotiations, Randy R. Reid
Tel: 416-326-6330; *Fax:* 416-326-4017
randy.r.reid@ontario.ca
Acting Director, Community Intiatives, Karma Call
karma.call@ontario.ca

Office of the Chief Administrative Officer - Corporate
Management Division
Whitney Block, #6450, 99 Wellesley St. West, 6th Fl.,
Toronto, ON M7A 1W3
Tel: 416-314-1939; *Fax:* 416-314-1901
Chief Administrative Officer, Paula Reid
Tel: 416-314-1939
paula.reid@ontario.ca
Acting Director, Strategic Human Resources Business, Tracy
Demal
Tel: 705-755-3131
tracy.demal@ontario.ca
Acting Director, Corporate Management, Esther Laquer
Tel: 416-212-1277
esther.laquer@ontario.ca

Strategic Policy & Planning Division
160 Bloor St. East, 4th Fl., Toronto, ON M7A 2E6
Tel: 416-326-4740; *Fax:* 416-326-4777
Assistant Deputy Minister, Jonathan Lebi
Tel: 416-212-2302
jonathan.lebi@ontario.ca
Director, Strategic Planning & Economic Policy, Matt Garrow
Tel: 416-314-1607
matt.garrow@ontario.ca
Acting Director, Strategic Initiatives & Social Policy, Stephanie
Prosen
Tel: 416-327-9632
stephanie.prosen@ontario.ca

Information & Privacy Commissioner of Ontario
(IPC)

#1400, 2 Bloor St. East, Toronto, ON M4W 1A8
Tel: 416-326-3333; *Fax:* 416-325-9195
Toll-Free: 800-387-0073
TTY: 416-325-7539
info@ipc.on.ca
www.ipc.on.ca
twitter.com/IPCinfoprivacy
www.facebook.com/IPCOntario
The IPC is the oversight body for Ontario's three provincial
freedom of information & protection of privacy statues, & is
responsible for resolving appeals when government
organizations refuse to grant access to information; investigating
privacy complaints related to government-held information;
ensuring government compliance with the acts; conducting
research on access & privacy issues & providing advice on
proposed government legislation & programs; educating the
public on Ontario's access, privacy & personal health information
laws & access & privacy issues; investigating complaints related
to personal health information; reviewing policies & procedures,
& ensuring compliance with the Personal Health Information
Protection Act.

Commissioner, Brian Beamish
Tel: 416-326-3333
commissioner@ipc.on.ca

Assistant Commissioner, Policy & Corporate Services,
David Goodis
Tel: 416-326-8723
david.goodis@ipc.on.ca

Assistant Commissioner, Tribunal Services, Sherry Liang
Tel: 416-326-3333
sherry.liang@ipc.on.ca

Office of the Integrity Commissioner (OICO)

#2100, 2 Bloor St. West, Toronto, ON M4W 3E2
Tel: 416-314-8983; *Fax:* 416-314-8987
Toll-Free: 866-884-4470
info@oico.on.ca
www.oico.on.ca
Other Communication: Alt. Emails: integrity.mail@oico.on.ca;
expenses@oico.on.ca
The Commissioner administers the Member's Integrity Act, 1994
as it applies to members of the Legislative Assembly &
Executive Council in Ontario, including the filing of Public
Disclosure Statements, & the right to conduct an inquiry if there
are reasonable & probable grounds to believe that the Act has
been contravened. The Commissioner also has responsiblity
under the Cabinet Ministers' and Opposition Leaders' Expenses
Review and Accountability Act, 2002.

Commissioner, Hon. David Wake
Tel: 416-314-9883
david.wake@oico.on.ca

Director, Cathryn Motherwell
Tel: 416-314-7811
cathryn.motherwell@oico.on.ca

General Counsel, Liliane Gingras
Tel: 416-314-1583
liliane.gingras@oico.on.ca

Lobbyists Registration Office
#2100, 2 Bloor St. West, Toronto, ON M4W 3E2
Tel: 416-327-4053; *Fax:* 416-327-4017
lobbyist.mail@oico.on.ca
www.oico.on.ca
Under the Lobbyists Registration Act, 1998, the Registrar is responsible for administering the lobbyist registration process, ensuring paid lobbyists report their lobbying of public office holders by filing a return; & ensuring public accessibility to the information contained in the lobbyist's registry.
Lobbyist Registrar, Hon. David Wake
Tel: 416-314-8983
lobbyist.registrar@oico.on.ca

Ontario Ministry of Infrastructure

777 Bay St., 5th Fl., Toronto, ON M5G 2C8
Tel: 416-327-4412
TTY: 416-325-3408
www.ontario.ca/page/ministry-infrastructure
Other Communication: Toll-Free TTY: 800-268-7095
The ministry was created in 2016 after a divison of the Ministry of Economic Growth, Development & Infrastructure. It supports the government's long-term infrastructure plan & works with all levels of government on various infrastructure projects, including those in small communities.

Minister, Hon. Kinga Surma
Tel: 416-327-4412

Deputy Minister, Chris Giannekos
Tel: 416-326-3880
chris.giannekos@ontario.ca

Parliamentary Assistant, Amarjot Sandhu
Tel: 416-326-7591

Associated Agencies, Boards & Commissions:
• **Infrastructure Ontario**
#2000, 1 Dundas St. West
Toronto, ON M5G 1Z3
Tel: 416-327-3937
Infrastructure Ontario is a Crown corporation dedicated to the renewal of Ontario's hospitals, courthouses, roads, bridges, water systems & other public assets.

• **Waterfront Toronto**
#1310, 20 Bay St.
Toronto, ON M5J 2N8
Tel: 416-214-1344; Fax: 416-214-4591

Community Hubs Division
Hearst Block, 900 Bay St., 3rd Fl., Toronto, ON M7A 2E1
Tel: 416-212-5419

Assistant Deputy Minister, Nancy Mudrinic
Tel: 416-327-4370
nancy.mudrinic2@ontario.ca
Director, Quantitative Policy & Research, Chris Monahan
Tel: 416-325-8695
chris.monahan2@ontario.ca
Director, Policy & Implementation, Dawn Palin Rokosh
Tel: 416-325-7673
dawn.palin.rokosh@ontario.ca

Corporate Services Division
Mowat Block, 900 Bay St., 5th Fl., Toronto, ON M7A 1L2
Tel: 416-325-6866; *Fax:* 416-314-7014
Toll-Free: 888-664-6008
TTY: 416-325-6707
Assistant Deputy Minister & Chief Administrative Officer, Robert Burns
Tel: 416-327-3682
robert.burns@ontario.ca
Director, Service Management & Facilities, Nelson Janicas
Tel: 416-314-3309
nelson.janicas@ontario.ca
Acting Director, Business Planning & Finance, Kate Johnstone
Tel: 416-327-1137
kate.johnstone@ontario.ca
Acting Director, Strategic Human Resources Business, Lawrence Wagner
Tel: 416-325-6599
lawrence.wagner@ontario.ca

Government Infrastructure Projects
College Park, 777 Bay St., 4th Fl., Toronto, ON M5G 2E5
Associate Deputy Minister, David Hallett
Tel: 416-327-2605
david.hallett@ontario.ca

Assistant Deputy Minister, Realty Division, Bruce Singbush
Tel: 416-326-1766
bruce.singbush@ontario.ca
Director, Realty Division - Realty Management, Maggie Allan
Tel: 416-212-1167
maggie.allan@ontario.ca
Director, Realty Division - Realty Policy, Trevor Bingler
Tel: 416-327-2900
trevor.bingler@ontario.ca
Acting Director, Realty Division - Realty Transformation, David McIntosh
Tel: 416-314-4385
david.mcintosh@ontario.ca
Director, Queen's Park Reconstruction Oversight - Office Transformation Oversight, Melody Robinson
Tel: 416-566-6011
melody.robinson@ontario.ca

Infrastructure Policy & Planning Division
Hearst Block, 900 Bay St., 3rd Fl., Toronto, ON M7A 2E1
Assistant Deputy Minister, Chris Giannekos
Tel: 416-325-4460
chris.giannekos@ontario.ca
Assistant Deputy Minister, Infrastructure Research & Financing, Grant Osborn
Tel: 416-212-1473
grant.osborn@ontario.ca
Assistant Deputy Minister, Infrastructure Policy Division, Adam Redish
Tel: 416-314-5148
adam.redish@ontario.ca
Acting Director, Policy & Planning, Kelly Brown
Tel: 416-325-7966
kelly.brown@ontario.ca
Director, Inter-Governmental Policy, Elizabeth Doherty
Tel: 416-212-8757
elizabeth.doherty@ontario.ca
Director, Capital Planning & Coordination, Trevor Fleck
Tel: 416-325-8559
trevor.fleck@ontario.ca
Director, Infrastructure Research, Vijay Gill
Tel: 416-314-0890
vijay.gill@ontario.ca

Ontario Ministry of Intergovernmental Affairs

Legislative Bldg., #223, 223 Queen's Park, Toronto, ON M7A 1A4
Tel: 416-326-1234
Toll-Free: 800-268-7095
TTY: 416-325-3408
www.ontario.ca/page/ministry-intergovernmental-affairs
The Ministry of Intergovernmental Affairs key responsibilities are: to provide strategic advice & analysis on matters of intergovernmental relations, international affairs & protocol; to work to enhance inter-ministerial collaboration; to support the Minister in ensuring the federal government treats Ontario fairly when it comes to health care, climate change, immigration & child care; to support the Premier in providing leadership in the Canadian federation & enhancing Ontario's international image & profile; & to lead the development of Ontario's overall intergovernmental strategy.

Minister, Hon. Doug Ford
doug.ford@pc.ola.org

Deputy Minister, Intergovernmental Affairs & Associate Secretary of the Cabinet, Lynn Betzner
Tel: 416-325-9698
lynn.betzner@ontario.ca

Parliamentary Assistant, Norm Miller
Tel: 416-325-3720
Norman.Miller@ontario.ca

Assistant Deputy Minister, Health, Social, Environment & National Institutions, Ernie Bartucci
Tel: 416-325-4804
ernie.bartucci@ontario.ca

Assistant Deputy Minister, Economic & Justice, Craig McFadyen
Tel: 416-325-4603
craig.mcfadyen@ontario.ca

Assistant Deputy Minister, Office of International Relations & Protocol & Chief of Protocol, Vacant

Ontario Ministry of Labour, Training & Skills Development

400 University Ave., 14th Fl., Toronto, ON M7A 1T7
Tel: 416-326-7160
Toll-Free: 800-531-5551
TTY: 866-567-8893
www.ontario.ca/page/ministry-labour-training-skills-development
Other Communication: Health & Safety Contact Centre:
877-202-0008
twitter.com/ONTatwork
www.facebook.com/OntarioAtWork
www.linkedin.com/company/ontario-ministry-of-labour
The Ministry aims to advances safe, fair & harmonious workplace practices that are essential to the social & economic well-being of the people of Ontario. Through the Ministry's key areas of occupational health & safety; employment rights & responsibilities; labour relations & internal administration, the ministry's mandate is to set, communicate & enforce workplace standards while encouraging greater workplace self-reliance. A range of specialized agencies, boards & commissions assist the Ministry in its work. Serviced by the Labour & Transportation I&IT Cluster.

Minister, Hon. Monte McNaughton
Tel: 416-326-7600
Minister.MLTSD@ontario.ca

Deputy Minister, Greg Meredith
greg.meredith@ontario.ca

Parliamentary Assistant, Deepak Anand
Deepak.Anand@ontario.ca

Acting Director, Legal Services, Roslyn Baichoo
roslyn.baichoo@ontario.ca

Director, Communications, Ian Ross
Tel: 647-244-3885
Ian.Ross@ontario.ca

Associated Agencies, Boards & Commissions:
• **Office of the Employer Advisor (OEA)**
505 University Ave., 20th Fl.
Toronto, ON M5G 2P1
Tel: 416-327-0020; *Fax:* 416-327-0726
Toll-free: 800-387-0774
www.employeradviser.ca
The OEA advises & represents employers with fewer than 100 employees in relation to worker's compensation issues at no cost to the employer.

• **Office of the Worker Advisor (OWA)**
#1300, 123 Edward St.
Toronto, ON M5G 1E2
Tel: 416-325-8570; *Fax:* 416-325-4830
Toll-free: 800-660-6769
TTY: 866-455-3092
owaweb@ontario.ca
www.owa.gov.on.ca
Other Communication: Toll-Free French: 800-661-6365; TTY: 866-455-4830
The OWA advises, represents & educates injured workers with Workplace Safety & Insurance Board (WSIB) claims through all stages of the Workplace Safety & Insurance System.

• **Ontario Labour Relations Board (OLRB)**
505 University Ave., 2nd Fl.
Toronto, ON M5G 2P1
Tel: 416-326-7500; *Fax:* 416-326-7531
Toll-free: 877-339-3335
TTY: 416-212-7036
www.olrb.gov.on.ca

• **Pay Equity Office**
#300, 180 Dundas St. West
Toronto, ON M7A 2S6
Tel: 416-314-1896; *Fax:* 416-314-8741
Toll-free: 800-387-8813
TTY: 855-253-8333
www.payequity.gov.on.ca
The Pay Equity Office investigates, attempts to settle, & resolves pay equity complaints & objections to pay equity plans by Order or Notice of Decision.

• **Public Service Appeal Boards (GSB)**
Dundas/Edward Ctr.
#600, 180 Dundas St. West
Toronto, ON M5G 1Z8
Tel: 416-326-1388; *Fax:* 416-326-1396
www.psab.gov.on.ca
The Public Service Appeal Boards is the administrative structure that supports the Grievance Settlement Board & the Public Service Grievance Board.

• Workplace Safety & Insurance Appeals Tribunal (WSIAT)
505 University Ave., 7th Fl.
Toronto, ON M5G 2P2
Tel: 416-314-8800; *Fax:* 416-326-5164
Toll-free: 888-618-8846
TTY: 416-314-1787
www.wsiat.on.ca
Formerly known as the Workers' Compensation Appeals Tribunal.

• Workplace Safety & Insurance Board
See Entry Name Index for detailed listing.

Corporate Management & Services Division
400 University Ave., 14th Fl., Toronto, ON M7A 1T7
Assistant Deputy Minister & Chief Administrative Officer, Susan Flanagan
Tel: 416-326-7305
susan.flanagan@ontario.ca
Director, Strategic Human Resources, Janis Bartley
Tel: 416-326-7215; *Fax:* 416-326-7241
janis.bartley@ontario.ca
Director, Corporate Services, Cordelia Clarke Julien
Tel: 416-212-7821
cordelia.clarkejulien@ontario.ca
Director, Finance & Administration, Patricia Perez
Tel: 416-326-7271; *Fax:* 416-326-9069
patricia.perez@ontario.ca

Labour Relations Solutions Division
400 University Ave., 14th Fl., Toronto, ON M7A 1T7
Tel: 416-326-0660; *Fax:* 416-325-7924
Assistant Deputy Minister, Mary Incognito
Tel: 416-325-3608
mary.incognito@ontario.ca
Director, Dispute Resolution Services, Dayna Firth
Tel: 416-326-7965
dayna.firth@ontario.ca

Operations Division
400 University Ave., 14th Fl., Toronto, ON M7A 1T7
Tel: 416-326-7606; *Fax:* 416-212-4455
Toll-Free: 800-531-5551
TTY: 866-567-8893
Assistant Deputy Minister, Peter Augruso
Tel: 416-326-7665
peter.augruso@ontario.ca
Director, Divisional Learning Unit, Ken Fox
Tel: 647-777-5112
ken.fox@ontario.ca
Acting Director, Operations Integration, Margaret Medeiros
Tel: 416-212-1132
margaret.medeiros@ontario.ca
Acting Director, Occupational Health & Safety, Leon Genesove
Tel: 416-326-2913
leon.genesove@ontario.ca
Acting Director, Employment Practices, Stephen McDonald
Tel: 416-326-7004
stephen.mcdonald@ontario.ca

Policy Division
400 University Ave., 14th Fl., Toronto, ON M7A 1T7
Assistant Deputy Minister, Marcelle Crouse
Tel: 416-326-7555
marcelle.crouse@ontario.ca
Director, Employment, Labour & Corporate Policy, David Beaulieu
Tel: 416-326-7641; *Fax:* 416-326-7650
david.beaulieu@ontario.ca
Director, Health & Safety Policy, Melissa Faber
Tel: 416-326-7628
melissa.faber@ontario.ca
Director, Corporate Policy & Special Projects, Careen Jones
Tel: 416-326-0809
careen.jones@ontario.ca

Prevention Office
400 University Ave., 14th Fl., Toronto, ON M7A 1T7
Tel: 416-212-3960; *Fax:* 416-314-5809
Associate Deputy Minister & Chief Prevention Officer, Ron Kelusky
ron.kelusky@ontario.ca
Corporate Risk Officer, Sujoy Dey
Tel: 416-212-9934
sujoy.dey@ontario.ca
Director, Training & Awareness & Strategy & Integration Branch, William Roy
william.h.roy@ontario.ca

Ontario Ministry of Long-Term Care

400 University Ave., 6th Fl., Toronto, ON M7A 1N3
Tel: 416-327-4327; *Fax:* 416-327-8497
Toll-Free: 800-268-1153
TTY: 800-387-5559
www.ontario.ca/page/ministry-long-term-care
The ministry was created in 2019 when it was separated from the Ministry of Health & Long-Term Care. It aims to improve long-term care for seniors in Ontario at various levels of care.

Minister, Hon. Rod Phillips
Tel: 416-325-6200
Rod.Phillips@ontario.ca

Deputy Minister, Nancy Matthews
Tel: 416-325-6200
nancy.matthews@ontario.ca

Parliamentary Assistant, Effie Triantafilopoulos
Tel: 416-205-8049
Effie.triantafilopoulos@ontario.ca

Acting Director, Communications Branch, Peter Spadoni
Tel: 416-272-2509
Peter.Spadoni@Ontario.ca

Ontario Ministry of Municipal Affairs & Housing

College Park, 777 Bay St., 17th Fl., Toronto, ON M7A 2J3
Tel: 416-585-7041; *Fax:* 416-585-4230
TTY: 866-220-2290
mininfo@ontario.ca
www.ontario.ca/page/ministry-municipal-affairs-housing
Other Communication: TTY: 416-585-6991
twitter.com/onmunicipal
The Ministry is responsible for providing provincial leadership in defining the framework for governance, finances & management for the local government systems; as well as leadership in the development & administration of the legislative & policy framework for land use planning. In June 2016 the Ministry was divided into two portfolios: Ministry of Municipal Affairs & Ministry of Housing. It was later recombined by Premier Doug Ford, in July 2018. Serviced by the Office of the Chief Information Officer, Community Services I&IT Cluster.

Minister, Hon. Steve Clark
Minister.MAH@ontario.ca

Deputy Minister, Kate Manson-Smith
Tel: 416-585-7100
kate.manson-smith@ontario.ca

Parliamentary Assistant, Jim McDonell
Jim.McDonell@ontario.ca

Director, Legal Services, Jeff Schelling
Tel: 416-585-6670
jeff.schelling@ontario.ca

Director, Communications, Burke Christian
Tel: 416-843-8312
burke.christian@ontario.ca

Business Management Division
College Park, 777 Bay St., 17th Fl., Toronto, ON M5G 2E5
Tel: 416-585-7062; *Fax:* 416-585-6191
Assistant Deputy Minister & Chief Administrative Officer, Mary Anne Covelli
Tel: 416-585-6670; *Fax:* 416-585-6191
maryanne.covelli@ontario.ca
Director, Controllership & Financial Planning, Jason Arandjelovic
Tel: 416-585-7448; *Fax:* 416-585-7328
jason.arandjelovic@ontario.ca
Director, Human Resources Strategies, Suzana Ristich
Tel: 416-585-6742
suzana.ristich@ontario.ca
Director, Corporate Services, Corwin Troje
Tel: 416-585-7321
corwin.troje@ontario.ca
Acting Executive Coordinator, Corporate Services, Nevila Rebi
Tel: 416-585-7353
nevila.rebi@ontario.ca
Executive Coordinator, Human Resources Strategies, Andrea Ubeysekera
Tel: 416-585-7358
andrea.ubeysekera@ontario.ca

Housing Division
College Park, 777 Bay St., 14th Fl., Toronto, ON M5G 2E5
Tel: 416-585-6738; *Fax:* 416-585-6800

Assistant Deputy Minister, Janet Hope
Tel: 416-585-6755
janet.hope@ontario.ca
Director, Housing Programs, Jim Adams
Tel: 416-585-7021
jim.adams@ontario.ca
Director, Housing Funding & Risk Management, Keith Extrance
Tel: 416-585-7524
keith.extance@ontario.ca
Director, Housing Policy, Carol Latimer
Tel: 416-585-6400; *Fax:* 416-585-7607
carol.latimer@ontario.ca

Local Government & Planning Policy Division
College Park, 777 Bay St., 13th Fl., Toronto, ON M5G 2E5
Tel: 416-585-6321; *Fax:* 416-585-6463
Assistant Deputy Minister, Kate Manson-Smith
Tel: 416-585-6320
kate.manson-smith@ontario.ca
Director, Municipal Finance Policy, Caspar Hall
Tel: 416-585-6951; *Fax:* 416-585-6315
caspar.hall@ontario.ca
Director, Intergovernmental Relations & Partnerships, Diane McArthur-Rodgers
Tel: 416-585-6047
diane.mcarthur-rodgers@ontario.ca
Director, Provincial Planning Policy, Laurie Miller
Tel: 416-585-6072; *Fax:* 416-585-6870
laurie.miller@ontario.ca
Director, Local Government Policy, Tanzeel Merchant
Tel: 416-585-7260
Tanzeel.Merchant@ontario.ca

Municipal Services Division
777 Bay St., 16th Fl., Toronto, ON M5G 2E5
Fax: 416-585-6445
Assistant Deputy Minister, Marcia Wallace
Tel: 416-585-6427
marcia.wallace@ontario.ca
Director, Building & Development, Hannah Evans
Tel: 416-585-6399
hannah.evans@ontario.ca
www.ontario.ca/buildingcode
Director, Building Services Transformation, Brenda J. Lewis
Tel: 416-585-6656
brenda.lewis@ontario.ca
www.ontario.ca/buildingcode
Director, Municipal Programs & Analytics, Dawn Palin Rokosh
Dawn.Palin.Rokosh@ontario.ca

Office of the Provincial Land & Development Facilitator
College Park, #2704, 777 Bay St., 27th Fl., Toronto, ON M7A 2J8
Tel: 416-325-0835; *Fax:* 416-325-0209
www.moi.gov.on.ca
Provincial Land & Development Facilitator, Paula Dill
Tel: 416-325-9764
paula.dill@ontario.ca

Ontario Growth Secretariat
College Park, #2304, 777 Bay St., Toronto, ON M5G 2E5
Tel: 416-325-1210; *Fax:* 416-325-7403
Toll-Free: 866-479-9781
www.placestogrow.ca
Assistant Deputy Minister, Cordelia Clarke Julien
Tel: 416-325-5803
Cordelia.ClarkeJulien@ontario.ca
Director, Partnerships & Consultation, Darren Cooney
Tel: 416-325-5799
darren.cooney@ontario.ca
Director, Growth Policy, Planning & Analysis, Charles O'Hara
Tel: 416-325-5794
charles.o'hara@ontario.ca

Ontario Ministry of Northern Development, Mines, Natural Resources & Forestry

Natural Resources Information & Support Centre, 300 Water St., Toronto, ON K9J 8M5
Toll-Free: 800-667-1940
TTY: 866-686-6072
Other Communication: URL:
www.ontario.ca/page/ministry-northern-development-mines-natural-resources-forestry
Secondary Address: 300 Water St.
Natural Resources Information & Support Centre (NRISC)
Peterborough, ON K9J 8M5
The Ministry manages & protects natural resources in the province for wise use by working with environmental organizations, private industries, fish & game associations, researchers, & other government agencies. The Ministry is responsible for the following areas: science & information resources; forest management; fish & wildlife management; land & waters management; Ontario Parks; aviation & forest fire

management; & geographic information.

In 2021, the Ministry of Northern Development & Mines & the Ministry of Natural Resources & Forestry merged to create the Ministry of Northern Development, Mines, Natural Resources & Forestry. It is serviced by the Office of the Chief Information Officer, Land & Resources I&IT Cluster.

Minister, Hon. Greg Rickford

Deputy Minister, Monique Rolf von den Baumen-Clark
Tel: 416-314-2150
deputy.ndmnrf@ontario.ca

Parliamentary Assistant, Natural Resources & Forestry,
Mike Harris
Tel: 416-326-6945
mike.harris@ontario.ca

Parliamentary Assistant, Northern Development & Mines,
Dave Smith
Tel: 705-930-7121
david.g.smith@ontario.ca

Acting Director, Legal Services, Donald J. Bennett
Tel: 416-327-0637
donald.bennett@ontario.ca

Director, Communications, Ken Fasciano
ken.fasciano@ontario.ca

Associated Agencies, Boards & Commissions:

• Academic & Experience Requirements Committee of the Association of Ontario Land Surveyors (AERC)
1043 McNicoll Ave.
Toronto, ON M1W 3W6
Tel: 416-491-9020; *Fax:* 416-491-2576

• Algonquin Forestry Authority - Huntsville
222 Main St. West
Huntsville, ON P1H 1Y1
Tel: 705-789-9647; *Fax:* 705-789-3353
info@algonquinforestry.on.ca
www.algonquinforestry.on.ca
Ensures the viability of the local forest industry while preserving the soil & water resources, fish & wildlife habitat & recreational areas in the park.

• Algonquin Forestry Authority - Pembroke
Victoria Centre
84 Isabella St., 2nd Fl.
Pembroke, ON K8A 5S5
Tel: 613-735-0173; *Fax:* 613-735-4192
info@algonquinforestry.on.ca
www.algonquinforestry.on.ca

• Council of the Association of Ontario Land Surveyors
1043 McNicoll Ave.
Toronto, ON M1W 3W6
Tel: 416-491-9020; *Fax:* 416-491-2576
Toll-free: 800-268-0718
www.aols.org

• Niagara Escarpment Commission
232 Guelph St.
Georgetown, ON L7G 4B1
Tel: 905-877-5191; *Fax:* 905-873-7452

• Ontario Fish & Wildlife Heritage Commission
Robinson Pl.
300 Water St., 5th Fl.
PO Box 7000
Peterborough, ON K9J 8M5
Tel: 705-755-1905; *Fax:* 705-755-1900

• Ontario Geographic Names Board
Robinson Place
300 Water St.
PO Box 7000
Peterborough, ON K9J 8M5
Tel: 705-755-2134
The Board investigates the background of geographic names & recommends names to be used on maps.

• Ontario Northland Transportation Commission (ONTC)
555 Oak St. East
North Bay, ON P1B 8L3
Tel: 705-472-4500; *Fax:* 705-476-5598
Toll-free: 800-363-7512
info@ontarionorthland.ca
www.ontarionorthland.ca
Other Communication: Marketing & Media, Email:
pr@ontarionorthland.ca
The commission provides motor coach, rail transportation (including the Polar Bear Express), & refurbishment services to northeastern Ontario.

• Owen Sound Transportation Company Ltd. (OSTC)
717875, Hwy. 6
Owen Sound, ON N4K 5N7
Tel: 519-376-8740
Toll-free: 800-265-3163
www.ontarioferries.com
The OSTC's goal is to provide vehicle & passenger ferry transportation in the province of Ontario, including services between Tobermory & Manitoulin Island & service to Pelee Island.

• Ottawa River Regulation Planning Board / Commission de planification de la régularisation de la rivière des Outaouais
351 St. Joseph Blvd
Hull, QC J8Y 3Z5
Tel: 613-997-1735
Toll-free: 800-778-1246
secretariat@ottawariver.ca
www.ottawariver.ca
Established under the terms of a Canada-Ontario-Québec Agreement, the board is responsible for the preparation & continuing review of policies, guidelines & criteria for the integrated management of the principal reservoirs of the Ottawa River Basin in order to reduce flood damages along the river, its tributaries & in the Montréal area. It is also responsible for the operation & coordination of inflow forecasting, flow routing & optimization models that will reduce flood damages while having the least possible impact on users of the basin.

• Rabies Advisory Committee
Trent University Science Complex
2140 East Bank Dr.
PO Box 4840
Peterborough, ON K9J 8N8
Tel: 705-755-2270
Established in 1979, the committee advises the Minister on the development of suitable vaccines against rabies & an effective system for vaccinating wild animals.

• Shibogama Interim Planning Board
PO Box 105
Wunnumin, ON P0V 2Z0
Tel: 807-442-2559; *Fax:* 807-442-2627
Advises the province on land use & resource development in an 11,131-square-kilometre area south of Big Trout Lake in northwestern Ontario.

• Windigo Interim Planning Board
PO Box 299
Sioux Lookout, ON P8T 1A3
Tel: 807-737-1585; *Fax:* 807-737-3133
Advises the province on land use & resource development in two areas totalling 15,959 square kilometres south of Big Trout Lake.

Office of the Chief Information Officer, Land & Resources I&IT Cluster
Whitney Block, #6601, 99 Wellesley St. West, 6th Fl., Toronto, ON M7A 1W3
Fax: 416-314-6091
The department works in collaboration with the Ministry of Indigenous Relations & Reconciliation.
Chief Information Officer, John DiMarco
Tel: 416-326-6954
john.dimarco@ontario.ca
Head, Cluster Management, Doug Green
Tel: 519-826-3236; *Fax:* 705-755-5552
doug.green@ontario.ca
Head, Cluster Operations, Uwe Helmer
Tel: 519-826-5160
uwe.helmer@ontario.ca
Head, Business Solutions Services, Asif Khan
Tel: 416-212-4821
asif.khan@ontario.ca

Corporate Management & Information Division
Whitney Block, #6540, 99 Wellesley St. West, 6th Fl., Toronto, ON M7A 1W3
Tel: 416-314-1900; *Fax:* 416-314-1994
Other Communication: Peterborough Fax: 705-755-5369
Assistant Deputy Minister, Paula Reid
Tel: 416-314-1939; *Fax:* 416-314-1994
paula.reid@ontario.ca
Director, Strategic Human Resources Business, Tracy Demal
Tel: 705-755-3131; *Fax:* 705-755-3120
tracy.demal@ontario.ca
300 Water St., 3rd Fl.
PO Box 7000
Peterborough, ON K9J 8M5 Canada
Director, Mapping & Information Resources, Steve Gregory
Tel: 705-755-2204; *Fax:* 705-755-2149
steve.gregory@ontario.ca
300 Water St., 3rd Fl.
PO Box 7000
Peterborough, ON K9J 8M5 Canada

Director, Strategic Management & Corporate Services, Andrew Flynn
Tel: 705-755-1857
andrew.flynn@ontario.ca

Forest Industry Division
Roberta Bondar Pl., #400, 70 Foster Dr., Sault Ste. Marie, ON P6A 6V5
Fax: 705-945-5977
Toll-Free: 800-667-1940
Assistant Deputy Minister, Kathleen McFadden
Tel: 705-945-6767
kathleen.mcfadden@ontario.ca
Director, Business Development, Wayne Barnes
Tel: 705-945-6795; *Fax:* 705-945-6796
wayne.barnes@ontario.ca
Director, Operations, David Hayhurst
Tel: 705-945-5733; *Fax:* 705-945-6667
david.hayhurst@ontario.ca
Director, Forest Tenure & Economics, Faye Johnson
Tel: 705-945-5860
faye.johnson@ontario.ca

Mines & Minerals Division
Willet Green Miller Centre, 933 Ramsey Lake Rd., Level B6, Sudbury, ON P3E 6B5
Tel: 705-670-5755; *Fax:* 705-670-5818
Toll-Free: 888-415-9845
The Division collects, analyzes & publishes valuable information about the state of the mining & mineral industries in Ontario, as well as specific information about the location & quality of mineral deposits. The field staff throughout the province provide consultative services to the industry through all phases of the mining sequence, & include resident geologists, mining recorders & mineral development officers.
Assistant Deputy Minister, Christine Kaszycki
Tel: 705-670-5820; *Fax:* 705-670-5818
christie.kaszycki@ontario.ca
Director, Indigenous Reltaions & Reconciliations, Bernie Hughes
Tel: 705-670-5743; *Fax:* 705-670-5818
bernie.hughes@ontario.ca
Director, Strategic Services, Jamesene King
Tel: 705-670-3003; *Fax:* 705-670-5818
jamesene.king@ontario.ca
Acting Manager, Finance & Administration, Therese Paradis
Tel: 705-670-5831
therese.paradis@ontario.ca

Mineral Development & Lands
Tel: 705-670-5787; *Fax:* 705-670-5803
Toll-Free: 888-415-9845
Director, Gordon MacKay
Tel: 705-670-5784
gordon.mackay@ontario.ca

Ontario Geological Survey
Tel: 705-670-5758; *Fax:* 705-670-5818
Toll-Free: 888-415-9845
Director, Jack Parker
Tel: 705-670-5924
jack.parker@ontario.ca
Senior Manager, Resident Geologist Program, Mark Smyk
Tel: 807-475-1107
mark.smyk@ontario.ca

Ring of Fire Secretariat
Tel: 705-670-5819; *Fax:* 705-670-5626
Toll-Free: 888-415-9845
Assistant Deputy Minister, Vacant
Director, Aboriginal Community & Stakeholder Relations, Lori Churchill
Tel: 705-670-5767
lori.churchill@ontario.ca
Director, General Operations, Strategic Policy Division, RoF Infrastructure Development Corporation, Fiona Mackintosh
Tel: 416-212-8207
fiona.mackintosh@ontario.ca

Northern Development Division
Roberta Bondar Place, #200, 70 Foster Dr., Sault Ste. Marie, ON P6A 6V8
Tel: 705-945-5900; *Fax:* 705-945-5931
Toll-Free: 800-461-2287
The Division is responsible for promoting business, industrial, community & regional economic development & diversification; improving access to social & health services for northerners; planning & coordinating an integrated transportation system to meet private & commercial transportation needs at local, regional & provincial levels; & coordinating the policies & programs of other ministries to ensure the special needs of northerners are addressed by government.
Assistant Deputy Minister, Helen Mulc
Tel: 705-945-6733; *Fax:* 705-945-5932
helen.mulc@ontario.ca

Executive Director, Northern Ontario Heritage Fund Corporation, Bruce Strapp
Tel: 705-945-6734; *Fax:* 705-564-7447
bruce.strapp@ontario.ca
Director, Transportation, Trade & Investment, Mark Speers
Tel: 705-945-6636
mark.speers@ontario.ca
Director, Strategic Iniatives, Sharon Tansley
Tel: 705-564-7115
sharon.tansley@ontario.ca

Area Offices

Kenora
#104, 810 Robertson St., Kenora, ON P9N 4J2
Tel: 807-468-2937; *Fax:* 807-468-2930
Manager, Christine Hansen
Tel: 807-468-2938
christine.hansen@ontario.ca

North Bay
#203, 447 McKeown Ave., North Bay, ON P1B 9S9
Tel: 705-494-4045; *Fax:* 705-494-4069
Manager, Theo Noel de Tilly
Tel: 705-494-4176
theo.noeldetilly@ontario.ca

Sault Ste Marie
Roberta Bondar Place, #200, 70 Foster Dr., Sault Ste Marie, ON P6A 6V8
Tel: 705-945-5914; *Fax:* 705-945-5931
Acting Manager, Leigh Colpitts
leigh.colpitts@ontario.ca

Sudbury
#601, 159 Cedar St., Sudbury, ON P3E 6A5
Tel: 705-564-7517; *Fax:* 705-564-7583
Manager, Theo Noel de Tilly
Tel: 705-564-7515
theo.noeldetilly@ontario.ca

Thunder Bay
Ontario Government Bldg., #332, 435 James St. South, Thunder Bay, ON P7E 6S7
Tel: 807-475-1648; *Fax:* 807-475-1589
Manager, Jamie Taylor
Tel: 807-475-1725
jamie.taylor@ontario.ca

Timmins
Ontario Government Complex, East Wing, 5520 Hwy. 101 East, PO Box 3060 South Porcupine, ON P0N 1H0
Tel: 705-235-1664; *Fax:* 705-235-1660
Manager, Brian Pountney
Tel: 705-235-1654
brian.pountney@ontario.ca

Regional Operations Division
Whitney Block, #6610, 99 Wellesley St. West, Toronto, ON M7A 1W3
Fax: 416-314-2629
Toll-Free: 800-667-1940
Other Communication: Peterborough Fax: 705-755-5073
Assistant Deputy Minister, Jennifer Barton
Tel: 705-875-8601
jennifer.barton@ontario.ca

Strategic Policy Division
#1305, 123 Edward St., 13th Fl., Toronto, ON M5G 1E2
Tel: 416-212-8202
Assistant Deputy Minister, Susan Capling
Tel: 416-314-3803
susan.capling@ontario.ca
Director, Corporate Policy Secretariat, Priya Tandon
Tel: 416-327-0302
priya.tandon@ontario.ca
Acting Director, Policy Coordination & Ring of Fire, Afsana Qureshi
Tel: 416-327-0110
afsana.qureshi@ontario.ca

Office of the Ombudsman

Bell Trinity Sq., South Tower, 483 Bay St., 10th Fl., Toronto, ON M5G 2C9
Tel: 416-586-3300; *Fax:* 416-586-3485
Toll-Free: 800-263-1830
TTY: 866-411-4211
info@ombudsman.on.ca
www.ombudsman.on.ca
Other Communication: Ligne sans frais: 800-387-2620 (Français)
twitter.com/ont_ombudsman
www.facebook.com/OntarioOmbudsman
www.linkedin.com/company/ontario-ombudsman
www.youtube.com/user/OntarioOmbudsman

An impartial body independent of government that investigates & resolves complaints about the administrative actions & decisions of provincial government organizations such as ministries, boards, agencies, commissions & tribunals. The Ombudsman is an Officer of the provincial Legislature & has jurisdiction over all provinical government organizations as an office of last resort. All available complaint & appeal procedures whenever possible should be used before the Ombudsman conducts an investigation. The Ombudsman decides cases based on independent investigations & works to find solutions that are acceptable to everyone involved.
In 2018, the Office of the Ombudsman assumed the duties of the Provincial Advocate for Children & Youth.

Ombudsman, Paul Dubé
Tel: 416-586-3300
pdube@ombudsman.on.ca

Deputy Ombudsman, Barbara Finlay
Tel: 416-586-3300
bfinlay@ombudsman.on.ca

General Counsel, Laura Pettigrew
Tel: 416-586-3325
lpettigrew@ombudsman.on.ca

General Counsel, Wendy Ray
Tel: 416-586-3513
wray@ombudsman.on.ca

Ontario Power Generation (OPG)

700 University Ave., Toronto, ON M5G 1X6
Tel: 416-592-2555
Toll-Free: 877-592-2555
webmaster@opg.com
www.opg.com
Other Communication: Media Relations Email: media@opg.com;
Investor Relations Email: investor.relations@opg.com
twitter.com/OntarioPowerGen
www.youtube.com/opgvideos
Mandate is to meet Ontario's requirements for electricity so as to result in the greatest overall benefit to the community & the lowest cost to the consumer, while operating in a safe & environmentally responsible manner. Assets include 2 nuclear power stations, 66 hydroelectric stations (including 29 small hydroelectric plants) & 241 dams on 24 river systems.

Chair, Wendy Kei

President & Chief Executive Officer, Ken Hartwick

President, Renewable Generation & Power Marketing, Mike Martelli, B.A.Sc., P.Eng.

President, Nuclear, Dominique Miniere

Chief Administrative Officer, Christopher F. Ginther

Chief Financial Officer & Senior Vice-President, Finance, John Mauti

Chief Nuclear Officer, Sean Granville

Chief Ethics Officer & Senior Vice-President, Law & General Counsel, Shelley Babin

Senior Vice-President, Corporate Business Development & Strategy, Nicolle Butcher

Senior Vice-President, Enterprise Projects, Dietmar Reiner, B.A.Sc., P.Eng.

Senior Vice-President, Corporate Affairs, Heather Ferguson

Ontario Ministry of Seniors & Accessibility

College Park, 777 Bay St., Toronto, ON M7A 1S5
Tel: 416-326-7076; *Fax:* 416-326-7078
Toll-Free: 888-910-1999
TTY: 800-387-5559
infoseniors@ontario.ca
www.ontario.ca/page/ministry-seniors-accessibility
twitter.com/seniorsON
www.facebook.com/SeniorsOntario
The Ministry (formerly known as Seniors Affairs, prior to the 2018 general election) advocates for, undertakes & supports policy initiatives that improve the quality of life for Ontario seniors, & public education efforts for & about Ontario seniors. The Ministry was established in 2016 from the former Ontario Seniors Secretariat, previously falling under the jurisdiction of the Ministry of Citizenship & Immigration.

Minister, Hon. Raymond Sung Joon Cho

Deputy Minister, Denise Allyson Cole
Tel: 416-314-3802
denise.cole@ontario.ca

Parliamentary Assistant, Daisy Wai
Tel: 416-314-0797

Accessibility for Ontarians with Disabilities Division
College Park, #601A & 601B, 777 Bay St., Toronto, ON M7A 2J4
Tel: 416-849-8276; *Fax:* 416-325-9620
Toll-Free: 866-515-2025
TTY: 416-325-3408
www.ontario.ca/accesson
accessibility@ontario.ca
The Accessibility Directorate is working to improve accessibility for people with disabilities in Ontario, aiming to reach its goals by 2025.
Assistant Deputy Minister, Ann Hoy
Tel: 416-325-5247
ann.hoy@ontario.ca

Accessibility Policy, Employment Strategy & Outreach Division
Macdonald Block, Niagara Room, 900 Bay St., 2nd Fl., Toronto, ON M7A 2A2
Assistant Deputy Minister, Susan Picarello
Tel: 416-327-7079
susan.picarello@ontario.ca

Regional & Corporate Services Division
400 University Ave., 2nd Fl., Toronto, ON M7A 2R9
Tel: 416-314-7311; *Fax:* 416-314-7313
Assistant Deputy Minister & Chief Administrative Officer, Maureen Buckley
Tel: 416-325-6278
maureen.buckley@ontario.ca

Ontario Solicitor General

George Drew Bldg., 25 Grosvenor St., 18th Fl., Toronto, ON M7A 1Y6
Tel: 416-326-5000; *Fax:* 416-325-6067
Toll-Free: 866-517-0571
TTY: 416-326-5511
mcscs.feedback@ontario.ca
www.mcscs.jus.gov.on.ca
Other Communication: TTY Toll-Free: 866-517-0572
The Ministry, known as Community Safety & Correctional Services until 2019, ensures that communities across the province are protected by safe, effective & accountable law enforcement & public safety systems. General responsibilities of the Ministry are as follows: correctional services; public safety & security; & policing services.

Solicitor General, Hon. Sylvia Jones
Tel: 416-326-5000
sylvia.jones@ontario.ca

Deputy Solicitor General, Correctional Services, Karen Ellis
Tel: 416-327-9734
karen.ellis@ontario.ca

Deputy Solicitor General, Community Safety, Mario Di Tommaso
Tel: 416-326-5060
mario.ditommaso@ontario.ca

Parliamentary Assistant, Christine Hogarth
christine.hogarth@ontario.ca

Chief Information Officer, Justice Technology Services Cluster, Catherine Emile
Tel: 416-574-6491
catherine.emile@ontario.ca

Director, Legal, Brian Loewen
Tel: 416-434-8436
brian.loewen@ontario.ca

Director, Communications, Stuart McGetrick
Tel: 647-963-0843
stuart.mcgetrick@ontario.ca

Associated Agencies, Boards & Commissions:

• Death Investigation Oversight Council (DIOC)
George Drew Bldg.
25 Grosvenor St., 15th Fl.
Toronto, ON M7A 1Y6
Tel: 416-212-4041
Toll-free: 855-240-3414
dioc@ontario.ca
www.dioc.gov.on.ca

• Fire Safety Commission
Place Nouveau Bldg.
5775 Yonge St., 7th Fl.
Toronto, ON M2M 4J1
Tel: 416-325-3100; *Fax:* 416-314-1217
info@firesafetycouncil.com
www.gov.on.ca/ofm

• Ontario Police Arbitration Commission (OPAC)
George Drew Bldg.
25 Grosvenor St., 15th Fl.
Toronto, ON M7A 1Y6
Tel: 416-314-3520; *Fax:* 416-314-3522
Toll-free: 866-517-0571
TTY: 416-326-5511
www.policearbitration.on.ca
Other Communication: Toll-Free TTY: 866-517-0572

Corporate Services Division
George Drew Bldg, North Side, 25 Grosvenor St., 18th Fl., Toronto, ON M7A 1Y6
Tel: 416-325-3257; *Fax:* 416-326-3149
Assistant Deputy Minister & Chief Administration Officer, Drew Vanderduim
Tel: 416-325-9208
drew.vanderduim@ontario.ca
Director, Facilities & Capital Planning, Robert Greene
Tel: 416-314-6683; *Fax:* 416-327-1470
robert.greene@ontario.ca
Acting Director, HR-Strategic Business Unit, Bart Nowak
Tel: 416-212-3555; *Fax:* 416-314-5559
bart.nowak@ontario.ca
Director, Business & Financial Planning, Joy Stevenson
Tel: 416-326-1016; *Fax:* 416-325-3465
joy.stevenson@ontario.ca

Correctional Services
George Drew Bldg, 25 Grosvenor St., 17th Fl., Toronto, ON M7A 1Y6
Assistant Deputy Minister, Community Services, Arlene Berday
Tel: 519-661-1694
arlene.berday@ontario.ca
Assistant Deputy Minister, Institutional Services, Christina Danylchenko
Tel: 416-327-9992; *Fax:* 416-314-6669
christina.danylchenko@ontario.ca
Assistant Deputy Minister, Operational Support, Shelley Unterlander
Tel: 416-327-0099
shelley.unterlander@ontario.ca
Director, Oversight & Investigations, Kevin West
Tel: 905-279-1882; *Fax:* 905-279-1295
kevin.west@ontario.ca
Acting Director, Field Operations & Corporate Support, Bob Cook
Tel: 416-494-3689
bob.cook@ontario.ca
Director, Programs & Operational Policy, Jennifer Oliver
Tel: 416-327-2329; *Fax:* 416-314-5987
jennifer.oliver@ontario.ca
Regional Director, Community Services, Barb Forbes
Tel: 519-675-7080
barb.forbes@ontario.ca
Acting Regional Director, Institutional Services, David W. Wilson
Tel: 519-661-1693
david.w.wilson@ontario.ca

Modernization Division
George Drew Bldg, 25 Grosvenor St., 15th Fl., Toronto, ON M7A 1Y6

Office of the Chief Coroner & Ontario Forensic Pathology Service
25 Morton Shulman Ave., Toronto, ON M3M 0B1
Chief Coroner for Ontario, Dr. Dirk Huyer
Tel: 647-329-1814
dirk.huyer@ontario.ca
Chief Legal Counsel, Prabhu Rajan
Tel: 416-329-1889
prabhu.rajan@ontario.ca
Chief Forensic Pathologist for Ontario &, Deputy Chief Coroner, Dr. Michael Pollanen
Tel: 416-329-1914; *Fax:* 416-314-4060
michael.pollanen@ontario.ca

Deputy Chief Coroner, Dr. Reuven Jhirad
Tel: 416-329-1830; *Fax:* 416-314-4030
reuven.jhirad@ontario.ca
Deputy Chief Coroner, Dr. James Sproule
Tel: 416-329-1812
james.sproule@ontario.ca
Deputy Chief Forensic Pathologist, Dr. Toby Rose
Tel: 647-329-1922; *Fax:* 647-329-1389
toby.rose@ontario.ca
Director, Operational Services, Martin Chicilo
Tel: 647-329-1880; *Fax:* 416-314-4060
martin.chicilo@ontario.ca

Office of the Fire Marshal & Emergency Management
25 Morton Shulman Ave., Toronto, ON M3M 0B1
Tel: 647-329-1100; *Fax:* 647-329-1143
www.ofm.gov.on.ca
Fire Marshal of Ontario & Chief of Emergency Management, Ross Nichols
Tel: 647-329-1200
ross.nichols@ontario.ca
Assistant Deputy Fire Marshal & Executive Officer, Tony Pacheco
Tel: 647-329-1203
tony.pacheco@ontario.ca
Deputy Fire Marshal, Fire Investigations & Field & Advisory Services, Jim Kay
Tel: 647-329-1210
jim.kay@ontario.ca
Acting Director, Administration & Business Services, Troy Fernandes
Tel: 647-329-1110
troy.fernandes@ontario.ca
Director, Emergency Management, Michael J. Morton
Tel: 647-329-1180
michael.j.morton@ontario.ca

Ontario Provincial Police
Lincoln M Alexander Bldg, 777 Memorial Ave, Orillia, ON L3V 7V3
Tel: 705-329-6111
Toll-Free: 888-310-1122
TTY: 888-310-1133
www.opp.ca
twitter.com/OPP_News
www.facebook.com/ontarioprovincialpolice
www.youtube.com/user/OPPCorpComm
Commissioner, Thomas Carrique

Public Safety Division
George Drew Bldg, 25 Grosvenor St., 12th Fl., Toronto, ON M7A 1Y6
Tel: 416-314-3377; *Fax:* 416-314-4037
Assistant Deputy Minister, Stephen Beckett
Tel: 416-325-3454
stephen.beckett@ontario.ca
Registrar & Director, Private Security & Investigative Services, Bruce Herridge
bruce.herridge@ontario.ca

Centre of Forensic Sciences
Tel: 647-329-1320; *Fax:* 647-329-1361
Director, Tony Tessarolo
Tel: 416-314-3224; *Fax:* 416-314-3225
tony.tessarolo@ontario.ca
Deputy Director, Support Services, Colette Blair
Tel: 647-329-1323
colette.blair@ontario.ca
Deputy Director, Scientific Services, Jonathan Newman
Tel: 416-314-3280
jonathan.newman@ontario.ca
Assistant Section Head, Northern Regional Forensic Laboratory, Vacant

Public Safety Training Division
25 Grosvenor St., 13th Fl., Toronto, ON M7A 1Y6
Acting Assistant Deputy Minister, Stephen Beckett
Tel: 416-325-3454
stephen.beckett@ontario.ca
Director, Ontario Police College, Paul Hebert
Tel: 519-773-4200
paul.hebert@ontario.ca
Deputy Director, Training, Ontario Police College, Catherine Bates
Tel: 519-773-4286
catherine.bates@ontario.ca
Deputy Director, Operations, Ontario Police College, Paul Hebert
Tel: 519-773-4271
paul.hebert@ontario.ca
Deputy Director, Transformation & Distance Learning, Ontario Police College, Vacant
Tel: 519-773-4560

Strategic Policy, Research & Innovation Design
George Drew Bldg, 25 Grosvenor St., 9th Fl., Toronto, ON M7A 1Y6
Tel: 416-212-4437; *Fax:* 416-212-4020
Assistant Deputy Minister, Debbie Conrad
Tel: 416-212-1266
debbie.conrad@ontario.ca
Director, Community Safety & Corrections Policy, Adriana Ibarguchi
Tel: 416-212-4025
adriana.ibarguchi@ontario.ca
Director, Research, Analytics & Innovation, Michael McBain
Tel: 416-325-3426
michael.mcbain@ontario.ca
Director, Community Safety & Intergovernmental Policy, Rebecca Ramsarran
Tel: 416-326-3252
rebecca.ramsarran@ontario.ca

Ontario Ministry of Transportation

777 Bay St., 5th Fl., Toronto, ON M7A 1Z8
Tel: 416-235-4686; *Fax:* 416-327-9185
Toll-Free: 800-268-4686
TTY: 866-471-8929
www.ontario.ca/page/ministry-transportation
Other Communication: Driver & Vehicle Licensing: 800-387-3445; Road Test Booking: 888-570-6110
twitter.com/ONtransport
www.facebook.com/OntarioTransportation
www.linkedin.com/company/ontario-ministry-of-transportation
The Ministry performs the following functions: planning, designing & building highways; performing environmental assessments; rehabilitating existing highways to increase their efficiency & safety; performing ongoing highway maintenance; developing standards, operational guidelines & policies relating to highways; & researching & introducing new technologies for more effective highway management. The Ministry commits to providing & promoting transportation services in a way that sustains a healthful environment through the Ministry's Statement of Environmental Values. The Ministry applies & integrates environmental concerns, along with prevailing social, economic, scientific & other considerations when conducting its business activities.

Minister, Hon. Caroline Mulroney
Tel: 416-327-9200
minister.mto@ontario.ca

Associate Minister, Transit-Oriented Communities, Hon. Stan Cho
stan.cho@ontario.ca

Deputy Minister, Laurie LaBlanc
Tel: 416-327-9162
laurie.leblanc@ontario.ca

Parliamentary Assistant, Vijay Thanigasalam
Tel: 416-327-9200

Acting Director, Communications Branch, Michael DeRuyter
Tel: 647-631-6138
michael.deruyter@ontario.ca

Director, Legal Services, Mary Gersht
Tel: 416-235-4406
mary.gersht@ontario.ca

Associated Agencies, Boards & Commissions:
• Metrolinx
97 Front St. West
Toronto, ON M5J 1E6
Tel: 416-874-5900; *Fax:* 416-869-1755
www.metrolinx.com
Metrolinx serves the Greater Toronto Area & Hamilton, & operates the following companies & programs: GO Transit; Union Pearson Express; PRESTO; Smart Commute; & the Transit Procurement Initiative (TPI).

• Ontario Highway Transport Board (OHTB)
151 Bloor St. West, 10th Fl.
Toronto, ON M5S 2T5
Tel: 416-326-6732; *Fax:* 416-326-6738
ohtb@mto.gov.on.ca
www.ohtb.gov.on.ca

Corporate Services Division
Garden City Tower, 301 St. Paul St., 6th Fl., St Catharines, ON L2R 7R4
Tel: 905-704-2693; *Fax:* 905-704-2445
Acting Director, Strategic Human Resources, Karen Balassarra
Tel: 905-704-2242
karen.baldassarra@ontario.ca

Acting Director, Finance, Virginia McKimm
 Tel: 905-704-2702; *Fax:* 905-704-2515
 virginia.mckimm@ontario.ca

Labour & Transportation I&IT Cluster
400 University Ave., 9th Fl., Toronto, ON M7A 1T7
 Tel: 416-327-3754; *Fax:* 416-327-3755
Chief Information Officer, Wynnann Rose
 Tel: 905-704-1267
 wynnann.rose@ontario.ca
Director, RUS Modernization IT Branch, Roman Corpuz
 Tel: 416-235-6798
 roman.corpuz@ontario.ca
Acting Director, .Net Solutions Delivery Centre, John Miniaci
 Tel: 905-704-3120
 john.miniaci@ontario.ca
Director, Road User Safety Solutions, Bob Stephens
 Tel: 416-235-5209; *Fax:* 416-235-5658
 bob.stephens@ontario.ca
Director, Information Management, Project Advisor & Labour
 Solutions, Daniel Young
 Tel: 416-326-3181; *Fax:* 416-325-0000
 daniel.young@ontario.ca

Policy & Planning Division
**Ferguson Block, 77 Wesley St., 3rd Fl., Toronto, ON M7A
1Z8**
 Tel: 416-327-8521; *Fax:* 416-327-8746
Assistant Deputy Minister, John Lieou
 Tel: 416-327-8521
 john.lieou@ontario.ca
Executive Director, Transit Policy & Programs, Vinay Shardar
 Tel: 416-585-7347
 vinay.sharda@ontario.ca
Director, Transportation Planning, Tija Dirks
 Tel: 416-585-7238; *Fax:* 416-585-7324
 tija.dirks@ontario.ca
Director, Strategic Policy & Transportation Economics, Elizabeth
 Kay-Zorowski
 Tel: 416-212-1893
 elizabeth.kay-zorowski@ontario.ca
Director, Transportation Policy, James Nowlan
 Tel: 416-585-7628
 james.nowlan@ontario.ca
Director, Indigenous Relations, Gurpeet Sidhu-Dhanoa
 Tel: 416-585-7315; *Fax:* 416-585-6876
 gurpreet.sidhu-dhanoa@ontario.ca

Provincial Highways Management Division
**Ferguson Block, 77 Wellesley St. West, 3rd Fl., Toronto, ON
M7A 1Z8**
 Tel: 416-327-9044; *Fax:* 416-327-9226
Assistant Deputy Minister, Linda McAusland
 Tel: 416-327-9044
 linda.mcausland@ontario.ca
Executive Director, Asset Management, Kevin Bentley
 Tel: 905-704-2299; *Fax:* 905-704-2562
 kevin.bentley@ontario.ca
Director, Highway Standards, Dan Remollino
 Tel: 905-704-2194; *Fax:* 905-704-2055
 dan.remollino@ontario.ca
Director, Investment Strategies, Shael Gwartz
 Tel: 905-704-2622
 shael.gwartz@ontario.ca
Director, Contract Management & Operations, Tony Tuinstra
 Tony.Tuinstra@ontario.ca
Director, Windsor Border Initiatives Implementation Group
 (BIIG), Vacant
Manager, Division Services, Cindy Lucas
 Tel: 905-704-2473
 cindy.lucas@ontario.ca

Road User Safety Division
Bldg A, 87 Sir William Hearst Ave., Toronto, ON M3M 0B4
 Tel: 416-235-2999; *Fax:* 416-235-4153
Assistant Deputy Minister, Kevin Byrnes
 kevin.byrnes@ontario.ca
Director, Licencing Services, Paul Brown
 Tel: 416-235-4392; *Fax:* 416-235-4378
 paul.h.brown@ontario.ca
Director, Safety Policy & Education, Maureen Tetzlaff
 maureen.tetzlaff@ontario.ca
Acting Director, Carrier Safety & Enforcement, Ian Freeman
 Tel: 416-235-2501; *Fax:* 905-704-2530
 ian.freeman@ontario.ca
Director, Program Development & Evaluation, Paul Harbottle
 Tel: 416-235-4559; *Fax:* 416-235-4111
 paul.harbottle@ontario.ca
Director, Regional Operations, Jeff Hudebine
 Tel: 416-235-3526; *Fax:* 416-235-4670
 jeff.hudebine@ontario.ca
Director, Organizational Development & Controllership, Barbara
 Maher

 Tel: 416-235-4864; *Fax:* 416-235-3939
 barbara.maher@ontario.ca
Director, Service Delivery Partnerships, Logan Purdy
 Tel: 416-235-4827
 logan.purdy@ontario.ca

Treasury Board Secretariat

315 Front St. West, 7th Fl., Toronto, ON M7A 0B8
 www.ontario.ca/page/treasury-board-secretariat
 Other Communication: General Inquiries, Phone: 416-327-2333
The Treasury Board Secretariat is involved in decision-making
related to capital; labour relations between the government, the
Ontario Public Service & the public sector; corporate policy &
agency governance; internal audit; internal human resources; &
information & information technology.

President, Treasury Board, Hon. Prabmeet Sarkaria
 Tel: 416-327-2333
 minister.tbs@ontario.ca

**Deputy Minister; Secretary, Treasury Board; Secretary,
Management Board of Cabinet,** Deborah Richardson
 Tel: 416-325-1607
 deborah.richardson2@ontario.ca

Parliamentary Assistant, Internal Audit, Rudy Cuzzetto
 Rudy.Cuzzetto@ontario.ca

Director, Legal Services, Len Hatzis
 Tel: 416-970-6591
 Len.Hatzis@ontario.ca

Director, Communications, Bryant J. Sullivan
 Tel: 647-330-5784
 Bryant.j.sullivan@ontario.ca

Associated Agencies, Boards & Commissions:
• **Conflict of Interest Commissioner**
#1802, 2 Bloor St. East
Toronto, ON M4W 3J5
Tel: 416-212-3606; *Fax:* 416-325-4330
Toll-free: 866-956-1191
coicommissioner@ontario.ca
www.coicommissioner.gov.on.ca
• **Ontario Pension Board (OPB)**
Sun Life Bldg.
#2200, 200 King St. West
Toronto, ON M5H 3X6
Tel: 416-364-8558; *Fax:* 416-364-7578
Toll-free: 800-668-6203
office.services@opb.ca
www.opb.ca
The OPB is the administrator of the Public Service Pension Plan.
• **OPSEU Pension Trust (OPTrust)**
#1200, 1 Adelaide St. East
Toronto, ON M5C 3A7
Tel: 416-681-6161; *Fax:* 416-681-6175
Toll-free: 800-637-0024
www.optrust.com
Other Communication: Member & Pensioner Services, Phone:
416-681-6100
• **Provincial Judges Pension Board**
c/o Ontario Pension Board
#2200, 200 King St. West
Toronto, ON M5H 3X6
Tel: 416-364-8558; *Fax:* 416-364-7578
Toll-free: 800-668-6203
Administers pension benefits associated with the pension plan
established for provincial judges.
• **Public Service Commission**
Whitney Block
99 Wellesley St. West, 5th Fl.
Toronto, ON M7A 1W4
Tel: 416-325-1750

Central Agencies I&IT Cluster
222 Jarvis St., 2nd Fl., Toronto, ON M7A 0B6
 Tel: 416-326-2700; *Fax:* 416-327-3347
Chief Information Officer, Ron Huxter
 Tel: 905-433-6890
 ron.huxter@ontario.ca

Centre for Leadership & Learning
#5320, 99 Wellesley St. West, 5th Fl., Toronto, ON M7A 1W4
 Tel: 416-325-1768; *Fax:* 416-325-6317
Chief Talent Officer, Diane McArthur
 Tel: 416-325-1777
 diane.mcarthur@ontario.ca
Director, Executive Programs & Services, Janet Hannah
 Tel: 416-325-8816
 janet.hannah@ontario.ca

Director, Corporate Leadership & Learning Branch, Judi
 Hartman
 Tel: 416-325-2802
 judi.hartman@ontario.ca
Director, Talent Management Branch, Chettie Legaspi
 Tel: 416-325-1617; *Fax:* 416-325-4996
 chettie.legaspi@ontario.ca

Centre for Public Sector Labour Relations & Compensation
**Ferguson Block, 77 Wellesley St. West, 5th Fl., Toronto, ON
M7A 1N3**
Associate Deputy Minister, Marc Rondeau
 Tel: 416-327-0132
 marc.rondeau@ontario.ca
Assistant Deputy Minister, Matt Siple
 matt.siple@ontario.ca
Acting Director, Labour Relations Policy & Strategic Initatives,
 Natasha Holland
 Tel: 416-325-1651
 natasha.holland@ontario.ca
Director, Negotiations, Mike Mously
 mike.mously@ontario.ca
Director, Employee Relations, Jennifer Price
 Tel: 416-327-0088
 jennifer.price@ontario.ca
Project Director, Corrections Labour Relations, Michaeal
 Villeneuve
 Tel: 416-325-1490
 michael.villeneuve@ontario.ca

Corporate Policy, Agency Governance & Open Government Division
77 Wellesley St. West, 13th Fl., Toronto, ON M7A 1N3
 Tel: 416-327-9262; *Fax:* 416-325-9577
Assistant Deputy Minister, Shawn Lawson
 Tel: 416-327-9223
 shawn.lawson@ontario.ca
Director, Public Appointments & Agency Governance, Olha
 Dobush
 Tel: 416-325-1345
 olha.dobush@ontario.ca
 www.pas.gov.on.ca

Corporate Services Division
**Whitney Block, 99 Wellesley St. West, 5th Fl., Toronto, ON
M7A 1W3**
 Tel: 416-212-8256; *Fax:* 416-327-2866
 Toll-Free: 888-745-8888
Assistant Deputy Minister & Chief Administrative Officer, Melanie
 Fraser
 Tel: 416-325-3821
 melanie.fraser@ontario.ca
Director, Service Management & Service Delivery Branch, Karl
 Cunningham
 Tel: 416-326-8896; *Fax:* 416-326-8932
 karl.cunningham@ontario.ca
Director, Business Planning & Financial Management, Anna Di
 Misa
 Tel: 416-327-2526; *Fax:* 416-327-3794
 anna.dimisa@ontario.ca
Director, Enterprise Services Strategic Business, Janette
 Jozefacki
 Tel: 416-892-0654
 janette.jozefacki@ontario.ca

Office of the Corporate Chief Information Officer (OCCIO)
**Ferguson Block, 77 Wellesley St. West, 8th Fl., Toronto, ON
M7A 1N3**
 Tel: 416-327-3442; *Fax:* 416-327-3264
Corporate Chief Information & Information Technology Officer,
 David Nicholl
 Tel: 416-327-9696
 david.nicholl@ontario.ca
Assistant Deputy Minister & Executive Lead,, Infrastructure
 Technology Services, Rocco Passero
 Tel: 416-326-3398
 rocco.passero@ontario.ca
Chief Information Officer, Enterprise Service Management, Fred
 Pitt
 Tel: 416-212-1624
 fred.pitt@ontario.ca
Head, Cyber Security Operations, Mohammad Qureshi
 Tel: 416-327-0413
 mohammad.qureshi@ontario.ca
Lead, Cluster Security Operations, Philippe Madore
 Tel: 416-212-9256
 philippe.madore@ontario.ca
Senior Manager, Training, Outreach & Reporting, Cat Pieri
 Tel: 416-212-6173; *Fax:* 416-326-1374
 cat.pieri@ontario.ca

Office of the Treasury Board
7 Queens Park Cres., 7th Fl., Toronto, ON M7A 1Y7
Tel: 416-325-2794; *Fax:* 416-325-1595
otb@ontario.ca

Acting Divisional Coordinator, Linda Sommer
Tel: 416-327-2062
linda.sommer@ontario.ca

Capital Expenditure Management Division
Tel: 416-325-9411

Assistant Deputy Minister, Russ Whitehead
russ.whitehead@ontario.ca
Director, Economic Infrastructure, Dorothy Cheung
Tel: 416-325-3391
dorothy.cheung@ontario.ca
Director, Social Infrastructure, Gladys Miu
Tel: 416-325-5311
gladys.miu@ontario.ca

Office of the Provincial Controller Division
Tel: 416-325-0535; *Fax:* 416-325-4843
askFMG@ontario.ca

Assistant Deputy Minister & Provincial Controller, Gary Wuschnakowski
Tel: 416-325-8017
Gary.Wuschnakowski@ontario.ca
Director, Operations Control & Management Reporting, Rodney Dewell
Tel: 416-327-3273
rod.dewell@ontario.ca
Director, Financial Management & Business Modernization Office, Bruce Foster
Tel: 416-212-6611
bruce.foster@ontario.ca
Director, Controllership Policy & Accounting Consultation, Khalida Noor
khalida.noor@ontario.ca

Planning & Performance Division
Tel: 416-326-1214

Assistant Deputy Minister, Shawn Lawson
Shawn.Lawson@ontario.ca
Acting Director, Centre of Excellence, Shannon Fenton
shannon.fenton@ontario.ca
Director, Planning & Coordination, Jody Hendry
jody.hendry@ontario.ca
Director, Corporate Policy & Accountability, Carol Pauker
carol.pauker@ontario.ca

Ontario Internal Audit Division
777 Bay St., 25th Fl., Toronto, ON M5G 2E5
Tel: 416-327-9512; *Fax:* 416-327-9486

Chief Internal Auditor & Assistant Deputy Minister, Richard Kennedy
Tel: 416-327-9319
richard.kennedy@ontario.ca
Executive Lead & Strategic Advisor, Audit Centre for Excellence, Marisa Fernandez
Tel: 416-212-6357
marisa.fernandez@ontario.ca

Women's Issues

#601D, 777 Bay St., 6th Fl., Toronto, ON M7A 2J4
www.ontario.ca/page/womens-issues
twitter.com/WomenON
Women's Issues (formerly Status of Women) provides focus for government action on issues of concern to women, in particular, preventing violence against women and promoting women's economic independence.
The Ministry was established in 2016 from the former Ontario Women's Directorate, previously falling under the jurisdiction of the Ministry of Citizenship & Immigration. It is now overseen by the Ministry of Children, Community & Social Services.

Associate Minister, Children & Women's Issues, Hon. Jane McKenna

Chief of Staff, Alexandra Hoene
Tel: 416-325-5225
alexandra.hoene@ontario.ca

Workplace Safety & Insurance Board (WSIB)

200 Front St. West, Ground Fl., Toronto, ON M5V 3J1
Tel: 416-344-1000; *Fax:* 416-344-4684
Toll-Free: 800-387-0750
TTY: 800-387-0050
www.wsib.on.ca
Other Communication: Toll-Free Fax: 888-313-7373; eServices Inquiries, Phone: 888-243-1569; Collections, Phone: 800-268-0929
Secondary Address: 120 King St. West Collections BranchPO Box 2099 LCD1 Sta. Hamilton, ON L8N 4C5
Alt. Fax: 905-521-4203
Other Communication: Toll-Free: 1-800-268-0929
twitter.com/wsib
www.linkedin.com/company/wsib
www.youtube.com/ontariowsib
The Workplace Safety & Insurance Board is involved in Ontario's occupational health & safety system. The Board's responsibilities are as follows: administering no-fault workplace insurance in Ontario for employers & workers; providing disability benefits; monitoring the quality of healthcare; & assisting workers who have been injured on the job or persons who have contracted an occupational disease in an early & safe return to work. The Board reports to the Minister of Labour.

Chair, Elizabeth Witmer
Tel: 416-344-3775

President & Chief Executive Officer, Thomas Teahen
thomas_teahen@wsib.on.ca

Government of Prince Edward Island

Seat of Government: Island Information Service, PO Box 2000 Charlottetown, PE C1A 7N8
Tel: 902-368-4000
Toll-Free: 800-236-5196
island@gov.pe.ca
www.princeedwardisland.ca
twitter.com/infopei
www.facebook.com/govpe
www.youtube.com/c/PrinceEdwardIslandGovernment
The Province of Prince Edward Island entered Confederation on July 1, 1873. It has a land area of 5,686.03 sq km, with a population of 142,907, according to the 2016 StatsCan census.

Office of the Lieutenant Governor

Government House, PO Box 846 Charlottetown, PE C1A 7L9
Tel: 902-368-5480; *Fax:* 902-368-5481
www.lgpei.ca
The Honourable Antoinette Perry was sworn in as the 42nd Lieutenant Governor of Prince Edward Island on October 20, 2017, at the Tignish Parish Centre. It was the first time in history that a Lieutenant Governor of PEI was sworn in outside of Charlottetown.

Lieutenant Governor, Hon. Antoinette Perry, OPEI

Office of the Premier

Shaw Bldg., 95 Rochford St. South, 5th Fl., PO Box 2000 Charlottetown, PE C1A 7N8
Tel: 902-368-4400; *Fax:* 902-368-4416
premier@gov.pe.ca
www.princeedwardisland.ca/en/information/office-premier
Honourable Dennis King is the thirty-third Premier of Prince Edward Island. After winning the 2019 general election, he was sworn in as premier on May 9, 2019, forming a minority government.

Premier; President, Executive Council; Minister responsible, Intergovernmental Affairs, Indigenous Relations, & Acadian & Francophone Affairs, Hon. Dennis King
premier@gov.pe.ca

Chief of Staff, Pamela Williams
pjwilliams@gov.pe.ca

Executive Council

Shaw Bldg., 5th Fl., PO Box 2000 Charlottetown, PE C1A 7N8
Tel: 902-368-4502; *Fax:* 902-368-6118
www.princeedwardisland.ca/en/topic/executive-council-office
The Executive Council of Prince Edward Island is made up of Ministers of the Crown. The role of the Executive Council is to decide upon the policy & direction that the government will take & to advise the Lieutenant Governor.

Premier; President, Executive Council; Minister responsible for Intergovernmental Affairs, Indigenous Relations, & Acadian & Francophone Affairs; Leader, Progressive Conservative Party of Prince Edward Island, Hon. Dennis King
Tel: 90- 36- 440
premier@gov.pe.ca

Deputy Premier; Minister, Finance, Hon. Darlene Compton
Tel: 902-368-4050
MinisterFinance@gov.pe.ca

Minister, Transportation & Infrastructure, Hon. James Aylward
Tel: 902-368-5120
jsjaylwardMinister@gov.pe.ca

Minister, Fisheries & Communities, Hon. Jamie Fox
Tel: 902-838-0983
MinisterFC@gov.pe.ca

Minister, Health & Wellness, Hon. Ernie Hudson
Tel: 902-368-5250
ehhudsonminister@gov.pe.ca

Minister, Education & Lifelong Learning; Minister responsible, Status of Women, Hon. Natalie Jameson
Tel: 902-368-4610
MinisterELL@gov.pe.ca

Minister, Economic Growth, Tourism & Culture, Hon. Matthew MacKay
Tel: 902-368-4230
MinisterEGTC@gov.pe.ca

Minister, Transportation, Infrastructure & Energy, Hon. Steven Myers
Tel: 902-620-3646
samyersMinister@gov.pe.ca

Minister, Social Development & Housing, Hon. Bradley G. Trivers
Tel: 902-620-3777
DeptSDH@gov.pe.ca

Minister, Agriculture & Land; Minister, Justice & Public Safety & Attorney General, Hon. Bloyce Thompson
Tel: 902-368-4820; *Fax:* 902-368-4846
MinisterAgLand@gov.pe.ca

Executive Council Office
Shaw Bldg., 95 Rochford St., 5th Fl., PO Box 2000 Charlottetown, PE C1A 7N8
Tel: 902-368-4502; *Fax:* 902-368-6118
DeptECO@gov.pe.ca
www.princeedwardisland.ca/en/topic/executive-council-office
It is the responsibility of the Executive Council Office to provide administrative services & advice to the Executive Council. Advice & support are also offered to the government's departments & agencies.
An important activity of the Executive Council Office is the provision of research & analysis on intergovernmental affairs. Advice is given related to social & economic policies.
The Executive Office is also involved in the coordination of traditional ceremonial or legal requirements, such as the swearing into office of Members of Cabinet or the Lieutenant Governor.

Premier; President, Executive Council; Minister responsible, Intergovernmental Affairs, Indigenous Relations, & Acadian & Francophone Affairs, Hon. Dennis King
Tel: 902-368-4400; *Fax:* 902-368-4416
premier@gov.pe.ca
Note: Web Site: www.gov.pe.ca/premier (Office of the Premier)
Deputy Minister, Christopher Gillis
Tel: 902-620-3198
wcgillis@gov.pe.ca
Note: Web Site: www.gov.pe.ca/premier (Office of the Premier)
Clerk of the Executive Council; Secretary to Cabinet, Dan Campbell
Tel: 902-368-4407; *Fax:* 902-368-6118
dmcampbell@gov.pe.ca
Clerk Assistant, Pamela Trainor
Tel: 902-368-4302; *Fax:* 902-368-6188
pjtrainor@gov.pe.ca
Chief of Protocol, Debbie Atkinson
Tel: 902-368-6889; *Fax:* 902-368-6118
djatkinson@gov.pe.ca

Cabinet Committee on Policy & Priorities
Chair, Hon. Jamie Fox
Tel: 902-838-0983
Vice-Chair, Hon. Bloyce Thompson
Tel: 902-368-4820

Treasury Board
The Executive Council Act established the Treasury Board as a committee of the Executive Council. The Board advises the Executive Council about budgetary & financial matters & the management of the Public Service.
Chair, Hon. Darlene Compton
Tel: 902-368-4050; *Fax:* 902-368-6575
dcomptonmla@assembly.pe.ca
Secretary to Treasury Board, Gordon MacFadyen

Prince Edward Island Legislative Assembly

197 Richmond St., PO Box 2000 Charlottetown, PE C1A 7N8
Tel: 902-368-5970; *Fax:* 902-368-5175
assembly@assembly.pe.ca
www.assembly.pe.ca
The Legislative Assembly of Prince Edward Island consists of the lawmakers & the offices & officials who support their work.

Office of the Clerk
197 Richmond St., 2nd Fl., PO Box 2000 Charlottetown, PE C1A 7N8
Tel: 902-368-5970; *Fax:* 902-368-5175
www.assembly.pe.ca/offices/assembly-administrative-offices/clerk

The Clerk of the Legislative Assembly is responsible for providing administrative support to the Speaker, the House, & its members. Decisions of the House are recorded by the Clerk & published in the Journals of the Legislative Assembly of Prince Edward Island.
Clerk of the Legislative Assembly, Joseph Jeffrey
Tel: 902-368-5970; *Fax:* 902-368-5175
jajeffrey@assembly.pe.ca
Deputy Clerk, Emily Doiron
Tel: 902-368-5972
emilydoiron@assembly.pe.ca
Committee Clerk, Alysha Campbell
Tel: 902-368-4320
alyshacampbell@assembly.pe.ca
Director, Communications & External Relations, JoAnne Holden
Tel: 902-368-4316; *Fax:* 902-368-5175
jdholden@assembly.pe.ca
Sergeant-at-Arms & Director, Security, Brian Weldon
bdweldon@assembly.pe.ca

Office of the Conflict of Interest Commissioner
197 Richmond St., 1st Fl., PO Box 2000 Charlottetown, PE C1A 7N8
Tel: 902-368-5970; *Fax:* 902-368-5175
www.assembly.pe.ca/offices/conflict-of-interest-commissioner
The Conflict of Interest Commissioner is an independent officer of the Legislative Assembly who administers the Conflict of Interest Act. To enhance public confidence in the Legislative Assembly, the Conflict of Interest Act ensures that Ministers & Members reconcile their private & public interests & conduct their responsibilities with integrity.
Commisioner, Conflict of Interest, Hon. Judy Burke, Q.C.
judyburke@assembly.pe.ca

Government Members' Office (Progressive Conservative)
Coles Bldg., 175 Richmond St., 3rd Fl., PO Box 338 Charlottetown, PE C1A 7K7
Tel: 902-368-4360; *Fax:* 902-368-4377
www.assembly.pe.ca/members/caucus-offices
Administrative support to government backbenchers is provided by the Government Members' Office.

Hansard
J. Angus MacLean Bldg., 180 Richmond St., 2nd Fl., PO Box 2000 Charlottetown, PE C1A 7L3
The published daily debates of Members in the House & in committees are known as Hansard. Staff of the Hansard office transcribe, publish, & index the debates.
Manager & Editor, Linda Henry
Tel: 902-368-5371; *Fax:* 902-368-5175
lmhenry@assembly.pe.ca

Office of the Information & Privacy Commissioner
J. Angus MacLean Bldg., 180 Richmond St., 2nd Fl., PO Box 2000 Charlottetown, PE C1A 7L3
The Information & Privacy Commissioner is appointed by the Legislature for a five year term. The Commissioner, who is an independent officer of the Legislative Assembly, reports annually to the Speaker of the Legislative Assembly about the work of the Office.
The Commissioner accepts Requests for Review from persons who are not satisfied with responses as a result of access to information requests made under the Freedom of Information &

Protection of Privacy Act. Upon conclusion of a review, the order of the Information & Privacy Commissioner is final. Applicants, the public body, or a third party may only apply to the Supreme Court of Prince Edward Island for judicial review.
The Commissioner also conducts investigations related to privacy complaints.
Commissioner, Information & Privacy, Denise N. Doiron
Tel: 902-368-4099; *Fax:* 902-368-5947
denisendoiron@assembly.pe.ca

Legislative Library & Research Service
J. Angus MacLean Bldg., 94 Great George St., PO Box 2000 Charlottetown, PE C1A 7N8
Tel: 902-620-3765; *Fax:* 902-620-3975
Opened in 2008, the Legislative Library supports members, committees, & house officers in their work. Non-partisan reports are provided by the research service.
Librarian, Research, Web Services & Print Design, Laura Morrell
lemorrell@assembly.pe.ca

Office of the Official Opposition (Green)
Coles Bldg., 175 Richmond St., 2nd Fl., PO Box 2000 Charlottetown, PE C1A 7N8
Tel: 902-620-3977
www.assembly.pe.ca/members/caucus-offices
Other Communication: Party URL: www.greenparty.pe.ca
twitter.com/PEIgreens
www.facebook.com/GreenPartyPEI
The Official Opposition raises concerns of Islanders & holds the government accountable for its policies & promises.
Leader, Green Party of PEI; Leader, Official Opposition, Hon. Peter Bevan-Baker
leader@peigreens.ca
Opposition House Leader, Michele Beaton
mlbeatonmla@assembly.pe.ca
Opposition Whip, Trish Altass
pdaltassmla@assembly.pe.ca

Office of the Speaker
197 Richmond St., 1st Fl., PO Box 2000 Charlottetown, PE C1A 7N8
Tel: 902-368-4310; *Fax:* 902-368-4473
At the beginning of each new General Assembly, a Speaker of the Legislative Assembly is elected by secret ballot. The following Members of the Legislative Assembly are ineligible to be the Speaker: the Premier, the Leader of the Opposition & leaders of other political parties in the Assembly, & Members of the Executive Council.
Speaker, Hon. Colin LaVie
crlaviemla@assembly.pe.ca
Deputy Speaker, Hal Perry
Tel: 902-368-4310; *Fax:* 902-368-4473
jhperrymla@assembly.pe.ca

Office of the Third Party (Liberal)
Basement, Coles Bldg., 175 Richmond St., PO Box 2890 Charlottetown, PE C1A 8C5
Tel: 902-368-4330; *Fax:* 902-368-4348
www.assembly.pe.ca/members/caucus-offices
Other Communication: Party URL: liberalpei.ca
twitter.com/peiliberalparty
www.facebook.com/PEILiberals
Interim Leader, Third Party, Sonny Gallant
Tel: 902-368-4801
sjgallantmla@assembly.pe.ca
Third Party House Leader, Gordon McNeilly
Tel: 902-368-4330
gamcneillyMLA@assembly.pe.ca
Third Party Whip, Robert Henderson
Tel: 902-368-4330
rlhendersonMLA@assembly.pe.ca

Sixty-sixth General Assembly - Prince Edward Island

Province House, 165 Richmond St., 1st Fl., PO Box 2000 Charlottetown, PE C1A 7N8
Tel: 902-368-5970; *Fax:* 902-368-5175
Toll-Free: 877-315-5518
www.assembly.pe.ca
twitter.com/peileg

Last General Election: April 23, 2019.
Next General Election: Oct. 2023.
Party Standings (Oct. 2021):
Progressive Conservative 14;
Green Party 8;
Liberal 4;
Vacant 1;
Total 27.
Salaries, Indemnities & Allowances (April 2020):
A Member of the Legislative Assembly's salary is $74,394.
In addition to this basic salary for each Member of the Legislative Assembly are the following additional salaries:

Premier $80,797;
Ministers $51,986;
Speaker $51,986;
Deputy Speaker $25,993;
Leader of the Opposition $51,986;
Government House Leader $14,081;
Opposition House Leader $7,009;
Third Party House Leader $4,626;
Government, Opposition & Third Party Whip $4,084;
Per-diem for committee meeting attendance: $109/day;
Leader of a Third Party $25,993.
The following is a list of Members of the Legislative Assembly, with their electoral district number & name, number of persons enumerated in the district for the 2019 provincial general election, party affiliation, & contact information. The general address for all Members of the Legislative Assembly is as follows: PO Box 2000, Charlottetown PE, C1A 7N8.
Members of the Legislative Assembly of Prince Edward Island
Trish Altass
Constituency: District #23 - Tyne Valley - Sherbrooke, Green Party of Canada
Tel: 902-620-3977
pdaltassMLA@assembly.pe.ca
www.assembly.pe.ca/members/trish-altass
twitter.com/AltassTrish, www.facebook.com/TrishAltassMLA
Minister, Transportation & Infrastructure, Hon. James Aylward
Constituency: District #6 - Stratford - Kinlock, PC
Tel: 902-368-5120; *Fax:* 902-368-5385
jsjaylwardmla@assembly.pe.ca
www.assembly.pe.ca/members/james-aylward
twitter.com/jsjaylward, www.facebook.com/JamesAylwardPC
Official Opposition House Leader, Michele Beaton
Constituency: District #5 - Mermaid - Stratford, Green Party of Canada
Tel: 902-620-3977
mlbeatonMLA@assembly.pe.ca
www.assembly.pe.ca/members/michele-beaton
twitter.com/beaton_michele,
www.facebook.com/MicheleBeatonMLA
Hannah Bell
Constituency: District #11 - Charlottetown - Belvedere, Green Party of Canada
Tel: 902-620-3977
hebellmla@assembly.pe.ca
www.assembly.pe.ca/members/hannah-bell
twitter.com/hannahbethbell,
www.facebook.com/hannahbellMLA
Zack Bell
Constituency: District #10 - Charlottetown - Winsloe, Progressive Conservative
Tel: 902-368-4360; *Fax:* 902-368-4377
zhbellmla@assembly.pe.ca
www.assembly.pe.ca/members/zack-bell
twitter.com/zackbellpei, www.facebook.com/ZackBellPEI
Note: Zack Bell was elected in a by-election held Nov. 18, 2020.
Karla Bernard
Constituency: District #12 - Charlottetown - Victoria Park, Green Party of Canada
Tel: 902-620-3977
kmbernardMLA@assembly.pe.ca
www.assembly.pe.ca/members/karla-bernard
twitter.com/karlabernardmla,
www.facebook.com/KarlaBernardMLA
Leader, Official Opposition; Leader, Green Party of Prince Edward Island, Hon. Peter Bevan-Baker
Constituency: District #17 - New Haven - Rocky Point, Green Party of Canada
Tel: 902-620-3977
psbevanbakermla@assembly.pe.ca
www.assembly.pe.ca/members/peter-bevan-baker
twitter.com/peterbevanbaker,
www.facebook.com/peter.bevanbaker
Deputy Premier; Minister, Finance, Hon. Darlene Compton
Constituency: District #4 - Belfast - Murray River, Progressive Conservative
Tel: 902-368-4050; *Fax:* 902-368-6575
dcomptonmla@assembly.pe.ca
www.assembly.pe.ca/members/darlene-compton
www.facebook.com/darlenecomptonpc
Cory Deagle
Constituency: District #3 - Montague - Kilmuir, Green Party of Canada
Tel: 902-368-4360; *Fax:* 902-368-4377
cfdeaglemla@assembly.pe.ca
www.assembly.pe.ca/members/cory-deagle
twitter.com/corydeaglepei
Minister, Fisheries & Communities, Hon. Jamie Fox
Constituency: District #19 - Borden - Kinkora, Progressive Conservative
Tel: 902-838-0983; *Fax:* 902-838-0972
jdfoxmla@assembly.pe.ca

www.assembly.pe.ca/members/jamie-fox
twitter.com/jamiedfox
Interim Third Party Leader, Sonny Gallant
Constituency: District #24 - Evangeline - Miscouche, Liberal
Tel: 902-368-4330
sjgallantmla@assembly.pe.ca
www.assembly.pe.ca/members/sonny-gallant
www.facebook.com/sonny.gallant
Ole Hammarlund
Constituency: District #13 - Charlottetown - Brighton, Green
Party of Canada
Tel: 902-620-3977
ohammarlundmla@assembly.pe.ca
www.assembly.pe.ca/members/ole-hammarlund
twitter.com/olehammarlund,
www.facebook.com/OleHammarlundMLA
Third Party Whip, Hon. Robert L. Henderson
Constituency: District #25 - O'Leary - Inverness, Liberal
Tel: 902-368-4330
rlhendersonmla@assembly.pe.ca
www.assembly.pe.ca/members/robert-henderson
Stephen Howard
Constituency: District #22 - Summerside - South Drive, Green
Party of Canada
Tel: 902-620-3977
sphowardmla@assembly.pe.ca
www.assembly.pe.ca/members/stephen-howard
www.facebook.com/SteveHowardMLA
Minister, Social Health & Wellness, Hon. Ernie Hudson
Constituency: District #26 - Alberton - Bloomfield, Progressive
Conservative
Tel: 902-368-5250; *Fax:* 902-368-4121
ehhudsonmla@assembly.pe.ca
www.assembly.pe.ca/members/ernie-hudson
Minister, Education & Lifelong Learning, Hon. Natalie Jameson
Constituency: District #9 - Charlottetown - Hillsborough Park,
Progressive Conservative
Tel: 902-368-4610; *Fax:* 902-368-4699
ngjamesonmla@assembly.pe.ca
www.assembly.pe.ca/members/natalie-jameson
twitter.com/NatalieJ_PEI,
www.facebook.com/nataliejamesonmla
Note: Natalie Jameson won the riding in a deferred election
held July 15, 2019. The election in the newly created riding
Charlottetown-Hillsborough Park was deferred after the death
of Green Party candidate Josh Underhay prior to the general
election.
Premier; President, Executive Council; Minister responsible,
Intergovernmental Affairs, Indigenous Relations, & Acadian &
Francophone Affairs; Leader, Progressive Conservative Party
of Prince Edward Island, Hon. Dennis King
Constituency: District #15 - Brackley - Hunter River,
Progressive Conservative
Tel: 902-368-4360; *Fax:* 902-368-4377
premier@gov.pe.ca
www.assembly.pe.ca/members/dennis-king
twitter.com/dennyking, www.facebook.com/DennisKingPC
Speaker, Hon. Colin LaVie
Constituency: District #1 - Souris - Elmira, Progressive
Conservative
Tel: 902-368-4310; *Fax:* 902-368-4473
crlavie@assembly.pe.ca
www.assembly.pe.ca/members/colin-lavie
Lynne Lund
Constituency: District #21 - Summerside - Wilmot, Green
Party of Canada
Tel: 902-620-3977
lglundmla@assembly.pe.ca
www.assembly.pe.ca/members/lynne-lund
twitter.com/lundlynne, www.facebook.com/LynneLund
Government House Leader, Sidney MacEwen
Constituency: District #7 - Morell - Donagh, Progressive
Conservative
Tel: 902-368-4360
smacewenmla@assembly.pe.ca
www.assembly.pe.ca/members/sidney-macewen
twitter.com/sidneymacewen
Minister, Economic Growth, Tourism & Culture, Hon. Matthew
MacKay
Constituency: District #20 - Kensington - Malpeque,
Progressive Conservative
Tel: 902-836-4360; *Fax:* 902-368-4377
mmackaymla@assembly.pe.ca
www.assembly.pe.ca/members/matthew-mackay
Third Party House Leader, Gordon McNeilly
Constituency: District #14 - Charlottetown - West Royalty,
Liberal
Tel: 902-368-4330
gamcneillymla@assembly.pe.ca
www.assembly.pe.ca/gordonmcneilly
twitter.com/gordmcneillypei,
www.facebook.com/GordMcNeillyPE

Minister, Environment, Energy & Climate Action, Hon. Steven
Myers
Constituency: District #2 - Georgetown - Pownal, Progressive
Conservative
Tel: 902-368-4360; *Fax:* 902-368-4377
samyers@assembly.pe.ca
www.assembly.pe.ca/members/steven-myers
twitter.com/stevenmyerspc
Deputy Speaker, Hal Perry
Constituency: District #27 - Tignish - Palmer Road, Liberal
Tel: 902-368-4330
jhperrymla@assembly.pe.ca
www.assembly.pe.ca/members/hal-perry
Minister, Agrilculture & Land; Minister, Justice & Public Safety;
Attorney General, Hon. Bloyce Thompson
Constituency: District #8 - Stanhope - Marshfield, Progressive
Conservative
Tel: 902-368-4360; *Fax:* 902-368-4846
bgthompsonmla@assembly.pe.ca
www.assembly.pe.ca/members/bloyce-thompson
twitter.com/BloyceThompson,
www.facebook.com/BloyceThompsonPEI
Minister, Social Development & Housing, Hon. Bradley G.
Trivers
Constituency: District #18 - Rustico - Emerald, PC
Tel: 902-368-4360; *Fax:* 902-368-4377
bgtriversmla@assembly.pe.ca
www.assembly.pe.ca/members/brad-trivers
twitter.com/bradtrivers, www.facebook.com/BradTriversPC,
www.linkedin.com/in/bradtrivers
Vacant
Constituency: District #16 - Cornwall - Meadowbank
Note: In August 2021, Heath MacDonald (L) resigned as the
district 16 MLA to run in the federal eletion.

Prince Edward Island Government Departments & Agencies

Prince Edward Island Department of Agriculture & Land

**Jones Bldg., 11 Kent St., 5th Fl., PO Box 2000
Charlottetown, PE C1A 7N8**
Tel: 902-368-4880; *Fax:* 902-368-4857
www.princeedwardisland.ca/en/topic/agriculture-and-land
twitter.com/AgInfoPEI
Formerly Agriculture & Fisheries, Prince Edward Island's
Department of Agriculture & Land provides programs & services
to the island's primary industries, including sustaining all
elements of agriculture, protecting the environment & natural
resources, & developing innovative products in food production.

Minister, Hon. Bloyce Thompson
Tel: 902-368-4820; *Fax:* 902-368-4846
MinisterAgLand@gov.pe.ca

Deputy Minister, Brian Matheson
Tel: 902-368-4830; *Fax:* 902-368-4846
bgmatheson@gov.pe.ca

Associated Agencies, Boards & Commissions:

• **Agricultural Insurance Corporation**
7 Gerald McCarville Drive
Kensington, PE C0B 1M0
Production insurance is administered by the Prince Edward
Island Agricultural Insurance Corporation. It provides production
risk protection to producers who may sustain crop losses due to
natural hazards.
Programs administered by the Corporation are as follows:
AgriStability, AgriInvest, AgriInsurance, & AgriRecovery.

• **Agricultural Insurance Corporation Appeal Board**

• **Animal Health Advisory Committee**

• **Farm Practices Review Board**
The Farm Practices Review Board is responsible for reviewing
concerns from the public about farm practices.

• **Grain Elevators Corporation**
62 Victoria St.
PO Box 250
Kensington, PE C0B 1M0
Tel: 902-836-8935; *Fax:* 902-836-8926
www.peigec.com
The Prince Edward Island Grain Elevators Corporation is a
leader in the province's cereal & protein sector.
For growers who want the pooled return, the Corporation
operates grain marketing pools. Producers may also sell part of
their crop to the Corporation at daily market prices.
Grain & products marketed throughout Prince Edward Island &
Atlantic Canada.

• **Marketing Council**
• **Natural Products Appeals Tribunal**
• **Pesticides Advisory Committee**
• **Veterinary College Advisory Council**
• **Veterinary Medical Association Licensing Board**

Land

www.princeedwardisland.ca/en/topic/land
The divison deals with building & development, invasive species,
land use planning, and shoreline stabilization. In addition, it
offers the following services: contractor licensing program;
environmental records review; online contaminated site search;
and handles complaints about unsightly properties.
Director, Land, Jim Young, P.Eng.
Tel: 902-368-5034
jjyoung@gov.pe.ca
Manager, Inspection Services, Glenda MacKinnon-Peters,
P.Eng.
Tel: 902-368-4874
gcmackinnon-peters@gov.pe.ca
Manager, Provincial Planning, Dale McKeigan
Tel: 902-620-3634
dfmckeigan@gov.pe.ca

Finance

Financial, administrative, & human resources services are
provided by the Finance.
Director, Mary Kinsman
Tel: 902-368-5741; *Fax:* 902-368-4857
makinsman@gov.pe.ca
Manager, Finance, Janet Doyle
Tel: 902-368-4837; *Fax:* 902-368-4857
jedoyle@gov.pe.ca
Manager, Human Resource Services, Erin Gauthier
Tel: 902-368-6694
ehgauthier@gov.pe.ca

Policy & Agriculture Resources

Jones Bldg., 11 Kent St., 5th Fl., Charlottetown, PE C1A 7N8
The Agriculture Policy & Regulatory Division oversees areas
such as the following: research; administration of industry
development programs; community pastures; on-farm food
safety; food quality; marketing legislation; domestic & foreign
trade; traceability; foreign animal disease; & emergency
preparedness.
Manager, Policy, Planning & FPT Relations, Bobby Cameron
Tel: 902-620-3483
bcameron@gov.pe.ca
Manager, Agriculture Industry Development, Lynda MacSwain
Tel: 902-368-4815
lemacswain@gov.pe.ca
Manager, Sustainable Agriculture, Barry Thompson
Tel: 902-368-6366
blthompson@gov.pe.ca

Prince Edward Island Analytical Laboratories

23 Innovation Way, Charlottetown, PE C1E 0B7
Tel: 902-368-4190
Prince Edward Island Analytical Laboratories include the Dairy
Laboratory, the Soil, Feed, & Water Chemistry Testing
Laboratory, & the Water Microbiology Laboratory.
The Dairy Laboratory works in support of the Prince Edward
Island Dairy Industry Act & Regulations. It also provides services
to VALACTA in Prince Edward Island, Nova Scotia, & New
Brunswick.
The Soil, Feed, & Water Chemistry Testing Laboratory provides
analytical information for farmers & the public.
Laboratory Manager, Lori C. Connolly-Brine
Tel: 902-368-3300; *Fax:* 902-368-6299
lcconnolly@gov.pe.ca
Laboratory Manager, Anna Marie MacFarlane
Tel: 902-368-4190; *Fax:* 902-569-7778
ammacfarlane@gov.pe.ca
New Initiatives Officer, Tim Lynch
Tel: 902-620-3300
txlynch@gov.pe.ca

Office of the Auditor General

**Shaw Bldg., 105 Rochford St. North, 2nd Fl., PO Box 2000
Charlottetown, PE C1A 7N8**
Tel: 902-368-4520; *Fax:* 902-368-4598
www.assembly.pe.ca/auditorgeneral
Accountability & best practices in government operations are
promoted by the Office of the Auditor General. Independent
audits & examinations are conducted by the Office of the Auditor
General for the Legislative Assembly of Prince Edward Island.

Auditor General, Darren Noonan, CPA, CA
dwnoonan@assembly.pe.ca

Audit Director, Gerri Russell, CPA, CA

Tel: 902-368-4526; *Fax:* 902-368-4598
gfrussell@assembly.pe.ca

Audit Director, Elvis Alisic, CPA, CA
Tel: 902-368-4522; *Fax:* 902-368-4598
ealisic@assembly.pe.ca

Prince Edward Island Cannabis Management Corporation / PEI Cannabis (PEICMC)

85 Belvedere Ave., Charlottetown, PE C1A 6B2
Tel: 902-368-5551
infopeicmc@peicannabiscorp.com
peicannabiscorp.com
Other Communication: Charlottetown Phone: 902-569-7758
twitter.com/PEICannabis
facebook.com/peicmc
www.instagram.com/peicannabis
The PEICMC is responsible for the distribution & sale of recreational cannabis in PEI, in partnership with the PEI Liquor Control Commission, & under the authority of the Cannabis Control Act. The corporation operates four retail locations across the island, & individuals may also purchase online.

Chair, Quentin Bevan

Chief Executive Officer, Andrew MacMillan
Tel: 902-368-5855
abmacmillan@liquorpei.com

Director, Cannabis Operations, Zach Currie
Tel: 902-368-5727
zrcurrie@liquorpei.com

Prince Edward Island Department of Economic Growth, Tourism & Culture

PO Box 2000 Charlottetown, PE C1A 7N8
Tel: 902-368-5540; *Fax:* 902-368-5277
tpswitch@gov.pe.ca
Other Communication: URL:
www.princeedwardisland.ca/en/topic/economic-development-and
-tourism
Prince Edward Island's Department of Economic Development & Tourism is engaged in the following activities: promoting tourism & special events; facilitating product development; managing infrastructure projects such as parks & golf courses; providing library services; promoting historic preservation & documentation; & encouraging cultural development.

Minister, Hon. Matthew MacKay
Tel: 902-368-4230; *Fax:* 902-620-3726
MinisterEGTC@gov.pe.ca

Deputy Minister, Erin McGrath-Gaudet
emcgrathgaudet@gov.pe.ca

Associated Agencies, Boards & Commissions:
• **Anne of Green Gables Licensing Authority Inc.**
94 Euston St.
PO Box 910
Charlottetown, PE C1A 7L9
Tel: 902-368-5961
Other Communication: Toronto Office, Phone: 416-971-7473
The Anne of Green Gables Licensing Authority Inc. controls the use of Anne of Green Gables & related trademarks, protects the integrity of Anne images, & preserves the legacy of L.M. Montgomery & her works. The authority is jointly owned by the Province of Prince Edward Island, Ruth Macdonald, & David Macdonald.
• **BIO|FOOD|TECH**
101 Belvedere Ave.
PO Box 2000
Charlottetown, PE C1A 7N8
Tel: 902-368-5548; *Fax:* 902-368-5549
Toll-free: 877-368-5548
biofoodtech@biofoodtech.ca
biofoodtechpei.ca
Formerly known as the PEI Food Technology Centre, BIO|FOOD|TECH operates as a contract research & analytical services company. It serves companies & entrepreneurs in the food & bioprocessing sectors.
• **Charlottetown Area Development Corporation (CADC)**
4 Pownal St.
PO Box 786
Charlottetown, PE C1A 7L9
Tel: 902-892-5341; *Fax:* 902-368-1935
www.cadcpei.com
The Charlottetown Area Development Corporation operates as a self-financed entity that aims to attract private sector development to the Greater Charlottetown area. To carry out its work, the Charlottetown Area Development Corporation partners

with the Province of Prince Edward Island, the City of Charlottetown, & the Town of Stratford.
• **Eastlink Centre Charlottetown**
46 Kensington Rd.
Charlottetown, PE C1A 5H7
Tel: 902-629-6600; *Fax:* 902-629-6650
www.eastlinkcentrepei.com
The Eastlink Centre Charlottetown is a multi-purpose facility.
• **Finance PEI**
94 Euston St., 2nd Fl.
Charlottetown, PE C1A 1R7
Tel: 902-368-6300; *Fax:* 902-368-6255
financepei@gov.pe.ca
financepei.ca
Finance PEI administers business financing programs for the provincial government.
• **Innovation PEI**
94 Euston St.
PO Box 910
Charlottetown, PE C1A 7L9
Tel: 902-368-6300; *Fax:* 902-368-6301
Toll-free: 800-563-3734
innovation@gov.pe.ca
www.innovationpei.com
Innovation PEI strives to advance economic development in Prince Edward Island. It promotes small business development, business improvement, employment creation, research, innovation, market access, & trade. Through the Island Prosperity Strategy, Innovation PEI focuses upon the following sectors: renewable energy, aerospace, information technology, & bioscience.
• **Island Investment Development Inc. (IIDI)**
94 Euston St., 2nd Fl.
PO Box 1176
Charlottetown, PE C1A 7M8
Tel: 902-620-3628; *Fax:* 902-368-5886
opportunitiespei@gov.pe.ca
The Island Investment Development Inc. is a crown corporation. Its business name is Immigration Services. The organization oversees the Prince Edward Island Provincial Nominee Program.
• **Tourism Advisory Council of Prince Edward Island (TAC)**
Shaw Bldg., 3rd Fl.
Rochford St.
PO Box 2000
Charlottetown, PE C1A 7N8
Tel: 902-368-5907
peitac@peitac.com
www.peitac.com
An industry advisory board to the Minister of Tourism & Culture, Prince Edward Island's Tourism Advisory Council features nineteen members. Members include senior provincial & federal government members & industry stakeholders who discuss the challenges of the tourism industry.
The Tourism Advisory Council works to ensure growing revenues in the tourism industry. To achieve this goal, the council partners with the Tourism Industry Association of PEI, Tourism PEI, & the Atlantic Canada Opportunities Agency.
The Minister of Tourism & Culture receives advice from the council about research initiatives, product development, & marketing.
• **Tourism Arbitration Board**
• **Tourism PEI Board**

Economic & Population Growth
#212, 176 Great George St., Charlottetown, PE C1A 4K9
Executive Director, Kal Whitnell
Tel: 902-368-4228; *Fax:* 902-368-4242
kbwhitnell@gov.pe.ca

Finance & Administration
Shaw Bldg., #95, 105 Rochford St., 5th Fl., Charlottetown, PE C1A 7N8
Director, Finance, Shannon Burke
Tel: 902-368-5875
slburke@gov.pe.ca
Director, Operations, Jennifer DeCoursey
Tel: 902-368-4084
jbdecoursey@gov.pe.ca

Labour & Industrial Relations
16 St. Peters Rd., Charlottetown, PE C1A 7N8
Director, Patricia H. McPhail
Tel: 902-569-0545
phmcphail@gov.pe.ca
Chief Employment Standards Officer, Robert G.S. Yeo
rgyeo@gov.pe.ca
Employer Advisor, Erinn Moore
egmoore@gov.pe.ca
Worker Advisor, Maureen A. Peters
mapeters@gov.pe.ca

Marketing Communications, Sales & Customer Relationship Management
#95, 105 Rochford St., Charlottetown, PE C1A 7N8
The role of the Marketing Communications, Sales & CRM Division is the promotion of Prince Edward Island as a tourist destination.
Director, Brenda Gallant
Tel: 902-368-6066; *Fax:* 902-368-4438
bgallant@gov.pe.ca
Manager, Visitor Services, Heather Pollard
Tel: 902-368-4441; *Fax:* 902-368-4438
hlpollard@gov.pe.ca
Manager, Trade & Sales, Craig Sulis
Tel: 902-368-5754; *Fax:* 902-368-4438
cdsulis@gov.pe.ca

Museum & Heritage Foundation
Beaconsfield, 2 Kent St., Charlottetown, PE C1A 1M6
Tel: 902-368-6600; *Fax:* 902-368-6608
mhpei@gov.pe.ca
www.peimuseum.com
twitter.com/PEIMUSEUM
www.facebook.com/PEIMuseum
www.flickr.com/photos/pei_museum
Governed by the Museum Act, the Prince Edward Island Museum & Heritage Foundation operates as a Schedule B Provincial Crown Corporation. The mandate of the registered charitable corporation is to collect, preserve, & interpret Prince Edward Island's human & natural heritage.
The following seven provincial museums & heritage sites across Prince Edward Island are administered by the organization for the benefit & enjoyment of the people of the province & tourists: Elmira Railway Museum; Basin Head Fisheries Museum; Orwell Corner Historic Village & Agricultural Museum; Beaconsfield Historic House; Eptek Art & Culture Centre; The Acadian Museum of Prince Edward Island; & Green Park Shipbuilding Museum & Yeo House. There are more than 90,000 artifacts in the Provincial Collection, which are the responsibility of the Foundation.
Chair, Carolyn McKillop
Tel: 902-368-6600; *Fax:* 902-368-6608
Executive Director, Matthew McRae

Strategic Initiatives
#95, 105 Rochford St., Charlottetown, PE C1A 7N8
The Strategic Initiatives Division works with regional tourism associations to help them prosper. Overseeing the development of support programs is a key activity.
The division is also responsible for the management of regulatory affairs related to the Highway Signage Act & the Tourism Industry Act. Examples of these responsibilities include special event signage, on-premise signage, licensing, & occupancy reports.
Advocating for the interests of the tourism industry is another part of the mandate for the Strategic Initiatives Division. The division has represented the tourism industry in areas such as the Atlantic Gateway Initiative & land use issues.
Director, Chris K. Jones
Tel: 902-368-6342; *Fax:* 902-368-4438
ckjones@gov.pe.ca
Manager, Tourism Development, Janet Wood
Tel: 902-368-5508; *Fax:* 902-368-4438
jewood@gov.pe.ca

Prince Edward Island Department of Education & Lifelong Learning

Holman Centre, #101, 250 Water St., Summerside, PE C1N 1B6
Tel: 902-438-4130; *Fax:* 902-438-4062
DeptELL@gov.pe.ca
Other Communication: URL:
www.princeedwardisland.ca/en/topic/education-and-lifelong-lear
ning
Formerly known as the Department of Education, Early Learning & Culture, & renamed after the 2019 general election. Oversees the following areas: Apprenticeship & certification; certification & professional development for teachers; continuing education; early childhood development; library services & archives; reports, publications, & statistics; schools in PEI; student assessment; student financial services; supports & services.

Minister, Hon. Natalie Jameson
Tel: 902-368-4610; *Fax:* 902-368-4699
MinisterELL@gov.pe.ca

Deputy Minister, Bethany MacLeod
Tel: 902-438-4876
brmacleod@gov.pe.ca

Chief Financial Officer, Karen Stanley
klstanley@gov.pe.ca

Associated Agencies, Boards & Commissions:

• Atlantic Provinces Special Education Authority (APSEA)
5940 South St.
Halifax, NS B3H 1S6
Tel: 902-424-8500; *Fax:* 902-423-8700
www.apsea.ca
The APSEA serves children & youth who are deaf, hard of hearing, deafblind, blind, or visually impaired. It is a cooperative agency between the Provincial Departments of Education of New Brunswick, Nova Scotia, & Prince Edward Island.

• Certification & Standards Board
www.gov.pe.ca/eecd/index.php3?number=1028331&
The APSEA serves children & youth who are deaf, hard of hearing, deafblind, blind, or visually impaired. It is a cooperative agency between the Provincial Departments of Education of New Brunswick, Nova Scotia, & Prince Edward Island.

• Child Care Facilities Board
Responsible for providing safe, good quality, & appropriate child care facilities.

• Children's Commissioner & Advocate
PO Box 2000
Summerside, PE C1A 7N8
Tel: 902-368-4508; *Fax:* 902-368-6118
voiceforchildren@gov.pe.ca
The Children's Commissioner & Advocate deals with issues that affect children, youth & families in Prince Edward Island.

• Education Negotiation Agency

• Fathers of Confederation Buildings Trust

• French Language School Board / La Commission scolaire de langue française de l'Île-du-Prince-Édouard
1596, rte 124
Abram-Village, PE C0B 2E0
Tel: 902-854-2975; *Fax:* 902-854-2981
cslf@edu.pe.ca
cslfipe.wordpress.com
Prince Edward Island's French Language School Board administers six schools.

• Heritage Places Advisory Board

• Island Regulatory & Appeals Commission (IRAC)
See Entry Name Index for detailed listing.

• Lucy Maud Montgomery Foundation

• Prince Edward Island School Athletic Association (PEISAA)
#101, 250 Water St.
Summerside, PE C1N 1B6
Tel: 902-438-4846
info@peisaa.pe.ca
www.peisaa.pe.ca
The Prince Edward Island Athletic Association was established as the governing body for all school sports in the province. The association is a member of the Canadian School Sport Federation & is affiliated with the National Federation of State High School Athletic Associations.

• Teachers' Superannuation Commission
c/o Pensions & Benefits
PO Box 2000
Charlottetown, PE C1A 7N8
www.peitsf.ca/index.php3?number=1017189

Corporate & Financial Services
250 Water St., Summerside, PE C1N 1B6
Oversees the following areas: finance & school board operations; program evaluation & student assessment; research & corporate services; technology in education; human resources; & the Office of the Registrar.
Director, Chris DesRoche
Tel: 902-388-8876
cmdesroche@gov.pe.ca
Manager, Human Resources, Kim Nickerson
Tel: 902-438-4881
kenickerson@edu.pe.ca
Manager, Addictions Programming, Shauna Reddin
Tel: 902-368-5053
smreddin@gov.pe.ca

Early Childhood Development
Responsible for the following services: early childhood development & kindergarten; child & student services; & English & French programs.
Director, Carolyn Simpson
Tel: 902-368-5509
cesimpson@edu.pe.ca
Manager, Early Learning & Child Care, Doreen Gillis
Tel: 902-368-6518
degillis@gov.pe.ca
Project Manager, Garth Waite
Tel: 902-438-4880
glwaite@gov.pe.ca

Education Services
Executive Director, John Cummings
Tel: 902-438-4879
jacummings@edu.pe.ca
Director, Imelda Arsenault
Tel: 902-438-4879
imarsenault@edu.pe.ca

English Education, Programs and Services
Director, Tamara Hubley-Little
Tel: 902-438-4886
thlittle@edu.pe.ca

French Innovation, Education & Programs
Director, French Programs, René Hurtubise
Tel: 902-438-4155
rvhurtubise@gov.pe.ca
Coordinator, French Cultural Programming, Cecile Arenault
Tel: 902-438-4859
ccarsenault@edu.pe.ca

Libraries & Archives
Shaw Bldg., #95, 105 Rochford St., Charlottetown, PE C1A 7N8
The Libraries & Archives Division acts as a liaison between the Prince Edward Island provincial government & organizations that represent the library, heritage, & cultural sectors.
Director, Kathleen Simmonds
Tel: 902-368-4784; *Fax:* 902-894-0342
kesimmonds@gov.pe.ca
Provincial Archivist, Public Archives & Records Offices, Jill MacMicken-Wilson
Tel: 902-368-4351; *Fax:* 902-368-6327
jswilson@gov.pe.ca
French Services Coordinator, Robyn Gallant
rngallant@gov.pe.ca

SkillsPEI
Atlantic Technology Centre, #212, 176 Great George St., Charlottetown, PE C1A 4K9
Tel: 902-368-6290; *Fax:* 902-368-6340
Toll-Free: 877-491-4766
www.skillspei.com
SkillsPEI manages the delivery of training & skills development programs. The programming is funded by the Labour Market Agreement & the Canada-Prince Edward Island Labour Market Development Agreement. Examples of programs include Training PEI, Employ PEI, Self Employ PEI, Community Internship, Immigrant Work Experience, & Labour Market Partnerships. SkillsPEI offices are located across Prince Edward Island.
Executive Director, Richard Gallant
Tel: 902-620-4244; *Fax:* 902-368-6340
rkgallant@gov.pe.ca
Manager, Service Delivery, Kings & Queens County, Blair Aitken
Tel: 902-368-4178; *Fax:* 902-368-6580
abaitken@gov.pe.ca
Manager, Service Delivery, Prince County, Nelda Praught
Tel: 902-438-4110; *Fax:* 902-438-4096
ndpraught@gov.pe.ca

Elections Prince Edward Island

Atlantic Technology Centre, #160, 176 Great George St., Charlottetown, PE C1A 4K3
Tel: 902-368-5895; *Fax:* 902-368-6500
Toll-Free: 888-234-8783
www.electionspei.ca
Elections Prince Edward Island provides information to electors & candidates. Guided by the Canadian Charter of Rights & Freedoms, Elections Prince Edward Island works to ensure that electors & candidates have the opportunity to exercise their democratic right.

Chief Electoral Officer, Tim G. Garrity
tggarrity@electionspei.ca

Deputy Chief Electoral Officer, Stephanie Roberts
saroberts@electionspei.ca

Prince Edward Island Department of Environment, Energy & Climate Action

Jones Bldg., 11 Kent St., 4th Fl., Charlottetown, PE C1A 7N8
Tel: 902-368-5044; *Fax:* 902-368-5830
Toll-Free: 866-368-5044
DeptEECA@gov.pe.ca
Other Communication: URL:
www.princeedwardisland.ca/en/topic/environment-energy-and-climate-action
Formerly the Department of Communities, Land & Environment, it was renamed after the 2019 general election. In 2021 it was renamed to the Department of Environment, Energy & Climate Action. It oversees areas such as: air quality; angling, hunting & trapping; climate change; approvals, licenses & permits; fish & wildlife; forests; & monitoring.

Minister, Hon. Steven Myers
Tel: 902-620-3646
samyersMinister@gov.pe.ca

Deputy Minister, Brad Colwill, CPA, CA
Tel: 902-620-3646; *Fax:* 902-368-5542
bccolwill@gov.pe.ca

Executive Director, Climate Change & Environment, Todd Dupuis
Tel: 902-368-5024; *Fax:* 902-368-5830
tdupuis@gov.pe.ca

Associated Agencies, Boards & Commissions:
• Boilers & Pressure Vessels Advisory Board
• Environmental Advisory Council
www.gov.pe.ca/environment/eac
The Environmental Advisory Council advises the Minister responsible for the environment about environmental concerns. Members of the council are appointed by the Lieutenant Governor in Council.
• Natural Areas Advisory Committee
• Power Engineers Board of Examiners
• Public Forest Council (PFC)
The Public Forest Council is made up of six private sector members & three public sector members, who are appointed by the Lieutenant Governor in Council. Council members foster discussion about the potential for provincial woodlands. The council is especially interested in non-traditional, non-consumptive uses of public forests.
• Species at Risk Advisory Committee
The Species at Risk Advisory Committee performs the following tasks: assessing the province's wildlife resources; advising the Minister of Environment, Energy, & Forestry about the species that should be listed at risk; analyzing the effects of land use on wildlife & their habitat; & making recommendations about the conservation of wildlife & its habitat.
• Wildlife Conservation Fund Advisory Committee

Climate Change & Environment
Jones Bldg., 11 Kent St., 4th Fl., PO Box 2000
Charlottetown, PE C1A 7N8
The Climate Change & Environment Division oversees programs that protect the province's environement, including the following elements: groundwater; inland surface water & coastal estuaries; drinking water; the ozone layer; & air quality.
The division is also involved in waste management activities, such as the handling of litter, beverage containers, hazardous wastes, used oil, petroleum storage tanks, lead-acid batteries, tires, & derelict vehicles.
Director, Special Projects, John Hughes
jshughes@gov.pe.ca
Director, Strategic Planning & Policy Development, Tony Sturz
Tel: 902-569-7529; *Fax:* 902-368-5830
avsturz@gov.pe.ca
Laboratory Manager, PEI Analytical Laboratories, Anna Marie MacFarlane
Tel: 902-368-4190; *Fax:* 902-569-7778
ammacfarlane@gov.pe.ca
Manager, Water & Air Quality, Bruce Raymond
Tel: 902-368-5054; *Fax:* 902-368-5830
bgraymond@gov.pe.ca
Manager, Drinking Water & Wastewater Management, George Somers
Tel: 902-368-5046; *Fax:* 902-368-5830
ghsomers@gov.pe.ca
Manager, Climate Change, Erin Taylor
Tel: 902-368-6111; *Fax:* 902-368-5830
eotaylor@gov.pe.ca
Manager, Environmental Land Management, Greg Wilson
Tel: 902-368-5274; *Fax:* 902-368-5830
gbwilson@gov.pe.ca

Finance & Corporate Services
Jones Bldg., 11 Kent St., 4th Fl., PO Box 2000
Charlottetown, PE C1A 7N8
Administrative services, human resources, & finances are the responsibilities of this division.
Acting Director, Michele Koughan
Tel: 902-368-5830
makoughan@gov.pe.ca
Acting Manager, Finance, Tiffany Bernard
tdbernard@gov.pe.ca
Manager, Human Resource Management, Michael Ready
mcready@gov.pe.ca

Forests, Fish, & Wildlife
J. Frank Gaudet Tree Nursery, 183 Upton Rd., PO Box 2000
Charlottetown, PE C1A 7N8
Tel: 902-368-4700; *Fax:* 902-368-4713

The Forests, Fish, & Wildlife Division oversees the following programs & services: the provincial forests; the private forest program; production development; resource inventory & modelling; & wildlife & fish.

Director, Kate E. MacQuarrie
Tel: 902-368-4705; *Fax:* 902-368-4713
kemacquarrie@gov.pe.ca
Manager, Fish & Wildlife, Brad Potter
Tel: 902-368-5111; *Fax:* 902-368-4713
bdpotter@gov.pe.ca
Manager, Production Development, Mary N. Myers
Tel: 902-368-4711; *Fax:* 902-368-4713
mnmyers@gov.pe.ca

Prince Edward Island Department of Finance

Shaw Bldg., 95 Rochford St. South, 2nd Fl., PO Box 2000
Charlottetown, PE C1A 7N8
Tel: 902-368-4040; *Fax:* 902-368-6575
DeptFinance@gov.pe.ca
www.princeedwardisland.ca/en/topic/finance

The Department of Finance facilitates the management of the Government of Prince Edward Island's human & financial resources.

Minister, Hon. Darlene Compton
Tel: 902-368-4050; *Fax:* 902-368-6575
MinisterFinance@gov.pe.ca

Deputy Minister, Dan Campbell, CFA
Tel: 902-368-4050; *Fax:* 902-368-6575
dmcampbell@gov.pe.ca

Associated Agencies, Boards & Commissions:
• **Atlantic Provinces Harness Racing Commission (APHRC)**
5 Gerald McCarville Dr.
PO Box 128
Kensington, PE C0B 1M0
Tel: 902-836-5500; *Fax:* 902-836-5320
www.atlanticphrc.ca

• **Classification Appeal Committee**
• **Lotteries Commission**
• **Maritime Geomatics Committee**
• **Northumberland Strait Crossing Advisory Group**
• **Prince Edward Island Liquor Control Commission**
See Entry Name Index for detailed listing.
• **Prince Edward Island Master Trust Advisory Board**
• **Public Service Commission (PSC)**
Shaw Bldg. North
105 Rochford St., 1st Fl.
PO Box 2000
Charlottetown, PE C1A 7N8
Tel: 902-368-4080; *Fax:* 902-368-4383
psc.gpei.ca
The independent & impartial agency coordinates human resources in the public sector of Prince Edward Island. All government departments & agencies, health authorities, & other public sector employers are served by Prince Edward Island's Public Service Commission. Examples of services include recruitment, selection, occupational health & safety, payroll & benefits administration, & the employee assistant program.

• **Self-Insurance & Risk Management Fund Advisory Committee**

Debt, Investment & Pension Management
Shaw Bldg. South, 95 Rochford St., 3rd Fl., PO Box 2000
Charlottetown, PE C1A 7N8
The Debt, Investment & Pension Management Division carries out the following responsibilities: provincial banking; sinking fund asset management; supervision of the pension fund managers; financial research; investment & debt management strategies; project financing; asset/liability management of crown corporations; & coordinating insurance of public debt.
Manager, Alan Silliker
Tel: 902-569-7666; *Fax:* 902-368-4077
agsilliker@gov.pe.ca
Officer, Investment, Ryan Bradley, MBA
Tel: 902-368-4167; *Fax:* 902-368-4077
rxbradley@gov.pe.ca

Economics, Statistics, & Federal Fiscal Relations
Shaw Bldg., 95 Rochford St., 2nd Fl., PO Box 2000
Charlottetown, PE C1A 7N8
The Economics, Statistics, & Federal Fiscal Relations Division is engaged in the following activities: offering economic policy, statistical, tax, & fiscal advice; providing a liaison with the federal government & the other provinces on fiscal arrangements; & responding to queries regarding statistical information.
Director, Nigel Burns
Tel: 902-368-4181; *Fax:* 902-368-4034
ndburns@gov.pe.ca

Interministerial Women's Secretariat
Jones Bldg., 11 Kent St., 2nd Fl., PO Box 2000
Charlottetown, PE C1A 7N8
The role of the Interministerial Women's Secretariat is to assist the Minister Responsible for the Status of Women to protect & promote gender equality.
Director, Michelle Harris-Genge
Tel: 902-368-5557; *Fax:* 902-892-0242
mdharris-genge@gov.pe.ca

Office of the Comptroller
Shaw Bldg., 95 Rochford St., 2nd Fl., PO Box 2000
Charlottetown, PE C1A 7N8
The Office of the Comptroller carries out the following responsibilities: operating the government's corporate accounting system; providing advice related to financial management; administering the corporate procurement service for departments & agencies; managing a corporate fleet information system; & producing the province's public accounts.
Comptroller, Gordon MacFadyen, CA
Tel: 902-368-4201; *Fax:* 902-368-6661
gsmacfadyen@gov.pe.ca
Manager, Procurement, Ian K. Burge
Tel: 902-368-4041; *Fax:* 902-368-5171
ikburge@gov.pe.ca
Manager, Financial Systems & Processing, Theresa A. DesRoches, CGA
Tel: 902-368-4225; *Fax:* 902-368-6661
tadesroches@gov.pe.ca
Manager, Accounting, Judy M. Killam
Tel: 902-368-4014; *Fax:* 902-368-6661
jmkillam@gov.pe.ca

Pensions & Benefits
Sullivan Bldg., 16 Fitzroy St., 3rd Fl., PO Box 2000
Charlottetown, PE C1A 7N8
The Pension & Benefits Division carries out the following responsibilities: financial management and policy development of pension and group insurance programs; & administering the pension program to retired employees.
Manager, Terry Hogan
Tel: 902-368-4002; *Fax:* 902-620-3096
tmhogan@gov.pe.ca
Senior Officer, Pensions & Benefits, Elmer Ramsay
Tel: 902-368-4164; *Fax:* 902-620-3096
erramsay@gov.pe.ca

Taxation & Property Records
Shaw Bldg., 95 Rochford St., 1st Fl., PO Box 2000
Charlottetown, PE C1A 7N8
Tel: 902-368-4070; *Fax:* 902-368-6164
www.taxandland.pe.ca
The role of the Taxation & Property Records Division is to ensure equity in the collection of provincial tax revenues & in the production of both provincial & municipal real property assessment rolls. Services are coordinated with federal, provincial, & municipal governments.
Provincial Tax Commissioner, Elizabeth (Beth) Gaudet
Tel: 902-368-4060; *Fax:* 902-368-6584
eagaudet@gov.pe.ca
Manager, Compliance & Tax Administration Services, Ryan Scott
Tel: 902-368-5137; *Fax:* 902-368-6164
scottryan@gov.pe.ca

Prince Edward Island Department of Fisheries & Communities

548 Main St., PO Box 1180 Montague, PE C0A 1R0
Tel: 902-838-0983; *Fax:* 902-838-0972
DeptFC@gov.pe.ca
www.princeedwardisland.ca/en/topic/fisheries-and-communities
The Department of Fisheries & Communities was created after the 2019 general election. It oversees aquaculture, marine fisheries & seafood services, municipalities, rural/regional development, and other supports & services.

Minister, Hon. Jamie Fox
Tel: 902-838-0983; *Fax:* 902-838-0972
MinisterFC@gov.pe.ca

Deputy Minister, Bob Creed
Tel: 902-838-0625
Toll-free: 877-407-0187; *Fax:* 902-838-0975
bdcreed@gov.pe.ca

Associated Agencies, Boards & Commissions:

• **Employment Development Agency**
548 Main St.
PO Box 1180
Montague, PE C0A 1R0
Tel: 902-838-0910; *Fax:* 902-838-0975
Toll-free: 877-407-0187

Aquaculture
Director, Neil MacNair
Tel: 902-838-0685
ngmacnair@gov.pe.ca
Manager, Kim Gill
klgill@gov.pe.ca

Marine Fisheries, Agri-Food, Seafood & Regulatory
Manager, Marine Fisheries, David MacEwan
Tel: 902-838-0635
dgmacewen@gov.pe.ca
Manager, Agri-food & Seafood Services, David McGuire
Tel: 902-838-0691
dpmcguire@gov.pe.ca
Seafood Marketing Officer, Kaley E. MacDonald
Tel: 902-838-0627
kemacdonald@gov.pe.ca

Municipal Affairs
Acting Director, Christine MacKinnon
Tel: 902-368-5282
cgmackinnon@gov.pe.ca
Manager, Samantha J. Murphy
Tel: 902-368-5892
sjmurphy@gov.pe.ca
Senior Municipal Officer, Danielle Gillan
Tel: 902-368-5582
dmgillan@gov.pe.ca

Rural Economic Development
Director, Amie Swallow MacDonald
Tel: 902-838-0662
aswallowmacdonald@gov.pe.ca
Administrative Financial Officer, Lisa Holland
Tel: 902-838-0963
laholland@gov.pe.ca

Prince Edward Island Department of Health & Wellness

Shaw Bldg., 105 Rochford St. North, 4th Fl., Charlottetown,
PE C1A 7N8
Tel: 902-368-6414; *Fax:* 902-368-4121
DeptHW@gov.pe.ca
www.princeedwardisland.ca/en/topic/health-and-wellness
The Department of Health & Wellness carries out the following responsibilities: ensuring quality health care to the citizens of Prince Edward Island; providing leadership in policy, programs, & operations; maintaining & improving the health of citizens; playing a leadership role in innovation; coordinating the implementation of the Healthy Living Strategy; providing regulatory services to the health system; acting as a central contact for Aboriginal organizations; & promoting cooperation on governmental matters related to Aboriginal affairs.

Minister, Hon. Ernie Hudson
Tel: 902-368-5250; *Fax:* 902-368-4121
ehhudsonminister@gov.pe.ca

Deputy Minister, Mark Spidel
Tel: 902-368-5290; *Fax:* 902-368-4121
maspidel@gov.pe.ca

Associated Agencies, Boards & Commissions:
• **Community Care Facilities & Nursing Homes Board**
Tel: 902-368-4953
The Board issues licenses to community care facilities & nursing homes.

• **Council of the Association of Registered Nurses of PEI (ARNPEI)**
#6, 161 Maypoint Rd.
Charlottetown, PE C1E 1X6
Tel: 902-368-3764; *Fax:* 902-368-1430
Toll-free: 844-843-3933
info@arnpei.ca
www.arnpei.ca

• **Council of the College of Physicians & Surgeons of PEI (CPSPEI)**
14 Paramount Dr.
Charlottetown, PE C1E 0C7
Tel: 902-566-3861; *Fax:* 902-566-3986
cpspei.ca

• **Council of the Denturist Society of PEI**
c/o Accu-Bite Denture Clinic
500 Main St.
PO Box 1589
Montague, PE C0A 1R0
Tel: 902-838-2350

• **Council of the PEI Chiropractic Association**
228 Grafton St.
Charlottetown, PE C1A 1L5
Tel: 902-894-4400; *Fax:* 902-894-3762
www.peichiropractic.ca

• **Council of the PEI College of Physiotherapists (PEICPT)**
PO Box 20078
Charlottetown, PE C1A 9E3
contact@peicpt.com
www.peicpt.com

• **Dental Council of PEI**
184 Belvedere Ave.
Charlottetown, PE C1A 2Z1
Tel: 902-628-8156; *Fax:* 902-892-0234
info@dcpei.ca
www.dcpei.ca

• **Dietitians Registration Board (PEIDRB)**
PO Box 362
Charlottetown, PE C1A 7K7
info@peidietitians.ca
www.peidietitians.ca

• **Dispensing Opticians Board**
• **Emergency Medical Services Board**
• **Financial Assistance Appeal Panel**
• **Health PEI**
See Entry Name Index for detailed listing.
• **Medical Advisory Committee**
• **Mental Health Review Board**
• **Nurse Practitioner Diagnostic & Therapeutics Committee**
• **Prince Edward Island College of Optometrists**
15 Ellis Rd.
Charlottetown, PE C1A 9B3
Tel: 902-368-3001; *Fax:* 902-628-6604
info@peico.ca
www.peico.ca

• **Prince Edward Island Funeral Services & Professions Board**
• **Prince Edward Island Licensed Practical Nurses Registration Board (PEILPNRB)**
#204, 155 Belvedere Ave.
Charlottetown, PE C1A 2Y9
Tel: 902-566-1512
peilpnrb.ca

• **Prince Edward Island Occupational Therapists Registration Board**
PO Box 2248 Central
Charlottetown, PE C1A 8B9
www.peiot.org/board-home-page

• **Prince Edward Island College of Pharmacists**
375 Trans Canada Hwy.
PO Box 208
Cornwall, PE C0A 1H0
Tel: 902-628-3561; *Fax:* 902-628-6946
info@pepharmacists.ca
www.pepharmacists.ca
The Prince Edward Island College of Pharmacists regulates the practice of pharmacy in Prince Edward Island. Its goal is to promote high standards of pharmaceutical service for the welfare of the public.

• **Prince Edward Island Psychologists Registration Board (PEIPRB)**
c/o Dept. of Psychology, UPEI
550 University Ave.
Charlottetown, PE C1A 4P3
Tel: 902-566-0549
www.peipsychology.org/peiprb

• **Prince Edward Island Sports Hall of Fame & Museum, Inc. Board**
40 Enman Cres.
Charlottetown, PE C1E 1E6
Tel: 902-393-5474
peisportshall@gmail.com

• **Pharmaceutical Information Program Advisory Committee**
• **Physician Resource Planning Committee**

Chief Public Health Office
Sullivan Bldg., 16 Fitzroy St., Charlottetown, PE C1A 7N8
Tel: 902-368-4996
The Chief Health Office administers & enforces the Public Health Act. The office also delivers services in the following areas:

environmental health, epidemiology, reproductive care, & vital statistics.
Chief Public Health Officer, Dr. Heather G. Morrison
Tel: 902-368-4996; *Fax:* 902-620-3354
hgmorrison@gov.pe.ca
Provincial Epidemiologist, Dr. Shamara Baidoobonso
Tel: 902-368-4943
sbaidoobonso@ihis.org

Finance & Corporate Management
The Finance & Corporate Management Division supports the Department of Health & Wellness in the areas of finances, human resources, communications, & the administration of the Freedom of Information & Protection of Privacy Act.
Director, Kevin Barnes
Tel: 902-368-4865; *Fax:* 902-368-4224
kcbarnes@gov.pe.ca

Health Policy & Programs
The Health Policy & Programs Division supports the Department of Health & Wellness. It includes the Health Recruitment & Retention section.
Director, Kevin Barnes
Tel: 902-368-4865; *Fax:* 902-368-4224
kcbarnes@gov.pe.ca

Sport, Recreation & Physical Activity
Tel: 902-368-4789; *Fax:* 902-368-4224
www.teampei.ca
twitter.com/Team_PEI
www.facebook.com/Team-PEI-Canada-Games-17635112905663 0
The main role of this division is to encourage citizens of Prince Edward Island to be active. Sport, recreation, & other physical activities are promoted.
Consultation services & grants are available for community, regional, & provincial groups.
Director, John Morrison
Tel: 902-894-0283; *Fax:* 902-368-4224
jwmorris@gov.pe.ca

Health PEI

16 Garfield St., PO Box 2000 Charlottetown, PE C1A 7N8
Tel: 902-368-6130; *Fax:* 902-368-6136
healthinput@gov.pe.ca
www.healthpei.ca
twitter.com/Health_PEI
When the Health Services Act was proclaimed in 2010, Health PEI took on responsibility for the operation & delivery of health services in the province.
The main goals of Health PEI are to improve access to quality health care across Prince Edward Island & to develop more consistent standards & practices for health services

Chair, Derek Key

Chief Executive Officer, Dr. Michael Gardam

Chief, Nursing, Allied Health & Patient Experience, Marion H. Dowling
Tel: 902-894-2356; *Fax:* 902-894-2416
mhdowling@gov.pe.ca

Executive Director, Quality & Safety, Rick Adams
Tel: 902-368-5804; *Fax:* 902-368-6136
radams@gov.pe.ca

Executive Director, Medical Affairs and Legal Services, Dr. André Celliers
acelliers@ihis.org

Executive Director, Human Resources, Tanya Tynski
Tel: 902-368-6257; *Fax:* 902-368-4969
tmtynski@gov.pe.ca

Corporate Services
Executive Director, Kellie C. Hawes
Tel: 902-368-6125; *Fax:* 902-368-6136
kchawes@ihis.org
Director, Materials Management, Todd G. Gillis
Tel: 902-894-2097; *Fax:* 902-894-2384
gtgillis@ihis.org
Director, eHealth Clinical Operations, Robin Laird
Tel: 902-620-3869; *Fax:* 902-620-3388
rlaird@ihis.org
Director, Facility & Capital Planning, Marsha Pyke
Tel: 902-620-3329; *Fax:* 902-368-6136
mlpyke@gov.pe.ca

Emergency Health Services, Long-Term Care & Hospital Services East
www.healthpei.ca/hospitals

Chief Administrative Officer, Jamie MacDonald
Tel: 902-894-2350; *Fax:* 902-894-2416
jamiemacdonald@gov.pe.ca
Director, Facilities Management, Kevin Barry
Tel: 902-894-2032; *Fax:* 902-894-2386
kpbarry@gov.pe.ca
Director, Support Services, Terry Campbell
Tel: 902-894-2353; *Fax:* 902-894-2416
tscampbell@gov.pe.ca
Director, Medical Affairs & Legal Services, Dr. Lori L. Ellis
Tel: 902-620-3692; *Fax:* 902-620-3072
llellis@gov.pe.ca
Director, Environmental Services, Ken Hughes
kjhughes@gov.pe.ca
Director, Long-Term Care, Andrew MacDougall
asmacdougall@gov.pe.ca
Director, Nursing, Queen Elizabeth Hospital & Community Hospitals East, Sandra MacKay
sgmackay@ihis.org
Acting Director, Provincial Diagnostic Imaging Services, Gailyne MacPherson
Tel: 902-894-2979; *Fax:* 902-894-2276
tgmacpherson@gov.pe.ca
Director, Support Services, Marsha Pyke
Tel: 902-438-4530; *Fax:* 902-438-4381
mlpyke@gov.pe.ca
Director, Hospital Services, Kelley Rayner
Tel: 902-894-2364; *Fax:* 902-894-2416
kjrayner@gov.pe.ca
Director, Pharmacy Services, Iain D. Smith
Tel: 902-894-0292; *Fax:* 902-894-2911
idsmith@gov.pe.ca
Director, Emergency Health & Planning Services, James Sullivan
Tel: 902-368-6719; *Fax:* 902-620-3072
jasullivan@gov.pe.ca

Family & Community Medicine & Hospital Services West
www.healthpei.ca/hospitals
Chief Administrative Officer, Arlene Gallant-Bernard
Tel: 902-438-4514; *Fax:* 902-438-4381
algallant-bernard@gov.pe.ca
Director, Hospital Services & Provincial Renal Program, Cheryl Banks
Tel: 902-438-4519
cabanks@gov.pe.ca
Director, Nursing, Cathy DesRoches
Tel: 902-438-4516
cddesroches@gov.pe.ca
Director, Primary Care & Chronic Disease, Anita A. MacKenzie
Tel: 902-569-7640; *Fax:* 902-569-0579
ahmackenzie@ihis.org
Director, Prince County Hospital Foundation, Heather Matheson
Tel: 902-432-2834; *Fax:* 902-432-2551
hematheson@ihis.org
Director, Home Care, Palliative & Geriatric Care, Mary Sullivan
Tel: 902-569-7646; *Fax:* 902-368-6136
mksullivan@gov.pe.ca

Mental Health & Addictions Services
www.healthpei.ca/mentalhealth
Other Communication: Island Helpline: 800-218-2885
Chief Administrative Officer, Verna Ryan
Tel: 902-368-6197; *Fax:* 902-569-0579
vryan@gov.pe.ca
Senior Director, Capital Planning, Wayne Walker
Tel: 902-368-6547
waynewalker@ihis.org
Acting Director, Nursing & Manager, Clinical Services, Tanya Machon
Tel: 902-368-5413; *Fax:* 902-368-4195
tdmachon@ihis.org

Prince Edward Island Human Rights Commission

53 Water St., PO Box 2000 Charlottetown, PE C1A 7N8
Tel: 902-368-4180; *Fax:* 902-368-4236
Toll-Free: 800-237-5031
contact@peihumanrights.ca
www.gov.pe.ca/humanrights
The Prince Edward Island Human Rights Act is administered & enforced by the Prince Edward Island Human Rights Commission.
The Commission receives, investigates, & settles & makes rulings on complaints. Other tasks of the Commission include the development of public information & educational programs & the provision of advice to the government about human rights issues.

Chair, John G. Rogers

Commissioner, Carmen de Pontbriand

Commissioner, Joanne Inges

Commissioner, George Lyle

Commissioner, Lori St. Onge

Commissioner, Maurice H.J. Rio

Executive Director, Brenda J. Picard, Q.C.
Tel: 902-368-4134; *Fax:* 902-368-4236
bpicard@peihumanrights.ca

Prince Edward Island Department of Justice & Public Safety

Shaw Bldg. South, 95 Rochford St., 4th Fl., PO Box 2000 Charlottetown, PE C1A 7N8
Tel: 902-368-4589; *Fax:* 902-368-5283
DeptJPS@gov.pe.ca
www.princeedwardisland.ca/en/topic/justice-and-public-safety
Other Communication: Corporations: 902-368-4550

Minister; Attorney General, Hon. Bloyce Thompson
Tel: 902-368-5152; *Fax:* 902-368-4910
MinisterJPS@gov.pe.ca

Acting Deputy Minister & Deputy Attorney General, Karen MacDonald
karenmacdonald@gov.pe.ca

Associated Agencies, Boards & Commissions:
• **Court Transcribers Examining Board**
• **Credit Union Deposit Insurance Corporation (CUDIC)**
#209, 281 University Ave.
Charlottetown, PE C1A 4M3
Tel: 902-628-6280; *Fax:* 902-628-8147
info@peicudic.com
www.peicudic.com
• **Employment Standards Board**
The Employment Standards Board listens to appeals from employers regarding alleged violations of the Employment Standards Act. The Employment Standards Board is also responsible for presenting recommendations about the Minimum Wage Order to the Lieutenant Governor in Council.
• **Judicial Remuneration Review Commission**
• **Labour Relations Board**
Sherwood Business Centre
161 St. Peters Rd.
PO Box 2000
Charlottetown, PE C1A 7N8
Tel: 902-368-5550; *Fax:* 902-368-5476
Toll-free: 800-333-4362
www.princeedwardisland.ca/en/topic/labour-relations-board
The Labour Relations Board works to resolve applications received from labour or management, in accordance with Prince Edward Island's Labour Act.
• **Law Society of Prince Edward Island Council (LSPEI)**
49 Water St.
PO Box 128
Charlottetown, PE C1A 7K2
Tel: 902-566-1666; *Fax:* 902-368-7557
lawsociety@lspei.pe.ca
lawsocietypei.ca
• **Prince Edward Island Criminal Code Review Board**
• **Prince Edward Island Human Rights Commission**
See Entry Name Index for detailed listing.
• **Prince Edward Island Workers Compensation Board**
See Entry Name Index for detailed listing.
• **Office of the Police Commissioner**
114 Kent St.
PO Box 427
Charlottetown, PE C1A 7K7
Tel: 902-368-7200; *Fax:* 902-368-1123
Toll-free: 877-541-7204
office@policecommissioner.pe.ca
www.policecommissioner.pe.ca
The Office of the Police Commissioner investigates & resolves complaints about the unprofessional conduct of police, other than the RCMP. Under the Police Act, a person who is 18 years of age & over, who has been directly affected by the conduct of municipal police officer, may make a complaint. The Office of the Police Commissioner also handles complaints about a chief of a municipal police service, a director or instructing officer at the Atlantic Police Academy, or a security police officer at the University of Prince Edward Island. The independent statutory office works to carry out its mission in a timely & impartial manner.
Persons must call the Office of the Police Commissioner to book an appointment.

• **Public Trustee Advisory Committee**
• **Supreme Court Finance Committee**
• **Victim Services Advisory Committee**
• **Workers Compensation Appeal Tribunal (WCAT)**
c/o Executive Council
95 Rochford St.
PO Box 2000
Charlottetown, PE C1A 7N8
Tel: 902-569-0545
Established under Prince Edward Island's Worker's Compensation Act, the Workers Compensation Appeal Tribunal operates as an independent quasi-judicial administrative tribunal. Workers or employers who are dissatisfied with a decision made by the Internal Reconsideration Officer can appeal it through the Workers Compensation Appeal Tribunal. The appeal body is the last level of appeal for workers' compensation matters.
The Office of the Workers Compensation Appeal Tribunal Coordinator is responsible for administrative duties related to the tribunal. The coordinator attends all hearings, but is not part of the decision making process.

Community & Correctional Services
Shaw Bldg., #95, 105 Rochford St., Charlottetown, PE C1A 7N8
The Community & Correctional Services Division provides community & custody programs to contribute to the rehabilitation of youth & adult offenders. The division also offers the following services: research; policy development; support services to the courts & victims of crime; crime prevention programs; & public education.
The work of the Community & Correctional Services Division is conducted by the following sections: Community Programs; Correctional Programs; Victim Services; & Clinical Services.
Director, Vacant
Provincial Manager, Community Programs, Gary Trainor
Tel: 902-368-5295; *Fax:* 902-368-4579
gjtrainor@gov.pe.ca
Provincial Manager, Victim Services, Susan Maynard
Tel: 902-368-4584; *Fax:* 902-368-4514
smaynard@gov.pe.ca
Provincial Manager, Custody Programs, Donna Myers
Tel: 902-569-7680; *Fax:* 902-569-7711
dfmyers@gov.pe.ca
Manager, Correctional Programs, Allan J. Curley
Tel: 902-569-7763; *Fax:* 902-569-7711
ajcurley@gov.pe.ca
Supervisor, Probation Services, Darlene Dawson
Tel: 902-368-4697; *Fax:* 902-368-4579
dndawson@gov.pe.ca
Acting Manager, Youth Justice Services, Philip Duffy
Tel: 902-368-4578; *Fax:* 902-368-4579
pvduffy@gov.pe.ca
Manager, Correctional Programs, Kim Kempton
Tel: 902-368-4885; *Fax:* 902-368-5834
kjkempton@gov.pe.ca
Manager, Prince Correctional Centre, Gordon Roche
Tel: 902-888-8209; *Fax:* 902-888-8464
gmroche@gov.pe.ca
Manager, Corporate Services, Denise M. Spenceley
Tel: 902-569-7681; *Fax:* 902-569-7711
dmspenceley@gov.pe.ca

Consumer, Corporate, & Insurance
Shaw Bldg., 95 Rochford St., 4th Fl., PO Box 2000 Charlottetown, PE C1A 7N8
Tel: 902-368-4550; *Fax:* 902-368-5283
The Consumer, Labour, & Financial Services Division consists of the following sections: Consumer Affairs; Corporations; Securities; Firearms Office; & Insurance & Real Estate.
The Consumer Affairs section administers the Lottery Schemes Order. It also responds to complaints & inquiries from consumers.
The Corporations section handles the registration of partnerships & business names. It also oversees the incorporation of companies, non-profit corporations, co-operatives, & credit unions.
The Securities Act is administered & enforced by the Securities Division.
The Gun Control Program is administered by the Firearms Office, in accordance with the Criminal Code of Canada & the federal Firearms Act. The Firearms Office is also responsible for the administration of the Private Investigators & Security Guards Act.
Under the supervision of the Superintendent of Insurance, the Insurance & Real Estate section administers the Fire Prevention Act, the Insurance Act, the Premium Tax Act, & the Real Estate Trading Act.
Director, Steve Dowling
Tel: 902-368-4551; *Fax:* 902-368-5283
sddowling@gov.pe.ca

Manager, Vital Statistics, Adam Peters
Tel: 902-368-5653; *Fax:* 902-368-5283
ajpeters@gov.pe.ca
Superintendent, Insurance, Robert Bradley
Tel: 902-368-6478; *Fax:* 902-368-5283
rabradley@gov.pe.ca
Corporations Officer, Corporation Section, Mary Roach
Tel: 902-368-4509; *Fax:* 902-368-5283
mvroach@gov.pe.ca

Family Law & Court Services
Director, Maintenance Enforcement Program, Norma I. Reardon
Tel: 902-368-6499; *Fax:* 902-368-6934
nireardon@gov.pe.ca
Public Trustee, Jessie M. Frost-Wicks
Tel: 902-368-4552; *Fax:* 902-368-5335
jmwicks@gov.pe.ca
Chief Sheriff, Court Services Section, Ron Dowling
Tel: 902-368-6055; *Fax:* 902-368-6571
rjdowling@gov.pe.ca

Legal & Policy Services
Director, Gary Demeulenaere
Tel: 902-368-4554
gdemeulenaere@gov.pe.ca
Chief Legislative Counsel, Peter F. Allison
Tel: 902-368-4553
pfallison@gov.pe.ca
Manager, Blair Barbour
Tel: 902-368-5010
Bwbarbour@gov.pe.ca

Legal Aid
40 Great George St., PO Box 2000 Charlottetown, PE C1A 7N8
The Legal Aid program in Prince Edward Island is staffed by lawyers who offer direct assistance to legal aid clients in the areas of family & criminal law. In order to be eligible for these legal services, potential clients are required to take a financial means test.
Funding of the family legal aid program is provided by the province of Prince Edward Island & the Prince Edward Island Law Foundation. Prince Edward Island & Canada fund the criminal legal aid program.
Director, W. Kent Brown, Q.C.
Tel: 902-368-6015; *Fax:* 902-368-6122
wkbrown@gov.pe.ca
Manager/Lawyer, Criminal Legal Aid, Summerside Location, Patricia L. Cheverie, Q.C.
Tel: 902-888-8220; *Fax:* 902-438-4071
tlcheverie@gov.pe.ca
Lawyer, Family Legal Aid, Charlottetown Location, Leslie A. Collins, Q.C.
Tel: 902-368-6540; *Fax:* 902-620-3083
lacollins@gov.pe.ca
Lawyer, Criminal Legal Aid, Charlottetown Location, Thane A. MacEachern, Q.C.
Tel: 902-368-6017; *Fax:* 902-368-6122
tamaceachern@gov.pe.ca

Public Safety
National Bank Tower, #600, 134 Kent St., Charlottetown, PE C1A 8R8
Tel: 902-894-0385; *Fax:* 902-368-6362
twitter.com/PEIPublicSafety
www.facebook.com/PEIPublicSafety
The Public Safety Division includes the following sections: 911 Administration Office; Emergency Measures Organization; Fire Marshal's Office; & the Office for Business Continuity Management Planning.
Director, 911 Administration, Aaron Campbell
Tel: 902-620-3632
acampbell@gov.pe.ca
Fire Marshal, Fire Marshal's Office, David Rossiter
Tel: 902-368-4869; *Fax:* 902-368-5526
derossiter@gov.pe.ca
Deputy Fire Marshal, Fire Marshal's Office, Robert Arsenault
Tel: 902-368-4893; *Fax:* 902-368-5526
robarsenault@gov.pe.ca
Chief Firearms Officer, Vivian Hayward
Tel: 902-368-4585; *Fax:* 902-368-5198
vdhayward@gov.pe.ca
Acting Provincial Coordinator, 911 Administration, Pat J. Kelly
Tel: 902-894-0299; *Fax:* 902-368-6362
pjkelly@gov.pe.ca
Provincial Emergency Management Coordinator, Emergency Measures Organization, Tanya Mullally
Tel: 902-368-5980; *Fax:* 902-368-6362
tlmullally@gov.pe.ca
Manager, Investigation & Enforcement, Wade MacKinnon
Tel: 902-368-4884; *Fax:* 902-368-5198
wjmackinnon@gov.pe.ca

Prince Edward Island Liquor Control Commission (PEILCC)

3 Garfield St., PO Box 967 Charlottetown, PE C1A 7M4
Tel: 902-368-5710; *Fax:* 902-368-5735
liquorpei.com
twitter.com/PEILiquor
www.facebook.com/liquorpei
www.instagram.com/peiliquor

Under the authority of the Liquor Control Act & Regulations, the Prince Edward Island Liquor Control Commission is responsible for managing the distribution of alcohol & regulating the sale & purchase of all alcoholic beverages. The crown corporation also administers the operation of seventeen retail liquor stores across the province. Licenses are issued by the commission for dining rooms, clubs, lounges, special premises, military canteens, & caterers & waiters.
As of 2018, the PEILCC is also responsible for the control & sale of cannabis in partnership with the Prince Edward Island Cannabis Management Corporation (PEICMC, or PEI Cannabis).

Chair, Quentin Bevan

Interim Chief Executive Officer, James MacLeod
jcmacleod@liquorpei.com

Chief Financial Officer, Carl Adams
Tel: 902-368-5718
cjadams@liquorpei.com

Prince Edward Island Regulatory & Appeals Commission (IRAC) / Commission de réglementation et d'appels

National Bank Tower, #501, 134 Kent St., PO Box 577
Charlottetown, PE C1A 7L1
Tel: 902-892-3501; *Fax:* 902-566-4076
Toll-Free: 800-501-6268
info@irac.pe.ca
www.irac.pe.ca

Prince Edward Island's Regulatory & Appeals Commission was established in 1991, with the amalgamation of the Office of the Director of Residential Property, the Public Utilities Commission, & the Land Use Commission.
Operating under the authority of the Island Regulatory & Appeals Commission Act, the Regulatory & Appeals Commission works at arms-length from the provincial government to administer statutes dealing with economic regulation. The quasi-judicial tribunal also listens to appeals dealing with property & revenue sales tax, land use, & unsightly premises.
The Regulatory & Appeals Commission reports to the Legislative Assembly of Prince Edward Island through the Minister of Education & Early Childhood Development.

Chair & Chief Executive Officer, J. Scott MacKenzie, Q.C.

Vice-Chair, Doug Clow, CPA, CA

Full-time Commissioner, John Broderick

Director, Regulatory Services, Allison MacEwen
amacewen@irac.pe.ca

Director, Residential Rental Property, Jennifer L. Perry
jperry@irac.pe.ca

Prince Edward Island Department of Social Development & Housing

Jones Bldg., 11 Kent St., 2nd Fl., PO Box 2000
Charlottetown, PE C1A 7N8
Tel: 902-620-3777; *Fax:* 902-368-4740
Toll-Free: 866-594-3777
DeptSDH@gov.pe.ca
www.gov.pe.ca/sss

Formerly the Department of Family & Human Services, & renamed after the 2019 general election. Oversees the following areas: Child & family; housing; people with disabilities; seniors; & supports & services.

Minister, Hon. Brad Trivers
Tel: 902-620-3777; *Fax:* 902-368-4740
MinisterSDH@gov.pe.ca

Deputy Minister, David Keedwell
Tel: 902-368-6520
dkeedwell@gov.pe.ca

Assistant Deputy Minister, Deborah Bradley
Tel: 902-368-4588
mdbradley@gov.pe.ca

Associated Agencies, Boards & Commissions:

- Alberton Housing Authority
- Charlottetown Area Housing Authority
- Disability Advisory Council

The 19 member Council is responsible for consulting with & advising the provincial government on legislation, policies, programs & services that affect people with disabilities.

- Georgetown Housing Authority
- Montague Housing Authority
- Mount Stewart Housing Authority
- O'Leary Housing Authority
- PEI Social Work Registration Board (PEISWRB)

81 Prince St.
Charlottetown, PE C1A 4R3
Tel: 902-368-7337; *Fax:* 902-368-7180
registrar@socialworkpei.ca
socialworkpei.ca

Regulatory body for the social work profession on Prince Edward Island, seeking to protect the public from preventable harm.

- Premier's Action Committee on Family Violence Prevention

c/o Child and Family Services Division
161 St. Peters Rd.
PO Box 2000
Charlottetown, PE C1A 7N8
Tel: 902-368-6712; *Fax:* 902-620-3362
www.stopfamilyviolence.pe.ca

- Seniors' Secretariat
- Social Assistance Appeal Board
- Souris Housing Authority
- Summerside Housing Authority
- Tignish Housing Authority

Child & Family Services

The Child & Family Services Division offers a wide range of programs & services to care for Prince Edward Island's children & families. Examples of programs include child protection, foster care, & adoption services.
Director, Sean Morrison
Tel: 902-368-5396; *Fax:* 902-368-4258
msmorrison@gov.pe.ca
Director, Child Protection, Wendy L. McCourt
Tel: 902-368-6515; *Fax:* 902-620-3776
wlmccourt@gov.pe.ca

Corporate Support & Seniors

Corporate Support & Seniors has responsibility for the Senior's Secretariat / the Office of Seniors, records information management, French Language Services, intergovernmental & external relations, & emergency social services.
Acting Director, Planning, Policy & Innovation, Jennifer Burgess
Tel: 902-368-5199; *Fax:* 902-894-0242
jmburgess@gov.pe.ca

Housing Services

The Housing Services Division is responsible for the following areas: finance, administration, human resources, communications, French language services, intergovernmental & external relations, records information management, & emergency social services.
Director, Sonya L. Cobb
Tel: 902-368-5973; *Fax:* 902-894-0242
slcobb@gov.pe.ca

Social Programs

The Social Programs Division provides services related to social assistance & disability support.
Acting Director, Patrick MacDonald
Tel: 902-368-5118
pwmacdonald@gov.pe.ca
Provincial Manager, Residential & Support Services, Joe Coade
Tel: 902-368-4634
jcoade@gov.pe.ca

Prince Edward Island Department of Transportation & Infrastructure

Jones Bldg., 11 Kent St., 3rd Fl., PO Box 2000
Charlottetown, PE C1A 7N8
Tel: 902-368-5100; *Fax:* 902-368-5395
DeptTIE@gov.pe.ca
Other Communication: URL:
www.princeedwardisland.ca/en/topic/transportation-and-infrastructure

Prince Edward Island's Department of Transportation & Infrastructure maintains & enhances transportation systems & services throughout the province to ensure the safe & efficient movement of people, goods, & services.
The department also works to provide necessary infrastructure for the efficient operation of government. The department is therefore involved in crown land management & building construction & maintenance.

Minister, Hon. James Aylward
Tel: 902-368-5120; *Fax:* 902-368-5395
jsjaylwardMinister@gov.pe.ca

Deputy Minister, Darren Chiasson, P.Eng.
Tel: 902-368-5130; *Fax:* 902-368-5385
ddchiasson@gov.pe.ca

Associated Agencies, Boards & Commissions:

- 100099 P.E.I. Inc.
- Advisory Council on the Status of Women

Sherwood Business Centre
161 St. Peter's Rd., Main Level
PO Box 2000
Charlottetown, PE C1A 7N8
Tel: 902-368-4510; *Fax:* 902-368-3269
info@peistatusofwomen.ca
www.gov.pe.ca/acsw

The Prince Edward Island Advisory Council on the Status of Women consists of nine members. Members are appointed by government to serve on the government advisory agency. The Council advises the Minister Responsible for the Status of Women & works to support equality & the participation of women in economic, political, legal, & cultural activities.

- C.V.C. Management Inc.
- Crown Building Corporation
- Island Waste Management Corporation (IWMC)

110 Watts Ave.
Charlottetown, PE C1E 2C1
Tel: 902-882-0525; *Fax:* 902-894-0331
Toll-free: 888-280-8111
info@iwmc.pe.ca
www.iwmc.pe.ca
Other Communication: Customer Service Fax: 902-882-0520

The Island Waste Management Corporation is a provincial Crown Corporation that was formed in 1999, according to the Environmental Act R.S.P.E.I. 1988, Cap. E-9. Conducting business throughout Prince Edward Island, the corporation administers & provides solid waste management services to both commercial & residential sectors.
One of the Island Waste Management Corporation's successful environmental programs is Waste Watch. Everyone in Prince Edward Island must separate waste into one of three categories: compost, marketable recyclable material, & waste. Waste Watch Drop-Off Centres also accept household hazardous waste free of charge.
In addition to operating the Waste Watch Drop-Off Centres, the Island Waste Management Corporation also operates or oversees the following facilities: Central Compost Facility, East Prince Waste Management Facility, & the Energy from Waste Facility.

- Land Surveyors Board of Examiners
- Prince Edward Island Energy Corporation

Sullivan Bldg.
16 Fitzroy St.
PO Box 2000
Charlottetown, PE C1A 7N8
www.peiec.ca

The Prince Edward Island Energy Corporation promotes the development, generation, transmission, & distribution of energy in an economic & efficient manner.

Access PEI

Charlottetown Office, 33 Riverside Dr., Charlottetown, PE C1A 7N8
Tel: 902-368-5200; *Fax:* 902-569-7560
accesspeicharlottetown@gov.pe.ca

Prince Edward Island Provincial Government services are available at government service centres, known as Access PEI locations. At the eight Access PEI centres across Prince Edward Island, citizens obtain information about the Provincial Government & its programs.
The Access PEI Centres are situated in the following places:
Alberton (902-853-8622);
Charlottetown (902-368-5200);
Montague (902-838-0600);
O'Leary (902-859-8800);
Souris' Johnny Ross Young Service Centre (902-687-7000);
Summerside (902-888-8000);
Tignish (902-882-7351); &
Wellington (902-854-7250).
Director, Mark Arsenault
mxarsenault@gov.pe.ca
Manager, Access PEI Summerside & PEI Wellington, Leah Smallwood
Tel: 902-888-8001; *Fax:* 902-888-8306
Other Communications: Access PEI Wellington:
accesspeiwellington@gov.pe.ca

Access PEI Summerside
120 Heather Moyse Dr.
Summerside, PE C1N 5Y8
Manager, Access PEI Montague & Access PEI Souris, Lori
Deveaux-MacKinnon
Tel: 902-687-7050; *Fax:* 902-687-7051
lmdeveaux@gov.pe.ca
Other Communications: Access PEI Souris, Email:
accesspeisouris@gov.pe.ca
Access PEI Souris, Johnny Ross Young Services Centre
15 Green St.
PO Box 550
Souris, PE C0A 2B0
Manager, Access PEI Alberton, Access PEI O'Leary, & Access
PEI Tignish, Martha Dawson
Tel: 902-859-8801; *Fax:* 902-859-8709
accesspeialberton@gov.pe.ca
Other Communications: Access PEI Tignish Email:
accesspeitignish@gov.pe.ca
Access PEI O'Leary
45 East Dr.
PO Box 8
O'Leary, PE C0B 1V0

Capital Projects

Jones Bldg., 11 Kent St., 3rd Fl., Charlottetown, PE C1A 7N8
The following sections make up the Capital Projects Division:
Engineering Services; Highway Construction; Materials Lab; &
Planning & Design. Staff take care of the design & construction
of highways & building infrastructure.
Director & Chief Engineer, Stephen J. Yeo, P.Eng.
Tel: 902-368-5105; *Fax:* 902-368-5425
sjyeo@gov.pe.ca
Manager, Materials Lab, Terry Kelly, P.Eng.
Tel: 902-676-7979; *Fax:* 902-676-7994
jtkelly@gov.pe.ca
Manager, Design & Bridge Maintenance, Darrell Evans, P.Eng.
Tel: 902-569-0578; *Fax:* 902-368-5395
djevans@gov.pe.ca
Manager, GIS-T, Dan MacDonald
Tel: 902-368-5158; *Fax:* 902-368-5425
wdmacdonald@gov.pe.ca
Manager, Traffic Data Collection & Analysis, Orooba H.
Mohammed
Tel: 902-368-5107; *Fax:* 902-368-5425
ohmohammed@gov.pe.ca

Energy & Minerals

Jones Bldg., 4th Fl., PO Box 2000 Charlottetown PE C1A
7N8
The Energy & Minerals Division is engaged in the following
activities: developing & managing energy policies & programs;
overseeing the development of mineral resources; & supporting
gas exploration.
Director, Kim Horrelt, P.Eng.
Tel: 902-894-0289; *Fax:* 902-894-0290
kdhorrelt@gov.pe.ca

Finance & Human Resources

Jones Bldg., 11 Kent St., 2nd Fl., Charlottetown, PE C1A
7N8
Director, Wendy L. MacDonald, CA
Tel: 902-368-5126; *Fax:* 902-368-5395
wlmacdonald@gov.pe.ca
Manager, Human Resources, Jason J. Rendell
Tel: 902-620-3356
jjrendell@gov.pe.ca

Highway Maintenance

Park St. & Riverside Dr. Provincial Headquarters, PO Box
2000 Charlottetown, PE C1A 7N8
The Highway Maintenance Division is responsible for the upkeep
of the total provincial highway system.
Acting Director, Stephen J. Szwarc
Tel: 902-368-5103
sjszwarc@gov.pe.ca
Acting Assistant Director, Matthew Fortier
Tel: 902-368-3286
mfortier@gov.pe.ca
Manager, Fleet, Wilfred J. MacDonald
Tel: 902-368-5222; *Fax:* 902-368-5994
wjmacdonald@gov.pe.ca

Highway Safety

33 Riverside Dr., Charlottetown, PE C1A 9R9
Safety issues from the province's highways are handled by the
Highway Safety Division.
Director & Registrar, Graham L. Miner
Tel: 902-368-5223; *Fax:* 902-368-5236
glminer@gov.pe.ca
Registrar of Motor Vehicles, Doug J. MacEwen
Tel: 902-368-5219; *Fax:* 902-368-5236
djmacewen@gov.pe.ca

Land & Environment

Jones Bldg., 11 Kent St., 3rd Fl., PO Box 2000
Charlottetown, PE C1A 7N8
The Land & Environment Division is responsible for provincial
lands. Environmental services are also provided by the Land &
Environment Division for projects related to transportation &
public works. Staff members ensure compliance with provincial &
federal environmental legislation & regulations during highway
construction & maintenance projects.
Director, Brian F. Thompson, P.Eng.
Tel: 902-368-5185; *Fax:* 902-368-5395
bfthompson@gov.pe.ca
Chief Surveyor, Wayne Tremblay
Tel: 902-368-5143; *Fax:* 902-620-3033
wltremblay@gov.pe.ca
Manager, Provincial Lands, Carol Craswell, BBA
Tel: 902-368-6119; *Fax:* 902-368-5395
cmcraswell@gov.pe.ca

Public Works & Planning

Jones Bldg., 11 Kent St., 3rd Fl., Charlottetown, PE C1A 7N8
The Public Works & Planning Division is engaged in the
following activities: analyzing long term transportation
requirements; planning & designing construction projects;
implementing major projects; & maintaining buildings.
Director, Alan Maynard, P.Eng.
Tel: 902-368-5147; *Fax:* 902-569-0590
aemaynard@gov.pe.ca
Manager, General Services, Shawn Heron
Tel: 902-368-5116; *Fax:* 902-368-5395
sjheron@gov.pe.ca
Manager, Building Maintenance & Accommodation, Holly Hinds
Tel: 902-368-4854; *Fax:* 902-368-5395
hahinds@gov.pe.ca
Manager, Building Construction Contract Administration, Kevin
Kennedy
Tel: 902-368-5148; *Fax:* 902-368-5395
kjkennedy@gov.pe.ca
Manager, Building Design & Construction, Tyler Richardson,
P.Eng.
Tel: 902-368-4249; *Fax:* 902-569-0590
ttrichardson@gov.pe.ca

Infrastructure Secretariat

#303, 75 Fitzroy St., PO Box 2000 Charlottetown, PE C1A
7N8
Fax: 902-620-3383
Toll-Free: 888-240-4411
cpei-infrastructure@gov.pe.ca
Infrastructure is a joint initiative between the Government of
Prince Edward Island & the Government of Canada.
Provincial Manager, Darlene Rhodenizer
Tel: 902-368-6213; *Fax:* 902-620-3383
dlrhodenizer@gov.pe.ca
Director, Infrastructure, Paul Godfrey, P. Eng.
Tel: 902-368-4849; *Fax:* 902-569-0590
jpgodfrey@gov.pe.ca

Prince Edward Island Workers' Compensation Board (WCB)

14 Weymouth St., PO Box 757 Charlottetown, PE C1A 7L7
Tel: 902-368-5680; *Fax:* 902-368-5696
Toll-Free: 800-237-5049
www.wcb.pe.ca
Other Communication: Customer Liaison Service, Toll-Free
Phone: 866-460-3074; Employer Services, Fax: 902-368-5705
The Workers Compensation Board of Prince Edward Island
operates as an independent, non-profit organization. Prince
Edward Island employers provide funding for the board. Both
workers & employers are served by the Workers Compensation
Board through the promotion of workplace health & safety & the
provision of workplace injury & illness insurance.

Chair, Stuart Affleck

Chief Executive Officer, Cheryl Paynter
Tel: 902-368-5688
cpaynter@wcb.pe.ca

Chief Financial Officer, Norman MacDonald
Tel: 902-620-3047
ncgmacdonald@wcb.pe.ca

Director, Corporate Services, Tory Kennedy
Tel: 902-894-0315
tkennedy@wcb.pe.ca

Director, Workplace Services, Kate Marshall
Tel: 902-368-6358
kmarshall@wcb.pe.ca

Director, Occupational Health & Safety, Danny Miller

Tel: 902-569-7713
jdmiller@wcb.pe.ca

Director, Finance, Tammy Turner
Tel: 902-368-4102
teturner@wcb.pe.ca

Gouvernement du Québec / Government of Québec

Siege du gouvernement: Hôtel du Parlement, 1045, rue des
Parlementaires, Québec, QC G1A 1A3
Tel: 418-644-4545
Ligne sans frais: 877-644-4545
TTY: 800-361-9596
www.quebec.ca
Autres nombres: Montréal, Tél: 514-644-4545
twitter.com/gouvqc
www.facebook.com/GouvQc
La Province de Québec est entrée dans la Confédération le 1ère
juillet, 1867. Terre: 1,356,625.27 kilomètres carrés; Population:
8,164,361 (2016).

Cabinet du Lieutenant-gouverneur / Office of the Lieutenant Governor

**Édifice André-Laurendeau, 1050, rue des Parlementaires
R.C., Québec, QC G1A 1A1**
Tél: 418-643-5385
Téléc: 418-644-4677
Ligne sans frais: 866-791-0766
infoCLG@mce.gouv.qc.ca
www.lieutenant-gouverneur.qc.ca
Rôles constitutionnels et cérémoniels: le lieutenant-gouverneur a
des pouvoirs constitutionnels d'un chef d'État et est le
fonctionnaire exécutif en chef de la province; il/elle donne une
suite légale à la politique déterminée par le gouvernement en ce
qui concerne la nomination du premier ministre, et les membres
du Conseil exécutif, la convocation, la prorogation et la
dissolution de l'Assemblée nationale, la ratification des décrets
du gouvernement, et la nomination des juges des cours de la
province; il/elle occupe le plus haut rang protocolaire du Québec
et il/elle a préséance sur tous les membres de la famille royale,
à l'exception de Sa Majesté qu'il/elle représente

Lieutenant-gouverneur, L'hon. J. Michel Doyon, c.r., LL.L.,
Ph.D., Ad.E.

Cabinet du premier ministre / Office of the Premier

**Édifice Honoré-Mercier, 835, boul René-Lévesque est, 3e
étage, Québec, QC G1A 1B4**
Tél: 418-643-5321
Téléc: 418-643-3924
www.quebec.ca/premier-ministre
Autres nombres: Alt. Tél: 514-873-3411

Premier ministre, L'hon. François Legault

Secrétaire général et greffier du Conseil exécutif, Yves
Ouellet
Tél: 418-643-7355

Ministère du Conseil exécutif / Executive Council

875, Grande Allée est, Québec, QC G1R 4Y8
Tél: 418-644-7600
communication@mce.gouv.qc.ca
www.quebec.ca/gouv/ministere/conseil-executif

**Premier ministre; Ministre responsable, jeunesse,
relations avec les Québécois anglophones, Internet
haute vitesse et des projets spéciaux de connectivité,**
L'hon. François Legault
Tél: 418-643-5321
Téléc: 418-643-3924

**Vice-première ministre; Ministre de la Sécurité publique;
Ministre responsable de la Capitale-Nationale,** L'hon.
Geneviève Guilbault

Ministre de l'Éducation, L'hon. Jean-François Roberge

Ministre de l'Enseignement supérieur, L'hon. Danielle
McCann

**Ministre de l'Économie et de l'Innovation; Ministre
responsable du Développement économique régional,**
L'hon. Pierre Fitzgibbon

Ministre des Finances, L'hon. Éric Girard

Ministre de la Santé et des Services sociaux, L'hon. Christian Dubé

Ministre de l'Environnement; Ministre responsable de la Lutte contre les changements climatiques; Ministre responsable, Lutte contre le racisme et de la région de Laval, L'hon. Benoît Charette

Ministre responsable des Aînés et des Proches aidants, L'hon. Marguerite Blais

Leader parlementaire; Ministre de la Justice; Ministre responsable de la Langue française, de la Laïcité et de la Réforme parlementaire et de la région de la Montérégie, L'hon. Simon Jolin-Barrette

Ministre des Transports; Ministre responsable de la région de l'Estrie, L'hon. François Bonnardel

Ministre responsable des Relations canadiennes et de la Francophonie canadienne, des Institutions démocratiques, de la Réforme électorale et de l'Administration gouvernementale et présidente du Conseil du trésor, L'hon. Sonia LeBel

Ministre de la Famille; Ministre responsable de la région de l'Outaouais, L'hon. Mathieu Lacombe

Ministre des Relations internationales et de la Francophonie; Ministre de l'Immigration, de la Francisation et de l'Intégration; Ministre responsable de la région des Laurentides, L'hon. Nadine Girault

Ministre déléguée aux Transports; Ministre responsable de la métropole et de la région de Montréal, L'hon. Chantal Rouleau

Ministre des Affaires municipales et de l'Habitation; Ministre de la région du Saguenay-Lac-Saint-Jean, L'hon. Andrée Laforest

Ministre de l'Agriculture, des Pêcheries et de l'Alimentation; Ministre responsable, région du Centre-du-Québec et de la région de la Chaudière-Appalaches, L'hon. André Lamontagne

Ministre de l'Énergie et des Ressources naturelles; Ministre responsable de la région de la Côte-Nord, région de la Côte-Nord et de la région de la Gaspésie-Iles-de-la-Madeleine, L'hon. Jonatan Julien

Ministre des Forêts, de la Faune et des Parcs; Ministre responsable de l'Abitibi-Témiscamingue et du Nord-du-Québec, L'hon. Pierre Dufour

Ministre de Travail, de l'Emploi et de la Solidarité sociale; Ministre responsable de la Mauricie, L'hon. Jean Boulet

Ministre de la Culture et des Communications, L'hon. Nathalie Roy

Ministre du Tourisme; Ministre responsable de la région du Bas-Saint-Laurent de la région de Lanaudière, L'hon. Caroline Proulx

Ministre responsable des Affaires autochtones, L'hon. Ian Lafrenière

Ministre déléguée à l'Éducation; Ministre responsable de la Condition féminine, L'hon. Isabelle Charest

Ministre délégué à la Santé et aux Services sociaux, L'hon. Lionel Carmant

Ministre délégué à la Transformation numérique gouvernementale; Leader parlementaire adjoint du gouvernement, Ministre responsable de l'Accès à l'information et de la Protection des renseignements personnels, L'hon. Éric Caire

Ministre déléguée à l'Économie, L'hon. Lucie Lecours

Cabinet du Conseil exécutif / Cabinet Office
875, Grande Allée est, Québec, QC G1R 4Y8
Tél: 418-644-7600
communic@mce.gouv.qc.ca
www.quebec.ca/gouv/ministere/conseil-executif
www.linkedin.com/company/mceqc
Secrétaire général et greffier du Conseil exécutif, Yves Ouellet
Tél: 418-643-7355

Secrétaire général associé, Secrétariat du comité ministériel des services aux citoyens et Bureau de lutte contre le racisme, Stéphane Dolbuc
Secrétaire générale associée, Secrétariat aux emplois supérieurs, Benoît Grenier
Secrétaire général associé, Secrétariat aux priorités et aux projets stratégiques, Carl Lessard
Secrétaire général associé, Secrétariat à la communication gouvernementale, Michel Léveillé
Secrétaire général associé, Secrétariat du comité ministériel de l'économie et de l'environnement, Geneviève Moisan

Comités ministériels / Cabinet Committees
875, Grande Allée est, Québec, QC G1R 4Y8
Tél: 418-643-7355
Téléc: 418-528-9552
quebec.ca/gouv/ministere/conseil-executif/comites-ministeriels
Présidente, Comité ministériel des services aux citoyens, L'hon. Danielle McCann
Président, Comité ministériel de l'économie et de l'environnement, L'hon. Nadine Girault
Présidente, Comité de législation, L'hon. Simon Jolin-Barrette
Président, Conseil du trésor, L'hon. Sonia LeBel

L'Assemblée nationale / National Assembly

Hôtel du Parlement, 1045, rue des Parlementaires, Québec, QC G1A 1A3
Tél: 418-643-7239
Téléc: 418-646-4271
Ligne sans frais: 866-337-8837
renseignements@assnat.qc.ca
www.assnat.qc.ca

Président de l'Assemblée nationale, Président de la Commission de l'Assemblée nationale, et la Sous-commission de la réforme parlementaire, l'hon. François Paradis
Tél: 418-643-2820
Téléc: 418-643-3423
presidentcabinet@assnat.qc.ca

Première vice-président, Marc Picard

Deuxième vice-présidente, Chantal Soucy

Troisième vice-président, Maryse Gaudreault

Leader parlementaire du gouvernement, L'hon. Simon Jolin-Barrette

Leader parlementaire adjoint du gouvernement, L'hon. Éric Caire

Leader parlementaire adjoint du gouvernement, Sébastien Schneeberger

Whip en chef du gouvernement, Éric Lefebvre

Whip adjoint du gouvernement, Geneviève Hébert

Whip adjointe du gouvernement, Sylvain Lévesque

Président du caucus du gouvernement, Mario Laframboise

Cabinet du chef de l'opposition officielle / Office of the Leader of the Official Opposition
Hôtel du Parlement, 1045, rue des Parlementaires, Québec, QC G1A 1A4
Ligne sans frais: 800-463-4575
info@plq.org
plq.org
twitter.com/liberalquebec
www.facebook.com/liberalquebec
Cheffe de l'opposition officielle, Dominique Anglade
chefopposition@assnat.qc.ca
Leader parlementaire de l'opposition officielle, André Fortin
Whip en chef de l'opposition officielle, Filomena Rotiroti
Présidente du caucus de l'opposition officielle, Pierre Arcand

Cabinet du chef du deuxième groupe d'opposition / Office of the Leader of the Second Opposition Group
Hôtel du Parlement, 1045, rue des Parlementaires, Québec, QC G1A 1A4
quebecsolidaire.net
twitter.com/quebecsolidaire
www.facebook.com/quebecsolidaire
Le parti politique n'a pas de chef élu, mais utilise des porte-parole comme représentants.
Chef du deuxième groupe d'opposition, Gabriel Nadeau-Dubois
Leader parlementaire du deuxième groupe d'opposition, Christine Labrie

Quarante-deuxième assemblée nationale / Forty-second National Assembly - Québec

Hôtel du Parlement, 1045, rue des Parlementaires, Québec, QC G1A 1A4
Tél: 418-643-7239
Téléc: 418-646-4271
Ligne sans frais: 866-337-8837
www.assnat.qc.ca
twitter.com/AssnatQc
www.facebook.com/AssnatQc
www.youtube.com/user/quebecassnat
La dernière élection générale: le 1 octobre 2018.
Depuis octobre 2021, la composition de l'Assemblée est la suivante:
Coalition Avenir Québec 75;
Parti Libéral du Québec 28;
Québec solidaire 10;
Parti québécois 7;
Parti conservateur du Québec 1;
Indépendant 4;
Total 125.
Salaires, indemnités, allocations (2021): indemnité annuelle: $95,704 et une allocation de dépenses de $18,179. En plus, le Premier ministre reçoit $100,489, et les ministres, le Leader parlementaire du gouvernement, le Président et le Chef de l'Opposition officielle $71,778.
Par la suite: membre, circonscription, allégeance politique, téléphone & télécopieur, courriel, (Adresse: Hôtel du Parlement, Québec, QC G1A 1A4)

Députés de l'Assemblée nationale
Simon Allaire
Circonscription électorale: Maskinongé *Nombre de constituants:* 44 239, CA
Tél: 418-644-0617
Simon.Allaire.MASK@assnat.qc.ca
Autres numéros: Circ. Tél: 819-228-9722; Téléc: 819-228-0040
Bureau de circonscription
429, boul St-Laurent
Louiseville, QC J5V 1H5
Cheffe de l'opposition officielle, Dominique Anglade
Circonscription électorale: Saint-Henri—Sainte-Anne *Nombre de constituants:* 55 994, Liberal
Tél: 581-628-1854
Dominique.Anglade.SHSA@assnat.qc.ca
Autres numéros: Circ. Tél: 514-933-8796; Téléc: 514-933-4986
Bureau de circonscription
3269, rue Saint-Jacques
Montréal, QC H4C 1G8
Président du caucus de l'opposition officielle, Pierre Arcand
Circonscription électorale: Mont-Royal-Outremont *Nombre de constituants:* 56 659, Liberal
Tél: 418-263-0702
Pierre.Arcand.MROU@assnat.qc.ca
Autres numéros: Circ. Tél: 514-341-1151; Téléc: 514-341-4777
Bureau de circonscription
#201, 5151, rue de la Savane
Montréal, QC H4P 1V1
Chef du troisième groupe d'opposition, Joël Arseneau
Circonscription électorale: Iles-de-la-Madeleine *Nombre de constituants:* 10 729, Parti Québécois
Tél: 418-644-1454
Joel.Arseneau.IDLM@assnat.qc.ca
Autres numéros: Circ. Tél: 418-986-4140; Téléc: 418-986-2577
Bureau de circonscription
625, ch Principal
Cap-aux-Meules, QC G4T 1G3
Mario Asselin
Circonscription électorale: Vanier-Les Rivières *Nombre de constituants:* 57 345, CA
Tél: 418-643-7719
Mario.Asselin.VANI@assnat.qc.ca
Autres numéros: Circ. Tél: 418-644-3107; Téléc: 418-643-9258
Bureau de circonscription
#11, 1170, boul Lebourgneuf
Québec, QC G2K 2E3
André Bachand
Circonscription électorale: Richmond *Nombre de constituants:* 60 502, CA
Tél: 418-263-0546
Ligne sans frais: 800-567-3596
Andre.Bachand.RICM@assnat.qc.ca
Bureau de circonscription
#111B, 1300, boul du Mi-Vallon
Sherbrooke, QC H3Z 1K9
Gaétan Barrette
Circonscription électorale: La Pinière *Nombre de constituants:* 54 534, Liberal

Tél: 581-628-1813
Gaetan.Barrette.LAPI@assnat.qc.ca
Autres numéros: Circ. Tél: 450-678-0611; Téléc:
450-678-1758
twitter.com/drgbarrette
Bureau de circonscription
#425, 6300, av Auteuil
Brossard, QC J4Z 3P2

Gilles Bélanger
Circonscription électorale: Orford *Nombre de constituants:* 43
367, CA
Tél: 418-644-3944
Ligne sans frais: 855-547-3911
Gilles.Belanger.ORFO@assnat.qc.ca
Autres numéros: Circ. Tél: 819-847-3911; Téléc:
818-847-4099
Bureau de circonscription
343, rue Principale ouest
Magog, QC J1X 2B1

Frantz Benjamin
Circonscription électorale: Viau *Nombre de constituants:* 41
646, Liberal
Tél: 581-628-1812
Frantz.Benjamin.VIAU@assnat.qc.ca
Autres numéros: Circ. Tél: 514-728-2474; Téléc:
514-728-2759
Bureau de circonscription
#202, 3333, rue Jarry est
Montréal, QC H1Z 2E5

Pascal Bérubé
Circonscription électorale: Matane-Matapédia *Nombre de
constituants:* 45 840, Parti Québécois
Tél: 418-644-0912
Ligne sans frais: 877-462-0371
Pascal.Berube.MATN@assnat.qc.ca
pq.org/deputes/pascal-berube
Autres numéros: Circ. Tél: 418-562-0371; Téléc:
418-562-7806
twitter.com/PascalBerube,
www.facebook.com/PascalBerubePQ,
www.linkedin.com/in/pascal-bérubé-94343736
Bureau de circonscription
121, av Fraser
Matane, QC G4W 3G8

David Birnbaum
Circonscription électorale: D'Arcy-McGee *Nombre de
constituants:* 55 726, Liberal
Tél: 418-528-1960
David.Birnbaum.DMG@assnat.qc.ca
Autres numéros: Circ. Tél: 514-488-7028; Téléc:
514-488-1713
Bureau de circonscription
#403, 5800, boul Cavendish
Côte-Saint-Luc, QC H4W 2T5

Ministre responsable des Aînés et des Proches aidants, L'hon.
Marguerite Blais
Circonscription électorale: Prévost *Nombre de constituants:*
45 347, CA
Tél: 418-266-7191
Téléc: 418-266-7199
Marguerite.Blais.PREV@assnat.qc.ca
Autres numéros: Circ. Tél: 450-224-4359; Téléc:
450-224-9605
Bureau de circonscription
#101, 2894, boul du Curé-Labelle
Prévost, QC J0R 1T0

Suzanne Blais
Circonscription électorale: Abitibi-Ouest *Nombre de
constituants:* 35 339, CA
Tél: 581-628-1857
Suzanne.Blais.ABOU@assnat.qc.ca
Autres numéros: Circ. Tél: 819-444-5007; Téléc:
819-444-5011
Bureau de circonscription
259, 1e av ouest
Amos, QC J9T 1V1

Ministre des Transports; Ministre responsable de la région de
l'Estrie, L'hon. François Bonnardel
Circonscription électorale: Granby *Nombre de constituants:*
52 468, CA
Tél: 418-643-6980
Téléc: 418-643-2033
Francois.Bonnardel.GRAN@assnat.qc.ca
Autres numéros: Circ. Tél: 450-372-9152; Téléc:
450-372-3040
twitter.com/fbonnardelCAQ,
www.facebook.com/Francois.Bonnardel.Granby
Bureau de circonscription
650, rue Principale
Granby, QC J2G 8L4

Ministre de Travail, de l'Emploi et de la Solidarité sociale;
Ministre responsable de la Mauricie, L'hon. Jean Boulet
Circonscription électorale: Trois-Rivières *Nombre de
constituants:* 54 187, CA

Tél: 418-643-4810
Téléc: 418-643-2802
Jean.Boulet.TRRI@assnat.qc.ca
Autres numéros: Circ. Tél: 819-371-6901; Téléc:
819-371-6648
Bureau de circonscription
#180, 1500, rue Royale
Trois-Rivières, QC G9A 6E6

Joëlle Boutin
Circonscription électorale: Jean-Talon, CA
Tél: 418-643-0223
Joelle.Boutin.JETA@assnat.qc.ca
joelleboutindeputee.com
Autres numéros: Circ. Tél: 819-371-6901; Téléc:
819-371-6648
twitter.com/joelleboutin,
www.facebook.com/joelleboutinjeantalon,
www.linkedin.com/in/joelleboutin
Bureau de circonscription
#310, 969, rte de l'Église
Québec, QC G1V 3V4

Robert Bussière
Circonscription électorale: Gatineau *Nombre de constituants:*
59 189, CA
Tél: 581-628-1802
Ligne sans frais: 866-315-0237
Robert.Bussiere.GATI@assnat.qc.ca
Autres numéros: Circ. Tél: 819-827-3868; Téléc:
819-827-0226
www.facebook.com/RobertBussiereGatineau
Bureau de circonscription
#250, 490, rte 105
Chelsea, QC J9B 1L2

Ministre délégué à la Transformation numérique
gouvernementale; Leader parlementaire adjoint du
gouvernement, Ministre responsable de l'Accès à
l'information et de la Protection des renseignements
personnels, L'hon. Éric Caire
Circonscription électorale: La Peltrie *Nombre de constituants:*
58 329, CA
Tél: 418-781-1737
Eric.Caire.LAPE@assnat.qc.ca
ericcaire.qc.ca
Autres numéros: Circ. Tél: 418-877-5260; Téléc:
418-877-6533
twitter.com/ericcaire, www.facebook.com/caire.coalition,
www.linkedin.com/in/ericcaire
Bureau de circonscription
#201, 5121, boul Chauveau ouest
Québec, QC G2E 5A6

Richard Campeau
Circonscription électorale: Bourget *Nombre de constituants:*
50 481, CA
Tél: 418-263-0691
Richard.Campeau.BOUR@assnat.qc.ca
Autres numéros: Circ. Tél: 514-251-8126; Téléc:
514-251-1064
www.facebook.com/RichardCampeauCAQ
Bureau de circonscription
#105, 6070, rue Sherbrooke est, 1e étage
Montréal, QC H1N 1C1

Ministre délégué à la Santé et aux Services sociaux, L'hon.
Lionel Carmant
Circonscription électorale: Taillon *Nombre de constituants:* 53
083, CA
Tél: 418-266-7181
Téléc: 418-266-7197
Lionel.Carmant.TAIL@assnat.qc.ca
Autres numéros: Circ. Tél: 450-463-3772; Téléc:
450-463-1527
twitter.com/carmantlionel,
www.facebook.com/LionelCarmantCAQ
Bureau de circonscription
498, boul Roland-Therrien
Longueuil, QC J4H 3V9

Vincent Caron
Circonscription électorale: Portneuf *Nombre de constituants:*
42 771, CA
Tél: 418-644-1473
Ligne sans frais: 855-383-0712
Vincent.Caron.PORT@assnat.qc.ca
Autres numéros: Circ. Tél: 418-337-4378; Téléc:
418-337-1582
www.facebook.com/VincentCaronPortneuf
Bureau de circonscription
118, rue Saint-Pierre
Saint-Raymond, QC G3L 1P6

Francine Charbonneau
Circonscription électorale: Mille-Iles *Nombre de constituants:*
44 374, Liberal
Tél: 581-628-1830
Francine.Charbonneau.MIIL@assnat.qc.ca
www.francinecharbonneau.ca
Autres numéros: Circ. Tél: 450-661-3595; Téléc:

450-661-6093
twitter.com/mille_iles
www.facebook.com/FCharbonneauMillelles,
www.linkedin.com/in/francine-charbonneau-744a8663
Bureau de circonscription
#303, 3131, boul da la Concorde est
Laval, QC H7E 4W4

Ministre déléguée à l'Éducation; Ministre responsable de la
Condition féminine, Hon. Isabelle Charest
Circonscription électorale: Brome-Missiquoi, CA
Tél: 418-266-3255
Ligne sans frais: 833-257-7410
Téléc: 418-646-7551
Isabelle.Charest.BRMI@assnat.qc.ca
Autres numéros: Circ. Tél: 450-266-7410; Téléc:
450-263-6584
twitter.com/isabellecharest,
www.facebook.com/IsabelleCharestBRMI
Bureau de circonscription
#205, 170, rue de Sherbrooke
Cowansville, QC J2K 3Y9

Ministre de l'Environnement et de la Lutte contre les
changements climatiques; Ministre responsable, Lutte contre
le racisme et de la région de Laval, L'hon. Benoit Charette
Circonscription électorale: Deux-Montagnes *Nombre de
constituants:* 48 440, CA
Tél: 418-521-3911
Téléc: 41- 64- 414
Benoit.Charette.DEMO@assnat.qc.ca
coalitionavenirquebec.org/fr/blog/equipe/benoit-charette
Autres numéros: Circ. Tél: 450-623-4963; Téléc:
450-623-7178
www.facebook.com/Charette.DeMo
Bureau de circonscription
#230, 477 - 25e av
Saint-Eustache, QC J7P 4Y1

MarieChantal Chassé
Circonscription électorale: Châteauguay *Nombre de
constituants:* 52 642, CA
Tél: 418-266-1101 ext: 72105
MarieChantal.Chasse.CHAT@assnat.qc.ca
Autres numéros: Circ. Tél: 450-699-4136; Téléc:
450-699-9056
www.facebook.com/MarieChantalChasseCAQ,
www.linkedin.com/in/mariechantalchasse
Bureau de circonscription
#98, 233, boul Saint-Jean-Baptiste
Châteauguay, QC J6K 3C3

Youri Chassin
Circonscription électorale: Saint-Jérôme *Nombre de
constituants:* 60 859, CA
Tél: 581-628-1174
Youri.Chassin.STJE@assnat.qc.ca
Autres numéros: Circ. Tél: 450-569-7436; Téléc:
450-569-7440
twitter.com/yourichassin, www.facebook.com/YouriChassin
Bureau de circonscription
#205, 227, rue Saint-Georges
Saint-Jérôme, QC J7Z 5A1

Enrico Ciccone
Circonscription électorale: Marquette *Nombre de constituants:*
46 740, Liberal
Tél: 418-628-1852
Enrico.Ciccone.MARQ@assnat.qc.ca
Autres numéros: Circ. Tél: 514-634-9720; Téléc:
514-634-1653
twitter.com/enricociccone,
www.facebook.com/enrico.ciccone.plq
Bureau de circonscription
#202, 655 - 32e av
Lachine, QC H8T 3G6

Sylvie D'Amours
Circonscription électorale: Mirabel *Nombre de constituants:*
56 903, CA
Ligne sans frais: 866-875-0487
Sylvie.DAmours.MIRA@assnat.qc.ca
coalitionavenirquebec.org/fr/blog/equipe/sylvie-damours
Autres numéros: Circ. Tél: 450-623-8376; Téléc:
450-623-2336
twitter.com/SylvieDAmours,
www.facebook.com/sdamoursmira
Bureau de circonscription
#101, 95, ch Principal
Saint-Joseph-du-Lac, QC J0N 1M0

Suzanne Dansereau
Circonscription électorale: Verchères *Nombre de constituants:*
59 769, CA
Tél: 581-628-1026
Ligne sans frais: 800-652-4419
Suzanne.Dansereau.VERC@assnat.qc.ca
Autres numéros: Circ. Tél: 450-652-4419; Téléc:
450-652-3713
www.facebook.com/SuzanneDansereauCAQ
Bureau de circonscription

#103, 1625, boul Lionel-Boulet
Varennes, QC J3X 1P7

Hélène David
Circonscription électorale: Marguerite-Bourgeoys *Nombre de constituants:* 53 442, Liberal
Tél: 581-628-1824
Helene.David.MABO@assnat.qc.ca
Autres numéros: Circ. Tél: 514-368-1818; Téléc: 514-368-1844
twitter.com/david_hlne, www.facebook.com/plq.helenedavid
Bureau de circonscription
#311, 7655, boul Newman
LaSalle, QC H8N 1X7

Leader parlementaire adjoint de l'opposition officielle, Monsef Derraji
Circonscription électorale: Nelligan *Nombre de constituants:* 58 249, Liberal
Tél: 581-628-1834
Monsef.Derraji.NELL@assnat.qc.ca
Autres numéros: Circ. Tél: 514-695-2440; Téléc: 514-695-8648
twitter.com/monsefderraji, www.facebook.com/derrajimonsef
Bureau de circonscription
#400, 3535, boul Saint-Charles
Kirkland, QC H9H 5B9

Catherine Dorion
Circonscription électorale: Taschereau *Nombre de constituants:* 49 619, QS
Tél: 581-628-1858
Catherine.Dorion.TASC@assnat.qc.ca
Autres numéros: Circ. Tél: 418-646-6090; Téléc: 418-646-6088
twitter.com/cathdorion, www.facebook.com/catherinedorionqs
Bureau de circonscription
#300, 275, rue du Parvis
Québec, QC G1K 6G7

Ministre de la Santé et des Services sociaux, L'hon. Christian Dubé
Circonscription électorale: La Prairie *Nombre de constituants:* 45 669, CA
Tél: 418-266-7171
Téléc: 418-266-7197
Christian.Dube.LAPR@assnat.qc.ca
Autres numéros: Circ. Tél: 450-619-7313; Téléc: 450-619-7519
twitter.com/cdube_sante, www.facebook.com/ChristianDubeLaPrairie
Bureau de circonscription
#306, 26, boul Taschereau
La Prairie, QC J5R 0R9

Ministre des Forêts, de la Faune et des Parcs; Ministre responsable de l'Abitibi-Témiscamingue et du Nord-du-Québec, L'hon. Pierre Dufour
Circonscription électorale: Abitibi-Est *Nombre de constituants:* 33 770, CA
Tél: 418-643-7295
Téléc: 418-643-4318
Pierre.Dufour.ABES@assnat.qc.ca
Autres numéros: Circ. Tél: 819-824-3333; Téléc: 819-824-4300
twitter.com/pdufourofficiel, www.facebook.com/PierreDufourDeputeAbitibiEst
Bureau de circonscription
#202, 888 - 3e av
Val-d'Or, QC J9P 5E6

Jean-Bernard Émond
Circonscription électorale: Richelieu *Nombre de constituants:* 44 346, CA
Tél: 418-263-0660
Ligne sans frais: 866-649-8832
Jean-Bernard.Emond.RICL@assnat.qc.ca
Autres numéros: Circ. Tél: 450-742-3781; Téléc: 450-742-7744
Bureau de circonscription
#100, 50, rue du Roi
Sorel-Tracy, QC J3P 4M7

Ministre de l'Économie et de l'Innovation; Ministre responsable du Développement économique régional, L'hon. Pierre Fitzgibbon
Circonscription électorale: Terrebonne *Nombre de constituants:* 57 776, CA
Tél: 418-691-5650
Téléc: 418-643-8553
Pierre.Fitzgibbon.TERR@assnat.qc.ca
Autres numéros: Circ. Tél: 450-964-3553; Téléc: 450-964-4634
www.linkedin.com/in/pierre-fitzgibbon-9241599
Bureau de circonscription
#101, 3455, boul de la Pinière
Terrebonne, QC J6X 0A1

Andrés Fontecilla
Circonscription électorale: Laurier-Dorion *Nombre de constituants:* 47 910, QS
Tél: 418-644-5987

Andres.Fontecilla.LADO@assnat.qc.ca
Autres numéros: Circ. Tél: 514-273-1412; Téléc: 514-273-3150
twitter.com/afontecillaqs, www.facebook.com/AFontecillaQS
Bureau de circonscription
#401, 529, rue Jarry est
Montréal, QC H2P 1V4

Leader parlementaire de l'opposition officielle, André Fortin
Circonscription électorale: Pontiac *Nombre de constituants:* 52 009, Liberal
Tél: 418-643-1275
Ligne sans frais: 866-988-7070
Téléc: 418-643-1906
Andre.Fortin.PONT@assnat.qc.ca
Autres numéros: Circ. Tél: 819-648-7070; Téléc: 819-648-2448
twitter.com/AvecAndreFortin, www.facebook.com/AvecAndreFortin, www.linkedin.com/in/andré-fortin-5393bb17
Bureau de circonscription
104, rue Front
PO Box 100
Campbell's Bay, QC J0X 1K0

Émilie Foster
Circonscription électorale: Charlevoix—Côte-de-Beaupré *Nombre de constituants:* 51 165, CA
Tél: 418-263-0701
Emilie.Foster.CHCB@assnat.qc.ca
Autres numéros: Circ. Tél: 418-827-5115; Téléc: 418-827-4300
twitter.com/milie_foster, www.facebook.com/EmilieFosterCAQ, www.linkedin.com/in/émilie-foster-492066165
Bureau de circonscription
#101, 10989, boul Sainte-Anne
Beaupré, QC G0A 1E0

Catherine Fournier
Circonscription électorale: Marie-Victorin *Nombre de constituants:* 47 044, Independent
Tél: 581-628-1028
Catherine.Fournier.MAVI@assnat.qc.ca

Troisième vice-président, Maryse Gaudreault
Circonscription électorale: Hull *Nombre de constituants:* 54 787, Liberal
Tél: 418-644-1007
Maryse.Gaudreault.HULL@assnat.qc.ca
marysegaudreault.com
Autres numéros: Circ. Tél: 819-772-3000; Téléc: 819-772-3265
twitter.com/mgaudreaulthull, www.facebook.com/maryse.gaudreault.14
Bureau de circonscription
#207, 259, boul Saint-Joseph
Gatineau, QC J8Y 6T1

Sylvain Gaudreault
Circonscription électorale: Jonquière *Nombre de constituants:* 45 091, Parti Québécois
Tél: 581-628-1853
Sylvain.Gaudreault.JONQ@assnat.qc.ca
sylvaingaudreault.org
Autres numéros: Circ. Tél: 418-547-0666; Téléc: 418-547-1166
twitter.com/sylvaingaudrea2, www.facebook.com/SylvainGaudreaultPQ
Bureau de circonscription
2240, rue Montpetit
Jonquière, QC G7X 6A3

Ruba Ghazal
Circonscription électorale: Mercier *Nombre de constituants:* 45 048, QS
Tél: 418-644-1430
Ruba.Ghazal.MERC@assnat.qc.ca
Autres numéros: Circ. Tél: 514-525-8877; Téléc: 514-521-0147
twitter.com/rubaghazalqs, www.facebook.com/RubaGhazalQS
Bureau de circonscription
#102, 1012, av du Mont-Royal est
Montréal, QC H2J 1X6

Ministre des Finances, L'hon. Éric Girard
Circonscription électorale: Groulx *Nombre de constituants:* 52 633, CA
Tél: 418-643-5270
Téléc: 418-646-1574
Eric.Girard.GROU@assnat.qc.ca
Autres numéros: Circ. Tél: 450-430-7890; Téléc: 450-430-4587
twitter.com/ericgirardmfq, www.facebook.com/EricGirardGroulx, www.linkedin.com/in/eric-girard-158734b1
Bureau de circonscription
#210, 204, boul du Curé-Labelle
Sainte-Thérèse, QC J7E 2X7

Éric Girard
Circonscription électorale: Lac-Saint-Jean *Nombre de constituants:* 42 954, CA
Tél: 418-263-0697
Eric.Girard.LSJ@assnat.qc.ca
Autres numéros: Circ. Tél: 418-668-6149; Téléc: 418-668-0684
www.facebook.com/EricGirardLacSaintJean
Bureau de circonscription
510A, rue Sacré-Coeur ouest
PO Box 2025
Alma, QC G8B 1L9

Ministre des Relations internationales et de la Francophonie; Ministre de l'Immigration, de la Francisation et de l'Intégration; Ministre responsable de la région des Laurentides, L'hon. Nadine Girault
Circonscription électorale: Bertrand *Nombre de constituants:* 50 158, CA
Tél: 418-649-2319
Ligne sans frais: 800-882-4757
Téléc: 418-643-4804
Nadine.Girault.BERR@assnat.qc.ca
Autres numéros: Circ. Tél: 819-321-1676; Téléc: 819-321-0048
twitter.com/nadinegirault
Bureau de circonscription
#101, 197, rue Principale est
Sainte-Agathe-des-Monts, QC J8C 1K5

Agnès Grondin
Circonscription électorale: Argenteuil *Nombre de constituants:* 47 351, CA
Tél: 418-528-6379
Ligne sans frais: 800-870-7964
Agnes.Grondin.ARGE@assnat.qc.ca
Autres numéros: Circ. Tél: 450-562-0785; Téléc: 450-562-0650
www.facebook.com/AgnesGrondinCAQ
Bureau de circonscription
512, rue Principale
Lachute, QC J8H 1Y3

Vice-première ministre; Ministre de la Sécurité publique; Ministre responsable de la Capitale-Nationale, L'hon. Geneviève Guilbault
Circonscription électorale: Louis-Hébert *Nombre de constituants:* 45 821, CA
Tél: 418-643-2112
Téléc: 418-646-6168
Genevieve.Guilbault.LOHE@assnat.qc.ca
Autres numéros: Circ. Tél: 418-528-0483; Téléc: 418-644-1253
twitter.com/gguilbaultcaq, www.facebook.com/GenevieveGuilbaultCAQ, www.linkedin.com/in/geneviève-guilbault-486b0293
Bureau de circonscription
#202, 810, rte Jean-Gauvin
Québec, QC G1X 0B6

Nancy Guillemette
Circonscription électorale: Roberval, CA
Tél: 418-266-1101 ext: 72107
Nancy.Guillemette.ROBE@assnat.qc.ca
Autres numéros: Circ. Tél: 418-275-5050; Téléc: 418-275-5519
twitter.com/guillemette_caq, www.facebook.com/NancyGuillemetteRoberval
Bureau de circonscription
#203, 729, boul St-Joseph
Roberval, QC G8H 2L4

Whip adjoint du gouvernement, Geneviève Hébert
Circonscription électorale: Saint-François *Nombre de constituants:* 57 290, CA
Tél: 418-263-0703
Genevieve.Hebert.SAFR@assnat.qc.ca
Autres numéros: Circ. Tél: 819-565-3667; Téléc: 819-565-8779
www.facebook.com/GenevieveHebertCoalitionAvenirQuebec
Bureau de circonscription
#203B, 373, rue King est, 2e étage
Sherbrooke, QC J1G 1B4

Véronique Hivon
Circonscription électorale: Joliette *Nombre de constituants:* 54 057, Parti Québécois
Tél: 418-263-0666
Veronique.Hivon.JOLI@assnat.qc.ca
veroniquehivon.org
Autres numéros: Circ. Tél: 450-752-6929; Téléc: 450-752-6935
twitter.com/vhivon, www.facebook.com/veroniquehivon, www.linkedin.com/in/véronique-hivon-b229674
Bureau de circonscription
970, rue Saint-Louis
Joliette, QC J6E 3A4

Claire Isabelle
Circonscription électorale: Huntingdon *Nombre de constituants:* 43 512, CA

Tél: 581-628-1806
Ligne sans frais: 866-540-9097
Claire.IsaBelle.HUNT@assnat.qc.ca
Autres numéros: Circ. Tél: 450-427-2150; Téléc:
450-427-2154
www.facebook.com/Claire.IsaBelle.Huntingdon
Bureau de circonscription
263, boul Saint-Joseph
Sainte-Martine, QC J0S 1V0

François Jacques
Circonscription électorale: Mégantic *Nombre de constituants:*
38 856, CA
Tél: 418-644-0711
Francois.Jacques.MEGA@assnat.qc.ca
Autres numéros: Circ. Tél: 819-583-4500; Téléc:
819-583-0926
www.facebook.com/FrancoisJacquesMEGA
Bureau de circonscription
#201, 5600, rue Frontenac
Lac-Mégantic, QC G6B 1H5

Chantale Jeannotte
Circonscription électorale: Labelle *Nombre de constituants:*
48 741, CA
Tél: 418-528-1349
Chantale.Jeannotte.LABE@assnat.qc.ca
Autres numéros: Circ. Tél: 819-429-5038; Téléc:
819-429-5331
www.facebook.com/ChantaleJeannotteCAQ
Bureau de circonscription
#202, 499, rue Charbonneau
Mont-Tremblant, QC J8E 3H4

Leader parlementaire; Ministre de la Justice; Ministre
responsable de la Langue française, de la Laïcité, de la
Réforme parlementaire et de la région de la Montérégie,
L'hon. Simon Jolin-Barrette
Circonscription électorale: Borduas *Nombre de constituants:*
57 897, CA
Tél: 418-263-0684
Téléc: 418-646-1614
sjb.BORD@assnat.qc.ca
Autres numéros: Circ. Tél: 450-464-5505; Téléc:
450-464-4335
twitter.com/sjb_caq
Bureau de circonscription
888, rue Laurier
Beloeil, QC J3G 4K7

Ministre de l'Énergie et des Ressources naturelles; Ministre
responsable de la région de la Côte-Nord, et de la
Gaspésie-Iles-de-la-Madeleine, L'hon. Jonatan Julien
Circonscription électorale: Charlesbourg *Nombre de
constituants:* 57 722, CA
Tél: 418-643-7295
Téléc: 418-643-4318
Jonatan.Julien.CHLB@assnat.qc.ca
Autres numéros: Circ. Tél: 418-644-9240; Téléc:
418-644-9266
www.facebook.com/JonatanJulienMinistre,
www.linkedin.com/in/jonatan-julien-74317a1ba
Bureau de circonscription, Carrefour Charlesbourg
#213, 8500, boul Henri-Bourassa
Québec, QC G1G 5X1

Gregory Kelley
Circonscription électorale: Jacques-Cartier *Nombre de
constituants:* 45 490, Liberal
Tél: 581-628-1809
Gregory.Kelley.JACA@assnat.qc.ca
Autres numéros: Circ. Tél: 514-697-7663; Téléc:
514-697-6499
twitter.com/gharperkelley,
www.facebook.com/AvecGregKelley
Bureau de circonscription, Place Scotia
#206, 620, boul Saint-Jean
Montréal, QC H9R 3K2

Leader parlementaire du deuxième groupe d'opposition,
Christine Labrie
Circonscription électorale: Sherbrooke *Nombre de
constituants:* 50 912, QS
Tél: 418-644-1467
Christine.Labrie.SHER@assnat.qc.ca
christinelabrie.quebec
Autres numéros: Circ. Tél: 819-569-5646; Téléc:
819-569-0229
twitter.com/christine_qs,
www.facebook.com/ChristineLabrieQS
Bureau de circonscription
#301, 230, rue King ouest
Sherbrooke, QC J1H 1P9

Stéphanie Lachance
Circonscription électorale: Bellechasse *Nombre de
constituants:* 43 947, CA
Tél: 581-628-1781
Ligne sans frais: 866-504-3294
Autres numéros: Circ. Tél: 418-883-1343; Téléc:
418-983-0186

www.facebook.com/StephanieLachanceBellechasse,
www.linkedin.com/in/stephanielachance
Bureau de circonscription
250A, rte 279
Saint-Lazare-de-Bellechasse, QC G0R 3J0

Ministre de la Famille; Ministre responsable de la région de
l'Outaouais, L'hon. Mathieu Lacombe
Circonscription électorale: Papineau *Nombre de constituants:*
60 137, CA
Tél: 418-643-2181
Ligne sans frais: 866-971-7974
Téléc: 418-643-7690
Mathieu.Lacombe.PAPI@assnat.qc.ca
Autres numéros: Circ. Tél: 819-986-9300; Téléc:
819-986-8629
twitter.com/lacombemathieu,
www.facebook.com/MathieuLacombeCAQ
Bureau de circonscription
564, av de Buckingham
Gatineau, QC J8L 2H1

Ministre des Affaires municipales et de l'Habitation; Ministre dela
région du Saguenay-Lac-Saint-Jean, L'hon. Andrée Laforest
Circonscription électorale: Chicoutimi *Nombre de
constituants:* 45 937, CA
Tél: 418-691-2050
Andree.Laforest.CHIC@assnat.qc.ca
Autres numéros: Circ. Tél: 418-543-7797; Téléc:
418-543-1355
twitter.com/andreelaforest,
www.facebook.com/AndreeLaforestCAQ
Bureau de circonscription
110, boul Barrette
Chicoutimi, QC G7H 7W8

Président du caucus du gouvernement, Mario Laframboise
Circonscription électorale: Blainville *Nombre de constituants:*
57 856, CA
Tél: 418-263-0613
Mario.Laframboise.BLAI@assnat.qc.ca
Autres numéros: Circ. Tél: 450-430-8086; Téléc:
450-430-9795
twitter.com/laframboisema,
www.facebook.com/Mario.Laframboise.blainville
Bureau de circonscription
#211, 369, boul Adolphe-Chapleau
Bois-des-Filion, QC J6Z 1H1

Ministre responsable des Affaires autochtones, L'hon. Ian
Lafrenière
Circonscription électorale: Vachon *Nombre de constituants:*
51 519, CA
Tél: 418-528-8407
Téléc: 418-646-9487
Ian.Lafreniere.VACHON@assnat.qc.ca
Autres numéros: Circ. Tél: 450-676-5086; Téléc:
450-676-0709
twitter.com/ianlafreniere,
www.facebook.com/IanLafreniereVachon
Bureau de circonscription
5610, ch de Chambly
Saint-Hubert, QC J3Y 7E5

Ministre de l'Agriculture, des Pêches; Ministre responsable de la
région du Centre-du-Québec et Chaudière-Appalaches,
L'hon. André Lamontagne
Circonscription électorale: Johnson *Nombre de constituants:*
57 123, CA
Tél: 418-380-2525
Téléc: 418-380-2184
Andre.Lamontagne.JOHN@assnat.qc.ca
coalitionavenirquebec.org/equipe/andre-lamontagne
Autres numéros: Circ. Tél: 819-474-7770; Téléc:
819-474-4492
twitter.com/andrelamontagn2,
www.facebook.com/andrelamontagnecaq
Bureau de circonscription
641, rue Saint-Pierre
Drummondville, QC J2C 3W6

Denis Lamothe
Circonscription électorale: Ungava *Nombre de constituants:*
28 314, CA
Tél: 418-644-1363
Ligne sans frais: 800-463-7122
Denis.Lamothe.UNGA@assnat.qc.ca
Autres numéros: Circ. Tél: 418-748-6046; Téléc:
418-748-3255
www.facebook.com/DenisLamotheCAQ
Bureau de circonscription
#12, 462 - 3e rue
Chibougamau, QC G8P 1N7

Lise Lavallée
Circonscription électorale: Repentigny *Nombre de
constituants:* 51 729, CA
Tél: 418-263-0612
Lise.Lavallee.REPE@assnat.qc.ca
Autres numéros: Circ. Tél: 450-581-6102; Téléc:
450-581-9173

www.facebook.com/lise.lavallee.repentigny
Bureau de circonscription
#102, 522, rue Notre-Dame
Repentigny, QC J6A 2T8

Harold LeBel
Circonscription électorale: Rimouski *Nombre de constituants:*
45 580, Independent
Tél: 581-628-1017
Harold.Lebel.RIMO@assnat.qc.ca
Autres numéros: Circ. Tél: 418-722-9787; Téléc:
418-725-0526
twitter.com/hlebelrimouski,
www.facebook.com/haroldrimouski
Bureau de circonscription
#400, 320, rue Saint-Germain est
Rimouski, QC G5L 1C2

Ministre responsable de l'Administration gouvernementale et
présidente du Conseil du trésor, des Relations canadiennes
et de la Francophonie canadienne, et des Institutions
démocratiques et de la Réforme électorale, L'hon. Sonia
LeBel
Circonscription électorale: Champlain *Nombre de
constituants:* 58 905, CA
Tél: 418-643-5926
Téléc: 418-643-7824
Sonia.LeBel.CHMP@assnat.qc.ca
Autres numéros: Circ. Tél: 819-694-4600; Téléc:
819-694-4606
twitter.com/slebel19, www.facebook.com/SoniaLeBelCAQ
Bureau de circonscription
#210, 580, rue Barkoff
Trois-Rivières, QC G8T 9T7

Isabelle Lecours
Circonscription électorale: Lotbinière-Frontenac *Nombre de
constituants:* 55 581, CA
Tél: 581-628-1822
Isabelle.Lecours.LOFR@assnat.qc.ca
Autres numéros: Circ. Tél: 418-332-3444; Téléc:
418-332-3445
www.facebook.com/IsabelleLecoursCAQ
Bureau de circonscription
257, rue Notre-Dame ouest
Thetford Mines, QC G6G 1J7

Ministre déléguée à l'Économie, L'hon. Lucie Lecours
Circonscription électorale: Les Plaines *Nombre de
constituants:* 40 009, CA
Tél: 418-691-5650
Téléc: 418-643-8553
Lucie.Lecours.LPLA@assnat.qc.ca
Autres numéros: Circ. Tél: 450-838-7493
www.facebook.com/LucieLecoursCAQ,
www.linkedin.com/in/lucie-lecours-83b97587
Bureau de circonscription
193, boul Sainte-Anne
Sainte-Anne-des-Plaines, QC J0N 1H0

Alexandre Leduc
Circonscription électorale: Hochelaga-Maisonneuve *Nombre
de constituants:* 42 934, QS
Tél: 581-814-1286
Alexandre.Leduc.HOCH@assnat.qc.ca
Autres numéros: Circ. Tél: 514-873-9309; Téléc:
514-873-5415
Bureau de circonscription
#300, 2030, boul Pie-IX
Montréal, QC H1V 2C8

Whip en chef du gouvernement, Éric Lefebvre
Circonscription électorale: Arthabaska *Nombre de
constituants:* 60 808, CA
Tél: 418-643-6018
Ligne sans frais: 800-463-1928
Téléc: 418-643-5462
Eric.Lefebvre.ARTH@assnat.qc.ca
Autres numéros: Circ. Tél: 819-758-7440; Téléc:
819-758-1583
Bureau de circonscription
#201, 21, rue de la Gare
Victoriaville, QC G6P 3Z3

Premier ministre; Ministre responsable, jeunesse, relations
avecles Québécois anglophones, Internet haute vitesse et
des projets spéciaux de connectivité, L'hon. François Legault
Circonscription électorale: L'Assomption *Nombre de
constituants:* 45 248, CA
Tél: 418-643-5321
Téléc: 41- 64- 185
flegault-asso@assnat.qc.ca
Autres numéros: Circ. Tél: 450-589-0226; Téléc:
450-589-3457
twitter.com/francoislegault,
www.facebook.com/FrancoisLegaultPremierMinistre
Bureau de circonscription
#208, 831, boul de l'Ange-Gardien nord
L'Assomption, QC J5W 1P5

Carlos J. Leitao
Circonscription électorale: Robert-Baldwin *Nombre de

constituants: 55 075, Liberal
Tél: 581-628-1848
CarlosJ.Leitao.ROBA@assnat.qc.ca
Autres numéros: Circ. Tél: 514-684-9000; Téléc:
514-683-7271
twitter.com/carlosjleitao, www.facebook.com/carlos.j.leitao.qc
Bureau de circonscription
#203, 3869, boul des Sources
Dollard-des-Ormeaux, Q H9B 2A2

Mathieu Lemay
Circonscription électorale: Masson *Nombre de constituants:*
46 214, CA
Tél: 418-643-5771
Mathieu.Lemay.MASS@assnat.qc.ca
coalitionavenirquebec.org/fr/blog/equipe/mathieu-lemay
Autres numéros: Circ. Tél: 450-966-0111; Téléc:
450-966-0115
www.facebook.com/Lemay.Masson
Bureau de circonscription
#108, 3101, ch Sainte-Marie
Mascouche, QC J7K 1P2

Louis Lemieux
Circonscription électorale: Saint-Jean *Nombre de constituants:* 60 761, CA
Tél: 418-644-1463
Louis.Lemieux.SAJE@assnat.qc.ca
Autres numéros: Circ. Tél: 450-346-3040; Téléc:
450-346-3340
Bureau de circonscription
188, rue Longueuil
Saint-Jean-sur-Richelieu, QC J3B 6P1

Émilise Lessard-Therrien
Circonscription électorale: Rouyn-Noranda—Témiscamingue
Nombre de constituants: 44 824, QS
Tél: 581-628-1851
Ligne sans frais: 866-268-4685
Emilise.Lessard-Therrien.RNT@assnat.qc.ca
Autres numéros: Circ. Tél: 819-763-3047; Téléc:
819-763-3050
Bureau de circonscription
#103, 170, av Principale
Rouyn-Noranda, QC J9X 4P7

Mathieu Lévesque
Circonscription électorale: Chapleau *Nombre de constituants:*
54 962, CA
Tél: 418-528-0390
Mathieu.Levesque.CHAP@assnat.qc.ca
Autres numéros: Circ. Tél: 819-246-4558; Téléc:
819-246-2970
Bureau de circonscription
#206, 195, boul Gréber
Gatineau, QC J8T 3R1

Whip adjointe du gouvernement, Sylvain Lévesque
Circonscription électorale: Chauveau *Nombre de constituants:*
56 405, CA
Tél: 581-628-1796
Sylvain.Levesque.CHAU@assnat.qc.ca
Autres numéros: Circ. Tél: 418-842-3330; Téléc:
418-842-6444
Bureau de circonscription
#201, 1680, av Lapierre, 2e étage
Québec, QC G3E 0G1

Jennifer Maccarone
Circonscription électorale: Westmount—Saint-Louis *Nombre de constituants:* 45 352, Liberal
Tél: 581-628-1843
Jennifer.Maccarone.WSL@assnat.qc.ca
Autres numéros: Circ. Tél: 514-395-2929; Téléc:
514-395-2955
Bureau de circonscription
#801, 1134, rue Sainte-Catherine ouest, 8e étage
Montréal, QC H3B 1H4

Vincent Marissal
Circonscription électorale: Rosemont *Nombre de constituants:*
53 596, QS
Tél: 581-628-1845
Vincent.Marissal.ROSE@assnat.qc.ca
Autres numéros: Circ. Tél: 514-593-7495; Téléc:
514-593-4264
Bureau de circonscription
3308, boul Rosemont
Montréal, QC H1X 1K2

Donald Martel
Circonscription électorale: Nicolet-Bécancour *Nombre de constituants:* 39 995, CA
Tél: 581-628-1849
Ligne sans frais: 855-333-3521
Donald.Martel.NICO@assnat.qc.ca
coalitionavenirquebec.org/fr/blog/equipe/donald-martel
Autres numéros: Circ. Tél: 819-233-3521; Téléc:
819-233-3529
twitter.com/domartell, www.facebook.com/MartelD.coalition
Bureau de circonscription

#202, 625, av Godefroy
Bécancour, QC G9H 1S3

Cheffe du deuxième groupe d'opposition, Manon Massé
Circonscription électorale: Sainte-Marie—Saint-Jacques
Nombre de constituants: 42 894, QS
Tél: 418-644-1632
Manon.Masse.SMSJ@assnat.qc.ca
manon.quebecsolidaire.net
Autres numéros: Circ. Tél: 514-525-2501; Téléc:
514-525-5637
twitter.com/ManonMasse_Qs,
www.facebook.com/QS.ManonMasse
Bureau de circonscription
#330, 533, rue Ontario est
Montréal, QC H2L 1N8

Ministre de l'Enseignement supérieur, L'hon. Danielle McCann
Circonscription électorale: Sanguinet *Nombre de constituants:*
42 016, CA
Tél: 418-781-6500
Danielle.McCann.SAGU@assnat.qc.ca
Autres numéros: Circ. Tél: 450-632-1164; Téléc:
450-632-2145
Bureau de circonscription
#200, 223, rue Sainte-Catherine
Saint-Constant, QC J5A 2H3

Isabelle Melançon
Circonscription électorale: Verdun *Nombre de constituants:*
49 826, Liberal
Tél: 581-628-1860
Isabelle.Melancon.VERD@assnat.qc.ca
Autres numéros: Circ. Tél: 514-766-7503; Téléc:
514-766-1136
twitter.com/isamelancon,
www.facebook.com/MelanconIsabelle,
www.linkedin.com/in/melanconisabelle
Bureau de circonscription
#301, 4110, rue Wellington
Verdun, QC H4G 1V7

L'hon. Nicole Ménard
Circonscription électorale: Laporte *Nombre de constituants:*
53 823, Liberal
Nicole.Menard.LAPO@assnat.qc.ca
Autres numéros: Circ. Tél: 450-672-1885; Téléc:
450-465-6046
twitter.com/Nicole_Menard,
www.facebook.com/nicole.menard.90
Bureau de circonscription
228, rue de Woodstock
Saint-Lambert, QC J4P 3R5

Marie Montpetit
Circonscription électorale: Maurice-Richard *Nombre de constituants:* 47 407, Liberal
Tél: 581-628-1828
Marie.Montpetit.CREM@assnat.qc.ca
Autres numéros: Circ. Tél: 514-387-6314; Téléc:
514-387-6462
twitter.com/Marie_Montpetit,
www.facebook.com/MontpetitMarie
Bureau de circonscription
1421, rue Fleury est
Montréal, QC H2C 1R9

Leader parlementaire du deuxième groupe d'opposition, Gabriel Nadeau-Dubois
Circonscription électorale: Gouin *Nombre de constituants:* 44 196, QS
Tél: 418-644-1632
Gabriel.Nadeau-Dubois.GOUI@assnat.qc.ca
Autres numéros: Circ. Tél: 514-864-6133; Téléc:
514-873-8998
twitter.com/gnadeaudubois,
www.facebook.com/GNadeauDubois
Bureau de circonscription
#201, 1453, rue Beaubien est
Montréal, QC H2G 3C6

Marie-Claude Nichols
Circonscription électorale: Vaudreuil *Nombre de constituants:*
58 504, Liberal
Tél: 418-646-7623
Marie-Claude.Nichols.VAUD@assnat.qc.ca
Autres numéros: Circ. Tél: 450-424-6666; Téléc:
450-424-9274
twitter.com/nicholsmariec,
www.facebook.com/deputemarieclaudenichols
Bureau de circonscription
416, boul Harwood
Vaudreuil-Dorion, QC J7V 7H4

Leader parlementaire du troisième groupe d'opposition, Martin Ouellet
Circonscription électorale: René-Lévesque *Nombre de constituants:* 32 944, Parti Québécois
Tél: 581-628-1002
Ligne sans frais: 866-268-4077
Martin.Ouellet.RELE@assnat.qc.ca
Autres numéros: Circ. Tél: 418-295-4001; Téléc:

418-295-4028
twitter.com/martinouellet_,
www.facebook.com/martinouelletpq
Bureau de circonscription
852, rue Bossé
Baie-Comeau, QC G5C 1L6

Guy Ouellette
Circonscription électorale: Chomedey *Nombre de constituants:* 57 131, Independent
Tél: 418-644-4050
Guy.Ouellette.CHOM@assnat.qc.ca
Autres numéros: Circ. Tél: 450-686-0166; Téléc:
450-686-7153
twitter.com/Guy0uellette,
www.linkedin.com/in/guy-ouellette-75275a2b
Bureau de circonscription
#201, 4599, boul Samson
Laval, QC H7W 2H2

Président de l'Assemblée nationale, L'hon. François Paradis
Circonscription électorale: Lévis *Nombre de constituants:* 48 200, CA
Tél: 418-643-2820
Téléc: 418-643-3423
Francois.Paradis.LEVI@assnat.qc.ca
Autres numéros: Circ. Tél: 418-833-5550; Téléc:
418-833-0999
twitter.com/fparadislevis
Bureau de circonscription
#210, 5955, rue Saint-Laurent
Lévis, QC G6V 3P5

Méganne Perry Mélançon
Circonscription électorale: Gaspé *Nombre de constituants:* 30 033, Parti Québécois
Tél: 418-263-0699
Ligne sans frais: 855-368-5827
Meganne.PerryMelancon.GASP@assnat.qc.ca
Autres numéros: Circ. Tél: 418-368-5827; Téléc:
418-368-6416
twitter.com/megannemelancon,
www.facebook.com/megannepm
Bureau de circonscription
#102, 11, rue de la Cathédrale
Gaspé, QC G4X 2V9

Première vice-président, Marc Picard
Circonscription électorale: Chutes-de-la-Chaudière *Nombre de constituants:* 57 523, CA
Tél: 418-643-2750
Téléc: 418-643-2942
Marc.Picard.CDLC@assnat.qc.ca
marcpicard.com
Autres numéros: Circ. Tél: 418-834-0015; Téléc:
418-834-0368
twitter.com/MarcPicardQc, www.facebook.com/marcpicard01
Bureau de circonscription
#230, 730, av Taniata
Lévis, QC G6Z 2C5

Marilyne Picard
Circonscription électorale: Soulanges *Nombre de constituants:* 56 258, CA
Tél: 581-628-1859
Ligne sans frais: 866-268-3607
Marilyne.Picard.SOUL@assnat.qc.ca
Autres numéros: Circ. Tél: 450-456-3816; Téléc:
450-456-3930
Bureau de circonscription
607, rte 201
Saint-Clet, QC J0P 1S0

Saul Polo
Circonscription électorale: Laval-des-Rapides *Nombre de constituants:* 55 678, Liberal
Tél: 418-263-0617
Saul.Polo.LDR@assnat.qc.ca
Autres numéros: Circ. Tél: 450-668-6077; Téléc:
450-668-6168
twitter.com/sauljpolo, www.facebook.com/SaulJPolo,
www.linkedin.com/in/saulpolo
Bureau de circonscription
#309, 400, boul Saint-Martin ouest
Laval, QC H7M 3Y8

Samuel Poulin
Circonscription électorale: Beauce-Sud *Nombre de constituants:* 48 992, CA
Tél: 418-263-0645
Ligne sans frais: 866-758-2641
Samuel.Poulin.BESU@assnat.qc.ca
Autres numéros: Circ. Tél: 418-226-4570; Téléc:
418-227-9664
Bureau de circonscription
#204, 1150 - 107e rue
Saint-Georges, QC G5Y 8C3

Ministre du Tourisme; Ministre responsable de la région de Lanaudière et de la région du Bas-Saint-Laurent, L'hon. Caroline Proulx
Circonscription électorale: Berthier *Nombre de constituants:*

58 335, CA
Tél: 418-528-8063
Ligne sans frais: 866-256-3898
Téléc: 418-528-8066
Caroline.Proulx.BERH@assnat.qc.ca
Autres numéros: Circ. Tél: 450-586-3171; Téléc:
450-586-2505
Bureau de circonscription
61, ch de Lavaltrie
Lavaltrie, QC J5T 2H4

Marie-Eve Proulx
Circonscription électorale: Côte-du-Sud *Nombre de constituants:* 49 881, CA
Ligne sans frais: 866-774-1893
Marie-Eve.Proulx.CDS@assnat.qc.ca
Autres numéros: Circ. Tél: 418-234-1893; Téléc:
418-234-1659
Bureau de circonscription, Édifice Amable-Bélanger
#206, 6, rue Saint-Jean-Baptiste est
Montmagny, QC G5V 1J7

Luc Provençal
Circonscription électorale: Beauce-Nord *Nombre de constituants:* 43 398, CA
Tél: 418-643-5016
Ligne sans frais: 800-463-2544
Luc.Provencal.BENO@assnat.qc.ca
Autres numéros: Circ. Tél: 418-387-2044; Téléc:
418-387-4250
Bureau de circonscription
452, boul Vachon nord
Sainte-Marie, QC G6E 1M1

Claude Reid
Circonscription électorale: Beauharnois *Nombre de constituants:* 47 666, CA
Tél: 418-644-7844
Claude.Reid.BEAU@assnat.qc.ca
Autres numéros: Circ. Tél: 450-377-3131; Téléc:
450-373-5272
Bureau de circonscription
#100, 157, rue Victoria
Salaberry-de-Valleyfield, QC J6T 1A5

Lorraine Richard
Circonscription électorale: Duplessis *Nombre de constituants:* 37 349, Parti Québécois
Tél: 418-643-2446
Ligne sans frais: 800-463-1644
Lorraine.Richard.DUPL@assnat.qc.ca
pq.org/deputes/lorraine-richard
Autres numéros: Circ. Tél: 418-968-5044; Téléc:
418-968-2541
twitter.com/lrichardpq,
www.facebook.com/LorraineRichardPQ
Bureau de circonscription
#202, 421, av Arnaud
Sept-Iles, QC G4R 3B3

Marwah Rizqy
Circonscription électorale: Saint-Laurent *Nombre de constituants:* 56 749, Liberal
Tél: 581-628-1844
Marwah.Rizqy.STLO@assnat.qc.ca
Autres numéros: Circ. Tél: 514-747-4050; Téléc:
514-747-5605
Bureau de circonscription
#312, 5255, boul Henri-Bourassa ouest, 3e étage
Montréal, QC H4R 2M6

Ministre de l'Éducation, L'hon. Jean-François Roberge
Circonscription électorale: Chambly *Nombre de constituants:* 50 699, CA
Tél: 418-644-0664
Téléc: 418-643-2640
Jean-Francois.Roberge.CHMB@assnat.qc.ca
Autres numéros: Circ. Tél: 418-658-5452; Téléc:
418-658-4417
twitter.com/jfrobergeqc, www.facebook.com/roberge.chambly,
www.linkedin.com/in/jean-françois-roberge-498b6523
Bureau de circonscription
2028, av Bourgogne
Chambly, QC J3L 1Z6

Paule Robitaille
Circonscription électorale: Bourassa-Sauvé *Nombre de constituants:* 48 592, Liberal
Tél: 581-628-1182
Paule.Robitaille.BOSA@assnat.qc.ca
Autres numéros: Circ. Tél: 514-328-6006; Téléc:
514-328-0763
Bureau de circonscription
#305, 5879, boul Henri-Bourassa est
Montréal, QC H1G 2V1

Whip en chef de l'opposition officielle, Filomena Rotiroti
Circonscription électorale: Jeanne-Mance—Viger *Nombre de constituants:* 50 660, Liberal
Tél: 418-643-2301
Téléc: 418-646-9284
Filomena.Rotiroti.JMV@assnat.qc.ca

Autres numéros: Circ. Tél: 514-326-0491; Téléc:
514-326-9837
twitter.com/FiloRotiroti, www.facebook.com/FiloRotiroti
Bureau de circonscription
#100, 5450, rue Jarry est
Montréal, QC H1P 1T9

Ministre déléguée aux Transports; Ministre responsable de la métropole et de la région de Montréal, L'hon. Chantal Rouleau
Circonscription électorale: Pointe-aux-Trembles *Nombre de constituants:* 41 148, CA
Tél: 418-643-6980
Téléc: 418-266-6645
Chantal.Rouleau.PAT@assnat.qc.ca
Autres numéros: Circ. Tél: 514-640-9085; Téléc:
514-640-0857
Bureau de circonscription
#100, 500, boul Saint-Jean-Baptiste
Montréal, QC H1B 3Z7

Jean Rousselle
Circonscription électorale: Vimont *Nombre de constituants:* 45 909, Liberal
Tél: 418-644-0877
Jean.Rousselle.VIMO@assnat.qc.ca
Autres numéros: Circ. Tél: 450-628-9269; Téléc:
450-963-7547
www.facebook.com/Jean.Rousselle.Vimont,
www.linkedin.com/in/jean-rousselle-520543158
Bureau de circonscription
#415, 4650, boul des Laurentides
Laval, QC H7K 2J4

Ministre de la Culture et des Communications, L'hon. Nathalie Roy
Circonscription électorale: Montarville *Nombre de constituants:* 53 315, CA
Tél: 418-380-2310
Téléc: 418-380-2311
Nathalie.Roy.MOTA@assnat.qc.ca
nathalieroy.org
Autres numéros: Circ. Tél: 450-641-2748; Téléc:
450-641-0689
twitter.com/NathalieRoyCAQ
www.facebook.com/nathalie.roy.montarville
Bureau de circonscription
#500, 1570, rue Ampère
Boucherville, QC J4B 7L4

Sylvain Roy
Circonscription électorale: Bonaventure *Nombre de constituants:* 35 530, Independent
Tél: 418-263-0359
Ligne sans frais: 800-490-3511
Sylvain.Roy.BONA@assnat.qc.ca
Autres numéros: Circ. Tél: 418-364-6153; Téléc:
418-364-7906
twitter.com/roy_bonaventure
Bureau de circonscription
314E, boul Perron
Carleton, QC G0C 1J0

Claire Samson
Circonscription électorale: Iberville *Nombre de constituants:* 48 072, Conservative Party
Tél: 418-644-1475
Ligne sans frais: 866-877-8522
Claire.Samson.IBER@assnat.qc.ca
Autres numéros: Circ. Tél: 450-346-1123; Téléc:
450-346-9068
Bureau de circonscription
327, 2e av
Saint-Jean-sur-Richelieu, QC J2X 2B5

Monique Sauvé
Circonscription électorale: Fabre *Nombre de constituants:* 53 670, Liberal
Tél: 418-263-0554
Monique.Sauve.FABR@assnat.qc.ca
Autres numéros: Circ. Tél: 450-689-5516; Téléc:
450-689-7842
twitter.com/monique_sauve,
www.facebook.com/Monique.Sauve.fabre
Bureau de circonscription
538, rue Principale
Laval, QC H7X 1C8

Leader parlementaire adjoint du gouvernement, Sébastien Schneeberger
Circonscription électorale: Drummond—Bois-Francs *Nombre de constituants:* 51 691, CA
Tél: 418-644-1052
Sebastien.Schneeberger.DRUM@assnat.qc.ca
Autres numéros: Circ. Tél: 819-475-4343; Téléc:
819-475-2354
www.facebook.com/Schneeberger.coalition
Bureau de circonscription
#203, 228, rue Hériot
Drummondville, QC J2C 1K1

Jean-François Simard
Circonscription électorale: Montmorency *Nombre de constituants:* 51 179, CA
Tél: 418-644-9600
Jean-Francois.Simard.MONT@assnat.qc.ca
Autres numéros: Circ. Tél: 418-660-6870; Téléc:
418-660-8988
Bureau de circonscription
#203, 2400, boul Louis-XIV
Québec, QC G1C 5Y8

Christopher Skeete
Circonscription électorale: Sainte-Rose *Nombre de constituants:* 53 080, CA
Tél: 418-263-0619
Christopher.Skeete.SARO@assnat.qc.ca
Autres numéros: Circ. Tél: 450-963-8272; Téléc:
450-963-7318
Bureau de circonscription
132, boul Sainte-Rose
Laval, QC H7L 1K4

Deuxième vice-présidente, Chantal Soucy
Circonscription électorale: Saint-Hyacinthe *Nombre de constituants:* 58 377, CA
Tél: 418-643-2810
Téléc: 418-643-3688
Chantal.Soucy.SAHY@assnat.qc.ca
chantalsoucy.ca
Autres numéros: Circ. Tél: 450-773-0550; Téléc:
450-773-6092
twitter.com/chantalsoucy2,
www.facebook.com/ChantalSoucyDeputee
Bureau de circonscription
#215, 2685, boul Casavant ouest
Saint-Hyacinthe, QC J2S 2B8

Christine St-Pierre
Circonscription électorale: Acadie *Nombre de constituants:* 49 838, Liberal
Tél: 581-628-1773
Christine.St-Pierre.ACAD@assnat.qc.ca
Autres numéros: Circ. Tél: 514-337-4278; Téléc:
514-337-0987
twitter.com/stpierre_ch,
www.facebook.com/Christine.StPierre.PLQ,
www.linkedin.com/in/christine-st-pierre-345b0053
Bureau de circonscription
#540, 1600, boul Henri-Bourassa ouest
Montréal, QC H3M 3E2

Marc Tanguay
Circonscription électorale: LaFontaine *Nombre de constituants:* 42 584, Liberal
Tél: 418-528-7413
Marc.Tanguay-LAFO@assnat.qc.ca
Autres numéros: Circ. Tél: 514-648-1007; Téléc:
514-648-4559
twitter.com/marc_tanguay
Bureau de circonscription
9094, boul Maurice-Duplessis
Montréal, QC H1E 7C2

Denis Tardif
Circonscription électorale: Rivière-du-Loup—Témiscouata *Nombre de constituants:* 50 261, CA
Tél: 581-628-1846
Ligne sans frais: 855-868-0822
Denis.Tardif.RDLT@assnat.qc.ca
Autres numéros: Circ. Tél: 418-868-0822; Téléc:
418-868-0826
Bureau de circonscription
#105, 320, boul de l'Hôtel-de-Ville
Rivière-du-Loup, QC G5R 5C6

Marie-Louise Tardif
Circonscription électorale: Laviolette-Saint-Maurice *Nombre de constituants:* 57 511, CA
Tél: 581-628-1818
Marie-Louise.Tardif.LASM@assnat.qc.ca
Autres numéros: Circ. Tél: 819-539-7292; Téléc:
819-539-8441
Bureau de circonscription
695, av de la Station
Shawinigan, QC G9N 1V9

L'hon. Lise Thériault
Circonscription électorale: Anjou—Louis-Riel *Nombre de constituants:* 43 666, Liberal
Tél: 581-628-1775
ltheriault-anjo@assnat.qc.ca
Autres numéros: Circ. Tél: 514-493-9630; Téléc:
514-493-9633
twitter.com/liset_alr, www.facebook.com/LiseTheriaultplq
Bureau de circonscription
#205, 7077, rue Beaubien est
Anjou, QC H1M 2Y2

Louis-Charles Thouin
Circonscription électorale: Rousseau *Nombre de constituants:* 41 944, CA
Tél: 418-263-0688

Ligne sans frais: 800-889-4401
Louis-Charles.Thouin.ROUS@assnat.qc.ca
Autres numéros: Circ. Tél: 450-302-4610
Bureau de circonscription
461, rue du Parc
Saint-Lin-Laurentides, QC J5M 3A2
François Tremblay
Circonscription électorale: Dubuc *Nombre de constituants:* 40
506, CA
Tél: 418-263-0615
Ligne sans frais: 877-380-8106
Francois.Tremblay.DUBU@assnat.qc.ca
Autres numéros: Circ. Tél: 418-544-8106; Téléc:
418-544-8167
Bureau de circonscription
439, rue Albert
La Baie, QC G7B 3L5
Kathleen Weil
Circonscription électorale: Notre-Dame-de-Grâce *Nombre de
constituants:* 48 076, Liberal
Tél: 581-628-1836
Kathleen.Weil.NDDG@assnat.qc.ca
Autres numéros: Circ. Tél: 514-489-7581; Téléc:
514-489-5426
twitter.com/Kathleen_Weil,
www.facebook.com/KathleenWeilNDG
Bureau de circonscription
#406, 5890, av Monkland
Montréal, QC H4A 1G2
Sol Zanetti
Circonscription électorale: Jean-Lesage *Nombre de
constituants:* 46 090, QS
Tél: 418-646-7635
Sol.Zanetti.JELE@assnat.qc.ca
Autres numéros: Circ. Tél: 418-648-6221; Téléc:
418-648-2061
Bureau de circonscription
#303, 1750, av De Vitré
Québec, QC G1J 1Z6

Ministères et organismes du gouvernement du Québec / Québec Government Departments & Agencies

Secrétariat aux affaires autochtones / Aboriginal Affairs

905, av Honoré-Mercier, 1e étage, Québec, QC G1R 5M6
Tél: 418-643-3166
Téléc: 418-646-4918
Autres nombres: URL:
www.quebec.ca/gouv/ministeres-et-organismes/secretariat-aux-a
ffaires-autochtones
www.facebook.com/AutochtonesQc

Ministre responsable, L'hon. Ian Lafrenière

Secrétaire générale associée, Marie-José Thomas

Secrétaire adjoint, Patrick Brunelle

Secrétaire exécutif et greffier, Jean-Daniel Thériault

Ministère des affaires municipales et Habitation / Municipal Affairs & Housing

Aile Chaveau, 10, rue Pierre-Olivier-Chauveau, Québec, QC G1R 4J3
Tél: 418-691-2015
Téléc: 418-643-7385
communications@mamrot.gouv.qc.ca
www.mamh.gouv.qc.ca
A la charge de conseiller le gouvernement & d'assurer la
coordination interministérielle dans ces domaines; a pour
mission de favoriser la mise en place & le maintien d'un cadre
de vie & de services municipaux de qualité pour des
citoyens/citoyennes; le développement des régions & des
milieux ruraux; & le progrès & le rayonnement de la métropole;
intervient auprès des municipalités locales, régionales de comté,
des communautés métropolitaines de Montréal & de Québec, &
de l'administration régionale Kativik

Ministre, L'hon. Andrée Laforest

**Ministre responsable de la Métropole, et de la région de
Montréal,** L'hon. Chantal Rouleau

Sous-ministre, Frédéric Guay
Tél: 418-691-2040
Téléc: 418-643-7708

Secrétariat général, Dominique Jodoin
Tél: 418-691-2040

**Sous-ministre adjoint, Urbanisme, aménagement du
territoire et habitation,** Daniel Gaudreau
Tél: 418-691-2040

**Sous-ministre adjointe, Secrétariat à la région
métropolitaine,** Manon Lecours
Tél: 514-873-8395
courrier.dam@mamot.gouv.qc.ca

Directeur général, Ressources financières et matérielles,
Raymond Sarrazin
Tél: 418-691-2040

Commissaire aux plaintes, Richard Villeneuve
Tél: 418-691-2071

**Agences, Conseils et Commissions Associés/
Associated Agencies, Boards & Commissions:**
**• Commission municipale du Québec (CMQ) / Québec
Municipal Commission**
Mezzanine, aile Chauveau
10, rue Pierre-Olivier-Chauveau
Québec, QC G1R 4J3
Tél: 418-691-2014
Téléc: 418-644-4676
Ligne sans frais: 866-353-6767
www.cmq.gouv.qc.ca
CMQ est un tribunal et un organisme administratif, d'enquête et
de conseil, spécialisé en matière municipale.
• Régie du logement du Québec / Québec Rental Board
Village Olympique
#2360, 5199, rue Sherbrooke est
Montréal, QC H1T 3X1
Tél: 514-873-2245
Téléc: 514-864-8077
Ligne sans frais: 800-683-2245
www.rdl.gouv.qc.ca
Autres numéros: Montréal, Laval & Longueuil: 514-864-8077
• Société d'habitation du Québec (SHQ) / Housing Québec
Aile St-Amable
1054, rue Louis-Alexandre-Taschereau, 3e étage
Québec, QC G1R 5E7
Téléc: 418-643-2533
Ligne sans frais: 800-463-4315
www.habitation.gouv.qc.ca

Infrastructures et finances municipales / Infrastructures & Municipal Financing

Sous-ministre adjoint, Jocelyn Savoie
Tél: 418-691-2040
Directeur général, Infrastructures, Jean-François Bellemare
Tél: 418-691-2005
Directrice générale, Finances municipales, Nancy Klein
Tél: 418-691-2007

Politiques / Policy

Sous-ministre adjoint, Nicolas Paradis
Tél: 418-691-2040
Directrice générale, Fiscalité et de l'évaluation foncière,
Geneviève Camiré
Tél: 418-691-2035
Directrice générale, Politiques, Jocelyn Savoie
Tél: 418-691-2039

Territoires / Regions

Sous-ministre adjoint, Martin Arsenault
Tél: 418-691-2040
Directrice générale, Opérations régionales, Jessy Baron
Tél: 418-691-2015

Ministère de l'Agriculture, des Pêcheries et de l'Alimentation du Québec (MAPAQ) / Agriculture, Fisheries & Food

200, ch Sainte-Foy, Québec, QC G1R 4X6
Tél: 418-380-2110
Ligne sans frais: 888-222-6272
www.mapaq.gouv.qc.ca
twitter.com/mapaquebec
www.facebook.com/mapaquebec
Le Ministère influence et appuie l'essor de l'industrie
bioalimentaire québécoise dans une perspective de
développement durable; réalise des interventions en production,
transformation, commercialisation & consommation des produits
agricoles, marins & alimentaires; & joue un rôle important en
matière de recherche & de développement, d'enseignement & de
formation

Ministre, L'hon. André Lamontagne

Sous-ministre, René Dufresne

**Directrice générale, Secrétariat et coordination
ministérielle,** Marie-Odile Koch

Directrice, Communications, Johanne Pelletier

**Agences, Conseils et Commissions Associés/
Associated Agencies, Boards & Commissions:**
**• Commission de protection du territoire agricole du
Québec (CPTAQ) / Agricultural Land Preservation
Commission**
200, ch Ste-Foy, 2e étage
Québec, QC G1R 4X6
Tél: 418-643-3314
Téléc: 418-643-2261
Ligne sans frais: 800-667-5294
info@cptaq.gouv.qc.ca
www.cptaq.gouv.qc.ca
**• Conseil des appellations réservées et des termes
valorisant (CARTV) / Council of Reserved Designations &
Added-Value Claims**
#4.03, 201 boul Crémazie est
Montréal, QC H2M 1L2
Tél: 514-864-8999
Téléc: 514-873-2580
info@cartv.gouv.qc.ca
www.cartv.gouv.qc.ca
**• La financière agricole de Québec (FADQ) / Farm Financial
Québec**
1400, boul Guillaume-Couture
Lévis, QC G6W 8K7
Tél: 418-838-5602
Téléc: 418-833-3871
Ligne sans frais: 800-749-3646
www.fadq.qc.ca
**• Régie des marchés agricoles et alimentaires du Québec
(RMAAQ) / Québec Agriculture & Food Marketing Board**
201, boul Crémazie est, 5e étage
Montréal, QC H2M 1L3
Tél: 514-873-4024
Téléc: 514-873-3984
rmaaqc@rmaaq.gouv.qc.ca
www.rmaaq.gouv.qc.ca

Services à la gestion / Management Services
Directeur général, Administration, Louis Gagnon

Développement régional et développement durable / Regional Development/Sustainable Development
Sous-ministre adjointe, Geneviève Masse
Directrice, Planification et programmes, Micheline Allard
Directeur, L'agriculture durable, Raynald Chassé
Directeur, Développement régional, Alain Fournier

Formation Bioalimentaire / Bio-food Training
Sous-ministre adjointe, Louise Leblanc

Pêches et aquaculture commerciales / Commercial Fishing & Aquaculture
Tél: 418-380-2136
Téléc: 418-380-2171
Sous-ministre adjoint, Abdoul Aziz Niang

Santé animale & inspection des aliments / Animal Health & Food Inspection
Tél: 418-380-2120
Téléc: 418-380-2169
Ligne sans frais: 800-463-5023
dgsaia@mapaq.gouv.qc.ca
Sous-ministre adjointe, Christine Barthe
Directrice générale, Développement et soutien à l'inspection,
Annie Lafrance
Directeur général, Inspection et bien-être animal, Daniel
Tremblay
#C 2.105, 2700, rue Einstein
Sainte-Foy, QC G1P 3W8 Canada

Transformation et aux politiques agroalimentaires / Transformation & Agri-Food Policy
Sous-ministre adjoint, Bernard Verret

Secrétariat à la Capitale-Nationale / National Capital Affairs

700, boul René-Lévesque est, 31e étage, Québec, QC G1R 5H1
Tél: 418-528-8549
Téléc: 418-528-8558
www.scn.gouv.qc.ca
twitter.com/SCN_Qc

Ministre responsable, L'hon. Geneviève Guibault

Sous-ministre associé, Alain Kirouac
Tel: 418-528-0784

Ministère de la Culture et Communications / Culture & Communications

225, Grande Allée est, Québec, QC G1R 5G5
Ligne sans frais: 888-380-8882
www.mcc.gouv.qc.ca
twitter.com/mccquebec
www.facebook.com/mccquebec

Ministre, L'hon. Nathalie Roy

Sous-ministre, Marie Gendron

Directrice, Communications & affaires publiques, Isabelle Hurtevent
Tél: 418-380-2363
Téléc: 418-380-2364
Caroline.Dorval@mcc.gouv.qc.ca

Directrice, Secrétariat général et bureau de la sous-ministre, Julie Lévesque
Tél: 418-380-2319 ext: 7127
julie.levesque@mcc.gouv.qc.ca

Directrice, Ressources humaines, Véronique Morin
Tél: 418-380-2329
Téléc: 418-380-2332
marc.tremblay@mcc.gouv.qc.ca

Agences, Conseils et Commissions Associés/ Associated Agencies, Boards & Commissions:
• **Secrétariat à la politique linguistique (SPL) / Secretariat for Language Policy**
225 Grande-Allée est, 4e étage, bloc A
Québec, QC G1R 5G5
Tél: 418-643-4248
Téléc: 418-646-7832
www.spl.gouv.qc.ca

Secrértariat à la politique linguistique / Secretariat for Language Policy
Sous-ministre associé, Claude Pinault

Développement culturel et patrimoine / Cultural Development & Heritage
Sous-ministre adjoint, Dominique Malack
Directeur général, Patrimoine et immobilisations, Martin Pineault
Directrice générale, Métropole, Danielle Dubé

Politiques et sociétés d'État / Policies & Crown Corporations
Sous-ministre adjoint, Ian Morissette
Directrice (par intérim), Centre de conservation du Québec, Élizabeth Carmichael

Organismes et Sociétés d'État/Associated Agencies, Boards & Commissions

Bibliothèque et Archives nationales du Québec (BAnQ) / National Library & Archives of Québec
475, boul de Maisonneuve est, Montréal, QC H2L 5C4
Tél: 514-873-1100
Téléc: 514-873-9312
Ligne sans frais: 800-363-9028
www.banq.qc.ca
twitter.com/_banq
www.facebook.com/banqweb20
instagram.com/banq_officiel
Président-directeur général, Jean-Louis Roy
Secrétaire générale et directrice, Affaires juridiques et de la commercialisation, Anne Milot

Conseil des arts et des lettres du Québec (CALQ) / Council for the Arts & Letters of Quebec
79, boul René-Lévesque, 3e étage, Québec, QC G1R 5N5
Tél: 418-643-1707
Téléc: 418-643-4558
Ligne sans frais: 800-608-3350
info@calq.gouv.qc.ca
www.calq.gouv.qc.ca
Secondary Address: #300, 1435, rue de Bleury
Montréal, QC H3A 2H7
Alt. Téléc: 514-864-4161
twitter.com/lecalq
www.facebook.com/lecalq
Présidente-directrice générale, Anne-Marie Jean
Tél: 514-864-4333
pdg@calq.gouv.qc.ca

Conseil du patrimoine culturel du Québec / Cultural Heritage Council of Québec
225, Grande Allée est, Québec, QC G1R 5G5
Tél: 418-643-8378
Téléc: 418-643-8591
Ligne sans frais: 844-701-0912
info@cpcq.gouv.qc.ca
www.cpcq.gouv.qc.ca
Présidente, Line Ouellet
Vice-présidente, Ann Mundy

Musée d'art contemporain de Montréal (MACM) / Montréal Museum of Contemporary Art
185, rue Sainte-Catherine ouest, Montréal, QC H2X 3X5
Tél: 514-847-6226
Téléc: 514-847-6292
info@macm.org
www.macm.org
twitter.com/macm
www.facebook.com/macmontreal
instagram.com/macmontreal
Directeur général et conservateur en chef; Directeur artistique et éducatif, John Zeppetelli

Musée de la civilisation (MCQ) / Museum of Civilisation
85, rue Dalhousie, CP 155 Succ B, Québec, QC G1K 8R2
Tél: 418-643-2158
Ligne sans frais: 866-710-8031
renseignements@mcq.org
www.mcq.org
twitter.com/mcqorg
www.facebook.com/mcqorg
instagram.com/mcqorg
Directeur général, Stéphan La Roche

Musée national des beaux-arts du Québec (MNBA) / National Museum of Fine Arts of Quebec
Parc des Champs-de-Bataille, 1, av Wolfe-Montcalm, Québec, QC G1R 5H3
Tél: 418-643-2150
Ligne sans frais: 866-220-2150
info@mnbaq.org
www.mnbaq.org
Secondary Address: 179 Grande Allée Ouest
Québec, QC G1R 2H1
twitter.com/mnbaq
www.facebook.com/mnbaq
instagram.com/mnbaq

Régie du cinéma (RCQ) / Film Board
#100, 390, rue Notre-Dame ouest, Montréal, QC H2Y 1T9
Tél: 514-873-2371
Téléc: 514-873-8874
Ligne sans frais: 800-463-2463
www.rcq.gouv.qc.ca
www.facebook.com/regieducinema

Société de développement des entreprises culturelles (SODEC) / Arts & Cultural Enterprise Development Commission
#800, 215, rue Saint-Jacques, Montréal, QC H2Y 1M6
Tél: 514-841-2200
Téléc: 514-841-8606
Ligne sans frais: 800-363-0401
info@sodec.gouv.qc.ca
www.sodec.gouv.qc.ca
Secondary Address: 36 1/2, rue St-Pierre
Québec, QC G1K 3Z6
Alt. Téléc: 418-643-8918
twitter.com/la_sodec
www.facebook.com/sodec.gouv.qc.ca
www.linkedin.com/company/sodec

Société de la Place des Arts de Montréal / Montréal Place des Arts Corporation
260, boul de Maisonneuve ouest, Montréal, QC H2X 1Y9
Tél: 514-285-4200
Téléc: 514-285-1968
info@placedesarts.com
placedesarts.com
twitter.com/place_des_arts
www.facebook.com/placedesarts
Président-Directeur général, Marc Blondeau

Société de télédiffusion du Québec (Télé-Québec) / Québec Broadcasting Corporation
1000, rue Fullum, Montréal, QC H2K 3L7
Tél: 514-521-2424
Téléc: 514-864-1970
info@telequebec.tv
www.telequebec.tv
twitter.com/telequebec
www.facebook.com/teleqc
instagram.com/telequebec

Directrice générale, Marie Collin

Société du Grand Théâtre de Québec / Grand Theatre of Québec
269, boul René-Lévesque est, Québec, QC G1R 2B3
Tél: 418-643-8111
Ligne sans frais: 877-643-8131
gtq@grandtheatre.qc.ca
www.grandtheatre.qc.ca
twitter.com/grandtheatreqc
www.facebook.com/grandtheatre
instagram.com/grandtheatreqc
Président-directeur général, Gaétan Morency

Ministère de l'Environnement et de la Lutte contre les changements climatiques / Environment & the Fight Against Climate Change

Édifice Marie-Guyart, 675, boul René-Lévesque est, 30e étage, Québec, QC G1R 5V7
Tél: 418-521-3830
Téléc: 418-646-5974
Ligne sans frais: 800-561-1616
relations.medias@mddelcc.gouv.qc.ca
www.environnement.gouv.qc.ca
twitter.com/MELCC_Qc
www.facebook.com/MELCCQuebec
www.linkedin.com/company/melcc
www.youtube.com/user/MDDEPQuebec

A pour mission d'assurer la protection de l'environnement & des écosystèmes naturels; de promouvoir le développement durable & d'assurer à la population un environnement sain en harmonie avec le développement économique & le progrès social du Québec

Ministre, L'hon. Benoit Charette

Sous-ministre, Marc Croteau

Directeur, Bureau des renseignements, de l'accès à l'information et des plaintes sur la qualité des services, Pascale Porlier

Directeur, Communications, Pauline Boissinot
Tél: 418-521-3823 ext: 4167

Directeur du cabinet, Hugo Delaney

Directrice, Affaires juridiques, Monique Rousseau
Tél: 418-521-3816 ext: 4547

Agences, Conseils et Commissions Associés/ Associated Agencies, Boards & Commissions:
• **Bureau d'audiences publiques sur l'environnement (BAPE) / Environmental Public Hearing Board**
Édifice Lomer-Gouin
#2.10, 575, rue Jacques-Parizeau
Québec, QC G1R 6A6
Tél: 418-643-7447
Téléc: 418-643-9474
Ligne sans frais: 800-463-4732
communication@bape.gouv.qc.ca
www.bape.gouv.qc.ca
• **Comité consultatif de l'environnement Kativik (CCEK) / Kativik Environmental Advisory Committee (KEAC)**
CP 930
Kuujjuaq, QC J0M 1C0
Tél: 819-964-2961
Téléc: 819-964-0694
keac-ccek@krg.ca
www.keac-ccek.ca
• **Société des établissements en plein air du Québec (SÉPAQ)**
Place de la Cité, Tour Cominar
#250, 2640, boul Laurier, 2e étage
Québec, QC G1V 5C2
Tel: 418-686-4875; Fax: 418-643-8177
Toll-free: 800-665-6527
inforeservation@sepaq.com
www.sepaq.com
• **Société québécoise de récupération et de recyclage (RECYC-QUÉBEC)**
#411, 300, rue Saint-Paul
Québec, QC G1K 7R1
Tél: 418-643-0394
Téléc: 418-643-6507
Ligne sans frais: 800-807-0678
info@recyc-quebec.gouv.qc.ca
www.recyc-quebec.gouv.qc.ca
Autres numéros: Relations médias:
medias@recyc-quebec.gouv.qc.ca

Contrôle environnemental et à la sécurité des barrages / Environmental Control & Dam Safety
Sous-ministre adjoint, Michel Rousseau
 Tél: 418-521-3860
Directeur, Sécurité des barrages, Michel Rhéaume

Centre de contrôle environnemental du Québec / Québec Centre for Environmental Control
Directeur, Enquêtes et du passif environnemental, Carl Bernier

Développement durable et à la qualité de l'environnement / Sustainable Development & Environmental Quality
Sous-ministre adjoint, Jacob Martin-Malus
Directeur général, Politiques du milieu terrestre, Mario Bérubé
Directeur général, Suivi de l'état de l'environnement, François Houde

Évaluations et aux autorisations environnementales / Assessments & Environmental Permits
Sous-ministre adjointe, Marie-Josée Lizotte
 Tél: 418-521-3861
Directeur général, L'évaluation environnementale et stratégique et responsable, consultation autochtone, Yves Rochon

Analyse et de l'expertise régionales / Regional Analysis & Expertise
La mission est d'assurer l'analyse & la délivrance d'autorisations environnementales & d'offrir une expertise professionnelle en matière d'environnement

Expertise et aux politiques de l'eau et de l'air / Water & Air Policies & Expertise
Sous-ministre adjointe, Guylaine Bouchard
Directeur général, Centre d'expertise en analyse environnementale du Québec, Claude Denis
Directrice générale, Politiques de l'eau, Marie-Claude Théberge

Lutte contre les changements climatiques / Fight Against Climate Change
Sous-ministre adjoint, Éric Théroux
Directrice générale, Réglementation carbone et des données d'émission, France Delisle

Services à la gestion / Administrative Services
Sous-ministre adjointe, Lise Lallemand
 Tél: 418-521-3860
Directrice générale, Technologies de l'information, Paule Tremblay
Directrice générale, Ressources financières et matérielles, Joëlle Jobin

Commission des droits de la personne et des droits de la jeunesse (CDPDJ) / Commission for Human Rights & the Rights of Youth

360, rue Saint-Jacques, 2e étage, Montréal, QC H2Y 1P5
 Tél: 514-873-5146
 Téléc: 514-873-6032
 Ligne sans frais: 800-361-6477
 information@cdpdj.qc.ca
 www.cdpdj.qc.ca
Autres nombres: TTY: 514-873-2648; Relations avec les médias: communications@cdpdj.qc.ca
 twitter.com/cdpdj1
 www.facebook.com/CDPDJ
A pour mission d'assurer la promotion et la respect des droits et libertés affirmés par la Charte des droits et libertés de la personne, par la Loi sur la protection de la jeunesse, et par la Loi sur les jeunes contrevenants.

Président (par intérim), Philippe-André Tessier

Secrétariat à la condition féminine / Status of Women Commission

905, av Honoré-Mercier, 3e étage, Québec, QC G1R 5M6
 Tél: 418-643-9052
 Téléc: 418-643-4991
 www.scf.gouv.qc.ca
 www.facebook.com/ConditionFeminineQc

Ministre responsable, Isabelle Charest

Sous-ministre associée, Catherine Ferembach

Directrice (par intérim), Régionalisation, Abdelouaheb Baalouch

Ministère de l'Économie et de l'Innovation / Economy & Innovation

710, Place D'Youville, 3e étage, Québec, QC G1R 4Y4
 Tél: 418-691-5950
 Téléc: 418-644-0118
 Ligne sans frais: 866-680-1884
 www.economie.gouv.qc.ca
Secondary Address: 380, rue Saint-Antoine Ouest, 5e étage
 Montréal, QC H2Y 3X7
 twitter.com/economie_quebec
 www.facebook.com/economieqc

Ministre; Ministre responsable du Développement économique régional, L'hon. Pierre Fitzgibbon

Ministre délégué à l'Économie, L'hon. Lucie Lecours

Sous-ministre, David Bahan

Directrice, Bureau du sous-ministre et Secrétariat général, Marie-Claude Lajoie

Directreur, Communications, Terry McKinnon

Directrice, Audit interne, Sylvie Plante

Agences, Conseils et Commissions Associés/ Associated Agencies, Boards & Commissions:
• **Centre de recherche industrielle du Québec (CRIQ) / Industrial Research Centre of Québec**
333, rue Franquet
Québec, QC G1P 4C7
Tél: 418-659-1550
Téléc: 418-652-2251
Ligne sans frais: 800-667-2386
infocriq@criq.qc.ca
www.criq.qc.ca
Recherche industrielle appliquée; services de RD pour des entreprises

• **Commission de l'éthique en science et en technologie (CEST) / Ethics of Science & Technology Commission**
#555, 888, rue Saint-Jean
Québec, QC G1R 5H6
Tél: 418-691-5989
Téléc: 418-646-0920
ethique@ethique.gouv.qc.ca
www.ethique.gouv.qc.ca

• **Coopérative régionale d'électricité de Saint-Jean-Baptiste-de-Rouville / Electric Cooperative of Saint-Jean-Baptiste-de-Rouville**
3113, rue Principale
Saint-Jean-Baptiste, QC J0L 1B0
Tél: 450-467-5583
Téléc: 450-467-0092
Ligne sans frais: 800-267-5583
info@coopsjb.com
www.coopsjb.com

• **Fonds de recherche du Québec - Société et culture / Québec Research Funds - Society & Culture**
#470, 140, Grande Allée est
Québec, QC G1R 5M8
Tél: 418-643-7582
frq.sc@frq.gouv.qc.ca
www.frqsc.gouv.qc.ca
Autres numéros: Montréal: 514-864-8355

• **Investissement Québec / Investment Québec**
#60, 1195, av Lavigerie
Québec, QC G1V 4N3
Tél: 418-643-5172
Téléc: 418-528-2063
Ligne sans frais: 844-474-6367
www.investquebec.com

• **Société du parc industriel et portuaire de Bécancour (SPIPB) / Industrial Park & Port Society of Bécancour**
1000, boul Arthur-Sicard
Bécancour, QC G9H 2Z8
Tél: 819-294-6656
Téléc: 819-294-9020
info@spipb.com
www.spipb.com

Commerce extérieur et Export Québec / Foreign Trade & Export Québec
Sous-ministre adjoint, Jean Séguin
Directeur, Marchés de l'Europe, de l'Afrique et du Moyen-Orient, Julien Cormier
Directeur, Marchés de l'Asie-Pacifique et de l'Océanie, Dominic Cousineau
Directeur, Marchés de l'Amérique du Nord, Yves Lafortune

Directrice, Marchés de l'Amérique latine et des Antilles, Marie-Josée Lapointe
Directeur, Coordination et stratégies commerciales, Isabelle Phaneuf

Industries stratégiques et projets économiques majeurs / Strategic Industries & Major Economic Projects
Sous-ministre adjoint, Mario Bouchard
Directeur général, Interventions stratégiques, Pierre Dupont
Directeur général, Développement des industries et Directeur, biens de consommation et commerce électronique, Richard Masse
Directeur, Transport et mobilité durable, Martin Aubé
Directrice, Technologies de l'information et des communications, Marie-Hélène Savard
Directrice, Sciences de la vie et investissement étranger, Vanessa Claveau
Directeur, Projets économiques majeurs, Raymond Jeudi
Directeur, Interventions financières, Alexandre Montelpare
Directreur, Produits industriels, Gabriel Audet

Politiques économiques / Economic Policies
Sous-ministre associé, Philippe Dubuisson
Directeur général, Politique commerciale, Jean-François Raymond
Directeur général, Politiques et affaires institutionnelles, François Maxime Langlois

Science et Innovation / Science & Innovation
Sous-ministre adjoint, Marie-Josée Blais
Directeur général, Marco Blouin
Directrice, Partenariats et programmes canadiens et internationaux, Barbara Béliveau
Directeur, Développement de la relève, André Doré
Directeur, Maillages et partenariats industriels, Martin Doyon
Directeur, Bureau de gestion des projets d'infrastructure, Josée Mayrand
Directrice, Soutien aux organisations, Denise Moranville

Services aux entreprises et affaires territoriales / Business Services & Regional Affairs
Sous-ministre adoint, Mario Limoges
Directeur général, Services aux entreprises et entrepreneuriat, Daniel Gagné
Directeur général, Affaires régionales et métropolitaines, Jacques La Rue
Directrice, Coordination et stratégies régionales, Monique Asselin
Directrice, Entreprises Québec et processus d'accompagnement, Jocelyn Bianki
Directeur, Développement des entreprises, Pierre Hébert
Directeur, Soutien à léntrepreneuriat et aux créneaux d'excellence, Alexandre Vézina

Ministère de l'Éducation et de l'Enseignement supérieur / Education & Higher Education

1035, rue de la Chevrotière, 28e étage, Québec, QC G1R 5A5
 Tél: 418-643-7095
 Téléc: 418-646-6561
 Ligne sans frais: 866-747-6626
 www.education.gouv.qc.ca
 twitter.com/educationqc
 www.facebook.com/quebeceducation
 www.facebook.com/enseignementsuperieurquebec

Ministre de l'Éducation, L'hon. Jean-François Roberge

Ministre de l'Enseignement supérieur, L'hon. Danielle McCann

Ministre déléguée à l'Éducation, L'hon. Isabelle Charest

Sous-ministre, Eric Blackburn

Directrice, Accès à l'information et plaintes, Ingrid Barakatt

Directrice, Vérification interne, Anne DeBlais

Directrice, Communications, Stéphanie Jourdain

Directrice, Affaires juridiques, Mélanie Paradis

Directrice, Coordination ministérielle et Secrétariat général, Stéphanie Vachon

Agences, Conseils et Commissions Associés/ Associated Agencies, Boards & Commissions:

• Comité consultatif sur l'accessibilité financière aux études (CCAFE) / Advisory Committee on Financial Accessibility for Education
1035, rue de la Chevrotière, 20e étage
Québec, QC G1R 5A5
Tél: 418-644-3468
www.ccafe.gouv.qc.ca
Autres numéros: Téléphone poste: 3972

• Commission consultative de l'enseignement privé (CCEP) / Consultative Committee on Private Education
1035, rue de la Chevrotière, 26e étage
Québec, QC G1R 5A5
Tél: 418-646-1249
www.education.gouv.qc.ca/organismes-relevant-du-ministre/ccep

• Commission d'évaluation de l'enseignement collégial (CEEC) / College Teachers Assessment Commission
#400, 888, rue St-Jean, 4e étage
Québec, QC G1R 5H6
Tél: 418-643-9938
Téléc: 418-643-9019
info@ceec.gouv.qc.ca
www.ceec.gouv.qc.ca

• Commission de l'éducation en langue anglaise (CELA) / Commission for English Language Education (ABEE)
600, rue Fullum, 11e étage
Montréal, QC H2K 4L1
Tél: 514-873-5656
Téléc: 514-864-4181
www.mels.gouv.qc.ca/cela/anglais.htm

• Commission de la capitale nationale du Québec (CCNQ)
Édifice Hector-Fabre
525, boul René-Lévesque est, RC
Québec, QC G1R 5S9
Tél: 418-528-0773
Téléc: 418-528-0833
Ligne sans frais: 800-442-0773
commission@capitale.gouv.qc.ca
www.capitale.gouv.qc.ca

• Conseil du statut de la femme / Status of Women Council
#300, 800, place D'Youville, 3e étage
Québec, QC G1R 6E2
Tél: 418-643-4326
Téléc: 418-643-8926
Ligne sans frais: 800-463-2851
csf@csf.gouv.qc.ca
www.csf.gouv.qc.ca

• Conseil supérieur de l'éducation / Superior Council of Education
#180, 1175, av Lavigerie
Québec, QC G1V 5B2
Tél: 418-643-3850
Téléc: 418-644-2530
conseil@cse.gouv.qc.ca
www.cse.gouv.qc.ca

• Institut de tourisme et d'hôtellerie du Québec (ITHQ) / Tourism & Hotel Institute of Québec
3535, rue Saint-Denis
Montréal, QC H2X 3P1
Tél: 514-282-5111
Ligne sans frais: 800-282-5111
info@ithq.qc.ca
www.ithq.qc.ca

• Institut national des mines du Québec (INMQ) / Québec National Institute of Mines
125, rue Self
Val-d'Or, QC J9P 3N2
Tél: 819-825-4667
Téléc: 819-825-4660
secretariat@inmq.qc.ca
www.inmq.gouv.qc.ca

Secrétariat à la Capitale-Nationale / Secretariat of the National Capital Region
Sous-ministre adjoint, Alain Kirouac
Tel: 418-528-0784

Secrétariat à la condition féminine / Status of Women Secretariat
Sous-ministre adjointe/Directrice (par intérim), Initiatives intersectorielles et mandats spéciaux, Catherine Ferembach
Tel: 418-646-8395

Aide financière aux études / Student Financial Aid
Sous-ministre adjoint, Jean-Claude Labelle
Directeur-général, Services de l'aide financière aux études, Martin Baron

Éducation préscolaire, enseignement primaire et secondaire / Preschool, Elementary & Secondary Education
Sous-ministre adjointe, Anne-Marie Lepage
Tél: 418-643-3810 ext: 3600

Directeur général, Services de soutien aux élèves, Yvon Doyle
Directrice générale, Services à l'enseignement, Geneviève LeBlanc
Directrice générale, Financement, Nathalie Parenteau

Enseignement supérieur / Higher Education
Sous-ministre adjoint/ Directeur (par intérim), affaires universitaires et interordres, Simon Bergeron
Directrice générale, Affaires collégiales, Esther Blais
Directeur général, Financement, Éric Fournier

Gouvernance des technologies, des infrastructures et des ressources / Governance of Technology, Infrastructure & Resources
Sous-ministre adjoint, François Bérubé
Directeur général, Infrastructures, Patrick Lachapelle
Directrice générale, Administration, Katlyn Langlois
Directrice générale, Transformation numérique et ressources informationnelles, Stéphane Lehoux
Directeur général adjoint, Systèmes et technologies, Jean Lauzier
Directeur général adjoint, Orientations, architecture et financement, Frédéric Potok

Loisir et sport / Sport & Recreation
Sous-ministre adjoint, Robert Bédard

Politiques et relations du travail dans les réseaux / Labour Relations & Network Policies
Sous-ministre adjoint, Nicolas Paradis
Directrice générale, Relations du travail, Monique D'Amours
Directeur général adjoint, Relations du travail, Richard Bernier
Directrice générale, Politiques et performance ministérielle, Anne Robitaille

Services aux anglophones, aux autochtones et à la diversité culturelles / Anglophone Services, Aboriginal Affairs & Cultural Diversity
Sous-ministre adjoint, Steven Colpitts

Directeur général des Élections du Québec / Chief Electoral Officer of Québec

Édifice René-Lévesque, 3460, rue de la Pérade, Québec, QC G1X 3Y5

Tél: 418-528-0422
Téléc: 418-643-7291
Ligne sans frais: 888-353-2846
TTY: 418-646-0644
info@electionsquebec.qc.ca
www.facebook.com/electionsquebec
www.linkedin.com/company/elections-quebec
instagram.com/electionsquebec

Directeur général des élections, Président de la commission de la représentation électorale, Pierre Reid
Tél: 418-644-1090 ext: 3207

Secrétaire général, Catherine Lagacé
Tél: 418-644-1090 ext: 3202

Agences, Conseils et Commissions Associés/ Associated Agencies, Boards & Commissions:

• Commission de la représentation électorale (CRE)
Édifice René-Lévesque
3460, rue de La Pérade
Québec, QC G1X 3Y5
Tél: 418-528-0422
Téléc: 418-643-7291
Ligne sans frais: 888-353-2846
TTY: 800-537-0644
info@electionsquebec.qc.ca
www2.electionsquebec.qc.ca/lacartechange

Ministère des Énergie et des Ressources naturelles (MERN) / Energy & Natural Resources

Service à la clientèle, 5700, 4e av ouest, #A301, Québec, QC G1H 6R1

Ligne sans frais: 866-248-6936
services.clientele@mern.gouv.qc.ca
mern.gouv.qc.ca
Autres nombres: Alt. courriel: renseignements@mern.gouv.qc.ca
twitter.com/mern_quebec
www.facebook.com/energieressourcesnaturelles
instagram.com/mern_quebec

Ministre, L'hon. Jonatan Julien

Sous-ministre, Marie-Josée Lizotte

Directrice, Communications, Nathalie Germain
Tél: 418-627-8609 ext: 3107

Agences, Conseils et Commissions Associés/ Associated Agencies, Boards & Commissions:

• Hydro Québec
See Entry Name Index for detailed listing.

• Régie de l'énergie / Energy Regulation Board
Tour de la Bourse
#2.55, 800, Place Victoria
Montréal, QC H4Z 1A2
Tél: 514-873-2452
Téléc: 514-873-2070
Ligne sans frais: 888-873-2452
secretariat@regie-energie.qc.ca
www.regie-energie.qc.ca
Autres numéros: Greffe: greffe@regie-energie.qc.ca; Centre de documentation: centre.doc@regie-energie.qc.ca
La Régie fixe les tarifs et les conditions de services destinés aux consommateurs québécois d'électricité et de gaz naturel.

• Société de développement de la Baie James (SDBJ) / James Bay Development Society
#10, 462, 3e rue
Chibougamau, QC G8P 1N7
Tél: 418-748-7777
Téléc: 418-748-6868
chi@sdbj.gouv.qc.ca
www.sdbj.gouv.qc.ca
Autres numéros: Matagami, Tél: 819-739-4717; Téléc: 819-739-4329; Courriel: mat@sdbj.gouv.qc.ca; Radisson, Tél: 819 638-8411; Téléc: 819 638-8838; Courriel: rad@sdbj.gouv.qc.ca
La SDBJ a pour mission de favoriser, dans une perspective de développement durable, le développement économique, la mise en valeur et l'exploitation des ressources naturelles du territoire de la Baie-James (autres que les ressources hydroélectriques relevant du mandat d'Hydro-Québec).

• Transition énergetique Québec (TEQ) / Energy Transition Québec
5700, 4e av ouest, #B406
Québec, QC G1H 6R1
Tél: 418-627-6379
Téléc: 418-643-5828
Ligne sans frais: 877-727-6655
transitionenergetique@teq.gouv.qc.ca
www.efficaciteenergetique.gouv.qc.ca
Autres numéros: Alt. courriel: renseignements@teq.gouv.qc.ca
Transition énergetique Québec (annoncée dans la Politique énergétique 2030) a été créée pour assurer la transition énergétique du Québec; sa mission est de soutenir, de stimuler et de promouvoir la transition, l'innovation et l'efficacité énergétiques ainsi que de coordonner la mise en ouvre de l'ensemble des programmes et des mesures nécessaires à l'atteinte des cibles énergétiques définies par le gouvernement.

Mandats stratégiques / Strategic Manadates
Directeur général, Marc Leduc
Tél: 418-627-6370 ext: 4693

Ressources financières et matérielles et gestion contractuelle / Financial & Material Resources & Contract Management
Directrice générale et Directrice (par intérim), Systèmes financiers et mandats spéciaux, et ressources matérielles et gestion contractuelle, Martine Allard

Ressources humaines et ressources informationnelles / Human Resources & Information Resources
Directrice générale, Jenny Côté
Directrice générale adjointe, Ressources informationelles, Julie Bélanger
Directrice générale adjointe (par intérim), Ressources humaines, et directrice, Gestion de la main-d'oeuvre, Isabelle Godbout

Énergie / Energy
#A301 - 5700, 4e av ouest, Québec, QC G1H 6R1
www.mern.gouv.qc.ca/energie
Autres nombres: Énergie: www.mern.gouv.qc.ca/energie
Secondary Address: 5700, 4e av ouest, #D327
Bureau de la sous-ministre associée aux Mines
Québec, QC G1H 6R1
www.facebook.com/quebecminesenergie
instagram.com/quebec_mines_energie
Sous-ministre associée, Luce Asselin
Tél: 418-627-6377 ext: 8172
Directrice générale (par intérim), Hydrocarbures et bioarburants, et Directrice, Bureau des hydrocarbures, Marie-Eve Bergeron
Tél: 418-627-6385 ext: 8131
Directeur général, Électricité, Louis Germain

Mines / Mines
#A301 - 5700, 4e av ouest, Québec, QC G1H 6R1
Tél: 418-627-6278
service.mines@mern.gouv.qc.ca
www.mern.gouv.qc.ca/energie
Autres nombres: Mines: www.mern.gouv.qc.ca/mines
Secondary Address: 5700, 4e av ouest, #D327
Bureau de la sous-ministre associée aux Mines
Québec, QC G1H 6R1
www.facebook.com/quebecminesenergie
instagram.com/quebec_mines_energie
Sous-ministre associée, Nathalie Camden
Directrice générale adjointe, Développement de l'industrie minière et directrice générale (par intérim), Gestion du milieu minier, Renée Garon
Directeur général adjoint, Géologie Québec, Robert Giguère
Directrice, Promotion et soutien aux opérations et Directrice (par intérim), Bureau de la connaissance géoscientifique du Québec, Andréa Amortegui
Directeur, Restauration des sites miniers, Yves Boutin
Directeur, Développement et contrôle de l'activité minière, Roch Gaudreau
Directrice, Affaires minières et coordination, Hélène Giroux
Directeur, Information géologique du Québec, Jean-Yves Labbé

Territoire
#E330 - 5700, 4e av ouest, Québec, QC G1H 6R1
Tél: 418-627-6297
Le Ministère favorise une utilisation du territoire qui rejoint les préoccupations économiques, sociales & environnementales des Québécois
Sous-ministre associé, Mario Gosselin
Tél: 418-627-6252 ext: 3082
Directeur général, Arpentage et cadastre, Julien Arsenault
Tél: 418-627-6267 ext: 2881
Directrice générale, Registre foncier, Stéphanie Cashman-Pelletier
Tél: 418-627-6350 ext: 2279
Directrice générale, Soutien aux opérations, Julie Sauvageau
Directeur général, Information géospatiale, Ricardo Binotto
information.geographique@mern.gouv.qc.ca

Foncier / Lands
Tél: 418-643-3582
Téléc: 418-528-8721
Ligne sans frais: 866-226-0977
info.foncier@mern.gouv.qc.ca
Autres nombres: Propriétaires touchés par la réforme du cadastre québécois, Tél: 418-627-8600; Ligne sans frais: 888-733-3720

Réseau régional / Regional Network
Ligne sans frais: 844-282-8277
droit.terre.publique@mern.gouv.qc.ca
mern.gouv.qc.ca/nous-joindre
Directeur général, Yves Robertson

Abitibi-Témiscamingue
70, av Québec, Rouyn-Noranda, QC J9X 6R1
Ligne sans frais: 844-282-8277
droit.terre.publique@mern.gouv.qc.ca

Bas-Saint-Laurent
#207 - 92, 2e rue ouest, Rimouski, QC G5L 8B3
Ligne sans frais: 844-282-8277
droit.terre.publique@mern.gouv.qc.ca

Côte-Nord
#RC 702, 625, boul Laflèche, Baie-Comeau, QC G5C 1C5
Ligne sans frais: 844-282-8277
droit.terre.publique@mern.gouv.qc.ca

Estrie-Montréal-Chaudière-Appalaches-Laval-Montérégie-Centre-du-Québec
545, boul Crémazie est, 8e étage, Montréal, QC H2M 2V1
Ligne sans frais: 844-282-8277
droit.terre.publique@mern.gouv.qc.ca

Gaspésie-îles-de-la-Madeleine
195, boul Perron est, Caplan, QC G0C 1H0
Ligne sans frais: 844-282-8277
droit.terre.publique@mern.gouv.qc.ca

Mauricie-Lanaudière
#207, 100, rue Laviolette, Trois-Rivières, QC G9A 5S9
Ligne sans frais: 844-282-8277
droit.terre.publique@mern.gouv.qc.ca

Nord-du-Québec
624, 3e rue, Chibougamau, QC G8P 1P1
Ligne sans frais: 844-282-8277
droit.terre.publique@mern.gouv.qc.ca

Outaouais-Laurentides
#RC 100, 16, impasse de la Gare-Talon, Gatineau, QC J8T 0B1
Ligne sans frais: 844-282-8277
droit.terre.publique@mern.gouv.qc.ca

Saguenay-Lac-Saint-Jean-Capitale-Nationale
3950, boul Harvey, 3e étage, Jonquière, QC G7X 8L6
Ligne sans frais: 844-282-8277
droit.terre.publique@mern.gouv.qc.ca

Ministère de la Famille / Family

Service des renseignements, 600, rue Fullum, 6e étage, Montréal, QC H2K 4S7
Ligne sans frais: 855-336-8568
www.mfa.gouv.qc.ca
twitter.com/famillequebec
www.facebook.com/famillequebec
A la suite de la formation du nouveau Conseil des ministres, le 19 septembre 2012, le volet Aînés relève désormais du ministère de la Santé et des Services sociaux.

Ministre, L'hon. Mathieu Lacombe

Ministre responsable des Aînés et des Proches aidants, L'hon. Marguerite Blais

Sous-ministre, Julie Blackburn

Secretariat général, Steeve Audet

Agences, Conseils et Commissions Associés/ Associated Agencies, Boards & Commissions:
• Curateur public du Québec / Québec Public Trustee
600, boul René-Lévesque ouest
Montréal, QC H3B 4W9
Tél: 514-873-4074
Ligne sans frais: 800-363-9020
www.curateur.gouv.qc.ca

• Retraite Québec / Retirement Québec
Place de la Cité, entrée 6
#548, 2600, boul Laurier
Québec, QC G1V 4T3
www.retraitequebec.gouv.qc.ca

Administration et des technologies / Administration & Technology
Directrice générale, Lynda Roy
Directeur général adjoint, Technologies de l'information, Luc Tremblay

Opérations régionales / Regional Operations
Sous-ministre adjointe, Chantal Castonguay

Politiques / Policies
Sous-ministre adjointe, France Dompierre

Secrétariat aux aînés / Seniors' Secretariat
www.mfa.gouv.qc.ca/fr/aines
Sous-ministre adjoint, Christian Barrette

Services de garde éducatifs à l'enfance / Educational Childcare Services
Sous-ministre adjointe, Carole Vézina

Ministère des Finances / Finance

12, rue Saint-Louis, Québec, QC G1R 5L3
Tél: 418-528-9323
Téléc: 418-646-1631
info@finances.gouv.qc.ca
www.finances.gouv.qc.ca

Ministre, L'hon. Éric Girard

Sous-ministre, Pierre Côté

Directeur, Affaires juridiques, Jean-François Lord

Directrice, Communications, Danielle-Josée Pelletier

Directeur du secrétariat général et de la coordination ministérielle; L'organisation du budget et de l'administration, David St-Martin

Agences, Conseils et Commissions Associés/ Associated Agencies, Boards & Commissions:
• Autorité des marchés financiers (AMF)
Tour de la Bourse
800, rue du Square-Victoria, 22e étage
CP 246
Montréal, QC H4Z 1G3
Tél: 514-395-0337
Téléc: 514-873-3090
Ligne sans frais: 877-525-0337
www.lautorite.qc.ca

• Caisse de dépôt et placement du Québec
Édifice Jacques-Parizeau
1000, place Jean-Paul-Riopelle
Montréal, QC H2Z 2B3
Tél: 514-842-3261
Téléc: 514-842-4833
Ligne sans frais: 866-330-3936
TTY: 514-847-2190
info@cdpq.com
cdpq.com

• Financement-Québec
12, rue Saint-Louis, 3e étage
Québec, QC G1R 5L3
Tél: 418-691-2203
Téléc: 418-644-6214
financement.regroupe@finances.gouv.qc.ca
www.finances.gouv.qc.ca/en/Financement_Quebec58.asp

• Institut de la statistique du Québec (BSQ) / Québec Statistics Office
200, ch Ste-Foy, 3e étage
Québec, QC G1R 5T4
Tél: 418-691-2401
Téléc: 418-643-4129
Ligne sans frais: 800-463-4090
www.stat.gouv.qc.ca

• Société de financement des infrastructures locales (SOFIL) / Local Infrastructure Financing Corporation
Ministère des Finances
12, rue Saint-Louis
Québec, QC G1R 5L3
Tél: 418-528-9323
Téléc: 418-646-1631
info@finances.gouv.qc.ca
www.sofil.gouv.qc.ca

• Société des alcools du Québec (SAQ) / Québec Liquor Corporation
7500, rue Tellier
Montréal, QC H1N 3W5
Tél: 514-254-2020
Ligne sans frais: 866-873-2020
www.saq.com

• Société des loteries du Québec / Québec Lotteries Corporation
500, rue Sherbrooke ouest
Montréal, QC H3A 3G6
Tél: 514-282-8000
Téléc: 514-873-8999
service_clientele@loto-quebec.com
lotoquebec.com

• Société Québécoise du Cannabis (SQDC) / Québec Cannabis Corporation
7500, rue Tellier
Montréal, QC H1N 3W5
Tél: 514-504-7732
Ligne sans frais: 888-551-2161
www.sqdc.ca
La Société québécoise du cannabis est une filiale de la Société des alcools du Québec; créée en juin 2018 à la suite de l'adoption de la Loi encadrant la Société québécoise du cannabis; constituée en tant que compagnie à fonds social.

• Tribunal administratif des marchés financiers (TMF) / Administrative Tribunal of Financial Markets
#16.40, 500, boul Réné-Lévesque ouest
Montréal, QC H2Z 1W7
Tél: 514-873-2211
Téléc: 514-873-2162
Ligne sans frais: 877-873-2211
secretariattmf@tmf.gouv.qc.ca
www.tmf.gouv.qc.ca

Contrôleur des finances / Financial Controller
Contrôleur des finances, Simon-Pierre Falardeau

Droit fiscal, optimisation des revenus et aux politiques locales et autochtones / Fiscal Law, Revenue Optimization & Aboriginal & Local Affairs
Sous-ministre adjoint, Marc Grandisson
Directeur, Impôts des entreprises et de l'intégrité, Luc Bilodeau
Directrice, Politiques locales et autochtones, Étienne Paré

Politiques aux particuliers et à l'économie / Social Policy & Economy
Sous-ministre adjointe, Julie Gingras
Directeur général, Politiques aux particuliers, Jean-Pierre Simard

Politiques budgétaire et financières / Budgetary Policy & Finances
Sous-ministre adjoint, Marc Sirois

Politiques fiscales aux enterprises, au développement économique et aux sociétés d'État / Tax Policies for Businesses, Economic Development & Crown Corporations
Sous-ministre adjoint, Bertrand Cayouette
Directeur, Taxation des entreprises, Nicolas Tremblay

Politiques relatives aux institutions financières et au droit corporatif / Policy Regarding Financial Institutions & Corporations
Sous-ministre adjoint, Richard Boivin
Directeur, Droit corporatif et de la solvabilité, François Bouchard

Relations fédérales-provinciales, dette, régimes de retraite, et opérations financières / Federal-Provincial Relations, Debt, Pension Plans & Financial Operations
Sous-ministre adjoint, Financement et la gestion de la dette, Alain Bélanger
Directeur général, Régimes de retraite et des projets spéciaux, Guy Émond
Directeur général, Opérations bancaires et financières et des relations avec les agences de notation, Gino Ouellet

Commission de la fonction publique / Public Service Commission

800, Place D'Youville, 7e étage, Québec, QC G1R 3P4
Tél: 418-643-1425
Téléc: 418-643-7264
Ligne sans frais: 800-432-0432
cfp@cfp.gouv.qc.ca
www.cfp.gouv.qc.ca

Présidente, Hélène Fréchette

Secrétaire général et directeur, Services administratifs, Richard Saint-Pierre

Directrice générale, Activités de surveillance et du greffe, Lucie Robitaille

Ministère des Forêts, Faune et Parcs / Forestry, Wildlife & Parks

Service à la clientèle, #A409 - 5700, 4e av ouest, Québec, QC G1H 6R1
Téléc: 418-644-6513
Ligne sans frais: 844-523-6738
services.clientele@mrnf.gouv.qc.ca
Autres nombres: SOS Braconnage, Tél: 800-463-2191; Courriel:
centralesos@mffp.gouv.qc.ca
twitter.com/MFFP_Quebec

Ministre, L'hon. Pierre Dufour

Sous-ministre, Mario Gosselin

Directeur général, Mandats stratégiques, Francis Forcier
Tel: 418-266-8178 ext: 4206

Directrice générale, Ressources financières et matérielles et gestion contractuelle, Martine Allard

Directrice générale, Ressources humaines et ressources informationnelles, Jenny Côté

Directrice, Conseil stratégique et moyens de communication, Geneviève Coderre

Agences, Conseils et Commissions Associés/ Associated Agencies, Boards & Commissions:

• Comité conjoint de chasse, de pêche et de piégeage / Hunting, Fishing & Trapping Coordinating Committee
#1420, 1080, Côte du Beaver Hall
Montréal, QC H2Z 1N8
Tél: 514-284-2151
Téléc: 514-284-0039
infohftcc@cccpp-hftcc.com
www.cccpp-hftcc.com

• Fondation de la faune du Québec / Québec Wildlife Foundation
#420, 1175, av Lavigerie
Québec, QC G1V 4P1
Tél: 418-644-7926
Téléc: 418-643-7655
Ligne sans frais: 877-639-0742
ffq@fondationdelafaune.qc.ca
www.fondationdelafaune.qc.ca
Non-profit organization whose mission is to enhance the value & promote the conservation of wildlife & its habitats.

• Société des établissements de plein air du Québec (Sépaq) / Québec Outdoor Enterprises Association
Place de la Cité, Tour Cominar
#1300, 2640, boul Laurier
Québec, QC G1V 5C2
Tél: 418-686-4875
Téléc: 418-643-8177
Ligne sans frais: 800-665-6527
inforeservation@sepaq.com
www.sepaq.com

Faune et des parcs / Wildlife & Parks
Autres nombres: Faune: www.mffp.gouv.qc.ca/faune; Parcs: www.mffp.gouv.qc.ca/parcs
Sous-ministre associée, Faune et aux parcs, Line Drouin
Directeur général adjoint, Gestion de la faune et des habitats, René Desaulniers
Directeur général adjoint, Protection de la faune, Philippe Laliberté

Forestier en chef / Chief Forester
845, boul Saint-Joseph, Roberval, QC G8H 2L4
Tél: 418-275-7770
Téléc: 418-275-8884
bureau@forestierenchef.gouv.qc.ca
www.forestierenchef.gouv.qc.ca
Secondary Address: #A-405, 5700, 4e Avenue ouest
Québec, QC G1H 6R1
Alt. Téléc: 418-644-7607
twitter.com/Forestierenchef
www.facebook.com/BFEC2012
Sous-ministre associé et Forestier en chef, Louis Pelletier

Forêts / Forests
#A-405, 5700, 4e Avenue ouest, Québec, G1H 6R1
Tél: 418-627-8652
Téléc: 418-528-1278
mffp.gouv.qc.ca/les-forets/forets-du-quebec
Sous-ministre associé, Ronald Brizard
Tél: 418-627-8652 ext: 4424
Directeur général, Conaissance et aménagement durable des forêts, Luc Tellier
Tél: 418-627-8650 ext: 4320
Directrice générale, Coordination, Linda Tremblay
Tél: 418-627-8662 ext: 4244
Directeur général, Attribution des bois et développement industriel, Alain Sénéchal
Tél: 418-627-8657 ext: 4127
Directrice générale, Bureau de mise en marché des bois, Vincent Auclair

Opérations régionales / Regional Operations
Sous-ministre associé, Daniel Richard
Tél: 418-627-8660 ext: 4651
Directeur général, Production de semences et de plants forestiers, Sébastien Desrochers
Tél: 418-627-8660 ext: 4651
Directeur général, Coordination de la gestion des forêts, François Provost
Tél: 418-627-8638 ext: 2055
Directeur général, Coordination de la gestion de la faune, Serge Tremblay
Tél: 418-627-8696 ext: 2042

Secteur centrale
#207, 100, rue Laviolette, Trois-Rivières, QC G9A 5S9
Tél: 819-371-6151
Téléc: 819-371-6978
centreduquebec@mffp.gouv.qc.ca
Autres nombres: Alt. Courriel:
capitale-nationale@mffp.gouv.qc.ca;
chaudiere-appalaches@mffp.gouv.qc.ca;
mauricie@mffp.gouv.qc.ca
Capitale-Nationale—Chaudière-Appalaches;
Mauricie—Centre-du-Québec
Directrice générale, Cécile Tremblay

Secteur métropolitain et sud et gestion des forêts
545, boul Crémazie est, 8e étage, Montréal, QC H2M 2V1
Tél: 514-873-2140
Téléc: 514-873-8983
estrie@mffp.gouv.qc.ca
Autres nombres: Alt. Courriel: montreal@mffp.gouv.qc.ca;
laval@mffp.gouv.qc.ca; monteregie@mffp.gouv.qc.ca
Estrie-Montréal-Montérégie-Laval
Directeur général, Jean-Philippe Détolle

Secteur nord-est
#RC 702, 625, boul Laflèche, Baie-Comeau, QC G5C 1C5
Tél: 418-295-4676
Téléc: 418-295-4682
cote-nord@mffp.gouv.qc.ca
Autres nombres: Alt. Courriel:
saguenay-lac-saint-jean@mffp.gouv.qc.ca
Côte-Nord; Saguenay—Lac-Saint-Jean

Directeur général, Alain Thibeault
Secteur nord-ouest
70, av Québec, Rouyn-Noranda, QC J9X 6R1
Tél: 819-763-3388
Téléc: 819-763-3216
abitibi-temiscamingue@mffp.gouv.qc.ca
Autres nombres: Alt. Courriel:
Nord-du-Quebec@mffp.gouv.qc.ca
Abitibi-Témiscamingue; Nord-du-Québec
Directeur général, Pierre Ménard
Secteur sud-est
#207 - 92, 2e rue ouest, Rimouski, QC G5L 8B3
Tél: 418-727-3710
Téléc: 418-727-3735
bas-saint-laurent@mffp.gouv.qc.ca
Autres nombres: Alt. Courriel:
gaspesie-iles-de-la-madeleine@mffp.gouv.qc.ca
Bas-Saint-Laurent; Gaspésie—Iles-de-la-Madeleine
Directeur général, Paul St-Laurent
Secteur sud-ouest
#RC 100, 16, impasse de la Gare-Talon, Gatineau, QC J8T 0B1
Tél: 819-246-4827
Téléc: 819-246-5049
outaouais@mffp.gouv.qc.ca
Autres nombres: Alt. Courriel: lanaudiere@mffp.gouv.qc.ca;
laurentides@mffp.gouv.qc.ca
Outaouais; Lanaudière—Laurentides
Directeur général, Martin Gingras

Hydro-Québec

Édifice Jean-Lesage, 75, boul René-Lévesque ouest, Montréal, QC H2Z 1A4
Tél: 514-385-7252
Ligne sans frais: 888-385-7252
www.hydroquebec.com
twitter.com/hydroquebec
www.facebook.com/hydroquebec1944
www.linkedin.com/company/hydro-quebec
instagram.com/hydroquebec

Président, Conseil d'administration, Michael D. Penner

Président-directeur général, Éric Martel

Président, Hydro-Québec TransÉnergie, Marc Boucher

Président, Hydro-Québec Distribution, Éric Filion

Président, Hydro-Québec Innovation, équipement et services partagés, Réal Laporte

Président, Hydro-Québec Production, David Murray

Vice-présidente exécutif et chef de la direction financière et du risque, Jean-Hugues Lafleur

Filiales/Subsidiaries

Société d'énergie de la Baie-James (SEBJ) / James Bay Energy
#1100, 800, de Maisonneuve est, Montréal, QC H2L 4L8
Tél: 514-286-2020
www.hydroquebec.com/sebj
Président-directeur général de la SEBJ et Président, Hydro-Québec Innovation, équipement et services partagés, Réal Laporte
Société de transmission électrique de Cedars Rapids limitée (CRT) / Cedars Rapids Transmission Co. Ltd
944, rue Principale, Rivière Beaudette, QC J0P 1R0
Tél: 450-269-3461
Téléc: 450-269-2889
admin@cedarsrapids.ca
www.hydroquebec.com/crt
Président-directeur général, Hydro-Québec, Éric Martel

Ministère de l'Immigration, de la Francisation et de l'Intégration / Immigration, Francization & Integration

285, rue Notre-Dame ouest, 4e étage, Montréal, QC H2Y 1T8
Ligne sans frais: 877-864-9191
www.immigration-quebec.gouv.qc.ca
Autres nombres: Téléscripteur: 866-227-5968
Secondary Address: #301, 800, boul de Maisonneuve est
Montréal, QC H2L 2L8
twitter.com/midi_qc
www.youtube.com/miccgouvqc

Ministre, L'hon. Nadine Girault

Sous-ministre, Benoit Dagenais

Directrice (par intérim), Communications, Christina Mirtcheva
Tél: 514-873-8624
Téléc: 514-873-7349

Francisation, diversité et inclusion / Francization, Diversity & Inclusion

Sous-ministre adjoint, Éric Gervais
Tél: 514-873-5132
Directeur général, Participation et partnerariats, Alain Dupont
Tél: 514-864-3511
Directrice générale, Politiques et programmes de francisation, de diversité et d'inclusion, Marie-Josée Lemay
Tél: 514-873-3280
Directeur, Services de francisation, Ghislain Beaudin
Tél: 514-940-1501
Directrice, Conformité des programmes et services, Manon Beauregard
Tél: 514-873-9290
Directeur, Programmes et services aux entreprises, Frederico Fonseca
Tél: 514-873-3280
Directeur, Société inclusive et interculturalisme, Irvine Henry
Tél: 514-940-1632
Directrice, Politiques et programmes de participation, Christine Rioux
Tél: 514-873-3280
Directeur, Intervention territoriale, Siham Zouali
Tél: 514-873-3255

Immigration et prospection / Immigration & Prospecting

Sous-ministre adjointe, Johanne Dumont
Tél: 514-873-9120
Directeur général, Opérations d'immigration, Louis Belanger
Tél: 514-873-2446
Directrice générale, Prospection et politiques et programmes d'immigration, et directrice (par intérim), Opérations de prospection et recrutement international, Nancy Carignan
Tél: 514-873-8624
Directrice, Enregistrement et évaluation comparative, Simona Gheorghe
Tél: 514-873-4260
Directeur, Immigration temporaire, Jonathan Guénette
Tél: 514-864-1165
Directrice (par intérim), Immigration familiale et humanitaire, Tihana Majcen
Tél: 514-864-9305
Directrice (par intérim), Politiques et programmes d'immigration et de prospection, Fanny Marcoux
Directeur, Immigration économique, Ivan Ruscitti
Directeur, Évaluation professionnelle et reconnaissance des compétences, Guillaume Vaillancourt
Tél: 514-873-2324

Performance, développement et soutien à la transformation / Performance, Development & Support for Transformation

Sous-ministre adjoint, Jacques Leroux
Tél: 514-873-5942
Directrice générale, Soutien à la transformation et développement, Maryse Faubert
Tél: 514-905-3261
Directrice générale, Planification et soutien à la performance, Charlotte Poirier
Tél: 514-873-8512
Directrice, Développement des stratégies de services en francisation et en intégration, Diane Bolduc
Tél: 514-940-1626
Directeur, Développement des stratégies de services en immigration, Réjean Charette
Tél: 514-873-9449
Directrice, Recherche et planification, Anne-Marie Fadel
Tél: 514-873-5914
Directrice, Portefeuille et soutien des projets et des programmes, Anne Pelletier
Tél: 514-873-9533
Directrice, Assurance-qualité, analyse et architecture d'affaires, Thérèse Trottier
Tél: 514-873-6440
Directeur, Évaluation de programme et analyses économiques, Raphael Vargas Benavente
Tél: 514-864-9896

Soutien à l'organisation / Organizational Support

Sous-ministre adjoint, Maroun Shaneen
Tél: 514-873-1627
Directrice générale, Technologies de l'information, Georgine Shum-Tim
Tél: 514-864-1854
Directeur général (par intérim), Administration, Denis Williams
Tél: 514-873-1565

Directeur, Services d'infrastructure et évolution des systèmes, Christian Boisvert
Tél: 514-873-1533
Directeur, Sécurité de l'information, Steve Bolduc
Tél: 514-873-2396
Directrice (par intérim), Relations avec la clientèle et Services d'accueil à l'aéroport, Karine Gilbert
Tél: 514-864-9818
Directrice, Ressources humaines, Suzie Melançon
Tél: 514-873-7172
Directeur, Soutien technologique à la clientèle, Kim-Tu Nguyen
Tél: 514-873-1533
Directeur (par intérim), Services communs et soutien aux projets, Tan Loc Nguyen
Tél: 514-873-1533

Ministère de la Justice / Justice

Édifice Louis-Philippe-Pigeon, 1200, rte de l'Église, Québec, QC G1V 4M1

Tél: 418-643-5140
Ligne sans frais: 866-536-5140
informations@justice.gouv.qc.ca
www.justice.gouv.qc.ca
Secondary Address: #11.39,, 1, rue Notre-Dame est, 11e étage
Palais de justice de Montréal
Montréal, QC
Alt. Téléc: 514-873-7174

Ministre, L'hon. Simon Jolin-Barrette

Sous-ministre, Line Drouin

Secrétaire, Sélection des candidats à la fonction de juge, Sonia Beaudoin
Tél: 418-643-4090 ext: 20600

Directeur général associé, Ressources humaines, Dany Blanchette
Tél: 418-646-7656 ext: 20040

Directeur, Communications, Caroline Dorval
Tél: 418-644-3947 ext: 20921

Directrice, Gestion budgétaire, financière et des contrats, Marie-Claude Fontaine
Tél: 418-646-1867 ext: 20084

Agences, Conseils et Commissions Associés/ Associated Agencies, Boards & Commissions:

• Commission des droits de la personne et des droits de la jeunesse (CDPDJ) / Commission for Human Rights & the Rights of Youth
See Entry Name Index for detailed listing.

• Commission des services juridiques (CSJ) / Legal Services Commission
Tour de l'Est
#1404, 2, Complexe Desjardins
CP 123
Montréal, QC H5B 1B3
Tél: 514-873-3562
Téléc: 514-864-2351
info@csj.qc.ca
www.csj.qc.ca

• Conseil de la justice administrative (CJA) / Administrative Justice Council
#4.30, 575, rue Jacques-Parizeau
Québec, QC G1R 2G4
Tél: 418-644-6279
Téléc: 418-528-8471
Ligne sans frais: 888-848-2581
plaintes@cja.gouv.qc.ca
www.cja.gouv.qc.ca

• Conseil de la magistrature
#RC.01, 300, boul Jean-Lesage
Québec, QC G1K 8K6
Tél: 418-644-2196
Téléc: 418-528-1581
information@cm.gouv.qc.ca
www.conseildelamagistrature.qc.ca
Le Conseil de la magistrature est un organisme indépendant.

• Directeur des poursuites criminelles et pénales (DPCP) / Criminal & Penal Prosecutions
Tour 1
#500, 2828, boul Laurier
Québec, QC G1V 0B9
Tél: 418-643-4085
Téléc: 418-643-7462
info@dpcp.gouv.qc.ca
www.dpcp.gouv.qc.ca

• Fonds d'aide aux actions collectifs (FAAC) / Assistance Fund for Collective Action
#10.30, 1, rue Notre-Dame est
Montréal, QC H2Y 1B6
Tél: 514-393-2087
Téléc: 514-864-2998
farc@justice.gouv.qc.ca
www.faac.justice.gouv.qc.ca

• Office de la protection du consommateur (OPC) / Consumer Protection Board
#450, 400, boul Jean-Lesage
Québec, QC G1K 8W4
Tél: 418-643-1484
Téléc: 418-528-0979
Ligne sans frais: 888-672-2556
www.opc.gouv.qc.ca

• Office des professions du Québec / Occupations Board
See Entry Name Index for detailed listing.

• Société québécoise d'information juridique (SOQUIJ) / Judicial Information Society of Québec
#600, 715, rue du Square-Victoria
Montréal, QC H2Y 2H7
Tél: 514-842-8745
Ligne sans frais: 800-363-6718
www.soquij.qc.ca

• Tribunal administratif du Québec / Administrative Tribunal of Québec
575, rue Jacques-Parizeau
Québec, QC G1R 5R4
Tél: 418-643-3418
Téléc: 418-643-5335
Ligne sans frais: 800-567-0278
tribunal.administratif@taq.gouv.qc.ca
www.taq.gouv.qc.ca

Affaires juridiques, législatives et l'access à la justice / Legal & Legislative Affairs & Access to Justice

Sous-ministre associé, Yan Paquette
Tel: 416-643-4228 ext: 21229
Directeur général associé, Affaires contentieuses, Jean-Yves Bernard
Tél: 514-393-2336 ext: 51467
Directeur général associé, Services aux ministères - jurisconsulte, François Bélanger
Tel: 418-266-4451 ext: 20835
Directrice générale associée, Services juridiques centraux, Lise Proulx
Tél: 418-266-4451 ext: 20700
Directrice générale associée, Direction du contentieux de la Procedure générale du Québec et de la transformation - volet PGQ, Diane Raîche
Tél: 418-266-4451 ext: 21321
Directeur général associé, Orientations, des politiques et de la législation ministérielle, Marc Samson
Tél: 418-646-5580 ext: 21230

Programme de transformation organisationnelle de la justice / Organizational Transformation of Justice Program

Sous-ministre associée, Patrick-Thierry Grenier
Tél: 418-646-8153 ext: 20018
Directrice, Affaires à la transformation, Céline Dufresne
Tél: 418-644-2330 ext: 21075

Services de justice / Justice Services

Sous-ministre associé, Pierre E. Rodrigue
Directeur général associé, Services judiciares de la Métropole, Paul Charbonneau
Tél: 514-393-2256 ext: 51796
Directrice générale associée, Services judiciares de la Capitale-Nationale et des régions, Marjorie Forgues
Tél: 418-649-3510 ext: 42322
Directeur général associé, Soutien de l'activité judiciare et de la gestion, Gaétan Rancourt
Tél: 418-644-7700 ext: 20155
Directeur général associé, Bureau des infractions et amendes, Jacques Vachon
Tél: 418-644-2330 ext: 21110

Technologies de l'information et des registres / Information Technologies & Registries

Sous-ministre associée, Mylène Martel
Tél: 418-528-2235 ext: 20003
Directrice général associé, Registres et certification, Christian G. Sirois
Directeur, Solutions d'affaires, Nicolas Charlebois
Tél: 418-646-6004 ext: 21777
Directeur, Services d'infrastructures technologiques et de la modernisation, Charles Émond
Tél: 418-646-2255 ext: 20011
Directrice, Gouvernance des projets et de l'architecture d'entreprise, Valérie Roy-Perreault
Tél: 418-643-8501 ext: 21309

Commission des normes, de l'équité, de la santé et de la sécurité du travail (CNESST) / Committee on Standards, Equity, Health & Safety at Work

524, rue Bourdages, Québec, QC G1M 1A1

Téléc: 418-266-4015
Ligne sans frais: 844-838-0808
www.cnesst.gouv.qc.ca
twitter.com/cnesst
www.facebook.com/cnesst
www.linkedin.com/company/cnesst

A pour mission de soutenir aux travailleurs & aux employeurs dans leurs démarches pour éliminer les dangers présents dans leur milieu de travail, inspecter des lieux de travail, & promouvoir la santé & sécurité du travail

Présidente & Chef de la direction, Manuelle Oudar

Vice-président, Opérations, Claude Beauchamp

Vice-présidente, Normes du travail, Martine Bégin

Vice-président, Communications, Pierre Hamelin

Vice-président, Finances, Bruno Labrecque

Vice-président, Partenariat et l'expertise-conseil, Claude Sicard

Office des professions du Québec (OPQ) / Occupations Board

800, Place D'Youville, 10e étage, Québec, QC G1R 5Z3

Tél: 418-643-6912
Téléc: 418-643-0973
Ligne sans frais: 800-643-6912
www.opq.gouv.qc.ca

Présidente, Diane Legault

Secrétaire, Guylaine Couture

Le Protecteur du Citoyen / Ombudsman

800, place D'Youville, 19e étage, Québec, QC G1R 3P4

Tél: 418-643-2688
Téléc: 418-643-8759
Ligne sans frais: 800-463-5070
TTY: 866-410-0901
protecteur@protecteurducitoyen.qc.ca
www.protecteurducitoyen.qc.ca
Secondary Address: #1000, 1080, côte du Beaver Hull, 10e étage
Montréal, QC H2Z 1S8
Alt. Téléc: 514-873-4640
twitter.com/pcitoyen
www.facebook.com/leprotecteurducitoyen

Protectrice du citoyen, Marie Rinfret

Vice-protecteur, Services aux citoyens et aux usagers, Claude Dussault

Vice-protectrice, Affaires institutionnelles et prévention, Hélène Vallières

Directrice, Ressources humaines et l'administration, Chantal Gagnon

Directrice, Communications, Joanne Trudel

Secrétariat du Québec aux relations canadiennes / Québec Secretariat for Canadian Relations

875, Grande Allée est, 3e étage, Québec, QC G1R 4Y8

Tél: 418-643-4011
Téléc: 418-528-0052
www.sqrc.gouv.qc.ca
www.facebook.com/sqrc.mce

Ministre responsable, L'hon. Sonia LeBel

Responsable, Centre de la francophonie des Amériques, Denis Desgagné

Secrétaire général associé, Jean-Stéphane Bernard

Secrétaire adjointe, Francophonie canadienne, Sylvie Lachance

Secrétaire adjointe, Relations intergouvernementales canadiennes, Suzanne Lévesque

Secrétaire adjoint, Relations intergouvernementales canadiennes, Artur J. Pires

Responsable, Bureau du Secrétaire général associé/Responsable de l'accès à l'information, Cynthia Jean
Chef de poste, Catherine Tadros

Ministère des Relations internationales et Francophonie / International Relations & La Francophonie

Édifice Hector-Fabre, 525, boul Réne-Lévesque est, Québec, QC G1R 5R9

Tél: 418-649-2300
Téléc: 418-649-2656
www.mrif.gouv.qc.ca
Autres nombres: www.linkedin.com/company/mriquebec
Secondary Address: 380, rue St-Antoine ouest
Montréal, QC H2Y 3X7
Alt. Téléc: 514-873-7468
twitter.com/mrif_quebec
www.facebook.com/mriquebec

Ministre, L'hon. Nadine Girault

Sous-ministre, Sylvie Barcelo

Secrétaire général, Relations fédérales-provinciales, Frédéric Tremblay

Administration / Administration
Directeur général, Marc Gagné
Tél: 418-649-2400 ext: 57917
Directeur, Technologies de l'information, Claude Crête
Tél: 418-649-2400 ext: 57452
Directeur, Ressources humaines, Louis Métivier
Tél: 418-649-2400 ext: 57049
Directrice, Ressources financières, contractuelles et immobilières, Karine Savoie
Tél: 418-649-2400 ext: 57974

Affaires bilatérales - États-Unis, Amériques et Asie-Pacifique / Bilateral Affairs - United States, Americas and Asia Pacific
Sous-ministre, Éric Marquis
Directeur, Amérique latine et Antilles, Marie-Josée Audet
Directeur, Asie-Pacifique, Anne Toussaint
Directeur, États-Unis, Jean-Pierre Forgues

Affaires bilatérales - Europe, Afrique et Moyen-Orient / Bilateral Affairs - Europe, Africa & the Middle East
Sous-ministre adjointe, Jean-François Bernier
Directeur général, Jean Saintonge
Tél: 418-649-2400 ext: 57234

Concertation de l'action internationale et Protocole / Coordination of International Action & Protocol
Sous-ministre adjointe, Johanne Whittom

Affaires francophones et multilatérales et partenariats / Francophone & Multilateral Affairs & Partnerships
Sous-ministre adjoint, Jean-François Bernier

Revenu Québec / Revenue Québec

3800, rue de Marly, Québec, QC G1X 4A5

Tél: 418-652-6831
Téléc: 418-646-0167
cabinet@revenuquebec.ca
www.revenuquebec.ca
Secondary Address: 150, rue Ste-Catherine ouest
Complexe Desjardins
Montréal, QC H5B 1A7
Alt. Téléc: 514-873-7502
twitter.com/revenuquebec
www.facebook.com/revenuquebec
www.linkedin.com/company/5473697

Ministre des Finances, L'hon. Eric Girard

Président du conseil d'administration, Florent Gagné

Bureau de président-directeur général / Office of the President/Director General
Président-directeur général, Carl Gauthier
Vice-président et directeur général, Traitement et des technologies, Patrice Alain
Vice-président et directeur général, Entreprises, Hajib Amachi
Vice-présidente et directrice générale, Direction générale des particuliers, Nicole Bourget
Vice-présidente et directrice générale, Recouvrement, Danièle Cantin

Vice-président et directeur général, Législation, René Martineau
Vice-présidente et directrice générale, Traitement des plaintes et de l'éthique, Joseé Morin
Vice-présidente et directrice générale, Ressources humaines et communications, Line Paulin
Vice-président et directeur général, Innovation et administration, Daniel Prud'homme

Ministère de la Santé et des Services sociaux / Health & Social Services

Direction des communications, 1075, ch Sainte-Foy, 15e étage, Québec, QC G1S 2M1

Tél: 418-644-4545
Ligne sans frais: 877-644-4545
TTY: 800-361-9596
www.msss.gouv.qc.ca
Autres nombres: Montréal: 514-644-4545

Ministre, L'hon. Christian Dubé

Ministre responsable des Aînés et des Proches aidants, L'hon. Marguerite Blais

Ministre délégué à la Santé et aux Services sociaux, L'hon. Lionel Carmant

Directrice, Cabinet du ministre, Denis Simard

Agences, Conseils et Commissions Associés/ Associated Agencies, Boards & Commissions:

• **Commissaire à la santé et au bien-être / Commissioner for Health & Welfare**
Bureau de Québec
1005, ch Ste-Fot, 1er étage
Québec, QC G1S 4N4
Tél: 418-266-5990
www.csbe.gouv.qc.ca

• **Héma-Québec**
4045, boul Côte-Vertu
Montréal, QC H4R 2W7
Tél: 514-832-5000
Téléc: 514-832-1025
Ligne sans frais: 888-666-4362
www.hema-quebec.qc.ca

• **Institut national d'excellence en santé et en services sociaux (INESSS) / National Institute for Excellence in Health & Social Services**
2535, boul Laurier, 5e étage
Québec, QC G1V 4M3
Tél: 418-643-1339
Téléc: 418-646-8349
inesss@inesss.qc.ca
www.inesss.qc.ca

• **Institut national de santé publique du Québec (INSPQ) / National Public Health Institute of Québec**
945, av Wolfe
Québec, QC G1V 5B3
Tél: 418-650-5115
info@inspq.qc.ca
www.inspq.qc.ca
Autres numéros: Poste: 5336

• **Modernisation des centres hospitaliers universitaires de Montréal, CHUM, CUSM, CHU Sainte-Justine / Modernization of Montréal's University Health Centres CHUM, MUHC & Sainte-Justine UHC**
#10.049, 2021, rue Union
Montréal, QC H3A 2S9
Tél: 514-864-9883
Téléc: 514-873-7362
info.construction3chu@msss.gouv.qc.ca
construction3chu.msss.gouv.qc.ca

• **Office des personnes handicapées du Québec / Office for Handicapped Persons**
309, rue Brock
Drummondville, QC J2B 1C5
Téléc: 819-475-8753
Ligne sans frais: 800-567-1465
TTY: 800-567-1477
info@ophq.gouv.qc.ca
www.ophq.gouv.qc.ca

• **Régie de l'assurance maladie du Québec (RAMQ) / Québec Health Insurance Board**
CP 6600
Québec, QC G1K 7T3
Tél: 418-646-4636
Ligne sans frais: 800-561-9749
www.ramq.gouv.qc.ca

• Secrétariat à l'accès aux services en langue anglaise et aux communautés culturelles / English Language & Cultural Communities Services Secretariat
475, boul de Maisonneuve est
Montréal, QC H2L 5C4
Tél: 514-873-5163
Téléc: 514-873-9876
www.msss.gouv.qc.ca/ministere/saslacc

• Urgences-santé Québec / Emergency Health Services Québec
6700, rue Jarry est
Montréal, QC H1P 0A4
Tél: 514-723-5600
info@urgences-sante.qc.ca
www.urgences-sante.qc.ca

Cabinet du Sous-ministre / Office of the Deputy Minister
Sous-ministre, Dominique Savoie
Directrice exécutive, Bureau du sous-ministre, Dominique Breton
  Tél: 418-266-8989
Directeur, Secrétariat général, André Giguère
  Tél: 418-266-8989
Directrice, Communications, Catherine Gauthier
  Tél: 418-266-8905
Directrice, Affaires juridiques, Patricia Lavoie
  Tél: 418-266-8950
Directrice, Audit interne, Isabelle Savard
  Tél: 418-266-8989

Coordination réseau et ministérielle / Network & Departmental Coordination
Sous-ministre adjoint, Pierre Lafleur
  Tél: 418-266-8850
Directeur général adjoint, Coordination, inspection et sécurité civile, Martin Simard
  Tél: 418-266-6822

Finances, l'allocation des ressources et budget / Finance, Resource Allocation & Budget
Sous-ministre adjoint, Pierre-Albert Coubat
Directeur général adjointe, Gestion financière et des politiques de financement réseau, Guylaine Lajoie
  Tél: 418-266-5920
Directrice générale adjointe, Gestion budgétaire et comptable ministérielle, Anne Martineau
  Tél: 418-266-6820
Directrice, Analyses financières des établissements publics et privés, Claudia Angers
  Tél: 418-266-5928
Directeur, Politiques de financement et de l'allocation des ressources, Normand Lantagne
  Tél: 418-266-7111
Directrice, Opérations budgétaires, Josée Veilleux
  Tél: 418-266-5975

Infrastructures, logistique, des équipements et de l'approvisionnement / Infrastructure, Logistics, Equipment & Supplies
Sous-ministre adjoint, Luc Desbiens
  Tél: 418-266-5830
Directrice, Ressources matérielles ministérielles, Marie-Claude Beauchamp
  Tél: 418-266-8760
Directeur, Conservation des infrastructures, Yves Charette
  Tél: 418-266-8814
Directrice, Projets immobiliers, Céline Drolet
  Tél: 418-266-7002

Planification, évaluation et qualité / Planning, Evaluation and Quality
Sous-ministre adjoint, Pierre Lafleur
Directrice générale adjointe (par intérim), Planification, évaluation et qualité, et directrice, Orientations stratégiques, Lynda Fortin
  Tél: 418-266-7025
Directeur (par intérim), Affaires pharmaceutiques et du médicament, Dominc Bélanger
  Tél: 418-266-8815
Directrice, L'évaluation, Marie-Claude Brunet
  Tél: 418-266-7505
Directrice, Affaires intergouvernementales et la coopération internationale, Valérie Fontaine
  Tél: 418-266-8740
Directrice, L'éthique et de la qualité, Geneviève Landry
  Tél: 418-266-7079
Directeur, Affaires autochtones, Martin Rhéaume
  Tél: 418-266-6811
Directrice, Recherche, transfert des connaissances et du secrétariat du bureau de l'innovation, Manon St-Pierre
  Tél: 418-266-7056

Personnel réseau et ministériel / Personal & Corporate Network
Directrice générale adjointe, Relations de travail et professionnelles; directrice (par intérim), Conditions d'exercice des professionnels de la santé et du personnel hors établissement, Josée Doyon
  Tél: 418-266-8408
Directeur général adjointe, Ressources humaines ministérielles et de la gestion contractuelle, Maryse Grondin
  Tél: 418-266-8717
Directeur, Gestion de la main-d'oeuvre, Mathieu Gagnon
  Tél: 418-266-8717
Directeur, Conditions de travail du personnel d'encadrement et de la classification, Yves Lapointe
  Tél: 418-266-8420
Directrice, Développement des personnes et de l'organisation, Mélany Ouellet
  Tél: 418-266-6878
Directrice, Relations professionnelles avec les fédérations médicales, Manon Paquin
  Tél: 418-266-8430
Directrice, Analyse et du soutient informationnel; directrice (par intérim), Soutient informationnel, Mélanie Rainville
  Tél: 418-266-8457

Santé publique / Public Health
Sous-ministre adjoint, Horacio Arruda
  Tél: 418-266-6700
Directeur général adjoint, Prévention et de la promotion de la santé, André Dontigny
  Tél: 418-266-6714
Directeur général adjoint, Protection de la santé publique, Yves Jalbert
  Tél: 418-266-6770
Directrice générale adjointe, Santé publique, Sylvie Poirier
  Tél: 418-266-6780
Directrice, Prévention clinique, santé dentaire et des dépistages, Cynthia Beaudoin
  Tél: 418-266-8876
Directeur, Légalisation du cannabis, Yovan Fillion
  Tél: 418-266-4593
Directrice, Prévention des infections transmissibles sexuellement et par le sang, Lise Guérard
  Tél: 514-873-9892
Directrice, Vigie sanitaire, Marlène Mercier
  Tél: 514-873-1580
Directrice, Promotion des saines habitudes de vie, Martine Pageau
  Tél: 418-266-6755
Directeur, Prévention et du contrôle des maladies infectieuses, Paul-Georges Rossi
  Tél: 418-266-6741
Directrice, Santé environnementale, Marion Schnebelen
  Tél: 418-266-4602
Directrice, Surveillance de l'état de santé, Julie Soucy
  Tél: 418-266-6775

Services hospitaliers, médecine spécialisée et universitaire / Hospital Services, Specialty & Academic Medicine
Sous-ministre adjointe, Lucie Opatrny
  Tél: 514-873-2071
Directrice générale adjointe, Services hospitaliers, Lucie Poitras
  Tél: 514-873-3010
Directrice, Soins et services infirmiers, Sylvie Dubois
  Tél: 418-266-8485
Directeur, L'organisation clinique et de la gestion des effectifs médicaux spécialisés, Martin Forgues
  Tél: 418-266-6946
Directrice (par intérim), Services mère-enfant, Sabrina Fortin
  Tél: 418-266-7161
Directeur, Biovigilance et de la biologie médicale, Denis Ouellet
  Tél: 418-266-6710

Services de proximité, des urgences et du préhospitalier / Local, Emergency & Pre-Hospital Services
Sous-ministre adjoint, Lucie Opatrny
Directeur général adjoint, Services de proximité intégrés, François Dubé
  Tél: 418-266-6969
Directeur, Services d'urgence, Pierre Bouchard
  Tél: 514-864-3215
Directeur, Services préhospitaliers d'urgence, André Lizotte
  Tél: 418-266-5806

Services sociaux / Social Services
Sous-ministre adjointe, Lyne Jobin
  Tél: 418-266-6800
Directrice générale adjointe, Services de santé mentale et de psychiatrie légale, Josée Lepage
Directrice générale adjointe, Services sociaux et services aux aînés, Natalie Rosebush
  Tél: 418-266-6855

Directrice, Secrétariat à l'adoption internationale, Josée-Anne Goupil
  Tél: 514-873-4747

Technologies de l'information / Information Technology
Sous-ministre associé et directeur (par intérim), Orientations et architecture, Richard Audet
  Tél: 418-529-4898
Directeur général adjoint, Licences et des actifs informationnels, Denis Deslauriers
  Tél: 514-597-2066
Directrice générale adjointe, Projets d'unification et des systèmes ministériels, Nathalie Surprenant
  Tél: 418-529-4898 ext: 452
Directeur général adjoint, Planification, coordination, et la sécurité, Dave Roussy
  Tél: 418-266-8498
Directrice générale adjointe, Opérations technologoqies, Agathe Tremblay
  Tél: 418-527-5211 ext: 6267
Directeur, Service de la bureautique et de la proximité, Christian Bolduc
  Tél: 418-527-5211 ext: 6237
Directeur, Gestion des licences et des actifs informationnels, Stéphane Brossard
  Tél: 514-596-2066 ext: 3353
Directrice, Intégration des solutions d'affaires et cliniques, Louise Fortin
  Tél: 418-266-7017
Directeur, Architecture, Boris Gueissaz-Teufel
  Tél: 418-529-4898 ext: 226
Directeur, Coordination des dossiers d'affaires, Claude Isabel
  Tél: 418-266-7104
Directrice, Mise en oeuvre des grands projets, Caroline Lemelin
  Tél: 418-529-4898 ext: 409
Directrice, Centre de services, Caroline Martin
  Tél: 418-527-5211 ext: 6243
Directrice, L'évolution et du developpement des infrastructures technologiques, François Martin
  Tél: 418-527-5211 ext: 6256

Ministère de la Sécurité publique / Public Security

Tour des Laurentides, 2525, boul Laurier, 5e étage, Québec, QC G1V 2L2
  Tél: 418-643-2112
  Téléc: 418-646-6168
  Ligne sans frais: 800-361-3795
  www.securitepublique.gouv.qc.ca
  Secondary Address: #11.87, 10, rue Saint-Antoine est
  Montréal, QC H2Y 1A2
  Alt. Téléc: 514-873-6597
A pour mission d'assurer la sécurité publique au Québec

  Ministre, L'hon. Geneviève Guilbault

  Sous-ministre, Brigitte Pelletier

Agences, Conseils et Commissions Associés/ Associated Agencies, Boards & Commissions:
• Bureau des enquêtes indépandantes / Office of Independent Investigations
#6.01, 201, Place Charles-Lemoyne
Longueuil, QC J4K 2T5
Tél: 450-640-1350
Téléc: 450-670-6386
www.bei.gouv.qc.ca

• Bureau du coroner / Office of the Coroner
Édifice le Delta 2
#390, 2875, boul Laurier
Québec, QC G1V 5B1
Téléc: 418-643-6174
Ligne sans frais: 888-267-6637
clientele.coroner@msp.gouv.qc.ca
www.coroner.gouv.qc.ca

• Comité de déontologie policière / Police Ethics Committee
Tour du Saint-Laurent
#A-200, 2525, boul Laurier, 2e étage
Québec, QC G1V 4Z6
Tél: 418-646-1936
Téléc: 418-528-0987
comite.deontologie@msp.gouv.qc.ca
www.deontologie-policiere.gouv.qc.ca/le-comite.html

• Commissaire à la déontologie policière / Police Ethics Commissioner
#1.06, 2535, boul Laurier
Québec, QC G1V 4M3
Tél: 418-643-7897
Téléc: 418-528-9473
Ligne sans frais: 877-237-7897
deontologie-policiere.quebec@msp.gouv.qc.ca
www.deontologie-policiere.gouv.qc.ca/le-commissaire

• **Commissaire à la lutte contre la corruption (Unité permanente anticorruption) (UPAC) / Commissioner in the Fight Against Corruption**
#3010, 2100, av Pierre-Dupuy
Montréal, QC H3C 3R5
Tél: 514-228-3098
Téléc: 514-873-0177
Ligne sans frais: 855-567-8722
www.upac.gouv.qc.ca

• **Commission québécoise des libérations conditionnelles (CQLC) / Parole Board**
#1.32A, 300, boul Jean-Lesage
Québec, QC G1K 8K6
Tél: 418-646-8300
Téléc: 418-643-7217
cqlc@cqlc.gouv.qc.ca
www.cqlc.gouv.qc.ca

• **École nationale de police du Québec (ENPQ) / National Police School of Québec**
350, rue Marguerite-d'Youville
Nicolet, QC J3T 1X4
Tél: 819-293-8631
Téléc: 819-293-8630
courriel@enpq.qc.ca
www.enpq.qc.ca

• **École nationale des pompiers du Québec (ENPQ) / Québec National Fire Fighters School**
Palais de justice de Laval
#3.08, 2800, boul Saint-Martin ouest
Laval, QC H7T 2S9
Tél: 450-680-6800
Téléc: 450-680-6818
Ligne sans frais: 866-680-3677
enpq@enpq.gouv.qc.ca
www.ecoledespompiers.qc.ca
Autres numéros: registrariat@enpq.gouv.qc.ca

• **Régie des alcools, des courses et des jeux (RACJ) / Liquor, Gaming & Racing Board**
560, boul Charest est
Québec, QC G1K 3J3
Tél: 418-643-7667
Téléc: 418-643-5971
Ligne sans frais: 800-363-0320

Services à la gestion / Administrative Services
Sous-ministre associé (par intérim), Sylvain Ayotte

Affaires policières / Police Services
Sous-ministre associé, Louis Morneau
Tél: 418-643-3500
Téléc: 418-643-0275
Directeur général adjoint, Pratiques policières, Samuel-Loubier Demers
Directeur général adjoint, L'organisation policière, Jean-Sébastien Dion
Directeur général adjoint, Sécurité de l'État, Jérôme Gagnon
Directeur général adjoint, Prévention et de la lutte contre la criminalité, Clément Robitaille
Directrice, La lutte contre la criminalité, Marie-Pierre Bérubé
Directeur, Renseignement, l'analyse et du soutien aux opérations, Dave Castegan
Directeur, Protection des personnalités, Karell Maguire
Directeur, Sécurité dans les palais de justice, Martin Maranda

Sécurité civile et sécurité incendie / Public Safety & Fire Services
Sous-ministre associé, Jean Bissonnette

Services correctionnels / Correctional Services
Sous-ministre associé, Jean-François Longtin
Tél: 418-643-3500
Téléc: 418-643-0275
Directrice générale adjointe, Est-Du-Québec, Marlène Langlois
Tél: 418-646-6777 ext: 50002
Directeur général adjoint, Montréal, Vince Parente
Directrice générale adjointe, Programmes, au conseil et à l'administration, Karine Pelletier
Directrice générale adjointe, Sécurité, Chantal Robert
Directeur général adjoint, Ouest-Du-Québec, Christian Thibault

Sûreté du Québec / Québec Provincial Police
Grand quartier général, 1701, rue Parthenais, Montréal, QC H2K 3S7
Tél: 514-598-4141
Téléc: 514-598-4242
www.sq.gouv.qc.ca
twitter.com/suretequebec
www.facebook.com/policesuretequebec
www.linkedin.com/company/s-ret-du-qu-bec
instagram.com/suretequebec
Directeur général, Martin Prud'homme

Directeur général adjoint (par intérim), Grande fonction de l'administration, Richard Moffet
Directeur général adjoint, Grande fonction de la surveillance du territoire, Mario Bouchard
Directeur général adjoint, Grande fonction des enquêtes criminelles, André Goulet

Ministère du Tourisme / Tourism

#400, 900, boul René-Lévesque est, Québec, QC G1R 2B5
Tél: 418-643-5959
Téléc: 418-646-8723
Ligne sans frais: 800-482-2433
relations.publiques@tourisme.gouv.qc.ca
www.quebec.ca/gouv/ministere/tourisme
twitter.com/tourisme_quebec
www.facebook.com/tourismeqc
www.linkedin.com/company/tourismequebec

Ministre, L'hon. Caroline Proulx

Sous-ministre, Manon Boucher

Secrétariat générale, Geneviève Morneau

Directeur, Communications, Terry McKinnon
Tél: 418-691-5698 ext: 5653

Agences, Conseils et Commissions Associés/ Associated Agencies, Boards & Commissions:
• **Régie des installations olympiques/Parc olympique Québec / Québec Olympic Park**
4141, av Pierre-De Coubertin
Montréal, QC H1V 3N7
Tél: 514-252-4141
Ligne sans frais: 877-997-0919
rio@rio.gouv.qc.ca
www.parcolympique.qc.ca

• **Société du Centre des congrès de Québec / Québec City Convention Centre**
900, boul René-Lévesque est, 2e étage
Québec, QC G1R 2B5
Tél: 418-644-4000
Téléc: 418-644-6455
Ligne sans frais: 888-679-4000
www.convention.qc.ca

• **Société du Palais des congrès de Montréal / Montréal City Convention Centre**
159, rue Saint-Antoine ouest, 9é étage
Montréal, QC H2Z 1H2
Tél: 418-871-8122
Téléc: 514-871-9389
Ligne sans frais: 800-268-8122
info@congresmtl.com
congresmtl.com

Services à la gestion / Administrative Services
Directeur général, Sylvain Bernier
Tél: 418-643-5959 ext: 3300

Partenariats d'affaires et aux services aux clientéles / Business Partnerships & Customer Relations
Sous-ministre adjointe, Francis Paradis
Tél: 418-643-5959 ext: 5002

Ministère des Transports / Ministry of Transport

#4.010, 500, boul René-Lévesque est, Québec, QC H2Z 1W7
Ligne sans frais: 888-355-0511
communications@mtq.gouv.qc.ca
www.transports.gouv.qc.ca
Autres nombres: Partout au Québec: 5-1-1; Au Ailleurs en Amérique du Nord: 888-355-0511
twitter.com/transports_qc
www.facebook.com/transportsqc

Ministre des Transports, L'hon. François Bonnardel

Ministre déléguée aux Transports, L'hon. Chantal Rouleau

Sous-ministre, Patrick Dubé
Tél: 418-643-6740

Agences, Conseils et Commissions Associés/ Associated Agencies, Boards & Commissions:
• **Commission des transports du Québec / Québec Transport Commission**
200, ch Sainte-Foy, 7e étage
Québec, QC G1R 5V5
Tél: 514-873-6424
Téléc: 418-644-8034
Ligne sans frais: 888-461-2433
courier@ctq.gouv.qc.ca
www.ctq.gouv.qc.ca

• **Réseau de transport métropolitain (Exo) (RTM)**
700, rue de la Gauchetière ouest, 26e étage
Montréal, QC H3B 5M2
Tél: 514-287-8726
Ligne sans frais: 888-702-8726
rtm.quebec/fr
Autres numéros: Exo: rtm.quebec/fr/essayezexo

• **Société de l'assurance automobile du Québec (SAAQ)**
333, boul Jean-Lesage
CP 19600 Terminus
Québec, QC G1K 8J6
Tél: 418-643-7620
Téléc: 418-644-0339
Ligne sans frais: 800-361-7620
TTY: 800-565-7763
www.saaq.gouv.qc.ca
Autres numéros: Montréal: 514-873-7620

• **Société des traversiers du Québec / Ferries Québec**
250, rue Saint-Paul
Québec, QC G1K 9K9
Tél: 418-643-2019
Téléc: 418-643-7308
Ligne sans frais: 877-787-7483
stq@traversiers.gouv.qc.ca
traversiers.com

• **Société du port ferroviaire Baie-Comeau-Haute-Rive (SOPOR) / Baie-Comeau-Haute-Rive Railway Station Society**
18, rte Maritime
Baie-Comeau, QC G4Z 2L6
Tél: 418-296-6785

Bureau de la sous-ministre / Office of the Deputy Minister
Sous-ministre, Patrick Dubé
Tél: 418-643-6740
Directeur général, Centre de gestion de l'équipement roulant, Richard Dionne
Tél: 418-643-5430
Directrice générale, Secrétariat général en mise en oeuvre de la transformation organisationelle, Debra Dollard
Tél: 418-643-6740
Directeur général, Exploitation et servies à la clientèle, Carl Gauthier
Tél: 418-643-5430
Directeur, Communications, Thierry Audin
Tél: 418-644-1537
Directrice, Affaires juridiques, Kathleen Laroche
Tél: 418-643-6937
Directeur, Enquêtes et audit interne, Martin St-Louis
Tél: 418-643-6840

Électrification des transports, à la sécurité et à la mobilité / Electrification of Transport, Safety & Mobility
Sous-ministre adjoint, Jérôme Unterberg
Tél: 418-528-0808
Directeur général (par intérim), Programmes d'aide, André G. Bernier
Tél: 418-644-5607
Directeur général, Securité et camionnage, Yanick Blouin
Tél: 418-528-0631
Directeur général, Transport terrestre des personnes, Martin Breault
Tél: 418-644-0324
Directrice générale, Politique de la mobilité durable et de l'électrification, Évangéline Lévesque
Tél: 418-644-0447
Directeur général (par intérim), Transport maritime, aérien et ferroviaire, Denis Simard
Tél: 418-643-1864

Gestion contractuelle et à la surveillance des marchés / Contract Management & Market Surveillance
Sous-ministre associée, Julie Blackburn
Tél: 418-528-0808
Directrice générale, Surveillance des marchés et application des règles contractuelles, Marie-Josée Fournier
Tél: 418-266-8084
Directrice générale, Expertise contractuelle, Nathalie Dion
Tél: 418-643-5473
Directeur général, Opérations contractuelles, Nathalie Hovington
Tél: 418-266-8084

Grands Projets Routiers / Major Road Projects
Sous-ministre associé (par intérim), Stéphan Deschênes
Directeur général, Grands projets routiers de Québec et de l'Est, Richard Charpentier
Tél: 418-830-2003
Directrice générale, Grands projets Turcot et tunnel Louis-Hippolyte-La Fontaine, Sandra Sultana
Tél: 514-873-3838

Ingénierie et aux infrastructures / Engineering & Infrastructure

Sous-ministre adjointe, Anne-Marie Leclerc
Tél: 418-528-0808
Directeur général, Structures, Steve Arsenault
Tél: 418-643-6906
Directeur général, Gestion des projets routiers et encadrement en exploitation, Éric Breton
Tél: 418-643-9298
Directeur général, Gestion des actifs routiers et de l'innovation, Stéphane Dallaire
Tél: 418-528-0808
Directrice générale, Laboratoire des chaussées, Yvon Villeneuve
Tél: 418-643-6618

Performance organisationnelle / Organizational Performance

Sous-ministre associé, Nikolas Ducharme
Tel: 418-528-0808
Directrice générale, Gestion des risques de amélioration continue, Chantal Garcia
Tél: 418-780-6119
Directrice générale, Planification, coordination et programmation, Joanne Laberge
Tél: 418-780-8862
Directeur général, Ressources informationelles, François Rousseau
Tél: 418-646-0700

Services à la gestion / Management Services

Sous-ministre associé, Jean Villeneuve
Tel: 418-528-0808
Directrice générale, Ressources humaines, Nathalie Diamond
Tel: 418-646-4157
Directeur général, Gestion des immeubles et services partagés, Jean-Sébastien Dumont
Tel: 418-780-6123
Directeur général, Technologies de l'information, Alexandre Poirier
Tel: 418-643-4431
Directrice générale, Finances, Lisa Roberge
Tel: 418-644-2182
Directrice générale, Expertise immobilière, Lise Talbot
Tel: 418-646-2182

Territoires / Territories

Sous-ministre associé, Vacant
Sous-ministre adjointe (par intérim), Région métropolitaine de Montréal; Directeur, Projets, Fadi Moubayed
Tél: 514-873-7781
Directeur général, Coordination territoriale, Carl Bélanger
Tél: 418-528-0808
Directeur général, Planification et gestion des infrastructures, Daniel Donais
Tél: 514-873-7781
Directeur général, Exploitation, Borislav Milisav
Tél: 514-873-7781
Directeur général, Suivi des projets et parcs routiers, Claude Morin
Tél: 514-266-6648
Directrice générale, Sécurité civile et veille opérationnelle, Céline Tremblay
Tél: 418-644-0529

Ministère du Travail, de l'Emploi et de la Solidarité sociale / Labour, Employment & Social Solidarity

150, rue Monseigneur-Ross, 5e étage, Québec, QC G4X 2S7
Tél: 514-873-4000
Ligne sans frais: 877-767-8773
www.mess.gouv.qc.ca
Autres nombres: Secrétariat du travail: www.travail.gouv.qc.ca
twitter.com/gouv_mtess
www.facebook.com/emploisolidaritesocialequebec

Ministre, L'hon. Jean Boulet

Sous-ministre, Carole Arav

Agences, Conseils et Commissions Associés/ Associated Agencies, Boards & Commissions:

• **Comité consultatif de lutte contre la pauvreté et l'exclusion sociale (CCLP) / Advisory Committee on the Fight Against Poverty & Social Exclusion**
425, rue Jacques-Parizeau, RC 145
Québec, QC G1R 4Z1
Tél: 418-528-9866
Téléc: 418-643-6623
infocclp@mess.gouv.qc.ca
www.cclp.gouv.qc.ca

• **Commission de la construction du Québec (CCQ) / Québec Construction Commission**
8485, av Christophe-Colomb
Montréal, QC H2M 0A7
www.ccq.org
Autres numéros: Employeurs: 877-973-5383; Travailleurs et le grand public: 888-842-8282

• **Commission de la santé et de la sécurité du travail (CSST) / Occupational Health & Safety Commission**
See Entry Name Index for detailed listing.

• **Commission des normes, de l'équité, de la santé et de la sécurité du travail (CNESST) / Committee on Standards, Equity, Health & Safety at Work**
See Entry Name Index for detailed listing.

• **Commission des partenaires du marché du travail (CPMT) / Labour Market Partnerships Commission**
Tour de la Place-Victoria
800, rue du Square-Victoria, 28e étage
CP 100
Montréal, QC H4Z 1B7
Tél: 514-873-5252
Ligne sans frais: 866-640-3059
partenaires@mess.gouv.qc.ca
www.cpmt.gouv.qc.ca

• **Conseil consultatif du travail et de la main d'oeuvre (CCTM) / Advisory Council on Labour & Manpower**
#17.100, 500, boul René-Lévesque ouest
Montréal, QC H2Z 1W7
Tél: 514-873-2880
Téléc: 514-873-1129
Autres numéros:
www.travail.gouv.qc.ca/a_propos/comite_consultatif_du_travail_ et_de_la_main_doeuvre.html

• **Conseil de gestion de l'assurance parentale (CGAP) / Management Board of Parental Insurance**
#104, 1122, Grande Allée ouest
Québec, QC G1S 1E5
Tél: 418-643-1009
Téléc: 418-643-6738
Ligne sans frais: 888-610-7727
www.cgap.gouv.qc.ca
Autres numéros: Régime fédéral d'assurance-emploi:
800-808-6352

• **Directeur de l'état civil / Vital Statistics**
2535, boul Laurier
Québec, QC G1V 5C5
Tél: 418-644-4545
Ligne sans frais: 877-644-4545
TTY: 800-361-9596
www.etatcivil.gouv.qc.ca
Autres numéros: Montréal: 514-644-4545

• **Office de la sécurité du revenu des chasseurs et piègeurs cris / Cree Hunters & Trappers Income Security Board**
Édifice Champlain
#1100, 2700, boul Laurier
Québec, QC G1V 4K5
Tél: 418-643-7300
Téléc: 418-643-6803
Ligne sans frais: 800-363-1560
courrier@osrcpc.ca
www.osrcpc.ca

• **Régie du bâtiment du Québec (RBQ) / Québec Construction Companies Board**
545, boul Crémazie est, 4e étage
Montréal, QC H2M 2V2
Tél: 514-873-0976
Ligne sans frais: 800-361-0761
www.rbq.gouv.qc.ca

• **Tribunal administratif du travail (TAT) / Administrative Court of Labour**
900, boul René-Lévesque est, 5e étage
Québec, QC G1R 6C9
Tél: 418-643-3208
Téléc: 418-643-8946
Ligne sans frais: 866-864-3646
www.tat.gouv.qc.ca
Le Tribunal administratif du travail remplace la Commission des lésions professionnelles et la Commission des relations du travail.

Secrétariat du travail / Secretariat of Labour

Sous-ministre associée, Anne Racine
Directeur général, Recherche et innovation en milieu de travail, Louis Tremblay
Tel: 418-646-1893

Développement et des partenariats de Services Québec / Services Québec Development & Partnerships

Sous-ministre adjointe, Francis Gauthier
Tel: 418-622-4000 ext: 1220

Régime québécois d'assurance parentale (RQAP) / Québec Parental Insurance Plan

19, rue Perreault ouest, 1e étage, Rouyn-Noranda, QC J9X 0A1
Tél: 418-643-7246
Ligne sans frais: 888-610-7727
www.rqap.gouv.qc.ca
Directeur général, Marc Lemieux
Tél: 418-528-7727 ext: 89144

Emploi-Québec / Employment Québec

Direction du Centre de communication avec la clientèle, 150, rue Monseigneur-Ross, 5e étage, Gaspé, QC G4X 2S7
Tél: 514-873-4000
Ligne sans frais: 877-767-8773
www.emploiquebec.gouv.qc.ca
twitter.com/emploi_quebec
www.facebook.com/emploiquebec
Sous-ministre associé et secrétaire générale de la CPMT, Roger Tremblay
Tél: 418-646-0425 ext: 88681
Directrice générale, Développement et reconaissance de la main-oeuvre, Isabelle Bemeur
Tél: 514-873-0800 ext: 35524
Directrice générale, Mesures et services d'emploi, Frédérique-Myriam Villemure
Tél: 418-646-0425 ext: 34009
Directeur général, Politiques d'emploi, planification et marché du travail, Richard St-Pierre
Tél: 514-864-3660
Directeur, Politiques d'emploi et stratégies, Pierre Berger
Tél: 514-873-0800 ext: 38766
Directeur, Mesures et services aux entreprises et placement, Guylaine Bilodeau
Tél: 418-646-0425 ext: 37384
Directeur, Soutien opérationnel au développement de la main-d'oeuvre, Reine Bohbot
Tél: 514-873-0800 ext: 43563
Directrice, Analyse et information sur le marchée du travail, Karine Dumont
Tél: 514-873-0800 ext: 38767
Directrice, Qualification professionnelle, Élise Martel
Tél: 514-873-0800 ext: 36422
Directrice, Qualification professionnelle, Marie-Josée Ouellet
Tél: 418-646-0425 ext: 82793

Opérations / Operations

Sous-ministre adjoint, Martin Bouchard
Tél: 418-646-0425 ext: 48481
Directeur général, Services téléphoniques, Serge Bouchard
Directeur général (par intérim), Opérations territoriales, Ghislain Laprise
Tél: 418-646-0425 ext: 88681
Directrice général, Soutien à la prestation de services, Anik Simard
Tél: 418-646-0425 ext: 37186

Recouvrement, de la révision et de la conformité / Recovery, Revision & Compliance

Sous-ministre adjoint, Jean Audet
Tél: 418-646-0425 ext: 42781
Directrice générale, Recouvrement, révision et recours administratifs, Esther Quirion
Tél: 418-644-0425 ext: 31774

Registres de l'État / State Registers

Sous-ministre adjointe, Marie-Claude Rioux
Tél: 418-643-3080 ext: 2781
Directeur général, Directeur de l'état civil, Hermel Grandmaison
Tél: 418-643-1447
Directeur général, Registraire des entreprises, Yves Pepin
Tél: 418-643-3080

Services à la gestion et ressources informationnelles / Administrative Services & Information Resources

Sous-ministre adjoint, Pierre E. Rodrigue
Tél: 418-646-0425 ext: 66816
Directeur général, Ressources humaines, Serge Bouchard
Tél: 418-646-0425 ext: 31825
Directrice générale, Ressources informationnelles, Nicole Boucher
Tél: 418-646-0425 ext: 65265
Directrice générale, Services à l'organisation, Lucie Pelletier
Tél: 418-646-0425 ext: 800088
Directeur général, Ressources financières et contractuelles, Etienne Sabourin
Tél: 418-646-0800 ext: 1492

Services Québec
Bureau de la qualité, 800, Place D'Youville, 20e étage, Québec, QC G1R 3P4

Tél: 418-644-4545
Ligne sans frais: 877-644-4545
TTY: 800-361-9596
www.mess.gouv.qc.ca/services-quebec
Autres nombres: Montréal: 514-644-4545
twitter.com/servicesquebec
www.facebook.com/servicesquebec
www.linkedin.com/company/services-qu-bec

Les Publications du Québec
1000, rte de l'Église, 5e étage, Québec, QC G1V 3V9

Tél: 418-643-5150
Téléc: 418-643-6177
Ligne sans frais: 800-463-2100
www.publicationsduquebec.gouv.qc.ca
Autres nombres: Téléc sans frais: 800-561-3479
www.facebook.com/publicationsquebec

Solidarité sociale et de l'analyse stratégique / Social Solidarity & Strategic Analysis
Sous-ministre adjointe, Chantal Maltais
Tél: 418-646-0425 ext: 35568
Directeur général, Assistance sociale, Daniel Jean
Tél: 418-646-9270 ext: 65780
Directeur général, Solidarité sociale et de l'action communautaire (par intérim), Stéphane Morin
Tél: 418-646-0425 ext: 80081

Secrétariat du Conseil du trésor / Treasury Board

875, Grande Allée est, 2e étage, secteur 800, Québec, QC G1R 5R8

Tél: 418-643-1529
Téléc: 418-643-9226
Ligne sans frais: 866-552-5158
communication@sct.gouv.qc.ca
www.tresor.gouv.qc.ca

Président du Conseil du trésor, L'hon. Sonia LeBel

Secrétaire, Éric Ducharme

Greffier (par intérim), Louis Tremblay
Tél: 418-643-0875 ext: 4201

Directeur, Communications, Jérôme Thibaudeau
Tél: 418-643-2001 ext: 4051

Agences, Conseils et Commissions Associés/ Associated Agencies, Boards & Commissions:

• Centre du services partagés du Québec (CSPQ) / Québec Shared Services Centre
875, Grande Allée est, 4e étage, section 4.550
Québec, QC G1R 5W5
Tél: 418-644-2777
Téléc: 418-644-0462
Ligne sans frais: 855-644-2777
cspq@cspq.gouv.qc.ca
www.cspq.gouv.qc.ca

• Commission de la fonction publique (Québec) / Public Service Commission
800, Place d'Youville, 7e étage
Québec, QC G1R 3P4
Tél: 418-643-1425
Téléc: 418-643-7264
Ligne sans frais: 800-432-0432
cfp@cfp.gouv.qc.ca
www.cfp.gouv.qc.ca
La Commission de la fonction publique: contribuons à assurer l'égalité d'accès des citoyennes et des citoyens à la fonction publique; la compétence des personnes qui y sont recrutées et promues; et l'impartialité et l'équité des décisions qui y sont prises en matière de gestion des ressources humaines.

• Société québécoise des infrastructures / Infrastructure
Édifice Marie-Fitzbach
1075, rue de l'Amérique-Française
Québec, QC G1R 5P8
Tél: 418-646-1766
Téléc: 418-646-6911
courrier@sqi.gouv.qc.ca
www.sqi.gouv.qc.ca
Autres numéros: Bureau des plaintes, Tél: 418-644-4542; Téléc: 418-528-2999; Courrier: plainte@sqi.gouv.qc.ca

Administration
Directrice générale (par intérim) et Directrice, Ressources humaines, France Normand
Tél: 418-643-0875 ext: 4401

Ressources informationnelles / Information Resources
Directeur général, Alexandre Mailhot
Tél: 418-643-0875 ext: 4350

Bureau de la gouvernance en gestion des ressources humaines / Governance & Human Resources Management
Directrice principale (par intérim), Farah Ouamara
Tél: 418-643-0875 ext: 4661
Directrice générale, Coordination et de la performance en gestion des RH, Michelle Rhéaume

Sous-secrétariat à la révision permanente des programmes et à l'application de la Loi sur l'administration publique / Permanent Review Programs & the Application of the Public Administration Act
Secrétaire associé, Reno Bernier
Tél: 418-643-0875 ext: 5301
Directeur général, Révision des programmes; Directeur (par intérim), Application des lignes directrices en matière de planification stratégique et de reddition de compte publique, Renée Berger
Directrice générale, Encadrement gouvernemental des fonctions d'évaluation de programmes et de vérification interne, Carole Blouin
Directeur général, Analyse, recherche et du partenariat stratégique, Daniel Otis

Sous-secrétariat à la négociation, aux relations de travail et à la rémunération globale / Negotiation, Labour Relations & Overall Compensation
Secrétaire associée, Édith Lapointe
Tél: 418-643-0875 ext: 4600

Sous-secrétariat aux infrastructures publiques / Public Infrastructure
Secrétaire associée, Marie-Claude Lavallée

Sous-secrétariat aux marchés publics / Public Markets
Tél: 418-643-1529
Téléc: 418-643-9226
marches.publics@sct.gouv.qc.ca
Directeur général (par intérim), Politiques de marchés publics, Robert Villeneuve
Tél: 418-643-0875 ext: 4938

Sous-secrétariat aux politiques budgétaires et aux programmes / Budget Policies & Programs
Secrétaire associé, Jean-François Lachaine
Tél: 418-643-0875 ext: 4501
Directrice générale, Programmes économiques, éducatifs et culturels, Anne Boucher
Tél: 418-643-0875 ext: 4554
Directeur général, Programmes administratifs, sociaux & de santé, Serge Garon
Tél: 418-643-0875 ext: 4536
Directeur général (par intérim), Politiques & opérations budgétaires, Jean-François Lachaine
Tél: 418-643-0875 ext: 4510

Sous-secrétariat du dirigeant principal de l'information / Office of the Chief Information Officer
Secrétaire associé, Benoît Boivin
Tél: 418-643-0875 ext: 5001
Directrice générale, Gouvernance des ressources informationnelles, Marcel Boudreault
Tél: 418-643-0875 ext: 5150
Directeur général, Orientations gouvernementales en ressources informationnelles, Christiane Langlois
Tél: 418-643-0875 ext: 5140

Vérificateur général du Québec / Auditor General

#300, 750, boul Charest est, Québec, QC G1K 9J6
Tél: 418-691-5900
Téléc: 418-644-4460
verificateur.general@vgq.qc.ca
www.vgq.gouv.qc.ca
Secondary Address: #1910, 770, rue Sherbrooke ouest
Montréal, QC H3A 1G1
Alt. Téléc: 514-873-7665
twitter.com/vgquebec
www.linkedin.com/company/10410640
Le Vérificateur général du Québec a pour mission de favoriser par la vérification le contrôle parlementaire sur les fonds et autres biens publics.

Vérificatrice générale, Guylaine Leclerc

Sous-vérificateur général, Serge Giguère, CPA auditeur, CA

Vérificateur général adjoint, Commissaire au développement durable, Paul Lanoie

---

Vérificateur général adjoint, Jean-Pierre Fiset, CPA auditeur, CA

Vérificatrice générale adjointe, Christine Roy

Government of Saskatchewan

Seat of Government: 2405 Legislative Dr., Regina, SK S4S 0B3

www.saskatchewan.ca
twitter.com/SKGov
www.facebook.com/SKGov

The Province of Saskatchewan entered Confederation on September 1, 1905. It has a land area of 588,243.54 sq km, & the StatsCan census population in 2016 was 1,098,352.

Office of the Lieutenant Governor

Government House, 4607 Dewdney Ave., Regina, SK S4T 1B7
Tel: 306-787-4070; *Fax:* 306-787-7716
lgo@ltgov.sk.ca
ltgov.sk.ca
Other Communication: Authentication of Documents, Phone: 306-787-2951
twitter.com/LGTomMolloy
www.facebook.com/LtGovSk
The position of the Lieutenant Governor is apolitical & non-partisan. His Honour the Honourable Russ Mirasty, Lieutenant Governor of Saskatchewan, is the representative of The Queen in Saskatchewan.
Some responsibilities of the Lieutenant Governor are as follows: presiding over the swearing in of the Premier, cabinet ministers, & the Chief Justice of Saskatchewan; delivering the Speech from the Throne; giving Royal Assent to acts of the Legislative Assembly; participating in commemorative ceremonies & provincial celebrations; & honouring achievements.

Lieutenant Governor of Saskatchewan, Hon. Russ Mirasty

Executive Director & Private Secretary, Heather Salloum
Tel: 306-787-4415
heather.salloum@gov.sk.ca

Office of the Premier

Legislative Bldg., #226, 2405 Legislative Dr., Regina, SK S4S 0B3
Tel: 306-787-9433; *Fax:* 306-787-0885
www.saskatchewan.ca/premier
Scott Moe was elected to be Saskatchewan's 15th Premier at a party convention held Jan. 27, 2018, following the resignation of former Premier Brad Wall.

Premier; President, Executive Council; Minister, Intergovernmental Affairs, Hon. Scott Moe
Tel: 306-787-9433; *Fax:* 306-787-0885
premier@gov.sk.ca

Deputy Minister, Cam Swan
Tel: 306-787-6338
cam.swan@gov.sk.ca

Provincial Secretary, Lyle Stewart
Tel: 306-787-4301; *Fax:* 306-787-1269
lyle.stewart@gov.sk.ca

Executive Council

Communications Services, Executive Council, #130, 3085 Albert St., Regina, SK S4S 0B1
Other Communication: Cabinet URL: www.saskatchewan.ca/government/government-structure/cabinet

Appointed by the Premier of Saskatchewan, each cabinet minister is responsible for a ministry or portfolio.

Premier; President, Executive Council; Minister, Intergovernmental Affairs, Hon. Scott Moe
Tel: 306-787-9433; *Fax:* 306-787-0885
premier@gov.sk.ca
www.premier.gov.sk.ca

Deputy Premier; Minister, Finance, Hon. Donna Harpauer
Tel: 306-787-6060; *Fax:* 306-787-6055
fin.minister@gov.sk.ca

Minister, Crown Investments Corporation; Minister, Labour Relations & Workplace Safety; Minister responsible, Saskatchewan Workers' Compensation Board & Crown corporations, including SaskEnergy, SGI, SaskPower, SaskTel, SaskGaming & SaskWater, Hon.

Don Morgan, Q.C.
Tel: 306-787-8824; *Fax:* 306-787-1232

Minister, SaskBuilds & Procurement; Minister responsible, Public Service Commission, Saskatchewan Liquor & Gaming Authority, Hon. Jim Reiter
Tel: 306-787-0942

Minister, Education, Hon. Dustin Duncan
Tel: 306-787-0393; *Fax:* 306-787-1669

Minister, Corrections & Policing; Minister responsible, Saskatchewan Public Safety Agency, Hon. Christine Tell
Tel: 306-787-0284
christine.tell@gov.sk.ca

Minister, Justice & Attorney General, Hon. Gordon Wyant, Q.C.
Tel: 306-787-5353

Minister, Trade & Export Development; Minister, Immigration & Career Training; Minister responsible, Innovation Saskatchewan; Minister responsible, Tourism Saskatchewan; Government House Leader, Hon. Jeremy Harrison
Tel: 30- 78- 868; *Fax:* 306-787-8677
minister.teic@gov.sk.ca

Minister of Agriculture; Minister responsible, Saskatchewan Crop Insurance Corporation, Hon. David Marit
Tel: 306-787-0338
minister.ag@gov.sk.ca

Minister, Energy & Resources, Hon. Bronwyn Eyre
Tel: 306-787-0804
ministerer@gov.sk.ca

Minister, Health, Hon. Paul Merriman
Tel: 306-787-7345

Minister, Advanced Education, Hon. Gene Makowsky
Tel: 306-798-0574

Minister, Environment, Hon. Warren Kaeding
Tel: 306-787-0393

Minister, Social Services, Hon. Lori Carr
Tel: 306-787-3661

Minister, Government Relations; Minister, First Nations, Métis Relations & Northern Affairs; Minister responsible, Provincial Capital Commission, Hon. Don McMorris
Tel: 306-787-7326

Minister, Parks, Culture & Sport; Minister, Status of Women, Hon. Laura Ross
Tel: 306-787-0354

Minister, Mental Health & Addictions; Minister, Seniors & Rural & Remote Health, Hon. Everett Hindley
Tel: 306-798-9014

Minister, Highways; Minister responsible, Saskatchewan Water Security Agency, Hon. Fred Bradshaw
Tel: 306-787-6447

Cabinet Secretariat
Legislative Bldg., #145, 2405 Legislative Dr., Regina, SK S4S 0B3
Tel: 306-787-6343; *Fax:* 306-787-8299
cabsec@ec.gov.sk.ca
The Cabinet Secretariat has the following responsibilities: supporting the Premier & President of the Executive Council; offering administrative support to the Cabinet; maintaining public records & employment contracts.
Assistant Cabinet Secretary & Clerk of the Executive Council, Paul Crozier
Tel: 306-787-9630; *Fax:* 306-787-8299
paul.crozier@gov.sk.ca

Office of the Chief of Staff to the Premier
Legislative Bldg., #110, 2405 Legislative Dr., Regina, SK S4S 0B3
Tel: 306-787-9433; *Fax:* 306-787-0883
Includes the Correspondence Unit, which handles daily correspondence to & from the Premier. The unit also processes requests for photographs of the Premier.
Chief of Staff to the Premier, Shannon Andrews
Tel: 306-787-0064
shannon.andrews@gov.sk.ca

Deputy Chief of Staff, Operations & Policy, Drew Dwernychuk
Tel: 306-787-5288
Drew.Dwernychuk@gov.sk.ca
Director, Policy & Research, Michelle Lang
Tel: 306-787-9120
michelle.lang@gov.sk.ca

Communications
Legislative Bldg., #110, 2405 Legislative Dr., Regina, SK S4S 0B3
Tel: 306-787-0425; *Fax:* 306-787-0883
The Communications Services branch administers the Communications Procurement Policy to government ministries, agencies, & Crowns. The Executive Director of Communications oversees communications to ensure information is provided to the media & the public in a timely & effective manner. Media relations staff provide assistance in the preparation & distribution of news releases.
Deputy Chief of Staff, Communications & External Relations, Jim Billington
Tel: 306-787-0425; *Fax:* 306-787-0883
jim.billington@gov.sk.ca

Office of the Deputy Minister to the Premier
Legislative Bldg., #135, 2405 Legislative Dr., Regina, SK S4S 0B3
Tel: 306-787-6337; *Fax:* 306-787-8338
The Office of the Deputy Minister to the Premier carries out the following key functions: supporting the Premier; providing coordination between the Cabinet, ministries, agencies, & Crown corporations; & handling appointments of senior executives for ministries.
Deputy Minister to the Premier & Cabinet Secretary, Cam Swan
Tel: 306-787-6338
cam.swan@gov.sk.ca

Cabinet Planning
Legislative Bldg., #37, 2405 Legislative Dr., Regina, SK S4S 0B3
Tel: 306-787-6344; *Fax:* 306-787-0012
The Cabinet Planning branch is involved in the following activities: offering research & advice about ministry & sectoral plans & policy proposals; providing policy analysis & secretariat support to the Premier, members of the Executive Council, & the Committee on Planning & Priorities; & participating in inter-ministry & inter-agency working groups.
Associate Deputy Minister, James Saunders
Tel: 306-787-6339
james.saunders@gov.sk.ca

Corporate Services
Legislative Bldg., #34, 2405 Legislative Dr., Regina, SK S4S 0B3
Tel: 306-787-7448; *Fax:* 306-787-0097
The Corporate Services branch of the Executive Council oversees the following areas: the ministry's budget; expense claims of cabinet ministers & ministry staff; human resource services; & information technology.
Executive Director, Kristen Fry
Tel: 306-787-2126
Kristen.Fry@gov.sk.ca

Intergovernmental Affairs
Legislative Bldg., #135, 2405 Legislative Dr., Regina, SK S4S 0B3
Tel: 306-787-4474
The Government of Saskatchewan's Intergovernmental Affairs manages the province's relationships with Canadian provincial & territorial governments, federal governments, & international jurisdictions.
The mission of Intergovernmental Affairs involves promoting the province's interests, securing access to markets for products from Saskatchewan, handling official protocol, managing the provincial honours & awards program, & overseeing Francophone affairs.
Associate Deputy Minister, Ashley Metz
Tel: 306-787-7962; *Fax:* 306-787-1269
ashley.metz@gov.sk.ca
Chief of Protocol & Secretary of the Saskatchewan Honours Advisory Council, Major Jason Quilliam, C.C.
Tel: 306-787-3109
Toll-free: 877-427-5505; *Fax:* 306-787-1269
jason.quilliam@gov.sk.ca

Provincial Secretary
#315, 3085 Albert St., Regina, SK S4S 0B1
Tel: 306-787-3001; *Fax:* 306-787-1269
The Provincial Secretary reports to the Premier. The work of the Provincial Secretary is to assist the Premier with protocol, events, & French language services.
Provincial Secretary, Lyle Stewart
Tel: 306-787-3001; *Fax:* 306-787-1269
lyle.stewart@gov.sk.ca

Office of the Clerk, Legislative Bldg., #239, 2405 Legislative Dr., Regina, SK S4S 0B3
info@legassembly.sk.ca
www.legassembly.sk.ca
Other Communication: Library Reference Questions, Email: reference@legassembly.sk.ca
twitter.com/SKLegAssembly
www.facebook.com/SKLegAssembly
The Legislative Assembly oversees the government & performs three major roles: a legislative role, an inquiry role, & a financial role.
Members of the Assembly may include the Premier, the Leader of the Opposition, House Leaders, & Whips. Officers of the House include the Speaker, Clerks, & the Sargeant-at-Arms. Some major legislative services are legislative library services, visitor services, the production of parliamentary publications, & communication & technology services.

Speaker, Legislative Assembly, Hon. Randy Weekes
Tel: 306-787-2282; *Fax:* 306-787-2283
speaker@legassembly.sk.ca
Legislative Bldg.
#203, 2405 Legislative Dr.
Regina, SK S4S 0B3

Clerk, Greg Putz
Tel: 306-787-2335; *Fax:* 306-787-0408
gputz@legassembly.sk.ca

Law Clerk; Parliamentary Counsel, Kenneth S. Ring, Q.C.
Tel: 306-787-2298; *Fax:* 306-787-0408
kring@legassembly.sk.ca

Sergeant-at-Arms, Terry Quinn
Tel: 306-787-8798
tquinn@legassembly.sk.ca

Chief Executive, Member & Corporate Services, Dawn Court
Tel: 306-787-6477; *Fax:* 306-798-2085
dcourt@legassembly.sk.ca

Legislative Librarian, Melissa Bennett
Tel: 306-787-2277; *Fax:* 306-787-1772
mbennett@legassembly.sk.ca
www.legassembly.sk.ca/library
Office of the Legislative Librarian, Legislative Bldg.
#234, 2405 Legislative Dr.
Regina, SK S4S 0B3

Government Caucus Office (Saskatchewan Party)
Legislative Bldg., #203, 2405 Legislative Dr., Regina, SK S4S 0B3
Tel: 306-787-4300; *Fax:* 306-787-3174
Toll-Free: 888-708-7780
info@skcaucus.com
www.skcaucus.com
twitter.com/SaskParty
www.facebook.com/SaskParty
Established in 1997, the Saskatchewan Party has been the province's governing party since 2007. Past leaders include Ken Krawetz (1997-1998), Elwin Hermanson (1998-2004), Lyle Stewart (2004) & Brad Wall (2004-2018), who was Premier for three terms.
Premier; President, Executive Council; Minister, Intergovernmental Affairs; Leader, Saskatchewan Party, Hon. Scott Moe
Tel: 306-787-9433; *Fax:* 306-787-0885
premier@gov.sk.ca
www.premier.gov.sk.ca
Government House Leader, Hon. Jeremy Harrison
Tel: 306-787-8687; *Fax:* 306-787-7977
jharrisonmla@sasktel.net
Government Whip, Greg Ottenbreit

Opposition Caucus Office (New Democratic Party)
Legislative Bldg., #265, 2405 Legislative Dr., Regina, SK S4S 0B3
Tel: 306-787-7388; *Fax:* 306-787-6247
caucus@ndpcaucus.sk.ca
www.ndpcaucus.sk.ca
Dwain Lingenfelter resigned as the leader of Saskatchewan's New Democratic Party after he lost his seat in the November 2011 provincial election. John Nilson, a veteran Member of the Legislative Assembly, took over as the interim leader of the party. Cam Broten became the new leader in March 2013, but lost his seat in the 2016 general election. Following the election, Trent Wotherspoon became the party's Interim Leader. He remained in that position until June 2017, when he resigned to focus on winning the permanent leadership in the May 2018 leadership election. Nicole Sarauer assumed the Interim position

until the convention, when Ryan Meili was elected to be the party's new permanent Leader.

Leader, Official Opposition; Leader, Saskatchewan New Democratic Party, Ryan Meili
Tel: 306-787-7388; *Fax:* 306-787-6247
saskatoonmeewasin@ndpcaucus.sk.ca

Deputy Leader, Official Opposition, Nicole Sarauer
Tel: 306-787-7388; *Fax:* 306-787-6247
reginadouglaspark@ndpcaucus.sk.ca

Opposition Caucus Chair, Carla Beck
Tel: 306-787-0633; *Fax:* 306-787-6247
reginalakeview@ndpcaucus.sk.ca

Deputy Opposition Caucus Chair, Matt Love
Tel: 306-787-7388
saskatooneastview@ndpcaucus.sk.ca

House Leader, Official Opposition, Vicki Mowat
Tel: 306-787-2563
saskatoonfairview@ndpcaucus.sk.ca

Deputy House Leader, Official Opposition, Aleana Young
Tel: 306-787-7388
reginauniversity@ndpcaucus.sk.ca

Opposition Whip, Doyle Vermette
Tel: 306-787-6340; *Fax:* 306-787-6247
cumberland@ndpcaucus.sk.ca

Standing Committees of the Legislative Assembly of Saskatchewan

Legislative Bldg., #7, 2405 Legislative Dr., Regina, SK S4S 0B3

Tel: 306-787-9930
committees@legassembly.sk.ca
www.legassembly.sk.ca/legislative-business/legislative-committees

Standing committees are established according to the permanent Rules of the Legislative Assembly. There are three categories of Standing Committees: Policy Field, House, & Scrutiny. The committees function for the duration of the legislature.

The following are the Standing Committees of the Legislative Assembly of Saskatchewan: Crown & Central Agencies; Economy; House Services; Human Services; Intergovernmental Affairs & Justice; Private Bills; Privileges; & Public Accounts.

Chair, Standing Committee on Crown & Central Agencies, Terry Dennis

Chair, Standing Committee on the Economy, Colleen Young

Chair, Standing Committee on House Services, Hon. Randy Weekes

Chair, Standing Committee on Human Services, Ken Cheveldayoff

Chair, Standing Committee on Intergovernmental Affairs & Justice, Mark Docherty

Chair, Standing Committee on Private Bills, Vicki Mowat

Chair, Standing Committee on Privileges, Hon. Randy Weekes

Chair, Standing Committee on Public Accounts, Trent Wotherspoon

---

Twenty-ninth Legislature - Saskatchewan

Legislative Bldg., 2405 Legislative Dr., Regina, SK S4S 0B3
www.legassembly.sk.ca
Other Communication: Legislative Library Reference Desk, Phone: 306-787-2276
twitter.com/SKLegAssembly
www.facebook.com/SKLegAssembly

Last General Election: Oct. 26, 2020.
Next General Election: 2024.
Party Standings (Oct. 2021):
Saskatchewan Party 47;
New Democratic Party 12;
Independent 1;
Vacant 1;
Total 61.
Salaries & Allowances of Members (April 2021):
Member of the Legislative Assembly, Annual Indemnity $100,668.
Additional Allowances:
Premier $67,506;
Deputy Premier $73,217.
Speaker $51,253;
Minister $51,253;
Leader of the Opposition $51,253;
Leader of the Third Party $25,626;
Government House Leader $14,978;
Opposition House Leader $14,978;
Third Party House Leader $7,490;
Government Whip $14,978;
Opposition Whip $14,978;
Third Party Whip $7,490;
Government Caucus Chair $14,978;
Opposition Caucus Chair $14,978;
Third Party Caucus Chair $7,490.
The following is a list of members, with their constituency, the number of electors in the constituency for the 2020 general election, party affiliation, & contact information:

Members of the Legislative Assembly of Saskatchewan

Opposition Caucus Chair, Carla Beck
Constituency: Regina Lakeview *No. of Constituents:* 12,268, New Democratic Party
Tel: 306-787-0633; *Fax:* 306-787-6247
reginalakeview@ndpcaucus.sk.ca
Other Communications: Constituency Phone: 306-522-1333; Fax: 306-522-1479
twitter.com/Carla4Lakeview,
www.facebook.com/carla4lakeview,
www.linkedin.com/in/carla-beck-35989858
Constituency Office
2213 Broad St.
Regina, SK S4P 1Y7

Steven Bonk
Constituency: Moosomin *No. of Constituents:* 12,878, Saskatchewan Party
stevenbonkmla@sasktel.net
Other Communications: Constituency Phone: 306-435-4005; Fax: 306-435-4008
Constituency Office
622 Main St.
PO Box 1038
Moosomin, SK S0G 3N0

Jennifer Bowes
Constituency: Saskatoon University *No. of Constituents:* 11,286, New Democratic Party
Tel: 306-787-7388
saskatoonuniversity@ndpcaucus.sk.ca
Other Communications: Constituency Phone: 306-956-0224
Constituency Office
#50, 2105 - 8th St. East
Saskatoon, SK S7H 0T8

Minister, Highways; Minister responsible, Saskatchewan Water Security Agency, Hon. Fred Bradshaw
Constituency: Carrot River Valley *No. of Constituents:* 12,409, Saskatchewan Party
Tel: 306-787-6447
Toll-free: 866-744-3977; *Fax:* 306-787-1736
fbradshaw.mla@sasktel.net
fredbradshaw.ca
Other Communications: Constituency Phone: 306-768-3977; Fax: 306-768-3979
Constituency Office
29 Main St.
PO Box 969
Carrot River, SK S0E 0L0

David Buckingham
Constituency: Saskatoon Westview *No. of Constituents:* 15,701, Saskatchewan Party
davidbuckinghammla@gmail.com
www.davidbuckinghammla.ca
Other Communications: Constituency Phone: 306-242-4440; Fax: 306-934-2867
twitter.com/dbuckinghamsk,
www.facebook.com/davidbuckinghamSW
Constituency Office
#14, 2345 Ave. C North
Saskatoon, SK S7L 5Z5

Minister, Social Services, Hon. Lori Carr
Constituency: Estevan *No. of Constituents:* 12,255, Saskatchewan Party
Tel: 306-787-0658
Toll-free: 866-284-7496; *Fax:* 306-787-0656
loricarrmla@sasktel.net
Other Communications: Constituency Phone: 306-634-7311; Fax: 306-634-7332
Constituency Office
1108 - 4th St.
Estevan, SK S4A 0W7

Minister, Central Services; Minister responsible, Public Service Commission, Hon. Ken Cheveldayoff
Constituency: Saskatoon Willowgrove *No. of Constituents:* 20,102, Saskatchewan Party
ken.cheveldayoff.mla@sasktel.net
www.cheveldayoff.com
Other Communications: Constituency Phone: 306-651-7100; Fax: 306-651-6008
twitter.com/kencheveld,
www.facebook.com/kencheveldayoffsk,
www.linkedin.com/in/ken-cheveldayoff-235942148
Constituency Office
1106A Central Ave. North
Saskatoon, SK S7N 2H1

Jeremy Cockrill
Constituency: The Battlefords *No. of Constituents:* 14,223, Saskatchewan Party
office@jeremycockrill.ca
Other Communications: Constituency Phone: 306-445-5195
twitter.com/jeremycockrill,
www.facebook.com/jeremy4thebattlefords,
www.linkedin.com/in/jeremycockrill
Constituency Office
1991 - 100th St.
North Battleford, SK S9A 0X2

Meara Conway
Constituency: Regina Elphinstone-Centre *No. of Constituents:* 12,813, New Democratic Party
Tel: 306-787-7388
reginaelphinstonecentre@ndpcaucus.sk.ca
Other Communications: Constituency Phone: 306-352-2002
twitter.com/mearaconwayndp,
www.facebook.com/mearaconwayNDP
Constituency Office
3510 - 5th Ave.
Regina, SK S4T 0M2

Terry Dennis
Constituency: Canora-Pelly *No. of Constituents:* 11,817, Saskatchewan Party
Canora.PellyMLA@sasktel.net
www.terrydennismla.com
Other Communications: Constituency Phone: 306-563-1363; Fax: 306-563-1365
Constituency Office
106 - 1st Ave. East
PO Box 838
Canora, SK S0A 0L0

Mark Docherty
Constituency: Regina Coronation Park *No. of Constituents:* 12,621, Saskatchewan Party
markdochertymla@sasktel.net
Other Communications: Constituency Phone: 306-359-3624; Fax: 306-787-3174
Constituency Office
1820 - 9th Ave. North
Regina, SK S4R 7T4

Ryan Domotor
Constituency: Cut Knife-Turtleford *No. of Constituents:* 13,003, Saskatchewan Party
domotor.mla@sasktel.net
Other Communications: Constituency Phone: 306-893-2619; Fax: 306-893-2660
www.linkedin.com/in/ryan-domotor-347150130
Constituency Office
#6, 116 - 1st Ave. West
PO Box 850
Maidstone, SK S0M 1M0

Minister, Education, Hon. Dustin Duncan
Constituency: Weyburn-Big Muddy *No. of Constituents:* 12,625, Saskatchewan Party
Tel: 306-787-7360
Toll-free: 877-842-4810; *Fax:* 396-787-6946
dduncan.mla@myaccess.ca
Other Communications: Constituency Phone: 306-842-4810; Fax: 306-842-4811
Constituency Office
28 - 4th St. NE
Weyburn, SK S4H 0X7

Minister, Energy & Resources, Hon. Bronwyn Eyre
Constituency: Saskatoon Stonebridge-Dakota *No. of Constituents:* 19,683, Saskatchewan Party
Tel: 306-787-0804; *Fax:* 306-798-2009
bronwyn.eyre.mla@sasktel.net
://www.bronwyneyremla.ca
Other Communications: Constituency Phone: 306-477-4740; Fax: 306-477-4744
www.facebook.com/BronwynEyreSSD
Constituency Office
#18, 102 Cope Cres.
Saskatoon, SK S7T 0X2

Muhammad Fiaz
Constituency: Regina Pasqua *No. of Constituents:* 18,884, Saskatchewan Party
mfiaz.mla@sasktel.net
Other Communications: Constituency Phone: 306-545-4555
twitter.com/fiazregina,
www.facebook.com/FiazMLAReginaPasqua,
www.linkedin.com/in/muhammad-fiaz-31282770
Note: Muhammad Fiaz is the first Muslim MLA in Saskatchewan history.
Constituency Office
#4, 4621 Rae St.
Regina, SK S4S 6K6

Ken Francis
Constituency: Kindersley *No. of Constituents:* 12,275, Saskatchewan Party
kfrancismla@gmail.com
www.saskparty.com/francis
Other Communications: Constituency Phone: 306-463-4446; Fax: 306-445-5195
www.facebook.com/kenfrancisforsaskpartycandidate
Constituency Office
#5, 1001 Main St.
PO Box 2620
Kindersley, SK S0L 1S0

Marv Friesen
Constituency: Saskatoon Riversdale *No. of Constituents:*
13,308, Saskatchewan Party
riversdale.mla@sasktel.net
marvfriesen.ca
Other Communications: Constituency Phone: 306-244-6278
www.facebook.com/MarvForRiversdale,
www.linkedin.com/in/marv-friesen-42989847
Constituency Office
2013 - 11th St. West
Saskatoon, SK S7M 4A7

Todd Goudy
Constituency: Melfort *No. of Constituents:* 12,494,
Saskatchewan Party
goudymla@gmail.com
Other Communications: Constituency Phone: 306-752-9500
www.facebook.com/ToddGoudyMelfort
Constituency Office
#14, 1121 Main St. North
PO Box 2800
Melfort, SK S0E 1A0

Gary Grewal
Constituency: Regina Northeast *No. of Constituents:* 12,879,
Saskatchewan Party
garygrewalmla@sasktel.net
Other Communications: Constituency Phone: 306-949-4900;
Fax: 306-949-4906
Constituency Office
1912 Prince of Wales Dr.
Regina, SK S4Z 1A4

Joe Hargrave
Constituency: Prince Albert Carlton *No. of Constituents:*
13,965, Saskatchewan Party
pacarltonmla@sasktel.net
www.saskparty.com/hargrave
Other Communications: Constituency Phone: 306-922-2828;
Fax: 306-922-0261
Constituency Office
#4, 406 South Industrial Dr.
Prince Albert, SK S6V 7L8

Deputy Premier; Minister, Finance, Hon. Donna Harpauer
Constituency: Humboldt-Watrous *No. of Constituents:* 12,736,
Saskatchewan Party
Tel: 306-787-6060
Toll-free: 800-682-9909; *Fax:* 306-787-6055
humboldtmla@sasktel.net
www.donnaharpauer.ca
Other Communications: Constituency Phone: 306-682-5141;
Fax: 306-683-5144
www.facebook.com/DonnaHarpauerHW
Constituency Office
632 - 9th St.
PO Box 2950
Humboldt, SK S0K 2A0

Daryl Harrison
Constituency: Cannington *No. of Constituents:* 12,599,
Saskatchewan Party
Toll-free: 833-670-4400
canningtonconstituency@sasktel.net
www.saskparty.com/darylharrison
Other Communications: Constituency Phone: 306-443-4400;
Fax: 306-443-4402
twitter.com/darylharrison20
Constituency Office
220 Centre St.
PO Box 130
Alida, SK S0C 0B0

Minister, Trade & Export Development; Minister, Immigration & Career Training; Minister responsible, Innovation Saskatchewan; Minister responsible, Tourism Saskatchewan; Government House Leader, Hon. Jeremy Harrison
Constituency: Meadow Lake *No. of Constituents:* 13,809,
Saskatchewan Party
Tel: 306-787-8687
Toll-free: 877-234-6669; *Fax:* 306-787-7977
jharrisonmla@sasktel.net
www.jeremyharrison.ca
Other Communications: Constituency Phone: 306-236-6669;
Fax: 306-236-6744
twitter.com/jharrisonmla,
www.linkedin.com/in/jeremy-harrison-61805b60
Constituency Office, North Entrance
201 - 2nd St. West
PO Box 848
Meadow Lake, SK S9X 1Y6

Minister, Mental Health & Addictions; Minister, Seniors & Rural & Remote Health, Everett Hindley
Constituency: Swift Current *No. of Constituents:* 12,630,
Saskatchewan Party
Tel: 306-798-9014; *Fax:* 306-798-9013
everettmla@sasktel.net
Other Communications: Constituency Phone: 306-778-2429
twitter.com/everetthindley,
www.facebook.com/everettswiftcurrrent

Constituency Office
42C Central Ave. North
Swift Current, SK S9H 0K7

Terry Jenson
Constituency: Martensville-Warman *No. of Constituents:*
18,131, Saskatchewan Party
office@terryjenson.ca
www.terryjenson.ca
Other Communications: Constituency Phone: 306-242-2111
twitter.com/tjenson33, www.facebook.com/terryjenson.mla
Constituency Office
#3G, 520 Central St. West
PO Box 2270
Warman, SK S0K 4S0

Minister, Environment, Hon. Warren Kaeding
Constituency: Melville-Saltcoats *No. of Constituents:* 12,714,
Saskatchewan Party
Tel: 306-787-6100; *Fax:* 306-787-3174
warrenkaedingmla@sasktel.net
www.warrenkaedingmla.ca
Other Communications: Constituency Phone: 306-728-3881;
Fax: 306-728-3883
twitter.com/wkaeding,
www.linkedin.com/in/warren-kaeding-35583165
Constituency Office
317E Main St.
PO Box 3215
Melville, SK S0A 2P0

Travis Keisig
Constituency: Last Mountain-Touchwood *No. of Constituents:*
11,943, Saskatchewan Party
lastmountaintouchwood.mla@sasktel.net
traviskeisig.ca
Other Communications: Constituency Phone: 306-334-3444
twitter.com/tkeisig, www.facebook.com/traviskeisigLMT
Constituency Office
110 Elgin St.
PO Box 928
Balcarres, SK S0G 0C0

Delbert Kirsch
Constituency: Batoche *No. of Constituents:* 11,886,
Saskatchewan Party
Toll-free: 877-256-4056
batochemla@sasktel.net
Other Communications: Constituency Phone: 306-256-3930;
Fax: 306-256-3924
Constituency Office
115 Main St.
PO Box 308
Cudworth, SK S0K 1B0

Lisa Lambert
Constituency: Saskatoon Churchill-Wildwood *No. of Constituents:* 12,700, Saskatchewan Party
mla@lisalambert.ca
www.saskparty.com/lambert
Other Communications: Constituency Phone: 306-373-7373;
Fax: 306-652-5938
twitter.com/lisalambert88,
www.linkedin.com/in/lisa-lambert-75a7478a
Constituency Office
#210A, 3929 - 8th St. East
Saskatoon, SK S7H 5M2

Greg Lawrence
Constituency: Moose Jaw Wakamow *No. of Constituents:*
12,918, Saskatchewan Party
greglawrencemla@sasktel.net
www.skcaucus.com/greg_lawrence
Other Communications: Constituency Phone: 306-694-1001;
Fax: 306-691-0486
Constituency Office
412 Lilloet St. West
Moose Jaw, SK S6H 7T1

Deputy Caucus Chair, Opposition, Matt Love
Constituency: Saskatoon Eastview *No. of Constituents:*
12,873, New Democratic Party
Tel: 306-787-7388
saskatooneastview@ndpcaucus.sk.ca
mattlovemla.ca
Other Communications: Constituency Phone: 306-664-6626
twitter.com/MattloveNDP, www.facebook.com/mattloveNDP
Constituency Office, Market Mall
#24, 2325 Preston Ave.
Saskatoon, SK S7J 2G2

Minister, Advanced Education, Hon. Gene Makowsky
Constituency: Regina Gardiner Park *No. of Constituents:*
12,448, Saskatchewan Party
Tel: 306-787-0341; *Fax:* 306-798-0263
gmakowsky.mla@sasktel.net
www.genemakowsky.ca
Other Communications: Constituency Phone: 306-545-4363
twitter.com/genemakowsky,
www.facebook.com/GeneAMakowsky
Constituency Office

1912 Prince of Wales Dr.
Regina, SK S4Z 1A4

Minister of Agriculture; Minister responsible, Saskatchewan Crop Insurance Corporation, Hon. David Marit
Constituency: Wood River *No. of Constituents:* 12,304,
Saskatchewan Party
Tel: 306-787-0338
Toll-free: 844-776-4200; *Fax:* 306-787-0630
mlawoodrider@sasktel.net
www.saskparty.com/marit
Other Communications: Constituency Phone: 306-642-4200;
Fax: 306-642-4207
twitter.com/david_marit
Constituency Office
108 - 1st Ave. West
PO Box 2097
Assiniboia, SK S0H 0B0

Tim McLeod
Constituency: Moose Jaw North *No. of Constituents:* 12,834,
Saskatchewan Party
mjnorthmla@sasktel.net
Other Communications: Constituency Phone: 306-692-8884
Constituency Office
#200, 99 Diefenbaker Dr.
Moose Jaw, SK S6J 0C2

Minister, Government Relations; Minister, First Nations, Métis Relations & Northern Affairs; Minister responsible, Provincial Capital Commission, Hon. Don McMorris
Constituency: Indian Head-Milestone *No. of Constituents:*
14,159, Saskatchewan Party
Tel: 306-787-6100
Toll-free: 877-337-3366; *Fax:* 306-787-0399
mcmorris.mla@sasktel.net
www.donmcmorris.ca
Other Communications: Constituency Phone: 306-771-2733;
Fax: 306-771-2574
Constituency Office
125 Railway St.
PO Box 720
Balgonie, SK S0G 0E0

Leader, Official Opposition; Leader, Saskatchewan New Democratic Party, Ryan Meili
Constituency: Saskatoon Meewasin *No. of Constituents:*
12,982, New Democratic Party
Tel: 306-787-7388; *Fax:* 306-787-6247
saskatoonmeewasin@ndpcaucus.sk.ca
Other Communications: Constituency Phone: 306-244-2280
twitter.com/ryanmeili
Constituency Office
814 - 3rd Ave. North
Saskatoon, SK S7K 2K2

Minister, Health, Hon. Paul Merriman
Constituency: Saskatoon Silverspring-Sutherland *No. of Constituents:* 13,470, Saskatchewan Party
Tel: 306-787-7345; *Fax:* 306-787-0237
office@paulmerriman.ca
www.skcaucus.com/paul_merriman
Other Communications: Constituency Phone: 306-244-5623;
Fax: 306-244-5626
twitter.com/merrimanpaul
Constituency Office
#211, 3521 - 8th St. East
Saskatoon, SK S7H 0W5

Derek Meyers
Constituency: Regina Walsh Acres *No. of Constituents:*
12,048, Saskatchewan Party
derekmeyersmla@sasktel.net
Other Communications: Constituency Phone: 306-522-1020
twitter.com/dmeyersYQR, www.facebook.com/dmeyersyqr
Constituency Office
1047 Devonshire Dr.
Regina, SK S4X 2X4

Premier; President, Executive Council; Minister, Intergovernmental Affairs; Leader, Saskatchewan Party, Hon. Scott Moe
Constituency: Rosthern-Shellbrook *No. of Constituents:*
12,210, Saskatchewan Party
Tel: 306-787-9433
Toll-free: 855-793-3422; *Fax:* 306-787-0885
scottmoe.mla@sasktel.net
Other Communications: Constituency Phone: 306-747-3422;
Fax: 306-747-3472
twitter.com/PremierScottMoe,
www.facebook.com/PremierScottMoe
Constituency Office
34 Main St.
PO Box 115
Shellbrook, SK S0J 2E0

Minister, Crown Investments Corporation; Minister, Labour Relations & Workplace Safety; Minister responsible, Saskatchewan Workers' Compensation Board & Crown corporations, including SaskEnergy, SGI, SaskPower, SaskTel, SaskGaming & SaskWater, Hon. Don Morgan, Q.C.
Constituency: Saskatoon Southeast *No. of Constituents:*

15,150, Saskatchewan Party
Tel: 306-787-8824; *Fax:* 306-787-1232
mla@donmorgan.ca
www.donmorgan.ca
Other Communications: Constituency Phone: 306-955-4755;
Fax: 306-955-4765
twitter.com/saskmla
Constituency Office
#109, 3502 Taylor St. East
Saskatoon, SK S7H 5H9

House Leader, Opposition, Vicki Mowat
Constituency: Saskatoon Fairview *No. of Constituents:*
14,952, New Democratic Party
Tel: 306-787-2563
saskatoonfairview@ndpcaucus.sk.ca
Other Communications: Constituency Phone: 306-664-1090
twitter.com/vicki_mowat_ndp,
www.facebook.com/VickiMowatNDP
Constituency Office
#16, 15 Worobetz Pl.
Saskatoon, SK S7L 6R4

Hugh Nerlien
Constituency: Kelvington-Wadena *No. of Constituents:*
12,014, Saskatchewan Party
Toll-free: 800-234-4134
nerlien.mla@sasktel.net
www.hughnerliensaskmla.ca
Other Communications: Constituency Phone: 306-278-2200;
Fax: 306-278-2208
twitter.com/hughnerlien, www.facebook.com/HughNerlien
Constituency Office
#102, 302 Pine St. West
PO Box 547
Porcupine Plain, SK S0E 1H0

Betty Nippi-Albright
Constituency: Saskatoon Centre *No. of Constituents:* 13,522,
New Democratic Party
Tel: 306-787-3388
saskatooncentre@ndpcaucus.sk.ca
www.ndpcaucus.sk.ca/bettynippialbright
Other Communications: Constituency Phone: 306-244-3555
twitter.com/bettynippi, www.facebook.com/BettyNDP
Constituency Office
#211, 220 - 20th St. West
Saskatoon, SK S7M 0W9

Government Whip, Greg Ottenbreit
Constituency: Yorkton *No. of Constituents:* 12,752,
Saskatchewan Party
yorkton.mla@sasktel.net
Other Communications: Constituency Phone: 306-783-7275;
Fax: 306-783-7273
twitter.com/GregOttenbreit,
www.facebook.com/gregottenbreitsk
Constituency Office
9 - 5th Ave. North
Yorkton, SK S3N 0Y9

Minister, SaskBuilds & Procurement; Minister responsible, Public
Service Commission, Saskatchewan Liquor & Gaming
Authority, Hon. Jim Reiter
Constituency: Rosetown-Elrose *No. of Constituents:* 12,049,
Saskatchewan Party
Tel: 306-787-0942
Toll-free: 855-762-2233; *Fax:* 306-787-8677
jimreitermla@sasktel.net
www.jimreiter.ca
Other Communications: Constituency Phone: 306-882-4105;
Fax: 306-882-4108
Constituency Office
215 Main St.
PO Box 278
Rosetown, SK S0L 2V0

Erika Ritchie
Constituency: Saskatoon Nutana *No. of Constituents:* 13,007,
New Democratic Party
Tel: 306-787-0974
saskatoonnutana@ndpcaucus.sk.ca
Other Communications: Constituency Phone: 306-664-6101;
Fax: 306-665-5633
twitter.com/erikaritchiendp,
www.facebook.com/ErikaRitchieSaskNDP,
www.linkedin.com/in/erikaritchie
Constituency Office
#104B, 733 Broadway Ave.
Saskatoon, SK S7N 1B3

Alana Ross
Constituency: Prince Albert Northcote *No. of Constituents:*
14,499, Saskatchewan Party
panorthcote.mla@sasktel.net
Other Communications: Constituency Phone: 306-763-7677;
Fax: 306-763-7678
Constituency Office
#7, 598 - 15th St. East
Prince Albert, SK S6V 1G2

Minister, Parks, Culture & Sport; Minister, Status of Women,
Hon. Laura Ross
Constituency: Regina Rochdale *No. of Constituents:* 17,122,
Saskatchewan Party
Tel: 306-787-0354; *Fax:* 306-798-0264
laurarossmla@sasktel.net
lauraross.ca
Other Communications: Constituency Phone: 306-545-6333;
Fax: 306-545-6112
twitter.com/laurarossmla, www.facebook.com/laurarossmla
Constituency Office
6859 Rochdale Blvd.
Regina, SK S4X 2Z2

Deputy Leader, Opposition, Nicole Sarauer
Constituency: Regina Douglas Park *No. of Constituents:*
12,950, New Democratic Party
Tel: 306-787-7388; *Fax:* 306-787-6247
reginadouglaspark@ndpcaucus.sk.ca
www.nicolesarauer.com
Other Communications: Constituency Phone: 306-522-2829;
Fax: 306-522-0296
twitter.com/nicolesarauer,
www.facebook.com/nicole4douglaspark,
www.linkedin.com/in/nicole-sarauer-a2594346
Constituency Office
2213 Broad St.
Regina, SK S4P 1Y7

Dana Skoropad
Constituency: Arm River *No. of Constituents:* 13,130,
Saskatchewan Party
armriver.mla@gmail.com
www.danaskoropad.ca
Other Communications: Constituency Phone: 306-567-2843
www.facebook.com/DanaSkoropadArmRiver
Constituency Office
121 Washington Ave.
Davidson, SK S0G 1A0

Douglas Steele
Constituency: Cypress Hills *No. of Constituents:* 12,630,
Saskatchewan Party
Toll-free: 844-672-1755
steelemla@sasktel.net
www.saskparty.com/steele
Other Communications: Constituency Phone: 306-672-1755;
Fax: 306-672-1756
twitter.com/DougSteeleSK
Constituency Office
4671 Price Ave.
PO Box 238
Gull Lake, SK S0N 1A0

Provincial Secretary, Hon. Lyle Stewart
Constituency: Lumsden-Morse *No. of Constituents:* 13,476,
Saskatchewan Party
Tel: 306-787-4558
lumsdenmorse.mla@sasktel.net
www.lylestewart.ca
Other Communications: Constituency Phone: 306-693-3229;
Fax: 306-693-3251
Constituency Office
#207, 310 Main St. North
Moose Jaw, SK S6H 3K1

Minister, Corrections & Policing; Minister responsible,
Saskatchewan Public Safety Agency, Hon. Christine Tell
Constituency: Regina Wascana Plains *No. of Constituents:*
17,900, Saskatchewan Party
Tel: 306-787-0284; *Fax:* 306-787-4304
christinetellmla@accesscomm.ca
www.christinetell.com
Other Communications: Constituency Phone: 306-205-2126;
Fax: 306-205-2127
Constituency Office
2318B Assiniboine Ave. East
Regina, SK S4V 2P5

Opposition Whip, Doyle Vermette
Constituency: Cumberland *No. of Constituents:* 14,533, New
Democratic Party
Tel: 306-787-6340
Toll-free: 877-702-2525; *Fax:* 306-787-6247
cumberland@ndpcaucus.sk.ca
www.ndpcaucus.sk.ca/vermette
Other Communications: Constituency Phone: 306-425-2525;
Fax: 306-425-2885
www.facebook.com/doyle.vermette
Constituency Office
215 La Ronge Ave.
PO Box 192
La Ronge, SK S0J 1L0

Speaker, Hon. Randy Weekes
Constituency: Biggar-Sask Valley *No. of Constituents:*
13,712, Saskatchewan Party
Tel: 306-787-2282
Toll-free: 877-948-4880
randyweekes.mla@accesscomm.ca
www.randyweekes.ca

Other Communications: Constituency Phone: 306-948-4880;
Fax: 306-948-4882
twitter.com/randyweekes,
www.linkedin.com/in/randy-weekes-8b2b025b
Constituency Office
106 - 3rd Ave. West
PO Box 1413
Biggar, SK S0K 0M0

Nadine Wilson
Constituency: Saskatchewan Rivers *No. of Constituents:*
12,211, Independent
Tel: 306-787-4300
Toll-free: 888-763-0615; *Fax:* 306-798-3174
saskatchewanrivers@sasktel.net
nadinewilson.ca
Other Communications: Constituency Phone: 306-763-0615;
Fax: 306-763-2503
www.facebook.com/nadinewilsonmla
Constituency Office
Site 16, RR#5
PO Box 4
Prince Albert, SK S6V 5R3

Trent Wotherspoon
Constituency: Regina Rosemont *No. of Constituents:* 13,401,
New Democratic Party
Tel: 306-787-0077; *Fax:* 306-787-6247
reginarosemont@ndpcaucus.sk.ca
www.trentwotherspoon.com
Other Communications: Constituency Phone: 306-565-2444;
Fax: 306-565-2952
twitter.com/WotherspoonT,
www.facebook.com/TrentWotherspoon
Constituency Office
6300 Dewdney Ave.
Regina, SK S4T 1E3

Minister, Justice & Attorney General, Hon. Gordon Wyant, Q.C.
Constituency: Saskatoon Northwest *No. of Constituents:*
11,820, Saskatchewan Party
Tel: 306-787-5353; *Fax:* 306-787-1232
g.wyant.mla@sasktel.net
gordonwyant.ca
Other Communications: Constituency Phone: 306-934-2847;
Fax: 306-934-2867
twitter.com/GordWyant, www.facebook.com/gordwyantsask
Constituency Office
#14, 2345 Ave. C North
Saskatoon, SK S7L 5Z5

Deputy House Leader, Opposition, Aleana Young
Constituency: Regina University *No. of Constituents:* 11,176,
New Democratic Party
Tel: 306-787-7388
reginauniversity@ndpcaucus.sk.ca
www.ndpcaucus.sk.ca/aleanayoung
Other Communications: Constituency Phone: 306-545-0300
twitter.com/AleanaYoung
Constituency Office
2213 Broad St.
Regina, SK S4P 1Y7

Colleen Young
Constituency: Lloydminster *No. of Constituents:* 15,397,
Saskatchewan Party
colleen.young@sasktel.net
www.saskparty.com/young
Other Communications: Constituency Phone: 306-825-5550;
Fax: 306-825-5552
Constituency Office
#2, 4304 - 40th Ave.
Lloydminster, SK S9V 2H1

Vacant
Constituency: Athabasca *No. of Constituents:* 9,136
Note: In August 2021, Bucky Belanger (N) resigned as the
Athabasca MLA to run in the federal election (L).

Saskatchewan Government Departments & Agencies

Saskatchewan Advanced Education (AE)

#1120, 2010 - 12th Ave., Regina, SK S4P 0M3
aeeinquiry@gov.sk.ca
www.saskatchewan.ca/advancededucation

The Ministry strives to create a vital, educated & skilled
workforce by focussing on the following areas: retaining
educated & skilled workers in Saskatchewan; providing
educational & training programs to develop a skilled workforce; &
promoting the province's opportunities to attract educated &
skilled workers from outside Saskatchewan & Canada. In
November 2007, a new provincial government resulted in the
reorganization of provincial government ministries. An expanded
Ministry of Advanced Education, Employment & Labour was
formed, & was subsequently changed to Advanced Education,
Employment & Immigration, then simply to Advanced Education.

Minister, Hon. Gene Makowsky
Tel: 306-787-0341
minister.ae@gov.sk.ca
Office of the Minister of Advanced Education, Legislative
Bldg.
#307, 2405 Legislative Dr.
Regina, SK S4S 0B3

Deputy Minister, Mark McLoughlin
Tel: 306-787-7071; *Fax:* 306-798-0975
mark.mcloughlin@gov.sk.ca

Associated Agencies, Boards & Commissions:

**• Saskatchewan Apprenticeship & Trade Certification
Commission**
2140 Hamilton St.
Regina, SK S4P 2E3
Tel: 306-787-2444; *Fax:* 306-787-5105
Toll-free: 877-363-0536
apprenticeship@gov.sk.ca
saskapprenticeship.ca

Corporate & Student Services
Tel: 306-787-3920; *Fax:* 306-787-7392
Assistant Deputy Minister, David Boehm
Tel: 306-787-0835; *Fax:* 306-787-7392
david.boehm@gov.sk.ca
Executive Director, Corporate Finance, Corinne Barnett
Tel: 306-787-5923
corinne.barnett@gov.sk.ca
Executive Director, Business Systems & Information
Management, Duane Rieger
Tel: 306-787-1421
duane.rieger@gov.sk.ca
Executive Director, Student & Support Services, Kirk Wosminity
Tel: 306-787-8064; *Fax:* 306-798-0193
Kirk.Wosminity@gov.sk.ca

International Education & Jurisdictional Initiatives
Executive Lead, Livia Castellanos
Tel: 306-526-7740
livia.castellanos@gov.sk.ca
Director, Danelle Reiss
Tel: 306-787-9428; *Fax:* 306-787-7537
Danelle.Reiss@gov.sk.ca

Sector Management & Relations
Executive Director, Mike Pestill
Tel: 306-787-2189; *Fax:* 306-798-3159
Mike.Pestill@gov.sk.ca
Director, Regional Colleges, Bond Ferguson
Tel: 306-787-5739; *Fax:* 306-798-3159
Bond.Ferguson@gov.sk.ca

Strategic Communications
Tel: 306-787-9478; *Fax:* 306-798-5021
Executive Director, Linsay Rabyj
Tel: 306-787-6041; *Fax:* 306-798-5021
linsay.rabyj3@gov.sk.ca

Saskatchewan Agriculture (AG)

Walter Scott Bldg., 3085 Albert St., Regina, SK S4S 0B1
Toll-Free: 866-457-2377
www.saskatchewan.ca/agriculture
The Ministry's mandate is to foster, in partnership with
individuals, communities, industry, & government, a
commercially viable, self-sufficient, & sustainable agricultural
sector in Saskatchewan. The Ministry addresses needs of
individual farmers & ranchers, encourages & develops higher
value production & processing, & promotes sustainable
economic development in rural areas of the province. Some
responsibilities are as follows: agri-business development
through provision of agriculture-based business experts &
technical support; agricultural research to promote development
& diversification; corporate services to support the Information
Technology Office & the Rural Economic Co-operative
Development; crop development; financial programs; inspection
& administration of regulations for food & crop protection, animal
disease surveillance, environmental reviews, licenses,
registrations, & complaint resolution; irrigation development;
promotion of sustainable use of Crown land; livestock
development; provision of food safety, quality, policy, regulatory,
market & business development programs; policy analysis,
strategies, & agricultural information services; & delivery of
Saskatchewan Crop Insurance Corporation programs &
services.

Minister, Hon. David Marit
ag.minister@gov.sk.ca
Office of the Minister of Agriculture, Legislative Bldg.
#334, 2405 Legislative Dr.
Regina, SK S4S 0B3

Deputy Minister, Rick Burton
Tel: 306-787-8077; *Fax:* 306-787-2393
rick.burton@gov.sk.ca

Assistant Deputy Minister, Programs, Lee Auten
Tel: 306-787-5170; *Fax:* 306-787-2393
lee.auten@gov.sk.ca

Assistant Deputy Minister, Policy, Paul Johnson
paul.johnson@gov.sk.ca

Assistant Deputy Minister, Regulatory & Innovation,
Penny McCall
Tel: 306-787-5247; *Fax:* 306-787-2393
Penny.McCall@gov.sk.ca

Executive Director, Programs Branch, Mark Anderson
Tel: 306-787-8510
mark.anderson@gov.sk.ca

Executive Director, Corporate Services, Michele Arscott
Tel: 306-787-5211
michele.arscott@gov.sk.ca

Executive Director, Crops & Irrigation Branch, Dianna
Emperingham
Tel: 306-787-8061; *Fax:* 306-787-0428
dianna.emperingham@gov.sk.ca

Executive Director, Agriculture Research Branch, Shawn
Gibson
Tel: 306-787-9768
shawn.gibson@gov.sk.ca

Executive Director, Policy Branch, Jonathan Greuel
Tel: 306-787-5834
jonathan.greuel2@gov.sk.ca

Executive Director, Communications, Angela Hall
Tel: 306-787-2359; *Fax:* 306-787-0216
angela.hall@gov.sk.ca

Executive Director, Trade & Value-Added Branch, James
Kettel
Tel: 306-787-5139; *Fax:* 306-787-5134
James.Kettel@gov.sk.ca

Executive Director, Livestock Branch, Venkata
Vakulabharanam
Tel: 306-787-8191; *Fax:* 306-787-1315
venkata.vakulabharanam@gov.sk.ca

Executive Director, Lands Branch, Grant Zalinko
Tel: 306-787-6607; *Fax:* 306-787-1315
grant.zalinko@gov.sk.ca

Director, Financial Services, Robert Pentland
Tel: 306-787-9272
robert.pentland2@gov.sk.ca

Associated Agencies, Boards & Commissions:

• Agri-Food Council
#315, 3085 Albert St.
Regina, SK S4S 0B1
Fax: 306-787-8599
The Agri-Food Council is an independent board appointed by the
provincial government. The Council is accountable to the
Minister of Agriculture for the supervision of all agencies
established under The Agri-Food Act, 2004.

• Agricultural Implements Board
#302, 3085 Albert St.
Regina, SK S4S 0B1
Fax: 306-787-8599

• Farmland Security Board
#315, 3988 Albert St.
Regina, SK S4S 3R1
Tel: 306-787-5047; *Fax:* 306-787-8599
www.farmland.gov.sk.ca

• Prairie Agricultural Machinery Institute (PAMI)
2215 - 8th Ave.
PO Box 1150
Humboldt, SK S0K 2A0
Tel: 306-682-5033; *Fax:* 306-682-5080
Toll-free: 800-567-7264
pami@pami.ca
pami.ca
PAMI works for the advancement of technology in agriculture
through research & development. Satellite offices are located in
Winnipeg, Saskatoon & Ottawa.

• Saskatchewan Crop Insurance Corporation (SCIC)
484 Prince William Dr.
PO Box 3000
Melville, SK S0A 2P0
Tel: 306-728-7200; *Fax:* 306-728-7202
Toll-free: 888-935-0000
customer.service@scic.gov.sk.ca
www.saskcropinsurance.com
Other Communication: AgriStability Call Centre, Toll-Free:
866-270-8450, Toll-Free Fax: 888-728-0440, Email:
agristability@scic.gov.sk.ca
The provincial Crown Corporation provides responsive & flexible
risk management tools. Crop insurance programs are as follows:
Multi-Peril Insurance; Organic Insurance; Forage Insurance; &
Weather Based Insurance.

• Saskatchewan Egg Producers (SEP)
#1, 123 Pinehouse Dr.
Saskatoon, SK S7K 5W1
Tel: 306-664-4131; *Fax:* 306-664-4140
info@saskegg.ca
www.saskegg.ca

• Saskatchewan Milk Marketing Board (SMMB)
470 Maxwell Cres.
Regina, SK S4N 6L7
Tel: 306-949-6999; *Fax:* 306-949-2605
info@saskmilk.ca
www.saskmilk.ca

• Saskatchewan Sheep Development Board (SSDB)
2213C Hanselman Crt.
Saskatoon, SK S7L 6A8
Tel: 306-933-5200; *Fax:* 306-933-7182
sheepdb@sasktel.net
www.sksheep.com

Saskatchewan Assessment Management Agency (SAMA)

#200, 2201 - 11th Ave., Regina, SK S4P 0J8
Tel: 306-924-8000; *Fax:* 306-924-8070
Toll-Free: 800-667-7262
info.request@sama.sk.ca
www.sama.sk.ca
Other Communication: Alt. Emails: roll.confn@sama.sk.ca
(Quality Assurance); revaluation.unit@sama.sk.ca (Revaluation);
industrial.unit@sama.sk.ca (Industrial)
SAMA is an independent agency with responsibility to develop &
maintain the province's assessment policies, standards &
procedures, audit assessments, & review & confirm municipal
assessment rolls & provide property valuation services to local
governments (municipalities & school boards).

Chair, Myron Knafelc

Chief Executive Officer, Irwin Blank

SaskBuilds & Procurement

1920 Rose St., Regina, SK S4P 0A9
Tel: 306-787-6911; *Fax:* 306-787-1061
cs.receptioncenturyplaza@gov.sk.ca
www.saskatchewan.ca/saskbuilds-procurement
SaskBuilds is a Crown corporation created in October 2012. In
2020, it was merged with Central Services to become
Saskbuilds & Procurement. Its mandate is to plan & manage
large-scale infrastructure projects that are high-cost ($100 million
or more), & that are high-priority for the province. These projects
will likely be candidates for alternative financing.
The Priority Saskatchewan branch was established in 2014,
intended to ensure that procurement across the provincial
government is fair, open, transparent, & based on international
best practice.

Minister, Hon. Jim Reiter
Tel: 306-787-0942
minister.sbp@gov.sk.ca

Deputy Minister, Kyle Toffan
Tel: 306-787-6520; *Fax:* 306-787-6547
kyle.toffan@gov.sk.ca

Chief Financial Officer, Jim Olson
Tel: 306-798-1228
jim.olson@gov.sk.ca

Executive Director, Communications, Lisa Danyluk
Tel: 306-535-2451
lisa.danyluk@gov.sk.ca

Corporate Strategy & Services
Tel: 306-787-1061

Executive Director, Corporate Operations, Daniel Hersche
Tel: 306-570-2093
daniel.hersche@gov.sk.ca
Executive Director, Corporate Strategy, Erik Lizee
Tel: 306-519-5014; *Fax:* 306-787-1061
erik.lizee2@gov.sk.ca

Information Technology Division
South Tower, 2045 Broad St., 4th Fl., Regina, SK S4P 3T7
Tel: 306-787-5000
inquiries@ito.gov.sk.ca
The work of the Information Technology Office is guided by The Information Technology Office Regulations, December 2004 & The Canadian Information Processing Society of Saskatchewan Act, 2005.
The following are some of the programs & services of the Information Technology Office: the procurement of information technology goods & services; corporate services, such as planning & communications; customer support; leadership on issues related to enterprise architecture; application management services; & operations such as the help desk.
Assistant Deputy Minister, Jason Wall
Tel: 306-519-0014
jason.wall@gov.sk.ca
Chief Information Officer, Vacant
Executive Director, Application Management Services, Atiq Ahmad
Tel: 306-787-1447
atiq.ahmad@gov.sk.ca
Executive Director, Strategic Architecture, Kelly Fuessel
Tel: 306-787-7894
kelly.fuessel@gov.sk.ca

Digital Strategy & Operations
Walter Scott Bldg., 2045 Broad St., 5th Fl., Regina, SK S4P 3T7
csweb@gov.sk.ca
Chief Digital Officer, Lisa Raddysh
Tel: 306-527-8240
lisa.raddysh@gov.sk.ca

Operations & Service Delivery
Fax: 306-787-1061
Assistant Deputy Minister, Troy Smith
Tel: 306-787-2433; *Fax:* 306-787-1061
troy.smith@gov.sk.ca
Executive Director, Commercial & Logistical Services, Derek Collins
Tel: 306-798-7103
derek.collins@gov.sk.ca

Building Services
Fax: 306-787-1061
Executive Director, Rob Clarke
Tel: 306-787-6332; *Fax:* 306-787-1980
rob.clarke@gov.sk.ca

Procurement Management
#720, 1855 Victoria Ave., Regina, SK S4P 3T2
Fax: 306-798-0626
Chief Procurement Officer, Kathryn Pollack
Tel: 306-798-1229
kathryn.pollack@gov.sk.ca
Associate Chief Procurement Officer, Glenn Deck
Tel: 306-787-1696
glenn.deck@gov.sk.ca
Director, Goods & Services Procurement, Joyce Sebastian
Tel: 306-798-1313
joyce.sebastian@gov.sk.ca
Director, Business Solutions & IT Procurement, Kathleen Stelter
Tel: 306-787-3391
kathleen.stelter@gov.sk.ca

Crown Investments Corporation of Saskatchewan (CIC)

#400, 2400 College Ave., Regina, SK S4P 1C8
Tel: 306-787-6851; *Fax:* 306-787-0294
www.cicorp.sk.ca
The holding company for the commercial Crown corporations of Saskatchewan is the Crown Investments Corporation.
The key functions of the Corporation are as follows: assisting the boards of Crown corporations to strengthen governance; overseeing the direction of Crown corporations to improve performance & accountability; managing CIC Asset Management Inc. & the Gradworks program; & overseeing funds established with the administrative coordination or financial assistance of the government.

Minister, Hon. Don Morgan, Q.C.
Office of the Minister of Crown Investments, Legislative Bldg.
#302, 2405 Legislative Dr.
Regina, SK S4S 0B3

President & CEO, Kent Campbell
Tel: 306-787-9085; *Fax:* 306-787-8125
kcampbell@cicorp.sk.ca

Vice-President & Chief Financial Officer, Cindy Ogilvie
Tel: 306-787-6246
cogilvie@cicorp.sk.ca

Vice-President, Crown Services, Brian Gyoerick
Tel: 306-787-1257; *Fax:* 306-787-0294
brian.gyoerick@gov.sk.ca

Executive Director, Communications, Joanne Johnson
Tel: 306-787-5889; *Fax:* 306-787-8125
jjohnson@cicorp.sk.ca

Crown Services Division
Tel: 306-787-5915; *Fax:* 306-787-0294
Vice-President, Brian Gyoerick
Tel: 306-787-1257; *Fax:* 306-787-0294
brian.gyoerick@gov.sk.ca
General Counsel & Corporate Secretary, Alan Fern
Tel: 306-787-0542
afern@cicorp.sk.ca
Executive Director, Crown Governance, Dale Bloom
Tel: 306-787-9357
dbloom@cicorp.sk.ca
Manager, Human Resources, Carla Stouffer
Tel: 306-787-5782; *Fax:* 306-787-8125
cstouffer@cicorp.sk.ca

Finance & Administration Division
Tel: 306-787-5937; *Fax:* 306-787-8030
Chief Financial Officer & Senior Vice-President, Cindy Ogilvie
Tel: 306-787-6246; *Fax:* 306-787-8030
cogilvie@cicorp.sk.ca
Executive Director, Performance Management & Financial Analysis, Kyla Hillmer
Tel: 306-787-7286; *Fax:* 306-787-8030
khillmer@cicorp.sk.ca

Saskatchewan Corrections, Policing & Public Safety

Legislative Bldg., #345, 2405 Legislative Dr., Regina, SK S4S 0B3
www.saskatchewan.ca/corrections-policing-and-public-safety
The Ministry promotes safe communities in Saskatchewan. Adult correction & young offender programs & services are delivered that serve individuals in conflict with the law. Public safety is also addressed through the following programs & services: protection & emergency planning & communication; monitoring of building standards; fire prevention & disaster assistance programs; & licensing & inspections services.

Minister, Hon. Christine Tell
Tel: 306-787-0284; *Fax:* 306-787-4304
ministercpps@gov.sk.ca

Deputy Minister, Dale Larsen
Tel: 306-787-8065; *Fax:* 306-787-0270
dale.larsen@gov.sk.ca

Executive Director, Communications, Noel Busse
Tel: 306-787-8959
Noel.busse@gov.sk.ca

Executive Director, Strategic Systems & Innovation, Monica Field
Tel: 306-798-1309
monica.field@gov.sk.ca

Access & Privacy Branch
#1510, 1855 Victoria Ave., Regina, SK S4P 3T2
Tel: 306-798-0222; *Fax:* 306-798-9007
accessprivacyjustice@gov.sk.ca
Executive Director, Aaron Orban
Tel: 306-787-3316; *Fax:* 306-798-9007
aaron.orban@gov.sk.ca
Director, Access to Information, Obeyaa Ampofo-Hunstad
Tel: 306-798-0334
obeyaa.ampofohunstad@gov.sk.ca
Director, Records Management, Bonnie Caven
Tel: 306-798-3299
bonnie.caven@gov.sk.ca
Director, Privacy Operations, Darren Hunter
Tel: 306-798-0446
darren.hunter6@gov.sk.ca

Community Engagement Division
1874 Scarth St., 12th Fl., Regina, SK S4P 4B3
Tel: 306-787-5787; *Fax:* 306-798-0270

Assistant Deputy Minister, Drew Wilby
Tel: 306-787-5883; *Fax:* 306-798-4064
Drew.Wilby@gov.sk.ca
Executive Director, Strategic Policy, Planning & Reporting, Elissa Aitken
Tel: 306-531-8520
elissa.aitken2@gov.sk.ca
Executive Director, Strategic Engagement, Gina Alexander
Tel: 306-539-4472; *Fax:* 306-787-0078
gina.alexander@gov.sk.ca
Executive Director, Research & Implementation Branch, Scott Harron
Tel: 306-787-3892; *Fax:* 306-798-0270
scott.harron@gov.sk.ca

Custody, Supervision & Rehabilitation Services
#700, 1874 Scarth St., Regina, SK S4P 4B3
Tel: 306-787-8958; *Fax:* 306-787-0676
Assistant Deputy Minister, Heather Scriver
Tel: 306-787-3571; *Fax:* 306-787-0676
heather.scriver@gov.sk.ca

Provincial Disaster Assistance Program
PO Box 227 Regina, SK S4S 0B1
Fax: 306-798-2318
Executive Director, Grant Hilsenteger
Tel: 306-798-8470; *Fax:* 306-798-2318
grant.hilsenteger@gov.sk.ca

Policing & Community Safety Services
1874 Scarth St., 12th Fl., Regina, SK S4P 4B3
Tel: 306-787-5787; *Fax:* 306-798-0270
Assistant Deputy Minister, Rob Cameron
Tel: 306-787-1978
rob.cameron@gov.sk.ca
Executive Director, Police Contracts & Financial Services, Rae Gallivan
Tel: 306-787-3572; *Fax:* 306-787-0136
Rae.Gallivan@gov.sk.ca
Executive Director, First Nations & Indigenous Policing Program, Cory Lerat
Tel: 306-798-0006; *Fax:* 306-787-0136
cory.lerat@gov.sk.ca

Saskatchewan Education (ED)

2220 College Ave., Regina, SK S4P 4V9
learning.inquiry@gov.sk.ca
www.saskatchewan.ca/education
The Ministry provides programs & services in the following key areas: early learning & child care, the pre-kindergarten to grade 12 education system, & the Provincial Library. In November 2007, a new provincial government resulted in the reorganization of provincial government ministries. The work of Saskatchewan Learning was merged into the newly named Ministry of Education.

Minister, Hon. Dustin Duncan
Tel: 306-787-7360
minister.edu@gov.sk.ca
Office of the Minister of Education, Legislative Bldg.
#361, 2405 Legislative Dr.
Regina, SK S4S 0B3

Deputy Minister, Donna Johnson
Tel: 306-787-2471; *Fax:* 306-787-1300
donna.johnson@gov.sk.ca

Assistant Deputy Minister, Susan Nedelcov-Anderson
Tel: 306-787-3222; *Fax:* 306-787-1300
susan.nedelcovanderson@gov.sk.ca

Assistant Deputy Minister, Gerry Craswell
Tel: 306-787-6056; *Fax:* 306-787-1300
Gerry.Craswell@gov.sk.ca

Assistant Deputy Minister, Rory Jensen
Tel: 306-787-6115; *Fax:* 306-787-1300
rory.jensen@gov.sk.ca

Acting Executive Director, Corporate Services, Sara Hawryluk
Tel: 306-787-3520; *Fax:* 306-798-5042
sara.hawryluk@gov.sk.ca

Executive Director, Communications & Sector Relations, Rosann Semchuk
Tel: 306-787-5609; *Fax:* 306-798-2045
rosann.semchuk@gov.sk.ca

Associated Agencies, Boards & Commissions:

• Teachers' Superannuation Commission
#129, 3085 Albert St.
Regina, SK S4S 0B1
Tel: 306-787-6440; *Fax:* 306-787-1939
Toll-free: 877-364-8202
mail@stsc.gov.sk.ca
www.stsc.gov.sk.ca

Early Years
2220 College Ave., 2nd Fl., Regina, SK S4P 4V9
Tel: 306-787-2004; *Fax:* 306-787-0277
Executive Director, Janet Mitchell
Tel: 306-787-0765; *Fax:* 306-787-0277
janet.mitchell@gov.sk.ca
Director, Child Care Operations, Samantha Ecarnot
Tel: 306-787-3740; *Fax:* 306-787-0277
Samantha.Ecarnot@gov.sk.ca
Director, Early Learning Supports, Cindy Jeanes
Tel: 306-787-3750; *Fax:* 306-798-3146
cindy.jeanes@gov.sk.ca
Director, Early Childhood Development, Tricia Wuschenny
Tel: 306-787-1617; *Fax:* 306-787-0277
tricia.wuschenny@gov.sk.ca

Education Funding
2220 College Ave., 7th Fl., Regina, SK S4P 4V9
Acting Executive Director, Shaylene Salazar
Tel: 306-787-6042
shaylene.salazar@gov.sk.ca
Director, Capital Funding & Programs, Yvonne Anderson
Tel: 306-787-5476
Yvonne.Anderson@gov.sk.ca
Director, Financial Analyst & Reporting, Kayla Edgerton
Tel: 306-787-6634
kayla.edgerton@gov.sk.ca
Acting Director, Education Financial Policy, Paul Lewis
Tel: 306-787-5192
paul.lewis@gov.sk.ca

Information Management & Support
2220 College Ave., 3rd Fl., Regina, SK S4P 4V9
Tel: 306-787-2494

Executive Director, Sheldon Ramstead
Tel: 306-787-6053; *Fax:* 306-787-0035
sheldon.ramstead@gov.sk.ca
Director & Registrar, Student & Educator Services, Shelley Lowes
Tel: 306-787-6039
shelley.lowes@gov.sk.ca

Provincial Library & Literacy Office
409A Park St., Regina, SK S4N 5B2
Tel: 306-787-2976; *Fax:* 306-787-2029
Provincial Librarian & Executive Director, Alison Hopkins
Tel: 306-787-2972; *Fax:* 306-787-2029
alison.hopkins@gov.sk.ca
Director, Public Library Planning, Julie Arie
Tel: 306-787-3005; *Fax:* 306-787-2029
julie.arie@gov.sk.ca
Director, Library Accountability & Administration, Flo Woods
Tel: 306-787-6262
flo.woods@gov.sk.ca

Strategic Policy & Planning Branch
2220 College Ave., 3rd Fl., Regina, SK S4P 4V9
Tel: 306-787-6769

Executive Director, Edith Nagy
Tel: 306-787-8246
edith.nagy@gov.sk.ca

Student Achievement & Supports
2220 College Ave., 7th Fl., Regina, SK S4P 4V9
Tel: 306-787-6000

Executive Director, Maria Chow
Tel: 306-787-6089
Maria.Chow@gov.sk.ca
Director, Student Supports, Kevin Kleisinger
Tel: 306-787-9042
kevin.kleisinger@gov.sk.ca
Director, Curriculum Unit, Delise Pitman
Tel: 306-785-5776
delise.pitman@gov.sk.ca
Acting Director, Assessment Unit, Wendy Sawatzky
Tel: 306-527-8605; *Fax:* 306-787-0945
wendy.sawatzky@gov.sk.ca

#301, 3303 Hillsdale St., Regina, SK S4S 6W9
Tel: 306-787-4000; *Fax:* 306-787-4052
Toll-Free: 877-958-8683
info@elections.sk.ca
www.elections.sk.ca
Other Communication: Toll-Free Fax: 866-678-4052
twitter.com/ElectionsSask

Chief Electoral Officer, Michael Boda
Tel: 306-787-4290; *Fax:* 306-787-4052
ceo@elections.sk.ca

Deputy Chief Electoral Officer, Corporate Services, Jennifer Colin
Tel: 306-787-4061; *Fax:* 306-787-4052
jennifer.colin@elections.sk.ca

Deputy Chief Electoral Officer, Electoral Operations, Jeff Kress
Tel: 306-787-0258; *Fax:* 306-787-4052
jeff.kress@elections.sk.ca

Senior Director, Outreach, Policy & Communications, Tim Kydd
Tel: 306-787-7355
tkydd@elections.sk.ca

Director, Information Technology, Jordan Arendt
Tel: 306-787-5768; *Fax:* 306-787-4052
jordan.arendt@elections.sk.ca

Director, Electoral Operations, Bonnie Schenher
Tel: 306-787-0156; *Fax:* 306-787-4052
bonnie.schenher@elections.sk.ca

#1000, 2103 - 11th Ave., Regina, SK S4P 3Z8
www.saskatchewan.ca/energy-and-resources
To build an innovative, diversified, & sustainable economy for Saskatchewan, the Ministry of Energy & Resources develops, implements, & promotes policies & programs related to the province's energy, mineral, & forestry sectors.
The following mineral resource databases are available: Saskatchewan Mineral Assessment Database; Saskatchewan Mineral Deposit Index; & Saskatchewan Kimberlite Indicator Minerals.

Minister, Hon. Bronwyn Eyre
Tel: 306-787-0804
ministerer@gov.sk.ca
Office of the Minister of Energy & Resources, Legislative Bldg.
#340, 2405 Legislative Dr.
Regina, SK S4S 0B3

Deputy Minister, Susanna Laaksonen-Craig
Tel: 306-787-9580; *Fax:* 306-787-2159
susanna.laaksonencraig@gov.sk.ca

Energy Regulation
Fax: 306-787-2478
Toll-Free: 855-219-9373
Executive Coordinator, Julie Dayman
Tel: 306-787-2592; *Fax:* 306-787-2478
julie.dayman@gov.sk.ca
Executive Director, Field Services, Bryce Jardine-Pelletier
Tel: 306-787-2318; *Fax:* 306-798-1004
bryce.jardinepelletier@gov.sk.ca
Director, Client Support, Janice Loseth
Tel: 306-798-9509
Janice.Loseth@gov.sk.ca
Director, Information Management, Erin Raaf
Tel: 306-798-9507
erin.raaf@gov.sk.ca
Director, Liability Management, Brad Wagner
Tel: 306-787-2348
Brad.Wagner@gov.sk.ca
Director, Regulatory Affairs, Scott Weaver
Tel: 306-787-2912; *Fax:* 306-787-2478
scott.weaver@gov.sk.ca
Director, Resource Management, Debby Westerman
Tel: 306-798-4210; *Fax:* 306-787-2478
Debby.Westerman@gov.sk.ca

Resource Development
Tel: 306-787-8178; *Fax:* 306-787-2198
Assistant Deputy Minister, Cory Hughes
Tel: 306-787-3524; *Fax:* 306-787-2198
Cory.Hughes@gov.sk.ca

Chief Geologist, Saskatchewan Geological Survey, Gary Delaney
Tel: 306-787-1160; *Fax:* 306-787-1284
gary.delaney@gov.sk.ca
Executive Director, Mineral Policy, Kirk Brecht
Tel: 306-535-8454; *Fax:* 306-798-0047
Kirk.Brecht@gov.sk.ca
Executive Director, Lands & Mineral Tenure, Jeremy Karwandy
Tel: 306-787-5385; *Fax:* 306-787-0620
jeremy.karwandy@gov.sk.ca
Executive Director, Energy Policy, Cullen Stewart
Tel: 306-787-2477; *Fax:* 306-787-2198
cullen.stewart@gov.sk.ca
Executive Director, Forestry Development - Prince Albert, Shane Vermette
Tel: 306-930-8701
shane.vermette@gov.sk.ca

Revenue & Business Systems
Tel: 306-787-2101; *Fax:* 306-798-2158
Acting Executive Director, Kim Olyowsky
Tel: 306-787-6508; *Fax:* 306-787-0083
kim.olyowsky@gov.sk.ca
Director, IRIS Management Services, Danette Flegel
Tel: 306-798-3068
Danette.Flegel@gov.sk.ca

3211 Albert St., Regina, SK S4S 5W6
Tel: 306-787-2584; *Fax:* 306-787-9544
Toll-Free: 800-567-4224
centre.inquiry@gov.sk.ca
www.saskatchewan.ca/environment
Other Communication: Firewatch Line: 800-667-9660; Spill Control Centre: 800-667-7525; TIPS (Turn in Poachers): 800-667-7561

Saskatchewan Environment protects & mananges the province's environmental & natural resources by offering the following programs & services: compliance & enforcement to protect the public's interests in the management of air, land, water & natural resources; protection & management of forest ecosystems; wildfire management; Green Strategy; environmental assessment; legislation, & policies to ensure that Crown land is used in ways that respect environmental, economic & social values; fishing & fisheries management; hunting management; licensing & guiding the trapping industry; protection of wildlife; recycling; waste management; & water resource & treatment plant operations management.

Minister, Hon. Warren Kaeding
Tel: 306-787-0393
env.minister@gov.sk.ca
Office of the Minister of the Environment, Legislative Bldg.
#348, 2405 Legislative Dr.
Regina, SK S4S 0B3

Deputy Minister, Sarah Harrison
Tel: 306-787-2930; *Fax:* 306-787-2947
sarah.harrison@gov.sk.ca

Executive Director, Communication & Client Service Branch, Paul Spasoff
Tel: 306-787-1020; *Fax:* 306-787-3941
paul.spasoff@gov.sk.ca

Associated Agencies, Boards & Commissions:
• Saskatchewan Conservation Data Centre (SKCDC)
Fish & Wildlife Branch, Ministry of Environment
3211 Albert St.
Regina, SK S4S 5W6
Tel: 306-787-7196; *Fax:* 306-787-9544
biodiversity.sk.ca
The SKCDC was formed as a co-operative venture between the province, The Nature Conservancy USA & The Nature Conservancy of Canada. The SKCDC gathers, interprets & distributes scientific information on the ecological status of provincial wild species & communities. The SKCDC is committed to conserving biological diversity; producing scientific reports & being the provincial clearinghouse for threatened & endangered species information.

Climate Change & Adaptation Division
3211 Albert St., 2nd Fl., Regina, SK S4S 5W6
Tel: 306-787-9016

Protects human health & ecosystem integrity.
Assistant Deputy Minister, David Brock
Tel: 306-787-6488
david.brock@gov.sk.ca
Executive Director, Climate Change, Aaron Wirth
Tel: 306-787-1023
aaron.wirth2@gov.sk.ca

given to Saskatchewan's northern municipalities through municipal management functions, training, & advisory services.
Executive Director, Brad Henry
Tel: 306-425-4322; Fax: 306-425-2401
brad.henry@gov.sk.ca
Director, Northern Planning, Administration & Sustainability, Dee Johns
Tel: 306-425-6642; Fax: 306-425-2401
dee.johns@gov.sk.ca

Policy & Program Services
1855 Victoria Ave., 15th Fl., Regina, SK S4P 3T2
Tel: 306-787-2653; Fax: 306-787-4161
Executive Director, Vacant
Director, Property Tax & Assessment, Abayomi Akintola
Tel: 306-787-2895
abayomi.akintola2@gov.sk.ca
Director, Policy & Business Intelligence, Jason Liggett
Tel: 306-533-7869
jason.liggett@gov.sk.ca
Director, Legislation & Regulations, Rod Nasewich
Tel: 306-798-7048
Rod.Nasewich@gov.sk.ca

Saskatchewan Health (HE)

T.C. Douglas Bldg., 3475 Albert St., Regina, SK S4S 6X6
Tel: 306-787-0146
Toll-Free: 800-667-7766
info@health.gov.sk.ca
www.saskatchewan.ca/health
Other Communication: Family Health Benefits: 800-266-0695;
HealthLine: 877-800-0002; Health Registration / Health Card: 800-667-7551; Prescription Drug Plan: 800-667-7581
Saskatchewan Health offers the following programs & services: continuing care to help people live independently; e-health & information systems for access to medical information; emergency services; health benefits; recruitment & retention of healthcare providers; promotion of mental health & treatment for mental illness & addictions; personal health services; prescription drug coverage; public health programs; privacy of health information; services for people with long term disabilities or illnesses; surgery & diagnostics initiatives; & vital statistics.

Minister, Hon. Paul Merriman
Tel: 306-787-7345
he.minister@gov.sk.ca
Office of the Minister of Health, Legislative Bldg.
#204, 2405 Legislative Dr.
Regina, SK S4S 0B3

Minister responsible, Mental Health & Addictions, Seniors & Rural & Remote Health, Hon. Everett Hindley
Tel: 306-798-9014
minister.rrhe@gov.sk.ca
Office of the Minister Responsible for Rural & Remote Health, Legislative Bldg.
#208, 2405 Legislative Dr.
Regina, SK S4S 0B3

Deputy Minister, Max Hendricks
Tel: 306-787-3041; Fax: 306-787-4533
max.hendricks@health.gov.sk.ca

Associate Deputy Minister, Denise Macza
Tel: 306-787-3186; Fax: 306-787-4533
Denise.Macza@health.gov.sk.ca

Assistant Deputy Minister, Rebecca Carter
Tel: 306-787-4695; Fax: 306-787-4533
Rebecca.Carter@health.gov.sk.ca

Assistant Deputy Minister, Billie-Jo Morrissette
Tel: 306-787-3147; Fax: 306-787-4533
billie-jo.morrissette@health.gov.sk.ca

Associated Agencies, Boards & Commissions:

• Health Quality Council
Atrium Bldg., Innovation Place
241, 111 Research Dr.
Saskatoon, SK S7N 3R2
Tel: 306-668-8810; Fax: 306-668-8820
info@hqc.sk.ca
www.saskhealthquality.ca
• eHealth Saskatchewan
2130 - 11th Ave.
Regina, SK S4P 0J5
Tel: 306-337-5000
Toll-free: 855-347-5465
www.ehealthsask.ca
Other Communication: Vital Statistics, Email:
vitalstatistics@ehealthsask.ca

eHealth Saskatchewan is mandated to develop & implement the provincial electronic health record. Vital Statistics services were transferred from the Information Services Corporation of Saskatchewan after it became a public company in 2013.

• Saskatchewan Health Research Foundation (SHRF)
Atrium Bldg., Innovation Place
#204, 111 Research Dr.
Saskatoon, SK S7N 3R2
Tel: 639-398-8400
Toll-free: 800-975-1699
info@shrf.ca
www.shrf.ca

Acute & Emergency Services Branch
Tel: 306-787-3204; Fax: 306-787-6113
Executive Director, Ingrid Kirby
Tel: 306-798-2655; Fax: 306-787-6113
ingrid.kirby@health.gov.sk.ca
Director, Quality & Continuous Improvement, Terry Blackmore
Tel: 306-787-3219; Fax: 306-787-6113
terry.blackmore@health.gov.sk.ca
Director, Hospitals & Specialized Services, Luke Jackiw
Tel: 306-787-3656
ljackiw@health.gov.sk.ca
Director, Cancer Services & EMS, Dave Morhart
Tel: 306-787-1129
dave.morhart@health.gov.sk.ca

Communications Branch
Tel: 306-787-3696; Fax: 306-787-8310
Toll-Free: 800-667-7766
Executive Director, Joan Petrie
Tel: 306-787-8433; Fax: 306-787-8310
joan.petrie@gov.sk.ca
Director, Program Services, Carolyn Hamilton
Tel: 306-787-2743; Fax: 306-787-8310
carolyn.hamilton@gov.sk.ca
Director, Media & Health Sector Relations, Karen Hill
Tel: 306-787-7296
karen.hill@health.gov.sk.ca

Community Care Branch
Tel: 306-787-7239; Fax: 306-787-7095
Executive Director, Brad Havervold
Tel: 306-787-6092; Fax: 306-787-7095
brad.havervold@health.gov.sk.ca
Director, Mental Health & Addictions, Jamie Ash
Tel: 306-787-5020; Fax: 306-787-7095
jamie.ash@health.gov.sk.ca
Director, Continuing Care & Rehabilitation, Denise Grad
Tel: 306-787-7901; Fax: 306-787-7095
denise.grad@health.gov.sk.ca
Director, Research, Evaluation & Central Support, Heather Murray
Tel: 306-787-3236; Fax: 306-787-7095
hmurray@health.gov.sk.ca
Director, Licensing, Dawn Skalicky-Souliere
Tel: 306-787-1718; Fax: 306-787-7095

Drug Plan & Extended Benefits Branch
Tel: 306-787-3317; Fax: 306-787-8679
Toll-Free: 800-667-7581
dpeb@health.gov.sk.ca
Executive Director, Nick Doulias
Tel: 306-787-3110
nick.doulias@health.gov.sk.ca
Director, Professional Practice, Arlene Kuntz
Tel: 306-787-3306
arlene.kuntz@health.gov.sk.ca
Director, Pharmaceutical Policy & Appropriateness, Rachel Cheruvallath
Tel: 306-798-2025
rachel.cheruvallath@health.gov.sk.ca
Director, Client Services, Extended Benefits & Policy, Sonja Orban
Tel: 306-787-3677; Fax: 306-787-8679
Director, Financial & Information Services, Jill Raddysh
Tel: 306-787-3031
jill.raddysh@health.gov.sk.ca

Financial Services Branch
Tel: 306-787-4923; Fax: 306-787-0218
Executive Director, Joy Vanstone
Tel: 306-787-5025; Fax: 306-787-0218
joy.vanstone@health.gov.sk.ca
Director, Health System Performance Management, Marcie Bellamy
Tel: 306-787-3330; Fax: 306-787-0218
Marcie.Bellamy@health.gov.sk.ca
Director, Operations & Internal Audit, Melanie DeMarni
Tel: 306-787-7738; Fax: 306-787-0218
melanie.demarni@health.gov.sk.ca
Director, Corporate & Health Partner Financial Services, Ksenia Regel

Tel: 306-787-2392; Fax: 306-787-0218
ksenia.regel@health.gov.sk.ca

Medical Services Branch
Tel: 306-787-3475; Fax: 306-787-3761
Toll-Free: 800-667-7523
Executive Director, James Turner
Tel: 306-787-3423; Fax: 306-787-3761
james.turner@health.gov.sk.ca
Director, Strategic Financial Planning & Support, Braden Giblett
Tel: 306-787-3461
braden.giblett@health.gov.sk.ca

Partnerships & Workforce Planning
Tel: 306-787-3143; Fax: 306-787-4534
Executive Director, Duane Mombourquette
Tel: 306-787-2869; Fax: 306-787-4534
duane.mombourquette@health.gov.sk.ca
Chief Nursing Officer, Liliana Canadic
Tel: 306-787-7195; Fax: 306-787-4534
Liliana.Canadic@health.gov.sk.ca
Director, Labour Relations, Jennifer Green
Tel: 306-787-0219; Fax: 306-787-4534
jennifer.green@health.gov.sk.ca
Director, Health Information & Privacy, Chantelle Probe
Tel: 306-787-0297; Fax: 306-787-4534
chantelle.probe@health.gov.sk.ca

Population Health Branch
Tel: 306-787-8847; Fax: 306-787-3237
Chief Medical Health Officer, Dr. Saqib Shahab
Deputy Chief Medical Health Officer, Dr. Julie Kryzanowski
Executive Director, Tami Denomie
Tel: 306-787-7110
tami.denomie@health.gov.sk.ca
Director, Surveillance & Epidemiology, Patty Beck
Tel: 306-787-1405
patty.beck@health.gov.sk.ca
Director, Health Promotion & Central Policy Support, Jillian Code
Tel: 306-787-5930; Fax: 306-787-3237
jillian.code@health.gov.sk.ca
Director, Disease Prevention, Suzanne Fedorowich
Tel: 306-787-1580
suzanne.fedorowich@health.gov.sk.ca
Director, Environmental Health, Nicole White
Tel: 306-787-7128; Fax: 306-787-3237
nicole.white@health.gov.sk.ca

Strategy & Innovation Branch
Tel: 306-787-7291; Fax: 306-787-2974
Executive Director, Pauline M. Rousseau
Tel: 306-787-3951; Fax: 306-787-2974
paulinem.rousseau@health.gov.sk.ca
Director, Continuous Improvement Office, Pam Herbert
Tel: 306-787-7507; Fax: 306-787-2974
pam.herbert@health.gov.sk.ca
Director, Health System Policy & Innovation, David Howland
Tel: 306-787-3163; Fax: 306-787-2974
david.howland@health.gov.sk.ca
Acting Director, Health System Planning, Doug Scott
Tel: 306-787-3432
doug.scott@health.gov.sk.ca

Saskatchewan Highways

Victoria Tower, 1855 Victoria Ave., Regina, SK S4P 3T2
Tel: 306-933-5186
MHI.CustomerService@gov.sk.ca
www.saskatchewan.ca/highways
twitter.com/skgovhwyhotline
www.facebook.com/SaskatchewanHighwayHotline
The Ministry of Highways is concerned with transportation in Saskatchewan as it relates to the social & economic development of the province. Business areas include ministry services & standards information, planning & policy development, & regional services.
The following are some programs & services offered through the Ministry: Urban Highway Connector Program; Adopt a Highway; Assistance to Motorists; Preservation Program; & Community Airport Partnership Program.

Minister, Hon. Fred Bradshaw
Tel: 306-787-6447
hi.minister@gov.sk.ca
Office of the Minister of Highways, Legislative Bldg.
#322, 2405 Legislative Dr.
Regina, SK S4S 0B3

Deputy Minister, Blair Wagar
Tel: 306-787-4949; Fax: 306-787-9777
blair.wagar@gov.sk.ca

Associated Agencies, Boards & Commissions:

• **Global Transportation Hub Authority**
#700, 1855 Victoria Ave.
Regina, SK S4P 3T2
Tel: 306-787-4842; *Fax:* 306-798-4600
inquiry@thegth.com
thegth.com
The Hub Authority was created in June 2009, & is the primary agency in charge of planning, developing, constructing & promoting the Global Transportation Hub - a transportation & logistics centre encompassing 2,000 acres of serviced land.

• **Highway Traffic Board (HTB)**
1621A McDonald St.
Regina, SK S4N 5R2
Fax: 306-798-0162
Toll-free: 855-775-8336
contactus.htb@gov.sk.ca
www.highwaytrafficboard.sk.ca
The Highway Traffic Board's mandate is to establish & to administer legislation relating to the safe & legal operations of private vehicles, the bus-truck industry & the short line rail industry in Saskatchewan, where specifically legislated to do so.

Design & Construction Division

Tel: 306-787-4904
Assistant Deputy Minister, Wayne Gienow
Tel: 306-787-1355; *Fax:* 306-787-9777
wayne.gienow@gov.sk.ca
Executive Director, Design Branch, Terri Arendt
Tel: 306-787-9418
terri.arendt@gov.sk.ca
Executive Director, Construction Branch, Rocky Boyko
Tel: 306-787-4808; *Fax:* 306-787-4910
rocky.boyko@gov.sk.ca
Executive Director, Bridge Branch, Doug Hansen
Tel: 306-953-3503
doug.hansen@gov.sk.ca
Executive Director, Project Support Office, Karl Lehmann
Tel: 306-371-6410
karl.lehmann@gov.sk.ca

Policy, Planning & Regulation Division

Tel: 306-787-4904
Executive Director, Transportation Policy & Programs Branch, Karri Kempf
Tel: 306-787-0049
karri.kempf@gov.sk.ca
Acting Director, Network Planning & Investment Branch, Doug Daniels
Tel: 306-230-6661; *Fax:* 306-933-7090
doug.daniels@gov.sk.ca
Chief, Saskatchewan Highway Patrol, Andy Landers
Tel: 306-787-4891; *Fax:* 306-787-0013

Saskatchewan Human Rights Commission (SHRC)

PO Box 6011 Saskatoon, SK S7K 4E4
Tel: 306-933-5952; *Fax:* 306-933-7863
Toll-Free: 800-667-9249
shrc@gov.sk.ca
saskatchewanhumanrights.ca
twitter.com/saskhumanrights
www.facebook.com/the.shrc
The Saskatchewan Human Rights Commission promotes & protects individual dignity & equal rights by discouraging & eliminating discrimination. The Commission's guide is The Saskatchewan Human Rights Code. The following are the principle functions of the Commission: approving equity programs; educating people & promoting human rights laws in Saskatchewan; & investigating complaints of discrimination.

Interim Chief Commissioner, Barry Wilcox, Q.C.
Tel: 306-933-5952; *Fax:* 306-933-7863
humanrights.commission@gov.sk.ca

Executive Director, Norma Gunningham-Kapphahn
Tel: 306-933-8284; *Fax:* 306-933-7863
norma.gunningham-kapphahn@gov.sk.ca

Saskatchewan Immigration & Career Training

#1000, 2103 - 11th Ave., Regina, SK S4P 3Z8
Fax: 306-787-7977
Other Communication: URL: www.saskatchewan.ca/government/government-structure/ministr ies/immigration-and-career-training
Secondary Address: 1945 Hamilton St., 12th Fl.
Regina, SK S4P 2C8
The Ministry assists individuals with preparing for, obtaining & maintaining employment, & also aids employers with developing, recruiting & retaining employees.

Minister, Hon. Jeremy Harrison

Tel: 306-787-8687
Minister.TED@gov.sk.ca

Deputy Minister, Clint Repski
Tel: 306-787-6846; *Fax:* 306-798-5022
clint.repski3@gov.sk.ca

Corporate Services

Tel: 306-787-9878; *Fax:* 306-787-8702
Chief Financial Officer, Denise Haas
Tel: 306-787-2756
denise.haas@gov.sk.ca
Executive Director, Finance & Operations, Andrea Terry Munro
Tel: 306-787-9694
andrea.terrymunro@gov.sk.ca
Executive Director, Modernization of Agreements, Programs & Services, Jan Kot
Tel: 306-787-8099
jan.kot@gov.sk.ca

Immigration, Employment & Career Development

Assistant Deputy Minister, Christa Ross
Tel: 306-529-7200
christa.ross@gov.sk.ca
Executive Director, Immigration Services, Anne McRorie
Tel: 306-570-2416
anne.mcrorie@gov.sk.ca
Director, Labour Market Services, Derrick Lepine
Tel: 306-570-8415
derrick.lepine@gov.sk.ca

Training & Employer Services

Assistant Deputy Minister, Darcy Smycniuk
Tel: 306-787-5984
Darcy.Smycniuk@gov.sk.ca

Information & Privacy Commissioner of Saskatchewan

#503, 1801 Hamilton St., Regina, SK S4P 4B4
Tel: 306-787-8350; *Fax:* 306-798-1603
Toll-Free: 877-748-2298
webmaster@oipc.sk.ca
oipc.sk.ca
twitter.com/saskipc

Information & Privacy Commissioner, Ron Kruzeniski, Q.C.
Tel: 306-537-4287; *Fax:* 306-798-1603
rkruzeniski@oipc.sk.ca

Executive Director, Compliance, Diane Aldridge
Tel: 306-537-2146; *Fax:* 306-798-1603
daldridge@oipc.sk.ca

Executive Director, Corporate Services, Pam Scott
Tel: 306-798-2261; *Fax:* 306-798-1603
pscott@oipc.sk.ca

Saskatchewan Justice & Attorney General

1874 Scarth St., Regina, SK S4P 4B3
www.saskatchewan.ca/justice

Minister & Attorney General, Hon. Gordon Wyant, Q.C.
Tel: 306-787-5353
jus.minister@gov.sk.ca
Office of the Minister of Justice & Attorney General, Legislative Bldg.
#355, 2405 Legislative Dr.
Regina, SK S4S 0B3

Deputy Minister, Justice; Deputy Attorney General, J. Glen Gardner, Q.C.
Tel: 306-787-5351; *Fax:* 306-787-3874
Glen.Gardner@gov.sk.ca

Executive Director, Communications, Noel Busse
Tel: 306-787-8959; *Fax:* 306-798-4064
noel.busse@gov.sk.ca

Executive Director, Access & Privacy Branch, Aaron Orban
Tel: 306-787-3316; *Fax:* 306-798-9007
aaron.orban@gov.sk.ca

Associated Agencies, Boards & Commissions:

• **Automobile Injury Appeal Commission**
#504, 2400 College Ave.
Regina, SK S4P 1C8
Tel: 306-798-5545; *Fax:* 306-798-5540
Toll-free: 866-798-5544
aiac@gov.sk.ca

• **Financial & Consumer Affairs Authority (FCAA)**
#601, 1919 Saskatchewan Dr.
Regina, SK S4P 4H2
Tel: 306-787-5645; *Fax:* 306-787-5899
Toll-free: 877-880-5550
consumerprotection@gov.sk.ca
fcaa.gov.sk.ca
Other Communication: Film Classification Board Inquiries, Email: skfilmclass@gov.sk.ca
The Financial & Consumer Affairs Authority (formerly known as the Saskatchewan Financial Services Commission (SFSC)) protects consumer & public interests & supports economic well-being through responsive financial marketplace regulation. The SFSC enhances consumer protection through licensing, registration, audit, complaint handling & enforcement activities pursuant to various provincial statutes.

• **Law Reform Commission of Saskatchewan**
c/o University of Saskatchewan, College of Law
#184, 15 Campus Dr.
Saskatoon, SK S7N 5A6
Tel: 306-966-1625; *Fax:* 306-966-5900
www.lawreformcommission.sk.ca
The Law Reform Commission of Saskatchewan was established by An Act to Establish a Law Reform Commission, proclaimed in force in November, 1973, & began functioning in February of 1974.

• **Legal Aid Saskatchewan**
#502, 201 - 21st St. East
Saskatoon, SK S7K 0B8
Tel: 306-933-5300; *Fax:* 306-933-6764
Toll-free: 800-667-3764
headoffice@legalaid.sk.ca
legalaid.sk.ca
The Saskatchewan Legal Aid Commission provides legal services to persons & organizations for criminal & civil matters where those persons & organizations are financially unable to secure these services from their own resources. The organization has been in existence since 1974.

• **Office of Residential Tenancies (ORT)**
#304, 1855 Victoria Ave.
Regina, SK S4P 3T2
Toll-free: 888-215-2222
ort@gov.sk.ca
www.saskatchewan.ca/ort

• **Provincial Mediation Board**
#304, 1855 Victoria Ave.
Regina, SK S4P 3T2
Tel: 306-787-5408
Toll-free: 877-787-5408
pmb@gov.sk.ca
www.saskatchewan.ca/pmb
The Provincial Mediation Board provides budgeting advice & counselling to individuals with personal debt problems. It may be able to arrange repayment plans with creditors. The Board also deals with problems of debtors related to property tax arrears, eviction of commercial tenants & residential mortgage foreclosures.

• **Public & Private Rights Board**
#23, 3085 Albert St.
Regina, SK S4S 0B1
Tel: 306-787-4071; *Fax:* 306-787-0088

• **Saskatchewan Human Rights Commission (SHRC)**
See Entry Name Index for detailed listing.

• **Saskatchewan Police College (SkPC)**
College West Bldg., University of Regina
#217, 3737 Wascana Pkwy.
Regina, SK S4S 0A2
Tel: 306-787-8870; *Fax:* 306-787-8876
www.saskatchewan.ca/residents/justice-crime-and-the-law

• **Saskatchewan Police Commission**
#1850, 1881 Scarth St.
Regina, SK S4P 4K9
Tel: 306-787-9292; *Fax:* 306-798-4908
The Commission promotes crime prevention, improved police relationships with communities, & effective policing throughout Saskatchewan by working closely with police services & Boards of Police Commissioners.

• **Saskatchewan Public Complaints Commission (PCC)**
#300, 1919 Saskatchewan Dr.
Regina, SK S4P 4H2
Tel: 306-787-6519; *Fax:* 306-787-6528
Toll-free: 866-256-6194
www.saskatchewan.ca/pcc
The Public Complaints Commission is a five-person, non-police body appointed by the government. It is mandated to investigate complaints against the police or of possible criminal offences by police officers, & to ensure that investigations are fair & thorough.

• Saskatchewan Review Board
220 - 19th St. East, 3rd Fl.
Saskatoon, SK S7K 0A2
Tel: 306-933-7892

The Saskatchewan Review Board was established under the Criminal Code of Canada to review decisions & orders regarding an accused person, where a verdict of not criminally responsible by reason of mental disorder or unfit to stand trial on account of mental disorder has been made.

Administrative Justice & Strategic Relations Division
#1000, 1874 Scarth St., Regina, SK S4P 4B3
Fax: 306-787-3411
Assistant Deputy Attorney General, Kylie Head, Q.C.
Tel: 306-787-8220; *Fax:* 306-787-3874
kylie.head@gov.sk.ca
Director, Office of Tribunal Counsel, Charita Ohashi
Tel: 306-787-9711; *Fax:* 306-787-0497
Charita.Ohashi@gov.sk.ca

Community Engagement Division
1874 Scarth St., 12th Fl., Regina, SK S4P 4B3
Tel: 306-787-5787; *Fax:* 306-798-0270
Assistant Deputy Minister, Drew Wilby
Tel: 306-787-5883; *Fax:* 306-798-4064
Drew.Wilby@gov.sk.ca
Executive Director, Strategic Policy, Planning & Reporting, Elissa Aitken
Tel: 306-531-8520
elissa.aitken2@gov.sk.ca
Executive Director, Strategic Engagement, Gina Alexander
Tel: 306-539-4472; *Fax:* 306-787-0078
gina.alexander@gov.sk.ca
Executive Director, Research & Implementation Branch, Scott Harron
Tel: 306-787-3892; *Fax:* 306-798-0270
scott.harron@gov.sk.ca
Director, Healthy Families, Jeffrey Dudar
Tel: 306-798-8066; *Fax:* 306-787-0078
Jeffrey.Dudar@gov.sk.ca
Director, Strategic Partnerships & Health Families, Carla Frohaug
Tel: 306-425-4603; *Fax:* 306-787-0078
Carla.Frohaug@gov.sk.ca

Corporate Services Branch
#1100, 1874 Scarth St., Regina, SK S4P 4B3
Fax: 306-787-5830
Assistant Deputy Minister, Dave Tulloch
Tel: 306-787-5472; *Fax:* 306-787-5830
dave.tulloch@gov.sk.ca
Acting Executive Director, Infrastructure & Support Services, Jill Zimmer
Tel: 306-798-1252; *Fax:* 306-787-5830
jill.zimmer2@gov.sk.ca

Court Services Division
#1010, 1874 Scarth St., Regina, SK S4P 4B3
Tel: 306-787-5359; *Fax:* 306-787-8737
Assistant Deputy Minister, Jan Turner
Tel: 306-787-5112; *Fax:* 306-787-8737
jan.turner@gov.sk.ca
Registrar, Court of Appeal, Amy Groothuis
Tel: 306-787-5382; *Fax:* 306-787-5815
agroothuis@sasklawcourts.ca
Court House
2425 Victoria Ave.
Regina, SK S4P 4W6
Senior Director, Court Operations & Services, Kim Kreklewetz
Tel: 306-787-5386
kim.kreklewetz2@gov.sk.ca
Senior Director, Strategic & Corporate Services, Curtis Kosolofski
Tel: 306-787-5972
curtis.kosolofski@gov.sk.ca
Senior Director, Legal & Policy Services, Audrey Olson
Tel: 306-798-2111
audrey.olson@gov.sk.ca
Senior Director, Sheriff Services, Barry Watson
Tel: 306-787-3584
barry.watson@gov.sk.ca

Justice Services Division
#1000, 1874 Scarth St., Regina, SK S4P 4B3
Fax: 306-787-3874
Assistant Deputy Attorney General, Shannon Williams
Tel: 306-787-6268; *Fax:* 306-787-3874
shannon.williams@gov.sk.ca
Chief Counsel, Criminal Justice System Review, Dale Tesarowski
Tel: 306-787-5469; *Fax:* 306-787-9008
306-787-9008

Saskatchewan Coroners Service
#1050, 2010 - 12th Ave., Regina, SK S4P 0M3
Tel: 306-787-5541; *Fax:* 306-787-5503
Toll-Free: 866-592-7845
coroner@gov.sk.ca
Secondary Address: #3, 2345 Ave. C North
Saskatoon, SK S7L 5Z5
Alt. Fax: 306-964-1896
ocoronernorthern@gov.sk.ca
Other Communication: Toll-Free Phone: 1-888-824-0491
Chief Coroner, Clive Weighill
Tel: 306-787-5541; *Fax:* 306-787-5503
clive.weighill@gov.sk.ca
Chief Forensic Pathologist, Dr. Shaun Ladham
Tel: 306-964-1677; *Fax:* 306-655-8399
shaun.ladham@saskatoonhealthregion.ca
Regional Supervising Coroner, Maureen Stinnen
Tel: 306-787-0401
Maureen.Stinnen@gov.sk.ca

Legal Services Division
#900,1874 Scarth St., Regina, SK S4P 4B3
Tel: 306-787-5224; *Fax:* 306-787-0581
Assistant Deputy Attorney General, Linda Zarzeczny, Q.C.
Tel: 306-787-8387; *Fax:* 306-787-0581
Linda.Zarzeczny@gov.sk.ca
Chief Legislative Crown Counsel, Alan Jacobson, Q.C.
Tel: 306-787-9346; *Fax:* 306-787-9111
Alan.Jacobson@gov.sk.ca
Director, Office of Public Registry Administration, Catherine Benning
Tel: 306-787-8391; *Fax:* 306-787-4732
Catherine.Benning@gov.sk.ca
Director, Constitutional Law Branch, Mitch McAdam, Q.C.
Tel: 306-787-7846; *Fax:* 306-787-9111
Mitch.McAdam@gov.sk.ca
Director, Legislative Services, Darcy McGovern, Q.C.
Tel: 306-787-5662; *Fax:* 306-787-9111
Darcy.McGovern@gov.sk.ca

Public Prosecutions
#300, 1874 Scarth St., Regina, SK S4P 4B3
Tel: 306-787-5490; *Fax:* 306-787-8878
Assistant Deputy Attorney General, Anthony Gerein, Q.C.
Director, High Risk Violent Offender Unit, Roger DeCorby
Director, Financial, Shari Parisian
Director, Appeals, Dean Sinclair, Q.C.

Strategic Systems & Innovation
1874 Scarth St., 12th Fl., Regina, SK S4P 4B3
Fax: 306-798-0270
Executive Director, Monica Field
Tel: 306-798-1309; *Fax:* 306-798-0270
monica.field@gov.sk.ca
Director, Business Intelligence & Data Analytics, Yashu Bither
Tel: 306-787-0469
yashu.bither@gov.sk.ca

Saskatchewan Labour Relations & Workplace Safety (LRWS)

#300, 1870 Albert St., Regina, SK S4P 4W1
Fax: 306-787-7404
www.saskatchewan.ca/lrws
The Ministry is responsible for labour standards, labour support services, labour relations, mediation, occupational health & safety, & workers' advocacy.

Minister, Hon. Don Morgan, Q.C.
Tel: 306-787-7339
cic.minister@gov.sk.ca
Office of the Minister of Labour Relation & Workplace Safety, Legislative Bldg.
#348, 2405 Legislative Dr.
Regina, SK S4S 0B3

Deputy Minister, Greg Tuer
Tel: 306-787-7424; *Fax:* 306-798-5190
greg.tuer2@gov.sk.ca

Executive Director, Corporate Services, Louise Usick
Tel: 306-787-8078; *Fax:* 306-798-5190
louise.usick@gov.sk.ca

Executive Director, Communications, Gladys Wasylenchuk
Tel: 306-787-2411
gladys.wasylenchuk@gov.sk.ca

Associated Agencies, Boards & Commissions:

• Labour Relations Board
#1600, 1920 Broad St.
Regina, SK S4P 3V2
Tel: 306-787-2406; *Fax:* 306-787-2664
www.sasklabourrelationsboard.com
An independent, quasi-judicial tribunal charged with the responsibility of adjudicating disputes that arise under The Trade Union Act, The Construction Industry Labour Relations Act, 1992 & The Health Labour Relations Reorganization Act.

• Office of the Workers' Advocate
#300, 1870 Albert St.
Regina, SK S4P 4W1
Fax: 306-787-0249
Toll-free: 877-787-2456
workersadvocate@gov.sk.ca
The Office of the Worker's Advocate provides free assistance to workers who are experiencing difficulties with workers' compensation claims. The Office offers information about the following programs & services: wage loss, benefits, survivor's benefits, medical aid, rehabilitation, & retraining. Working with advocacy groups & unions, The Office of the Worker's Advocate strives to improve service to injured workers. Workers' Compensation Board (WCB) decisions about claims can be reviewed & appealed.

• Saskatchewan Workers' Compensation Board
See Entry Name Index for detailed listing.

Programs Division
Assistant Deputy Minister, Sameema Haque
Tel: 306-787-5634; *Fax:* 306-798-5190
sameema.haque@gov.sk.ca
Acting Executive Director, Occupational Health & Safety Division, Joel Bender
Tel: 306-787-4481; *Fax:* 306-787-2208
joel.bender@gov.sk.ca
Executive Director, Employment Standards, Glen McRorie
Tel: 306-933-5087; *Fax:* 306-933-5444
Glen.McRorie@gov.sk.ca
Executive Director, Labour Relations & Mediation, Pete Suderman
Tel: 306-787-9106; *Fax:* 306-787-1064
pete.suderman@gov.sk.ca

Saskatchewan Liquor & Gaming Authority (SLGA)

2500 Victoria Ave., PO Box 5054 Regina, SK S4P 3M3
Tel: 306-787-5563
inquiry@slga.gov.sk.ca
www.slga.com
Other Communication: Cannabis Permits & Licences:
www.slga.com/permits-and-licences/cannabis-permits;
cannabisbranch@slga.gov.sk.ca
The Treasury Board Crown Corporation is responsible for the distribution, control, & regulation of liquor & most gaming across Saskatchewan. As of 2018, its mandate expanded to include recreational cannabis.

Minister responsible, Hon. Jim Reiter, Q.C.
Tel: 306-787-0942; *Fax:* 306-787-8677
Minister.sbp@gov.sk.ca

President & CEO, Susan Ross
Tel: 306-787-1737; *Fax:* 306-787-8439
sross@slga.gov.sk.ca

Registrar, Licensing Commission, Karen Mondor
Tel: 306-787-1746; *Fax:* 306-798-0653
kmondor@slga.gov.sk.ca

Director, Communications, Stephanie Choma
Tel: 306-787-1799
schoma@slga.gov.sk.ca

Corporate Services & Gaming Operations Division
Tel: 306-787-9902; *Fax:* 306-787-8439
Vice-President, Charlene Callander
Tel: 306-536-8132
ccallander@slga.gov.sk.ca

SLGA Retail Inc.
Vice-President, Greg Mildenberger
Tel: 306-787-1222; *Fax:* 306-787-8201
gmildenberger@slga.gov.sk.ca
Acting Senior Director, Liquor Operations, Jim Selinger
Tel: 306-787-4237
jselinger@slga.gov.sk.ca

Liquor Wholesale & Distribution Division
Vice-President, Greg Gettle
Tel: 306-533-3466
ggettle@slga.gov.sk.ca

Senior Director, Customer Relations, Warren Fry
Tel: 306-787-5360
wfry@slga.gov.sk.ca

Regulatory Services Division
Tel: 306-787-1780; Fax: 306-787-8981
Vice-President, Fiona Cribb
Tel: 306-787-4705
fcribb@slga.gov.sk.ca

Ombudsman Saskatchewan

#500, 2103 - 11th Ave., Regina, SK S4P 3Z8
Tel: 306-787-6211; Fax: 306-787-9090
Toll-Free: 800-667-9787
ombreg@ombudsman.sk.ca
ombudsman.sk.ca
Secondary Address: #500, 350 - 3rd Ave. North
Saskatoon, SK S7K 6G7
Alt. Fax: 306-933-8406
ombsktn@ombudsman.sk.ca
The Ombudsman is an Officer of the Legislative Assembly with the authority to investigate complaints received from members of the public who believe the government administration has dealt with them unfairly. Government administration includes any department, branch, board, agency or commission responsible to the Crown & any public servant in Saskatchewan. The Ombudsman was established by the Ombudsman & Children's Advocate Act.

Ombudsman, Mary McFadyen, B.A., LL.B., LL.M.
Tel: 306-787-6211; Fax: 306-787-9090
ombreg@ombudsman.sk.ca

Deputy Ombudsman, Saskatoon Office, Renee Gavigan
Tel: 306-933-6767; Fax: 306-933-8406
rgavigan@ombudsman.sk.ca

Deputy Ombudsman, Regina Office, Mike Halayka
Tel: 306-787-6142
mhalayka@ombudsman.sk.ca

Saskatchewan Opportunities Corporation (SOCO)

Innovation Place, #114, 15 Innovation Blvd., Saskatoon, SK S7N 2X8
Tel: 306-933-6295; Fax: 306-933-8215
saskatoon@innovationplace.com
www.innovationplace.com
The Opportunities Corporation aims to support Saskatchewan's technology sector through the development & operation of research parks. The corporation operates under the business name Innovation Place.

Minister responsible, Hon. Don Morgan, Q.C.
cic.minister@gov.sk.ca

Acting President & CEO, Brent Sukenik
Tel: 306-933-6258; Fax: 306-933-8215
bsukenik@innovationplace.com

Acting Chief Financial Officer & Vice-President, Corporate Services, Trevor Cross
Tel: 306-361-7565; Fax: 306-933-8215

Saskatchewan Parks, Culture & Sport (PCS)

3211 Albert St., 1st Fl., Regina, SK S4S 5W6
Tel: 306-787-5729; Fax: 306-798-0033
pcs.info@gov.sk.ca
www.saskatchewan.ca/pcs
The Ministry is concerned with Saskatchewan's quality of life, tourism, & economic growth.
The following are some of the goals of the Ministry of Parks, Culture, & Sport: to enhance the province's parks by offering recreational activities & focussing upon natural resources that appeal to residents & visitors; to conserve heritage resources & ecosystems; to protect the province's history & culture; to promote Saskatchewan's cultural & artistic communities; & to encourage residents to be healthy & active through participation in sports & recreational events.
Some of the programs & services available through the Ministry include the Developers' Online Screening Tool, the provision of Archaeological/Palaeontological Permits, the maintenance of the Saskatchewan Register of Heritage Property, the operation of the Royal Saskatchewan Museum, competitive games information, the operation of the Canadian Sport Centre Saskatchewan, & the Active Families Benefit.
Ministry publications available through the provincial government's publication centre include the annual Parks Guide, A Physically Active Saskatchewan: A Strategy to get Saskatchewan People in Motion, & Conserving Your Historic Places.

Minister, Hon. Laura Ross
minister.pcs@gov.sk.ca

Deputy Minister, Twyla MacDougall
Tel: 306-787-5050; Fax: 306-798-0033
twyla.macdougall@gov.sk.ca

Associated Agencies, Boards & Commissions:

• Conexus Arts Centre
200A Lakeshore Dr.
Regina, SK S4S 7L3
Tel: 306-565-4500; Fax: 306-565-3274
Toll-free: 800-667-8497
reception@conexusartscentre.ca
www.conexusartscentre.ca
Formerly known as the Saskatchewan Centre of the Arts, the Conexus Arts Centre is a performing arts & theatre complex. The Centre's mandate is to provide facilities, services, & programs to educate & entertain the people of Saskatchewan.

• Provincial Capital Commission (PCC)
PO Box 7111
Regina, SK S4P 3S7
Tel: 306-522-3661; Fax: 306-565-2742
www.saskatchewan.ca/provincial-capital-commission
The Provincial Capital Commission aims to provide education about the history of Saskatchewan. The Commission creates tourism & economic development opportunities, through the preservation & promotion of the province's heritage & culture. The PCC assumed responsibility for the Wascana Centre Authority (WCA) in the spring of 2017.
The following Acts & Regulations guide the work of the Provincial Capital Commission:
Air, Army, Sea, & Navy League Cadets Recognition Day Act;
Archives Act, 2004;
Culture & Recreation Act, 1993;
Government House Foundation Regulations;
Heritage Property Act;
Historic Properties Foundations Act;
Provincial Capital Commission Regulations;
National Peacekeepers Recognition Day Act;
Recognition of John George Diefenbaker Day Act;
Recognition of Telemiracle Week Act;
Saskatchewan Centre of the Arts Act, 2000;
Saskatchewan Heritage Foundation Act;
Tartan Day Act;
Tommy Douglas Day Act;
Wascana Centre Act.

• Royal Saskatchewan Museum (RSM)
2445 Albert St.
Regina, SK S4P 4W7
Tel: 306-787-2815; Fax: 306-787-2820
info@royalsaskmuseum.ca
royalsaskmuseum.ca
The Royal Saskatchewan Museum in Regina presents Saskatchewan's geological & natural history, as well as a look at First Nations' cultures of the past& present.

• Saskatchewan Archives Board
See Entry Name Index for detailed listing.

• Saskatchewan Arts Board (SK Arts)
1355 Broad St.
Regina, SK S4R 7V1
Tel: 306-787-4056
Toll-free: 800-667-7526
info@sk-arts.ca
sk-arts.ca

• Saskatchewan Heritage Foundation
3211 Albert St., 1st Fl.
Regina, SK S4S 5W6
www.saskheritagefoundation.com
The Saskatchewan Heritage Foundation was established by provincial legislation as an agent of the Crown. Its mission is to conserve heritage resources for the benefit of present & future generations.

• Saskatchewan Science Centre
2903 Powerhouse Dr.
Regina, SK S4N 0A1
Tel: 306-791-7914
Toll-free: 800-667-6300
info@sasksciencecentre.com
www.sasksciencecentre.com
Other Communication: Administration: 306-791-7900; Media: 306-791-7917

• Wanuskewin Heritage Park
RR#4 Penner Rd.
Saskatoon, SK S7K 3J7
Tel: 306-931-6767
wanuskewin.com

• Western Development Museum (WDM)
Curatorial Centre
2935 Lorne Ave.
Saskatoon, SK S7J 5A6
Tel: 306-934-1400
Toll-free: 800-363-6345
info@wdm.ca
wdm.ca
There are locations in Moose Jaw (50 Diefenbaker Dr., Moose Jaw, SK S6J 1L9), North Battleford (PO Box 183, Hwy. 16 & 40, North Battleford, SK S9A 2Y1), Saskatoon (2610 Lorne Ave. South, Saskatoon, SK S7J 0S6), & Yorkton (PO Box 98, Hwy. 16 West, Yorkton, SK S3N 2V6).

Communications Branch
Tel: 306-787-0346; Fax: 306-798-0033
Other Communication: Inquiry Line: 306-787-5729
Executive Director, Brooke Lochbaum
Tel: 306-550-5927
brooke.lochbaum@gov.sk.ca

Parks Division
Tel: 306-787-5729; Fax: 306-787-7000
parks.info@gov.sk.ca
Other Communication: Sask Parks, URL:
www.tourismsaskatchewan.com/places-to-go/provincial-parks
www.facebook.com/saskparks
www.instagram.com/saskparks
Responsibilities of the Parks division include planning, managing & operating the provincial park system.
Saskatchewan has a provincial parks & protected areas network encompassing 1.4 million hectares, in 34 provincial parks, 8 historic sites, 24 protected areas & 129 recreation sites. The Ministry provides programs & services to conserve, protect, & enhance the province's natural & cultural resources in its parks & protected areas.
Assistant Deputy Minister, Jennifer Johnson
Jennifer.Johnson@gov.sk.ca
Executive Director, Visitor Experiences Branch, Robin Campese
Tel: 306-798-3308; Fax: 306-787-7000
robin.campese@gov.sk.ca
Executive Director, Infrastructure & Capital Planning, Byron Davis
Tel: 306-787-3035
Byron.Davis@gov.sk.ca
Executive Director, Parks Operations, Dan French
Tel: 306-798-0181; Fax: 306-787-7000
dan.french@gov.sk.ca
Executive Director, Park Management Services, Michael Roth
Tel: 306-787-2948; Fax: 306-787-0069
Michael.Roth@gov.sk.ca
Director, Safety & Training, Jason Lessard
Tel: 306-221-2632; Fax: 306-933-7930
Jason.Lessard@gov.sk.ca

Stewardship Division
Tel: 306-798-0697; Fax: 306-798-0033
The Stewardship Division is responsible for advancing sport, recreation & heritage conservation, oversight of the Saskatchewan Heritage Foundation & the Royal Saskatchewan Museum.
Heritage conservation involves the protection of the province's heritage legacy, through inventories, research, & consultative services. Resources are available to help municipalities manage their historic places. One program is known as Main Street Saskatchewan, which works to revitalize historic downtown commercial districts.
Assistant Deputy Minister, Candace Caswell
Tel: 306-798-3905; Fax: 306-798-0033
candace.caswell@gov.sk.ca
Executive Director, Sport, Recreation, & Stewardship, Darin Banadyga
Tel: 306-787-0685
darin.banadyga@gov.sk.ca
Executive Director, Francophone Affairs, Charles-Henri Warren
Tel: 306-787-8035
charles-henri.warren@gov.sk.ca
www.pcs.gov.sk.ca/culture
Acting Director, Heritage Conservation Branch, Tom Richards
Tel: 306-787-5772; Fax: 306-787-0069
tom.richards@gov.sk.ca
www.pcs.gov.sk.ca/heritage

Strategic & Corporate Services Branch
Tel: 306-787-4928; Fax: 306-798-0033
Acting Executive Director, Jennifer Fink
Tel: 306-787-5717
jennifer.fink@gov.sk.ca
Director, Financial Services, Myron Soloduk
Tel: 306-787-5896
myron.soloduk3@gov.sk.ca

Provincial Archives of Saskatchewan

PO Box 1665 Regina, SK S4P 3C6
Tel: 306-787-4068; *Fax:* 306-787-1975
www.saskarchives.com
Secondary Address: 2440 Broad St.
Regina, SK S4P 0A5

The Provincial Archives (formerly the Saskatchewan Archives Board) is a joint university-government agency, which was established under legislation. The Archives collects official records of the Government of Saskatchewan, as well as documentary material from local government & private sources.

Chair, Louise Greenberg
Tel: 306-787-4073
boardchair@archives.gov.sk.ca

Provincial Archivist, Carol Radford-Grant
Tel: 306-798-4018
cradfordgrant@archives.gov.sk.ca

Director, Archival Services, Nadine Charabin
Tel: 306-787-4073
ncharabin@archives.gov.sk.ca

Director, Corporate Services, Darren Cranfield
Tel: 306-787-8686
dcranfield@archives.gov.sk.ca

Director, Information Management Services, Anna Stoszek
Tel: 306-787-0700
astoszek@archives.gov.sk.ca

Saskatchewan Power Corporation (SaskPower)

2025 Victoria Ave., Regina, SK S4P 0S1
Toll-Free: 888-757-6937
www.saskpower.com
Other Communication: Media phone: 306-536-2886
twitter.com/SaskPower
www.facebook.com/saskpower
www.linkedin.com/company/saskpower

A Crown Corporation which provides services to over 490,000 customers over 652,000 square kilometres of diverse terrain in Saskatchewan; operates 18 generating facilities including three coal-fired power stations, seven hydroelectric stations, six natural gas stations, & two wind facilities; capacity of 3,513 megawatts. The SaskPower Environmental policy maintains a commitment to environmental responsibility. The policy includes compliance with relevant environmental legislation, regulations & corporate environmental committees; continual improvement of environmental management systems & prevention of pollution. SaskPower's management system is ISO 14001 registered.

Minister responsible, Hon. Don Morgan, Q.C.

President & CEO, Mike Marsh
Tel: 306-566-3271
mmarsh@saskpower.com

Vice-President, Asset Management, Planning & Sustainability, Tim Eckel
Tel: 306-566-3727
teckel@saskpower.com

Vice-President, Transmission & Industrial Services, Kory Hayko
Tel: 306-566-2174
khayko@saskpower.com

Chief Financial Officer & Vice-President, Finance & Business Performance, Troy King
Tel: 306-566-2872
tking@saskpower.com

Vice-President, Power Production, Howard Matthews
Tel: 306-566-3565
hmatthews@saskpower.com

Vice-President, Human Resources & Safety, Kathy McCrum
Tel: 306-566-2058
kmccrum@saskpower.com

Vice-President, Supply Chain, Grant Ring
Tel: 306-566-3577
gring@saskpower.com

Vice-President, Distribution & Customer Services, Shawn Schmidt
Tel: 306-934-7797
sschmidt@saskpower.com

Chief Information Officer & Vice-President, Technology & Security, Brad Strom
Tel: 306-566-2146
bstrom@saskpower.com

Vice-President, Corporate & Regulatory Affairs; General Counsel & Assistant Secretary, Rachelle Verret Morphy, Q.C.
Tel: 306-566-3139
rverretmor@saskpower.com

NorthPoint Energy Solutions Inc.
2025 Victoria Ave., Regina, SK S4P 0S1
www.northpointenergy.com
NorthPoint Energy is the wholly owned marketing subsidiary of SaskPower, & operates a 24/7 electrical energy trading desk.
President & CEO, Kory Hayko
Tel: 306-566-2174
khayko@northpointenergy.com

Provincial Auditor Saskatchewan

Chateau Tower, #1500, 1920 Broad St., Regina, SK S4P 3V2
Tel: 306-787-6398; *Fax:* 306-787-6383
info@auditor.sk.ca
auditor.sk.ca
twitter.com/ProvAuditorSK
www.linkedin.com/company/provincial-auditor-of-saskatchewan

The Provincial Auditor is the auditor of public money managed by the Government of Saskatchewan. The Provincial Auditor Act gives the Provincial Auditor the responsibility, authority & independence to audit & publicly report on all government organizations.

Acting Provincial Auditor, Tara Clemett
Tel: 306-787-6313
clemett@auditor.sk.ca

Deputy Provincial Auditor & Chief Operating Officer, Angèle Borys
Tel: 306-787-6326
borys@auditor.sk.ca

Deputy Provincial Auditor, Kelly Deis
Tel: 306-787-0027
deis@auditor.sk.ca

Deputy Provincial Auditor, Carolyn O'Quinn
Tel: 306-787-9686
oquinn@auditor.sk.ca

Deputy Provincial Auditor, Trevor St. John
Tel: 306-787-6305
stjohn@auditor.sk.ca

Saskatchewan Research Council (SRC)

#125, 15 Innovation Blvd., Saskatoon, SK S7N 2X8
Tel: 306-933-5400; *Fax:* 306-933-7446
www.src.sk.ca
twitter.com/srcnews
www.facebook.com/saskresearchcouncil
www.linkedin.com/company/saskatchewan-research-council-src
www.youtube.com/c/saskresearchcouncil

Research activities include: gas emissions testing; indoor environment testing; groundwater pesticides testing; indoor air quality & source testing for rayon & asbestos; spray drift research; vegetation studies for range, forestry, conservation; aquatic monitoring & assessment methods; climate impact assessment for environmental economic & urban stormwater management; development of plant bioassays for assessing the effects of hazardous materials in aquatic ecosystems; radiochemistry, chromatographic analysis, water analysis; parenting verification centre for the Canadian livestock industry; develops the optimum engine & fuel system for natural gas operation; bioprocessing technology; emulsions research; studies to support mineral exploration; analyses various sample material used in mineral exploration; geoenvironmental research. SRC's Biofuels Test Centre opened in September, 2006.

President & CEO, Mike Crabtree
Tel: 306-933-5402; *Fax:* 306-933-7519
mike.crabtree@src.sk.ca

Vice-President, Organizational Effectiveness, Toby Arnold
Tel: 306-385-4020; *Fax:* 306-933-7896
arnold@src.sk.ca

Vice-President, Finance, Ryan Hill
Tel: 306-385-4077; *Fax:* 306-933-7446

Vice-President, Environment, Jesse Merilees
Tel: 306-385-4203; *Fax:* 306-933-7446

Vice-President, Mining & Energy, Craig Murray
Tel: 306-385-4200; *Fax:* 306-933-7446

Vice-President, Communications, Growth Services & Risk, Wanda Nyirfa
Tel: 306-385-4196

Saskatchewan Social Services (SS)

1920 Broad St., Regina, SK S4P 3V6
Tel: 306-787-3800
socialservicesinquiry@gov.sk.ca
www.saskatchewan.ca/social-services

The Ministry works with citizens in the following areas: income support; child & family services; supports for persons with disabilities; affordable housing; economic independence; & active involvement in the labour market & the community. In November 2007, a new provincial government resulted in the reorganization of provincial government ministries. The work of Saskatchewan Community Resources was merged into the newly named Ministry of Social Services.

Minister, Hon. Lori Carr
Tel: 306-787-3661
ss.minister@gov.sk.ca

Deputy Minister, Tracey Smith
Tel: 306-787-3491; *Fax:* 306-787-1032
tracey.smith@gov.sk.ca

Executive Director, Communications, Julianne Jack
Tel: 306-787-4274; *Fax:* 306-787-8669
jjack3@gov.sk.ca

Executive Director, Strategic Management Branch, David Loewen
Tel: 306-787-9074
david.loewen@gov.sk.ca

Executive Director, Program Support, Chad Ryan
Tel: 306-535-1249
Chad.Ryan@gov.sk.ca

Executive Director, Enterprise Projects & Information Technology Branch, Tracy Sawatzky
Tel: 306-798-3352; *Fax:* 306-798-5550
Tracy.sawatzky@gov.sk.ca

Acting Executive Director, Finance, Rhiannon Shaw
Tel: 306-787-3575; *Fax:* 306-787-3575
rhiannon.shaw@gov.sk.ca

Child & Family Programs
Tel: 306-787-7300; *Fax:* 306-787-0925
Executive Director, Indigenous Services, Janice Colquhoun
Tel: 306-787-2245; *Fax:* 306-787-0925
janice.colquhoun@gov.sk.ca
Executive Director, Program & Service Design, Joel Kilbride
Tel: 306-787-3090; *Fax:* 306-787-1600
Joel.Kilbride@gov.sk.ca
Executive Director, Community Services, Mitch Tremblay
Tel: 306-787-9109; *Fax:* 306-787-0925
mitch.tremblay@gov.sk.ca
Acting Executive Director, Service Delivery, Isla Wilcox
Tel: 306-953-2624
tobie.eberhardt@gov.sk.ca
Director, Indigenous Services, Marcel St. Onge
Tel: 306-933-6050; *Fax:* 306-933-5887
marcel.st.onge@gov.sk.ca

Disability Programs
Tel: 306-798-0660
Toll-Free: 866-221-5200
Assistant Deputy Minister, Louise Michaud
Tel: 306-787-3450; *Fax:* 306-787-1032
louise.michaud@gov.sk.ca
Executive Director, Community Living Service Delivery (CLSD), Bob Martinook
Tel: 306-787-1348; *Fax:* 306-798-4450
bob.martinook@gov.sk.ca
Executive Director, Program & Service Design, Sterling Snider
Sterling.Snider@gov.sk.ca
Executive Director, Office of Disability Issues, Daryl Stubel
Tel: 306-787-3670
daryl.stubel@gov.sk.ca

Housing Programs
Tel: 306-787-4177; *Fax:* 306-798-3110
Toll-Free: 800-667-7567

Executive Director, Governance & Innovation, Dianne Baird
Tel: 306-787-8569; *Fax:* 306-798-3110
dianne.baird@gov.sk.ca

Executive Director, Program & Service Design, Sean Burnett
Tel: 306-787-1998; *Fax:* 306-798-3110
sean.burnett@gov.sk.ca

Executive Director, Housing Operations, Roger Parenteau
Tel: 306-933-8464; *Fax:* 306-933-8411
roger.parenteau@gov.sk.ca

Income Assistance Programs

Fax: 306-798-4040
Toll-Free: 866-221-5200

Assistant Deputy Minister, Devon Exner
Tel: 306-787-1383; *Fax:* 306-787-1032
devon.exner@gov.sk.ca

Executive Director, Program & Service Design, Doris Morrow
Tel: 306-787-2165; *Fax:* 306-798-0743
doris.morrow2@gov.sk.ca

Executive Director, Income Assistance Service Delivery, Jeff Redekop
Tel: 306-787-9013; *Fax:* 306-798-4450
jeff.redekop@gov.sk.ca

Director, Program Effectiveness, Lynette Halvorsen
Tel: 306-787-7318; *Fax:* 306-798-0743
lynette.halvorsen@gov.sk.ca

Director, Program Design & Operational Policy, Tim Helfrich
Tel: 306-787-5061; *Fax:* 306-798-0743

Director, Operational Effectiveness, Sabrina Randall
Tel: 306-787-3261
Sabrina.Randall@gov.sk.ca

Saskatchewan Telecommunications (SaskTel)

2121 Saskatchewan Dr., Regina, SK S4P 3Y2
Toll-Free: 800-727-5835
corporate.comments@sasktel.sk.ca
www.sasktel.com
twitter.com/sasktel
www.facebook.com/SaskTel
www.linkedin.com/company/sasktel
www.youtube.com/sasktel

The provincial Crown Corporation delivers full service telecommunications to the people of Saskatchewan. Services are as follows: competitive voice, data, dial-up, & high speed internet; entertainment & multimedia services; security; web hosting; text & messaging services; & cellular & wireless data services.

Minister responsible, Hon. Don Morgan, Q.C.
Tel: 306-787-7339
cic.minister@gov.sk.ca

Chair, Grant Kook

Acting President & CEO, Doug Burnett
Tel: 306-777-2283
doug.burnett@sasktel.com

Chief Information Officer, Jim Dundas
Tel: 306-777-2327

Chief Financial Officer, Charlene Gavel
Tel: 306-777-3185

Vice-President, Business Sales & Solutions, David Ekstrand
Tel: 306-931-5915

Vice-President, Consumer Sales & Solutions, Keith Jeannot
Tel: 306-777-0363

Vice-President, Corporate Counsel & Regulatory Affairs, Doug Kosloski
Tel: 306-777-1900

Vice-President, Customer Services, Greg Meister
Tel: 306-931-6456

Director, Corporate Communications, Michelle Englot
Tel: 306-777-4476
michelle.englot@sasktel.com

Saskatchewan Trade & Export Development

#1000, 2103 - 11th Ave., Regina, SK S4P 3Z8
www.saskatchewan.ca/ted

Saskatchewan's Ministry of Trade & Export Development (formerly Economy) seeks to advance economic growth & opportunity in Saskatchewan by attracting investment & growing export markets.

Minister, Hon. Jeremy Harrison
Tel: 306-787-8687
Minister.TED@gov.sk.ca
Office of the Minister of Economy, Legislative Bldg.
#346, 2405 Legislative Dr.
Regina, SK S4S 0B3

Deputy Minister, Jodi Banks
Tel: 306-787-0306
Jodi.Banks@gov.sk.ca

Associated Agencies, Boards & Commissions:

• Surface Rights Board of Arbitration
#102, 113 - 2nd Ave. East
PO Box 1597
Kindersley, SK S0L 1S0
Tel: 306-463-5447; *Fax:* 306-463-5449
surfacerightsboard@gov.sk.ca

Governed by The Surface Rights Acquisition & Compensation Act, the Surface Rights Board of Arbitration is a last resort when an occupant or landowner & an oil, gas or potash operator are unable to reach an agreement.

Marketing & Communications

2103 - 11th Ave., 2nd Fl., Regina, SK S4P 3Z8
Executive Director, Tyler Lynch
Tel: 306-787-7967
tyler.lynch2@gov.sk.ca

Economic Development

2103 - 11th Ave., 4th Fl., Regina, SK S4P 3Z8
Tel: 306-787-0917; *Fax:* 306-787-7559

Assistant Deputy Minister, Kirk Westgard
Tel: 306-787-0370
Kirk.Westgard@gov.sk.ca

Director, Lead & Prospect Generation, Derek Burden
Tel: 306-787-2225; *Fax:* 306-787-7559
derek.burden@gov.sk.ca

Director, Planning, Bryan Dilling
Tel: 306-230-5374; *Fax:* 306-933-8244
bryan.dilling@gov.sk.ca

Director, Indigenous Economic Development, Matt Smith
Tel: 306-798-9679; *Fax:* 306-787-7559
matt.smith@gov.sk.ca

Strategic Policy & Competitiveness

2103 - 11th Ave., 4th Fl., Regina, SK S4P 3Z8
Fax: 306-787-7559

Assistant Deputy Minister, Cammy Colpitts
Tel: 306-787-0572
cammy.colpitts@gov.sk.ca

Executive Director, Strategic Policy & Planning, Kareen Holtby
Tel: 306-787-0950
kareen.holtby@gov.sk.ca

Executive Director, Trade Policy, Rob Swallow
Tel: 306-798-6098
rob.swallow@gov.sk.ca

Director, Financial Programs, Rene Descottes
Tel: 306-798-1277
rene.descottes3@gov.sk.ca

Director, Regulatory Modernization, Tracey McMurchy
Tel: 306-787-8865; *Fax:* 306-787-8865
tracey.mcmurchy2@gov.sk.ca

Tourism Saskatchewan

#189, 1621 Albert St., Regina, SK S4P 2S5
Tel: 306-787-9600; *Fax:* 306-787-6293
Toll-Free: 877-237-2273
travel.info@tourismsask.com
www.tourismsaskatchewan.com
twitter.com/Saskatchewan
www.facebook.com/TourismSaskatchewan
www.instagram.com/tourismsask

Tourism Saskatchewan is a Crown corporation responsible for promoting & developing tourism in the province of Saskatchewan. Tourism training opportunities are available through the Saskatchewan Tourism Education Council (STEC).

Chief Executive Officer, Jonathan Potts
Tel: 306-787-0570
jonathan.potts@tourismsask.com

Chief Financial Officer & Executive Director, Corporate Services, Kathy Rintoul
Tel: 306-787-1535
kathy.rintoul@tourismsask.com

Executive Director, Destination & Workforce Development, Tracy Breher
Tel: 306-933-5905
tracy.breher@tourismsask.com

Acting Executive Director, Marketing & Communications, Amy McInnis
Tel: 306-787-2199

Saskatchewan Water Corporation (SaskWater)

#200, 111 Fairford St. East, Moose Jaw, SK S6H 1C8
Fax: 306-694-3207
Toll-Free: 888-230-1111
communications@saskwater.com
www.saskwater.com

SaskWater, a provincial Crown corporation, is Saskatchewan's water utility service provider. Lines of business are as follows: supply of potable & non-potable water; treatment & management of wastewater; & certified operations & maintenance. SaskWater is responsible for designing, building, & operating transmission, regional, & stand-alone water supply & wastewater systems. All systems must meet regulatory requirements.

Minister responsible, Hon. Don Morgan, Q.C.

President, Doug Matthies
Tel: 306-694-3903
doug.matthies@saskwater.com

Vice-President, Corporate & Customer Service, Jacquie Gibney
Tel: 306-694-3916; *Fax:* 306-694-3207
jacquie.gibney@saskwater.com

Vice-President, Operations & Engineering Division, Eric Light
Tel: 306-694-3920
eric.light@saskwater.com

Saskatchewan Water Security Agency (WSA)

#400, 111 Fairford St. East, Moose Jaw, SK S6H 7X9
Tel: 306-694-3900; *Fax:* 306-694-3105
comm@wsask.ca
www.wsask.ca
Other Communication: Provincial Water Inquiry Line, Toll-Free:
866-727-5420
www.linkedin.com/company/water-security-agency-of-saskatche
wan

Saskatchewan Water Security Agency (formerly known as Saskatchewan Watershed Authority) was created in 2012 to coincide with the release of the 25 Year Saskatchewan Water Security Plan. The agency is a Crown corporation that is responsible for managing water resources in Saskatchewan, & to work to ensure reliable water supplies & safe drinking water sources.

The following regulations are administered by the Saskatchewan Watershed Authority: Conservation & Development; Drainage Control; Ground Water; & Reservoir Development Area.

Minister responsible, Hon. Fred Bradshaw

Acting President & CEO, Shawn Jaques
Tel: 306-694-3162; *Fax:* 306-787-0780
shawn.jaques@wsask.ca

Chief Engineer & Senior Vice-President, Technical Services, John Fahlman
Tel: 306-690-6515; *Fax:* 306-694-3944
john.fahlman@wsask.ca

Vice-President, Financial Services, Laurier Donais
Tel: 306-527-4406
laurier.donais@wsask.ca

Vice-President, Agriculture Services, Kevin France
Tel: 306-519-3552
kevin.france@wsask.ca

Executive Director, Communications, Patrick Boyle
Tel: 306-631-6997; *Fax:* 306-694-3105
patrick.boyle@wsask.ca

Acting Executive Director, Environmental & Municipal Management Services, Jeff Paterson
Tel: 306-531-6840
jeff.paterson@wsask.ca

Saskatchewan Workers' Compensation Board

#200, 1881 Scarth St., Regina, SK S4P 4L1
Tel: 306-787-4370; *Fax:* 306-787-4311
Toll-Free: 800-667-7590
webmaster@wcbsask.com
www.wcbsask.com
Other Communication: Injury Reports: 800-787-9288; Health
Care Provider Inquiries: internet_healthcare@wcbsask.com;
Appeal Fax: 306-787-1116
Secondary Address: 115 - 24th St. East
Saskatoon, SK S7K 1L5
twitter.com/saskwcb
www.facebook.com/SaskWCB
www.youtube.com/c/SaskWorkersCompensationBoard
The Saskatchewan's Workers' Compensation Board was created
by the following provincial legislation in Saskatchewan: the
Workers' Compensation Act 1979, General Regulations, &
Exclusion Regulations. The Board is an independent body that
administers a no-fault compensation system to protect
employers and workers against the result of work injuries. The
WCB provides financial protection, medical benefits, &
rehabilitation services to injured workers & their dependents in
cases of injury or death arising from, & in the course of,
employment.

Minister responsible, Hon. Don Morgan, Q.C.
Tel: 306-787-5353; *Fax:* 306-787-1232
jus.minister@gov.sk.ca

Chair, Gordon Dobrowolsky
Tel: 306-787-4379; *Fax:* 306-787-0213
GDobrowolsky@wcbsask.com

Chief Executive Officer, Phil Germain
Tel: 306-787-4441
pgermain@wcbsask.com

Chief Financial Officer, Crystal Nett
Tel: 306-787-0260
cnett@wcbsask.com

Vice-President, Transformation Program, Stuart
Cunningham
Tel: 306-787-4440
scunningham@wcbsask.com

Vice-President, Prevention & Employer Services, Kevin
Mooney
Tel: 306-787-1161
kmooney@wcbsask.com

Vice-President, Operations Executive, Jennifer
Norleen-Beltel
Tel: 306-787-4397
jnorleenbeitel@wcbsask.com

Government of the Yukon Territory

Seat of Government: PO Box 2703 Whitehorse, YT Y1A 2C6
Tel: 867-667-5811
Toll-Free: 800-661-0408
TTY: 867-393-7460
inquiry.desk@yukon.ca
yukon.ca
Other Communication: Alt. Phone: 867-667-5812
twitter.com/yukongov
www.facebook.com/yukongov
www.linkedin.com/company/yukon-government
www.youtube.com/user/yukongovernment
Yukon was created as a separate territory June 13, 1898. It has
an area of 474,712.68 sq km, & StatsCan's census in 2016
showed the population was 35,874.
A federally appointed Commissioner (similar to a provincial
Lieutenant-Governor) oversees federal interests in the territory,
but the day-to-day operation of the government rests with the
wholly elected executive council (cabinet). The territorial
legislature has power to make acts on generally all matters of a
local nature in the territory, including the imposition of local
taxes, property & civil rights & the administration of justice,
education & health & social services. Legislative powers vested
in the provinces but not available to the territory include control
of unoccupied Crown land, renewable & non-renewable
resources (except wildlife & sport fisheries) & the power to
amend the Yukon Act, a federal statute.

Office of the Commissioner of Yukon

Taylor House, 412 Main St., Whitehorse, YT Y1A 2B7
Tel: 867-667-5121
commissioner@yukon.ca
commissionerofyukon.ca
www.facebook.com/OfficeOfTheCommissionerOfYukon

The Yukon Territory is governed by a commissioner appointed
for a 5-year term by the federal government, a government
leader, an executive council functionaing as a cabinet, & a
legislative assembly. The Yukon Act provides for the
establishment of a commissioner & the elected legislative
assembly.

Commissioner of Yukon, Hon. Angélique Bernard

Office of the Premier

2071 - 2nd Ave., PO Box 2703 Whitehorse, YT Y1A 2C6
yukon.ca/en/office-premier
Premier Sandy Silver was first elected to the Yukon Legislative
Assembly in the general election for the 33rd Legislative
Assembly on October 11, 2011. He was re-elected in the general
election for the 34th Legislative Assembly on November 7, 2016,
& in the general election for the 35th Legislative Assembly on
April 12, 2021. In addition to his duties as Premier, he also
serves as Minister responsible for the Executive Council Office &
Minister of Finance.

**Premier, Yukon Territory; Leader, Yukon Liberal Party;
Minister of the Executive Council Office; Minister,
Finance,** Hon. Sandy Silver, Liberal
Tel: 867-393-7142
sandy.silver@yukon.ca

Principal Secretary, Jason Cunning
Tel: 867-393-7466
Jason.Cunning@yukon.ca

Chief of Staff, Jasmina Randhawa
Tel: 867-393-7007
Jasmina.Randhawa@yukon.ca

Executive Council

2071 - 2nd Ave., PO Box 2703 Whitehorse, YT Y1A 2C6
eco@yukon.ca
yukon.ca/en/premiers-team
The Executive Council of Yukon Territory is selected by the
Honourable Sandy Silver, Premier. Members of Yukon's cabinet
are members of the Yukon Liberal Party, following its victory in
the April 2021 general election.

**Premier; Leader, Yukon Liberal Party; Minister of the
Executive Council Office; Minister, Finance,** Hon. Sandy
Silver
Tel: 867-393-7142
sandy.silver@yukon.ca

**Deputy Premier; Minister, Justice; Minister, Health &
Social Services,** Hon. Tracy-Anne McPhee
Tel: 867-393-7488
Tracy.McPhee@yukon.ca

**Minister, Environment; Minister, Highways & Public
Works,** Hon. Nils Clarke
Tel: 867-333-1007
nils.clarke@yukon.ca

**Minister, Education; Minister Responsible, Women's
Directorate,** Hon. Jeanie McLean
Tel: 867-393-7494
Jeanie.McLean@yukon.ca

**Minister, Community Services; Minister Responsible,
Yukon Workers' Compensation Health & Safety Board,**
Hon. Richard Mostyn
Tel: 867-393-7482
Richard.Mostyn@yukon.ca

**Minister, Tourism & Culture; Minister, Economic
Development; Minister Responsible, Yukon Housing
Corporation; Yukon Liquor Corporation; Yukon Lottery
Commission,** Hon. Ranj Pillai
Tel: 867-393-7418
Ranj.Pillai@yukon.ca

**Minister, Energy, Mines & Resources; Minister, Public
Service Commission; Minister Responsible, Yukon
Development Corporation; Yukon Energy Corporation;
French Language Services Directorate,** Hon. John
Streicker
Tel: 867-393-7467
John.Streicker@yukon.ca

Executive Council Office

2071 - 2nd Ave., Whitehorse, YT Y1A 2C6
Premier; Minister, Hon. Sandy Silver
Tel: 867-393-7142
sandy.silver@yukon.ca

Deputy Minister, Stephen Mills
Tel: 867-667-8609
Stephen.Mills@yukon.ca
Assistant Deputy Minister, Strategic Corporate Services, Jeff
Ford
Tel: 867-667-8081
Jeff.Ford@yukon.ca
Assistant Deputy Minister, Aboriginal Relations, Brian
MacDonald
Tel: 867-667-8127
Brian.MacDonald@yukon.ca

Government Inquiry Office

**Government of Yukon Administration Bldg., 2071 - 2nd Ave.,
PO Box 2703 Whitehorse, YT Y1A 2C6**
Tel: 867-393-6930
Toll-Free: 800-661-0408
inquiry.desk@yukon.ca
yukon.ca/en/contact-government
Other Communication: Alternate Phone: 867-393-6931

Yukon Legislative Assembly

2071 - 2nd Ave., PO Box 2703 Whitehorse, YT Y1A 2C6
Tel: 867-667-5498
yla@yukon.ca
yukonassembly.ca

Speaker, Hon. Jeremy Harper
Tel: 867-667-5800
Jeremy.Harper@yukon.ca

Deputy Speaker; Chair, Committee of the Whole, Annie
Blake
Tel: 867-393-7050
Annie.Blake@yla.gov.yk.ca

Clerk (Deputy Minister), Dan Cable
Tel: 867-667-5498
Dan.Cable@yukon.ca

Deputy Clerk, Linda Kolody
Tel: 867-667-5499
Linda.Kolody@yukon.ca

Clerk of Committees, Allison Lloyd
Tel: 867-667-5494
Allison.Lloyd@yukon.ca

Government Caucus Office (Liberal Party)

108 Elliott St., PO Box 183 Whitehorse, YT Y1A 6C4
Tel: 867-668-7677
info@ylp.ca
www.ylp.ca
twitter.com/YukonLiberal
www.facebook.com/yukonliberals
Hon. Mr. Silver has been leader of the Yukon Liberal Party since
February 2014. He was Leader of the Third Party in the
Legislative Assembly from August 17, 2012 to the end of the
33rd Legislative Assembly. Hon. Mr. Silver's appointment as
Premier took effect on December 3, 2016.
Leader, Yukon Liberal Party; Premier, Yukon Territory, Hon.
Sandy Silver
Tel: 867-393-7142
sandy.silver@yukon.ca
Government House Leader, Hon. Tracy-Anne McPhee
Tel: 867-393-7488
Tracy.McPhee@yukon.ca
President, Vacant
president@ylp.ca

Office of the Official Opposition (Yukon Party)

PO Box 31113 Whitehorse, YT Y1A 5P7
Tel: 867-668-6505
info@yukonparty.ca
www.yukonparty.ca
twitter.com/yukonparty
www.facebook.com/YukonParty
www.instagram.com/yukonparty
Yukon's Liberal Party won a majority government in the
November 2016 election, moving the Yukon Party to opposition
status. Since May 2020, Currie Dixon has been Lead of the
Yukon Party.
Leader, Official Opposition; Leader, Yukon Party, Currie Dixon
Official Opposition House Leader, Scott Kent
Tel: 867-393-7104; *Fax:* 867-393-6982
scott.kent@yla.gov.yk.ca

Office of the Leader of the Third Party (New Democratic Party)
PO Box 31516 Whitehorse, YT Y1A 6K8

Tel: 867-668-2203
yukon@ndp.ca
www.yukonndp.ca
twitter.com/YukonNDP
www.facebook.com/YukonNDP

Kate White has been leader of the Yukon New Democratic Party, the current official Third Party, since May 2019.

Leader, Yukon New Democratic Party; House Leader, Third Party, Kate White
Tel: 867-393-7001; *Fax:* 867-393-6499
kate.white@yla.gov.yk.ca

Standing Committees of the Yukon Legislative Assembly
yukonassembly.ca/committees

The following are the Standing Committees of the Yukon Legislative Assembly: Members' Services Board; Public Accounts; Rules, Elections & Privileges; Statuatory Instruments; & Appointments to Major Government Boards & Committees.

Clerk of Committees, Allison Lloyd
Tel: 867-667-5494
Allison.Lloyd@yukon.ca

Chair, Members' Services Board, Hon. Jeremy Harper
Constituency: Riverdale North, Liberal

Chair, Public Accounts Committee, Hon. Currie Dixon
Constituency: Pelly-Nisutlin, Yukon Party

Chair, Rules, Elections & Privileges Committee, Hon. Richard Mostyn
Constituency: Porter Creek Centre, Liberal

Chair, Statutory Instruments Committee, Vacant
Constituency: Copperbelt North, Liberal

Chair, Appointments to Major Government Boards & Committees, Hon. Nils Clarke
Constituency: Copperbelt North, Liberal

Thirty-fifth Legislative Assembly - Yukon Territory

Yukon Legislative Assembly Office, 2071 - 2nd Ave., PO Box 2703 Whitehorse, YT Y1A 2C6

yukonassembly.ca

Last General Election: April 12, 2021.
Next General Election: 2025.
Party Standings (Oct. 2021):
Liberal Party 8;
Yukon Party 8;
New Democratic Party 3;
Total Seats 19.
Salaries, Indemnities, & Allowances (2021):
Members' indemnity $82,130, plus $20,527 expense allowances for both Whitehorse & rural members;
Ministers $44,224;
Premier $66,282;
Leader of the Opposition $44,224;
Leader of the Third Party $21,967;
Speaker $41,076;
Deputy Speaker $16,405.
Members of the 35th Legislative Assembly are listed with their constituency, number of electors on the list for the most recent election, party affiliation, & contact information. The address for all Members of the Yukon Legislative Assembly is as follows: PO Box 2703, Whitehorse, YT, Y1A 2C6.

Members of the Legislative Assembly of Yukon Territory

Deputy Speaker; Chair, Committee of the Whole, Annie Blake
Constituency: Vuntut Gwitchin *No. of Constituents:* 156, New Democratic Party
Tel: 867-393-7050; *Fax:* 867-393-6499
Annie.Blake@yla.gov.yk.ca

Official Opposition Deputy House Leader, Brad Cathers
Constituency: Lake Laberge *No. of Constituents:* 1,277, Yukon Party
Tel: 867-669-8625; *Fax:* 867-393-6982
brad.cathers@yla.gov.yk.ca

Minister, Highways & Public Works; Minister, Environment, Hon. Nils Clarke
Constituency: Riverdale North *No. of Constituents:* 1,124, Liberal
Tel: 867-333-1007; *Fax:* 867-393-7135
nils.clarke@yukon.ca

Yvonne Clarke
Constituency: Porter Creek Centre *No. of Constituents:* 1,681, Liberal
Tel: 867-393-7104; *Fax:* 867-393-6982
Yvonne.Clarke@yla.gov.yk.ca

Leader, Yukon Party; Leader, Official Opposition, Currie Dixon
Constituency: Copperbelt North *No. of Constituents:* 1,381, Yukon Party
Tel: 867-393-7104; *Fax:* 867-393-6982
Currie.Dixon@yla.gov.yk.ca

Stacey Hassard
Constituency: Pelly-Nisutlin *No. of Constituents:* 713, Yukon Party
Tel: 867-393-7104; *Fax:* 867-393-6982
Stacey.Hassard@yla.gov.yk.ca

Speaker, Hon. Jeremy Harper
Constituency: Mayo-Tatchun *No. of Constituents:* 632, Liberal
Tel: 867-667-5800; *Fax:* 867-393-7135
Jeremy.Harper@yukon.ca

Wade Istchenko
Constituency: Kluane *No. of Constituents:* 782, Yukon Party
Tel: 867-393-7104; *Fax:* 867-393-6982
wade.istchenko@yla.gov.yk.ca

House Leader, Official Opposition, Scott Kent
Constituency: Copperbelt South *No. of Constituents:* 1,274, Yukon Party
Tel: 867-393-7104; *Fax:* 867-393-6982
scott.kent@yla.gov.yk.ca

Minister, Education; Minister Responsible, Women's Directorate, Hon. Jeanie McLean
Constituency: Mountainview *No. of Constituents:* 1,052, Liberal
Tel: 867-393-7494; *Fax:* 867-393-7135
jeanie.mclean@yukon.ca

Patti McLeod
Constituency: Watson Lake *No. of Constituents:* 550, Yukon Party
Tel: 867-393-7104; *Fax:* 867-393-6982
patti.mcleod@yla.gov.yk.ca

Deputy Premier; House Leader, Government; Minister, Justice; Minister, Health & Social Services, Hon. Tracy-Anne McPhee
Constituency: Riverdale South *No. of Constituents:* 1,056, Liberal
Tel: 867-393-7488; *Fax:* 867-393-7135
tracy.mcphee@yukon.ca

Minister, Community Services; Minister Responsible, Workers' Compensation Health & Safety Board, Hon. Richard Mostyn
Constituency: Whitehorse West *No. of Constituents:* 1,003, Liberal
Tel: 867-393-7482; *Fax:* 867-393-7135
richard.mostyn@yukon.ca

Minister, Tourism & Culture; Minister, Economic Development; Minister Responsible, Yukon Housing Corporation; Yukon Liquor Corporation; Yukon Lottery Commission, Hon. Ranj Pillai
Constituency: Porter Creek South *No. of Constituents:* 655, Liberal
Tel: 867-393-7418; *Fax:* 867-393-7135
ranj.pillai@yukon.ca

Premier, Yukon Territory; Leader, Yukon Liberal Party; Minister of the Executive Council Office; Minister, Finance, Hon. Sandy Silver
Constituency: Klondike *No. of Constituents:* 1,114, Liberal
Tel: 867-393-7142; *Fax:* 867-393-7135
sandy.silver@yukon.ca

Minister, Energy, Mines & Resources; Public Service Commission; Minister Responsible, Yukon Development Corporation; Yukon Energy Corporation; French Language Services Directorate, Hon. John Streicker
Constituency: Mount Lorne - Southern Lakes *No. of Constituents:* 1,144, Liberal
Tel: 867-393-7467; *Fax:* 867-393-7135
john.streicker@yukon.ca

Deputy Chair, Committee of the Whole; House Leader, Third Party, Emily Tredger
Constituency: Whitehorse Centre *No. of Constituents:* 1,059, New Democratic Party
Tel: 867-393-7050; *Fax:* 867-393-6499
Emily.Tredger@yla.gov.yk.ca

Geraldine Van Bibber
Constituency: Porter Creek North *No. of Constituents:* 1,143, Yukon Party
Tel: 867-393-7104; *Fax:* 867-393-6982
geraldine.vanbibber@yla.gov.yk.ca

Leader, Yukon New Democratic Party, Kate White
Constituency: Takhini - Kopper King *No. of Constituents:* 1,205, New Democratic Party
Tel: 867-393-7001; *Fax:* 867-393-6499
kate.white@yla.gov.yk.ca

Yukon Territory Government Departments & Agencies

Yukon Child & Youth Advocate Office

#19, 2070 Second Ave., Whitehorse, YT Y1A 1B1
Tel: 867-456-5575; *Fax:* 867-456-5574
Toll-Free: 800-661-0408
info@ycao.ca
www.ycao.ca
twitter.com/ytycao
www.facebook.com/ytycao

Yukon Child & Youth Advocate, Annette King
annette.king@ycao.ca

Deputy Child & Youth Advocate, Bengie Clethero
bengie.clethero@ycao.ca

Yukon Community Services

PO Box 2703 Whitehorse, YT Y1A 2C6
Tel: 867-667-5811; *Fax:* 867-393-6295
Toll-Free: 800-661-0408
TTY: 867-393-7460
yukon.ca/en/department-community-services
twitter.com/CSYukon

The main purpose of the department is to serve Yukoners & their communities by providing access to services to strengthen communities. The department focuses on community affairs & municipal relations within government on behalf of Yukon communities & acts as a liaison between community groups & government departments.

Minister, Hon. Richard Mostyn
richard.mostyn@yukon.ca

Deputy Minister, Matt King
Tel: 867-456-6512
Matt.King@yukon.ca

Director, Communications, Aisha Montgomery
Tel: 867-456-6580
Aisha.Montgomery@yukon.ca

Associated Agencies, Boards & Commissions:

• Assessment Appeal Board
PO Box 2703
Whitehorse, YT Y1A 2C6
Tel: 867-667-5268; *Fax:* 867-667-8276

• Assessment Review Boards
PO Box 2703
Whitehorse, YT Y1A 2C6
Tel: 867-667-5268; *Fax:* 867-667-8276
Responsible for Central, Centraleast, North, Southeast & Southwest regions.

• Building Standards Board
Tel: 867-667-5445

• Council for the Association of Professional Engineers of Yukon
Tel: 867-667-6727; *Fax:* 867-668-2142

• Electrical Safety Standards Board
Tel: 867-456-6596

• Employment Standards Board
Tel: 687-667-5944
Toll-free: 800-661-0408

• Licensed Practical Nurses Advisory Committee
Tel: 867-332-7295
Toll-free: 800-661-0408

• Licensed Practical Nurses Discipline Panel
Tel: 867-332-7295
Toll-free: 800-661-0408

• Physiotherapists Advisory Committee
Tel: 867-332-7295
Toll-free: 800-661-0408

• Private Investigators & Security Agencies Review Board
Tel: 867-332-7295
Toll-free: 800-661-0408

• Registered Psychiatric Nurses Advisory Committee
Tel: 867-332-7295
Toll-free: 800-661-0408

• Whitehorse Public Library Board
Tel: 867-667-8062; *Fax:* 867-393-6333
Toll-free: 800-661-0408
whitehorse.library@yukon.ca

• Yukon Lottery Appeal Board
Tel: 867-332-7295
Other Communication: Toll-Free Phone: 800-661-0408, ext. 5111

• Yukon Medical Council
Tel: 867-667-3774; *Fax:* 867-393-6483
ymc@yukon.ca

• Yukon Municipal Board
Tel: 867-334-7472

• Yukon Recreaction Advisory Committee
Tel: 867-667-5254; *Fax:* 867-393-6416
sportrec@yukon.ca

Community Development Division
Fax: 867-393-6258

The branch assists, advises & organizes municipal & unincorporated communities, provides funding by administering

the comprehensive municipal grants & grants in lieu of taxes, assesses properties, collects property taxes & administers the Rural Electrification & Telecommunication program & the Home Owner Grant program. The branch collaborates with communities for the planning, design, & construction of land development projects & includes residential, rural residential, commercial, industrial, & cottage lots. The branch is responsible for regulatory approvals & design, managing construction capital works projects, such as upgrading roads, water & sewage treatment facilities & solid waste disposal sites & assists communities in developing land use plans, working closely with the Yukon Municipal Board & the Association of Yukon Communities. The branch is responsible for the operation of Yukon Government owned facilities for water supply & distribution, sewage treatment & solid waste disposal.
Assistant Deputy Minister, Andrea Buckley
 Tel: 867-667-3534
 Andrea.Buckley@yukon.ca
Director, Operations & Programs, Dave Albisser
 Tel: 867-667-6191
 Dave.Albisser@yukon.ca
Acting Director, Sport & Recreation Branch, Marie Cairns
 Tel: 867-667-5608
 Marie.Cairns@yukon.ca
Director, Infrastructure Development, Mark Roberts
 Mark.Roberts@yukon.ca
Director, Public Libraries, Melissa Yu Schott
 Tel: 867-335-8600
 Melissa.YuSchott@yukon.ca

Corporate Policy & Consumer Affairs Division
Berska Bldg., 307 Black St., 2nd Fl., Whitehorse, YT Y1A 2N1
Assistant Deputy Minister, Vacant
Director, Professional Licensing & Regulatory Affairs, Stephanie Connolly
 Tel: 867-667-5257
 Stephanie.Connolly@yukon.ca
Director, Property Assessment & Taxation Branch, Kelly Eby
 Tel: 867-667-5234
 Kelly.Eby@yukon.ca
Director, Employment Standards & Residential Tenancies, Jaime Mellott
 Tel: 867-667-5944
 Jaime.Mellott@yukon.ca
Director, Corporate Affairs, Fred Pretorius
 Tel: 867-667-5225
 Fred.Pretorius@yukon.ca

Protective Services
91788 Alaska Hwy., Whitehorse, YT Y1A 5X7
 Fax: 867-456-6589
Assistant Deputy Minister, Damien Burns
 Tel: 867-667-5717
 Damien.Burns@yukon.ca
Chief Mechanical Inspector, Blair Rawlings
 Tel: 867-667-5765
 Blair.Rawlings@yukon.ca
Chief Mechanical Inspector, Michael Smith
 Tel: 867-456-3975
 Michael.Smith@yukon.ca
Acting Director, Building Safety Standards Branch, Hector Lang
 Tel: 867-456-6596
 Hector.Lang@yukon.ca

Emergency Measures Organization (EMO)
 Tel: 867-667-5220; Fax: 867-393-6266
 emo.yukon@yukon.ca
 Other Communication: Toll-Free Phone: 800-661-0408, ext. 5220
Responsible for coordinating the Territory's preparedness for, response to, & recovery from, major emergencies & disasters. EMO provides authority to ensure that contingency plans are in place to deal with foreseeable risks & hazards. The EMO is divided into 13 geographical preparedness areas, mirroring the RCMP detachment boundaries. Eight of these areas have incorporated Municipalities that have appointed a Municipal EMO Coordinator to chair the local Emergency Planning Committee. In the remaining areas, the Emergency Measures Branch appoints a co-ordinator.

Emergency Medical Services (EMS)
 Tel: 867-456-3943
Director, Gerard Dinn
 Tel: 867-456-6591
 Gerard.Dinn@yukon.ca

Fire & Life Safety / Fire Marshal's Office
91790 Alaska Hwy., PO Box 2703 C-20 Whitehorse, YT Y1A 2C6
 Tel: 867-456-6517
 CS.FMO@yukon.ca
The Fire Marshal's Office works to reduce the loss of life & property due to fire & is responsible for public education & fire fighter training, as well as for funding & administering volunteer

fire departments in Yukon unincorporated communities. Staff carry out fire & life safety inspections on hotels, motels, public assembly buildings, schools, day care centers, homes for special care, restaurants, etc. throughout Yukon. The Office inspects & permits underground fuel storage tank installations.
Director, Fire & Life Safety, Diarmuid O'Donovan
 Tel: 867-667-5220
 Diarmuid.O'Donovan@yukon.ca

Wildland Fire Management
91790 Alaska Hwy., Whitehorse, YT Y1A 5X7
 Tel: 867-456-3845
 Other Communication: Toll-Free Phone: 800-661-0408, ext. 3845
Director, Wildland Fire Management, Lisa Walker
 Tel: 867-332-3037
 Lisa.Walker@yukon.ca

Yukon Development Corporation (YDC)
#234, 2180 - 2nd Ave., Whitehorse, YT Y1A 5N6
 Tel: 867-456-3995
 ydc-admin@yukon.ca
 yukon.ca/en/yukon-development-corporation
The YDC assists with implementation of energy policies from the Department of Energy, Mines & Resources, by designing & delivering related energy programs. It facilitates the generation, production, transmission & distribution of energy in a manner consistent with sustainable development. YDC has investments in electricity & related energy infrastructure & acts as the primary vehicle for delivery of territorial energy programs & services. YDC owns two subsidiary corporations, Yukon Energy Corporation, YEC, & the Energy Solutions Centre Inc., ESC. YEC is the primary producer & transmitter of electrical energy in the territory & operates under the Yukon Utilities Board & the Public Utilities Act. ESC provides technical services, promotes efficiency & renewable energy technologies, co-ordinates & delivers federal & territorial energy programs to households, businesses, institutions, First Nation & public governments.

 Minister responsible, Hon. John Streicker
 john.streicker@yukon.ca

 Chair, Mike Pemberton

 President & CEO, Justin Ferbey
 Tel: 867-393-7191
 Justin.Ferbey@ydc.yk.ca

 Corporate Secretary, Allyn Walton
 Allyn.Walton@yukon.ca

Yukon Energy Corporation
2 Miles Canyon Rd., PO Box 5920 Whitehorse, YT Y1A 6S7
 Tel: 867-393-5300
 Toll-Free: 866-926-3749
 communications@yec.yk.ca
 yukonenergy.ca
 Other Communication: Public & Community Relations, Phone: 867-393-5333; Business Development, Phone: 867-393-5398
 twitter.com/yukonenergy
 www.facebook.com/yukonenergy
 www.youtube.com/user/yukonsenergyfuture
The YEC distributes electricity to wholesale & industrial customers. YEC acts in an environmentally responsible manner while developing & maintaining energy infrastructure & services consistent with the principles of sustainable development. Sources of energy include solar power, wind power, geo-thermal power, hydro power & diesel power. YEC is also involved in fish ladder & hatchery.
Minister responsible, Hon. John Streicker
 john.streicker@yukon.ca
President & CEO, Andrew Hall

Yukon Economic Development
303 Alexander St., Whitehorse, YT Y1A 2L5
 Toll-Free: 800-661-0408
 ecdev@yukon.ca
 yukon.ca/en/department-of-economic-development
The Department works with the Yukon business community & with other governments to support business development, trade & investment opportunities, & partnerships for the development of the Yukon economy. It co-ordinates & facilitates the Yukon Government's economic development agenda. The Department is focused on creating a positive business climate in Yukon & is committed to First Nation business development in the territory.

 Minister, Hon. Ranj Pillai
 ranjpillai@yukon.ca

 Deputy Minister, Justin Ferbey
 Tel: 867-393-7191
 Justin.Ferbey@ydc.yk.ca

Assistant Deputy Minister, Operations, Helen Booth
 Tel: 867-667-8416
 Helen.Booth@yukon.ca

Director, Human Resources, Charmaine Cheung
 Tel: 867-667-8838
 Charmaine.Cheung@yukon.ca

Acting Director, Business & Industry Development, Lise Farynowski
 Tel: 867-667-3430
 Lise.Farynowski@yukon.ca

Director, Finance & Information Management Branch, Beth Fricke
 Tel: 867-667-5933
 Beth.Fricke@yukon.ca

Director, Technology & Innovation, Candy Poon
 Tel: 867-667-8073
 Candy.Poon@yukon.ca

Associated Agencies, Boards & Commissions:
• Business Incentive Review Committee
 Tel: 867-393-7014; Fax: 867-393-6944
 bip.office@yukon.ca
 Other Communication: Toll-Free Phone: 800-661-0408, ext. 7014

Yukon Education
1000 Lewes Blvd., Whitehorse, YT Y1A 3H9
 Tel: 867-667-5141; Fax: 867-393-6254
 edu-communications@yukon.ca
 yukon.ca/en/department-education
 Other Communication: Toll-Free Phone: 800-661-0408, ext. 5141
The Yukon has 28 public schools (14 in Whitehorse, 14 in other communities) & two private schools. The public schools are administered directly by the Department of Education, although elected school council officials are gradually assuming more powers under the 1990 Education Act, & may evolve into school boards in the near future. In 1996, the Yukon Francophone School Board was created, becoming Yukon's first school board. Curriculum is largely based on that of British Columbia, with flexibility for locally developed courses, particularly from a First Nations perspective (approximately one-third of the Yukon's students are of First Nations ancestry). Instruction is English-based for the majority of students. French & Indigenous languages are widely offered as second language instruction. French Immersion & French First Language education is offered in Whitehorse.

 Minister, Hon. Jeanie McLean
 Jeanie.McLean@yukon.ca

 Deputy Minister, Nicole Morgan
 Tel: 867-667-5126
 Nicole.Morgan@yukon.ca

 Director, Human Resources, Stephanie Boyle
 Tel: 867-471-0906
 Stephanie.Boyle@yukon.ca

 Director, Finance, Systems & Administration, Jackie McBride-Dickson
 Tel: 867-333-6376
 Jackie.McBride-Dickson@yukon.ca

Associated Agencies, Boards & Commissions:
• Apprentice Advisory Board
 Tel: 867-667-5141; Fax: 867-667-8555
• Education Appeal Tribunal
 Tel: 867-667-5900; Fax: 867-393-3904
 registrar@yeat.ca
• Students Financial Assistance Committee
 Tel: 867-667-5141; Fax: 867-667-8555
 Toll-free: 800-661-0408
• Teacher Certification Board
 Tel: 867-667-8631
• Teacher Qualification Board
 Tel: 867-456-5598; Fax: 867-667-5435
 Toll-free: 800-661-0408

• Teacher Profession Appeal Board
• **Yukon University Board of Governors**
500 University Dr.
PO Box 2799
Whitehorse, YT Y1A 5K4
Tel: 867-668-8800
Toll-free: 800-661-0504
www.yukonu.ca

First Nation Initiatives

Tel: 867-456-6752; *Fax:* 867-393-6339
Other Communication: Toll-Free Phone: 800-661-0408, ext.
6752
Assistant Deputy Minister, Lori Duncan
Lori.Duncan@yukon.ca
Coordinator, First Nation Programs & Partnerships, Danielle
Sheldon
Tel: 867-332-0647
Danielle.Sheldon@yukon.ca

Policy & Partnerships

Assistant Deputy Minister, Kelli Taylor
Tel: 867-456-6787
Kelli.Taylor@yukon.ca
Executive Director, Commission Scolaire Francophone du
Yukon, Marc Champagne
Tel: 867-667-8680
Marc.Champagne@yukon.ca
Director, Training Programs, Suzan Davy
Tel: 867-667-5129
Suzan.Davy@yukon.ca
Director, Performance & Analytics, Gabriel Stetkiewicz
Tel: 867-333-0105
Gabriel.Stetkiewicz@yukon.ca
Director, Curriculum & Assessment, Paula Thompson
Tel: 867-456-5545
Paula.Thompson@yukon.ca

Schools & Student Services

Tel: 867-667-5906
edu-pslm@yukon.ca
yukon.ca/en/department-education
Other Communication: Toll-Free Phone: 800-661-0408, ext.
5906
Assistant Deputy Minister, Shawn Kitchen
Tel: 867-667-5129
Shawn.Kitchen@yukon.ca
Director, Student Support Services, Karen Campbell
Tel: 867-667-5986
Karen.Campbell@yukon.ca
Director, Operations, Chris Hanlin
Tel: 867-667-3483
Chris.Hanlin@yukon.ca
Director, Information Technology & Support Services, Tony
Vivone
Tel: 867-667-3717
Tony.Vivone@yukon.ca
Superintendent, Area 1, Paul McFadyen
Paul.McFadyen@yukon.ca
Superintendent, Area 2, Penny Prysnuk
Tel: 867-667-3747
Penny.Prysnuk@yukon.ca
Superintendent, Area 3, Kim Ramsay
Kim.Ramsay@yukon.ca

Elections Yukon

**Yukon Government Bldg., PO Box 2703 Whitehorse, YT Y1A
2C6**
Tel: 867-667-8683; *Fax:* 867-393-6977
Toll-Free: 866-668-8683
info@electionsyukon.ca
electionsyk.ca
twitter.com/ElectionsYukon
www.facebook.com/ElectionsYukon
www.instagram.com/electionsyt
Elections Yukon is responsible for the administration of elections
of members to the Yukon Legislative Assembly.

Chief Electoral Officer, H. Maxwell Harvey
Maxwell.Harvey@electionsyukon.ca

Yukon Energy, Mines & Resources (EMR)

PO Box 2703 Whitehorse, YT Y1A 2C6
Tel: 867-667-3123; *Fax:* 867-393-7421
Toll-Free: 800-661-0408
emr@yukon.ca
yukon.ca/en/department-energy-mines-resources
twitter.com/EMRYukon
The territory has extensive mineral deposits, oil & gas potential,
with two producing gas wells, which rank among the top
producing wells in Canada, forest reserves & local

manufacturing of wood products, such as furniture, wood
laminate stock & lumber. The territory has abundant & diverse
energy resources due to the presence of fossil fuel reserves,
numerous lakes & rivers, windy & mountainous terrain, broad
forest cover & sunny conditions. The Yukon is one of the few
places left in Canada where Crown land can be obtained for
agricultural purposes.

Minister, Hon. John Streicker
john.streicker@yukon.ca

Deputy Minister, John Bailey
Tel: 867-456-3837
John.Bailey@yukon.ca

**Acting Assistant Deputy Minister, Client Services &
Partnerships,** Lyle Dinn
Tel: 867-667-5636
Lyle.Dinn@yukon.ca

Director, Human Resources, Jim Brown
Tel: 867-667-3549
Jim.Brown@yukon.ca

Director, Corporate Services, Ross McLachlan
Tel: 867-456-3960
Ross.McLachlan@yukon.ca

Director, Strategic Alliances, Nathan Millar
Tel: 867-456-3807
Nathan.Millar@yukon.ca

Director, Compliance Monitoring & Inspection, Briar
Young
Tel: 867-667-3136
Briar.Young@yukon.ca

Associated Agencies, Boards & Commissions:

• **Agriculture Industry Advisory Committee**
Tel: 867-667-5838; *Fax:* 867-393-6222
• **Regional Land Use Planning Commissions**
#201, 307 Jarvis St.
Whitehorse, YT Y1A 2H3
Tel: 867-667-7397; *Fax:* 867-667-4624
planyukon.ca
• **Yukon Land Use Planning Council**
#201, 307 Jarvis St.
Whitehorse, YT Y1A 2H3
Tel: 867-667-7397; *Fax:* 867-667-4624
planyukon.ca
• **Yukon Minerals Advisory Board**
Tel: 867-633-7952; *Fax:* 867-456-3899
mining@yukon.ca

Energy, Corporate Policy & Communications

Assistant Deputy Minister, Shirley Abercrombie
Tel: 867-667-5496
Shirley.Abercrombie@yukon.ca
Director, Communications, Jesse Devost
Tel: 867-667-5307
Jesse.Devost@yukon.ca

Oil, Gas & Mineral Resources

Tel: 867-667-5026
oilandgas@yukon.ca
Other Communication: Toll-Free Phone: 800-661-0408, ext.
5026
Assistant Deputy Minister, Stephen Mead
Tel: 867-332-5512
Stephen.Mead@yukon.ca
Director, Oil & Gas Resources, Derek Fraser
Tel: 867-667-5026
Derek.Fraser@yukon.ca
Director, Assessment & Abandoned Mines, Heather Mills
Heather.Mills@yukon.ca
Director, Mineral Resources, Todd Powell
Tel: 867-667-3126
Todd.Powell@yukon.ca

Yukon Geological Survey

Tel: 867-455-2808; *Fax:* 867-667-3198
geology@yukon.ca
yukon.ca/en/science-and-natural-resources/geology
Other Communication: Toll-Free Phone: 800-661-0408, ext.
2808
www.facebook.com/YukonGeologicalSurvey
Director, Carolyn Relf
Tel: 867-667-8892
Carolyn.Relf@yukon.ca

Sustainable Resources

Assistant Deputy Minister, Ed van Randen
Tel: 867-456-3827
Ed.vanRanden@yukon.ca
Director, Land Management, Matt Ball
Tel: 867-393-6334
Matt.Ball@yukon.ca
Director, Land Planning, Jerome McIntyre
Tel: 867-667-3530
Jerome.McIntyre@yukon.ca
Director, Agriculture, Bobbie Milnes
Tel: 867-667-5287
Bobbie.Milnes@yukon.ca

Yukon Environment

10 Burns Rd., Whitehorse, YT Y1A 2C6
Tel: 867-667-5652; *Fax:* 867-393-7197
environmentyukon@yukon.ca
yukon.ca/en/department-environment
Other Communication: Toll-Free Phone: 800-661-0408, ext.
5652
twitter.com/ENV_Yukon
www.youtube.com/user/environmentyukon
The department is responsible for legislation, regulations
licensing, management, policies, programs, services, education
& information regarding the natural environment in three
program areas: fish & wildlife, environmental protection &
assessment & parks & protection areas. The department's
branches educate resource users & the general public, develop
& enforce policies, regulations, & legislation & assist other
departments in the sustainable use & management of the
territory's natural resources. The department supports land
claims negotiations & assists in implementing land claims
agreements. The department represents the Yukon government
at national & global environmental forums on issues such as
climate change & biodiversity conservation. Through the
Environmental Awareness Fund the government provides
funding to assist registered non-government organizations to
promote environmental education or awareness, resource
planning & sustainable development in the Yukon.

Minister, Hon. Nils Clarke
nils.clarke@yukon.ca

Deputy Minister, Manon Moreau
Manon.Moreau@yukon.ca

Associated Agencies, Boards & Commissions:

• **Alsek Renewable Resources Council (ARRC)**
PO Box 2077
Haines Junction, YT Y0B 1L0
Tel: 867-634-2524; *Fax:* 867-634-2527
admin@alsekrrc.ca
www.alsekrrc.ca
Renewable Resource Councils provide a voice for local
community members in managing renewable resources, such as
fish, wildlife & forests. The ARRC was formed in 1995 with the
signing of the Champagne & Aishihik First Nations (CAFN) Final
Agreement.

• **Carcross / Tagish Renewable Resources Council (CTRRC)**
PO Box 70
Tagish, YT Y0B 1T0
Tel: 867-399-4923; *Fax:* 867-399-4978
carcrosstagishrrc@gmail.com
yfwmb.ca/renewable-resource-councils/carcrosstagish
• **Carmacks Renewable Resource Council (CRRC)**
PO Box 122
Carmacks, YT Y0B 1C0
Tel: 867-863-6838; *Fax:* 867-863-6429
carmacksrrc@northwestel.net
yfwmb.ca/renewable-resource-councils/carmacks
• **Concession & Compensation Review Board**
Tel: 867-667-5336; *Fax:* 867-393-6213
The Board makes recommendations to the Minister concerning
the issuance, revocation, cancellation or suspension of outfitting
& trapping concession.
• **Dän Keyi Renewable Resource Council (DKRRC)**
PO Box 50
Burwash Landing, YT Y0B 1V0
Tel: 867-841-5820; *Fax:* 867-841-5821
dankeyirrc@northwestel.net
yfwmb.ca/renewable-resource-councils/dankeyi
• **Dawson District Renewable Resource Council (DDRRC)**
PO Box 1380
Dawson City, YT Y0B 1G0
Tel: 867-993-6976; *Fax:* 867-993-6093
dawsonrrc@northwestel.net
yfwmb.ca/renewable-resource-councils/dawson

• Laberge Renewable Resource Council (LRRC)
3A Glacier Rd.
Whitehorse, YT Y1A 5S7
Tel: 867-393-3940
labergerrc@northwestel.net
yfwmb.ca/renewable-resource-councils/laberge

• Mackenzie River Basin Board
Tel: 780-217-4832
ec.cbm-mrbb.ec@ec.gc.ca
www.mrbb.ca
The governments of Canada, British Columbia, Alberta, Saskatchewan, Yukon & the Northwest Territories signed the Mackenzie River Basin Transboundary Waters Master Agreement in 1997. The agreement commits the aforementioned governments to work closely together to inform about & advocate for the maintenance of the ecological integrity of the Mackenzie watershed.

• Mayo District Renewable Resources Council (MDRRC)
PO Box 249
Mayo, YT Y0B 1M0
Tel: 867-996-2942; Fax: 867-996-2948
mayorrc@northwestel.net
yfwmb.ca/renewable-resource-councils/mayo

• Outfitter Quota Appeal Committee
Tel: 867-667-5336; Fax: 867-393-6213
The Committee provides recommendations to the Minister of Environment to help resolve outfitting quota disputes faced by Yukon outfitters.

• Porcupine Caribou Management Board
Tel: 867-633-4780; Fax: 867-393-3904
dlemke@pcmb.ca
The Board provides advice & makes recommendations to governments & traditional caribou users for the conservation & management of the Porcupine Caribou herd & its habitat.

• Selkirk Renewable Resources Council (SRRC)
PO Box 32
Pelly Crossing, YT Y0B 1P0
Tel: 867-537-3937; Fax: 867-537-3938
selkirkrrc@northwestel.net
yfwmb.ca/renewable-resource-councils/selkirk

• Teslin Renewable Resource Council (TRRC)
PO Box 186
Teslin, YT Y0A 1B0
Tel: 867-390-2323; Fax: 867-390-2919
teslinrrc@northwestel.net
yfwmb.ca/renewable-resource-councils/teslin

• Wilderness Tourism Licensing Appeal Board
Tel: 867-667-3048; Fax: 867-393-6223
The Board assess appeals made by applicants if the registrar refuses to grant an operating licence or cancels or suspends an operating licence for wilderness tourism activities.

• Yukon Fish & Wildlife Management Board (YFWMB)
409 Black St., 2nd Fl.
PO Box 31104
Whitehorse, YT Y1A 5P7
Tel: 867-667-3754; Fax: 867-393-6947
officemanager@yfwmb.ca
yfwmb.ca
The Board focuses its efforts on territorial policies, legislation & other measures to help guide management of fish & wildlife, conserve habitat & enhance the renewable resources economy. The Board influences management decisions through public education & by making recommendations to Yukon, federal & First Nations governments.
The Board works in conjunction with the territory's Renewable Resources Councils (RRCs), which are local management bodies in the Yukon established in areas where individual land claim agreements have been signed. RRCs provide strong input into planning & regulation by the territorial, federal & First Nations governments. RRCs also play an important advisory role to the YFWMB by raising awareness of specific issues & providing local & traditional information.

Corporate Services & Climate Change
Tel: 867-456-5544; Fax: 867-456-5543
climatechange@yukon.ca
The Secretariat has the lead role in ensuring Yukon government actions support a healthy & resilient Yukon in a changing climate. It strives to identify needs, opportunities & priorities; promote & support action; & monitor & report on progress.
Assistant Deputy Minister, Amanda MacDonald
Tel: 867-667-5634
Amanda.MacDonald@yukon.ca
Director, Policy & Planning, Diane Gunter
Tel: 867-334-3257
Diane.Gunter@yukon.ca
Director, Finance, Jeston Innes
Tel: 867-332-3007
Jeston.Innes@yukon.ca

Acting Director, Communications & Public Engagement, Ash Kayseas
Tel: 867-332-0219
Ash.Kayseas@yukon.ca
Director, Human Resources, Matt Lackowicz
Tel: 867-334-3699
Matt.Lackowicz@yukon.ca
Director, Client, Business & Technology Solutions, Sasha Sywulsky
Tel: 867-334-6616
Sasha.Sywulsky@yukon.ca
Director, Climate Change Secretariat, Rebecca Turpin
Tel: 867-332-2420
Rebecca.Turpin@yukon.ca

Environmental Sustainability
The Secretariat has the lead role in ensuring Yukon government actions support a healthy & resilient Yukon in a changing climate. It strives to identify needs, opportunities & priorities; promote & support action; & monitor & report on progress.
Assistant Deputy Minister, Christine Cleghorn
Tel: 867-667-5634
Christine.Cleghorn@yukon.ca
Chief Veterinary Officer, Mary Vanderkop
Tel: 867-456-5582
Mary.Vanderkop@yukon.ca

Conservation Officer Services
Tel: 867-667-8005; Fax: 867-393-6206
coservices@yukon.ca
The Branch provides environmental education, environmental youth camps & projects, provides hunting, fishing & trapping licences, provides hunter & trapper education, resource management support, wildlife safety for the public & provides enforcement & compliance.
Director, Gordon Hitchcock
Tel: 867-667-8005
Gordon.Hitchcock@yukon.ca

Environmental Protection & Assessment
Tel: 867-667-3227; Fax: 867-393-6213
envprot@yukon.ca
Formed in 1994, the Branch is responsible for development of regulations & standards under the Environment Act & programs associated with everyday waste management, contaminated sites, air quality & pesticides. The Branch is also responsible for monitoring & inspection of permits, spill cleanup & environmental assessments of development projects, recycling education & promotion, public education & awareness.
Director, Bryna Cable
Tel: 867-667-8177
Bryna.Cable@yukon.ca

Fish & Wildlife Branch
Tel: 867-667-5715; Fax: 867-393-6263
fish.wildlife@yukon.ca
Other Communication: Toll-Free Phone: 800-661-0408, ext. 5715
The Branch maintains the ecosystem based on sound management of fish, wildlife & their habitats, preserves the sustainability of fish & wildlife populations, works with First Nations & community relations to preserve & enhance the ecosystem, develops management plans, provides policy & planning, collects, assesses & disseminates natural resource data & provides public education for resource users.
Director, Marc Cattet
Tel: 867-667-5715
Marc.Cattet@yukon.ca

Water Resources Branch
Tel: 867-667-3171; Fax: 867-667-3195
water.resources@yukon.ca
Director, Heather Jirousek
Tel: 867-667-3145
Heather.Jirousek@yukon.ca

Yukon Parks Branch
Tel: 867-667-5648; Fax: 867-393-6223
yukon.parks@yukon.ca
Director, Mike Etches
Tel: 867-332-4591
Mike.Etches@yukon.ca

Yukon Finance

PO Box 2703 Whitehorse, YT Y1A 2C6
Tel: 867-667-5343; Fax: 867-393-6217
fininfo@yukon.ca
yukon.ca/en/department-finance

Premier; Minister, Hon. Sandy Silver
sandy.silver@yukon.ca

Deputy Minister, Scott Thompson

Tel: 867-667-9017
Scott.Thompson@yukon.ca

Comptroller, Raffaelo (Ralph) D'Alessandro
Tel: 867-332-5079
RaffaeloRalph.D'Alessandro@yukon.ca

Economics, Fiscal Policy & Statistics
Other Communication: Yukon Bureau of Statistics, Email: ybsinfo@yukon.ca; Phone: 867-667-5640; Fax: 867-393-6203
Assistant Deputy Minister, Clarke LaPrairie
Tel: 867-332-0559
Clarke.Laprairie@yukon.ca
Director, Fiscal Policy, Sonny Jose
Tel: 867-667-5303
Sonny.Jose@yukon.ca
Director, Business & Economic Research, Kailer Mullet
Tel: 867-667-8515
Kailer.Mullet@yukon.ca
Director, Yukon Bureau of Statistics, Bishnu Saha
Tel: 867-667-5463
Bishnu.Saha@yukon.ca

Financial Operations & Revenue Services
Fax: 867-393-6217
Assistant Deputy Minister, Ian Davis
Tel: 867-332-2411
Ian.Davis@yukon.ca
Director, Investments & Debt Services, Rebecca Edzerza
Tel: 867-332-2813
Rebecca.Edzerza@yukon.ca
Director, Financial Systems, Gritt Hoffmann
Tel: 867-334-5628
Gritt.Hoffmann@yukon.ca
Director, Financial Operations & Tax Administration, Johanna Smith
Tel: 867-335-4353
Johanna.Smith@yukon.caa

Management Board Secretariat
Assistant Deputy Minister, Jessica Schultz
Tel: 867-332-1294
Jessica.Schultz@yukon.ca
Director, Management Board Analysis, Jamie McAllister
Tel: 867-332-4944
Jamie.McAllister@yukon.ca
Director, Budgets, Glen Traverse
Tel: 867-332-2020
Glen.Traverse@yukon.ca

Yukon French Language Services Directorate

305 Jarvis St., 3rd Fl., PO Box 2703 Whitehorse, YT Y1A 2C6
Tel: 867-667-8260; Fax: 867-393-6226
info.dsf-flsd@yukon.ca
yukon.ca/en/french-language-services-directorate
The French Language Services Directorate does not provide services directly to the public; rather, it supports the Yukon's government departments & corporations in meeting the Languages Act requirements.

Minister responsible, Hon. John Streicker
john.streicker@yukon.ca

Director, Andre Bourcier
Tel: 867-667-3735
Andre.Bourcier@yukon.ca

Associated Agencies, Boards & Commissions:
• Advisory Committee on French Language Services
Tel: 867-667-8970; Fax: 867-393-6226
Other Communication: Toll-Free Phone: 800-611-0408, ext. 8970

Yukon Health & Social Services

PO Box 2703 Whitehorse, YT Y1A 2C6
Tel: 867-667-3673; Fax: 867-667-3096
Toll-Free: 800-661-0408
hss@yukon.ca
www.hss.gov.yk.ca
twitter.com/HSSYukon
www.facebook.com/yukonhss
www.youtube.com/user/hssyukongovernment
Committed to quality health & social services for Yukoners by helping individuals acquire the skills to live responsible, healthy & independent lives; & providing a range of accessible, affordable services that assist individuals, families & communities to reach their full potential.

Minister, Hon. Tracy-Anne McPhee
tracy.mcphee@yukon.ca

Deputy Minister, Stephen Samis
Stephen.Samis@yukon.ca

Chief Medical Officer of Health, Vacant

Director, Communications & Social Marketing, Patricia Living
Tel: 867-667-3673
Patricia.Living@yukon.ca

Director, Human Resources, Sonya Parsons
Tel: 867-334-1743
Sonya.Parsons@yukon.ca

Associated Agencies, Boards & Commissions:
• **Capability & Consent Board**
Tel: 867-633-7614; *Fax:* 867-633-6954
• **Social Assistance Review Committee**
Tel: 867-667-5669; *Fax:* 867-667-5819
• **Yukon Advisory Committee on Nursing**
Tel: 867-668-8721; *Fax:* 867-668-8899
• **Yukon Child Care Board**
Tel: 867-667-6966
This advisory body makes recommendations to the Minister of Health & Social Services, on any issues that pertain to child care.
• **Yukon Hospital Corporation Board of Trustees**
5 Hospital Rd.
Whitehorse, YT Y1A 3H7
Tel: 867-393-3732; *Fax:* 867-393-8707
yukonhospitals.ca/node/255
• **Yukon Joint Management Committee**
Tel: 867-393-6461; *Fax:* 867-667-3096

Continuing Care
#201, 1 Hospital Rd., Whitehorse, YT Y1A 3H7
Tel: 867-667-5945; *Fax:* 867-456-6545
hssweb@yukon.ca
Provides residential, home care & regional therapy services for citizens.
Acting Assistant Deputy Minister, Sharon Specht
Tel: 867-667-5945
Sharon.Specht@yukon.ca
Acting Director, Clinical Psychology, Emma Eaton
Emma.Eaton@yukon.ca
Director, Care & Community, Cathy McNeil
Tel: 867-456-6839
Cathy.McNeil@yukon.ca
Acting Director, Extended Care Services, Brigitte Poirier
Tel: 867-667-9398
Brigitte.Poirier@yukon.ca
Acting Director, Safety & Clinical Excellence, Sheryl-Ann Wasson
Tel: 867-667-8750
Sheryl-Ann.Wasson@yukon.ca

Corporate Services
Tel: 867-667-8541; *Fax:* 867-393-6457
Plays a key role in ensuring that Yukon residents have accurate, up-to-date information about the territory's health & social programs, services & systems.
Assistant Deputy Minister, Karen Chan
Tel: 867-667-8309
Karen.Chan@yukon.ca
Chief Information Officer; Director, Information Services Branch, Jennifer Potvin
Jennifer.Potvin@yukon.ca
Director, Finance & Administration, Madeleine Davidson
Madeleine.Davidson@yukon.ca
Director, Policy & Program Development, Caitlin Kerwin
Tel: 867-667-5688
Caitlin.Kerwin@yukon.ca
Director, Strategic Finance & Corporate Services, Andrea McIntyre
Andrea.McIntyre@yukon.ca

Health Services
#201, 1 Hospital Rd., Whitehorse, YT Y1A 3H7
Tel: 867-667-3096; *Fax:* 867-667-3096
Responsible for a variety of health care, disease prevention & treatment services which assist eligible Yukon residents in attaining maximum individual independence within their community.
Acting Assistant Deputy Minister, Mary Vanstone
Mary.Vanstone@yukon.ca
Acting Director, Insured Health & Hearing Services, Marguerite Fenske
Tel: 867-667-5620
Marguerite.Fenske@yukon.ca

Acting Director, Community Health Programs, Benton Foster
Tel: 867-667-8340
Benton.Foster@yukon.ca
Director, Public Health, Cathy Stannard
Tel: 867-335-1010
Cathy.Stannard@yukon.ca
Director, Community Nursing, Sheila Thompson
Tel: 867-667-8325
Sheila.Thompson@yukon.ca

Social Services
Tel: 867-667-8343; *Fax:* 867-667-3742
Consists of Family & Children's Services, Program Support, Social Supports, Mental Wellness & Substance Use.
Assistant Deputy Minister, Shehnaz Ali
Tel: 867-667-8343
Shehnaz.Ali@yukon.ca
Director, Social Supports, Kaila deBoer
Tel: 867-667-3705
Kaila.deBoer@yukon.caa
Director, Community & Program Support, Stephen Doyle
Tel: 867-332-3074
Stephen.Doyle@yukon.ca
Director, Family & Children's Services Branch, Geraldine MacDonald
Tel: 867-667-3471
Geraldine.MacDonald@yukon.ca
Manager, Disability Services, Wendy McIntire-Cowx
Tel: 867-667-8843
Wendy.McIntire-Cowx@yukon.ca

Yukon Highways & Public Works

PO Box 2703 Whitehorse, YT Y1A 2C6
Tel: 867-667-3732; *Fax:* 867-393-6218
hpw-info@yukon.ca
yukon.ca/en/department-highways-public-works
Other Communication: Toll-Free Phone: 800-661-0408, ext. 3732
The Department of Highways & Public Works is responsible for ensuring safe & efficient public highways, airstrips, buildings & information systems.

Minister, Hon. Nils Clarke
Nils.Clarke@yukon.ca

Deputy Minister, Paul McConnell
Tel: 867-667-3732
Paul.McConnell@yukon.caa

Assistant Deputy Minister, Scott Milton
Tel: 867-334-5139
Scott.Milton@yukon.ca

Director, Human Resources, Nathalie Dugas
Tel: 867-332-3179
Nathalie.Dugas@yukon.ca

Director, Capital Planning Office, Derek Parker
Tel: 867-332-6636
Derek.Parker@yukon.ca

Associated Agencies, Boards & Commissions:
• **Bid Challenge Committee**
Tel: 867-667-3680; *Fax:* 867-667-5479
• **Driver Control Board**
Tel: 867-667-5623; *Fax:* 867-393-6963
Other Communication: Toll-Free Phone: 800-661-0408, ext. 5623
• **National Safety Code Review Board**

Corporate Services
Tel: 867-667-3732; *Fax:* 867-393-6218
hpw-info@yukon.ca
Other Communication: Toll-Free Phone: 800-661-0408, ext. 3732
Assistant Deputy Minister, Catherine Harwood
Tel: 867-667-5128
Catherine.Harwood@yukon.ca
Director, Supply Services, Shanna Epp
Tel: 867-667-5289
Shanna.Epp@yukon.ca
Director, Policy & Communications, Cassandra Kelly
Tel: 867-332-6517
Cassandra.Kelly@yukon.ca
Director, Corporate Finance, Risk & Safety, Jody Woodland
Tel: 867-667-9037
Jody.Woodland@yukon.ca

Information & Communications Technology
Tel: 867-667-5196
Other Communication: Toll-Free Phone: 800-661-0408, ext. 5196

Assistant Deputy Minister & Chief Information Officer, Sean McLeish
Tel: 867-667-3712
Sean.McLeish@yukon.ca
Director, E-Services for Citizens, Mark Burns
Tel: 867-332-6275
Mark.Burns@yukon.ca
Director, Information, Technology & Client Solutions, George Harvey
Tel: 867-332-1756
George.Harvey@yukon.ca
Director, Service Innovation & Support, Terri McLeod
Tel: 867-667-9515
Terri.McLeod@yukon.ca
Director, Corporate Information Management, Jeff Sunstrum
Tel: 867-667-9523
Jeff.Sunstrum@yukon.ca

Property Management Division (PMD)
Tel: 867-667-8721
Other Communication: Toll-Free Phone: 800-661-0408, ext. 8721
Acting Assistant Deputy Minister, Richard Gorczyca
Tel: 867-336-1080
Richard.Gorczyca@yukon.ca
Superintendent, Operations, Facilities Management & Regional Services, Glenn Lemoine
Tel: 867-667-8882
Glenn.Lemoine@yukon.ca
Chief Security Guard, Facilities Management, Chris Schneider
Tel: 867-334-5898
Chris.Schneider@yukon.ca
Director, Capital Development, Joanna Magee
Tel: 867-333-6529
Joanna.Magee@yukon.ca
Director, Facilities Management & Regional Services, Shannon Trott
Tel: 867-336-0272
Shannon.Trott@yukon.ca
Director, Realty & Capital Asset Planning, Scott Whitehead
Tel: 416-648-2550
Scott.Whitehead@yukon.ca
Manager, Finance, Donna Sibley
Tel: 867-667-3706
Donna.Sibley@yukon.ca

Transportation
Tel: 867-667-5196; *Fax:* 867-393-6218
Other Communication: Toll-Free Phone: 800-661-0408, ext. 5196
Assistant Deputy Minister, Sherri Young
Tel: 867-667-8006
Sherri.Young@yukon.ca
Executive Director, Transportation Engineering, Paul Murchison
Tel: 867-393-6207
Paul.Murchison@yukon.ca
Director, Transportation Planning, Colin Nickerson
Tel: 867-335-1455
Colin.Nickerson@yukon.ca
Director, Transport Services; Registrar, Motor Vehicles, Ryan Parry
Tel: 867-667-5833
Ryan.Parry@yukon.ca
Supervisor, Operations, Transportation Maintenance, Dan Ewashen
Dan.Ewashen@yukon.ca

Aviation
Tel: 867-667-8440; *Fax:* 867-667-8446
YXY@yukon.ca
Other Communication: Toll-Free Phone: 800-661-0408, ext. 8440
The Aviation branch operates 4 airports & 25 aerodromes, & manages the NAV CANADA's Yukon Community Aerodrome Radio Station (CARS) program.
Director, Aviation Land Development, Clint Ireland
Tel: 867-332-1554
Clint.Ireland@yukon.ca
Director, Aviation, Leah Stone
Tel: 867-667-9044
Leah.Stone@yukon.ca
Superintendent, Yukon Airports, Denis Robinson
Tel: 867-334-6445
Denis.Robinson@yukon.ca
Superintendent, Safety & Security, Christopher Bradshaw
Tel: 867-332-1557
Christopher.Bradshaw@yukon.ca

Yukon Housing Corporation

410G Jarvis St., PO Box 2703 Whitehorse, YT Y1A 2H5
Tel: 867-667-5712; *Fax:* 867-393-7597
ykhouse@yukon.ca
yukon.ca/en/yukon-housing-corporation
Other Communication: Toll-Free Phone: 800-661-0408, ext.
5759
Links families, communities & the housing industry with
programs & services that work to support the housing needs of
Yukoners.

Minister responsible, Hon. Ranj Pillai
ranj.pillai@yukon.ca

President, Mary Cameron
Tel: 867-667-5155
Mary.Cameron@yukon.ca

Acting Vice-President, Corporate Services, Philippe Mollet
Tel: 867-667-5155
Philippe.Mollet@yukon.ca

Director, Information Management & Technology, Linh Ho
Tel: 867-332-5668
Linh.Ho@yukon.ca

Director, Finance & Risk Management, Marcel
HolderRobinson
Tel: 867-667-8773
Marcel.HolderRobinson@yukon.ca

Director, Capital Development & Maintenance, Darren
Stahl
Tel: 867-667-3439
Darren.Stahl@yukon.ca

Director, Housing Operations, Eva Wieckowski
Tel: 867-456-6172
Eva.Wieckowski@yukon.ca

Associated Agencies, Boards & Commissions:
• **Carcross Housing Advisory Board**
Tel: 867-821-4281; *Fax:* 867-821-3806
• **Carmacks Housing Advisory Board**
Tel: 867-996-2358; *Fax:* 867-996-2417
• **Dawson City Housing Advisory Board**
Tel: 867-993-5478; *Fax:* 867-993-5814
• **Faro Housing Advisory Board**
Tel: 867-994-3113; *Fax:* 867-944-3174
• **Haines Junction Housing Advisory Board**
Tel: 867-634-2202; *Fax:* 867-634-2416
• **Mayo Housing Advisory Board**
Tel: 867-996-2358; *Fax:* 867-996-2417
• **Ross River Housing Advisory Board**
Tel: 867-969-2347; *Fax:* 867-969-2002
• **Teslin Housing Advisory Board**
Tel: 867-390-2024; *Fax:* 867-390-2207
• **Watson Lake Housing Advisory Board**
Tel: 867-536-7304; *Fax:* 867-536-7356
• **Whitehorse Housing Advisory Board**
Tel: 867-667-3892; *Fax:* 867-393-6386

Yukon Justice

**Andrew Philipsen Law Centre, 2134 - 2nd Ave., PO Box 2703
Whitehorse, YT Y1A 2C6**
Tel: 867-667-3033; *Fax:* 867-667-5200
justice@yukon.ca
yukon.ca/en/department-justice
Other Communication: Court Services, Email:
courtservices@yukon.ca

Minister, Hon. Tracy-Anne McPhee
tracy.mcphee@yukon.ca

Deputy Minister, John Phelps
Tel: 867-667-5959
John.Phelps@yukon.ca

Director, Finance, Systems, Administration & Records,
Luda Ayzenberg
Tel: 867-667-5615
Luda.Ayzenberg@yukon.ca

Director, Court Services, Mark Daniels
Tel: 867-667-3440
Mark.Daniels@yukon.ca

Director, Human Resources, Amanda Ho
Tel: 867-667-8212
Amanda.Ho@yukon.ca

Director, Regulatory Services, Michele McDonnell
Tel: 867-667-5942
Michele.McDonnell@yukon.ca

Director, Policy & Communications, Patricia Randell
Tel: 867-667-3508
Patricia.Randell@yukon.ca

Sheriff, Court Services, Andrew Hyde
Tel: 867-667-5365
Andrew.Hyde@yukon.ca

Clerk, Supreme Court, Edwige Graham
Tel: 867-667-5938
Edwige.Graham@yukon.ca

Registrar, Yukon Courts, Justin Gorczyca
Tel: 867-456-3821
Justin.Gorczyca@yukon.ca

Associated Agencies, Boards & Commissions:
• **Auxiliary Police Advisory Committee**
Tel: 867-667-5596
Other Communication: Toll-Free Phone: 800-661-0408, ext.
5596
• **Comunity Advisory Board**
Tel: 867-667-8297
Other Communication: Toll-Free Phone: 800-661-0408, ext.
8297
• **Crime Prevention & Victim Services Trust Board of
Trustees**
Tel: 867-667-8746; *Fax:* 867-393-6240
Other Communication: Toll-Free Phone: 800-661-0408, ext.
8746
• **Human Rights Panel of Adjudicators**
409 Black St.
Whitehorse, YT Y1A 2N2
Tel: 867-688-5767
registrar@yhrpa.ca
yhrpa.ca
• **Judicial Council**
PO Box 31222
Whitehorse, YT Y1A 5P7
Tel: 867-667-5438; *Fax:* 867-393-6400
www.yukoncourts.ca/en/who-we-are/judicial-council
Other Communication: Toll-Free Phone: 800-661-0408, ext.
5438
The Council makes recommendations respecting appointments
of judges& justices, & deals with formal complaints respecting
judges & justices. It makes recommendations respecting the
efficiency, uniformity & quality of judicial services provided by the
Territorial Court or the Justice of the Peace Court. It also
performs other duties requested by the Minister.
• **Law Society of Yukon - Discipline Committee**
#304, 104 Elliott St.
Whitehorse, YT Y1A 0M2
Tel: 867-668-4231; *Fax:* 867-667-7556
info@lawsocietyyukon.com
lawsocietyyukon.com/discipline
This adjudicative committee conducts inquiries & investigations
into matters regarding the conduct of a member or a
student-at-law.
• **Law Society of Yukon - Executive**
#304, 104 Elliott St.
Whitehorse, YT Y1A 0M2
Tel: 867-668-4231; *Fax:* 867-667-7556
info@lawsocietyyukon.com
lawsocietyyukon.com
This regulatory society serves & protects the public interest in
the administration of justice.
• **Mediation Board**
Tel: 867-456-3821
Other Communication: Toll-Free Phone: 800-661-0408, ext.
3821
• **Yukon Human Rights Commission**
#215, 305 Main St.
Whitehorse, YT Y1A 2B4
Tel: 867-667-6226; *Fax:* 867-667-2662
Toll-free: 800-661-0535
info@yukonhumanrights.ca
yukonhumanrights.ca
The Commission administers the Human Rights Act, hears
complaints & arranges for adjudication if required. Promotes &

coordinates public education & research programs in the area of
human rights.
• **Yukon Law Foundation Board of Directors**
PO Box 31789
Whitehorse, YT Y1A 6L3
Tel: 867-667-7500; *Fax:* 867-393-3904
execdir@yukonlawfoundation.com
www.yukonlawfoundation.com
• **Yukon Legal Services Society**
#203, 2131 - 2nd Ave.
Whitehorse, YT Y1A 1C3
Tel: 867-667-5210; *Fax:* 867-667-8649
intake@legalaid.yk.ca
legalaid.yk.ca
• **Yukon Police Council**
Yukon Police Council Secretariat'
PO Box 2703 J-10
Whitehorse, YT Y1A 2C6
Tel: 867-393-6475
yukonpolicecouncil@yukon.ca
yukon.ca/en/yukon-police-council
• **Yukon Review Board**
Tel: 867-667-3596; *Fax:* 867-393-6212
yukonreviewboard@yukon.ca
Other Communication: Toll-Free Phone: 800-661-0408, ext.
3596
• **Yukon Utilities Board**
PO Box 31728
Whitehorse, YT Y1A 6L3
Tel: 867-667-5058; *Fax:* 867-667-5059
yub@utilitiesboard.yk.ca
yukonutilitiesboard.yk.ca
This regulatory board consists of three to five members
appointed by the Government of Yukon. It receives its mandate
from the Public Utilities Act & Regulations.

Community Justice & Public Safety Division
**Prospector Bldg., 301 Jarvis St., 2nd Fl., PO Box 2703
Whitehorse, YT Y1A 2C6**
Acting Assistant Deputy Minister, Jeff Simons
Tel: 867-393-7077
Jeff.Simons@yukon.ca
Director, Corrections, Andrea Monteiro
Tel: 867-667-8294
Andrea.Monteiro@yukon.ca
Director, Victim Services, Lareina Twardochleb
Tel: 867-667-5962
Lareina.Twardochleb@yukon.ca

Legal Services
**Andrew A. Philipsen Law Centre, 2134 - 2nd Ave., 2nd Fl.,
PO Box 2703 Whitehorse, YT Y1A 2C6**
Tel: 867-667-5764; *Fax:* 867-393-6379
legalservices@yukon.ca
Other Communication: Toll-Free Phone: 800-661-0408, ext.
5764
Assistant Deputy Minister; Assistant Deputy Attorney General,
Mark Pindera
Tel: 867-667-3469
Mark.Radke@yukon.ca
Chief Legislative Counsel, Rebecca Veinott
Tel: 867-667-5776
Rebecca.Veinott@yukon.ca
Chief Negotiator; Director, Negotiations Collaborations &
Partnerships, Ruby Porter
Tel: 867-393-6371
Ruby.Porter@yukon.ca

Yukon Liquor Corporation

9031 Quartz Rd., Whitehorse, YT Y1A 4P9
Tel: 867-667-5245; *Fax:* 867-393-6306
yukon.liquor@yukon.ca
yukon.ca/en/yukon-liquor-corporation
Other Communication: Toll-Free Phone: 800-661-0408, ext.
5245
The Yukon Liquor Corporation is responsible for the purchase,
distribution, & responsible sale of liquor products in the territory.
As of 2018, its mandate also expanded to include non-medical
cannabis.

Minister responsible, Hon. Ranj Pillai
ranj.pillai@yukon.ca

Deputy Minister, Dennis Berry
Tel: 867-667-5708
Dennis.Berry@yukon.ca

Director, Finance & Information Management, Luzelle
Nagel

Tel: 867-333-1856
Luzelle.Nagel@yukon.ca

Director, Policy & Communications, Amelie Quirke-Tomlins
Tel: 867-667-8924
Amelie.Quirke-Tomlins@yukon.ca

Director, Regulatory Services, Will Tewnion
Tel: 867-332-6510
Will.Tewnion@yukon.ca

Manager, Warehouse, Raymond Sherwood
Tel: 867-335-7626
Raymond.Sherwood@yukon.ca

Supervisor, Sales & Distribution, Teresa Rudolph
Tel: 867-667-3113
Teresa.Rudolph@yukon.ca

Associated Agencies, Boards & Commissions:
• **Yukon Liquor Board**
9031 Quartz Rd.
Whitehorse, YT Y1A 4P9
Tel: 867-667-5265
yukon.ca/en/learn-about-yukon-liquor-board
Other Communication: Toll-Free Phone: 800-661-0408, ext.
5265

Lotteries Yukon

#101, 205 Hawkins St., Whitehorse, YT Y1A 1X3
Tel: 867-633-7890
Toll-Free: 800-661-0555
lotteriesyukon@yukon.ca
lotteriesyukon.com
Other Communication: Sales, Phone: 867-633-7891; Funding
Programs: 867-633-7892
The Yukon Lottery Commission is appointed to provide conduct
& management of interjurisdictional lotteries, & is responsible for
allocating profits from the sale of lottery tickets to the areas of
art, sport, & recreation throughout the territory.

Minister Responsible, Hon. Ranj Pillai
Ranj.Pillai@yukon.ca

Associated Agencies, Boards & Commissions:
• **Yukon Lottery Commission**
#101, 205 Hawkins St.
Whitehorse, YT Y1A 1X3
Tel: 867-633-7890
Toll-free: 800-661-0555
lotteriesyukon@yukon.ca

Yukon Ombudsman, Information & Privacy Commissioner

3162 - 3rd Ave., Main Fl., Whitehorse, YT Y1A 1G3
Tel: 867-667-8468; *Fax:* 867-667-8469
info@yukonombudsman.ca
www.yukonombudsman.ca
Other Communication: Toll-Free Phone: 800-661-0408, ext.
8468
twitter.com/yukonombipcpidc

Ombudsman, Information & Privacy Commissioner, Diane
McLeod-McKay
diane.mcleod-mckay@yukonombudsman.ca

Yukon Public Service Commission

2071 - 2nd Ave., PO Box 2703 Whitehorse, YT Y1A 2C6
Tel: 867-667-5653; *Fax:* 867-667-5755
pscwebsite@yukon.ca
yukon.ca/en/public-service-commission
Other Communication: Toll-Free Phone: 800-661-0408, ext.
5653

This central agency has a mandate to provide human resource
advice & support services to Yukon government departments &
employees, to act as the employer on behalf of the Yukon
government & to establish & maintain human resource
legislation, policies & collective agreements.

Minister responsible, Hon. John Streicker
john.streicker@yukon.ca

**Assistant Deputy Minister, Human Resource Service
Centre,** Kim Runions
Tel: 867-667-5250
Kim.Runions@yukon.ca

Assistant Deputy Minister, People & Culture, Lisa Wykes
Tel: 867-667-9511
Lisa.Wykes@yukon.ca

Public Service Commissioner, Paul Moore
Tel: 867-667-5252
Paul.Moore@yukon.ca

Acting Director, Finance & Administration, Loretta Boorse
Tel: 867-667-8222
Loretta.Boorse@yukon.ca

Acting Director, Compensation & Classification, Lienke
deVries-Clarke
Tel: 867-667-9417
Lienke.deVries-Clarke@yukon.ca

Director, Human Resource Management Systems, Satnam
Gill
Tel: 867-456-3976
Satnam.Gill@yukon.ca

Director, Diversity & Inclusion, Jordan Holway
Tel: 867-667-9450
Jordan.Holway@yukon.ca

Director, Organizational Development, Desiree Hombert
Tel: 867-667-8267
Desiree.Hombert@yukon.ca

Director, Respectful Workplace Office, Jodi-Lyn Newnham
Tel: 867-667-8134
Jodi-Lyn.Newnham@yukon.ca

Director, Employee Relations, Jeananne Nicloux
Tel: 867-667-5197
Jeananne.Nicloux@yukon.ca

Yukon Tourism & Culture

PO Box 2703 Whitehorse, YT Y1A 2C6
Tel: 867-393-7048
yukon.ca/en/department-tourism-culture
twitter.com/insideyukon
The department focuses on business, tourism, cultural industries
& technology / telecommunications to develop & promote
economic capacity & entrepreneurial skills to stimulate economy.
The department works with the Yukon's diverse arts
communities to foster creativity & quality of life & with heritage
interests to preserve & interpret heritage resources.

Minister, Hon. Ranj Pillai
ranj.pillai@yukon.ca

Deputy Minister, Valerie Royle
Valerie.Royle@yukon.ca

Associated Agencies, Boards & Commissions:
• **Advanced Artists Award Jury**
PO Box 2703 L-3
Whitehorse, YT Y1A 2C6
Tel: 867-667-8789
artsfund@yukon.ca
Other Communication: Toll-Free Phone: 800-661-0408, ext.
8789

• **Yukon Arts Advisory Council**
Tel: 867-667-3535; *Fax:* 867-393-7400
Other Communication: Toll-Free Phone: 800-661-0408, ext.
3535

• **Yukon Arts Centre Corporation Board of Directors**
Tel: 867-667-8575; *Fax:* 867-393-6300
Other Communication: Toll-Free Phone: 800-661-0408, ext.
8575

• **Yukon Geographical Place Names Board**
PO Box 31164
Whitehorse, YT Y1A 5P7
Tel: 867-667-2200
yukonplacenames@yknet.ca
yukonplacenames.ca

• **Yukon Heritage Resources Board**
PO Box 31115
Whitehorse, YT Y1A 5P7
Tel: 867-668-7150
www.yhrb.ca

• **Yukon Historic Resources Appeal Board**
Tel: 867-667-5363; *Fax:* 867-667-6456
Other Communication: Toll-Free Phone: 800-661-0408, ext.
5363

Corporate Services
Provides a range of central support services within the
Department of Tourism & Culture. These include human
resources, information technology, administration, information
management & finance.

Acting Director, Kate Olynyk
Tel: 867-667-9063
Kate.Olynyk@yukon.ca
Acting Director, Tim Sellars
Tel: 867-667-3009
Tim.Sellars@yukon.ca

Cultural Services
Tel: 867-667-8589; *Fax:* 867-393-6456
Dedicated to the preservation, development, interpretation of
Yukon's heritage resources & to fostering the growth & mpact of
the territory's visual, literary & performing arts.
Director, Jennifer Meurer
Tel: 867-667-8592
Jennifer.Meurer@yukon.ca
Yukon Archaeologist, Ty Heffner
Tel: 867-667-3771
Ty.Heffner@yukon.ca
Territorial Archivist, David Schlosser
Tel: 867-667-5275
David.Schlosser@yukon.ca
Yukon Paleontologist, Grant Zazula
Tel: 867-667-8089
Grant.Zazula@yukon.ca
Private Records Archivist, Lesley Buchan
Tel: 867-667-5641; *Fax:* 867-393-6253
Lesley.Buchan@yukon.ca

Strategic Initiatives
Provides legislative & policy support for Tourism & Culture &
coordinates the communications efforts of the department.
Assistant Deputy Minister, Strategic Initiatives, Jonathan Parker
Tel: 867-667-3016
Jonathan.Parker@yukon.ca

Tourism Services
Tel: 867-667-3053; *Fax:* 867-393-7005
industryservices@yukon.ca
Engages in tourism marketing, product development, & research
in order to bring the scenic natural beauty and rich & diverse
cultural heritage of Yukon to the attention of potential visitors.
Director, Pierre Germain
Tel: 867-667-3087
Pierre.Germain@yukon.ca

Yukon Women's Directorate

#1, 404 Hason St., PO Box 2703 Whitehorse, YT Y1A 2C6
Tel: 867-667-3030
yukon.ca/en/womens-directorate
www.facebook.com/womensdirectorate

Minister responsible, Hon. Jeanie McLean
jeanie.mclean@yukon.ca

Director, Hillary Aitken
Tel: 867-667-5182
Hillary.Aitken@yukon.ca

Associated Agencies, Boards & Commissions:
• **Yukon Advisory Council on Women's Issues**
Tel: 867-667-3030; *Fax:* 867-393-6270
Other Communication: Toll-Free Phone: 800-661-0408, ext.
3030

Yukon Workers' Compensation Health & Safety Board (YWCHSB)

401 Strickland St., Whitehorse, YT Y1A 5N8
Tel: 867-667-5645; *Fax:* 867-393-6279
Toll-Free: 800-661-0443
worksafe@yukon.ca
www.wcb.yk.ca

The YWCHSB administers workers' compensation &
occupational health & safety in the Yukon.

Minister responsible, Hon. Richard Mostyn
richard.mostyn@yukon.ca

President & CEO, Kurt Dieckmann
Tel: 867-667-8983
Kurt.Dieckmann@wcb.yk.ca

Chief Financial Officer; Vice-President, Operations, Jim
Stephens
Tel: 867-689-0970; *Fax:* 867-393-6279
Jim.Stephens@wcb.yk.ca

Chief Mine Safety Officer, Michael Henney
Tel: 867-667-8739
Michael.Henney@wcb.yk.ca

Director, Corporate Services, Catherine Jones

Tel: 867-667-8695
Catherine.Jones@wcb.yk.ca

Director, Occupational Health & Safety, Bruce Milligan
Tel: 867-667-3726
Bruce.Milligan@wcb.yk.ca

Acting Director, Human Resources, Danielle Ouellette

Tel: 867-667-5013
Danielle.Ouellette@yukon.ca

Director, Claimant Services, Susanne Wirth
Tel: 867-332-2438
Susanne.Wirth@wcb.yk.ca

Associated Agencies, Boards & Commissions:

• Workers' Compensation Appeal Tribunal
456 Range Rd.
Whitehorse, YT Y1A 3A2
Tel: 867-667-8731; *Fax:* 867-393-7030
tribunal@yukonwcat.ca
www.yukonwcat.ca
Other Communication: Toll-Free Phone: 800-661-0443, ext. 8731

The Queen & Royal Family

The House of Windsor

In 1917 the late King George V, by Proclamation, changed the House name of the Royal Family from Saxe-Coburg-Gotha to the House of Windsor.

THE QUEEN. - Elizabeth the Second, (Elizabeth Alexandra Mary, of Windsor) by the Grace of God, of the United Kingdom, Canada and Her other Realms and Territories Queen; Head of the Commonwealth, Defender of the Faith, Succeeded to the throne February 6th, 1952, and was crowned June 2nd, 1953, at Westminster Abbey. Her Majesty, the elder daughter of the late King George VI and Queen Elizabeth The Queen Mother, was born at 17 Bruton St., London, W.1, on April 21st, 1926, married November 20th, 1947, H.R.H. The Prince Philip, Duke of Edinburgh, Earl of Merioneth and Baron Greenwich, P.C., K.G., K.T., O.M., G.B.E., A.C., Q.S.O.

THE CHILDREN of Queen Elizabeth and H.R.H. The Prince Philip, Duke of Edinburgh are:

H.R.H. Prince Charles Philip Arthur George, Prince of Wales and Earl of Chester, Duke of Cornwall and Duke of Rothesay, Earl of Carrick and Baron Renfrew, Lord of the Isles, and Prince and Great Steward of Scotland, K.G., K.T., G.C.B., O.M., A.K., Q.S.O., C.C., P.C., A.D.C., born November 14th, 1948. Married July 29th, 1981. Marriage dissolved 1996. The Lady Diana Spencer (died August 31st, 1997) and has issue. Prince William, Prince of Wales, Duke of Cambridge, Earl of Strathearn and Baron Carrickfergus, K.G., K.T., P.C., A.D.C.(P), born June 21st, 1982 (married April 29, 2011, Catherine Middleton, H.R.H. The Duchess of Cambridge, and has issue, Prince George of Cambridge, born July 22, 2013, Princess Charlotte of Cambridge, born May 2, 2015, and Prince Louis of Cambridge, born April 23, 2018); and Prince Henry of Wales, Duke of Sussex, Earl of Dumbarton and Baron Kilkeel, K.C.V.O., A.D.C., born September 15th, 1984 (married May 19, 2018, Meghan Markle, The Duchess of Sussex, and has issue, Archie Harrison Mountbatten-Windsor, born May 6, 2019, and Lilibet Mountbatten-Windsor, born June 4, 2021). Prince Charles married April 9th, 2005 Camilla Parker Bowles (H.R.H. The Duchess of Cornwall).

H.R.H. The Princess Royal, Anne Elizabeth Alice Louise, K.G., K.T., G.C.V.O., G.C.St.J., Q.S.O., G.C.L., C.D., born August 15th, 1950. Married 1st November 14th, 1973 Captain Mark Anthony Peter Phillips, C.V.O., A.D.C.(P) and has issue, Peter Phillips born November 15th, 1977 and Zara Phillips born May 15th, 1981. Marriage dissolved 1992. Married 2nd December 12th, 1993 Vice-Admiral Sir Timothy James Hamilton Laurence, K.C.V.O., C.B., A.D.C.(P)

H.R.H. The Prince Andrew Albert Christian Edward, K.G., G.C.V.O., C.D., A.D.C.(P), Duke of York, Earl of Inverness and Baron Killyleagh, born February 19th, 1960, married July 23rd, 1986 Miss Sarah Margaret Ferguson and has issue, Princess Beatrice of York, born August 8th, 1988, and Princess Eugenie of York, born March 23rd, 1990. Marriage dissolved 1996.

H.R.H. The Prince Edward Antony Richard Louis, K.G., G.C.V.O., C.D., A.D.C.(P), Earl of Wessex, and Viscount Severn, born March 10th, 1964, married June 19, 1999 Miss Sophie Rhys-Jones and has issue, Lady Louise Windsor, born November 8, 2003, and James, Viscount Severn, born December 17, 2007.

THE LATE GEORGE VI. - George VI succeeded to the Throne December 11th, 1936; and was crowned at Westminster Abbey, May 12th, 1937. Second son of King George V and Queen Mary, he was born at York Cottage, Sandringham, on December 14th, 1895, married, April 26th, 1923, Lady Elizabeth Bowes-Lyon, daughter of the Earl and Countess of Strathmore and Kinghorne. As Heir Presumptive succeeded to the Throne on the abdication of Edward VIII.

QUEEN ELIZABETH, THE QUEEN MOTHER - born August 4th, 1900, daughter of the 14th Earl of Strathmore and Kinghorne; married, April 26th, 1923. Died March 30th, 2002.

THE ISSUE of the late King George VI and Queen Elizabeth are:

The reigning Sovereign, Elizabeth the Second (elder daughter).

The Princess Margaret (Rose), Countess of Snowdon, C.I., G.C.V.O., born August 21st, 1930, married Antony Charles Robert Armstrong-Jones, G.C.V.O., (since created Earl of Snowdon) May 6th, 1960, and has issue, Viscount Linley, born November 3rd, 1961 and the Lady Sarah Frances Elizabeth Armstrong-Jones, born May 1st, 1964. Marriage dissolved 1978. Died February 9th, 2002.

SUCCESSION-The order stands:
The Prince of Wales
The Duke of Cambridge
Prince George of Cambridge
Princess Charlotte of Cambridge
Prince Louis of Cambridge
The Duke of Sussex
Master Archie Mountbatten-Windsor
Miss Lilibet Mountbatten-Windsor
The Duke of York, Prince Andrew
Princess Beatrice of York
Princess Eugenie of York

Master August Brooksbank
The Earl of Wessex, Prince Edward
James, Viscount Severn
The Lady Louise Mountbatten-Windsor
The Princess Royal, Princess Anne
Mr. Peter Phillips
Miss Savannah Phillips
Miss Isla Phillips
Miss Zara Tindall
Miss Mia Grace Tindall
Miss Lena Tindall
Master Lucas Tindall
Earl of Snowdon, David Armstrong-Jones
Viscount Linley, Charles Armstrong-Jones
Lady Margarita Armstrong-Jones
Lady Sarah Chatto
Master Samuel Chatto
Master Arthur Chatto
The Duke of Gloucester, Prince Richard
Earl of Ulster, Alexander Windsor
Lord Culloden (Xan Windsor)
Lady Cosima Windsor
Lady Davina Lewis
Miss Senna Lewis
Miss Tane Lewis
The Lady Rose Gilman
Miss Lyla Gilman
Master Rufus Gilman
The Duke of Kent, Prince Edward
The Earl of St. Andrews, George Windsor
Lady Amelia Windsor
Master Albert Windsor
Master Leopold Windsor
Master Louis Windsor
Lady Helen Taylor
Master Columbus Taylor
Master Cassius Taylor
Miss Eloise Taylor
Miss Estella Taylor
Prince Michael of Kent
The Lord Frederick Windsor
Miss Maud Windsor
Miss Isabella Windsor
Lady Gabriella Windsor
Princess Alexandra, The Hon. Lady Ogilvy
Mr. James Ogilvy
Master Alexander Ogilvy
Miss Flora Ogilvy
Miss Marina Ogilvy
Master Christian Mowatt
Miss Zenouska Mowatt

NOTES

1. The Sucession was governed by the Act of Settlement 1701 (12 & 13 Will 3 c 2) which limited the succession to the Throne to the heirs, being Protestants, of Princess Sophia of Hanover, granddaughter of King James I. Section 6 (4) of the Legitimacy Act of 1959 (Nothing in this Act affects the succession to the Throne) was also relevant.

2. The Bill of Rights and the Act of Settlement were amended by the Succession to the Crown Act (2003), ending the system of male primogeniture, and applying to those born after Oct. 28, 2011. The Act also ended provisions stating that those who marry Roman Catholics are ineligible for inclusion in the line of succession. These changes came into effect in March 2015.

HER MAJESTY'S HOUSEHOLD

Lord Chamberlain, The Earl Peel, G.C.V.O., P.C., D.L.
Private Secretary to The Queen, The Rt. Hon. Edward Young, C.V.O.
Keeper of the Privy Purse, Sir Michael Stevens, K.C.V.O.
The Lord Chamberlain has the general supervision of the Royal Household.

The Commonwealth

The Commonwealth of Nations is a voluntary association of 53 independent member countries representing over 2.4 billion people around the world - in Africa, the Americas, Asia, the Caribbean, Europe & the Pacific. It promotes good governance, democracy, sustainable economic & social development, the rule of law & human rights. These & other principles are enshrined in the Harare Commonwealth Declaration of 1991.

There are three principal international organizations of the Commonwealth:

THE COMMONWEALTH SECRETARIAT

Marlborough House, Pall Mall, London SW1Y 5HX, UK, +44 (0)20 7747 6500; Fax: +44 (0)20 7930 0827, URL: www.thecommonwealth.org
The Rt. Hon. Patricia Scotland, Q.C. (Dominica), Commonwealth Secretary-General
Dr. Arjoon Suddhoo, Commonwealth Deputy Secretary

Lolita Applewhaite, Chief of Staff, Office of the Secretary General
Matt Patterson, Official Spokesperson, Director, Communicaitons & Public Affairs, 44 (0) 20 7747 6235, media@commonwealth.int

THE COMMONWEALTH FOUNDATION

Marlborough House, Pall Mall, London SW1Y 5HY, UK, +44 (0)20 7830 3783; Fax: +44 (0)20 7839 8157, Email: foundation@commonwealth.int, URL: www.commonwealthfoundation.org
The Commonwealth Foundation is an international organization established by heads of government, and is the Commonwealth agency for civil society.

THE COMMONWEALTH OF LEARNING (COL)

#2500, 4710 Kingsway, Burnaby BC V5H 4M2, 604-775-8200; Fax: 604-775-8210, Email: info@col.org, URL: www.col.org
The Commonwealth of Learning's focus is in strengthening institutions in developing Commonwealth countries that are striving to provide affordable education to larger numbers of their citizens.

Member States

(showing capital, population (2018) & date of membership. Dates for Australia, Canada & New Zealand are those on which Dominion Status was acquired):

Antigua & Barbuda - St. John's; 96, 290; Nov. 1, 1981
Australia - Canberra; 25, 000, 000; Jan. 1, 1901
- External territories: Norfolk Island, Coral Sea Islands Territory, Australian Antarctic Territory, Heard Island & McDonald Islands, Cocos (Keeling) Islands, Christmas Island, Territory of Ashmore & Cartier Islands
The Bahamas - Nassau; 385, 640; July 10, 1973
Bangladesh - Dhaka; 161, 000, 000; Mar. 26, 1972
Barbados - Bridgetown; 287, 000; Nov. 30, 1966
Belize - Belmopan; 383, 070; Sept. 21, 1981
Botswana - Gaborone; 2, 300, 000; Sept. 30, 1966
Brunei Darussalam - Bandar Seri Begawan; 428, 960; Feb. 23, 1984
Cameroon - Yaoundé; 25, 000, 000; May 20, 1995
Canada - Ottawa; 37, 000, 000; July 1, 1867
Cyprus - Nicosia; 1, 189, 265; Oct. 1, 1961
Dominica - Roseau; 72, 000; Nov. 3, 1978
Fiji Islands - Suva; 883, 480; Oct. 10, 1997 N.B. Fiji Islands was suspended from the councils of the Commonwealth in May 2000 following the overthrow of its democratically elected government.It was suspended again in 2006 after another coup, but reinstated in 2014 after elections were held.
Gambia, The - Banjul; 2, 300, 000; Feb. 8, 2018 (previously member 1965-2013, rejoined in 2018)
Ghana - Accra; 30, 000, 000; Mar. 6, 1957
Grenada - St. George's; 111, 450; Feb. 7, 1974
Guyana - Georgetown; 779, 000; Feb. 23, 1966
India - New Delhi; 1, 353, 00, 000; Jan. 26, 1947
Jamaica - Kingston; 2, 900, 000; Aug. 6, 1962
Kenya - Nairobi; 51, 000, 000; Dec. 12, 1963
Kingdom of eSwatini (formerly Swaziland) - Mbabane; 1, 100, 000; Sept. 6, 1968
Kiribati - Tarawa; 102, 000; July 12, 1979
Lesotho - Maseru; 2, 100, 000; Oct. 4, 1966
Malawi - Lilongwe; 18, 000, 000; July 6, 1964
Malaysia - Kuala Lumpur; 32, 000, 000; Aug. 31, 1957
Malta - Valletta; 485, 000; Mar. 31, 1964
Mauritius - Port Louis; 1, 265, 300; Mar. 12, 1968
Mozambique - Maputo; 29, 000, 000; June 25, 1995
Namibia - Windhoek; 2, 500, 000; Mar. 21, 1990
Nauru - Nauru; 13, 000; Jan. 31, 1968 N.B. Member in Arrears until 2011.
New Zealand - Wellington; 4, 800, 000; Sept. 26, 1907 - Includes the territories of Tokelau & the Ross Dependency (Antarctic). Self-governing countries in free association with New Zealand: Cook Islands & Niue.
Nigeria - Abuja; 212, 000, 000; Oct. 1, 1960
Pakistan - Islamabad; 182, 143, 000; Mar. 23, 1989 (previously member 1947-1972; rejoined in 1989) N.B. Pakistan was suspended from participation in the councils of the Commonwealth in October 1999 following a military coup, but was reinstated in 2004.
Rwanda - Kigali; 12, 000, 000; Nov. 2009
Papua New Guinea - Port Moresby; 8, 600, 000; Sept. 16, 1975
Saint Lucia - Castries; 182, 000; Feb. 22, 1979
St. Kitts & Nevis - Basseterre; 52, 000; Sept. 19, 1983
St. Vincent & The Grenadines - Kingstown; 110, 000; Oct. 27, 1979
Samoa - Apia; 196, 000; June 1, 1970
Seychelles - Victoria; 96, 762; June 18, 1976
Sierra Leone - Freetown; 7, 700, 000; Apr. 27, 1961
Singapore - Singapore; 5, 600, 000; Aug. 9, 1965
Solomon Islands - Honiara; 652, 860; July 7, 1978
South Africa - Pretoria; 58, 000, 000; 1931 - Left Commonwealth 1961, rejoined 1994
Sri Lanka - Colombo; 22, 000, 000; Feb. 4, 1948

Tonga - Nuku'alofa; 103, 200; June 4, 1970
Trinidad & Tobago - Port of Spain; 1, 400, 000; Aug. 31, 1962
Tuvalu - Funafuti; 11, 500; Oct. 1, 1978
Uganda - Kampala; 43, 000, 000; Oct. 9, 1962
United Kingdom - London; 66, 000, 000
- Overseas territories: Akrotiri and Dhekelia, Anguilla, Bermuda,
  British Antarctic Territory, British Indian Ocean Territory,
  British Virgin Islands, Cayman Islands, Falkland Islands,
  Gibraltar, Montserrat, Pitcairn (incl. Henderson, Ducie & Oeno
  Islands), St. Helena & St. Helena Dependencies (Ascension &
  Tristan da Cunha), South Georgia & the South Sandwich
  Islands, & Turks & Caicos Islands
United Republic of Tanzania - Dodoma;
56, 000, 000; Dec. 9, 1961
Vanuatu - Port Vila; 292, 680; July 30, 1980
Zambia - Lusaka; 17, 000, 000; Oct. 24, 1964

La Francophonie

ORGANISATION INTERNATIONALE DE LA FRANCOPHONIE
Secrétariat général, 19-21, av Bosquet, 75007 Paris, France
(33) 1 44 37 33 25; Téléc: (33) 1 45 79 14 98; URL:
www.francophonie.org
Louise Mushikiwabo (Rwanda), Secrétaire général

Member States

(showing member name, population (2021), national holiday):

Albanie (République d'), 3, 088 M, 11 janvier et 28 novembre
Andorre (Principauté), 0, 085 M, 8 septembre
Arménie (République d'), 3, 011 M, 23 août
Belgique (Royaume de), 11, 778 M, 21 juillet
Bénin (République du), 13, 301 M, 1er août
Bulgarie (République de), 6, 919 M, 3 mars
Burkina Faso, 21, 382 M, 11 décembre
Burundi (République du), 12, 241 M, 1er juillet
Cambodge (Royaume du), 17, 304 M, 7 janvier - 17 avril
Cameroun (République du), 28, 524 M, 20 mai
Canada, 37, 943 M, 1er juillet
Canada - Nouveau-Brunswick (Province du), 0, 747 M, 15 août
Canada - Québec (Province du), 8, 164 M, 24 juin
Cap-Vert (République du), 0, 589 M, 5 juillet
Centrafricaine (République), 5, 357 M, 1er décembre
Chypre, 1, 281 M, 1er octobre
Communauté française de Belgique (Wallonie-Bruxelles), 4, 200
M, 27 septembre
Comores (Union des), 0, 864 M, 6 juillet
Congo (République du), 5, 417 M, 15 août
Congo (République démocratique du Congo), 105, 044 M, 30
juin
Côte d'Ivoire (République de), 28, 088 M, 7 août
Djibouti (République de), 0, 938 M, 27 juin
Dominique (Commonwealth de la), 0, 074 M, 3 novembre
Égypte (République arabe d'), 106, 437 M, 23 juillet
France (République française), 68, 084 M, 14 juillet
Gabon (République gabonaise), 2, 284 M, 17 août
Ghana, 32, 372 M, 6 mars
Grèce, 10, 569 M, 25 mars
Guinée (République de), 12, 877 M, 2 octobre
Guinée-Bissau (République de), 1, 976 M, 24 septembre
Guinée-équatoriale (République de), 0, 857 M, 12 octobre
Haïti (République d'), 11, 198 M, 1er janvier
Laos (République démocratique populaire Lao), 7, 574 M, 2
décembre
Liban (République libanaise), 5, 261 M, 22 novembre
Luxembourg (Grand-Duché de), 0, 639 M, 23 juin
Macédoine (ARY), 2, 128 M, 8 septembre
Madagascar (République de), 27, 534 M, 26 juin
Mali (République du), 20, 137 M, 22 septembre
Maroc (Royaume du), 36, 561 M, 30 juillet
Maurice (République de), 1, 386 M, 12 mars
Mauritanie (République islamique de), 4, 079 M, 28 novembre
Moldavie, 3, 323 M, 27 août
Monaco (Principauté de), 0, 031 M, 19 novembre
Niger (République du), 23, 605 M, 18 décembre
Nouvelle-Calédonie, 0, 293 M, 14 juillet
Qatar (État du), 2, 479 M, 18 décembre
Roumanie, 21, 230 M, 1er décembre
Rwanda (République rwandaise), 12, 943 M, 1er juillet
Sainte-Lucie, 0, 166 M, 22 février
Sao Tomé et Principe (République démocratique de), 0, 213 M,
12 juillet
Sénégal (République du), 16, 082 M, 4 avril
Seychelles (République des), 0, 096 M, 18 juin
Suisse (Confédération), 10, 261 M, 1er août
Tchad (République du), 17, 414 M, 11 janvier
Togo (République du), 8, 283 M, 13 janvier et 27 avril
Tunisie (République tunisienne), 11, 811 M, 20 mars
Vanuatu (République du), 0, 303 M, 30 juillet
Vietnam (République socialiste du), 102, 789 M, 2 septembre

Canadian Permanent Missions Abroad

Canadian Delegation to the Organization for Security & Cooperation in Europe
Laurenzerberg 2, Vienna, Austria
011 43 1 531-38-3000,
vosce@international.gc.ca
www.international.gc.ca/world-monde/international_relations-rela
tions_internationales/osce/index.aspx
Jocelyn Kinnear, Ambassador & Permanent Representative

Canadian Joint Delegation to NATO (North Atlantic Treaty Organization)
Léopold III Blvd., Brussels, 1110 Belgium
32 (0)2 707 3831,
mailbox.tribunal@hq.nato.int
www.international.gc.ca/world-monde/international_relations-rela
tions_internationales/nato-otan/index.aspx
David Angell, Ambassador & Permanent Representative of
Canada
Lieutenant-General Frances J. Allen, Military Representative of
Canada, CMM, CD

Mission of Canada to the European Union, Brussels
Avenue des Arts 58, Brussels, 1000 Belgium
32 (0)2 741 0611, Fax: 32 (0)2 741 0643,
breu@international.gc.ca
www.canadainternational.gc.ca/eu-ue/index.aspx
Ailish Campbell, Ambassador
Hon. Stéphane Dion, Special Envoy

NORAD (North American Aerospace Defense Command)
**NORAD Public Affairs, Peterson AFB, #B-016, 250
Vandenberg, Colorado Springs, 80914-3808 USA**
719-554-6889,
n-nc.peterson.n-ncspecialstaff.mbx.usnorthcom-pa-omb@mail.m
il, pa@forces.gc.ca
www.norad.mil
Glen D. Vanherck, Commander, Gen. USA, USAF
Alain Pelletier, Deputy Commander, Lt.-Gen. RCAF

Organization for Economic Cooperation & Development
2, rue André Pascal, Paris, F-75775 France
331-45-24-82-00, Fax: 331-45-24-85-00,
www.oecd.org
Madeleine Chenette, Ambassador & Permanent Representative
of Canada
Mathias Cormann, Secretary-General
Juan Yermo, Chief of Staff

Permanent Mission of Canada to the Organization of American States
501 Pennsylvania Ave. NW, Washington, DC 20001 USA
202-448-6556,
prmoasg@international.gc.ca
www.international.gc.ca/world-monde/international_relations-rela
tions_internationales/oas-oea
Hugh Adsett, Ambassador & Permanent Representative of
Canada

UN: Permanent Delegation of Canada to the UN Educational, Scientific & Cultural Organization (UNESCO)
1, rue Miollis, Paris, 75015 France
331-44-43-25-71, Fax: 331-44 43-25-79,
pesco@international.gc.ca
www.international.gc.ca/world-monde/international_relations-rela
tions_internationales/unesco/index.aspx
Natasha Power Cayer, Ambassador & Permanent Delegate
Maria Mourani, Representative of the Quebec Government

UN: Permanent Mission of Canada to the Food & Agriculture Organization (FAO)
Via Zara 30, Rome, 00198 Italy
39-06-85-444-1; Fax: 39-06-85-444-3916,
rperm@international.gc.ca, fao-hq@fao.org
www.fao.org
Alexandra Bugailiskis, Permanent Representative
Gloria Wiseman, Deputy Permanent Representative
Mi Nguyen, Deputy Permanent Representative

UN: Permanent Mission of Canada to the International Civil Aviation Organization (ICAO)
999, boul Robert-Bourassa, Montréal, QC H3C 5H7 Canada
514-283-3530
canada@icao.int; icaohq@icao.int
www.icao.int
Fang Liu, Secretary General
Salvatore Sciacchitano, President of the Council
Captain Claude Hurley, FRAeS, Permanent Representative

UN: Permanent Mission of Canada to the International Organizations in Vienna
**United Nations Office at Vienna, Vienna International
Centre, PO Box 500, Wagramer Strasse 5, 1400 Vienna,
Austria**
43-1-26060, Fax: 43-1-263-3389,
www.unvienna.org
Heidi Hulan, Permanent Representative & Ambassador

UN: Permanent Mission of Canada to the Office of the United Nations in Nairobi
**c/o High Commission of Canada in Kenya, PO Box 1013,
Nairobi, 00621 Kenya**
254-20-366-3000, Fax: 254-20-366-3900,
nrobi@international.gc.ca
www.unhabitat.org, www.unep.org
This office is responsible for relations to the United Nations
Centre for Human Settlements (UN-Habitat) and to the United
Nations Environment Programme (UNEP).

UN: Permanent Mission of Canada to the United Nations
466 Lexington Ave., 20th Fl., New York, NY 10017
212-848-1100, Fax: 212-848-1195,
canada.un@international.gc.ca
www.international.gc.ca/world-monde/international_relations-rela
tions_internationales/un-onu/index.aspx
Hon. Robert Rae, Ambassador & Permanent
Representative-Designate of Canada to the United Nations in
New York
Leslie E. Norton, Ambassador & Permanent Representative of
Canada to the United Nations in Geneva

UN: Permanent Mission of Canada to the World Trade Organization, the UN and the Conference on Disarmament
5, av de l'Ariana, Geneva, 1202 Switzerland
41-22-919-9200, Fax: 41-22-919-9233,
genev-ag@international.gc.ca
www.international.gc.ca/genev/index.aspx
Stephen de Boer, Ambassador & Permanent Representative to
the World Trade Organization
Leslie E. Norton, Ambassador & Permanent Representative to
the United Nations

Diplomatic & Consular Representatives in Canada

Islamic State of Afghanistan
**Embassy of the Islamic Republic of Afghanistan, 240 Argyle
Ave.,
Ottawa, ON K2P 1B9**
Tel: 613-563-4223; *Fax:* 613-563-4962
contact@afghanembassy.ca
www.ottawa.mfa.af
www.facebook.com/afghanistan.embassyottawa
His Excellency M. Hassan Soroosh Y., Ambassador
Sayed Mujtaba Ahmadi, Minister-Counsellor
Mohammad Azim Wardak, Counsellor

Republic of Albania
**Embassy of Albania (to Canada), #302, 130 Albert St.,
Ottawa, ON K1P 5G4**
Tel: 613-236-3053; *Fax:* 613-236-0804
embassy.ottawa@mfa.gov.al
www.ambasadat.gov.al/canada/en
His Excellency Ermal Muca, Ambassador
Arlinda Dega, First Secretary

People's Democratic Republic of Algeria
**Embassy of Algeria, 500 Wilbrod St.,
Ottawa, ON K1N 6N2**
Tel: 613-789-8505; *Fax:* 613-789-1406
info@embassyalgeria.ca
www.ambalgott.com
Other contact information: Alt. Email: ambalgcan@rogers.com
His Excellency Larbi El Hadj Ali, Ambassador
Faiza Latrous, Minister-Counsellor
Abdenacer Kateb, Counsellor
Arezki Ouamri, Counsellor

Principality of Andorra
**Permanent Mission of Andorra to the UN, Two United
Nations Plaza, 27th Fl.,
New York, NY 10017 USA**
Tel: 212-750-8064; *Fax:* 212-750-6630
andorra@un.int
Her Excellency Elisenda Vives Balmana, Permanent
Representative
Joan Josep Lopez Lavado, Second Secretary

Republic of Angola
Embassy of the Republic of Angola, #2100, 2108 - 16th St. NW,
Washington, DC 20009
Tel: 202-785-1156; *Fax:* 202-822-9049
Angola@angola.org
angola.org
Angola closed its embassy in Ottawa in 2018.
His Excellency Joaquim do Espirito Santo, Ambassador

Anguilla
See: Organization of the Eastern Caribbean States

Antigua & Barbuda
See: Organization of the Eastern Caribbean States

Argentine Republic
Embassy of the Argentine Republic, 81 Metcalfe St., 7th Fl.,
Ottawa, ON K1P 6K7
Tel: 613-236-2351; *Fax:* 613-235-2659
ecana@mrecic.gov.ar
ecana.cancilleria.gob.ar/en
www.facebook.com/Argen tinaEnCanada
Her Excellency Josefina Martinez Gramuglia, Ambassador
Pedro Alchourron, Deputy Head of Mission
Maria Florencia Furbatto, Secretary, Public Diplomacy
Pablo Castagnino, Counsellor, Trade & Economic, Cooperation & Innovation Section
Sebastián Carrau, Administrative Attaché

Republic of Armenia
Embassy of the Republic of Armenia, 7 Delaware Ave.,
Ottawa, ON K2P 0Z2
Tel: 613-234-3710; *Fax:* 613-234-2144
armcanadaembassy@mfa.am
canada.mfa.am
Her Excellency Anahit Harutyunyan, Ambassador
Ara Mkrtchian, Counsellor

Aruba
See: Republic of Venezuela

Commonwealth of Australia
Australian High Commission, #1301, 50 O'Connor St.,
Ottawa, ON K1P 6L2
Tel: 613-236-0841; *Fax:* 613-786-7621
www.canada.embassy.gov.au
twitter.com/AusHCCanada
www.facebook.com/Aus traliaInCanada
Other contact information: Alt. URL: canada.highcommission.gov.au
Her Excellency Natasha Smith, High Commissioner
Katherine Ruiz-Avila, Deputy High Commissioner
Grayson Perry, Consul General & Senior Trade & Investment Commissioner
Kevin M. Lamb, Post Manager & Honorary Consul, Australian Consulate & Trade Commission

Republic of Austria
Embassy of Austria, 445 Wilbrod St.,
Ottawa, ON K1N 6M7
Tel: 613-789-1444; *Fax:* 613-789-3431
ottawa-ob@bmaa.gv.at
www.bmeia.gv.at/oeb-ottawa
www.facebook.com/austr iaincanada
Her Excellency Sylvia Meier-Kajbic, Ambassador
Hannes Machor, Deputy Head of Mission
Christian Grinschgl, Counsellor & Consul

Republic of Azerbaijan
Embassy of Azerbaijan (to Canada), #1203, 275 Slater St.,
Ottawa, ON K1P 5H9
Tel: 613-288-0497; *Fax:* 613-230-8089
reception@azembassy.ca
www.ottawa.mfa.gov.az
twitter.com/AzEmbCanada
www.facebook.com/185253704851295
Fuad Aliyev, Chargé d'Affaires, a.i.

Autonomous Region of the Azores
See: Portuguese Republic

Commonwealth of the Bahamas
High Commission for the Commonwealth of The Bahamas, #415, 99 Bank St.,
Ottawa, ON K1P 6B9
Tel: 613-232-1724; *Fax:* 613-232-0097
ottawa-mission@bahighco.com
www.bahighco.ca
His Excellency Alvin Alfred Smith, High Commissioner
Chanelle Patrice Brown, Counsellor & Consul
Nestor Thurgood Grachion Sands, Second Secretary & Vice-Consul

Kingdom of Bahrain
Embassy of Bahrain (to Canada), 3502 International Dr. NW,
Washington, DC 20008 USA
Tel: 202-342-1111; *Fax:* 202-362-2192
ambsecretary@bahrainembassy.org
www.youtube.com/bahrainvideo
twitter.com/bahdiplomatic
His Excellency Shaikh Abdulla bin Rashed bin Abdulla Alkhalifa, High Commissioner

Barbados
High Commission for Barbados, #470, 55 Metcalfe St.,
Ottawa, ON K1P 6L5
Tel: 613-236-9517; *Fax:* 613-230-4362
ottawa@foreign.gov.bb
www.foreign.gov.bb
Vacant, High Commissioner
Joanna Esme N. Benn-Griffith, First Secretary

Republic of Belarus
Embassy of the Republic of Belarus, #600, 130 Albert St.,
Ottawa, ON K1P 5G4
Tel: 613-233-9994; *Fax:* 613-233-8500
canada@mfa.gov.by
canada.mfa.gov.by
instagram.com/BelarusMFA
twitter.com/BelarusMFA
www.facebook.com/Belar usEmbassy.Canada
Evgeny Russak, Minister-Counsellor & Chargé d'affaires, a.i.
Andrei Martsyanu, Counsellor

Kingdom of Belgium
Embassy of Belgium, #820, 360 Albert St.,
Ottawa, ON K1R 7X7
Tel: 613-236-7267; *Fax:* 613-236-7882
ottawa@diplobel.fed.be
diplomatie.belgium.be/canada
www.facebook.com/B elEmbassyOttawa
His Excellency Patrick Van Gheel, Ambassador
Arnaud Gaspart, Deputy Head of Mission, Political & Economic Affairs

Belize
High Commission for Belize (to Canada), 2535 Massachusetts Ave. NW,
Washington, DC 20008 USA
Tel: 202-332-9636; *Fax:* 202-332-6888
reception.usa@mfa.gov.bz
www.belizeembassyusa.mfa.gov.bz
twitter.com/M FABelize
www.facebook.com/embassy.belize.94
His Excellency Daniel Gutierez, Ambassador

Republic of Benin
Embassy of Benin, 470 Somerset St. W,
Ottawa, ON K1R 5J8
Tel: 613-233-4429; *Fax:* 613-233-8952
ambassade@benin.ca
www.benin.ca
His Excellency René Koto Sounon, Ambassador

Kingdom of Bhutan
Permanent Mission of the Kingdom of Bhutan to the UN, 343 East 43rd St.,
New York, NY 10017 USA
Tel: 212-682-2268; *Fax:* 212-661-0551
bhutan@un.int
www.mfa.gov.bt/pmbny
Her Excellency Doma Tshering, Permanent Representative

Plurinational State of Bolivia
Embassy of Bolivia, #416, 130 Albert St.,
Ottawa, ON K1P 5G4
Tel: 613-236-5730; *Fax:* 613-236-1312
bolivianembassy@bellnet.ca
bolivianembassy.ca
www.facebook.com/BolEnCa nada
Sorka Jannet Copa Romero, Diplomatic Agent

Bosnia & Herzegovina
Embassy of Bosnia & Herzegovina, 17 Blackburn Ave.,
Ottawa, ON K1N 8A2
Tel: 613-236-0028; *Fax:* 613-236-1139
info@bhembassy.ca
www.ambasadabih.ca
twitter.com/AmbasadaBiH
His Excellency Marko Milisav, Ambassador
Zlatko Aksamija, Counsellor

Republic of Botswana
High Commission for Botswana (to Canada), #1531, 1533 New Hampshire Ave. NW,
Washington, DC 20036 USA
Tel: 202-244-4990; *Fax:* 202-244-4164
info@botswanaembassy.org
www.botswanaembassy.org
www.facebook.com/Bots wana.Government
His Excellency Onkokame Kitso Mokaila, Ambassador
Wame Phetlhu, Minister-Counsellor
Thato Matlho, First Secretary

Federative Republic of Brazil
Embassy of Brazil, 450 Wilbrod St.,
Ottawa, ON K1N 6M8
Tel: 613-237-1090; *Fax:* 613-237-6144
brasemb.ottawa@itamaraty.gov.br
ottawa.itamaraty.gov.br/en-us
www.face book.com/EmbaixadaBrasilOttawa
Other contact information: Consular E-mail:
consular.ottawa@itamaraty.gov.br
His Excellency Pedro Henrique Lopes Borio, Ambassador
Jose Raphael Lopes Mendes de Azerado, Minister-Counsellor
Davino Ribeiro de Sena, Counsellor
Clarissa Souza Della Nina, Counsellor

British Virgin Islands
See: Organization of the Eastern Caribbean States

Brunei Darussalam
High Commission of Brunei Darussalam, 395 Laurier Ave. East,
Ottawa, ON K1N 6R4
Tel: 613-234-5656; *Fax:* 613-234-4397
ottawa.canada@mfa.gov.bn
Other contact information: Alt. Email: bhco@bellnet.ca
His Excellency PG Kamal Bashah PG Ahmad, High Commissioner
Muhd Ali-Azri Mohd Alipah, Second Secretary
Dk Rabiatul Haziqah PG Yunus, Third Secretary

Republic of Bulgaria
Embassy of the Republic of Bulgaria, 325 Stewart St.,
Ottawa, ON K1N 6K5
Tel: 613-789-3215; *Fax:* 613-789-3524
Embassy.Ottawa@mfa.bg
www.mfa.bg/embassies/canada
Other contact information: Alt. Email: embgottawa@hotmail.com
Her Excellency Svetlana Sashova Stoycheva-Etropolski, Ambassador
Antoniya Aleksieva, Second Secretary
Stanislav Dimitrov Stanoev, Second Secretary & Consul
Marieta Spassova, Second Secretary

Burkina Faso
Embassy of Burkina Faso, 48 Range Rd.,
Ottawa, ON K1N 8J4
Tel: 613-238-4796; *Fax:* 613-238-3812
contact@ambabf-ca.org
ambabf-ca.org
Other contact information: Alt. Email:
ambassadeur.burkina@sympatico.ca
His Excellency Athanase Boudo, Ambassador
Yacouba Damoue, Counsellor, Cultural Affairs
Severine Bationo Kanssono, First Counsellor
Issaka Bonkoungou, Second Counsellor

Republic of Burundi
Embassy of Burundi, #410, 350 Albert St.,
Ottawa, ON K1R 1A4
Tel: 613-234-9000; *Fax:* 613-234-4030
ambabottawa@yahoo.ca

Kingdom of Cambodia
Permanent Mission of the Kingdom of Cambodia to the UN, 327 East 58 St.,
New York, NY 10022 USA
Tel: 212-336-0777; *Fax:* 212-759-7672
cambodia@un.int
www.facebook.com/CambodiaUN

Republic of Cameroon
High Commission for Cameroon, 170 Clemow Ave.,
Ottawa, ON K1S 2B4
Tel: 613-236-1522; *Fax:* 613-236-3885
cameroun@rogers.com
www.hc-cameroon-ottawa.org
Philippe Aime Landry Fouda Tsilla Otto, First Counsellor & Chargé d'affaires, a.i.
Michel Foumane Adoumou, Counsellor, Cultural
Sabine Viviane Ndolo Balock Epse Fouda Tsilla, Second Counsellor
Marguerite Abeng Bilongo Epse Esso, First Secretary
Daniel Armand Ze Mbarga, Second Secretary

Republic of Cabo Verde
Embassy of Cabo Verde (to Canada), 3415 Massachusetts Ave. NW,
Washington, DC 20007 USA
Tel: 202-965-6820; *Fax:* 202-965-1207
embassy@caboverdeus.net
www.embcv-usa.gov.cv
www.facebook.com/Embaixad aCaboVerdeWashingtonDC
His Excellency Jose Luis Livramento, Ambassador

Central African Republic
Embassy of Central African Republic (to Canada), 2704 Ontario Rd. NW,
Washington, DC 20009 USA
Tel: 202-483-7800; *Fax:* 202-332-9893
centrafricwashington@yahoo.com
www.usrcaembassy.org
His Excellency Martial Ndoubou, Ambassador

Republic of Chad
Embassy of Chad, #802, 350 Sparks St.,
Ottawa, ON K1R 7S8
Tel: 613-680-3322; *Fax:* 613-695-6622
info@chadembassy.ca
www.chadembassy.ca
His Excellency Mahamat Ali Adoum, Ambassador
Mahamat Itno Nassour Bahar, First Secretary

Republic of Chile
Embassy of Chile, #1413, 50 O'Connor St.,
Ottawa, ON K1P 6L2
Tel: 613-235-4402; *Fax:* 613-235-1176
chile.gob.cl/canada
His Excellency Raul Eduardo Fernandez Daza, Ambassador
Sebatián Molina Medina, First Secretary, smolina@minrel.gob.cl
Andrea Droppelmann Valenzuela, First Secretary
Julio Figueroa Puente, First Secretary

People's Republic of China
Embassy of China, 515 St. Patrick St.,
Ottawa, ON K1N 5H3
Tel: 613-789-3434; *Fax:* 613-789-1911
consulate.can@gmail.com
ca.china-embassy.org
twitter.com/ChinaEmbOttaw a
His Excellency Peiwu Cong, Ambassador
Mingjain Chen, Minister-Counsellor
Jiwen Sun, Minister-Counsellor
Changxue Yu, Minister-Counsellor
Shan Bai, Counsellor
Jin Hou, Counsellor
Lihua Hu, Counsellor
Yihong Tao, Counsellor
Zongbing Wang, Counsellor
Mingxuan Wang, Counsellor
Fan Yang, Counsellor
Haitao Zhang, Counsellor

Republic of Colombia
Embassy of Colombia, #1002, 360 Albert St.,
Ottawa, ON K1R 7X7
Tel: 613-230-3760; *Fax:* 613-230-4416
cottawa@cancilleria.gov.co
ottawa.consulado.gov.co
www.youtube.com/CancilleriaCol
twitter.com/CancilleriaCol
www.facebook .com/CancilleriaCol
His Excellency Jorge Alberto Julian Londono De La Cuesta, Ambassador
Monica Beltran Espitia, Minister

Union of the Comoros
Permanent Mission of the Comoros to the UN, #418, 866 UN Plaza,
New York, NY 10017 USA
Tel: 212-750-1637; *Fax:* 212-750-1657
comoros@un.int
www.un.int/comoros
His Excellency Issimail Chanfi, Permanent Representative

Republic of the Congo
Embassy of the Congo (to Canada), 1720 - 16th St. NW,
Washington, DC 20009 USA
Tel: 202-726-5500; *Fax:* 202-726-1860
info@ambacongo-us.org
www.ambacongo-us.org
twitter.com/ambacongous
w ww.facebook.com/ambacongous
His Excellency Serge Mombouli, Ambassador

Democratic Republic of the Congo
Embassy of the Democratic Republic of the Congo, 18 Range Rd.,
Ottawa, ON K1N 8J3
Tel: 613-230-6582
ambardcongocan@rogers.com
www.ambardcongocanada.ca
Lohaka Yemba, Minister-Counsellor & Chargé d'affaires, a.i.

Republic of Costa Rica
Embassy of Costa Rica, #701, 350 Sparks St.,
Ottawa, ON K1R 7S8
Tel: 613-562-2855; *Fax:* 613-562-2582
embcr-ca@rree.go.cr
www.costaricaembassy.com
www.facebook.com/13115864 6950387
His Excellency Mauricio Ortíz Ortíz, Ambassador, mortiz@rree.go.cr
Ana Marcela Calderón Garbanzo, Counsellor & Consul, mcalderon@rree.go.cr

Republic of Côte d'Ivoire
Embassy of Côte d'Ivoire, 9 Marlborough Ave.,
Ottawa, ON K1N 8E6
Tel: 613-236-9919; *Fax:* 613-563-8287
ambci.info@rogers.com
www.canada.diplomatie.gouv.ci
His Excellency Bafetigue Ouattara, Ambassador
Monnet Julien Adou, First Counsellor
Marie-Ange Flore Elloh Nee Aouely, First Secretary
Gouegone Florentin Vole Bi, First Secretary

Republic of Croatia
Embassy of Croatia, 229 Chapel St.,
Ottawa, ON K1N 7Y6
Tel: 613-562-7820; *Fax:* 613-562-7821
croemb.ottawa@mvep.hr
ca.mvep.hr
www.youtube.com/mveprh; www.flickr.com/photos/mvep_rh
twitter.com/MVEP_hr
www.facebook.com/MVEP.hr
His Excellency Vice Skracic, Ambassador
Diana Strkalj, Minister-Counsellor
Jelena Peric, Counsellor

Republic of Cuba
Embassy of Cuba, 388 Main St.,
Ottawa, ON K1S 1E3
Tel: 613-563-0141; *Fax:* 613-563-0068
embacuba@embacubacanada.net
misiones.minrex.gob.cu/en/canada
twitter.c om/EmbacubaCanada
www.facebook.com/EmbacubaCanada
Her Excellency Josefina De La Caridad Vidal Ferreiro, Ambassador
Giuvel Orozco Ortega, Counsellor & Deputy Head of Mission, 613-563-0141, dhmission@embacubacanada.net
José Anselmo López Perera, Minister-Counsellor, ministercounsellor@embacubacanada.net
Victor Daniel Alvarez Garcia, Counsellor, Political, consejero@embacubacanada.net
Victor Daniel Alvarez Garcia, Counsellor
Cristina Ramos Moreno, Counsellor, Economic & Commercial, ecounsellor@embacubacanada.net

Republic of Cyprus
High Commission for the Repulic of Cyprus (to Canada), #1002, 150 Metcalfe St.,
Ottawa, ON K2P 1P1
Tel: 613-563-9763; *Fax:* 613-563-1953
ottawahighcom@mfa.gov.cy
His Excellency Vasilios Philippou, High Commissioner

Czech Republic
Embassy of the Czech Republic, 251 Cooper St.,
Ottawa, ON K2P 0G2
Tel: 613-562-3875; *Fax:* 613-562-3878
ottawa@embassy.mzv.cz
www.mzv.cz/ottawa
His Excellency Borek Lizec, Ambassador
Jiri Borcel, Deputy Head of Mission
Milena Levickova, Consul
Jan Kubacka, Second Secretary

Kingdom of Denmark
Royal Danish Embassy, #450, 47 Clarence St.,
Ottawa, ON K1N 9K1
Tel: 613-562-1811; *Fax:* 613-562-1812
ottamb@um.dk
canada.um.dk
twitter.com/denmarkincanada
Her Excellency Hanne Fugl Eskjaer, Ambassador
Louise De Brass, Minister-Counsellor & Deputy Head of Mission

Republic of Djibouti
Embassy of the Republic of Djibouti (to Canada), #515, 1156 - 15th St. NW,
Washington, DC 20005 USA
Tel: 202-331-0270; *Fax:* 202-331-0302
info@djiboutiembassyus.org
www.djiboutiembassyus.org
twitter.com/AmbDo ualeh
His Excellency Mohamed Siad Douale, Ambassador
Ismail Mohamed Djama, Counsellor, imdjama@djiboutiembassyus.org

Commonwealth of Dominica
See: Organization of the Eastern Caribbean States

Dominican Republic
Embassy of the Dominican Republic, #1605, 130 Albert St.,
Ottawa, ON K1P 5G4
Tel: 613-569-9893; *Fax:* 613-569-8673
info@drembassy.org
dominicanembassycanada.gob.do
Her Excellency Michelle Cohen De Friedlander, Ambassador
Erika Ylonca Alvarez Rodriguez, Minister-Counsellor
Enrique Alberto Pina Serra, Minister-Counsellor
Wendy Teresa Goico Campagna, Counsellor
Orly David Perez Medina, Counsellor
Iris Joseline Pujol Rodriguez, Counsellor

Republic of Ecuador
Embassy of the Republic of Ecuador, #230, 99 Bank St.,
Ottawa, ON K1P 6B9
Tel: 613-563-8206; *Fax:* 613-235-5776
embassy@embassyecuador.ca
www.embassyecuador.ca
twitter.com/EmbajadaEc uCAN
www.facebook.com/embajadaecuador.encanada
His Excellency Juan Diego Stacey Moreno, Ambassador
Cruskaya Elizabeth Moreano Cruz, Minister
Marco Torres Jaramillo, Second Secretary
Christian Bernardo Oquendo Sanchez, Second Secretary

Arab Republic of Egypt
Embassy of the Arab Republic of Egypt, #1100, 150 Metcalfe St.,
Ottawa, ON K2P 1P1
Tel: 613-234-4931; *Fax:* 613-234-9347
egyptembottawa@gmail.com
His Excellency Ahmed Mahmoud A. Abu Zeid, Ambassador
Sherif Abdelaziz Bedeir Hussein, Counsellor
Rehab Abdelhak Ali Shawer, Counsellor
Sherif Badrawy M.M. Elbadrawy, Second Secretary
Mahmoud Abdelhakim A. Ahmed, Third Secretary

Republic of El Salvador
Embassy of El Salvador, 209 Kent St.,
Ottawa, ON K2P 1Z8
Tel: 613-238-2939; *Fax:* 613-238-6940
elsalvadorottawa@rree.gob.sv
www.youtube.com/user/cancilleria1
twitter.com/cancilleriasv
www.facebo ok/ministerio.exteriores.sv
His Excellency Ricardo Alfonso Cisneros Rodriguez, Ambassador

Republic of Equatorial Guinea
Permanent Mission of the Republic of Equatorial Guinea to the UN, 242 East 51st St.,
New York, NY 10022 USA
Tel: 212-223-2324; *Fax:* 212-223-2366
equatorialguineamission@yahoo.com
www.un.int/equatorialguinea
His Excellency Anatolio Ndong Mba, Permanent Representative

State of Eritrea
Embassy of Eritrea (to Canada), 1708 New Hampshire Ave. NW,
Washington, DC 20009 USA
Tel: 202-319-1991; *Fax:* 202-319-1304
embassyeritrea@embassyeritrea.org
www.embassyeritrea.org

Republic of Estonia
Embassy of Estonia, 168 Daly Ave.,
Ottawa, ON K1N 6E9
Tel: 613-789-4222; *Fax:* 613-789-9555
embassy.ottawa@mfa.ee
ottawa.mfa.ee
www.facebook.com/estemb.ottawa
His Excellency Toomas Lukk, Ambassador
Anee-Ly Ader, Consul

Kingdom of eSwatini
High Commission for eSwatini (to Canada), 1712 New Hampshire Ave. NW,
Washington, DC 20009 USA
Tel: 202-234-5002; *Fax:* 202-234-8254
His Excellency Abednego Mandla Ntshangase, High Commissioner

Federal Democratic Republic of Ethiopia
Embassy of Federal Democratic Republic of Ethiopia, #1501, 275 Slater St.,
Ottawa, ON K1P 5H9
Tel: 613-235-6637; *Fax:* 613-565-9175
info@ethioembassycanada.org
ethioembassycanada.org
twitter.com/mfaethi opia
www.facebook.com/MFAEthiopia
Her Excellency Nasise Challi Jira, Ambassador
Legesse Geremew Haile, Deputy Head of Mission
Merga Feyissa Tufa, Minister, Diaspora Affairs
Muktar Kedir, Minister-Counsellor
Gebretinsae Berhe, Minister-Counsellor, Consular Affairs

European Union
Delegation of the European Union to Canada, #1900, 150 Metcalfe St.,
Ottawa, ON K2P 1P1
Tel: 613-238-6464; *Fax:* 613-238-5191
Delegation-Canada@eeas.europa.eu
eeas.europa.eu/delegations/canada_en
twitter.com/EUinCanada
www.facebook.com/EUinCanada
Her Excellency Melita Gabric, Ambassador & Head of Delegation
Eva Palatova, First Counsellor & Head, Political & Public Affairs
Jakub Urbanik, Counsellor, Political & Public Affairs Section
Delphine Sallard, Minister-Counsellor & Head, Trade & Economic Section
Maud Labat, First Counsellor, Coordination of Trade Affairs

Republic of the Fiji Islands
High Commission for the Republic of the Fiji Islands (to Canada), #200, 1707 L St. NW,
Washington, DC 20036 USA
Tel: 202-337-8320; *Fax:* 202-466-8325
info@fijiembassydc.com
www.fijiembassydc.com
twitter.com/fiji_embassy
www.facebook.com/FijiEmbassyWashingtonDC
Aporosa Babakobau, Research/Consular Officer,
ababakobau@fijiembassydc.com

Republic of Finland
Embassy of Finland, #850, 55 Metcalfe St.,
Ottawa, ON K1P 6L5
Tel: 613-288-2233; *Fax:* 613-288-2244
embassy@finland.ca
www.finland.ca
twitter.com/FinlandinCanada
www.fa cebook.com/FinnishEmbassyOttawa
His Excellency Roy Kennet Eriksson, Ambassador
Kaisa Heikkila, Deputy Head of Mission

French Republic
Embassy of France, 42 Sussex Dr.,
Ottawa, ON K1M 2C9
Tel: 613-789-1795; *Fax:* 613-562-3735
politique@ambafrance-ca.org
ca.ambafrance.org
youtube.com/user/Ambafracanada;
instagram.com/franceaucanada
twitter.com/franceaucanada
www.facebook.com/ambassadefrance.canada
Her Excellency Kareen Géraldine M.L. Rispal, Ambassador
Frank Marchetti, Minister-Counsellor
Xavier Bonnet, Counsellor
Thibault Alexis Decruyenaere, Counsellor

Gabonese Republic
Embassy of Gabon, #103, 2283, boul Saint-Laurent,
Ottawa, ON K1G 5A2
Tel: 613-608-6064
info@ambassadegabon.ca
www.ambassadegabon.ca
His Excellency Sosthène Ngokila, Ambassador
Rosine Engone Ep Oliveira, First Counsellor
Genevieve Betoe, Counsellor
Roger Nlome, Counsellor

Republic of the Gambia
High Commission for Gambia (to Canada), 5630 - 16th St. NW,
Washington, DC 20011 USA
Tel: 202-785-1399
info@gambiaembassydc.us
His Excellency Dawda D. Fadera, High Commissioner

Georgia
Embassy of Georgia, #940, 340 Albert St.,
Ottawa, ON K1R 7Y6
Tel: 613-421-0460; *Fax:* 613-680-0394
ottawa.emb@mfa.gov.ge
canada.mfa.gov.ge
His Excellency Konstantine Kavtaradze, Ambassador
Nino Kharadze, Minister-Counsellor

Federal Republic of Germany
Embassy of the Federal Republic of Germany, 1 Waverley St.,
Ottawa, ON K2P 0T8
Tel: 613-232-1101; *Fax:* 613-594-9330
info@ottawa.diplo.de
www.canada.diplo.de
www.instagram.com/germanyincanada
twitter.com/GermanyInCanada
www.face book.com/GermanyInCanada
Her Excellency Sabine Anne Sparwasser, Ambassador
Gerhard Friedrich Schlaudraff, Minister & Deputy Head of Mission
Markus Gerhard Brill, Minister-Counsellor
Michael Martin Bartholmei, First Secretary
Manuel Furtwangler, First Secretary
Christin Furtwangler Maier, First Secretary
Timm Benjamin Wolfgang Hermann Boettcher, First Secretary

Republic of Ghana
High Commission for Ghana, 1 Clemow Ave.,
Ottawa, ON K1S 2A9
Tel: 613-236-0871; *Fax:* 613-236-0874
ottawa@mfa.gov.gh
www.ghc-ca.com
Noble Mawutor Kudzo Alifo, Minister & Acting High Commissioner
Yvonne Danquah, Minister-Counsellor, Consular
Benyamin Y. Tanko, Minister-Counsellor, Chancery & Diaspora
Mawutor Alifo, Minister, Trade & Investment
Rita Akyaa Agyekum, First Secretary
George Nii Okai Okine, First Secretary
Doris Addo, Second Secretary, Administration
Elvis Kwame Arhinful, Second Secretary

Grenada
See: Organization of the Eastern Caribbean States

Republic of Guatemala
Embassy of Guatemala, #1010, 130 Albert St.,
Ottawa, ON K1P 5G4
Tel: 613-233-7237; *Fax:* 613-233-0135
embassy1@embaguate-canada.com
www.canada.minex.gob.gt
Other contact information: Alt. E-mail:
consular@embaguate-canada.com
Her Excellency Guisela Atalida Godinez Sazo, Ambassador
Alejandro Fajardo Estrada, Minister-Counsellor,
afajardo@minex.gob.gt
Allan Daniel Peréz Hernández, First Secretary,
adperez@minex.gob.gt

Republic of Guinea
Embassy of Guinea, 483 Wilbrod St.,
Ottawa, ON K1N 6N1
Tel: 613-789-8444; *Fax:* 613-789-7560
ambassadeguinee@bellnet.ca
Other contact information: Alt. Email:
ambagui.canada@maegn.net
Lounceny Conde, Chargé d'affaires, a.i.
Alhassane Diabate, First Secretary
Brig. Gen. Bachir Diallo, Defence Attaché

Republic of Guinea-Bissau
Permanent Mission of the Republic of Guinea-Bissau to the UN, 336 East 45th St., 13th Fl.,
New York, NY 10017 USA
Tel: 212-896-8311; *Fax:* 212-896-8313
guinea-bissau@un.int
www.un.int/guineabissau
His Excellency Joao Soares Da Gama, Permanent Representative

Co-operative Republic of Guyana
High Commission for the Republic of Guyana, #800, 151 Slater St.,
Ottawa, ON K1P 5H3
Tel: 613-235-7249; *Fax:* 613-235-1447
guyanahcott@rogers.com
www.guyanamissionottawa.org/welcome.html
Marsha Andrea Caddett, Counsellor & Chargé d'affaires, a.i.

Republic of Haiti
Embassy of Haiti, #1110, 85 Albert St.,
Ottawa, ON K1P 6A4
Tel: 613-238-1628; *Fax:* 613-238-2986
info@ambassade-haiti.ca
ambassade-haiti.ca
www.facebook.com/3719436795 43938
His Excellency Wien Weibert Arthus, Ambassador
Ann-Kathryne Lassegue, Minister-Counsellor
Maria Alexandra Georges, Counsellor
Nesly Numa, Counsellor
Marjorie Latortue Presume, First Secretary

Hellenic Republic / Greece
Embassy of Greece, 80 MacLaren St.,
Ottawa, ON K2P 0K6
Tel: 613-238-6271; *Fax:* 613-238-5676
gremb.otv@mfa.gr
www.mfa.gr/canada/en/the-embassy
twitter.com/GreeceIn Canada
www.facebook.com/Greeceincanada
Her Excellency Konstantina Athanassiadou, Ambassador
Christina Valassopoulou, Deputy Head of Mission & First Counsellor, Political Section
Dimitra Schina, First Secretary, Economic & Commercial Affairs
Lt. Col. Stefanos Ampouleris, Defence Attaché

Holy See / Vatican
Apostolic Nunciature, 724 Manor Ave.,
Ottawa, ON K1M 0E3
Tel: 613-746-4914; *Fax:* 613-746-4786
nuntiatura@nuntiatura.ca
www.nuntiatura.ca
His Excellency Most Rev. Ivan Jurkovic, Apostolic Nuncio
Monsignor Matjaz Roter, First Secretary & Chargé d'affaires, a.i.

Republic of Honduras
Embassy of Honduras, #805, 130 Albert St.,
Ottawa, ON K1P 5G4
Tel: 613-233-8900; *Fax:* 613-232-0193
ambassador@embassyhonduras.hn
embajadahondurasencanada.hn
www.facebook .com/embajada.encanada
Her Excellency Sofia Lastenia Cerrato Rodriguez, Ambassador
Tania Vanessa Maria A. Casco Rubi, First Secretary

Hungary
Embassy of Hungary, 299 Waverly St.,
Ottawa, ON K2P 0V9
Tel: 613-230-2717; *Fax:* 613-230-7560
mission.ott@mfa.gov.hu
ottawa.mfa.gov.hu
www.facebook.com/HunEmbassy.O ttawa
Her Excellency Maria Eva Vass-Salazar, Ambassador-designate
Mark Horvath, First Counsellor & Chargé d'affaires, a.i.
Gabor Simon, Counsellor & Consul
Gergely Bodnar, First Secretary
Katalin Oroszi, First Secretary
Zoltan Jatekos, Second Secretary
Dorottya Judit Deak-Stifner, Third Secretary, Cultural & Consular Affairs

Iceland
Embassy of Iceland, Constitution Square, #710, 360 Albert St.,
Ottawa, ON K1R 7X7
Tel: 613-482-1944; *Fax:* 613-482-1945
icemb.ottawa@utn.stjr.is
www.government.is/diplomatic-missions/embassy-o f-iceland-in-ottawa
twitter.com/iceincan
www.facebook.com/IcelandInCan ada
His Excellency Hlynur Gudjonsson, Ambassador

Republic of India
High Commission of India, 10 Springfield Rd.,
Ottawa, ON K1M 1C9
Tel: 613-744-3751; *Fax:* 613-744-0913
hicomind@hciottawa.ca
www.hciottawa.gov.in
twitter.com/HCI_Ottawa
ww w.facebook.com/MEAINDIA
His Excellency Ajay Bisaria, High Commissioner,
hc.ottawa@mea.gov.in

Anshuman Gaur, Deputy High Commissioner,
dhc.ottawa@mea.gov.in
Rajeev Madaan, Counsellor, pol.ottawa@mea.gov.in

Republic of Indonesia
Embassy of Indonesia, 55 Parkdale Ave.,
Ottawa, ON K1Y 1E5
Tel: 613-724-1100; *Fax:* 613-724-1105
publicaffairs@indonesia-ottawa.org
kemlu.go.id/ottawa
www.youtube.com/user/kbriottawa
twitter.com/KBRI_Ottawa
www.facebook.com/kbri.ottawa.5
Yulastiawarman Zakaria, Minister & Chargé d'affaires, a.i.
Iwan Nur Hidayat, Counsellor
Sam Aryadi, First Secretary
Adde Anindyawati, Second Secretary

Islamic Republic of Iran
Embassy of the Islamic Republic of Iran, 245 Metcalfe St.,
Ottawa, ON K2P 2K2
Canada suspended diplomatic relations with Iran in September
2012.

Republic of Iraq
Embassy of Iraq, 189 Laurier Ave. East,
Ottawa, ON K1N 6P1
Tel: 613-236-9177; *Fax:* 613-236-9641
media@iqemb.ca
www.mofa.gov.iq/ottawa
His Excellency Wadee Batti Hanna Albatti, Ambassador
Intisar Talib Dawood Al-Juboori, Third Secretary

Republic of Ireland
Embassy of Ireland, #1105, 130 Albert St.,
Ottawa, ON K1P 5G4
Tel: 613-233-6281; *Fax:* 613-233-5835
embassyofireland@rogers.com
www.dfa.ie/irish-embassy/canada
twitter.co m/IrlEmbCanada
His Excellency Eamonn McKee, Ambassador
John Boylan, Deputy Head of Mission
Michael Declan Hurley, First Secretary
Laura Ann Finlay, Second Secretary

State of Israel
Embassy of Israel, #1005, 50 O'Connor St.,
Ottawa, ON K1P 6L2
Tel: 613-750-7500; *Fax:* 613-750-7555
info@ottawa.mfa.gov.il
embassies.gov.il/ottawa
twitter.com/IsraelinCan ada
www.facebook.com/IsraelinCanada
Ohad Nakash Kaynar, Chargé d'affaires, a.i.
Yaakov Moshe Lemann, Counsellor
Orly Aharona Erlich, First Secretary
Bar Segal, Second Secretary
Col. Amos Nachmani, Defence Attaché

Italian Republic
Embassy of Italy, 275 Slater St., 21st Fl.,
Ottawa, ON K1P 5H9
Tel: 613-232-2401; *Fax:* 613-233-1484
ambasciata.ottawa@esteri.it
ambottawa.esteri.it/ambasciata_ottawa/it
www.flickr.com/photos/ambitaliaottawa
twitter.com/ItalyinCanada
www.facebook.com/ambottawa
His Excellency Andrea Ferrari, Ambassador,
segreteria.ottawa@esteri.it
Gaia La Cognata, Deputy Head of Mission,
ambasciata.ottawa@esteri.it
Nicoletta Gomiero, First Secretary, consolare.ottawa@esteri.it
Benedetto Reitano, First Secretary, Economic & Commercial
Affairs

Ivory Coast
See: **Republic of Côte d'Ivoire**

Jamaica
Jamaican High Commission, The Burnside Bldg., #809, 350
Sparks St.,
Ottawa, ON K1R 7S8
Tel: 613-233-9311; *Fax:* 613-233-0611
jamaica@jhcottawa.ca
www.jhcottawa.ca
Her Excellency Sharon Miller, High Commissioner
Dana-Leigh Gienda Anderson, Counsellor

Japan
Embassy of Japan, 255 Sussex Dr.,
Ottawa, ON K1N 9E6
Tel: 613-241-8541; *Fax:* 613-241-2232
infocul@ot.mofa.go.jp
www.ca.emb-japan.go.jp
www.instagram.com/japaninottawa
twitter.com/JapaninCanada
www.facebook.com/infoculEmbassyofJapanCA
His Excellency Yasuhisa Kawamura, Ambassador
Namika Fujikawa, Counsellor
Ken Fujita, Counsellor
Shunichi Inoue, Counsellor
Yoshifuru Yokoyama, Counsellor
Aya Okada, Second Counsellor

Hashemite Kingdom of Jordan
Embassy of Jordan, #701, 100 Bronson Ave.,
Ottawa, ON K1R 6G8
Tel: 613-238-8090; *Fax:* 613-232-3341
ottawa@fm.gov.jo
www.embassyofjordan.ca
His Excellency Majed Alqatarneh, Ambassador
Ismael Maddallah Suliman Maaytah, Minister & Deputy Head of
Mission
Omar El-Atoum, Counsellor

Republic of Kazakhstan
Embassy of the Republic of Kazakhstan, #1603-1064, 150
Metcalfe St.,
Ottawa, ON K2P 1P1
Tel: 613-695-8055; *Fax:* 613-695-8755
ottawa@mfa.kz
mfa.gov.kz/en/ottawa
twitter.com/KZEmbassyCA
www.faceb ook.com/232463933540282
Other contact information: Alt. E-mail:
kazakhembassy@gmail.com
His Excellency Akylbek Kamaldinov, Ambassador
Murat Rustemov, Counsellor
Dinazat Kassymova, First Secretary
Talgat Ketebayev, First Secretary
Indira Kurmanbekova, First Secretary

Republic of Kenya
High Commission for Kenya, 415 Laurier Ave. East,
Ottawa, ON K1N 6R4
Tel: 613-563-1773; *Fax:* 613-233-6599
balozi@kenyahighcommission.ca
www.kenyahighcommission.ca
www.facebook .com/kenyahighcommissionottawa
His Excellency Immaculate Nduku Musili Wambua, High
Commissioner
Stella Musembi, First Counsellor
Abdishakur Sheikh Hussein Noor, First Counsellor
John Musembi Mutinda, First Secretary

Republic of Korea
Embassy of Korea, 150 Boteler St.,
Ottawa, ON K1N 5A6
Tel: 613-244-5010; *Fax:* 613-244-5034
canada@mofa.go.kr
can-ottawa.mofa.go.kr
www.youtube.com/user/koreanembassycanada
twitter.com/koremb_canada
www .facebook.com/embassyofkorea.canada
His Excellency Keung Ryong Chang, Ambassador
Dong-Ok Lee, Minister & Consul General
Bum Soo Kwak, Minister
Seokhwan Yang, Counsellor
Col. Keunsik Moon, Defence Attaché

Democratic People's Republic of Korea
Permanent Mission of Democratic People's Republic of
Korea to the UN, 820 - 2 Ave., 13th Fl.,
New York, NY 10017 USA
Tel: 212-972-3105; *Fax:* 212-972-3154
bizpibf7@verizon.net
His Excellency Kim Song, Permanent Representative

Republic of Kosovo
Embassy of the Republic of Kosovo (to Canada), 470
Somerset St. West,
Ottawa, ON K1R 5J8
Tel: 613-569-2828; *Fax:* 613-569-4848
embassy.canada@rks-gov.net
www.ambasada-ks.net/ca
twitter.com/MFAKOSOV O
www.facebook.com/MFAKosovo
His Excellency Adriatik Kryeziu, Ambassador
Blerta Ademi Beqiri, First Counsellor

State of Kuwait
Embassy of Kuwait, 333 Sussex Dr.,
Ottawa, ON K1N 1J9
Tel: 613-780-9999; *Fax:* 613-237-4444
info@kuwaitembassy.ca
kuwaitembassy.ca
Her Excellency Reem Mohammad Khaled Zaid Al Khaled,
Ambassador
Yaseen Almajed, Deputy Head of Mission
Hamad Aldhafeeri, First Secretary
Yaseen Almajed, Second Secretary
Habeeb Rashed Aldawila, Third Secretary

Kyrgyz Republic
Embassy of the Kyrgyz Republic (to Canada), 2360
Masachussets. Ave. NW,
Washington, DC 20008 USA
Tel: 202-449-9822; *Fax:* 202-449-8275
info@kgembassy.org
www.youtube.com/user/kgembassyusa
www.facebook.com/kgembassyusa
His Excellency Bolot Otunbaev, Ambassador

Lao People's Democratic Republic
Embassy of the Lao People's Democratic Republic (to
Canada), 2222 S St. NW,
Washington, DC 20008 USA
Tel: 202-332-6416; *Fax:* 202-332-4923
embasslao@gmail.com
www.laoembassy.com
His Excellency Khamphan Anlavan, Ambassador

Republic of Latvia
Embassy of the Republic of Latvia, #1200, 350 Sparks St.,
Ottawa, ON K1R 7S8
Tel: 613-238-6014; *Fax:* 613-238-7044
embassy.canada@mfa.gov.lv
www.mfa.gov.lv/ottawa
www.flickr.com/photos/latvianmfa
twitter.com/LV_EmbassyCA
www.facebook .com/EmbassyOfLatviaInCanada
His Excellency Karlis Eihenbaums, Ambassador
Inga Skruzmane, Counsellor
Katrina Kjaspere, Third Secretary

Lebanese Republic
Embassy of Lebanon, 640 Lyon St.,
Ottawa, ON K1S 3Z5
Tel: 613-236-5825; *Fax:* 613-232-1609
info@lebanonembassy.ca
www.lebanonembassy.ca
His Excellency Fadi Ziadeh, Ambassador,
ambassador@lebanonembassy.ca

Kingdom of Lesotho
High Commission for the Kingdom of Lesotho, #1820, 130
Albert St.,
Ottawa, ON K1P 5G4
Tel: 613-234-0770; *Fax:* 636-234-5665
lesotho.ottawa@bellnet.ca
Molebatseng Lydiah Makhata, Counsellor & Chargé d'affaires,
a.i.

Republic of Liberia
Embassy of the Republic of Liberia (to Canada), 5201 - 16th
St. NW,
Washington, DC 20011 USA
Tel: 202-723-0437; *Fax:* 202-723-0436
www.liberianembassyus.org
www.facebook.com/liberianembassyus
Her Excellency George S.W. Patten, Ambassador

State of Libya
Embassy of the State of Libya, #710, 170 Laurier Ave. West,
Ottawa, ON K1P 5V5
Tel: 613-842-7519; *Fax:* 613-842-8627
info@embassyoflibya.ca
embassyoflibya.ca
Omar Alghanai, Counsellor & Chargé d'affaires, a.i.
Tarek Alnajeh, Counsellor
Fateh Benelhaj, Counsellor

Liechtenstein
See: **Swiss Confederation**

Republic of Lithuania
Embassy of Lithuania, #1600, 150 Metcalfe St.,
Ottawa, ON K2P 1P1
Tel: 613-567-5458; *Fax:* 613-567-5315
amb.ca@urm.lt
ca.mfa.lt
His Excellency Darius Skusevicius, Ambassador
Kristina Seniavskiene, Counsellor
Inga Miskinyte, Third Secretary

Grand Duchy of Luxembourg
Embassy of Luxembourg (to Canada), 2200 Massachusetts Ave. NW,
Washington, DC 20008 USA

Tel: 202-265-4171; Fax: 202-328-8270
washington.amb@mae.etat.lu
washington.mae.lu
His Excellency Nicole Bintner-Bakshian, Ambassador

Republic of Macedonia
Embassy of the Republic of Macedonia, #1006, 130 Albert St.,
Ottawa, ON K1P 5G4

Tel: 613-234-3882; Fax: 613-233-1852
ottawa@mfa.gov.mk
www.mfa.gov.mk/ottawa/index.php/en
Dimitar Blazhevski, Counsellor & Chargé d'affaires, a.i.

Republic of Madagascar
Embassy of Madagascar, 3 Raymond St.,
Ottawa, ON K1R 1A3

Tel: 613-537-0505; Fax: 613-537-2882
ambamadcanada@bellnet.ca
www.madagascar-embassy.ca
Sahondra Harilala Rakotoniaina, Counsellor & Chargé d'affaires, a.i.
Lanto Lydie Noelle Rajernerson, Counsellor
Vahintsoa Mirella Ramanandraibe, Counsellor

Republic of Malawi
High Commission for Malawi (to Canada), 2408 Massachussetts Ave. NW,
Washington, DC 20008 USA

Tel: 202-721-0270; Fax: 202-721-0288
malawidc@aol.com
www.malawiembassy-dc.org
His Excellency Edward Yakobe Sawerengera, Ambassador

Malaysia
High Commission for Malaysia, 60 Boteler St.,
Ottawa, ON K1N 8Y7

Tel: 613-241-5182; Fax: 613-241-5214
mwottawa@kln.gov.my
www.kln.gov.my/web/can_ottawa
www.facebook.com/Mal awakil.Ottawa
Her Excellency Anizan Binti Adnin, High Commissioner
Suresh Kumar K Rengasamy, Minister-Counsellor
Muhammad Muhaimin Bin Rasidi, Second Secretary
Zainul Akmar Binti Ahmad, Second Secretary

Republic of Maldives
Permanent Mission of the Republic of Maldives to the UN,
#202E, 801 - 2 Ave.,
New York, NY 10017 USA

Tel: 212-599-6194; Fax: 212-661-6405
info@maldivesmission.com
maldivesmission.com
twitter.com/MVPMNY
Her Excellency Thilmeeza Hussain, High Commissioner

Republic of Mali
Embassy of Mali, 50 Goulburn Ave.,
Ottawa, ON K1N 8C8

Tel: 613-232-1501; Fax: 613-232-7429
ambassade@ambamali.ca
www.ambamali.ca
Her Excellency Fatima Meite, Ambassador
Cherif Mohamed Kanoute, First Counsellor
Fatoumata Sylla Maiga, Second Counsellor

Republic of Malta
High Commission for Malta (to Canada), 2017 Connecticut Ave. NW,
Washington, DC 20008 USA

Tel: 202-462-3611; Fax: 202-387-5470
maltaembassy.washington@gov.mt
foreignaffairs.gov.mt/en/Embassies/Me_Uni ted_States
His Excellency Keith Azzopardi, Ambassador

Republic of the Marshall Islands
Embassy of the Republic of the Marshall Islands (to Canada), 2433 Massachusetts Ave. NW,
Washington, DC 20008 USA

Tel: 202-234-5414; Fax: 202-232-3236
info@rmiembassyus.org
His Excellency Gerald M. Zackios, Ambassador

Islamic Republic of Mauritania
Permanent Mission of the Islamic Republic of Mauritania to the UN, 116 East 38th St.,
New York, NY 10016 USA

Tel: 212-252-0113; Fax: 212-252-0175
mauritaniamission@gmail.com
www.un.int/mauritania

His Excellency Sidi Mohamed Boubacar, Permanent Representative

Republic of Mauritius
High Commission for Mauritius (to Canada), 1709 N St. NW,
Washington, DC 20036 USA

Tel: 202-244-1491; Fax: 202-966-0983
mauritius.embassy@verizon.net
Other contact information: Alt. E-mail:
washingtonemb@govmu.org

United Mexican States
Embassy of Mexico, #1000, 45 O'Connor St.,
Ottawa, ON K1P 1A4

Tel: 613-233-8988; Fax: 613-235-9123
infocan@sre.gob.mx
embamex.sre.gob.mx/canada
www.flickr.com/photos/embamexcan
twitter.com/embamexcan
www.facebook.c om/embamexcan
His Excellency Juan Jose Ignacio Gomez Camacho,
Ambassador, aambassadorcan@sre.gob.mx
Arturo Hernandez Basave, Deputy Head of Mission,
ahernandezb@sre.gob.mx
Jacqueline Marquez Rojano, Minister
Dulce Maria Valle Alvarez, Minister
Juan Gabriel Morales Morales, Counsellor
Maria Cristina Oropeza Zorrilla, Counsellor

Republic of Moldova
Embassy of the Republic of Moldova, #801, 275 Slater St.,
Ottawa, ON K1P 5H9

Tel: 613-695-6167; Fax: 613-695-6164
ottawa@mfa.md
canada.mfa.gov.md
www.facebook.com/MoldovainCanada
His Excellency Emil Druc, Ambassador, emil.druc@mfa.gov.md
Petru Alexei, Counsellor

Principality of Monaco
Embassy of the Principality of Monaco (to Canada), 888 - 17th St. NW,
Washington, DC 20006 USA

Tel: 202-234-1530; Fax: 202-244-7656
info@monacodc.org
monacodc.org/canadahome.html
twitter.com/MonacoEmbas syDC
www.facebook.com/EmbassyofMonacoDC
Her Excellency Maguy Maccario Doyle, Ambassador

Mongolia
Embassy of Mongolia, 132 Stanley Ave.,
Ottawa, ON K1M 1N9

Tel: 613-569-3830; Fax: 613-569-3916
ottawa@mfa.gov.mn
ottawa.embassy.mn
www.facebook.com/mfamongoliaMN
His Excellency Ariunbold Yadmaa, Ambassador,
mongolia@rogers.com
Munkh-Ulzii Tserendorj, Deputy Chief of Mission,
dcm.mongolia@rogers.com
Battushig Zanabazar, Counsellor
Zolzaya Dorjtsoo, Second Secretary
Zolzaya Sanjmyatav, Third Secretary

Montenegro
Embassy of Montenegro (to Canada), 1610 New Hampshire Ave. NW,
Washington, DC 20009

Tel: 202-234-6108; Fax: 202-234-6109
usa@mfa.gov.me
His Excellency Nebojsa Kaludjerovic, Ambassador
Andelka Rogac, Deputy Head of Mission
Milena Veljovic, Second Secretary

Montserrat
See: Organization of the Eastern Caribbean States

Kingdom of Morocco
Embassy of Morocco, 38 Range Rd.,
Ottawa, ON K1N 8J4

Tel: 613-236-7391; Fax: 613-236-6164
sifamaot@bellnet.ca
Her Excellency Souriya Otmani, Ambassador
Jamila Antra, Minister
Abdollah Lkahya, Minister-Counsellor
Mohammed Larbi Bouchara, Counsellor
Houda Zemmouri, Counsellor, Economic Affairs

Republic of Mozambique
High Commission of the Republic of Mozambique (to Canada), 1525 New Hampshire Ave. NW,
Washington, DC 20036 USA

Tel: 202-293-7146; Fax: 202-835-0245
washington.dc@embamoc.gov.mz
usa.embamoc.gov.mz
His Excellency Carlos Dos Santos, High Commissioner
Aristides De J.M.A.D.G. Adriano, Minister-Counsellor

Republic of the Union of Myanmar
Embassy of the Republic of the Union of Myanmar, 336 Island Park Dr.,
Ottawa, ON K1Y 0A7

Tel: 613-232-9990
meottawa@rogers.com
www.meottawa.org
His Excellency U Hau Khan Sum, Ambassador
Aye Mya Hman, Minister-Counsellor
Htun Aye, First Secretary
Soe Wuttye Htoo, Second Secretary

Republic of Namibia
High Commission for Namibia (to Canada), 1605 New Hampshire Ave. NW,
Washington, DC 20009 USA

Tel: 202-986-0540; Fax: 202-986-0443
info@namibianembassyusa.org
www.namibianembassyusa.org
Her Excellency Margaret Mensah-Williams, High Commissioner

Federal Democratic Republic of Nepal
Embassy of Nepal, 408 Queen St.,
Ottawa, ON K1R 5A7

Tel: 613-680-5513; Fax: 613-422-5149
nepalembassy@rogers.com
ca.nepalembassy.gov.np
www.youtube.com/mofa; www.flickr.com/photos/mofanepal
twitter.com/nepal_of
facebook.com/100009732422934
Other contact information: Alt. E-mail: eonottawa@mofa.gov.np
His Excellency Bhrigu Dhungana, Ambassador
Prakash Adhikari, Deputy Chief of Mission
Sharad Adhikari, Third Secretary

Kingdom of the Netherlands
Embassy of the Netherlands, #2020, 350 Albert St.,
Ottawa, ON K1R 1A4

Tel: 613-237-5031; Fax: 613-237-6471
ott@minbuza.nl
www.netherlandsworldwide.nl/countries/canada
twitter.co m/NLinCanada
www.facebook.com/thenetherlandsincanada
Her Excellency Goverdina Christina Coppoolase, Ambassador
Jaap Jan Speelman, Deputy Head of Mission
Regina Maria Alida T. Aalders, Counsellor
L.Col. Antonius C.L. Maria Linssen, Defence, Military, Naval & Air Attaché

New Zealand
New Zealand High Commission, #1401, 150 Elgin St.,
Ottawa, ON K2P 1L4

Tel: 613-238-5991; Fax: 613-238-5707
info@nzhcottawa.org
www.mfat.govt.nz
twitter.com/NZinOttawa
www.face book.com/219970494714908
His Excellency Martin Wilfred Harvey, High Commissioner
Amy Louise Tisdall, Deputy High Commissioner
Emma Rennie, Second Secretary
Lt. Col. Scott Barrie Cordwell, Defence Adviser

Republic of Nicaragua
Embassy of Nicaragua (to Canada), 1627 New Hamphire Ave. NW,
Washington, DC 20009 USA

Tel: 202-939-6570; Fax: 202-939-6545
mperalta@cancilleria.gob.ni
consuladodenicaragua.com
His Excellency Maurizio Gelli, Ambassador

Republic of Niger
Embassy of Niger (to Canada), 2204 R St. NW,
Washington, DC 20008 USA

Tel: 202-483-4224; Fax: 202-483-3169
communication@embassyofniger.org
www.embassyofniger.org
His Excellency Abdallah Wafy, Ambassador

Kasozi Helen Kayiza, Minister-Counsellor
Sam Muzoora Muhwezi, Second Counsellor

Ukraine
Embassy of Ukraine, 310 Somerset St. West,
Ottawa, ON K2P 0J9

Tel: 613-230-2961; Fax: 613-230-2400
emb_ca@ukremb.ca
canada.mfa.gov.ua
twitter.com/UkrEmb_inCanada
www.facebook.com/UkraineInCanada
His Excellency Andrii Shevchenko, Ambassador
Yurii Nykytiuk, Minister-Counsellor
Oleksii Liashenko, Counsellor
Petro Petrenko, Counsellor
Oles Gryban, First Secretary
Oleh Khavroniuk, First Secretary

United Arab Emirates
Embassy of the United Arab Emirates, 125 Boteler St.,
Ottawa, ON K1N 0A4

Tel: 613-565-7272; Fax: 613-565-8007
ottawaEMB.reception@mofaic.gov.ae
twitter.com/uaeembassyca
His Excellency Fahad Saeed M.A. Alraqbani, Ambassador
Mohamed R.M. Alfandi Alshamsi, Second Secretary

United Kingdom of Great Britain & Northern Ireland
British High Commission, 80 Elgin St.,
Ottawa, ON K1P 5K7

Tel: 613-237-1530; Fax: 613-232-0738
ukincanada@fco.gov.uk
www.gov.uk/world/canada
www.instagram.com/ukincanada
twitter.com/ukincanada
www.facebook.com/u kincanada
Her Excellency Susannah Goshko, High Commissioner CMG
David Reed, Deputy Head of Mission MBE
Martin Robert Thursfield, Counsellor
Andrew Michael Barr, First Secretary
Nancy Olivia Bellers-Ivison, First Secretary
Samuel James Jeremy, First Secretary
Catriona Grace Blyth Little, First Secretary
Alexander James Partridge, First Secretary
James Richard Prior, First Secretary
Sonal Lavji Rathod, First Secretary
Brig. Doug Gibson, Defence Adviser

United States of America
Embassy of the United States of America, 490 Sussex Dr.,
Ottawa, ON K1N 1G8

Tel: 613-238-5335; Fax: 613-688-3082
ca.usembassy.gov
www.youtube.com/user/USEmbassyOttawa
twitter.com/usembassyottawa
www.f acebook.com/canada.usembassy
Arnold Anthony Chacon, Chargé d'affaires, a.i.
Katherine Ann Brucker, Deputy Head of Mission
Karen Kyung Won Choe-Fichte, Minister-Counsellor
Eric Allan Fichte, Minister-Counsellor
Holly Sue Higgins, Minister-Counsellor
Brian Richard Naranjo, Minister-Counsellor
James Cornelius Rigassio, Minister-Counsellor

Eastern Republic of Uruguay
Embassy of Uruguay, #800, 55 Metcalfe St.,
Ottawa, ON K1P 6L5

Tel: 613-234-2727
urucanada@mrree.gub.uy
www.embassyofuruguay.ca
His Excellency Martin Alejandro Vidal Delgado, Ambassador
Trilce Gervaz Muniz, Second Secretary

Republic of Uzbekistan
Embassy of the Republic of Uzbekistan, 1746
Massachusetts Ave. NW,
Washington, DC 20036 USA

Tel: 202-887-5300; Fax: 202-293-6804
info.washington@mfa.uz
www.uzbekistan.org
His Excellency Javlon Vakhabov, Ambassador

Republic of Venezuela
Embassy of Venezuela, 32 Range Rd.,
Ottawa, ON K1N 8J4

Tel: 613-235-5151; Fax: 613-235-3205
embve.caotw@mppre.gob.ve
www.misionvenezuela.org
Luis Augusto Acuna Cedeno, Chargé d'affaires

Socialist Republic of Vietnam
Embassy of Vietnam, 55 Mackay St.,
Ottawa, ON K1M 2B2

Tel: 613-236-0772; Fax: 613-236-2704
vietnamembassy@rogers.com
www.vietnamembassy.ca
His Excellency Cao Phong Pham, Ambassador
Houng Tra Nguyen, Minister-Counsellor
Thi Thu Huong Do, Counsellor, Commerce
Hoang Yen Vu, Counsellor

Republic of Yemen
Embassy of the Republic of Yemen, 54 Chamberlain Ave.,
Ottawa, ON K1S 1V9

Tel: 613-729-6627; Fax: 613-729-8915
yeminfo@yemenembassy.ca
www.yemenembassy.ca
www.facebook.com/205072892 918967
His Excellency Jamal Abdullah Yahya Al-Sallal, Ambassador,
Ambassador@yemenembassy.ca
Abdulhakim Alhamadi, Minister & Deputy Head of Mission
Rafat Hassan Mohamed Abdullah, Minister
Khaldon Yaseen Saeed Noman, Counsellor

Republic of Zambia
High Commission for Zambia (to Canada), #900, 130 Albert St.,
Ottawa, ON K1P 5G4

Tel: 613-232-4400; Fax: 613-232-4410
zhc.ottawa@bellnet.ca
www.zambiahighcommission.ca
His Excellency Felix Mfula, High Commissioner
Evaristo D. Kasunga, Deputy Head of Mission
Charlotte Mulenga Chansa-Mutanga, First Secretary, Economic
& Trade
Brian Malama, First Secretary
Grace Chintu Ng'andu, First Secretary, Education
Winston Bwalya, Second Secretary, Accounts
Jennifer Konjela Manda, Third Secretary

Republic of Zimbabwe
Embassy for the Republic of Zimbabwe, 332 Somerset St.
West,
Ottawa, ON K2P 0J9

Tel: 613-421-1242; Fax: 613-422-7403
zimottawa@zimfa.gov.zw
www.zimembassyottawa.com
His Excellency Ruth Masodzi Chikwira, Ambassador
Ruvimbo Miriro Mbudzi, Counsellor, Political Affairs
Herbert Garikai Nyathi, Counsellor
Lawrencia Mariga, Second Secretary
Ebar Zvipo Nyamasvisva, Third Secretary

Canadian Diplomatic & Consular Representatives Abroad

Islamic State of Afghanistan
Embassy of Canada, House 256, St. 15, Wazir-Akbar-Khan,
Kabul, Afghanistan

kabul@international.gc.ca
www.international.gc.ca/afghanistan
twitter.com/CanEmbAFG
www.facebook .com/CanadainAfghanistan
Other contact information: Tel: 93 (0) 701 108 800; Fax: 93 (0)
701 108 805
Canada temporarily closed its embassy in Afghanistan and
suspended diplomatic relations in August 2021, after the Taliban
seized control of Kabul.
Reid Sirrs, Ambassador

Republic of Albania
See: **Italian Republic**

twitter.com/canadainalbania

People's Democratic Republic of Algeria
Embassy of Canada, PO Box 464 Ben Aknon, 18 Mustapha
Khalef St.,
Algiers, 16306 Algeria

alger@international.gc.ca
www.algerie.gc.ca
twitter.com/CanadaAlgeria
www.facebook.com/CanadaAlgeria
Other contact information: Phone: 213 (0) 770-083-000; Fax:
213 (0) 770-083-070
Christopher Wilkie, Ambassador

American Samoa
See: **New Zealand**
High Commission of Australia, PO Box 704, Beach Rd.,
Apia, Samoa

samoa.embassy.gov.au/apia/home.html
Other contact information: Tel: 68 5 23 411; Fax: 68 5 23 159

Under the Canada-Australia Consular Services Sharing
Agreement, the High Commission of Australia will serve
Canadians abroad.
Sara Moriarty, Australian High Commissioner

Principality of Andorra
See: **Kingdom of Spain**

People's Republic of Angola
See: **Republic of Zimbabwe**

Anguilla
See: **Barbados**

Antigua & Barbuda
See: **Barbados**

Argentine Republic
Embassy of Canada, Tagle 2828,
Buenos Aires, C1425EEH Argentine

bairs-webmail@international.gc.ca
www.argentina.gc.ca
twitter.com/CanadaArgentina
www.facebook.com/CanadaInArgentina
Other contact information: Tel: 54 (11) 4808-1000; Fax: 54 (11)
4808-1111
David Usher, Ambassador

Republic of Armenia
See: **Russian Federation**

Aruba
See: **Kingdom of the Netherlands**

Commonwealth of Australia
High Commission of Canada, Commonwealth Ave.,
Canberra, ACT 2600 Australia

cnbra@international.gc.ca
www.australia.gc.ca
twitter.com/canadadownunder
www.facebook.com/CanadaDownUnder
Other contact information: Phone: (02) 6270-4000; Fax: (02)
6270-4060
Mark Glauser, High Commissioner

Republic of Austria
Embassy of Canada, Laurenzerberg 2,
Vienna, A-1010 Austria

vienn@international.gc.ca
www.austria.gc.ca
twitter.com/CanAmbAustria
www.facebook.com/CanadainAustria
Other contact information: Phone: 43 (1) 531-38-3000; Fax: 43
(1) 531-38-3321
Heidi Alberta Hulan, Ambassador

Republic of Azerbaijan
See: **Republic of Turkey**

Autonomous Region of the Azores
See: **Portuguese Republic**

Commonwealth of the Bahamas
See: **Jamaica**

info@cdnbahamas.com

Kingdom of Bahrain
See: **Kingdom of Saudi Arabia**

People's Republic of Bangladesh
High Commission of Canada, PO Box 569, United Nations
Road, Baridhara,
Dhaka, 1212 Bangladesh

dhakag@international.gc.ca
www.bangladesh.gc.ca
twitter.com/CanHCBangladesh
www.facebook.com/CanadaInBangladesh
Other contact information: Phone: 880 2 5566 8444; Fax: 880 2
5566 8423
Benoit Préfontaine, High Commissioner

Barbados
High Commission of Canada, PO Box 404, Bishop's Court
Hill,
Bridgetown, BB11113 Barbados

Tel: 246-429-3550; Fax: 246-437-7436
bdgtn@international.gc.ca
www.barbados.gc.ca
twitter.com/CanHCBarbados
www.facebook.com/CanadaInBarbados
Lilian Chatterjee, High Commissioner

Republic of Belarus
See: Republic of Poland

Kingdom of Belgium
Embassy of Canada, 58, av des Arts,
Brussels, 1000 Belgium

bru@international.gc.ca
www.belgium.gc.ca
twitter.com/CanEmbBELUX
Other contact information: Phone: 32 2 741 0611; Fax: 32 2 741 0643

Alain Gendron, Ambassador

Belize
See: Republic of Guatemala
The Renaissance Tower of Belize,
Belize City, Belize

Tel: 501-223-1060; *Fax:* 501-223-0060
belize-city@international.gc.ca
twitter.com/CanadainBelize
www.faceboo k.com/CanadainBelize

Republic of Benin
See: Burkina Faso

Bermuda
See: United States of America

Kingdom of Bhutan
See: Republic of India

Republic of Bolivia
See: Republic of Peru
Embassy of Canada (Program Office), Plaza España
(Sopocachi), 2678, Calle Victor Sanjinez, Edificio Barcelona,
2nd Fl,
La Paz, Bolivia

lapaz@international.gc.ca
twitter.com/CanadaBolivia
www.facebook.com/CanadaPeruBolivia
Other contact information: Phone: 591 (2) 241-5141; Fax: 591 (2) 241-4453

Bonaire
See: Republic of Colombia

Bosnia & Herzegovina
See: Hungary

Republic of Botswana
See: Republic of Zimbabwe

Federative Republic of Brazil
Embassy of Canada, SES-Av. das Naçoes - Qd. 803 - Lote 16,
Brasilia, D.F., 70410-900 Brazil

brslag@international.gc.ca
www.brazil.gc.ca
twitter.com/canadabrazil
www.facebook.com/CanadainBrazil
Other contact information: Tel: (5561) 3424-5400; Fax: (5561) 3424-5490

Jennifer May, Ambassador

British Virgin Islands
See: Barbados

Brunei Darussalam
High Commission of Canada, PO Box 2808,
Bandar Seri Begawan, BS8675 Brunei Darussalam
bsbgn@international.gc.ca
www.facebook.com/CanadainBruneiDarussalam
Other contact information: Tel: 673 (2) 22-00-43; Fax: 673 (2) 22-00-40

Jeanette Stovel, High Commissioner

Republic of Bulgaria
See: Republic of Romania

Burkina Faso
Embassy of Canada, PO Box 548, 316 Professeur Ki-Zerbo St.,
Ouagadougou, Burkina Faso
ouaga@international.gc.ca
www.burkinafaso.gc.ca
twitter.com/CanEmbBFA
www.facebook.com/CanEmbBFA
Other contact information: Phone: 226 25 49 08 00; Fax: 226 25 49 08 10

Carol McQueen, Ambassador

Republic of Burundi
See: Republic of Kenya

bujumbura@canadaconsulate.ca

Kingdom of Cambodia
See: Thailand

twitter.com/CanadaCambodia
www.facebook.com/CanadainCambodia

Republic of Cameroon
High Commission of Canada, PO Box 572,
Yaoundé, Cameroon

yunde@international.gc.ca
www.cameroon.gc.ca
twitter.com/CanadaCameroon
www.facebook.com/CanadainCameroon
Other contact information: Phone: 237 222 50 39 04; Fax: 237 222 50 39 11

Richard Bale, High Commissioner

Canada-ASEAN Business Council (CABC)
10 Anson Road #12-08 International Plaza, 079903
Singapore

support@canasean.com
www.canasean.com
twitter.com/CAN_ASEAN
www.facebook.com/CANASEAN

Diedrah Kelly, Ambassador
Andrew Doherty, Contact, Canada Office,
andrew.doherty@canasean.com
Greg Ross, Contact, greg.ross@canasean.com

Canary Islands
See: Kingdom of Spain

Republic of Cabo Verde
See: Republic of Senegal

Cayman Islands
See: Jamaica

Central African Republic
See: Republic of Cameroon

Republic of Chad
See: Republic of The Sudan

Republic of Chile
Embassy of Canada, Nueva Tajamar 481, Torre Norte, 12th Fl.,
Santiago, Chile

stago.general@international.gc.ca
www.chile.gc.ca
twitter.com/CanEmbChile
www.facebook.com/CanadainChile
Other contact information: Tel: 56 (2) 2652-3800; Fax: 56 (2) 2652-3912

Michael Gort, Ambassador

People's Republic of China
Embassy of Canada, 19 Dong Zhi Men Wai St., Chao Yang Dist.,
Beijing, 100600 China

beijing-pa@international.gc.ca
www.china.gc.ca
twitter.com/CanadaChina
Other contact information: Tel: 86 (10) 5139-4000; Fax: 86 (10) 5139-4448

Dominic Barton, Ambassador

Republic of Colombia
Embassy of Canada, PO Box 110067, Carrera 7, No. 114-33,
Bogotá, Colombia

bgota@international.gc.ca
www.colombia.gc.ca
twitter.com/CanadaColombia
www.facebook.com/CanadainColombia
Other contact information: Tel: 57 (1) 657-9800; Fax: 57 (1) 657-9912

Marcel Lebleu, Ambassador

Union of the Comoros
See: United Republic of Tanzania

Democratic Republic of the Congo
Embassy of Canada, PO Box 8341,
Kinshasa, 1 Congo (Kinshasa)

knsha@international.gc.ca
www.canadainternational.gc.ca/congo
twitter.com/CanadaDRC
www.facebook .com/CanadainDRCongo
Other contact information: Tel: 243-996-021-500; Fax: 243-996-021-510

Nicolas Simard, Ambassador

Cook Islands
See: New Zealand

Republic of Costa Rica
Embassy of Canada, PO Box 351-1007 Centro Colón,
San José, Costa Rica

sjcra@international.gc.ca
www.costarica.gc.ca
www.facebook.com/CanEmbCRHNNI
Other contact information: Tel: 506 2242-4400; Fax: 506 2242-4410

James K. Hill, Ambassador

Republic of Côte d'Ivoire
Embassy of Canada, Immeuble Trade Centre, PO Box 4104,
23, av Nogues, 6th & 7th Fls., Le Plateau,
Abidjan, Ivory Coast

abdjn@international.gc.ca
www.canadainternational.gc.ca/cotedivoire
twitter.com/canembci
www.fac ebook.com/canadaincotedivoire
Other contact information: Tel: 225-20 30 07 00; Fax: 225-20 30 07 20

Claude Demers, Ambassador

Republic of Croatia
Embassy of Canada, Prilaz Gjure Dezelica 4,
Zagreb, 10 000 Croatia

zagrb@international.gc.ca
www.croatia.gc.ca
twitter.com/CanadaCroatia
www.facebook.com/CanadainCroatia
Other contact information: Tel: 385-1-488-1200; Fax: 385-1-488-1230

Alan Bowman, Ambassador

Republic of Cuba
Embassy of Canada, Calle 30, No. 518, Esquina 7a, Miramar,

Havana, Cuba

havan@international.gc.ca
www.cuba.gc.ca
twitter.com/CanEmbCuba
Other contact information: Tel: 53-7-204-2516; Fax: 53-7-204-2044

In April 2018, the Embassy of Canada in Havana, Cuba, was declared an unaccompanied post by the Canadian foreign service, in response to ongoing unexplained health issues affecting staff.
Timothy Zuniga-Brown, Chargé d'affaires

Republic of Cyprus
See: Hellenic Republic / Greece

Czech Republic
Embassy of Canada, Ve Struhach 95/2,
Prague, 160 00 Czech Republic

canada@canada.cz
www.czechrepublic.gc.ca
twitter.com/canembcz
www.facebook.com/KanadaCZ
Other contact information: Tel: 420 272 101 800; Fax: 420 272 101 890

Ayesha Patricia Rekhi, Ambassador

Kingdom of Denmark
Embassy of Canada, Kristen Bernikowsgade 1,
Copenhagen, K-1105 Denmark

copen@international.gc.ca
www.denmark.gc.ca
twitter.com/CanadaDenmark
Other contact information: Tel: 45-33-48-32-00; Fax: 45-33-48-32-20

Emi Furuya, Ambassador

Republic of Djibouti
See: Federal Democratic Republic of Ethiopia

Commonwealth of Dominica
See: Barbados

Dominican Republic
Embassy of Canada, Torre Citigroup en Acrópolis Center,
PO Box 2054, Av. Winston Churchill 1099, piso 18,
Santo Domingo, Dominican Republic

Tel: 809-262-3100; *Fax:* 809-262-3155
sdmgo@international.gc.ca
www.dominicanrepublic.gc.ca
twitter.com/CanE mbDR
www.facebook.com/CanEmbDR

Christine Laberge, Ambassador

Republic of Ecuador
PO Box 17-11-6512,
Quito, EC170514 Ecuador

quito@international.gc.ca
www.ecuador.gc.ca
twitter.com/CanadaEcuador
www.facebook.com/CanadainEcuador
Other contact information: Tel: (011 593 2) 2455-499; Fax: (011
593 2) 2277-672

Sylvie Bédard, Ambassador

Arab Republic of Egypt
Nile City Towers, South Tower, 2005 (A) Corniche El Nile,
18th Fl.,
Cairo, 11221 Egypt

cairo@international.gc.ca
www.egypt.gc.ca
twitter.com/CanEmbEgypt
www.facebook.com/CanadaEgypt
Other contact information: Tel: 20 2 2461-2200; Fax: 20 2
2461-2201

Louis Dumas, Ambassador

Republic of El Salvador
Embassy of Canada, Edificio Centro Financiero Gigante,
Alameda Roosevelt y 63 Avenida Sur, Nivel Lobby 2, Loca,
San Salvador, El Salvador

ssal@international.gc.ca
www.elsalvador.gc.ca
twitter.com/CanEmbSV
www.facebook.com/CanadainElSalvador
Other contact information: Tel: 503-2279-4655; Fax:
503-2279-0765

Karolina Guay, Ambassador

England
See: United Kingdom of Great Britain & Northern
Ireland

Republic of Equatorial Guinea
See: Federal Republic of Nigeria

Eritrea
See: Republic of The Sudan

Republic of Estonia
Embassy of Canada, Toom Kooli 13, 2nd Fl.,
Tallinn, 15186 Estonia

Tel: 372-627-3311; *Fax:* 372-627-3312
tallinn@canada.ee
www.international.gc.ca/country-pays/estonia-estonie
twitter.com/CanadaEstonia

Kevin Rex, Ambassador

Kingdom of eSwatini
See: Republic of Mozambique

Federal Democratic Republic of Ethiopia
Embassy of Canada, PO Box 1130,
Addis Ababa, Ethiopia

addis@international.gc.ca
www.canadainternational.gc.ca/ethiopia-ethiopie
www.facebook.com/CanadaE thiopia
Other contact information: Tel: 251-11-317-0000; Fax:
251-11-317-0040

Stéphane Jobin, Ambassador

European Union
The Mission of Canada to the European Union, 58, av des
Arts,
Brussels, 1000 Belgium

breu@international.gc.ca
www.canadainternational.gc.ca/eu-ue
twitter.com/Canada2EU
Other contact information: Tel: 32 0(2) 741 0660; Fax: 32 0(2)
741 0629

Ailish Campbell, Ambassador
Hon. Stéphane Dion, Special Envoy
Michelle Cooper, Counsellor & Section Head, Agriculture,
Fisheries & Environment,
michelle.cooper@international.gc.ca

Republic of the Fiji Islands
See: New Zealand

Republic of Finland
Embassy of Canada, PO Box 779,
Helsinki, 00101 Finland

hsnki@international.gc.ca
www.finland.gc.ca
twitter.com/CanEmbFinland
Other contact information: Tel: 358-9-228-530; Fax:
358-9-2285-3385

Jason Tolland, Ambassador

French Republic
Embassy of Canada, 130, rue du Faubourg Saint-Honoré,
Paris, 75008 France

www.france.gc.ca
twitter.com/CanEmbFrance
www.facebook.com/CanEmbFrance
Other contact information: Tel: 33-1-44-43-29-00; Fax:
33-1-44-43-29-99

Amy Baker, Chargée d'Affaires

Gabonese Republic
See: Republic of Cameroon

Republic of the Gambia
See: Republic of Senegal

Georgia
See: Republic of Turkey

Federal Republic of Germany
Embassy of Canada, Leipziger Platz 17,
Berlin, D-10117 Germany

www.germany.gc.ca
twitter.com/CanEmbGermany
www.facebook.com/CanadainGermany
Other contact information: Tel: 49-30-20-312-0

Hon. Stéphane Dion, Ambassador

Republic of Ghana
High Commission of Canada, PO Box 1639, 42
Independence Ave.,
Accra, Ghana

accra@international.gc.ca
www.canadainternational.gc.ca/ghana
twitter.com/CanHCGhana
www.faceboo k.com/CanadainGhana
Other contact information: Tel: 011 233 302 211521; Fax: 011
233 302 211523

Kati Csaba, High Commissioner

Grenada
See: Barbados

Republic of Guatemala
Embassy of Canada, PO Box 400,
Guatemala City, Guatemala

gtmla@international.gc.ca
www.guatemala.gc.ca
twitter.com/canembguatemala
www.facebook.com/CanadainGuatemala
Other contact information: Tel: 502 2363-4348; Fax: 502
2365-1210

Rita Rudaitis-Renaud, Ambassador

Republic of Guinea-Bissau
See: Republic of Senegal

Co-operative Republic of Guyana
High Commission of Canada, PO Box 10880,
Georgetown, Guyana

Tel: 592-227-2081; *Fax:* 592-225-8380
grgtn@international.gc.ca
www.guyana.gc.ca
twitter.com/canambguyana
www.facebook.com/CanadainGuyanaandSuriname

Mark Berman, High Commissioner

Republic of Haiti
PO Box 826, Delmas Rd.,
Port-au-Prince, Haiti

prnce@international.gc.ca
www.haiti.gc.ca
twitter.com/CanEmbHaiti
www.facebook.com/CanadainHaiti
Other contact information: Tel: 011 (509) 2249-9000; Fax: 011
(509) 2249-9920

Stuart Savage, Ambassador

Hellenic Republic / Greece
Embassy of Canada, 48 Ethnikis Antistaseos St.,
Chalandri, 152 31 Athens Greece

athns@international.gc.ca
www.greece.gc.ca
twitter.com/canadagreece
www.facebook.com/CanadainGreece
Other contact information: Tel: 30-210-727-3400; Fax:
30-210-727-3480

Mark Allen, Ambassador

Holy See / Vatican
Embassy of Canada, Via della Conciliazione 4/D,
Rome, 00193 Italy

vatcn@international.gc.ca
www.canadainternational.gc.ca/holy_see-saint_siege
twitter.com/CanadaHol ySee
Other contact information: Tel: 39-06-6830-7316; Fax:
39-06-6880-6283

Dennis Savoie, Ambassador

Republic of Honduras
See: Republic of Costa Rica
Embassy of Canada (Program Office), PO Box 3552,
Tegucigalpa, Honduras

tglpa@international.gc.ca
www.canadainternational.gc.ca/costa_rica
www.facebook.com/CanEmbCRHNNI
Other contact information: Tel: 504 2232 4551; Fax: 504 2239
7767

James K. Hill, Ambassador

Hungary
Embassy of Canada, Ganz U. 12-14,
Budapest, 1027 Hungary

bpest@international.gc.ca
www.hungary.gc.ca
twitter.com/CanadaHungary
www.facebook.com/CanadainHungary
Other contact information: Tel: 36-1-392-3360; Fax:
36-1-392-3390

Caroline Charette, Ambassador

Iceland
Embassy of Canada, PO Box 1510, Túngata 14,
Reykjavik, 121 Iceland

Tel: 354-575-6500; *Fax:* 354-575-6501
rkjvk@international.gc.ca
www.canadainternational.gc.ca/iceland-islande
twitter.com/CanadaIceland
www.facebook.com/CanadaIceland

Jeannette Menzies, Ambassador

Republic of India
High Commission of Canada, 7/8 Shantipath, Chanakyapuri,

New Delhi, 110021 India

delhi@international.gc.ca
www.international.gc.ca/country-pays/india-inde
www.youtube.com/user/CanadaInIndia
twitter.com/CanadaInIndia
www.faceb ook.com/CanadainIndia
Other contact information: Tel: 91-11-4178-2000; Fax:
91-11-4178-2020

Nadir Patel, High Commissioner

Republic of Indonesia
Embassy of Canada, PO Box 8324/JKS.MP,
Jakarta, 12084 Indonesia

canadianembassy.jkrta@international.gc.ca
www.indonesia.gc.ca
www.instagram.com/CanadaInIndonesia
twitter.com/CanEmbIndonesia
www.fa cebook.com/CanadainIndonesia
Other contact information: Tel: 62-21-2550-7800; Fax:
62-21-2550-7811

Cameron MacKay, Ambassador

Republic of Iraq
Embassy of Canada, British Embassy Compound,
International Zone,
Baghdad, Iraq

BGHDD.Consular@international.gc.ca
www.Canada.ca/Canada-And-Iraq
twitter.com/CanadainIraq
Other contact information: Phone: 964-782-783 5084
Due to the security situation in Iraq, the Canadian government
only provides limited consular assistance to Canadian citizens, &
does not provide in-person consular services.
Ulric Shannon, Ambassador

Republic of Ireland
Embassy of Canada, 7-8 Wilton Terrace,
Dublin, 2 Ireland

dubln@international.gc.ca
www.ireland.gc.ca
twitter.com/CanadaIreland
Other contact information: Tel: 353-1-234-4000; Fax:
353-1-234-4001

Nancy Smyth, Ambassador

State of Israel
Embassy of Canada, PO Box 9442,
Tel Aviv, 61093 Israel

taviv@international.gc.ca
www.israel.gc.ca
twitter.com/CanEmbIsrael
www.facebook.com/CanadainIsrael
Other contact information: Tel: (011 972 3) 636-3300; Fax: (011 972 3) 636-3380

Lisa Stadelbauer, Ambassador

Italian Republic
Embassy of Canada, Via Zara 30,
Rome, 00198 Italy

www.italy.gc.ca
twitter.com/CanadainItaly
www.facebook.com/CanadainItaly
Other contact information: Tel: (011-39) 06-85444-1; Fax: (011-39) 06-85444-3913

Alexandra Bugailiskis, Ambassador

Jamaica
High Commission of Canada, PO Box 1500,
Kingston, 10 Jamaica

Tel: 876-926-1500; *Fax:* 876-733-3493
kngtn@international.gc.ca
www.jamaica.gc.ca
twitter.com/CanadaJamaica
www.facebook.com/CanadainJamaica
Emina Tudakovic, High Commissioner

Japan
Embassy of Canada, 3-38 Akasaka, 7-chome Minato-ku,
Tokyo, 107-8503 Japan

www.japan.gc.ca
twitter.com/CanEmbJapan
www.facebook.com/canembjapan
Other contact information: Tel: 81-3-5412-6200; Fax: 81-3-5412-6291

Ian G. McKay, Ambassador

Hashemite Kingdom of Jordan
Embassy of Canada, PO Box 815403, 133 Zaharan St.,
Amman, 11180 Jordan

amman@international.gc.ca
www.jordan.gc.ca
twitter.com/CanadainIraq
www.facebook.com/canadainjordan
Other contact information: Tel: 962-6-590-1500; Fax: 962-6-590-1501

Donica Pottie, Ambassador

Republic of Kazakhstan
Embassy of Canada, 13/1 Kabanbay Batyr St.,
Astana, 010000 Kazakhstan

astnag@international.gc.ca
www.canadainternational.gc.ca/kazakhstan
twitter.com/CanEmbKZ
www.face book.com/CanadainKazakhstan
Other contact information: Tel: 7-7172-47-55-77; Fax: 7-7172-47-55-87

Nicholas Brousseau, Ambassador

Republic of Kenya
High Commission of Canada, PO Box 1013,
Nairobi, 00621 Kenya

nairobi@international.gc.ca
www.canadainternational.gc.ca/kenya
twitter.com/CanHCKenya
Other contact information: Tel: 254-20-366-3000; Fax: 254-20-366-3900

Vacant, High Commissioner

Republic of Kiribati
See: New Zealand

Republic of Korea
Embassy of Canada, 21 Jeongdong-gil, Jung-gu,
Seoul, 04518 Korea

seoul@international.gc.ca
www.korea.gc.ca
instagram.com/CanadaKorea
twitter.com/CanEmbKorea
www.facebook.com/CanadainKorea
Other contact information: Tel: 82-2-3783-6000; Fax: 82-2-3783-6239

Michael Danagher, Ambassador

State of Kuwait
Embassy of Canada, PO Box 25281,
Kuwait City, 13113 Kuwait

kwait@international.gc.ca
www.kuwait.gc.ca
twitter.com/CanadaKuwait
Other contact information: Tel: 965-2256-3025; Fax: 965-2256-0173

Louis-Pierre Émond, Ambassador

Kyrgyz Republic
See: Republic of Kazakhstan

Republic of Latvia
Embassy of Canada, 20/22 Baznicas St., 6th Fl.,
Riga, LV-1010 Latvia

riga@international.gc.ca
www.latvia.gc.ca
twitter.com/CanadaLatvia
Other contact information: Tel: 371-6781-3945; Fax: 371-6781-3960

Kevin Rex, Ambassador

Lebanese Republic
Embassy of Canada, PO Box 60163,
Jal El Dib, Lebanon

berut@international.gc.ca
www.lebanon.gc.ca
twitter.com/canadalebanon
www.facebook.com/CanadainJordan
Other contact information: Tel: 961-4-726-700; Fax: 961-4-726-703

Chantal Chastenay, Ambassador

Kingdom of Lesotho
See: Republic of South Africa

Republic of Liberia
See: Republic of Côte d'Ivoire

State of Libya
See: Republic of Tunisia
The Canadian embassy in Libya closed in 2014 due to security concerns. It temporarily relocated to Tunisia.
Hilary Childs-Adams, Ambassador

Principality of Liechtenstein
See: Swiss Confederation

Republic of Lithuania
Embassy of Canada, Business Center 2000, Jogailos St. 4,
Vilnius, LT-01116 Lithuania

vilnius@canada.lt
www.balticstates.gc.ca
twitter.com/CanadaLithuania
www.facebook.com/CanadaLithuania
Other contact information: Tel: 370-5249-0950; Fax: 370-5249-7865

Kevin Rex, Ambassador

Grand Duchy of Luxembourg
See: Kingdom of Belgium

Macao
See: People's Republic of China

Republic of Macedonia
See: Serbia

Democratic Republic of Madagascar
See: Republic of South Africa

Republic of Malawi
See: Republic of Mozambique

Federation of Malaysia
PO Box 10990,
Kuala Lumpur, 50732 Malaysia

klmpr@international.gc.ca
www.malaysia.gc.ca
twitter.com/CanadaMalaysia
www.facebook.com/CanadaMalaysia
Other contact information: Tel: 6-03-2718-3333; Fax: 6-03-2718-3399

Julia Bentley, High Commissioner

Republic of Maldives
See: Democratic Socialist Republic of Sri Lanka

Republic of Mali
Embassy of Canada, PO Box 198,
Bamako, Mali

bmakog@international.gc.ca
www.mali.gc.ca
twitter.com/CanEmbMali
www.facebook.com/canadainmali
Other contact information: Tel: 223-4498-0450; Fax: 223-4498-0455

Michael Elliot, Ambassador

Republic of Malta
See: Italian Republic

Marshall Islands
See: Commonwealth of Australia

Islamic Republic of Mauritania
See: Kingdom of Morocco

Republic of Mauritius
See: Republic of South Africa

United Mexican States
Embassy of Canada, Schiller 529, Col. Bosque de
Chapultepec, Del. Miguel H,
Mexico City, 11580 Mexico

mex@international.gc.ca
www.mexico.gc.ca
twitter.com/CanEmbMexico
www.facebook.com/CanadainMexico
Other contact information: Tel: 52-57-24-7900; Fax: 52-57-24-7980

Graeme C. Clark, Ambassador

Federated States of Micronesia
See: Commonwealth of Australia

Republic of Moldova
See: Republic of Romania

Principality of Monaco
See: French Republic

Mongolia
Embassy of Canada, PO Box 1028,
Ulaanbaatar, 14200 Mongolia

ulaan@international.gc.ca
www.mongolia.gc.ca
twitter.com/CanadaMongolia
www.facebook.com/CanadaMongolia
Other contact information: Tel: 976-11-332-500; Fax: 976-11-32-515

Catherine Ivkoff, Ambassador

Montenegro
See: Serbia

Montserrat
See: Barbados

Kingdom of Morocco
Embassy of Canada, PO Box 2040,
Rabat-Ryad, 10000 Morocco

rabat@international.gc.ca
www.morocco.gc.ca
twitter.com/CanEmbMorocco
www.facebook.com/CanadainMorocco
Other contact information: Tel: 212-537-54-4949; Fax: 212-537-54-4853

Nell Stewart, Ambassador

Republic of Mozambique
High Commission of Canada, Avenida Kenneth Kaunda 1138,
Maputo, Mozambique

mputo@international.gc.ca
www.canadainternational.gc.ca/mozambique
twitter.com/CanHCMozambique
w ww.facebook.com/CanadainMozambique
Other contact information: Tel: 258-21-244-200; Fax: 258-21-492-667

Caroline Delany, High Commissioner

Republic of the Union of Myanmar
Embassy of Canada, Centrepoint Towers, 9th Fl., 65 Sule Pagoda Rd.,
Yangon, Burma

YNGON@international.gc.ca
www.international.gc.ca/country-pays/myanmar
www.facebook.com/CanadainBurma
Other contact information: Tel: 95-1-384-805; Fax: 95-1-384-806
François Lafrenière, Ambassador

Republic of Namibia
See: Republic of South Africa

Nauru
See: Commonwealth of Australia

Federal Democratic Republic of Nepal
See: Republic of India

Kingdom of the Netherlands
Embassy of Canada, Sophialaan 7,
The Hague, 2514 JP The Netherlands

hague@international.gc.ca
www.netherlands.gc.ca
twitter.com/CanAmbNL
www.facebook.com/CanadainNetherlands
Other contact information: Tel: 31-70-311-1600; Fax:
31-70-311-1620
Lisa Helfand, Ambassador

New Caledonia
See: Commonwealth of Australia

New Zealand
High Commission of Canada, PO Box 8047,
Wellington, 6143 New Zealand

wlgtn@international.gc.ca
www.newzealand.gc.ca
twitter.com/CanHCNZ
Other contact information: Tel: 64-4-473-9577; Fax:
64-4-471-2082
Joanne Lemay, High Commissioner

Republic of Nicaragua
See: Republic of Costa Rica
Embassy of Canada (Program Office), PO Box 25, De Los Pipitos, 2 Blocks West, El Nogal Street No. 25, ,
Managua, Nicaragua

mngua@international.gc.ca
www.facebook.com/CanEmbCRHNNI
Other contact information: Tel: 505-2268-0433; Fax:
505-2268-0437
James K. Hill, Ambassador

Republic of Niger
See: Republic of Mali

Federal Republic of Nigeria
High Commission of Canada, Central Business District
Abuja, PO Box 5144, 13010G, Palm close, Diplomatic Dr.,
Abuja, Nigeria

abuja@international.gc.ca
www.canadainternational.gc.ca/nigeria
twitter.com/CanHCNigeria
Other contact information: Tel: 234-9-461-2900; Fax:
234-9-461-2901
Philip Baker, High Commissioner

Northern Ireland
See: United Kingdom of Great Britain & Northern Ireland

Northern Marianas
See: Commonwealth of Australia

Kingdom of Norway
Embassy of Canada, Wergelandsveien 7,
Oslo, 0244 Norway

oslo@international.gc.ca
www.norway.gc.ca
twitter.com/CanadaNorway
www.facebook.com/CanadaNorway
Other contact information: Tel: 47-2299-5300; Fax:
47-2299-5301
Patrick Parisot, Ambassador

Sultanate of Oman
See: Kingdom of Saudi Arabia

Islamic Republic of Pakistan
High Commission of Canada, PO Box 1042,
Islamabad, Pakistan

isbad@internationl.gc.ca
www.pakistan.gc.ca
twitter.com/canhcpakistan
www.facebook.com/CanadainPakistan
Other contact information: Tel: 92-51-208-6000; Fax:
92-51-208-6900
Wendy Gilmour, High Commissioner

Republic of Palau
See: Commonwealth of Australia

Republic of Panama
Estafeta World Trade Center, PO Box 0832-2446,
Panama City, Panama

panam@international.gc.ca
www.panama.gc.ca
twitter.com/CanEmbPanama
www.facebook.com/canada.pa
Other contact information: Tel: (011 507) 264-2500; Fax: (011
507) 294-2514
Lilly Nicholls, Ambassador

Papua New Guinea
See: Commonwealth of Australia

Republic of Paraguay
See: Argentine Republic

twitter.com/CanEmbParaguay
www.facebook.com/CanadainParaguay

Republic of Peru
Embassy of Canada, PO Box 18-1126 Miraflores,
Lima, Peru

Tel: 511-319-3200; *Fax:* 511-446-4912
lima@international.gc.ca
www.peru.gc.ca
twitter.com/CanadaPeru
www.facebook.com/CanadaPeruBolivia
Other contact information: Tel: 51-1-319-3200; Fax:
51-1-446-4912
Ralph Jansen, Ambassador

Republic of the Philippines
PO Box 2168 Makati Central, 1261 Philippines

manil@international.gc.ca
www.philippines.gc.ca
twitter.com/CanEmbPH
www.facebook.com/CanEmbPH
Other contact information: Tel: 63-2-857-9000; Fax:
63-2-843-1082
Peter MacArthur, Ambassador

Republic of Poland
Embassy of Canada, ul. Jana Matejiki 1/5,
Warsaw, 00-481 Poland

wsaw@international.gc.ca
www.poland.gc.ca
twitter.com/CanadaPoland
www.facebook.com/CanadainPoland
Other contact information: Tel: 48-22-584-3100; Fax:
48-22-584-3192
Leslie Scanlon, Ambassador

Portuguese Republic
Embassy of Canada, Avenida da Liberdade, 198-200, 3rd Fl.,

Lisbon, 1269-121 Portugal

lsbon@international.gc.ca
www.portugal.gc.ca
www.facebook.com/CanadainPortugal
Other contact information: Tel: 351-21-316-4600; Fax:
351-21-316-4693
Lisa Rice Madan, Ambassador

Puerto Rico
See: United States of America

State of Qatar
Embassy of Canada, PO Box 24876, Doha Qatar

dohag@international.gc.ca
www.canadainternational.gc.ca/qatar
www.facebook.com/CanadainQatar
Other contact information: Tel: 974-4419-9000; Fax:
974-4419-9035
Stefanie McCollum, Ambassador

Republic of Romania
Embassy of Canada, Sector 1, #1, 3 Tuberozelor St.,
Bucharest, 011411 Romania

bucst@international.gc.ca
www.romania.gc.ca
twitter.com/canadaromania
www.facebook.com/CanadaRomania
Other contact information: Tel: 40-21-307-5000; Fax:
40-21-307-5010
Annick Goulet, Ambassador

Russian Federation
Embassy of Canada, 23 Starokonyushenny Pereulok,
Moscow, 119002 Russia

mosco@international.gc.ca
www.russia.gc.ca
twitter.com/CanadaRussia
Other contact information: Tel: 7-495-925-6000; Fax:
7-495-925-6025
Alison LeClaire, Ambassador

Republic of Rwanda
Embassy of Canada, PO Box 1117,
Kigali, Rwanda

kgali@international.gc.ca
www.canadainternational.gc.ca/kenya
twitter.com/CanadainRwanda
Other contact information: Tel: 250-252-573-210; Fax:
250-252-572-719

Saint Kitts & Nevis
See: Barbados

Saint Lucia
See: Barbados

Saint Vincent & the Grenadines
See: Barbados

Saint-Pierre & Miquelon
See: French Republic

Samoa
See: New Zealand
High Commission of Australia, PO Box 704, Beach Rd.,
Apia, Samoa

samoa.embassy.gov.au/apia/home.html
Other contact information: Tel: 68 5 23 411; Fax: 68 5 23 159
Under the Canada-Australia Consular Services Sharing
Agreement, the High Commission of Australia will serve
Canadians abroad.
Sara Moriarty, Australian High Commissioner

Republic of San Marino
See: Italian Republic

Democratic Republic of Sao Tomé & Principe
See: Federal Republic of Nigeria

Kingdom of Saudi Arabia
Embassy of Canada, PO Box 94321,
Riyadh, 11693 Saudi Arabia

ryadh@international.gc.ca
www.saudiarabia.gc.ca
twitter.com/CanEmbSA
Other contact information: Tel: 966-11-488-2288; Fax:
966-11-482-5670
Ambassador Dennis Horak was expelled from Saudi Arabia on
Aug. 6, 2018, over criticism of the kingdom's arrest of women's
right activists.

Scotland
See: United Kingdom of Great Britain & Northern
Ireland

Republic of Senegal
Embassy of Canada, PO Box 3373,
Dakar, Senegal

dakar@international.gc.ca
www.senegal.gc.ca
twitter.com/CanEmbSenegal
www.facebook.com/canadainsenegal
Other contact information: Tel: 221-33-889-4700; Fax:
221-33-889-4720
Vacant, Ambassador

Republic of Serbia
Embassy of Canada, Kneza Milosa 75,
Belgrade, 111711 Serbia

bgrad@international.gc.ca
www.serbia.gc.ca
twitter.com/CanadaSerbia
www.facebook.com/CanadainSerbia
Other contact information: Tel: 381-11-306-3000; Fax:
381-11-306-3042

Giles Norman, Ambassador

Republic of Seychelles
See: United Republic of Tanzania

Republic of Sierra Leone
See: Republic of Ghana

Republic of Singapore
High Commission of Canada, One George Street, #11-01,
049145 Singapore

spore@international.gc.ca
www.singapore.gc.ca
twitter.com/CanHCSingapore
www.facebook.com/canadainsingapore
Other contact information: Tel: 65-6854-5900; Fax:
65-6854-5930

Lynn McDonald, High Commissioner

Slovak Republic
Embassy of Canada, Mostova 2, Carlton Savoy Building,
Bratislava, 81102 Slovak Republic

brtsv@international.gc.ca
www.canadainternational.gc.ca/austria-autriche
twitter.com/canadaslovaki a
www.facebook.com/CanadainSlovakia
Other contact information: Tel: 421-259-204-031; Fax:
421-254-434-227

Ambassador resides in Prague, Czech Republic
Heidi Alberta Hulan, Ambassador

Republic of Slovenia
See: Republic of Hungary

Solomon Islands
See: Commonwealth of Australia

Somali Democratic Republic
See: Republic of Kenya

Republic of South Africa
High Commission of Canada, Private Bag X13, Hatfield,
Pretoria, 0028 South Africa

pret@international.gc.ca
www.canadainternational.gc.ca/southafrica-afriquedusud
twitter.com/CanHC ZA
www.facebook.com/CanadainSouthAfrica
Other contact information: Tel: 27-12-422-3000; Fax:
27-12-422-3052

Sandra McCardell, High Commissioner

Republic of South Sudan
Embassy of Canada, Joint Embassy Compound, Airport
Ave.,
Juba, South Sudan

juba-g@international.gc.ca
www.canadainternational.gc.ca/south_sudan-soudan_du_sud
twitter.com/canh ckenya
Other contact information: Tel: 916 726 304; 925 787 916; 925
806 831

Jenny Hill, Ambassador

Kingdom of Spain
Embassy of Canada, Torre Espacio, Paseo de la Castellana
259D,
Madrid, 28046 Spain

mdrid@international.gc.ca
www.spain.gc.ca
twitter.com/CanEmbSpain
www.facebook.com/CanadainSpain
Other contact information: Tel: 34-91-382-8400; Fax:
34-91-382-8490

Wendy Drukier, Ambassador

Democratic Socialist Republic of Sri Lanka
High Commission of Canada, PO Box 1006, 33A, 5th Lane,
Colpetty,
Colombo, 3 Sri Lanka

colomboconsul@international.gc.ca
www.srilanka.gc.ca
twitter.com/CanHCSriLanka
www.facebook.com/canadainsrilanka
Other contact information: Tel: 94-11-532-6232; Fax:
94-11-532-6296

David McKinnon, High Commissioner

Republic of The Sudan
Embassy of Canada, PO Box 10503,
Khartouom, Sudan

khrtm@international.gc.ca
www.canadainternational.gc.ca/sudan-soudan
www.facebook.com/CanadainSuda n
Other contact information: Tel: 249-156-550-500; Fax:
249-156-550-501

Adrian Norfolk, Ambassador

Republic of Suriname
See: Republic of Guyana

Kingdom of Sweden
Embassy of Canada, PO Box 16129, Klarabergsgatan 23,
Stockholm, 10323 Sweden

stkhm@international.gc.ca
www.sweden.gc.ca
twitter.com/CanadaSweden
Other contact information: Tel: 46-8-453-3000; Fax:
46-8-453-3016

Vacant, Ambassador

Swiss Confederation
Embassy of Canada, PO Box 234, Kirchenfeldstrasse 88,
Bern 6, CH-3000 Switzerland

bern@international.gc.ca
www.switzerland.gc.ca
twitter.com/CanSwitzerland
Other contact information: Tel: 41-31-357-3200; Fax:
41-31-357-3210

Susan Bincoletto, Ambassador

Syrian Arab Republic
See: Lebanon

Republic of China (ROC) / Taiwan
Canadian Trade Office, #6F Hua-Hsin Bldg., 1 SongZhi Rd.,
Xinyi District,
Taipei, 11047 Taiwan

tapei@international.gc.ca
www.canada.org.tw
www.facebook.com/CTOTEnFr
Other contact information: Tel: 886-2-8723-3000; Fax:
886-2-8723-3592

Jordan Reeves, Executive Director

Republic of Tajikistan
See: Republic of Kazakhstan

United Republic of Tanzania
High Commission of Canada, PO Box 1022, 26 Garden
Ave./38 Mirambo St.,
Dar-es-Salaam, Tanzania

dslam@international.gc.ca
www.tanzania.gc.ca
twitter.com/CanadaTanzania
www.facebook.com/CanadainTanzania
Other contact information: Tel: 255-22-216-3300; Fax:
255-22-211-6897

Pamela O'Donnell, High Commissioner

Kingdom of Thailand
Embassy of Canada, PO Box 2090,
Bangkok, 10501 Thailand

bngkk@international.gc.ca
www.thailand.gc.ca
twitter.com/canadathailand
www.facebook.com/canadainthailand
Other contact information: Tel: 66-0-2646-4300; Fax:
66-0-2646-4336

Sarah Taylor, Ambassador

Togolese Republic
See: Republic of Ghana

Kingdom of Tonga
See: New Zealand

Republic of Trinidad & Tobago
High Commission of Canada, PO Box 1246,
Port of Spain, Trinidad & Tobago

Tel: 868-622-6232; *Fax:* 868-628-2581
pspan@international.gc.ca
www.trinidadandtobago.gc.ca
twitter.com/Cana daTandT
www.facebook.com/hccanada.tt

Kumar Gupta, High Commissioner

Republic of Tunisia
Embassy of Canada, PO Box 48, 1053 Les Berges du Lac II,
Tunis, Tunisia

tunis-ag@international.gc.ca
www.canadainternational.gc.ca/tunisia-tunisie
twitter.com/CanadaTunisia
www.facebook.com/CanadainTunisia
Other contact information: Tel: 216-70-010-200; Fax:
216-70-010-393

The Canadian Embassy in Libya temporarily relocated to Tunisia
in 2014, due to ongoing security concerns.
Patrice Cousineau, Ambassador to Tunisia

Republic of Turkey
Embassy of Canada, Cinnah Caddesi 58, Cankaya,
Ankara, 06690 Turkey

ankra@international.gc.ca
www.turkey.gc.ca
twitter.com/CanEmbTurkey
www.facebook.com/CanEmbTurkey
Other contact information: Tel: 90-312-409-2700; Fax:
90-312-409-2712

Jamal Khokhar, Ambassador

Turkmenistan
See: Republic of Turkey

Turks & Caicos Islands
See: Jamaica

Republic of Tuvalu
See: New Zealand

Republic of Uganda
See: Republic of Kenya

twitter.com/canadainuganda

Ukraine
Embassy of Canada, 13A Kostelna St.,
Kyiv, 01901 Ukraine

kyiv@international.gc.ca
www.ukraine.gc.ca
twitter.com/CanEmbUkraine
www.facebook.com/CanadainUkraine
Other contact information: Tel: 380-44-590-3100; Fax:
380-44-590-3134

Larisa Galadza, Ambassador

United Arab Emirates
Embassy of Canada, PO Box 6970,
Abu Dhabi, United Arab Emirates

abdbi@international.gc.ca
www.canadainternational.gc.ca/uae-eau
twitter.com/CanadainUAE
www.face book.com/CanadainUAE
Other contact information: Tel: 971-2-694-0300; Fax:
971-2-694-0399

Marcy Grossman, Ambassador

United Kingdom of Great Britain & Northern Ireland
High Commission of Canada, Canada House, Trafalgar
Square,
London, SW1Y 5BJ UK

ldn.consular@international.gc.ca
unitedkingdom.gc.ca
twitter.com/CanadianUK
www.facebook.com/CanadaintheUK
Other contact information: Phone: 44 (0) 207 004 6000; Fax: 44
(0) 207 004 6053

Ralph Goodale, High Commissioner

United States of America
Embassy of Canada, 501 Pennsylvannia Ave. NW,
Washington, DC 20001 USA

Tel: 202-682-1740; *Fax:* 202-682-7726
ccs.scc@international.gc.ca
www.washington.gc.ca
twitter.com/CanEmbUSA

Kirsten Hillman, Ambassador
Denis Stevens, Deputy Head of Mission

Eastern Republic of Uruguay
Embassy of Canada, #102, Plaza Independencia 749,
Montevideo, 11100 Uruguay

mvdeo@international.gc.ca
www.uruguay.gc.ca
twitter.com/CanEmbUruguay
www.facebook.com/CanadainUruguay
Other contact information: Tel: 598-2-902-2030; Fax:
598-2-902-2029

Vacant, Ambassador

Republic of Uzbekistan
See: **Russian Federation**

Republic of Vanuatu
See: **Commonwealth of Australia**

Republic of Venezuela
Embassy of Canada, PO Box 62302,
Caracas, 1060A Venezuela

crcas@international.gc.ca
www.venezuela.gc.ca
twitter.com/CanEmbVenezuela
www.facebook.com/CanadainVenezuela
Other contact information: Tel: 58-212-600-3000; Fax:
58-212-263-8326

Socialist Republic of Vietnam
Embassy of Canada, 31 Huong Vuong St.,
Hanoi, Vietnam

hanoi@international.gc.ca
www.vietnam.gc.ca
twitter.com/CanEmbVietnam
www.facebook.com/canadainvietnam
Other contact information: Tel: 84-4-3734-5000; Fax:
84-4-3734-5049

Deborah Paul, Ambassador

Wales
See: **United Kingdom of Great Britain & Northern Ireland**

Republic of Yemen
See: **Kingdom of Saudi Arabia**

Republic of Zambia
High Commission of Canada, PO Box 31313, 5210
Independance Ave.,
Lusaka, Zambia

lsaka@international.gc.ca
www.tanzania.gc.ca
twitter.com/canadazambia
www.facebook.com/canadainzambia
Other contact information: Tel: 260-211-25-08-33; Fax:
260-211-25-41-76

Pamela O'Donnell, High Commissioner

Republic of Zimbabwe
Embassy of Canada, PO Box 1430, 45 Baines Ave.,
Harare, Zimbabwe

hrare@international.gc.ca
www.zimbabwe.gc.ca
twitter.com/CanEmbZimbabwe
www.facebook.com/CanadaZimbabwe
Other contact information: Tel: 263 86 7700 8600; Fax: 263 86
7700 8624

Tanatsiwa Vurayai, Ambassador

SECTION 8
GOVERNMENT:
MUNICIPAL

Listings in this section are arranged by province and are as current as possible at time of publication. For appointments made and results of elections held after publication, please refer to Canada's Information Resource Centre (CIRC), if your library subscribes to this online database. Each provincial section includes a district map, notes concerning local government structure and elections, and the following categories:

Counties & Municipal Districts

Major Municipalities

Other Municipalities

ALBERTA

The major legislation concerning municipal government in Alberta is the Municipal Government Act.

Municipal government in Alberta is rural, urban or specialized. Rural municipal governments are organized into Municipal Districts, with Specialized Municipalities created to meet the unique needs of a specific municipality. Elected councils are responsible for the welfare and interests of the municipalities. Two other rural categories are Improvement Districts and Special Areas, which are geographically large, sparsely populated areas for which the provincial government levies and collects all taxes and provides services.

Urban municipalities include Summer Villages, Villages, Towns and Cities. These are fully autonomous municipal units, each with an elected council. They are responsible for providing all municipal services within their corporate limits and for levying taxes and rates.

In addition to the above forms of municipal government there are eight Metis Settlements established under the Metis Settlements Act.

Types of Municipalities that may be formed:

Municipal District: A majority of the buildings used as dwellings are on parcels of land with an area of at least 1,850 square metres and there is a population of 1,000 or more.

Village: A majority of the buildings are on parcels of land smaller than 1,850 square metres and there is a population of 300 or more.

Town: A majority of the buildings are on parcels of land smaller than 1,850 square metres and there is a population of 1,000 or more.

City: A majority of the buildings are on parcels of land smaller than 1,850 square metres and there is a population of 10,000 or more.

Specialized Municipality: An area in which the Minister is satisfied that a type of municipality (as listed above) does not meet the needs of the proposed municipality; to provide for a form of local government that, in the opinion of the Minister, will provide for the orderly development of the municipality to a type of municipality (as listed above), or to another form of specialized municipality; an area in which the Minister is satisfied for any other reason that it is appropriate in the circumstances to form a specialized municipality.

Incorporation and changes in status are determined by the Lieutenant Governor in Council (Provincial Cabinet) on the recommendation of the Minister of Municipal Affairs. It is not necessary to change status by reason of population change. Elections are held in October. As of 2013, terms of office are now four years (2021, 2025, etc.).

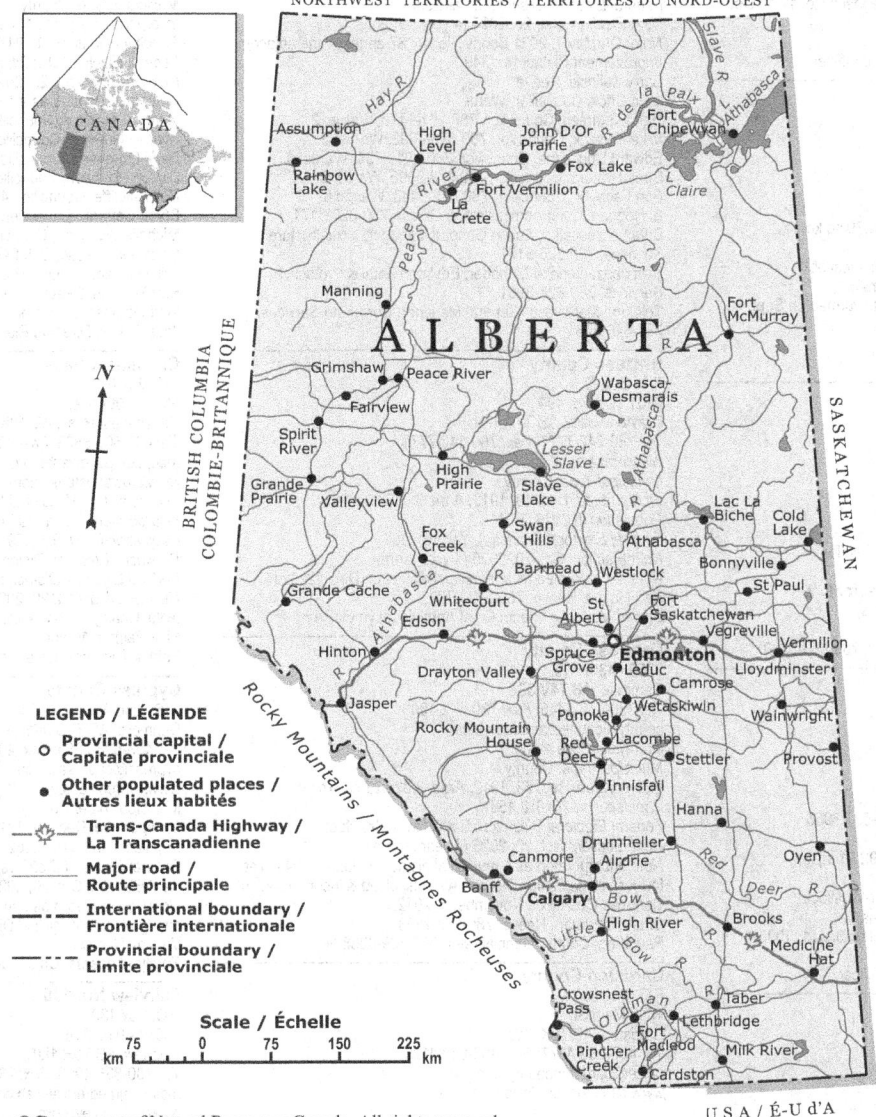

Alberta

Counties & Municipal Districts in Alberta

Acadia No. 34
P.O. Box 30
9 Main St.
Acadia Valley, AB T0J 0A0
Tel: 403-972-3808; *Fax:* 403-972-3833
md34@mdacadia.ab.ca
www.mdacadia.ab.ca
Municipal Type: Municipal District
Incorporated: Dec. 9, 1913; *Area:* 1,076.26 sq km
Population in 2016: 493
Federal Electoral District(s): Battle River-Crowfoot
Next Election: Oct. 20, 2025 (4 year terms)
Peter Rafa, Reeve
Jason Wallsmith, Chief Administrative Officer

Athabasca County
3602 - 48th Ave.
Athabasca, AB T9S 1M8
Tel: 780-675-2273; *Fax:* 780-675-5512
info@athabascacounty.com
www.athabascacounty.com
Municipal Type: County
Incorporated: Dec. 18, 1913; *Area:* 6,126.43 sq km
Population in 2016: 7,869
Federal Electoral District(s): Lakeland
Next Election: Oct. 20, 2025 (4 year terms)
Note: Incorporated as a municipal district on Dec. 14, 1914. Name changed from The County of Athabasca No. 12 on Dec. 1, 2009.
Vacant, Reeve
Dawn Phillips, Acting Chief Administrative Officer

Barrhead County No. 11
5306 - 49th St.
Barrhead, AB T7N 1N5
Tel: 780-674-3331; *Fax:* 780-674-2777
info@countybarrhead.ab.ca
www.countybarrhead.ab.ca
Municipal Type: County
Incorporated: Dec. 18, 1913; *Area:* 2,404.70 sq km
Population in 2016: 6,288
Federal Electoral District(s): Peace River-Westlock
Next Election: Oct. 20, 2025 (4 year terms)
Note: The County of Barrhead No. 11 was formed on Sept. 26, 1958.
Doug Drozd, Reeve, 780-674-4404
Debbie Oyarzun, County Manager

Beaver County
P.O. Box 140
5120 - 50th St.
Ryley, AB T0B 4A0
Tel: 780-663-3730; *Fax:* 780-663-3602
administration@beaver.ab.ca
www.beaver.ab.ca
Municipal Type: County
Incorporated: Feb. 1, 1943; *Area:* 3,319.1 sq km
Population in 2016: 5,905
Federal Electoral District(s): Battle River-Crowfoot
Next Election: Oct. 20, 2025 (4 year terms)
Vacant, Reeve
Robert Beck, Chief Administrative Officer, 780-663-3730

Big Lakes County
P.O. Box 239
5305 - 56th St.
High Prairie, AB T0G 1E0
Tel: 780-523-5955; *Fax:* 780-523-4227
biglakes@biglakescounty.ca
www.biglakescounty.ca
Other Information: Toll-Free Phone: 866-523-5955
Municipal Type: Municipal District
Incorporated: Dec. 18, 1913; *Area:* 13,892.91 sq km
Population in 2016: 5,612
Federal Electoral District(s): Peace River-Westlock
Next Election: Oct. 20, 2025 (4 year terms)
Note: Incorporated as a municipal district on Jan. 1, 1995.
Ken Matthews, Reeve
Jordan Panasiuk, Chief Administrative Officer

Bighorn No. 8
P.O. Box 310
Exshaw, AB T0L 2C0
Tel: 403-673-3611; *Fax:* 403-673-3895
bighorn@mdbighorn.ca
www.mdbighorn.ca

Municipal Type: Municipal District
Incorporated: April 1, 1945; *Area:* 2,767.94 sq km
Population in 2016: 1,334
Federal Electoral District(s): Banff-Airdrie; Foothills
Next Election: Oct. 20, 2025 (4 year terms)
Note: Incorporated as a municipal district on Jan. 1, 1988.
Vacant, Reeve
Robert Ellis, Chief Administrative Officer

Birch Hills County
P.O. Box 157
4601 - 50th St.
Wanham, AB T0H 3P0
Tel: 780-694-3793; *Fax:* 780-694-3788
info@birchhillscounty.com
www.birchhillscounty.com
Municipal Type: County
Incorporated: Dec. 18, 1913; *Area:* 2,856.69 sq km
Population in 2016: 1,553
Federal Electoral District(s): Peace River-Westlock
Next Election: Oct. 20, 2025 (4 year terms)
Gerald Manzulenko, Reeve
Rick Bastow, Chief Administrative Officer, 780-507-2502

Bonnyville No. 87
P.O. Box 1010
4905 - 50th Ave.
Bonnyville, AB T9N 2J7
Tel: 888-886-3171; *Fax:* 780-826-4524
www.md.bonnyville.ab.ca
Municipal Type: Municipal District
Incorporated: Dec. 14, 1914; *Area:* 6,064.73 sq km
Population in 2016: 13,575
Federal Electoral District(s): Lakeland
Next Election: Oct. 20, 2025 (4 year terms)
Note: On May 1, 2021 Bonnyville No. 87 annexed the adjacent Improvement District No. 349.
Barry Kalinski, Reeve
Josh Crick, Councillor, Wards: 1
Darcy Skarsen, Councillor, 780-201-3478, Wards: 2
Mike Krywiak, Councillor, 780-573-6093, Wards: 3
Edward Duchesne, Councillor, 780-201-5734, Wards: 4
Dana Swigart, Councillor, 780-573-9095, Wards: 5
Ben Fadeyiw, Councillor, 780-826-1462, Wards: 6
Al Hoggan, Chief Administrative Officer, 780-826-3171
Bryan e Bespalko, Acting General Manager, Infrastructure Services, 780-826-3171
Matt Janz, General Manager, Environmental & Protective Services, 780-826-3951
Tolulope Maraiyesa, General Manager, Corporate Services, 780-826-3951

Brazeau County
P.O. Box 77
7401 Twp Rd. 494
Drayton Valley, AB T7A 1R1
Tel: 780-542-7777; *Fax:* 780-542-7770
www.brazeau.ab.ca
Municipal Type: County
Incorporated: Dec. 18, 1913; *Area:* 3,015.83 sq km
Population in 2016: 7,771
Federal Electoral District(s): Yellowhead
Next Election: Oct. 20, 2025 (4 year terms)
Note: Incorporated as a municipal district on Dec. 13, 1915.
Bart Guyon, Reeve, 780-542-8777
Shawn McKerry, Interim Chief Administrative Officer

Camrose County
3755 - 43rd Ave.
Camrose, AB T4V 3S8
Tel: 780-672-4446; *Fax:* 780-672-1008
county@county.camrose.ab.ca
county.camrose.ab.ca
Municipal Type: County
Incorporated: Dec. 23, 1912; *Area:* 3,324.21 sq km
Population in 2016: 8,458
Federal Electoral District(s): Battle River-Crowfoot
Next Election: Oct. 20, 2025 (4 year terms)
Note: Incorporated as a municipal district on Jan. 1, 1944. The former Village of New Norway was dissolved & incorporated into Camrose County on November 1, 2012.
Cindy Trautman, Reeve, 780-373-2503
Paul King, County Administrator, 587-769-0388

Cardston County
P.O. Box 580
1050 Main St.
Cardston, AB T0K 0K0
Tel: 403-653-4977; *Fax:* 403-653-1126
office@cardstoncounty.com
www.cardstoncounty.com

Municipal Type: County
Incorporated: Dec. 18, 1913; *Area:* 3,414.87 sq km
Population in 2016: 4,481
Federal Electoral District(s): Medicine Hat-Cardston-Warner
Next Election: Oct. 20, 2025 (4 year terms)
Note: Incorporated as a municipal district on Jan. 1, 1946.
Vacant, Reeve
Murray Millward, Chief Administrative Officer, 403-653-4977

Clear Hills County
P.O. Box 240
Worsley, AB T0H 3W0
Tel: 780-685-3925; *Fax:* 780-685-3960
info@clearhillscounty.ca
clearhillscounty.ca
Municipal Type: County
Incorporated: Dec. 18, 1913; *Area:* 15,112.69 sq km
Population in 2016: 2,023
Federal Electoral District(s): Grande Prairie-Mackenzie
Next Election: Oct. 20, 2025 (4 year terms)
Note: Incorporated as a municipal district on Jan. 1, 1995. Name changed from The Municipal District of Clear Hills No. 21 on Jan. 1, 2006.
Jason Ruecker, Reeve, 780-835-0398
Allan Rowe, Chief Administrative Officer

Clearwater County
P.O. Box 550
4340 - 47th Ave.
Rocky Mountain House, AB T4T 1A4
Tel: 403-845-4444; *Fax:* 403-845-7330
admin@clearwatercounty.ca
www.clearwatercounty.ca
Municipal Type: County
Incorporated: April 1, 1945; *Area:* 18,682.45 sq km
Population in 2016: 11,947
Federal Electoral District(s): Yellowhead
Next Election: Oct. 20, 2025 (4 year terms)
Note: Incorporated as a municipal district on Jan. 1, 1985.
Gennifer Mehlhaf, Councillor, Wards: 1
Sydney Graham, Councillor, Wards: 2
Daryl Lougheed, Councillor, 403-729-2335, Wards: 3
Jordon Northcott, Councillor, Wards: 4
Neil Ratcliffe, Councillor, 403-845-7120, Wards: 5
Bryan Cermak, Councillor, Wards: 6
Michelle Swanson, Councillor, 403-846-4410, Wards: 7
Christopher Read, Chief Administrative Officer
Erik Hansen, Director, Public Works Infrastructure
Kurt Magnus, Director, Public Works Operations
Matt Martinson, Director, Agriculture & Community Services
Jose Reyes, Director, Planning & Development

Crowsnest Pass
P.O. Box 600
8502 - 19th Ave.
Crowsnest Pass, AB T0K 0E0
Tel: 403-562-8833; *Fax:* 403-563-5474
reception@crowsnestpass.com
www.crowsnestpass.com
Municipal Type: Regional Municipality
Incorporated: Jan. 1, 1979; *Area:* 373.07 sq km
Population in 2016: 5,589
Provincial Electoral District(s): Livingstone-Macleod
Federal Electoral District(s): Foothills
Next Election: Oct. 20, 2025 (4 year terms)
Note: Changed from a town to a specialized municipality in 2008.
Blair Painter, Mayor
Patrick Thosmas, Chief Administrative Officer

Cypress County
816 - 2nd Ave.
Dunmore, AB T1B 0K3
Tel: 403-526-2888; *Fax:* 403-526-8958
cypress@cypress.ab.ca
www.cypress.ab.ca
Municipal Type: County
Incorporated: Dec. 18, 1913; *Area:* 13,166.13 sq km
Population in 2016: 7,662
Federal Electoral District(s): Medicine Hat-Cardston-Warner
Next Election: Oct. 20, 2025 (4 year terms)
Note: Incorporated as a municipal district on Jan. 1, 1985. Name changed from Municipal District of Cypress on Nov. 1, 1998.
Vacant, Reeve
Tarolyn Aaserud, Chief Administrative Officer

Fairview No. 136
P.O. Box 189
10957 - 91st Ave.
Fairview, AB T0H 1L0
Tel: 780-835-4903; *Fax:* 780-835-3131
mdinfo@medfairview.ab.ca
www.mdfairview.com

Municipal Type: Municipal District
Incorporated: Dec. 18, 1913; *Area:* 1,390.66 sq km
Population in 2016: 1,604
Federal Electoral District(s): Peace River-Westlock
Next Election: Oct. 20, 2025 (4 year terms)
Note: Incorporated as a municipal district on Dec. 9, 1914.
Vacant, Reeve
Sandra Fox, Chief Administrative Officer, 780-835-4903

Flagstaff County
P.O. Box 358
12435 Township Rd. 442
Sedgewick, AB T0B 4C0
Tel: 780-384-4100; *Fax:* 780-384-3635
county@flagstaff.ab.ca
www.flagstaff.ab.ca
Other Information: Toll-Free Phone: 877-387-4100
Municipal Type: County
Incorporated: Dec. 9, 1912; *Area:* 4,066.92 sq km
Population in 2016: 3,738
Federal Electoral District(s): Battle River-Crowfoot
Next Election: Oct. 20, 2025 (4 year terms)
Don Kroetch, Reeve
Shelly Armstrong, Chief Administrative Officer

Foothills No. 31
P.O. Box 5605
309 Macleod Trail
High River, AB T1V 1M7
Tel: 403-652-2341; *Fax:* 403-652-7880
www.mdfoothills.com
Municipal Type: Municipal District
Incorporated: Dec. 23, 1912; *Area:* 3,636.80 sq km
Population in 2016: 22,766
Federal Electoral District(s): Foothills
Next Election: Oct. 20, 2025 (4 year terms)
Note: Incorporated as a municipal district on Jan. 1, 1944.
Robert Siewert, Councillor, Wards: 1
Delilah Miller, Councillor, Wards: 2
Barbara Castell, Councillor, Wards: 3
Suzanne Oel, Councillor, 403-931-2711, Wards: 4
Alan Alger, Councillor, Wards: 5
Don Waldorf, Councillor, Wards: 6
R.D. McHugh, Councillor, Wards: 7
Ryan Payne, Chief Administrative Officer
Rick Saulnier, Fire Chief

Forty Mile County No. 8
P.O. Box 160
Foremost, AB T0K 0X0
Tel: 403-867-3530
info@fortymile.ab.ca
www.40mile.ca
Municipal Type: County
Incorporated: Dec. 9, 1912; *Area:* 7,229.84 sq km
Population in 2016: 3,581
Federal Electoral District(s): Medicine Hat-Cardston-Warner
Next Election: Oct. 20, 2025 (4 year terms)
Stacey Barrows, Reeve, 403-867-2607
Keith Bodin, Chief Administrative Officer

Grande Prairie County No. 1
10001 - 84th Ave.
Clairmont, AB T0H 0W0
Tel: 780-532-9722; *Fax:* 780-539-9880
info@countygp.ab.ca
www.countygp.ab.ca
Municipal Type: County
Incorporated: Dec. 9, 1912; *Area:* 5,802.21 sq km
Population in 2016: 22,303
Federal Electoral District(s): Grande Prairie-Mackenzie
Next Election: Oct. 20, 2025 (4 year terms)
Note: Incorporated as a county on Jan. 1, 1951.
Amanda Frayn, Councillor, Wards: 1
Kurt Balderston, Councillor, Wards: 2
Leanne Beaupre, Councillor, 780-814-3121, Fax: 780-402-3809, Wards: 3
Steve Zimmerman, Councillor, Wards: 4
Bob Marshall, Councillor, 780-933-2053, Wards: 5
Peter Harris, Councillor, 780-933-3074, Wards: 6
Brian Peterson, Councillor, Wards: 7
Karen Rosvold, Councillor, 780-831-0902, Wards: 8
Robert Chrenek, Councillor, Wards: 9
Joulia Whittleton, Chief Administrative Officer, 780-532-9722
Nick Lapp, Director, Planning & Development, 780-532-9727
Dale Van Volkingburgh, Director, Public Works, 780-532-9727
Megan Beson, Acting Manager, Legislative Services, 780-532-9727
Dan Verdun, Fire Chief, 780-532-9727

Greenview No. 16
P.O. Box 1079
Valleyview, AB T0H 3N0
Tel: 780-524-7600; *Fax:* 780-524-4307
info@mdgreenview.ab.ca
mdgreenview.ab.ca
Other Information: Toll-Free Phone: 888-524-7601
Municipal Type: Municipal District
Incorporated: Jan. 1, 1969; *Area:* 32,994.14 sq km
Population in 2017: 5,583
Federal Electoral District(s): Grande Prairie-Mackenzie; Peace River-Westlock; Yellowhead
Next Election: Oct. 20, 2025 (4 year terms)
Note: Incorporated as a municipal district on Jan. 1, 1994.
Vacant, Reeve
Stacey Wabick, Interim Chief Administration Officer

Jasper
P.O. Box 520
303 Pyramid Lake Rd.
Jasper, AB T0E 1E0
Tel: 780-852-3356; *Fax:* 780-852-4019
www.jasper-alberta.com
Municipal Type: Regional Municipality
Incorporated: Aug. 31, 1995; *Area:* 925.52 sq km
Population in 2016: 4,590
Provincial Electoral District(s): West Yellowhead
Federal Electoral District(s): Yellowhead
Next Election: Oct. 20, 2025 (4 year terms)
Note: Incorporated as a specialized municipality on July 20, 2001.
Richard Ireland, Mayor
Bill Given, Chief Administrative Officer, 780-852-6501

Kneehill County
P.O. Box 400
1600 - 2nd St. NE
Three Hills, AB T0M 2A0
Tel: 866-443-5541; *Fax:* 403-443-5115
office@kneehillcounty.com
www.kneehillcounty.com
Other Information: Toll-Free Phone: 866-443-5541
Municipal Type: County
Incorporated: Dec. 9, 1912; *Area:* 3,380.04 sq km
Population in 2016: 5,001
Federal Electoral District(s): Battle River-Crowfoot
Next Election: Oct. 20, 2025 (4 year terms)
Jerry Wittstock, Reeve
Mike Haugen, Chief Administrative Officer

Lac La Biche County
P.O. Box 1679
Lac La Biche, AB T0A 2C0
Tel: 780-623-1747; *Fax:* 780-623-2039
main.office@laclabichecounty.com
www.laclabichecounty.com
Other Information: Toll-Free Phone: 877-806-5632
Municipal Type: County
Incorporated: Aug. 1, 2007; *Area:* 16,300 sq km
Population in 2016: 8,330
Federal Electoral District(s): Fort McMurray-Cold Lake
Next Election: Oct. 20, 2025 (4 year terms)
Note: The Town of Lac La Biche & Lakeland County amalgamated on August 1, 2007 to create Lac La Biche County. It was changed from a municipal district to a specialized municipality in September 2017.
Paul Reutov, Mayor
Ken Van Buul, Chief Administrative Officer

Lac Ste. Anne County
P.O. Box 219
Sangudo, AB T0E 2A0
Tel: 780-785-3411; *Fax:* 780-785-2359
lsac@lsac.ca
lsac.ca
Other Information: Toll-Free Phone: 866-880-5722
Municipal Type: County
Incorporated: Jan. 1, 1944; *Area:* 2,850.38 sq km
Population in 2016: 10,889
Federal Electoral District(s): Sturgeon River-Parkland
Next Election: Oct. 20, 2025 (4 year terms)
Lorne Olsvik, Councillor, 780-967-5360, Wards: 1
Nick Gelych, Councillor, 780-903-9393, Wards: 2
George Vaughan, Councillor, 780-967-3469, Wards: 3
Steve Hoyda, Councillor, 780-674-8080, Wards: 4
Joe Blakeman, Councillor, 780-918-1916, Wards: 5
Harvey W. Hagman, Councillor, Wards: 6
Lloyd Giebelhaus, Councillor, 780-785-2095, Wards: 7
Mike Primeau, County Manager
Trista Court, General Manager, Community & Protective Services
Joe Duplessie, General Manager, Utilities & Special Projects

Randy Schroeder, Fire Chief

Lacombe County
RR#3
Lacombe, AB T4L 2N3
Tel: 403-782-6601; *Fax:* 403-782-3820
info@lacombecounty.com
www.lacombecounty.com
Municipal Type: County
Incorporated: Jan. 1, 1944; *Area:* 2,765.16 sq km
Population in 2016: 10,343
Federal Electoral District(s): Red Deer-Lacombe
Next Election: Oct. 20, 2025 (4 year terms)
Note: Incorporated as a county on Jan. 1, 1961.
John Ireland, Councillor, 403-392-3981, Wards: 1
Brenda Knight, Councillor, 403-788-2168, Wards: 2
Barb Shepherd, Councillor, 403-340-9724, Wards: 3
Dwayne West, Councillor, Wards: 4
Kenneth Weenink, Councillor, Wards: 5
Allan Wilson, Councillor, Wards: 6
Dana Kreil, Councillor, 403-746-3607, Wards: 7
Tim Timmons, County Manager
Keith Boras, Director, Community Services, 403-782-6601
Bill Cade, Director, Operations, 403-782-6601
Dale Freitag, Director, Planning Services, 403-782-6601
Michael Minchin, Director, Corporate Services, 403-782-6601
Drayton Bussiere, Fire Chief, 403-782-8959

Lamont County
Administration Bldg.
5303 - 50th Ave.
Lamont, AB T0B 2R0
Tel: 780-895-2233; *Fax:* 780-895-7404
info@lamontcounty.ca
www.lamontcounty.ca
Municipal Type: County
Incorporated: Dec. 23, 1912; *Area:* 2,400.78 sq km
Population in 2016: 3,899
Federal Electoral District(s): Lakeland
Next Election: Oct. 20, 2025 (4 year terms)
Note: Incorporated as a county on Jan. 1, 1968.
Wayne Woldanski, Reeve
Stephen Hill, Chief Administrative Officer

Leduc County
#101, 1101 - 5th St.
Nisku, AB T9E 2X3
Tel: 780-955-3555; *Fax:* 780-955-3444
communications@leduc-county.com
www.leduc-county.com
Other Information: Toll-Free Phone: 800-379-9052
Municipal Type: County
Incorporated: Jan. 1, 1944; *Area:* 2,601.49 sq km
Population in 2016: 13,780
Federal Electoral District(s): Edmonton-Wetaskiwin
Next Election: Oct. 20, 2025 (4 year terms)
Note: Incorporated as a county on Jan. 1, 1964.
Tanni Doblanko, Mayor, 780-955-4565, Wards: 5
Rick Smith, Councillor, 780-955-4561, Wards: 1
Kelly-Lynn Lewis, Councillor, 780-955-4562, Wards: 2
Kelly Vandenberghe, Councillor, 780-955-4563, Wards: 3
Larry Wanchuk, Councillor, 780-955-4564, Wards: 4
Glenn Belozer, Councillor, 780-955-4566, Wards: 6
Ray Scobie, Councillor, 780-955-4567, Wards: 7
Duane Coleman, County Manager, 780-955-6400
Rick Thomas, Deputy County Manager, 780-955-6415
Grant Bain, Director, Planning & Development, 780-979-2113
Garett Broadbent, Director, Road Operations & Agricultural Services, 780-955-6404
Des Mrygold, Director, Engineering & Utilities, 780-955-6418
Dean Ohnysty, Director, Community Services, 780-955-4535
Keven Lefebvre, Fire Chief, 780-955-7099

Lesser Slave River No. 124
P.O. Box 722
3000 - 15th Ave. SE
Slave Lake, AB T0G 2A0
Tel: 780-849-4888; *Fax:* 780-849-4939
info@mdlsr.ca
www.mdlsr.ca
Other Information: Toll-Free Phone: 866-449-4888
Municipal Type: Municipal District
Incorporated: Jan. 1, 1969; *Area:* 10,075.88 sq km
Population in 2016: 2,803
Federal Electoral District(s): Peace River-Westlock
Next Election: Oct. 20, 2025 (4 year terms)
Note: Incorporated as a municipal district on Jan. 1, 1995.
Murray Kerik, Reeve
Barbara Miller, Chief Administrative Officer

Lethbridge County

#100, 905 - 4th Ave. South
Lethbridge, AB T1J 4E4
Tel: 403-328-5525; *Fax:* 403-328-5602
mailbox@lethcounty.ca
www.lethcounty.ca
Other Information: Toll-Free Phone: 855-728-5525
Municipal Type: County
Incorporated: Jan. 1, 1954; *Area:* 2,836.64 sq km
County or District: Lethbridge No. 26; *Population in 2016:* 10,353
Federal Electoral District(s): Lethbridge
Next Election: Oct. 20, 2025 (4 year terms)
Note: Incorporated as a county on Jan 1, 1964.
Lorne Hickey, Reeve, Wards: 1
Tory Campbell, Councillor, Wards: 2
Mark Sayers, Councillor, Wards: 3
John Kuerbis, Councillor, Wards: 4
Vacant, Councillor, Wards: 5
Klaas VanderVeen, Councillor, Wards: 6
Morris Zeinstra, Councillor, Wards: 7
Ann Mitchell, Chief Administrative Officer
Jeremy Wickson, Director, Public Operations
Darren Gillies, Supervisor, Public Works

Mackenzie County

P.O. Box 640
4511 - 46th Ave.
Fort Vermilion, AB T0H 1N0
Tel: 780-927-3718; *Fax:* 780-927-4266
office@mackenziecounty.com
www.mackenziecounty.com
Other Information: Toll-Free Phone: 877-927-0677
Municipal Type: Regional Municipality
Incorporated: Jan. 1, 1995; *Area:* 80,484.42 sq km
Population in 2016: 11,171
Federal Electoral District(s): Grande Prairie-Mackenzie
Next Election: Oct. 20, 2025 (4 year terms)
Note: Incorporated as a specialized municipality on June 23, 1999. Name changed from The Municipal District of Mackenzie No. 23 to Mackenzie County in 2007.
Josh Knelsen, Councillor, 780-926-7405, Wards: 1
Darrell Derksen, Councillor, Wards: 2
Peter F. Braun, Councillor, 780-926-6238, Fax: 780-928-2683, Wards: 3
David Driedger, Councillor, Wards: 4
Ernest Peters, Councillor, Wards: 5
Garrell Smith, Councillor, Wards: 6
Cameron Cardinal, Councillor, Wards: 7
Walter Sarapuk, Councillor, Wards: 8
Jacqueline Bateman, Councillor, 780-926-3388, Wards: 9
Lisa Wardley, Councillor, 780-841-5799, Wards: 10
Lenard Racher, Chief Administrative Officer
Jennifer Batt, Director, Finance
Don Roberts, Director, Community Services
Jeff Simpson, Director, Operations, 780-928-3983
Fred Wiebe, Director, Utilities
Caitlin Smith, Manager, Planning & Development

Minburn County No. 27

P.O. Box 550
4909 - 50th St.
Vegreville, AB T9C 1R6
Tel: 780-632-2082; *Fax:* 780-632-6296
info@minburncounty.ab.ca
www.minburncounty.ab.ca
Municipal Type: County
Incorporated: Jan. 30, 1942; *Area:* 2,911.14 sq km
Population in 2016: 3,188
Federal Electoral District(s): Lakeland
Next Election: Oct. 20, 2025 (4 year terms)
Note: Incorporated as a county on Jan. 1, 1965.
Vacant, Reeve
Brent Williams, Chief Administrative Officer

Mountain View County

P.O. Box 100
1408 Twp Rd. 320
Didsbury, AB T0M 0W0
Tel: 403-335-3311; *Fax:* 403-335-9207
info@mvcounty.com
www.mountainviewcounty.com
Other Information: Toll-Free Phone: 877-264-9754
Municipal Type: County
Incorporated: Dec. 9, 1912; *Area:* 3,782.64 sq km
Population in 2016: 13,074
Federal Electoral District(s): Red Deer-Mountain View
Next Election: Oct. 20, 2025 (4 year terms)
Note: Incorporated as a county on Jan. 1, 1961.
Dwayne Fulton, Councillor, 403-606-8925, Wards: 1
Greg Harris, Councillor, 403-586-6267, Wards: 2
Alan Miller, Councillor, Wards: 3

Gord Krebs, Councillor, Wards: 4
Angela Aalbers, Councillor, 403-507-1057, Wards: 5
Peggy Johnson, Councillor, 403-586-6273, Wards: 6
Jennifer Lutz, Councillor, Wards: 7
Jeff Holmes, Chief Administrative Officer, 403-335-3311
Margaretha Bloem, Director, Planning & Development Services, 403-335-3311
Lorianne Marshall, Director, Corporate Services, 403-335-3311
Ryan Morrison, Director, Operational Services & Municipal Energy Management, 403-335-3311

Newell County

P.O. Box 130
183037 Range Rd. 145
Brooks, AB T1R 1B2
Tel: 403-362-3266; *Fax:* 888-361-7921
administration@newellmail.ca
www.countyofnewell.ab.ca
Municipal Type: County
Incorporated: Feb. 10, 1948; *Area:* 5,903.47 sq km
Population in 2016: 7,524
Federal Electoral District(s): Bow River
Next Election: Oct. 20, 2025 (4 year terms)
Note: Incorporated as a county on Jan. 1, 1953. The Village of Tilley was dissolved on August 31, 2013, & its lands became part of the County of Newell.
Vacant, Reeve
Matt Fenske, Chief Administrative Officer

Northern Lights County

P.O. Box 10
600 - 7th Ave. NW
Manning, AB T0H 2M0
Tel: 780-836-3348; *Fax:* 780-836-3663
info@countyofnorthernlights.com
www.countyofnorthernlights.com
Other Information: Toll-Free Phone: 888-525-3481
Municipal Type: County
Incorporated: Dec. 18, 1913; *Area:* 20,745.45 sq km
Population in 2016: 4,200
Federal Electoral District(s): Grande Prairie-Mackenzie
Next Election: Oct. 20, 2025 (4 year terms)
Note: Incorporated as a municipal district on April 1, 1995.
Terry Ungarian, Reeve
Theresa Van Oort, Chief Administrative Officer, 780-836-3348

Northern Sunrise County

P.O. Box 1300
135 Sunrise Rd.
Peace River, AB T8S 1Y9
Tel: 780-624-0013; *Fax:* 780-624-0023
general@northernsunrise.net
northernsunrise.net
Municipal Type: County
Incorporated: Dec. 18, 1913; *Area:* 21,141.25 sq km
Population in 2016: 1,891
Federal Electoral District(s): Peace River-Westlock
Next Election: Oct. 20, 2025 (4 year terms)
Note: Incorporated as a municipal district on April 1, 1994.
Carolyn Kolebaba, Reeve
Peter Thomas, Chief Administrative Officer

Opportunity No. 17

P.O. Box 60
2077 Mistassiniy Rd. North
Wabasca, AB T0G 2K0
Tel: 780-891-3778; *Fax:* 780-891-4283
info@mdopportunity.ab.ca
www.mdopportunity.ab.ca
Other Information: Toll-Free Phone: 888-891-3778
Municipal Type: Municipal District
Incorporated: Dec. 18, 1913; *Area:* 29,140.78 sq km
Population in 2016: 3,181
Federal Electoral District(s): Fort McMurray-Cold Lake; Peace River-Westlock
Next Election: Oct. 20, 2025 (4 year terms)
Note: Incorporated as a municipal district on Aug. 1, 1995.
Vacant, Reeve
Chad Tullis, Chief Administrative Officer

Paintearth County No. 18

P.O. Box 509
1 Crowfoot Crossing
Castor, AB T0C 0X0
Tel: 403-882-3211; *Fax:* 403-882-3560
www.countypaintearth.ca
Municipal Type: County
Incorporated: Dec. 8, 1913; *Area:* 3,287.24 sq km
Population in 2016: 2,012
Federal Electoral District(s): Battle River-Crowfoot
Next Election: Oct. 20, 2025 (4 year terms)
Note: Incorporated as a county on Jan. 1, 1962.

Vacant, Reeve
Michael Simpson, Chief Administrative Officer, 403-741-6203

Parkland County

53109A Hwy. 779
Parkland County, AB T7Z 1R1
Tel: 780-968-8888; *Fax:* 780-968-8413
hello@parklandcounty.com
www.parklandcounty.com
Other Information: Toll-Free Phone: 888-880-0858
Municipal Type: County
Incorporated: March 1, 1918; *Area:* 2,390.23 sq km
Population in 2016: 32,097
Federal Electoral District(s): Sturgeon River-Parkland; Yellowhead
Next Election: Oct. 20, 2025 (4 year terms)
Note: Incorporated as a county on Jan. 1, 1969.
Allan Gamble, Mayor
Sally Kucher Johnson, Councillor, Wards: 1
Kristina Kowalski, Councillor, Wards: 2
Phyllis Kobasiuk, Councillor, 780-968-8422, Fax: 780-968-8430, Wards: 3
Natalie Birnie, Councillor, Wards: 4
Rob Wiedeman, Councillor, Wards: 5
Allan William Hoefsloot, Councillor, Wards: 6
Laura Swain, Interim Chief Administrative Officer
Brian Cornforth, Fire Chief

Peace No. 135

P.O. Box 34
5239 - 52nd Ave.
Berwyn, AB T0H 0E0
Tel: 780-338-3845; *Fax:* 780-338-2222
info@mdpeace.com
mdpeace.com
Other Information: Alt. Phone: 780-338-3846
Municipal Type: Municipal District
Incorporated: Dec. 11, 1916; *Area:* 851.92 sq km
Population in 2016: 1,747
Federal Electoral District(s): Peace River-Westlock
Next Election: Oct. 20, 2025 (4 year terms)
Robert Willing, Reeve
Barbara Johnson, Chief Administrative Officer

Pincher Creek No. 9

P.O. Box 279
1037 Herron Ave.
Pincher Creek, AB T0K 1W0
Tel: 403-627-3130; *Fax:* 403-627-5070
info@mdpinchercreek.ab.ca
mdpinchercreek.ab.ca
Municipal Type: Municipal District
Incorporated: Jan. 1, 1944; *Area:* 3,482.26 sq km
Population in 2016: 9,965
Federal Electoral District(s): Foothills
Next Election: Oct. 20, 2025 (4 year terms)
Vacant, Reeve
Troy MacCulloch, Chief Administrative Officer

Ponoka County

4205 Hwy. 2A
Ponoka, AB T4J 1V9
Tel: 403-783-3333; *Fax:* 403-783-6965
ponokacounty@ponokacounty.com
www.ponokacounty.com
Municipal Type: County
Incorporated: Jan. 1, 1944; *Area:* 2,807.94 sq km
Population in 2016: 9,806
Federal Electoral District(s): Red Deer-Lacombe
Next Election: Oct. 20, 2025 (4 year terms)
Note: Incorporated as a county on July 1, 1999.
Paul McLauchlin, Reeve
Charlie Cutforth, Chief Administrative Officer

Provost No. 52

P.O. Box 300
4504 - 53rd Ave.
Provost, AB T0B 3S0
Tel: 780-753-2434; *Fax:* 780-753-6432
mdprovost@mdprovost.ca
mdprovost.ca
Municipal Type: Municipal District
Incorporated: Dec. 9, 1912; *Area:* 3,625.2 sq km
Population in 2016: 2,205
Federal Electoral District(s): Battle River-Crowfoot
Next Election: Oct. 20, 2025 (4 year terms)
Allan Murray, Reeve, 780-753-6531
Tyler Lawrason, Administrator

Ranchland No. 66
P.O. Box 1060
Nanton, AB T0L 1R0
Tel: 403-646-3131; *Fax:* 403-646-3141
admin@ranchland66.com
mdranchland.ca
Municipal Type: Municipal District
Incorporated: Jan. 1, 1969; *Area:* 2,639.16 sq km
Population in 2016: 92
Federal Electoral District(s): Foothills
Next Election: Oct. 20, 2025 (4 year terms)
Note: Incorporated as a municipal district on Jan. 1, 1995.
Ron Davis, Reeve
Robert Strauss, Chief Administrative Officer

Red Deer County
Red Deer County Centre
38106 Range Rd. 275
Red Deer County, AB T4S 2L9
Tel: 403-350-2150; *Fax:* 403-346-9840
info@rdcounty.ca
www.rdcounty.ca
Municipal Type: County
Incorporated: Jan. 1, 1944; *Area:* 3,691.85 sq km
Population in 2016: 19,541
Federal Electoral District(s): Red Deer-Lacombe; Red
Deer-Mountain View
Next Election: Oct. 20, 2025 (4 year terms)
Note: Incorporated as a county on Jan. 1, 1963.
James Wood, Mayor, 403-773-2215
Philip Massier, Councillor, 403-749-2956, Wards: 1
Lonny Kennett, Councillor, Wards: 2
Dana Depalme, Councillor, 403-872-1547, Wards: 3
Connie Huelsman, Councillor, 403-224-3037, Wards: 4
Brent Ramsay, Councillor, Wards: 5
Christine Moore, Councillor, 403-314-4084, Wards: 6
Curtis Herzberg, County Manager, 403-350-2152
Marty Campbell, Director, Operations Services, 403-350-2163
Dave Dittrick, Director, Planning & Development, 403-357-5395
Heather Surkan, Director, Corporate Services, 403-350-2159
Dave Laurin, Fire Chief, 403-343-6667

Rocky View County
262075 Rocky View Point
Calgary, AB T4A 0X2
Tel: 403-230-1401; *Fax:* 403-277-5977
questions@rockyview.ca
www.rockyview.ca
Municipal Type: County
Incorporated: Feb. 1, 1943; *Area:* 3,836.33 sq km
Population in 2016: 39,407
Federal Electoral District(s): Banff-Airdrie; Bow River; Foothills
Next Election: Oct. 20, 2025 (4 year terms)
Kevin Hanson, Councillor, Wards: 1
Don Kochan, Councillor, Wards: 2
Crystal Kissel, Councillor, Wards: 3
Samanntha Wright, Councillor, Wards: 4
Greg Boehlke, Councillor, Wards: 5
Sunny Samra, Councillor, Wards: 6
Al Schule, Councillor, Wards: 7
Kent Robinson, Acting Chief Administrative Officer
Brock Beach, Acting Executive Director, Community
Development Services
Grant Kaiser, Executive Director, Community & Business
Cheryl Schultz, Director, Corporate & Strategic Planning
Kristyn Smigelski, Acting Manager, Agriculture & Environment
Barry Woods, Manager, Financial Services
Randy Smith, Fire Chief

Saddle Hills County
P.O. Box 69
Spirit River, AB T0H 3G0
Tel: 780-864-3760; *Fax:* 780-864-3904
admin@saddlehills.ab.ca
www.saddlehills.ab.ca
Other Information: Toll-Free Phone: 888-864-3760
Municipal Type: County
Incorporated: April 1, 1945; *Area:* 5,836.94 sq km
Population in 2016: 2,225
Federal Electoral District(s): Grande Prairie-Mackenzie
Next Election: Oct. 20, 2025 (4 year terms)
Note: Incorporated as a municipal district on Jan. 1, 1995.
Alvin Hubert, Reeve
Cary Merritt, Chief Administrative Officer

St. Paul County No. 19
5015 - 49th Ave.
St Paul, AB T0A 3A4
Tel: 780-645-3301; *Fax:* 780-645-3104
countysp@county.stpaul.ab.ca
www.county.stpaul.ab.ca

Municipal Type: County
Incorporated: Jan. 30, 1942; *Area:* 3,297.74 sq km
Population in 2016: 6,036
Federal Electoral District(s): Lakeland
Next Election: Oct. 20, 2025 (4 year terms)
Glen Ockerman, Reeve
Sheila Kitz, Chief Administrative Officer

Smoky Lake County
P.O. Box 310
4612 McDougall Dr.
Smoky Lake, AB T0A 3C0
Tel: 780-656-3730; *Fax:* 780-656-3768
county@smokylakecounty.ab.ca
www.smokylakecounty.ab.ca
Other Information: Toll-Free Phone: 888-656-3730
Municipal Type: County
Incorporated: May 3, 1922; *Area:* 3,412.81 sq km
Population in 2016: 4,107
Federal Electoral District(s): Lakeland
Next Election: Oct. 20, 2025 (4 year terms)
Vacant, Reeve
Gene Sobolewski, Chief Administrative Officer

Smoky River No. 130
P.O. Box 210
701 Main St.
Falher, AB T0H 1M0
Tel: 780-837-2221; *Fax:* 780-837-2453
admin@mdsmokyriver.com
www.mdsmokyriver.com
Municipal Type: Municipal District
Incorporated: Dec. 18, 1913; *Area:* 2,842.82 sq km
Population in 2016: 2,023
Federal Electoral District(s): Peace River-Westlock
Next Election: Oct. 20, 2025 (4 year terms)
Note: Incorporated as a municipal district on Jan. 1, 1952.
Robert Brochu, Reeve
Rita Therriault, Chief Administrative Officer

Spirit River No. 133
P.O. Box 389
4202 - 50th St.
Spirit River, AB T0H 3G0
Tel: 780-864-3500; *Fax:* 780-864-4303
mdsr133@mdspiritriver.ab.ca
www.mdspiritriver.ab.ca
Municipal Type: Municipal District
Incorporated: Dec. 18, 1913; *Area:* 684.14 sq km
Population in 2016: 700
Federal Electoral District(s): Grande Prairie-Mackenzie
Next Election: Oct. 20, 2025 (4 year terms)
Note: Incorporated as a municipal district on Dec. 11, 1916.
Vacant, Reeve
Dan Dibbelt, Chief Administrative Officer

Starland County
P.O. Box 249
217 Railway Ave. North
Morrin, AB T0J 2B0
Tel: 403-772-3793; *Fax:* 403-772-3807
info@starlandcounty.com
www.starlandcounty.com
Municipal Type: County
Incorporated: Dec. 9, 1912; *Area:* 2,557.7 sq km
Population in 2016: 2,066
Federal Electoral District(s): Battle River-Crowfoot
Next Election: Oct. 20, 2025 (4 year terms)
Steven Wannstrom, Reeve
Shirley J. Bremer, Chief Administrative Officer, 403-772-3793,
Fax: 403-772-3807

Stettler County No. 6
P.O. Box 1270
6602 - 44th Ave.
Stettler, AB T0C 2L0
Tel: 403-742-4441; *Fax:* 403-742-1277
info@stettlercounty.ca
www.stettlercounty.ca
Municipal Type: County
Incorporated: Dec. 9, 1912; *Area:* 4,008.72 sq km
Population in 2016: 5,322
Federal Electoral District(s): Battle River-Crowfoot
Next Election: Oct. 20, 2025 (4 year terms)
Larry Clarke, Reeve
Yvette Cassidy, Chief Administrative Officer

Strathcona County
2001 Sherwood Dr.
Sherwood Park, AB T8A 3W7
Tel: 780-464-8111; *Fax:* 780-464-8050
info@strathcona.ca
www.strathcona.ca
Municipal Type: Regional Municipality
Incorporated: Jan. 1, 1962; *Area:* 1,182.78 sq km
Population in 2016: 98,044
Federal Electoral District(s): Sherwood Park-Fort Saskatchewan
Next Election: Oct. 20, 2025 (4 year terms)
Note: Incorporated as a specialized municipality on Jan. 1, 1996.
Rod Frank, Mayor
Robert Parks, Councillor, Wards: 1
Dave Anderson, Councillor, Wards: 2
Lorne Harvey, Councillor, Wards: 3
Bill Tonita, Councillor, Wards: 4
Aaron C. Nelson, Councillor, Wards: 5
Corey-Ann Hartwick, Councillor, Wards: 6
Glen Lawrence, Councillor, Wards: 7
Katie Berghofer, Councillor, Wards: 8
Darrell Reid, Chief Commissioner, 780-464-8100
Jennifer Cannon, Chief Financial Officer, 780-464-8068
Jason Chance, Associate Commissioner, Corporate Services,
780-400-2085
Stacy Fedechko, Associate Commissioner, Infrastructure
Planning Services, 780-464-8409
Gord Johnston, Associate Commissioner, Community Services,
780-464-8291, Fax: 780-417-7143
Jeff Hutton, Fire Chief

Sturgeon County
9613 - 100th St.
Morinville, AB T8R 1L9
Tel: 780-939-4321
sturgeonmail@sturgeoncounty.ca
www.sturgeoncounty.ca
Other Information: Toll-Free Phone: 866-939-9303
Municipal Type: County
Incorporated: Feb. 1, 1943; *Area:* 2,090.13 sq km
Population in 2016: 20,495
Federal Electoral District(s): Sturgeon River-Parkland
Next Election: Oct. 20, 2025 (4 year terms)
Alanna Hnatiw, Mayor
Dan Derouin, Councillor, Wards: 1
Kristin Toms, Councillor, Wards: 2
Matthew McLennan, Councillor, Wards: 3
Neal Comeau, Councillor, Wards: 4
Deanna Stang, Councillor, Wards: 5
Ronald Shaw, Councillor, Wards: 6
Reegan McCullough, Chief Administrative Officer, 780-939-8345
Scott MacDougall, Chief Operations Officer, 780-939-8337
Travis Peter, Director, Development Services, 780-939-8344
Jesse Sopko, Director, Corporate Services, 780-939-8377

Taber
4900B - 50th St.
Taber, AB T1G 1T2
Tel: 403-223-3541; *Fax:* 403-223-1799
dkrizsan@mdtaber.ab.ca
www.mdtaber.ab.ca
Municipal Type: Municipal District
Incorporated: April 1, 1945; *Area:* 4,204.38 sq km
Population in 2016: 7,098
Federal Electoral District(s): Bow River
Next Election: Oct. 20, 2025 (4 year terms)
Vacant, Reeve
Arlos Crofts, Chief Administrative Officer

Thorhild County
P.O. Box 10
801 - 1st St.
Thorhild, AB T0A 3J0
Tel: 780-398-3741; *Fax:* 780-398-3748
www.thorhildcounty.com
Other Information: Toll-Free Phone: 877-398-3777
Municipal Type: County
Incorporated: Jan. 1, 1955; *Area:* 1,998.38 sq km
Population in 2016: 3,254
Federal Electoral District(s): Lakeland
Next Election: Oct. 20, 2025 (4 year terms)
Note: Thorhild County No. 7 was changed to Thorhild County on
March 20, 2013.
Vacant, Reeve
Ryan Maier, Interim Chief Administrative Officer

Two Hills County No. 21
P.O. Box 490
4818 - 50th Ave.
Two Hills, AB T0B 4K0
Tel: 780-657-3358; *Fax:* 780-657-3504
info@thcounty.ab.ca
www.thcounty.ab.ca
Other Information: Toll-Free Phone: 877-657-3359
Municipal Type: County
Incorporated: Jan. 1, 1944; *Area:* 2,630.95 sq km
Population in 2016: 3,322
Federal Electoral District(s): Lakeland
Next Election: Oct. 20, 2025 (4 year terms)
Note: Incorporated as a county on Jan. 1, 1963.
Donald Gulayec, Reeve
Sally Dary, Chief Administrative Officer

Vermilion River County
P.O. Box 69
4912 - 50th Ave.
Kitscoty, AB T0B 2P0
Tel: 780-846-2244
office@county24.com
vermilion-river.com
Municipal Type: County
Incorporated: Jan. 1, 1944; *Area:* 5,518.71 sq km
Population in 2016: 8,267
Federal Electoral District(s): Lakeland
Next Election: Oct. 20, 2025 (4 year terms)
Note: Name changed from Vermilion River No. 24 County on Sept. 13, 2006.
Dale Swyripa, Reeve
Harold Northcott, Chief Administrative Officer

Vulcan County
P.O. Box 180
102 Centre St.
Vulcan, AB T0L 2B0
Tel: 403-485-2241; *Fax:* 403-485-2920
reception@vulcancounty.ab.ca
vulcancounty.ab.ca
Municipal Type: County
Incorporated: April 1, 1945; *Area:* 5,430.06 sq km
Population in 2016: 3,984
Federal Electoral District(s): Bow River
Next Election: Oct. 20, 2025 (4 year terms)
Note: Incorporated as a county on Jan. 1, 1951.
Jason Schneider, Reeve, 403-485-1803
Nels Peterson, Chief Administrative Officer

Wainwright No. 61
717 - 14th Ave.
Wainwright, AB T9W 1B3
Tel: 780-842-4454; *Fax:* 780-842-2463
info@mdwainwright.ca
www.mdwainwright.ca
Municipal Type: Municipal District
Incorporated: Jan. 30, 1942; *Area:* 4,154.74 sq km
Population in 2016: 4,479
Federal Electoral District(s): Battle River-Crowfoot
Next Election: Oct. 20, 2025 (4 year terms)
Bob Barss, Reeve, 780-754-2195
Kelly Buchinski, Municipal Administrator

Warner County No. 5
P.O. Box 90
300 County Rd.
Warner, AB T0K 2L0
Tel: 403-642-3635; *Fax:* 403-642-3631
admin@warnercounty.ca
www.warnercounty.ca
Other Information: Toll-Free Phone: 888-642-2241
Municipal Type: County
Incorporated: Dec. 9, 1912; *Area:* 4,517.67 sq km
Population in 2016: 3,847
Federal Electoral District(s): Medicine Hat-Cardston-Warner
Next Election: Oct. 20, 2025 (4 year terms)
Ross Ford, Reeve, 403-344-3053, Fax: 403-344-3055
Shawn Hathaway, Chief Administrative Officer

Westlock County
10336 - 106th St.
Westlock, AB T7P 2G1
Tel: 780-349-3346; *Fax:* 780-349-2012
info@westlockcounty.com
www.westlockcounty.com
Other Information: Toll-Free Phone: 877-349-5880
Municipal Type: County
Incorporated: Feb. 1, 1943; *Area:* 3,174.6 sq km
Population in 2016: 7,220
Federal Electoral District(s): Peace River-Westlock
Next Election: Oct. 20, 2025 (4 year terms)

Jared Stitsen, Reeve
Kayleena Spiess, Chief Administrative Officer

Wetaskiwin County No. 10
P.O. Box 6960
Wetaskiwin, AB T9A 2G5
Tel: 780-352-3321; *Fax:* 780-352-3486
www.county.wetaskiwin.ab.ca
Municipal Type: County
Incorporated: Dec. 13, 1915; *Area:* 3,132.06 sq km
Population in 2016: 11,181
Federal Electoral District(s): Edmonton-Wetaskiwin
Next Election: Oct. 20, 2025 (4 year terms)
Note: Incorporated as a county on Jan. 1, 1958.
Bill Krahn, Councillor, 780-352-6930, Wards: 1
Lynn Marie Carwell, Councillor, Wards: 2
Dale Woitt, Councillor, 780-352-7429, Wards: 3
Josh Bishop, Councillor, 780-352-6830, Wards: 4
Ken Adair, Councillor, 780-352-6318, Wards: 5
Kathy Rooyakkers, Councillor, Wards: 6
Lyle Seely, Councillor, 780-388-3894, Wards: 7
Rod Hawken, Chief Administrative Officer, 780-352-3321
David Blades, Director, Planning & Economic Development, 780-361-6235
Eric Hofbauer, Director, Finance, 780-361-6228
Geoff Lynch, Director, Leisure & Community Services, 780-361-6227

Wheatland County
242006 Range Rd. 243
Wheatland County, AB T1P 2C4
Tel: 403-934-3321; *Fax:* 403-934-4889
admin@wheatlandcounty.ca
wheatlandcounty.ca
Municipal Type: County
Incorporated: April 1, 1945; *Area:* 4,550.92 sq km
Population in 2016: 8,788
Federal Electoral District(s): Bow River
Next Election: Oct. 20, 2025 (4 year terms)
Note: Incorporated as a county on Jan. 1, 1961.
Glenn Koester, Reeve, 403-533-2228
Alan Parkin, Chief Administrative Officer

Willow Creek No. 26
P.O. Box 550
#273129 Secondary Hwy. 520 West
Claresholm, AB T0L 0T0
Tel: 403-625-3351; *Fax:* 403-625-3886
md26@mdwillowcreek.com
mdwillowcreek.com
Other Information: Toll-Free Phone: 888-337-3351
Municipal Type: Municipal District
Incorporated: Jan. 1, 1944; *Area:* 4,560.22 sq km
Population in 2016: 5,179
Federal Electoral District(s): Foothills
Note: The town of Granum was dissolved as of Feb. 1, 2020, & became part of the MD of Willow Creek.
Maryanne Sandberg, Reeve, 403-553-2141
Derrick Kriszan, Chief Administrative Officer

Wood Buffalo
9909 Franklin Ave.
Fort McMurray, AB T9H 2K4
Tel: 780-743-7000
www.rmwb.ca
Other Information: Toll-Free Phone: 800-973-9663
Municipal Type: Regional Municipality
Incorporated: April 1, 1995; *Area:* 61,777.65 sq km
Population in 2016: 71,589
Federal Electoral District(s): Fort McMurray-Cold Lake
Next Election: Oct. 20, 2025 (4 year terms)
Note: Incorporated as a specialized municipality on April 1, 1995.
Sandy Bowman, Mayor
Ken Ball, Councillor, Wards: 1
Funky Banjoko, Councillor, Wards: 1
Lance Bussieres, Councillor, Wards: 1
M. Shafiq Dogar, Councillor, Wards: 1
Allan Grandison, Councillor, Wards: 1
Keith McGrath, Councillor, Wards: 1
Kendrick Cardinal, Councillor, Wards: 2
Loretta Eva Waquan, Councillor, Wards: 2
Stu Wigle, Councillor, Wards: 3
Jane Stroud, Councillor, Wards: 4
Jamie Doyle, Chief Administrative Officer, 780-743-7023, Fax: 780-743-7099

Woodlands County
P.O. Box 60
1 Woodlands Lane
Whitecourt, AB T7S 1N3
Tel: 780-778-8400
woodlands@woodlands.ab.ca
woodlands.ab.ca
Other Information: Toll-Free Phone: 888-870-6315
Municipal Type: County
Incorporated: Jan. 1, 1969; *Area:* 7,668.11 sq km
Population in 2016: 4,754
Federal Electoral District(s): Peace River-Westlock
Next Election: Oct. 20, 2025 (4 year terms)
Note: Incorporated as a municipal district on Jan. 1, 1994.
Vacant, Mayor
Gordon Frank, Chief Administrative Officer

Yellowhead County
2716 - 1st Ave.
Edson, AB T7E 1N9
Tel: 780-723-4800; *Fax:* 780-723-5066
info@yellowheadcounty.ab.ca
yhcounty.ca
Other Information: Toll-Free Phone: 800-665-6030
Municipal Type: County
Incorporated: Jan. 1, 1994; *Area:* 22,293.16 sq km
Population in 2016: 10,995
Federal Electoral District(s): Yellowhead
Next Election: Oct. 20, 2025 (4 year terms)
Wade Williams, Mayor
Patrick Soroka, Councillor, Wards: 1. Evansburg & Area
Anthony Giezen, Councillor, 780-325-2459, Wards: 2. Wildwood & Area
Penny Lowe, Councillor, 780-795-2500, Wards: 3. Nilton/Carrot Creek Area
David Russell, Councillor, 780-693-2209, Wards: 4. Peers/Rosevear/Shiningbank
Shawn Berry, Councillor, 780-723-2606, Wards: 5. Wolf Creek/Pinedale Area
Brigitte Lemieux, Councillor, Wards: 6. Edson Area
Dawn Mitchell, Councillor, 780-725-1174, Wards: 7. Edson West
Ken Groat, Councillor, Wards: 8. Hinton/Cadomin/Robb
Luc Mercier, Chief Administrative Officer
Deborah Juch, Director, Community Services
Jeffrey Morrison, Director, Corporate Services
Don O'Quinn, Director, Infrastructure & Planning Services
Brent Shepherd, Manager, Planning & Development

Major Municipalities in Alberta

Airdrie
400 Main St. SE
Airdrie, AB T4B 3C3
Tel: 403-948-8800; *Fax:* 403-948-6567
www.airdrie.ca
Other Information: Toll-Free Phone: 888-247-3743
Municipal Type: City
Incorporated: Sept. 10, 1909; *Area:* 84.57 sq km
Population in 2016: 61,581
Provincial Electoral District(s): Airdrie-Cochrane; Airdrie-East
Federal Electoral District(s): Banff-Airdrie
Next Election: Oct. 20, 2025 (4 year terms)
Note: Incorporated as a city on Jan. 1, 1985.
Peter Brown, Mayor, 403-948-8820
Darrell Belyk, Councillor, 403-862-8643
Ronald (Ron) Chapman, Councillor, 403-992-4604
Alfred (Al) Jones, Councillor
Candice Kolson, Councillor, 403-828-1448
Tina Petrow, Councillor
Heather Spearman, Councillor
Paul Schulz, Chief Administrative Officer, 403-948-8800, Fax: 403-948-6567

Beaumont
5600 - 49th St.
Beaumont, AB T4X 1A1
Tel: 780-929-8782; *Fax:* 780-929-8729
administrator@beaumont.ab.ca
www.beaumont.ab.ca
Municipal Type: City
Incorporated: Jan. 1, 1973; *Area:* 10.47 sq km
County or District: Leduc County; *Population in 2016:* 17,396
Provincial Electoral District(s): Leduc-Beaumont
Federal Electoral District(s): Edmonton-Wetaskiwin
Next Election: Oct. 20, 2025 (4 year terms)
Note: Incorporated as a town on Jan 1, 1980.
Bill Daneluik, Mayor
Kathy Barnhart, Councillor, 780-721-5504
Catherine McCook, Councillor
Ashley Miller, Councillor

Sam Munckhof-Swain, Councillor, 780-690-0031
Rene Tessier, Councillor
Steven Van Nieuwkerk, Councillor, 780-991-0871
Mike Schwirtz, Chief Administrative Officer, 780-929-8782

Brooks
P.O. Box 879
201 - 1st Ave. West
Brooks, AB T1R 0Z6
Tel: 403-362-3333; *Fax:* 403-362-4787
brookscommunications@brooks.ca
www.brooks.ca
Municipal Type: City
Incorporated: July 14, 1910; *Area:* 18.59 sq km
Population in 2016: 14,451
Provincial Electoral District(s): Brooks-Medicine Hat
Federal Electoral District(s): Bow River
Next Election: Oct. 20, 2025 (4 year terms)
Note: Incorporated as a city on Sept. 1, 2005.
John Petrie, Mayor
Joel Goodnough, Councillor
Mohammed Idriss, Councillor
Ray Juska, Councillor
Jon Nesbitt, Councillor
Bill Prentice, Councillor
Marissa Wardrop, Councillor
Alan Martens, Chief Administrative Officer
Don Saari, Manager, Works & Utilities, 403-362-3146
Shelley Thomas, Manager, Finance
Kevin Swanson, Fire Chief
Kelly Attwell, Supervisor, Facilities
Phil Lunn, Supervisor, Parks, 403-362-0271
Natacha Entz, Officer, Planning & Development Services

Calgary
P.O. Box 2100 M
800 Macleod Trail SE
Calgary, AB T2P 2M5
Tel: 403-268-2489; *Fax:* 403-538-6111
311contactus@calgary.ca
www.calgary.ca
Other Information: TTY: 403-268-4889
Municipal Type: City
Incorporated: Nov. 7, 1884; *Area:* 825.56 sq km
Population in 2016: 1,239,220
Provincial Electoral District(s): Cal.-Acadia; Cal.-Beddington; Cal.-Bow; Cal.-Buffalo; Cal.-Cross; Cal.-Currie; Cal.-East; Cal.-Edgemont; Cal.-Elbow; Cal.-Falconridge; Cal.-Fish Creek; Cal.-Foothills; Cal.-Glenmore; Cal.-Hays; Cal.-Klein; Cal.-Lougheed; Cal.-McCall; Cal.-Mountain View; Cal.-North; Cal.-North East; Cal.-N.W.; Cal.-Peigan; Cal.-Shaw; Cal.-S.E.; Cal.-Varsity; Cal.-West
Federal Electoral District(s): Calgary Centre; Calgary Confederation; Calgary Forest Lawn; Calgary Heritage; Calgary Midnapore; Calgary Nose Hill; Calgary Rocky Ridge; Calgary Shepard; Calgary Signal Hill; Calgary Skyview
Next Election: Oct. 20, 2025 (4 year terms)
Note: Incorporated as a city on Jan. 1, 1894.
Jyoti Gondek, Mayor
Sonya Sharp, Councillor, Wards: 1
Jennifer Wyness, Councillor, Wards: 2
Jasmine Mian, Councillor, Wards: 3
Sean Chu, Councillor, 403-268-2430, Fax: 403-268-8091, Wards: 4
Raj Dhaliwal, Councillor, Wards: 5
Richard Pootmans, Councillor, Wards: 6
Terry Wong, Councillor, Wards: 7
Courtney Walcott, Councillor, Wards: 8
Gian-Carlo Carra, Councillor, 403-268-5330, Fax: 403-268-8091, Wards: 9
Andre Chabot, Councillor, Wards: 10
Kourtney Branagan, Councillor, Wards: 11
Evan Spencer, Councillor, Wards: 12
Dan McLean, Councillor, Wards: 13
Peter Demong, Councillor, 403-268-1653, Fax: 403-268-3823, Wards: 14
Vacant, City Clerk
David Duckworth, City Manager, 403-268-2109
Carla Male, Chief Financial Officer, 403-268-1689
Stuart Dalgleish, General Manager, Planning & Development, 403-268-2601
Doug Morgan, General Manager, Transportation, 403-537-7800
Michael Thompson, General Manager, Utilities & Environmental Protection
Mark Neufeld, Chief of Police
Steve Dongworth, Fire Chief, 403-287-4255
Christopher Collier, Director, Environmental & Safety Management, 403-268-1012
Mark Lavallee, Director, Human Resources, 403-268-2201
Rick Valdarchi, Director, Waste & Recycling Services, 403-268-6474

Camrose
City Hall
5204 - 50th Ave.
Camrose, AB T4V 0S8
Tel: 780-672-4426; *Fax:* 780-672-2469
admin@camrose.ca
www.camrose.ca
Municipal Type: City
Incorporated: May 4, 1905; *Area:* 42.62 sq km
Population in 2016: 18,742
Provincial Electoral District(s): Camrose
Federal Electoral District(s): Battle River-Crowfoot
Next Election: Oct. 20, 2025 (4 year terms)
Note: Incorporated as a city on Jan. 1, 1955.
PJ Stasko, Mayor
Lucas Banack, Councillor
Lana Broker, Councillor
David R. Francoeur, Councillor
Agnes Hoveland, Councillor, 780-678-3027
Kevin Hycha, Councillor, 780-678-3027
DJ Ilg, Councillor
Don Rosland, Councillor
Malcolm Boyd, City Manager, 780-678-3027, Fax: 780-672-2469
Travis Bouck, General Manager, Financial Services, 780-672-4426, Fax: 780-672-2469
Ryan Poole, General Manager, Community Services, 780-672-9195
Dean LaGrange, Police Chief, 780-672-8300
Peter Krich, Fire Chief, 780-672-2906, Fax: 780-672-1384

Chestermere
105 Marina Rd.
Chestermere, AB T1X 1V7
Tel: 403-207-7050; *Fax:* 403-569-0512
info@chestermere.ca
www.chestermere.ca
Municipal Type: City
Incorporated: April 1, 1977; *Area:* 32.94 sq km
County or District: Rocky View County; *Population in 2016:* 19,887
Provincial Electoral District(s): Chestermere-Strathmore
Federal Electoral District(s): Bow River
Next Election: Oct. 20, 2025 (4 year terms)
Note: Incorporated as a town on March 1, 1993.
Jeff Colvin, Mayor
Shannon Dean, Councillor
Mel Foat, Councillor
Blaine Funk, Councillor
Stephen Hanley, Councillor
Sandeep (Sandy) Johal-Watt, Councillor
Ritesh Dalip Narayan, Councillor
Bernie Morton, Chief Administrative Officer

Cochrane
P.O. Box 10
101 RancheHouse Rd.
Cochrane, AB T4C 2K8
Tel: 403-851-2500; *Fax:* 403-932-6032
info@cochrane.ca
www.cochrane.ca
Municipal Type: City
Incorporated: June 17, 1903; *Area:* 29.83 sq km
County or District: Rocky View County; *Population in 2016:* 25,853
Provincial Electoral District(s): Airdrie-Cochrane
Federal Electoral District(s): Banff-Airdrie
Next Election: Oct. 20, 2025 (4 year terms)
Note: Incorporated as a town on Feb. 15, 1971.
Jeff Genung, Mayor
Marni Fedeyko, Councillor
Susan Flowers, Councillor
Tara McFadden, Councillor
Morgan Nagel, Councillor
Alex Reed, Councillor
Patrick Wilson, Councillor
Mike Derricott, Chief Administrative Officer
Shawn Polley, Fire Chief

Cold Lake
5513 - 48th Ave.
Cold Lake, AB T9M 1A1
Tel: 780-594-4494; *Fax:* 780-594-3480
city@coldlake.com
www.coldlake.com
Municipal Type: City
Incorporated: Dec. 31, 1953; *Area:* 59.92 sq km
Population in 2016: 14,961
Provincial Electoral District(s): Bonnyville-Cold Lake-St Paul
Federal Electoral District(s): Fort McMurray-Cold Lake
Next Election: Oct. 20, 2025 (4 year terms)
Note: Incorporated as a city on Oct. 1, 2000.

Craig Copeland, Mayor, 780-573-9897
Ryan Bailey, Councillor
Victoria Lefebvre, Councillor, 780-573-3136
Bob Mattice, Councillor
William (Bill) Charles Parker, Councillor
Adele Richardson, Councillor
Chris Vining, Councillor, 780-573-3658
Kevin Nagoya, Chief Administrative Officer

Edmonton
City Hall
1 Sir Winston Churchill Sq., 3rd Fl.
Edmonton, AB T5J 2R7
Tel: 780-442-5311; *Fax:* 780-496-5618
311@edmonton.ca
www.edmonton.ca
Other Information: TTY: 780-944-5555
Municipal Type: City
Incorporated: Jan. 9, 1892; *Area:* 685.25 sq km
Population in 2016: 932,546
Provincial Electoral District(s): Ed.-Beverly-Clareview; Ed.-Castle Downs; Ed.-City Centre; Ed.-Decore; Ed.-Ellerslie; Ed.-Glenora; Ed.-Gold Bar; Ed.-Highlands-Norwood; Ed.-Manning; Ed.-McClung; Ed.-Meadows; Ed.-Mill Woods; Ed.-N.W.; Ed.-Riverview; Ed.-Rutherford; Ed.-South; Ed.-S.W.; Ed.-Strathcona; Ed.-West Henday; Ed.-Whitemud
Federal Electoral District(s): Edmonton Griesbach; Edmonton Centre; Edmonton Manning; Edmonton Mill Woods; Edmonton Riverbend; Edmonton Strathcona; Edmonton West; Edmonton-Wetaskiwin; St. Albert-Edmonton
Next Election: Oct. 20, 2025 (4 year terms)
Note: Incorporated as a city on Oct. 08, 1904.
Amarjeet Sohi, Mayor
Erin Rutherford, Councillor, Wards: Anirniq
Aaron Paquette, Councillor, Fax: 780-496-8113, Wards: Dene
Jennifer Rice, Councillor, Wards: Ipiihkoohkanipiaohtsi
Keren Tang, Councillor, Wards: Karhiio
Ashley Salvador, Councillor, Wards: Métis
Andrew Knack, Councillor, 780-496-8122, Fax: 780-496-8113, Wards: Nakota Isga
Anne Stevenson, Councillor, Wards: O-day'min
Michael Janz, Councillor, Wards: papastew
Tim Cartmell, Councillor, Fax: 780-496-8113, Wards: pihêsiwin
Sarah Hamilton, Councillor, Fax: 780-496-8113, Wards: sipiwiyiniwak
Jo-Anne Wright, Councillor, Wards: Sspomitapi
Karen Principe, Councillor, Wards: tastawiyiniwak
Andre Corbould, City Manager, 780-496-8222
Gord Cebryk, Deputy City Manager, City Operations, 780-496-2808
Catrin Owen, Deputy City Manager, Communications & Engagement, 780-423-7401
Stephanie McCabe, Deputy City Manager, Urban Form & Corporate Strategic Development, 780-984-3109
Rob Smyth, Deputy City Manager, Citizen Services, 780-496-5804
Stacey Padbury, Acting Chief Financial Officer, 780-496-5487
Joe Zatylny, Fire Chief
Dale McFee, Police Chief

Fort Saskatchewan
10005 - 102nd St.
Fort Saskatchewan, AB T8L 2C5
Tel: 780-992-6200; *Fax:* 780-998-4774
info@fortsask.ca
www.fortsask.ca
Municipal Type: City
Incorporated: March 1, 1899; *Area:* 48.18 sq km
Population in 2016: 24,149
Provincial Electoral District(s): Fort Saskatchewan-Vegreville
Federal Electoral District(s): Sherwood Park-Fort Saskatchewan
Next Election: Oct. 20, 2025 (4 year terms)
Note: Incorporated as a city on July 1, 1985.
Gale Katchur, Mayor, 780-992-6232, Fax: 780-998-4774
Jibs Abitoye, Councillor, 780-200-6863
Gordon Harris, Councillor, 780-934-4903
Brian Kelly, Councillor, 780-991-4575
Lisa Makin, Councillor, 780-340-0054
Patrick Noyen, Councillor
Dennis Thompson, Councillor
Troy Fleming, City Manager, 780-992-6212
Richard Gagnon, Director, Public Works, 780-992-6212
Bettina Ryan, Director, People Services, 780-992-6624
Craig Thomas, Director, Planning & Development, 780-997-6696
Diane Yanch, Director, Culture & Recreation, 780-992-6261
Todd Martens, Fire Chief, 780-992-6235

Grande Prairie
P.O. Box 4000
10205 - 98th St.
Grande Prairie, AB T8V 6V3
Tel: 780-538-0300; *Fax:* 780-539-1056
info@cityofgp.com
www.cityofgp.com
Municipal Type: City
Incorporated: April 30, 1914; *Area:* 132.73 sq km
Population in 2016: 63,166
Provincial Electoral District(s): Grande Prairie; Grande
Prairie-Wapiti
Federal Electoral District(s): Grande Prairie-Mackenzie
Next Election: Oct. 20, 2025 (4 year terms)
Note: Incorporated as a city on Jan. 1, 1958.
Jackie Clayton, Mayor, 780-538-0300
Grant Berg, Councillor
Gladys Blackmore, Councillor
Wendy Bosch, Councillor
Dylan Bressey, Councillor, 780-402-4166
John Lehners, Councillor
Mike O'Connor, Councillor
Kevin P. O'Toole, Councillor, 780-933-0925
Chris Thiessen, Councillor, 780-831-1328
Horacio Galanti, City Manager
Preben Bossen, Fire Chief

High River
309B MacLeod Trail SW
High River, AB T1V 1Z5
Tel: 403-652-2110; *Fax:* 403-652-2396
www.highriver.ca
Municipal Type: City
Incorporated: Dec. 5, 1901; *Area:* 21.39 sq km
County or District: Municipal District of Foothills No. 31;
Population in 2016: 13,584
Provincial Electoral District(s): Livingstone-Macleod
Federal Electoral District(s): Foothills
Next Election: Oct. 20, 2025 (4 year terms)
Note: Incorporated as a town on Feb. 12, 1906.
Craig L. Snodgrass, Mayor
Jamie (James) Barton, Councillor
Jenny Jones, Councillor
Kelly Rianne Killick-Smit, Councillor
Jamie Kinghorn, Councillor
Michael Nychyk, Councillor
Brenda Walsh, Councillor
Chris Prosser, Chief Administrative Officer
Nicole Chepil, Director, Corporate Services
Reiley McKerracher, Director, Engineering, Parks & Recreation
& Operational Services

Lacombe
5432 - 56th Ave.
Lacombe, AB T4L 1E9
Tel: 403-782-6666; *Fax:* 403-782-5655
webmaster@lacombe.ca
lacombe.ca
Municipal Type: City
Incorporated: July 28, 1896; *Area:* 20.81 sq km
Population in 2016: 13,057
Provincial Electoral District(s): Lacombe-Ponoka
Federal Electoral District(s): Red Deer-Lacombe
Next Election: Oct. 20, 2025 (4 year terms)
Note: Incorporated as a town on May 5, 1902.
Grant Creasey, Mayor
Scott Dallas, Councillor
Don Gullekson, Councillor
Thalia Hibbs, Councillor
Cora Hoekstra, Councillor
Reuben Konnik, Councillor
Chris Ross, Councillor
Matthew Goudy, Chief Administrative Officer
Dennis Cole, Fire Chief

Leduc
1 Alexandra Park
Leduc, AB T9E 4C4
Tel: 780-980-7177; *Fax:* 780-980-7127
info@leduc.ca
www.leduc.ca
Municipal Type: City
Incorporated: Dec. 15, 1899; *Area:* 42.44 sq km
Population in 2016: 29,993
Provincial Electoral District(s): Leduc-Beaumont
Federal Electoral District(s): Edmonton-Wetaskiwin
Next Election: Oct. 20, 2025 (4 year terms)
Note: Incorporated as a city on Sept. 01, 1983.
Bob Young, Mayor, 780-916-3547
Beverly Beckett, Councillor, 780-940-5186
Glen Finstad, Councillor, 780-493-1583

Bill Hamilton, Councillor, 780-991-9979
Lars Hansen, Councillor, 780-937-4588
Ryan Pollard, Councillor
Laura Tillack, Councillor, 780-243-8455
Derek Prohar, City Manager

Lethbridge
City Hall
910 - 4th Ave. South
Lethbridge, AB T1J 0P6
Tel: 403-329-7355; *Fax:* 403-320-7575
info@lethbridge.ca
www.lethbridge.ca
Municipal Type: City
Incorporated: Nov. 29, 1890; *Area:* 122.09 sq km
Population in 2016: 92,729
Provincial Electoral District(s): Lethbridge-East; Lethbridge-West
Federal Electoral District(s): Lethbridge
Next Election: Oct. 20, 2025 (4 year terms)
Note: Incorporated as a city on May 9, 1906.
Blaine E. Hyggen, Mayor
Mark Campbell, Councillor, 403-360-0808
Jeff Carlson, Councillor, 403-360-7550
Belinda Crowson, Councillor, 403-320-4276
Rajko Dodic, Councillor
John Middleton-Hope, Councillor
Joe Paladino, Councillor
Ryan Parker, Councillor, 403-360-8880
Jenn Schmidt-Rempel, Councillor
Craig Dalton, City Manager
Hailey Pinkesn, City Treasurer
Brian Loewen, City Solicitor, 403-320-3903, Fax: 403-320-4195
Jason Elliott, Manager, People & Culture
Mike Fox, Director, Community Services
Marc Rathwell, Chief, Fire & Emergency Services

Lloydminster
City Hall
4420 - 50th Ave.
Lloydminster, AB T9V 0W2
Tel: 780-875-6184; *Fax:* 780-871-8345
info@lloydminster.ca
www.lloydminster.ca
Municipal Type: City
Incorporated: Nov. 25, 1903; *Area:* 24.04 sq km
Population in 2016: 31,410
Provincial Electoral District(s):
Vermilion-Lloydminster-Wainwright
Federal Electoral District(s): Lakeland
Next Election: Oct. 20, 2025 (4 year terms)
Note: Population figure represents both the Alberta &
Saskatchewan populations. Incorporated as a city on Jan. 1,
1958.
Gerald Aalbers, Mayor
Aaron Buckingham, Councillor
Michael Diachuk, Councillor
Glenn Fagnan, Councillor
Lorelee Marin, Councillor
Jonathan Torresan, Councillor
Jason Whiting, Councillor
Dion Pollard, City Manager, 780-875-6184
Leigh Sawicki, Fire Chief

Medicine Hat
580 - 1st St. SE
Medicine Hat, AB T1A 8E6
Tel: 403-529-8111; *Fax:* 403-529-8182
www.medicinehat.ca
Municipal Type: City
Incorporated: May 31, 1894; *Area:* 112.04 sq km
Population in 2016: 63,260
Provincial Electoral District(s): Brooks-Medicine Hat;
Cypress-Medicine Hat
Federal Electoral District(s): Medicine Hat-Cardston-Warner
Next Election: Oct. 20, 2025 (4 year terms)
Note: Incorporated as a city on May 9, 1906.
Linnsie Clark, Mayor
Robert Dumanowski, Councillor, 403-502-4348
Cassi Hider, Councillor
Darren Hirsch, Councillor, 403-504-3325
Allison Knodel, Councillor
Andy McGrogan, Councillor
Ramona Karen Robins, Councillor
Shila Sharps, Councillor
Alison Van Dyke, Councillor
Angela Cruickshank, City Clerk, 403-529-8234
Robert Nicolay, Chief Administrative Officer
Benjamin Bullock, City Solicitor, 403-529-8303
Brian Mastel, Managing Director, Public Services, 403-529-8230
Dennis Egert, Managing Director, Corporate Services,
403-529-8228
Brian Stauth, Fire Chief

Okotoks
P.O. Box 20 Main
Okotoks, AB T1S 1K1
Tel: 403-938-4404; *Fax:* 403-938-7387
www.okotoks.ca
Municipal Type: City
Incorporated: Oct. 25, 1899; *Area:* 19.63 sq km
County or District: Municipal District of Foothills No. 31;
Population in 2016: 28,881
Provincial Electoral District(s): Highwood
Federal Electoral District(s): Foothills
Next Election: Oct. 20, 2025 (4 year terms)
Note: Incorporated as a town on June 1, 1904.
Tanya Thorn, Mayor
Cheryl Actemichuk, Councillor
Oliver Hallmark, Councillor
Ken Heemeryck, Councillor, 403-512-6985
Gord Lang, Councillor
Brent Robinson, Councillor
Rachel Swendseid, Councillor
Elaine Vincent, Chief Administrative Officer, 403-938-8900

Red Deer
City Hall
P.O. Box 5008
Red Deer, AB T4N 3T4
Tel: 403-342-8111; *Fax:* 403-346-6195
feedback@reddeer.ca
www.reddeer.ca
Municipal Type: City
Incorporated: May 31, 1894; *Area:* 104.73 sq km
Population in 2016: 100,418
Provincial Electoral District(s): Red Deer-North; Red Deer-South
Federal Electoral District(s): Red Deer-Lacombe; Red
Deer-Mountain View
Next Election: Oct. 20, 2025 (4 year terms)
Note: Incorporated as a city on March 25, 1913.
Ken Johnston, Mayor
Kraymer Barnstable, Councillor
Bruce Buruma, Councillor
Michael Dawe, Councillor, 403-357-4631
Victor Doerksen, Councillor
Vesna Higham, Councillor
Cindy Jefferies, Councillor
Lawrence Lee, Councillor, 403-318-8862, Fax: 403-346-6195
Dianne Wyntjes, Councillor, 403-505-4256, Fax: 403-346-6195
Tara Lodewyk, Interim City Manager, 403-342-8156
Ken McMullen, Acting General Manager, Development &
Protective Services, 403-356-2455
Lisa Perkins, General Manager, Corporate & Employee
Services, 403-309-8489
Sarah Tittemore, General Manager, Community Services,
403-342-8308

St. Albert
5 St Anne St.
St Albert, AB T8N 3Z9
Tel: 780-459-1500; *Fax:* 780-460-2394
stalbert@stalbert.ca
stalbert.ca
Municipal Type: City
Incorporated: Dec. 7, 1899; *Area:* 48.45 sq km
Population in 2016: 65,589
Provincial Electoral District(s): Morinville-St Albert; St Albert
Federal Electoral District(s): St. Albert-Edmonton
Next Election: Oct. 20, 2025 (4 year terms)
Note: Incorporated as a city on Jan. 1, 1977.
Catherine (Cathy) Heron, Mayor
Shelley Biermanski, Councillor
Wes Brodhead, Councillor, 780-915-9622, Fax: 780-459-1591
Sheena Hughes, Councillor, 780-240-9889, Fax: 780-459-1591
Natalie Joly, Councillor, 780-459-1697, Fax: 780-459-1591
Mike Killick, Councillor
Ken MacKay, Councillor, 780-459-1697, Fax: 780-459-1591
Kevin Scoble, Chief Administrative Officer

Spruce Grove
315 Jespersen Ave.
Spruce Grove, AB T7X 3E8
Tel: 780-962-2611; *Fax:* 780-962-2526
info@sprucegrove.org
www.sprucegrove.org
Municipal Type: City
Incorporated: March 14, 1907; *Area:* 32.20 sq km
Population in 2016: 34,066
Provincial Electoral District(s): Spruce Grove-Stony Plain
Federal Electoral District(s): Sturgeon River-Parkland
Next Election: Oct. 20, 2025 (4 year terms)
Note: Incorporated as a city on March 1, 1986.
Jeff Acker, Mayor
Danielle Carter, Councillor

Jan Gillett, Councillor
Stuart Houston, Councillor
Dave Oldham, Councillor
Reid MacDonald, Councillor
Erin Stevenson, Councillor
Dean Screpnek, City Manager
Robert Kosterman, Fire Chief

Stony Plain
4905 - 51st Ave.
Stony Plain, AB T7Z 1Y1
Tel: 780-963-2151; *Fax:* 780-963-2197
info@stonyplain.com
www.stonyplain.com
Municipal Type: City
Incorporated: March 14, 1907; *Area:* 35.72 sq km
County or District: Parkland County; *Population in 2016:* 17,189
Provincial Electoral District(s): Spruce Grove-Stony Plain
Federal Electoral District(s): Sturgeon River-Parkland
Next Election: Oct. 20, 2025 (4 year terms)
Note: Incorporated as a town on Dec. 10, 1908
William Choy, Mayor
Justin Anderson, Councillor
Pat Hansard, Councillor
Justin Laurie, Councillor
Melanie Loyns, Councillor
Eric Meyer, Councillor
Harold Pawlechko, Councillor
Thomas Goulden, Town Manager
Jennifer Boleski, General Manager, Corporate Services
Karl Hill, General Manager, Community & Protective Services
Ian McKay, General Manager, Planning & Infrastructure

Strathmore
P.O. Box 2280
1 Parklane Dr.
Strathmore, AB T1P 1K2
Tel: 403-934-3133; *Fax:* 403-934-4713
webadmin@strathmore.ca
strathmore.ca
Municipal Type: City
Incorporated: March 20, 1908; *Area:* 27.40 sq km
County or District: Wheatland County; *Population in 2016:*
13,756
Provincial Electoral District(s): Chestermere-Strathmore
Federal Electoral District(s): Bow River
Next Election: Oct. 20, 2025 (4 year terms)
Note: Incorporated as a town on July 6, 1911.
Pat Fule, Mayor, 403-324-3314
Melissa Langmaid, Councillor
Debbie Mitzner, Councillor
Jason Montgomery, Councillor, 403-901-7244
Denise Peterson, Councillor, 403-901-5606
Richard Wegener, Councillor
Brent Wiley, Councillor
Douglas Lagore, Chief Administrative Officer
Mel Tiede, Director, Corporate Services
Bas Owel, Acting Fire Chief

Sylvan Lake
5012 - 48th Ave.
Sylvan Lake, AB T4S 1G6
Tel: 403-887-2141; *Fax:* 403-887-3660
tsl@sylvanlake.ca
www.sylvanlake.ca
Municipal Type: City
Incorporated: Dec. 30, 1912; *Area:* 23.26 sq km
County or District: Red Deer County; *Population in 2016:* 14,816
Provincial Electoral District(s): Innisfail-Sylvan Lake
Federal Electoral District(s): Red Deer-Lacombe
Next Election: Oct. 20, 2025 (4 year terms)
Note: Incorporated as a town on May 20, 1946.
Megan Hanson, Mayor
Kjeryn Dakin, Councillor
Kendall Kloss, Councillor
Tim Mearns, Councillor
Graham Parsons, Councillor
Jas Payne, Councillor
Theresa Rilling, Councillor
Wally Ferris, Chief Administrative Officer
Kim Devlin, Director, Planning & Development
Ron Lebsack, Director, Parks & Protective Services
Darren Moore, Director, Corporate Services

Wetaskiwin
P.O. Box 6210
4705 - 50th Ave.
Wetaskiwin, AB T9A 2E9
Tel: 780-361-4400; *Fax:* 780-361-4402
www.wetaskiwin.ca
Other Information: Toll-Free Phone: 800-989-6899

Municipal Type: City
Incorporated: Dec. 4, 1899; *Area:* 18.31 sq km
Population in 2016: 12,655
Provincial Electoral District(s): Maskwacis-Wetaskiwin
Federal Electoral District(s): Edmonton-Wetaskiwin
Next Election: Oct. 20, 2025 (4 year terms)
Note: Incorporated as a city on May 9, 1906.
Tyler Gandam, Mayor
Karen Aberle, Councillor
Gabrielle Blatz, Councillor
Dean Billingsley, Councillor
Bill Elliot, Councillor
Kevin Lonsdale, Councillor
Wayne Neilson, Councillor
Sue Howard, City Manager
Alan Harris, Director, Corporate Services, 780-361-4406
Jamie Wilkinson, Fire Chief, 780-361-4429

Other Municipalities in Alberta

Acme
P.O. Box 299
615A Pacific Ave.
Acme, AB T0M 0A0
Tel: 403-546-3783; *Fax:* 403-546-3014
clerk@acme.ca
www.acme.ca
Municipal Type: Village
Incorporated: July 7, 1910; *Area:* 2.47 sq km
County or District: Kneehill County; *Population in 2016:* 653
Provincial Electoral District(s): Olds-Didsbury-Three Hills
Federal Electoral District(s): Bow River
Next Election: Oct. 20, 2025 (4 year terms)
Bruce McLeod, Mayor
Deb Sedrovic, Municipal Clerk

Alberta Beach
P.O. Box 278
4935 - 50th Ave.
Alberta Beach, AB T0E 0A0
Tel: 780-924-3181; *Fax:* 780-924-3313
abofficea@albertabeach.com
www.albertabeach.com
Municipal Type: Village
Incorporated: Aug. 23, 1920; *Area:* 1.98 sq km
County or District: Lac Ste. Anne County; *Population in 2016:*
1,018
Provincial Electoral District(s): Lac Ste Anne-Parkland
Federal Electoral District(s): Yellowhead
Next Election: Oct. 20, 2025 (4 year terms)
Note: Status changed to a village on Nov. 25, 1998.
Jim Benedict, Mayor
Kathy Skwarchuck, Chief Administrative Officer

Alix
P.O. Box 87
4849 - 50th St.
Alix, AB T0C 0B0
Tel: 403-747-2495; *Fax:* 403-747-3663
info@villageofalix.ca
www.villageofalix.ca
Municipal Type: Village
Incorporated: June 3, 1907; *Area:* 3.15 sq km
County or District: Lacombe County; *Population in 2016:* 734
Provincial Electoral District(s): Lacombe-Ponoka
Federal Electoral District(s): Red Deer-Lacombe
Next Election: Oct. 20, 2025 (4 year terms)
Rob Fehr, Mayor
Wendy Menage, Municipal Clerk

Alliance
P.O. Box 149
Alliance, AB T0B 0A0
Tel: 780-879-3911; *Fax:* 780-879-2235
info@villageofalliance.ca
www.villageofalliance.ca
Municipal Type: Village
Incorporated: Aug. 26, 1918; *Area:* 0.64 sq km
County or District: Flagstaff County; *Population in 2016:* 154
Provincial Electoral District(s):
Vermilion-Lloydminster-Wainwright
Federal Electoral District(s): Battle River-Crowfoot
Next Election: Oct. 20, 2025 (4 year terms)
Leslie Ganshirt, Mayor
Carmen Frank, Chief Administrative Officer

Amisk
5005 - 50th St.
Amisk, AB T0B 0B0
Tel: 780-856-3980
village@amisk.ca
www.amisk.ca
Municipal Type: Village
Incorporated: Jan. 1, 1956; *Area:* 0.76 sq km
County or District: Municipal District of Provost No. 52;
Population in 2016: 204
Provincial Electoral District(s):
Vermilion-Lloydminster-Wainwright
Federal Electoral District(s): Battle River-Crowfoot
Next Election: Oct. 20, 2025 (4 year terms)
Bill Rock, Mayor
Kathy Ferguson, Chief Administration Officer

Andrew
P.O. Box 180
5021 - 50th St.
Andrew, AB T0B 0C0
Tel: 780-365-3687; *Fax:* 780-365-2061
andrew@mcsnet.ca
www.andrewab.com
Municipal Type: Village
Incorporated: June 24, 1930; *Area:* 1.23 sq km
County or District: Lamont County; *Population in 2016:* 425
Provincial Electoral District(s): Fort Saskatchewan-Vegreville
Federal Electoral District(s): Lakeland
Next Election: Oct. 20, 2025 (4 year terms)
Gary Leppek, Mayor

Argentia Beach
P.O. Box 100
605 - 2nd Ave.
Ma-Me-O Beach, AB T0C 1X0
Tel: 780-586-2494; *Fax:* 780-586-3567
argentiabeach.ca
Other Information: Alt. URL: svofficepl.com
Municipal Type: Summer Village
Incorporated: Jan. 1, 1967; *Area:* 0.69 sq km
County or District: Wetaskiwin County No. 10; *Population in
2016:* 27
Provincial Electoral District(s): Drayton Valley-Devon
Federal Electoral District(s): Edmonton-Wetaskiwin
Next Election: Summer 2025 (4 year terms)
Donald Oborowsky, Mayor
Sylvia Roy, Chief Administrative Officer

Arrowwood
P.O. Box 36
22 Center St.
Arrowwood, AB T0L 0B0
Tel: 403-534-3821
vlgarrw@telusplanet.net
villageofarrowwood.ca
Municipal Type: Village
Incorporated: May 13, 1926; *Area:* 0.66 sq km
County or District: Vulcan County; *Population in 2016:* 208
Federal Electoral District(s): Bow River
Next Election: Oct. 20, 2025 (4 year terms)
Matt Crane, Mayor
Cristopher Northcott, Chief Administrative Officer

Athabasca
4705 - 49th Ave.
Athabasca, AB T9S 1B7
Tel: 780-675-2063; *Fax:* 780-675-4242
town@athabasca.ca
www.athabasca.ca
Municipal Type: Town
Incorporated: May 18, 1905; *Area:* 16.98 sq km
County or District: Athabasca County; *Population in 2016:* 2,965
Provincial Electoral District(s): Athabasca-Barrhead-Westlock
Federal Electoral District(s): Lakeland
Next Election: Oct. 20, 2025 (4 year terms)
Note: Incorporated as a town on Aug. 4, 1913.
Robert Balay, Mayor
Rachel Ramey, Chief Administrative Officer

Banff
P.O. Box 1260
110 Bear St.
Banff, AB T1L 1A1
Tel: 403-762-1200; *Fax:* 403-762-1260
comments@banff.ca
www.banff.ca
Municipal Type: Town
Incorporated: Jan. 1, 1990; *Area:* 4.85 sq km
County or District: Improvement District No. 9 (Banff); *Population
in 2016:* 7,851
Provincial Electoral District(s): Banff-Kananaskis

Federal Electoral District(s): Banff-Airdrie
Next Election: Oct. 20, 2025 (4 year terms)
Corrie DiManno, Mayor
Kelly Gibson, Town Manager

Barnwell
P.O. Box 159
612 Heritage Rd.
Barnwell, AB T0K 0B0
Tel: 403-223-4018; *Fax:* 403-223-2373
barnwell@platinum.ca
barnwell.ca
Municipal Type: Village
Incorporated: Jan. 1, 1980; *Area:* 0.9 sq km
County or District: Municipal District of Taber; *Population in 2016:* 947
Provincial Electoral District(s): Taber-Warner
Federal Electoral District(s): Bow River
Next Election: Oct. 20, 2025 (4 year terms)
Del Bodnarek, Mayor
Rachel Schortinghuis, Chief Administrative Officer

Barons
P.O. Box 129
Barons, AB T0L 0G0
Tel: 403-757-3633; *Fax:* 403-757-2599
barons@xplornet.com
barons.ca
Municipal Type: Village
Incorporated: May 6, 1910; *Area:* 0.68 sq km
County or District: Lethbridge County; *Population in 2016:* 341
Federal Electoral District(s): Lethbridge
Next Election: Oct. 20, 2025 (4 year terms)
Vacant, Mayor
Laurie Beck, Chief Administrative Officer

Barrhead
P.O. Box 4189
5014 - 50th Ave.
Barrhead, AB T7N 1A2
Tel: 780-674-3301; *Fax:* 780-674-5648
town@barrhead.ca
www.barrhead.ca
Municipal Type: Town
Incorporated: Nov. 14, 1927; *Area:* 8.1 sq km
County or District: Barrhead County No. 11; *Population in 2016:* 4,579
Provincial Electoral District(s): Athabasca-Barrhead-Westlock
Federal Electoral District(s): Peace River-Westlock
Next Election: Oct. 20, 2025 (4 year terms)
Note: Proclaimed as a town on Nov. 26, 1946.
Dave McKenzie, Mayor
Edward LeBlanc, Chief Administrative Officer

Bashaw
P.O. Box 510
5011 - 52nd Ave.
Bashaw, AB T0B 0H0
Tel: 780-372-3911; *Fax:* 780-372-2335
admin@townofbashaw.com
townofbashaw.com
Municipal Type: Town
Incorporated: Aug. 18, 1911; *Area:* 2.84 sq km
County or District: Camrose County; *Population in 2016:* 830
Federal Electoral District(s): Battle River-Crowfoot
Next Election: Oct. 20, 2025 (4 year terms)
Note: Incorporated as a town on May 1, 1964.
Robert McDonald, Mayor
Theresa Fuller, Chief Administrative Officer

Bassano
P.O. Box 299
502 - 2nd Ave.
Bassano, AB T0J 0B0
Tel: 403-641-3788; *Fax:* 403-641-2585
town@bassano.ca
bassano.ca
Municipal Type: Town
Incorporated: Dec. 28, 1909; *Area:* 5.16 sq km
County or District: Newell County; *Population in 2016:* 1,206
Provincial Electoral District(s): Brooks-Medicine Hat
Federal Electoral District(s): Bow River
Next Election: Oct. 20, 2025 (4 year terms)
Note: Incorporated as a town on Jan. 16, 1911.
Vacant, Mayor

Bawlf
P.O. Box 40
203 Hanson St.
Bawlf, AB T0B 0J0
Tel: 780-373-3797; *Fax:* 780-373-3798
customerservice@bawlf.com
www.villageofbawlf.com
Municipal Type: Village
Incorporated: Oct. 12, 1906; *Area:* 0.96 sq km
County or District: Camrose County; *Population in 2016:* 422
Federal Electoral District(s): Battle River-Crowfoot
Next Election: Oct. 20, 2025 (4 year terms)
Vacant, Mayor
Erin Smyl, Acting Chief Administrative Officer

Beaverlodge
P.O. Box 30
1016 - 4th Ave.
Beaverlodge, AB T0H 0C0
Tel: 780-354-2201; *Fax:* 780-354-2207
town@beaverlodge.ca
beaverlodge.ca
Municipal Type: Town
Incorporated: July 31, 1929; *Area:* 5.58 sq km
County or District: Grande Prairie County No. 1; *Population in 2016:* 2,465
Provincial Electoral District(s): Grande Prairie-Wapiti
Federal Electoral District(s): Grande Prairie-Mackenzie
Next Election: Oct. 20, 2025 (4 year terms)
Note: Incorporated as a town on Jan. 24, 1956.
Gary Rycroft, Mayor
Jeff Johnston, Chief Administrative Officer

Beiseker
P.O. Box 349
700 - 1st Ave.
Beiseker, AB T0M 0G0
Tel: 403-947-3774; *Fax:* 403-947-2146
beiseker@beiseker.com
www.beiseker.com
Municipal Type: Village
Incorporated: Feb. 23, 1921; *Area:* 2.84 sq km
County or District: Rocky View County; *Population in 2016:* 819
Provincial Electoral District(s): Olds-Didsbury-Three Hills
Federal Electoral District(s): Bow River
Next Election: Oct. 20, 2025 (4 year terms)
Vacant, Mayor
Jo-Anne Lambert, Chief Administrative Officer
Doug Hawkins, Director, Infrastructure Services

Bentley
P.O. Box 179
Bentley, AB T0C 0J0
Tel: 403-748-4044; *Fax:* 403-748-3213
info@townofbentley.ca
www.townofbentley.ca
Municipal Type: Town
Incorporated: March 17, 1915; *Area:* 2.3 sq km
County or District: Lacombe County; *Population in 2016:* 1,078
Provincial Electoral District(s): Rimbey-Rocky Mountain House-Sundre
Federal Electoral District(s): Red Deer-Lacombe
Next Election: Oct. 20, 2025 (4 year terms)
Note: Incorporated as a town on Jan. 1, 2001.
Greg Rathjen, Mayor
Marc Fortais, Chief Administrative Officer

Berwyn
P.O. Box 250
5006 - 51st St.
Berwyn, AB T0H 0E0
Tel: 780-338-3922; *Fax:* 780-338-2224
cao@berwyn.ca
berwyn.ca
Municipal Type: Village
Incorporated: Nov. 28, 1936; *Area:* 1.66 sq km
County or District: Municipal District of Peace No. 135; *Population in 2016:* 538
Provincial Electoral District(s): Central Peace-Notley
Federal Electoral District(s): Peace River-Westlock
Next Election: Oct. 20, 2025 (4 year terms)
Ken Montie, Mayor
Heather Fawcett, Municipal Clerk

Betula Beach
P.O. Box 157
Site 1, RR#1
Onoway, AB T0E 1V0
Tel: 780-914-0997
administration@betulabeach.ca
www.betulabeach.ca

Municipal Type: Summer Village
Incorporated: Jan. 1, 1960; *Area:* 0.18 sq km
County or District: Parkland County; *Population in 2016:* 16
Federal Electoral District(s): Yellowhead
Next Election: Summer 2025 (4 year terms)
Rob Dickie, Mayor
Susan Evans, Chief Administrative Officer

Big Valley
P.O. Box 236
29 - 1st Ave. South
Big Valley, AB T0J 0G0
Tel: 403-876-2269; *Fax:* 403-876-2223
info@villagebigvalley.ca
www.villageofbigvalley.ca
Municipal Type: Village
Incorporated: July 28, 1914; *Area:* 1.84 sq km
County or District: Stettler County No. 6; *Population in 2016:* 346
Provincial Electoral District(s): Drumheller-Stettler
Federal Electoral District(s): Battle River-Crowfoot
Next Election: Oct. 20, 2025 (4 year terms)
Vacant, Mayor

Birch Cove
P.O. Box 7
#19, RR 1
Gunn, AB T0E 1A0
Tel: 780-446-1426
birchcove.ca
Municipal Type: Summer Village
Incorporated: Dec. 31, 1988; *Area:* 0.29 sq km
County or District: Lac Ste. Anne County; *Population in 2016:* 45
Federal Electoral District(s): Sturgeon River-Parkland
Next Election: Summer 2025 (4 year terms)
Eugene Dugan, Mayor
Dennis Evans, Municipal Administrator

Birchcliff
Bay 8, 14 Thevenaz Industrial Tr.
Sylvan Lake, AB T4S 1W2
Tel: 403-887-2822; *Fax:* 403-887-2897
www.sylvansummervillages.ca/birchcliff.html
Municipal Type: Summer Village
Incorporated: Jan. 1, 1972; *Area:* 0.98 sq km
County or District: Lacombe County; *Population in 2016:* 117
Provincial Electoral District(s): Innisfail-Sylvan Lake
Federal Electoral District(s): Red Deer-Lacombe
Next Election: Summer 2025 (4 year terms)
Roger Dufresne, Mayor
Tanner Evans, Chief Administrative Officer

Bittern Lake
P.O. Box 5
Bittern Lake, AB T0C 0L0
Tel: 780-672-7373; *Fax:* 780-672-2353
www.villageofbitternlake.ca
Municipal Type: Village
Incorporated: Nov. 21, 1904; *Area:* 6.64 sq km
County or District: Camrose County; *Population in 2016:* 220
Provincial Electoral District(s): Maskwacis-Wetaskiwin
Federal Electoral District(s): Battle River-Crowfoot
Next Election: Oct. 20, 2025 (4 year terms)
Vacant, Mayor
Jill Tinson, Chief Administrative Officer

Black Diamond
P.O. Box 10
301 Centre Ave. West
Black Diamond, AB T0L 0H0
Tel: 403-933-4348; *Fax:* 403-933-5865
info@town.blackdiamond.ab.ca
www.town.blackdiamond.ab.ca
Municipal Type: Town
Incorporated: May 8, 1929; *Area:* 3.21 sq km
County or District: Municipal District of Foothills No. 31; *Population in 2016:* 2,700
Provincial Electoral District(s): Highwood
Federal Electoral District(s): Foothills
Next Election: Oct. 20, 2025 (4 year terms)
Note: Incorporated as a town on Jan 1, 1956.
Brendan Kelly, Mayor
Sharlene Brown, Chief Administrative Officer

Blackfalds
P.O. Box 220
5018 Waghorn St.
Blackfalds, AB T0M 0J0
Tel: 403-885-4677; *Fax:* 403-885-4610
info@blackfalds.com
www.blackfalds.com
Municipal Type: Town
Incorporated: June 17, 1904; *Area:* 8.4 sq km

County or District: Lacombe County; *Population in 2016:* 9,328
Provincial Electoral District(s): Lacombe-Ponoka
Federal Electoral District(s): Red Deer-Lacombe
Next Election: Oct. 20, 2025 (4 year terms)
Note: Incorporated as a town on April 1, 1980.
Jamie Hoover, Mayor
Myron Thompson, Chief Administrative Officer

Bon Accord
P.O. Box 779
5025 - 50th Ave.
Bon Accord, AB T0A 0K0
Tel: 780-921-3550; *Fax:* 780-921-3585
info@bonaccord.ca
www.bonaccord.ca
Municipal Type: Town
Incorporated: Jan. 1, 1964; *Area:* 2.11 sq km
County or District: Sturgeon County; *Population in 2016:* 1,529
Provincial Electoral District(s): Morinville-St Albert
Federal Electoral District(s): Sturgeon River-Parkland
Next Election: Oct. 20, 2025 (4 year terms)
Note: Incorporated as a town on Nov. 20, 1979.
Holden Brian, Mayor
Joyce Pierce, Chief Administrative Officer

Bondiss
724 Baptiste Dr.
West Baptiste, AB T9S 1R8
Tel: 780-675-9270
www.bondiss.com
Municipal Type: Summer Village
Incorporated: Jan. 1, 1983; *Area:* 1.33 sq km
County or District: Athabasca County; *Population in 2016:* 110
Provincial Electoral District(s): Athabasca-Barrhead-Westlock
Federal Electoral District(s): Lakeland
Next Election: Summer 2025 (4 year terms)
April Clark, Mayor
Edwin Tomaszyk, Chief Administrative Officer

Bonnyville
4917 - 49th Ave.
Bonnyville, AB T9N 2J7
Tel: 780-826-3496; *Fax:* 780-826-4806
town.bonnyville.ab.ca
Other Information: Toll-free Phone: 866-826-3496
Municipal Type: Town
Incorporated: Sept. 19, 1929; *Area:* 14.1 sq km
County or District: Municipal District of Bonnyville No. 87;
Population in 2016: 5,417
Provincial Electoral District(s): Bonnyville-Cold Lake-St Paul
Federal Electoral District(s): Lakeland
Next Election: Oct. 20, 2025 (4 year terms)
Note: Proclaimed as a town on Feb. 3, 1948.
Elisa Brosseau, Mayor
Bill Rogers, Chief Administrative Officer

Bonnyville Beach
P.O. Box 6439 Main
Bonnyville, AB T9N 2G9
Tel: 780-826-2925; *Fax:* 780-812-2904
admin@bonnyvillebeach.com
www.bonnyvillebeach.com
Municipal Type: Summer Village
Incorporated: Jan 1, 1958; *Area:* 0.38 sq km
County or District: Municipal District of Bonnyville No. 87;
Population in 2016: 84
Provincial Electoral District(s): Bonnyville-Cold Lake-St Paul
Federal Electoral District(s): Lakeland
Next Election: Summer 2025 (4 year terms)
Grant Ferbey, Mayor

Botha
P.O. Box 160
Botha, AB T0C 0N0
Tel: 403-742-5079; *Fax:* 403-742-6586
vlbotha@xplornet.com
Municipal Type: Hamlet
Incorporated: Sept. 5, 1911; *Area:* 1.09 sq km
County or District: Stettler County No. 6; *Population in 2016:* 204
Provincial Electoral District(s): Drumheller-Stettler
Federal Electoral District(s): Battle River-Crowfoot
Note: Botha was dissolved from village status effective Sept. 1, 2017, becoming a hamlet within Stettler County No. 6.

Bow Island
P.O. Box 100
52 Centre St.
Bow Island, AB T0K 0G0
Tel: 403-545-2522; *Fax:* 403-545-6642
townoffice@bowisland.com
www.bowisland.com

Municipal Type: Town
Incorporated: June 14, 1910; *Area:* 5.92 sq km
County or District: Forty Mile County No. 8; *Population in 2016:* 1,983
Provincial Electoral District(s): Taber-Warner
Federal Electoral District(s): Medicine Hat-Cardston-Warner
Next Election: Oct. 20, 2025 (4 year terms)
Note: Incorporated as a town on Feb. 1, 1912.
Gordon Reynolds, Mayor
Dave Matz, Chief Administrative Officer

Bowden
P.O. Box 338
2101 - 20th Ave.
Bowden, AB T0M 0K0
Tel: 403-224-3395; *Fax:* 403-224-2244
info@bowden.ca
www.bowden.ca
Municipal Type: Town
Incorporated: June 17, 1904; *Area:* 1.9 sq km
County or District: Red Deer County; *Population in 2016:* 1,240
Provincial Electoral District(s): Innisfail-Sylvan Lake
Federal Electoral District(s): Red Deer-Mountain View
Next Election: Oct. 20, 2025 (4 year terms)
Note: Incorporated as a town on Sept. 1, 1981.
Robb Stuart, Mayor
Greg Skotheim, Chief Administrative Officer

Boyle
P.O. Box 9
4800 - 3rd St. South
Boyle, AB T0A 0M0
Tel: 780-689-3643; *Fax:* 780-689-3998
admin@boylealberta.com
www.boylealberta.com
Municipal Type: Village
Incorporated: Dec. 31, 1953; *Area:* 4.1 sq km
County or District: Athabasca County; *Population in 2016:* 845
Provincial Electoral District(s): Athabasca-Barrhead-Westlock
Federal Electoral District(s): Lakeland
Next Election: Oct. 20, 2025 (4 year terms)
Colin Derko, Mayor
Warren Griffin, Chief Executive Officer

Breton
P.O. Box 480
Breton, AB T0C 0P0
Tel: 780-696-3636; *Fax:* 780-696-3590
admin@breton.ca
www.breton.ca
Municipal Type: Village
Incorporated: Jan. 1, 1957; *Area:* 1.73 sq km
County or District: Brazeau County; *Population in 2016:* 574
Provincial Electoral District(s): Drayton Valley-Devon
Federal Electoral District(s): Yellowhead
Next Election: Oct. 20, 2025 (4 year terms)
Vacant, Mayor
Terri Wiebe, Chief Administrative Officer

Bruderheim
P.O. Box 280
5017 Queen St.
Bruderheim, AB T0B 0S0
Tel: 780-796-3731; *Fax:* 780-796-3037
info@bruderheim.ca
www.bruderheim.ca
Municipal Type: Town
Incorporated: May 29, 1908; *Area:* 4.23 sq km
County or District: Lamont County; *Population in 2016:* 1,308
Provincial Electoral District(s): Fort Saskatchewan-Vegreville
Federal Electoral District(s): Lakeland
Next Election: Oct. 20, 2025 (4 year terms)
Note: Incorporated as a town on Sept. 17, 1980.
Karl Hauch, Mayor
Patty Podoborozny, Chief Administrative Officer

Burnstick Lake
P.O. Box 501
Caroline, AB T0M 0M0
Tel: 403-304-3591
burnstick8@gmail.com
www.burnsticklakesummervillage.ca
Municipal Type: Summer Village
Incorporated: Dec. 31, 1991; *Area:* 0.18 sq km
County or District: Clearwater County
Provincial Electoral District(s): Rimbey-Rocky Mountain
House-Sundre
Federal Electoral District(s): Yellowhead
Next Election: Summer 2025 (4 year terms)
Harold Esche, Mayor
Therese Kleeberger, Chief Administrative Officer

Calmar
P.O. Box 750
4901 - 50th Ave.
Calmar, AB T0C 0V0
Tel: 780-985-3604; *Fax:* 780-985-3039
info@calmar.ca
www.calmar.ca
Other Information: Toll-Free Phone: 877-922-5627
Municipal Type: Town
Incorporated: Jan. 1, 1949; *Area:* 4.34 sq km
County or District: Leduc County; *Population in 2016:* 2,228
Provincial Electoral District(s): Drayton Valley-Devon
Federal Electoral District(s): Edmonton-Wetaskiwin
Next Election: Oct. 20, 2025 (4 year terms)
Note: Incorporated as a town on Jan. 19, 1954.
Sean Carnahan, Mayor
Kathy Krawchuk, Town Manager

Canmore
902 - 7th Ave.
Canmore, AB T1W 3K1
Tel: 403-678-1500; *Fax:* 403-678-1534
www.canmore.ca
Municipal Type: Town
Incorporated: Jan. 1, 1965; *Area:* 69.43 sq km
Population in 2016: 13,992
Provincial Electoral District(s): Banff-Kananaskis
Federal Electoral District(s): Banff-Airdrie
Next Election: Oct. 20, 2025 (4 year terms)
Note: Incorporated as a town on June 1, 1966.
Sean Krausert, Mayor
Tanya Foubert, Councillor
Wade Graham, Councillor
Jeff Hilstad, Councillor, Fax: 403-678-1524
Jeff Mah, Councillor
Karen Marra, Councillor, Fax: 403-678-1524
Joanna McCallum, Councillor, 403-678-3098, Fax: 403-678-1524
Lisa de Soto, Chief Administrative Officer, 403-678-1535
Sally Caudill, General Manager, Municipal Services, 403-678-1520
Whitney Smithers, General Manager, Infrastructure, 403-678-1514
Walter Gahler, Fire Chief, 403-678-5555

Carbon
238 Hillside Ave.
Carbon, AB T0M 0L0
Tel: 403-572-3244; *Fax:* 403-572-3778
office@villageofcarbon.com
www.villageofcarbon.com
Municipal Type: Village
Incorporated: Nov. 18, 1912; *Area:* 2 sq km
County or District: Kneehill County; *Population in 2016:* 454
Provincial Electoral District(s): Olds-Didsbury-Three Hills
Federal Electoral District(s): Bow River
Next Election: Oct. 20, 2025 (4 year terms)
Bryan Peever, Mayor
Vanessa Van der Meer, Chief Administrative Officer

Cardston
P.O. Box 280
67 - 3rd Ave. West
Cardston, AB T0K 0K0
Tel: 403-653-3366; *Fax:* 403-653-2499
info@cardston.ca
www.cardston.ca
Municipal Type: Town
Incorporated: Dec. 29, 1898; *Area:* 8.64 sq km
County or District: Cardston County; *Population in 2016:* 3,585
Provincial Electoral District(s): Cardston-Siksika
Federal Electoral District(s): Medicine Hat-Cardston-Warner
Next Election: Oct. 20, 2025 (4 year terms)
Note: Incorporated as a town on July 2, 1901.
Maggie Kronen, Mayor, 403-653-2553
Jeff Shaw, Chief Administrative Officer

Carmangay
119 Carman St.
Carmangay, AB T0L 0N0
Tel: 403-643-3595; *Fax:* 403-643-2007
admin@villageofcarma.ca
villageofcarmangay.ca
Municipal Type: Village
Incorporated: Jan. 20, 1910; *Area:* 1.86 sq km
County or District: Vulcan County; *Population in 2016:* 242
Provincial Electoral District(s): Cardston-Siksika
Federal Electoral District(s): Bow River
Next Election: Oct. 20, 2025 (4 year terms)
Stacey Hovde, Mayor

Caroline

P.O. Box 148
Caroline, AB T0M 0M0
Tel: 403-722-3781
info@villageofcaroline.com
villageofcaroline.com
Municipal Type: Village
Incorporated: Dec. 31, 1951; *Area:* 1.98 sq km
County or District: Clearwater County; *Population in 2016:* 512
Provincial Electoral District(s): Rimbey-Rocky Mountain House-Sundre
Federal Electoral District(s): Yellowhead
Next Election: Oct. 20, 2025 (4 year terms)
John Rimmer, Mayor
Craig Curtis, Chief Administrative Officer

Carstairs

P.O. Box 370
844 Centre St.
Carstairs, AB T0M 0N0
Tel: 403-337-3341; *Fax:* 403-337-3343
www.carstairs.ca
Municipal Type: Town
Incorporated: May 15, 1903; *Area:* 5 sq km
County or District: Mountain View County; *Population in 2016:* 4,077
Provincial Electoral District(s): Olds-Didsbury-Three Hills
Federal Electoral District(s): Red Deer-Mountain View
Next Election: Oct. 20, 2025 (4 year terms)
Note: Incorporated as a town on Sept. 1, 1966.
Lance Colby, Mayor, 403-337-3697
Carl McDonnell, Chief Administrative Officer

Castle Island

7 Delwood Pl.
St Albert, AB T8N 6Y5
Tel: 780-418-8348
svcastle@telus.net
summervillageofcastleisland.com
Municipal Type: Summer Village
Incorporated: Jan. 1, 1955; *Area:* 0.05 sq km
County or District: Lac Ste. Anne County; *Population in 2016:* 10
Federal Electoral District(s): Yellowhead
Next Election: Summer 2025 (4 year terms)
Vacant, Mayor
Shelley Marsh, Chief Administrative Officer

Castor

P.O. Box 479
4901 - 50th Ave.
Castor, AB T0C 0X0
Tel: 403-882-3215; *Fax:* 403-882-2700
www.castor.ca
Municipal Type: Town
Incorporated: Nov. 26, 1909; *Area:* 2.72 sq km
County or District: Paintearth County No. 18; *Population in 2016:* 929
Provincial Electoral District(s): Drumheller-Stettler
Federal Electoral District(s): Battle River-Crowfoot
Next Election: Oct. 20, 2025 (4 year terms)
Note: Incorporated as a town on June 27, 1910.
Richard Elhard, Mayor
Christopher Robblee, Chief Administrative Officer

Cereal

P.O. Box 160
Cereal, AB T0J 2J0
Tel: 403-326-3823; *Fax:* 403-326-3826
Municipal Type: Hamlet
Incorporated: Aug. 19, 1914; *Area:* 0.95 sq km
County or District: Special Area No. 3; *Population in 2016:* 111
Provincial Electoral District(s): Drumheller-Stettler
Federal Electoral District(s): Battle River-Crowfoot
Note: On Jan. 1, 2021, Cereal relinquished its village status to become a Hamlet.

Champion

135 Main St.
Champion, AB T0L 0R0
Tel: 403-897-3833
www.villageofchampion.ca
Municipal Type: Village
Incorporated: May 27, 1911; *Area:* 0.88 sq km
County or District: Vulcan County; *Population in 2016:* 317
Provincial Electoral District(s): Cardston-Siksika
Federal Electoral District(s): Bow River
Next Election: Oct. 20, 2025 (4 year terms)
James F. Smith, Mayor
Patrick Bergen, Chief Administrative Officer

Chauvin

P.O. Box 160
216 Main St.
Chauvin, AB T0B 0V0
Tel: 780-858-3881; *Fax:* 780-858-2125
info@villageofchauvin.ca
www.villageofchauvin.ca
Municipal Type: Village
Incorporated: Dec. 30, 1912; *Area:* 2.32 sq km
County or District: Municipal District of Wainwright No. 61; *Population in 2016:* 335
Provincial Electoral District(s): Vermilion-Lloydminster-Wainwright
Federal Electoral District(s): Battle River-Crowfoot
Next Election: Oct. 20, 2025 (4 year terms)
Vacant, Mayor
Martina Skinner, Interim Chief Administrative Officer

Chipman

P.O. Box 176
Chipman, AB T0B 0W0
Tel: 780-363-3982; *Fax:* 780-363-2386
chipmanab@mcsnet.ca
www.chipmanab.ca
Municipal Type: Village
Incorporated: Oct. 21, 1913; *Area:* 0.62 sq km
County or District: Lamont County; *Population in 2016:* 274
Provincial Electoral District(s): Fort Saskatchewan-Vegreville
Federal Electoral District(s): Lakeland
Next Election: Oct. 20, 2025 (4 year terms)
Vacant, Mayor
Pat Tomkow, Chief Administrative Officer

Claresholm

P.O. Box 1000
111 - 55th Ave. West
Claresholm, AB T0L 0T0
Tel: 403-625-3381; *Fax:* 403-625-3869
info@claresholm.ca
www.claresholm.ca
Municipal Type: Town
Incorporated: May 30, 1903; *Area:* 8.3 sq km
County or District: Municipal District of Willow Creek No. 26; *Population in 2016:* 3,780
Provincial Electoral District(s): Livingstone-Macleod
Federal Electoral District(s): Foothills
Next Election: Oct. 20, 2025 (4 year terms)
Note: Incorporated as a town on Aug. 31, 1905.
Chelsae Petrovic, Mayor
Abe Tinney, Chief Administrative Officer

Clive

P.O. Box 90
5115 - 50th St.
Clive, AB T0C 0Y0
Tel: 403-784-3366; *Fax:* 403-784-2012
admin@clive.ca
clive.ca
Municipal Type: Village
Incorporated: Jan. 9, 1912; *Area:* 2.12 sq km
County or District: Lacombe County; *Population in 2017:* 715
Provincial Electoral District(s): Lacombe-Ponoka
Federal Electoral District(s): Red Deer-Lacombe
Next Election: Oct. 20, 2025 (4 year terms)
Luci Henry, Mayor
Carla Kenny, Chief Administrative Officer

Clyde

P.O. Box 190
4812 - 50th St.
Clyde, AB T0G 0P0
Tel: 780-348-5356
admin@villageofclyde.ca
www.villageofclyde.ca
Municipal Type: Village
Incorporated: Jan. 28, 1914; *Area:* 1.36 sq km
County or District: Westlock County; *Population in 2016:* 430
Federal Electoral District(s): Peace River-Westlock
Next Election: Oct. 20, 2025 (4 year terms)
vacant, Mayor
Ron Cust, Chief Administrative Officer

Coaldale

1920 - 17th St.
Coaldale, AB T1M 1M1
Tel: 403-345-1300; *Fax:* 403-345-1311
office@coaldale.ca
www.coaldale.ca
Municipal Type: Town
Incorporated: Dec. 27, 1919; *Area:* 7.95 sq km
County or District: Lethbridge County; *Population in 2016:* 8,215
Provincial Electoral District(s): Taber-Warner

Federal Electoral District(s): Lethbridge
Next Election: Oct. 20, 2025 (4 year terms)
Note: Incorporated as a town on Jan. 7, 1952.
Jack Van Rijn, Mayor
Kalen Hastings, Chief Administrative Officer

Coalhurst

P.O. Box 456
100 - 51st Ave.
Coalhurst, AB T0L 0V0
Tel: 403-381-3033; *Fax:* 403-381-2924
main@town.coalhurst.ab.ca
www.town.coalhurst.ab.ca
Municipal Type: Town
Incorporated: Dec. 17, 1913; *Area:* 1.64 sq km
County or District: Lethbridge County; *Population in 2016:* 2,668
Provincial Electoral District(s): Cardston-Siksika
Federal Electoral District(s): Lethbridge
Next Election: Oct. 20, 2025 (4 year terms)
Note: Incorporated as a town on June 1, 1995.
Lyndsay Montina, Mayor
R.K. (Kim) Hauta, Chief Administrative Officer

Consort

P.O. Box 490
4901 - 50th Ave.
Consort, AB T0C 1B0
Tel: 403-577-3623; *Fax:* 403-577-2024
info@consort.ca
www.consort.ca
Municipal Type: Village
Incorporated: Sept. 23, 1912; *Area:* 2.63 sq km
Population in 2016: 729
Provincial Electoral District(s): Drumheller-Stettler
Federal Electoral District(s): Battle River-Crowfoot
Next Election: Oct. 20, 2025 (4 year terms)
Vacant, Mayor
Barbara Kulyk, Chief Administrative Officer

Coronation

P.O. Box 219
5015 Victoria Ave.
Coronation, AB T0C 1C0
Tel: 403-578-3679; *Fax:* 403-578-3020
admin@town.coronation.ab.ca
town.coronation.ab.ca
Municipal Type: Town
Incorporated: Dec. 16, 1911; *Area:* 3.73 sq km
County or District: Paintearth County No. 18; *Population in 2016:* 940
Provincial Electoral District(s): Drumheller-Stettler
Federal Electoral District(s): Battle River-Crowfoot
Next Election: Oct. 20, 2025 (4 year terms)
Note: Incorporated as a town on April 29, 1912.
Mark Stannard, Mayor
Quinton Flint, Chief Administrative Officer

Coutts

P.O. Box 236
Coutts, AB T0K 0N0
Tel: 403-344-3848; *Fax:* 403-344-4360
vilcoutt@telus.net
www.couttsalberta.com
Municipal Type: Village
Incorporated: Jan. 1, 1960; *Area:* 0.98 sq km
County or District: Warner County No. 5; *Population in 2016:* 245
Provincial Electoral District(s): Taber-Warner
Federal Electoral District(s): Medicine Hat-Cardston-Warner
Next Election: Oct. 20, 2025 (4 year terms)
Jim Willett, Mayor
Lori Rolfe, Chief Administrative Officer

Cowley

P.O. Box 40
Cowley, AB T0K 0P0
Tel: 403-628-3808; *Fax:* 403-628-2807
vilcowow@shaw.ca
cowley.ca
Municipal Type: Village
Incorporated: Aug. 16, 1906; *Area:* 1.4 sq km
County or District: Municipal District of Pincher Creek No. 9; *Population in 2016:* 209
Provincial Electoral District(s): Livingstone-Macleod
Federal Electoral District(s): Foothills
Next Election: Oct. 20, 2025 (4 year terms)
Cindy Cornish, Chief Administrative Officer

Cremona
P.O. Box 10
205 - 1st St. East
Cremona, AB T0M 0R0
Tel: 403-637-3762; *Fax:* 403-637-2101
inquiry@cremona.ca
cremona.ca
Municipal Type: Village
Incorporated: Jan. 1, 1955; *Area:* 0.68 sq km
County or District: Mountain View County; *Population in 2016:*
444
Provincial Electoral District(s): Olds-Didsbury-Three Hills
Federal Electoral District(s): Red Deer-Mountain View
Next Election: Oct. 20, 2025 (4 year terms)
Timothy Hagen, Mayor
Rudy Friesen, Chief Administrative Officer

Crossfield
P.O. Box 500
1005 Ross St.
Crossfield, AB T0M 0S0
Tel: 403-946-5565; *Fax:* 403-946-4523
town@crossfieldalberta.com
www.crossfieldalberta.com
Municipal Type: Town
Incorporated: June 3, 1907; *Area:* 4.8 sq km
County or District: Rocky View County; *Population in 2016:*
2,983
Provincial Electoral District(s): Olds-Didsbury-Three Hills
Federal Electoral District(s): Banff-Airdrie
Next Election: Oct. 20, 2025 (4 year terms)
Note: Incorporated as a town on Aug. 1, 1980.
Kim Harris, Mayor
Merel Jarvis, Interim Chief Administrative Officer

Crystal Springs
P.O. Box 100
605 - 2nd Ave.
Ma-Me O Beach, AB T0C 1X0
Tel: 780-586-2494; *Fax:* 780-586-3567
crystalsprings.ca
Municipal Type: Summer Village
Incorporated: Jan. 1, 1957; *Area:* 0.58 sq km
County or District: Wetaskiwin County No. 10; *Population in
2016:* 51
Provincial Electoral District(s): Drayton Valley-Devon
Federal Electoral District(s): Edmonton-Wetaskiwin
Next Election: Summer 2025 (4 year terms)
Ian Rawlinson, Mayor
Sylvia Roy, Chief Administrative Officer

Czar
P.O. Box 30
Czar, AB T0B 0Z0
Tel: 780-857-3740; *Fax:* 780-857-2353
www.villageofczar.ca
Municipal Type: Village
Incorporated: Nov. 12, 1917; *Area:* 1.18 sq km
County or District: Municipal District of Provost No. 52;
Population in 2016: 202
Federal Electoral District(s): Battle River-Crowfoot
Next Election: Oct. 20, 2025 (4 year terms)
Vacant, Mayor
Bobbi Usselman, Chief Administrative Officer

Daysland
P.O. Box 610
5130 - 50th St.
Daysland, AB T0B 1A0
Tel: 780-374-3767; *Fax:* 780-374-2455
info@daysland.com
daysland.com
Municipal Type: Town
Incorporated: April 23, 1906; *Area:* 1.75 sq km
County or District: Flagstaff County; *Population in 2016:* 824
Provincial Electoral District(s): Camrose
Federal Electoral District(s): Battle River-Crowfoot
Next Election: Oct. 20, 2025 (4 year terms)
Note: Incorporated as a town on April 2, 1907.
Wayne Button, Mayor
Rod Krips, Chief Administrative Officer

Delburne
P.O. Box 341
Delburne, AB T0M 0V0
Tel: 403-749-3606; *Fax:* 403-749-2800
village@delburne.ca
www.delburne.ca
Municipal Type: Village
Incorporated: Jan. 17, 1913; *Area:* 1.32 sq km
County or District: Red Deer County; *Population in 2016:* 892
Provincial Electoral District(s): Innisfail-Sylvan Lake

Federal Electoral District(s): Red Deer-Mountain View
Next Election: Oct. 20, 2025 (4 year terms)
Bill Chandler, Mayor
Karen Fegan, Chief Administrative Officer

Delia
P.O. Box 206
Delia, AB T0J 0W0
Tel: 403-364-3787
delia.ca
Municipal Type: Village
Incorporated: July 20, 1914; *Area:* 1.31 sq km
County or District: Starland County; *Population in 2016:* 216
Provincial Electoral District(s): Drumheller-Stettler
Federal Electoral District(s): Battle River-Crowfoot
Next Election: Oct. 20, 2025 (4 year terms)
David Sisley, Mayor
William Huff, Interim Chief Administrative Officer

Devon
1 Columbia Ave. West
Devon, AB T9G 1A1
Tel: 780-987-8300; *Fax:* 780-987-4778
information@devon.ca
www.devon.ca
Municipal Type: Town
Incorporated: Dec. 31, 1949; *Area:* 8.63 sq km
Population in 2016: 6,578
Provincial Electoral District(s): Drayton Valley-Devon
Federal Electoral District(s): Edmonton-Wetaskiwin; Yellowhead
Next Election: Oct. 20, 2025 (4 year terms)
Note: Incorporated as a town on Feb. 24, 1950.
Jeff Craddock, Mayor
Tony Kulbisky, Chief Administrative Officer

Dewberry
P.O. Box 30
22 Centre St.
Dewberry, AB T0B 1G0
Tel: 780-847-3053; *Fax:* 780-847-3057
Municipal Type: Hamlet
Incorporated: Jan. 1, 1957; *Area:* 0.84 sq km
County or District: Vermilion River County; *Population in 2016:*
186
Provincial Electoral District(s):
Vermilion-Lloydminster-Wainwright
Federal Electoral District(s): Lakeland
Note: On Jan. 1, 2021 Dewberry relinquished its village to
become a hamlet of Vermilion River County.

Didsbury
P.O. Box 790
2037 - 19th Ave.
Didsbury, AB T0M 0W0
Tel: 403-335-3391; *Fax:* 403-335-9794
inquiries@didsbury.ca
www.didsbury.ca
Municipal Type: Town
Incorporated: Dec. 24, 1901; *Area:* 5.47 sq km
County or District: Mountain View County; *Population in 2016:*
5,268
Provincial Electoral District(s): Olds-Didsbury-Three Hills
Federal Electoral District(s): Red Deer-Mountain View
Next Election: Oct. 20, 2025 (4 year terms)
Note: Incorporated as a town on Sept. 27, 1906.
Rhonda Hunter, Mayor
Ethan Gorner, Chief Administrative Officer

Donalda
P.O. Box 160
5001 Main St.
Donalda, AB T0B 1H0
Tel: 403-883-2345; *Fax:* 403-883-2022
village.donalda.ab.ca
Municipal Type: Village
Incorporated: Dec. 30, 1912; *Area:* 0.99 sq km
County or District: Stettler County No. 6; *Population in 2016:* 219
Provincial Electoral District(s): Drumheller-Stettler
Federal Electoral District(s): Battle River-Crowfoot
Next Election: Oct. 20, 2025 (4 year terms)
Vacant, Mayor
Kristie Vallet, Chief Administrative Officer

Donnelly
P.O. Box 200
Donnelly, AB T0H 1G0
Tel: 780-925-3835; *Fax:* 780-925-2100
admin@donnelly.ca
donnelly.ca
Municipal Type: Village
Incorporated: Jan. 1, 1956; *Area:* 1.04 sq km
County or District: Municipal District of Smoky River No. 130;

Population in 2016: 342
Provincial Electoral District(s): Central Peace-Notley
Federal Electoral District(s): Peace River-Westlock
Next Election: Oct. 20, 2025 (4 year terms)
Myrna Lanctot, Mayor
Matthew Ferris, Chief Administrative Officer

Drayton Valley
P.O. Box 6837
5120 - 52nd St.
Drayton Valley, AB T7A 1A1
Tel: 780-514-2200; *Fax:* 780-542-5753
info@draytonvalley.ca
www.draytonvalley.ca
Municipal Type: Town
Incorporated: Jan. 1, 1956; *Area:* 12.27 sq km
County or District: Brazeau County; *Population in 2016:* 7,235
Provincial Electoral District(s): Drayton Valley-Devon
Federal Electoral District(s): Yellowhead
Next Election: Oct. 20, 2025 (4 year terms)
Note: Incorporated as a town on June 1, 1956.
Nancy Dodds, Mayor
Annette Driessen, Interim Chief Administrative Officer

Drumheller
224 Centre St.
Drumheller, AB T0J 0Y4
Tel: 403-823-6300; *Fax:* 403-823-7739
communications@drumheller.ca
www.dinosaurvalley.ca
Municipal Type: Town
Incorporated: May 15, 1913; *Area:* 107.93 sq km
Population in 2016: 7,982
Provincial Electoral District(s): Drumheller-Stettler
Federal Electoral District(s): Battle River-Crowfoot
Next Election: Oct. 20, 2025 (4 year terms)
Note: Incorporated as a town on March 2, 1916.
Heather Joanne Colberg, Mayor
Darryl Drohomerski, Chief Administrative Officer

Duchess
P.O. Box 158
103 - 2nd St. East
Duchess, AB T0J 0Z0
Tel: 403-378-4452; *Fax:* 403-378-3860
administration@villageofduchess.com
www.villageofduchess.com
Municipal Type: Village
Incorporated: May 12, 1921; *Area:* 1.89 sq km
County or District: Newell County; *Population in 2016:* 1,085
Provincial Electoral District(s): Brooks-Medicine Hat
Federal Electoral District(s): Bow River
Next Election: Oct. 20, 2025 (4 year terms)
Vacant, Mayor
Yvonne Cosh, Chief Administrative Officer

Eckville
P.O. Box 578
5023 - 51st Ave.
Eckville, AB T0M 0X0
Tel: 403-746-2171; *Fax:* 403-746-2900
info@eckville.com
www.eckville.com
Municipal Type: Town
Incorporated: Nov. 3, 1921; *Area:* 1.58 sq km
County or District: Lacombe County; *Population in 2016:* 1,125
Provincial Electoral District(s): Rimbey-Rocky Mountain
House-Sundre
Federal Electoral District(s): Red Deer-Lacombe
Next Election: Oct. 20, 2025 (4 year terms)
Note: Incorporated as a town on July 1, 1966.
Colleen Ebden, Mayor
Jack Ramsden, Chief Administrative Officer

Edberg
P.O. Box 160
Edberg, AB T0B 1J0
Tel: 780-877-3999; *Fax:* 780-877-2562
vledberg@syban.net
villageofedberg.com
Municipal Type: Village
Incorporated: Feb. 4, 1930; *Area:* 0.36 sq km
County or District: Camrose County; *Population in 2016:* 151
Federal Electoral District(s): Battle River-Crowfoot
Next Election: Oct. 20, 2025 (4 year terms)
Vacant, Mayor
Courtney Wold, Chief Administrative Officer

Edgerton

P.O. Box 57
5037 - 50th Ave.
Edgerton, AB T0B 1K0
Tel: 780-755-3933; *Fax:* 780-755-3750
info@edgerton.ca
www.edgerton.ca
Municipal Type: Village
Incorporated: Sept. 11, 1917; *Area:* 1.22 sq km
County or District: Municipal District of Wainwright No. 61;
Population in 2016: 384
Provincial Electoral District(s):
Vermilion-Lloydminster-Wainwright
Federal Electoral District(s): Battle River-Crowfoot
Next Election: Oct. 20, 2025 (4 year terms)
Vacant, Mayor
Wes Laporte, Chief Administrative Officer

Edson

P.O. Box 6300
605 - 50th St.
Edson, AB T7E 1T7
Tel: 780-723-4401; *Fax:* 780-723-8617
www.townofedson.ca
Municipal Type: Town
Incorporated: Jan. 9, 1911; *Area:* 29.54 sq km
County or District: Yellowhead County; *Population in 2016:* 8,414
Provincial Electoral District(s): West Yellowhead
Federal Electoral District(s): Yellowhead
Next Election: Oct. 20, 2025 (4 year terms)
Note: Incorporated as a town on Sept. 21, 1911.
Kevin Zahara, Mayor
Christine Beveridge, Chief Administrative Officer

Elk Point

P.O. Box 448
Elk Point, AB T0A 1A0
Tel: 780-724-3810; *Fax:* 780-724-2762
town@elkpoint.ca
www.elkpoint.ca
Municipal Type: Town
Incorporated: May 31, 1938; *Area:* 4.88 sq km
County or District: St. Paul County No. 19; *Population in 2016:* 1,452
Provincial Electoral District(s): Bonnyville-Cold Lake-St Paul
Federal Electoral District(s): Lakeland
Next Election: Oct. 20, 2025 (4 year terms)
Note: Incorporated as a town on Jan. 1, 1962.
Parrish Chi-Kin Tung, Mayor
Ken Gwozdz, Chief Administrative Officer

Elnora

P.O. Box 629
Elnora, AB T0M 0Y0
Tel: 403-773-3922
elnoraab@gmail.com
www.villageofelnora.com
Municipal Type: Village
Incorporated: July 22, 1929; *Area:* 0.69 sq km
County or District: Red Deer County; *Population in 2016:* 298
Provincial Electoral District(s): Innisfail-Sylvan Lake
Federal Electoral District(s): Red Deer-Mountain View
Next Election: Oct. 20, 2025 (4 year terms)
Vacant, Mayor
Sharon Wesgate, Chief Administrative Officer

Empress

P.O. Box 159
6 - 3rd Ave.
Empress, AB T0J 1E0
Tel: 403-565-3938; *Fax:* 403-565-2010
voe14@villageofempress.com
villageofempress.com
Municipal Type: Village
Incorporated: Feb. 5, 1914; *Area:* 1.75 sq km
Population in 2016: 135
Provincial Electoral District(s): Drumheller-Stettler
Federal Electoral District(s): Battle River-Crowfoot
Next Election: Oct. 20, 2025 (4 year terms)
Vacant, Mayor
Debbie Ross, Chief Administrative Officer

Fairview

P.O. Box 730
Fairview, AB T0H 1L0
Tel: 780-835-5461; *Fax:* 780-835-3576
reception@fairview.ca
www.fairview.ca
Municipal Type: Town
Incorporated: March 28, 1929; *Area:* 9.65 sq km
County or District: Municipal District of Fairview No. 136;
Population in 2016: 2,998

Provincial Electoral District(s): Central Peace-Notley
Federal Electoral District(s): Peace River-Westlock
Next Election: Oct. 20, 2025 (4 year terms)
Note: Incorporated as a town on April 25, 1949.
Gordon MacLeod, Mayor
Daryl Greenhill, Chief Administrative Officer

Falher

P.O. Box 155
11 Central Ave. SW
Falher, AB T0H 1M0
Tel: 780-837-2247; *Fax:* 780-837-2647
info@falher.ca
falher.ca
Municipal Type: Town
Incorporated: Sept. 05, 1923; *Area:* 2.87 sq km
County or District: Municipal District of Smoky River No. 130;
Population in 2016: 1,047
Provincial Electoral District(s): Central Peace-Notley
Federal Electoral District(s): Peace River-Westlock
Next Election: Oct. 20, 2025 (4 year terms)
Note: Incorporated as a town on Jan. 1, 1955.
Donna Buchinski, Mayor
James Bell, Chief Administrative Officer

Ferintosh

P.O. Box 160
Ferintosh, AB T0B 1M0
Tel: 780-877-3767; *Fax:* 780-877-2338
Municipal Type: Hamlet
Incorporated: Jan. 9, 1911; *Area:* 0.62 sq km
County or District: Camrose County; *Population in 2016:* 202
Federal Electoral District(s): Battle River-Crowfoot
Note: On Jan. 1, 2020 it relinquished its village status to become
a hamlet of Camrose County.

Foremost

P.O. Box 159
301 Main St.
Foremost, AB T0K 0X0
Tel: 403-867-3733; *Fax:* 403-867-2031
vlg4most@telusplanet.net
www.foremostalberta.com
Municipal Type: Village
Incorporated: Dec. 31, 1950; *Area:* 1.74 sq km
County or District: Forty Mile County No. 8; *Population in 2016:* 541
Provincial Electoral District(s): Taber-Warner
Federal Electoral District(s): Medicine Hat-Cardston-Warner
Next Election: Oct. 20, 2025 (4 year terms)
Vacant, Mayor
Marilynn Hirsche, Interim Municipal Administrator

Forestburg

P.O. Box 210
Forestburg, AB T0B 1N0
Tel: 780-582-3668; *Fax:* 780-582-2233
reception@forestburg.ca
www.forestburg.ca
Municipal Type: Village
Incorporated: Aug. 21, 1919; *Area:* 2.19 sq km
County or District: Flagstaff County; *Population in 2016:* 875
Provincial Electoral District(s): Camrose
Federal Electoral District(s): Battle River-Crowfoot
Next Election: Oct. 20, 2025 (4 year terms)
Blaise Young, Mayor
Dwight Dibben, Chief Administrative Officer

Fort Macleod

P.O. Box 1420
Fort MacLeod, AB T0L 0Z0
Tel: 403-553-4425; *Fax:* 403-553-2426
admin@fortmacleod.com
fortmacleod.com
Municipal Type: Town
Incorporated: Dec. 31, 1892; *Area:* 23.34 sq km
County or District: Municipal District of Willow Creek No. 26;
Population in 2016: 2,967
Provincial Electoral District(s): Livingstone-Macleod
Federal Electoral District(s): Foothills
Next Election: Oct. 20, 2025 (4 year terms)
Brent Feyter, Mayor
Sue Keenan, Chief Administrative Officer

Fox Creek

P.O. Box 149
102 Kaybob Dr.
Fox Creek, AB T0H 1P0
Tel: 780-622-3896; *Fax:* 780-622-4247
info@foxcreek.ca
foxcreek.ca

Municipal Type: Town
Incorporated: July 19, 1967; *Area:* 11.54 sq km
County or District: Municipal District of Greenview No. 16;
Population in 2016: 1,971
Provincial Electoral District(s): Central Peace-Notley
Federal Electoral District(s): Peace River-Westlock
Next Election: Oct. 20, 2025 (4 year terms)
Sheila Gilmour, Mayor
Kristen Milne, Chief Administrative Officer

Gadsby

P.O. Box 80
Gadsby, AB T0C 1K0
Tel: 403-574-3793; *Fax:* 403-574-2369
Municipal Type: Hamlet
Incorporated: May 6, 1910; *Area:* 0.82 sq km
County or District: Stettler County No. 6; *Population in 2016:* 40
Provincial Electoral District(s): Drumheller-Stettler
Federal Electoral District(s): Battle River-Crowfoot
Note: On Feb. 1, 2020 the village dissolved to become a hamlet
of County of Stettler No. 6.

Galahad

c/o Flagstaff County Office
P.O. Box 358
12435 TWP Rd. 442
Sedgewick, AB T0B 4C0
Tel: 780-384-4100
Municipal Type: Hamlet
Incorporated: March 5, 1918; *Area:* 0.6 sq km
County or District: Flagstaff County
Federal Electoral District(s): Battle River-Crowfoot
Note: On January 1, 2016, Galahad became a hamlet within
Flagstaff County.

Ghost Lake

PO Box 19554, RPO South Cranston
Calgary, AB T3M 0V4
Tel: 403-510-8083; *Fax:* 403-206-7209
admin@ghostlake.ca
ghostlake.ca
Municipal Type: Summer Village
Incorporated: Dec. 31, 1953; *Area:* 0.63 sq km
County or District: Municipal District of Bighorn No. 8; *Population in 2016:* 82
Provincial Electoral District(s): Banff-Kananaskis
Federal Electoral District(s): Banff-Airdrie
Next Election: Summer 2025 (4 year terms)
John Walsh, Mayor
Sherri Bureyko, Chief Administrative Officer

Gibbons

P.O. Box 68
4807 - 50th Ave.
Gibbons, AB T0A 1N0
Tel: 780-923-3331; *Fax:* 780-923-3691
gov@gibbons.ca
www.gibbons.ca
Municipal Type: Town
Incorporated: Jan. 1, 1959; *Area:* 6.46 sq km
County or District: Sturgeon County; *Population in 2016:* 3,159
Provincial Electoral District(s): Morinville-St Albert
Federal Electoral District(s): Sturgeon River-Parkland
Next Election: Oct. 20, 2025 (4 year terms)
Note: Incorporated as a town on April 1, 1977.
Dan Deck, Mayor
Farrell O'Malley, Chief Administrative Officer

Girouxville

4804 - 50th St.
Girouxville, AB T0H 1S0
Tel: 780-323-4270; *Fax:* 780-323-4110
girouxvl@serbernet.com
girouxville.ca
Municipal Type: Village
Incorporated: Dec. 31, 1951; *Area:* 0.58 sq km
County or District: Municipal District of Smoky River No. 130;
Population in 2016: 219
Provincial Electoral District(s): Central Peace-Notley
Federal Electoral District(s): Peace River-Westlock
Next Election: Oct. 20, 2025 (4 year terms)
Alain Dion, Mayor
Estelle Girard, Chief Administrative Officer

Glendon

P.O. Box 177
Glendon, AB T0A 1P0
Tel: 780-635-3807; *Fax:* 780-635-2100
admin@villageofglendon.ca
villageofglendon.ca
Municipal Type: Village
Incorporated: Jan. 1, 1956; *Area:* 1.98 sq km

County or District: Municipal District of Bonnyville No. 87;
Population in 2016: 493
Provincial Electoral District(s): Bonnyville-Cold Lake-St Paul
Federal Electoral District(s): Lakeland
Next Election: Oct. 20, 2025 (4 year terms)
Vacant, Mayor
Melody Kwiatkowski, Chief Administrative Officer

Glenwood
P.O. Box 1084
Glenwood, AB T0K 2R0
Tel: 403-626-3233; *Fax:* 403-626-3234
office@glenwood.ca
www.glenwood.ca
Municipal Type: Village
Incorporated: Jan. 1, 1961; *Area:* 1.46 sq km
County or District: Cardston County; *Population in 2017:* 316
Provincial Electoral District(s): Cardston-Siksika
Federal Electoral District(s): Foothills
Next Election: Oct. 20, 2025 (4 year terms)
Vacant, Mayor
Carrie Kinahan, Chief Administrative Officer

Golden Days
605 - 2nd Ave.
Ma-Me O Beach, AB T0k 1x0
Tel: 780-586-2494; *Fax:* 780-586-3567
information@svofficepl.com
goldendays.ca
Municipal Type: Summer Village
Incorporated: Jan. 1, 1965; *Area:* 2.27 sq km
County or District: Leduc County; *Population in 2016:* 160
Provincial Electoral District(s): Drayton Valley-Devon
Federal Electoral District(s): Edmonton-Wetaskiwin
Next Election: Summer 2025 (4 year terms)
Richard Tooke, Mayor
Sylvia Roy, Chief Administrative Officer

Grande Cache
10002 Shand Ave.
Grande Cache, AB T0E 0Y0
Tel: 780-827-3362
Municipal Type: Hamlet
Incorporated: Sept. 1, 1966; *Area:* 35.48 sq km
County or District: Municipal District of Greenview No. 16;
Population in 2016: 3,571
Provincial Electoral District(s): West Yellowhead
Federal Electoral District(s): Yellowhead
Note: On Jan 1., 2019 the town dissolved to become a hamlet of
Municipal District of Greenview No. 16.

Grandview
P.O. Box 100
605 - 2nd Ave.
Ma-Me O Beach, AB T0C 1X0
Tel: 780-586-2494; *Fax:* 780-586-3567
information@svofficepl.com
grandview.ca
Municipal Type: Summer Village
Incorporated: Jan. 1, 1967; *Area:* 0.8 sq km
County or District: Wetaskiwin County No. 10; *Population in 2016:* 114
Provincial Electoral District(s): Drayton Valley-Devon
Federal Electoral District(s): Edmonton-Wetaskiwin
Next Election: Summer 2025 (4 year terms)
Don Davidson, Mayor
Sylvia Roy, Chief Administrative Offcier

Grimshaw
P.O. Box 377
5005 - 53rd Ave.
Grimshaw, AB T0H 1W0
Tel: 780-332-4626; *Fax:* 780-332-1250
info@grimshaw.ca
www.grimshaw.ca
Municipal Type: Town
Incorporated: Feb. 18, 1930; *Area:* 7.21 sq km
County or District: Municipal District of Peace No. 135;
Population in 2016: 2,718
Provincial Electoral District(s): Peace River
Federal Electoral District(s): Peace River-Westlock
Next Election: Oct. 20, 2025 (4 year terms)
Note: Incorporated as a town on Feb. 2, 1953.
Wendy Wald, Mayor
Brian Allen, Chief Administrative Officer

Gull Lake
P.O. Box 5
RR#1, Site 2
Lacombe, AB T4L 2N1
Tel: 403-784-2966; *Fax:* 888-241-6027
admin@summervillageofgulllake.com
www.summervillageofgulllake.com
Municipal Type: Summer Village
Incorporated: Sept. 1, 1993; *Area:* 0.7 sq km
County or District: Lacombe County; *Population in 2016:* 176
Provincial Electoral District(s): Lacombe-Ponoka
Federal Electoral District(s): Red Deer-Lacombe
Next Election: Summer 2025 (4 year terms)
Doug Francoeur, Mayor
Therese Kleeberger, Chief Administrative Officer

Half Moon Bay
Bay 8, 14 Thevenaz Indsutrial Trail
Sylvan Lake, AB T4S 2J5
Tel: 403-887-2822; *Fax:* 403-887-2897
information@sylvansummervillages.ca
www.sylvansummervillages.ca/half-moon-bay.html
Municipal Type: Summer Village
Incorporated: Jan. 1, 1978; *Area:* 0.17 sq km
County or District: Lacombe County; *Population in 2016:* 42
Provincial Electoral District(s): Rocky Mountain House
Federal Electoral District(s): Red Deer-Lacombe
Next Election: Summer 2025 (4 year terms)
Jonathan Johnston, Mayor
Tanner Evans, Chief Administrative Officer

Halkirk
P.O. Box 126
Halkirk, AB T0C 1M0
Tel: 403-884-2464; *Fax:* 403-884-2113
halkirk@syban.net
www.halkirk.ca
Municipal Type: Village
Incorporated: Feb. 10, 1912; *Area:* 0.65 sq km
County or District: Paintearth County No. 18; *Population in 2016:*
112
Provincial Electoral District(s): Drumheller-Stettler
Federal Electoral District(s): Battle River-Crowfoot
Next Election: Oct. 20, 2025 (4 year terms)
Thomas Schmidt, Mayor
Marcy Renschler, Chief Administrative Officer

Hanna
P.O. Box 430
202 - 1st St. West
Hanna, AB T0J 1P0
Tel: 403-854-4433
admin@hanna.ca
hanna.ca
Municipal Type: Town
Incorporated: Dec. 31, 1912; *Area:* 8.39 sq km
Population in 2016: 2,559
Provincial Electoral District(s): Drumheller-Stettler
Federal Electoral District(s): Battle River-Crowfoot
Next Election: Oct. 20, 2025 (4 year terms)
Note: Incorporated as a town on April 14, 1914.
Vacant, Mayor
Kim Neill, Chief Administrative Officer

Hardisty
P.O. Box 10
4807 - 49th St.
Hardisty, AB T0B 1V0
Tel: 780-888-3623; *Fax:* 780-888-2200
town.office@hardisty.ca
www.hardisty.ca
Municipal Type: Town
Incorporated: Dec. 11, 1906; *Area:* 5.48 sq km
County or District: Flagstaff County; *Population in 2016:* 554
Federal Electoral District(s): Battle River-Crowfoot
Next Election: Oct. 20, 2025 (4 year terms)
Note: Incorporated as a town on Nov. 9, 1910.
Vacant, Mayor
Jackie Fenton, Interim Chief Administrative Officer

Hay Lakes
P.O. Box 40
Hay Lakes, AB T0B 1W0
Tel: 780-878-3200
office@villageofhaylakes.com
www.villageofhaylakes.com
Municipal Type: Village
Incorporated: April 17, 1928; *Area:* 0.58 sq km
County or District: Camrose County; *Population in 2016:* 495
Federal Electoral District(s): Battle River-Crowfoot
Next Election: Oct. 20, 2025 (4 year terms)
Vacant, Mayor

K. Shannon Yearwood, Chief Administrative Officer

Heisler
P.O. Box 60
Heisler, AB T0B 2A0
Tel: 780-889-3774; *Fax:* 780-889-2280
administration@villageofheisler.ca
www.villageofheisler.ca
Municipal Type: Village
Incorporated: July 27, 1920; *Area:* 0.75 sq km
County or District: Flagstaff County; *Population in 2016:* 160
Provincial Electoral District(s): Battle River-Crowfoot
Next Election: Oct. 20, 2025 (4 year terms)
Bonita Wood, Mayor
Heidi Rohe, Chief Administrative Officer

High Level
10511 - 103rd St.
High Level, AB T0H 1Z0
Tel: 780-926-2201; *Fax:* 780-926-2899
town@highlevel.ca
www.highlevel.ca
Municipal Type: Town
Incorporated: June 1, 1965; *Area:* 31.99 sq km
County or District: Mackenzie County; *Population in 2016:* 3,159
Provincial Electoral District(s): Peace River
Federal Electoral District(s): Grande Prairie-Mackenzie
Next Election: Oct. 20, 2025 (4 year terms)
Crystal McAteer, Mayor, 780-841-5729
Clark McAskile, Chief Administrative Officer, 780-821-4001

High Prairie
P.O. Box 179
4806 - 53rd Ave.
High Prairie, AB T0G 1E0
Tel: 780-523-3388; *Fax:* 780-523-5930
reception@highprairie.ca
www.highprairie.ca
Municipal Type: Town
Incorporated: April 6, 1945; *Area:* 6.39 sq km
County or District: Municipal District of Big Lakes; *Population in 2016:* 2,564
Provincial Electoral District(s): Lesser Slave Lake
Federal Electoral District(s): Peace River-Westlock
Next Election: Oct. 20, 2025 (4 year terms)
Note: Incorporated as a town on Jan. 10, 1950.
Brian Panasiuk, Mayor
Rod Risling, Chief Administrative Officer

Hill Spring
P.O. Box 40
Hill Spring, AB T0K 1E0
Tel: 403-626-3876; *Fax:* 403-626-2333
office@hillspring.ca
hillspring.ca
Municipal Type: Village
Incorporated: Jan. 1, 1961; *Area:* 1.11 sq km
County or District: Cardston County; *Population in 2016:* 162
Provincial Electoral District(s): Cardston-Siksika
Federal Electoral District(s): Foothills
Next Election: Oct. 20, 2025 (4 year terms)
Dwight Davis, Mayor
Janet Edwards, Chief Administrative Officer

Hines Creek
P.O. Box 421
212 - 10th St.
Hines Creek, AB T0H 2A0
Tel: 780-494-3690; *Fax:* 780-494-3605
hinescreek.com
Municipal Type: Village
Incorporated: Dec. 31, 1951; *Area:* 4.37 sq km
County or District: Clear Hills County; *Population in 2016:* 346
Provincial Electoral District(s): Central Peace-Notley
Federal Electoral District(s): Grande Prairie-Mackenzie
Next Election: Oct. 20, 2025 (4 year terms)
Hazel Reintjes, Mayor
Leanne Walmsley, Chief Administrative Officer

Hinton
131 Civic Centre Rd., 2nd Fl.
Hinton, AB T7V 2E5
Tel: 780-865-6000; *Fax:* 780-865-5706
info@hinton.ca
www.hinton.ca
Municipal Type: Town
Incorporated: Nov. 1, 1956; *Area:* 25.76 sq km
County or District: Yellowhead County; *Population in 2016:* 9,882
Provincial Electoral District(s): West Yellowhead
Federal Electoral District(s): Yellowhead
Next Election: Oct. 20, 2025 (4 year terms)
Marcel Michaels, Mayor

Emily Olsen, Chief Administrative Officer, 780-865-6003

Holden
P.O. Box 357
Holden, AB T0B 2C0
Tel: 780-688-3928; *Fax:* 780-688-2091
vholden@telusplanet.net
holden.ca
Municipal Type: Village
Incorporated: April 14, 1909; *Area:* 1.7 sq km
County or District: Beaver County; *Population in 2016:* 350
Federal Electoral District(s): Battle River-Crowfoot
Next Election: Oct. 20, 2025 (4 year terms)
Vacant, Mayor
Amanda Cox, Chief Administrative Officer

Horseshoe Bay
P.O. Box 1778
St Paul, AB T0A 3A0
Tel: 780-645-4677
svhorseshoebay@gmail.com
www.svhorseshoebay.com
Municipal Type: Summer Village
Incorporated: Jan. 1, 1985; *Area:* 1.04 sq km
County or District: St. Paul County No. 19; *Population in 2016:*
49
Provincial Electoral District(s): Fort McMurray-Lac La Biche
Federal Electoral District(s): Lakeland
Next Election: Summer 2025 (4 year terms)
Gary Burns, Mayor, 780-464-2011
Norman Briscoe, Chief Administrative Officer

Hughenden
P.O. Box 26
33 McKenzie Ave.
Hughenden, AB T0B 2E0
Tel: 780-856-3830; *Fax:* 780-856-2034
hughenden@xplornet.com
hughendenab.ca
Municipal Type: Village
Incorporated: Dec. 27, 1917; *Area:* 0.78 sq km
County or District: Municipal District of Provost No. 52;
Population in 2016: 243
Federal Electoral District(s): Battle River-Crowfoot
Next Election: Oct. 20, 2025 (4 year terms)
Vacant, Mayor
Richard A. Lavoie, Chief Administrative Officer

Hussar
P.O. Box 100
109 - 1st Ave.
Hussar, AB T0J 1S0
Tel: 403-787-3766; *Fax:* 888-800-4937
office@villageofhussar.ca
www.villageofhussar.ca
Municipal Type: Village
Incorporated: April 20, 1928; *Area:* 1.05 sq km
County or District: Wheatland County; *Population in 2016:* 190
Provincial Electoral District(s): Chestermere-Strathmore
Federal Electoral District(s): Bow River
Next Election: Oct. 20, 2025 (4 year terms)
Tim Frank, Mayor
Kate Brandt, Chief Administrative Officer

Hythe
P.O. Box 219
10011 - 100th St.
Hythe, AB T0H 2C0
Tel: 780-356-3888
Municipal Type: Hamlet
Incorporated: Aug. 31, 1929; *Area:* 4.12 sq km
County or District: Grande Prairie County No. 1; *Population in
2016:* 827
Provincial Electoral District(s): Grande Prairie-Wapiti
Federal Electoral District(s): Grande Prairie-Mackenzie
Note: On July 1, 2021 the village dissolved & became a hamlet
of Grande Prairie County No. 1.

Innisfail
4943 - 53rd St.
Innisfail, AB T4G 1A1
Tel: 403-227-3376; *Fax:* 403-227-4045
townhall@innisfail.ca
innisfail.ca
Municipal Type: Town
Incorporated: Dec. 15, 1899; *Area:* 13.02 sq km
County or District: Red Deer County; *Population in 2016:* 7,847
Provincial Electoral District(s): Innisfail-Sylvan Lake
Federal Electoral District(s): Red Deer-Mountain View
Next Election: Oct. 20, 2025 (4 year terms)
Note: Incorporated as a town on Nov. 20, 1903.
Jean Barclay, Mayor

Todd Becker, Chief Administrative Officer

Innisfree
5116 - 50th Ave.
Innisfree, AB T0B 2G0
Tel: 780-592-3886; *Fax:* 780-592-3729
admin@innisfree.ca
www.villageofinnisfree.ca
Municipal Type: Village
Incorporated: March 11, 1911; *Area:* 1.27 sq km
County or District: Minburn County No. 27; *Population in 2016:*
193
Provincial Electoral District(s):
Vermilion-Lloydminster-Wainwright
Federal Electoral District(s): Lakeland
Next Election: Oct. 20, 2025 (4 year terms)
Vacant, Mayor
Brooke Magosse, Chief Administrative Officer

Irma
P.O. Box 419
4919 - 50th St.
Irma, AB T0B 2H0
Tel: 780-754-3665; *Fax:* 780-754-3668
info@irma.ca
irma.ca
Municipal Type: Village
Incorporated: May 30, 1912; *Area:* 1.11 sq km
County or District: Municipal District of Wainwright No. 61;
Population in 2016: 521
Provincial Electoral District(s):
Vermilion-Lloydminster-Wainwright
Federal Electoral District(s): Battle River-Crowfoot
Next Election: Oct. 20, 2025 (4 year terms)
Vacant, Mayor
Rudolf Liebenberg, Chief Administrative Officer

Irricana
P.O. Box 100
222 - 2nd St.
Irricana, AB T0M 1B0
Tel: 403-935-4672; *Fax:* 403-935-4270
irricana@irricana.com
townofirricana.ca
Municipal Type: Town
Incorporated: June 9, 1911; *Area:* 3.18 sq km
County or District: Rocky View County; *Population in 2016:*
1,216
Provincial Electoral District(s): Olds-Didsbury-Three Hills
Federal Electoral District(s): Bow River
Next Election: Oct. 20, 2025 (4 year terms)
Note: Incorporated as a town on June 9, 2005.
Frank Friesen, Mayor
Barrie Hutchinson, Chief Administrative Officer, 403-935-4672

Island Lake
P.O. Box 8
Alberta Beach, AB T0E 0A0
Tel: 780-967-0271; *Fax:* 780-967-0431
svislandlake@wildwillowenterprises.com
www.islandlake.ca
Municipal Type: Summer Village
Incorporated: Jan. 1, 1958; *Area:* 1.45 sq km
County or District: Athabasca County; *Population in 2016:* 228
Provincial Electoral District(s): Athabasca-Barrhead-Westlock
Federal Electoral District(s): Lakeland
Next Election: Summer 2025 (4 year terms)
Chad Newton, Mayor
Wendy Wildman, Chief Administrative Officer

Island Lake South
899 Village Mews
Sherwood Park, AB T8A 4L9
Tel: 780-239-7323; *Fax:* 780-416-6353
myislandlakesouth.com
Municipal Type: Summer Village
Incorporated: Jan. 1, 1983; *Area:* 0.63 sq km
County or District: Athabasca County; *Population in 2016:* 61
Provincial Electoral District(s): Athabasca-Barrhead-Westlock
Federal Electoral District(s): Lakeland
Next Election: Summer 2025 (4 year terms)
Thomas Tarrant, Mayor, 780-218-3804
Kim Bancroft, Chief Administrative Officer

Itaska Beach
10 Norwood Close
Wetaskiwin, AB T9A 0C8
Tel: 780-312-0928
www.itaska.ca
Municipal Type: Summer Village
Incorporated: June 30, 1953; *Area:* 0.28 sq km
County or District: Leduc County; *Population in 2016:* 23

Provincial Electoral District(s): Drayton Valley-Devon
Federal Electoral District(s): Edmonton-Wetaskiwin
Next Election: Summer 2025 (4 year terms)
David Alton, Mayor
June Boyda, Chief Administrative Officer

Jarvis Bay
Bay 8, 14 Thevenaz Industrial Trial
Sylvan Lake, AB T4S 1W2
Tel: 403-887-2822; *Fax:* 403-887-2897
info@sylvansummervillages.ca
www.sylvansummervillages.ca/jarvis-bay.html
Municipal Type: Summer Village
Incorporated: Jan. 1, 1986; *Area:* 0.55 sq km
County or District: Red Deer County; *Population in 2016:* 213
Provincial Electoral District(s): Innisfail-Sylvan Lake
Federal Electoral District(s): Red Deer-Lacombe
Next Election: Summer 2025 (4 year terms)
Julie Maplethorpe, Mayor, 403-304-0446
Tanner Evans, Chief Administrative Officer

Kapasiwin
P.O. Box 157
RR#1, Site 1
Onoway, AB T0E 1V0
Tel: 780-914-0997
info@kapasiwinalberta.com
www.kapasiwinalberta.com
Municipal Type: Summer Village
Incorporated: Oct. 25, 1913; *Area:* 0.31 sq km
County or District: Parkland County; *Population in 2016:* 10
Provincial Electoral District(s): Spruce Grove-Stony Plain
Federal Electoral District(s): Yellowhead
Next Election: Summer 2025 (4 year terms)
Note: Incorporated as a summer village on Sept. 01, 1993.
Tim Wiles, Mayor
Emily House, Chief Administrative Officer

Killam
P.O. Box 189
4923 - 50th St.
Killam, AB T0B 2L0
Tel: 780-385-3977; *Fax:* 780-385-2120
tkillam@telusplanet.net
www.town.killam.ab.ca
Municipal Type: Town
Incorporated: Dec. 29, 1906; *Area:* 4.53 sq km
County or District: Flagstaff County; *Population in 2016:* 989
Federal Electoral District(s): Battle River-Crowfoot
Next Election: Oct. 20, 2025 (4 year terms)
Note: Incorporated as a town on May 1, 1965.
Ben Kellert, Mayor
Kimberly Borgel, Chief Administrative Officer

Kitscoty
P.O. Box 128
Kitscoty, AB T0B 2P0
Tel: 780-846-2221; *Fax:* 780-846-2213
info@vokitscoty.ca
vokitscoty.ca
Municipal Type: Village
Incorporated: March 22, 1911; *Area:* 1.54 sq km
County or District: Vermilion River County; *Population in 2016:*
925
Provincial Electoral District(s):
Vermilion-Lloydminster-Wainwright
Federal Electoral District(s): Lakeland
Next Election: Oct. 20, 2025 (4 year terms)
Daryl Frank, Mayor
Sharon Williams, Chief Administrative Officer

Lakeview
P.O. Box 157
RR#1, Site 1
Onoway, AB T0E 1V0
Tel: 780-914-0997
administration@lakeview.ca
www.lakeview.ca
Municipal Type: Summer Village
Incorporated: Oct. 25, 1913; *Area:* 0.33 sq km
County or District: Parkland County; *Population in 2016:* 30
Provincial Electoral District(s): Spruce Grove-Stony Plain
Federal Electoral District(s): Yellowhead
Next Election: Summer 2025 (4 year terms)
Earle Robertson, Mayor
Emily House, Chief Administrative Officer

Lamont
5307 - 50th Ave.
Lamont, AB T0B 2R0
Tel: 780-895-2010
general@lamont.ca
www.lamont.ca
Municipal Type: Town
Incorporated: June 14, 1910; *Area:* 4.59 sq km
County or District: Lamont County; *Population in 2016:* 1,774
Provincial Electoral District(s): Fort Saskatchewan-Vegreville
Federal Electoral District(s): Lakeland
Next Election: Oct. 20, 2025 (4 year terms)
Note: Incorporated as a town on May 31, 1968.
Kirk Perrin, Mayor
Dawn Nielsen, Interim Chief Administrative Officer

Larkspur
899 Village Mews
Sherwood Park, AB T8A 4L9
Tel: 780-239-7323; *Fax:* 780-416-6353
gmbancroft@shaw.ca
www.svlarkspur.ca
Municipal Type: Summer Village
Incorporated: Jan. 1, 1985; *Area:* 0.22 sq km
County or District: Westlock County; *Population in 2016:* 40
Federal Electoral District(s): Peace River-Westlock
Next Election: Summer 2025 (4 year terms)
Greg Drechsler, Mayor, 780-499-3018
Kim Bancroft, Chief Administrative Officer

Legal
P.O. Box 390
5021 - 50th St.
Legal, AB T0G 1L0
Tel: 780-961-3773; *Fax:* 780-961-4133
main@legal.ca
www.legal.ca
Municipal Type: Town
Incorporated: Feb. 20, 1914; *Area:* 2.55 sq km
County or District: Sturgeon County; *Population in 2016:* 1,345
Provincial Electoral District(s): Morinville-St Albert
Federal Electoral District(s): Sturgeon River-Parkland
Next Election: Oct. 20, 2025 (4 year terms)
Note: Incorporated as a town on Jan. 1, 1998.
Carol Tremblay, Mayor
Robert Proulx, Chief Administrative Officer

Linden
P.O. Box 213
109 Central Ave. East
Linden, AB T0M 1J0
Tel: 403-546-3888; *Fax:* 403-546-2112
cao@linden.ca
www.linden.ca
Municipal Type: Village
Incorporated: Jan. 1, 1964; *Area:* 2.56 sq km
County or District: Kneehill County; *Population in 2016:* 828
Provincial Electoral District(s): Olds-Didsbury-Three Hills
Federal Electoral District(s): Bow River
Next Election: Oct. 20, 2025 (4 year terms)
Kelly Klassen, Mayor
Sarah Hardy, Municipal Clerk

Lomond
113 Centre St.
Lomond, AB T0L 1G0
Tel: 403-792-3611; *Fax:* 403-792-3300
villageoflomond.ca
Municipal Type: Village
Incorporated: Feb. 16, 1916; *Area:* 1.28 sq km
County or District: Vulcan County; *Population in 2016:* 166
Provincial Electoral District(s): Cardston-Siksika
Federal Electoral District(s): Bow River
Next Election: Oct. 20, 2025 (4 year terms)
Brad Koch, Mayor
Tracy Doram, Chief Administrative Officer

Longview
P.O. Box 147
128 Morrison Rd.
Longview, AB T0L 1H0
Tel: 403-558-3922; *Fax:* 403-558-3743
info@village.longview.ab.ca
village.longview.ab.ca
Municipal Type: Village
Incorporated: Jan. 1, 1964; *Area:* 1.09 sq km
County or District: Municipal District of Foothills No. 31;
Population in 2016: 307
Provincial Electoral District(s): Livingstone-Macleod
Federal Electoral District(s): Foothills
Next Election: Oct. 20, 2025 (4 year terms)
Vacant, Mayor

Dale Harrison, Chief Administrative Officer

Lougheed
P.O. Box 5
5004 - 50th St.
Lougheed, AB T0B 2V0
Tel: 780-386-3970; *Fax:* 780-386-2136
info@lougheed.ca
lougheed.ca
Municipal Type: Village
Incorporated: Nov. 7, 1911; *Area:* 1.13 sq km
County or District: Flagstaff County; *Population in 2016:* 256
Federal Electoral District(s): Battle River-Crowfoot
Next Election: Oct. 20, 2025 (4 year terms)
Vacant, Mayor
Karen O'Connor, Chief Administrative Officer

Magrath
P.O. Box 520
55 South 1 St. West
Magrath, AB T0K 1J0
Tel: 403-758-3212; *Fax:* 403-758-6333
info@magrath.ca
www.magrath.ca
Municipal Type: Town
Incorporated: Aug. 20, 1901; *Area:* 4.97 sq km
County or District: Cardston County; *Population in 2016:* 2,374
Provincial Electoral District(s): Cardston-Siksika
Federal Electoral District(s): Medicine Hat-Cardston-Warner
Next Election: Oct. 20, 2025 (4 year terms)
Note: Incorporated as a town on July 24, 1907.
Byrne Cook, Mayor
James Suffredine, Chief Administrative Officer

Ma-Me-O Beach
P.O. Box 100
605 - 2nd Ave.
Ma-Me-O Beach, AB T0C 1X0
Tel: 780-586-2494; *Fax:* 780-586-3567
information@svofficepl.com
mameobeach.ca
Municipal Type: Summer Village
Incorporated: Dec. 31, 1948; *Area:* 0.65 sq km
County or District: Wetaskiwin County No. 10; *Population in 2016:* 110
Provincial Electoral District(s): Drayton Valley-Devon
Federal Electoral District(s): Edmonton-Wetaskiwin
Next Election: Summer 2025 (4 year terms)
Christine Holmes, Mayor, 587-768-0268
Sylvia Roy, Chief Administrative Officer
Greg Rycroft, Mayor
April Doll, Chief Administrative Officer

Manning
P.O. Box 125
Manning, AB T0H 2M0
Tel: 780-836-3606; *Fax:* 780-836-3570
info@manning.ca
manning.ca
Municipal Type: Town
Incorporated: Dec. 31, 1951; *Area:* 3.42 sq km
County or District: Northern Lights County; *Population in 2016:* 1,183
Provincial Electoral District(s): Peace River
Federal Electoral District(s): Grande Prairie-Mackenzie
Next Election: Oct. 20, 2025 (4 year terms)
Note: Incorporated as a town on Jan. 1, 1957.

Mannville
P.O. Box 180
5127 - 50th St.
Mannville, AB T0B 2W0
Tel: 780-763-3500; *Fax:* 780-763-3643
info@mannville.com
mannville.com
Municipal Type: Village
Incorporated: Dec. 29, 1906; *Area:* 2.15 sq km
County or District: Minburn County No. 27; *Population in 2016:* 828
Provincial Electoral District(s): Vermilion-Lloydminster-Wainwright
Federal Electoral District(s): Lakeland
Next Election: Oct. 20, 2025 (4 year terms)
Rex Smith, Mayor
Jody Quickstad, Chief Administrative Officer

Marwayne
P.O. Box 113
210 - 2nd Ave. South
Marwayne, AB T0B 2X0
Tel: 780-847-3962; *Fax:* 780-847-3324
admin@marwayne.ca
www.marwayne.ca
Municipal Type: Village
Incorporated: Dec. 31, 1952; *Area:* 1.15 sq km
County or District: Vermilion River County; *Population in 2016:* 565
Provincial Electoral District(s): Vermilion-Lloydminster-Wainwright
Federal Electoral District(s): Lakeland
Next Election: Oct. 20, 2025 (4 year terms)
Cheryle Eikeland, Mayor
Shannon Harrower, Chief Administrative Officer

Mayerthorpe
P.O. Box 420
4911 Denny Hay Dr.
Mayerthorpe, AB T0E 1N0
Tel: 780-786-2416; *Fax:* 780-786-4590
admin@mayerthorpe.ca
www.mayerthorpe.ca
Municipal Type: Town
Incorporated: March 5, 1927; *Area:* 4.78 sq km
County or District: Lac Ste. Anne County; *Population in 2016:* 1,320
Provincial Electoral District(s): Lac Ste Anne-Parkland
Federal Electoral District(s): Yellowhead
Next Election: Oct. 20, 2025 (4 year terms)
Note: Incorporated as a town on March 20, 1961.
Janet Jabush, Mayor
Karen St. Martin, Chief Administrative Officer

McLennan
P.O. Box 356
19 - 1st Ave. NW
McLennan, AB T0H 2L0
Tel: 780-324-3065; *Fax:* 780-324-2288
admin@mclennan.ca
www.mclennan.ca
Municipal Type: Town
Incorporated: Feb. 1, 1944; *Area:* 3.58 sq km
County or District: Municipal District of Smoky River No. 130; *Population in 2016:* 701
Provincial Electoral District(s): Central Peace-Notley
Federal Electoral District(s): Peace River-Westlock
Next Election: Oct. 20, 2025 (4 year terms)
Note: Incorporated as a town on Feb. 11, 1948.
Jason Doris, Mayor
Lorraine Willier, Chief Administrative Officer

Mewatha Beach
899 Village Mews
Sherwood Park, AB T8A 4L9
Tel: 780-239-7323; *Fax:* 780-416-6353
www.mymewathabeach.com
Municipal Type: Summer Village
Incorporated: Jan. 1, 1978; *Area:* 0.78 sq km
County or District: Athabasca County; *Population in 2016:* 90
Provincial Electoral District(s): Athabasca-Barrhead-Westlock
Federal Electoral District(s): Lakeland
Next Election: Summer 2025 (4 year terms)
Dennis Tomuschat, Mayor, 780-689-7676
Kim Bancroft, Chief Administrative Officer

Milk River
P.O. Box 270
240 Main St.
Milk River, AB T0K 1M0
Tel: 403-647-3773; *Fax:* 403-647-3772
main@milkriver.ca
www.milkriver.ca
Municipal Type: Town
Incorporated: July 11, 1916; *Area:* 2.39 sq km
County or District: Warner County No. 5; *Population in 2016:* 827
Provincial Electoral District(s): Taber-Warner
Federal Electoral District(s): Medicine Hat-Cardston-Warner
Next Election: Oct. 20, 2025 (4 year terms)
Note: Incorporated as a town on Feb. 7, 1956.
Larry Liebett, Mayor
Jon Hood, Chief Administrative Officer

Millet
P.O. Box 270
4528 - 51st St.
Millet, AB T0C 1Z0
Tel: 780-387-4554; *Fax:* 780-387-4459
millet@millet.ca
www.millet.ca

Municipal Type: Town
Incorporated: June 17, 1903; *Area:* 3.74 sq km
County or District: Wetaskiwin County No. 10; *Population in 2016:* 1,945
Provincial Electoral District(s): Maskwacis-Wetaskiwin
Federal Electoral District(s): Edmonton-Wetaskiwin
Next Election: Oct. 20, 2025 (4 year terms)
Note: Incorporated as a town on Sept. 1, 1983.
Doug Peel, Mayor
Lisa Schoening, Chief Administrative Officer

Milo

P.O. Box 65
Milo, AB T0L 1L0
Tel: 403-599-3883; *Fax:* 403-599-2201
admin@villageofmilo.ca
villageofmilo.ca
Municipal Type: Village
Incorporated: May 7, 1931; *Area:* 0.48 sq km
County or District: Vulcan County; *Population in 2016:* 91
Provincial Electoral District(s): Cardston-Siksika
Federal Electoral District(s): Bow River
Next Election: Oct. 20, 2025 (4 year terms)
Scott Schroeder, Mayor
Wendy Hingley, Chief Administrative Officer

Minburn

c/o Minburn County No. 27
P.O. Box 550
4909 - 50th St.
Vegreville, AB T9C 1R6
info@minburncounty.ab.ca
www.minburncounty.ab.ca
Municipal Type: Hamlet
Incorporated: June 24, 1919; *Area:* 0.73 sq km
County or District: Minburn County No. 27
Provincial Electoral District(s):
Vermilion-Lloydminster-Wainwright
Federal Electoral District(s): Lakeland
Note: Minburn was dissolved from village status to become a hamlet on July 1, 2015.

Morinville

10125 - 100th Ave.
Morinville, AB T8R 1L6
Tel: 780-939-4361; *Fax:* 780-939-5633
info@morinville.ca
www.morinville.ca
Municipal Type: Town
Incorporated: Aug. 24, 1901; *Area:* 11.34 sq km
County or District: Sturgeon County; *Population in 2016:* 9,848
Provincial Electoral District(s): Morinville-St Albert
Federal Electoral District(s): Sturgeon River-Parkland
Next Election: Oct. 20, 2025 (4 year terms)
Note: Incorporated as a town on April 21, 1911.
Simon Boersma, Mayor
Stephane Labonne, Chief Administrative Officer

Morrin

P.O. Box 149
Morrin, AB T0J 2B0
Tel: 403-772-3870; *Fax:* 403-772-2123
morrin@netago.ca
morrin.ca
Municipal Type: Village
Incorporated: April 16, 1920; *Area:* 0.82 sq km
County or District: Starland County; *Population in 2016:* 240
Provincial Electoral District(s): Drumheller-Stettler
Federal Electoral District(s): Battle River-Crowfoot
Next Election: Oct. 20, 2025 (4 year terms)
Vacant, Mayor
Annette Plachner, Chief Administrative Officer

Mundare

P.O. Box 348
5128 - 50th St.
Mundare, AB T0B 3H0
Tel: 780-764-3929
info@mundare.ca
www.mundare.ca
Municipal Type: Town
Incorporated: March 6, 1907; *Area:* 3 sq km
County or District: Lamont County; *Population in 2016:* 852
Provincial Electoral District(s): Fort Saskatchewan-Vegreville
Federal Electoral District(s): Lakeland
Next Election: Oct. 20, 2025 (4 year terms)
Note: Incorporated as a town on Jan. 4, 1951.
Cheryl Calanoiu, Mayor
Colin Zyla, Chief Administrative Officer

Munson

P.O. Box 10
Munson, AB T0J 2C0
Tel: 403-823-6987; *Fax:* 403-823-9883
munson@netago.ca
Municipal Type: Village
Incorporated: May 5, 1911; *Area:* 2.6 sq km
County or District: Starland County; *Population in 2016:* 192
Provincial Electoral District(s): Drumheller-Stettler
Federal Electoral District(s): Battle River-Crowfoot
Next Election: Oct. 20, 2025 (4 year terms)
Steve Hayes, Mayor
Lyle Cawiezel, Chief Administrative Officer

Myrnam

P.O. Box 278
5007 - 50th St.
Myrnam, AB T0B 3K0
Tel: 780-366-3910; *Fax:* 780-366-2246
admin@myrnam.ca
myrnam.ca
Municipal Type: Village
Incorporated: Aug. 22, 1930; *Area:* 2.76 sq km
County or District: Two Hills County No. 21; *Population in 2016:* 339
Provincial Electoral District(s): Fort McMurray-Lac La Biche
Federal Electoral District(s): Lakeland
Next Election: Oct. 20, 2025 (4 year terms)
Donna Rudolf, Mayor
Gary Dupuis, Chief Administrative Officer

Nakamun Park

P.O. Box 1250
Onoway, AB T0E 1V0
Tel: 780-460-7226; *Fax:* 780-419-2476
www.svnakamun.com
Municipal Type: Summer Village
Incorporated: Jan. 1, 1966; *Area:* 0.41 sq km
County or District: Lac Ste. Anne County; *Population in 2016:* 96
Federal Electoral District(s): Sturgeon River-Parkland
Next Election: Summer 2025 (4 year terms)
Marge Hanssen, Mayor
Dwight Moskalyk, Chief Administrative Officer

Nampa

9902 - 102nd Ave.
Nampa, AB T0H 2R0
Tel: 780-322-3852; *Fax:* 780-322-2100
cao@nampa.ca
nampa.ca
Municipal Type: Village
Incorporated: Jan. 1, 1958; *Area:* 1.86 sq km
County or District: Northern Sunrise County; *Population in 2016:* 364
Provincial Electoral District(s): Peace River
Federal Electoral District(s): Peace River-Westlock
Next Election: Oct. 20, 2025 (4 year terms)
Vacant, Mayor
Dianne Roshuk, Chief Administrative Officer

Nanton

P.O. Box 609
1907 - 21st Ave.
Nanton, AB T0L 1R0
Tel: 403-646-2029; *Fax:* 403-646-2653
www.nanton.ca
Other Information: Toll-Free Phone: 877-365-3901
Municipal Type: Town
Incorporated: June 22, 1903; *Area:* 4.25 sq km
County or District: Municipal District of Willow Creek No. 26; *Population in 2016:* 2,130
Provincial Electoral District(s): Livingstone-Macleod
Federal Electoral District(s): Foothills
Next Election: Oct. 20, 2025 (4 year terms)
Note: Incorporated as a town on Aug. 9, 1907.
Jennifer Handley, Mayor
Neil Smith, Chief Administrative Officer

Nobleford

P.O. Box 67
906 Highway Ave.
Nobleford, AB T0L 1S0
Tel: 403-824-3555; *Fax:* 403-824-3553
admin@nobleford.ca
nobleford.ca
Municipal Type: Town
Incorporated: Feb. 28, 1918; *Area:* 1.17 sq km
County or District: Lethbridge County; *Population in 2016:* 1,278
Provincial Electoral District(s): Cardston-Siksika
Federal Electoral District(s): Lethbridge
Next Election: Oct. 20, 2025 (4 year terms)

Note: Nobleford was changed from a Village to a Town on Feb. 21, 2018.
Vacant, Mayor

Norglenwold

Bay 8, 14 Thevenaz Industrial Trail
Sylvan Lake, AB T4S 2J5
Tel: 403-887-2822; *Fax:* 403-887-2897
info@sylvansummervillages.ca
www.sylvansummervillages.ca/norglenwold
Municipal Type: Summer Village
Incorporated: Jan. 1, 1965; *Area:* 0.67 sq km
County or District: Red Deer County; *Population in 2016:* 273
Provincial Electoral District(s): Innisfail-Sylvan Lake
Federal Electoral District(s): Red Deer-Lacombe
Next Election: Summer 2025 (4 year terms)
Cyril Gurevitch, Mayor
Tanner Evans, Chief Administrative Officer

Norris Beach

P.O. Box 100
605 - 2nd Ave.
Ma-Me-O Beach, AB T0C 1X0
Tel: 780-586-2494
information@svofficepl.ca
norrisbeach.ca
Municipal Type: Summer Village
Incorporated: Dec. 31, 1988; *Area:* 0.16 sq km
County or District: Wetaskiwin County No. 10; *Population in 2016:* 38
Provincial Electoral District(s): Drayton Valley-Devon
Federal Electoral District(s): Edmonton-Wetaskiwin
Next Election: Summer 2025 (4 year terms)
Brian Keeler, Mayor, 780-887-5232
Sylvia Roy, Chief Administrative Officer

Olds

4512 - 46th St.
Olds, AB T4H 1R5
Tel: 403-556-6981; *Fax:* 403-556-6537
admin@olds.ca
www.olds.ca
Municipal Type: Town
Incorporated: May 26, 1896; *Area:* 11.05 sq km
County or District: Mountain View County; *Population in 2016:* 9,185
Provincial Electoral District(s): Olds-Didsbury-Three Hills
Federal Electoral District(s): Red Deer-Mountain View
Next Election: Oct. 20, 2025 (4 year terms)
Note: Incorporated as a town on July 01, 1905.
Judy Dahl, Mayor
Michael Merritt, Chief Administrative Officer

Onoway

P.O. Box 540
4812 - 51st St.
Onoway, AB T0E 1V0
Tel: 780-967-5338; *Fax:* 780-967-3226
info@onoway.com
www.onoway.com
Municipal Type: Town
Incorporated: June 25, 1923; *Area:* 3.34 sq km
County or District: Lac Ste. Anne County; *Population in 2016:* 1,029
Federal Electoral District(s): Sturgeon River-Parkland
Next Election: Oct. 20, 2025 (4 year terms)
Note: Incorporated as a town on Sept. 1, 2005.
Judy Tracy, Mayor, 587-783-7141
Wendy Wildman, Chief Administrative Officer

Oyen

P.O. Box 360
201 Main St.
Oyen, AB T0J 2J0
Tel: 403-664-3511; *Fax:* 403-664-3712
townoffice@townofoyen.com
townofoyen.com
Municipal Type: Town
Incorporated: Jan. 17, 1913; *Area:* 4.93 sq km
Population in 2016: 1,001
Provincial Electoral District(s): Drumheller-Stettler
Federal Electoral District(s): Battle River-Crowfoot
Next Election: Oct. 20, 2025 (4 year terms)
Note: Incorporated as a town on Sept. 1, 1965.
Douglas A. Jones, Mayor, 403-664-0560
Steve Kuhn, Interim Chief Administrative Officer

Paradise Valley

P.O. Box 24
109 Main St.
Paradise Valley, AB T0B 3R0
Tel: 780-745-2287; *Fax:* 780-745-2287
villageofpv@mcsnet.ca
villageofparadisevalley.ca
Municipal Type: Village
Incorporated: Jan. 1, 1964; *Area:* 0.57 sq km
County or District: Vermilion River County; *Population in 2016:* 179
Provincial Electoral District(s):
Vermilion-Lloydminster-Wainwright
Federal Electoral District(s): Lakeland
Next Election: Oct. 20, 2025 (4 year terms)
Mary Arnold, Mayor
James Warren, Chief Administrative Officer

Parkland Beach

P.O. Box 130
9 Parkland Beach Rd. NW
Rimbey, AB T0C 2J0
Tel: 403-843-2055; *Fax:* 888-470-2762
admin@parklandbeachsv.ca
parklandbeachsv.ca
Municipal Type: Summer Village
Incorporated: Jan. 1, 1984; *Area:* 0.93 sq km
County or District: Ponoka County; *Population in 2016:* 153
Provincial Electoral District(s): Rimbey-Rocky Mountain
House-Sundre
Federal Electoral District(s): Red Deer-Lacombe
Next Election: Summer 2025 (4 year terms)
Marc Mousseau, Mayor
Cyril Fortney, Chief Administrative Officer

Peace River

P.O. Box 6600
9911 - 100th St.
Peace River, AB T8S 1S4
Tel: 780-624-2574; *Fax:* 780-624-4664
info@peaceriver.ca
peaceriver.ca
Municipal Type: Town
Incorporated: June 2, 1914; *Area:* 24.87 sq km
Population in 2016: 6,842
Provincial Electoral District(s): Peace River
Federal Electoral District(s): Peace River-Westlock; Grande
Prairie-Mackenzie
Next Election: Oct. 20, 2025 (4 year terms)
Note: Incorporated as a town on Dec. 1, 1919.
Elaine Manzer, Mayor
Christopher Parker, Chief Administrative Officer

Pelican Narrows

P.O. Box 7878
Bonnyville, AB T9N 2J2
Tel: 780-614-4496
pelicanarrows@gmail.com
pelicannarrowsab.ca
Municipal Type: Summer Village
Incorporated: July 1, 1979; *Area:* 0.7 sq km
County or District: Municipal District of Bonnyville No. 87;
Population in 2016: 151
Provincial Electoral District(s): Bonnyville-Cold Lake-St Paul
Federal Electoral District(s): Lakeland
Next Election: Summer 2025 (4 year terms)
Ashley Homseth, Mayor
Shirley Yuschyshyn, Chief Administrative Officer

Penhold

P.O. Box 10
1 Waskasoo Ave.
Penhold, AB T0M 1R0
Tel: 403-886-4567; *Fax:* 403-886-4039
info@townofpenhold.ca
www.townofpenhold.ca
Municipal Type: Town
Incorporated: May 4, 1904; *Area:* 2.35 sq km
County or District: Red Deer County; *Population in 2016:* 3,277
Provincial Electoral District(s): Innisfail-Sylvan Lake
Federal Electoral District(s): Red Deer-Mountain View
Next Election: Oct. 20, 2025 (4 year terms)
Note: Incorporated as a town on Sept. 1, 1980.
Mike Yargeau, Mayor
Richard Binnendyk, Chief Administrative Officer

Picture Butte

P.O. Box 670
120 - 4th St. North
Picture Butte, AB T0K 1V0
Tel: 403-732-4555; *Fax:* 403-732-4334
info@picturebutte.ca
www.picturebutte.ca
Municipal Type: Town
Incorporated: Feb. 4, 1943; *Area:* 2.9 sq km
County or District: Lethbridge County; *Population in 2016:* 1,810
Provincial Electoral District(s): Cardston-Siksika
Federal Electoral District(s): Lethbridge
Next Election: Oct. 20, 2025 (4 year terms)
Note: Incorporated as a town on Jan. 1, 1960.
Cathy Moore, Mayor
Keith Davis, Chief Administrative Officer

Pincher Creek

P.O. Box 159
962 St John Ave.
Pincher Creek, AB T0K 1W0
Tel: 403-627-3156; *Fax:* 403-627-4784
reception@pinchercreek.ca
www.pinchercreek.ca
Municipal Type: Town
Incorporated: Aug. 18, 1898; *Area:* 8.84 sq km
County or District: Municipal District of Pincher Creek No. 9;
Population in 2016: 3,642
Provincial Electoral District(s): Livingstone-Macleod
Federal Electoral District(s): Foothills
Next Election: Oct. 20, 2025 (4 year terms)
Note: Incorporated as a town on May 12, 1906.
Don Anderberg, Mayor
Laurie Wilgosh, Chief Administrative Officer

Point Allison

P.O. Box 221
Wabamun, AB T0E 2K0
Tel: 780-984-2773
svpointalison@outlook.com
svpointalison.com
Municipal Type: Summer Village
Incorporated: Dec. 31, 1950; *Area:* 0.16 sq km
County or District: Parkland County; *Population in 2016:* 10
Provincial Electoral District(s): Spruce Grove-Stony Plain
Federal Electoral District(s): Yellowhead
Next Election: Summer 2025 (4 year terms)
C. Gordon Wilson, Mayor, 780-892-2984
Brenda Bennett, Chief Administrative Officer

Ponoka

#200, 5604 - 50th St.
Ponoka, AB T4J 1G5
Tel: 403-783-4431; *Fax:* 403-783-6745
town@ponoka.ca
www.ponoka.ca
Municipal Type: Town
Incorporated: Oct. 19, 1900; *Area:* 13.05 sq km
County or District: Ponoka County; *Population in 2016:* 7,229
Provincial Electoral District(s): Lacombe-Ponoka
Federal Electoral District(s): Red Deer-Lacombe
Next Election: Oct. 20, 2025 (4 year terms)
Note: Incorporated as a town on Oct. 15, 1904.
Kevin Ferguson, Mayor
Sandra Lund, Chief Administrative Officer, 403-783-0130

Poplar Bay

P.O. Box 100
605 - 2nd Ave.
Ma-Me-O Beach, AB T0C 1X0
Tel: 780-586-2494; *Fax:* 780-586-3567
information@svofficepl.com
poplarbay.ca
Municipal Type: Summer Village
Incorporated: Jan. 1, 1967; *Area:* 0.76 sq km
County or District: Wetaskiwin County No. 10; *Population in 2016:* 103
Provincial Electoral District(s): Drayton Valley-Devon
Federal Electoral District(s): Edmonton-Wetaskiwin
Next Election: Summer 2025 (4 year terms)
Fraser Hubbard, Mayor, 403-612-5272
Sylvia Roy, Chief Administrative Officer

Provost

P.O. Box 449
4904 - 51st Ave.
Provost, AB T0B 3S0
Tel: 780-753-2217; *Fax:* 780-753-6889
info@townofprovost.ca
provost.ca
Municipal Type: Town
Incorporated: Jan. 20, 1910; *Area:* 4.93 sq km
County or District: Municipal District of Provost No. 52;
Population in 2016: 1,998
Provincial Electoral District(s): Drumheller-Stettler
Federal Electoral District(s): Battle River-Crowfoot
Next Election: Oct. 20, 2025 (4 year terms)
Note: Incorporated as a town on Dec. 29, 1952.
Peggy McFayden, Mayor
David Connauton, Chief Administrative Officer, 780-753-2261

Rainbow Lake

P.O. Box 149
Rainbow Lake, AB T0H 2Y0
Tel: 780-956-3934; *Fax:* 780-956-3570
admin@rainbowlake.ca
rainbowlake.ca
Municipal Type: Town
Incorporated: Sept. 1, 1966; *Area:* 11.04 sq km
County or District: Mackenzie County; *Population in 2016:* 795
Provincial Electoral District(s): Peace River
Federal Electoral District(s): Grande Prairie-Mackenzie
Next Election: Oct. 20, 2025 (4 year terms)
Michelle Farris, Mayor, 780-926-3373
Dan Fletcher, Chief Administrative Officer, 780-956-3934

Raymond

P.O. Box 629
15 Broadway St.
Raymond, AB T0K 2S0
Tel: 403-752-3322; *Fax:* 403-752-4379
contact@raymond.ca
raymond.ca
Municipal Type: Town
Incorporated: May 30, 1902; *Area:* 4.75 sq km
County or District: Warner County No. 5; *Population in 2016:* 3,708
Provincial Electoral District(s): Taber-Warner
Federal Electoral District(s): Medicine Hat-Cardston-Warner
Next Election: Oct. 20, 2025 (4 year terms)
Note: Incorporated as a town on July 1, 1903.
Jim Depew, Mayor
Kurtis Pratt, Chief Administrative Officer

Redcliff

P.O. Box 40
1 - 3rd St. NE
Redcliff, AB T0J 2P0
Tel: 403-548-3618; *Fax:* 403-548-6623
redcliff@redcliff.ca
redcliff.ca
Municipal Type: Town
Incorporated: Oct. 29, 1910; *Area:* 10.51 sq km
County or District: Cypress County; *Population in 2016:* 5,600
Provincial Electoral District(s): Brooks-Medicine Hat
Federal Electoral District(s): Medicine Hat-Cardston-Warner
Next Election: Oct. 20, 2025 (4 year terms)
Note: Incorporated as a town on Aug. 5, 1912.
Dwight Kilpatrick, Mayor
Phyllis Forsyth, Chief Administrative Officer

Redwater

P.O. Box 397
4924 - 47th St.
Redwater, AB T0A 2W0
Tel: 780-942-3519; *Fax:* 780-942-4321
redwater@redwater.ca
www.redwater.ca
Municipal Type: Town
Incorporated: Dec. 31, 1949; *Area:* 7.95 sq km
County or District: Sturgeon County; *Population in 2016:* 2,053
Provincial Electoral District(s): Morinville-St Albert
Federal Electoral District(s): Sturgeon River-Parkland
Next Election: Oct. 20, 2025 (4 year terms)
Note: Incorporated as a town on Dec. 31, 1950.
David McRae, Mayor
Nawaz Panhwer, Interim Town Manager, 780-942-3519

Rimbey

P.O. Box 350
4938 - 50th Ave.
Rimbey, AB T0C 2J0
Tel: 403-843-2113; *Fax:* 403-843-6599
generalinfo@rimbey.com
www.rimbey.com
Municipal Type: Town
Incorporated: June 13, 1919; *Area:* 11.34 sq km
County or District: Ponoka County; *Population in 2016:* 2,567
Provincial Electoral District(s): Rimbey-Rocky Mountain
House-Sundre
Federal Electoral District(s): Red Deer-Lacombe
Next Election: Oct. 20, 2025 (4 year terms)
Note: Incorporated as a town on Dec. 13, 1948.
Rick Pankiw, Mayor

Lori Hills, Chief Administrative Officer, 403-843-2113

Rochon Sands
1 Hall St.
Rochon Sands, AB T0C 3B0
Tel: 403-742-4717; *Fax:* 403-742-4771
info@rochonsands.net
www.rochonsands.net
Municipal Type: Summer Village
Incorporated: May 17, 1929; *Area:* 2.32 sq km
County or District: Stettler County No. 6; *Population in 2016:* 86
Provincial Electoral District(s): Drumheller-Stettler
Federal Electoral District(s): Battle River-Crowfoot
Next Election: Summer 2025 (4 year terms)
Dan Hiller, Mayor
Melissa Beebe, Chief Administrative Officer

Rocky Mountain House
P.O. Box 1509
5116 - 50th Ave.
Rocky Mountain House, AB T4T 1B2
Tel: 403-845-2866; *Fax:* 403-845-3230
town@rockymtnhouse.com
www.rockymtnhouse.com
Municipal Type: Town
Incorporated: May 15, 1913; *Area:* 12.44 sq km
County or District: Clearwater County; *Population in 2016:* 6,635
Provincial Electoral District(s): Rimbey-Rocky Mountain
House-Sundre
Federal Electoral District(s): Yellowhead
Next Election: Oct. 20, 2025 (4 year terms)
Note: Incorporated as a town on Aug. 31, 1939.
Debbie Baich, Mayor
Dean Krause, Chief Administrative Officer

Rockyford
110 Main St.
Rockyford, AB T0J 2R0
Tel: 403-533-3950; *Fax:* 403-533-3744
village@rockyford.ca
www.rockyford.ca
Municipal Type: Village
Incorporated: March 28, 1919; *Area:* 1.05 sq km
County or District: Wheatland County; *Population in 2016:* 316
Provincial Electoral District(s): Chestermere-Strathmore
Federal Electoral District(s): Bow River
Next Election: Oct. 20, 2025 (4 year terms)
Darcy J. Burke, Mayor
Elaine Macdonald, Administrator

Rosalind
P.O. Box 181
Rosalind, AB T0B 3Y0
Tel: 780-375-3996; *Fax:* 780-375-3997
rosalindvillage@xplornet.com
villageofrosalind.ca
Municipal Type: Village
Incorporated: Jan. 1, 1966; *Area:* 0.59 sq km
County or District: Camrose County; *Population in 2016:* 188
Federal Electoral District(s): Battle River-Crowfoot
Next Election: Oct. 20, 2025 (4 year terms)
James McTavish, Mayor
Nancy Friend, Chief Administrative Officer

Rosemary
P.O. Box 128
Rosemary, AB T0J 2W0
Tel: 403-378-4246; *Fax:* 403-378-3144
rosemary.admin@eidnet.org
www.rosemary.ca
Municipal Type: Village
Incorporated: Dec. 31, 1951; *Area:* 0.56 sq km
County or District: Newell County; *Population in 2016:* 396
Provincial Electoral District(s): Chestermere-Strathmore
Federal Electoral District(s): Bow River
Next Election: Oct. 20, 2025 (4 year terms)
Vacant, Mayor
Sharon Zacharias, Chief Administrative Officer

Ross Haven
P.O. Box 7
Site 19, RR#1
Gunn, AB T0E 1A0
Tel: 780-999-6654
rosshaven.ca
Municipal Type: Summer Village
Incorporated: Jan. 1, 1962; *Area:* 0.7 sq km
County or District: Lac Ste. Anne County; *Population in 2016:* 160
Federal Electoral District(s): Yellowhead
Next Election: Summer 2025 (4 year terms)
Ray Hutscal, Mayor

Tony Sonnleitner, Chief Administrative Officer

Rycroft
P.O. Box 360
Rycroft, AB T0H 3A0
Tel: 780-765-3652; *Fax:* 780-765-2002
rycroft@rycroft.ca
rycroft.ca
Municipal Type: Village
Incorporated: March 15, 1944; *Area:* 1.69 sq km
County or District: Municipal District of Spirit River No. 133;
Population in 2016: 612
Provincial Electoral District(s): Central Peace-Notley
Federal Electoral District(s): Grande Prairie-Mackenzie
Next Election: Oct. 20, 2025 (4 year terms)
Vacant, Mayor
Peter Thomas, Chief Administrative Officer

Ryley
P.O. Box 230
5005 - 50th St.
Ryley, AB T0B 4A0
Tel: 780-663-3653; *Fax:* 780-663-3541
info@ryley.ca
www.ryley.ca
Municipal Type: Village
Incorporated: April 2, 1910; *Area:* 1.97 sq km
County or District: Beaver County; *Population in 2016:* 483
Federal Electoral District(s): Battle River-Crowfoot
Next Election: Oct. 20, 2025 (4 year terms)
Vacant, Mayor
Glen Hamilton-Brown, Chief Administrative Officer

St. Paul
P.O. Box 1480
5101 - 50th St.
St Paul, AB T0A 3A0
Tel: 780-645-4481; *Fax:* 780-645-5076
townhall@town.stpaul.ab.ca
www.stpaul.ca
Municipal Type: Town
Incorporated: June 14, 1912; *Area:* 6.86 sq km
County or District: St. Paul County No. 19; *Population in 2016:* 5,827
Provincial Electoral District(s): Bonnyville-Cold Lake-St Paul
Federal Electoral District(s): Lakeland
Next Election: Oct. 20, 2025 (4 year terms)
Note: Incorporated as a town on Dec. 15, 1936.
Vacant, Mayor
Steven Jeffrey, Chief Administrative Officer

Sandy Beach
RR#1, Site 1, Comp 63
Onoway, AB T0E 1V0
Tel: 780-967-2873; *Fax:* 780-967-2813
svsandyb@xplornet.ca
www.summervillageofsandybeach.ca
Municipal Type: Summer Village
Incorporated: Jan. 1, 1956; *Area:* 2.43 sq km
County or District: Lac Ste. Anne County; *Population in 2016:* 278
Federal Electoral District(s): Sturgeon River-Parkland; Lakeland
Next Election: Summer 2025 (4 year terms)
Denise Lambert, Mayor
Rudolf Liebenberg, Chief Administrative Officer

Seba Beach
P.O. Box 190
Seba Beach, AB T0E 2B0
Tel: 780-797-3863; *Fax:* 587-305-0103
svseba@telusplanet.net
www.sebabeach.ca
Municipal Type: Summer Village
Incorporated: Aug. 2, 1920; *Area:* 0.66 sq km
County or District: Parkland County; *Population in 2016:* 169
Provincial Electoral District(s): Spruce Grove-Stony Plain
Federal Electoral District(s): Yellowhead
Next Election: Summer 2025 (4 year terms)
Rick MacPhee, Mayor
Martino Verhaeghe, Chief Administrative Officer

Sedgewick
P.O. Box 129
4818 - 47th St.
Sedgewick, AB T0B 4C0
Tel: 780-384-3504; *Fax:* 780-384-3545
reception@sedgewick.ca
sedgewick.ca
Municipal Type: Town
Incorporated: March 6, 1907; *Area:* 2.6 sq km
County or District: Flagstaff County; *Population in 2016:* 811
Federal Electoral District(s): Battle River-Crowfoot

Next Election: Oct. 20, 2025 (4 year terms)
Note: Incorporated as town on May 1, 1966.
Stephen Levy, Mayor
Jim Fedyk, Chief Administrative Officer

Sexsmith
P.O. Box 420
9927 - 100th St.
Sexsmith, AB T0H 3C0
Tel: 780-568-3681; *Fax:* 780-568-2200
admin@sexsmith.ca
www.sexsmith.ca
Municipal Type: Town
Incorporated: April 12, 1929; *Area:* 3.43 sq km
County or District: Grande Prairie County No. 1; *Population in 2016:* 2,620
Provincial Electoral District(s): Grande Prairie-Wapiti
Federal Electoral District(s): Grande Prairie-Mackenzie
Next Election: Oct. 20, 2025 (4 year terms)
Note: Incorporated as a town on Oct. 15, 1979.
Vacant, Mayor
Rachel Wueschner, Chief Administrative Officer

Silver Beach
P.O. Box 619 29
Thorsby, AB T0C 2P0
Tel: 780-389-4409
www.silverbeach.ca
Municipal Type: Summer Village
Incorporated: Dec. 31, 1953; *Area:* 0.66 sq km
County or District: Wetaskiwin County No. 10; *Population in 2016:* 65
Provincial Electoral District(s): Drayton Valley-Devon
Federal Electoral District(s): Edmonton-Wetaskiwin
Next Election: Summer 2025 (4 year terms)
David Rolf, Mayor
June Boyda, Chief Administrative Officer

Silver Sands
P.O. Box 8
Alberta Beach, AB T0E 0A0
Tel: 587-873-5765; *Fax:* 780-967-0431
administration@wildwillowenterprises.com
www.summervillageofsilversands.com
Municipal Type: Summer Village
Incorporated: Jan. 1, 1969; *Area:* 2.35 sq km
County or District: Lac Ste. Anne County; *Population in 2016:* 160
Federal Electoral District(s): Yellowhead
Next Election: Summer 2025 (4 year terms)
Bernie Poulin, Mayor
Wendy Wildman, Chief Administrative Officer

Slave Lake
P.O. Box 1030
10 Main St. SW
Slave Lake, AB T0G 2A0
Tel: 780-849-8000; *Fax:* 780-849-2633
town@slavelake.ca
www.slavelake.ca
Municipal Type: Town
Incorporated: Jan. 1, 1961; *Area:* 14.18 sq km
County or District: Municipal District of Lesser Slave River No. 124; *Population in 2016:* 6,651
Provincial Electoral District(s): Lesser Slave Lake
Federal Electoral District(s): Peace River-Westlock
Next Election: Oct. 20, 2025 (4 year terms)
Note: Incorporated as a town on Aug. 2, 1965.
Tyler Warman, Mayor, 780-805-4045
Kim David, Chief Administrative Officer

Smoky Lake
56 Wheatland Ave.
Smoky Lake, AB T0A 3C0
Tel: 780-656-3674
town@smokylake.ca
www.smokylake.ca
Municipal Type: Town
Incorporated: March 26, 1923; *Area:* 4.2 sq km
County or District: Smoky Lake County; *Population in 2016:* 964
Provincial Electoral District(s): Athabasca-Barrhead-Westlock
Federal Electoral District(s): Lakeland
Next Election: Oct. 20, 2025 (4 year terms)
Note: Incorporated as a town on Feb. 1, 1962.
Amy Cherniwchan, Mayor
Gene Sobolewski, Chief Administrative Officer

South Baptiste
724 Baptiste Dr.
West Baptiste, AB T9S 1R8
Tel: 780-675-9270
www.southbaptiste.com

Municipal Type: Summer Village
Incorporated: Jan. 1, 1983; *Area:* 1.05 sq km
County or District: Athabasca County; *Population in 2016:* 66
Provincial Electoral District(s): Athabasca-Barrhead-Westlock
Federal Electoral District(s): Lakeland
Next Election: Summer 2025 (4 year terms)
Blaine Page, Mayor
Edwin Tomaszyk, Chief Administrative Officer

South View
P.O. Box 8
Alberta Beach, AB T0E 0A0
Tel: 587-873-5765; *Fax:* 780-967-0431
administration@wildwillowenterprises.com
www.summervillageofsouthview.com
Municipal Type: Summer Village
Incorporated: Jan. 1, 1970; *Area:* 0.69 sq km
County or District: Lac Ste. Anne County; *Population in 2016:* 67
Federal Electoral District(s): Yellowhead
Next Election: Summer 2025 (4 year terms)
Sandra Benford, Mayor
Wendy Wildman, Chief Administrative Officer

Spirit River
P.O. Box 130
Spirit River, AB T0H 3G0
Tel: 780-864-3998; *Fax:* 780-864-3433
www.townofspiritriver.ca
Municipal Type: Town
Incorporated: June 13, 1916; *Area:* 2.81 sq km
County or District: Municipal District of Spirit River No. 133;
Population in 2016: 995
Provincial Electoral District(s): Central Peace-Notley
Federal Electoral District(s): Grande Prairie-Mackenzie
Next Election: Oct. 20, 2025 (4 year terms)
Note: Incorporated as a town on Sept. 18, 1951.
Vacant, Mayor
Deedra Deveau, Chief Administrative Officer

Spring Lake
990 Bauer Ave.
Spring Lake, AB T7Z 2S9
Tel: 780-963-4211; *Fax:* 780-963-4260
villageoffice@springlakealberta.com
www.springlakealberta.com
Municipal Type: Village
Incorporated: Jan. 1, 1959; *Area:* 2.12 sq km
County or District: Parkland County; *Population in 2016:* 699
Provincial Electoral District(s): Spruce Grove-Stony Plain
Federal Electoral District(s): Sturgeon River-Parkland
Next Election: Oct. 20, 2025 (4 year terms)
Note: Incorporated as a village on Jan. 1, 1999.
Vacant, Mayor
Emily House, Chief Administrative Officer

Standard
P.O. Box 249
Standard, AB T0J 3G0
Tel: 403-644-3968
www.villageofstandard.ca
Municipal Type: Village
Incorporated: April 29, 1922; *Area:* 2.34 sq km
County or District: Wheatland County; *Population in 2016:* 353
Provincial Electoral District(s): Chestermere-Strathmore
Federal Electoral District(s): Bow River
Next Election: Oct. 20, 2025 (4 year terms)
Vacant, Mayor
Yvette April, Chief Administrative Officer

Stavely
P.O. Box 249
5001 - 50th Ave.
Stavely, AB T0L 1Z0
Tel: 403-549-3761; *Fax:* 403-549-3743
info@stavely.ca
stavely.ca
Municipal Type: Town
Incorporated: Oct. 16, 1903; *Area:* 1.62 sq km
County or District: Municipal District of Willow Creek No. 26;
Population in 2016: 541
Provincial Electoral District(s): Livingstone-Macleod
Federal Electoral District(s): Foothills
Next Election: Oct. 20, 2025 (4 year terms)
Note: Incorporated as a town on May 25, 1912.
Gentry Hall, Mayor
Candice Greig, Chief Administrative Officer

Stettler
P.O. Box 280
5031 - 50th St.
Stettler, AB T0C 2L0
Tel: 403-742-8305; *Fax:* 403-742-1404
townoffice@stettler.net
www.stettler.net
Municipal Type: Town
Incorporated: June 30, 1906; *Area:* 9.5 sq km
County or District: Stettler County No. 6; *Population in 2016:*
5,952
Provincial Electoral District(s): Drumheller-Stettler
Federal Electoral District(s): Battle River-Crowfoot
Next Election: Oct. 20, 2025 (4 year terms)
Note: Incorporated as a town on Nov. 23, 1906.
Vacant, Mayor
Greg Switenky, Chief Administrative Officer

Stirling
P.O. Box 360
229 - 4th Ave.
Stirling, AB T0K 2E0
Tel: 403-756-3379; *Fax:* 403-756-2262
office@stirling.ca
stirling.ca
Municipal Type: Village
Incorporated: Sept. 3, 1901; *Area:* 2.64 sq km
County or District: Warner County No. 5; *Population in 2016:* 978
Provincial Electoral District(s): Taber-Warner
Federal Electoral District(s): Medicine Hat-Cardston-Warner
Next Election: Oct. 20, 2025 (4 year terms)
Trevor Lewington, Mayor
Scott Donselaar, Chief Administrative Officer

Strome
c/o Flagstaff County Office
P.O. Box 358
Sedgewick, AB T0B 4C0
Tel: 780-384-4100; *Fax:* 780-384-3635
Municipal Type: Hamlet
Incorporated: Feb. 3, 1910; *Area:* 0.92 sq km
County or District: Flagstaff County
Federal Electoral District(s): Battle River-Crowfoot
Note: On January 1, 2016, Strome became a hamlet within
Flagstaff County.

Sunbreaker Cove
Bay 8, 14 Thevenaz Industrial Trail
Sylvan Lake, AB T4S 2J3
Tel: 403-887-2822; *Fax:* 403-887-2897
info@sylvansummervillages.ca
www.sylvansummervillages.ca/sunbreaker-cove.html
Municipal Type: Summer Village
Incorporated: Dec. 31, 1990; *Area:* 0.49 sq km
County or District: Lacombe County; *Population in 2016:* 81
Provincial Electoral District(s): Rimbey-Rocky Mountain
House-Sundre
Federal Electoral District(s): Red Deer-Lacombe
Next Election: Summer 2025 (4 year terms)
Teresa Beets, Mayor, 403-605-0641
Tanner Evans, Chief Administrative Officer

Sundance Beach
P.O. Box 28
Site 1, RR#1 South
Thorsby, AB T0C 2P0
Tel: 780-389-4409
info@sundancebeach.ca
www.sundancebeach.ca
Municipal Type: Summer Village
Incorporated: Jan. 1, 1970; *Area:* 0.42 sq km
County or District: Leduc County; *Population in 2016:* 73
Provincial Electoral District(s): Drayton Valley-Devon
Federal Electoral District(s): Edmonton-Wetaskiwin
Next Election: Summer 2025 (4 year terms)
Brian Waterhouse, Mayor
June Boyda, Chief Administrative Officer

Sundre
P.O. Box 420
Sundre, AB T0M 1X0
Tel: 403-638-3551; *Fax:* 403-638-2100
townmail@sundre.com
www.sundre.com
Municipal Type: Town
Incorporated: Dec. 31, 1949; *Area:* 7.65 sq km
County or District: Mountain View County; *Population in 2016:*
2,729
Provincial Electoral District(s): Rimbey-Rocky Mountain
House-Sundre
Federal Electoral District(s): Red Deer-Mountain View

Next Election: Oct. 20, 2025 (4 year terms)
Note: Incorporated as a town on Jan. 1, 1956.
Richard Warnock, Mayor
Linda Nelson, Chief Administrative Officer

Sunrise Beach
P.O. Box 1197
Onoway, AB T0E 1V0
Tel: 780-967-0271; *Fax:* 780-967-0431
svsunrisebeach@wildwillowenterprises.com
www.summervillageofsunrisebeach.ca
Municipal Type: Summer Village
Incorporated: Dec. 31, 1988; *Area:* 1.72 sq km
County or District: Lac Ste. Anne County; *Population in 2016:*
135
Federal Electoral District(s): Sturgeon River-Parkland
Next Election: Summer 2025 (4 year terms)
Jon Ethier, Mayor
Wendy Wildman, Chief Administrative Officer

Sunset Beach
899 Village Mews
Sherwood Park, AB T8A 4L9
Tel: 780-239-7323; *Fax:* 780-416-6353
svsunsetbeach@wildwillowenterprises.com
summervillageofsunsetbeach.com
Municipal Type: Summer Village
Incorporated: May 1, 1977; *Area:* 0.99 sq km
County or District: Athabasca County; *Population in 2016:* 49
Provincial Electoral District(s): Athabasca-Barrhead-Westlock
Federal Electoral District(s): Lakeland
Next Election: Summer 2025 (4 year terms)
Mark Lindskoog, Mayor
Kim Bancroft, Chief Administrative Officer

Sunset Point
P.O. Box 596
Alberta Beach, AB T0E 0A0
Tel: 780-665-5866; *Fax:* 780-967-5651
office@sunsetpoint.ca
sunsetpoint.ca
Municipal Type: Summer Village
Incorporated: Jan. 1, 1959; *Area:* 1.11 sq km
County or District: Lac Ste. Anne County; *Population in 2016:*
169
Federal Electoral District(s): Yellowhead
Next Election: Summer 2025 (4 year terms)
Gwen Jones, Mayor
Matthew Ferris, Chief Administrative Officer

Swan Hills
P.O. Box 149
5536 Main St.
Swan Hills, AB T0G 2C0
Tel: 780-333-4477; *Fax:* 780-333-4547
info@townofswanhills.com
www.townofswanhills.com
Municipal Type: Town
Incorporated: Sept. 1, 1959; *Area:* 25.44 sq km
County or District: Municipal District of Big Lakes; *Population in
2016:* 1,301
Provincial Electoral District(s): Athabasca-Barrhead-Westlock
Federal Electoral District(s): Peace River-Westlock
Next Election: Oct. 20, 2025 (4 year terms)
Craig Wilson, Mayor
Bill Lewis, Chief Administrative Officer

Taber
4900A - 50th St.
Taber, AB T1G 1T1
Tel: 403-223-5500; *Fax:* 403-223-5530
town@taber.ca
www.taber.ca
Municipal Type: Town
Incorporated: March 15, 1905; *Area:* 15.09 sq km
County or District: Municipal District of Taber; *Population in
2016:* 8,428
Provincial Electoral District(s): Taber-Warner
Federal Electoral District(s): Bow River
Next Election: Oct. 20, 2025 (4 year terms)
Note: Incorporated as a town on July 1, 1907.
Andrew Prokop, Mayor, 403-223-5500
Gary Scherer, Chief Administrative Officer

Thorsby
P.O. Box 297
4917 Hankin St.
Thorsby, AB T0C 2P0
Tel: 780-789-3935; *Fax:* 780-789-3779
info@thorsby.ca
www.thorsby.ca

Municipal Type: Town
Incorporated: Dec. 31, 1949; *Area:* 2.92 sq km
County or District: Leduc County; *Population in 2016:* 985
Provincial Electoral District(s): Drayton Valley-Devon
Federal Electoral District(s): Yellowhead
Next Election: Oct. 20, 2025 (4 year terms)
Note: Thorsby was changed from a village to a town in December 2016.
Hostyn Darryl, Mayor
Tamara Sloboda, Chief Administrative Officer

Three Hills
P.O. Box 610
232 Main St.
Three Hills, AB T0M 2A0
Tel: 403-443-5822; *Fax:* 403-443-2616
info@threehills.ca
www.threehills.ca
Municipal Type: Town
Incorporated: June 14, 1912; *Area:* 5.63 sq km
County or District: Kneehill County; *Population in 2016:* 3,212
Provincial Electoral District(s): Olds-Didsbury-Three Hills
Federal Electoral District(s): Battle River-Crowfoot
Next Election: Oct. 20, 2025 (4 year terms)
Note: Incorporated as a town on Jan. 1, 1929.
Raymond Wildeman, Mayor
Ryan Leuzinger, Chief Administrative Officer

Tofield
P.O. Box 30
5407 - 50th St.
Tofield, AB T0B 4J0
Tel: 780-662-3269; *Fax:* 780-662-3929
tofieldadmin@tofieldalberta.ca
tofieldalberta.ca
Municipal Type: Town
Incorporated: Sept. 9, 1907; *Area:* 6.01 sq km
County or District: Beaver County; *Population in 2016:* 2,081
Provincial Electoral District(s): Camrose
Federal Electoral District(s): Battle River-Crowfoot
Next Election: Oct. 20, 2025 (4 year terms)
Note: Incorporated as a town on Sept. 10, 1909.
Debora Lynn Dueck, Mayor
Cindy Neufeld, Chief Administrative Officer, 780-662-3269

Trochu
P.O. Box 340
222 Northfield Rd.
Trochu, AB T0M 2C0
Tel: 403-442-3085; *Fax:* 403-442-2528
town.trochu.ab.ca
Municipal Type: Town
Incorporated: May 5, 1911; *Area:* 2.82 sq km
County or District: Kneehill County; *Population in 2016:* 1,058
Provincial Electoral District(s): Olds-Didsbury-Three Hills
Federal Electoral District(s): Battle River-Crowfoot
Next Election: Oct. 20, 2025 (4 year terms)
Note: Incorporated as a town on Aug. 1, 1962.
Barry Kletke, Mayor
Carl Peterson, Chief Administrative Officer

Turner Valley
P.O. Box 330
514 Windsor Ave. NW
Turner Valley, AB T0L 2A0
Tel: 403-933-4944; *Fax:* 403-933-5377
admin@turnervalley.ca
turnervalley.ca
Municipal Type: Town
Incorporated: Feb. 25, 1930
County or District: Municipal District of Foothills No. 31;
Population in 2016: 2,559
Provincial Electoral District(s): Highwood
Federal Electoral District(s): Foothills
Next Election: Oct. 20, 2025 (4 year terms)
Note: Incorporated as a town on Sept.1, 1977.
Barry Crane, Mayor
Shawn Patience, Chief Administrative Officer

Two Hills
P.O. Box 630
4712 - 50th St.
Two Hills, AB T0B 4K0
Tel: 780-657-3395; *Fax:* 780-657-2158
info@townoftwohills.com
townoftwohills.com
Municipal Type: Town
Incorporated: June 4, 1929; *Area:* 3.31 sq km
County or District: Two Hills County No. 21; *Population in 2016:* 1,352
Provincial Electoral District(s): Fort Saskatchewan-Vegreville
Federal Electoral District(s): Lakeland

Next Election: Oct. 20, 2025 (4 year terms)
Note: Incorporated as a town on Jan. 1, 1955.
Leonard Ewanishan, Mayor
Gerren Saskiw, Chief Administrative Officer

Val Quentin
P.O. Box 7
Site 19, RR#1
Gunn, AB T0E 1A0
Tel: 780-446-1426
valquentin.ca
Municipal Type: Summer Village
Incorporated: Jan. 1, 1966; *Area:* 0.3 sq km
County or District: Lac Ste. Anne County; *Population in 2016:* 252
Federal Electoral District(s): Yellowhead
Next Election: Summer 2025 (4 year terms)
Roger Montpellier, Mayor
Dennis Evans, Municipal Administrator

Valleyview
4909 - 50th St.
Valleyview, AB T0H 3N0
Tel: 780-524-5150; *Fax:* 780-524-2727
info@valleyview.ca
valleyview.ca
Municipal Type: Town
Incorporated: Jan. 1, 1955; *Area:* 4.57 sq km
County or District: Municipal District of Greenview No. 16;
Population in 2016: 1,863
Provincial Electoral District(s): Central Peace-Notley
Federal Electoral District(s): Peace River-Westlock
Next Election: Oct. 20, 2025 (4 year terms)
Note: Incorporated as a town on Feb. 5, 1957.
Vern Lymburner, Mayor
Ben Berlinguette, Chief Administrative Officer

Vauxhall
P.O. Box 509
223 - 5th St. North
Vauxhall, AB T0K 2K0
Tel: 403-654-2174; *Fax:* 403-654-4110
town.vauxhall.ab.ca
Municipal Type: Town
Incorporated: Dec. 31, 1949; *Area:* 2.88 sq km
County or District: Municipal District of Taber; *Population in 2016:* 1,222
Provincial Electoral District(s): Cardston-Siksika
Federal Electoral District(s): Bow River
Next Election: Oct. 20, 2025 (4 year terms)
Note: Incorporated as a town on Jan. 1, 1961.
Margaret Plumtree, Mayor
Cris Burns, Chief Administrative Officer

Vegreville
P.O. Box 640
4829 - 50th St.
Vegreville, AB T9C 1R7
Tel: 780-632-2606; *Fax:* 780-632-3088
vegtown@vegreville.com
www.vegreville.com
Municipal Type: Town
Incorporated: April 4, 1906; *Area:* 13.49 sq km
County or District: Minburn County No. 27; *Population in 2016:* 5,708
Provincial Electoral District(s): Fort Saskatchewan-Vegreville
Federal Electoral District(s): Lakeland
Next Election: Oct. 20, 2025 (4 year terms)
Note: Incorporated as a town on Aug 15, 1906.
Timothy MacPhee, Mayor
Cliff Craig, Town Manager

Vermilion
5021 - 49th Ave.
Vermilion, AB T9X 1X1
Tel: 780-853-5358; *Fax:* 780-853-4910
info@vermilion.ca
www.vermilion.ca
Municipal Type: Town
Incorporated: Feb. 17, 1906; *Area:* 13.69 sq km
County or District: Vermilion River County; *Population in 2016:* 4,084
Provincial Electoral District(s):
Vermilion-Lloydminster-Wainwright
Federal Electoral District(s): Lakeland
Next Election: Oct. 20, 2025 (4 year terms)
Note: Incorporated as a town on Aug. 27, 1906.
Gregory Throndson, Mayor
George Rogers, Chief Administrative Officer

Veteran
P.O. Box 439
Veteran, AB T0C 2S0
Tel: 403-575-3954; *Fax:* 403-575-3954
villageofveteran@gmail.com
villageofveteran.ca
Municipal Type: Village
Incorporated: June 30, 1914; *Area:* 0.84 sq km
Population in 2016: 207
Provincial Electoral District(s): Drumheller-Stettler
Federal Electoral District(s): Battle River-Crowfoot
Next Election: Oct. 20, 2025 (4 year terms)
Jerry Wipf, Mayor
Debbie Johnstone, Chief Administrative Officer

Viking
P.O. Box 369
Viking, AB T0B 4N0
Tel: 780-336-3466; *Fax:* 780-336-2660
webinfo@viking.ca
viking.ca
Municipal Type: Town
Incorporated: Feb. 5, 1909; *Area:* 3.76 sq km
County or District: Beaver County; *Population in 2016:* 1,083
Provincial Electoral District(s): Camrose
Federal Electoral District(s): Battle River-Crowfoot
Next Election: Oct. 20, 2025 (4 year terms)
Note: Incorporated as a town on Nov. 10, 1952.
Laura Yakiwchuk, Mayor
Don McLeod, Chief Administrative Officer

Vilna
P.O. Box 10
Vilna, AB T0A 3L0
Tel: 780-636-3620; *Fax:* 780-636-3022
vilna@mcsnet.ca
www.vilna.ca
Municipal Type: Village
Incorporated: June 23, 1923; *Area:* 0.9 sq km
County or District: Smoky Lake County; *Population in 2016:* 290
Provincial Electoral District(s): Fort McMurray-Lac La Biche
Federal Electoral District(s): Lakeland
Next Election: Oct. 20, 2025 (4 year terms)
Vacant, Mayor
Earla Wagar, Interim Chief Administrative Officer

Vulcan
P.O. Box 360
321 - 2nd St. South
Vulcan, AB T0L 2B0
Tel: 403-485-2417; *Fax:* 403-485-2914
admin@townofvulcan.ca
townofvulcan.ca
Municipal Type: Town
Incorporated: Dec. 23, 1912; *Area:* 6.58 sq km
County or District: Vulcan County; *Population in 2016:* 1,917
Provincial Electoral District(s): Cardston-Siksika
Federal Electoral District(s): Bow River
Next Election: Oct. 20, 2025 (4 year terms)
Note: Incorporated as a town on Jun 15, 1921.
Thomas Grant, Mayor
Kim Fath, Chief Administrative Officer

Wabamun
c/o Parkland County
53109A Hwy. 779
Parkland County, AB T7Z 1R1
Tel: 780-892-2699
Municipal Type: Hamlet
Incorporated: July 18, 1912; *Area:* 3.58 sq km
County or District: Parkland County; *Population in 2016:* 682
Provincial Electoral District(s): Spruce Grove-Stony Plain
Federal Electoral District(s): Yellowhead
Note: On Jan. 1, 2021 it relinquished its village status to become a hamlet of Parkland County. This was the second time since 1946, having incorporated as a village once again in 1980.

Wainwright
1018 - 2nd Ave.
Wainwright, AB T9W 1R1
Tel: 780-842-3381; *Fax:* 780-842-2898
receptionist@wainwright.ca
wainwright.ca
Municipal Type: Town
Incorporated: March 25, 1909; *Area:* 8.55 sq km
County or District: Municipal District of Wainwright No. 61;
Population in 2016: 6,270
Provincial Electoral District(s):
Vermilion-Lloydminster-Wainwright
Federal Electoral District(s): Battle River-Crowfoot
Next Election: Oct. 20, 2025 (4 year terms)
Note: Incorporated as town on July 14, 1910.

Bruce Pugh, Mayor
Karrie Gau, Chief Administrative Officer

Waiparous
PO Box 19554, RPO South Cranston
Calgary, AB T3M 0V4
Tel: 403-510-8083; *Fax:* 403-206-7209
admin@waiparous.ca
waiparous.ca
Municipal Type: Summer Village
Incorporated: Jan. 1, 1986; *Area:* 0.41 sq km
County or District: Municipal District of Bighorn No. 8; *Population in 2016:* 49
Provincial Electoral District(s): Banff-Kananaskis
Federal Electoral District(s): Banff-Airdrie
Next Election: Summer 2025 (4 year terms)
Matt Sundal, Mayor
Sherri Bureyko, Chief Administrative Officer

Warburg
P.O. Box 29
5212 - 50th Ave.
Warburg, AB T0C 2T0
Tel: 780-848-2841; *Fax:* 780-848-2296
village@warburg.ca
www.warburg.ca
Municipal Type: Village
Incorporated: Dec. 31, 1953; *Area:* 2.08 sq km
County or District: Leduc County; *Population in 2016:* 766
Provincial Electoral District(s): Drayton Valley-Devon
Federal Electoral District(s): Yellowhead
Next Election: Oct. 20, 2025 (4 year terms)
Dwayne Edward Mayr, Mayor
Chris Pankewitz, Chief Administrative Officer

Warner
P.O. Box 88
210 - 3rd Ave.
Warner, AB T0K 2L0
Tel: 403-642-3877; *Fax:* 403-642-2011
admin@warner.ca
www.warner.ca
Municipal Type: Village
Incorporated: Nov. 12, 1908; *Area:* 1.15 sq km
County or District: Warner County No. 5; *Population in 2016:* 373
Provincial Electoral District(s): Taber-Warner
Federal Electoral District(s): Medicine Hat-Cardston-Warner
Next Election: Oct. 20, 2025 (4 year terms)
Tyler Lindsay, Mayor
Jon Hood, Chief Administrative Officer

Waskatenau
P.O. Box 99
5008 - 51st St.
Waskatenau, AB T0A 3P0
Tel: 780-358-2208
info@waskatenau.ca
www.waskatenau.ca
Municipal Type: Village
Incorporated: May 19, 1932; *Area:* 0.6 sq km
County or District: Smoky Lake County; *Population in 2016:* 186
Federal Electoral District(s): Lakeland
Next Election: Oct. 20, 2025 (4 year terms)
Casey Caron, Mayor
Bernice Macyk, Chief Administrative Officer

Wembley
P.O. Box 89
9940 - 101st St.
Wembley, AB T0H 3S0
Tel: 780-766-2269; *Fax:* 780-766-2868
info@wembley.ca
www.wembley.ca
Municipal Type: Town
Incorporated: Jan. 3, 1928; *Area:* 3.63 sq km
County or District: Grande Prairie County No. 1; *Population in 2016:* 1,516
Provincial Electoral District(s): Grande Prairie-Wapiti
Federal Electoral District(s): Grande Prairie-Mackenzie
Next Election: Oct. 20, 2025 (4 year terms)
Note: Incorporated as a town on Aug. 1, 1980.
Kelly Peterson, Mayor
Noreen Zhang, Chief Administrative Officer

West Baptiste
945 Baptiste Dr.
West Baptiste, AB T9S 1R8
Tel: 780-675-3900; *Fax:* 780-675-4174
svwestbaptiste.ca
Municipal Type: Summer Village
Incorporated: Jan. 1, 1983; *Area:* 0.6 sq km
County or District: Athabasca County; *Population in 2016:* 38

Provincial Electoral District(s): Athabasca-Barrhead-Westlock
Federal Electoral District(s): Lakeland
Next Election: Summer 2025 (4 year terms)
Keith Wilson, Mayor
Vivian Driver, Chief Administrative Officer

West Cove
721 Valking Rd.
West Cove, AB T0E 0A2
Tel: 780-967-0271; *Fax:* 780-967-0431
svwestcove@outlook.com
www.westcove.ca
Municipal Type: Summer Village
Incorporated: Jan. 1, 1963; *Area:* 1.21 sq km
County or District: Lac Ste. Anne County; *Population in 2016:* 149
Federal Electoral District(s): Yellowhead
Next Election: Summer 2025 (4 year terms)
Ren Giesbrecht, Mayor
Wendy Wildman, Chief Administrative Officer

Westlock
10003 - 106th St.
Westlock, AB T7P 2K3
Tel: 780-349-4444; *Fax:* 780-349-4436
info@westlock.ca
www.westlock.ca
Other Information: Toll-Free Phone: 866-349-4445
Municipal Type: Town
Incorporated: March 13, 1916; *Area:* 9.64 sq km
County or District: Westlock County; *Population in 2016:* 5,101
Provincial Electoral District(s): Athabasca-Barrhead-Westlock
Federal Electoral District(s): Peace River-Westlock
Next Election: Oct. 20, 2025 (4 year terms)
Note: Incorporated as a town on Jan. 7, 1947.
Vacant, Mayor
Simone Wiley, Chief Administrative Officer

Whispering Hills
899 Village Mews
Sherwood Park, AB T8A 4L9
Tel: 780-239-7323; *Fax:* 780-416-6353
mywhisperinghills.com
Municipal Type: Summer Village
Incorporated: Jan. 1, 1983; *Area:* 1.73 sq km
County or District: Athabasca County; *Population in 2016:* 142
Provincial Electoral District(s): Athabasca-Barrhead-Westlock
Federal Electoral District(s): Lakeland
Next Election: Summer 2025 (4 year terms)
Curtis Schoepp, Mayor, 780-220-4897
Kim Bancroft, Chief Administrative Officer

White Sands
P.O. Box 119
Stettler, AB T0C 2L0
Tel: 403-742-4717; *Fax:* 403-742-1404
townoffice@stettler.net
www.whitesandsab.ca
Municipal Type: Summer Village
Incorporated: Jan. 1, 1980; *Area:* 1.6 sq km
County or District: Stettler County No. 6; *Population in 2016:* 120
Provincial Electoral District(s): Drumheller-Stettler
Federal Electoral District(s): Battle River-Crowfoot
Next Election: Summer 2025 (4 year terms)
Lorne Thurston, Mayor
Melissa Beebe, Chief Administrative Officer

Whitecourt
P.O. Box 509
5004 - 52nd Ave.
Whitecourt, AB T7S 1N6
Tel: 780-778-2273; *Fax:* 780-778-4166
administration@whitecourt.ca
www.whitecourt.ca
Municipal Type: Town
Incorporated: Jan. 1, 1959; *Area:* 26.14 sq km
County or District: Woodlands County; *Population in 2016:* 10,204
Provincial Electoral District(s): West Yellowhead
Federal Electoral District(s): Peace River-Westlock
Next Election: Oct. 20, 2025 (4 year terms)
Note: Incorporated as a town on Aug. 15, 1961.
Tom Pickard, Mayor
Peter Smyl, Chief Administrative Officer

Willingdon
P.O. Box 210
Willingdon, AB T0B 4R0
Tel: 780-367-2337; *Fax:* 780-367-2167
Municipal Type: Hamlet
Incorporated: Aug. 31, 1928; *Area:* 0.97 sq km
County or District: Two Hills County No. 21; *Population in 2016:*

319
Provincial Electoral District(s): Fort McMurray-Lac La Biche
Federal Electoral District(s): Lakeland
Note: Willingdon was dissolved from village status effective Sept. 1, 2017, becoming part of Two Hills County No. 21.

Yellowstone
P.O. Box 8
Alberta Beach, AB T0E 0A0
Tel: 587-873-5765; *Fax:* 780-967-0431
administration@wildwillowenterprises.com
www.summervillageofyellowstone.com
Municipal Type: Summer Village
Incorporated: Jan. 1, 1965; *Area:* 0.28 sq km
County or District: Lac Ste. Anne County; *Population in 2016:* 137
Federal Electoral District(s): Yellowhead
Next Election: Summer 2025 (4 year terms)
Don Bauer, Mayor
Wendy Wildman, Chief Administrative Officer

Youngstown
P.O. Box 99
Youngstown, AB T0J 3P0
Tel: 403-779-3873; *Fax:* 403-779-3875
info@youngstown.ca
youngstown.ca
Municipal Type: Village
Incorporated: March 8, 1913; *Area:* 1 sq km
Population in 2016: 154
Provincial Electoral District(s): Drumheller-Stettler
Federal Electoral District(s): Battle River-Crowfoot
Next Election: Oct. 20, 2025 (4 year terms)
Robert Blagen, Mayor
Emma Garlock, Municipal Administrator

Improvement Districts in Alberta

Improvement District No. 12 (Jasper National Park)
Municipal Services Branch
10155 - 102nd St., 17th Fl.
Edmonton, AB T5J 4L4
Tel: 780-422-8110
lgsmail@gov.ab.ca
Municipal Type: Improvement Districts
Incorporated: April 1, 1945; *Area:* 10,181.58 sq. km
Population in 2016: 53
Federal Electoral District(s): Yellowhead
Troy Shewchuk, Interim Chief Administrative Officer

Improvement District No. 13 (Elk Island)
Municipal Services Branch
10155 - 102nd St., 17th Fl.
Edmonton, AB T5J 4L4
Tel: 780-422-8110
lgsmail@gov.ab.ca
Municipal Type: Improvement Districts
Incorporated: April 1, 1958; *Area:* 165.28 sq. km
Federal Electoral District(s): Lakeland
Troy Shewchuk, Interim Chief Administrative Officer

Improvement District No. 24 (Wood Buffalo)
Municipal Services Branch
10155 - 102nd St., 17th Fl.
Edmonton, AB T5J 4L4
Tel: 780-422-8110
lgsmail@gov.ab.ca
Municipal Type: Improvement Districts
Incorporated: Jan. 1, 1967; *Area:* 165.28 sq km.
Population in 2017: 648
Federal Electoral District(s): Peace River-Westlock
Troy Shewchuk, Interim Chief Administrative Officer

Improvement District No. 25 (Willmore Wilderness)
Municipal Services Branch
10155 - 102nd St., 17th Fl.
Edmonton, AB T5J 4L4
Tel: 780-422-8110
lgsmail@gov.ab.ca
Municipal Type: Improvement Districts
Incorporated: Jan. 2, 1994; *Area:* 4,604.97 sq. km
Federal Electoral District(s): Yellowhead
Troy Shewchuk, Interim Chief Administrative Officer

Improvement District No. 4 (Waterton)
P.O. Box 629
Raymond, AB T0K 2S0
Tel: 403-859-2042
admin@id4waterton.ca
id4waterton.ca
Municipal Type: Improvement Districts
Incorporated: Jan. 1, 1944; *Area:* 480.58 sq. km

Population in 2016: 105
Federal Electoral District(s): Foothills
Next Election: Oct. 20, 2025 (4 year terms)
Ken Black, Chair
J. Scott Barton, Chief Administrative Officer

Improvement District No. 9 (Banff)
P.O. Box 58
103 Village Rd.
Lake Louise, AB T0L 1E0
Tel: 403-522-2606
info@improvementdistrict9.ca
improvementdistrict9.ca
Municipal Type: Improvement Districts
Incorporated: April 1, 1945; *Area:* 6,782.26 sq. km
Population in 2016: 1,028
Federal Electoral District(s): Banff-Airdrie
Dave Schebek, Chair
Danielle Morine, Chief Administrative Officer

Kananaskis Improvement District
P.O. Box 70
Kananaskis, AB T0L 2H0
Tel: 403-591-7774; *Fax:* 403-591-7123
info@kananaskisid.ca
www.kananaskisid.ca
Municipal Type: Improvement Districts
Incorporated: April 1, 1945; *Area:* 4,210.72 sq km
Population in 2017: 221
Federal Electoral District(s): Banff-Airdrie; Foothills
Next Election: Oct. 20, 2025 (4 year terms)
Melanie Gnyp, Chair
Kieran Dowling, Acting Chief Administrative Officer

Metis Settlements in Alberta

Buffalo Lake
P.O. Box 16
Caslan, AB T0A 0R0
Tel: 780-689-2170; *Fax:* 780-689-2024
reception@blmetis.ca
buffalolakems.ca
Municipal Type: Metis Settlements
Area: 336.97 sq km
Population in 2016: 712
Federal Electoral District(s): Grande Prairie-Mackenzie
Next Election: Oct. 20, 2025 (4 year terms)

Stanley Delorme, Chair
Brenda Blyan, Administrator

East Prairie
P.O. Box 1289
High Prairie, AB T0G 1E0
Tel: 780-535-056; *Fax:* 780-523-2777
Municipal Type: Metis Settlements
Area: 333.87 sq km
Population in 2016: 304
Provincial Electoral District(s): Lesser Slave Lake
Federal Electoral District(s): Peace River-Westlock
Next Election: Oct. 20, 2025 (4 year terms)
Peter Patenaude, Chair

Elizabeth
P.O. Box 420
Cold Lake, AB T9M 1P1
Tel: 780-594-5028; *Fax:* 780-594-5452
elizabethms.ca
Municipal Type: Metis Settlements
Population in 2016: 653
Federal Electoral District(s): Lakeland
Next Election: Oct. 20, 2025 (4 year terms)
Irene Zimmer, Chair
Sharna Collins, Administrator

Fishing Lake
5102 - 50th St.
Sputinow, AB T0A 3G0
Tel: 780-943-2202; *Fax:* 780-943-2575
reception@flms.ca
flms.ca
Municipal Type: Metis Settlements
Area: 355.74 sq km
Population in 2016: 446
Provincial Electoral District(s): Bonnyville-Cold Lake-St Paul
Federal Electoral District(s): Fort McMurray-Cold Lake
Next Election: Oct. 20, 2025 (4 year terms)
Karen Telford, Chair

Gift Lake
P.O. Box 60
Gift Lake, AB T0G 1B0
Tel: 780-767-3794
info@giftlakemetis.ca
giftlakemetis.ca
Municipal Type: Metis Settlements
Area: 811.30 sq km

Population in 2016: 658
Provincial Electoral District(s): Lesser Slave Lake
Federal Electoral District(s): Peace River-Westlock
Next Election: Oct. 20, 2025 (4 year terms)
Howard Shaw, Chair
Tammy Anderson, Administrator

Kikino
General Delivery
Kikino, AB T0A 2B0
Tel: 780-623-7868; *Fax:* 780-623-7080
kirecreation@mcsnet.ca
Municipal Type: Metis Settlements
Area: 442.92 sq km
Population in 2016: 934
Provincial Electoral District(s): Fort McMurray-Lac La Biche
Federal Electoral District(s): Lakeland
Next Election: Oct. 20, 2025 (4 year terms)
Dean Thompson, Chair

Paddle Prairie
P.O. Box 58
Paddle Prairie, AB T0H 2W0
Tel: 780-981-2227; *Fax:* 780-981-3737
admin@paddleprairie.com
paddleprairiemetis.com
Municipal Type: Metis Settlements
Area: 1716.72 sq km
Population in 2016: 544
Provincial Electoral District(s): Peace River
Federal Electoral District(s): Grande Prairie-Mackenzie
Next Election: Oct. 20, 2025 (4 year terms)
Alden Armstrong, Chair
Lorraine Poitras, Administrator

Peavine
P.O. Box 4
High Prairie, AB T0G 1E0
Tel: 780-523-2557; *Fax:* 780-523-2626
Municipal Type: Metis Settlements
Area: 817.13 sq km
Population in 2016: 607
Provincial Electoral District(s): Lesser Slave Lake
Federal Electoral District(s): Peace River-Westlock
Next Election: Oct. 20, 2025 (4 year terms)
Ken Noskey, Chair

BRITISH COLUMBIA

Incorporated municipalities in British Columbia include Villages, Towns, Cities, and District Municipalities as well as one Indian Government District, one Resort Municipality, two Mountain Resort Municipalities, and one Island Municipality. Twenty-seven regional districts (plus one administered by the provincial government) provide services to unincorporated areas and member municipalities.

Municipal elections in all municipalities are held on the 3rd Saturday of October. Election terms are four years (2018, 2022, etc.).

Legislation: The Local Government Act, excluding the City of Vancouver, which is regulated under the provisions of the Vancouver Charter.

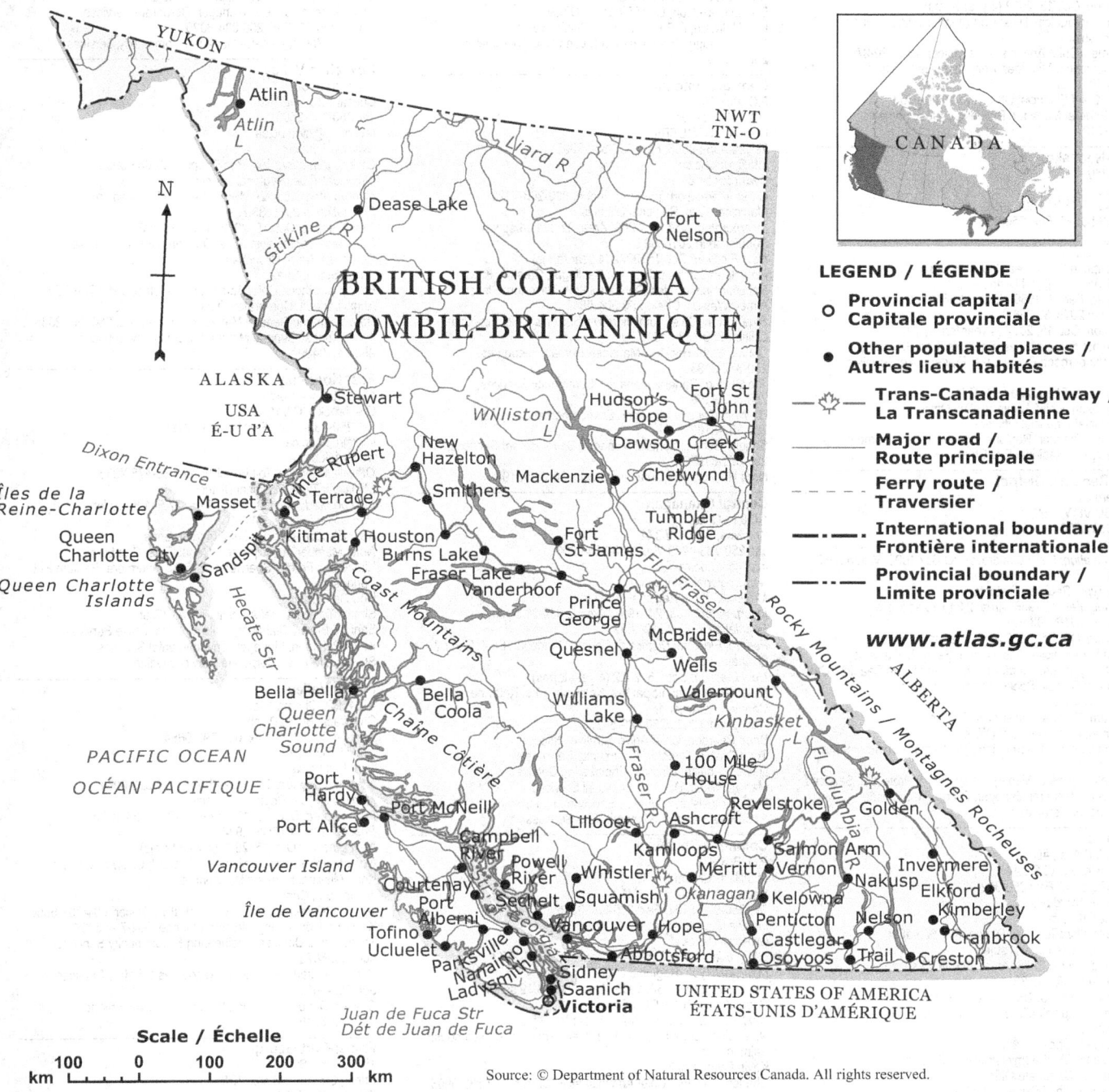

LEGEND / LÉGENDE
- ○ Provincial capital / Capitale provinciale
- ● Other populated places / Autres lieux habités
- Trans-Canada Highway / La Transcanadienne
- Major road / Route principale
- Ferry route / Traversier
- International boundary / Frontière internationale
- Provincial boundary / Limite provinciale

www.atlas.gc.ca

Source: © Department of Natural Resources Canada. All rights reserved.

British Columbia

Counties & Municipal Districts in British Columbia

Alberni-Clayoquot
3008 - 5 Ave.
Port Alberni, BC V9Y 2E3
Tel: 250-720-2700; *Fax:* 250-723-1327
mailbox@acrd.bc.ca
www.acrd.bc.ca
Municipal Type: Regional Districts
Incorporated: April 21, 1966; *Area:* 6,589.15 sq km
Population in 2016: 31,981
Next Election: Oct. 15, 2022 (4 year terms)
Note: Member municipalities: Port Alberni; Tofino; Ucluelet.
John Jack, Chair
Doug Holmes, Chief Administrative Officer, 250-720-2705
Wendy Thompson, Manager, Administrative Services, 250-720-2706
Teri Fong, Chief Financial Officer, 250-720-2707
Mike Irg, General Manager, Planning & Development, 250-720-2710

Bulkley-Nechako
P.O. Box 820
37, 3rd Ave.
Burns Lake, BC V0J 1E0
Tel: 250-692-3195; *Fax:* 250-692-3305
inquiries@rdbn.bc.ca
www.rdbn.bc.ca
Other Information: Toll-Free Phone: 800-320-3339
Municipal Type: Regional Districts
Incorporated: Feb. 1, 1966; *Area:* 73,361.00 sq km
Population in 2016: 37,896
Next Election: Oct. 15, 2022 (4 year terms)
Note: Member municipalities: Smithers; Fort St. James; Housten; Vanderhoof; Burns Lake; Fraser Lake; Granisle; Telkwa.
Gerry Thiessen, Chair, 250-567-4711
Curtis Helgesen, Chief Administrative Officer
John Iles, Chief Financial Officer
Nellie Davis, Manager, Regional Economic Development
Jason Blackwell, Regional Fire Chief

Capital Regional District
625 Fisgard St.
Victoria, BC V8W 1R7
Tel: 250-360-3000
www.crd.bc.ca
Other Information: Mailing address: PO Box 1000, Victoria, BC V8W 2S6
Municipal Type: Regional Districts
Incorporated: Feb. 1, 1966; *Area:* 2,340.49 sq km
Population in 2016: 383,991
Next Election: Oct. 15, 2022 (4 year terms)
Note: Member municipalities: Central Saanich; Colwood; Esquimalt; Highlands; Langford; Metchosin; North Saanich; Oak Bay; Saanich; Sidney; Sooke; Victoria; View Royal.
Colin Plant, Chair
Bob Lapham, Chief Administrative Officer
Nelson Chan, Chief Financial Officer
Larissa Hutcheson, General Manager, Parks & Environmental Services
Kevin Lorette, General Manager, Planning & Protective Services
Kristen Morley, General Manager, Corporate Services
Ted Robbins, General Manager

Cariboo
180 North 3rd Ave., #D
Williams Lake, BC V2G 2A4
Tel: 250-392-3351; *Fax:* 250-392-2812
mailbox@cariboord.bc.ca
www.cariboord.bc.ca
Other Information: Toll-Free Phone: 800-665-1636
Municipal Type: Regional Districts
Incorporated: July 9, 1968; *Area:* 80,609.75 sq km
Population in 2016: 61,988
Next Election: Oct. 15, 2022 (4 year terms)
Note: Member municipalities: 100 Mile House; Quesnel; Wells; Williams Lake.
Margo Wagner, Chair
John MacLean, Chief Administrative Officer
Alice Johnston, Corporate Officer
Kevin Erickson, Chief Financial Officer
Virgil Hoefels, Chief Building Official
Charles Boulet, Manager, Environmental Services
Darron Campbell, Manager, Community Services

Central Coast
P.O. Box 186
626 Cliff St.
Bella Coola, BC V0T 1C0
Tel: 250-799-5291; *Fax:* 250-799-5750
info@ccrd-bc.ca
www.ccrd-bc.ca
Municipal Type: Regional Districts
Incorporated: July 16, 1968; *Area:* 24,556.35 sq km
Population in 2016: 3,319
Next Election: Oct. 15, 2022 (4 year terms)
Note: Member municipalities: Bella Coola Valley; Ocean Falls; Denny Island; Bella Bella; Oweekeno.
Reginald Moody-Humchitt, Chair, 250-799-5291
Darla Blake, Chief Administrative Officer
Donna Mikkelson, Chief Financial Officer
Ken McIlwain, R.P.F., Manager, Public Works
Cheryl Waugh, Transportation & Land Use Coordinator, 250-799-5291

Central Kootenay
P.O. Box 590
202 Lakeside Dr.
Nelson, BC V1L 5R4
Tel: 250-352-6665; *Fax:* 250-352-9300
info@rdck.bc.ca
www.rdck.bc.ca
Other Information: Toll-Free Phone: 800-268-7325
Municipal Type: Regional Districts
Incorporated: Nov. 30, 1965; *Area:* 22,094.94 sq km
Population in 2016: 59,517
Next Election: Oct. 15, 2022 (4 year terms)
Note: Member municipalities: Castlegar; Creston; Kaslo; Nakusp; Nelson; New Denver; Salmo; Silverton; Slocan.
Aimee Watson, Chair, 250-304-5842
Stuart Horn, Chief Administrative Officer & Chief Financial Officer, 250-352-8184
Connie Saari-Heckley, Manager, Human Resources, 250-352-8193
Joe Chirico, General Manager, Community Services, 250-352-8158
Uli Wolf, General Manager, Environmental Services, 250-352-8163
Sangita Sudan, General Manager, Development Services, 250-352-8157
Nora Hannon, Regional Fire Chief, 250-352-8198

Central Okanagan
1450 KLO Rd.
Kelowna, BC V1W 3Z4
Tel: 250-763-4918; *Fax:* 250-763-0606
info@cord.bc.ca
www.regionaldistrict.com
Municipal Type: Regional Districts
Incorporated: Aug. 24, 1967; *Area:* 2,904.86 sq km
Population in 2016: 194,882
Federal Electoral District(s): Central Okanagan East; Central Okanagan West
Next Election: Oct. 15, 2022 (4 year terms)
Note: Member municipalities: Kelowna; West Kelowna; Lake Country; Peachland.
Gail Given, Chair, 250-469-8677
Brian Reardon, Chief Administrative Officer
Todd Cashin, Director, Community Services
David Komaike, Director, Engineering Services
Marilyn Rilkoff, Director, Financial Services
Peter Rotheisler, Manager, Environmental Services
Ross Kotscherofski, Manager, Fire Services

Columbia-Shuswap
P.O. Box 978
555 Harbourfront Dr. NE
Salmon Arm, BC V1E 3M1
Tel: 250-832-8194; *Fax:* 250-832-3375
inquiries@csrd.bc.ca
www.csrd.bc.ca
Other Information: Toll-Free Phone: 888-248-2773
Municipal Type: Regional Districts
Incorporated: Nov. 30, 1965; *Area:* 28,929.19 sq km
Population in 2016: 51,366
Next Election: Oct. 15, 2022 (4 year terms)
Note: Member municipalities: Golden; Revelstoke; Sicamous; Salmon Arm.
Kevin Flynn, Chair
Charles Hamilton, Chief Administrative Officer, 250-833-5905
Gerald Christie, Manager, Development Services, 250-833-5919
Jodi Pierce, Manager, Financial Services, 250-833-5907
Sean Coubrough, Coordinator, Fire Services, 250-833-5955

Comox Valley
600 Comox Rd.
Courtenay, BC V9N 3P6
Tel: 250-334-6000; *Fax:* 250-334-4358
www.comoxvalleyrd.ca
Other Information: Toll-Free Phone: 800-331-6007
Municipal Type: Regional Districts
Incorporated: Aug. 19, 1965; *Area:* 1,699.90 sq km
Population in 2016: 66,527
Next Election: Oct. 15, 2022 (4 year terms)
Note: Member municipalities: Comox; Courtenay; Cumberland.
Jesse Ketler, Chair, 250-336-2291
Russell Dyson, Chief Administrative Officer, 250-334-6055, Fax: 250-334-4358
Beth Dunlop, Corporate Financial Officer
Jake Martens, General Manager, Corporate Services, 250-334-6029, Fax: 250-334-6029
Doug DeMarzo, General Manager, Community Services

Cowichan Valley
175 Ingram St.
Duncan, BC V9L 1N8
Tel: 250-746-2500
reception@cvrd.bc.ca
www.cvrd.bc.ca
Other Information: Toll-Free Phone: 800-665-3955
Municipal Type: Regional Districts
Incorporated: Sept. 26, 1967; *Area:* 3,474.52 sq km
Population in 2016: 83,739
Next Election: Oct. 15, 2022 (4 year terms)
Note: Member municipalities: Duncan; Ladysmith; Lake Cowichan; North Cowichan.
Aaron Stone, Chair
Brian Carruthers, Chief Administrative Officer, 250-746-2500
Angie Legault, Corporate Officer
Hamid Hatami, General Manager, Engineering, 250-746-2538
John Elzinga, General Manager, Community Services, 250-746-0400

East Kootenay
19 - 24th Ave. South
Cranbrook, BC V1C 3H8
Tel: 250-489-2791; *Fax:* 250-489-3498
info@rdek.bc.ca
www.rdek.bc.ca
Other Information: Toll-Free Phone: 888-478-7335
Municipal Type: Regional Districts
Incorporated: Nov. 30, 1965; *Area:* 27,541.84 sq km
Population in 2016: 60,439
Next Election: Oct. 15, 2022 (4 year terms)
Note: Member municipalities: Canal Flats; Cranbrook; Kimberley; Fernie; Sparwood; Elkford; Invermere; Radium Hot Springs.
Rob Gay, Chair
Shawn Tomlin, Chief Administrative Officer
Sanford Brown, Manager, Building & Protective Services
Kevin Paterson, Manager, Environmental Services
Shannon Moskal, Corporate Services Officer

Fraser Valley
#1, 45950 Cheam Ave.
Chilliwack, BC V2P 1N6
Tel: 604-702-5000; *Fax:* 604-792-9684
info@fvrd.bc.ca
www.fvrd.bc.ca
Other Information: Toll-Free Phone: 800-528-0061
Municipal Type: Regional Districts
Incorporated: Dec. 12, 1995; *Area:* 13,335.28 sq km
Population in 2016: 295,934
Next Election: Oct. 15, 2022 (4 year terms)
Note: Member municipalities: Abbotsford; Chilliwack; Hope; Kent; Mission; Harrison Hot Springs.
Jason Lum, Chair
Jennifer Kinneman, Chief Administrative Officer, 604-702-5056
Kristy Hodson, Acting Director, Finance, 604-702-5037
Tareq Islam, Director, Engineering & Community Services, 604-702-5026
Raf Jamil, Manager, Human Resources & Safety Services, 604-702-5031
Graham Daneluz, Director, Planning & Development, 604-702-5046

Fraser-Fort George
155 George St.
Prince George, BC V2L 1P8
Tel: 250-960-4400
district@rdffg.bc.ca
www.rdffg.bc.ca
Other Information: Toll-Free Phone: 800-667-1959
Municipal Type: Regional Districts
Incorporated: March 8, 1967; *Area:* 50,676.10 sq km
Population in 2016: 94,506

Next Election: Oct. 15, 2022 (4 year terms)
Note: Member municipalities: McBride; Mackenzie; Prince George; Valemount.
Art Kaehn, Chair
Jim Martin, Chief Administrative Officer

Kitimat-Stikine
#300, 4545 Lazelle Ave.
Terrace, BC V8G 4E1
Tel: 250-615-6100; *Fax:* 250-635-9222
info@rdks.bc.ca
www.rdks.bc.ca
Other Information: Toll-Free Phone: 800-663-3208
Municipal Type: Regional Districts
Incorporated: Sept. 14, 1967; *Area:* 104,464.61 sq km
Population in 2016: 37,367
Next Election: Oct. 15, 2022 (4 year terms)
Note: Member municipalities: Kitimat; Terrace; Stewart; Hazelton; New Hazelton.
Philip Germuth, Chair
Ron Poole, Chief Administrative Officer
Yvonne Koerner, Chief Financial Officer
Erin Blaney, Interim Coordinator, Environmental Services
Steve Prouse, Director, Works & Services

Kootenay Boundary
#202, 843 Rossland Ave.
Trail, BC V1R 4S8
Tel: 250-368-9148; *Fax:* 250-368-3990
rdkb.com
Other Information: Toll-Free Phone: 800-355-7352 (BC only)
Municipal Type: Regional Districts
Incorporated: Feb. 22, 1966; *Area:* 8,084.52 sq km
Population in 2016: 31,447
Next Election: Oct. 15, 2022 (4 year terms)
Note: Member municipalities: Fruitvale; Grand Forks; Greenwood; Midway; Montrose; Rossland; Trail; Warfield.
Diane Langman, Chair
Mark Andison, Chief Administrative Officer
Barb Ihlen, General Manager, Finance
Goran Denkovski, Manager, Infrastructure & Sustainability
Daniel Derby, Regional Fire Chief

Metro Vancouver
4330 Kingsway
Burnaby, BC V5H 4G8
Tel: 604-432-6200; *Fax:* 604-436-6901
icentre@metrovancouver.org
www.metrovancouver.org
Municipal Type: Regional Districts
Incorporated: June 29, 1967; *Area:* 2,882.68 sq km
Population in 2016: 2,463,431
Next Election: Oct. 15, 2022 (4 year terms)
Note: Member municipalities: Anmore; Belcarra; Bowen Island; Burnaby; Coquitlam; Delta; Langley; Lions Bay; New Westminster; North Vancouver; Pitt Meadows; Port Coquitlam; Port Moody; Richmond; Surrey; Vancouver; West Vancouver; White Rock.
Sav Dhaliwal, Chair
Jerry Dobrovolny, Commissioner & Chief Administrative Officer
Chris Plagnol, Corporate Officer
Dean Rear, Chief Financial Officer
Paul Henderson, General Manager, Solid Waste Services
Jessica Beverly, Corporate Solicitor & General Manager, Corporate Services
Marilyn Towill, General Manager, Water Services
Neal Carley, General Manager, Parks & Environment
Rav Chhina, General Manager, Human Resources

Mount Waddington
P.O. Box 729
2044 McNeill Rd.
Port McNeill, BC V0N 2R0
Tel: 250-956-3301; *Fax:* 250-956-3232
info@rdmw.bc.ca
www.rdmw.bc.ca
Other Information: Alternate Phone: 250-956-3161
Municipal Type: Regional Districts
Incorporated: June 13, 1966; *Area:* 20,244.27 sq km
Next Election: Oct. 15, 2022 (4 year terms)
Note: Member municipalities: Alert Bay; Port Alice; Port Hardy; Port McNeill.
Andrew Hory, Chair
Greg Fletcher, Administrator
Patrick Donaghy, Manager, Operations
Pat English, Manager, Economic Development

Nanaimo
6300 Hammond Bay Rd.
Nanaimo, BC V9T 6N2
Tel: 250-390-4111; *Fax:* 250-390-4163
corpsrv@rdn.bc.ca
www.rdn.bc.ca
Other Information: Toll-Free Phone: 877-607-4111
Municipal Type: Regional Districts
Incorporated: Aug. 24, 1967; *Area:* 2,038.04 sq km
Population in 2016: 155.698
Next Election: Oct. 15, 2022 (4 year terms)
Note: Member municipalities: Nanaimo; Lantzville; Parksville; Qualicum Beach.
Ian Thorpe, Chair
Phyllis Carlyle, Chief Administrative Officer

North Coast
#14, 342 - 3rd Ave. West
Prince Rupert, BC V8J 1L5
Tel: 250-624-2002
info@ncrdbc.com
www.ncrdbc.com
Municipal Type: Regional Districts
Incorporated: Aug. 17, 1967; *Area:* 19,775.41 sq km
Population in 2016: 18,122
Next Election: Oct. 15, 2022 (4 year terms)
Note: Member municipalities: Prince Rupert; Port Edward; Queen Charlotte; Port Clemens; Masset.
Barry Pages, Chair, 250-626-3995, Fax: 250-626-5503
Daniel Fish, Chief Administrative Officer, 250-624-2002

North Okanagan
9848 Aberdeen Rd.
Coldstream, BC V1B 2K9
Tel: 250-550-3700; *Fax:* 250-550-3701
info@rdno.ca
www.rdno.ca
Municipal Type: Regional Districts
Incorporated: Nov. 9, 1965; *Area:* 7,502.60 sq km
Population in 2016: 84,354
Next Election: Oct. 15, 2022 (4 year terms)
Note: Member municipalities: Enderby; Armstrong; Spallumcheen; Vernon; Coldstream; Lumby.
Kevin Acton, Chair
David Sewell, Chief Administrative Officer

Northern Rockies
P.O. Box 399
5319 - 50th Ave. South
Fort Nelson, BC V0C 1R0
Tel: 250-774-2541; *Fax:* 250-774-6794
justask@northernrockies.ca
www.northernrockies.ca
Municipal Type: Regional Districts
Incorporated: Oct. 31, 1987; *Area:* 85,148.87 sq km
Population in 2016: 4,831
Next Election: Oct. 15, 2022 (4 year terms)
Note: Member municipality: Fort Nelson; Tetsa River; Toad River.
Gary Foster, Mayor
Randy McLean, Chief Administrative Officer, 250-774-2541
Scott Barry, Director, Public Works, 250-774-2541
Erin La Vale, Director, Human Resources, 250-774-2541
Jack Stevenson, Director, Community Development & Planning, 250-774-2541
Harvey Woodland, Director, Recreation, 250-774-2541
Toni Thurbide, Director, Finance, 250-774-2541
Terry Cavaliere, Chief Building Inspector, 250-774-2541
Jaylene Arnold, Economic Development & Tourism Officer, 250-774-2541

Okanagan-Similkameen
101 Martin St.
Penticton, BC V2A 5J9
Tel: 250-492-0237
info@rdos.bc.ca
www.rdos.bc.ca
Other Information: Toll-Free Phone: 877-610-3737
Municipal Type: Regional Districts
Incorporated: March 4, 1966; *Area:* 10,411.68 sq km
Population in 2016: 83,022
Next Election: Oct. 15, 2022 (4 year terms)
Note: Member municipalities: Penticton; Summerland; Oliver; Osoyoos; Princeton; Keremeos.
Karla Kozakevich, Chair
Bill Newell, Chief Administrative Officer, 250-492-0237
John Kurvink, Chief Financial Officer, 250-490-4230
Mark Wood, General Manager, Community Services, 250-490-4132
Lisa Bloomfield, Manager, Engineering, 250-490-4229

Peace River
P.O. Box 810
1981 Alaska Ave.
Dawson Creek, BC V1G 4H8
Tel: 250-784-3200; *Fax:* 250-784-3201
prrd.dc@prrd.bc.ca
prrd.bc.ca
Other Information: Toll-Free Phone: 800-670-7773
Municipal Type: Regional Districts
Incorporated: Oct. 31, 1987; *Area:* 117,387.55 sq km
Population in 2016: 62,942
Next Election: Oct. 15, 2022 (4 year terms)
Note: Member municipalities: Dawson Creek; Fort St. John; Chetwynd; Hudson's Hope; Tumbler Ridge; Pouce Coupe; Taylor.
Brad Sperling, Chair
Shawn Dahlen, Chief Administrative Officer
Teri Vetter, Chief Financial Officer
Paulo Eichelberger, General Manager, Environmental Services
Trish Morgan, General Manager, Community Services

qathet
#202, 4675 Marine Ave.
Powell River, BC V8A 2M4
Tel: 604-485-2260; *Fax:* 604-485-2216
administration@qathet.ca
www.qathet.ca
Municipal Type: Regional Districts
Incorporated: Dec. 19, 1967; *Area:* 5,075.33 sq km
Population in 2016: 20,070
Next Election: Oct. 15, 2022 (4 year terms)
Note: Name changed to qathet Regional District in 2018 to avoid confusion with the City of Powell River. Member municipality: Powell River.
Patrick Brabazon, Chair
Al Radke, Chief Administrative Officer

Squamish-Lillooet
P.O. Box 219
1350 Aster St.
Pemberton, BC V0N 2L0
Tel: 604-894-6371; *Fax:* 604-894-6526
info@slrd.bc.ca
www.slrd.bc.ca
Other Information: Toll-Free Phone: 800-298-7753
Municipal Type: Regional Districts
Incorporated: Oct. 3, 1968; *Area:* 16,311.62 sq km
Population in 2016: 42,665
Next Election: Oct. 15, 2022 (4 year terms)
Note: Member municipalities: Squamish; Whistler; Pemberton; Lillooet.
Tony Rainbow, Chair

Strathcona
#301, 990 Cedar St.
Campbell River, BC V9W 7Z8
Tel: 250-830-6700; *Fax:* 250-830-6710
www.strathconard.ca
Other Information: Toll-Free Phone: 877-830-2990
Municipal Type: Regional Districts
Incorporated: Feb. 15, 2008; *Area:* 18,278.06 sq km
Population in 2016: 44,671
Next Election: Oct. 15, 2022 (4 year terms)
Note: Member municipalities: Campbell River; Gold River; Sayward; Tahsis; Zeballos.
Michele Babchuk, Chair, 250-830-6700
David Leitch, Chief Administrative Officer, 250-830-6703

Sunshine Coast
1975 Field Rd.
Sechelt, BC V0N 3A1
Tel: 604-885-6800; *Fax:* 604-885-7909
info@scrd.ca
www.scrd.ca
Other Information: Toll-Free Phone: 800-687-5753
Municipal Type: Regional Districts
Incorporated: Jan. 4, 1967; *Area:* 3,773.73 sq km
Population in 2016: 29,970
Next Election: Oct. 15, 2022 (4 year terms)
Note: Member municipalities: Sechelt; Gibsons.
Lori Pratt, Chair
Dean McKinley, Chief Administrative Officer

Thompson-Nicola
#300, 465 Victoria St.
Kamloops, BC V2C 2A9
Tel: 250-377-8673; *Fax:* 250-372-5048
admin@tnrd.ca
www.tnrd.ca
Other Information: Toll-Free Phone: 877-377-8673
Municipal Type: Regional Districts
Incorporated: Nov. 24, 1967; *Area:* 44,449.42 sq km

Population in 2016: 132,663
Next Election: Oct. 15, 2022 (4 year terms)
Note: Member municipalities: Ashcroft; Barriere; Cache Creek;
Chase; Clearwater; Clinton; Kamloops; Logan Lake; Lytton;
Merritt; Sun Peaks.
Kenneth Gillis, Chair
Randy Diehl, Interim Chief Administrative Officer, 250-377-8673
Ron Storie, Director, Community Services, 250-377-8673
Doug Rae, Director, Finance, 250-378-7050
Jason Tomlin, Manager, Fire Protection Services, 250-377-2598

Major Municipalities in British Columbia

Abbotsford
32315 South Fraser Way
Abbotsford, BC V2T 1W7
Tel: 604-853-2281; *Fax:* 604-853-1934
www.abbotsford.ca
Municipal Type: City
Incorporated: Jan. 1, 1995; *Area:* 375.55 sq km
County or District: Fraser Valley; *Population in 2016:* 141,397
Provincial Electoral District(s): Abbotsford-Mission; Abbotsford
South; Abbotsford West
Federal Electoral District(s): Abbotsford; Langley-Aldergrove;
Mission-Matsqui-Fraser Canyon
Next Election: Oct. 15, 2022 (4 year terms)
Henry Braun, Mayor, 604-864-5500, Fax: 604-853-1934
Bruce Banman, Councillor, 604-851-4168
Les Barkman, Councillor, 604-851-4168
Sandy Blue, Councillor, 604-851-4168
Kelly Chahal, Councillor, 604-851-4168
Brenda Falk, Councillor, 604-851-4168
Dave Loewen, Councillor, 604-851-4168
Patricia Ross, Councillor, 604-851-4168
Ross Siemens, Councillor, 604-851-4168
Peter Sparanese, City Manager, 604-864-5501
Rob Isaac, General Manager, Engineering & Regional Utilities,
604-864-5685
Mary Morrison-Clark, General Manager, Parks, Recreation &
Culture, 604-859-3134
Mark Neill, Acting General Manager, Planning & Development,
604-864-5513
Don Beer, Fire Chief, 604-853-3566

Burnaby
4949 Canada Way
Burnaby, BC V5G 1M2
Tel: 604-294-7944
www.burnaby.ca
Municipal Type: City
Incorporated: Sept. 22, 1892; *Area:* 90.61 sq km
County or District: Metro Vancouver; *Population in 2016:*
232,755
Provincial Electoral District(s): Burnaby-Edmonds; Burnaby
North; Burnaby-Deer Lake; Burnaby-Lougheed
Federal Electoral District(s): Burnaby North-Seymour; Burnaby
South; New Westminster-Burnaby
Next Election: Oct. 15, 2022 (4 year terms)
Mike Hurley, Mayor
Pietro Calendrino, Councillor
Sav Dhaliwal, Councillor
Dan Johnson, Councillor
Colleen Jordan, Councillor
Joe Keithley, Councillor
Paul McDonell, Councillor
Nick Volkow, Councillor
James Wang, Councillor
Lambert S.H. Chu, City Manager, 604-294-7101
Dave Critchley, Director, Public Safety & Community Services
Dipak Dattani, Director, Corporate Services
Dave Ellenwood, Director, Parks, Recreation & Cultural Services
Leon Gous, Director, Engineering
Noreen Kassam, Director, Finance
Ed Kozak, Director, Planning & Building
Joe Robertson, Fire Chief

Campbell River
301 St. Ann's Rd.
Campbell River, BC V9W 4C7
Tel: 250-286-5700
info@campbellriver.ca
www.campbellriver.ca
Municipal Type: City
Incorporated: June 24, 1947; *Area:* 143 sq km
County or District: Strathcona; *Population in 2016:* 32,588
Provincial Electoral District(s): North Island
Federal Electoral District(s): North Island-Powell River
Next Election: Oct. 15, 2022 (4 year terms)
Andy Adams, Mayor, 250-286-5708
Michele Babchuk, Councillor

Charlie Cornfield, Councillor
Kermit Dahl, Councillor
Colleen Evans, Councillor
Ron Kerr, Councillor
Claire Moglove, Councillor
Deborah Sargent, City Manager, 250-286-5740
Ron Neufeld, Deputy City Manager, 250-286-5765
Ron Bowles, General Manager, Community Development,
250-286-5759
Dave Morris, General Manager, Asset & Operations,
250-286-5739
Alaina Maher, Manager, Finance, 250-286-5780
Colleen Tillapaugh, Manager, Human Resources, 250-286-5795
Lynn Wark, Manager, Recreation & Culture, 250-923-7911
Thomas Doherty, Fire Chief

Chilliwack
8550 Young Rd
Chilliwack, BC V2P 8A4
Tel: 604-792-9311; *Fax:* 604-795-8443
info@chilliwack.com
www.chilliwack.com
Municipal Type: City
Incorporated: Jan. 1, 1980; *Area:* 261.65 sq km
County or District: Fraser Valley; *Population in 2016:* 83,788
Provincial Electoral District(s): Chilliwack; Chilliwack-Kent
Federal Electoral District(s): Chilliwack-Hope
Next Election: Oct. 15, 2022 (4 year terms)
Kenneth Popove, Mayor
Chris Kloot, Councillor
Sue Knott, Councillor
Jason Lum, Councillor
Bud R. Mercer, Councillor
Jeff E. Shields, Councillor
Harv H. Westeringh, Councillor
Peter Monteith, Chief Administrative Officer, 604-793-2903, Fax:
604-792-2561
Chris Crossman, Deputy CAO & Director, Development &
Regulatory Enforcement Services, 604-793-2999
David Blain, Director, Planning & Engineering, 604-793-2907
Jennifer Kooistra, Director, Corporate Services, 604-793-2986
Glen MacPherson, Director, Operations, 604-793-2810
Glen Savard, Director, Finance, 604-793-2920
Ian Josephson, Fire Chief, 604-792-8713

Colwood
3300 Wishart Rd.
Victoria, BC V9C 1R1
Tel: 250-478-5541; *Fax:* 250-478-7516
colwood.ca
Municipal Type: City
Incorporated: June 24, 1985; *Area:* 17.67 sq km
County or District: Capital; *Population in 2016:* 16,859
Provincial Electoral District(s): Esquimalt-Metchosin
Federal Electoral District(s): Esquimalt-Saanich-Sooke
Next Election: Oct. 15, 2022 (4 year terms)
Rob C. Martin, Mayor, 250-216-6639, Fax: 250-478-7516
Michael S. Baxter, Councillor
Cynthia Day, Councillor, 250-478-5999
Dean Jantzen, Councillor
Doug Kobayashi, Councillor
Gordie Logan, Councillor
Stewart Parkinson, Councillor
Robert Earl, Chief Administrative Officer
Iain Bourhill, Director, Long Range Planning & Sustainability
Nikki Hoglund, Director, Public Works
Alan Thomas, Director, Finance
Selina Williams, Director, Corporate Services
John Cassidy, Fire Chief

Comox
Town Hall
1809 Beaufort Ave.
Comox, BC V9M 1R9
Tel: 250-339-2202; *Fax:* 250-339-7110
town@comox.ca
www.comox.ca
Municipal Type: City
Incorporated: Jan. 14, 1946; *Area:* 16.74 sq km
County or District: Comox Valley; *Population in 2016:* 14,028
Provincial Electoral District(s): Courtenay-Comox
Federal Electoral District(s): North Island-Powell River
Next Election: Oct. 15, 2022 (4 year terms)
Russ Arnott, Mayor
Alex Bissinger, Councillor
Ken Grant, Councillor
Stephanie McGowan, Councillor
Pat McKenna, Councillor
Nicole Minions, Councillor
Maureen Swift, Councillor
Jordan Wall, Chief Administrative Officer
Clive Freundlich, Director, Finance

Ted Hagmeier, Director, Recreation
Shelley Ashfield, Municipal Engineer
Gord Schreiner, Fire Chief

Coquitlam
3000 Guildford Way
Coquitlam, BC V3B 7N2
Tel: 604-927-3000
www.coquitlam.ca
Municipal Type: City
Incorporated: July 25, 1891; *Area:* 122.30 sq km
County or District: Metro Vancouver; *Population in 2016:*
139,284
Provincial Electoral District(s): Port Coquitlam; Port
Moody-Coquitlam
Federal Electoral District(s): Coquitlam-Port Coquitlam; Port
Moody-Coquitlam
Next Election: Oct. 15, 2022 (4 year terms)
Richard Stewart, Mayor, 604-927-3001
Brent Asmundson, Councillor
Craig Hodge, Councillor
Steve Kim, Councillor
Trish Mandewo, Councillor
Dennis Marsden, Councillor, 604-306-0686
Teri Towner, Councillor, 604-617-6042
Chris Wilson, Councillor
Bonita Zarrillo, Councillor
Peter Steblin, City Manager, 604-927-3006
Jaime Boan, General Manager, Engineering & Public Works,
604-927-3504
Michelle Hunt, General Manager, Finance & Technology,
604-927-3531
Jim McIntyre, General Manager, Planning & Development
Jim Ogloff, Fire Chief, 604-927-6400

Courtenay
830 Cliffe Ave.
Courtenay, BC V9N 2J7
Tel: 250-334-4441; *Fax:* 250-334-4241
info@courtenay.ca
www.courtenay.ca
Municipal Type: City
Incorporated: Jan. 1, 1915; *Area:* 32.41 sq km
County or District: Comox Valley; *Population in 2016:* 25,599
Provincial Electoral District(s): Courtenay-Comox
Federal Electoral District(s): Courtenay-Alberni; North
Island-Powell River
Next Election: Oct. 15, 2022 (4 year terms)
Bob Wells, Mayor
Will Cole-Hamilton, Councillor
David Frisch, Councillor
Doug Hillian, Councillor
Melanie McCollum, Councillor
Wendy Morin, Councillor
Manno Theos, Councillor
David Allen, Chief Administrative Officer, 250-703-4854
Don Bardonnex, Fire Chief

Cranbrook
40 - 10th Ave. South
Cranbrook, BC V1C 2M8
Tel: 250-426-4211; *Fax:* 250-426-4026
info@cranbrook.ca
www.cranbrook.ca
Other Information: Toll-Free Phone: 800-728-2728
Municipal Type: City
Incorporated: Nov. 1, 1905; *Area:* 32.00 sq km
County or District: East Kootenay; *Population in 2016:* 20,047
Provincial Electoral District(s): Kootenay East
Federal Electoral District(s): Kootenay-Columbia
Next Election: Oct. 15, 2022 (4 year terms)
Lee Pratt, Mayor, 250-489-0200
Norma Blissett, Councillor
John Hudak, Councillor
Wesly Graham, Councillor
Ron Popoff, Councillor
Mike Peabody, Councillor
Wayne Price, Councillor
Ron Fraser, Interim Chief Administrative Officer
Derrick Anderson, Director, Public Works
Chris New, Director, Community Services
Charlotte Osborne, Director, Finance & Computer Services
Scott Driver, Director, Fire & Emergency Services

Dawson Creek
P.O. Box 150
10105 - 12A St.
Dawson Creek, BC V1G 4G4
Tel: 250-784-3600; *Fax:* 250-782-3203
admin@dawsoncreek.ca
www.dawsoncreek.ca
Other Information: General Fax: 250-782-3352

Municipal Type: City
Incorporated: May 26, 1936; *Area:* 24.37 sq km
County or District: Peace River; *Population in 2016:* 12,178
Provincial Electoral District(s): Peace River South
Federal Electoral District(s): Prince George-Peace River-Northern Rockies
Next Election: Oct. 15, 2022 (4 year terms)
Dale Bumstead, Mayor, 250-784-3616, Fax: 250-782-3203
Jerimy Earl, Councillor, 250-219-0482
Paul Gevatkoff, Councillor, 250-782-8792
Amy Kaempf, Councillor, 250-784-4145
Charlie Parslow, Councillor, 250-782-1783
Shaely Wilbur, Councillor, 250-719-9492
Blair Lekstrom, Chief Administrative Officer, 250-784-3683, Fax: 250-782-3203
Flavia Rossi Donovan, Chief Financial Officer, 250-784-3624, Fax: 250-782-3352
Kevin Henderson, General Manager, Development Services, 250-784-3622, Fax: 250-782-3352
Ross deBoer, General Manager, Community Services, 250-784-3605, Fax: 250-782-3203
Bob Fulton, Fire Chief, 250-782-9898, Fax: 250-784-3638

Fort St. John
10631 - 100th St.
Fort St John, BC V1J 3Z5
Tel: 250-787-8150; *Fax:* 250-787-8181
info@fortstjohn.ca
www.fortstjohn.ca
Municipal Type: City
Incorporated: Dec. 31, 1947; *Area:* 26.27 sq km
County or District: Peace River; *Population in 2016:* 20,155
Provincial Electoral District(s): Peace River North
Federal Electoral District(s): Prince George-Peace River-Northern Rockies
Next Election: Oct. 15, 2022 (4 year terms)
Lori Ackerman, Mayor, 250-787-8160
Trevor Bolin, Councillor, 250-262-7334
Becky Grimsrud, Councillor
Lilia Hansen, Councillor, 250-261-3148
Gord Klassen, Councillor
Byron Stewart, Councillor
Tony Zabinsky, Councillor
Dianne Hunter, City Manager, 250-787-8150
Moira Green, General Manager, Community Services, 250-787-5787
Victor Shopland, General Manager, Integrated Services, 250-787-8162
David Joy, General Manager, Corporate Services, 250-794-3300
Darrell Blades, Fire Chief, 250-787-8000

Kamloops
City Hall
7 Victoria St. West
Kamloops, BC V2C 1A2
Tel: 250-828-3311
info@kamloops.ca
www.kamloops.ca
Municipal Type: City
Incorporated: Oct. 17, 1967; *Area:* 299.25 sq km
County or District: Thompson-Nicola; *Population in 2016:* 90,280
Provincial Electoral District(s): Kamloops-North Thompson; Kamloops-South Thompson
Federal Electoral District(s): Kamloops-Thompson-Cariboo
Next Election: Oct. 15, 2022 (4 year terms)
Kenneth Christian, Mayor, 250-828-3494
Dale Bass, Councillor, 250-320-2840
Dieter Dudy, Councillor, 250-318-9369
Sadie Hunter, Councillor, 250-318-2207
Mike O'Reilly, Councillor, 250-819-3165
Bill Sarai, Councillor, 250-819-8527
Kathy Sinclair, Councillor, 250-320-5467
Arjun Singh, Councillor, 250-320-6532
Denis Walsh, Councillor, 250-299-5454
David Trawin, Chief Administrative Officer, 250-828-3498
Kathy Humphrey, Director, Corporate Services
Jen Fretz, Director, Civic Operations
Byron McCorkell, Director, Community & Protective Services
Mike Adams, Fire Chief

Kelowna
City Hall
1435 Water St.
Kelowna, BC V1Y 1J4
Tel: 250-469-8500; *Fax:* 250-862-3399
ask@kelowna.ca
www.kelowna.ca
Municipal Type: City
Incorporated: May 4, 1905; *Area:* 211.85 sq km
County or District: Central Okanagan; *Population in 2016:* 127,380
Provincial Electoral District(s): Kelowna-Mission; Kelowna-Lake Country; Kelowna West
Federal Electoral District(s): Central Okanagan-Similkameen-Nicola; Kelowna-Lake Country
Next Election: Oct. 15, 2022 (4 year terms)
Colin Basran, Mayor, 250-469-8980
Maxine DeHart, Councillor, 250-469-8865
Ryan Donn, Councillor, 250-469-8674
Gail Given, Councillor, 250-469-8677
Charlie Hodge, Councillor, 250-469-8896
Brad Sieben, Councillor, 250-215-4377
Mohini Singh, Councillor, 250-469-8949
Luke Stack, Councillor, 250-878-4990
Loyal Woolridge, Councillor, 250-863-0149
Doug Gilchrist, City Manager
Joe Creron, Deputy City Manager, Operations
Ian Wilson, Manager, Infrastructure Operations
Travis Whiting, Fire Chief

Langford
877 Goldstream Ave., 2nd Fl.
Victoria, BC V9B 2X8
Tel: 250-478-7882
www.cityoflangford.ca
Other Information: Alt. Phone: 250-478-7770
Municipal Type: City
Incorporated: Dec. 8, 1992; *Area:* 39.94 sq km
County or District: Capital; *Population in 2016:* 35,342
Provincial Electoral District(s): Langford-Juan de Fuca
Federal Electoral District(s): Cowichan-Malahat-Langford
Next Election: Oct. 15, 2022 (4 year terms)
Stewart Young, Mayor
Denise Blackwell, Councillor
Matthew Sahlstrom, Councillor
Lanny Seaton, Councillor
Norma Stewart, Councillor
Lillian Szpak, Councillor
Roger Wade, Councillor
Jim Bowden, Administrator
Michelle Mahovlich, Director, Engineering
Matthew Baldwin, City Planner

Langley
20399 Douglas Cres.
Langley, BC V3A 4B3
Tel: 604-514-2800; *Fax:* 604-530-4371
info@langleycity.ca
city.langley.bc.ca
Municipal Type: City
Incorporated: March 15, 1955; *Area:* 10.22 sq km
County or District: Metro Vancouver; *Population in 2016:* 25,888
Provincial Electoral District(s): Langley
Federal Electoral District(s): Cloverdale-Langley City; Langley-Aldergrove
Next Election: Oct. 15, 2022 (4 year terms)
Val van den Broek, Mayor
Paul Albrecht, Councillor
Teri James, Councillor
Gayle Martin, Councillor
Nathan Pachal, Councillor
Rudy Storteboom, Councillor
Rosemary Wallace, Councillor
Francis Cheung, Chief Administrative Officer

Nanaimo
455 Wallace St.
Nanaimo, BC V9R 5J6
Tel: 250-754-4251
legislativeservices.office@nanaimo.ca
www.nanaimo.ca
Municipal Type: City
Incorporated: Dec. 24, 1874; *Area:* 90.76 sq km
County or District: Nanaimo; *Population in 2016:* 90,504
Provincial Electoral District(s): Nanaimo-North Cowichan; Nanaimo
Federal Electoral District(s): Courtenay-Alberni; Nanaimo-Ladysmith
Next Election: Oct. 15, 2022 (4 year terms)
Leonard Krog, Mayor, 250-755-4400
Sheryl Armstrong, Councillor, 250-668-6748
Don Bonner, Councillor, 250-755-6146
Tyler Brown, Councillor, 250-713-5781
Ben Geselbracht, Councillor, 250-713-4173
Erin Hemmens, Councillor, 250-268-4552
Zeni Maartman, Councillor, 250-668-9107
Ian Thorpe, Councillor, 250-713-9135
Jim Turley, Councillor, 250-668-5226
Jake Rudolph, Chief Administrative Officer, 250-755-4401
Laura Mercer, Director, Finance
Richard Harding, General Manager, Parks, Recreation & Environment, 250-755-7516
Dale Lindsay, General Manager, Development Services, 250-755-4493

Karen Fry, Fire Chief, 250-755-4583

Nelson
#101, 310 Ward St.
Nelson, BC V1L 5S4
Tel: 250-352-5511; *Fax:* 250-352-2131
www.nelson.ca
Municipal Type: City
Incorporated: March 18, 1897; *Area:* 11.95 sq km
County or District: Central Kootenay; *Population in 2016:* 10,572
Provincial Electoral District(s): Nelson-Creston
Federal Electoral District(s): Kootenay-Columbia
Next Election: Oct. 15, 2022 (4 year terms)
John Dooley, Mayor
Brittny Anderson, Councillor
Rik Logtenberg, Councillor
Janice Morrison, Councillor
Keith Page, Councillor
Calvin Renwick, Councillor
Jesse Woodward, Councillor
Kevin Cormack, City Manager, 250-352-8203
Colin McClure, Chief Financial Officer, 250-352-8235
Pam Mierau, Manager, Development Services, 250-352-8217
Len MacCharles, Fire Chief, 250-352-8264

New Westminster
511 Royal Ave.
New Westminster, BC V3L 1H9
Tel: 604-521-3711; *Fax:* 604-521-3895
info@newwestcity.ca
www.newwestcity.ca
Municipal Type: City
Incorporated: July 16, 1860; *Area:* 15.63 sq km
County or District: Metro Vancouver; *Population in 2016:* 70,996
Provincial Electoral District(s): New Westminster
Federal Electoral District(s): New Westminster-Burnaby
Next Election: Oct. 15, 2022 (4 year terms)
Jonathan Cote, Mayor
Chinu Das, Councillor
Patrick Johnstone, Councillor
Jaimie McEvoy, Councillor
Nadine Nakagawa, Councillor
Chuck Puchmayr, Councillor
Mary Trentadue, Councillor
Lisa Spitale, Chief Administrative Officer
Colleen Ponzini, Chief Financial Officer
Richard Fong, Director, Human Resources
Emilie Adin, Director, Development Services
Jim Lowrie, Director, Engineering Services
Rod Carle, General Manager, Electric Utility
Tim Armstrong, Fire Chief, Fire & Rescue Services

North Vancouver
141 West 14th St.
North Vancouver, BC V7M 1H9
Tel: 604-985-7761; *Fax:* 604-985-9417
info@cnv.org
www.cnv.org
Municipal Type: City
Incorporated: May 13, 1907; *Area:* 11.85 sq km
County or District: Metro Vancouver; *Population in 2016:* 52,898
Provincial Electoral District(s): N. Vancouver-Lonsdale; N. Vancouver-Seymour
Federal Electoral District(s): North Vancouver; Burnaby North-Seymour
Next Election: Oct. 15, 2022 (4 year terms)
Linda Buchanan, Mayor
Holly Back, Councillor
Don Bell, Councillor
Angela Girard, Councillor
Tina Hu, Councillor
Jessica McIlroy, Councillor
Tony Valente, Councillor
Leanne McCarthy, Chief Administrative Officer, 604-990-4242
Mark Jefferson, Director, Human Resources, 604-990-4241
Douglas Pope, City Engineer, 604-983-7337
Ben Themens, Director, Finance, 604-983-7312
Jeff Klochnyk, Manager, Public Works, 604-983-7391
Greg Schalk, Fire Chief

Parksville
P.O. Box 1390
100 Jensen Ave. East
Parksville, BC V9P 2H3
Tel: 250-248-6144; *Fax:* 250-248-6650
info@parksville.ca
www.parksville.ca
Municipal Type: City
Incorporated: June 19, 1945; *Area:* 14.56 sq km
County or District: Nanaimo; *Population in 2016:* 12,514
Provincial Electoral District(s): Parksville-Qualicum

Federal Electoral District(s): Courtenay-Alberni
Next Election: Oct. 15, 2022 (4 year terms)
Ed Mayne, Mayor
Mark Chandler, Councillor
Adam Fras, Councillor
Al Greir, Councillor
Doug O'Brien, Councillor
Teresa Patterson, Councillor
Marilyn Wilson, Councillor
Keeva Kehler, Chief Administrative Officer, 250-954-4660
Lucky Butterworth, Director, Finance, 250-954-3063
Joe Doxey, Acting Director, Engineering
Blaine Russell, Director, Community Planning & Building, 250-954-4673
Marc Norris, Fire Chief, 250-954-4695

Penticton
171 Main St.
Penticton, BC V2A 5A9
Tel: 250-490-2400; *Fax:* 250-490-2402
ask@penticton.ca
www.penticton.ca
Municipal Type: City
Incorporated: Jan. 1, 1909; *Area:* 42.10 sq km
County or District: Okanagan-Similkameen; *Population in 2016:* 33,761
Provincial Electoral District(s): Penticton
Federal Electoral District(s): South Okanagan-West Kootenay
Next Election: Oct. 15, 2022 (4 year terms)
John Vassilaki, Mayor
Julius Bloomfield, Councillor
Jake Kimberley, Councillor
Frank Regehr, Councillor
Katie Robinson, Councillor
Judy Sentes, Councillor
Campbell Watt, Councillor
Donny van Dyk, Chief Administrative Officer, 250-490-2407
Jim Bauer, Chief Financial Officer, 250-490-2480
Bregje Kozak, Director, Recreation & Facilities, 250-490-2579
Blake Laven, Director, Development Services, 250-490-2528
Kerri Lockwood, Director, People & Safety Strategy, 250-490-2470
Larry Watkinson, Fire Chief, 250-490-2309

Pitt Meadows
Municipal Hall
12007 Harris Rd.
Pitt Meadows, BC V3Y 2B5
Tel: 604-465-5454; *Fax:* 604-465-2404
info@pittmeadows.bc.ca
www.pittmeadows.bc.ca
Municipal Type: City
Incorporated: April 25, 1914; *Area:* 86.51 sq km
County or District: Metro Vancouver; *Population in 2016:* 18,573
Provincial Electoral District(s): Maple Ridge-Pitt Meadows
Federal Electoral District(s): Pitt Meadows-Maple Ridge
Next Election: Oct. 15, 2022 (4 year terms)
Note: Effective Jan. 1, 2007, Pitt Meadows' designation was changed from a district to a city.
Bill Dingwall, Mayor
Mike Hayes, Councillor
Nicole MacDonald, Councillor
Bob Meachen, Councillor
Tracy Miyashita, Councillor, 604-250-2336
Gwen O'Connell, Councillor
Anena Simpson, Councillor
Mark Roberts, Chief Administrative Officer, 604-465-2449
Cheryl Harding, Director, Financial Services, 604-465-2461
Samantha Maki, Director, Operations & Engineering
Stephanie St. Jean, Director, Corporate Services, 604-465-2448
Mike Larson, Fire Chief, 604-465-2401

Port Alberni
4850 Argyle St.
Port Alberni, BC V9Y 1V8
Tel: 250-723-2146; *Fax:* 250-723-1003
citypa@portalberni.ca
www.portalberni.ca
Municipal Type: City
Incorporated: Oct. 28, 1967; *Area:* 19.76 sq km
County or District: Alberni-Clayoquot; *Population in 2016:* 17,678
Provincial Electoral District(s): Mid Island-Pacific Rim
Federal Electoral District(s): Courtenay-Alberni
Next Election: Oct. 15, 2022 (4 year terms)
Sharie Minions, Mayor, 250-735-9444
Ron Corbeil, Councillor
Debbie Haggard, Councillor
Ron Paulson, Councillor
Helen Poon, Councillor
Cindy Solda, Councillor
Dan Washington, Councillor
Tim Pley, Chief Administrative Officer, 250-720-2824

Andrew McGifford, Director, Finance, 250-720-2821
Wilf Taekema, Director, Engineering & Public Works, 250-720-2838
Mike Owens, Fire Chief, 250-720-2540

Port Coquitlam
2580 Shaughnessy St.
Port Coquitlam, BC V3C 2A8
Tel: 604-927-5411; *Fax:* 604-927-5360
info@portcoquitlam.ca
www.portcoquitlam.ca
Municipal Type: City
Incorporated: March 7, 1913; *Area:* 29.17 sq km
County or District: Metro Vancouver; *Population in 2016:* 58,612
Provincial Electoral District(s): Port Coquitlam
Federal Electoral District(s): Coquitlam-Port Coquitlam
Next Election: Oct. 15, 2022 (4 year terms)
Brad West, Mayor, 604-927-5410
Steve Darling, Councillor, 604-788-7391
Laura Dupont, Councillor, 604-328-8026
Nancy McCurrach, Councillor, 604-837-9484
Darrell Penner, Councillor, 604-941-9823
Glenn Pollock, Councillor, 604-771-4415
Dean Washington, Councillor, 604-317-7045
Kristen Dixon, Chief Administrative Officer
Forrest Smith, Director, Engineering & Public Works
Lisa Grant, Director, Development Services
Steve Traviss, Director, Human Resources, 604-927-5417
Robin Wishart, Director, Corporate Support, 604-927-5302
Karen Grommada, Director, Finance
Robert Kipps, Fire Chief

Port Moody
P.O. Box 36
100 Newport Dr.
Port Moody, BC V3H 3E1
Tel: 604-469-4500; *Fax:* 604-469-4550
info@portmoody.ca
www.portmoody.ca
Municipal Type: City
Incorporated: March 11, 1913; *Area:* 25.89 sq km
County or District: Metro Vancouver; *Population in 2016:* 33,551
Provincial Electoral District(s): Port Moody-Coquitlam
Federal Electoral District(s): Port Moody-Coquitlam
Next Election: Oct. 15, 2022 (4 year terms)
Rob Vagramov, Mayor, 604-469-4515
Diana Dilworth, Councillor, 604-469-4516
Meghan Lahti, Councillor, 604-469-4586
Amy Lubik, Councillor, 604-469-4584
Hunter Madsen, Councillor, 604-469-4585
Steve Milani, Councillor, 604-469-4517
Zoe Royer, Councillor, 604-469-4518
Tim Savoie, City Manager
Ron Coulson, Fire Chief

Powell River
6910 Duncan St.
Powell River, BC V8A 1V4
Tel: 604-485-6291; *Fax:* 604-485-8644
info@powellriver.ca
www.powellriver.ca
Municipal Type: City
Incorporated: Oct. 15, 1955; *Area:* 28.91 sq km
County or District: Powell River; *Population in 2016:* 13,57
Provincial Electoral District(s): Powell River-Sunshine Coast
Federal Electoral District(s): Courtenay-Alberni; North Island-Powell River
Next Election: Oct. 15, 2022 (4 year terms)
David Formosa, Mayor, 604-485-8601
George Doubt, Councillor, 604-414-9383
Cindy Elliott, Councillor, 604-223-0054
Maggie Hathaway, Councillor
CaroleAnn Leishman, Councillor
Jim Palm, Councillor
Rob Southcott, Councillor
Russell Brewer, Chief Administrative Officer
Terry Peters, Fire Chief

Prince George
City Hall
1100 Patricia Blvd.
Prince George, BC V2L 3V9
Tel: 250-561-7600
cityclerk@city.pg.bc.ca
princegeorge.ca
Municipal Type: City
Incorporated: March 6, 1915; *Area:* 318.26 sq km
County or District: Fraser-Fort George; *Population in 2016:* 74,003
Provincial Electoral District(s): Pr. George-Valemount; Pr. George-Mackenzie
Federal Electoral District(s): Cariboo-Prince George; Prince

George-Peace River-Northern Rockies
Next Election: Oct. 15, 2022 (4 year terms)
Lyn Hall, Mayor, 250-561-7609
Frank Everitt, Councillor
Garth Frizzell, Councillor, 250-613-2363
Murry Krause, Councillor
Terri McConnachie, Councillor
Cori Ramsay, Councillor
Kyle Sampson, Councillor
Susan Scott, Councillor
Brian Skakun, Councillor
Kathleen Soltis, City Manager
Gina Layte Liston, Director, Engineering & Public Works
Kris Dalio, Director, Finance
Ian Whitman, General Manager, Planning & Development
Ian Wells, General Manager, Planning & Development
John Iverson, Fire Chief

Prince Rupert
424 - 3rd Ave. West
Prince Rupert, BC V8J 1L7
Tel: 250-627-0934; *Fax:* 250-627-0999
cityhall@princerupert.ca
www.princerupert.ca
Municipal Type: City
Incorporated: March 10, 1910; *Area:* 66.28 sq km
County or District: Skeena-Queen Charlotte; *Population in 2016:* 12,220
Provincial Electoral District(s): North Coast
Federal Electoral District(s): Skeena-Bulkley Valley
Next Election: Oct. 15, 2022 (4 year terms)
Lee Brain, Mayor, 250-627-0930
Nick Adey, Councillor
Barry Cunningham, Councillor
Blair Mirau, Councillor
Wade Niesh, Councillor
Gurvinder Randhawa, Councillor
Reid Skelton-Morven, Councillor
Robert Long, City Manager
Zeno Krekic, City Planner
Corinne Bomben, Chief Financial Officer, 250-627-0934
David Geronazzo, Director, Parks, Recreation & Heritage
Dave Mckenzie, Fire Chief, 250-624-5115

Quesnel
410 Kinchant St.
Quesnel, BC V2J 7J5
Tel: 250-992-2111; *Fax:* 250-992-2206
cityhall@quesnel.ca
www.quesnel.ca
Municipal Type: City
Incorporated: March 21, 1928; *Area:* 35.39 sq km
County or District: Cariboo; *Population in 2016:* 9,879
Provincial Electoral District(s): Cariboo North
Federal Electoral District(s): Cariboo-Prince George
Next Election: Oct. 15, 2022 (4 year terms)
Bob Simpson, Mayor
Scott Elliott, Councillor
Tony Goulet, Councillor
Ron Paull, Councillor
Laurey-Anne Roodenburg, Councillor
Martin Runge, Councillor
Mitch Vik, Councillor
Byron Johnson, Chief Administrative Officer
Kari Bolton, Director, Corporate & Financial Services
Chris Coben, Director, Infrastructure & Capital Works
Matt Thomas, Director, Public Works Operations
Sylvian Gauthier, Fire Chief & Director, Emergency Services

Richmond
6911 No. 3 Rd.
Richmond, BC V6Y 2C1
Tel: 604-276-4000
infocentre@richmond.ca
www.richmond.ca
Other Information: TTY: 604-276-4311
Municipal Type: City
Incorporated: Nov. 10, 1879; *Area:* 129.27 sq km
County or District: Metro Vancouver; *Population in 2016:* 198,309
Provincial Electoral District(s): Richmond North Centre; Richmond-Queensborough; Richmond South Centre; Richmond-Steveston
Federal Electoral District(s): Richmond Centre; Steveston-Richmond East
Next Election: Oct. 15, 2022 (4 year terms)
Malcolm D. Brodie, Mayor
Chak Au, Councillor
Carol Day, Councillor
Kelly Greene, Councillor
Alexa Loo, Councillor
Bill McNulty, Councillor

Linda McPhail, Councillor
Harold Steves, Councillor
Michael Wolfe, Councillor
George Duncan, Chief Administrative Officer, 604-276-4336,
Fax: 604-276-4222
Serena Lusk, General Manager, Community Services,
604-276-4068
Cecilia Achiam, General Manager, Community Safety,
604-276-4104
Joe Erceg, General Manager, Planning & Development,
604-276-4214
John Irving, P. Eng., General Manager, Engineering & Public
Works, 604-276-4140, Fax: 604-276-4222
Andrew Nazareth, General Manager, Finance & Corporate
Services, 604-276-4095
Laurie Bachynski, Director, Human Resources, 604-276-4105
Tim Wilkinson, Fire Chief

Salmon Arm
P.O. Box 40
500 - 2nd Ave. NE
Salmon Arm, BC V1E 4N2
Tel: 250-803-4000; *Fax:* 250-803-4041
www.salmonarm.ca
Municipal Type: City
Incorporated: May 15, 1905; *Area:* 155.28 sq km
County or District: Columbia-Shuswap; *Population in 2016:*
17,706
Provincial Electoral District(s): Shuswap
Federal Electoral District(s): North Okanagan-Shuswap
Next Election: Oct. 15, 2022 (4 year terms)
Alan Harrison, Mayor, 250-803-4034
Debbie Cannon, Councillor, 250-803-4075
Chad Eliason, Councillor, 250-803-4072
Kevin Flynn, Councillor, 250-803-4073
Tim Lavery, Councillor, 250-803-4076
Sylvia Lindgren, Councillor, 250-803-4078
Louise Wallace-Richmond, Councillor, 250-803-4077
Carl Bannister, Chief Administrative Officer, 250-803-4033
Chelsea Van de Cappelle, Chief Financial Officer, 250-803-4032
Robert Niewenhuizen, Director, Engineering & Public Works,
250-803-4017
Darin Gerow, Manager, Roads & Parks, 250-803-4088
Brad Shirley, Fire Chief, 250-803-4060

Surrey
14245 - 56th Ave.
Surrey, BC V3X 3A2
Tel: 604-591-4011; *Fax:* 604-591-8731
www.surrey.ca
Municipal Type: City
Incorporated: Nov. 10, 1879; *Area:* 316.41 sq km
County or District: Metro Vancouver; *Population in 2016:*
517,887
Provincial Electoral District(s): Surrey-Cloverdale; Surrey-Green
Timbers; Surrey-Newton; Surrey-Panorama; Surrey-Whalley;
Surrey-White Rock; Surrey-Guildford; Surrey-Fleetwood
Federal Electoral District(s): Cloverdale-Langley City;
Fleetwood-Port Kells; South Surrey-White Rock; Surrey Centre;
Surrey-Newton
Next Election: Oct. 15, 2022 (4 year terms)
Doug McCallum, Mayor, 604-591-4126
Linda Annis, Councillor, 604-502-6037
Doug Elford, Councillor, 604-502-6033
Laura Guerra, Councillor, 604-502-6034
Brenda Locke, Councillor, 604-502-6032
Mandeep Nagra, Councillor, 604-502-6039
Allison Patton, Councillor, 604-502-6036
Steve Pettigrew, Councillor, 604-502-6038
Jack Singh Hundial, Councillor, 604-502-6035
Vince Lalonde, City Manager, 604-591-4122, Fax: 604-591-4357
Laurie Cavan, General Manager, Parks, Recreation & Culture,
604-598-5760, Fax: 604-598-5781
Jean Lamontagne, General Manager, Planning & Development,
604-591-4441, Fax: 604-591-2507
Scott Neuman, General Manager, Engineering, 604-591-4042,
Fax: 604-591-8693
Kam Grewal, General Manager, Finance
Larry Thomas, Fire Chief, 604-541-4011

Terrace
3215 Eby St.
Terrace, BC V8G 2X8
Tel: 250-635-6311; *Fax:* 250-638-4777
www.terrace.ca
Municipal Type: City
Incorporated: Dec. 31, 1927; *Area:* 57.36 sq km
County or District: Kitimat-Stikine; *Population in 2016:* 11,643
Provincial Electoral District(s): Skeena
Federal Electoral District(s): Skeena-Bulkley Valley
Next Election: Oct. 15, 2022 (4 year terms)
Carol Leclerc, Mayor

Sean Bujtas, Councillor
Lynne Christiansen, Councillor
James Cordeiro, Councillor
Brian Downie, Councillor
Jessica McCallum-Miller, Councillor
Evan Ramsay, Councillor
Heather Avison, Chief Administrative Officer, 250-638-4722
David Block, Director, Development Services, 250-615-4028
Lori Greenlaw, Director, Finance, 250-638-4731
Rob Schibli, Director, Public Works, 250-615-4043
John Klie, Fire Chief, 250-638-4742

Vancouver
453 West 12th Ave.
Vancouver, BC V5Y 1V4
Tel: 604-873-7000
info@vancouver.ca
www.vancouver.ca
Municipal Type: City
Incorporated: November 15, 2008; *Area:* 114.97 sq km
County or District: Metro Vancouver; *Population in 2016:*
631,486
Provincial Electoral District(s): Vancouver-Fairview; Vanc.-False
Creek; Vanc.-Fraserview; Vanc.-Hastings; Vanc. Kensington;
Vanc.-Kingsway; Vanc.-Langara; Vanc.-Mount Pleasant;
Vanc.-Point Grey; Vanc.-Quilchena; Vanc.-West End
Federal Electoral District(s): Vancouver Centre; Vancouver East;
Vancouver Granville; Vancouver Kingsway; Vancouver Quadra;
Vancouver South
Next Election: Oct. 15, 2022 (4 year terms)
Kennedy Stewart, Mayor
Rebecca Bligh, Councillor, 604-873-7249
Christine Boyle, Councillor, 604-873-7242
Adriane Carr, Councillor, 604-873-7245, Fax: 604-873-7750
Melissa De Genova, Councillor, 604-873-7244, Fax:
604-873-7750
Lisa Dominato, Councillor, 604-873-7248
Pete Fry, Councillor, 604-873-7246
Colleen Hardwick, Councillor, 604-873-7240
Sarah Kirby-Yung, Councillor, 604-873-7247
Jean Swanson, Councillor, 604-873-7243
Michael Wiebe, Councillor, 604-873-7241
Paul Mochrie, City Manager
Patrice Impey, Chief Financial Officer, 604-873-7610
Nick Kassam, General Manager, Real Estate & Facilities
Management, 604-871-6859
Malcolm Bromley, General Manager, Parks & Recreation,
604-257-8448
Lon LaClaire, General Manager, Engineering Services
Rena Kendall-Craden, Director, Communications, 604-673-8121
Gil Kelley, General Manager, Planning, Urban Design &
Sustainability, 604-873-7456
Jessie Adcock, General Manager, Development, Buildings &
Licensing, 604-873-7160
Darrell Reid, Fire Chief/General Manager, Vancouver Fire &
Rescue Services

Vernon
3400 - 30th St.
Vernon, BC V1T 5E6
Tel: 250-545-1361; *Fax:* 250-545-7876
admin@vernon.ca
www.vernon.ca
Municipal Type: City
Incorporated: Dec. 30, 1892; *Area:* 96.05 sq km
County or District: North Okanagan; *Population in 2016:* 40,116
Provincial Electoral District(s): Vernon-Monashee
Federal Electoral District(s): North Island-Powell River; North
Okanagan-Shuswap
Next Election: Oct. 15, 2022 (4 year terms)
Victor Cumming, Mayor
Scott Anderson, Councillor
Kelly Fehr, Councillor
Kari Gares, Councillor
Akbal Mund, Councillor
Dalvir Nahal, Councillor
Brian Quiring, Councillor
Will Pearce, Chief Administrative Officer
Patti Bridal, Director, Corporate Services
Doug Ross, Director, Recreation Services
James Rice, Manager, Public Works
Scott Hemstad, Deputy Fire Chief

Victoria
1 Centennial Sq.
Victoria, BC V8W 1P6
Tel: 250-385-5711; *Fax:* 250-361-0214
www.victoria.ca
Municipal Type: City
Incorporated: Aug. 2, 1862; *Area:* 19.47 sq km
County or District: Capital Regional District; *Population in 2016:*
85,792

Provincial Electoral District(s): Victoria-Beacon Hill;
Victoria-Swan Lake; In Greater Victoria: Esquimalt-Metchosin;
Saanich South; Saanich North & the Islands; and Langford-Juan
de Fuca
Federal Electoral District(s): Victoria
Next Election: Oct. 15, 2022 (4 year terms)
Lisa Helps, Mayor, 250-361-0200
Marianne Alto, Councillor, 250-361-0216
Sharmarke Dubow, Councillor, 250-361-0223
Ben Isitt, Councillor, 250-882-9302
Jeremy Loveday, Councillor, 250-361-0218
Sarah Potts, Councillor, 250-361-0221
Charlayne Thornton-Joe, Councillor, 250-361-0219
Geoff Young, Councillor, 250-361-0220
Jocelyn Jenkins, City Manager, 250-361-0563
Jodi Jensen, Head, Human Resources, 250-361-0362
Thomas Soulliere, Director, Parks, Recreation & Facilities,
250-361-0631
Karen Hoese, Director, Sustainable Planning & Community
Development
Susanne Thompson, Director, Finance, 250-361-0280
Paul Bruce, Fire Chief, 250-920-3380

West Kelowna
2760 Cameron Rd.
West Kelowna, BC V1Z 2T6
Tel: 778-797-1000; *Fax:* 778-797-1001
info@westkelownacity.ca
www.westkelownacity.ca
Municipal Type: City
Incorporated: Dec. 6, 2007; *Area:* 123.53 sq km
County or District: Central Okanagan; *Population in 2016:*
32,655
Provincial Electoral District(s): Kelowna West
Federal Electoral District(s): Central
Okanagan-Similkameen-Nicola
Next Election: Oct. 15, 2022 (4 year terms)
Gord Milsom, Mayor
Rick de Jong, Councillor
Doug Findlater, Councillor
Jason Friesen, Councillor
Stephen Johnston, Councillor
Carol Zanon, Councillor
Jayson Zilkie, Councillor
Paul Gipps, Chief Administrative Officer

White Rock
15322 Buena Vista Ave.
White Rock, BC V4B 1Y6
Tel: 604-541-2100; *Fax:* 604-541-2118
webmaster@whiterockcity.ca
www.whiterockcity.ca
Municipal Type: City
Incorporated: April 15, 1957; *Area:* 5.12 sq km
County or District: Metro Vancouver; *Population in 2016:* 19,952
Provincial Electoral District(s): Surrey-White Rock
Federal Electoral District(s): South Surrey-White Rock
Next Election: Oct. 15, 2022 (4 year terms)
Darryl A. Walker, Mayor, 604-541-2131
David Chesney, Councillor
Helen Fathers, Councillor
Erika Johanson, Councillor
Scott Kristjanson, Councillor
Anthony Manning, Councillor
Christopher Trevelyan, Councillor
Guillermo Ferrero, Chief Administrative Officer
Tracey Arthur, Director, Corporate Administration
Jim Gordon, Director, Engineering & Municipal Operations
Colleen Ponzini, Director, Financial Services
Eric Stepura, Director, Recreation & Culture
Jacquie Johnstone, Director, Human Resources, 604-541-2157
Chris Zota, Manager, Information Technology, 604-541-2113
Phil Lemire, Fire Chief, 604-541-2122

Williams Lake
450 Mart St.
Williams Lake, BC V2G 1N3
Tel: 250-392-2311; *Fax:* 250-392-4408
corporateservices@williamslake.ca
www.williamslake.ca
Municipal Type: City
Incorporated: March 15, 1929; *Area:* 33.13 sq km
County or District: Cariboo; *Population in 2016:* 10,753
Provincial Electoral District(s): Cariboo North; Cariboo-Chilcotin
Federal Electoral District(s): Cariboo-Prince George
Next Election: Oct. 15, 2022 (4 year terms)
Walt Lloyd Cobb, Mayor, 250-392-2311
Sheila Boehm, Councillor
Ivan Bonnell, Councillor
Marnie Brenner, Councillor
Scott Douglas Nelson, Councillor
Jason Ryll, Councillor

Craig Robert Smith, Councillor
Milo MacDonald, Chief Administrative Officer
Ashley Williston, Manager, Human Resources, 250-392-1795
Gary Muraca, Director, Municipal Services
Vitali Kozubenko, Chief Financial Officer, Financial Services,
250-392-1777
Erick Peterson, Fire Chief

Other Municipalities in British Columbia

100 Mile House
P.O. Box 340
385 South Birch Ave.
100 Mile House, BC V0K 2E0
Tel: 250-395-2434; *Fax:* 250-395-3625
district@dist100milehouse.bc.ca
www.100milehouse.com
Municipal Type: District
Incorporated: July 27, 1965; *Area:* 51.34 sq km
County or District: Cariboo; *Population in 2016:* 1,980
Provincial Electoral District(s): Cariboo-Chilcotin
Federal Electoral District(s): Kamloops-Thomson-Cariboo
Next Election: Oct. 15, 2022 (4 year terms)
Mitch Campsall, Mayor
Roy Scott, Chief Administrative Officer, Corporate Administration

Alert Bay
P.O. Box 2800
15 Maple Rd.
Alert Bay, BC V0N 1A0
Tel: 250-974-5213; *Fax:* 250-974-5470
officeclerk@alertbay.ca
www.alertbay.ca
Municipal Type: Village
Incorporated: Jan. 14, 1946; *Area:* 1.78 sq km
County or District: Mount Waddington; *Population in 2016:* 489
Provincial Electoral District(s): North Island
Federal Electoral District(s): North Island-Powell River
Next Election: Oct. 15, 2022 (4 year terms)
Dennis Buchanan, Mayor
Justin Beadle, Chief Administrative Officer
Pete Nelson-Smith, Public Works Superintendent

Anmore
2697 Sunnyside Rd.
Anmore, BC V3H 3C8
Tel: 604-469-9877; *Fax:* 604-469-0537
village.hall@anmore.com
www.anmore.com
Municipal Type: Village
Incorporated: Dec. 7, 1987; *Area:* 27.42 sq km
County or District: Metro Vancouver; *Population in 2016:* 2,210
Provincial Electoral District(s): Port Moody-Coquitlam
Federal Electoral District(s): Port Moody-Coquitlam
Next Election: Oct. 15, 2022 (4 year terms)
John McEwen, Mayor, 604-461-3384, Fax: 604-469-0537
Juli Kolby, Chief Administrative Officer
Kevin Dicken, Manager, Public Works

Armstrong
P.O. Box 40
3570 Bridge St.
Armstrong, BC V0E 1B0
Tel: 250-546-3023; *Fax:* 250-546-3710
info@cityofarmstrong.bc.ca
www.cityofarmstrong.bc.ca
Municipal Type: Town
Incorporated: March 31, 1913; *Area:* 5.24 sq km
County or District: North Okanagan; *Population in 2016:* 5,114
Provincial Electoral District(s): Shuswap
Federal Electoral District(s): North Okanagan-Shuswap
Next Election: Oct. 15, 2022 (4 year terms)
Chris Pieper, Mayor, 250-550-7239
Melinda Stickney, Chief Administrative Officer
Tim Perepolkin, Manager, Public Works

Ashcroft
P.O. Box 129
Ashcroft, BC V0K 1A0
Tel: 250-453-9161; *Fax:* 250-453-9664
admin@ashcroftbc.ca
www.ashcroftbc.ca
Other Information: Toll-Free Phone: 877-453-9161
Municipal Type: Village
Incorporated: June 27, 1952; *Area:* 51.45 sq km
County or District: Thompson-Nicola; *Population in 2016:* 1,558
Provincial Electoral District(s): Fraser-Nicola
Federal Electoral District(s): Mission-Matsqui-Fraser Canyon
Next Election: Oct. 15, 2022 (4 year terms)
Barbara H. Roden, Mayor

Michelle Allen, Chief Administrative Officer

Barriere
P.O. Box 219
4936 Barriere Town Rd.
Barriere, BC V0E 1E0
Tel: 250-672-9751; *Fax:* 250-672-9708
inquiry@barriere.ca
www.barriere.ca
Other Information: Toll-Free Phone: 866-672-9751
Municipal Type: District
Incorporated: Dec. 4 2007; *Area:* 6.17 sq km
County or District: Thompson-Nicola; *Population in 2016:* 1,713
Provincial Electoral District(s): Kamloops-North Thompson
Federal Electoral District(s): Kamloops-Thompson-Cariboo
Next Election: Oct. 15, 2022 (4 year terms)
Ward Stamer, Mayor
Colleen Hannigan, Chief Administrative Officer, 250-672-9751

Belcarra
4084 Bedwell Bay Rd.
Belcarra, BC V3H 4P8
Tel: 604-937-4100; *Fax:* 604-939-5034
belcarra@belcarra.ca
www.belcarra.ca
Municipal Type: Village
Incorporated: Aug. 22, 1979; *Area:* 5.46 sq km
County or District: Metro Vancouver; *Population in 2016:* 643
Provincial Electoral District(s): Port Moody-Coquitlam
Federal Electoral District(s): Port Moody-Coquitlam
Next Election: Oct. 15, 2022 (4 year terms)
Vacant, Mayor
Lorna Dysart, Chief Administrative Officer, 604-937-4101

Bowen Island
981 Artisan Lane
Bowen Island, BC V0N 1G0
Tel: 604-947-4255; *Fax:* 604-947-0193
bim@bimbc.ca
www.bimbc.ca
Municipal Type: Island Municipality
Incorporated: Dec. 4, 1999; *Area:* 49.94 sq km
County or District: Metro Vancouver; *Population in 2016:* 3,680
Provincial Electoral District(s): West Vancouver-Sea to Sky
Federal Electoral District(s): West Vancouver-Sunshine
Coast-Sea to Sky Country
Next Election: Oct. 15, 2022 (4 year terms)
Gary Ander, Mayor
Kathy Lalonde, Chief Administrative Officer, 604-947-4255
Bob Robinson, Superintendent, Public Works, 604-947-4255

Burns Lake
P.O. Box 570
Burns Lake, BC V0J 1E0
Tel: 250-692-7587; *Fax:* 250-692-3059
village@burnslake.org
www.burnslake.org
Other Information: Fire Hall Phone: 250-692-3664
Municipal Type: Village
Incorporated: Dec. 6, 1923; *Area:* 7.17 sq km
County or District: Bulkley-Nechako; *Population in 2016:* 1,779
Provincial Electoral District(s): Nechako Lakes
Federal Electoral District(s): Skeena-Bulkley Valley
Next Election: Oct. 15, 2022 (4 year terms)
Note: Mayor Strimbold resigned September 15, 2016. A
by-election is planned for December.
Dolores D. Funk, Mayor
Sheryl Worthing, Chief Administrative Officer
Cameron Harthing, City Clerk, 250-692-7587
Rick Martin, Director, Public Works, 250-692-7587
Jim McBride, Fire Chief & Director, Protective Services,
250-692-7587

Cache Creek
P.O. Box 7
Cache Creek, BC V0K 1H0
Tel: 250-457-6237; *Fax:* 250-457-9192
admin@cachecreek.info
www.cachecreekvillage.com
Municipal Type: Village
Incorporated: Nov. 28, 1967; *Area:* 10.57 sq km
County or District: Thompson-Nicola; *Population in 2016:* 963
Provincial Electoral District(s): Fraser-Nicola
Federal Electoral District(s): Mission-Matsqui-Fraser Canyon
Next Election: Oct. 15, 2022 (4 year terms)
Santo Talarico, Mayor
Keir Gervais, Chief Administrative Officer

Canal Flats
P.O. Box 159
8853 Grainger Rd.
Canal Flats, BC V0B 1B0
Tel: 250-349-5462; *Fax:* 250-349-5460
village@canalflats.ca
www.canalflats.com
Municipal Type: Village
Incorporated: June 29, 2004; *Area:* 10.84 sq km
County or District: East Kootenay; *Population in 2016:* 668
Provincial Electoral District(s): Columbia River-Revelstoke
Federal Electoral District(s): Kootenay-Columbia
Next Election: Oct. 15, 2022 (4 year terms)
Karl Sterzer, Mayor
Brian Woodward, Chief Administrative Officer, 250-349-5462

Castlegar
460 Columbia Ave.
Castlegar, BC V1N 1G7
Tel: 250-365-7227; *Fax:* 250-365-4810
castlegar@castlegar.ca
www.castlegar.ca
Municipal Type: Town
Incorporated: Jan. 1, 1974; *Area:* 19.8 sq km
County or District: Central Kootenay; *Population in 2016:* 8,039
Provincial Electoral District(s): Kootenay West
Federal Electoral District(s): South Okanagan-West Kootenay
Next Election: Oct. 15, 2022 (4 year terms)
Bruno Tassone, Mayor
Sue L. Heaton-Sherstobitoff, Councillor
Cherryl MacLeod, Councillor
Maria J. McFaddin, Councillor
Bergen A. Price, Councillor
Dan H. Rye, Councillor
Florio M. Vassilakakis, Councillor
John Malcolm, Chief Administrative Officer
Phil Markin, Director, Development Services
Chris Barlow, Director, Transportation & Civic Works
Carolyn Rempel, Director, Corporate Services

Central Saanich
1903 Mt. Newton Cross Rd.
Saanichton, BC V8M 2A9
Tel: 250-652-4444; *Fax:* 250-652-0135
www.centralsaanich.ca
Municipal Type: District
Incorporated: Dec. 12, 1950; *Area:* 41.33 sq km
County or District: Capital; *Population in 2016:* 16,814
Provincial Electoral District(s): Saanich North & the Islands
Federal Electoral District(s): Saanich-Gulf Islands
Next Election: Oct. 15, 2022 (4 year terms)
Ryan Windsor, Mayor
Christopher R. Graham, Councillor
Carl Jensen, Councillor
Zeb King, Councillor
Gord Newton, Councillor
Niall Paltiel, Councillor
Bob L. Thompson, Councillor
Paul Murray, Interim Chief Administrative Officer
Brian Barnett, Director, Engineering & Public Works
Jarret Matanowitsch, Director, Planning & Building Services
Chris Vrabel, Fire Chief, 250-544-4238

Chase
P.O. Box 440
826 Okanagan Ave.
Chase, BC V0E 1M0
Tel: 250-679-3238; *Fax:* 250-679-3070
chase@chasebc.ca
www.chasebc.ca
Municipal Type: Village
Incorporated: April 22, 1969; *Area:* 3.75 sq km
County or District: Thompson-Nicola; *Population in 2016:* 2,286
Provincial Electoral District(s): Kamloops-South Thompson
Federal Electoral District(s): North Okanagan-Shuswap
Next Election: Oct. 15, 2022 (4 year terms)
Rod Crowe, Mayor
Joni Heinrich, Chief Administrative Officer

Chetwynd
P.O. Box 357
5400 North Access Rd.
Chetwynd, BC V0C 1J0
Tel: 250-401-4100; *Fax:* 250-401-4101
d-chet@gochetwynd.com
www.gochetwynd.com
Municipal Type: District
Incorporated: Sept. 25, 1962; *Area:* 64.32 sq km
County or District: Peace River; *Population in 2016:* 2,503
Provincial Electoral District(s): Peace River South
Federal Electoral District(s): Prince George-Peace

River-Northern Rockies
Next Election: Oct. 15, 2022 (4 year terms)
Allen G. Courtoreille, Mayor
Doug Fleming, Chief Administrative Officer, 250-401-4103
Paul Gordon, Director, Engineering & Public Works,
250-401-4111

Clearwater
P.O. Box 157
132 Clearwater Station Rd.
Clearwater, BC V0E 1N0
Tel: 250-674-2257; *Fax:* 250-674-2173
admin@docbc.ca
www.districtofclearwater.com
Municipal Type: District
Incorporated: Dec. 7 2007; *Area:* 60 sq km
County or District: Thompson-Nicola; *Population in 2016:* 2,324
Provincial Electoral District(s): Kamloops-North Thompson
Federal Electoral District(s): Kamloops-Thompson-Cariboo
Next Election: Oct. 15, 2022 (4 year terms)
Merlin Blackwell, Mayor
Leslie Groulx, Chief Administrative Officer, 250-674-2257
Bruce Forsyth, Superindendent, Public Works

Clinton
P.O. Box 309
1423 Cariboo Hwy.
Clinton, BC V0K 1K0
Tel: 250-459-2261; *Fax:* 250-459-2227
admin@village.clinton.bc.ca
www.village.clinton.bc.ca
Municipal Type: Village
Incorporated: July 16, 1963; *Area:* 4.36 sq km
County or District: Thompson-Nicola; *Population in 2016:* 641
Provincial Electoral District(s): Fraser-Nicola
Federal Electoral District(s): Kamloops-Thompson-Cariboo
Next Election: Oct. 15, 2022 (4 year terms)
Susan Swan, Mayor
Tom Dall, Chief Administrative Officer, 250-459-2261

Coldstream
9901 Kalamalka Rd.
Coldstream, BC V1B 1L6
Tel: 250-545-5304; *Fax:* 250-545-4733
info@districtofcoldstream.ca
www.districtofcoldstream.ca
Municipal Type: District
Incorporated: Dec. 21, 1906; *Area:* 67.25 sq km
County or District: North Okanagan; *Population in 2016:* 10,648
Provincial Electoral District(s): Vernon-Monashee
Federal Electoral District(s): North Okanagan-Shuswap
Next Election: Oct. 15, 2022 (4 year terms)
Jim Garlick, Mayor, 250-307-9490
Trevor Seibel, Chief Administrative Officer
Michael Baker, Director, Infrastructure Services, 250-545-5304
Mike Reiley, Director, Development Services, 250-545-5304

Creston
P.O. Box 1339
#238, 10th Ave. North
Creston, BC V0B 1G0
Tel: 250-428-2214; *Fax:* 250-428-9164
info@creston.ca
www.creston.ca
Municipal Type: Town
Incorporated: May 14, 1924; *Area:* 8.48 sq km
County or District: Central Kootenay; *Population in 2016:* 5,351
Provincial Electoral District(s): Nelson-Creston
Federal Electoral District(s): Kootenay-Columbia
Next Election: Oct. 15, 2022 (4 year terms)
Ron Toyota, Mayor, 250-428-2214
Lou Varela, Town Manager, 250-428-2214, Fax: 250-428-9164
Ross Beddoes, Director, Municipal Services, 250-428-2214,
Fax: 250-428-9164

Cumberland
P.O. Box 340
2673 Dunsmuir Ave.
Cumberland, BC V0R 1S0
Tel: 250-336-2291; *Fax:* 250-336-2321
info@cumberland.ca
www.cumberlandbc.net
Municipal Type: Village
Incorporated: Jan. 1, 1898; *Area:* 29.13 sq km
County or District: Comox Valley; *Population in 2016:* 3,753
Provincial Electoral District(s): Mid Island-Pacific Rim
Federal Electoral District(s): Courtenay-Alberni
Next Election: Oct. 15, 2022 (4 year terms)
Leslie Baird, Mayor, 250-336-3001
Sundance Topham, Chief Administrative Officer, 250-336-3002

Delta
4500 Clarence Taylor Cres.
Delta, BC V4K 3E2
Tel: 604-946-4141
www.delta.ca
Municipal Type: District
Incorporated: Nov. 10, 1879; *Area:* 180.20 sq km
County or District: Metro Vancouver; *Population in 2016:*
102,238
Provincial Electoral District(s): Delta North; Delta South
Federal Electoral District(s): Delta
Next Election: Oct. 15, 2022 (4 year terms)
George Harvie, Mayor
Dan Copeland, Councillor
Alicia Guichon, Councillor
Lois Jackson, Councillor
Jeannie Kanakos, Councillor, 604-591-1995
Dylan Kruger, Councillor
Bruce McDonald, Councillor, 604-596-8345
Sean McGill, City Manager
Ken Kuntz, Director, Parks, Recreation & Culture, 604-952-3537
Steven Lan, Director, 604-946-3260
Paul Scholfield, Fire Chief, 604-946-8541

Duncan
200 Craig St.
Duncan, BC V9L 1W3
Tel: 250-746-6126; *Fax:* 250-746-6129
duncan@duncan.ca
www.duncan.ca
Municipal Type: Town
Incorporated: March 4, 1912; *Area:* 2.05 sq km
County or District: Cowichan Valley; *Population in 2016:* 4,944
Provincial Electoral District(s): Cowichan Valley
Federal Electoral District(s): Cowichan-Malahat-Langford
Next Election: Oct. 15, 2022 (4 year terms)
Michelle Staples, Mayor
Peter de Verteuil, Chief Administrative Officer, 250-746-6126
Abbas Farahbakhsh, Director, Public Works, 250-746-6126

Elkford
P.O. Box 340
Elkford, BC V0B 1H0
Tel: 250-865-4000; *Fax:* 250-865-4001
info@elkford.ca
www.elkford.ca
Municipal Type: District
Incorporated: July 16, 1971; *Area:* 101.59 sq km
County or District: East Kootenay; *Population in 2016:* 2,499
Provincial Electoral District(s): Kootenay East
Federal Electoral District(s): Kootenay-Columbia
Next Election: Oct. 15, 2022 (4 year terms)
Dean McKerracher, Mayor, 250-865-4000
Curtis Helgesen, Chief Administrative Officer, 250-865-4004
Bernie Van Tighem, Director, Fire Rescue & Emergency
Services, 250-865-4020

Enderby
P.O. Box 400
619 Cliff Ave.
Enderby, BC V0E 1V0
Tel: 250-838-7230; *Fax:* 250-838-6007
enderbycity@sunwave.net
www.cityofenderby.com
Municipal Type: Town
Incorporated: March 1, 1905; *Area:* 4.23 sq km
County or District: North Okanagan; *Population in 2016:* 2,964
Provincial Electoral District(s): Shuswap
Federal Electoral District(s): North Okanagan-Shuswap
Next Election: Oct. 15, 2022 (4 year terms)
Greg McCune, Mayor
Tate Bengtson, Chief Administrative Officer, 250-838-7230

Esquimalt
1229 Esquimalt Rd.
Victoria, BC V9A 3P1
Tel: 250-414-7100; *Fax:* 250-414-7111
info@esquimalt.ca
www.esquimalt.ca
Municipal Type: Township
Incorporated: Sept. 1, 1912; *Area:* 7.08 sq km
County or District: Capital; *Population in 2016:* 17,655
Provincial Electoral District(s): Esquimalt-Metchosin
Federal Electoral District(s): Esquimalt-Saanich-Sooke
Next Election: Oct. 15, 2022 (4 year terms)
Barbara Desjardins, Mayor, 250-414-7100
Ken Armour, Councillor
Meagan Brame, Councillor
Jacob Helliwell, Councillor
Lynda Hundleby, Councillor
Tim Morrison, Councillor
Jane Vermeulen, Councillor

Laurie Hurst, Chief Administrative Officer, 250-414-7133
Ian Irvine, Director, Financial Services, 250-414-7141
Scott Hartman, Director, Parks & Recreation, 250-412-8509
Bill Brown, Director, Development Services, 250-414-7146
Blair McDonald, Director, Community Safety Services
Chris Jancowski, Fire Chief

Fernie
P.O. Box 190
#501, 3rd Ave.
Fernie, BC V0B 1M0
Tel: 250-423-6817; *Fax:* 250-423-3034
cityhall@fernie.ca
www.fernie.ca
Municipal Type: Town
Incorporated: July 28, 1904; *Area:* 16.05 sq km
County or District: East Kootenay; *Population in 2016:* 5,249
Provincial Electoral District(s): Kootenay East
Federal Electoral District(s): Kootenay-Columbia
Next Election: Oct. 15, 2022 (4 year terms)
Ange Qualizza, Mayor
Norm McInniss, Chief Administrative Officer, 250-423-2225
Ted Ruiter, Director, 250-423-4226

Fort Nelson
P.O. Box 399
5319 - 50th Ave.
Fort Nelson, BC V0C 1R0
Tel: 250-774-2541
justask@northernrockies.ca
www.northernrockies.ca
Municipal Type: Town
Incorporated: Oct. 31, 1987; *Area:* 13.26 sq km
County or District: Northern Rockies; *Population in 2016:* 3,366
Provincial Electoral District(s): Peace River North
Federal Electoral District(s): Prince George-Peace
River-Northern Rockies
Next Election: Oct. 15, 2022 (4 year terms)
Gary Foster, Mayor
Scott Barry, Chief Administrative Officer

Fort St. James
P.O. Box 640
477 Stuart Dr. West
Fort St James, BC V0J 1P0
Tel: 250-996-8233; *Fax:* 250-996-2248
district@fortstjames.ca
www.fortstjames.ca
Municipal Type: District
Incorporated: Dec. 19, 1952; *Area:* 22.1 sq km
County or District: Bulkley-Nechako; *Population in 2016:* 1,598
Provincial Electoral District(s): Nechako Lakes
Federal Electoral District(s): Skeena-Bulkley Valley
Next Election: Oct. 15, 2022 (4 year terms)
Beverley Playfair, Mayor
Kelley Williams, Acting Chief Administrative Officer
David Stewart, Public Works Superintendent, 250-996-7161

Fraser Lake
P.O. Box 430
210 Carrier Cres.
Fraser Lake, BC V0J 1S0
Tel: 250-699-6257; *Fax:* 250-699-6469
village@fraserlake.ca
www.fraserlake.ca
Municipal Type: Village
Incorporated: Sept. 27, 1966; *Area:* 3.9 sq km
County or District: Bulkley-Nechako; *Population in 2016:* 988
Provincial Electoral District(s): Nechako Lakes
Federal Electoral District(s): Skeena-Bulkley Valley
Next Election: Oct. 15, 2022 (4 year terms)
Sarrah A. Storey, Mayor
Rodney J. Holland, Chief Administrative Officer & Director,
Corporate Services, 250-699-6257
Vern Hilman, Director, Public Works, 250-699-6562

Fruitvale
P.O. Box 370
1947 Beaver St.
Fruitvale, BC V0G 1L0
Tel: 250-367-7551; *Fax:* 250-367-9267
info@village.fruitvale.bc.ca
www.village.fruitvale.bc.ca
Municipal Type: Village
Incorporated: Nov. 4, 1952; *Area:* 36.86 sq km
County or District: Kootenay Boundary; *Population in 2016:*
1,920
Provincial Electoral District(s): Kootenay West
Federal Electoral District(s): South Okanagan-West Kootenay
Next Election: Oct. 15, 2022 (4 year terms)
Stephen J. Morissette, Mayor
Lila Cresswell, Chief Administrative Officer, 250-367-7551

Gibsons

P.O. Box 340
474 South Fletcher Rd.
Gibsons, BC V0N 1V0
Tel: 604-886-2274; *Fax:* 604-886-9735
info@gibsons.ca
www.gibsons.ca
Municipal Type: Town
Incorporated: March 4, 1929; *Area:* 4.33 sq km
County or District: Sunshine Coast; *Population in 2016:* 4,605
Provincial Electoral District(s): Powell River-Sunshine Coast
Federal Electoral District(s): West Vancouver-Sunshine Coast-Sea to Sky Country
Next Election: Oct. 15, 2022 (4 year terms)
Bill Beamish, Mayor
Emanuel Machado, Chief Administrative Officer, 604-886-2274
Andre Boel, Director, Planning
Greg Foss, Director, Public Works
Wendy Gilbertson, Director, Parks
Dave Newman, Director, Engineering

Gold River

P.O. Box 610
499 Muchalat Dr.
Gold River, BC V0P 1G0
Tel: 250-283-2202; *Fax:* 250-283-7500
villageofgoldriver@cablerocket.com
www.villageofgoldriver.com
Municipal Type: Village
Incorporated: Aug. 26, 1965; *Area:* 10.51 sq km
County or District: Strathcona; *Population in 2016:* 1,212
Provincial Electoral District(s): North Island
Federal Electoral District(s): North Island-Powell River
Next Election: Oct. 15, 2022 (4 year terms)
Brad Unger, Mayor, 250-283-2615
Larry Plourde, Chief Administrative Officer, 250-283-2202
Mick Mann, Public Works Supervisor & Manager, Parks & Rec

Golden

P.O. Box 350
Golden, BC V0A 1H0
Tel: 250-344-2271; *Fax:* 250-344-6577
enquiries@town.golden.bc.ca
www.golden.ca
Municipal Type: Town
Incorporated: June 26, 1957; *Area:* 11.02 sq km
County or District: Columbia-Shuswap; *Population in 2016:* 3,708
Provincial Electoral District(s): Columbia River-Revelstoke
Federal Electoral District(s): Kootenay-Columbia
Next Election: Oct. 15, 2022 (4 year terms)
Ron Oszust, Mayor, 250-344-2271
Jon Wilsgard, Chief Administrative Officer, 250-344-2271

Grand Forks

P.O. Box 220
7217 - 4th St.
Grand Forks, BC V0H 1H0
Tel: 250-442-8266; *Fax:* 250-442-8000
info@citinfo@grandforks.ca
www.grandforks.ca
Municipal Type: Town
Incorporated: April 15, 1897; *Area:* 10.44 sq km
County or District: Kootenay Boundary; *Population in 2016:* 4,049
Provincial Electoral District(s): Boundary-Similkameen
Federal Electoral District(s): South Okanagan-West Kootenay
Next Election: Oct. 15, 2022 (4 year terms)
Brian Taylor, Mayor
Diane Heinrich, Chief Administrative Officer, 250-442-8266

Granisle

P.O. Box 128
Granisle, BC V0J 1W0
Tel: 250-697-2248; *Fax:* 250-697-2306
general@villageofgranisle.ca
www.villageofgranisle.ca
Municipal Type: Village
Incorporated: June 29, 1971; *Area:* 40.21 sq km
County or District: Bulkley-Nechako; *Population in 2016:* 303
Provincial Electoral District(s): Nechako Lakes
Federal Electoral District(s): Skeena-Bulkley Valley
Next Election: Oct. 15, 2022 (4 year terms)
Linda McGuire, Mayor, 250-697-2248
Sharon Smith, Chief Administrative Officer, 250-697-2428
Blaine Maughan, Manager, Public Works, 250-697-2429

Greenwood

P.O. Box 129
202 Government Ave.
Greenwood, BC V0H 1J0
Tel: 250-445-6644; *Fax:* 250-445-6441
info@greenwoodcity.com
www.greenwoodcity.com
Municipal Type: Town
Incorporated: July 12, 1897; *Area:* 2.52 sq km
County or District: Kootenay Boundary; *Population in 2016:* 665
Provincial Electoral District(s): Boundary-Similkameen
Federal Electoral District(s): South Okanagan-West Kootenay
Next Election: Oct. 15, 2022 (4 year terms)
Ed I. Smith, Mayor, 250-445-6644
Wendy Higashi, Chief Administrative Officer, 250-445-6644
Randy Smith, Superintendent of Public Works

Harrison Hot Springs

P.O. Box 160
495 Hot Springs Rd.
Harrison Hot Springs, BC V0M 1K0
Tel: 604-796-2171; *Fax:* 604-796-2192
info@harrisonhotsprings.ca
www.harrisonhotsprings.ca
Municipal Type: Village
Incorporated: May 27, 1949; *Area:* 5.47 sq km
County or District: Fraser Valley; *Population in 2016:* 1,468
Provincial Electoral District(s): Chilliwack-Kent
Federal Electoral District(s): Mission-Matsqui-Fraser Canyon
Next Election: Oct. 15, 2022 (4 year terms)
Leo Facio, Mayor, 604-796-2171
Madeline McDonald, Chief Administrative Officer, 604-796-2171

Hazelton

P.O. Box 40
Hazelton, BC V0J 1Y0
Tel: 250-842-5991; *Fax:* 250-842-5152
info@hazelton.ca
www.hazelton.ca
Municipal Type: Village
Incorporated: Feb. 15, 1956; *Area:* 2.85 sq km
County or District: Kitimat-Stikine; *Population in 2016:* 313
Provincial Electoral District(s): Stikine
Federal Electoral District(s): Skeena-Bulkley Valley
Next Election: Oct. 15, 2022 (4 year terms)
Dennis Sterritt, Mayor
Tanalee Hesse, Chief Administrative Officer, 250-842-5991

Highlands

1980 Millstream Rd.
Victoria, BC V9B 6H1
Tel: 250-474-1773; *Fax:* 250-474-3677
www.highlands.bc.ca
Municipal Type: District
Incorporated: Dec. 7, 1993; *Area:* 37.87 sq km
County or District: Capital; *Population in 2016:* 2,225
Provincial Electoral District(s): Langford-Juan de Fuca
Federal Electoral District(s): Cowichan-Malahat-Langford
Next Election: Oct. 15, 2022 (4 year terms)
Kenneth Williams, Mayor
Christopher D. Coates, Chief Administrative Officer

Hope

325 Wallace St.
Hope, BC V0X 1L0
Tel: 604-869-5671; *Fax:* 604-869-2275
info@hope.ca
www.hope.ca
Municipal Type: District Municipality
Incorporated: April 6, 1929; *Area:* 41.42 sq km
County or District: Fraser Valley; *Population in 2016:* 6,181
Provincial Electoral District(s): Fraser-Nicola
Federal Electoral District(s): Chilliwack-Hope
Next Election: Oct. 15, 2022 (4 year terms)
Peter Robb, Mayor
John Fortoloczky, Chief Administrative Officer, 604-869-5607
Scott Misumi, Director, Community Development, 604-869-5607
Ian Vaughan, Director, Operations, 604-869-2333

Houston

P.O. Box 370
3367 - 12th St.
Houston, BC V0J 1Z0
Tel: 250-845-2238; *Fax:* 250-845-3429
doh@houston.ca
www.houston.ca
Municipal Type: District
Incorporated: March 4, 1957; *Area:* 72.83 sq km
County or District: Bulkley-Nechako; *Population in 2016:* 2,993
Provincial Electoral District(s): Fraser-Nicola
Federal Electoral District(s): Skeena-Bulkley Valley
Next Election: Oct. 15, 2022 (4 year terms)
Shane Brienen, Mayor, 250-845-8842
Michael D. Gavin, Chief Administrative Officer, 250-845-2238
Ryan Coltura, Director, 250-845-7420

Hudson's Hope

P.O. Box 330
9904 Dudley Dr.
Hudson's Hope, BC V0C 1V0
Tel: 250-783-9901; *Fax:* 250-783-5741
district@hudsonshope.ca
www.hudsonshope.ca
Municipal Type: District
Incorporated: Nov. 16, 1965; *Area:* 869.43 sq km
County or District: Peace River; *Population in 2016:* 1,015
Provincial Electoral District(s): Peace River North
Federal Electoral District(s): Prince George-Peace River-Northern Rockies
Next Election: Oct. 15, 2022 (4 year terms)
Dave Heiberg, Mayor
Chris Cvik, Chief Administrative Officer

Invermere

P.O. Box 339
914 - 8th Ave.
Invermere, BC V0A 1K0
Tel: 250-342-9281; *Fax:* 250-342-2934
info@invermere.net
www.invermere.net
Municipal Type: District
Incorporated: May 22, 1951; *Area:* 10.18 sq km
County or District: East Kootenay; *Population in 2016:* 3,391
Provincial Electoral District(s): Columbia River-Revelstoke
Federal Electoral District(s): Kootenay-Columbia
Next Election: Oct. 15, 2022 (4 year terms)
Allen Miller, Mayor
Christopher Prosser, Chief Administrative Officer, 250-342-9281
Rory Hromadnik, Director, Development Services

Kaslo

P.O. Box 576
312 Fourth St.
Kaslo, BC V0G 1M0
Tel: 250-353-2311; *Fax:* 250-353-7767
admin@kaslo.ca
www.kaslo.ca
Municipal Type: Village
Incorporated: Aug. 14, 1893; *Area:* 2.8 sq km
County or District: Central Kootenay; *Population in 2016:* 968
Provincial Electoral District(s): Nelson-Creston
Federal Electoral District(s): Kootenay-Columbia
Next Election: Oct. 15, 2022 (4 year terms)
Suzan Hewat, Mayor, 250-353-2311
Neil Smith, Chief Administrative Officer, 250-353-2311

Kent

P.O. Box 70
7170 Cheam Ave.
Agassiz, BC V0M 1A0
Tel: 604-796-2235; *Fax:* 604-796-9854
www.district.kent.bc.ca
Municipal Type: District
Incorporated: Jan. 1, 1895; *Area:* 166.51 sq km
County or District: Fraser Valley; *Population in 2016:* 6,067
Provincial Electoral District(s): Chilliwack-Kent
Federal Electoral District(s): Mission-Matsqui-Fraser Canyon
Next Election: Oct. 15, 2022 (4 year terms)
Sylvia Pranger, Mayor
Wallace Mah, Chief Administrative Officer, 604-796-2235
Darcey Kohuch, Director, Development Services
Mick Thiessen, Director, Engineering Services

Keremeos

P.O. Box 160
702 - 4th St.
Keremeos, BC V0X 1N0
Tel: 250-499-2711; *Fax:* 250-499-5477
town@keremeos.ca
www.keremeos.ca
Municipal Type: Village
Incorporated: Oct. 30, 1956; *Area:* 2.11 sq km
County or District: Okanagan-Similkameen; *Population in 2016:* 1,502
Provincial Electoral District(s): Boundary-Similkameen
Federal Electoral District(s): Central Okanagan-Similkameen-Nicola
Next Election: Oct. 15, 2022 (4 year terms)
Manfred Bauer, Mayor
Marg Coulson, Chief Administrative Officer

Kimberley
340 Spokane St.
Kimberley, BC V1A 2E8
Tel: 250-427-5311; *Fax:* 250-427-5252
info@citinfo@kimberley.ca
www.kimberley.ca
Municipal Type: Town
Incorporated: March 29, 1944; *Area:* 58.31 sq km
County or District: East Kootenay; *Population in 2016:* 7,425
Provincial Electoral District(s): Columbia River-Revelstoke
Federal Electoral District(s): Kootenay-Columbia
Next Election: Oct. 15, 2022 (4 year terms)
Don McCormick, Mayor, 250-432-5460
Scott Sommerville, Chief Administrative Officer
Janyce Bampton, Human Resources Officer, 250-427-9656

Kitimat
270 City Centre
Kitimat, BC V8C 2H7
Tel: 250-632-8900; *Fax:* 250-632-4995
feedback@kitimat.ca
www.kitimat.ca
Municipal Type: District
Incorporated: March 31, 1953; *Area:* 241.01 sq km
County or District: Kitimat-Stikine; *Population in 2016:* 8,131
Provincial Electoral District(s): Skeena
Federal Electoral District(s): Skeena-Bulkley Valley
Next Election: Oct. 15, 2022 (4 year terms)
Philip Germuth, Mayor, 250-632-8920
Edwin Empinado, Councillor, 250-639-9749
Mario Feldhoff, Councillor, 250-639-5662
Rob Goffinet, Councillor, 250-632-1451
Lani Gibson, Councillor, 250-639-2293
Terry Marleau, Councillor, 250-279-0946
Mark Zielinski, Councillor, 250-639-3946
Warren Waycheshen, Chief Administrative Officer, 250-632-8916
Mike Dewar, Director, Economic Development, 250-632-8921
Martin Gould, Director, Leisure Services, 250-632-8913
Cam McCulley, Director, Operations, 250-632-8935
Gwendolyn Sewell, Director, Community Planning & Development, 250-632-8912
Trent Bossence, Fire Chief, 250-632-8942

Ladysmith
Town Hall
P.O. Box 220 Main
410 Esplanade
Ladysmith, BC V9G 1A2
Tel: 250-245-6400; *Fax:* 250-245-6411
info@ladysmith.ca
www.ladysmith.ca
Municipal Type: Town
Incorporated: June 3, 1904; *Area:* 12.18 sq km
County or District: Cowichan Valley; *Population in 2016:* 8,537
Provincial Electoral District(s): Nanaimo-North Cowichan
Federal Electoral District(s): Nanaimo-Ladysmith
Next Election: Oct. 15, 2022 (4 year terms)
Aaron Stone, Mayor, 250-245-6400
Amanda Jacobson, Councillor
Robert Johnson, Councillor
Tricia McKay, Councillor
Donald Paterson, Councillor
Marsh Stevens, Councillor
Jeff Virtanen, Councillor
Guillermo Ferror, City Manager, 250-245-6401
Sandy Bowden, Director, Corporate Services
Felicity Adams, Director, Development Services
John Manson, Director, Infrastructure Services
Clayton Postings, Director, Parks, Recreation & Culture
Karen Cousins, Manager, Human Resources, 250-245-6412

Lake Country
10150 Bottom Wood Lake Rd.
Lake Country, BC V4V 2M1
Tel: 250-766-5650; *Fax:* 250-766-0116
admin@lakecountry.bc.ca
www.lakecountry.bc.ca
Municipal Type: District
Incorporated: May 2, 1995; *Area:* 122.16 sq km
County or District: Central Okanagan; *Population in 2016:* 12,922
Provincial Electoral District(s): Kelowna-Lake Country
Federal Electoral District(s): Kelowna-Lake Country
Next Election: Oct. 15, 2022 (4 year terms)
James Baker, Mayor
Alberto De Feo, Chief Administrative Officer, 250-766-6671
Holly Flinkman, Manager, Human Resources, 250-766-5650
Michael J. Mercer, Director, Engineering & Environmental Services, 250-766-5650

Lake Cowichan
P.O. Box 860
39 South Shore Rd.
Lake Cowichan, BC V0R 2G0
Tel: 250-749-6681; *Fax:* 250-749-3900
general@lakecowichan.ca
www.town.lakecowichan.bc.ca
Municipal Type: Town
Incorporated: Aug. 19, 1944; *Area:* 8.25 sq km
County or District: Cowichan Valley; *Population in 2016:* 3,226
Provincial Electoral District(s): Cowichan Valley
Federal Electoral District(s): Cowichan-Malahat-Langford
Next Election: Oct. 15, 2022 (4 year terms)
Rod Peters, Mayor
Joseph A. Fernandez, Chief Administrative Officer
Nagi Rizk, Superintendent, Public Works & Engineering Services, 250-749-6244

Langley
20338 - 65 Ave.
Langley, BC V2Y 3J1
Tel: 604-534-3211
info@tol.ca
www.tol.ca
Municipal Type: Township
Incorporated: April 26, 1873; *Area:* 308.03 sq km
County or District: Metro Vancouver; *Population in 2016:* 117,285
Provincial Electoral District(s): Langely; Langley East
Federal Electoral District(s): Cloverdale-Langley City; Langley-Aldergrove
Next Election: Oct. 15, 2022 (4 year terms)
Jack Froese, Mayor, 604-533-6000
Petrina Arnason, Councillor
David Davis, Councillor
Steve Ferguson, Councillor
Margaret Kunst, Councillor
Bob Long, Councillor
Kim Richter, Councillor
Blair Whitmarsh, Councillor
Eric Woodward, Councillor
Mark Bakken, Chief Administrative Officer
Stephen Gamble, Fire Chief

Lantzville
P.O. Box 100
7192 Lantzville Rd.
Lantzville, BC V0R 2H0
Tel: 250-390-4006; *Fax:* 250-390-5188
district@lantzville.ca
www.lantzville.ca
Municipal Type: District
Incorporated: June 25, 2003; *Area:* 27.87 sq km
County or District: Nanaimo; *Population in 2016:* 3,605
Provincial Electoral District(s): Parksville-Qualicum
Federal Electoral District(s): Nanaimo-Ladysmith
Next Election: Oct. 15, 2022 (4 year terms)
Mark Swain, Mayor
Twyla Graff, Chief Administrative Officer
Fred Spears, Director, Public Works, 250-390-4006

Lillooet
P.O. Box 610
615 Main St.
Lillooet, BC V0K 1V0
Tel: 250-256-4289; *Fax:* 250-256-4288
cityhall@lillooetbc.ca
lillooetbc.ca
Municipal Type: District
Incorporated: Dec. 31, 1946; *Area:* 27.83 sq km
County or District: Squamish-Lillooet; *Population in 2016:* 2,275
Provincial Electoral District(s): Fraser-Nicola
Federal Electoral District(s): Mission-Matsqui-Fraser Canyon
Next Election: Oct. 15, 2022 (4 year terms)
Peter Busse, Mayor
Michael Roy, Chief Administrative Officer
Wayne Robinson, Director, Recreation
Jodi Pawloski, Supervisor, Public Works

Lions Bay
P.O. Box 141
400 Centre Rd.
Lions Bay, BC V0N 2E0
Tel: 604-921-9333; *Fax:* 604-921-6643
reception@lionsbay.ca
www.lionsbay.ca
Municipal Type: Village
Incorporated: Dec. 17, 1970; *Area:* 2.55 sq km
County or District: Metro Vancouver; *Population in 2016:* 1,334
Provincial Electoral District(s): West Vancouver-Sea to Sky
Federal Electoral District(s): West Vancouver-Sunshine Coast-Sea to Sky Country
Next Election: Oct. 15, 2022 (4 year terms)
Ron McLaughlin, Mayor
Peter Dejong, Chief Administrative Officer, 604-921-9333
Nikii Hoglund, Manager, Public Works & Services

Logan Lake
P.O. Box 190
1 Opal Dr.
Logan Lake, BC V0K 1W0
Tel: 250-523-6225; *Fax:* 250-523-6678
districtofloganlake@loganlake.ca
www.loganlake.ca
Municipal Type: District
Incorporated: Nov. 10, 1970; *Area:* 325.4 sq km
County or District: Thompson-Nicola; *Population in 2016:* 1,993
Provincial Electoral District(s): Fraser-Nicola
Federal Electoral District(s): Central Okanagan-Similkameen-Nicola
Next Election: Oct. 15, 2022 (4 year terms)
Robin Smith, Mayor
Randy Diehl, Chief Administrative Officer, 250-523-6225
Jeff Carter, Director, Public Works & Recreation

Lumby
P.O. Box 430
1775 Glencaird St.
Lumby, BC V0E 2G0
Tel: 250-547-2171; *Fax:* 250-547-6894
info@lumby.ca
www.lumby.ca
Municipal Type: Village
Incorporated: Dec. 20, 1955; *Area:* 5.27 sq km
County or District: North Okanagan; *Population in 2016:* 1,833
Provincial Electoral District(s): Vernon-Monashee
Federal Electoral District(s): North Okanagan-Shuswap
Next Election: Oct. 15, 2022 (4 year terms)
Kevin Acton, Mayor, 250-547-2171
Tom Kadla, Chief Administrative Officer
Dave Manson, Superintendent, Public Works, Parks & Recreation

Lytton
P.O. Box 100
380 Main St.
Lytton, BC V0K 1Z0
Tel: 250-455-2355; *Fax:* 250-455-2142
hotspot@lytton.ca
www.lytton.ca
Municipal Type: Village
Incorporated: May 3, 1945; *Area:* 6.71 sq km
County or District: Thompson-Nicola; *Population in 2016:* 249
Provincial Electoral District(s): Fraser-Nicola
Federal Electoral District(s): Mission-Matsqui-Fraser Canyon
Next Election: Oct. 15, 2022 (4 year terms)
Jan Polderman, Mayor
Rebecca Anderson, Chief Administrative Officer

Mackenzie
P.O. Box 340
1 Mackenzie Blvd.
Mackenzie, BC V0J 2C0
Tel: 250-997-3221; *Fax:* 250-997-5186
info@district.mackenzie.bc.ca
www.district.mackenzie.bc.ca
Municipal Type: District
Incorporated: May 19, 1966; *Area:* 159.09 sq km
County or District: Fraser-Fort George; *Population in 2016:* 3,714
Provincial Electoral District(s): Prince George Mackenzie
Federal Electoral District(s): Prince George-Peace River-Northern Rockies
Next Election: Oct. 15, 2022 (4 year terms)
Joan Atkinson, Mayor
Dean McKinley, Chief Administrative Officer, 250-997-3221
Gord Petersen, Director, Community Services, 250-997-3221

Maple Ridge
11995 Haney Pl.
Maple Ridge, BC V2X 6A9
Tel: 604-463-5221; *Fax:* 604-467-7329
www.mapleridge.ca
Municipal Type: District
Incorporated: Sept. 12, 1874; *Area:* 266.78 sq km
County or District: Metro Vancouver; *Population in 2016:* 82,256
Provincial Electoral District(s): Maple Ridge-Pitt Meadows; Maple Ridge-Mission
Federal Electoral District(s): Pitt Meadows-Maple Ridge
Next Election: Oct. 15, 2022 (4 year terms)
Mike Morden, Mayor
Judy Dueck, Councillor
Kiersten Duncan, Councillor
Chelsa Meadus, Councillor
Gordy Robson, Councillor

Ryan Svendsen, Councillor
Ahmed Yousef, Councillor
Al Horsman, Chief Administrative Officer, 604-467-7430
Trevor Thompson, Chief Financial Officer, 604-467-7472
James Storey, Director, Engineering Operations, 604-463-9581
Valoree Richmond, Acting Director, Parks & Facilities,
604-467-7346
Danielle Pope, Director, Recreation & Community Services,
604-467-7447
Howard Exner, Fire Chief, 604-476-3055

Masset
P.O. Box 68
Masset, BC V0T 1M0
Tel: 250-626-3995; *Fax:* 250-626-3968
vom@mhtv.ca
www.massetbc.com
Municipal Type: Village
Incorporated: May 11, 1961; *Area:* 19.45 sq km
County or District: Skeena-Queen Charlotte; *Population in 2016:*
793
Provincial Electoral District(s): North Coast
Federal Electoral District(s): Skeena-Bulkley Valley
Next Election: Oct. 15, 2022 (4 year terms)
Barry Pages, Mayor
Trevor Jarvis, Chief Administrative Officer, 250-626-3995
Ralph Lamorie, Supervisor of Works, 250-626-3995

McBride
P.O. Box 519
100 Robson Centre
McBride, BC V0J 2E0
Tel: 250-569-2229; *Fax:* 250-569-3276
www.mcbride.ca
Municipal Type: Village
Incorporated: April 7, 1932; *Area:* 4.43 sq km
County or District: Fraser-Fort George; *Population in 2016:* 616
Provincial Electoral District(s): Prince George-Valemount
Federal Electoral District(s): Prince George-Peace
River-Northern Rockies
Next Election: Oct. 15, 2022 (4 year terms)
Gene P. Runtz, Mayor
Kelley Williams, Chief Administrative Officer

Merritt
P.O. Box 189
2185 Voght St.
Merritt, BC V1K 1B8
Tel: 250-378-4224; *Fax:* 250-378-2600
info@merritt.ca
www.merritt.ca
Municipal Type: Town
Incorporated: April 1, 1911; *Area:* 24.94 sq km
County or District: Thompson-Nicola; *Population in 2016:* 7,139
Provincial Electoral District(s): Fraser-Nicola
Federal Electoral District(s): Central
Okanagan-Similkameen-Nicola
Next Election: Oct. 15, 2022 (4 year terms)
Linda A. Brown, Mayor
Scott Hildebrand, Chief Administrative Officer, 250-378-4224

Metchosin
4450 Happy Valley Rd.
Victoria, BC V9C 3Z3
Tel: 250-474-3167; *Fax:* 250-474-6298
info@metchosin.ca
www.metchosin.ca
Municipal Type: District
Incorporated: Dec. 3, 1984; *Area:* 71.32 sq km
County or District: Capital; *Population in 2016:* 4,708
Provincial Electoral District(s): Esquimalt-Metchosin
Federal Electoral District(s): Esquimalt-Saanich-Sooke
Next Election: Oct. 15, 2022 (4 year terms)
John Ranns, Mayor, 250-474-3167
Lisa Urlacher, Chief Administrative Officer, 250-474-3167

Midway
P.O. Box 160
661 Eighth Ave.
Midway, BC V0H 1M0
Tel: 250-449-2222; *Fax:* 250-449-2258
midwaybc@shaw.ca
www.midwaybc.ca
Municipal Type: Village
Incorporated: May 25, 1967; *Area:* 12.16 sq km
County or District: Kootenay Boundary; *Population in 2016:* 649
Provincial Electoral District(s): Boundary-Similkameen
Federal Electoral District(s): South Okanagan-West Kootenay
Next Election: Oct. 15, 2022 (4 year terms)
Martin Fromme, Mayor
Penny Feist, Chief Administrative Officer, 250-449-2222

Mission
P.O. Box 20
8645 Stave Lake St.
Mission, BC V2V 4L9
Tel: 604-820-3700; *Fax:* 604-820-3715
info@mission.ca
www.mission.ca
Municipal Type: District
Incorporated: June 2, 1892; *Area:* 227.65 sq km
County or District: Fraser Valley; *Population in 2016:* 38,833
Provincial Electoral District(s): Maple Ridge-Mission
Federal Electoral District(s): Mission-Matsqui-Fraser Canyon;
Pitt Meadows-Maple Ridge
Next Election: Oct. 15, 2022 (4 year terms)
Pam Alexis, Mayor, 604-820-3702, Fax: 604-826-1363
Cal Crawford, Councillor
Mark Davies, Councillor
Jag Gill, Councillor
Carol Hamilton, Councillor
Ken Herar, Councillor
Danny Plecas, Councillor
Mike Younie, Chief Administrative Officer, 604-820-3704
Tracy Kyle, Director, Engineering & Public Works, 604-820-3739
Mark Goddard, Fire Chief, 604-820-5395

Montrose
P.O. Box 510
565 - 11th Ave.
Montrose, BC V0G 1P0
Tel: 250-367-7234; *Fax:* 250-367-7288
admin@montrose.ca
www.montrose.ca
Municipal Type: Village
Incorporated: June 22, 1956; *Area:* 1.53 sq km
County or District: Kootenay Boundary; *Population in 2016:* 996
Provincial Electoral District(s): Kootenay West
Federal Electoral District(s): South Okanagan-West Kootenay
Next Election: Oct. 15, 2022 (4 year terms)
Mike Walsh, Mayor
Larry Plotnikoff, Chief Administrative Officer, 250-367-7234

Nakusp
P.O. Box 280
91 - 1st St. NW
Nakusp, BC V0G 1R0
Tel: 250-265-3689; *Fax:* 250-265-3788
info@nakusp.com
www.nakusp.com
Municipal Type: Village
Incorporated: Nov. 24, 1964; *Area:* 8 sq km
County or District: Central Kootenay; *Population in 2016:* 1,130
Provincial Electoral District(s): Kootenay West
Federal Electoral District(s): South Okanagan-West Kootenay
Next Election: Oct. 15, 2022 (4 year terms)
Tom Zeleznik, Mayor
Laurie Taylor, Chief Administrative Officer, 250-265-3689

New Denver
P.O. Box 40
115 Slocan Ave.
New Denver, BC V0G 1S0
Tel: 250-358-2316; *Fax:* 250-358-7251
office@newdenver.ca
www.newdenver.ca
Municipal Type: Village
Incorporated: Jan. 12, 1929; *Area:* 1.1 sq km
County or District: Central Kootenay; *Population in 2016:* 473
Provincial Electoral District(s): Kootenay West
Federal Electoral District(s): South Okanagan-West Kootenay
Next Election: Oct. 15, 2022 (4 year terms)
Leonard Casley, Mayor
Bruce Woodbury, Chief Administrative Officer, 250-358-2316

New Hazelton
P.O. Box 340
3026 Bowser St.
New Hazelton, BC V0J 2J0
Tel: 250-842-6571; *Fax:* 250-842-6077
info@newhazelton.ca
www.newhazelton.ca
Municipal Type: District
Incorporated: Dec. 15, 1980; *Area:* 25.64 sq km
County or District: Kitimat-Stikine; *Population in 2016:* 580
Provincial Electoral District(s): Stikine
Federal Electoral District(s): Skeena-Bulkley Valley
Next Election: Oct. 15, 2022 (4 year terms)
Marilyn Lowry, Mayor
Wendy Hunt, Chief Administrative Officer, 250-842-6571

North Cowichan
P.O. Box 278
7030 Trans Canada Hwy.
Duncan, BC V9L 3X4
Tel: 250-746-3100; *Fax:* 250-746-3133
info@northcowichan.ca
www.northcowichan.ca
Municipal Type: District
Incorporated: June 18, 1873; *Area:* 195.56 sq km
County or District: Cowichan Valley; *Population in 2016:* 29,676
Provincial Electoral District(s): Nanaimo-North Cowichan
Federal Electoral District(s): Cowichan-Malahat-Langford
Next Election: Oct. 15, 2022 (4 year terms)
Al Siebring, Mayor
Rob Douglas, Councillor
Christopher Justice, Councillor
Tek Manhas, Councillor
Kate Marsh, Councillor
Rosalie Sawrie, Councillor
Debra Toporowski, Councillor
Ted Swabey, Chief Administrative Officer, 250-746-3117
David Conway, Director, Engineering, 250-746-3103
Don Stewart, Director, Parks & Recreation, 250-746-3193
Mark Frame, General Manager, Financial Services
Martin Drakeley, Manager, Fire & Bylaw Services, 250-746-3266

North Saanich
1620 Mills Rd.
North Saanich, BC V8L 5S9
Tel: 250-656-0781; *Fax:* 250-656-3155
admin@northsaanich.ca
www.northsaanich.ca
Municipal Type: District
Incorporated: Aug. 19, 1965; *Area:* 37.27 sq km
County or District: Capital; *Population in 2016:* 11,249
Provincial Electoral District(s): Saanich North & the Islands
Federal Electoral District(s): Saanich-Gulf Islands
Next Election: Oct. 15, 2022 (4 year terms)
Geoff Orr, Mayor, 250-655-5451
Heather Gartshore, Councillor, 250-656-0974
Jack McClintock, Councillor, 250-888-4890
Patricia Pearson, Councillor, 250-888-7202
Brett Smyth, Councillor, 250-656-1520
Celia Stock, Councillor, 250-655-3437
Murray Weisenberger, Councillor, 778-351-2213
Tim Tanton, Chief Administrative Officer, 250-655-5452
Brian Green, Director, Planning & Community Services,
250-655-5471
Curt Kingsley, Director, Corporate Services, 250-655-5453
Stephanie Munro, Director, Financial Services, 250-655-5495
Eymond Toupin, Director, Infrastructure Services, 250-655-5461
John Trelford, Director, Emergency Services, 250-656-1931

North Vancouver
355 West Queens Rd.
North Vancouver, BC V7N 4N5
Tel: 604-990-2311
infoweb@dnv.org
www.dnv.org
Municipal Type: District Municipality
Incorporated: Aug. 10, 1891; *Area:* 160.76 sq km
County or District: Metro Vancouver; *Population in 2016:* 85,395
Provincial Electoral District(s): N. Vancouver-Lonsdale; N.
Vancouver-Seymour
Federal Electoral District(s): North Vancouver; Burnaby
North-Seymour
Next Election: Oct. 15, 2022 (4 year terms)
Mike Little, Mayor
Jordan Back, Councillor
Matthew Bond, Councillor
Megan Curren, Councillor
Betty Forbes, Councillor
Jim Hanson, Councillor
Lisa Muri, Councillor
David Stuart, Chief Administrative Officer, 604-990-2209
Brian Hutchinson, Fire Chief

Oak Bay
2167 Oak Bay Ave.
Victoria, BC V8R 1G2
Tel: 250-598-3311; *Fax:* 250-598-9108
www.oakbay.ca
Municipal Type: District
Incorporated: July 2, 1906; *Area:* 10.53 sq km
County or District: Capital; *Population in 2016:* 18,094
Provincial Electoral District(s): Oak Bay-Gordon Head
Federal Electoral District(s): Victoria
Next Election: Oct. 15, 2022 (4 year terms)
Kevin Murdoch, Mayor, 250-896-4983
Andrew Appleton, Councillor, 778-533-4604
Hazel Braithwaite, Councillor, 250-595-8200

Cairine Green, Councillor, 250-896-5412
Tara Ney, Councillor, 250-592-1966
Esther Paterson, Councillor, 778-679-7057
Eric Zhelka, Councillor, 250-704-8641
Lou Varela, Chief Administrative Officer, 250-598-3311, Fax: 250-598-9108
Debbie Carter, Director, Corporate Services, 250-598-3311, Fax: 250-598-9108
Ray Herman, Director, Parks & Recreation Services, 250-370-7102, Fax: 250-370-7127
Daniel Horan, Director, Engineering & Public Works, 250-598-3311
Darren Hughes, Fire Chief, 250-592-9121, Fax: 250-598-2749

Oliver
P.O. Box 638
35016 - 97th St.
Oliver, BC V0H 1T0
Tel: 250-485-6200; *Fax:* 250-498-4466
admin@oliver.ca
www.oliver.ca
Municipal Type: Town
Incorporated: Dec. 31, 1945; *Area:* 4.95 sq km
County or District: Okanagan-Similkameen; *Population in 2016:* 4,928
Provincial Electoral District(s): Boundary-Similkameen
Federal Electoral District(s): South Okanagan-West Kootenay
Next Election: Oct. 15, 2022 (4 year terms)
Martin Johansen, Mayor
Cathy Cowans, Chief Administrative Officer
Carol Sheridan, Director, Recreation & Community Services

Osoyoos
P.O. Box 3010
8707 Main St.
Osoyoos, BC V0H 1V0
Tel: 250-495-6515; *Fax:* 250-495-2400
info@osoyoos.ca
www.osoyoos.ca
Other Information: Toll-Free Phone: 888-495-6515
Municipal Type: Town
Incorporated: Jan. 14, 1946; *Area:* 8.76 sq km
County or District: Okanagan-Similkameen; *Population in 2016:* 5,085
Provincial Electoral District(s): Boundary-Similkameen
Federal Electoral District(s): South Okanagan-West Kootenay
Next Election: Oct. 15, 2022 (4 year terms)
Sue McKortoff, Mayor
Barry Romanko, Chief Administrative Officer

Peachland
5806 Beach Ave.
Peachland, BC V0H 1X7
Tel: 250-767-2647; *Fax:* 250-767-3433
info@peachland.ca
www.peachland.ca
Municipal Type: District
Incorporated: Jan. 1, 1909; *Area:* 15.98 sq km
County or District: Central Okanagan; *Population in 2016:* 5,428
Provincial Electoral District(s): Penticton
Federal Electoral District(s): Central Okanagan-Similkameen-Nicola
Next Election: Oct. 15, 2022 (4 year terms)
Cindy Fortin, Mayor
Elsie Lemke, Chief Administrative Officer, 250-767-2647

Pemberton
P.O. Box 100
7400 Prospect St.
Pemberton, BC V0N 2L0
Tel: 604-894-6135; *Fax:* 604-894-6136
admin@pemberton.ca
www.pemberton.ca
Municipal Type: Village
Incorporated: July 20, 1956; *Area:* 4.45 sq km
County or District: Squamish-Lillooet; *Population in 2016:* 2,574
Provincial Electoral District(s): West Vancouver-Sea to Sky
Federal Electoral District(s): West Vancouver-Sunshine Coast-Sea to Sky Country
Next Election: Oct. 15, 2022 (4 year terms)
Michael Richman, Mayor
Nikki Gilmore, Chief Administrative Officer, 604-894-6135
Jeff Westlake, Public Works Supervisor, 604-894-6135

Port Alice
P.O. Box 130
1061 Marine Dr.
Port Alice, BC V0N 2N0
Tel: 250-284-3391; *Fax:* 250-284-3416
info@portalice.ca
www.portalice.ca

Municipal Type: Village
Incorporated: June 16, 1965; *Area:* 7.65 sq km
County or District: Mount Waddington; *Population in 2016:* 664
Provincial Electoral District(s): North Island
Federal Electoral District(s): North Island-Powell River
Next Election: Oct. 15, 2022 (4 year terms)
Kevin Cameron, Mayor
Madeline McDonald, Chief Administrative Officer

Port Clements
P.O. Box 198
36 Cedar Ave. West
Port Clements, BC V0T 1R0
Tel: 250-557-4295; *Fax:* 250-557-4568
deputy@portclements.ca
www.portclements.com
Municipal Type: Village
Incorporated: Dec. 31, 1975; *Area:* 13.59 sq km
County or District: Skeena-Queen Charlotte; *Population in 2016:* 282
Provincial Electoral District(s): North Coast
Federal Electoral District(s): Skeena-Bulkley Valley
Next Election: Oct. 15, 2022 (4 year terms)
Douglas Daugert, Mayor
Kim Mushynsky, Chief Administrative Officer
Sean O'Donoghue, Superintendent, Public Works

Port Edward
P.O. Box 1100
770 Pacific Ave.
Port Edward, BC V0V 1G0
Tel: 250-628-3667; *Fax:* 250-628-9225
info@portedward.ca
www.portedward.ca
Municipal Type: District
Incorporated: June 29, 1966; *Area:* 168.12 sq km
County or District: Skeena-Queen Charlotte; *Population in 2016:* 467
Provincial Electoral District(s): North Coast
Federal Electoral District(s): Skeena-Bulkley Valley
Next Election: Oct. 15, 2022 (4 year terms)
Knut Bjorndal, Mayor
Bob Payette, Chief Administrative Officer

Port Hardy
P.O. Box 68
7360 Columbia St.
Port Hardy, BC V0N 2P0
Tel: 250-949-6665; *Fax:* 250-949-7433
general@porthardy.ca
www.porthardy.ca
Municipal Type: District
Incorporated: May 5, 1966; *Area:* 40.81 sq km
County or District: Mount Waddington; *Population in 2016:* 4,132
Provincial Electoral District(s): North Island
Federal Electoral District(s): North Island-Powell River
Next Election: Oct. 15, 2022 (4 year terms)
Dennis Dugas, Mayor
Allison McCarrick, Chief Administrative Officer, 250-949-6665
Adrian Maas, Director, Financial Services
Jeff Long, Director, Corporate & Development Services, 250-949-6665

Port McNeill
P.O. Box 728
1775 Grenville Pl.
Port McNeill, BC V0N 2R0
Tel: 250-956-3111; *Fax:* 250-956-4300
reception@portmcneill.ca
www.portmcneill.ca
Municipal Type: Town
Incorporated: Feb. 18, 1966; *Area:* 7.74 sq km
County or District: Mount Waddington; *Population in 2016:* 2,337
Provincial Electoral District(s): North Island
Federal Electoral District(s): North Island-Powell River
Next Election: Oct. 15, 2022 (4 year terms)
Gaby Wickstrom, Mayor
Sue Harvey, Administrator

Pouce Coupé
P.O. Box 190
5011 - 49 Ave.
Pouce Coupé, BC V0C 2C0
Tel: 250-786-5794; *Fax:* 250-786-5257
admin@poucecoupe.ca
www.poucecoupe.ca
Municipal Type: Village
Incorporated: Jan. 5, 1932; *Area:* 2.06 sq km
County or District: Peace River; *Population in 2016:* 792
Provincial Electoral District(s): Peace River South
Federal Electoral District(s): Prince George-Peace

River-Northern Rockies
Next Election: Oct. 15, 2022 (4 year terms)
Lorraine Michetti, Mayor
Christopher Leggett, Chief Administrative Officer

Princeton
P.O. Box 670
169 Bridge St.
Princeton, BC V0X 1W0
Tel: 250-295-3135; *Fax:* 250-295-3477
admin@princeton.ca
www.princeton.ca
Municipal Type: Town
Incorporated: Sept. 11, 1951; *Area:* 10.25 sq km
County or District: Okanagan-Similkameen; *Population in 2016:* 2,828
Provincial Electoral District(s): Boundary-Similkameen
Federal Electoral District(s): Central Okanagan-Similkameen-Nicola
Next Election: Oct. 15, 2022 (4 year terms)
Spencer Coyne, Mayor
Rick Zerr, Chief Administrative Officer
Kevin Huey, Director, Infrastructure & Parks

Qualicum Beach
P.O. Box 130
#201, 660 Primrose St.
Qualicum Beach, BC V9K 1S7
Tel: 250-752-6921; *Fax:* 250-752-1243
qbtown@qualicumbeach.com
www.qualicumbeach.com
Municipal Type: Town
Incorporated: May 5, 1942; *Area:* 18 sq km
County or District: Nanaimo; *Population in 2016:* 9,943
Provincial Electoral District(s): Parksville-Qualicum
Federal Electoral District(s): Courtenay-Alberni
Next Election: Oct. 15, 2022 (4 year terms)
Brian S. Wiese, Mayor
Daniel Sailland, Chief Administrative Officer, 250-752-6921
Al Cameron, Superintendent, Public Works, Parks & Buildings, 250-752-6921
Luke Sales, Director, Planning & Approving Officer
Bob Weir, Director, Engineering, Utilities & Airport

Queen Charlotte
P.O. Box 580
903A Oceanview Dr.
Queen Charlotte, BC V0T 1S0
Tel: 250-559-4765; *Fax:* 250-559-4742
office@queencharlotte.ca
www.queencharlotte.ca
Municipal Type: Village
Incorporated: Dec. 7, 2005; *Area:* 37.28 sq km
County or District: Skeena-Queen Charlotte; *Population in 2016:* 852
Provincial Electoral District(s): North Coast
Federal Electoral District(s): Skeena-Bulkley Valley
Next Election: Oct. 15, 2022 (4 year terms)
Kris Olsen, Mayor
Lori Wiedeman, Chief Administrative Officer, 250-559-4765

Radium Hot Springs
P.O. Box 340
Radium Hot Springs, BC V0A 1M0
Tel: 250-347-6455; *Fax:* 250-347-9068
www.radiumhotsprings.ca
Municipal Type: Village
Incorporated: Dec. 10, 1990; *Area:* 6.31 sq km
County or District: East Kootenay; *Population in 2016:* 776
Provincial Electoral District(s): Columbia River-Revelstoke
Federal Electoral District(s): Kootenay-Columbia
Next Election: Oct. 15, 2022 (4 year terms)
Clara Reinhardt, Mayor
Mark Read, Chief Administrative Officer/Clerk/Approving Officer

Revelstoke
P.O. Box 170
216 Mackenzie Ave.
Revelstoke, BC V0E 2S0
Tel: 250-837-2161; *Fax:* 250-837-4930
admin@revelstoke.ca
www.cityofrevelstoke.com
Municipal Type: Town
Incorporated: March 1, 1899; *Area:* 31.9 sq km
County or District: Columbia-Shuswap; *Population in 2016:* 7,547
Provincial Electoral District(s): Columbia River-Revelstoke
Federal Electoral District(s): Kootenay-Columbia
Next Election: Oct. 15, 2022 (4 year terms)
Gary Sulz, Mayor
Laurie Donato, Director, Parks, Recreation & Culture
Mike Thomas, Director, Engineering & Development Services

Warfield

555 Schofield Hwy.
Trail, BC V1R 2G7
Tel: 250-368-8202; *Fax:* 250-368-9354
warfieldadmin@shawlink.ca
www.warfield.ca
Municipal Type: Village
Incorporated: Dec. 8, 1952; *Area:* 1.9 sq km
County or District: Kootenay Boundary; *Population in 2016:*
1,680
Provincial Electoral District(s): Kootenay West
Federal Electoral District(s): South Okanagan-West Kootenay
Next Election: Oct. 15, 2022 (4 year terms)
Diane Langman, Mayor, 250-368-8202
Jackie Patridge, CAO/Clerk/Treasurer
Teresa Mandoli, Director, Parks & Recreation

Wells

P.O. Box 219
Wells, BC V0K 2R0
Tel: 250-994-3330; *Fax:* 250-994-3331
wells@goldcity.net
www.wells.ca
Municipal Type: District
Incorporated: June 29, 1998; *Area:* 159.15 sq km
County or District: Cariboo; *Population in 2016:* 217
Provincial Electoral District(s): Cariboo North
Federal Electoral District(s): Cariboo-Prince George
Next Election: Oct. 15, 2022 (4 year terms)
Gabe Fourchalk, Mayor
Katrina Leckovic, Chief Administrative Officer, 250-994-3330
Dennis Manuel, Fire Chief & Superintendent, Public Works,
250-994-3330

West Vancouver

750 - 17th St.
West Vancouver, BC V7V 3T3
Tel: 604-925-7000; *Fax:* 604-925-5999
info@westvancouver.ca
www.westvancouver.ca
Municipal Type: District
Incorporated: March 15, 1912; *Area:* 87.26 sq km
County or District: Metro Vancouver; *Population in 2016:* 42,473

Provincial Electoral District(s): West Vancouver-Sea to Sky;
West Vancouver-Capilano
Federal Electoral District(s): West Vancouver-Sunshine
Coast-Sea to Sky Country
Next Election: Oct. 15, 2022 (4 year terms)
Mary-Ann Booth, Mayor
Craig Cameron, Councillor
Nora Gambioli, Councillor
Peter Lambur, Councillor
Bill Soporovich, Councillor
Sharon Thompson, Councillor
Marcus Wong, Councillor
Nina Leemhuis, Chief Administrative Officer, 604-925-7002
Jim Bailey, Director, Planning & Development Services,
604-925-7058
Andy Kwan, Acting Director, Engineering & Transportation
Services, 604-925-7027
Isabel Gordon, Director, Financial Services, 604-921-2902
Anne Mooi, Director, Parks, Culture & Community Services,
604-925-7235
Dave Clark, Fire Chief, 604-925-7396

Whistler

4325 Blackcomb Way
Whistler, BC V0N 1B4
Tel: 604-932-5535; *Fax:* 604-935-8109
info@whistler.ca
www.whistler.ca
Municipal Type: Resort Municipality
Incorporated: Sept. 6, 1975; *Area:* 161.71 sq km
County or District: Squamish-Lillooet; *Population in 2016:* 11,854
Provincial Electoral District(s): West Vancouver-Sea to Sky
Federal Electoral District(s): West Vancouver-Sunshine
Coast-Sea to Sky Country
Next Election: Oct. 15, 2022 (4 year terms)
Jack Crompton, Mayor
Mike Furey, Chief Administrative Officer, 604-935-8181
Jan Jansen, General Manager, Resort Experience,
604-932-8177
Norm McPhail, General Manager, Corporate & Community
Services

Joe Paul, General Manager, Infrastructure Services & Approving
Officer, 604-935-8193
Mike Kirkegaard, Director, Planning, 604-935-8163
Denise Wood, Director, Human Resources, 604-935-8217

Zeballos

P.O. Box 127
Zeballos, BC V0P 2A0
Tel: 250-761-4229; *Fax:* 250-761-4331
adminzeb@recn.ca
www.zeballos.com
Municipal Type: Village
Incorporated: June 27, 1952; *Area:* 130 sq km
County or District: Strathcona; *Population in 2016:* 107
Provincial Electoral District(s): North Island
Federal Electoral District(s): North Island-Powell River
Next Election: Oct. 15, 2022 (4 year terms)
Julie Colborne, Mayor
Eileen Lovestrom, Chief Administrative Officer
Mike Atchison, Fire Chief & Superintendent, Public Works

Indian Government District in British Columbia

Sechelt

P.O. Box 740
5555 Sunshine Coast Hwy.
Sechelt, BC V0N 3A0
Tel: 604-885-2273; *Fax:* 604-885-4324
hello@shishalm.com
www.shishalh.com
Other Information: Toll-Free Phone: 866-885-2275
Municipal Type: Metis Settlements
Incorporated: March 17, 1988; *Area:* 10.95 sq km
Population in 2016: 10,216
Next Election: Oct. 15, 2022 (4 year terms)
Henry Warren Paull, Chief
Nadine Hoehne, Chief Adminsitrative Officer, 604-885-2273

MANITOBA

All municipalities in Manitoba (except Winnipeg, which is governed by the City of Winnipeg Act) come under authority of the Manitoba Municipal Act.

In Manitoba there are no counties or regional governments; there are only urban and rural municipalities. Incorporation of a new municipality requires a population of at least 1,000 residents and a population density of at least 400 residents per square kilometre for an urban municipality and a population density of less than 400 residents per square kilometre for a rural municipality. Urban municipalities may be called cities, towns, villages or urban municipalities. The population requirement for a city is at least 7,500 residents.

Municipal elections are held every four years on the fourth Wednesday of October (2018, 2022, etc.). As of January 1, 2015, the province amalgamated municipalities with populations of fewer than 1,000, merging neighbouring municipalities and reducing the total number of municipalities in the province from 197 to 137.

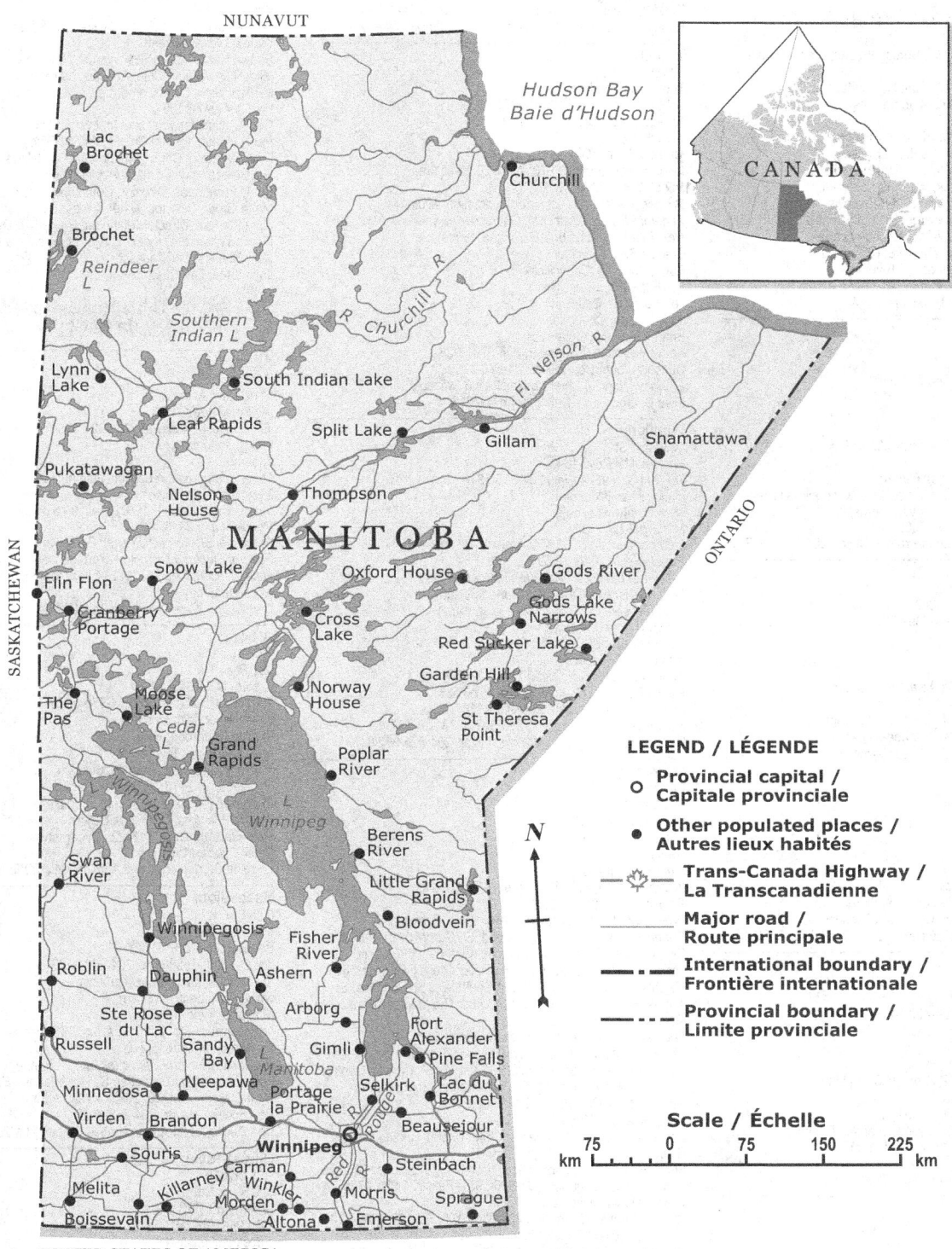

Source: © Department of Natural Resources Canada. All rights reserved.

Manitoba

Major Municipalities in Manitoba

Brandon
410 - 9th St.
Brandon, MB R7A 6A2
Tel: 204-729-2186; *Fax:* 204-729-8244
www.brandon.ca
Municipal Type: City
Incorporated: May 3, 1882; *Area:* 77.41 sq km
Population in 2016: 48,859
Provincial Electoral District(s): Spruce Woods; Brandon East; Brandon West
Federal Electoral District(s): Brandon-Souris
Next Election: Oct. 26, 2022 (4 year terms)
Rick Chrest, Mayor
Jeff Fawcett, Councillor, Wards: 1. Assiniboine
Kris Desjarlais, Councillor, Wards: 2. Rosser
Barry Cullen, Councillor, Wards: 3. Victoria
Shaun Cameron, Councillor, Wards: 4. University
John LoRegio, Councillor, Wards: 5. Meadows
Bruce Luebke, Councillor, Wards: 6. South Centre
Shawn Berry, Councillor, Wards: 7. Linden Lanes
Ron W. Brown, Councillor, Wards: 8. Richmond
Glen Parker, Councillor, Wards: 9. Riverview
Jan Chaboyer, Councillor, Wards: 10. Green Acres
Scott McDonald, Fire Chief, 204-729-2404

Flin Flon
20 - 1st Ave.
Flin Flon, MB R8A 0T7
Tel: 204-684-7511; *Fax:* 204-681-7530
info@flinflon.ca
www.cityofflinflon.ca
Municipal Type: City
Incorporated: Jan. 1, 1933; *Area:* 13.88 sq km
Population in 2016: 4,982
Provincial Electoral District(s): Flin Flon
Federal Electoral District(s): Churchill-Keewatinook Aski
Next Election: Oct. 26, 2022 (4 year terms)
Cal Huntley, Mayor, 204-681-7508
Glenna Daschuk, Chief Administrative Officer, 204-681-7503

Portage la Prairie
97 Saskatchewan Ave. East
Portage la Prairie, MB R1N 0L8
Tel: 204-239-8337; *Fax:* 204-239-1532
info@city-plap.com
www.city-plap.com
Municipal Type: City
Incorporated: Jan. 3, 1907; *Area:* 24.68 sq km
Population in 2016: 13,304
Provincial Electoral District(s): Portage la Prairie
Federal Electoral District(s): Portage-Lisgar
Next Election: Oct. 26, 2022 (4 year terms)
Irvine A. Ferris, Mayor
Brent Budz, Councillor
Melissa Draycott, Councillor
Ryan Espey, Councillor
Sherilyn Knox, Councillor
Preston Meier, Councillor
Wayne Wall, Councillor
Nathan Peto, City Manager
Jocelyn Lequier-Jobin, Director, Operations
Cathie McFarlane, Director, Corporate Services
Phil Carpenter, Fire Chief, 204-239-8340; Fax: 204-239-5154

Selkirk
200 Eaton Ave.
Selkirk, MB R1A 0W6
Tel: 204-785-4900; *Fax:* 204-482-5448
info@cityofselkirk.com
myselkirk.ca
Municipal Type: City
Incorporated: June 5, 1882; *Area:* 24.87 sq km
Population in 2016: 10,278
Provincial Electoral District(s): Selkirk
Federal Electoral District(s): Selkirk-Interlake-Eastman
Next Election: Oct. 26, 2022 (4 year terms)
Larry Johannson, Mayor
Duane Nicol, Chief Administrative Officer

Steinbach
225 Reimer Ave.
Steinbach, MB R5G 2J1
Tel: 204-326-9877; *Fax:* 204-346-6235
www.steinbach.ca
Municipal Type: City
Incorporated: Jan. 3, 1946; *Area:* 25.57 sq km

Population in 2016: 15,829
Provincial Electoral District(s): Steinbach
Federal Electoral District(s): Provencher
Next Election: Oct. 26, 2022 (4 year terms)
Earl Funk, Mayor, 204-346-6234
Jack Hiebert, Councillor
Bill Hiebert, Councillor
Damian Penner, Councillor
Susan Penner, Councillor, 204-346-1896
Jac Siemens, Councillor, 204-326-2697
Michael Zwaagstra, Councillor, 204-320-9502
Troy Warkentin, Chief Administrative Officer, 204-345-6529
Randy Reimer, Department Head, Public Works, 204-346-6215

Thompson
226 Mystery Lake Rd.
Thompson, MB R8N 1S6
Tel: 204-677-7910; *Fax:* 204-677-7936
communications@thompson.ca
www.thompson.ca
Municipal Type: City
Incorporated: Jan. 5, 1970; *Area:* 20.79 sq km
Population in 2016: 13,678
Provincial Electoral District(s): Thompson; Midland
Federal Electoral District(s): Churchill-Keewatinook Aski
Next Election: Oct. 26, 2022 (4 year terms)
Colleen Smook, Mayor
Earl Colbourne, Councillor
Les Ellsworth, Councillor
Jeff Fountain, Councillor
Judy Kolada, Councillor
Brian Lundmark, Councillor
Kathy Valentino, Councillor, 204-679-0035
Duncan Wong, Councillor, 204-679-2728
Anthony McInnis, Chief Administrative Officer
Mike Bourgon, Fire Chief, 204-677-7916

Winkler
185 Main St.
Winkler, MB R6W 1B4
Tel: 204-325-9524; *Fax:* 204-325-5915
info@cityofwinkler.ca
www.cityofwinkler.ca
Municipal Type: City
Incorporated: Jan. 6, 1954; *Area:* 17.02 sq km
Population in 2016: 12,591
Provincial Electoral District(s): Morden-Winkler
Federal Electoral District(s): Portage-Lisgar
Next Election: Oct. 26, 2022 (4 year terms)
Martin Harder, Mayor
Karina Bueckert, Councillor
Don Fehr, Councillor
Andrew Froese, Councillor, 204-362-4928
Michael Grenier, Councillor, 204-362-7728
Marvin Plett, Councillor, 204-362-4148
Henry Siemens, Councillor, 204-362-3178
Barb Dyck, Chief Administrative Officer, 204-325-9524

Winnipeg
City Hall
510 Main St.
Winnipeg, MB R3B 1B9
311@winnipeg.ca
www.winnipeg.ca
Municipal Type: City
Incorporated: Nov. 8, 1873; *Area:* 464.33 sq km
Population in 2016: 705,244
Provincial Electoral District(s): Assiniboia; Burrows; Charleswood; Concordia; Elmwood; Ft. Garry-Riverview; Ft. Richmond; Ft. Rouge; Ft. Whyte; Kildonan; Kirkfield Park; Logan; Minto; Point Douglas; Radisson; Riel; River East; River Heights; Rossmere; Seine River; Southdale; St. Boniface; St. James; St. Johns; St. Norbert; St. Vital; The Maples; Transcona; Tuxedo; Tyndall Park; Wollseley
Federal Electoral District(s): Charleswood-St. James-Assiniboia-Headingley; Elmwood-Transcona; Kildonan-St. Paul; Saint Boniface-Saint Vital; Winnipeg Centre; Winnipeg North; Winnipeg South; Winnipeg South Centre
Next Election: Oct. 26, 2022 (4 year terms)
Brian Bowman, Mayor
Kevin Klein, Councillor, Wards: Charleswood-Tuxedo-Whyte Ridge
Sherri Rollins, Councillor, Wards: Fort Rouge-East Fort Garry
Cindy Gilroy, Councillor, 204-986-5951, Fax: 204-986-3725, Wards: Daniel McIntyre
Jason Schreyer, Councillor, 204-986-5195, Fax: 204-986-3725, Wards: Elmwood-East Kildonan
Ross Eadie, Councillor, 204-986-5188, Fax: 204-986-3726, Wards: Mynarski
Jeff Browaty, Councillor, 204-986-5196, Fax: 204-986-3725, Wards: North Kildonan

Devi Sharma, Councillor & Speaker, 204-986-5264, Fax: 204-986-7806, Wards: Old Kildonan
Vivian Santos, Councillor, Wards: Point Douglas
John Orlikow, Councillor, 204-986-5236, Fax: 204-986-3725, Wards: River Heights-Fort Garry
Matt Allard, Councillor, 204-396-4636, Fax: 204-986-3725, Wards: St. Boniface
Markus Chambers, Councillor, Wards: St. Nortbert-Seine River
Scott Gillingham, Councillor, 204-986-5848, Fax: 204-986-4320, Wards: St. James
Brian Mayes, Councillor, 204-986-5088, Fax: 204-986-3725, Wards: St. Vital
Janice Lukes, Councillor, 204-986-6824, Fax: 204-986-3725, Wards: Waverly West
Shawn Nason, Councillor, Wards: Transcona
Mike Ruta, Interim Chief Administrative Officer
Michael Jack, Chief Corporate Services Officer, 204-986-2566, Fax: 204-947-9155
Glen Cottick, Interim Chief Innovation Officer
Paul Olafson, Interim Chief Financial Officer
Dave Wardrop, Chief Transportation & Utilities Officer
Jim Berezowsky, Director, Public Works
Cindy Fernandes, Director, Community Services
Moira Greer, Director, Water & Waste
John Kiernan, Director, Planning, Property & Development
Felicia Wiltshire, Director, Customer Service & Communications
Kelly Sheilds, City Assessor
John Lane, Fire Chief

Other Municipalities in Manitoba

Altona
P.O. Box 1630
111 Centre Ave. East
Altona, MB R0G 0B0
Tel: 204-324-6468; *Fax:* 204-324-1550
info@altona.ca
altona.ca
Other Information: reception@altona.ca
Municipal Type: Town
Incorporated: Jan. 1, 1956; *Area:* 9.46 sq km
Population in 2016: 4,212
Provincial Electoral District(s): Borderland
Federal Electoral District(s): Portage-Lisgar
Next Election: Oct. 26, 2022 (4 year terms)
Al Friesen, Mayor
Dan Gagne, Chief Administrative Officer

Arborg
P.O. Box 159
337 River Rd.
Arborg, MB R0C 0A0
Tel: 204-376-2647; *Fax:* 204-376-5379
townofarborg@mymts.net
www.townofarborg.com
Municipal Type: Town
Incorporated: 1964; *Area:* 2.26 sq km
Population in 2016: 1,232
Provincial Electoral District(s): Interlake-Gimli
Federal Electoral District(s): Selkirk-Interlake-Eastman
Next Election: Oct. 26, 2022 (4 year terms)
Peter Dueck, Mayor
Lorraine Bardarson, Chief Administrative Officer

Beausejour
P.O. Box 1028
639 Park Ave.
Beausejour, MB R0E 0C0
Tel: 204-268-7550; *Fax:* 204-268-3107
townoffice@townofbeausejour.com
www.townofbeausejour.ca
Municipal Type: Town
Incorporated: Jan. 2, 1912; *Area:* 5.35 sq km
Population in 2016: 3,219
Provincial Electoral District(s): Lac du Bonnet
Federal Electoral District(s): Selkirk-Interlake-Eastman
Next Election: Oct. 26, 2022 (4 year terms)
Ray Schirle, Mayor, 204-268-3022
Don Dowle, Chief Administrative Officer, 204-268-7553

Bifrost-Riverton
P.O. Box 70
329 River Rd.
Arborg, MB R0C 0A0
Tel: 204-376-2391; *Fax:* 204-376-2742
bifrost@mymts.net
rmbifrost.com
Other Information: Alternate Phone: 204-378-2281
Municipal Type: Municipality
Incorporated: Jan. 4, 1908; *Area:* 1,643.69 sq km

Population in 2016: 3,378
Provincial Electoral District(s): Interlake-Gimli
Federal Electoral District(s): Selkirk-Interlake-Eastman
Next Election: Oct. 26, 2022 (4 year terms)
Note: The RM of Bifrost & the Village of Riverton amalgamated to form the new Municipality of Bifrost-Riverton on Jan. 1, 2015.
Brian N. Johnson, Reeve
Cindy Stansell, Chief Administrative Officer

Boissevain-Morton
P.O. Box 490
420 South Railway Ave.
Boissevain, MB R0K 0E0
Tel: 204-534-2433; *Fax:* 204-534-3710
admin@boissevain.ca
www.boissevain.ca
Municipal Type: Municipality
Incorporated: 1906; *Area:* 1092.65 sq km
Population in 2016: 2,353
Provincial Electoral District(s): Turtle Mountain
Federal Electoral District(s): Brandon-Souris
Next Election: Oct. 26, 2022 (4 year terms)
Note: The Town of Boissevain & the RM of Morton amalgamated to form the new Municipality of Boissevain-Morton on Jan. 1, 2015.
Judy Swanson, Mayor
Leo Poulin, Chief Administrative Officer

Brenda-Waskada
P.O. Box 40
33 Railway Ave.
Waskada, MB R0M 2E0
Tel: 204-673-2401; *Fax:* 204-673-2663
office@brendawaskada.ca
www.waskada.org
Municipal Type: Municipality
Area: 766.77 sq km
Population in 2016: 674
Provincial Electoral District(s): Turtle Mountain
Federal Electoral District(s): Brandon-Souris
Next Election: Oct. 26, 2022 (4 year terms)
Note: The RM of Brenda & the Village of Waskada amalgamated to form the new Municipality of Brenda-Waskada on Jan. 1, 2015.
Jordan Morningstar, Head of Council
Diane Woodworth, Chief Administrative Officer

Carberry
P.O. Box 130
316 - 4th Ave.
Carberry, MB R0K 0H0
Tel: 204-834-6600; *Fax:* 204-834-6604
town@townofcarberry.ca
www.townofcarberry.ca
Municipal Type: Town
Incorporated: Jan. 1, 1905; *Area:* 4.79 sq km
Population in 2016: 1,738
Provincial Electoral District(s): Agassiz
Federal Electoral District(s): Dauphin-Swan River-Neepawa
Next Election: Oct. 26, 2022 (4 year terms)
Stuart Olmstead, Mayor, 204-834-2524
Sandra Jones, Chief Administrative Officer

Carman
P.O. Box 160
12 - 2nd Ave. SW
Carman, MB R0G 0J0
Tel: 204-745-2443; *Fax:* 204-745-2903
info@townofcarman.com
www.carmanmanitoba.ca
Municipal Type: Town
Incorporated: Jan. 1, 1905; *Area:* 4.12 sq km
Population in 2016: 3,164
Provincial Electoral District(s): Midland
Federal Electoral District(s): Portage-Lisgar
Next Election: Oct. 26, 2022 (4 year terms)
Brent Owen, Mayor
Cheryl Young, Chief Administrative Officer

Cartwright-Roblin
P.O. Box 9
485 Curwen St.
Cartwright, MB R0K 0L0
Tel: 204-529-2363; *Fax:* 204-529-2288
www.cartwrightroblin.ca
Municipal Type: Municipality
Incorporated: Jan. 5, 1948; *Area:* 718.01 sq km
Population in 2016: 1,308
Provincial Electoral District(s): Swan River; Turtle Mountain
Federal Electoral District(s): Brandon-Souris
Next Election: Oct. 26, 2022 (4 year terms)
Note: The RM of Roblin & the Village of Cartwright amalgamated

to form the new Rural Municipality of Cartwright-Roblin on Jan. 1, 2015.
Jamie Dousselaere, Head of Council
Colleen Mullin, Chief Administrative Officer

Churchill
P.O. Box 459
180 LaVerendrye Blvd.
Churchill, MB R0B 0E0
Tel: 204-675-8871; *Fax:* 204-675-2934
townofchurchill@churchill.ca
www.churchill.ca
Municipal Type: Town
Incorporated: Jan. 4, 1997; *Area:* 53.96 sq km
Population in 2016: 899
Provincial Electoral District(s): Thompson
Federal Electoral District(s): Churchill-Keewatinook Aski
Next Election: Oct. 26, 2022 (4 year terms)
Michael Spence, Mayor
Cory Young, Chief Executive Officer

Clanwilliam-Erickson
P.O. Box 40
45 Main St.
Erickson, MB R0J 0P0
Tel: 204-636-2431; *Fax:* 204-636-2516
admin@ericksonmb.ca
www.ericksonmb.ca
Municipal Type: Municipality
Incorporated: Jan. 3, 1884; *Area:* 352.08 sq km
Population in 2016: 870
Provincial Electoral District(s): Riding Mountain
Federal Electoral District(s): Dauphin-Swan River-Neepawa
Next Election: Oct. 26, 2022 (4 year terms)
Note: The Town of Erickson & the RM of Clanwilliam amalgamated to form the new Municipality of Clanwilliam-Erickson on Jan. 1, 2015.
Victor Baraniuk, Mayor, 204-636-2470
Quinn Greavett, Chief Administrative Officer

Dauphin
100 Main St. South
Dauphin, MB R7N 1K3
Tel: 204-622-3200; *Fax:* 204-622-3290
info@dauphin.ca
www.dauphin.ca
Other Information: Toll-Free Phone: 877-566-5669
Municipal Type: Town
Incorporated: Jan. 7, 1898; *Area:* 12.65 sq km
Population in 2016: 8,457
Provincial Electoral District(s): Dauphin
Federal Electoral District(s): Dauphin-Swan River-Neepawa
Next Election: Oct. 26, 2022 (4 year terms)
Allen Dowhan, Mayor
Brad D. Collett, Chief Administrative Officer, 204-622-3213, Fax: 204-622-3291

Dunnottar
P.O. Box 321
44 Whytewold Rd.
Matlock, MB R0C 2B0
Tel: 204-389-4962; *Fax:* 204-389-4966
info@dunnottar.ca
www.dunnottar.ca
Municipal Type: Resort Village
Area: 2.79 sq km
Population in 2016: 763
Provincial Electoral District(s): Interlake-Gimli
Federal Electoral District(s): Selkirk-Interlake-Eastman
Next Election: July 22, 2022 (4 year terms)
Richard Gamble, Mayor
J.M. Thevenot, Chief Administrative Officer

Emerson-Franklin
P.O. Box 66
115 Waddell Ave. East
Dominion City, MB R0A 0H0
Tel: 204-427-2557; *Fax:* 204-427-2224
info@emersonfranklin.com
www.emersonfranklin.com
Municipal Type: Municipality
Area: 975.62 sq km
Population in 2016: 2,537
Provincial Electoral District(s): Borderland; Turtle Mountain
Federal Electoral District(s): Provencher
Next Election: Oct. 26, 2022 (4 year terms)
Note: The RM of Franklin & the Town of Emerson amalgamated to form the new Municipality of Emerson-Franklin on Jan. 1, 2015.
David Carlson, Reeve
Tracey French, Chief Administrative Officer

Ethelbert
P.O. Box 115
56 - 2nd Ave.
Ethelbert, MB R0L 0T0
Tel: 204-742-3212; *Fax:* 204-742-3642
rmethelbert@inetlink.ca
Municipal Type: Municipality
Incorporated: Jan. 1, 1905; *Area:* 1,134.5 sq km
Population in 2017: 607
Provincial Electoral District(s): Swan River
Federal Electoral District(s): Dauphin-Swan River-Neepawa
Next Election: Oct. 26, 2022 (4 year terms)
Note: The RM of Ethelbert & the Village of Ethelbert amalgamated to form the new Municipality of Ethelbert on Jan. 1, 2015.
Arlene Rehaluk, Head of Council
Loretta Woytkiewicz, Chief Administrative Officer

Gilbert Plains
P.O. Box 220
201 Main St. North
Gilbert Plains, MB R0L 0X0
Tel: 204-548-2326; *Fax:* 204-548-2564
gilbertplainsmunicipality@mymts.net
www.gilbertplains.com
Other Information: rmofgp3@mymts.net
Municipal Type: Municipality
Incorporated: Jan. 3, 1901; *Area:* 1,049.14 sq km
Population in 2016: 1,470
Provincial Electoral District(s): Dauphin
Federal Electoral District(s): Dauphin-Swan River-Neepawa
Next Election: Oct. 26, 2022 (4 year terms)
Note: The RM of Gilbert Plains & the Town of Gilbert Plains amalgamated to form the new Municipality of Gilbert Plains on Jan. 1, 2015.
Blake Price, Head of Council
Leanne McKay, Chief Administrative Officer

Gillam
P.O. Box 100
323 Railway Ave.
Gillam, MB R0B 0L0
Tel: 204-652-3150; *Fax:* 204-652-3199
information@townofgillam.com
www.townofgillam.com
Municipal Type: Town
Area: 1,996.35 sq km
Population in 2016: 1,265
Provincial Electoral District(s): Thompson
Federal Electoral District(s): Churchill-Keewatinook Aski
Next Election: Oct. 26, 2022 (4 year terms)
Dwayne Forman, Mayor
Jackie Clayton, Chief Administrative Officer

Glenboro-South Cypress
P.O. Box 219
618 Railway Ave.
Glenboro, MB R0K 0X0
Tel: 204-827-2252; *Fax:* 204-827-2123
caormsc@mts.net
glenboro.com
Municipal Type: Municipality
Incorporated: Jan. 7, 1881; *Area:* 1,095.08 sq km
Population in 2016: 1,565
Provincial Electoral District(s): Spruce Woods
Federal Electoral District(s): Brandon-Souris
Next Election: Oct. 26, 2022 (4 year terms)
Note: The Village of Glenboro & the RM of South Cypress amalgamated to form the new Municipality of Glenboro-South Cypress on Jan. 1, 2015.
Trevor Drinkwater, Mayor
Darren Myers, Chief Administrative Officer

Glenella-Lansdowne
P.O. Box 10
50 Main St. North
Glenella, MB R0J 0V0
Tel: 204-352-4281; *Fax:* 204-352-4100
rmofglen@inetlink.ca
glenella.ca
Other Information: Alternate Phone: 204-368-2202
Municipal Type: Municipality
Incorporated: Jan. 5, 1920; *Area:* 1263.43 sq km
Population in 2016: 1,181
Provincial Electoral District(s): Agassiz
Federal Electoral District(s): Dauphin-Swan River-Neepawa
Next Election: Oct. 26, 2022 (4 year terms)
Note: The RM of Glenella & the RM of Lansdowne amalgamated to form the new Municipality of Glenella-Lansdowne on Jan. 1, 2015.
Richard Funk, Reeve
Wendy Wutzke, Chief Administrative Officer

Grand Rapids
P.O. Box 301
200 Grand Rapids Dr.
Grand Rapids, MB R0C 1E0
Tel: 204-639-2260; *Fax:* 204-639-2475
towngra@xplornet.ca
Municipal Type: Town
Incorporated: Jan. 2, 1962; *Area:* 85.95 sq km
Population in 2016: 268
Provincial Electoral District(s): The Pas-Kameesak
Federal Electoral District(s): Churchill-Keewatinook Aski
Next Election: Oct. 26, 2022 (4 year terms)
Robert Buck, Mayor
Bernard Beardy, Chief Administrative Officer

Grandview
P.O. Box 219
531 Main St. North
Grandview, MB R0L 0Y0
Tel: 204-546-5250; *Fax:* 204-546-5269
grandview@mymts.net
www.grandviewmanitoba.com
Municipal Type: Municipality
Incorporated: Jan. 3, 1901; *Area:* 1,152.5 sq km
Population in 2016: 1,482
Provincial Electoral District(s): Dauphin
Federal Electoral District(s): Dauphin-Swan River-Neepawa
Next Election: Oct. 26, 2022 (4 year terms)
Note: The RM of Grandview & the Town of Grandview amalgamated to form the new Municipality of Grandview on Jan. 1, 2015.
Kevin Edmonson, Mayor
Vacant, Chief Administrative Officer

Grassland
P.O. Box 399
209 Airdrie St.
Hartney, MB R0M 0X0
Tel: 204-858-2590; *Fax:* 204-858-2681
hartney@mts.net
Municipal Type: Municipality
Incorporated: Jan. 6, 1897
Population in 2016: 1,561
Provincial Electoral District(s): Turtle Mountain
Federal Electoral District(s): Brandon-Souris
Next Election: Oct. 26, 2022 (4 year terms)
Note: The RM of Cameron, the Town of Hartney & the RM of Whitewater amalgamated to form the new Municipality of Grassland on Jan. 1, 2015.
Blair Woods, Reeve
Brad Coe, Chief Administrative Officer

Hamiota
P.O. Box 100
75 Maple Ave. East
Hamiota, MB R0M 0T0
Tel: 204-764-3050; *Fax:* 204-764-3055
info@hamiota.com
www.hamiota.com
Municipal Type: Municipality
Incorporated: 1907; *Area:* 3.38 sq km
Population in 2016: 1,225
Provincial Electoral District(s): Riding Mountain
Federal Electoral District(s): Dauphin-Swan River-Neepawa
Next Election: Oct. 26, 2022 (4 year terms)
Note: The RM of Hamiota & the Town of Hamiota amalgamated to form the new Municipality of Hamiota on Jan. 1, 2015.
Larry Oakden, Reeve
Tristant Urquhart, Chief Administrative Officer

Harrison Park
P.O. Box 190
43 Gateway St.
Onanole, MB R0J 1N0
Tel: 204-848-7614; *Fax:* 204-848-2082
admin@harrisonpark.ca
harrisonpark.ca
Municipal Type: Municipality
Incorporated: Jan. 6, 1954; *Area:* 793.38 sq km
Population in 2016: 1,622
Provincial Electoral District(s): Riding Mountain
Federal Electoral District(s): Dauphin-Swan River-Neepawa
Next Election: Oct. 26, 2022 (4 year terms)
Note: The RM of Harrison & the RM of Park amalgamated to form the new Municipality of Harrison Park on Jan. 1, 2015.
Jason Potter, Reeve
Chad Davies, Chief Administrative Officer

Killarney-Turtle Mountain
P.O. Box 10
415 Broadway Ave.
Killarney, MB R0K 1G0
Tel: 204-523-7247; *Fax:* 204-523-4637
info@killarney.ca
www.killarney.ca
Municipal Type: Municipality
Incorporated: Jan. 1, 1882; *Area:* 925.13 sq km
Population in 2016: 3,429
Provincial Electoral District(s): Turtle Mountain
Federal Electoral District(s): Brandon-Souris
Next Election: Oct. 26, 2022 (4 year terms)
Note: The municipalities of Killarney & Turtle Mountain amalgamated to form one entity effective Jan. 1, 2007.
Rick Pauls, Mayor
Karen Patterson, Chief Administrative Officer

Lac du Bonnet
P.O. Box 339
84 - 2nd St.
Lac du Bonnet, MB R0E 1A0
Tel: 204-345-8693; *Fax:* 204-345-8694
townldb@mts.net
townoflacdubonnet.com
Municipal Type: Town
Incorporated: Jan. 4, 1947; *Area:* 2.25 sq km
Population in 2016: 1,089
Provincial Electoral District(s): Lac du Bonnet
Federal Electoral District(s): Selkirk-Interlake-Eastman
Next Election: Oct. 26, 2022 (4 year terms)
Gordon Peters, Mayor
Darcey Wittig, Chief Administrative Officer

Leaf Rapids
Town Centre Complex
P.O. Box 340
Leaf Rapids, MB R0B 1W0
Tel: 204-473-2436; *Fax:* 204-473-2566
reception@townofleafrapids.ca
Municipal Type: Town
Incorporated: Jan. 5, 1976; *Area:* 1,272.87 sq km
Population in 2016: 582
Provincial Electoral District(s): Flin Flon
Federal Electoral District(s): Churchill-Keewatinook Aski
Next Election: Oct. 26, 2022 (4 year terms)
Ervin Bighetty Jr., Mayor
Spencer Sprowler, Chief Administrative Officer

Lorne
P.O. Box 10
307 - 3rd St.
Somerset, MB R0G 2L0
Tel: 204-744-2133; *Fax:* 204-744-2349
rmlorne@mymts.net
www.rmoflorne.ca
Municipal Type: Municipality
Incorporated: Jan. 5, 1880; *Area:* 906.82 sq km
Population in 2016: 3,041
Provincial Electoral District(s): Turtle Mountain
Federal Electoral District(s): Portage-Lisgar
Next Election: Oct. 26, 2022 (4 year terms)
Note: The RM of Lorne, the Village of Notre Dame de Lourdes & the Village of Somerset amalgamated to form the new Municipality of Lorne on Jan. 1, 2015.
Aurel Pantel, Reeve
Shannon Gaultier, Chief Administrative Officer

Louise
P.O. Box 310
26 South Railway Ave. East
Crystal City, MB R0K 0N0
Tel: 204-873-2591; *Fax:* 204-873-2459
rmlouise@inetlink.ca
Other Information: fina@louisemb.net
Municipal Type: Municipality
Incorporated: Jan. 5, 1880; *Area:* 932.67 sq km
Population in 2016: 1,918
Provincial Electoral District(s): Turtle Mountain
Federal Electoral District(s): Brandon-Souris
Next Election: Oct. 26, 2022 (4 year terms)
Note: The RM of Louise, the Town of Pilot Mound & the Village of Crystal City amalgamated to form the new Municipality of Louise on Jan. 1, 2015.
Murray McIntyre, Reeve
Penny Burton, Chief Administrative Officer

Lynn Lake
P.O. Box 100
503 Sherritt Ave.
Lynn Lake, MB R0B 0W0
Tel: 204-356-2418; *Fax:* 204-356-8297
info@lynnlake.ca
www.lynnlake.ca
Municipal Type: Town
Incorporated: 1950; *Area:* 910.23 sq km
Population in 2016: 494
Provincial Electoral District(s): Flin Flon
Federal Electoral District(s): Churchill-Keewatinook Aski
Next Election: Oct. 26, 2022 (4 year terms)
Jim Shortt, Mayor
James Fielder, Chief Administrative Officer

McCreary
P.O. Box 338
432 - 1st Ave.
McCreary, MB R0J 1B0
Tel: 204-835-2309; *Fax:* 204-835-2649
mccreary@mymts.net
www.exploremccreary.com
Municipal Type: Municipality
Incorporated: Jan. 6, 1909; *Area:* 522.69 sq km
Population in 2016: 892
Provincial Electoral District(s): Dauphin
Federal Electoral District(s): Dauphin-Swan River-Neepawa
Next Election: Oct. 26, 2022 (4 year terms)
Note: The RM of McCreary & the Village of McCreary amalgamated to form the new Municipality of McCreary on Jan. 1, 2015.
Mike Gawaziuk, Reeve
Wendy Turko, Chief Administrative Officer

Melita
P.O. Box 364
79 Main St.
Melita, MB R0M 1L0
Tel: 204-522-3413; *Fax:* 204-522-3587
meladmin@mymts.net
www.melitamb.ca
Other Information: tofmel@mts.net
Municipal Type: Town
Incorporated: Jan. 2, 1906; *Area:* 2.96 sq km
Population in 2016: 1,042
Provincial Electoral District(s): Turtle Mountain
Federal Electoral District(s): Brandon-Souris
Next Election: Oct. 26, 2022 (4 year terms)
William Holden, Mayor
Sandra Anderson, Chief Administrative Officer

Minitonas-Bowsman
P.O. Box 9
311 Main St.
Minitonas, MB R0L 1G0
Tel: 204-525-4461; *Fax:* 204-525-4857
minitonas-bowsman.ca
Municipal Type: Municipality
Incorporated: Jan. 3, 1901; *Area:* 1,197.67 sq km
Population in 2016: 1,653
Provincial Electoral District(s): Swan River
Federal Electoral District(s): Dauphin-Swan River-Neepawa
Next Election: Oct. 26, 2022 (4 year terms)
Note: The RM of Minitonas, the Town of Minitonas & the Village of Bowsman amalgamated to form the new Municipality of Minitonas-Bowsman on Jan. 1, 2015.
Walter Pacamaniuk, Reeve
Kasey Chartrand, Chief Administrative Officer

Minnedosa
P.O. Box 426
103 Main St. South
Minnedosa, MB R0J 1E0
Tel: 204-867-2727; *Fax:* 204-867-2686
minnedosa@minnedosa.com
www.discoverminnedosa.com
Municipal Type: Town
Incorporated: Jan. 5, 1948; *Area:* 15.26 sq km
Population in 2016: 2,449
Provincial Electoral District(s): Riding Mountain
Federal Electoral District(s): Dauphin-Swan River-Neepawa
Next Election: Oct. 26, 2022 (4 year terms)
Pat Skatch, Mayor
Cindy Marzoff, Chief Administrative Officer

Morden
#100, 195 Stephen St.
Morden, MB R6M 1V3
Tel: 204-822-4434; *Fax:* 204-822-6494
info@mordenmb.com
www.mordenmb.com

Municipal Type: Town
Incorporated: Jan. 1, 1882; *Area:* 12.44 sq km
Population in 2016: 8,668
Provincial Electoral District(s): Morden-Winkler
Federal Electoral District(s): Portage-Lisgar
Next Election: Oct. 26, 2022 (4 year terms)
Brandon Burley, Mayor
John Scarce, Chief Administrative Officer

Morris
P.O. Box 28
#1, 380 Stampede Grounds
Morris, MB R0G 1K0
Tel: 204-746-2531; *Fax:* 204-746-6009
info@townofmorris.ca
townofmorris.ca
Municipal Type: Town
Incorporated: Jan. 2, 1883; *Area:* 6.1 sq km
Population in 2016: 1,885
Provincial Electoral District(s): Midland
Federal Electoral District(s): Portage-Lisgar
Next Election: Oct. 26, 2022 (4 year terms)
Scott Crick, Mayor
Brigitte Doerksen, Chief Administrative Officer

Neepawa
P.O. Box 339
275 Hamilton St.
Neepawa, MB R0J 1H0
Tel: 204-476-7600; *Fax:* 204-476-7624
neepawa@wcgwave.ca
www.neepawa.ca
Municipal Type: Town
Incorporated: Jan. 2, 1883; *Area:* 17.57 sq km
Population in 2016: 4,609
Provincial Electoral District(s): Aggasiz
Federal Electoral District(s): Dauphin-Swan River-Neepawa
Next Election: Oct. 26, 2022 (4 year terms)
Blake McCutcheon, Mayor
Colleen Synchyshyn, Chief Administrative Officer, 204-476-7603

Niverville
P.O. Box 267
86 Main St.
Niverville, MB R0A 1E0
Tel: 204-388-4600; *Fax:* 204-388-6110
feedback@whereyoubelong.ca
www.whereyoubelong.ca
Municipal Type: Town
Incorporated: Jan. 4, 1969; *Area:* 8.79 sq km
Population in 2016: 4,610
Provincial Electoral District(s): Springfield-Ritchot
Federal Electoral District(s): Provencher
Next Election: Oct. 26, 2022 (4 year terms)
Myron Dyck, Mayor
G. Jim Buys, Chief Administrative Officer

Norfolk Treherne
P.O. Box 30
215 Broadway St.
Treherne, MB R0G 2V0
Tel: 204-723-2044; *Fax:* 204-723-2719
info@treherne.ca
www.treherne.ca
Municipal Type: Municipality
Area: 726.76 sq km
Population in 2016: 1,751
Provincial Electoral District(s): Agassiz
Federal Electoral District(s): Portage-Lisgar
Next Election: Oct. 26, 2022 (4 year terms)
Note: The Town of Treherne & the RM of South Norfolk amalgamated to form the new Municipality of Norfolk-Treherne on Jan. 1, 2015.
Will Eert, Reeve
Jackie Jenkinson, Chief Administrative Officer

North Cypress-Langford
P.O. Box 130
316 - 4th Ave.
Carberry, MB R0K 0H0
Tel: 204-834-6600; *Fax:* 204-834-6604
ncl@rmofnorthcypress.ca
www.townofcarberry.ca
Municipal Type: Municipality
Incorporated: Jan. 1, 1882; *Area:* 1,199.92 sq km
Population in 2016: 2,745
Provincial Electoral District(s): Agassiz
Federal Electoral District(s): Dauphin-Swan River-Neepawa
Next Election: Oct. 26, 2022 (4 year terms)
Note: The RM of Langford & the RM of North Cypress amalgamated to form the new RM of North Cypress-Langford on Jan. 1, 2015.

Robert Adriaansen, Reeve
Sandra Jones, Chief Administrative Officer

North Norfolk
P.O. Box 190
27 Hampton St. East
MacGregor, MB R0H 0R0
Tel: 204-685-2211; *Fax:* 204-685-2616
office@northnorfolk.ca
northnorfolk.ca
Municipal Type: Municipality
Incorporated: Jan. 4, 1947; *Area:* 1,160.76 sq km
Population in 2016: 3,853
Provincial Electoral District(s): Agassiz
Federal Electoral District(s): Dauphin-Swan River-Neepawa
Next Election: Oct. 26, 2022 (4 year terms)
Note: The RM of North Norfolk & the Town of MacGregor amalgamated to form the new Municipality of North Norfolk on Jan. 1, 2015.
Gerald Barber, Mayor
Valorie Unrau, Chief Administrative Officer

Oakland-Wawanesa
P.O. Box 28
54 Main St.
Nesbitt, MB R0K 1P0
Tel: 204-824-2666; *Fax:* 204-824-2374
adminassist@oakland-wawanesa.ca
oakland-wawanesa.ca
Municipal Type: Municipality
Incorporated: Jan. 2, 1883; *Area:* 575.21 sq km
Population in 2016: 1,690
Provincial Electoral District(s): Portage la Prairie; Spruce Woods
Federal Electoral District(s): Brandon-Souris
Next Election: Oct. 26, 2022 (4 year terms)
Note: The RM of Oakland & the Village of Wawanesa amalgamated to form the new Municipality of Oakland-Wawanesa on Jan. 1, 2015.
David Kreklewich, Mayor
Joni Swidnicki, Chief Administrative Officer

The Pas
P.O. Box 870
81 Edwards Ave.
The Pas, MB R9A 1K8
Tel: 204-627-1100; *Fax:* 204-623-5506
info@townofthepas.ca
www.townofthepas.com
Municipal Type: Town
Incorporated: Jan. 2, 1912; *Area:* 47.83 sq km
Population in 2016: 5,369
Provincial Electoral District(s): The Pas-Kameesak
Federal Electoral District(s): Churchill-Keewatinook Aski
Next Election: Oct. 26, 2022 (4 year terms)
Herb Jacques, Mayor
Randi Salamanowicz, Chief Administrative Officer, 204-627-1109

Pembina
P.O. Box 189
360 PTH 3
Manitou, MB R0G 1G0
Tel: 204-242-2838; *Fax:* 204-242-2798
admin@pembina.ca
pembina.ca
Municipal Type: Municipality
Incorporated: Jan. 4, 1890; *Area:* 1,114.76 sq km
Population in 2016: 2,347
Provincial Electoral District(s): Turtle Mountain
Federal Electoral District(s): Portage-Lisgar
Next Election: Oct. 26, 2022 (4 year terms)
Note: The RM of Pembina & the Town of Manitou amalgamated to form the new Municipality of Pembina on Jan. 1, 2015.
Glen Shiskoski, Head of Council
Wes Unrau, Chief Administrative Officer

Powerview-Pine Falls
P.O. Box 220
277B Main St.
Powerview, MB R0E 1P0
Tel: 204-367-8483; *Fax:* 204-367-4747
infopvpf@mymts.net
www.powerview-pinefalls.com
Municipal Type: Town
Incorporated: Jan. 2, 1951; *Area:* 5.05 sq km
Population in 2016: 1,316
Provincial Electoral District(s): Lac du Bonnet
Federal Electoral District(s): Selkirk-Interlake-Eastman
Next Election: Oct. 26, 2022 (4 year terms)
Don MacLellan, Mayor
Sharon Desiatnyk, Chief Administrative Officer

Prairie View
P.O. Box 70
678 Main St.
Birtle, MB R0M 0C0
Tel: 204-842-3403; *Fax:* 204-842-3496
info@myprairieview.ca
myprairieview.ca
Other Information: Alternate Phone: 204-567-3683
Municipal Type: Municipality
Incorporated: Jan. 3, 1884
Population in 2016: 2,088
Provincial Electoral District(s): Point Douglas
Federal Electoral District(s): Dauphin-Swan River-Neepawa
Next Election: Oct. 26, 2022 (4 year terms)
Note: The Town of Birtle, the RM of Birtle & the RM of Miniota amalgamated to form the new Prairie View Municipality on Jan. 1, 2015.
Linda Clark, Reeve, 204-567-3847
Tina Collier, Chief Administrative Officer

Rhineland
P.O. Box 270
109 - 3rd Ave. NE
Altona, MB R0G 0B0
Tel: 204-324-5357; *Fax:* 204-324-1516
info@rhinelandmb.ca
www.rmofrhineland.com
Municipal Type: Municipality
Incorporated: Jan. 3, 1884; *Area:* 953.42 sq km
Population in 2016: 5,945
Provincial Electoral District(s): Borderland
Federal Electoral District(s): Portage-Lisgar
Next Election: Oct. 26, 2022 (4 year terms)
Note: The RM of Rhineland, the Town of Gretna & the Town of Plum Coulee amalgamated to form the new Municipality of Rhineland on Jan. 1, 2015.
Don Wiebe, Reeve
Michael Rempel, Chief Administrative Officer

Riverdale
P.O. Box 520
670 - 2nd Ave.
Rivers, MB R0K 1X0
Tel: 204-328-5250; *Fax:* 204-328-5374
bonnierivers@mymts.net
riversdaly.ca
Other Information: Alternate Phone: 204-328-5300
Municipal Type: Municipality
Area: 570.42 sq km
Population in 2016: 2,133
Provincial Electoral District(s): Spruce Woods
Federal Electoral District(s): Dauphin-Swan River-Neepawa
Next Election: Oct. 26, 2022 (4 year terms)
Note: The Town of Rivers & the RM of Daly amalgamated to form the new Riverdale Municipality on Jan. 1, 2015.
Todd Gill, Mayor
Kat Bridgeman, Chief Administrative Officer

Roblin
P.O. Box 998
125 - 1st Ave. NW
Roblin, MB R0L 1P0
Tel: 204-937-8333; *Fax:* 204-937-4382
info@roblin.ca
www.roblinmanitoba.com
Municipal Type: Municipality
Incorporated: Jan. 3, 1884; *Area:* 735.12 sq km
Population in 2016: 3,214
Provincial Electoral District(s): Swan River; Turtle Mountain
Federal Electoral District(s): Dauphin-Swan River-Neepawa
Next Election: Oct. 26, 2022 (4 year terms)
Note: The RM of Hillsburg, the RM of Shell River & the Town of Roblin amalgamated to form the new Municipality of Hillsburg-Roblin-Shell River on Jan. 1, 2015.
Robert Misko, Mayor
Twyla Ludwig, Chief Administrative Officer

Rossburn
P.O. Box 100
43 Main St. North
Rossburn, MB R0J 1V0
Tel: 204-859-2779; *Fax:* 204-859-2959
municipaloffice@rossburn.ca
www.rossburn.ca
Municipal Type: Municipality
Incorporated: Jan. 4, 1913; *Area:* 3.43 sq km
Population in 2016: 976
Provincial Electoral District(s): Swan River
Federal Electoral District(s): Dauphin-Swan River-Neepawa
Next Election: Oct. 26, 2022 (4 year terms)
Note: The RM of Rossburn & the Town of Rossburn

amalgamated to form the new Rossburn Municipality on Jan. 1, 2015.
Kerry Lawless, Head of Council
Cheryl Melnyk, Chief Administrative Officer

Russell-Binscarth
P.O. Box 10
178 Main St. North
Russell, MB R0J 1W0
Tel: 204-773-2253; *Fax:* 204-773-3370
info@mrbgov.com
russellbinscarth.com
Municipal Type: Municipality
Incorporated: Jan. 4, 1913; *Area:* 3.15 sq km
Population in 2016: 2,442
Provincial Electoral District(s): Swan River
Federal Electoral District(s): Dauphin-Swan River-Neepawa
Next Election: Oct. 26, 2022 (4 year terms)
Note: The RM of Russell, Town of Russell & Village of Binscarth amalgamated to form the new Municipality of Russell-Binscarth on Jan. 1, 2015.
Cheryl Kingdon-Chartier, Mayor
Shawn Stuckey, Chief Administrative Officer

Ste. Anne
30 Dawson Rd., Unit B
Ste. Anne, MB R5H 1B5
Tel: 204-422-5293; *Fax:* 204-422-5459
town@steannemb.ca
www.steannemb.ca
Municipal Type: Town
Incorporated: Jan. 3, 1963; *Area:* 4.23 sq km
Population in 2016: 2,114
Provincial Electoral District(s): Dawson Trail
Federal Electoral District(s): Provencher
Next Election: Oct. 26, 2022 (4 year terms)
Richard Pelletier, Mayor
Marc Darker, Chief Administrative Officer

Ste. Rose
P.O. Box 30
722 Central Ave.
Ste. Rose du Lac, MB R0L 1S0
Tel: 204-447-2229; *Fax:* 204-447-2875
sterose@mts.net
www.sterose.ca
Municipal Type: Municipality
Incorporated: Jan. 5, 1920; *Area:* 2.53 sq km
Population in 2016: 1,712
Provincial Electoral District(s): Dauphin
Federal Electoral District(s): Dauphin-Swan River-Neepawa
Next Election: Oct. 26, 2022 (4 year terms)
Note: The Town of Ste. Rose du Lac & the RM of St. Rose amalgamated to form the new Municipality of Ste. Rose on Jan. 1, 2015.
Robert Brunel, Mayor
Marlene M. Bouchard, Chief Administrative Officer

St. Pierre-Jolys
P.O. Box 218
555 Hébert St.
St Pierre-Jolys, MB R0A 1V0
Tel: 204-433-7832; *Fax:* 204-433-7053
info@villagestpierrejolys.ca
www.stpierrejolys.com
Municipal Type: Village
Incorporated: Jan. 4, 1947; *Area:* 2.6 sq km
Population in 2016: 1,170
Provincial Electoral District(s): La Verendrye
Federal Electoral District(s): Provencher
Next Election: Oct. 26, 2022 (4 year terms)
Raymond Maynard, Mayor
Janine Wiebe, Chief Administrative Officer

Snow Lake
P.O. Box 40
113 Elm St.
Snow Lake, MB R0B 1M0
Tel: 204-358-2551; *Fax:* 204-358-2112
snowlake_office@mymts.net
snowlake.com
Municipal Type: Town
Incorporated: 1947; *Area:* 1,211.89 sq km
Population in 2016: 899
Provincial Electoral District(s): Flin Flon
Federal Electoral District(s): Churchill-Keewatinook Aski
Next Election: Oct. 26, 2022 (4 year terms)
Peter Roberts, Mayor
Ross Gilmore, Chief Administrative Officer

Souris-Glenwood
P.O. Box 518
100 - 2nd St. South
Souris, MB R0K 2C0
Tel: 204-483-5200; *Fax:* 204-483-5203
tnsouris@mymts.net
www.sourismanitoba.com
Municipal Type: Municipality
Incorporated: Jan. 6, 1904; *Area:* 3.64 sq km
Population in 2016: 2,562
Provincial Electoral District(s): Spruce Woods
Federal Electoral District(s): Brandon-Souris
Next Election: Oct. 26, 2022 (4 year terms)
Note: The RM of Glenwood & the Town of Souris amalgamated to form the new Municipality of Souris-Glenwood on Jan. 1, 2015.
Darryl Jackson, Mayor
Charlotte Parham, Chief Administrative Officer

Stonewall
P.O. Box 250
293 Main St.
Stonewall, MB R0C 2Z0
Tel: 204-467-7979; *Fax:* 204-467-7999
info@stonewall.ca
www.stonewall.ca
Municipal Type: Town
Incorporated: Jan. 4, 1908; *Area:* 6.02 sq km
Population in 2016: 4,809
Provincial Electoral District(s): Lakeside
Federal Electoral District(s): Selkirk-Interlake-Eastman
Next Election: Oct. 26, 2022 (4 year terms)
Clive Hinds, Mayor
Wally Melnyk, Chief Administrative Officer

Swan River
P.O. Box 879
439 Main St.
Swan River, MB R0L 1Z0
Tel: 204-734-4586; *Fax:* 204-734-5166
main@townsr.ca
www.swanrivermanitoba.ca
Municipal Type: Town
Incorporated: Jan. 4, 1908; *Area:* 6.89 sq km
Population in 2016: 4,014
Provincial Electoral District(s): Swan River
Federal Electoral District(s): Dauphin-Swan River-Neepawa
Next Election: Oct. 26, 2022 (4 year terms)
Lance Jacobson, Mayor
Julie Fothergill, Chief Administrative Officer

Swan Valley West
P.O. Box 610
216 Main St. West
Swan River, MB R0L 1Z0
Tel: 204-734-3344; *Fax:* 204-734-3701
munswanvalleywest.ca
Municipal Type: Municipality
Incorporated: Jan. 3, 1901; *Area:* 1,719.58 sq km
Population in 2016: 2,829
Provincial Electoral District(s): Swan River
Federal Electoral District(s): Dauphin-Swan River-Neepawa
Next Election: Oct. 26, 2022 (4 year terms)
Note: The RM of Swan River & the Village of Benito amalgamated to form the new Municipality of Swan Valley West on Jan. 1, 2015.
William Galloway, Reeve
Betty Nemetchuk, Acting Chief Administrative Officer

Teulon
P.O. Box 69
44 - 4th Ave. SE
Teulon, MB R0C 3B0
Tel: 204-886-2314; *Fax:* 204-886-3918
info@teulon.ca
www.teulon.ca
Municipal Type: Town
Incorporated: Jan. 4, 1919; *Area:* 3.2 sq km
Population in 2016: 1,201
Provincial Electoral District(s): Lakeside
Federal Electoral District(s): Selkirk-Interlake-Eastman
Next Election: Oct. 26, 2022 (4 year terms)
Debbie Kozyra, Mayor
Doreen Steg, Chief Administrative Officer

Two Borders
P.O. Box 429
138 Main St.
Melita, MB R0M 1L0
Tel: 204-522-3263; *Fax:* 204-522-8706
info@twoborders.ca

Municipal Type: Municipality
Area: 2,304.46 sq km
Population in 2016: 1,175
Federal Electoral District(s): Brandon-Souris
Next Election: Oct. 26, 2022 (4 year terms)
Note: The RM of Albert, the RM of Arthur & the RM of Edward amalgamated to form the new Municipality of Two Borders on Jan. 1, 2015.
Debbie McMeechan, Reeve
Grace Carr, Chief Administrative Officer

Victoria Beach
#705, 1661 Portage Ave.
Winnipeg, MB R3J 3T7
Tel: 204-774-4263; *Fax:* 204-774-9834
vicbeach@mymts.net
rmofvictoriabeach.ca
Municipal Type: Resort Village
Incorporated: Jan. 4, 1902; *Area:* 20.28 sq km
Population in 2016: 398
Provincial Electoral District(s): Lac du Bonnet
Federal Electoral District(s): Selkirk-Interlake-Eastman
Next Election: July 22, 2022 (4 year terms)
Penny McMorris, Reeve
Andrew Glassco, Chief Administrative Officer

Virden
P.O. Box 310
236 Wellington St. West
Virden, MB R0M 2C0
Tel: 204-748-2440; *Fax:* 204-748-2501
info@virden.ca
www.virden.ca
Municipal Type: Town
Incorporated: Jan. 6, 1904; *Area:* 8.56 sq km
Population in 2016: 3,322
Provincial Electoral District(s): Riding Mountain
Federal Electoral District(s): Brandon-Souris
Next Election: Oct. 26, 2022 (4 year terms)
Murray Wright, Mayor
Rhonda Stewart, Chief Administrative Officer

West Interlake
P.O. Box 10
10 Main St.
Eriksdale, MB R0C 0W0
Tel: 204-739-2666; *Fax:* 204-739-2073
info@rmofwestinterlake.com
www.rmofwestinterlake.com
Other Information: admineriksdale@rmofwestinterlake.com
Municipal Type: Municipality
Incorporated: Jan. 6, 1904; *Area:* 784.76 sq km
Population in 2016: 2,162
Provincial Electoral District(s): Interlake-Gimli
Federal Electoral District(s): Selkirk-Interlake-Eastman
Next Election: Oct. 26, 2022 (4 year terms)
Note: The RM of Eriksdale & the RM of Siglunes amalgamated to form the new RM of West Interlake on Jan. 1, 2015.
Arnthor (Art) Jonasson, Reeve, 204-768-0004
Larissa Love, Chief Administrative Officer

Westlake-Gladstone
P.O. Box 150
14 Dennis St. East
Gladstone, MB R0J 0T0
Tel: 204-385-2332; *Fax:* 204-385-2391
info@westlake-gladstone.ca
westlake-gladstone.ca
Municipal Type: Municipality
Incorporated: Jan. 1, 1882; *Area:* 2.43 sq km
Population in 2016: 3,154
Provincial Electoral District(s): Agassiz
Federal Electoral District(s): Dauphin-Swan River-Neepawa
Next Election: Oct. 26, 2022 (4 year terms)
Note: The Town of Gladstone, the RM of Lakeview & the RM of Westbourne amalgamated to form the new Municipality of WestLake-Gladstone on Jan. 1, 2015.
Scott Kinley, Mayor
Coralie Smith, Chief Administrative Officer

Winnipeg Beach
P.O. Box 160
29 Robinson Ave.
Winnipeg Beach, MB R0C 3G0
Tel: 204-389-2698; *Fax:* 204-389-2019
info@winnipegbeach.ca
www.winnipegbeach.ca
Municipal Type: Resort Village
Incorporated: Jan. 5, 1914; *Area:* 3.88 sq km
Population in 2016: 1,145
Provincial Electoral District(s): Interlake-Gimli

Federal Electoral District(s): Selkirk-Interlake-Eastman
Next Election: July 22, 2022 (4 year terms)
Tony Pimentel, Mayor
Kerry Lawless, Chief Administrative Officer

Rural Municipalities in Manitoba

Alexander
P.O. Box 100
1 Bouvier Trail
St Georges, MB R0E 1V0
Tel: 204-367-6170; *Fax:* 204-367-2257
info@rmalexander.com
rmalexander.com
Municipal Type: Rural Municipalities
Incorporated: Jan. 2, 1945; *Area:* 1,568.66 sq km
Population in 2016: 3,333
Provincial Electoral District(s): Lac du Bonnet; Spruce Woods
Federal Electoral District(s): Brandon-Souris;
Selkirk-Interlake-Eastman
Next Election: Oct. 26, 2022 (4 year terms)
Jack Brisco, Reeve
Scott Spicer, Chief Administrative Officer

Alonsa
P.O. Box 127
20 Railway Ave.
Alonsa, MB R0H 0A0
Tel: 204-767-2054; *Fax:* 204-767-2044
rmalonsa@inetlink.ca
rmofalonsa.com
Municipal Type: Rural Municipalities
Area: 2,977.50 sq km
Population in 2016: 1,247
Provincial Electoral District(s): Dauphin
Federal Electoral District(s): Dauphin-Swan River-Neepawa
Next Election: Oct. 26, 2022 (4 year terms)
Stan Asham, Reeve
Pamela Sul, Chief Administrative Officer

Argyle
P.O. Box 40
132 - 2nd St. North
Baldur, MB R0K 0B0
Tel: 204-535-2176; *Fax:* 204-535-2505
rmofargyle@mymts.net
Municipal Type: Rural Municipalities
Incorporated: Jan. 1, 1882; *Area:* 770.44 sq km
Population in 2016: 1,025
Provincial Electoral District(s): Lakeside; Turtle Mountain
Federal Electoral District(s): Brandon-Souris
Next Election: Oct. 26, 2022 (4 year terms)
Daniel Martens, Reeve
Barbara Bramwell, Chief Administrative Officer

Armstrong
P.O. Box 69
55 Hwy. 17
Inwood, MB R0C 1P0
Tel: 204-278-3377; *Fax:* 204-278-3437
www.rmofarmstrong.com
Municipal Type: Rural Municipalities
Incorporated: Dec. 5, 1944; *Area:* 1,864.96 sq km
Population in 2016: 1,792
Provincial Electoral District(s): Interlake-Gimli
Federal Electoral District(s): Selkirk-Interlake-Eastman
Next Election: Oct. 26, 2022 (4 year terms)
Susan Smerchanski, Reeve
Corlie Larson, Chief Administrative Officer

Brokenhead
P.O. Box 490
72013 Rd. 42 East
Beausejour, MB R0E 0C0
Tel: 204-268-6700; *Fax:* 204-268-1504
admin@rmofbrokenhead.ca
www.ourhomeyourhome.ca/rm-of-brokenhead
Municipal Type: Rural Municipalities
Incorporated: Jan. 2, 1900; *Area:* 750.54 sq km
Population in 2016: 5,122
Provincial Electoral District(s): Lac du Bonnet; Red River North
Federal Electoral District(s): Selkirk-Interlake-Eastman
Next Election: Oct. 26, 2022 (4 year terms)
Brad Saluk, Reeve, 204-268-5540
Sue Sutherland, Chief Administrative Officer

La Broquerie
P.O. Box 130
123 Simard St.
La Broquerie, MB R0A 0W0
Tel: 204-424-5251; *Fax:* 204-424-5193
reception@rmlabroquerie.ca
www.labroquerie.com
Municipal Type: Rural Municipalities
Incorporated: Jan. 2, 1883; *Area:* 8.05 sq km
Population in 2016: 6,076
Provincial Electoral District(s): La Verendrye
Federal Electoral District(s): Provencher
Next Election: Oct. 26, 2022 (4 year terms)
Lewis Weiss, Reeve
Anne Burns, Chief Administrative Officer

Cartier
P.O. Box 117
28 Provincial Rd. 248 South
Elie, MB R0H 0H0
Tel: 204-353-2214; *Fax:* 204-353-2335
admin@rm-cartier.mb.ca
www.rm-cartier.mb.ca
Municipal Type: Rural Municipalities
Incorporated: Jan. 5, 1914; *Area:* 553.42 sq km
Population in 2016: 3,368
Provincial Electoral District(s): Lakeside
Federal Electoral District(s): Portage-Lisgar
Next Election: Oct. 26, 2022 (4 year terms)
Dale Fossay, Reeve, 204-735-2317
Virginia Beckwith, Chief Administrative Officer

Coldwell
P.O. Box 90
35 Main St.
Lundar, MB R0C 1Y0
Tel: 204-762-5421; *Fax:* 204-762-5177
coldwell@mymts.net
www.lundar.ca
Municipal Type: Rural Municipalities
Incorporated: Jan. 4, 1913; *Area:* 901.84 sq km
Population in 2016: 1,254
Provincial Electoral District(s): Interlake-Gimli
Federal Electoral District(s): Selkirk-Interlake-Eastman
Next Election: Oct. 26, 2022 (4 year terms)
Brian Sigfusson, Reeve
Nicole Christensen, Chief Administrative Officer

Cornwallis
P.O. Box 10 500
RR#5
Brandon, MB R7A 5Y5
Tel: 204-725-8686; *Fax:* 204-725-3659
info@gov.cornwallis.mb.ca
www.gov.cornwallis.mb.ca
Municipal Type: Rural Municipalities
Incorporated: Jan. 3, 1884; *Area:* 500.82 sq km
Population in 2016: 4,520
Provincial Electoral District(s): Spruce Woods
Federal Electoral District(s): Brandon-Souris
Next Election: Oct. 26, 2022 (4 year terms)
Bill Courtice, Reeve
Donna Anderson, Chief Administrative Officer

Dauphin
P.O. Box 574
Hwy. 20A East
Dauphin, MB R7N 2V4
Tel: 204-638-4531; *Fax:* 204-638-7598
info@rmofdauphin.ca
www.rmofdauphin.ca
Municipal Type: Rural Municipalities
Area: 1,516.1 sq km
Population in 2016: 2,388
Provincial Electoral District(s): Dauphin
Federal Electoral District(s): Dauphin-Swan River-Neepawa
Next Election: Oct. 26, 2022 (4 year terms)
Ronald E. Ryz, Reeve
Laura Murray, Chief Administrative Officer

De Salaberry
P.O. Box 40
466 Sabourin St.
St Pierre Jolys, MB R0A 1V0
Tel: 204-433-7406; *Fax:* 204-433-7063
info@rmdesalaberry.mb.ca
www.rmdesalaberry.mb.ca
Municipal Type: Rural Municipalities
Incorporated: Jan. 2, 1883; *Area:* 670.29 sq km
Population in 2016: 3,580
Provincial Electoral District(s): La Verendrye

Federal Electoral District(s): Provencher
Next Election: Oct. 26, 2022 (4 year terms)
Darrek Curé, Reeve
Kristine Shields, Chief Administrative Officer

Deloraine-Winchester
P.O. Box 387
129 Broadway St.
Deloraine, MB R0M 0M0
Tel: 204-747-2572; *Fax:* 204-747-2927
admin@delowin.ca
delowin.ca
Municipal Type: Rural Municipalities
Incorporated: Jan. 6, 1904; *Area:* 727.83 sq km
Population in 2016: 1,489
Provincial Electoral District(s): Turtle Mountain
Federal Electoral District(s): Brandon-Souris
Next Election: Oct. 26, 2022 (4 year terms)
Note: The RM of Winchester & the Town of Deloraine
amalgamated to form the new Rural Municipality of
Deloraine-Winchester on Jan. 1, 2015.
Gordon Weidenhamer, Head of Council
Pamela Hainsworth, Chief Administrative Officer

Dufferin
P.O. Box 100
12 - 2nd Ave. SW
Carman, MB R0G 0J0
Tel: 204-745-2301; *Fax:* 204-745-6348
info@rmofdufferin.com
www.rmofdufferin.com
Municipal Type: Rural Municipalities
Incorporated: Feb. 7, 1880; *Area:* 915.72 sq km
Population in 2016: 2,435
Provincial Electoral District(s): Midland
Federal Electoral District(s): Portage-Lisgar
Next Election: Oct. 26, 2022 (4 year terms)
George Gray, Reeve
Sharla Murray, Chief Administrative Officer

East St. Paul
#1, 3021 Birds Hill Rd.
East St Paul, MB R2E 1A7
Tel: 204-668-8112; *Fax:* 204-668-1987
info@eaststpaul.com
www.eaststpaul.com
Municipal Type: Rural Municipalities
Incorporated: May 2, 1916; *Area:* 42.1 sq km
Population in 2016: 9,372
Provincial Electoral District(s): Red River North
Federal Electoral District(s): Kildonan-St. Paul
Next Election: Oct. 26, 2022 (4 year terms)
Shelley Hart, Reeve
Sheila Mowat, Chief Administrative Officer

Ellice-Archie
P.O. Box 67
318 Railway Ave.
McAuley, MB R0M 1H0
Tel: 204-722-2053; *Fax:* 204-722-2027
rmarchie@mts.net
www.rmarchie.com
Municipal Type: Rural Municipalities
Incorporated: Jan. 2, 1883; *Area:* 1153.33 sq km
Population in 2016: 887
Federal Electoral District(s): Dauphin-Swan River-Neepawa
Next Election: Oct. 26, 2022 (4 year terms)
Note: The RM of Archie, the RM of Ellis & the Village of St.
Lazare amalgamated to form the new Rural Municipality of
Ellice-Archie on Jan. 1, 2015.
Barry Lowes, Reeve
Trisha Huberdeau, Chief Administrative Officer

Elton
General Delivery
Forrest, MB R0K 0W0
Tel: 204-728-7834; *Fax:* 204-725-1865
elton@info.ca
www.rmofelton.ca
Municipal Type: Rural Municipalities
Incorporated: Jan. 2, 1883; *Area:* 571.85 sq km
Population in 2016: 1,273
Provincial Electoral District(s): Spruce Woods
Federal Electoral District(s): Dauphin-Swan River-Neepawa
Next Election: Oct. 26, 2022 (4 year terms)
Ross Farley, Reeve
Kathleen E.I. Steele, Chief Administrative Officer

Fisher
P.O. Box 280
30 Tache St.
Fisher Branch, MB R0C 0Z0
Tel: 204-372-6393; *Fax:* 204-372-8470
rmoffisher@mts.net
rmoffisher.com
Municipal Type: Rural Municipalities
Incorporated: Jan. 2, 1945; *Area:* 1,481.35 sq km
Population in 2016: 1,708
Provincial Electoral District(s): Interlake-Gimli
Federal Electoral District(s): Selkirk-Interlake-Eastman
Next Election: Oct. 26, 2022 (4 year terms)
Shannon Pyziak, Reeve
Linda Tremblay, Chief Administrative Officer

Gimli
P.O. Box 1246
62 - 2nd St.
Gimli, MB R0C 1B0
Tel: 264-642-6650; *Fax:* 204-642-6660
gimli@rmgimli.com
www.gimli.ca
Other Information: Toll-Free Phone: 866-642-6650
Municipal Type: Rural Municipalities
Incorporated: Jan. 7, 1887; *Area:* 319.25 sq km
Population in 2016: 6,181
Provincial Electoral District(s): Interlake-Gimli
Federal Electoral District(s): Selkirk-Interlake-Eastman
Next Election: Oct. 26, 2022 (4 year terms)
Lynn Greenberg, Mayor
Joann King, Chief Administrative Officer

Grahamdale
P.O. Box 160
23 Government Rd.
Moosehorn, MB R0C 2E0
Tel: 204-768-2858; *Fax:* 204-768-3374
info@grahamdale.ca
www.grahamdale.ca
Municipal Type: Rural Municipalities
Incorporated: Jan. 2, 1945; *Area:* 2,384.62 sq km
Population in 2016: 1,359
Provincial Electoral District(s): Interlake-Gimli
Federal Electoral District(s): Selkirk-Interlake-Eastman
Next Election: Oct. 26, 2022 (4 year terms)
Clifford Halaburda, Reeve
Shelly Schwitek, Chief Administrative Officer

Grey
P.O. Box 99
27 Church Ave. East
Elm Creek, MB R0G 0N0
Tel: 204-436-2014; *Fax:* 204-436-2543
info@rmofgrey.ca
www.rmofgrey.ca
Municipal Type: Rural Municipalities
Incorporated: Jan. 2, 1906; *Area:* 958.49 sq km
Population in 2016: 2,648
Provincial Electoral District(s): Midland
Federal Electoral District(s): Portage-Lisgar
Next Election: Oct. 26, 2022 (4 year terms)
Note: The RM of Grey & the Village of St. Claude amalgamated
to form the new RM of Grey on Jan. 1, 2015.
Raymond Franzmann, Reeve
Kim Arnal, Chief Administrative Officer

Hanover
28 Westland Dr.
Mitchell, MB R5G 1N4
Tel: 204-326-4488; *Fax:* 204-326-4830
general@hanovermb.ca
www.hanovermb.ca
Municipal Type: Rural Municipalities
Incorporated: Jan. 7, 1881; *Area:* 741.52 sq km
Population in 2016: 15,733
Provincial Electoral District(s): Steinbach; La Verendrye;
Springfield-Ritchot
Federal Electoral District(s): Provencher
Next Election: Oct. 26, 2022 (4 year terms)
Stan Toews, Reeve
Travis Doerksen, Councillor, Wards: 1
Brian Esau, Councillor, Wards: 2
Bob Brandt, Councillor, Wards: 3
John Giesbrecht, Councillor, Wards: 4
Darrin Warkentin, Councillor, Wards: 5
Jim Funk, Councillor, Wards: 6
Luc Lahaie, Chief Administrative Officer
Derek Decru, Chief Financial Officer
Rob Driedger, Manager, Engineering & Utilities
Wes Fehr, Manager, Public Works & Operations
Jason Peters, Manager, Recreation & Community Services

Paul Wiebe, Fire Chief

Headingley
#1, 126 Bridge Rd.
Headingley, MB R4H 1G9
Tel: 204-837-5766; *Fax:* 204-831-7207
admin@rmofheadingley.ca
www.rmofheadingley.ca
Municipal Type: Rural Municipalities
Incorporated: Jan. 4, 1992; *Area:* 106.96 sq km
Population in 2016: 3,579
Provincial Electoral District(s): Roblin
Federal Electoral District(s): Charleswood-St.
James-Assiniboia-Headingley
Next Election: Oct. 26, 2022 (4 year terms)
John Mauseth, Reeve
Chris Fulsher, Chief Administrative Officer

Kelsey
P.O. Box 578
264 Fischer Ave.
The Pas, MB R9A 1K6
Tel: 204-623-7474; *Fax:* 204-623-4546
rmkelsey@mts.net
rmofkelsey.ca
Municipal Type: Rural Municipalities
Incorporated: Jan. 7, 1944; *Area:* 867.64 sq km
Population in 2016: 2,424
Provincial Electoral District(s): The Pas-Kameesak
Federal Electoral District(s): Churchill-Keewatinook Aski
Next Election: Oct. 26, 2022 (4 year terms)
Rodney Berezowecki, Reeve
Jerry Hlady, Chief Administrative Officer

Lac du Bonnet
P.O. Box 100
4187 Provincial Trunk Hwy. 317
Lac du Bonnet, MB R0E 1A0
Tel: 204-345-2619; *Fax:* 204-345-6716
rmldb@lacdubonnet.com
rmoflacdubonnet.com
Municipal Type: Rural Municipalities
Incorporated: Jan. 2, 1917; *Area:* 1,100.17 sq km
Population in 2016: 3,121
Provincial Electoral District(s): Lac du Bonnet
Federal Electoral District(s): Selkirk-Interlake-Eastman
Next Election: Oct. 26, 2022 (4 year terms)
Loren Schinkel, Reeve
Tannis Lodge, Chief Administrative Officer

Lakeshore
P.O. Box 220
714 Main St.
Rorketon, MB R0L 1R0
Tel: 204-732-2333; *Fax:* 204-732-2557
info@rmoflakeshore.ca
www.rmoflakeshore.ca
Other Information: Alternate Phone: 204-733-2423
Municipal Type: Rural Municipalities
Incorporated: Jan. 5, 1914; *Area:* 761.64 sq km
Population in 2016: 1,363
Provincial Electoral District(s): Dauphin
Federal Electoral District(s): Dauphin-Swan River-Neepawa
Next Election: Oct. 26, 2022 (4 year terms)
Note: The RM of Lawrence & the RM of Ochre River
amalgamated to form the new RM of Lakeshore on Jan. 1, 2015.
Carmen Hannibal, Reeve
Donna Ainscough, Chief Administrative Officer

Macdonald
P.O. Box 100
161 Mandan Dr.
Sanford, MB R0G 2J0
Tel: 204-736-2255; *Fax:* 204-736-4335
info@rmofmacdonald.com
rmofmacdonald.com
Municipal Type: Rural Municipalities
Incorporated: Jan. 7, 1881; *Area:* 1,156.62 sq km
Population in 2016: 7,162
Provincial Electoral District(s): Midland
Federal Electoral District(s): Portage-Lisgar
Next Election: Oct. 26, 2022 (4 year terms)
Bradley Erb, Reeve
Daryl Hrehirchuk, Chief Administrative Officer

Minto-Odanah
P.O. Box 1197
49 Main St. South
Minnedosa, MB R0J 1E0
Tel: 204-867-3282; *Fax:* 204-867-1937
mintoodanah@wcgwave.ca

Municipal Type: Rural Municipalities
Incorporated: Jan. 5, 1903; *Area:* 363.65 sq km
Population in 2016: 1,189
Provincial Electoral District(s): Turtle Mountain
Federal Electoral District(s): Dauphin-Swan River-Neepawa
Next Election: Oct. 26, 2022 (4 year terms)
Note: The RM of Minto & the RM of Odanah amalgamated to
form the new RM of Minto-Odanah on Jan. 1, 2015.
Doug Dowsett, Reeve
Aaren Robertson, Chief Administrative Officer

Montcalm
P.O. Box 300
46 - 1st St. East
Letellier, MB R0G 1C0
Tel: 204-737-2271; *Fax:* 204-737-2326
info@rmofmontcalm.com
rmofmontcalm.com
Municipal Type: Rural Municipalities
Incorporated: Jan. 1, 1882; *Area:* 469.41 sq km
Population in 2016: 1,260
Provincial Electoral District(s): Borderland
Federal Electoral District(s): Provencher
Next Election: Oct. 26, 2022 (4 year terms)
Paul Gilmore, Reeve
Jolene Bird, Chief Administrative Officer

Morris
P.O. Box 518
207 Main St. North
Morris, MB R0G 1K0
Tel: 204-746-7300; *Fax:* 204-746-8801
info@rmofmorris.ca
www.rmofmorris.ca
Municipal Type: Rural Municipalities
Incorporated: Jan. 5, 1880; *Area:* 1,041.15 sq km
Population in 2016: 3,047
Provincial Electoral District(s): Midland
Federal Electoral District(s): Portage-Lisgar
Next Election: Oct. 26, 2022 (4 year terms)
Ralph Groening, Reeve
Larry Driedger, Chief Administrative Officer

Mossey River
P.O. Box 370
130 - 2nd St.
Winnipegosis, MB R0L 2G0
Tel: 204-656-4791; *Fax:* 204-656-4751
assistantcao.mrm@outlook.com
mosseyrivermunicipality.com
Municipal Type: Rural Municipalities
Incorporated: Jan. 6, 1915; *Area:* 2.5 sq km
Population in 2016: 1,145
Provincial Electoral District(s): Dauphin
Federal Electoral District(s): Dauphin-Swan River-Neepawa
Next Election: Oct. 26, 2022 (4 year terms)
Note: The RM of Mossey River & the Village of Winnipegosis
amalgamated to form the new RM of Mossey River on Jan. 1,
2015.
Ron Kostyshyn, Head of Council
Kevin Drewniak, Chief Administrative Officer

Mountain
P.O. Box 155
200 Drury Ave.
Birch River, MB R0L 0E0
Tel: 204-236-4222; *Fax:* 204-236-4773
rmmountn@mymts.net
rmofmountain.com
Municipal Type: Rural Municipalities
Area: 2607.69 sq km
Population in 2016: 978
Federal Electoral District(s): Dauphin-Swan River-Neepawa
Next Election: Oct. 26, 2022 (4 year terms)
Robert (Bob) Hanson, Reeve
Paige Larocque, Chief Administrative Officer

Mystery Lake
C/O The Town of Lynn Lake
P.O. Box 100
Lynn Lake, MB R8N 1N1
Tel: 204-356-4201; *Fax:* 204-356-8297
lgdmlake@gmail.com
Municipal Type: Local Goverment District
Incorporated: Jan. 1, 1956; *Area:* 3,464.06 sq km
Federal Electoral District(s): Churchill-Keewatinook Aski
Jim Fielder, Resident Administrator

Oakview

P.O. Box 179
10 Cochrane St.
Oak River, MB R0K 1T0
Tel: 204-566-2146; *Fax:* 204-566-2126
oakviewcao@mymts.net
rmofoakview.ca
Municipal Type: Rural Municipalities
Incorporated: Jan. 3, 1884
Population in 2016: 1,626
Provincial Electoral District(s): Riding Mountain
Federal Electoral District(s): Dauphin-Swan River-Neepawa
Next Election: Oct. 26, 2022 (4 year terms)
Note: The RM of Blanshard, the RM of Saskatchewan & the Town of Rapid City amalgamated to form the new Rural Municipality of Oakview on Jan. 1, 2015.
Brent Fortune, Reeve
Diane Kuculym, Chief Administrative Officer

Pinawa

P.O. Box 100
36 Burrows Rd.
Pinawa, MB R0E 1L0
Tel: 204-753-5100; *Fax:* 204-753-2770
townoffice@pinawa.com
www.pinawa.com
Municipal Type: Local Goverment District
Incorporated: Jan. 3, 1963; *Area:* 128.47 sq km
Population in 2016: 1,504
Provincial Electoral District(s): Lac du Bonnet
Federal Electoral District(s): Selkirk-Interlake-Eastman
Next Election: Oct. 26, 2022 (4 year terms)
Blair Skinner, Mayor
Gisele Smith, Resident Administrator

Piney

P.O. Box 48
6092 Boundary St.
Vassar, MB R0A 2J0
Tel: 204-437-2284; *Fax:* 204-437-2556
office@rmofpiney.mb.ca
www.rmofpiney.mb.ca
Other Information: Alternate Phone: 204-437-2060
Municipal Type: Rural Municipalities
Area: 2,433.77 sq km
Population in 2016: 1,726
Provincial Electoral District(s): La Verendrye
Federal Electoral District(s): Provencher
Next Election: Oct. 26, 2022 (4 year terms)
Wayne Anderson, Reeve
Martin Van Osch, Chief Administrative Officer

Pipestone

P.O. Box 99
401 - 3rd Ave.
Reston, MB R0M 1X0
Tel: 204-877-3327; *Fax:* 204-877-3999
accounts@rmofpipestone.com
www.rmofpipestone.com
Municipal Type: Rural Municipalities
Incorporated: Jan. 6, 1897; *Area:* 1,147.35 sq km
Population in 2016: 1,458
Provincial Electoral District(s): Riding Mountain
Federal Electoral District(s): Brandon-Souris
Next Election: Oct. 26, 2022 (4 year terms)
Archie McPherson, Reeve
Michelle Halls, Chief Administrative Officer

Portage la Prairie

35 Tupper St. South
Portage la Prairie, MB R1N 1W7
Tel: 204-857-3821; *Fax:* 204-239-0069
info@rmofportage.ca
www.rmofportage.ca
Municipal Type: Rural Municipalities
Incorporated: Jan. 4, 1879; *Area:* 1,964.32 sq km
Population in 2016: 6,975
Provincial Electoral District(s): Portage la Prairie
Federal Electoral District(s): Portage-Lisgar
Next Election: Oct. 26, 2022 (4 year terms)
Kameron W. Blight, Reeve
Nettie Neudorf, Chief Administrative Officer

Prairie Lakes

P.O. Box 100
211 - 3rd St.
Belmont, MB R0K 0C0
Tel: 204-537-2241; *Fax:* 204-537-2364
admin@rmofprairielakes.ca
www.rmofprairielakes.ca
Municipal Type: Rural Municipalities
Incorporated: Jan. 2, 1906; *Area:* 485.56 sq km

Population in 2016: 1,453
Provincial Electoral District(s): Fort Garry; Turtle Mountain
Federal Electoral District(s): Brandon-Souris
Next Election: Oct. 26, 2022 (4 year terms)
Note: The RM of Strathcona & the RM of Riverside amalgamated to form the new RM of Prairie Lakes on Jan. 1, 2015.
J. W. Garth Stephenson, Reeve
Tracy Lockhart, Chief Administrative Officer

Reynolds

P.O. Box 46
46044 Hwy. 11
Hadashville, MB R0E 0X0
Tel: 204-426-5305; *Fax:* 204-426-5552
admin@rmofreynolds.com
www.rmofreynolds.com
Municipal Type: Rural Municipalities
Incorporated: Jan. 2, 1945; *Area:* 3,573.31 sq km
Population in 2016: 1,338
Provincial Electoral District(s): Lac du Bonnet
Federal Electoral District(s): Provencher
Next Election: Oct. 26, 2022 (4 year terms)
Trudy Turchyn, Reeve
Yann Boissonneault, Chief Administrative Officer

Riding Mountain West

P.O. Box 110
118 Main St.
Inglis, MB R0J 0X0
Tel: 204-564-2589; *Fax:* 204-564-2643
info@rmwest.ca
www.rmwest.ca
Municipal Type: Rural Municipalities
Incorporated: Jan. 6, 1999; *Area:* 1,622.55 sq km
Population in 2016: 1,420
Federal Electoral District(s): Dauphin-Swan River-Neepawa
Next Election: Oct. 26, 2022 (4 year terms)
Note: The RM of Shellmouth-Boulton & the RM of Silver Creek amalgamated to form the new RM of Riding Mountain West on Jan. 1, 2015.
Grant Boryskavich, Reeve
Erna Hall, Chief Administrative Officer

Ritchot

352 Main St.
St Adolphe, MB R5A 1B9
Tel: 204-883-2293; *Fax:* 204-883-2674
info@ritchot.com
www.ritchot.com
Municipal Type: Rural Municipalities
Incorporated: Jan. 4, 1890; *Area:* 333.53 sq km
Population in 2016: 6,679
Provincial Electoral District(s): Springfield-Ritchot
Federal Electoral District(s): Provencher; Winnipeg South
Next Election: Oct. 26, 2022 (4 year terms)
Chris Ewen, Mayor
Mitch Duval, Chief Administrative Officer

Rockwood

P.O. Box 902
285 Main St.
Stonewall, MB R0C 2Z0
Tel: 204-467-2272; *Fax:* 204-467-5329
info@rockwood.ca
www.rockwood.ca
Municipal Type: Rural Municipalities
Incorporated: Jan. 7, 1881; *Area:* 1,199.76 sq km
Population in 2016: 7,823
Provincial Electoral District(s): Lakeside
Federal Electoral District(s): Selkirk-Interlake-Eastman
Next Election: Oct. 26, 2022 (4 year terms)
J. Wesley Taplin, Reeve
Chris Luellman, Chief Administrative Officer

Roland

P.O. Box 119
45 - 3rd St.
Roland, MB R0G 1T0
Tel: 204-343-2061; *Fax:* 204-343-2001
www.rmofroland.com
Municipal Type: Rural Municipalities
Incorporated: Jan. 4, 1908; *Area:* 485.06 sq km
Population in 2016: 1,129
Provincial Electoral District(s): Midland
Federal Electoral District(s): Portage-Lisgar
Next Election: Oct. 26, 2022 (4 year terms)
Michael Pfrimmer, Reeve
Kristi Olson, Chief Administrative Officer

Rosedale

P.O. Box 100
282 Hamilton St.
Neepawa, MB R0J 1H0
Tel: 204-476-5414; *Fax:* 204-476-5431
rosedale@mts.net
rmrosedale.com
Municipal Type: Rural Municipalities
Incorporated: Jan. 3, 1884; *Area:* 865.58 sq km
Population in 2016: 1,672
Provincial Electoral District(s): Selkirk
Federal Electoral District(s): Dauphin-Swan River-Neepawa
Next Election: Oct. 26, 2022 (4 year terms)
Michael Porrok, Reeve
Kara Sylvester, Chief Administrative Officer

Rosser

P.O. Box 131
0077E - PR #221
Rosser, MB R0H 1E0
Tel: 204-467-5711; *Fax:* 204-467-5958
info@rmofrosser.com
www.rmofrosser.com
Municipal Type: Rural Municipalities
Incorporated: Jan. 1, 1893; *Area:* 441.43 sq km
Population in 2016: 1,372
Provincial Electoral District(s): Lakeside
Federal Electoral District(s): Selkirk-Interlake-Eastman
Next Election: Oct. 26, 2022 (4 year terms)
Frances Smee, Reeve
Larry Wandowich, Chief Administrative Officer

St. Andrews

P.O. Box 130
500 Railway Ave.
Clandeboye, MB R0C 0P0
Tel: 204-738-2264; *Fax:* 204-738-2500
info@rmofstandrews.com
www.rmofstandrews.com
Other Information: Toll-Free Phone: 866-738-2264
Municipal Type: Rural Municipalities
Incorporated: Jan. 5, 1880; *Area:* 752.22 sq km
Population in 2016: 11,913
Provincial Electoral District(s): Selkirk
Federal Electoral District(s): Selkirk-Interlake-Eastman
Next Election: Oct. 26, 2022 (4 year terms)
Joy Sul, Mayor
Matthew Prychun, Councillor, Wards: 1
Kristin Hoebee, Councillor, Wards: 2
Darryl Pohl, Councillor, Wards: 3
Russ Garvie, Councillor, Wards: 4
John Preun, Councillor, Wards: 5
Laurie Hunt, Councillor, Wards: 6
DJ Sigmundson, Chief Administrative Officer
Ron Hahlweg, Manager, Public Works

St. Clements

P.O. Box 2
1043 Kittson Rd., Grp 35, RR# 1
East Selkirk, MB R0E 0M0
Tel: 204-482-3300; *Fax:* 204-482-3098
info@rmofstclements.com
www.rmofstclements.com
Municipal Type: Rural Municipalities
Incorporated: July 7, 1883; *Area:* 728.67 sq km
Population in 2016: 10,876
Provincial Electoral District(s): Red River North
Federal Electoral District(s): Selkirk-Interlake-Eastman
Next Election: Oct. 26, 2022 (4 year terms)
Debbie Fiebelkorn, Mayor
DJ Sigmundson, Chief Administrative Officer

Ste. Anne

P.O. Box 6
395 Traverse St., Grp 50, RR# 1
Ste. Anne, MB R5H 1R1
Tel: 204-422-5929; *Fax:* 204-422-9723
info@rmofsteanne.com
www.rmofsteanne.com
Municipal Type: Rural Municipalities
Incorporated: Feb. 3, 1881; *Area:* 477.65 sq km
Population in 2016: 5,003
Provincial Electoral District(s): Dawson Trail
Federal Electoral District(s): Provencher
Next Election: Oct. 26, 2022 (4 year terms)
Paul Saindon, Reeve
Jennifer Blatz, Chief Administrative Officer

St. François Xavier
1060 Hwy. 26
St François Xavier, MB R4L 1A5
Tel: 204-864-2092; *Fax:* 204-864-2390
info@rm-stfrancois.mb.ca
www.rm-stfrancois.mb.ca
Municipal Type: Rural Municipalities
Incorporated: Jan. 5, 1880; *Area:* 204.55 sq km
Population in 2016: 1,411
Provincial Electoral District(s): Lakeside
Federal Electoral District(s): Portage-Lisgar
Next Election: Oct. 26, 2022 (4 year terms)
Rick Van Wyk, Reeve
Holly Krysko, Chief Administrative Officer

St. Laurent
P.O. Box 220
Lot 825, Provincial Trunk Hwy. 6
St Laurent, MB R0C 2S0
Tel: 204-646-2259; *Fax:* 204-646-2705
rmstlaur@mymts.net
www.rmofstlaurent.ca
Municipal Type: Rural Municipalities
Incorporated: Jan. 1, 1882; *Area:* 462.51 sq km
Population in 2016: 1,338
Provincial Electoral District(s): Interlake-Gimli
Federal Electoral District(s): Selkirk-Interlake-Eastman
Next Election: Oct. 26, 2022 (4 year terms)
Cheryl Smith, Reeve
Hilda Zotter, Chief Administrative Officer

Sifton
P.O. Box 100
293 - 2nd Ave. West
Oak Lake, MB R0M 1P0
Tel: 204-855-2423; *Fax:* 204-855-2836
cao_sifton@mymts.net
Municipal Type: Rural Municipalities
Incorporated: Jan. 3, 1884; *Area:* 768.11 sq km
Population in 2016: 1,256
Provincial Electoral District(s): Dauphin
Federal Electoral District(s): Dauphin-Swan River-Neepawa;
Brandon-Souris
Next Election: Oct. 26, 2022 (4 year terms)
Note: The RM of Sifton & the RM of Oak Lake amalgamated to
form the new RM of Sifton on Jan. 1, 2015.
Cyril Druwe, Reeve
Lon Turner, Chief Administrative Officer

Springfield
P.O. Box 219
100 Springfield Centre Dr.
Oakbank, MB R0E 1J0
Tel: 204-444-3321; *Fax:* 204-444-2137
info@rmofspringfield.ca
www.rmofspringfield.ca
Municipal Type: Rural Municipalities
Incorporated: Jan. 4, 1873; *Area:* 1,100.92 sq km
Population in 2016: 15,342
Provincial Electoral District(s): Dawson Trail; Springfield-Ritchot
Federal Electoral District(s): Provencher
Next Election: Oct. 26, 2022 (4 year terms)
Tiffany Fell, Mayor
Glen Fuhl, Councillor, Wards: 1
Howard Bredin, Councillor, Wards: 2
Rick Wilson, Councillor, Wards: 3
Valerie Ralke, Councillor, Wards: 4
Peter Williams, Councillor, Wards: 5
Colleen Draper, Chief Administrative Officer
Dan Doucet, Director, Planning & Development
Blaine Moffat, Director, Public Works
Doug Murray, Director, Facilities & Special Projects Manager
Shawn Wilkinson, Director, Community Services
Garth Cook, Interim Fire Chief

Stanley
P.O. Box 1600
23111 Provincial Trunk Hwy. 14W
Morden, MB R6W 4B5
Tel: 204-325-4101; *Fax:* 204-325-4008
info@rmofstanley.ca
www.rmofstanley.ca
Municipal Type: Rural Municipalities
Incorporated: Nov. 7, 1890; *Area:* 835.59 sq km
Population in 2016: 9,038
Provincial Electoral District(s): Borderland; Morden-Winkler

Federal Electoral District(s): Portage-Lisgar
Next Election: Oct. 26, 2022 (4 year terms)
Morris Olafson, Reeve
Dale Toews, Chief Administrative Officer

Stuartburn
P.O. Box 59
108 Main St. North
Vita, MB R0A 2K0
Tel: 204-425-3218; *Fax:* 204-425-3513
inquiries@rmofstuartburn.com
www.rmofstuartburn.com
Municipal Type: Rural Municipalities
Incorporated: Jan. 4, 1997; *Area:* 1,161.65 sq km
Population in 2016: 1,648
Provincial Electoral District(s): La Verendrye
Federal Electoral District(s): Provencher
Next Election: Oct. 26, 2022 (4 year terms)
David Kiansky, Reeve
Lucie Maynard, Chief Administrative Officer

Taché
P.O. Box 100
28007 Mun 52N
Lorette, MB R0A 0Y0
Tel: 204-878-3321; *Fax:* 204-878-9977
info@rmtache.ca
rmtache.ca
Municipal Type: Rural Municipalities
Incorporated: Jan. 5, 1880; *Area:* 581.52 sq km
Population in 2016: 11,568
Provincial Electoral District(s): Dawson Trail
Federal Electoral District(s): Provencher
Next Election: Oct. 26, 2022 (4 year terms)
Justin Denis Bohémier, Mayor
Christine Hutlet, Chief Administrative Officer, 204-878-3321

Thompson
P.O. Box 190
531 Norton Ave.
Miami, MB R0G 1H0
Tel: 204-435-2114; *Fax:* 204-435-2067
rmthomp@mts.net
www.rmofthompson.com
Municipal Type: Rural Municipalities
Incorporated: Jan. 6, 1909; *Area:* 528.57 sq km
Population in 2016: 13,678
Provincial Electoral District(s): Thompson; Midland
Federal Electoral District(s): Portage-Lisgar
Next Election: Oct. 26, 2022 (4 year terms)
Brian Callum, Reeve
Nicole Enns, Chief Administrative Officer

Victoria
P.O. Box 40
130 Broadway St.
Holland, MB R0G 0X0
Tel: 204-526-2423; *Fax:* 204-526-2028
rm.office@rmofvictoria.com
rmofvictoria.com
Municipal Type: Rural Municipalities
Incorporated: Jan. 4, 1902; *Area:* 697.63 sq km
Population in 2016: 1,514
Provincial Electoral District(s): Lac du Bonnet
Federal Electoral District(s): Brandon-Souris
Next Election: Oct. 26, 2022 (4 year terms)
Raymond Huggart, Reeve
Ivan Bruneau, Chief Administrative Officer

Wallace-Woodworth
P.O. Box 2200
154023-PR 257
Virden, MB R0M 2C0
Tel: 204-748-1239; *Fax:* 204-748-3450
info@wallace-woodworth.com
www.wallace-woodworth.com
Municipal Type: Rural Municipalities
Incorporated: Jan. 6, 1909; *Area:* 1,148.75 sq km
Population in 2016: 2,948
Provincial Electoral District(s): Riding Mountain
Federal Electoral District(s): Brandon-Souris; Dauphin-Swan
River-Neepawa
Next Election: Oct. 26, 2022 (4 year terms)
Note: The RM of Wallace, the RM of Woodworth & the Village of
Elkhorn amalgamated to form the new RM of
Wallace-Woodworth on Jan. 1, 2015.

Clayton Canart, Reeve
Garth Mitchell, Chief Administrative Officer

West St. Paul
3550 Main St.
West St Paul, MB R4A 5A3
Tel: 204-338-0306; *Fax:* 204-334-9362
info@weststpaul.com
www.weststpaul.com
Municipal Type: Rural Municipalities
Incorporated: Jan. 7, 1916; *Area:* 87.66 sq km
Population in 2016: 5,368
Provincial Electoral District(s): McPhillips
Federal Electoral District(s): Kildonan-St. Paul
Next Election: Oct. 26, 2022 (4 year terms)
Cheryl Christian, Reeve
Brent Olynyk, Chief Administrative Officer

Whitehead
P.O. Box 107
517 - 2nd Ave.
Alexander, MB R0K 0A0
Tel: 204-752-2261; *Fax:* 204-752-2129
rmwhitehead@mymts.net
www.rmofwhitehead.ca
Municipal Type: Rural Municipalities
Incorporated: Jan. 2, 1883; *Area:* 562.82 sq km
Population in 2016: 1,661
Provincial Electoral District(s): Spruce Woods
Federal Electoral District(s): Brandon-Souris
Next Election: Oct. 26, 2022 (4 year terms)
Allan Sutherland, Reeve
Cindy Izzard, Chief Administrative Officer

Whitemouth
P.O. Box 248
47 Railway Ave.
Whitemouth, MB R0E 2G0
Tel: 204-348-2221; *Fax:* 204-348-2576
rmwhite@mymts.net
www.rmwhitemouth.com
Municipal Type: Rural Municipalities
Incorporated: Jan. 1, 1905; *Area:* 703.02 sq km
Population in 2016: 1,557
Provincial Electoral District(s): Lac du Bonnet
Federal Electoral District(s): Provencher
Next Election: Oct. 26, 2022 (4 year terms)
Walter Amerongen, Reeve
Colleen Johnson, Chief Administrative Officer

Woodlands
P.O. Box 10
57 Railway Ave.
Woodlands, MB R0C 3H0
Tel: 204-383-5679; *Fax:* 204-383-5169
admin@rmwoodlands.ca
www.rmwoodlands.info
Municipal Type: Rural Municipalities
Incorporated: Jan. 5, 1880; *Area:* 1,160.45 sq km
Population in 2016: 3,416
Provincial Electoral District(s): Lakeside
Federal Electoral District(s): Selkirk-Interlake-Eastman
Next Election: Oct. 26, 2022 (4 year terms)
Lori Schellekens, Reeve
Adam Turner, Chief Administrative Officer

Yellowhead
P.O. Box 278
306 Elm St.
Shoal Lake, MB R0J 1Z0
Tel: 204-759-2565; *Fax:* 204-759-2740
info@yellowheadmunicipality.ca
yellowheadmunicipality.ca
Other Information: info@yhgov.net
Municipal Type: Rural Municipalities
Area: 1,110.72 sq km
Population in 2016: 1,948
Provincial Electoral District(s): Riding Mountain
Federal Electoral District(s): Dauphin-Swan River-Neepawa
Next Election: Oct. 26, 2022 (4 year terms)
Note: The Municipality of Shoal Lake & the RM of Strathclair
amalgamated to form the new RM of Yellowhead on Jan. 1,
2015.
Mervin Starzyk, Mayor
Nadine Gapka, Chief Administrative Officer

NEW BRUNSWICK

The provincial government of New Brunswick provides all services of a municipal nature for the rural area of the province, while municipalities provide these services to their residents. For the rural area, an advisory committee may be elected at public meetings biennially to assist and advise the Minister. Municipal councils are elected to look after the affairs of the municipalities.

Acts of the legislature governing municipalities are the Local Governance Act, the Community Planning Act, the Community Funding Act, the Control of Municipalities Act, the Municipal Capital Borrowing Act, the Municipal Debentures Act, and the Municipal Thoroughfare Easements Act.

Population requirements for incorporation of municipalities are 10,000 for cities and 1,500 for towns. There are no specified requirements for villages.

Municipal elections are held every four years on the second Monday in May (2020, 2024, etc.).

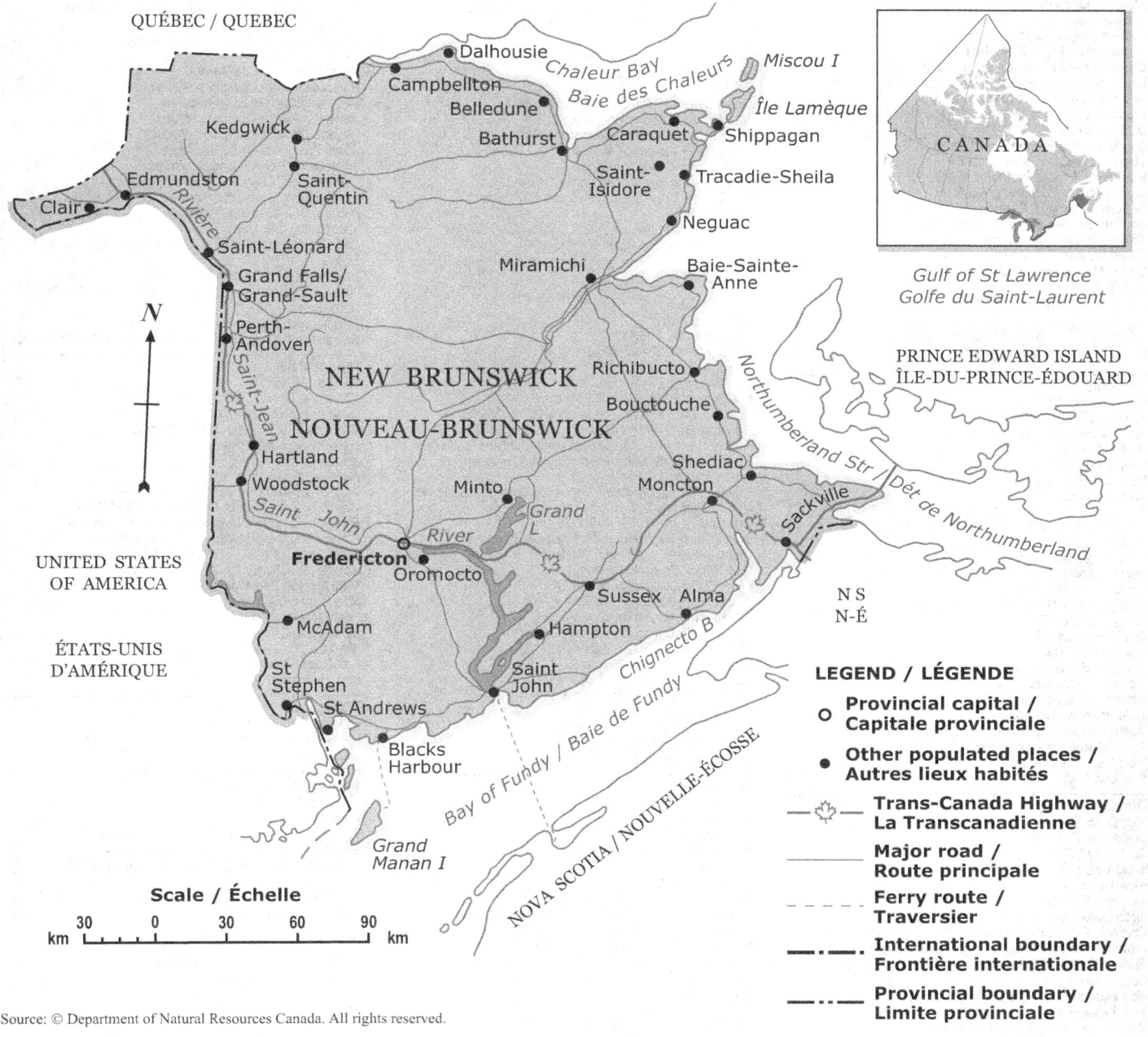

New Brunswick

Counties & Municipal Districts in New Brunswick

Tracadie
CP 3600 Main
3267, rue Principale
Tracadie-Sheila, NB E1X 1G5
Tél: 506-394-4020; *Téléc:* 506-394-4025
info@tracadienb.ca
tracadienb.ca
Entité municipal: Regional Municipality
Incorporation: July 1, 2014; *Area:* 6.03 sq km
Comté ou district: Gloucester; *Population au 2016:* 16,114
Circonscription(s) électorale(s) provinciale(s): Tracadie-Sheila
Circonscription(s) électorale(s) fédérale(s): Acadie-Bathurst
Prochaines élections: May 10, 2021 (4 year terms)
Denis Losier, Maire
Chantal Mazerolle, Conseillère, Wards: 1
Yolan Thomas, Conseiller, Wards: 2
Rita Benoit, Conseillère, Wards: 3
Joanne Doiron, Conseillère, Wards: 4
Réaldine Robichaud, Conseillère, Wards: 5
Geoffrey Saulnier, Conseiller, Wards: 6
Thérèse Brideau, Conseillère, Wards: 7
Gilbert McLaughlin, Conseiller, Wards: 7
Dianna May Savoie, Conseillère, Wards: 8
Joey Thibodeau, Greffier municipal
Daniel Hachey, Directeur général

Major Municipalities in New Brunswick

Bathurst
150 St George St.
Bathurst, NB E2A 1B5
Tel: 506-548-0400; *Fax:* 506-548-0581
city@bathurst.ca
www.bathurst.ca
Municipal Type: City
Area: 92.04 sq km
County or District: Gloucester; *Population in 2016:* 11,897
Provincial Electoral District(s): Bathurst West-Beresford;
Bathurst East-Nepisiguit-Saint-Isidore
Federal Electoral District(s): Acadie-Bathurst
Next Election: May 10, 2021 (4 year terms)
Kim Chamberlain, Mayor
Rickey Hondas, Deputy Mayor & Councillor
Penny Anderson, Councillor
Stephen J. Brunet, Councillor
Dale Knowles, Councillor
Jean-François Leblanc, Councillor
Stephen Legacy, Councillor
Michael Willet, Councillor
Todd Pettigrew, City Manager
Matthew Abernethy, Director, Engineering & Operations
Paul Thériault, Director, Recreation & Tourism
Marc Arsenault, Fire Chief
Stephane Roy, Police Chief

Dieppe
333, av Acadie
Dieppe, NB E1A 1G9
Tel: 506-877-7900
info@dieppe.ca
www.dieppe.ca
Municipal Type: City
Incorporated: Jan. 1, 1952; *Area:* 54.05 sq km
County or District: Westmorland; *Population in 2016:* 25,384
Provincial Electoral District(s): Shediac Bay-Dieppe; Dieppe
Federal Electoral District(s): Moncton-Riverview-Dieppe;
Beauséjour
Next Election: May 10, 2021 (4 year terms)
Yvon Lapierre, Mayor
Mélyssa Boudreau, Councillor-at-Large
Corinne Gocbout, Councillor-at-Large
Josée Turgeon-Roy, Councillor-at-Large
Jean-Marc Brideau, Councillor, Wards: 1
Lise LeBouthillier, Councillor, Wards: 2
Marc Lanteigne, Councillor, Wards: 3
Ernest Thibodeau, Councillor, Wards: 4
Paul Gaudet, Councillor, Wards: 5
Marc Melanson, Chief Administrative Officer

Edmundston
7 Canada Rd.
Edmundston, NB E3V 1T7
Tel: 506-739-2115; *Fax:* 506-737-6820
communication@edmundston.ca
edmundston.ca
Municipal Type: City
Area: 106.85 sq km
County or District: Madawaska; *Population in 2016:* 16,580
Provincial Electoral District(s): Edmundston-Madawaska Centre;
Madawaska Les Lacs-Edmundston
Federal Electoral District(s): Madawaska-Restigouche
Next Election: May 10, 2021 (4 year terms)
Eric Marquis, Mayor
Sylvie Morneau, Councillor, Wards: 1
Aldéo Nadeau, Councillor, Wards: 1
Éric Desjardins, Councillor, Wards: 2
Denise Landry-Nadeau, Councillor, Wards: 2
Eric Morneault, Councillor, Wards: 3
Diane Bélanger-Nadeau, Councillor, Wards: 3
Karen Power, Councillor, Wards: 4
Eric McGuire, Councillor, Wards: 4
Marc Michaud, Chief Administrative Officer
Paul Dionne, Director, Public Works & Environment,
506-739-2103
Christine Lavoie, Director, Arts & Culture, 506-739-2127
Rino Francoeur, Fire Chief, 506-739-2117

Fredericton
City Hall
P.O. Box 130
397 Queen St.
Fredericton, NB E3B 4Y7
Tel: 506-460-2020; *Fax:* 506-460-2042
www.fredericton.ca
Municipal Type: City
Incorporated: 1848; *Area:* 132.57 sq km
County or District: York; *Population in 2016:* 58,220
Provincial Electoral District(s): Oromocto-Lincoln;
Fredericton-Grand Lake; New Maryland-Sunbury; Fredericton
South; Fredericton North; Fredericton-York; Fredericton
West-Hanwell
Federal Electoral District(s): Fredericton; Tobique-Mactaquac
Next Election: May 10, 2021 (4 year terms)
Kate Rogers, Mayor, 506-460-2125
Greg Ericson, Deputy Mayor & Councillor, Wards: 8
Margo Sheppard, Councillor, Wards: 1
Mark Peters, Councillor, Wards: 2
Bruce Grandy, Councillor, Wards: 3
Jocelyn Pike, Councillor, Wards: 4
Steven Hicks, Councillor, Wards: 5
Eric Megarity, Councillor, Wards: 6
Kevin Darrah, Councillor, Wards: 7
Ruth Breen, Councillor, Wards: 9
Cassandra Blackmore, Councillor, Wards: 10
Jason LeJeune, Councillor, Wards: 11
Henri Mallet, Councillor, Wards: 12
Chris MacPherson, Chief Administrative Officer
Alicia Keating, Acting City Treasurer
Dwayne Killingbeck, Fire Chief

Miramichi
City Hall
141 Henry St.
Miramichi, NB E1V 2N5
Tel: 506-623-2200; *Fax:* 506-623-2201
www.miramichi.org
Municipal Type: City
Incorporated: Jan. 1, 1995; *Area:* 179.47 sq km
County or District: Northumberland; *Population in 2016:* 17,537
Provincial Electoral District(s): Miramichi Bay-Neguac;
Miramichi; Southwest Miramichi-Bay du Vin
Federal Electoral District(s): Miramichi-Grand Lake
Next Election: May 10, 2021 (4 year terms)
Adam Lordon, Mayor
Paddy Quinn, Deputy Mayor
Veronique Arsenault, Councillor
Chad Duplessie, Councillor
Jason Harris, Councillor
Sam Johnston, Councillor
Brian King, Councillor
Ryan Somers, Councillor
Tara Ross-Robinson, Councillor
Rhonda Ripley, Clerk
Nancy Gormon, Treasurer
Michael Noel, City Manager
Darren Row, Director, Engineering
Mary Savage, Director, Human Resources
Jay Shanahan, Director, Public Works

Moncton / Ville de Moncton
655 Main St.
Moncton, NB E1C 1E8
Tel: 506-853-3333; *Fax:* 506-389-5904
info@moncton.ca
www.moncton.ca
Municipal Type: City
Incorporated: 1890; *Area:* 141.92 sq km
County or District: Westmorland; *Population in 2016:* 71,889
Provincial Electoral District(s): Moncton East; Moncton Centre;
Moncton South; Moncton Northwest; Moncton Southwest
Federal Electoral District(s): Moncton-Riverview-Dieppe;
Beauséjour; Fundy Royal
Next Election: May 10, 2021 (4 year terms)
Dawn Arnold, Mayor
Charles Léger, Deputy Mayor
Monique LeBlanc, Councillor-at-Large
Marty Kingston, Councillor-at-Large
Shawn Crossman, Councillor, Wards: 1
Paulette Thériault, Councillor, Wards: 1
Daniel Bourgeois, Councillor, Wards: 2
Bryan David Butler, Councillor, Wards: 3
Dave Steeves, Councillor, Wards: 3
Susan Edgett, Councillor, Wards: 4
Paul Richard, Councillor, Wards: 4
Marc Landry, City Manager
Catherine Dallaire, General Manager, Recreation, Culture &
Events
Laurann Hanson, General Manager, Corporate Services
Jack MacDonald, General Manager, Sustainable Growth &
Development
Jacques Jacques, General Manager, Finance
Conrad Landry, Fire Chief, 506-857-8800, Fax: 506-856-4353

Quispamsis
P.O. Box 21085
12 Landing Ct.
Quispamsis, NB E2E 4Z4
Tel: 506-849-5778; *Fax:* 506-849-5799
quispamsis@quispamsis.ca
quispamsis.ca
Municipal Type: City
Area: 57.21 sq km
County or District: Kings; *Population in 2016:* 18,245
Provincial Electoral District(s): Hampton; Quispamsis
Federal Electoral District(s): Fundy Royal
Next Election: May 10, 2021 (4 year terms)
Libby O'Hara, Mayor
Mary Schryer, Deput Mayor
Mike Biggar, Councillor
Noah Donovan, Councillor
Kerrie Luck, Councillor
Kirk Miller, Councillor
Emil Olsen, Councillor
Beth Thompson, Councillor

Riverview
30 Honour House Ct.
Riverview, NB E1C3Y9
Tel: 506-387-2020
info@townofriverview.ca
www.townofriverview.ca
Municipal Type: City
Area: 35.45 sq km
County or District: Albert; *Population in 2016:* 19,667
Provincial Electoral District(s): Riverview; Albert
Federal Electoral District(s): Moncton-Riverview-Dieppe; Fundy
Royal
Next Election: May 10, 2021 (4 year terms)
Andrew J. LeBlanc, Mayor
Jeremy Thorne, Deputy Mayor
Cecile Cassista, Councillor-at-Large
Russell Hayward, Councillor-at-Large
Heath Johnson, Councillor-at-Large
Sarah Murphy, Councillor, Wards: 1
John Coughlan, Councillor, Wards: 2
Wayne Bennett, Councillor, Wards: 4
Colin Smith, Chief Administrative Officer
Robin True, Fire Chief

Rothesay
70 Hampton Rd.
Rothesay, NB E2E 5L5
Tel: 506-848-6600; *Fax:* 506-848-6677
rothesay@rothesay.ca
www.rothesay.ca
Municipal Type: City
Incorporated: Jan. 1, 1998; *Area:* 34.72 sq km
County or District: Kings; *Population in 2016:* 11,659
Provincial Electoral District(s): Rothesay

Federal Electoral District(s): Saint John-Rothesay; Fundy Royal
Next Election: May 10, 2021 (4 year terms)
Nancy Grant, Mayor
Matt Alexander, Deputy Mayor
Helen Boyle, Councillor
Dave Brown, Councillor
Peter J. Lewis, Councillor
Tiffany Mackay French, Councillor
Bill McGuire, Councillor
Don Shea, Councillor
John Jarvie, Town Manager

Saint John
City Hall
P.O. Box 1971
15 Market Sq.
Saint John, NB E2L 4L1
Tel: 506-649-6000
saintjohn.ca
Municipal Type: City
Incorporated: May 18, 1785; *Area:* 315.96 sq km
County or District: Saint John; *Population in 2016:* 65,575
Provincial Electoral District(s): Hampton; Saint John East;
Portland-Simonds; Saint John Harbour; Saint John Lancaster;
Fundy-The Isles-Saint John West
Federal Electoral District(s): Saint John-Rothesay
Next Election: May 10, 2021 (4 year terms)
Donna Noade Reardon, Mayor
John MacKenzie, Deputy Mayor, Wards: 2
Brent Harris, Councillor-at-Large
Gary Sullivan, Councillor-at-Large
Joanna Killen, Councillor, Wards: 1
Greg J. Norton, Councillor, Wards: 1
Barry Ogden, Councillor, Wards: 2
David Hickey, Councillor, Wards: 3
Gerry Lowe, Councillor, Wards: 3
Paula Radwan, Councillor, Wards: 4
Greg Stewart, Councillor, Wards: 4
John Collin, City Manager, 506-658-2913, Fax: 506-658-2802
Kevin Fudge, CFO & Chief
Jacqueline Hamilton, Commissioner, Growth & Community
Development, 506-658-2835, Fax: 506-658-2837
Kevin Clifford, Fire Chief

Other Municipalities in New Brunswick

Alma
8 School St.
Alma, NB E4H 1L2
Tel: 506-887-6123; *Fax:* 506-887-6124
villageofalma@gmail.com
www.villageofalma.ca
Municipal Type: Village
Area: 47.64 sq km
County or District: Albert; *Population in 2016:* 213
Provincial Electoral District(s): Albert
Federal Electoral District(s): Fundy Royal
Next Election: May 10, 2021 (4 year terms)
Andrew Casey, Mayor
Kim Beers, Clerk-Treasurer

Aroostook
383 Main St.
Aroostook, NB E7H 2Z4
Tel: 506-273-6443; *Fax:* 506-273-3025
varoostk@nb.aibn.com
Municipal Type: Village
Area: 2.24 sq km
County or District: Victoria; *Population in 2016:* 306
Provincial Electoral District(s): Carleton-Victoria
Federal Electoral District(s): Tobique-Mactaquac
Next Election: May 10, 2021 (4 year terms)
Darryl David Demmings, Mayor

Atholville
247, rue Notre-Dame
Atholville, NB E3N 4T1
Tél: 506-789-2944; *Téléc:* 506-789-2925
atholvillecouncil@gmail.com
www.atholville.ca
Entité municipal: Village
Incorporation: 1966; *Area:* 10.25 sq km
Comté ou district: Restigouche; *Population au 2016:* 3,570
Circonscription(s) électorale(s) provinciale(s): Restigouche West
Circonscription(s) électorale(s) fédérale(s):
Madawaska-Restigouche
Prochaines élections: May 10, 2021 (4 year terms)
Jean-Guy Levesque, Mayor
Nicole LeBrun, Chief Administrative Officer

Balmoral
CP 2531
1447, av des Pionniers
Balmoral, NB E8E 2W7
Tél: 506-826-6060; *Téléc:* 506-826-6037
vilbal@nbnet.nb.ca
balmoralnb.com
Entité municipal: Village
Incorporation: 1972; *Area:* 43.51 sq km
Comté ou district: Restigouche; *Population au 2016:* 1,674
Circonscription(s) électorale(s) provinciale(s): Restigouche West
Circonscription(s) électorale(s) fédérale(s):
Madawaska-Restigouche
Prochaines élections: May 10, 2021 (4 year terms)
Guy Chiasson, Maire
Marie-Claude Keeley, Directrice générale

Bas-Caraquet
8185, rue St-Paul
Bas-Caraquet, NB E1W 6C4
Tél: 506-726-2776; *Téléc:* 506-726-2770
municipalite@bascaraquet.com
www.bascaraquet.com
Entité municipal: Village
Area: 31 sq km
Comté ou district: Gloucester; *Population au 2016:* 1,305
Circonscription(s) électorale(s) provinciale(s): Caraquet
Circonscription(s) électorale(s) fédérale(s): Acadie-Bathurst
Prochaines élections: May 10, 2021 (4 year terms)
Roger R. Chiasson, Maire
Richard Frigault, Directeur général

Bath
161 School St.
Bath, NB E7J 1C3
Tel: 506-278-5293; *Fax:* 506-278-5932
bath@nbnet.nb.ca
www.villageofbath.ca
Municipal Type: Village
Area: 2.03 sq km
County or District: Carleton; *Population in 2016:* 476
Provincial Electoral District(s): Carleton-Victoria
Federal Electoral District(s): Tobique-Mactaquac
Next Election: May 10, 2021 (4 year terms)
Troy F.J. Stone, Mayor

Belledune
P.O. Box 1006
2330 Main St.
Belledune, NB E8G 2X9
Tel: 506-522-3700; *Fax:* 506-522-3704
info@belledune.com
belledune.com
Municipal Type: Village
Incorporated: Jan. 1, 1968; *Area:* 189.03 sq km
County or District: Gloucester; *Population in 2016:* 1,417
Provincial Electoral District(s): Restigouche-Chaleur
Federal Electoral District(s): Acadie-Bathurst
Next Election: May 10, 2021 (4 year terms)
Paul A. Arseneault, Mayor
Landon Lee, Chief Administrative Officer

Beresford
#2, 855, rue Principale
Beresford, NB E8K 1T3
Tél: 506-542-2727; *Téléc:* 506-542-2702
info@beresford.ca
beresford.ca
Entité municipal: Town
Area: 19.2 sq km
Comté ou district: Gloucester; *Population au 2016:* 4,288
Circonscription(s) électorale(s) provinciale(s): Bathurst
West-Beresford
Circonscription(s) électorale(s) fédérale(s): Acadie-Bathurst
Prochaines élections: May 10, 2021 (4 year terms)
Edgar Aubé, Maire
Marc-André Godin, Directeur général

Bertrand
#1, 651, boul des Acadiens
Bertrand, NB E1W 1G5
Tél: 506-726-2442; *Téléc:* 506-726-2449
info@villagedebertrand.ca
www.villagedebertrand.ca
Entité municipal: Village
Area: 46.45 sq km
Comté ou district: Gloucester; *Population au 2016:* 1,166
Circonscription(s) électorale(s) provinciale(s): Caraquet
Circonscription(s) électorale(s) fédérale(s): Acadie-Bathurst
Prochaines élections: May 10, 2021 (4 year terms)
Yvon Godin, Maire
Joël Thibodeau, Directeur général

Blacks Harbour
65 Wallace Cove Rd.
Blacks Harbour, NB E5H 1G9
Tel: 506-456-4870; *Fax:* 506-456-4872
info@blacksharbour.ca
blacksharbour.ca
Municipal Type: Village
Area: 8.9 sq km
County or District: Charlotte; *Population in 2016:* 894
Provincial Electoral District(s): Fundy-The Isles-Saint John West
Federal Electoral District(s): New Brunswick Southwest
Next Election: May 10, 2021 (4 year terms)
John D. Craig, Mayor
Deborah Johnson, Chief Administrative Officer

Blackville
12 South Bartholomew Rd.
Blackville, NB E9B 1N2
Tel: 506-843-6337; *Fax:* 506-843-6043
blackvl@nb.sympatico.ca
www.villageofblackville.com
Municipal Type: Village
Area: 21.73 sq km
County or District: Northumberland; *Population in 2016:* 958
Provincial Electoral District(s): Southwest Miramichi-Bay du Vin
Federal Electoral District(s): Miramichi-Grand Lake
Next Election: May 10, 2021 (4 year terms)
Ian Fortune, Mayor

Bouctouche
30, rue Évangéline
Bouctouche, NB E4S 3E4
Tél: 506-743-7000; *Téléc:* 506-743-7261
ville@bouctouche.ca
www.villedebouctouche.ca
Entité municipal: Town
Area: 18.34 sq km
Comté ou district: Kent; *Population au 2016:* 2,361
Circonscription(s) électorale(s) provinciale(s): Kent South
Circonscription(s) électorale(s) fédérale(s): Beauséjour
Prochaines élections: May 10, 2021 (4 year terms)
Aldéo Saulnier, Maire
Emilie Doiron Gaudet, Directrice générale et greffière,
506-743-7000

Cambridge-Narrows
Municipal Bldg.
6 Municipal Lane
Cambridge-Narrows, NB E4C 4P4
Tel: 506-488-3155; *Fax:* 506-488-1018
office@nbnet.nb.ca
cambridge-narrows.ca
Municipal Type: Village
Area: 106.94 sq km
County or District: Queens; *Population in 2016:* 562
Provincial Electoral District(s): Gagetown-Petitcodiac
Federal Electoral District(s): New Brunswick Southwest
Next Election: May 10, 2021 (4 year terms)
Doug Richardson, Mayor

Campbellton
Campbellton City Centre
P.O. Box 100
76 Water St.
Campbellton, NB E3N 3G1
Tel: 506-789-2700; *Fax:* 506-759-7403
info@campbellton.org
www.campbellton.org
Municipal Type: Town
Incorporated: 1889; *Area:* 18.66 sq km
County or District: Restigouche; *Population in 2016:* 6,883
Provincial Electoral District(s): Campbellton-Dalhousie
Federal Electoral District(s): Madawaska-Restigouche
Next Election: May 10, 2021 (4 year terms)
Ian Comeau, Mayor
Manon Cloutier, Chief Administrative Officer

Canterbury
199 Main St.
Canterbury, NB E6H 1M6
Tel: 506-279-6248; *Fax:* 506-279-9019
canterbury@anb.aibn.com
Municipal Type: Village
Area: 5.34 sq km
County or District: York; *Population in 2016:* 336
Provincial Electoral District(s): Carleton-York
Federal Electoral District(s): Tobique-Mactaquac
Next Election: May 10, 2021 (4 year terms)
Tanya Marie Cloutier, Mayor
Susan Patterson, Clerk

Cap-Pelé
2647, ch Acadie
Cap-Pelé, NB E4N 1C2
Tél: 506-577-2030; *Téléc:* 506-577-2035
info@cap-pele.com
cap-pele.com
Entité municipal: Village
Incorporation: 1969; *Area:* 23.78 sq km
Comté ou district: Westmorland; *Population au 2016:* 2,425
Circonscription(s) électorale(s) provinciale(s):
Shediac-Beaubassin-Cap-Pelé
Circonscription(s) électorale(s) fédérale(s): Beauséjour
Prochaines élections: May 10, 2021 (4 year terms)
Serge J. Léger, Maire
Stéphane Dallaire, Directeur général

Caraquet
CP 5695
10, rue du Colisée
Caraquet, NB E1W 1B7
Tél: 506-726-2727; *Téléc:* 506-726-2660
ville@caraquet.ca
caraquet.ca
Entité municipal: Town
Incorporation: Nov. 15, 1961; *Area:* 68.26 sq km
Comté ou district: Gloucester; *Population au 2016:* 4,248
Circonscription(s) électorale(s) provinciale(s): Caraquet
Circonscription(s) électorale(s) fédérale(s): Acadie-Bathurst
Prochaines élections: May 10, 2021 (4 year terms)
Bernard Thériault, Maire
Marc Duguay, Directeur général

Centreville
836 Central St.
Centreville, NB E7K 2E7
Tel: 506-276-3671; *Fax:* 506-276-9891
voc@rogers.com
www.villageofcentreville.ca
Municipal Type: Village
Area: 2.69 sq km
County or District: Carleton; *Population in 2016:* 557
Provincial Electoral District(s): Carleton-Victoria
Federal Electoral District(s): Tobique-Mactaquac; New
Brunswick Southwest
Next Election: May 10, 2021 (4 year terms)
Michael John Stewart, Mayor
Andrea Callahan, Administrator

Charlo
614, rue Chaleur
Charlo, NB E8E 2G6
Tél: 506-684-7850
info@villagecharlo.com
www.villagecharlo.com
Entité municipal: Village
Incorporation: 1966; *Area:* 30.75 sq km
Comté ou district: Restigouche; *Population au 2016:* 1,310
Circonscription(s) électorale(s) provinciale(s):
Campbellton-Dalhousie
Circonscription(s) électorale(s) fédérale(s):
Madawaska-Restigouche
Prochaines élections: May 10, 2021 (4 year terms)
Gaétan Pelletier, Maire
Lilianne Cayouette, Directrice générale

Chipman
#1, 10 Civic Ct.
Chipman, NB E4A 2H9
Tel: 506-339-6601; *Fax:* 506-339-6197
www.chipmannb.org
Municipal Type: Village
Area: 19.58 sq km
County or District: Queens; *Population in 2016:* 1,104
Provincial Electoral District(s): Fredericton-Grand Lake
Federal Electoral District(s): Miramichi-Grand Lake
Next Election: May 10, 2021 (4 year terms)
Keith V. West, Mayor
Michelle Dickinson, Clerk

Dalhousie
#1, 111 Hall St.
Dalhousie, NB E8C 1X2
Tel: 506-684-7600; *Fax:* 506-684-7613
reception@dalhousie.ca
www.dalhousie.ca
Municipal Type: Town
Incorporated: 1905; *Area:* 14.51 sq km
County or District: Restigouche; *Population in 2016:* 3,126
Provincial Electoral District(s): Campbellton-Dalhousie
Federal Electoral District(s): Madawaska-Restigouche
Next Election: May 10, 2021 (4 year terms)
Normand Gerard Pelletier, Mayor

Gilles Legacy, Clerk/Treasurer

Doaktown
8 Miramichi St.
Doaktown, NB E9C 1C8
Tel: 506-365-7970; *Fax:* 506-365-7111
doaktown@nb.aibn.com
www.discoverdoaktown.com
Municipal Type: Village
Area: 28.74 sq km
County or District: Northumberland; *Population in 2016:* 792
Provincial Electoral District(s): Southwest Miramichi-Bay du Vin
Federal Electoral District(s): Miramichi-Grand Lake
Next Election: May 10, 2021 (4 year terms)
Caroline St. Pierre Taylor, Mayor
Marilyn E. Price, Clerk-Administrator

Dorchester
4984 Main St.
Dorchester, NB E4K 2Z1
Tel: 506-379-3030; *Fax:* 506-379-3033
www.dorchester.ca
Municipal Type: Village
Area: 5.74 sq km
County or District: Westmorland; *Population in 2016:* 1,096
Provincial Electoral District(s): Memramcook-Tantramar
Federal Electoral District(s): Beauséjour
Next Election: May 10, 2021 (4 year terms)
Debbie Darlene Wiggins-Colwell, Mayor

Drummond
1413, ch Tobique
Drummond, NB E3Y 1H7
Tél: 506-475-4000; *Téléc:* 506-475-4010
info@drummondnb.com
www.drummondnb.com
Entité municipal: Village
Area: 8.91 sq km
Comté ou district: Victoria; *Population au 2016:* 737
Circonscription(s) électorale(s) provinciale(s): Victoria-La Vallée
Circonscription(s) électorale(s) fédérale(s): Tobique-Mactaquac
Prochaines élections: May 10, 2021 (4 year terms)
France Roussel, Maire
Annie Gagné, Directrice générale

Eel River Crossing
20, rue Savoie
Eel River Crossing, NB E8E 1T8
Tél: 506-826-6080; *Téléc:* 506-826-6088
erc@ercvillage.com
eelriverdundee.ca
Entité municipal: Village
Area: 17.43 sq km
Population au 2016: 1,953
Circonscription(s) électorale(s) provinciale(s):
Campbellton-Dalhousie
Circonscription(s) électorale(s) fédérale(s):
Madawaska-Restigouche
Prochaines élections: May 10, 2021 (4 year terms)
Note: Also Known As: Eel River Dundee
Mario Pelletier, Maire
Kim Bujold, Directrice générale

Florenceville-Bristol
19 Station Rd.
Florenceville-Bristol, NB E7L 3J8
Tel: 506-392-6013; *Fax:* 506-392-5211
office@florencevillebristol.ca
www.florencevillebristol.ca
Municipal Type: Village
Incorporated: 2008
County or District: Carleton; *Population in 2016:* 1,604
Provincial Electoral District(s): Carleton-Victoria
Federal Electoral District(s): Tobique-Mactaquac
Next Election: May 10, 2021 (4 year terms)
Note: The villages of Florenceville & Bristol amalgamated to
create the municipality of Florenceville-Bristol.
Karl E. Curtis, Mayor
Sarah Pacey, Chief Administrative Officer

Fredericton Junction
102 Wilsey Rd.
Fredericton Junction, NB E5L 1W7
Tel: 506-368-2628; *Fax:* 506-368-1900
fredjct@nb.aibn.com
frederictonjunction.ca
Municipal Type: Village
Area: 23.86 sq km
County or District: Sunbury; *Population in 2016:* 704
Provincial Electoral District(s): New Maryland-Sunbury
Federal Electoral District(s): New Brunswick Southwest
Next Election: May 10, 2021 (4 year terms)

John B. Bigger, Mayor
Cindy Ogden, Chief Administrative Officer

Gagetown
41 Front St.
Gagetown, NB E5M 1A1
Tel: 506-488-3567; *Fax:* 506-488-3543
clerk@villageofgagetown.ca
www.villageofgagetown.ca
Municipal Type: Village
Incorporated: 1966; *Area:* 49.48 sq km
County or District: Queens; *Population in 2016:* 711
Provincial Electoral District(s): Gagetown-Petitcodiac
Federal Electoral District(s): New Brunswick Southwest
Next Election: May 10, 2021 (4 year terms)
Derek Pleadwell, Mayor
Robert White, Chief Administrative Officer

Le Goulet
1295, rue Principale
Le Goulet, NB E8S 2E9
Tél: 506-336-3272; *Téléc:* 506-336-3281
www.legoulet.ca
Entité municipal: Village
Incorporation: May 12, 1986; *Area:* 5.46 sq km
Comté ou district: Gloucester; *Population au 2016:* 793
Circonscription(s) électorale(s) provinciale(s):
Lamèque-Shippagan-Miscou
Circonscription(s) électorale(s) fédérale(s): Acadie-Bathurst
Prochaines élections: May 10, 2021 (4 year terms)
Paul-Aimé Mallet, Maire
Alvine Bulger, Directeur général

Grand Bay-Westfield
P.O. Box 3001
Grand Bay-Westfield, NB E5K 4V3
Tel: 506-738-6400
administration@towngbw.ca
grandbaywestfield.ca
Municipal Type: Town
Incorporated: 1998; *Area:* 59.73 sq km
County or District: Kings; *Population in 2016:* 4,964
Provincial Electoral District(s): Kings Centre
Federal Electoral District(s): New Brunswick Southwest
Next Election: May 10, 2021 (4 year terms)
Brittany Merrifield, Mayor
John Enns-Wind, Chief Administrative Officer

Grand Falls / Grand-Sault
#200, 131, rue Pleasant
Grand-Sault, NB E3Z 1G6
Tel: 506-475-7777; *Fax:* 506-475-7779
vgs-tgf@nb.aibn.com
www.grandfallsnb.com
Municipal Type: Town
Area: 18.06 sq km
County or District: Victoria; *Population in 2016:* 5,326
Provincial Electoral District(s): Victoria-La Vallée
Federal Electoral District(s): Tobique-Mactaquac
Next Election: May 10, 2021 (4 year terms)
Barry Manuel, Mayor
Peter Michaud, Chief Administrative Officer-Clerk

Grand Manan
P.O. Box 1310
Grand Manan, NB E5G 4E9
Tel: 506-662-3442
info@grandmanannb.com
www.grandmanannb.com
Other Information: Toll-Free Phone: 888-525-1655
Municipal Type: Village
Incorporated: May 8, 1995; *Area:* 150.78 sq km
County or District: Charlotte; *Population in 2016:* 2,360
Provincial Electoral District(s): Fundy-The Isles-Saint John West
Federal Electoral District(s): New Brunswick Southwest
Next Election: May 10, 2021 (4 year terms)
Bonnie H. Morse, Mayor

Grande-Anse
393, rue Acadie
Grande-Anse, NB E8N 1E2
Tél: 506-732-3242; *Téléc:* 506-732-3217
info@grande-anse.net
www.grande-anse.net
Entité municipal: Village
Incorporation: 1968; *Area:* 24.42 sq km
Comté ou district: Gloucester; *Population au 2016:* 899
Circonscription(s) électorale(s) provinciale(s): Caraquet
Circonscription(s) électorale(s) fédérale(s): Acadie-Bathurst
Prochaines élections: May 10, 2021 (4 year terms)
Thérèse Haché, Maire
Henri Battah, Directeur général

Hampton

P.O. Box 1066
648 Main St.
Hampton, NB E5N 8H1
Tel: 506-832-6065
info@townofhampton.ca
www.townofhampton.ca
Municipal Type: Town
Area: 21 sq km
County or District: Kings; *Population in 2016:* 4,282
Provincial Electoral District(s): Hampton
Federal Electoral District(s): Fundy Royal
Next Election: May 10, 2021 (4 year terms)
Robert Doucet, Mayor
Richard Malone, Town Manager

Hanwell

5 Nature Park Dr.
Hanwell, NB E3E 0G7
Tel: 506-460-1177
hanwell.nb.ca
Municipal Type: Community
Incorporated: May 27, 2014
County or District: York; *Population in 2016:* 4,750
Provincial Electoral District(s): Fredericton West-Hanwell
Federal Electoral District(s): New Brunswick Southwest
Next Election: May 10, 2021 (4 year terms)
Dave Morrison, Mayor
Terri Parker, Clerk-Treasurer

Hartland

#1, 31 Orser St.
Hartland, NB E7P 1R4
Tel: 506-375-4357; *Fax:* 506-596-0226
office@townofhartland.com
townofhartland.ca
Municipal Type: Town
Area: 9.63 sq km
County or District: Carleton; *Population in 2016:* 957
Provincial Electoral District(s): Carleton
Federal Electoral District(s): Tobique-Mactaquac
Next Election: May 10, 2021 (4 year terms)
Tracey D. DeMerchant, Mayor
David Hutten, Chief Administrative Officer

Harvey

58 Hanselpacker Rd.
Harvey, NB E6K 1A3
Tel: 506-366-6240
village.harvey@rogers.com
www.village.harvey-station.nb.ca
Municipal Type: Village
Incorporated: Nov. 9, 1966; *Area:* 2.46 sq km
County or District: York; *Population in 2016:* 333
Provincial Electoral District(s): Carleton-York
Federal Electoral District(s): New Brunswick Southwest; Fundy Royal
Next Election: May 10, 2021 (4 year terms)
Winston Gamblin, Mayor

Hillsborough

#1, 2849 Main St.
Hillsborough, NB E4H 2X7
Tel: 506-734-3733; *Fax:* 506-734-3711
hillsboroughnb@rogers.com
villageofhillsborough.ca
Municipal Type: Village
Incorporated: 1966; *Area:* 12.98 sq km
County or District: Albert; *Population in 2016:* 1,277
Provincial Electoral District(s): Albert
Federal Electoral District(s): Fundy Royal
Next Election: May 10, 2021 (4 year terms)
Robert R. Rochon, Mayor
Shari Kaster, Administrator-Clerk

Kedgwick

114, rue Notre-Dame
Kedgwick, NB E8B 1H8
Tél: 506-284-2160; *Téléc:* 506-284-2859
crkedgwick@bellaliant.com
Entité municipal: Village
Area: 4.28 sq km
Comté ou district: Restigouche; *Population au 2016:* 1,003
Circonscription(s) électorale(s) provinciale(s): Restigouche West
Circonscription(s) électorale(s) fédérale(s): Madawaska-Restigouche
Prochaines élections: May 10, 2021 (4 year terms)
Eric Gagnon, Maire

Lac-Baker

69, rue de la Pointe
Lac Baker, NB E7A 1J1
Tel: 506-992-6060; *Fax:* 506-992-6061
Municipal Type: Village
Area: 4.02 sq km
County or District: Madawaska; *Population in 2016:* 690
Provincial Electoral District(s): Madawaska Les Lacs-Edmundston
Federal Electoral District(s): Madawaska-Restigouche
Next Election: May 10, 2021 (4 year terms)
Roseline Pelletier, Mayor

Lamèque

CP 2037
44, rue du Pêcheur Nord
Lamèque, NB E8T 3N4
Tél: 506-344-3222; *Téléc:* 506-344-3266
info@lameque.ca
www.lameque.ca
Entité municipal: Town
Area: 12.45 sq km
Comté ou district: Gloucester; *Population au 2016:* 1,285
Circonscription(s) électorale(s) provinciale(s): Shippagan-Lamèque-Miscou
Circonscription(s) électorale(s) fédérale(s): Acadie-Bathurst
Prochaines élections: May 10, 2021 (4 year terms)
Jules Haché, Maire
Dave Brown, Directeur général

Maisonnette

1512, rue Châtillon
Maisonnette, NB E8N 1S4
Tél: 506-726-2717; *Téléc:* 506-726-2718
info@maisonnette.ca
www.maisonnette.ca
Entité municipal: Village
Incorporation: May 12, 1986; *Area:* 12.88 sq km
Comté ou district: Gloucester; *Population au 2016:* 495
Circonscription(s) électorale(s) provinciale(s): Caraquet
Circonscription(s) électorale(s) fédérale(s): Acadie-Bathurst
Prochaines élections: May 10, 2021 (4 year terms)
Anthony Poirier, Maire

McAdam

146 Saunders Rd.
McAdam, NB E6J 1L2
Tel: 506-784-2293
mcadamnb.com
Municipal Type: Village
Area: 14.47 sq km
County or District: York; *Population in 2016:* 1,151
Provincial Electoral District(s): Charlotte-Campobello
Federal Electoral District(s): New Brunswick Southwest
Next Election: May 10, 2021 (4 year terms)
Kenneth Stannix, Mayor
Ann Donahue, Clerk-Treasurer

Meductic

320 Rte. 165
Meductic, NB E6H 1J5
Tel: 506-272-2098; *Fax:* 506-272-1883
www.meductic.ca
Municipal Type: Village
Area: 5.57 sq km
County or District: York; *Population in 2016:* 173
Provincial Electoral District(s): Carleton-York
Federal Electoral District(s): Tobique-Mactaquac
Next Election: May 10, 2021 (4 year terms)
Lance Royden Graham, Mayor
Lana Sharpe, Clerk-Treasurer

Memramcook

540, rue Centrale
Memramcook, NB E4K 3S6
Tél: 506-758-4078; *Téléc:* 506-758-4079
village@memramcook.com
memramcook.com
Entité municipal: Village
Incorporation: 1995; *Area:* 185.71 sq km
Comté ou district: Westmorland; *Population au 2016:* 4,778
Circonscription(s) électorale(s) provinciale(s): Memramcook-Tantramar
Circonscription(s) électorale(s) fédérale(s): Beauséjour
Prochaines élections: May 10, 2021 (4 year terms)
Maxime Bourgeois, Maire
Monique Bourque, Directrice générale et greffière

Millville

39 Howland Ridge Rd.
Millville, NB E6E 1Y3
Tel: 506-575-4144; *Fax:* 506-463-8262
villageofmillville@nb.aibn.com
www.millvillenb.com
Municipal Type: Village
Area: 12.16 sq km
County or District: York; *Population in 2016:* 273
Provincial Electoral District(s): Carleton-York
Federal Electoral District(s): Tobique-Mactaquac
Next Election: May 10, 2021 (4 year terms)
Beverly Herbert Forbes, Mayor
Natalie Hill, Clerk-Treasurer

Minto

420 Pleasant Dr.
Minto, NB E4B 2T3
Tel: 506-327-3383; *Fax:* 506-327-3041
www.villageofminto.ca
Municipal Type: Village
Area: 31.53 sq km
County or District: Sunbury-Queens; *Population in 2016:* 2,305
Provincial Electoral District(s): Fredericton-Grand Lake
Federal Electoral District(s): Miramichi-Grand Lake
Next Election: May 10, 2021 (4 year terms)
Erica Barnett, Mayor
Wendy Flowers, Clerk

Nackawic

115 Otis Dr.
Nackawic, NB E6G 2P1
Tel: 506-575-2241; *Fax:* 506-575-2035
townhall@nackawic.com
nackawic.com
Municipal Type: Town
Area: 8.4 sq km
County or District: York; *Population in 2016:* 941
Provincial Electoral District(s): Carleton-York
Federal Electoral District(s): Tobique-Mactaquac
Next Election: May 10, 2021 (4 year terms)
Ian Kitchen, Mayor
Randy Wilson, Chief Administrative Officer

Néguac

#1, 1175, rue Principale
Néguac, NB E9G 1T1
Tél: 506-776-3950; *Téléc:* 506-776-3975
info@neguac.com
www.neguac.com
Entité municipal: Village
Incorporation: Aug. 23, 1967; *Area:* 26.69 sq km
Comté ou district: Northumberland; *Population au 2016:* 1,684
Circonscription(s) électorale(s) provinciale(s): Miramichi Bay-Neguac
Circonscription(s) électorale(s) fédérale(s): Miramichi-Grand Lake
Prochaines élections: May 10, 2021 (4 year terms)
Georges Rhéal Savoie, Maire
Jeannot Doiron, Directeur général

New Maryland

584 New Maryland Hwy.
New Maryland, NB E3C 1K1
Tel: 506-451-8508; *Fax:* 506-450-1605
office@vonm.ca
www.vonm.ca
Municipal Type: Village
Incorporated: 1991; *Area:* 21.24 sq km
County or District: York; *Population in 2016:* 4,174
Provincial Electoral District(s): New Maryland-Sunbury
Federal Electoral District(s): Fredericton; New Brunswick Southwest
Next Election: May 10, 2021 (4 year terms)
Judy E. Wilson-Shee, Mayor
Cynthia Geldart, Chief Administrative Officer-Clerk

Nigadoo

#1, 385, rue Principale
Nigadoo, NB E8K 3R6
Tél: 506-542-2626; *Téléc:* 506-542-2678
info@nigadoo.net
nigadoo.ca
Entité municipal: Village
Incorporation: 1967; *Area:* 7.69 sq km
Comté ou district: Gloucester; *Population au 2016:* 963
Circonscription(s) électorale(s) provinciale(s): Restigouche-Chaleur
Circonscription(s) électorale(s) fédérale(s): Acadie-Bathurst
Prochaines élections: May 10, 2021 (4 year terms)
Charles Henri Doucet, Maire

Norton
10 Municipal St.
Norton, NB E5T 0C8
Tel: 506-839-3011; *Fax:* 506-839-3015
www.villageofnorton.com
Municipal Type: Village
Area: 75.35 sq km
County or District: Kings; *Population in 2016:* 1,382
Provincial Electoral District(s): Kings Centre
Federal Electoral District(s): Fundy Royal
Next Election: May 10, 2021 (4 year terms)
Ann-Marie Snyder, Mayor
Anita Pollock, Clerk

Oromocto
4 Doyle Dr.
Oromocto, NB E2V 2V3
Tel: 506-357-4400; *Fax:* 506-357-2266
gengov@oromocto.ca
www.oromocto.ca
Municipal Type: Town
Area: 22.37 sq km
County or District: Sunbury; *Population in 2016:* 9,223
Provincial Electoral District(s): Oromocto-Lincoln
Federal Electoral District(s): Fredericton
Next Election: May 10, 2021 (4 year terms)
Robert Powell, Mayor
Richard Isabelle, Chief Administrative Officer-Clerk

Paquetville
1094, rue du Parc
Paquetville, NB E8R 1J4
Tél: 506-764-2500; *Téléc:* 506-764-2504
info@villagepaquetville.com
villagepaquetville.com
Entité municipal: Village
Incorporation: 1966; *Area:* 9.4 sq km
Comté ou district: Gloucester; *Population au 2016:* 720
Circonscription(s) électorale(s) provinciale(s): Caraquet
Circonscription(s) électorale(s) fédérale(s): Acadie-Bathurst
Prochaines élections: May 10, 2021 (4 year terms)
Luc Robichaud, Maire
Ghislain Comeau, Directeur général

Perth-Andover
1131 West Riverside Dr.
Perth-Andover, NB E7H 5G5
Tel: 506-273-4959
www.perth-andover.com
Municipal Type: Village
Incorporated: 1966; *Area:* 8.89 sq km
County or District: Victoria; *Population in 2016:* 1,590
Provincial Electoral District(s): Carleton-Victoria
Federal Electoral District(s): Tobique-Mactaquac
Next Election: May 10, 2021 (4 year terms)
Marianne Bell, Mayor
Daniel Dionne, Chief Administrative Officer

Petitcodiac
P.O. Box 2507
63 Main St.
Petitcodiac, NB E4Z 6H4
Tel: 506-756-3140; *Fax:* 506-756-3142
vop@nbnet.nb.ca
www.petitcodiac.ca
Municipal Type: Village
Area: 17.22 sq km
County or District: Westmorland; *Population in 2016:* 1,383
Provincial Electoral District(s): Gagetown-Petitcodiac
Federal Electoral District(s): Fundy Royal
Next Election: May 10, 2021 (4 year terms)
Daniel Pollock, Mayor

Petit-Rocher
582, rue Principale
Petit-Rocher, NB E8J 1S5
Tél: 506-542-2686; *Téléc:* 506-542-2708
petit-rocher@nb.aibn.com
www.petit-rocher.ca
Entité municipal: Village
Area: 4.49 sq km
Comté ou district: Gloucester; *Population au 2016:* 1,897
Circonscription(s) électorale(s) provinciale(s):
Restigouche-Chaleur
Circonscription(s) électorale(s) fédérale(s): Acadie-Bathurst
Prochaines élections: May 10, 2021 (4 year terms)
Rachel Boudreau, Maire
Magali Courtin, Directrice générale

Plaster Rock
159 Main St.
Plaster Rock, NB E7G 2H2
Tel: 506-356-6070; *Fax:* 506-356-6081
office@plasterrockvillage.com
plasterrockvillage.com
Municipal Type: Village
Area: 3.09 sq km
County or District: Victoria; *Population in 2016:* 1,023
Provincial Electoral District(s): Carleton-Victoria
Federal Electoral District(s): Tobique-Mactaquac
Next Election: May 10, 2021 (4 year terms)
Tom Eagles, Mayor
Patty St. Peter, Clerk-Manager, 506-356-6071

Pointe-Verte
375, rue Principale
Pointe-Verte, NB E8J 2S8
Tél: 506-542-2606; *Téléc:* 506-542-2638
info@pointeverte.net
pointe-verte.ca
Entité municipal: Village
Area: 13.79 sq km
Comté ou district: Gloucester; *Population au 2016:* 886
Circonscription(s) électorale(s) provinciale(s):
Restigouche-Chaleur
Circonscription(s) électorale(s) fédérale(s): Acadie-Bathurst
Prochaines élections: May 10, 2021 (4 year terms)
Maxime Lejeun, Maire
Donna Landry-Haché, Directrice générale

Port Elgin
9 East Main St.
Port Elgin, NB E4M 2X8
Tel: 506-538-2120; *Fax:* 506-538-2126
info@villageofportelgin.com
villageofportelgin.com
Municipal Type: Village
Incorporated: 1922; *Area:* 2.61 sq km
County or District: Westmorland; *Population in 2016:* 408
Provincial Electoral District(s): Memramcook-Tantramar
Federal Electoral District(s): Beauséjour
Next Election: May 10, 2021 (4 year terms)
Jason Davis Stokes, Mayor

Rexton
82 Main St.
Rexton, NB E4W 5N4
Tel: 506-523-6921; *Fax:* 506-523-7383
villageofrexton@nb.aibn.com
www.villageofrexton.com
Municipal Type: Village
Incorporated: Nov. 9, 1966; *Area:* 6.14 sq km
County or District: Kent; *Population in 2016:* 830
Provincial Electoral District(s): Kent North
Federal Electoral District(s): Beauséjour
Next Election: May 10, 2021 (4 year terms)
Wayne Carpenter, Mayor
Shane Thomson, General Manager

Richibucto
#1, 9235, rue Main
Richibucto, NB E4W 4B4
Tél: 506-523-7870; *Téléc:* 506-523-7850
reception@richibucto.org
www.richibucto.org
Entité municipal: Town
Incorporation: 1967; *Area:* 11.83 sq km
Comté ou district: Kent; *Population au 2016:* 1,266
Circonscription(s) électorale(s) provinciale(s): Kent North
Circonscription(s) électorale(s) fédérale(s): Beauséjour
Prochaines élections: May 10, 2021 (4 year terms)
Stella M. Richard, Maire

Riverside-Albert
5823 King St.
Riverside-Albert, NB E4H 4B4
Tel: 506-882-3022
villra@nbnet.nb.ca
www.riverside-albert.ca
Municipal Type: Village
Area: 3.41 sq km
County or District: Albert; *Population in 2016:* 350
Provincial Electoral District(s): Albert
Federal Electoral District(s): Fundy Royal
Next Election: May 10, 2021 (4 year terms)
Jim Campbell, Mayor
Deborah Murray-Butland, Clerk

Rivière-Verte
78, rue Principale
Rivière-Verte, NB E7C 2T8
Tél: 506-263-1060; *Téléc:* 506-263-1065
info@riviere-verte.ca
riviere-verte.ca
Entité municipal: Village
Area: 7 sq km
Comté ou district: Madawaska; *Population au 2016:* 724
Circonscription(s) électorale(s) provinciale(s):
Edmundston-Madawaska Centre
Circonscription(s) électorale(s) fédérale(s):
Madawaska-Restigouche
Prochaines élections: May 10, 2021 (4 year terms)
Lisa Parent, Maire
Parise Pelletier, Secrétaire municipale

Rogersville
10989, rue Principale
Rogersville, NB E4Y 2L6
Tél: 506-775-2080; *Téléc:* 506-775-2090
rogervil@nbnet.nb.ca
www.rogersvillenb.com
Entité municipal: Village
Incorporation: Nov. 9, 1966; *Area:* 7.23 sq km
Comté ou district: Kent; *Population au 2016:* 1,166
Circonscription(s) électorale(s) provinciale(s): Kent North
Circonscription(s) électorale(s) fédérale(s): Miramichi-Grand Lake
Prochaines élections: May 10, 2021 (4 year terms)
Pierrette F. Robichaud, Mairesse
Angèle McCaie, Directrice générale

Sackville
P.O. Box 6191
31C Main St.
Sackville, NB E4L 1G6
Tel: 506-364-4930; *Fax:* 506-364-4976
info@sackville.com
www.sackville.com
Other Information: Toll-Free Phone: 800-249-2020
Municipal Type: Town
Incorporated: Jan. 1903; *Area:* 74.32 sq km
County or District: Westmorland; *Population in 2016:* 5,331
Provincial Electoral District(s): Memramcook-Tantramar
Federal Electoral District(s): Beauséjour
Next Election: May 10, 2021 (4 year terms)
Shawn Mesheau, Mayor
Jamie Burke, Chief Administrative Officer

Saint-André
492, ch de l'Église
Saint-André, NB E3Y 2Y6
Tél: 506-473-7580; *Téléc:* 506-473-7585
vilstand@nb.aibn.com
www.saintandrenb.ca
Entité municipal: Village
Area: 3.72 sq km
Comté ou district: Madawaska; *Population au 2016:* 772
Circonscription(s) électorale(s) provinciale(s): Victoria-La Vallée
Circonscription(s) électorale(s) fédérale(s): Tobique-Mactaquac
Prochaines élections: May 10, 2021 (4 year terms)
Marcel Levesques, Maire
John Morrisey, Greffier/Secrétaire municipal/Directeur général

St. Andrews
212 Water St.
St Andrews, NB E5B 1B4
Tel: 506-529-5120; *Fax:* 506-529-5183
town@townofstandrews.ca
www.townofstandrews.ca
Municipal Type: Town
Area: 8.35 sq km
County or District: Charlotte; *Population in 2016:* 11,913
Provincial Electoral District(s): Charlotte-Campobello
Federal Electoral District(s): New Brunswick Southwest
Next Election: May 10, 2021 (4 year terms)
Brad Henderson, Mayor
Chris Spear, Chief Administrative Officer & Treasurer

Saint-Antoine
300, 4556, rue Principale
Saint-Antoine, NB E4V 1P8
Tél: 506-525-4020; *Téléc:* 506-525-4027
village@saint-antoine.ca
saint-antoine.ca
Entité municipal: Village
Area: 6.43 sq km
Comté ou district: Kent; *Population au 2016:* 1,733
Circonscription(s) électorale(s) provinciale(s): Kent South
Circonscription(s) électorale(s) fédérale(s): Beauséjour
Prochaines élections: May 10, 2021 (4 year terms)

Jean-Pierre Richard, Maire
Vicky Williams, Directrice générale et greffière

Sainte-Anne-de-Madawaska
75 Principale St.
Sainte-Anne-de-Madawaska, NB E7E 1A8
Tél: 506-445-2449; *Téléc:* 506-445-2405
ste-anne@nb.aibn.com
Entité municipal: Village
Area: 9.19 sq km
Comté ou district: Madawaska; *Population au 2016:* 957
Circonscription(s) électorale(s) provinciale(s): Madawaska Les Lacs-Edmundston
Circonscription(s) électorale(s) fédérale(s):
Madawaska-Restigouche
Prochaines élections: May 10, 2021 (4 year terms)
Sylvie Girard, Maire

Sainte-Marie-Saint-Raphaël
1541, boul de la Mer
Sainte-Marie-Saint-Raphaël, NB E8T 1P5
Tél: 506-344-3210; *Téléc:* 506-344-3213
info@ste-marie-st-raphael.ca
ste-marie-st-raphael.ca
Entité municipal: Village
Incorporation: May 12, 1986; *Area:* 15.61 sq km
Comté ou district: Gloucester; *Population au 2016:* 879
Circonscription(s) électorale(s) provinciale(s):
Lamèque-Shippagan-Miscou
Circonscription(s) électorale(s) fédérale(s): Acadie-Bathurst
Prochaines élections: May 10, 2021 (4 year terms)
Bernard Savoie, Maire
Caroline Ethier, Directrice Générale

St. George
1 School St.
St George, NB E5C 3N2
Tel: 506-755-4320; *Fax:* 506-755-4329
www.townofstgeorge.com
Municipal Type: Town
Incorporated: Oct. 17, 1904; *Area:* 16.13 sq km
County or District: Charlotte; *Population in 2016:* 1,517
Provincial Electoral District(s): Fundy-The Isles-Saint John West
Federal Electoral District(s): New Brunswick Southwest
Next Election: May 10, 2021 (4 year terms)
John Detorakis, Mayor
Jason Gaudet, Chief Administration Officer
Louis LeBouthillier, Maire
Vanessa Haché Breau, Directrice Générale

Saint-Isidore
3906, boul des Fondateurs
Saint-Isidore, NB E8M 1C2
Tel: 506-358-6005; *Fax:* 506-358-6010
info@saintisidore.ca
saintisidore.ca
Municipal Type: Village
Incorporated: June 1, 1991; *Area:* 22.58 sq km
Population in 2016: 764
Provincial Electoral District(s): Bathurst
East-Nepisiguit-Saint-Isidore
Federal Electoral District(s): Acadie-Bathurst
Next Election: May 10, 2021 (4 year terms)

Saint-Léolin
117, rue des Prés
Saint-Léolin, NB E8N 2P9
Tél: 506-732-3266
villagesaintleolin.ca
Entité municipal: Village
Area: 19.78 sq km
Comté ou district: Gloucester; *Population au 2016:* 647
Circonscription(s) électorale(s) provinciale(s): Caraquet
Circonscription(s) électorale(s) fédérale(s): Acadie-Bathurst
Prochaines élections: May 10, 2021 (4 year terms)
Joseph Lanteigne, Maire
Nadia Michon, Secrétaire-greffière

Saint-Léonard
564, rue St-Jean
Saint-Léonard, NB E7E 2B5
Tél: 506-423-3111; *Téléc:* 506-423-3115
info@saint-leonard.ca
saint-leonard.ca
Entité municipal: Town
Incorporation: 1920; *Area:* 5.2 sq km
Comté ou district: Madawaska; *Population au 2016:* 1,300
Circonscription(s) électorale(s) provinciale(s): Victoria-La Vallée
Circonscription(s) électorale(s) fédérale(s):
Madawaska-Restigouche
Prochaines élections: May 10, 2021 (4 year terms)
Lise Anne Roussel, Maire

Saint-Louis-de-Kent
10511, rue Principale
Saint-Louis-de-Kent, NB E4X 1A6
Tél: 506-876-3420; *Téléc:* 506-876-3477
info@st-louis-de-kent.ca
www.st-louis-de-kent.ca
Entité municipal: Village
Area: 2 sq km
Comté ou district: Kent; *Population au 2016:* 856
Circonscription(s) électorale(s) provinciale(s): Kent North
Circonscription(s) électorale(s) fédérale(s): Beauséjour
Prochaines élections: May 10, 2021 (4 year terms)
Danielle Andrée Dugas, Mairesse

St. Martins
P.O. Box 123
St Martins, NB E5R 2H1
Tel: 506-833-2010; *Fax:* 506-833-2008
vilstmar@nbnet.nb.ca
stmartinscanada.com
Municipal Type: Village
Incorporated: Nov. 9, 1967; *Area:* 2.29 sq km
County or District: Saint John; *Population in 2016:* 276
Provincial Electoral District(s): Sussex-Fundy-St. Martins
Federal Electoral District(s): Fundy Royal
Next Election: May 10, 2021 (4 year terms)
Bette Ann M. Chatterton, Mayor
Darcy Hutchinson, Clerk

Saint-Quentin
10, rue Deschênes
Saint-Quentin, NB E8A 1M1
Tél: 506-235-2425; *Téléc:* 506-235-1952
ville@saintquentin.nb.ca
www.saintquentin.nb.ca
Entité municipal: Town
Incorporation: 1947; *Area:* 4.3 sq km
Comté ou district: Restigouche; *Population au 2016:* 2,194
Circonscription(s) électorale(s) provinciale(s): Restigouche West
Circonscription(s) électorale(s) fédérale(s):
Madawaska-Restigouche
Prochaines élections: May 10, 2021 (4 year terms)
Note: Proclaimed as a town in 1992.
Nicole Somers, Maire
Suzanne Coulombe, Directrice générale et greffière

St. Stephen
22 Budd Ave.
St Stephen, NB E3L 1E9
Tel: 506-466-7700
info@chocolatetown.ca
town.ststephen.nb.ca
Municipal Type: Town
County or District: Charlotte; *Population in 2016:* 4,415
Provincial Electoral District(s): Charlotte-Campobello
Federal Electoral District(s): New Brunswick Southwest
Next Election: May 10, 2021 (4 year terms)
Allan L. MacEachern, Mayor
Jeff Renaud, Chief Administrative Officer

Salisbury
56, rue Douglas
Salisbury, NB E4J 3E3
Tel: 506-372-3230; *Fax:* 506-372-3225
vilsalisbury@nb.aibn.com
salisburynb.ca
Municipal Type: Village
Incorporated: 1966; *Area:* 13.68 sq km
County or District: Westmorland; *Population in 2016:* 2,284
Provincial Electoral District(s): Albert
Federal Electoral District(s): Fundy Royal
Next Election: May 10, 2021 (4 year terms)
Robert Campbell, Mayor
Dianne Ayles, Clerk-Administrator

Shediac
#300, 290, rue Main
Shediac, NB E4P 2E3
Tél: 506-532-7000; *Téléc:* 506-532-6156
info@shediac.org
shediac.ca
Entité municipal: Town
Area: 11.97 sq km
Comté ou district: Westmorland; *Population au 2016:* 6,664
Circonscription(s) électorale(s) provinciale(s): Shediac
Bay-Dieppe; Shediac-Beaubassin-Cap-Pelé
Circonscription(s) électorale(s) fédérale(s): Beauséjour
Prochaines élections: May 10, 2021 (4 year terms)
Roger Caissie, Maire
Gilles Belleau, Directeur général, 506-531-2227

Shippagan
200, av Hôtel de Ville
Shippagan, NB E8S 1M1
Tél: 506-336-3900; *Téléc:* 506-336-3901
info@shippagan.ca
www.shippagan.ca
Entité municipal: Town
Incorporation: 1947; *Area:* 9.94 sq km
Comté ou district: Gloucester; *Population au 2016:* 2,580
Circonscription(s) électorale(s) provinciale(s):
Lamèque-Shippagan-Miscou
Circonscription(s) électorale(s) fédérale(s): Acadie-Bathurst
Prochaines élections: May 10, 2021 (4 year terms)
Note: Proclaimed as a town in 1958.
Kassim Doumbia, Maire
Jules DeSylva, Directeur général

Stanley
20 Main St.
Stanley, NB E6B 1A2
Tel: 506-367-3245
vstanley@nbnet.nb.ca
Municipal Type: Village
Area: 17.34 sq km
County or District: York; *Population in 2016:* 412
Provincial Electoral District(s): Fredericton-York
Federal Electoral District(s): Tobique-Mactaquac
Next Election: May 10, 2021 (4 year terms)
Jeffery H. MacFarlane, Mayor

Sussex
524 Main St.
Sussex, NB E4E 3E4
Tel: 506-432-4540; *Fax:* 506-432-4566
townofsussex@sussex.ca
sussex.ca
Municipal Type: Town
Incorporated: 1904; *Area:* 9.03 sq km
County or District: Kings; *Population in 2016:* 4,282
Provincial Electoral District(s): Sussex-Fundy-St. Martins
Federal Electoral District(s): Fundy Royal
Next Election: May 10, 2021 (4 year terms)
Marc Thorne, Mayor
Scott Hatcher, Chief Administrative Officer

Sussex Corner
1067 Main St.
Sussex Corner, NB E4E 3A1
Tel: 506-433-5184; *Fax:* 506-433-3785
village@sussexcorner.com
sussexcorner.com
Municipal Type: Village
Incorporated: 1966; *Area:* 9.43 sq km
County or District: Kings; *Population in 2016:* 1,461
Provincial Electoral District(s): Sussex-Fundy-St. Martins
Federal Electoral District(s): Fundy Royal
Next Election: May 10, 2021 (4 year terms)
Wayne A. Wilkins, Mayor
Robby Obermeier, Clerk-Treasurer

Tide Head
6 Mountain St.
Tide Head, NB E3N 4J9
Tel: 506-789-6550
viltide@nb.sympatico.ca
tidehead.ca
Municipal Type: Village
Area: 19.57 sq km
County or District: Restigouche; *Population in 2016:* 938
Provincial Electoral District(s): Restigouche West
Federal Electoral District(s): Madawaska-Restigouche
Next Election: May 10, 2021 (4 year terms)
Allan Dickson, Mayor
Angie Irvine, Clerk-Administrator

Tracy
4435 Heritage Dr.
Tracy, NB E5L 1C1
Tel: 506-368-2878; *Fax:* 506-368-1014
villageoftracy@rogers.com
Municipal Type: Village
Area: 29.36 sq km
County or District: Sunbury; *Population in 2016:* 608
Provincial Electoral District(s): New Maryland-Sunbury
Federal Electoral District(s): New Brunswick-Southwest
Next Election: May 10, 2021 (4 year terms)
Dale W. Mowry, Mayor

Upper Miramichi
6094 Route 8
Boiestown, NB E6A 1M7
Tel: 506-369-9810; Fax: 506-369-8180
uppermiramichi1@nb.aibn.com
www.uppermiramichi.ca
Municipal Type: Community
County or District: Northumberland; *Population in 2016:* 2,218
Provincial Electoral District(s): Southwest Miramichi-Bay du Vin
Federal Electoral District(s): Miramichi-Grand Lake
Next Election: May 10, 2021 (4 year terms)
M.A. Douglas Munn, Mayor
Mary Hunter, Clerk

Woodstock
824 Main St.
Woodstock, NB E7M 2E8
Tel: 506-325-4600; *Fax:* 506-325-4308
townhall@town.woodstock.nb.ca
www.town.woodstock.nb.ca

Municipal Type: Town
Incorporated: 1856; *Area:* 13.41 sq km
County or District: Carleton; *Population in 2016:* 5,228
Provincial Electoral District(s): Carleton
Federal Electoral District(s): Tobique-Mactaquac
Next Election: May 10, 2021 (4 year terms)
Arthur L. Slipp, Mayor
Ken Anthony, Chief Administrative Officer

Rural Municipalities in New Brunswick

Haut-Madawaska
3851, rue Prinicipale
Baker Brook, NB E7A 2A1
Tél: 506-258-3030; *Téléc:* 506-258-3017
info@haut-madawaska.com
haut-madawaska.com
Entité municipal: Rural Municipalities
Incorporation: 2017

Comté ou district: Madawaska; *Population au 2016:* 3,714
Circonscription(s) électorale(s) provinciale(s): Madawaska Les Lacs-Edmundston
Circonscription(s) électorale(s) fédérale(s):
Madawaska-Restigouche
Prochaines élections: May 10, 2021 (4 year terms)
Note: Amalgamation of the villages of Baker Brook, Clair, Saint-François de Madawaska & Saint-Hilaire.
Jean-Pierre Ouellet, Maire
Pierre Milliard, Directeur général

NEWFOUNDLAND & LABRADOR

The provincial government of Newfoundland and Labrador exercises control over the activities of all municipalities in accordance with the Executive Council Act and the Municipal Affairs Act. Under the provisions of the Municipalities Act, the Department exercises a certain degree of financial and administrative control over all municipalities with the exception of the cities of St. John's, Corner Brook and Mount Pearl. The towns incorporated under the Municipalities Act do not require ministerial approval of their annual budgets, but the Department employs Municipal Analysts to oversee municipal activities. The province assumes responsibility for public health, welfare and law enforcement which are elsewhere generally considered to be municipal functions.

The cities and towns incorporated in Newfoundland are authorized to levy taxes and to provide a wide range of municipal services and to make appropriate bylaws or regulations for the implementation and administration of these services.

City and town councils in Newfoundland are elected on the last Tuesday in September every four years (2021, 2025, etc.).

LEGEND / LÉGENDE

○ Provincial capital / Capitale provinciale
● Other populated places / Autres lieux habités
━🍁━ Trans-Canada Highway / La Transcanadienne
──── Major road / Route principale
─ ─ ─ Ferry route / Traversier
━·━·━ International boundary / Frontière internationale
━··━··━ Provincial boundary / Limite provinciale

Scale / Échelle
100   0   100   200   300
km   km

Newfoundland & Labrador

Major Municipalities in Newfoundland & Labrador

Conception Bay South
P.O. Box 14040 Manuels
11 Remembrance Sq.
Conception Bay South, NL A1W 3J1
Tel: 709-834-6500; *Fax:* 709-834-8337
info@conceptionbaysouth.ca
www.conceptionbaysouth.ca
Other Information: After Hours Emergency: 709-834-6529
Municipal Type: City
Incorporated: Sept. 1, 1971; *Area:* 59.10 sq km
Population in 2016: 26,199
Provincial Electoral District(s): Conception Bay South;
Topsail—Paradise; Harbour Main
Federal Electoral District(s): Avalon
Next Election: Sept. 30, 2025 (4 year terms)
Darrin Bent, Mayor
Shelley Moores, Councillor, Wards: 1
Andrea Gosse, Councillor, Wards: 2
Gerard Tilley, Councillor, Wards: 3
Melissa Hardy, Councillor, Wards: 4
Joshua Barrett, Councillor-at-Large
Christine Butler, Councillor-at-Large
Paul Connors, Councillor-at-Large
Rex Hillier, Councillor-at-Large
Dan Noseworthy, Chief Administrative Officer

Corner Brook
City Hall
P.O. Box 1080
5 Park St.
Corner Brook, NL A2H 6E1
Tel: 709-637-1666; *Fax:* 709-637-1625
city.hall@cornerbrook.com
www.cornerbrook.com
Municipal Type: City
Incorporated: April 27, 1955; *Area:* 148.26 sq km
Population in 2016: 19,806
Provincial Electoral District(s): Humber—Bay of Islands; Corner Brook
Federal Electoral District(s): Long Range Mountains
Next Election: Sept. 30, 2025 (4 year terms)
Note: Provincial Electoral Districts formerly Humber East, Humber West.
Jim Parsons, Mayor
Bill Griffin, Deputy Mayor
Linda Chaisson, Councillor
Vaughn Granter, Councillor
Pamela Gill, Councillor
Pam Keeping, Councillor
Charles Pender, Councillor
Rodney Cumby, City Manager, 709-637-1532
Donald Burden, Director, Public Works, Water & Wastewater
Darren Charters, Director, Community, Engineering, Development & Planning
Dale Park, Director, Finance & Administration
Krista Rose, Manager, Human Resources
Deon Rumbolt, Manager, Development & Planning
Craig Harnum, Deputy Fire Chief

Grand Falls-Windsor
P.O. Box 439
5 High St.
Grand Falls-Windsor, NL A2A 2J8
Tel: 709-489-0407
www.grandfallswindsor.com
Municipal Type: City
Incorporated: Jan. 1, 1991; *Area:* 54.67 sq km
Population in 2016: 14,171
Provincial Electoral District(s): Grand Falls-Windsor—Buchans; Exploits
Federal Electoral District(s): Coast of Bays—Central—Notre Dame
Next Election: Sept. 30, 2025 (4 year terms)
Note: Provincial Electoral Districts formerly Grand Falls-Buchans; Windsor-Springdale.
Barry Manuel, Mayor
Mike Browne, Deputy Mayor
Amy Coady-Davis, Councillor
Holly Dwyer, Councillor
Bob (Flipper) Hiscock, Councillor
Andrew Little, Councillor
Dave Noel, Councillor
Darren Finn, Chief Administrative Officer
Keith Antle, Director, Community Services
Nelson Chatman, Director, Public Works & Development
Steve Gosse, Director, Corporate Services

Vince J. MacKenzie, Fire Chief

Mount Pearl
3 Centennial St.
Mount Pearl, NL A1N 1G4
Tel: 709-748-1000; *Fax:* 709-748-1150
info@mountpearl.ca
www.mountpearl.ca
Municipal Type: City
Incorporated: Jan. 11, 1955; *Area:* 15.76 sq km
Population in 2016: 22,957
Provincial Electoral District(s): Mount Pearl North; Mount Pearl—Southlands
Federal Electoral District(s): St. John's South—Mount Pearl
Next Election: Sept. 30, 2025 (4 year terms)
Dave Aker, Mayor
Jim Locke, Deputy Mayor
Bill Antle, Councillor
Isabelle Fry, Councillor
Chelsea Lane, Councillor
Nicole Kieley, Councillor
Mark Rice, Councillor
Mona Lewis, City Clerk
Steve Kent, Chief Administrative Officer
Gerry Antle, Director, Infrastructure & Public Works
Jason Collins, Director, Community Development
Cassie Pittman, Director, Corporate Services
Stephanie Hynes, Manager, Finance
Janice Mullins, Manager, Human Resources

Paradise
28 McNamara Dr.
Paradise, NL A1L 0A6
Tel: 709-782-1400; *Fax:* 709-782-3603
info@paradise.ca
www.paradise.ca
Municipal Type: City
Incorporated: Feb. 1, 1992; *Area:* 29.24 sq km
Population in 2016: 21,389
Provincial Electoral District(s): Conception Bay East—Bell Island; Mount Scio
Federal Electoral District(s): Avalon
Next Election: Sept. 30, 2025 (4 year terms)
Dan Bobbett, Mayor
Glen Carew, Councillor
Elizabeth Laurie, Councillor
Patrick Martin, Councillor
Kimberly Street, Councillor
Deborah Quilty, Councillor
Larry Vaters, Councillor
Lisa Niblock, Chief Administrative Officer
Conrad Freake, Director, Recreation & Community Services
Chris Milley, Director, Infrastructure & Engineering
Terrilynn Smith, Director, Corporate Services
Nelson Whalen, Director, Public Works

St. John's
P.O. Box 908
St. John's, NL A1C 5M2
Tel: 709-754-2489; *Fax:* 709-576-8474
access@stjohns.ca
www.stjohns.ca
Municipal Type: City
Incorporated: Aug. 7, 1921; *Area:* 445.88 sq km
Population in 2016: 108,860
Provincial Electoral District(s): St. John's East—Quidi Vidi; St. John's Centre; St. John's West; Virginia Waters—Pleasantville; Mount Pearl North; Cape St. Francis
Federal Electoral District(s): St. John's East; St. John's South—Mount Pearl
Next Election: Sept. 30, 2025 (4 year terms)
Danny Breen, Mayor
Sheilagh O'Leary, Deputy Mayor
Jill Bruce, Councillor, Wards: 1
Ophelia Ravencroft, Councillor, Wards: 2
Jamie Korab, Councillor, Wards: 3
Ian Froude, Councillor, Wards: 4
Carl Ridgeley, Councillor, Wards: 5
Maggie Burton, Councillor-at-Large
Ron Ellsworth, Councillor-at-Large
Debbie Hanlon, Councillor-at-Large
Sandy Hickman, Councillor-at-Large
Kevin Breen, City Manager, 709-576-8207
Ken O'Brien, Chief Municipal Planner, Planning, Development & Engineering, 709-576-8220
Sherry Colford, Fire Chief, St. John's Regional Fire Department

Other Municipalities in Newfoundland & Labrador

Admirals Beach
P.O. Box 196 Site 4
Admirals Beach, NL A0B 3A0
Tel: 709-521-2671; *Fax:* 709-521-2671
townadmiralsbeach@outlook.com
Municipal Type: Town
Incorporated: Jan. 16, 1968; *Area:* 24.42 sq km
Population in 2016: 135
Provincial Electoral District(s): Placentia—St. Mary's
Federal Electoral District(s): Avalon
Next Election: Sept. 30, 2025 (4 year terms)
Theresa Bungay, Mayor
Mary Dobbin, Clerk

Anchor Point
P.O. Box 117
Anchor Point, NL A0K 1A0
Tel: 709-456-2011; *Fax:* 709-456-2364
anchorpoint@nf.aibn.com
Other Information: Alt. Phone: 709-456-2689
Municipal Type: Town
Incorporated: Sept. 10, 1974; *Area:* 2.41 sq km
Population in 2016: 314
Provincial Electoral District(s): St. Barbe—L'Anse aux Meadows
Federal Electoral District(s): Long Range Mountains
Next Election: Sept. 30, 2025 (4 year terms)
Gerry Gros, Mayor
Sharon Gaulton, Clerk

L'Anse au Clair
P.O. Box 83
L'Anse au Clair, NL A0K 3K0
Tel: 709-931-2481
townoflanseauclair@hotmail.com
www.lanseauclair.ca
Municipal Type: Town
Incorporated: June 2, 1970; *Area:* 61.92 sq km
Population in 2016: 216
Provincial Electoral District(s): Cartwright—L'Anse au Clair
Federal Electoral District(s): Labrador
Next Election: Sept. 30, 2025 (4 year terms)
Chad Letto, Mayor
Loretta Griffin, Clerk

L'Anse au Loup
P.O. Box 101
L'Anse au Loup, NL A0K 3L0
Tel: 709-927-5573; *Fax:* 709-927-5263
lanseauloup@nf.aibn.com
www.lanseauloup.ca
Municipal Type: Town
Incorporated: April 11, 1975; *Area:* 3.48 sq km
Population in 2016: 558
Provincial Electoral District(s): Cartwright—L'Anse au Clair
Federal Electoral District(s): Labrador
Next Election: Sept. 30, 2025 (4 year terms)
Vacant, Mayor
Janice Normore, Clerk

Appleton
P.O. Box 31 Site 4
Appleton, NL A0G 2K0
Tel: 709-679-2289; *Fax:* 709-679-5552
townofappleton@personainternet.com
Municipal Type: Town
Incorporated: Feb. 27, 1962; *Area:* 6.39 sq km
Population in 2016: 574
Provincial Electoral District(s): Gander
Federal Electoral District(s): Coast of Bays—Central—Notre Dame
Next Election: Sept. 30, 2025 (4 year terms)
Garrett Watton, Mayor
Pat Barnes, Clerk

Aquaforte
General Delivery
Aquaforte, NL A0A 1A0
Tel: 709-363-2233; *Fax:* 709-363-2232
aquafortecouncil@bellaliant.com
Municipal Type: Town
Incorporated: April 25, 1972; *Area:* 6.82 sq km
Population in 2016: 80
Provincial Electoral District(s): Ferryland
Federal Electoral District(s): Avalon
Next Election: Sept. 30, 2025 (4 year terms)
Deborah Windsor, Mayor
Christina Payne, Clerk

Arnold's Cove
P.O. Box 270
Arnold's Cove, NL A0B 1A0
Tel: 709-463-2323; *Fax:* 709-463-2326
townofarnoldscove@nf.aibn.com
www.townofarnoldscove.ca
Other Information: Alt. Phone: 709-463-8082
Municipal Type: Town
Incorporated: June 3, 1967; *Area:* 4.93 sq km
Population in 2016: 949
Provincial Electoral District(s): Placentia West—Bellevue
Federal Electoral District(s): Bonavista—Burin—Trinity
Next Election: Sept. 30, 2025 (4 year terms)
Basil Daley, Mayor
Angela Gale, Clerk

Avondale
P.O. Box 59
Avondale, NL A0A 1B0
Tel: 709-229-4201; *Fax:* 709-229-4446
townofavondale@eastlink.ca
Municipal Type: Town
Incorporated: Nov. 26, 1974; *Area:* 29.93 sq km
Population in 2016: 641
Provincial Electoral District(s): Harbour Main
Federal Electoral District(s): Avalon
Next Election: Sept. 30, 2025 (4 year terms)
Owen Mahoney, Mayor
Maureen Lewis, Clerk

Badger
P.O. Box 130 Town Office
Badger, NL A0H 1A0
Tel: 709-539-2406; *Fax:* 709-539-5262
info@townofbadger.ca
www.townofbadger.ca
Municipal Type: Town
Incorporated: Sept. 24, 1963; *Area:* 1.96 sq km
Population in 2016: 704
Provincial Electoral District(s): Grand Falls-Windsor—Buchans
Federal Electoral District(s): Coast of Bays—Central—Notre Dame
Next Election: Sept. 30, 2025 (4 year terms)
Ed Card, Mayor
Pansy Hurley, Town Clerk & Manager

Baie Verte
P.O. Box 218
32 Hwy. 410
Baie Verte, NL A0K 1B0
Tel: 709-532-8222; *Fax:* 709-532-4134
info@townofbaieverte.ca
www.townofbaieverte.ca
Municipal Type: Town
Incorporated: April 29, 1958; *Area:* 371.07 sq km
Population in 2016: 1,313
Provincial Electoral District(s): Baie Verte—Green Bay
Federal Electoral District(s): Coast of Bays—Central—Notre Dame
Next Election: Sept. 30, 2025 (4 year terms)
Shawn Russell, Mayor

Baine Harbour
General Delivery
Baine Harbour, NL A0E 1A0
Tel: 709-443-2980; *Fax:* 709-443-2355
bhrtc@bellaliant.net
Municipal Type: Town
Incorporated: Dec. 1, 1970; *Area:* 4.82 sq km
Population in 2016: 124
Provincial Electoral District(s): Placentia West—Bellevue
Federal Electoral District(s): Bonavista—Burin—Trinity
Next Election: Sept. 30, 2025 (4 year terms)
Harold Kenway, Mayor
Claudia King, Clerk

Bauline
2 Memorial Park Pl.
Bauline, NL A1K 0M5
Tel: 709-335-2483; *Fax:* 709-335-2053
info@townofbauline.ca
townofbauline.com
Municipal Type: Town
Incorporated: July 1, 1988; *Area:* 15.95 sq km
Population in 2016: 452
Provincial Electoral District(s): Cape St. Francis
Federal Electoral District(s): St. John's East
Next Election: Sept. 30, 2025 (4 year terms)
Craig LeGrow, Mayor
Craig Drover, Town Manager

Bay Bulls
P.O. Box 70
2 Southside Rd.
Bay Bulls, NL A0A 1C0
Tel: 709-334-3454; *Fax:* 709-334-3477
info@townofbaybulls.com
www.townofbaybulls.com
Municipal Type: Town
Incorporated: Jan. 1, 1986; *Area:* 30.74 sq km
Population in 2016: 1,500
Provincial Electoral District(s): Ferryland
Federal Electoral District(s): St. John's South—Mount Pearl
Next Election: Sept. 30, 2025 (4 year terms)
Harold Mullowney, Mayor
Jennifer Aspell, Town Manager

Bay de Verde
P.O. Box 10
71-75 Rte. 70
Bay de Verde, NL A0A 1E0
Tel: 709-587-2260
info@baydeverde.com
www.baydeverde.com
Municipal Type: Town
Incorporated: Aug. 22, 1950; *Area:* 13.28 sq km
Population in 2016: 392
Provincial Electoral District(s): Carbonear—Trinity—Bay de Verde
Federal Electoral District(s): Bonavista—Burin—Trinity
Next Election: Sept. 30, 2025 (4 year terms)
Gerard Murphy, Mayor
Renee Froude, Town Clerk & Manager

Bay L'Argent
P.O. Box 29
Bay L'Argent, NL A0E 1B0
Tel: 709-461-2606; *Fax:* 709-461-2608
townofbaylargent@nf.aibn.com
Municipal Type: Town
Incorporated: July 13, 1971; *Area:* 3.56 sq km
Population in 2016: 241
Provincial Electoral District(s): Burin—Grand Bank
Federal Electoral District(s): Bonavista—Burin—Trinity
Next Election: Sept. 30, 2025 (4 year terms)
Note: Provincial Electoral District formerly Bellevue.
Rhonda Baker, Mayor
Viola Pardy, Clerk

Bay Roberts
P.O. Box 114
321 Water St.
Bay Roberts, NL A0A 1G0
Tel: 709-786-2126; *Fax:* 709-786-2128
www.bayroberts.com
Municipal Type: Town
Incorporated: Feb. 17, 1951; *Area:* 23.92 sq km
Population in 2016: 6,012
Provincial Electoral District(s): Harbour Grace—Port de Grave
Federal Electoral District(s): Avalon
Next Election: Sept. 30, 2025 (4 year terms)
Walter Yetman, Mayor
Christine Bradbury, Clerk

Baytona
P.O. Box 29
110 Main St.
Baytona, NL A0G 2J0
Tel: 709-659-6101; *Fax:* 709-659-6101
thetownofbaytona@eastlink.ca
Municipal Type: Town
Incorporated: Aug. 1, 1975; *Area:* 15.38 sq km
Population in 2016: 262
Provincial Electoral District(s): Lewisporte—Twillingate
Federal Electoral District(s): Coast of Bays—Central—Notre Dame
Next Election: Sept. 30, 2025 (4 year terms)
Rex Quinlan, Mayor
Diana Lewis, Clerk

Beachside
112 Bayview Rd.
Beachside, NL A0J 1T0
Tel: 709-267-5251; *Fax:* 709-267-5251
townofbeachside@gmail.com
Municipal Type: Town
Incorporated: July 7, 1961; *Area:* 2.61 sq km
Population in 2016: 132
Provincial Electoral District(s): Baie Verte—Green Bay
Federal Electoral District(s): Coast of Bays—Central—Notre Dame
Next Election: Sept. 30, 2025 (4 year terms)
Nancy Webber Bowers, Mayor

Joan Power, Clerk

Bellburns
P.O. Box 16 Site 4
Bellburns, NL A0K 1H0
Tel: 709-898-2468; *Fax:* 709-898-2468
bellburns.tripod.com
Municipal Type: Town
Incorporated: May 13, 1969; *Area:* 7.39 sq km
Population in 2016: 53
Provincial Electoral District(s): Humber—Gros Morne
Federal Electoral District(s): Long Range Mountains
Next Election: Sept. 30, 2025 (4 year terms)
Note: Provincial Electoral District formerly St. Barbe.
Denise House, Mayor
Pauline House, Clerk

Belleoram
P.O. Box 29
Belleoram, NL A0H 1B0
Tel: 709-881-6161; *Fax:* 709-881-6161
belleoram1946@yahoo.ca
Municipal Type: Town
Incorporated: March 19, 1946; *Area:* 2.1 sq km
Population in 2016: 374
Provincial Electoral District(s): Fortune Bay—Cape La Hune
Federal Electoral District(s): Coast of Bays—Central—Notre Dame
Next Election: Sept. 30, 2025 (4 year terms)
Steward May, Mayor
Janice Keeping, Clerk

Birchy Bay
P.O. Box 40
Birchy Bay, NL A0G 1E0
Tel: 709-659-3221; *Fax:* 709-659-2121
office@birchybay.ca
Other Information: Alt. Phone: 709-659-3500
Municipal Type: Town
Incorporated: Aug. 27, 1974; *Area:* 49.52 sq km
Population in 2016: 550
Provincial Electoral District(s): Lewisporte—Twillingate
Federal Electoral District(s): Coast of Bays—Central—Notre Dame
Next Election: Sept. 30, 2025 (4 year terms)
Ewen Quinlan, Mayor
Cynthia Baker, Clerk

Bird Cove
67 Michael's Dr.
Bird Cove, NL A0K 1L0
Tel: 709-247-2256; *Fax:* 709-247-2254
tobc@nf.aibn.com
Municipal Type: Town
Incorporated: April 15, 1977; *Area:* 9.39 sq km
Population in 2016: 179
Provincial Electoral District(s): St. Barbe—L'Anse aux Meadows
Federal Electoral District(s): Long Range Mountains
Next Election: Sept. 30, 2025 (4 year terms)
Andre Myers, Mayor
Irene Myers, Clerk

Bishop's Cove
P.O. Box 70 Site 3
Bishop's Cove, NL A0A 3X1
Tel: 709-594-3001; *Fax:* 709-594-3002
bishopscove@eastlink.ca
Other Information: Alt. Phone: 709-589-2852
Municipal Type: Town
Incorporated: June 24, 1969; *Area:* 1.89 sq km
Population in 2016: 287
Provincial Electoral District(s): Harbour Grace—Port de Grave
Federal Electoral District(s): Avalon
Next Election: Sept. 30, 2025 (4 year terms)
Gary N. Smith, Mayor
Irene Menchions, Clerk

Bishop's Falls
445 Main St.
Bishops Falls, NL A0H 1C0
Tel: 709-258-6581; *Fax:* 709-258-6346
info@bishopsfalls.ca
www.bishopsfalls.ca
Municipal Type: Town
Incorporated: Nov. 1, 1961; *Area:* 28.12 sq km
Population in 2016: 3,156
Provincial Electoral District(s): Exploits
Federal Electoral District(s): Coast of Bays—Central—Notre Dame
Next Election: Sept. 30, 2025 (4 year terms)
Bryan King, Mayor
Dan Oldford, Town Clerk

Next Election: Sept. 30, 2025 (4 year terms)
Note: Provincial Electoral District formerly Humber Valley.
Melvin Rideout Sr., Mayor
Tracey Hewitt, Clerk

Cottlesville
P.O. Box 10
12 Luke's Arm Rd.
Cottlesville, NL A0G 1S0
Tel: 709-629-3505; *Fax:* 709-629-7411
towncottlesville@eastlink.ca
Municipal Type: Town
Incorporated: Oct. 24, 1972; *Area:* 11.17 sq km
Population in 2016: 271
Provincial Electoral District(s): Lewisporte—Twillingate
Federal Electoral District(s): Coast of Bays—Central—Notre Dame
Next Election: Sept. 30, 2025 (4 year terms)
Note: Provincial Electoral District formerly Twillingate-Fogo.
Rodney Wheeler, Mayor
Shelly Abbott, Clerk

Cow Head
P.O. Box 40
Cow Head, NL A0K 2A0
Tel: 709-243-2446; *Fax:* 709-243-2590
townofcowhead@bellalliant.com
www.cowhead.ca
Municipal Type: Town
Incorporated: Feb. 1, 1964; *Area:* 17.84 sq km
Population in 2016: 428
Provincial Electoral District(s): Humber—Gros Morne
Federal Electoral District(s): Long Range Mountains
Next Election: Sept. 30, 2025 (4 year terms)
Note: Provincial Electoral District formerly St. Barbe.
Adrian Payne, Mayor
Terri-Lynn Payne, Clerk

Cox's Cove
P.O. Box 100
Cox's Cove, NL A0L 1C0
Tel: 709-688-2900; *Fax:* 709-688-2929
coxscove@eastlink.ca
Municipal Type: Town
Incorporated: Nov. 11, 1969; *Area:* 7.21 sq km
Population in 2016: 688
Provincial Electoral District(s): Humber—Bay of Islands
Federal Electoral District(s): Long Range Mountains
Next Election: Sept. 30, 2025 (4 year terms)
Terry Wells, Mayor
Tina Sheppard, Clerk

Crow Head
P.O. Box 250
Crow Head, NL A0G 4M0
Tel: 709-884-5651; *Fax:* 709-884-2344
Municipal Type: Town
Incorporated: Sept. 13, 1960; *Area:* 2.98 sq km
Population in 2016: 177
Provincial Electoral District(s): Lewisporte—Twillingate
Federal Electoral District(s): Coast of Bays—Central—Notre Dame
Next Election: Sept. 30, 2025 (4 year terms)
Note: Provincial Electoral District formerly Twillingate & Fogo.
John Hamlyn, Mayor
Meta J. Hamlyn, Clerk

Cupids
P.O. Box 99
199 Seaforrest Dr.
Cupids, NL A0A 2B0
Tel: 709-528-4428; *Fax:* 709-528-4430
townofcupids@eastlink.ca
townofcupids.ca
Municipal Type: Town
Incorporated: April 13, 1965; *Area:* 11.02 sq km
Population in 2016: 743
Provincial Electoral District(s): Harbour Main
Federal Electoral District(s): Avalon
Next Election: Sept. 30, 2025 (4 year terms)
Carl Butler, Mayor
Ivy King, Clerk

Daniel's Harbour
P.O. Box 68
Daniel's Harbour, NL A0K 2C0
Tel: 709-898-2300; *Fax:* 709-898-2311
townofdanielshr@eastlink.ca
Municipal Type: Town
Incorporated: March 9, 1965; *Area:* 8.19 sq km
Population in 2016: 253
Provincial Electoral District(s): Humber—Gros Morne

Federal Electoral District(s): Long Range Mountains
Next Election: Sept. 30, 2025 (4 year terms)
Note: Provincial Electoral District formerly St. Barbe.
Ross Humber, Mayor
Melda Hann, Clerk

Deer Lake
34 Reid's Lane
Deer Lake, NL A8A 2A2
Tel: 709-635-2451; *Fax:* 709-635-5857
deerlakeec@nf.aibn.com
deerlake.ca
Municipal Type: Town
Incorporated: May 27, 1950; *Area:* 73.23 sq km
Population in 2016: 5,249
Provincial Electoral District(s): Humber—Gros Morne
Federal Electoral District(s): Long Range Mountains
Next Election: Sept. 30, 2025 (4 year terms)
Note: Provincial Electoral District formerly Humber Valley.
Michael Goosney, Mayor
Lori Humphrey, Town Clerk, 709-635-0110

Dover
P.O. Box 10
113-115 Wellington Rd.
Dover, NL A0G 1X0
Tel: 709-537-2139; *Fax:* 709-537-2190
townofdover@persona.ca
www.townofdover.ca
Municipal Type: Town
Incorporated: July 13, 1971; *Area:* 11.55 sq km
Population in 2016: 662
Provincial Electoral District(s): Fogo Island—Cape Freels
Federal Electoral District(s): Bonavista—Burin—Trinity
Next Election: Sept. 30, 2025 (4 year terms)
Note: Provincial Electoral District formerly Terra Nova.
Tony R. Keats, Mayor
Yvonne Collins, Clerk

Duntara
P.O. Box 15
Duntara, NL A0C 1M0
Tel: 709-447-3122
Municipal Type: Town
Incorporated: Nov. 14, 1961; *Area:* 17.78 sq km
Population in 2016: 30
Provincial Electoral District(s): Bonavista
Federal Electoral District(s): Bonavista—Burin—Trinity
Next Election: Sept. 30, 2025 (4 year terms)
Vacant , Mayor

Eastport
P.O. Box 119
Eastport, NL A0G 1Z0
Tel: 709-677-2161; *Fax:* 709-677-2144
info@eastport.ca
eastport.ca
Municipal Type: Town
Incorporated: Oct. 20, 1959; *Area:* 18.64 sq km
Population in 2016: 501
Provincial Electoral District(s): Terra Nova
Federal Electoral District(s): Bonavista—Burin—Trinity
Next Election: Sept. 30, 2025 (4 year terms)
Vacant, Mayor
Chantal Lynch, Town Clerk & Manager

Elliston
P.O. Box 115
Elliston, NL A0C 1N0
Tel: 709-468-2649; *Fax:* 709-468-2867
town_elliston@yahoo.ca
www.townofelliston.ca
Municipal Type: Town
Incorporated: June 15, 1965; *Area:* 10.05 sq km
Population in 2016: 308
Provincial Electoral District(s): Bonavista
Federal Electoral District(s): Bonavista—Burin—Trinity
Next Election: Sept. 30, 2025 (4 year terms)
Derek Martin, Mayor
Donna Chaulk, Clerk

Embree
P.O. Box 81
Embree, NL A0G 2A0
Tel: 709-535-8712; *Fax:* 709-535-8716
Municipal Type: Town
Incorporated: Sept. 28, 1971; *Area:* 18.16 sq km
Population in 2016: 701
Provincial Electoral District(s): Lewisporte—Twillingate
Federal Electoral District(s): Coast of Bays—Central—Notre Dame
Next Election: Sept. 30, 2025 (4 year terms)

Harold Nippard, Mayor
Maxine Lane, Clerk

Englee
P.O. Box 160
Englee, NL A0K 2J0
Tel: 709-866-2711; *Fax:* 709-866-2357
engleeoffice@bellaliant.com
www.engleenl.ca
Other Information: Alt. Phone: 709-457-7492
Municipal Type: Town
Incorporated: Dec. 23, 1948; *Area:* 28.76 sq km
Population in 2016: 527
Provincial Electoral District(s): St. Barbe—L'Anse aux Meadows
Federal Electoral District(s): Long Range Mountains
Next Election: Sept. 30, 2025 (4 year terms)
Note: Provincial Electoral District formerly The Straits & White Bay North.
Stephanie Fillier, Mayor
Samantha Brenton, Clerk

English Harbour East
General Delivery
English Harbour East, NL A0E 1M0
Tel: 709-245-4556; *Fax:* 709-245-4556
Municipal Type: Town
Incorporated: Feb. 5, 1974; *Area:* 3.2 sq km
Population in 2016: 139
Provincial Electoral District(s): Placentia West—Bellevue
Federal Electoral District(s): Bonavista—Burin—Trinity
Next Election: Sept. 30, 2025 (4 year terms)
Maxine Hackett, Mayor
Sheena Bolt, Clerk

Fermeuse
General Delivery
Fermeuse, NL A0A 2G0
Tel: 709-363-2400; *Fax:* 709-363-2308
townoffermeuse@gmail.com
Other Information: Alt. Phone: 709-363-2918
Municipal Type: Town
Incorporated: Nov. 28, 1967; *Area:* 38.73 sq km
Population in 2016: 325
Provincial Electoral District(s): Ferryland
Federal Electoral District(s): Avalon
Next Election: Sept. 30, 2025 (4 year terms)
Perry Oates, Mayor
Marsha Kenny, Clerk

Ferryland
P.O. Box 75
Ferryland, NL A0A 2H0
Tel: 709-432-2127; *Fax:* 709-432-2209
town.ferryland@nf.aibn.com
www.ferryland.com
Municipal Type: Town
Incorporated: Oct. 19, 1971; *Area:* 13.62 sq km
Population in 2016: 414
Provincial Electoral District(s): Ferryland
Federal Electoral District(s): St. John's South—Mount Pearl
Next Election: Sept. 30, 2025 (4 year terms)
Note: Federal Electoral District formerly Avalon.
Vacant, Mayor
Doris Kavanagh, Clerk

Flatrock
663 Wind Gap Rd.
Flatrock, NL A1K 1C7
Tel: 709-437-6312; *Fax:* 709-437-6311
info@townofflatrock.com
www.townofflatrock.com
Other Information: Alt. Phone: 709-437-6334
Municipal Type: Town
Incorporated: Oct. 31, 1975; *Area:* 18.12 sq km
Population in 2016: 1,683
Provincial Electoral District(s): Cape St. Francis
Federal Electoral District(s): St. John's East
Next Election: Sept. 30, 2025 (4 year terms)
Darrin Thorne, Mayor, 709-437-5654
Dianne Stamp, Clerk

Fleur de Lys
P.O. Box 9
Fleur de Lys, NL A0K 2M0
Tel: 709-253-3131; *Fax:* 709-253-2146
townoffleurdelysgmail.com
Municipal Type: Town
Incorporated: April 18, 1967; *Area:* 39.77 sq km
Population in 2016: 244
Provincial Electoral District(s): Baie Verte—Green Bay
Federal Electoral District(s): Coast of Bays—Central—Notre

Dame
Next Election: Sept. 30, 2025 (4 year terms)
Joy Walsh, Mayor
Jackie Walsh, Clerk

Flower's Cove
P.O. Box 149
Flower's Cove, NL A0K 2N0
Tel: 709-456-2124; *Fax:* 709-456-2086
townofflowerscove@nf.aibn.net
www.townofflowerscove.com
Municipal Type: Town
Incorporated: Dec. 12, 1961; *Area:* 7.64 sq km
Population in 2016: 270
Provincial Electoral District(s): St. Barbe—L'Anse aux Meadows
Federal Electoral District(s): Long Range Mountains
Next Election: Sept. 30, 2025 (4 year terms)
Note: Provincial Electoral District formerly The Straits & White Bay North.
Keith Billard, Mayor
Sandra Way, Clerk

Fogo Island
6 Centre Island Rd. South, Hwy. 333
Fogo Island Centre, NL A0G 2X0
Tel: 709-266-1320; *Fax:* 709-266-1323
info@townoffogoisland.ca
www.townoffogoisland.ca
Other Information: Alt. Phone: 709-266-1321
Municipal Type: Town
Incorporated: March 1, 2011; *Area:* 237.65 sq km
Population in 2016: 2,244
Provincial Electoral District(s): Fogo Island—Cape Freels
Federal Electoral District(s): Coast of Bays—Central—Notre Dame
Next Election: Sept. 30, 2025 (4 year terms)
Note: Provincial Electoral District formerly The Isles of Notre Dame. Effective Dec. 2010, the towns of Fogo, Joe Batt's Arm-Barr'd Islands-Shoal Bay, Seldom-Little Seldom, Tilting & Fogo Island Region amalgamated to form the new Town of Fogo Island.
Wayne Collins, Mayor
Bruce Pomeroy, Chief Administrative Officer, 709-266-1320

Forteau
P.O. Box 99
Forteau, NL A0K 2P0
Tel: 709-931-2241; *Fax:* 709-931-2037
forteautowncouncil@hotmail.com
Municipal Type: Town
Incorporated: Dec. 7, 1971; *Area:* 7.44 sq km
Population in 2016: 409
Provincial Electoral District(s): Cartwright—L'Anse au Clair
Federal Electoral District(s): Labrador
Next Election: Sept. 30, 2025 (4 year terms)
James Roberts, Mayor
Heather Jordan, Town Clerk

Fortune
Temple St.
Fortune, NL A0E 1P0
Tel: 709-832-2810; *Fax:* 709-832-2210
townoffortune@eastlink.ca
www.townoffortune.ca
Municipal Type: Town
Incorporated: Sept. 3, 1946; *Area:* 54.85 sq km
Population in 2016: 1,401
Provincial Electoral District(s): Burin—Grand Bank
Federal Electoral District(s): Bonavista—Burin—Trinity
Next Election: Sept. 30, 2025 (4 year terms)
Vacant, Mayor
Lacey Symes, Clerk

Fox Cove-Mortier
P.O. Box 17 25
Burin, NL A0E 1E0
Tel: 709-891-1500; *Fax:* 709-891-1999
Municipal Type: Town
Incorporated: June 2, 1970; *Area:* 25.6 sq km
Population in 2016: 295
Provincial Electoral District(s): Burin—Grand Bank
Federal Electoral District(s): Bonavista—Burin—Trinity
Next Election: Sept. 30, 2025 (4 year terms)
Wanda Antle, Mayor
Gladys Kavanagh, Town Manager & Clerk

Fox Harbour
P.O. Box 64
Fox Harbour, NL A0B 1V0
Tel: 709-227-2271; *Fax:* 709-227-2817
Municipal Type: Town
Incorporated: Oct. 13, 1964; *Area:* 19.78 sq km

Population in 2016: 252
Provincial Electoral District(s): Placentia—St. Mary's
Federal Electoral District(s): Avalon
Next Election: Sept. 30, 2025 (4 year terms)
Brian Quilty, Mayor
Audrey Rolls, Clerk

Frenchman's Cove
P.O. Box 20
Frenchman's Cove, NL A0E 1R0
Tel: 709-826-2190; *Fax:* 709-826-2362
townoffrenchmanscove@persona.ca
Municipal Type: Town
Incorporated: May 28, 1974; *Area:* 68.55 sq km
Population in 2016: 169
Provincial Electoral District(s): Burin—Grand Bank; Humber—Bay of Islands
Federal Electoral District(s): Bonavista—Burin—Trinity; Long Range Mountains
Next Election: Sept. 30, 2025 (4 year terms)
Leslie Cluett, Mayor
Candace Savoury, Clerk

Gallants
4 Main St.
Gallants, NL A0L 1G0
Tel: 709-646-3881; *Fax:* 709-646-2857
Municipal Type: Town
Incorporated: Aug. 16, 1966; *Area:* 6.34 sq km
Population in 2016: 50
Provincial Electoral District(s): St. George's—Humber
Federal Electoral District(s): Long Range Mountains
Next Election: Sept. 30, 2025 (4 year terms)
Note: Provincial Electoral District formerly Humber West.
Cater Glover, Mayor
Georgina Robinson, Clerk

Gambo
P.O. Box 250
4 Centennial Rd.
Gambo, NL A0G 1T0
Tel: 709-674-4476
www.townofgambo.com
Municipal Type: Town
Incorporated: July 10, 1962; *Area:* 92.07 sq km
Population in 2016: 1,978
Provincial Electoral District(s): Gander
Federal Electoral District(s): Bonavista—Burin—Trinity
Next Election: Sept. 30, 2025 (4 year terms)
Note: Provincial Electoral District formerly Terra Nova.
Darren Dyke, Mayor
Lorne Greene, Town Clerk & Manager, 709-674-4476

Gander
P.O. Box 280
100 Elizabeth Dr.
Gander, NL A1V 1G7
Tel: 709-651-2930; *Fax:* 709-256-5809
info@gandercanada.com
www.gandercanada.com
Municipal Type: Town
Incorporated: Dec. 28, 1954; *Area:* 104.25 sq km
Population in 2016: 11,688
Provincial Electoral District(s): Gander
Federal Electoral District(s): Coast of Bays—Central—Notre Dame
Next Election: Sept. 30, 2025 (4 year terms)
Percy Farwell, Mayor
Tara Pollett, Deputy Mayor
Gina Brown, Councillor
Bettina Ford, Councillor
Sheldon Handcock, Councillor
Wilson Hoffe, Councillor
Pat Woodford, Councillor
Brad Hefford, Town Clerk, 709-651-5901
Dermot Chafe, Chief Administrative Officer
Tony Barron, Director, Municipal Works
James Blackwood, Director, Engineering
Kelly Hiscock, Acting Director, Finance
R.J. Locke, Director, Economic Development
Nicole Newell, Director, Recreation & Community Services
Harold Lowe, Fire Chief

Garnish
P.O. Box 70
Garnish, NL A0E 1T0
Tel: 709-826-2330; *Fax:* 709-826-2173
www.townofgarnish.com
Municipal Type: Town
Incorporated: Aug. 25, 1971; *Area:* 39.11 sq km
Population in 2016: 568
Provincial Electoral District(s): Burin—Grand Bank

Federal Electoral District(s): Bonavista—Burin—Trinity
Next Election: Sept. 30, 2025 (4 year terms)
Gregory Day, Mayor
Ruth Cluett, Clerk

Gaskiers-Point La Haye
P.O. Box 434
St Mary's, NL A0B 3B0
Tel: 709-525-2430; *Fax:* 709-525-2431
townofgaskiers@nf.aibn.com
Municipal Type: Town
Incorporated: Aug. 25, 1970; *Area:* 23.81 sq km
Population in 2016: 232
Provincial Electoral District(s): Placentia—St. Mary's
Federal Electoral District(s): Avalon
Next Election: Sept. 30, 2025 (4 year terms)
Johnny Critch, Mayor
Jeanette Critch, Clerk

Gaultois
P.O. Box 101
Gaultois, NL A0H 1N0
Tel: 709-841-6546; *Fax:* 709-841-3521
townofgaultois@hotmail.com
townofgaultois.weebly.com
Municipal Type: Town
Incorporated: Jan. 1, 1962; *Area:* 4.33 sq km
Population in 2016: 136
Provincial Electoral District(s): Fortune Bay—Cape La Hune
Federal Electoral District(s): Coast of Bays—Central—Notre Dame
Next Election: Sept. 30, 2025 (4 year terms)
Gordon Hunt, Mayor
Marcella Drover, Clerk

Gillams
P.O. Box 3968
RR#2
Corner Brook, NL A2H 6B9
Tel: 709-783-2800; *Fax:* 709-783-2671
townofgillams@nf.aibn.com
www.gillams.net
Municipal Type: Town
Incorporated: Aug. 17, 1971; *Area:* 6.7 sq km
Population in 2016: 410
Provincial Electoral District(s): Humber—Bay of Islands
Federal Electoral District(s): Long Range Mountains
Next Election: Sept. 30, 2025 (4 year terms)
Patricia Penney, Mayor
Shelly Penney, Clerk

Glenburnie-Birchy Head-Shoal Brook
General Delivery
Birchy Head, NL A0K 1K0
Tel: 709-453-7220; *Fax:* 709-453-7220
gbstownoffice@eastlink.ca
www.townofgbs.com
Municipal Type: Town
Incorporated: Sept. 1, 1978; *Area:* 6.57 sq km
Population in 2016: 224
Provincial Electoral District(s): Humber—Gros Morne
Federal Electoral District(s): Long Range Mountains
Next Election: Sept. 30, 2025 (4 year terms)
Note: Provincial Electoral District formerly Humber Valley.
William Anderson, Mayor
Myrna Goosney, Clerk

Glenwood
P.O. Box 130
Glenwood, NL A0G 2K0
Tel: 709-679-2159; *Fax:* 709-679-5470
townofglenwood@hotmail.com
Municipal Type: Town
Incorporated: June 12, 1962; *Area:* 6.92 sq km
Population in 2016: 778
Provincial Electoral District(s): Gander
Federal Electoral District(s): Coast of Bays—Central—Notre Dame
Next Election: Sept. 30, 2025 (4 year terms)
Jason Kinden, Mayor
Susan Gillingham, Town Manager & Clerk

Glovertown
P.O. Box 224
10 Station Rd.
Glovertown, NL A0G 2L0
Tel: 709-533-2351; *Fax:* 709-533-2225
glovertowncounc@eastlink.ca
www.glovertown.net
Municipal Type: Town
Incorporated: Dec. 28, 1954; *Area:* 70.33 sq km
Population in 2016: 2,083

Provincial Electoral District(s): Terra Nova
Federal Electoral District(s): Bonavista—Burin—Trinity
Next Election: Sept. 30, 2025 (4 year terms)
Douglas Churchill, Mayor
Joanne Perry, Clerk

Goose Cove East
P.O. Box 8
St Anthony, NL A0K 4S0
Tel: 709-454-8393; *Fax:* 709-454-8393
Municipal Type: Town
Incorporated: Oct. 19, 1971; *Area:* 2.69 sq km
Population in 2016: 174
Provincial Electoral District(s): St. Barbe—L'Anse aux Meadows
Federal Electoral District(s): Long Range Mountains
Next Election: Sept. 30, 2025 (4 year terms)
Note: Provincial Electoral District formerly The Straits-White Bay North.
Marie Reardon, Mayor
Patricia Reardon, Clerk

Grand Bank
P.O. Box 640
56 Main St.
Grand Bank, NL A0E 1W0
Tel: 709-832-1600; *Fax:* 709-832-1636
townofgrandbank@townofgrandbank.net
www.townofgrandbank.com
Other Information: Alt. Phone: 709-832-1601
Municipal Type: Town
Incorporated: Dec. 28, 1943; *Area:* 16.97 sq km
Population in 2016: 2,310
Provincial Electoral District(s): Burin—Grand Bank
Federal Electoral District(s): Bonavista—Burin—Trinity
Next Election: Sept. 30, 2025 (4 year terms)
Rex Matthews, Mayor
Sheila Dolimount, Clerk

Grand Le Pierre
P.O. Box 35
Grand Le Pierre, NL A0E 1Y0
Tel: 709-662-2702; *Fax:* 709-662-2076
towncouncilglp@hotmail.ca
Municipal Type: Town
Incorporated: June 17, 1969; *Area:* 153.59 sq km
Population in 2016: 235
Provincial Electoral District(s): Placentia West—Bellevue
Federal Electoral District(s): Bonavista—Burin—Trinity
Next Election: Sept. 30, 2025 (4 year terms)
Glen Bolt, Mayor
Donna Fizzard, Clerk

Greenspond
P.O. Box 100
Greenspond, NL A0G 2N0
Tel: 709-269-3111; *Fax:* 709-269-3191
greenspond@eastlink.ca
Municipal Type: Town
Incorporated: Aug. 15, 1951; *Area:* 2.85 sq km
Population in 2016: 266
Provincial Electoral District(s): Fogo Island—Cape Freels
Federal Electoral District(s): Bonavista—Burin—Trinity
Next Election: Sept. 30, 2025 (4 year terms)
Note: Provincial Electoral District formerly Bonavista North.
Roxanne Hounsell, Mayor
Clyde Bragg, Town Clerk

Hampden
P.O. Box 9
Hampden, NL A0K 2Y0
Tel: 709-455-4212; *Fax:* 709-455-2117
townofhampden@eastlink.ca
Municipal Type: Town
Incorporated: Dec. 8, 1959; *Area:* 32.97 sq km
Population in 2016: 429
Provincial Electoral District(s): Humber—Gros Morne
Federal Electoral District(s): Long Range Mountains
Next Election: Sept. 30, 2025 (4 year terms)
Note: Provincial Electoral District formerly Humber Valley.
Calvin Wilton, Mayor
Sabrina Fudge, Clerk

Hant's Harbour
P.O. Box 40
Hant's Harbour, NL A0B 1Y0
Tel: 709-586-2741; *Fax:* 709-586-2680
info@hantsharbour.ca
www.hantsharbour.net
Municipal Type: Town
Incorporated: Oct. 13, 1970; *Area:* 32.31 sq km
Population in 2016: 329
Provincial Electoral District(s): Carbonear—Trinity—Bay de

Verde
Federal Electoral District(s): Bonavista—Burin—Trinity
Next Election: Sept. 30, 2025 (4 year terms)
Donald Green, Mayor
Betty Tuck, Clerk

Happy Adventure
P.O. Box 1 Site 2
Happy Adventure, NL A0G 1Z0
Tel: 709-677-2593; *Fax:* 709-677-2594
happyadventure@nf.aibn.com
Municipal Type: Town
Incorporated: May 10, 1960; *Area:* 9.62 sq km
Population in 2016: 200
Provincial Electoral District(s): Terra Nova
Federal Electoral District(s): Bonavista—Burin—Trinity
Next Election: Sept. 30, 2025 (4 year terms)
Carl Turner, Mayor
Judy Powell, Clerk

Happy Valley-Goose Bay
P.O. Box 40 B
212 Hamilton River Rd.
Happy Valley-Goose Bay, NL A0P 1E0
Tel: 709-896-3321; *Fax:* 709-896-9454
pr@townhvgb.com
www.happyvalley-goosebay.com
Municipal Type: Town
Incorporated: March 15, 1955; *Area:* 305.85 sq km
Population in 2016: 8,109
Provincial Electoral District(s): Lake Melville
Federal Electoral District(s): Labrador
Next Election: Sept. 30, 2025 (4 year terms)
George Andrews, Mayor

Harbour Breton
P.O. Box 130
Harbour Breton, NL A0H 1P0
Tel: 709-885-2354; *Fax:* 709-885-2095
harbourbreton@nf.aibn.com
www.harbourbreton.com
Municipal Type: Town
Incorporated: Dec. 16, 1952; *Area:* 13.74 sq km
Population in 2016: 1,634
Provincial Electoral District(s): Fortune Bay—Cape La Hune
Federal Electoral District(s): Coast of Bays—Central—Notre Dame
Next Election: Sept. 30, 2025 (4 year terms)
Georgina Ollerhead, Mayor
Bernice Herritt, Town Manager & Clerk

Harbour Grace
P.O. Box 310
112 Water St.
Harbour Grace, NL A0A 2M0
Tel: 709-596-3631; *Fax:* 709-596-1991
thg@nf.sympatico.ca
www.hrgrace.ca
Municipal Type: Town
Incorporated: July 10, 1945; *Area:* 33.71 sq km
Population in 2016: 2,995
Provincial Electoral District(s): Harbour Grace—Port de Grave
Federal Electoral District(s): Avalon
Next Election: Sept. 30, 2025 (4 year terms)
Don Coombs, Mayor
Amy Parsons, Town Clerk

Harbour Main-Chapel's Cove-Lakeview
P.O. Box 40
362 Conception Bay Hwy.
Harbour Main, NL A0A 2P0
Tel: 709-229-6822; *Fax:* 709-229-6234
hmcouncil@eastlink.ca
Other Information: Alt. Phone: 709-229-6887
Municipal Type: Town
Incorporated: June 1, 1965; *Area:* 21.05 sq km
Population in 2016: 1,067
Provincial Electoral District(s): Harbour Main
Federal Electoral District(s): Avalon
Next Election: Sept. 30, 2025 (4 year terms)
Mike Doyle, Mayor
Rhonda Dalton, Clerk

Hare Bay
P.O. Box 130
Hare Bay, NL A0G 2P0
Tel: 709-537-2187; *Fax:* 709-537-2987
harebaytowncouncil@bellaliant.com
www.townofharebay.com
Municipal Type: Town
Incorporated: Oct. 20, 1964; *Area:* 34.06 sq km
Population in 2016: 969

Provincial Electoral District(s): Fogo Island—Cape Freels
Federal Electoral District(s): Bonavista—Burin—Trinity
Next Election: Sept. 30, 2025 (4 year terms)
Note: Provincial Electoral District formerly Terra Nova.
Tanya Collins, Mayor
June Linehan, Clerk

Hawke's Bay
P.O. Box 58
Hawke's Bay, NL A0K 3B0
Tel: 709-248-5216; *Fax:* 709-248-5201
hbcouncil@nf.aibn.com
Municipal Type: Town
Incorporated: Aug. 21, 1956; *Area:* 46.55 sq km
Population in 2016: 315
Provincial Electoral District(s): St. Barbe—L'Anse aux Meadows
Federal Electoral District(s): Long Range Mountains
Next Election: Sept. 30, 2025 (4 year terms)
Garcien Plowman, Mayor
Nina Dredge, Clerk

Heart's Content
P.O. Box 31
154 Main Rd.
Hearts Content, NL A0B 1Z0
Tel: 709-583-2491; *Fax:* 709-583-2226
heartscontent@persona.ca
www.heartscontent.ca
Municipal Type: Town
Incorporated: Aug. 25, 1967; *Area:* 62.81 sq km
Population in 2016: 340
Provincial Electoral District(s): Carbonear—Trinity—Bay de Verde
Federal Electoral District(s): Bonavista—Burin—Trinity
Next Election: Sept. 30, 2025 (4 year terms)
Fred Cumby, Mayor
Alice Cumby, Clerk

Heart's Delight-Islington
395 Main Rd.
Hearts Delight, NL A0B 2A0
Tel: 709-588-2708; *Fax:* 709-588-2235
info@townofhdi.ca
townofhdi.ca
Municipal Type: Town
Incorporated: Oct. 24, 1972; *Area:* 27.27 sq km
Population in 2016: 674
Provincial Electoral District(s): Carbonear—Trinity—Bay de Verde
Federal Electoral District(s): Bonavista—Burin—Trinity
Next Election: Sept. 30, 2025 (4 year terms)
Clayton Branton, Mayor
Kim Reid, Clerk

Heart's Desire
P.O. Box 10
Hearts Desire, NL A0B 2B0
Tel: 709-588-2280; *Fax:* 709-588-2343
townofheartsdesire@persona.ca
Municipal Type: Town
Incorporated: Sept. 28, 1971; *Area:* 17.27 sq km
Population in 2016: 213
Provincial Electoral District(s): Carbonear—Trinity—Bay de Verde
Federal Electoral District(s): Bonavista—Burin—Trinity
Next Election: Sept. 30, 2025 (4 year terms)
Francis St. George, Mayor
Eleanor Andrews, Clerk

Hermitage-Sandyville
P.O. Box 160
Hermitage, NL A0H 1S0
Tel: 709-883-2343; *Fax:* 709-883-2150
hermitage-sandyville.ca
Municipal Type: Town
Incorporated: Oct. 22, 1960; *Area:* 28.91 sq km
Population in 2016: 422
Provincial Electoral District(s): Fortune Bay—Cape La Hune
Federal Electoral District(s): Coast of Bays—Central—Notre Dame
Next Election: Sept. 30, 2025 (4 year terms)
Stephen Crewe, Mayor
Josie Simms, Clerk

Holyrood
P.O. Box 100
34 Salmonier Line
Holyrood, NL A0A 2R0
Tel: 709-229-7252; *Fax:* 709-229-7269
info@holyrood.ca
holyrood.ca

Municipal Type: Town
Incorporated: March 23, 1969; *Area:* 125.57 sq km
Population in 2016: 2,463
Provincial Electoral District(s): Harbour Main
Federal Electoral District(s): Avalon
Next Election: Sept. 30, 2025 (4 year terms)
Note: Provincial Electoral District formerly Conception Bay South.
Gary Goobie, Mayor
Gary Corbett, Chief Administrative Officer

Hopedale
P.O. Box 190
Hopedale, NL A0P 1G0
Tel: 709-933-3864; *Fax:* 709-933-3800
Other Information: Alt. Phone: 709-933-3871
Municipal Type: Town
Incorporated: Sept. 30, 1969; *Area:* 3.36 sq km
Population in 2016: 574
Provincial Electoral District(s): Torngat Mountains
Federal Electoral District(s): Labrador
Next Election: Sept. 30, 2025 (4 year terms)
Marjorie Flowers, Mayor
Jillian Mitsuk, Clerk

Howley
P.O. Box 40
Howley, NL A0K 3E0
Tel: 709-635-5555
howleynl@hotmail.com
Municipal Type: Town
Incorporated: Feb. 4, 1958; *Area:* 19.91 sq km
Population in 2016: 205
Provincial Electoral District(s): Humber—Gros Morne
Federal Electoral District(s): Long Range Mountains
Next Election: Sept. 30, 2025 (4 year terms)
Note: Provincial Electoral District formerly Humber Valley.
Wayne Ronald Bennett, Mayor

Hughes Brook
46 Lidstone's Dr.
Hughes Brook, NL A2H 4A1
Tel: 709-783-2921; *Fax:* 709-783-3039
info@hughesbrook.com
www.hughesbrook.com
Municipal Type: Town
Incorporated: July 25, 1975; *Area:* 1.6 sq km
Population in 2016: 255
Provincial Electoral District(s): Humber—Bay of Islands
Federal Electoral District(s): Long Range Mountains
Next Election: Sept. 30, 2025 (4 year terms)
Freeman Parsons, Mayor
Amanda Bennett, Clerk

Humber Arm South
P.O. Box 10
Benoit's Cove, NL A0L 1A0
Tel: 709-789-2981; *Fax:* 709-789-2918
townofhumberarmsouth@hotmail.com
Municipal Type: Town
Incorporated: June 15, 1971; *Area:* 65.05 sq km
Population in 2016: 1,599
Provincial Electoral District(s): Humber—Bay of Islands
Federal Electoral District(s): Long Range Mountains
Next Election: Sept. 30, 2025 (4 year terms)
Vacant, Mayor
Marion Evoy, Town Manager & Clerk

Indian Bay
10-18 Municipal Cres.
Indian Bay, NL A0G 2V0
Tel: 709-678-2727; *Fax:* 709-678-2727
toib1971@gmail.com
Municipal Type: Town
Incorporated: Oct. 19, 1971; *Area:* 86.24 sq km
Population in 2016: 175
Provincial Electoral District(s): Fogo Island—Cape Freels
Federal Electoral District(s): Bonavista—Burin—Trinity
Next Election: Sept. 30, 2025 (4 year terms)
Note: Provincial Electoral District formerly Bonavista North.
Christa Lane, Mayor
Triffie Parsons, Clerk

Irishtown-Summerside
183 Main St.
Irishtown, NL A2H 4A1
Tel: 709-783-2146; *Fax:* 709-783-3220
townofirishtownsummerside@bellaliant.com
Municipal Type: Town
Incorporated: Jan. 1, 1991; *Area:* 11.89 sq km
Population in 2016: 1,418
Provincial Electoral District(s): Bay of Islands

Federal Electoral District(s): Long Range Mountains
Next Election: Sept. 30, 2025 (4 year terms)
Barry Wheeler, Mayor
Rita Blanchard, Clerk

Isle aux Morts
P.O. Box 110
11 Legallais St.
Isle-aux-Morts, NL A0M 1J0
Tel: 709-698-3441; *Fax:* 709-698-3449
info@isleauxmorts.ca
www.isleauxmorts.ca
Municipal Type: Town
Incorporated: Nov. 5, 1956; *Area:* 7.66 sq km
Population in 2016: 664
Provincial Electoral District(s): Burgeo—La Poile
Federal Electoral District(s): Long Range Mountains
Next Election: Sept. 30, 2025 (4 year terms)
Nelson Lillington, Mayor
Lydia Francis, Clerk

Jackson's Arm
P.O. Box 10
Jacksons Arm, NL A0K 3H0
Tel: 709-459-3122; *Fax:* 709-459-3173
townofjackson@explornet.ca
Municipal Type: Town
Incorporated: June 19, 1982; *Area:* 7.02 sq km
Population in 2016: 284
Provincial Electoral District(s): Humber—Gros Morne
Federal Electoral District(s): Long Range Mountains
Next Election: Sept. 30, 2025 (4 year terms)
Randell House, Mayor
Carmel Wicks, Clerk

Keels
P.O. Box 30
Keels, NL A0C 1R0
Fax: 709-447-3155
Municipal Type: Town
Incorporated: June 14, 1966; *Area:* 6.54 sq km
Population in 2016: 51
Provincial Electoral District(s): Bonavista
Federal Electoral District(s): Bonavista—Burin—Trinity
Next Election: Sept. 30, 2025 (4 year terms)
Annie Fitzgerald, Mayor
Eileen Mesh, Clerk

King's Cove
P.O. Box 22
Kings Cove, NL A0C 1S0
Tel: 709-447-3146
communityofkingscove@gmail.com
Municipal Type: Town
Incorporated: June 14, 1966; *Area:* 21.48 sq km
Population in 2016: 90
Provincial Electoral District(s): Bonavista
Federal Electoral District(s): Bonavista—Burin—Trinity
Next Election: Sept. 30, 2025 (4 year terms)
Mike Ricketts, Mayor
Nora Ricketts, Clerk

King's Point
P.O. Box 10
Kings Point, NL A0J 1H0
Tel: 709-268-3838; *Fax:* 709-268-3856
kpcouncil@eastlink.ca
www.townofkingspoint.com
Municipal Type: Town
Incorporated: Oct. 1, 1957; *Area:* 46.31 sq km
Population in 2016: 659
Provincial Electoral District(s): Baie Verte
Federal Electoral District(s): Coast of Bays—Central—Notre Dame
Next Election: Sept. 30, 2025 (4 year terms)
Perry Gillingham, Mayor
Marie Cumming, Clerk

Kippens
2 Juniper Ave.
Kippens, NL A2N 3H8
Tel: 709-643-5281; *Fax:* 709-643-9773
admin@kippens.ca
www.kippens.ca
Municipal Type: Town
Incorporated: Dec. 31, 1968; *Area:* 14.32 sq km
Population in 2016: 2,008
Provincial Electoral District(s): Stephenville—Port au Port
Federal Electoral District(s): Long Range Mountains
Next Election: Sept. 30, 2025 (4 year terms)
Debbie Brake-Patten, Mayor
Debbie Cormier, Clerk

Labrador City
P.O. Box 280
Labrador City, NL A2V 2K5
Tel: 709-944-2621; *Fax:* 709-944-6353
labradorwest.com
Municipal Type: Town
Incorporated: June 27, 1961; *Area:* 38.83 sq km
Population in 2016: 7,220
Provincial Electoral District(s): Labrador West
Federal Electoral District(s): Labrador
Next Election: Sept. 30, 2025 (4 year terms)
Vacant, Mayor
Cathy Etsell, Town Manager

Lamaline
P.O. Box 40
Lamaline, NL A0E 2C0
Tel: 709-857-2341; *Fax:* 709-857-2210
lamalinecouncil1@outlook.com
Municipal Type: Town
Incorporated: April 24, 1963; *Area:* 81.69 sq km
Population in 2016: 267
Provincial Electoral District(s): Burin—Grand Bank
Federal Electoral District(s): Bonavista—Burin—Trinity
Next Election: Sept. 30, 2025 (4 year terms)
Katherine Hillier, Mayor
Barbara King, Clerk

Lark Harbour
P.O. Box 40
Lark Harbour, NL A0L 1H0
Tel: 709-681-2270; *Fax:* 709-681-2900
larkharbourtowncouncil@nf.aibn.com
yorkharbourlarkharbour.com
Municipal Type: Town
Incorporated: Jan. 22, 1974; *Area:* 12.92 sq km
Population in 2016: 522
Provincial Electoral District(s): Bay of Islands
Federal Electoral District(s): Long Range Mountains
Next Election: Sept. 30, 2025 (4 year terms)
Vacant, Mayor
Patti Lynn MacDonald, Co-Clerk
Nicola Parker, Co-Clerk

Lawn
P.O. Box 29
Lawn, NL A0E 2E0
Tel: 709-873-2439; *Fax:* 709-873-3006
townoflawn@eastlink.ca
www.townoflawn.com
Municipal Type: Town
Incorporated: Sept. 30, 1952; *Area:* 3.61 sq km
Population in 2016: 624
Provincial Electoral District(s): Burin—Grand Bank
Federal Electoral District(s): Bonavista—Burin—Trinity
Next Election: Sept. 30, 2025 (4 year terms)
John Strang, Mayor
Arlette Strang, Clerk

Leading Tickles
P.O. Box 39
Leading Tickles West, NL A0H 1T0
Tel: 709-483-2180; *Fax:* 709-483-2185
leadingtickles@nf.aibn.com
Municipal Type: Town
Incorporated: July 11, 1961; *Area:* 26.73 sq km
Population in 2016: 292
Provincial Electoral District(s): Exploits
Federal Electoral District(s): Coast of Bays—Central—Notre Dame
Next Election: Sept. 30, 2025 (4 year terms)
Florence Parsons, Mayor
Mary Ann Cooke, Clerk

Lewin's Cove
P.O. Box 40
Lewins Cove, NL A0E 2G0
Tel: 709-894-4777; *Fax:* 709-894-4952
townoflewinscove@bellaliant.com
Municipal Type: Town
Incorporated: May 1, 1973; *Area:* 6.52 sq km
Population in 2016: 544
Provincial Electoral District(s): Burin—Grand Bank
Federal Electoral District(s): Bonavista—Burin—Trinity
Next Election: Sept. 30, 2025 (4 year terms)
John Moore, Mayor
Barbara Mullett, Clerk

Lewisporte
P.O. Box 219
Lewisporte, NL A0G 3A0
Tel: 709-535-2737; *Fax:* 709-535-2695
info@lewisportecanada.com
lewisporte.ca
Municipal Type: Town
Incorporated: July 2, 1946; *Area:* 36.91 sq km
Population in 2016: 3,409
Provincial Electoral District(s): Lewisporte—Twillingate
Federal Electoral District(s): Coast of Bays—Central—Notre Dame
Next Election: Sept. 30, 2025 (4 year terms)
Krista Freake, Mayor
Elizabeth Elliott, Acting Clerk

Little Bay
P.O. Box 40
Little Bay, NL A0J 1J0
Tel: 709-267-3200; *Fax:* 709-267-3200
townoflittebay@gmail.com
Municipal Type: Town
Incorporated: April 19, 1966; *Area:* 1.45 sq km
Population in 2016: 105
Provincial Electoral District(s): Baie Verte—Green Bay
Federal Electoral District(s): Coast of Bays-Central-Notre Dame
Next Election: Sept. 30, 2025 (4 year terms)
Phyllis Simms, Mayor
Joan Power, Clerk

Little Bay East
P.O. Box 15
Little Bay East, NL A0E 2J0
Tel: 709-461-2724; *Fax:* 709-461-2724
Municipal Type: Town
Incorporated: April 27, 1979; *Area:* 1.48 sq km
Population in 2016: 127
Provincial Electoral District(s): Burin—Grand Bank
Federal Electoral District(s): Bonavista—Burin—Trinity
Next Election: Sept. 30, 2025 (4 year terms)
Cora Scott, Mayor
Gail Clarke, Clerk

Little Burnt Bay
P.O. Box 40
Little Burnt Bay, NL A0G 3B0
Tel: 709-535-6415; *Fax:* 709-535-6490
lbbtowncouncil@bellaliant.com
Municipal Type: Town
Incorporated: Sept. 19, 1975; *Area:* 8.5 sq km
Population in 2016: 281
Provincial Electoral District(s): Lewisporte—Twillingate
Federal Electoral District(s): Coast of Bays—Central—Notre Dame
Next Election: Sept. 30, 2025 (4 year terms)
Laverne Suppa, Mayor
Maisie Wells, Clerk

Logy Bay-Middle Cove-Outer Cove
744 Logy Bay Rd.
Logy Bay, NL A1K 3B5
Tel: 709-726-7930; *Fax:* 709-726-2178
office@lbmcoc.ca
lbmcoc.ca
Municipal Type: Town
Incorporated: Sept. 1, 1986; *Area:* 16.98 sq km
Population in 2016: 2,221
Provincial Electoral District(s): Cape St. Francis
Federal Electoral District(s): St. John's East
Next Election: Sept. 30, 2025 (4 year terms)
Bert Hickey, Mayor
Janine Walsh, Town Clerk & Manager, 709-726-7930

Long Harbour-Mount Arlington Heights
P.O. Box 40
Long Harbour, NL A0B 2J0
Tel: 709-228-2920; *Fax:* 709-228-2900
towncouncil@longharbour.net
longharbour.net
Municipal Type: Town
Incorporated: Oct. 22, 1968; *Area:* 18.41 sq km
Population in 2016: 185
Provincial Electoral District(s): Placentia West—Bellevue
Federal Electoral District(s): Bonavista—Burin—Trinity
Next Election: Sept. 30, 2025 (4 year terms)
Gary Keating, Mayor
Juanita Gosse, Clerk

Lord's Cove
P.O. Box 21
Site 11
Lord's Cove, NL A0E 2C0
Tel: 709-857-2316
Municipal Type: Town
Incorporated: May 17, 1966; *Area:* 30.91 sq km
Population in 2016: 162
Provincial Electoral District(s): Burin—Grand Bank
Federal Electoral District(s): Bonavista—Burin—Trinity
Next Election: Sept. 30, 2025 (4 year terms)
Bob Hennebury, Mayor
Eileen Harnett, Clerk

Lourdes
P.O. Box 29
Lourdes, NL A0N 1R0
Tel: 709-642-5812; *Fax:* 709-642-5558
townoflourdes@yahoo.ca
Municipal Type: Town
Incorporated: July 17, 1969; *Area:* 8.1 sq km
Population in 2016: 465
Provincial Electoral District(s): Stephenville—Port au Port
Federal Electoral District(s): Long Range Mountains
Next Election: Sept. 30, 2025 (4 year terms)
Anne Bullen, Mayor
Angela Young, Clerk

Lumsden
P.O. Box 100
Lumsden, NL A0G 3E0
Tel: 709-530-2309
townoflumsden@nf.aibn.com
Municipal Type: Town
Incorporated: April 16, 1968; *Area:* 20.43 sq km
Population in 2016: 501
Provincial Electoral District(s): Fogo Island—Cape Freels
Federal Electoral District(s): Bonavista—Burin—Trinity
Next Election: Sept. 30, 2025 (4 year terms)
Vacant, Mayor
Jeanie Stokes, Clerk

Lushes Bight-Beaumont-Beaumont North
P.O. Box 40
Beaumont, NL A0J 1A0
Tel: 709-264-3271; *Fax:* 709-264-3191
beaumont@xplornet.ca
Municipal Type: Town
Incorporated: Oct. 15, 1968; *Area:* 34.38 sq km
Population in 2016: 168
Provincial Electoral District(s): Baie Verte—Green Bay
Federal Electoral District(s): Coast of Bays—Central—Notre Dame
Next Election: Sept. 30, 2025 (4 year terms)
Daniel Veilleux, Mayor
Nancy Rideout, Clerk

Main Brook
P.O. Box 130
Main Brook, NL A0K 3N0
Tel: 709-865-6561; *Fax:* 709-865-3279
townofmainbrook@nf.aibn.com
townofmainbrook.ca
Municipal Type: Town
Incorporated: June 1, 1948; *Area:* 28.51 sq km
Population in 2016: 243
Provincial Electoral District(s): St. Barbe—L'Anse aux Meadows
Federal Electoral District(s): Long Range Mountains
Next Election: Sept. 30, 2025 (4 year terms)
Barbe Genge, Mayor
Sherry Reid, Clerk

Makkovik
P.O. Box 132
Makkovik, NL A0P 1J0
Tel: 709-923-2221; *Fax:* 709-923-2126
info@makkovik.ca
www.makkovik.ca
Municipal Type: Town
Incorporated: April 7, 1970; *Area:* 1.97 sq km
Population in 2016: 377
Provincial Electoral District(s): Torngat Mountains
Federal Electoral District(s): Labrador
Next Election: Sept. 30, 2025 (4 year terms)
Herbert R. Jacque, Mayor
Doreen Winters, Clerk

Mary's Harbour
P.O. Box 134
Mary's Harbour, NL A0K 3P0
Tel: 709-921-6281; *Fax:* 709-921-6255
maryshbr@nf.aibn.com

Municipal Type: Town
Incorporated: April 11, 1975; *Area:* 38.16 sq km
Population in 2016: 377
Provincial Electoral District(s): Cartwright—L'Anse au Clair
Federal Electoral District(s): Labrador
Next Election: Sept. 30, 2025 (4 year terms)
Alton Rumbolt, Mayor
Glenys Rumbolt, Clerk

Marystown
P.O. Box 1118
Marystown, NL A0E 2M0
Tel: 709-279-1661; *Fax:* 709-279-2862
info@townofmarystown.ca
marystown.ca
Municipal Type: Town
Incorporated: Dec. 18, 1951; *Area:* 61.97 sq km
Population in 2016: 5,316
Provincial Electoral District(s): Placentia West—Bellevue
Federal Electoral District(s): Bonavista—Burin—Trinity
Next Election: Sept. 30, 2025 (4 year terms)
Brian Keating, Mayor
Petrina Power, Acting Town Clerk, 709-279-1661

Massey Drive
85 Massey Dr.
Massey Drive, NL A2H 7A2
Tel: 709-634-2742; *Fax:* 709-634-2899
info@masseydrive.com
masseydrive.com
Municipal Type: Town
Incorporated: Sept. 28, 1971; *Area:* 2.48 sq km
Population in 2016: 1,632
Provincial Electoral District(s): St. George's—Humber
Federal Electoral District(s): Long Range Mountains
Next Election: Sept. 30, 2025 (4 year terms)
Vacant, Mayor
Rodger Hunt, Town Manager/Clerk

McIvers
P.O. Box 4375
RR#2
Corner Brook, NL A2H 6B9
Tel: 709-688-2603; *Fax:* 709-688-2680
mcivers.ca
Municipal Type: Town
Incorporated: June 15, 1971; *Area:* 12.06 sq km
Population in 2016: 538
Provincial Electoral District(s): Bay of Islands
Federal Electoral District(s): Long Range Mountains
Next Election: Sept. 30, 2025 (4 year terms)
Susan Park-White, Mayor
Jerrilynn Lovell, Clerk

Meadows
11 Community Hall Rd.
Corner Brook, NL A2H 6B9
Tel: 709-783-2339; *Fax:* 709-783-2501
townofmeadows@nf.aibn.com
www.townofmeadows.com
Municipal Type: Town
Incorporated: Jan. 13, 1970; *Area:* 3.79 sq km
Population in 2016: 626
Provincial Electoral District(s): Bay of Islands
Federal Electoral District(s): Long Range Mountains
Next Election: Sept. 30, 2025 (4 year terms)
Jamie Brake, Mayor
Sandra Legge, Clerk

Middle Arm
P.O. Box 51
Middle Arm, NL A0K 3R0
Tel: 709-252-2521; *Fax:* 709-252-2400
townofmiddlearm@nf.aibn.com
Municipal Type: Town
Incorporated: Nov. 29, 1966; *Area:* 25.19 sq km
Population in 2016: 474
Provincial Electoral District(s): Baie Verte—Green Bay
Federal Electoral District(s): Coast of Bays—Central—Notre Dame
Next Election: Sept. 30, 2025 (4 year terms)
Neville Robinson, Mayor, 709-252-2136
Loretta Budgell, Clerk

Miles Cove
General Delivery
Miles Cove, NL A0J 1L0
Tel: 709-652-3685; *Fax:* 709-652-3695
mctownhall@hotmail.com
Municipal Type: Town
Incorporated: Sept. 22, 1970; *Area:* 4.03 sq km
Population in 2016: 104

Provincial Electoral District(s): Baie Verte—Green Bay
Federal Electoral District(s): Coast of Bays—Central—Notre Dame
Next Election: Sept. 30, 2025 (4 year terms)
Melvin Morey, Mayor
Charles Harris, Clerk

Millertown
P.O. Box 56
Millertown, NL A0H 1V0
Tel: 709-852-6216
townofmillertown@nf.aibn.com
www.townofmillertown.com
Municipal Type: Town
Incorporated: Dec. 15, 1959; *Area:* 3.24 sq km
Population in 2016: 81
Provincial Electoral District(s): Grand Falls-Windsor—Buchans
Federal Electoral District(s): Coast of Bays—Central—Notre Dame
Next Election: Sept. 30, 2025 (4 year terms)
Barbara Sheppard, Mayor
Deborah Eliott, Clerk

Milltown-Head of Bay d'Espoir
P.O. Box 70
Milltown, NL A0H 1W0
Tel: 709-882-2232; *Fax:* 709-882-2636
townofmill@bellaliant.com
Municipal Type: Town
Incorporated: Dec. 16, 1952; *Area:* 25.02 sq km
Population in 2016: 749
Provincial Electoral District(s): Fortune Bay—Cape La Hune
Federal Electoral District(s): Coast of Bays—Central—Notre Dame
Next Election: Sept. 30, 2025 (4 year terms)
Jerry Kearley, Mayor
Anita Garland, Clerk

Ming's Bight
P.O. Box 61
Site 1
Ming's Bight, NL A0K 3S0
Tel: 709-254-6516; *Fax:* 709-254-7461
townmingsbight@outlook.com
Municipal Type: Town
Incorporated: June 6, 1970; *Area:* 3.78 sq km
Population in 2016: 319
Provincial Electoral District(s): Baie Verte—Green Bay
Federal Electoral District(s): Coast of Bays—Central—Notre Dame
Next Election: Sept. 30, 2025 (4 year terms)
Danny Regular, Mayor
Roxanne Dicks, Clerk

Morrisville
P.O. Box 19
Morrisville, NL A0H 1W0
Tel: 709-538-3138; *Fax:* 709-882-2831
Municipal Type: Town
Incorporated: June 1, 1971; *Area:* 14.26 sq km
Population in 2016: 101
Provincial Electoral District(s): Fortune Bay—Cape La Hune
Federal Electoral District(s): Coast of Bays—Central—Notre Dame
Next Election: Sept. 30, 2025 (4 year terms)
Shawn Nash, Mayor
Kristen Kendell, Clerk

Mount Carmel-Mitchells Brook-St. Catherines
408 Main Rd. North
Mount Carmel, NL A0B 2M0
Tel: 709-521-2040; *Fax:* 709-521-2258
townclerk@townofmountcarmel.ca
townofmountcarmel.ca
Municipal Type: Town
Incorporated: Oct. 6, 1970; *Area:* 61.55 sq km
Population in 2016: 349
Provincial Electoral District(s): Placentia—St. Mary's
Federal Electoral District(s): Avalon
Next Election: Sept. 30, 2025 (4 year terms)
Eugene McDonald, Mayor
Stacey Dean, Clerk

Mount Moriah
P.O. Box 31
Mount Moriah, NL A0L 1J0
Tel: 709-785-5232; *Fax:* 709-785-5332
mountmoriah@nl.rogers.com
Municipal Type: Town
Incorporated: Oct. 12, 1971; *Area:* 15.71 sq km
Population in 2016: 746
Provincial Electoral District(s): Bay of Islands

Federal Electoral District(s): Long Range Mountains
Next Election: Sept. 30, 2025 (4 year terms)
Joseph Park, Mayor
Carol Skeard, Clerk

Musgrave Harbour
P.O. Box 159
Musgrave Harbour, NL A0G 3J0
Tel: 709-655-2119; *Fax:* 709-655-2064
musgravetowncouncil@nf.aibn.com
www.musgraveharbour.com
Municipal Type: Town
Incorporated: Jan. 1, 1954; *Area:* 69.94 sq km
Population in 2016: 990
Provincial Electoral District(s): Fogo Island—Cape Freels
Federal Electoral District(s): Bonavista—Burin—Trinity
Next Election: Sept. 30, 2025 (4 year terms)
Bill Smith, Mayor
Kim Osbourne, Clerk

Musgravetown
P.O. Box 129
Musgravetown, NL A0C 1Z0
Tel: 709-467-2726; *Fax:* 709-467-2109
townofmusg@nf.aibn.com
Municipal Type: Town
Incorporated: March 1, 1974; *Area:* 13.63 sq km
Population in 2016: 564
Provincial Electoral District(s): Terra Nova
Federal Electoral District(s): Bonavista—Burin—Triniity
Next Election: Sept. 30, 2025 (4 year terms)
Jim Brown, Mayor
Linda Fitzgerald, Clerk

Nain
P.O. Box 400
Nain, NL A0P 1L0
Tel: 709-922-2842; *Fax:* 709-922-2295
nainicg@nf.aibn.com
Municipal Type: Town
Incorporated: Nov. 24, 1970; *Area:* 94.58 sq km
Population in 2016: 1,125
Provincial Electoral District(s): Torngat Mountains
Federal Electoral District(s): Labrador
Next Election: Sept. 30, 2025 (4 year terms)
Julius (Joe) Dicker, Mayor
Karen Dicker, Clerk

New Perlican
P.O. Box 130
New Perlican, NL A0B 2S0
Tel: 709-583-2500; *Fax:* 709-583-2554
townofnewperlican@persona.ca
Municipal Type: Town
Incorporated: Sept. 28, 1971; *Area:* 24.47 sq km
Population in 2016: 186
Provincial Electoral District(s): Carbonear—Trinity—Bay de Verde
Federal Electoral District(s): Bonavista—Burin—Trinity
Next Election: Sept. 30, 2025 (4 year terms)
Eric Hiscock, Mayor
Shelly Burrage, Clerk

New-Wes-Valley
P.O. Box 64
Badger's Quay, NL A0G 1B0
Tel: 709-536-2010
info@townofnewwesvalley.ca
townofnewwesvalley.ca
Municipal Type: Town
Incorporated: Jan. 1, 1992; *Area:* 133.59 sq km
Population in 2016: 2,172
Provincial Electoral District(s): Fogo Island—Cape Freels
Federal Electoral District(s): Bonavista—Burin—Trinity
Next Election: Sept. 30, 2025 (4 year terms)
Note: Incorporating Valleyfield, Badger's Quay, Pool's Island, Brookfield Wesleyville, Pound Cove, Templeman & Newton. Provincial Electoral District formerly Bonavista North.
Curtis Roebotham, Mayor
Elizabeth Hall, Town Clerk

Nippers Harbour
P.O. Box 10
Nippers Harbour, NL A0K 3T0
Tel: 709-255-4583; *Fax:* 709-255-4583
towncouncil@aibn.nf.com
Municipal Type: Town
Incorporated: Nov. 10, 1964; *Area:* 1.93 sq km
Population in 2016: 85
Provincial Electoral District(s): Baie Verte—Green Bay
Federal Electoral District(s): Coast of Bays—Central—Notre

Dame
Next Election: Sept. 30, 2025 (4 year terms)
Ted Noble, Mayor
Beth Prole, Clerk

Norman's Cove-Long Cove
P.O. Box 70
Normans Cove, NL A0B 2T0
Tel: 709-592-2490; *Fax:* 709-592-2106
townofnclc@eastlink.ca
Municipal Type: Town
Incorporated: June 2, 1970; *Area:* 19.98 sq km
Population in 2016: 666
Provincial Electoral District(s): Placentia West—Bellevue
Federal Electoral District(s): Bonavista—Burin—Trinity
Next Election: Sept. 30, 2025 (4 year terms)
Henry Brenton, Mayor
Jessica Reid, Clerk

Norris Arm
P.O. Box 70
Norris Arm, NL A0G 3M0
Tel: 709-653-2519; *Fax:* 709-653-2163
townofnorrisarm@gmail.com
Municipal Type: Town
Incorporated: April 20, 1971; *Area:* 41.49 sq km
Population in 2016: 737
Provincial Electoral District(s): Exploits
Federal Electoral District(s): Coast of Bays—Central—Notre Dame
Next Election: Sept. 30, 2025 (4 year terms)
Ross Rowsell, Mayor
Tracy Atwood, Clerk

Norris Point
P.O. Box 119
Norris Point, NL A0K 3V0
Tel: 709-458-2896; *Fax:* 709-458-2883
info@norrispoint.ca
www.norrispoint.ca
Municipal Type: Town
Incorporated: Oct. 25, 1960; *Area:* 4.91 sq km
Population in 2016: 670
Provincial Electoral District(s): Humber—Gros Morne
Federal Electoral District(s): Long Range Mountains
Next Election: Sept. 30, 2025 (4 year terms)
Joseph Reid, Mayor
Jennifer Samms, Clerk

North River
P.O. Box 104
North River, NL A0A 3C0
Tel: 709-786-6216; *Fax:* 709-786-1955
townofnorthriver@bellaliant.com
www.townofnorthriver.com
Municipal Type: Town
Incorporated: Aug. 11, 1964; *Area:* 4.32 sq km
Population in 2016: 570
Provincial Electoral District(s): Harbour Main
Federal Electoral District(s): Avalon
Next Election: Sept. 30, 2025 (4 year terms)
Joanne Morrissey, Mayor
Sheila Hall, Clerk

North West River
P.O. Box 100
North West River, NL A0P 1M0
Tel: 709-497-8533; *Fax:* 709-497-8228
manager@townofnwr.ca
www.townofnwr.ca
Municipal Type: Town
Incorporated: March 11, 1958; *Area:* 3.2 sq km
Population in 2016: 547
Provincial Electoral District(s): Lake Melville
Federal Electoral District(s): Labrador
Next Election: Sept. 30, 2025 (4 year terms)
David Kieser, Mayor
Cardella MacAulay, Clerk

Northern Arm
P.O. Box 2006
Northern Arm, NL A0H 1E0
Tel: 709-257-3482; *Fax:* 709-257-3482
contact@townofnorthernarm.ca
www.townofnorthernarm.ca
Municipal Type: Town
Incorporated: July 18, 1972; *Area:* 25.64 sq km
Population in 2016: 426
Provincial Electoral District(s): Exploits
Federal Electoral District(s): Coast of Bays—Central—Notre Dame
Next Election: Sept. 30, 2025 (4 year terms)

Lloyd Hunter, Mayor
Lisa Gosse, Clerk

Old Perlican
P.O. Box 39
Old Perlican, NL A0A 3G0
Tel: 709-587-2266; *Fax:* 709-587-2261
info@townofoldperlican.ca
www.townofoldperlican.ca
Municipal Type: Town
Incorporated: March 30, 1971; *Area:* 14.47 sq km
Population in 2016: 633
Provincial Electoral District(s): Carbonear—Trinity—Bay de Verde
Federal Electoral District(s): Bonavista—Burin—Trinity
Next Election: Sept. 30, 2025 (4 year terms)
Harvey Button, Mayor
Sonya Durdle, Clerk

Pacquet
97 Main St.
Pacquet, NL A0K 3X0
Tel: 709-251-5496; *Fax:* 709-251-5497
pacquet@eastlink.ca
Municipal Type: Town
Incorporated: June 12, 1962; *Area:* 14.48 sq km
Population in 2016: 164
Provincial Electoral District(s): Baie Verte—Green Bay
Federal Electoral District(s): Coast of Bays—Central—Notre Dame
Next Election: Sept. 30, 2025 (4 year terms)
Vera Norman, Mayor
Tanya Greenham, Clerk

Parker's Cove
General Delivery
Parker's Cove, NL A0E 1H0
Tel: 709-443-2216; *Fax:* 709-443-2216
council@eatlink.ca
Municipal Type: Town
Incorporated: Jan. 25, 1966; *Area:* 4.85 sq km
Population in 2016: 248
Provincial Electoral District(s): Placentia West—Bellevue
Federal Electoral District(s): Bonavista—Burin—Trinity
Next Election: Sept. 30, 2025 (4 year terms)
Harold Murphy, Mayor
Jennifer Murphy, Clerk

Parson's Pond
P.O. Box 39
Parson's Pond, NL A0K 3Z0
Tel: 709-243-2564; *Fax:* 709-243-2500
towncouncilpp@nf.aibn.com
Municipal Type: Town
Incorporated: March 29, 1966; *Area:* 12.63 sq km
Population in 2016: 345
Provincial Electoral District(s): Humber—Gros Morne
Federal Electoral District(s): Long Range Mountains
Next Election: Sept. 30, 2025 (4 year terms)
Brenda Biggin, Mayor
Blanche Thornhill, Clerk

Pasadena
18 - 10th Ave.
Pasadena, NL A0L 1K0
Tel: 709-686-2075; *Fax:* 709-686-2507
info@pasadena.ca
pasadena.ca
Municipal Type: Town
Incorporated: Oct. 25, 1955; *Area:* 49.16 sq km
Population in 2016: 3,620
Provincial Electoral District(s): St. George's—Humber
Federal Electoral District(s): Long Range Mountains
Next Election: Sept. 30, 2025 (4 year terms)
Darren Gardner, Mayor
Sharon Brown, Clerk

Peterview
P.O. Box 10
Peterview, NL A0H 1Y0
Tel: 709-257-2926; *Fax:* 709-257-2926
townofpeterview@nf.aibn.com
www.peterview.ca
Municipal Type: Town
Incorporated: June 12, 1962; *Area:* 6.72 sq km
Population in 2016: 828
Provincial Electoral District(s): Exploits
Federal Electoral District(s): Coast of Bays—Central—Notre Dame
Next Election: Sept. 30, 2025 (4 year terms)
James Samson, Mayor, 709-257-4223
Chris Torraville, Clerk

Petty Harbour-Maddox Cove
P.O. Box 434
35 Main Rd.
Petty Harbour, NL A0A 3H0
Tel: 709-368-3959; *Fax:* 709-368-3994
www.pettyharbourmaddoxcove.ca
Municipal Type: Town
Incorporated: March 25, 1969; *Area:* 4.51 sq km
Population in 2016: 960
Provincial Electoral District(s): Ferryland
Federal Electoral District(s): St. John's South—Mount Pearl
Next Election: Sept. 30, 2025 (4 year terms)
Sam Lee, Mayor
Mandy Dinn, Clerk

Pilley's Island
P.O. Box 70
Pilleys Island, NL A0J 1M0
Tel: 709-652-3555; *Fax:* 709-652-3852
pilleysisland@eastlink.ca
Municipal Type: Town
Incorporated: April 11, 1975; *Area:* 34.67 sq km
Population in 2016: 294
Provincial Electoral District(s): Baie Verte—Green Bay
Federal Electoral District(s): Coast of Bays—Central—Notre Dame
Next Election: Sept. 30, 2025 (4 year terms)
Terry Hoskins, Mayor
Glenda Gale, Clerk

Pinware
P.O. Box 73
Pinware, NL A0K 5S0
Tel: 709-927-5422; *Fax:* 709-927-5422
clerk@pinware-labrador.ca
Municipal Type: Town
Incorporated: May 18, 1978; *Area:* 4.37 sq km
Population in 2016: 88
Provincial Electoral District(s): Cartwright—L'Anse au Clair
Federal Electoral District(s): Labrador
Next Election: Sept. 30, 2025 (4 year terms)
Didier Naulleau, Mayor

Placentia
P.O. Box 99
Placentia, NL A0B 2Y0
Tel: 709-227-2151; *Fax:* 709-227-2323
townofplacentia@placentia.ca
www.placentia.ca
Municipal Type: Town
Incorporated: Nov. 6, 1945; *Area:* 58.05 sq km
Population in 2016: 3,496
Provincial Electoral District(s): Placentia—St. Mary's
Federal Electoral District(s): Avalon
Next Election: Sept. 30, 2025 (4 year terms)
Bernard Power, Mayor
Robert Beaupertuis, Chief Administrative Officer

Point au Gaul
P.O. Box 30
Site 8
Point au Gaul, NL A0E 2C0
Tel: 709-857-2211
towncouncilpag@hotmail.com
Municipal Type: Town
Incorporated: Jan. 4, 1966; *Area:* 3.84 sq km
Population in 2016: 88
Provincial Electoral District(s): Burin—Grand Bank
Federal Electoral District(s): Bonavista—Burin—Trinity
Next Election: Sept. 30, 2025 (4 year terms)
Lewis Dodge, Mayor
Theresa Dodge, Clerk

Point Lance
P.O. Box 15
Point Lance, NL A0B 1E0
Tel: 709-338-2186; *Fax:* 709-338-2186
pointlance@bellaliant.net
Municipal Type: Town
Incorporated: Dec. 7, 1971; *Area:* 29.14 sq km
Population in 2016: 102
Provincial Electoral District(s): Placentia—St. Mary's
Federal Electoral District(s): Avalon
Next Election: Sept. 30, 2025 (4 year terms)
Melvin Careen, Mayor
Jane Power, Clerk

Point Leamington
P.O. Box 39
Point Leamington, NL A0H 1Z0
Tel: 709-484-3421; *Fax:* 709-484-3556
ptleamington@nf.aibn.com
www.townofpointleamington.ca
Municipal Type: Town
Incorporated: Aug. 25, 1970; *Area:* 28.81 sq km
Population in 2016: 591
Provincial Electoral District(s): Exploits
Federal Electoral District(s): Coast of Bays—Central—Notre Dame
Next Election: Sept. 30, 2025 (4 year terms)
Wilf Mercer, Mayor
Wanda Ryan, Clerk

Point May
P.O. Box 19
Point May, NL A0E 2C0
Tel: 709-857-2640; *Fax:* 709-857-2640
Municipal Type: Town
Incorporated: Dec. 4, 1962; *Area:* 64.89 sq km
Population in 2016: 231
Provincial Electoral District(s): Burin—Grand Bank
Federal Electoral District(s): Bonavista—Burin—Trinity
Next Election: Sept. 30, 2025 (4 year terms)
Lawrence Harnett, Mayor
Janice Cousins, Clerk

Point of Bay
P.O. Box 9
Point of Bay, NL A0H 2A0
Tel: 709-257-3171; *Fax:* 709-257-3192
Municipal Type: Town
Incorporated: April 18, 1967; *Area:* 21.94 sq km
Population in 2016: 154
Provincial Electoral District(s): Exploits
Federal Electoral District(s): Coast of Bays—Central—Notre Dame
Next Election: Sept. 30, 2025 (4 year terms)
Edward Cameron, Mayor
Sybil Boone, Clerk

Pool's Cove
P.O. Box 10
Pools Cove, NL A0H 2B0
Tel: 709-665-3371; *Fax:* 709-665-3372
thetownofpoolscove@hotmail.com
Municipal Type: Town
Incorporated: Nov. 25, 1969; *Area:* 2.64 sq km
Population in 2016: 193
Provincial Electoral District(s): Fortune Bay—Cape La Hune
Federal Electoral District(s): Coast of Bays—Central—Notre Dame
Next Election: Sept. 30, 2025 (4 year terms)
Dwayne Williams, Mayor
Branda Williams, Clerk

Port Anson
P.O. Box 62
General Delivery
Port Anson, NL A0J 1N0
Tel: 709-652-3683; *Fax:* 709-652-3680
townofportanson@hotmail.com
Municipal Type: Town
Incorporated: Dec. 12, 1961; *Area:* 7.69 sq km
Population in 2016: 130
Provincial Electoral District(s): Baie Verte—Green Bay
Federal Electoral District(s): Coast of Bays—Central—Notre Dame
Next Election: Sept. 30, 2025 (4 year terms)
Shawn Burton, Mayor
Cynthia Rowsell, Clerk

Port au Choix
P.O. Box 89
119 Fisher St.
Port au Choix, NL A0K 4C0
Tel: 709-861-3409; *Fax:* 709-861-3061
info@townofportauchoix.ca
www.townofportauchoix.ca
Municipal Type: Town
Incorporated: July 26, 1966; *Area:* 35.61 sq km
Population in 2016: 789
Provincial Electoral District(s): St. Barbe—L'Anse aux Meadows
Federal Electoral District(s): Long Range Mountains
Next Election: Sept. 30, 2025 (4 year terms)
Donald Spence, Mayor
Lizeta Gould, Town Clerk & Manager

Port au Port East
P.O. Box 160
Port au Port East, NL A0N 1T0
Tel: 709-648-2731; *Fax:* 709-648-9481
portauporteast@gmail.com
portauporteast.com
Municipal Type: Town
Incorporated: Dec. 16, 1952; *Area:* 24.76 sq km
Population in 2016: 579
Provincial Electoral District(s): Stephenville—Port au Port
Federal Electoral District(s): Long Range Mountains
Next Election: Sept. 30, 2025 (4 year terms)
James Cashin, Mayor
Florence Barter, Clerk

Port au Port West-Aguathuna-Felix Cove
P.O. Box 89
Aguathuna, NL A0N 1T0
Tel: 709-648-2891; *Fax:* 709-648-9292
papwaf@nf.aibn.com
Municipal Type: Town
Incorporated: Oct. 6, 1970; *Area:* 16.72 sq km
Population in 2016: 449
Provincial Electoral District(s): Stephenville—Port au Port
Federal Electoral District(s): Long Range Mountains
Next Election: Sept. 30, 2025 (4 year terms)
Chalsie Kook-Marche, Mayor
Vanessa Glasgow, Clerk

Port Blandford
P.O. Box 70
Port Blandford, NL A0C 2G0
Tel: 709-543-2170; *Fax:* 709-543-2153
info@portblandford.com
portblandford.com
Municipal Type: Town
Incorporated: Sept. 28, 1971; *Area:* 50.56 sq km
Population in 2016: 601
Provincial Electoral District(s): Terra Nova
Federal Electoral District(s): Bonavista—Burin—Trinity
Next Election: Sept. 30, 2025 (4 year terms)
Chad Holloway, Mayor
Vida Greening, Clerk & Manager

Port Hope Simpson
P.O. Box 130
Port Hope Simpson, NL A0K 4E0
Tel: 709-960-0236; *Fax:* 709-960-0387
porthopesimpson@nf.aibn.com
Municipal Type: Town
Incorporated: May 1, 1973; *Area:* 32.52 sq km
Population in 2016: 412
Provincial Electoral District(s): Cartwright—L'Anse au Clair
Federal Electoral District(s): Labrador
Next Election: Sept. 30, 2025 (4 year terms)
Margaret Burden, Mayor
Marilyn Parr Penney, Clerk

Port Kirwan
P.O. Box 40
Site 2
Port Kirwan, NL A0A 2G0
Fax: 709-363-2114
Municipal Type: Town
Incorporated: June 15, 1965; *Area:* 9.19 sq km
Population in 2016: 52
Provincial Electoral District(s): Ferryland
Federal Electoral District(s): Avalon
Next Election: Sept. 30, 2025 (4 year terms)
Eugene Brothers, Mayor
Dana Boland, Clerk

Port Rexton
P.O. Box 55
Port Rexton, NL A0C 2H0
Tel: 709-464-2006
info@townofportrexton.com
www.townofportrexton.com
Municipal Type: Town
Incorporated: April 22, 1969; *Area:* 11.78 sq km
Population in 2016: 340
Provincial Electoral District(s): Bonavista
Federal Electoral District(s): Bonavista—Burin—Trinity
Next Election: Sept. 30, 2025 (4 year terms)
Dean Bailey, Mayor
Lois Long, Clerk

Port Saunders
P.O. Box 39
Port Saunders, NL A0K 4H0
Tel: 709-861-3105; *Fax:* 709-861-2137
info@townofportsaunders.ca
www.townofportsaunders.ca
Municipal Type: Town
Incorporated: Aug. 21, 1956; *Area:* 38.81 sq km
Population in 2016: 674
Provincial Electoral District(s): St. Barbe—L'Anse aux Meadows
Federal Electoral District(s): Long Range Mountains
Next Election: Sept. 30, 2025 (4 year terms)
Tony Ryan, Mayor
Judy Quinlan, Clerk

Portugal Cove South
P.O. Box 8
Site 11
Trepassey, NL A0A 4B0
Tel: 709-438-2092; *Fax:* 709-438-2090
townofpcs@live.ca
Municipal Type: Town
Incorporated: Aug. 6, 1963; *Area:* 1.14 sq km
Population in 2016: 150
Provincial Electoral District(s): Ferryland
Federal Electoral District(s): Avalon
Next Election: Sept. 30, 2025 (4 year terms)
Clarence Molloy, Mayor
Ida Perry, Clerk

Portugal Cove-St. Philip's
1119 Thorburn Rd.
Portugal Cove-St Philips, NL A1M 1T6
Tel: 709-895-8000; *Fax:* 709-895-3780
pcsp@pcsp.ca
www.pcsp.ca
Municipal Type: Town
Incorporated: Feb. 1, 1992; *Area:* 57.35 sq km
Population in 2016: 8,147
Provincial Electoral District(s): Conception Bay East—Bell Island
Federal Electoral District(s): St. John's East
Next Election: Sept. 30, 2025 (4 year terms)
Carol McDonald, Mayor
Claudine Murray, Town Clerk

Postville
P.O. Box 74
Postville, NL A0P 1N0
Tel: 709-479-9830; *Fax:* 709-479-9888
communitycouncil@nf.aibn.com
Municipal Type: Town
Incorporated: Aug. 1, 1975; *Area:* 1.96 sq km
Population in 2016: 177
Provincial Electoral District(s): Torngat Mountains
Federal Electoral District(s): Labrador
Next Election: Sept. 30, 2025 (4 year terms)
Diane Gear, Mayor
Melanie Gear, Clerk

Pouch Cove
P.O. Box 59
Pouch Cove, NL A0A 3L0
Tel: 709-335-2848; *Fax:* 709-335-2840
info@pouchcove.ca
pouchcove.ca
Municipal Type: Town
Incorporated: Dec. 22, 1970; *Area:* 58.34 sq km
Population in 2016: 2,069
Provincial Electoral District(s): Cape St. Francis
Federal Electoral District(s): St. John's East
Next Election: Sept. 30, 2025 (4 year terms)
Joedy Wall, Mayor
Pamela Wall, Town Clerk, 709-335-2848

Raleigh
P.O. Box 119
Raleigh, NL A0K 4J0
Tel: 709-452-4461; *Fax:* 709-452-2135
townofraleigh@nf.aibn.com
Municipal Type: Town
Incorporated: Oct. 2, 1973; *Area:* 11.12 sq km
Population in 2016: 177
Provincial Electoral District(s): St. Barbe—L'Anse aux Meadows
Federal Electoral District(s): Long Range Mountains
Next Election: Sept. 30, 2025 (4 year terms)
Angela Taylor, Clerk

Ramea
P.O. Box 69
Ramea, NL A0N 2J0
Tel: 709-625-2280; *Fax:* 709-625-2010
rameatowncouncil@gmail.com

Municipal Type: Town
Incorporated: March 20, 1951; *Area:* 1.89 sq km
Population in 2016: 447
Provincial Electoral District(s): Burgeo—La Poile
Federal Electoral District(s): Long Range Mountains
Next Election: Sept. 30, 2025 (4 year terms)
Clyde Dominie, Mayor
Minnie Organ, Clerk

Red Bay
P.O. Box 108
Red Bay, NL A0K 4K0
Tel: 709-920-2197; *Fax:* 709-920-2103
redbaytowncouncil@nf.aibn.com
Municipal Type: Town
Incorporated: May 22, 1973; *Area:* 1.58 sq km
Population in 2016: 169
Provincial Electoral District(s): Cartwright—L'Anse au Clair
Federal Electoral District(s): Labrador
Next Election: Sept. 30, 2025 (4 year terms)
Wanita Stone, Mayor
Alice Moores, Clerk

Red Harbour
P.O. Box 5
Red Harbour PB, NL A0E 2R0
Tel: 709-443-2599; *Fax:* 709-443-2599
townofredharbour@yahoo.ca
Municipal Type: Town
Incorporated: Nov. 9, 1969; *Area:* 11.35 sq km
Population in 2016: 189
Provincial Electoral District(s): Placentia West—Bellevue
Federal Electoral District(s): Bonavista—Burin—Trinity
Next Election: Sept. 30, 2025 (4 year terms)
Cory Miller, Mayor
Kevin Paddle, Clerk

Reidville
2 Community Sq.
Reidville, NL A8A 2V7
Tel: 709-635-5232; *Fax:* 709-635-4498
townofreidville@nf.aibn.com
reidville-nl.ca
Municipal Type: Town
Incorporated: Oct. 3, 1975; *Area:* 58.41 sq km
Population in 2016: 509
Provincial Electoral District(s): Humber—Gros Morne
Federal Electoral District(s): Long Range Mountains
Next Election: Sept. 30, 2025 (4 year terms)
Roger Barrett, Mayor
Connie Reid, Clerk

Rencontre East
P.O. Box 33
Rencontre East, NL A0H 2C0
Tel: 709-848-3171; *Fax:* 709-848-4194
townofrencontreeast@hotmail.com
Municipal Type: Town
Incorporated: 0eb. 8, 1972; *Area:* 2.62 sq km
Population in 2016: 139
Provincial Electoral District(s): Fortune Bay—Cape La Hune
Federal Electoral District(s): Coast of Bays—Central—Notre Dame
Next Election: Sept. 30, 2025 (4 year terms)
Peter Giovannini, Mayor
Krystal Gillard, Clerk

Renews-Cappahayden
P.O. Box 40
Renews, NL A0A 3N0
Tel: 709-363-2500; *Fax:* 709-363-2143
townofrenewscappahayden@nf.aibn.com
Municipal Type: Town
Incorporated: Sept. 19, 1967; *Area:* 127.84 sq km
Population in 2016: 301
Provincial Electoral District(s): Ferryland
Federal Electoral District(s): Avalon
Next Election: Sept. 30, 2025 (4 year terms)
Ben Boland, Mayor
Susan Sheehan, Clerk

Rigolet
P.O. Box 69
Rigolet, NL A0P 1P0
Tel: 709-947-3382; *Fax:* 709-947-3360
town.clerk@rigolet.ca
www.townofrigolet.com
Municipal Type: Town
Incorporated: Jan. 7, 1977; *Area:* 3.61 sq km
Population in 2016: 305
Provincial Electoral District(s): Torngat Mountains

Federal Electoral District(s): Labrador
Next Election: Sept. 30, 2025 (4 year terms)
Jack Shiwak, Mayor
Ashley Shivwak, Clerk

River of Ponds
P.O. Box 10
River of Ponds, NL A0K 4M0
Tel: 709-225-3161; *Fax:* 709-225-3162
townofriverofponds@nf.aibn.com
Municipal Type: Town
Incorporated: May 26, 1970; *Area:* 4.69 sq km
Population in 2016: 215
Provincial Electoral District(s): St. Barbe—L'Anse aux Meadows
Federal Electoral District(s): Long Range Mountains
Next Election: Sept. 30, 2025 (4 year terms)
Eric Patey, Mayor
Valerie House, Clerk

Riverhead
P.O. Box 14
Site 5, RR#1
St Marys, NL A0B 3B0
Tel: 709-525-2600; *Fax:* 709-525-2106
Municipal Type: Town
Incorporated: Dec. 20, 1966; *Area:* 105.6 sq km
Population in 2016: 185
Provincial Electoral District(s): Placentia—St. Mary's
Federal Electoral District(s): Avalon
Next Election: Sept. 30, 2025 (4 year terms)
Sheila Lee, Mayor
Janet Barron, Clerk

Robert's Arm
P.O. Box 10
Roberts Arm, NL A0J 1R0
Tel: 709-652-3331
townofrobertsarm@eastlink.ca
www.robertsarm.com
Municipal Type: Town
Incorporated: Sept. 7, 1954; *Area:* 35.79 sq km
Population in 2016: 805
Provincial Electoral District(s): Baie Verte—Green Bay
Federal Electoral District(s): Coast of Bays—Central—Notre Dame
Next Election: Sept. 30, 2025 (4 year terms)
Lori Miller, Mayor
Ada Rowsell, Administrator

Rocky Harbour
P.O. Box 24
Rocky Harbour, NL A0K 4N0
Tel: 709-458-2376; *Fax:* 709-458-2293
rockyharbour@msn.com
www.rockyharbour.ca
Municipal Type: Town
Incorporated: April 5, 1966; *Area:* 12.08 sq km
Population in 2016: 947
Provincial Electoral District(s): Humber—Gros Morne
Federal Electoral District(s): Long Range Mountains
Next Election: Sept. 30, 2025 (4 year terms)
Tony Major, Mayor
Debbie Reid, Clerk

Roddickton-Bide Arm
P.O. Box 10
Roddickton, NL A0K 4P0
Tel: 709-457-2413; *Fax:* 709-457-2663
roddickton@nf.aibn.com
roddickton.bidearm.ca
Municipal Type: Town
Incorporated: April 7, 1953; *Area:* 47.71 sq km
Population in 2016: 999
Provincial Electoral District(s): St. Barbe—L'Anse aux Meadows
Federal Electoral District(s): Long Range Mountains
Next Election: Sept. 30, 2025 (4 year terms)
Sheila Fitzgerald, Mayor
Jenny Gardiner, Clerk

Rose Blanche-Harbour Le Cou
P.O. Box 159
Rose Blanche, NL A0M 1P0
Tel: 709-956-2540; *Fax:* 709-956-2541
townofroseblanche@nf.aibn.com
Municipal Type: Town
Incorporated: Aug. 25, 1971; *Area:* 4.44 sq km
Population in 2016: 394
Provincial Electoral District(s): Burgeo—La Poile
Federal Electoral District(s): Long Range Mountains
Next Election: Sept. 30, 2025 (4 year terms)
Clayton Durnford, Mayor
Tammy Farrell, Clerk

Rushoon
P.O. Box 25
Rushoon, NL A0E 2S0
Tel: 709-443-2572; *Fax:* 709-443-2572
townofrushoon@bellaliant.com
Municipal Type: Town
Incorporated: Jan. 18, 1966; *Area:* 6.15 sq km
Population in 2016: 245
Provincial Electoral District(s): Placentia West—Bellevue
Federal Electoral District(s): Bonavista—Burin—Trinity
Next Election: Sept. 30, 2025 (4 year terms)
Jill Mulrooney, Mayor
Jackie Gaulton, Clerk

St. Alban's
P.O. Box 10
St Albans, NL A0H 2E0
Tel: 709-538-3132; *Fax:* 709-538-3683
st.albans@nf.aibn.com
stalbans.ca
Municipal Type: Town
Incorporated: Sept. 1, 1953; *Area:* 20.85 sq km
Population in 2016: 1,186
Provincial Electoral District(s): Fortune Bay—Cape La Hune
Federal Electoral District(s): Coast of Bays—Central—Notre Dame
Next Election: Sept. 30, 2025 (4 year terms)
Gail Hoskins, Mayor
Sandra Cox, Clerk

St. Anthony
P.O. Box 430
St Anthony, NL A0K 4S0
Tel: 709-454-3454; *Fax:* 709-454-4154
stanthony@nf.aibn.com
www.stanthony.ca
Municipal Type: Town
Incorporated: July 18, 1945; *Area:* 37.02 sq km
Population in 2016: 2,258
Provincial Electoral District(s): St. Barbe—L'Anse aux Meadows
Federal Electoral District(s): Long Range Mountains
Next Election: Sept. 30, 2025 (4 year terms)
Brad Johannessen, Mayor
Judy Patey, Clerk

St. Bernard's-Jacques Fontaine
P.O. Box 70
St Bernards, NL A0E 2T0
Tel: 709-461-2257; *Fax:* 709-461-2179
townofsbjf@eastlink.ca
Municipal Type: Town
Incorporated: Nov. 21, 1967; *Area:* 16.44 sq km
Population in 2016: 433
Provincial Electoral District(s): Burin—Grand Bank
Federal Electoral District(s): Bonavista—Burin—Trinity
Next Election: Sept. 30, 2025 (4 year terms)
Barry Hodder, Mayor
Pauline Smith, Clerk

St. Brendan's
P.O. Box 54
St Brendans, NL A0G 3V0
Tel: 709-669-4271; *Fax:* 709-669-4271
Municipal Type: Town
Incorporated: Sept. 1, 1953; *Area:* 10.14 sq km
Population in 2016: 145
Provincial Electoral District(s): Terra Nova
Federal Electoral District(s): Bonavista—Burin—Trinity
Next Election: Sept. 30, 2025 (4 year terms)
Veronica Broomfield, Mayor
Rita White, Clerk

St. Bride's
37 Main St.
St Brides, NL A0B 2Z0
Tel: 709-337-2160; *Fax:* 709-337-2160
Municipal Type: Town
Incorporated: May 2, 1972; *Area:* 5.84 sq km
Population in 2016: 252
Provincial Electoral District(s): Placentia—St. Mary's
Federal Electoral District(s): Avalon
Next Election: Sept. 30, 2025 (4 year terms)
Eugene Manning, Mayor
Joan Morrissey, Clerk

St. George's
P.O. Box 250
St Georges, NL A0N 1Z0
Tel: 709-647-3283; *Fax:* 709-647-3180
info@townofstgeorges.com
www.townofstgeorges.com

Municipal Type: Town
Incorporated: May 18, 1965; *Area:* 25.83 sq km
Population in 2016: 1,203
Provincial Electoral District(s): St. George's—Humber
Federal Electoral District(s): Long Range Mountains
Next Election: Sept. 30, 2025 (4 year terms)
Daniel Conway, Mayor
Jocelyn Butt, Town Manager & Clerk

St. Jacques-Coomb's Cove
P.O. Box 102
English Harbour West, NL A0H 1M0
Tel: 709-888-6141; *Fax:* 709-888-6102
sjcctc@gmail.com
Municipal Type: Town
Incorporated: Nov. 15, 1971; *Area:* 83.76 sq km
Population in 2016: 588
Provincial Electoral District(s): Fortune Bay—Cape La Hune
Federal Electoral District(s): Coast of Bays—Central—Notre Dame
Next Election: Sept. 30, 2025 (4 year terms)
Cyril Brown, Mayor
Joan Sheppard, Clerk

St. Joseph's
P.O. Box 9
St Josephs, NL A0B 3A0
Tel: 709-521-2440; *Fax:* 709-521-2440
towncouncilstjosephs@gmail.com
Municipal Type: Town
Incorporated: Aug. 18, 1970; *Area:* 32.31 sq km
Population in 2016: 115
Provincial Electoral District(s): Placentia—St. Mary's
Federal Electoral District(s): Avalon
Next Election: Sept. 30, 2025 (4 year terms)
Tony Reardon, Clerk

St. Lawrence
P.O. Box 128
St Lawrence, NL A0E 2V0
Tel: 709-873-2222; *Fax:* 709-873-3352
townofstlawrence@nf.aibn.com
www.townofstlawrence.com
Municipal Type: Town
Incorporated: Nov. 15, 1949; *Area:* 35.5 sq km
Population in 2016: 1,192
Provincial Electoral District(s): Burin—Grand Bank
Federal Electoral District(s): Bonavista—Burin—Trinity
Next Election: Sept. 30, 2025 (4 year terms)
Paul Pike, Mayor
Andrea Kettle, Clerk

St. Lewis
P.O. Box 106
St Lewis, NL A0K 4W0
Tel: 709-939-2282; *Fax:* 709-939-2210
stlewistownoffice@nf.aibn.com
Municipal Type: Town
Incorporated: July 17, 1981; *Area:* 9.25 sq km
Population in 2016: 194
Provincial Electoral District(s): Cartwright—L'Anse au Clair
Federal Electoral District(s): Labrador
Next Election: Sept. 30, 2025 (4 year terms)
Helen Poole, Mayor
Lorraine Poole, Clerk

St. Lunaire-Griquet
P.O. Box 9
St Lunaire-Griquet, NL A0K 2X0
Tel: 709-623-2323; *Fax:* 709-623-2170
stlunaire.griquet@nf.aibn.com
Municipal Type: Town
Incorporated: June 10, 1958; *Area:* 16.68 sq km
Population in 2016: 604
Provincial Electoral District(s): St. Barbe—L'Anse aux Meadows
Federal Electoral District(s): Long Range Mountains
Next Election: Sept. 30, 2025 (4 year terms)
Dale Colbourne, Mayor
Linda Hillier, Clerk

St. Mary's
P.O. Box 348
St Marys, NL A0B 3B0
Tel: 709-525-2586
townofstmarys@nf.aibn.com
Municipal Type: Town
Incorporated: Dec. 13, 1966; *Area:* 37.05 sq km
Population in 2016: 347
Provincial Electoral District(s): Placentia—St. Mary's
Federal Electoral District(s): Avalon
Next Election: Sept. 30, 2025 (4 year terms)
Keith Bowen, Mayor

Patricia Walsh, Clerk

St. Pauls
P.O. Box 9
St Pauls, NL A0K 4Y0
Tel: 709-243-2279; *Fax:* 709-243-2299
townofstpauls@nf.aibn.com
Municipal Type: Town
Incorporated: July 30, 1968; *Area:* 5.35 sq km
Population in 2016: 238
Provincial Electoral District(s): Humber—Gros Morne
Federal Electoral District(s): Long Range Mountains
Next Election: Sept. 30, 2025 (4 year terms)
Melvin Reid, Mayor
Monica Pittman, Clerk

St. Shott's
General Delivery
St Shott's, NL A0A 3R0
Tel: 709-438-2817; *Fax:* 709-438-2617
Municipal Type: Town
Incorporated: May 21, 1963; *Area:* 1.14 sq km
Population in 2016: 66
Provincial Electoral District(s): Ferryland
Federal Electoral District(s): Avalon
Next Election: Sept. 30, 2025 (4 year terms)
Madonna Hewitt, Mayor
Corinna Watson, Clerk

St. Vincent's-St. Stephen's-Peter's River
P.O. Box 39
St Vincents, NL A0B 3C0
Tel: 709-525-2540; *Fax:* 709-525-2110
svstpr@nf.aibn.com
Municipal Type: Town
Incorporated: Aug. 1, 1971; *Area:* 87.5 sq km
Population in 2016: 313
Provincial Electoral District(s): Placentia—St. Mary's
Federal Electoral District(s): Avalon
Next Election: Sept. 30, 2025 (4 year terms)
Edward Raymond, Mayor
Linda Gibbons, Clerk

Salmon Cove
P.O. Box 240
Salmon Cove, NL A0A 3S0
Tel: 709-596-2101; *Fax:* 709-596-1170
townofsalmoncove@nf.aibn.com
www.salmoncove.ca
Municipal Type: Town
Incorporated: Aug. 27, 1974; *Area:* 4.21 sq km
Population in 2016: 680
Provincial Electoral District(s): Carbonear—Trinity—Bay de Verde
Federal Electoral District(s): Bonavista—Burin—Trinity
Next Election: Sept. 30, 2025 (4 year terms)
Gordon King, Mayor
Donette Morris, Clerk

Salvage
General Delivery
Salvage, NL A0G 3X0
Tel: 709-677-3535; *Fax:* 709-677-3535
Municipal Type: Town
Incorporated: Oct. 24, 1972; *Area:* 15.86 sq km
Population in 2016: 124
Provincial Electoral District(s): Terra Nova
Federal Electoral District(s): Bonavista—Burin—Trinity
Next Election: Sept. 30, 2025 (4 year terms)
Gordon Janes, Mayor
Beverly Hunter, Clerk

Sandringham
43-47 Main St.
Sandringham, NL A0G 3Y0
Tel: 709-677-2317; *Fax:* 709-677-3836
townofsandringham@yahoo.ca
sandringhamnl.weebly.com
Municipal Type: Town
Incorporated: April 30, 1968; *Area:* 9.6 sq km
Population in 2016: 229
Provincial Electoral District(s): Terra Nova
Federal Electoral District(s): Bonavista—Burin—Trinity
Next Election: Sept. 30, 2025 (4 year terms)
Glenn Arnold, Mayor
Audrey Penney, Clerk

Sandy Cove
P.O. Box 37
Site 8
Eastport, NL A0G 1Z0
Tel: 709-677-2731; *Fax:* 709-677-2731
sandycove@bellaliant.com
www.sandycovenl.com
Municipal Type: Town
Incorporated: Sept. 18, 1956; *Area:* 9.01 sq km
Population in 2016: 122
Provincial Electoral District(s): Terra Nova; Bonavista
Federal Electoral District(s): Bonavista—Burin—Trinity
Next Election: Sept. 30, 2025 (4 year terms)
Julia Whelan, Mayor
Anne Benger, Clerk

La Scie
P.O. Box 130
La Scie, NL A0K 3M0
Tel: 709-675-2266; *Fax:* 709-675-2168
townoflascie@eastlink.ca
Municipal Type: Town
Incorporated: May 25, 1955; *Area:* 29.14 sq km
Population in 2016: 872
Provincial Electoral District(s): Baie Verte—Green Bay
Federal Electoral District(s): Coast of Bays—Central—Notre Dame
Next Election: Sept. 30, 2025 (4 year terms)
Derek Tilley, Mayor
Chasity Andrews, Clerk

Seal Cove (White Bay)
P.O. Box 119
Seal Cove (White Bay), NL A0K 5E0
Tel: 709-531-2550; *Fax:* 709-531-2551
sealcovewb@nf.aibn.com
Municipal Type: Town
Incorporated: Dec. 16, 1958; *Area:* 10.79 sq km
Population in 2016: 303
Provincial Electoral District(s): Baie Verte—Green Bay
Federal Electoral District(s): Coast of Bays—Central—Notre Dame
Next Election: Sept. 30, 2025 (4 year terms)
Steward Pinken, Mayor
Patricia Rice, Clerk

Seal Cove Fortune Bay
P.O. Box 156
Seal Cove Fortune Bay, NL A0H 2G0
Tel: 709-851-4431; *Fax:* 709-851-6174
sealcovecc@nf.aibn.com
Municipal Type: Town
Incorporated: Jan. 25, 1972; *Area:* 2.42 sq km
Population in 2016: 242
Provincial Electoral District(s): Fortune Bay—Cape La Hune
Federal Electoral District(s): Coast of Bays—Central—Notre Dame
Next Election: Sept. 30, 2025 (4 year terms)
Albert Loveless, Mayor
Emily Loveless, Clerk

Small Point-Adam's Cove-Blackhead-Broad Cove
P.O. Box 160
Broad Cove, NL A0A 1L0
Tel: 709-598-2610; *Fax:* 709-598-2618
Municipal Type: Town
Incorporated: Oct. 24, 1972; *Area:* 22.22 sq km
Population in 2016: 387
Provincial Electoral District(s): Carbonear—Trinity—Bay de Verde
Federal Electoral District(s): Bonavista—Burin—Trinity
Next Election: Sept. 30, 2025 (4 year terms)
Leslie Gover, Mayor
Beverley Reynolds, Clerk

South Brook
P.O. Box 63
South Brook, NL A0J 1S0
Tel: 709-657-2206; *Fax:* 709-657-2202
townofsbrk@yahoo.ca
Municipal Type: Town
Incorporated: July 6, 1965; *Area:* 9.07 sq km
Population in 2016: 482
Provincial Electoral District(s): Baie Verte—Green Bay
Federal Electoral District(s): Coast of Bays—Central—Notre Dame; Long Range Mountains
Next Election: Sept. 30, 2025 (4 year terms)
Donald Higdon, Mayor
Janice Canning, Clerk

South River
P.O. Box 40
South River, NL A0A 3W0
Tel: 709-786-6761; *Fax:* 709-786-6760
townofsouthriver@persona.com
www.townofsouthriver.ca
Municipal Type: Town
Incorporated: June 7, 1966; *Area:* 6.06 sq km
Population in 2016: 647
Provincial Electoral District(s): Harbour Main
Federal Electoral District(s): Avalon
Next Election: Sept. 30, 2025 (4 year terms)
Scott Rose, Mayor
Marjorie Dawson, Clerk

Southern Harbour
P.O. Box 10
Southern Harbour PB, NL A0B 3H0
Tel: 709-463-2329; *Fax:* 709-463-2208
twnsouthernhr@nf.aibn.com
Municipal Type: Town
Incorporated: Aug. 20, 1968; *Area:* 5.41 sq km
Population in 2016: 369
Provincial Electoral District(s): Placentia West—Bellevue
Federal Electoral District(s): Bonavista—Burin—Trinity
Next Election: Sept. 30, 2025 (4 year terms)
Joseph Brewer, Mayor
Kelsie Emberley, Clerk

Spaniard's Bay
P.O. Box 190
Spaniards Bay, NL A0A 3X0
Tel: 709-786-3568; *Fax:* 709-786-7273
spaniardsbay@persona.ca
townofspaniardsbay.ca
Municipal Type: Town
Incorporated: June 8, 1965; *Area:* 65.73 sq km
Population in 2016: 2,653
Provincial Electoral District(s): Harbour Grace—Port de Grave
Federal Electoral District(s): Avalon
Next Election: Sept. 30, 2025 (4 year terms)
Paul Brazil, Mayor
Tony Ryan, Clerk & Manager

Springdale
P.O. Box 57
Springdale, NL A0J 1T0
Tel: 709-673-3439; *Fax:* 709-673-4969
info@townofspringdale.ca
www.townofspringdale.ca
Municipal Type: Town
Incorporated: Oct. 23, 1961; *Area:* 17.6 sq km
Population in 2016: 2,971
Provincial Electoral District(s): Baie Verte—Green Bay
Federal Electoral District(s): Coast of Bays—Central—Notre Dame
Next Election: Sept. 30, 2025 (4 year terms)
Dave Edison, Mayor
Daphne Earle, Clerk & Manager

Steady Brook
P.O. Box 117
Steady Brook, NL A2H 2N2
Tel: 709-634-7601; *Fax:* 709-634-7547
www.steadybrook.com
Municipal Type: Town
Incorporated: April 7, 1953; *Area:* 1.22 sq km
Population in 2016: 444
Provincial Electoral District(s): St. George's—Humber
Federal Electoral District(s): Long Range Mountains
Next Election: Sept. 30, 2025 (4 year terms)
Donna Thistle, Mayor
Renee Burden, Clerk & Manager

Stephenville
P.O. Box 420
Stephenville, NL A2N 2Z5
Tel: 709-643-8360; *Fax:* 709-643-2770
contactus@stephenville.ca
www.townofstephenville.com
Municipal Type: Town
Incorporated: Oct. 1, 1952; *Area:* 35.69 sq km
Population in 2016: 6,623
Provincial Electoral District(s): Stephenville—Port au Port
Federal Electoral District(s): Long Range Mountains
Next Election: Sept. 30, 2025 (4 year terms)
Tom Rose, Mayor
Jennifer Brake, Clerk

Stephenville Crossing
P.O. Box 68
Stephenville Crossing, NL A0N 2C0
Tel: 709-646-2600; *Fax:* 709-646-2065
www.thetownofstephenvillecrossing.com
Municipal Type: Town
Incorporated: Oct. 20, 1958; *Area:* 31.2 sq km
Population in 2016: 1,719
Provincial Electoral District(s): St. George's—Humber
Federal Electoral District(s): Long Range Mountains
Next Election: Sept. 30, 2025 (4 year terms)
Lisa Lucas, Mayor
Yvonne Young, Clerk

Summerford
P.O. Box 59
Summerford, NL A0G 4E0
Tel: 709-629-3419; *Fax:* 709-629-7532
townofsummerford@nf.aibn.com
Municipal Type: Town
Incorporated: Sept. 28, 1971; *Area:* 16.06 sq km
Population in 2016: 906
Provincial Electoral District(s): Lewisporte—Twillingate
Federal Electoral District(s): Coast of Bays—Central—Notre Dame
Next Election: Sept. 30, 2025 (4 year terms)
Kevin Barnes, Mayor
Vicky Anstey, Clerk

Sunnyside
P.O. Box 89
Sunnyside, NL A0B 3J0
Tel: 709-472-4506; *Fax:* 709-472-4182
townofsunnyside@eastlink.ca
Municipal Type: Town
Incorporated: March 10, 1970; *Area:* 37.95 sq km
Population in 2016: 396
Provincial Electoral District(s): Placentia West—Bellevue
Federal Electoral District(s): Bonavista—Burin—Trinity
Next Election: Sept. 30, 2025 (4 year terms)
Robert Snook, Mayor
G. Philip Smith, Clerk

Terra Nova
1 River Rd.
Terra Nova, NL A0C 1L0
Tel: 709-265-6543; *Fax:* 709-265-6533
townofterranova@nf.aibn.com
Municipal Type: Town
Incorporated: Sept. 13, 1960; *Area:* 2.46 sq km
Population in 2016: 73
Provincial Electoral District(s): Terra Nova
Federal Electoral District(s): Bonavista—Burin—Trinity
Next Election: Sept. 30, 2025 (4 year terms)
Cynthia Osmond, Mayor
Thelma Greening, Clerk

Terrenceville
P.O. Box 100
Terrenceville, NL A0E 2X0
Tel: 709-662-2204; *Fax:* 709-662-2071
terrencevilletownoffice@nf.aibn.com
Municipal Type: Town
Incorporated: Aug. 15, 1972; *Area:* 14.5 sq km
Population in 2016: 482
Provincial Electoral District(s): Placentia West—Bellevue
Federal Electoral District(s): Bonavista—Burin—Trinity
Next Election: Sept. 30, 2025 (4 year terms)
Sheila Cox, Mayor
Joan Rideout, Clerk

Tilt Cove
P.O. Box 22
Tilt Cove, NL A0K 3M0
Tel: 709-675-2641
Municipal Type: Town
Incorporated: March 4, 1969; *Area:* 3.1 sq km
Population in 2016: 5
Provincial Electoral District(s): Baie Verte—Green Bay
Federal Electoral District(s): Coast of Bays—Central—Notre Dame
Next Election: Sept. 30, 2025 (4 year terms)
Donald Collins, Mayor
Margaret Collins, Clerk

Torbay
P.O. Box 1160
1288 Torbay Rd.
Torbay, NL A1K 1K4
Tel: 709-437-6532; *Fax:* 709-437-1309
info@torbay.ca
torbay.ca

Municipal Type: Town
Incorporated: Oct. 24, 1972; *Area:* 34.88 sq km
Population in 2016: 7,899
Provincial Electoral District(s): Cape St. Francis
Federal Electoral District(s): St. John's East
Next Election: Sept. 30, 2025 (4 year terms)
Craig Scott, Mayor, 709-437-6532
Dawn Chaplin, Chief Administration Officer

Traytown
1 Poplar Lane
Traytown, NL A0G 4K0
Tel: 709-533-2156; *Fax:* 709-533-2155
townoftraytown@eastlink.ca
traytown.net
Municipal Type: Town
Incorporated: June 15, 1971; *Area:* 13.31 sq km
Population in 2016: 267
Provincial Electoral District(s): Terra Nova
Federal Electoral District(s): Bonavista—Burin—Trinity
Next Election: Sept. 30, 2025 (4 year terms)
Shannon Carter, Mayor
Sarah Patten, Clerk

Trepassey
P.O. Box 129
Trepassey, NL A0A 4B0
Tel: 709-438-2641; *Fax:* 709-438-2749
townoftrepassey2@hotmail.com
Municipal Type: Town
Incorporated: Aug. 1, 1967; *Area:* 55.81 sq km
Population in 2016: 481
Provincial Electoral District(s): Ferryland
Federal Electoral District(s): Avalon
Next Election: Sept. 30, 2025 (4 year terms)
Joan Power, Mayor
Valerie Wilson, Acting Clerk

Trinity
P.O. Box 42
Trinity, NL A0C 2S0
Tel: 709-464-3836; *Fax:* 709-464-3836
counciltrinity@netscape.net
www.townoftrinity.com
Municipal Type: Town
Incorporated: May 13, 1969; *Area:* 12.92 sq km
Population in 2016: 169
Provincial Electoral District(s): Bonavista
Federal Electoral District(s): Bonavista—Burin—Trinity
Next Election: Sept. 30, 2025 (4 year terms)
Jim Miller, Mayor
Linda Sweet, Clerk

Trinity Bay North
P.O. Box 91
Port Union, NL A0C 2J0
Tel: 709-469-2571; *Fax:* 709-469-3444
info@trinitybaynorth.com
www.trinitybaynorth.com
Municipal Type: Town
Incorporated: Jan. 1, 2005; *Area:* 14.28 sq km
Population in 2016: 1,819
Provincial Electoral District(s): Bonavista
Federal Electoral District(s): Bonavista—Burin—Trinity
Next Election: Sept. 30, 2025 (4 year terms)
Note: Effective Jan. 1, 2005, the towns of Catalina, Port Union, & Melrose amalgamated to form the new town of Trinity Bay North. Little Catalina was included on Oct. 1, 2010.
Shelly Blackmore, Mayor
Valerie Rogers, Clerk

Triton
P.O. Box 10
Triton, NL A0J 1V0
Tel: 709-263-2264; *Fax:* 709-263-2381
townoftriton@eastlink.ca
www.townoftriton.ca
Municipal Type: Town
Incorporated: March 11, 1958; *Area:* 7.55 sq km
Population in 2016: 983
Provincial Electoral District(s): Baie Verte—Green Bay
Federal Electoral District(s): Coast of Bays—Central—Notre Dame
Next Election: Sept. 30, 2025 (4 year terms)
Jason Roberts, Mayor
Marcus Vincent, Clerk

Trout River
P.O. Box 89
Trout River, NL A0K 5P0
Tel: 709-451-5376; *Fax:* 709-451-2127
townclerk@townoftroutriver.com
townoftroutriver.com
Municipal Type: Town
Incorporated: April 12, 1966; *Area:* 5.91 sq km
Population in 2016: 552
Provincial Electoral District(s): Humber—Gros Morne
Federal Electoral District(s): Long Range Mountains
Next Election: Sept. 30, 2025 (4 year terms)
Horace Crocker, Mayor
Lorraine Barnes, Clerk

Twillingate
P.O. Box 220
Twillingate, NL A0G 4M0
Tel: 709-884-2438; *Fax:* 709-884-5278
hello@townoftwillingate.ca
townoftwillingate.ca
Municipal Type: Town
Incorporated: Jan. 1, 1992; *Area:* 25.74 sq km
Population in 2016: 2,196
Provincial Electoral District(s): Lewisporte—Twillingate
Federal Electoral District(s): Coast of Bays—Central—Notre Dame
Next Election: Sept. 30, 2025 (4 year terms)
Vacant, Mayor
Jonathan Galgay, Clerk

Upper Island Cove
P.O. Box 149
Upper Island Cove, NL A0A 4E0
Tel: 709-589-2503; *Fax:* 709-589-2522
townoffice@upperislandcove.ca
upperislandcove.ca
Municipal Type: Town
Incorporated: Oct. 19, 1965; *Area:* 7.85 sq km
Population in 2016: 1,561
Provincial Electoral District(s): Harbour Grace—Port de Grave
Federal Electoral District(s): Avalon
Next Election: Sept. 30, 2025 (4 year terms)
Philip Lundrigan, Mayor
Dorothy Mercer, Clerk

Victoria
P.O. Box 130
Victoria, NL A0A 4G0
Tel: 709-596-3783; *Fax:* 709-596-5020
townofvictoria@nf.aibn.com
Municipal Type: Town
Incorporated: 1971; *Area:* 17.64 sq km
Population in 2016: 1,800
Provincial Electoral District(s): Carbonear—Trinity—Bay de Verde
Federal Electoral District(s): Avalon
Next Election: Sept. 30, 2025 (4 year terms)
Barry Dooley, Mayor
Shelly Butt, Clerk

Wabana
P.O. Box 1229
Wabana, NL A0A 4H0
Tel: 709-488-2990; *Fax:* 709-488-3181
info@townofwabana.net
www.townofwabana.net
Municipal Type: Town
Incorporated: Aug. 28, 1950; *Area:* 14.5 sq km
Population in 2016: 2,146
Provincial Electoral District(s): Conception Bay East—Bell Island
Federal Electoral District(s): St. John's East
Next Election: Sept. 30, 2025 (4 year terms)
Gary Gosine, Mayor
Jenna Vokey, Town Clerk

Wabush
P.O. Box 190
Wabush, NL A0R 1B0
Tel: 709-282-5696; *Fax:* 709-282-5142
labradorwest.com
Municipal Type: Town
Incorporated: April 11, 1967; *Area:* 46.25 sq km
Population in 2016: 1,906
Provincial Electoral District(s): Labrador West
Federal Electoral District(s): Labrador
Next Election: Sept. 30, 2025 (4 year terms)
Ronald Barron, Mayor
Charie Perry, Town Manager

West St. Modeste
P.O. Box 78
West St Modeste, NL A0K 5S0
Tel: 709-927-5583; *Fax:* 709-927-5898
townofweststmodeste@hotmail.ca
Municipal Type: Town
Incorporated: Aug. 1, 1975; *Area:* 7.78 sq km
Population in 2016: 111
Provincial Electoral District(s): Cartwright—L'Anse au Clair
Federal Electoral District(s): Labrador
Next Election: Sept. 30, 2025 (4 year terms)
Agnes Pike, Mayor
Sandra O'Dell, Clerk

Westport
P.O. Box 29
Westport, NL A0K 5R0
Tel: 709-224-5501; *Fax:* 709-224-5501
westportnl@gmail.com
Municipal Type: Town
Incorporated: July 18, 1967; *Area:* 5.13 sq km
Population in 2016: 195
Provincial Electoral District(s): Baie Verte—Green Bay
Federal Electoral District(s): Coast of Bays—Central—Notre Dame
Next Election: Sept. 30, 2025 (4 year terms)
Sadie Hewitt, Mayor
Peggy Randell, Clerk

Whitbourne
P.O. Box 119
Whitbourne, NL A0B 3K0
Tel: 709-759-2780; *Fax:* 709-759-2016
info@whitbournenl.com
whitbournenl.com
Municipal Type: Town
Incorporated: April 16, 1968; *Area:* 21.41 sq km
Population in 2016: 890
Provincial Electoral District(s): Placentia—St. Mary's
Federal Electoral District(s): Bonavista—Burin—Trinity
Next Election: Sept. 30, 2025 (4 year terms)
Hilda Whelan, Mayor
Crystal Peddle, Clerk

Whiteway
420 Main St.
Whiteway, NL A0B 3L0
Tel: 709-588-2948; *Fax:* 709-588-2985
townofwhiteway@eastlink.ca
Municipal Type: Town
Incorporated: Oct. 3, 1975; *Area:* 22.64 sq km

Population in 2016: 373
Provincial Electoral District(s): Carbonear—Trinity—Bay de Verde
Federal Electoral District(s): Bonavista—Burin—Trinity
Next Election: Sept. 30, 2025 (4 year terms)
Justin Mahoney, Mayor
Erica Jackson, Clerk

Winterland
P.O. Box 10
Winterland, NL A0E 2Y0
Tel: 709-279-3701; *Fax:* 709-279-3702
townofwinterland@hotmail.com
www.townofwinterland.com
Municipal Type: Town
Incorporated: Nov. 24, 1970; *Area:* 54.34 sq km
Population in 2016: 390
Provincial Electoral District(s): Burin—Grand Bank
Federal Electoral District(s): Bonavista—Burin—Trinity
Next Election: Sept. 30, 2025 (4 year terms)
Ches Kenway, Mayor
Marlyese Simms, Clerk

Winterton
P.O. Box 59
Winterton, NL A0B 3M0
Tel: 709-583-2010; *Fax:* 709-583-2099
info@winterton.ca
www.winterton.ca
Municipal Type: Town
Incorporated: April 15, 1964; *Area:* 10.52 sq km
Population in 2016: 450
Provincial Electoral District(s): Carbonear—Trinity—Bay de Verde
Federal Electoral District(s): Bonavista—Burin—Trinity
Next Election: Sept. 30, 2025 (4 year terms)
Mark Sheppard, Mayor
Suzanne Coates, Clerk

Witless Bay
P.O. Box 130
Witless Bay, NL A0A 4K0
Tel: 709-334-3407; *Fax:* 709-334-2377
townofwitlessbay@nl.rogers.com
www.witlessbay.ca
Municipal Type: Town
Incorporated: Jan. 1, 1986; *Area:* 17.49 sq km
Population in 2016: 1,619
Provincial Electoral District(s): Ferryland
Federal Electoral District(s): St. John's South—Mount Pearl
Next Election: Sept. 30, 2025 (4 year terms)

René Estrada, Mayor
Geraldine Caul, Clerk

Woodstock
19 Park St.
Woodstock, NL A0K 5X0
Tel: 709-251-3176; *Fax:* 709-251-3176
townofwoodstock@nf.aibn.com
Municipal Type: Town
Incorporated: Sept. 29, 1970; *Area:* 10.09 sq km
Population in 2016: 190
Provincial Electoral District(s): Baie Verte—Green Bay
Federal Electoral District(s): Coast of Bays—Central—Notre Dame
Next Election: Sept. 30, 2025 (4 year terms)
Kirk Simms, Mayor
Tracey Decker, Clerk

Woody Point
P.O. Box 100
Woody Point, NL A0K 1P0
Tel: 709-453-2273; *Fax:* 709-453-2270
woodypoint.net
Municipal Type: Town
Incorporated: March 27, 1956; *Area:* 2.91 sq km
Population in 2016: 282
Provincial Electoral District(s): Humber—Gros Morne
Federal Electoral District(s): Long Range Mountains
Next Election: Sept. 30, 2025 (4 year terms)
Vacant, Mayor
Jacqueline Blanchard, Clerk

York Harbour
P.O. Box 179
136-138 Main St.
York Harbour, NL A0L 1L0
Tel: 709-681-2280; *Fax:* 709-681-2799
yorkharbourcouncil@nf.aibn.com
www.yorkharbourlarkharbour.com
Municipal Type: Town
Incorporated: June 27, 1972; *Area:* 3.9 sq km
Population in 2016: 344
Provincial Electoral District(s): Humber—Bay of Islands
Federal Electoral District(s): Long Range Mountains
Next Election: Sept. 30, 2025 (4 year terms)
Charles Kendell, Mayor
Michelle Sheppard, Clerk

NORTHWEST TERRITORIES

The Department of Municipal and Community Affairs is responsible for the following legislation regarding municipalities in the Territory: Business License Act; Charter Communities Act; Cities, Towns and Villages Act; Civil Emergency Measures Act; Community Planning and Development Act; Consumer Protection Act; Cost of Credit Disclosure Act; Dog Act; Film Classification Act; Fire Prevention Act; Hamlets Act; Home Owner's Property Tax Rebate Act; Local Authorities Elections Act; Lotteries Act; Property Assessment and Taxation Act; Real Estate Agent's Licensing Act; Senior Citizens and Disabled Persons Property Tax Relief Act; Tłı̨chǫ Community Government Act; Western Canada Lottery Act.

Incorporation as a city, town or village is determined by the value of all assessable land. Incorporation values: Village, $10 million; Town, $50 million; City, $200 million. All tax-based. Hamlets and Charter Communities may request tax-based status.

Local Authorities Elections: three years for cities, towns and villages; two years/staggered terms for hamlets and settlements; two to three years for charter communities. The Minister may extend or shorten terms on applications. Except for settlement councils, heads of councils are elected by separate ballot. First Nations conduct their own electoral process.

Heads of Councils: Mayor, K'wati, Ehk'Wahtide, Chief, Chairperson.

First Nations provide municipal services as the main governing authority in several communities. On March 13, 2014, the Charter Community of Déline voted in favour of self-government. The Déline Gotine Government began operating in September 2016, and is responsible for matters such as health care, justice and adoption.

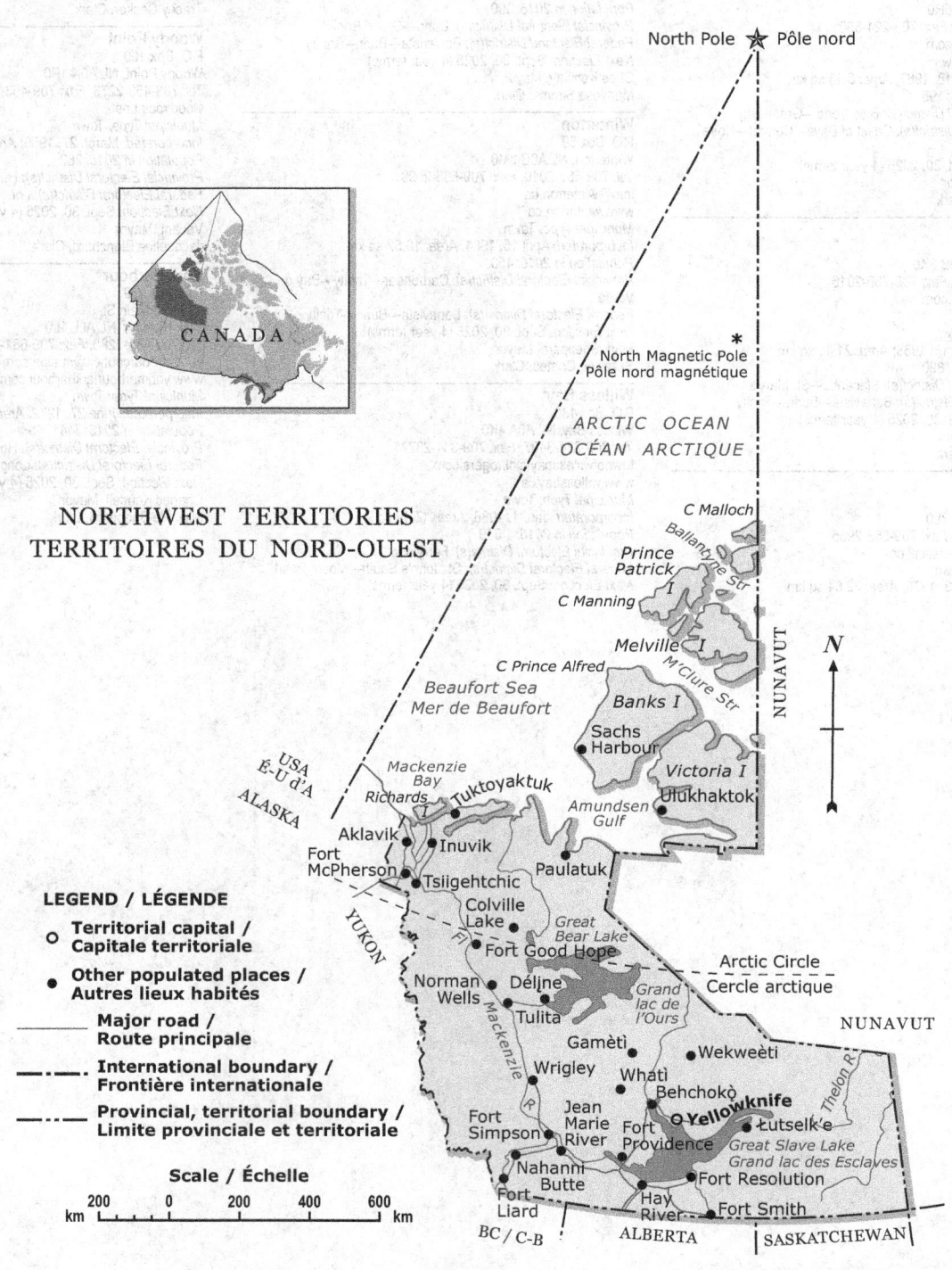

www.atlas.gc.ca

Northwest Territories

Major Municipalities in Northwest Territories

Yellowknife
P.O. Box 580
4807 - 52nd St.
Yellowknife, NT X1A 2N4
Tel: 867-920-5600; *Fax:* 867-920-5649
communications@yellowknife.ca
www.yellowknife.ca
Municipal Type: City
Incorporated: Jan. 1, 1970; *Area:* 105.22 sq km
Population in 2016: 19,569
Provincial Electoral District(s): Yellowknife South; Yellowknife Centre; Frame Lake; Great Slave; Weledeh; Kam Lake, Range Lake
Federal Electoral District(s): Northwest Territories
Next Election: Oct. 2022 (4 year terms)
Rebecca Alty, Mayor
Niels Konge, Councillor
Shauna Morgan, Councillor
Julian Morse, Councillor
Cynthia Mufandaedza, Councillor
Steve Payne, Councillor
Rommel Silverio, Councillor
Stacie Smith, Councillor
Robin Williams, Councillor
Debbie Gillard, City Clerk, 867-920-5646
Sheila Bassi-Kellett, City Manager, 867-920-5693
Chris Greencorn, Director, Public Works, 867-920-5637
Jennifer Hunt-Poitras, Director, Public Safety, 867-920-5661
Grant White, Director, Community Services, 867-920-5624
Sharolynn Woodward, Director, Corporate Services, 867-920-5666
John Fredericks, Fire Chief, 867-766-5501

Other Municipalities in Northwest Territories

Aklavik
P.O. Box 88
Aklavik, NT X0E 0A0
Tel: 867-978-2351; *Fax:* 867-978-2434
www.aklavik.ca
Municipal Type: Hamlet
Incorporated: Jan. 1, 1974; *Area:* 8.16 sq km
Population in 2016: 590
Provincial Electoral District(s): Mackenzie Delta
Federal Electoral District(s): Northwest Territories
Next Election: Dec. 13, 2021
Andrew Charlie, Mayor
Fred Behrens, Senior Administrative Officer

Behchokò
P.O. Box 68
Behchokò, NT X0E 0Y0
Tel: 867-392-6500; *Fax:* 867-392-6139
www.tlicho.ca/community/behchoko
Municipal Type: Tlicho Community Government
Area: 75.08 sq km
Population in 2016: 1,874
Provincial Electoral District(s): Monfwi
Federal Electoral District(s): Northwest Territories
Clifford Daniels, Chief
Graeme Drew, Senior Administrative Officer

Colville Lake
Behdzi Ahda First Nation
P.O. Box 53
Colville Lake, NT X0E 1L0
Tel: 867-709-2200; *Fax:* 867-709-2202
behdziahda.com
Municipal Type: Settlement Corporation
Incorporated: Nov. 30, 1995; *Area:* 128.3 sq km
Population in 2016: 129
Provincial Electoral District(s): Sahtu
Federal Electoral District(s): Northwest Territories
Wilbert Kochon, Chief
Joseph Kochon, Senior Administrative Officer

Déline
P.O. Box 156
Déline, NT X0E 0G0
Tel: 867-589-8100; *Fax:* 867-589-8101
info@gov.deline.ca
www.deline.ca
Municipal Type: Charter Community
Incorporated: April 1, 1993; *Area:* 79.33 sq km
Population in 2016: 533

Provincial Electoral District(s): Sahtu
Federal Electoral District(s): Northwest Territories
Note: Déline sets its election date through its community charter. On March 13, 2014, the community voted in favour of self-government. Once approved, the Déline Got'ine Government will be formed.
Leeroy Andre, Ekw'atide (Chief), 867-586-8100
Paulina Roche, Chief Executive Officer, 867-589-8100

Dettah
Yellowknives Dene First Nation
P.O. Box 2514
Yellowknife, NT X1A 2P8
Tel: 867-873-4307; *Fax:* 867-873-5969
dettahadmin@ykdene.com
ykdene.com
Municipal Type: First Nations/Governing Authority
Area: 1.34 sq km
Population in 2016: 219
Provincial Electoral District(s): Tu Nedhé-Wiilideh
Federal Electoral District(s): Northwest Territories
Edward Sangris, Chief of Dettah, 867-873-4307
Ernest Betsina, Chief of Ndilo, 867-673-8951, Fax: 867-873-8545
Jason Snaggs, Chief Executive Officer

Enterprise
526 Robin Rd.
Enterprise, NT X0E 0R1
Tel: 867-984-3491; *Fax:* 867-984-3400
Municipal Type: Hamlet
Incorporated: July 1, 1988; *Area:* 286.9 sq km
Population in 2016: 106
Provincial Electoral District(s): Deh Cho
Federal Electoral District(s): Northwest Territories
Next Election: Dec. 13, 2021
Winnifred Cadieux, Mayor
Tammy Neal, Senior Administrative Officer

Fort Good Hope
K'asho Got'ine Charter Community
P.O. Box 80
Fort Good Hope, NT X0E 0H0
Tel: 867-598-2231; *Fax:* 867-598-2024
Other Information: Alternate Phone: 867-598-2232
Municipal Type: Charter Community
Incorporated: April 1, 1995; *Area:* 47.14 sq km
Population in 2016: 516
Provincial Electoral District(s): Sahtu
Federal Electoral District(s): Northwest Territories
Note: Fort Good Hope sets its election date through its community charter.
Wilfred Glenn McNeely Jr., Chief
Ben Coffie, Senior Administrative Officer

Fort Liard
General Delivery
Fort Liard, NT X0G 0A0
Tel: 867-770-4104
hamlet@fortliard.com
www.fortliard.com
Municipal Type: Hamlet
Incorporated: April 1, 1987; *Area:* 67.96 sq km
Population in 2016: 500
Provincial Electoral District(s): Nahendeh
Federal Electoral District(s): Northwest Territories
Next Election: Dec. 13, 2021
Genevieve McLeod, Mayor
John W. McKee, Interim Senior Administrative Officer

Fort McPherson
P.O. Box 57
Fort McPherson, NT X0E 0J0
Tel: 867-952-2428; *Fax:* 867-952-2725
www.fortmcpherson.ca
Municipal Type: Hamlet
Incorporated: Nov. 1, 1986; *Area:* 53.06 sq km
Population in 2016: 700
Provincial Electoral District(s): Mackenzie Delta
Federal Electoral District(s): Northwest Territories
Next Election: Dec. 13, 2021
William Koe, Mayor
Morag Macpherson, Senior Administrative Officer

Fort Providence
P.O. Box 290
Fort Providence, NT X0E 0L0
Tel: 867-699-3441; *Fax:* 867-699-3360
Municipal Type: Hamlet
Incorporated: Jan. 1, 1987; *Area:* 256.33 sq km
Population in 2016: 695
Provincial Electoral District(s): Deh Cho

Federal Electoral District(s): Northwest Territories
Next Election: Dec. 13, 2021
Danny Beaulieu, Mayor
Susan Christie, Senior Administrative Officer

Fort Resolution
General Delivery
P.O. Box 197
Fort Resolution, NT X0E 0M0
Tel: 867-394-4556; *Fax:* 867-394-5415
Municipal Type: Settlement Corporation
Incorporated: April 1, 1988; *Area:* 455.06 sq km
Population in 2016: 470
Provincial Electoral District(s): Tu Nedhé-Wiilideh
Federal Electoral District(s): Northwest Territories
Todd Francis, Interim Senior Administrative Officer

Fort Simpson
P.O. Box 438
Fort Simpson, NT X0E 0N0
Tel: 867-695-2253; *Fax:* 867-695-2005
fortsimpson.com
Municipal Type: Village
Incorporated: Jan. 1, 1973; *Area:* 78.32 sq km
Population in 2016: 1,202
Provincial Electoral District(s): Nahendeh
Federal Electoral District(s): Northwest Territories
Next Election: Oct. 21, 2024 (3 year terms)
Sean Whelly, Mayor
Darrell White, Senior Administrative Officer

Fort Smith
P.O. Box 147
174 McDougal Rd.
Fort Smith, NT X0E 0P0
Tel: 867-872-8400; *Fax:* 867-872-8401
townoffortsmith@fortsmith.ca
www.fortsmith.ca
Municipal Type: Town
Incorporated: Oct. 1, 1966; *Area:* 92.79 sq km
Population in 2016: 2,542
Provincial Electoral District(s): Thebacha
Federal Electoral District(s): Northwest Territories
Next Election: Oct. 21, 2024 (3 year terms)
Sean Whelly, Mayor
Cynthia White, Senior Administrative Officer

Gamètì
Gamètì First Nation
P.O. Box 1
Gamètì, NT X0E 1R0
Tel: 867-997-3441; *Fax:* 867-997-3411
www.tlicho.ca/community/gameti
Municipal Type: Tlicho Community Government
Incorporated: Aug. 4, 2005; *Area:* 9.18 sq km
Population in 2016: 278
Provincial Electoral District(s): Monfwi
Federal Electoral District(s): Northwest Territories
David Wedawin, Chief
Memory Murefu, Senior Administrative Officer

Hay River
#100, 62 Woodland Dr.
Hay River, NT X0E 1G1
Tel: 867-874-6522; *Fax:* 867-874-3237
townhall@hayriver.com
hayriver.com
Municipal Type: Town
Incorporated: June 16, 1963; *Area:* 132.58 sq km
Population in 2016: 3,528
Provincial Electoral District(s): Hay River North; Hay River South
Federal Electoral District(s): Northwest Territories
Next Election: Oct. 21, 2024 (3 year terms)
Kandis Jameson, Mayor
Glenn Smith, Senior Administrative Officer, 867-874-6522

Inuvik
P.O. Box 1160
2 Firth St.
Inuvik, NT X0E 0T0
Tel: 867-777-8600; *Fax:* 867-777-8601
info@inuvik.ca
www.inuvik.ca
Municipal Type: Town
Incorporated: Jan. 1, 1979; *Area:* 49.76 sq km
Population in 2016: 3,243
Provincial Electoral District(s): Inuvik Twin Lakes; Inuvik Boot Lake
Federal Electoral District(s): Northwest Territories
Next Election: Oct. 21, 2024 (3 year terms)
Clarence Wood, Mayor
Grant Hood, Senior Administrative Officer, 867-777-8608

Jean Marie River

Tthets'ek'ehdeli First Nation
General Delivery
Jean Marie River, NT X0E 0N0
Tel: 867-809-2000; *Fax:* 867-809-2002
jmrfn.com
Municipal Type: First Nations/Governing Authority
Area: 37.26 sq km
Population in 2016: 77
Provincial Electoral District(s): Nahendeh
Federal Electoral District(s): Northwest Territories
Stanley Sanguez, Chief
Brenda McDonald, Senior Administrative Officer

Kakisa

Ka'a'gee Tu First Nation
P.O. Box 4428
Hay River, NT X0E 1G4
Tel: 867-825-2000; *Fax:* 867-825-2002
Municipal Type: First Nations/Governing Authority
Area: 94.82 sq km
Population in 2016: 36
Provincial Electoral District(s): Deh Cho
Federal Electoral District(s): Northwest Territories
Lloyd Chicot, Chief
Ruby Simba, Council Manager

Katlodeeche

Katlodeeche First Nation
P.O. Box 3060
Hay River, NT X0E 1G4
Tel: 867-874-6701; *Fax:* 867-874-3229
receptionist@katlodeeche.com
katlodeeche.com
Municipal Type: Reserve
Area: 134.21 sq km
Population in 2016: 309
Provincial Electoral District(s): Deh Cho
Federal Electoral District(s): Northwest Territories
Note: Also known as Hay River Reserve or Hay River Dene 1.
Katlodeeche may also be spelled K'atl'odeeche.
Roy Fabian, Chief, 867-674-6701
Peter Groenen, Senior Administrative Officer, 867-874-6701

Lutselk'e

Lutselk'e Dene Band
P.O. Box 28
Lutselk'e, NT X0E 1A0
Tel: 867-370-7000; *Fax:* 867-370-3010
Municipal Type: First Nations/Governing Authority
Area: 43.01 sq km
Population in 2016: 303
Provincial Electoral District(s): Tu Nedhé-Wiilideh
Federal Electoral District(s): Northwest Territories
Note: Lutselk'e may also be spelled Lutsel K'e.
Darryl Marlowe, Chief
Hanna Catholique, Administrator

Nahanni Butte

Nahanni Butte Dene Band
General Delivery
Nahanni Butte, NT X0E 0N0
Tel: 867-602-2900; *Fax:* 867-602-2910
Municipal Type: First Nations/Governing Authority
Area: 78.96 sq km
Population in 2016: 87
Provincial Electoral District(s): Nahendeh
Federal Electoral District(s): Northwest Territories
Peter Marcellais, Chief
Vacant , Band Manager

Norman Wells

P.O. Box 5
3 Mackenzie Dr.
Norman Wells, NT X0E 0V0
Tel: 867-587-3700
towninformation@normanwells.com
www.normanwells.com

Municipal Type: Town
Incorporated: April 12, 1992; *Area:* 93.28 sq km
Population in 2016: 778
Provincial Electoral District(s): Sahtu
Federal Electoral District(s): Northwest Territories
Next Election: Oct. 21, 2024 (3 year terms)
Vacant, Mayor
Cathy Clarke, Town Manager

Paulatuk

P.O. Box 98
Paulatuk, NT X0E 1N0
Tel: 867-580-3531; *Fax:* 867-580-3703
Municipal Type: Hamlet
Incorporated: April 1, 1987; *Area:* 66.76 sq km
Population in 2016: 265
Provincial Electoral District(s): Nunakput
Federal Electoral District(s): Northwest Territories
Next Election: Dec. 13, 2021
Ray Ruben, Sr., Mayor
John Holland, Senior Administrative Officer

Sachs Harbour

General Delivery
P.O. Box 90
Sachs Harbour, NT X0E 0Z0
Tel: 867-690-4351; *Fax:* 867-690-4802
Municipal Type: Hamlet
Incorporated: April 1, 1986; *Area:* 290.94 sq km
Population in 2016: 103
Provincial Electoral District(s): Nunakput
Federal Electoral District(s): Northwest Territories
Next Election: Dec. 13, 2021
Floyd Lennie, Mayor
Betty Haogak, Senior Administrative Officer

Trout Lake

Sambaa K'e Dene Band
P.O. Box 10
Trout Lake, NT X0E 1Z0
Tel: 867-206-2800; *Fax:* 867-206-2828
Municipal Type: First Nations/Governing Authority
Area: 119.42 sq km
Population in 2016: 88
Provincial Electoral District(s): Nahendeh
Federal Electoral District(s): Northwest Territories
Dolphus Jumbo, Chief
Ruby Jumbo, Band Manager

Tsiigehtchic

General Delivery
Tsiigehtchic, NT X0E 0B0
Tel: 867-953-3201; *Fax:* 867-953-3302
Municipal Type: Charter Community
Incorporated: June 21, 1993; *Area:* 48.98 sq km
Population in 2016: 172
Provincial Electoral District(s): Mackenzie Delta
Federal Electoral District(s): Northwest Territories
Note: Tsiigehtchic sets its election date through its community charter.
Phillip Blake, Chief
Grant Scott, Senior Administrative Officer

Tuktoyaktuk

P.O. Box 120
Tuktoyaktuk, NT X0E 1C0
Tel: 867-977-2286; *Fax:* 867-977-2110
www.tuktoyaktuk.ca
Municipal Type: Hamlet
Incorporated: April 1, 1970; *Area:* 11.07 sq km
Population in 2016: 898
Provincial Electoral District(s): Nunakput
Federal Electoral District(s): Northwest Territories
Next Election: Dec. 13, 2021
Merven Gruben, Mayor
Shawn Stuckey, Senior Administrative Officer

Tulita

General Delivery
P.O. Box 91
Tulita, NT X0E 0K0
Tel: 867-588-4471; *Fax:* 867-588-4908
tulita2019@outlook.com
discovertulita.ca
Municipal Type: Hamlet
Incorporated: April 1, 1984; *Area:* 51.74 sq km
Population in 2016: 477
Provincial Electoral District(s): Sahtü
Federal Electoral District(s): Northwest Territories
Next Election: Dec. 13, 2021
Rocky Norwegian Sr., Mayor
Don Smeltzer, Interim Senior Administrative Officer

Ulukhaktok

P.O. Box 157
Ulukhaktok, NT X0E 0S0
Tel: 867-396-8000; *Fax:* 867-396-8001
Municipal Type: Hamlet
Incorporated: April 1, 1984; *Area:* 124.43 sq km
Population in 2016: 396
Provincial Electoral District(s): Nunakput
Federal Electoral District(s): Northwest Territories
Next Election: Dec. 13, 2021
Note: Formerly known as Holman.
Laverna Klengenberg, Mayor
Mike Rudkin, Senior Administrative Officer

Wekweeti

Community Government of Wekweeti
P.O. Box 69
Wekweeti, NT X0E 1W0
Tel: 867-713-2010; *Fax:* 867-713-2030
www.tlicho.ca/community/wekweeti
Municipal Type: Tlicho Community Government
Incorporated: Aug. 4, 2005; *Area:* 14.66 sq km
Population in 2016: 129
Provincial Electoral District(s): Monfwi
Federal Electoral District(s): Northwest Territories
Charlie Football, Chief
LeeAnn Rabesca, Senior Administrative Officer

Whatì

Community Government of Whatì
P.O. Box 71
Whatì, NT X0E 1P0
Tel: 867-573-3401; *Fax:* 867-573-3018
www.tlicho.ca/community/whati
Municipal Type: Tlicho Community Government
Incorporated: Aug. 4, 2005; *Area:* 15.18 sq km
Population in 2016: 470
Provincial Electoral District(s): Monfwi
Federal Electoral District(s): Western Arctic
Note: Formerly known as Lac La Martre.
Alfonz Nitsiza, Chief
Lisa Nitsiza, Senior Administrative Officer

Wrigley

Pehdzeh Ki First Nation
General Delivery
Wrigley, NT X0E 1E0
Tel: 867-581-3321; *Fax:* 867-581-3229
info@pkfn.ca
pkfn.ca
Municipal Type: First Nations/Governing Authority
Area: 55.83 sq km
Population in 2016: 119
Provincial Electoral District(s): Nahendeh
Federal Electoral District(s): Northwest Territories
Lloyd Moses, Chief
Kelly Pennycook, Band Manager

NOVA SCOTIA

Nova Scotia is geographically divided into 18 counties. Twelve of these constitute separate municipalities (four are regional municipalities). The remaining six are each divided into two districts and each of these constitutes a separate municipality. Thus there are 20 rural municipalities. Within each of these areas are 25 autonomous incorporated towns and other local organizations with limited jurisdiction, including school boards, boards of school trustees, village commissions, local service commissions, rural fire districts and other special purpose forms.

Incorporation of a town is governed by the Municipal Government Act, Sections 371 to 382 (dissolution is governed by Sections 394 to 402).

The organization of municipalities and villages is governed by the Municipal Government Act. Additional regulation is provided by the Municipal Finance Corporation Act.

All general and special municipal elections, including elections for school board members, are governed by the Municipal Elections Act. The term of office for mayors, councillors, aldermen, and elective school board members is four years. Elections take place on the third Saturday in October in every four years (2020, 2024, etc.).

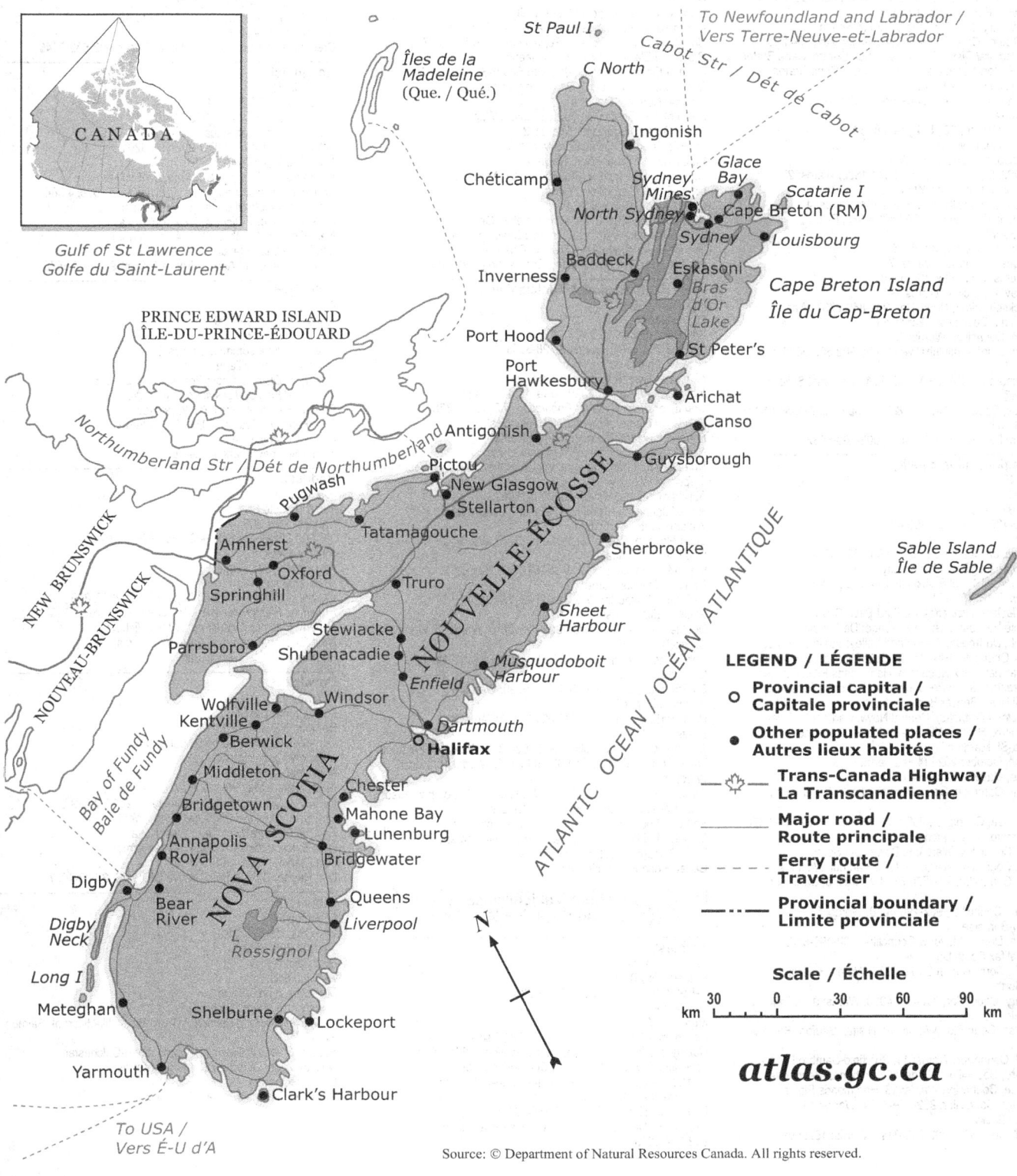

Source: © Department of Natural Resources Canada. All rights reserved.

Nova Scotia

Counties & Municipal Districts in Nova Scotia

Cape Breton
320 Esplanade
Sydney, NS B1P 7B9
Tel: 902-563-5005; *Fax:* 902-564-0481
cbrm@cbrm.ns.ca
www.cbrm.ns.ca
Other Information: Citizen Service Centre, Phone: 902-563-5080
Municipal Type: Regional Municipality
Incorporated: Aug. 1, 1995; *Area:* 2,430.06 sq km
County or District: Cape Breton; *Population in 2016:* 94,285
Provincial Electoral District(s): Cape Breton Centre; Cape Breton East; Cape Breton North; Cape Breton Nova; Cape Breton South; Cape Breton-The Lakes
Federal Electoral District(s): Cape Breton-Canso; Sydney-Victoria
Next Election: October 2024 (4 year terms)
Amanda McDougall, Mayor
Gordon MacDonald, Councillor, Wards: 1
Earlene MacMullin, Councillor, 902-574-1822, Wards: 2
Cyril MacDonald, Councillor, Wards: 3
Steve Gillespie, Councillor, 902-539-2144, Wards: 4
Eldon MacDonald, Councillor, 902-539-0588, Fax: 902-564-1036, Wards: 5
Glenn Paruch, Councillor, Wards: 6
Steve Parsons, Councillor, Wards: 7
James Edwards, Councillor, Wards: 8
Kenny Tracey, Councillor, Wards: 9
Darren Bruckschwaiger, Councillor, 902-849-2737, Wards: 10
Darren O'Quinn, Councillor, Wards: 11
Lorne Green, Councillor, Wards: 12
Marie Walsh, Chief Administrative Officer, 902-563-5009, Fax: 902-564-0481
Demetri Kachafanas, BA, BBA, LLB, LLM, Regional Solicitor, 902-563-5047
Michael Ruus, Director, Planning & Development, 902-563-5027, Fax: 902-564-0481
Michael Seth, Director, Fire Services, 902-563-5132

Halifax Regional Municipality
P.O. Box 1749
1841 Argyle St.
Halifax, NS B3J 3A5
Tel: 902-490-4000; *Fax:* 902-490-4208
www.halifax.ca
Other Information: Toll-Free Phone: 800-835-6428
Municipal Type: Regional Municipality
Incorporated: April 1, 1996; *Area:* 5,490.35 sq km
Population in 2016: 403,171
Provincial Electoral District(s): Bedford-Birch Cove; Cole Harbour; Cole Harbour-Eastern Passage; Dartmouth E.; Dartmouth N.; Dartmouth S.-Portland Valley; Eastern Shore; Hlfx Atlantic; Hlfx Chebucto; Hlfx Citadel-Sable Island; Hlfx-Clayton Park; Hlfx Fairview; Hlfx Needham; Hammonds Plains-Upper Sackville; Preston; Sackville-Cobequid; Timberlea-Prospect; Waverly-Fall River-Beaver Bank
Federal Electoral District(s): Central Nova; Dartmouth-Cole Harbour; Halifax; Halifax West; Sackville-Preston-Chezzetcook; South Shore-St. Margaret's
Next Election: October 2024 (4 year terms)
Mike Savage, Mayor, 902-490-4010
Cathy Deagle Gammon, Councillor, Wards: 1. Waverly-Fall River
David Hendsbee, Councillor, 902-889-3553, Fax: 902-829-3620, Wards: 2. Preston-Chezzetcook
Becky Kent, Councillor, Wards: 3. Dartmouth South
Trish Purdy, Councillor, Wards: 4. Cole Harbour-Westphal
Sam Austin, Councillor, 902-576-6814, Wards: 5. Dartmouth Centre
Tony Mancini, Councillor, 902-490-4050, Wards: 6. Harbourview-Burnside
Waye Mason, Deputy Mayor & Councillor, 902-490-8462, Wards: 7. Halifax South Downtown
Lindell Smith, Councillor, 902-579-6975, Wards: 8. Halifax Peninsula North
Shawn Cleary, Councillor, 902-490-4090, Wards: 9. Halifax West Armdale
Kathryn Morse, Councillor, Wards: 10. Halifax-Bedford Basin West
Patty Cuttell, Councillor, Wards: 11. Spryfield-Sambro Loop
Iona Stoddard, Councillor, Wards: 12. Timberlea-Beechville
Pam Lovelace, Councillor, Wards: 13. Hammonds Plains
Lisa Blackburn, Councillor, 902-579-7164, Wards: 14. Middle/Upper Sackville
Paul Russell, Councillor, 902-240-0441, Wards: 15. Lower Sackville

Tim Outhit, Councillor, 902-490-5679, Fax: 902-490-5681, Wards: 16. Bedford-Wentworth
Jacques Dubé, Chief Administrative Officer
Jason Fraser, Chief Finacial Officer
Breton Murphy, Manager, Public Affairs, 902-490-6198
Kenneth Stuebing, Fire Chief

Queens
P.O. Box 1264
249 White Point Rd.
Liverpool, NS B0T 1K0
Tel: 902-354-3453; *Fax:* 902-354-7473
www.regionofqueens.com
Municipal Type: Regional Municipality
Incorporated: April 1, 1996; *Area:* 2,386.58 sq km
County or District: Queens; *Population in 2016:* 10,307
Provincial Electoral District(s): Queens
Federal Electoral District(s): South Shore-St. Margaret's
Next Election: October 2024 (4 year terms)
Darlene Norman, Mayor
Kevin Muise, Councillor, 902-683-2207, Wards: 1
Ralph Gidney, Councillor, Wards: 2
Maddie Charlton, Councillor, Wards: 3
Vicki Amirault, Councillor, Wards: 4
Jack Fancy, Councillor, 902-350-3905, Wards: 5
David Fiske, Councillor, Wards: 6
Carl Hawkes, Councillor, Wards: 7
Richard MacLellan, Chief Administrative Officer
Jill Cruikshank, Director, Economic Development
Jennifer Keating-Hubley, Director, Finance
Brad Rowter, P. Eng, Director, Engineering and Works

West Hants Regional Municipality
P.O. Box 3000
76 Morison Dr.
Windsor, NS B0N 2T0
Tel: 902-798-8391; *Fax:* 902-798-8553
www.westhants.ca
Municipal Type: Regional Municipality
Incorporated: April 1, 2020; *Area:* 1,244.09 sq km
County or District: Hants; *Population in 2016:* 15,358
Provincial Electoral District(s): Hants West
Federal Electoral District(s): Kings-Hants
Next Election: October 2024 (4 year terms)
Note: Created from the amalgamation of the District of West Hants & Town of Windsor.
Abraham Zebian, Mayor, 902-790-1566
Rupert Jannasch, Councillor, 902-633-2358, Wards: 1. Walton-Centre Burlington
Scott McLean, Councillor, 902-790-3100, Wards: 2. Cogmagun-Avondale
Mark McLean, Councillor, 902-757-3559, Wards: 3. Newport-Sweets Corner
Jeff Hartt, Councillor, 902-798-7743, Wards: 4. St.Croix-Ellershouse
Debbie Francis, Councillor, 902-798-2710, Wards: 5. Wentworth Creek-Three Mile
Bob Morton, Councillor, 902-790-6490, Wards: 6. Panuke Lake-Garlands Crossi
Ed Sherman, Councillor, 902-792-0690, Wards: 7. Vaughan-Upper Falmouth
Paul Morton, Councillor, 902-684-9415, Wards: 8. Hantsport-Mount Denson
Richard Murphy, Councillor, 902-792-1882, Wards: 9. Falmouth
Laurie Murley, Councillor, 902-790-3121, Wards: 10. North Windsor
Jim Ivey, Councillor, 902-791-0371, Wards: 11. South Windsor
Mark Phillips, Chief Administrative Officer
Kathy Kehoe, Director, Community Development
Madelyn LeMay, Director, Planning & Development
Todd Richard, Director, Public Works
Carlee Rochon, Director, Finance

Other Municipalities in Nova Scotia

Amherst
98 East Victoria St.
Amherst, NS B4H 1X6
Tel: 902-667-3352; *Fax:* 902-667-3356
www.amherst.ca
Municipal Type: Town
Incorporated: Dec. 18, 1889; *Area:* 12.02 sq km
County or District: Cumberland; *Population in 2016:* 9,413
Provincial Electoral District(s): Cumberland North
Federal Electoral District(s): Cumberland-Colchester
Next Election: October 2024 (4 year terms)
David Paul Kogon, Mayor, 902-694-2214
Gregory D. Herrett, CA, Chief Administrative Officer, 902-667-6513

Annapolis Royal
P.O. Box 310
285 St. George St.
Annapolis Royal, NS B0S 1A0
Tel: 902-532-2043; *Fax:* 902-532-7443
admin@annapolisroyal.com
www.annapolisroyal.com
Other Information: Toll-Free Phone: 877-522-1110
Municipal Type: Town
Incorporated: Nov. 29, 1892; *Area:* 2.04 sq km
County or District: Annapolis; *Population in 2016:* 491
Provincial Electoral District(s): Annapolis
Federal Electoral District(s): West Nova
Next Election: October 2024 (4 year terms)
Amery Boyer, Mayor
Gregory Barr, Chief Administrative Officer, 902-532-3146

Antigonish
274 Main St.
Antigonish, NS B2G 2C4
Tel: 902-863-2351; *Fax:* 902-863-0460
www.townofantigonish.ca
Other Information: Alt. Fax 902-863-9201
Municipal Type: Town
Incorporated: Jan. 9, 1889; *Area:* 5.15 sq km
County or District: Antigonish; *Population in 2016:* 4,364
Provincial Electoral District(s): Antigonish
Federal Electoral District(s): Central Nova
Next Election: October 2024 (4 year terms)
Laurie Boucher, Mayor, 902-867-5577
J. Lawrence, Chief Administrative Officer, 902-867-5576

Aylesford
P.O. Box 91
Aylesford, NS B0P 1C0
Tel: 902-847-0827
aylesfordvillagecommission@eastlink.ca
Municipal Type: Village
County or District: Kings; *Population in 2016:* 833
Provincial Electoral District(s): Kings West
Federal Electoral District(s): West Nova
Next Election: October 2024 (4 year terms)
Rhonda Carey, Chair
Trudie Spinney, Clerk-Treasurer

Baddeck
P.O. Box 63
495 Chebucto St.
Baddeck, NS B0E 1B0
Tel: 902-295-3666; *Fax:* 902-295-1729
www.baddeck.com
Municipal Type: Village
Area: 2.08 sq km
County or District: Victoria; *Population in 2016:* 826
Provincial Electoral District(s): Victoria-The Lakes
Federal Electoral District(s): Sydney-Victoria
Next Election: October 2024 (4 year terms)
Erin Bradley, Clerk-Treasurer

Berwick
P.O. Box 130
236 Commercial St.
Berwick, NS B0P 1E0
Tel: 902-538-8068; *Fax:* 902-538-3724
www.town.berwick.ns.ca
Municipal Type: Town
Incorporated: May 25, 1923; *Area:* 6.8 sq km
County or District: Kings; *Population in 2016:* 2,509
Provincial Electoral District(s): Kings West
Federal Electoral District(s): West Nova
Next Election: October 2024 (4 year terms)
Don Clarke, Mayor, 902-583-4008
Don Regan, Chief Administrative Officer, 902-583-4007

Bible Hill
67 Pictou Rd.
Bible Hill, NS B2N 2R9
Tel: 902-893-8083
clerk@biblehill.ca
www.biblehill.ca
Municipal Type: Village
County or District: Colchester
Provincial Electoral District(s): Truro-Bible Hill-Millbrook-Salmon River
Federal Electoral District(s): Cumberland-Colchester
Next Election: October 2024 (4 year terms)
Lois MacCormick, Chair
Robert Christianson, Clerk/Treasurer

Bridgewater
60 Pleasant St.
Bridgewater, NS B4V 3X9
Tel: 902-543-4651; *Fax:* 902-543-6876
www.bridgewater.ca
Municipal Type: Town
Incorporated: Feb. 13, 1899; *Area:* 13.6 sq km
County or District: Lunenburg; *Population in 2016:* 8,532
Provincial Electoral District(s): Lunenburg West
Federal Electoral District(s): South Shore-St. Margaret's
Next Election: October 2024 (4 year terms)
David Mitchell, Mayor, 902-541-4364
Ken Smith, Chief Administrative Officer, 902-541-4363, Fax: 902-543-4651

Canning
P.O. Box 9
977 J Jordan Rd.
Canning, NS B0P 1H0
Tel: 902-582-3768; *Fax:* 902-582-3068
village.canning@xcountry.tv
canning.ca
Municipal Type: Village
Area: 1.86 sq km
County or District: Kings; *Population in 2016:* 731
Provincial Electoral District(s): Kings North
Federal Electoral District(s): Kings-Hants
Next Election: October 2024 (4 year terms)
Angela Cruickshank, Chair
Ruth Pearson, Clerk/Treasurer

Clark's Harbour
P.O. Box 260
2648 Main St.
Clarks Harbour, NS B0W 1P0
Tel: 902-745-2390; *Fax:* 902-745-1772
www.clarksharbour.com
Municipal Type: Town
Incorporated: March 4, 1919; *Area:* 2.9 sq km
County or District: Shelburne; *Population in 2016:* 758
Provincial Electoral District(s): Shelburne
Federal Electoral District(s): South Shore-St. Margaret's
Next Election: October 2024 (4 year terms)
Rex Stoddard, Mayor
Jennifer Jones, Clerk, 902-745-2390

Cornwallis Square
P.O. Box 129
1415 County Home Rd.
Waterville, NS B0P 1V0
Tel: 902-538-0325; *Fax:* 902-538-1683
Municipal Type: Village
County or District: Kings
Provincial Electoral District(s): Kings North
Federal Electoral District(s): Kings-Hants
Next Election: October 2024 (4 year terms)
Simon Holleman, Chair
William Farrell, Clerk, 902-538-0325

Digby
P.O. Box 579
147 First Ave.
Digby, NS B0V 1A0
Tel: 902-245-4769; *Fax:* 902-245-2121
townhall@digby.ca
www.digby.ca
Municipal Type: Town
Incorporated: Feb. 28, 1890; *Area:* 3.14 sq km
County or District: Digby; *Population in 2016:* 2,060
Provincial Electoral District(s): Digby-Annapolis
Federal Electoral District(s): West Nova
Next Election: October 2024 (4 year terms)
Ben Cleveland, Mayor, 902-247-0484
Tom Ossinger, Chief Administrative Officer, 902-245-4769, Fax: 902-245-2121

Freeport
P.O. Box 31
Freeport, NS B0V 1B0
Tel: 902-839-2144
Municipal Type: Village
County or District: Digby; *Population in 2016:* 223
Provincial Electoral District(s): Digby-Annapolis
Federal Electoral District(s): West Nova
Next Election: October 2024 (4 year terms)

Greenwood
P.O. Box 1068
904 Central Ave.
Greenwood, NS B0P 1N0
Tel: 902-765-8788; *Fax:* 902-765-4369
villageoffice@greenwoodns.ca
www.greenwoodnovascotia.com
Municipal Type: Village
County or District: Kings
Provincial Electoral District(s): Kings West
Federal Electoral District(s): Central Nova; West Nova
Next Election: October 2024 (4 year terms)
Note: As of 2011, Statistics Canada shows that the Designated Place known as Kingston - Greenwood has an area of 14.50 sq km, & a population of 6,595.
Brian Banks, Chair
Marian Elsworth, Clerk-Treasurer, 902-765-8788

Havre Boucher
1318 Catejack Rd.
Havre Boucher, NS B0P 1P0
hbcdra@gmail.com
www.havreboucher.com
Municipal Type: Village
County or District: Antigonish; *Population in 2016:* 309
Provincial Electoral District(s): Antigonish
Federal Electoral District(s): Cape Breton-Canso
Next Election: October 2024 (4 year terms)

Hebbville
47 Catidian Pl., RR#4
Bridgewater, NS B4V 2W3
Tel: 902-543-5786; *Fax:* 902-543-7006
info@villageofhebbville.ca
www.villageofhebbville.ca
Municipal Type: Village
County or District: Lunenburg; *Population in 2016:* 802
Provincial Electoral District(s): Lunenburg West
Federal Electoral District(s): South Shore-St. Margaret's
Next Election: October 2024 (4 year terms)
Russell Barrier, Chair, 902-543-1155

Kentville
354 Main St.
Kentville, NS B4N 1K6
Tel: 902-679-2500; *Fax:* 902-679-2375
kentville.ca
Municipal Type: Town
Incorporated: May 1, 1886; *Area:* 17.35 sq km
County or District: Kings; *Population in 2016:* 6,271
Provincial Electoral District(s): Kings North
Federal Electoral District(s): Kings-Hants
Next Election: October 2024 (4 year terms)
Sandra Snow, Mayor
Mark Phillips, Chief Administrative Officer, 902-679-2501

Kingston
P.O. Box 254
671 Main St.
Kingston, NS B0P 1R0
Tel: 902-765-2800; *Fax:* 902-765-0807
info@kingstonnovascotia.ca
www.kingstonnovascotia.ca
Municipal Type: Village
Incorporated: 1957
County or District: Kings; *Population in 2016:* 2,913
Provincial Electoral District(s): Kings West
Federal Electoral District(s): West Nova
Next Election: October 2024 (4 year terms)
Note: As of 2011, Statistics Canada shows that the Designated Place known as Kingston - Greenwood has an area of 14.50 sq km, & a population of 6,595.
Mike McCleave, Clerk-Treasurer

Lawrencetown
P.O. Box 38
12 Prince St.
Lawrencetown, NS B0S 1M0
Tel: 902-584-3082; *Fax:* 902-584-3878
villageclerk@lawrencetownnovascotia.ca
www.lawrencetownnovascotia.ca
Municipal Type: Village
Area: 5.62 sq km
County or District: Annapolis; *Population in 2016:* 516
Provincial Electoral District(s): Annapolis
Federal Electoral District(s): West Nova
Next Election: October 2024 (4 year terms)
Brian K. Reid, Chair, 902-584-3992
Melissa Roscoe, Clerk-Treasurer, 902-584-3082, Fax: 902-584-3878

Lockeport
P.O. Box 189
26 North St.
Lockeport, NS B0T 1L0
Tel: 902-656-2216; *Fax:* 902-656-2935
townoflockeport@ns.sympatico.ca
www.lockeport.ns.ca
Municipal Type: Town
Incorporated: Feb. 26, 1907; *Area:* 2.32 sq km
County or District: Shelburne; *Population in 2016:* 531
Provincial Electoral District(s): Queens-Shelburne
Federal Electoral District(s): South Shore-St. Margaret's
Next Election: October 2024 (4 year terms)
Cory Nickerson, Mayor

Lunenburg
P.O. Box 129
119 Cumberland St.
Lunenburg, NS B0J 2C0
Tel: 902-634-4410; *Fax:* 902-634-4416
explorelunenburg@ns.sympatico.ca
www.explorelunenburg.ca
Municipal Type: Town
Incorporated: Oct. 29, 1888; *Area:* 4.01 sq km
County or District: Lunenburg; *Population in 2016:* 2,263
Provincial Electoral District(s): Lunenburg
Federal Electoral District(s): South Shore-St. Margaret's
Next Election: October 2024 (4 year terms)
Matt Risser, Mayor
Beatrice Renton, Chief Administrative Officer, 902-634-4410

Mahone Bay
P.O. Box 530
493 Main St.
Mahone Bay, NS B0J 2E0
Tel: 902-624-8327; *Fax:* 902-624-8069
clerk@townofmahonebay.ca
www.townofmahonebay.ca
Municipal Type: Town
Incorporated: March 31, 1919; *Area:* 3.13 sq km
County or District: Lunenburg; *Population in 2016:* 1,036
Provincial Electoral District(s): Lunenburg
Federal Electoral District(s): South Shore-St. Margaret's
Next Election: October 2024 (4 year terms)
David Devenne, Mayor
Jim Wentzell, Chief Administrative Officer, 902-624-8327, Fax: 902-624-8069

Middleton
P.O. Box 340
131 Commercial St.
Middleton, NS B0S 1P0
Tel: 902-825-4841; *Fax:* 902-825-6460
billingclerk@town.middleton.ns.ca
www.discovermiddleton.ca
Municipal Type: Town
Incorporated: May 31, 1909; *Area:* 5.44 sq km
County or District: Annapolis; *Population in 2016:* 1,832
Provincial Electoral District(s): Annapolis
Federal Electoral District(s): West Nova
Next Election: October 2024 (4 year terms)
Sylvestor Atkinson, Mayor, 902-825-4758
Rachel Turner, Chief Administrative Officer, 902-825-3559, Fax: 902-825-6460

Mulgrave
P.O. Box 129
457 MacLeod St.
Mulgrave, NS B0E 2G0
Tel: 902-747-2243; *Fax:* 902-747-2585
www.townofmulgrave.ca
Municipal Type: Town
Incorporated: Dec. 1, 1923; *Area:* 17.81 sq km
County or District: Guysborough; *Population in 2016:* 722
Provincial Electoral District(s): Guysborough-Eastern Shore-Tracadie
Federal Electoral District(s): Cape Breton-Canso
Next Election: October 2024 (4 year terms)
Ron Chisholm, Mayor
Darlene Berthier Sampson, Chief Administrative Officer

New Glasgow
P.O. Box 7
111 Provost St.
New Glasgow, NS B2H 5E1
Tel: 902-755-7788; *Fax:* 902-755-6242
www.newglasgow.ca
Municipal Type: Town
Incorporated: May 6, 1875; *Area:* 9.93 sq km
County or District: Pictou; *Population in 2016:* 9,075
Provincial Electoral District(s): Pictou Centre

Federal Electoral District(s): Central Nova
Next Election: October 2024 (4 year terms)
Nancy Dicks, Mayor, 902-755-8340
Lisa M. MacDonald, Chief Administrative Officer, 902-755-8333

New Minas
9489 Commercial St.
New Minas, NS B4N 3G3
Tel: 902-681-6972; *Fax:* 902-681-0779
www.newminas.com
Municipal Type: Village
Incorporated: Sept. 1, 1968
County or District: Kings; *Population in 2016:* 4,000
Provincial Electoral District(s): Kings South
Federal Electoral District(s): Kings-Hants
Next Election: October 2024 (4 year terms)
Dave Chaulk, Chair, 902-681-2387
Brenda Stimpson, Clerk-Treasurer, 902-681-0292

Oxford
P.O. Box 338
105 Lower Main St.
Oxford, NS B0M 1P0
Tel: 902-447-2170; *Fax:* 902-447-2485
townhall@town.oxford.ns.ca
www.town.oxford.ns.ca
Municipal Type: Town
Incorporated: April 19, 1904; *Area:* 10.76 sq km
County or District: Cumberland; *Population in 2016:* 1,190
Provincial Electoral District(s): Cumberland South
Federal Electoral District(s): Cumberland-Colchester
Next Election: October 2024 (4 year terms)
Gregory Henley, Mayor
Rachel Jones, Chief Administrative Officer, 902-447-2130

Pictou
P.O. Box 640
40 Water St.
Pictou, NS B0K 1H0
Tel: 902-485-4372; *Fax:* 902-485-8110
info@townofpictou.ca
www.townofpictou.com
Municipal Type: Town
Incorporated: May 4, 1874; *Area:* 7.94 sq km
County or District: Pictou; *Population in 2016:* 3,186
Provincial Electoral District(s): Pictou West
Federal Electoral District(s): Central Nova
Next Election: October 2024 (4 year terms)
Jim Ryan, Mayor, 902-485-8748
Scott Conrod, Chief Administrative Officer, 902-485-4372

Port Hawkesbury
606 Reeves St.
Port Hawkesbury, NS B9A 2R7
Tel: 902-625-0116; *Fax:* 902-625-0040
www.townofporthawkesbury.ca
Municipal Type: Town
Incorporated: Jan. 22, 1889; *Area:* 8.11 sq km
County or District: Inverness; *Population in 2016:* 3,214
Provincial Electoral District(s): Cape Breton-Richmond
Federal Electoral District(s): Cape Breton-Canso
Next Election: October 2024 (4 year terms)
Brenda Chisholm Beaton, Mayor, 902-302-9371
Maris Freimanis, Chief Administrative Officer, 902-625-7890,
Fax: 902-625-0040

Port Williams
P.O. Box 153
1045 Main St.
Port Williams, NS B0P 1T0
Tel: 902-542-4411; *Fax:* 902-542-4566
villageoffice@portwilliams.com
www.portwilliams.com
Municipal Type: Village
County or District: Kings; *Population in 2016:* 1,186
Provincial Electoral District(s): Kings North
Federal Electoral District(s): Kings-Hants
Next Election: October 2024 (4 year terms)
Lewis Benedict, Chair, 902-542-9519
Darlene Robertson, Clerk, 902-542-4411, Fax: 902-542-4566

Pugwash
P.O. Box 220
124 Water St.
Pugwash, NS B0K 1L0
Tel: 902-243-2946; *Fax:* 902-243-2126
villagecommission@pugwashvillage.com
www.pugwashvillage.com
Municipal Type: Village
Area: 9.83 sq km
County or District: Cumberland; *Population in 2016:* 736
Provincial Electoral District(s): Cumberland North

Federal Electoral District(s): Cumberland-Colchester
Next Election: October 2024 (4 year terms)
Roger Mundle, Chair
Lisa Betts, Clerk-Treasurer, 902-243-2946

River Hebert
2724 Taylor Rd.
River Hebert, NS B0L 1G0
Tel: 902-251-2250
Municipal Type: Village
County or District: Cumberland; *Population in 2016:* 453
Provincial Electoral District(s): Cumberland South
Federal Electoral District(s): Cumberland-Colchester
Next Election: October 2024 (4 year terms)

St. Peter's
P.O. Box 452
60 Denys St.
St Peters, NS B0E 3B0
Tel: 902-535-2155; *Fax:* 902-535-2330
info@visitstpeters.com
www.visitstpeters.com
Municipal Type: Village
County or District: Richmond
Provincial Electoral District(s): Cape Breton-Richmond
Federal Electoral District(s): Cape Breton-Canso
Next Election: October 2024 (4 year terms)

Shelburne
P.O. Box 670
168 Water St.
Shelburne, NS B0T 1W0
Tel: 902-875-2991; *Fax:* 902-875-3932
townofshelburnens@town.shelburne.ns.ca
www.town.shelburne.ns.ca
Municipal Type: Town
Incorporated: April 4, 1907; *Area:* 9 sq km
County or District: Shelburne; *Population in 2016:* 1,743
Provincial Electoral District(s): Shelburne
Federal Electoral District(s): South Shore-St. Margaret's
Next Election: October 2024 (4 year terms)
Harold Locke, Mayor
Ken Smith, Interim Chief Administrative Officer, 902-875-2991

Stellarton
P.O. Box 2200
250 Foord St.
Stellarton, NS B0K 1S0
Tel: 902-752-2114; *Fax:* 902-755-4105
town.office@stellarton.ca
www.stellarton.ca
Municipal Type: Town
Incorporated: Oct. 22, 1889; *Area:* 8.99 sq km
County or District: Pictou; *Population in 2016:* 4,208
Provincial Electoral District(s): Pictou Centre
Federal Electoral District(s): Central Nova
Next Election: October 2024 (4 year terms)
Danny MacGillivray, Mayor
Joyce Eaton, Town Clerk, 902-752-2114

Stewiacke
P.O. Box 8
295 George St.
Stewiacke, NS B0N 2J0
Tel: 902-639-2231; *Fax:* 902-639-2221
town@stewiacke.net
www.stewiacke.net
Municipal Type: Town
Incorporated: Aug. 30, 1906; *Area:* 17.67 sq km
County or District: Colchester; *Population in 2016:* 1,373
Provincial Electoral District(s): Colchester-Musqodoboit Valley
Federal Electoral District(s): Cumberland-Colchester
Next Election: October 2024 (4 year terms)
George Lloy, Mayor
Dale A. Bogle, Chief Administrative Officer, 902-639-2231

Tatamagouche
229 Main St., 2nd Fl.
Tatamagouche, NS B0K 1V0
Tel: 902-657-3696
villageoftatamagouche.com
Municipal Type: Village
Area: 8.04 sq km
County or District: Colchester; *Population in 2016:* 755
Provincial Electoral District(s): Colchester North
Federal Electoral District(s): Cumberland-Colchester
Next Election: October 2024 (4 year terms)
Peter Pope, Chair, 902-957-1300

Tiverton
P.O. Box 16
RR#1
Tiverton, NS B0V 1G0
Tel: 902-839-2369
Municipal Type: Village
County or District: Digby; *Population in 2016:* 725
Provincial Electoral District(s): Digby-Annapolis
Federal Electoral District(s): West Nova
Next Election: October 2024 (4 year terms)

Trenton
P.O. Box 328
120 Main St.
Trenton, NS B0K 1X0
Tel: 902-752-5311; *Fax:* 902-752-0090
trenton@town.trenton.ns.ca
www.town.trenton.ns.ca
Municipal Type: Town
Incorporated: March 18, 1911; *Area:* 6 sq km
County or District: Pictou; *Population in 2016:* 2,474
Provincial Electoral District(s): Pictou Centre
Federal Electoral District(s): Central Nova
Next Election: October 2024 (4 year terms)
Donald Hussher, Mayor
Wayne Teasdale, Chief Administrative Officer

Truro
695 Prince St.
Truro, NS B2N 1G5
Tel: 902-895-4484; *Fax:* 902-893-0501
inquiries@truro.ca
www.truro.ca
Municipal Type: Town
Incorporated: May 6, 1875; *Area:* 34.49 sq km
County or District: Colchester; *Population in 2016:* 12,261
Provincial Electoral District(s): Truro-Bible Hill-Millbrook-Salmon
River
Federal Electoral District(s): Cumberland-Colchester
Next Election: October 2024 (4 year terms)
W.R. (Bill) Mills, Mayor, 902-956-1401
Alison Graham-Fulmore, Councillor, Wards: 1
Wayne Talbot, Councillor, 902-956-1407, Wards: 1
Jim Flemming, Councillor, Wards: 2
Bill Thomas, Councillor, Wards: 2
Juliana Barnard, Councillor, Wards: 3
Cathy Hinton, Councillor, 902-956-1406, Wards: 3
Mike Dolter, Chief Administrative Officer, 902-895-4484, Fax:
902-893-0501

Westport
The Spouter Inn
P.O. Box 1192
263 Water St.
Westport, NS B0V 1H0
Tel: 902-839-2219; *Fax:* 902-839-2219
www.brierisland.com/experiences/village-of-westport
Municipal Type: Village
County or District: Digby; *Population in 2016:* 218
Provincial Electoral District(s): Clare-Digby
Federal Electoral District(s): West Nova
Next Election: October 2024 (4 year terms)

Westville
P.O. Box 923
2042 Queen St.
Westville, NS B0K 2A0
Tel: 902-396-1500; *Fax:* 902-396-3986
www.westville.ca
Municipal Type: Town
Incorporated: Aug. 20, 1894; *Area:* 14.39 sq km
County or District: Pictou; *Population in 2016:* 3,628
Provincial Electoral District(s): Pictou East
Federal Electoral District(s): Central Nova
Next Election: October 2024 (4 year terms)
Lennie White, Mayor
Kelly Rice, Chief Administrative Officer, 902-396-1500

Weymouth
P.O. Box 121
5108 Hwy. 1
Weymouth, NS B0W 3T0
Tel: 902-837-4976; *Fax:* 902-837-5397
www.weymouthnovascotia.com
Municipal Type: Village
County or District: Digby
Provincial Electoral District(s): Digby-Annapolis
Federal Electoral District(s): West Nova
Next Election: October 2024 (4 year terms)
Irwin Gaudett, Chair
Murray Betts, Clerk/Treasurer, 902-837-4976

Wolfville
359 Main St.
Wolfville, NS B4P 1A1
Tel: 902-542-5767; *Fax:* 902-542-4789
wolfville.ca
Municipal Type: Town
Incorporated: March 4, 1893; *Area:* 6.45 sq km
County or District: Kings; *Population in 2016:* 4,195
Provincial Electoral District(s): Kings South
Federal Electoral District(s): Kings-Hants
Next Election: October 2024 (4 year terms)
Wendy Donovan, Mayor
Erin Beaudin, Chief Administrative Officer, 902-542-4494, Fax:
902-542-4789

Yarmouth
400 Main St.
Yarmouth, NS B5A 1G2
Tel: 902-742-2521; *Fax:* 902-742-6244
admin@townofyarmouth.ca
www.townofyarmouth.ca
Municipal Type: Town
Incorporated: Aug. 6, 1890; *Area:* 10.56 sq km
County or District: Yarmouth; *Population in 2016:* 6,518
Provincial Electoral District(s): Yarmouth
Federal Electoral District(s): West Nova
Next Election: October 2024 (4 year terms)
Pam Mood, Mayor, 902-742-8565, Fax: 902-742-6244
Jeffrey Gushue, Chief Administrative Officer, 902-742-8565,
Fax: 902-742-6244

Rural Municipalities in Nova Scotia

Annapolis County
P.O. Box 100
752 St George St.
Annapolis Royal, NS B0S 1A0
Tel: 902-532-2331; *Fax:* 902-532-2096
www.annapoliscounty.ca
Other Information: Alt. Phone: 902-825-2005
Municipal Type: Rural Municipalities
Incorporated: April 17, 1879; *Area:* 3,189.14 sq km
County or District: Annapolis; *Population in 2016:* 20,591
Provincial Electoral District(s): Annapolis; Digby-Annapolis
Federal Electoral District(s): West Nova
Next Election: October 2024 (4 year terms)
Note: The Town of Bridgetown dissolved on April 1, 2015 & was
folded into Annapolis County.
Bruce Prout, Councillor, Wards: 1
Brian Connell, Councillor, Wards: 2
Alan Parish, Councillor, Wards: 3
Clyde Barteaux, Councillor, Wards: 4
Lynn A. Longmire, Councillor, Wards: 5
Alex Morrison, Councillor, Wards: 6
David Hudson, Councillor, Wards: 7
Michael Gunn, Councillor, Wards: 8
Wendy Sheridan, Councillor, Wards: 9
Brad Redden, Councillor, Wards: 10
Diane LeBlanc, Councillor, Wards: 11
John Ferguson, Chief Administrative Officer

Antigonish County
285 Beech Hill Rd. RR #6
Antigonish, NS B2G 0B4
Tel: 902-863-1117; *Fax:* 902-863-5751
www.antigonishcounty.ns.ca
Municipal Type: Rural Municipalities
Incorporated: April 17, 1879; *Area:* 1,457.99 sq km
County or District: Antigonish; *Population in 2016:* 19,301
Provincial Electoral District(s): Antigonish
Federal Electoral District(s): Central Nova
Next Election: October 2024 (4 year terms)
Owen McCarron, Warden & Councillor, Wards: 6. St. Andrews
Hugh D. Stewart, Deputy Warden & Councillor, Wards: 3. St.
Joseph's
Mary MacLellan, Councillor, Wards: 1. Arisaig
Donnie MacDonald, Councillor, Wards: 2. North Grant/Colverville
Shawn Brophy, Councillor, Wards: 4. Fringe Area West
Remi Deveau, Councillor, Wards: 5. Pomquet
John Dunbar, Councillor, Wards: 7. Heatherton/Afton
Gary Mattie, Councillor, Wards: 8. Tracadie/Monestary
Harris MacNamara, Councillor, Wards: 9. Linwood/Havre
Boucher
Bill MacFarlane, Councillor, Wards: 10. Fringe Area South
Glenn Horne, Clerk/Treasurer
Allison Duggan, Director, Finance
Marlene Melanson, Director, Recreation
Daryl Myers, Director, Public Works, 902-863-5004

Argyle District
P.O. Box 10
27 Courthouse Rd.
Tusket, NS B0W 3M0
Tel: 902-648-2311; *Fax:* 902-648-0367
admin@munargyle.com
www.munargyle.com
Municipal Type: Rural Municipalities
Incorporated: April 17, 1879; *Area:* 1,527.1 sq km
County or District: Yarmouth; *Population in 2016:* 7,899
Provincial Electoral District(s): Argyle
Federal Electoral District(s): West Nova
Next Election: October 2024 (4 year terms)
Richard Donaldson, Warden & Councillor, 902-643-2047, Wards:
6
Alain Muise, Chief Administrative Officer, 902-648-3293

Barrington District
P.O. Box 100
2447 Hwy. 3
Barrington, NS B0W 1E0
Tel: 902-637-2015; *Fax:* 902-637-2075
www.barringtonmunicipality.com
Municipal Type: Rural Municipalities
Incorporated: April 17, 1879; *Area:* 631.94 sq km
County or District: Shelburne; *Population in 2016:* 6,646
Provincial Electoral District(s): Argyle-Barrington
Federal Electoral District(s): South Shore-St. Margaret's
Next Election: October 2024 (4 year terms)
Eddie Nickerson, Warden/Councillor, 902-635-1682, Wards: 4
Rob Frost, Chief Administrative Officer, 902-637-2015, Fax:
902-637-2075

Chester District
P.O. Box 369
151 King St.
Chester, NS B0J 1J0
Tel: 902-275-3554; *Fax:* 902-275-4771
www.chester.ca
Municipal Type: Rural Municipalities
Incorporated: April 17, 1879; *Area:* 1,122.11 sq km
County or District: Lunenburg; *Population in 2016:* 10,310
Provincial Electoral District(s): Chester-St. Margaret's
Federal Electoral District(s): South Shore-St. Margaret's
Next Election: October 2024 (4 year terms)
Allen Webber, Warden, 902-275-2536, Wards: 4
Floyd Shatford, Deputy Warden, 902-857-9817, Wards: 2
Marshal Hector, Councillor, 902-277-2982, Wards: 1
Danielle Barkhouse, Councillor, 902-277-1624, Wards: 3
Abdella Assaff, Councillor, 902-277-2765, Wards: 5
Tina Connors, Councillor, 902-679-4461, Wards: 6
Sharon Church, Councillor, 902-277-1301, Wards: 7
Dan McDougall, Chief Administrative Officer, 902-275-3554,
Fax: 902-275-4771
Pam Myra, Municipal Clerk, 902-275-3554, Fax: 902-275-4771
Malcolm Pitman, Treasurer/Director of Finance, Finance,
902-275-3554
Chad Haughn, Director, Recreation & Parks, 902-275-3490, Fax:
902-275-3630

Clare District
P.O. Box 458
1185 Hwy. 1
Little Brook, NS B0W 1Z0
Tel: 902-769-2031; *Fax:* 902-769-3773
www.clarenovascotia.com
Municipal Type: Rural Municipalities
Incorporated: April 17, 1879; *Area:* 852.82 sq km
County or District: Digby; *Population in 2016:* 8,018
Provincial Electoral District(s): Clare
Federal Electoral District(s): West Nova
Next Election: October 2024 (4 year terms)
Ronnie LeBlanc, Warden & Councillor, 902-769-8006
Stéphane Cyr, Chief Administrative Officer, 902-769-2031, Fax:
902-769-3773

Colchester County
P.O. Box 697
1 Church St.
Truro, NS B2N 5E7
Tel: 902-897-3160; *Fax:* 902-843-4066
www.colchester.ca
Other Information: Toll-Free Phone: 866-728-5144
Municipal Type: Rural Municipalities
Incorporated: April 17, 1879; *Area:* 3,628.12 sq km
County or District: Colchester; *Population in 2016:* 50,585
Provincial Electoral District(s): Colchester North; Truro-Bible
Hill-Millbrook-Salmon River
Federal Electoral District(s): Cumberland-Colchester
Next Election: October 2024 (4 year terms)
Christine Blair, Mayor, 902-897-3184, Fax: 902-843-4066
Eric Boutilier, Councillor, 902-890-5866, Wards: 1

Laurie Sandeson, Councillor, Wards: 2
Geoff Stewart, Councillor, 902-673-3039, Wards: 3
Mike Cooper, Councillor, 902-671-2854, Wards: 4
Tim Johnson, Councillor, Wards: 5
Karen MacKenzie, Councillor, 902-895-8930, Wards: 6
Michael Gregory, Councillor, 902-305-4002, Wards: 7
Lisa Patton, Councillor, Wards: 8
Marie Benoit, Councillor, Wards: 9
Tom Taggart, Councillor, 902-647-2025, Wards: 10
Wade Parker, Councillor, 902-893-5448, Wards: 11
Rob Simonds, Chief Administrative Officer, 902-897-3184
Craig Burgess, Director, Recreation
Scott Fraser, Director, Corporate Services
Crawford Macpherson, Director, Community Development
Michelle Newell, Director, Public Works

Cumberland County
E.D. Fullerton Municipal Bldg.
1395 Blair Lake Rd., RR#6
Amherst, NS B4H 3Y4
Tel: 902-667-2313; *Fax:* 902-667-1352
info@cumberlandcounty.ns.ca
www.cumberlandcounty.ns.ca
Other Information: Toll-Free Phone: 888-756-6262
Municipal Type: Rural Municipalities
Incorporated: April 17, 1879; *Area:* 4,277.86 sq km
County or District: Cumberland; *Population in 2016:* 30,005
Provincial Electoral District(s): Cumberland North; Cumberland
South
Federal Electoral District(s): Cumberland-Colchester
Next Election: October 2024 (4 year terms)
Note: The town of Springhill dissolved on April 1st 2015 & was
folded into the Municipality of Cumberland County.
Murray Scott, Mayor
Fred Gould, Councillor, Wards: 1
Rod Gilroy, Councillor, Wards: 2
Jennifer Houghtaling, Councillor, Wards: 3
Kathy Redmond, Councillor, Wards: 4
Angela McCormick, Councillor, Wards: 5
Mark Joseph, Councillor, Wards: 6
Dale Porter, Councillor, Wards: 7
Carrie Goodwin, Councillor, Wards: 8
Rennie Bugley, Chief Administrative Officer
Steve Ferguson, Director, Community Development
Andrew MacDonald, Director, Finance
Justin Waugh-Cress, Director, Engineering & Operations,
902-667-2313

Digby District
P.O. Box 429
Digby, NS B0V 1A0
Tel: 902-245-4777; *Fax:* 902-245-5748
administration@municipality.digby.ns.ca
www.digbydistrict.ca
Municipal Type: Rural Municipalities
Incorporated: April 17, 1879; *Area:* 1,655.93 sq km
County or District: Digby; *Population in 2016:* 7,107
Provincial Electoral District(s): Digby-Annapolis
Federal Electoral District(s): West Nova
Next Election: October 2024 (4 year terms)
Jimmy MacAlpine, Warden & Councillor, Wards: 1
Linda Fraser, Chief Administrative Officer

East Hants District
P.O. Box 190
#230, 15 Commerce Ct.
Elmsdale, NS B2S 3K5
Tel: 902-883-2299; *Fax:* 888-684-5912
info@easthants.ca
www.easthants.ca
Other Information: Toll-Free Phone: 866-758-2299
Municipal Type: Rural Municipalities
Incorporated: April 17, 1879; *Area:* 1,786.56 sq km
County or District: Hants; *Population in 2016:* 22.453
Provincial Electoral District(s): Hants East
Federal Electoral District(s): Kings-Hants
Next Election: October 2024 (4 year terms)
Sandra Garden-Cole, Councillor, Wards: 1. Enfield
Norval Mitchell, Councillor, Wards: 2. Elmsdale-Belnan
Eldon Hebb, Councillor, 902-883-2047, Wards: 3. Milford-Nine
Mile River
Ian Knockwood, Councillor, Wards: 4. Shubenacadie
Keith Ryno, Councillor, 902-261-2533, Wards: 5.
Maitland-MacPhees Corner
Wayne Greene, Councillor, 902-369-2629, Wards: 6.
Walton-Noel-Kennetcook
John MacDonald, Councillor, Wards: 7. Lantz-Milford
Michael Perry, Councillor, 902-701-0633, Wards: 8. Mount
Uniacke
Elie Moussa, Councillor, 902-403-4588, Wards: 9. South-East
Uniacke
Tim Isenor, Councillor, Wards: 10. Enfield-Grand Lake

Eleanor Roulston, Councillor, 902-632-2573, Wards: 11.
Rawdon-Gore
Kim Ramsay, Chief Administrative Officer, 902-883-7098
Adam Clarkson, Director, Parks, Recreation & Culture
Jesse Hulsman, Director, Infrastructure & Operations
John Woodford, Director, Planning & Development,
902-883-7098

Guysborough District
Municipal Bldg.
P.O. Box 79
33 Pleasant St.
Guysborough, NS B0H 1N0
Tel: 902-533-3705; *Fax:* 902-533-2749
www.municipality.guysborough.ns.ca
Other Information: Alt. Phone: 902-533-3508
Municipal Type: Rural Municipalities
Incorporated: April 17, 1879; *Area:* 2,111.42 sq km
County or District: Guysborough; *Population in 2016:* 7,625
Provincial Electoral District(s): Guysborough-Eastern
Shore-Tracadie
Federal Electoral District(s): Cape Breton-Canso
Next Election: October 2024 (4 year terms)
Vernon Pitts, Warden, 902-533-3705
Barry Carroll, Chief Administrative Officer, 902-533-3705

Inverness County
Municipal Bldg.
P.O. Box 179
375 Main St.
Port Hood, NS B0E 2W0
Tel: 902-787-2274; *Fax:* 902-787-3110
www.invernesscounty.ca
Municipal Type: Rural Municipalities
Incorporated: April 17, 1879; *Area:* 3,831.17 sq km
County or District: Inverness; *Population in 2016:* 17,235
Provincial Electoral District(s): Inverness
Federal Electoral District(s): Cape Breton-Canso;
Sydney-Victoria
Next Election: October 2024 (4 year terms)
Alfred Poirier, Councillor, 902-224-0097, Wards: 1
Laurie Cranton, Councillor, 902-248-2726, Wards: 2
Bonny MacIsaac, Councillor, Wards: 3
John MacLennan, Councillor, Wards: 4
Lynn Chisholm, Councillor, Wards: 5
Catherine L. Gillis, Councillor, Wards: 6
Keith MacDonald, Chief Administrative Officer, 902-787-3500,
Fax: 902-787-3110
Donna MacDonald, Director, Recreation & Tourism,
902-787-3506, Fax: 902-787-3110
Tanya Tibbo, Director, Finance, 902-787-3511, Fax:
902-787-3110

Kings County
P.O. Box 100
87 Cornwallis St.
Kentville, NS B4N 3W3
Tel: 902-678-6141; *Fax:* 902-678-9279
inquiry@countyofkings.ca
www.countyofkings.ca
Other Information: Toll-Free Phone: 888-337-2999
Municipal Type: Rural Municipalities
Incorporated: April 17, 1879; *Area:* 2,126.71 sq km
County or District: Kings; *Population in 2016:* 60,600
Provincial Electoral District(s): Kings North; Kings South; Kings
West
Federal Electoral District(s): Kings-Hants; West Nova
Next Election: October 2024 (4 year terms)
Peter Muttart, Mayor
Dean Tupper, Councillor, Wards: 1
Lexie Burgess, Councillor, Wards: 2
Dick Killam, Councillor, Wards: 3
Martha Armstrong, Councillor, Wards: 4
Tim Harding, Councillor, Wards: 5
Joel Hirtle, Councillor, Wards: 6
Emily Lutz, Councillor, Wards: 7
Jim Winsor, Councillor, Wards: 8
Peter Allen, Councillor, Wards: 9
Scott Conrod, Chief Administrative Officer, 902-690-6131, Fax:
902-678-9279
Scott Quinn, Director, EPW, Lands & Parks Services,
902-690-6194
Greg Barr, Director, Finance & IT, 902-690-6136

Lunenburg District
P.O. Box 200
210 Aberdeen Rd.
Bridgewater, NS B4V 4G8
Tel: 902-543-8181; *Fax:* 902-543-7123
info@modl.ca
www.modl.ca
Municipal Type: Rural Municipalities
Incorporated: April 17, 1879; *Area:* 1,759.59 sq km
County or District: Lunenburg; *Population in 2016:* 24,863
Provincial Electoral District(s): Chester-St. Margaret's
Lunenburg; Lunenburg West
Federal Electoral District(s): South Shore-St. Margaret's
Next Election: October 2024 (4 year terms)
Carolyn Bolivar-Geston, Mayor, 902-541-1326
Leitha Haysom, Councillor, Wards: 1
Martin Bell, Councillor, 902-543-7090, Wards: 2
Wendy Oickle, Councillor, Wards: 3
Pam Hubley, Councillor, Wards: 4
Cathy Moore, Councillor, 902-644-2922, Wards: 5
Sandra Statton, Councillor, Wards: 6
Michelle Greek, Councillor, Wards: 7
Kacy DeLong, Councillor, Wards: 8
Reid Whynot, Councillor, 902-766-0418, Wards: 9
Chasidy Veinotte, Councillor, Wards: 10
Tom MacEwan, Chief Administrative Officer, 902-541-1320, Fax:
902-543-7123
Jeff Merrill, Director, Planning & Development, 902-541-1340
Stephen Pace, Director, Engineering, Project Management &
Public Works, 902-541-1339
Elana Wentzell, Director, Finance, 902-541-1332

Pictou County
46 Municipal Dr.
Pictou, NS B0K 1H0
Tel: 902-485-4311; *Fax:* 902-485-6475
www.county.pictou.ns.ca
Other Information: Alt. Phone: 902-752-1530
Municipal Type: Rural Municipalities
Incorporated: April 17, 1879; *Area:* 2,846.28 sq km
County or District: Pictou; *Population in 2016:* 43,748
Provincial Electoral District(s): Pictou Centre; Pictou East; Pictou
West
Federal Electoral District(s): Central Nova
Next Election: October 2024 (4 year terms)
Robert Parker, Warden & Councillor, Wards: 6
Wayne Murray, Deputy Warden & Councillor, Wards: 5
Don Butler, Councillor, Wards: 1
Deborah Wadden, Councillor, Wards: 2
Darla MacKeil, Councillor, Wards: 3
Mary Wooldridge-Elliot, Councillor, Wards: 4
David Parker, Councillor, Wards: 7
Larry Turner, Councillor, Wards: 8
Peter Boyles, Councillor, Wards: 9
Randy Palmer, Councillor, Wards: 10
Andy Thompson, Councillor, Wards: 11
Chester Dewar, Councillor, Wards: 12
Brian Cullen, Chief Administrative Officer, 902-485-4311, Fax:
902-485-6475

Richmond County
P.O. Box 120
2357 Hwy. 206
Arichat, NS B0E 1A0
Tel: 902-226-2400; *Fax:* 902-226-1510
www.richmondcounty.ca
Other Information: Toll-Free Phone: 800-567-2600
Municipal Type: Rural Municipalities
Incorporated: April 17, 1879; *Area:* 1,249.33 sq km
County or District: Richmond; *Population in 2016:* 8,694
Provincial Electoral District(s): Cape Breton-Richmond
Federal Electoral District(s): Cape Breton-Canso
Next Election: October 2024 (4 year terms)
Shawn Samson, Councillor, Wards: 1
Michael Diggdon, Councillor, Wards: 2
Melanie Sampson, Councillor, Wards: 3
Amanda Mombourquette, Councillor, Wards: 4
Brent Sampson, Councillor, Wards: 5
Don Marchand, Chief Adminstrative Officer, 902-226-3970, Fax:
902-226-1510
Chris Boudreau, Director, Public Works
Jason Martell, Director, Finance

St. Mary's District
P.O. Box 296
8296 Hwy. #7
Sherbrooke, NS B0J 3C0
Tel: 902-522-2049; *Fax:* 902-522-2309
www.saint-marys.ca
Other Information: Alt. Phone: 902-522-2496
Municipal Type: Rural Municipalities
Incorporated: April 17, 1879; *Area:* 1,909.59 sq km
County or District: Guysborough; *Population in 2016:* 2,233
Provincial Electoral District(s): Guysborough-Eastern
Shore-Tracadie
Federal Electoral District(s): Central Nova
Next Election: October 2024 (4 year terms)
David Gillis, Clerk, 902-522-2049, Fax: 902-522-2309
Marvin MacDonald, Chief Administrative Officer, 902-522-2049,
Fax: 902-522-2309

Shelburne District
P.O. Box 280
136 Hammond St.
Shelburne, NS B0T 1W0
Tel: 902-875-3544; *Fax:* 902-875-1278
www.municipalityofshelburne.ca
Other Information: Alt. Phone: 902-875-3083
Municipal Type: Rural Municipalities
Incorporated: April 17, 1879; *Area:* 1,818.49 sq km
County or District: Shelburne; *Population in 2016:* 4,288
Provincial Electoral District(s): Shelburne
Federal Electoral District(s): South Shore-St. Margaret's
Next Election: October 2024 (4 year terms)
Doris Townsend, Councillor, Wards: 1
Penny Smith, Councillor, Wards: 2
Sherry Thorburn-Irvine, Councillor, Wards: 3
Terry McIntyre, Councillor, Wards: 4
Heidi Wagner, Councillor, Wards: 5
Ron Coole, Councillor, Wards: 6
Dale Richardson, Councillor, Wards: 7
Trudy Payne, Chief Administrative Officer, 902-875-3544

Victoria County
495 Chebucto St.
Baddeck, NS B0E 1B0
Tel: 902-295-3231; *Fax:* 902-295-3331
www.victoriacounty.com
Municipal Type: Rural Municipalities
Incorporated: April 17, 1879; *Area:* 2,870.85 sq km
County or District: Victoria; *Population in 2016:* 7,089
Provincial Electoral District(s): Victoria-The Lakes
Federal Electoral District(s): Sydney-Victoria
Next Election: October 2024 (4 year terms)
Bruce Morrison, Warden, 902-565-8229, Fax: 902-295-1311,
Wards: 3
Leanne MacEachen, Chief Administrative Officer, 902-295-3654,
Fax: 902-295-3331

Yarmouth District
932 Hwy 1
Hebron, NS B5A 5Z5
Tel: 902-742-7159; *Fax:* 902-742-3164
admin@district.yarmouth.ns.ca
www.district.yarmouth.ns.ca
Municipal Type: Rural Municipalities
Incorporated: April 17, 1879; *Area:* 586.65 sq km
County or District: Yarmouth; *Population in 2016:* 9,845
Provincial Electoral District(s): Yarmouth
Federal Electoral District(s): West Nova
Next Election: October 2024 (4 year terms)
John Cunningham, Councillor, 902-742-7159, Fax:
902-742-3164, Wards: 1
Daniel Allen, Councillor, 902-742-7159, Fax: 902-742-3164,
Wards: 2
Sheri Hurlburt, Councillor, Wards: 3
Patti Durkee, Councillor, 902-742-7159, Fax: 902-742-3164,
Wards: 4
Trevor Cunningham, Councillor, 902-742-7159, Fax:
902-742-3164, Wards: 5
Loren Cushing, Councillor, 902-742-7159, Fax: 902-742-3164,
Wards: 6
Nick Hilton, Councillor, Wards: 7
Victoria Brooks, Chief Administrative Officer

NUNAVUT

The Department of Community and Government Services has legislative responsibility for Territorial Acts and Regulations. Some of these include: Area Development; Business Licenses; Cities, Towns and Villages; Commissioner's Land; Community Employees Benefits Program Transfer; Conflict of Interest; Consumer Protection; Curfew; Dog; Emergency Measures; Film Classification; Fire Safety; Hamlet; Homeowners Property Tax Rebate; Local Authorities Election; Lotteries; Pawnbrokers and Second-hand Dealers; Planning; Property Assessments and Taxation; Real Estate Agents Licensing; Religious Societies Land; Residential Tenancies; Senior Citizens and Disabled Persons Property Tax Relief Act; Settlement; Technical Standards and Safety; Western Canada Lottery.

Incorporation as a city, town or village is determined by the value of all assessable land. Incorporation values: Village, $10 million; Town, $50 million; City, $200 million, all tax-based. Hamlets may request tax-based status. There are 24 hamlets and one city in Nunavut.

Starting in October 2019, municipal elections in Nunavut will be held every four years, on the 4th Monday in October.

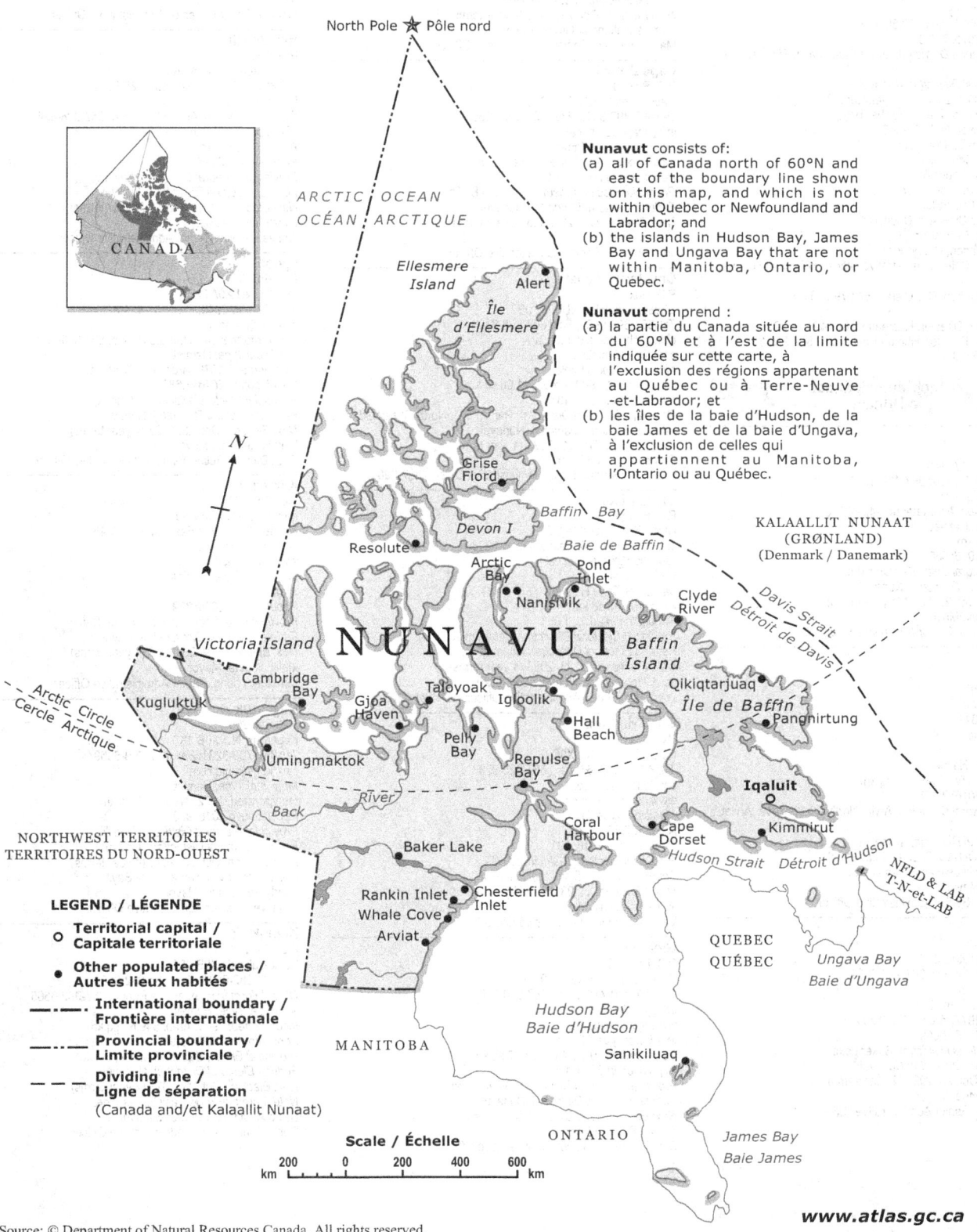

Nunavut consists of:
(a) all of Canada north of 60°N and east of the boundary line shown on this map, and which is not within Quebec or Newfoundland and Labrador; and
(b) the islands in Hudson Bay, James Bay and Ungava Bay that are not within Manitoba, Ontario, or Quebec.

Nunavut comprend :
(a) la partie du Canada située au nord du 60°N et à l'est de la limite indiquée sur cette carte, à l'exclusion des régions appartenant au Québec ou à Terre-Neuve-et-Labrador; et
(b) les îles de la baie d'Hudson, de la baie James et de la baie d'Ungava, à l'exclusion de celles qui appartiennent au Manitoba, l'Ontario ou au Québec.

LEGEND / LÉGENDE

○ Territorial capital / Capitale territoriale

● Other populated places / Autres lieux habités

—··— International boundary / Frontière internationale

—·— Provincial boundary / Limite provinciale

— — Dividing line / Ligne de séparation (Canada and/et Kalaallit Nunaat)

Scale / Échelle

200 0 200 400 600
km   km

www.atlas.gc.ca

Nunavut

Major Municipalities in Nunavut

Iqaluit
P.O. Box 460
Iqaluit, NU X0A 0H0
Tel: 867-979-5600; *Fax:* 867-979-5922
admin@city.iqaluit.nu.ca
www.city.iqaluit.nu.ca
Municipal Type: City
Incorporated: 2001; *Area:* 52.50 sq km
Population in 2016: 7,740
Provincial Electoral District(s): Iqaluit East; Iqaluit West; Iqaluit Centre
Federal Electoral District(s): Nunavut
Next Election: Oct. 23, 2023 (4 year terms)
Note: Formerly known as Frobisher Bay.
Kenny Bell, Mayor, 867-979-5667
Joanasie Akumalik, Councillor
Solomon Awa, Councillor
Sheila Flaherty, Councillor
Malaiya Lucassie, Councillor
Simon Nattaq, Councillor
Janet Pitsiulaaq Brewster, Councillor
Kyle Sheppard, Councillor
Romeyn Stevenson, Councillor
Amy Elgersma, Chief Administrative Officer, 867-979-5667, Fax: 867-979-0228
Tammy Ernst-Doiron, City Clerk, 867-979-5634, Fax: 867-979-0228
Stephanie Clark, Director, Recreation, 867-975-8532
Robyn Mackey, Director, Human Resources, 867-975-8506, Fax: 867-979-5210

Other Municipalities in Nunavut

Arctic Bay
P.O. Box 150
Arctic Bay, NU X0A 0A0
Tel: 867-439-9917; *Fax:* 867-439-8767
recep_ap@qiniq.com
Other Information: Alternate: 867-439-9918
Municipal Type: Hamlet
Area: 247.5 sq km
Population in 2016: 868
Provincial Electoral District(s): Quttiktuq
Federal Electoral District(s): Nunavut
Next Election: Oct. 23, 2023 (4 year terms)
Moses Oyukuluk, Mayor
Deborah Johnson, Senior Administrative Officer

Arviat
P.O. Box 150
613 3rd Avenue
Arviat, NU X0C 0E0
Tel: 867-857-2841
reception@arviat.ca
www.arviat.ca
Municipal Type: Hamlet
Incorporated: 1977; *Area:* 132 sq km
Population in 2016: 2,657
Provincial Electoral District(s): Arviat North-Whale Cove; Arviat South
Federal Electoral District(s): Nunavut
Next Election: Oct. 23, 2023 (4 year terms)
Note: Formerly known as Eskimo Point.
Bob Leonard, Mayor
Steve England, Senior Administrative Officer

Baker Lake
P.O. Box 149
Baker Lake, NU X0C 0A0
Tel: 867-793-2874; *Fax:* 867-793-2509
www.bakerlake.ca
Municipal Type: Hamlet
Incorporated: 1977; *Area:* 182.22 sq km
Population in 2016: 2,069
Provincial Electoral District(s): Baker Lake
Federal Electoral District(s): Nunavut
Next Election: Oct. 23, 2023 (4 year terms)
Richard Aksawnee, Mayor
Sheldon Dorey, Senior Administrative Officer

Cambridge Bay
P.O. Box 16
23 Kamotik Rd.
Cambridge Bay, NU X0B 0C0
Tel: 867-983-4650; *Fax:* 867-983-2193
frontdesk@cambridgebay.ca
www.cambridgebay.ca
Municipal Type: Hamlet
Incorporated: 1984; *Area:* 202.2 sq km
Population in 2016: 1,766
Provincial Electoral District(s): Cambridge Bay
Federal Electoral District(s): Nunavut
Next Election: Oct. 23, 2023 (4 year terms)
Pamela Hakongak Gross, Mayor
Marla Limousin, Senior Administrative Officer

Cape Dorset
P.O. Box 30
Cape Dorset, NU X0A 0C0
Tel: 867-897-8943; *Fax:* 867-897-8030
info@capedorset.ca
Municipal Type: Hamlet
Incorporated: 1982; *Area:* 9.74 sq km
Population in 2016: 1,441
Provincial Electoral District(s): South Baffin
Federal Electoral District(s): Nunavut
Next Election: Oct. 23, 2023 (4 year terms)
Vacant, Mayor
John Hussey, Senior Administrative Officer

Chesterfield Inlet
P.O. Box 10
Chesterfield Inlet, NU X0C 0B0
Tel: 867-898-9951; *Fax:* 867-898-9108
clerk@chesterfield-inlet.ca
chesterfield-inlet.ca
Municipal Type: Hamlet
Incorporated: 1980; *Area:* 141.08 sq km
Population in 2016: 437
Provincial Electoral District(s): Rankin Inlet North-Chesrfield Inlet
Federal Electoral District(s): Nunavut
Next Election: Oct. 23, 2023 (4 year terms)
Barney Aggark, Mayor
Paul Sammurtok, Senior Administrative Officer, 867-898-9926

Clyde River
P.O. Box 89
Clyde River, NU X0A 0E0
Tel: 867-924-6220; *Fax:* 867-924-6293
reception@clyderiver.ca
clyderiver.ca
Municipal Type: Hamlet
Area: 106.48 sq km
Population in 2016: 1,053
Provincial Electoral District(s): Uqqummiut
Federal Electoral District(s): Nunavut
Next Election: Oct. 23, 2023 (4 year terms)
Jerry Natanine, Mayor, 867-924-6220
John Ivey, Senior Administrative Officer, 867-924-6220

Coral Harbour
P.O. Box 30
Coral Harbour, NU X0C 0C0
Tel: 867-925-8867; *Fax:* 867-925-8233
coraledo@qiniq.com
www.coralharbour.ca
Municipal Type: Hamlet
Area: 137.83 sq km
Population in 2016: 891
Provincial Electoral District(s): Aivilik
Federal Electoral District(s): Nunavut
Next Election: Oct. 23, 2023 (4 year terms)
Willie Nakoolak, Mayor
Vacant, Senior Administrative Officer

Gjoa Haven
P.O. Box 200
Gjoa Haven, NU X0B 1J0
Tel: 867-360-7141; *Fax:* 867-360-6309
edogjoa@qiniq.com
www.gjoahaven.net
Municipal Type: Hamlet
Incorporated: 1981; *Area:* 28.47 sq km
Population in 2016: 1,324
Provincial Electoral District(s): Gjoa Haven
Federal Electoral District(s): Nunavut
Next Election: Oct. 23, 2023 (4 year terms)
Megan Porter, Mayor
David Stockley, Senior Administrative Officer

Grise Fiord
P.O. Box 77
Grise Fiord, NU X0A 0J0
Tel: 867-980-9959; *Fax:* 867-980-9052
gfeafao@qiniq.com
Municipal Type: Hamlet
Incorporated: 1987; *Area:* 332.7 sq km
Population in 2016: 129
Provincial Electoral District(s): Quttiktuq
Federal Electoral District(s): Nunavut
Next Election: Oct. 23, 2023 (4 year terms)
Meeka Kigutak, Mayor
Marjorie Dobson, Senior Administrative Officer

Hall Beach
P.O. Box 3
Hall Beach, NU X0A 0K0
Tel: 867-928-8829; *Fax:* 867-928-8871
fino_hbhamlet@qiniq.com
Other Information: Alternate Phone: 867-928-8945
Municipal Type: Hamlet
Area: 16.82 sq km
Population in 2016: 848
Provincial Electoral District(s): Amittuq
Federal Electoral District(s): Nunavut
Next Election: Oct. 23, 2023 (4 year terms)
Jayko Simonie, Mayor
James Langille, Senior Administrative Officer

Igloolik
P.O. Box 30
Igloolik, NU X0A 0L0
Tel: 867-934-8940; *Fax:* 867-934-8757
igloolik@magma.ca
Other Information: Alternate Phone: 867-934-8830
Municipal Type: Hamlet
Incorporated: 1976; *Area:* 102.87 sq km
Population in 2016: 1,682
Provincial Electoral District(s): Amittuq
Federal Electoral District(s): Nunavut
Next Election: Oct. 23, 2023 (4 year terms)
Merlyn Recinos, Mayor
Gord Dinney, Acting Senior Administrative Officer

Kimmirut
P.O. Box 120
Kimmirut, NU X0A 0N0
Tel: 867-939-2247; *Fax:* 867-939-2045
cedkimm@qiniq.com
www.kimmirut.ca
Municipal Type: Hamlet
Area: 2.27 sq km
Population in 2016: 389
Provincial Electoral District(s): South Baffin
Federal Electoral District(s): Nunavut
Next Election: Oct. 23, 2023 (4 year terms)
Maliktuk Lyta, Mayor
Kimberly Young, Senior Administrative Officer

Kugaaruk
P.O. Box 205
Kugaaruk, NU X0B 1K0
Tel: 867-769-6281; *Fax:* 867-769-6069
sao_kug@qiniq.com
Municipal Type: Hamlet
Incorporated: 1972; *Area:* 4.97 sq km
Population in 2016: 933
Provincial Electoral District(s): Netsilik
Federal Electoral District(s): Nunavut
Next Election: Oct. 23, 2023 (4 year terms)
Note: Formerly known as Pelly Bay.
Teddy Apsaktaun, Mayor
John Ivey, Senior Administrative Officer

Kugluktuk
P.O. Box 271
Kugluktuk, NU X0B 0E0
Tel: 867-982-6500; *Fax:* 867-982-3060
Other Information: Alternate Phone: 867-982-6505
Municipal Type: Hamlet
Incorporated: 1981; *Area:* 549.61 sq km
Population in 2016: 1,491
Provincial Electoral District(s): Kugluktuk
Federal Electoral District(s): Nunavut
Next Election: Oct. 23, 2023 (4 year terms)
Note: Formerly known as Coppermine.
David Audlatak Nivingalok, Mayor
Don LeBlanc, Senior Administrative Officer

Naujaat
P.O. Box 10
Naujaat, NU X0C 0H0
Tel: 867-462-9952; *Fax:* 867-462-4144
edorepulse@qiniq.com
www.repulsebay.ca
Municipal Type: Hamlet
Incorporated: 1978; *Area:* 423.74 sq km
Population in 2016: 1,082
Provincial Electoral District(s): Aivilik
Federal Electoral District(s): Nunavut
Next Election: Oct. 23, 2023 (4 year terms)
Note: Residents of Repulse Bay voted on May 12, 2014, to change the Hamlet's name to Naujaat, which is the community's Inuktitut name, meaning "Nesting place for seagulls."
Alan Robinson, Mayor
Rob Hedley, Senior Administrative Officer

Pangnirtung
P.O. Box 253
Pangnirtung, NU X0A 0R0
Tel: 867-473-8953; *Fax:* 867-473-8832
pang_reception@qiniq.com
www.pangnirtung.ca
Other Information: pangedo@qiniq.com
Municipal Type: Hamlet
Incorporated: 1972; *Area:* 7.54 sq km
Population in 2016: 1,481
Provincial Electoral District(s): Pangnirtung
Federal Electoral District(s): Nunavut
Next Election: Oct. 23, 2023 (4 year terms)
Hezakiah Oshutapik, Mayor
Ron Ladd, Senior Administrative Officer

Pond Inlet
P.O. Box 180
801 Tuqaarvik St.
Pond Inlet, NU X0A 0S0
Tel: 867-899-8934; *Fax:* 867-899-8940
info@pondinlet.ca
www.pondinlet.ca
Other Information: Alternate Phone: 867-899-8935
Municipal Type: Hamlet
Area: 173.36 sq km
Population in 2016: 1,617
Provincial Electoral District(s): Tununiq
Federal Electoral District(s): Nunavut
Next Election: Oct. 23, 2023 (4 year terms)

Joshua Arreak, Mayor
Vacant, Senior Administrative Officer

Qikiqtarjuaq
P.O. Box 4
Qikiqtarjuaq, NU X0A 0B0
Tel: 867-927-8832; *Fax:* 867-927-8120
munqik@qiniq.com
Other Information: Alternate Phone: 867-927-8178
Municipal Type: Hamlet
Area: 130.65 sq km
Population in 2016: 598
Provincial Electoral District(s): Uqqummiut
Federal Electoral District(s): Nunavut
Next Election: Oct. 23, 2023 (4 year terms)
Note: Formerly Broughton Island.
Harry Alookie, Mayor
Geela Kooneeliusie, Senior Administrative Officer

Rankin Inlet
P.O. Box 310
Rankin Inlet, NU X0C 0G0
Tel: 867-645-2895; *Fax:* 867-645-2146
www.rankininlet.ca
Municipal Type: Hamlet
Incorporated: 1975; *Area:* 20.24 sq km
Population in 2016: 2,842
Provincial Electoral District(s): Rankin Inlet North-Chesterfield Inlet; Rankin Inlet South
Federal Electoral District(s): Nunavut
Next Election: Oct. 23, 2023 (4 year terms)
Harry Towtongie, Mayor
Justin Merritt, Senior Administrative Officer

Resolute Bay
P.O. Box 60
Resolute Bay, NU X0A 0V0
Tel: 867-252-3616; *Fax:* 867-252-3749
cedorb@qiniq.com
Municipal Type: Hamlet
Incorporated: 1987; *Area:* 116.89 sq km
Population in 2016: 198
Provincial Electoral District(s): Quttiktuq
Federal Electoral District(s): Nunavut
Next Election: Oct. 23, 2023 (4 year terms)
Note: Also called Resolute.
Mark Amarualik, Mayor
Angela Idlout, Senior Administrative Officer

Sanikiluaq
P.O. Box 157
Sanikiluaq, NU X0A 0W0
Tel: 867-266-7900; *Fax:* 867-266-7924
www.sanikiluaq.ca
Municipal Type: Hamlet
Incorporated: 1976; *Area:* 114.98 sq km
Population in 2016: 882
Provincial Electoral District(s): Hudson Bay
Federal Electoral District(s): Nunavut
Next Election: Oct. 23, 2023 (4 year terms)
Johnnie Cookie, Mayor
Michael Rowan, Senior Administrative Officer, 867-266-7910

Taloyoak
P.O. Box 8
Taloyoak, NU X0B 1B0
Tel: 867-561-6341; *Fax:* 867-561-5057
edotalo@qiniq.com
Municipal Type: Hamlet
Incorporated: 1981; *Area:* 37.65 sq km
Population in 2016: 1,029
Provincial Electoral District(s): Nattilik
Federal Electoral District(s): Nunavut
Next Election: Oct. 23, 2023 (4 year terms)
Note: Formerly known as Spence Bay.
Chuck Pizzo-Lyall, Mayor
Greg Holitzki, Senior Administrative Officer, 867-561-6341, Fax: 897-561-5057

Whale Cove
P.O. Box 120
Whale Cove, NU X0C 0J0
Tel: 867-896-9961; *Fax:* 867-896-9109
cedo@whalecove.ca
www.whalecove.ca
Municipal Type: Hamlet
Incorporated: 1976; *Area:* 283.65 sq km
Population in 2016: 435
Provincial Electoral District(s): Arviat North-Whale Cove
Federal Electoral District(s): Nunavut
Next Election: Oct. 23, 2023 (4 year terms)
Percy Kabloona, Mayor
Ian Copeland, Senior Administrative Officer

ONTARIO

There are two types of municipal government structures in Ontario: two-tier municipalities, which consist of upper-tier municipalities, known as either regions or counties, plus their constituent lower-tier municipalities; and single-tier municipalities.

One-half of Ontario's population lives in the single-tier cities of Toronto, Ottawa and Hamilton and in areas with a regional system of government. The regional system was created for the more densely populated areas of this province. Regions have more servicing responsibilities than a county, and while there are variations, services usually provided by regions include arterial roads, transit, policing, sewer and water systems, waste disposal, region-wide land use planning and development, health and social services. Lower-tier municipalities within regions are generally responsible for local roads, fire protection, tax collection, garbage collection, recreation and local land use planning. All municipalities in a region participate in the regional system.

Counties exist only in southern Ontario. Lower-tier municipalities (known as cities, towns, villages, townships) within counties provide the majority of municipal services to their residents. The services provided by county governments are usually limited to arterial roads, health and social services and county land use planning. Local municipalities raise taxes for their own purposes, as well as for upper-tier and school board purposes.

Generally, membership of the upper-tier council comprises representatives from the lower tiers, although heads of council can be directly elected.

Single-tier municipalities exist across Ontario and include separated municipalities that are located within a county but are not part of the county for municipal purposes (e.g. City of Windsor, Town of Smiths Falls, Township of Pelee). Single-tier municipalities also include all northern municipalities (e.g. City of Thunder Bay, Town of Blind River, Township of Cockburn Island). Single-tier municipalities also include those former counties or regional municipalities that have amalgamated into single-tier municipalities (e.g. Municipality of Chatham-Kent, County of Prince Edward, County of Brant, City of Kawartha Lakes, City of Toronto, City of Hamilton, City of Ottawa, City of Greater Sudbury, Haldimand County, Norfolk County). Single-tier municipalities have responsibilities for their residents.

The more populated areas are incorporated into municipalities; roughly 33,000 people (not including aboriginal peoples on reserves) live in areas not incorporated as municipalities. Services in the northern regions have been structured to optimize efficiencies in service delivery. District Social Service Administration Boards deliver core services in social assistance, child care and social housing, and may also provide optional health services, land ambulances and public health. Some services in a limited number of unincorporated areas are provided by local service boards and local roads which are funded by the province.

Under the Municipal Elections Act, local government elections are held on the fourth Monday in October, for a four-year term (2018, 2022, etc.).

Ontario

Counties & Municipal Districts in Ontario

Brant
P.O. Box 160
26 Park Ave.
Burford, ON N0E 1A0
Tel: 519-449-2451; *Fax:* 519-449-2454
info@brant.ca
www.brant.ca
Other Information: Toll-Free Phone: 888-250-2295
Municipal Type: County
Incorporated: Jan. 1, 1999; *Area:* 843.25 sq km
Population in 2016: 36,707
Provincial Electoral District(s): Brantford-Brant; Cambridge; Oxford
Federal Electoral District(s): Brantford-Brant
Next Election: Oct. 24, 2022 (4 year terms)
David Bailey, Mayor
John MacAlpine, Councillor, Wards: 1
John Wheat, Councillor, Wards: 1
Steve Howes, Councillor, Wards: 2
Marc Laferriere, Councillor, Wards: 2
John Bell, Councillor, Wards: 3
John Peirce, Councillor, Wards: 3
Robert Chambers, Councillor, Wards: 4
David Miller, Councillor, Wards: 4
Brian Coleman, Councillor, Wards: 5
Joan Gatward, Councillor, Wards: 5
Heather Boyd, Clerk & Director, Council Services
Michael Bradley, Chief Administrative Officer
Heather Mifflin, Treasurer & Director, Finance
Kathy Ballantyne, Director, Parks & Facilities, 519-442-1818
Alex Davidson, Director, Water
Pam Duesling, General Manager, Development Services, 519-442-6324
Robert Walton, General Manager, Operations
Geoff Hayman, Fire Chief, 519-442-4500

Bruce
P.O. Box 70
30 Park St.
Walkerton, ON N0G 2V0
Tel: 519-881-1291
info@brucecounty.on.ca
www.brucecounty.on.ca
Municipal Type: County
Area: 4,090.20 sq km
Population in 2016: 68,147
Next Election: Oct. 24, 2022 (4 year terms)
Steve Hammell, Councillor, Wards: Arran Elderslie
Mitch Twolan, Councillor, Wards: Huron-Kinloss
Chris Peabody, Councillor, Wards: Brockton
Anne Eadie, Councillor, Wards: Kincardine
Luke Charbonneau, Councillor, Wards: Saugeen Shores
Milton McIver, Councillor, Wards: Northern Bruce Peninsula
Janice Jackson, Councillor, Wards: South Bruce Peninsula
Robert Buckle, Councillor, Wards: South Bruce
Sandra Datars Bere, Chief Administrative Officer
Edward Henley, Director, Corporate Services
Kara Van Myall, Director, Planning & Development

Dufferin
55 Zina St.
Orangeville, ON L9W 1E5
Tel: 519-941-2816; *Fax:* 519-941-4565
info@dufferincounty.ca
www.dufferincounty.ca
Other Information: Toll-Free Phone: 877-941-6991
Municipal Type: County
Incorporated: Jan. 24, 1881; *Area:* 1,486.44 sq km
Population in 2016: 61,735
Next Election: Oct. 24, 2022 (4 year terms)
Darren White, Warden, Wards: Melancthon
Steve Anderson, Councillor, Wards: Shelburne
Sandy Brown, Councillor, Wards: Orangeville
John Creelman, Councillor, Wards: Mono
Bob Currie, Councillor, Wards: Amaranth
Guy Gardhouse, Councillor, Wards: East Garafraxa
Chris Gerrits, Councillor, Wards: Amaranth
Earl Hawkins, Councillor, Wards: Mulmur
Janet Horner, Councillor, Wards: Mulmur
Andy Macintosh, Councillor, Wards: Orangeville
Wade Mills, Councillor, Wards: Shelburne
Philip Rentsch, Councillor, Wards: Grand Valley
Laura Ryan, Councillor, Wards: Mono
Steve Soloman, Councillor, Wards: Grand Valley
Sonya Pritchard, Chief Administrative Officer
Aimee Raves, Acting Treasurer

Scott Burns, Director, Public Works

Durham
P.O. Box 623
605 Rossland Rd. East
Whitby, ON L1N 6A3
Tel: 905-668-7711
info@durham.ca
www.durham.ca
Other Information: Toll-Free Phone: 800-372-1102
Municipal Type: Regional Municipality
Incorporated: Jan. 1, 1974; *Area:* 2,523.80 sq km
Population in 2016: 645,862
Next Election: Oct. 24, 2022 (4 year terms)
Note: Durham Region elected its first chair in 2014.
John Henry, Regional Chair
Shaun Collier, Councillor, Wards: Ajax
Marilyn Crawford, Councillor, Wards: Ajax
Sterling Lee, Councillor, Wards: Ajax
Joanne Dies, Councillor, Wards: Ajax
Debbie Bath-Hadden, Councillor, Wards: Brock
Ted Smith, Councillor, Wards: Brock
Adrian Foster, Councillor, Wards: Clarington
Joe Neal, Councillor, Wards: Clarington
Granville Anderson, Councillor, Wards: Clarington
Dan Carter, Councillor, Wards: Oshawa
John Neal, Councillor, Wards: Oshawa
Tito-Dante Marimpietri, Councillor, Wards: Oshawa
Bob Chapman, Councillor, Wards: Oshawa
Rick Kerr, Councillor, Wards: Oshawa
Brian Nicholson, Councillor, Wards: Oshawa
Dave Ryan, Councillor, Wards: Pickering
Kevin Ashe, Councillor, Wards: Pickering
Bill McLean, Councillor, Wards: Pickering
David Pickles, Councillor, Wards: Pickering
Bobbie Drew, Councillor, Wards: Scugog
Wilma Wotten, Councillor, Wards: Scugog
Dave Barton, Councillor, Wards: Uxbridge
Gord Highet, Councillor, Wards: Uxbridge
Don Mitchell, Councillor, Wards: Whitby
Elizabeth Roy, Councillor, Wards: Whitby
Chris Leahy, Councillor, Wards: Whitby
Steve Yamada, Councillor, Wards: Whitby
Rhonda Mulcahy, Councillor, Wards: Whitby
Elaine Baxter-Trahair, Chief Administrative Officer
Nancy Taylor, Treasurer & Commissioner, Finance
Brian Bridgeman, Commissioner, Planning & Economic Development
Stella Danos-Papaconstantinou, Commissioner, Social Services
Susan Siopis, Commissioner, Works
Robert Kyle, Medical Officer of Health, Fax: 905-666-3327
Warren Leonard, Director, Durham Emergency Management, 905-430-2792, Fax: 905-430-8635

Elgin
450 Sunset Dr.
St Thomas, ON N5R 5V1
Tel: 519-631-1460
www.elgincounty.ca
Municipal Type: County
Incorporated: 1852; *Area:* 1,881.03 sq km
Population in 2016: 88,978
Next Election: Oct. 24, 2022 (4 year terms)
Note: Restructuring of the county occurred in 1998.
Dave Mennill, Warden, Wards: Malahide
Duncan McPhail, Deputy Warden, Wards: West Elgin
Mary French, Councillor, Wards: Aylmer
Ed Ketchabaw, Councillor, Wards: Bayham
Sally Martyn, Councillor, Wards: Central Elgin
Tom Marks, Councillor, Wards: Central Elgin
Bob Purcell, Councillor, Wards: Dutton/Dunwich
Dominique Giguère, Councillor, Wards: Malahide
Grant Jones, Councillor, Wards: Southwold
Julie Gonyou, Chief Administrative Officer

Essex
360 Fairview Ave. West
Essex, ON N8M 1Y6
Tel: 519-776-6441; *Fax:* 519-776-4455
www.countyofessex.on.ca
Municipal Type: County
Incorporated: 1999; *Area:* 1,850.90 sq km
Population in 2016: 398,953
Next Election: Oct. 24, 2022 (4 year terms)
Aldo DiCarlo, Councillor, Wards: Amherstburg
Leo Meloche, Councillor, Wards: Amherstburg
Larry Snively, Councillor, Wards: Essex
Richard Meloche, Councillor, Wards: Essex
Nelson Santos, Councillor, Wards: Kingsville
Gord Queen, Councillor, Wards: Kingsville
Tom Bain, Councillor, Wards: Lakeshore
Tracey Bailey, Councillor, Wards: Lakeshore

Marc A. Bondy, Councillor, Wards: LaSalle
Crystal Meloche, Councillor, Wards: LaSalle
Hilda MacDonald, Councillor, Wards: Leamington
Larry Verbeke, Councillor, Wards: Leamington
Gary McNamara, Councillor, Wards: Tecumseh
Joe Bachetti, Councillor, Wards: Tecumseh
Robert Maisonville, Chief Administrative Officer

Frontenac
2069 Battersea Rd., RR#1
Glenburnie, ON K0H 1S0
Tel: 613-548-9400; *Fax:* 613-546-8460
www.frontenaccounty.ca
Municipal Type: County
Incorporated: Jan. 1, 1998; *Area:* 3,787.76 sq km
Population in 2016: 150,475
Next Election: Oct. 24, 2022 (4 year terms)
Ron Higgins, Councillor, Wards: North Frontenac
Frances Smith, Councillor, Wards: Central Frontenac
Ron Vandewal, Councillor, Wards: South Frontenac
Denis Doyle, Councillor, Wards: Frontenac Islands
Kelly Pender, Chief Administrative Officer
Jannette Amini, Clerk & Manager, Legislative Services
Paul Charbonneau, Chief of Paramedics & Director, Emergency & Transportation Services
Joe Gallivan, Director, Planning & Economic Development
Mark Podgers, Community Emergency Management Coordinator

Grey
County Administration Bldg.
595 - 9th Ave. East
Owen Sound, ON N4K 3E3
Tel: 519-376-2205
www.grey.ca
Other Information: Toll-Free Phone: 800-567-4739
Municipal Type: County
Incorporated: Jan. 1, 1852; *Area:* 4,513.50 sq km
Population in 2016: 93,830
Next Election: Oct. 24, 2022 (4 year terms)
Paul McQueen, Warden, Wards: Grey Highlands
Scott Mackey, Councillor, Wards: Chatsworth
Brian Gamble, Councillor, Wards: Chatsworth
Dwight Burley, Councillor, Wards: Georgian Bluffs
Sue Carleton, Councillor, Wards: Georgian Bluffs
Aakash Desai, Councillor, Wards: Grey Highlands
Sue Paterson, Councillor, Wards: Hanover
Selwyn Hicks, Councillor, Wards: Hanover
Barb Clumpus, Councillor, Wards: Meaford
Shirley Keaveney, Councillor, Wards: Meaford
Ian Boddy, Councillor, Wards: Owen Sound
Brian O'Leary, Councillor, Wards: Owen Sound
John Woodbury, Councillor, Wards: Southgate
Brian Milne, Councillor, Wards: Southgate
Alar Soever, Councillor, Wards: The Blue Mountains
Rob Potter, Councillor, Wards: The Blue Mountains
Christine Robinson, Councillor, Wards: West Grey
Tom Hutchinson, Councillor, Wards: West Grey
Heather Morrison, Clerk
Kim Wingrove, Chief Administrative Officer
Kevin Weppler, Director, Corprate Services
Barb Fedy, Director, Social Services
Randy Scherzer, Director, Planning & Development

Haldimand
Cayuga Administration Bldg.
P.O. Box 400
45 Munsee St. North
Cayuga, ON N0A 1E0
Tel: 905-318-5932; *Fax:* 905-772-3542
www.haldimandcounty.on.ca
Municipal Type: County
Incorporated: Jan. 1, 2001; *Area:* 1,251.54 sq km
Population in 2016: 45,608
Provincial Electoral District(s): Haldimand-Norfolk
Federal Electoral District(s): Haldimand-Norfolk
Next Election: Oct. 24, 2022 (4 year terms)
Ken Hewitt, Mayor
Stewart Patterson, Councillor, Wards: 1
John Metcalfe, Councillor, Wards: 2
Dan Lawrence, Councillor, Wards: 3
Tony Dalimonte, Councillor, Wards: 4
Rob Shirton, Councillor, Wards: 5
Bernie Corbett, Councillor, Wards: 6
Craig Manley, Chief Administrative Officer
Cathy Case, General Manager, Corporate Services
Mike Evers, General Manager, Community & Development Services
Philip Mete, General Manager, Public Works

Haliburton
P.O. Box 399
11 Newcastle St.
Minden, ON K0M 2K0
Tel: 705-286-1333; *Fax:* 705-286-4829
info@county.haliburton.on.ca
www.haliburtoncounty.ca
Municipal Type: County
Incorporated: Jan. 1, 2001; *Area:* 4,076.08 sq km
Population in 2016: 18,062
Next Election: Oct. 24, 2022 (4 year terms)
Carol Moffatt, Councillor, Wards: Algonquin Highlands
Liz Danielsen, Councillor, Wards: Algonquin Highlands
Andrea Roberts, Councillor, Wards: Dysart et al
Patrick Kennedy, Councillor, Wards: Dysart et al
Dave Burton, Councillor, Wards: Highlands East
Cecil Ryall, Councillor, Wards: Highlands East
Brent Devolin, Councillor, Wards: Minden Hills
Lisa Schell, Councillor, Wards: Minden Hills
Mike Rutter, Chief Administrative Officer & County Clerk
Elaine Taylor, Treasurer
Craig Douglas, Director, Public Works
Charlsey White, Director, Planning

Halton
1151 Bronte Rd.
Oakville, ON L6M 3L1
Tel: 905-825-6000; *Fax:* 905-825-9010
accesshalton@halton.ca
www.halton.ca
Other Information: Toll-Free Phone: 866-442-5866; TTY:
905-827-9833
Municipal Type: Regional Municipality
Incorporated: Jan. 1, 1974; *Area:* 964.05 sq km
Population in 2016: 548,435
Next Election: Oct. 24, 2022 (4 year terms)
Gary Carr, Regional Chair
Marianne Meed Ward, Councillor, Wards: Burlington Mayor
Kelvin Galbraith, Councillor, Wards: Burlington 1
Lisa Kearns, Councillor, Wards: Burlington 2
Rory Nisan, Councillor, Wards: Burlington 3
Shawna Stolte, Councillor, Wards: Burlington 4
Paul Sharman, Councillor, Wards: Burlington 5
Angelo Bentivegna, Councillor, Wards: Burlington 6
Rick Bonnette, Councillor, Wards: Halton Hills Mayor
Clark Somerville, Councillor, Wards: Halton Hills 1 & 2
Jane Fogal, Councillor, Wards: Halton Hills 3 & 4
Gordon A. Krantz, Councillor, Wards: Milton Mayor
Colin Best, Councillor, Wards: Milton 1
Rick Malboeuf, Councillor, Wards: Milton 2
Mike Cluett, Councillor, Wards: Milton 3
Zeeshan Hamid, Councillor, Wards: Milton 4
Rob Burton, Councillor, Wards: Oakville Mayor
Sean O'Meara, Councillor, Wards: Oakville 1
Cathy Duddeck, Councillor, Wards: Oakville 2
Dave Gittings, Councillor, Wards: Oakville 3
Allan Elgar, Councillor, Wards: Oakville 4
Jeff Knoll, Councillor, Wards: Oakville 5
Tom Adams, Councillor, Wards: Oakville 6
Pavan Parmar, Councillor, Wards: Oakville 7
Jane MacCaskill, Chief Administrative Officer
Cyndy Winslow, Acting Regional Treasurer & Commissioner,
Finance

Hastings
County Administration Bldg.
P.O. Box 4400
235 Pinnacle St.
Belleville, ON K8N 3A9
Tel: 613-966-1319; *Fax:* 613-966-2574
www.hastingscounty.com
Other Information: Toll-Free Phone: 800-510-3306
Municipal Type: County
Incorporated: 1850; *Area:* 6,103.92 sq km
Population in 2016: 136,445
Next Election: Oct. 24, 2022 (4 year terms)
Bob Mullin, Councillor, Wards: Stirling-Rawdon
Paul Jenkins, Councillor, Wards: Bancroft
Bonnie Adams, Councillor, Wards: Carlow/Mayo
Tom Deline, Councillor, Wards: Centre Hastings
Dan Johnston, Councillor, Wards: Deseronto
Dennis Purcell, Councillor, Wards: Faraday
Vic A. Bodnar, Councillor, Wards: Hastings Highlands
Carl Stefanski, Councillor, Wards: Limerick
Loyde Blackburn, Councillor, Wards: Madoc
Jan O'Neill, Councillor, Wards: Marmora & Lake
Libby Clarke, Councillor, Wards: Tudor & Cashel
Jo-Anne Albert, Councillor, Wards: Tweed
Rick Phillips, Councillor, Wards: Tyendinaga
Barbara Shaw, Councillor, Wards: Wollaston
James Pine, Chief Administrative Officer

Justin Harrow, Director, Planning
Sue Horwood, Director, Finance
Shaune Lightfoot, Director, Human Resources

Huron
1 Courthouse Sq.
Goderich, ON N7A 1M2
Tel: 519-524-8394; *Fax:* 519-524-2044
huronadmin@huroncounty.ca
www.huroncounty.ca
Other Information: Toll-Free Phone: 888-524-8394 (in 519 area)
Municipal Type: County
Area: 3,399.27 sq km
Population in 2016: 59,297
Next Election: Oct. 24, 2022 (4 year terms)
Glen McNeil, Councillor, Wards: Ashfield-Colborne-Wawanosh
Roger Watt, Councillor, Wards: Ashfield-Colborne-Wawanosh
Paul Klopp, Councillor, Wards: Bluewater
Jim Fergusson, Councillor, Wards: Bluewater
Jim Ginn, Councillor, Wards: Central Huron
David Jewitt, Councillor, Wards: Central Huron
John Grace, Councillor, Wards: Goderich
Myles Murdock, Councillor, Wards: Goderich
Doug Harding, Councillor, Wards: Howick
Bernie MacLellan, Councillor, Wards: Huron East
Robert Fisher, Councillor, Wards: Huron East
Jamie Heffer, Councillor, Wards: Morris-Turnberry
Bernie Bailey, Councillor, Wards: North Huron
George Finch, Councillor, Wards: South Huron
Jim Dietrich, Councillor, Wards: South Huron
Susan Cronin, Clerk
Meighan Wark, Chief Administrative Officer
Steve Lund, Director, Operations
Sandra Weber, Director, Planning

Lambton
P.O. Box 3000
789 Broadway St.
Wyoming, ON N0N 1T0
Tel: 519-845-0801; *Fax:* 519-845-3160
administration@county-lambton.on.ca
www.lambtononline.com
Other Information: Toll-Free Phone: 866-324-6912
Municipal Type: County
Incorporated: 1853; *Area:* 3,002.25 sq km
Population in 2016: 126,638
Next Election: Oct. 24, 2022 (4 year terms)
Bill Weber, Warden, Wards: Lambton Shores
David Ferguson, Councillor, Wards: Brooke-Alvinston
Alan Broad, Councillor, Wards: Dawn-Euphemia
Kevin Marriott, Councillor, Wards: Enniskillen
Ian Veen, Councillor, Wards: Oil Springs
Brad Loosley, Councillor, Wards: Petrolia
Lonny Napper, Councillor, Wards: Plympton-Wyoming
Bev Hand, Councillor, Wards: Point Edward
Mike Bradley, Councillor, Wards: Sarnia
Steve Arnold, Councillor, Wards: St. Clair
Jackie Rombouts, Councillor, Wards: Warwick
Stephane Thiffeault, Clerk & General Manager, Corporate
Services
Ron Van Horne, Chief Administrative Officer
Jason Cole, General Manager, Infrastructure & Development
Services
Larry Palarchio, General Manager, Finance, Facilities & Court
Services
Matt Deline, Manager, Public Works
Ben Puzanov, Manager, Planning & Development Services

Lanark
County Administration Bldg.
99 Christie Lake Rd.
Perth, ON K7H 3C6
Tel: 613-267-4200; *Fax:* 613-267-2964
info@lanarkcounty.ca
www.county.lanark.on.ca
Other Information: Toll-Free Phone: 888-952-6275
Municipal Type: County
Incorporated: Jan. 1st 1998; *Area:* 3,035.64 sq km
Population in 2016: 68,698
Next Election: Oct. 24, 2022 (4 year terms)
Brian Campbell, Warden, Wards: Tay Valley
Richard Kidd, Councillor, Wards: Beckwith
Sharon Mousseau, Councillor, Wards: Beckwith
Douglas Black, Councillor, Wards: Carleton Place
Sean Redmond, Councillor, Wards: Carleton Place
Steve Fournier, Councillor, Wards: Drummond/North Elmsley
Peter McLaren, Councillor, Wards: Lanark Highlands
John Hall, Councillor, Wards: Lanark Highlands
Christa Lowry, Councillor, Wards: Mississippi Mills
John Levi, Councillor, Wards: Mississippi Mills
Bill Dobson, Councillor, Wards: Montague
Klaas Van Der Meer, Councillor, Wards: Montague

John Fenik, Councillor, Wards: Perth
Ed McPherson, Councillor, Wards: Perth
Barrie Crampton, Councillor, Wards: Tay Valley
Leslie Drynan, Clerk & Deputy Chief Administrative Officer
Kurt Greaves, Chief Administrative Officer
Emily Hollington, Director, Social Services
Terry McCann, Director, Public Works

Lennox & Addington
97 Thomas St. East
Napanee, ON K7R 3S9
Tel: 613-354-4883; *Fax:* 613-354-3112
www.lennox-addington.on.ca
Municipal Type: County
Area: 2,839.68 sq km
Population in 2016: 42,888
Next Election: Oct. 24, 2022 (4 year terms)
Ric Bresee, Councillor, Wards: Loyalist
Jim Hegadorn, Councillor, Wards: Loyalist
Henry Hogg, Councillor, Wards: Addington Highlands
Marg Isbester, Councillor, Wards: Greater Napanee
Max Kaiser, Councillor, Wards: Greater Napanee
Eric Smith, Councillor, Wards: Stone Mills
John Wise, Councillor, Wards: Stone Mills
Brenda Orchard, Chief Administrative Officer, 613-354-4883
Mark Day, Director, Financial Services, 613-354-4883
Stephen Paul, Director, Community & Development Services,
613-354-4883
Mark Schjerning, Chief, Emergency Services, 613-354-4883

Middlesex
399 Ridout St. North
London, ON N6A 2P1
Tel: 519-434-7321; *Fax:* 519-434-0638
www.middlesex.ca
Municipal Type: County
Area: 3,317.27 sq km
Population in 2016: 455,526
Next Election: Oct. 24, 2022 (4 year terms)
Kurtis Smith, Councillor, Wards: Adelaide Metcalfe
Mary Ann Hendrikx, Councillor, Wards: Adelaide Metcalfe
Cathy Burghardt-Jesson, Councillor, Wards: Lucan Biddulph
Dave Manders, Councillor, Wards: Lucan Biddulph
Aina DeViet, Councillor, Wards: Middlesex Centre
John Brennan, Councillor, Wards: Middlesex Centre
Brian Ropp, Councillor, Wards: North Middlesex
Adrian Cornelissen, Councillor, Wards: North Middlesex
Allan Mayhew, Councillor, Wards: Southwest Middlesex
Marigay Wilkins, Councillor, Wards: Southwest Middlesex
Joanne Vanderheyden, Councillor, Wards: Strathroy-Caradoc
Brad Richards, Councillor, Wards: Strathroy-Caradoc
Alison Warwick, Councillor, Wards: Thames Centre
Kelly Elliott, Councillor, Wards: Thames Centre
Diane Brewer, Councillor, Wards: Newbury
Kathy Bunting, Clerk
Bill Rayburn, Chief Administrative Officer
Cindy Howard, General Manager, Finance & Community
Services
Cara Finn, Director, Economic Development
Chris Traini, County Engineer
Doug Spettigue, Human Resource Officer
Durk Vanderwerff, Director, Planning

Muskoka
70 Pine St.
Bracebridge, ON P1L 1N3
Tel: 705-645-2231; *Fax:* 705-645-5319
www.muskoka.on.ca
Municipal Type: Regional Municipality
Incorporated: Jan. 1, 1971; *Area:* 3,940.48 sq km
Population in 2016: 60,599
Next Election: Oct. 24, 2022 (4 year terms)
Graydon Smith, Councillor, Wards: Bracebridge Mayor
Steven Clement, Councillor, Wards: Bracebridge
Rick Maloney, Councillor, Wards: Bracebridge
Don Smith, Councillor, Wards: Bracebridge
Peter Koetsier, Councillor, Wards: Georgian Bay Mayor
Peter Cooper, Councillor, Wards: Georgian Bay 2 & 4
Paul Wiancko, Councillor, Wards: Georgian Bay 1 & 3
Paul Kelly, Councillor, Wards: Gravenhurst Mayor
Sandy Cairns, Councillor, Wards: Gravenhurst
John Gordon, Councillor, Wards: Gravenhurst
Heidi Lorenz, Councillor, Wards: Gravenhurst
Scott Aitchison, Councillor, Wards: Huntsville Mayor
Nancy Alcock, Councillor, Wards: Huntsville
Helena Renwick, Councillor, Wards: Huntsville
Brian Thompson, Councillor, Wards: Huntsville
Terry Glover, Councillor, Wards: Lake of Bays Mayor
Mike Peppard, Councillor, Wards: Lake of Bays Franklin/Sinclair
Robert Lacroix, Councillor, Wards: Lake of Bays Ridout/McLean
Phil Harding, Councillor, Wards: Muskoka Lakes Mayor
Ruth-Ellen Nishikawa, Councillor, Wards: Muskoka Lakes A

Allen Edwards, Councillor, Wards: Muskoka Lakes B
Frank Jaglowitz, Councillor, Wards: Muskoka Lakes C
Amy Black, District Clerk
Michael Duben, Chief Administrative Officer
Samantha Hastings, Commissioner, Planning & Economic Development
Fred Jahn, Commissioner, Engineering & Public Works
Julie Stevens, Commissioner, Finance & Corporate Services

Niagara
P.O. Box 1042
1815 Sir Isaac Brock Way
Thorold, ON L2V 4T7
Tel: 905-980-6000
www.niagararegion.ca
Other Information: Toll-Free Phone: 800-263-7215
Municipal Type: Regional Municipality
Incorporated: Jan. 1, 1970; *Area:* 1,854.23 sq km
Population in 2016: 447,346
Next Election: Oct. 24, 2022 (4 year terms)
Wayne H. Redekop, Councillor, Wards: Fort Erie
Jeff A. Jordan, Councillor, Wards: Grimsby
Sandra Easton, Councillor, Wards: Lincoln
Jim Diodati, Councillor, Wards: Niagara Falls
Betty Disero, Councillor, Wards: Niagara-on-the-Lake
Marvin Junkin, Councillor, Wards: Pelham
Bill Steele, Councillor, Wards: Port Colborne
Walter Sendzik, Councillor, Wards: St. Catharines
Terry Ugulini, Councillor, Wards: Thorold
Kevin Gibson, Councillor, Wards: Wainfleet
Frank Campion, Councillor, Wards: Welland
David Bylsma, Councillor, Wards: West Lincoln
Ron Tripp, Acting Chief Administrative Officer
Todd Harrison, Commissioner, Enterprise Resource Management Services
Adrienne Jugley, Commissioner, Community Services
Rino Mostacci, Commissioner, Planning & Development Services
Bruce Zvaniga, Interim Commissioner, Public Works
Kevin Smith, Regional Fire Chief

Norfolk County
50 Colborne St. South
Simcoe, ON N3Y 4N5
Tel: 519-426-5870; *Fax:* 519-426-8573
askus@norfolkcounty.ca
www.norfolkcounty.on.ca
Municipal Type: County
Incorporated: Jan. 1, 2001; *Area:* 1,607.55 sq km
Population in 2016: 64,044
Provincial Electoral District(s): Haldimand-Norfolk
Federal Electoral District(s): Haldimand-Norfolk
Next Election: Oct. 24, 2022 (4 year terms)
Kristal Chopp, Mayor
Tom Masschaele, Councillor, Wards: 1
Roger Geysens, Councillor, Wards: 2
Michael J. Columbus, Councillor, Wards: 3
Chris Van Paassen, Councillor, Wards: 4
Ian Rabbitts, Councillor, Wards: 5
Ryan J. Taylor, Councillor, Wards: 5
Amy Martin, Councillor, Wards: 6
Kim Huffman, Councillor, Wards: 7
Jason Burgess, Chief Administrative Officer
Jason Godby, Interim General Manager, Public Works
Gord Stilwell, Fire Chief

Northumberland
555 Courthouse Rd.
Cobourg, ON K9A 5J6
Tel: 905-372-3329; *Fax:* 905-372-1746
www.northumberlandcounty.ca
Other Information: Toll-Free Phone: 800-354-7050
Municipal Type: County
Area: 1,905.15 sq km
Population in 2016: 85,598
Next Election: Oct. 24, 2022 (4 year terms)
Bill Cane, Councillor, Wards: Hamilton
Gail Latchford, Councillor, Wards: Alnwick/Haldimand
Brian Ostrander, Councillor, Wards: Brighton
John Henderson, Councillor, Wards: Cobourg
Mandy Martin, Councillor, Wards: Cramahe
Bob Sanderson, Councillor, Wards: Port Hope
Robert Crate, Councillor, Wards: Trent Hills
Nancy MacDonald, Clerk & Manager, Legislative Services
Jennifer Moore, Chief Administrative Officer
Lisa Ainsworth, Director, Corporate Services
Dan Borowec, Director, Economic Development, Land Use Planning & Tourism
Glenn Dees, Director, Finance

Peel
10 Peel Centre Dr.
Brampton, ON L6T 4B9
Tel: 905-791-7800
www.peelregion.ca
Other Information: Toll-Free Phone: 888-919-7800
Municipal Type: Regional Municipality
Incorporated: Oct. 15, 1973; *Area:* 1,246.95 sq km
Population in 2016: 1,381,739
Next Election: Oct. 24, 2022 (4 year terms)
Patrick Brown, Councillor, Wards: Brampton Mayor
Paul Vicente, Councillor, Wards: Brampton 1 & 5
Michael Paul Palleschi, Councillor, Wards: Brampton 2 & 6
Martin Medeiros, Councillor, Wards: Brampton 3 & 4
Pat Fortini, Councillor, Wards: Brampton 7 & 8
Gurpreet Singh Dhillon, Councillor, Wards: Brampton 9 & 10
Allan Thompson, Councillor, Wards: Caledon Mayor
Ian Sinclair, Councillor, Wards: Caledon 1
Johanna Downey, Councillor, Wards: Caledon 2
Jennifer Innis, Councillor, Wards: Caledon 3 & 4
Annette Groves, Councillor, Wards: Caledon 5
Bonnie Crombie, Councillor, Wards: Mississauga Mayor
Stephen Dasko, Councillor, Wards: Mississauga 1
Karen Ras, Councillor, Wards: Mississauga 2
Chris Fonseca, Councillor, Wards: Mississauga 3
John Kovac, Councillor, Wards: Mississauga 4
Carolyn Parrish, Councillor, Wards: Mississauga 5
Ron Starr, Councillor, Wards: Mississauga 6
Dipika Damerla, Councillor, Wards: Mississauga 7
Matt Mahoney, Councillor, Wards: Mississauga 8
Pat Saito, Councillor, Wards: Mississauga 9
Sue McFadden, Councillor, Wards: Mississauga 10
George Carlson, Councillor, Wards: Mississauga 11
Kathryn Lockyer, Regional Clerk
Nancy Polsinelli, Chief Administrative Officer
Stephen VanOfwegen, Chief Financial Officer & Commissioner, Finance
Kathryn Lockyer, Acting Commissioner, Corporate Services
Andrew Farr, Acting Commissioner, Public Works

Perth
Courthouse
1 Huron St.
Stratford, ON N5A 5S4
Tel: 519-271-0531; *Fax:* 519-271-6265
www.perthcounty.ca
Other Information: Toll-Free Phone: 800-463-8275
Municipal Type: County
Incorporated: Jan. 1850; *Area:* 2,218.52 sq km
Population in 2016: 76,796
Next Election: Oct. 24, 2022 (4 year terms)
Note: Restructuring occurred in Jan. 1998.
Jim Aitcheson, Warden, Wards: Perth South
Todd Kasenberg, Councillor, Wards: North Perth
Doug Kellum, Councillor, Wards: North Perth
Rhonda Ehgoetz, Councillor, Wards: Perth East
Hugh McDermid, Councillor, Wards: Perth East
Daryl Herlick, Councillor, Wards: Perth East
Robert Wilhelm, Councillor, Wards: Perth South
Walter McKenzie, Councillor, Wards: West Perth
Douglas Eidt, Councillor, Wards: West Perth
Tyler Sager, Clerk & Manager, Legisative Services
Lori Wolfe, Interim Chief Administrative Officer
Corey Bridges, Treasurer & Manager, Finance
Marion McKeen, Manager, Human Resources
Sally McMullen, Manager, Planning & Development
Todd KcKone, Coordinator, Emergency Management

Peterborough
County Court House
470 Water St.
Peterborough, ON K9H 3M3
Tel: 705-743-0380; *Fax:* 705-876-1730
info@ptbocounty.ca
www.ptbocounty.ca
Other Information: Toll-Free Phone: 800-710-9586
Municipal Type: County
Area: 3,848.20 sq km
Population in 2016: 138,236
Next Election: Oct. 24, 2022 (4 year terms)
Rodger Bonneau, Councillor, Wards: Asphodel-Norwood
Lori Burtt, Councillor, Wards: Asphodel-Norwood
Scott McFadden, Councillor, Wards: Cavan Monaghan
Matthew Graham, Councillor, Wards: Cavan Monaghan
J. Murray Jones, Councillor, Wards: Douro-Dummer
Karl Moher, Councillor, Wards: Douro-Dummer
Jim Martin, Councillor, Wards: Havelock-Belmont-Methuen
David Gerow, Councillor, Wards: Havelock-Belmont-Methuen
Carolyn Amyotte, Councillor, Wards: North Kawartha
Jim Whelan, Councillor, Wards: North Kawartha
Joe Taylor, Councillor, Wards: Otonabee-South Monaghan

Bonnie Clark, Councillor, Wards: Otonabee-South Monaghan
Andy Mitchell, Councillor, Wards: Selwyn
Sherry Senis, Councillor, Wards: Selwyn
Janet Clarkson, Councillor, Wards: Trent Lakes
Ron Windover, Councillor, Wards: Trent Lakes
Troy Speck, Chief Administrative Officer
Sheridan Graham, Director, Corporate Projects & Services
Grant Murphy, Director, Infrastructure Services
Mary Spence, Director, Human Resources
Bryan Weir, Director, Planning

Prince Edward County
332 Main St.
Picton, ON K0K 2T0
Tel: 613-476-2148; *Fax:* 613-476-8356
info@pecounty.on.ca
www.thecounty.ca
Municipal Type: County
Incorporated: Jan. 1, 1998; *Area:* 1,050.49 sq km
Population in 2016: 24,735
Provincial Electoral District(s): Bay of Quinte
Federal Electoral District(s): Bay of Quinte
Next Election: Oct. 24, 2022 (4 year terms)
Steve Ferguson, Mayor
Kate McNaughton, Councillor, Wards: 1. Picton
Phil St. Jean, Councillor, Wards: 1. Picton
Brad Nieman, Councillor, Wards: 2. Bloomfield-Hallowell
Phil Prinzen, Councillor, Wards: 2. Bloomfield-Hallowell
Mike Harper, Councillor, Wards: 3. Wellington
Andreas H. Bolik, Councillor, Wards: 4. Ameliasburgh
Janice Maynard, Councillor, Wards: 4. Ameliasburgh
Bill McMahon, Councillor, Wards: 4. Ameliasburgh
Jamie Forrester, Councillor, Wards: 5. Athol
Bill Roberts, Councillor, Wards: 6. Sophiasburgh
Ernest Margetson, Councillor, Wards: 7. Hillier
Stewart Scott Bailey, Councillor, Wards: 8. North Marysburgh
John Hirsch, Councillor, Wards: 9. South Marysburgh
Catalina Blumenberg, Clerk
Marcia Wallace, Chief Administrative Officer
Amanda Carter, Director, Finance
Todd Davis, Acting Director, Community Development & Strategic Initiatives
Pat Heffernan, Acting Director, Operations
Peter Moyer, Director, Development Services
Susan Thomas, Manager, Human Resources
Scott Manlow, Fire Chief

Renfrew
9 International Dr.
Pembroke, ON K8A 6W5
Tel: 613-735-7288; *Fax:* 613-735-2081
info@countyofrenfrew.on.ca
www.countyofrenfrew.on.ca
Other Information: Toll-Free Phone: 800-273-0183
Municipal Type: County
Incorporated: June 8, 1861; *Area:* 7,448.57 sq km
Population in 2016: 102,394
Next Election: Oct. 24, 2022 (4 year terms)
Michael Donohue, Councillor, Wards: Admaston Bromley
Jennifer Murphy, Councillor, Wards: Bonnechere Valley
Sheldon Keller, Councillor, Wards: Brudenell, Lyndoch, Raglan
Glenn Doncaster, Councillor, Wards: Deep River
Debbi Grills, Councillor, Wards: Head, Clara, Maria
David Bennett, Councillor, Wards: Horton
Janice Visneskie Moore, Councillor, Wards: Killaloe, Hagarty, Richards
John Reinwald, Councillor, Wards: Laurentian Hills
Debbie Robinson, Councillor, Wards: Laurentian Valley
Brian Hunt, Councillor, Wards: Greater Madawaska
Kim Love, Councillor, Wards: Madawaska Valley
Tom Peckett, Councillor, Wards: McNab/Braeside
James Brose, Councillor, Wards: North Algona Wilberforce
Bob Sweet, Councillor, Wards: Petawawa
Peter Emon, Councillor, Wards: Renfrew
Cathy Regier, Councillor, Wards: White Water Region
Paul Moreau, Chief Administrative Officer & Clerk

Simcoe
County of Simcoe Administration Centre
1110 Hwy. 26
Midhurst, ON L0L 1X0
Tel: 705-726-9300; *Fax:* 705-719-4626
info@simcoe.ca
www.simcoe.ca
Other Information: Toll-Free Phone: 866-893-9300
Municipal Type: County
Incorporated: Jan. 1, 1850; *Area:* 4,859.64 sq km
Population in 2016: 479,650
Next Election: Oct. 24, 2022 (4 year terms)
Floyd Pinto, Councillor, Wards: Adjala-Tosorontio
Bob Meadows, Councillor, Wards: Adjala-Tosorontio
Rob Keffer, Councillor, Wards: Bradford West Gwillimbury

James Leduc, Councillor, Wards: Bradford West Gwillimbury
Doug Measures, Councillor, Wards: Clearview
Barry Burton, Councillor, Wards: Clearview
Brian Saunderson, Councillor, Wards: Collingwood
Keith Hull, Councillor, Wards: Collingwood
Sandie Macdonald, Councillor, Wards: Essa
Michael Smith, Councillor, Wards: Essa
Lynn Dollin, Councillor, Wards: Innisfil
Daniel Davidson, Councillor, Wards: Innisfil
Stewart M. Strathearn, Councillor, Wards: Midland
Mike Ross, Councillor, Wards: Midland
Rick Milne, Councillor, Wards: New Tecumseth
Richard Norcross, Councillor, Wards: New Tecumseth
Harry Hughes, Councillor, Wards: Oro-Medonte
Scott Jermey, Councillor, Wards: Oro-Medonte
Douglas Leroux, Councillor, Wards: Penetanguishene
Anita Dubeau, Councillor, Wards: Penetanguishene
Basil Clarke, Councillor, Wards: Ramara
John O'Donnell, Councillor, Wards: Ramara
Mike Burkett, Councillor, Wards: Severn
Jane Dunlop, Councillor, Wards: Severn
Don Allen, Councillor, Wards: Springwater
Jennifer Coughlin, Councillor, Wards: Springwater
Ted Walker, Councillor, Wards: Tay
Jim Crawford, Councillor, Wards: Tay
George Cornell, Councillor, Wards: Tiny
Steffen Walma, Councillor, Wards: Tiny
Brian Smith, Councillor, Wards: Wasaga Beach
Nina Bifolchi, Councillor, Wards: Wasaga Beach
Mark Aitken, Chief Administrative Officer
Lealand Sibbick, Treasurer
David Parks, Director, Planning, Development & Tourism
Michael Moffatt, Director, Human Resources

Waterloo
Regional Administration Bldg.
P.O. Box 9051 C
150 Frederick St.
Kitchener, ON N2G 4J3
Tel: 519-575-4400; *Fax:* 519-575-4481
regionalinquiries@regionofwaterloo.ca
www.regionofwaterloo.ca
Municipal Type: Regional Municipality
Incorporated: Jan. 1, 1973; *Area:* 1,368.92 sq km
Population in 2016: 535,153
Next Election: Oct. 24, 2022 (4 year terms)
Karen Redman, Regional Chair & Councillor
Kathryn McGarry, Councillor, Wards: Cambridge
Karl Kiefer, Councillor, Wards: Cambridge
Helen Jowett, Councillor, Wards: Cambridge
Berry Vrbanovic, Councillor, Wards: Kitchener
Tom Galloway, Councillor, Wards: Kitchener
Elizabeth Clarke, Councillor, Wards: Kitchener
Michael D. Harris, Councillor, Wards: Kitchener
Geoff Lorentz, Councillor, Wards: Kitchener
Sue Foxton, Councillor, Wards: North Dumfries
Dave Jaworsky, Councillor, Wards: Waterloo
Jim Erb, Councillor, Wards: Waterloo
Sean Strickland, Councillor, Wards: Waterloo
Joe Nowak, Councillor, Wards: Wellesley
Les Armstrong, Councillor, Wards: Wilmot
Sandy Shantz, Councillor, Wards: Woolwich
Kris Fletcher, Regional Clerk & Director, Council & Administrative Services
Bruce Lauckner, Chief Administrative Officer
Craig Dyer, Chief Financial Officer
Thomas Schmidt, Commissioner, Transportation & Environmental Services
Jane Albright, Commissioner, Human Resources & Citizen Services

Wellington
74 Woolwich St.
Guelph, ON N1H 3T9
Tel: 519-837-2600; *Fax:* 519-837-1909
www.wellington.ca
Other Information: Toll-Free Phone: 800-663-0750
Municipal Type: County
Incorporated: Jan. 1, 1852; *Area:* 2,660.57 sq km
Population in 2016: 222,726
Next Election: Oct. 24, 2022 (4 year terms)
Note: The council of the County of Wellington is comprised of the mayors of its seven municipalities, plus nine elected county ward councillors.
Kelly Linton, Councillor, Wards: Centre Wellington
Allan Alls, Councillor, Wards: Erin
Chris White, Councillor, Wards: Guelph/Eramosa
Gregg Davidson, Councillor, Wards: Mapleton
George Bridge, Councillor, Wards: Minto
James Seeley, Councillor, Wards: Puslinch
Andy Lennox, Councillor, Wards: Wellington North

David Anderson, Councillor, Wards: 1
Earl Campbell, Councillor, Wards: 2
Campbell Cork, Wards: 3
Stephen O'Neill, Councillor, Wards: 4
Mary Lloyd, Councillor, Wards: 5
Diane Ballantyne, Councillor, Wards: 6
Don McKay, Councillor, Wards: 7
Doug Breen, Councillor, Wards: 8
Jeff Duncan, Councillor, Wards: 9
Scott Wilson, Chief Administrative Officer
Kenneth DeHart, Treasurer
Susan Farrelly, Director, Human Resources
Aldo Salis, Director, Planning & Development

York
17250 Yonge St.
Newmarket, ON L3Y 6Z1
Tel: 905-895-1231
www.york.ca
Other Information: Toll-Free Phone: 877-464-9675
Municipal Type: Regional Municipality
Incorporated: Jan. 1, 1971; *Area:* 1,762.13 sq km
Population in 2016: 1,109,909
Next Election: Oct. 24, 2022 (4 year terms)
Wayne Emmerson, Chair & CEO
Tom Mrakas, Councillor, Wards: Aurora
Virginia Hackson, Councillor, Wards: East Gwillimbury
Margaret Quirk, Councillor, Wards: Georgina
Robert Grossi, Councillor, Wards: Georgina
Steve Pellegrini, Councillor, Wards: King
Frank Scarpitti, Councillor, Wards: Markham
Don Hamilton, Councillor, Wards: Markham
Jack Heath, Councillor, Wards: Markham
Joe Li, Councillor, Wards: Markham
Jim Jones, Councillor, Wards: Markham
John Taylor, Councillor, Wards: Newmarket
Tom Vegh, Councillor, Wards: Newmarket
David Barrow, Councillor, Wards: Richmond Hill
Joe Dipaola, Councillor, Wards: Richmond Hill
Carmine Perrelli, Councillor, Wards: Richmond Hill
Maurizio Bevilacqua, Councillor, Wards: Vaughan
Mario Ferri, Councillor, Wards: Vaughan
Gino Rosati, Councillor, Wards: Vaughan
Linda D. Jackson, Councillor, Wards: Vaughan
Ian Lovatt, Councillor, Wards: Whitchurch-Stouffville
Bruce Macgregor, Chief Administrative Officer
Laura Mirabella, Regional Treasurer & Commissioner, Finance
Dino Basso, Commissioner, Corporate Services
Paul Jankowski, Commissioner, Transportation
Erin Mahoney, Commissioner, Environmental Services
Katherine Chislett, Commissioner, Community & Health Services
Paul Freeman, Chief Planner, Planning & Economic Development
Karim Kurji, Medical Officer of Health & Director, Public Health Programs

---

Major Municipalities in Ontario

Ajax
65 Harwood Ave. South
Ajax, ON L1S 2H9
Tel: 905-683-4550; *Fax:* 905-683-1061
contactus@ajax.ca
www.ajax.ca
Other Information: TTY: 866-460-4489
Municipal Type: City
Incorporated: 1955; *Area:* 67.00 sq km
County or District: Durham Regional Municipality; *Population in 2016:* 119,677
Provincial Electoral District(s): Ajax
Federal Electoral District(s): Ajax
Next Election: Oct. 24, 2022 (4 year terms)
Shaun Collier, Mayor
Marilyn Crawford, Regional Councillor, Wards: 1
Sterling Lee, Regional Councillor, Wards: 2
Joanne Dies, Regional Councillor, Wards: 3
Rob Tyler-Morin, Councillor, Wards: 1
Ashmeed Khan, Councillor, Wards: 2
Lisa Bower, Councillor, Wards: 3
Shane Baker, Chief Administrative Officer
Dave Meredith, Director, Operations & Environmental Services
Tracey Vaughan, Director, Recreation, Culture & Community Development
Dave Lang, Fire Chief

Barrie
P.O. Box 400
70 Collier St.
Barrie, ON L4M 4T5
Tel: 705-726-4242; *Fax:* 705-739-4243
servicebarrie@barrie.ca
www.barrie.ca
Other Information: TTY: 705-792-7910
Municipal Type: City
Incorporated: 1853; *Area:* 99.04 sq km
County or District: Simcoe; *Population in 2016:* 141,434
Provincial Electoral District(s): Barrie-Innisfil;
Barrie-Springwater-Oro-Medonte
Federal Electoral District(s): Barrie-Innisfil;
Barrie-Springwater-Oro-Medonte
Next Election: Oct. 24, 2022 (4 year terms)
Jeff Lehman, Mayor, 705-792-7900
Clare Riepma, Councillor, Wards: 1
Keenan Aylwin, Councillor, Wards: 2
Ann-Marie Kungl, Councillor, Wards: 3
Barry Ward, Councillor, 705-739-4268, Wards: 4
Robert Thomson, Councillor, Wards: 5
Natalie Harris, Councillor, Wards: 6
Gary Harvey, Councillor, Wards: 7
Jim Harris, Councillor, Wards: 8
Sergio Morales, Councillor, 705-739-4256, Wards: 9
Mike McCann, Councillor, 705-739-4290, Wards: 10
Michael Prowse, Chief Administrative Officer
Craig Millar, Director, Finance, 705-739-4232
Rick Pews, Director, Corporate Facilities, 705-739-4220
Steve Lee Young, Manager, Recreation, 705-739-4220
Cory Mainprize, Fire Chief

Belleville
City Hall
169 Front St.
Belleville, ON K8N 2Y8
Tel: 613-968-6481; *Fax:* 613-967-3206
www.belleville.ca
Other Information: TTY: 613-967-3768; Toll-Free Phone:
877-968-6481
Municipal Type: City
Area: 247.25 sq km
County or District: Hastings; *Population in 2016:* 50,716
Provincial Electoral District(s): Bay of Quinte; Hastings-Lennox and Addington
Federal Electoral District(s): Bay of Quinte; Hastings-Lennox and Addington
Next Election: Oct. 24, 2022 (4 year terms)
Mitch Panciuk, Mayor
Pat Culhane, Councillor, Wards: 1
Sean Kelly, Councillor, Wards: 1
Chris Malette, Councillor, Wards: 1
Kelly McCaw, Councillor, Wards: 1
Garnet Thompson, Councillor, Wards: 1
Ryan Williams, Councillor, Wards: 1
Paul Carr, Councillor, Wards: 2
Bill Sandison, Councillor, Wards: 2
Matt MacDonald, City Clerk, 613-967-3256
Rod Bovay, Chief Administrative Officer, 613-967-3268
Stephen Ashton, Director, Engineering & Development Services, 613-968-6481, Fax: 613-967-3262
Carol Hinze, Director, Finance, 613-967-3270
Mark Fluhrer, Director, Recreation, Culture & Community Services, 613-967-3217
Perry Decola, General Manager, Environmental Services, 613-966-3657
Joseph D. Reid, General Manager, Transportation & Operations, 613-967-3313
Mark MacDonald, Fire Chief, 613-771-3075

Bradford West Gwillimbury
Administration Centre
P.O. Box 100
#7 & #8, 100 Dissette St.
Bradford, ON L3Z 2A7
Tel: 905-775-5366; *Fax:* 905-775-0153
www.townofbwg.com
Municipal Type: City
Incorporated: 1857; *Area:* 201.04 sq km
County or District: Simcoe; *Population in 2016:* 35,325
Provincial Electoral District(s): York-Simcoe
Federal Electoral District(s): York-Simcoe
Next Election: Oct. 24, 2022 (4 year terms)
Note: Incorporated as a town in 1960.
Rob Keffer, Mayor, 905-775-5366
James Leduc, Deputy Mayor & Councillor, 905-775-5366
Raj Sandhu, Councillor, 905-775-5366, Wards: 1
Gary Baynes, Councillor, 905-775-5366, Wards: 2
Gary R. Lamb, Councillor, 905-775-5366, Wards: 3
Ron Orr, Councillor, 905-775-5366, Wards: 4

Peter Ferragine, Councillor, 905-775-5366, Wards: 5
Mark Contois, Councillor, 905-775-5366, Wards: 6
Peter Dykie, Jr., Councillor, 905-775-5366, Wards: 7
Geoff McKnight, Chief Administrative Officer, 905-775-5366
Ian Goodfellow, Director, Finance, 905-775-5303
Joe Gratrix, Manager, Water, 905-775-5369
Ryan Windle, Manager, Community Planning, 905-778-2055
Kevin Gallant, Fire Chief, 905-775-7311

Brampton
2 Wellington St. West
Brampton, ON L6Y 4R2
Tel: 905-874-2000; *Fax:* 905-874-2119
city.hall@brampton.ca
www.brampton.ca
Other Information: E-mail, Economic Development:
edo@brampton.ca
Municipal Type: City
Incorporated: Jan. 1, 1974; *Area:* 266.36 sq km
County or District: Peel Reg. Mun.; *Population in 2016:* 593,638
Provincial Electoral District(s): Brampton Centre; Brampton East;
Brampton North; Brampton South; Brampton West
Federal Electoral District(s): Brampton Centre; Brampton East,
Brampton West; Brampton South
Next Election: Oct. 24, 2022 (4 year terms)
Patrick Brown, Mayor
Paul Vicente, Regional Councillor, Wards: 1 & 5
Michael Paul Palleschi, Regional Councillor, Wards: 2 & 6
Martin Medeiros, Regional Councillor, Wards: 3 & 4
Pat Fortini, Regional Councillor, Wards: 7 & 8
Gurpreet Singh Dhillon, Regional Councillor, Wards: 9 & 10
Rowena Santos, City Councillor, Wards: 1 & 5
Doug Whillans, City Councillor, Wards: 2 & 6
Jeff Bowman, City Councillor, Wards: 3 & 4
Charmaine Williams, City Councillor, Wards: 7 & 8
Harkirat Singh, City Councillor, Wards: 9 & 10
David Barrick, Chief Administrative Officer
Bill Boyes, Fire Chief

Brantford
City Hall
P.O. Box 818
100 Wellington Sq.
Brantford, ON N3T 5R7
Tel: 519-759-4150
www.brantford.ca
Municipal Type: City
Incorporated: May 31, 1877; *Area:* 72.44 sq km
County or District: Brant; *Population in 2016:* 97,496
Provincial Electoral District(s): Brantford-Brant
Federal Electoral District(s): Brantford-Brant
Next Election: Oct. 24, 2022 (4 year terms)
Kevin Davis, Mayor
Jan Vander Stelt, Councillor, Wards: 1
Rick Weaver, Councillor, Wards: 1
John Sless, Councillor, Wards: 2
John K. Utley, Councillor, Wards: 2
Greg Martin, Councillor, Wards: 3
Dan McCreary, Councillor, Wards: 3
Cheryl Lynn Antoski, Councillor, Wards: 4
Richard Carpenter, Councillor, Wards: 4
Brian Van Tilborg, Councillor, Wards: 5
Joshua Wall, Councillor, Wards: 5
Brian Hutchings, Chief Administrative Officer
Josephine Atanas, General Manager, Health & Human Services
Catherine Brubacher, General Manager, Corporate Services
Inderjit Hans, General Manager, Public Works
Paul Moore, General Manager, Community Development
Todd Binkley, Acting Fire Chief

Brockville
Victoria Bldg.
P.O. Box 5000
1 King St. West
Brockville, ON K6V 7A5
Tel: 613-342-8772; *Fax:* 613-342-8780
info@brockville.com
www.brockville.com
Other Information: Tourism, Email:
tourism@brockvillechamber.com
Municipal Type: City
Area: 20.85 sq km
County or District: Leeds & Grenville; *Population in 2016:* 21,346
Provincial Electoral District(s): Leeds-Grenville-Thousand
Islands and Rideau Lakes
Federal Electoral District(s): Leeds-Grenville-Thousand Islands
and Rideau Lakes
Next Election: Oct. 24, 2022 (4 year terms)
Jason Baker, Mayor
Leigh Zachary Baker Bursey, Councillor
Jeffrey Earle, Councillor
Jane Fullarton, Councillor

Larry Journal, Councillor
Mike Kalivas, Councillor
Nathalie Lavergne, Councillor
Cameron Wales, Councillor
Matt Wren, Councillor
Sandra M. MacDonald, City Clerk, 613-342-8772
Janette Loveys, City Manager, 613-342-8772
Rob Nolan, Acting Director, Planning, 613-342-8772
Peter Raabe, Director, Environmental Services, 613-342-8772
Krista Vandewal, Manager, Human Resources, 613-342-8772
Ghislain Pigeon, Fire Chief, 613-498-1261

Burlington
City Hall
P.O. Box 5013
426 Brant St.
Burlington, ON L7R 3Z6
Tel: 905-335-7600; *Fax:* 905-335-7881
city@burlington.ca
www.burlington.ca
Other Information: Toll-Free Phone: 877-213-3609
Municipal Type: City
Incorporated: 1914; *Area:* 185.66 sq km
County or District: Halton Regional Municipality; *Population in 2016:* 183,314
Provincial Electoral District(s): Burlington; Milton; Oakville
North-Burlington
Federal Electoral District(s): Burlington; Milton; Oakville
North-Burlington
Next Election: Oct. 24, 2022 (4 year terms)
Note: Incorporated as a city in 1974.
Marianne Meed Ward, Mayor
Kelvin Galbraith, Councillor, Wards: 1
Lisa Kearns, Councillor, Wards: 2
Rory Nisan, Councillor, Wards: 3
Shawna Stolte, Councillor, Wards: 4
Paul Sharman, Councillor, Wards: 5
Angelo Bentivegna, Councillor, Wards: 6
Tim Commisso, City Manager

Cambridge
P.O. Box 669
50 Dickson St.
Cambridge, ON N1R 5W8
Tel: 519-623-1340; *Fax:* 519-740-3011
questions@cambridge.ca
www.cambridge.ca
Other Information: TTY: 519-623-6691
Municipal Type: City
Incorporated: Jan. 1973; *Area:* 113.01 sq km
County or District: Waterloo Regional Municipality; *Population in 2016:* 129,920
Provincial Electoral District(s): Cambridge; Kitchener
South-Hespeler
Federal Electoral District(s): Cambridge
Next Election: Oct. 24, 2022 (4 year terms)
Kathryn McGarry, Mayor
Donna Reid, Councillor, 519-740-4517, Wards: 1
Mike Devine, City Councillor, 519-740-4517, Wards: 2
Mike Mann, City Councillor, 519-740-4517, Wards: 3
Jan Liggett, City Councillor, 519-740-4517, Wards: 4
Pam Wolf, City Councillor, 519-740-4517, Wards: 5
Shannon Adshade, City Councillor, 519-740-4517, Wards: 6
Nicholas Ermeta, City Councillor, 519-740-4517, Wards: 8
Helen Jowett, Regional Councillor
Karl Kiefer, Regional Councillor
David Calder, City Manager, 519-740-4683
Neil Main, Fire Chief, 519-627-6001

Clarence-Rockland
1560 Laurier St.
Rockland, ON K4K 1P7
Tel: 613-446-6022; *Fax:* 613-446-1497
www.clarence-rockland.com
Municipal Type: City
Incorporated: Jan. 1, 1998; *Area:* 297.71 sq km
County or District: Prescott & Russell; *Population in 2016:* 24,512
Provincial Electoral District(s): Glengarry-Prescott-Russell
Federal Electoral District(s): Glengarry-Prescott-Russell
Next Election: Oct. 24, 2022 (4 year terms)
Note: Amalgamation of the Town of Rockland & the Township of
Clarence.
Michel Levert, Deputy Mayor; Acting Mayor
Samuel Cardarelli, Councillor, Wards: 1
Mario Zanth, Councillor, Wards: 2
Carl Grimard, Councillor, Wards: 3
Don Bouchard, Councillor, Wards: 4
André J. Lalonde, Councillor, Wards: 5
Christian Simard, Councillor, Wards: 6
Diane Choinière, Councillor, Wards: 8
Monique Ouellet, Clerk

Helen Collier, Chief Administrative Officer
Pierre Boucher, Director, Community Services
Phil Cormier, Interim Manager, Environment & Water
Yves Rousselle, Manager, Supply & Processes
Pierre Voisine, Fire Chief

Cornwall
P.O. Box 877
360 Pitt St.
Cornwall, ON K6H 5T9
Tel: 613-930-2787; *Fax:* 613-932-8145
www.cornwall.ca
Municipal Type: City
Incorporated: 1834; *Area:* 61.56 sq km
County or District: Stormont, Dundas & Glengarry; *Population in 2016:* 46,589
Provincial Electoral District(s): Stormont-Dundas-South
Glengarry
Federal Electoral District(s): Stormont-Dundas-South Glengarry
Next Election: Oct. 24, 2022 (4 year terms)
Note: Incorporated as a city in 1945.
Vacant, Mayor
Todd Bennett, Councillor
Eric Bergeron, Councillor
Maurice Dupelle, Councillor
Syd Gardiner, Councillor
Glen Garry Grant, Councillor
Carilyne Hébert, Councillor
Dean Hollingsworth, Councillor
Elaine MacDonald, Councillor
Claude McIntosh, Councillor
Justin Towndale, Councillor
Maureen Adams, Chief Administrative Officer, 613-930-2787
Tracey Bailey, General Manager, Financial Services &
Treasurer, 613-930-2787
Mark Boileau, General Manager, Development & Recreation,
613-930-2787
Geoff Clarke, General Manager, Corporate Services,
613-930-2787
Bill de Wit, General Manager, Infrastructure & Municipal Works,
613-930-2787
Jeff Weber, Fire Chief, 613-930-2787

Dryden
30 Van Horne Ave.
Dryden, ON P8N 2A7
Tel: 807-223-2225; *Fax:* 807-223-3999
generalinquiries@dryden.ca
www.dryden.ca
Other Information: Phone, Administration: 807-223-1147
Municipal Type: City
Area: 66.19 sq km
County or District: Kenora; *Population in 2016:* 7,749
Provincial Electoral District(s): Kenora-Rainy River
Federal Electoral District(s): Kenora
Next Election: Oct. 24, 2022 (4 year terms)
Greg Wilson, Mayor, 807-223-6119
Roger Nesnitt, Chief Administrative Officer, 807-223-1194

Elliot Lake
45 Hillside Dr. North
Elliot Lake, ON P5A 1X5
Tel: 705-848-2287
www.cityofelliotlake.com
Municipal Type: City
Area: 714.65 sq km
County or District: Algoma District; *Population in 2016:* 10,741
Provincial Electoral District(s): Algoma-Manitoulin
Federal Electoral District(s): Algoma-Manitoulin-Kapuskasing
Next Election: Oct. 24, 2022 (4 year terms)
Dan Marchisella, Mayor
Luc Cyr, Councillor
Sandy Finamore, Councillor
Norman Mann, Councillor
Chris Patrie, Councillor
Ed Pearce, Councillor
Tom Turner, Councillor
Daniel Gagnon, Chief Administrative Officer, 705-848-2287
John Thomas, Fire Chief

Erin
5684 Trafalgar Rd.
Hillsburgh, ON N0B 1Z0
Tel: 519-855-4407; *Fax:* 519-855-4821
info@erin.ca
www.erin.ca
Other Information: Toll-Free Phone: 877-818-2888
Municipal Type: City
Incorporated: 1997; *Area:* 297.76 sq km
County or District: Wellington; *Population in 2016:* 11,439
Provincial Electoral District(s): Wellington-Halton Hills

Federal Electoral District(s): Wellington-Halton Hills
Next Election: Oct. 24, 2022 (4 year terms)
Allan Alls, Mayor
John Brennan, Councillor
Jamie Cheyne, Councillor
Mike Robins, Councillor
Rob Smith, Councillor
Jeff Duncan, County Councillor
Nathan Hyde, Chief Administrative Officer
Ursula D'Angelo, Director, Finance
Paul Evans, Chief Building Official
Jim Sawkins, Fire Chief

Greater Sudbury / Grand Sudbury
Tom Davies Square
P.O. Box 5000 A
200 Brady St.
Sudbury, ON P3A 5P3
Tel: 705-671-2489; *Fax:* 705-671-8118
311@greatersudbury.ca
www.greatersudbury.ca
Other Information: TTY: 705-688-3919
Municipal Type: City
Incorporated: Jan. 1, 2001; *Area:* 3,228.35 sq km
Population in 2016: 161,521
Provincial Electoral District(s): Nickel Belt; Sudbury;
Timiskaming-Cochrane
Federal Electoral District(s): Nickel Belt; Sudbury
Next Election: Oct. 24, 2022 (4 year terms)
Brian Bigger, Mayor
Mark Signoretti, Councillor, Wards: 1
Michael Vagnini, Councillor, Wards: 2
Gerry Montpellier, Councillor, Wards: 3
Geoff McCausland, Councillor, Wards: 4
Robert Kirwan, Councillor, Wards: 5
René Lapierre, Councillor, Wards: 6
Mike Jakubo, Councillor, Wards: 7
Al Sizer, Councillor, Wards: 8
Deb McIntosh, Councillor, Wards: 9
Fern Cormier, Councillor, Wards: 10
Bill Leduc, Councillor, Wards: 11
Joscelyne Landry-Altmann, Councillor, Wards: 12
Ed Archer, Chief Administrative Officer
Tony Cecutti, P. Eng, General Manager, Growth & Infrastructure
Ron Henderson, General Manager, Citizen Services
Guido Mazza, Director & Chief Building Official, Building
Services
Darrel McAloney, Deputy Fire Chief

Guelph
City Hall
1 Carden St.
Guelph, ON N1H 3A1
Tel: 519-822-1260; *Fax:* 519-763-1269
info@guelph.ca
www.guelph.ca
Other Information: TTY: 519-826-9771
Municipal Type: City
Incorporated: 1879; *Area:* 87.22 sq km
County or District: Wellington; *Population in 2016:* 131,794
Provincial Electoral District(s): Guelph
Federal Electoral District(s): Guelph; Wellington-Halton Hills
Next Election: Oct. 24, 2022 (4 year terms)
Cam Guthrie, Mayor
Bob Bell, Councillor, 519-803-5543, Wards: 1
Dan Gibson, Councillor, 519-822-1260, Wards: 1
Rodrigo Goller, Councillor, Wards: 2
James Gordon, Councillor, 519-822-1260, Wards: 2
Phil Allt, Councillor, 519-822-1260, Wards: 3
June Hofland, Councillor, 519-822-1260, Wards: 3
Christine Billings, Councillor, 519-826-0567, Wards: 4
Mike Salisbury, Councillor, 519-822-1260, Wards: 4
Cathy Downer, Councillor, 519-822-1260, Wards: 5
Leanne Piper, Councillor, 519-822-1260, Wards: 5
Mark MacKinnon, Councillor, 519-829-5137, Wards: 6
Dominique O'Rourke, Councillor, Wards: 6
Scott Stewart, Chief Administrative Officer, 519-822-1260
Colleen Clack, Deputy Chief Administrative Officer, Public
Services, 519-822-1260
Trevor Lee, Deputy Chief Administrative Officer, Corporate
Services, 519-822-1260
Scott Stewart, Deputy Chief Administrative Officer,
Infrastructure, Development & Enterprise Services,
519-822-1260
John Osborne, Fire Chief, 519-824-6590

Hamilton
71 Main St. West
Hamilton, ON L8P 4Y5
Tel: 905-546-2489; *Fax:* 905-546-2095
askcity@hamilton.ca
www.hamilton.ca

Municipal Type: City
Incorporated: 1846; *Area:* 1,117.29 sq km
Population in 2016: 536,917
Provincial Electoral District(s): Flamborough-Glanbrook;
Hamilton Centre; Hamilton East-Stoney Creek; Hamilton
Mountain; Hamilton West-Ancaster-Dundas
Federal Electoral District(s): Flamborough-Glanbrook; Hamilton
Centre; Hamilton East-Stoney Creek; Hamilton Mountain;
Hamilton West-Ancaster-Dundas
Next Election: Oct. 24, 2022 (4 year terms)
Note: Incorporated as a city on Jan. 1, 2001.
Fred Eisenberger, Mayor
Maureen Wilson, Councillor, Wards: 1
Jason Farr, Councillor, Wards: 2
Nrinder Nann, Councillor, Wards: 3
Sam Merulla, Councillor, Wards: 4
Chad Collins, Councillor, Wards: 5
Tom Jackson, Councillor, Wards: 6
Esther Pauls, Councillor, Wards: 7
John-Paul Danko, Councillor, Wards: 8
Brad Clark, Councillor, Wards: 9
Maria Pearson, Councillor, Wards: 10
Brenda Johnson, Councillor, Wards: 11
Lloyd Ferguson, Councillor, Wards: 12
Arlene Vanderbeek, Councillor, Wards: 13
Terry Whitehead, Councillor, Wards: 14
Judi Partridge, Councillor, Wards: 15
Janette Smith, City Manager
Paul Johnson, General Manager, Healthy & Safe Communities
Dan McKinnon, General Manager, Public Works
Jason Thorne, General Manager, Planning & Economic
Development
Mike Zegarac, General Manager, Finance & Corporate Services
Dave Duncliffe, Fire Chief

Innisfil
2101 Innisfil Beach Rd.
Innisfil, ON L9S 1A1
Tel: 705-436-3710
inquiry@innisfil.ca
www.innisfil.ca
Other Information: Toll-Free Phone: 888-436-3710
Municipal Type: City
Incorporated: 1850; *Area:* 262.71 sq km
County or District: Simcoe; *Population in 2016:* 36,566
Provincial Electoral District(s): Barrie-Innisfil
Federal Electoral District(s): Barrie-Innisfil
Next Election: Oct. 24, 2022 (4 year terms)
Lynn Dollin, Mayor
Daniel Davidson, Deputy Mayor
Kevin Eisses, Councillor, Wards: 1
William Van Berkel, Councillor, Wards: 2
Donna Orsatti, Councillor, Wards: 3
Alex Waters, Councillor, Wards: 4
Kenneth Fowler, Councillor, Wards: 5
Carolyn Payne, Councillor, Wards: 6
Rob Nicol, Councillor, Wards: 7
Jason Reynar, Chief Administrative Officer
Danny Rodgers, Chief Building Official
Tom Raeburn, Fire Chief

Kawartha Lakes
P.O. Box 9000
26 Francis St.
Lindsay, ON K9V 5R8
Tel: 705-324-9411; *Fax:* 705-324-8110
www.kawarthalakes.ca
Other Information: Toll-Free Phone: 888-822-2225
Municipal Type: City
Incorporated: Jan. 1, 2001; *Area:* 3,084.38 sq km
Population in 2016: 75,423
Provincial Electoral District(s): Haliburton-Kawartha Lakes-Brock
Federal Electoral District(s): Haliburton-Kawartha Lakes-Brock
Next Election: Oct. 24, 2022 (4 year terms)
Note: Formerly the County of Victoria.
Andy Letham, Mayor
Emmett Yeo, Councillor, Wards: 1
Kathleen Seymour-Fagan, Councillor, Wards: 2
Doug Elmslie, Councillor, Wards: 3
Andrew Veale, Councillor, Wards: 4
Pat Dunn, Councillor, Wards: 5
Ron Ashmore, Councillor, Wards: 6
Patrick O'Reilly, Councillor, Wards: 7
Tracy Richardson, Councillor, Wards: 8
Ron Taylor, Chief Administrative Officer
Bryan Robinson, Director, Public Works
Craig Shanks, Director, Community Services
Rod Sutherland, Director, Human Services
Mark Pankhurst, Fire Chief

Kenora
1 Main St. South
Kenora, ON P9N 3X2
Tel: 807-467-2000; *Fax:* 807-467-2045
service@kenora.ca
www.kenora.ca
Municipal Type: City
Area: 211.59 sq km
County or District: Kenora District; *Population in 2016:* 15,096
Provincial Electoral District(s): Kenora-Rainy River
Federal Electoral District(s): Kenora
Next Election: Oct. 24, 2022 (4 year terms)
Dan Reynard, Mayor
Mort Goss, Councillor
Rory McMillan, Councillor
Andrew Poirier, Councillor
Kirsi Ralko, Councillor
Sharon Smith, Councillor
Chris Van Walleghem, Councillor
Heather Kasprick, Clerk
Karen Brown, Chief Administrative Officer
Charlotte Edie, Treasurer
Josh Nelson, Manager, Recreation & Tourism
Jeff Hawley, Manager, Operations & Infrastructure
Kevin Robertson, Chief Building Official
Marco Vogrig, Municipal Engineer
Todd Skene, Fire Chief

Kingston
City Hall
216 Ontario St.
Kingston, ON K7L 2Z3
Tel: 613-546-0000; *Fax:* 613-546-5232
www.cityofkingston.ca
Other Information: TTY: 613-546-4889
Municipal Type: City
Incorporated: Jan. 1, 1998; *Area:* 451.19 sq km
County or District: Frontenac; *Population in 2016:* 123,798
Provincial Electoral District(s): Kingston & the Islands;
Lanark-Frontenac-Kingston
Federal Electoral District(s): Kingston & the Islands;
Lanark-Frontenac-Kingston
Next Election: Oct. 24, 2022 (4 year terms)
Bryan Paterson, Mayor
Gary Oosterhof, Councillor, Wards: 1. Countryside
Simon Chapelle, Councillor, Wards: 2. Loyalist-Cataraqui
Lisa Osanic, Councillor, Wards: 3. Collins-Bayridge
Wayne Hill, Councillor, Wards: 4. Lakeside
Bridget Doherty, Councillor, Wards: 5. Portsmouth
Robert Kiley, Councillor, Wards: 6. Trillium
Mary Rita Holland, Councillor, Wards: 7. Kingscourt-Rideau
Jeff McLaren, Councillor, Wards: 8. Meadowbrook-Strathcona
Jim Neill, Councillor, Wards: 9. Williamsville
Peter Stroud, Councillor, Wards: 10. Sydenham
Rob Hutchison, Councillor, Wards: 11. King's Town
Ryan Boehme, Councillor, Wards: 12. Pittsburgh
Lanie Hurdle, Chief Administrative Officer, 613-546-4291
Desiree Kennedy, Treasurer & Director, Financial Services,
613-546-4291
Paul MacLatchy, Director, Environment, 613-546-4291
Bill Linnen, Acting Director, Public Works, 613-546-4291
Shawn Armstrong, Fire Chief

Kingsville
2021 Division Rd. North
Kingsville, ON N9Y 2Y9
Tel: 519-733-2305; *Fax:* 519-733-8108
www.kingsville.ca
Other Information: kingsvilleworks@kingsville.ca
Municipal Type: City
Incorporated: 1874; *Area:* 246.83 sq km
County or District: Essex; *Population in 2016:* 21,552
Provincial Electoral District(s): Essex
Federal Electoral District(s): Essex
Next Election: Oct. 24, 2022 (4 year terms)
Note: Incorporated as a town in 1901. Restructuring occurred in
1999.
Nelson Santos, Mayor
Gord Queen, Deputy Mayor & Councillor
Kimberly DeYong, Councillor
Tony Gaffan, Councillor
Laura Lucier, Councillor
Thomas Neufeld, Councillor
Larry Patterson, Councillor
Vacant , Chief Administrative Officer
Chuck Parsons, Fire Chief

Kitchener

City Hall
P.O. Box 1118
200 King St. West
Kitchener, ON N2G 4G7
Tel: 519-741-2345
www.kitchener.ca
Other Information: TTY: 866-969-9994
Municipal Type: City
Incorporated: June 9, 1912; *Area:* 136.77 sq km
County or District: Waterloo Regional Municipality; *Population in 2016:* 233,222
Provincial Electoral District(s): Kitchener Centre; Kitchener-Conestoga; Kitchener South-Hespeler; Waterloo
Federal Electoral District(s): Kitchener Centre; Kitchener-Conestoga; Kitchener South-Hespeler; Waterloo
Next Election: Oct. 24, 2022 (4 year terms)
Berry Vrbanovic, Mayor, 519-741-2300
Scott Davey, Councillor, Wards: 1
Dave Schnider, Councillor, Wards: 2
John Gazzola, Councillor, Wards: 3
Christine Michaud, Councillor, Wards: 4
Kelly Galloway-Sealock, Councillor, Wards: 5
Paul Singh, Councillor, Wards: 6
Bil Ioannidis, Councillor, Wards: 7
Margaret Johnston, Councillor, Wards: 8
Debbie Chapman, Councillor, Wards: 9
Sarah Marsh, Councillor, Wards: 10
Dan Chapman, Chief Administrative Officer, 519-741-2200
Alain Pinard, Director, Planning
Jon Rehill, Fire Chief

Lincoln

4800 South Service Rd.
Beamsville, ON L0R 1B1
Tel: 905-563-8205; *Fax:* 905-563-6566
info@lincoln.ca
www.lincoln.ca
Municipal Type: City
Incorporated: Jan. 1, 1970; *Area:* 162.81 sq km
County or District: Niagara Reg. Mun.; *Population in 2016:* 23,787
Provincial Electoral District(s): Niagara West
Federal Electoral District(s): Niagara West
Next Election: Oct. 24, 2022 (4 year terms)
Note: Amalgamation of the Town of Beamsville, the Township of Clinton, & part of the Township of Louth.
Sandra Easton, Mayor
Dianne Rintjema, Councillor, Wards: 1
Adam Thomas Russell, Councillor, Wards: 1
Tony G. Brunet, Councillor, Wards: 2
John D. Pachereva, Councillor, Wards: 2
Paul MacPherson, Councillor, Wards: 3
Mike Mikolic, Councillor, Wards: 3
Greg Reimer, Councillor, Wards: 4
Lynn Timmers, Councillor, Wards: 4
Michael Kirkopoulos, Chief Administrative Officer
Angela Cifani, Director, Finance & Administration
Kathleen Dale, Director, Planning & Development
Dave Graham, Director, Public Works
David Warden, Manager, Facilities & Parks
Greg Hudson, Fire Chief

London

City Hall
P.O. Box 5035
300 Dufferin Ave.
London, ON N6A 4L9
Tel: 519-661-2489; *Fax:* 519-661-4892
askcity@london.ca
www.london.ca
Municipal Type: City
Incorporated: 1855; *Area:* 420.35 sq km
County or District: Middlesex; *Population in 2016:* 383,151
Provincial Electoral District(s): Elgin-Middlesex-London; London-Fanshawe; London North Centre; London West
Federal Electoral District(s): Elgin-Middlesex-London; Lambton-Kent-Middlesex; London North Centre; London West; London-Fanshawe
Next Election: Oct. 24, 2022 (4 year terms)
Ed Holder, Mayor
Michael Van Holst, Councillor, Wards: 1
Shawn Lewis, Councillor, Wards: 2
Mo Mohamed Salih, Councillor, Wards: 3
Jesse Helmer, Councillor, Wards: 4
Maureen Cassidy, Councillor, Wards: 5
Phil Squire, Councillor, Wards: 6
Josh Morgan, Councillor, Wards: 7
Steve Lehman, Councillor, Wards: 8
Anna Hopkins, Councillor, Wards: 9
Paul Van Meerbergen, Councillor, Wards: 10

Stephen Turner, Councillor, Wards: 11
Elizabeth Peloza, Councillor, Wards: 12
Arielle Kayabaga, Councillor, Wards: 13
Steve Hillier, Councillor, Wards: 14
Cathy Saunders, City Clerk, 519-661-2489
Lynne Livingstone, City Manager, 519-661-2489
Anna Lisa Barbon, CFO, City Treasurer & Managing Director, Corporate Services, 519-661-2489
Gregg Barrett, City Planner, 519-661-2489
Michael Goldrup, Director, People Services, 519-661-2489
Scott Stafford, Managing Director, Parks & Recreation, 519-661-2489
Lori Hamer, Fire Chief, 519-661-2489

Markham

Markham Civic Centre
101 Town Centre Blvd.
Markham, ON L3R 9W3
Tel: 905-477-7000; *Fax:* 905-415-7504
customerservice@markham.ca
www.markham.ca
Other Information: Customer Service, Phone: 905-477-5530
Municipal Type: City
Incorporated: Jan. 1, 1971; *Area:* 212.35 sq km
County or District: York Reg. Mun.; *Population in 2016:* 328,966
Provincial Electoral District(s): Markham-Stouffville; Markham-Thornhill; Markham-Unionville; Richmond Hill; Thornhill
Federal Electoral District(s): Markham-Stouffville; Markham-Thornhill; Markham-Unionville; Richmond Hill; Thornhill
Next Election: Oct. 24, 2022 (4 year terms)
Frank Scarpitti, Mayor, 905-475-4702
Don Hamilton, Deputy Mayor & Regional Councillor
Jack Heath, Regional Councillor, 905-475-4872
Jim Jones, Regional Councillor, 905-479-7757
Joe Li, Regional Councillor, 905-479-7749
Keith Irish, Councillor, Wards: 1
Alan Ho, Councillor, Wards: 2
Reid McAlpine, Councillor, Wards: 3
Karen Rea, Councillor, Wards: 4
Andrew Keyes, Councillor, Wards: 5
Amanda Collucci, Councillor, Wards: 6
Khalid Usman, Councillor, Wards: 7
Isa Lee, Councillor, Wards: 8
Kimberly Kitteringham, City Clerk, 905-475-4729
Andy Taylor, Chief Administrative Officer
Arvin Prasad, Commissioner, Development Services
Trinela Cane, Commissioner, Corporate Services
Nasir Kenea, Chief Information Officer
Dave Decker, Fire Chief

Mississauga

Civic Centre
300 City Centre Dr.
Mississauga, ON L5B 3C1
Tel: 905-615-4311; *Fax:* 905-615-4081
public.info@mississauga.ca
www.mississauga.ca
Other Information: TTY: 905-896-5151
Municipal Type: City
Incorporated: Jan. 1, 1974; *Area:* 292.43 sq km
County or District: Peel Reg. Mun.; *Population in 2016:* 721,599
Provincial Electoral District(s): Mississauga Centre; Mississauga East-Cooksville; Mississauga-Erin Mills; Mississauga-Lakeshore; Mississauga-Malton; Mississauga-Streetsville
Federal Electoral District(s): Mississauga Centre; Mississauga East-Cooksville; Mississauga-Erin Mills; Mississauga-Lakeshore; Mississauga-Malton; Mississauga-Streetsville
Next Election: Oct. 24, 2022 (4 year terms)
Bonnie Crombie, Mayor
Stephen Dasko, Councillor, Wards: 1
Karen Ras, Councillor, 905-896-5200, Wards: 2
Chris Fonseca, Councillor, 905-896-5300, Wards: 3
John Kovac, Councillor, 905-896-5400, Wards: 4
Carolyn Parrish, Councillor, 905-896-5500, Wards: 5
Ron Starr, Councillor, 905-896-5600, Wards: 6
Dipika Damerla, Councillor, 905-896-5700, Wards: 7
Matt Mahoney, Councillor, 905-896-5800, Wards: 8
Pat Saito, Councillor, 905-896-5900, Wards: 9
Sue McFadden, Councillor, 905-896-5010, Wards: 10
George Carlson, Councillor, 905-896-5011, Wards: 11
Diana Rusnov, City Clerk & Director, Legislative Services
Paul Mitcham, City Manager
Gary Kent, Commissioner, Corporate Services
Shari Lichterman, Commissioner, Community Services
Andrew Whittmore, Commissioner, Planning & Building
Tim Beckett, Fire Chief

Mississippi Mills

P.O. Box 400
3131 Old Perth Rd., RR#2
Almonte, ON K0A 1A0
Tel: 613-256-2064; *Fax:* 613-256-4887
town@mississippimills.ca
www.mississippimills.ca
Municipal Type: City
Incorporated: Jan. 1, 1998; *Area:* 519.58 sq km
County or District: Lanark; *Population in 2016:* 13,163
Provincial Electoral District(s): Lanark-Frontenac-Kingston
Federal Electoral District(s): Lanark-Frontenac-Kingston
Next Election: Oct. 24, 2022 (4 year terms)
Note: Merger of the Town of Almonte with the townships of Ramsay & Pakenham.
Christa Lowry, Mayor
Ricky Minnille, Deputy Mayor
John Dalgity, Councillor, Wards: Almonte
Jan Maydan, Councillor, Wards: Almonte
Denzil Ferguson, Councillor, Wards: Pakenham
Cynthia Guerard, Councillor, Wards: Ramsay
Bev Holmes, Councillor, Wards: Ramsay
Jeanne Harfield, Town Clerk, 613-256-2064
Ken Kelly, Chief Administrative Officer, 613-256-2064
Rhonda Whitmarsh, Treasurer, 613-256-2064
Chad Brown, Fire Chief

Newmarket

P.O. Box 328
395 Mulock Dr.
Newmarket, ON L3Y 4X7
Tel: 905-895-5193; *Fax:* 905-953-5100
info@newmarket.ca
www.newmarket.ca
Municipal Type: City
Incorporated: 1857; *Area:* 38.45 sq km
County or District: York Regional Municipality; *Population in 2016:* 84,224
Provincial Electoral District(s): Newmarket-Aurora
Federal Electoral District(s): Newmarket-Aurora
Next Election: Oct. 24, 2022 (4 year terms)
Note: Incorporated as a town in 1880.
John Taylor, Mayor
Tom Vegh, Deputy Mayor
Grace Simon, Councillor, Wards: 1
Victor Woodhouse, Councillor, Wards: 2
Jane Twinney, Councillor, Wards: 3
Trevor Morrison, Councillor, Wards: 4
Bob Kwapis, Councillor, Wards: 5
Kelly Broome, Councillor, Wards: 6
Christina Bisanz, Councillor, Wards: 7
Lisa Lyons, Clerk & Director, Legislative Services
Jag Sharma, Chief Administrative Officer
Mike Mayes, Treasurer & Director, Financial Services
Ian McDougall, Commissioner, Community Services
Peter Noehammer, Commissioner, Development & Infrastructure
Chris Kalimootoo, Director, Public Works Services
Rick Nethery, Director, Planning & Building Services
Ian Laing, Fire Chief, Central York Fire Services

Niagara Falls

City Hall
P.O. Box 1023
4310 Queen St.
Niagara Falls, ON L2E 6X5
Tel: 905-356-7521; *Fax:* 905-356-9083
www.niagarafalls.ca
Municipal Type: City
Incorporated: Jan. 1, 1904; *Area:* 209.73 sq km
County or District: Niagara Reg. Mun.; *Population in 2016:* 88,071
Provincial Electoral District(s): Niagara Falls
Federal Electoral District(s): Niagara Falls
Next Election: Oct. 24, 2022 (4 year terms)
Jim Diodati, Mayor
Wayne Campbell, Councillor, 905-358-9643
Chris Dabrowski, Councillor
Carolynn Ioannoni, Councillor, 905-359-5690
Vince A. Kerrio, Councillor, 905-358-4534
Lori Lococo, Councillor
Victor Pietrangelo, Councillor, 905-353-1808
Mike Strange, Councillor, 289-696-1916
Wayne Thomson, Councillor, 905-359-2238
Anne Angelone, Regional Councillor
Bob Gale, Regional Councillor, 905-321-4253
Barbara Greenwood, Regional Councillor
Peter Nicholson, Regional Councillor
Ken Todd, Chief Administrative Officer
Serge Felicetti, Director, Business Development
Alex Herlovich, Director, Planning, Building & Development
Geoffrey Holman, Director, Municipal Works

Jim Boutilier, Fire Chief

North Bay
City Hall
P.O. Box 360
200 McIntyre St. East
North Bay, ON P1B 8H8
Tel: 705-474-0400; *Fax:* 705-495-4353
customerservice@cityofnorthbay.ca
www.cityofnorthbay.ca
Other Information: Toll-Free Phone: 800-465-1882
Municipal Type: City
Incorporated: 1925; *Area:* 319.11 sq km
County or District: Nipissing District; *Population in 2016:* 51,553
Provincial Electoral District(s): Nipissing
Federal Electoral District(s): Nipissing-Timiskaming
Next Election: Oct. 24, 2022 (4 year terms)
Al McDonald, Mayor
Mike Anthony, Councillor
Mac Bain, Councillor
Johanne Brousseau, Councillor
Mark R. King, Councillor
Chris Mayne, Councillor
Dave Mendecino, Councillor
Scott Robertson, Councillor
Marcus Tignelli, Councillor
Bill Vrebosch, Councillor
Tanya G. Vrebosch, Councillor
Karen McIsaac, City Clerk
David Euler, Chief Administrative Officer
John Severino, City Engineer
Lea Janisse, Chief Human Resources & Information Officer
Karin Pratte, Senior Environment & Facilities Engineer
Jason Whiteley, Fire Chief

Orillia
Administration Office
#300, 50 Andrew St. South
Orillia, ON L3V 7T5
Tel: 705-325-1311; *Fax:* 705-325-5178
help@orillia.ca
www.orillia.ca
Municipal Type: City
Incorporated: 1867; *Area:* 28.58 sq km
County or District: Simcoe; *Population in 2016:* 31,166
Provincial Electoral District(s): Simcoe North
Federal Electoral District(s): Simcoe North
Next Election: Oct. 24, 2022 (4 year terms)
Note: Incorporated as a town in 1875 & as a city in 1969.
Steve Clarke, Mayor
David Campbell, Councillor, Wards: 1
Ted Emond, Councillor, Wards: 1
Ralph Cipolla, Councillor, Wards: 2
Rob Kloostra, Councillor, Wards: 2
Mason Ainsworth, Councillor, Wards: 3
Jay Fallis, Councillor, Wards: 3
Pat Hehn, Councillor, Wards: 4
Tim Lauer, Councillor, Wards: 4
Gayle Jackson, City Clerk & Chief Administrative Officer, 705-329-7232
Jim Lang, City Treasurer
Lori Bolton, Director, Human Resources
Ian Sugden, Director, Development Services & Engineering
Ray Merkley, General Manager, Community Services
Andrew Schell, General Manager, Environment & Infrastructure Services
Brent Thomas, Acting Fire Chief, 705-325-5889

Oshawa
City Hall
50 Centre St. South
Oshawa, ON L1H 3Z7
Tel: 905-436-3311; *Fax:* 905-436-5642
service@oshawa.ca
www.oshawa.ca
Other Information: Toll-Free Phone: 800-667-4292; TTY: 905-436-5627
Municipal Type: City
Incorporated: March 8, 1924; *Area:* 145.64 sq km
County or District: Durham Reg. Mun.; *Population in 2016:* 159,458
Provincial Electoral District(s): Durham; Oshawa
Federal Electoral District(s): Durham; Oshawa
Next Election: Oct. 24, 2022 (4 year terms)
Dan Carter, Mayor
John Neal, Regional & City Councillor, Wards: 1
Tito-Dante Marimpietri, Regional & City Councillor, Wards: 2
Bob Chapman, Regional & City Councillor, Wards: 3
Rick Kerr, Regional & City Councillor, Wards: 4
Brian Nicholson, Regional & City Councillor, Wards: 5
Rosemary McConkey, City Councillor, Wards: 1
Jane Hurst, City Councillor, Wards: 2

Bradley J. Marks, City Councillor, Wards: 3
Derek Giberson, City Councillor, Wards: 4
John Gray, City Councillor, Wards: 5
Paul Ralph, Chief Administrative Officer, 905-436-3311, Fax: 905-436-5623
Tracy Adams, Commissioner, Corporate Services
Ron Diskey, Commissioner, Community Services
Warren Munro, Commissioner, Development Services
Anthony Ambra, Director, Engineering Services
Derrick Clark, Fire Chief

Ottawa
City Hall
110 Laurier Ave. West
Ottawa, ON K1P 1J1
Tel: 613-580-2400; *Fax:* 613-560-1380
info@ottawa.ca
www.ottawa.ca
Other Information: Toll-Free Phone: 866-261-9799
Municipal Type: City
Incorporated: Jan. 1, 1855; *Area:* 2,790.30 sq km
Population in 2016: 934,243
Provincial Electoral District(s): Carleton;
Glengarry-Prescott-Russell; Kanata-Carleton; Nepean; Orléans;
Ottawa Centre; Ottawa South; Ottawa-Vanier; Ottawa
West-Nepean
Federal Electoral District(s): Carleton;
Glengarry-Prescott-Russell; Kanata-Carleton; Nepean; Orléans;
Ottawa Centre; Ottawa South; Ottawa West-Nepean;
Ottawa-Vanier
Next Election: Oct. 24, 2022 (4 year terms)
Jim Watson, Mayor, 613-580-2496
Matthew Luloff, Councillor, 613-580-2471, Wards: 1. Orléans
Laura Dudas, Councillor, 613-580-2472, Wards: 2. Innes
Jan Harder, Councillor, 613-580-2473, Wards: 3. Barrhaven
Jenna Sudds, Councillor, 613-580-2474, Wards: 4. Kanata North
Eli El-Chantiry, Councillor, 613-580-2475, Wards: 5. West Carleton-March
Glen Gower, Councillor, 613-580-2476, Wards: 6. Stittsville
Theresa Kavanagh, Councillor, 613-580-2477, Wards: 7. Bay
Rick Chiarelli, Councillor, 613-580-2478, Wards: 8. College
Keith Egli, Councillor, 613-580-2479, Wards: 9. Knoxdale-Merivale
Diane Deans, Councillor, 613-580-2480, Wards: 10. Gloucester-Southgate
Tim Tierney, Councillor, 613-580-2481, Wards: 11. Beacon Hill-Cyrville
Mathieu Fleury, Councillor, 613-580-2482, Wards: 12. Rideau-Vanier
Rawlson King, Councillor, 613-580-2483, Wards: 13. Rideau-Rockcliffe
Catherine McKenney, Councillor, 613-580-2484, Wards: 14. Somerset
Jeff Leiper, Councillor, 613-580-2485, Wards: 15. Kitchissippi
Riley Brockington, Councillor, 613-580-2486, Wards: 16. River
Shawn Menard, Councillor, 613-580-2487, Wards: 17. Capital
Jean Cloutier, Councillor, 613-580-2488, Wards: 18. Alta Vista
Vacant , Councillor, Wards: 19. Cumberland
George Darouze, Councillor, 613-580-2490, Wards: 20. Osgoode
Scott Moffatt, Councillor, 613-580-2491, Wards: 21. Rideau-Goulbourn
Carol Anne Meehan, Councillor, 613-580-2751, Wards: 22. Gloucester-South Nepean
Allan Hubley, Councillor, 613-580-2752, Wards: 23. Kanata South
M. Rick O'Connor, City Clerk & Solicitor, 613-580-2424
Steve Kanellakos, City Manager, 613-580-2424
Wendy Stephanson, City Treasurer, 613-580-2424
Dan Chenier, General Manager, Recreation, Cultural & Facility Services, 613-580-2424
Donna Gray, General Manager, Community & Social Services
Kevin Wylie, General Manager, Public Works & Environmental Services, 613-580-2424
Vera Etches, Medical Officer of Health
Kim Ayotte, Fire Chief
Peter Sloly, Police Chief

Owen Sound
City Hall
808 - 2nd Ave. East
Owen Sound, ON N4K 2H4
Tel: 519-376-1440
cityadmin@owensound.ca
www.owensound.ca
Municipal Type: City
Incorporated: Jan. 1, 2001; *Area:* 24.27 sq km
County or District: Grey; *Population in 2016:* 21,341
Provincial Electoral District(s): Bruce-Grey-Owen Sound
Federal Electoral District(s): Bruce-Grey-Owen Sound
Next Election: Oct. 24, 2022 (4 year terms)

Ian Boddy, Mayor
Brian O'Leary, Deputy Mayor
Travis Dodd, Councillor
Scott Greig, Councillor
Brock Hamley, Councillor
Marion Koepke, Councillor
Carol Merton, Councillor
John A. Tamming, Councillor
Richard Thomas, Councillor
Tim Simmonds, City Manager, 519-376-4440
Kate Allan, Director, Corporate Services, 519-376-4440
Pam Coulter, Director, Community Services, 519-376-4440
Dennis Kefalas, Director, Public Works & Engineering, 519-376-4440
Doug Barfoot, Fire Chief, 519-376-2512

Pembroke
1 Pembroke St. East
Pembroke, ON K8A 3J5
Tel: 613-735-6821; *Fax:* 613-735-3660
pembroke@pembroke.ca
www.pembroke.ca
Municipal Type: City
Incorporated: 1877; *Area:* 14.56 sq km
County or District: Renfrew; *Population in 2016:* 13,882
Provincial Electoral District(s): Renfrew-Nipissing-Pembroke
Federal Electoral District(s): Renfrew-Nipissing-Pembroke
Next Election: Oct. 24, 2022 (4 year terms)
Note: Incorporated as a city in 1971.
Michael LeMay, Mayor
Ron Gervais, Deputy Mayor & Councillor
Brian Abdallah, Councillor
Ed Jacyno, Councillor
Patricia Lafreniere, Councillor
Andrew Plummer, Councillor
Christine Reavie, Councillor
Terry Lapierre, Chief Administrative Officer, 613-735-6821
Angela Lochtie, Treasurer
Ron Conroy, Manager, Recreation
Brian Lewis, Manager, Operations
Colleen Sauriol, Manager, Planning, Building & By-law Enforcement
Mark Schultz, Chief Building Official
Daniel Herback, Fire Chief

Petawawa
1111 Victoria St.
Petawawa, ON K8H 2E6
Tel: 613-687-5536; *Fax:* 613-687-5973
email@petawawa.ca
www.petawawa.ca
Municipal Type: City
Incorporated: July 1, 1997; *Area:* 166.69 sq km
County or District: Renfrew; *Population in 2016:* 17,187
Provincial Electoral District(s): Renfrew-Nipissing-Pembroke
Federal Electoral District(s): Renfrew-Nipissing-Pembroke
Next Election: Oct. 24, 2022 (4 year terms)
Note: Amalgamation of Petawawa Village & Petawawa Township.
Robert Sweet, Mayor
James Carmody, Councillor
Matthew McLean, Councillor
Tom Mohns, Councillor
Murray Rutz, Councillor
Theresa Sabourin, Councillor
Gary Serviss, Councillor
Daniel Scissons, Chief Administrative Officer & Clerk
Annette Mantifel, Treasurer
Levi Junop, Chief Building Official
David Unrau, Director, Public Works
Steve Knott, Fire Chief

Peterborough
500 George St. North
Peterborough, ON K9H 3R9
Tel: 705-742-7777
www.peterborough.ca
Other Information: Toll-Free Phone: 855-738-3755
Municipal Type: City
Incorporated: 1850; *Area:* 64.25 sq km
County or District: Peterborough; *Population in 2016:* 81,032
Provincial Electoral District(s): Peterborough-Kawartha
Federal Electoral District(s): Northumberland-Peterborough
South; Peterborough-Kawartha
Next Election: Oct. 24, 2022 (4 year terms)
Diane Therrien, Mayor
Lesley Parnell, Councillor, Wards: 1. Otonabee
Kim Zippel, Councillor, Wards: 1. Otonabee
Henry Clarke, Councillor, Wards: 2. Monaghan
Don Vassiliadis, Councillor, Wards: 2. Monaghan
Kemi Akapo, Councillor, Wards: 3. Town
Dean Pappas, Councillor, Wards: 3. Town

Gary Baldwin, Councillor, Wards: 4. Ashburnham
Keith G. Riel, Councillor, Wards: 4. Ashburnham
Andrew Beamer, Councillor, Wards: 5. Northcrest
Stephen Wright, Councillor, Wards: 5. Northcrest
Sandra Clancy, Chief Administrative Officer
Richard Freymond, Treasurer
Sheldon Laidman, Commissioner, Community Services
David Potts, Director, Legal Services
Cathy Robertson, Fire Chief

Pickering
1 The Esplanade
Pickering, ON L1V 6K7
Tel: 905-420-2222
www.pickering.ca
Other Information: Toll-Free Phone: 866-683-2760; TTY:
905-420-1739
Municipal Type: City
Incorporated: 1849; *Area:* 231.55 sq km
County or District: Durham Reg. Mun.; *Population in 2016:*
91,771
Provincial Electoral District(s): Pickering-Uxbridge
Federal Electoral District(s): Ajax; Pickering-Uxbridge
Next Election: Oct. 24, 2022 (4 year terms)
Note: Incorporated as a town in 1974 & as a city in 2000.
Dave Ryan, Mayor, 905-420-4600, Fax: 905-420-6064
Kevin Ashe, Regional Councillor, Wards: 1
Maurice Brenner, City Councillor, Wards: 1
Bill McLean, Regional Councillor, Wards: 2
Ian Cumming, City Councillor, Wards: 2
David Pickles, Regional Councillor, Wards: 3
Shaheen Butt, City Councillor, Wards: 3
Susan Cassel, City Clerk, 905-420-4660
Tony Prevedel, Chief Administrative Officer, 905-420-4648
Paul Bigioni, City Solicitor & Director, Corporate Services,
905-420-4660
Kyle Bentley, Chief Building Official & Director, City
Development, 902-420-4660
Brian Duffield, Director, Community Services, 905-420-4660
Richard Holborn, Director, Engineering Services, 905-420-4660
Catherine Rose, Chief Planner, 905-420-4660
John Hagg, Fire Chief, 905-420-4660

Port Colborne
66 Charlotte St.
Port Colborne, ON L3K 3C8
Tel: 905-835-2900; *Fax:* 905-834-5746
www.portcolborne.ca
Municipal Type: City
Incorporated: 1870; *Area:* 121.96 sq km
County or District: Niagara Reg. Mun.; *Population in 2016:*
18,306
Provincial Electoral District(s): Niagara Centre
Federal Electoral District(s): Niagara Centre
Next Election: Oct. 24, 2022 (4 year terms)
Note: Incorporated as a town in 1918 & as a city in 1966.
Bill Steele, Mayor
Barbara Butters, Regional Councillor
Mark Bagu, Councillor, Wards: 1
Donna Kalailieff, Councillor, Wards: 1
Eric Beauregard, Councillor, Wards: 2
Angie Desmarais, Councillor, Wards: 2
Gary Bruno, Councillor, Wards: 3
Frank M. Danch, Councillor, Wards: 3
Ron Bodner, Councillor, Wards: 4
Harry Wells, Councillor, Wards: 4
Scott Luey, Chief Administrative Officer, 905-835-2900
Dan Aquilina, Director, Planning & Development, 905-835-2900
Bryan Boles, Director, Corporate Services
Chris Lee, Director, Engineering & Operations, 905-835-2901
Todd Rogers, Chief Building Official, 905-835-2901
Darlene Suddard, Supervisor, Environmental Compliance,
905-835-5079
Thomas Cartwright, Fire Chief, 905-834-4512

Quinte West
P.O. Box 490
7 Creswell Dr.
Trenton, ON K8V 5R6
Tel: 613-392-2841; *Fax:* 613-392-5608
www.quintewest.ca
Other Information: Toll-Free Phone: 866-485-2841
Municipal Type: City
Incorporated: Jan. 1, 1998; *Area:* 494.02 sq km
County or District: Hastings; *Population in 2016:* 43,577
Provincial Electoral District(s): Bay of Quinte;
Northumberland-Peterborough South
Federal Electoral District(s): Bay of Quinte
Next Election: Oct. 24, 2022 (4 year terms)
Note: Amalgamation of the former municipalities of Trenton,
Sidney, Murray & Frankford.
Jim Harrison, Mayor

Sally Freeman, Councillor, Wards: 1
Michael Kotsovos, Councillor, Wards: 1
Fred Kuypers, Councillor, Wards: 1
David O'Neil, Councillor, Wards: 1
Leslie Roseblade, Councillor, Wards: 1
Terry Cassidy, Councillor, Wards: 2
Allan DeWitt, Councillor, Wards: 2
Don Kuntze, Councillor, Wards: 2
Karen Sharpe, Councillor, Wards: 2
Jim Alyea, Councillor, Wards: 3
David McCue, Councillor, Wards: 3
Lynda Reid, Councillor, Wards: 4
Kevin Heath, Clerk & Manager, Corporate Services,
613-392-2841
Charlie Murphy, Chief Administrative Officer, 613-392-2841
David Clazie, Treasurer & Director, Corporate & Financial
Services, 613-392-2841
Chris Angelo, Director, Public Works & Environmental Services,
613-392-2841
Brian Jardine, Director, Planning & Development Services,
613-392-2841
Tim Colasante, Manager, Engineering Services, 613-392-2841
Lori Coxwell-Duncan, Manager, Human Resources,
613-392-2841
John Whelan, Fire Chief, 613-392-2841

Richmond Hill
225 East Beaver Creek Rd.
Richmond Hill, ON L4B 3P4
Tel: 905-771-8800; *Fax:* 905-771-2500
access@richmondhill.ca
www.richmondhill.ca
Municipal Type: City
Incorporated: 1873; *Area:* 101.11 sq km
County or District: York Reg. Mun.; *Population in 2016:* 195,022
Provincial Electoral District(s): Aurora-Oak Ridges-Richmond
Hill; Richmond Hill
Federal Electoral District(s): Aurora-Oak Ridges-Richmond Hill;
Richmond Hill
Next Election: Oct. 24, 2022 (4 year terms)
Joe DiPaola, Acting Mayor; Deputy Mayor; Regional & Local
Councillor
Carmine Perrelli, Regional & Local Councillor
Greg Beros, Councillor, Wards: 1
Tom Muench, Councillor, Wards: 2
Castro Liu, Councillor, Wards: 3
David West, Councillor, Wards: 4
Karen Cilevitz, Councillor, Wards: 5
Godwin Chan, Councillor, Wards: 6
Neil Garbe, Chief Administrative Officer
David Dexter, Acting Treasurer & Commissioner, Corporate &
Financial Services, 905-771-2484
Kevin Kwan, Commissioner, Planning & Regulatory Services
Italo Brutto, Commissioner, Environment & Infrastructure
Services
Darlene Joslin, Director, Recreation & Culture
Steve Kraft, Fire Chief

St. Catharines
City Hall
P.O. Box 3012
50 Church St.
St Catharines, ON L2R 7C2
Tel: 905-688-5600; *Fax:* 905-682-3631
www.stcatharines.ca
Other Information: TTY: 905-688-4889
Municipal Type: City
Incorporated: 1876; *Area:* 96.13 sq km
County or District: Niagara Reg. Mun.; *Population in 2016:*
133,113
Provincial Electoral District(s): Niagara Centre; Niagara West;
St. Catharines
Federal Electoral District(s): Niagara Centre; Niagara West; St.
Catharines
Next Election: Oct. 24, 2022 (4 year terms)
Walter Sendzik, Mayor
Lori Littleton, Councillor, Wards: 1. Merritton
Greg Miller, Councillor, Wards: 1. Merritton
Matthew J. Harris, Councillor, Wards: 2. St. Andrew's
Joseph Kushner, Councillor, Wards: 2. St. Andrew's
Sal Sorrento, Councillor, Wards: 3. St. George's
Kevin Townsend, Councillor, Wards: 3. St. George's
Karrie Porter, Councillor, Wards: 4. St. Patrick's
Mathew D. Siscoe, Councillor, Wards: 4. St. Patrick's
Dawn Dodge, Councillor, Wards: 5. Grantham
Bill Phillips, Councillor, Wards: 5. Grantham
Carlos Garcia, Councillor, Wards: 6. Port Dalhousie
Bruce Williamson, Councillor, Wards: 6. Port Dalhousie
Sandie Bellows, Regional Councillor
George Darte, Regional Councillor
Brian Heit, Regional Councillor

Laura Ip, Regional Councillor
Tim Rigby, Regional Councillor
Bonnie Nistico-Dunk, City Clerk
Shelley Chemnitz, Chief Administrative Officer
Jeff McCormick, Fire Chief

St. Thomas
City Hall
P.O. Box 520
545 Talbot St.
St Thomas, ON N5P 3V7
Tel: 519-631-1680
info@stthomas.ca
www.stthomas.ca
Other Information: TTY: 519-631-3836
Municipal Type: City
Incorporated: March 4, 1881; *Area:* 35.63 sq km
County or District: Elgin; *Population in 2016:* 38,909
Provincial Electoral District(s): Elgin-Middlesex-London
Federal Electoral District(s): Elgin-Middlesex-London
Next Election: Oct. 24, 2022 (4 year terms)
Joe Preston, Mayor
Lori Baldwin-Sands, Councillor
Gary Clarke, Councillor
Jim Herbert, Councillor
Jeff Kohler, Councillor
Steve Peters, Councillor
Joan Rymal, Councillor
Mark Tinlin, Councillor
Stephen Wookey, Councillor
Wendell Graves, Chief Administrative Officer, 519-631-1680
Graham Dart, Director, Human Resources
Patrick Keenan, Director, Planning & Building Services,
529-631-1680
Ross Tucker, Director, Parks, Recreation & Property,
519-633-2560
Bob Davidson, Fire Chief

Sarnia
City Hall
P.O. Box 3018
255 North Christina St.
Sarnia, ON N7T 7N2
Tel: 519-332-0330; *Fax:* 519-332-3995
www.sarnia.ca
Other Information: TTY: 519-332-2664
Municipal Type: City
Incorporated: May 7, 1914; *Area:* 164.85 sq km
County or District: Lambton; *Population in 2016:* 71,594
Provincial Electoral District(s): Sarnia-Lambton
Federal Electoral District(s): Sarnia-Lambton
Next Election: Oct. 24, 2022 (4 year terms)
Mike Bradley, Mayor
Margaret Bird, City & County Councillor
Dave Boushy, City & County Councillor
Mike Stark, City & County Councillor
Brian White, City & County Councillor
Terry Burrell, City Councillor
Nathan Colquhoun, City Councillor
Bill Dennis, City Councillor
George Vandenberg, City Councillor
Dianne Gould-Brown, City Clerk, 519-332-0330
Chris Carter, Chief Administrative Officer, 519-332-0330
Stacey Forfar, General Manager, Community Services,
519-332-0330
David Jackson, General Manager, Engineering & Operations,
519-332-0330
David Logan, General Manager, Corporate Services
Brian Arnold, Fire Chief, 519-332-0330

Sault Ste. Marie
Civic Centre
P.O. Box 580
99 Foster Dr.
Sault Ste Marie, ON P6A 5N1
Tel: 705-759-2500; *Fax:* 705-759-2310
info@cityssm.on.ca
www.cityssm.on.ca
Other Information: TTY: 877-688-5528
Municipal Type: City
Incorporated: 1912; *Area:* 223.24 sq km
County or District: Algoma District; *Population in 2016:* 73,368
Provincial Electoral District(s): Sault Ste. Marie
Federal Electoral District(s): Sault Ste. Marie
Next Election: Oct. 24, 2022 (4 year terms)
Christian Provenzano, Mayor
Paul Christian, Councillor, Wards: 1
Sandra Hollingsworth, Councillor, Wards: 1
Luke Dufour, Councillor, Wards: 2
Lisa Vezeau-Allen, Councillor, Wards: 2
Donna Hilsinger, Councillor, Wards: 3
Matthew Shoemaker, Councillor, Wards: 3

Marchy Bruni, Councillor, Wards: 4
Rick Niro, Councillor, Wards: 4
Corey Gardi, Councillor, Wards: 5
Matthew Scott, Councillor, Wards: 5
Rachel Tyczinski, City Clerk, 705-759-5391
Malcolm White, Chief Administrative Officer, 705-759-5347
Larry Girardi, Deputy Chief Administration Officer, Public Works & Transportation
Tom Vair, Deputy Chief Administrative Officer, Community Development & Enterprise Services
Donald McConnell, Director, Planning & Enterprise Services
Peter Johnson, Fire Chief, 705-949-3333

Stratford
City Hall
P.O. Box 818
1 Wellington St.
Stratford, ON N5A 6W1
Tel: 519-271-0250; *Fax:* 519-273-5041
www.stratfordcanada.ca
Other Information: TTY: 519-271-5241
Municipal Type: City
Incorporated: 1854; *Area:* 28.28 sq km
County or District: Perth; *Population in 2016:* 31,465
Provincial Electoral District(s): Perth-Wellington
Federal Electoral District(s): Perth-Wellington
Next Election: Oct. 24, 2022 (4 year terms)
Note: Incorporated as a city in 1886.
Daniel Mathieson, Mayor, 519-271-0251
Brad Beatty, Councillor
Graham Bunting, Councillor
Jo-Dee Burbach, Councillor
Tom Clifford, Councillor
Dave Gaffney, Councillor
Bonnie Henderson, Councillor
Danielle Ingram, Councillor
Martin Ritsma, Councillor
Cody Sebben, Councillor
Kathy Vassilakos, Councillor
Joan Thomson, Chief Administrative Officer, 519-271-0250
Ed Dujlovic, Director, Infrastructure & Development Services, 519-271-0250
Richard Young, Fire Chief

Temiskaming Shores
Temiskaming Shores Administration Office
P.O. Box 2050
325 Farr Ave.
Haileybury, ON P0J 1K0
Tel: 705-672-3363; *Fax:* 705-672-2911
www.temiskamingshores.ca
Municipal Type: City
Incorporated: Jan. 1, 2004; *Area:* 178.11 sq km
County or District: Timiskaming District; *Population in 2016:* 9,920
Provincial Electoral District(s): Timiskaming-Cochrane
Federal Electoral District(s): Nipissing-Timiskaming
Next Election: Oct. 24, 2022 (4 year terms)
Note: Amalgamation of the Town of Haileybury, the Town of New Liskeard & the Township of Dymond.
Carman Kidd, Mayor, 705-672-3363
Jesse Foley, Councillor
Patricia Hewitt, Councillor
Douglas Jelly, Councillor
Jeff Laferriere, Councillor
Mike McArthur, Councillor
Danny Whalen, Councillor
David Treen, Clerk, 705-672-3363
Christopher W. Oslund, City Manager, 705-672-3363
Laura Lee McLeod, Treasurer, 705-672-3363
Tammie Caldwell, Director, Recreation, 705-672-3363
Doug Walsh, Director, Public Works, 705-672-3363
Paul Allair, Superintendent, Parks & Facilities, 705-647-5728
Darrell Phaneuf, Superintendent, Environmental Services, 705-672-3363
James Sheppard, Superintendent, Transportation Services, 705-672-3363
Tim Uttley, Fire Chief, 705-672-3363

Thorold
Thorold City Hall
P.O. Box 1044
3540 Schmon Pkwy.
Thorold, ON L2V 4A7
Tel: 905-227-6613; *Fax:* 905-227-5590
www.thorold.com
Other Information: TTY: 905-227-6206
Municipal Type: City
Incorporated: 1798; *Area:* 82.99 sq km
County or District: Niagara Reg. Mun.; *Population in 2016:* 18,801
Provincial Electoral District(s): Niagara Centre

Federal Electoral District(s): Niagara Centre
Next Election: Oct. 24, 2022 (4 year terms)
Note: Incorporated as a village in 1850, as a town in 1875, as a new town (amalgamating the Township of Thorold & the Town of Thorold) in 1970, & as a city in 1975.
Terry Ugulini, Mayor
Tim Whalen, Regional Councillor
Nella Dekker, Councillor
Carmen Derose, Councillor
Jim Handley, Councillor
John Kenny, Councillor
Anthony Longo, Councillor
Fred Neale, Councillor
Ken Sentance, Councillor
Victoria Wilson, Councillor
Manoj Dilwaria, Chief Administrative Officer
Terry Dixon, Fire Chief

Thunder Bay
City Hall
P.O. Box 800
500 Donald St. East
Thunder Bay, ON P7C 5K4
Tel: 807-625-2230; *Fax:* 807-623-5468
www.thunderbay.ca
Other Information: TTY: 807-622-2225
Municipal Type: City
Incorporated: Jan 1, 1970; *Area:* 328.36 sq km
County or District: Thunder Bay District; *Population in 2016:* 107,909
Provincial Electoral District(s): Thunder Bay-Atikokan; Thunder Bay-Superior North
Federal Electoral District(s): Thunder Bay-Rainy River; Thunder Bay-Superior North
Next Election: Oct. 24, 2022 (4 year terms)
Bill Mauro, Mayor
Mark Bentz, Councillor at Large
Trevor Giertuga, Councillor at Large
Rebecca Johnson, Councillor at Large
Aldo. V. Ruberto, Councillor at Large
Peng You, Councillor at Large
Andrew Foulds, Councillor, Wards: Current River
Albert Aiello, Councillor, Wards: McIntyre
Brian Hamilton, Councillor, Wards: McKellar
Cody Fraser, Councillor, Wards: Neebing
Shelby Ch'ng, Councillor, Wards: Northwood
Brian McKinnon, Councillor, Wards: Red River
Kristin Oliver, Councillor, Wards: Westfort
Norm Gale, City Manager
Karen Lewis, Director, Corporate Strategic Services, 807-625-3859, Fax: 807-625-0181
Kelly Robertson, General Manager, Community Services, 807-625-2964, Fax: 807-625-3258
Kerri Marshall, General Manager, Infrastructure & Operations
John Hay, Fire Chief, 807-625-2101

Tillsonburg
Customer Service Centre
10 Lisgar Ave.
Tillsonburg, ON N4G 5A5
Tel: 519-842-9200; *Fax:* 519-688-0759
www.tillsonburg.ca
Municipal Type: City
Incorporated: 1872; *Area:* 22.33 sq km
County or District: Oxford; *Population in 2016:* 15,872
Provincial Electoral District(s): Oxford
Federal Electoral District(s): Oxford
Next Election: Oct. 24, 2022 (4 year terms)
Stephen Molnar, Mayor, 519-688-3009
Dave Beres, Councillor
Penny Esseltine, Councillor
Deb Gilvesy, Councillor
Pete Luciani, Councillor
Chris Parker, Councillor
Chris Rosehart, Councillor
Sheena Pawliwec, Interim Treasurer, 519-688-3009
Ashley Andrews, Manager, Human Resources, 519-688-3009
Andrea Brown, Manager, Programs & Services, 519-688-3009
Carl Kristensen, Interim Manager, Parks & Facilities, 519-688-3009
Dan Locke, Manager, Public Works, 519-688-3009
Brad Lemaich, Fire Chief, 519-688-3009

Timmins
220 Algonquin Blvd. East
Timmins, ON P4N 1B3
Tel: 705-264-1331; *Fax:* 705-360-2674
www.timmins.ca
Municipal Type: City
Incorporated: 1973; *Area:* 2,978.83 sq km
County or District: Cochrane District; *Population in 2016:* 41,788
Provincial Electoral District(s): Timmins

Federal Electoral District(s): Timmins-James Bay
Next Election: Oct. 24, 2022 (4 year terms)
George Pirie, Mayor
Rock Whissell, Councillor, Wards: 1
Mickey Auger, Councillor, Wards: 2
Joe Campbell, Councillor, Wards: 3
John P. Curley, Councillor, Wards: 4
Michelle Boileau, Councillor, Wards: 5
Andrew Marks, Councillor, Wards: 5
Kristin Murray, Councillor, Wards: 5
Noella Rinaldo, Councillor, Wards: 5
Dave Landers, Chief Administrative Officer
Tom Laughren, Fire Chief

Toronto
City Hall
100 Queen St. West
Toronto, ON M5H 2N2
Tel: 416-392-2489; *Fax:* 416-338-0685
311@toronto.ca
www.toronto.ca
Other Information: TTY: 416-338-0889
Municipal Type: City
Incorporated: March 6, 1834; *Area:* 630.20 sq km
Population in 2016: 2,731,571
Provincial Electoral District(s): Bchs-E. York; Davenport; Don V. E.; Don V N.; Don V. W.; Eglinton-Lawrence; Etob. Ctr; Etob.-Lkshore; Etob. N.; Humber River-Blk Creek; Parkdale-High Pk.; Scarb.-Agincourt; Scarb. Ctr; Scarb.-Guildwood; Scarb. N.; Scarb.-Rouge Pk.; Scarb. SW.; Spad.-Fort York; To. Ctr; To.-Danforth; To.-St. Paul's; Univ.-Rosedale; Willowdale; York Ctr.; York S.-Weston
Federal Electoral District(s): Beaches-East York; Davenport; Don V. W.; Don.V.N.; Eglinton-Lawrence; Etob. Centre; Etob. N.; Etob.-Lakeshore; Humber River-Black Creek; Parkdale-High Park; Scarb. Ctr.; Scarb.N.; Scarb. SW.; Scarb.-Agincourt; Scarb.-Guildwood; Scarb.-Rouge Park; Spadina-Ft. York; Tor. Ctr.; Tor.-Danforth; To.-St.Paul's; University-Rosedale; Willowdale, York Ctr.; York S.-Weston
Next Election: Oct. 24, 2022 (4 year terms)
Note: Incorporated as a city on Jan. 1, 1998, & comprising the 6 former municipalities of: Etobicoke; North York; York; East York; Scarborough; & Old Toronto.
In 2018, Premier Doug Ford reduced the size of Toronto council from 47 to 25 seats.
John Tory, Mayor
Michael Ford, Councillor, Wards: 1. Etobicoke North
Stephen Holyday, Councillor, Wards: 2. Etobicoke Centre
Mark Grimes, Councillor, Wards: 3. Etobicoke-Lakeshore
Gord Perks, Councillor, Wards: 4. Parkdale-High Park
Frances Nunziata, Councillor, Wards: 5. York South-Weston
James Pasternak, Councillor, Wards: 6. York Centre
Anthony Perruzza, Councillor, Wards: 7. Humber River-Black Creek
Mike Colle, Councillor, Wards: 8. Eglinton-Lawrence
Ana Bailao, Councillor, Wards: 9. Davenport
Joe Cressy, Councillor, Wards: 10. Spadina-Fort York
Mike Layton, Councillor, Wards: 11. University-Rosedale
Josh Matlow, Councillor, Wards: 12. Toronto-St. Paul's
Kristyn Wong-Tam, Councillor, Wards: 13. Toronto Centre
Paula Fletcher, Councillor, Wards: 14. Toronto-Danforth
Jaye Robinson, Councillor, Wards: 15. Don Valley West
Denzil Minnan-Wong, Councillor, Wards: 16. Don Valley East
Shelley Carroll, Councillor, Wards: 17. Don Valley North
John Filion, Councillor, Wards: 18. Willowdale
Brad Bradford, Councillor, Wards: 19. Beaches-East York
Gary Crawford, Councillor, Wards: 20. Scarborough Southwest
Michael Thompson, Councillor, Wards: 21. Scarborough Centre
Nick Mantas, Councillor, Wards: 22. Scarborough-Agincourt
Cynthia Lai, Councillor, Wards: 23. Scarborough North
Paul Ainslie, Councillor, Wards: 24. Scarborough-Guildwood
Jennifer McKelvie, Councillor, Wards: 25. Scarborough-Rouge Park
Ulli S. Watkiss, City Clerk, 416-392-8010, Fax: 416-392-2980
Chris Murray, City Manager, 416-392-3551, Fax: 416-392-1827
Wendy Walberg, City Solicitor, 416-392-8047
Tracy Cook, Deputy City Manager, Infrastructure & Development Services, 416-338-7200, Fax: 416-392-4540
Giuliana Carbone, Deputy City Manager, Community & Social Services, 416-338-7205, Fax: 416-395-0388
Josie Scioli, Deputy City Manager, Corporate Services, 416-392-3974
Heather Taylor, Chief Financial Officer, 416-392-8773, Fax: 416-397-5236
Omo Akintan, Chief People Officer, 416-392-8703
Rob Meikle, Chief Information Officer, 416-392-8421, Fax: 416-696-4244
Will Johnston, Chief Building Official & Executive Director, Toronto Building, 416-397-4446
Abigail Bond, Executive Director, Housing Secretariat, 416-392-0054, Fax: 416-392-0548

Carleton Grant, Executive Director, Municipal Licensing & Standards, 416-392-8445, Fax: 416-397-5463
Tom Azouz, General Manager, Employment & Social Services, 416-392-8952, Fax: 416-392-4214
Barbara Gray, General Manager, Transportation Services, 416-392-8431, Fax: 416-392-4455
Matt Keliher, General Manager, Solid Waste Management Services, 416-392-4715, Fax: 416-392-4754
Shanley McNamee, General Manager, Children's Services, 416-392-8134, Fax: 416-392-4576
Janie Romoff, General Manager, Parks, Forestry, & Recreation, 416-392-8182, Fax: 416-392-8565
Gord McEachen, Acting Chief, Toronto Paramedic Services, 416-392-2205, Fax: 416-392-2115
Matthew Pegg, Fire Chief & General Manager, Fire Services, 416-338-9051, Fax: 416-338-9060
Mark Saunders, Chief of Police, Toronto Police Services
Eileen de Villa, Medical Officer of Health

Vaughan
2141 Major Mackenzie Dr.
Vaughan, ON L6A 1T1
Tel: 905-832-2281; *Fax:* 905-832-8535
www.vaughan.ca
Other Information: Automated Tel.: 905-832-8585; TTY: 866-534-0545
Municipal Type: City
Incorporated: Jan. 1, 1971; *Area:* 273.56 sq km
County or District: York Regional Municipality; *Population in 2016:* 306,233
Provincial Electoral District(s): King-Vaughan; Thornhill; Vaughan-Woodbridge
Federal Electoral District(s): King-Vaughan; Thornhill; Vaughan-Woodbridge
Next Election: Oct. 24, 2022 (4 year terms)
Maurizio Bevilacqua, Mayor
Mario Ferri, Deputy Mayor, Local & Regional Councillor
Linda D. Jackson, Local & Regional Councillor
Gino Rosati, Local & Regional Councillor
Marilyn Iafrate, Councillor, Wards: 1
Tony Carella, Councillor, Wards: 2
Rosanna DeFrancesca, Councillor, Wards: 3
Sandra Yeung Racco, Councillor, Wards: 4
Alan Shefman, Councillor, Wards: 5
Todd Coles, City Clerk
Vacant , City Manager
Michael Coroneos, Treasurer, CFO & Deputy City Manager, Corporate Services, 905-832-2281
Zoran Postic, Deputy City Manager, Public Works, 905-832-2281
Mary Reali, Deputy City Manager, Community Services, 905-832-8585
Jason Schmidt-Shoukri, Deputy City Manager, Planning & Growth Management, 905-832-2281
Jamie Bronsema, Director, Parks Delivery, 905-303-2069
Michael Genova, Director, Corporate & Strategic Communications
Deryn Bentley, Fire Chief

Wasaga Beach
30 Lewis St.
Wasaga Beach, ON L9Z 1A1
Tel: 705-429-3844; *Fax:* 705-429-7603
www.wasagabeach.com
Municipal Type: City
Incorporated: 1947; *Area:* 58.64 sq km
County or District: Simcoe; *Population in 2016:* 20,675
Provincial Electoral District(s): Simcoe-Grey
Federal Electoral District(s): Simcoe-Grey
Next Election: Oct. 24, 2022 (4 year terms)
Note: Incorporated as a village in 1951 & as a town in 1974.
Nina Bifolchi, Mayor
Sylvia Bray, Deputy Mayor & Councillor
Joe Belanger, Councillor
David Foster, Councillor
Mark Kinney, Councillor
George Watson, Councillor
Stan Wells, Councillor
Dina Lundy, Town Clerk
George Vadeboncoeur, Chief Administrative Officer
Jocelyn Lee, Treasurer
Kevin Lalonde, Director, Public Works
Chris Roos, Director, Recreation, Events & Facilities
Mike McWilliam, Fire Chief

Waterloo
City Hall
P.O. Box 337 Waterloo
100 Regina St. South
Waterloo, ON N2J 4A8
Tel: 519-886-1550; *Fax:* 519-747-8500
www.waterloo.ca
Other Information: TTY: 866-786-3941
Municipal Type: City
Incorporated: Jan. 15, 1857; *Area:* 64.02 sq km
County or District: Waterloo Regional Municipality; *Population in 2016:* 104,986
Provincial Electoral District(s): Waterloo
Federal Electoral District(s): Waterloo
Next Election: Oct. 24, 2022 (4 year terms)
Note: Incorporated as a town in 1876 & as a city on Jan 1, 1948.
Dave Jaworsky, Mayor
Sandra Hanmer, Councillor, Wards: 1
Royce Bodaly, Councillor, Wards: 2
Angela Vieth, Councillor, Wards: 3
Diane Freeman, Councillor, Wards: 4
Jen Vasic, Councillor, Wards: 5
Jeff Henry, Councillor, Wards: 6
Tenille Bonoguore, Councillor, Wards: 7
Olga Smith, City Clerk, 519-747-8705, Fax: 519-747-8510
Tim Anderson, Chief Administrative Officer, 519-747-8702, Fax: 519-747-8500
Keshwer Patel, Chief Financial Officer & Commissioner, Corporate Services, 519-747-8722
Mark Dykstra, Commissioner, Community Services
Cameron Rapp, Commissioner, Integrated Planning & Public Works
Richard Hepditch, Fire Chief

Welland
60 East Main St.
Welland, ON L3B 3X4
Tel: 905-735-1700; *Fax:* 905-732-1919
www.welland.ca
Municipal Type: City
Incorporated: July 24, 1858; *Area:* 81.04 sq km
County or District: Niagara Regional Municipality; *Population in 2016:* 52,293
Provincial Electoral District(s): Niagara Centre
Federal Electoral District(s): Niagara Centre
Next Election: Oct. 24, 2022 (4 year terms)
Note: Incorporated as a town on Jan. 1, 1878 & as a city on July 1, 1917.
Frank Campion, Mayor
Mary Ann Grimaldi, Councillor, Wards: 1
Adam Moote, Councillor, Wards: 1
David McLeod, Councillor, Wards: 2
Leo Van Vliet, Councillor, Wards: 2
John Chiocchio, Councillor, Wards: 3
Lucas Spinosa, Councillor, Wards: 3
Tony DiMarco, Councillor, Wards: 4
Bryan Green, Councillor, Wards: 4
Claudette Richard, Councillor, Wards: 5
Graham Speck, Councillor, Wards: 5
Bonnie Fokkens, Councillor, Wards: 6
Jim Larouche, Councillor, Wards: 6
Pat Chiocchio, Regional Councillor
Leanna Villella, Regional Councillor
Gary Long, Chief Administrative Officer
Steve Zorbas, Chief Financial Officer & General Manager, Corporate Services, 905-735-1700
Brian Kennedy, Fire Chief

Whitby
575 Rossland Rd. East
Whitby, ON L1N 2M8
Tel: 905-668-5803; *Fax:* 905-686-7005
info@whitby.ca
www.whitby.ca
Other Information: TTY: 905-430-1942
Municipal Type: City
Incorporated: 1855; *Area:* 146.66 sq km
County or District: Durham Reg. Mun.; *Population in 2016:* 128,377
Provincial Electoral District(s): Whitby
Federal Electoral District(s): Whitby
Next Election: Oct. 24, 2022 (4 year terms)
Don Mitchell, Mayor
Steve Lee, Councillor, Wards: 1. North
Deidre Newman, Councillor, Wards: 2. West
JoAnne Drumm, Councillor, Wards: 3. Centre
Maleeha Shahid, Councillor, Wards: 4. East
Chris Leahy, Regional Councillor
Rhonda Mulcahy, Regional Councillor
Elizabeth Roy, Regional Councillor
Steve Yamada, Regional Councillor

Matthew Gaskell, Chief Administrative Officer
Dave Speed, Fire Chief

Whitchurch-Stouffville
111 Sandiford Dr.
Stouffville, ON L4A 0Z8
Tel: 905-640-1900; *Fax:* 905-640-7957
www.townofws.com
Other Information: Toll-Free Phone: 855-642-8696
Municipal Type: City
Incorporated: 1877; *Area:* 206.22 sq km
County or District: York Reg. Mun.; *Population in 2016:* 45,837
Provincial Electoral District(s): Markham-Stouffville
Federal Electoral District(s): Markham-Stouffville
Next Election: Oct. 24, 2022 (4 year terms)
Note: Incorporated as a town in 1971, with the amalgamation of Whitchurch Township & the Village of Stouffville.
Iain Lovatt, Mayor
Ken Ferdinands, Councillor, 905-640-1910, Wards: 1
Maurice Smith, Councillor, 905-640-1910, Wards: 2
Hugo T. Kroon, Councillor, 905-640-1910, Wards: 3
Rick Upton, Councillor, 905-640-1910, Wards: 4
Richard Bartley, Councillor, Wards: 5
Sue Sherban, Councillor, Wards: 6
Rob Adams, Chief Administrative Officer
Brian Kavanagh, Director, Public Works, 905-640-1910
Haiqing Xu, Director, Development Services, 905-640-1910
Marilou Murray, Director, Leisure & Community Services, 905-640-1910
William Snowball, Fire Chief, 905-640-9595

Windsor
City Hall
350 City Hall Sq. West
Windsor, ON N9A 6S1
Tel: 519-255-2489; *Fax:* 519-256-3311
311@city.windsor.on.ca
www.citywindsor.ca
Other Information: Toll-Free Phone: 877-746-4311
Municipal Type: City
Incorporated: 1854; *Area:* 146.38 sq km
County or District: Essex; *Population in 2016:* 217,188
Provincial Electoral District(s): Windsor-Tecumseh; Windsor West
Federal Electoral District(s): Windsor-Tecumseh; Windsor-West
Next Election: Oct. 24, 2022 (4 year terms)
Note: Incorporated as a town in 1858 & as a city in 1892.
Drew Dilkens, Mayor
Fred Francis, Councillor, Wards: 1
Fabio Costante, Councillor, Wards: 2
Rino Bortolin, Councillor, Wards: 3
Chris Holt, Councillor, Wards: 4
Ed Sleiman, Councillor, Wards: 5
Jo-Anne Gignac, Councillor, Wards: 6
Vacant , Councillor, Wards: 7
Gary Kaschak, Councillor, Wards: 8
Kieran McKenzie, Councillor, Wards: 9
Jim Morrison, Councillor, Wards: 10
Onorio Colucci, Chief Administrative Officer, 519-255-6349, Fax: 519-255-1861
Shelby Askin Hager, City Solicitor
Thom Hunt, MCIP, RPP, City Planner
Mark Winterton, P. Eng., City Engineer & Corporate Leader, Environmental Protection & Infrastructure Services
Stephen Laforet, Fire Chief

Woodstock
City Hall
P.O. Box 1539
500 Dundas St.
Woodstock, ON N4S 7W5
Tel: 519-539-1291; *Fax:* 519-539-3275
info@cityofwoodstock.ca
www.cityofwoodstock.ca
Other Information: TTY: 519-539-7268
Municipal Type: City
Incorporated: Jan. 1, 1851; *Area:* 48.97 sq km
County or District: Oxford; *Population in 2016:* 40,902
Provincial Electoral District(s): Oxford
Federal Electoral District(s): Oxford
Next Election: Oct. 24, 2022 (4 year terms)
Note: Incorporated as a city on July 1, 1901.
Trevor T. Birtch, Mayor, 519-539-2382
Deb A. Tait, City & County Councillor, 519-421-7449
Sandra J. Talbot, City & County Councillor, 519-788-0639
Jerry Acchione, City Councillor, 519-532-2381
Ron Fraser, City Councillor
Connie Lauder, City Councillor, 519-532-2590
Mark Schadenberg, City Councillor
David Creery, Chief Administrative Officer
Len Magyar, Commissioner, Development
Harold deHaan, City Engineer

Jeff Slager, Fire Chief

Other Municipalities in Ontario

Addington Highlands
P.O. Box 89
72 Flinton St.
Flinton, ON K0H 1P0
Tel: 613-336-2286; *Fax:* 613-336-2847
Other Information: Toll-Free Phone: 844-666-2286
Municipal Type: Township
Area: 1,328.32 sq km
County or District: Lennox & Addington; *Population in 2016:* 2,323
Provincial Electoral District(s): Hastings-Lennox and Addington
Federal Electoral District(s): Hastings-Lennox and Addington
Next Election: Oct. 24, 2022 (4 year terms)
Henry Hogg, Reeve
Christine Reed, Chief Administrative Officer & Clerk-Treasurer

Adelaide Metcalfe
2340 Egremont Dr., RR#5
Strathroy, ON N7G 3H6
Tel: 519-247-3687; *Fax:* 519-247-3411
info@adelaidemetcalfe.on.ca
www.adelaidemetcalfe.on.ca
Other Information: Toll-Free Phone: 866-525-8878
Municipal Type: Township
Incorporated: Jan. 1, 2001; *Area:* 331.46 sq km
County or District: Middlesex; *Population in 2016:* 2,990
Provincial Electoral District(s): Lambton-Kent-Middlesex
Federal Electoral District(s): Lambton-Kent-Middlesex
Next Election: Oct. 24, 2022 (4 year terms)
Note: Amalgamation of the former Township of Adelaide & the Township of Metcalfe.
Kurtis Smith, Mayor
Cathy Case, Chief Administrative Officer & Treasurer

Adjala-Tosorontio
7855 Sideroad 30, RR#1
Alliston, ON L9R 1V1
Tel: 705-434-5055; *Fax:* 705-434-5051
www.adjtos.ca
Municipal Type: Township
Incorporated: Jan. 1, 1994; *Area:* 372.34 sq km
County or District: Simcoe; *Population in 2016:* 10,975
Provincial Electoral District(s): Simcoe-Grey
Federal Electoral District(s): Simcoe-Grey
Next Election: Oct. 24, 2022 (4 year terms)
Note: Amalgamation of the former Township of Adjala & the former Township of Tosorontio.
Floyd Pinto, Mayor
Bob Meadows, Deputy Mayor & Councillor
Annette Bays, Councillor, Wards: 1
Jonathan Pita, Councillor, Wards: 2
Ronald O'Leary, Councillor, Wards: 3
Deborah Hall-Chancey, Councillor, Wards: 4
Scott W. Anderson, Councillor, Wards: 5
John Krayetski, Fire Chief, 705-434-5055, Fax: 705-434-5051

Admaston / Bromley
477 Stone Rd., RR#2
Renfrew, ON K7V 3Z5
Tel: 613-432-2885; *Fax:* 613-432-4052
info@admastonbromley.com
www.admastonbromley.com
Municipal Type: Township
Incorporated: Jan. 1, 2000; *Area:* 524.06 sq km
County or District: Renfrew; *Population in 2016:* 2,935
Provincial Electoral District(s): Renfrew-Nipissing-Pembroke
Federal Electoral District(s): Renfrew-Nipissing-Pembroke
Next Election: Oct. 24, 2022 (4 year terms)
Note: Amalgamation of Admaston Township & Bromley Township.
Michael Donohue, Mayor
Annette Gilchrist, Clerk-Treasurer

Alberton
#B2, RR#1
Fort Frances, ON P9A 3M2
Tel: 807-274-6053; *Fax:* 807-274-8449
alberton@jam21.net
www.alberton.ca
Municipal Type: Township
Area: 116.66 sq km
County or District: Rainy River District; *Population in 2016:* 969
Provincial Electoral District(s): Kenora-Rainy River
Federal Electoral District(s): Thunder Bay-Rainy River
Next Election: Oct. 24, 2022 (4 year terms)
Mike Ford, Reeve

Dawn Hayes, Chief Administrative Officer & Clerk-Treasurer

Alfred & Plantagenet
P.O. Box 350
205 Old Hwy. 17
Plantagenet, ON K0B 1L0
Tel: 613-673-4797; *Fax:* 613-673-4812
info@alfred-plantagenet.com
www.alfred-plantagenet.com
Municipal Type: Township
Incorporated: Jan. 1, 1997; *Area:* 392.31 sq km
County or District: Prescott & Russell; *Population in 2016:* 9,680
Provincial Electoral District(s): Glengarry-Prescott-Russell
Federal Electoral District(s): Glengarry-Prescott-Russell
Next Election: Oct. 24, 2022 (4 year terms)
Note: Amalgamation of the Township of Alfred, the Village of Alfred, the Township of North Plantagenet & the Village of Plantagenet.
Stéphane Sarrazin, Mayor
Marc Daigneault, Chief Administrative Officer & Clerk, 613-673-4797

Algoma
c/o Algoma District Svs. Administration Bd.
1 Collver Rd., RR#1
Thessalon, ON P0R 1L0
Tel: 705-842-3370; *Fax:* 705-842-3747
info@adsab.on.ca
www.adsab.on.ca
Municipal Type: District
Area: 48,814.88 sq km
Population in 2016: 114,094
Provincial Electoral District(s): Algoma-Manitoulin
Federal Electoral District(s): Algoma-Manitoulin-Kapuskasing
Keith Bell, Chief Administrative Officer, 705-842-3370

Algonquin Highlands
1123 North Shore Rd., RR#2
Algonquin Highlands, ON K0M 1J1
Tel: 705-489-2379; *Fax:* 705-489-3491
info@algonquinhighlands.ca
www.algonquinhighlands.ca
Other Information: Phone, Dorset Satellite Office: 705-766-2211
Municipal Type: Township
Area: 1,007.20 sq km
County or District: Haliburton; *Population in 2016:* 2,351
Provincial Electoral District(s): Haliburton-Kawartha Lakes-Brock
Federal Electoral District(s): Haliburton-Kawartha Lakes-Brock
Next Election: Oct. 24, 2022 (4 year terms)
Carol Moffatt, Mayor
Angela Bird, Chief Administrative Officer & Deputy Clerk

Alnwick-Haldimand
P.O. Box 70
10836 County Rd. No. 2
Grafton, ON K0K 2G0
Tel: 905-349-2822; *Fax:* 905-349-3259
alnhald@alnwickhaldimand.ca
www.alnwickhaldimand.ca
Other Information: Phone, Roseneath Satellite Office: 905-352-3949
Municipal Type: Township
Area: 398.45 sq km
County or District: Northumberland; *Population in 2016:* 6,869
Provincial Electoral District(s): Northumberland-Peterborough South
Federal Electoral District(s): Northumberland-Peterborough South
Next Election: Oct. 24, 2022 (4 year terms)
John Logel, Mayor
Robin van de Moosdyk, Chief Administrative Officer, 905-349-2822

Amaranth
374028 - 6th Line
Amaranth, ON L9W 2Z3
Tel: 519-941-1007; *Fax:* 519-941-1802
township@amaranth-eastgary.ca
www.amaranth-eastgary.ca
Municipal Type: Township
Incorporated: Jan. 2, 1854; *Area:* 264.58 sq km
County or District: Dufferin; *Population in 2016:* 4,079
Provincial Electoral District(s): Dufferin-Caledon
Federal Electoral District(s): Dufferin-Caledon
Next Election: Oct. 24, 2022 (4 year terms)
Bob Currie, Mayor
Susan M. Stone, A.M.C.T., Chief Administrative Officer & Clerk-Treasurer, 519-941-1007

Amherstburg
271 Sandwich St. South
Amherstburg, ON N9V 2A5
Tel: 519-736-0012; *Fax:* 519-736-5403
www.amherstburg.ca
Other Information: TTY: 519-736-9860
Municipal Type: Town
Incorporated: 1851; *Area:* 185.61 sq km
County or District: Essex; *Population in 2016:* 21,936
Provincial Electoral District(s): Essex
Federal Electoral District(s): Essex
Next Election: Oct. 24, 2022 (4 year terms)
Note: Incorporated as a town in 1878.
Aldo DiCarlo, Mayor
Leo Meloche, Deputy Mayor
Peter Courtney, Councillor
Donald McArthur, Councillor
Michael Prue, Councillor
Marc Renaud, Councillor
Patricia Simone, Councillor
Giovanni (John) Miceli, Chief Administrative Officer, 519-736-0012
Antonietta Giofu, Director, Engineering & Public Works, 519-736-3664
Cheryl Horrobin, Director, Corporate Services
Dan Beaulieu, Manager, Environmental Services, 519-736-3664
Todd Hewitt, Manager, Engineering & Operations, 519-736-3664
Bruce Montone, Fire Chief, 519-736-0091

The Archipelago
9 James St.
Parry Sound, ON P2A 1T4
Tel: 705-746-4243; *Fax:* 705-746-7301
info@thearchipelago.on.ca
www.thearchipelago.on.ca
Municipal Type: Township
Incorporated: April 1, 1980; *Area:* 606.14 sq km
County or District: Parry Sound District; *Population in 2016:* 531
Provincial Electoral District(s): Parry Sound-Muskoka
Federal Electoral District(s): Parry Sound-Muskoka
Next Election: Oct. 24, 2022 (4 year terms)
Note: Amalgamation of the Township of Georgian Bay South Archipelago & the Township of Georgian Bay North Archipelago.
Bert Liverance, Reeve
John Fior, Chief Administrative Officer, 705-746-4243

Armour
Municipal Office
P.O. Box 533
56 Ontario St.
Burk's Falls, ON P0A 1C0
Tel: 705-382-3332; *Fax:* 705-382-2068
info@armourtownship.ca
www.armourtownship.ca
Other Information: Alternative Phone: 705-382-2954
Municipal Type: Township
Area: 164.64 sq km
County or District: Parry Sound District; *Population in 2016:* 1,414
Provincial Electoral District(s): Parry Sound-Muskoka
Federal Electoral District(s): Parry Sound-Muskoka
Next Election: Oct. 24, 2022 (4 year terms)
Bob MacPhail, Reeve, 705-636-7678
Wendy Whitwell, Clerk-Administrator

Armstrong
P.O. Box 546
35-10th St.
Earlton, ON P0J 1E0
Tel: 705-563-2375; *Fax:* 705-563-2093
www.armstrongtownship.com
Municipal Type: Township
Area: 90.20 sq km
County or District: Timiskaming District; *Population in 2016:* 1,166
Provincial Electoral District(s): Timiskaming-Cochrane
Federal Electoral District(s): Timmins-James Bay
Next Election: Oct. 24, 2022 (4 year terms)
Jean Marc Boileau, Mayor
Reynald Rivard, Clerk-Treasurer, 705-563-2375

Arnprior
P.O. Box 130
105 Elgin St. West
Arnprior, ON K7S 0A8
Tel: 613-623-4231; *Fax:* 613-623-8091
arnprior@arnprior.ca
www.arnprior.ca
Municipal Type: Town
Area: 13.07 sq km
County or District: Renfrew; *Population in 2016:* 8,795
Provincial Electoral District(s): Renfrew-Nipissing-Pembroke

Federal Electoral District(s): Renfrew-Nipissing-Pembroke
Next Election: Oct. 24, 2022 (4 year terms)
Walter Stack, Mayor
Michael Wildman, Chief Administrative Officer, 613-623-4231

Arran-Elderslie
P.O. Box 70
1925 Bruce Rd. 10
Chesley, ON N0G 1L0
Tel: 519-363-3039; Fax: 519-363-2203
info@arran-elderslie.ca
www.arran-elderslie.com
Municipal Type: Municipality
Area: 460.07 sq km
County or District: Bruce; Population in 2016: 6,803
Provincial Electoral District(s): Bruce-Grey-Owen Sound
Federal Electoral District(s): Bruce-Grey-Owen Sound
Next Election: Oct. 24, 2022 (4 year terms)
Steve Hammell, Mayor
Peggy Rouse, Clerk, 519-363-3039

Ashfield-Colborne-Wawanosh
82133 Council Line, RR#5
Goderich, ON N7A 3Y2
Tel: 519-524-4669; Fax: 519-524-1951
www.acwtownship.ca
Municipal Type: Township
Area: 586.97 sq km
County or District: Huron; Population in 2016: 5,422
Provincial Electoral District(s): Huron-Bruce
Federal Electoral District(s): Huron-Bruce
Next Election: Oct. 24, 2022 (4 year terms)
Glen McNeil, Reeve
Mark Becker, Administrator & Clerk Treasurer, 519-524-4669

Asphodel-Norwood
P.O. Box 29
2357 County Rd. 45
Norwood, ON K0L 2V0
Tel: 705-639-5343; Fax: 705-639-1880
www.asphodelnorwood.com
Municipal Type: Township
Incorporated: 1998; Area: 161.02 sq km
County or District: Peterborough; Population in 2016: 4,109
Provincial Electoral District(s): Northumberland-Peterborough
South
Federal Electoral District(s): Northumberland-Peterborough
South
Next Election: Oct. 24, 2022 (4 year terms)
Note: Amalgamation of the Village of Norwood & the Township of
Asphodel.
Rodger Bonneau, Mayor
Candice White, Chief Administrative Officer & Clerk-Treasurer

Assiginack
P.O. Box 238
156 Arthur St.
Manitowaning, ON P0P 1N0
Tel: 705-859-3196; Fax: 705-859-3010
info@assiginack.ca
www.assiginack.ca
Other Information: Toll-Free Phone: 800-540-0179
Municipal Type: Township
Area: 226.72 sq km
County or District: Manitoulin District; Population in 2016: 1,013
Provincial Electoral District(s): Algoma-Manitoulin
Federal Electoral District(s): Algoma-Manitoulin-Kapuskasing
Next Election: Oct. 24, 2022 (4 year terms)
David Ham, Mayor
Alton Hobbs, Clerk-Treasurer

Athens
P.O. Box 189
1 Main St. West
Athens, ON K0E 1B0
Tel: 613-924-2044; Fax: 613-924-2091
athens@ripnet.com
www.athenstownship.ca
Municipal Type: Township
Incorporated: 2001; Area: 127.88 sq km
County or District: Leeds & Grenville; Population in 2016: 3,013
Provincial Electoral District(s): Leeds-Grenville-Thousand
Islands and Rideau Lakes
Federal Electoral District(s): Leeds-Grenville-Thousand Islands
and Rideau Lakes
Next Election: Oct. 24, 2022 (4 year terms)
Herb Scott, Mayor
Darlene Noonan, Chief Administrative Officer & Clerk-Treasurer,
613-924-2044, Fax: 613-924-2091

Atikokan
P.O. Box 1330
120 Marks St.
Atikokan, ON P0T 1C0
Tel: 807-597-1234; Fax: 807-597-6186
info@atikokan.ca
www.atikokan.ca
Municipal Type: Town
Area: 319.52 sq km
County or District: Rainy River District; Population in 2016: 2,753
Provincial Electoral District(s): Thunder Bay-Atikokan
Federal Electoral District(s): Thunder Bay-Rainy River
Next Election: Oct. 24, 2022 (4 year terms)
Dennis Brown, Mayor, 807-597-2540
Angela Sharbot, Chief Administrative Officer, 801-597-1234

Augusta
3560 County Rd. 26, RR#2
Prescott, ON K0E 1T0
Tel: 613-925-4231; Fax: 613-925-3499
www.augusta.ca
Municipal Type: Township
Area: 314.66 sq km
County or District: Leeds & Grenville; Population in 2016: 7,353
Provincial Electoral District(s): Leeds-Grenville-Thousand
Islands and Rideau Lakes
Federal Electoral District(s): Leeds-Grenville-Thousand Islands
and Rideau Lakes
Next Election: Oct. 24, 2022 (4 year terms)
Doug Malanka, Mayor
Ray Morrison, Chief Administrative Officer & Treasurer,
613-825-4231

Aurora
P.O. Box 1000
100 John Way West
Aurora, ON L4G 6J1
Tel: 905-727-1375; Fax: 905-726-4732
info@aurora.ca
www.aurora.ca
Other Information: Alt. Phone: 905-727-3123; TTY:
905-726-4766
Municipal Type: Town
Area: 49.85 sq km
County or District: York Regional Municipality; Population in
2016: 55,445
Provincial Electoral District(s): Aurora-Oak Ridges-Richmond
Hill; Newmarket-Aurora
Federal Electoral District(s): Newmarket-Aurora; Aurora-Oak
Ridges-Richond Hill
Next Election: Oct. 24, 2022 (4 year terms)
Tom Mrakas, Mayor
Wendy Gaertner, Councillor
John Gallo, Councillor
Rachel Gilliland, Councillor
Sandra Humfryes, Councillor
Harold Kim, Councillor
Michael Thompson, Councillor
Doug Nadorozny, Chief Administrative Officer
Allan Downey, Director, Parks & Recreation, 905-727-3123
David Waters, Director, Planning & Development Services,
905-727-1375, Fax: 905-726-4736
Ryan Schell, Fire Chief, Central York Fire Services

Aylmer
46 Talbot St. West
Aylmer, ON N5H 1J7
Tel: 519-773-3164; Fax: 519-765-1446
www.aylmer.ca
Municipal Type: Town
Area: 6.26 sq km
County or District: Elgin; Population in 2016: 7,492
Provincial Electoral District(s): Elgin-Middlesex-London
Federal Electoral District(s): Elgin-Middlesex-London
Next Election: Oct. 24, 2022 (4 year terms)
Mary French, Mayor
Jennifer Reynaert, Chief Administrative Officer

Baldwin
P.O. Box 7095
11 Spooner St.
McKerrow, ON P0P 1M0
Tel: 705-869-0225; Fax: 705-869-5049
baldwin.ca
Municipal Type: Township
Area: 83.20 sq km
County or District: Sudbury District; Population in 2016: 620
Provincial Electoral District(s): Algoma-Manitoulin
Federal Electoral District(s): Algoma-Manitoulin-Kapuskasing
Next Election: Oct. 24, 2022 (4 year terms)
Vern Gorham, Mayor
Karin Bates, Chief Administrative Officer & Clerk

Bancroft
P.O. Box 790
8 Hastings Heritage Way
Bancroft, ON K0L 1C0
Tel: 613-332-3331; Fax: 613-332-0384
info@bancroft.ca
www.bancroft.ca
Municipal Type: Town
Incorporated: 1904; Area: 229.51 sq km
County or District: Hastings; Population in 2016: 3,881
Provincial Electoral District(s): Hastings-Lennox and Addington
Federal Electoral District(s): Hastings-Lennnox and Addington
Next Election: Oct. 24, 2022 (4 year terms)
Paul Jenkins, Mayor, 613-332-1041
Hazel Lambe, Chief Administrative Officer & Clerk

Bayham
P.O. Box 160
56169 Heritage Line
Straffordville, ON N0J 1Y0
Tel: 519-866-5521; Fax: 519-866-3884
bayham@bayham.on.ca
www.bayham.on.ca
Municipal Type: Municipality
Area: 244.97 sq km
County or District: Elgin; Population in 2016: 7,396
Provincial Electoral District(s): Elgin-Middlesex-London
Federal Electoral District(s): Elgin-Middlesex-London
Next Election: Oct. 24, 2022 (4 year terms)
Ed Ketchabaw, Mayor
Paul Shipway, Chief Administrative Officer & Clerk

Beckwith
1702 - 9th Line Beckwith, RR#2
Carleton Place, ON K7C 3P2
Tel: 613-257-1539; Fax: 613-257-8996
twp.beckwith.on.ca
Other Information: Toll-Free Phone: 800-535-4532
Municipal Type: Township
Area: 240.47 sq km
County or District: Lanark; Population in 2016: 7,644
Provincial Electoral District(s): Lanark-Frontenac-Kingston
Federal Electoral District(s): Lanark-Frontenac-Kingston
Next Election: Oct. 24, 2022 (4 year terms)
Richard Kidd, Reeve, 613-257-5409
Ross Trimble, Acting Clerk Administrator

Billings
Municipal Office
P.O. Box 34
15 Old Mill Rd.
Kagawong, ON P0P 1J0
Tel: 705-282-2611; Fax: 705-282-3199
billingsadmin@billingstwp.ca
billingstwp.ca
Municipal Type: Township
Incorporated: 1884; Area: 209.64 sq km
County or District: Manitoulin District; Population in 2016: 603
Provincial Electoral District(s): Algoma-Manitoulin
Federal Electoral District(s): Algoma-Manitoulin-Kapuskasing
Next Election: Oct. 24, 2022 (4 year terms)
J. Ian Anderson, Mayor
Katherine McDonald, Chief Administrative Officer &
Clerk-Treasurer, 705-282-2611

Black River-Matheson
P.O. Box 601
429 Park Lane
Matheson, ON P0K 1N0
Tel: 705-273-2313
reception@blackriver-matheson.com
www.blackriver-matheson.com
Municipal Type: Township
Area: 1,163.45 sq km
County or District: Cochrane District; Population in 2016: 2,438
Provincial Electoral District(s): Timiskaming-Cochrane
Federal Electoral District(s): Timmins-James Bay
Next Election: Oct. 24, 2022 (4 year terms)
Gilles Laderoute, Mayor
Heather Smith, Clerk-Treasurer, 705-273-2313

Blandford-Blenheim
P.O. Box 100
47 Wilmot St. South
Drumbo, ON N0J 1G0
Tel: 519-463-5347; Fax: 519-463-5881
generalmail@blandfordblenheim.ca
www.blandfordblenheim.ca
Municipal Type: Township
Area: 382.33 sq km
County or District: Oxford; Population in 2016: 7,399
Provincial Electoral District(s): Oxford

Federal Electoral District(s): Oxford
Next Election: Oct. 24, 2022 (4 year terms)
Mark Peterson, Mayor
Rodger Mordue, Chief Administrative Officer & Clerk,
519-463-5347, Fax: 519-463-5881

Blind River
P.O. Box 640
11 Hudson St.
Blind River, ON P0R 1B0
Tel: 705-356-2251; *Fax:* 705-356-7343
info@blindriver.ca
www.blindriver.ca
Municipal Type: Town
Incorporated: 1906; *Area:* 525.65 sq km
County or District: Algoma District; *Population in 2016:* 3,472
Provincial Electoral District(s): Algoma-Manitoulin
Federal Electoral District(s): Algoma-Manitoulin-Kapuskasing
Next Election: Oct. 24, 2022 (4 year terms)
Sally Hagman, Mayor
Kathryn Scott, Clerk Administrator, 705-356-2251, Fax:
705-356-7343

The Blue Mountains
P.O. Box 310
32 Mill St.
Thornbury, ON N0H 2P0
Tel: 519-599-3131; *Fax:* 519-599-7723
info@town.thebluemountains.on.ca
www.thebluemountains.ca
Other Information: Toll-Free Phone: 888-258-6867
Municipal Type: Town
Incorporated: Jan. 1, 2001; *Area:* 287.24 sq km
County or District: Grey; *Population in 2016:* 7,025
Provincial Electoral District(s): Simcoe-Grey
Federal Electoral District(s): Simcoe-Grey
Next Election: Oct. 24, 2022 (4 year terms)
Note: Amalgamation of Collingwood & Thornbury.
Alar Soever, Mayor
Shawn Everitt, Interim Chief Administrative Officer,
519-599-3131

Bluewater
P.O. Box 250
14 Mill Ave.
Zurich, ON N0M 2T0
Tel: 519-236-4351; *Fax:* 519-236-4329
info@municipalityofbluewater.ca
www.municipalityofbluewater.ca
Other Information: Toll-Free Phone: 877-236-4351
Municipal Type: Municipality
Area: 417.00 sq km
County or District: Huron; *Population in 2016:* 7,136
Provincial Electoral District(s): Huron-Bruce
Federal Electoral District(s): Huron-Bruce
Next Election: Oct. 24, 2022 (4 year terms)
Paul Klopp, Mayor
Kyle Pratt, Chief Administrative Officer, 519-236-4351

Bonfield
365 Hwy. 531
Bonfield, ON P0H 1E0
Tel: 705-776-2641; *Fax:* 705-776-1154
webmaster@bonfieldtownship.org
bonfieldtownship.com
Municipal Type: Township
Incorporated: 1975; *Area:* 208.38 sq km
County or District: Nipissing District; *Population in 2016:* 1,975
Provincial Electoral District(s): Nipissing
Federal Electoral District(s): Nipissing-Timiskaming
Next Election: Oct. 24, 2022 (4 year terms)
Randall McLaren, Mayor
Peter M Johnston, Chief Administrative Officer & Clerk

Bonnechere Valley
P.O. Box 100
49 Bonnechere St. East
Eganville, ON K0J 1T0
Tel: 613-628-3101; *Fax:* 613-628-1336
admin@eganville.com
www.bonncherevalleytwp.com
Municipal Type: Township
Incorporated: Jan. 1, 2001; *Area:* 593.75 sq km
County or District: Renfrew; *Population in 2016:* 3,674
Provincial Electoral District(s): Renfrew-Nipissing-Pembroke
Federal Electoral District(s): Renfrew-Nipissing-Pembroke
Next Election: Oct. 24, 2022 (4 year terms)
Note: Amalgamation of Eganville Village, Grattan Township,
Sebastopol Township & Algona South Township.
Jennifer Murphy, Mayor, 613-433-0956
Bryan Martin, Chief Administrative Officer, 613-628-3101

Bracebridge
1000 Taylor Ct.
Bracebridge, ON P1L 1R6
Tel: 705-645-5264; *Fax:* 705-645-1262
www.bracebridge.ca
Other Information: Fax, Public Works: 705-645-7525
Municipal Type: Town
Area: 628.22 sq km
County or District: Muskoka Dist. Mun.; *Population in 2016:*
16,010
Provincial Electoral District(s): Parry Sound-Muskoka
Federal Electoral District(s): Parry Sound-Muskoka
Next Election: Oct. 24, 2022 (4 year terms)
Graydon Smith, Mayor, 705-644-3253
Chris Wilson, Councillor, 705-394-4027, Wards: Bracebridge
Archie Buie, Councillor, 705-645-9545, Wards: Draper
Andrew Struthers, Councillor, Wards: Macaulay
Mark Quemby, Councillor, 705-646-7676, Wards:
Monck/Muskoka
Barb McMurray, Councillor, 705-645-3706, Wards: Oakley
Steven Clement, District Councillor, 705-645-5325
Rick Maloney, District Councillor
Don Smith, District Councillor, 705-644-3525
John Sisson, Chief Administrative Officer, 705-645-6319, Fax:
705-645-1262
Cheryl Kelley, Director, Planning & Development, 705-645-6319
Stephen Rettie, Director, Finance, 519-645-5264
Geoff Carleton, Director, Public Works, 705-645-6319
Murray Medley, Fire Chief, 705-465-8258

Brethour
P.O. Box 537
51476 Brethour Rd.
Belle Vallee, ON P0J 1A0
Tel: 705-647-1712; *Fax:* 705-647-6851
brethour@parolink.net
Municipal Type: Township
Area: 82.08 sq km
County or District: Timiskaming District; *Population in 2016:* 97
Provincial Electoral District(s): Timiskaming-Cochrane
Federal Electoral District(s): Timmins-James Bay
Next Election: Oct. 24, 2022 (4 year terms)
David White, Reeve
Cathy Beach, Clerk-Treasurer

Brighton
P.O. Box 189
35 Alice St.
Brighton, ON K0K 1H0
Tel: 613-475-0670; *Fax:* 613-475-3453
www.brighton.ca
Municipal Type: Municipality
Area: 222.71 sq km
County or District: Northumberland; *Population in 2016:* 11,844
Provincial Electoral District(s): Northumberland-Peterborough
South
Federal Electoral District(s): Northumberland-Peterborough
South
Next Election: Oct. 24, 2022 (4 year terms)
Brian Ostrander, Mayor
Laura Vink, Deputy Mayor
Ron Anderson, Councillor
Mark Bateman, Councillor
Doug Leblanc, Councillor
Emily Rowley, Councillor
Mary Tadman, Councillor
Bob Casselman, Chief Administrative Officer, 613-475-0670
Preston Parkinson, Director, Public Works & Infrastructure,
613-475-1162
Jim Millar, Director, Parks & Recreation, 613-475-0302
Linda Widdifield, Director, Finance & Administrative Services,
613-475-0670
Rick Caddick, Fire Chief, 613-475-1744, Fax: 613-475-1385

Brock
P.O. Box 10
1 Cameron St. East
Cannington, ON L0E 1E0
Tel: 705-432-2355; *Fax:* 705-432-3487
brock@townshipofbrock.ca
www.townshipofbrock.ca
Other Information: Toll-Free Phone: 866-223-7668
Municipal Type: Township
Incorporated: 1973; *Area:* 423.34 sq km
County or District: Durham Reg. Mun.; *Population in 2016:*
11,642
Provincial Electoral District(s): Haliburton-Kawartha Lakes-Brock
Federal Electoral District(s): Haliburton-Kawartha Lakes-Brock
Next Election: Oct. 24, 2022 (4 year terms)
Debbie Bath-Hadden, Mayor
Ted Smith, Regional Coucillor, 705-357-2427

Michael Jubb, Councillor, Wards: 1
Claire Doble, Councillor, Wards: 2
Walter Schummer, Councillor, Wards: 3
Cria Pettingill, Councillor, Wards: 4
Lynn Campbell, Councillor, 705-357-0013, Wards: 5
Ralph Walton, Chief Administrative Officer, 705-432-2355
Rick Harrison, Fire Chief

Brockton
P.O. Box 68
100 Scott St.
Walkerton, ON N0G 2V0
Tel: 519-881-2223; *Fax:* 519-881-2991
info@brockton.ca
www.brockton.ca
Other Information: Toll-Free Phone: 877-885-8084
Municipal Type: Municipality
Incorporated: Jan. 1, 1999; *Area:* 565.18 sq km
County or District: Bruce; *Population in 2016:* 9,461
Provincial Electoral District(s): Huron-Bruce
Federal Electoral District(s): Huron-Bruce
Next Election: Oct. 24, 2022 (4 year terms)
Note: Amalgamation of the Town of Walkerton, Township of
Brant, & the Township of Greenock.
Chris Peabody, Mayor
Sonya Watson, Chief Administrative Officer & Clerk,
519-881-2223

Brooke-Alvinston
P.O. Box 28
3236 River St.
Alvinston, ON N0N 1A0
Tel: 519-898-2173; *Fax:* 519-898-5653
info@brookealvinston.com
www.brookealvinston.com
Other Information: Toll-Free Phone, Enforcement Unit:
866-344-9119
Municipal Type: Municipality
Area: 311.31 sq km
County or District: Lambton; *Population in 2016:* 2,411
Provincial Electoral District(s): Lambton-Kent-Middlesex
Federal Electoral District(s): Lambton-Kent-Middlesex
Next Election: Oct. 24, 2022 (4 year terms)
David Ferguson, Mayor
Janet Denkers, Clerk-Administrator, 519-898-2173, Fax:
519-878-5653

Bruce Mines
P.O. Box 220
9126 Hwy. 17 East
Bruce Mines, ON P0R 1C0
Tel: 705-785-3493; *Fax:* 705-785-3170
brucemines@bellnet.ca
www.brucemines.ca
Municipal Type: Town
Incorporated: 1903; *Area:* 6.22 sq km
County or District: Algoma District; *Population in 2016:* 582
Provincial Electoral District(s): Algoma-Manitoulin
Federal Electoral District(s): Algoma-Manitoulin-Kapuskasing
Next Election: Oct. 24, 2022 (4 year terms)
Lory Patteri, Mayor
Donna Brunke, Town Clerk

Brudenell, Lyndoch & Raglan
P.O. Box 40
42 Burnt Bridge Rd.
Palmer Rapids, ON K0J 2E0
Tel: 613-758-2061; *Fax:* 613-758-2235
info@blrtownship.ca
www.blrtownship.ca
Municipal Type: Township
Incorporated: Jan. 1, 1999; *Area:* 706.24 sq km
County or District: Renfrew; *Population in 2016:* 1,503
Provincial Electoral District(s): Renfrew-Nipissing-Pembroke
Federal Electoral District(s): Renfrew-Nipissing-Pembroke
Next Election: Oct. 24, 2022 (4 year terms)
Sheldon Keller, Mayor, 613-758-2360
Michelle Mantifel, Clerk-Treasurer

Burk's Falls
P.O. Box 160
172 Ontario St.
Burk's Falls, ON P0A 1C0
Tel: 705-382-3138; *Fax:* 705-382-2273
www.burksfalls.net
Municipal Type: Village
Incorporated: 1890; *Area:* 3.07 sq km
County or District: Parry Sound District; *Population in 2016:* 981
Provincial Electoral District(s): Parry Sound-Muskoka
Federal Electoral District(s): Parry Sound-Muskoka
Next Election: Oct. 24, 2022 (4 year terms)
Cathy Still, Reeve

Nicky Kunkel, Clerk

Burpee & Mills
8 Bailey Line Rd.
Evansville, ON P0P 1E0
Tel: 705-282-0624; *Fax:* 705-282-0624
burpeemills@vianet.ca
www.burpeemills.com
Municipal Type: Township
Area: 218.49 sq km
County or District: Manitoulin District; *Population in 2016:* 343
Provincial Electoral District(s): Algoma-Manitoulin
Federal Electoral District(s): Algoma-Manitoulin-Kapuskasing
Next Election: Oct. 24, 2022 (4 year terms)
Ken Noland, Reeve
Bonnie J. Bailey, Clerk-Treasurer

Caledon
Town Hall
6311 Old Church Rd.
Caledon, ON L7C 1J6
Tel: 905-584-2272; *Fax:* 905-584-4325
info@caledon.ca
www.caledon.ca
Other Information: Toll-Free Phone: 888-225-3366
Municipal Type: Town
Incorporated: Jan. 1, 1974; *Area:* 688.16 sq km
County or District: Peel Regional Municipality; *Population in 2016:* 66,502
Provincial Electoral District(s): Dufferin-Caledon
Federal Electoral District(s): Dufferin-Caledon
Next Election: Oct. 24, 2022 (4 year terms)
Allan Thompson, Mayor, 905-584-2272
Ian Sinclair, Regional Councillor, Wards: 1
Johanna Downey, Regional Councillor, 416-434-4102, Wards: 2
Jennifer Innis, Regional Councillor, 416-697-8280, Wards: 3 & 4
Annette Groves, Regional Councillor, 416-434-3256, Wards: 5
Lynn Kiernan, Area Councillor, Wards: 1
Christina Early, Area Councillor, Wards: 2
Nick deBoer, Area Councillor, 416-357-3524, Wards: 3 & 4
Tony Rosa, Area Councillor, Wards: 5
Carey Herd, Chief Administrative Officer, 905-584-2272
Laura Hall, Acting General Manager, Corporate Services
Peggy Tollett, General Manager, Community Services
Fuwing Wong, General Manager, Finance & Infrastructure Services
Darryl Bailey, Fire Chief

Callander, Municipality of
P.O. Box 100
280 Main St. North
Callander, ON P0H 1H0
Tel: 705-752-1410; *Fax:* 705-752-3116
www.mycallander.ca
Municipal Type: Municipality
Area: 105.98 sq km
County or District: Parry Sound District; *Population in 2016:* 3,863
Provincial Electoral District(s): Nipissing
Federal Electoral District(s): Nipissing-Timiskaming
Next Election: Oct. 24, 2022 (4 year terms)
Note: Formerly North Himsworth Township.
Hector Lavigne, Mayor, 705-845-5010
Mike Purcell, Chief Administration Officer, 705-752-1410

Calvin
1355 Peddlers Dr., RR#2
Mattawa, ON P0H 1V0
Tel: 705-744-2700; *Fax:* 705-744-0309
administration@calvintownship.ca
www.calvintownship.ca
Municipal Type: Municipality
Area: 139.17 sq km
County or District: Nipissing District; *Population in 2016:* 516
Provincial Electoral District(s): Nipissing
Federal Electoral District(s): Nipissing-Timiskaming
Next Election: Oct. 24, 2022 (4 year terms)
Ian Pennell, Mayor
Lynda Kovacs, Clerk-Treasurer, 705-744-2700

Carleton Place
175 Bridge St.
Carleton Place, ON K7C 2V8
Tel: 613-257-6200; *Fax:* 613-257-8170
info@carletonplace.ca
www.carletonplace.ca
Municipal Type: Town
Area: 9.05 sq km
County or District: Lanark; *Population in 2016:* 10,644
Provincial Electoral District(s): Lanark-Frontenac-Kingston
Federal Electoral District(s): Lanark-Frontenac-Kingston
Next Election: Oct. 24, 2022 (4 year terms)

Douglas Black, Mayor
Diane Smithson, Chief Administrative Officer, 613-257-6255

Carling
2 West Carling Bay Rd., RR#1
Nobel, ON P0G 1G0
Tel: 705-342-5856; *Fax:* 705-342-9527
clerksoffice@carling.ca
www.carlingtownship.ca
Municipal Type: Township
Area: 248.85 sq km
County or District: Parry Sound District; *Population in 2016:* 1,125
Provincial Electoral District(s): Parry Sound-Muskoka
Federal Electoral District(s): Parry Sound-Muskoka
Next Election: Oct. 24, 2022 (4 year terms)
Mike Konoval, Mayor
Kevin McLlwain, Chief Administrative Officer & Clerk, 705-342-5856

Carlow / Mayo
General Delivery, 3987 Boulter Rd.
Boulter, ON K0L 1G0
Tel: 613-332-1760; *Fax:* 613-332-2175
clerk@carlowmayo.ca
www.carlowmayo.ca
Municipal Type: Township
Incorporated: Jan. 1, 2001; *Area:* 390.79 sq km
County or District: Hastings; *Population in 2016:* 864
Provincial Electoral District(s): Hastings-Lennox and Addington
Federal Electoral District(s): Hastings-Lennox and Addington
Next Election: Oct. 24, 2022 (4 year terms)
Note: Amalgamation of the former townships of Carlow & Mayo.
Bonnie Adams, Reeve
Arlene Cox, Clerk-Administrator

Casey
P.O. Box 460
6 Lachapelle St.
Belle Vallee, ON P0J 1A0
Tel: 705-647-7257; *Fax:* 705-647-6373
harlytwp@parolink.net
casey.ca
Other Information: Alternate Phone: 705-647-5439
Municipal Type: Township
Incorporated: 1909; *Area:* 80.86 sq km
County or District: Timiskaming District; *Population in 2016:* 368
Provincial Electoral District(s): Timiskaming-Cochrane
Federal Electoral District(s): Timmins-James Bay
Next Election: Oct. 24, 2022 (4 year terms)
Guy Labonté, Reeve
Michel Lachapelle, Clerk-Treasurer

Casselman
P.O. Box 710
751 St. Jean St.
Casselman, ON K0A 1M0
Tel: 613-764-3139; *Fax:* 613-764-5709
info@casselman.ca
www.casselman.ca
Municipal Type: Village
Area: 5.12 sq km
County or District: Prescott & Russell; *Population in 2016:* 3,548
Provincial Electoral District(s): Glengarry-Prescott-Russell
Federal Electoral District(s): Glengarry-Prescott-Russell
Next Election: Oct. 24, 2022 (4 year terms)
Daniel Lafleur, Mayor
Daniel Gatien, Chief Administrative Officer, 613-764-3139

Cavan Monaghan
988 County Rd. 10, RR#3
Millbrook, ON L0A 1G0
Tel: 705-932-2929; *Fax:* 705-932-3458
info@cavanmonaghan.net
www.cavanmonaghan.net
Other Information: Toll-Free Phone: 877-906-5556
Municipal Type: Township
Area: 306.33 sq km
County or District: Peterborough; *Population in 2016:* 8,829
Provincial Electoral District(s): Haliburton-Kawartha Lakes-Brock
Federal Electoral District(s): Haliburton-Kawartha Lakes-Brock
Next Election: Oct. 24, 2022 (4 year terms)
Note: Formerly The Corporation of the Township of Cavan-Millbrook-North Monaghan.
Scott McFadden, Mayor
Yvette Hurley, Chief Administrative Officer, 705-932-9326

Central Elgin
450 Sunset Dr.
St Thomas, ON N5R 5V1
Tel: 519-631-4860; *Fax:* 519-631-4036
www.centralelgin.org

Municipal Type: Municipality
Area: 280.33 sq km
County or District: Elgin; *Population in 2016:* 12,607
Provincial Electoral District(s): Elgin-Middlesex-London
Federal Electoral District(s): Elgin-Middlesex-London
Next Election: Oct. 24, 2022 (4 year terms)
Sally Martyn, Mayor
Tom Marks, Deputy Mayor
Colleen Row, Councillor, Wards: 1
Dennis Crevits, Councillor, Wards: 2
Karen Cook, Councillor, Wards: 3
Bill Fehr, Councillor, Wards: 4
Fiona Roberts, Councillor, Wards: 5
Donald Leitch, Chief Administrative Officer & Clerk
Karen Harris, Treasurer & Director, Finance
Chris McDonough, Fire Chief

Central Frontenac
P.O. Box 89
1084 Elizabeth S.
Sharbot Lake, ON K0H 2P0
Tel: 613-279-2935; *Fax:* 613-279-2422
township@centralfrontenac.com
www.centralfrontenac.com
Municipal Type: Township
Incorporated: Jan. 1, 1998; *Area:* 1,025.20 sq km
County or District: Frontenac; *Population in 2016:* 4,373
Provincial Electoral District(s): Lanark-Frontenac-Kingston
Federal Electoral District(s): Lanark-Frontenac-Kingston
Next Election: Oct. 24, 2022 (4 year terms)
Frances Smith, Mayor
Cathy MacMunn, Clerk Administrator, 613-279-2935

Central Huron
P.O. Box 400
23 Albert St.
Clinton, ON N0M 1L0
Tel: 519-482-3997; *Fax:* 519-482-9183
www.centralhuron.com
Municipal Type: Municipality
Incorporated: Jan. 1, 2001; *Area:* 449.58 sq km
County or District: Huron; *Population in 2016:* 7,576
Provincial Electoral District(s): Huron-Bruce
Federal Electoral District(s): Huron-Bruce
Next Election: Oct. 24, 2022 (4 year terms)
Note: Amalgamation of the Town of Clinton, the Township of Hullett, & the Township of Goderich.
Jim Ginn, Mayor, 519-524-2522, Fax: 519-524-2755
Steve Doherty, Chief Administrative Officer, 519-482-3997

Central Manitoulin
P.O. Box 187
6020 Hwy. 542
Mindemoya, ON P0P 1S0
Tel: 705-377-5726; *Fax:* 705-377-5585
centralm@amtelecom.net
www.centralmanitoulin.ca
Other Information: Economic Dev.: centralecdev@amtelecom.net
Municipal Type: Municipality
Area: 431.11 sq km
County or District: Manitoulin District; *Population in 2016:* 2,084
Provincial Electoral District(s): Algoma-Manitoulin
Federal Electoral District(s): Algoma-Manitoulin-Kapuskasing
Next Election: Oct. 24, 2022 (4 year terms)
Richard Stephens, Mayor
Ruth Frawley, Chief Administrative Officer & Clerk, 705-377-5726

Centre Hastings
P.O. Box 900
7 Furnace St.
Madoc, ON K0K 2K0
Tel: 613-473-4030; *Fax:* 613-473-5444
www.centrehastings.com
Municipal Type: Municipality
Area: 222.86 sq km
County or District: Hastings; *Population in 2016:* 4,774
Provincial Electoral District(s): Hastings-Lennox and Addington
Federal Electoral District(s): Hastings-Lennox and Addington
Next Election: Oct. 24, 2022 (4 year terms)
Tom Deline, Mayor
Christine Martin, Chief Administrative Officer & Treasurer, 613-849-5908

Centre Wellington
P.O. Box 10
1 MacDonald Sq.
Elora, ON N0B 1S0
Tel: 519-846-9691; *Fax:* 519-846-2190
www.centrewellington.ca

Municipal Type: Township
Area: 407.54 sq km
County or District: Wellington; *Population in 2016:* 28,191
Provincial Electoral District(s): Wellington-Halton Hills
Federal Electoral District(s): Wellington-Halton Hills
Next Election: Oct. 24, 2022 (4 year terms)
Kelly Linton, Mayor
Ian Macrae, Councillor, Wards: 1
Kirk McElwain, Councillor, Wards: 2
Bob Foster, Councillor, Wards: 3
Neil Dunsmore, Councillor, Wards: 4
Stephen Kitras, Councillor, Wards: 5
Steven VanLeeuwen, Councillor, Wards: 6
Andy Goldie, Chief Administrative Officer
Mark Bradey, Deputy Treasurer & Manager, Finance
Colin Baker, Managing Director, Infrastructure Services
Sandra Schulz, Manager, Human Resources

Chamberlain
467501 Chamberlain Rd. 5, RR#3
Englehart, ON P0J 1H0
Tel: 705-544-8088; *Fax:* 705-544-1118
www.chamberlaintownship.com
Municipal Type: Township
Incorporated: 1908; *Area:* 110.59 sq km
County or District: Timiskaming District; *Population in 2016:* 332
Provincial Electoral District(s): Timiskaming-Cochrane
Federal Electoral District(s): Timmins-James Bay
Next Election: Oct. 24, 2022 (4 year terms)
Kerry Stewart, Reeve
Calvin Rodgers, Clerk-Treasurer & CAO

Champlain
948 Pleasant Corner Rd. East
Vankleek Hill, ON K0B 1R0
Tel: 613-678-3003; *Fax:* 613-678-3363
info@champlain.ca
www.champlain.ca
Municipal Type: Township
Incorporated: Jan. 1, 1998; *Area:* 207.27 sq km
County or District: Prescott & Russell; *Population in 2016:* 8,706
Provincial Electoral District(s): Glengarry-Prescott-Russell
Federal Electoral District(s): Glengarry-Prescott-Russell
Next Election: Oct. 24, 2022 (4 year terms)
Note: Amalgamation of the Village of L'Orignal, the Township of West Hawkesbury, the Township of Longueuil & the Village of Vankleek Hill.
Normand Riopel, Mayor
Paula Knudsen, Chief Administrative Officer-Treasurer

Chapleau
Civic Centre
P.O. Box 129
20 Pine St. West
Chapleau, ON P0M 1K0
Tel: 705-864-1330; *Fax:* 705-864-1824
www.chapleau.ca
Municipal Type: Township
Area: 14.22 sq km
County or District: Sudbury District; *Population in 2016:* 1,964
Provincial Electoral District(s): Algoma-Manitoulin
Federal Electoral District(s): Algoma-Manitoulin-Kapuskasing
Next Election: Oct. 24, 2022 (4 year terms)
Michael J. Levesque, Mayor
Chelsea Swearengen, Chief Administrative Officer

Chapple
P.O. Box 4
Barwick, ON P0W 1A0
Tel: 807-487-2354; *Fax:* 807-487-2406
info@chapple.on.ca
www.chapple.on.ca
Other Information: chapple@tbaytel.net
Municipal Type: Township
Area: 527.94 sq km
County or District: Rainy River District; *Population in 2016:* 638
Provincial Electoral District(s): Kenora-Rainy River
Federal Electoral District(s): Thunder Bay-Rainy River
Next Election: Oct. 24, 2022 (4 year terms)
Rilla Race, Reeve
Peggy Johnson, Chief Administrative Officer & Clerk-Treasurer

Charlton & Dack
287237 Sprucegrove Rd. RR#2
Englehart, ON P0J 1H0
Tel: 705-544-7525; *Fax:* 705-544-2369
dack@ntl.sympatico.ca
www.charltonanddack.com
Municipal Type: Municipality
Incorporated: Jan. 1, 2003; *Area:* 92.72 sq km
County or District: Timiskaming District; *Population in 2016:* 686
Provincial Electoral District(s): Timiskaming-Cochrane

Federal Electoral District(s): Timmins-James Bay
Next Election: Oct. 24, 2022 (4 year terms)
Note: Amalgamation of the Town of Charlton & the Township of Dack.
Merrill Bond, Reeve
Dan Thibeault, Clerk-Treasurer & Chief Administrative Officer

Chatham-Kent
Civic Centre
P.O. Box 640
315 King St. West
Chatham, ON N7M 5K8
Tel: 519-360-1998; *Fax:* 519-436-3204
ckinfo@chatham-kent.ca
www.chatham-kent.ca
Other Information: Toll-Free Phone: 800-714-7497
Municipal Type: Municipality
Incorporated: Jan. 1, 1998; *Area:* 2,457.90 sq km
Population in 2016: 101,647
Provincial Electoral District(s): Chatham-Kent-Leamington; Lambton-Kent-Middlesex
Federal Electoral District(s): Chatham-Kent-Leamington; Lambton-Kent-Middlesex
Next Election: Oct. 24, 2022 (4 year terms)
Note: Formerly the County of Kent.
Darrin Canniff, Mayor
Mark Authier, Councillor, Wards: 1
Melissa Harrigan, Councillor, Wards: 1
Anthony Ceccacci, Councillor, Wards: 2
Mary Clare Latimer, Councillor, Wards: 2
Trevor Thompson, Councillor, Wards: 2
Steve Pinsonneault, Councillor, Wards: 3
John Wright, Councillor, Wards: 3
Joe Faas, Councillor, Wards: 4
Jamie McGrail, Councillor, Wards: 4
Aaron Hall, Councillor, Wards: 5
Carmen McGregor, Councillor, Wards: 5
Michael Bondy, Councillor, Wards: 6
Marjorie Crew, Councillor, Wards: 6
Amy Finn, Councillor, Wards: 6
Karen Kirkwood-Whyte, Councillor, Wards: 6
Brock McGregor, Councillor, Wards: 6
Douglas Sulman, Councillor, Wards: 6
Don Shropshire, Chief Administrative Officer
John Norton, Chief Legal Officer
Gord Quinton, Chief Financial Officer
Thomas Kelly, General Manager, Infrastructure & Engineering Services
Chris Case, Fire Chief

Chatsworth
316837, Hwy. 6, RR#1
Chatsworth, ON N0H 1G0
Tel: 519-794-3232; *Fax:* 519-794-4499
office@chatsworth.ca
www.chatsworth.ca
Municipal Type: Township
Incorporated: Jan. 1, 2001; *Area:* 596.19 sq km
County or District: Grey; *Population in 2016:* 6,630
Provincial Electoral District(s): Bruce-Grey-Owen Sound
Federal Electoral District(s): Bruce-Grey-Owen Sound
Next Election: Oct. 24, 2022 (4 year terms)
Note: Amalgamation of the Townships of Holland & Sullivan & the Village of Chatsworth.
Scott Mackey, Mayor
Patty Sinnamon, Chief Administrative Officer & Clerk, 519-794-3232

Chisholm
2847 Chiswick Line, RR#4
Powassan, ON P0H 1Z0
Tel: 705-724-3526; *Fax:* 705-724-5099
info@chisholm.ca
www.chisholm.ca
Municipal Type: Township
Incorporated: 1912; *Area:* 206.73 sq km
County or District: Nipissing District; *Population in 2016:* 1,291
Provincial Electoral District(s): Nipissing
Federal Electoral District(s): Nipissing-Timiskaming
Next Election: Oct. 24, 2022 (4 year terms)
Leo Jobin, Mayor
Alice Lauzon, Acting Clerk-Treasurer

Clarington
40 Temperance St.
Bowmanville, ON L1C 3A6
Tel: 905-623-3379; *Fax:* 905-623-6506
info@clarington.net
www.clarington.net
Other Information: Toll-Free Phone: 800-563-1195
Municipal Type: Municipality
Area: 611.40 sq km

County or District: Durham Reg. Mun.; *Population in 2016:* 92,013
Provincial Electoral District(s): Durham; Northumberland-Peterborough South
Federal Electoral District(s): Durham
Next Election: Oct. 24, 2022 (4 year terms)
Adrian Foster, Mayor
Joe Neal, Regional Councillor, Wards: 1 & 2
Granville Anderson, Regional Councillor, Wards: 3 & 4
Janice Jones, Councillor, Wards: 1
Ron Hooper, Councillor, Wards: 2
Corinna Traill, Councillor, Wards: 3
Margaret Zwart, Councillor, Wards: 4
Anne Greentree, Municipal Clerk
Andy Allison, Chief Administrative Officer
Trevor Pinn, Treasurer & Director, Finance
Stephen Blake, Acting Director, Operations
George Acorn, Acting Director, Community Services
Ron Albright, Director, Engineering & Building Services
Faye Langmaid, Acting Director, Planning Services
Gord Weir, Fire Chief

Clearview
P.O. Box 200
217 Gideon St.
Stayner, ON L0M 1S0
Tel: 705-428-6230; *Fax:* 705-428-0288
www.clearview.ca
Municipal Type: Township
Area: 557.10 sq km
County or District: Simcoe; *Population in 2016:* 14,151
Provincial Electoral District(s): Simcoe-Grey
Federal Electoral District(s): Simcoe-Grey
Next Election: Oct. 24, 2022 (4 year terms)
Doug Measures, Mayor
Barry Burton, Deputy Mayor & Councillor
Phyllis Dineen, Councillor, Wards: 1
Doug McKechnie, Councillor, Wards: 2
John Broderick, Councillor, Wards: 3
Robert Walker, Councillor, Wards: 4
Thom Paterson, Councillor, Wards: 5
Connie Leishman, Councillor, Wards: 6
John Lamers, Councillor, Wards: 7
Pamela Fettes, Clerk
Steve Sage, Chief Administrative Officer
Kelly McDonald, Treasurer & Director, Finance
Terry Vachon, General Manager, Culture & Recreation
Mara Burton, Director, Community Services
Mike Rawn, Director
Roree Payment, Director

Cobalt
P.O. Box 70
18 Silver St.
Cobalt, ON P0J 1C0
Tel: 705-679-8877; *Fax:* 705-679-5050
cobalt@cobalt.ca
www.cobalt.ca
Municipal Type: Town
Area: 2.08 sq km
County or District: Timiskaming District; *Population in 2016:* 1,128
Provincial Electoral District(s): Timiskaming-Cochrane
Federal Electoral District(s): Nipissing-Timiskaming
Next Election: Oct. 24, 2022 (4 year terms)
George Othmer, Mayor
Michelle Larose, Chief Administrative Officer

Cobourg
55 King St. West
Cobourg, ON K9A 2M2
Tel: 905-372-4301; *Fax:* 905-372-7421
webmaster@cobourg.ca
www.cobourg.ca
Other Information: Toll-Free Phone: 888-262-6874
Municipal Type: Town
Area: 22.36 sq km
County or District: Northumberland; *Population in 2016:* 19,440
Provincial Electoral District(s): Northumberland-Peterborough South
Federal Electoral District(s): Northumberland-Peterborough South
Next Election: Oct. 24, 2022 (4 year terms)
John Henderson, Mayor
Suzanne Séguin, Deputy Mayor & Councillor
Nicole Beatty, Councillor
Aaron Burchat, Councillor
Adam Bureau, Councillor
Emily Chorley, Councillor
Brian Darling, Councillor
Ian Davey, Interim Chief Administrative Officer, 905-372-4301
Mike Vilneff, Fire Chief

Cochrane
P.O. Box 490
171 - 4 Ave.
Cochrane, ON P0L 1C0
Tel: 705-272-4361; *Fax:* 705-272-6068
townhall@cochraneontario.com
www.cochraneontario.com
Municipal Type: Town
Incorporated: 1910; *Area:* 539.12 sq km
County or District: Cochrane District; *Population in 2016:* 5,321
Provincial Electoral District(s): Timiskaming-Cochrane
Federal Electoral District(s): Timmins-James Bay
Next Election: Oct. 24, 2022 (4 year terms)
Denis Clement, Mayor
Jean-Pierre Ouellette, Chief Administrative Officer & Clerk

Cochrane
c/o CDSSAB
500 Algonquin Blvd. East
Cochrane, ON P4N 1B7
Tel: 705-268-7722; *Fax:* 705-268-8302
www.cdssab.on.ca
Municipal Type: District
Area: 141,268.51 sq km
Population in 2016: 79,682
Brian Marks, Chief Administrative Officer, Cochrane District
Social Services Administration Board, 705-268-7722, Fax:
705-268-8290

Cockburn Island
P.O. Box 209
Spanish, ON P0P 2A0

Municipal Type: Township
Area: 171.04 sq km
County or District: Manitoulin District
Provincial Electoral District(s): Algoma-Manitoulin
Federal Electoral District(s): Algoma-Manitoulin-Kapuskasing
Next Election: Oct. 24, 2022 (4 year terms)
Brenda Jones, Reeve
Brent St. Denis, Clerk-Treasurer

Coleman
Municipal Complex
937907 Marsh Bay Rd.
Coleman, ON P0J 1C0
Tel: 705-679-8833; *Fax:* 705-679-8300
toc@ontera.net
www.colemantownship.ca
Municipal Type: Township
Incorporated: 1906; *Area:* 178.89 sq km
County or District: Timiskaming District; *Population in 2016:* 595
Provincial Electoral District(s): Timiskaming-Cochrane
Federal Electoral District(s): Nipissing-Timiskaming
Next Election: Oct. 24, 2022 (4 year terms)
Dan Cleroux, Mayor, 705-679-5678
Logan Belanger, Chief Administrative Officer

Collingwood
P.O. Box 157
97 Hurontario St.
Collingwood, ON L9Y 3Z5
Tel: 705-445-1030; *Fax:* 705-445-2448
townhall@collingwood.ca
www.collingwood.ca
Municipal Type: Town
Incorporated: 1858; *Area:* 33.78 sq km
County or District: Simcoe; *Population in 2016:* 21,793
Provincial Electoral District(s): Simcoe-Grey
Federal Electoral District(s): Simcoe-Grey
Next Election: Oct. 24, 2022 (4 year terms)
Brian Saunderson, Mayor
Keith Hull, Deputy Mayor & Councillor
Steve Berman, Councillor
Tina Comi, Councillor
Deb Doherty, Councillor
Yvonne Hamlin, Councillor
Kathy Jeffery, Councillor
Bob Madigan, Councillor
Mariane McLeod, Councillor
Sonya Skinner, Acting Chief Administrative Officer,
705-445-1030
Marjory Leonard, Treasurer, 705-445-1030
Greg Miller, Chief Building Official
Adam Farr, Director, Planning & Building Services
Daniel Cole, Manager, Public Works, 705-445-1351
Wendy Martin, Manager, Parks, 705-444-2500
Ross Parr, Fire Chief, 705-445-3920

Conmee
RR#1
Kakabeka Falls, ON P0T 1W0
Tel: 807-475-5229; *Fax:* 807-475-4793
info@conmee.com
www.conmee.com
Other Information: conmee@tbaytel.net
Municipal Type: Township
Area: 169.13 sq km
County or District: Thunder Bay District; *Population in 2016:* 819
Provincial Electoral District(s): Thunder Bay-Atikokan
Federal Electoral District(s): Thunder Bay-Rainy River
Next Election: Oct. 24, 2022 (4 year terms)
Kevin Holland, Mayor
Patricia Maxwell, Clerk

Cramahe
P.O. Box 357
1 Toronto St.
Colborne, ON K0K 1S0
Tel: 905-355-2821; *Fax:* 905-355-3430
www.visitcramahe.ca
Other Information: Toll-Free Phone: 877-272-4263
Municipal Type: Township
Area: 202.16 sq km
County or District: Northumberland; *Population in 2016:* 6,355
Provincial Electoral District(s): Northumberland-Peterborough
South
Federal Electoral District(s): Northumberland-Peterborough
South
Next Election: Oct. 24, 2022 (4 year terms)
Mandy Martin, Mayor
Craig Brooks, Chief Administrative Officer & Clerk,
905-355-2821

Dawn-Euphemia
4591 Lambton Line, RR#4
Dresden, ON N0P 1M0
Tel: 519-692-5148; *Fax:* 519-692-5511
admin@dawneuphemia.on.ca
www.dawneuphemia.ca
Municipal Type: Township
Area: 445.12 sq km
County or District: Lambton; *Population in 2016:* 1,967
Provincial Electoral District(s): Lambton-Kent-Middlesex
Federal Electoral District(s): Lambton-Kent-Middlesex
Next Election: Oct. 24, 2022 (4 year terms)
Alan Broad, Mayor
Donna Clermont, Administrator-Clerk

Dawson
P.O. Box 427
211 Fourth St.
Rainy River, ON P0W 1L0
Tel: 807-852-3529; *Fax:* 807-852-3529
dawsomtwp@tbaytel.net
dawsontownship.weebly.com
Municipal Type: Township
Area: 339.50 sq km
County or District: Rainy River District; *Population in 2016:* 468
Provincial Electoral District(s): Kenora-Rainy River
Federal Electoral District(s): Thunder Bay-Rainy River
Next Election: Oct. 24, 2022 (4 year terms)
Bill Langner, Mayor
Patrick W. Giles, Clerk-Treasurer

Deep River
P.O. Box 400
100 Deep River Rd.
Deep River, ON K0J 1P0
Tel: 613-584-2000; *Fax:* 613-584-3237
townmail@deepriver.ca
www.deepriver.ca
Municipal Type: Town
Area: 50.13 sq km
County or District: Renfrew; *Population in 2016:* 4,109
Provincial Electoral District(s): Renfrew-Nipissing-Pembroke
Federal Electoral District(s): Renfrew-Nipissing-Pembroke
Next Election: Oct. 24, 2022 (4 year terms)
Suzanne D'Eon, Mayor
Ric McGee, Chief Administrative Officer & Clerk, 613-584-2000

Deseronto
P.O. Box 310
331 Main St.
Deseronto, ON K0K 1X0
Tel: 613-396-2440; *Fax:* 613-396-3141
admin@deseronto.ca
www.deseronto.ca
Municipal Type: Town
Incorporated: 1889; *Area:* 2.51 sq km
County or District: Hastings; *Population in 2016:* 1,774

Provincial Electoral District(s): Hastings-Lennox and Addington
Federal Electoral District(s): Hastings-Lennox and Addington
Next Election: Oct. 24, 2022 (4 year terms)
Dan Johnston, Mayor
Ellen Hamel, Chief Administrative Officer/Clerk

Dorion
170 Dorion Loop Rd., RR#1
Dorion, ON P0T 1K0
Tel: 807-857-2289; *Fax:* 807-857-2203
office@doriontownship.ca
www.doriontownship.ca
Municipal Type: Township
Area: 212.11 sq km
County or District: Thunder Bay District; *Population in 2016:* 316
Provincial Electoral District(s): Thunder Bay-Superior North
Federal Electoral District(s): Thunder Bay-Superior North
Next Election: Oct. 24, 2022 (4 year terms)
Ed Chambers, Reeve
Mavis Harris, Clerk-Treasurer

Douro-Dummer
P.O. Box 92
894 South St.
Warsaw, ON K0L 3A0
Tel: 705-652-8392; *Fax:* 705-652-5044
info@dourodummer.on.ca
www.dourodummer.on.ca
Other Information: Toll-Free Phone: 800-899-8785
Municipal Type: Township
Area: 458.95 sq km
County or District: Peterborough; *Population in 2016:* 6,709
Provincial Electoral District(s): Peterborough-Kawartha
Federal Electoral District(s): Peterborough-Kawartha
Next Election: Oct. 24, 2022 (4 year terms)
J. Murray Jones, Mayor, 705-652-6325
David Clifford, Chief Administrative Officer, 705-652-8392

Drummond-North Elmsley
310 Port Elmsley Rd., RR#5
Perth, ON K7H 3L7
Tel: 613-267-6500; *Fax:* 613-267-2083
admin@dnetownship.ca
www.dnetownship.ca
Municipal Type: Township
Incorporated: 1998; *Area:* 366.13 sq km
County or District: Lanark; *Population in 2016:* 7,773
Provincial Electoral District(s): Lanark-Frontenac-Kingston
Federal Electoral District(s): Lanark-Frontenac-Kingston
Next Election: Oct. 24, 2022 (4 year terms)
Note: Amalgamation of the Townships of Drummond & North
Elmsley.
Steve Fournier, Reeve
Cindy Halcrow, Clerk-Administrator

Dubreuilville
P.O. Box 367
23 Pine St.
Dubreuilville, ON P0S 1B0
Tel: 705-884-2340; *Fax:* 705-884-2626
township@dubreuilville.ca
www.dubreuilville.ca
Municipal Type: Township
Incorporated: 1978; *Area:* 89.50 sq km
County or District: Algoma District; *Population in 2016:* 613
Provincial Electoral District(s): Algoma-Manitoulin
Federal Electoral District(s): Algoma-Manitoulin-Kapuskasing
Next Election: Oct. 24, 2022 (4 year terms)
Beverly Nantel, Mayor
Shelley Casey, Chief Administrative Officer & Clerk,
705-884-2340

Dutton-Dunwich
P.O. Box 329
199 Currie Rd.
Dutton, ON N0L 1J0
Tel: 519-762-2204; *Fax:* 519-762-2278
info@duttondunwich.on.ca
www.duttondunwich.on.ca
Municipal Type: Municipality
Area: 294.58 sq km
County or District: Elgin; *Population in 2016:* 3,866
Provincial Electoral District(s): Elgin-Middlesex-London
Federal Electoral District(s): Elgin-Middlesex-London
Next Election: Oct. 24, 2022 (4 year terms)
Bob Purcell, Mayor
Laurie Spence-Bannerman, Chief Administrative Officer

Dysart et al

P.O. Box 389
135 Maple Ave.
Haliburton, ON K0M 1S0
Tel: 705-457-1740; *Fax:* 705-457-1964
info@dysartetal.ca
www.dysartetal.ca
Municipal Type: Municipality
Incorporated: Jan. 7, 1867; *Area:* 1,485.98 sq km
County or District: Haliburton; *Population in 2016:* 6,280
Provincial Electoral District(s): Haliburton-Kawartha Lakes-Brock
Federal Electoral District(s): Haliburton-Kawartha Lakes-Brock
Next Election: Oct. 24, 2022 (4 year terms)
Andrea Roberts, Mayor
Tamara Wilbee, Chief Administrative Officer

Ear Falls

P.O. Box 309
2 Willow Cres.
Ear Falls, ON P0V 1T0
Tel: 807-222-3624; *Fax:* 807-222-2384
eftownship@ear-falls.com
www.ear-falls.com
Municipal Type: Township
Area: 330.96 sq km
County or District: Kenora District; *Population in 2016:* 995
Provincial Electoral District(s): Kiiwetinoong
Federal Electoral District(s): Kenora
Next Election: Oct. 24, 2022 (4 year terms)
Kevin Kahoot, Mayor
Kimberly Ballance, Clerk-Treasurer & Administrator,
807-222-3624

East Ferris

390 Hwy. 94
Corbeil, ON P0H 1K0
Tel: 705-752-2740
municipality@eastferris.ca
eastferris.ca
Municipal Type: Municipality
Area: 155.17 sq km
County or District: Nipissing District; *Population in 2016:* 4,750
Provincial Electoral District(s): Nipissing
Federal Electoral District(s): Nipissing-Timiskaming
Next Election: Oct. 24, 2022 (4 year terms)
Pauline Rochefort, Mayor
Jason Trottier, Treasurer & Interim Chief Administrative Officer,
705-752-2740

East Garafraxa

374028 6th Line, RR#3
Amaranth, ON L0N 1N0
Tel: 519-941-1007; *Fax:* 519-941-1802
www.eastgarafraxa.ca
Municipal Type: Township
Incorporated: Jan. 1, 1869; *Area:* 166.07 sq km
County or District: Dufferin; *Population in 2016:* 2,579
Provincial Electoral District(s): Dufferin-Caledon
Federal Electoral District(s): Dufferin-Caledon
Next Election: Oct. 24, 2022 (4 year terms)
Guy Gardhouse, Mayor
Susan M. Stone, AMCT, Chief Administrative Officer &
Clerk-Treasurer, 519-941-1007

East Gwillimbury

19000 Leslie St.
Sharon, ON L0G 1V0
Tel: 905-478-4282; *Fax:* 905-478-2808
customerservice@eastgwillimbury.ca
www.eastgwillimbury.ca
Municipal Type: Town
Incorporated: 1850; *Area:* 245.04 sq km
County or District: York Regional Municipality; *Population in 2016:* 23,991
Provincial Electoral District(s): Newmarket-Aurora; York-Simcoe
Federal Electoral District(s): Newmarket-Aurora; York-Simcoe
Next Election: Oct. 24, 2022 (4 year terms)
Virginia Hackson, Mayor, 905-478-4283
Loralea Carruthers, Councillor, Wards: 1
Terry E. Foster, Councillor, Wards: 1
Tara Roy-DiClemente, Councillor, Wards: 2
Joe Persechini, Councillor, Wards: 2
Scott Crone, Councillor, Wards: 3
Cathy Morton, Councillor, Wards: 3
Thomas R. Webster, Chief Administrative Officer
Aaron Karmazyn, General Manager, Community Parks,
Recreation & Culture
Mike Molinari, General Manager, Community Infrastructure &
Environmental Services
Marco Ramunno, General Manager, Development Services
Mark Valcic, General Manager, Corporate Services
Rob McKenzie, Fire Chief

East Hawkesbury

P.O. Box 340
5151 County Rd. 14
St Eugene, ON K0B 1P0
Tel: 613-674-2170; *Fax:* 613-674-2989
www.easthawkesbury.ca
Municipal Type: Township
Incorporated: Jan. 1, 1850; *Area:* 235.01 sq km
County or District: Prescott & Russell; *Population in 2016:* 3,296
Provincial Electoral District(s): Glengarry-Prescott-Russell
Federal Electoral District(s): Glengarry-Prescott-Russell
Next Election: Oct. 24, 2022 (4 year terms)
Robert Kirby, Mayor, 613-632-4841, Fax: 613-632-4841
Luc Lalonde, Chief Administrative Officer & Clerk-Treasurer

East Zorra-Tavistock

P.O. Box 100
90 Loveys St.
Hickson, ON N0J 1L0
Tel: 519-462-2697; *Fax:* 519-462-2961
ezt@ezt.ca
ezt.ca
Municipal Type: Township
Area: 242.30 sq km
County or District: Oxford; *Population in 2016:* 7,129
Provincial Electoral District(s): Oxford
Federal Electoral District(s): Oxford
Next Election: Oct. 24, 2022 (4 year terms)
Don McKay, Mayor, 519-532-2500
Ruth Coursey, Interim Chief Administrative Officer,
519-462-2697

Edwardsburgh / Cardinal

P.O. Box 129
18 Centre St.
Spencerville, ON K0E 1X0
Tel: 613-658-3055; *Fax:* 613-658-3445
www.twpec.ca
Other Information: Toll-Free Phone: 866-848-9099
Municipal Type: Township
Area: 311.25 sq km
County or District: Leeds & Grenville; *Population in 2016:* 7,093
Provincial Electoral District(s): Leeds-Grenville-Thousand
Islands and Rideau Lakes
Federal Electoral District(s): Leeds-Grenville-Thousand Islands
and Rideau Lakes
Next Election: Oct. 24, 2022 (4 year terms)
Patrick Sayeau, Mayor, 613-657-1087
Debra McKinstry, Chief Administrative Officer & Clerk,
613-658-3055

Elizabethtown-Kitley

6544 New Dublin Rd., RR#2
Addison, ON K0E 1A0
Tel: 613-345-7480; *Fax:* 613-345-7235
mail@ektwp.ca
www.elizabethtown-kitley.on.ca
Other Information: Toll-Free Phone: 800-492-3175
Municipal Type: Township
Area: 557.71 sq km
County or District: Leeds & Grenville; *Population in 2016:* 9,854
Provincial Electoral District(s): Leeds-Grenville-Thousand
Islands and Rideau Lakes
Federal Electoral District(s): Leeds-Grenville-Thousand Islands
and Rideau Lakes
Next Election: Oct. 24, 2022 (4 year terms)
Brant Burrow, Mayor
Earl Brayton, Councillor
Christine Eady, Councillor
Tom Linton, Councillor
Susan Prettejohn, Councillor
Eleanor Leacock Renaud, Councillor
Rob Smith, Councillor
Yvonne L. Robert, Administrator-Clerk, 613-345-7480
Jim Donovan, Fire Chief, 613-498-2460

Emo

P.O. Box 520
39 Roy St.
Emo, ON P0W 1E0
Tel: 807-482-2378; *Fax:* 807-482-2741
township@emo.ca
www.emo.ca
Municipal Type: Township
Incorporated: 1899; *Area:* 203.09 sq km
County or District: Rainy River District; *Population in 2016:* 1,333
Provincial Electoral District(s): Kenora-Rainy River
Federal Electoral District(s): Thunder Bay-Rainy River
Next Election: Oct. 24, 2022 (4 year terms)
Harold McQuaker, Mayor
Bridget Foster, Chief Administrative Officer & Clerk-Treasurer

Englehart

P.O. Box 399
61 Fifth Ave.
Englehart, ON P0J 1H0
Tel: 705-544-2244; *Fax:* 705-544-8737
englehrt@ntl.sympatico.ca
www.englehart.ca
Municipal Type: Town
Incorporated: 1908; *Area:* 3.02 sq km
County or District: Timiskaming District; *Population in 2016:* 1,479
Provincial Electoral District(s): Timiskaming-Cochrane
Federal Electoral District(s): Timmins-James Bay
Next Election: Oct. 24, 2022 (4 year terms)
Nina Wallace, Mayor
Shawn LaCarte, Clerk Administrator

Enniskillen

4465 Rokeby Line, RR#1
Petrolia, ON N0N 1R0
Tel: 519-882-2490; *Fax:* 519-882-3335
www.enniskillen.ca
Municipal Type: Township
Area: 338.16 sq km
County or District: Lambton; *Population in 2016:* 2,796
Provincial Electoral District(s): Sarnia-Lambton
Federal Electoral District(s): Sarnia-Lambton
Next Election: Oct. 24, 2022 (4 year terms)
Kevin Marriott, Mayor
Duncan McTavish, Administrator-Clerk

Espanola

#2, 100 Tudhope St.
Espanola, ON P5E 1S6
Tel: 705-869-1540; *Fax:* 705-869-0083
www.espanola.ca
Municipal Type: Town
Incorporated: March 1, 1958; *Area:* 82.37 sq km
County or District: Sudbury District; *Population in 2016:* 4,996
Provincial Electoral District(s): Algoma-Manitoulin
Federal Electoral District(s): Algoma-Manitoulin-Kapuskasing
Next Election: Oct. 24, 2022 (4 year terms)
Jill Beer, Mayor
Cynthia Townsend, Chief Administrative Officer & Treasurer,
705-869-1540

Essa

5786 County Rd. 21
Utopia, ON L0M 1T0
Tel: 705-424-9770; *Fax:* 705-424-2367
www.essatownship.on.ca
Other Information: TTY: 705-424-5302
Municipal Type: Township
Incorporated: 1850; *Area:* 280.03 sq km
County or District: Simcoe; *Population in 2016:* 21,083
Provincial Electoral District(s): Simcoe-Grey
Federal Electoral District(s): Barrie-Innisfil; Simcoe-Grey
Next Election: Oct. 24, 2022 (4 year terms)
Sandie Macdonald, Mayor
Michael Smith, Deputy Mayor & Councillor
Keith White, Councillor, Wards: 1
Henry Sander, Councillor, Wards: 2
Ron Henderson, Councillor, Wards: 3
Colleen Healey-Dowdall, Chief Administrative Officer
Jason Coleman, Manager, Parks & Recreation
Aimee Powell, Manager, Planning & Development
Carol Traynor, Manager, Finance
Cynthia Ross Tustin, Fire Chief

Essex

33 Talbot St. South
Essex, ON N8M 1A8
Tel: 519-776-7336; *Fax:* 519-776-8811
www.essex.ca
Municipal Type: Town
Incorporated: 1883; *Area:* 277.97 sq km
County or District: Essex; *Population in 2016:* 20,427
Provincial Electoral District(s): Essex
Federal Electoral District(s): Essex
Next Election: Oct. 24, 2022 (4 year terms)
Note: Incorporated as a town in 1890. Restructuring occurred in 1999.
Larry Snively, Mayor
Richard Meloche, Deputy Mayor
Morley Bowman, Councillor, Wards: 1
Joe Garon, Councillor, Wards: 1
Kim Verbeek, Councillor, Wards: 2
Steve Bjorkman, Councillor, Wards: 3
Chris Vander Doelen, Councillor, Wards: 3
Sherry Bondy, Councillor, Wards: 4
Chris Nepszy, Chief Administrative Officer
Kevin Girard, Director, Infastructure & Development

Rick Arnel, Fire Chief

Evanturel
P.O. Box 209
245453 Hwy. 569
Englehart, ON P0J 1H0
Tel: 705-544-8200; *Fax:* 705-544-8206
evanturelclerk@parolink.net
www.evanturel.com
Municipal Type: Township
Incorporated: Jan. 1, 1904; *Area:* 89.31 sq km
County or District: Timiskaming District; *Population in 2016:* 449
Provincial Electoral District(s): Timiskaming-Cochrane
Federal Electoral District(s): Timmins-James Bay
Next Election: Oct. 24, 2022 (4 year terms)
Derek Mundle, Reeve
Amy Vickery-Menard, Clerk-Treasurer

Faraday
P.O. Box 929
29860 Hwy. 28 South
Bancroft, ON K0L 1C0
Tel: 613-332-3638; *Fax:* 613-332-3006
office@faraday.ca
www.faraday.ca
Municipal Type: Township
Area: 219.62 sq km
County or District: Hastings; *Population in 2016:* 1,401
Provincial Electoral District(s): Hastings-Lennox and Addington
Federal Electoral District(s): Hastings-Lennox and Addington
Next Election: Oct. 24, 2022 (4 year terms)
Dennis Purcell, Reeve
Dawn Switzer, Clerk-Treasurer & Tax Collector

Fauquier-Strickland
P.O. Box 40
25 Grzela Rd.
Fauquier, ON P0L 1G0
Tel: 705-339-2521; *Fax:* 705-339-2421
info@fauquierstrickland.com
fauquierstrickland.com
Municipal Type: Township
Area: 1,013.25 sq km
County or District: Cochrane District; *Population in 2016:* 536
Provincial Electoral District(s): Mushkegowuk-James Bay
Federal Electoral District(s): Algoma-Manitoulin-Kapuskasing
Next Election: Oct. 24, 2022 (4 year terms)
Madeleine Tremblay, Mayor
Robert Courchesne, Administrator & Clerk-Treasurer

Fort Erie
1 Municipal Centre Dr.
Fort Erie, ON L2A 2S6
Tel: 905-871-1600; *Fax:* 905-871-4022
www.forterie.on.ca
Other Information: Fax, Corporate Services: 905-871-9984
Municipal Type: Town
Incorporated: 1857; *Area:* 166.27 sq km
County or District: Niagara Regional Municipality; *Population in 2016:* 30,710
Provincial Electoral District(s): Niagara Falls
Federal Electoral District(s): Niagara Falls
Next Election: Oct. 24, 2022 (4 year terms)
Wayne Redekop, Mayor
George McDermott, Councillor, Wards: 1
Nick Dubanow, Councillor, Wards: 2
Kimberly Zanko, Councillor, Wards: 3
Marina Butler, Councillor, Wards: 4
Don Lubberts, Councillor, Wards: 5
Ann-Marie Noyes, Councillor, Wards: 6
Tom Insinna, Regional Councillor
Tom Kuchyt, Chief Administrative Officer, 905-871-1600
Jonathan Janzen, Director, Corporate Services, 905-871-1600
George Stojanovic, Manager, Roads & Fleet, 905-871-1600
Ed Melanson, Fire Chief

Fort Frances
320 Portage Ave.
Fort Frances, ON P9A 3P9
Tel: 807-274-5323; *Fax:* 807-274-8479
town@fort-frances.com
www.fortfrances.com
Municipal Type: Town
Incorporated: 1903; *Area:* 25.51 sq km
County or District: Rainy River District; *Population in 2016:* 7,739
Provincial Electoral District(s): Kenora-Rainy River
Federal Electoral District(s): Thunder Bay-Rainy River
Next Election: Oct. 24, 2022 (4 year terms)
June Caul, Mayor
Doug Brown, Chief Administrative Officer, 807-274-5323

French River, Municipality of / Municipalité de la Rivière des Français
P.O. Box 156
#1, 44 St. Christophe St.
Noëlville, ON P0M 2N0
Tel: 705-898-2294; *Fax:* 705-898-2181
webmaster@frenchriver.ca
www.frenchriver.ca
Municipal Type: Municipality
Incorporated: Jan. 1, 1999; *Area:* 735.48 sq km
County or District: Sudbury District; *Population in 2016:* 2,662
Provincial Electoral District(s): Nickle Belt;
Timiskaming-Cochrane
Federal Electoral District(s): Nickel Belt
Next Election: Oct. 24, 2022 (4 year terms)
Gisele Pageau, Mayor
Marc Gagnon, Chief Administrative Officer, 705-898-2294

Front of Yonge
P.O. Box 130
1514 County Rd. 2
Mallorytown, ON K0E 1R0
Tel: 613-923-2251; *Fax:* 613-923-2421
admin@frontofyonge.com
www.mallorytown.ca
Other Information: Phone, Public Works: 613-923-5074
Municipal Type: Township
Area: 128.47 sq km
County or District: Leeds & Grenville; *Population in 2016:* 2,607
Provincial Electoral District(s): Leeds-Grenville-Thousand Islands and Rideau Lakes
Federal Electoral District(s): Leeds-Grenville-Thousand Islands and Rideau Lakes
Next Election: Oct. 24, 2022 (4 year terms)
Roger Haley, Mayor
Jennifer Ault, Clerk

Frontenac Islands
P.O. Box 130
1191 County Rd. 96
Wolfe Island, ON K0H 2Y0
Tel: 613-385-2216; *Fax:* 613-385-1032
frontenacislands.ca
Other Information: Phone, Howe Island Office: 613-544-6348
Municipal Type: Township
Incorporated: Jan. 1, 1998; *Area:* 175.04 sq km
County or District: Frontenac; *Population in 2016:* 1,760
Provincial Electoral District(s): Kingston & the Islands
Federal Electoral District(s): Kingston & the Islands
Next Election: Oct. 24, 2022 (4 year terms)
Note: Amalgamation of Howe Island & Wolfe Island.
Denis Doyle, Mayor, 613-385-2763
Darlene Plumley, AMCT, Chief Administrative Officer & Clerk

Gananoque
Town Hall
P.O. Box 100
30 King St. East
Gananoque, ON K7G 2T6
Tel: 613-382-2149; *Fax:* 613-382-8587
www.gananoque.ca
Municipal Type: Town
Area: 7.03 sq km
County or District: Leeds & Grenville; *Population in 2016:* 5,159
Provincial Electoral District(s): Leeds-Grenville-Thousand Islands and Rideau Lakes
Federal Electoral District(s): Leeds-Grenville-Thousand Islands and Rideau Lakes
Next Election: Oct. 24, 2022 (4 year terms)
Ted Lojko, Mayor
Shellee Fournier, Chief Administrative Officer & Human Resources, 613-382-2149

Gauthier
P.O. Box 65
92 McPherson St.
Dobie, ON P0K 1B0
Tel: 705-568-8951; *Fax:* 705-568-8951
Municipal Type: Township
Area: 88.41 sq km
County or District: Timiskaming District; *Population in 2016:* 138
Provincial Electoral District(s): Timiskaming-Cochrane
Federal Electoral District(s): Timmins-James Bay
Next Election: Oct. 24, 2022 (4 year terms)
Marie Savarie, Reeve
Dianne Quinn, Clerk-Treasurer

Georgian Bay
99 Lone Pine Rd.
Port Severn, ON L0K 1S0
Tel: 705-538-2337; *Fax:* 705-538-1850
www.gbtownship.com
Other Information: Toll-Free Phone: 800-567-0187
Municipal Type: Township
Area: 547.61 sq km
County or District: Muskoka District Municipality; *Population in 2016:* 2,499
Provincial Electoral District(s): Parry Sound-Muskoka
Federal Electoral District(s): Parry Sound-Muskoka
Next Election: Oct. 24, 2022 (4 year terms)
Peter Koetsier, Mayor
Laurie Kennard, Chief Administrative Officer, 705-538-2337

Georgian Bluffs
177964 Grey Rd. 18, RR#3
Owen Sound, ON N4K 5N5
Tel: 519-376-2729; *Fax:* 519-372-1620
office@georgianbluffs.on.ca
www.georgianbluffs.on.ca
Municipal Type: Township
Incorporated: Jan. 1, 2001; *Area:* 604.37 sq km
County or District: Grey; *Population in 2016:* 10,479
Provincial Electoral District(s): Bruce-Grey-Owen Sound
Federal Electoral District(s): Bruce-Grey-Owen Sound
Next Election: Oct. 24, 2022 (4 year terms)
Note: Amalgamation of the Townships of Derby, Keppel & Sarawak.
Dwight Burley, Mayor
Sue Carleton, Deputy Mayor & Councillor
Carol Barfoot, Councillor
Cathy Moore Coburn, Councillor
Grant Pringle, Councillor
Paul Sutherland, Councillor
Ryan Thompson, Councillor
Anne Marie Shaw, Interim Chief Administrative Officer
Tim Lewis, Chief Building Official, 519-376-2729
Tyler Jahnke, Director, Operations
Kassandra Rocca, Director, Finances

Georgina
Georgina Civic Centre
26557 Civic Centre Rd., RR#2
Keswick, ON L4P 3G1
Tel: 905-476-4301; *Fax:* 905-476-8100
info@georgina.ca
www.georgina.ca
Other Information: Alt. Phone: 705-437-2210
Municipal Type: Town
Area: 287.75 sq km
County or District: York Reg. Mun.; *Population in 2016:* 45,418
Provincial Electoral District(s): York-Simcoe
Federal Electoral District(s): York-Simcoe
Next Election: Oct. 24, 2022 (4 year terms)
Note: Amalgamation of the Village of Keswick, the Township of Georgina & Village of Sutton.
Margaret Quirk, Mayor
Robert Grossi, Regional Councillor
Mike Waddington, Councillor, Wards: 1
Dan Fellini, Councillor, Wards: 2
Dave Neeson, Councillor, Wards: 3
Frank Sebo, Councillor, Wards: 4
David A. Harding, Councillor, Wards: 5
David Reddon, Chief Administrative Officer, 905-476-4301
Rob Flindall, Director, Operations
Harold Lenters, Director, Development Services, 905-476-4301
Rob Wheater, Director, Corporate Services
Bev Moffat, Manager, Human Resources
Ron Jenkins, Fire Chief

Gillies
1092 Hwy. 595, RR#1
Kakabeka Falls, ON P0T 1W0
Tel: 807-475-3185; *Fax:* 807-473-0767
gillies@tbaytel.net
www.gilliestownship.com
Municipal Type: Township
Area: 93.05 sq km
County or District: Thunder Bay District; *Population in 2016:* 474
Provincial Electoral District(s): Thunder Bay-Atikokan
Federal Electoral District(s): Thunder Bay-Rainy River
Next Election: Oct. 24, 2022 (4 year terms)
Wendy Wright, Reeve
Jenna Hakala, Clerk

Goderich

Municipal Office, Town Hall
57 West St.
Goderich, ON N7A 2K5
Tel: 519-524-8344; *Fax:* 519-524-7209
townhall@goderich.ca
www.goderich.ca
Municipal Type: Town
Area: 8.64 sq km
County or District: Huron; *Population in 2016:* 7,628
Provincial Electoral District(s): Huron-Bruce
Federal Electoral District(s): Huron-Bruce
Next Election: Oct. 24, 2022 (4 year terms)
John Grace, Mayor
Larry J. McCabe, Chief Administrative Officer

Gordon / Barrie Island

P.O. Box 680
29 Noble Side Rd.
Gore Bay, ON P0P 1H0
Tel: 705-282-2702; *Fax:* 705-282-2722
adminoffice@gordonbarrieisland.ca
www.gordonbarrieisland.ca
Municipal Type: Municipality
Incorporated: Jan. 1, 2009; *Area:* 267.77 sq km
County or District: Manitoulin District; *Population in 2016:* 490
Provincial Electoral District(s): Algoma-Manitoulin
Federal Electoral District(s): Algoma-Manitoulin-Kapuskasing
Next Election: Oct. 24, 2022 (4 year terms)
Note: Amalgamation of the former Township of Gordon & Allan West & the Township of Barrie Island.
Lee Hayden, Reeve
Carrie Lewis, Chief Administrative Officer & Clerk-Treasurer

Gore Bay

P.O. Box 590
15 Water St.
Gore Bay, ON P0P 1H0
Tel: 705-282-2420; *Fax:* 705-282-3076
www.gorebay.ca
Municipal Type: Town
Incorporated: 1890; *Area:* 5.23 sq km
County or District: Manitoulin District; *Population in 2016:* 867
Provincial Electoral District(s): Algoma-Manitoulin
Federal Electoral District(s): Algoma-Manitoulin-Kapuskasing
Next Election: Oct. 24, 2022 (4 year terms)
Dan Osborne, Mayor
Annette Clarke, Chief Administrative Officer & Clerk, 705-282-2420

Grand Valley

5 Main St. North
Grand Valley, ON L9W 5S6
Tel: 519-928-5652; *Fax:* 519-928-2275
mail@townofgrandvalley.ca
www.townofgrandvalley.ca
Municipal Type: Town
Incorporated: Dec. 27, 1880; *Area:* 158.2 sq km
County or District: Dufferin; *Population in 2016:* 2,956
Provincial Electoral District(s): Dufferin-Caledon
Federal Electoral District(s): Dufferin-Caledon
Next Election: Oct. 24, 2022 (4 year terms)
Note: Amalgamation of the Township of East Luther & the Village of Grand Valley on Jan. 1, 1995.
Steve Soloman, Mayor
Jane M. Wilson, Chief Administrative Officer & Clerk-Treasurer, 519-928-5652

Gravenhurst

3 - 5 Pineridge Gate
Gravenhurst, ON P1P 1Z3
Tel: 705-687-3412; *Fax:* 705-687-7016
reception@gravenhurst.ca
www.gravenhurst.ca
Municipal Type: Town
Area: 518.06 sq km
County or District: Muskoka District Municipality; *Population in 2016:* 12,311
Provincial Electoral District(s): Parry Sound-Muskoka
Federal Electoral District(s): Parry Sound-Muskoka
Next Election: Oct. 24, 2022 (4 year terms)
Paul Kelly, Mayor
Sandy Cairns, District Councillor
John Gordon, District Councillor
Heidi Lorenz, District Councillor
Penny Varney, Councillor, Wards: 1
Jo Morphy, Councillor, Wards: 2
Steven Klinck, Councillor, Wards: 3
Terry Pilger, Councillor, Wards: 4
Graeme Murray, Councillor, Wards: 5
Glen Davies, Chief Administrative Officer, 705-687-6774
Scott Lucas, Director, Community Growth & Development

Val Sequeira, Director, Corporate Services
Andrew Stacey, Director, Infrastructure Services
Larry Brassard, Fire Chief

Greater Madawaska

P.O. Box 180
19 Parnell St.
Calabogie, ON K0J 1H0
Tel: 613-752-2222; *Fax:* 613-752-2617
admin@greatermadawaska.com
www.greatermadawaska.com
Other Information: Toll-Free Phone: 800-347-7224
Municipal Type: Township
Incorporated: Jan. 1, 2001; *Area:* 1,035.59 sq km
County or District: Renfrew; *Population in 2016:* 2,518
Provincial Electoral District(s): Renfrew-Nipissing-Pembroke
Federal Electoral District(s): Renfrew-Nipissing-Pembroke
Next Election: Oct. 24, 2022 (4 year terms)
Note: Amalgamation of Bagot, Blythfield & Brougham Township & Griffith & Matawatchan Township.
Brian Hunt, Mayor
Allison Hotzhauer, Chief Administrative Officer & Clerk-Treasurer, 613-572-2222

Greater Napanee

P.O. Box 97
124 John St.
Napanee, ON K7R 3L4
Tel: 613-354-3351; *Fax:* 613-354-6545
info@greaternapanee.com
www.greaternapanee.com
Municipal Type: Town
Area: 461.17 sq km
County or District: Lennox-Addington; *Population in 2016:* 15,892
Provincial Electoral District(s): Hastings-Lennox and Addington
Federal Electoral District(s): Hastings-Lennox & Addington
Next Election: Oct. 24, 2022 (4 year terms)
Marg Isbester, Mayor
Max Kaiser, Deputy Mayor
John McCormack, Councillor, Wards: 1
Terry Richardson, Councillor, Wards: 2
Dave Pinnell, Councillor, Wards: 3
Bob Norrie, Councillor, Wards: 4
Ellen Johnson, Councillor, Wards: 5
Raymond Callery, Chief Administrative Officer, 613-354-3351
Paul Dowber, Treasurer & General Manager, Financial Services, 613-354-3351
Jeff Cuthill, Director, Capital Works, 613-354-5931
Charles McDonald, Chief Building Official & Director, Operational Audits, 613-354-3351
Wayne Taylor, Director, Public Works & Facilities, 613-354-5931
Rob Serson, Fire Chief, 613-354-3415

Greenstone, Municipality of

P.O. Box 70
1800 Main St.
Geraldton, ON P0T 1M0
Tel: 807-854-1100; *Fax:* 807-854-1947
www.greenstone.ca
Other Information: Toll-Free Phone: 866-462-2064
Municipal Type: Municipality
Area: 2,767.19 sq km
County or District: Thunder Bay; *Population in 2016:* 4,636
Provincial Electoral District(s): Thunder Bay-Superior North
Federal Electoral District(s): Thunder Bay-Superior North
Next Election: Oct. 24, 2022 (4 year terms)
Renald Beaulieu, Mayor
Mark Wright, Chief Administrative Officer, 807-854-1100

Grey Highlands, Municipality of

P.O. Box 409
#1, 206 Toronto St. South
Markdale, ON N0C 1H0
Tel: 519-986-1216; *Fax:* 519-986-3643
info@greyhighlands.ca
www.greyhighlands.ca
Other Information: Toll-Free Phone: 888-342-4059
Municipal Type: Municipality
Incorporated: Jan. 1, 2001; *Area:* 882.51 sq km
County or District: Grey; *Population in 2016:* 9,804
Provincial Electoral District(s): Bruce-Grey-Owen Sound
Federal Electoral District(s): Bruce-Grey-Owen Sound
Next Election: Oct. 24, 2022 (4 year terms)
Note: Amalgamation of Flesherton, Artemesia, Euphrasia, Markdale & Osprey.
Paul McQueen, Mayor
Rob Adams, Chief Administrative Officer, 519-986-2811

Grimsby

160 Livingston Ave.
Grimsby, ON L3M 4G3
Tel: 905-945-9634; *Fax:* 905-945-5010
www.grimsby.ca
Municipal Type: Town
Area: 68.93 sq km
County or District: Niagara Reg. Mun.; *Population in 2016:* 27,314
Provincial Electoral District(s): Niagara West
Federal Electoral District(s): Niagara West
Next Election: Oct. 24, 2022 (4 year terms)
Jeff Jordan, Mayor
Reg Freake, Alderman, Wards: 1
Kevin Ritchie, Alderman, Wards: 1
Dave Kadwell, Alderman, Wards: 2
Lianne Vardy, Alderman, Wards: 2
John Dunstall, Alderman, Wards: 3
Randy Vaine, Alderman, Wards: 3
Dorothy Bothwell, Alderman, Wards: 4
Dave Sharpe, Alderman, Wards: 4
Stephen Gruninger, CGA, Town Treasurer
Sarah Sweeney, CGA, Director, Recreation, Facilities & Culture
Bill Thomson, Interim Fire Chief

Guelph / Eramosa

P.O. Box 700
8348 Wellington Rd. 124
Rockwood, ON N0B 2K0
Tel: 519-856-9951; *Fax:* 519-856-2240
general@get.on.ca
www.get.on.ca
Other Information: Toll-Free Phone: 800-267-1465
Municipal Type: Township
Incorporated: Jan. 1, 1999; *Area:* 291.67 sq km
County or District: Wellington; *Population in 2016:* 12,854
Provincial Electoral District(s): Wellington-Halton Hills
Federal Electoral District(s): Wellington-Halton Hills
Next Election: Oct. 24, 2022 (4 year terms)
Note: Amalgamation of the Townships of Guelph, Eramosa, Pilkington & Nichol.
Chris White, Mayor
Bruce Dickieson, Councillor, Wards: 1
Corey Woods, Councillor, Wards: 2
Louise Marshall, Councillor, Wards: 3
Mark Bouwmeester, Councillor, Wards: 4
Amanda Knight, Clerk & Director, Legislative Services
Ian Roger, Chief Administrative Officer
Linda Cheyne, Director, Finance
Robin Milne, Director, Parks & Recreation
Harry Niemi, Director, Public Works
Jim Petrik, Fire Chief

Halton Hills

Civic Centre
1 Halton Hills Dr.
Georgetown, ON L7G 5G2
Tel: 905-873-2600; *Fax:* 905-873-2347
www.haltonhills.ca
Other Information: Toll-free phone: 877-712-2205
Municipal Type: Town
Area: 276.27 sq km
County or District: Halton Reg. Mun.; *Population in 2016:* 61,161
Provincial Electoral District(s): Wellington-Halton Hills
Federal Electoral District(s): Wellington-Halton Hills
Next Election: Oct. 24, 2022 (4 year terms)
Rick Bonnette, Mayor, 905-873-2601
Clark Somerville, Regional Councillor, Wards: 1 & 2
Jane Fogal, Regional Councillor, 905-877-5806, Wards: 3 & 4
Jon Hurst, Councillor, 519-853-2015, Wards: 1
Michael Albano, Councillor, 519-853-3465, Wards: 1
Ted Brown, Councillor, 905-877-2323, Wards: 2
Bryan Lewis, Councillor, 905-877-5380, Wards: 2
Moya Johnson, Councillor, 905-877-3755, Wards: 3
Wendy Farrow-Reed, Councillor, Wards: 3 & 4
Bob Inglis, Councillor, 905-873-9124, Wards: 4
Ann Lawlor, Councillor, 905-877-5662, Wards: 4
Brent Marshall, Chief Administrative Officer, 905-873-2601
Brent Marshall, Fire Chief, 905-877-1133

Hamilton

P.O. Box 1060
8285 Majestic Hills Dr.
Cobourg, ON K9A 4W5
Tel: 905-342-2810; *Fax:* 905-342-2818
info@hamiltontownship.ca
www.hamiltontownship.ca
Municipal Type: Township
Area: 256.08 sq km
County or District: Northumberland; *Population in 2016:* 10,942
Provincial Electoral District(s): Northumberland-Peterborough

South
Federal Electoral District(s): Northumberland-Peterborough South
Next Election: Oct. 24, 2022 (4 year terms)
Bill Cane, Mayor
Scott Jibb, Deputy Mayor & Councillor
Mark Lovshin, Councillor
Pat McCourt, Councillor
Larry Williamson, Councillor
Kate Surerus, Clerk
Arthur Anderson, Chief Administrative Officer
Nusrat Ahmed, Treasurer
Don Hamly, Foreman, Public Works
Kelly Serson, Fire Chief & Director, Emergency Services

Hanover
341 - 10th St.
Hanover, ON N4N 1P5
Tel: 519-364-2780; *Fax:* 519-364-6456
civic@hanover.ca
www.hanover.ca
Municipal Type: Town
Incorporated: Jan. 1, 2001; *Area:* 9.80 sq km
County or District: Grey; *Population in 2016:* 7,688
Provincial Electoral District(s): Bruce-Grey-Owen Sound
Federal Electoral District(s): Bruce-Grey-Owen Sound
Next Election: Oct. 24, 2022 (4 year terms)
Sue Paterson, Mayor, 519-364-2780
Brian Tocheri, Chief Administrative Officer & Clerk, 519-364-2780

Harley
903303 Hanbury Rd., RR#2
New Liskeard, ON P0J 1P0
Tel: 705-647-5439; *Fax:* 705-647-6373
harleytwp@parolink.net
www.harley.ca
Municipal Type: Township
Incorporated: 1904; *Area:* 92.30 sq km
County or District: Timiskaming District; *Population in 2016:* 551
Provincial Electoral District(s): Timiskaming-Cochrane
Federal Electoral District(s): Timmins-James Bay
Next Election: Oct. 24, 2022 (4 year terms)
Pauline Archambault, Reeve
Michel Lachapelle, Clerk-Treasurer

Harris
782156 Balls Rd. RR#3
New Liskeard, ON P0J 1P0
Tel: 705-647-5094; *Fax:* 705-647-0041
harris@parolink.net
harristownship.weebly.com
Municipal Type: Township
Area: 49.88 sq km
County or District: Timiskaming District; *Population in 2016:* 545
Provincial Electoral District(s): Timiskaming-Cochrane
Federal Electoral District(s): Timmins-James Bay
Next Election: Oct. 24, 2022 (4 year terms)
Chantal Despres, Reeve
Anita Herd, Clerk-Treasurer

Hastings Highlands
P.O. Box 130
33011 Hwy. 62 North
Maynooth, ON K0L 2S0
Tel: 613-338-2811; *Fax:* 613-338-3292
info@hastingshighlands.ca
www.hastingshighlands.ca
Other Information: Toll-Free Phone: 877-338-2818
Municipal Type: Municipality
Area: 972.35 sq km
County or District: Hastings; *Population in 2016:* 4,078
Provincial Electoral District(s): Hastings-Lennox and Addington
Federal Electoral District(s): Hastings-Lennox and Addington
Next Election: Oct. 24, 2022 (4 year terms)
Vic A. Bodnar, Mayor
Pat Pilgrim, Chief Administrative Officer & Clerk, 613-338-2811

Havelock-Belmont-Methuen
P.O. Box 10
1 Ottawa St. East
Havelock, ON K0L 1Z0
Tel: 705-778-2308; *Fax:* 705-778-5248
havbelmet@hbmtwp.ca
www.hbmtwp.ca
Other Information: Toll-Free Phone: 877-767-2795
Municipal Type: Township
Area: 542.73 sq km
County or District: Peterborough; *Population in 2016:* 4,530
Provincial Electoral District(s): Peterborough-Kawartha
Federal Electoral District(s): Peterborough-Kawartha
Next Election: Oct. 24, 2022 (4 year terms)

Jim Martin, Mayor
Pat Kemp, Chief Administrative Officer, 705-778-2308

Hawkesbury
600 Higginson St.
Hawkesbury, ON K6A 1H1
Tel: 613-632-0106
www.hawkesbury.ca
Municipal Type: Town
Area: 9.62 sq km
County or District: Prescott & Russell; *Population in 2016:* 10,263
Provincial Electoral District(s): Glengarry-Prescott-Russell
Federal Electoral District(s): Glengarry-Prescott-Russell
Next Election: Oct. 24, 2022 (4 year terms)
Paula Assaly, Mayor
Lawrence Bogue, Councillor
André Chamaillard, Councillor
Raymond Campbell, Councillor
Robert Lefebvre, Councillor
Yves Paquette, Councillor
Antonios Tsourounakis, Councillor
Christine Groulx, Clerk
Daniel Gatien, Chief Administrative Officer
Daniel Gascon, Fire Chief

Head, Clara & Maria
15 Township Hall Rd.
Stonecliffe, ON K0J 2K0
Tel: 613-586-2526; *Fax:* 613-586-2596
hcminfocfischer@gmail.com
www.townshipsofheadclaramaria.ca
Municipal Type: Township
Area: 728.38 sq km
County or District: Renfrew; *Population in 2016:* 248
Provincial Electoral District(s): Renfrew-Nipissing-Pembroke
Federal Electoral District(s): Renfrew-Nipissing-Pembroke
Next Election: Oct. 24, 2022 (4 year terms)
Debbi Grills, Mayor
Melinda Reith, Municipal Clerk

Hearst
Town Hall
P.O. Box 5000
925 Alexandra St.
Hearst, ON P0L 1N0
Tel: 705-362-4341; *Fax:* 705-362-5902
townofhearst@hearst.ca
www.hearst.ca
Municipal Type: Town
Incorporated: 1922; *Area:* 98.52 sq km
County or District: Cochrane District; *Population in 2016:* 5,070
Provincial Electoral District(s): Mushkegowuk-James Bay
Federal Electoral District(s): Algoma-Manitoulin-Kapuskasing
Next Election: Oct. 24, 2022 (4 year terms)
Roger Sigouin, Mayor
Yves Morrissette, Chief Administrative Officer, 705-372-2817

Highlands East, Municipality of
P.O. Box 295
County Rd. 648
Wilberforce, ON K0L 3C0
Tel: 705-448-2981; *Fax:* 705-448-2532
info@highlandseast.ca
www.highlandseast.ca
Municipal Type: Municipality
Incorporated: Jan. 1, 2001; *Area:* 704.63 sq km
County or District: Haliburton; *Population in 2016:* 3,343
Provincial Electoral District(s): Haliburton-Kawartha Lakes-Brock
Federal Electoral District(s): Haliburton-Kawartha Lakes-Brock
Next Election: Oct. 24, 2022 (4 year terms)
Note: Amalgamation of the Townships of Bicroft, Cardiff, Glamorgan & Monmouth.
Dave Burton, Mayor, 705-448-9355
Shannon Hunter, CMO, Chief Administrative Officer & Treasurer, 705-448-2981

Hilliard
P.O. Box 8
RR#3
Thornloe, ON P0J 1S0
Tel: 705-563-2593; *Fax:* 705-563-8303
twphill@parolink.net
Municipal Type: Township
Area: 91.38 sq km
County or District: Timiskaming District; *Population in 2016:* 223
Provincial Electoral District(s): Timiskaming-Cochrane
Federal Electoral District(s): Timmins-James Bay
Next Election: Oct. 24, 2022 (4 year terms)
Morgan Carson, Reeve
Alex Regele, Clerk-Treasurer

Hilton
2983 Base Line
Hilton Beach, ON P0R 1G0
Tel: 705-246-2472; *Fax:* 705-246-0132
admin@hiltontownship.ca
www.hiltontownship.ca
Other Information: Phone, Roads: 705-246-1781
Municipal Type: Township
Incorporated: 1883; *Area:* 115.82 sq km
County or District: Algoma District; *Population in 2016:* 307
Provincial Electoral District(s): Algoma-Manitoulin
Federal Electoral District(s): Algoma-Manitoulin-Kapuskasing
Next Election: Oct. 24, 2022 (4 year terms)
Rodney Wood, Reeve
Valerie Obarymskyj, Clerk-Treasurer

Hilton Beach
P.O. Box 25
3100 Bowker St.
Hilton Beach, ON P0R 1G0
Tel: 705-246-2242; *Fax:* 705-246-2913
info@hiltonbeach.com
www.hiltonbeach.com
Municipal Type: Village
Area: 2.62 sq km
County or District: Algoma District; *Population in 2016:* 171
Provincial Electoral District(s): Algoma-Manitoulin
Federal Electoral District(s): Algoma-Manitoulin-Kapuskasing
Next Election: Oct. 24, 2022 (4 year terms)
Robert Hope, Mayor
Peggy Cramp, Clerk & Treasurer

Hornepayne
P.O. Box 370
68 Front St.
Hornepayne, ON P0M 1Z0
Tel: 807-868-2020; *Fax:* 807-868-2787
www.townshipofhornepayne.ca
Municipal Type: Township
Area: 204.07 sq km
County or District: Algoma District; *Population in 2016:* 980
Provincial Electoral District(s): Algoma-Manitoulin
Federal Electoral District(s): Algoma-Manitoulin-Kapuskasing
Next Election: Oct. 24, 2022 (4 year terms)
Cheryl T. Fort, Mayor
Gail Jaremy, Chief Administration Office & Clerk, 807-868-2020

Horton
2253 Johnston Rd., RR#5
Renfrew, ON K7V 3Z8
Tel: 613-432-6271; *Fax:* 613-432-7298
www.hortontownship.ca
Municipal Type: Township
Area: 158.51 sq km
County or District: Renfrew; *Population in 2016:* 2,887
Provincial Electoral District(s): Renfrew-Nipissing-Pembroke
Federal Electoral District(s): Renfrew-Nipissing-Pembroke
Next Election: Oct. 24, 2022 (4 year terms)
David Bennett, Mayor
Suzanne Klatt, Chief Administrative Officer & Clerk

Howick
44816 Harriston Rd.
Gorrie, ON N0G 1X0
Tel: 519-335-3208; *Fax:* 519-335-6208
howick.ca
Municipal Type: Township
Area: 287.06 sq km
County or District: Huron; *Population in 2016:* 3,873
Provincial Electoral District(s): Huron-Bruce
Federal Electoral District(s): Huron-Bruce
Next Election: Oct. 24, 2022 (4 year terms)
Doug Harding, Reeve
Carol Watson, Clerk

Hudson
903303 Hanbury Rd., RR#2
New Liskeard, ON P0J 1P0
Tel: 705-647-5439; *Fax:* 705-647-6373
harleytwp@parolink.net
www.hudson.ca
Municipal Type: Township
Area: 90.37 sq km
County or District: Timiskaming District; *Population in 2016:* 503
Provincial Electoral District(s): Timiskaming-Cochrane
Federal Electoral District(s): Timmins-James Bay
Next Election: Oct. 24, 2022 (4 year terms)
Larry Craig, Reeve
Michel Lachapelle, Clerk-Treasurer

Huntsville
37 Main St. East
Huntsville, ON P1H 1A1
Tel: 705-789-1751; *Fax:* 705-788-5153
help@huntsville.ca
www.huntsville.ca
Municipal Type: Town
Area: 710.01 sq km
County or District: Muskoka Dist. Mun.; *Population in 2016:* 19,816
Provincial Electoral District(s): Parry Sound-Muskoka
Federal Electoral District(s): Parry Sound-Muskoka
Next Election: Oct. 24, 2022 (4 year terms)
Karin Terziano, Mayor
Nancy Alcock, District Councillor, 705-789-4399
Brian Thompson, District Councillor
Tim Withey, District Councillor, 705-571-0770
Bob Stone, Councillor, Wards: 1
Jonathan Wiebe, Councillor, Wards: 2
Jason FitzGerald, Councillor, 705-385-1838, Wards: 3, 4 & 5
Daniel Armour, Councillor, 705-789-7958, Wards: 6
Denise Corry, Chief Administrative Officer, 705-789-1751
Kristin Maxwell, Director, Development Services, 705-789-1751
Lorrie O'Brien, Director, Community Services, 705-789-6421
Stephen Hernen, Fire Chief, 705-789-1751

Huron East, Municipality of
P.O. Box 610
72 Main St. South
Seaforth, ON N0K 1W0
Tel: 519-527-0160; *Fax:* 519-527-2561
www.huroneast.com
Other Information: Toll-Free Phone: 888-868-7513
Municipal Type: Municipality
Incorporated: Jan. 1, 2001; *Area:* 669.22 sq km
County or District: Huron; *Population in 2016:* 9,138
Provincial Electoral District(s): Huron-Bruce
Federal Electoral District(s): Huron-Bruce
Next Election: Oct. 24, 2022 (4 year terms)
Note: Amalgamation of the Town of Seaforth, the Village of Brussels & the Townships of Grey, McKillop & Tuckersmith.
Bernie MacLellan, Mayor, 519-233-7489, Fax: 519-233-3405
Brad Knight, Chief Administrative Officer & Clerk-Administrator

Huron Shores
P.O. Box 460
7 Bridge St.
Iron Bridge, ON P0R 1H0
Tel: 705-843-2033; *Fax:* 705-843-2035
email@huronshores.ca
www.huronshores.ca
Municipal Type: Municipality
Area: 457.35 sq km
County or District: Algoma District; *Population in 2016:* 1,664
Provincial Electoral District(s): Algoma-Manitoulin
Federal Electoral District(s): Algoma-Manitoulin-Kapuskasing
Next Election: Oct. 24, 2022 (4 year terms)
Georges Bilodeau, Mayor
Deborah Tonelli, AMCT, Administrator-Clerk

Huron-Kinloss
P.O. Box 130
21 Queen St.
Ripley, ON N0G 2R0
Tel: 519-395-3735; *Fax:* 519-395-4107
info@huronkinloss.com
www.huronkinloss.com
Municipal Type: Township
Incorporated: 1999; *Area:* 440.76 sq km
County or District: Bruce; *Population in 2016:* 7,069
Provincial Electoral District(s): Huron-Bruce
Federal Electoral District(s): Huron-Bruce
Next Election: Oct. 24, 2022 (4 year terms)
Note: Amalgamation of the Village of Lucknow & the Townships of Ripley-Huron & Kinloss.
Mitch Twolan, Mayor, 519-395-0717
Mary Rose Walden, Chief Administrative Officer, 519-395-3735

Ignace
P.O. Box 248
34 Hwy. 17 West
Ignace, ON P0T 1T0
Tel: 807-934-2202; *Fax:* 807-934-2864
administration@town.ignace.on.ca
www.town.ignace.on.ca
Municipal Type: Township
Incorporated: 1908; *Area:* 72.82 sq km
County or District: Kenora District; *Population in 2016:* 1,202
Provincial Electoral District(s): Kenora-Rainy River
Federal Electoral District(s): Kenora
Next Election: Oct. 24, 2022 (4 year terms)
Donald Cunningham, Mayor

Marshalina Reader, Chief Administrative Officer & Clerk

Ingersoll
130 Oxford St., 2nd Fl.
Ingersoll, ON N5C 2V5
Tel: 519-485-0120; *Fax:* 519-485-3543
info@ingersoll.ca
www.ingersoll.ca
Municipal Type: Town
Area: 12.75 sq km
County or District: Oxford; *Population in 2016:* 12,757
Provincial Electoral District(s): Oxford
Federal Electoral District(s): Oxford
Next Election: Oct. 24, 2022 (4 year terms)
Ted J. Comiskey, Mayor
Fred Freeman, Deputy Mayor & Councillor
Michael Bowman, Councillor
Rick Eus, Councillor
Gordon Lesser, Councillor
Brian Petrie, Councillor
Kristy Van Kooten-Bossence, Councillor
William Tigert, Chief Administrative Officer, 519-485-0120
Ramesh Umatt, Director, Engineering
Kyle Stefanovic, Director, Recreation
Doug Wituik, Manager, Public Works
John Holmes, Fire Chief

Iroquois Falls
P.O. Box 230
253 Main St.
Iroquois Falls, ON P0K 1G0
Tel: 705-232-5700; *Fax:* 705-232-4241
www.iroquoisfalls.com
Other Information: Alternate Phone: 705-232-6357
Municipal Type: Town
Area: 600.01 sq km
County or District: Cochrane District; *Population in 2016:* 4,537
Provincial Electoral District(s): Timiskaming-Cochrane
Federal Electoral District(s): Timmins-James Bay
Next Election: Oct. 24, 2022 (4 year terms)
Pat Britton, Mayor
Linda McLean, Clerk-Administrator

James
P.O. Box 10
372 Third St.
Elk Lake, ON P0J 1G0
Tel: 705-678-2237; *Fax:* 705-678-2495
elklake@ntl.sympatico.ca
www.elklake.ca
Municipal Type: Township
Incorporated: 1909; *Area:* 86.36 sq km
County or District: Timiskaming District; *Population in 2016:* 420
Provincial Electoral District(s): Timiskaming-Cochrane
Federal Electoral District(s): Timmins-James Bay
Next Election: Oct. 24, 2022 (4 year terms)
Terry Fiset, Reeve
Myrna J. Hayes, Clerk-Treasurer

Jocelyn
3670 5th Side Rd. RR#1
Hilton Beach, ON P0R 1J0
Tel: 705-246-2025; *Fax:* 705-246-3282
admin@jocelyn.ca
www.jocelyn.ca
Municipal Type: Township
Area: 131.45 sq km
County or District: Algoma District; *Population in 2016:* 313
Provincial Electoral District(s): Algoma-Manitoulin
Federal Electoral District(s): Algoma-Manitoulin-Kapuskasing
Next Election: Oct. 24, 2022 (4 year terms)
Mark Henderson, Reeve
Janet Boucher, Clerk-Treasurer

Johnson
P.O. Box 160
1 Johnson Dr.
Desbarats, ON P0R 1E0
Tel: 705-782-6601; *Fax:* 705-782-6780
people@johnsontownship.ca
johnsontownship.ca
Municipal Type: Township
Area: 120.27 sq km
County or District: Algoma District; *Population in 2016:* 751
Provincial Electoral District(s): Algoma-Manitoulin
Federal Electoral District(s): Algoma-Manitoulin-Kapuskasing
Next Election: Oct. 24, 2022 (4 year terms)
Blaine Mersereau, Mayor
Ruth Kelso, Clerk & Chief Administrative Officer

Joly
P.O. Box 519
871 Forest Lake Rd.
Sundridge, ON P0A 1Z0
Tel: 705-384-5428; *Fax:* 705-384-0845
office@townshipofjoly.com
www.townshipofjoly.com
Municipal Type: Township
Area: 194.73 sq km
County or District: Parry Sound District; *Population in 2016:* 304
Provincial Electoral District(s): Parry Sound-Muskoka
Federal Electoral District(s): Parry Sound-Muskoka
Next Election: Oct. 24, 2022 (4 year terms)
Tim Bryson, Mayor
Leanne Crozier, Clerk-Treasurer

Kapuskasing
Civic Centre
88 Riverside Dr.
Kapuskasing, ON P5N 1B3
Tel: 705-335-2341; *Fax:* 705-337-1741
general@kapuskasing.ca
www.kapuskasing.ca
Municipal Type: Town
Incorporated: 1921; *Area:* 84.37 sq km
County or District: Cochrane District; *Population in 2016:* 8,292
Provincial Electoral District(s): Mushkegowuk-James Bay
Federal Electoral District(s): Algoma-Manitoulin-Kapuskasing
Next Election: Oct. 24, 2022 (4 year terms)
David Plourde, Mayor
Guylain Baril, Chief Administrative Officer

Kearney
P.O. Box 38
8 Main St.
Kearney, ON P0A 1M0
Tel: 705-636-7752; *Fax:* 705-636-0527
admin@townofkearney.ca
townofkearney.ca
Municipal Type: Town
Incorporated: 1908; *Area:* 532.00 sq km
County or District: Parry Sound District; *Population in 2016:* 882
Provincial Electoral District(s): Parry Sound-Muskoka
Federal Electoral District(s): Parry Sound-Muskoka
Next Election: Oct. 24, 2022 (4 year terms)
Carol Ballantyne, Mayor
Brenda Fraser, Clerk Administrator

Kenora
c/o Kenora District Services Board
#1, 211 Princess St.
Dryden, ON P8N 3L5
Tel: 807-223-2100; *Fax:* 807-223-6500
kdsb@kdsb.on.ca
www.kdsb.on.ca
Municipal Type: District
Area: 407,268.65 sq km
Population in 2016: 65,533
Barry Baltessen, Chair, Kenora District Services Board
Henry Wall, Chief Administrative Officer

Kerns
903303 Hanbury Rd., RR#2
New Liskeard, ON P0J 1P0
Tel: 705-647-5439; *Fax:* 705-647-6373
harleytwp@parolink.net
www.kerns.ca
Municipal Type: Township
Incorporated: 1904; *Area:* 90.64 sq km
County or District: Timiskaming District; *Population in 2016:* 358
Provincial Electoral District(s): Timiskaming-Cochrane
Federal Electoral District(s): Timmins-James Bay
Next Election: Oct. 24, 2022 (4 year terms)
Terry Phillips, Reeve
Michel Lachapelle, Clerk-Treasurer

Killaloe, Hagarty & Richards
P.O. Box 39
1 John St.
Killaloe, ON K0J 2A0
Tel: 613-757-2300; *Fax:* 613-757-3634
info@khrtownship.ca
www.killaloe-hagarty-richards.ca
Municipal Type: Township
Incorporated: July 1, 2000; *Area:* 396.80 sq km
County or District: Renfrew; *Population in 2016:* 2,420
Provincial Electoral District(s): Renfrew-Nipissing-Pembroke
Federal Electoral District(s): Renfrew-Nipissing-Pembroke
Next Election: Oct. 24, 2022 (4 year terms)
Note: Amalgamation of the Township of Hagarty & Richards & the former Village of Killaloe.
Janice Visneskie Moore, Mayor

Lorna Hudder, Chief Administrative Officer & Clerk-Treasurer

Killarney, Municipality of
32 Commissioner St.
Killarney, ON P0M 2A0
Tel: 705-287-2424; *Fax:* 705-287-2660
inquiries@municipalityofkillarney.ca
www.municipalityofkillarney.ca
Other Information: Toll-Free Phone: 888-597-2721
Municipal Type: Municipality
Incorporated: Jan. 1, 1999; *Area:* 1,653.32 sq km
County or District: Sudbury District; *Population in 2016:* 386
Provincial Electoral District(s): Algoma-Manitoulin; Nickel Belt
Federal Electoral District(s): Nickel Belt
Next Election: Oct. 24, 2022 (4 year terms)
Virginia Rook, Mayor, 705-857-1100
Candy Beauvais, Clerk-Treasurer, 705-287-2424

Kincardine
1475 Concession 5, RR#5
Kincardine, ON N2Z 2X6
Tel: 519-396-3468; *Fax:* 519-396-8288
info@kincardine.net
www.kincardine.net
Municipal Type: Municipality
Area: 537.94 sq km
County or District: Bruce; *Population in 2016:* 11,389
Provincial Electoral District(s): Huron-Bruce
Federal Electoral District(s): Huron-Bruce
Next Election: Oct. 24, 2022 (4 year terms)
Anne Eadie, Mayor
Marie Wilson, Deputy Mayor
Maureen Couture, Councillor, Wards: 1
Gerry Glover, Councillor, Wards: 1
Bill Stewart, Councillor, Wards: 2
Randy Roppel, Councillor, Wards: 3
Dave Cuyler, Councillor-at-Large
Laura Haight, Councillor-at-Large
Doug Kennedy, Councillor-at-Large
Sharon Chambers, Chief Administrative Officer
Roxana Baumann, Director, Finance
Michele Barr, Director, Building & Planning
Karen Kieffer, Director, Recreation
Adam Weishar, Director, Public Works
Kevin McNeilly, Fire Chief

King
2075 King Rd.
King City, ON L7B 1A1
Tel: 905-833-5321; *Fax:* 905-833-2300
customerservice@king.ca
www.king.ca
Municipal Type: Township
Incorporated: 1850; *Area:* 333.25 sq km
County or District: York Reg. Mun.; *Population in 2016:* 24,512
Provincial Electoral District(s): King-Vaughan; York-Simcoe
Federal Electoral District(s): King-Vaughan; York-Simcoe
Next Election: Oct. 24, 2022 (4 year terms)
Steve Pellegrini, Mayor
Jordan Alexander Cescolini, Councillor, Wards: 1
David Boyd, Councillor, Wards: 2
Jakob Schneider, Councillor, Wards: 3
Bill Cober, Councillor, Wards: 4
Debbie Schaefer, Councillor, Wards: 5
Avia Eek, Councillor, Wards: 6
Daniel Kostopoulos, Chief Administrative Officer
Allan Evelyn, Director, Finance
Peter Angelo, Director, Engineering, Public Works & Building
Chris Fasciano, Director, Parks, Recreation & Culture
Cara Tuch, Manager, Human Resources
Jim Wall, Fire Chief

Kirkland Lake
P.O. Box 1757
3 Kirkland St. West
Kirkland Lake, ON P2N 3P4
Tel: 705-567-9361; *Fax:* 705-567-3535
kirklandlake.ca
Municipal Type: Town
Incorporated: 1972; *Area:* 262.13 sq km
County or District: Timiskaming District; *Population in 2016:* 7,981
Provincial Electoral District(s): Timiskaming-Cochrane
Federal Electoral District(s): Timmins-James Bay
Next Election: Oct. 24, 2022 (4 year terms)
Note: Formerly known as the Township of Teck.
Patrick Kiely, Mayor
Wilfred Hass, Interim Chief Administrative Officer, 705-567-9361

Laird
3 Pumpkin Point Rd., RR#4
Echo Bay, ON P0S 1C0
Tel: 705-248-2395; *Fax:* 705-248-1138
lairdtwp@soonet.ca
www.lairdtownship.ca
Municipal Type: Township
Incorporated: 1891; *Area:* 102.48 sq km
County or District: Algoma District; *Population in 2016:* 1,047
Provincial Electoral District(s): Algoma-Manitoulin
Federal Electoral District(s): Algoma-Manitoulin-Kapuskasing
Next Election: Oct. 24, 2022 (4 year terms)
Richard (Dick) Beitz, Mayor
Phyllis L. MacKay, Clerk-Treasurer, Tax Collector & License Issuing Officer

Lake of Bays
1012 Dwight Beach Rd., RR#1
Dwight, ON P0A 1H0
Tel: 705-635-2272; *Fax:* 705-635-2132
contact@lakeofbays.on.ca
www.lakeofbays.on.ca
Other Information: Toll-Free Phone: 877-566-0005
Municipal Type: Township
Incorporated: 1971; *Area:* 677.91 sq km
County or District: Muskoka Dist. Mun.; *Population in 2016:* 3,167
Provincial Electoral District(s): Parry Sound-Muskoka
Federal Electoral District(s): Parry Sound-Muskoka
Next Election: Oct. 24, 2022 (4 year terms)
Note: Amalgamation of the former Townships of Franklin, Ridout, McLean & Sinclair/Finlayson.
Terry Glover, Mayor
Michelle Percival, Chief Administrative Officer

Lake of the Woods
P.O. Box 427
211-4th St.
Rainy River, ON P0W 1L0
Tel: 807-852-3529; *Fax:* 807-852-3529
lakeofthewoodstwp@tbaytel.net
www.lakeofthewoods.ca
Municipal Type: Township
Incorporated: Jan. 1, 1998; *Area:* 751.31 sq km
County or District: Rainy River District; *Population in 2016:* 230
Provincial Electoral District(s): Kenora-Rainy River
Federal Electoral District(s): Thunder Bay-Rainy River
Next Election: Oct. 24, 2022 (4 year terms)
Note: Amalgamation of the Township of Morson & McCrosson-Tovell.
Colleen Fadden, Mayor
Patrick W. Giles, Clerk-Treasurer

Lakeshore
419 Notre Dame St.
Belle River, ON N0R 1A0
Tel: 519-728-2700; *Fax:* 519-728-9530
www.lakeshore.ca
Municipal Type: Town
Incorporated: 1999; *Area:* 530.33 sq km
County or District: Essex; *Population in 2016:* 36,611
Provincial Electoral District(s): Chatham-Kent-Leamington; Essex
Federal Electoral District(s): Essex
Next Election: Oct. 24, 2022 (4 year terms)
Note: Amalgamation of the former Town of Belle River & the former Townships of Maidstone, Rochester, Tilbury North & Tilbury West.
Tom Bain, Mayor
Tracey Bailey, Deputy Mayor & Councillor
Steven Wilder, Councillor, Wards: 1
Len Janisse, Councillor, Wards: 2
Kelsey Santarossa, Councillor, Wards: 3
John Kerr, Councillor, Wards: 4
Kirk Walstedt, Councillor, Wards: 5
Linda McKinlay, Councillor, Wards: 6
Truper McBride, Chief Administrative Officer
Rosanna Pellerito, Director, Finance
Tammie Ryall, Director, Community & Development Services
Nelson Cavacas, Director, Engineering & Infrastructure Services
Albert Dionne, Manager, Public Works
Don Williamson, Fire Chief

Lambton Shores
P.O. Box 610
7883 Amtelecom Pkwy.
Forest, ON N0N 1J0
Tel: 519-786-2335; *Fax:* 519-786-2135
info@lambtonshores.ca
www.lambtonshores.ca
Other Information: Toll-Free Phone: 866-943-1400
Municipal Type: Municipality
Incorporated: 2001; *Area:* 331.20 sq km
County or District: Lambton; *Population in 2016:* 10,631
Provincial Electoral District(s): Lambton-Kent-Middlesex
Federal Electoral District(s): Lambton-Kent-Middlesex
Next Election: Oct. 24, 2022 (4 year terms)
Note: Amalgamation of the Towns of Bosanquet & Forest, & the Villages of Thedford, Arkona & Grand Bend.
Bill Weber, Mayor, 519-649-6885
Doug Cook, Deputy Mayor & Councillor
Dave Maguire, Councillor, 519-238-8687, Wards: 1
Dan Sageman, Councillor, 519-494-4028, Wards: 2
Lorie Scott, Councillor, Wards: 3
Ronn E. Dodge, Councillor, 519-786-2581, Wards: 4
Rick Goodhand, Councillor, 519-786-5055, Wards: 5
Dave Marsh, Councillor, Wards: 6
Jeff Wilcox, Councillor, 519-520-8163, Wards: 7
Kevin Williams, Chief Administrative Officer, 519-786-2335, Fax: 519-786-2135
Janet Ferguson, Treasurer, 519-238-8461, Fax: 519-238-8577
Stephen McAuley, Director, Community Services, 519-243-1400
Will Nywening, Senior Planner, 519-243-1400, Fax: 519-786-2135
Randy Lovie, Chief Building Official, 519-786-2335
Lawrence Swift, Fire Chief, 519-243-1400

Lanark Highlands
P.O. Box 340
75 George St.
Lanark, ON K0G 1K0
Tel: 613-259-2398; *Fax:* 613-259-2291
www.lanarkhighlands.ca
Other Information: Toll-Free Phone: 800-239-4695
Municipal Type: Township
Incorporated: July 1, 1997; *Area:* 1,048.83 sq km
County or District: Lanark; *Population in 2016:* 5,338
Provincial Electoral District(s): Lanark-Frontenac-Kingston
Federal Electoral District(s): Lanark-Frontenac-Kingston
Next Election: Oct. 24, 2022 (4 year terms)
Note: Amalgamation of North West Lanark Township & Darling Township.
Peter McLaren, Mayor
Allison Vereyken, Clerk Administrator & Deputy Treasurer, 613-259-2398

Larder Lake
P.O. Box 40
69-4th Ave.
Larder Lake, ON P0K 1L0
Tel: 705-643-2158; *Fax:* 705-643-2311
www.larderlake.ca
Municipal Type: Township
Area: 229.52 sq km
County or District: Timiskaming District; *Population in 2016:* 730
Provincial Electoral District(s): Timiskaming-Cochrane
Federal Electoral District(s): Timmins-James Bay
Next Election: Oct. 24, 2022 (4 year terms)
Patricia Quinn, Mayor
Dwight McTaggart, Clerk-Treasurer/CAO

LaSalle
5950 Malden Rd.
Lasalle, ON N9H 1S4
Tel: 519-969-7770; *Fax:* 519-969-4469
www.lasalle.ca
Municipal Type: Town
Incorporated: 1924; *Area:* 65.35 sq km
County or District: Essex; *Population in 2016:* 30,180
Provincial Electoral District(s): Essex
Federal Electoral District(s): Essex
Next Election: Oct. 24, 2022 (4 year terms)
Note: Dissolved into Township of Sandwich West in 1959. Status & name change to Town of LaSalle in 1991.
Marc A. Bondy, Mayor
Crystal Meloche, Deputy Mayor & Councillor
Michael Akpata, Councillor, 519-969-7770
Mark Carrick, Councillor
Sue Desjarlais, Councillor, 519-969-7770
Jeff Renaud, Councillor, 519-969-7770
Anita Riccio-Spagnuolo, Councillor
Agatha Robertson, Clerk
Joe Millicia, Chief Administrative Officer, 519-969-7770
Dale Langlois, Treasurer
Peter Marra, Director, Public Works, 519-969-7770
Larry Silani, Director, Development & Strategic Initiatives, 519-969-7770
Dave Sutton, Fire Chief, 519-966-0744

Latchford

P.O. Box 10
10 Main St.
Latchford, ON P0J 1N0
Tel: 705-676-2416; *Fax:* 705-676-2121
www.latchford.ca
Municipal Type: Town
Incorporated: 1907; *Area:* 153.53 sq km
County or District: Timiskaming District; *Population in 2016:* 313
Provincial Electoral District(s): Timiskaming-Cochrane
Federal Electoral District(s): Nipissing-Timiskaming
Next Election: Oct. 24, 2022 (4 year terms)
George Lefebvre, Mayor
Jaime Allen, Clerk, 705-676-2416

Laurentian Hills

34465 Hwy. 17, Point Alexander, RR#1
Deep River, ON K0J 1P0
Tel: 613-584-3114; *Fax:* 613-584-3285
info@laurentianhills.ca
www.laurentianhills.ca
Municipal Type: Town
Incorporated: Jan. 1, 2000; *Area:* 642.03 sq km
County or District: Renfrew; *Population in 2016:* 2,961
Provincial Electoral District(s): Renfrew-Nipissing-Pembroke
Federal Electoral District(s): Renfrew-Nipissing-Pembroke
Next Election: Oct. 24, 2022 (4 year terms)
Note: Amalgamation of the United Townships of Rolph,
Buchanan, Wylie & McKay & the Village of Chalk River.
John Reinwald, Mayor
Sherry Batten, Chief Administrative Officer & Clerk

Laurentian Valley

460 Witt Rd., RR#4
Pembroke, ON K8A 6W5
Tel: 613-735-6291; *Fax:* 613-735-5820
info@lvtownship.ca
www.lvtownship.ca
Municipal Type: Township
Incorporated: Jan. 1, 2000; *Area:* 551.43 sq km
County or District: Renfrew; *Population in 2016:* 9,387
Provincial Electoral District(s): Renfrew-Nipissing-Pembroke
Federal Electoral District(s): Renfrew-Nipissing-Pembroke
Next Election: Oct. 24, 2022 (4 year terms)
Note: Amalgamation of the former Townships of
Stafford-Pembroke & Alice & Fraser.
Steve Bennett, Mayor
Dean Sauriol, Chief Administrative Officer & Clerk,
613-735-6291, Fax: 613-735-5820

Leamington

111 Erie St. North
Leamington, ON N8H 2Z3
Tel: 519-326-5761; *Fax:* 519-326-2481
info@leamington.ca
www.leamington.ca
Other Information: Public Works, Email:
publicworks@leamington.ca
Municipal Type: Municipality
Incorporated: 1874; *Area:* 262.01 sq km
County or District: Essex; *Population in 2016:* 27,595
Provincial Electoral District(s): Chatham-Kent-Leamington
Federal Electoral District(s): Chatham-Kent-Leamington
Next Election: Oct. 24, 2022 (4 year terms)
Note: Incorporated as a town in 1890. Restructuring occurred in
1999.
Hilda MacDonald, Mayor
Larry Verbeke, Deputy Mayor & Councillor
Bill Dunn, Councillor
John Hammond, Councillor
John Jacobs, Councillor
Paul Tiessen, Councillor
Tim Wilkinson, Councillor
Peter Neufeld, Chief Administrative Officer

Leeds & Grenville

#100, 25 Central Ave. West
Brockville, ON K6V 4N6
Tel: 613-342-3840; *Fax:* 613-342-2101
www.leedsgrenville.com
Other Information: Toll-Free Phone: 800-770-2170
Municipal Type: United County
Area: 3,382.89 sq km
Population in 2016: 100,546
Next Election: Oct. 24, 2022 (4 year terms)
Herb Scott, Councillor, Wards: Athens
Doug Malanka, Councillor, Wards: Augusta
Patrick Sayeau, Councillor, Wards: Edwardsburgh Cardinal
Brant Burrow, Councillor, Wards: Elizabethtown-Kitley
Roger Haley, Councillor, Wards: Front of Yonge
Corinna Smith-Gatcke, Councillor, Wards: Leeds & the
Thousand Islands

Doug Struthers, Councillor, Wards: Merrickville-Wolford
Nancy Peckford, Councillor, Wards: North Grenville
Arie Hoogenboom, Councillor, Wards: Rideau Lakes
Robin Jones, Councillor, Wards: Westport
Andy Brown, Chief Administrative Officer

Leeds & The Thousand Islands

P.O. Box 280
1233 Prince St.
Lansdowne, ON K0E 1L0
Tel: 613-659-2415; *Fax:* 613-659-3619
www.leeds1000islands.ca
Other Information: Toll-Free Phone: 866-220-2327
Municipal Type: Township
Incorporated: Jan. 1, 2001; *Area:* 612.45 sq km
County or District: Leeds & Grenville; *Population in 2016:* 9,465
Provincial Electoral District(s): Leeds-Grenville-Thousand
Islands and Rideau Lakes
Federal Electoral District(s): Leeds-Grenville-Thousand Islands
and Rideau Lakes
Next Election: Oct. 24, 2022 (4 year terms)
Note: Amalgamation of Front of Leeds & Lansdowne, Rear of
Leeds & Lansdowne & Front of Escott.
Corinna Smith-Gatcke, Mayor
Greg Borduas, Chief Administrative Officer, 613-659-2415

Limerick

89 Limerick Lake Rd., RR#2
Gilmour, ON K0L 1W0
Tel: 613-474-2863; *Fax:* 613-474-0478
assistant@township.limerick.on.ca
www.township.limerick.on.ca
Municipal Type: Township
Incorporated: 1887; *Area:* 205.37 sq km
County or District: Hastings; *Population in 2016:* 346
Provincial Electoral District(s): Hastings-Lennox and Addington
Federal Electoral District(s): Hastings-Lennox and Addington
Next Election: Oct. 24, 2022 (4 year terms)
Carl Stefanski, Reeve
Jennifer Trumble, Chief Administrative Officer & Clerk-Treasurer,
613-474-2863

Loyalist

P.O. Box 70
263 Main St.
Odessa, ON K0H 2H0
Tel: 613-386-7351; *Fax:* 613-386-3833
info@loyalist.ca
www.loyalisttownship.ca
Municipal Type: Township
Incorporated: 1998; *Area:* 341.02 sq km
County or District: Lennox & Addington; *Population in 2016:*
16,971
Provincial Electoral District(s): Hastings-Lennox and Addington
Federal Electoral District(s): Hastings-Lennox and Addington
Next Election: Oct. 24, 2022 (4 year terms)
Note: Amalgamation of the Townships of Ernestown, Amherst
Island & the Village of Bath.
Ric Bresee, Mayor
Jim Hegadorn, Deputy Mayor
Nathan Townend, Councillor, Wards: 1
Carol Parks, Councillor, Wards: 2
Mike Budarick, Councillor, Wards: 3
Ron Gordon, Councillor, Wards: 3
Penny Porter, Councillor, Wards: 3
Steven Silver, Chief Administrative Officer
Lorie McFarland, Director, Community & Customer Services
David Thompson, Director, Infrastructure Services
Murray Beckel, Chief Planner & Director, Planning &
Development Services
Fred Stephenson, Fire Chief

Lucan Biddulph

P.O. Box 190
270 Main St.
Lucan, ON N0M 2J0
Tel: 519-227-4491; *Fax:* 519-227-4998
www.lucanbiddulph.on.ca
Municipal Type: Township
Incorporated: Jan. 1, 1999; *Area:* 169.14 sq km
County or District: Middlesex; *Population in 2016:* 4,700
Provincial Electoral District(s): Lambton-Kent-Middlesex
Federal Electoral District(s): Lambton-Kent-Middlesex
Next Election: Oct. 24, 2022 (4 year terms)
Note: Amalgamation of the Village of Lucan and the Township of
Biddulph.
Cathy Burghardt-Jesson, Mayor
Ron Reymer, Chief Administrative Officer & Clerk, 519-227-4491

MacDonald, Meredith & Aberdeen Additional

P.O. Box 10
208 Church St.
Echo Bay, ON P0S 1C0
Tel: 705-248-2441; *Fax:* 705-248-3091
twpmacd@onlink.net
www.echobay.ca
Municipal Type: Township
Incorporated: 1899; *Area:* 161.73 sq km
County or District: Algoma District; *Population in 2016:* 1,609
Provincial Electoral District(s): Algoma-Manitoulin
Federal Electoral District(s): Algoma-Manitoulin-Kapuskasing
Next Election: Oct. 24, 2022 (4 year terms)
Lynn Watson, Mayor
Lynne Duguay, Clerk Administrator

Machar

P.O. Box 70
73 Municipal Rd. North
South River, ON P0A 1X0
Tel: 705-386-7741; *Fax:* 705-386-0765
www.machartownship.net
Municipal Type: Township
Area: 184.35 sq km
County or District: Parry Sound District; *Population in 2016:* 882
Provincial Electoral District(s): Parry Sound-Muskoka
Federal Electoral District(s): Parry Sound-Muskoka
Next Election: Oct. 24, 2022 (4 year terms)
Lynda Carleton, Mayor
Brenda Paul, AMCT, Clerk Administrator

Machin

P.O. Box 249
75 Spruce St.
Vermilion Bay, ON P0V 2V0
Tel: 807-227-2633; *Fax:* 807-227-5443
www.visitmachin.com
Municipal Type: Township
Area: 291.81 sq km
County or District: Kenora District; *Population in 2016:* 971
Provincial Electoral District(s): Kenora-Rainy River
Federal Electoral District(s): Kenora
Next Election: Oct. 24, 2022 (4 year terms)
Gord Griffiths, Mayor
Tammy Rob, Clerk-Treasurer

Madawaska Valley

P.O. Box 1000
85 Bay St.
Barry's Bay, ON K0J 1B0
Tel: 613-756-2747; *Fax:* 613-756-0553
info@madawaskavalley.ca
www.madawaskavalley.ca
Other Information: Toll-Free Phone: 866-222-8699
Municipal Type: Township
Incorporated: Jan. 1, 2001; *Area:* 672.51 sq km
County or District: Renfrew; *Population in 2016:* 4,123
Provincial Electoral District(s): Renfrew-Nipissing-Pembroke
Federal Electoral District(s): Renfrew-Nipissing-Pembroke
Next Election: Oct. 24, 2022 (4 year terms)
Note: Amalgamation of Barry's Bay Village, Radcliffe Township &
Sherwood, Jones & Burns Township.
Kim Love, Mayor
Suzanne Klatt, Chief Administrative Officer & Clerk,
613-756-2747, Fax: 613-756-0553

Madoc

P.O. Box 503
15651 Hwy. 62, RR#2
Madoc, ON K0K 2K0
Tel: 613-473-2677; *Fax:* 613-473-5580
www.madoc.ca
Municipal Type: Township
Incorporated: 1850; *Area:* 277.97 sq km
County or District: Hastings; *Population in 2016:* 2,078
Provincial Electoral District(s): Hastings-Lennox and Addington
Federal Electoral District(s): Hastings-Lennox and Addington
Next Election: Oct. 24, 2022 (4 year terms)
Loyde Blackburn, Reeve
Cassandra Boniface, Clerk-Treasurer

Magnetawan, Municipality of

P.O. Box 70
4304 Hwy. 520
Magnetawan, ON P0A 1P0
Tel: 705-387-3947; *Fax:* 705-387-4875
info@magnetawan.com
www.magnetawan.com
Municipal Type: Municipality
Incorporated: July 4, 1997; *Area:* 531.53 sq km
County or District: Parry Sound District; *Population in 2016:*
1,390

Provincial Electoral District(s): Parry Sound-Muskoka
Federal Electoral District(s): Parry Sound-Muskoka
Next Election: Oct. 24, 2022 (4 year terms)
Sam Dunnett, Mayor
Andrew Farnsworth, Clerk-Administrator, 705-387-3947

Malahide
87 John St. South
Aylmer, ON N5H 2C3
Tel: 519-773-5344; *Fax:* 519-773-5334
malahide@malahide.ca
www.malahide.ca
Municipal Type: Township
Incorporated: Jan. 1, 1998; *Area:* 395.05 sq km
County or District: Elgin; *Population in 2016:* 9,292
Provincial Electoral District(s): Elgin-Middlesex-London
Federal Electoral District(s): Elgin-Middlesex-London
Next Election: Oct. 24, 2022 (4 year terms)
Note: Amalgamation of the Township of Malahide, Village of
Springfield & Township of South Dorchester.
Dave Mennill, Mayor, 519-773-8850
Michelle M. Casavecchia-Somers, Chief Administrative Officer &
Clerk, 519-773-5344

Manitoulin
c/o Manitoulin-Sudbury District Svs. Board
210 Mead Blvd.
Espanola, ON P5E 1R9
Tel: 705-862-7850
www.msdsb.net
Municipal Type: District
Area: 3,107.23 sq km
Population in 2016: 13,255
Provincial Electoral District(s): Algoma-Manitoulin
Federal Electoral District(s): Algoma-Manitoulin-Kapuskasing
Note: Incorporates the towns of Gore Bay, & Northeastern
Manitoulin & the Islands; communities in the townships of
Assiginack, Barrie Island, Billing, Burpe & Mills, Central
Manitoulin, Cockburn Island, Gordon, & Tehkummah; & First
Nations reserves

Manitouwadge
1 Mississauga Rd.
Manitouwadge, ON P0T 2C0
Tel: 807-826-3227; *Fax:* 807-826-4592
admin@manitouwadge.ca
www.manitouwadge.ca
Municipal Type: Township
Area: 352.07 sq km
County or District: Thunder Bay District; *Population in 2016:*
1,937
Provincial Electoral District(s): Algoma-Manitoulin
Federal Electoral District(s): Thunder Bay-Superior North
Next Election: Oct. 24, 2022 (4 year terms)
John MacEachern, Mayor
Margaret Hartling, Chief Administrative Officer &
Clerk-Treasurer, 807-826-3227

Mapleton
P.O. Box 160
7275 Sideroad 16
Drayton, ON N0G 1P0
Tel: 519-638-3313; *Fax:* 519-638-5113
www.mapleton.ca
Other Information: Toll-Free Phone: 800-385-7248
Municipal Type: Township
Incorporated: Jan. 1, 1999; *Area:* 534.87 sq km
County or District: Wellington; *Population in 2016:* 10,527
Provincial Electoral District(s): Perth-Wellington
Federal Electoral District(s): Perth-Wellington
Next Election: Oct. 24, 2022 (4 year terms)
Note: Amalgamation of the Townships of Maryborough & Peel &
the Village of Drayton.
Gregg Davidson, Mayor
Manny Baron, Chief Administrative Officer, 519-638-3313

Marathon
P.O. Box TM
4 Hemlo Dr.
Marathon, ON P0T 2E0
Tel: 807-229-1340; *Fax:* 807-229-1999
info@marathon.ca
www.marathon.ca
Municipal Type: Town
Area: 170.54 sq km
County or District: Thunder Bay District; *Population in 2016:*
3,273
Provincial Electoral District(s): Thunder Bay-Superior North
Federal Electoral District(s): Thunder Bay-Superior North
Next Election: Oct. 24, 2022 (4 year terms)
Richard Dumas, Mayor

Daryl Skworchinski, Chief Administrative Officer & Clerk,
807-229-1340

Markstay-Warren, Municipality of
P.O. Box 79
21 Main St. South
Markstay, ON P0M 2G0
Tel: 705-853-4536; *Fax:* 705-853-4964
info@markstay-warren.ca
www.markstay-warren.ca
Other Information: Toll-Free Phone: 866-710-1065
Municipal Type: Municipality
Incorporated: Jan. 1, 1999; *Area:* 512.78 sq km
County or District: Sudbury District; *Population in 2016:* 2,656
Provincial Electoral District(s): Timiskaming-Cochrane
Federal Electoral District(s): Nickel Belt
Next Election: Oct. 24, 2022 (4 year terms)
Note: Amalgamation of the Towns of Warren, Markstay & the
Townships of Awrey, Street, Hawley, Loughrin & Henry.
Stephen Salonin, Mayor
Celine Anderson, Chief Administrative Officer & Clerk,
705-853-4536

Marmora & Lake, Municipality of
P.O. Box 459
12 Bursthall St.
Marmora, ON K0K 2M0
Tel: 613-472-2629; *Fax:* 613-472-5330
www.marmoraandlake.ca
Other Information: Toll-Free Phone: 866-518-2282
Municipal Type: Municipality
Area: 557.08 sq km
County or District: Hastings; *Population in 2016:* 3,953
Provincial Electoral District(s): Hastings-Lennox and Addington
Federal Electoral District(s): Hastings-Lennox and Addington
Next Election: Oct. 24, 2022 (4 year terms)
Jan O'Neill, Mayor
Typhany Choinard, Chief Adminsitrative Officer, 613-472-2629

Matachewan
P.O. Box 177
Matachewan, ON P0K 1M0
Tel: 705-565-2274; *Fax:* 705-565-2564
township@ntl.sympatico.ca
www.matachewan.com
Municipal Type: Township
Area: 543.58 sq km
County or District: Timiskaming District; *Population in 2016:* 225
Provincial Electoral District(s): Timiskaming-Cochrane
Federal Electoral District(s): Timmins-James Bay
Next Election: Oct. 24, 2022 (4 year terms)
Anne Commando-Dubé, Mayor
Anne Kmyta, Chief Administrative Officer & Clerk-Treasurer

Mattawa
P.O. Box 390
160 Water St.
Mattawa, ON P0H 1V0
Tel: 705-744-5611; *Fax:* 705-744-0104
info@mattawa.ca
mattawa.ca
Municipal Type: Town
Area: 3.66 sq km
County or District: Nipissing District; *Population in 2016:* 1,993
Provincial Electoral District(s): Nipissing
Federal Electoral District(s): Nipissing-Timiskaming
Next Election: Oct. 24, 2022 (4 year terms)
Dean Backer, Mayor
Raymond Belanger, Chief Administrative Officer & Treasurer

Mattawan
P.O. Box 610
947 Hwy. 533
Mattawa, ON P0H 1V0
Tel: 705-744-5680; *Fax:* 705-744-4141
mattawan@xplornet.ca
Municipal Type: Township
Area: 201.00 sq km
County or District: Nipissing District; *Population in 2016:* 161
Provincial Electoral District(s): Nipissing
Federal Electoral District(s): Nipissing-Timiskaming
Next Election: Oct. 24, 2022 (4 year terms)
Peter Murphy, Mayor
Deborah Miller, Clerk-Treasurer

Mattice-Val Côté
P.O. Box 129
500 Hwy. 11
Mattice, ON P0L 1T0
Tel: 705-364-6511; *Fax:* 705-364-6431
matticevalcote.ca

Municipal Type: Township
Area: 414.00 sq km
County or District: Cochrane District; *Population in 2016:* 648
Provincial Electoral District(s): Mushkegowuk-James Bay
Federal Electoral District(s): Algoma-Manitoulin-Kapuskasing
Next Election: Oct. 24, 2022 (4 year terms)
Marc Dupuis, Mayor
Guylaine Coulombe, Chief Administrative Officer & Clerk

McDougall
5 Barager Blvd., RR#3
McDougall, ON P2A 2W9
Tel: 705-342-5252; *Fax:* 705-342-5573
thazzard@mcdougall.ca
www.mcdougall.ca
Municipal Type: Municipality
Incorporated: May 1, 1872; *Area:* 268.48 sq km
County or District: Parry Sound District; *Population in 2016:*
2,702
Provincial Electoral District(s): Parry Sound-Muskoka
Federal Electoral District(s): Parry Sound-Muskoka
Next Election: Oct. 24, 2022 (4 year terms)
Dale Robinson, Mayor
Tim Hunt, Chief Administrative Officer

McGarry
P.O. Box 99
27 Webster St.
Virginiatown, ON P0K 1X0
Tel: 705-634-2145; *Fax:* 705-634-2700
admin@mcgarry.ca
www.mcgarry.ca
Municipal Type: Township
Area: 86.67 sq km
County or District: Timiskaming District; *Population in 2016:* 609
Provincial Electoral District(s): Timiskaming-Cochrane
Federal Electoral District(s): Timmins-James Bay
Next Election: Oct. 24, 2022 (4 year terms)
Matt Reimer, Mayor
Sylvie Côté, Clerk-Treasurer

McKellar
P.O. Box 69
701 Hwy. 124
McKellar, ON P0G 1C0
Tel: 705-389-2842; *Fax:* 705-389-1244
www.township.mckellar.on.ca
Municipal Type: Township
Incorporated: 1873; *Area:* 180.88 sq km
County or District: Parry Sound District; *Population in 2016:*
1,111
Provincial Electoral District(s): Parry Sound-Muskoka
Federal Electoral District(s): Parry Sound-Muskoka
Next Election: Oct. 24, 2022 (4 year terms)
Peter Hopkins, Reeve
Tammy Wylie, AMCT, Clerk Administrator, 705-389-2842

McMurrich / Monteith
P.O. Box 70
31 William St.
Sprucedale, ON P0A 1Y0
Tel: 705-685-7901; *Fax:* 705-685-7393
www.mcmurrichmonteith.com
Municipal Type: Township
Area: 277.92 sq km
County or District: Parry Sound District; *Population in 2016:* 824
Provincial Electoral District(s): Parry Sound-Muskoka
Federal Electoral District(s): Parry Sound-Muskoka
Next Election: Oct. 24, 2022 (4 year terms)
Ron Walton, Reeve
Cheryl Marshall, Clerk

McNab / Braeside
2508 Russett Dr., RR#2
Arnprior, ON K7S 3G8
Tel: 613-623-5756; *Fax:* 613-623-9138
info@mcnabbraeside.com
www.mcnabbraeside.com
Other Information: Toll-Free Phone: 800-957-4621
Municipal Type: Township
Incorporated: Jan. 1, 1998; *Area:* 255.76 sq km
County or District: Renfrew; *Population in 2016:* 7,178
Provincial Electoral District(s): Renfrew-Nipissing-Pembroke
Federal Electoral District(s): Renfrew-Nipissing-Pembroke
Next Election: Oct. 24, 2022 (4 year terms)
Note: Amalgamation of Braeside Village & McNab Township.
Thomas Peckett, Mayor, 613-623-5756
Lindsey Lee, Chief Administrative Officer & Clerk, 613-623-5756

Meaford
21 Trowbridge St. West
Meaford, ON N4L 1A1
Tel: 519-538-1060; *Fax:* 519-538-5240
www.meaford.ca
Other Information: Alternate Fax: 519-538-1556
Municipal Type: Municipality
Incorporated: Jan. 1, 2001; *Area:* 588.57 sq km
County or District: Grey; *Population in 2016:* 10,991
Provincial Electoral District(s): Bruce-Grey-Owen Sound
Federal Electoral District(s): Bruce-Grey-Owen Sound
Next Election: Oct. 24, 2022 (4 year terms)
Note: Formerly the Town of Georgian Highlands. Amalgamation of Sydenham, St. Vincent & Meaford.
Barb Clumpus, Mayor
Shirley Keaveney, Deputy Mayor
Steve Bartley, Councillor
Tony Bell, Councillor
Harley Greenfield, Councillor
Ross Kentner, Councillor
Paul Vickers, Councillor
Matt Smith, Clerk & Director, Legislative Services
Robert Armstrong, Chief Administrative Officer & Director, Development Services
Rick Carefoot, Chief Building Official
John deHooge, Fire Chief

Melancthon
157101 Hwy. 10, RR#6
Melancthon, ON L9V 2E6
Tel: 519-925-5525; *Fax:* 519-925-1110
info@melancthontownship.ca
www.melancthontownship.ca
Municipal Type: Township
Incorporated: Jan. 1, 1853; *Area:* 310.79 sq km
County or District: Dufferin; *Population in 2016:* 3,008
Provincial Electoral District(s): Dufferin-Caledon
Federal Electoral District(s): Dufferin-Caledon
Next Election: Oct. 24, 2022 (4 year terms)
Darren White, Mayor
Denise B. Holmes, Chief Administrative Officer & Clerk

Merrickville-Wolford
P.O. Box 340
317 Brock St. West
Merrickville, ON K0G 1N0
Tel: 613-269-4791; *Fax:* 613-269-3095
reception@merrickville-wolford.ca
www.merrickville-wolford.ca
Municipal Type: Village
Area: 214.55 sq km
County or District: Leeds-Grenville; *Population in 2016:* 3,067
Provincial Electoral District(s): Leeds-Grenville-Thousand Islands and Rideau Lakes
Federal Electoral District(s): Leeds-Grenville-Thousand Islands and Rideau Lakes
Next Election: Oct. 24, 2022 (4 year terms)
Doug Struthers, Mayor
Arie Hoogenboom, Acting Chief Administrative Officer & Clerk-Treasurer, 613-269-4791

Middlesex Centre
10227 Ilderton Rd., RR#2
Ilderton, ON N0M 2A0
Tel: 519-666-0190; *Fax:* 519-666-0271
cormans@middlesexcentre.on.ca
www.middlesexcentre.on.ca
Other Information: Toll-Free Phone: 800-220-8968
Municipal Type: Township
Incorporated: Jan. 1, 1998; *Area:* 588.11 sq km
County or District: Middlesex; *Population in 2016:* 17,262
Provincial Electoral District(s): Lambton-Kent-Middlesex
Federal Electoral District(s): Lambton-Kent-Middlesex
Next Election: Oct. 24, 2022 (4 year terms)
Note: Amalgamation of the former Townships of Delaware, Lobo, & London.
Aina DeViet, Mayor
John Brennan, Deputy Mayor
Debbie Heffernan, Councillor, Wards: 1
Wayne Shipley, Councillor, Wards: 2
Hugh Aerts, Councillor, Wards: 3
Derek Silva, Councillor, Wards: 4
Brad Scott, Councillor, Wards: 5
Ann Wright, Clerk
Michael Di Lullo, Chief Administrative Officer
Robert Cascaden, Director, Public Works & Engineering
Arnie Marsman, Chief Building Official & Director, Planning & Development Services
Colin Toth, Fire Chief

Midland
575 Dominion Ave.
Midland, ON L4R 1R2
Tel: 705-526-4275; *Fax:* 705-526-9971
admin@midland.ca
www.midland.ca
Other Information: TTY: 705-526-4276, ext. 2824
Municipal Type: Town
Area: 35.34 sq km
County or District: Simcoe; *Population in 2016:* 16,864
Provincial Electoral District(s): Simcoe North
Federal Electoral District(s): Simcoe North
Next Election: Oct. 24, 2022 (4 year terms)
Stewart Strathearn, Mayor
Mike Ross, Deputy Mayor
Jim Downer, Councillor, Wards: 1
Jonathan G. Main, Councillor, Wards: 1
Beth Prost, Councillor, Wards: 1
Bill Gordon, Councillor, Wards: 2
Carole McGinn, Councillor, Wards: 2
Cody Oschefski, Councillor, Wards: 2
Cher Cunningham, Councillor, Wards: 3
Karen Desroches, Clerk
David Denault, Chief Administrative Officer
Michael Jeremy, Chief Financial Officer
Terry Paquette, Chief Building Official
Paul Ryan, Fire Chief

Milton
150 Mary St.
Milton, ON L9T 6Z5
Tel: 905-878-7252; *Fax:* 905-878-6995
www.milton.ca
Municipal Type: Town
Incorporated: 1857; *Area:* 363.22 sq km
County or District: Halton Regional Municipality; *Population in 2016:* 110,128
Provincial Electoral District(s): Milton
Federal Electoral District(s): Milton
Next Election: Oct. 24, 2022 (4 year terms)
Gordon A. Krantz, Mayor, 905-878-7252
Colin Best, Regional Councillor, Wards: 1
Rick Malbeouf, Regional Councillor, Wards: 2
Mike Cluett, Regional Councillor, Wards: 3
Zeeshan Hamid, Regional Councillor, Wards: 4
Kristina Tesser Derksen, Town Councillor, Wards: 1
John Challinor, Town Councillor, Wards: 2
Rick Di Lorenzo, Town Councillor, Wards: 3
Sameera Ali, Town Councillor, Wards: 4
Troy McHarg, Clerk
Andrew Siltala, Chief Administrative Officer, 905-878-7252
Glen Cowan, Chief Financial Officer
John Brophy, Acting Commissioner, Engineering Services
Kristene Scott, Commissioner, Community Services
Kevin Foster, Acting Fire Chief

Minden Hills
P.O. Box 359
7 Milne St.
Minden, ON K0M 2K0
Tel: 705-286-1260; *Fax:* 705-286-4917
admin@mindenhills.ca
www.mindenhills.ca
Other Information: Treasury/Bldg./By-law/Planning, Fax: 705-286-6005
Municipal Type: Township
Area: 878.27 sq km
County or District: Haliburton; *Population in 2016:* 6,088
Provincial Electoral District(s): Haliburton-Kawartha Lakes-Brock
Federal Electoral District(s): Haliburton-Kawartha Lakes-Brock
Next Election: Oct. 24, 2022 (4 year terms)
Brent Devolin, Mayor
Lorrie Blanchard, CAO/Treasurer, 705-286-1260

Minto
5941 Hwy. 89
Harriston, ON N0G 1Z0
Tel: 519-338-2511; *Fax:* 519-338-2005
town.minto.on.ca
Municipal Type: Town
Area: 300.69 sq km
County or District: Wellington; *Population in 2016:* 8,671
Provincial Electoral District(s): Perth-Wellington
Federal Electoral District(s): Perth-Wellington
Next Election: Oct. 24, 2022 (4 year terms)
George Bridge, Mayor
Bill White, Chief Administrative Officer & Clerk, 519-338-2511

Mono
347209 Mono Centre Rd., RR#1
Mono, ON L9W 6S3
Tel: 519-941-3599; *Fax:* 519-941-9490
info@townofmono.com
www.townofmono.com
Municipal Type: Town
Incorporated: June 1, 1999; *Area:* 277.83 sq km
County or District: Dufferin; *Population in 2016:* 8,609
Provincial Electoral District(s): Dufferin-Caledon
Federal Electoral District(s): Dufferin-Caledon
Next Election: Oct. 24, 2022 (4 year terms)
Laura Ryan, Mayor
Mark Early, Chief Administrative Officer & Clerk, 519-941-3599

Montague
P.O. Box 755
6547 Roger Stevens Dr.
Smiths Falls, ON K7A 4W6
Tel: 613-283-7478; *Fax:* 613-283-3112
info@township.montague.on.ca
www.township.montague.on.ca
Municipal Type: Township
Area: 279.66 sq km
County or District: Lanark; *Population in 2016:* 3,761
Provincial Electoral District(s): Lanark-Frontenac-Kingston
Federal Electoral District(s): Lanark-Frontenac-Kingston
Next Election: Oct. 24, 2022 (4 year terms)
Bill Dobson, Reeve
Jasmin Ralph, Clerk Administrator

Moonbeam
P.O. Box 330
53 St. Aubin Ave.
Moonbeam, ON P0L 1V0
Tel: 705-367-2244; *Fax:* 705-367-2610
moonbeam@moonbeam.ca
www.moonbeam.ca
Municipal Type: Township
Area: 235.58 sq km
County or District: Cochrane District; *Population in 2016:* 1,231
Provincial Electoral District(s): Mushkegowuk-James Bay
Federal Electoral District(s): Algoma-Manitoulin-Kapuskasing
Next Election: Oct. 24, 2022 (4 year terms)
Nicole Fortier Levesque, Mayor
Carole Gendron, Clerk-Treasurer, 705-367-2244

Moosonee
P.O. Box 727
5 First St.
Moosonee, ON P0L 1Y0
Tel: 705-336-2993; *Fax:* 705-336-2426
www.moosonee.ca
Municipal Type: Town
Area: 546.72 sq km
County or District: Cochrane District; *Population in 2016:* 1,481
Provincial Electoral District(s): Mushkegowuk-James Bay
Federal Electoral District(s): Timmins-James Bay
Next Election: Oct. 24, 2022 (4 year terms)
Wayne Taipale, Mayor
Shannon MacGillivray, Chief Administrative Officer

Morley
P.O. Box 40
Stratton, ON P0W 1N0
Tel: 807-483-5455; *Fax:* 807-483-5882
townshipofmorley@gmail.com
www.townshipofmorley.ca
Municipal Type: Township
Incorporated: 1903; *Area:* 390.61 sq km
County or District: Rainy River District; *Population in 2016:* 481
Provincial Electoral District(s): Kenora-Rainy River
Federal Electoral District(s): Thunder Bay-Rainy River
Next Election: Oct. 24, 2022 (4 year terms)
George Heyens, Reeve
Teresa Desserre, CMO, Clerk-Treasurer

Morris-Turnberry
P.O. Box 310
41342 Morris Rd., RR#4
Brussels, ON N0G 1H0
Tel: 519-887-6137; *Fax:* 519-887-6424
mail@morristurnberry.ca
www.morristurnberry.ca
Municipal Type: Municipality
Incorporated: Jan. 1, 2001; *Area:* 376.56 sq km
County or District: Huron; *Population in 2016:* 3,496
Provincial Electoral District(s): Huron-Bruce
Federal Electoral District(s): Huron-Bruce
Next Election: Oct. 24, 2022 (4 year terms)
Note: Amalgamation of the Township of Morris & the Township of Turnberry.

Jamie Heffer, Mayor
Nancy Michie, Administrator & Clerk-Treasurer, 519-887-6137

Mulmur
758070 2nd Line East, RR#2
Mulmur, ON L0M 1M0
Tel: 705-466-3341; *Fax:* 705-466-2922
info@mulmur.ca
mulmur.ca
Other Information: Toll-Free Phone: 866-472-0417 (In 519 area code)
Municipal Type: Township
Incorporated: 1851; *Area:* 286.77 sq km
County or District: Dufferin; *Population in 2016:* 3,478
Provincial Electoral District(s): Dufferin-Caledon
Federal Electoral District(s): Dufferin-Caledon
Next Election: Oct. 24, 2022 (4 year terms)
Janet Horner, Mayor
Terry M. Horner, AMCT, Chief Administrative Officer & Clerk, 705-466-3341

Muskoka Lakes
P.O. Box 129
1 Bailey St.
Port Carling, ON P0B 1J0
Tel: 705-765-3156; *Fax:* 705-765-6755
www.muskokalakes.ca
Municipal Type: Township
Incorporated: Jan. 1971; *Area:* 794.26 sq km
County or District: Muskoka Dist. Mun.; *Population in 2016:* 6,588
Provincial Electoral District(s): Parry Sound-Muskoka
Federal Electoral District(s): Parry Sound-Muskoka
Next Election: Oct. 24, 2022 (4 year terms)
Phil Harding, Mayor
Steve McDonald, Chief Administrative Officer

Nairn & Hyman
64 McIntyre St.
Nairn Centre, ON P0M 2L0
Tel: 705-869-4232
information@nairncentre.ca
nairncentre.ca
Municipal Type: Township
Incorporated: 1896; *Area:* 160.82 sq km
County or District: Sudbury District; *Population in 2016:* 342
Provincial Electoral District(s): Algoma-Manitoulin
Federal Electoral District(s): Algoma-Manitoulin-Kapuskasing
Next Election: Oct. 24, 2022 (4 year terms)
Laurier P. Falldien, Mayor
Robert Deschene, Chief Administrative Officer & Clerk-Treasurer

The Nation
958 Rte. 500 West
Casselman, ON K0A 1M0
Tel: 613-764-5444; *Fax:* 613-764-3310
www.nationmun.ca
Other Information: Toll-Free Phone: 800-475-2855
Municipal Type: Municipality
Incorporated: Jan. 1, 1998; *Area:* 658.32 sq km
County or District: Prescott & Russell; *Population in 2016:* 12,808
Provincial Electoral District(s): Glengarry-Prescott-Russell
Federal Electoral District(s): Glengarry-Prescott-Russell
Next Election: Oct. 24, 2022 (4 year terms)
Note: Amalgamation of the Townships of Cambridge, South Plantagenet, Caledonia & the Village of St. Isidore.
François St. Amour, Mayor
Marie-Noelle Lanthier, Councillor, Wards: 1
Alain Mainville, Councillor, Wards: 2
Danik Forgues, Councillor, Wards: 3
Francis Biere, Councillor, Wards: 4
Josée Brizard, Clerk
Cécile Maisonneuve, Treasurer
Marc Legault, Director, Public Works
Todd Bayly, Chief Building Official
Tobias Hovey, Fire Chief

Neebing, Municipality of
4766 Hwy. 61
Neebing, ON P7L 0B5
Tel: 807-474-5331; *Fax:* 807-474-5332
neebing@neebing.org
www.neebing.org
Municipal Type: Municipality
Area: 877.27 sq km
County or District: Thunder Bay District; *Population in 2016:* 2,055
Provincial Electoral District(s): Thunder Bay-Atikokan
Federal Electoral District(s): Thunder Bay-Rainy River
Next Election: Oct. 24, 2022 (4 year terms)
Erwin Butikofer, Mayor

Rosalie Evans, Solicitor-Clerk

New Tecumseth
Town Administration Centre
P.O. Box 910
10 Wellington St. East
Alliston, ON L9R 1A1
Tel: 705-435-6219; *Fax:* 705-435-2873
newtecumseth.ca
Other Information: Alternative Phone: 905-729-0057
Municipal Type: Town
Incorporated: Jan. 1991; *Area:* 274.21 sq km
County or District: Simcoe; *Population in 2016:* 32,242
Provincial Electoral District(s): Simcoe-Grey
Federal Electoral District(s): Simcoe-Grey
Next Election: Oct. 24, 2022 (4 year terms)
Rick Milne, Mayor
Richard Norcross, Deputy Mayor
Wayne Noye, Councillor, Wards: 1
Michael Beattie, Councillor, Wards: 2
Paul Foster, Councillor, Wards: 3
Fran Sainsbury, Councillor, Wards: 4
Donna Jebb, Councillor, Wards: 5
Stephanie Maclellan, Councillor, Wards: 6
Shira Harrison McIntyre, Councillor, Wards: 7
Alan Lacey, Councillor, Wards: 8
Cindy Maher, Clerk & Director, Administrative Services
Blaine Parkin, Chief Administrative Officer, 705-435-3900
Bruce Hoppe, Director, Planning & Development
Chad Horan, Director, Public Works
John Henry, Treasurer & Director, Finance
Rick Vatri, Director, Engineering
Dan Heydon, Fire Chief

Newbury
P.O. Box 130
22910 Hagerty Rd.
Newbury, ON N0L 1Z0
Tel: 519-693-4941; *Fax:* 519-693-4340
office@newbury.ca
www.newbury.ca
Municipal Type: Village
Incorporated: 1873; *Area:* 1.77 sq km
County or District: Middlesex; *Population in 2016:* 466
Provincial Electoral District(s): Lambton-Kent-Middlesex
Federal Electoral District(s): Lambton-Kent-Middlesex
Next Election: Oct. 24, 2022 (4 year terms)
Diane Brewer, Reeve
Betty D. Gordon, Clerk-Treasurer

Niagara-on-the-Lake
P.O. Box 100
1593 Four Mile Creek Rd.
Virgil, ON L0S 1T0
Tel: 905-468-3266; *Fax:* 905-468-2959
info@notl.org
www.notl.org
Municipal Type: Town
Area: 132.81 sq km
County or District: Niagara Reg. Mun.; *Population in 2016:* 17,511
Provincial Electoral District(s): Niagara Falls
Federal Electoral District(s): Niagara Falls
Next Election: Oct. 24, 2022 (4 year terms)
Betty Disero, Mayor
Gary Zalepa Jr., Regional Councillor
Norm Arsenault, Councillor
Allan Bisback, Councillor
Gary Burroughs, Councillor
Clare Cameron, Councillor
Wendy Cheropita, Councillor
Stuart McCormack, Councillor
Erwin Wiens, Councillor
John Wiens, Councillor
Peter Todd, Town Clerk
Sheldon Randall, Interim Chief Administrative Officer
Craig Larmour, Director, Community & Development Services
Kevin Turcotte, Acting Director, Operations
Jeff Vyse, Manager, Public Works
Rob Grimwood, Fire Chief

Nipigon
P.O. Box 160
52 Front St.
Nipigon, ON P0T 2J0
Tel: 807-887-3135; *Fax:* 807-887-3564
info@nipigon.net
www.nipigon.net
Other Information: E-mail, Recreation Inquiries:
nipigonrec@shaw.ca
Municipal Type: Township
Area: 109.11 sq km

County or District: Thunder Bay District; *Population in 2016:* 1,642
Provincial Electoral District(s): Thunder Bay-Superior North
Federal Electoral District(s): Thunder Bay-Superior North
Next Election: Oct. 24, 2022 (4 year terms)
Richard Harvey, Mayor
Lindsay Mannila, Chief Administrative Officer, 807-887-3135

Nipissing
45 Beatty St.
Nipissing, ON P0H 1W0
Tel: 705-724-2144; *Fax:* 705-724-5385
www.nipissingtownship.com
Municipal Type: Township
Area: 393.80 sq km
County or District: Parry Sound District; *Population in 2016:* 1,707
Provincial Electoral District(s): Nipissing
Federal Electoral District(s): Nipissing-Timiskaming
Next Election: Oct. 24, 2022 (4 year terms)
Tom Piper, Mayor, 705-492-4890
Charles H. Barton, Chief Administrative Officer & Clerk

Nipissing
District Social Services Administration Bd.
P.O. Box 750
200 McIntyre St. East
North Bay, ON P1B 8J8
info@dnssab.on.ca
www.dnssab.on.ca
Municipal Type: District
Area: 17,103.78 sq km
Population in 2016: 83,150
Mark King, Chair, District of Nipissing Social Services Administration Board
Catherine Matheson, Chief Administrative Officer, District of Nipissing Social Services Administration Board, 705-474-2151, Fax: 705-474-7155

North Algona Wilberforce
1091 Shaw Woods Rd., RR#1
Eganville, ON K0J 1T0
Tel: 613-628-2080; *Fax:* 613-628-3341
naw@nalgonawil.com
www.nalgonawil.com
Municipal Type: Township
Incorporated: Jan. 1, 1999; *Area:* 378.98 sq km
County or District: Renfrew; *Population in 2016:* 2,915
Provincial Electoral District(s): Renfrew-Nipissing-Pembroke
Federal Electoral District(s): Renfrew-Nipissing-Pembroke
Next Election: Oct. 24, 2022 (4 year terms)
Note: Amalgamation of North Algona Township & Wilberforce Township.
James Brose, Mayor
Andrew Sprunt, Chief Administrative Officer & Operations Manager, 613-628-2080

North Dumfries
P.O. Box 1060
2958 Greenfield Rd.
Ayr, ON N0B 1E0
Tel: 519-632-8800; *Fax:* 519-632-8700
township@northdumfries.ca
www.northdumfries.ca
Other Information: TTY: 519-621-9595
Municipal Type: Township
Area: 187.43 sq km
County or District: Waterloo Regional Municipality; *Population in 2016:* 10,215
Provincial Electoral District(s): Cambridge
Federal Electoral District(s): Cambridge
Next Election: Oct. 24, 2022 (4 year terms)
Sue Foxton, Mayor, 519-632-8800
Andrew McNeely, Chief Administrative Officer, 519-632-8800

North Dundas
P.O. Box 489
636 St. Lawrence St.
Winchester, ON K0C 2K0
Tel: 613-774-2105; *Fax:* 613-774-5699
info@northdundas.com
www.northdundas.com
Other Information: Toll-Free Phone: 800-795-0437
Municipal Type: Township
Incorporated: Jan. 1, 1998; *Area:* 503.08 sq km
County or District: Stormont, Dundas & Glengarry; *Population in 2016:* 11,278
Provincial Electoral District(s): Stormont-Dundas-South Glengarry
Federal Electoral District(s): Stormont-Dundas-South Glengarry
Next Election: Oct. 24, 2022 (4 year terms)

Municipal Type: Town
Incorporated: 1970; *Area:* 126.43 sq km
County or District: Niagara Reg. Mun.; *Population in 2016:*
17,110
Provincial Electoral District(s): Niagara West
Federal Electoral District(s): Niagara West
Next Election: Oct. 24, 2022 (4 year terms)
Marvin Junkin, Mayor
Marianne Stewart, Councillor, Wards: 1
Ron Kore, Councillor, Wards: 2
John Wink, Councillor, Wards: 2
Lisa Haun, Councillor, Wards: 3
Robert Hildebrandt, Councillor, Wards: 3
Diana Huson, Regional Councillor
Nancy J. Bozzato, Clerk
David Cribbs, Chief Administrative Officer, 905-892-2607
Jason Marr, Director, Public Works, 905-892-2607
Barb Wiens, Director, Planning & Development, 905-892-2607
Bob Lymburner, Fire Chief, 905-892-2607

Penetanguishene
P.O. Box 5009
10 Robert St. West
Penetanguishene, ON L9M 2G2
Tel: 705-549-7453; *Fax:* 705-549-3743
www.penetanguishene.ca
Other Information: Public Works, Phone: 705-549-7992
Municipal Type: Town
Incorporated: Feb. 22, 1882; *Area:* 25.58 sq km
County or District: Simcoe; *Population in 2016:* 8,962
Provincial Electoral District(s): Simcoe North
Federal Electoral District(s): Simcoe North
Next Election: Oct. 24, 2022 (4 year terms)
Douglas R. Leroux, Mayor
Jeff Lees, Chief Administrative Officer

Perry
P.O. Box 70
1695 Emsdale Rd.
Emsdale, ON P0A 1J0
Tel: 705-636-5941; *Fax:* 705-636-5759
info@townshipofperry.ca
www.townshipofperry.ca
Municipal Type: Township
Area: 187.22 sq km
County or District: Parry Sound District; *Population in 2016:*
2,454
Provincial Electoral District(s): Parry Sound-Muskoka
Federal Electoral District(s): Parry Sound-Muskoka
Next Election: Oct. 24, 2022 (4 year terms)
Norm Hofstetter, Mayor, 705-788-3151
Beth Morton, Clerk & Planning Administrator

Perth
Town Hall
80 Gore St. East
Perth, ON K7H 1H9
Tel: 613-267-3311; *Fax:* 613-267-5635
www.perth.ca
Municipal Type: Town
Area: 12.25 sq km
County or District: Lanark; *Population in 2016:* 5,930
Provincial Electoral District(s): Lanark-Frontenac-Kingston
Federal Electoral District(s): Lanark-Frontenac-Kingston
Next Election: Oct. 24, 2022 (4 year terms)
John Fenik, Mayor, 613-267-3311
John deRosenroll, Chief Administrative Officer, 613-326-3129

Perth East
P.O. Box 455
25 Mill St. East
Milverton, ON N0K 1M0
Tel: 519-595-2800; *Fax:* 519-595-2801
www.pertheast.ca
Municipal Type: Township
Area: 712.14 sq km
County or District: Perth; *Population in 2016:* 12,261
Provincial Electoral District(s): Perth-Wellinton
Federal Electoral District(s): Perth-Wellington
Next Election: Oct. 24, 2022 (4 year terms)
Note: Amalgamation of North Easthope Township, South
Easthope Township, Ellice Township, Village of Milverton &
Mornington Township.
Rhonda Ehgoetz, Mayor
Hugh McDermid, Deputy Mayor
Amanda Brodhagen, Councillor, Wards: Ellice
Jerry Smith, Councillor, Wards: Milverton
Jeremy Matheson, Councillor, Wards: Mornington
Daryl Herlick, Councillor, Wards: North Easthope
Andrew MacAlpine, Councillor, Wards: South Easthope
Theresa Campbell, Municipal Clerk, 519-595-2800
Glenn Schwendinger, Chief Administrative Officer, 519-595-2800

Rhonda Fischer, Treasurer, 519-595-2800
Jon Crummer, Acting Chief Building Official, 519-595-2800
Wes Kuepfer, Manager, Public Works & Parks, 519-595-2800
Bill Hunter, Fire Chief, 519-595-2800

Perth South
3191 Rd. 122
St Pauls, ON N0K 1V0
Tel: 519-271-0619; *Fax:* 519-271-0647
www.perthsouth.ca
Other Information: Toll-Free Phone: 866-771-0619
Municipal Type: Township
Area: 393.14 sq km
County or District: Perth; *Population in 2016:* 3,810
Provincial Electoral District(s): Perth-Wellington
Federal Electoral District(s): Perth-Wellington
Next Election: Oct. 24, 2022 (4 year terms)
Note: Amalgamation of Blanshard Township & Downie Township.
Robert Wilhelm, Mayor, 519-225-2304
Lizet Scott, Clerk, 519-271-0619

Petrolia
P.O. Box 1270
411 Greenfield St.
Petrolia, ON N0N 1R0
Tel: 519-882-2350; *Fax:* 519-882-3373
petrolia@petrolia.ca
town.petrolia.on.ca
Other Information: After Hours Emergency, Phone:
519-882-2351
Municipal Type: Town
Area: 12.68 sq km
County or District: Lambton; *Population in 2016:* 5,742
Provincial Electoral District(s): Sarnia-Lambton
Federal Electoral District(s): Sarnia-Lambton
Next Election: Oct. 24, 2022 (4 year terms)
Brad Loosley, Mayor
Rick Charlebois, Chief Administrative Officer & Treasurer

Pickle Lake
P.O. Box 340
2 Anne St. South
Pickle Lake, ON P0V 3A0
Tel: 807-928-2034; *Fax:* 807-928-2708
reception@picklelake.org
www.picklelake.ca
Other Information: Toll-Free Phone: 800-565-9189
Municipal Type: Township
Incorporated: Dec. 1980; *Area:* 252.18 sq km
County or District: Kenora District; *Population in 2016:* 388
Provincial Electoral District(s): Kiiwetinoong
Federal Electoral District(s): Kenora
Next Election: Oct. 24, 2022 (4 year terms)
Dwight Monck, Mayor
Jamie Hussey, Acting Clerk-Treasurer, 807-928-2034

Plummer Additional
38 Railway Cres., RR#2
Bruce Mines, ON P0R 1C0
Tel: 705-785-3479; *Fax:* 705-785-3135
plumtwsp@onlink.net
www.plummertownship.ca
Municipal Type: Township
Area: 220.30 sq km
County or District: Algoma District; *Population in 2016:* 660
Provincial Electoral District(s): Algoma-Manitoulin
Federal Electoral District(s): Algoma-Manitoulin-Kapuskasing
Next Election: Oct. 24, 2022 (4 year terms)
Beth West, Mayor
Vicky Goertzen-Cooke, Clerk-Treasurer

Plympton-Wyoming
P.O. Box 250
546 Niagara St.
Wyoming, ON N0N 1T0
Tel: 519-845-3939; *Fax:* 519-845-0597
www.plympton-wyoming.com
Other Information: Toll-Free Phone: 877-313-3939
Municipal Type: Town
Incorporated: Jan. 1, 2001; *Area:* 318.78 sq km
County or District: Lambton; *Population in 2016:* 7,795
Provincial Electoral District(s): Sarnia-Lambton
Federal Electoral District(s): Sarnia-Lambton
Next Election: Oct. 24, 2022 (4 year terms)
Note: Amalgamation of the Village of Wyoming & the Township
of Plympton.
Lonny Napper, Mayor
Carolyn Tripp, Chief Administrative Officer

Point Edward
Municipal Office
135 Kendall St.
Point Edward, ON N7V 4G6
Tel: 519-337-3021; *Fax:* 519-337-5963
info@villageofpointedward.com
www.villageofpointedward.com
Municipal Type: Village
Incorporated: 1878; *Area:* 3.28 sq km
County or District: Lambton; *Population in 2016:* 2,037
Provincial Electoral District(s): Sarnia-Lambton
Federal Electoral District(s): Sarnia-Lambton
Next Election: Oct. 24, 2022 (4 year terms)
Bev Hand, Mayor
Jim Burns, Chief Administrative Officer & Clerk

Port Hope
Town Hall
56 Queen St.
Port Hope, ON L1A 3Z9
Tel: 905-885-4544; *Fax:* 905-885-7698
admin@porthope.ca
www.porthope.ca
Municipal Type: Municipality
Incorporated: March 6, 1834; *Area:* 278.87 sq km
County or District: Northumberland; *Population in 2016:* 16,753
Provincial Electoral District(s): Northumberland-Peterborough
South
Federal Electoral District(s): Northumberland-Peterborough
South
Next Election: Oct. 24, 2022 (4 year terms)
Bob Sanderson, Mayor
Les Andrews, Councillor, Wards: 1
Laurie Carr, Councillor, Wards: 1
Jeff Lees, Councillor, Wards: 1
Wendy Meadows, Councillor, Wards: 1
John Bickle, Councillor, Wards: 2
Vicki Mink, Councillor, Wards: 2
Brian Gilmer, Clerk & Director, Corporate Services,
905-885-4544
David Baxter, Director, Finance, 905-885-4544
Jim McCormack, Director, Parks, Recreation & Culture,
905-885-8760
Ken Andrus, Chief Building Official, 905-885-2431
C. Ryan Edgar, Fire Chief, 905-753-2230

Powassan, Municipality of
P.O. Box 250
466 Main St.
Powassan, ON P0H 1Z0
Tel: 705-724-2813; *Fax:* 705-724-5533
info@powassan.net
www.powassan.net
Municipal Type: Municipality
Incorporated: Nov. 30, 1904; *Area:* 224.56 sq km
County or District: Parry Sound District; *Population in 2016:*
3,455
Provincial Electoral District(s): Nipissing
Federal Electoral District(s): Nipissing-Timiskaming
Next Election: Oct. 24, 2022 (4 year terms)
Peter McIsaac, Mayor, 705-491-0374
Maureen Lang, Clerk-Treasurer, 795-724-2813, Fax:
705-724-5533

Prescott
P.O. Box 160
360 Dibble St. West
Prescott, ON K0E 1T0
Tel: 613-925-2812; *Fax:* 613-925-4381
info@prescott.ca
www.prescott.ca
Other Information: admin@prescott.ca
Municipal Type: Town
Area: 4.93 sq km
County or District: Leeds & Grenville; *Population in 2016:* 4,222
Provincial Electoral District(s): Leeds-Grenville-Thousand
Islands and Rideau Lakes
Federal Electoral District(s): Leeds-Grenville-Thousand Islands
and Rideau Lakes
Next Election: Oct. 24, 2022 (4 year terms)
Brett Todd, Mayor
Matthew Armstrong, Chief Administrative Officer & Treasurer,
613-925-2812

Prescott & Russell
P.O. Box 303
59 Court St.
L'Orignal, ON K0B 1K0
Tel: 613-675-4661; *Fax:* 613-675-2519
www.prescott-russell.on.ca
Other Information: Toll-Free Phone: 800-667-6307

Municipal Type: United County
Incorporated: 1820; *Area:* 2,004.47 sq km
Population in 2016: 89,333
Next Election: Oct. 24, 2022 (4 year terms)
Stéphane Sarrazin, Councillor, Wards: Alfred and Plantagenet
Daniel Lafleur, Councillor, Wards: Casselman
Normand Riopel, Councillor, Wards: Champlain
Robert Kirby, Councillor, Wards: East Hawkesbury
Paula Assaly, Councillor, Wards: Hawkesbury
François St-Amour, Councillor, Wards: The Nation
Pierre Leroux, Councillor, Wards: Russell
Stéphane P. Parisien, Chief Administrative Officer & Clerk,
613-675-4661

Prince
3042 2nd Line West
Prince Township, ON P6A 6K4
Tel: 705-779-2992; *Fax:* 705-779-2725
www.princetwp.ca
Municipal Type: Township
Area: 85.30 sq km
County or District: Algoma District; *Population in 2016:* 1,010
Provincial Electoral District(s): Algoma Manitoulin
Federal Electoral District(s): Sault Ste Marie
Next Election: Oct. 24, 2022 (4 year terms)
Ken Lamming, Mayor, 705-779-2875
Peggy Greco, Chief Administrative Officer & Clerk-Treasurer,
705-779-2992

Puslinch
7404 Wellington Rd. 34, RR#3
Puslinch, ON N0B 2J0
Tel: 519-763-1226; *Fax:* 519-763-5846
admin@puslinch.ca
www.puslinch.ca
Municipal Type: Township
Incorporated: Jan. 1, 1850; *Area:* 214.62 sq km
County or District: Wellington; *Population in 2016:* 7,336
Provincial Electoral District(s): Wellington-Halton Hills
Federal Electoral District(s): Wellington-Halton Hills; Guelph
Next Election: Oct. 24, 2022 (4 year terms)
James Seeley, Mayor
Karen Landry, Chief Administrative Officer & Clerk-Treasurer,
519-763-1226

Rainy River
P.O. Box 488
201 Atwood Ave.
Rainy River, ON P0W 1L0
Tel: 807-852-3978; *Fax:* 807-852-3553
rainyriver@tbaytel.net
www.rainyriver.ca
Other Information: Alternate Phone: 807-852-3244
Municipal Type: Town
Incorporated: 1904; *Area:* 3.11 sq km
County or District: Rainy River District; *Population in 2016:* 807
Provincial Electoral District(s): Kenora-Rainy River
Federal Electoral District(s): Thunder Bay-Rainy River
Next Election: Oct. 24, 2022 (4 year terms)
Deborah Ewald, Mayor
Veldron Vogan, Chief Administrative Officer

Rainy River
District Social Services Administration Bd.
450 Scott St.
Fort Frances, ON P9A 1H2
Tel: 807-274-5349; *Fax:* 807-274-0678
www.rrdssab.ca
Other Information: Toll-Free Phone: 800-265-5349
Municipal Type: District
Area: 15,486.75 sq km
Population in 2016: 20,110
Vacant, Chair, Rainy River District Social Services
Administration Board
Dan McCormick, Chief Administrative Officer, Rainy River
District Social Services Administration Board

Ramara
Ramara Administration Building
P.O. Box 130
2297 Hwy. 12
Brechin, ON L0K 1B0
Tel: 705-484-5374; *Fax:* 705-484-0441
ramara@ramara.ca
www.ramara.ca
Other Information: Toll-Free Phone: 800-663-4054 (for 689
exchange)
Municipal Type: Township
Area: 418.82 sq km
County or District: Simcoe; *Population in 2016:* 9,488
Provincial Electoral District(s): Simcoe North

Federal Electoral District(s): Simcoe North
Next Election: Oct. 24, 2022 (4 year terms)
Basil Clarke, Mayor
Janice McKinnon, Chief Administrative Officer, 705-484-5374

Red Lake
P.O. Box 1000
2 Fifth St.
Balmertown, ON P0V 1C0
Tel: 807-735-2096; *Fax:* 866-681-2954
municipality@redlake.ca
redlake.ca
Municipal Type: Municipality
Incorporated: July 1, 1998; *Area:* 610.06 sq km
County or District: Kenora District; *Population in 2016:* 4,107
Provincial Electoral District(s): Kiiwetinoong
Federal Electoral District(s): Kenora
Next Election: Oct. 24, 2022 (4 year terms)
Note: Amalgamation of the former Unorganized Territory of
Madsen, the Township of Red Lake, & the Township of Golden.
Fred Mota, Mayor
Mark Vermette, Chief Administrative Officer, 807-735-2096

Red Rock
P.O. Box 447
42 Salls St.
Red Rock, ON P0T 2P0
Tel: 807-886-2245; *Fax:* 807-886-2793
info@redrocktownship.com
www.redrocktownship.com
Other Information: Phone, Public Works: 807-886-2524
Municipal Type: Township
Area: 62.21 sq km
County or District: Thunder Bay District; *Population in 2016:* 895
Provincial Electoral District(s): Thunder Bay-Superior North
Federal Electoral District(s): Thunder Bay-Superior North
Next Election: Oct. 24, 2022 (4 year terms)
Gary Nelson, Mayor, 807-886-2503
Nancy Gladun, Chief Administrative Officer

Renfrew
127 Raglan St. South
Renfrew, ON K7V 1P8
Tel: 613-432-4848; *Fax:* 613-432-7245
info@renfrew.ca
www.renfrew.ca
Municipal Type: Town
Area: 12.78 sq km
County or District: Renfrew; *Population in 2016:* 8,223
Provincial Electoral District(s): Renfrew-Nipissing-Pembroke
Federal Electoral District(s): Renfrew-Nipissing-Pembroke
Next Election: Oct. 24, 2022 (4 year terms)
Don Eady, Mayor, 613-432-4848
Kim R. Bulmer, Town Clerk, 613-432-4848

Rideau Lakes
1439 County Rd. 8
Delta, ON K0E 1G0
Tel: 613-928-2251; *Fax:* 613-928-3097
info@twprideaulakes.on.ca
www.twprideaulakes.on.ca
Other Information: Toll-Free Phone: 800-928-2250
Municipal Type: Township
Incorporated: Jan. 1, 1998; *Area:* 729.22 sq km
County or District: Leeds-Grenville; *Population in 2016:* 10,326
Provincial Electoral District(s): Leeds-Grenville-Thousand
Islands and Rideau Lakes
Federal Electoral District(s): Leeds-Grenville-Thousand Islands
and Rideau Lakes
Next Election: Oct. 24, 2022 (4 year terms)
Note: Amalgamation of the former Townships of North Crosby,
South Crosby, Bastard & South Burgess, South Elmsley & the
Village of Newboro.
Arie Hoogenboom, Mayor
Carolyn Bresee, Councillor, Wards: 1
Cathy Livingston, Councillor, Wards: 1
Jeff Banks, Councillor, Wards: 2
Marcia Maxwell, Councillor, Wards: 2
Joan Delaney, Councillor, Wards: 3
Claire Gunnewiek, Councillor, Wards: 3
Bob Lavoie, Councillor, Wards: 4
Ronald J. Pollard, Councillor, Wards: 4
Mary Ellen Truelove, Clerk, 613-928-2251
Mike Dwyer, Chief Administrative Officer, 613-928-2251
Cynthia Laprade, Treasurer, 613-928-2251
Susan Dunfield, Manager, Community & Leisure Services,
613-928-2251
Mel Bursey, Chief Building Official, 613-928-2251
Dan Chant, Roads Coordinator & Drainage Superintendent,
613-928-2251
Steve Fournier, Interim Fire Chief, 613-928-2251

Russell
717 Notre Dame St.
Embrun, ON K0A 1W1
Tel: 613-443-3066; *Fax:* 613-443-1042
www.russell.ca
Municipal Type: Township
Area: 199.11 sq km
County or District: Prescott & Russell; *Population in 2016:*
16,520
Provincial Electoral District(s): Glengarry-Prescott-Russell
Federal Electoral District(s): Glengarry-Prescott-Russell
Next Election: Oct. 24, 2022 (4 year terms)
Pierre Leroux, Mayor
Andre Brisson, Councillor
Jamie Laurin, Councillor
Cindy Saucier, Councillor
Mike Tarnowski, Councillor
Joanne Camiré-Laflamme, Municipal Clerk
Jean Leduc, Chief Administrative Officer, 613-443-3066
Bruce Armstrong, Fire Chief, 613-445-3326

Ryerson
28 Midlothian Rd., RR#1
Burks Falls, ON P0A 1C0
Tel: 705-382-3232; *Fax:* 705-382-3286
admin@ryersontownship.ca
www.ryersontownship.ca
Municipal Type: Township
Area: 187.92 sq km
County or District: Parry Sound District; *Population in 2016:* 648
Provincial Electoral District(s): Parry Sound-Muskoka
Federal Electoral District(s): Parry Sound-Muskoka
Next Election: Oct. 24, 2022 (4 year terms)
George Sterling, Reeve
Judy Kosowan, Chief Administrative Officer & Clerk-Treasurer

Sables-Spanish Rivers
P.O. Box 5
Site 1, 11 Birch Lake Rd. RR#3
Massey, ON P0P 1P0
Tel: 705-865-2646; *Fax:* 705-865-2736
inquiries@sables-spanish.ca
www.sables-spanish.ca
Municipal Type: Township
Incorporated: July 1998; *Area:* 815.21 sq km
County or District: Sudbury District; *Population in 2016:* 3,214
Provincial Electoral District(s): Algoma-Manitoulin
Federal Electoral District(s): Algoma-Manitoulin-Kapuskasing
Next Election: Oct. 24, 2022 (4 year terms)
Leslie Gamble, Mayor, 705-865-2655
Kim Sloss, Clerk-Administrator, 705-865-2646

St.-Charles, Municipality of
P.O. Box 70
2 King St. East
St-Charles, ON P0M 2W0
Tel: 705-867-2032; *Fax:* 705-867-5789
www.stcharlesontario.ca
Other Information: Toll-Free Phone: 877-867-2032
Municipal Type: Municipality
Area: 321.75 sq km
County or District: Sudbury District; *Population in 2016:* 1,269
Provincial Electoral District(s): Timiskaming-Cochrane
Federal Electoral District(s): Nickel Belt
Next Election: Oct. 24, 2022 (4 year terms)
Paul Schoppmann, Mayor, 705-867-2032
Denis Turcot, Chief Administrative Officer, 705-867-2032

St. Clair
Civic Centre
1155 Emily St.
Mooretown, ON N0N 1M0
Tel: 519-867-2021; *Fax:* 519-867-5509
webmaster@stclairtownship.ca
stclairtownship.ca
Municipal Type: Township
Area: 619.17 sq km
County or District: Lambton; *Population in 2016:* 14,086
Provincial Electoral District(s): Sarnia-Lambton
Federal Electoral District(s): Sarnia-Lambton
Next Election: Oct. 24, 2022 (4 year terms)
Steve Arnold, Mayor, 519-381-7440
Steve Miller, Deputy Mayor
Pat Brown, Councillor, Wards: 1
Jim DeGurse, Councillor, Wards: 1
Tracy Kingston, Councillor, Wards: 1
Rose Atkins, Councillor, Wards: 2
Bill Myers, Councillor, Wards: 2
Jeff Baranek, City Clerk, 519-867-2021
John Rodey, MCIP, RPP, Chief Administrative Officer,
519-867-2021, Fax: 519-867-5509
Walt Anderson, Fire Chief

St. Joseph

P.O. Box 187
1669 Arthur St.
Richards Landing, ON P0R 1J0
Tel: 705-246-2625; *Fax:* 705-246-3142
www.stjosephtownship.com
Municipal Type: Township
Area: 129.12 sq km
County or District: Algoma District; *Population in 2016:* 1,240
Provincial Electoral District(s): Algoma-Manitoulin
Federal Electoral District(s): Algoma-Manitoulin-Kapuskasing
Next Election: Oct. 24, 2022 (4 year terms)
Jody Wildman, Mayor, 705-297-0592
Carol O. Trainor, A.M.C.T., Clerk Administrator

St. Marys

P.O. Box 998
175 Queen St. East, 2nd Fl.
St Marys, ON N4X 1B6
Tel: 519-284-2340; *Fax:* 519-284-3881
www.townofstmarys.com
Municipal Type: Town
Area: 12.45 sq km
County or District: Perth; *Population in 2016:* 7,265
Provincial Electoral District(s): Perth-Wellington
Federal Electoral District(s): Perth-Wellington
Next Election: Oct. 24, 2022 (4 year terms)
Al Strathdee, Mayor, 519-284-2340
Brent Kittmer, Chief Administrative Officer & Clerk, 519-284-2340

Saugeen Shores

P.O. Box 820
600 Tomlinson Dr.
Port Elgin, ON N0H 2C0
Tel: 519-832-2008; *Fax:* 519-832-2140
www.saugeenshores.ca
Municipal Type: Town
Area: 171.05 sq km
County or District: Bruce; *Population in 2016:* 13,715
Provincial Electoral District(s): Huron-Bruce
Federal Electoral District(s): Huron-Bruce
Next Election: Oct. 24, 2022 (4 year terms)
Luke Charbonneau, Mayor
Don Matheson, Deputy Mayor
Mike Myatt, Vice-Deputy Mayor
Kristan Shrider, Councillor, Wards: Port Elgin
Jami Smith, Councillor, Wards: Port Elgin
Matt Carr, Councillor, Wards: Saugeen
Dave Myette, Councillor, Wards: Saugeen
Cheryl Grace, Councillor, Wards: Southampton
John Rich, Councillor, Wards: Southampton
Linda White, Clerk, 519-832-2008
David Smith, Chief Administrative Officer, 519-832-2008
Adam Stanley, Manager, Engineering Services, 519-832-2008
Phil Eagleson, Fire Chief, 519-389-6120

Schreiber

P.O. Box 40
204 Alberta St.
Schreiber, ON P0T 2S0
Tel: 807-824-2711; *Fax:* 807-824-3231
info@schreiber.ca
www.schreiber.ca
Municipal Type: Township
Area: 36.80 sq km
County or District: Thunder Bay District; *Population in 2016:* 1,059
Provincial Electoral District(s): Thunder Bay-Superior North
Federal Electoral District(s): Thunder Bay-Superior North
Next Election: Oct. 24, 2022 (4 year terms)
Dave Hamilton, Mayor
Don McArthur, Chief Administrative Officer & Clerk, 807-824-2711

Scugog

P.O. Box 780
181 Perry St.
Port Perry, ON L9L 1A7
Tel: 905-985-7346; *Fax:* 905-985-9914
mail@scugog.ca
www.scugog.ca
Municipal Type: Township
Area: 474.71 sq km
County or District: Durham Regional Municipality; *Population in 2016:* 21,617
Provincial Electoral District(s): Durham
Federal Electoral District(s): Durham
Next Election: Oct. 24, 2022 (4 year terms)
Bobbie Drew, Mayor
Wilma Wotten, Regional Councillor
Ian McDougall, Councillor, Wards: 1

Janna Guido, Councillor, 905-809-7345, Wards: 2
Angus Ross, Councillor, Wards: 3
Deborah Kiezebrink, Councillor, Wards: 4
Lance Brown, Councillor, Wards: 5
Paul Allore, Chief Administrative Officer, 905-985-7346
Dianne Valentim, Treasurer & Director, Finance
Carol Coleman, Director, Community Services
Kevin Heritage, Director, Development Services
Mark Berney, Fire Chief, 905-985-2384

Seguin

5 Humphrey Dr., RR#2
Seguin, ON P2A 2W8
Tel: 705-732-4300; *Fax:* 705-732-6347
info@seguin.ca
www.seguin.ca
Other Information: Toll-Free Phone: 877-473-4846
Municipal Type: Township
Incorporated: May 8, 1997; *Area:* 595.68 sq km
County or District: Parry Sound District; *Population in 2016:* 4,304
Provincial Electoral District(s): Parry Sound-Muskoka
Federal Electoral District(s): Parry Sound-Muskoka
Next Election: Oct. 24, 2022 (4 year terms)
Ann MacDiarmid, Mayor
Chris Madej, Chief Administrative Officer, 705-732-4300

Selwyn

P.O. Box 270
1310 Centre Line, RR#4
Bridgenorth, ON K0L 1H0
Tel: 705-292-9507; *Fax:* 705-292-8964
info@selwyntownship.ca
www.selwyntownship.ca
Municipal Type: Township
Area: 315.69 sq km
County or District: Peterborough; *Population in 2016:* 17,060
Provincial Electoral District(s): Peterborough-Kawartha
Federal Electoral District(s): Peterborough-Kawartha
Next Election: Oct. 24, 2022 (4 year terms)
Andy Mitchell, Mayor
Sherry Senis, Deputy Mayor
Donna Ballantyne, Councillor, Wards: Ennismore
Anita Locke, Councillor, Wards: Lakefield
Gerry Herron, Councillor, Wards: Smith
Angela Chittick, Clerk
Janice Lavalley, Chief Administrative Officer
R. Lane Vance, Treasurer & Manager, Financial Services
Mike Richardson, Manager, Recreation
Rick Dunford, Manager, Public Works
Robert Lamarre, Manager, Building & Planning
Gord Jopling, Fire Chief

Severn

P.O. Box 159
1024 Hurlwood Lane
Orillia, ON L3V 6J3
Tel: 705-325-2315; *Fax:* 705-327-5818
info@townshipofsevern.com
www.townshipofsevern.com
Municipal Type: Township
Incorporated: Jan. 1, 1994; *Area:* 549.75 sq km
County or District: Simcoe; *Population in 2016:* 13,477
Provincial Electoral District(s): Simcoe North
Federal Electoral District(s): Simcoe North
Next Election: Oct. 24, 2022 (4 year terms)
Mike Burkett, Mayor
Jane Dunlop, Deputy Mayor
Mark Taylor, Councillor, Wards: 1
Judith Cox, Councillor, Wards: 2
John Betsworth, Councillor, Wards: 3
Ron Stevens, Councillor, Wards: 4
Sarah Valiquette-Thompson, Councillor, Wards: 5
Laurie Kennard, Chief Administrative Officer, 705-325-2315, Wards: 5
Andrew Plunkett, Treasurer & Director, Corporate Services, 705-325-2315
Derek Burke, Director, Public Works, 705-325-2315
Andrea Woodrow, Director, Planning & Development, 705-325-2315
Tim Cranney, Fire Chief, 705-325-2315

Shelburne

Town of Shelburne Municipal Office
203 Main St. East
Shelburne, ON L0N 1S0
Tel: 519-925-2600; *Fax:* 519-925-6134
www.townofshelburne.on.ca
Municipal Type: Town
Incorporated: March 22, 1879; *Area:* 6.56 sq km
County or District: Dufferin; *Population in 2016:* 8,126
Provincial Electoral District(s): Dufferin-Caledon

Federal Electoral District(s): Dufferin-Caledon
Next Election: Oct. 24, 2022 (4 year terms)
Note: Incorporated as a town on Dec. 31, 1976.
Wade Mills, Mayor
Denyse Morrissey, Chief Administrative Officer, 519-925-2600

Shuniah

420 Leslie Ave.
Thunder Bay, ON P7A 1X8
Tel: 807-683-4545; *Fax:* 807-683-6982
shuniah@shuniah.org
www.shuniah.org
Other Information: Toll-Free Phone: 855-683-4545
Municipal Type: Municipality
Incorporated: 1873; *Area:* 570.99 sq km
County or District: Thunder Bay District; *Population in 2016:* 2,798
Provincial Electoral District(s): Thunder Bay-Superior North
Federal Electoral District(s): Thunder Bay-Superior North
Next Election: Oct. 24, 2022 (4 year terms)
Wendy Landry, Mayor, 807-346-9330
Paul Greenwood, Chief Administrative Officer, 807-683-4543

Sioux Lookout, Municipality of

P.O. Box 158
25-5th Ave.
Sioux Lookout, ON P8T 1A4
Tel: 807-737-2700
admin@siouxlookout.ca
www.siouxlookout.ca
Municipal Type: Municipality
Incorporated: 1912; *Area:* 378.12 sq km
County or District: Kenora District; *Population in 2016:* 5,272
Provincial Electoral District(s): Kiiwetinoong
Federal Electoral District(s): Kenora
Next Election: Oct. 24, 2022 (4 year terms)
Doug Lawrance, Mayor
Ann Mitchell, Chief Administrative Officer, 807-737-2700

Sioux Narrows-Nestor Falls

P.O. Box 417
5521 Hwy. 71
Sioux Narrows, ON P0X 1N0
Tel: 807-226-5241; *Fax:* 807-226-5712
www.snnf.ca
Municipal Type: Township
Area: 1,223.12 sq km
County or District: Kenora District; *Population in 2016:* 567
Provincial Electoral District(s): Kenora-Rainy River
Federal Electoral District(s): Kenora
Next Election: Oct. 24, 2022 (4 year terms)
Norbert Dufresne, Mayor
Wanda Kabel, Chief Administrative Officer

Smiths Falls

77 Beckwith St. North
Smiths Falls, ON K7A 2B8
Tel: 613-283-4124
info@smithsfalls.ca
www.smithsfalls.ca
Municipal Type: Town
Incorporated: 1854; *Area:* 9.66 sq km
County or District: Lanark; *Population in 2016:* 8,780
Provincial Electoral District(s): Lanark-Frontenac-Kingston
Federal Electoral District(s): Lanark-Frontenac-Kingston
Next Election: Oct. 24, 2022 (4 year terms)
Note: Incorporated as a town on Jan. 1, 1883. In Dec. 1902, the Town of Smiths Falls became the Separated Town of Smiths Falls.
Shawn James Pankow, Mayor
Malcom Morris, Chief Administrative Officer, 613-283-4124

Smooth Rock Falls

P.O. Box 249
142 First St.
Smooth Rock Falls, ON P0L 2B0
Tel: 705-338-2717; *Fax:* 705-338-2584
townhall@townsrf.ca
www.smoothrockfalls.ca
Municipal Type: Town
Incorporated: 1929; *Area:* 200.10 sq km
County or District: Cochrane District; *Population in 2016:* 1,330
Provincial Electoral District(s): Mushkegowuk-James Bay
Federal Electoral District(s): Algoma-Manitoulin-Kapuskasing
Next Election: Oct. 24, 2022 (4 year terms)
Michel Arseneault, Mayor
Luc Denault, Chief Administrative Officer & Director of Economic Development, 705-338-2717

South Algonquin
P.O. Box 217
7 - 3rd Ave.
Whitney, ON K0J 2M0
Tel: 613-637-2650; *Fax:* 613-637-5368
info@southalgonquin.ca
www.southalgonquin.ca
Other Information: Toll-Free Phone: 888-307-3187
Municipal Type: Township
Area: 873.43 sq km
County or District: Nipissing District; *Population in 2016:* 1,096
Provincial Electoral District(s): Renfrew-Nipissing-Pembroke
Federal Electoral District(s): Renfrew-Nipissing-Pembroke
Next Election: Oct. 24, 2022 (4 year terms)
Jane A.E. Dumas, Mayor, 613-637-5261
Holly Hayes, Chief Administrative Officer & Clerk-Treasurer,
613-637-2650, Fax: 613-637-5368

South Bruce
P.O. Box 540
21 Gordon St. East
Teeswater, ON N0G 2S0
Tel: 519-392-6623; *Fax:* 519-392-6266
www.town.southbruce.on.ca
Municipal Type: Municipality
Incorporated: 1999; *Area:* 487.48 sq km
County or District: Bruce; *Population in 2016:* 5,639
Provincial Electoral District(s): Huron-Bruce
Federal Electoral District(s): Huron-Bruce
Next Election: Oct. 24, 2022 (4 year terms)
Note: Amalgamation of the Village of Mildmay, the Township of
Carrick, the Village of Teeswater, & the Township of Culross.
Robert Buckle, Mayor
Leanne Martin, Chief Administrative Officer & Clerk

South Bruce Peninsula
P.O. Box 310
315 George St.
Wiarton, ON N0H 2T0
Tel: 519-534-1400; *Fax:* 519-534-4862
admin@southbrucepeninsula.com
www.southbrucepeninsula.com
Other Information: Toll-Free Phone: 877-534-1400
Municipal Type: Town
Area: 531.9 sq km
County or District: Bruce; *Population in 2016:* 8,416
Provincial Electoral District(s): Bruce-Grey-Owen Sound
Federal Electoral District(s): Bruce-Grey-Owen Sound
Next Election: Oct. 24, 2022 (4 year terms)
Janice Jackson, Mayor, 519-422-2552
Brad McRoberts, Chief Administrative Officer, 519-534-1400

South Dundas
P.O. Box 160
4296 County Rd. 31
Williamsburg, ON K0C 2H0
Tel: 613-535-2673; *Fax:* 613-535-2099
mail@southdundas.com
www.southdundas.com
Other Information: Toll-Free Phone: 800-265-0619
Municipal Type: Township
Area: 521.06 sq km
County or District: Stormont, Dundas & Glengarry; *Population in 2016:* 10,833
Provincial Electoral District(s): Stormont-Dundas-South
Glengarry
Federal Electoral District(s): Stormont-Dundas-South Glengarry
Next Election: Oct. 24, 2022 (4 year terms)
Steven Byvelds, Mayor
Kirsten Gardner, Deputy Mayor
Donald William Lewis, Councillor
Archie Mellan, Councillor
Lloyd Wells, Councillor
Brenda Brunt, Clerk
Shannon Geraghty, Chief Administrative Officer
Sarah McMillan, Treasurer
Jeff Hyndman, Director, Transportation
Nicole Lowey, Chief Building Official
Cameron Morehouse, Fire Chief

South Frontenac
P.O. Box 100
4432 George St.
Sydenham, ON K0H 2T0
Tel: 613-376-3027; *Fax:* 613-376-6657
www.southfrontenac.net
Other Information: Toll-Free Phone: 800-559-5862
Municipal Type: Township
Incorporated: Jan. 1, 1998; *Area:* 971.56 sq km
County or District: Frontenac; *Population in 2016:* 18,646
Provincial Electoral District(s): Lanark-Frontenac-Kingston

Federal Electoral District(s): Lanark-Frontenac-Kingston
Next Election: Oct. 24, 2022 (4 year terms)
Ron Vandewal, Mayor
Pat Barr, Councillor, Wards: Bedford
Alan Revill, Councillor, Wards: Bedford
Randy Ruttan, Councillor, Wards: Loughborough
Ross Sutherland, Councillor, Wards: Loughborough
Ray Leonard, Councillor, Wards: Portland
Doug Morey, Councillor, Wards: Portland
Norm Roberts, Councillor, Wards: Storrington
Ronald Sleeth, Councillor, Wards: Storrington
Neil Carbone, Chief Administrative Officer, 613-376-3027
Louise Fragnito, Treasurer, 613-376-3027
Mark Segsworth, Manager, Public Works, 613-376-3027
Darcy Knott, Fire Chief, 613-376-3027

South Glengarry
6 Oak St.
Lancaster, ON K0C 1N0
Tel: 613-347-1166
info@southglengarry.com
www.southglengarry.com
Municipal Type: Township
Incorporated: Jan. 1, 1998; *Area:* 605.36 sq km
County or District: Stormont, Dundas & Glengarry; *Population in 2016:* 13,150
Provincial Electoral District(s): Stormont-Dundas-South
Glengarry
Federal Electoral District(s): Stormont-Dundas-South Glengarry
Next Election: Oct. 24, 2022 (4 year terms)
Frank Prevost, Mayor
Lyle Warden, Deputy Mayor
Stephanie Jaworski, Councillor
Martin Lang, Councillor
Sam McDonell, Councillor
Kelli Campeau, Clerk, 613-347-1166
Tim Mills, Chief Administrative Officer, 613-347-1166
Lachlan McDonald, Treasurer & Manager, Corporate Services,
613-347-1166
Ewen MacDonald, General Manager, Infrastructure Services,
613-347-1166, Fax: 613-347-3411
Gary Poupart, Chief Building Official & Director, Development,
613-347-1166
Dave Robertson, Fire Chief, Development, 613-347-2500

South Huron
P.O. Box 759
322 Main St. South
Exeter, ON N0M 1S6
Tel: 519-235-0310; *Fax:* 519-235-3304
info@southhuron.ca
www.southhuron.ca
Other Information: Toll-Free Phone: 877-204-0747
Municipal Type: Municipality
Incorporated: 2001; *Area:* 425.41 sq km
County or District: Huron; *Population in 2016:* 10,096
Provincial Electoral District(s): Huron-Bruce
Federal Electoral District(s): Huron-Bruce
Next Election: Oct. 24, 2022 (4 year terms)
George Finch, Mayor
Jim Dietrich, Deputy Mayor
Dianne Faubert, Councillor, Wards: 1
Marissa Vaughan, Councillor, Wards: 1
Aaron Neeb, Councillor, Wards: 2
Barb Willard, Councillor, Wards: 2
Ted Oke, Councillor, Wards: 3
Dan Best, Chief Administrative Officer, 519-235-0310
Don Giberson, Director, Infrastructure & Development
Sandy Becker, Manager, Financial Services
Scott Currie, Manager, Community Services
Dwayne McNab, Chief Building Official & Manager, Development
Services
Jeremy Becker, Fire Chief

South River
P.O. Box 310
63 Marie St.
South River, ON P0A 1X0
Tel: 705-386-2573; *Fax:* 705-386-0702
info@southriverontario.com
www.southriverontario.com
Municipal Type: Village
Incorporated: 1907; *Area:* 4.15 sq km
County or District: Parry Sound District; *Population in 2016:* 1,114
Provincial Electoral District(s): Parry Sound-Muskoka
Federal Electoral District(s): Parry Sound-Muskoka
Next Election: Oct. 24, 2022 (4 year terms)
Jim Coleman, Mayor
Susan Arnold, Administrator & Clerk

South Stormont
P.O. Box 84
2 Mille Roches Rd.
Long Sault, ON K0C 1P0
Tel: 613-534-8889; *Fax:* 613-534-2280
info@southstormont.ca
www.southstormont.ca
Other Information: Toll-Free Phone: 800-265-3915
Municipal Type: Township
Area: 447.58 sq km
County or District: Stormont, Dundas & Glengarry; *Population in 2016:* 13,110
Provincial Electoral District(s): Stormont-Dundas-South
Glengarry
Federal Electoral District(s): Stormont-Dundas-South Glengarry
Next Election: Oct. 24, 2022 (4 year terms)
Bryan McGillis, Mayor
David Smith, Deputy Mayor
Andrew Guindon, Councillor
Jennifer MacIsaac, Councillor
Cindy Woods, Councillor
Debi LucasSwitzer, Chief Administrative Officer, 613-534-8889
Cindy Piche, Treasurer & Director, Finance, 613-534-8889
Ross Gellately, Director, Public Works, 613-534-8889
Peter Young, Director, Planning, Building & Economic
Development, 613-534-8889
Gilles Crepeau, Fire Chief, 613-534-8889

Southgate
185667 Grey Rd. 9, RR#1
Dundalk, ON N0C 1B0
Tel: 519-923-2110; *Fax:* 519-923-9262
info@southgate.ca
www.southgate.ca
Other Information: Toll-Free Phone: 888-560-6607
Municipal Type: Township
Incorporated: Jan. 1, 2001; *Area:* 644.38 sq km
County or District: Grey; *Population in 2016:* 7,354
Provincial Electoral District(s): Bruce-Grey-Owen Sound
Federal Electoral District(s): Bruce-Grey-Owen Sound
Next Election: Oct. 24, 2022 (4 year terms)
Note: Amalgamation of the Village of Dundalk, the Township of
Proton & the Township of Egremont.
John Woodbury, Mayor
Dave Milliner, Chief Adminstrative Officer, 519-923-9262

Southwest Middlesex, Municipality of
P.O. Box 218
153 McKellar St.
Glencoe, ON N0L 1M0
Tel: 519-287-2015; *Fax:* 519-287-2359
www.southwestmiddlesex.ca
Municipal Type: Municipality
Incorporated: Jan. 1, 2001; *Area:* 427.88 sq km
County or District: Middlesex; *Population in 2016:* 5,723
Provincial Electoral District(s): Lambton-Kent-Middlesex
Federal Electoral District(s): Lambton-Kent-Middlesex
Next Election: Oct. 24, 2022 (4 year terms)
Note: Amalgamation of the Villages of Glencoe & Wardsville &
the Townships of Ekfrid & Mosa.
Allan Mayhew, Mayor
Jill Bellchamber-Glazier, Chief Administrative Officer & Clerk,
519-287-2015

South-West Oxford
312915 Dereham Line
Mount Elgin, ON N0J 1N0
Tel: 519-485-0477; *Fax:* 519-485-2932
generaladmin@swox.org
www.swox.org
Other Information: Phone, Works Department: 519-877-2702
Municipal Type: Township
Area: 370.73 sq km
County or District: Oxford; *Population in 2016:* 7,664
Provincial Electoral District(s): Oxford
Federal Electoral District(s): Oxford
Next Election: Oct. 24, 2022 (4 year terms)
David Mayberry, Mayor, 519-532-2917
Mary Ellen Greb, Chief Administrative Officer, 519-485-0477

Southwold
General Delivery
35663 Fingal Line
Fingal, ON N0L 1K0
Tel: 519-769-2010; *Fax:* 519-769-2837
southwold@southwold.ca
www.southwold.ca
Municipal Type: Township
Area: 301.74 sq km
County or District: Elgin; *Population in 2016:* 4,421
Provincial Electoral District(s): Elgin-Middlesex-London

Federal Electoral District(s): Elgin-Middlesex-London
Next Election: Oct. 24, 2022 (4 year terms)
Grant Jones, Mayor
Lisa Higgs, Chief Administrative Officer, Clerk & Deputy Treasurer

Spanish

P.O. Box 70
8 Trunk Rd.
Spanish, ON P0P 2A0
Tel: 705-844-2300; *Fax:* 705-844-2622
info@townofspanish.com
www.townofspanish.com
Municipal Type: Town
Area: 108.67 sq km
County or District: Algoma District; *Population in 2016:* 712
Provincial Electoral District(s): Algoma-Manitoulin
Federal Electoral District(s): Algoma-Manitoulin-Kapuskasing
Next Election: Oct. 24, 2022 (4 year terms)
Note: Formerly the Township of Shedden. Effective Oct. 1, 2004, the name was changed to the Town of Spanish.
Jocelyne Bishop, Mayor
Pam Lortie, Chief Administrative Officer & Treasurer

Springwater

Township of Springwater Administrative Ctr.
2231 Nursery Rd.
Minesing, ON L0L 1Y2
Tel: 705-728-4784; *Fax:* 705-728-6957
www.springwater.ca
Municipal Type: Township
Incorporated: Jan. 1, 1994; *Area:* 536.28 sq km
County or District: Simcoe; *Population in 2016:* 19,059
Provincial Electoral District(s): Barrie-Springwater-Oro-Medonte
Federal Electoral District(s): Barrie-Springwater-Oro-Medonte
Next Election: Oct. 24, 2022 (4 year terms)
Don Allen, Mayor
Jennifer Coughlin, Deputy Mayor
George Cabral, Councillor, Wards: 1
Perry Ritchie, Councillor, Wards: 2
Wanda Maw-Chapman, Councillor, Wards: 3
Anita Moore, Councillor, Wards: 4
Jack Hanna, Councillor, Wards: 5
Jeff Schimdt, Chief Administrative Officer, 705-728-4784
Jane Corbeil, Treasurer & Director, Finance, 705-728-4784
Heather Coleman, Director, Public Works, 705-728-4784
Jeff Kirk, Director, Fire & Emergency Services, 705-728-4784

Stirling-Rawdon

P.O. Box 40
2529 Stirling-Marmora Rd.
Stirling, ON K0K 3E0
Tel: 613-395-3380; *Fax:* 613-395-0864
info@stirling-rawdon.com
www.stirling-rawdon.com
Municipal Type: Township
Area: 282.33 sq km
County or District: Hastings; *Population in 2016:* 4,882
Provincial Electoral District(s): Hastings-Lennox and Addington
Federal Electoral District(s): Hastings-Lennox and Addington
Next Election: Oct. 24, 2022 (4 year terms)
Bob Mullin, Mayor
Roxanne Hearns, Chief Administrative Officer & Treasurer, 613-395-3380

Stone Mills

4504 County Rd. 4
Centreville, ON K0K 1N0
Tel: 613-378-2475; *Fax:* 613-378-0033
Municipal Type: Township
Incorporated: Jan. 1, 1998; *Area:* 709.17 sq km
County or District: Lennox-Addington; *Population in 2016:* 7,702
Provincial Electoral District(s): Hastings-Lennox and Addington
Federal Electoral District(s): Hastings-Lennox and Addington
Next Election: Oct. 24, 2022 (4 year terms)
Note: Amalgamation of the former Township of Camden East, Township of Sheffield & Village of Newburgh.
Eric Smith, Reeve
Bryan Brooks, Chief Administrative Officer & Municipal Clerk, 613-378-2475

Stormont, Dundas & Glengarry

26 Pitt St.
Cornwall, ON K6J 3P2
Tel: 613-932-1515; *Fax:* 613-936-2913
info@sdgcounties.ca
www.sdgcounties.ca
Other Information: Toll-Free Phone: 800-267-7158
Municipal Type: United County
Area: 3,309.87 sq km
Population in 2016: 113,429
Next Election: Oct. 24, 2022 (4 year terms)

Tony Fraser, Councillor, Wards: North Dundas
Allan Armstrong, Councillor, Wards: North Dundas
Jamie MacDonald, Councillor, Wards: North Glengarry
Carma Williams, Councillor, Wards: North Glengarry
Jim Wert, Councillor, Wards: North Stormont
Francois Landry, Councillor, Wards: North Stormont
Steven Byvelds, Councillor, Wards: South Dundas
Kirsten Gardner, Councillor, Wards: South Dundas
Frank Prevost, Councillor, Wards: South Glengarry
Lyle Warden, Councillor, Wards: South Glengarry
Bryan McGillis, Councillor, Wards: South Stormont
David Smith, Councillor, Wards: South Stormont
Helen Thomson, Clerk
Tim J. Simpson, Chief Administrative Officer
Rebecca Russell, Treasurer & Director, Financial Services
Benjamin de Haan, Director, Transportation & Planning
Trevor Baker, Manager, Operations

Strathroy-Caradoc

52 Frank St.
Strathroy, ON N7G 2R4
Tel: 519-245-1070; *Fax:* 519-245-6353
general@strathroy-caradoc.ca
www.strathroy-caradoc.ca
Municipal Type: Township
Incorporated: 2001; *Area:* 270.77 sq km
County or District: Middlesex; *Population in 2016:* 20,867
Provincial Electoral District(s): Lambton-Kent-Middlesex
Federal Electoral District(s): Lambton-Kent-Middlesex
Next Election: Oct. 24, 2022 (4 year terms)
Note: Amalgamation of the Town of Strathroy & the Township of Caradoc.
Joanne Vanderheyden, Mayor, 519-245-1105, Fax: 519-245-6353
Brad Richards, Deputy Mayor, 519-245-1105, Fax: 519-245-6353
Marie Baker, Councillor, 519-245-8696, Fax: 519-245-0076, Wards: 1
John G. Brennan, Councillor, 519-245-2680, Wards: 1
Frank Kennes, Councillor, Wards: 1
Steve Pelkman, Councillor, Wards: 1
Larry Cowan, Councillor, Wards: 2
Neil Flegel, Councillor, Wards: 2
Sandi Hipple, Councillor, Wards: 2
Fred Tranquilli, Chief Administrative Officer & Clerk
Brian George, Fire Chief

Strong

P.O. Box 1120
28 Municipal Lane
Sundridge, ON P0A 1Z0
Tel: 705-384-5819; *Fax:* 705-384-5892
www.strongtownship.com
Other Information: Alternate Phone: 705-384-5852
Municipal Type: Township
Area: 159.93 sq km
County or District: Parry Sound District; *Population in 2016:* 1,439
Provincial Electoral District(s): Parry Sound-Muskoka
Federal Electoral District(s): Parry Sound-Muskoka
Next Election: Oct. 24, 2022 (4 year terms)
Kelly Elik, Mayor
Caitlin Haggart, Clerk-Administrator, 705-384-5819

Sudbury District

c/o Manitoulin-Sudbury District Services Bd
210 Mead Blvd.
Espanola, ON P5E 1R9
www.msdsb.net
Municipal Type: District
Area: 40,204.77 sq km
Population in 2016: 21,546
Provincial Electoral District(s): Algoma-Manitoulin; Nickel Belt
Federal Electoral District(s): Nickel Belt; Algoma-Manitoulin-Kapuskasing
Les Gamble, Board Chair, Manitoulin-Sudbury District Services Board
Fern Dominelli, Chief Administrative Officer, Manitoulin-Sudbury District Services Board, 705-862-7850, Fax: 705-862-7866

Sundridge

P.O. Box 129
110 Main St.
Sundridge, ON P0A 1Z0
Tel: 705-384-5316; *Fax:* 705-384-7874
admin@sundridge.ca
www.sundridge.ca
Municipal Type: Village
Incorporated: 1889; *Area:* 2.30 sq km
County or District: Parry Sound District; *Population in 2016:* 961
Provincial Electoral District(s): Parry Sound-Muskoka

Federal Electoral District(s): Parry Sound-Muskoka
Next Election: Oct. 24, 2022 (4 year terms)
Lyle Hall, Mayor
Karen Fraser, Clerk-Administrator

Tarbutt & Tarbutt Additional

27 Barr Rd. South
Desbarats, ON P0R 1E0
Tel: 705-782-6776; *Fax:* 705-782-4274
tarbutttownship@bellnet.ca
www.tarbutt.ca
Municipal Type: Township
Incorporated: 1889; *Area:* 52.82 sq km
County or District: Algoma District; *Population in 2016:* 534
Provincial Electoral District(s): Algoma-Manitoulin
Federal Electoral District(s): Algoma-Manitoulin-Kapuskasing
Next Election: Oct. 24, 2022 (4 year terms)
Chris Burton, Mayor, 705-782-4294
Glenn Martin, Clerk-Treasurer

Tay

P.O. Box 100
450 Park St.
Victoria Harbour, ON L0K 2A0
Tel: 705-534-7248; *Fax:* 705-534-4493
www.tay.ca
Municipal Type: Township
Area: 139.07 sq km
County or District: Simcoe; *Population in 2016:* 10,033
Provincial Electoral District(s): Simcoe North
Federal Electoral District(s): Simcoe North
Next Election: Oct. 24, 2022 (4 year terms)
Ted Walker, Mayor
Gerard LaChapelle, Deputy Mayor
Paul Raymond, Councillor, Wards: 1
Sandy Talbot, Councillor, Wards: 1
Jeff Bumstead, Councillor, Wards: 2
Mary Warnock, Councillor, Wards: 2
Barry Norris, Councillor, Wards: 3
Cyndi Bonneville, Municipal Clerk, 705-534-7248
Lindsay Barron, Chief Administrative Officer, 705-534-7248
Brian Thomas, Fire Chief, 705-534-7248

Tay Valley

217 Harper Rd., RR#4
Perth, ON K7H 3C6
Tel: 613-267-5353; *Fax:* 613-264-8516
www.tayvalleytwp.ca
Other Information: Toll-Free Phone: 800-810-0161
Municipal Type: Township
Area: 550.01 sq km
County or District: Lanark; *Population in 2016:* 5,665
Provincial Electoral District(s): Lanark-Frontenac-Kingston
Federal Electoral District(s): Lanark-Frontenac-Kingston
Next Election: Oct. 24, 2022 (4 year terms)
Note: Formerly the Township of Bathurst Burgess Sherbrooke.
Brian Campbell, Reeve
Larry Donaldson, Chief Administrative Officer

Tecumseh

917 Lesperance Rd.
Tecumseh, ON N8N 1W9
Tel: 519-735-2184; *Fax:* 519-735-6712
www.tecumseh.ca
Municipal Type: Town
Incorporated: 1921; *Area:* 94.64 sq km
County or District: Essex; *Population in 2016:* 23,229
Provincial Electoral District(s): Windsor-Tecumseh
Federal Electoral District(s): Windsor-Tecumseh
Next Election: Oct. 24, 2022 (4 year terms)
Note: Restructuring occurred in 1999.
Gary McNamara, Mayor
Joe Bachetti, Deputy Mayor & Councillor, 519-979-3339
Andrew Dowie, Councillor, 226-773-1910, Wards: 1
William Altenhof, Councillor, 519-818-1067, Wards: 2
Rico Tonial, Councillor, Wards: 3
Brian Houston, Councillor, Wards: 4
Tania Jobin, Councillor, Wards: 5
Laura Moy, Clerk & Director, Corporate Services, 519-735-2184
Margaret Misek-Evans, Chief Administrative Officer, 519-735-2184
Tom Kitsos, Chief Financial Officer & Director, Financial Services
Paul Anthony, Director, Parks & Recreation, 519-735-4756
Shaun Fuerth, Director, Information & Communications Services, 519-735-4756
Brian Hillman, Director, Planning & Building Services, 519-735-2184
Phil Bartnik, Director, Public Works & Environmental Services, 519-735-2184
Wade Bondy, Fire Chief, 519-979-4941

Tehkummah

Municipal Building
456 Hwy. 542A
Tehkummah, ON P0P 2C0
Tel: 705-859-3293; *Fax:* 705-859-2605
twptehk@amtelecom.net
www.manitoulin-island.com/tehkummah
Municipal Type: Township
Incorporated: 1881; *Area:* 132.69 sq km
County or District: Manitoulin District; *Population in 2016:* 436
Provincial Electoral District(s): Algoma-Manitoulin
Federal Electoral District(s): Algoma-Manitoulin-Kapuskasing
Next Election: Oct. 24, 2022 (4 year terms)
David Jaggard, Reeve

Temagami

P.O. Box 220
Temagami, ON P0H 2H0
Tel: 705-569-3421; *Fax:* 705-569-2834
visit@temagami.ca
www.temagami.ca
Municipal Type: Municipality
Incorporated: Jan. 1, 1998; *Area:* 1,905.92 sq km
County or District: Nipissing District; *Population in 2016:* 802
Provincial Electoral District(s): Timiskaming-Cochrane
Federal Electoral District(s): Nipissing-Timiskaming
Next Election: Oct. 24, 2022 (4 year terms)
Dan O'Mara, Mayor
Patrick Cormier, Chief Administrative Officer, 705-569-3421

Terrace Bay

P.O. Box 40
1 Selkirk Ave.
Terrace Bay, ON P0T 2W0
Tel: 807-825-3315; *Fax:* 807-825-9576
info@terracebay.ca
www.terracebay.ca
Municipal Type: Township
Incorporated: Sept. 1, 1947; *Area:* 152.82 sq km
County or District: Thunder Bay District; *Population in 2016:* 1,611
Provincial Electoral District(s): Thunder Bay-Superior North
Federal Electoral District(s): Thunder Bay-Superior North
Next Election: Oct. 24, 2022 (4 year terms)
Note: Incorporated as a municipality on July 1, 1959.
George (Jody) Davis, Mayor
Jonathan Hall, Chief Administrative Officer & Clerk, 807-825-3315

Thames Centre

4305 Hamilton Rd.
Dorchester, ON N0L 1G3
Tel: 519-268-7334; *Fax:* 519-268-3928
inquiries@thamescentre.on.ca
www.thamescentre.on.ca
Other Information: Toll-Free Phone: 866-425-7306
Municipal Type: Municipality
Incorporated: Jan. 1, 2001; *Area:* 433.99 sq km
County or District: Middlesex; *Population in 2016:* 13,191
Provincial Electoral District(s): Elgin-Middlesex-London
Federal Electoral District(s): Elgin-Middlesex-London
Next Election: Oct. 24, 2022 (4 year terms)
Note: Amalgamation of the former Township of West Nissouri & the Township of North Dorchester.
Alison Warwick, Mayor
Kelly Elliott, Deputy Mayor
Thomas Heeman, Councillor, Wards: 1
Chris Patterson, Councillor, Wards: 2
Paul Hunter, Councillor, Wards: 3
Tena Michiels, Clerk, 519-268-7334
Mike Henry, Chief Administrative Officer, 519-268-7334
Kim Grogan, Treasurer & Director, Financial Services, 519-268-7334
Carlos Reyes, Director, Public Works, 519-268-7334
Ken Armstrong, Fire Chief

Thessalon

P.O. Box 220
187 Main St.
Thessalon, ON P0R 1L0
Tel: 705-842-2217; *Fax:* 705-842-2572
townthess@bellnet.ca
www.thessalon.ca
Municipal Type: Town
Area: 4.52 sq km
County or District: Algoma District; *Population in 2016:* 1,286
Provincial Electoral District(s): Algoma-Manitoulin
Federal Electoral District(s): Algoma-Manitoulin-Kapuskasing
Next Election: Oct. 24, 2022 (4 year terms)
Bill Rosenberg, Mayor
Robert P. MacLean, Clerk-Treasurer

Thornloe

P.O. Box 546
35-10th St.
Earlton, ON P0J 1E0
Tel: 705-563-2375; *Fax:* 705-563-2093
Municipal Type: Village
Area: 6.59 sq km
County or District: Timiskaming District; *Population in 2016:* 112
Provincial Electoral District(s): Timiskaming-Cochrane
Federal Electoral District(s): Timmins-James Bay
Next Election: Oct. 24, 2022 (4 year terms)
Earl Read, Reeve
Reynald Rivard, Clerk-Treasurer

Thunder Bay

District Social Services Administration Bd.
231 May St. South
Thunder Bay, ON P7E 1B5
Tel: 807-766-2111; *Fax:* 807-345-7921
contact-us@tbdssab.ca
www.tbdssab.ca
Municipal Type: District
Area: 103,722.82 sq km
Population in 2016: 146,048
Lucy Kloosterhuis, Chair, District of Thunder Bay Social Services Administration Board
Bill Bradica, Chief Administrative Officer, District of Thunder Bay Social Services Administration Board, 807-766-2103, Fax: 807-345-6146

Timiskaming

District Social Services Administrative Bd.
P.O. Box 310
29 Duncan Ave. North
Kirkland Lake, ON P2N 3H7
Tel: 705-567-9366
www.dtssab.com
Other Information: Toll-Free Phone: 888-544-5555
Municipal Type: District
Area: 13,303.30 sq km
Population in 2016: 32,251
Doug Jelly, Chair, District of Timiskaming Social Services Administration Board
Kelly Black, Chief Administrative Officer, District of Timiskaming Social Services Administration Board, 705-567-9366, Fax: 705-567-3908

Tiny

130 Balm Beach Rd. West, RR#1
Tiny, ON L0L 2J0
Tel: 705-526-4204; *Fax:* 705-526-2372
www.tiny.ca
Other Information: Toll-Free Phone: 866-939-8469
Municipal Type: Township
Area: 336.93 sq km
County or District: Simcoe; *Population in 2016:* 11,787
Provincial Electoral District(s): Simcoe North
Federal Electoral District(s): Simcoe North
Next Election: Oct. 24, 2022 (4 year terms)
George Cornell, Mayor
Steffen Walma, Deputy Mayor
Cindy Hastings, Councillor
Tony Mintoff, Councillor
Gibb Wishart, Councillor
Doug Luker, Chief Administrative Officer, 705-526-4204
Doug Taylor, Director of Finance & Administration, 705-526-4204
Tim Leitch, Director of Public Works, 705-526-4204
Shawn Persaud, Director of Planning & Development, 705-526-4204
Ray Millar, Fire Chief/Manager of Emergency Services, 705-322-1161
Steven Harvey, Chief Municipal Law Enforcement Officer, 705-526-4136

Trent Hills

P.O. Box 1030
66 Front St. South
Campbellford, ON K0L 1L0
Tel: 705-653-1900; *Fax:* 705-653-5203
info@trenthills.ca
www.trenthills.ca
Other Information: Public Works Emergency, Phone: 705-653-2610
Municipal Type: Municipality
Area: 511.95 sq km
County or District: Northumberland; *Population in 2016:* 12,900
Provincial Electoral District(s): Northumberland-Peterborough South
Federal Electoral District(s): Northumberland-Peterborough South
Next Election: Oct. 24, 2022 (4 year terms)
Robert Crate, Mayor, 705-761-2278
Gene Brahaney, Councillor, Wards: 1. Campbellford/Seymour
Catherine Redden, Councillor, 705-653-2046, Wards: 1. Campbellford/Seymour
Rick English, Councillor, 705-924-2590, Wards: 2. Percy
Ken Tully, Councillor, 705-696-2480, Wards: 2. Percy
Michael Metcalf, Councillor, 905-269-7816, Wards: 3. Hastings
Doug Irwon, Clerk & Director, Legislative Services, 705-653-1900
Lynn Phillips, Chief Administrative Officer, 705-653-1900
Valerie Nesbitt, Treasurer & Director, Finance, 705-653-1900
Scott White, General Manager, Infrastructure Renewal & Public Works Administration, 705-653-1900
Jim Peters, Director, Planning & Development, 705-653-1900
Tim Blake, Fire Chief, 705-653-1900

Trent Lakes

760 County Rd. 36
Trent Lakes, ON K0M 1A0
Tel: 705-738-3800; *Fax:* 705-738-3801
info@trentlakes.ca
www.trentlakes.ca
Other Information: Toll-Free Phone: 800-374-4009
Municipal Type: Municipality
Area: 861.32 sq km
County or District: Peterborough; *Population in 2016:* 5,397
Provincial Electoral District(s): Peterborough-Kawartha
Federal Electoral District(s): Peterborough-Kawartha
Next Election: Oct. 24, 2022 (4 year terms)
Note: Formerly the Township of Galway-Cavendish & Harvey. Renamed in 2013.
Janet Clarkson, Mayor
Lois O'Neill-Jackson, Chief Administrative Officer & Economic Development Officer, 705-738-3800

Tudor & Cashel

P.O. Box 436
371 Weslemkoon Lake Rd., RR#2
Gilmour, ON K0L 1W0
Tel: 613-474-2583; *Fax:* 613-474-0664
www.tudorandcashel.com
Other Information: Toll-Free Phone: 855-474-2583
Municipal Type: Township
Incorporated: 1869; *Area:* 445.66 sq km
County or District: Hastings; *Population in 2016:* 586
Provincial Electoral District(s): Hastings-Lennox and Addington
Federal Electoral District(s): Hastings-Lennox and Addington
Next Election: Oct. 24, 2022 (4 year terms)
Libby Clarke, Reeve
Bernice Crocker, Chief Administrative Officer

Tweed

P.O. Box 729
255 Metcalf St.
Tweed, ON K0K 3J0
Tel: 613-478-2535; *Fax:* 613-478-6457
info@twp.tweed.on.ca
www.tweed.ca
Municipal Type: Municipality
Incorporated: 1998; *Area:* 953.47 sq km
County or District: Hastings; *Population in 2016:* 6,044
Provincial Electoral District(s): Hastings-Lennox and Addington
Federal Electoral District(s): Hastings-Lennox and Addington
Next Election: Oct. 24, 2022 (4 year terms)
Jo-Anne Albert, Mayor
Betty Gallagher, Chief Administrative Officer & Clerk-Treasurer

Tyendinaga

859 Melrose Rd., RR#1
Shannonville, ON K0K 3A0
Tel: 613-396-1944; *Fax:* 613-396-2080
info@tyendinagatownship.com
www.tyendinagatownship.com
Municipal Type: Township
Area: 312.92 sq km
County or District: Hastings; *Population in 2016:* 4,297
Provincial Electoral District(s): Hastings-Lennox and Addington
Federal Electoral District(s): Hastings-Lennox and Addington
Next Election: Oct. 24, 2022 (4 year terms)
Rick Phillips, Reeve, 613-477-3129
Steve Mercer, Clerk-Treasurer

Uxbridge

P.O. Box 190
51 Toronto St. South
Uxbridge, ON L9P 1T1
Tel: 905-852-9181; *Fax:* 905-852-9674
info@town.uxbridge.on.ca
www.town.uxbridge.on.ca
Municipal Type: Township
Incorporated: 1872; *Area:* 420.95 sq km
County or District: Durham Reg. Mun.; *Population in 2016:*

21,176
Provincial Electoral District(s): Pickering-Uxbridge
Federal Electoral District(s): Pickering-Uxbridge
Next Election: Oct. 24, 2022 (4 year terms)
Note: Incorporated as a town in 1885, & town became part of
Uxbridge Township in 1973.
Dave Barton, Mayor
Gord Highet, Regional Councillor
Pamela Beach, Councillor, Wards: 1
Gary Ruona, Councillor, Wards: 2
Bruce Garrod, Councillor, Wards: 3
Willie Popp, Councillor, Wards: 4
Todd Snooks, Councillor, Wards: 5
Debbie Leroux, Clerk & Director, Legislative Services,
905-852-9181, Fax: 905-852-9674
Kristi Honey, Chief Administrative Officer, 905-852-9181, Fax:
905-852-9674
Ben Kester, C.E.T., Director, Public Works, 905-852-9181, Fax:
905-852-9674
Amanda Ferraro, Director, Parks, Recreation & Culture,
905-852-0095
Tom Dion, Fire Chief

Val Rita-Harty
P.O. Box 100
2 Eglise Ave.
Val Rita, ON P0L 2G0
Tel: 705-335-6146; *Fax:* 705-337-6292
administration@valharty.ca
www.valharty.ca
Municipal Type: Township
Area: 381.18 sq km
County or District: Cochrane District; *Population in 2016:* 762
Provincial Electoral District(s): Mushkegowuk-James Bay
Federal Electoral District(s): Algoma-Manitoulin-Kapuskasing
Next Election: Oct. 24, 2022 (4 year terms)
Johanne Baril, Mayor
Guillaume Richy, Chief Administrative Officer

La Vallée
P.O. Box 99
56 Church Rd.
Devlin, ON P0W 1C0
Tel: 807-486-3452; *Fax:* 807-486-3863
lavalley@nwonet.net
www.lavallee.ca
Municipal Type: Township
Area: 237.84 sq km
County or District: Rainy River District; *Population in 2016:* 938
Provincial Electoral District(s): Kenora-Rainy River
Federal Electoral District(s): Thunder Bay-Rainy River
Next Election: Oct. 24, 2022 (4 year terms)
Ken McKinnon, Reeve
Patti McDowall, Municipal Clerk-Treasurer

Wainfleet
P.O. Box 40
31940 Hwy. 3
Wainfleet, ON L0S 1V0
Tel: 905-899-3463; *Fax:* 905-899-2340
www.wainfleet.ca
Municipal Type: Township
Area: 217.31 sq km
County or District: Niagara Reg. Mun.; *Population in 2016:* 6,372
Provincial Electoral District(s): Niagara West
Federal Electoral District(s): Niagara West
Next Election: Oct. 24, 2022 (4 year terms)
Kevin Gibson, Mayor
William Kolasa, Chief Administrative Officer & Clerk,
905-899-3463

Warwick
6332 Nauvoo Rd.
Watford, ON N0M 2S0
Tel: 519-849-3926; *Fax:* 519-849-6136
info@warwicktownship.ca
www.warwicktownship.ca
Other Information: Toll-Free Phone: 877-849-3962
Municipal Type: Township
Incorporated: 1998; *Area:* 290.20 sq km
County or District: Lambton; *Population in 2016:* 3,692
Provincial Electoral District(s): Lambton-Kent-Middlesex
Federal Electoral District(s): Lambton-Kent-Middlesex
Next Election: Oct. 24, 2022 (4 year terms)
Jackie Rombouts, Mayor
Amanda Gubbels, Administrator-Clerk

Wawa
P.O. Box 500
40 Broadway Ave.
Wawa, ON P0S 1K0
Tel: 705-856-2244; *Fax:* 705-856-2120
info@wawa.cc
wawa.cc
Other Information: Toll-Free Phone: 800-367-9292
Municipal Type: Municipality
Area: 416.21 sq km
County or District: Algoma District; *Population in 2016:* 2,905
Provincial Electoral District(s): Algoma-Manitoulin
Federal Electoral District(s): Algoma-Manitoulin-Kapuskasing
Next Election: Oct. 24, 2022 (4 year terms)
Ron Rody, Mayor
Chris Wray, Chief Administrative Officer & Clerk-Treasurer,
705-856-2244

Wellesley
Administration Office
4639 Lobsinger Line, RR#1
St Clements, ON N0B 2M0
Tel: 519-699-4611; *Fax:* 519-699-4540
www.township.wellesley.on.ca
Municipal Type: Township
Area: 277.76 sq km
County or District: Waterloo Regional Municipality; *Population in
2016:* 11,260
Provincial Electoral District(s): Kitchener-Conestoga
Federal Electoral District(s): Kitchener-Conestoga
Next Election: Oct. 24, 2022 (4 year terms)
Joe Nowak, Mayor
Rik Louwagie, Chief Administrative Officer

Wellington North
P.O. Box 125
7490 Sideroad 7 West
Kenilworth, ON N0G 2E0
Tel: 519-848-3620
township@wellington-north.com
www.wellington-north.com
Other Information: Toll-Free Phone: 866-848-3620
Municipal Type: Township
Incorporated: Jan. 1, 1999; *Area:* 526.21 sq km
County or District: Wellington; *Population in 2016:* 11,914
Provincial Electoral District(s): Perth-Wellington
Federal Electoral District(s): Perth-Wellington
Next Election: Oct. 24, 2022 (4 year terms)
Note: Amalgamation of the Township of Arthur, Arthur Village,
the Township of West Luther & the Town of Mount Forest.
Andy Lennox, Mayor
Dan Yake, Councillor, Wards: 1
Sherry Burke, Councillor, Wards: 2
Lisa Hern, Councillor, Wards: 3
Steve McCabe, Councillor, Wards: 4
Karen Wallace, Clerk & Director, Legislative Services
Michael Givens, Chief Administrative Officer
Darren Jones, Chief Building Official
Chanda Riggi, Manager, Human Resources
Chris Harrow, Fire Chief

West Elgin
P.O. Box 490
22413 Hoskins Line
Rodney, ON N0L 2C0
Tel: 519-785-0560; *Fax:* 519-785-0644
westelgin@westelgin.net
www.westelgin.net
Municipal Type: Municipality
Area: 322.48 sq km
County or District: Elgin; *Population in 2016:* 4,995
Provincial Electoral District(s): Elgin-Middlesex-London
Federal Electoral District(s): Elgin-Middlesex-London
Next Election: Oct. 24, 2022 (4 year terms)
Duncan McPhail, Mayor
Genevieve Scharback, CMO, Chief Administrative Officer &
Clerk, 519-785-0560

West Grey
402813 Grey Rd., RR#2
Durham, ON N0G 1R0
Tel: 519-369-2200; *Fax:* 519-369-5962
info@westgrey.com
www.westgrey.com
Other Information: Toll-Free Phone: 800-538-9647
Municipal Type: Municipality
Incorporated: Jan 1, 2001; *Area:* 876.16 sq km
County or District: Grey; *Population in 2016:* 12,518
Provincial Electoral District(s): Bruce-Grey-Owen Sound
Federal Electoral District(s): Bruce-Grey-Owen Sound
Next Election: Oct. 24, 2022 (4 year terms)

Note: Amalgamation of Bentinck, Glenelg, Normanby, Neustadt
& Durham.
Christine Robinson, Mayor
Tom Hutchinson, Deputy Mayor
Beth Hamilton, Councillor
Rebecca Hergert, Councillor
Doug Hutchinson, Councillor
Geoffrey Shea, Councillor
Stephen Townsend, Councillor
Genevieve Scharback, Clerk, 519-369-2200
Laura Johnston, Chief Administrative Officer, 519-369-2200
Kerri Mighton, Treasurer & Director, Finance, 519-369-2200
Vance Czerwinski, Director, Infrastructure & Public Works,
519-369-2200
Phil Schwartz, Fire Chief, 519-269-2505

West Lincoln
P.O. Box 400
318 Canborough St.
Smithville, ON L0R 2A0
Tel: 905-957-3346; *Fax:* 905-957-3219
www.westlincoln.ca
Other Information: TTY: 905-957-0680
Municipal Type: Township
Incorporated: Jan. 1, 1970; *Area:* 387.81 sq km
County or District: Niagara Reg. Mun.; *Population in 2016:*
14,500
Provincial Electoral District(s): Niagara West
Federal Electoral District(s): Niagara West
Next Election: Oct. 24, 2022 (4 year terms)
Note: Amalgamation of the former Townships of South Grimsby,
Caistor, & Gainsborough.
David Bylsma, Mayor
Mike Rehner, Councillor, Wards: 1
Jason Trombetta, Councillor, Wards: 1
Christopher Coady, Councillor, Wards: 2
Harold Jonker, Councillor, Wards: 2
Cheryl Ganann, Councillor, Wards: 3
William Reilly, Councillor, Wards: 3
Albert Witteveen, Regional Councillor
Joanne Scrime, Clerk
Beverly Hendry, Chief Administrative Officer
Dennis Fisher, Fire Chief, 905-957-3346

West Nipissing
Municipal Office
#101, 225 Holditch St.
Sturgeon Falls, ON P2B 1T1
Tel: 705-753-2250; *Fax:* 705-753-3950
www.westnipissingouest.ca
Municipal Type: Municipality
Area: 1,993.63 sq km
County or District: Nipissing District; *Population in 2016:* 14,364
Provincial Electoral District(s): Nipissing; Timiskaming-Cochrane
Federal Electoral District(s): Nickel Belt
Next Election: Oct. 24, 2022 (4 year terms)
Joanne Savage, Mayor, 705-753-2250, Fax: 705-753-3950
Lise Sénécal, Councillor, Wards: 1
Léo Malette, Councillor, 705-753-3568, Wards: 2
Yvon Duhaime, Councillor, 705-499-6439, Wards: 3
Dan Roveda, Councillor, Wards: 4
Christopher Fisher, Councillor, Wards: 5
Ronald Larabie, Councillor, 705-758-6899, Wards: 6
Jeremy Séguin, Councillor, Wards: 7
Denis Sénécal, Councillor, Wards: 8
Jean-Pierre (Jay) Barbeau, Chief Administrative Officer,
705-753-2250
Shawn Remillard, Manager, Public Works, 705-753-2250
Stephan Poulin, Director, Economic Development & Community
Services, 705-753-2250
Alain Bazinet, Chief Building Official & Officer, Property
Maintenance, 705-753-2250
Richard Maranda, Fire Chief, 705-753-1171

West Perth, Municipality of
P.O. Box 609
169 St. David St.
Mitchell, ON N0K 1N0
Tel: 519-348-8429; *Fax:* 519-348-8935
info@westperth.com
www.westperth.com
Municipal Type: Municipality
Area: 579.36 sq km
County or District: Perth; *Population in 2016:* 8,865
Provincial Electoral District(s): Perth-Wellington
Federal Electoral District(s): Perth-Wellington
Next Election: Oct. 24, 2022 (4 year terms)
Note: Amalgamation of Fullarton Township, Hibbert Township,
Logan Township & the Town of Mitchell.
Walter McKenzie, Mayor, 519-348-4236
Carla Preston, Municipal Clerk, 519-348-8429

Westport

P.O. Box 68
30 Bedford St.
Westport, ON K0G 1X0
Tel: 613-273-2191; *Fax:* 613-273-3460
info@villageofwestport.ca
www.villageofwestport.ca
Municipal Type: Village
Incorporated: 1904; *Area:* 1.68 sq km
County or District: Leeds & Grenville; *Population in 2016:* 590
Provincial Electoral District(s): Leeds-Grenville-Thousand Islands and Rideau Lakes
Federal Electoral District(s): Leeds-Grenville-Thousand Islands and Rideau Lakes
Next Election: Oct. 24, 2022 (4 year terms)
Robin Patricia Jones, Mayor
Paul Snider, Chief Administrative Officer & Clerk

White River

P.O. Box 307
102 Durham St.
White River, ON P0M 3G0
Tel: 807-822-2450; *Fax:* 807-822-2719
info@whiteriver.ca
www.whiteriver.ca
Municipal Type: Township
Area: 96.78 sq km
County or District: Algoma District; *Population in 2016:* 645
Provincial Electoral District(s): Algoma-Manitoulin
Federal Electoral District(s): Algoma-Manitoulin-Kapuskasing
Next Election: Oct. 24, 2022 (4 year terms)
Angelo Bazzoni, Mayor
Tina Forsyth, Chief Administrative Officer & Treasurer, 807-822-2450

Whitestone

General Delivery
21 Church St.
Dunchurch, ON P0A 1G0
Tel: 705-389-2466; *Fax:* 705-389-1855
deputy@whitestone.ca
www.whitestone.ca
Municipal Type: Municipality
Incorporated: 2000; *Area:* 957.93 sq km
County or District: Parry Sound District; *Population in 2016:* 916
Provincial Electoral District(s): Parry Sound-Muskoka
Federal Electoral District(s): Parry Sound-Muskoka
Next Election: Oct. 24, 2022 (4 year terms)
Chris Armstrong, Mayor, 705-389-3721
Michelle Hendry, Chief Administrative Officer & Clerk, 705-389-2466

Whitewater Region

P.O. Box 40
44 Main St.
Cobden, ON K0J 1K0
Tel: 613-646-2282; *Fax:* 613-646-2283
info@whitewaterregion.ca
www.whitewaterregion.ca
Other Information: Toll-Free Phone: 877-646-2282
Municipal Type: Township
Incorporated: Jan. 1, 2001; *Area:* 539.51 sq km
County or District: Renfrew; *Population in 2016:* 7,009
Provincial Electoral District(s): Renfrew-Nipissing-Pembroke
Federal Electoral District(s): Renfrew-Nipissing-Pembroke
Next Election: Oct. 24, 2022 (4 year terms)
Note: Amalgamation of Beachburg Village, Cobden Village, Westmeath Township & Ross Township.
Michael Moore, Mayor
Cathy Regier, Reeve
Robert Tremblay, Chief Administrative Officer & Clerk

Wilmot

60 Snyder's Rd. West
Baden, ON N3A 1A1
Tel: 519-634-8444; *Fax:* 519-634-5522
www.wilmot.ca
Other Information: Toll-Free Phone: 800-469-5576
Municipal Type: Township
Area: 263.78 sq km
County or District: Waterloo Regional Municipality; *Population in 2016:* 20,545
Provincial Electoral District(s): Kitchener-Conestoga
Federal Electoral District(s): Kitchener-Conestoga
Next Election: Oct. 24, 2022 (4 year terms)
Les Armstrong, Mayor, Fax: 519-662-2764
Angie Hallman, Councillor, Wards: 1
Cheryl Gordijk, Councillor, Wards: 2
Barry Fisher, Councillor, 519-634-8916, Wards: 3
Jeff Gerber, Councillor, Wards: 4
Jennifer Pfenning, Councillor, Wards: 4
Grant Whittington, Chief Administrative Officer, 519-634-8444, Fax: 519-634-5522
Rod Leeson, Fire Chief, 519-634-8444

Wollaston

P.O. Box 99
90 Wollaston Lake Rd.
Coe Hill, ON K0L 1P0
Tel: 613-337-5731; *Fax:* 613-337-5789
wollaston@bellnet.ca
www.wollastontownship.ca
Municipal Type: Township
Incorporated: 1880; *Area:* 219.14 sq km
County or District: Hastings; *Population in 2016:* 670
Provincial Electoral District(s): Hastings-Lennox and Addington
Federal Electoral District(s): Hastings-Lennox and Addington
Next Election: Oct. 24, 2022 (4 year terms)
Barbara Shaw, Reeve
Jennifer Cohen, Clerk & Deputy Treasurer

Woolwich

P.O. Box 158
24 Church St. West
Elmira, ON N3B 2Z6
Tel: 519-669-1647; *Fax:* 519-669-1820
www.woolwich.ca
Other Information: Toll-Free Phone: 877-969-0094
Municipal Type: Township
Incorporated: Jan. 1, 1973; *Area:* 326.15 sq km
County or District: Waterloo Regional Municipality; *Population in 2016:* 25,006
Provincial Electoral District(s): Kitchener-Conestoga
Federal Electoral District(s): Kitchener-Conestoga
Next Election: Oct. 24, 2022 (4 year terms)
Sandy Shantz, Mayor
Scott McMillan, Councillor, Wards: 1
Patrick Merlihan, Councillor, Wards: 1
Fred Redekop, Councillor, Wards: 2
Murray Martin, Councillor, Wards: 3
Larry Shantz, Councillor, Wards: 3
David Brenneman, Chief Administrative Officer, 519-669-1647
Richard Petherick, Treasurer & Director, Finance, 519-669-1647
Ann McArthur, Director, Recreation & Facilities Services, 519-669-1647
Jared Puppe, Director, Infrastructure Services, 519-669-1647
Dale Martin, Township Fire Chief, 519-669-1647

Zorra

Municipal Office
P.O. Box 306
274620 - 27th Line, RR#3
Ingersoll, ON N5C 3K5
Tel: 519-485-2490; *Fax:* 519-485-2520
admin@zorra.on.ca
www.zorra.on.ca
Other Information: Toll-Free Phone: 888-699-3868
Municipal Type: Township
Area: 528.94 sq km
County or District: Oxford; *Population in 2016:* 8,138
Provincial Electoral District(s): Oxford
Federal Electoral District(s): Oxford
Next Election: Oct. 24, 2022 (4 year terms)
Marcus Ryan, Mayor
Don MacLeod, Chief Administrative Officer, 519-485-2490

PRINCE EDWARD ISLAND

Enabling legislation in P.E.I. includes the Charlottetown Area Municipalities Act, the City of Summerside Act, and the Municipalities Act. The first two provide governance for the cities of Charlottetown and Summerside, while the third provides the framework for 59 municipalities, consisting of 1 resort municipality, 2 cities, 10 towns, and 46 regional municipalities. There are no population considerations for incorporation of a municipality, but a petition must be made by at least 25 residents of an area indicating their desire to incorporate; stating the boundaries of the area, whether it is to be a town or a community, and the services which are to be provided.

Elections are held every four years on the first Monday of November (2018, 2022, etc.).

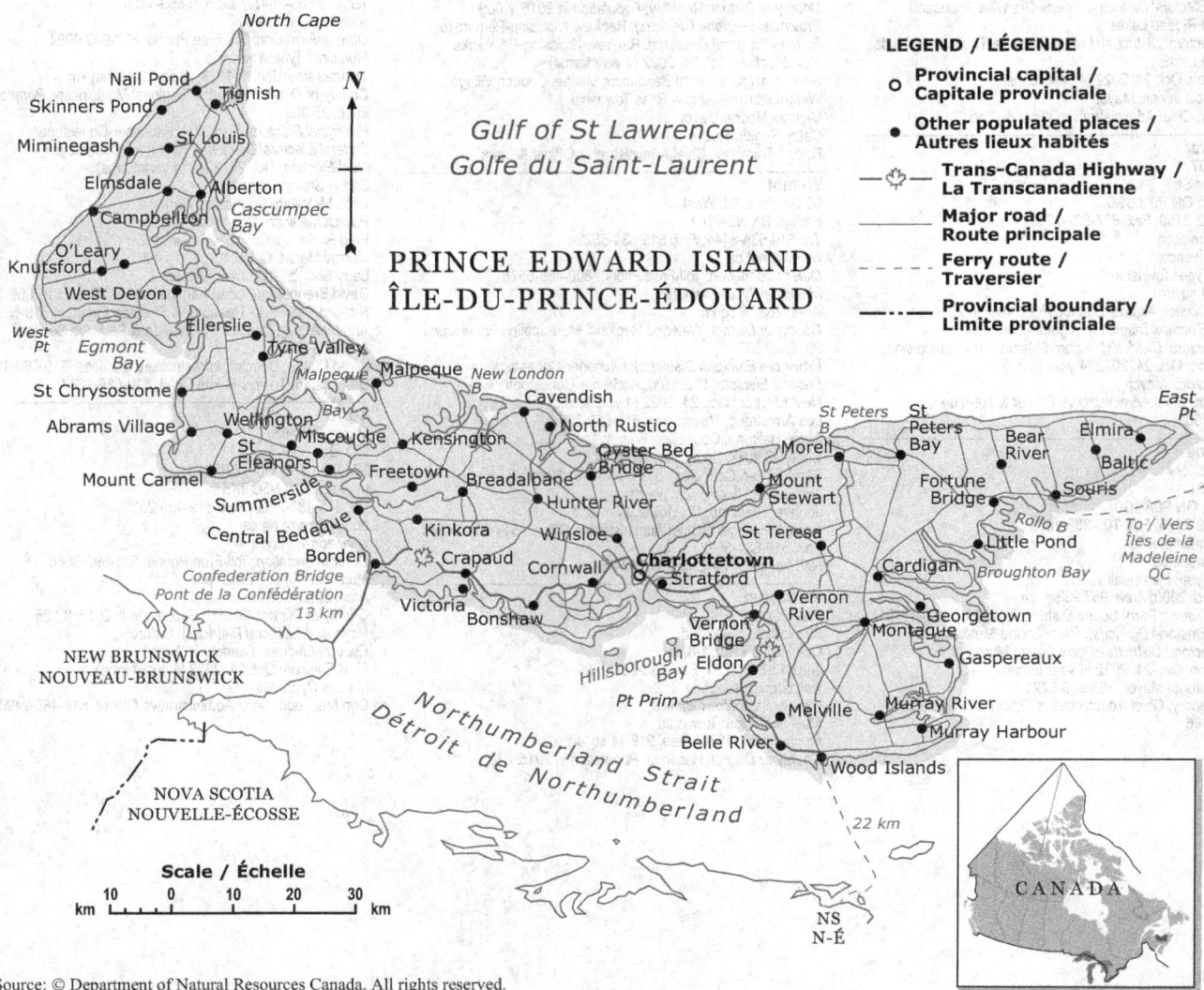

LEGEND / LÉGENDE

○ Provincial capital / Capitale provinciale
● Other populated places / Autres lieux habités
— Trans-Canada Highway / La Transcanadienne
— Major road / Route principale
--- Ferry route / Traversier
—·— Provincial boundary / Limite provinciale

Source: © Department of Natural Resources Canada. All rights reserved.

Prince Edward Island

Major Municipalities in Prince Edward Island

Charlottetown
P.O. Box 98
199 Queen St.
Charlottetown, PE C1A 7K2
Tel: 902-566-5548; *Fax:* 902-566-4701
www.charlottetown.ca
Municipal Type: City
Incorporated: 1855; *Area:* 44.34 sq km
County or District: Hillsborough; *Population in 2016:* 36,094
Provincial Electoral District(s): Charlottetown-Sherwood;
Charlottetown-Parkdale; Charlottetown-Victoria Park;
Charlottetown-Brighton; Charlottetown-Lewis Point
Federal Electoral District(s): Charlottetown
Next Election: Nov. 7, 2022 (4 year terms)
Philip Brown, Mayor, 902-566-5548, Fax: 902-566-4701
Alanna Jankov, Councillor, Wards: 1
Terry MacLeod, Councillor, 902-566-5548, Fax: 902-455-4701,
Wards: 2. Belvedere
Mike Duffy, Councillor, 902-566-5548, Fax: 902-566-4701,
Wards: 3. Brighton
Mitchell G. Tweel, B.A., Councillor, 902-566-5548, Fax:
902-566-4701, Wards: 4. St. Avard's
Kevin Ramsay, Councillor, 902-566-5548, Fax: 902-566-4701,
Wards: 5. Spring Park
Bob Doiron, Councillor, 902-566-5548, Fax: 902-566-4701,
Wards: 6. Mount Edward
Greg Rivard, Councillor, 902-566-5548, Fax: 902-566-4701,
Wards: 7. Beach Grove
Jason E. Coady, Councillor, 902-566-5548, Fax: 902-566-4701,
Wards: 8. Highfield
Julie McCabe, Councillor, 902-566-5548, Wards: 9. Stonepark
Terry Bernard, Councillor, 902-566-5548, Fax: 902-566-4701,
Wards: 10. Falconwood
Peter Kelly, Chief Administrative Officer, 902-566-5548, Fax:
902-566-4701
Donna Waddell, Director, Corporate Services
Scott Adams, Manager, Public Works
Frank Quinn, Manager, Parks & Recreation
Randy MacDonald, Fire Chief

Summerside
275 Fitzroy St.
Summerside, PE C1N 1H9
Tel: 902-432-1230; *Fax:* 902-436-9296
contactus@city.summerside.pe.ca
www.summerside.ca
Municipal Type: City
Incorporated: 1995; *Area:* 28.49 sq km
County or District: Egmont; *Population in 2016:* 14,829
Provincial Electoral District(s): Wilmot-Summerside; St.
Eleanors-Summerside
Federal Electoral District(s): Egmont
Next Election: Nov. 7, 2022 (4 year terms)
Basil Stewart, Mayor, 902-432-1246
Norma McColeman, Deputy Mayor & Councillor, 902-786-8476,
Wards: 6. Centre East-Downtown
Bruce MacDougall, Councillor, 902-437-3602, Wards: 1. St.
Eleanor's-Bayview
Justin Doiron, Councillor, 902-786-7354, Wards: 2. St.
Eleanors-Slemon Park
Barb Ramsay, Councillor, 902-786-8243, Wards: 3.
Summerside-North
Cory Snow, Councillor, 902-786-6440, Wards: 4. Clifton/Market
Greg Campbell, Councillor, 902-786-7902, Wards: 5.
Hillcrest-Platte River
Brian McFeely, Councillor, 902-439-3326, Wards: 7.
Greenhouse-Three Oaks
Carrie Adams, Councillor, 902-439-9080, Wards: 8. Wilmot
Rob Philpott, Chief Administrative Officer, 902-439-8055
Kristen Dunsford, Acting Director, Financial Services,
902-432-9184
JP Desrosiers, Director, Community Services, 902-432-1234
Michael Thususka, Director, Economic Development,
902-432-0103
Ron Enman, Fire Chief, 902-432-4434

Other Municipalities in Prince Edward Island

Abrams Village
8938 Rte. 11
Wellington, PE C0B 2E0
Tel: 902-854-2255; *Fax:* 902-854-2266
abvillage@bellaliant.com

Municipal Type: Community
Incorporated: 1974; *Area:* 1.26 sq km
Population in 2016: 272
Provincial Electoral District(s): Evangeline-Miscouche
Federal Electoral District(s): Egmont
Next Election: Nov. 7, 2022 (4 year terms)
Roger Gallant, Chairperson
Pierre Arsenault, Chief Administrative Officer

Afton
1552 Rte. 19
New Dominion, PE C0A 1H6
Tel: 902-675-2567
afton.cic@gmail.com
Municipal Type: Community
Incorporated: 1974
Provincial Electoral District(s): Kellys Cross-Cumberland
Federal Electoral District(s): Malpeque
Next Election: Nov. 7, 2022 (4 year terms)
Note: According to the 2016 census, falls within Lot 65 (pop.
2,347; 84.53 sq. km.).
Brian Hogan, Chairperson
Beverley McIsaac, Chief Administrative Officer

Alberton
P.O. Box 153
3 Emma Dr.
Alberton, PE C0B 1B0
Tel: 902-853-2720; *Fax:* 902-853-2314
info@townofalberton.ca
www.townofalberton.ca
Municipal Type: Town
Incorporated: May 1913; *Area:* 4.52 sq km
County or District: Egmont; *Population in 2016:* 1,145
Provincial Electoral District(s): Alberton-Roseville
Federal Electoral District(s): Egmont
Next Election: Nov. 7, 2022 (4 year terms)
David Gordon, Mayor
Susan Wallace-Flynn, Chief Administrative Officer

Alexandra
1550 Pownal Rd.
Alexandra, PE C1B 1P6
Tel: 902-569-4760
sgw@hotmail.com
Municipal Type: Community
Incorporated: 1972
County or District: Cardigan
Provincial Electoral District(s): Vernon River-Stratford
Federal Electoral District(s): Cardigan
Next Election: Nov. 7, 2022 (4 year terms)
Note: According to the 2016 census, falls within Lot 49 (pop.
1,096; 95.15 sq. km.).
Glen Beaton, Mayor
Sheila Whiteway, Chief Administrative Officer

Annandale-Little Pond-Howe Bay
2547 Annadale Rd., Rte 310
Souris, PE C0A 2B0
Tel: 902-583-3156
littleponders@gmail.com
Municipal Type: Community
Incorporated: 1975
County or District: Cardigan
Provincial Electoral District(s): Georgetown-St. Peters
Federal Electoral District(s): Cardigan
Next Election: Nov. 7, 2022 (4 year terms)
Note: According to the 2016 census, falls within Lot 56 (pop.
328; 81.24 sq. km.).
Edwin McKie, Mayor
Paul MacDonald, Chief Administrative Officer

Bedeque & Area
P.O. Box 3892
933 Callbeck St.
Central Bedeque, PE C0B 1G0
Tel: 902-439-0733
Municipal Type: Community
Incorporated: 1978; *Area:* 2.53 sq km
County or District: Malpeque; *Population in 2016:* 302
Provincial Electoral District(s): Borden-Kinkora
Federal Electoral District(s): Malpeque
Next Election: Nov. 7, 2022 (4 year terms)
Ron Rayner, Chairperson
Nicole Desroches, Chief Administrative Officer

Belfast
3278 Rte. 1
South Pinette, PE C0A 1B0
Tel: 902-659-2989; *Fax:* 902-659-2813
ruralmunicipalityofbelfast@gmail.com
ruralmunicipalityofbelfast.com

Municipal Type: Community
Incorporated: 1972
County or District: Cardigan
Provincial Electoral District(s): Belfast-Murray River
Federal Electoral District(s): Cardigan
Next Election: Nov. 7, 2022 (4 year terms)
Note: According to the 2016 census, falls within Lot 57 (pop.
974; 96.60 sq. km.).
Jill Walsh, Mayor
Janice MacDonald, Chief Administrative Officer

Bonshaw
P.O. Box 40049
West Royalty
Charlottetown, PE C1E 0J2
Tel: 902-626-9623
bonshawcc@gmail.com
Municipal Type: Community
Incorporated: 1977
County or District: Malpeque
Provincial Electoral District(s): Kellys Cross-Cumberland
Federal Electoral District(s): Malpeque
Next Election: Nov. 7, 2022 (4 year terms)
Note: According to the 2016 census, falls within Lot 30 (pop.
849; 86.14 sq. km.).
Art Ortenburger, Chairperson
Horatio Toledo, Chief Administrative Officer

Borden-Carleton
P.O. Box 89
167 Industrial Dr.
Borden-Carleton, PE C0B 1X0
Tel: 902-437-2225; *Fax:* 902-437-2610
bcadmin@borden-carleton.ca
www.borden-carleton.ca
Municipal Type: Community
Incorporated: July 1, 1995; *Area:* 12.99 sq km
County or District: Malpeque; *Population in 2016:* 724
Provincial Electoral District(s): Borden-Kinkora
Federal Electoral District(s): Malpeque
Next Election: Nov. 7, 2022 (4 year terms)
Charles MacKenzie, Mayor
Anytra Eterovich, Chief Administrative Officer

Brackley
14 Union Rd.
Brackley, PE C1E 3J6
Tel: 902-368-8274
mecbrackley@gmail.com
www.brackleypei.ca
Municipal Type: Community
Incorporated: 1983; *Area:* 8.79 sq km
County or District: Malpeque; *Population in 2016:* 372
Provincial Electoral District(s): York-Oyster Bed
Federal Electoral District(s): Malpeque
Next Election: Nov. 7, 2022 (4 year terms)
Note: On Dec. 15, 2017 the Community of Winsloe South & the
Community of Brackley amalgamated to become the Rural
Municipality of Brackley.
Brandon McKenna, Mayor
Maureen Cudmore, Chief Administrative Officer

Breadalbane
20 Grafton St.
Breadalbane, PE C0A 1E0
Tel: 902-964-2730
Municipal Type: Community
Incorporated: 1991; *Area:* 12.55 sq km
Population in 2016: 167
Provincial Electoral District(s): Rustico-Emerald
Federal Electoral District(s): Malpeque
Next Election: Nov. 7, 2022 (4 year terms)
Margo Dooks, Chairperson
Kim MacLeod, Chief Administrative Officer

Brudenell
415 Brudenell Point Rd., RR#5
Montague, PE C0A 1R0
Tel: 902-838-4160; *Fax:* 902-838-3517
www.brudenellpei.com
Municipal Type: Community
Incorporated: 1973
County or District: Cardigan
Provincial Electoral District(s): Montague-Kilmuir
Federal Electoral District(s): Cardigan
Next Election: Nov. 7, 2022 (4 year terms)
Note: According to the 2016 census, falls within Lot 52 (pop.
740; 82.17 sq. km.).
Edward MacAulay, Mayor, Three Rivers
Linda Barry, Chief Administrative Officer

Cardigan

P.O. Box 40
358 Shore Rd.
Cardigan, PE C0A 1G0
Tel: 902-583-2198; *Fax:* 902-583-3198
admin@cardigan.ca
www.villageofcardigan.ca
Municipal Type: Community
Incorporated: 1954; *Area:* 5.12 sq km
County or District: Cardigan; *Population in 2016:* 269
Provincial Electoral District(s): Georgetown-St. Peters
Federal Electoral District(s): Cardigan
Next Election: Nov. 7, 2022 (4 year terms)
Edward MacAulay, Mayor, Three Rivers
Andrew Rowe, Chief Administrative Officer

Central Kings

P.O. Box 10
Bridgetown, RR#5
Cardigan, PE C0A 1G0
Tel: 902-583-2248
centralkings@hotmail.com
Municipal Type: Community
Incorporated: 1975
Provincial Electoral District(s): Georgetown-St. Peters
Federal Electoral District(s): Cardigan
Next Election: Nov. 7, 2022 (4 year terms)
Note: According to the 2016 census, falls within Lot 55 (pop.
398; 86.76 sq. km.).
Craig Jackson, Chairperson
Micheline Downe, Chief Administrative Officer, 902-593-2248,
Fax: 902-687-3733

Central Prince

P.O. Box 13
Ellerslie, PE C0B 1J0
Tel: 902-303-9446
centralprince@outlook.com
Municipal Type: Community
Incorporated: 1977
County or District: Egmont
Provincial Electoral District(s): Tyne Valley-Linkletter
Federal Electoral District(s): Egmont
Next Election: Nov. 7, 2022 (4 year terms)
Note: The communities of Ellerslie-Bideford & Lady Slipper
amalgamated into the new community of Central Prince on Sept.
28, 2018.
Rod Millar, Mayor
Ian Millar, Chief Administrative Officer

Clyde River

P.O. Box 644
Cornwall, PE C0A 1H0
Tel: 902-675-4747
clyderiver.cic@pei.sympatico.ca
clyderiverpei.com
Municipal Type: Community
Incorporated: 1974; *Area:* 16.52 sq km
County or District: Malpeque; *Population in 2016:* 653
Provincial Electoral District(s): Kelleys Cross-Cumberland
Federal Electoral District(s): Malpeque
Next Election: Nov. 7, 2022 (4 year terms)
Hilda Colodey, Chairperson, 902-675-3171
Bruce Brine, Chief Administrative Officer

Cornwall

P.O. Box 430
39 Lowther Dr.
Cornwall, PE C0A 1H0
Tel: 902-566-2354; *Fax:* 902-566-5228
town@cornwallpe.ca
www.cornwallpe.ca
Municipal Type: Town
Incorporated: 1995; *Area:* 28.19 sq km
County or District: Malpeque; *Population in 2016:* 5,348
Provincial Electoral District(s): Cornwall-Meadowbank
Federal Electoral District(s): Malpeque
Next Election: Nov. 7, 2022 (4 year terms)
Minerva McCourt, Mayor, 902-566-3791
Kevin Coady, Chief Administrative Officer

Crapaud

P.O. Box 30
Crapaud, PE C0A 1J0
Tel: 902-658-2558; *Fax:* 902-658-2450
crapaudadmin@pei.aibn.com
www.communityofcrapaud.com
Municipal Type: Community
Incorporated: 1950; *Area:* 2.15 sq km
County or District: Malpeque; *Population in 2016:* 319
Provincial Electoral District(s): Kellys Cross-Cumberland

Federal Electoral District(s): Malpeque
Next Election: Nov. 7, 2022 (4 year terms)
Neila Auld, Mayor
Eddie MacKenzie, Chief Administrative Officer, 902-658-2558

Darlington

2476 Johnstons Rd.
Darlington, PE C0A 1Y0
Tel: 902-621-0076
Municipal Type: Community
Incorporated: 1983
County or District: Malpeque
Provincial Electoral District(s): Rustico-Emerald
Federal Electoral District(s): Malpeque
Next Election: Nov. 7, 2022 (4 year terms)
Note: According to the 2016 census, falls within Lot 23 (pop.
984; 70.65 sq. km.) & Lot 31 (pop. 1,767; 68.60 sq. km.).
Matthew Sanford, Chairperson
Carolyn Sanford, Chief Administrative Officer

Eastern Kings

85 Munns Rd., RR#2
Bothwell, PE C0A 2B0
Tel: 902-357-2894; *Fax:* 902-357-2607
easternkingspe@gmail.com
www.easternkingspei.com
Municipal Type: Community
Incorporated: 1974
County or District: Cardigan
Provincial Electoral District(s): Souris-Elmira
Federal Electoral District(s): Cardigan
Next Election: Nov. 7, 2022 (4 year terms)
Note: According to the 2016 census, falls within Lot 47 (pop.
474; 89.85 sq. m.).
Grace Cameron, Mayor
Horatio Toledo, Chief Administrative Officer

Georgetown

P.O. Box 89
36 Kent St.
Georgetown, PE C0B 1L0
Tel: 902-652-2924; *Fax:* 902-652-2701
georgetown@pei.sympatico.ca
www.georgetown.ca
Municipal Type: Town
Incorporated: 1912; *Area:* 1.59 sq km
County or District: Cardigan; *Population in 2016:* 555
Provincial Electoral District(s): Georgetown-St. Peters
Federal Electoral District(s): Cardigan
Next Election: Nov. 7, 2022 (4 year terms)
Edward MacAulay, Mayor, Three Rivers
Dorothy Macdonald, Chief Administrative Officer

Greenmount-Montrose

260 Hardy Rd.
Alberton, PE C0B 1B0
Tel: 902-853-2235
greenmountmontrosemunicipality.wordpress.com
Municipal Type: Community
Incorporated: 1977
County or District: Egmont
Provincial Electoral District(s): Alberton-Roseville
Federal Electoral District(s): Egmont
Next Election: Nov. 7, 2022 (4 year terms)
Note: According to the 2016 census, falls within Lot 3 (pop. 774;
86.69 sq. km.).
Leroy Hiltz, Chairperson
Dave Pizio, Chief Administrative Officer

Hampshire

1001 Rte. 225
North Wiltshire, PE C0A 1Y0
Tel: 902-964-3376
communityofhampshire@gmail.com
Other Information: 902-393-6290
Municipal Type: Community
Incorporated: 1974
County or District: Malpeque
Provincial Electoral District(s): West Royalty-Springvale
Federal Electoral District(s): Malpeque
Next Election: Nov. 7, 2022 (4 year terms)
Note: According to the 2016 census, falls within Lot 31 (pop.
1,767; 68.60 sq. km.).
Gordon Lank, Chairperson
Donna Butler, Chief Administrative Officer

Hazelbrook

P.O. Box 1023
101 Kent St.
Charlottetown, PE C1A 1M0
Tel: 902-892-5819; *Fax:* 902-892-5760
ccouncil@communityofhazelbrook.com
www.communityofhazelbrook.com
Other Information: 902-629-8602
Municipal Type: Community
Incorporated: 1974
County or District: Cardigan
Provincial Electoral District(s): Vernon River-Stratford
Federal Electoral District(s): Cardigan
Next Election: Nov. 7, 2022 (4 year terms)
Note: According to the 2016 census, falls within Lot 48 (pop.
2,045; 71.97 sq. km.).
Brian Gallant, Chairperson
Ruth Copeland, Chief Administrative Officer

Hunter River

P.O. Box 154
Hunter River, PE C0A 1N0
Tel: 902-621-2170; *Fax:* 902-621-0836
admin.hunter.river@gmail.com
Municipal Type: Community
Incorporated: 1974; *Area:* 5.97 sq km
County or District: Malpeque; *Population in 2016:* 356
Provincial Electoral District(s): Rustico-Emerald
Federal Electoral District(s): Malpeque
Next Election: Nov. 7, 2022 (4 year terms)
Terry McGrath, Chairperson
Sarah Weeks, Chief Administrative Officer

Kensington

P.O. Box 418
55 Victoria St. East
Kensington, PE C0B 1M0
Tel: 902-836-3781; *Fax:* 902-836-3741
mail@townofkensington.com
kensington.ca
Municipal Type: Town
Incorporated: 1914; *Area:* 3.01 sq km
County or District: Malpeque; *Population in 2016:* 1,619
Provincial Electoral District(s): Kensington-Malpeque
Federal Electoral District(s): Malpeque
Next Election: Nov. 7, 2022 (4 year terms)
Rowan Caseley, Mayor
Geoff Baker, Chief Administrative Officer

Kingston

P.O. Box 648 Cornwall
Cornwall, PE C0A 1H0
Tel: 902-675-3670; *Fax:* 902-368-1239
thecouncil@kingstonpei.ca
kingstonpei.ca
Municipal Type: Community
Incorporated: 1974
County or District: Malpeque
Provincial Electoral District(s): Kellys Cross-Cumberland
Federal Electoral District(s): Malpeque
Next Election: Nov. 7, 2022 (4 year terms)
Note: According to the 2016 census, falls within Lot 31 (pop.
1,767; 68.60 sq. km.).
Alan Miller, Chairperson
Dianne Dowling, Chief Administrative Officer

Kinkora

P.O. Box 38
45 Anderson St.
Kinkora, PE C0B 1N0
Tel: 902-887-2868; *Fax:* 902-887-3514
communityofkinkora@eastlink.ca
www.kinkorapei.com
Municipal Type: Community
Incorporated: 1955; *Area:* 3.82 sq km
County or District: Malpeque; *Population in 2016:* 336
Provincial Electoral District(s): Borden-Kinkora
Federal Electoral District(s): Malpeque
Next Election: Nov. 7, 2022 (4 year terms)
Vacant, Mayor
Tina Harvey, Chief Administrative Officer

Linkletter

1670 Rte. 11
Linkletter, PE C1N 4J8
Tel: 902-724-0914
communityoflinkletter@gmail.com
communityoflinkletter.wordpress.com
Municipal Type: Community
Incorporated: 1972; *Area:* 9.08 sq km
County or District: Egmont; *Population in 2016:* 310
Provincial Electoral District(s): Tyne Valley-Linkletter

Federal Electoral District(s): Egmont
Next Election: Nov. 7, 2022 (4 year terms)
David Buell, Mayor
Kari Reynolds, Chief Administrative Officer

Lorne Valley
415 Brudenell Point Rd., RR#4
Montague, PE C0A 1R0
Tel: 902-838-4160
Municipal Type: Community
Incorporated: 1978
County or District: Cardigan
Provincial Electoral District(s): Georgetown-St. Peters
Federal Electoral District(s): Cardigan
Next Election: Nov. 7, 2022 (4 year terms)
Note: According to the 2016 census, falls within Lot 52 (pop. 740; 82.17 sq. km.).
Vacant, Mayor
Linda Barry, Chief Administrative Officer

Lot 11 & Area
P.O. Box 40
Ellerslie, PE C0B 1J0
Tel: 902-831-2962
admin@lot11andarea.org
www.lot11andarea.org
Other Information: 902-439-4331
Municipal Type: Community
Incorporated: 1982; *Area:* 89.33
County or District: Egmont; *Population in 2016:* 495
Provincial Electoral District(s): O'Leary-Inverness;
Alberton-Roseville
Federal Electoral District(s): Egmont
Next Election: Nov. 7, 2022 (4 year terms)
Susan Milligan, Chair
Lisa Smith, Chief Administrative Officer

Lower Montague
179A Lower Montague Rd., RR#2
Montague, PE C0A 1R0
Tel: 902-838-5405; *Fax:* 902-838-3617
administrator@lowermontague.ca
www.lowermontague.ca
Municipal Type: Community
Incorporated: 1974
County or District: Cardigan
Provincial Electoral District(s): Montague-Kilmuir
Federal Electoral District(s): Cardigan
Next Election: Nov. 7, 2022 (4 year terms)
Note: According to the 2016 census, falls within Lot 59 (pop. 1,186; 79.08 sq. km.).
Edward MacAulay, Mayor
Melda Patterson-Jones, Chief Administrative Officer

Malpeque Bay
P.O. Box 405
Kensington, PE C0B 1M0
Tel: 902-836-5029
communityofmalpequebay@gmail.com
www.malpequebay.ca
Other Information: themccarvills@gmail.com
Municipal Type: Community
Incorporated: 1973
County or District: Malpeque
Provincial Electoral District(s): Kensington-Malpeque
Federal Electoral District(s): Malpeque
Next Election: Nov. 7, 2022 (4 year terms)
Note: According to the 2016 census, falls within Lot 18 (pop. 1,062; 92.98 sq. km.).
Jamie Crozier, Chair
Joanne McCarvill, Chief Administrative Officer

Meadowbank
P.O. Box 1162
Cornwall, PE C0A 1H0
Tel: 902-388-1592
communityofmeadowbank@gmail.com
Municipal Type: Community
Incorporated: 1974; *Area:* 9.29 sq km
County or District: Malpeque; *Population in 2016:* 355
Provincial Electoral District(s): Cornwall-Meadowbank
Federal Electoral District(s): Malpeque
Next Election: Nov. 7, 2022 (4 year terms)
Helen Smith-MacPhail, Chair
Cheryl Champion, Chief Administrative Officer

Miltonvale Park
7B New Glasgow Rd., Rte. 224
North Milton, PE C1E 0S7
Tel: 902-368-3090; *Fax:* 902-368-1152
admin@miltonvalepark.com
www.miltonvalepark.com

Municipal Type: Community
Incorporated: 1974; *Area:* 35.45 sq km
County or District: Malpeque; *Population in 2016:* 1,148
Provincial Electoral District(s): West Royalty-Springvale
Federal Electoral District(s): Malpeque
Next Election: Nov. 7, 2022 (4 year terms)
Hal Parker, Chair
Shari MacDonald, Chief Administrative Officer

Miminegash
11334 Rte. 14
Miminegash, PE C0B 1S0
Tel: 902-882-3223; *Fax:* 902-882-2179
ebbsfleet41@gmail.com
Municipal Type: Community
Incorporated: 1968; *Area:* 1.90 sq km
County or District: Egmont; *Population in 2016:* 148
Provincial Electoral District(s): Alberton-Roseville
Federal Electoral District(s): Egmont
Next Election: Nov. 7, 2022 (4 year terms)
Audrey Callaghan, Chair
LouAnne Gallant, Chief Administrative Officer

Miscouche
P.O. Box 70
30 School St.
Miscouche, PE C0B 1T0
Tel: 902-436-4962; *Fax:* 902-436-4963
communityofmiscouche@pei.aibn.com
miscouche.ca
Municipal Type: Community
Incorporated: 1957; *Area:* 3.45 sq km
County or District: Egmont; *Population in 2016:* 873
Provincial Electoral District(s): Evangeline-Miscouche
Federal Electoral District(s): Egmont
Next Election: Nov. 7, 2022 (4 year terms)
Albert Gallant, Mayor
Michelle Perry, Chief Administrative Officer, 902-436-4962

Montague
P.O. Box 546
24 Queens Rd.
Montague, PE C0A 1R0
Tel: 902-838-2528; *Fax:* 902-838-3392
townhall@montaguepei.ca
www.montaguepei.ca
Other Information: jhaley@montaguepei.ca
Municipal Type: Town
Incorporated: 1917; *Area:* 3.16 sq km
County or District: Cardigan; *Population in 2016:* 1,961
Provincial Electoral District(s): Montague-Kilmuir
Federal Electoral District(s): Cardigan
Next Election: Nov. 7, 2022 (4 year terms)
Edward MacAulay, Mayor, Three Rivers
Andrew Daggett, Chief Administrative Officer

Morell
P.O. Box 173
25 Sunset Cres.
Morell, PE C0A 1S0
Tel: 902-961-2900; *Fax:* 902-739-2900
morellcommunity@eastlink.ca
www.morellpei.com
Municipal Type: Community
Incorporated: 1953; *Area:* 1.46 sq km
County or District: Cardigan; *Population in 2016:* 297
Provincial Electoral District(s): Morell-Mermaid
Federal Electoral District(s): Cardigan
Next Election: Nov. 7, 2022 (4 year terms)
David MacAdam, Chair
Jennifer Phelan, Chief Administrative Officer

Mount Stewart
P.O. Box 143
Mount Stewart, PE C0A 1T0
Tel: 902-676-2881; *Fax:* 902-731-3111
mountstewart@eastlink.ca
mountstewartpei.wordpress.com
Municipal Type: Community
Incorporated: 1953; *Area:* 1.22 sq km
County or District: Cardigan; *Population in 2016:* 209
Provincial Electoral District(s): Morell-Mermaid
Federal Electoral District(s): Cardigan
Next Election: Nov. 7, 2022 (4 year terms)
Jay Doucette, Mayor
Christine Watts, Chief Administrative Officer

Murray Harbour
P.O. Box 72
27 Park St.
Murray Harbour, PE C0A 1V0
Tel: 902-962-3835
villoffice@eastlink.ca
Other Information: office@murrayharbour.ca
Municipal Type: Community
Incorporated: 1953; *Area:* 3.89 sq km
County or District: Cardigan; *Population in 2016:* 258
Provincial Electoral District(s): Belfast-Murray River
Federal Electoral District(s): Cardigan
Next Election: Nov. 7, 2022 (4 year terms)
Paul White, Mayor
Mark Tiller, Chief Administrative Officer

Murray River
P.O. Box 266
11179 Shore Rd.
Murray River, PE C0A 1W0
Tel: 902-962-2820; *Fax:* 902-962-3671
mrvillage@bellaliant.net
www.murrayriverpei.com
Other Information: www.murrayriver.ca
Municipal Type: Community
Incorporated: 1955; *Area:* 1.47 sq km
County or District: Cardigan; *Population in 2016:* 304
Provincial Electoral District(s): Belfast-Murray River
Federal Electoral District(s): Cardigan
Next Election: Nov. 7, 2022 (4 year terms)
Patricia Bray, Chair, 902-962-3593
Dianne MacDonald, Chief Administrative Officer

New Haven-Riverdale
P.O. Box 309 Cornwall
Cornwall, PE C0A 1H0
newhavenriverdalecc.ca
Municipal Type: Community
Incorporated: 1974
County or District: Malpeque
Provincial Electoral District(s): Kellys Cross-Cumberland
Federal Electoral District(s): Malpeque
Next Election: Nov. 7, 2022 (4 year terms)
Note: According to the 2016 census, falls within Lot 31 (pop. 1,767; 68.60 sq. km.).
Claus Brodersen, Chair, 902-675-3765
Bonnie MacLean, Chief Administrative Officer, 902-675-7000

North Rustico
P.O. Box 38
106 Riverside Dr.
North Rustico, PE C0A 1X0
Tel: 902-963-3211; *Fax:* 902-963-3321
northrustico@pei.aibn.com
www.northrustico.ca
Municipal Type: Community
Incorporated: 1954; *Area:* 2.41 sq km
County or District: Malpeque; *Population in 2016:* 607
Provincial Electoral District(s): Rustico-Emerald
Federal Electoral District(s): Malpeque
Next Election: Nov. 7, 2022 (4 year terms)
Anne Kirk, Mayor
Patsy Gamauf, Chief Administrative Officer

North Shore
2120 Covehead Rd., Rte. 25
York, PE C0A 1P0
Tel: 902-672-2600; *Fax:* 902-672-1766
www.stanhopecovehead.pe.ca
Municipal Type: Community
Incorporated: 1974
County or District: Malpeque
Provincial Electoral District(s): York-Oyster Bed
Federal Electoral District(s): Malpeque
Next Election: Nov. 7, 2022 (4 year terms)
Note: The communities of Pleasant Grove, Grand Tracadie & North Shore amalgamated into North Shore on Sept. 28, 2018.
Gerard Watts, Mayor
Jonathan MacLean, Chief Administrative Officer

North Wiltshire
1605 Kinkora Rd.
North Wiltshire, PE C0A 1Y0
Tel: 902-621-1908
Municipal Type: Community
Incorporated: 1974
County or District: Egmont
Provincial Electoral District(s): Kelleys Cross-Cumberland
Federal Electoral District(s): Malpeque
Next Election: Nov. 7, 2022 (4 year terms)
Note: According to the 2016 census, falls within Lot 31 (pop. 1,767; 68.60 sq. km.).

Robert Bertram, Chair
Charlene Waddell, Chief Administrative Officer

Northport
P.O. Box 466
Alberton, PE C0B 1B0
Tel: 902-856-2831
Municipal Type: Community
Incorporated: 1974
County or District: Egmont
Provincial Electoral District(s): Alberton-Roseville
Federal Electoral District(s): Egmont
Next Election: Nov. 7, 2022 (4 year terms)
Note: According to the 2016 census, falls within Lot 2 (pop. 1,457; 85.83 sq. km.) & Lot 5 (pop. 1,285; 80.92 sq. km.).
Wendy McNeill, Chair
Hillary Gallant, Chief Administrative Officer

O'Leary
P.O. Box 130
18 Community St.
O'Leary, PE C0B 1V0
Tel: 902-859-3311; *Fax:* 902-859-2341
olearyadm@eastlink.ca
www.townofoleary.com
Municipal Type: Town
Incorporated: 1951; *Area:* 1.68 sq km
County or District: Egmont; *Population in 2016:* 815
Provincial Electoral District(s): O'Leary-Inverness
Federal Electoral District(s): Egmont
Next Election: Nov. 7, 2022 (4 year terms)
Eric Gavin, Mayor
Beverley Shaw, Chief Administrative Officer

Resort Municipality
7591 Cawnpore Lane, RR#2
Hunter River, PE C0A 1N0
Tel: 902-963-2698; *Fax:* 902-963-2932
resort@pei.aibn.com
resortmunicipalitypei.com
Other Information: resortmunicipal@eastlink.ca
Municipal Type: Community
Incorporated: 1990; *Area:* 37.79 sq km
Population in 2016: 328
Provincial Electoral District(s): Rustico-Emerald
Federal Electoral District(s): Malpeque
Next Election: Aug. 2022
Note: Comprised of Stanley Bridge, Hope River, Bayview, Cavendish & North Rustico.
Matthew Jelley, Mayor
Brenda MacDonald, Chief Administrative Officer

St. Felix
P.O. Box 22
Tignish, PE C0B 2B0
Tel: 902-882-4015
Municipal Type: Community
Incorporated: 1977
County or District: Egmont
Provincial Electoral District(s): Tignish-Palmer Road
Federal Electoral District(s): Egmont
Next Election: Nov. 7, 2022 (4 year terms)
Note: According to the 2016 census, falls within Lot 2 (pop. 1,457; 85.83 sq. km.).
Vance Keough, Mayor
Joanne Gaudette, Chief Administrative Officer, Fax: 902-882-3443

St. Louis
P.O. Box 40
St Louis, PE C0B 1Z0
Tel: 902-856-2203
Municipal Type: Community
Incorporated: 1964; *Area:* 0.62
County or District: Egmont; *Population in 2016:* 66
Provincial Electoral District(s): Tignish-Palmer Road
Federal Electoral District(s): Egmont
Next Election: Nov. 7, 2022 (4 year terms)
Everett (Sonny) Wedge, Chair
Shaunda Hanlon, Chief Administrative Officer

St. Nicholas
3699 St. Nicholas
Miscouche, PE C0B 1T0
Tel: 902-432-4368
Municipal Type: Community
Incorporated: 1991
Provincial Electoral District(s): Evangeline-Miscouche
Federal Electoral District(s): Egmont
Next Election: Nov. 7, 2022 (4 year terms)
Note: According to the 2016 census, falls within Lot 17 (pop. 575; 51.41 sq. km.).

Jason Woodbury, Mayor
Vacant, Chief Administrative Officer

St. Peter's Bay
P.O. Box 51
5599 St. Peter's Rd.
St Peter's Bay, PE C0A 2A0
Tel: 902-961-2268; *Fax:* 902-961-3148
stpeters@eastlink.ca
www.stpetersbaycommunity.com
Municipal Type: Community
Incorporated: 1953; *Area:* 4.27 sq km
County or District: Cardigan; *Population in 2016:* 237
Provincial Electoral District(s): Georgetown-St. Peters
Federal Electoral District(s): Cardigan
Next Election: Nov. 7, 2022 (4 year terms)
Ron MacInnis, Chair
Mary Burge, Chief Administrative Officer

Sherbrooke
P.O. Box 1344
Summerside, PE C1N 4K2
Tel: 902-436-7005; *Fax:* 902-436-9170
Municipal Type: Community
Incorporated: 1972; *Area:* 8.85 sq km
Population in 2016: 159
Provincial Electoral District(s): Kensington-Malpeque
Federal Electoral District(s): Egmont
Next Election: Nov. 7, 2022 (4 year terms)
Ron Chappell, Chair
Peggy Kilbride, Chief Administrative Officer

Souris
P.O. Box 628
75 Main St.
Souris, PE C0A 2B0
Tel: 902-687-2157; *Fax:* 902-687-4426
www.sourispei.com
Municipal Type: Town
Incorporated: 1910; *Area:* 3.47 sq km
County or District: Cardigan; *Population in 2016:* 1,053
Provincial Electoral District(s): Souris-Elmira
Federal Electoral District(s): Cardigan
Next Election: Nov. 7, 2022 (4 year terms)
Jo-Anne Dunphy, Interim Mayor & Deputy Mayor
Shelley LaVie, Chief Administrative Officer, 902-687-2157

Souris West
P.O. Box 690
Souris, PE C0A 2B0
Tel: 902-687-2602
Municipal Type: Community
Incorporated: 1972
County or District: Cardigan
Provincial Electoral District(s): Souris-Elmira
Federal Electoral District(s): Cardigan
Next Election: Nov. 7, 2022 (4 year terms)
Note: According to the 2016 census, falls within Lot 44 (pop. 772; 76.89 sq. km.).
Pat O'Connor, Chair
Cathy Williams, Chief Administrative Officer

Stratford
234 Shakespeare Dr.
Stratford, PE C1B 2V8
Tel: 902-569-1995; *Fax:* 902-569-5000
info@townofstratford.ca
townofstratford.ca
Municipal Type: Town
Incorporated: April 1, 1995; *Area:* 22.53 sq km
Population in 2016: 9,706
Provincial Electoral District(s): Stratford-Kinlock; Vernon River-Stratford
Federal Electoral District(s): Cardigan
Next Election: Nov. 7, 2022 (4 year terms)
Steve Ogden, Mayor
Robert Hughes, P.Eng, Chief Administrative Officer, 902-569-6251

Tignish
P.O. Box 57
209 Phillip St.
Tignish, PE C0B 2B0
Tel: 902-882-2600; *Fax:* 902-882-2414
townoftignish.ca
Municipal Type: Community
Incorporated: 1952; *Area:* 5.87 sq km
County or District: Egmont; *Population in 2016:* 719
Provincial Electoral District(s): Tignish-Pamler Road
Federal Electoral District(s): Egmont
Next Election: Nov. 7, 2022 (4 year terms)
Allan McInnis, Chair

Chancey Gaudette, Chief Administrative Officer

Tignish Shore
RR#1
Tignish, PE C0B 2B0
Tel: 902-853-3931
Other Information: 902-882-3811
Municipal Type: Community
Incorporated: 1975
Provincial Electoral District(s): Tignish-Pamler Road
Federal Electoral District(s): Egmont
Next Election: Nov. 7, 2022 (4 year terms)
Note: According to the 2016 census, falls within Lot 1 (pop. 1,670; 95.96 sq. km.).
Ronnie McRae, Chair
Donna MacKay, Chief Administrative Officer

Tyne Valley
P.O. Box 39
Tyne Valley, PE C0B 2C0
Tel: 902-831-2938
rmoftynevalley@gmail.com
Municipal Type: Community
Incorporated: 1966; *Area:* 1.72 sq km
County or District: Egmont; *Population in 2016:* 249
Provincial Electoral District(s): Cascumpec-Grand River
Federal Electoral District(s): Egmont
Next Election: Nov. 7, 2022 (4 year terms)
Jeffery Noye, Mayor
Marie Barlow, Chief Administrative Officer

Union Road
P.O. Box 20114
161 St. Peters Rd.
Charlottetown, PE C1A 9E3
Tel: 902-629-8602
admin@communityofunionroadpei.com
www.communityofunionroadpei.com
Municipal Type: Community
Incorporated: 1977; *Area:* 9.97 sq km
County or District: Malpeque; *Population in 2016:* 204
Provincial Electoral District(s): York-Oyster Bed
Federal Electoral District(s): Malpeque; Cardigan
Next Election: Nov. 7, 2022 (4 year terms)
Fern Yeo, Chair, 902-368-8207
Ruth Copeland, Chief Administrative Officer, 902-892-5819

Valleyfield
1783 Queens Rd.
Lyndale, PE C0A 1R0
Tel: 902-838-4447; *Fax:* 902-838-3649
Municipal Type: Community
Incorporated: 1974
County or District: Cardigan
Provincial Electoral District(s): Montague-Kilmuir; Belfast-Murray River
Federal Electoral District(s): Cardigan
Next Election: Nov. 7, 2022 (4 year terms)
Note: According to the 2016 census, falls within Lot 57 (pop. 974; 96.60 sq. km.) & Lot 59 (pop. 1,186; 79.08 sq. km.).
Vacant, Mayor
Margaret Campion, Chief Administrative Officer

Victoria
P.O. Box 7
Victoria, PE C0A 2G0
Tel: 902-658-2541
Municipal Type: Community
Incorporated: 1951; *Area:* 1.46 sq km
County or District: Malpeque; *Population in 2016:* 74
Provincial Electoral District(s): Kellys Cross-Cumberland
Federal Electoral District(s): Malpeque
Next Election: Nov. 7, 2022 (4 year terms)
Ian W. Dennison, Mayor
Hilary Price, Chief Administrative Officer

Warren Grove
P.O. Box 963
7 Mill Rd.
Cornwall, PE C0A 1H0
communityofwarrengrove@gmail.com
www.communityofwarrengrove.com
Municipal Type: Community
Incorporated: 1985; *Area:* 10.18 sq km
County or District: Malpeque; *Population in 2016:* 356
Provincial Electoral District(s): North River-Rice Point
Federal Electoral District(s): Malpeque
Next Election: Nov. 7, 2022 (4 year terms)
Trevor Sanderson, Chair
Norma Mayhew, Chief Administrative Officer, 902-393-5971

Wellington
P.O. Box 26
Wellington, PE C0B 2E0
Tel: 902-854-2920
office@wellingtonpei.ca
wellingtonpei.ca
Other Information: info@wellingtonpei.ca
Municipal Type: Community
Incorporated: 1959; *Area:* 1.78 sq km
County or District: Egmont; *Population in 2016:* 415
Provincial Electoral District(s): Evangeline-Miscouche
Federal Electoral District(s): Egmont
Next Election: Nov. 7, 2022 (4 year terms)
Alcide Bernard, Mayor
Giselle Bernard, Chief Administrative Officer

West River
1144 St. Catherines Rd.
St Catherines, PE C0A 1H1
Tel: 902-393-3840; *Fax:* 902-367-1147
Municipal Type: Community
Incorporated: 1974
County or District: Malpeque
Provincial Electoral District(s): Kellys Cross-Cumberland
Federal Electoral District(s): Malpeque
Next Election: Nov. 7, 2022 (4 year terms)
Note: According to the 2016 census, falls within Lot 65 (pop. 2,347; 84.53 sq. km.).
Eric MacArthur, Chair
Bill Grant, Chief Administrative Officer, 902-569-1792

York
P.O. Box 8910
669 Rte. 25
York, PE C0A 1P0
Tel: 902-367-6475; *Fax:* 902-569-1132
yorkmunicipality@gmail.com
yorkmunicipality.wixsite.com/website
Municipal Type: Community
Incorporated: 1986
Provincial Electoral District(s): York-Oyster Bed
Federal Electoral District(s): Malpeque
Next Election: Nov. 7, 2022 (4 year terms)
Note: According to the 2016 census, falls within Lot 34 (pop. 2,847; 91.93 sq. km.).
Richard Furlong, Mayor
Heather Idt, Chief Administrative Officer

QUÉBEC

Québec legislation recognizes two levels of municipal organization: the local and the regional.

Major municipal reform has reduced the number of local municipalities from nearly 1,400 in 1998 to 1,110 as of 2016. Of this number, 227 fall under the jurisdiction of the Cities and Towns Act (RSQ, chap. C-19). Nine of them have over 100,000 inhabitants and account for 53% of the Québec population. There are also 883 municipalities that are governed by the Municipal Code of Québec, 14 northern villages that fall under the Act Respecting Northern Villages and the Kativik Regional Government, and 9 villages governed by the Cree Villages and the Naskapi Village Act.

The regional level of municipal territorial organization includes the Montréal and Québec City metropolitan communities, the 87 regional county municipalities (RCMs), and the Kativik Regional Government. The metropolitan communities and RCMs are made up of local municipalities. RCMs may also include unorganized territories.

The regional organizations were created to ensure that issues that go beyond local boundaries were handled at the regional or metropolitan level. Although their structures, operation and powers vary, they are based on identical principles. The Montréal and Québec City metropolitan communities are responsible at their level for land use planning, economic development, international economic promotion, artistic and cultural development, regional orientations in public transit, waste management planning, establishing a tax base sharing program, as well as for determining and financing regional facilities, infrastructures, activities, and services. RCMs also meet regional needs, including land use planning and the pooling of services. In addition, they exercise certain powers in the areas of economic development, public security and the environment. The Kativik Regional Government is in charge of local administration, police, transport, communications and labour force training and use, and may also set minimum standards by ordinance for things like house and building construction.

Eight local municipalities belong neither to a metropolitan community nor to one of the regional county municipalities. They do, however, wield some of the same powers as RCMs. This also holds true for six other cities, which although situated within one of the two metropolitan communities, nonetheless exercise certain of the powers of an RCM.

Eight cities are divided into boroughs. The boroughs have consultative and decision-making powers, are responsible for delivering certain neighbourhood services, and are represented by an elected borough council. Elections in the province are held every four years on the first Sunday of November (2021, 2025, etc.).

Source: © Department of Natural Resources Canada. All rights reserved.

Québec

Major Municipalities in Québec

Alma
140, rue St-Joseph sud
Alma, QC G8B 3R1
Tél: 418-669-5000; *Téléc:* 418-669-5029
info@ville.alma.qc.ca
www.ville.alma.qc.ca
Entité municipal: City
Incorporation: 21 février 2001; *Area:* 196,54 km2
Comté ou district: Lac-Saint-Jean-Est; *Population au 2016:* 30,776
Circonscription(s) électorale(s) provinciale(s): Lac-St-Jean
Circonscription(s) électorale(s) fédérale(s): Lac-Saint-Jean
Prochaines élections: 7e novembre 2021
Marc Asselin, Maire
Olivier Larouche, Conseiller, Wards: 1. Delisle
Jocelyn Fradette, Conseiller, Wards: 2. Isle-Maligne Albert-Naud
François Carrier, Conseiller, Wards: 3. Melançon
Frédéric Tremblay, Conseiller, Wards: 4. Damase-Boulanger
Véronique Fortin, Conseillère, Wards: 5. Saint-Pierre
Sylvie Beaumont, Conseillère, Wards: 6. Champagnat
Audrée Villeneuve, Conseillère, Wards: 7. Scott
Alain Fortin, Conseiller, Wards: 8. Signay-Labarre
Jean Paradis, Greffier
Sylvain Duchesne, Directeur général, 418-669-5001
Karine Morel, Directrice, Travaux publics, 418-669-5001
Alain Tremblay, Directeur, Ressources humaines, 418-669-5001
Denis Verrette, Directeur, Urbanisme, 418-669-5031
Maxime Fortin, Directeur, Prévention des incendies, 418-669-5001

Amos
182, 1e rue est
Amos, QC J9T 2G1
Tél: 819-732-3254; *Téléc:* 819-727-9792
infos@amos.quebec
amos.quebec
Entité municipal: City
Incorporation: 17 janvier 1987; *Area:* 430,29 km2
Comté ou district: Abitibi; *Population au 2016:* 12,823
Circonscription(s) électorale(s) provinciale(s): Abitibi-Ouest
Circonscription(s) électorale(s) fédérale(s):
Abitibi-Témiscamingue
Prochaines élections: 7e novembre 2021
Sébastien D'Astous, Maire
Yvon Leduc, Conseiller, Wards: 1
Martin Roy, Conseiller, Wards: 2
Nathalie Michaud, Conseillère, Wards: 3
Pierre Deshaires, Conseiller, Wards: 4
Mario Brunet, Conseiller, Wards: 5
Micheline Godbout, Conseillère, Wards: 6
Claudyne Maurice, Greffière
Guy Nolet, Directeur général
Guy Béchard, Directeur, Service sécurité d'incendie
Richard Michaud, Directeur, Services administratif et financier

L'Ancienne-Lorette
1575, rue Turmel
L'Ancienne-Lorette, QC G2E 3J5
Tél: 418-872-9811; *Téléc:* 418-641-6019
info@lancienne-lorette.org
lancienne-lorette.org
Entité municipal: City
Incorporation: 1er janvier 2006; *Area:* 7,72 km2
Comté ou district: Communauté métropolitaine de Québec;
Population au 2016: 16,543
Circonscription(s) électorale(s) provinciale(s): La Peltrie
Circonscription(s) électorale(s) fédérale(s): Louis-Saint-Laurent
Prochaines élections: 7e novembre 2021
Gaétan Pageau, Maire
Josée Ossio, Conseiller, 418-871-0758, Wards: 1.
Saint-Jacques
André Laliberté, Conseiller, 418-864-7545, Wards: 2.
Notre-Dame
Vacant, Conseiller, Wards: 3. Saint-Paul
Charles Guérard, Conseiller, 418-871-7774, Wards: 4.
Saint-Oliver
Sylvie Papillon, Conseillère, 418-977-4028, Wards: 5.
Saint-Jean-Baptiste
Sylvie Falardeau, Conseillère, 418-872-6949, Wards: 6. des Pins
Marie-Hélène Savard, Greffière
André Rousseau, Directeur général
Anick Marceau, Trésorière
Éric Ferland, Directeur, Travaux publics

L'Assomption
781, rang du Bas-de-L'Assomption Nord
L'Assomption, QC J5W 2H1
Tél: 450-589-5671; *Téléc:* 450-589-4512
bureauducitoyen@ville.lassomption.qc.ca
www.ville.lassomption.qc.ca
Entité municipal: City
Incorporation: 1er juillet 2000; *Area:* 98,99 km2
Comté ou district: L'Assomption; Communauté métropolitaine de Montréal; *Population au 2016:* 22,429
Circonscription(s) électorale(s) provinciale(s): L'Assomption
Circonscription(s) électorale(s) fédérale(s): Repentigny
Prochaines élections: 7e novembre 2021
Sébastien Nadeau, Maire
Nathalie Ayotte, Conseillère, Wards: 1. Hector-Charland
Pierre-Étienne Thériault, Conseiller, Wards: 2. Wilfrid Laurier
François Moreau, Conseiller, Wards: 3.
Joseph-Édouard-Faribault
Nicole Martel, Conseillère, Wards: 4. Pierre-LeSueur
Chantal Brien, Conseillère, Wards: 5. Louis-Michel-Viger
Marc-André Desjardins, Conseiller, Wards: 6. Louis-Laberge
Michel Gagnon, Conseiller, Wards: 7. Albert-Racette
Fernanrd Gendron, Conseiller, Wards: 8. Maurice-Lafortune
Serge Geoffrion, Directeur général
Sophie Laurin, Trésorier, 450-589-5671, Fax: 450-589-4512
Jean-Charles Drapeau, Directeur, Service de la qualité de vie
Michel Doré, Directeur, Service de sécurité incendie

Baie-Comeau
19, av Marquette
Baie-Comeau, QC G4Z 1K5
Tél: 418-296-4931
vbc@ville.baie-comeau.qc.ca
www.ville.baie-comeau.qc.ca
Entité municipal: City
Incorporation: 23 juin 1982; *Area:* 336,59 km2
Comté ou district: Manicouagan; *Population au 2016:* 21,536
Circonscription(s) électorale(s) provinciale(s): René-Lévesque
Circonscription(s) électorale(s) fédérale(s): Manicouagan
Prochaines élections: 7e novembre 2021
Yves Montigny, Maire
Sylvain Girard, Conseiller, Wards: Saint-Sacrement
Réjean Girard, Conseiller, Wards: Mgr-Bélanger
Alain Charest, Conseiller, Wards: Trudel
Mario Quinn, Conseiller, Wards: N.-A.-Labrie
Alain Choinard, Conseiller, Wards: La Chasse
Onil Lévesque, Conseiller, Wards: Saint-Nom-de-Marie
Viviane Richard, Conseillère, Wards: Saint-Amélie
Martine Salomon, Conseillère, Wards: Saint-George
Annick Tremblay, Greffière, 418-296-8109, Fax: 418-296-8151
François Corriveau, Directeur général, 418-296-8104, Fax: 418-296-8121
Jeanie Caron, Trésorière et directrice, Finances, 418-296-8128, Fax: 418-296-8349
Ghislain Gauthier, Directeur, Travaux publics et gestion de l'eau, 418-296-4931, Fax: 418-296-3095
Carl Prévéreault, Directeur, Culture et loisirs, 418-296-8362, Fax: 418-296-8323
Alain Miville, Directeur, Sécurité publique - Protection incendie, 418-589-1504, Fax: 418-589-1582

Beaconsfield
303, boul Beaconsfield
Beaconsfield, QC H9W 4A7
Tél: 514-428-4400
info@beaconsfield.ca
www.beaconsfield.ca
Entité municipal: City
Incorporation: 1er janvier 2006; *Area:* 11,03 km2
Comté ou district: Communauté métropolitaine de Montréal;
Population au 2016: 19,324
Circonscription(s) électorale(s) provinciale(s): Jacques-Cartier
Circonscription(s) électorale(s) fédérale(s): Lac-Saint-Louis
Prochaines élections: 7e novembre 2021
Georges Bourelle, Maire, 514-428-4410
Dominique Godin, Conseiller, 514-249-8843, Wards: 1
Karen Messier, Conseillère, 514-428-8975, Wards: 2
Rob Mercuri, Conseiller, 514-448-1349, Wards: 3
David Newell, Conseiller, 514-630-4274, Wards: 4
Roger Moss, Conseiller, 514-426-2144, Wards: 5
Al Gardner, Conseiller, 514-428-4400, Wards: 6
Nathalie Libersan-Laniel, Greffière
Patrice Boileau, Directeur général

Beauharnois
#100, 660, rue Ellice
Beauharnois, QC J6N 1Y1
Tél: 450-429-3546; *Téléc:* 450-429-2478
reception@ville.beauharnois.qc.ca
ville.beauharnois.qc.ca
Entité municipal: City
Incorporation: 1er janvier 2002; *Area:* 69,31 km2
Comté ou district: Beauharnois-Salaberry; Communauté métropolitaine de Montréal; *Population au 2016:* 12,884
Circonscription(s) électorale(s) provinciale(s): Beauharnois
Circonscription(s) électorale(s) fédérale(s): Salaberry-Suroît
Prochaines élections: 7e novembre 2021
Bruno Tremblay, Maire
Jocelyne Rajotte, Conseillère, Wards: 1
Roxanne Poissant, Conseillère, Wards: 2
Richard Dubuc, Conseiller, Wards: 4
Alain Savard, Conseiller, Wards: 5
Linda Toulouse, Conseillère, Wards: 6
Karen Loko, Greffière, 450-429-3546
Alain Gravel, Directeur général
Guylaine Côte, Directrice, Finances
Jean-Maurice Marleau, Directeur, Sécurité incendie et civile
Michel Morneau, Directeur, Occupation du territoire et à l'aménagement urbain

Bécancour
1295, av Nicolas-Perrot
Bécancour, QC G9H 1A1
Tél: 819-294-6500; *Téléc:* 819-294-6535
info@ville.becancour.qc.ca
www.becancour.net
Entité municipal: City
Incorporation: 17 octobre 1965; *Area:* 440,68 km2
Comté ou district: Bécancour; *Population au 2016:* 13,031
Circonscription(s) électorale(s) provinciale(s): Nicolet-Bécancour
Circonscription(s) électorale(s) fédérale(s):
Bécancour-Nicolet-Saurel
Prochaines élections: 7e novembre 2021
Jean-Guy Dubois, Maire
Fernand Croteau, Conseiller, Wards: 1. Bécancour
Raymond St-Onge, Conseiller, Wards: 2. Sainte-Gertrude
Pierre Moras, Conseiller, Wards: 3. Gentilly
Mario Gagné, Conseiller, Wards: 4. Précieux-Sang
Denis Vouligny, Conseiller, Wards: 5. Saint-Grégoire
Carmen Lampron-Pratte, Conseillère, Wards: 6. Sainte-Angèle
Isabelle Auger St-Yves, Greffière
Jean-Marc Dirouard, Directeur général
James McCulloch, Directeur, Travaux publics
Luc Desmarais, Directeur, Service de sécurité incendie

Beloeil
777, rue Laurier
Beloeil, QC J3G 4S9
Tél: 450-467-2835; *Téléc:* 450-464-5445
info@beloeil.ca
beloeil.ca
Entité municipal: City
Incorporation: 9e décembre 1903; *Area:* 24,40 km2
Comté ou district: La Vallée-du-Richelieu; Communauté métropolitaine de Montréal; *Population au 2016:* 22,458
Circonscription(s) électorale(s) provinciale(s): Borduas
Circonscription(s) électorale(s) fédérale(s): Beloeil-Chambly
Prochaines élections: 7e novembre 2021
Diane Lavoie, Mairesse, 450-467-2835
Louise Allie, Conseillère, 450-446-4201, Wards: 1
Renée Trudel, Conseillère, 514-718-2317, Wards: 2
Odette Martin, Conseillère, 450-536-2586, Wards: 3
Luc Cossette, Conseiller, 514-820-8395, Wards: 4
Guy Bédard, Conseiller, 450-446-7837, Wards: 5
Pierre Verret, Conseiller, 450-467-0630, Wards: 6
Réginald Gagnon, Conseillère, 514-569-4500, Wards: 7
Jean-Yves Labadie, Conseiller, 450-446-0347, Wards: 8
Marilyne Tremblay, Greffière
Martine Vallières, Directrice générale, 450-467-2835
Claudia De Courval, Directrice, Service de l'ingénierie
Dany Dolan, Directeur, Travaux publics

Blainville
1000, ch du Plan-Bouchard
Blainville, QC J7C 3S9
Tél: 450-434-5200; *Téléc:* 450-434-8295
accueil@blainville.ca
blainville.ca
Entité municipal: City
Incorporation: 1er juillet 1968; *Area:* 55,16 km2
Comté ou district: Thérèse-De Blainville; Communauté métropolitaine de Montréal; *Population au 2016:* 56,863
Circonscription(s) électorale(s) provinciale(s): Blainville; Groulx
Circonscription(s) électorale(s) fédérale(s): Thérèse-De Blainville
Prochaines élections: 7e novembre 2021
Richard Perreault, Maire
Liza Poulin, Conseillère, Wards: 1. Fontainebleau
Stéphane Dufour, Conseiller, Wards: 2. Côte-Saint-Louis
Serge Paquette, Conseiller, Wards: 3. Saint-Rédempteur
Guy Frigon, Conseiller, Wards: 4. Plan-Bouchard
Jean-François Pinard, Conseiller, Wards: 5.
Notre-Dame-de-l'Assomption

Danielle Landreville, Conseillère, Wards: 3
Richard Leduc, Conseiller, Wards: 4
Yves Liard, Conseiller, Wards: 5
Patrick Lasalle, Conseiller, Wards: 6
Patrick Bonin, Conseiller, Wards: 7
Alexandre Martel, Conseiller, Wards: 8
Mylène Mayer, Directrice, Greffe et affaires juridiques, 450-960-8998
Gaétan Béchard, Directeur général, 450-753-8031
Julie Bourgie, Trésorerie et Directrice, Finances, 450-753-8185
Carl Gauthier, Directeur, Incendies, 450-753-8154

Kirkland
17200, boul Hymus
Kirkland, QC H9J 3Y8
Tél: 514-694-4100; *Téléc:* 514-630-2711
www.ville.kirkland.qc.ca
Entité municipal: City
Incorporation: 1er janvier 2006; *Area:* 9,63 km2
Comté ou district: Communauté métropolitaine de Montréal;
Population au 2016: 20,151
Circonscription(s) électorale(s) provinciale(s): Nelligan
Circonscription(s) électorale(s) fédérale(s): Lac-Saint-Louis
Prochaines élections: 7e novembre 2021
Michel Gibson, Maire, 514-694-4100
Michael Brown, Conseiller, 514-694-4100, Wards: 1. Timberlea
Luciano Piciacchia, Conseiller, 514-694-4100, Wards: 2. Holleuffer
Samuel Rother, Conseiller, 514-694-4100, Wards: 3. Brunswick
Domenico Zito, Conseiller, 514-694-4100, Wards: 4. Lacey Green Ouest
Stephen Bouchard, Conseiller, 514-694-4100, Wards: 5. Lacey Green Est
John Morson, Conseiller, 514-694-4100, Wards: 6. Canvin
Paul Dufort, Conseiller, 514-694-4100, Wards: 7. Saint-Charles
André Allard, Conseiller, 514-694-4100, Wards: 8. Summerhill
Annie Riendeau, Greffière et directrice, Affaires juridiques, 514-694-4100
Joe Sanalitro, Directeur général, 514-694-4100
Nadine Bassila, Trésorière et directrice, Services administratifs, 514-694-4100
Lise Labrosse, Directrice, Communications et relations publiques, 514-694-4100
Bruno Possa, Directeur, Travaux publics, 514-694-4100
Sam Tock, Directeur, Ingénierie, 514-694-4100

Lachute
380, rue Principale
Lachute, QC J8H 1Y2
Tél: 450-562-3781; *Téléc:* 450-562-1431
lachute@ville.lachute.qc.ca
www.ville.lachute.qc.ca
Entité municipal: City
Incorporation: 30 avril 1966; *Area:* 109,96 km2
Comté ou district: Argenteuil; *Population au 2016:* 12,862
Circonscription(s) électorale(s) provinciale(s): Argenteuil
Circonscription(s) électorale(s) fédérale(s): Argenteuil-La Petite-Nation
Prochaines élections: 7e novembre 2021
Carl Péloquin, Maire
Patrick Cadieux, Conseiller, Wards: 1
Serge Lachance, Conseiller, Wards: 2
Denis Richer, Conseiller, Wards: 3
Alain Lanoue, Conseiller, Wards: 4
Guylaine Desforges, Conseiller, Wards: 5
Hugo Lajoie, Conseiller, Wards: 6
Lynda-Ann Murray, Greffière et directrice, Affaires juridiques
Benoît Gravel, Directeur général, 450-562-3781
Nathalie Derouin, Trésorière, 450-562-3781
Pascal Larocque, Directeur, Travaux publics, 450-562-3781
Alain St-Jacques, Directeur, Sécurité incendie, 450-562-3781

Laval
Hôtel de Ville
CP 422 St-Martin
1, Place du Souvenir
Laval, QC H7V 3Z4
Tél: 450-978-8000; *Téléc:* 450-978-5943
info@laval.ca
www.laval.ca
Entité municipal: City
Incorporation: 6e août 1965; *Area:* 247,23 km2
Comté ou district: Communauté métropolitaine de Montréal;
Population au 2016: 422,993
Circonscription(s) électorale(s) provinciale(s): Chomedey; Fabre; Laval-des-Rapides; Mille-Îles; Sainte-Rose; Vimont
Circonscription(s) électorale(s) fédérale(s): Alfred-Pellan; Bécancour-Nicolet-Saurel; Laval-Les Îles; Marc-Aurèle-Fortin; Vimy
Prochaines élections: 7e novembre 2021
Marc Demers, Maire
Éric Morasse, Conseiller, Wards: 1. Saint-François

Paolo Galati, Conseiller, Wards: 2. Saint-Vincent-de-Paul
Christiane Yoakim, Conseiller, Wards: 3. Val-des-Arbres
Stéphane Boyer, Conseiller, Wards: 4. Duvernay-Pont-Viau
Daniel Hébert, Conseiller, Wards: 5. Marigot
Sandra Desmeules, Conseiller, Wards: 6. Concorde-Bois-de-Boulogne
Aram Elagoz, Conseiller, Wards: 7. Renaud
Michel Poissant, Conseiller, Wards: 8. Vimont
David De Cotis, Conseiller, Wards: 9. Saint-Bruno
Jocelyne Frédéric-Gauthier, Conseillère, Wards: 10. Auteuil
Isabella Tassoni, Conseiller, Wards: 11. Laval-des-Rapides
Sandra El-Helou, Conseiller, Wards: 12. Souvenir-Labelle
Vasilios Karidogiannis, Conseiller, Wards: 13. Abord-à-Plouffe
Aglaia Revelakis, Conseillère, Wards: 14. Chomedey
Aline Dib, Conseillère, Wards: 15. Saint-Martin
Ray Khalil, Conseiller, Wards: 16. Sainte-Dorothée
Nicholas Borne, Conseiller, Wards: 17. Laval-les-Îles
Yannick Langlois, Conseiller, Wards: 18. Orée-des-bois
Michel Trottier, Conseiller, Wards: 19. Marc-Aurèle-Fortin
Claude Larochelle, Conseiller, Wards: 20. Fabreville
Virginie Dufour, Conseillère, Wards: 21. Sainte-Rose
Jacques Ulysse, Directeur général, 450-978-3676
Pierre Beaudet, Trésorier
René Daigneault, Directeur, Sécurité d'incendie, 450-662-4450

Lavaltrie
1370, rue Notre-Dame
Lavaltrie, QC J0K 1H0
Tél: 450-586-2921; *Téléc:* 450-586-4060
www.ville.lavaltrie.qc.ca
Entité municipal: City
Incorporation: 16 mai 2001; *Area:* 68,39 km2
Comté ou district: D'Autray; *Population au 2016:* 13,657
Circonscription(s) électorale(s) provinciale(s): Berthier
Circonscription(s) électorale(s) fédérale(s): Berthier-Maskinongé
Prochaines élections: 7e novembre 2021
Christian Goulet, Maire, 450-586-2921
Denis Moreau, Conseiller, Wards: 1. Terrasses
Pascal Tremblay, Conseiller, Wards: 2. Rivière
Isabelle Charette, Conseillère, Wards: 3. Chemin du Roy
Jocelyn Guévremont, Conseiller, Wards: 4. Érablière
Danielle Perreault, Conseillère, Wards: 5. Boisé
Robert Pellerin, Conseiller, Wards: 6. Golf
Lisette Falker, Conseillère, Wards: 7. Chasse-galerie
Gaétan Bérard, Conseiller, Wards: 8. Saint-Antoine
Marc-Olivier Breault, Directeur général, 450-586-2921
Marc-André Desjardins, Trésorier et directeur, Services administratifs, 450-586-2921
Antoine Lagimonière, Directeur, Travaux publics, 450-586-2921

Lévis
2175, ch du Fleuve
Lévis, QC G6W 7W9
Tél: 418-839-2002; *Téléc:* 418-839-5548
levis@ville.levis.qc.ca
www.ville.levis.qc.ca
Entité municipal: City
Incorporation: 1er janvier 2002; *Area:* 449,05 km2
Comté ou district: Communauté métropolitaine de Québec;
Population au 2016: 143,414
Circonscription(s) électorale(s) provinciale(s): Bellechasse; Chutes-de-la-Chaudière; Lévis
Circonscription(s) électorale(s) fédérale(s): Bellechasse-Les Etchemins-Lévis; Lévis-Lotbinière
Prochaines élections: 7e novembre 2021
Gilles Lehouillier, Maire
Mario Fortier, Conseiller, Wards: 1
Clément Genest, Conseiller, Wards: 2
Isabelle Demers, Conseillère, Wards: 3
Réjean Lamontagne, Conseiller, Wards: 4
Karine Lavertu, Conseillère, Wards: 5
Michel Turner, Conseiller, Wards: 6
Guy Dumoulin, Conseiller, Wards: 7
Karine Laflamme, Conseillère, Wards: 8
Brigitte Duchesneau, Conseillère, Wards: 9
Steve Dorval, Conseiller, Wards: 10
Serge Côté, Conseiller, Wards: 11
Janet Jones, Conseillère, Wards: 12
Amélie Landry, Conseillère, Wards: 13
Fleur Paradis, Conseillère, Wards: 14
Ann Jeffrey, Conseillère, Wards: 15
Marlyne Turgeon, Greffière
Simon Rousseau, Directeur général
Dominic Deslauriers, Directerice générale adjointe, Développement durable
Christian Tanguay, Directeur général adjoint, Services administratifs
Jean-Claude Belles-Isles, Directeur, Environnement
Gaétan Drouin, Directeur par interim, Infrastructures
Luc de la Durantaye, Directeur, Sécurité incendie

Longueuil
4250, ch de la Savane
Longueuil, QC J3Y 9G4
Tél: 450-463-7311
311@longueuil.quebec
longueuil.quebec
Entité municipal: City
Incorporation: 1er janvier 2002; *Area:* 115,75 km2
Comté ou district: Communauté métropolitaine de Montréal;
Population au 2016: 239,700
Circonscription(s) électorale(s) provinciale(s): Laporte; Marie-Victorin; Taillon; Vachon
Circonscription(s) électorale(s) fédérale(s):
Longueuil-Charles-LeMoyne; Longueuil-Saint-Hubert; Montarville
Prochaines élections: 7e novembre 2021
Sylvie Parent, Mairesse
Michel Lanctôt, Conseiller, Wards: Antoinette-Robidoux
Benoît L'Ecuyer, Conseiller, Wards: Boisé-Du Tremblay
Monique Bastien, Conseillère, Wards: Coteau-Rouge
Tommy Théberge, Conseiller, Wards: Explorateurs
Steve Gagnon, Conseiller, Wards: Fatima-du Parcours-du-Cerf
Xavier Léger, Conseiller, Wards: Georges-Dor
Colette Éthier, Conseillère, Wards: LeMoyne-de Jacques-Cartier
Jonathan Tabarah, Conseiller, Wards: Parc-Michel-Chartrand
Eric Bouchard, Conseiller, Wards: Saint-Charles
Peter Doonan, Conseiller, Wards: Greenfield Park
Robert Myles, Conseiller, Wards: Greenfield Park
Wade Wilson, Conseiller, Wards: Greenfield Park
Éric Beaulieu, Conseiller, Wards: Iberville
Jacques Lemire, Conseiller, Wards: Laflèche
Jean-François Boivin, Conseiller, Wards: Maraîchers
Jacques E. Poitras, Conseiller, Wards: Parc-de-la-Cité
Nathalie Boisclair, Conseillère, Wards: Vieux-Saint-Hubert-de Savane
Sophie Deslauriers, Greffière
Patrick Savard, Directeur général
Luc Labelle, Directeur général adjoint, Services corporatifs
Marie-Chantal Verrier, Directerice générale adjointe, Développement durable
Jean Melançon, Directeur, Sécurité incendie

Magog
7, rue Principale est
Magog, QC J1X 1Y4
Tél: 819-843-6501; *Téléc:* 819-843-1091
www.magog.qc.ca
Entité municipal: City
Incorporation: 9e octobre 2002; *Area:* 144,47 km2
Comté ou district: Memphrémagog; *Population au 2016:* 26,669
Circonscription(s) électorale(s) provinciale(s): Orford
Circonscription(s) électorale(s) fédérale(s): Brome-Missisquoi; Compton-Stanstead
Prochaines élections: 7e novembre 2021
Note: Depuis le 9 oct., le canton de Magog, le village d'Omerville & la ville de Magog sont regroupés pour former la nouvelle ville de Magog.
Vicki-May Hamm, Mairesse, 819-843-2880
Jean-François Rompré, Conseiller, 819-868-2086, Wards: 1. La Rivière
Bertrand Bilodeau, Conseiller, 819-843-7250, Wards: 2. Omerville
Yvon Lamontagne, Conseiller, 819-843-1146, Wards: 3. Des Sommets
Samuel Côté, Conseiller, 819-843-3663, Wards: 4. Du Marais
Nathalie Bélanger, Conseillère, 819-620-4134, Wards: 5. Canton Ouest
Diane Pelletier, Conseillère, 819-843-3244, Wards: 6. Des Pionniers
Nathalie Pelletier, Conseillère, 819-843-1108, Wards: 7. Centre
Jacques Laurendeau, Conseiller, 819-868-0256, Wards: 8. Monseigneur Vel
Sylvianne Lavigne, Greffière, 819-843-6501
Jean-François D'Amour, Directeur général
Manon Courchesne, Trésorière, 819-843-6501
Marco Prévost, Directeur, Environnement et Infrastructures municipales, 819-843-7106
Sylvain Arteau, Directeur, Sécurité incendie

Marieville
682, rue Saint-Charles
Marieville, QC J3M 1P9
Tél: 450-460-4444; *Téléc:* 450-460-2770
administration@ville.marieville.qc.ca
www.ville.marieville.qc.ca
Entité municipal: City
Incorporation: 14 juin 2000; *Area:* 63,23 km2
Comté ou district: Rouville; *Population au 2016:* 10,725
Circonscription(s) électorale(s) provinciale(s): Iberville
Circonscription(s) électorale(s) fédérale(s): Beloeil-Chambly
Prochaines élections: 7e novembre 2021

Sylvaine Lapointe, Conseiller, Wards: 1
Geneviève Létourneau, Conseillère, Wards: 2
Cynthia Vallée, Conseillère, Wards: 3
Monic Paquette, Conseillère, Wards: 4
Louis Bienvenu, Conseiller, Wards: 5
Gilbert Lefort, Conseiller, Wards: 6
Mélanie Calgaro, Greffière
Francine Tétreault, Directrice générale
Isabelle Laurin, Trésorière
Sylvain Gagnon, Directeur, Travaux publics
Robert Dubuc, Directeur, Protection contre les incendies

Mascouche
3034, ch Ste-Marie
Mascouche, QC J7K 1P1
Tél: 450-474-4133; *Téléc:* 450-474-6401
info@ville.mascouche.qc.ca
mascouche.ca
Entité municipal: City
Incorporation: 1er juillet 1855; *Area:* 107,00 km2
Comté ou district: Les Moulins; Communauté métropolitaine de
Montréal; *Population au 2016:* 46,692
Circonscription(s) électorale(s) provinciale(s): Masson
Circonscription(s) électorale(s) fédérale(s): Montcalm
Prochaines élections: 7e novembre 2021
Guillaume Tremblay, Maire, 450-474-4133
Roger Côté, Conseiller, 450-966-0784, Wards: 1. Louis-Hébert
Eugène Jolicoeur, Conseiller, 514-809-5115, Wards: 2. Le Gardeur
Louise Forest, Conseillère, 450-474-0488, Wards: 3. Le Gardeur
Stéphane Handfield, Conseiller, 514-942-3610, Wards: 4. La
Vérendrye
Bertrand Lefebvre, Conseiller, 514-713-1958, Wards: 5. Du
Coteau
Don Monahan, Conseiller, 450-474-6435, Wards: 6. Des
Hauts-Bois
Anny Mailloux, Conseillère, 514-886-5709, Wards: 7. Du Rucher
Gabriel Michaud, Conseiller, 514-531-7762, Wards: 8. Du
Manoir
Raynald Martel, Greffier, 450-474-4133
Pratte André, Directeur général par intérim, 450-474-4133
Luce Jacques, Trésorier, 450-474-4133
François Gosselin, Directeur, Travaux publics, 450-474-4133
Jean-Pierre Boudreau, Directeur, Service sécurité d'incendie,
450-474-4133

Matane
230, av St-Jérôme
Matane, QC G4W 3A2
Tél: 418-562-2333; *Téléc:* 418-562-4869
reception@ville.matane.qc.ca
www.ville.matane.qc.ca
Entité municipal: City
Incorporation: 26 septembre 2001; *Area:* 196,08 km2
Comté ou district: La Matanie; *Population au 2016:* 14,311
Circonscription(s) électorale(s) provinciale(s): Matane-Matapédia
Circonscription(s) électorale(s) fédérale(s): Avignon-La
Mitis-Matane-Matapédia
Prochaines élections: 7e novembre 2021
Jérôme Landry, Maire
Eddy Métivier, Conseiller, Wards: 1
Jean-Pierre Levasseur, Conseiller, Wards: 2
Nelson Gagnon, Conseiller, Wards: 3
Annie Veillette, Conseillère, Wards: 4
Steven Levesque, Conseiller, Wards: 5
Steve Girard, Conseiller, Wards: 6
Marie-Claude Gagnon, Greffière
Nicolas Leclerc, Directeur général
Marie Pelletier, Trésorière et directrice, Services financiers
Jérôme Caron, Directeur, Génie et de l'environnement
Martin Gilbert, Directeur, Service des loisirs, de la culture et de
la vie communautaire

Mercier
869, boul St-Jean-Baptiste, 2e étage
Mercier, QC J6R 2L3
Tél: 450-691-6090; *Téléc:* 450-691-6529
info@ville.mercier.qc.ca
www.ville.mercier.qc.ca
Entité municipal: City
Incorporation: 1er juillet 1855; *Area:* 46,08 km2
Comté ou district: Roussillon; Communauté métropolitaine de
Montréal; *Population au 2016:* 13,115
Circonscription(s) électorale(s) provinciale(s): Châteauguay
Circonscription(s) électorale(s) fédérale(s): Châteauguay-Lacolle
Prochaines élections: 7e novembre 2021
Lise Michaud, Mairesse
Stéphane Roy, Conseiller, Wards: 1
Johanne Anderson, Conseillère, Wards: 2
Judith Prud'homme, Conseillère, Wards: 3
Philippe Drolet, Conseiller, Wards: 4
Louis Cimon, Conseiller, Wards: 5
Martin Laplaine, Conseiller, Wards: 6

Denis Ferland, Greffier
René Chalifoux, Directeur général
Michel Brousseau, Directeur, Travaux publics
Jean-Pierre Roy, Directeur, Urbanisme et environnement
Éric Steingue, Directeur, Sécurité incendie

Mirabel
14111, rue Saint-Jean
Mirabel, QC J7J 1Y3
Tél: 450-475-8653
communications@mirabel.ca
mirabel.ca
Entité municipal: City
Incorporation: 1er janvier 1971; *Area:* 485,07 km2
Comté ou district: Communauté métropolitaine de Montréal;
Population au 2016: 50,513
Circonscription(s) électorale(s) provinciale(s): Mirabel
Circonscription(s) électorale(s) fédérale(s): Mirabel
Prochaines élections: 7e novembre 2021
Jean Bouchard, Maire
Michel Lauzon, Conseiller, Wards: 1
Guylaine Coursol, Conseillère, Wards: 2
Robert Charron, Conseiller, Wards: 3
François Bélanger, Conseiller, Wards: 4
Patrick Charbonneau, Conseiller, Wards: 5
Isabelle Gauthier, Conseillère, Wards: 6
Francine Charles, Conseillère, Wards: 7
Marc Laurin, Conseiller, Wards: 8
Suzanne Mireault, Greffière, 450-475-2002
Mario Boily, Directeur général, 450-475-2000, Fax:
450-475-2013
Jeannic D'Aoust, Trésorier, 450-475-2003
Christine Chartier, Directrice, Équipement et des travaux publics,
450-475-2005
Jérôme Duguay, Directeur, Environnement, 450-475-2006
Carolyne Lapierre, Directrice, Loisirs, la culture et la vie,
450-475-8656
Geneviève Cauden, Directrice, Génie, 450-475-2004
Dominic Noiseux, Directeur, Aménagement et de l'urbanisme,
450-475-2007
Joël Laviolette, Directeur, Sécurité incendie, 450-475-2010

Mont-Laurier
300, boul Albiny-Paquette
Mont-Laurier, QC J9L 1J9
Tél: 819-623-1221; *Téléc:* 819-623-4840
info@villemontlaurier.qc.ca
www.villemontlaurier.qc.ca
Entité municipal: City
Incorporation: 8e janvier 2003; *Area:* 591,27 km2
Comté ou district: Antoine-Labelle; *Population au 2016:* 14,116
Circonscription(s) électorale(s) provinciale(s): Labelle
Circonscription(s) électorale(s) fédérale(s): Laurentides-Labelle
Prochaines élections: 7e novembre 2021
Note: Dès le 8 janvier 2003, la ville de Mont-Laurier regroupe les
municipalités de Des Ruisseaux & Saint-Aimé-du-Lac-des-Iles.
Daniel Bourdon, Maire
Denis Ethier, Conseiller, Wards: 1
Élaine Brière, Conseillère, Wards: 2
Isabelle Nadon, Conseillère, Wards: 3
Yves Desjardins, Conseiller, Wards: 5
Stéphanie Lelièvre, Greffière
François Leduc, Directeur général
Johanne Nantel, Trésorière, 819-623-1221
Julie Richer, Directrice, Aménagement du territoire et
urbanisme, 819-623-1221
Mario Hamel, Directeur, Service des incendies

Montmagny
143, rue St-Jean-Baptiste est
Montmagny, QC G5V 1K4
Tél: 418-248-3361; *Téléc:* 418-248-0923
info@ville.montmagny.qc.ca
www.ville.montmagny.qc.ca
Entité municipal: City
Incorporation: 2e avril 1966; *Area:* 124,51 km2
Comté ou district: Montmagny; *Population au 2016:* 11,255
Circonscription(s) électorale(s) provinciale(s): Côte-du-Sud
Circonscription(s) électorale(s) fédérale(s):
Montmagny-L'Islet-Kamouraska-Rivière-du-Loup
Prochaines élections: 7e novembre 2021
Rémy Langevin, Maire
Gaston Morin, Conseiller, Wards: 1
Jessy Croteau, Conseiller, Wards: 2
Yves Gendrau, Conseiller, Wards: 3
Bernard Boulet, Conseiller, Wards: 4
Sylvie Boulet, Conseillère, Wards: 5
Marc Langlois, Conseiller, Wards: 6
Félix Michaud, Directeur général, 418-248-3362

Montréal
275, rue Notre-Dame est
Montréal, QC H2Y 1C6
Tél: 514-872-3142; *Téléc:* 514-872-5655
montreal.ca
Entité municipal: City
Incorporation: 1er janvier 2002; *Area:* 365,65 km2
Comté ou district: Communauté métropolitaine de Montréal;
Population au 2016: 1,704,694
Circonscription(s) électorale(s) provinciale(s):
Acadie;Anjou-Louis-Riel;Bourassa-Sauvé;Bourget;Crémazie;D'A
rcy-McGee;Gouin;Hochelaga-Maisonneuve;Jeanne-Mance-Viger
;LaFontaine;Laurier-Dorion;Marguerite-Bourgeoys;Mercier;Marq
uette;Mont-Royal;Nelligan;Notre-Dame-de-Grâce;Outremont;Poi
nte-aux-Trembles;Robert-Baldwin;Rosemont;St-Henri-Ste-Anne;
St-Laurent;Ste-Marie-St-Jacques;Westmount-St-Louis;Verdun;Vi
au
Circonscription(s) électorale(s) fédérale(s): Ahuntsic-Cartierville;
Bourassa; Dorval-Lachine-LaSalle; Hochelaga; Honoré-Mercier;
La Pointe-de-l'Île; LaSalle-Émard-Verdun; Lac-St-Louis;
Laurier-Ste-Marie; Mount Royal;
Notre-Dame-de-Grâce-Westmount; Outremont; Papineau;
Pierrefonds-Dollard; Rosemont-La Petite-Patrie; St-Laurent;
St-Léonard-St Michel; Ville-Marie-Le Sud Ouest-Île-des-Soeurs
Prochaines élections: 7e novembre 2021
Valérie Plante, Mairesse
Cathy Wong, Conseillère de la Ville et Présidente du conseil de
la Ville, Wards: Ville-Marie
Effie Giannou, Conseillère de la Ville, Wards:
Ahuntsic-Cartierville
Nathalie Goulet, Conseillère de la Ville, Wards:
Ahuntsic-Cartierville
Jérôme Normand, Conseiller de la Ville, Wards:
Ahuntsic-Cartierville
Hadrien Parizeau, Conseiller de la Ville, Wards:
Ahuntsic-Cartierville
Émilie Thuillier, Conseiller de la Ville et Mairesse
d'arrondissement, Wards: Ahuntsic-Cartierville
Andrée Hénault, Conseillère de la Ville, Wards: Anjou
Luis Miranda, Conseiller de la Ville et Maire d'arrondissement,
Wards: Anjou
Christian Arseneault, Conseiller de la Ville, Wards:
Côte-des-Neiges-N.D.-de-Grâce
Peter McQueen, Conseiller de la Ville, Wards:
Côte-des-Neiges-N.D.-de-Grâce
Sue Montgomery, Conseillère de la Ville et Mairesse
d'arrondissement, Wards: Côte-des-Neiges-N.D.-de-Grâce
Lionel Perez, Conseiller de la Ville, Wards:
Côte-des-Neiges-N.D.-de-Grâce
Magda Popeanu, Conseillère de la Ville, Wards:
Côte-des-Neiges-N.D.-de-Grâce
Marvin Rotrand, Conseiller de la Ville, Wards:
Côte-des-Neiges-N.D.-de-Grâce
Norman Marinacci, Conseiller de la Ville et Maire
d'arrondissement, Wards: L'Ile-Bizard-Sainte-Geneviève
Micheline Rouleau, Conseillère de la Ville, Wards: Lachine
Maja Vodanovic, Conseillère de la Ville et Mairesse
d'arrondissement, Wards: Lachine
Manon Barbe, Conseillère de la Ville et Mairesse
d'arrondissement, Wards: LaSalle
Richard Deschamps, Conseiller de la Ville, Wards: LaSalle
Lise Zarac, Conseillère de la Ville, Wards: LaSalle
Luc Rabouin, Conseiller de la Ville et Maire d'arrondissement,
Wards: Le Plateau—Mont-Royal
Marianne Giguère, Conseillère de la Ville, Wards: Le
Plateau—Mont-Royal
Alex Norris, Conseiller de la Ville, Wards: Le
Plateau—Mont-Royal
Richard Ryan, Conseiller de la Ville, Wards: Le
Plateau—Mont-Royal
Benoit Dorais, Conseiller de la Ville et Maire d'arrondissement,
Wards: Le Sud-Ouest
Craig Sauvé, Conseiller de la Ville, Wards: Le Sud-Ouest
Anne-Marie Sigouin, Conseillère de la Ville, Wards: Le
Sud-Ouest
Karine Boivin Roy, Conseillère de la Ville, Wards:
Mercier-Hochelaga-Maisonneuve
Éric Alan Caldwell, Conseiller de la Ville, Wards:
Mercier-Hochelaga-Maisonneuve
Laurence Lavigne Lalonde, Conseillère de la Ville, Wards:
Mercier-Hochelaga-Maisonneuve
Pierre Lessard-Blais, Conseiller de la Ville et Maire
d'arrondissement, Wards: Mercier-Hochelaga-Maisonneuve
Suzie Miron, Conseillère de la Ville, Wards:
Mercier-Hochelaga-Maisonneuve
Christine Black, Conseillère de la Ville et Mairesse
d'arrondissement, Wards: Montréal-Nord
Chantal Rossi, Conseillère de la Ville, Wards: Montréal-Nord
Abdelhaq Sari, Conseiller de la Ville, Wards: Montréal-Nord
Philipe Tomlinson, Conseiller de la Ville et Maire
d'arrondissement, Wards: Outremont

Dimitrios Jim Beis, Conseiller de la Ville et Maire d'arrondissement, Wards: Pierrefonds-Roxboro
Catherine Clément-Talbot, Conseillère de la Ville, Wards: Pierrefonds-Roxboro
Benoit Langevin, Conseiller de la Ville, Wards: Pierrefonds-Roxboro
Suzanne Décarie, Conseillère de la Ville, Wards: Rivière-des-Prairies
Richard Guay, Conseiller de la Ville, Wards: Rivière-des-Prairies
Giovanni Rapanà, Conseiller de la Ville, Wards: Rivière-des-Prairies
Chantal Rouleau, Conseillère de la Ville et Mairesse d'arrondissement, Wards: Rivière-des-Prairies
François William Croteau, Conseiller de la Ville et Maire d'arrondissement, Wards: Rosemont—La Petite-Patrie
Christine Gosselin, Conseillère de la Ville, Wards: Rosemont—La Petite-Patrie
François Limoges, Conseiller de la Ville, Wards: Rosemont—La Petite-Patrie
Jocelyn Pauzé, Conseiller de la Ville, Wards: Rosemont—La Petite-Patrie
Stephanie Watt, Conseillère de la Ville, Wards: Rosemont—La Petite-Patrie
Alan DeSousa, Conseiller de la Ville et Maire d'arrondissement, Wards: Saint-Laurent
Francesco Miele, Conseiller de la Ville, Wards: Saint-Laurent
Aref Salem, Conseiller de la Ville, Wards: Saint-Laurent
Michel Bissonnet, Conseiller de la Ville et Maire d'arrondissement, Wards: Saint-Léonard
Patricia R. Lattanzio, Conseillère de la Ville, Wards: Saint-Léonard
Dominic Perri, Conseiller de la Ville, Wards: Saint-Léonard
Sterling Downey, Conseiller de la Ville, Wards: Verdun
Marie-Josée Parent, Conseillère de la Ville, Wards: Verdun
Jean-François Parenteau, Conseiller de la Ville et Maire d'arrondissement, Wards: Verdun
Robert Beaudry, Conseiller de la Ville, Wards: Ville-Marie
Sophie Mauzerolle, Conseillère de la Ville, Wards: Ville-Marie
Frantz Benjamin, Conseiller de la Ville, Wards: Villeray-St.-Michel-Parc-Ext.
Mary Deros, Conseillère de la Ville, Wards: Villeray-St.-Michel-Parc-Ext.
Rosannie Filato, Conseillère de la Ville, Wards: Villeray-St.-Michel-Parc-Ext.
Giuliana Fumagalli, Conseillère de la Ville et Mairesse d'arrondissement, Wards: Villeray-St.-Michel-Parc-Ext.
Sylvain Ouellet, Conseiller de la Ville, Wards: Villeray-St.-Michel-Parc-Ext.
Emmanuel Tani-Moore, Greffier
Serge Lamontagne, Directeur général
Diane Bouchard, Directrice, Ressources humaines
Yves Courchesne, Directeur, Finances
Laurent Laroche, Directeur, Environnement
Bruno Lachance, Directeur, Sécurité incendie

Mont-Royal
90, av Roosevelt
Mont-Royal, QC H3R 1Z5
Tél: 514-734-2900; *Téléc:* 514-734-3080
info@ville.mont-royal.qc.ca
www.ville.mont-royal.qc.ca
Entité municipal: City
Incorporation: 1er janvier 2006; *Area:* 7,53 km2
Comté ou district: Communauté métropolitaine de Montréal;
Population au 2016: 20,276
Circonscription(s) électorale(s) provinciale(s): Mont-Royal
Circonscription(s) électorale(s) fédérale(s): Mont-Royal
Prochaines élections: 7e novembre 2021
Philippe Roy, Maire, 514-734-2914, Fax: 514-734-3072
Joseph Daoura, Conseiller, Wards: 1
Minh-Diem Le Thi, Conseillère, Wards: 2
Erin Kennedy, Conseillère, Wards: 3
John Miller, Conseiller, Wards: 4
Michelle Setlakwe, Conseiller, Wards: 5
Jonathan Lang, Conseiller, Wards: 6
Alexandre Verdy, Greffier et directeur, Affairs publiques, 514-734-2988
Ava L. Couch, Directrice générale, 514-734-2915
Nathalie Rhéaume, Trésorière, 514-734-3015
Isabel Tardif, Directrice, Services Techniques, 514-734-3034, Fax: 514-734-3084

Mont-Saint-Hilaire
100, rue du Centre-Civique
Mont-Saint-Hilaire, QC J3H 3M8
Tél: 450-467-2854
information@villemsh.ca
www.ville.mont-saint-hilaire.qc.ca
Entité municipal: City
Incorporation: 12 mars 1966; *Area:* 44,19 km2
Comté ou district: La Vallée-du-Richelieu; Communauté

métropolitaine de Montréal; *Population au 2016:* 18,585
Circonscription(s) électorale(s) provinciale(s): Borduas
Circonscription(s) électorale(s) fédérale(s): Beloeil-Chambly
Prochaines élections: 7e novembre 2021
Yves Corriveau, Maire
Brigitte Minier, Conseiller, Wards: 1. Déboulis
Emile Gilbert, Conseiller, Wards: 2. Patriotes
Jean-Pierre Brault, Conseiller, Wards: 3. Rouville
Sylvain Houle, Conseiller, Wards: 4. Piémont
Louis Toner, Conseiller, Wards: 6. Montagne
Anne-Marie Piérard, Greffière
Daniel-Éric St-Onge, Directeur général
Sylvie Laplame, Trésorière et directrice, Finances, 450-467-2854
Jean Lanciault, Directeur, Ingénierie, 450-467-2854
Francis Leblanc, Directeur, Travaux publics, 450-467-2854
Jean Clément, Directeur, Sécurité incendie, 450-467-2854

Notre-Dame-de-l'Ile-Perrot
21, rue de l'Église
Notre-Dame-de-l'Ile-Perrot, QC J7V 8P4
Tél: 514-453-4128; *Téléc:* 514-453-8961
info@ndip.org
www.ndip.org
Entité municipal: City
Incorporation: 14 avril 1984; *Area:* 28,21 km2
Comté ou district: Vaudreuil-Soulanges; Communauté
métropolitaine de Montréal; *Population au 2016:* 10,654
Circonscription(s) électorale(s) provinciale(s): Vaudreuil
Circonscription(s) électorale(s) fédérale(s): Vaudreuil-Soulanges
Prochaines élections: 7e novembre 2021
Danie Deschênes, Mairesse
Natalia Pereira, Conseillère, Wards: 1
Bruno Roy, Conseiller, Wards: 2
Daniel Lauzon, Conseiller, Wards: 3
Bernard Groulx, Conseiller, Wards: 4
Normand Pigeon, Conseiller, Wards: 5
Jean Fournel, Conseiller, Wards: 6
Catherine Fortier-Pesant, Greffière et directrice, Services juridiques
Katherine-Erika Vincent, Directrice générale
Guillaume Laforest, Trésorier et directeur, Financiers
Mélissa Arbour LaSalle, Directrice, Urbanisme
Isabelle Roy, Directrice, Services techniques

Pincourt
919, ch Duhamel
Pincourt, QC J7V 4G8
Tél: 514-453-8981; *Téléc:* 514-453-8401
information@villepincourt.qc.ca
www.villepincourt.qc.ca
Entité municipal: City
Incorporation: 1er janvier 1950; *Area:* 7,11 km2
Comté ou district: Vaudreuil-Soulanges; Communauté
métropolitaine de Montréal; *Population au 2016:* 14,558
Circonscription(s) électorale(s) provinciale(s): Vaudreuil
Circonscription(s) électorale(s) fédérale(s): Vaudreuil-Soulanges;
Lévis-Lotbinière;Terrebonne
Prochaines élections: 7e novembre 2021
Yvan Cardinal, Maire
Alexandre Wolford, Conseiller, Wards: 1
Denise Bergeron, Conseillère, Wards: 2
Sam Ierfino, Conseiller, Wards: 3
Diane Boyer, Conseillère, Wards: 4
Claudine Girouard-Morel, Conseiller, Wards: 5
René Lecavalier, Conseiller, Wards: 6
Etienne Bergevin Byette, Directeur général et greffier, 514-453-8981
Nathalie Boisvert, Directrice, Finances, 514-453-8981
Line St-Onge, Directrice, Travaux publics et infrastructures, 514-453-8981
Richard Dubois, Directeur, Aménagement du territoire, 514-453-8981
Simon Grenier, Directeur, Loisirs et via communautaire, 514-453-8981
Yanick Bernier, Directeur, Urgence et de sécurité incendie, 514-453-8981

Pointe-Claire
451, boul Saint-Jean
Pointe-Claire, QC H9R 3J3
Tél: 514-630-1200
communications@pointe-claire.ca
www.ville.pointe-claire.qc.ca
Entité municipal: City
Incorporation: 1er janvier 2006; *Area:* 18,90 km2
Comté ou district: Communauté métropolitaine de Montréal;
Population au 2016: 31,380
Circonscription(s) électorale(s) provinciale(s): Jacques-Cartier
Circonscription(s) électorale(s) fédérale(s): Lac-Saint-Louis
Prochaines élections: 7e novembre 2021
John Belvedere, Maire, 514-630-1207

Claude Cousineau, Conseiller, 514-630-1288, Wards: 1. Cedar/Le Village
Paul Bissonnette, Conseiller, 514-630-1289, Wards: 2. Lakeside
Kelly Thorstad-Cullen, Conseillère, 514-630-1290, Wards: 3. Valois
Tara Stainforth, Conseillère, 514-630-1291, Wards: 4. Cedar Park Heights
Cynthia Homan, Conseillère, 514-630-1292, Wards: 5. Lakeside Heights
David Webb, Conseiller, 514-630-1293, Wards: 6. Seigniory
Eric Stork, Conseiller, 514-630-1294, Wards: 7. Northview
Brent Cowan, Conseiller, 514-630-1295, Wards: 8. Oneida
Caroline Thibault, Greffière, 514-630-1228
Robert F. Weemaes, Directeur général, 514-630-1237
Daniel Séguin, Trésorier
Joanne Poirier, Directrice, Urbanisme
Erik Rolland, Directeur, Travaux publics

La Prairie
#400, 170, boul Taschereau
La Prairie, QC J5R 5H6
Tél: 450-444-6600; *Téléc:* 450-444-6636
info@ville.laprairie.qc.ca
www.ville.laprairie.qc.ca
Entité municipal: City
Incorporation: 30 mars 1846; *Area:* 43,68 km2
Comté ou district: Roussillon; Communauté métropolitaine de Montréal; *Population au 2016:* 24,110
Circonscription(s) électorale(s) provinciale(s): La Prairie
Circonscription(s) électorale(s) fédérale(s): La Prairie
Prochaines élections: 7e novembre 2021
Donat Serres, Maire
Allen Scott, Conseiller, Wards: 1. Milice
Christian Caron, Conseiller, Wards: 2. Christ-Roi
Ian Rajotte, Conseiller, Wards: 3. Vieux La Prairie
Marie Eve Plante-Hébert, Conseillère, Wards: 4. Citière
Julie Gauthier, Conseillère, Wards: 5. Clairière
Pierre Vocino, Conseiller, Wards: 6. Magdeleine
Paule Fontaine, Conseillère, Wards: 7. Bataille
Denis Girard, Conseiller, Wards: 8. Briqueterie
Sandra Hardy, Directrice générale, 450-444-6619

Prévost
2870, boul du Curé-Labelle
Prévost, QC J0R 1T0
Tél: 450-224-8888; *Téléc:* 450-224-8323
servicecitoyen@ville.prevost.qc.ca
www.ville.prevost.qc.ca
Entité municipal: City
Incorporation: 20 janvier 1973; *Area:* 24,58 km2
Comté ou district: La Rivière-du-Nord; *Population au 2016:* 13,002
Circonscription(s) électorale(s) provinciale(s): Bertrand
Circonscription(s) électorale(s) fédérale(s): Rivière-du-Nord
Prochaines élections: 7e novembre 2021
Paul Germain, Maire
Joey Leckman, Conseiller, - - 8, Wards: 1
Pier-Luc Laurin, Conseillère, Wards: 2
Michel Morin, Conseiller, Wards: 3
Michèle Guay, Conseillère, Wards: 4
Sara Dupras, Conseillère, Wards: 5
Pierre Daigneault, Conseiller, Wards: 6
Caroline Dion, Greffier, 450-224-8888
Laurent Laberge, Directeur général et directeur, Ressources humaines, 450-224-8888
Catherine Nadeau-Jobin, Trésorière
Danielle Cyr, Directeur, Urbanisme et relation citoyen

Québec
Hôtel de Ville
CP 700 Haute-Ville
2, rue des Jardins
Québec, QC G1R 4S9
Tél: 418-641-6010; *Téléc:* 418-641-6357
311@ville.quebec.qc.ca
www.ville.quebec.qc.ca
Entité municipal: City
Incorporation: 1er janvier 2002; *Area:* 453,38 km2
Comté ou district: Communauté métropolitaine de Québec;
Population au 2016: 531,902
Circonscription(s) électorale(s) provinciale(s): Charlesbourg;
Chauveau; Jean-Lesage; La Peltrie; Louis-Hébert;
Montmorency; Taschereau; Vanier-Les Rivières
Circonscription(s) électorale(s) fédérale(s): Beauport-Limoilou;
Beauport—Côte-de-Beaupré—Île d'Orléans—Charlevoix;
Charlesbourg—Haute-Saint-Charles; Louis-Hébert; Québec
Prochaines élections: 7e novembre 2021
Régis Labeaume, Maire, 418-641-6434
Stevens Mélançon, Conseiller, 418-641-6080, Wards: Chute-Montmorency-Seigneurial
Jérémie Ernould, Conseiller, 418-641-6501, Wards: Robert-Giffard

Jean-François Gosselin, Conseiller, 418-641-6385, Wards: Sainte-Thérèse-de-Lisieux
Michelle Morin-Doyle, Conseillère, 418-641-6080, Wards: Louis-XIV
Patrick Voyer, Conseiller, 418-641-6080, Wards: Monts
Vincent Dufresne, Conseiller, 418-641-6401, Wards: Saint-Rodrigue
Jean Rousseau, Conseillère, 418-641-6411, Wards: Cap-aux-Diamants
Suzanne Verreault, Conseillère, 418-641-6411, Wards: Limoilou
Geneviève Hamelin, Conseillère, 418-641-6411, Wards: Maizerets-Lairet
Yvon Bussières, Conseiller, 418-641-6101, Wards: Montcalm-Saint-Sacrement
Pierre-Luc Lachance, Conseiller, 418-641-6080, Wards: Saint-Roch-Saint-Sauveur
Steeve Verret, Conseiller, 418-641-6080, Wards: Lac-Saint-Charles—Saint-Émile
Raymond Dion, Conseiller, 418-641-6701, Wards: Loretteville-Les Châtels
Sylvain Légaré, Conseiller, 418-641-6701, Wards: Val-Bélair
Dominique Tanguay, Conseillère, 418-641-6201, Wards: Les Saules
Patrick Paquet, Conseiller, 274-141-6080, Wards: Neufchâtel-Lebourgneuf
Alicia Despins, Conseillère, 418-641-6080, Wards: Vanier-Duberger
Marie-Josée Savard, Conseillère, 418-641-6301, Wards: Cap-Rouge-Laurentien
Rémy Normand, Conseiller, 418-641-6080, Wards: Plateau
Anne Corriveau, Conseillère, 418-641-6301, Wards: Pointe-de-Sainte-Foy
Émilie Villeneuve, Conseiller, 418-641-6301, Wards: Saint-Louis-Sillery
Sylvain Ouellet, Greffier
Luc Monty, Directeur général, 418-641-6373
Gilles Dufour, Directeur général adjoint, Eau, environnement et équipements d'utilité publique
Cindy Gendron, Directeur, Ressources humaines, 418-641-6234
Daniel Lessard, Directeur, Ingénierie, 418-641-6217
Marie-Christine Magnan, Directrice, Communications, 418-641-6651
Daniel Maranda, Directeur, Service des approvisionnements, 418-641-6164
Chantal Pineault, Directrice, Services des finances, 418-641-6203
Christian Paradis, Directeur, Protection contre l'incendie, 418-641-6231

Rawdon
3647, rue Queen
Rawdon, QC J0K 1S0
Tél: 450-834-2596; *Téléc:* 450-834-3031
info@rawdon.ca
www.rawdon.ca
Entité municipal: City
Incorporation: 28 mai 1998; *Area:* 186,27 km2
Comté ou district: Matawinie; *Population au 2016:* 11,057
Circonscription(s) électorale(s) provinciale(s): Rousseau
Circonscription(s) électorale(s) fédérale(s): Joliette
Prochaines élections: 7e novembre 2021
Bruno Guilbault, Maire
Marco Bellefeuille, Conseiller, Wards: 1
Josianne Girard, Conseillère, Wards: 2
Raymond Rougeau, Conseiller, Wards: 3
Renald Breault, Conseiller, Wards: 4
Kimberly St. Denis, Conseillère, Wards: 5
Stéphanie Labelle, Conseillère, Wards: 6
Caroline Gray, Greffière
François Dauphin, Directeur général
Carole Landry, Directrice, Finances
Hugo Lebreux, Directeur, Travaux publics
Christian Fortin, Directeur, Sécurité d'incendie

Repentigny
435, boul Iberville
Repentigny, QC J6A 2B6
Tél: 450-470-3000; *Téléc:* 450-470-3082
communication@repentigny.ca
repentigny.ca
Entité municipal: City
Incorporation: 1er juin 2002; *Area:* 61,23 km2
Comté ou district: L'Assomption; Communauté métropolitaine de Montréal; *Population au 2016:* 84,285
Circonscription(s) électorale(s) provinciale(s): L'Assomption; Repentigny
Circonscription(s) électorale(s) fédérale(s): Repentigny
Prochaines élections: 7e novembre 2021
Chantal Deschamps, Mairesse, 450-470-3103
Josée Mailhot, Conseillère, 450-585-3410, Wards: 1
Georges Robinson, Conseiller, 450-654-9746, Wards: 2

Denyse Peltier, Conseillère, 450-581-5733, Wards: 3
Cécile Hénault, Conseillère, 450-654-3046, Wards: 4
Eric Chartré, Conseiller, 514-743-9961, Wards: 5
Sylvain Benoit, Conseiller, 514-602-4793, Wards: 6
Raymond Hénault, Conseiller, 450-581-0319, Wards: 7
Jennifer Robillard, Conseiller, 450-585-6497, Wards: 8
Jean Langlois, Conseiller, 450-721-6699, Wards: 9
Kevin Buteau, Conseiller, 514-266-2987, Wards: 10
Chantal Routhier, Conseillère, 450-582-7711, Wards: 11
Stéphane Machabée, Conseiller, 450-585-3221, Wards: 12
Louis-André Garceau, Greffier, 450-470-3130
David Legault, Directeur général, 450-470-3110
Marie-Josée Boissonneault, Trésorière, 450-470-3200
Daniel Galarneau, Directeur, Travaux publics, 450-470-3800
Valérie Prévost, Directrice, Loisirs, culture et vie communautaire, 450-470-3400
Jean Bartolo, Directeur, Incendie, 450-470-3620

Rimouski
CP 710
205, av de la Cathédrale
Rimouski, QC G5L 7C7
Tél: 418-723-3313; *Téléc:* 418-724-3183
communications@rimouski.ca
rimouski.ca
Entité municipal: City
Incorporation: 1er janvier 2002; *Area:* 339,64 km2
Comté ou district: Rimouski-Neigette; *Population au 2016:* 48,664
Circonscription(s) électorale(s) provinciale(s): Rimouski
Circonscription(s) électorale(s) fédérale(s): Rimouski-Neigette-Témiscouata-Les Basques
Prochaines élections: 7e novembre 2021
Marc Parent, Maire
Sébastien Bolduc, Conseiller, Wards: 1. Sacré-Coeur
Rodrigue Joncas, Conseiller, Wards: 2. Nazareth
Jennifer Murray, Conseillère, Wards: 3. Saint-Germain
Cécilia Michaud, Conseillère, Wards: 4. Rimouski-Est
Jacques Lévesque, Conseiller, Wards: 5. Pointe-au-Père
Grégory Thorez, Conseiller, Wards: 6. Sainte-Odile
Jocelyn Pelletier, Conseiller, Wards: 7. Saint-Robert
Karol Francis, Conseiller, Wards: 8. Terrasse Arthur-Buies
Simon St-Pierre, Conseiller, Wards: 9. Saint-Pie-X
Dave Dumas, Conseiller, Wards: 10. Sainte-Blanche/Mont-Lebel
Virginie Proulx, Conseillère, Wards: 11. Le Bic
Julien Rochefort-Girard, Greffière
Claude Périnet, Directeur général
Patrick Caron, Directeur, Travaux publics
Rémi Fiola, Directeur, Génie et environnement
Sylvain St-Pierre, Directeur, Finances
Jean-Sébastien Meunier, Directeur, sécurité incendie

Rivière-du-Loup
CP 37
65, rue de l'Hôtel-de-Ville
Rivière-du-Loup, QC G5R 3Y7
Tél: 418-867-6700; *Téléc:* 418-862-2817
ville@villerdl.ca
www.villerdl.ca
Entité municipal: City
Incorporation: 30 décembre 1998; *Area:* 84,11 km2
Comté ou district: Rivière-du-Loup; *Population au 2016:* 19,507
Circonscription(s) électorale(s) provinciale(s): Rivière-du-Loup-Témiscouata
Circonscription(s) électorale(s) fédérale(s): Montmagny-L'Islet-Kamouraska-Rivière-du-Loup
Prochaines élections: 7e novembre 2021
Sylvie Vignet, Mairesse
Steeve Drapeau, Conseiller, Wards: Estuaire
Jacques Minville, Conseiller, Wards: Fraserville
André Beaulieu, Conseiller, Wards: Plaine
Gérald Plourde, Conseiller, Wards: Pointe
Mario Bastille, Conseiller, Wards: Rivière
Nelson Lepage, Conseiller, Wards: Saint-Patrice
Desjardins Caroline, Greffier
Denis Lagacé, Directeur général
Jacques Moreau, Trésorier et directeur, Finances, 418-867-6711
Pascale Boucher, Directrice, Ressources humaines, 418-867-6641
Éric Bérubé, Directeur, Sécurité incendie, 418-862-5901

Roberval
851, boul St-Joseph
Roberval, QC G8H 2L6
Tél: 418-275-0202; *Téléc:* 418-275-5031
vroberval@roberval.ca
www.roberval.ca
Entité municipal: City
Incorporation: 23 décembre 1976; *Area:* 151,85 km2
Comté ou district: Le Domaine-du-Roy; *Population au 2016:* 10,046
Circonscription(s) électorale(s) provinciale(s): Roberval

Circonscription(s) électorale(s) fédérale(s): Lac-St-Jean
Prochaines élections: 7e novembre 2021
Sabin Côté, Maire
Damien Côté, Conseiller, Wards: 1
Marie-Eve Lebel, Conseillère, Wards: 2
Gaston Langevin, Conseiller, Wards: 3
Nicole Bilodeau, Conseillère, Wards: 4
Germain Maltais, Conseiller, Wards: 5
Claudie Gauthier, Conseiller, Wards: 6
Luc R. Bouchard, Greffe et directeur, Affaires juridiques, 418-275-0202
Nathalie Samson, Directrice générale
Nancy Boutin, Trésorière, 418-275-0202
Jean-Luc Gagnon, Directeur, Travaux publics, l'ingénierie et de l'hygiène du milieu, 418-275-0202
Guy Mailhiot, Directeur, Service de sécurité incendie, 418-275-0202

Rosemère
100, rue Charbonneau
Rosemère, QC J7A 3W1
Tél: 450-621-3500; *Téléc:* 450-621-7601
info@ville.rosemere.qc.ca
ville.rosemere.qc.ca
Entité municipal: City
Incorporation: 1er janvier 1947; *Area:* 10,84 km2
Comté ou district: Thérèse-De Blainville; Communauté métropolitaine de Montréal; *Population au 2016:* 13,958
Circonscription(s) électorale(s) provinciale(s): Groulx
Circonscription(s) électorale(s) fédérale(s): Rivière-des-Mille-îles
Prochaines élections: 7e novembre 2021
Eric Westram, Maire
Marie-Hélène Fortin, Conseiller, Wards: 1
Melissa Monk, Conseillère, Wards: 2
Stéphanie Nantel, Conseillère, Wards: 3
René Villeneuve, Conseiller, Wards: 4
Hélène Akzam, Conseillère, Wards: 5
Philip Panet-Raymond, Conseiller, Wards: 6
Catherine Blais-Adam, Greffière, 450-621-3500
Guy Benedetti, Directeur général, 450-621-3500
Justine Asselin, Directrice, Finances, 450-621-3500
Simon Coulombe, Directeur, Travaux publics, 450-621-3500
Claude Guérin, Directeur, Loisirs et vie communautaire
Nathalie Legault, Directrice, Développement durable du territoire, 450-621-3500
Isabelle Rivest, Directrice, Ressources humaines, 450-621-3500

Rouyn-Noranda
CP 220
100, rue Taschereau est
Rouyn-Noranda, QC J9X 5C3
Tél: 819-797-7110; *Téléc:* 819-797-7108
info@rouyn-noranda.ca
www.ville.rouyn-noranda.qc.ca
Entité municipal: City
Incorporation: 1er janvier 2002; *Area:* 6435,64 km2
Population au 2016: 42,334
Circonscription(s) électorale(s) provinciale(s): Rouyn-Noranda—Témiscamingue; Abitibi-Est
Circonscription(s) électorale(s) fédérale(s): Abitibi-Témiscamingue
Prochaines élections: 7e novembre 2021
Diane Dallaire, Mairesse
Sylvie Turgeon, Conseillère, Wards: 2. Rouyn-Noranda-Ouest
André Philippon, Conseiller, Wards: 3. Rouyn-Sud
Claudette Carignan, Conseillère, Wards: 4. Centre-Ville
Denise Lavalée, Conseillère, Wards: 5. Noranda
Daniel Marcotte, Conseiller, Wards: 6. L'Université
Luc Lacroix, Conseiller, Wards: 7. Granada/Bellecombe
François Cotnoir, Conseiller, Wards: 8. Marie-Victorin/Du Sourire
Samuelle Ramsay-Houle, Conseillère, Wards: 9. Évain
Cédric Laplante, Conseiller, Wards: 10. Kekeko
Benjamin Tremblay, Conseiller, Wards: 11. McWatters/Cadillac
Stéphane Girard, Conseiller, Wards: 12. Auguebelle
Angèle Tousignant, Greffière, 819-797-7110
Huguette Lemay, Directrice générale, 819-797-7110
Hélène Piuze, Trésorière et directrice, Finances et services administratifs, 819-797-7110
Yves Blanchette, Directeur, Travaux publics et services techniques
Stéphane Lacombe, Directeur, Gestion des eaux et de l'environnement du territoire
Stephen Valade, Directeur, Sécurité incendie, 819-797-7124

Saguenay
CP 8060
201, rue Racine est
Chicoutimi, QC G7H 5B8
Tél: 418-698-3000; *Téléc:* 418-541-4524
info@ville.saguenay.qc.ca
ville.saguenay.ca

Circonscription(s) électorale(s) fédérale(s): Beauce
Prochaines élections: 7e novembre 2021
Claude Morin, Maire
Serge Thomassin, Conseiller, Wards: 1
Tom Redmond, Conseiller, Wards: 2
Jean Perron, Conseiller, Wards: 3
Esther Fortin, Conseillère, Wards: 4
Manon Bougie, Conseillère, Wards: 5
Jean-Pierre Fortier, Conseiller, Wards: 6
Solange Thibodeau, Conseillère, Wards: 7
Renaud Fortier, Conseiller, Wards: 8
Isabelle Beaulieu, Greffière
Claude Poulin, Directeur général
Sylvain Veilleux, Directeur, Service des incendies

Saint-Hyacinthe
700, av de l'Hôtel-de-Ville
Saint-Hyacinthe, QC J2S 5B2
Tél: 450-778-8300
communications@ville.st-hyacinthe.qc.ca
www.st-hyacinthe.ca
Entité municipal: City
Incorporation: 27 décembre 2001; *Area:* 188,97 km2
Comté ou district: Les Maskoutains; *Population au 2016:* 55,648
Circonscription(s) électorale(s) provinciale(s): St-Hyacinthe
Circonscription(s) électorale(s) fédérale(s): St-Hyacinthe—Bagot
Prochaines élections: 7e novembre 2021
Claude Corbeil, Maire, 450-778-8302, Fax: 450-778-5800
Donald Côté, Conseiller, Wards: 1. Sainte-Rosalie
Pierre Thériault, Conseiller, Wards: 2. Yamaska
Stéphanie Messier, Conseillère, Wards: 3. Saint-Joseph
Bernard Barré, Conseiller, Wards: 4. La Providence
André Beauregard, Conseiller, Wards: 5. Douville
Linda Roy, Conseillère, Wards: 6. Saint-Thomas-d'Aquin
Annie Pelletier, Conseillère, Wards: 7. Saint-Sacrement
Claire Gagné, Conseillère, Wards: 8. Bois-Joli
David Bousquet, Conseiller, Wards: 9. Sacré-Coeur
Jeannot Caron, Conseiller, Wards: 10. Cascades
Crystel Poirier, Greffière
Louis Bilodeau, Directeur général, 450-778-8303

Saint-Jean-sur-Richelieu
CP 1025
188, rue Jacques-Cartier nord
Saint-Jean-sur-Richelieu, QC J3B 7B2
Tél: 450-357-2100; *Téléc:* 450-357-2285
info@sjsr.ca
sjsr.ca
Entité municipal: City
Incorporation: 24 janvier 2001; *Area:* 226,63 km2
Comté ou district: Le Haut-Richelieu; *Population au 2016:* 95,114
Circonscription(s) électorale(s) provinciale(s): Iberville; St-Jean
Circonscription(s) électorale(s) fédérale(s): Saint-Jean
Prochaines élections: 7e novembre 2021
Alain Laplante, Maire, 450-357-2095, Fax: 450-357-2079
Mélanie Dufresne, Conseillère, 514-714-8410, Wards: 1
Justin Bessette, Conseiller, 514-718-5675, Wards: 2
Michel Gendron, Conseiller, 450-346-2392, Wards: 3
Jean Fontaine, Conseiller, 450-346-3063, Wards: 4
François Auger, Conseiller, 514-432-3951, Wards: 5
Patricia Poissant, Conseillère, 450-741-1236, Wards: 6
Christiane Marcoux, Conseillère, 450-347-5277, Wards: 7
Marco Savard, Conseiller, 450-349-0473, Wards: 8
Yvan Berthelot, Conseiller, 450-349-0685, Wards: 9
Ian Langlois, Conseiller, 450-515-3259, Wards: 10
Claire Charbonneau, Conseillère, 450-348-0463, Wards: 11
Maryline Charbonneau, Conseillère, 450-349-6661, Wards: 12
Pierre Archambault, Greffier, 450-357-2077, Fax: 450-357-2362
François Vaillancourt, Directeur général, 450-357-2383
Manon Tourigny, Trésorière, 450-357-2392

Saint-Jérôme
300, rue Parent
Saint-Jérôme, QC J7Z 7Z7
Tél: 450-436-1511
info@vsj.ca
www.vsj.ca
Entité municipal: City
Incorporation: 1er janvier 2002; *Area:* 90,44 km2
Comté ou district: La Rivière-du-Nord; *Population au 2016:* 74,347
Circonscription(s) électorale(s) provinciale(s): Saint-Jérôme
Circonscription(s) électorale(s) fédérale(s): Rivière-du-Nord
Prochaines élections: 7e novembre 2021
Stéphane Maher, Maire, 450-436-1512
Benoit Beaulieu, Conseiller, 514-234-7226, Wards: 1
Mylène Laframboise, Conseillère, 450-304-3301, Wards: 2
François Poirier, Conseiller, 450-275-7742, Wards: 3
Érik Bak, Conseiller, 450-848-1445, Wards: 4
Bernard Bougie, Conseiller, 450-431-7227, Wards: 5
Benoît Delage, Conseiller, 450-436-6134, Wards: 6
Chantale Lambert, Conseillère, 450-512-2916, Wards: 7

Johanne Dicaire, Conseillère, 450-432-7927, Wards: 8
Sophie St-Gelais, Conseillère, 450-280-9843, Wards: 9
Janice Bélair-Rolland, Conseillère, 450-432-7662, Wards: 10
Gilles Robert, Conseiller, 450-512-9391, Wards: 11
Nathalie Lasalle, Conseillère, 450-712-3037, Wards: 12
Marie-Josée Larocque, Greffière
Yvan Patenaude, Directeur général
Luc Chaput, Chef de division, Opérations sécurité incendie

Saint-Lambert
55, av Argyle
Saint-Lambert, QC J4P 2H3
Tél: 450-672-4444
info.citoyens@saint-lambert.ca
www.saint-lambert.ca
Entité municipal: City
Incorporation: 1er janvier 2006; *Area:* 7,59 km2
Comté ou district: Communauté métropolitaine de Montréal;
Population au 2016: 21,861
Circonscription(s) électorale(s) provinciale(s): Laporte
Circonscription(s) électorale(s) fédérale(s):
Brossard-Saint-Lambert
Prochaines élections: 7e novembre 2021
Pierre Brodeur, Maire, 450-466-3235
Francis Le Chatelier, Conseiller, 450-671-3532, Wards: 1
Philippe Glorieux, Conseiller, 514-513-8768, Wards: 2
Bernard Rodrigue, Conseiller, 514-436-5407, Wards: 3
Julie Bourgoin, Conseiller, 438-883-0328, Wards: 4
Loïc Blancquaert, Conseiller, 450-923-2416, Wards: 5
Brigitte Marcotte, Conseiller, 450-465-8712, Wards: 6
David Bowles, Conseiller, 450-812-6237, Wards: 7
France Désaulniers, Conseillère, 450-923-7219, Wards: 8
Martine Savard, Greffière
Georges Pichet, Directeur général
Maxime Marquis, Trésorier

Saint-Lazare
1960, ch Ste-Angélique
Saint-Lazare, QC J7T 3A3
Tél: 450-424-8000
info@ville.saint-lazare.qc.ca
ville.saint-lazare.qc.ca
Entité municipal: City
Incorporation: 29 décembre 1875; *Area:* 66,80 km2
Comté ou district: Vaudreuil-Soulanges; Communauté
métropolitaine de Montréal; *Population au 2016:* 19,889
Circonscription(s) électorale(s) provinciale(s): Soulanges
Circonscription(s) électorale(s) fédérale(s): Vaudreuil-Soulanges
Prochaines élections: 7e novembre 2021
Robert Grimaudo, Maire, 450-424-8000
Geneviève Lachance, Conseillère, 450-424-8000, Wards: 1
Pamela Tremblay, Conseillère, 450-424-8000, Wards: 2
Vacant , Conseiller, Wards: 3
Michel Poitras, Conseiller, 450-424-8000, Wards: 4
Richard Chartrand, Conseiller, 450-424-8000, Wards: 5
Brian Trainor, Conseiller, 450-424-8000, Wards: 6
Nathaly Rayneault, Greffière
Hervé Rivet, Directeur général
Dominic Léger, Trésorier

Saint-Lin-Laurentides
900, 12e av
Saint-Lin-Laurentides, QC J5M 2W2
Tél: 450-439-3130; *Téléc:* 450-439-1525
info@saint-lin-laurentides.com
www.saint-lin-laurentides.com
Entité municipal: City
Incorporation: 1er mars 2000; *Area:* 118,36 km2
Comté ou district: Montcalm; *Population au 2016:* 20,786
Circonscription(s) électorale(s) provinciale(s): Rousseau
Circonscription(s) électorale(s) fédérale(s): Montcalm
Prochaines élections: 7e novembre 2021
Patrick Massé, Maire, 450-439-3130
Luc Cyr, Conseiller, Wards: 1
Mathieu Maisonneuve, Conseiller, Wards: 2
Mario Chrétien, Conseiller, Wards: 3
Jean-Luc Arène, Conseiller, Wards: 4
Benoit Venne, Conseiller, Wards: 5
Pierre Lortie, Conseiller, Wards: 6
Richard Dufort, Greffier & directeur général, 450-439-3130
Sylvain Martel, Directeur, Finances, 450-439-3130
Alain Martel, Directeur, Travaux publics
Robert Marsolais, Directeur, Urbanisme, 450-439-3130
Julien Albert, Chef de division, Service de sécurité incendie,
514-561-7417

Salaberry-de-Valleyfield
61, rue Ste-Cécile
Salaberry-de-Valleyfield, QC J6T 1L8
Tél: 450-370-4300
communications@ville.valleyfield.qc.ca
www.ville.valleyfield.qc.ca

Entité municipal: City
Incorporation: 24 avril 2002; *Area:* 107,13 km2
Comté ou district: Beauharnois-Salaberry; *Population au 2016:*
40,745
Circonscription(s) électorale(s) provinciale(s): Beauharnois
Circonscription(s) électorale(s) fédérale(s): Salaberry-Suroît
Prochaines élections: 7e novembre 2021
Miguel Lemieux, Maire, 450-370-4819
Lyne Lefebvre, Conseillère, 450-373-0954, Wards: 1. Grande-île
Jason Grenier, Conseiller, 450-377-2774, Wards: 2. Nitro
Jean-Marc Rochon, Conseiller, 450-377-8597, Wards: 3.
Georges-Leduc
France Gingras, Conseillère, 450-373-8195, Wards: 4.
Champlain
Guillaume Massicotte, Conseiller, 450-747-3899, Wards: 5. La
Baie
Jacques Smith, Conseiller, 450-371-4975, Wards: 6.
Robert-Cauchon
Patrick Rancourt, Conseiller, 450-370-1717, Wards: 7.
Jules-Léger
Normand Amesse, Conseiller, 450-371-6895, Wards: 8.
Saint-Timothée
Kim Verdant Dumouchel, Greffière, 450-370-4304, Fax:
450-370-4388
Manon Bernard, Directrice générale, 450-370-4800, Fax:
450-370-4343
Michel Décosse, Trésorier, 450-370-4320, Fax: 450-370-4316
Stéphane Bellefeuille, Directeur, Eau, environnement et travaux
publics, 450-370-4820, Fax: 450-370-4370
Martin Pharand, Directeur, Urbanisme, 450-370-4310, Fax:
450-370-4772
Michel Ménard, Directeur, Sécurité incendie, 450-370-4750, Fax:
450-370-4755

Sept-îles
546, av De Quen
Sept-îles, QC G4R 2R4
Tél: 418-962-2525
communications@septiles.ca
www.ville.sept-iles.qc.ca
Entité municipal: City
Incorporation: 12 février 2003; *Area:* 1 762,92 km2
Comté ou district: Sept-Rivières; *Population au 2016:* 25,400
Circonscription(s) électorale(s) provinciale(s): Duplessis
Circonscription(s) électorale(s) fédérale(s): Manicouagan
Prochaines élections: 7e novembre 2021
Note: En 1970, Clarke City est fusionnée à Sept-Iles; le 12 fév.,
2003, Moisie & Gallix sont fusionnées à Sept-Iles.
Réjean Porlier, Maire
Gervais Gagné, Conseiller, Wards: 1. Ste-Marguerite
Guylaine Lejeune, Conseillère, Wards: 2. Ferland
Jean Masse, Conseiller, Wards: 3. L'Anse
Denis Miousse, Conseiller, Wards: 4. Marie-Immaculée
Marie-Claude Quessy-Légaré, Conseillère, Wards: 5. Vieux-Quai
Élisabeth Chevalier, Conseillère, Wards: 6. Mgr-Blanche
Charlotte Audet, Conseillère, Wards: 7. Jacques-Cartier
Michel Bellavance, Conseiller, Wards: 8. Sainte-Famille
Dominic Elsliger Ouellet, Conseiller, Wards: 9. Moisie-Plages
Valérie Haince, Greffière
Patrick Gwilliam, Directeur général
Suzy Lévesque, Trésorier et Directrice, Finances
Michel Tardif, Directeur, Services techniques
Denis Tétreault, Directeur, Urbanisme
Denis Jutras, Directeur, Sécurité incendie

Shawinigan
CP 400
550, av de l'Hôtel-de-Ville
Shawinigan, QC G9N 6V3
Tél: 819-536-7200
information@shawinigan.ca
www.shawinigan.ca
Entité municipal: City
Incorporation: 1er janvier 2002; *Area:* 734,84 km2
Population au 2016: 49,349
Circonscription(s) électorale(s) provinciale(s): Saint-Maurice;
Laviolette
Circonscription(s) électorale(s) fédérale(s):
Saint-Maurice-Champlain
Prochaines élections: 7e novembre 2021
Note: 8 nouveaux districts seront en vigueur lors des élections
municipal de nov/09.
Michel Angers, Maire, 819-536-7211
Josette Allard-Gignac, Conseillère, 819-537-4727, Wards:
Almaville
Martin Asselin, Conseiller, 819-533-5953, Wards: Boisés
Jacinthe Campagna, Conseillère, 819-539-8462, Wards: Cité
Jean-Yves Tremblay, Conseiller, 819-536-7211, Wards: Hêtres
Claude Grenier, Conseiller, 819-539-9474, Wards: Montagnes
Nancy Déziel, Conseillère, 819-247-8508, Wards: Rivière
Lucie de Bons, Conseillère, 819-538-7348, Wards: Rocher

Guy Arseneault, Conseiller, 819-536-7010, Wards: Val-Mauricie
Chantal Doucet, Greffière, 819-536-7211
Yves Vincent, Directeur général, 819-536-7211

Sherbrooke
CP 610
191, rue du Palais
Sherbrooke, QC J1H 5H9
Tél: 819-823-8000
communications@sherbrooke.ca
www.sherbrooke.ca
Entité municipal: City
Incorporation: 1er janvier 2002; *Area:* 353,76 km2
Population au 2016: 161,323
Circonscription(s) électorale(s) provinciale(s): St-François;
Sherbrooke; Richmond
Circonscription(s) électorale(s) fédérale(s): Sherbrooke
Prochaines élections: 7e novembre 2021
Steve Lussier, Maire, 819-821-5969
Nicole Bergeron, Conseillère, Wards: Rock-Forest—Saint-Élie
Annie Godbout, Conseillère, Wards: Rock-Forest—Saint-Élie
Julien Lachance, Conseiller, Wards: Rock-Forest—Saint-Élie
Pierre Tremblay, Conseiller, Wards: Rock-Forest—Saint-Élie
Pierre Avard, Conseiller, Wards: Fleurimont
Danielle Berthold, Conseillère, Wards: Fleurimont
Vincent Boutin, Conseiller, Wards: Fleurimont
Rémi Demers, Conseiller, Wards: Fleurimont
Claude Charron, Conseiller, Wards: Lennoxville
Bertrand Collins, Conseiller, Wards: Lennoxville
Jennifer Garfat, Conseillère, Wards: Lennoxville
Évelyne Beaudin, Conseillère, Wards:
Jacques-Cartier/Mont-Bellevue
Marc Denault, Conseiller, Wards: Jacques-Cartier/Mont-Bellevue
Chantal L'Ésperance, Conseillère, Wards:
Jacques-Cartier/Mont-Bellevue
Paul Gingues, Conseiller, Wards: Jacques-Cartier/Mont-Bellevue
Karine Godbout, Conseillère, Wards:
Jacques-Cartier/Mont-Bellevue
Line Chabot, Greffière
Daniel Picard, Directeur général, 819-823-8000, Fax:
819-823-5121
Nathalie Lapierre, Trésorier, 819-821-5490, Fax: 819-822-6091
Stéphane Simoneau, Directeur, Sécurité d'incendie,
819-822-6098, Fax: 819-821-5516

Sorel-Tracy
CP 368
71, rue Charlotte
Sorel-Tracy, QC J3P 7K1
Tél: 450-780-5600; *Téléc:* 450-780-5625
info@ville.sorel-tracy.qc.ca
www.ville.sorel-tracy.qc.ca
Entité municipal: City
Incorporation: 15 mars 2000; *Area:* 57,46 km2
Comté ou district: Pierre-De Saurel; *Population au 2016:* 34,755
Circonscription(s) électorale(s) provinciale(s): Richelieu
Circonscription(s) électorale(s) fédérale(s):
Bécancour-Nicolet-Saurel
Prochaines élections: 7e novembre 2021
Serge Péloquin, Maire
Olivier Picard, Conseiller, 450-780-5600, Wards: 1. Bourgchemin
Sylvie Labelle, Conseillère, 450-746-2536, Wards: 2. Richelieu
Martin Lajeunesse, Conseiller, 450-746-8987, Wards: 3.
Saint-Laurent
Jocelyn Mondou, Conseiller, 450-881-6738, Wards: 4.
Vieux-Sorel
Alain Maher, Conseiller, 450-743-8749, Wards: 5. Faubourg
Benoit Guèvremont, Conseiller, 450-780-5600, Wards: 6.
Gouverneurs
Patrick Péloquin, Conseiller, 450-780-5600, Wards: 7. Patriotes
Dominique Ouellet, Conseillère, 450-780-1248, Wards: 8.
Pierre-De Saurel
René Chevalier, Greffier, 450-780-5600
Carlo Fleury, Directeur général
Vicky Bussière, Trésorière et directrice, Finances, 450-780-5600
David Gagné, Directeur, Travaux publics, 450-780-5600

Terrebonne
775, rue St-Jean-Baptiste
Terrebonne, QC J6W 1B5
Tél: 450-961-2001; *Téléc:* 450-471-4482
information@ville.terrebonne.qc.ca
www.ville.terrebonne.qc.ca
Entité municipal: City
Incorporation: 27 juin 2001; *Area:* 154,12 km2
Comté ou district: Les Moulins; Communauté métropolitaine de
Montréal; *Population au 2016:* 111,575
Circonscription(s) électorale(s) provinciale(s): L'Assomption;
Terrebonne; Masson
Circonscription(s) électorale(s) fédérale(s): Terrebonne
Prochaines élections: 7e novembre 2021
Marc-André Plante, Maire, 450-961-2001

Brigitte Villeneuve, Conseillère, 450-478-5929, Wards: 1
Nathalie Bellavance, Conseillère, 450-478-7440, Wards: 2
Dany St-Pierre, Conseiller, 450-477-7565, Wards: 3
Réal Leclerc, Conseiller, 450-433-1310, Wards: 4
Serge Gagnon, Conseiller, 514-647-5266, Wards: 5
Éric Fortin, Conseiller, 450-492-1266, Wards: 6
Yan Maisonneuve, Conseiller, 450-964-0467, Wards: 7
Caroline Desbiens, Conseillère, 450-471-0763, Wards: 8
Simon Paquin, Conseiller, 450-704-4972, Wards: 9
Robert Morin, Conseiller, 450-961-0594, Wards: 10
Nathalie Richard, Conseillère, 450-471-2071, Wards: 11
André Fontaine, Conseiller, 450-492-4212, Wards: 12
Jacques Demers, Conseiller, 450-471-5653, Wards: 13
Robert Brisebois, Conseiller, 450-964-7269, Wards: 14
Nathalie LePage, Conseillère, 514-781-1915, Wards: 14
Marc-André Michaud, Conseiller, 450-654-6446, Wards: 16
Jean-François Milot, Greffier
Alain Marcoux, Directeur général
Nathalie Reniers, Trésorier
Sylvain Dufresne, Directeur, Incendie

Thetford Mines
CP 489
144, rue Notre-Dame sud
Thetford Mines, QC G6G 5T3
Tél: 418-335-2981; *Téléc:* 418-335-7089
infos@villethetford.ca
www.villethetford.ca
Entité municipal: City
Incorporation: 17 octobre 2001; *Area:* 226,32 km2
Comté ou district: Les Appalaches; *Population au 2016:* 25,403
Circonscription(s) électorale(s) provinciale(s):
Lotbinière-Frontenac
Circonscription(s) électorale(s) fédérale(s): Mégantic-L'Érable
Prochaines élections: 7e novembre 2021
Marc-Alexandre Brousseau, Maire
Josée Perreault, Conseillère, 418-423-7387, Wards: 1. Black
Lake
Michel Verreault, Conseiller, 418-332-3600, Wards: 2. Black
Lake-Mitchell/Lacs
Adam Patry, Conseiller, 418-338-1394, Wards: 3. Thetford
Mines
Yvan Corriveau, Conseiller, 418-335-2592, Wards: 4. Thetford
Mines
Jean-François Delisle, Conseiller, 418-334-0763, Wards: 5.
Thetford Mines
Hélène Martin, Conseillère, 418-338-1249, Wards: 6. Thetford
Mines
Yves Bergeron, Conseiller, 418-338-4770, Wards: 8. Thetford
Mines
Lise Delisle, Conseillère, 418-338-5313, Wards: 9. Thetford-Sud
Edith Girard, Greffier, 418-335-2981
Marie-Eve Mercier, Directrice général, 418-335-2981
Alexandre Meilleur, Directeur, Travaux publics, 418-335-2981
Kyle Landry, Directeur, Sécurité incendie, 418-338-9183

Trois-Rivières
CP 368
1325, place de l'Hôtel-de-Ville
Trois-Rivières, QC G9A 5H3
Tél: 819-374-2002
311@v3r.net
www.v3r.net
Entité municipal: City
Incorporation: 1er janvier 2002; *Area:* 289,32 km2
Population au 2016: 134,413
Circonscription(s) électorale(s) provinciale(s): Trois-Rivières;
Maskinongé; Champlain
Circonscription(s) électorale(s) fédérale(s): Trois-Rivières;
Berthier-Maskinongé; Saint-Maurice-Champlain
Prochaines élections: 7e novembre 2021
Jean Lamarche, Maire
Pierre Montreuil, Conseiller, Wards: Carmel
Maryse Bellemare, Conseillère, Wards: Chavigny
Pierre-Luc Fortin, Conseiller, Wards: Estacades
Sabrina Roy, Conseillère, Wards: Madeleine
Denis Roy, Conseiller, Wards: Marie-de-l'Incarnation
Valérie Renaud-Martin, Conseillère, Wards: Carrefours
François Belisle, Conseiller, Wards: Pointe-du-lac
Luc Tremblay, Conseiller, Wards: Châteaudun
Michel Cormier, Conseiller, Wards: St-Louis-de-France
Mariannick Mercure, Conseillère, Wards: Forges
Daniel Cournoyer, Conseiller, Wards: Ste-Marthe
Dany Carpentier, Conseiller, Wards: La-Vérendrye
Claude Ferron, Conseiller, Wards: Rivières
Ginette Bellemare, Conseillère, Wards: Richelieu
Daniel Cournoyer, Conseiller, Wards: Sainte-Marthe
Yolaine Tremblay, Greffière
France Cinq-Mars, Directrice générale et directrice, Finances
Claude Bélisle, Directeur, Ressources humaines
Sophie Desfossés, Directeur, Loisirs et communautaires

Robert Dussault, Directeur, Aménagement et développement
urbain
Ghislain Lachance, Directeur, Travaux publics

La Tuque
375, rue St-Joseph
La Tuque, QC G9X 1L5
Tél: 819-676-5091; *Téléc:* 819-523-5419
infoservice@ville.latuque.qc.ca
ville.latuque.qc.ca
Entité municipal: City
Incorporation: 26 mars 2003; *Area:* 25 112,41 km2
Population au 2016: 11,001
Circonscription(s) électorale(s) provinciale(s): Laviolette
Circonscription(s) électorale(s) fédérale(s):
St-Maurice-Champlain
Prochaines élections: 7e novembre 2021
Note: Dès le 26 mars 2003, la nouvelle ville de La Tuque
regroupe La Tuque, les municipalités de La Croche, La
Bostonnais, & Lac-Édouard, le village de Parent, & 8 autres
territoires.
Pierre-David Tremblay, Maire
Éric Chagnon, Conseiller, Wards: 1. Parent
René Mercure, Conseiller, Wards: 2. Croche/Couronee rurale
Luc Martel, Conseiller, Wards: 3. Jacques-Buteux
Roger Mantha, Conseiller, Wards: 4. Polyvalente
Jean Duchesneau, Conseiller, Wards: 5. Bel-Air/Centre-ville
Caroline Bérubé, Conseillère, Wards: 6. Aéroport
Jean-Sébastien Poirier, Greffier et directeur, Service du greffe et
de l'urbanisme, 819-523-8200
Marco Lethiecq, Directeur général, 819-523-8200
Christine Gervais, Trésorière et directrice, Service des finances
et de la trésorerie, 819-523-8200
Hélène Pelletier, Directrice adjointe, Infrastructures, travaux
publics urbains et forestiers, 819-523-8200
André Vézina, Directeur, Sécurité d'incendie, 819-523-9797

Val-d'Or
855, 2e av
Val-d'Or, QC J9P 4P4
Tél: 819-824-9613
info@ville.valdor.qc.ca
www.ville.valdor.qc.ca
Entité municipal: City
Incorporation: 1er janvier 2002; *Area:* 3 550,70 km2
Comté ou district: La Vallée-de-l'Or; *Population au 2016:* 32,491
Circonscription(s) électorale(s) provinciale(s): Abitibi-Est
Circonscription(s) électorale(s) fédérale(s):
Abitibi-Baie-James-Nunavik-Eeyou
Prochaines élections: 7e novembre 2021
Pierre Corbeil, Maire
Denis Giguère, Conseillère, Wards: 1. Lac Blouin-Centre-ville
Karen Busque, Conseillère, Wards: 2. Paquinville-Fatima
Eveline Laverdière, Conseillère, Wards: 3. Belvédère
Céline Brindamour, Conseillère, Wards: 4. Sullivan
Léandre Gervais, Conseiller, Wards: 5. Val-Senneville-Vassan
Sylvie Hébert, Conseillère, Wards: 6. Bourlamaque-Louvicourt
Lisyanne Morin, Conseillère, Wards: 7. Lemoine-Baie-Carrière
Robert Quesnel, Conseiller, Wards: 8. Dubuisson
Annie Lafond, Greffière, 819-824-9613
Sophie Gareau, Directrice générale, 819-824-9613
Chantale Gilbert, Trésorière, 819-824-9613
Diane Boudoul, Directrice, Ressources humaines, 819-824-9613
Daniel Turcottee, ing., Directeur, Travaux publics, 819-824-3802
Éric Hébert, ing., Directeur, Sécurité incendie, 819-825-7201

Val-des-Monts
1, rte du Carrefour
Val-des-Monts, QC J8N 4E9
Tél: 819-457-9400; *Téléc:* 819-457-4141
administration@val-des-monts.net
www.val-des-monts.net
Entité municipal: City
Incorporation: 1er janvier 1975; *Area:* 441,84 km2
Comté ou district: Les Collines-de-l'Outaouais; *Population au
2016:* 11,582
Circonscription(s) électorale(s) provinciale(s): Gatineau
Circonscription(s) électorale(s) fédérale(s): Pontiac
Prochaines élections: 7e novembre 2021
Jacques Laurin, Maire, 819-457-9400
Jean Tourangeau, Conseiller, Wards: 1
Pauline Lafrenière, Conseillère, 819-671-2529, Wards: 2
Claude Bergeron, Conseiller, 819-671-0501, Wards: 3
Benjamin Campin, Conseiller, 819-457-9648, Wards: 4
Joëlle Gauthier, Conseillère, 819-661-7807, Wards: 5
Michel B. Gauthier, Conseiller, 819-457-2732, Wards: 6
Patricia Fillet, Directrice générale et secrétaire-trésorière,
819-457-9400
Mireille Brazeau, Directrice, Ressources humaines,
819-457-9400
Nour Eddine El Guemri, Directeur, Travaux publics,
819-457-9400

Camille Lemire-Monette, Directeur, Loisirs, culture et vie communautaire, 819-457-9400
André Turcotte, Directeur, Environnement et urbanisme, 819-457-9400
Francis Lacharité, Directeur, Sécurité incendie, 819-457-9400

Varennes
175, rue Ste-Anne
Varennes, QC J3X 1T5
Tél: 450-652-9888; *Téléc:* 450-652-2655
citoyens@ville.varennes.qc.ca
ville.varennes.qc.ca
Entité municipal: City
Incorporation: 26 août 1972; *Area:* 94,41 km2
Comté ou district: Marguerite-D'Youville; Communauté métropolitaine de Montréal; *Population au 2016:* 21,257
Circonscription(s) électorale(s) provinciale(s): Verchères
Circonscription(s) électorale(s) fédérale(s): Pierre-Boucher-Les Patriotes-Verchères
Prochaines élections: 7e novembre 2021
Martin Damphousse, Maire
Marc-André Savaria, Conseiller, Wards: 1. Guillaudière
Genevieve Labrecque, Conseillère, Wards: 2. Sitière
Mélanie Simoneau, Conseiller, Wards: 3. Langloiserie
Denis Le Blanc, Conseiller, Wards: 4. Notre-Dame
Benoit Duval, Conseiller, Wards: 5. Petite Prairie
Natalie Parent, Conseillère, Wards: 6. Seigneuries
Gaétan Marcil, Conseiller, Wards: 7. Saint-Charles
Brigitte Collin, Conseillère, Wards: 8. Martigny
Marc Giard, Greffier, 450-652-9888
Sébastien Roy, Directeur général, 450-652-9888
Rémi Dubois, Trésorier, 450-652-9888
Bruno Gravel, Directeur, Travaux publics, 450-652-9888
Alain Rouette, Directeur, Ingénierie, 450-652-9888
Dominic Scully, Directeur, Urbanisme

Vaudreuil-Dorion
#200, 2555, rue Dutrisac
Vaudreuil-Dorion, QC J7V 7E6
Tél: 450-455-3371; *Téléc:* 450-424-8540
courriel@ville.vaudreuil-dorion.qc.ca
www.ville.vaudreuil-dorion.qc.ca
Entité municipal: City
Incorporation: 16 mars 1994; *Area:* 72,73 km2
Comté ou district: Vaudreuil-Soulanges; Communauté métropolitaine de Montréal; *Population au 2016:* 38,117
Circonscription(s) électorale(s) provinciale(s): Vaudreuil
Circonscription(s) électorale(s) fédérale(s): Vaudreuil-Soulanges
Prochaines élections: 7e novembre 2021
Guy Pilon, Maire
Josée Clément, Conseiller, Wards: 1. Quinchien
François Séguin, Conseiller, Wards: 2. Harwood
Jasmine Sharma, Conseillère, Wards: 3. Bâtisseurs
Céline Chartier, Conseillère, Wards: 4. Seigneurie
Diane Morin, Conseillère, Wards: 5. Chenaux
Gabriel Parent, Conseiller, Wards: 6. Cité-des-Jeunes
Paul M. Normand, Conseiller, Wards: 7. Carrefour
Paul Dumoulin, Conseiller, Wards: 8. Baie
Jean St-Antoine, Greffier
Olivier Van Neste, Directeur général, 450-455-3371
Marco Pilon, Trésorier et directeur général adjoint, 450-455-3371
Isabelle Bureau, Directrice, Ressources humaines, 450-455-3371
Christine Ouimet, Directrice, Génie et de l'environnement
Terry Rousseau, Directeur, Sécurité incendie, 450-455-3371

Victoriaville
CP 370
1, rue Notre-Dame ouest
Victoriaville, QC G6P 6T2
Tél: 819-758-1571; *Téléc:* 819-758-9292
info@victoriaville.ca
www.victoriaville.ca
Entité municipal: City
Incorporation: 23 juin 1993; *Area:* 84,23 km2
Comté ou district: Arthabaska; *Population au 2016:* 46,130
Circonscription(s) électorale(s) provinciale(s): Arthabaska
Circonscription(s) électorale(s) fédérale(s):
Richmond-Arthabaska
Prochaines élections: 7e novembre 2021
André Bellavance, Maire, 819-350-7910
Caroline Pilon, Conseillère, 819-758-2096, Wards: 1. Parc-de-l'Amitié
Benoit Gauthier, Conseiller, 819-758-1370, Wards: 2. Parc-de-l'Île
Patrick Paulin, Conseiller, 819-758-8214, Wards: 3. Charles-Édouard-Mailhot
Alexandre Côté, Conseiller, 819-752-1320, Wards: 4. Sainte-Famille
Yanick Poisson, Conseiller, 819-758-7330, Wards: 5. Parc-Terre-des-Jeunes
Marc Morin, Conseiller, 819-758-1864, Wards: 6. Parc-Victoria

Yannick Fréchette, Conseiller, 819-752-5454, Wards: 7. Sainte-Victoire
Chantal Moreau, Conseillère, 819-357-7821, Wards: 8. Arthabaska-Nord
Michael Provencher, Conseiller, 819-357-4025, Wards: 9. Arthabaska-Ouest
Sophie Lambert, Conseillère, 819-357-8573, Wards: 10. Arthabaska-Est
Yves Arcand, Greffier
François Pépin, Directeur général
Serge Cyr, Directeur, Service de l'environnement, 819-758-0651

Westmount
4333, rue Sherbrooke ouest
Westmount, QC H3Z 1E2
Tél: 514-989-5200
info@westmount.org
westmount.org
Entité municipal: City
Incorporation: 1er janvier 2006; *Area:* 4,04 km2
Comté ou district: Communauté métropolitaine de Montréal; *Population au 2016:* 20,312
Circonscription(s) électorale(s) provinciale(s): Westmount-Saint-Louis
Circonscription(s) électorale(s) fédérale(s): Notre-Dame-de-Grâce-Westmount
Prochaines élections: 7e novembre 2021
Christina M. Smith, Mairesse
Anitra Bostock, Conseillère, Wards: 1
Philip A. Cutler, Conseiller, Wards: 2
Jeff Shamie, Conseiller, Wards: 3
Conrad Peart, Conseiller, Wards: 4
Marina Brzeski, Conseillère, Wards: 5
Mary Gallery, Conseillère, Wards: 6
Cynthia Lulham, Conseillère, Wards: 7
Kathleen Kez, Conseillère, Wards: 8
Andrew Brownstein, Greffier et directeur, Services juridiques, 514-989-5318, Fax: 514-989-5270
Duncan E. Campbell, Directeur général par intérim, 514-989-5263, Fax: 514-989-5481
Julie Mandeville, Trésorière et directrice, Finances, 514-989-5234, Fax: 514-989-5480
David Lapointe, Directeur, Sports et loisirs, 514-989-5353, Fax: 514-989-5486
Michel Larue, Directeur, Aménagement urbain, 514-989-5219, Fax: 514-989-5270
Gregory McBain, Directeur, Sécurité publique, 514-989-5222, Fax: 514-989-5487

Other Municipalities in Québec

Abercorn
10, ch des Églises ouest
Abercorn, QC J0E 1B0
Tél: 450-538-2664; *Téléc:* 450-538-6295
info@abercorn.ca
municipalites-du-quebec.ca/abercorn/bienvenue.php
Entité municipal: Village
Incorporation: 25 juin 1929; *Area:* 26,72 km2
Comté ou district: Brome-Missisquoi; *Population au 2016:* 334
Circonscription(s) électorale(s) provinciale(s): Brome-Missisquoi
Circonscription(s) électorale(s) fédérale(s): Brome-Missisquoi
Prochaines élections: 7e novembre 2021
Guy Gravel, Maire
Pierre Bell, Directeur général

Abitibi
582, 10e av ouest
Amos, QC J9T 2H3
Tél: 819-732-5356; *Téléc:* 819-732-9607
mrc@mrcabitibi.qc.ca
mrcabitibi.qc.ca
Entité municipal: Regional County Municipality
Incorporation: 1er janvier 1983; *Area:* 7679,36 km2
Population au 2016: 24,639
Note: 17 municipalités & 2 autres territoires.
Josée Couillard, Directrice générale, 819-732-5356

Abitibi-Ouest
11, 5e av est
La Sarre, QC J9Z 1K7
Tél: 819-339-5671; *Téléc:* 819-339-5400
mrcao@mrcao.qc.ca
www.mrcao.qc.ca
Entité municipal: Regional County Municipality
Incorporation: 1er janvier 1982; *Area:* 3334,92 km2
Population au 2016: 20,538
Note: 21 municipalités & 2 autres territoires.
Jaclin Bégin, Préfet
Normand Lagrange, Directeur général, 819-339-5671

Acton
1037, rue Beaugrand
Acton Vale, QC J0H 1A0
Tél: 450-546-3256; *Téléc:* 450-546-0525
info@mrcacton.qc.ca
mrcacton.qc.ca
Entité municipal: Regional County Municipality
Incorporation: 1er janvier 1982; *Area:* 579,80 km2
Population au 2016: 15,594
Note: 8 municipalités.
Jean-Marie Laplante, Préfet
Chantal Lavigne, Directrice générale et secrétaire-trésorière

Acton Vale
1025, rue Boulay
Acton Vale, QC J0H 1A0
Tél: 450-546-2703; *Téléc:* 450-546-4865
actonvale@ville.actonvale.qc.ca
ville.actonvale.qc.ca
Entité municipal: Town
Incorporation: 26 janvier 2000; *Area:* 91,10 km2
Comté ou district: Acton; *Population au 2016:* 7,656
Circonscription(s) électorale(s) provinciale(s): Johnson
Circonscription(s) électorale(s) fédérale(s): St-Hyacinthe-Bagot
Prochaines élections: 7e novembre 2021
Éric Charbonneau, Maire
Claudine Babineau, Greffière

Adstock
35, rue Principale ouest
Adstock, QC G0N 1S0
Tél: 418-422-2135; *Téléc:* 418-422-2134
info@adstock.ca
www.adstock.ca
Entité municipal: Municipality
Incorporation: 24 octobre 2001; *Area:* 290,30 km2
Comté ou district: Les Appalaches; *Population au 2016:* 2,806
Circonscription(s) électorale(s) provinciale(s): Lotbinière-Frontenac
Circonscription(s) électorale(s) fédérale(s): Mégantic-L'Érable
Prochaines élections: 7e novembre 2021
Pascal Binet, Maire, 418-422-2135
Julie Lemelin, Directrice générale, 418-422-2135

Aguanish
CP 47
106, rte Jacques-Cartier
Aguanish, QC G0G 1A0
Tél: 418-533-2323; *Téléc:* 418-533-2012
info@mun.aguanish.org
www.aguanish.org
Entité municipal: Municipality
Incorporation: 1er janvier 1957; *Area:* 586,40 km2
Comté ou district: Minganie; *Population au 2016:* 245
Circonscription(s) électorale(s) provinciale(s): Duplessis
Circonscription(s) électorale(s) fédérale(s): Manicouagan
Prochaines élections: 7e novembre 2021
Léonard Labrie, Maire
Marlène Blais, Directrice générale, 418-533-2323

Akulivik
CP 50
Akulivik, QC J0M 1V0
Tél: 819-496-2222; *Téléc:* 819-496-2200
www.nvakulivik.ca
Entité municipal: Northern Village
Incorporation: 29 décembre 1979; *Area:* 77,03 km2
Comté ou district: Administration régionale Kativik; *Population au 2016:* 633
Circonscription(s) électorale(s) provinciale(s): Ungava
Circonscription(s) électorale(s) fédérale(s): Abitibi-Baie-James-Nunavik-Eeyou
Mark Qumak, Maire
Lydia Nappatuk, Secrétaire-trésorière

Albanel
160, rue Principale
Albanel, QC G8M 3J5
Tél: 418-279-5250; *Téléc:* 418-279-3147
info@albanel.ca
albanel.ca
Entité municipal: Municipality
Incorporation: 11 avril 1990; *Area:* 198,11 km2
Comté ou district: Maria-Chapdelaine; *Population au 2016:* 2,262
Circonscription(s) électorale(s) provinciale(s): Roberval
Circonscription(s) électorale(s) fédérale(s): Lac-Saint-Jean
Prochaines élections: 7e novembre 2021
Francine Chiasson, Mairesse
Stéphanie Marceau, Directrice générale, 418-279-5250

Albertville
1058, rue Principale
Albertville, QC G0J 1A0
Tél: 418-756-3554; *Téléc:* 418-756-3552
albertville@mrcmatapedia.quebec
www.municipalite-albertville.ca
Entité municipal: Municipality
Incorporation: 29 novembre 1930; *Area:* 103,24 km2
Comté ou district: La Matapédia; *Population au 2016:* 226
Circonscription(s) électorale(s) provinciale(s): Matane-Matapédia
Circonscription(s) électorale(s) fédérale(s): Avignon-La
Mitis-Matane-Matapédia
Prochaines élections: 7e novembre 2021
Martin Landry, Maire
Mélissa Hébert, Directrice générale

Alleyn-et-Cawood
10, ch Jondée
Danford Lake, QC J0X 1P0
Tél: 819-467-2941; *Téléc:* 819-467-3133
admin@alleyn-cawood.ca
www.alleyn-cawood.ca
Entité municipal: Municipality
Incorporation: 1er janvier 1877; *Area:* 314,83 km2
Comté ou district: Pontiac; *Population au 2016:* 172
Circonscription(s) électorale(s) provinciale(s): Pontiac
Circonscription(s) électorale(s) fédérale(s): Pontiac
Prochaines élections: 7e novembre 2021
Carl Mayer, Maire
Isabelle Cardinal, Directrice générale

Amherst
CP 30
124, rue St-Louis
Amherst, QC J0T 2L0
Tél: 819-681-3372
amherst@municipalite.amherst.qc.ca
municipalite.amherst.qc.ca
Entité municipal: Township
Incorporation: 9e mars 1887; *Area:* 230,22 km2
Comté ou district: Les Laurentides; *Population au 2016:* 1,484
Circonscription(s) électorale(s) provinciale(s): Labelle
Circonscription(s) électorale(s) fédérale(s): Laurentides-Labelle
Prochaines élections: 7e novembre 2021
Jean-Guy Galipeau, Maire
Marc St-Pierre, Directeur général et secrétaire-trésorier,
819-681-3372

Amqui
20, promenade Marcel-Rioux
Amqui, QC G5J 1A1
Tél: 418-629-4242; *Téléc:* 418-629-4090
info@amqui.ca
www.ville.amqui.qc.ca
Entité municipal: Town
Incorporation: 16 janvier 1991; *Area:* 121.17 km2
Comté ou district: La Matapédia; *Population au 2016:* 6,178
Circonscription(s) électorale(s) provinciale(s): Matane-Matapédia
Circonscription(s) électorale(s) fédérale(s): Avignon-La
Mitis-Matane-Matapédia
Prochaines élections: 7e novembre 2021
Pierre D'Amours, Maire
Vincent Paradis, Greffier

L'Ange-Gardien
1177, rte 315
L'Ange-Gardien, QC J8L 0L4
Tél: 819-986-7470; *Téléc:* 819-986-8349
info@municipalitedelangegardien.com
municipalitedelangegardien.com
Entité municipal: Municipality
Incorporation: 17 mai 1979; *Area:* 218,25 km2
Comté ou district: Les Collines-de-l'Outaouais; Communauté
métropolitaine de Québec; *Population au 2016:* 5,464
Circonscription(s) électorale(s) provinciale(s): Papineau
Circonscription(s) électorale(s) fédérale(s): Argenteuil-La
Petite-Nation; Beauport-Côte-de-Beaupré-île
d'Orléans-Charlevoix; Shefford
Prochaines élections: 7e novembre 2021
Marc Louis-Seize, Maire
Alain Descarreaux, Directeur général

L'Ange-Gardien
6355, av Royale
L'Ange-Gardien, QC G0A 2K0
Tél: 418-822-1555; *Téléc:* 418-822-2526
info@langegardien.qc.ca
langegardien.qc.ca
Entité municipal: Municipality
Incorporation: 1er juillet 1855; *Area:* 53,63 km2
Comté ou district: La Côte-de-Beaupré; *Population au 2016:*
3,695

Ange-Gardien
Circonscription(s) électorale(s) provinciale(s):
Charlevoix-Côte-de-Beaupré
Circonscription(s) électorale(s) fédérale(s):
Beauport—Côte-de-Beaupré—île d'Orléans—Charlevoix
Prochaines élections: 7e novembre 2021
Pierre Lefrançois, Maire
Lise Drouin, Directrice générale, 418-822-1555

Ange-Gardien
249, rue St-Joseph
Ange-Gardien, QC J0E 1E0
Tél: 450-293-7575; *Téléc:* 450-293-6635
info@municipalite.ange-gardien.qc.ca
www.municipalite.ange-gardien.qc.ca
Entité municipal: Municipality
Incorporation: 31 décembre 1997; *Area:* 90,23 km2
Comté ou district: Rouville; *Population au 2016:* 2,699
Circonscription(s) électorale(s) provinciale(s): Iberville
Circonscription(s) électorale(s) fédérale(s): Shefford
Prochaines élections: 7e novembre 2021
Yvan Pinsonneault, Maire
Brigitte Vachon, Directrice générale

L'Anse-Saint-Jean
3, rue du Couvent
L'Anse-Saint-Jean, QC G0V 1J0
Tél: 418-272-2633; *Téléc:* 418-544-3078
info@lanse-saint-jean.ca
municipal.lanse-saint-jean.ca
Entité municipal: Municipality
Incorporation: 1er janvier 1859; *Area:* 506,14 km2
Comté ou district: Le Fjord-du-Saguenay; *Population au 2016:*
1,201
Circonscription(s) électorale(s) provinciale(s): Dubuc
Circonscription(s) électorale(s) fédérale(s): Chicoutimi-Le Fjord
Prochaines élections: 7e novembre 2021
Lucien Martel, Maire
Jonathan Desbiens, Directeur général

Antoine-Labelle
425, rue du Pont
Mont-Laurier, QC J9L 2R6
Tél: 819-623-3485; *Téléc:* 819-623-5052
administration@mrc-antoine-labelle.qc.ca
www.mrc-antoine-labelle.qc.ca
Entité municipal: Regional County Municipality
Incorporation: 1er janvier 1983; *Area:* 14 976,99 km2
Population au 2016: 35,243
Note: 17 municipalités & 11 autres territoires.
Gilbert Pilote, Préfet
Mylène Mayer, Directrice générale et secrétaire-trésorière

Les Appalaches
233, boul Frontenac ouest
Thetford Mines, QC G6G 6K2
Tél: 418-423-2757; *Téléc:* 418-423-5122
info@mrcdesappalaches.ca
www.mrcdesappalaches.ca
Entité municipal: Regional County Municipality
Incorporation: 1er janvier 1982; *Area:* 1912,49 km2
Population au 2016: 42,346
Note: 19 municipalités.
Paul Vachon, Préfet
Louis Laferrière, Directeur générale, 418-332-2757

Argenteuil
430, rue Grace
Lachute, QC J8H 1M6
Tél: 450-562-2474; *Téléc:* 450-562-1911
mrc@argenteuil.qc.ca
argenteuil.qc.ca
Entité municipal: Regional County Municipality
Incorporation: 1er janvier 1983; *Area:* 1252,97 km2
Population au 2016: 32,389
Note: 9 municipalités.
Scott Pearce, Préfet
Marc Carrière, Directeur général

Armagh
5, rue de la Salle
Armagh, QC G0R 1A0
Tél: 418-466-2916; *Téléc:* 418-466-2409
info@armagh.ca
armagh.ca
Entité municipal: Municipality
Incorporation: 29 décembre 1993; *Area:* 168,04 km2
Comté ou district: Bellechasse; *Population au 2016:* 1,488
Circonscription(s) électorale(s) provinciale(s): Bellechasse
Circonscription(s) électorale(s) fédérale(s): Bellechasse-Les
Etchemins-Lévis
Prochaines élections: 7e novembre 2021
Sarto Roy, Maire

Sylvie Vachon, Directrice générale et Secrétaire-trésorière

Arthabaska
150, rue Notre-Dame ouest
Victoriaville, QC G6P 1R9
Tél: 819-752-2444; *Téléc:* 819-752-3623
info@mrc-arthabaska.qc.ca
www.regionvictoriaville.com/page/1320/mrc-darthabaska.aspx
Entité municipal: Regional County Municipality
Incorporation: 1er janvier 1982; *Area:* 1890,18 sq km
Population au 2016: 72,014
Circonscription(s) électorale(s) fédérale(s):
Richmond-Arthabaska
Note: 24 municipalités.
Alain St-Pierre, Préfet
Frédérick Michaud, Directeur général, 819-752-2444

Arundel
2, rue du Village
Arundel, QC J0T 1A0
Tél: 819-681-3390; *Téléc:* 819-687-8760
info@arundel.ca
arundel.ca
Entité municipal: Township
Incorporation: 1er janvier 1878; *Area:* 64,20 km2
Comté ou district: Les Laurentides; *Population au 2016:* 563
Circonscription(s) électorale(s) provinciale(s): Argenteuil
Circonscription(s) électorale(s) fédérale(s): Laurentides-Labelle
Prochaines élections: 7e novembre 2021
Pascale Blais, Mairesse
France Bellefleur, Directrice générale

L'Ascension
59, rue de l'Hôtel-de-Ville
L'Ascension, QC J0T 1W0
Tél: 819-275-3027
informationsgenerales@municipalite-lascension.qc.ca
www.municipalite-lascension.qc.ca
Entité municipal: Municipality
Incorporation: 23 septembre 1905; *Area:* 340,85 km2
Comté ou district: Antoine-Labelle; *Population au 2016:* 791
Circonscription(s) électorale(s) provinciale(s): Labelle
Circonscription(s) électorale(s) fédérale(s): Laurentides-Labelle;
Lac-Saint-Jean
Prochaines élections: 7e novembre 2021
Luc St-Denis, Maire
Hélène Beauchamp, Directrice générale, 819-275-3027

L'Ascension-de-Notre-Seigneur
CP 100
1000, 1e rue est
L'Ascension-de-Notre-Seigneur, QC G0W 1Y0
Tél: 418-347-3482; *Téléc:* 418-347-4253
info@ville.ascension.qc.ca
www.ville.ascension.qc.ca
Entité municipal: Parish (Paroisse)
Incorporation: 25 février 1919; *Area:* 131,93 km2
Comté ou district: Lac-Saint-Jean-Est; *Population au 2016:*
1,987
Circonscription(s) électorale(s) provinciale(s): Lac-St-Jean
Circonscription(s) électorale(s) fédérale(s): Lac-St-Jean
Prochaines élections: 7e novembre 2021
Louis Ouellet, Maire
Normand Desgagné, Directeur général, 418-347-3482

L'Ascension-de-Patapédia
70, rue Principale
L'Ascension-de-Patapédia, QC G0J 1R0
Tél: 418-299-2024; *Téléc:* 418-299-2027
munic@globetrotter.net
matapedialesplateaux.com
Entité municipal: Municipality
Incorporation: 1er janvier 1968; *Area:* 95,93 km2
Comté ou district: Avignon; *Population au 2016:* 164
Circonscription(s) électorale(s) provinciale(s): Bonaventure
Circonscription(s) électorale(s) fédérale(s): Avignon-La
Mitis-Matane-Matapédia
Prochaines élections: 7e novembre 2021
Guy Richard, Maire
Vianney Arseneault, Directeur général

Ascot Corner
5655, rte 112
Ascot-Corner, QC J0B 1A0
Tél: 819-560-8560; *Téléc:* 819-560-8561
ascot.corner@hsfqc.ca
ascot-corner.com
Other Information: Sans frais: 877-562-5436
Entité municipal: Municipality
Incorporation: 28 mars 1901; *Area:* 81,83 km2
Comté ou district: Le Haut-Saint-François; *Population au 2016:*
3,158

Circonscription(s) électorale(s) provinciale(s): Mégantic
Circonscription(s) électorale(s) fédérale(s): Compton-Stanstead
Prochaines élections: 7e novembre 2021
Nathale Bresse, Mairesse
Jonathan Piché, Directeur général, 819-560-8560

L'Assomption
300A, rue Dorval
L'Assomption, QC J5W 3A1
Tél: 450-589-2288; *Téléc:* 450-589-9430
info@mrclassomption.qc.ca
www.mrclassomption.qc.ca
Entité municipal: Regional County Municipality
Incorporation: 1er janvier 1983; *Area:* 255,65 km2
Population au 2016: 124,759
Note: 6 municipalités.
Chantal Deschamps, Préfète
Joffrey Bouchard, Directeur général, 450-589-2288

Aston-Jonction
1300, rue Principale
Aston-Jonction, QC G0Z 1A0
Tél: 819-489-1158; *Téléc:* 819-489-0158
www.aston-jonction.ca
Entité municipal: Municipality
Incorporation: 26 mars 1997; *Area:* 26,22 km2
Comté ou district: Nicolet-Yamaska; *Population au 2016:* 424
Circonscription(s) électorale(s) provinciale(s): Nicolet-Bécancour
Circonscription(s) électorale(s) fédérale(s):
Bécancour-Nicolet-Saurel
Prochaines élections: 7e novembre 2021
Marc-André Gosselin, Maire
Martine Lebeau, Directrice générale

Auclair
681, rue du Clocher
Auclair, QC G0L 1A0
Tél: 418-899-2834; *Téléc:* 418-899-6958
info@municipaliteauclair.ca
www.municipaliteauclair.ca
Entité municipal: Municipality
Incorporation: 1er janvier 1954; *Area:* 105,44 km2
Comté ou district: Témiscouata; *Population au 2016:* 448
Circonscription(s) électorale(s) provinciale(s):
Rivière-du-Loup-Témiscouata
Circonscription(s) électorale(s) fédérale(s):
Rimouski-Neigette-Témiscouata-Les Basques
Prochaines élections: 7e novembre 2021
Bruno Bonesso, Maire
Josée Dubé, Directeur général

Audet
266, rue Principale
Audet, QC G0Y 1A0
Tél: 819-583-1596; *Téléc:* 819-583-5938
munaudet@axion.ca
munaudet.qc.ca
Entité municipal: Municipality
Incorporation: 26 novembre 1903; *Area:* 135,05 km2
Comté ou district: Le Granit; *Population au 2016:* 734
Circonscription(s) électorale(s) provinciale(s): Mégantic
Circonscription(s) électorale(s) fédérale(s): Mégantic-L'Érable
Prochaines élections: 7e novembre 2021
Jean-Marc Grondin, Maire
France Larochelle, Directrice générale

Aumond
664, rue Principale
Aumond, QC J0W 1W0
Tél: 819-449-4006; *Téléc:* 819-449-7448
info@aumond.ca
www.aumond.ca
Entité municipal: Township
Incorporation: 12 décembre 1877; *Area:* 214,74 km2
Comté ou district: La Vallée-de-la-Gatineau; *Population au 2016:* 754
Circonscription(s) électorale(s) provinciale(s): Gatineau
Circonscription(s) électorale(s) fédérale(s): Pontiac
Prochaines élections: 7e novembre 2021
Alphée Moreau, Maire
Julie Cardinal, Directrice générale

Aupaluk
CP 5
Aupaluk, QC J0M 1X0
Tél: 819-491-7070; *Téléc:* 819-491-7035
Entité municipal: Northern Village
Incorporation: 2e février 1980; *Area:* 30,20 km2
Comté ou district: Administration régionale Kativik; *Population au 2016:* 209
Circonscription(s) électorale(s) provinciale(s): Ungava

Circonscription(s) électorale(s) fédérale(s):
Abitibi-Baie-James-Nunavik-Eeyou
George Eetook, Maire
Eva Grey, Secrétaire-trésorière

Austin
21, ch Millington
Austin, QC J0B 1B0
Tél: 819-843-2388; *Téléc:* 819-843-8211
info@municipalite.austin.qc.ca
municipalite.austin.qc.ca
Entité municipal: Municipality
Incorporation: 5 novembre 1938; *Area:* 73,78 km2
Comté ou district: Memphrémagog; *Population au 2016:* 1,485
Circonscription(s) électorale(s) provinciale(s): Orford
Circonscription(s) électorale(s) fédérale(s): Brome-Missisquoi
Prochaines élections: 7e novembre 2021
Lisette Maillé, Mairesse
Manon Fortin, Directrice générale

Authier
457, rue de la Montée
Authier, QC J0Z 1C0
Tél: 819-782-3093; *Téléc:* 819-782-3203
authier@mrcao.qc.ca
authier.ao.ca
Entité municipal: Municipality
Incorporation: 20 septembre 1918; *Area:* 143,42 km2
Comté ou district: Abitibi-Ouest; *Population au 2016:* 268
Circonscription(s) électorale(s) provinciale(s): Abitibi Ouest
Circonscription(s) électorale(s) fédérale(s):
Abitibi-Témiscamingue
Prochaines élections: 7e novembre 2021
Marcel Cloutier, Maire
Rachel Barbe, Directrice générale

Authier-Nord
452, rue Principale
Authier-Nord, QC J0Z 1E0
Tél: 819-782-3914; *Téléc:* 819-782-3916
authier-nord@mrcao.qc.ca
authier-nord.ao.ca
Entité municipal: Municipality
Incorporation: 1er janvier 1983; *Area:* 279,94 km2
Comté ou district: Abitibi-Ouest; *Population au 2016:* 300
Circonscription(s) électorale(s) provinciale(s): Abitibi-Ouest
Circonscription(s) électorale(s) fédérale(s):
Abitibi-Témiscamingue
Prochaines élections: 7e novembre 2021
Alain Gagnon, Maire
Élise Gagnon, Directrice générale

L'Avenir
545, rue Principale
L'Avenir, QC J0C 1B0
Tél: 819-394-2422; *Téléc:* 819-394-2222
info@municipalitelavenir.qc.ca
www.municipalitelavenir.qc.ca
Entité municipal: Municipality
Incorporation: 23 décembre 1976; *Area:* 97,72 km2
Comté ou district: Drummond; *Population au 2016:* 1,307
Circonscription(s) électorale(s) provinciale(s): Johnson
Circonscription(s) électorale(s) fédérale(s): Drummond
Prochaines élections: 7e novembre 2021
Jean Parenteau, Maire
Suzie Lemire, Directrice générale

Avignon
CP 5030
102, rue Nadeau
Carleton-sur-Mer, QC G0C 2Z0
Tél: 418-364-2000; *Téléc:* 418-364-2002
info@mrcavignon.com
www.mrcavignon.com
Entité municipal: Regional County Municipality
Incorporation: 18 mars 1981; *Area:* 3487,51 km2
Population au 2016: 14,461
Note: 11 municipalités & 2 autres territoires.
Guy Gallant, Préfet
David Bourdages, Directeur général, 418-364-2000

Ayer's Cliff
958, rue Main
Ayer's Cliff, QC J0B 1C0
Tél: 819-838-5006; *Téléc:* 819-838-4411
info@ayerscliff.ca
ayerscliff.ca
Entité municipal: Village
Incorporation: 24 février 1909; *Area:* 5,52 km2
Comté ou district: Memphrémagog; *Population au 2016:* 1,047
Circonscription(s) électorale(s) provinciale(s): Orford

Circonscription(s) électorale(s) fédérale(s): Compton-Stanstead
Prochaines élections: 7e novembre 2021
Vincent Gérin, Maire
Bastien Lefebvre, Directeur général

Baie-D'Urfé
20410, ch Lakeshore
Baie-D'Urfé, QC H9X 1P7
Tél: 514-457-5324; *Téléc:* 514-457-5671
info@baie-durfe.qc.ca
baie-durfe.qc.ca
Entité municipal: Town
Incorporation: 1er janvier 2006; *Area:* 6,03 km2
Comté ou district: Communauté métropolitaine de Montréal; *Population au 2016:* 3,823
Circonscription(s) électorale(s) provinciale(s): Jacques-Cartier
Circonscription(s) électorale(s) fédérale(s): Lac-Saint-Louis
Prochaines élections: 7e novembre 2021
Maria Tutino, Mairesse
Tania Lê, Greffière

Baie-des-Sables
CP 39
20, rue du Couvent
Baie-des-Sables, QC G0J 1C0
Tél: 418-772-6218; *Téléc:* 418-772-6455
baiedessables@lamatanie.ca
municipalite.baiedessables.ca
Entité municipal: Municipality
Incorporation: 1er janvier 1859; *Area:* 65,19 km2
Comté ou district: La Matanie; *Population au 2016:* 628
Circonscription(s) électorale(s) provinciale(s): Matane-Matapédia
Circonscription(s) électorale(s) fédérale(s): Avignon-La
Mitis-Matane-Matapédia
Prochaines élections: 7e novembre 2021
Denis Santerre, Maire
Adam Coulombe, Directeur général

Baie-du-Febvre
CP 10
298, rte Marie-Victorin
Baie-du-Febvre, QC J0G 1A0
Tél: 450-783-6422; *Téléc:* 450-783-6423
municipalite@baie-du-febvre.net
www.baie-du-febvre.net
Entité municipal: Municipality
Incorporation: 26 mars 1983; *Area:* 97,21 km2
Comté ou district: Nicolet-Yamaska; *Population au 2016:* 988
Circonscription(s) électorale(s) provinciale(s): Nicolet-Bécancour
Circonscription(s) électorale(s) fédérale(s):
Bécancour-Nicolet-Saurel
Prochaines élections: 7e novembre 2021
Claude Lefebvre, Maire
Maryse Baril, Directrice générale

Baie-Johan-Beetz
15A, rue Johan-Beetz
Baie-Johan-Beetz, QC G0G 1B0
Tél: 418-539-0125; *Téléc:* 418-539-0205
info@baiejohanbeetz.qc.ca
www.baiejohanbeetz.qc.ca
Entité municipal: Municipality
Incorporation: 1er janvier 1966; *Area:* 360,47 km2
Comté ou district: Minganie; *Population au 2016:* 86
Circonscription(s) électorale(s) provinciale(s): Duplessis
Circonscription(s) électorale(s) fédérale(s): Manicouagan
Prochaines élections: 7e novembre 2021
Martin Côté, Maire
Myriam Lafleur, Directrice générale

Baie-Sainte-Catherine
CP 10
308, rue Leclerc
Baie-Sainte-Catherine, QC G0T 1A0
Tél: 418-620-5020; *Téléc:* 418-620-5021
municipalite@baiestecatherine.com
www.baiestecatherine.com
Entité municipal: Municipality
Incorporation: 4e novembre 1903; *Area:* 236,37 km2
Comté ou district: Charlevoix-Est; *Population au 2016:* 206
Circonscription(s) électorale(s) provinciale(s):
Charlevoix-Côte-de-Beaupré
Circonscription(s) électorale(s) fédérale(s):
Beauport—Côte-de-Beaupré—Île d'Orléans—Charlevoix
Prochaines élections: 7e novembre 2021
Donald Kenny, Maire
Mariève Bouchard, Directrice-générale

Baie-Saint-Paul
15, rue Forget
Baie-Saint-Paul, QC G3Z 3G1
Tél: 418-435-2205; *Téléc:* 418-435-2688
ville@baiesaintpaul.com
www.baiesaintpaul.com
Entité municipal: Town
Incorporation: 3e janvier 1996; *Area:* 546,48 km2
Comté ou district: Charlevoix; *Population au 2016:* 7,146
Circonscription(s) électorale(s) provinciale(s):
Charlevoix-Côte-de-Beaupré
Circonscription(s) électorale(s) fédérale(s):
Beauport—Côte-de-Beaupré—Île d'Orléans—Charlevoix
Prochaines élections: 7e novembre 2021
Jean Fortin, Maire
Émilien Bouchard, Greffier

Baie-Trinité
CP 100
28, rte 138
Baie-Trinité, QC G0H 1A0
Tél: 418-939-2231; *Téléc:* 418-939-2616
directiongenerale@baie-trinite.quebec
baie-trinite.quebec
Entité municipal: Village
Incorporation: 1er janvier 1955; *Area:* 424,38 km2
Comté ou district: Manicouagan; *Population au 2016:* 407
Circonscription(s) électorale(s) provinciale(s): René-Lévesque
Circonscription(s) électorale(s) fédérale(s): Manicouagan
Prochaines élections: 7e novembre 2021
Marc Tremblay, Maire
Guy Bouchard, Greffier

Barkmere
199, ch de Barkmere
Barkmere, QC J0T 1A0
Tél: 819-681-3374; *Téléc:* 819-681-3375
www.barkmere.ca
Entité municipal: Village
Incorporation: 24 mars 1926; *Area:* 17,99 km2
Comté ou district: Les Laurentides; *Population au 2016:* 58
Circonscription(s) électorale(s) provinciale(s): Argenteuil
Circonscription(s) électorale(s) fédérale(s): Laurentides-Labelle
Prochaines élections: 7e novembre 2021
Luc Trépanier, Maire
Paul Gélinas, Directeur général

Barnston-Ouest
2080, ch de Way's Mills
Ayer's Cliff, QC J0B 1C0
Tél: 819-838-4334; *Téléc:* 819-838-1717
barnston.ouest@xittel.ca
www.barnston-ouest.ca
Entité municipal: Municipality
Incorporation: 1er janvier 1946; *Area:* 99,48 km2
Comté ou district: Coaticook; *Population au 2016:* 816
Circonscription(s) électorale(s) provinciale(s): Saint-François
Circonscription(s) électorale(s) fédérale(s): Compton-Stanstead
Prochaines élections: 7e novembre 2021
Johnny Piszar, Maire
Sonia Tremblay, Directrice générale

Barraute
481, 8e Av
Barraute, QC J0Y 1A0
Tél: 819-734-6574; *Téléc:* 819-734-5186
mun.barraute@cableamos.com
www.municipalitedebarraute.com
Entité municipal: Municipality
Incorporation: 5e janvier 1994; *Area:* 497,46 km2
Comté ou district: Abitibi; *Population au 2016:* 1,968
Circonscription(s) électorale(s) provinciale(s): Abitibi-Ouest
Circonscription(s) électorale(s) fédérale(s):
Abitibi-Témiscamingue
Prochaines élections: 7e novembre 2021
Yvan Roy, Maire
Alain Therrien, Directeur général

Les Basques
#400, 2, rue Jean-Rioux
Trois-Pistoles, QC G0L 4K0
Tél: 418-851-3206; *Téléc:* 418-851-3171
mrc@mrcdesbasques.com
www.tourismelesbasques.com/la-mrc
Entité municipal: Regional County Municipality
Incorporation: 1er avril 1981
Population au 2016: 8,694
Note: 11 municipalités & 1 autre territoire.
Bertin Denis, Préfet
Claude Dahl, Directeur général et secrétaire-trésorier,
418-851-3206

Batiscan
795, rue Principale
Batiscan, QC G0X 1A0
Tél: 418-362-2421
municipalite@batiscan.ca
www.batiscan.ca
Entité municipal: Municipality
Incorporation: 1er juillet 1855; *Area:* 43,34 km2
Comté ou district: Les Chenaux; *Population au 2016:* 903
Circonscription(s) électorale(s) provinciale(s): Champlain
Circonscription(s) électorale(s) fédérale(s):
St-Maurice-Champlain
Prochaines élections: 7e novembre 2021
Christian Fortin, Maire
Henriette Rivard Desbiens, Conseillère, Wards: 1
Monique Drouin, Conseillère, Wards: 2
Yves Gagnon, Conseiller, Wards: 3
Pierre Châteauneuf, Conseiller, Wards: 4
Sylvain Dussault, Conseiller, Wards: 5
René Proteau, Conseiller, Wards: 5
Pierre Massicotte, Directeur général

Béarn
CP 369
28, 2e rue nord
Béarn, QC J0Z 1G0
Tél: 819-726-4121; *Téléc:* 819-726-2121
www.mrctemiscamingue.org/mrct/liste-des-municipalites/bearn
Entité municipal: Municipality
Incorporation: 3e octobre 1912; *Area:* 501,79 km2
Comté ou district: Témiscamingue; *Population au 2016:* 690
Circonscription(s) électorale(s) provinciale(s):
Rouyn-Noranda-Témiscamingue
Circonscription(s) électorale(s) fédérale(s):
Abitibi-Témiscamingue
Prochaines élections: 7e novembre 2021
Luc Lalonde, Maire
Lynda Gaudet, Directrice générale

Beauce-Sartigan
2727, boul Dionne
Saint-Georges, QC G5Y 3Y1
Tél: 418-228-8418; *Téléc:* 418-228-3709
informations.generales@mrcbeaucesartigan.com
mrcbeaucesartigan.com
Entité municipal: Regional County Municipality
Incorporation: 1er janvier 1982; *Area:* 1954,50 km2
Population au 2016: 52,406
Note: 16 municipalités.
Normand Roy, Préfet
Éric Paquet, Directeur général, 418-228-8418

Beauceville
540, boul Renault
Beauceville, QC G5X 1N1
Tél: 418-774-9137; *Téléc:* 418-774-9141
beauceville@ville.beauceville.qc.ca
ville.beauceville.qc.ca
Entité municipal: Town
Incorporation: 25 février 1998; *Area:* 164,55 km2
Comté ou district: Robert-Cliche; *Population au 2016:* 6,281
Circonscription(s) électorale(s) provinciale(s): Beauce-Nord
Circonscription(s) électorale(s) fédérale(s): Beauce
Prochaines élections: 7e novembre 2021
Luc Provençal, Maire
Paméla Lavoie-Savard, Greffière

Beauharnois-Salaberry
2, rue Ellice
Beauharnois, QC J6N 1W6
Tél: 450-225-0870; *Téléc:* 450-225-0872
info@mrcbhs.ca
www.mrc-beauharnois-salaberry.com
Entité municipal: Regional County Municipality
Incorporation: 1er janvier 1982; *Area:* 471,26 km2
Population au 2016: 64,320
Note: 7 municipalités.
Maude Laberge, Préfete
Linda Phaneuf, Directrice générale, 450-225-0870

Beaulac-Garthby
96, rte 112
Beaulac-Garthby, QC G0Y 1B0
Tél: 418-458-2375; *Téléc:* 418-458-1127
munbeaulacadm@sogetel.net
www.beaulac-garthby.com
Entité municipal: Municipality
Incorporation: 15 mars 2000; *Area:* 75,67 km2
Comté ou district: Les Appalaches; *Population au 2016:* 905
Circonscription(s) électorale(s) provinciale(s): Mégantic
Circonscription(s) électorale(s) fédérale(s): Mégantic-L'Érable
Prochaines élections: 7e novembre 2021

Isabelle Gosselin, Mairesse, 418-458-1175
Josée Leblond, Directrice générale

Beaumont
48, ch du Domaine
Beaumont, QC G0R 1C0
Tél: 418-833-3369
info@beaumont-qc.com
beaumont-qc.com
Entité municipal: Municipality
Incorporation: 1er juillet 1855; *Area:* 44,70 km2
Comté ou district: Bellechasse; *Population au 2016:* 2,942
Circonscription(s) électorale(s) provinciale(s): Bellechasse
Circonscription(s) électorale(s) fédérale(s): Bellechasse-Les
Etchemins-Lévis
Prochaines élections: 7e novembre 2021
David Christopher, Maire
Carl Pelletier, Directeur général

Beaupré
10995, rue des Montagnards
Beaupré, QC G0A 1E0
Tél: 418-827-4541; *Téléc:* 418-827-3818
mairie@villedebeaupre.com
www.villedebeaupre.com
Entité municipal: Town
Incorporation: 23 avril 1928; *Area:* 22,96 km2
Comté ou district: La Côte-de-Beaupré; Communauté
métropolitaine de Québec; *Population au 2016:* 3,752
Circonscription(s) électorale(s) provinciale(s):
Charlevoix-Côte-de-Beaupré
Circonscription(s) électorale(s) fédérale(s):
Beauport—Côte-de-Beaupré—Île d'Orléans—Charlevoix
Prochaines élections: 7e novembre 2021
Pierre Renaud, Maire
Johanne Gagnon, Greffière

Bécancour
#1, 3689, boul Bécancour
Bécancour, QC G9H 3W7
Tél: 819-298-2070; *Téléc:* 819-298-2041
info@mrcbecancour.qc.ca
www.mrcbecancour.qc.ca
Other Information: Sans frais: 866-441-0404
Entité municipal: Regional County Municipality
Incorporation: 1er janvier 1982; *Area:* 1144,67 km2
Population au 2016: 20,404
Note: 12 municipalités.
Mario Lyonnais, Préfet
Daniel Béliveau, Directeur général, 819-298-3300

Bedford
237, rte 202 est
Canton de Bedford, QC J0J 1A0
Tél: 450-248-7576; *Téléc:* 450-248-0135
municipalite@cantondebedford.ca
www.cantondebedford.ca
Entité municipal: Township
Incorporation: 4e mars 1919; *Area:* 31,98 km2
Comté ou district: Brome-Missisquoi; *Population au 2016:* 687
Circonscription(s) électorale(s) provinciale(s): Brome-Missisquoi
Circonscription(s) électorale(s) fédérale(s): Brome-Missisquoi
Prochaines élections: 7e novembre 2021
Gilles St-Jean, Maire
Manon Blanchet, Directrice générale

Bedford
1, rue Principale
Bedford, QC J0J 1A0
Tél: 450-248-2440
administration@ville.bedford.qc.ca
ville.bedford.qc.ca
Entité municipal: Town
Incorporation: 21 novembre 1866; *Area:* 4,25 km2
Comté ou district: Brome-Missisquoi; *Population au 2016:* 2,560
Circonscription(s) électorale(s) provinciale(s): Brome-Missisquoi
Circonscription(s) électorale(s) fédérale(s): Brome-Missisquoi
Prochaines élections: 7e novembre 2021
Yves Lévesque, Maire
Richard Joyal, Directeur général

Bégin
126, rue Brassard
Bégin, QC G0V 1B0
Tél: 418-672-4270; *Téléc:* 418-673-2117
info@begin.ca
www.begin.ca
Entité municipal: Municipality
Incorporation: 8e février 1922; *Area:* 191,50 km2
Comté ou district: Le Fjord-du-Saguenay; *Population au 2016:*
818
Circonscription(s) électorale(s) provinciale(s): Dubuc

Circonscription(s) électorale(s) fédérale(s): Jonquière
Prochaines élections: 7e novembre 2021
Gérald Savard, Maire
Mireille Bergeron, Directrice générale

Belcourt
219, rue Communautaire
Belcourt, QC J0Y 2M0
Tél: 819-737-8894; *Téléc:* 819-737-4084
info@munbelcourt.ca
munbelcourt.ca
Entité municipal: Municipality
Incorporation: 24 octobre 1918; *Area:* 411,05 km2
Comté ou district: La Vallée-de-l'Or; *Population au 2016:* 225
Circonscription(s) électorale(s) provinciale(s): Abitibi-Est
Circonscription(s) électorale(s) fédérale(s):
Abitibi-Baie-James-Nunavik-Eeyou
Prochaines élections: 7e novembre 2021
Carol Nolet, Maire
Nathalie Lizotte, Directrice générale

Bellechasse
100, rue Monseigneur-Bilodeau
Saint-Lazare-de-Bellechasse, QC G0R 3J0
Tél: 418-883-3347; *Téléc:* 418-883-2555
info@mrcbellechasse.qc.ca
www.mrcbellechasse.qc.ca
Entité municipal: Regional County Municipality
Incorporation: 1er janvier 1982; *Area:* 1751,06 km2
Population au 2016: 37,233
Note: 20 municipalités.
Clément Fillion, Préfet
Alain Vallières, Directrice générale

Belleterre
265, 1e av
Belleterre, QC J0Z 1L0
Tél: 819-722-2122; *Téléc:* 819-722-2527
villedebelleterre@mrctemiscamingue.qc.ca
www.villebelleterre.com
Entité municipal: Village
Incorporation: 13 mai 1942; *Area:* 551,02 km2
Comté ou district: Témiscamingue; *Population au 2016:* 313
Circonscription(s) électorale(s) provinciale(s):
Rouyn-Noranda-Témiscamingue
Circonscription(s) électorale(s) fédérale(s):
Abitibi-Témiscamingue
Prochaines élections: 7e novembre 2021
Bruno Boyer, Maire
Josée Rivard, Directrice générale

Les Bergeronnes
424, rue de la Mer
Les Bergeronnes, QC G0T 1G0
Tél: 418-232-6244; *Téléc:* 418-232-6602
info@bergeronnes.com
bergeronnes.com
Entité municipal: Municipality
Incorporation: 29 décembre 1999; *Area:* 274,26 km2
Comté ou district: La Haute-Côte-Nord; *Population au 2016:* 661
Circonscription(s) électorale(s) provinciale(s): René-Lévesque
Circonscription(s) électorale(s) fédérale(s): Manicouagan
Prochaines élections: 7e novembre 2021
Francis Bouchard, Maire
Véronique Lapointe, Directrice générale

Berry
274, rte 399
Berry, QC J0Y 2G0
Tél: 819-732-1815; *Téléc:* 819-732-3289
direction.berry@mrcabitibi.qc.ca
municipalites-du-quebec.ca/berry
Entité municipal: Municipality
Incorporation: 1er janvier 1982; *Area:* 577,33 km2
Comté ou district: Abitibi; *Population au 2016:* 538
Circonscription(s) électorale(s) provinciale(s): Abitibi-Ouest
Circonscription(s) électorale(s) fédérale(s):
Abitibi-Témiscamingue
Prochaines élections: 7e novembre 2021
Raymond Doré, Maire
Marie-Eve Strzelec, Directrice générale

Berthier-sur-Mer
5, rue du Couvent
Berthier-sur-Mer, QC G0R 1E0
Tél: 418-259-7343
info@berthiersurmer.ca
berthiersurmer.ca
Entité municipal: Municipality
Incorporation: 1er juillet 1855; *Area:* 26,92 km2
Comté ou district: Montmagny; *Population au 2016:* 1,555
Circonscription(s) électorale(s) provinciale(s): Côte-du-Sud

Circonscription(s) électorale(s) fédérale(s):
Montmagny-L'Islet-Kamouraska-Rivière-du-Loup
Prochaines élections: 7e novembre 2021
Richard Galibois, Maire
Martin Turgeon, Directeur général

Berthierville
588, rue De Montcalm
Berthierville, QC J0K 1A0
Tél: 450-836-7035
info@ville.berthierville.qc.ca
www.ville.berthierville.qc.ca
Entité municipal: Town
Incorporation: 14 avril 1852; *Area:* 6,89 km2
Comté ou district: D'Autray; *Population au 2016:* 4,189
Circonscription(s) électorale(s) provinciale(s): Berthier
Circonscription(s) électorale(s) fédérale(s): Berthier-Maskinongé
Prochaines élections: 7e novembre 2021
Suzanne Nantel, Mairesse
Sylvie Dubois, Directrice générale et greffière

Béthanie
1321, ch de Béthanie
Béthanie, QC J0H 1E1
Tél: 450-548-2826
bethanie@cooptel.qc.ca
municipalitedebethanie.ca
Entité municipal: Municipality
Incorporation: 2e mars 1920; *Area:* 46,87 km2
Comté ou district: Acton; *Population au 2016:* 322
Circonscription(s) électorale(s) provinciale(s): Johnson
Circonscription(s) électorale(s) fédérale(s): St-Hyacinthe-Bagot
Prochaines élections: 7e novembre 2021
Boniface Dalle-Vedove, Maire
Yan Zurbach, Directeur général

Biencourt
CP 70
5, rue Berger
Biencourt, QC G0K 1T0
Tél: 418-499-2423; *Téléc:* 418-499-2708
info@biencourt.ca
www.biencourt.ca
Entité municipal: Municipality
Incorporation: 1er janvier 1947; *Area:* 187,34 km2
Comté ou district: Témiscouata; *Population au 2016:* 464
Circonscription(s) électorale(s) provinciale(s):
Rivière-du-Loup-Témiscouata
Circonscription(s) électorale(s) fédérale(s):
Rimouski-Neigette-Témiscouata-Les Basques
Prochaines élections: 7e novembre 2021
Daniel Boucher, Maire
Julie Vaillancourt, Directrice générale

Blanc-Sablon
CP 400
1149, boul Dr.-Camille-Marcoux
Blanc-Sablon, QC G0G 1W0
Tél: 418-461-2707; *Téléc:* 418-461-2529
info@blancsablon.com
Entité municipal: Municipality
Incorporation: 1er janvier 1990; *Area:* 247,94 km2
Comté ou district: Le Golfe-du-Saint-Laurent; *Population au 2016:* 1,112
Circonscription(s) électorale(s) provinciale(s): Duplessis
Circonscription(s) électorale(s) fédérale(s): Manicouagan
Prochaines élections: 7e novembre 2021
Wanda Beadoin, Mairesse
Lianda Joncas, Directrice générale

Blue Sea
CP 99
10, rue Principale
Blue Sea, QC J0X 1C0
Tél: 819-463-2261; *Téléc:* 819-463-4345
info@bluesea.ca
www.bluesea.ca
Entité municipal: Municipality
Incorporation: 31 janvier 1921; *Area:* 74,21 km2
Comté ou district: La Vallée-de-la-Gatineau; *Population au 2016:* 639
Circonscription(s) électorale(s) provinciale(s): Gatineau
Circonscription(s) électorale(s) fédérale(s): Pontiac
Prochaines élections: 7e novembre 2021
Laurent Fortin, Maire
Christian Michel, Directeur général

Boileau
702, ch de Boileau
Boileau, QC J0V 1N0
Tél: 819-687-3436; *Téléc:* 819-687-3745
info@boileau.ca
boileau.ca
Entité municipal: Municipality
Incorporation: 8e mars 1882; *Area:* 136,33 km2
Comté ou district: Papineau; *Population au 2016:* 335
Circonscription(s) électorale(s) provinciale(s): Papineau
Circonscription(s) électorale(s) fédérale(s): Argenteuil-La Petite-Nation
Prochaines élections: 7e novembre 2021
Robert Meyer, Maire
Cathy Viens, Directrice générale, 819-687-3436

Boischatel
45, rue Bédard
Boischatel, QC G0A 1H0
Tél: 418-822-4500; *Téléc:* 418-822-4512
info@boischatel.net
www.boischatel.ca
Entité municipal: Municipality
Incorporation: 3e avril 1920; *Area:* 20,45
Comté ou district: La Côte-de-Beaupré; Communauté métropolitaine de Québec; *Population au 2016:* 7,587
Circonscription(s) électorale(s) provinciale(s):
Charlevoix-Côte-de-Beaupré
Circonscription(s) électorale(s) fédérale(s):
Beauport—Côte-de-Beaupré—Île d'Orléans—Charlevoix
Prochaines élections: 7e novembre 2021
Benoit Bouchard, Maire
Carl Michaud, Directeur général

Bois-des-Filion
375, boul Adophe-Chapleau
Bois-des-Filion, QC J6Z 1H1
Tél: 450-621-1460; *Téléc:* 450-621-8483
ville@villebdf.ca
villebdf.ca
Entité municipal: Town
Incorporation: 1er janvier 1949; *Area:* 4,39 km2
Comté ou district: Thérèse-De Blainville; *Population au 2016:* 9,636
Circonscription(s) électorale(s) provinciale(s): Blainville
Circonscription(s) électorale(s) fédérale(s): Thérèse-De Blainville
Prochaines élections: 7e novembre 2021
Gilles Blanchette, Maire
Marie-Renée Houde, Greffière

Bois-Franc
466, rte 105
Bois-Franc, QC J9E 3A9
Tél: 819-449-2252; *Téléc:* 819-449-4407
info@bois-franc.ca
www.bois-franc.ca
Entité municipal: Municipality
Incorporation: 17 novembre 1920; *Area:* 72,25 km2
Comté ou district: La Vallée-de-la-Gatineau; *Population au 2016:* 421
Circonscription(s) électorale(s) provinciale(s): Gatineau
Circonscription(s) électorale(s) fédérale(s): Pontiac
Prochaines élections: 7e novembre 2021
Julie Jolivette, Mairesse
Annie Pelletier, Directrice générale

Bolton-Est
858, rte Missisquoi
Bolton-Est, QC J0E 1G0
Tél: 450-292-3444; *Téléc:* 450-292-4224
info@boltonest.ca
www.boltonest.ca
Entité municipal: Municipality
Incorporation: 28 décembre 1876; *Area:* 79,71 km2
Comté ou district: Memphrémagog; *Population au 2016:* 940
Circonscription(s) électorale(s) provinciale(s): Orford
Circonscription(s) électorale(s) fédérale(s): Brome-Missisquoi
Prochaines élections: 7e novembre 2021
Jacques Drolet, Maire
Mélisa Camiré, Directrice générale et secrétaire-trésorière, 450-292-3444

Bolton-Ouest
9, ch Town Hall
Bolton-Ouest, QC J0E 2T0
Tél: 450-242-2704; *Téléc:* 450-242-2705
reception@bolton-ouest.ca
bolton-ouest.ca
Entité municipal: Municipality
Incorporation: 28 décembre 1876; *Area:* 101,15 km2
Comté ou district: Brome-Missisquoi; *Population au 2016:* 630
Circonscription(s) électorale(s) provinciale(s): Brome-Missisquoi

Circonscription(s) électorale(s) fédérale(s): Brome-Missisquoi
Prochaines élections: 7e novembre 2021
Jacques Drolet, Maire
Jean-François Grandmont, Directeur général

Bonaventure
127, av de Louisbourg
Bonaventure, QC G0C 1E0
Tél: 418-534-2313
info@villebonaventure.ca
villebonaventure.ca
Entité municipal: Town
Incorporation: 1er janvier 1884; *Area:* 104,35 km2
Comté ou district: Bonaventure; *Population au 2016:* 2,706
Circonscription(s) électorale(s) provinciale(s): Bonaventure
Circonscription(s) électorale(s) fédérale(s): Gaspésie—Les
îles-de-la-Madeleine
Prochaines élections: 7e novembre 2021
Roch Audet, Maire
François Bouchard, Directeur général

Bonaventure
CP 310
51, rue Notre-Dame
New Carlisle, QC G0C 1Z0
Tél: 418-752-6601; *Téléc:* 418-752-6657
info@mrcbonaventure.com
mrcbonaventure.com
Entité municipal: Regional County Municipality
Incorporation: 8e avril 1981; *Area:* 4379,40 km2
Population au 2016: 17,660
Note: 13 municipalités & 1 autre territoire.
Éric Dubé, Préfet
François Bujold, Directeur général, 581-357-0126

Bonne-Espérance
CP 40
100, rue Whiteley
Rivière-Saint-Paul, QC G0G 2P0
Tél: 418-379-2911; *Téléc:* 418-379-2959
info@bonneesperance.ca
www.bonneesperance.ca
Entité municipal: Municipality
Incorporation: 1er janvier 1990; *Area:* 646,73 km2
Comté ou district: Le Golfe-du-Saint-Laurent; *Population au
2016:* 681
Circonscription(s) électorale(s) provinciale(s): Duplessis
Circonscription(s) électorale(s) fédérale(s): Manicouagan
Prochaines élections: 7e novembre 2021
Roderick Fequet, Maire
Leslie Woodland, Directrice générale

Bonsecours
557, rue du Couvent
Bonsecours, QC J0E 1H0
Tél: 450-532-3139; *Téléc:* 450-532-3953
municipalite@bonsecours.ca
municipalites-du-quebec.ca/bonsecours
Entité municipal: Municipality
Incorporation: 20 mars 1905; *Area:* 60,46 km2
Comté ou district: Le Val-Saint-François; *Population au 2016:*
608
Circonscription(s) électorale(s) provinciale(s): Orford
Circonscription(s) électorale(s) fédérale(s): Shefford
Prochaines élections: 7e novembre 2021
Jacques David, Maire
Nathalie Noël, Directrice générale

La Bostonnais
15, rue de l'Église
La Bostonnais, QC G9X 0A7
Tél: 819-523-5830; *Téléc:* 819-523-5776
secr.munlabostonnais@tlb.sympatico.ca
www.labostonnais.ca
Entité municipal: Municipality
Incorporation: 1er janvier 2006; *Area:* 287,09 km2
Population au 2016: 635
Circonscription(s) électorale(s) provinciale(s): Laviolette
Circonscription(s) électorale(s) fédérale(s):
Saint-Maurice-Champlain
Prochaines élections: 7e novembre 2021
Michel Sylvain, Maire
Michelle Cantin, Greffière

Bouchette
CP 59
36, rue Principale
Bouchette, QC J0X 1E0
Tél: 819-465-2555; *Téléc:* 819-465-2318
info@bouchette.ca
www.bouchette.ca

Entité municipal: Municipality
Incorporation: 22 mars 1980; *Area:* 123,44 km2
Comté ou district: La Vallée-de-la-Gatineau; *Population au 2016:*
731
Circonscription(s) électorale(s) provinciale(s): Gatineau
Circonscription(s) électorale(s) fédérale(s): Pontiac
Prochaines élections: 7e novembre 2021
Gilles Bastien, Maire
Claudia Lacroix, Directrice générale

Bowman
214, rte 307
Bowman, QC J0X 3C0
Tél: 819-454-2421; *Téléc:* 819-454-2133
commisadm@bowman.ca
www.bowman.ca
Entité municipal: Municipality
Incorporation: 27 juin 1913; *Area:* 129,30 km2
Comté ou district: Papineau; *Population au 2016:* 658
Circonscription(s) électorale(s) provinciale(s): Papineau
Circonscription(s) électorale(s) fédérale(s): Argenteuil-La
Petite-Nation
Prochaines élections: 7e novembre 2021
Pierre Labonté, Maire
Daisy Constantineau, Directrice générale

Brébeuf
217, rte 323
Brébeuf, QC J0T 1B0
Tél: 819-425-9833; *Téléc:* 819-425-6611
secretariat@brebeuf.ca
brebeuf.ca
Entité municipal: Parish (Paroisse)
Incorporation: 4e juin 1910; *Area:* 36,25 km2
Comté ou district: Les Laurentides; *Population au 2016:* 976
Circonscription(s) électorale(s) provinciale(s): Labelle
Circonscription(s) électorale(s) fédérale(s): Avignon-La
Mitis-Matane-Matapédia; Laurentides-Labelle
Prochaines élections: 7e novembre 2021
Marc L'Heureux, Maire
Pascal Caron, Directeur général

Brigham
118, av des Cèdres
Brigham, QC J2K 4K4
Tél: 450-263-5942; *Téléc:* 450-263-8380
info@brigham.ca
brigham.ca
Entité municipal: Municipality
Incorporation: 1er juillet 1855; *Area:* 86,92 km2
Comté ou district: Brome-Missisquoi; *Population au 2016:* 2,306
Circonscription(s) électorale(s) provinciale(s): Brome-Missisquoi
Circonscription(s) électorale(s) fédérale(s): Brome-Missisquoi
Prochaines élections: 7e novembre 2021
Steven Neil, Maire
Pierre Lefebvre, Directeur général

Bristol
32, ch d'Aylmer
Bristol, QC J0X 1G0
Tél: 819-647-5555; *Téléc:* 819-647-2424
info@bristolmunicipality.qc.ca
bristolmunicipality.qc.ca
Entité municipal: Municipality
Incorporation: 1er juillet 1855; *Area:* 207,19 km2
Comté ou district: Pontiac; *Population au 2016:* 1,036
Circonscription(s) électorale(s) provinciale(s): Pontiac
Circonscription(s) électorale(s) fédérale(s): Pontiac
Prochaines élections: 7e novembre 2021
Brent Orr, Maire
Christina Peck, Directrice générale

Brome
330, ch Stagecoach
Brome, QC J0E 1K0
Tél: 450-243-0489; *Téléc:* 450-243-1091
admin@bromevillage.ca
bromevillage.ca
Entité municipal: Village
Incorporation: 20 juin 1923; *Area:* 11,57 km2
Comté ou district: Brome-Missisquoi; *Population au 2016:* 296
Circonscription(s) électorale(s) provinciale(s): Brome-Missisquoi
Circonscription(s) électorale(s) fédérale(s): Brome-Missisquoi
Prochaines élections: 7e novembre 2021
Leon Thomas Selby, Maire
Francis Bergeron, Directeur général

Brome-Missisquoi
749, rue Principale
Cowansville, QC J2K 1J8
Tél: 450-266-4900; *Téléc:* 450-266-6141
administration@mrcbm.qc.ca
mrcbm.qc.ca
Entité municipal: Regional County Municipality
Incorporation: 1er janvier 1983; *Area:* 1652,08 km2
Population au 2016: 58,314
Note: 21 municipalités.
Patrick Melchior, Préfet
Robert Desmarais, Directeur général, 450-266-4900

Bromont
88, boul de Bromont
Bromont, QC J2L 1A1
Tél: 450-534-2021; *Téléc:* 450-534-1025
ville@bromont.com
www.bromont.net
Entité municipal: Town
Incorporation: 27 janvier 1973; *Area:* 114,13 km2
Comté ou district: Brome-Missisquoi; *Population au 2016:* 9,041
Circonscription(s) électorale(s) provinciale(s): Brome-Missisquoi
Circonscription(s) électorale(s) fédérale(s): Brome-Missisquoi
Prochaines élections: 7e novembre 2021
Louis Villeneuve, Maire
Éric Sévigny, Directeur général

Brownsburg-Chatham
300, rue de l'Hôtel-de-Ville
Brownsburg-Chatham, QC J8G 3B4
Tél: 450-533-6687; *Téléc:* 450-533-5795
info@brownsburgchatham.ca
www.brownsburgchatham.ca
Other Information: Sans frais: 866-533-6687
Entité municipal: Town
Incorporation: 6e octobre 1999; *Area:* 247,40 km2
Comté ou district: Argenteuil; *Population au 2016:* 7,122
Circonscription(s) électorale(s) provinciale(s): Argenteuil
Circonscription(s) électorale(s) fédérale(s): Argenteuil-La
Petite-Nation
Prochaines élections: 7e novembre 2021
Catherine Trickey, Mairesse
Pierre-Alain Bouchard, Greffier et directeur, Service juridique

Bryson
833, rue Principale
Bryson, QC J0X 1H0
Tél: 819-648-5940; *Téléc:* 819-648-5297
bryson@mrcpontiac.qc.ca
Entité municipal: Municipality
Incorporation: 1er janvier 1873; *Area:* 3,65 km2
Comté ou district: Pontiac; *Population au 2016:* 697
Circonscription(s) électorale(s) provinciale(s): Pontiac
Circonscription(s) électorale(s) fédérale(s): Pontiac;
Salaberry-Suroît
Prochaines élections: 7e novembre 2021
Alain Gagnon, Maire
Tracey Hérault, Directrice générale

Bury
528, rue Main
Bury, QC J0B 1J0
Tél: 819-560-8414
information.bury@hsfqc.ca
municipalitedebury.qc.ca
Entité municipal: Municipality
Incorporation: 1er juillet 1855; *Area:* 234,39 km2
Comté ou district: Le Haut-Saint-François; *Population au 2016:*
1,174
Circonscription(s) électorale(s) provinciale(s): Mégantic
Circonscription(s) électorale(s) fédérale(s): Compton-Stanstead
Prochaines élections: 7e novembre 2021
Walter Dougherty, Maire
Louise Brière, Directrice générale

Cacouna
415, rue St-Georges
Cacouna, QC G0L 1G0
Tél: 418-867-1781; *Téléc:* 418-867-5677
municipalite@cacouna.ca
cacouna.ca
Entité municipal: Municipality
Incorporation: 22 mars 2006; *Area:* 62,80 km2
Comté ou district: Rivière-du-Loup; *Population au 2016:* 1,803
Circonscription(s) électorale(s) provinciale(s):
Rivière-du-Loup-Témiscouata
Circonscription(s) électorale(s) fédérale(s):
Montmagny-L'Islet-Kamouraska-Rivière-du-Loup
Prochaines élections: 7e novembre 2021
Ghislaine Daris, Mairesse, 418-867-1781
Félix Bérubé, Directeur général, 418-867-1781

Calixa-Lavallée
771, ch de la Beauce
Calixa-Lavallée, QC J0L 1A0
Tél: 450-583-6470; *Téléc:* 450-583-5508
info@calixa-lavallee.ca
www.calixa-lavallee.ca
Entité municipal: Parish (Paroisse)
Incorporation: 24 juillet 1878; *Area:* 32,21 km2
Comté ou district: Marguerite-D'Youville; Communauté
métropolitaine de Montréal; *Population au 2016:* 523
Circonscription(s) électorale(s) provinciale(s): Verchères
Circonscription(s) électorale(s) fédérale(s): Pierre-Boucher-Les
Patriotes-Verchères
Prochaines élections: 7e novembre 2021
Daniel Plouffe, Maire
Suzanne Francoeur, Directrice générale

Campbell's Bay
CP 157
Campbell's Bay, QC J0X 1K0
Tél: 819-648-5811; *Téléc:* 819-648-2045
info@campbellsbay.ca
campbellsbay.ca
Entité municipal: Municipality
Incorporation: 23 février 1904; *Area:* 3,55 km2
Comté ou district: Pontiac; *Population au 2016:* 744
Circonscription(s) électorale(s) provinciale(s): Pontiac
Circonscription(s) électorale(s) fédérale(s): Pontiac
Prochaines élections: 7e novembre 2021
Maurice Beauregard, Maire
Sarah Bertrand, Directrice générale

Caniapiscau
CP 2025
100, rue le Carrefour
Fermont, QC G0G 1J0
Tél: 418-287-5339; *Téléc:* 418-287-3420
mrc@caniapiscau.net
caniapiscau.net
Entité municipal: Regional County Municipality
Incorporation: 1er janvier 1982; *Area:* 34 056,77
Population au : 3,142
Circonscription(s) électorale(s) fédérale(s): Manicouagan
Note: 2 municipalités & 4 autre territoire.
Martin St-Laurent, Préfet
Jimmy Morneau, Directeur général

Cantley
8, ch River
Cantley, QC J8V 2Z9
Tél: 819-827-3434; *Téléc:* 819-827-4328
municipalite@cantley.ca
cantley.ca
Entité municipal: Municipality
Incorporation: 1er janvier 1989; *Area:* 128,36 km2
Comté ou district: Les Collines-de-l'Outaouais; *Population au 2016:* 10,699
Circonscription(s) électorale(s) provinciale(s): Gatineau
Circonscription(s) électorale(s) fédérale(s): Pontiac
Prochaines élections: 7e novembre 2021
Madeleine Brunette, Mairesse
Aimé Sabourin, Conseiller, 819-457-1008, Wards: 1. Monts
Jocelyne Lapierre, Conseillère, 819-827-0256, Wards: 2. Prés
Jean-Benoît Trahan, Conseiller, 819-485-1728, Wards: 3. Rive
Sarah Plamondon, Conseillère, 819-610-0728, Wards: 4. Parcs
Louis Simon Joanisse, Conseiller, 819-664-2717, Wards: 5.
Érables
Jean-Nicolas De Bellefeuille, Conseiller, 819-414-5459, Wards:
6. Lacs
Stéphane Parent, Greffier, 819-827-3434
Stéphane Parent, Directeur général
Diane Forgues, Directrice, Ressources humaines

Cap-Chat
CP 279
53, rue Notre-Dame
Cap-Chat, QC G0J 1E0
Tél: 418-786-5537
ville.capchat@globetrotter.net
ville.cap-chat.ca
Entité municipal: Town
Incorporation: 15 mars 2000; *Area:* 182,05 km2
Comté ou district: La Haute-Gaspésie; *Population au 2016:* 2,476
Circonscription(s) électorale(s) provinciale(s): Gaspé
Circonscription(s) électorale(s) fédérale(s): Gaspésie—Les
Îles-de-la-Madeleine
Prochaines élections: 7e novembre 2021
Marie Gratton, Mairesse
Yves Roy, Directeur général et greffier

Caplan
CP 360
17, boul Perron est
Caplan, QC G0C 1H0
Tél: 418-388-2075; *Téléc:* 418-388-2429
caplan@globetrotter.net
www.municipalitecaplan.com
Entité municipal: Municipality
Incorporation: 1er janvier 1875; *Area:* 85,31 km2
Comté ou district: Bonaventure; *Population au 2016:* 2,024
Circonscription(s) électorale(s) provinciale(s): Bonaventure
Circonscription(s) électorale(s) fédérale(s): Gaspésie—Les
Îles-de-la-Madeleine
Prochaines élections: 7e novembre 2021
Lise Castilloux, Mairesse
Pamela Dow, Directrice générale

Cap-Saint-Ignace
180, place de l'Église
Cap-Saint-Ignace, QC G0R 1H0
Tél: 418-246-5631; *Téléc:* 418-246-5663
adjointe@capsaintignace.ca
www.capsaintignace.ca
Entité municipal: Municipality
Incorporation: 1er juillet 1855; *Area:* 204,71 km2
Comté ou district: Montmagny; *Population au 2016:* 3,089
Circonscription(s) électorale(s) provinciale(s): Côte-du-Sud
Circonscription(s) électorale(s) fédérale(s):
Montmagny-L'Islet-Kamouraska-Rivière-du-Loup
Prochaines élections: 7e novembre 2021
Jocelyne Caron, Mairesse
Sophie Boucher, Directrice générale

Cap-Santé
194, rte 138
Cap-Santé, QC G0A 1L0
Tél: 418-285-1207
info@capsante.qc.ca
capsante.qc.ca
Entité municipal: Town
Incorporation: 1er juillet 1855; *Area:* 54,53 km2
Comté ou district: Portneuf; *Population au 2016:* 3,400
Circonscription(s) électorale(s) provinciale(s): Portneuf
Circonscription(s) électorale(s) fédérale(s):
Portneuf-Jacques-Cartier
Prochaines élections: 7e novembre 2021
Denis Jobin, Maire
Nancy Sirois, Directrice générale, 418-285-1207

Carignan
#210, 2379, ch de Chambly
Carignan, QC J3L 4N4
Tél: 450-658-1066; *Téléc:* 450-658-2676
info@villedecarignan.org
www.carignan.quebec
Entité municipal: Town
Incorporation: 1er juillet 1855; *Area:* 62,27 km2
Comté ou district: La Vallée-du-Richelieu; Communauté
métropolitaine de Montréal; *Population au 2016:* 9,462
Circonscription(s) électorale(s) provinciale(s): Chambly
Circonscription(s) électorale(s) fédérale(s): Beloeil-Chambly;
Saint-Maurice-Champlain
Prochaines élections: 7e novembre 2021
Patrick Marquès, Maire
Eve Poulin, Greffière

Carleton-sur-Mer
629, boul Perron
Carleton, QC G0C 1J0
Tél: 418-364-7073; *Téléc:* 418-364-6011
info@carletonsurmer.com
carletonsurmer.com
Entité municipal: Town
Incorporation: 4e octobre 2000; *Area:* 221,42 km2
Comté ou district: Avignon; *Population au 2016:* 4,073
Circonscription(s) électorale(s) provinciale(s): Bonaventure
Circonscription(s) électorale(s) fédérale(s): Avignon-La
Mitis-Matane-Matapédia
Prochaines élections: 7e novembre 2021
Mathieu Lapointe, Maire
Antoine Audet, Directeur général et greffier

Cascapédia-Saint-Jules
75, rte Gallagher
Cascapédia-Saint-Jules, QC G0C 1T0
Tél: 418-392-4042; *Téléc:* 418-392-6004
www.cascapediastjules.com
Entité municipal: Municipality
Incorporation: 2e juin 1999; *Area:* 163,45 km2
Comté ou district: Bonaventure; *Population au 2016:* 730
Circonscription(s) électorale(s) provinciale(s): Bonaventure
Circonscription(s) électorale(s) fédérale(s):

Gaspésie—Îles-de-la-Madeleine
Prochaines élections: 7e novembre 2021
Gaetan (Guy) Boudreau, Maire
Susan Legouffe, Directrice générale

Causapscal
1, rue St-Jacques nord
Causapscal, QC G0J 1J0
Tél: 418-756-3444; *Téléc:* 418-756-3344
reception@causapscal.quebec
www.causapscal.net
Entité municipal: Town
Incorporation: 31 décembre 1997; *Area:* 161,60 km2
Comté ou district: La Matapédia; *Population au 2016:* 2,304
Circonscription(s) électorale(s) provinciale(s): Matane-Matapédia
Circonscription(s) électorale(s) fédérale(s): Avignon-La
Mitis-Matane-Matapédia
Prochaines élections: 7e novembre 2021
André Fournier, Maire
Laval Robichaud, Directeur général

Cayamant
6, ch Lachapelle
Lac-Cayamant, QC J0X 1Y0
Tél: 819-463-3587
info@cayamant.ca
www.cayamant.ca
Entité municipal: Municipality
Incorporation: 10 octobre 1906; *Area:* 389.07 km2
Comté ou district: La Vallée-de-la-Gatineau; *Population au 2016:*
821
Circonscription(s) électorale(s) provinciale(s): Gatineau
Circonscription(s) électorale(s) fédérale(s): Pontiac
Prochaines élections: 7e novembre 2021
Nicolas Malette, Maire
Julie Jetté, Directrice général

Les Cèdres
1060, ch du Fleuve
Les Cèdres, QC J7T 1A1
Tél: 450-452-4651; *Téléc:* 450-452-4605
info@ville.lescedres.qc.ca
www.ville.lescedres.qc.ca
Entité municipal: Municipality
Incorporation: 9 mars 1985; *Area:* 77,71 km2
Comté ou district: Vaudreuil-Soulanges; Communauté
métropolitaine de Montréal; *Population au 2016:* 6,777
Circonscription(s) électorale(s) provinciale(s): Soulanges
Circonscription(s) électorale(s) fédérale(s): Vaudreuil-Soulanges;
Hull-Aylmer
Prochaines élections: 7e novembre 2021
Raymond Larouche, Maire
Jimmy Poulin, Directeur général

Chambord
1526, rue Principale
Chambord, QC G0W 1G0
Tél: 418-342-6274; *Téléc:* 418-342-8438
info@chambord.ca
chambord.ca
Entité municipal: Municipality
Incorporation: 8e décembre 1973; *Area:* 121,49 km2
Comté ou district: Le Domaine-du-Roy; *Population au 2016:*
1,765
Circonscription(s) électorale(s) provinciale(s): Roberval
Circonscription(s) électorale(s) fédérale(s): Lac-Saint-Jean
Prochaines élections: 7e novembre 2021
Luc Chiasson, Maire
Grant Baergen, Directeur général, 418-342-6274

Champlain
CP 250
819, rue Notre-Dame
Champlain, QC G0X 1C0
Tél: 819-295-3979; *Téléc:* 819-295-3032
municipalite.champlain@infoteck.qc.ca
www.municipalite.champlain.qc.ca
Entité municipal: Municipality
Incorporation: 11 décembre 1982; *Area:* 58,30 km2
Comté ou district: Les Chenaux; *Population au 2016:* 1,735
Circonscription(s) électorale(s) provinciale(s): Champlain
Circonscription(s) électorale(s) fédérale(s): Lac-Saint-Jean
Prochaines élections: 7e novembre 2021
Guy Simon, Maire
Jean Houde, Directeur général

Champneuf
12, 6e av nord
Champneuf, QC J0Y 1E0
Tél: 819-754-2053; *Téléc:* 819-754-5749
munichampneuf@hotmail.com
www.champneuf.ca

Entité municipal: Municipality
Incorporation: 1er janvier 1964; *Area:* 242,81 km2
Comté ou district: Abitibi; *Population au 2016:* 123
Circonscription(s) électorale(s) provinciale(s): Abitibi-Ouest
Circonscription(s) électorale(s) fédérale(s):
Abitibi-Témiscamingue
Prochaines élections: 7e novembre 2021
Rosaire Guénette, Maire
Josée Beauregard, Directrice générale

Chandler
CP 459
35, rue Commerciale ouest
Chandler, QC G0C 1K0
Tél: 418-689-2221; *Téléc:* 418-689-3073
hdvchan@villechandler.com
www.villedechandler.com
Entité municipal: Town
Incorporation: 27 juin 2001; *Area:* 419,34 km2
Comté ou district: Le Rocher-Percé; *Population au 2016:* 7,546
Circonscription(s) électorale(s) provinciale(s): Bonaventure
Circonscription(s) électorale(s) fédérale(s): Gaspésie—Les
Îles-de-la-Madeleine
Prochaines élections: 7e novembre 2021
Louisette Langlois, Mairesse
Roch Giroux, Greffier et directeur général

Chapais
CP 380
145, boul Springer
Chapais, QC G0W 1H0
Tél: 418-745-2511; *Téléc:* 418-745-3871
info@villedechapais.com
villedechapais.com
Entité municipal: Village
Incorporation: 16 novembre 1955; *Area:* 63,71 km2
Population au 2016: 1,499
Circonscription(s) électorale(s) provinciale(s): Ungava
Circonscription(s) électorale(s) fédérale(s):
Abitibi-Baie-James-Nunavik-Eeyou;
Montmagny-L'Islet-Kamouraska-Rivière-du-Loup
Prochaines élections: 7e novembre 2021
Steve Gamache, Maire
Mariève Bernier, Greffière

Charette
390, rue St-Édouard
Charette, QC G0X 1E0
Tél: 819-221-2095; *Téléc:* 819-221-3493
municipalitecharette@sogetel.net
www.municipalite-charette.ca
Entité municipal: Municipality
Incorporation: 9e février 1918; *Area:* 41,88 km2
Comté ou district: Maskinongé; *Population au 2016:* 953
Circonscription(s) électorale(s) provinciale(s): Maskinongé
Circonscription(s) électorale(s) fédérale(s): Berthier-Maskinongé
Prochaines élections: 7e novembre 2021
Claude Boulanger, Maire
Patricia Adam, Directrice générale, 819-221-2095

Charlemagne
84, rue du Sacré-Coeur
Charlemagne, QC J5Z 1W8
Tél: 450-581-2541; *Téléc:* 450-581-0597
info@ville.charlemagne.qc.ca
www.ville.charlemagne.qc.ca
Entité municipal: Town
Incorporation: 13 novembre 1906; *Area:* 2,19 km2
Comté ou district: L'Assomption; Communauté métropolitaine de
Montréal; *Population au 2016:* 5,913
Circonscription(s) électorale(s) provinciale(s): L'Assomption
Circonscription(s) électorale(s) fédérale(s): Repentigny
Prochaines élections: 7e novembre 2021
Normand Grenier, Maire
Olivier Goyet, Greffier et Directeur général par intérim

Charlevoix
4, place de l'Église
Baie-Saint-Paul, QC G3Z 1T2
Tél: 418-435-2639; *Téléc:* 418-435-2666
mrc@charlevoix.net
www.mrc-charlevoix.com
Entité municipal: Regional County Municipality
Incorporation: 1er janvier 1982; *Area:* 1763,22
Population au 2016: 12,997
Note: 6 municipalités & 1 autre territoire.
Claudette Simard, Préfet
Karine Horvath, Directrice générale, 418-435-2639

Charlevoix-Est
172, boul Notre-Dame
Clermont, QC G4A 1G1
Tél: 418-439-3947; *Téléc:* 418-439-2502
direction@mrccharlevoixest.ca
mrccharlevoixest.ca
Entité municipal: Regional County Municipality
Incorporation: 1er janvier 1982; *Area:* 2307,23 km2
Population au 2016: 15,509
Note: 7 municipalités & 2 autres territoires.
Sylvain Tremblay, Préfet
Pierre Girard, Directeur général, 418-439-3947

Chartierville
27, rue St-Jean-Baptiste
Chartierville, QC J0B 1K0
Tél: 819-560-8522; *Téléc:* 819-560-8523
chartierville.ca
Entité municipal: Municipality
Incorporation: 1er janvier 1879; *Area:* 142,05 km2
Comté ou district: Le Haut-Saint-François; *Population au 2016:*
276
Circonscription(s) électorale(s) provinciale(s): Mégantic
Circonscription(s) électorale(s) fédérale(s): Compton-Stanstead
Prochaines élections: 7e novembre 2021
Denis Dion, Maire
Paméla Blais, Directrice générale

Château-Richer
8006, av Royale
Château-Richer, QC G0A 1N0
Tél: 418-824-4294; *Téléc:* 418-824-3277
info@chateauricher.qc.ca
www.chateauricher.qc.ca
Entité municipal: Town
Incorporation: 1er juillet 1855; *Area:* 229,55 km2
Comté ou district: La Côte-de-Beaupré; Communauté
métropolitaine de Québec; *Population au 2016:* 4,126
Circonscription(s) électorale(s) provinciale(s):
Charlevoix-Côte-de-Beaupré
Circonscription(s) électorale(s) fédérale(s):
Beauport—Côte-de-Beaupré—île d'Orléans—Charlevoix
Prochaines élections: 7e novembre 2021
Jean Robitaille, Maire
Jean-François Gervais, Greffier et responsable, Urbanisme

Chazel
752, 1e av ouest
Chazel, QC J0Z 1N0
Tél: 819-333-4758; *Téléc:* 819-333-3818
chazel@mrcao.qc.ca
chazel.ao.ca
Entité municipal: Municipality
Incorporation: 19 février 1938; *Area:* 133,96 km2
Comté ou district: Abitibi-Ouest; *Population au 2016:* 289
Circonscription(s) électorale(s) provinciale(s): Abitibi-Ouest
Circonscription(s) électorale(s) fédérale(s):
Abitibi-Témiscamingue
Prochaines élections: 7e novembre 2021
Daniel Favreau, Maire
Priscillia Lefebvre, Directrice générale

Chelsea
100, ch d'Old Chelsea
Chelsea, QC J9B 1C1
Tél: 819-827-1124; *Téléc:* 819-827-2672
info@chelsea.ca
www.chelsea.ca
Entité municipal: Municipality
Incorporation: 1er janvier 1875; *Area:* 113,77 km2
Comté ou district: Les Collines-de-l'Outaouais; *Population au
2016:* 6,909
Circonscription(s) électorale(s) provinciale(s): Gatineau
Circonscription(s) électorale(s) fédérale(s): Pontiac
Prochaines élections: 7e novembre 2021
Caryl Green, Mairesse
John-David McFaul, Directeur général

Les Chenaux
630, rue Principale
Saint-Luc-de-Vincennes, QC G0X 3K0
Tél: 819-840-0704; *Téléc:* 819-295-5117
info@mrcdeschenaux.ca
www.mrcdeschenaux.ca
Entité municipal: Regional County Municipality
Incorporation: 1er janvier 2002
Population au 2016: 18,617
Circonscription(s) électorale(s) fédérale(s): Trois-Rivières
Note: 10 municipalités.
Gérard Bruneau, Préfet
Patrick Baril, Directeur général, 819-840-0704

Chénéville
63, rue de l'Hôtel-de-Ville
Chénéville, QC J0V 1E0
Tél: 819-428-3583; *Téléc:* 819-428-4838
reception@ville-cheneville.com
www.ville.cheneville.qc.ca
Entité municipal: Municipality
Incorporation: 21 août 1996; *Area:* 66,76 km2
Comté ou district: Papineau; *Population au 2016:* 764
Circonscription(s) électorale(s) provinciale(s): Papineau
Circonscription(s) électorale(s) fédérale(s): Argenteuil-La
Petite-Nation
Prochaines élections: 7e novembre 2021
Gilles Tremblay, Maire
Krystelle Dagenais, Directrice générale

Chertsey
333, av de l'Amitié
Chertsey, QC J0K 3K0
Tél: 450-882-2920; *Téléc:* 450-882-3333
general@chertsey.ca
www.municipalite.chertsey.qc.ca
Entité municipal: Municipality
Incorporation: 13 novembre 1991; *Area:* 288,43 km2
Comté ou district: Matawinie; *Population au 2016:* 4,696
Circonscription(s) électorale(s) provinciale(s): Rousseau
Circonscription(s) électorale(s) fédérale(s): Joliette
Prochaines élections: 7e novembre 2021
François Quenneville, Maire
Linda Paquette, Directrice générale

Chesterville
486, rue de l'Accueil
Chesterville, QC G0P 1J0
Tél: 819-382-2059; *Téléc:* 819-382-2073
info@chesterville.net
www.chesterville.net
Entité municipal: Municipality
Incorporation: 18 décembre 1982; *Area:* 116,69 km2
Comté ou district: Arthabaska; *Population au 2016:* 922
Circonscription(s) électorale(s) provinciale(s):
Drummond-Bois-Francs
Circonscription(s) électorale(s) fédérale(s):
Richmond-Arthabaska
Prochaines élections: 7e novembre 2021
Maryse Beauchesne, Mairesse
Joanne Giguère, Directrice générale

Chibougamau
650, 3e rue
Chibougamau, QC G8P 1P1
Tél: 418-748-2688; *Téléc:* 418-748-6562
directiongenerale@ville.chibougamau.qc.ca
www.ville.chibougamau.qc.ca
Entité municipal: Town
Incorporation: 8e novembre 1952; *Area:* 698,13 km2
Population au 2016: 7,504
Circonscription(s) électorale(s) provinciale(s): Ungava
Circonscription(s) électorale(s) fédérale(s):
Abitibi-Baie-James-Nunavik-Eeyou
Prochaines élections: 7e novembre 2021
Manon Cyr, Mairesse
Marc Gauthier, Greffier

Chichester
CP 158
75, rue Notre-Dame
Chapeau, QC J0X 1M0
Tél: 819-689-2266; *Téléc:* 819-689-5619
chichester@mrcpontiac.qc.ca
www.chichestermunicipality.com
Entité municipal: Township
Incorporation: 1er janvier 1857; *Area:* 221,14 km2
Comté ou district: Pontiac; *Population au 2016:* 328
Circonscription(s) électorale(s) provinciale(s): Pontiac
Circonscription(s) électorale(s) fédérale(s): Pontiac
Prochaines élections: 7e novembre 2021
Donald Gagnon, Maire
Alicia Jones, Directrice générale

Chisasibi
CP 150
1, rue Riverside
Chisasibi, QC J0M 1E0
Tél: 819-855-2878; *Téléc:* 819-855-2875
info@chisasibi.ca
chisasibi.ca
Entité municipal: Villages Cris
Incorporation: 28 juin 1978; *Area:* 491,64 km2
Circonscription(s) électorale(s) provinciale(s): Ungava
Circonscription(s) électorale(s) fédérale(s):
Abitibi-Baie-James-Nunavik-Eeyou

Circonscription(s) électorale(s) fédérale(s): Mégantic-L'Érable
Prochaines élections: 7e novembre 2021
Jacques Lessard, Maire
Matthieu Levasseur, Directeur général

Disraéli
8306, rte 112
Disraéli, QC G0N 1E0
Tél: 418-449-5329; *Téléc:* 418-449-5459
info@paroissedisraeli.com
www.paroissedisraeli.com
Entité municipal: Parish (Paroisse)
Incorporation: 1er janvier 1883; *Area:* 92,56 km2
Comté ou district: Les Appalaches; *Population au 2016:* 1,123
Circonscription(s) électorale(s) provinciale(s): Mégantic
Circonscription(s) électorale(s) fédérale(s): Mégantic-L'Érable
Prochaines élections: 7e novembre 2021
Jacynthe Patry, Mairesse
Rock Sadoine, Directeur général

Dixville
251, ch Parker
Dixville, QC J0B 1P0
Tél: 819-849-3037; *Téléc:* 819-849-9520
secretariat@dixville.ca
www.dixville.ca
Entité municipal: Municipality
Incorporation: 27 septembre 1995; *Area:* 76,65 km2
Comté ou district: Coaticook; *Population au 2016:* 696
Circonscription(s) électorale(s) provinciale(s): St-François
Circonscription(s) électorale(s) fédérale(s): Compton-Stanstead
Prochaines élections: 7e novembre 2021
François Bouchard, Mairesse
Sylvain Benoit, Directeur général

Le Domaine-du-Roy
901, boul St-Joseph
Roberval, QC G8H 2L8
Tél: 418-275-5044; *Téléc:* 418-275-4049
info@mrcdomaineduroy.ca
mrcdomaineduroy.ca
Entité municipal: Regional County Municipality
Incorporation: 1er janvier 1983; *Area:* 17 803,47 km2
Population au 2016: 31,285
Note: 9 municipalités & 1 autre territoire.
Yanick Baillargeon, Préfet
Mario Gagnon, Directeur général, 450-275-5044

Donnacona
138, av Pleau
Donnacona, QC G3M 1A1
Tél: 418-285-0110; *Téléc:* 418-285-0020
info@villededonnacona.com
villededonnacona.com
Entité municipal: Town
Incorporation: 21 janvier 1967; *Area:* 20,13 km2
Comté ou district: Portneuf; *Population au 2016:* 7,200
Circonscription(s) électorale(s) provinciale(s): Portneuf
Circonscription(s) électorale(s) fédérale(s):
Portneuf-Jacques-Cartier
Prochaines élections: 7e novembre 2021
Jean-Claude Léveillée, Maire
Pierre-Luc Gignac, Greffier

La Doré
4998, rue des Peupliers
La Doré, QC G8J 1G9
Tél: 418-256-3545; *Téléc:* 418-256-3496
info@ladore.ca
www.ladore.ca
Entité municipal: Parish (Paroisse)
Incorporation: 16 mars 1906; *Area:* 289,80 km2
Comté ou district: Le Domaine-du-Roy; *Population au 2016:*
1,365
Circonscription(s) électorale(s) provinciale(s): Roberval
Circonscription(s) électorale(s) fédérale(s): Lac-St-Jean
Prochaines élections: 7e novembre 2021
Yanick Baillargeon, Maire
Stéphanie Gagnon, Directrice générale

Dosquet
2, rue Mgr. Chouinard
Dosquet, QC G0S 1H0
Tél: 418-728-3653; *Téléc:* 418-728-3338
mundosquet@videotron.ca
www.municipalitededosquet.com
Entité municipal: Municipality
Incorporation: 9e février 1918; *Area:* 65,09 km2
Comté ou district: Lotbinière; *Population au 2016:* 944
Circonscription(s) électorale(s) provinciale(s):
Lotbinière-Frontenac

Circonscription(s) électorale(s) fédérale(s): Lévis-Lotbinière
Prochaines élections: 7e novembre 2021
Yvan Charest, Maire
Jolyane Houle, Directrice générale

Drummond
436, rue Lindsay
Drummondville, QC J2B 1G6
Tél: 819-477-2230; *Téléc:* 819-477-8442
info@mrcdrummond.qc.ca
www.mrcdrummond.qc.ca
Entité municipal: Regional County Municipality
Incorporation: 1er janvier 1982; *Area:* 1600,26 km2
Population au 2016: 103,397
Note: 18 municipalités.
Carole Côté, Préfète
Gabriel Rioux, Directeur général, 819-477-2230

Dudswell
167, rue Main
Bishopton, QC J0B 1G0
Tél: 819-560-8484; *Téléc:* 819-560-8485
municipalite.dudswell@hsfqc.ca
municipalitededudswell.ca
Entité municipal: Municipality
Incorporation: 11 octobre 1995; *Area:* 218,61 km2
Comté ou district: Le Haut-Saint-François; *Population au 2016:*
1,727
Circonscription(s) électorale(s) provinciale(s): Mégantic
Circonscription(s) électorale(s) fédérale(s): Compton-Stanstead
Prochaines élections: 7e novembre 2021
Mariane Paré, Mairesse
Solange Masson, Directrice générale, 819-560-8484

Duhamel
1890, rue Principale
Duhamel, QC J0V 1G0
Tél: 819-428-7100
info@municipalite.duhamel.qc.ca
municipalite.duhamel.qc.ca
Entité municipal: Municipality
Incorporation: 15 août 1936; *Area:* 434,57 km2
Comté ou district: Papineau; *Population au 2016:* 430
Circonscription(s) électorale(s) provinciale(s): Papineau
Circonscription(s) électorale(s) fédérale(s): Argenteuil-La Petite
Nation
Prochaines élections: 7e novembre 2021
David Pharand, Maire
Julie Ricard, Directrice générale

Duhamel-Ouest
361, rte 101 sud
Duhamel-Ouest, QC J9V 1A2
Tél: 819-629-2522; *Téléc:* 819-629-2422
municipalites-du-quebec.ca/duhamel-ouest
Entité municipal: Municipality
Incorporation: 20 février 1911; *Area:* 91,47 km2
Comté ou district: Témiscamingue; *Population au 2016:* 878
Circonscription(s) électorale(s) provinciale(s):
Rouyn-Noranda-Témiscamingue
Circonscription(s) électorale(s) fédérale(s):
Abitibi-Témiscamingue
Prochaines élections: 7e novembre 2021
Guy Abel, Maire
Lise Perron, Directrice générale

Dundee
3296, montée Smallman
Dundee, QC J0S 1L0
Tél: 450-264-4674; *Téléc:* 450-264-8044
info@cantondundee.ca
www.cantondundee.ca
Entité municipal: Township
Incorporation: 1er juillet 1855; *Area:* 69,45 km2
Comté ou district: Le Haut-Saint-Laurent; *Population au 2016:*
387
Circonscription(s) électorale(s) provinciale(s): Huntingdon
Circonscription(s) électorale(s) fédérale(s): Salaberry-Suroît
Prochaines élections: 7e novembre 2021
Linda Gagnon, Mairesse
Christian Genest, Directeur général

Dunham
CP 70
3777, rue Principale
Dunham, QC J0E 1M0
Tél: 450-295-2418; *Téléc:* 450-295-2182
accueil@ville.dunham.qc.ca
www.ville.dunham.qc.ca
Entité municipal: Town
Incorporation: 25 septembre 1971; *Area:* 194,06 km2
Comté ou district: Brome-Missisquoi; *Population au 2016:* 3,432

Circonscription(s) électorale(s) provinciale(s): Brome-Missisquoi
Circonscription(s) électorale(s) fédérale(s): Brome-Missisquoi
Prochaines élections: 7e novembre 2021
Pierre Janecek, Maire
Valérie Beaudoin, Greffier

Duparquet
86, rue Principale
Duparquet, QC J0Z 1W0
Tél: 819-948-2266; *Téléc:* 819-948-2466
duparquet@mrcao.qc.ca
duparquet.ao.ca
Entité municipal: Village
Incorporation: 13 avril 1933; *Area:* 123,57 km2
Comté ou district: Abitibi-Ouest; *Population au 2016:* 666
Circonscription(s) électorale(s) provinciale(s): Abitibi-Ouest
Circonscription(s) électorale(s) fédérale(s):
Abitibi-Témiscamingue
Prochaines élections: 7e novembre 2021
Gilbert Rivard, Maire
Chantal Poirier, Directrice générale

Dupuy
1, 7e av ouest
Dupuy, QC J0Z 1X0
Tél: 819-783-2595; *Téléc:* 819-783-2192
dupuy@mrcao.qc.ca
www.dupuy.ao.ca
Entité municipal: Municipality
Incorporation: 20 septembre 1918; *Area:* 122,68 km2
Comté ou district: Abitibi-Ouest; *Population au 2016:* 931
Circonscription(s) électorale(s) provinciale(s): Abitibi-Ouest
Circonscription(s) électorale(s) fédérale(s):
Abitibi-Témiscamingue
Prochaines élections: 7e novembre 2021
Normand Lagrange, Maire
Marie-Josée Céleste, Greffière

La Durantaye
539, rue du Piedmont
La Durantaye, QC G0R 1W0
Tél: 418-884-3465; *Téléc:* 418-884-3048
bureau@munladurantaye.qc.ca
www.munladurantaye.qc.ca
Entité municipal: Parish (Paroisse)
Incorporation: 4e août 1910; *Area:* 35,00 km2
Comté ou district: Bellechasse; *Population au 2016:* 755
Circonscription(s) électorale(s) provinciale(s): Bellechasse
Circonscription(s) électorale(s) fédérale(s): Bellechasse-Les
Etchemins-Lévis
Prochaines élections: 7e novembre 2021
Yvon Dumont, Maire
Cindy Breton, Directrice générale

Durham-Sud
33, rue Principale
Durham-Sud, QC J0H 2C0
Tél: 819-858-2044; *Téléc:* 819-858-2929
mun@durham-sud.com
www.durham-sud.com
Entité municipal: Municipality
Incorporation: 1er novembre 1975; *Area:* 92,67 km2
Comté ou district: Drummond; *Population au 2016:* 1,043
Circonscription(s) électorale(s) provinciale(s): Johnson
Circonscription(s) électorale(s) fédérale(s): Drummond
Prochaines élections: 7e novembre 2021
Michel Noël, Maire
Linda Thomas, Directrice générale

East Angus
200, rue Saint-Jean est
East Angus, QC J0B 1R0
Tél: 819-560-8600; *Téléc:* 819-560-8611
info.eastangus@hsfqc.ca
eastangus.ca
Entité municipal: Town
Incorporation: 14 mars 1912; *Area:* 7,89 km2
Comté ou district: Le Haut-Saint-François; *Population au 2016:*
3,659
Circonscription(s) électorale(s) provinciale(s): Mégantic
Circonscription(s) électorale(s) fédérale(s): Compton-Stanstead
Prochaines élections: 7e novembre 2021
Lyne Boulanger, Mairesse
David Fournier, Directeur général, 819-560-8600

East Broughton
600, 10e av sud
East Broughton, QC G0N 1H0
Tél: 418-427-2608; *Téléc:* 418-427-3414
reception@municipaliteeastbroughton.com
www.municipaliteeastbroughton.com

Entité municipal: Municipality
Incorporation: 5e janvier 1994; *Area:* 8,87 km2
Comté ou district: Les Appalaches; *Population au 2016:* 2,199
Circonscription(s) électorale(s) provinciale(s):
Lotbinière-Frontenac
Circonscription(s) électorale(s) fédérale(s): Mégantic-L'Érable
Prochaines élections: 7e novembre 2021
François Baril, Maire, 418-427-2608
Manon Vachon, Directrice générale, 418-427-2608

East Farnham
228, rue Principale
East Farnham, QC J2K 4T5
Tél: 450-263-4252; *Téléc:* 450-263-6131
eastfarnham@videotron.ca
www.municipalite.eastfarnham.qc.ca
Entité municipal: Village
Incorporation: 27 août 1914; *Area:* 5,03 km2
Comté ou district: Brome-Missisquoi; *Population au 2016:* 554
Circonscription(s) électorale(s) provinciale(s): Brome-Missisquoi
Circonscription(s) électorale(s) fédérale(s): Brome-Missisquoi
Prochaines élections: 7e novembre 2021
Sylvie Dionne-Raymond, Mairesse
Madelyn Marcoux, Directrice générale

East Hereford
15, rue de l'Église
East Hereford, QC J0B 1S0
Tél: 819-844-2463
www.easthereford.ca
Entité municipal: Municipality
Incorporation: 1er juillet 1855; *Area:* 72,19 km2
Comté ou district: Coaticook; *Population au 2016:* 269
Circonscription(s) électorale(s) provinciale(s): St-François
Circonscription(s) électorale(s) fédérale(s): Compton-Stanstead
Prochaines élections: 7e novembre 2021
Benoit Lavoie, Maire
Marie-Eve Breton, Directrice générale

Eastmain
147, rue Shabow
Eastmain, QC J0M 1W0
Tél: 819-977-0211; *Téléc:* 819-977-0281
info@eastmain.ca
eastmain.ca
Entité municipal: Villages Cris
Incorporation: 28 juin 1978; *Area:* 147,66 km2
Population au 2016: 866
Circonscription(s) électorale(s) provinciale(s): Ungava
Circonscription(s) électorale(s) fédérale(s):
Abitibi-Baie-James-Nunavik-Eeyou
Edward Gilpin, Maire

Eastman
160, ch George-Bonnallie
Eastman, QC J0E 1P0
Tél: 450-297-3440; *Téléc:* 450-297-3448
info@eastman.quebec
eastman.quebec
Entité municipal: Municipality
Incorporation: 30 mai 2001; *Area:* 73,69 km2
Comté ou district: Memphrémagog; *Population au 2016:* 1,843
Circonscription(s) électorale(s) provinciale(s): Orford
Circonscription(s) électorale(s) fédérale(s): Brome-Missisquoi
Prochaines élections: 7e novembre 2021
Yvon Laramée, Maire
Marc-Antoine Bazinet, Directeur général

Les Éboulements
2335, route du Fleuve
Les Éboulements, QC G0A 2M0
Tél: 418-489-2988
municipalite@leseboulements.com
www.leseboulements.com
Entité municipal: Municipality
Incorporation: 19 septembre 2001; *Area:* 156,49 km2
Comté ou district: Charlevoix; *Population au 2016:* 1,331
Circonscription(s) électorale(s) provinciale(s):
Charlevoix-Côte-de-Beaupré
Circonscription(s) électorale(s) fédérale(s):
Beaupré—Côte-de-Beaupré—Île d'Orléans—Charlevoix
Prochaines élections: 7e novembre 2021
Pierre Tremblay, Maire
Linda Gauthier, Directrice générale

Egan-Sud
95, rte 105
Egan-Sud, QC J9E 3A9
Tél: 819-449-1702; *Téléc:* 819-449-7423
info@egan-sud.ca
www.egan-sud.ca

Entité municipal: Municipality
Incorporation: 17 novembre 1920; *Area:* 50,62 km2
Comté ou district: La Vallée-de-la-Gatineau; *Population au 2016:* 504
Circonscription(s) électorale(s) provinciale(s): Gatineau
Circonscription(s) électorale(s) fédérale(s): Pontiac
Prochaines élections: 7e novembre 2021
Neil Gagnon, Maire
Mariette Rochon, Directrice générale

Elgin
933, ch de la 2e Concession
Elgin, QC J0S 2E0
Tél: 450-264-2320; *Téléc:* 450-264-6846
www.municipalites-du-quebec.ca/elgin
Entité municipal: Township
Incorporation: 1er juillet 1855; *Area:* 69,61 km2
Comté ou district: Le Haut-Saint-Laurent; *Population au 2016:* 394
Circonscription(s) électorale(s) provinciale(s): Huntingdon
Circonscription(s) électorale(s) fédérale(s): Salaberry-Suroît
Prochaines élections: 7e novembre 2021
Deborah Stewart, Mairesse
Guylaine Carrière, Directrice générale

Entrelacs
2351, ch d'Entrelacs
Entrelacs, QC J0T 2E0
Tél: 450-228-2529; *Téléc:* 450-228-4866
info@entrelacs.com
www.entrelacs.com
Entité municipal: Municipality
Incorporation: 1er janvier 1860; *Area:* 49,05 km2
Comté ou district: Matawinie; *Population au 2016:* 928
Circonscription(s) électorale(s) provinciale(s): Bertrand
Circonscription(s) électorale(s) fédérale(s): Joliette
Prochaines élections: 7e novembre 2021
Sylvain Breton, Maire
Martine Guindon, Directrice générale

L'Épiphanie
66, rue Notre-Dame
L'Épiphanie, QC J5X 1A1
Tél: 450-588-5515; *Téléc:* 450-588-6171
info@lepiphanie.ca
www.lepiphanie.ca
Entité municipal: Town
Incorporation: 30 juin 1967; *Area:* 2,30 km2
Comté ou district: L'Assomption; *Population au 2016:* 5,493
Circonscription(s) électorale(s) provinciale(s): L'Assomption
Circonscription(s) électorale(s) fédérale(s): Montcalm
Prochaines élections: 7e novembre 2021
Valérie Plante, Mairesse
Guylaine Comtois, Directrice générale et greffière

L'Érable
1783, av St-Édouard
Plessisville, QC G6L 3S7
Tél: 819-362-2333; *Téléc:* 819-362-9150
mrc@erable.ca
www.erable.ca/mrc
Entité municipal: Regional County Municipality
Incorporation: 1er janvier 1982; *Area:* 1287,86 km2
Population au 2016: 23,425
Note: 11 municipalités.
Jocelyn Bédard, Préfet
Raphaël Teyssier, Directeur général, 819-362-2333

Les Escoumins
2, rue Sirois
Les Escoumins, QC G0T 1K0
Tél: 418-233-2766; *Téléc:* 418-233-3273
administration.muni@escoumins.ca
www.escoumins.ca
Entité municipal: Municipality
Incorporation: 5 mai 1863; *Area:* 271,47 km2
Comté ou district: La Haute-Côte-Nord; *Population au 2016:* 1,891
Circonscription(s) électorale(s) provinciale(s): René-Lévesque
Circonscription(s) électorale(s) fédérale(s): Manicouagan
Prochaines élections: 7e novembre 2021
Andre Desrosiers, Maire
Andrée Lessard, Directrice générale

Escuminac
13, rue de l'Église
Pointe-à-la-Garde, QC G0C 2M0
Tél: 418-788-5644; *Téléc:* 418-788-2613
munescuminac@globetrotter.net
www.escuminac.org
Entité municipal: Municipality
Incorporation: 10 octobre 1907; *Area:* 108,20 km2

Comté ou district: Avignon; *Population au 2016:* 544
Circonscription(s) électorale(s) provinciale(s): Bonaventure
Circonscription(s) électorale(s) fédérale(s): Avignon-La
Mitis-Matane-Matapédia
Prochaines élections: 7e novembre 2021
Robert Bruce Wafer, Maire
Hervé Esch, Directeur général

Esprit-Saint
121, rue Principale
Esprit-Saint, QC G0K 1A0
Tél: 418-779-2716; *Téléc:* 418-779-2716
muni.esprit@globetrotter.net
www.municipalite.esprit-saint.qc.ca
Entité municipal: Municipality
Incorporation: 13 mai 1972; *Area:* 169,40 km2
Comté ou district: Rimouski-Neigette; *Population au 2016:* 341
Circonscription(s) électorale(s) provinciale(s): Rimouski
Circonscription(s) électorale(s) fédérale(s):
Rimouski-Neigette-Témiscouata-Les Basques
Prochaines élections: 7e novembre 2021
Réjean Morissette, Maire
Diane Ouellet, Directrice générale

Estérel
115, ch Dupuis
Estérel, QC J0T 1E0
Tél: 450-228-3232; *Téléc:* 450-228-3737
info@villedesterel.com
www.villedesterel.com
Other Information: Sans frais: 877-928-3232
Entité municipal: Village
Incorporation: 1er janvier 2006; *Area:* 12,57 km2
Comté ou district: Les Pays-d'en-Haut; *Population au 2016:* 196
Circonscription(s) électorale(s) provinciale(s): Bertrand
Circonscription(s) électorale(s) fédérale(s): Laurentides—Labelle
Prochaines élections: 7e novembre 2021
Joseph Dydzak, Maire
Luc Lafontaine, Directeur général

Les Etchemins
1137, rte 277
Lac-Etchemin, QC G0R 1S0
Tél: 418-625-9000; *Téléc:* 418-625-9005
mrc@mrcetchemins.qc.ca
www.mrcetchemins.qc.ca
Entité municipal: Regional County Municipality
Incorporation: 1er janvier 1982; *Area:* 1810,05 km2
Population au 2016: 16,536
Note: 13 muncipalités.
Richard Couët, Préfet
Vacant, Directrice générale

Farnham
477, rue de l'Hôtel-de-Ville
Farnham, QC J2N 2H3
Tél: 450-293-3178; *Téléc:* 450-293-2989
administration@ville.farnham.qc.ca
www.ville.farnham.qc.ca
Entité municipal: Town
Incorporation: 8e mars 2000; *Area:* 92,26 km2
Comté ou district: Brome-Missisquoi; *Population au 2016:* 8,909
Circonscription(s) électorale(s) provinciale(s): Brome-Missisquoi
Circonscription(s) électorale(s) fédérale(s): Brome-Missisquoi
Prochaines élections: 7e novembre 2021
Patrick Melchior, Maire
Marielle Benoit, Greffière

Fassett
19, rue Gendron
Fassett, QC J0V 1H0
Tél: 819-423-6943; *Téléc:* 819-423-5388
www.village-fassett.com
Entité municipal: Municipality
Incorporation: 1er juillet 1855; *Area:* 12,49 km2
Comté ou district: Papineau; *Population au 2016:* 431
Circonscription(s) électorale(s) provinciale(s): Papineau
Circonscription(s) électorale(s) fédérale(s): Argenteuil-La
Petite-Nation
Prochaines élections: 7e novembre 2021
Éric Trépanier, Maire
Chantal Laroche, Directrice générale

Ferland-et-Boilleau
461, rte 381
Ferland-et-Boilleau, QC G0V 1H0
Tél: 418-676-2282; *Téléc:* 418-676-3092
municipalite@munfb.ca
www.ferlandetboilleau.ca
Entité municipal: Municipality
Incorporation: 1er janvier 1978; *Area:* 383,51 km2
Comté ou district: Le Fjord-du-Saguenay; *Population au 2016:*

540
Circonscription(s) électorale(s) provinciale(s): Dubuc
Circonscription(s) électorale(s) fédérale(s): Chicoutimi-Le Fjord
Prochaines élections: 7e novembre 2021
Hervé Simard, Maire
Réal Lavoie, Directeur général

Ferme-Neuve
125, 12e rue
Ferme-Neuve, QC J0W 1C0
Tél: 819-587-3400; *Téléc:* 819-587-4733
reception@munfn.ca
municipalite.ferme-neuve.qc.ca
Entité municipal: Municipality
Incorporation: 24 décembre 1997; *Area:* 793,44 km2
Comté ou district: Antoine-Labelle; *Population au 2016:* 2,706
Circonscription(s) électorale(s) provinciale(s): Labelle
Circonscription(s) électorale(s) fédérale(s): Laurentides-Labelle
Prochaines élections: 7e novembre 2021
Gilbert Pilote, Maire
Bernadette Ouellette, Directrice générale et secrétaire trésorière,
819-587-3400

Fermont
CP 2010
100, place Daviault
Fermont, QC G0G 1J0
Tél: 418-287-5411; *Téléc:* 418-287-5413
administration@villedefermont.qc.ca
www.villedefermont.qc.ca
Entité municipal: Town
Incorporation: 15 octobre 1974; *Area:* 476,89 km2
Comté ou district: Caniapiscau; *Population au 2016:* 2,474
Circonscription(s) électorale(s) provinciale(s): Duplessis
Circonscription(s) électorale(s) fédérale(s): Manicouagan
Prochaines élections: 7e novembre 2021
Martin St-Laurent, Maire
Marie Philippe Couture, Greffière

Le Fjord-du-Saguenay
3110, boul Martel
Saint-Honoré, QC G0V 1L0
Tél: 418-673-1705; *Téléc:* 418-673-7205
reception@mrc-fjord.qc.ca
www.mrc-fjord.qc.ca
Other Information: Sans frais: 888-673-1705
Entité municipal: Regional County Municipality
Incorporation: 18e février 2002; *Area:* 41 361,06 km2
Population au 2016: 21,600
Note: 13 municipalités & 3 autres territoires. Le chiffre de la
population de recensement et la superficie géographique sont
ceux de la division de recensement du Saguenay-et-son-Fjord.
Gérald Savard, Préfet
Christine Dufour, Directrice générale

Forestville
1, 2e av
Forestville, QC G0T 1E0
Tél: 418-587-2285; *Téléc:* 418-587-6212
forestville@forestville.ca
ville.forestville.ca
Entité municipal: Town
Incorporation: 5e janvier 1980; *Area:* 195,05 km2
Comté ou district: La Haute-Côte-Nord; *Population au 2016:*
3,081
Circonscription(s) électorale(s) provinciale(s): René-Lévesque
Circonscription(s) électorale(s) fédérale(s): Manicouagan
Prochaines élections: 7e novembre 2021
Micheline Anctil, Mairesse
Lison Huard, Greffière par intérim

Fort-Coulonge
134, rue Principale
Fort-Coulonge, QC J0X 1V0
Tél: 819-683-2259; *Téléc:* 819-683-3627
administration@fortcoulonge.qc.ca
www.fortcoulonge.qc.ca
Entité municipal: Village
Incorporation: 15 décembre 1888; *Area:* 3,10 km2
Comté ou district: Pontiac; *Population au 2016:* 1,433
Circonscription(s) électorale(s) provinciale(s): Pontiac
Circonscription(s) électorale(s) fédérale(s): Pontiac
Prochaines élections: 7e novembre 2021
Gaston Allard, Maire
Naomie Rivet, Directrice générale

Fortierville
198, rue de la Fabrique
Fortierville, QC G0S 1J0
Tél: 819-287-5922; *Téléc:* 819-287-0322
municipalite@fortierville.com
www.fortierville.com

Entité municipal: Municipality
Incorporation: 3e juin 1998; *Area:* 44,55 km2
Comté ou district: Bécancour; *Population au 2016:* 669
Circonscription(s) électorale(s) provinciale(s): Nicolet-Bécancour
Circonscription(s) électorale(s) fédérale(s):
Bécancour-Nicolet-Saurel
Prochaines élections: 7e novembre 2021
Julie Pressé, Mairesse
Annie Jacques, Directrice générale

Fossambault-sur-le-Lac
145, rue Gingras
Fossambault-sur-le-Lac, QC G0A 3M0
Tél: 418-875-3133; *Téléc:* 418-875-3544
info@fossambault.com
fossambault-sur-le-lac.com
Entité municipal: Village
Incorporation: 10 mars 1949; *Area:* 11,53 km2
Comté ou district: La Jacques-Cartier; Communauté
métropolitaine de Québec; *Population au 2016:* 1,960
Circonscription(s) électorale(s) provinciale(s): La Peltrie
Circonscription(s) électorale(s) fédérale(s):
Portneuf-Jacques-Cartier
Prochaines élections: 7e novembre 2021
Jean Perron, Maire
Jacques Arsenault, Greffier

Frampton
107, rue Ste-Anne
Frampton, QC G0R 1M0
Tél: 418-479-5363; *Téléc:* 418-479-5364
administration@frampton.ca
www.nouvellebeauce.com/frampton
Entité municipal: Municipality
Incorporation: 1er juillet 1855; *Area:* 151,30 km2
Comté ou district: La Nouvelle-Beauce; *Population au 2016:*
1,239
Circonscription(s) électorale(s) provinciale(s): Beauce-Nord
Circonscription(s) électorale(s) fédérale(s): Beauce
Prochaines élections: 7e novembre 2021
Jacques Soucy, Maire, 418-479-5363
Mélanie Jacques, Directrice générale, 418-479-5363

Franklin
1670, rte 202
Franklin, QC J0S 1E0
Tél: 450-827-2538; *Téléc:* 450-827-2640
info@municipalitedefranklin.ca
www.municipalitedefranklin.ca
Entité municipal: Municipality
Incorporation: 31 mars 1973; *Area:* 112,60 km2
Comté ou district: Le Haut-Saint-Laurent; *Population au 2016:*
1,636
Circonscription(s) électorale(s) provinciale(s): Huntingdon
Circonscription(s) électorale(s) fédérale(s): Salaberry-Suroît
Prochaines élections: 7e novembre 2021
Douglas Brooks, Maire
Louis-Alexandre Monast, Directeur général

Franquelin
CP 10
14, rue des Érables
Franquelin, QC G0H 1E0
Tél: 418-296-1406; *Téléc:* 418-296-6946
administration@municipalitefranquelin.ca
municipalites-du-quebec.ca/franquelin
Entité municipal: Municipality
Incorporation: 1er janvier 1978; *Area:* 446,08 km2
Comté ou district: Manicouagan; *Population au 2016:* 313
Circonscription(s) électorale(s) provinciale(s): René-Lévesque
Circonscription(s) électorale(s) fédérale(s): Manicouagan
Prochaines élections: 7e novembre 2021
Steeve Grenier, Maire
Martine Morin, Directrice générale

Frelighsburg
2, place de l'Hôtel-de-Ville
Frelighsburg, QC J0J 1C0
Tél: 450-298-5133; *Téléc:* 450-298-5557
frelighsburg.com
Entité municipal: Municipality
Incorporation: 28 septembre 1985; *Area:* 123,58 km2
Comté ou district: Brome-Missisquoi; *Population au 2016:* 1,111
Circonscription(s) électorale(s) provinciale(s): Brome-Missisquoi
Circonscription(s) électorale(s) fédérale(s): Brome-Missisquoi
Prochaines élections: 7e novembre 2021
Jean Lévesque, Maire
Anne Pouleur, Directrice générale

Frontenac
2430, rue St-Jean
Frontenac, QC G6B 2S1
Tél: 819-583-3295; *Téléc:* 819-583-0855
adm@municipalitefrontenac.qc.ca
municipalitefrontenac.qc.ca
Entité municipal: Municipality
Incorporation: 1er janvier 1882; *Area:* 223,68 km2
Comté ou district: Le Granit; *Population au 2016:* 1,734
Circonscription(s) électorale(s) provinciale(s): Mégantic
Circonscription(s) électorale(s) fédérale(s): Mégantic-L'Érable
Prochaines élections: 7e novembre 2021
Gaby Gendron, Maire
Bruno Turmel, Directeur général

Fugèreville
33B, rue Principale
Fugèreville, QC J0Z 2A0
Tél: 819-748-3241; *Téléc:* 819-748-2422
Entité municipal: Municipality
Incorporation: 5e février 1904; *Area:* 156,98 km2
Comté ou district: Témiscamingue; *Population au 2016:* 326
Circonscription(s) électorale(s) provinciale(s):
Rouyn-Noranda-Témiscamingue
Circonscription(s) électorale(s) fédérale(s):
Abitibi-Témiscamingue
Prochaines élections: 7e novembre 2021
André Pâquet, Maire
Claudette Lachance, Directrice générale

Gallichan
CP 38
168, ch Gallichan
Gallichan, QC J0Z 2B0
Tél: 819-787-6092; *Téléc:* 819-787-6015
gallichan@mrcao.qc.ca
gallichan.ao.ca
Entité municipal: Municipality
Incorporation: 1er janvier 1958; *Area:* 73,89 km2
Comté ou district: Abitibi-Ouest; *Population au 2016:* 468
Circonscription(s) électorale(s) provinciale(s): Abitibi-Ouest
Circonscription(s) électorale(s) fédérale(s):
Abitibi-Témiscamingue
Prochaines élections: 7e novembre 2021
Henri Bourque, Maire
Johanne Shink, Directrice générale

Girardville
180, rue Principale
Girardville, QC G0W 1R0
Tél: 418-258-3293; *Téléc:* 418-258-3473
info@ville.girardville.qc.ca
ville.girardville.qc.ca
Entité municipal: Municipality
Incorporation: 11 novembre 1921; *Area:* 124,52 km2
Comté ou district: Maria-Chapdelaine; *Population au 2016:* 988
Circonscription(s) électorale(s) provinciale(s): Roberval
Circonscription(s) électorale(s) fédérale(s): Lac-St-Jean
Prochaines élections: 7e novembre 2021
Michel Perreault, Maire
Denis Desmeules, Directeur général

Godbout
CP 248
Godbout, QC G0H 1G0
Tél: 418-568-7581; *Téléc:* 418-568-7401
mgodbout144@hotmail.com
www.municipalitegodbout.ca
Entité municipal: Village
Incorporation: 1er janvier 1955; *Area:* 161,60 km2
Comté ou district: Manicouagan; *Population au 2016:* 265
Circonscription(s) électorale(s) provinciale(s): René-Lévesque
Circonscription(s) électorale(s) fédérale(s): Manicouagan
Prochaines élections: 7e novembre 2021
Jean-Yves Bouffard, Maire
Martine Morin, Directrice générale

Godmanchester
2282, ch Ridge
Godmanchester, QC J0S 1H0
Tél: 450-264-4116; *Téléc:* 450-264-9749
info@godmanchester.ca
godmanchester.ca
Entité municipal: Township
Incorporation: 1er juillet 1855; *Area:* 138,80 km2
Comté ou district: Le Haut-Saint-Laurent; *Population au 2016:*
1,394
Circonscription(s) électorale(s) provinciale(s): Huntingdon
Circonscription(s) électorale(s) fédérale(s): Salaberry-Suroît
Prochaines élections: 7e novembre 2021
Pierre Poirier, Maire
Élaine Duhème, Directrice générale

Gore
9, ch Cambria
Lakefield, QC J0V 1K0
Tél: 450-562-2025
info@cantondegore.qc.ca
www.cantondegore.qc.ca
Entité municipal: Township
Incorporation: 1er juillet 1855; *Area:* 92,68 km2
Comté ou district: Argenteuil; *Population au 2016:* 1,904
Circonscription(s) électorale(s) provinciale(s): Argenteuil
Circonscription(s) électorale(s) fédérale(s): Argenteuil-La
Petite-Nation; Richmond-Arthabaska
Prochaines élections: 7e novembre 2021
Scott Pearce, Maire
Julie Boyer, Directrice générale, 450-562-2025

Gouvernement régional d'Eeyou Istchee Baie-James
CP 819
Matagami, QC J0Y 2A0
Tél: 819-739-2030; *Téléc:* 819-739-2713
gouvernement@greibj-eijbrg.ca
www.greibj.ca
Other Information: Sans frais: 888-739-4991
Entité municipal: Municipality
Incorporation: 14 juillet 1971; *Area:* 297 355,46 km2
Population au 2016: 1,589
Circonscription(s) électorale(s) provinciale(s): Ungava
Circonscription(s) électorale(s) fédérale(s):
Abitibi-Baie-James-Nunavik-Eeyou
Note: As of July 24, 2012, the Municipalité de Baie-James was
replaced by the Eeyou Istchee James Bay Regional
Government, which is comprised of 11 Cree representatives &
11 representatives from surrounding non-aboriginal
communities.
Matthew Coon Come, Président
Johanne Lacasse, Directrice générale

Gracefield
CP 329
351, rte 105
Gracefield, QC J0X 1W0
Tél: 819-463-3458; *Téléc:* 819-463-4236
info@gracefield.ca
www.gracefield.ca
Entité municipal: Town
Incorporation: 13 mars 2002; *Area:* 386,84 km2
Comté ou district: La Vallée-de-la-Gatineau; *Population au 2016:*
2,462
Circonscription(s) électorale(s) provinciale(s): Gatineau
Circonscription(s) électorale(s) fédérale(s): Pontiac
Prochaines élections: 7e novembre 2021
Note: Formerly known as Wright-Gracefield-Northfield.
Réal Rochon, Maire
Sylvain Hubert, Directeur général et greffier

Grande-Rivière
CP 188
108, rue de l'Hôtel de Ville
Grande-Rivière, QC G0C 1V0
Tél: 418-385-2282
villegr@globetrotter.net
www.ville.grande-riviere.qc.ca
Entité municipal: Town
Incorporation: 21 septembre 1974; *Area:* 87,86 km2
Comté ou district: Le Rocher-Percé; *Population au 2016:* 3,408
Circonscription(s) électorale(s) provinciale(s): Gaspé
Circonscription(s) électorale(s) fédérale(s): Gaspésie—Les
Îles-de-la-Madeleine
Prochaines élections: 7e novembre 2021
Gino Cyr, Maire
Marilyn Morin, Greffière

Grandes-Piles
630, 4e av
Grandes-Piles, QC G0X 1H0
Tél: 819-538-9708
info@grandespiles.qc.ca
www.grandespiles.qc.ca
Entité municipal: Village
Incorporation: 10 août 1885; *Area:* 120,61 km2
Comté ou district: Mékinac; *Population au 2016:* 415
Circonscription(s) électorale(s) provinciale(s): Laviolette
Circonscription(s) électorale(s) fédérale(s):
St-Maurice-Champlain
Prochaines élections: 7e novembre 2021
Michel Germain, Maire
Pierre Beauséjour, Directeur général

Grande-Vallée
3, rue St-François-Xavier est
Grande-Vallée, QC G0E 1K0
Tél: 418-393-2161
municipalite@grande-vallee.ca
grande-vallee.ca
Entité municipal: Municipality
Incorporation: 15 septembre 1927; *Area:* 144,50 km2
Comté ou district: La Côte-de-Gaspé; *Population au 2016:* 1,057
Circonscription(s) électorale(s) provinciale(s): Gaspé
Circonscription(s) électorale(s) fédérale(s): Gaspésie—Les
Îles-de-la-Madeleine; Joliette
Prochaines élections: 7e novembre 2021
Noel Richard, Maire
Ghislaine Bouthillette, Directrice générale

Grand-Métis
70, ch Kempt
Grand-Métis, QC G0J 1Z0
Tél: 418-775-6485; *Téléc:* 418-775-3591
grandmetis@mitis.qc.ca
www.municipalite.grand-metis.qc.ca
Entité municipal: Municipality
Incorporation: 13 septembre 1855; *Area:* 25,55 km2
Comté ou district: La Mitis; *Population au 2016:* 167
Circonscription(s) électorale(s) provinciale(s): Matane-Matapédia
Circonscription(s) électorale(s) fédérale(s): Avignon-La
Mitis-Matane-Matapédia
Prochaines élections: 7e novembre 2021
Rodrigue Roy, Maire
Chantal Tremblay, Directrice générale

Grand-Remous
1508, rte Transcanadienne
Grand-Remous, QC J0W 1E0
Tél: 819-438-2877; *Téléc:* 819-438-2364
info@grandremous.ca
www.grandremous.ca
Entité municipal: Municipality
Incorporation: 29 avril 1937; *Area:* 355,89 km2
Comté ou district: La Vallée-de-la-Gatineau; *Population au 2016:*
1,161
Circonscription(s) électorale(s) provinciale(s): Gatineau
Circonscription(s) électorale(s) fédérale(s): Pontiac
Prochaines élections: 7e novembre 2021
Jocelyne Lyrette, Mairesse
Jean-Marie Gauthier, Directrice générale, 819-438-2877

Grand-Saint-Esprit
5410, rte Principale
Grand-Saint-Esprit, QC J0G 1B0
Tél: 819-289-2410; *Téléc:* 819-289-2029
municipalite@grandsaintesprit.qc.ca
grandsaintesprit.qc.ca
Entité municipal: Municipality
Incorporation: 14 mai 1938; *Area:* 27,23 km2
Comté ou district: Nicolet-Yamaska; *Population au 2016:* 476
Circonscription(s) électorale(s) provinciale(s): Nicolet-Bécancour
Circonscription(s) électorale(s) fédérale(s):
Bécancour-Nicolet-Saurel
Prochaines élections: 7e novembre 2021
Julien Boudreault, Maire
Frédérick Marcotte, Directeur général

Le Granit
5600, rue Frontenac
Lac-Mégantic, QC G6B 1H5
Tél: 819-583-0181; *Téléc:* 819-583-5327
secretariat@mrcgranit.qc.ca
www.mrcgranit.qc.ca
Other Information: Ligne sans frais: 888-783-0181
Entité municipal: Regional County Municipality
Incorporation: 26 mai 1982; *Area:* 2735,21 km2
Population au 2016: 21,462
Note: 20 municipalités.
Marielle Fecteau, Préfet
Sonia Cloutier, Directrice générale

Grenville
21, rue Tri-Jean
Grenville, QC J0V 1J0
Tél: 819-242-2146; *Téléc:* 819-242-5891
info@grenville.ca
grenville.ca
Entité municipal: Village
Incorporation: 1er janvier 1876; *Area:* 2,87 km2
Comté ou district: Argenteuil; *Population au 2016:* 1,711
Circonscription(s) électorale(s) provinciale(s): Argenteuil
Circonscription(s) électorale(s) fédérale(s): Argenteuil-La
Petite-Nation; Jonquière
Prochaines élections: 7e novembre 2021
Luc Grondin, Maire

Alain Léveillé, Directeur général

Grenville-sur-la-Rouge
88, rue des Érables
Grenville-sur-la-Rouge, QC J0V 1B0
Tél: 819-242-8762; *Téléc:* 819-242-9341
info@gslr.ca
www.grenvillesurlarouge.ca
Entité municipal: Municipality
Incorporation: 24 avril 2002; *Area:* 317,65 km2
Comté ou district: Argenteuil; *Population au 2016:* 2,824
Circonscription(s) électorale(s) provinciale(s): Argenteuil
Circonscription(s) électorale(s) fédérale(s): Argenteuil-La
Petite-Nation
Prochaines élections: 7e novembre 2021
Tom Arnold, Maire
Marc Beaulieu, Directeur général

Gros-Mécatina
CP 9
30, rte Mecatina
La Tabatière, QC G0G 1T0
Tél: 418-773-2263; *Téléc:* 418-773-2696
mungrosmecatina@xplornet.com
Entité municipal: Municipality
Incorporation: 1er janvier 1994; *Area:* 790,07 km2
Comté ou district: Le Golfe-du-Saint-Laurent; *Population au*
2016: 428
Circonscription(s) électorale(s) provinciale(s): Duplessis
Circonscription(s) électorale(s) fédérale(s): Manicouagan
Prochaines élections: 7e novembre 2021
Randy Jones, Maire
Krystle Willcott, Directeur général

Grosse-Île
#1, 006, ch Jerry
Grosse-Île, QC G4T 6B9
Tél: 418-985-2510; *Téléc:* 418-985-2297
info@mungi.ca
www.mungi.ca
Entité municipal: Municipality
Incorporation: 1er janvier 2006; *Area:* 37,59 km2
Population au 2016: 465
Circonscription(s) électorale(s) provinciale(s):
Îles-de-la-Madeleine
Circonscription(s) électorale(s) fédérale(s):
Gaspésie—Îles-de-la-Madeleine
Prochaines élections: 7e novembre 2021
Rose Elmonde Clarke, Mairesse
Janice Turnbull, Directrice générale, 418-985-2510

Grosses-Roches
CP 69
122, rue de la Mer
Grosses-Roches, QC G0J 1K0
Tél: 418-733-4273; *Téléc:* 418-733-4273
grossesroches@lamatanie.ca
municipalite.grossesroches.ca
Entité municipal: Municipality
Incorporation: 19 août 1939; *Area:* 64,00 km2
Comté ou district: La Matanie; *Population au 2016:* 306
Circonscription(s) électorale(s) provinciale(s): Matane-Matapédia
Circonscription(s) électorale(s) fédérale(s): Avignon-La
Mitis-Matane-Matapédia
Prochaines élections: 7e novembre 2021
Victoire Morin, Mairesse
Linda Imbeault, Directrice générale

La Guadeloupe
#100, 763 - 14e av
La Guadeloupe, QC G0M 1G0
Tél: 418-459-3342; *Téléc:* 418-459-3507
info@munlaguadeloupe.qc.ca
www.munlaguadeloupe.qc.ca
Entité municipal: Village
Incorporation: 6e août 1929; *Area:* 32,88 km2
Comté ou district: Beauce-Sartigan; *Population au 2016:* 1,707
Circonscription(s) électorale(s) provinciale(s): Beauce-Sud
Circonscription(s) électorale(s) fédérale(s): Beauce
Prochaines élections: 7e novembre 2021
Carl Boilard, Maire
Christine Lacroix, Directrice générale, 418-459-3342

Guérin
#101, 516, rue St-Gabriel ouest
Guérin, QC J0Z 2E0
Tél: 819-784-7011; *Téléc:* 819-784-7012
mun.guerin@mrctemiscamingue.qc.ca
Entité municipal: Township
Incorporation: 8e novembre 1911; *Area:* 190,23 km2
Comté ou district: Témiscamingue; *Population au 2016:* 320
Circonscription(s) électorale(s) provinciale(s):

Yves Boissonneault, Maire
Marie-Pier Pelletier, Directrice générale, 418-453-2512

Irlande
157, ch Gosford
Irlande, QC G6H 2N7
Tél: 418-428-9216; *Téléc:* 418-428-4262
mundirlande@bellnet.ca
www.mundirlande.qc.ca
Entité municipal: Municipality
Incorporation: 1er juillet 1855; *Area:* 109,54 km2
Comté ou district: Les Appalaches; *Population au 2016:* 884
Circonscription(s) électorale(s) provinciale(s):
Lotbinière-Frontenac
Circonscription(s) électorale(s) fédérale(s): Gaspésie—Les
Îles-de-la-Madeleine; Mégantic-L'Érable
Prochaines élections: 7e novembre 2021
Jean-François Hamel, Maire
François Roberge, Directeur général

L'Ile-d'Anticosti
25B, ch des Forestiers
Port-Menier, QC G0G 2Y0
Tél: 418-535-0311
administration@ile-anticosti.org
municipalite-anticosti.org
Entité municipal: Municipality
Incorporation: 1er janvier 1984; *Area:* 7 953,20 km2
Comté ou district: Minganie; *Population au 2016:* 218
Circonscription(s) électorale(s) provinciale(s): Duplessis
Circonscription(s) électorale(s) fédérale(s): Manicouagan
Prochaines élections: 7e novembre 2021
John Pineault, Maire
Mathieu Gravel, Directeur général par intérim

L'Ile-du-Grand-Calumet
CP 130
8, rue Brizard
L'Ile-du-Grand-Calumet, QC J0X 1J0
Tél: 819-648-5965; *Téléc:* 819-648-2659
admin@lidgc.ca
île-du-grand-calumet.ca
Entité municipal: Municipality
Incorporation: 1er juillet 1855; *Area:* 132,57 km2
Comté ou district: Pontiac; *Population au 2016:* 626
Circonscription(s) électorale(s) provinciale(s): Pontiac
Circonscription(s) électorale(s) fédérale(s): Pontiac
Prochaines élections: 7e novembre 2021
Serge Newberry, Maire
Élaine Déry, Directrice générale

L'Isle-aux-Allumettes
CP 100
75, rue Notre-Dame
L'Isle-aux-Allumettes, QC J0X 1M0
Tél: 819-689-2266; *Téléc:* 819-689-5619
lisle-aux-allumettes@mrcpontiac.qc.ca
www.isle-aux-allumettes.com
Entité municipal: Municipality
Incorporation: 30 décembre 1998; *Area:* 186,02 km2
Comté ou district: Pontiac; *Population au 2016:* 1,334
Circonscription(s) électorale(s) provinciale(s): Pontiac
Circonscription(s) électorale(s) fédérale(s): Pontiac
Prochaines élections: 7e novembre 2021
Winston Sunstrum, Maire
Alicia Jones, Directrice générale

L'Isle-aux-Coudres
1026, ch des Coudriers
L'Isle-aux-Coudres, QC G0A 3J0
Tél: 418-760-1060; *Téléc:* 418-760-1061
contact@municipaliteiac.ca
www.municipaliteiac.ca
Entité municipal: Municipality
Incorporation: 23 août 2000; *Area:* 30,16 km2
Comté ou district: Charlevoix; *Population au 2016:* 1,143
Circonscription(s) électorale(s) provinciale(s):
Charlevoix-Côte-de-Beaupré
Circonscription(s) électorale(s) fédérale(s):
Beauport—Côte-de-Beaupré—Île d'Orléans—Charlevoix
Prochaines élections: 7e novembre 2021
Dominique Tremblay, Maire
Pamela Harvey, Directrice générale, 418-760-1060

L'Islet
284, boul Nilus-Leclerc
L'Islet, QC G0R 2C0
Tél: 418-247-3060; *Téléc:* 418-247-5085
info@lislet.com
www.lislet.com
Entité municipal: Municipality
Incorporation: 1er janvier 2000; *Area:* 120,20 km2

Comté ou district: L'Islet; *Population au 2016:* 3,827
Circonscription(s) électorale(s) provinciale(s): Côte-du-Sud
Circonscription(s) électorale(s) fédérale(s):
Montmagny-L'Islet-Kamouraska-Rivière-du-Loup
Prochaines élections: 7e novembre 2021
Jean-François Pelletier, Maire
Marie-Josée Bernier, Directrice générale, 418-247-3060

L'Islet
34A, rue Fortin
Saint-Jean-Port-Joli, QC G0R 3G0
Tél: 418-598-3076; *Téléc:* 418-598-6880
administration@mrclislet.com
mrclislet.com
Entité municipal: Regional County Municipality
Incorporation: 1er janvier 1982; *Area:* 2100,02 km2
Population au 2016: 17,798
Note: 14 municipalités.
René Laverdière, Préfet
Patrick Hamelin, Directeur général, 418-598-3076

L'Isle-Verte
141, rue St-Jean-Baptiste
L'Isle-Verte, QC G0L 1K0
Tél: 418-898-2812; *Téléc:* 418-898-2788
www.municipalite.lisle-verte.qc.ca
Entité municipal: Municipality
Incorporation: 9 février 2000; *Area:* 117,63 km2
Comté ou district: Rivière-du-Loup; *Population au 2016:* 1,294
Circonscription(s) électorale(s) provinciale(s):
Rivière-du-Loup-Témiscouata
Circonscription(s) électorale(s) fédérale(s):
Montmagny-L'Islet-Kamouraska-Rivière-du-Loup
Prochaines élections: 7e novembre 2021
Ginette Caron, Mairesse
Guy Bérubé, Directeur général

Ivry-sur-le-Lac
601, ch de la Gare
Ivry-sur-le-Lac, QC J8C 2Z8
Tél: 819-321-2332; *Téléc:* 819-321-3089
info@ivry-sur-le-lac.qc.ca
www.ivry-sur-le-lac.qc.ca
Entité municipal: Municipality
Incorporation: 1er janvier 2006; *Area:* 29,67 km2
Comté ou district: Les Laurentides; *Population au 2016:* 387
Circonscription(s) électorale(s) provinciale(s): Bertrand
Circonscription(s) électorale(s) fédérale(s): Laurentides-Labelle
Prochaines élections: 7e novembre 2021
Daniel Charette, Maire
Josiane Alarie, Directrice générale, 819-321-2332

Ivujivik
CP 20
Ivujivik, QC J0M 1H0
Tél: 819-922-9940; *Téléc:* 819-922-3045
Entité municipal: Northern Village
Incorporation: 27 juin 1981; *Area:* 35,21 km2
Comté ou district: Administration régionale Kativik; *Population au
2016:* 414
Circonscription(s) électorale(s) provinciale(s): Ungava
Circonscription(s) électorale(s) fédérale(s):
Abitibi-Baie-James-Nunavik-Eeyou
Tivi Iyaituk, Maire
Uqittuk Iyaituk, Secrétaire-trésorier

La Jacques-Cartier
60, rue St-Patrick
Shannon, QC G3S 1P8
Tél: 418-844-2160; *Téléc:* 418-844-2664
mrcjc@mrc.jacques-cartier.com
mrc.jacques-cartier.com
Entité municipal: Regional County Municipality
Incorporation: 1er avril 1981; *Area:* 3195.75 km2
Population au 2016: 43,485
Note: 9 municipalités & 1 autre territoire.
Claude Lebel, Préfet
Sandra Boucher, Directrice générale et secrétaire-trésorière

Les Jardins-de-Napierville
1767, rue Principale
Saint-Michel, QC J0L 2J0
Tél: 450-454-0559; *Téléc:* 450-454-0560
info@mrcjardinsdenapierville.ca
mrcjardinsdenapierville.ca
Entité municipal: Regional County Municipality
Incorporation: 1er janvier 1982; *Area:* 803,07 km2
Population au 2016: 27,870
Circonscription(s) électorale(s) provinciale(s): Huntingdon
Circonscription(s) électorale(s) fédérale(s):
Beauharnois-Salaberry
Note: 11 municipalités.

Paul Viau, Préfet
Rémi Raymond, Directeur général, 450-454-0559

Joliette
632, rue de Lanaudière
Joliette, QC J6E 3M7
Tél: 450-759-2237; *Téléc:* 450-759-2597
information@mrcjoliette.qc.ca
mrcjoliette.qc.ca
Entité municipal: Regional County Municipality
Incorporation: 1er janvier 1982; *Area:* 418,12 km2
Population au 2016: 66,550
Note: 10 municipalités.
Alain Bellemare, Préfet
Nancy Fortier, Directrice générale et secrétaire-trésorière,
450-759-2237

Kamouraska
67, av Morel
Kamouraska, QC G0L 1M0
Tél: 418-492-6523; *Téléc:* 418-492-9789
info@kamouraska.ca
www.kamouraska.ca
Entité municipal: Municipality
Incorporation: 25 avril 1987; *Area:* 43,86 km2
Comté ou district: Kamouraska; *Population au 2016:* 616
Circonscription(s) électorale(s) provinciale(s): Côte-du-Sud
Circonscription(s) électorale(s) fédérale(s):
Montmagny-L'Islet-Kamouraska-Rivière-du-Loup
Prochaines élections: 7e novembre 2021
Gilles A. Michaud, Maire
Mychelle Lévesque, Directrice générale

Kamouraska
235, rue Rochette
Saint-Pascal, QC G0L 3Y0
Tél: 418-492-1660; *Téléc:* 418-492-2220
accueil@mrckamouraska.com
www.mrckamouraska.com
Entité municipal: Regional County Municipality
Incorporation: 1er janvier 1982; *Area:* 2244,73 km2
Population au 2016: 21,073
Note: 17 municipalités & 2 autres territoires.
Yvon Soucy, Préfet
Jean Lachance, Directeur général et secrétaire-trésorier

Kangiqsualujjuaq
CP 120
Kangiqsualujjuaq, QC J0M 1N0
Tél: 819-337-5270; *Téléc:* 819-337-5200
Entité municipal: Northern Village
Incorporation: 2e février 1980; *Area:* 35,05 km2
Comté ou district: Administration régionale Kativik; *Population au
2016:* 942
Circonscription(s) électorale(s) provinciale(s): Ungava
Circonscription(s) électorale(s) fédérale(s):
Abitibi-Baie-James-Nunavik-Eeyou
Hilda Snowball, Mairesse
Tommy Annanack, Secrétaire-trésorier

Kangiqsujuaq
CP 60
901, ch Sinaitia
Kangiqsujuaq, QC J0M 1K0
Tél: 819-338-3342; *Téléc:* 819-338-3237
Entité municipal: Northern Village
Incorporation: 20 septembre 1980; *Area:* 12,60 km2
Comté ou district: Administration régionale Kativik; *Population au
2016:* 750
Circonscription(s) électorale(s) provinciale(s): Ungava
Circonscription(s) électorale(s) fédérale(s):
Abitibi-Baie-James-Nunavik-Eeyou
Charlie Arngak, Maire
Pasa Kiatainaq, Secrétaire-trésorière

Kangirsuk
CP 90
Kangirsuk, QC J0M 1A0
Tél: 819-935-4388; *Téléc:* 819-935-4287
manager@kangirsuk.ca
Entité municipal: Northern Village
Incorporation: 17 janvier 1981; *Area:* 57,42 km2
Comté ou district: Administration régionale Kativik; *Population au
2016:* 567
Circonscription(s) électorale(s) provinciale(s): Ungava
Circonscription(s) électorale(s) fédérale(s):
Abitibi-Baie-James-Nunavik-Eeyou
Noah Eetook, Maire
Joseph Annahatak, Secrétaire-trésorier

Kawawachikamach
1009, rue Naskapi
Kawawachikamach, QC G0G 2Z0
Tél: 418-585-2686; *Téléc:* 418-585-3130
kawawa@naskapi.ca
www.naskapi.ca
Entité municipal: Villages Naskapi
Incorporation: 10 septembre 1981; *Area:* 33,37 km2
Comté ou district: Administration régionale Kativik; *Population au 2016:* 601
Circonscription(s) électorale(s) provinciale(s): Duplessis
Circonscription(s) électorale(s) fédérale(s): Manicouagan
Noah Swappie, Maire
John Mameamskum, Directeur général

Kazabazua
CP 10
30, ch Begley
Kazabazua, QC J0X 1X0
Tél: 819-467-2852; *Téléc:* 819-467-3872
infos@kazabazua.ca
www.kazabazua.ca
Entité municipal: Municipality
Incorporation: 1er janvier 1862; *Area:* 175,09 km2
Comté ou district: La Vallée-de-la-Gatineau; *Population au 2016:* 945
Circonscription(s) électorale(s) provinciale(s): Gatineau
Circonscription(s) électorale(s) fédérale(s): Pontiac
Prochaines élections: 7e novembre 2021
Robert Bergeron, Maire
Pierre Vaillancourt, Directeur général

Kiamika
3, ch Valiquette
Kiamika, QC J0W 1G0
Tél: 819-585-3225; *Téléc:* 819-585-3992
info@kiamika.ca
www.kiamika.ca
Entité municipal: Municipality
Incorporation: 3e janvier 1898; *Area:* 339,92 km2
Comté ou district: Antoine-Labelle; *Population au 2016:* 757
Circonscription(s) électorale(s) provinciale(s): Labelle
Circonscription(s) électorale(s) fédérale(s): Laurentides-Labelle
Prochaines élections: 7e novembre 2021
Michel Dion, Maire
Bergeron Marc-André, Directeur général

Kingsbury
370, rue du Moulin
Kingsbury, QC J0B 1X0
Tél: 819-826-2527; *Téléc:* 819-826-2520
www.kingsbury.ca
Entité municipal: Village
Incorporation: 7e juillet 1896; *Area:* 6,18 km2
Comté ou district: Le Val-Saint-François; *Population au 2016:* 138
Circonscription(s) électorale(s) provinciale(s): Richmond
Circonscription(s) électorale(s) fédérale(s): Richmond-Arthabaska
Prochaines élections: 7e novembre 2021
Pierre-Luc Gagnon, Maire
Yves Barthe, Directeur général

Kingsey Falls
CP 270
15, rue Caron
Kingsey Falls, QC J0A 1B0
Tél: 819-363-3810; *Téléc:* 819-363-3819
www.kingseyfalls.ca
Entité municipal: Town
Incorporation: 31 décembre 1997; *Area:* 69,64 km2
Comté ou district: Arthabaska; *Population au 2016:* 1,947
Circonscription(s) électorale(s) provinciale(s): Drummond-Bois-Francs
Circonscription(s) électorale(s) fédérale(s): Richmond-Arthabaska
Prochaines élections: 7e novembre 2021
Micheline Pinard-Lampron, Mairesse
Anne Lemieux, Directrice générale et greffière, 819-363-3838

Kinnear's Mills
120, rue des Églises
Kinnear's Mills, QC G0N 1K0
Tél: 418-424-3377; *Téléc:* 418-424-0119
info@kinnearsmills.com
www.kinnearsmills.com
Entité municipal: Municipality
Incorporation: 1er juillet 1855; *Area:* 93,70 km2
Comté ou district: Les Appalaches; *Population au 2016:* 350
Circonscription(s) électorale(s) provinciale(s): Lotbinière-Frontenac

Circonscription(s) électorale(s) fédérale(s): Mégantic-L'Érable
Prochaines élections: 7e novembre 2021
Paul Vachon, Maire
Claudette Perreault, Directrice générale

Kipawa
15, rue Principale
Kipawa, QC J0Z 2H0
Tél: 819-627-3500; *Téléc:* 819-627-1067
kipawa@kipawa.ca
www.kipawa.ca
Entité municipal: Municipality
Incorporation: 1er janvier 1985; *Area:* 36,59 km2
Comté ou district: Témiscamingue; *Population au 2016:* 516
Circonscription(s) électorale(s) provinciale(s): Rouyn-Noranda-Témiscamingue
Circonscription(s) électorale(s) fédérale(s): Abitibi-Témiscamingue
Prochaines élections: 7e novembre 2021
Norman Young, Maire
Samir Boumerzoug, Directrice générale

Kuujjuaq
CP 210
Kuujjuaq, QC J0M 1C0
Tél: 819-964-2943; *Téléc:* 819-964-2980
Entité municipal: Northern Village
Incorporation: 29 décembre 1979; *Area:* 292,84 km2
Comté ou district: Administration régionale Kativik; *Population au 2016:* 2,754
Circonscription(s) électorale(s) provinciale(s): Ungava
Circonscription(s) électorale(s) fédérale(s): Abitibi-Baie-James-Nunavik-Eeyou
Tunu Napartuk, Maire
Ian D. Robertson, Secrétaire-trésorier

Kuujjuarapik
CP 360
412, av St-Edmund
Kuujjuarapik, QC J0M 1G0
Tél: 819-929-3360; *Téléc:* 819-929-3453
Entité municipal: Northern Village
Incorporation: 7e juin 1980; *Area:* 8,16 km2
Comté ou district: Administration régionale Kativik; *Population au 2016:* 686
Circonscription(s) électorale(s) provinciale(s): Ungava
Circonscription(s) électorale(s) fédérale(s): Abitibi-Baie-James-Nunavik-Eeyou
Lucassie Inukpuk, Maire
Pierre Roussel, Secrétaire-trésorier

Labelle
1, rue du Pont
Labelle, QC J0T 1H0
Tél: 819-681-3371; *Téléc:* 819-686-3820
info@municipalite.labelle.qc.ca
municipalite.labelle.qc.ca
Entité municipal: Municipality
Incorporation: 27 janvier 1973; *Area:* 198,47 km2
Comté ou district: Les Laurentides; *Population au 2016:* 2,477
Circonscription(s) électorale(s) provinciale(s): Labelle
Circonscription(s) électorale(s) fédérale(s): Laurentides-Labelle
Prochaines élections: 7e novembre 2021
Robert Bergeron, Maire
Claire Coulombe, Directrice générale, 819-681-3371

Labrecque
3425, rue Ambroise
Labrecque, QC G0W 2S0
Tél: 418-481-2022; *Téléc:* 418-481-1210
municipalite@ville.labrecque.qc.ca
www.ville.labrecque.qc.ca
Entité municipal: Municipality
Incorporation: 6 octobre 1925; *Area:* 153,07 km2
Comté ou district: Lac-Saint-Jean-Est; *Population au 2016:* 1,321
Circonscription(s) électorale(s) provinciale(s): Lac-St-Jean
Circonscription(s) électorale(s) fédérale(s): Jonquière; Portneuf-Jacques-Cartier
Prochaines élections: 7e novembre 2021
Eric Simard, Maire
Tommy Larouche, Directeur général

Lac-au-Saumon
36, rue Bouillon
Lac-au-Saumon, QC G0J 1M0
Tél: 418-778-3378; *Téléc:* 418-778-3706
lacausaumon@mrcmatapedia.quebec
municipalites-du-quebec.ca/lac-au-saumon
Entité municipal: Municipality
Incorporation: 17 décembre 1997; *Area:* 81,08 km2
Comté ou district: La Matapédia; *Population au 2016:* 1,450

Circonscription(s) électorale(s) provinciale(s): Matane-Matapédia
Circonscription(s) électorale(s) fédérale(s): Avignon-La Mitis-Matane-Matapédia
Prochaines élections: 7e novembre 2021
Gérard Grenier, Maire
Karine Dostie, Directrice générale

Lac-aux-Sables
820, rue St-Alphonse
Lac-aux-Sables, QC G0X 1M0
Tél: 418-336-2331; *Téléc:* 418-336-2500
lac-aux-sables@regionmekinac.com
lac-aux-sables.qc.ca
Entité municipal: Parish (Paroisse)
Incorporation: 24 avril 1899; *Area:* 271,58 km2
Comté ou district: Mékinac; *Population au 2016:* 1,292
Circonscription(s) électorale(s) provinciale(s): Laviolette
Circonscription(s) électorale(s) fédérale(s): St-Maurice-Champlain
Prochaines élections: 7e novembre 2021
Yvon Bourassa, Maire
Valérie Cloutier, Directrice générale, 418-336-2331

Lac-Beauport
65, ch du Tour-du-Lac
Lac-Beauport, QC G3B 0A1
Tél: 418-849-7141; *Téléc:* 418-849-0361
info@lacbeauport.net
lac-beauport.quebec
Entité municipal: Municipality
Incorporation: 1er juillet 1855; *Area:* 61,79 km2
Comté ou district: La Jacques-Cartier; Communauté métropolitaine de Québec; *Population au 2016:* 7,801
Circonscription(s) électorale(s) provinciale(s): Chauveau
Circonscription(s) électorale(s) fédérale(s): Portneuf-Jacques-Cartier
Prochaines élections: 7e novembre 2021
Michel Beaulieu, Maire
Richard Labrecque, Directeur général

Lac-Bouchette
249, rue Principale
Lac-Bouchette, QC G0W 1V0
Tél: 418-348-6306; *Téléc:* 418-348-9477
munilac@lac-bouchette.com
municipalites-du-quebec.ca/lac-bouchette
Entité municipal: Municipality
Incorporation: 25 septembre 1971; *Area:* 909,69 km2
Comté ou district: Le Domaine-du-Roy; *Population au 2016:* 1,196
Circonscription(s) électorale(s) provinciale(s): Roberval
Circonscription(s) électorale(s) fédérale(s): Lac-St-Jean; Argenteuil-La Petite-Nation
Prochaines élections: 7e novembre 2021
Ghislaine M.-Hudon, Mairesse
Jean-Pierre Tremblay, Directeur général

Lac-Brome
122, ch Lakeside
Lac-Brome, QC J0E 1V0
Tél: 450-243-6111; *Téléc:* 450-243-5300
reception@lacbrome.ca
ville.lac-brome.qc.ca
Entité municipal: Town
Incorporation: 2 janvier 1971; *Area:* 207,29 km2
Comté ou district: Brome-Missisquoi; *Population au 2016:* 5,495
Circonscription(s) électorale(s) provinciale(s): Brome-Missisquoi
Circonscription(s) électorale(s) fédérale(s): Brome-Missisquoi
Prochaines élections: 7e novembre 2021
Richard Burcombe, Maire
Gilbert Arel, Directeur général, 450-243-6111

Lac-Delage
24, rue du Pied-des-Pentes
Lac-Delage, QC G3C 5A4
Tél: 418-848-2417; *Téléc:* 418-848-1948
ville@lacdelage.qc.ca
www.lacdelage.qc.ca
Entité municipal: Village
Incorporation: 11 février 1959; *Area:* 1,59 km2
Comté ou district: La Jacques-Cartier; Communauté métropolitaine de Québec; *Population au 2016:* 638
Circonscription(s) électorale(s) provinciale(s): Chauveau
Circonscription(s) électorale(s) fédérale(s): Portneuf-Jacques-Cartier
Prochaines élections: 7e novembre 2021
Guy Rochette, Maire
Josée Desmeules, Directrice générale

Lac-des-Aigles
73, rue Principale
Lac-des-Aigles, QC G0K 1V0
Tél: 418-779-2300; *Téléc:* 418-779-3024
info@lacdesaigles.ca
www.lacdesaigles.ca
Entité municipal: Municipality
Incorporation: 1er janvier 1948; *Area:* 86,67 km2
Comté ou district: Témiscouata; *Population au 2016:* 512
Circonscription(s) électorale(s) provinciale(s):
Rivière-du-Loup-Témiscouata
Circonscription(s) électorale(s) fédérale(s):
Rimouski-Neigette-Témiscouata-Les Basques
Prochaines élections: 7e novembre 2021
Pierre Bossé, Maire
Francine Beaulieu, Directrice générale

Lac-des-Écorces
672, boul St-François
Lac-des-Écorces, QC J0W 1H0
Tél: 819-585-4600; *Téléc:* 819-585-4610
adm@lacdesecorces.ca
www.lacdesecorces.ca
Entité municipal: Municipality
Incorporation: 10 octobre 2002; *Area:* 144,90 km2
Comté ou district: Antoine-Labelle; *Population au 2016:* 2,734
Circonscription(s) électorale(s) provinciale(s): Labelle
Circonscription(s) électorale(s) fédérale(s): Laurentides-Labelle
Prochaines élections: 7e novembre 2021
Note: On October 10, 2002, the Municipality of Beaux-Rivages, the Village of Lac-des-Écorces & the Village of Val-Barrette amalgamated to create the new Municipality of Beaux-Rivages-Lac-des-Écorces-Val-Barrette. The name changed to Lac-des-Écorces in 2003
Pierre Flamand, Maire
Linda Fortier, Directrice générale, 819-585-4600

Lac-des-Plages
2053, ch Tour-du-Lac
Lac-des-Plages, QC J0T 1K0
Tél: 819-426-2391; *Téléc:* 819-426-2085
admin@lacdesplages.com
lacdesplages.com
Entité municipal: Municipality
Incorporation: 1er janvier 1950; *Area:* 152,94 km2
Comté ou district: Papineau; *Population au 2016:* 431
Circonscription(s) électorale(s) provinciale(s): Papineau
Circonscription(s) électorale(s) fédérale(s): Argenteuil-La Petite-Nation
Prochaines élections: 7e novembre 2021
Louis Venne, Maire
Denis Dagenais, Directeur général, 819-426-2391

Lac-des-Seize-Iles
47, rue de l'Église
Lac-des-Seize-Iles, QC J0T 2M0
Tél: 450-226-3117; *Téléc:* 450-226-1461
info@lac-des-seize-iles.com
www.lac-des-seize-iles.ca
Entité municipal: Municipality
Incorporation: 19 février 1914; *Area:* 8,96 km2
Comté ou district: Les Pays-d'en-Haut; *Population au 2016:* 172
Circonscription(s) électorale(s) provinciale(s): Argenteuil
Circonscription(s) électorale(s) fédérale(s): Argenteuil-La Petite-Nation
Prochaines élections: 7e novembre 2021
René Pelletier, Maire
Sophie Bélanger, Directrice générale par intérim

Lac-Drolet
685, rue Principale
Lac-Drolet, QC G0Y 1C0
Tél: 819-549-2332; *Téléc:* 819-549-2626
info@lacdrolet.ca
lacdrolet.ca
Entité municipal: Municipality
Incorporation: 1er janvier 1885; *Area:* 124,42 km2
Comté ou district: Le Granit; *Population au 2016:* 1,021
Circonscription(s) électorale(s) provinciale(s): Mégantic
Circonscription(s) électorale(s) fédérale(s): Mégantic-L'Érable
Prochaines élections: 7e novembre 2021
Rock Couët, Maire
Joannie Poirier, Directrice générale

Lac-du-Cerf
19, ch de l'Église
Lac-du-Cerf, QC J0W 1S0
Tél: 819-597-2424; *Téléc:* 819-597-4036
taxation@lac-du-cerf.ca
www.lac-du-cerf.info
Entité municipal: Municipality
Incorporation: 1er janvier 1955; *Area:* 73,29 km2

Comté ou district: Antoine-Labelle; *Population au 2016:* 435
Circonscription(s) électorale(s) provinciale(s): Labelle
Circonscription(s) électorale(s) fédérale(s): Laurentides-Labelle
Prochaines élections: 7e novembre 2021
Danielle Ouimet, Mairesse
Jacinthe Valiquette, Directrice générale

Lac-Édouard
195, rue Principale
Lac-Édouard, QC G0X 3N0
Tél: 819-653-2238
infos@lacedouard.ca
www.lacedouard.ca
Entité municipal: Municipality
Incorporation: 1er janvier 2006; *Area:* 916,50 km2
Population au 2016: 191
Circonscription(s) électorale(s) provinciale(s): Laviolette
Circonscription(s) électorale(s) fédérale(s):
Saint-Maurice-Champlain
Prochaines élections: 7e novembre 2021
Larry Bernier, Maire
Mélanie Dagenais, Directrice générale

Lac-Etchemin
208, 2e av
Lac-Etchemin, QC G0R 1S0
Tél: 418-625-4521; *Téléc:* 418-625-3175
munetchemin@sogetel.net
www.lac-etchemin.ca
Entité municipal: Municipality
Incorporation: 10 octobre 2001; *Area:* 157,21 km2
Comté ou district: Les Etchemins; *Population au 2016:* 3,822
Circonscription(s) électorale(s) provinciale(s): Bellechasse
Circonscription(s) électorale(s) fédérale(s): Bellechasse-Les Etchemins-Lévis
Prochaines élections: 7e novembre 2021
Camil Turmel, Maire
Laurent Rheault, Directeur général

Lac-Frontière
22, rue de l'Église
Lac-Frontière, QC G0R 1T0
Tél: 418-245-3553; *Téléc:* 418-245-3552
info@lac-frontiere.ca
www.lac-frontiere.ca
Entité municipal: Municipality
Incorporation: 7 février 1916; *Area:* 50,13 km2
Comté ou district: Montmagny; *Population au 2016:* 184
Circonscription(s) électorale(s) provinciale(s): Côte-du-Sud
Circonscription(s) électorale(s) fédérale(s):
Montmagny-L'Islet-Kamouraska-Rivière-du-Loup
Prochaines élections: 7e novembre 2021
Alain Robert, Maire
Denise Mercier, Directrice générale

Lac-Mégantic
#200, 5527, rue Frontenac
Lac-Mégantic, QC G6B 1H6
Tél: 819-583-2441; *Téléc:* 819-583-5920
info@ville.lac-megantic.qc.ca
www.ville.lac-megantic.qc.ca
Entité municipal: Town
Incorporation: 14 mars 1907; *Area:* 21,95 km2
Comté ou district: Le Granit; *Population au 2016:* 5,654
Circonscription(s) électorale(s) provinciale(s): Mégantic
Circonscription(s) électorale(s) fédérale(s): Mégantic-L'Érable
Prochaines élections: 7e novembre 2021
Julie Morin, Mairesse
Nancy Roy, Greffière, 819-583-2441

Lacolle
1, rue de l'Église sud
Lacolle, QC J0J 1J0
Tél: 450-246-3201; *Téléc:* 450-246-4412
info@lacolle.com
www.lacolle.com
Entité municipal: Municipality
Incorporation: 13 septembre 2001; *Area:* 49,42 km2
Comté ou district: Le Haut-Richelieu; *Population au 2016:* 2,596
Circonscription(s) électorale(s) provinciale(s): Huntingdon
Circonscription(s) électorale(s) fédérale(s): Saint-Jean
Prochaines élections: 7e novembre 2021
Jacques Lemaistre-Caron, Maire
Jean-Pierre Cayer, Directeur général et secrétaire-trésorier, 450-246-3201

Lac-Poulin
CP 1019
208, rte 271
Lac-Poulin, QC G0M 1P0
Tél: 418-228-7585; *Téléc:* 418-222-6931
munlacpoulin@globetrotter.net

Entité municipal: Village
Incorporation: 5 mars 1959; *Area:* 0,88 km2
Comté ou district: Beauce-Sartigan; *Population au 2016:* 147
Circonscription(s) électorale(s) provinciale(s): Beauce-Sud
Circonscription(s) électorale(s) fédérale(s): Beauce
Prochaines élections: 7e novembre 2021
Manon Veilleux, Mairesse
Odette Poulin, Directrice générale

Lac-Saguay
257A, rte 117
Lac-Saguay, QC J0W 1L0
Tél: 819-278-3972; *Téléc:* 819-278-0260
info@lacsaguay.qc.ca
www.lacsaguay.qc.ca
Entité municipal: Village
Incorporation: 1er juillet 1951; *Area:* 172,97 km2
Comté ou district: Antoine-Labelle; *Population au 2016:* 459
Circonscription(s) électorale(s) provinciale(s): Labelle
Circonscription(s) électorale(s) fédérale(s): Laurentides-Labelle
Prochaines élections: 7e novembre 2021
Francine Asselin-Bélisle, Mairesse
Richard Gagnon, Directeur général

Lac-Sainte-Marie
CP 97
106, ch de Lac-Ste-Marie
Lac-Sainte-Marie, QC J0X 1Z0
Tél: 819-467-5437; *Téléc:* 819-467-3691
municipalite@lac-sainte-marie.com
lac-sainte-marie.com
Entité municipal: Municipality
Incorporation: 1er janvier 1872; *Area:* 208,81 km2
Comté ou district: La Vallée-de-la-Gatineau; *Population au 2016:* 566
Circonscription(s) électorale(s) provinciale(s): Gatineau
Circonscription(s) électorale(s) fédérale(s): Pontiac
Prochaines élections: 7e novembre 2021
Gary Lachapelle, Maire
Yvon Blanchard, Directeur général

Lac-Saint-Jean-Est
625, rue Bergeron ouest
Alma, QC G8B 1V3
Tél: 418-668-3023; *Téléc:* 418-668-5112
info@mrclac.qc.ca
www.mrclacsaintjeanest.qc.ca
Entité municipal: Regional County Municipality
Incorporation: 1er janvier 1982; *Area:* 2779,97 km2
Population au 2016: 52,741
Note: 14 municipalités & 4 autres territoires.
André Paradis, Préfet
Sabin Larouche, Directeur général et secrétaire trésorier

Lac-Saint-Joseph
360, ch Thomas-Maher
Lac-St-Joseph, QC G3N 0A7
Tél: 418-875-3355; *Téléc:* 418-875-0444
info@villelacstjoseph.com
www.villelacstjoseph.com
Entité municipal: Village
Incorporation: 10 juin 1936; *Area:* 33,69 km2
Comté ou district: La Jacques-Cartier; Communauté métropolitaine de Québec; *Population au 2016:* 260
Circonscription(s) électorale(s) provinciale(s): La Peltrie
Circonscription(s) électorale(s) fédérale(s):
Portneuf-Jacques-Cartier
Prochaines élections: 7e novembre 2021
Michael Croteau, Maire
Vivian Viviers, Directrice générale

Lac-Saint-Paul
388, rue Principale
Lac-Saint-Paul, QC J0W 1K0
Tél: 819-587-4283; *Téléc:* 819-587-4892
secretaire@lac-saint-paul.ca
www.lac-saint-paul.ca
Entité municipal: Municipality
Incorporation: 11 septembre 1922; *Area:* 171,57 km2
Comté ou district: Antoine-Labelle; *Population au 2016:* 481
Circonscription(s) électorale(s) provinciale(s): Labelle
Circonscription(s) électorale(s) fédérale(s): Laurentides-Labelle
Prochaines élections: 7e novembre 2021
Colette Quevillon, Mairesse
Guillaume Ratelle, Directeur général, 819-587-4283

Lac-Sergent
1525, ch du Club Nautique
Lac-Sergent, QC G0A 2J0
Tél: 418-875-4854; *Téléc:* 418-875-3805
lac-sergent@derytele.com
www.villelacsergent.com

Entité municipal: Village
Incorporation: 25 février 1921; *Area:* 3,76 km2
Comté ou district: Portneuf; *Population au 2016:* 497
Circonscription(s) électorale(s) provinciale(s): Portneuf
Circonscription(s) électorale(s) fédérale(s):
Portneuf-Jacques-Cartier
Prochaines élections: 7e novembre 2021
Yves Bédard, Maire
Marie Tremblay, Directrice générale et greffière par intérim

Lac-Simon
849, ch du Tour-du-Lac
Chénéville, QC J0V 1E0
Tél: 819-428-3906; *Téléc:* 819-428-3455
mun@lac-simon.net
www.lac-simon.net
Entité municipal: Municipality
Incorporation: 1er janvier 1881; *Area:* 97,48 km2
Comté ou district: Papineau; *Population au 2016:* 944
Circonscription(s) électorale(s) provinciale(s): Papineau
Circonscription(s) électorale(s) fédérale(s): Argenteuil-La
Petite-Nation; Abitibi-Baie-James-Nunavik-Eeyou;
Laurentides-Labelle
Prochaines élections: 7e novembre 2021
Jean-Paul Descoeurs, Maire
Louise Sisla, Directrice générale et secrétaire-trésorière,
819-428-3906

Lac-Supérieur
1281, ch du Lac-Supérieur
Lac-Supérieur, QC J0T 1J0
Tél: 819-681-3370; *Téléc:* 819-688-3010
info@muni.lacsuperieur.qc.ca
www.muni.lacsuperieur.qc.ca
Entité municipal: Municipality
Incorporation: 1er janvier 1881; *Area:* 367,21 km2
Comté ou district: Les Laurentides; *Population au 2016:* 1,888
Circonscription(s) électorale(s) provinciale(s): Labelle
Circonscription(s) électorale(s) fédérale(s): Laurentides-Labelle
Prochaines élections: 7e novembre 2021
Steve Perreault, Maire, 819-681-3370
Steve Deschenes, Directeur général, 819-681-3370

Lac-Tremblant-Nord
1984, ch du Village
Mont-Tremblant, QC J8E 1K4
Tél: 819-425-8154; *Téléc:* 819-425-9208
info@lac-tremblant-nord.qc.ca
lac-tremblant-nord.qc.ca
Entité municipal: Municipality
Incorporation: 1er janvier 2006; *Area:* 20,90 km2
Comté ou district: Les Laurentides; *Population au 2016:* 42
Circonscription(s) électorale(s) provinciale(s): Labelle
Circonscription(s) électorale(s) fédérale(s): Laurentides-Labelle
Prochaines élections: 7e novembre 2021
Kimberly Meyer, Mairesse
Stephanie Carriere, Directrice générale

Laforce
CP 25
703, ch du Village
Laforce, QC J0Z 2J0
Tél: 819-722-2461; *Téléc:* 819-722-2462
laforce.ca
Entité municipal: Municipality
Incorporation: 1er janvier 1979; *Area:* 439,48 km2
Comté ou district: Témiscamingue; *Population au 2016:* 231
Circonscription(s) électorale(s) provinciale(s):
Rouyn-Noranda-Témiscamingue
Circonscription(s) électorale(s) fédérale(s):
Abitibi-Témiscamingue
Prochaines élections: 7e novembre 2021
Gérald Charron, Maire
Daniel Lizotte, Directeur général

Lamarche
100, rue Principale
Lamarche, QC G0W 1X0
Tél: 418-481-2861; *Téléc:* 418-481-1412
mun.lamarche@ville.lamarche.qc.ca
municipalitelamarche.ca
Entité municipal: Municipality
Incorporation: 1er janvier 1967; *Area:* 82,71 km2
Comté ou district: Lac-Saint-Jean-Est; *Population au 2016:* 514
Circonscription(s) électorale(s) provinciale(s): Lac-St-Jean
Circonscription(s) électorale(s) fédérale(s): Jonquière
Prochaines élections: 7e novembre 2021
Lise Garon, Mairesse
Myriam Lessard, Directrice générale

Lambton
230, rue du Collège
Lambton, QC G0M 1H0
Tél: 418-486-7438
lambton.ca
Entité municipal: Municipality
Incorporation: 23 décembre 1976; *Area:* 108,72 km2
Comté ou district: Le Granit; *Population au 2016:* 1,617
Circonscription(s) électorale(s) provinciale(s): Mégantic
Circonscription(s) électorale(s) fédérale(s): Mégantic-L'Érable
Prochaines élections: 7e novembre 2021
Ghislain Breton, Maire
Marcelle Paradis, Directrice générale, 418-486-7438

Landrienne
158, av Principale est
Landrienne, QC J0Y 1V0
Tél: 819-732-4357; *Téléc:* 819-732-3866
info@landrienne.com
www.landrienne.com
Entité municipal: Township
Incorporation: 15 juillet 1918; *Area:* 277,38 km2
Comté ou district: Abitibi; *Population au 2016:* 967
Circonscription(s) électorale(s) provinciale(s): Abitibi-Ouest
Circonscription(s) électorale(s) fédérale(s):
Abitibi-Témiscamingue
Prochaines élections: 7e novembre 2021
Guy Baril, Maire
Mario Tardif, Directeur général

Lanoraie
57, rue Laroche
Lanoraie, QC J0K 1E0
Tél: 450-887-1100
info@lanoraie.ca
www.lanoraie.ca
Entité municipal: Municipality
Incorporation: 6 décembre 2000; *Area:* 103,08 km2
Comté ou district: D'Autray; *Population au 2016:* 4,787
Circonscription(s) électorale(s) provinciale(s): Berthier
Circonscription(s) électorale(s) fédérale(s): Berthier-Maskinongé
Prochaines élections: 7e novembre 2021
Gérard Jean, Maire
Marc-André Maheu, Directeur général, 450-887-1100

Lantier
CP 39
118, croissant des Trois-Lacs
Lantier, QC J0T 1V0
Tél: 819-326-2674; *Téléc:* 819-326-5204
municipalite.lantier.qc.ca
Entité municipal: Municipality
Incorporation: 1er janvier 1948; *Area:* 48,51 km2
Comté ou district: Les Laurentides; *Population au 2016:* 834
Circonscription(s) électorale(s) provinciale(s): Bertrand
Circonscription(s) électorale(s) fédérale(s): Laurentides-Labelle
Prochaines élections: 7e novembre 2021
Richard Forget, Maire
Benoit Charbonneau, Directeur général, 819-326-2674

Larouche
#205, 610, rue Lévesque
Larouche, QC G0W 1Z0
Tél: 418-695-2201; *Téléc:* 418-693-2119
info@larouche.ca
www.larouche.ca
Entité municipal: Municipality
Incorporation: 21 mars 1922; *Area:* 85,21 km2
Comté ou district: Le Fjord-du-Saguenay; *Population au 2016:*
1,486
Circonscription(s) électorale(s) provinciale(s): Lac-St-Jean
Circonscription(s) électorale(s) fédérale(s): Jonquière
Prochaines élections: 7e novembre 2021
Réjean Bédard, Maire
Martin Gagné, Directeur général, 418-695-2201

Latulipe-et-Gaboury
1B, rue Principale est
Latulipe-et-Gaboury, QC J0Z 2N0
Tél: 819-747-4281; *Téléc:* 819-747-2194
latulipeetgaboury.net
Entité municipal: Township
Incorporation: 18 novembre 1924; *Area:* 270,42 km2
Comté ou district: Témiscamingue; *Population au 2016:* 295
Circonscription(s) électorale(s) provinciale(s):
Rouyn-Noranda-Témiscamingue
Circonscription(s) électorale(s) fédérale(s):
Abitibi-Témiscamingue
Prochaines élections: 7e novembre 2021
France Marion, Maire
Julie Gilbert, Directrice générale

Launay
843, rue des Pionniers
Launay, QC J0Y 1W0
Tél: 819-796-2545; *Téléc:* 819-796-2546
canton.launay@cableamos.com
www.launay.ca
Entité municipal: Township
Incorporation: 18 mai 1921; *Area:* 258,51 km2
Comté ou district: Abitibi; *Population au 2016:* 218
Circonscription(s) électorale(s) provinciale(s): Abitibi-Ouest
Circonscription(s) électorale(s) fédérale(s):
Abitibi-Témiscamingue
Prochaines élections: 7e novembre 2021
Claude Lamoureux, Maire
Manon Lampron, Directrice générale

Les Laurentides
1255, ch des Lacs
Saint-Faustin-Lac-Carré, QC J0T 1J2
Tél: 819-425-5555; *Téléc:* 819-688-6590
adm@mrclaurentides.qc.ca
mrclaurentides.qc.ca
Entité municipal: Regional County Municipality
Incorporation: 1er janvier 1983; *Area:* 2479,05 km2
Population au 2016: 45,902
Note: 20 municipalités.
Denis Chalifoux, Préfet
Nancy Pelletier, Directrice générale

Laurier-Station
121, rue St-André
Laurier-Station, QC G0S 1N0
Tél: 418-728-3852; *Téléc:* 418-728-4801
info@ville.laurier-station.qc.ca
www.ville.laurier-station.qc.ca
Entité municipal: Village
Incorporation: 1er janvier 1951; *Area:* 12,16 km2
Comté ou district: Lotbinière; *Population au 2016:* 2,573
Circonscription(s) électorale(s) provinciale(s):
Lotbinière-Frontenac
Circonscription(s) électorale(s) fédérale(s): Lévis-Lotbinière
Prochaines élections: 7e novembre 2021
Pierrette Trépanier, Mairesse
Frédérick Corneau, Directeur général, 418-728-3852

Laurierville
140, rue Grenier
Laurierville, QC G0S 1P0
Tél: 819-365-4646; *Téléc:* 819-365-4200
info@laurierville.ca
www.laurierville.net
Entité municipal: Municipality
Incorporation: 26 novembre 1997; *Area:* 108,05 km2
Comté ou district: L'Érable; *Population au 2016:* 1,346
Circonscription(s) électorale(s) provinciale(s): Arthabaska
Circonscription(s) électorale(s) fédérale(s): Mégantic-L'Érable
Prochaines élections: 7e novembre 2021
Marc Simoneau, Maire
Réjean Gingras, Directeur général, 819-365-4646

Laverlochère-Angliers
CP 159
11A, rue Principale sud
Laverlochère, QC J0Z 2P0
Tél: 819-765-5111; *Téléc:* 819-765-2564
www.laverlochere-angliers.org
Entité municipal: Municipality
Incorporation: 1 jan 2018; *Area:* 403,29 km2
Comté ou district: Témiscamingue; *Population au 2016:* 978
Circonscription(s) électorale(s) provinciale(s):
Rouyn-Noranda-Témiscamingue
Circonscription(s) électorale(s) fédérale(s):
Abitibi-Témiscamingue
Prochaines élections: 7e novembre 2021
Note: Créée 1 jan 2018 par la fusion de Laverlochère et
Angliers.
Daniel Barrette, Maire
Yan Bergeron, Directeur général

Lawrenceville
2100, rue Dandenault
Lawrenceville, QC J0E 1W0
Tél: 450-535-6398; *Téléc:* 450-535-6537
info@lawrenceville.ca
lawrenceville.ca
Entité municipal: Village
Incorporation: 27 avril 1905; *Area:* 16,74 km2
Comté ou district: Le Val-Saint-François; *Population au 2016:*
635
Circonscription(s) électorale(s) provinciale(s): Orford
Circonscription(s) électorale(s) fédérale(s): Shefford
Prochaines élections: 7e novembre 2021

Derek Grilli, Maire
François Paquette, Directeur général

Lebel-sur-Quévillon
CP 430
500, place Quévillon
Lebel-sur-Quévillon, QC J0Y 1X0
Tél: 819-755-4826; *Téléc:* 819-755-8124
ville@lsq.quebec
www.lsq.quebec
Entité municipal: Town
Incorporation: 6 août 1965; *Area:* 40,89 km2
Population au 2016: 2,187
Circonscription(s) électorale(s) provinciale(s): Ungava
Circonscription(s) électorale(s) fédérale(s):
Abitibi-Baie-James-Nunavik-Eeyou
Prochaines élections: 7e novembre 2021
Alain Poirier, Maire
Anne Audet, Greffière, 819-755-4826

Leclercville
1014, rue de l'Église
Leclercville, QC G0S 2K0
Tél: 819-292-2331; *Téléc:* 819-599-0550
mun.leclercville@videotron.ca
www.munleclercville.qc.ca
Entité municipal: Municipality
Incorporation: 26 janvier 2000; *Area:* 136,50 km2
Comté ou district: Lotbinière; *Population au 2016:* 473
Circonscription(s) électorale(s) provinciale(s):
Lotbinière-Frontenac
Circonscription(s) électorale(s) fédérale(s): Lévis-Lotbinière
Prochaines élections: 7e novembre 2021
Marcel Richard, Maire
Lucie Beaudoin, Directrice générale

Lefebvre
186, 10e rang
Lefebvre, QC J0H 2C0
Tél: 819-394-2782; *Téléc:* 819-394-2186
info@municipalite-lefebvre.ca
municipalites-du-quebec.ca/lefebvre
Entité municipal: Municipality
Incorporation: 10 octobre 1922; *Area:* 66,19 km2
Comté ou district: Drummond; *Population au 2016:* 904
Circonscription(s) électorale(s) provinciale(s): Johnson
Circonscription(s) électorale(s) fédérale(s): Drummond
Prochaines élections: 7e novembre 2021
François Parenteau, Maire
Julie Yergeau, Directrice générale

Le-Golfe-du-Saint-Laurent
CP 77
#400, 29, ch d'Aylmer Sound
Chevery, QC G0G 1G0
Tél: 418-787-2020; *Téléc:* 418-787-0052
info@mrcgsl.ca
mrcgsl.ca
Entité municipal: Regional County Municipality
Incorporation: 7er juillet 2010; *Area:* 40 819 km2
Population au 2016: 3,522
Note: 5 municipalités & 1 autre territoire non organisé.
Armand Joncas, Préfet
Karine Monger, Directrice générale

Lejeune
CP 40
69, rue de la Grande-Coulée
Lejeune, QC G0L 1S0
Tél: 418-855-2428; *Téléc:* 418-855-2428
info@municipalitelejeune.ca
www.municipalitelejeune.com
Entité municipal: Municipality
Incorporation: 1er janvier 1964; *Area:* 270,79 km2
Comté ou district: Témiscouata; *Population au 2016:* 262
Circonscription(s) électorale(s) provinciale(s):
Rivière-du-Loup-Témiscouata
Circonscription(s) électorale(s) fédérale(s):
Rimouski-Neigette-Témiscouata-Les Basques
Prochaines élections: 7e novembre 2021
Pierre Daigneault, Maire
Claudine Castonguay, Directrice générale

Lemieux
530, rue de l'Église
Lemieux, QC G0X 1S0
Tél: 819-283-2506; *Téléc:* 819-283-2029
info@municipalitelemieux.ca
www.municipalitelemieux.ca
Entité municipal: Municipality
Incorporation: 14 août 1922; *Area:* 74,75 km2
Comté ou district: Bécancour; *Population au 2016:* 301

Circonscription(s) électorale(s) provinciale(s): Nicolet-Bécancour
Circonscription(s) électorale(s) fédérale(s):
Bécancour-Nicolet-Saurel; Portneuf-Jacques-Cartier
Prochaines élections: 7e novembre 2021
Jean-Louis Belisle, Maire
Caroline Simoneau, Directrice générale

Léry
1, rue de l'Hôtel-de-Ville
Léry, QC J6N 1E8
Tél: 450-692-6861; *Téléc:* 450-692-6881
villedelery@videotron.ca
www.lery.ca
Entité municipal: Town
Incorporation: 1er juin 1914; *Area:* 10,53 km2
Comté ou district: Roussillon; Communauté métropolitaine de
Montréal; *Population au 2016:* 2,318
Circonscription(s) électorale(s) provinciale(s): Châteauguay
Circonscription(s) électorale(s) fédérale(s): Châteauguay-Lacolle
Prochaines élections: 7e novembre 2021
Walter Letham, Maire
Dale Stewart, Directeur général

Lingwick
72, rte 108
Lingwick, QC J0B 2Z0
Tél: 819-560-8422
canton.lingwick@hsfqc.ca
cantondelingwick.com
Entité municipal: Township
Incorporation: 1er juillet 1855; *Area:* 243,48 km2
Comté ou district: Le Haut-Saint-François; *Population au 2016:*
428
Circonscription(s) électorale(s) provinciale(s): Mégantic
Circonscription(s) électorale(s) fédérale(s): Compton-Stanstead
Prochaines élections: 7e novembre 2021
Martin Loubier, Maire
Josée Bolduc, Directrice générale

Litchfield
CP 340
1362, rte 148
Campbell's Bay, QC J0X 1K0
Tél: 819-648-5511; *Téléc:* 819-648-5575
litchfield@mrcpontiac.qc.ca
www.litchfield-qc.ca
Entité municipal: Municipality
Incorporation: 1er juillet 1855; *Area:* 202,18 km2
Comté ou district: Pontiac; *Population au 2016:* 459
Circonscription(s) électorale(s) provinciale(s): Pontiac
Circonscription(s) électorale(s) fédérale(s): Pontiac
Prochaines élections: 7e novembre 2021
Colleen Larivière, Mairesse
Julie Bertrand, Directrice générale

Lochaber
259, montée du Gore
Lochaber, QC J0X 3B0
Tél: 819-985-3291; *Téléc:* 819-985-3487
cantonlochaber.ca
Entité municipal: Township
Incorporation: 1er juillet 1855; *Area:* 60,70 km2
Comté ou district: Papineau; *Population au 2016:* 415
Circonscription(s) électorale(s) provinciale(s): Papineau
Circonscription(s) électorale(s) fédérale(s): Argenteuil-La
Petite-Nation
Prochaines élections: 7e novembre 2021
Alain Gamache, Maire
Marie-Agnès Lacoste, Directrice générale

Lochaber-Partie-Ouest
1361, montée du Quatre
Lochaber-Partie-Ouest, QC J0X 3B0
Tél: 819-281-1551; *Téléc:* 819-281-1991
adjointe@lochaber-ouest.ca
www.lochaber-ouest.ca
Entité municipal: Township
Incorporation: 20 avril 1891; *Area:* 57,45 km2
Comté ou district: Papineau; *Population au 2016:* 856
Circonscription(s) électorale(s) provinciale(s): Papineau
Circonscription(s) électorale(s) fédérale(s): Argenteuil-La
Petite-Nation
Prochaines élections: 7e novembre 2021
Pierre Renaud, Maire
Alain Hotte, Directeur général

Longue-Pointe-de-Mingan
878, ch du Roi
Longue-Pointe-de-Mingan, QC G0G 1V0
Tél: 418-949-2053; *Téléc:* 418-949-2166
www.longuepointedemingan.ca

Entité municipal: Municipality
Incorporation: 1er janvier 1966; *Area:* 387,81 km2
Comté ou district: Minganie; *Population au 2016:* 434
Circonscription(s) électorale(s) provinciale(s): Duplessis
Circonscription(s) électorale(s) fédérale(s): Manicouagan
Prochaines élections: 7e novembre 2021
Martin Beaudin, Maire
Nader Ghabi, Directeur général

Longue-Rive
3, rue de l'Église
Longue-Rive, QC G0T 1Z0
Tél: 418-231-2344
longuerive.ca
Entité municipal: Municipality
Incorporation: 28 mai 1997; *Area:* 312,77 km2
Comté ou district: La Haute-Côte-Nord; *Population au 2016:*
1,026
Circonscription(s) électorale(s) provinciale(s): René-Lévesque
Circonscription(s) électorale(s) fédérale(s): Manicouagan
Prochaines élections: 7e novembre 2021
Donald Perron, Maire
Chantale Otis, Directrice générale

Lorraine
33, boul De Gaulle
Lorraine, QC J6Z 3W9
Tél: 450-621-8550; *Téléc:* 450-621-4763
reception@ville.lorraine.qc.ca
ville.lorraine.qc.ca
Entité municipal: Town
Incorporation: 4e février 1960; *Area:* 5,92 km2
Comté ou district: Thérèse-De Blainville; Communauté
métropolitaine de Montréal; *Population au 2016:* 9,352
Circonscription(s) électorale(s) provinciale(s): Blainville
Circonscription(s) électorale(s) fédérale(s): Thérèse-De Blainville
Prochaines élections: 7e novembre 2021
Jean Comtois, Maire, 450-965-8717
Annie Chagnon, Greffière, 450-621-8550

Lorrainville
CP 218
2, rue St-Jean-Baptiste est
Lorrainville, QC J0Z 2R0
Tél: 819-625-2167
lorrainville@lorrainville.ca
municipalites-du-quebec.ca/lorrainville
Entité municipal: Municipality
Incorporation: 16 février 1994; *Area:* 87,94 km2
Comté ou district: Témiscamingue; *Population au 2016:* 1,272
Circonscription(s) électorale(s) provinciale(s):
Rouyn-Noranda-Témiscamingue
Circonscription(s) électorale(s) fédérale(s):
Abitibi-Témiscamingue
Prochaines élections: 7e novembre 2021
Simon Gélinas, Maire
Francyne Bleau, Directrice générale

Lotbinière
7440, rue Marie-Victorin
Lotbinière, QC G0S 1S0
Tél: 418-796-2103; *Téléc:* 418-796-2198
info@municipalite.lotbiniere.qc.ca
www.municipalite.lotbiniere.qc.ca
Entité municipal: Municipality
Incorporation: 1er janvier 1979; *Area:* 79,94 km2
Comté ou district: Lotbinière; *Population au 2016:* 812
Circonscription(s) électorale(s) provinciale(s):
Lotbinière-Frontenac
Circonscription(s) électorale(s) fédérale(s): Lévis-Lotbinière
Prochaines élections: 7e novembre 2021
Jean Bergeron, Maire
Sandra Bélanger, Directrice générale

Lotbinière
6375, rue Garneau
Sainte-Croix, QC G0S 2H0
Tél: 418-926-3407; *Téléc:* 418-926-3409
info@mrclotbiniere.org
www.mrclotbiniere.org
Entité municipal: Regional County Municipality
Incorporation: 1 janvier 1982; *Area:* 1662,27 km2
Population au 2016: 31,741
Note: 18 municipalités.
Normand Côté, Préfet
Stéphane Bergeron, Directeur général, 418-926-3407

Louiseville
105, av St-Laurent
Louiseville, QC J5V 1J6
Tél: 819-228-9437; *Téléc:* 819-228-2263
hoteldeville@louiseville.ca
louiseville.ca
Entité municipal: Town
Incorporation: 31 décembre 1988; *Area:* 63,85 km2
Comté ou district: Maskinongé; *Population au 2016:* 7,152
Circonscription(s) électorale(s) provinciale(s): Maskinongé
Circonscription(s) électorale(s) fédérale(s): Berthier-Maskinongé
Prochaines élections: 7e novembre 2021
Yvon Deshaies, Maire
Maude-Andrée Pelletier, Greffière, 819-228-9437

Low
CP 100
4A, ch d'Amour
Low, QC J0X 2C0
Tél: 819-422-3528; *Téléc:* 819-422-3796
reception@lowquebec.ca
www.lowquebec.ca
Entité municipal: Township
Incorporation: 1er janvier 1858; *Area:* 261,17 km2
Comté ou district: La Vallée-de-la-Gatineau; *Population au 2016:* 982
Circonscription(s) électorale(s) provinciale(s): Gatineau
Circonscription(s) électorale(s) fédérale(s): Pontiac
Prochaines élections: 7e novembre 2021
Carole Robert, Mairesse
Joanne Owens, Directrice générale

Lyster
2375, rue Bécancour
Lyster, QC G0S 1V0
Tél: 819-389-5787; *Téléc:* 819-389-5981
info@lyster.ca
lyster.ca
Entité municipal: Municipality
Incorporation: 18 septembre 1976; *Area:* 167,57 km2
Comté ou district: L'Érable; *Population au 2016:* 1,605
Circonscription(s) électorale(s) provinciale(s): Arthabaska
Circonscription(s) électorale(s) fédérale(s): Mégantic-L'Érable
Prochaines élections: 7e novembre 2021
Sylvain Labrecque, Maire
Suzy Côté, Directrice générale

Macamic
70, rue Principale
Macamic, QC J0Z 2S0
Tél: 819-782-4604; *Téléc:* 819-782-4283
macamic@mrcao.qc.ca
www.villemacamic.qc.ca
Entité municipal: Town
Incorporation: 6 mars 2002; *Area:* 202,70 km2
Comté ou district: Abitibi-Ouest; *Population au 2016:* 2,751
Circonscription(s) électorale(s) provinciale(s): Abitibi-Ouest
Circonscription(s) électorale(s) fédérale(s): Abitibi-Témiscamingue
Prochaines élections: 7e novembre 2021
Lina Lafrenière, Mairesse
Evelyne Bruneau, Directrice générale, 819-782-4604

La Macaza
53, rue des Pionniers
La Macaza, QC J0T 1R0
Tél: 819-275-2077; *Téléc:* 819-275-3429
info@munilamacaza.ca
www.munilamacaza.ca
Entité municipal: Municipality
Incorporation: 1er janvier 2006; *Area:* 163.48 km2
Comté ou district: Antoine-Labelle; *Population au 2016:* 1,150
Circonscription(s) électorale(s) provinciale(s): Labelle
Circonscription(s) électorale(s) fédérale(s): Laurentides-Labelle
Prochaines élections: 7e novembre 2021
Céline Beauregard, Mairesse
Caroline Dupuis, Directrice générale par intérim, 819-275-2077

Maddington Falls
86, rte 261 nord
Maddington, QC G0Z 1C0
Tél: 819-367-2577; *Téléc:* 819-367-3137
reception@maddington.ca
www.maddington.ca
Entité municipal: Township
Incorporation: 11 janvier 1902; *Area:* 23,84 km2
Comté ou district: Arthabaska; *Population au 2016:* 413
Circonscription(s) électorale(s) provinciale(s): Nicolet-Bécancour
Circonscription(s) électorale(s) fédérale(s): Richmond-Arthabaska
Prochaines élections: 7e novembre 2021
Ghislain Brûlé, Maire

Stéphanie Hinse, Directrice générale

Malartic
901, rue Royale
Malartic, QC J0Y 1Z0
Tél: 819-757-3611; *Téléc:* 819-757-3084
info@ville.malartic.qc.ca
malartic.quebec
Entité municipal: Town
Incorporation: 28 avril 1939; *Area:* 148,85 km2
Comté ou district: La Vallée-de-l'Or; *Population au 2016:* 3,377
Circonscription(s) électorale(s) provinciale(s): Abitibi-Est
Circonscription(s) électorale(s) fédérale(s): Abitibi-Baie-James-Nunavik-Eeyou
Prochaines élections: 7e novembre 2021
Martin Ferron, Maire
Gérald Laprise, Directeur général

La Malbaie
515, boul de Comporté
La Malbaie, QC G5A 1L9
Tél: 418-665-3747
ville@ville.lamalbaie.qc.ca
www.ville.lamalbaie.qc.ca
Entité municipal: Town
Incorporation: 1er décembre 1999; *Area:* 459,24 km2
Comté ou district: Charlevoix-Est; *Population au 2016:* 8,271
Circonscription(s) électorale(s) provinciale(s): Charlevoix-Côte-de-Beaupré
Circonscription(s) électorale(s) fédérale(s): Beauport—Côte-de-Beaupré—Île d'Orléans—Charlevoix
Prochaines élections: 7e novembre 2021
Michel Couturier, Maire
Valérie Bouchard, Greffière

Mandeville
162, rue Desjardins
Mandeville, QC J0K 1L0
Tél: 450-835-2055; *Téléc:* 450-835-7795
mandeville@intermonde.net
www.mandeville.ca
Entité municipal: Municipality
Incorporation: 20 avril 1904; *Area:* 322,73 km2
Comté ou district: D'Autray; *Population au 2016:* 2,189
Circonscription(s) électorale(s) provinciale(s): Berthier
Circonscription(s) électorale(s) fédérale(s): Berthier-Maskinongé
Prochaines élections: 7e novembre 2021
Francine Bergeron, Mairesse
Hélène Plourde, Directrice générale

Manicouagan
768, rue Bossé
Baie-Comeau, QC G5C 1L6
Tél: 418-589-9594; *Téléc:* 418-589-6383
info@mrcmanicouagan.qc.ca
www.mrcmanicouagan.qc.ca
Entité municipal: Regional County Municipality
Incorporation: 1er avril 1981; *Area:* 35 705,48 km2
Population au 2016: 31,027
Note: 8 municipalités & 1 autre territoire.
Marcel Furlong, Préfet, 418-589-9594
Lise Fortin, Directrice générale, 418-589-9594

Maniwaki
186, rue Principale sud
Maniwaki, QC J9E 1Z9
Tél: 819-449-2800; *Téléc:* 819-449-7078
maniwaki@ville.maniwaki.qc.ca
www.ville.maniwaki.qc.ca
Entité municipal: Town
Incorporation: 15 mars 1904; *Area:* 5,98 km2
Comté ou district: La Vallée-de-la-Gatineau; *Population au 2016:* 3,853
Circonscription(s) électorale(s) provinciale(s): Gatineau
Circonscription(s) électorale(s) fédérale(s): Pontiac
Prochaines élections: 7e novembre 2021
Francine Fortin, Mairesse
Louise Pelletier, Greffière, 819-449-2822

Manseau
200, rue Roux
Manseau, QC G0X 1V0
Tél: 819-356-2450
information@manseau.ca
municipalites-du-quebec.ca/manseau
Entité municipal: Municipality
Incorporation: 31 décembre 1997; *Area:* 104,64 km2
Comté ou district: Bécancour; *Population au 2016:* 816
Circonscription(s) électorale(s) provinciale(s): Nicolet-Bécancour
Circonscription(s) électorale(s) fédérale(s): Bécancour-Nicolet-Saurel
Prochaines élections: 7e novembre 2021

Guy St-Pierre, Maire
Nadine Watters, Directrice générale

Mansfield-et-Pontefract
300, rue Principale
Mansfield-et-Pontefract, QC J0X 1R0
Tél: 819-683-2944; *Téléc:* 819-683-3590
mansfield@mrcpontiac.qc.ca
www.mansfield-pontefract.com
Entité municipal: Municipality
Incorporation: 1er janvier 1868; *Area:* 477,44 km2
Comté ou district: Pontiac; *Population au 2016:* 2,285
Circonscription(s) électorale(s) provinciale(s): Pontiac
Circonscription(s) électorale(s) fédérale(s): Pontiac
Prochaines élections: 7e novembre 2021
Gilles Dionne, Maire
Éric Rochon, Directeur général

Marguerite-D'Youville
609, rte Marie-Victorin
Verchères, QC J0L 2R0
Tél: 450-583-3301; *Téléc:* 450-583-3592
infomrc@margueritedyouville.ca
margueritedyouville.ca
Entité municipal: Regional County Municipality
Incorporation: 1er janvier 1982; *Area:* 346,04 km2
Population au 2016: 77,550
Note: 6 municipalités.
Suzanne Roy, Préfète
Sylvain Berthiaume, Directeur général, 450-583-3301

Maria
545, boul Perron
Maria, QC G0C 1Y0
Tél: 418-759-3883
info@mariaquebec.ca
www.mariaquebec.com
Entité municipal: Municipality
Incorporation: 1er juillet 1855; *Area:* 95,09 km2
Comté ou district: Avignon; *Population au 2016:* 2,615
Circonscription(s) électorale(s) provinciale(s): Bonaventure
Circonscription(s) électorale(s) fédérale(s): Avignon-La Mitis-Matane-Matapédia
Prochaines élections: 7e novembre 2021
Christian Leblanc, Maire
Thomas Romagné, Directeur général, 581-358-3202

Maria-Chapdelaine
173, boul St-Michel
Dolbeau-Mistassini, QC G8L 4N9
Tél: 418-276-2131; *Téléc:* 418-276-7043
portail@mrcmaria.ca
www.mrcdemaria-chapdelaine.ca
Other Information: Sans frais: 800-776-2131
Entité municipal: Regional County Municipality
Incorporation: 1er janvier 1983; *Area:* 36 786,21 km2
Population au 2016: 24,793
Note: 12 municipalités & 2 autres territoires.
Luc Simard, Préfet, 418-276-2131
Marie-Claude Fortin, Directrice générale et secrétaire-trésorière, 418-276-2131

Maricourt
1195, 3e rang nord
Maricourt, QC J0E 1Y0
Tél: 450-532-2243
info@maricourt.ca
maricourt.ca
Entité municipal: Municipality
Incorporation: 1er janvier 1864; *Area:* 61,16 km2
Comté ou district: Le Val-Saint-François; *Population au 2016:* 416
Circonscription(s) électorale(s) provinciale(s): Richmond
Circonscription(s) électorale(s) fédérale(s): Shefford
Prochaines élections: 7e novembre 2021
Robert Ledoux, Maire
Nancy Daigle, Directrice générale, 450-532-2243

Marsoui
CP 130
8, rte Principale est
Marsoui, QC G0E 1S0
Tél: 418-288-5552; *Téléc:* 418-288-5104
municipalite.marsoui@globetrotter.net
Entité municipal: Village
Incorporation: 1er janvier 1950; *Area:* 181,75 km2
Comté ou district: La Haute-Gaspésie; *Population au 2016:* 275
Circonscription(s) électorale(s) provinciale(s): Gaspé
Circonscription(s) électorale(s) fédérale(s): Gaspésie—Les îles-de-la-Madeleine
Prochaines élections: 7e novembre 2021
Ghislain Deschenes, Maire

Colette Vaillancourt, Directrice générale

Marston
158, rte 263 sud
Marston, QC G0Y 1G0
Tél: 819-583-0435; *Téléc:* 819-583-6604
secretariat@munmarston.qc.ca
www.munmarston.qc.ca
Entité municipal: Township
Incorporation: 1er janvier 1874; *Area:* 71,91 km2
Comté ou district: Le Granit; *Population au 2016:* 705
Circonscription(s) électorale(s) provinciale(s): Mégantic
Circonscription(s) électorale(s) fédérale(s): Mégantic-L'Érable
Prochaines élections: 7e novembre 2021
Claude Roy, Maire
Francine Veilleux, Directrice générale

Martinville
233, rue Principale est
Martinville, QC J0B 2A0
Tél: 819-835-5390; *Téléc:* 819-835-0171
martinville@axion.ca
municipalites-du-quebec.ca/martinville
Entité municipal: Municipality
Incorporation: 21 décembre 1895; *Area:* 47,69 km2
Comté ou district: Coaticook; *Population au 2016:* 436
Circonscription(s) électorale(s) provinciale(s): St-François
Circonscription(s) électorale(s) fédérale(s): Compton-Stanstead
Prochaines élections: 7e novembre 2021
Réjean Masson, Maire
Julie Létourneau, Directrice générale

La Martre
9, av du Phare
La Martre, QC G0E 2H0
Tél: 418-288-5605; *Téléc:* 418-288-5144
lamartre@globetrotter.net
www.la-martre.ca
Entité municipal: Municipality
Incorporation: 18 décembre 1923; *Area:* 175,46 km2
Comté ou district: La Haute-Gaspésie; *Population au 2016:* 243
Circonscription(s) électorale(s) provinciale(s): Gaspé
Circonscription(s) électorale(s) fédérale(s): Gaspésie-Les Îles-de-la-Madeleine
Prochaines élections: 7e novembre 2021
Yves Sohier, Maire
France Bergeron, Directrice générale

Maskinongé
154, boul Ouest, rte 138
Maskinongé, QC J0K 1N0
Tél: 819-227-2243; *Téléc:* 819-227-2097
www.mun-maskinonge.ca
Entité municipal: Municipality
Incorporation: 25 avril 2001; *Area:* 73,10 km2
Comté ou district: Maskinongé; *Population au 2016:* 2,319
Circonscription(s) électorale(s) provinciale(s): Maskinongé
Circonscription(s) électorale(s) fédérale(s): Berthier-Maskinongé
Prochaines élections: 7e novembre 2021
Roger Michaud, Maire
France Gervais, Directrice générale

Maskinongé
651, boul St-Laurent est
Louiseville, QC J5V 1J1
Tél: 819-228-9461; *Téléc:* 819-228-2193
mrcinfo@mrc-maskinonge.qc.ca
mrcmaskinonge.ca
Entité municipal: Regional County Municipality
Incorporation: 1er janvier 1982; *Area:* 2384,76 km2
Population au 2016: 36,316
Note: 17 municipalités.
Robert Lalonde, Préfet
Pascale Plante, Directrice générale et secrétaire-trésorière, 819-228-9461

Les Maskoutains
805, av du Palais
Saint-Hyacinthe, QC J2S 5C6
Tél: 450-774-3141; *Téléc:* 450-774-7161
admin@mrcmaskoutains.qc.ca
www.mrcmaskoutains.qc.ca
Entité municipal: Regional County Municipality
Incorporation: 1er janvier 1982; *Area:* 1302,90 km2
Population au 2016: 87,099
Note: 17 municipalités.
Francine Morin, Préfète
André Charron, Directeur général

Massueville
246, rue Bonsecours
Massueville, QC J0G 1K0
Tél: 450-788-2957; *Téléc:* 450-788-2050
info@massueville.net
www.massueville.net
Entité municipal: Village
Incorporation: 25 mars 1903; *Area:* 1,55 km2
Comté ou district: Pierre-De Saurel; *Population au 2016:* 529
Circonscription(s) électorale(s) provinciale(s): Richelieu
Circonscription(s) électorale(s) fédérale(s): Bécancour-Nicolet-Saurel
Prochaines élections: 7e novembre 2021
Denis Marion, Maire
France Saint-Pierre, Directrice générale

Matagami
CP 160
195, boul Matagami
Matagami, QC J0Y 2A0
Tél: 819-739-2541; *Téléc:* 819-739-4278
matagami@matagami.com
matagami.com
Entité municipal: Town
Incorporation: 1er avril 1963; *Area:* 75,03 km2
Population au 2016: 1,453
Circonscription(s) électorale(s) provinciale(s): Ungava
Circonscription(s) électorale(s) fédérale(s): Abitibi-Baie-James-Nunavik-Eeyou
Prochaines élections: 7e novembre 2021
René Dubé, Maire
Pierre Deslauriers, Greffier et trésorier

La Matanie
158, rue Soucy, 2e étage
Matane, QC G4W 2E3
Tél: 418-562-6734; *Téléc:* 418-562-7265
mrcdelamatanie@lamatanie.ca
www.lamatanie.ca
Entité municipal: Regional County Municipality
Incorporation: 1er janvier 1982
Population au 2016: 17,926
Note: 11 municipalités & 1 autre territoire.
Andrew Turcotte, Préfet
Line Ross, Directrice générale

Matapédia
8, rue Macdonell
Matapédia, QC G0J 1V0
Tél: 418-865-2917
info@matapedia.ca
matapedialesplateaux.com/citoyens/matapedia
Entité municipal: Municipality
Incorporation: 4e novembre 1905; *Area:* 71,55 km2
Comté ou district: Avignon; *Population au 2016:* 645
Circonscription(s) électorale(s) provinciale(s): Bonaventure
Circonscription(s) électorale(s) fédérale(s): Avignon-La Mitis-Matane-Matapédia
Prochaines élections: 7e novembre 2021
Nicole Lagacé, Mairesse
Geneviève Moffatt, Directrice générale et secrétaire trésorière

La Matapédia
420, rte 132 ouest
Amqui, QC G5J 2G6
Tél: 418-629-2053; *Téléc:* 418-629-3195
administration@mrcmatapedia.quebec
www.mrcmatapedia.qc.ca
Entité municipal: Regional County Municipality
Incorporation: 1er janvier 1982; *Area:* 5374,57 km2
Population au 2016: 17,925
Note: 18 municipalités & 7 autres territoires.
Chantale Lavoie, Préfète
Steve Ouellet, Directeur général et secrétaire-trésorier, 418-629-2053

Matawinie
3184, 1e av
Rawdon, QC J0K 1S0
Tél: 450-834-5441
info@matawinie.org
mrcmatawinie.org
Other Information: Sans frais: 800-264-5441
Entité municipal: Regional County Municipality
Incorporation: 1er janvier 1982; *Area:* 9528,17 km2
Population au 2016: 50,435
Note: 15 municipalités & 12 autres territoires.
Sylvain Breton, Préfet
Réal Brassard, Directeur général, 450-834-5441

Mayo
20, ch McAlendin
Gatineau, QC J8L 4J7
Tél: 819-986-3199; *Téléc:* 819-986-8881
www.mayo.ca
Entité municipal: Municipality
Incorporation: 1er août 1864; *Area:* 73,25 km2
Comté ou district: Papineau; *Population au 2016:* 601
Circonscription(s) électorale(s) provinciale(s): Papineau
Circonscription(s) électorale(s) fédérale(s): Argenteuil-La Petite-Nation
Prochaines élections: 7e novembre 2021
Robert Betrand, Maire
Martin Cousineau, Directeur général, 819-986-3199

McMasterville
255, boul Constable
McMasterville, QC J3G 6N9
Tél: 450-467-3580; *Téléc:* 450-467-2493
info@mcmasterville.ca
www.mcmasterville.ca
Entité municipal: Municipality
Incorporation: 31 juillet 1917; *Area:* 3,12 km2
Comté ou district: La Vallée-du-Richelieu; Communauté métropolitaine de Montréal; *Population au 2016:* 5,698
Circonscription(s) électorale(s) provinciale(s): Borduas
Circonscription(s) électorale(s) fédérale(s): Beloeil-Chambly
Prochaines élections: 7e novembre 2021
Martin Dulac, Maire
Sébastien Gagnon, Directrice générale

Les Méchins
108, rte des Fonds
Les Méchins, QC G0J 1T0
Tél: 418-729-3952; *Téléc:* 418-729-3585
info@lesmechins.com
www.lesmechins.com
Entité municipal: Municipality
Incorporation: 27 novembre 1982; *Area:* 443,40 km2
Comté ou district: La Matanie; *Population au 2016:* 987
Circonscription(s) électorale(s) provinciale(s): Matane-Matapédia
Circonscription(s) électorale(s) fédérale(s): Avignon-La Mitis-Matane-Matapédia
Prochaines élections: 7e novembre 2021
Dominic Roy, Maire
Laurie Ross, Directrice générale, 418-729-3952

Mékinac
560, rue Notre-Dame
Saint-Tite, QC G0X 3H0
Tél: 418-365-5151; *Téléc:* 418-365-7377
mrcmekinac@mrcmekinac.com
www.mrcmekinac.com
Entité municipal: Regional County Municipality
Incorporation: 1 janvier 1982; *Area:* 5222,10 km2
Population au 2016: 12,358
Note: 10 municipalités & 4 autres territoires.
Bernard Thompson, Préfet
Nathalie Groleau, Directrice générale, 418-365-5151

Melbourne
1257, rte 243
Melbourne, QC J0B 2B0
Tél: 819-826-3555; *Téléc:* 819-826-3981
admin.melcan@bellnet.ca
melbournecanton.ca
Entité municipal: Township
Incorporation: 1er juillet 1855; *Area:* 174,06 km2
Comté ou district: Le Val-Saint-François; *Population au 2016:* 1,063
Circonscription(s) électorale(s) provinciale(s): Richmond
Circonscription(s) électorale(s) fédérale(s): Richmond-Arthabaska
Prochaines élections: 7e novembre 2021
James Johnston, Maire
Cindy Jones, Directrice générale

Memphrémagog
#200, 455, rue MacDonald
Magog, QC J1X 1M2
Tél: 819-843-9292; *Téléc:* 819-843-7295
info@mrcmemphremagog.com
www.mrcmemphremagog.com
Entité municipal: Regional County Municipality
Incorporation: 1er janvier 1982; *Area:* 1319,29 km2
Population au 2016: 50,415
Note: 17 municipalités.
Jacques Demers, Préfet
Guy Jauron, Directeur général, 819-843-9292

Messines
70, rue Principale
Messines, QC J0X 2J0
Tél: 819-465-2323; *Téléc:* 819-465-2943
info@messines.ca
www.messines.ca
Entité municipal: Municipality
Incorporation: 19 août 1921; *Area:* 111,97 km2
Comté ou district: La Vallée-de-la-Gatineau; *Population au 2016:*
1,609
Circonscription(s) électorale(s) provinciale(s): Gatineau
Circonscription(s) électorale(s) fédérale(s): Pontiac
Prochaines élections: 7e novembre 2021
Ronald Cross, Maire
Jim Smith, Directeur général, 819-465-2323

Métabetchouan—Lac-à-la-Croix
87, rue St-André
Métabetchouan—Lac-à-la-Croix, QC G8G 1A1
Tél: 418-349-2060; *Téléc:* 418-349-2395
courrier@ville.metabetchouan.qc.ca
www.ville.metabetchouan.qc.ca
Entité municipal: Town
Incorporation: 6 janvier 1999; *Area:* 187,23 km2
Comté ou district: Lac-Saint-Jean-Est; *Population au 2016:*
3,985
Circonscription(s) électorale(s) provinciale(s): Lac-St-Jean
Circonscription(s) électorale(s) fédérale(s): Lac-St-Jean
Prochaines élections: 7e novembre 2021
André Fortin, Maire
Mario Bouchard, Greffier

Métis-sur-Mer
138, rue Principale
Métis-sur-Mer, QC G0J 1S0
Tél: 418-936-3255; *Téléc:* 418-936-3117
metissurmer@mitis.qc.ca
www.ville.metis-sur-mer.qc.ca
Entité municipal: Village
Incorporation: 4 juillet 2002; *Area:* 48,60 km2
Comté ou district: La Mitis; *Population au 2016:* 587
Circonscription(s) électorale(s) provinciale(s): Matane-Matapédia
Circonscription(s) électorale(s) fédérale(s): Avignon-La
Mitis-Matane-Matapédia
Prochaines élections: 7e novembre 2021
Carolle-Anne Dubé, Mairesse
Stéphane Marcheterre, Directeur général et secrétaire-trésorier,
418-936-3255

Milan
CP 54
403, rang Ste-Marie
Milan, QC G0Y 1E0
Tél: 819-657-4527; *Téléc:* 819-657-2987
munmilan@axion.ca
www.munmilan.qc.ca
Entité municipal: Municipality
Incorporation: 1er juin 1948; *Area:* 129,52 km2
Comté ou district: Le Granit; *Population au 2016:* 299
Circonscription(s) électorale(s) provinciale(s): Mégantic
Circonscription(s) électorale(s) fédérale(s): Mégantic-L'Érable
Prochaines élections: 7e novembre 2021
Jacques Bergeron, Maire
Sylvia Roy, Directrice générale

Mille-Isles
1262, ch de Mille-Isles
Mille-Isles, QC J0R 1A0
Tél: 450-438-2958; *Téléc:* 450-438-6157
info@mille-isles.ca
mille-isles.ca
Entité municipal: Municipality
Incorporation: 1er juillet 1855; *Area:* 59,82 km2
Comté ou district: Argenteuil; *Population au 2016:* 1,567
Circonscription(s) électorale(s) provinciale(s): Argenteuil
Circonscription(s) électorale(s) fédérale(s): Argenteuil-La
Petite-Nation; Rivière-du-Nord
Prochaines élections: 7e novembre 2021
Michel Boyer, Maire
Pierre-Luc Nadeau, Directeur général et secrétaire-trésorier,
450-438-2958

La Minerve
6, rue Mailloux
La Minerve, QC J0T 1S0
Tél: 819-681-3380; *Téléc:* 819-274-2031
info@municipalite.laminerve.qc.ca
www.municipalite.laminerve.qc.ca
Entité municipal: Municipality
Incorporation: 30 décembre 1892; *Area:* 278,49 km2
Comté ou district: Les Laurentides; *Population au 2016:* 1,205
Circonscription(s) électorale(s) provinciale(s): Labelle

Circonscription(s) électorale(s) fédérale(s): Laurentides-Labelle
Prochaines élections: 7e novembre 2021
Jean Pierre Monette, Maire
Suzanne Sauriol, Directrice générale

Minganie
1303, rue de la Digue
Havre-Saint-Pierre, QC G0G 1P0
Tél: 418-538-2732; *Téléc:* 418-538-3711
info@mrc.minganie.org
mrc.minganie.org
Other Information: Sans frais: 866-538-2732
Entité municipal: Regional County Municipality
Incorporation: 1er janvier 1982; *Area:* 7 923 km2
Population au 2016: 6,035
Note: 8 municipalités & 2 communautés innues.
Luc Noël, Préfet
Nathalie de Grandpré, Directrice générale, 418-538-2732

Mistissini
187, ch Main
Mistissini, QC G0W 1C0
Tél: 418-923-3461
info@mistissini.ca
mistissini.ca
Entité municipal: Villages Cris
Incorporation: 28 juin 1978; *Area:* 859,88 km2
Population au 2016: 3,523
Circonscription(s) électorale(s) provinciale(s): Ungava
Circonscription(s) électorale(s) fédérale(s):
Abitibi-Baie-James-Nunavik-Eeyou
Thomas Neeposh, Maire
Titus Shecapio, Directeur général

La Mitis
300, av du Sanatorium
Mont-Joli, QC G5H 1V7
Tél: 418-775-8445; *Téléc:* 418-775-9303
mrcmitis@mitis.qc.ca
lamitis.ca
Entité municipal: Regional County Municipality
Incorporation: 1er janvier 1982; *Area:* 2281,25 km2
Population au 2016: 18,210
Note: 16 municipalités & 2 autres territoires.
Bruno Paradis, Préfet
Marcel Moreau, Directeur général, 418-775-8445

Moffet
CP 89
14C, rue Principale
Moffet, QC J0Z 2W0
Tél: 819-747-6116; *Téléc:* 819-747-6117
moffet.ca
Entité municipal: Municipality
Incorporation: 1er janvier 1953; *Area:* 343,00 km2
Comté ou district: Témiscamingue; *Population au 2016:* 187
Circonscription(s) électorale(s) provinciale(s):
Rouyn-Noranda-Témiscamingue
Circonscription(s) électorale(s) fédérale(s):
Abitibi-Témiscamingue
Prochaines élections: 7e novembre 2021
Alexandre Binette, Maire
Linda Roy, Directrice générale

Montcalm
10, rue de l'Hôtel-de-Ville
Montcalm, QC J0T 2V0
Tél: 819-681-3383
www.municipalite.montcalm.qc.ca
Entité municipal: Municipality
Incorporation: 6e mars 1907; *Area:* 119,98 km2
Comté ou district: Les Laurentides; *Population au 2016:* 628
Circonscription(s) électorale(s) provinciale(s): Argenteuil
Circonscription(s) électorale(s) fédérale(s): Laurentides-Labelle;
Montcalm; Québec
Prochaines élections: 7e novembre 2021
Steven Larose, Maire
Michael Doyle, Directeur général

Montcalm
1540, rue Albert
Sainte-Julienne, QC J0K 2T0
Tél: 450-831-2182
info@mrcmontcalm.com
www.mrcmontcalm.com
Other Information: Sans frais: 888-242-2412
Entité municipal: Regional County Municipality
Incorporation: 1er janvier 1982; *Area:* 711,02 km2
Population au 2016: 52,596
Note: 10 municipalités.
Pierre La Salle, Préfet
Nicolas Rousseau, Directrice générale, 450-831-2182

Mont-Carmel
22, rue de la Fabrique
Mont-Carmel, QC G0L 1W0
Tél: 418-498-2050
info@mont-carmel.ca
www.mont-carmel.ca
Entité municipal: Municipality
Incorporation: 1er juillet 1855; *Area:* 429,03 km2
Comté ou district: Kamouraska; *Population au 2016:* 1,127
Circonscription(s) électorale(s) provinciale(s): Côte-du-Sud
Circonscription(s) électorale(s) fédérale(s):
Montmagny-L'Islet-Kamouraska-Rivière-du-Loup
Prochaines élections: 7e novembre 2021
Pierre Saillant, Maire
Maryse Lizotte, Directrice générale et secrétaire-trésorière,
418-498-2050

Montcerf-Lytton
18, rue Principale nord
Montcerf-Lytton, QC J0W 1N0
Tél: 819-449-4578; *Téléc:* 819-449-7310
infos@montcerf-lytton.com
www.montcerf-lytton.com
Entité municipal: Municipality
Incorporation: 19 septembre 2001; *Area:* 360,05 km2
Comté ou district: La Vallée-de-la-Gatineau; *Population au 2016:*
636
Circonscription(s) électorale(s) provinciale(s): Gatineau
Circonscription(s) électorale(s) fédérale(s): Pontiac
Prochaines élections: 7e novembre 2021
Alain Fortin, Maire
Natacha Wacquiez, Directrice générale, 819-449-4578

Montebello
550, rue Notre-Dame
Montebello, QC J0V 1L0
Tél: 819-423-5123; *Téléc:* 819-423-5703
reception@montebello.ca
www.montebello.ca
Entité municipal: Municipality
Incorporation: 29 août 1878; *Area:* 8,62 km2
Comté ou district: Papineau; *Population au 2016:* 983
Circonscription(s) électorale(s) provinciale(s): Papineau
Circonscription(s) électorale(s) fédérale(s): Argenteuil-La Petite
Nation
Prochaines élections: 7e novembre 2021
Martin Deschênes, Maire
Nicolas Le Mat, Directeur général, 819-423-5123

Mont-Joli
40, av de l'Hôtel-de-Ville
Mont-Joli, QC G5H 1W8
Tél: 418-775-7285; *Téléc:* 418-775-6320
mont-joli@ville.mont-joli.qc.ca
ville.mont-joli.qc.ca
Entité municipal: Town
Incorporation: 13 juin 2001; *Area:* 24,20 km2
Comté ou district: La Mitis; *Population au 2016:* 6,281
Circonscription(s) électorale(s) provinciale(s): Matane-Matapédia
Circonscription(s) électorale(s) fédérale(s): Avignon-La
Mitis-Matane-Matapédia
Prochaines élections: 7e novembre 2021
Martin Soucy, Maire
Kathleen Bossé, Greffière, 418-775-7285

Montmagny
#300, 6, rue St-Jean-Baptiste est
Montmagny, QC G5V 1N5
Tél: 418-248-5985; *Téléc:* 418-248-4624
mrc@montmagny.com
www.montmagny.com
Entité municipal: Regional County Municipality
Incorporation: 1er janvier 1982; *Area:* 1698,13 km2
Population au 2016: 22,698
Note: 14 municipalités.
Jocelyne Caron, Préfet
Nancy Labrecque, Directrice générale, 418-248-5985

Montpellier
4, rue du Bosquet
Montpellier, QC J0V 1M0
Tél: 819-428-3663; *Téléc:* 819-428-1221
reception@montpellier.ca
montpellier.ca
Entité municipal: Municipality
Incorporation: 11 octobre 1920; *Area:* 249,14 km2
Comté ou district: Papineau; *Population au 2016:* 985
Circonscription(s) électorale(s) provinciale(s): Papineau
Circonscription(s) électorale(s) fédérale(s): Argenteuil-La
Petite-Nation
Prochaines élections: 7e novembre 2021
Stéphane Séguin, Maire

Manon Lanthier, Directrice générale, 819-428-3663

Montréal-Est
11370, rue Notre-Dame, 5e étage
Montréal-Est, QC H1B 2W6
Tél: 514-905-2000
servicescitoyens@montreal-est.ca
ville.montreal-est.qc.ca
Entité municipal: Town
Incorporation: 1er janvier 2006; *Area:* 12,24 km2
Comté ou district: Communauté métropolitaine de Montréal;
Population au 2016: 3,850
Circonscription(s) électorale(s) provinciale(s):
Pointe-aux-Trembles
Circonscription(s) électorale(s) fédérale(s): La Pointe-de-l'île
Prochaines élections: 7e novembre 2021
Robert Coutu, Maire
Roch Sergerie, Greffier

Montréal-Ouest
50, av Westminster sud
Montréal-Ouest, QC H4X 1Y7
Tél: 514-481-8125; *Téléc:* 514-481-4554
info@montreal-west.ca
montreal-west.ca
Entité municipal: Town
Incorporation: 1er janvier 2006; *Area:* 1,37 km2
Comté ou district: Communauté métropolitaine de Montréal;
Population au 2016: 5,050
Circonscription(s) électorale(s) provinciale(s):
Notre-Dame-de-Grâce
Circonscription(s) électorale(s) fédérale(s):
Notre-Dame-de-Grâce-Westmount
Prochaines élections: 7e novembre 2021
Beny Masella, Maire
Claude Gilbert, Greffier

Mont-Saint-Grégoire
1, boul du Frère-André
Mont-Saint-Grégoire, QC J0J 1K0
Tél: 450-347-5376; *Téléc:* 450-347-9200
www.mmsg.ca
Entité municipal: Municipality
Incorporation: 21 décembre 1994; *Area:* 79,97 km2
Comté ou district: Le Haut-Richelieu; *Population au 2016:* 3,077
Circonscription(s) électorale(s) provinciale(s): Iberville
Circonscription(s) électorale(s) fédérale(s): Saint-Jean
Prochaines élections: 7e novembre 2021
Suzanne Boulais, Mairesse
Murielle Papineau, Directrice générale, 450-347-5376

Mont-Saint-Michel
94, rue de l'Église
Mont-Saint-Michel, QC J0W 1P0
Tél: 819-587-3093; *Téléc:* 819-587-3781
info@montsaintmichel.ca
www.montsaintmichel.ca
Entité municipal: Municipality
Incorporation: 11 septembre 1928; *Area:* 139,02 km2
Comté ou district: Antoine-Labelle; *Population au 2016:* 503
Circonscription(s) électorale(s) provinciale(s): Labelle
Circonscription(s) électorale(s) fédérale(s): Laurentides-Labelle
Prochaines élections: 7e novembre 2021
André-Marcel Évéquoz, Maire
Laurence Tardif, Directrice générale

Mont-Saint-Pierre
102, rue Prudent-Cloutier
Mont-Saint-Pierre, QC G0E 1V0
Tél: 418-797-2898; *Téléc:* 418-797-2307
mont-st-pierre@globetrotter.net
municipalites-du-quebec.ca/mont-st-pierre
Entité municipal: Village
Incorporation: 1er janvier 1947; *Area:* 52,39 km2
Comté ou district: La Haute-Gaspésie; *Population au 2016:* 155
Circonscription(s) électorale(s) provinciale(s): Gaspé
Circonscription(s) électorale(s) fédérale(s): Gaspésie—Les
îles-de-la-Madeleine; Mirabel
Prochaines élections: 7e novembre 2021
Magella Emond, Maire
Colette Réhel, Directeur général

Mont-Tremblant
1145, rue de St-Jovite
Mont-Tremblant, QC J8E 1V1
Tél: 819-425-8614; *Téléc:* 819-425-2528
info@villedemont-tremblant.qc.ca
www.villedemont-tremblant.qc.ca
Entité municipal: Town
Incorporation: 22 novembre 2000; *Area:* 235,06 km2
Comté ou district: Les Laurentides; *Population au 2016:* 9,646
Circonscription(s) électorale(s) provinciale(s): Labelle

Circonscription(s) électorale(s) fédérale(s): Laurentides-Labelle
Prochaines élections: 7e novembre 2021
Luc Brisebois, Maire
Claudine Fréchette, Greffière

La Morandière
204, rte 397
La Morandière, QC J0Y 1S0
Tél: 819-734-6143; *Téléc:* 819-734-6143
lamo@cableamos.com
www.lamorandiere.ca
Entité municipal: Municipality
Incorporation: 1er janvier 1983; *Area:* 410,40 km2
Comté ou district: Abitibi; *Population au 2016:* 207
Circonscription(s) électorale(s) provinciale(s): Abitibi-Ouest
Circonscription(s) électorale(s) fédérale(s):
Abitibi-Témiscamingue
Prochaines élections: 7e novembre 2021
Alain Lemay, Maire
Sandra Hardy, Directrice générale

Morin-Heights
567, ch du Village
Morin-Heights, QC J0R 1H0
Tél: 450-226-3232; *Téléc:* 450-226-8786
municipalite@morinheights.com
www.morinheights.com
Entité municipal: Municipality
Incorporation: 1er juillet 1855; *Area:* 56,66 km2
Comté ou district: Les Pays-d'en-Haut; *Population au 2016:*
4,145
Circonscription(s) électorale(s) provinciale(s): Argenteuil
Circonscription(s) électorale(s) fédérale(s): Argenteuil-La
Petite-Nation
Prochaines élections: 7e novembre 2021
Timothy Watchorn, Maire
Hugo Lépine, Directeur général, 450-226-3232

La Motte
CP 644
349, ch St-Luc
La Motte, QC J0Y 1T0
Tél: 819-732-2878; *Téléc:* 819-727-4248
municipalite.lamotte@cableamos.com
municipalitedelamotte.ca
Entité municipal: Municipality
Incorporation: 30 mai 1921; *Area:* 176,90 km2
Comté ou district: Abitibi; *Population au 2016:* 453
Circonscription(s) électorale(s) provinciale(s): Abitibi-Ouest
Circonscription(s) électorale(s) fédérale(s):
Abitibi-Témiscamingue
Prochaines élections: 7e novembre 2021
Louis-Joseph Fecteau-Lefebvre, Maire
Rachel Cossette, Directrice générale

Les Moulins
CP 204
710, boul des Seigneurs, 2e étage
Terrebonne, QC J6W 1T6
Tél: 450-471-9576; *Téléc:* 450-471-8193
info@mrclesmoulins.ca
www.mrclesmoulins.ca
Entité municipal: Regional County Municipality
Incorporation: 1er janvier 1982; *Area:* 261,13 km2
Population au 2016: 158,267
Note: 2 municipalités.
Guillaume Tremblay, Préfet
Claude Robichaud, Directeur général, 450-471-9576

Mulgrave-et-Derry
560, av de Buckingham
Gatineau, QC J8L 2H1
Tél: 819-986-9519; *Téléc:* 819-986-9954
administration@mulgrave-derry.ca
www.mulgrave-derry.ca
Entité municipal: Municipality
Incorporation: 1er janvier 1870; *Area:* 293,75 km2
Comté ou district: Papineau; *Population au 2016:* 369
Circonscription(s) électorale(s) provinciale(s): Papineau
Circonscription(s) électorale(s) fédérale(s): Argenteuil-La
Petite-Nation
Prochaines élections: 7e novembre 2021
Michael Kane, Maire
Isabelle Cusson, Directrice générale

Murdochville
CP 1120
635, 5e rue
Murdochville, QC G0E 1W0
Tél: 418-784-2536; *Téléc:* 418-784-2607
ville@murdochville.com
murdochville.com

Circonscription(s) électorale(s) fédérale(s): Laurentides-Labelle
Entité municipal: Village
Incorporation: 15 juillet 1953; *Area:* 61,37 km2
Comté ou district: La Côte-de-Gaspé; *Population au 2016:* 651
Circonscription(s) électorale(s) provinciale(s): Gaspé
Circonscription(s) électorale(s) fédérale(s): Gaspésie—Les
îles-de-la-Madeleine
Prochaines élections: 7e novembre 2021
Délisca Roussy, Mairesse
Jean-Pierre Cassivi, Greffier

Namur
996, rue du Centenaire
Namur, QC J0V 1N0
Tél: 819-426-2457; *Téléc:* 819-426-3074
namur.ca
Entité municipal: Municipality
Incorporation: 1er janvier 1964; *Area:* 56,76 km2
Comté ou district: Papineau; *Population au 2016:* 572
Circonscription(s) électorale(s) provinciale(s): Papineau
Circonscription(s) électorale(s) fédérale(s): Argenteuil-La
Petite-Nation
Prochaines élections: 7e novembre 2021
Gilbert Dardel, Maire
Marie-Pier Lalonde Girard, Directrice générale, 819-426-2457

Nantes
1244, rue Principale
Nantes, QC G0Y 1G0
Tél: 819-547-3655; *Téléc:* 819-547-3755
municipalites-du-quebec.ca/nantes
Entité municipal: Municipality
Incorporation: 1er janvier 1874; *Area:* 119,30 km2
Comté ou district: Le Granit; *Population au 2016:* 1,377
Circonscription(s) électorale(s) provinciale(s): Mégantic
Circonscription(s) électorale(s) fédérale(s): Mégantic-L'Érable
Prochaines élections: 7e novembre 2021
Jacques Breton, Maire
Lucie Lortitch, Directrice générale

Napierville
260, rue de l'Église
Napierville, QC J0J 1L0
Tél: 450-245-7210; *Téléc:* 450-245-7691
www.napierville.ca
Entité municipal: Village
Incorporation: 1er janvier 1873; *Area:* 4,37 km2
Comté ou district: Les Jardins-de-Napierville; *Population au
2016:* 3,899
Circonscription(s) électorale(s) provinciale(s): Huntingdon
Circonscription(s) électorale(s) fédérale(s): Châteauguay-Lacolle
Prochaines élections: 7e novembre 2021
Chantale Pelletier, Mairesse
Julie Archambault, Directrice générale

Natashquan
29, ch d'en-Haut
Natashquan, QC G0G 2E0
Tél: 418-726-3362; *Téléc:* 418-726-3698
info@natashquan.org
www.natashquan.org
Entité municipal: Township
Incorporation: 16 septembre 1907; *Area:* 197,60 km2
Comté ou district: Minganie; *Population au 2016:* 263
Circonscription(s) électorale(s) provinciale(s): Duplessis
Circonscription(s) électorale(s) fédérale(s): Manicouagan
Prochaines élections: 7e novembre 2021
André Barrette, Maire
Denis Landry, Directeur général

Nédélec
CP 70
33, rue Principale
Nédélec, QC J0Z 2Z0
Tél: 819-784-3311; *Téléc:* 819-784-2126
nedelec@mrctemiscamingue.qc.ca
municipalite.nedelec.qc.ca
Entité municipal: Township
Incorporation: 1er février 1909; *Area:* 374,10 km2
Comté ou district: Témiscamingue; *Population au 2016:* 356
Circonscription(s) électorale(s) provinciale(s):
Rouyn-Noranda-Témiscamingue
Circonscription(s) électorale(s) fédérale(s):
Abitibi-Témiscamingue
Prochaines élections: 7e novembre 2021
Lyne Ash, Mairesse
Nathalie Arsenault, Directrice générale

Nemaska
32, rue Machishteweyaau
Nemaska, QC J0Y 3B0
Tél: 819-673-2512; *Téléc:* 819-673-2542
nation@nemaska.ca
www.nemaska.com
Entité municipal: Villages Cris
Incorporation: 28 juin 1978; *Area:* 98,49 km2
Population au 2016: 760
Circonscription(s) électorale(s) provinciale(s): Ungava
Circonscription(s) électorale(s) fédérale(s):
Abitibi-Baie-James-Nunavik-Eeyou
Thomas Jolly, Maire
Georges Wapachee, Directeur général

Neuville
230, rue du Père-Rhéaume
Neuville, QC G0A 2R0
Tél: 418-876-2280; *Téléc:* 418-876-3349
mun@ville.neuville.qc.ca
www.ville.neuville.qc.ca
Entité municipal: Town
Incorporation: 2 janvier 1997; *Area:* 71,99 km2
Comté ou district: Portneuf; *Population au 2016:* 4,392
Circonscription(s) électorale(s) provinciale(s): Portneuf
Circonscription(s) électorale(s) fédérale(s):
Portneuf-Jacques-Cartier
Prochaines élections: 7e novembre 2021
Bernard Gaudreau, Maire
Lisa Kennedy, Greffier

New Carlisle
CP 40
138, boul Gérard-D.-Levesque
New Carlisle, QC G0C 1Z0
Tél: 418-752-3141; *Téléc:* 418-752-3140
newcarlisle@globetrotter.net
new-carlisle.com
Entité municipal: Municipality
Incorporation: 1er février 1877; *Area:* 67,77 km2
Comté ou district: Bonaventure; *Population au 2016:* 1,388
Circonscription(s) électorale(s) provinciale(s): Bonaventure
Circonscription(s) électorale(s) fédérale(s):
Gaspésie-Îles-de-la-Madeleine
Prochaines élections: 7e novembre 2021
Stephen Chatterton, Maire
Denise Dallain, Directrice générale

New Richmond
99, place Suzanne-Guité
New Richmond, QC G0C 2B0
Tél: 418-392-7000; *Téléc:* 418-392-5331
villenewrichmond.com
Entité municipal: Town
Incorporation: 1er juillet 1855; *Area:* 171,34 km2
Comté ou district: Bonaventure; *Population au 2016:* 3,706
Circonscription(s) électorale(s) provinciale(s): Bonaventure
Circonscription(s) électorale(s) fédérale(s):
Gaspésie—Îles-de-la-Madeleine
Prochaines élections: 7e novembre 2021
Éric Dubé, Maire
Céline Leblanc, Greffière

Newport
1452, rte 212
Newport, QC J0B 1M0
Tél: 819-560-8565
municipalite.newport@hsfqc.ca
www.municipalitenewport.com
Entité municipal: Municipality
Incorporation: 1er janvier 2006; *Area:* 271,12 km2
Comté ou district: Le Haut-Saint-François; *Population au 2016:* 733
Circonscription(s) électorale(s) provinciale(s): Mégantic
Circonscription(s) électorale(s) fédérale(s): Compton-Stanstead
Prochaines élections: 7e novembre 2021
Lionel Roy, Maire
Lise Houle, Directrice générale

Nicolet
180, rue Monseigneur-Panet
Nicolet, QC J3T 1S6
Tél: 819-293-6901; *Téléc:* 819-293-6767
communication@nicolet.ca
nicolet.ca
Entité municipal: Town
Incorporation: 27 décembre 2000; *Area:* 95,93 km2
Comté ou district: Nicolet-Yamaska; *Population au 2016:* 8,169
Circonscription(s) électorale(s) provinciale(s): Nicolet-Bécancour
Circonscription(s) électorale(s) fédérale(s):
Bécancour-Nicolet-Saurel
Prochaines élections: 7e novembre 2021

Geneviève Dubois, Mairesse
Jacinthe Vallée, Greffière

Nicolet-Yamaska
#257, 1, rue de Mgr-Courchesne
Nicolet, QC J3T 2C1
Tél: 819-293-2997; *Téléc:* 819-293-5367
mrcny@mrcny.qc.ca
mrcnicolet-yamaska.qc.ca
Entité municipal: Regional County Municipality
Incorporation: 1 janvier 1982; *Area:* 1007,09 km2
Population au 2016: 23,159
Note: 16 municipalités.
Geneviève Dubois, Préfète
Michel Côté, Directeur général, 819-519-2997

Nominingue
2110, ch du Tour-du-Lac
Nominingue, QC J0W 1R0
Tél: 819-278-3384; *Téléc:* 819-278-4967
reception@municipalitenominingue.ca
www.municipalitenominingue.ca
Entité municipal: Municipality
Incorporation: 30 octobre 1971; *Area:* 307,48 km2
Comté ou district: Antoine-Labelle; *Population au 2016:* 2,137
Circonscription(s) électorale(s) provinciale(s): Labelle
Circonscription(s) électorale(s) fédérale(s): Laurentides-Labelle
Prochaines élections: 7e novembre 2021
Georges Décarie, Maire
François St-Amour, Directeur général

Normandin
1048, rue St-Cyrille
Normandin, QC G8M 4R9
Tél: 418-274-2004; *Téléc:* 418-274-7171
admin@ville.normandin.qc.ca
ville.normandin.qc.ca
Entité municipal: Town
Incorporation: 10 mars 1979; *Area:* 212,46 km2
Comté ou district: Maria-Chapdelaine; *Population au 2016:* 3,033
Circonscription(s) électorale(s) provinciale(s): Roberval
Circonscription(s) électorale(s) fédérale(s): Lac-St-Jean
Prochaines élections: 7e novembre 2021
Mario Fortin, Maire
Lyne Groleau, Directrice générale et greffière, 418-274-2004

Normétal
59, 1re rue
Normétal, QC J0Z 3A0
Tél: 819-788-2550; *Téléc:* 819-788-2730
normetal@mrcao.qc.ca
normetal.ao.ca
Entité municipal: Municipality
Incorporation: 1er janvier 1945; *Area:* 55,68 km2
Comté ou district: Abitibi-Ouest; *Population au 2016:* 808
Circonscription(s) électorale(s) provinciale(s): Abitibi-Ouest
Circonscription(s) électorale(s) fédérale(s):
Abitibi-Témiscamingue
Prochaines élections: 7e novembre 2021
Roger Lévesque, Maire
Lyne Blanchet, Directrice générale

North Hatley
3125, ch Capelton
North Hatley, QC J0B 2C0
Tél: 819-842-2754; *Téléc:* 819-842-4501
info@northhatley.org
www.northhatley.org
Entité municipal: Village
Incorporation: 25 octobre 1897; *Area:* 3,35 km2
Comté ou district: Memphrémagog; *Population au 2016:* 632
Circonscription(s) électorale(s) provinciale(s): Orford
Circonscription(s) électorale(s) fédérale(s): Compton-Stanstead
Prochaines élections: 7e novembre 2021
Michael Page, Maire
Benoit Tremblay, Directeur général

Notre-Dame-Auxiliatrice-de-Buckland
4340, rue Principale
Buckland, QC G0R 1G0
Tél: 418-789-3119; *Téléc:* 418-789-3535
info@buckland.qc.ca
www.buckland.qc.ca
Entité municipal: Parish (Paroisse)
Incorporation: 1er janvier 1885; *Area:* 94,95 km2
Comté ou district: Bellechasse; *Population au 2016:* 768
Circonscription(s) électorale(s) provinciale(s): Bellechasse
Circonscription(s) électorale(s) fédérale(s): Bellechasse-Les
Etchemins-Lévis
Prochaines élections: 7e novembre 2021
Jean-Yves Turmel, Maire
Jocelyne Nadeau, Directrice générale

Notre-Dame-de-Bonsecours
220A, rue Bonsecours
Montebello, QC J0V 1L0
Tél: 819-423-5575; *Téléc:* 819-423-5571
mun@ndbonsecours.com
www.ndbonsecours.com
Entité municipal: Municipality
Incorporation: 7 mars 1918; *Area:* 264,97 km2
Comté ou district: Papineau; *Population au 2016:* 301
Circonscription(s) électorale(s) provinciale(s): Papineau
Circonscription(s) électorale(s) fédérale(s): Argenteuil-La
Petite-Nation
Prochaines élections: 7e novembre 2021
Carol Fortier, Maire
Lorraine Briand, Directrice générale

Notre-Dame-de-Ham
25, rue de l'Église
Notre-Dame-de-Ham, QC G0P 1C0
Tél: 819-344-5806; *Téléc:* 819-344-5807
info@notre-dame-de-ham.ca
www.notre-dame-de-ham.ca
Entité municipal: Municipality
Incorporation: 7 octobre 1898; *Area:* 32,30 km2
Comté ou district: Arthabaska; *Population au 2016:* 411
Circonscription(s) électorale(s) provinciale(s):
Drummond-Bois-Francs
Circonscription(s) électorale(s) fédérale(s):
Richmond-Arthabaska
Prochaines élections: 7e novembre 2021
Luce Périard, Mairesse
Louise Côté, Directrice générale

Notre-Dame-de-la-Merci
1900, montée de la Réserve
Notre-Dame-de-la-Merci, QC J0T 2A0
Tél: 819-424-2113; *Téléc:* 819-424-7347
info@mun-ndm.ca
www.mun-ndm.ca
Entité municipal: Municipality
Incorporation: 1er janvier 1950; *Area:* 249,92 km2
Comté ou district: Matawinie; *Population au 2016:* 905
Circonscription(s) électorale(s) provinciale(s): Bertrand
Circonscription(s) électorale(s) fédérale(s): Joliette
Prochaines élections: 7e novembre 2021
Isabelle Parent, Mairesse
Chantal Soucy, Directrice générale

Notre-Dame-de-la-Paix
267, rue Notre-Dame
Notre-Dame-de-la-Paix, QC J0V 1P0
Tél: 819-522-6610; *Téléc:* 819-522-6710
www.notredamedelapaix.qc.ca
Entité municipal: Municipality
Incorporation: 3 octobre 1902; *Area:* 106,62 km2
Comté ou district: Papineau; *Population au 2016:* 648
Circonscription(s) électorale(s) provinciale(s): Papineau
Circonscription(s) électorale(s) fédérale(s): Argenteuil-La
Petite-Nation
Prochaines élections: 7e novembre 2021
Simon Deschambault, Maire
Chantal Delisle, Directrice générale

Notre-Dame-de-la-Salette
CP 59
45, rue des Saules
Notre-Dame-de-la-Salette, QC J0X 2L0
Tél: 819-766-2533; *Téléc:* 819-766-2983
salette@muni-ndsalette.qc.ca
www.muni-ndsalette.qc.ca
Entité municipal: Municipality
Incorporation: 17 mai 1979; *Area:* 115,49 km2
Comté ou district: Les Collines-de-l'Outaouais; *Population au 2016:* 727
Circonscription(s) électorale(s) provinciale(s): Papineau
Circonscription(s) électorale(s) fédérale(s): Argenteuil-La
Petite-Nation
Prochaines élections: 7e novembre 2021
Denis Légaré, Maire
Claude Sarrazin, Directeur général et secrétaire-trésorier,
819-766-2533

Notre-Dame-de-Lorette
22, rue Principale
Notre-Dame-de-Lorette, QC G0W 1B0
Tél: 418-276-1934; *Téléc:* 418-276-1934
Entité municipal: Municipality
Incorporation: 1er janvier 1966; *Area:* 335,82 km2
Comté ou district: Maria-Chapdelaine; *Population au 2016:* 189
Circonscription(s) électorale(s) provinciale(s): Roberval
Circonscription(s) électorale(s) fédérale(s): Lac-St-Jean
Prochaines élections: 7e novembre 2021

Martine Joanisse, Directrice générale, 819-427-5511

Parisville
975, rte Principale ouest
Parisville, QC G0S 1X0
Tél: 819-292-2222; *Téléc:* 819-292-1514
info@municipalite.parisville.qc.ca
www.municipalite.parisville.qc.ca
Entité municipal: Parish (Paroisse)
Incorporation: 18 mars 1901; *Area:* 35,54 km2
Comté ou district: Bécancour; *Population au 2016:* 530
Circonscription(s) électorale(s) provinciale(s): Nicolet-Bécancour
Circonscription(s) électorale(s) fédérale(s):
Bécancour-Nicolet-Saurel
Prochaines élections: 7e novembre 2021
Maurice Grimard, Maire
Dominique Lapointe, Directrice générale

Paspébiac
CP 130
5, boul Gérard-D.-Levesque est
Paspébiac, QC G0C 2K0
Tél: 418-752-2277; *Téléc:* 418-752-6566
villepaspebiac.ca
Entité municipal: Town
Incorporation: 20 août 1997; *Area:* 94,47 km2
Comté ou district: Bonaventure; *Population au 2016:* 3,164
Circonscription(s) électorale(s) provinciale(s): Bonaventure
Circonscription(s) électorale(s) fédérale(s):
Gaspésie—îles-de-la-Madeleine
Prochaines élections: 7e novembre 2021
Regent Bastien, Maire
Daniel Langlois, Directeur général

La Patrie
18, rue Chartier
La Patrie, QC J0B 1Y0
Tél: 819-560-8535; *Téléc:* 819-560-8536
muni.lapatrie@hsfqc.ca
www.lapatrie.ca
Entité municipal: Municipality
Incorporation: 24 décembre 1997; *Area:* 204,82 km2
Comté ou district: Le Haut-Saint-François; *Population au 2016:* 768
Circonscription(s) électorale(s) provinciale(s): Mégantic
Circonscription(s) électorale(s) fédérale(s): Compton-Stanstead
Prochaines élections: 7e novembre 2021
Johanne Delage, Mairesse
France Dumont, Directrice générale

Les Pays-d'en-Haut
1014, rue Valiquette
Sainte-Adèle, QC J8B 2M3
Tél: 450-229-6637; *Téléc:* 450-229-5203
info@mrcpdh.org
lespaysdenhaut.com
Entité municipal: Regional County Municipality
Incorporation: 1er janvier 1983; *Area:* 683,46 km2
Population au 2016: 41,877
Note: 10 municipalités.
André Genest, Préfet
Jackline Williams, Directrice générale, 450-229-6637

La Pêche
1, rue Principale ouest
La Pêche, QC J0X 2W0
Tél: 819-456-2161; *Téléc:* 819-456-4534
reception@villelapeche.qc.ca
www.villelapeche.qc.ca
Entité municipal: Municipality
Incorporation: 1er janvier 1975; *Area:* 585,93 km2
Comté ou district: Les Collines-de-l'Outaouais; *Population au 2016:* 7,863
Circonscription(s) électorale(s) provinciale(s): Gatineau
Circonscription(s) électorale(s) fédérale(s): Pontiac
Prochaines élections: 7e novembre 2021
Guillaume Lamoureaux, Maire
Marco Déry, Directeur général

Percé
CP 99
137, rte 132 ouest
Percé, QC G0C 2L0
Tél: 418-782-2933; *Téléc:* 418-782-5487
renseignements@ville.perce.qc.ca
ville.perce.qc.ca
Entité municipal: Town
Incorporation: 1er janvier 1971; *Area:* 431,37 km2
Comté ou district: Le Rocher-Percé; *Population au 2016:* 3,103
Circonscription(s) électorale(s) provinciale(s): Gaspé
Circonscription(s) électorale(s) fédérale(s):

Gaspésie—îles-de-la-Madeleine
Prochaines élections: 7e novembre 2021
Cathy Poirier, Mairesse
Gemma Vibert, Greffière

Péribonka
312, rue Édouard-Niquet
Péribonka, QC G0W 2G0
Tél: 418-374-2967; *Téléc:* 418-374-2355
www.peribonka.ca
Entité municipal: Municipality
Incorporation: 19 septembre 1908; *Area:* 111,33 km2
Comté ou district: Maria-Chapdelaine; *Population au 2016:* 515
Circonscription(s) électorale(s) provinciale(s): Roberval
Circonscription(s) électorale(s) fédérale(s): Lac-St-Jean
Prochaines élections: 7e novembre 2021
Ghislain Goulet, Maire
Steve Harvey, Directeur général

Petite-Rivière-Saint-François
CP 10
1067, rue Principale
Petite-Rivière-Saint-François, QC G0A 2L0
Tél: 418-760-1050; *Téléc:* 418-760-1051
info@petiteriviere.com
www.petiteriviere.com
Entité municipal: Municipality
Incorporation: 1er juillet 1855; *Area:* 134,31 km2
Comté ou district: Charlevoix; *Population au 2016:* 814
Circonscription(s) électorale(s) provinciale(s):
Charlevoix-Côte-de-Beaupré
Circonscription(s) électorale(s) fédérale(s):
Beauport—Côte-de-Beaupré—île d'Orléans—Charlevoix
Prochaines élections: 7e novembre 2021
Gérald Maltais, Maire
Stéphane Simard, Directeur général, 418-760-1050

Petite-Vallée
45, rue Principale
Petite-Vallée, QC G0E 1Y0
Tél: 418-393-2949
petitevallee.ca
Entité municipal: Municipality
Incorporation: 1er janvier 1957; *Area:* 39,94 km2
Comté ou district: La Côte-de-Gaspé; *Population au 2016:* 170
Circonscription(s) électorale(s) provinciale(s): Gaspé
Circonscription(s) électorale(s) fédérale(s):
Gaspésie—îles-de-la-Madeleine
Prochaines élections: 7e novembre 2021
Noel-marie Clavat, Maire
Simon Côté, Directeur général

Petit-Saguenay
35, ch du Quai
Petit-Saguenay, QC G0V 1N0
Tél: 418-272-2323; *Téléc:* 418-544-3077
petit-saguenay.com
Entité municipal: Municipality
Incorporation: 12 août 1919; *Area:* 334,57 km2
Comté ou district: Le Fjord-du-Saguenay; *Population au 2016:* 634
Circonscription(s) électorale(s) provinciale(s): Dubuc
Circonscription(s) électorale(s) fédérale(s): Chicoutimi-Le Fjord
Prochaines élections: 7e novembre 2021
Philôme LaFrance, Maire
Lisa Houde, Directrice générale

Piedmont
670, rue Principale
Piedmont, QC J0R 1K0
Tél: 450-227-1888; *Téléc:* 450-227-6716
info@piedmont.ca
www.piedmont.ca
Entité municipal: Municipality
Incorporation: 22 septembre 1923; *Area:* 24,56 km2
Comté ou district: Les Pays-d'en-Haut; *Population au 2016:* 2,950
Circonscription(s) électorale(s) provinciale(s): Bertrand
Circonscription(s) électorale(s) fédérale(s): Laurentides-Labelle
Prochaines élections: 7e novembre 2021
Nathalie Rochon, Mairesse
Hugo Allaire, Directeur général et greffier, 450-227-1888

Pierre-De Saurel
50, rue du Fort
Sorel-Tracy, QC J3P 7X7
Tél: 450-743-2703; *Téléc:* 450-743-7313
info@mrcpierredesaurel.com
www.mrcpierredesaurel.com
Entité municipal: Regional County Municipality
Incorporation: 1er janvier 1982; *Area:* 597,55 km2

Population au 2016: 51,025
Note: 12 municipalités.
Gilles Salvas, Préfet
Denis Boisvert, Directeur général et secrétaire-trésorier

Pierreville
CP 300
26, rue Ally
Pierreville, QC J0G 1J0
Tél: 450-568-2139; *Téléc:* 450-568-0689
info@municipalitepierreville.qc.ca
pierreville.net
Entité municipal: Municipality
Incorporation: 13 juin 2001; *Area:* 78,63 km2
Comté ou district: Nicolet-Yamaska; *Population au 2016:* 2,143
Circonscription(s) électorale(s) provinciale(s): Nicolet-Bécancour
Circonscription(s) électorale(s) fédérale(s):
Bécancour-Nicolet-Saurel
Prochaines élections: 7e novembre 2021
Éric Descheneaux, Maire
Lyne Boisvert, Directrice générale

Pike River
CP 93
548, rte 202
St-Pierre-de-Véronne, QC J0J 1P0
Tél: 450-248-2120; *Téléc:* 450-248-4772
info@pikeriver.com
www.pikeriver.ca
Entité municipal: Municipality
Incorporation: 3 avril 1912; *Area:* 40,81 km2
Comté ou district: Brome-Missisquoi; *Population au 2016:* 517
Circonscription(s) électorale(s) provinciale(s): Brome-Missisquoi
Circonscription(s) électorale(s) fédérale(s): Brome-Missisquoi
Prochaines élections: 7e novembre 2021
Martin Bellefroid, Maire
Lucie Riendeau, Directrice générale

Piopolis
403, rue Principale
Piopolis, QC G0Y 1H0
Tél: 819-583-3953; *Téléc:* 819-583-1467
info@piopolis.quebec
www.piopolis.quebec
Entité municipal: Municipality
Incorporation: 1er janvier 1880; *Area:* 103,17 km2
Comté ou district: Le Granit; *Population au 2016:* 358
Circonscription(s) électorale(s) provinciale(s): Mégantic
Circonscription(s) électorale(s) fédérale(s): Mégantic-L'Érable
Prochaines élections: 7e novembre 2021
Peter Manning, Maire
Emmanuelle Fredette, Directrice générale, 819-583-3953

Plaisance
275, rue Desjardins
Plaisance, QC J0V 1S0
Tél: 819-427-5363; *Téléc:* 819-427-5015
info@villeplaisance.com
ville.plaisance.qc.ca
Entité municipal: Municipality
Incorporation: 31 octobre 1900; *Area:* 36,15 km2
Comté ou district: Papineau; *Population au 2016:* 1,088
Circonscription(s) électorale(s) provinciale(s): Papineau
Circonscription(s) électorale(s) fédérale(s): Argenteuil-La Petite-Nation
Prochaines élections: 7e novembre 2021
Christian Pilon, Maire
Benoit Hébert, Directeur général, 819-427-5363

Plessisville
CP 245
290, rte 165 sud
Plessisville, QC G6L 2Y7
Tél: 819-362-2712; *Téléc:* 819-362-9185
info@paroisseplessisville.com
www.paroisseplessisville.com
Entité municipal: Parish (Paroisse)
Incorporation: 1er juillet 1855; *Area:* 141,50 km2
Comté ou district: L'Érable; *Population au 2016:* 2,663
Circonscription(s) électorale(s) provinciale(s): Arthabaska
Circonscription(s) électorale(s) fédérale(s): Mégantic-L'Érable
Prochaines élections: 7e novembre 2021
Alain Dubois, Maire
Johanne Dubois, Directrice générale, 819-362-2712

Plessisville
1700, rue St-Calixte
Plessisville, QC G6L 1R3
Tél: 819-362-3284; *Téléc:* 819-362-6421
info@plessisville.quebec
plessisville.quebec

Entité municipal: Town
Incorporation: 27 avril 1855; *Area:* 4,40 km2
Comté ou district: L'Érable; *Population au 2016:* 6,551
Circonscription(s) électorale(s) provinciale(s): Arthabaska
Circonscription(s) électorale(s) fédérale(s): Mégantic-L'Érable
Prochaines élections: 7e novembre 2021
Mario Fortin, Maire
Denis Beaudoin, Directeur général par intérim, 819-362-3284

La Pocatière
412, 9e rue
La Pocatière, QC G0R 1Z0
Tél: 418-856-3394; *Téléc:* 418-856-5465
communication@lapocatiere.ca
www.lapocatiere.ca
Entité municipal: Town
Incorporation: 1er janvier 1960; *Area:* 21,63 km2
Comté ou district: Kamouraska; *Population au 2016:* 4,120
Circonscription(s) électorale(s) provinciale(s): Côte-du-Sud
Circonscription(s) électorale(s) fédérale(s):
Montmagny-L'Islet-Kamouraska-Rivière-du-Loup
Prochaines élections: 7e novembre 2021
Sylvain Hudon, Maire
Cédrick Gagnon, Greffière

Pohénégamook
1309, rue Principale
Pohénégamook, QC G0L 1J0
Tél: 418-859-2222; *Téléc:* 418-859-3465
pohenegamook.net
Entité municipal: Town
Incorporation: 3 novembre 1973; *Area:* 340,44 km2
Comté ou district: Témiscouata; *Population au 2016:* 2,582
Circonscription(s) électorale(s) provinciale(s):
Rivière-du-Loup-Témiscouata
Circonscription(s) électorale(s) fédérale(s):
Rimouski-Neigette-Témiscouata-Les Basques
Prochaines élections: 7e novembre 2021
Louise Labonté, Mairesse
Simon Grenier, Directeur général, 418-863-7722

Pointe-à-la-Croix
CP 159
139, boul Inter-Provincial
Pointe-à-la-Croix, QC G0C 1L0
Tél: 418-788-2011; *Téléc:* 418-788-2916
info@pointe-a-la-croix.com
pointe-a-la-croix.com
Entité municipal: Municipality
Incorporation: 7 mai 1983; *Area:* 390,96 km2
Comté ou district: Avignon; *Population au 2016:* 1,391
Circonscription(s) électorale(s) provinciale(s): Bonaventure
Circonscription(s) électorale(s) fédérale(s): Avignon-La
Mitis-Matane-Matapédia
Prochaines élections: 7e novembre 2021
Pascal Bujold, Maire
Stéphanie Clark, Directrice générale, 418-788-2011

Pointe-aux-Outardes
471, ch Principal
Pointe-aux-Outardes, QC G0H 1M0
Tél: 418-567-2203; *Téléc:* 418-567-4409
municipalite@pointe-aux-outardes.ca
www.pointe-aux-outardes.ca
Entité municipal: Village
Incorporation: 1er janvier 1964; *Area:* 76,42 km2
Comté ou district: Manicouagan; *Population au 2016:* 1,332
Circonscription(s) électorale(s) provinciale(s): René-Lévesque
Circonscription(s) électorale(s) fédérale(s): Manicouagan
Prochaines élections: 7e novembre 2021
Serge Deschênes, Maire
Dania Hovington, Directrice générale

Pointe-Calumet
300, av Basile-Routhier
Pointe-Calumet, QC J0N 1G2
Tél: 450-473-5930; *Téléc:* 450-473-6571
info@pointe-calumet.ca
www.pointe-calumet.ca
Entité municipal: Municipality
Incorporation: 12 février 1953; *Area:* 4,62 km2
Comté ou district: Deux-Montagnes; Communauté
métropolitaine de Montréal; *Population au 2016:* 6,428
Circonscription(s) électorale(s) provinciale(s): Mirabel
Circonscription(s) électorale(s) fédérale(s): Mirabel
Prochaines élections: 7e novembre 2021
Sonia Fontaine, Mairesse
Chantal Pilon, Directrice générale

Pointe-des-Cascades
105, ch du Fleuve
Pointe-des-Cascades, QC J0P 1M0
Tél: 450-455-3414; *Téléc:* 450-455-9671
reception@pointe-des-cascades.com
www.pointe-des-cascades.com
Entité municipal: Village
Incorporation: 1er mai 1961; *Area:* 2,68 km2
Comté ou district: Vaudreuil-Soulanges; Communauté
métropolitaine de Montréal; *Population au 2016:* 1,481
Circonscription(s) électorale(s) provinciale(s): Soulanges
Circonscription(s) électorale(s) fédérale(s): Vaudreuil-Soulanges
Prochaines élections: 7e novembre 2021
Gilles Santerre, Maire
Anne-Marie Duval, Directrice générale

Pointe-Fortune
694, rue du Tisseur
Pointe-Fortune, QC J0P 1N0
Tél: 450-451-5178; *Téléc:* 450-451-4649
municipalite@pointefortune.ca
pointefortune.ca
Entité municipal: Village
Incorporation: 28 août 1880; *Area:* 8,26 km2
Comté ou district: Vaudreuil-Soulanges; *Population au 2016:* 580
Circonscription(s) électorale(s) provinciale(s): Soulanges
Circonscription(s) électorale(s) fédérale(s): Vaudreuil-Soulanges
Prochaines élections: 7e novembre 2021
François Bélanger, Maire
Jean-Charles Filion, Directeur général

Pointe-Lebel
382, rue Granier
Pointe-Lebel, QC G0H 1N0
Tél: 418-589-8073; *Téléc:* 418-589-6154
www.pointe-lebel.com
Entité municipal: Village
Incorporation: 1er janvier 1964; *Area:* 85,17 km2
Comté ou district: Manicouagan; *Population au 2016:* 1,918
Circonscription(s) électorale(s) provinciale(s): René-Lévesque
Circonscription(s) électorale(s) fédérale(s): Manicouagan
Prochaines élections: 7e novembre 2021
Normand Morin, Maire
Christian Matte, Directeur général, 418-589-8073

Pontiac
2024, rte 148
Pontiac, QC J0X 2G0
Tél: 819-455-2401; *Téléc:* 819-455-9756
info@municipalitepontiac.ca
municipalitepontiac.com
Other Information: Sans frais: 888-455-2401
Entité municipal: Municipality
Incorporation: 1er janvier 1975; *Area:* 448,15 km2
Comté ou district: Les Collines-de-l'Outaouais; *Population au
2016:* 5,850
Circonscription(s) électorale(s) provinciale(s): Pontiac
Circonscription(s) électorale(s) fédérale(s): Pontiac
Prochaines élections: 7e novembre 2021
Joanne Labadie, Mairesse
Pierre Said, Directeur général

Pontiac
602, rte 301
Campbell's Bay, QC J0X 1K0
Tél: 819-648-5689; *Téléc:* 819-648-5810
mrc@mrcpontiac.qc.ca
www.mrcpontiac.qc.ca
Entité municipal: Regional County Municipality
Incorporation: 1er janvier 1983; *Area:* 12 991,82 km2
Population au 2016: 14,251
Note: 18 municipalités & 1 autre territoire.
Jane Toller, Préfète, 819-648-5689
Bernard Roy, Directeur général, 819-648-5689

Pont-Rouge
189, rue Dupont
Pont-Rouge, QC G3H 1N4
Tél: 418-873-4481; *Téléc:* 418-873-3494
info@ville.pontrouge.qc.ca
www.ville.pontrouge.qc.ca
Entité municipal: Town
Incorporation: 3 janvier 1996; *Area:* 121,20 km2
Comté ou district: Portneuf; *Population au 2016:* 9,240
Circonscription(s) électorale(s) provinciale(s): Portneuf
Circonscription(s) électorale(s) fédérale(s):
Portneuf-Jacques-Cartier
Prochaines élections: 7e novembre 2021
Ghislain Langlais, Maire
Esther Godin, Greffière

Portage-du-Fort
24, rue de l'Église
Portage-du-Fort, QC J0X 2T0
Tél: 819-647-2767; *Téléc:* 819-647-2768
portage-du-fort@mrcpontiac.qc.ca
portage-du-fort.com
Entité municipal: Village
Incorporation: 1er janvier 1863; *Area:* 4,23 km2
Comté ou district: Pontiac; *Population au 2016:* 234
Circonscription(s) électorale(s) provinciale(s): Pontiac
Circonscription(s) électorale(s) fédérale(s): Pontiac
Prochaines élections: 7e novembre 2021
Lynne Cameron, Mairesse
Lisa Dagenais, Directrice générale

Port-Cartier
40, av Parent
Port-Cartier, QC G5B 2G5
Tél: 418-766-2343; *Téléc:* 418-766-6236
communications@villeport-cartier.com
villeport-cartier.com
Entité municipal: Town
Incorporation: 19 février 2003; *Area:* 1 102.09 km2
Comté ou district: Sept-Rivières; *Population au 2016:* 6,799
Circonscription(s) électorale(s) provinciale(s): Duplessis
Circonscription(s) électorale(s) fédérale(s): Manicouagan
Prochaines élections: 7e novembre 2021
Alain Thibault, Maire
Natacha Dupuis-Carrier, Greffière

Port-Daniel—Gascons
494, rte 132
Port-Daniel—Gascons, QC G0C 2N0
Tél: 418-396-5225; *Téléc:* 418-396-5588
munpdg.ca
Entité municipal: Municipality
Incorporation: 17 janvier 2001; *Area:* 301,60 km2
Comté ou district: Le Rocher-Percé; *Population au 2016:* 2,210
Circonscription(s) électorale(s) provinciale(s): Bonaventure
Circonscription(s) électorale(s) fédérale(s):
Gaspésie—Îles-de-la-Madeleine
Prochaines élections: 7e novembre 2021
Henri Grenier, Maire
Marlyne Cyr, Directrice générale

Portneuf
655A, av de l'Église
Portneuf, QC G0A 2Y0
Tél: 418-286-3844; *Téléc:* 418-286-4304
info@villedeportneuf.com
villedeportneuf.com
Entité municipal: Town
Incorporation: 4 juillet 2002; *Area:* 109,39 km2
Comté ou district: Portneuf; *Population au 2016:* 3,187
Circonscription(s) électorale(s) provinciale(s): Portneuf
Circonscription(s) électorale(s) fédérale(s):
Portneuf-Jacques-Cartier
Prochaines élections: 7e novembre 2021
Mario Alain, Maire
France Marcotte, Greffière, 418-286-3844

Portneuf
185, rte 138
Cap-Santé, QC G0A 1L0
Tél: 418-285-3744; *Téléc:* 418-285-1703
portneuf@mrc-portneuf.qc.ca
portneuf.ca
Other Information: Sans frais: 877-285-3746
Entité municipal: Regional County Municipality
Incorporation: 1er janvier 1982; *Area:* 3923,70 km2
Population au 2016: 53,008
Note: 18 municipalités & 3 autres territoires.
Bernard Gaudreau, Préfet
Josée Frenette, Directrice générale

Portneuf-sur-Mer
CP 98
170, rue Principale
Portneuf-sur-Mer, QC G0T 1P0
Tél: 418-238-2642; *Téléc:* 418-238-5319
infos@portneuf-sur-mer.ca
www.portneuf-sur-mer.ca
Entité municipal: Municipality
Incorporation: 12 septembre 1902; *Area:* 183,60 km2
Comté ou district: La Haute-Côte-Nord; *Population au 2016:* 598
Circonscription(s) électorale(s) provinciale(s): René-Lévesque
Circonscription(s) électorale(s) fédérale(s): Manicouagan
Prochaines élections: 7e novembre 2021
Gontran Tremblay, Maire
Simon Thériault, Directeur général, 418-238-2642

Potton
2, rue de Vale Perkins
Mansonville, QC J0E 1X0
Tél: 450-292-3313; *Téléc:* 450-292-5555
info@potton.ca
potton.ca
Entité municipal: Township
Incorporation: 1er juillet 1855; *Area:* 260,96 km2
Comté ou district: Memphrémagog; *Population au 2016:* 1,852
Circonscription(s) électorale(s) provinciale(s): Orford
Circonscription(s) électorale(s) fédérale(s): Brome-Missisquoi
Prochaines élections: 7e novembre 2021
Jacques Marcoux, Maire
Martin Maltais, Directeur général

Poularies
990, rue Principale
Poularies, QC J0Z 3E0
Tél: 819-782-5159; *Téléc:* 819-782-5063
poularies@mrcao.qc.ca
poularies.ao.ca
Entité municipal: Municipality
Incorporation: 7 mai 1924; *Area:* 170,07 km2
Comté ou district: Abitibi-Ouest; *Population au 2016:* 682
Circonscription(s) électorale(s) provinciale(s): Abitibi-Ouest
Circonscription(s) électorale(s) fédérale(s):
Abitibi-Témiscamingue
Prochaines élections: 7e novembre 2021
Pierre Godbout, Maire
Katy Rivard, Directrice générale

Preissac
6, rue des Rapides
Preissac, QC J0Y 2E0
Tél: 819-732-4938; *Téléc:* 819-732-4909
info@preissac.com
preissac.com
Entité municipal: Municipality
Incorporation: 1er janvier 1979; *Area:* 428,26 km2
Comté ou district: Abitibi; *Population au 2016:* 835
Circonscription(s) électorale(s) provinciale(s): Abitibi-Ouest
Circonscription(s) électorale(s) fédérale(s):
Abitibi-Témiscamingue
Prochaines élections: 7e novembre 2021
Stephan Lavoie, Maire
Gérard Pétrin, Directeur général

La Présentation
772, rue Principale
La Présentation, QC J0H 1B0
Tél: 450-796-2317; *Téléc:* 450-796-1707
secretaire@municipalitelapresentation.qc.ca
www.municipalitelapresentation.qc.ca
Entité municipal: Parish (Paroisse)
Incorporation: 1er juillet 1855; *Area:* 94,40 km2
Comté ou district: Les Maskoutains; *Population au 2016:* 2,540
Circonscription(s) électorale(s) provinciale(s): Saint-Hyacinthe
Circonscription(s) électorale(s) fédérale(s): St-Hyacinthe-Bagot
Prochaines élections: 7e novembre 2021
Claude Roger, Maire
Josiane Marchand, Directrice générale et Secrétaire-trésorière

Price
18, rue Fournier
Price, QC G0J 1Z0
Tél: 418-775-2144; *Téléc:* 418-775-2459
price@mitis.qc.ca
www.municipaliteprice.com
Entité municipal: Village
Incorporation: 3 mars 1926; *Area:* 2,58 km2
Comté ou district: La Mitis; *Population au 2016:* 1,759
Circonscription(s) électorale(s) provinciale(s): Matane-Matapédia
Circonscription(s) électorale(s) fédérale(s): Avignon-La
Mitis-Matane-Matapédia
Prochaines élections: 7e novembre 2021
Bruno Paradis, Maire
Martin Normand, Directeur général, 418-775-2144

Princeville
50, rue St-Jacques ouest
Princeville, QC G6L 4Y5
Tél: 819-364-3333; *Téléc:* 819-364-5198
info@villedeprinceville.qc.ca
villedeprinceville.qc.ca
Entité municipal: Town
Incorporation: 23 février 2000; *Area:* 195,26 km2
Comté ou district: L'Érable; *Population au 2016:* 6,001
Circonscription(s) électorale(s) provinciale(s): Arthabaska
Circonscription(s) électorale(s) fédérale(s): Mégantic-L'Érable
Prochaines élections: 7e novembre 2021
Gilles Fortier, Maire
Olivier Milot, Greffier

Puvirnituq
CP 150
Puvirnituq, QC J0M 1P0
Tél: 819-988-2825; *Téléc:* 819-988-2751
www.nvpuvirnituq.ca
Entité municipal: Northern Village
Incorporation: 2 septembre 1989; *Area:* 86,30 km2
Comté ou district: Administration régionale Kativik; *Population au 2016:* 1,779
Circonscription(s) électorale(s) provinciale(s): Ungava
Circonscription(s) électorale(s) fédérale(s):
Abitibi-Baie-James-Nunavik-Eeyou
Levi Amarualik, Maire
Sarah Beaulne, Secrétaire-trésorière

Quaqtaq
CP 107
Quaqtaq, QC J0M 1J0
Tél: 819-492-9912; *Téléc:* 819-492-9935
www.nvquaqtaq.ca
Entité municipal: Northern Village
Incorporation: 1er novembre 1980; *Area:* 26,41 km2
Comté ou district: Administration régionale Kativik; *Population au 2016:* 403
Circonscription(s) électorale(s) provinciale(s): Ungava
Circonscription(s) électorale(s) fédérale(s):
Abitibi-Baie-James-Nunavik-Eeyou
Robert Deer Sr, Maire
Sammy Tukkiapik, Secrétaire-trésorier

Racine
145, rte 222
Racine, QC J0E 1Y0
Tél: 450-532-2876
reception@racine.ca
municipalite.racine.qc.ca
Entité municipal: Municipality
Incorporation: 15 février 1995; *Area:* 105,82 km2
Comté ou district: Le Val-Saint-François; *Population au 2016:* 1,323
Circonscription(s) électorale(s) provinciale(s): Richmond
Circonscription(s) électorale(s) fédérale(s): Jonquière; Shefford
Prochaines élections: 7e novembre 2021
Christian Massé, Maire
Lyne Gaudreau, Directrice générale

Ragueneau
523, rte 138
Ragueneau, QC G0H 1S0
Tél: 418-567-2345; *Téléc:* 418-567-2344
ragueneau@municipalite.ragueneau.qc.ca
municipalite.ragueneau.qc.ca
Entité municipal: Parish (Paroisse)
Incorporation: 7 mars 1951; *Area:* 185,55 km2
Comté ou district: Manicouagan; *Population au 2016:* 1,343
Circonscription(s) électorale(s) provinciale(s): René-Lévesque
Circonscription(s) électorale(s) fédérale(s): Manicouagan
Prochaines élections: 7e novembre 2021
Joseph Imbeault, Maire
Marie-France Imbeault, Directrice générale, 418-567-2345

Rapide-Danseur
535, rue du Village
Rapide-Danseur, QC J0Z 3G0
Tél: 819-948-2152; *Téléc:* 819-948-2265
rapide-danseur@mrcao.qc.ca
rapide-danseur.ao.ca
Entité municipal: Municipality
Incorporation: 1er janvier 1981; *Area:* 175,56 km2
Comté ou district: Abitibi-Ouest; *Population au 2016:* 328
Circonscription(s) électorale(s) provinciale(s): Abitibi-Ouest
Circonscription(s) électorale(s) fédérale(s):
Abitibi-Témiscamingue
Prochaines élections: 7e novembre 2021
Alain Gagnon, Maire
Lucie Gravel, Directrice générale

Rapides-des-Joachims
48, rue de l'Église
Rapides-des-Joachims, QC J0X 3M0
Tél: 613-586-2532; *Téléc:* 613-586-2720
rapides-des-joachims@mrcpontiac.qc.ca
municipalites-du-quebec/rapides-des-joachims
Entité municipal: Municipality
Incorporation: 1er janvier 1955; *Area:* 242,81 km2
Comté ou district: Pontiac; *Population au 2016:* 156
Circonscription(s) électorale(s) provinciale(s): Pontiac
Circonscription(s) électorale(s) fédérale(s): Pontiac
Prochaines élections: 7e novembre 2021
James Gibson, Maire
Sylvain Bégin, Directeur général

La Rédemption
CP 39
68, rue Soucy
La Rédemption, QC G0J 1P0
Tél: 418-776-5311; *Téléc:* 418-776-5711
redemption@mitis.qc.ca
municipalite.laredemption.qc.ca
Entité municipal: Parish (Paroisse)
Incorporation: 1er janvier 1956; *Area:* 117,17 km2
Comté ou district: La Mitis; *Population au 2016:* 432
Circonscription(s) électorale(s) provinciale(s): Matane-Matapédia
Circonscription(s) électorale(s) fédérale(s): Avignon-La
Mitis-Matane-Matapédia
Prochaines élections: 7e novembre 2021
Sonia Bérubé, Maire
Raphaël Rioux, Directeur général

La Reine
1, 3e av ouest
La Reine, QC J0Z 2L0
Tél: 819-947-5271; *Téléc:* 819-947-5271
lareine@mrcao.qc.ca
lareine.ao.ca
Entité municipal: Municipality
Incorporation: 19 septembre 1981; *Area:* 97,93 km2
Comté ou district: Abitibi-Ouest; *Population au 2016:* 339
Circonscription(s) électorale(s) provinciale(s): Abitibi-Ouest
Circonscription(s) électorale(s) fédérale(s):
Abitibi-Témiscamingue
Prochaines élections: 7e novembre 2021
Jean-Guy Boulet, Maire
Daniel Céleste, Directeur général

Rémigny
1304, ch de l'Église
Rémigny, QC J0Z 3H0
Tél: 819-761-2421; *Téléc:* 819-761-2422
mun.remigny@mrctemiscamingue.qc.ca
www.municipaliteremigny.qc.ca
Entité municipal: Municipality
Incorporation: 1er janvier 1978; *Area:* 896,26 km2
Comté ou district: Témiscamingue; *Population au 2016:* 280
Circonscription(s) électorale(s) provinciale(s):
Rouyn-Noranda-Témiscamingue
Circonscription(s) électorale(s) fédérale(s):
Abitibi-Témiscamingue
Prochaines élections: 7e novembre 2021
Isabelle Coderre, Mairesse
Lorraine McLean, Directrice générale

Richelieu
200, boul Richelieu
Richelieu, QC J3L 3R4
Tél: 450-658-1157; *Téléc:* 450-658-5096
info@ville.richelieu.qc.ca
ville.richelieu.qc.ca
Entité municipal: Town
Incorporation: 15 mars 2000; *Area:* 30,98 km2
Comté ou district: Rouville; Communauté métropolitaine de
Montréal; *Population au 2016:* 5,236
Circonscription(s) électorale(s) provinciale(s): Chambly
Circonscription(s) électorale(s) fédérale(s): Beloeil-Chambly
Prochaines élections: 7e novembre 2021
Jacques Ladouceur, Maire
Roxanne Veilleux, Greffière

Richmond
745, rue Gouin
Richmond, QC J0B 2H0
Tél: 819-826-3789; *Téléc:* 819-826-2813
commis@ville.richmond.qc.ca
www.ville.richmond.qc.ca
Entité municipal: Town
Incorporation: 29 décembre 1999; *Area:* 6,92 km2
Comté ou district: Le Val-Saint-François; *Population au 2016:* 3,232
Circonscription(s) électorale(s) provinciale(s): Richmond
Circonscription(s) électorale(s) fédérale(s):
Richmond-Arthabaska
Prochaines élections: 7e novembre 2021
Bertrand Ménard, Maire
Rémi-Mario Mayette, Directeur général, 819-826-3789

Rigaud
33, St-Jean-Baptiste ouest
Rigaud, QC J0P 1P0
Tél: 450-451-0869; *Téléc:* 450-451-4227
rigaud@ville.rigaud.qc.ca
www.ville.rigaud.qc.ca
Entité municipal: Municipality
Incorporation: 29 novembre 1995; *Area:* 99,23 km2
Comté ou district: Vaudreuil-Soulanges; *Population au 2016:*

7,777
Circonscription(s) électorale(s) provinciale(s): Soulanges
Circonscription(s) électorale(s) fédérale(s): Vaudreuil-Soulanges
Prochaines élections: 7e novembre 2021
Hans Gruenwald Jr., Maire
Camille Primeau, Greffière, 450-451-0869

Rimouski-Neigette
#200, 23, rue de l'Évêché ouest
Rimouski, QC G5L 4H4
Tél: 418-724-5154; *Téléc:* 418-725-4567
administration@mrc-rn.ca
www.mrcrimouskineigette.qc.ca
Entité municipal: Regional County Municipality
Incorporation: 26 mai 1982; *Area:* 2715,17 km2
Population au 2016: 56,650
Note: 9 municipalités & 1 autre territoire.
Francis St-Pierre, Préfet, 418-724-5154
Jean-Maxime Dubé, Directeur général, 418-724-5154

Ripon
#101, 31, rue Coursol
Ripon, QC J0V 1V0
Tél: 819-983-2000; *Téléc:* 819-983-1327
info@ripon.ca
ripon.ca
Entité municipal: Municipality
Incorporation: 3 mai 2000; *Area:* 131,47 km2
Comté ou district: Papineau; *Population au 2016:* 1,542
Circonscription(s) électorale(s) provinciale(s): Papineau
Circonscription(s) électorale(s) fédérale(s): Argenteuil-La Petite-Nation
Prochaines élections: 7e novembre 2021
Luc Desjardins, Maire
Sébastien Gauthier, Directeur général, 819-983-2000

Ristigouche-Partie-Sud-Est
35, ch Kempt
Ristigouche-Sud-Est, QC G0J 1V0
Tél: 418-788-5769
ristigouchesudest@globetrotter.net
ristigouche.ca
Entité municipal: Township
Incorporation: 30 juin 1906; *Area:* 51,70 km2
Comté ou district: Avignon; *Population au 2016:* 171
Circonscription(s) électorale(s) provinciale(s): Bonaventure
Circonscription(s) électorale(s) fédérale(s): Avignon-La Mitis-Matane-Matapédia
Prochaines élections: 7e novembre 2021
François Boulay, Maire
Hervé Esch, Directeur général

Rivière-à-Claude
520, rue Principale est
Rivière-à-Claude, QC G0E 1Z0
Tél: 418-797-2422; *Téléc:* 418-797-2455
munirac@globetrotter.net
Entité municipal: Municipality
Incorporation: 18 décembre 1923; *Area:* 156,28 km2
Comté ou district: La Haute-Gaspésie; *Population au 2016:* 128
Circonscription(s) électorale(s) provinciale(s): Gaspé
Circonscription(s) électorale(s) fédérale(s): Gaspésie—Les Îles-de-la-Madeleine
Prochaines élections: 7e novembre 2021
Réjean Normand, Maire
Roselle Castonguay, Directrice générale

Rivière-à-Pierre
CP 648
830, rue Principale
Rivière-à-Pierre, QC G0A 3A0
Tél: 418-323-2112; *Téléc:* 418-323-2111
admin@riviereapierre.com
riviereapierre.com
Entité municipal: Municipality
Incorporation: 11 octobre 1897; *Area:* 522,47 km2
Comté ou district: Portneuf; *Population au 2016:* 584
Circonscription(s) électorale(s) provinciale(s): Portneuf
Circonscription(s) électorale(s) fédérale(s): Portneuf-Jacques-Cartier
Prochaines élections: 7e novembre 2021
Andrée St-Laurent, Mairesse
Mélanie Vézina, Directrice générale

Rivière-au-Tonnerre
CP 129
472, rue Jacques Cartier
Rivière-au-Tonnerre, QC G0G 2L0
Tél: 418-465-2255; *Téléc:* 418-465-2956
info@riviere-au-tonnerre.ca
riviere-au-tonnerre.ca

Entité municipal: Municipality
Incorporation: 14 décembre 1925; *Area:* 619,24 km2
Comté ou district: Minganie; *Population au 2016:* 279
Circonscription(s) électorale(s) provinciale(s): Duplessis
Circonscription(s) électorale(s) fédérale(s): Manicouagan
Prochaines élections: 7e novembre 2021
Lorenza Beaudin, Mairesse
Josée Poulin, Directrice générale, 418-465-2255

Rivière-Beaudette
663, ch de la Frontière
Rivière-Beaudette, QC J0P 1R0
Tél: 450-269-2931; *Téléc:* 450-269-2815
munrivbeaudette@qc.aira.com
riviere-beaudette.com
Entité municipal: Municipality
Incorporation: 17 janvier 1990; *Area:* 18,68 km2
Comté ou district: Vaudreuil-Soulanges; *Population au 2016:* 2,097
Circonscription(s) électorale(s) provinciale(s): Soulanges
Circonscription(s) électorale(s) fédérale(s): Salaberry-Suroît
Prochaines élections: 7e novembre 2021
Patrick Bousez, Maire
Céline Chayer, Directrice générale, 450-269-2931

Rivière-Bleue
32, rue des Pins est
Rivière-Bleue, QC G0L 2B0
Tél: 418-893-5559; *Téléc:* 418-893-5530
info@riviere-bleue.ca
www.riviere-bleue.ca
Entité municipal: Municipality
Incorporation: 14 juin 1975; *Area:* 173,59 km2
Comté ou district: Témiscouata; *Population au 2016:* 1,230
Circonscription(s) électorale(s) provinciale(s): Rivière-du-Loup-Témiscouata
Circonscription(s) électorale(s) fédérale(s): Rimouski-Neigette-Témiscouata-Les Basques
Prochaines élections: 7e novembre 2021
Claude H. Pelletier, Maire
Claudie Levasseur, Directrice générale, 418-893-5559

Rivière-du-Loup
310, rue St-Pierre
Rivière-du-Loup, QC G5R 3V3
Tél: 418-867-2485; *Téléc:* 418-867-3100
www.riviereduloup.ca
Entité municipal: Regional County Municipality
Incorporation: 1 janvier 1982; *Area:* 1277,15 km2
Population au 2016: 33,958
Note: 13 municipalités.
Michel Lagacé, Préfet
Jocelyn Villeneuve, Directeur générale, 418-867-2485

La Rivière-du-Nord
349, rue Labelle
Saint-Jérôme, QC J7Z 5L2
Tél: 450-436-9321; *Téléc:* 450-436-1977
info@mrcrdn.qc.ca
mrcrdn.qc.ca
Entité municipal: Regional County Municipality
Incorporation: 1er janvier 1983; *Area:* 451,02 km2
Population au 2016: 128,170
Note: 5 municipalités.
Bruno Laroche, Préfet
Roger Hotte, Directeur général

Rivière-Éternité
418, rue Principale
Rivière-Éternité, QC G0V 1P0
Tél: 418-272-2860; *Téléc:* 418-544-3085
municipalite@riviere-eternite.com
riviere-eternite.com
Entité municipal: Municipality
Incorporation: 20 juillet 1974; *Area:* 474,52 km2
Comté ou district: Le Fjord-du-Saguenay; *Population au 2016:* 413
Circonscription(s) électorale(s) provinciale(s): Dubuc
Circonscription(s) électorale(s) fédérale(s): Chicoutimi-Le Fjord
Prochaines élections: 7e novembre 2021
Rémi Gagné, Maire
Sandra Côté, Directrice générale

Rivière-Héva
740, rte St-Paul nord
Rivière-Héva, QC J0Y 2H0
Tél: 819-735-3521; *Téléc:* 819-735-4251
info@mun-r-h.com
www.riviere-heva.com
Entité municipal: Municipality
Incorporation: 1er janvier 1982; *Area:* 426,17 km2
Comté ou district: La Vallée-de-l'Or; *Population au 2016:* 1,419

Circonscription(s) électorale(s) provinciale(s): Abitibi-Est
Circonscription(s) électorale(s) fédérale(s): Abitibi-Baie-James-Nunavik-Eeyou
Prochaines élections: 7e novembre 2021
Réjean Guay, Maire
Nathalie Savard, Directrice générale

Rivière-Ouelle
133, rte 132
Rivière-Ouelle, QC G0L 2C0
Tél: 418-856-3829
info@riviereouelle.ca
riviereouelle.ca
Entité municipal: Municipality
Incorporation: 1er juillet 1855; *Area:* 57,78 km2
Comté ou district: Kamouraska; *Population au 2016:* 970
Circonscription(s) électorale(s) provinciale(s): Côte-du-Sud
Circonscription(s) électorale(s) fédérale(s): Montmagny-L'Islet-Kamouraska-Rivière-du-Loup
Prochaines élections: 7e novembre 2021
Louis-Georges Simard, Maire
Denise Fournier, Directrice générale

Rivière-Rouge
25, rue L'Annonciation sud
Rivière-Rouge, QC J0T 1T0
Tél: 819-275-2929; *Téléc:* 819-275-3676
info@riviere-rouge.ca
www.riviere-rouge.ca
Entité municipal: Town
Incorporation: 18 décembre 2002; *Area:* 455,65 km2
Comté ou district: Antoine-Labelle; *Population au 2016:* 4,322
Circonscription(s) électorale(s) provinciale(s): Labelle
Circonscription(s) électorale(s) fédérale(s): Laurentides-Labelle
Prochaines élections: 7e novembre 2021
Denis Charette, Maire
Katia Morin, Greffière

Rivière-Saint-Jean
434 rue Saint-Jean
Rivière-Saint-Jean, QC G0G 2N0
Tél: 418-949-2464; *Téléc:* 418-949-2489
magpiest-jean@globetrotter.net
municipalites-du-quebec.ca/riviere-st-jean
Entité municipal: Municipality
Incorporation: 1er janvier 1966; *Area:* 522,92 km2
Comté ou district: Minganie; *Population au 2016:* 215
Circonscription(s) électorale(s) provinciale(s): Duplessis
Circonscription(s) électorale(s) fédérale(s): Manicouagan
Prochaines élections: 7e novembre 2021
Josée Brunet, Mairesse
Karine Chouinard, Directrice générale

Robert-Cliche
111A, 107e Rue
Beauceville, QC G5X 2P9
Tél: 418-774-9828; *Téléc:* 418-774-4057
mrcrc@beaucerc.com
www.beaucerc.com
Entité municipal: Regional County Municipality
Incorporation: 1 janvier 1982; *Area:* 840,10 km2
Population au 2016: 19,125
Note: 10 municipalités.
Jonathan Bolduc, Préfet
Jacques Bussières, Directeur général

Rochebaucourt
20, rue du Chanoine-Girard
Rochebaucourt, QC J0Y 2J0
Tél: 819-754-2083; *Téléc:* 819-754-5417
muniroche@cableamos.com
mun-rochebaucourt.ca
Entité municipal: Municipality
Incorporation: 1er janvier 1983; *Area:* 184,95 km2
Comté ou district: Abitibi; *Population au 2016:* 131
Circonscription(s) électorale(s) provinciale(s): Abitibi-Ouest
Circonscription(s) électorale(s) fédérale(s): Abitibi-Témiscamingue
Prochaines élections: 7e novembre 2021
Marc-Antoine Pelletier, Maire
Nathalie Lyrette, Directrice générale

Rocher-Percé
#101, 129, boul René-Lévesque ouest
Chandler, QC G0C 1K0
Tél: 418-689-4313; *Téléc:* 418-689-5807
mrc@rocherperce.qc.ca
www.mrcrocherperce.qc.ca
Other Information: Sans frais: 888-689-3185
Entité municipal: Regional County Municipality
Incorporation: 1 avril 1981; *Area:* 3076,80 km2
Population au 2016: 17,282

Circonscription(s) électorale(s) fédérale(s): Lac-Saint-Jean
Note: 5 municipalités & 1 autre territoire.
Nadia Minassian, Préfete
Christine Roussy, Directrice générale

Roquemaure
15, rue Raymond est
Roquemaure, QC J0Z 3K0
Tél: 819-787-6311; *Téléc:* 819-787-6383
roquemaure@mrcao.qc.ca
roquemaure.ao.ca
Entité municipal: Municipality
Incorporation: 1er janvier 1952; *Area:* 120,86 km2
Comté ou district: Abitibi-Ouest; *Population au 2016:* 395
Circonscription(s) électorale(s) provinciale(s): Abitibi-Ouest
Circonscription(s) électorale(s) fédérale(s):
Abitibi-Témiscamingue
Prochaines élections: 7e novembre 2021
Léo Plourde, Maire
Line Boudreault, Directrice générale, 819-787-6311

Rougemont
61, ch de Marieville
Rougemont, QC J0L 1M0
Tél: 450-469-3790; *Téléc:* 450-469-0309
reception@rougemont.ca
www.rougemont.ca
Entité municipal: Municipality
Incorporation: 26 janvier 2000; *Area:* 43,92 km2
Comté ou district: Rouville; *Population au 2016:* 2,755
Circonscription(s) électorale(s) provinciale(s): Iberville
Circonscription(s) électorale(s) fédérale(s): Shefford
Prochaines élections: 7e novembre 2021
Michel Arseneault, Maire
Kathia Joseph, Directrice générale, 450-469-3790

Roussillon
#200, 260, rue Saint-Pierre
Saint-Constant, QC J5A 2A5
Tél: 450-638-1221; *Téléc:* 450-638-4499
admin@mrcroussillon.qc.ca
roussillon.ca
Entité municipal: Regional County Municipality
Incorporation: 1er janvier 1982; *Area:* 423,82 km2
Population au 2016: 171,443
Note: 11 municipalités.
Christian Ouellet, Préfet
Gilles Marcoux, Directeur générale, 450-638-1221

Rouville
#100, 500 rue Desjardins
Marieville, QC J3M 1E1
Tél: 450-460-2127; *Téléc:* 450-460-7169
info@mrcrouville.qc.ca
mrcrouville.qc.ca
Entité municipal: Regional County Municipality
Incorporation: 1er janvier 1982; *Area:* 483.12 sq km
Population au 2016: 36,536
Note: 8 municipalités.
Jacques Ladouceur, Préfet
Anne-Marie Dion, Directrice générale, 450-460-2127

Roxton
216, rang Ste-Geneviève
Roxton Falls, QC J0H 1E0
Tél: 450-548-2500; *Téléc:* 450-548-2412
info@cantonderoxton.qc.ca
www.cantonderoxton.qc.ca
Entité municipal: Township
Incorporation: 1er juillet 1855; *Area:* 149,00 km2
Comté ou district: Acton; *Population au 2016:* 1,086
Circonscription(s) électorale(s) provinciale(s): Johnson
Circonscription(s) électorale(s) fédérale(s): St-Hyacinthe-Bagot
Prochaines élections: 7e novembre 2021
Stéphane Beauchemin, Maire
Caroline Choquette, Directrice générale

Roxton Falls
26, rue du Marché
Roxton Falls, QC J0H 1E0
Tél: 450-548-5790; *Téléc:* 450-548-5881
roxton@roxtonfalls.ca
roxtonfalls.ca
Entité municipal: Village
Incorporation: 1er janvier 1863; *Area:* 4,93 km2
Comté ou district: Acton; *Population au 2016:* 1,305
Circonscription(s) électorale(s) provinciale(s): Johnson
Circonscription(s) électorale(s) fédérale(s): St-Hyacinthe-Bagot
Prochaines élections: 7e novembre 2021
Jean-Marie Laplante, Maire
Julie Gagné, Directrice générale

Roxton Pond
901, rue St-Jean
Roxton Pond, QC J0E 1Z0
Tél: 450-372-6875; *Téléc:* 450-372-1205
infomun@roxtonpond.ca
www.roxtonpond.ca
Entité municipal: Municipality
Incorporation: 17 décembre 1997; *Area:* 97,78 km2
Comté ou district: La Haute-Yamaska; *Population au 2016:* 3,809
Circonscription(s) électorale(s) provinciale(s): Johnson
Circonscription(s) électorale(s) fédérale(s): Shefford
Prochaines élections: 7e novembre 2021
Pierre Fontaine, Maire
François Giasson, Directeur général

Sacré-Coeur
88, rue Principale nord
Sacré-Coeur, QC G0T 1Y0
Tél: 418-236-4621; *Téléc:* 418-236-9144
info@sacre-coeur.ca
www.sacre-coeur.ca
Entité municipal: Municipality
Incorporation: 30 juin 1976; *Area:* 307,99 km2
Comté ou district: La Haute-Côte-Nord; *Population au 2016:* 1,803
Circonscription(s) électorale(s) provinciale(s): René-Lévesque
Circonscription(s) électorale(s) fédérale(s): Manicouagan; Rimouski-Neigette-Témiscouata-Les Basques
Prochaines élections: 7e novembre 2021
Lise Boulianne, Mairesse
Jeannot Lepage, Directeur général, 418-236-4621

Sacré-Coeur-de-Jésus
4118, rte 112
East Broughton, QC G0N 1G0
Tél: 418-427-3447; *Téléc:* 418-427-4774
info@sacrecoeurdejesus.qc.ca
municipalites-du-quebec.ca/sacre-coeur-de-jesus
Entité municipal: Parish (Paroisse)
Incorporation: 11 décembre 1889; *Area:* 104,64 km2
Comté ou district: Les Appalaches; *Population au 2016:* 521
Circonscription(s) électorale(s) provinciale(s):
Lotbinière-Frontenac
Circonscription(s) électorale(s) fédérale(s): Mégantic-L'Érable
Prochaines élections: 7e novembre 2021
Guy Roy, Maire
Sylvie Mercier, Directrice générale

Saint-Adalbert
15, rue du Collège
Saint-Adalbert, QC G0R 2M0
Tél: 418-356-5271; *Téléc:* 418-356-5271
mstadalb@globetrotter.net
www.saintadalbert.qc.ca
Entité municipal: Municipality
Incorporation: 26 août 1911; *Area:* 217,41 km2
Comté ou district: L'Islet; *Population au 2016:* 510
Circonscription(s) électorale(s) provinciale(s): Côte-du-Sud
Circonscription(s) électorale(s) fédérale(s):
Montmagny-L'Islet-Kamouraska-Rivière-du-Loup
Prochaines élections: 7e novembre 2021
René Laverdière, Maire
Magguy Mathault, Directrice générale

Saint-Adelme
138, rue Principale
Saint-Adelme, QC G0J 2B0
Tél: 418-733-4044; *Téléc:* 418-733-4111
st-adelme@mrcdematane.qc.ca
municipalite.st-adelme.ca
Entité municipal: Parish (Paroisse)
Incorporation: 9 septembre 1933; *Area:* 100,64 km2
Comté ou district: La Matanie; *Population au 2016:* 692
Circonscription(s) électorale(s) provinciale(s): Matane-Matapédia
Circonscription(s) électorale(s) fédérale(s): Avignon-La Mitis-Matane-Matapédia
Prochaines élections: 7e novembre 2021
Jean-Roland Lebrun, Maire
Annick Hudon, Directrice générale

Saint-Adelphe
150, rue Baillargeon
Saint-Adelphe-de-Champlain, QC G0X 2G0
Tél: 418-322-5721; *Téléc:* 418-322-5434
st-adelphe@regionmekinac.com
www.st-adelphe.qc.ca
Entité municipal: Parish (Paroisse)
Incorporation: 19 octobre 1891; *Area:* 137,45 km2
Comté ou district: Mékinac; *Population au 2016:* 922
Circonscription(s) électorale(s) provinciale(s): Laviolette
Circonscription(s) électorale(s) fédérale(s):

Saint-Maurice-Champlain
Prochaines élections: 7e novembre 2021
Paul Labranche, Maire
Daniel Bacon, Directeur général

Saint-Adolphe-d'Howard
1881, ch du Village
Saint-Adolphe-d'Howard, QC J0T 2B0
Tél: 819-327-2044; *Téléc:* 819-327-2282
info@stah.ca
www.stadolphedhoward.qc.ca
Entité municipal: Municipality
Incorporation: 1er janvier 1883; *Area:* 138,18 km2
Comté ou district: Les Pays-d'en-Haut; *Population au 2016:* 3,509
Circonscription(s) électorale(s) provinciale(s): Argenteuil
Circonscription(s) électorale(s) fédérale(s): Argenteuil-La Petite-Nation
Prochaines élections: 7e novembre 2021
Claude Charbonneau, Maire
Sylvain Boulianne, Directeur général par intérim, 819-327-2044

Saint-Adrien
1589, rue Principale
Saint-Adrien, QC J0A 1C0
Tél: 819-828-2872; *Téléc:* 819-828-0442
municipalite@st-adrien.com
www.st-adrien.com
Entité municipal: Municipality
Incorporation: 1er janvier 1879; *Area:* 98,71 km2
Comté ou district: Les Sources; *Population au 2016:* 522
Circonscription(s) électorale(s) provinciale(s): Richmond
Circonscription(s) électorale(s) fédérale(s):
Richmond-Arthabaska
Prochaines élections: 7e novembre 2021
Pierre Therrien, Maire
Maryse Ducharme, Directrice générale

Saint-Adrien-d'Irlande
152, rue Municipale
Saint-Adrien-d'Irlande, QC G0N 1M0
Tél: 418-335-2585; *Téléc:* 418-335-4040
stadriendirlande.ca
Entité municipal: Municipality
Incorporation: 1er janvier 1873; *Area:* 53,19 km2
Comté ou district: Les Appalaches; *Population au 2016:* 399
Circonscription(s) électorale(s) provinciale(s):
Lotbinière-Frontenac
Circonscription(s) électorale(s) fédérale(s): Mégantic-L'Érable
Prochaines élections: 7e novembre 2021
Rock Côté, Maire
Ghislaine Leblanc, Directrice générale

Saint-Agapit
1080, av Bergeron
Saint-Agapit, QC G0S 1Z0
Tél: 418-888-4620; *Téléc:* 418-888-4791
info@st-agapit.qc.ca
st-agapit.qc.ca
Entité municipal: Municipality
Incorporation: 14 avril 1979; *Area:* 65,44 km2
Comté ou district: Lotbinière; *Population au 2016:* 4,280
Circonscription(s) électorale(s) provinciale(s):
Lotbinière-Frontenac
Circonscription(s) électorale(s) fédérale(s): Lévis-Lotbinière
Prochaines élections: 7e novembre 2021
Yves Gingras, Maire
Claude Fortin, Directeur général, 418-888-4620

Saint-Aimé
398, montée Sainte-Victoire
Saint-Aimé, QC J0G 1K0
Tél: 450-788-2737; *Téléc:* 450-788-3337
direction@saintaime.qc.ca
www.saintaime.qc.ca
Entité municipal: Municipality
Incorporation: 1er juillet 1855; *Area:* 60,57 km2
Comté ou district: Pierre-De Saurel; *Population au 2016:* 461
Circonscription(s) électorale(s) provinciale(s): Richelieu
Circonscription(s) électorale(s) fédérale(s):
Bécancour-Nicolet-Saurel
Prochaines élections: 7e novembre 2021
Denis Benoit, Maire
Karine Lussier, Directrice générale

Saint-Aimé-des-Lacs
119, rue Principale
Saint-Aimé-des-Lacs, QC G0T 1S0
Tél: 418-439-2229; *Téléc:* 418-439-1475
info@saintaimedeslacs.ca
www.saintaimedeslacs.ca

Entité municipal: Municipality
Incorporation: 1er janvier 1950; *Area:* 92,00 km2
Comté ou district: Charlevoix-Est; *Population au 2016:* 1,095
Circonscription(s) électorale(s) provincial(s):
Charlevoix-Côte-de-Beaupré
Circonscription(s) électorale(s) fédérale(s):
Beauport—Côte-de-Beaupré—île d'Orléans—Charlevoix
Prochaines élections: 7e novembre 2021
Claire Gagnon, Mairesse
Suzanne Gaudreault, Directrice générale

Saint-Aimé-du-Lac-des-îles
871, ch Diotte
Saint-Aimé-du-Lac-des-îles, QC J0W 1J0
Tél: 819-597-2047; *Téléc:* 819-597-2554
info@saint-aime-du-lac-des-iles.ca
www.saint-aime-du-lac-des-iles.ca
Entité municipal: Municipality
Incorporation: 1er janvier 2006; *Area:* 163,74 km2
Comté ou district: Antoine-Labelle; *Population au 2016:* 790
Circonscription(s) électorale(s) provincial(s): Labelle
Circonscription(s) électorale(s) fédérale(s): Laurentides-Labelle
Prochaines élections: 7e novembre 2021
Luc Diotte, Maire
Gisèle Lépine-Pilotte, Directrice générale, 819-597-2047

Saint-Alban
241 rue Principalee
Saint-Alban, QC G0A 3B0
Tél: 418-268-8026; *Téléc:* 418-268-5073
info@st-alban.qc.ca
st-alban.qc.ca
Entité municipal: Municipality
Incorporation: 31 décembre 1991; *Area:* 149,04 km2
Comté ou district: Portneuf; *Population au 2016:* 1,198
Circonscription(s) électorale(s) provincial(s): Portneuf
Circonscription(s) électorale(s) fédérale(s):
Portneuf-Jacques-Cartier
Prochaines élections: 7e novembre 2021
Deny Lépine, Maire
Vincent Lévesque Dostie, Directeur général

Saint-Albert
1245, rue Principale
Saint-Albert, QC J0A 1E0
Tél: 819-353-3300; *Téléc:* 819-353-3313
reception@munstalbert.ca
www.munstalbert.ca
Entité municipal: Municipality
Incorporation: 1er janvier 1864; *Area:* 69,49 km2
Comté ou district: Arthabaska; *Population au 2016:* 1,601
Circonscription(s) électorale(s) provincial(s):
Drummond-Bois-Francs
Circonscription(s) électorale(s) fédérale(s):
Richmond-Arthabaska
Prochaines élections: 7e novembre 2021
Alain St-Pierre, Maire
Suzanne Crête, Directrice générale

Saint-Alexandre
453, rue St-Denis
Saint-Alexandre, QC J0J 1S0
Tél: 450-346-6641; *Téléc:* 450-346-0538
info@saint-alexandre.ca
www.saint-alexandre.ca
Entité municipal: Municipality
Incorporation: 17 septembre 1988; *Area:* 76,45 km2
Comté ou district: Le Haut-Richelieu; *Population au 2016:* 2,469
Circonscription(s) électorale(s) provincial(s): Iberville
Circonscription(s) électorale(s) fédérale(s): Saint-Jean
Prochaines élections: 7e novembre 2021
Luc Mercier, Maire
Francine Perras, Directrice générale, 450-346-6641

Saint-Alexandre-de-Kamouraska
629, rte 289
Saint-Alexandre-de-Kamouraska, QC G0L 2G0
Tél: 418-495-2440; *Téléc:* 418-495-2659
info@stalexkamouraska.com
www.stalexkamouraska.com
Entité municipal: Municipality
Incorporation: 1er juillet 1855; *Area:* 111,31 km2
Comté ou district: Kamouraska; *Population au 2016:* 2,109
Circonscription(s) électorale(s) provincial(s): Côte-du-Sud
Circonscription(s) électorale(s) fédérale(s):
Montmagny-L'Islet-Kamouraska-Rivière-du-Loup
Prochaines élections: 7e novembre 2021
Anita Ouellet-Castonguay, Mairesse
Armand Comeau, Directeur général

Saint-Alexandre-des-Lacs
17, rue de l'Église
Saint-Alexandre-des-Lacs, QC G0J 2C0
Tél: 418-778-3532; *Téléc:* 418-778-1315
stalexandre@mrcmatapedia.quebec
www.saintalexandredeslacs.com
Entité municipal: Parish (Paroisse)
Incorporation: 1er janvier 1965; *Area:* 90,07 km2
Comté ou district: La Matapédia; *Population au 2016:* 327
Circonscription(s) électorale(s) provinciale(s): Matane-Matapédia
Circonscription(s) électorale(s) fédérale(s): Avignon-La
Mitis-Matane-Matapédia
Prochaines élections: 7e novembre 2021
Nelson Pilote, Maire
Caroline Savoie, Directrice générale

Saint-Alexis
#100, 258, rue Principale
Saint-Alexis, QC J0K 1T0
Tél: 450-839-7277
info@st-alexis.com
st-alexis.com
Entité municipal: Municipality
Incorporation: 19 décembre 2012; *Area:* 43,02 km2
Comté ou district: Montcalm; *Population au 2016:* 1,308
Circonscription(s) électorale(s) provinciale(s): Rousseau
Circonscription(s) électorale(s) fédérale(s): Montcalm;
Avignon-La Mitis-Matane-Matapédia
Prochaines élections: 7e novembre 2021
Robert Perreault, Maire
Chantal Duval, Directeur général, 450-839-7277

Saint-Alexis-de-Matapédia
190, rue Principale
Saint-Alexis-de-Matapédia, QC G0J 2E0
Tél: 418-299-2030
plateau1@globetrotter.qc.ca
matapedialesplateaux.com
Entité municipal: Municipality
Incorporation: 1er juillet 1855; *Area:* 84,09 km2
Comté ou district: Avignon; *Population au 2016:* 500
Circonscription(s) électorale(s) provinciale(s): Bonaventure
Circonscription(s) électorale(s) fédérale(s): Avignon-La
Mitis-Matane-Matapédia
Prochaines élections: 7e novembre 2021
Cynthia Dufour, Maire
Lise Pitre, Directrice générale

Saint-Alexis-des-Monts
101, rue de l'Hôtel-de-Ville
Saint-Alexis-des-Monts, QC J0K 1V0
Tél: 819-265-2046; *Téléc:* 819-265-2481
info@saint-alexis-des-monts.ca
saint-alexis-des-monts.ca
Entité municipal: Parish (Paroisse)
Incorporation: 21 avril 1984; *Area:* 1 048,39 km2
Comté ou district: Maskinongé; *Population au 2016:* 2,981
Circonscription(s) électorale(s) provinciale(s): Maskinongé
Circonscription(s) électorale(s) fédérale(s): Berthier-Maskinongé
Prochaines élections: 7e novembre 2021
Michel Bourassa, Maire
Sylvie Clément, Directrice générale, 819-265-2046

Saint-Alfred
9, rte du Cap
Saint-Alfred, QC G0M 1L0
Tél: 418-774-2068; *Téléc:* 418-774-2068
municipalitestalfred@sogetel.net
www.st-alfred.qc.ca
Entité municipal: Municipality
Incorporation: 1er janvier 1950; *Area:* 43,52 km2
Comté ou district: Robert-Cliche; *Population au 2016:* 492
Circonscription(s) électorale(s) provinciale(s): Beauce-Nord
Circonscription(s) électorale(s) fédérale(s): Beauce
Prochaines élections: 7e novembre 2021
Jean-Roch Veilleux, Maire
Émilie Gagné, Directrice générale

Saint-Alphonse
127, rue Principale est
Saint-Alphonse, QC G0C 2V0
Tél: 418-388-5214; *Téléc:* 418-388-2435
st-alphonsemuni@globetrotter.net
www.st-alphonsegaspesie.com
Entité municipal: Municipality
Incorporation: 9 mai 1902; *Area:* 112,07 km2
Comté ou district: Bonaventure; *Population au 2016:* 699
Circonscription(s) électorale(s) provinciale(s): Bonaventure
Circonscription(s) électorale(s) fédérale(s): Joliette; Shefford;
Gaspésie-îles-de-la-Madeleine
Prochaines élections: 7e novembre 2021
Gérard Porlier, Maire

Reina Goulet, Directrice générale

Saint-Alphonse-de-Granby
360, rue Principale
Saint-Alphonse-de-Granby, QC J0E 2A0
Tél: 450-375-4570; *Téléc:* 450-375-4717
infos@st-alphonse.qc.ca
st-alphonse.qc.ca
Entité municipal: Parish (Paroisse)
Incorporation: 30 décembre 1890; *Area:* 50,14 km2
Comté ou district: La Haute-Yamaska; *Population au 2016:*
3,094
Circonscription(s) électorale(s) provinciale(s): Brome-Missisquoi
Circonscription(s) électorale(s) fédérale(s): Shefford
Prochaines élections: 7e novembre 2021
Marcel Gaudreault, Maire
Annie Lessard, Directrice générale

Saint-Alphonse-Rodriguez
101, rue de la Plage
Saint-Alphonse-Rodriguez, QC J0K 1W0
Tél: 450-883-2264; *Téléc:* 450-883-0833
info@munsar.ca
www.municipalite.saintalphonserodriguez.qc.ca
Entité municipal: Municipality
Incorporation: 1er juillet 1855; *Area:* 97,78 km2
Comté ou district: Matawinie; *Population au 2016:* 3,162
Circonscription(s) électorale(s) provinciale(s): Berthier
Circonscription(s) électorale(s) fédérale(s): Joliette
Prochaines élections: 7e novembre 2021
Isabelle Perreault, Mairesse
Elyse Bellerose, Directrice générale, 450-883-2264

Saint-Ambroise
330, rue Gagnon
Saint-Ambroise, QC G7P 2P9
Tél: 418-672-4765
info@st-ambroise.qc.ca
st-ambroise.qc.ca
Entité municipal: Municipality
Incorporation: 25 septembre 1971; *Area:* 149,83 km2
Comté ou district: Le Fjord-du-Saguenay; *Population au 2016:*
3,781
Circonscription(s) électorale(s) provinciale(s): Dubuc
Circonscription(s) électorale(s) fédérale(s): Jonquière
Prochaines élections: 7e novembre 2021
Monique Gagnon, Mairesse
Carolle Perron, Directrice générale

Saint-Ambroise-de-Kildare
CP 57
850, rue Principale
Kildare, QC J0K 1C0
Tél: 450-755-4782; *Téléc:* 450-755-4784
info@saintambroise.ca
www.saintambroise.ca
Entité municipal: Parish (Paroisse)
Incorporation: 1er juillet 1855; *Area:* 67,72 km2
Comté ou district: Joliette; *Population au 2016:* 3,856
Circonscription(s) électorale(s) provinciale(s): Joliette
Circonscription(s) électorale(s) fédérale(s): Joliette
Prochaines élections: 7e novembre 2021
François Desrochers, Maire
René Charbonneau, Directeur général, 450-755-4782

Saint-Anaclet-de-Lessard
318, rue Principale ouest
Saint-Anaclet, QC G0K 1H0
Tél: 418-723-2816; *Téléc:* 418-723-0436
municipalite@stanaclet.qc.ca
stanaclet.qc.ca
Entité municipal: Parish (Paroisse)
Incorporation: 9 mai 1859; *Area:* 126,77 km2
Comté ou district: Rimouski-Neigette; *Population au 2016:* 3,071
Circonscription(s) électorale(s) provinciale(s): Rimouski
Circonscription(s) électorale(s) fédérale(s):
Rimouski-Neigette-Témiscouata-Les Basques
Prochaines élections: 7e novembre 2021
Francis St-Pierre, Maire
Louise-Anne Belzile, Directrice générale, 418-723-2816

Saint-André
122A, rue Principale
Saint-André-de-Kamouraska, QC G0L 2H0
Tél: 418-493-2085; *Téléc:* 418-493-2373
munand@bellnet.ca
www.standredekamouraska.ca
Entité municipal: Municipality
Incorporation: 14 février 1987; *Area:* 70,65 km2
Comté ou district: Kamouraska; *Population au 2016:* 658
Circonscription(s) électorale(s) provinciale(s): Côte-du-Sud
Circonscription(s) électorale(s) fédérale(s):

Montmagny-L'Islet-Kamouraska-Rivière-du-Loup
Prochaines élections: 7e novembre 2021
Gervais Darisse, Maire
Nathalie Blais, Directrice générale

Saint-André-Avellin
119, rue Principale
Saint-André-Avellin, QC J0V 1W0
Tél: 819-983-2318; *Téléc:* 819-983-2344
info@st-andre-avellin.com
www.ville.st-andre-avellin.qc.ca
Entité municipal: Municipality
Incorporation: 17 décembre 1997; *Area:* 137,99 km2
Comté ou district: Papineau; *Population au 2016:* 3,749
Circonscription(s) électorale(s) provinciale(s): Papineau
Circonscription(s) électorale(s) fédérale(s): Argenteuil-La
Petite-Nation
Prochaines élections: 7e novembre 2021
Jean-René Carrière, Maire
Nathalie Piret, Directrice générale, 819-983-2318

Saint-André-d'Argenteuil
10, rue de la Mairie
Saint-André-d'Argenteuil, QC J0V 1X0
Tél: 450-537-3527; *Téléc:* 450-537-3070
info@stada.ca
stada.ca
Entité municipal: Municipality
Incorporation: 29 décembre 1999; *Area:* 97,80 km2
Comté ou district: Argenteuil; *Population au 2016:* 3,020
Circonscription(s) électorale(s) provinciale(s): Argenteuil
Circonscription(s) électorale(s) fédérale(s): Argenteuil-La
Petite-Nation
Prochaines élections: 7e novembre 2021
Marc-Olivier Labelle, Maire
Benoît Grimard, Directeur général

Saint-André-de-Restigouche
163, rue Principale
Saint-André-de-Restigouche, QC G0J 2G0
Tél: 418-865-2234
m.st.and.restigouche@globetrotter.net
matapedialesplateaux.com
Entité municipal: Municipality
Incorporation: 1er juillet 1855; *Area:* 144,54 km2
Comté ou district: Avignon; *Population au 2016:* 161
Circonscription(s) électorale(s) provinciale(s): Bonaventure
Circonscription(s) électorale(s) fédérale(s): Avignon-La
Mitis-Matane-Matapédia
Prochaines élections: 7e novembre 2021
Doris Deschênes, Mairesse
Johannie Tremblay, Directrice générale

Saint-André-du-Lac-Saint-Jean
11, rue du Collège
Saint-André-du-Lac-Saint-Jean, QC G0W 2K0
Tél: 418-349-8167
municipalite@standredulac.qc.ca
municipalites-du-quebec.ca/st-andre-du-lac-st-jean
Entité municipal: Village
Incorporation: 29 novembre 1969; *Area:* 145,56 km2
Comté ou district: Le Domaine-du-Roy; *Population au 2016:* 467
Circonscription(s) électorale(s) provinciale(s): Roberval
Circonscription(s) électorale(s) fédérale(s): Lac-St-Jean
Prochaines élections: 7e novembre 2021
Gérald Duchesne, Maire
Maude Tremblay, Directrice générale

Saint-Anicet
335, av Jules-Léger
Saint-Anicet, QC J0S 1M0
Tél: 450-264-2555; *Téléc:* 450-264-2395
info@stanicet.com
stanicet.com
Entité municipal: Parish (Paroisse)
Incorporation: 1er juillet 1855; *Area:* 135,33 km2
Comté ou district: Le Haut-Saint-Laurent; *Population au 2016:* 2,626
Circonscription(s) électorale(s) provinciale(s): Huntingdon
Circonscription(s) électorale(s) fédérale(s): Salaberry-Suroît
Prochaines élections: 7e novembre 2021
Gino Moretti, Maire
Denis Lévesque, Directeur général, 450-264-2555

Saint-Anselme
134, rue Principale
Saint-Anselme, QC G0R 2N0
Tél: 418-885-4977; *Téléc:* 418-885-9834
municipalite@st-anselme.ca
www.st-anselme.ca
Entité municipal: Municipality
Incorporation: 7 janvier 1998; *Area:* 74,27 km2

Comté ou district: Bellechasse; *Population au 2016:* 3,938
Circonscription(s) électorale(s) provinciale(s): Bellechasse
Circonscription(s) électorale(s) fédérale(s): Bellechasse-Les
Etchemins-Lévis
Prochaines élections: 7e novembre 2021
Yves Turgeon, Maire
Louis Felteau, Directeur général

Saint-Antoine de l'Isle-aux-Grues
107, ch de la Volière
L'Isle-aux-Grues, QC G0R 1P0
Tél: 418-248-8060; *Téléc:* 418-248-7955
www.isle-aux-grues.com
Entité municipal: Parish (Paroisse)
Incorporation: 1er janvier 1860; *Area:* 25,43 km2
Comté ou district: Montmagny; *Population au 2016:* 144
Circonscription(s) électorale(s) provinciale(s): Côte-du-Sud
Circonscription(s) électorale(s) fédérale(s):
Montmagny-L'Islet-Kamouraska-Rivière-du-Loup
Prochaines élections: 7e novembre 2021
Pierre Gariepy, Maire
Hélène Painchaud, Directrice générale

Saint-Antoine-de-Tilly
CP 10
3870, ch de Tilly
Saint-Antoine-de-Tilly, QC G0S 2C0
Tél: 418-886-2441; *Téléc:* 418-886-2075
info@saintantoinedetilly.com
www.saintantoinedetilly.com
Entité municipal: Municipality
Incorporation: 1er juillet 1855; *Area:* 60,20 km2
Comté ou district: Lotbinière; *Population au 2016:* 1,598
Circonscription(s) électorale(s) provinciale(s):
Lotbinière-Frontenac
Circonscription(s) électorale(s) fédérale(s): Lévis-Lotbinière
Prochaines élections: 7e novembre 2021
Christian Richard, Maire
Diane Laroche, Directrice générale, 418-886-2441

Saint-Antoine-sur-Richelieu
1060, rue des Ormes
Saint-Antoine-sur-Richelieu, QC J0L 1R0
Tél: 450-787-3497; *Téléc:* 450-787-2852
municipalite@sasr.ca
saint-antoine-sur-richelieu.ca
Entité municipal: Municipality
Incorporation: 6 novembre 1982; *Area:* 65,74 km2
Comté ou district: La Vallée-du-Richelieu; *Population au 2016:* 1,694
Circonscription(s) électorale(s) provinciale(s): Borduas
Circonscription(s) électorale(s) fédérale(s): Pierre-Boucher-Les
Patriotes-Verchères
Prochaines élections: 7e novembre 2021
Chantal Denis, Mairesse
Véronique Piché, Directrice générale

Saint-Antonin
261, rue Principale
Saint-Antonin, QC G0L 2J0
Tél: 418-862-1056; *Téléc:* 418-862-3268
reception@st-antonin.ca
www.municipalitedesaintantonin.qc.ca
Entité municipal: Parish (Paroisse)
Incorporation: 30 août 1856; *Area:* 176,09 km2
Comté ou district: Rivière-du-Loup; *Population au 2016:* 4,049
Circonscription(s) électorale(s) provinciale(s):
Rivière-du-Loup-Témiscouata
Circonscription(s) électorale(s) fédérale(s):
Montmagny-L'Islet-Kamouraska-Rivière-du-Loup
Prochaines élections: 7e novembre 2021
Michel Nadeau, Maire, 418-862-1056
Jessie Jessie, Directrice générale, 418-862-1056

Saint-Apollinaire
11, rue Industrielle
Saint-Apollinaire, QC G0S 2E0
Tél: 418-881-3996; *Téléc:* 418-881-4152
municipalite@st-apollinaire.com
www.st-apollinaire.com
Entité municipal: Municipality
Incorporation: 6 avril 1974; *Area:* 96,95 km2
Comté ou district: Lotbinière; *Population au 2016:* 6,110
Circonscription(s) électorale(s) provinciale(s):
Lotbinière-Frontenac
Circonscription(s) électorale(s) fédérale(s): Lévis-Lotbinière
Prochaines élections: 7e novembre 2021
Bernard Ouellet, Maire, 418-881-3996
Martine Couture, Directrice générale, 418-881-3996

Saint-Armand
414, ch Luke
Saint-Armand, QC J0J 1T0
Tél: 450-248-2344; *Téléc:* 450-248-3820
info@municipalite.saint-armand.qc.ca
www.municipalite.saint-armand.qc.ca
Entité municipal: Municipality
Incorporation: 3 février 1999; *Area:* 83,21 km2
Comté ou district: Brome-Missisquoi; *Population au 2016:* 1,205
Circonscription(s) électorale(s) provinciale(s): Brome-Missisquoi
Circonscription(s) électorale(s) fédérale(s): Brome-Missisquoi
Prochaines élections: 7e novembre 2021
Brent Chamberlin, Maire
Michèle Bertrand, Directrice générale, 450-248-2344

Saint-Arsène
63, rue de l'Église
Saint-Arsène, QC G0L 2K0
Tél: 418-867-2205; *Téléc:* 418-867-2025
commisadm@saint-arsene.ca
www.municipalite.saint-arsene.qc.ca
Entité municipal: Parish (Paroisse)
Incorporation: 1er juillet 1855; *Area:* 70,94 km2
Comté ou district: Rivière-du-Loup; *Population au 2016:* 1,230
Circonscription(s) électorale(s) provinciale(s):
Rivière-du-Loup-Témiscouata
Circonscription(s) électorale(s) fédérale(s):
Montmagny-L'Islet-Kamouraska-Rivière-du-Loup
Prochaines élections: 7e novembre 2021
Mario Lebel, Maire
Marc-Antoine Goulet, Directeur général, 418-867-2205

Saint-Athanase
6081, ch de l'Église
Saint-Athanase, QC G0L 2L0
Tél: 418-863-7706; *Téléc:* 418-863-7707
info@saint-athanase.com
www.saint-athanase.com
Entité municipal: Municipality
Incorporation: 1er janvier 1955; *Area:* 292,89 km2
Comté ou district: Témiscouata; *Population au 2016:* 317
Circonscription(s) électorale(s) provinciale(s):
Rivière-du-Loup-Témiscouata
Circonscription(s) électorale(s) fédérale(s):
Rimouski-Neigette-Témiscouata-Les Basques
Prochaines élections: 7e novembre 2021
André St-Pierre, Maire
Marc Leblanc, Directeur général

Saint-Aubert
14, rue des Loisirs
Saint-Aubert, QC G0R 2R0
Tél: 418-598-3368; *Téléc:* 418-598-3369
administration@saint-aubert.net
saint-aubert.net
Entité municipal: Municipality
Incorporation: 1er juillet 1857; *Area:* 98,59 km2
Comté ou district: L'Islet; *Population au 2016:* 1,474
Circonscription(s) électorale(s) provinciale(s): Côte-du-Sud
Circonscription(s) électorale(s) fédérale(s):
Montmagny-L'Islet-Kamouraska-Rivière-du-Loup
Prochaines élections: 7e novembre 2021
Ghislain Deschenes, Maire
Gilles Piché, Directeur général

Saint-Augustin
CP 279
Saint-Augustin, QC G0G 2R0
Tél: 418-947-2404; *Téléc:* 418-947-2533
www.saintaugustin.ca
Entité municipal: Municipality
Incorporation: 1er janvier 1993; *Area:* 1 252,77 km2
Comté ou district: Le Golfe-du-Saint-Laurent; *Population au 2016:* 445
Circonscription(s) électorale(s) provinciale(s): Duplessis
Circonscription(s) électorale(s) fédérale(s): Lac-Saint-Jean;
Manicouagan; Mirabel
Prochaines élections: 7e novembre 2021
Driscoll Martin Gladys, Maire
Corain Driscoll, Directrice générale

Saint-Augustin
686, rue Principale
Saint-Augustin, QC G0W 1K0
Tél: 418-374-2147
comptabilite@staugustinlacstjean.ca
staugustinlacstjean.ca
Entité municipal: Parish (Paroisse)
Incorporation: 14 mai 1925; *Area:* 104,56 km2
Comté ou district: Maria-Chapdelaine; *Population au 2016:* 351
Circonscription(s) électorale(s) provinciale(s): Roberval

Circonscription(s) électorale(s) fédérale(s): Lac-St-Jean
Prochaines élections: 7e novembre 2021
Philippe Lapointe, Maire
Nathalie Meunier, Directrice générale par intérim, 418-374-2147

Saint-Augustin-de-Woburn
590, rue St-Augustin
Woburn, QC G0Y 1R0
Tél: 819-544-4211; *Téléc:* 819-544-9236
adm.woburn@axion.ca
www.saintaugustindewoburn.com
Entité municipal: Parish (Paroisse)
Incorporation: 13 janvier 1900; *Area:* 281,40 km2
Comté ou district: Le Granit; *Population au 2016:* 692
Circonscription(s) électorale(s) provinciale(s): Mégantic
Circonscription(s) électorale(s) fédérale(s): Mégantic-L'Érable
Prochaines élections: 7e novembre 2021
Guy Brousseau, Maire
Gaétane Allard, Directrice générale

Saint-Barnabé
70, rue Duguay
Saint-Barnabé, QC G0X 2K0
Tél: 819-264-2085; *Téléc:* 819-264-2079
reception@saint-barnabe.ca
www.saint-barnabe.ca
Entité municipal: Parish (Paroisse)
Incorporation: 1er juillet 1855; *Area:* 58,83 km2
Comté ou district: Maskinongé; *Population au 2016:* 1,196
Circonscription(s) électorale(s) provinciale(s): Maskinongé
Circonscription(s) électorale(s) fédérale(s): Berthier-Maskinongé
Prochaines élections: 7e novembre 2021
Michel Lemay, Maire
Martin Beaudry, Directeur général

Saint-Barnabé-Sud
251, rang de Michaudville
Saint-Barnabé-Sud, QC J0H 1G0
Tél: 450-792-3030; *Téléc:* 450-792-3759
info@saintbarnabesud.ca
saintbarnabesud.ca
Entité municipal: Municipality
Incorporation: 1er juillet 1855; *Area:* 57,22 km2
Comté ou district: Les Maskoutains; *Population au 2016:* 861
Circonscription(s) électorale(s) provinciale(s): St-Hyacinthe
Circonscription(s) électorale(s) fédérale(s): St-Hyacinthe-Bagot
Prochaines élections: 7e novembre 2021
Alain Jobin, Maire
Linda Normandeau, Directrice générale

Saint-Barthélemy
1980, rue Bonin
Saint-Barthélémy, QC J0K 1X0
Tél: 450-885-3511; *Téléc:* 450-836-5220
municipalite@saint-barthelemy.ca
www.saint-barthelemy.ca
Entité municipal: Parish (Paroisse)
Incorporation: 1er juillet 1855; *Area:* 105.70 km2
Comté ou district: D'Autray; *Population au 2016:* 1,934
Circonscription(s) électorale(s) provinciale(s): Berthier
Circonscription(s) électorale(s) fédérale(s): Berthier-Maskinongé
Prochaines élections: 7e novembre 2021
Robert Sylvestre, Maire
Julie Maurice, Directrice générale, 450-885-3511

Saint-Basile
20, rue St-Georges
Saint-Basile, QC G0A 3G0
Tél: 418-329-2204; *Téléc:* 418-329-2788
info@saintbasile.qc.ca
saintbasile.qc.ca
Entité municipal: Town
Incorporation: 1er mars 2000; *Area:* 98,84 km2
Comté ou district: Portneuf; *Population au 2016:* 2,631
Circonscription(s) électorale(s) provinciale(s): Portneuf
Circonscription(s) électorale(s) fédérale(s):
Portneuf-Jacques-Cartier
Prochaines élections: 7e novembre 2021
Guillaume Vézina, Maire
Jean Richard, Directeur général

Saint-Benjamin
CP 100
440, av du Collège
Saint-Benjamin, QC G0M 1N0
Tél: 418-594-8156
munstbenjamin@aclcable.ca
www.st-benjamin.qc.ca
Entité municipal: Municipality
Incorporation: 9 janvier 1897; *Area:* 111,57 km2
Comté ou district: Les Etchemins; *Population au 2016:* 987
Circonscription(s) électorale(s) provinciale(s): Beauce-Sud

Circonscription(s) électorale(s) fédérale(s): Beauce
Prochaines élections: 7e novembre 2021
Martine Boulet, Mairesse
Isabelle Beaudoin, Directrice générale

Saint-Benoît-du-Lac
1, rue Principale
Saint-Benoît-du-Lac, QC J0B 2M0
Tél: 819-843-4080; *Téléc:* 819-843-0256
municipalite@stbenoitdulac.com
www.abbaye.ca
Entité municipal: Municipality
Incorporation: 16 mars 1939; *Area:* 2,18 km2
Comté ou district: Memphrémagog; *Population au 2016:* 32
Circonscription(s) électorale(s) provinciale(s): Orford
Circonscription(s) électorale(s) fédérale(s): Brome-Missisquoi
Prochaines élections: 7e novembre 2021
André Laberge, Administrateur
Patrick Flageole, Directeur général

Saint-Benoît-Labre
216, rte 271
Saint-Benoît-Labre, QC G0M 1P0
Tél: 418-228-9250; *Téléc:* 418-228-0518
info@saintbenoitlabre.com
saintbenoitlabre.qc.ca
Entité municipal: Municipality
Incorporation: 4 janvier 1894; *Area:* 85,64 km2
Comté ou district: Beauce-Sartigan; *Population au 2016:* 1,630
Circonscription(s) électorale(s) provinciale(s): Beauce-Sud
Circonscription(s) électorale(s) fédérale(s): Beauce
Prochaines élections: 7e novembre 2021
Éric Rouillard, Maire
Édith Quirion, Directrice générale, 418-228-9250

Saint-Bernard
CP 70
1512, rue St-Georges
Saint-Bernard, QC G0S 2G0
Tél: 418-475-6060; *Téléc:* 418-475-6069
info@saint-bernard.quebec
municipalite-saint-bernard.com
Entité municipal: Municipality
Incorporation: 9 mai 1987; *Area:* 90,15 km2
Comté ou district: La Nouvelle-Beauce; *Population au 2016:* 2,321
Circonscription(s) électorale(s) provinciale(s): Beauce-Nord
Circonscription(s) électorale(s) fédérale(s): Beauce
Prochaines élections: 7e novembre 2021
André Gagnon, Maire
Marie-Eve Parent, Directrice générale

Saint-Bernard-de-Lacolle
116, rang St-Claude
Saint-Bernard-de-Lacolle, QC J0J 1V0
Tél: 450-246-3348; *Téléc:* 450-246-4380
info@mun-sbdl.ca
www.municipalite-de-saint-bernard-de-lacolle.ca
Entité municipal: Parish (Paroisse)
Incorporation: 1er juillet 1855; *Area:* 113,52 km2
Comté ou district: Les Jardins-de-Napierville; *Population au 2016:* 1,549
Circonscription(s) électorale(s) provinciale(s): Huntingdon
Circonscription(s) électorale(s) fédérale(s): Châteauguay-Lacolle
Prochaines élections: 7e novembre 2021
Robert Duteau, Maire
Jocelyne Blanchet, Directrice générale

Saint-Bernard-de-Michaudville
390, rue Principale
Saint-Bernard-de-Michaudville, QC J0H 1C0
Tél: 450-792-3190; *Téléc:* 450-792-3591
saintbernarddemichaudville.qc.ca
Entité municipal: Municipality
Incorporation: 31 août 1908; *Area:* 66,05 km2
Comté ou district: Les Maskoutains; *Population au 2016:* 586
Circonscription(s) électorale(s) provinciale(s): Richelieu
Circonscription(s) électorale(s) fédérale(s): St-Hyacinthe-Bagot
Prochaines élections: 7e novembre 2021
Francine Morin, Mairesse
Émilie Petitclerc, Directrice générale, 450-792-3190

Saint-Blaise-sur-Richelieu
795, rue des Loisirs
Saint-Blaise-sur-Richelieu, QC J0J 1W0
Tél: 450-291-5944; *Téléc:* 450-291-3832
info@st-blaise.ca
www.st-blaise.ca
Entité municipal: Municipality
Incorporation: 20 juin 1892; *Area:* 69,64 km2
Comté ou district: Le Haut-Richelieu; *Population au 2016:* 2,066
Circonscription(s) électorale(s) provinciale(s): Saint-Jean

Circonscription(s) électorale(s) fédérale(s): Saint-Jean
Prochaines élections: 7e novembre 2021
Jacques Desmarais, Maire
Sophie Loubert, Directrice générale

Saint-Bonaventure
1155, rue Principale
Saint-Bonaventure, QC J0C 1C0
Tél: 819-396-2335
info@saint-bonaventure.ca
www.saint-bonaventure.ca
Entité municipal: Municipality
Incorporation: 1er janvier 1867; *Area:* 78,81 km2
Comté ou district: Drummond; *Population au 2016:* 1,031
Circonscription(s) électorale(s) provinciale(s): Nicolet-Bécancour
Circonscription(s) électorale(s) fédérale(s): Drummond;
Louis-Saint-Laurent
Prochaines élections: 7e novembre 2021
Guy Lavoie, Maire
Jessy Grenier, Directrice générale

Saint-Boniface
140, rue Guimont
Saint-Boniface, QC G0X 2L0
Tél: 819-535-3811; *Téléc:* 819-535-1242
info@ville.saint-boniface.ca
municipalitesaint-boniface.ca
Entité municipal: Municipality
Incorporation: 1er janvier 1962; *Area:* 108,54 km2
Comté ou district: Maskinongé; *Population au 2016:* 4,832
Circonscription(s) électorale(s) provinciale(s): St-Maurice
Circonscription(s) électorale(s) fédérale(s): Berthier-Maskinongé
Prochaines élections: 7e novembre 2021
Pierre Desaulniers, Maire
Julie Galarneau, Directrice générale

Saint-Bruno
563, av St-Alphonse
Saint-Bruno, QC G0W 2L0
Tél: 418-343-2303; *Téléc:* 418-343-2662
info@ville.saint-bruno.qc.ca
www.ville.saint-bruno.qc.ca
Entité municipal: Municipality
Incorporation: 12 juillet 1975; *Area:* 78,07 km2
Comté ou district: Lac-Saint-Jean-Est; *Population au 2016:* 2,801
Circonscription(s) électorale(s) provinciale(s): Lac-St-Jean
Circonscription(s) électorale(s) fédérale(s): Lac-St-Jean;
Chicoutimi-Le Fjord; Montarville
Prochaines élections: 7e novembre 2021
François Claveau, Maire
Rachel Bourget, Directeur général, 418-343-2303

Saint-Bruno-de-Guigues
6, rue Principale sud
Saint-Bruno-de-Guigues, QC J0Z 2G0
Tél: 819-728-2186
www.guigues.ca
Entité municipal: Municipality
Incorporation: 3 octobre 1912; *Area:* 125,70 km2
Comté ou district: Témiscamingue; *Population au 2016:* 1,154
Circonscription(s) électorale(s) provinciale(s):
Rouyn-Noranda-Témiscamingue
Circonscription(s) électorale(s) fédérale(s):
Abitibi-Témiscamingue
Prochaines élections: 7e novembre 2021
Carmen Côté, Mairesse
Serge Côté, Directeur général

Saint-Bruno-de-Kamouraska
CP 10
4, rue du Couvent
Saint-Bruno-de-Kamouraska, QC G0L 2M0
Tél: 418-492-2612; *Téléc:* 418-492-9076
www.stbrunokamouraska.ca
Entité municipal: Municipality
Incorporation: 1er janvier 1887; *Area:* 188,96 km2
Comté ou district: Kamouraska; *Population au 2016:* 541
Circonscription(s) électorale(s) provinciale(s): Côte-du-Sud
Circonscription(s) électorale(s) fédérale(s):
Montmagny-L'Islet-Kamouraska-Rivière-du-Loup
Prochaines élections: 7e novembre 2021
Richard Caron, Maire
Maryse Ouellet, Directrice générale

Saint-Calixte
6230, rue de l'Hôtel-de-Ville
Saint-Calixte, QC J0K 1Z0
Tél: 450-222-2782; *Téléc:* 450-222-2789
reception@mscalixte.qc.ca
saint-calixte.ca

Entité municipal: Municipality
Incorporation: 1er juillet 1855; *Area:* 143,63 km2
Comté ou district: Montcalm; *Population au 2016:* 6,046
Circonscription(s) électorale(s) provinciale(s): Rousseau
Circonscription(s) électorale(s) fédérale(s): Montcalm
Prochaines élections: 7e novembre 2021
Michel Jasmin, Maire
Mathieu-Charles Leblanc, Directeur général

Saint-Camille
85, rue Desrivières
Saint-Camille, QC J0A 1G0
Tél: 819-828-3222; *Téléc:* 819-828-3723
saint-camille.ca
Other Information: info@saint-camille.ca
Entité municipal: Township
Incorporation: 1er janvier 1860; *Area:* 83,09 km2
Comté ou district: Les Sources; *Population au 2016:* 529
Circonscription(s) électorale(s) provinciale(s): Richmond
Circonscription(s) électorale(s) fédérale(s):
Richmond-Arthabaska
Prochaines élections: 7e novembre 2021
Philippe Pagé, Maire
Julie Vaillancourt, Directrice générale, 819-828-3222

Saint-Camille-de-Lellis
217, rue Principale
Saint-Camille-de-Lellis, QC G0R 2S0
Tél: 418-595-2233; *Téléc:* 418-595-2238
www.saint-camille.net
Entité municipal: Parish (Paroisse)
Incorporation: 11 janvier 1904; *Area:* 251,92 km2
Comté ou district: Les Etchemins; *Population au 2016:* 752
Circonscription(s) électorale(s) provinciale(s): Bellechasse
Circonscription(s) électorale(s) fédérale(s): Bellechasse-Les
Etchemins-Lévis
Prochaines élections: 7e novembre 2021
Adélard Couture, Maire
Nicole Mathieu, Directrice générale, 418-595-2233

Saint-Casimir
CP 220
220, boul de la Montagne
Saint-Casimir, QC G0A 3L0
Tél: 418-339-2543; *Téléc:* 418-339-3105
info@saint-casimir.com
www.saint-casimir.com
Entité municipal: Municipality
Incorporation: 21 juin 2000; *Area:* 66,55 km2
Comté ou district: Portneuf; *Population au 2016:* 1,430
Circonscription(s) électorale(s) provinciale(s): Portneuf
Circonscription(s) électorale(s) fédérale(s): Portneuf-Jacques
Cartier
Prochaines élections: 7e novembre 2021
Dominic Tessier Perry, Maire
René Savard, Directeur général

Saint-Célestin
510, rue Marquis
Saint-Célestin, QC J0C 1G0
Tél: 819-229-3745; *Téléc:* 819-229-1386
info@saint-celestin.net
municipalites-du-quebec.ca/st-celestin
Entité municipal: Municipality
Incorporation: 1er juillet 1864; *Area:* 77,13 km2
Comté ou district: Nicolet-Yamaska; *Population au 2016:* 575
Circonscription(s) électorale(s) provinciale(s): Nicolet-Bécancour
Circonscription(s) électorale(s) fédérale(s):
Bécancour-Nicolet-Saurel
Prochaines élections: 7e novembre 2021
Michaël Bergeron, Maire
Gisèle Plourde, Directrice générale

Saint-Célestin
510, rue Marquis
Saint-Célestin, QC J0C 1G0
Tél: 819-229-3642; *Téléc:* 819-229-1149
info@village-st-celestin.net
village-st-celestin.net
Entité municipal: Village
Incorporation: 25 novembre 1896; *Area:* 1,41 km2
Comté ou district: Nicolet-Yamaska; *Population au 2016:* 831
Circonscription(s) électorale(s) provinciale(s): Nicolet-Bécancour
Circonscription(s) électorale(s) fédérale(s): Bécancour-Nicolet-Saurel
Prochaines élections: 7e novembre 2021
Raymond Noël, Maire
Pascale Lamoureux, Directrice générale

Saint-Césaire
1111, av St-Paul
Saint-Césaire, QC J0L 1T0
Tél: 450-469-3108
administration@ville.saint-cesaire.qc.ca
www.ville.saint-cesaire.qc.ca
Entité municipal: Town
Incorporation: 26 janvier 2000; *Area:* 83,20 km2
Comté ou district: Rouville; *Population au 2016:* 5,877
Circonscription(s) électorale(s) provinciale(s): Iberville
Circonscription(s) électorale(s) fédérale(s): Shefford
Prochaines élections: 7e novembre 2021
Guy Benjamin, Maire
Isabelle François, Directrice générale et greffière, 450-469-3108

Saint-Charles-de-Bellechasse
2815, av Royale
Saint-Charles-de-Bellechasse, QC G0R 2T0
Tél: 418-887-6600; *Téléc:* 418-887-6779
info@saint-charles.ca
www.saint-charles.ca
Entité municipal: Municipality
Incorporation: 22 décembre 1993; *Area:* 93,34 km2
Comté ou district: Bellechasse; *Population au 2016:* 2,396
Circonscription(s) électorale(s) provinciale(s): Bellechasse
Circonscription(s) électorale(s) fédérale(s): Bellechasse-Les
Etchemins-Lévis
Prochaines élections: 7e novembre 2021
Martin Lacasse, Maire
Jean-François Comeau, Directeur général

Saint-Charles-de-Bourget
357, 2e rang
Saint-Charles-de-Bourget, QC G0V 1G0
Tél: 418-672-2624; *Téléc:* 418-673-2118
info@stcharlesdebourget.ca
www.stcharlesdebourget.ca
Entité municipal: Municipality
Incorporation: 29 septembre 1885; *Area:* 62,03 km2
Comté ou district: Le Fjord-du-Saguenay; *Population au 2016:*
736
Circonscription(s) électorale(s) provinciale(s): Dubuc
Circonscription(s) électorale(s) fédérale(s): Jonquière
Prochaines élections: 7e novembre 2021
Bernard St-Gelais, Maire
Audrey Thibeault, Directrice générale, 418-672-2624

Saint-Charles-Garnier
38, rue Principale
Saint-Charles-Garnier, QC G0K 1K0
Tél: 418-798-4305; *Téléc:* 418-798-4499
stcharles@mitis.qc.ca
www.municipalite.saint-charles-garnier.qc.ca
Entité municipal: Parish (Paroisse)
Incorporation: 1er janvier 1966; *Area:* 84,77 km2
Comté ou district: La Mitis; *Population au 2016:* 240
Circonscription(s) électorale(s) provinciale(s): Matane-Matapédia
Circonscription(s) électorale(s) fédérale(s): Avignon-La
Mitis-Matane-Matapédia
Prochaines élections: 7e novembre 2021
Jean-Pierre Bélanger, Maire
Frédérick Lee, Directeur général et secrétaire-trésorier

Saint-Charles-sur-Richelieu
405, ch des Patriotes
Saint-Charles-sur-Richelieu, QC J0H 2G0
Tél: 450-584-3484
info@saint-charles-sur-richelieu.ca
saint-charles-sur-richelieu.ca
Entité municipal: Municipality
Incorporation: 22 mars 1995; *Area:* 65,00 km2
Comté ou district: La Vallée-du-Richelieu; *Population au 2016:*
1,717
Circonscription(s) électorale(s) provinciale(s): Borduas
Circonscription(s) électorale(s) fédérale(s): Pierre-Boucher-Les
Patriotes-Verchères
Prochaines élections: 7e novembre 2021
Marc Lavigne, Maire, 514-973-9512
Vacant, Directrice générale

Saint-Christophe-d'Arthabaska
418, av Pie-X
Saint-Christophe-d'Arthabaska, QC G6R 0M9
Tél: 819-357-9031
www.saint-christophe-darthabaska.ca
Entité municipal: Parish (Paroisse)
Incorporation: 1er juillet 1855; *Area:* 69,00 km2
Comté ou district: Arthabaska; *Population au 2016:* 3,021
Circonscription(s) électorale(s) provinciale(s): Arthabaska
Circonscription(s) électorale(s) fédérale(s):
Richmond-Arthabaska
Prochaines élections: 7e novembre 2021

Michel Larochelle, Maire
Katherine Beaudoin, Directrice générale

Saint-Chrysostome
624, rue Notre-Dame, 2e étage
Saint-Chrysostome, QC J0S 1R0
Tél: 450-826-3911; *Téléc:* 450-826-0568
www.mun-sc.ca
Entité municipal: Municipality
Incorporation: 29 septembre 1999; *Area:* 100.40 km2
Comté ou district: Le Haut-Saint-Laurent; *Population au 2016:*
2,645
Circonscription(s) électorale(s) provinciale(s): Huntingdon
Circonscription(s) électorale(s) fédérale(s): Salaberry-Suroît
Prochaines élections: 7e novembre 2021
Gilles Dagenais, Maire
Manuel Bouthillette, Directeur général

Saint-Claude
295, rte de l'Église
Saint-Claude, QC J0B 2N0
Tél: 819-845-7795; *Téléc:* 819-845-2479
www.municipalite.st-claude.ca
Entité municipal: Municipality
Incorporation: 15 novembre 1912; *Area:* 119,08 km2
Comté ou district: Le Val-Saint-François; *Population au 2016:*
1,185
Circonscription(s) électorale(s) provinciale(s): Richmond
Circonscription(s) électorale(s) fédérale(s):
Richmond-Arthabaska
Prochaines élections: 7e novembre 2021
Hervé Provencher, Maire
France Lavertu, Directrice générale, 819-845-7795

Saint-Clément
25A, rue St-Pierre
Saint-Clément, QC G0L 2N0
Tél: 418-963-2258; *Téléc:* 418-963-2619
www.st-clement.ca
Entité municipal: Municipality
Incorporation: 1er janvier 1885; *Area:* 86,84 km2
Comté ou district: Les Basques; *Population au 2016:* 460
Circonscription(s) électorale(s) provinciale(s):
Rivière-du-Loup-Témiscouata
Circonscription(s) électorale(s) fédérale(s):
Rimouski-Neigette-Témiscouata-Les Basques
Prochaines élections: 7e novembre 2021
Éric Blanchard, Maire
Line Caron, Directrice générale

Saint-Cléophas
356, rue Principale
Saint-Cléophas, QC G0J 3N0
Tél: 418-536-3023; *Téléc:* 418-536-1349
stcleophas@mrcmatapedia.quebec
www.stcleophas.com
Entité municipal: Parish (Paroisse)
Incorporation: 19 mai 1921; *Area:* 97,44 km2
Comté ou district: La Matapédia; *Population au 2016:* 333
Circonscription(s) électorale(s) provinciale(s): Matane-Matapédia
Circonscription(s) électorale(s) fédérale(s): Avignon-La
Mitis-Matane-Matapédia
Prochaines élections: 7e novembre 2021
Jean-Paul Bélanger, Maire
Katie St-Pierre, Directrice générale

Saint-Cléophas-de-Brandon
750, rue Principale
Saint-Cléophas-de-Brandon, QC J0K 2A0
Tél: 450-889-5683
www.st-cleophas.qc.ca
Entité municipal: Municipality
Incorporation: 7 octobre 1897; *Area:* 15,34 km2
Comté ou district: D'Autray; *Population au 2016:* 227
Circonscription(s) électorale(s) provinciale(s): Berthier
Circonscription(s) électorale(s) fédérale(s): Berthier-Maskinongé
Prochaines élections: 7e novembre 2021
Denis Gamelin, Maire
Francine Rainville, Directrice générale

Saint-Clet
4, rue du Moulin
Saint-Clet, QC J0P 1S0
Tél: 450-456-3363
st-clet@videotron.ca
www.st-clet.com
Entité municipal: Municipality
Incorporation: 31 août 1974; *Area:* 39,32 km2
Comté ou district: Vaudreuil-Soulanges; *Population au 2016:*
1,779
Circonscription(s) électorale(s) provinciale(s): Soulanges

Circonscription(s) électorale(s) fédérale(s): Salaberry-Suroît
Prochaines élections: 7e novembre 2021
Daniel Beaupré, Maire
Nathalie Pharand, Directrice générale

Saint-Côme
1673, 55e rue
Saint-Côme, QC J0K 2B0
Tél: 450-883-2726; *Téléc:* 450-883-6431
info@stcomelanaudiere.ca
www.stcomelanaudiere.ca
Entité municipal: Municipality
Incorporation: 1er janvier 1873; *Area:* 165,18 km2
Comté ou district: Matawinie; *Population au 2016:* 2,193
Circonscription(s) électorale(s) provinciale(s): Berthier
Circonscription(s) électorale(s) fédérale(s): Joliette
Prochaines élections: 7e novembre 2021
Martin Bordeleau, Maire
Marie-Claude Couture, Directrice générale

Saint-Côme—Linière
1408, rue Principale
Saint-Côme—Linière, QC G0M 1J0
Tél: 418-685-3825; *Téléc:* 418-685-2566
info@stcomeliniere.com
www.stcomeliniere.com
Entité municipal: Municipality
Incorporation: 13 avril 1994; *Area:* 150,67 km2
Comté ou district: Beauce-Sartigan; *Population au 2016:* 3,239
Circonscription(s) électorale(s) provinciale(s): Beauce-Sud
Circonscription(s) électorale(s) fédérale(s): Beauce
Prochaines élections: 7e novembre 2021
Yvon Paquet, Maire
Maryane Bélanger, Directeur général

Saint-Cuthbert
1891, rue Principale
Saint-Cuthbert, QC J0K 2C0
Tél: 450-836-4852; *Téléc:* 450-836-4833
st-cuthbert.qc.ca
Entité municipal: Municipality
Incorporation: 7 janvier 1998; *Area:* 132,28 km2
Comté ou district: D'Autray; *Population au 2016:* 1,862
Circonscription(s) électorale(s) provinciale(s): Berthier
Circonscription(s) électorale(s) fédérale(s): Berthier-Maskinongé
Prochaines élections: 7e novembre 2021
Bruno Vadnais, Maire
Larry Drapeau, Directeur général

Saint-Cyprien
Complexe Sportif Louis-Santerre
101B, rue Collin
Saint-Cyprien, QC G0L 2P0
Tél: 418-963-2730; *Téléc:* 418-963-3490
reception@saintcyprien.ca
www.saintcyprien.ca
Entité municipal: Municipality
Incorporation: 1er janvier 1883; *Area:* 138,16 km2
Comté ou district: Rivière-du-Loup; *Population au 2016:* 1,066
Circonscription(s) électorale(s) provinciale(s):
Rivière-du-Loup-Témiscouata
Circonscription(s) électorale(s) fédérale(s):
Montmagny-L'Islet-Kamouraska-Rivière-du-Loup;
Bellechasse-Les Etchemins-Lévis
Prochaines élections: 7e novembre 2021
Michel Lagacé, Maire
Frédéric d'Andrieu, Directeur général, 418-963-2730

Saint-Cyprien
512, rte de l'Église
Saint-Cyprien-des-Etchemins, QC G0R 1B0
Tél: 418-383-5274; *Téléc:* 418-383-5269
corpmun@sogetel.net
www.st-cyprien.qc.ca
Entité municipal: Parish (Paroisse)
Incorporation: 22 février 1918; *Area:* 93,52 km2
Comté ou district: Les Etchemins; *Population au 2016:* 490
Circonscription(s) électorale(s) provinciale(s): Bellechasse
Circonscription(s) électorale(s) fédérale(s): Bellechasse-Les
Etchemins-Lévis
Prochaines élections: 7e novembre 2021
Rejean Bédard, Maire
Sonia Baillargeon, Directrice générale

Saint-Cyprien-de-Napierville
121, rang Cyr
Saint-Cyprien-de-Napierville, QC J0J 1L0
Tél: 450-245-3658; *Téléc:* 450-987-0165
info@st-cypriendenapierville.ca
www.st-cypriendenapierville.ca
Entité municipal: Municipality
Incorporation: 1er juillet 1855; *Area:* 97,45 km2

Comté ou district: Les Jardins-de-Napierville; *Population au 2016:* 1,927
Circonscription(s) électorale(s) provinciale(s): Huntingdon
Circonscription(s) électorale(s) fédérale(s): Châteauguay-Lacolle
Prochaines élections: 7e novembre 2021
Jean Cheney, Maire
James L. Lacroix, Directeur général

Saint-Cyrille-de-Lessard
282, rue Principale
Saint-Cyrille-de-Lessard, QC G0R 2W0
Tél: 418-247-5186; *Téléc:* 418-247-7086
info@st-cyrille-de-lessard.ca
www.st-cyrille-de-lessard.ca
Entité municipal: Parish (Paroisse)
Incorporation: 1er juillet 1855; *Area:* 230,79 km2
Comté ou district: L'Islet; *Population au 2016:* 718
Circonscription(s) électorale(s) provinciale(s): Côte-du-Sud
Circonscription(s) électorale(s) fédérale(s):
Montmagny-L'Islet-Kamouraska-Rivière-du-Loup
Prochaines élections: 7e novembre 2021
Denise Deschênes, Mairesse
Carole St-Hilaire, Directrice générale par intérim

Saint-Cyrille-de-Wendover
4055, rue Principale
Saint-Cyrille-de-Wendover, QC J1Z 1C8
Tél: 819-397-4226; *Téléc:* 819-397-5505
municipalite@stcyrille.qc.ca
www.stcyrille.qc.ca
Entité municipal: Municipality
Incorporation: 6 septembre 1905; *Area:* 110,39 km2
Comté ou district: Drummond; *Population au 2016:* 4,723
Circonscription(s) électorale(s) provinciale(s):
Drummond-Bois-Francs
Circonscription(s) électorale(s) fédérale(s): Drummond
Prochaines élections: 7e novembre 2021
Hélène Laroche, Mairesse
Lucie Roberge, Directrice générale

Saint-Damase
115, rue St-Étienne
Saint-Damase, QC J0H 1J0
Tél: 450-797-3341; *Téléc:* 450-797-3543
info@st-damase.qc.ca
www.st-damase.qc.ca
Entité municipal: Municipality
Incorporation: 5 octobre 2001; *Area:* 79,70 km2
Comté ou district: Les Maskoutains; *Population au 2016:* 2,473
Circonscription(s) électorale(s) provinciale(s): St-Hyacinthe
Circonscription(s) électorale(s) fédérale(s): St-Hyacinthe-Bagot;
Saint-Hyacinthe-Bagot
Prochaines élections: 7e novembre 2021
Note: Effective October 10, 2001, the Village & Parish of
St-Damase amalgamated to create the Municipality of
St-Damase.
Christian Martin, Maire
Johanne Beauregard, Directrice générale, 450-797-3341

Saint-Damase
18, av du Centenaire
Sainte-Damase, QC G0J 2J0
Tél: 418-776-2103; *Téléc:* 418-776-2183
stdamase@mrcmatapedia.quebec
Entité municipal: Parish (Paroisse)
Incorporation: 31 décembre 1885; *Area:* 116,69 km2
Comté ou district: La Matapédia; *Population au 2016:* 426
Circonscription(s) électorale(s) provinciale(s): Matane-Matapédia
Circonscription(s) électorale(s) fédérale(s): Avignon-La
Mitis-Matane-Matapédia
Prochaines élections: 7e novembre 2021
Vacant, Maire
Vanessa Ruest-Vignola, Directrice générale

Saint-Damase-de-L'Islet
15, rue de la Rivière
Saint-Damase-de-L'Islet, QC G0R 2X0
Tél: 418-598-9370; *Téléc:* 418-598-9396
st-damase@globetrotter.net
saintdamasedelislet.com
Entité municipal: Municipality
Incorporation: 9 novembre 1898; *Area:* 247,71 km2
Comté ou district: L'Islet; *Population au 2016:* 552
Circonscription(s) électorale(s) provinciale(s): Côte-du-Sud
Circonscription(s) électorale(s) fédérale(s):
Montmagny-L'Islet-Kamouraska-Rivière-du-Loup
Prochaines élections: 7e novembre 2021
Gaétan Lord, Maire
Dany Marois, Directrice générale

Saint-Damien
6850, ch Montauban
Saint-Damien, QC J0K 2E0
Tél: 888-835-3419; *Téléc:* 450-835-5538
infos@st-damien.com
www.st-damien.com
Other Information: Sans frais: 888-835-3419
Entité municipal: Parish (Paroisse)
Incorporation: 6 septembre 1870; *Area:* 255,87 km2
Comté ou district: Matawinie; *Population au 2016:* 2,094
Circonscription(s) électorale(s) provinciale(s): Berthier
Circonscription(s) électorale(s) fédérale(s): Berthier-Maskinongé
Prochaines élections: 7e novembre 2021
Daniel Monette, Maire
Éric Gélinas, Directeur général, 418-835-3419

Saint-Damien-de-Buckland
75, rte St-Gérard
Saint-Damien-de-Buckland, QC G0R 2Y0
Tél: 418-789-2526; *Téléc:* 418-789-2125
info@saint-damien.com
saint-damien.com
Entité municipal: Parish (Paroisse)
Incorporation: 20 décembre 1890; *Area:* 82,07 km2
Comté ou district: Bellechasse; *Population au 2016:* 1,956
Circonscription(s) électorale(s) provinciale(s): Bellechasse
Circonscription(s) électorale(s) fédérale(s): Bellechasse-Les
Etchemins-Lévis
Prochaines élections: 7e novembre 2021
Sébastien Bourget, Maire
Vincent Drouin, Directeur général, 418-789-2526

Saint-David
16, rue Saint-Charles
Saint-David, QC J0G 1L0
Tél: 450-789-2288
info@stdavid.qc.ca
www.stdavid.qc.ca
Entité municipal: Municipality
Incorporation: 1er juillet 1855; *Area:* 92,90 km2
Comté ou district: Pierre-De Saurel; *Population au 2016:* 817
Circonscription(s) électorale(s) provinciale(s): Richelieu
Circonscription(s) électorale(s) fédérale(s):
Bécancour-Nicolet-Saurel
Prochaines élections: 7e novembre 2021
Michel Blanchard, Maire
Sylvie Letendre, Directrice générale

Saint-David-de-Falardeau
140, boul St-David
Saint-David-de-Falardeau, QC G0V 1C0
Tél: 418-673-4647; *Téléc:* 418-673-3266
info@villefalardeau.ca
www.villefalardeau.ca
Entité municipal: Municipality
Incorporation: 1er janvier 1948; *Area:* 400,30 km2
Comté ou district: Le Fjord-du-Saguenay; *Population au 2016:*
2,768
Circonscription(s) électorale(s) provinciale(s): Dubuc
Circonscription(s) électorale(s) fédérale(s): Jonquière
Prochaines élections: 7e novembre 2021
Catherine Morissette, Mairesse
Daniel Hudon, Directeur général, 418-673-4647

Saint-Denis-De La Bouteillerie
5, rte 287
Saint-Denis, QC G0L 2R0
Tél: 418-498-2968; *Téléc:* 418-498-2948
munstdenis.com
Entité municipal: Municipality
Incorporation: 1er juillet 1855; *Area:* 33,64 km2
Comté ou district: Kamouraska; *Population au 2016:* 517
Circonscription(s) électorale(s) provinciale(s): Côte-du-Sud
Circonscription(s) électorale(s) fédérale(s):
Montmagny-L'Islet-Kamouraska-Rivière-du-Loup
Prochaines élections: 7e novembre 2021
Jean Dallaire, Maire
Anne Desjardins, Directrice générale

Saint-Denis-de-Brompton
CP 120
2050, rue Ernest-Camiré
Saint-Denis-de-Brompton, QC J0B 2P0
Tél: 819-846-2744; *Téléc:* 819-846-0915
info@sddb.ca
sddb.ca
Entité municipal: Municipality
Incorporation: 6 mars 1935; *Area:* 70,39 km2
Comté ou district: Le Val-Saint-François; *Population au 2016:*
4,054
Circonscription(s) électorale(s) provinciale(s): Richmond
Circonscription(s) électorale(s) fédérale(s):

Richmond-Arthabaska
Prochaines élections: 7e novembre 2021
Jean-Luc Beauchemin, Maire
Liane Boisvert, Directrice générale

Saint-Denis-sur-Richelieu
129, av Yamaska
Saint-Denis-sur-Richelieu, QC J0H 1K0
Tél: 450-787-2244; *Téléc:* 450-787-2635
info@msdsr.com
www.stdenissurrichelieu.com
Entité municipal: Municipality
Incorporation: 24 décembre 1997; *Area:* 84,67 km2
Comté ou district: La Vallée-du-Richelieu; *Population au 2016:* 2,308
Circonscription(s) électorale(s) provinciale(s): Borduas
Circonscription(s) électorale(s) fédérale(s): Pierre-Boucher-Les Patriotes-Verchères
Prochaines élections: 7e novembre 2021
Ginette Thibault, Mairesse
Jonathan Lessard, Directeur général

Saint-Didace
380, rue Principale
Saint-Didace, QC J0K 2G0
Tél: 450-835-4184; *Téléc:* 450-836-0115
info@saint-didace.com
saint-didace.com
Entité municipal: Parish (Paroisse)
Incorporation: 27 août 1863; *Area:* 100,50 km2
Comté ou district: D'Autray; *Population au 2016:* 652
Circonscription(s) électorale(s) provinciale(s): Berthier
Circonscription(s) électorale(s) fédérale(s): Berthier-Maskinongé
Prochaines élections: 7e novembre 2021
Yves Germain, Maire
Chantale Dufort, Directrice générale, 450-835-4184

Saint-Dominique
467, rue Deslandes
Saint-Dominique, QC J0H 1L0
Tél: 450-774-9939
recep@st-dominique.ca
municipalite.saint-dominique.qc.ca
Entité municipal: Municipality
Incorporation: 1er juillet 1855; *Area:* 70,48 km2
Comté ou district: Les Maskoutains; *Population au 2016:* 2,553
Circonscription(s) électorale(s) provinciale(s): St-Hyacinthe
Circonscription(s) électorale(s) fédérale(s): St-Hyacinthe-Bagot; Vaudreuil-Soulanges
Prochaines élections: 7e novembre 2021
Robert Houle, Maire
Christine Massé, Directrice générale, 450-774-9939

Saint-Dominique-du-Rosaire
235, rue Principale
Saint-Dominique-du-Rosaire, QC J0Y 2K0
Tél: 819-727-9544
mun.stdomrosaire@cableamos.com
municipalites-du-quebec.ca/st-dominique-du-rosaire
Entité municipal: Municipality
Incorporation: 1er janvier 1978; *Area:* 482,89 km2
Comté ou district: Abitibi; *Population au 2016:* 450
Circonscription(s) électorale(s) provinciale(s): Abitibi-Ouest
Circonscription(s) électorale(s) fédérale(s): Abitibi-Témiscamingue
Prochaines élections: 7e novembre 2021
Christian Legault, Maire
Nathalie Boire, Directrice générale

Saint-Donat
194, av du Mont-Comi
Saint-Donat-de-Rimouski, QC G0K 1L0
Tél: 418-739-4634
www.saintdonat.ca
Entité municipal: Parish (Paroisse)
Incorporation: 10 mars 1869; *Area:* 95,58 km2
Comté ou district: La Mitis; *Population au 2016:* 876
Circonscription(s) électorale(s) provinciale(s): Matane-Matapédia
Circonscription(s) électorale(s) fédérale(s): Avignon-La Mitis-Matane-Matapédia
Prochaines élections: 7e novembre 2021
André Lechasseur, Maire
Julie Williamson, Directrice générale, 418-775-4634

Saint-Donat
490, rue Principale
Saint-Donat, QC J0T 2C0
Tél: 819-424-2383; *Téléc:* 819-424-5020
info@saint-donat.ca
www.saint-donat.ca
Entité municipal: Municipality
Incorporation: 19 février 1904; *Area:* 352,33 km2

Comté ou district: Matawinie; *Population au 2016:* 3,888
Circonscription(s) électorale(s) provinciale(s): Bertrand
Circonscription(s) électorale(s) fédérale(s): Joliette; Avignon-La Mitis-Matane-Matapédia
Prochaines élections: 7e novembre 2021
Joé Deslauriers, Maire
Stéphanie Russell, Greffière et directrice générale

Sainte-Agathe-de-Lotbinière
2540, rue Saint-Pierre
Sainte-Agathe-de-Lotbinière, QC G0S 2A0
Tél: 418-599-2605; *Téléc:* 418-599-2905
info@steagathedelotbiniere.com
www.steagathedelotbiniere.com
Entité municipal: Municipality
Incorporation: 3 février 1999; *Area:* 166,99 km2
Comté ou district: Lotbinière; *Population au 2016:* 1,168
Circonscription(s) électorale(s) provinciale(s): Lotbinière-Frontenac
Circonscription(s) électorale(s) fédérale(s): Lévis-Lotbinière
Prochaines élections: 7e novembre 2021
Gilbert Breton, Maire
Amélie Fournier, Directrice générale, 418-599-2605

Sainte-Angèle-de-Mérici
CP 129
23, rue de la Fabrique
Sainte-Angèle-de-Mérici, QC G0J 2H0
Tél: 418-775-7733; *Téléc:* 418-775-5722
steangele@mitis.qc.ca
municipalite.sainte-angele-de-merici.qc.ca
Entité municipal: Municipality
Incorporation: 26 avril 1989; *Area:* 107,81 km2
Comté ou district: La Mitis; *Population au 2016:* 953
Circonscription(s) électorale(s) provinciale(s): Matane-Matapédia
Circonscription(s) électorale(s) fédérale(s): Avignon-La Mitis-Matane-Matapédia
Prochaines élections: 7e novembre 2021
Michel Côté, Maire
Alain Thibault, Directeur général par intérim

Sainte-Angèle-de-Monnoir
5, ch du Vide
Sainte-Angèle-de-Monnoir, QC J0L 1P0
Tél: 450-460-7838; *Téléc:* 450-460-3853
info@sainte-angele-de-monnoir.ca
www.sainte-angele-de-monnoir.ca
Entité municipal: Parish (Paroisse)
Incorporation: 15 mars 1865; *Area:* 44,84 km2
Comté ou district: Rouville; *Population au 2016:* 1,823
Circonscription(s) électorale(s) provinciale(s): Iberville
Circonscription(s) électorale(s) fédérale(s): Shefford
Prochaines élections: 7e novembre 2021
Denis Paquin, Maire
Pierrettee Gendron, Directrice générale

Sainte-Angèle-de-Prémont
2451, rue Camirand
Sainte-Angèle-de-Prémont, QC J0K 1R0
Tél: 819-268-5526; *Téléc:* 819-268-5536
info@sainte-angele.ca
www.sainte-angele-de-premont.ca
Entité municipal: Municipality
Incorporation: 28 août 1917; *Area:* 37,72 km2
Comté ou district: Maskinongé; *Population au 2016:* 596
Circonscription(s) électorale(s) provinciale(s): Maskinongé
Circonscription(s) électorale(s) fédérale(s): Berthier-Maskinongé
Prochaines élections: 7e novembre 2021
Barbara Paillé, Mairesse
Isabelle Plante, Directeur général, 819-268-5526

Sainte-Anne-de-Beaupré
9336, av Royale
Sainte-Anne-de-Beaupré, QC G0A 3C0
Tél: 418-827-3191; *Téléc:* 418-827-8275
info@sainteannedebeaupre.com
www.sainteannedebeaupre.com
Entité municipal: Town
Incorporation: 27 janvier 1973; *Area:* 62,35 km2
Comté ou district: La Côte-de-Beaupré; Communauté métropolitaine de Québec; *Population au 2016:* 2,880
Circonscription(s) électorale(s) provinciale(s): Charlevoix-Côte-de-Beaupré
Circonscription(s) électorale(s) fédérale(s): Beauport—Côte-de-Beaupré—Île d'Orléans—Charlevoix
Prochaines élections: 7e novembre 2021
Jacques Bouchard, Maire
Frédéric Drolet-Gervais, Directeur général

Sainte-Anne-de-Bellevue
109, rue Sainte-Anne
Sainte-Anne-de-Bellevue, QC H9X 1M2
Tél: 514-457-5500; *Téléc:* 514-457-6087
info@sadb.qc.ca
ville.sainte-anne-de-bellevue.qc.ca
Entité municipal: Town
Incorporation: 1er janvier 2006; *Area:* 10,48 km2
Comté ou district: Communauté métropolitaine de Montréal; *Population au 2016:* 4,958
Circonscription(s) électorale(s) provinciale(s): Jacques-Cartier
Circonscription(s) électorale(s) fédérale(s): Lac-Saint-Louis
Prochaines élections: 7e novembre 2021
Paola Hawa, Mairesse
Catherine Blais-Adam, Greffière

Sainte-Anne-de-la-Pérade
200, rue Principale
Sainte-Anne-de-la-Pérade, QC G0X 2J0
Tél: 418-325-2841; *Téléc:* 418-325-3070
municipalite@sadlp.ca
sadlp.ca
Entité municipal: Municipality
Incorporation: 10 mai 1989; *Area:* 109,52 km2
Comté ou district: Les Chenaux; *Population au 2016:* 2,019
Circonscription(s) électorale(s) provinciale(s): Champlain
Circonscription(s) électorale(s) fédérale(s): St-Maurice-Champlain
Prochaines élections: 7e novembre 2021
Diane Aubut, Mairesse
Jacques Taillefer, Directeur général, 418-325-2841

Sainte-Anne-de-la-Pocatière
395, ch des Sables est
Sainte-Anne-de-la-Pocatière, QC G0R 1Z0
Tél: 418-856-3192; *Téléc:* 418-856-9936
paroisse@ste-anne-de-la-pocatiere.com
www.ste-anne-de-la-pocatiere.com
Entité municipal: Parish (Paroisse)
Incorporation: 1er juillet 1855; *Area:* 54,91 km2
Comté ou district: Kamouraska; *Population au 2016:* 1,636
Circonscription(s) électorale(s) provinciale(s): Côte-du-Sud
Circonscription(s) électorale(s) fédérale(s): Montmagny-L'Islet-Kamouraska-Rivière-du-Loup
Prochaines élections: 7e novembre 2021
Rosaire Ouellet, Maire
Isabelle Michaud, Directrice générale

Sainte-Anne-de-la-Rochelle
142, rue Principale est
Sainte-Anne-de-la-Rochelle, QC J0E 2B0
Tél: 450-539-1654; *Téléc:* 579-439-2048
mun@sadlr.quebec
steannedelarochelle.ca
Entité municipal: Municipality
Incorporation: 1er juillet 1855; *Area:* 61,99 km2
Comté ou district: Le Val-Saint-François; *Population au 2016:* 598
Circonscription(s) électorale(s) provinciale(s): Orford
Circonscription(s) électorale(s) fédérale(s): Shefford
Prochaines élections: 7e novembre 2021
Louis Coutu, Maire
Majella René, Directrice générale

Sainte-Anne-de-Sabrevois
1218, rte 133
Sabrevois, QC J0J 2G0
Tél: 450-347-0066; *Téléc:* 450-347-4040
info@sabrevois.info
sainte-anne-de-sabrevois.com
Entité municipal: Parish (Paroisse)
Incorporation: 1er mars 1888; *Area:* 44,73 km2
Comté ou district: Le Haut-Richelieu; *Population au 2016:* 2,039
Circonscription(s) électorale(s) provinciale(s): Iberville
Circonscription(s) électorale(s) fédérale(s): Saint-Jean
Prochaines élections: 7e novembre 2021
Jacques Lavallée, Maire
Fredy Serreyn, Directeur général, 450-347-0066

Sainte-Anne-des-Lacs
773, ch de Ste-Anne-des-Lacs
Sainte-Anne-des-Lacs, QC J0R 1B0
Tél: 450-224-2675; *Téléc:* 450-224-8672
www.sadl.qc.ca
Entité municipal: Parish (Paroisse)
Incorporation: 28 mars 1946; *Area:* 25,23 km2
Comté ou district: Les Pays-d'en-Haut; *Population au 2016:* 3,611
Circonscription(s) électorale(s) provinciale(s): Bertrand
Circonscription(s) électorale(s) fédérale(s): Laurentides-Labelle
Prochaines élections: 7e novembre 2021
Monique Monette Laroche, Mairesse

Jean-Philippe Gadbois, Directeur général, 450-224-2675

Sainte-Anne-des-Monts
6, 1e av ouest
Sainte-Anne-des-Monts, QC G4V 1A1
Tél: 418-763-5511; *Téléc:* 418-763-3473
villesadm.net
villesadm.net
Entité municipal: Town
Incorporation: février 2000; *Area:* 264,09 km2
Comté ou district: La Haute-Gaspésie; *Population au 2016:*
6,437
Circonscription(s) électorale(s) provinciale(s): Gaspé
Circonscription(s) électorale(s) fédérale(s): Gaspésie—Les
îles-de-la-Madeleine
Prochaines élections: 7e novembre 2021
Simon Deschênes, Maire
Sylvie Lepage, Greffière, 418-763-5511

Sainte-Anne-de-Sorel
1685, ch du Chenal-du-Moine
Sainte-Anne-de-Sorel, QC J3P 5N3
Tél: 450-742-1616; *Téléc:* 450-742-1118
info@sainteannedesorel.ca
www.sainteannedesorel.ca
Entité municipal: Municipality
Incorporation: 14 mai 1877; *Area:* 38,40 km2
Comté ou district: Pierre-De Saurel; *Population au 2016:* 2,771
Circonscription(s) électorale(s) provinciale(s): Richelieu
Circonscription(s) électorale(s) fédérale(s):
Bécancour-Nicolet-Saurel
Prochaines élections: 7e novembre 2021
Michel Péloquin, Maire
Maxime Dauplaise, Directeur général

Sainte-Anne-du-Lac
1, rue St-François-Xavier
Sainte-Anne-du-Lac, QC J0W 1V0
Tél: 819-586-2110; *Téléc:* 819-586-2203
municipalite@steannedulac.ca
www.municipalite.sainte-anne-du-lac.qc.ca
Entité municipal: Municipality
Incorporation: 30 décembre 1976; *Area:* 322,59 km2
Comté ou district: Antoine-Labelle; *Population au 2016:* 575
Circonscription(s) électorale(s) provinciale(s): Labelle
Circonscription(s) électorale(s) fédérale(s): Laurentides-Labelle;
Mégantic-L'Érable
Prochaines élections: 7e novembre 2021
Annick Brault, Mairesse
Lise Lapointe, Directrice générale

Sainte-Apolline-de-Patton
105, rte de l'Église
Sainte-Apolline-de-Patton, QC G0R 2P0
Tél: 418-469-3031
info@sainteapollinedepatton.ca
www.sainteapollinedepatton.ca
Entité municipal: Parish (Paroisse)
Incorporation: 14 décembre 1909; *Area:* 256,81 km2
Comté ou district: Montmagny; *Population au 2016:* 542
Circonscription(s) électorale(s) provinciale(s): Côte-du-Sud
Circonscription(s) électorale(s) fédérale(s):
Montamgny-L'Islet-Kamouraska-Rivière-du-Loup
Prochaines élections: 7e novembre 2021
Lucien Lavoie, Maire
Caroline Dancause, Directrice générale

Sainte-Aurélie
151A, ch des Bois Francs
Sainte-Aurélie, QC G0M 1M0
Tél: 418-593-3021
munsteau@sogetel.net
www.ste-aurelie.qc.ca
Entité municipal: Municipality
Incorporation: 3 avril 1909; *Area:* 78,23 km2
Comté ou district: Les Etchemins; *Population au 2016:* 847
Circonscription(s) électorale(s) provinciale(s): Beauce-Sud
Circonscription(s) électorale(s) fédérale(s): Beauce
Prochaines élections: 7e novembre 2021
René Allen, Maire
Stéphane Hétu, Directeur général, 418-593-3021

Sainte-Barbe
470, ch de l'Église
Sainte-Barbe, QC J0S 1P0
Tél: 450-371-2504; *Téléc:* 450-371-2575
info@ste-barbe.com
www.ste-barbe.com
Entité municipal: Municipality
Incorporation: 12 juin 1882; *Area:* 40,16 km2
Comté ou district: Le Haut-Saint-Laurent; *Population au 2016:*
1,324

Circonscription(s) électorale(s) provinciale(s): Huntingdon
Circonscription(s) électorale(s) fédérale(s): Salaberry-Suroît
Prochaines élections: 7e novembre 2021
Louise Lebrun, Mairesse
Chantal Girouard, Directrice générale

Sainte-Béatrix
861, rue de l'Église
Sainte-Béatrix, QC J0K 1Y0
Tél: 450-883-2245
www.sainte-beatrix.com
Entité municipal: Municipality
Incorporation: 11 mai 1864; *Area:* 83,05 km2
Comté ou district: Matawinie; *Population au 2016:* 1,955
Circonscription(s) électorale(s) provinciale(s): Berthier
Circonscription(s) électorale(s) fédérale(s): Joliette
Prochaines élections: 7e novembre 2021
Serge Perrault, Maire
Gérard Cossette, Directrice générale, 450-883-2245

Sainte-Brigide-d'Iberville
555, rue Principale
Sainte-Brigide-d'Iberville, QC J0J 1X0
Tél: 450-293-7511; *Téléc:* 450-293-1077
info@sainte-brigide.qc.ca
www.sainte-brigide.qc.ca
Entité municipal: Municipality
Incorporation: 1er juillet 1855; *Area:* 70,56 km2
Comté ou district: Le Haut-Richelieu; *Population au 2016:* 1,402
Circonscription(s) électorale(s) provinciale(s): Iberville
Circonscription(s) électorale(s) fédérale(s): Saint-Jean
Prochaines élections: 7e novembre 2021
Patrick Bonvouloir, Maire
Christianne Pouliot, Directrice générale

Sainte-Brigitte-de-Laval
414, av Ste-Brigitte
Sainte-Brigitte-de-Laval, QC G0A 3K0
Tél: 418-825-2515; *Téléc:* 418-825-3114
mairie@sbdl.net
sbdl.net
Entité municipal: Town
Incorporation: 11 février 1875; *Area:* 108,79 km2
Comté ou district: La Jacques-Cartier; Communauté
métropolitaine de Québec; *Population au 2016:* 7,348
Circonscription(s) électorale(s) provinciale(s): Montmorency
Circonscription(s) électorale(s) fédérale(s): Portneuf-Jacques
Cartier
Prochaines élections: 7e novembre 2021
Carl Thomassin, Maire
Maude Simard, Greffière, 418-825-2515

Sainte-Brigitte-des-Saults
319, rue Principale
Sainte-Brigitte-des-Saults, QC J0C 1E0
Tél: 819-336-4460; *Téléc:* 819-336-4410
reception@stebrigittedessaults.ca
www.saintebrigittedessaults.ca
Entité municipal: Parish (Paroisse)
Incorporation: 9 mars 1878; *Area:* 70,79
Comté ou district: Drummond; *Population au 2016:* 723
Circonscription(s) électorale(s) provinciale(s): Nicolet-Bécancour
Circonscription(s) électorale(s) fédérale(s): Drummond
Prochaines élections: 7e novembre 2021
Jean-Guy Hébert, Maire
Manon Lemaire, Directrice générale

Sainte-Catherine-de-Hatley
35, ch de North Hatley
Sainte-Catherine-de-Hatley, QC J0B 1W0
Tél: 819-843-1935; *Téléc:* 819-843-8527
secretariat@saintecatherinedehatley.ca
www.sainte-catherine-de-hatley.ca
Entité municipal: Municipality
Incorporation: 28 mars 1901; *Area:* 86,37 km2
Comté ou district: Memphrémagog; *Population au 2016:* 2,479
Circonscription(s) électorale(s) provinciale(s): Orford
Circonscription(s) électorale(s) fédérale(s): Compton-Stanstead
Prochaines élections: 7e novembre 2021
Jacques Demers, Maire
Josiane Hudon, Directeur général

Sainte-Catherine-de-la-Jacques-Cartier
2, rue Laurier
Ste-Catherine-de-la-J-Cartier, QC G3N 1W1
Tél: 418-875-2758; *Téléc:* 418-875-2170
info@villescjc.com
www.villescjc.com
Entité municipal: Town
Incorporation: 1er juillet 1855; *Area:* 121,06 km2
Comté ou district: La Jacques-Cartier; Communauté
métropolitaine de Québec; *Population au 2016:* 7,706

Circonscription(s) électorale(s) provinciale(s): La Peltrie
Circonscription(s) électorale(s) fédérale(s):
Portneuf-Jacques-Cartier
Prochaines élections: 7e novembre 2021
Pierre Dolbec, Maire
Marcel Grenier, Directeur général et greffier

Sainte-Cécile-de-Lévrard
219, rue Principale
Sainte-Cécile-de-Lévrard, QC G0X 2M0
Tél: 819-263-2104; *Téléc:* 819-263-1043
info@stececiledelevrard.com
stececiledelevrard.com
Entité municipal: Parish (Paroisse)
Incorporation: 11 septembre 1908; *Area:* 32,32 km2
Comté ou district: Bécancour; *Population au 2016:* 372
Circonscription(s) électorale(s) provinciale(s): Nicolet-Bécancour
Circonscription(s) électorale(s) fédérale(s):
Bécancour-Nicolet-Saurel
Prochaines élections: 7e novembre 2021
Simon Brunelle, Maire
Amélie Hardy Demers, Directrice générale

Sainte-Cécile-de-Milton
112, rue Principale
Sainte-Cécile-de-Milton, QC J0E 2C0
Tél: 450-378-1942; *Téléc:* 450-378-1942
mun@miltonqc.ca
www.stececiledemilton.qc.ca
Entité municipal: Township
Incorporation: 1er janvier 1864; *Area:* 73,03 km2
Comté ou district: La Haute-Yamaska; *Population au 2016:*
2,160
Circonscription(s) électorale(s) provinciale(s): Johnson
Circonscription(s) électorale(s) fédérale(s): Shefford
Prochaines élections: 7e novembre 2021
Paul Sarrazin, Maire
Yves Tanguay, Directeur général, 450-378-1942

Sainte-Cécile-de-Whitton
4554, rue Principale
Sainte-Cécile-de-Whitton, QC G0Y 1J0
Tél: 819-583-0770; *Téléc:* 819-583-0518
info@stececiledewhitton.qc.ca
www.stececiledewhitton.qc.ca
Entité municipal: Municipality
Incorporation: 19 septembre 1889; *Area:* 146,56 km2
Comté ou district: Le Granit; *Population au 2016:* 863
Circonscription(s) électorale(s) provinciale(s): Mégantic
Circonscription(s) électorale(s) fédérale(s): Mégantic-L'Érable
Prochaines élections: 7e novembre 2021
Diane Turgeon, Maire
Nicole Dominigue, Directrice générale

Sainte-Christine
646, 1e rang ouest
Sainte-Christine, QC J0H 1H0
Tél: 819-858-2828; *Téléc:* 819-858-9191
secretariat@ste-christine.com
ste-christine.com
Entité municipal: Parish (Paroisse)
Incorporation: 8 janvier 1894; *Area:* 92,16 km2
Comté ou district: Acton; *Population au 2016:* 730
Circonscription(s) électorale(s) provinciale(s): Johnson
Circonscription(s) électorale(s) fédérale(s): St-Hyacinthe-Bagot
Prochaines élections: 7e novembre 2021
Jean-Marc Ménard, Maire
Caroline Lamothe, Directrice-générale

Sainte-Christine-d'Auvergne
80, rue Principale
Sainte-Christine-d'Auvergne, QC G0A 1A0
Tél: 418-329-3304
sca.quebec
Entité municipal: Municipality
Incorporation: 10 avril 1896; *Area:* 144,28 km2
Comté ou district: Portneuf; *Population au 2016:* 704
Circonscription(s) électorale(s) provinciale(s): Portneuf
Circonscription(s) électorale(s) fédérale(s): Portneuf-Jacques
Cartier
Prochaines élections: 7e novembre 2021
Raymond Francoeur, Maire, 418-931-5040
July Bédard, Directrice générale, 418-329-3304

Sainte-Claire
135, rue Principale
Sainte-Claire, QC G0R 2V0
Tél: 418-883-3314; *Téléc:* 418-883-3845
administration@ste-claire.ca
ste-claire.ca
Entité municipal: Municipality
Incorporation: 1er octobre 1977; *Area:* 88,06 km2

Comté ou district: Bellechasse; *Population au 2016:* 3,362
Circonscription(s) électorale(s) provinciale(s): Bellechasse
Circonscription(s) électorale(s) fédérale(s): Bellechasse-Les Etchemins-Lévis
Prochaines élections: 7e novembre 2021
Denise Dulac, Mairesse
Luc Harveyr, Directeur général

Sainte-Clotilde
2452, ch de l'Église
Sainte-Clotilde, QC J0L 1W0
Tél: 450-826-3129; *Téléc:* 450-826-3217
info@ste-clotilde.ca
ste-clotilde.ca
Entité municipal: Municipality
Incorporation: 2 avril 1885; *Area:* 78,39 km2
Comté ou district: Les Jardins-de-Napierville; *Population au 2016:* 1,622
Circonscription(s) électorale(s) provinciale(s): Huntingdon
Circonscription(s) électorale(s) fédérale(s): Châteauguay-Lacolle
Prochaines élections: 7e novembre 2021
Andre Chenail, Maire
Amélie Latendresse, Directrice générale

Sainte-Clotilde-de-Beauce
307B, rue du Couvent
Sainte-Clotilde-de-Beauce, QC G0N 1C0
Tél: 418-427-2637; *Téléc:* 418-427-4303
info@ste-clotilde.com
www.ste-clotilde.ca
Entité municipal: Municipality
Incorporation: 19 novembre 1938; *Area:* 60,42 km2
Comté ou district: Les Appalaches; *Population au 2016:* 549
Circonscription(s) électorale(s) provinciale(s): Beauce-Sud
Circonscription(s) électorale(s) fédérale(s): Mégantic-L'Érable
Prochaines élections: 7e novembre 2021
Gérald Grenier, Maire
Brigitte Blais, Directrice générale

Sainte-Clotilde-de-Horton
CP 29
17, rte 122
Sainte-Clotilde-de-Horton, QC J0A 1H0
Tél: 819-336-5344; *Téléc:* 819-336-5440
info@steclotildehorton.ca
steclotildehorton.ca
Entité municipal: Municipality
Incorporation: 26 mars 1997; *Area:* 114,75 km2
Comté ou district: Arthabaska; *Population au 2016:* 1,569
Circonscription(s) électorale(s) provinciale(s): Drummond-Bois-Francs
Circonscription(s) électorale(s) fédérale(s): Richmond-Arthabaska
Prochaines élections: 7e novembre 2021
Simon Boucher, Maire
Matthieu Levasseur, Directeur général

Sainte-Croix
6310, rue Principale
Sainte-Croix, QC G0S 2H0
Tél: 418-926-3494; *Téléc:* 418-926-2570
sainte.croix@ville-sainte-croix.ca
www.ville.sainte-croix.qc.ca
Entité municipal: Municipality
Incorporation: 5 octobre 2001; *Area:* 69,86 km2
Comté ou district: Lotbinière; *Population au 2016:* 2,516
Circonscription(s) électorale(s) provinciale(s): Lotbinière-Frontenac
Circonscription(s) électorale(s) fédérale(s): Lévis-Lotbinière
Prochaines élections: 7e novembre 2021
Jacques Gauthier, Maire
France Dubuc, Directrice générale, 418-926-3494

Saint-Edmond-de-Grantham
1393, rue Notre-Dame-de-Lourdes
Saint-Edmond-de-Grantham, QC J0C 1K0
Tél: 819-395-2562; *Téléc:* 819-395-2666
municipalite@st-edmond-de-grantham.qc.ca
www.st-edmond-de-grantham.qc.ca
Entité municipal: Parish (Paroisse)
Incorporation: 9 février 1918; *Area:* 48,30 km2
Comté ou district: Drummond; *Population au 2016:* 762
Circonscription(s) électorale(s) provinciale(s): Johnson
Circonscription(s) électorale(s) fédérale(s): Drummond
Prochaines élections: 7e novembre 2021
Robert Corriveau, Maire
Donald Brideau, Directeur général

Saint-Edmond-les-Plaines
561, ch Principale
Saint-Edmond-les-Plaines, QC G0W 2M0
Tél: 418-274-3069
admin@stedmond.ca
stedmond.ca
Entité municipal: Municipality
Incorporation: 3 septembre 1938; *Area:* 84,41 km2
Comté ou district: Maria-Chapdelaine; *Population au 2016:* 381
Circonscription(s) électorale(s) provinciale(s): Roberval
Circonscription(s) électorale(s) fédérale(s): Lac-Saint-Jean
Prochaines élections: 7e novembre 2021
Rodrigue Cantin, Maire
Pascale Deschesnes, Directrice générale

Saint-Édouard
CP 230
405C, montée Lussier
Saint-Édouard, QC J0L 1Y0
Tél: 450-454-6333
info@saintedouard.ca
www.saintedouard.ca
Entité municipal: Municipality
Incorporation: 1er juillet 1855; *Area:* 52,69 km2
Comté ou district: Les Jardins-de-Napierville; *Population au 2016:* 1,321
Circonscription(s) électorale(s) provinciale(s): Huntingdon
Circonscription(s) électorale(s) fédérale(s): Châteauguay-Lacolle
Prochaines élections: 7e novembre 2021
Ronald Lécuyer, Maire
Catherine Rochefort, Directrice générale, 450-454-6333

Saint-Édouard-de-Fabre
620, rue de l'Église
Saint-Édouard-de-Fabre, QC J0Z 1Z0
Tél: 819-634-4441
admfabre@mrctemiscamingue.qc.ca
municipalites-du-quebec.ca/st-edouard-de-fabre
Entité municipal: Parish (Paroisse)
Incorporation: 3 octobre 1912; *Area:* 191,91 km2
Comté ou district: Témiscamingue; *Population au 2016:* 628
Circonscription(s) électorale(s) provinciale(s): Rouyn-Noranda-Témiscamingue
Circonscription(s) électorale(s) fédérale(s): Abitibi-Témiscamingue
Prochaines élections: 7e novembre 2021
Mario Drouin, Maire
Aline Desjardins, Directrice générale

Saint-Édouard-de-Lotbinière
2485, rue Principale
Saint-Édouard-de-Lotbinière, QC G0S 1Y0
Tél: 418-796-2971; *Téléc:* 418-796-2228
info@st-edouard.com
www.municipalite.st-edouard.qc.ca
Entité municipal: Parish (Paroisse)
Incorporation: 1er décembre 1862; *Area:* 98,43 km2
Comté ou district: Lotbinière; *Population au 2016:* 1,194
Circonscription(s) électorale(s) provinciale(s): Lotbinière-Frontenac
Circonscription(s) électorale(s) fédérale(s): Lévis-Lotbinière
Prochaines élections: 7e novembre 2021
Denise Poulin, Maire
Marie-Josée Lévesque, Directrice générale

Saint-Édouard-de-Maskinongé
3851, rue Notre-Dame
Saint-Édouard-de-Maskinongé, QC J0K 2H0
Tél: 819-268-2833
municipalitestedouard@sogetel.net
municipalites-du-quebec.ca/st-edouard-de-maskinonge
Entité municipal: Municipality
Incorporation: 1er janvier 1950; *Area:* 52,84 km2
Comté ou district: Maskinongé; *Population au 2016:* 712
Circonscription(s) électorale(s) provinciale(s): Maskinongé
Circonscription(s) électorale(s) fédérale(s): Berthier-Maskinongé
Prochaines élections: 7e novembre 2021
Réal Normandin, Maire
Chantal Hamelin, Directrice générale, 819-268-2833

Sainte-Edwidge-de-Clifton
1439, ch Favreau
Sainte-Edwidge-de-Clifton, QC J0B 2R0
Tél: 819-849-7740; *Téléc:* 819-849-4212
info@ste-edwidge.ca
www.ste-edwidge.ca
Entité municipal: Township
Incorporation: 21 décembre 1895; *Area:* 101,80 km2
Comté ou district: Coaticook; *Population au 2016:* 504
Circonscription(s) électorale(s) provinciale(s): St-François
Circonscription(s) électorale(s) fédérale(s): Compton-Stanstead
Prochaines élections: 7e novembre 2021

Bernard Marion, Maire
Brigitte Desruisseaux, Directrice générale

Sainte-Élisabeth
2270, rue Principale
Sainte-Élisabeth, QC J0K 2J0
Tél: 450-759-2875
communications@ste-elisabeth.qc.ca
www.ste-elisabeth.qc.ca
Entité municipal: Municipality
Incorporation: 1er juillet 1855; *Area:* 82,96 km2
Comté ou district: D'Autray; *Population au 2016:* 1,459
Circonscription(s) électorale(s) provinciale(s): Berthier
Circonscription(s) électorale(s) fédérale(s): Berthier-Maskinongé
Prochaines élections: 7e novembre 2021
Louis Bérard, Maire
Catherine Haulard, Directrice générale

Sainte-Élizabeth-de-Warwick
243, rue Principale
Sainte-Élizabeth-de-Warwick, QC J0A 1M0
Tél: 819-358-5162; *Téléc:* 819-358-9192
info@sainte-elizabeth-de-warwick.ca
www.sainte-elizabeth-de-warwick.ca
Entité municipal: Municipality
Incorporation: 18 mai 1887; *Area:* 51,96 km2
Comté ou district: Arthabaska; *Population au 2016:* 372
Circonscription(s) électorale(s) provinciale(s): Drummond-Bois-Francs
Circonscription(s) électorale(s) fédérale(s): Richmond-Arthabaska
Prochaines élections: 7e novembre 2021
Jeannine Moisan, Mairesse
Daniel René, Directeur général

Sainte-Émélie-de-l'Énergie
460, rue de la Mairie
Sainte-Émélie-de-l'Énergie, QC J0K 2K0
Tél: 450-886-3823; *Téléc:* 450-886-9175
info@steemelie.ca
steemelie.ca
Entité municipal: Municipality
Incorporation: 10 juin 1884; *Area:* 150,95 km2
Comté ou district: Matawinie; *Population au 2016:* 1,567
Circonscription(s) électorale(s) provinciale(s): Berthier
Circonscription(s) électorale(s) fédérale(s): Joliette
Prochaines élections: 7e novembre 2021
Martin Héroux, Maire
Mathieu Robillard, Directeur général, 450-886-3823

Sainte-Eulalie
757, rue des Bouleaux
Sainte-Eulalie, QC G0Z 1E0
Tél: 819-225-4345; *Téléc:* 819-225-4078
info@sainte-eulalie.ca
www.municipalite.sainte-eulalie.qc.ca
Entité municipal: Municipality
Incorporation: 1er juillet 1864; *Area:* 86,35 km2
Comté ou district: Nicolet-Yamaska; *Population au 2016:* 894
Circonscription(s) électorale(s) provinciale(s): Nicolet-Bécancour
Circonscription(s) électorale(s) fédérale(s): Bécancour-Nicolet-Saurel
Prochaines élections: 7e novembre 2021
Gilles Bédard, Maire
Fabiola Aubry, Directrice générale

Sainte-Euphémie-sur-Rivière-du-Sud
220, rue Principal est
Ste-Euphémie-sur-Rivière-du-Su, QC G0R 2Z0
Tél: 418-469-3427
mun_ste-euphemie@videotron.ca
municipalites-du-quebec.ca/ste-euphemie
Entité municipal: Municipality
Incorporation: 20 juillet 1907; *Area:* 92,38 km2
Comté ou district: Montmagny; *Population au 2016:* 320
Circonscription(s) électorale(s) provinciale(s): Côte-du-Sud
Circonscription(s) électorale(s) fédérale(s): Montmagny-L'Islet-Kamouraska-Rivière-du-Loup
Prochaines élections: 7e novembre 2021
Denis Giroux, Maire
Jacquelin Fraser, Directeur général

Sainte-Famille-de-l'Ile-d'Orléans
2478, ch Royal
Sainte-Famille, QC G0A 3P0
Tél: 418-829-3572; *Téléc:* 418-829-2513
info@munstefamille.org
ste-famille.iledorleans.com
Entité municipal: Municipality
Incorporation: 1er juillet 1855; *Area:* 48,76 km2
Comté ou district: L'Île-d'Orléans; Communauté métropolitaine de Québec; *Population au 2016:* 938

Circonscription(s) électorale(s) provinciale(s):
Charlevoix-Côte-de-Beaupré
Circonscription(s) électorale(s) fédérale(s):
Beauport—Côte-de-Beaupré—Île d'Orléans—Charlevoix
Prochaines élections: 7e novembre 2021
Jean-Pierre Turcotte, Maire
Sylvie Beaulieu, Directrice générale

Sainte-Félicité
5, rte de l'Église nord
Sainte-Félicité, QC G0R 4P0
Tél: 418-359-2321
mun.ste-felicite@globetrotter.net
ste-felicite.ca
Entité municipal: Municipality
Incorporation: 1er janvier 1950; *Area:* 94,81 km2
Comté ou district: L'Islet; *Population au 2016:* 389
Circonscription(s) électorale(s) provinciale(s): Côte-du-Sud
Circonscription(s) électorale(s) fédérale(s):
Montmagny-l'Islet-Kamouraska-Rivière-du-Loup
Prochaines élections: 7e novembre 2021
Alphé St-Pierre, Maire
Julie Bélanger, Directrice générale

Sainte-Félicité
151, rue Saint-Joseph
Sainte-Félicité, QC G0J 2K0
Tél: 418-733-4628; *Téléc:* 418-733-8377
ste-felicite@lamatanie.ca
www.sainte-felicite.com
Entité municipal: Municipality
Incorporation: 10 janvier 1996; *Area:* 91,38 km2
Comté ou district: La Matanie; *Population au 2016:* 1,065
Circonscription(s) électorale(s) provinciale(s): Matane-Matapédia
Circonscription(s) électorale(s) fédérale(s): Avignon-La
Mitis-Matane-Matapédia
Prochaines élections: 7e novembre 2021
Andrew Turcotte, Maire
Yves Chassé, Directeur général

Sainte-Flavie
775, rte Flavie-Drapeau
Sainte-Flavie, QC G0J 2L0
Tél: 418-775-7050; *Téléc:* 418-775-5672
info@sainte-flavie.net
www.sainte-flavie.net
Entité municipal: Parish (Paroisse)
Incorporation: 1er juillet 1855; *Area:* 38,52 km2
Comté ou district: La Mitis; *Population au 2016:* 884
Circonscription(s) électorale(s) provinciale(s): Matane-Matapédia
Circonscription(s) électorale(s) fédérale(s): Avignon-La
Mitis-Matane-Matapédia
Prochaines élections: 7e novembre 2021
Jean-François Fortin, Maire
Julie Dubé, Directrice générale, 418-775-7050

Sainte-Florence
6, rue des Loisirs
Sainte-Florence, QC G0J 2M0
Tél: 418-756-3491; *Téléc:* 418-756-5079
administration@sainte-florence.org
www.sainte-florence.org
Entité municipal: Municipality
Incorporation: 12 avril 1911; *Area:* 103,57 km2
Comté ou district: La Matapédia; *Population au 2016:* 384
Circonscription(s) électorale(s) provinciale(s): Matane-Matapédia
Circonscription(s) électorale(s) fédérale(s): Avignon-La
Mitis-Matane-Matapédia
Prochaines élections: 7e novembre 2021
Carol Poitras, Maire
Stéphanie Cormier, Directrice générale

Sainte-Françoise
563, 10e-et-11e rang est
Sainte-Françoise-de-Lotbinière, QC G0S 2N0
Tél: 819-287-5755; *Téléc:* 819-287-5838
municipalite@ste-francoise.com
ste-francoise.com
Entité municipal: Municipality
Incorporation: 1er janvier 1947; *Area:* 87,04 km2
Comté ou district: Bécancour; *Population au 2016:* 449
Circonscription(s) électorale(s) provinciale(s): Nicolet-Bécancour
Circonscription(s) électorale(s) fédérale(s):
Bécancour-Nicolet-Saurel; Rimouski-Neigette-Témiscouata-Les
Basques
Prochaines élections: 7e novembre 2021
Mario Lyonnais, Maire
Carine Neault, Directrice générale

Sainte-Françoise
156, rue Jérémie-Beaulieu
Sainte-Françoise, QC G0L 3B0
Tél: 418-851-1502; *Téléc:* 418-851-0926
municipal@ste-francoise.qc.ca
www.sainte-francoise.org
Entité municipal: Parish (Paroisse)
Incorporation: 6 décembre 1873; *Area:* 88,88 km2
Comté ou district: Les Basques; *Population au 2016:* 386
Circonscription(s) électorale(s) provinciale(s):
Rivière-du-Loup-Témiscouata
Circonscription(s) électorale(s) fédérale(s):
Rimouski-Neigette-Témiscouata-Les Basques
Prochaines élections: 7e novembre 2021
Simon Lavoie, Maire
Véronique Pelletier, Directrice générale

Sainte-Geneviève-de-Batiscan
30, rue St-Charles
Sainte-Geneviève-de-Batiscan, QC G0X 2R0
Tél: 418-362-2078; *Téléc:* 418-362-2111
municipalite@stegenevieve.ca
stegenevieve.ca
Entité municipal: Parish (Paroisse)
Incorporation: 1er juillet 1855; *Area:* 97,82 km2
Comté ou district: Les Chenaux; *Population au 2016:* 1,006
Circonscription(s) électorale(s) provinciale(s): Champlain
Circonscription(s) électorale(s) fédérale(s):
St-Maurice-Champlain
Prochaines élections: 7e novembre 2021
Christian Gendron, Maire
François Hénault, Directeur général

Sainte-Geneviève-de-Berthier
400, rang de la Rivière-Bayonne sud
Sainte-Geneviève-de-Berthier, QC J0K 1A0
Tél: 450-836-4333
info@stegenevievedeberthier.ca
municipalites-du-quebec.ca/sainte-genevieve-de-berthier
Entité municipal: Municipality
Incorporation: 1er juillet 1855; *Area:* 67,62 km2
Comté ou district: D'Autray; *Population au 2016:* 2,280
Circonscription(s) électorale(s) provinciale(s): Berthier
Circonscription(s) électorale(s) fédérale(s): Berthier-Maskinongé
Prochaines élections: 7e novembre 2021
Richard Giroux, Maire
Marie-Pier Aubuchon, Directrice générale

Sainte-Germaine-Boulé
199A, ch J.-Alfred-Roy
Sainte-Germaine-Boulé, QC J0Z 1M0
Tél: 819-787-6221; *Téléc:* 819-787-2560
direction@saintegermaineboule.ca
www.saintegermaineboule.com
Entité municipal: Municipality
Incorporation: 1er janvier 1954; *Area:* 110,33 km2
Comté ou district: Abitibi-Ouest; *Population au 2016:* 986
Circonscription(s) électorale(s) provinciale(s): Abitibi-Ouest
Circonscription(s) électorale(s) fédérale(s):
Abitibi-Témiscamingue
Prochaines élections: 7e novembre 2021
Jaclin Bégin, Maire
Gisèle Bisson-Lapointe, Directrice générale

Sainte-Gertrude-Manneville
2, rue de l'École
Sainte-Gertrude-Manneville, QC J0Y 2L0
Tél: 819-727-2244
stegertman@cableamos.com
municipalites-du-quebec.ca/ste-gertrude-manneville
Entité municipal: Municipality
Incorporation: 1er janvier 1980; *Area:* 318,80 km2
Comté ou district: Abitibi; *Population au 2016:* 787
Circonscription(s) électorale(s) provinciale(s): Abitibi-Ouest
Circonscription(s) électorale(s) fédérale(s):
Abitibi-Témiscamingue
Prochaines élections: 7e novembre 2021
Pascal Rheault, Maire
Sandra Boutin, Directrice générale

Sainte-Hedwidge
1090, rue Principale
Sainte-Hedwidge, QC G0W 2R0
Tél: 418-275-3020
municipalites-du-quebec.ca/ste-hedwidge
Entité municipal: Municipality
Incorporation: 10 mars 1909; *Area:* 462,77 km2
Comté ou district: Le Domaine-du-Roy; *Population au 2016:* 846
Circonscription(s) électorale(s) provinciale(s): Roberval
Circonscription(s) électorale(s) fédérale(s): Lac-St-Jean
Prochaines élections: 7e novembre 2021
Gilles Toulouse, Maire

Jimmy Morin, Directeur général

Sainte-Hélène-de-Bagot
421, 4e av
Sainte-Hélène-de-Bagot, QC J0H 1M0
Tél: 450-791-2455; *Téléc:* 450-791-2550
mun@saintehelenedebagot.com
www.saintehelenedebagot.com
Entité municipal: Municipality
Incorporation: 9 juilllet 1977; *Area:* 72,53 km2
Comté ou district: Les Maskoutains; *Population au 2016:* 1,688
Circonscription(s) électorale(s) provinciale(s): Johnson
Circonscription(s) électorale(s) fédérale(s): St-Hyacinthe-Bagot
Prochaines élections: 7e novembre 2021
Stephan Hebert, Maire
Sylvie Viens, Directrice générale, 450-791-2455

Sainte-Hélène-de-Chester
440, rue de l'Église
Sainte-Hélène-de-Chester, QC G0O 1H0
Tél: 819-382-2650
municipalite@sainte-helene-de-chester.ca
municipalites-du-quebec.ca/sainte-helene-de-chester
Entité municipal: Municipality
Incorporation: 1er janvier 1859; *Area:* 83,68 km2
Comté ou district: Arthabaska; *Population au 2016:* 374
Circonscription(s) électorale(s) provinciale(s):
Drummond-Bois-Francs
Circonscription(s) électorale(s) fédérale(s):
Richmond-Arthabaska
Prochaines élections: 7e novembre 2021
Lionel Fréchette, Maire
Chantal Baril, Directrice générale

Sainte-Hélène-de-Kamouraska
531, rue de l'Église sud
Sainte-Hélène, QC G0L 3J0
Tél: 418-492-6830; *Téléc:* 418-492-1854
developpement@sainte-helene.net
sainte-helene.net
Entité municipal: Municipality
Incorporation: 1er juillet 1855; *Area:* 60,56 km2
Comté ou district: Kamouraska; *Population au 2016:* 918
Circonscription(s) électorale(s) provinciale(s): Côte-du-Sud
Circonscription(s) électorale(s) fédérale(s):
Montmagny-L'Islet-Kamourask-Rivière-du-Loup
Prochaines élections: 7e novembre 2021
Louise Hémond, Mairesse
Cédric Lauzon, Directrice générale, 418-492-6830

Sainte-Hélène-de-Mancebourg
451, rang 2e-et-3e
Mancebourg, QC J0Z 2T0
Tél: 819-333-5766; *Téléc:* 819-333-9514
mancebourg@mrcao.qc.ca
ste-helene.ao.ca
Entité municipal: Parish (Paroisse)
Incorporation: 10 mai 1941; *Area:* 68,71 km2
Comté ou district: Abitibi-Ouest; *Population au 2016:* 373
Circonscription(s) électorale(s) provinciale(s): Abitibi-Ouest
Circonscription(s) électorale(s) fédérale(s):
Abitibi-Témiscamingue
Prochaines élections: 7e novembre 2021
Florent Bédard, Maire
Sylvie Boutin-Bergeron, Directrice générale

Sainte-Hénédine
111, rue Principale
Sainte-Hénédine, QC G0S 2R0
Tél: 418-935-7125; *Téléc:* 418-935-3113
info@ste-henedine.com
www.ste-henedine.com
Entité municipal: Parish (Paroisse)
Incorporation: 1er juillet 1855; *Area:* 51,54
Comté ou district: La Nouvelle-Beauce; *Population au 2016:*
1,271
Circonscription(s) électorale(s) provinciale(s): Beauce-Nord
Circonscription(s) électorale(s) fédérale(s): Beauce
Prochaines élections: 7e novembre 2021
Michel Duval, Maire
Yvon Marcoux, Directeur général

Sainte-Irène
362, rue de la Fabrique
Sainte-Irène, QC G0J 2P0
Tél: 418-629-5705; *Téléc:* 418-629-3220
www.sainteirene.com
Entité municipal: Parish (Paroisse)
Incorporation: 1er janvier 1953; *Area:* 135,25
Comté ou district: La Matapédia; *Population au 2016:* 327
Circonscription(s) électorale(s) provinciale(s): Matane-Matapédia
Circonscription(s) électorale(s) fédérale(s): Avignon-La

Mitis-Matane-Matapédia
Prochaines élections: 7e novembre 2021
Jérémie Gagnon, Maire
Mario Lavoie, Directeur général par interim

Sainte-Jeanne-d'Arc
321, rue Principale
Sainte-Jeanne-d'Arc, QC G0J 2T0
Tél: 418-775-5660; *Téléc:* 418-775-5666
stejeanne@mitis.qc.ca
www.municipalite.sainte-jeanne-darc.qc.ca
Entité municipal: Parish (Paroisse)
Incorporation: 30 janvier 1922; *Area:* 110,55 km2
Comté ou district: La Mitis; *Population au 2016:* 280
Circonscription(s) électorale(s) provinciale(s): Matane-Matapédia
Circonscription(s) électorale(s) fédérale(s): Avignon-La Mitis-Matane-Matapédia
Prochaines élections: 7e novembre 2021
Maurice Chrétien, Maire
Louise Boivin, Directrice générale

Sainte-Jeanne-d'Arc
378, rue François-Bilodeau
Sainte-Jeanne-d'Arc, QC G0W 1E0
Tél: 418-276-3166
info@stejeannedarc.qc.ca
www.stejeannedarc.qc.ca
Entité municipal: Village
Incorporation: 24 janvier 1970; *Area:* 269,17 km2
Comté ou district: Maria-Chapdelaine; *Population au 2016:* 1,050
Circonscription(s) électorale(s) provinciale(s): Roberval
Circonscription(s) électorale(s) fédérale(s): Lac-St-Jean
Prochaines élections: 7e novembre 2021
Denise Lamontagne, Mairesse
Vacant, Directeur général

Sainte-Julienne
2450, rue Victoria
Sainte-Julienne, QC J0K 2T0
Tél: 450-831-2688; *Téléc:* 450-831-4433
municipalite@sainte-julienne.com
www.sainte-julienne.com
Other Information: Sans frais: 800-690-2688
Entité municipal: Municipality
Incorporation: 1er juillet 1855; *Area:* 99,61 km2
Comté ou district: Montcalm; *Population au 2016:* 9,953
Circonscription(s) électorale(s) provinciale(s): Rousseau
Circonscription(s) électorale(s) fédérale(s): Montcalm
Prochaines élections: 7e novembre 2021
Jean-Pierre Charron, Maire
Nathalie Girard, Directrice générale

Sainte-Justine
167, rte 204
Sainte-Justine, QC G0R 1Y0
Tél: 418-383-5397; *Téléc:* 418-383-5398
reception@stejustine.net
www.stejustine.net
Entité municipal: Municipality
Incorporation: 1er janvier 1870; *Area:* 126,30 km2
Comté ou district: Les Etchemins; *Population au 2016:* 1,820
Circonscription(s) électorale(s) provinciale(s): Bellechasse
Circonscription(s) électorale(s) fédérale(s): Bellechasse-Etchemins-Lévis
Prochaines élections: 7e novembre 2021
Christian Chabot, Maire
Gilles Vézina, Directeur général

Sainte-Justine-de-Newton
2627, rue Principale
Sainte-Justine-de-Newton, QC J0P 1T0
Tél: 450-764-3573; *Téléc:* 450-764-3180
ste-justine@oricom.ca
www.sainte-justine-de-newton.ca
Entité municipal: Municipality
Incorporation: 1er juillet 1855; *Area:* 84,63 km2
Comté ou district: Vaudreuil-Soulanges; *Population au 2016:* 922
Circonscription(s) électorale(s) provinciale(s): Soulanges
Circonscription(s) électorale(s) fédérale(s): Salaberry-Suroît
Prochaines élections: 7e novembre 2021
Denis Ranger, Maire
Vacant, Directeur général

Saint-Élie-de-Caxton
52, ch des Loisirs
Saint-Élie, QC G0X 2N0
Tél: 819-221-2839; *Téléc:* 819-221-4039
info@st-elie-de-caxton.ca
www.st-elie-de-caxton.ca
Entité municipal: Municipality
Incorporation: 12 avril 1865; *Area:* 118,11 km2
Comté ou district: Maskinongé; *Population au 2016:* 1,836

Circonscription(s) électorale(s) provinciale(s): Maskinongé
Circonscription(s) électorale(s) fédérale(s): Berthier-Maskinongé
Prochaines élections: 7e novembre 2021
Robert Gauthier, Maire, 819-221-2839
Benoît Gauthier, Directeur général, 819-221-2839

Saint-Éloi
183, rue Principale
Saint-Éloi, QC G0L 2V0
Tél: 418-898-2734; *Téléc:* 418-898-2305
st-eloi@st-eloi.qc.ca
www.st-eloi.qc.ca
Entité municipal: Parish (Paroisse)
Incorporation: 1er juillet 1855; *Area:* 66,11 km2
Comté ou district: Les Basques; *Population au 2016:* 286
Circonscription(s) électorale(s) provinciale(s): Rivière-du-Loup-Témiscouata
Circonscription(s) électorale(s) fédérale(s): Rimouski-Neigette-Témiscouata-Les Basques
Prochaines élections: 7e novembre 2021
Mario St-Louis, Maire
Annie Roussel, Directrice générale

Sainte-Louise
80, rte de la Station
Sainte-Louise, QC G0R 3K0
Tél: 418-354-2509; *Téléc:* 418-354-7730
info@saintelouise.qc.ca
www.saintelouise.qc.ca
Entité municipal: Parish (Paroisse)
Incorporation: 11 décembre 1860; *Area:* 76,60 km2
Comté ou district: L'Islet; *Population au 2016:* 671
Circonscription(s) électorale(s) provinciale(s): Côte-du-Sud
Circonscription(s) électorale(s) fédérale(s): Montmagny-L'Islet-Kamouraska-Rivière-du-Loup
Prochaines élections: 7e novembre 2021
Normand Dubé, Maire
Roxanne Desrosiers, Directrice générale

Saint-Elphège
245, rang St-Antoine
Saint-Elphege, QC J0G 1J0
Tél: 450-568-0288
mun.stelphege@sogetel.net
municipalites-du-quebec.ca/saint-elphege
Entité municipal: Parish (Paroisse)
Incorporation: 12 mars 1886; *Area:* 40,55 km2
Comté ou district: Nicolet-Yamaska; *Population au 2016:* 270
Circonscription(s) électorale(s) provinciale(s): Nicolet-Bécancour
Circonscription(s) électorale(s) fédérale(s): Bécancour-Nicolet-Saurel
Prochaines élections: 7e novembre 2021
Mario Lefebvre, Maire
Yolaine Lampron, Directrice générale

Sainte-Luce
1, rue Langlois
Sainte-Luce, QC G0K 1P0
Tél: 418-739-4317; *Téléc:* 418-739-4823
sainte-luce@sainteluce.ca
sainteluce.ca
Entité municipal: Municipality
Incorporation: 29 octobre 2001; *Area:* 73,05 km2
Comté ou district: La Mitis; *Population au 2016:* 2,801
Circonscription(s) électorale(s) provinciale(s): Matane-Matapédia
Circonscription(s) électorale(s) fédérale(s): Avignon-La Mitis-Matane-Matapédia
Prochaines élections: 7e novembre 2021
Maïté Blanchette Vézina, Mairesse
Stéphane Forest, Directeur général

Sainte-Lucie-de-Beauregard
21, rte des Chutes
Sainte-Lucie-de-Beauregard, QC G0R 3L0
Tél: 418-223-3122; *Téléc:* 418-223-3121
ste-lucie@globetrotter.net
www.saintelucidebeauregard.net
Entité municipal: Municipality
Incorporation: 18 novembre 1924; *Area:* 82,24 km2
Comté ou district: Montmagny; *Population au 2016:* 280
Circonscription(s) électorale(s) provinciale(s): Côte-du-Sud
Circonscription(s) électorale(s) fédérale(s): Montmagny-L'Islet-Kamouraska-Rivière-du-Loup
Prochaines élections: 7e novembre 2021
Louis Lachance, Maire
Bianca Deschênes, Directrice générale

Sainte-Lucie-des-Laurentides
2121, ch des Hauteurs
Sainte-Lucie-des-Laurentides, QC J0T 2J0
Tél: 819-326-3198; *Téléc:* 819-326-0592
info@msldl.ca
msldl.ca
Entité municipal: Municipality
Incorporation: 1er janvier 1874; *Area:* 109,76 km2
Comté ou district: Les Laurentides; *Population au 2016:* 1,256
Circonscription(s) électorale(s) provinciale(s): Bertrand
Circonscription(s) électorale(s) fédérale(s): Laurentides-Labelle
Prochaines élections: 7e novembre 2021
Anne Guylaine Legault, Mairesse
Jacques Brisebois, Directeur général par intérim

Saint-Elzéar
148, ch Principal
Saint-Elzéar-de-Bonaventure, QC G0C 2W0
Tél: 418-534-2611
muni@saintelzear.net
www.saintelzear.net
Entité municipal: Municipality
Incorporation: 1er janvier 1965; *Area:* 203,58 km2
Comté ou district: Bonaventure; *Population au 2016:* 458
Circonscription(s) électorale(s) provinciale(s): Bonaventure
Circonscription(s) électorale(s) fédérale(s): Gaspésie—Îles-de-la-Madeleine; Beauce
Prochaines élections: 7e novembre 2021
Marie-Louis Bourages, Maire
Marjolaine St-Pierre, Directrice générale

Saint-Elzéar
597, rue des Érables
Saint-Elzéar, QC G0S 2J1
Tél: 418-387-2534
administration@st-elzear.ca
st-elzear.ca
Entité municipal: Municipality
Incorporation: 30 novembre 1994; *Area:* 87,07 km2
Comté ou district: La Nouvelle-Beauce; *Population au 2016:* 2,400
Circonscription(s) électorale(s) provinciale(s): Beauce-Nord
Circonscription(s) électorale(s) fédérale(s): Beauce
Prochaines élections: 7e novembre 2021
Carl Marcoux, Maire
Mathieu Genest, Directeur général, 418-387-2534

Saint-Elzér-de-Témiscouata
209, rue de l'Église
Saint-Elzér-de-Témiscouata, QC G0L 2W0
Tél: 418-854-7690
admin@saintelzear.ca
saintelzear.ca
Entité municipal: Municipality
Incorporation: 19 novembre 1938; *Area:* 151,34 km2
Comté ou district: Témiscouata; *Population au 2016:* 321
Circonscription(s) électorale(s) provinciale(s): Rivière-du-Loup-Témiscouata
Circonscription(s) électorale(s) fédérale(s): Rimouski-Neigette-Témiscouata-Les Basques
Prochaines élections: 7e novembre 2021
Carmen Massé, Mairesse
Denise Dubé, Directrice générale

Sainte-Madeleine
850, rue St-Simon
Sainte-Madeleine, QC J0H 1S0
Tél: 450-795-3822; *Téléc:* 450-795-3736
administration@stemadeleine.quebec
www.stemadeleine.quebec
Entité municipal: Village
Incorporation: 30 décembre 1919; *Area:* 5,37 km2
Comté ou district: Les Maskoutains; *Population au 2016:* 2,233
Circonscription(s) électorale(s) provinciale(s): Borduas
Circonscription(s) électorale(s) fédérale(s): St-Hyacinthe-Bagot
Prochaines élections: 7e novembre 2021
André Lefebvre, Maire
Carl Simard, Directeur général

Sainte-Madeleine-de-la-Rivière-Madeleine
104, rte Principale
Madeleine-Centre, QC G0E 1P0
Tél: 418-393-2428; *Téléc:* 418-393-2869
munste-madeleine@globetrotter.net
stemadeleine.ca
Entité municipal: Municipality
Incorporation: 27 février 1915; *Area:* 263,34 km2
Comté ou district: La Haute-Gaspésie; *Population au 2016:* 289
Circonscription(s) électorale(s) provinciale(s): Gaspé
Circonscription(s) électorale(s) fédérale(s): Gaspésie—Les Îles-de-la-Madeleine
Prochaines élections: 7e novembre 2021

Circonscription(s) électorale(s) provinciale(s): Lac-St-Jean
Circonscription(s) électorale(s) fédérale(s): Lac-St-Jean
Prochaines élections: 7e novembre 2021
Émile Hudon, Maire
Dany Dallaire, Directeur général, 418-345-8001

Saint-Gédéon-de-Beauce
127A, 1e av sud
Saint-Gédéon-de-Beauce, QC G0M 1T0
Tél: 418-582-3341; *Téléc:* 418-582-6016
stgedeon@globetrotter.net
www.st-gedeon-de-beauce.qc.ca
Entité municipal: Municipality
Incorporation: 12 février 1003; *Area:* 197,52 km2
Comté ou district: Beauce-Sartigan; *Population au 2016:* 2,205
Circonscription(s) électorale(s) provinciale(s): Beauce-Sud
Circonscription(s) électorale(s) fédérale(s): Beauce
Prochaines élections: 7e novembre 2021
Note: Effective October 12, 2003, the Municipality of
St-Gédéon-de-Beauce & the Parish of St-Gédéon amalgamated
to create the new Municipality of St-Gédéon-de-Beauce.
Alain Quirion, Maire
Erika Ouellet, Directeur général, 418-582-3341

Saint-Georges-de-Clarenceville
1350, ch Middle
Saint-Georges-de-Clarenceville, QC J0J 1B0
Tél: 450-294-2464; *Téléc:* 450-294-2016
info@clarenceville.qc.ca
www.clarenceville.qc.ca
Entité municipal: Municipality
Incorporation: 27 décembre 1989; *Area:* 63,46 km2
Comté ou district: Le Haut-Richelieu; *Population au 2016:* 1,103
Circonscription(s) électorale(s) provinciale(s): Iberville
Circonscription(s) électorale(s) fédérale(s): Brome-Missisquoi
Prochaines élections: 7e novembre 2021
Renée Rouleau, Mairesse
Sonia Côté, Directrice générale, 450-294-2464

Saint-Georges-de-Windsor
527, rue Principale
Saint-Georges-de-Windsor, QC J0A 1J0
Tél: 819-828-2716; *Téléc:* 819-828-0213
www.st-georges-de-windsor.org
Entité municipal: Municipality
Incorporation: 30 novembre 2009; *Area:* 127,66 km2
Comté ou district: Les Sources; *Population au 2016:* 958
Circonscription(s) électorale(s) provinciale(s): Richmond
Circonscription(s) électorale(s) fédérale(s):
Richmond-Arthabaska
Prochaines élections: 7e novembre 2021
René Perreault, Maire
Armande Perreault, Directrice générale

Saint-Gérard-Majella
444, rang St-Antoine
Saint-Gérard-Majella, QC J0G 1X0
Tél: 450-789-5777; *Téléc:* 450-789-1188
saintgerardmajella.ca
Entité municipal: Parish (Paroisse)
Incorporation: 18 février 1907; *Area:* 38,32 km2
Comté ou district: Pierre-De Saurel; *Population au 2016:* 242
Circonscription(s) électorale(s) provinciale(s): Richelieu
Circonscription(s) électorale(s) fédérale(s):
Bécancour-Nicolet-Saurel; Repentigny
Prochaines élections: 7e novembre 2021
Georges-Henri Parenteau, Maire
Anny Boisjoli, Directeur général

Saint-Germain
146, rang des Côtes
Saint-Germain, QC G0L 3G0
Tél: 418-492-9771; *Téléc:* 418-492-9772
info@munsaintgermain.ca
www.munsaintgermain.ca
Entité municipal: Parish (Paroisse)
Incorporation: 29 juin 1893; *Area:* 28,60 km2
Comté ou district: Kamouraska; *Population au 2016:* 286
Circonscription(s) électorale(s) provinciale(s): Côte-du-Sud
Circonscription(s) électorale(s) fédérale(s):
Montmagny-L'Islet-Kamouraska-Rivière-du-Loup
Prochaines élections: 7e novembre 2021
Daniel Laplante, Maire
Hélène B.-Bernier, Directrice générale

Saint-Germain-de-Grantham
233, ch Yamaska
Saint-Germain-de-Grantham, QC J0C 1K0
Tél: 819-395-5496
reception@st-germain.info
st-germain.info

Entité municipal: Municipality
Incorporation: 22 février 1995; *Area:* 87,46 km2
Comté ou district: Drummond; *Population au 2016:* 4,917
Circonscription(s) électorale(s) provinciale(s): Johnson
Circonscription(s) électorale(s) fédérale(s): Drummond
Prochaines élections: 7e novembre 2021
Nathacha Tessier, Mairesse
Nathalie Lemoine, Directrice générale

Saint-Gervais
150, rue Principale
Saint-Gervais, QC G0R 3C0
Tél: 418-887-6116; *Téléc:* 418-887-6312
info@saint-gervais.ca
saint-gervais.ca
Entité municipal: Municipality
Incorporation: 1er juillet 1855; *Area:* 89,36 km2
Comté ou district: Bellechasse; *Population au 2016:* 2,153
Circonscription(s) électorale(s) provinciale(s): Bellechasse
Circonscription(s) électorale(s) fédérale(s): Bellechasse-Les
Etchemins-Lévis
Prochaines élections: 7e novembre 2021
Manon Goulet, Maire
Johanne Simms, Directrice générale

Saint-Gilbert
110, rue Principale
Saint-Gilbert, QC G0A 3T0
Tél: 418-268-8194; *Téléc:* 418-268-6466
saint-gilbert@globetrotter.net
www.saint-gilbert.ca
Entité municipal: Parish (Paroisse)
Incorporation: 27 avril 1893; *Area:* 37,46 km2
Comté ou district: Portneuf; *Population au 2016:* 296
Circonscription(s) électorale(s) provinciale(s): Portneuf
Circonscription(s) électorale(s) fédérale(s):
Portneuf-Jacques-Cartier
Prochaines élections: 7e novembre 2021
Léo Gignac, Maire
Christian Fontaine, Directeur général

Saint-Gilles
165, rue O'Hurley
Saint-Gilles, QC G0S 2P0
Tél: 418-888-3198; *Téléc:* 418-888-5145
info@stgilles.net
www.st-gilles.qc.ca
Entité municipal: Municipality
Incorporation: 1er juillet 1855; *Area:* 177,43 km2
Comté ou district: Lotbinière; *Population au 2016:* 2,525
Circonscription(s) électorale(s) provinciale(s):
Lotbinière-Frontenac
Circonscription(s) électorale(s) fédérale(s): Lévis-Lotbinière
Prochaines élections: 7e novembre 2021
Robert Samson, Maire
Martel Raynald, Directeur général

Saint-Godefroi
CP 157
109C, rte 132
Saint-Godefroi, QC G0C 3C0
Tél: 418-752-6316; *Téléc:* 418-752-6396
stgodefroi@navigue.com
municipalitestgodefroi.com
Entité municipal: Township
Incorporation: 16 décembre 1913; *Area:* 63,52 km2
Comté ou district: Bonaventure; *Population au 2016:* 380
Circonscription(s) électorale(s) provinciale(s): Bonaventure
Circonscription(s) électorale(s) fédérale(s):
Gaspésie—Îles-de-la-Madeleine
Prochaines élections: 7e novembre 2021
Genade Grenier, Maire
Céline Roussy, Directrice générale

Saint-Guillaume
106, rue St-Jean-Baptiste
Saint-Guillaume, QC J0C 1L0
Tél: 819-396-2403; *Téléc:* 819-396-0184
www.municipalite-st-guillaume.qc.ca
Entité municipal: Municipality
Incorporation: 8 novembre 1995; *Area:* 87,88 km2
Comté ou district: Drummond; *Population au 2016:* 1,476
Circonscription(s) électorale(s) provinciale(s): Nicolet-Bécancour
Circonscription(s) électorale(s) fédérale(s): Drummond
Prochaines élections: 7e novembre 2021
Robert Julien, Maire
Diane Martineau, Directrice générale

Saint-Guy
52, rue Principal
Saint-Guy, QC G0K 1W0
Tél: 418-963-2601
bureau@saintguy.ca
st-guy.qc.ca
Entité municipal: Municipality
Incorporation: 1er janvier 1958; *Area:* 139,82 km2
Comté ou district: Les Basques; *Population au 2016:* 54
Circonscription(s) électorale(s) provinciale(s):
Rivière-du-Loup-Témiscouata
Circonscription(s) électorale(s) fédérale(s):
Rimouski-Neigette-Témiscouata-Les Basques
Prochaines élections: 7e novembre 2021
Maxime Dupont, Maire
Stéphane Lacam-Gitareu, Directeur général

Saint-Henri
219, rue Commerciale
Saint-Henri, QC G0R 3E0
Tél: 418-882-2401
info@saint-henri.ca
www.saint-henri.ca
Entité municipal: Municipality
Incorporation: 9 octobre 1976; *Area:* 122,57 km2
Comté ou district: Bellechasse; *Population au 2016:* 5,611
Circonscription(s) électorale(s) provinciale(s): Bellechasse
Circonscription(s) électorale(s) fédérale(s): Bellechasse-Les
Etchemins-Lévis
Prochaines élections: 7e novembre 2021
Germain Caron, Maire
Jérôme Fortier, Directeur général, 418-882-2401

Saint-Henri-de-Taillon
430, rue Hotel-de-Ville
Saint-Henri-de-Taillon, QC G0W 2X0
Tél: 418-347-3243
municipalite@ville.st-henri-de-taillon.qc.ca
ville.st-henri-de-taillon.qc.ca
Entité municipal: Municipality
Incorporation: 12 août 1903; *Area:* 61,45 km2
Comté ou district: Lac-Saint-Jean-Est; *Population au 2016:* 821
Circonscription(s) électorale(s) provinciale(s): Lac-St-Jean
Circonscription(s) électorale(s) fédérale(s): Lac-St-Jean
Prochaines élections: 7e novembre 2021
André Paradis, Maire
Mario Morissette, Directeur général, 418-347-3243

Saint-Herménégilde
816, rue Principale
Saint-Herménégilde, QC J0B 2W0
Tél: 819-849-4443; *Téléc:* 819-849-6924
municipalite@st-hermenegilde.qc.ca
www.st-hermenegilde.qc.ca
Entité municipal: Municipality
Incorporation: 12 octobre 1985; *Area:* 166,42 km2
Comté ou district: Coaticook; *Population au 2016:* 670
Circonscription(s) électorale(s) provinciale(s): St-François
Circonscription(s) électorale(s) fédérale(s): Compton-Stanstead
Prochaines élections: 7e novembre 2021
Gérard Duteau, Maire
Johanne Le Buis, Directrice générale

Saint-Hilaire-de-Dorset
847, rue Principale
Saint-Hilaire-de-Dorset, QC G0M 1G0
Tél: 418-459-6872; *Téléc:* 418-459-6882
munsthilaire@telstep.net
www.sthilairededorset.ca
Entité municipal: Parish (Paroisse)
Incorporation: 12 avril 1916; *Area:* 187,13 km2
Comté ou district: Beauce-Sartigan; *Population au 2016:* 95
Circonscription(s) électorale(s) provinciale(s): Beauce-Sud
Circonscription(s) électorale(s) fédérale(s): Beauce
Prochaines élections: 7e novembre 2021
Ghislain Jacques, Maire
Cathy Payeur, Directrice générale

Saint-Hilarion
306, ch Cartier nord
Saint-Hilarion, QC G0A 3V0
Tél: 418-489-2995; *Téléc:* 418-457-3805
municipalite@sainthilarion.ca
www.sainthilarion.ca
Entité municipal: Parish (Paroisse)
Incorporation: 1er juillet 1855; *Area:* 100,31 km2
Comté ou district: Charlevoix; *Population au 2016:* 1,127
Circonscription(s) électorale(s) provinciale(s):
Charlevoix-Côte-de-Beaupré
Circonscription(s) électorale(s) fédérale(s):
Beauport—Côte-de-Beaupré—Île d'Orléans—Charlevoix
Prochaines élections: 7e novembre 2021

Patrick Lavoie, Maire
Nathalie Lavoie, Directrice générale, 418-489-2995

Saint-Hippolyte
2253, ch des Hauteurs
Saint-Hippolyte, QC J8A 1A1
Tél: 450-563-2505
municipalite@saint-hippolyte.ca
saint-hippolyte.ca
Entité municipal: Municipality
Incorporation: 1er juillet 1855; *Area:* 120,72 km2
Comté ou district: La Rivière-du-Nord; *Population au 2016:* 9,113
Circonscription(s) électorale(s) provinciale(s): Bertrand
Circonscription(s) électorale(s) fédérale(s): Rivière-du-Nord
Prochaines élections: 7e novembre 2021
Bruno Laroche, Maire
Mathieu Meunier, Directeur général par intérim, 450-563-2505

Saint-Honoré
3611, boul Martel
Saint-Honoré, QC G0V 1L0
Tél: 418-673-3405
admin@ville.sthonore.qc.ca
www.ville.sthonore.qc.ca
Entité municipal: Municipality
Incorporation: 16 décembre 1972; *Area:* 189,54 km2
Comté ou district: Jonquière; *Population au 2016:* 5,757
Circonscription(s) électorale(s) provinciale(s): Dubuc
Circonscription(s) électorale(s) fédérale(s): Jonquière
Prochaines élections: 7e novembre 2021
Bruno Tremblay, Maire
Stéphane Leclerc, Directeur général

Saint-Honoré-de-Shenley
499, rue Principale
Saint-Honoré-de-Shenley, QC G0M 1V0
Tél: 418-485-6738; *Téléc:* 418-485-6171
sthonoredeshenley.com
Entité municipal: Municipality
Incorporation: 19 avril 2000; *Area:* 134,00 km2
Comté ou district: Beauce-Sartigan; *Population au 2016:* 1,483
Circonscription(s) électorale(s) provinciale(s): Beauce-Sud
Circonscription(s) électorale(s) fédérale(s): Beauce
Prochaines élections: 7e novembre 2021
Dany Quirion, Maire
Pier-Olivier Busque, Directeur général, 418-485-6738

Saint-Honoré-de-Témiscouata
99, rue Principale
Saint-Honoré-de-Témiscouata, QC G0L 3K0
Tél: 418-497-2588; *Téléc:* 418-497-1656
admin@sainthonoredetemiscouata.ca
www.sainthonoredetemiscouata.ca
Entité municipal: Municipality
Incorporation: 1er janvier 1881; *Area:* 263,20 km2
Comté ou district: Témiscouata; *Population au 2016:* 741
Circonscription(s) électorale(s) provinciale(s):
Rivière-du-Loup-Témiscouata
Circonscription(s) électorale(s) fédérale(s):
Rimouski-Neigette-Témiscouata-Les Basques
Prochaines élections: 7e novembre 2021
Richard F. Dubé, Maire
Michael Marmen, Directeur général, 418-497-2588

Saint-Hubert-de-Rivière-du-Loup
10, rue Saint-Rosaire
Saint-Hubert-Rivière-du-Loup, QC G0L 3L0
Tél: 418-497-3394; *Téléc:* 418-497-1187
communications@sthubertrdl.qc.ca
www.municipalite.saint-hubert-de-riviere-du-loup.qc.ca
Entité municipal: Municipality
Incorporation: 4 janvier 1894; *Area:* 192,76 km2
Comté ou district: Rivière-du-Loup; *Population au 2016:* 1,279
Circonscription(s) électorale(s) provinciale(s):
Rivière-du-Loup-Témiscouata
Circonscription(s) électorale(s) fédérale(s):
Montmagny-L'Islet-Kamouraska-Rivière-du-Loup
Prochaines élections: 7e novembre 2021
Gilles Couture, Maire
Sylvie Samson, Directrice générale, 418-497-3394

Saint-Hugues
#103, 171, rue Saint-Germain
Saint-Hugues, QC J0H 1N0
Tél: 450-794-2030; *Téléc:* 450-794-2474
reception@st-hugues.com
saint-hugues.com
Entité municipal: Municipality
Incorporation: 6 novembre 1982; *Area:* 84,71 km2
Comté ou district: Les Maskoutains; *Population au 2016:* 1,327
Circonscription(s) électorale(s) provinciale(s): St-Hyacinthe

Circonscription(s) électorale(s) fédérale(s): St-Hyacinthe-Bagot
Prochaines élections: 7e novembre 2021
Richard Veilleux, Maire
Carole Thibault, Directrice générale, 450-794-2030

Saint-Ignace-de-Loyola
25, rue Laforest
Saint-Ignace-de-Loyola, QC J0K 2P0
Tél: 450-836-3376
info@stignacedeloyola.qc.ca
www.stignacedeloyola.qc.ca
Entité municipal: Municipality
Incorporation: 11 février 1897; *Area:* 36,16 km2
Comté ou district: D'Autray; *Population au 2016:* 2,049
Circonscription(s) électorale(s) provinciale(s): Berthier
Circonscription(s) électorale(s) fédérale(s): Berthier-Maskinongé
Prochaines élections: 7e novembre 2021
Jean-Luc Barthe, Maire
Mélanie Messier, Directrice générale, 450-836-337

Saint-Ignace-de-Stanbridge
692, rang de l'Église nord
Saint-Ignace-de-Stanbridge, QC J0J 1Y0
Tél: 450-296-4467; *Téléc:* 450-296-4461
stignace@videotron.ca
www.saint-ignace-de-stanbridge.com
Entité municipal: Municipality
Incorporation: 21 mars 1889; *Area:* 69,43 km2
Comté ou district: Brome-Missisquoi; *Population au 2016:* 676
Circonscription(s) électorale(s) provinciale(s): Brome-Missisquoi
Circonscription(s) électorale(s) fédérale(s): Brome-Missisquoi
Prochaines élections: 7e novembre 2021
Dominique Martel, Maire
Marie-Josée Lamothe, Directrice générale

Saint-Irénée
350, rue Principale
Saint-Irénée, QC G0T 1V0
Tél: 418-620-5015; *Téléc:* 418-620-5017
secretaire@saintirenee.ca
saintirenee.ca
Entité municipal: Parish (Paroisse)
Incorporation: 1er juillet 1855; *Area:* 60,38 km2
Comté ou district: Charlevoix-Est; *Population au 2016:* 641
Circonscription(s) électorale(s) provinciale(s):
Charlevoix-Côte-de-Beaupré
Circonscription(s) électorale(s) fédérale(s):
Beauport—Côte-de-Beaupré—Île d'Orléans—Charlevoix
Prochaines élections: 7e novembre 2021
Odile Comeau, Maire
Marie-Claude Lavoie, Directrice générale, 418-620-5015

Saint-Isidore
671, rue St-Régis
Saint-Isidore, QC J0L 2A0
Tél: 450-454-3919
www.municipalite.saint-isidore.qc.ca
Entité municipal: Parish (Paroisse)
Incorporation: 1er juillet 1855; *Area:* 52,32 km2
Comté ou district: Roussillon; Communauté métropolitaine de Montréal; *Population au 2016:* 2,608
Circonscription(s) électorale(s) provinciale(s): Châteauguay
Circonscription(s) électorale(s) fédérale(s): Châteauguay-Lacolle
Prochaines élections: 7e novembre 2021
Sylvain Payant, Maire
Sébastien Carignan-Cervera, Directeur général

Saint-Isidore
128, rte Coulombe
Saint-Isidore, QC G0S 2S0
Tél: 418-882-5670; *Téléc:* 418-882-5902
info@saint-isidore.net
www.saint-isidore.net
Entité municipal: Municipality
Incorporation: 22 septembre 1993; *Area:* 102,65 km2
Comté ou district: La Nouvelle-Beauce; *Population au 2016:* 2,880
Circonscription(s) électorale(s) provinciale(s): Beauce-Nord
Circonscription(s) électorale(s) fédérale(s): Beauce
Prochaines élections: 7e novembre 2021
Turgeon Réal, Maire
Marc-Antoine Tremblay, Directeur général

Saint-Isidore-de-Clifton
66, ch Auckland
Saint-Isidore-de-Clifton, QC J0B 2X0
Tél: 819-658-3637; *Téléc:* 819-560-8559
stic@hsfqc.ca
www.st-isidore-clifton.qc.ca
Entité municipal: Municipality
Incorporation: 24 décembre 1997; *Area:* 177,30 km2
Comté ou district: Le Haut-Saint-François; *Population au 2016:*

695
Circonscription(s) électorale(s) provinciale(s): Mégantic
Circonscription(s) électorale(s) fédérale(s): Compton-Stanstead
Prochaines élections: 7e novembre 2021
Yann Vallières, Maire
Sarah Lévesque, Directrice générale

Saint-Jacques
16, rue Maréchal
Saint-Jacques, QC J0K 2R0
Tél: 450-839-3671; *Téléc:* 450-839-2387
info@st-jacques.org
www.st-jacques.org
Entité municipal: Municipality
Incorporation: 20 mai 1998; *Area:* 67,26 km2
Comté ou district: Montcalm; *Population au 2016:* 3,971
Circonscription(s) électorale(s) provinciale(s): Joliette
Circonscription(s) électorale(s) fédérale(s): Montcalm
Prochaines élections: 7e novembre 2021
Josyanne Forest, Maire, 450-839-3671
Josée Favreau, Directrice générale, 450-839-3671

Saint-Jacques-de-Leeds
405, rue Principale
Saint-Jacques-de-Leeds, QC G0N 1J0
Tél: 418-424-3321; *Téléc:* 418-424-0126
info@saintjacquesdeleeds.ca
www.saintjacquesdeleeds.ca
Entité municipal: Municipality
Incorporation: 23 septembre 1929; *Area:* 80,57 km2
Comté ou district: Les Appalaches; *Population au 2016:* 685
Circonscription(s) électorale(s) provinciale(s):
Lotbinière-Frontenac
Circonscription(s) électorale(s) fédérale(s): Mégantic-L'Érable
Prochaines élections: 7e novembre 2021
Philippe Chabot, Maire, 418-424-3321
Sonia Tardif, Directrice générale, 418-424-3321

Saint-Jacques-le-Majeur-de-Wolfestown
877, rte 263
Saint-Jacques-le-Majeur, QC G0N 1E0
Tél: 418-449-1531; *Téléc:* 418-449-1876
stjacqueslemajeur@hotmail.com
www.st-jacques-le-majeur-de-wolfestown.ca
Entité municipal: Parish (Paroisse)
Incorporation: 30 septembre 1909; *Area:* 58,79 km2
Comté ou district: Les Appalaches; *Population au 2016:* 188
Circonscription(s) électorale(s) provinciale(s):
Lotbinière-Frontenac
Circonscription(s) électorale(s) fédérale(s): Mégantic-L'Érable
Prochaines élections: 7e novembre 2021
Steven Laprise, Maire
France Moisan, Directrice générale

Saint-Jacques-le-Mineur
91, rue Principale
Saint-Jacques-le-Mineur, QC J0J 1Z0
Tél: 450-347-5446
info@sjlm.ca
www.saint-jacques-le-mineur.ca
Entité municipal: Municipality
Incorporation: 1er juillet 1855; *Area:* 67,19 km2
Comté ou district: Les Jardins-de-Napierville; *Population au 2016:* 1,690
Circonscription(s) électorale(s) provinciale(s): Huntingdon
Circonscription(s) électorale(s) fédérale(s): Châteauguay-Lacolle
Prochaines élections: 7e novembre 2021
Lise Sauriol, Mairesse
Isabelle Arcoite, Directrice générale, 450-347-5446

Saint-Janvier-de-Joly
729, rue des Loisirs
Saint-Janvier-de-Joly, QC G0S 1M0
Tél: 418-728-2984; *Téléc:* 418-728-2997
administration@municipalitedejoly.com
www.municipalitedejoly.com
Entité municipal: Municipality
Incorporation: 1er janvier 1944; *Area:* 109,73 km2
Comté ou district: Lotbinière; *Population au 2016:* 984
Circonscription(s) électorale(s) provinciale(s):
Lotbinière-Frontenac
Circonscription(s) électorale(s) fédérale(s): Lévis-Lotbinière
Prochaines élections: 7e novembre 2021
Bernard Fortier, Maire
Mélanie Boilard, Directrice générale, 418-728-2984

Saint-Jean-Baptiste
3041, rue Principale
Saint-Jean-Baptiste, QC J0L 2B0
Tél: 450-467-3456; *Téléc:* 450-467-8813
info@msjb.qc.ca
www.msjb.qc.ca

Entité municipal: Municipality
Incorporation: 1er juillet 1855; *Area:* 72,41 km2
Comté ou district: La Vallée-du-Richelieu; Communauté
métropolitaine de Montréal; *Population au 2016:* 3,107
Circonscription(s) électorale(s) provinciale(s): Borduas
Circonscription(s) électorale(s) fédérale(s): Beloeil-Chambly;
Montmagny-L'Islet-Kamouraska-Rivière-du-Loup; Québec
Prochaines élections: 7e novembre 2021
Marilyn Nadeau, Mairesse
Martin St-Gelais, Directeur général

Saint-Jean-de-Brébeuf
844, rue de l'Église
Saint-Jean-de-Brébeuf, QC G6G 0A1
Tél: 418-453-7774; *Téléc:* 418-453-2339
sjdb@bellnet.ca
www.st-jean-de-brebeuf.ca
Entité municipal: Municipality
Incorporation: 1er janvier 1946; *Area:* 79,18 km2
Comté ou district: Les Appalaches; *Population au 2016:* 372
Circonscription(s) électorale(s) provinciale(s):
Lotbinière-Frontenac
Circonscription(s) électorale(s) fédérale(s): Mégantic-L'Érable
Prochaines élections: 7e novembre 2021
Ghislain Hamel, Maire
Élaine Vachon, Directrice générale

Saint-Jean-de-Cherbourg
1, 8e rang
Saint-Jean-de-Cherbourg, QC G0J 2R0
Tél: 418-733-8177; *Téléc:* 418-733-8177
www.st-jeandecherbourg.ca
Entité municipal: Parish (Paroisse)
Incorporation: 1er mai 1954; *Area:* 114,05 km2
Comté ou district: La Matanie; *Population au 2016:* 86
Circonscription(s) électorale(s) provinciale(s): Matane-Matapédia
Circonscription(s) électorale(s) fédérale(s): Avignon-La
Mitis-Matane-Matapédia
Prochaines élections: 7e novembre 2021
Francine Ouellet Leclerc, Mairesse
Jacinthe Imbeault, Directrice générale

Saint-Jean-de-Dieu
32, rue Principale sud
Saint-Jean-de-Dieu, QC G0L 3M0
Tél: 418-963-3529; *Téléc:* 418-963-2903
secretariat1@saintjeandedieu.ca
www.saintjeandedieu.ca
Entité municipal: Municipality
Incorporation: 1er janvier 1865; *Area:* 152,38 km2
Comté ou district: Les Basques; *Population au 2016:* 1,596
Circonscription(s) électorale(s) provinciale(s):
Rivière-du-Loup-Témiscouata
Circonscription(s) électorale(s) fédérale(s):
Rimouski-Neigette-Témisouata-Les Basques
Prochaines élections: 7e novembre 2021
Alain Bélanger, Maire
Daniel Dufour, Directeur général, 418-963-3529

Saint-Jean-de-l'île-d'Orléans
8, ch des Côtes
Saint-Jean-de-l'île-d'Orléans, QC G0A 3W0
Tél: 418-829-2206; *Téléc:* 418-829-0997
administration@stjeanio.ca
st-jean.iledorleans.com
Entité municipal: Municipality
Incorporation: 1er juillet 1855; *Area:* 43,63 km2
Comté ou district: L'Île-d'Orléans; Communauté métropolitaine
de Québec; *Population au 2016:* 1,059
Circonscription(s) électorale(s) provinciale(s):
Charlevoix-Côte-de-Beaupré
Circonscription(s) électorale(s) fédérale(s):
Beauport—Côte-de-Beaupré—Île d'Orléans—Charlevoix
Prochaines élections: 7e novembre 2021
Jean-Claude Pouliot, Maire
Chantal Daigle, Directrice générale

Saint-Jean-de-la-Lande
810, rue Principale
Saint-Jean-de-la-Lande, QC G0L 3N0
Tél: 418-853-3703; *Téléc:* 418-853-3475
info@saintjeandelalande.ca
www.saintjeandelalande.ca
Entité municipal: Municipality
Incorporation: 1er janvier 1965; *Area:* 107,05 km2
Comté ou district: Témiscouata; *Population au 2016:* 248
Circonscription(s) électorale(s) provinciale(s):
Rivière-du-Loup-Témiscouata
Circonscription(s) électorale(s) fédérale(s):
Rimouski-Neigette-Témisouata-Les Basques
Prochaines élections: 7e novembre 2021
Jean-Marc Belzile, Maire

Luc Grandmaison, Directeur général

Saint-Jean-de-Matha
65, rue Lessard
Saint-Jean-de-Matha, QC J0K 2S0
Tél: 450-886-3867; *Téléc:* 450-886-3398
info@matha.ca
municipalitestjeandematha.com
Other Information: Sans frais: 877-886-3867
Entité municipal: Municipality
Incorporation: 1er juillet 1855; *Area:* 109,36 km2
Comté ou district: Matawinie; *Population au 2016:* 4,450
Circonscription(s) électorale(s) provinciale(s): Berthier
Circonscription(s) électorale(s) fédérale(s): Berthier-Maskinongé
Prochaines élections: 7e novembre 2021
Martin Rondeau, Maire
Philippe Morin, Directeur général, 450-886-3867

Saint-Jean-Port-Joli
7, place de l'Église
Saint-Jean-Port-Joli, QC G0R 3G0
Tél: 418-598-3084; *Téléc:* 418-598-3085
munisjpj@globetrotter.net
saintjeanportjoli.com
Entité municipal: Municipality
Incorporation: 1er juillet 1855; *Area:* 69,37 km2
Comté ou district: L'Islet; *Population au 2016:* 3,407
Circonscription(s) électorale(s) provinciale(s): Côte-du-Sud
Circonscription(s) électorale(s) fédérale(s):
Montmagny-L'Islet-Kamouraska-Rivière-du-Loup
Prochaines élections: 7e novembre 2021
Normand Caron, Maire
Stéphen Lord, Directeur général

Saint-Joachim
172, rue de l'Église
Saint-Joachim, QC G0A 3X0
Tél: 418-827-3755; *Téléc:* 418-827-8574
reception@saintjoachim.qc.ca
www.saintjoachim.qc.ca
Entité municipal: Parish (Paroisse)
Incorporation: 1er juillet 1855; *Area:* 42,51 km2
Comté ou district: La Côte-de-Beaupré; Communauté
métropolitaine de Québec; *Population au 2016:* 1,441
Circonscription(s) électorale(s) provinciale(s):
Charlevoix-Côte-de-Beaupré
Circonscription(s) électorale(s) fédérale(s):
Beauport—Côte-de-Beaupré—île d'Orléans—Charlevoix
Prochaines élections: 7e novembre 2021
Marc Dubeau, Maire
Nadia Duchesne, Directrice générale

Saint-Joachim-de-Shefford
615, rue Principale
Saint-Joachim-de-Shefford, QC J0E 2G0
Tél: 450-539-3201; *Téléc:* 450-539-3145
mairie@st-joachim.ca
st-joachim.ca
Entité municipal: Municipality
Incorporation: 10 juin 1884; *Area:* 127,09 km2
Comté ou district: La Haute-Yamaska; *Population au 2016:*
1,301
Circonscription(s) électorale(s) provinciale(s): Johnson
Circonscription(s) électorale(s) fédérale(s): Shefford
Prochaines élections: 7e novembre 2021
René Beauregard, Maire
France Lagrandneur, Directrice générale, 450-539-3201

Saint-Joseph-de-Beauce
843, av du Palais
Saint-Joseph-de-Beauce, QC G0S 2V0
Tél: 418-397-4358; *Téléc:* 418-397-5715
info@vsjb.ca
www.vsjb.ca
Entité municipal: Town
Incorporation: 27 janvier 1999; *Area:* 114,87 km2
Comté ou district: Robert-Cliche; *Population au 2016:* 4,858
Circonscription(s) électorale(s) provinciale(s): Beauce-Nord
Circonscription(s) électorale(s) fédérale(s): Beauce
Prochaines élections: 7e novembre 2021
Pierre Gilbert, Maire
Danielle Maheu, Greffière, 418-397-4358

Saint-Joseph-de-Coleraine
88, av St-Patrick
Saint-Joseph-de-Coleraine, QC G0N 1B0
Tél: 418-423-4000; *Téléc:* 418-423-4150
administration@coleraine.qc.ca
www.coleraine.qc.ca
Entité municipal: Municipality
Incorporation: 11 novembre 1891; *Area:* 126,99 km2
Comté ou district: Les Appalaches; *Population au 2016:* 1,762

Circonscription(s) électorale(s) provinciale(s):
Lotbinière-Frontenac
Circonscription(s) électorale(s) fédérale(s): Mégantic-L'Érable
Prochaines élections: 7e novembre 2021
Gaston Nadeau, Maire
Martin Cadorette, Directeur général, 418-423-4000

Saint-Joseph-de-Kamouraska
140A, rte de l'Église
Saint-Joseph-de-Kamouraska, QC G0L 3P0
Tél: 418-493-2214
secretariat@stjosephkam.ca
www.stjosephkam.ca
Entité municipal: Parish (Paroisse)
Incorporation: 14 janvier 1924; *Area:* 85,58 km2
Comté ou district: Kamouraska; *Population au 2016:* 391
Circonscription(s) électorale(s) provinciale(s): Côte-du-Sud
Circonscription(s) électorale(s) fédérale(s):
Montmagny-L'Islet-Kamouraska-Rivière-du-Loup
Prochaines élections: 7e novembre 2021
Nancy St-Pierre, Mairesse
Marie-Eve Blache-Gagné, Directrice générale, 418-493-2214

Saint-Joseph-de-Lepage
70, rue de la Rivière
Saint-Joseph-de-Lepage, QC G5H 3N8
Tél: 418-775-4171; *Téléc:* 418-775-3004
stjoseph@mitis.qc.ca
www.municipalite.saint-joseph-de-lepage.qc.ca
Entité municipal: Parish (Paroisse)
Incorporation: 29 septembre 1873; *Area:* 30,91 km2
Comté ou district: La Mitis; *Population au 2016:* 523
Circonscription(s) électorale(s) provinciale(s): Matane-Matapédia
Circonscription(s) électorale(s) fédérale(s): Avignon-La
Mitis-Matane-Matapédia
Prochaines élections: 7e novembre 2021
Magella Roussel, Mairesse
Tammy Caron, Directrice générale

Saint-Joseph-des-Érables
139, rue Ste-Christine, #P5
Saint-Joseph-des-Érables, QC G0S 2V0
Tél: 418-397-4772
municipalite@stjosephdeserables.com
www.stjosephdeserables.com
Entité municipal: Municipality
Incorporation: 26 novembre 2009; *Area:* 51,56 km2
Comté ou district: Robert-Cliche; *Population au 2016:* 410
Circonscription(s) électorale(s) provinciale(s): Beauce-Nord
Circonscription(s) électorale(s) fédérale(s): Beauce
Prochaines élections: 7e novembre 2021
Jeannot Roy, Maire
Marie-Josée Mathieu, Directrice générale

Saint-Joseph-de-Sorel
700, rue Montcalm
Saint-Joseph-de-Sorel, QC J3R 1C9
Tél: 450-742-3744; *Téléc:* 450-742-1315
ville@vsjs.ca
www.vsjs.ca
Entité municipal: Village
Incorporation: 1er mai 1907; *Area:* 1,38 km2
Comté ou district: Pierre-De Saurel; *Population au 2016:* 1,642
Circonscription(s) électorale(s) provinciale(s): Richelieu
Circonscription(s) électorale(s) fédérale(s):
Bécancour-Nicolet-Saurel
Prochaines élections: 7e novembre 2021
Vincent Deguise, Maire
Martin Valois, Directeur général

Saint-Joseph-du-Lac
1110, ch Principal
Saint-Joseph-du-Lac, QC J0N 1M0
Tél: 450-623-1072; *Téléc:* 450-623-2889
info@sjdl.qc.ca
sjdl.qc.ca
Entité municipal: Municipality
Incorporation: 1er juillet 1855; *Area:* 41,32 km2
Comté ou district: Deux-Montagnes; Communauté
métropolitaine de Montréal; *Population au 2016:* 6,687
Circonscription(s) électorale(s) provinciale(s): Mirabel
Circonscription(s) électorale(s) fédérale(s): Mirabel
Prochaines élections: 7e novembre 2021
Benoit Proulx, Maire
Stéphane Guiguère, Directeur général

Saint-Jude
940, rue du Centre
Saint-Jude, QC J0H 1P0
Tél: 450-792-3855; *Téléc:* 450-792-3828
munstjude@mrcmaskoutains.qc.ca
www.saint-jude.ca

Entité municipal: Municipality
Incorporation: 1er juillet 1855; *Area:* 77,36 km2
Comté ou district: Les Maskoutains; *Population au 2016:* 1,214
Circonscription(s) électorale(s) provinciale(s): Richelieu
Circonscription(s) électorale(s) fédérale(s): St-Hyacinthe-Bagot
Prochaines élections: 7e novembre 2021
Yves de Bellefeuille, Maire
Julie Clément, Directrice générale

Saint-Jules
390, rte Principale
Saint-Jules, QC G0N 1R0
Tél: 418-397-5444; *Téléc:* 418-397-5007
info@st-jules.qc.ca
www.st-jules.qc.ca
Entité municipal: Parish (Paroisse)
Incorporation: 28 mai 1919; *Area:* 55,74 km2
Comté ou district: Robert-Cliche; *Population au 2016:* 539
Circonscription(s) électorale(s) provinciale(s): Beauce-Nord
Circonscription(s) électorale(s) fédérale(s): Beauce
Prochaines élections: 7e novembre 2021
Ghislaine Doyon, Mairesse
Gina Lessard, Directrice générale

Saint-Julien
787, ch St-Julien
Saint-Julien, QC G0N 1B0
Tél: 418-423-4295
municipalite@st-julien.ca
www.st-julien.ca
Entité municipal: Municipality
Incorporation: 1er juillet 1855; *Area:* 81,72 km2
Comté ou district: Les Appalaches; *Population au 2016:* 376
Circonscription(s) électorale(s) provinciale(s):
Lotbinière-Frontenac
Circonscription(s) électorale(s) fédérale(s): Mégantic-L'Érable
Prochaines élections: 7e novembre 2021
Jacques Laprise, Maire
Martin Cloutier, Directeur général

Saint-Just-de-Bretenières
CP 617
205, rue Principale
Saint-Just-de-Bretenières, QC G0R 3H0
Tél: 418-244-3637; *Téléc:* 418-244-3636
info@saintjustdebretenieres.com
www.saintjustdebretenieres.com
Entité municipal: Municipality
Incorporation: 27 mai 1918; *Area:* 132,63 km2
Comté ou district: Montmagny; *Population au 2016:* 668
Circonscription(s) électorale(s) provinciale(s): Côte-du-Sud
Circonscription(s) électorale(s) fédérale(s):
Montmagny-L'Islet-Kamouraska-Rivière-du-Loup
Prochaines élections: 7e novembre 2021
Donald Gilbert, Maire
Josée Poulin, Directrice générale

Saint-Juste-du-Lac
28, ch Principal
Saint-Juste-du-Lac, QC G0L 3R0
Tél: 418-899-2855; *Téléc:* 418-899-2938
info@saintjustedulac.com
www.saintjustedulac.com
Entité municipal: Municipality
Incorporation: 23 mai 1923; *Area:* 167,10 km2
Comté ou district: Témiscouata; *Population au 2016:* 561
Circonscription(s) électorale(s) provinciale(s):
Rivière-du-Loup-Témiscouata
Circonscription(s) électorale(s) fédérale(s):
Montmagny-L'Islet-Kamouraska-Rivière-du-Loup
Prochaines élections: 7e novembre 2021
Michel Normand, Maire
Dominique Létourneau, Directrice générale

Saint-Justin
1281, rue Gérin
Saint-Justin, QC J0K 2V0
Tél: 819-227-2838
info@saint-justin.ca
municipalites-du-quebec.ca/saint-justin
Entité municipal: Municipality
Incorporation: 1er juillet 1855; *Area:* 78,62 km2
Comté ou district: Maskinongé; *Population au 2016:* 973
Circonscription(s) électorale(s) provinciale(s): Maskinongé
Circonscription(s) électorale(s) fédérale(s): Berthier-Maskinongé
Prochaines élections: 7e novembre 2021
François Gagnon, Maire
Thomas Gravel, Directeur général

Saint-Lambert
509, rte 5e-au-8e Rang
Saint-Lambert, QC J0Z 1V0
Tél: 819-788-2491; *Téléc:* 819-788-2491
st-lambert@mrcao.qc.ca
Entité municipal: Parish (Paroisse)
Incorporation: 14 mai 1938; *Area:* 100,23 km2
Comté ou district: Abitibi-Ouest; *Population au 2016:* 194
Circonscription(s) électorale(s) provinciale(s): Abitibi-Ouest
Circonscription(s) électorale(s) fédérale(s):
Abitibi-Témiscamingue
Prochaines élections: 7e novembre 2021
Diane Provost, Mairesse
Nataly Morin, Directrice générale

Saint-Lambert-de-Lauzon
1200, rue du Pont
Saint-Lambert-de-Lauzon, QC G0S 2W0
Tél: 418-889-9715; *Téléc:* 418-889-0660
info@mun-sldl.ca
mun-sldl.ca
Entité municipal: Municipality
Incorporation: 1er juillet 1855; *Area:* 106,88 km2
Comté ou district: La Nouvelle-Beauce; *Population au 2016:* 6,647
Circonscription(s) électorale(s) provinciale(s): Beauce-Nord
Circonscription(s) électorale(s) fédérale(s): Lévis-Lotbinière
Prochaines élections: 7e novembre 2021
Olivier Dumais, Maire
Éric Boisvert, Directeur général, 418-889-9715

Saint-Laurent-de-l'île-d'Orléans
6822, ch Royal
St-Laurent-de-l'île-d'Orléans, QC G0A 3Z0
Tél: 418-828-2322; *Téléc:* 418-828-2170
info@saintlaurentio.com
stlaurentio.com
Entité municipal: Municipality
Incorporation: 1er juillet 1855; *Area:* 35,86 km2
Comté ou district: L'île-d'Orléans; Communauté métropolitaine de Québec; *Population au 2016:* 1,532
Circonscription(s) électorale(s) provinciale(s):
Charlevoix-Côte-de-Beaupré
Circonscription(s) électorale(s) fédérale(s):
Beauport—Côte-de-Beaupré—île d'Orléans—Charlevoix
Prochaines élections: 7e novembre 2021
Debbie Deslauriers, Mairesse
Michelle Moisan, Directrice générale, 418-828-2322

Saint-Lazare-de-Bellechasse
116, rue de la Fabrique
Saint-Lazare-de-Bellechasse, QC G0R 3J0
Tél: 418-883-3841; *Téléc:* 418-883-2551
munstlaz@globetrotter.net
www.st-lazare.qc.com
Entité municipal: Municipality
Incorporation: 1er juillet 1855; *Area:* 85,91 km2
Comté ou district: Bellechasse; *Population au 2016:* 1,288
Circonscription(s) électorale(s) provinciale(s): Bellechasse
Circonscription(s) électorale(s) fédérale(s): Bellechasse-Les Etchemins-Lévis
Prochaines élections: 7e novembre 2021
Martin J. Côté, Maire
Patrick Côté, Directeur général, 418-883-3841

Saint-Léandre
2005, rue de l'Église
Saint-Léandre, QC G0J 2V0
Tél: 418-737-4973; *Téléc:* 418-737-4876
st-leandre@lamatanie.ca
www.st-leandre.ca
Entité municipal: Parish (Paroisse)
Incorporation: 20 mars 1912; *Area:* 105,01 km2
Comté ou district: La Matanie; *Population au 2016:* 400
Circonscription(s) électorale(s) provinciale(s): Matane-Matapédia
Circonscription(s) électorale(s) fédérale(s): Avignon-La Mitis-Matane-Matapédia
Prochaines élections: 7e novembre 2021
Steve Castonguay, Maire
André Marcil, Directeur général

Saint-Léonard-d'Aston
444, rue de l'Exposition
Saint-Léonard-d'Aston, QC J0C 1M0
Tél: 819-399-2596
reception@saint-leonard-daston.net
saint-leonard-daston.net
Entité municipal: Municipality
Incorporation: 13 avril 1994; *Area:* 82,59 km2
Comté ou district: Nicolet-Yamaska; *Population au 2016:* 2,331
Circonscription(s) électorale(s) provinciale(s): Nicolet-Bécancour
Circonscription(s) électorale(s) fédérale(s):

Bécancour-Nicolet-Saurel
Prochaines élections: 7e novembre 2021
Laurent Marcotte, Maire
Galina Papantcheva, Directrice générale

Saint-Léonard-de-Portneuf
260, rue Pettigrew
Saint-Léonard-de-Portneuf, QC G0A 4A0
Tél: 418-337-6741
saintleonard@derytele.com
municipalites-du-quebec.ca/saint-leonard-de-portneuf
Entité municipal: Municipality
Incorporation: 22 juillet 1899; *Area:* 142,00 km2
Comté ou district: Portneuf; *Population au 2016:* 1,145
Circonscription(s) électorale(s) provinciale(s): Portneuf
Circonscription(s) électorale(s) fédérale(s):
Portneuf-Jacques-Cartier
Prochaines élections: 7e novembre 2021
Denis Langlois, Maire
Nancy Clavet, Directeur général

Saint-Léon-de-Standon
CP 130
100A, rue St-Pierre
Saint-Léon-de-Standon, QC G0R 4L0
Tél: 418-642-5034; *Téléc:* 418-642-2570
administration@standon.ca
www.stleondestandon.qc.ca
Entité municipal: Parish (Paroisse)
Incorporation: 1er janvier 1874; *Area:* 136,94 km2
Comté ou district: Bellechasse; *Population au 2016:* 1,127
Circonscription(s) électorale(s) provinciale(s): Bellechasse
Circonscription(s) électorale(s) fédérale(s): Bellechasse-Les Etchemins-Lévis
Prochaines élections: 7e novembre 2021
Bernard Morin, Maire
Michel Lacasse, Directeur général

Saint-Léon-le-Grand
8A, place de l'Église
Saint-Léon-le-Grand, QC G0J 2W0
Tél: 418-743-2914; *Téléc:* 418-743-2914
stleonlegrand@mrcmatapedia.quebec
municipalite.saint-leon-le-grand.qc.ca
Entité municipal: Parish (Paroisse)
Incorporation: 12 août 1903; *Area:* 128,47 km2
Comté ou district: La Matapédia; *Population au 2016:* 953
Circonscription(s) électorale(s) provinciale(s): Matane-Matapédia
Circonscription(s) électorale(s) fédérale(s): Avignon-La Mitis-Matane-Matapédia
Prochaines élections: 7e novembre 2021
Jean-Côme Lévesque, Maire
Jean-Noël Barriault, Directeur général

Saint-Léon-le-Grand
52, rue de la Fabrique
Saint-Léon-le-Grand, QC J0K 2W0
Tél: 819-228-3236; *Téléc:* 819-228-8088
hoteldeville@st-leon.com
www.st-leon.com
Entité municipal: Parish (Paroisse)
Incorporation: 1er juillet 1855; *Area:* 76,11 km2
Comté ou district: Maskinongé; *Population au 2016:* 928
Circonscription(s) électorale(s) provinciale(s): Maskinongé
Circonscription(s) électorale(s) fédérale(s): Berthier-Maskinongé
Prochaines élections: 7e novembre 2021
Robert Lalonde, Maire
Andrée Ricard, Directrice générale, 819-228-3236

Saint-Liboire
#102, 151, rue Gabriel
Saint-Liboire, QC J0H 1R0
Tél: 450-793-2811; *Téléc:* 450-793-4428
reception@st-liboire.ca
www.st-liboire.ca
Entité municipal: Municipality
Incorporation: 17 août 1994; *Area:* 73,86 km2
Comté ou district: Les Maskoutains; *Population au 2016:* 3,062
Circonscription(s) électorale(s) provinciale(s): St-Hyacinthe
Circonscription(s) électorale(s) fédérale(s): St-Hyacinthe-Bagot
Prochaines élections: 7e novembre 2021
Claude Vadnais, Maire
France Desjardins, Directrice générale

Saint-Liguori
750, rue Principale
Saint-Liguori, QC J0K 2X0
Tél: 450-753-3570; *Téléc:* 450-753-4638
info@saint-liguori.com
www.saint-liguori.com
Entité municipal: Parish (Paroisse)
Incorporation: 1er juillet 1855; *Area:* 50,70 km2

Comté ou district: Montcalm; *Population au 2016:* 1,943
Circonscription(s) électorale(s) provinciale(s): Joliette
Circonscription(s) électorale(s) fédérale(s): Montcalm
Prochaines élections: 7e novembre 2021
Ghislaine Pomerleau, Maire
Simon Franche, Directeur général

Saint-Louis
765B, rue St-Joseph
Saint-Louis, QC J0G 1K0
Tél: 450-788-2631; *Télec:* 450-788-2231
mstlouis@mrcmaskoutains.qc.ca
www.saint-louis.ca
Entité municipal: Municipality
Incorporation: 29 août 1881; *Area:* 47,27 km2
Comté ou district: Les Maskoutains; *Population au 2016:* 712
Circonscription(s) électorale(s) provinciale(s): Richelieu
Circonscription(s) électorale(s) fédérale(s): St-Hyacinthe-Bagot
Prochaines élections: 7e novembre 2021
Stéphane Bernier, Maire
Pascale Dalcourt, Directrice générale

Saint-Louis-de-Blandford
80-1, rue Principale
Saint-Louis-de-Blandford, QC G0Z 1B0
Tél: 819-364-7007; *Télec:* 819-364-2781
info@saint-louis-de-blandford.ca
www.saint-louis-de-blandford.ca
Entité municipal: Municipality
Incorporation: 1er juillet 1855; *Area:* 105,85 km2
Comté ou district: Arthabaska; *Population au 2016:* 1,011
Circonscription(s) électorale(s) provinciale(s): Arthabaska
Circonscription(s) électorale(s) fédérale(s):
Richmond-Arthabaska
Prochaines élections: 7e novembre 2021
Yvon Barrette, Maire
Stéphanie Hinse, Directrice générale

Saint-Louis-de-Gonzague
108, rue de l'Église
Saint-Louis-de-Gonzague, QC G0R 2L0
Tél: 418-267-5931; *Télec:* 418-267-5930
munstlouis@sogetel.net
www.st-louisdegonzague.qc.ca
Entité municipal: Municipality
Incorporation: 17 mars 1923; *Area:* 118,02 km2
Comté ou district: Les Etchemins; *Population au 2016:* 374
Circonscription(s) électorale(s) provinciale(s): Bellechasse
Circonscription(s) électorale(s) fédérale(s): Bellechasse-Les
Etchemins-Lévis
Prochaines élections: 7e novembre 2021
Lucie Gagnon, Mairesse
Vicky Giguère, Directrice générale

Saint-Louis-de-Gonzague
140, rue Principale
Saint-Louis-de-Gonzague, QC J0S 1T0
Tél: 450-371-0523
info@sldg.ca
sldg.ca
Entité municipal: Parish (Paroisse)
Incorporation: 1er juillet 1855; *Area:* 79,83 km2
Comté ou district: Beauharnois-Salaberry; *Population au 2016:*
1,481
Circonscription(s) électorale(s) provinciale(s): Beauharnois
Circonscription(s) électorale(s) fédérale(s): Salaberry-Suroît
Prochaines élections: 7e novembre 2021
Yves Daoust, Maire
Dany Michaud, Directrice générale et secrétaire-trésorière,
450-371-0523

Saint-Louis-de-Gonzague-du-Cap-Tourmente
CP 460 Haute-Ville
Québec, QC G1R 4R7
Tél: 418-692-3981; *Télec:* 418-692-4345
Entité municipal: Parish (Paroisse)
Incorporation: 1er janvier 1917; *Area:* 0,42 km2
Comté ou district: La Côte-de-Beaupré; Communauté
métropolitaine de Québec; *Population au 2016:* 5
Circonscription(s) électorale(s) provinciale(s):
Charlevoix-Côte-de-Beaupré
Circonscription(s) électorale(s) fédérale(s):
Beauport—Côte-de-Beaupré—Île d'Orléans—Charlevoix
Prochaines élections: 7e novembre 2021
Jacques Roberge, Administrateur

Saint-Louis-du-Ha!-Ha!
95, rue St-Charles
Saint-Louis-du-Ha!-Ha!, QC G0L 3S0
Tél: 418-854-2260; *Télec:* 418-854-0717
municipalite@saintlouisduhaha.com
saintlouisduhaha.com

Entité municipal: Parish (Paroisse)
Incorporation: 14 juillet 1874; *Area:* 112,25 km2
Comté ou district: Témiscouata; *Population au 2016:* 1,292
Circonscription(s) électorale(s) provinciale(s):
Rivière-du-Loup-Témiscouata
Circonscription(s) électorale(s) fédérale(s):
Rimouski-Neigette-Témiscouata-Les Basques
Prochaines élections: 7e novembre 2021
Sonia Larrivée, Mairesse
Dominique Michaud, Directrice générale

Saint-Luc-de-Bellechasse
115, rue de la Fabrique
Saint-Luc-de-Bellechasse, QC G0R 1L0
Tél: 418-636-2176; *Télec:* 418-636-2175
www.st-luc-bellechasse.qc.ca
Entité municipal: Municipality
Incorporation: 12 août 1921; *Area:* 162,01 km2
Comté ou district: Les Etchemins; *Population au 2016:* 438
Circonscription(s) électorale(s) provinciale(s): Bellechasse
Circonscription(s) électorale(s) fédérale(s): Bellechasse-Les
Etchemins-Lévis
Prochaines élections: 7e novembre 2021
Denis Laflamme, Maire
Huguette Lavigne, Directrice générale

Saint-Luc-de-Vincennes
600, rue Principale
Saint-Luc-de-Vincennes, QC G0X 3K0
Tél: 819-295-3782; *Télec:* 819-295-3782
municipalite@stlucdevincennes.com
stlucdevincennes.com
Entité municipal: Municipality
Incorporation: 19 janvier 1865; *Area:* 53,67 km2
Comté ou district: Les Chenaux; *Population au 2016:* 545
Circonscription(s) électorale(s) provinciale(s): Champlain
Circonscription(s) électorale(s) fédérale(s):
St-Maurice-Champlain
Prochaines élections: 7e novembre 2021
Jean-Claude Milot, Maire
Francis Dubreuil, Directeur général

Saint-Lucien
5350, 7e rang
Saint-Lucien, QC J0C 1N0
Tél: 819-397-4679; *Télec:* 819-397-2732
bureaumunicipal@saint-lucien.ca
www.saint-lucien.ca
Entité municipal: Municipality
Incorporation: 11 novembre 1907; *Area:* 111,29 km2
Comté ou district: Drummond; *Population au 2016:* 1,647
Circonscription(s) électorale(s) provinciale(s):
Drummond-Bois-Francs
Circonscription(s) électorale(s) fédérale(s): Drummond
Prochaines élections: 7e novembre 2021
Diane Bourgeois, Mairesse
Alain St-Vincent-Rioux, Directeur général

Saint-Ludger
212, rue La Salle
Saint-Ludger, QC G0M 1W0
Tél: 819-548-5408; *Télec:* 819-548-5743
info@st-ludger.qc.ca
st-ludger.qc.ca
Entité municipal: Municipality
Incorporation: 25 février 1998; *Area:* 127,64 km2
Comté ou district: Le Granit; *Population au 2016:* 1,071
Circonscription(s) électorale(s) provinciale(s): Beauce-Sud
Circonscription(s) électorale(s) fédérale(s): Mégantic-L'Érable
Prochaines élections: 7e novembre 2021
Bernard Therrien, Maire
Julie Létourneau, Directrice générale, 819-548-5408

Saint-Ludger-de-Milot
739, rue Gaudreault
Saint-Ludger-de-Milot, QC G0W 2B0
Tél: 418-373-2266; *Télec:* 418-373-2554
administration@ville.st-ludger-de-milot.qc.ca
www.ville.st-ludger-de-milot.qc.ca
Entité municipal: Municipality
Incorporation: 1er janvier 1948; *Area:* 108,75 km2
Comté ou district: Lac-Saint-Jean-Est; *Population au 2016:* 651
Circonscription(s) électorale(s) provinciale(s): Lac-St-Jean
Circonscription(s) électorale(s) fédérale(s): Lac-St-Jean
Prochaines élections: 7e novembre 2021
Marc Laliberté, Maire
Rita Ouellet, Directrice générale, 418-373-2266

Saint-Magloire
13, rue de la Caisse
Saint-Magloire, QC G0R 3M0
Tél: 418-257-4421; *Télec:* 581-500-3061
stmagloire@sogetel.net
www.saint-magloire.com
Entité municipal: Municipality
Incorporation: 1er janvier 1875; *Area:* 208,68 km2
Comté ou district: Les Etchemins; *Population au 2016:* 676
Circonscription(s) électorale(s) provinciale(s): Bellechasse
Circonscription(s) électorale(s) fédérale(s): Bellechasse-Les
Etchemins-Lévis
Prochaines élections: 7e novembre 2021
Marielle Lemieux, Maire
Dany Robert, Directrice générale

Saint-Majorique-de-Grantham
1962, boul St-Joseph ouest
Saint-Majorique-de-Grantham, QC J2B 8A8
Tél: 819-478-7058; *Télec:* 819-478-8479
info@st-majorique.ca
st-majoriquedegrantham.qc.ca
Entité municipal: Parish (Paroisse)
Incorporation: 13 juillet 1901; *Area:* 57,62 km2
Comté ou district: Drummond; *Population au 2016:* 1,388
Circonscription(s) électorale(s) provinciale(s): Johnson
Circonscription(s) électorale(s) fédérale(s): Drummond
Prochaines élections: 7e novembre 2021
Line Fréchette, Mairesse
Emilie Trottier, Directrice générale

Saint-Malachie
610, 7e rue
Saint-Malachie, QC G0R 3N0
Tél: 418-642-2102; *Télec:* 418-642-2231
contact@st-malachie.qc.ca
www.st-malachie.qc.ca
Entité municipal: Parish (Paroisse)
Incorporation: 1er juin 1874; *Area:* 101,06 km2
Comté ou district: Bellechasse; *Population au 2016:* 1,517
Circonscription(s) électorale(s) provinciale(s): Bellechasse
Circonscription(s) électorale(s) fédérale(s): Bellechasse-Les
Etchemins-Lévis
Prochaines élections: 7e novembre 2021
Denis Laflamme, Maire
Hélène Bissonnette, Directrice générale

Saint-Malo
228, rte 253 sud
Saint-Malo, QC J0B 2Y0
Tél: 819-658-2174; *Télec:* 819-658-1169
info@saint-malo.ca
www.saint-malo.ca
Entité municipal: Municipality
Incorporation: 1er janvier 1870; *Area:* 131,93 km2
Comté ou district: Coaticook; *Population au 2016:* 475
Circonscription(s) électorale(s) provinciale(s): St-François
Circonscription(s) électorale(s) fédérale(s): Compton-Stanstead
Prochaines élections: 7e novembre 2021
Benoit Roy, Maire
Édith Rouleau, Directrice générale

Saint-Marc-de-Figuery
162, ch des Prés
Saint-Marc-de-Figuery, QC J0Y 1J0
Tél: 819-732-8501; *Télec:* 819-732-4324
municipalite@saint-marc-de-figuery.org
www.saint-marc-de-figuery.org
Entité municipal: Parish (Paroisse)
Incorporation: 10 novembre 1926; *Area:* 81,83 km2
Comté ou district: Abitibi; *Population au 2016:* 834
Circonscription(s) électorale(s) provinciale(s): Abitibi-Ouest
Circonscription(s) électorale(s) fédérale(s):
Abitibi-Témiscamingue
Prochaines élections: 7e novembre 2021
Daniel Rose, Maire
Martine Lachaine, Directrice générale par intérim

Saint-Marc-des-Carrières
965, av Bona-Dussault
Saint-Marc-des-Carrières, QC G0A 4B0
Tél: 418-268-3862; *Télec:* 418-268-8776
info@villestmarc.com
st-marc-des-carrieres.qc.ca
Entité municipal: Town
Incorporation: 24 octobre 1918; *Area:* 17,27 km2
Comté ou district: Portneuf; *Population au 2016:* 2,911
Circonscription(s) électorale(s) provinciale(s): Portneuf
Circonscription(s) électorale(s) fédérale(s):
Portneuf-Jacques-Cartier
Prochaines élections: 7e novembre 2021
Maryon Leclerc, Maire

Marc-Eddy Jonathas, Directeur général

Saint-Marc-du-Lac-Long
18A, rue de l'Église
Saint-Marc-du-Lac-Long, QC G0L 1T0
Tél: 418-893-2643; *Téléc:* 418-893-7228
admin@saintmarcdulaclong.ca
saintmarcdulaclong.ca
Entité municipal: Parish (Paroisse)
Incorporation: 11 juin 1938; *Area:* 148,85 km2
Comté ou district: Témiscouata; *Population au 2016:* 397
Circonscription(s) électorale(s) provinciale(s):
Rivière-du-Loup-Témiscouata
Circonscription(s) électorale(s) fédérale(s):
Rimouski-Neigette-Témiscouata-Les Basques
Prochaines élections: 7e novembre 2021
Marcel Dubé, Maire
Sylvie Dumont, Directrice générale, 418-893-2643

Saint-Marcel
48, ch Taché est
Saint-Marcel, QC G0R 3R0
Tél: 418-356-2691; *Téléc:* 418-356-2820
info@saintmarcel.qc.ca
www.saintmarcel.qc.ca
Entité municipal: Municipality
Incorporation: 30 juillet 1904; *Area:* 179,04 km2
Comté ou district: L'Islet; *Population au 2016:* 428
Circonscription(s) électorale(s) provinciale(s): Côte-du-Sud
Circonscription(s) électorale(s) fédérale(s):
Montmagny-L'Islet-Kamouraska-Rivière-du-Loup
Prochaines élections: 7e novembre 2021
Eddy Morin, Maire
Sonia Bisson, Directrice générale

Saint-Marcel-de-Richelieu
117, rue Saint-Louis
Saint-Marcel-de-Richelieu, QC J0H 1T0
Tél: 450-794-2832; *Téléc:* 450-794-1140
munst-marcel@mrcmaskoutains.qc.ca
saintmarcelderichelieu.ca
Entité municipal: Municipality
Incorporation: 1er juillet 1855; *Area:* 51,28 km2
Comté ou district: Les Maskoutains; *Population au 2016:* 497
Circonscription(s) électorale(s) provinciale(s): Richelieu
Circonscription(s) électorale(s) fédérale(s): St-Hyacinthe-Bagot
Prochaines élections: 7e novembre 2021
Robert Beauchamp, Maire
Julie Hébert, Directrice générale

Saint-Marcellin
336, rte 234
Saint-Marcellin, QC G0K 1R0
Tél: 418-798-4382; *Téléc:* 418-798-4383
munstmar@globetrotter.net
www.st-marcellin.qc.ca
Entité municipal: Parish (Paroisse)
Incorporation: 19 novembre 1924; *Area:* 117,56 km2
Comté ou district: Rimouski-Neigette; *Population au 2016:* 353
Circonscription(s) électorale(s) provinciale(s): Rimouski
Circonscription(s) électorale(s) fédérale(s):
Rimouski-Neigette-Témiscouata-Les Basques
Prochaines élections: 7e novembre 2021
Paul-Émile Lévesque, Maire
Nathalie Chouinard, Directrice générale

Saint-Marc-sur-Richelieu
102, rue de la Fabrique
Saint-Marc-sur-Richelieu, QC J0L 2E0
Tél: 450-584-2258; *Téléc:* 450-584-2795
info@smsr.quebec
smsr.quebec
Entité municipal: Municipality
Incorporation: 1er juillet 1855; *Area:* 60,99 km2
Comté ou district: La Vallée-du-Richelieu; *Population au 2016:*
2,172
Circonscription(s) électorale(s) provinciale(s): Borduas
Circonscription(s) électorale(s) fédérale(s): Pierre-Boucher-Les
Patriotes-Verchères
Prochaines élections: 7e novembre 2021
Michel Robert, Maire
Sylvie Burelle, Directrice générale, 450-584-2258

Saint-Martin
131, 1e av est
Saint-Martin, QC G0M 1B0
Tél: 418-382-5035; *Téléc:* 418-382-5561
administration@st-martin.qc.ca
st-martin.qc.ca
Entité municipal: Parish (Paroisse)
Incorporation: 12 octobre 1911; *Area:* 118,06 km2
Comté ou district: Beauce-Sartigan; *Population au 2016:* 2,477

Circonscription(s) électorale(s) provinciale(s): Beauce-Sud
Circonscription(s) électorale(s) fédérale(s): Beauce
Prochaines élections: 7e novembre 2021
Éric Giguère, Maire
Simon Leclerc, Directeur général

Saint-Mathias-sur-Richelieu
300, ch des Patriotes
Saint-Mathias-sur-Richelieu, QC J3L 6Z5
Tél: 450-658-2841; *Téléc:* 450-447-1416
info@st-mathias.org
www.saint-mathias-sur-richelieu.org
Entité municipal: Municipality
Incorporation: 1er juillet 1855; *Area:* 47,15 km2
Comté ou district: Rouville; Communauté métropolitaine de
Montréal; *Population au 2016:* 4,531
Circonscription(s) électorale(s) provinciale(s): Chambly
Circonscription(s) électorale(s) fédérale(s): Beloeil-Chambly
Prochaines élections: 7e novembre 2021
Jocelyne G. Deswarte, Mairesse
Philippe Gaudet, Ggreffier et dDirecteur général, 450-658-2841

Saint-Mathieu
299, ch St-Édouard
Saint-Mathieu, QC J0L 2H0
Tél: 450-632-9528; *Téléc:* 450-632-9544
info@municipalite.saint-mathieu.qc.ca
municipalite.saint-mathieu.qc.ca
Entité municipal: Municipality
Incorporation: 1er août 1917; *Area:* 31,43 km2
Comté ou district: Roussillon; Communauté métropolitaine de
Montréal; *Population au 2016:* 2,156
Circonscription(s) électorale(s) provinciale(s): Sanguinet
Circonscription(s) électorale(s) fédérale(s): La Prairie;
Rimouski-Neigette-Témiscouata-Les Basques
Prochaines élections: 7e novembre 2021
Lise Poissant, Mairesse
Ginette Roy, Directrice générale par intérim, 450-632-9528

Saint-Mathieu-d'Harricana
203, ch Lanoix
Saint-Mathieu-d'Harricana, QC J0Y 1M0
Tél: 819-727-9557; *Téléc:* 819-727-2052
accueil@stmathieudharricana.com
stmathieudharricana.com
Entité municipal: Municipality
Incorporation: 1er janvier 1943; *Area:* 106,71 km2
Comté ou district: Abitibi; *Population au 2016:* 739
Circonscription(s) électorale(s) provinciale(s): Abitibi-Ouest
Circonscription(s) électorale(s) fédérale(s):
Abitibi-Témiscamingue
Prochaines élections: 7e novembre 2021
Martin Roch, Maire
Anne-Renée Jacob, Directrice générale, 819-727-9557

Saint-Mathieu-de-Beloeil
5000, rue des Loisirs
Saint-Mathieu-de-Beloeil, QC J3G 2C9
Tél: 450-467-7490
reception@stmathieudebeloeil.ca
stmathieudebeloeil.ca
Entité municipal: Municipality
Incorporation: 1er juillet 1855; *Area:* 39,41 km2
Comté ou district: La Vallée-du-Richelieu; Communauté
métropolitaine de Montréal; *Population au 2016:* 2,619
Circonscription(s) électorale(s) provinciale(s): Borduas
Circonscription(s) électorale(s) fédérale(s): Pierre-Boucher-Les
Patriotes-Verchères
Prochaines élections: 7e novembre 2021
Normand Teasdale, Maire
Lyne Rivard, Directrice générale, 450-467-7490

Saint-Mathieu-de-Rioux
1, rue du Moulin
Saint-Mathieu-de-Rioux, QC G0L 3T0
Tél: 418-738-2953; *Téléc:* 418-738-2454
admin@mstmr.ca
www.stmathieuderioux.qc.ca
Entité municipal: Parish (Paroisse)
Incorporation: 18 août 1865; *Area:* 107,82 km2
Comté ou district: Les Basques; *Population au 2016:* 639
Circonscription(s) électorale(s) provinciale(s):
Rivière-du-Loup-Témiscouata
Circonscription(s) électorale(s) fédérale(s):
Rimouski-Neigette-Témiscouata-Les Basques
Prochaines élections: 7e novembre 2021
Roger Martin, Maire
Gino Dubé, Directeur général

Saint-Mathieu-du-Parc
561, ch Déziel
Saint-Mathieu-du-Parc, QC G0X 1N0
Tél: 819-299-3830; *Téléc:* 819-532-2415
info@saint-mathieu-du-parc.ca
saint-mathieu-du-parc.ca
Entité municipal: Municipality
Incorporation: 30 juin 1886; *Area:* 220,15 km2
Comté ou district: Maskinongé; *Population au 2016:* 1,338
Circonscription(s) électorale(s) provinciale(s): St-Maurice
Circonscription(s) électorale(s) fédérale(s): Berthier-Maskinongé
Prochaines élections: 7e novembre 2021
Josée Magny, Mairesse
Anne-Claude Hébert-Moreau, Directrice générale

Saint-Maurice
2510, rang St-Jean
Saint-Maurice, QC G0X 2X0
Tél: 819-374-4525; *Téléc:* 819-374-9132
infocitoyens@st-maurice.ca
www.st-maurice.ca
Entité municipal: Parish (Paroisse)
Incorporation: 1er juillet 1855; *Area:* 91,34 km2
Comté ou district: Les Chenaux; *Population au 2016:* 3,286
Circonscription(s) électorale(s) provinciale(s): Champlain
Circonscription(s) électorale(s) fédérale(s):
St-Maurice-Champlain
Prochaines élections: 7e novembre 2021
Gérard Bruneau, Maire
Andrée Neault, Directrice générale

Saint-Maxime-du-Mont-Louis
1, 1e av ouest
Saint-Maxime-du-Mont-Louis, QC G0E 1T0
Tél: 418-797-2310; *Téléc:* 418-797-2928
info@st-maxime.qc.ca
st-maxime.qc.ca
Entité municipal: Municipality
Incorporation: 10 juin 1884; *Area:* 233,63 km2
Comté ou district: La Haute-Gaspésie; *Population au 2016:*
1,134
Circonscription(s) électorale(s) provinciale(s): Gaspé
Circonscription(s) électorale(s) fédérale(s): Gaspésie—Les
îles-de-la-Madeleine
Prochaines élections: 7e novembre 2021
Guy Bernatchez, Maire
Dany Bergeron, Directeur général, 418-797-2310

Saint-Médard
51A, rue Principale est
Saint-Médard, QC G0L 3V0
Tél: 418-963-6276
admin@st-medard.qc.ca
municipalites-du-quebec.ca/st-medard
Entité municipal: Municipality
Incorporation: 1er janvier 1949; *Area:* 75,28 km2
Comté ou district: Les Basques; *Population au 2016:* 209
Circonscription(s) électorale(s) provinciale(s):
Rivière-du-Loup-Témiscouata
Circonscription(s) électorale(s) fédérale(s):
Rimouski-Neigette-Témiscouata-Les Basques
Prochaines élections: 7e novembre 2021
Louis-Philippe Sirois, Maire
Nancy Rioux, Directrice générale

Saint-Michel
1700, rue Principale
Saint-Michel, QC J0L 2J0
Tél: 450-454-4502; *Téléc:* 450-454-7508
info@mst-michel.ca
municipalite-saint-michel.ca
Entité municipal: Municipality
Incorporation: 1er juillet 1855; *Area:* 59,98 km2
Comté ou district: Les Jardins-de-Napierville; *Population au
2016:* 3,186
Circonscription(s) électorale(s) provinciale(s): Huntingdon
Circonscription(s) électorale(s) fédérale(s): Châteauguay-Lacolle
Prochaines élections: 7e novembre 2021
Jean-Guy Hamelin, Maire
Daniel Prince, Directeur général et secrétaire-trésorier,
450-454-4502

Saint-Michel-de-Bellechasse
129, rte 132 est
Saint-Michel-de-Bellechasse, QC G0R 3S0
Tél: 418-884-2865
info@stmicheldebellechasse.ca
www.saintmicheldebellechasse.com
Entité municipal: Municipality
Incorporation: 1er juillet 1855; *Area:* 43,52 km2
Comté ou district: Bellechasse; *Population au 2016:* 1,813
Circonscription(s) électorale(s) provinciale(s): Bellechasse

Circonscription(s) électorale(s) fédérale(s): Bellechasse-Les Etchemins-Lévis
Prochaines élections: 7e novembre 2021
Éric Tessier, Maire
Bernard Caouette, Directeur général

Saint-Michel-des-Saints
441, rue Brassard
Saint-Michel-des-Saints, QC J0K 3B0
Tél: 450-886-4502; *Téléc:* 450-833-6081
info@smds.quebec
smds.quebec
Other Information: Sans frais: 877-833-6941
Entité municipal: Municipality
Incorporation: 3 mars 1979; *Area:* 501,61 km2
Comté ou district: Matawinie; *Population au 2016:* 2,359
Circonscription(s) électorale(s) provinciale(s): Berthier
Circonscription(s) électorale(s) fédérale(s): Joliette
Prochaines élections: 7e novembre 2021
Réjean Gouin, Maire
Sébastien Gariépy, Directeur général, 450-886-4502

Saint-Michel-du-Squatec
CP 280
150, rue St-Joseph
Saint-Michel-du-Squatec, QC G0L 4H0
Tél: 418-855-2185; *Téléc:* 418-855-2935
info@squatec.qc.ca
www.squatec.qc.ca
Entité municipal: Municipality
Incorporation: 16 avril 1928; *Area:* 362,03 km2
Comté ou district: Témiscouata; *Population au 2016:* 1,113
Circonscription(s) électorale(s) provinciale(s):
Rivière-du-Loup-Témiscouata
Circonscription(s) électorale(s) fédérale(s):
Rimouski-Neigette-Témiscouata-Les Basques
Prochaines élections: 7e novembre 2021
André Chouinard, Maire
Nadia Sheink, Directrice générale

Saint-Modeste
312, rue Principale
Saint-Modeste, QC G0L 3W0
Tél: 418-867-2352; *Téléc:* 418-867-5359
municipalite@saint-modeste.ca
www.municipalite.saint-modeste.qc.ca
Entité municipal: Municipality
Incorporation: 1er juillet 1855; *Area:* 110,02 km2
Comté ou district: Rivière-du-Loup; *Population au 2016:* 1,162
Circonscription(s) électorale(s) provinciale(s):
Rivière-du-Loup-Témiscouata
Circonscription(s) électorale(s) fédérale(s):
Montmagny-L'Islet-Kamouraska-Rivière-du-Loup
Prochaines élections: 7e novembre 2021
Louis-Marie Bastille, Maire
Alain Vila, Directeur général, 418-867-2352

Saint-Moïse
117B, rue Principale
Saint-Moïse, QC G0J 2Z0
Tél: 418-776-2833; *Téléc:* 418-776-2835
stmoise@mrcmatapedia.quebec
st-moise.com
Entité municipal: Parish (Paroisse)
Incorporation: 1er janvier 1878; *Area:* 109,93 km2
Comté ou district: La Matapédia; *Population au 2016:* 580
Circonscription(s) électorale(s) provinciale(s): Matane-Matapédia
Circonscription(s) électorale(s) fédérale(s): Avignon-La
Mitis-Matane-Matapédia
Prochaines élections: 7e novembre 2021
Paul Lepage, Maire
Nadine Beaulieu, Directrice générale

Saint-Narcisse
353, rue Notre-Dame
Saint-Narcisse, QC G0X 2Y0
Tél: 418-328-8645; *Téléc:* 418-328-4348
municipalite@saint-narcisse.com
www.saint-narcisse.com
Entité municipal: Parish (Paroisse)
Incorporation: 1er juillet 1855; *Area:* 106,85 km2
Comté ou district: Les Chenaux; *Population au 2016:* 1,832
Circonscription(s) électorale(s) provinciale(s): Champlain
Circonscription(s) électorale(s) fédérale(s):
St-Maurice-Champlain
Prochaines élections: 7e novembre 2021
Guy Veillette, Maire
Stéphane Bourassa, Directeur général

Saint-Narcisse-de-Beaurivage
400, rue Principale
Saint-Narcisse-de-Beaurivage, QC G0S 1W0
Tél: 418-475-6842; *Téléc:* 418-475-6880
saintnarcisse@globetrotter.net
www.saintnarcissedebeaurivage.ca
Entité municipal: Parish (Paroisse)
Incorporation: 1er mai 1874; *Area:* 61,93 km2
Comté ou district: Lotbinière; *Population au 2016:* 1,106
Circonscription(s) électorale(s) provinciale(s):
Lotbinière-Frontenac
Circonscription(s) électorale(s) fédérale(s): Lévis-Lotbinière
Prochaines élections: 7e novembre 2021
Denis Dion, Maire
Dany Lehoux, Directrice générale

Saint-Narcisse-de-Rimouski
7, rue du Pavillon
Saint-Narcisse-de-Rimouski, QC G0K 1S0
Tél: 418-735-2638; *Téléc:* 418-735-6021
renseignements@saintnarcisse.net
saintnarcisse.net
Entité municipal: Parish (Paroisse)
Incorporation: 13 février 1922; *Area:* 163,41 km2
Comté ou district: Rimouski-Neigette; *Population au 2016:* 961
Circonscription(s) électorale(s) provinciale(s): Rimouski
Circonscription(s) électorale(s) fédérale(s):
Rimouski-Neigette-Témiscouata-Les Basques
Prochaines élections: 7e novembre 2021
Robert Duchesne, Maire
Gilles Lepage, Directeur général

Saint-Nazaire
174, rue Principale
Saint-Nazaire, QC G0W 2V0
Tél: 418-662-4154; *Téléc:* 418-662-5467
info@ville.saint-nazaire.qc.ca
ville.saint-nazaire.qc.ca
Entité municipal: Municipality
Incorporation: 23 septembre 1905; *Area:* 145,00 km2
Comté ou district: Lac-Saint-Jean-Est; *Population au 2016:*
2,073
Circonscription(s) électorale(s) provinciale(s): Lac-St-Jean
Circonscription(s) électorale(s) fédérale(s): Jonquière
Prochaines élections: 7e novembre 2021
Jules Bouchard, Maire
Pierre-Yves Tremblay, Directeur général, 418-662-4154

Saint-Nazaire-d'Acton
750, rue des Loisirs
Saint-Nazaire-d'Acton, QC J0H 1V0
Tél: 819-392-2347; *Téléc:* 819-392-2039
stnazairedacton.ca
Entité municipal: Parish (Paroisse)
Incorporation: 8 janvier 1894; *Area:* 58,05 km2
Comté ou district: Acton; *Population au 2016:* 884
Circonscription(s) électorale(s) provinciale(s): Johnson
Circonscription(s) électorale(s) fédérale(s): St-Hyacinthe-Bagot
Prochaines élections: 7e novembre 2021
Pierre Laflamme, Maire
Guylaine Bourgoin, Directrice générale

Saint-Nazaire-de-Dorchester
61A, rue Principale
Saint-Nazaire, QC G0R 3T0
Tél: 418-642-1305
municipalite@st-nazaire.ca
saint-nazaire-de-dorchester.org
Entité municipal: Parish (Paroisse)
Incorporation: 9 mars 1906; *Area:* 51,59 km2
Comté ou district: Bellechasse; *Population au 2016:* 363
Circonscription(s) électorale(s) provinciale(s): Bellechasse
Circonscription(s) électorale(s) fédérale(s): Bellechasse-Les
Etchemins-Lévis
Prochaines élections: 7e novembre 2021
Clément Fillion, Maire
Joanie Bolduc Pelchat, Directrice générale

Saint-Nérée-de-Bellechasse
1990, rte Principale
Saint-Nérée, QC G0R 3V0
Tél: 418-243-2735
muneree@stneree.ca
www.st-neree.qc.ca
Entité municipal: Municipality
Incorporation: 29 mars 1887; *Area:* 75,78 km2
Comté ou district: Bellechasse; *Population au 2016:* 742
Circonscription(s) électorale(s) provinciale(s): Bellechasse
Circonscription(s) électorale(s) fédérale(s): Bellechasse-Les
Etchemins-Lévis
Prochaines élections: 7e novembre 2021
Pascal Fournier, Maire

Michaël Couture, Directeur général

Saint-Noël
19A, rue Turcotte
Saint-Noël, QC G0J 3A0
Tél: 418-776-2936; *Téléc:* 418-776-5521
stnoel@mrcmatapedia.quebec
www.st-noel.com
Entité municipal: Village
Incorporation: 2 octobre 1906; *Area:* 45,85 km2
Comté ou district: La Matapédia; *Population au 2016:* 398
Circonscription(s) électorale(s) provinciale(s): Matane-Matapédia
Circonscription(s) électorale(s) fédérale(s): Avignon-La
Mitis-Matane-Matapédia
Prochaines élections: 7e novembre 2021
Daniel Carrier, Maire
Manon Caron, Directrice générale

Saint-Norbert
4, rue Laporte
Saint-Norbert, QC J0K 3C0
Tél: 450-836-4700; *Téléc:* 450-836-4004
municipalite@saint-norbert.net
saint-norbert.net
Entité municipal: Parish (Paroisse)
Incorporation: 1er juillet 1855; *Area:* 74,78 km2
Comté ou district: D'Autray; *Population au 2016:* 1,003
Circonscription(s) électorale(s) provinciale(s): Berthier
Circonscription(s) électorale(s) fédérale(s): Berthier-Maskinongé
Prochaines élections: 7e novembre 2021
Michel Lafontaine, Maire
Caroline Gagnon, Directrice générale, 450-836-4700

Saint-Norbert-d'Arthabaska
44, rue Landry
Saint-Norbert-d'Arthabaska, QC G0P 1B0
Tél: 819-369-9318; *Téléc:* 819-369-8686
municipalite@saint-norbert-darthabaska.ca
saint-norbert-darthabaska.ca
Entité municipal: Municipality
Incorporation: 30 novembre 1994; *Area:* 102,93 km2
Comté ou district: Arthabaska; *Population au 2016:* 1,157
Circonscription(s) électorale(s) provinciale(s): Arthabaska
Circonscription(s) électorale(s) fédérale(s):
Richmond-Arthabaska
Prochaines élections: 7e novembre 2021
Jean-François Pinard, Maire
Guylaine Trottier, Directrice générale

Saint-Octave-de-Métis
201A, rue de l'Église
Saint-Octave-de-Métis, QC G0J 3B0
Tél: 418-775-2996; *Téléc:* 418-775-0099
municipalites-du-quebec.ca/st-octave-de-metis
Entité municipal: Parish (Paroisse)
Incorporation: 25 avril 1908; *Area:* 75,32 km2
Comté ou district: La Mitis; *Population au 2016:* 511
Circonscription(s) électorale(s) provinciale(s): Matane-Matapédia
Circonscription(s) électorale(s) fédérale(s): Avignon-La
Mitis-Matane-Matapédia
Prochaines élections: 7e novembre 2021
Martin Reid, Maire
Ginette Roy, Directrice générale par intérim

Saint-Odilon-de-Cranbourne
111, rue de l'Hôtel-de-Ville
Saint-Odilon, QC G0S 3A0
Tél: 418-464-4801; *Téléc:* 418-464-4800
info@saint-odilon.qc.ca
www.saint-odilon.qc.ca
Entité municipal: Parish (Paroisse)
Incorporation: 1er juillet 1855; *Area:* 130,58 km2
Comté ou district: Robert-Cliche; *Population au 2016:* 1,374
Circonscription(s) électorale(s) provinciale(s): Beauce-Nord
Circonscription(s) électorale(s) fédérale(s): Beauce
Prochaines élections: 7e novembre 2021
Denise Roy, Mairesse
Dominique Giguère, Directrice générale

Saint-Omer
243, rang des Pelletier
Saint-Omer, QC G0R 4R0
Tél: 418-356-5634; *Téléc:* 418-356-2965
municipalitest-omer@globetrotter.net
www.st-omer.qc.ca
Entité municipal: Municipality
Incorporation: 1er janvier 1954; *Area:* 122,48 km2
Comté ou district: L'Islet; *Population au 2016:* 277
Circonscription(s) électorale(s) provinciale(s): Côte-du-Sud
Circonscription(s) électorale(s) fédérale(s):
Montmagny-L'Islet-Kamouraska-Rivière-du-Loup
Prochaines élections: 7e novembre 2021

Clément Fortin, Maire
Tina Godin, Directrice générale

Saint-Onésime-d'Ixworth
12, rue de l'Église
Saint-Onésime-d'Ixworth, QC G0R 3W0
Tél: 418-856-3018
municipalite@stonesime.com
st-onesime.ca
Entité municipal: Municipality
Incorporation: 13 mai 1895; *Area:* 102,89 km2
Comté ou district: Kamouraska; *Population au 2016:* 560
Circonscription(s) électorale(s) provinciale(s): Côte-du-Sud
Circonscription(s) électorale(s) fédérale(s):
Montmagny-L'Islet-Kamouraska-Rivière-du-Loup
Prochaines élections: 7e novembre 2021
Benoit Politto, Maire
Nancy Lizotte, Directrice générale et secrétaire-trésorière

Saint-Ours
2531, rue Immaculée-Conception
Saint-Ours, QC J0G 1P0
Tél: 450-785-2203; *Téléc:* 450-785-2254
admin@saintours.qc.ca
ville.saintours.qc.ca
Entité municipal: Village
Incorporation: 17 avril 1991; *Area:* 59,31 km2
Comté ou district: Pierre-De Saurel; *Population au 2016:* 1,669
Circonscription(s) électorale(s) provinciale(s): Richelieu
Circonscription(s) électorale(s) fédérale(s):
Bécancour-Nicolet-Saurel
Prochaines élections: 7e novembre 2021
Sylvain Dupuis, Maire
Carole Dulude, Directrice générale

Saint-Pacôme
27, rue St-Louis
Saint-Pacôme, QC G0L 3X0
Tél: 418-852-2356; *Téléc:* 418-852-2977
info@st-pacome.ca
www.st-pacome.ca
Entité municipal: Municipality
Incorporation: 5 janvier 1980; *Area:* 29,15 km2
Comté ou district: Kamouraska; *Population au 2016:* 1,598
Circonscription(s) électorale(s) provinciale(s): Côte-du-Sud
Circonscription(s) électorale(s) fédérale(s):
Montmagny-L'Islet-Kamouraska-Rivière-du-Loup
Prochaines élections: 7e novembre 2021
Robert Bérubé, Maire
Andréane Collard-Simard, Directrice générale, 418-852-2356

Saint-Pamphile
3, rte Elgin sud
Saint-Pamphile, QC G0R 3X0
Tél: 418-356-5501; *Téléc:* 418-356-5502
saintpamphile.ca
Entité municipal: Town
Incorporation: 21 janvier 1888; *Area:* 137,77 km2
Comté ou district: L'Islet; *Population au 2016:* 2,400
Circonscription(s) électorale(s) provinciale(s): Côte-du-Sud
Circonscription(s) électorale(s) fédérale(s):
Montmagny-L'Islet-Kamouraska-Rivière-du-Loup
Prochaines élections: 7e novembre 2021
Mario Leblanc, Maire
Alexandra Dupont, Directrice générale

Saint-Pascal
465, rue Taché
Saint-Pascal, QC G0L 3Y0
Tél: 418-492-2312
hoteldeville@villestpascal.com
villesaintpascal.qc.ca
Entité municipal: Town
Incorporation: 1er mars 2000; *Area:* 59,69 km2
Comté ou district: Kamouraska; *Population au 2016:* 3,468
Circonscription(s) électorale(s) provinciale(s): Côte-du-Sud
Circonscription(s) électorale(s) fédérale(s):
Montmagny-L'Islet-Kamouraska-Rivière-du-Loup
Prochaines élections: 7e novembre 2021
Rénald Bernier, Maire
Louise Saint-Pierre, Greffière, 418-492-2312

Saint-Patrice-de-Beaurivage
#100, 486, rue Principale
Saint-Patrice-de-Beaurivage, QC G0S 1B0
Tél: 418-596-2362; *Téléc:* 418-596-2430
st.patrice@globetrotter.net
www.ville.saint-patrice-de-beaurivage.qc.ca
Entité municipal: Municipality
Incorporation: 29 septembre 1984; *Area:* 85,55 km2
Comté ou district: Lotbinière; *Population au 2016:* 1,036
Circonscription(s) électorale(s) provinciale(s):

Lotbinière-Frontenac
Circonscription(s) électorale(s) fédérale(s): Lévis-Lotbinière
Prochaines élections: 7e novembre 2021
Claude Fortin, Maire
Annie Gagnon, Directrice générale

Saint-Patrice-de-Sherrington
300, rue St-Patrice
Saint-Patrice-de-Sherrington, QC J0L 2N0
Tél: 450-454-4959; *Téléc:* 450-454-5677
info@sherr.ca
st-patrice-sherrington.com
Entité municipal: Municipality
Incorporation: 1er juillet 1855; *Area:* 92,62 km2
Comté ou district: Les Jardins-de-Napierville; *Population au 2016:* 1,960
Circonscription(s) électorale(s) provinciale(s): Huntingdon
Circonscription(s) électorale(s) fédérale(s): Châteauguay-Lacolle
Prochaines élections: 7e novembre 2021
Yves Boyer, Maire
Clément Costanza, Directeur général

Saint-Paul
10, ch Delangis
Saint-Paul, QC J0K 3E0
Tél: 450-759-4040; *Téléc:* 450-759-6396
reception@saintpaul.quebec
saintpaul.quebec
Entité municipal: Municipality
Incorporation: 1er juillet 1855; *Area:* 49,11 km2
Comté ou district: Joliette; *Population au 2016:* 5,891
Circonscription(s) électorale(s) provinciale(s): Joliette
Circonscription(s) électorale(s) fédérale(s): Joliette
Prochaines élections: 7e novembre 2021
Alain Bellemare, Maire
Richard B. Morasse, Directeur général, 450-759-4040

Saint-Paul-d'Abbotsford
926, rue Principale est
Saint-Paul-d'Abbotsford, QC J0E 1A0
Tél: 450-379-5408; *Téléc:* 450-379-9905
info@saintpauldabbotsford.qc.ca
www.saintpauldabbotsford.qc.ca
Entité municipal: Municipality
Incorporation: 1er juillet 1855; *Area:* 79,57 km2
Comté ou district: Rouville; *Population au 2016:* 2,890
Circonscription(s) électorale(s) provinciale(s): Iberville
Circonscription(s) électorale(s) fédérale(s): Shefford
Prochaines élections: 7e novembre 2021
Robert Vyncke, Maire
Jean-Raphaël Cloutier, Directeur général, 450-379-5408

Saint-Paul-de-l'île-aux-Noix
959, rue Principale
Saint-Paul-de-l'île-aux-Noix, QC J0J 1G0
Tél: 450-291-3166; *Téléc:* 450-291-5930
info@ileauxnoix.qc.ca
www.ileauxnoix.com
Entité municipal: Municipality
Incorporation: 18 novembre 1898; *Area:* 29,66 km2
Comté ou district: Le Haut-Richelieu; *Population au 2016:* 1,980
Circonscription(s) électorale(s) provinciale(s): Huntingdon
Circonscription(s) électorale(s) fédérale(s): Saint-Jean
Prochaines élections: 7e novembre 2021
Claude Leroux, Maire
Edith Letourneau, Directrice générale, 450-291-3166

Saint-Paul-de-la-Croix
1A, rue du Parc
Saint-Paul-de-la-Croix, QC G0L 3Z0
Tél: 418-898-2031; *Téléc:* 418-898-2322
munstpaul@st-paul-de-la-croix.qc.ca
municipalite.saint-paul-de-la-croix.qc.ca
Entité municipal: Parish (Paroisse)
Incorporation: 1er janvier 1873; *Area:* 78,45 km2
Comté ou district: Rivière-du-Loup; *Population au 2016:* 309
Circonscription(s) électorale(s) provinciale(s):
Rivière-du-Loup-Témiscouata
Circonscription(s) électorale(s) fédérale(s):
Montmagny-L'Islet-Kamouraska-Rivière-du-Loup
Prochaines élections: 7e novembre 2021
Simon Périard, Maire
Hélène Malenfant, Directrice générale

Saint-Paul-de-Montminy
309, 4e av
Saint-Paul-de-Montminy, QC G0R 3Y0
Tél: 418-469-3120; *Téléc:* 418-469-3358
info@stpauldemontminy.com
www.stpauldemontminy.com
Entité municipal: Municipality
Incorporation: 1er janvier 1862; *Area:* 162,89 km2

Comté ou district: Montmagny; *Population au 2016:* 785
Circonscription(s) électorale(s) provinciale(s): Côte-du-Sud
Circonscription(s) électorale(s) fédérale(s):
Montmagny-L'Islet-Kamouraska-Rivière-du-Loup
Prochaines élections: 7e novembre 2021
Alain Talbot, Maire
Jacquelin Fraser, Directeur général

Saint-Paulin
2873, rue Laflèche
Saint-Paulin, QC J0K 3G0
Tél: 819-268-2026; *Téléc:* 819-268-2890
municipalite@saint-paulin.ca
st-paulin.qc.ca
Entité municipal: Municipality
Incorporation: 27 février 1988; *Area:* 95,67 km2
Comté ou district: Maskinongé; *Population au 2016:* 1,497
Circonscription(s) électorale(s) provinciale(s): Maskinongé
Circonscription(s) électorale(s) fédérale(s): Berthier-Maskinongé
Prochaines élections: 7e novembre 2021
Serge Dubé, Maire
Ghislain Lemay, Directeur général

Saint-Philémon
820, rue Therrien
Saint-Philémon, QC G0R 4A0
Tél: 418-469-2890; *Téléc:* 418-469-2726
info@saintphilemon.com
www.saintphilemon.com
Entité municipal: Parish (Paroisse)
Incorporation: 1er janvier 1867; *Area:* 146,54 km2
Comté ou district: Bellechasse; *Population au 2016:* 714
Circonscription(s) électorale(s) provinciale(s): Bellechasse
Circonscription(s) électorale(s) fédérale(s): Bellechasse-Les
Etchemins-Lévis
Prochaines élections: 7e novembre 2021
Daniel Pouliot, Maire
Julie Saint-Laurent, Directrice générale

Saint-Philibert
376, rue Principale
Saint-Philibert, QC G0M 1X0
Tél: 418-228-8759; *Téléc:* 418-228-0432
infos@st-philibert.qc.ca
www.st-philibert.qc.ca
Entité municipal: Municipality
Incorporation: 25 février 1921; *Area:* 57,18 km2
Comté ou district: Beauce-Sartigan; *Population au 2016:* 369
Circonscription(s) électorale(s) provinciale(s): Beauce-Sud
Circonscription(s) électorale(s) fédérale(s): Beauce
Prochaines élections: 7e novembre 2021
Jean-Guy Plante, Maire
Maryse Nadeau, Directrice générale

Saint-Philippe
#201, 175, ch Sanguinet
Saint-Philippe, QC J0L 2K0
Tél: 450-659-7701; *Téléc:* 450-659-7702
info@ville.saintphilippe.quebec
ville.saintphilippe.quebec
Entité municipal: Municipality
Incorporation: 1er juillet 1855; *Area:* 61,95 km2
Comté ou district: Roussillon; Communauté métropolitaine de
Montréal; *Population au 2016:* 6,320
Circonscription(s) électorale(s) provinciale(s): La Prairie
Circonscription(s) électorale(s) fédérale(s): La Prairie
Prochaines élections: 7e novembre 2021
Johanne Beaulac, Mairesse
Martin Lelièvre, Directeur général

Saint-Philippe-de-Néri
CP 130
11A, côte de l'Église
Saint-Philippe-de-Néri, QC G0L 4A0
Tél: 418-498-2744; *Téléc:* 418-498-2193
munic.s.phil.neri@qc.aira.com
www.stphilippedeneri.org
Entité municipal: Parish (Paroisse)
Incorporation: 29 décembre 1875; *Area:* 32,68 km2
Comté ou district: Kamouraska; *Population au 2016:* 832
Circonscription(s) électorale(s) provinciale(s): Côte-du-Sud
Circonscription(s) électorale(s) fédérale(s):
Montmagny-L'Islet-Kamouraska-Rivière-du-Loup
Prochaines élections: 7e novembre 2021
Frédéric Liztotte, Maire
Pierre Leclerc, Directeur général

Saint-Pie
77, rue St-Pierre
Saint-Pie, QC J0H 1W0
Tél: 450-772-2488; *Téléc:* 450-772-2233
st-pie@villest-pie.ca
www.villest-pie.ca
Entité municipal: Town
Incorporation: 28 février 2003; *Area:* 107,49 km2
Comté ou district: Les Maskoutains; *Population au 2016:* 5,607
Circonscription(s) électorale(s) provinciale(s): St-Hyacinthe
Circonscription(s) électorale(s) fédérale(s): St-Hyacinthe-Bagot
Prochaines élections: 7e novembre 2021
Note: Effective February 28, 2003, the Parish & the Village of
St-Pie amalgamated to create the new City of St-Pie.
Mario St-Pierre, Maire
Annick Lafontaine, Greffière, 450-772-2488

Saint-Pie-de-Guire
435, rue Principale
Saint-Pie-de-Guire, QC J0G 1R0
Tél: 450-784-2278; *Téléc:* 450-784-0133
info@stpiedeguire.ca
stpiedeguire.ca
Entité municipal: Parish (Paroisse)
Incorporation: 14 juin 1866; *Area:* 51,32 km2
Comté ou district: Drummond; *Population au 2016:* 450
Circonscription(s) électorale(s) provinciale(s): Nicolet-Bécancour
Circonscription(s) électorale(s) fédérale(s): Drummond
Prochaines élections: 7e novembre 2021
Benoît Bourque, Maire
Annick Vincent, Directrice générale

Saint-Pierre
485, ch du Village-de-St-Pierre nord
Joliette, QC J6E 0H2
Tél: 450-756-2592
villagestpierre@videotron.ca
villagestpierre.org
Entité municipal: Village
Incorporation: 24 avril 1922; *Area:* 9,80 km2
Comté ou district: Joliette; *Population au 2016:* 276
Circonscription(s) électorale(s) provinciale(s): Joliette
Circonscription(s) électorale(s) fédérale(s): Joliette
Prochaines élections: 7e novembre 2021
Roland Charest, Maire
Édith Gagné, Directrice générale

Saint-Pierre-Baptiste
525, rte de l'Église
Saint-Pierre-Baptiste, QC G0P 1K0
Tél: 418-453-2286
info@saintpierrebaptiste.qc.ca
www.saintpierrebaptiste.qc.ca
Entité municipal: Parish (Paroisse)
Incorporation: 1er janvier 1874; *Area:* 81,77 km2
Comté ou district: L'Érable; *Population au 2016:* 527
Circonscription(s) électorale(s) provinciale(s): Arthabaska
Circonscription(s) électorale(s) fédérale(s): Mégantic-L'Érable
Prochaines élections: 7e novembre 2021
Donald Lamontagne, Maire
Marc Fournier, Directeur général

Saint-Pierre-de-Broughton
29, rue de la Fabrique
Saint-Pierre-de-Broughton, QC G0N 1T0
Tél: 418-424-3572; *Téléc:* 418-424-0389
info@saintpierredebroughton.ca
www.ville.st-pierre-de-broughton.qc.ca
Entité municipal: Municipality
Incorporation: 12 octobre 1974; *Area:* 150,46 km2
Comté ou district: Les Appalaches; *Population au 2016:* 898
Circonscription(s) électorale(s) provinciale(s):
Lotbinière-Frontenac
Circonscription(s) électorale(s) fédérale(s): Mégantic-L'Érable
Prochaines élections: 7e novembre 2021
France Laroche, Mairesse, 418-424-3572
Alain Paré, Directeur général, 418-424-3572

Saint-Pierre-de-l'île-d'Orléans
515, rte des Prêtres
Saint-Pierre-île-d'Orléans, QC G0A 4E0
Tél: 418-828-2855; *Téléc:* 418-828-0724
info@stpierreio.ca
st-pierre.iledorleans.com
Entité municipal: Municipality
Incorporation: 1er juillet 1855; *Area:* 31,38 km2
Comté ou district: L'île-d'Orléans; Communauté métropolitaine
de Québec; *Population au 2016:* 1,993
Circonscription(s) électorale(s) provinciale(s):
Charlevoix-Côte-de-Beaupré
Circonscription(s) électorale(s) fédérale(s):

Beauport—Côte-de-Beaupré—île d'Orléans—Charlevoix
Prochaines élections: 7e novembre 2021
Sylvain Bergeron, Maire
Nicolas St-Gelais, Directeur général, 418-828-2855

Saint-Pierre-de-Lamy
115, rte de l'Église
Saint-Pierre-de-Lamy, QC G0L 4B0
Tél: 418-497-2447; *Téléc:* 418-497-2447
admin@saintpierredelamy.ca
municipalites-du-quebec.org/saint-pierre-de-lamy
Entité municipal: Municipality
Incorporation: 4 juin 1977; *Area:* 110,69 km2
Comté ou district: Témiscouata; *Population au 2016:* 117
Circonscription(s) électorale(s) provinciale(s):
Rivière-du-Loup-Témiscouata
Circonscription(s) électorale(s) fédérale(s):
Rimouski-Neigette-Témiscouata-Les Basques
Prochaines élections: 7e novembre 2021
Jean-Pierre Ouellet, Maire
Mireille Plourde, Directrice générale

Saint-Pierre-de-la-Rivière-du-Sud
645, 2e av
St-Pierre-de-la-Rivière-du-Sud, QC G0R 4B0
Tél: 418-248-8277; *Téléc:* 418-248-7068
info@stpierrerds.ca
stpierrerds.ca
Entité municipal: Parish (Paroisse)
Incorporation: 1er juillet 1855; *Area:* 91,08 km2
Comté ou district: Montmagny; *Population au 2016:* 907
Circonscription(s) électorale(s) provinciale(s): Côte-du-Sud
Circonscription(s) électorale(s) fédérale(s):
Montmagny-L'Islet-Kamouraska-Rivière-du-Loup
Prochaines élections: 7e novembre 2021
Alain Fortier, Maire
Karine Lachance, Directrice générale

Saint-Pierre-les-Becquets
110, rue des Loisirs
Saint-Pierre-les-Becquets, QC G0X 2Z0
Tél: 819-263-2622
municipalite@st-pierre-les-becquets.qc.ca
st-pierre-les-becquets.qc.ca
Entité municipal: Municipality
Incorporation: 22 février 1986; *Area:* 48,09 km2
Comté ou district: Bécancour; *Population au 2016:* 1,137
Circonscription(s) électorale(s) provinciale(s): Nicolet-Bécancour
Circonscription(s) électorale(s) fédérale(s):
Bécancour-Nicolet-Saurel
Prochaines élections: 7e novembre 2021
Éric Dupont, Maire
Martine Lafond, Directrice générale

Saint-Placide
281, montée St-Vincent
Saint-Placide, QC J0V 2B0
Tél: 450-258-2305; *Téléc:* 450-258-3059
info@saintplacide.ca
saintplacide.ca
Entité municipal: Municipality
Incorporation: 3 août 1994; *Area:* 42,98 km2
Comté ou district: Deux-Montagnes; *Population au 2016:* 1,686
Circonscription(s) électorale(s) provinciale(s): Mirabel
Circonscription(s) électorale(s) fédérale(s): Mirabel
Prochaines élections: 7e novembre 2021
Richard Labonté, Maire
Mathieu Dessureault, Directeur général

Saint-Polycarpe
1263, ch Élie-Auclair
Saint-Polycarpe, QC J0P 1X0
Tél: 450-265-3777; *Téléc:* 450-265-3010
stpolycarpe.ca
Entité municipal: Municipality
Incorporation: 31 décembre 1988; *Area:* 70,00 km2
Comté ou district: Vaudreuil-Soulanges; *Population au 2016:*
2,224
Circonscription(s) électorale(s) provinciale(s): Soulanges
Circonscription(s) électorale(s) fédérale(s): Salaberry-Suroît
Prochaines élections: 7e novembre 2021
Jean-Yves Poirier, Maire
Anne-Marie Duval, Directrice générale

Saint-Prime
599, rue Principale
Saint-Prime, QC G8J 1T2
Tél: 418-251-2116; *Téléc:* 418-251-2823
info@saint-prime.ca
www.saint-prime.ca
Entité municipal: Municipality
Incorporation: 29 juin 1968; *Area:* 147,48 km2

Comté ou district: Le Domaine-du-Roy; *Population au 2016:*
2,753
Circonscription(s) électorale(s) provinciale(s): Roberval
Circonscription(s) électorale(s) fédérale(s): Lac-Saint-Jean
Prochaines élections: 7e novembre 2021
Lucien Boivin, Maire
Caroline Bergeron, Directrice générale, 418-251-2116

Saint-Prosper
2025, 29e rue
Saint-Prosper, QC G0M 1Y0
Tél: 418-594-8135; *Téléc:* 418-594-8865
info@saint-prosper.com
www.saint-prosper.com
Entité municipal: Municipality
Incorporation: 26 septembre 1887; *Area:* 133,65 km2
Comté ou district: Les Etchemins; *Population au 2016:* 3,590
Circonscription(s) électorale(s) provinciale(s): Beauce-Sud
Circonscription(s) électorale(s) fédérale(s): Beauce
Prochaines élections: 7e novembre 2021
Richard Couët, Maire
Dany Desjardins, Directeur général, 418-594-8135

Saint-Prosper-de-Champlain
375, rue St-Joseph
Saint-Prosper, QC G0X 3A0
Tél: 418-840-0461; *Téléc:* 418-328-4267
municipalite@st-prosper.ca
www.st-prosper.ca
Entité municipal: Municipality
Incorporation: 1er juillet 1855; *Area:* 94,02 km2
Comté ou district: Les Chenaux; *Population au 2016:* 530
Circonscription(s) électorale(s) provinciale(s): Champlain
Circonscription(s) électorale(s) fédérale(s):
St-Maurice-Champlain
Prochaines élections: 7e novembre 2021
René Gravel, Maire
Sandra Turcotte, Directrice générale

Saint-Raphaël
19, av Chanoine-Audet
Saint-Raphaël, QC G0R 4C0
Tél: 418-243-2853
info@saint-raphael.ca
www.saint-raphael.ca
Entité municipal: Municipality
Incorporation: 8 décembre 1993; *Area:* 121,65 km2
Comté ou district: Bellechasse; *Population au 2016:* 2,390
Circonscription(s) électorale(s) provinciale(s): Bellechasse
Circonscription(s) électorale(s) fédérale(s): Bellechasse-Les
Etchemins-Lévis
Prochaines élections: 7e novembre 2021
Gilles Breton, Maire
Johnny Louis Jean, Directeur général

Saint-Raymond
375, rue St-Joseph
Saint-Raymond, QC G3L 1A1
Tél: 418-337-2202; *Téléc:* 418-337-2203
info@villesaintraymond.com
villesaintraymond.coma
Entité municipal: Town
Incorporation: 29 mars 1995; *Area:* 670,33 km2
Comté ou district: Portneuf; *Population au 2016:* 10,221
Circonscription(s) électorale(s) provinciale(s): Portneuf
Circonscription(s) électorale(s) fédérale(s):
Portneuf-Jacques-Cartier
Prochaines élections: 7e novembre 2021
Daniel Dion, Maire
Chantal Plamandon, Greffière

Saint-Rémi
105, rue de la Mairie
Saint-Rémi, QC J0L 2L0
Tél: 450-454-3993
info@ville.saint-remi.qc.ca
www.saint-remi.ca
Entité municipal: Town
Incorporation: 20 septembre 1975; *Area:* 78,35 km2
Comté ou district: Les Jardins-de-Napierville; *Population au
2016:* 8,061
Circonscription(s) électorale(s) provinciale(s): Sanguinet
Circonscription(s) électorale(s) fédérale(s): Châteauguay-Lacolle
Prochaines élections: 7e novembre 2021
Sylvie Gagnon-Breton, Mairesse
Patrice De Repentigny, Greffier

Saint-Rémi-de-Tingwick
1461, rue Principale
Saint-Rémi-de-Tingwick, QC J0A 1K0
Tél: 819-359-2731; *Téléc:* 819-359-3532
info@st-remi-tingwick.qc.ca
www.st-remi-tingwick.qc.ca
Entité municipal: Municipality
Incorporation: 1er janvier 1882; *Area:* 73,03 km2
Comté ou district: Arthabaska; *Population au 2016:* 458
Circonscription(s) électorale(s) provinciale(s):
Drummond-Bois-Francs
Circonscription(s) électorale(s) fédérale(s):
Richmond-Arthabaska
Prochaines élections: 7e novembre 2021
Mario Nolin, Maire
Anouk Wilsey, Directrice générale, 819-359-2731

Saint-René
778, rte Principale
Saint-René, QC G0M 1Z0
Tél: 418-382-5226
www.st-rene.ca
Entité municipal: Parish (Paroisse)
Incorporation: 1er janvier 1945; *Area:* 61,55 km3
Comté ou district: Beauce-Sartigan; *Population au 2016:* 745
Circonscription(s) électorale(s) provinciale(s): Beauce-Sud
Circonscription(s) électorale(s) fédérale(s): Beauce
Prochaines élections: 7e novembre 2021
Luc Paquet, Maire
Fanhui Kong, Directrice générale

Saint-René-de-Matane
CP 58
178, av St-René
Saint-René-de-Matane, QC G0J 3E0
Tél: 418-224-3306; *Téléc:* 418-224-3259
www.saintrene.ca
Entité municipal: Municipality
Incorporation: 18 décembre 1982; *Area:* 255,26 km2
Comté ou district: La Matanie; *Population au 2016:* 965
Circonscription(s) électorale(s) provinciale(s): Matane-Matapédia
Circonscription(s) électorale(s) fédérale(s): Avignon-La
Mitis-Matane-Matapédia
Prochaines élections: 7e novembre 2021
Rémi Fortin, Maire
Yvette Boulay, Directrice générale

Saint-Robert
666, ch de St-Robert
Saint-Robert, QC J0G 1S0
Tél: 450-782-2844; *Téléc:* 450-782-2733
info@saintrobert.qc.ca
www.saintrobert.qc.ca
Entité municipal: Municipality
Incorporation: 17 octobre 1857; *Area:* 64,98 km2
Comté ou district: Pierre-De Saurel; *Population au 2016:* 1,803
Circonscription(s) électorale(s) provinciale(s): Richelieu
Circonscription(s) électorale(s) fédérale(s):
Bécancour-Nicolet-Saurel
Prochaines élections: 7e novembre 2021
Gilles Salvas, Maire
Nathalie Lussier, Directrice générale

Saint-Robert-Bellarmin
10, rue Nadeau
Saint-Robert-Bellarmin, QC G0M 2E0
Tél: 418-582-3420; *Téléc:* 418-582-0052
www.st-robertbellarmin.qc.ca
Entité municipal: Municipality
Incorporation: 1er janvier 1949; *Area:* 236,75 km2
Comté ou district: Le Granit; *Population au 2016:* 575
Circonscription(s) électorale(s) provinciale(s): Beauce-Sud
Circonscription(s) électorale(s) fédérale(s): Mégantic-L'Érable
Prochaines élections: 7e novembre 2021
Jeannot Lachance, Maire
Suzanne Lescomb, Directrice générale

Saint-Roch-de-l'Achigan
7, rue du Dr.-Wilfrid-Locat
Saint-Roch-de-l'Achigan, QC J0K 3H0
Tél: 450-588-2326; *Téléc:* 450-588-4478
reception@sra.quebec
www.sra.quebec
Entité municipal: Municipality
Incorporation: 1er juillet 1855; *Area:* 80,29 km2
Comté ou district: Montcalm; *Population au 2016:* 5,147
Circonscription(s) électorale(s) provinciale(s): Rousseau
Circonscription(s) électorale(s) fédérale(s): Montcalm
Prochaines élections: 7e novembre 2021
Yves Prud'Homme, Maire
Marie-Josée Masson, Directrice générale, 450-588-2326

Saint-Roch-de-Mékinac
1216, rue Principale
Saint-Roch-de-Mékinac, QC G0X 2E0
Tél: 819-646-5635; *Téléc:* 819-646-5010
st-roch@regionmekinac.com
www.strochdemekinac.com
Entité municipal: Parish (Paroisse)
Incorporation: 2 novembre 2009; *Area:* 145,11 km2
Comté ou district: Mékinac; *Population au 2016:* 302
Circonscription(s) électorale(s) provinciale(s): Laviolette
Circonscription(s) électorale(s) fédérale(s):
St-Maurice-Champlain
Prochaines élections: 7e novembre 2021
Guy Dessureault, Maire
Sylvie Genois, Directrice générale, 819-646-5635

Saint-Roch-de-Richelieu
1111, rue du Parc
Saint-Roch-de-Richelieu, QC J0L 2M0
Tél: 450-785-2755; *Téléc:* 450-785-3098
info@saintrochderichelieu.com
saintrochderichelieu.qc.ca
Entité municipal: Municipality
Incorporation: 4 juin 1859; *Area:* 34,48 km2
Comté ou district: Pierre-De Saurel; *Population au 2016:* 2,188
Circonscription(s) électorale(s) provinciale(s): Richelieu
Circonscription(s) électorale(s) fédérale(s):
Bécancour-Nicolet-Saurel
Prochaines élections: 7e novembre 2021
Michel Beck, Maire
Reynald Castonguay, Directeur général, 450-785-2755

Saint-Roch-des-Aulnaies
1009, rte de la Seigneurie
Saint-Roch-des-Aulnaies, QC G0R 4E0
Tél: 418-354-2892; *Téléc:* 418-354-2059
muniroch@saintrochdesaulnaies.ca
www.saintrochdesaulnaies.ca
Entité municipal: Parish (Paroisse)
Incorporation: 1er juillet 1855; *Area:* 49,30 km2
Comté ou district: L'Islet; *Population au 2016:* 917
Circonscription(s) électorale(s) provinciale(s): Côte-du-Sud
Circonscription(s) électorale(s) fédérale(s):
Montmagny-L'Islet-Kamouraska-Rivière-du-Loup
Prochaines élections: 7e novembre 2021
André Simard, Maire
Stève Dionne, Directeur général

Saint-Roch-Ouest
270, rte 125
Saint-Roch-Ouest, QC J0K 3H0
Tél: 450-588-6060; *Téléc:* 450-588-0975
info@saint-roch-ouest.ca
www.saint-roch-ouest.ca
Entité municipal: Municipality
Incorporation: 4 juin 1921; *Area:* 20,17 km2
Comté ou district: Montcalm; *Population au 2016:* 266
Circonscription(s) électorale(s) provinciale(s): Rousseau
Circonscription(s) électorale(s) fédérale(s): Montcalm
Prochaines élections: 7e novembre 2021
Pierre Mercier, Maire
Sherron Kollar, Directrice générale

Saint-Romain
290, rue Principale
Saint-Romain, QC G0Y 1L0
Tél: 418-486-7374; *Téléc:* 418-486-7875
municipalite@st-romain.ca
www.st-romain.ca
Entité municipal: Municipality
Incorporation: 1er janvier 1858; *Area:* 112,30 km2
Comté ou district: Le Granit; *Population au 2016:* 691
Circonscription(s) électorale(s) provinciale(s): Mégantic
Circonscription(s) électorale(s) fédérale(s): Mégantic-L'Érable
Prochaines élections: 7e novembre 2021
Jean-Luc Fillion, Maire
Nicole Chicoine, Directrice générale

Saint-Rosaire
208, 6e rang
Saint-Rosaire, QC G0Z 1K0
Tél: 819-752-6178; *Téléc:* 819-752-3959
info@strosaire.ca
www.strosaire.ca
Entité municipal: Parish (Paroisse)
Incorporation: 23 mai 1896; *Area:* 109,66 km2
Comté ou district: Arthabaska; *Population au 2016:* 843
Circonscription(s) électorale(s) provinciale(s): Arthabaska
Circonscription(s) électorale(s) fédérale(s):
Richmond-Arthabaska
Prochaines élections: 7e novembre 2021
Harold Poisson, Maire

Julie Roberge, Directrice générale

Saint-Samuel
140, rue de l'Église
Saint-Samuel, QC G0Z 1G0
Tél: 819-353-1242; *Téléc:* 819-353-1499
info@saint-samuel.ca
www.saint-samuel.ca
Entité municipal: Municipality
Incorporation: 9 mars 1878; *Area:* 43,20 km2
Comté ou district: Arthabaska; *Population au 2016:* 744
Circonscription(s) électorale(s) provinciale(s):
Drummond-Bois-Francs
Circonscription(s) électorale(s) fédérale(s):
Richmond-Arthabaska
Prochaines élections: 7e novembre 2021
Denis Lampron, Maire
Sarah Richard, Directrice générale

Saints-Anges
494, av Principale
Saints-Anges, QC G0S 3E0
Tél: 418-253-5230; *Téléc:* 418-253-5613
info@saintsanges.com
Entité municipal: Parish (Paroisse)
Incorporation: 29 décembre 1880; *Area:* 68,70 km2
Comté ou district: La Nouvelle-Beauce; *Population au 2016:*
1,157
Circonscription(s) électorale(s) provinciale(s): Beauce-Nord
Circonscription(s) électorale(s) fédérale(s): Beauce
Prochaines élections: 7e novembre 2021
Carole Santerre, Mairesse
Caroline Bisson, Directrice générale

Saint-Sauveur
1, place de la Mairie
Saint-Sauveur, QC J0R 1R6
Tél: 450-227-4633; *Téléc:* 866-313-6267
administration@ville.saint-sauveur.qc.ca
www.ville.saint-sauveur.qc.ca
Entité municipal: Town
Incorporation: 11 septembre 2002; *Area:* 47,91 km2
Comté ou district: Les Pays-d'en-Haut; *Population au 2016:*
10,231
Circonscription(s) électorale(s) provinciale(s): Bertrand
Circonscription(s) électorale(s) fédérale(s): Laurentides-Labelle
Prochaines élections: 7e novembre 2021
Note: Effective September 9, 2002, the Parish of St-Sauveur &
the Village of St-Sauveur-des-Monts amalgamated to create the
City of St-Sauveur.
Jacques Gariépy, Maire
Marie-Pier Pharand, Greffière

Saint-Sébastien
582, rue Principale
Saint-Sébastien, QC G0Y 1M0
Tél: 819-652-2727; *Téléc:* 819-652-2584
info@st-sebastien.com
www.st-sebastien.com
Entité municipal: Municipality
Incorporation: 15 mars 1975; *Area:* 91,98 km2
Comté ou district: Le Granit; *Population au 2016:* 657
Circonscription(s) électorale(s) provinciale(s): Mégantic
Circonscription(s) électorale(s) fédérale(s): Mégantic-L'Érable
Prochaines élections: 7e novembre 2021
France Bisson, Mairesse
Martine Rouleau, Directrice générale

Saint-Sébastien
CP 126
176, rue Dussault
Saint-Sébastien, QC J0J 2C0
Tél: 450-346-4205; *Téléc:* 450-346-4207
info@municipalite-saint-sebastien.ca
www.paroisse-saint-sebastien.ca
Entité municipal: Municipality
Incorporation: 17 février 1865; *Area:* 63,29 km2
Comté ou district: Le Haut-Richelieu; *Population au 2016:* 718
Circonscription(s) électorale(s) provinciale(s): Iberville
Circonscription(s) électorale(s) fédérale(s): Brome-Missisquoi
Prochaines élections: 7e novembre 2021
Martin Thibert, Maire
Joance Martin, Directrice générale

Saint-Sévère
59, rue Principale
Saint-Sévère, QC G0X 3B0
Tél: 819-264-5656; *Téléc:* 819-519-9800
direction@saint-severe.ca
www.st-severe.ca
Entité municipal: Parish (Paroisse)
Incorporation: 1er juillet 1855; *Area:* 31,87 km2

Comté ou district: Maskinongé; *Population au 2016:* 302
Circonscription(s) électorale(s) provinciale(s): Maskinongé
Circonscription(s) électorale(s) fédérale(s): Berthier-Maskinongé
Prochaines élections: 7e novembre 2021
Jean-Yves St-Arnaud, Maire
Marie-Andrée Cadorette, Directeur général

Saint-Séverin
900, rue des Lacs
Saint-Séverin, QC G0N 1V0
Tél: 418-426-2423; *Téléc:* 418-426-1274
www.st-severin.qc.ca
Entité municipal: Parish (Paroisse)
Incorporation: 24 décembre 1875; *Area:* 58,93 km2
Comté ou district: Robert-Cliche; *Population au 2016:* 278
Circonscription(s) électorale(s) provinciale(s): Beauce-Nord
Circonscription(s) électorale(s) fédérale(s): Beauce
Prochaines élections: 7e novembre 2021
Jean-Paul Cloutier, Maire
Marie Giguère, Directrice générale

Saint-Séverin
1986, place du Centre
Saint-Séverin, QC G0X 2B0
Tél: 418-365-5844; *Téléc:* 418-365-7544
st-severin@regionmekinac.com
st-severin.ca
Entité municipal: Parish (Paroisse)
Incorporation: 11 avril 1890; *Area:* 61,61 km2
Comté ou district: Mékinac; *Population au 2016:* 846
Circonscription(s) électorale(s) provinciale(s): Laviolette
Circonscription(s) électorale(s) fédérale(s):
St-Maurice-Champlain
Prochaines élections: 7e novembre 2021
Julie Trépanier, Mairesse
Jocelyn St-Amant, Directeur général

Saint-Siméon
CP 98
502, rue St-Laurent
Saint-Siméon, QC G0T 1X0
Tél: 418-620-5010; *Téléc:* 418-620-5011
info@saintsimeon.ca
www.saintsimeon.ca
Entité municipal: Municipality
Incorporation: 25 avril 2001; *Area:* 284,14 km2
Comté ou district: Charlevoix-Est; *Population au 2016:* 1,227
Circonscription(s) électorale(s) provinciale(s):
Charlevoix-Côte-de-Beaupré
Circonscription(s) électorale(s) fédérale(s):
Beauport—Côte-de-Beaupré—Île d'Orléans—Charlevoix
Prochaines élections: 7e novembre 2021
Sylvain Tremblay, Maire
Sylvie Foster, Directrice générale

Saint-Siméon
300, rue Alexis-Poirier
Saint-Siméon, QC G0C 3A0
Tél: 418-534-2155; *Téléc:* 418-534-3830
administration@stsimeon.ca
www.stsimeon.ca
Entité municipal: Parish (Paroisse)
Incorporation: 29 octobre 1914; *Area:* 56,87 km2
Comté ou district: Bonaventure; *Population au 2016:* 1,171
Circonscription(s) électorale(s) provinciale(s): Bonaventure
Circonscription(s) électorale(s) fédérale(s):
Gaspésie—Îles-de-la-Madeleine
Prochaines élections: 7e novembre 2021
Denis Gauthier, Maire
Nathalie Arsenault, Directrice générale

Saint-Simon
CP 40
30, rue de l'Église
Saint-Simon, QC G0L 4C0
Tél: 418-738-2896
admin@st-simon.qc.ca
www.st-simon.qc.ca
Entité municipal: Parish (Paroisse)
Incorporation: 1er juillet 1855; *Area:* 75,01 km2
Comté ou district: Les Basques; *Population au 2016:* 426
Circonscription(s) électorale(s) provinciale(s):
Rivière-du-Loup-Témiscouata
Circonscription(s) électorale(s) fédérale(s):
Rimouski-Neigette-Témiscouata-Les Basques
Prochaines élections: 7e novembre 2021
Wilfrid Lepage, Maire
Nancy Dubé, Directrice générale

Saint-Simon
49, rue du Couvent
Saint-Simon-de-Bagot, QC J0H 1Y0
Tél: 450-798-2276; *Téléc:* 450-798-2498
info@saint-simon.ca
saint-simon.ca
Entité municipal: Municipality
Incorporation: 1er juillet 1855; *Area:* 69,07 km2
Comté ou district: Les Maskoutains; *Population au 2016:* 1,413
Circonscription(s) électorale(s) provinciale(s): St-Hyacinthe
Circonscription(s) électorale(s) fédérale(s): St-Hyacinthe-Bagot
Prochaines élections: 7e novembre 2021
Simon Giard, Maire
Johanna Godin, Directrice générale, 450-798-2276

Saint-Simon-les-Mines
3338, rue Principale
Saint-Simon-les-Mines, QC G0M 1K0
Tél: 418-774-3317; *Téléc:* 418-774-3362
info@sslm.ca
www.sslm.ca
Entité municipal: Municipality
Incorporation: 1er juin 1950; *Area:* 47,45 km2
Comté ou district: Beauce-Sartigan; *Population au 2016:* 549
Circonscription(s) électorale(s) provinciale(s): Beauce-Sud
Circonscription(s) électorale(s) fédérale(s): Beauce
Prochaines élections: 7e novembre 2021
Martin St-Laurent, Maire
Véronique Fortin, Directrice générale

Saint-Sixte
28, rue Principale
Saint-Sixte, QC J0X 3B0
Tél: 819-983-3155; *Téléc:* 819-983-3409
www.saintsixte.ca
Entité municipal: Municipality
Incorporation: 7 février 1893; *Area:* 85,33 km2
Comté ou district: Papineau; *Population au 2016:* 469
Circonscription(s) électorale(s) provinciale(s): Papineau
Circonscription(s) électorale(s) fédérale(s): Argenteuil-La
Petite-Nation
Prochaines élections: 7e novembre 2021
André Bélisle, Maire
Michel Tardif, Directeur général

Saints-Martyrs-Canadiens
13, ch du Village
Saints-Martyrs-Canadiens, QC G0Y 1A1
Tél: 819-344-5171; *Téléc:* 819-344-2298
info@saints-martyrs-canadiens.ca
www.saints-martyrs-canadiens.ca
Entité municipal: Parish (Paroisse)
Incorporation: 1er janvier 1943; *Area:* 111,67 km2
Comté ou district: Arthabaska; *Population au 2016:* 254
Circonscription(s) électorale(s) provinciale(s):
Drummond-Bois-Francs
Circonscription(s) électorale(s) fédérale(s):
Richmond-Arthabaska
Prochaines élections: 7e novembre 2021
André Henri, Maire
Thérèse Lemay, Directrice générale

Saint-Stanislas
1302, rue Principale
Saint-Stanislas, QC G0X 3E0
Tél: 819-840-0703; *Téléc:* 418-328-4121
municipalite@saint-stanislas.ca
www.saint-stanislas.ca
Entité municipal: Municipality
Incorporation: 17 avril 1976; *Area:* 89,48 km2
Comté ou district: Les Chenaux; *Population au 2016:* 1,010
Circonscription(s) électorale(s) provinciale(s): Champlain
Circonscription(s) électorale(s) fédérale(s):
St-Maurice-Champlain
Prochaines élections: 7e novembre 2021
Luc Pellerin, Maire
Marie-Claude Jean, Directrice générale

Saint-Stanislas
953, rue Principale
Saint-Stanislas, QC G8L 7B4
Tél: 418-276-4476; *Téléc:* 418-276-4476
admin@st-stanislas.qc.ca
st-stanislas.com
Entité municipal: Municipality
Incorporation: 24 octobre 1931; *Area:* 153,48 km2
Comté ou district: Maria-Chapdelaine; *Population au 2016:* 373
Circonscription(s) électorale(s) provinciale(s): Roberval
Circonscription(s) électorale(s) fédérale(s): Lac-Saint-Jean
Prochaines élections: 7e novembre 2021
Mario Biron, Maire
Caroline Gagnon, Directrice générale

Saint-Stanislas-de-Kostka
221, rue Centrale
Saint-Stanislas-de-Kostka, QC J0S 1W0
Tél: 450-373-8944; *Téléc:* 450-373-8949
info@st-stanislas-de-kostka.ca
st-stanislas-de-kostka.ca
Entité municipal: Municipality
Incorporation: 1er juillet 1855; *Area:* 57,72 km2
Comté ou district: Beauharnois-Salaberry; *Population au 2016:*
1,654
Circonscription(s) électorale(s) provinciale(s): Beauharnois
Circonscription(s) électorale(s) fédérale(s): Salaberry-Suroît
Prochaines élections: 7e novembre 2021
Caroline Huot, Mairesse
Éric Beaulieu, Directrice générale

Saint-Sulpice
1089, rue Notre-Dame
Saint-Sulpice, QC J5W 1G1
Tél: 450-589-4450; *Téléc:* 450-589-9647
info@st-sulpice.com
www.municipalitesaintsulpice.com
Entité municipal: Parish (Paroisse)
Incorporation: 1er juillet 1855; *Area:* 36,36 km2
Comté ou district: L'Assomption; Communauté métropolitaine de
Montréal; *Population au 2016:* 3,439
Circonscription(s) électorale(s) provinciale(s): Repentigny
Circonscription(s) électorale(s) fédérale(s): Repentigny
Prochaines élections: 7e novembre 2021
Michel Champagne, Maire
Chantal Bédard, Directrice générale

Saint-Sylvère
756A, rue Principale
Saint-Sylvère, QC G0Z 1H0
Tél: 819-285-2075; *Téléc:* 819-285-2040
info@saint-sylvere.ca
saint-sylvere.ca
Entité municipal: Municipality
Incorporation: 18 septembre 1976; *Area:* 86,31 km2
Comté ou district: Bécancour; *Population au 2016:* 791
Circonscription(s) électorale(s) provinciale(s): Nicolet-Bécancour
Circonscription(s) électorale(s) fédérale(s):
Bécancour-Nicolet-Saurel
Prochaines élections: 7e novembre 2021
Adrien Pellerin, Maire
Sandra Ricard, Directrice générale

Saint-Sylvestre
423B, rue Principale
Saint-Sylvestre, QC G0S 3C0
Tél: 418-596-2384; *Téléc:* 418-596-2375
info@st-sylvestre.org
www.st-sylvestre.org
Entité municipal: Municipality
Incorporation: 4 décembre 1996; *Area:* 147,18 km2
Comté ou district: Lotbinière; *Population au 2016:* 1,019
Circonscription(s) électorale(s) provinciale(s):
Lotbinière-Frontenac
Circonscription(s) électorale(s) fédérale(s): Lévis-Lotbinière
Prochaines élections: 7e novembre 2021
Mario Grenier, Maire
Marie-Lyne Rousseau, Directrice générale

Saint-Télesphore
1425, rte 340
Saint-Télesphore, QC J0P 1Y0
Tél: 450-269-2999; *Téléc:* 450-269-2257
info@st-telesphore.ca
saint-telesphore.com
Entité municipal: Municipality
Incorporation: 10 avril 1877; *Area:* 60,33 km2
Comté ou district: Vaudreuil-Soulanges; *Population au 2016:* 759
Circonscription(s) électorale(s) provinciale(s): Soulanges
Circonscription(s) électorale(s) fédérale(s): Salaberry-Suroît
Prochaines élections: 7e novembre 2021
Yvon Bériault, Maire
Micheline Déry, Directrice générale

Saint-Tharcisius
55, rue Principale
Saint-Tharcisius, QC G0J 3G0
Tél: 418-629-4727; *Téléc:* 418-629-4727
sttharcisius@mrcmatapedia.quebec
saint-tharcisius.ca
Entité municipal: Parish (Paroisse)
Incorporation: 4 décembre 2009; *Area:* 79,11 km2
Comté ou district: La Matapédia; *Population au 2016:* 315
Circonscription(s) électorale(s) provinciale(s): Matapédia
Circonscription(s) électorale(s) fédérale(s): Avignon-La
Mitis-Matane-Matapédia
Prochaines élections: 7e novembre 2021

Jocelyn Jean, Maire
Caroline Lapointe, Directrice générale

Saint-Théodore-d'Acton
1661, rue Principale
Saint-Théodore-d-Acton, QC J0H 1Z0
Tél: 450-546-2634
mun.st-theodore@mrcacton.qc.ca
st-theodore.com
Entité municipal: Municipality
Incorporation: 1er janvier 1864; *Area:* 82,90 km2
Comté ou district: Acton; *Population au 2016:* 1,519
Circonscription(s) électorale(s) provinciale(s): Johnson
Circonscription(s) électorale(s) fédérale(s): St-Hyacinthe-Bagot
Prochaines élections: 7e novembre 2021
Guy Bond, Maire
Marc Lévesque, Directrice générale

Saint-Théophile
CP 10
629, rue Principale
Saint-Théophile, QC G0M 2A0
Tél: 418-597-3998; *Téléc:* 418-597-3015
info@sainttheophile.qc.ca
www.sainttheophile.qc.ca
Entité municipal: Municipality
Incorporation: 28 juin 1975; *Area:* 428,35 km2
Comté ou district: Beauce-Sartigan; *Population au 2016:* 713
Circonscription(s) électorale(s) provinciale(s): Beauce-Sud
Circonscription(s) électorale(s) fédérale(s): Beauce
Prochaines élections: 7e novembre 2021
Clément Létourneau, Maire
Martin Chaput, Directeur général, 418-597-3998

Saint-Thomas
1240, rte 158
Saint-Thomas, QC J0K 3L0
Tél: 450-759-3405
municipalite@saintthomas.qc.ca
www.saintthomas.qc.ca
Entité municipal: Municipality
Incorporation: 1er juillet 1855; *Area:* 94,80 km2
Comté ou district: Joliette; *Population au 2016:* 3,249
Circonscription(s) électorale(s) provinciale(s): Joliette
Circonscription(s) électorale(s) fédérale(s): Joliette
Prochaines élections: 7e novembre 2021
Marc Corriveau, Maire
Danielle Lambert, Directrice générale, 450-759-3405

Saint-Thomas-Didyme
9, av du Moulin
Saint-Thomas-Didyme, QC G0W 1P0
Tél: 418-274-3638; *Téléc:* 418-274-4176
info@stthomasdidyme.qc.ca
stthomasdidyme.qc.ca
Entité municipal: Municipality
Incorporation: 11 mai 1923; *Area:* 339,79 km2
Comté ou district: Maria-Chapdelaine; *Population au 2016:* 676
Circonscription(s) électorale(s) provinciale(s): Roberval
Circonscription(s) électorale(s) fédérale(s): Lac-Saint-Jean
Prochaines élections: 7e novembre 2021
Denis Tremblay, Maire
Gabrielle Fortin-Darveau, Directrice générale, 418-274-3638

Saint-Thuribe
238, rue Principale
Saint-Thuribe, QC G0A 4H0
Tél: 418-339-2171
info@st-thuribe.net
municipalites-du-quebec.ca/st-thuribe
Entité municipal: Parish (Paroisse)
Incorporation: 14 février 1898; *Area:* 50,93 km2
Comté ou district: Portneuf; *Population au 2016:* 286
Circonscription(s) électorale(s) provinciale(s): Portneuf
Circonscription(s) électorale(s) fédérale(s):
Portneuf-Jacques-Cartier
Prochaines élections: 7e novembre 2021
Jacques Delisle, Maire
Annie Frenette, Directrice générale, 418-339-2171

Saint-Tite
540, rue Notre-Dame
Saint-Tite, QC G0X 3H0
Tél: 418-365-5143; *Téléc:* 418-365-4020
info@villest-tite.com
villest-tite.com
Entité municipal: Town
Incorporation: 23 décembre 1998; *Area:* 91,33 km2
Comté ou district: Mékinac; *Population au 2016:* 3,673
Circonscription(s) électorale(s) provinciale(s): Laviolette
Circonscription(s) électorale(s) fédérale(s):

St-Maurice-Champlain
Prochaines élections: 7e novembre 2021
Annie Pronovost, Mairesse
Julie Marchand, Greffière

Saint-Tite-des-Caps
5, rue Leclerc
Saint-Tite-des-Caps, QC G0A 4J0
Tél: 418-823-2239; *Téléc:* 418-823-2527
info@sainttitedescaps.com
sainttitedescaps.com
Entité municipal: Municipality
Incorporation: 24 décembre 1872; *Area:* 129,21 km2
Comté ou district: La Côte-de-Beaupré; Communauté
métropolitaine de Québec; *Population au 2016:* 1,473
Circonscription(s) électorale(s) provinciale(s):
Charlevoix-Côte-de-Beaupré
Circonscription(s) électorale(s) fédérale(s):
Beauport—Côte-de-Beaupré—Île d'Orléans—Charlevoix
Prochaines élections: 7e novembre 2021
Majella Pichette, Maire
Marc Lachance, Directeur général

Saint-Ubalde
427B, boul Chabot
Saint-Ubalde, QC G0A 4L0
Tél: 418-277-2124
info@saintubalde.com
saintubalde.com
Entité municipal: Municipality
Incorporation: 3 mars 1973; *Area:* 140,72 km2
Comté ou district: Portneuf; *Population au 2016:* 1,412
Circonscription(s) électorale(s) provinciale(s): Portneuf
Circonscription(s) électorale(s) fédérale(s):
Portneuf-Jacques-Cartier
Prochaines élections: 7e novembre 2021
Guy Germain, Maire
Christine Genest, Directrice générale

Saint-Ulric
128, av Ulric-Tessier
Saint-Ulric, QC G0J 3H0
Tél: 418-737-4341; *Téléc:* 418-737-9242
st-ulric@lamatanie.ca
st-ulric.ca
Entité municipal: Municipality
Incorporation: 12 janvier 2000; *Area:* 120,65 km2
Comté ou district: La Matanie; *Population au 2016:* 1,585
Circonscription(s) électorale(s) provinciale(s): Matane-Matapédia
Circonscription(s) électorale(s) fédérale(s): Avignon-La
Mitis-Matane-Matapédia
Prochaines élections: 7e novembre 2021
Pierre Lagacé, Maire
Louise Coll, Directrice générale, 418-737-4341

Saint-Urbain
917, rue St-Édouard
Saint-Urbain, QC G0A 4K0
Tél: 418-639-2467; *Téléc:* 418-639-1056
munsturb@sainturbain.qc.ca
www.sainturbain.qc.ca
Entité municipal: Parish (Paroisse)
Incorporation: 1er juillet 1855; *Area:* 334,83 km2
Comté ou district: Charlevoix; *Population au 2016:* 1,373
Circonscription(s) électorale(s) provinciale(s):
Charlevoix-Côte-de-Beaupré
Circonscription(s) électorale(s) fédérale(s):
Beauport—Côte-de-Beaupré—Île d'Orléans—Charlevoix
Prochaines élections: 7e novembre 2021
Claudette Simard, Mairesse
Gilles Gagnon, Directeur général

Saint-Urbain-Premier
204, rue Principale
Saint-Urbain-Premier, QC J0S 1Y0
Tél: 450-427-3987; *Téléc:* 450-427-2056
sainturbainpremier@videotron.ca
www.saint-urbain-premier.com
Entité municipal: Municipality
Incorporation: 1er juillet 1855; *Area:* 53,29
Comté ou district: Beauharnois-Salaberry; *Population au 2016:*
1,264
Circonscription(s) électorale(s) provinciale(s): Huntingdon
Circonscription(s) électorale(s) fédérale(s): Châteauguay-Lacolle
Prochaines élections: 7e novembre 2021
Réjean Beaulieu, Maire
Charles Whissell, Directeur général par intérim

Saint-Valentin
790, ch de la Quatrième-Ligne
Saint-Valentin, QC J0J 2E0
Tél: 450-291-5422; *Téléc:* 450-291-5327
administration@municipalite.saint-valentin.qc.ca
municipalite.saint-valentin.qc.ca
Entité municipal: Municipality
Incorporation: 1er juillet 1855; *Area:* 39,28 km2
Comté ou district: Le Haut-Richelieu; *Population au 2016:* 447
Circonscription(s) électorale(s) provinciale(s): Huntingdon
Circonscription(s) électorale(s) fédérale(s): Saint-Jean
Prochaines élections: 7e novembre 2021
Pierre Chamberland, Maire
Brigitte Garceau, Directrice générale

Saint-Valère
2, rue du Parc
Saint-Valère, QC G0P 1M0
Tél: 819-353-3450; *Téléc:* 819-353-3459
reception@msvalere.qc.ca
www.msvalere.qc.ca
Entité municipal: Municipality
Incorporation: 1er janvier 1862; *Area:* 108,11 km2
Comté ou district: Arthabaska; *Population au 2016:* 1,263
Circonscription(s) électorale(s) provinciale(s): Arthabaska
Circonscription(s) électorale(s) fédérale(s):
Richmond-Arthabaska
Prochaines élections: 7e novembre 2021
Marc Plante, Maire
Jocelyn Jutras, Directeur général

Saint-Valérien
181, rte Centrale
Saint-Valérien-de-Rimouski, QC G0L 4E0
Tél: 418-736-5047; *Téléc:* 418-736-5922
info@municipalite.saint-valerien.qc.ca
municipalite.saint-valerien.qc.ca
Entité municipal: Parish (Paroisse)
Incorporation: 19 juin 1885; *Area:* 145,27 km2
Comté ou district: Rimouski-Neigette; *Population au 2016:* 816
Circonscription(s) électorale(s) provinciale(s): Rimouski
Circonscription(s) électorale(s) fédérale(s):
Rimouski-Neigette-Témiscouata-Les Basques
Prochaines élections: 7e novembre 2021
Robert Savoie, Maire
Marie-Paule Cimon, Directrice générale, 418-736-5047

Saint-Valérien-de-Milton
960, ch de Milton
Saint-Valérien-de-Milton, QC J0H 2B0
Tél: 450-549-2463; *Téléc:* 450-549-2993
administration.st-valerien@mrcmaskoutains.qc.ca
www.st-valerien-de-milton.qc.ca
Entité municipal: Municipality
Incorporation: 1er janvier 1864; *Area:* 107,01 km2
Comté ou district: Les Maskoutains; *Population au 2016:* 1,793
Circonscription(s) électorale(s) provinciale(s): Johnson
Circonscription(s) électorale(s) fédérale(s): St-Hyacinthe-Bagot
Prochaines élections: 7e novembre 2021
Daniel Paquette, Maire
Caroline Lamothe, Directrice générale, 450-549-2463

Saint-Vallier
367, av de l'Église
Saint-Vallier, QC G0R 4J0
Tél: 418-884-2559; *Téléc:* 418-884-2454
svallier@globetrotter.net
www.stvallierbellechasse.qc.ca
Entité municipal: Municipality
Incorporation: 10 mars 1993; *Area:* 45,03 km2
Comté ou district: Bellechasse; *Population au 2016:* 1,061
Circonscription(s) électorale(s) provinciale(s): Bellechasse
Circonscription(s) électorale(s) fédérale(s): Bellechasse-Les
Etchemins-Lévis
Prochaines élections: 7e novembre 2021
Christian Lacasse, Maire
Claire St-Laurent, Directrice générale, 418-884-2559

Saint-Venant-de-Paquette
5, ch du Village
Saint-Venant-de-Paquette, QC J0B 1S0
Tél: 819-658-3660; *Téléc:* 819-658-0985
stvenant@axion.ca
www.saint-venant-de-paquette.org
Entité municipal: Municipality
Incorporation: 11 juin 1917; *Area:* 58,80 km2
Comté ou district: Coaticook; *Population au 2016:* 97
Circonscription(s) électorale(s) provinciale(s): St-François
Circonscription(s) électorale(s) fédérale(s): Compton-Stanstead
Prochaines élections: 7e novembre 2021
Henri Pariseau, Maire
Roland Gascon, Directeur général

Saint-Vianney
170, av Centrale
Saint-Vianney, QC G0J 3J0
Tél: 418-629-4082; *Téléc:* 418-629-4821
stvianney@mrcmatapedia.qc.ca
www.saint-vianney.net
Entité municipal: Municipality
Incorporation: 27 août 1926; *Area:* 145,99 km2
Comté ou district: La Matapédia; *Population au 2016:* 441
Circonscription(s) électorale(s) provinciale(s): Matane-Matapédia
Circonscription(s) électorale(s) fédérale(s): Avignon-La
Mitis-Matane-Matapédia
Prochaines élections: 7e novembre 2021
Georges Guénard, Maire
Mélanie Champagne, Directrice générale

Saint-Victor
287, rue Marchand
Saint-Victor, QC G0M 2B0
Tél: 418-588-6854; *Téléc:* 418-588-6855
administration@st-victor.qc.ca
st-victor.qc.ca
Entité municipal: Municipality
Incorporation: 31 décembre 1996; *Area:* 120,34 km2
Comté ou district: Robert-Cliche; *Population au 2016:* 2,448
Circonscription(s) électorale(s) provinciale(s): Beauce-Nord
Circonscription(s) électorale(s) fédérale(s): Beauce
Prochaines élections: 7e novembre 2021
Jonathan V. Bolduc, Maire
Félix Nunez, Directeur général par intérim

Saint-Wenceslas
1055, rue Richard
Saint-Wenceslas, QC G0Z 1J0
Tél: 819-224-7784; *Téléc:* 819-224-4036
mun.stwen@sogetel.net
www.municipalitestwenceslas.com
Entité municipal: Municipality
Incorporation: 11 octobre 1995; *Area:* 79,67 km2
Comté ou district: Nicolet-Yamaska; *Population au 2016:* 1,157
Circonscription(s) électorale(s) provinciale(s): Nicolet-Bécancour
Circonscription(s) électorale(s) fédérale(s):
Bécancour-Nicolet-Saurel
Prochaines élections: 7e novembre 2021
Réal Deschênes, Maire
Carole Hélie, Directrice générale, 819-224-7784

Saint-Zacharie
735, 15e rue
Saint-Zacharie, QC G0M 2C0
Tél: 418-593-3185; *Téléc:* 418-593-3085
munzac@sogetel.net
www.st-zacharie.qc.ca
Entité municipal: Municipality
Incorporation: 18 avril 1990; *Area:* 186,77 km2
Comté ou district: Les Etchemins; *Population au 2016:* 1,653
Circonscription(s) électorale(s) provinciale(s): Beauce-Sud
Circonscription(s) électorale(s) fédérale(s): Beauce
Prochaines élections: 7e novembre 2021
Joey Cloutier, Maire
Brigitte Larivière, Dirctrice générale

Saint-Zénon
6101, rue Principale
Saint-Zénon, QC J0K 3N0
Tél: 450-884-5987; *Téléc:* 450-884-5285
municipalite@st-zenon.net
www.st-zenon.org
Entité municipal: Municipality
Incorporation: 7 octobre 1895; *Area:* 465,23 km2
Comté ou district: Matawinie; *Population au 2016:* 1,120
Circonscription(s) électorale(s) provinciale(s): Berthier
Circonscription(s) électorale(s) fédérale(s): Joliette
Prochaines élections: 7e novembre 2021
Richard Rondeau, Maire
Julie Martin, Directrice générale

Saint-Zénon-du-Lac-Humqui
146, rte 195
Lac-Humqui, QC G0J 1N0
Tél: 418-743-2177; *Téléc:* 418-743-2177
info@lachumqui.com
www.lachumqui.com
Entité municipal: Parish (Paroisse)
Incorporation: 28 avril 1920; *Area:* 113,42 km2
Comté ou district: La Matapédia; *Population au 2016:* 359
Circonscription(s) électorale(s) provinciale(s): Matane-Matapédia
Circonscription(s) électorale(s) fédérale(s): Avignon-La
Mitis-Matane-Matapédia
Prochaines élections: 7e novembre 2021
Gino Canuel, Maire
Maryline Pronovost, Directrice générale

Saint-Zéphirin-de-Courval
1232, rang St-Pierre
Saint-Zéphirin-de-Courval, QC J0G 1V0
Tél: 450-564-2188; *Téléc:* 450-564-2339
reception@saint-zephirin.ca
www.saint-zephirin.ca
Entité municipal: Parish (Paroisse)
Incorporation: 1er juillet 1855; *Area:* 71,97 km2
Comté ou district: Nicolet-Yamaska; *Population au 2016:* 700
Circonscription(s) électorale(s) provinciale(s): Nicolet-Bécancour
Circonscription(s) électorale(s) fédérale(s):
Bécancour-Nicolet-Saurel
Prochaines élections: 7e novembre 2021
Mathieu Lemire, Maire
Hélène Chassé, Directrice générale

Saint-Zotique
1250, rue Principale
Saint-Zotique, QC J0P 1Z0
Tél: 450-267-9335; *Téléc:* 450-267-0907
infost-zo@st-zotique.com
st-zotique.com
Entité municipal: Municipality
Incorporation: 27 mai 1967; *Area:* 25,10 km2
Comté ou district: Vaudreuil-Soulanges; *Population au 2016:*
7,934
Circonscription(s) électorale(s) provinciale(s): Soulanges
Circonscription(s) électorale(s) fédérale(s): Salaberry-Suroît
Prochaines élections: 7e novembre 2021
Yvon Chiasson, Maire
Jean-François Messier, Directeur général, 450-267-9335

Salluit
74, rue Aqqutituqaq
Salluit, QC J0M 1S0
Tél: 819-255-8953; *Téléc:* 819-255-8802
www.nvsalluit.ca
Entité municipal: Northern Village
Incorporation: 29 décembre 1979; *Area:* 14,66 km2
Comté ou district: Administration régionale Kativik; *Population au
2016:* 1,483
Circonscription(s) électorale(s) provinciale(s): Ungava
Circonscription(s) électorale(s) fédérale(s):
Abitibi-Baie-James-Nunavik-Eeyou
Paulusie Saviadjuk, Maire
Susie P. Alaku, Secrétaire-trésorière

La Sarre
201, rue Principale
La Sarre, QC J9Z 1Y3
Tél: 819-333-2282; *Téléc:* 819-333-3090
info@ville.lasarre.qc.ca
www.ville.lasarre.qc.ca
Other Information: Sans Frais: 888-330-2282
Entité municipal: Town
Incorporation: 19 avril 1980; *Area:* 148,50 km2
Comté ou district: Abitibi-Ouest; *Population au 2016:* 7,282
Circonscription(s) électorale(s) provinciale(s): Abitibi-Ouest
Circonscription(s) électorale(s) fédérale(s):
Abitibi-Témiscamingue
Prochaines élections: 7e novembre 2021
Yves Dubé, Maire
Valérie Fournier, Greffière

Sayabec
3, rue Keable
Sayabec, QC G0J 3K0
Tél: 418-536-5440; *Téléc:* 418-536-5572
sayabec@mrcmatapedia.quebec
municipalitesayabec.com
Entité municipal: Municipality
Incorporation: 24 décembre 1982; *Area:* 130,73 km2
Comté ou district: La Matapédia; *Population au 2016:* 1,594
Circonscription(s) électorale(s) provinciale(s): Matane-Matapédia
Circonscription(s) électorale(s) fédérale(s): Avignon-La
Mitis-Matane-Matapédia
Prochaines élections: 7e novembre 2021
Marcel Belzile, Maire
Joël Charest, Directeur général, 418-536-5440

Schefferville
505, rue Fleming
Schefferville, QC G0G 2T0
Tél: 418-585-2471; *Téléc:* 418-585-2256
schefferville1.info@gmail.com
ville-schefferville.ca
Other Information: Sans frais: 855-817-5699
Entité municipal: Village
Incorporation: 1er août 1955; *Area:* 27,33 km2
Comté ou district: Caniapiscau; *Population au 2016:* 155
Circonscription(s) électorale(s) provinciale(s): Duplessis

Circonscription(s) électorale(s) fédérale(s): Manicouagan
Prochaines élections: 7e novembre 2021
Ghislain Lévesque, Administrateur
Jean Dionne, Directeur général

Scotstown
101, ch Victoria ouest
Scotstown, QC J0B 3B0
Tél: 819-560-8433; *Téléc:* 819-560-8434
ville.scotstown@hsfgc.ca
scotstown.net
Entité municipal: Village
Incorporation: 24 juin 1892; *Area:* 11,46 km2
Comté ou district: Le Haut-Saint-François; *Population au 2016:*
472
Circonscription(s) électorale(s) provinciale(s): Mégantic
Circonscription(s) électorale(s) fédérale(s): Compton-Stanstead
Prochaines élections: 7e novembre 2021
Dominique Boisvert, Maire
Monique Polard, Directrice générale

Scott
1070, rte du Président-Kennedy
Scott, QC G0S 3G0
Tél: 418-387-2037; *Téléc:* 418-387-1837
info@municipalitescott.com
www.municipalitescott.com
Entité municipal: Municipality
Incorporation: 29 mars 1995; *Area:* 31,31 km2
Comté ou district: La Nouvelle-Beauce; *Population au 2016:*
2,352
Circonscription(s) électorale(s) provinciale(s): Beauce-Nord
Circonscription(s) électorale(s) fédérale(s): Beauce
Prochaines élections: 7e novembre 2021
Clément Marcoux, Maire
Marie-Michèle Benoit, Directrice générale

Senneterre
100, rue le Portage
Senneterre, QC J0Y 2M0
Tél: 819-737-2842; *Téléc:* 819-737-4668
info@paroissesenneterre.qc.ca
www.paroissesenneterre.qc.ca
Entité municipal: Parish (Paroisse)
Incorporation: 23 mars 1923; *Area:* 568,88 km2
Comté ou district: La Vallée-de-l'Or; *Population au 2016:* 1,192
Circonscription(s) électorale(s) provinciale(s): Abitibi-Est
Circonscription(s) électorale(s) fédérale(s):
Abitibi-Baie-James-Nunavik-Eeyou
Prochaines élections: 7e novembre 2021
Jacline Rouleau, Mairesse
Mélanie Hébert, Directrice générale

Senneterre
551, 10e av
Senneterre, QC J0Y 2M0
Tél: 819-737-2296; *Téléc:* 819-737-4215
info@ville.senneterre.qc.ca
ville.senneterre.qc.ca
Entité municipal: Town
Incorporation: 13 juin 1919; *Area:* 14 889,93 km2
Comté ou district: La Vallée-de-l'Or; *Population au 2016:* 2,868
Circonscription(s) électorale(s) provinciale(s): Abitibi-Est
Circonscription(s) électorale(s) fédérale(s):
Abitibi-Baie-James-Nunavik-Eeyou
Prochaines élections: 7e novembre 2021
Jean-Maurice Matte, Maire
Hélène Veillette, Greffière, 819-737-2296

Senneville
35, ch de Senneville
Senneville, QC H9X 1B8
Tél: 514-457-6020; *Téléc:* 514-457-0447
info@villagesenneville.qc.ca
villagesenneville.qc.ca
Entité municipal: Town
Incorporation: 1er janvier 2006; *Area:* 7,53 km2
Comté ou district: Communauté métropolitaine de Montréal;
Population au 2016: 921
Circonscription(s) électorale(s) provinciale(s): Jacques-Cartier
Circonscription(s) électorale(s) fédérale(s): Lac-Saint-Louis
Prochaines élections: 7e novembre 2021
Julie Brisebois, Mairesse
Francine Crête, Greffière

Sept-Rivières
1166, boul Laure
Sept-îles, QC G4R 3L7
Tél: 418-962-1900; *Téléc:* 418-962-3365
info@mrc.septrivieres.qc.ca
www.septrivieres.qc.ca

Entité municipal: Regional County Municipality
Incorporation: 18 mars 1981; *Area:* 100 868,87 km2
Population au 2016: 39,322
Note: 2 municipalités & 2 autres territoires.
Alain Thibault, Préfet
Alain Lapierre, Directeur général, 418-962-1900

Shannon
50, rue St-Patrick
Shannon, QC G0A 4N0
Tél: 418-844-3778; *Téléc:* 418-844-2111
ville@shannon.ca
shannon.ca
Entité municipal: Municipality
Incorporation: 1er janvier 1947; *Area:* 63,78 km2
Comté ou district: La Jacques-Cartier; Communauté
métropolitaine de Québec; *Population au 2016:* 6,031
Circonscription(s) électorale(s) provinciale(s): La Peltrie
Circonscription(s) électorale(s) fédérale(s):
Portneuf-Jacques-Cartier
Prochaines élections: 7e novembre 2021
Mike-James Noonan, Maire
Gaétan Bussières, Directeur général

Shawville
CP 339
350, rue Main
Shawville, QC J0X 2Y0
Tél: 819-647-2979; *Téléc:* 819-647-6895
info@town.shawville.qc.ca
www.town.shawville.qc.ca
Entité municipal: Municipality
Incorporation: 1er janvier 1874; *Area:* 5,39 km2
Comté ou district: Pontiac; *Population au 2016:* 1,587
Circonscription(s) électorale(s) provinciale(s): Pontiac
Circonscription(s) électorale(s) fédérale(s): Pontiac
Prochaines élections: 7e novembre 2021
Sandra A. Murray, Mairesse
Crystal Webb, Directrice générale, 819-647-2979

Sheenboro
59, ch de Sheenboro
Sheenboro, QC J0X 2Z0
Tél: 819-689-5022; *Téléc:* 819-689-2408
www.sheenboro.ca
Entité municipal: Municipality
Incorporation: 1er janvier 1860; *Area:* 570,92 km2
Comté ou district: Pontiac; *Population au 2016:* 141
Circonscription(s) électorale(s) provinciale(s): Pontiac
Circonscription(s) électorale(s) fédérale(s): Pontiac
Prochaines élections: 7e novembre 2021
Doris Ranger, Mairesse
Ashlee Poirier, Directrice générale

Shefford
245, ch Picard
Shefford, QC J2M 1J2
Tél: 450-539-2258; *Téléc:* 450-539-4951
info@cantonshefford.qc.ca
cantonshefford.qc.ca
Entité municipal: Township
Incorporation: 1er juillet 1855; *Area:* 118,28 km2
Comté ou district: La Haute-Yamaska; *Population au 2016:*
6,947
Circonscription(s) électorale(s) provinciale(s): Brome-Missisquoi
Circonscription(s) électorale(s) fédérale(s): Shefford
Prochaines élections: 7e novembre 2021
Éric Chagnon, Maire
Sylvie Gougeon, Directrice générale, 450-539-2258

Shigawake
180, rte 132
Shigawake, QC G0C 3E0
Tél: 418-752-2474; *Téléc:* 418-752-7474
shigawake@navigue.com
municipalityshigawake.com
Entité municipal: Municipality
Incorporation: 15 décembre 1924; *Area:* 76,82 km2
Comté ou district: Bonaventure; *Population au 2016:* 292
Circonscription(s) électorale(s) provinciale(s): Bonaventure
Circonscription(s) électorale(s) fédérale(s):
Gaspésie—Îles-de-la-Madeleine
Prochaines élections: 7e novembre 2021
Colette Dow, Mairesse
Maria Marroquin, Directrice général

Les Sources
309, rue Chassé
Asbestos, QC J1T 2B4
Tél: 819-879-6661
mrc.info@mrcdessources.com
mrcdessources.com

Entité municipal: Regional County Municipality
Incorporation: 1er janvier 1982; *Area:* 787,13 km2
Population au 2016: 14,286
Note: 7 municipalités.
Hughes Grimard, Préfet
Frédéric Marcotte, Directeur général et secrétaire-trésorier,
819-879-6661

Stanbridge East
12, rue Maple
Stanbridge East, QC J0J 2H0
Tél: 450-248-3188; *Téléc:* 450-248-7744
stanbridge@axion.ca
stanbridgeeast.ca
Entité municipal: Municipality
Incorporation: 1er juillet 1855; *Area:* 49,54 km2
Comté ou district: Brome-Missisquoi; *Population au 2016:* 866
Circonscription(s) électorale(s) provinciale(s): Brome-Missisquoi
Circonscription(s) électorale(s) fédérale(s): Brome-Missisquoi
Prochaines élections: 7e novembre 2021
Gregory Vaughan, Maire
Nicole Blinn, Directrice générale

Stanbridge Station
229, ch Principal
Stanbridge Station, QC J0J 2J0
Tél: 450-248-2125; *Téléc:* 450-248-1125
stanbridgestation46030@gmail.com
www.stanbridge-station.ca
Entité municipal: Municipality
Incorporation: 21 mars 1889; *Area:* 18,07 km2
Comté ou district: Brome-Missisquoi; *Population au 2016:* 274
Circonscription(s) électorale(s) provinciale(s): Brome-Missisquoi
Circonscription(s) électorale(s) fédérale(s): Brome-Missisquoi
Prochaines élections: 7e novembre 2021
Gilles Rioux, Maire
Bertrand Déry, Directeur général

Stanstead
425, rue Dufferin
Stanstead, QC J0B 3E2
Tél: 819-876-7181; *Téléc:* 819-876-5560
info@stanstead.ca
www.stanstead.ca
Entité municipal: Town
Incorporation: 15 février 1995; *Area:* 22,00 km2
Comté ou district: Memphrémagog; *Population au 2016:* 2,788
Circonscription(s) électorale(s) provinciale(s): Orford
Circonscription(s) électorale(s) fédérale(s): Compton-Stanstead
Prochaines élections: 7e novembre 2021
Philip Dutil, Maire
Jean-Charles Bellemare, Directeur général

Stanstead
778, ch Sheldon
Stanstead, QC J1X 3W4
Tél: 819-876-2948; *Téléc:* 819-876-7007
info@cantonstanstead.ca
www.cantonstanstead.ca
Entité municipal: Township
Incorporation: 1er juillet 1855; *Area:* 113,37 km2
Comté ou district: Memphrémagog; *Population au 2016:* 1,036
Circonscription(s) électorale(s) provinciale(s): Orford
Circonscription(s) électorale(s) fédérale(s): Compton-Stanstead
Prochaines élections: 7e novembre 2021
Francine Caron Markwell, Mairesse
Josiane Hudon, Directrice générale, 819-876-2948

Stanstead-Est
7015, rte 143
Stanstead-Est, QC J0B 3E0
Tél: 819-876-7292; *Téléc:* 819-876-7170
info@stansteadest.ca
stansteadest.ca
Entité municipal: Municipality
Incorporation: 16 juillet 1932; *Area:* 114,58 km2
Comté ou district: Coaticook; *Population au 2016:* 584
Circonscription(s) électorale(s) provinciale(s): St-François
Circonscription(s) électorale(s) fédérale(s): Compton-Stanstead
Prochaines élections: 7e novembre 2021
Gilbert Ferland, Maire
Claudine Tremblay, Directrice générale

Stoke
403, rue Principale
Stoke, QC J0B 3G0
Tél: 819-878-3790; *Téléc:* 819-878-3804
reception@stoke.ca
stoke.ca
Entité municipal: Municipality
Incorporation: 1er janvier 1864; *Area:* 255,46 km2
Comté ou district: Le Val-Saint-François; *Population au 2016:*

2,955
Circonscription(s) électorale(s) provinciale(s): Mégantic
Circonscription(s) électorale(s) fédérale(s): Compton-Stanstead
Prochaines élections: 7e novembre 2021
Luc Cayer, Maire
Anne Turcotte, Directrice générale, 819-878-3790

Stoneham-et-Tewkesbury
325, ch du Hibou
Stoneham-et-Tewkesbury, QC G3C 1R8
Tél: 418-848-2381; *Téléc:* 418-848-1748
info@villestoneham.com
www.villestoneham.com
Entité municipal: Township
Incorporation: 1er juillet 1855; *Area:* 670,67 km2
Comté ou district: La Jacques-Cartier; Communauté
métropolitaine de Québec; *Population au 2016:* 8,359
Circonscription(s) électorale(s) provinciale(s): Chauveau
Circonscription(s) électorale(s) fédérale(s):
Portneuf-Jacques-Cartier
Prochaines élections: 7e novembre 2021
Claude Lebel, Maire
Louis Desrosiers, Directeur général, 418-848-2381

Stornoway
507, rte 108 ouest
Stornoway, QC G0Y 1N0
Tél: 819-652-2800; *Téléc:* 819-652-2105
administration@munstornoway.qc.ca
www.munstornoway.qc.ca
Entité municipal: Municipality
Incorporation: 1er janvier 1858; *Area:* 180,40 km2
Comté ou district: Le Granit; *Population au 2016:* 530
Circonscription(s) électorale(s) provinciale(s): Mégantic
Circonscription(s) électorale(s) fédérale(s): Mégantic-L'Érable
Prochaines élections: 7e novembre 2021
Mario Lachance, Maire
Lynda Fillion, Directrice générale

Stratford
165, av Centrale nord
Stratford, QC G0Y 1P0
Tél: 418-443-2307; *Téléc:* 418-443-2603
mun.stratford@stratford.quebec
stratford.quebec
Entité municipal: Township
Incorporation: 1er janvier 1874; *Area:* 120,89 km2
Comté ou district: Le Granit; *Population au 2016:* 945
Circonscription(s) électorale(s) provinciale(s): Mégantic
Circonscription(s) électorale(s) fédérale(s): Mégantic-L'Érable
Prochaines élections: 7e novembre 2021
Denis Lalumière, Maire
William Leclerc Bellavance, Directeur général

Stukely-Sud
101, place de la Mairie
Stukely-Sud, QC J0E 2J0
Tél: 450-297-3407; *Téléc:* 450-297-3759
info@stukely-sud.com
stukely-sud.com
Entité municipal: Village
Incorporation: 19 septembre 1934; *Area:* 63,31 km2
Comté ou district: Memphrémagog; *Population au 2016:* 1,058
Circonscription(s) électorale(s) provinciale(s): Orford
Circonscription(s) électorale(s) fédérale(s): Brome-Missisquoi
Prochaines élections: 7e novembre 2021
Patrick Leblond, Maire
Louisette Tremblay, Directrice générale

Sutton
11, rue Principale sud
Sutton, QC J0E 2K0
Tél: 450-538-2290; *Téléc:* 450-538-0930
ville@sutton.ca
sutton.ca
Entité municipal: Town
Incorporation: 4 juillet 2002; *Area:* 245,95 km2
Comté ou district: Brome-Missisquoi; *Population au 2016:* 4,012
Circonscription(s) électorale(s) provinciale(s): Brome-Missisquoi
Circonscription(s) électorale(s) fédérale(s): Brome-Missisquoi
Prochaines élections: 7e novembre 2021
Michel Lafrance, Maire
Pascal Smith, Directeur général

Tadoussac
197, rue des Pionniers
Tadoussac, QC G0T 2A0
Tél: 418-235-4744; *Téléc:* 418-235-4433
ville@tadoussac.com
tadoussac.com
Entité municipal: Village
Incorporation: 10 octobre 1899; *Area:* 53,96 km2

Comté ou district: La Haute-Côte-Nord; *Population au 2016:* 799
Circonscription(s) électorale(s) provinciale(s): René-Lévesque
Circonscription(s) électorale(s) fédérale(s): Manicouagan
Prochaines élections: 7e novembre 2021
Charles Breton, Maire
Marie-Claude Guérin, Directrice générale

Taschereau
52, rue Morin
Taschereau, QC J0Z 3N0
Tél: 819-796-2219; *Téléc:* 819-796-2220
taschereau@mrcao.qc.ca
taschereau.ao.ca
Entité municipal: Municipality
Incorporation: 27 décembre 2001; *Area:* 250,72 km2
Comté ou district: Abitibi-Ouest; *Population au 2016:* 963
Circonscription(s) électorale(s) provinciale(s): Abitibi-Ouest
Circonscription(s) électorale(s) fédérale(s):
Abitibi-Témiscamingue
Prochaines élections: 7e novembre 2021
Lucien Côté, Maire
Chantal Martel, Directrice générale, 819-796-2219

Tasiujaq
CP 54
Tasiujaq, QC J0M 1T0
Tél: 819-633-9924; *Téléc:* 819-633-5026
www.nvtasiujaq.ca
Entité municipal: Northern Village
Incorporation: 2 février 1980; *Area:* 66,54 km2
Comté ou district: Administration régionale Kativik; *Population au 2016:* 369
Circonscription(s) électorale(s) provinciale(s): Ungava
Circonscription(s) électorale(s) fédérale(s):
Abitibi-Baie-James-Nunavik-Eeyou
Billy Cain, Maire
Chelsey Mesher, Secrétaire-trésorière

Témiscaming
20, rue Humphrey
Témiscaming, QC J0Z 3R0
Tél: 819-627-3273; *Téléc:* 819-627-3019
ville.temiscaming@temiscaming.net
temiscaming.net
Entité municipal: Town
Incorporation: 26 mars 1988; *Area:* 718,49 km2
Comté ou district: Témiscamingue; *Population au 2016:* 2,431
Circonscription(s) électorale(s) provinciale(s):
Rouyn-Noranda-Témiscamingue
Circonscription(s) électorale(s) fédérale(s):
Abitibi-Témiscamingue
Prochaines élections: 7e novembre 2021
Yves Ouellet, Maire
Sophie Lamarche, Directrice générale, 819-627-3273

Témiscamingue
#209, 21, rue Notre-Dame-de-Lourdes
Ville-Marie, QC J9V 1X8
Tél: 819-629-2829; *Téléc:* 819-629-3472
mrct@mrctemiscamingue.qc.ca
www.mrctemiscamingue.org
Other Information: Sans frais: 855-622-6728
Entité municipal: Regional County Municipality
Incorporation: 15 avril 1981; *Area:* 16 420,32 km2
Population au 2016: 15,980
Note: 20 municipalités & 2 autres territoires.
Claire Bolduc, Préfète, 819-629-2829
Lyne Gironne, Directrice générale, 819-629-2829

Témiscouata
#101, 5, rue de l'Hôtel de Ville
Notre-Dame-du-Lac, QC G0L 1X0
Tél: 418-899-6725; *Téléc:* 418-899-2000
admin@mrctemis.ca
www.mrctemiscouata.qc.ca
Other Information: Sans frais: 877-303-6725
Entité municipal: Regional County Municipality
Incorporation: 1 janvier 1982; *Area:* 3 904,03 km2
Population au 2016: 19,574
Note: 19 municipalités.
Guylaine Sirois, Préfète, 418-899-6725
Jacky Ouellet, Directeur général, 418-899-6725

Témiscouata-sur-le-Lac
861, rue Commerciale nord
Témiscouata-sur-le-Lac, QC G0L 1E0
Tél: 418-854-2116; *Téléc:* 418-854-0118
info@temiscouatasurlelac.ca
temiscouatasurlelac.ca
Entité municipal: Town
Incorporation: 5e mai 2010; *Area:* 218,80 km2
Comté ou district: Témiscouata; *Population au 2016:* 4,910

Circonscription(s) électorale(s) provinciale(s):
Rivière-du-Loup-Témiscouata
Circonscription(s) électorale(s) fédérale(s):
Rimouski-Neigette—Témiscouata—Les Basques
Prochaines élections: 7e novembre 2021
Note: Le 5e mai 2010, les villes de Cabano et
Notre-Dame-du-Lac ont été amalgamé sous le nom de
Témiscouata-sur-le-Lac.
Gilles Garon, Maire
Chantal-Karen Caron, Directeur général

Terrasse-Vaudreuil
74, 7e av
Terrasse-Vaudreuil, QC J7V 3M9
Tél: 514-453-8120; *Téléc:* 514-453-1180
info@terrasse-vaudreuil.ca
www.terrasse-vaudreuil.ca
Entité municipal: Municipality
Incorporation: 1er janvier 1952; *Area:* 1,06 km2
Comté ou district: Vaudreuil-Soulanges; *Communauté
métropolitaine de Montréal; Population au 2016:* 1,986
Circonscription(s) électorale(s) provinciale(s): Vaudreuil
Circonscription(s) électorale(s) fédérale(s): Vaudreuil-Soulanges
Prochaines élections: 7e novembre 2021
Michel Bourdeau, Jr., Maire
Ronald Kelley, Directeur général, 514-453-8120

Thérèse-de-Blainville
#304, 201, Curé Labelle
Sainte-Thérèse, QC J7E 2X6
Tél: 450-621-5546; *Téléc:* 450-621-2628
reception@mrc-tdb.org
mrc-tdb.org
Entité municipal: Regional County Municipality
Incorporation: 26 mai 1982; *Area:* 207,20 km2
Population au 2016: 157,103
Note: 7 municipalités.
Richard Perreault, Préfet
Kamal El-Batal, Directeur général

Thorne
775, rte 366
Ladysmith, QC J0X 2A0
Tél: 819-647-3206; *Téléc:* 819-647-2086
thorne@mrcpontiac.qc.ca
www.thornequebec.ca
Entité municipal: Municipality
Incorporation: 1er janvier 1860; *Area:* 175,55 km2
Comté ou district: Pontiac; *Population au 2016:* 448
Circonscription(s) électorale(s) provinciale(s): Pontiac
Circonscription(s) électorale(s) fédérale(s): Pontiac
Prochaines élections: 7e novembre 2021
Karen Daly Kelly, Mairesse
Stacy Lafleur, Directrice générale

Thurso
161, rue Galipeau
Thurso, QC J0X 3B0
Tél: 819-985-2000; *Téléc:* 819-985-0134
info@villethurso.ca
www.ville.thurso.qc.ca
Entité municipal: Town
Incorporation: 16 janvier 1886; *Area:* 6,28 km2
Comté ou district: Papineau; *Population au 2016:* 2,818
Circonscription(s) électorale(s) provinciale(s): Papineau
Circonscription(s) électorale(s) fédérale(s): Argenteuil-La
Petite-Nation
Prochaines élections: 7e novembre 2021
Benoit Lauzon, Maire
Jasmin Gibeau, Greffier et directeur général

Tingwick
12, rue de l'Hôtel-de-Ville
Tingwick, QC J0A 1L0
Tél: 819-359-2454; *Téléc:* 819-359-2233
www.tingwick.ca
Entité municipal: Municipality
Incorporation: 12 décembre 1981; *Area:* 169,66 km2
Comté ou district: Arthabaska; *Population au 2016:* 1,410
Circonscription(s) électorale(s) provinciale(s):
Drummond-Bois-Francs
Circonscription(s) électorale(s) fédérale(s):
Richmond-Arthabaska
Prochaines élections: 7e novembre 2021
Réal Fortin, Maire
Chantale Ramsay, Directrice générale, 819-359-2454

Tourville
#100, 962, rue des Trembles
Tourville, QC G0R 4M0
Tél: 418-359-2106; *Téléc:* 418-359-3671
municipal.tourville@globetrotter.net
www.muntourville.qc.ca
Entité municipal: Municipality
Incorporation: 14 novembre 1918; *Area:* 164,73 km2
Comté ou district: L'Islet; *Population au 2016:* 589
Circonscription(s) électorale(s) provinciale(s): Côte-du-Sud
Circonscription(s) électorale(s) fédérale(s):
Montmagny-L'Islet-Kamouraska-Rivière-du-Loup
Prochaines élections: 7e novembre 2021
Benoit Dubé, Maire
Normand Blier, Directeur général

Trécesson
330, rue Sauvé
Trécesson, QC J0Y 2S0
Tél: 819-732-8524
municipalite@trecesson.ca
www.municipalitedetrecesson.com
Entité municipal: Township
Incorporation: 15 juillet 1918; *Area:* 197,10 km2
Comté ou district: Abitibi; *Population au 2016:* 1,223
Circonscription(s) électorale(s) provinciale(s): Abitibi-Ouest
Circonscription(s) électorale(s) fédérale(s):
Abitibi-Témiscamingue
Prochaines élections: 7e novembre 2021
Jacques Grenier, Maire
Chantal Poliquin, Directrice générale, 819-732-8524

Très-Saint-Rédempteur
769, rte Principale
Très-Saint-Rédempteur, QC J0P 1P0
Tél: 450-451-5203
recep@tressaintredempteur.ca
www.tressaintredempteur.ca
Entité municipal: Municipality
Incorporation: 30 décembre 1880; *Area:* 26,05 km2
Comté ou district: Vaudreuil-Soulanges; *Population au 2016:* 898
Circonscription(s) électorale(s) provinciale(s): Soulanges
Circonscription(s) électorale(s) fédérale(s): Salaberry-Suroît
Prochaines élections: 7e novembre 2021
Julie Lemieux, Mairesse
Jean-Charles Filion, Directeur général par intérim, 450-451-5203

Très-Saint-Sacrement
1180, rte 203
Howick, QC J0S 1G0
Tél: 450-825-0192; *Téléc:* 450-825-0193
mun-trst@videotron.ca
www.tres-st-sacrement.ca
Entité municipal: Parish (Paroisse)
Incorporation: 2 avril 1885; *Area:* 97,53 km2
Comté ou district: Le Haut-Saint-Laurent; *Population au 2016:* 1,186
Circonscription(s) électorale(s) provinciale(s): Huntingdon
Circonscription(s) électorale(s) fédérale(s): Salaberry-Suroît
Prochaines élections: 7e novembre 2021
Agnes McKell, Mairesse
Suzanne Côté, Directrice générale

Tring-Jonction
247, rue Notre-Dame
Tring-Jonction, QC G0N 1X0
Tél: 418-426-2497
info@tringjonction.qc.ca
www.tringjonction.qc.ca
Entité municipal: Village
Incorporation: 21 novembre 1918; *Area:* 27,50 km2
Comté ou district: Robert-Cliche; *Population au 2016:* 1,401
Circonscription(s) électorale(s) provinciale(s): Beauce-Nord
Circonscription(s) électorale(s) fédérale(s): Beauce
Prochaines élections: 7e novembre 2021
Mario Groleau, Maire
Jonathan Paquet, Directeur général

La Trinité-des-Monts
12, rue Principale ouest
La Trinité-des-Monts, QC G0K 1B0
Tél: 418-779-2421; *Téléc:* 418-779-2454
muntrinite@mrc-rn.ca
la-trinite-des-monts.ca
Entité municipal: Parish (Paroisse)
Incorporation: 1er janvier 1965; *Area:* 234,23 km2
Comté ou district: Rimouski-Neigette; *Population au 2016:* 223
Circonscription(s) électorale(s) provinciale(s): Rimouski
Circonscription(s) électorale(s) fédérale(s):
Rimouski-Neigette-Témiscouata-Les Basques
Prochaines élections: 7e novembre 2021
Yves Detroz, Maire

Nadia Lavoie, Directrice générale

Trois-Pistoles
5, rue Notre-Dame est
Trois-Pistoles, QC G0L 4K0
Tél: 418-851-1995; *Téléc:* 418-851-3567
administration@ville-trois-pistoles.ca
ville-trois-pistoles.ca
Entité municipal: Town
Incorporation: 9 mars 1916; *Area:* 7,64 km2
Comté ou district: Les Basques; *Population au 2016:* 3,246
Circonscription(s) électorale(s) provinciale(s):
Rivière-du-Loup-Témiscouata
Circonscription(s) électorale(s) fédérale(s):
Rimouski-Neigette-Témiscouata-Les Basques
Prochaines élections: 7e novembre 2021
Jean Pierre Rioux, Maire
Pascale Rioux, Directrice générale, 418-851-1995

Trois-Rives
258, ch St-Joseph
Trois-Rives, QC G0X 2C0
Tél: 819-646-5686; *Téléc:* 819-646-5688
trois-rives@regionmekinac.com
trois-rives.com
Entité municipal: Municipality
Incorporation: 2 septembre 1972; *Area:* 602,57 km2
Comté ou district: Mékinac; *Population au 2016:* 396
Circonscription(s) électorale(s) provinciale(s): Laviolette
Circonscription(s) électorale(s) fédérale(s):
St-Maurice-Champlain
Prochaines élections: 7e novembre 2021
Lucien Mongrain, Maire
Nicole Léveillé, Directrice générale

Ulverton
151, rte 143
Ulverton, QC J0B 2B0
Tél: 819-826-5049; *Téléc:* 819-826-5181
municipaliteulverton.ca
Entité municipal: Municipality
Incorporation: 1er juillet 1855; *Area:* 51,31 km2
Comté ou district: Le Val-Saint-François; *Population au 2016:* 418
Circonscription(s) électorale(s) provinciale(s): Richmond
Circonscription(s) électorale(s) fédérale(s):
Richmond-Arthabaska
Prochaines élections: 7e novembre 2021
J. Pierre Bordua, Maire
Vicki Turgeon, Directrice générale

Umiujaq
CP 108
Umiujaq, QC J0M 1Y0
Tél: 819-331-7000; *Téléc:* 819-331-7057
www.nvumiujaq.ca
Entité municipal: Northern Village
Incorporation: 20 décembre 1986; *Area:* 28,59 km2
Comté ou district: Administration régionale Kativik; *Population au 2016:* 442
Circonscription(s) électorale(s) provinciale(s): Ungava
Circonscription(s) électorale(s) fédérale(s):
Abitibi-Baie-James-Nunavik-Eeyou
Louisa Tookalook, Maire
Sam Nuktie, Secrétaire-trésorier

Upton
810, rue Lanoie
Upton, QC J0H 2E0
Tél: 450-549-5611; *Téléc:* 450-549-5045
info@upton.ca
www.upton.ca
Entité municipal: Municipality
Incorporation: 25 février 1998; *Area:* 54,80 km2
Comté ou district: Acton; *Population au 2016:* 2,092
Circonscription(s) électorale(s) provinciale(s): Johnson
Circonscription(s) électorale(s) fédérale(s): St-Hyacinthe-Bagot
Prochaines élections: 7e novembre 2021
Guy Lapointe, Maire
Caroline Dubois, Directrice générale par intérim

Val-Alain
648, rue Principale
Val-Alain, QC G0S 3H0
Tél: 819-744-3222
info@val-alain.com
www.val-alain.com
Entité municipal: Municipality
Incorporation: 1er janvier 1950; *Area:* 102,32 km2
Comté ou district: Lotbinière; *Population au 2016:* 924
Circonscription(s) électorale(s) provinciale(s):
Lotbinière-Frontenac

Circonscription(s) électorale(s) fédérale(s): Lévis-Lotbinière
Prochaines élections: 7e novembre 2021
Daniel Turcotte, Maire
Claudia Daigle, Directrice générale, 418-744-3222

Val-Brillant
11, rue St-Pierre ouest
Val-Brillant, QC G0J 3L0
Tél: 418-742-3212
valbrillant@mrcmatapedia.quebec
municipalites-du-quebec.ca/val-brillant
Entité municipal: Municipality
Incorporation: 20 décembre 1986; *Area:* 78,04 km2
Comté ou district: La Matapédia; *Population au 2016:* 927
Circonscription(s) électorale(s) provinciale(s): Matane-Matapédia
Circonscription(s) électorale(s) fédérale(s): Avignon-La Mitis-Matane-Matapédia
Prochaines élections: 7e novembre 2021
Jacques Pelletier, Maire
Nancy Paquet, Directrice générale

Valcourt
5583, ch de l'Aéroport
Valcourt, QC J0E 2L0
Tél: 450-532-2688; *Téléc:* 450-532-5570
info@cantonvalcourt.qc.ca
cantonvalcourt.qc.ca
Entité municipal: Township
Incorporation: 1er juillet 1855; *Area:* 80,68 km2
Comté ou district: Le Val-Saint-François; *Population au 2016:* 1,044
Circonscription(s) électorale(s) provinciale(s): Richmond
Circonscription(s) électorale(s) fédérale(s): Shefford
Prochaines élections: 7e novembre 2021
Patrice Desmarais, Maire
Holly Hunter, Directrice générale, 450-532-2688

Valcourt
1155, rue St-Joseph
Valcourt, QC J0E 2L0
Tél: 450-532-3313; *Téléc:* 450-532-3424
ville.valcourt@valcourt.ca
www.valcourt.ca
Entité municipal: Town
Incorporation: 19 octobre 1929; *Area:* 5,42 km2
Comté ou district: Le Val-Saint-François; *Population au 2016:* 2,165
Circonscription(s) électorale(s) provinciale(s): Richmond
Circonscription(s) électorale(s) fédérale(s): Shefford
Prochaines élections: 7e novembre 2021
Renald Chênevert, Maire
Lydia Laquerre, Greffière, 450-532-3313

Val-David
2579, rue de l'Église
Val-David, QC J0T 2N0
Tél: 819-324-5678
info@valdavid.com
valdavid.com
Entité municipal: Village
Incorporation: 10 mai 1921; *Area:* 42,82 km2
Comté ou district: Les Laurentides; *Population au 2016:* 4,917
Circonscription(s) électorale(s) provinciale(s): Bertrand
Circonscription(s) électorale(s) fédérale(s): Laurentides-Labelle
Prochaines élections: 7e novembre 2021
Kathy Poulin, Mairesse
Sophie Charpentier, Directrice générale, 819-324-5678

Val-des-Bois
595, rte 309
Val-des-Bois, QC J0X 3C0
Tél: 819-454-2280; *Téléc:* 819-454-2211
mun@val-des-bois.ca
val-des-bois.ca
Entité municipal: Municipality
Incorporation: 1er janvier 1885; *Area:* 225,42 km2
Comté ou district: Papineau; *Population au 2016:* 865
Circonscription(s) électorale(s) provinciale(s): Papineau
Circonscription(s) électorale(s) fédérale(s): Argenteuil-La Petite-Nation
Prochaines élections: 7e novembre 2021
Roland Montpetit, Maire
Anick Morin, Directrice générale, 819-454-2280

Val-des-Lacs
349, ch de Val-des-Lacs
Val-des-Lacs, QC J0T 2P0
Tél: 819-326-5624; *Téléc:* 819-326-7065
info@val-des-lacs.ca
municipalite.val-des-lacs.qc.ca
Entité municipal: Municipality
Incorporation: 6 février 1932; *Area:* 127,00 km2

Comté ou district: Les Laurentides; *Population au 2016:* 744
Circonscription(s) électorale(s) provinciale(s): Bertrand
Circonscription(s) électorale(s) fédérale(s): Laurentides-Labelle
Prochaines élections: 7e novembre 2021
Jean-Philippe Martin, Maire
Nathalie Paquet, Directrice générale, 819-326-5624

Val-des-Sources
345, boul Saint-Luc
Asbestos, QC J1T 2W4
Tél: 819-879-7171
infovaldessources@valdessources.ca
valdessources.ca
Entité municipal: Town
Incorporation: 8e décembre 1999; *Area:* 30,41 km2
Comté ou district: Les Sources; *Population au 2016:* 6,786
Circonscription(s) électorale(s) provinciale(s): Richmond
Circonscription(s) électorale(s) fédérale(s):
Richmond-Arthabaska
Prochaines élections: 7e novembre 2021
Note: Anciennement nommée Asbestos jusqu'en 2020.
Hugues Grimard, Maire
Georges-André Gagné, Directeur général

Val-Joli
500, rte 249
Val-Joli, QC J1S 2L5
Tél: 819-845-7663; *Téléc:* 819-845-4399
secretariat@val-joli.ca
val-joli.ca
Entité municipal: Municipality
Incorporation: 1er juillet 1855; *Area:* 91,64 km2
Comté ou district: Le Val-Saint-François; *Population au 2016:* 1,619
Circonscription(s) électorale(s) provinciale(s): Richmond
Circonscription(s) électorale(s) fédérale(s):
Richmond-Arthabaska
Prochaines élections: 7e novembre 2021
Rolland Camiré, Maire
Marie-Céline Corbeil, Directrice générale

La Vallée-de-l'Or
42, place Hammond
Val-d'Or, QC J9P 3A9
Tél: 819-825-7733; *Téléc:* 819-825-4137
info@mrcvo.qc.ca
mrcvo.qc.ca
Entité municipal: Regional County Municipality
Incorporation: 8e avril 1981; *Area:* 24 292,04 km2
Population au 2016: 43,226
Note: 6 municipalités & 4 autres territoires.
Martin Ferron, Préfet
Christian Riopel, Directeur général

La Vallée-de-la-Gatineau
7, rue de la Polyvalente
Gracefield, QC J0X 1W0
Tél: 819-463-3241; *Téléc:* 819-463-3632
info@mrcvg.qc.ca
www.mrcvg.qc.ca
Entité municipal: Regional County Municipality
Incorporation: 1er janvier 1983; *Area:* 12 480,50 km2
Population au 2016: 20,182
Note: 17 municipalités & 5 autres territoires.
Chantal Lamarche, Préfete, 819-463-3241
Chantal Rondeau, Directrice générale, 819-463-3241

La Vallée-du-Richelieu
#100, 255, boul Laurier
McMasterville, QC J3G 0B7
Tél: 450-464-0339; *Téléc:* 450-464-3827
info@mrcvr.ca
www.mrcvr.ca
Entité municipal: Regional County Municipality
Incorporation: 1er janvier 1982; *Area:* 588,60 km2
Population au 2016: 124,420
Note: 13 municipalités.
Diane Lavoie, Préfete
Evelyne D'Avignon, Directrice générale et secrétaire-trésorière, 450-464-0339

Vallée-Jonction
259, boul Jean-Marie Rousseau
Vallée-Jonction, QC G0S 3J0
Tél: 418-253-5515; *Téléc:* 418-253-6731
info@valleejonction.qc.ca
www.valleejonction.qc.ca
Entité municipal: Municipality
Incorporation: 22 mars 1989; *Area:* 25,35 km2
Comté ou district: La Nouvelle-Beauce; *Population au 2016:* 1,875
Circonscription(s) électorale(s) provinciale(s): Beauce-Nord

Circonscription(s) électorale(s) fédérale(s): Beauce
Prochaines élections: 7e novembre 2021
Réal Bisson, Maire
Julie Cliche, Directrice générale

Val-Morin
6120, rue Morin
Val-Morin, QC J0T 2R0
Tél: 819-322-5670; *Téléc:* 819-322-3923
municipalite@val-morin.ca
www.val-morin.ca
Entité municipal: Municipality
Incorporation: 27 juin 1922; *Area:* 39,42 km2
Comté ou district: Les Laurentides; *Population au 2016:* 2,870
Circonscription(s) électorale(s) provinciale(s): Bertrand
Circonscription(s) électorale(s) fédérale(s): Laurentides-Labelle
Prochaines élections: 7e novembre 2021
Donna Salvati, Maire
Caroline Nielly, Directrice générale

Val-Racine
2991, ch St-Léon
Val-Racine, QC G0Y 1E0
Tél: 819-657-4790; *Téléc:* 819-657-4790
info@val-racine.com
municipalite.val-racine.qc.ca
Entité municipal: Municipality
Incorporation: 26 avril 1907; *Area:* 116,23 km2
Comté ou district: Le Granit; *Population au 2016:* 178
Circonscription(s) électorale(s) provinciale(s): Mégantic
Circonscription(s) électorale(s) fédérale(s): Mégantic-L'Érable
Prochaines élections: 7e novembre 2021
Pierre Brosseau, Maire
Chantal Grégoire, Directrice générale

Le Val-Saint-François
CP 3160
810, montée du Parc
Richmond, QC J0B 2H0
Tél: 819-826-6505
mrc@val-saint-francois.qc.ca
www.val-saint-francois.qc.ca
Entité municipal: Regional County Municipality
Incorporation: 26 mai 1982; *Area:* 1403,43 km2
Population au 2016: 30,686
Note: 18 municipalités.
Luc Cayer, Préfet
Vacant, Directeur général, 819-826-6505

Val-Saint-Gilles
801, rue Principale
Val-Saint-Gilles, QC J0Z 3T0
Tél: 819-333-2158; *Téléc:* 819-333-3116
valstgilles@mrcao.qc.ca
valst-gilles.ao.ca
Entité municipal: Municipality
Incorporation: 1er avril 1939; *Area:* 109,74 km2
Comté ou district: Abitibi-Ouest; *Population au 2016:* 157
Circonscription(s) électorale(s) provinciale(s): Abitibi-Ouest
Circonscription(s) électorale(s) fédérale(s):
Abitibi-Témiscamingue
Prochaines élections: 7e novembre 2021
Réjean Lambert, Maire
Sylvie Lambert, Directrice générale

Vaudreuil-Soulanges
420, av Saint-Charles
Vaudreuil-Dorion, QC J7V 2N1
Tél: 450-455-5753; *Téléc:* 450-455-0145
info@mrcvs.ca
mrcvs.ca
Entité municipal: Regional County Municipality
Incorporation: 14 avril 1982; *Area:* 855,56 km2
Population au 2016: 149,349
Note: 23 municipalités.
Patrick Bousez, Préfet, 450-455-5753
Guy-Lin Beaudoin, Directeur général, 450-455-5753

Vaudreuil-sur-le-Lac
44, rue de l'Église
Vaudreuil-sur-le-Lac, QC J7V 8P3
Tél: 450-455-1133; *Téléc:* 450-455-8614
communications@vsll.ca
www.vsll.ca
Entité municipal: Village
Incorporation: 29 mai 1920; *Area:* 1,39 km2
Comté ou district: Vaudreuil-Soulanges; Communauté
métropolitaine de Montréal; *Population au 2016:* 1,341
Circonscription(s) électorale(s) provinciale(s): Vaudreuil
Circonscription(s) électorale(s) fédérale(s): Vaudreuil-Soulanges
Prochaines élections: 7e novembre 2021
Claude Pilon, Maire

Carolyn Ayoub, Directrice générale par intérim, 450-455-1133

Venise-en-Québec
237, 16e av ouest
Venise-en-Québec, QC J0J 2K0
Tél: 450-346-4260
information@venise-en-quebec.ca
veniseenquebec.ca
Entité municipal: Municipality
Incorporation: 1er janvier 1950; *Area:* 13,23 km2
Comté ou district: Le Haut-Richelieu; *Population au 2016:* 1,634
Circonscription(s) électorale(s) provinciale(s): Iberville
Circonscription(s) électorale(s) fédérale(s): Brome-Missisquoi
Prochaines élections: 7e novembre 2021
Jacques Landry, Maire
Frédéric Martineau, Directeur général

Verchères
581, rte Marie-Victorin
Verchères, QC J0L 2R0
Tél: 450-583-3307; *Téléc:* 450-583-3637
ville.vercheres.qc.ca
Entité municipal: Municipality
Incorporation: 18 septembre 1971; *Area:* 72,57 km2
Comté ou district: Marguerite-D'Youville; Communauté
métropolitaine de Montréal; *Population au 2016:* 5,835
Circonscription(s) électorale(s) provinciale(s): Verchères
Circonscription(s) électorale(s) fédérale(s): Pierre-Boucher-Les
Patriotes-Verchères
Prochaines élections: 7e novembre 2021
Alexandre Bélisle, Maire
Luc Forcier, Directeur général

Ville-Marie
Édifice Gérard-Caron
21, rue St-Gabriel sud
Ville-Marie, QC J9V 1A1
Tél: 819-629-2881; *Téléc:* 819-629-3215
info@villevillemarie.org
www.ville-marie.ca
Entité municipal: Town
Incorporation: 13 octobre 1897; *Area:* 5,84 km2
Comté ou district: Témiscamingue; *Population au 2016:* 2,584
Circonscription(s) électorale(s) provinciale(s):
Rouyn-Noranda-Témiscamingue
Circonscription(s) électorale(s) fédérale(s):
Abitibi-Témiscamingue
Prochaines élections: 7e novembre 2021
Michel Roy, Maire
Martin Lecomte, Directeur général, 819-629-2881

Villeroy
398, rue Principale
Villeroy, QC G0S 3K0
Tél: 819-385-4605
info@municipalitevilleroy.ca
municipalitevilleroy.ca
Entité municipal: Municipality
Incorporation: 22 septembre 1924; *Area:* 102,15 km2
Comté ou district: L'Érable; *Population au 2016:* 457
Circonscription(s) électorale(s) provinciale(s): Arthabaska
Circonscription(s) électorale(s) fédérale(s): Mégantic-L'Érable
Prochaines élections: 7e novembre 2021
Éric Chartier, Maire
Joannie Lamothe, Directrice générale

La Visitation-de-l'Île-Dupas
113, rue de l'Église
La Visitation-de-l'Île-Dupas, QC J0K 2P0
Tél: 450-836-6019
admin@ile-dupas.ca
ile-dupas.ca
Entité municipal: Municipality
Incorporation: 1er juillet 1855; *Area:* 30,60 km2
Comté ou district: D'Autray; *Population au 2016:* 626
Circonscription(s) électorale(s) provinciale(s): Berthier
Circonscription(s) électorale(s) fédérale(s): Berthier-Maskinongé
Prochaines élections: 7e novembre 2021
Marie-Pier Aubuchon, Mairesse
Nancy Guertin, Directrice générale

La Visitation-de-Yamaska
21, rue Principale
La Visitation, QC J0G 1C0
Tél: 450-564-2818; *Téléc:* 450-564-9923
info@lavisitationdeyamaska.net
lavisitationdeyamaska.net
Entité municipal: Municipality
Incorporation: 2 février 1899; *Area:* 42,71 km2
Comté ou district: Nicolet-Yamaska; *Population au 2016:* 327
Circonscription(s) électorale(s) provinciale(s): Nicolet-Bécancour
Circonscription(s) électorale(s) fédérale(s):

Bécancour-Nicolet-Saurel; Bas-Richelieu
Prochaines élections: 7e novembre 2021
Sylvain Laplante, Maire
Suzanne Bibeau, Directrice générale

Waltham
69, rue de l'Hôtel-de-Ville
Waltham, QC J0X 3H0
Tél: 819-683-3027; *Téléc:* 819-683-1815
municipalite.waltham@mrcpontiac.qc.ca
www.municipalitedewaltham.ca
Entité municipal: Municipality
Incorporation: 1er janvier 1859; *Area:* 374,22 km2
Comté ou district: Pontiac; *Population au 2016:* 378
Circonscription(s) électorale(s) provinciale(s): Pontiac
Circonscription(s) électorale(s) fédérale(s): Pontiac
Prochaines élections: 7e novembre 2021
David Rochon, Maire
Fernand Roy, Directeur général

Warden
172, rue Principale
Warden, QC J0E 2M0
Tél: 450-539-1349
info@village.warden.gc.ca
municipalites-du-quebec.ca/warden
Entité municipal: Village
Incorporation: 31 mars 1916; *Area:* 5,46 km2
Comté ou district: La Haute-Yamaska; *Population au 2016:* 363
Circonscription(s) électorale(s) provinciale(s): Brome-Missisquoi
Circonscription(s) électorale(s) fédérale(s): Shefford
Prochaines élections: 7e novembre 2021
Philip Tétrault, Maire
Robert Désilets, Directeur général

Warwick
8, rue de l'Hôtel-de-Ville
Warwick, QC J0A 1M0
Tél: 819-358-4300
reception@villedewarwick.quebec
villedewarwick.quebec
Entité municipal: Town
Incorporation: 15 mars 2000; *Area:* 109,84 km2
Comté ou district: Arthabaska; *Population au 2016:* 4,635
Circonscription(s) électorale(s) provinciale(s):
Drummond-Bois-Francs
Circonscription(s) électorale(s) fédérale(s):
Richmond-Arthabaska
Prochaines élections: 7e novembre 2021
Diego Scalzo, Maire
Lise Lemieux, Directrice générale

Waskaganish
CP 60
70, rue Waskaganish
Waskaganish, QC J0M 1R0
Tél: 819-895-8650; *Téléc:* 819-895-8901
waskaganish.ca
Entité municipal: Villages Cris
Area: 502,26
Population au 2016: 2,196
Circonscription(s) électorale(s) provinciale(s): Ungava
Circonscription(s) électorale(s) fédérale(s):
Abitibi-Baie-James-Nunavik-Eeyou
Darlene Cheechoo, Mairesse
Susan Esau, Secrétaire-Trésorière

Waswanipi
1, rue Chief Louis Gull
Waswanipi, QC J0Y 3C0
Tél: 819-753-2587; *Téléc:* 819-753-2555
info@waswanipi.com
www.waswanipi.com
Entité municipal: Villages Cris
Area: 419,85
Population au 2016: 1,759
Circonscription(s) électorale(s) provinciale(s): Ungava
Circonscription(s) électorale(s) fédérale(s):
Abitibi-Baie-James-Nunavik-Eeyou
Marcel Happyjack, Maire
Jonathan Sutherland, Directeur général

Waterloo
417, rue de la Cour
Waterloo, QC J0E 2N0
Tél: 450-539-2282; *Téléc:* 450-539-3257
administration@ville.waterloo.gc.ca
ville.waterloo.qc.ca
Entité municipal: Town
Incorporation: 1er janvier 1867; *Area:* 12,24 km2
Comté ou district: La Haute-Yamaska; *Population au 2016:*
4,410

Circonscription(s) électorale(s) provinciale(s): Brome-Missisquoi
Circonscription(s) électorale(s) fédérale(s): Shefford
Prochaines élections: 7e novembre 2021
Jean-Marie Lachapelle, Maire
Louis Verhoef, Greffier et directeur général, 450-539-2282

Waterville
170, rue Principale sud
Waterville, QC J0B 3H0
Tél: 819-837-2456
adm@waterville.ca
www.waterville.ca
Entité municipal: Village
Incorporation: 1er janvier 1876; *Area:* 44,10 km2
Comté ou district: Coaticook; *Population au 2016:* 2,121
Circonscription(s) électorale(s) provinciale(s): St-François
Circonscription(s) électorale(s) fédérale(s): Compton-Stanstead
Prochaines élections: 7e novembre 2021
Nathalie Dupuis, Mairesse
Nathalie Isabelle, Directrice générale

Weedon
520, 2e av
Weedon, QC J0B 3J0
Tél: 819-560-8550
adm.weedon@hsfgc.ca
weedon.ca
Entité municipal: Municipality
Incorporation: 9 février 2000; *Area:* 216,42 km2
Comté ou district: Le Haut-Saint-François; *Population au 2016:* 2,670
Circonscription(s) électorale(s) provinciale(s): Mégantic
Circonscription(s) électorale(s) fédérale(s): Compton-Stanstead
Prochaines élections: 7e novembre 2021
Richard Tanguay, Maire
Marie-Claude Cloutier, Directrice générale

Wemindji
21, ch Hilltop
Wemindji, QC J0M 1L0
Tél: 819-978-0264; *Téléc:* 819-978-0258
www.wemindji.ca
Entité municipal: Villages Cris
Incorporation: 28 juin 1978; *Area:* 388,15 km2
Population au 2016: 1,444
Circonscription(s) électorale(s) provinciale(s): Ungava
Circonscription(s) électorale(s) fédérale(s):
Abitibi-Baie-James-Nunavik-Eeyou
Dennis Georgekish, Maire
Stella L. Gilpin, Directrice générale

Wentworth
175, ch Louisa
Wentworth, QC J8H 0C7
Tél: 450-562-0701; *Téléc:* 450-562-0703
info@wentworth.ca
www.wentworth.ca
Entité municipal: Township
Incorporation: 1er juillet 1855; *Area:* 87,69 km2
Comté ou district: Argenteuil; *Population au 2016:* 533
Circonscription(s) électorale(s) provinciale(s): Argenteuil
Circonscription(s) électorale(s) fédérale(s): Argenteuil-La
Petite-Nation
Prochaines élections: 7e novembre 2021
Jason Morrison, Maire
Natalie Black, Directrice générale

Wentworth-Nord
3488, rte Principale
Wentworth-Nord, QC J0T 1Y0
Tél: 450-226-2416; *Téléc:* 450-226-2109
info@wentworth-nord.ca
wentworth-nord.ca
Other Information: Sans frais: 800-770-2416
Entité municipal: Municipality
Incorporation: 1er janvier 1958; *Area:* 156,48 km2
Comté ou district: Les Pays-d'en-Haut; *Population au 2016:* 1,381
Circonscription(s) électorale(s) provinciale(s): Argenteuil
Circonscription(s) électorale(s) fédérale(s): Argenteuil-La
Petite-Nation
Prochaines élections: 7e novembre 2021
François Ghali, Maire
Marie-France Matteau, Directrice générale

Westbury
168, rte 112
Westbury, QC J0B 1R0
Tél: 819-560-8450; *Téléc:* 819-560-8451
info@cantonwestbury.com
cantonwestbury.com
Entité municipal: Township
Incorporation: 16 août 1858; *Area:* 55,75 km2
Comté ou district: Le Haut-Saint-François; *Population au 2016:* 1,006
Circonscription(s) électorale(s) provinciale(s): Mégantic
Circonscription(s) électorale(s) fédérale(s): Compton-Stanstead
Prochaines élections: 7e novembre 2021
Gray Forster, Maire
Nathalie Audet, Directrice générale

Whapmagoostui
CP 390
Whapmagoostui, QC J0M 1G0
Tél: 819-929-3384; *Téléc:* 819-929-3203
info@whapmagoostuifn.ca
www.whapmagoostuifn.ca
Entité municipal: Villages Cris
Incorporation: 28 juillet 1978; *Area:* 189,88 km2
Population au 2016: 984
Circonscription(s) électorale(s) provinciale(s): Ungava
Circonscription(s) électorale(s) fédérale(s):
Abitibi-Baie-James-Nunavik-Eeyou
Stanley George, Maire
Robert Wynne, Directeur général

Wickham
893, rue Moreau
Wickham, QC J0C 1S0
Tél: 819-398-6878; *Téléc:* 819-398-7166
www.wickham.ca
Entité municipal: Municipality
Incorporation: 23 décembre 1972; *Area:* 98,79 km2
Comté ou district: Drummond; *Population au 2016:* 2,541
Circonscription(s) électorale(s) provinciale(s): Johnson
Circonscription(s) électorale(s) fédérale(s): Drummond
Prochaines élections: 7e novembre 2021
Carole Côté, Mairesse
Réal Dulmaine, Directeur général

Windsor
CP 90
#230, 11, rue St-Georges
Windsor, QC J1S 2L7
Tél: 819-845-7888; *Téléc:* 819-845-7606
info@villedewindsor.qc.ca
www.villedewindsor.qc.ca
Entité municipal: Town
Incorporation: 29 décembre 1999; *Area:* 14,56 km2
Comté ou district: Le Val-Saint-François; *Population au 2016:* 5,419
Circonscription(s) électorale(s) provinciale(s): Richmond
Circonscription(s) électorale(s) fédérale(s):
Richmond-Arthabaska
Prochaines élections: 7e novembre 2021
Sylvie Bureau, Mairesse
Edwin John Sullivan, Greffier

Wotton
396, rue Monseigneur-L'Heureux
Wotton, QC J0A 1N0
Tél: 819-828-2112; *Téléc:* 819-828-3594
reception@wotton.ca
www.wotton.ca
Entité municipal: Municipality
Incorporation: 10 mars 1993; *Area:* 143,78 km2
Comté ou district: Les Sources; *Population au 2016:* 1,430
Circonscription(s) électorale(s) provinciale(s): Richmond
Circonscription(s) électorale(s) fédérale(s):
Richmond-Arthabaska
Prochaines élections: 7e novembre 2021
Jocelyn Dion, Maire
Marcel Boisvert, Directeur général par intérim

Yamachiche
366, rue Ste-Anne
Yamachiche, QC G0X 3L0
Tél: 819-296-3795; *Téléc:* 819-296-3542
hoteldeville@yamachiche.ca
www.yamachiche.ca
Entité municipal: Municipality
Incorporation: 26 décembre 1987; *Area:* 106,47 km2
Comté ou district: Maskinongé; *Population au 2016:* 2,830
Circonscription(s) électorale(s) provinciale(s): Maskinongé
Circonscription(s) électorale(s) fédérale(s): Berthier-Maskinongé
Prochaines élections: 7e novembre 2021
Paul Carbonneau, Maire
Marie-France Boisvert, Directrice générale

Yamaska
100, rue Guilbault
Yamaska, QC J0G 1X0
Tél: 450-789-2489; *Téléc:* 450-789-2970
info@yamaska.ca
www.yamaska.ca
Entité municipal: Municipality
Incorporation: 19 décembre 2001; *Area:* 72,80 km2
Comté ou district: Pierre-De Saurel; *Population au 2016:* 1,687
Circonscription(s) électorale(s) provinciale(s): Richelieu
Circonscription(s) électorale(s) fédérale(s):
Bécancour-Nicolet-Saurel
Prochaines élections: 7e novembre 2021
Diane De Tonnancourt, Mairesse
Suzanne Francoeur, Directrice générale

SASKATCHEWAN

Acts governing the municipal system in Saskatchewan are The Urban Municipality Act, 1984; The Municipalities Act; and The Northern Municipalities Act, 2010. In southern Saskatchewan there are 775 incorporated municipalities; 452 are urban municipalities, which include 16 cities; 147 towns; 248 villages and 41 resort villages. Of the 775, 296 are rural municipalities. In northern Saskatchewan, there are 25 incorporated municipalities: 2 northern towns; 11 northern villages and 11 northern hamlets. Unincorporated areas of the province include hamlets and organized hamlets within rural municipalities. There are 144 organized hamlets as defined by The Municipalities Act. Unincorporated areas of northern Saskatchewan are part of the Northern Saskatchewan Administration District (NSAD); there are 11 northern settlements within the NSAD.

Elections in Saskatchewan occur every four years. For cities, (southern) towns and villages, elections occur on the fourth Wednesday of October. For resort villages, elections occur on the last Saturday of July, and for northern municipalities, elections occur on either the second last Wednesday in September, the last Wednesday in September or the first Wednesday in October (as decided upon by Council).

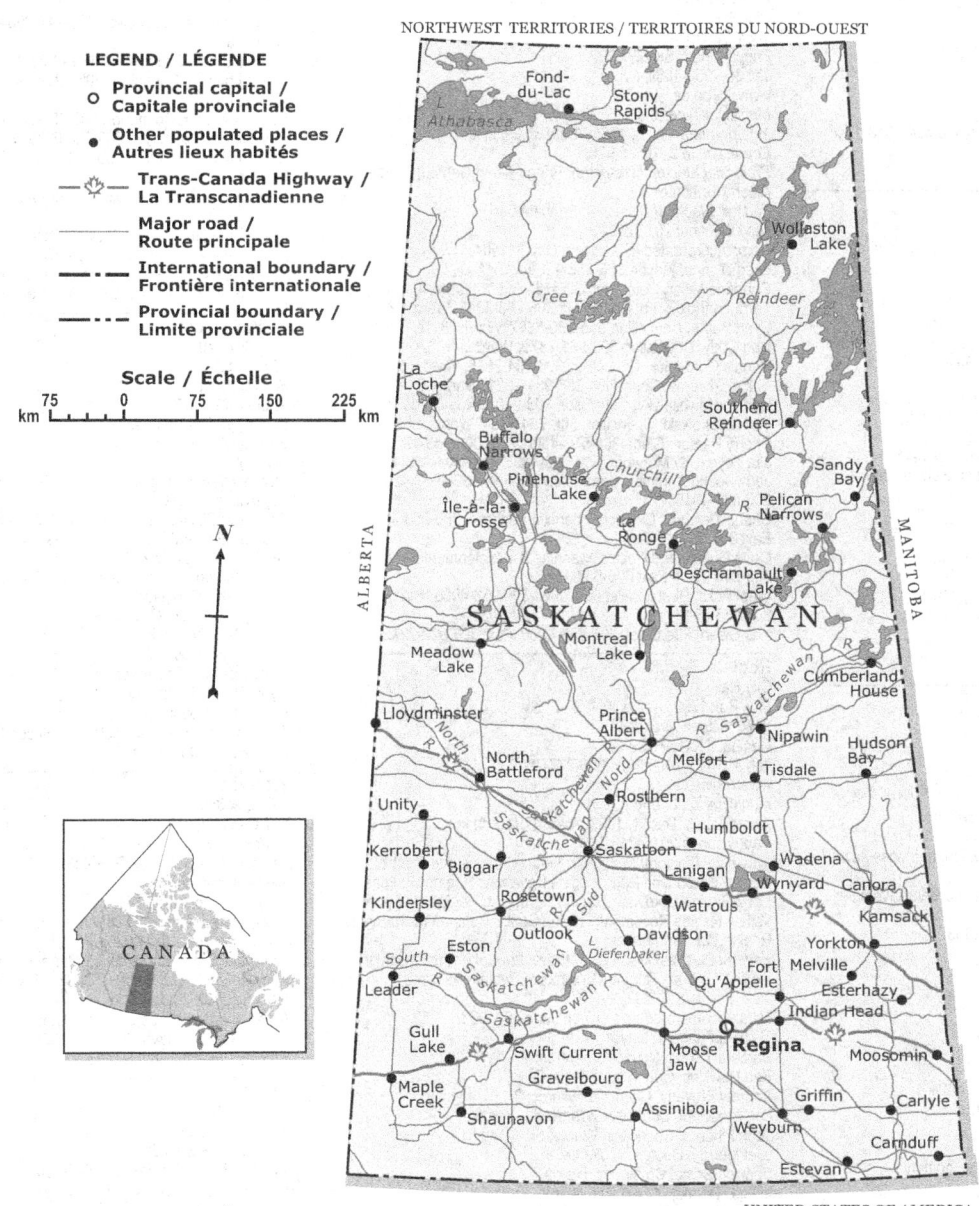

Saskatchewan

Major Municipalities in Saskatchewan

Estevan
1102 - 4th St.
Estevan, SK S4A 0W7
Tel: 306-634-1800; *Fax:* 306-634-9790
www.estevan.ca
Municipal Type: City
Incorporated: Nov. 2, 1899; *Area:* 18,85 sq km
Population in 2016: 11,483
Provincial Electoral District(s): Estevan
Federal Electoral District(s): Souris-Moose Mountain
Next Election: 2022/2024
Note: Incorporated as city on March 1, 1957.
Roy Ludwig, Mayor, 306-634-3050
Travis Frank, Councillor
Greg Hoffort, Councillor
Trevor Knibbs, Councillor
Dennis Moore, Councillor
Shelly Veroba, Councillor
Lyle Yanish, Councillor
Jeff Ward, City Manager & City Treasurer, 306-634-1813, Fax: 306-634-9790
Dale Feser, Fire Chief, 306-634-1856

Lloydminster
City Hall
4420 - 50th Ave.
Lloydminster, SK T9V 0W2
Tel: 780-875-6184; *Fax:* 780-871-8345
info@lloydminster.ca
www.lloydminster.ca
Municipal Type: City
Incorporated: Nov. 25, 1903; *Area:* 18.28 sq km
Population in 2016: 31,410
Provincial Electoral District(s): Lloydminster
Federal Electoral District(s): Battlefords-Lloydminster
Next Election: Oct. 23, 2024 (4 year terms)
Note: Population figure represents both the Alberta & Saskatchewan populations. Incorporated as a city on Jan. 1, 1958.
Gerald Aalbers, Mayor
Aaron Buckingham, Councillor
Michael Diachuk, Councillor
Glenn Fagnan, Councillor
Lorelee Marin, Councillor
Jonathan Torresan, Councillor
Jason Whiting, Councillor
Dion Pollard, City Manager, 780-875-6184
Leigh Sawicki, Fire Chief

Moose Jaw
228 Main St. North
Moose Jaw, SK S6H 3J8
Tel: 306-694-4400; *Fax:* 306-694-4480
www.moosejaw.ca
Municipal Type: City
Incorporated: Jan. 19, 1884; *Area:* 50,68 sq km
Population in 2016: 33,890
Provincial Electoral District(s): Moose Jaw North; Moose Jaw Wakamow
Federal Electoral District(s): Moose Jaw-Lake Centre-Lanigan
Next Election: 2022/2024
Note: Incorporated as a city on Nov. 20, 1903.
Dawn Luhning, Acting Mayor; Councillor
Heather Eby, Councillor
Crystal Froese, Councillor
Scott McMann, Councillor
Don Mitchell, Councillor
Brian Swanson, Councillor
Chris Warren, Councillor
Myron Gulka-Tiechko, City Clerk, 306-694-4421
James Puffalt, City Manager, 306-694-4427
Brian Acker, Director, Financial Services
Derek Blais, Director, Parks & Recreation
Michelle Sanson, Director, Planning & Development
Rod Montgomery, Fire Chief

North Battleford
P.O. Box 460
1291 - 101st St.
North Battleford, SK S9A 2Y6
Tel: 306-445-1700; *Fax:* 306-694-4480
reception@cityofnb.ca
www.cityofnb.ca
Municipal Type: City
Incorporated: March 21, 1906; *Area:* 33,55 sq km
Population in 2016: 14,315

Provincial Electoral District(s): The Battlefords
Federal Electoral District(s): Battlefords-Lloydminster
Next Election: 2022/2024
Note: Proclaimed as a city on May 1, 1913.
Ryan Bater, Mayor
Don Buglas, Councillor
Kelli Hawtin, Councillor
Greg Lightfoot, Councillor
Kent Lindgren, Councillor
Kevin Steinborn, Councillor
Len Taylor, Councillor
Randy Patrick, City Manager
Steve Brown, Director, Finance
Cheryl Deneire, Director, Leisure Services
Stewart Schafer, Director, Infrastructure Services
Debbie Wohlberg, Director, Legislative Services
Lindsay Holm, Fire Chief

Prince Albert
City Hall
1084 Central Ave.
Prince Albert, SK S6V 7P3
Tel: 306-953-4884
www.citypa.ca
Municipal Type: City
Incorporated: Oct. 8, 1885; *Area:* 67,29 sq km
Population in 2016: 35,926
Provincial Electoral District(s): Prince Albert Carlton; Prince Albert Northcote
Federal Electoral District(s): Prince Albert
Next Election: 2022/2024
Note: Incorporated as a city on Oct. 8, 1904.
Greg Dionne, Mayor, 306-953-4300
Charlene Miller, Councillor, 306-764-3690, Wards: 1
Terra Lennox-Zepp, Councillor, 306-763-3818, Wards: 2
Evert Botha, Councillor, 306-980-5387, Wards: 3
Don Cody, Councillor, 306-961-7870, Wards: 4
Dennis Ogrodnick, Councillor, 306-764-2655, Wards: 5
Blake Edwards, Councillor, 306-961-2921, Wards: 6
Dennis Nowoselsky, Councillor, 306-940-6848, Wards: 7
Ted Zurakowski, Councillor, 306-764-6461, Wards: 8
Sherry Person, Clerk, 306-953-4305, Fax: 306-953-4313
Jim Toye, City Manager, 306-953-4395, Fax: 306-953-4396
Jody Boulet, Director, Community Services, 306-953-4800, Fax: 306-953-4915
Cheryl Tkachuk, Director, Financial Services, 306-953-4350, Fax: 306-953-4347
Craig Guidinger, Director, Planning & Development Services, 306-953-4370, Fax: 306-953-4380
Wes Hicks, Director, Public Works, 306-953-4900, Fax: 306-953-4915
Kris Olsen, Fire Chief, 306-953-4200, Fax: 306-922-2272

Regina
City Hall
P.O. Box 1790
2476 Victoria Ave.
Regina, SK S4P 3C8
Tel: 306-777-7000; *Fax:* 306-777-7609
www.regina.ca
Municipal Type: City
Incorporated: Dec. 1, 1883; *Area:* 179,97 sq km
Population in 2016: 215,106
Provincial Electoral District(s): Regina Elphinstone-Centre; Regina Coronation Park; Regina Dewdney; Regina Douglas Park; Regina Lakeview; Regina Northeast; Regina Qu'Appelle Valley; Regina Rosemont; Regina South; Regina Walsh Acres; Regina Wascana Plains
Federal Electoral District(s): Moose Jaw-Lake Centre-Lanigan; Regina-Lewvan; Regina-Qu'Appelle; Regina-Wascana
Next Election: 2022/2024
Note: Incorporated as a city on June 19, 1903.
Michael Fougere, Mayor
Barbara Young, Councillor, Wards: 1
Bob Hawkins, Councillor, Wards: 2
Andrew Stevens, Councillor, Wards: 3
Lori Bresciani, Councillor, Wards: 4
John Findura, Councillor, Wards: 5
Joel Murray, Councillor, Wards: 6
Sharron Bryce, Councillor, Wards: 7
Mike O'Donnell, Councillor, Wards: 8
Jason Mancinelli, Councillor, Wards: 9
Jerry Flegel, Councillor, Wards: 10
Chris Holden, City Manager
Layne Jackson, Fire Chief

Saskatoon
City Hall
222 - 3rd Ave. North
Saskatoon, SK S7K 0J5
Tel: 306-975-3200
www.saskatoon.ca

Municipal Type: City
Incorporated: Nov. 16, 1901; *Area:* 228,13 sq km
Population in 2016: 246,376
Provincial Electoral District(s): Saskatoon Centre; Saskatoon Eastview; Saskatoon Fairview; Saskatoon Greystone; Saskatoon Massey Place; Saskatoon Meewasin; Saskatoon Northwest; Saskatoon Nutana; Saskatoon Riversdale; Saskatoon Silver Springs; Saskatoon Southeast; Saskatoon Sutherland
Federal Electoral District(s): Carlton Trail-Eagle Creek; Saskatoon West; Saskatoon-Grasswood; Saskatoon-University
Next Election: 2022/2024
Note: Incorporated as a city on May 26, 1906.
Charlie Clark, Mayor, 306-975-3202, Fax: 306-975-3144
Darren Hill, Councillor, 306-227-4322, Wards: 1
Hilary Gough, Councillor, 306-717-4533, Wards: 2
Ann Iwanchuk, Councillor, 306-380-6870, Wards: 3
Troy Davies, Councillor, 306-361-0201, Fax: 306-664-2112, Wards: 4
Randy Donauer, Councillor, 306-244-6634, Fax: 306-244-6637, Wards: 5
Cynthia Block, Councillor, 306-244-2228, Wards: 6
Mairin Loewen, Councillor, 306-229-5298, Fax: 306-975-2784, Wards: 7
Sarina Gersher, Councillor, 306-250-9256, Wards: 8
Bev Dubois, Councillor, 306-220-5075, Wards: 9
Zach Jeffries, Councillor, 306-249-5513, Wards: 10
Vacant, City Manager
Patricia Warwick, City Solicitor, 306-975-3270, Fax: 306-975-7828
Kerry Tarasoff, Chief Financial Officer
Randy Grauer, General Manager, Community Services
Jeff Jorgenson, General Manager, Transportation & Utilities
Morgan Hackl, Fire Chief, Fire & Protective Services

Swift Current
P.O. Box 340
177 - 1st Ave. NE
Swift Current, SK S9H 3W1
Tel: 306-778-2777
admin@swiftcurrent.ca
www.swiftcurrent.ca
Municipal Type: City
Incorporated: Feb. 4, 1904; *Area:* 29,31 sq km
Population in 2016: 16,604
Provincial Electoral District(s): Swift Current
Federal Electoral District(s): Cypress Hills-Grasslands
Next Election: 2022/2024
Note: Incorporated as a city on Jan. 15, 1914.
Denis Perrault, Mayor
George Bowditch, Councillor
Bruce Deg, Councillor
Pat Friesen, Councillor
Chris Martens, Councillor
Ryan Plewis, Councillor
Ron Toles, Councillor
Tim Marcus, Chief Administrative Officer, 306-778-2723
Ryan Hunter, Fire Chief

Warman
P.O. Box 340
107 Central St. West
Warman, SK S0K 4S0
Tel: 306-933-2133; *Fax:* 306-933-1987
www.warman.ca
Municipal Type: City
Incorporated: Aug. 3, 1906; *Area:* 13.03 sq km
Population in 2016: 11,020
Provincial Electoral District(s): Martensville
Federal Electoral District(s): Carlton Trail-Eagle Creek
Next Election: 2022/2024
Note: Incorporated as a city on October 27th, 2012.
Sheryl Spence, Mayor, 306-385-2336
Stanley Westby, City Manager

Weyburn
P.O. Box 370
157 - 3rd St. NE
Weyburn, SK S4H 2K6
Tel: 306-848-3200; *Fax:* 306-842-2001
questions@weyburn.ca
www.weyburn.ca
Municipal Type: City
Incorporated: Oct. 22, 1900; *Area:* 15.78 sq km
Population in 2016: 10,870
Provincial Electoral District(s): Weyburn-Big Muddy
Federal Electoral District(s): Souris-Moose Mountain
Next Election: 2022/2024
Note: Incorporated as a city on Sept. 1, 1913.
Marcel Roy, Mayor
Winston Bailey, Councillor, 306-842-1614
Jeffrey Chessall, Councillor

Dick Michel, Councillor, 306-842-6479
Jeff Richards, Councillor
Mel Van Betuw, Councillor
Brad Wheeler, Councillor
Donette Ritcher, City Clerk, 306-848-3209
Robert (Bob) Smith, City Manager
Sean Abram, Director, Engineering, 306-848-3232
Laura Missal, Director, Finance, 306-848-3214
Mathew Warren, Director, Leisure Services, 306-848-3217
Greg Button, Manager, Facilities, 306-848-3270
Claude Morin, Superintendent, Public Works, 306-848-3294,
Fax: 306-842-1766
Simon Almond, Fire Chief
Marlo Pritchard, Police Chief

Yorkton
P.O. Box 400
37 - 3rd Ave. North
Yorkton, SK S3N 2W3
Tel: 306-786-1700; *Fax:* 306-786-6880
www.yorkton.ca
Municipal Type: City
Incorporated: July 11, 1894; *Area:* 36.32 sq km
Population in 2016: 16,343
Provincial Electoral District(s): Yorkton
Federal Electoral District(s): Yorkton-Melville
Next Election: 2022/2024
Note: Incorporated as a city on Feb. 1, 1928.
Bob Maloney, Mayor, 306-786-1701
Ken Chyz, Councillor, 306-621-5687
Randy Goulden, Councillor, 306-783-8707
Quinn Haider, Councillor, 306-641-5334
Mitch Hipssley, Councillor, 306-782-4911
Aaron Kienle, Councillor, 306-621-9349
Darcy Zaharia, Councillor, 306-621-9660
Lonnie Kaal, City Manager, 306-786-1703
Michael Buchholzer, Director, Environmental Services,
306-828-2470
Michael Eger, Director, Planning, Building & Development,
306-786-1758
Trent Mandzuk, Director, Public Works, 306-786-1760
Darcy McLeod, Director, Community Development, Parks &
Recreation, 306-786-1750
Ashley Stradeski, Director, Finance, 306-786-1721
Trevor Morrissey, Fire Chief, Fire Protective Services,
306-786-1798

Other Municipalities in Saskatchewan

Abbey
P.O. Box 210
Abbey, SK S0N 0A0
Tel: 306-689-2412; *Fax:* 306-689-2901
rm229@sasktel.net
www.rm229.com
Municipal Type: Village
Incorporated: Sept. 2, 1913; *Area:* 0.77 sq km
Population in 2016: 129
Provincial Electoral District(s): Cypress Hills
Federal Electoral District(s): Cypress Hills-Grasslands
Next Election: 2022/2024
Bruce Walker, Mayor
Dianne Scriven, Administrator

Aberdeen
401C Main St.
Aberdeen, SK S0K 0A0
Tel: 306-253-4311; *Fax:* 306-253-4201
townaberdeen@sasktel.net
www.aberdeen.ca
Municipal Type: Town
Incorporated: March 13, 1907; *Area:* 1.95 sq km
Population in 2016: 622
Provincial Electoral District(s): Humboldt
Federal Electoral District(s): Carlton Trail-Eagle Creek
Next Election: 2022/2024
Note: Proclaimed as town on Nov. 1, 1988.
Bruce Voldeng, Mayor
Susan Thompson, Chief Administrative Officer

Abernethy
P.O. Box 189
Abernethy, SK S0A 0A0
Tel: 306-333-2271; *Fax:* 306-333-2276
village@abernethy.ca
www.abernethy.ca
Municipal Type: Village
Incorporated: July 26, 1904; *Area:* 1.03 sq km
Population in 2016: 204
Provincial Electoral District(s): Last Mountain-Touchwood

Federal Electoral District(s): Regina-Qu'Appelle
Next Election: 2022/2024
Janet Englot, Mayor
Sheree Emmerson, Administrator

Air Ronge
123 Cessna St. West
Air Ronge, SK S0J 3G0
Tel: 306-425-2107; *Fax:* 306-425-3108
nvoar@sasktel.net
www.airronge.ca
Municipal Type: Northern Village
Incorporated: Oct. 1, 1983; *Area:* 6.00 sq km
Population in 2016: 1,106
Provincial Electoral District(s): Cumberland
Federal Electoral District(s): Desnethé-Missinippi-Churchill River
Next Election: 2022/2024
Gordon Stomp, Mayor
Charmayne Szatkowski, Administrator

Alameda
P.O. Box 36
Alameda, SK S0C 0A0
Tel: 306-489-2077; *Fax:* 306-489-4602
townofalameda@sasktel.net
www.townofalameda.ca
Municipal Type: Town
Incorporated: Dec. 29, 1898; *Area:* 2.55 sq km
Population in 2016: 369
Provincial Electoral District(s): Cannington
Federal Electoral District(s): Souris-Moose Mountain
Next Election: 2022/2024
Note: Proclaimed as town on April 15, 1907.
Wade Duncan, Mayor
Lynne Hewitt, Administrator

Albertville
P.O. Box 83
212 St James Ave. South
Albertville, SK S0J 0A0
Tel: 306-929-2110; *Fax:* 306-929-4744
albertville@inet2000.com
Municipal Type: Village
Incorporated: Jan. 1, 1986; *Area:* 1.11 sq km
Population in 2016: 86
Provincial Electoral District(s): Saskatchewan Rivers
Federal Electoral District(s): Prince Albert
Next Election: 2022/2024
Christopher Dunn, Mayor
Audrey Veer, Administrator

Alice Beach
P.O. Box 70
Dilke, SK S0G 1C0
Tel: 306-519-3939
rvab@sasktel.net
Municipal Type: Resort Village
Area: 0.71 sq km
Population in 2016: 51
Provincial Electoral District(s): Thunder Creek
Federal Electoral District(s): Moose Jaw-Lake Centre-Lanigan
Next Election: 2022/2024
Ronald Ziegler, Mayor
Darlene Mann, Administrator

Alida
P.O. Box 6
Alida, SK S0C 0B0
Tel: 306-443-2228; *Fax:* 306-443-2568
villageofalida@sasktel.net
Municipal Type: Village
Incorporated: Feb. 19, 1926; *Area:* 0.35 sq km
Population in 2016: 120
Provincial Electoral District(s): Cannington
Federal Electoral District(s): Souris-Moose Mountain
Next Election: 2022/2024
James Boettcher, Mayor
Kathy Anthony, Administrator

Allan
P.O. Box 159
224 Main St.
Allan, SK S0K 0C0
Tel: 306-257-3272; *Fax:* 306-257-3337
townofallan@sasktel.net
www.allan.ca
Municipal Type: Town
Incorporated: June 9, 1910; *Area:* 1.78 sq km
Population in 2016: 644
Provincial Electoral District(s): Humboldt
Federal Electoral District(s): Moose Jaw-Lake Centre-Lanigan

Next Election: 2022/2024
Note: Proclaimed as town on Dec. 1, 1965.
Rob Vogelgesang, Mayor
Christine Dyck, Administrator

Alvena
P.O. Box 8
Alvena, SK S0K 0E0
Tel: 306-943-2101; *Fax:* 306-943-2139
villageofalvena@yahoo.ca
Municipal Type: Village
Incorporated: July 1, 1936; *Area:* 0.43 sq km
Population in 2016: 60
Provincial Electoral District(s): Batoche
Federal Electoral District(s): Carlton Trail-Eagle Creek
Next Election: 2022/2024
Ernie Sawitsky, Mayor
Pamela Hilkewich, Clerk

Annaheim
P.O. Box 130
Annaheim, SK S0K 0G0
Tel: 306-598-2006; *Fax:* 306-598-2008
villageofannaheim@sasktel.net
villageofannaheim.com
Municipal Type: Village
Incorporated: April 1, 1977; *Area:* 0.78 sq km
Population in 2016: 210
Provincial Electoral District(s): Melfort
Federal Electoral District(s): Carlton Trail-Eagle Creek
Next Election: 2022/2024
Mike Bold, Mayor
Debra Parry, Administrator

Antler
P.O. Box 70
Redvers, SK S0C 2H0
Tel: 306-452-3263; *Fax:* 306-452-3518
rm61@sasktel.net
Municipal Type: Village
Incorporated: March 15, 1905; *Area:* 0.72 sq km
Population in 2016: 40
Provincial Electoral District(s): Cannington
Federal Electoral District(s): Souris-Moose Mountain
Next Election: 2022/2024
Ron Henderson, Reeve
Melissa Roberts, Administrator

Aquadeo
P.O. Box 501
1006 Hwy. 4 North
Cochin, SK S0M 0L0
Tel: 306-386-2942; *Fax:* 306-386-2544
aquadeoadmin@gmail.com
www.aquadeo.net
Municipal Type: Resort Village
Area: 0.74 sq km
Population in 2016: 111
Provincial Electoral District(s): Cut Knife-Turtleford
Federal Electoral District(s): Battlefords-Lloydminster
Next Election: 2022/2024
Cameron Duncan, Mayor, 306-386-3112
Amber Loeppky, Administrator

Arborfield
P.O. Box 95
Arborfield, SK S0E 0A0
Tel: 306-769-0101; *Fax:* 306-769-8301
townarborfield@sasktel.net
www.arborfieldsk.ca
Municipal Type: Town
Incorporated: June 16, 1933; *Area:* 0.88 sq km
Population in 2016: 312
Provincial Electoral District(s): Carrot River Valley
Federal Electoral District(s): Prince Albert
Next Election: 2022/2024
Note: Proclaimed as town on June 1, 1950.
Ashley Gray, Mayor
Lisa Hamelin, Administrator

Archerwill
P.O. Box 130
Archerwill, SK S0E 0B0
Tel: 306-323-2161; *Fax:* 306-323-2106
villageofarcherwill@sasktel.net
Municipal Type: Village
Incorporated: Jan. 1, 1947; *Area:* 0.83 sq km
Population in 2016: 166
Provincial Electoral District(s): Kelvington-Wadena
Federal Electoral District(s): Yorkton-Melville
Next Election: 2022/2024
Jody Hagenes, Mayor

Geraldine Fountain, Administrator

Arcola
P.O. Box 359
127 Main St.
Arcola, SK S0C 0G0
Tel: 306-455-2212; *Fax:* 306-455-2445
admin@townofarcola.ca
www.townofarcola.ca
Municipal Type: Town
Incorporated: April 11, 1901; *Area:* 2.59 sq km
Population in 2016: 657
Provincial Electoral District(s): Cannington
Federal Electoral District(s): Souris-Moose Mountain
Next Election: 2022/2024
Note: Proclaimed as town on Nov. 20, 1903.
Harry Laurent, Mayor
Christie Hislop, Administrator

Arran
P.O. Box 40
Arran, SK S0A 0B0
Tel: 306-595-4521; *Fax:* 306-595-4531
rm331@sasktel.net
Municipal Type: Village
Incorporated: Sept. 21, 1916; *Area:* 0.69 sq km
Population in 2016: 25
Provincial Electoral District(s): Canora-Pelly
Federal Electoral District(s): Yorkton-Melville
Next Election: 2022/2024
Rick Nahnybida, Mayor
Yvonne Bilsky, Administrator

Asquith
P.O. Box 160
535 Main St.
Asquith, SK S0K 0J0
Tel: 306-329-4341; *Fax:* 306-329-4969
town.asquith@sasktel.net
www.townofasquith.com
Municipal Type: Town
Incorporated: Dec. 10, 1907; *Area:* 1.23 sq km
Population in 2016: 639
Provincial Electoral District(s): Biggar
Federal Electoral District(s): Carlton Trail-Eagle Creek
Next Election: 2022/2024
Note: Proclaimed as a town on Aug. 15, 1908.
Gail Erhart, Mayor
Holly Cross, Chief Administrative Officer

Assiniboia
P.O. Box 1470
131 Third Ave. West
Assiniboia, SK S0H 0B0
Tel: 306-642-3382; *Fax:* 306-642-5622
townoffice@assiniboia.net
www.assiniboia.net
Municipal Type: Town
Incorporated: Dec. 19, 1912; *Area:* 3.78 sq km
Population in 2016: 2,389
Provincial Electoral District(s): Wood River
Federal Electoral District(s): Cypress Hills-Grasslands
Next Election: 2022/2024
Note: Proclaimed as a town on Oct. 1, 1913.
Bob Himbeault, Mayor
Carol White, Chief Administrative Officer

Atwater
P.O. Box 17
Atwater, SK S0A 0C0
Tel: 306-793-2193
villageofatwater@gmail.com
Municipal Type: Village
Incorporated: Aug. 12, 1910; *Area:* 1.79 sq km
Population in 2016: 30
Provincial Electoral District(s): Melville-Saltcoats
Federal Electoral District(s): Yorkton-Melville
Next Election: 2022/2024
James Ferguson, Mayor
Sheila Shivak, Clerk

Avonlea
P.O. Box 209
203 Main St.
Avonlea, SK S0H 0C0
Tel: 306-868-2221; *Fax:* 306-868-2040
avonlea@sasktel.net
www.villageofavonlea.com
Municipal Type: Village
Incorporated: Feb. 10, 1912; *Area:* 0.96 sq km
Population in 2016: 393
Provincial Electoral District(s): Indian Head-Milestone

Federal Electoral District(s): Moose Jaw-Lake Centre-Lanigan
Next Election: 2022/2024
Marlyn Stevens, Mayor
Jaimie Paranuik, Administrator

Aylesbury
P.O. Box 151
316 Main St.
Aylesbury, SK S0G 0B0
Tel: 306-734-2250; *Fax:* 306-734-2257
rm222@sasktel.net
Municipal Type: Village
Incorporated: March 31, 1910; *Area:* 1.28 sq km
Population in 2016: 40
Provincial Electoral District(s): Thunder Creek
Federal Electoral District(s): Moose Jaw-Lake Centre-Lanigan
Next Election: 2022/2024
Douglas Watt, Mayor
Sarah Wells, Administrator

Aylsham
P.O. Box 64
Aylsham, SK S0E 0C0
Tel: 306-862-9415
villageofaylsham@sasktel.net
Municipal Type: Village
Incorporated: Aug. 4, 1947; *Area:* 0.48 sq km
Population in 2016: 65
Provincial Electoral District(s): Carrot River Valley
Federal Electoral District(s): Prince Albert
Next Election: 2022/2024
Elizabeth F. Archer, Mayor
Tammy Gray, Clerk

Balcarres
P.O. Box 130
209 Main St.
Balcarres, SK S0G 0C0
Tel: 306-334-2566; *Fax:* 306-334-2907
balcarrestown@sasktel.net
www.townofbalcarres.ca
Municipal Type: Town
Incorporated: Nov. 21, 1904; *Area:* 1.57 sq km
Population in 2016: 587
Provincial Electoral District(s): Last Mountain-Touchwood
Federal Electoral District(s): Regina-Qu'Appelle
Next Election: 2022/2024
Note: Proclaimed as a town on Jan. 1, 1951.
Dwight Dixon, Mayor
Bev Gelech, Administrator

Balgonie
P.O. Box 310
129 South Railway St. East
Balgonie, SK S0G 0E0
Tel: 306-771-2284; *Fax:* 306-771-2899
townofbalgonie@sasktel.net
www.townofbalgonie.ca
Municipal Type: Town
Incorporated: April 20, 1903; *Area:* 3.15 sq km
Population in 2016: 1,765
Provincial Electoral District(s): Indian Head-Milestone
Federal Electoral District(s): Regina-Qu'Appelle
Next Election: 2022/2024
Note: Proclaimed as a town on Jan. 1, 1951.
Frank Thauberger, Mayor
Valerie Hubbard, Administrator

Bangor
P.O. Box 35
Bangor, SK S0A 0E0
Tel: 306-728-4084
Municipal Type: Village
Incorporated: June 8, 1911; *Area:* 1.65 sq km
Population in 2016: 38
Provincial Electoral District(s): Melville-Saltcoats
Federal Electoral District(s): Yorkton-Melville
Next Election: 2022/2024
Jerome Bomberak, Mayor
Joan C. Bomberak, Clerk

Battleford
P.O. Box 40
Battleford, SK S0M 0E0
Tel: 306-937-6200; *Fax:* 306-937-2450
reception@battleford.ca
www.battleford.ca
Municipal Type: Town
Incorporated: Jan. 6, 1899; *Area:* 23.33 sq km
Population in 2016: 4,429
Provincial Electoral District(s): The Battlefords
Federal Electoral District(s): Battlefords-Lloydminster

Next Election: 2022/2024
Note: Proclaimed as a town on June 15, 1904.
Derek Mahon, Mayor
John Enns-Wind, Administrator

Bear Creek
P.O. Box 69
Buffalo Narrows, SK S0M 0J0
Tel: 306-235-1726; *Fax:* 306-235-1727
Municipal Type: NS
Population in 2016: 33
Provincial Electoral District(s): Athabasca
Federal Electoral District(s): Desnethé-Missinippi-Churchill River
Next Election: 2022/2024
Dean Herman, Chair
Bruce Leier, Advisor

Beatty
P.O. Box 60
Beatty, SK S0J 0C0
Tel: 306-752-2028; *Fax:* 306-752-5687
villageofbeatty@sasktel.net
Municipal Type: Village
Incorporated: March 31, 1921; *Area:* 0.82 sq km
Population in 2016: 60
Provincial Electoral District(s): Melfort
Federal Electoral District(s): Prince Albert
Next Election: 2022/2024
Harvey Rainville, Mayor
Linda Logan, Clerk

Beauval
P.O. Box 19
Lavoie St.
Beauval, SK S0M 0G0
Tel: 306-288-2110; *Fax:* 306-288-2348
admin.beauval@sasktel.net
Municipal Type: Northern Village
Incorporated: Oct. 1, 1983; *Area:* 6.71 sq km
Population in 2016: 640
Provincial Electoral District(s): Athabasca
Federal Electoral District(s): Desnethé-Missinippi-Churchill River
Next Election: 2022/2024
Nick Daigneault, Mayor
Lydia Gauthier, Clerk

Beaver Flat
P.O. Box 991
Swift Current, SK S9H 3X1
Tel: 306-778-7638
rvbeaverflat@gmail.com
www.beaverflatsk.ca
Municipal Type: Resort Village
Area: 0.92 sq km
Population in 2016: 72
Provincial Electoral District(s): Thunder Creek
Federal Electoral District(s): Cypress Hills-Grasslands
Next Election: 2022/2024
Bill Bresett, Mayor
Dianne Hahn, Clerk

Beechy
P.O. Box 153
Beechy, SK S0L 0C0
Tel: 306-859-2205; *Fax:* 306-859-2290
info@beechysask.ca
www.beechysask.ca
Municipal Type: Village
Incorporated: May 11, 1925; *Area:* 1.06 sq km
Population in 2016: 228
Provincial Electoral District(s): Rosetown-Elrose
Federal Electoral District(s): Cypress Hills-Grasslands
Next Election: 2022/2024
Curtis Turner, Mayor
Carrie James, Administrator

Belle Plaine
P.O. Box 63
Belle Plaine, SK S0G 0G0
Tel: 306-345-1200
villageofbelleplaine@xplornet.com
Municipal Type: Village
Incorporated: Aug. 12, 1910; *Area:* 1.34 sq km
Population in 2016: 85
Provincial Electoral District(s): Thunder Creek
Federal Electoral District(s): Moose Jaw-Lake Centre-Lanigan
Next Election: 2022/2024
Edwin Siemens, Mayor
Leane Johnston, Administrator

Bengough
P.O. Box 188
181 Main St.
Bengough, SK S0C 0K0
Tel: 306-268-2927; *Fax:* 306-268-2988
town.bengough@sasktel.net
www.bengough.com
Municipal Type: Town
Incorporated: March 15, 1912; *Area:* 1.07 sq km
Population in 2016: 332
Provincial Electoral District(s): Weyburn-Big Muddy
Federal Electoral District(s): Souris-Moose Mountain
Next Election: 2022/2024
Note: Proclaimed as a town on April 1, 1958.
Dennis Mazenc, Mayor
Penny Nergard, Administrator

Bethune
P.O. Box 209
507 Main St.
Bethune, SK S0G 0H0
Tel: 306-638-3188; *Fax:* 306-638-3102
villageofbethune@sasktel.net
www.villageofbethune.com
Municipal Type: Village
Incorporated: Aug. 2, 1912; *Area:* 1.04 sq km
Population in 2016: 399
Provincial Electoral District(s): Thunder Creek
Federal Electoral District(s): Moose Jaw-Lake Centre-Lanigan
Next Election: 2022/2024
Doug Patience, Mayor
Rodney Audette, Administrator

Bienfait
P.O. Box 220
Bienfait, SK S0C 0M0
Tel: 306-388-2969; *Fax:* 306-388-2449
bienfait@sasktel.net
www.bienfait.ca
Municipal Type: Town
Incorporated: April 16, 1912; *Area:* 3.09 sq km
Population in 2016: 762
Provincial Electoral District(s): Estevan
Federal Electoral District(s): Souris-Moose Mountain
Next Election: 2022/2024
Note: Proclaimed as a town on March 1, 1957.
Paul Carroll, Mayor
Laurel Gilroy, Administrator

Big River
P.O. Box 220
Big River, SK S0J 0E0
Tel: 306-469-2112; *Fax:* 306-469-4856
bigriver@sasktel.net
www.bigriver.ca
Municipal Type: Town
Incorporated: Aug. 18, 1923; *Area:* 2.11 sq km
Population in 2016: 700
Provincial Electoral District(s): Saskatchewan Rivers
Federal Electoral District(s): Desnethé-Missinippi-Churchill River
Next Election: 2022/2024
Note: Proclaimed as a town on Oct. 1, 1966.
Rob Buckingham, Mayor
Noreen Olsen, Administrator

Big Shell
P.O. Box 130
Shell Lake, SK S0J 2G0
Tel: 306-427-2188; *Fax:* 306-427-1203
villagebigshell@gmail.com
Municipal Type: Resort Village
Area: 1.02 sq km
Population in 2016: 48
Provincial Electoral District(s): Rosthern-Shellbrook
Federal Electoral District(s): Desnethé-Missinippi-Churchill River
Next Election: 2022/2024
Jim Wilkie, Mayor
Tara Bueckert, Administrator

Biggar
P.O. Box 489
202 - 3rd Ave. West
Biggar, SK S0K 0M0
Tel: 306-948-3317; *Fax:* 306-948-5134
townoffice@townofbiggar.com
www.townofbiggar.com
Municipal Type: Town
Incorporated: May 18, 1909; *Area:* 15.75
Population in 2016: 2,226
Provincial Electoral District(s): Biggar
Federal Electoral District(s): Carlton-Eagle Creek

Next Election: 2022/2024
Note: Proclaimed as a town on Nov. 1, 1911.
Raymond Sadler, Mayor
Barb Barteski, Administrator

Birch Hills
P.O. Box 206
Birch Hills, SK S0J 0G0
Tel: 306-749-2232; *Fax:* 306-749-2545
birchhills@town.sasktel.net
www.birchhills.ca
Municipal Type: Town
Incorporated: July 19, 1907; *Area:* 1.82 sq km
Population in 2016: 1,033
Provincial Electoral District(s): Batoche
Federal Electoral District(s): Prince Albert
Next Election: 2022/2024
Note: Proclaimed as a town on Aug. 1, 1960.
Dale Pratt, Mayor
Tara Gariepy, Administrator

Bird's Point
P.O. Box 1019
169 Currie Ave.
Whitewood, SK S0G 5C0
Tel: 306-793-4552; *Fax:* 306-793-2017
rvbirdspoint@sasktel.net
Municipal Type: Resort Village
Area: 0.58 sq km
Population in 2016: 112
Provincial Electoral District(s): Melville-Saltcoats
Federal Electoral District(s): Yorkton-Melville
Next Election: 2022/2024
Kelly Bear, Mayor
Lila Sippola, Administrator

Bjorkdale
P.O. Box 27
213B Forest View
Bjorkdale, SK S0E 0E0
Tel: 306-886-2167; *Fax:* 306-886-2181
villageofbjorkdale@live.com
www.villageofbjorkdale.ca
Municipal Type: Village
Incorporated: April 1, 1968; *Area:* 1.39 sq km
Population in 2016: 201
Provincial Electoral District(s): Kelvington-Wadena
Federal Electoral District(s): Yorkton-Melville
Next Election: 2022/2024
James Majewski, Mayor, 306-886-2181
Lorraine Fleming, Acting Administrator, 306-886-2167, Fax:
306-886-2181

Black Point
P.O. Box 640
La Loche, SK S0M 1G0
Tel: 306-822-2727; *Fax:* 306-822-2268
Municipal Type: Northern Hamlet
Population in 2016: 43
Provincial Electoral District(s): Athabasca
Federal Electoral District(s): Desnethé-Missinippi-Churchill River
Next Election: 2022/2024
Annette Petit, Mayor
Heather Montgrand, Clerk

Bladworth
P.O. Box 90
Bladworth, SK S0G 0J0
Tel: 306-567-5564; *Fax:* 306-567-4730
davidsoncd@sasktel.net
Municipal Type: Village
Incorporated: July 27, 1906; *Area:* 0.84 sq km
Population in 2016: 65
Provincial Electoral District(s): Arm River-Watrous
Federal Electoral District(s): Moose Jaw-Lake Centre-Lanigan
Next Election: 2022/2024
Barkley Prpick, Mayor
Sheila Sinclair, Clerk

Blaine Lake
P.O. Box 10
Blaine Lake, SK S0J 0J0
Tel: 306-497-2531; *Fax:* 306-497-2511
blainelake@sasktel.net
www.blainelake.ca
Municipal Type: Town
Incorporated: March 15, 1912; *Area:* 1.75 sq km
Population in 2016: 499
Provincial Electoral District(s): Rosthern-Shellbrook
Federal Electoral District(s): Carlton Trail-Eagle Creek
Next Election: 2022/2024
Note: Proclaimed as a town on March 1, 1954.

Allan Sorenson, Mayor
Anna Brad, Administrator

Borden
P.O. Box 210
200 Shepard St.
Borden, SK S0K 0N0
Tel: 306-997-2134; *Fax:* 306-997-2201
office@bordensask.ca
www.bordensask.ca
Municipal Type: Village
Incorporated: July 19, 1907; *Area:* 0.76 sq km
Population in 2016: 287
Provincial Electoral District(s): Biggar
Federal Electoral District(s): Carlton Trail-Eagle Creek
Next Election: 2022/2024
Jamie Brandrick, Mayor
Jennifer King, Administrator

Brabant Lake
c/o Government Relations
P.O. Box 5000
La Ronge, SK S0J 1L0
Tel: 306-758-4888; *Fax:* 306-758-4888
Other Information: Toll-Free Phone: 800-663-1555
Municipal Type: NS
Population in 2016: 62
Provincial Electoral District(s): Athabasca
Federal Electoral District(s): Desnethé-Missinippi-Churchill River
Next Election: 2022/2024
Gideon Cook, Chair
Valerie Antoniuk, Advisor, 306-425-4323

Bracken
P.O. Box 41
Bracken, SK S0N 0G0
Tel: 306-293-2119
Municipal Type: Village
Incorporated: Jan. 4, 1926; *Area:* 0.60 sq km
Population in 2016: 20
Provincial Electoral District(s): Wood River
Federal Electoral District(s): Cypress Hills-Grasslands
Next Election: 2022/2024
Susan Wiens, Mayor
Monique Fehr, Administrator

Bradwell
P.O. Box 100
Bradwell, SK S0K 0P0
Tel: 306-257-4141; *Fax:* 306-257-3303
rm343@sasktel.net
Municipal Type: Village
Incorporated: July 13, 1910; *Area:* 0.42 sq km
Population in 2016: 166
Provincial Electoral District(s): Humboldt
Federal Electoral District(s): Moose Jaw-Lake Centre-Lanigan
Next Election: 2022/2024
Ken Hartz, Mayor
R. Doran Scott, Administrator

Bredenbury
P.O. Box 87
Bredenbury, SK S0A 0H0
Tel: 306-898-2055; *Fax:* 306-898-2333
bredenbury@sasktel.net
www.townofbredenbury.ca
Municipal Type: Town
Incorporated: May 3, 1911; *Area:* 4.80 sq km
Population in 2016: 372
Provincial Electoral District(s): Melville-Saltcoats
Federal Electoral District(s): Yorkton-Melville
Next Election: 2022/2024
Note: Proclaimed as a town on May 1, 1913.
Jonas St. Marie, Mayor
Kim Varga, Administrator

Briercrest
P.O. Box 25
Briercrest, SK S0H 0K0
Tel: 306-799-2066; *Fax:* 306-799-2067
villageofbriercrest@sasktel.net
villageofbriercrest.ca
Municipal Type: Village
Incorporated: April 17, 1912; *Area:* 0.62 sq km
Population in 2016: 159
Provincial Electoral District(s): Indian Head-Milestone
Federal Electoral District(s): Moose Jaw-Lake Centre-Lanigan
Next Election: 2022/2024
Ray Briggs, Mayor
Linda Senchuk, Administrator

Broadview
P.O. Box 430
524 Main St.
Broadview, SK S0G 0K0
Tel: 306-696-2533; Fax: 306-696-3573
town.of.broadview@sasktel.net
www.broadview.ca
Municipal Type: Town
Incorporated: Dec. 29, 1898; *Area:* 2.45 sq km
Population in 2016: 552
Provincial Electoral District(s): Moosomin
Federal Electoral District(s): Souris-Moose Mountain
Next Election: 2022/2024
Note: Proclaimed as a town on May 15, 1907.
Carol Mills, Mayor
Mervin J. Schmidt, Administrator

Brock
P.O. Box 70
Brock, SK S0L 0H0
Tel: 306-379-2116
brockadmin@sasktel.net
Municipal Type: Village
Incorporated: July 7, 1910; *Area:* 0.74 sq km
Population in 2016: 142
Provincial Electoral District(s): Rosetown-Elrose
Federal Electoral District(s): Cypress Hills-Grasslands
Next Election: 2022/2024
Vance Brost, Mayor
Charlotte Helfrich, Administrator

Broderick
P.O. Box 29
Broderick, SK S0H 0L0
Tel: 306-867-8578
villageofbroderick@yourlink.ca
Municipal Type: Village
Incorporated: Sept. 13, 1909; *Area:* 0.91 sq km
Population in 2016: 85
Provincial Electoral District(s): Rosetown-Elrose
Federal Electoral District(s): Moose Jaw-Lake Centre-Lanigan
Next Election: 2022/2024
Arlin Simonson, Mayor
Shannon Pederson, Clerk

Brownlee
P.O. Box 89
Brownlee, SK S0H 0M0
Tel: 306-759-2302
Municipal Type: Village
Incorporated: Dec. 29, 1908; *Area:* 2.42 sq km
Population in 2016: 55
Provincial Electoral District(s): Thunder Creek
Federal Electoral District(s): Moose Jaw-Lake Centre-Lanigan
Next Election: 2022/2024
Michael Worotniak, Mayor
Jackie Leggott, Clerk

Bruno
P.O. Box 370
Bruno, SK S0K 0S0
Tel: 306-369-2514; *Fax:* 306-369-2878
bruno@sasktel.net
www.townofbruno.wordpress.com
Municipal Type: Town
Incorporated: March 9, 1909; *Area:* 0.95 sq km
Population in 2016: 611
Provincial Electoral District(s): Humboldt
Federal Electoral District(s): Carlton Trail-Eagle Creek
Next Election: 2022/2024
Note: Proclaimed as a town on Jan. 1, 1962.
Dale Glessman, Mayor
Colette Radcliffe, Administrator

B-Say-Tah
P.O. Box 908
842 Broadway St.
Fort Qu'Appelle, SK S0G 1S0
Tel: 306-332-6449; *Fax:* 306-332-2923
bsaytah@sasktel.net
www.bsaytah.ca
Municipal Type: Resort Village
Area: 1.33 sq km
Population in 2016: 156
Provincial Electoral District(s): Indian Head-Milestone
Federal Electoral District(s): Regina-Qu'Appelle
Next Election: 2022/2024
Isaac Sneath, Mayor
Richelle Haanstra, Administrator

Buchanan
P.O. Box 479
300 Central Ave.
Buchanan, SK S0A 0J0
Tel: 306-592-2144; *Fax:* 306-592-4471
buchananvillage@sasktel.net
Municipal Type: Village
Incorporated: June 11, 1907; *Area:* 1.29 sq km
Population in 2016: 218
Provincial Electoral District(s): Canora-Pelly
Federal Electoral District(s): Yorkton-Melville
Next Election: 2022/2024
Garry Kupchinski, Mayor
Candace Loshka, Administrator

Buena Vista
1050 Grand Ave.
Buena Vista, SK S2V 1A2
Tel: 306-729-4385; *Fax:* 306-729-4518
buenavista@sasktel.net
www.buenavista.ca
Other Information: After Hours Emergency: 306-729-3239
Municipal Type: Village
Incorporated: Nov. 18, 1983; *Area:* 3.61 sq km
Population in 2016: 612
Provincial Electoral District(s): Thunder Creek
Federal Electoral District(s): Moose Jaw-Lake Centre-Lanigan
Next Election: 2022/2024
Bill Dinu, Mayor, 306-729-3201
Lorna Davies, Administrator

Buffalo Narrows
P.O. Box 98
1 - 1491 Pedersen Ave.
Buffalo Narrows, SK S0M 0J0
Tel: 306-235-4225; *Fax:* 306-235-4699
villageofbuffalo@sasktel.net
www.buffalonarrows.com
Municipal Type: Northern Village
Incorporated: Oct. 1, 1983; *Area:* 34.10 sq km
Population in 2016: 1,110
Provincial Electoral District(s): Athabasca
Federal Electoral District(s): Desnethé-Missinippi-Churchill River
Next Election: 2022/2024
Robert Woods, Mayor
Therese Chartier, Administrator

Bulyea
P.O. Box 37
Bulyea, SK S0G 0L0
Tel: 306-725-4936
info@bulyea.com
www.bulyea.com
Municipal Type: Village
Incorporated: March 9, 1909; *Area:* 1.28 sq km
Population in 2016: 113
Provincial Electoral District(s): Last Mountain-Touchwood
Federal Electoral District(s): Moose Jaw-Lake Centre-Lanigan
Next Election: 2022/2024
Terry Myers, Mayor
Jenna Johnson, Administrator, 306-725-4936

Burstall
P.O. Box 250
428 Martin St.
Burstall, SK S0N 0H0
Tel: 306-679-2000; *Fax:* 306-679-2275
burstall@sasktel.net
www.burstall.ca
Municipal Type: Town
Incorporated: May 31, 1921; *Area:* 1.11 sq km
Population in 2016: 378
Provincial Electoral District(s): Cypress Hills
Federal Electoral District(s): Cypress Hills-Grasslands
Next Election: 2022/2024
Note: Proclaimed as a town on Nov. 1, 1976.
Tegan Bodnarchuk, Mayor
Lucein Stuebing, Administrator

Cabri
P.O. Box 200
202 Centre St.
Cabri, SK S0N 0J0
Tel: 306-587-2500; *Fax:* 306-587-2392
townofcabri@sasktel.net
www.cabri.ca
Municipal Type: Town
Incorporated: May 13, 1912; *Area:* 1.33 sq km
Population in 2016: 390
Provincial Electoral District(s): Cypress Hills
Federal Electoral District(s): Cypress Hills-Grasslands

Next Election: 2022/2024
Note: Proclaimed as a town on April 16, 1917.
David Gossard, Mayor
Janelle Anderson, Chief Administrative Officer

Cadillac
P.O. Box 189
Cadillac, SK S0N 0K0
Tel: 306-785-2100; *Fax:* 306-785-2101
v.cadillac@sasktel.net
Municipal Type: Village
Incorporated: July 2, 1914; *Area:* 1.05 sq km
Population in 2016: 92
Provincial Electoral District(s): Wood River
Federal Electoral District(s): Cypress Hills-Grasslands
Next Election: 2022/2024
Bryce Evesque, Mayor
Betty Moller, Clerk

Calder
P.O. Box 47
Calder, SK S0A 0K0
Tel: 306-742-2158; *Fax:* 306-742-2158
caldervillage@sasktel.net
Municipal Type: Village
Incorporated: Jan. 18, 1911; *Area:* 0.75 sq km
Population in 2016: 90
Provincial Electoral District(s): Melville-Saltcoats
Federal Electoral District(s): Yorkton-Melville
Next Election: 2022/2024
Ivan Sobkow, Mayor
Sharon Wonchulanko, Clerk

Camsell Portage
c/o Government Relations
P.O. Box 5000
La Ronge, SK S0J 1L0
Tel: 306-425-4321; *Fax:* 306-425-2401
Other Information: Toll-Free Phone: 800-663-1555
Municipal Type: NS
Area: 5.10
Population in 2016: 10
Provincial Electoral District(s): Athabasca
Federal Electoral District(s): Desnethé-Missinippi-Churchill River
Next Election: 2022/2024
Claire Larocque, Chair
Sandra Galambos, Advisor

Candle Lake
P.O. Box 114
20 Hwy. 265
Candle Lake, SK S0J 3E0
Tel: 306-929-2236; *Fax:* 306-929-2201
rvcandlelakeoffice@sasktel.net
www.candlelakeresort.ca
Municipal Type: Resort Village
Area: 63.32 sq km
Population in 2016: 840
Provincial Electoral District(s): Saskatchewan Rivers
Federal Electoral District(s): Desnethé-Missinippi-Churchill River
Next Election: 2022/2024
John G. Quinn, Mayor
Joan Corneil, Administrator

Canora
P.O. Box 717
418 Main St.
Canora, SK S0A 0L0
Tel: 306-563-5773; *Fax:* 306-563-4336
townofcanora@sasktel.net
www.canora.com
Municipal Type: Town
Incorporated: April 8, 1905; *Area:* 7.31 sq km
Population in 2016: 2,024
Provincial Electoral District(s): Canora-Pelly
Federal Electoral District(s): Yorkton-Melville
Next Election: 2022/2024
Note: Proclaimed as a town on Nov. 1, 1910.
Gina Rakochy, Mayor, 303-563-4314
Michael Mykytyshyn, Chief Administrative Officer, 306-563-6466

Canwood
P.O. Box 172
651 Main St.
Canwood, SK S0J 0K0
Tel: 306-468-2016; *Fax:* 306-468-2805
canwood.town@sasktel.net
www.canwood.ca
Municipal Type: Village
Incorporated: July 18, 1916; *Area:* 2.56 sq km
Population in 2016: 332
Provincial Electoral District(s): Rosthern-Shellbrook

Federal Electoral District(s): Desnethé-Missinippi-Churchill River
Next Election: 2022/2024
Robert Thompson, Mayor, 306-468-2266
Erin Robertson, Administrator, 303-468-2016

Carievale
P.O. Box 88
128 Broadway St.
Carievale, SK S0C 0P0
Tel: 306-928-2033; *Fax:* 306-928-2021
village.carievale@sasktel.net
Municipal Type: Village
Incorporated: March 14, 1903; *Area:* 0.88 sq km
Population in 2016: 240
Provincial Electoral District(s): Cannington
Federal Electoral District(s): Souris-Moose Mountain
Next Election: 2022/2024
Michael Wolf, Mayor
Elaine Lowdon, Administrator

Carlyle
P.O. Box 10
Carlyle, SK S0C 0R0
Tel: 306-453-2363; *Fax:* 306-453-6380
towncarlyle@sasktel.net
www.townofcarlyle.com
Municipal Type: Town
Incorporated: March 13, 1902; *Area:* 3.03 sq km
Population in 2016: 1,508
Provincial Electoral District(s): Cannington
Federal Electoral District(s): Souris-Moose Mountain
Next Election: 2022/2024
Note: Proclaimed as a town on Jan. 1, 1906.
Wayne Orsted, Mayor
Huguette Lutz, Chief Administrative Officer

Carmichael
P.O. Box 420
Gull Lake, SK S0N 1A0
Tel: 306-672-3501; *Fax:* 306-672-3879
rm109@sasktel.net
Municipal Type: Village
Incorporated: May 25, 1917; *Area:* 0.67 sq km
Population in 2016: 58
Provincial Electoral District(s): Cypress Hills
Federal Electoral District(s): Cypress Hills-Grasslands
Next Election: 2022/2024
Miles C. Wells, Mayor
Natasha Brown, Clerk

Carnduff
P.O. Box 100
1312 Railway Ave.
Carnduff, SK S0C 0S0
Tel: 306-482-3300; *Fax:* 306-482-3422
info@carnduff.ca
www.carnduff.ca
Municipal Type: Town
Incorporated: March 29, 1899; *Area:* 2.05 sq km
Population in 2016: 1,099
Provincial Electoral District(s): Cannington
Federal Electoral District(s): Souris-Moose Mountain
Next Election: 2022/2024
Note: Proclaimed as a town on Aug. 12, 1905.
Ross Apperley, Mayor, 306-482-7775
Annette Brown, Administrator

Caronport
P.O. Box 550
Caronport, SK S0H 0S0
Tel: 306-756-2225; *Fax:* 306-756-5007
vcoffice@sasktel.net
Municipal Type: Village
Incorporated: Jan. 1, 1988; *Area:* 1.90 sq km
Population in 2016: 994
Provincial Electoral District(s): Thunder Creek
Federal Electoral District(s): Cypress Hills-Grasslands
Next Election: 2022/2024
Darryl Tunall, Mayor
Pat Peecock, Administrator

Carrot River
P.O. Box 147
Carrot River, SK S0E 0L0
Tel: 306-768-2515; *Fax:* 306-768-2930
t.carrotriver@sasktel.net
www.carrotriver.ca
Municipal Type: Town
Incorporated: Nov. 6, 1941; *Area:* 1.46 sq km
Population in 2016: 973
Provincial Electoral District(s): Carrot River Valley
Federal Electoral District(s): Prince Albert

Next Election: 2022/2024
Note: Proclaimed as a town on April 1, 1948.
Robert Gagne, Mayor
Kevin Trew, Administrator

Central Butte
P.O. Box 10
Central Butte, SK S0H 0T0
Tel: 306-796-2288; *Fax:* 306-796-4627
townofcentralbutte@sasktel.net
www.centralbutte.ca
Municipal Type: Town
Incorporated: April 9, 1915; *Area:* 2.24 sq km
Population in 2016: 372
Provincial Electoral District(s): Thunder Creek
Federal Electoral District(s): Cypress Hills-Grasslands
Next Election: 2022/2024
Note: Proclaimed as a town on July 1, 1967.
Reg Stewart, Mayor
Kyle Van Den Bosch, Administrator

Ceylon
P.O. Box 188
Ceylon, SK S0C 0T0
Tel: 306-454-2202; *Fax:* 306-454-2627
rmgap39@sasktel.net
Municipal Type: Village
Incorporated: Sept. 26, 1911; *Area:* 0.75 sq km
Population in 2016: 111
Provincial Electoral District(s): Weyburn-Big Muddy
Federal Electoral District(s): Souris-Moose Mountain
Next Election: 2022/2024
Kurt McCurry, Mayor
Velvet Muxlow, Administrator

Chamberlain
P.O. Box 8
Chamberlain, SK S0G 0R0
Tel: 306-638-4680; *Fax:* 306-638-3108
Municipal Type: Village
Incorporated: Jan. 31, 1911; *Area:* 0.70 sq km
Population in 2016: 90
Provincial Electoral District(s): Thunder Creek
Federal Electoral District(s): Moose Jaw-Lake Centre-Lanigan
Next Election: 2022/2024
Shaun Ackerman, Mayor
Sarah Wells, Administrator

Chaplin
P.O. Box 210
Chaplin, SK S0H 0V0
Tel: 306-395-2221; *Fax:* 306-395-2555
village.chaplin@sasktel.net
www.chaplin.ca
Municipal Type: Village
Incorporated: Oct. 8, 1912; *Area:* 1.26 sq km
Population in 2016: 229
Provincial Electoral District(s): Thunder Creek
Federal Electoral District(s): Cypress Hills-Grasslands
Next Election: 2022/2024
Gary Adrian, Mayor
Brittany Hornbrook, Administrator

Chitek Lake
P.O. Box 70
219 Pine St.
Chitek Lake, SK S0J 0L0
Tel: 306-984-2353; *Fax:* 306-984-1178
rvchitek@sasktel.net
www.rvchiteklake.com
Municipal Type: Resort Village
Area: 2.54 sq km
Population in 2016: 138
Provincial Electoral District(s): Meadow Lake
Federal Electoral District(s): Desnethé-Missinippi-Churchill River
Next Election: 2022/2024
Douglas Struhar, Mayor
Cindy Larson, Administrator

Choiceland
P.O. Box 279
100 Railway Ave. East
Choiceland, SK S0J 0M0
Tel: 306-428-2070; *Fax:* 306-428-2071
choiceland.town@sasktel.net
choiceland.ca
Municipal Type: Town
Incorporated: Sept. 8, 1944; *Area:* 1.12 sq km
Population in 2016: 359
Provincial Electoral District(s): Saskatchewan Rivers
Federal Electoral District(s): Prince Albert

Next Election: 2022/2024
Note: Proclaimed as a town on Jan. 1, 1979.
Robert Mardell, Mayor
Holly Toews, Administrator

Chorney Beach
P.O. Box 328
Foam Lake, SK S0A 1A0
Tel: 306-272-3359; *Fax:* 306-272-3738
chorneybeach@gmail.com
Municipal Type: Resort Village
Area: 0.17 sq km
Population in 2016: 24
Provincial Electoral District(s): Kelvington-Wadena
Federal Electoral District(s): Yorkton-Melville
Next Election: 2022/2024
Peter Olson, Mayor
Bethalyn Rusch, Clerk

Christopher Lake
P.O. Box 163
Christopher Lake, SK S0J 0N0
Tel: 306-982-4242; *Fax:* 306-982-4242
vilchris@sasktel.net
www.villageofchristopherlake.com
Municipal Type: Village
Incorporated: March 1, 1985; *Area:* 3.47 sq km
Population in 2016: 289
Provincial Electoral District(s): Saskatchewan Rivers
Federal Electoral District(s): Desnethé-Missinippi-Churchill River
Next Election: 2022/2024
Denis Daughton, Mayor, 306-982-4686
Jeannie Rip, Administrator, 306-982-4242

Churchbridge
P.O. Box 256
116 Vincent Ave.
Churchbridge, SK S0A 0M0
Tel: 306-896-2240; *Fax:* 306-896-2910
churchbridge@sasktel.net
www.churchbridge.com
Municipal Type: Town
Incorporated: Sept. 17, 1903; *Area:* 2.76 sq km
Population in 2016: 896
Provincial Electoral District(s): Melville-Saltcoats
Federal Electoral District(s): Yorkton-Melville
Next Election: 2022/2024
Note: Proclaimed as a town on March 1, 1964.
Jim Gallant, Mayor
Carla Kaeding, Administrator

Clavet
P.O. Box 68
9 Main St.
Clavet, SK S0K 0Y0
Tel: 306-933-2425; *Fax:* 306-933-1995
clavetvillage@sasktel.net
www.villageofclavet.com
Municipal Type: Village
Incorporated: Dec. 21, 1908; *Area:* 0.61 sq km
Population in 2016: 410
Provincial Electoral District(s): Humboldt
Federal Electoral District(s): Moose Jaw-Lake Centre-Lanigan
Next Election: 2022/2024
Spencer Beaulieu, Mayor
Bev Dovell, Administrator

Climax
P.O. Box 30
Climax, SK S0N 0N0
Tel: 306-293-2128; *Fax:* 306-293-2702
villageofclimax@sasktel.net
Municipal Type: Village
Incorporated: Dec. 11, 1923; *Area:* 1.00 sq km
Population in 2016: 195
Provincial Electoral District(s): Cypress Hills
Federal Electoral District(s): Cypress Hills-Grasslands
Next Election: 2022/2024
Nancy Kirk, Mayor
Shawna Bertram, Administrator

Cochin
P.O. Box 160
Cochin, SK S0M 0L0
Tel: 306-386-2333; *Fax:* 306-386-2305
cochinadmin@sasktel.net
www.cochin.ca
Municipal Type: Resort Village
Incorporated: 1915; *Area:* 1.35 sq km
Population in 2016: 118
Provincial Electoral District(s): Cut Knife-Turtleford

Federal Electoral District(s): Battlefords-Lloydminster
Next Election: 2022/2024
Harvey Walker, Mayor
Linda Sandwick, Administrator

Coderre
P.O. Box 9
Coderre, SK S0H 0X0
Tel: 306-394-2070
vil.of.coderre@sasktel.net
Municipal Type: Village
Incorporated: Aug. 26, 1925; Area: 0.85 sq km
Population in 2016: 30
Provincial Electoral District(s): Wood River
Federal Electoral District(s): Cypress Hills-Grasslands
Next Election: 2022/2024
Leonard Lepine, Mayor
Patti Verville, Administrator

Codette
P.O. Box 100
Codette, SK S0E 0P0
Tel: 306-862-9551; Fax: 306-862-2432
villageofcodette@sasktel.net
www.codette.ca
Municipal Type: Village
Incorporated: March 9, 1929; Area: 0.37 sq km
Population in 2016: 198
Provincial Electoral District(s): Carrot River Valley
Federal Electoral District(s): Prince Albert
Next Election: 2022/2024
Kevin Hess, Mayor, 306-862-8781
Eunice Rudy, Administrator, 306-862-9551

Cole Bay
P.O. Box 80
Canoe Rd.
Cole Bay, SK S0M 0M0
Tel: 306-829-4232; Fax: 306-829-4312
Municipal Type: Northern Village
Incorporated: Jan. 1, 1990; Area: 4.95 sq km
Population in 2016: 170
Provincial Electoral District(s): Athabasca
Federal Electoral District(s): Desnethé-Missinippi-Churchill River
Next Election: 2022/2024
Harold Aubichon, Mayor
Delphine Bouvier, Clerk

Coleville
P.O. Box 249
Coleville, SK S0L 0K0
Tel: 306-965-2281; Fax: 306-965-2466
rm320@sasktel.net
www.colevillesk.ca
Other Information: Alt. E-mail: rmoakassist@sasktel.net
Municipal Type: Village
Incorporated: July 1, 1953; Area: 1.27 sq km
Population in 2016: 305
Provincial Electoral District(s): Kindersley
Federal Electoral District(s): Battlefords-Lloydminster
Next Election: 2022/2024
Darwin Whitfield, Mayor
Gillian Lund, Administrator

Colonsay
P.O. Box 190
100 Jura St.
Colonsay, SK S0K 0Z0
Tel: 306-255-2313; Fax: 306-255-2291
town.colonsay@sasktel.net
www.townofcolonsay.ca
Municipal Type: Town
Incorporated: Oct. 6, 1910; Area: 2.46 sq km
Population in 2016: 451
Provincial Electoral District(s): Humboldt
Federal Electoral District(s): Moose Jaw-Lake Centre-Lanigan
Next Election: 2022/2024
Note: Proclaimed as a town on Jan. 1, 1977.
James Gray, Mayor
Maureen Moen, Administrator

Conquest
P.O. Box 250
202 Coulthard St.
Conquest, SK S0L 0L0
Tel: 306-856-2114; Fax: 306-856-2114
conquest@sasktel.net
Municipal Type: Village
Incorporated: Oct. 24, 1911; Area: 1 sq km
Population in 2016: 160
Provincial Electoral District(s): Rosetown-Elrose

Federal Electoral District(s): Carlton Trail-Eagle Creek
Next Election: 2022/2024
Marc Norris, Mayor
Bobbi Jones, Administrator

Consul
P.O. Box 185
Consul, SK S0N 0P0
Tel: 306-299-2030; Fax: 306-299-2031
consul@sasktel.net
Municipal Type: Village
Incorporated: June 12, 1917; Area: 0.65 sq km
Population in 2016: 73
Provincial Electoral District(s): Cypress Hills
Federal Electoral District(s): Cypress Hills-Grasslands
Next Election: 2022/2024
Linda Brown, Mayor
Yvonne Leismeister, Administrator

Coronach
P.O. Box 90
Coronach, SK S0H 0Z0
Tel: 306-267-2150; Fax: 306-267-2296
townoffice@coronach.ca
www.coronach.ca
Municipal Type: Town
Incorporated: Feb. 3, 1928; Area: 2.33 sq km
Population in 2016: 643
Provincial Electoral District(s): Weyburn-Big Muddy
Federal Electoral District(s): Souris-Moose Mountain
Next Election: 2022/2024
Note: Proclaimed as a town on Jan. 1, 1977.
Trevor Schnell, Mayor
Catherine MacKay-Wilson, Administrator

Coteau Beach
219 Greaves Ct.
Saskatoon, SK S7W 1A8
Tel: 306-649-2440
coteaubeach@sasktel.net
www.resortvillageofcoteau.ca
Municipal Type: Resort Village
Incorporated: 1969; Area: 0.54 sq km
Population in 2016: 48
Provincial Electoral District(s): Rosetown-Elrose
Federal Electoral District(s): Cypress Hills-Grasslands
Next Election: 2022/2024
Jeff Sopczak, Mayor
Trudy Eggleston, Clerk, 306-649-2440

Craik
P.O. Box 60
Craik, SK S0G 0V0
Tel: 306-734-2250; Fax: 306-734-2688
townofcraik@craik.ca
www.craik.ca
Municipal Type: Town
Incorporated: Oct. 22, 1903; Area: 5.41 sq km
Population in 2016: 392
Provincial Electoral District(s): Thunder Creek
Federal Electoral District(s): Moose Jaw-Lake Centre-Lanigan
Next Election: 2022/2024
Note: Proclaimed as a town on Aug. 1, 1907.
David Ashdown, Mayor
Sarah Wells, Administrator

Craven
P.O. Box 30
Craven, SK S0G 0W0
Tel: 306-731-3452; Fax: 306-731-3162
villageofcraven@sasktel.net
www.villageofcraven.com
Municipal Type: Village
Incorporated: April 11, 1905; Area: 1.16 sq km
Population in 2016: 214
Provincial Electoral District(s): Last Mountain-Touchwood
Federal Electoral District(s): Moose Jaw-Lake Centre-Lanigan
Next Election: 2022/2024
Adri Vandeven, Mayor
Wendy Dunn, Administrator

Creelman
P.O. Box 177
Creelman, SK S0G 0X0
Tel: 306-433-2011; Fax: 306-433-2011
creelmanvillage@sasktel.net
Municipal Type: Village
Incorporated: April 6, 1906; Area: 1.14 sq km
Population in 2016: 113
Provincial Electoral District(s): Cannington
Federal Electoral District(s): Souris-Moose Mountain
Next Election: 2022/2024

Gordon Kolish, Mayor
Vernna Wiggins, Administrator

Creighton
P.O. Box 100
300 - 1st St. East
Creighton, SK S0P 0A0
Tel: 306-688-8253; Fax: 306-688-4764
townofcreighton@sasktel.net
www.townofcreighton.ca
Municipal Type: Northern Town
Incorporated: Oct. 1, 1983; Area: 14.39 sq km
Population in 2016: 1,402
Provincial Electoral District(s): Cumberland
Federal Electoral District(s): Desnethé-Missinippi-Churchill River
Next Election: 2022/2024
Bruce Fidler, Mayor
Paula Muench, Administrator

Cudworth
P.O. Box 69
223 Main St.
Cudworth, SK S0K 1B0
Tel: 306-256-3492; Fax: 306-256-3515
town.cudworth@sasktel.net
www.townofcudworth.com
Municipal Type: Town
Incorporated: Oct. 23, 1911; Area: 2.21 sq km
Population in 2016: 814
Provincial Electoral District(s): Batoche
Federal Electoral District(s): Carlton Trail-Eagle Creek
Next Election: 2022/2024
Note: Proclaimed as a town on Oct. 1, 1961.
Harold Mueller, Mayor
Yvonne Gobolos, Administrator

Cumberland House
P.O. Box 190
Cumberland St.
Cumberland House, SK S0E 0S0
Tel: 306-888-2066; Fax: 306-888-2103
northernvillageofchouse@sasktel.net
Municipal Type: Northern Village
Incorporated: Oct. 1, 1983; Area: 15.69 sq km
Population in 2016: 671
Provincial Electoral District(s): Cumberland
Federal Electoral District(s): Desnethé-Missinippi-Churchill River
Next Election: 2022/2024
Kelvin McKay, Mayor
Marcie Fiddler, Clerk
Jacqueline Fleury, Administrator

Cupar
P.O. Box 397
Cupar, SK S0G 0Y0
Tel: 306-723-4324; Fax: 306-723-4644
townofcupar1@sasktel.net
www.townofcupar.com
Municipal Type: Town
Incorporated: March 21, 1906; Area: 0.80 sq km
Population in 2016: 564
Provincial Electoral District(s): Last Mountain-Touchwood
Federal Electoral District(s): Regina-Qu'Appelle
Next Election: 2022/2024
Note: Proclaimed as a town on Jan. 1, 1961.
Steve Boha, Mayor
Karen Herman, Administrator

Cut Knife
P.O. Box 70
Cut Knife, SK S0M 0N0
Tel: 306-398-2363; Fax: 306-398-2839
webmaster@townofcutknife.ca
www.townofcutknife.ca
Municipal Type: Town
Incorporated: May 17, 1912; Area: 1.99 sq km
Population in 2016: 573
Provincial Electoral District(s): Cut Knife-Turtleford
Federal Electoral District(s): Battlefords-Lloydminster
Next Election: 2022/2024
Note: Proclaimed as a town on Aug. 1, 1968.
Gwenn Kaye, Mayor
Tammy Martin, Administrator

Dafoe
P.O. Box 142
Dafoe, SK S0K 1C0
Tel: 306-554-3250
Municipal Type: Village
Incorporated: May 28, 1920; Area: 0.80 sq km
Population in 2016: 15
Provincial Electoral District(s): Rosetown-Elrose

Federal Electoral District(s): Regina-Qu'Appelle
Next Election: 2022/2024
Bob Pilkey, Mayor
Lana M. Bolt, Clerk

Dalmeny
P.O. Box 400
301 Railway Ave.
Dalmeny, SK S0K 1E0
Tel: 306-254-2133; Fax: 306-254-2142
dalmenytownoffice@sasktel.net
www.dalmeny.ca
Municipal Type: Town
Incorporated: June 17, 1912; Area: 2.27 sq km
Population in 2016: 1,826
Provincial Electoral District(s): Weyburn-Big Muddy
Federal Electoral District(s): Carlton Trail-Eagle Creek
Next Election: 2022/2024
Note: Proclaimed as a town on April 1, 1983.
Jon Kroeker, Mayor
Jim Weninger, Administrator

Davidson
P.O. Box 340
206 Washington Ave.
Davidson, SK S0G 1A0
Tel: 306-567-2040; Fax: 306-567-4730
townofdavidson@sasktel.net
www.townofdavidson.com
Municipal Type: Town
Incorporated: March 7, 1904; Area: 4.49 sq km
Population in 2016: 1,048
Provincial Electoral District(s): Arm River-Watrous
Federal Electoral District(s): Moose Jaw-Lake Centre-Lanigan
Next Election: 2022/2024
Note: Proclaimed as a town on Nov. 15, 1906.
Clayton Schneider, Mayor
Gary Edom, Administrator

Debden
P.O. Box 400
204 - 2nd Ave. East
Debden, SK S0J 0S0
Tel: 306-724-2040; Fax: 306-724-4458
villagedebden@sasktel.net
www.debden.net
Municipal Type: Village
Incorporated: June 7, 1922; Area: 1.39 sq km
Population in 2016: 337
Provincial Electoral District(s): Saskatchewan Rivers
Federal Electoral District(s): Desnethé-Missinippi-Churchill River
Next Election: 2022/2024
Rod Fisher, Mayor
Tamara Couture, Administrator

Delisle
P.O. Box 40
201 - 1st St. West
Delisle, SK S0L 0P0
Tel: 306-493-2242; Fax: 306-493-2263
delisle@sasktel.net
www.townofdelisle.com
Municipal Type: Town
Incorporated: Dec. 29, 1908; Area: 2.35 sq km
Population in 2016: 1,038
Provincial Electoral District(s): Biggar
Federal Electoral District(s): Carlton Trail-Eagle Creek
Next Election: 2022/2024
Note: Proclaimed as a town on Nov. 1, 1913.
Dave Anderchek, Mayor, 306-493-2258
Mark Dubkowski, Administrator

Denare Beach
P.O. Box 70
512 - 7th Ave.
Denare Beach, SK S0P 0B0
Tel: 306-362-2054; Fax: 306-362-2257
denarebeach@aski.ca
www.denarebeach.net
Municipal Type: Northern Village
Incorporated: April 1, 1984; Area: 5.84 sq km
Population in 2016: 779
Provincial Electoral District(s): Cumberland
Federal Electoral District(s): Desnethé-Missinippi-Churchill River
Next Election: 2022/2024
Carl Lentowicz, Mayor
Meredith Norman, Administrator

Denholm
P.O. Box 71
Denholm, SK S0M 0R0
Tel: 306-446-0478

Municipal Type: Village
Incorporated: June 25, 1912; Area: 0.33 sq km
Population in 2016: 88
Provincial Electoral District(s): Biggar
Federal Electoral District(s): Battlefords-Lloydminster
Next Election: 2022/2024
Donna Oborowsky, Mayor
Lila Yuhasz, Clerk

Denzil
P.O. Box 100
Denzil, SK S0L 0S0
Tel: 306-358-2118; Fax: 306-358-4828
villageofdenzil@sasktel.net
www.villageofdenzil.com
Municipal Type: Village
Incorporated: May 3, 1911; Area: 0.55 sq km
Population in 2016: 143
Provincial Electoral District(s): Kindersley
Federal Electoral District(s): Battlefords-Lloydminster
Next Election: 2022/2024
Murray Sieben, Mayor
Kathy Reschny, Administrator

Descharme Lake
c/o Government Relations
P.O. Box 69
Buffalo Narrows, SK S0M 0J0
Tel: 306-235-1726; Fax: 306-235-1727
Municipal Type: NS
Population in 2016: 5
Provincial Electoral District(s): Athabasca
Federal Electoral District(s): Desnethé-Missinippi-Churchill River
Next Election: 2022/2024
John Frank Sylvestre, Chair
Bruce Leier, Advisor

Dilke
P.O. Box 100
Devon St.
Dilke, SK S0G 1C0
Tel: 306-488-4866; Fax: 306-488-4866
dilke@canwan.com
Municipal Type: Village
Incorporated: Dec. 30, 1912; Area: 1.28 sq km
Population in 2016: 98
Provincial Electoral District(s): Thunder Creek
Federal Electoral District(s): Moose Jaw-Lake Centre-Lanigan
Next Election: 2022/2024
Arnold Ball, Mayor
Colleen R. Duesing, Clerk

Dinsmore
P.O. Box 278
100 Main St.
Dinsmore, SK S0L 0T0
Tel: 306-846-2220; Fax: 306-846-2999
dinsmore@sasktel.net
www.dinsmore.ca
Municipal Type: Village
Incorporated: Nov. 3, 1913; Area: 2.59 sq km
Population in 2016: 289
Provincial Electoral District(s): Rosetown-Elrose
Federal Electoral District(s): Carlton Trail-Eagle Creek
Next Election: 2022/2024
Jim Main, Mayor, 306-846-2248
Kirsten Raffos, Administrator

Disley
R.R.#1
Lumsden, SK S0G 3C0
Tel: 306-731-3355
villageofdisley@gmail.com
Municipal Type: Village
Incorporated: June 24, 1907; Area: 0.65 sq km
Population in 2016: 67
Provincial Electoral District(s): Thunder Creek
Federal Electoral District(s): Moose Jaw-Lake Centre-Lanigan
Next Election: 2022/2024
Gord Wilson, Mayor
Rhonda Woelk, Administrator

Dodsland
P.O. Box 400
Dodsland, SK S0L 0V0
Tel: 306-356-0011; Fax: 306-356-0012
villageofdodsland@yourlink.ca
Municipal Type: Village
Incorporated: Aug. 23, 1913; Area: 2.93 sq km
Population in 2016: 215
Provincial Electoral District(s): Rosetown-Elrose

Federal Electoral District(s): Battlefords-Lloydminster
Next Election: 2022/2024
Joey Straza, Mayor
Amy Sittler, Administrator

Dore Lake
P.O. Box 608
Dore Ave.
Big River, SK S0J 0E0
Tel: 306-832-4528; Fax: 306-832-4525
northern.dore@sasktel.net
Municipal Type: Northern Hamlet
Incorporated: Jan. 11, 1985; Area: 8.03 sq km
Population in 2016: 30
Provincial Electoral District(s): Athabasca
Federal Electoral District(s): Desnethé-Missinippi-Churchill River
Next Election: 2022/2024
Bobby Buffin, Mayor
Hilda McKay, Administrator

Dorintosh
P.O. Box 40
301 1st St. East
Dorintosh, SK S0M 0T0
Tel: 306-236-5166
vill.dor@sasktel.net
Municipal Type: Village
Incorporated: Jan. 1, 1989; Area: 143.7 sq km
Population in 2016: 134
Provincial Electoral District(s): Meadow Lake
Federal Electoral District(s): Desnethé-Missinippi-Churchill River
Next Election: 2022/2024
Derek Osborne, Mayor
Nicole Neufeld, Administrator

Drake
P.O. Box 18
125 Francis St.
Drake, SK S0K 1H0
Tel: 306-363-2109; Fax: 306-363-2102
villageofdrake@sasktel.net
www.drake.ca
Municipal Type: Village
Incorporated: Sept. 19, 1910; Area: 0.72 sq km
Population in 2016: 197
Provincial Electoral District(s): Arm River-Watrous
Federal Electoral District(s): Moose Jaw-Lake Centre-Lanigan
Next Election: 2022/2024
Peter Nicholson, Mayor, 306-363-2021
Stuart Jantz, Administrator, 306-363-2109

Drinkwater
P.O. Box 66
Drinkwater, SK S0H 1G0
Tel: 306-693-5093; Fax: 306-693-4410
villageofdrinkwater@sasktel.net
Municipal Type: Village
Incorporated: June 7, 1904; Area: 2.64 sq km
Population in 2016: 70
Provincial Electoral District(s): Indian Head-Milestone
Federal Electoral District(s): Moose Jaw-Lake Centre-Lanigan
Next Election: 2022/2024
Ryan Briggs, Mayor
Colleen Loos, Clerk

Dubuc
P.O. Box 126
Dubuc, SK S0A 0R0
Tel: 306-877-2172; Fax: 306-877-0044
villageofdubuc@sasktel.net
Municipal Type: Village
Incorporated: May 29, 1905; Area: 0.63 sq km
Population in 2016: 61
Provincial Electoral District(s): Melville-Saltcoats
Federal Electoral District(s): Yorkton-Melville
Next Election: 2022/2024
Peter Nielsen, Mayor
Janet Siever, Clerk

Duck Lake
P.O. Box 430
Duck Lake, SK S0K 1J0
Tel: 306-467-2277; Fax: 306-467-4434
town.ducklake@sasktel.net
www.ducklake.ca
Municipal Type: Town
Incorporated: Dec. 29, 1898; Area: 2.86 sq km
Population in 2016: 569
Provincial Electoral District(s): Batoche
Federal Electoral District(s): Carlton Trail-Eagle Creek
Next Election: 2022/2024
Note: Proclaimed as a town on Nov. 1, 1911.

Gainsborough
P.O. Box 120
Gainsborough, SK S0C 0Z0
Tel: 306-685-2010; Fax: 306-685-2161
rm.1@sasktel.net
Municipal Type: Village
Incorporated: May 25, 1894; *Area:* 1.95 km
Population in 2016: 254
Provincial Electoral District(s): Cannington
Federal Electoral District(s): Souris-Moose Mountain
Next Election: 2022/2024
Victor Huish, Mayor
Erin McMillen, Administrator

Garson Lake
c/o Government Relations
P.O. Box 69
Buffalo Narrows, SK S0M 0J0
Tel: 403-799-8556; Fax: 306-235-1727
Municipal Type: NS
Population in 2016: 10
Provincial Electoral District(s): Athabasca
Federal Electoral District(s): Desnethé-Missinippi-Churchill River
Next Election: 2022/2024
Dora Laprise, Chair
Bruce Leier, Advisor

Gerald
P.O. Box 155
Gerald, SK S0A 1B0
Tel: 306-745-6786; Fax: 306-745-6590
vofger@sasktel.net
Municipal Type: Village
Incorporated: March 25, 1953; *Area:* 0.80 sq km
Population in 2016: 136
Provincial Electoral District(s): Melville-Saltcoats
Federal Electoral District(s): Yorkton-Melville
Next Election: 2022/2024
Trevor Rieger, Mayor
Susan Gawryluk, Administrator

Gladmar
P.O. Box 8
Gladmar, SK S0C 1A0
Tel: 306-869-2212
Municipal Type: Village
Incorporated: Feb. 15, 1968; *Area:* 0.55 sq km
Population in 2016: 57
Provincial Electoral District(s): Weyburn-Big Muddy
Federal Electoral District(s): Souris-Moose Mountain
Next Election: 2022/2024

Glaslyn
P.O. Box 279
172 Main St.
Glaslyn, SK S0M 0Y0
Tel: 306-342-2144; Fax: 306-342-2135
villageofglaslyn@sasktel.net
glaslyn.ca
Municipal Type: Village
Incorporated: April 16, 1929; *Area:* 1.97 sq km
Population in 2016: 387
Provincial Electoral District(s): Cut Knife-Turtleford
Federal Electoral District(s): Battlefords-Lloydminster
Next Election: 2022/2024
Ken Morrison, Mayor
Kate Clarke, Administrator

Glen Ewen
P.O. Box 99
Glen Ewen, SK S0C 1C0
Tel: 306-925-2211; Fax: 306-925-2210
office@villageofglenewen.com
www.villageofglenewen.com
Municipal Type: Village
Incorporated: March 24, 1904; *Area:* 2.77 sq km
Population in 2016: 154
Provincial Electoral District(s): Cannington
Federal Electoral District(s): Souris-Moose Mountain
Next Election: 2022/2024
Glen Lewis, Mayor
Myrna-Jean Babbings, Administrator

Glen Harbour
P.O. Box 280
212 Main St.
Nokomis, SK S0G 3R0
Tel: 306-545-5170; Fax: 306-528-2083
rvglenharbour@sasktel.net
www.resortvillageofglenharbour.ca
Municipal Type: Resort Village
Area: 0.35 sq km

Population in 2016: 67
Provincial Electoral District(s): Last Mountain-Touchwood
Federal Electoral District(s): Moose Jaw-Lake Centre-Lanigan
Next Election: 2022/2024
Tim Selinger, Mayor
Kevin Kleckner, Administrator

Glenavon
104 Main St.
Glenavon, SK S0G 1Y0
Tel: 306-429-2110; Fax: 306-429-2260
rmchester125@sasktel.net
Municipal Type: Village
Incorporated: April 13, 1910; *Area:* 1.32 sq km
Population in 2016: 182
Provincial Electoral District(s): Moosomin
Federal Electoral District(s): Souris-Moose Mountain
Next Election: 2022/2024
Blair Arnott, Mayor
James Hoff, Administrator

Glenside
P.O. Box 99
Glenside, SK S0H 1T0
Tel: 306-867-8932
villageofglenside@xplornet.com
Municipal Type: Village
Incorporated: March 30, 1911; *Area:* 0.77 sq km
Population in 2016: 76
Provincial Electoral District(s): Rosetown-Elrose
Federal Electoral District(s): Moose Jaw-Lake Centre-Lanigan
Next Election: 2022/2024
Kerry Greig, Mayor
Shannon Pederson, Clerk

Golden Prairie
P.O. Box 9
Golden Prairie, SK S0N 0Y0
Tel: 306-662-2883; Fax: 306-662-3954
rm141@sasktel.net
Municipal Type: Village
Incorporated: April 15, 1942; *Area:* 0.41 sq km
Population in 2016: 30
Provincial Electoral District(s): Cypress Hills
Federal Electoral District(s): Cypress Hills-Grasslands
Next Election: 2022/2024
Delmar Beck, Mayor
Melinda Hammer, Administrator

Goodeve
P.O. Box 160
Main St.
Goodeve, SK S0A 1C0
Tel: 306-876-4633
villageofgoodeve@sasktel.net
Municipal Type: Village
Incorporated: Aug. 18, 1910; *Area:* 2.62 sq km
Population in 2016: 40
Provincial Electoral District(s): Last Mountain-Touchwood
Federal Electoral District(s): Yorkton-Melville
Next Election: 2022/2024
Craig Sawchuk, Mayor
Angela Romanson, Administrator

Goodsoil
P.O. Box 176
Goodsoil, SK S0M 1A0
Tel: 306-238-2094; Fax: 306-238-2098
villageofgoodsoil@sasktel.net
www.villageofgoodsoil.com
Municipal Type: Village
Incorporated: Jan. 1, 1960; *Area:* 1.76 sq km
Population in 2016: 282
Provincial Electoral District(s): Meadow Lake
Federal Electoral District(s): Desnethé-Missinippi-Churchill River
Next Election: 2022/2024
John Purves, Mayor
Fred Puffer, Administrator

Goodwater
P.O. Box 280
Weyburn, SK S4H 2K1
Tel: 306-456-2566; Fax: 306-456-2440
rm37@sasktel.net
Municipal Type: Village
Incorporated: May 8, 1911; *Area:* 0.59 sq km
Population in 2016: 30
Provincial Electoral District(s): Estevan
Federal Electoral District(s): Souris-Moose Mountain
Next Election: 2022/2024
Greg Collins, Mayor
Kevin Melle, Administrator

Govan
P.O. Box 160
Main St.
Govan, SK S0G 1Z0
Tel: 306-484-2011
govan@sasktel.net
Municipal Type: Town
Incorporated: Aug. 21, 1907; *Area:* 1.35 sq km
Population in 2016: 194
Provincial Electoral District(s): Arm River-Watrous
Federal Electoral District(s): Moose Jaw-Lake Centre-Lanigan
Next Election: 2022/2024
Note: Proclaimed as a town on Nov. 1, 1911.
Del Skoropata, Mayor
Kelly Holbrook, Administrator

Grand Coulee
P.O. Box 72
GBS 200, RR#2
Regina, SK S4P 2Z2
Tel: 306-352-8694; Fax: 306-352-6659
grandcoulee.cap@sasktel.net
www.grandcoulee.ca
Municipal Type: Village
Incorporated: April 10, 1908; *Area:* 1.75 sq km
Population in 2016: 649
Provincial Electoral District(s): Regina Qu'Appelle Valley
Federal Electoral District(s): Moose Jaw-Lake Centre-Lanigan
Next Election: 2022/2024
Walter Botkin, Mayor
Tobi Duck, Administrator

Grandview Beach
3111 Kanuka Pl.
Regina, SK S4V 2C6
Tel: 306-789-6040
grandview@sasktel.net
Municipal Type: Resort Village
Area: 0.25 sq km
Population in 2016: 35
Provincial Electoral District(s): Thunder Creek
Federal Electoral District(s): Moose Jaw-Lake Centre-Lanigan
Next Election: 2022/2024
Jake Hutton, Mayor
Gail Meyer, Administrator

Gravelbourg
P.O. Box 359
209 Main St.
Gravelbourg, SK S0H 1X0
Tel: 306-648-3301; Fax: 306-648-3400
www.gravelbourg.ca
Municipal Type: Town
Incorporated: Dec. 30, 1912; *Area:* 3.23 sq km
Population in 2016: 1,083
Provincial Electoral District(s): Wood River
Federal Electoral District(s): Cypress Hills-Grasslands
Next Election: 2022/2024
Note: Proclaimed as a town on Nov. 1, 1916.
Dan Lamarre, Mayor
Ward P. Minifie, Chief Administrative Officer

Grayson
P.O. Box 9
Grayson, SK S0A 1E0
Tel: 306-794-2011
villageofgrayson@sasktel.net
Municipal Type: Village
Incorporated: April 19, 1906; *Area:* 1.47 sq km
Population in 2016: 211
Provincial Electoral District(s): Melville-Saltcoats
Federal Electoral District(s): Yorkton-Melville
Next Election: 2022/2024
Tyson Lowenberg, Mayor
Colleen Stinson, Administrator

Green Lake
P.O. Box 128
Green Lake, SK S0M 1B0
Tel: 306-832-2131; Fax: 306-832-2124
green.lake@sasktel.net
www.nvgreenlake.ca
Municipal Type: Northern Village
Incorporated: Oct. 1, 1983; *Area:* 121.92 sq km
Population in 2016: 429
Provincial Electoral District(s): Athabasca
Federal Electoral District(s): Desnethé-Missinippi-Churchill River
Next Election: 2022/2024
Rod Wolfe, Mayor, 306-832-2224
Tina Rasmussen, Administrator

Greig Lake
P.O. Box 334
Elrose, SK S0L 0Z0
Tel: 306-378-2351; *Fax:* 306-378-2338
Municipal Type: Resort Village
Area: 0.14 sq km
Population in 2016: 10
Provincial Electoral District(s): Meadow Lake
Federal Electoral District(s): Desnethé-Missinippi-Churchill River
Next Election: 2022/2024
Dale Brander, Mayor
Joan Tatomir, Administrator

Grenfell
P.O. Box 1120
800 Desmond St.
Grenfell, SK S0G 2B0
Tel: 306-697-2815; *Fax:* 306-697-2484
townofgrenfell@sasktel.net
www.grenfell.com
Municipal Type: Town
Incorporated: April 12, 1894; *Area:* 3.17 sq km
Population in 2016: 1,099
Provincial Electoral District(s): Moosomin
Federal Electoral District(s): Souris-Moose Mountain
Next Election: 2022/2024
Note: Proclaimed as a town on Nov. 1, 1911.
Lloyd Gwilliam, Mayor
Nicole Monchamp, Administrator

Gull Lake
P.O. Box 150
2378 Proton Ave.
Gull Lake, SK S0N 1A0
Tel: 306-672-3361; *Fax:* 306-672-3777
gulllaketown@sasktel.net
www.gulllakesk.ca
Municipal Type: Town
Incorporated: Jan. 12, 1909; *Area:* 2.5 sq km
Population in 2016: 1,046
Provincial Electoral District(s): Cypress Hills
Federal Electoral District(s): Cypress Hills-Grasslands
Next Election: 2022/2024
Note: Proclaimed as a town on Nov. 1, 1911.
Blake Campbell, Mayor
Dawnette Peterson, Administrator

Hafford
P.O. Box 220
Hafford, SK S0J 1A0
Tel: 306-549-2331; *Fax:* 306-549-2338
town.administrator@hafford.ca
www.hafford.ca
Municipal Type: Town
Incorporated: Dec. 16, 1913; *Area:* 0.80 sq km
Population in 2016: 407
Provincial Electoral District(s): Rosthern-Shellbrook
Federal Electoral District(s): Carlton Trail-Eagle Creek
Next Election: 2022/2024
Note: Proclaimed as a town on Jan. 1, 1981.
Ron Kowalchuk, Mayor
John Sawyshyn, Administrator

Hague
P.O. Box 180
206 Main St.
Hague, SK S0K 1X0
Tel: 306-225-2155; *Fax:* 306-225-4410
town.hague@sasktel.net
www.townofhague.com
Municipal Type: Town
Incorporated: Aug. 25, 1903; *Area:* 1.03 sq km
Population in 2016: 874
Provincial Electoral District(s): Martensville
Federal Electoral District(s): Carlton Trail-Eagle Creek
Next Election: 2022/2024
Note: Proclaimed as a town on Nov. 1, 1991.
Patricia Wagner, Mayor
Deanna Braun, Chief Administrative Officer

Halbrite
P.O. Box 10
Halbrite, SK S0C 1H0
Tel: 306-891-9990; *Fax:* 306-458-2657
halbrite@sasktel.net
Municipal Type: Village
Incorporated: Feb. 26, 1904; *Area:* 1.20 sq km
Population in 2016: 119
Provincial Electoral District(s): Estevan
Federal Electoral District(s): Souris-Moose Mountain
Next Election: 2022/2024
Dwayne Carlson, Mayor

Lloyd Muma, Administrator

Hanley
P.O. Box 270
Hanley, SK S0G 2E0
Tel: 306-544-2223; *Fax:* 306-544-2261
townoffice@townofhanley.ca
www.townofhanley.ca
Municipal Type: Town
Incorporated: April 27, 1905; *Area:* 2.65 sq km
Population in 2016: 511
Provincial Electoral District(s): Arm River-Watrous
Federal Electoral District(s): Moose Jaw-Lake Centre-Lanigan
Next Election: 2022/2024
Note: Proclaimed as a town on Dec. 1, 1906.
Marvin Gerbrandt, Mayor, 306-544-2802
Darice Carlson, Administrator

Harris
P.O. Box 124
Harris, SK S0L 1K0
Tel: 306-656-2122; *Fax:* 306-656-2123
villageofharris@sasktel.net
harris.ca
Municipal Type: Village
Incorporated: Aug. 10, 1909; *Area:* 0.72 sq km
Population in 2016: 193
Provincial Electoral District(s): Rosetown-Elrose
Federal Electoral District(s): Carlton Trail-Eagle Creek
Next Election: 2022/2024
Ron Genest, Mayor
Rhonda Leonard, Clerk

Hawarden
P.O. Box 7
Hawarden, SK S0H 1Y0
Tel: 306-855-2020
villageofhawarden@xplornet.com
Municipal Type: Village
Incorporated: July 16, 1909; *Area:* 1.24 sq km
Population in 2016: 52
Provincial Electoral District(s): Arm River-Watrous
Federal Electoral District(s): Moose Jaw-Lake Centre-Lanigan
Next Election: 2022/2024
Charley S. Edwards, Mayor
Barabara J. Martin, Clerk

Hazenmore
P.O. Box 36
Hazenmore, SK S0N 1C0
Tel: 306-264-3218
villageofhazenmore@hotmail.com
Municipal Type: Village
Incorporated: Aug. 20, 1913; *Area:* 0.80 sq km
Population in 2016: 70
Provincial Electoral District(s): Wood River
Federal Electoral District(s): Cypress Hills-Grasslands
Next Election: 2022/2024
Gary Loverin, Mayor
Barb Switzer, Administrator

Hazlet
P.O. Box 150
Hazlet, SK S0N 1E0
Tel: 306-678-2131; *Fax:* 306-678-2132
hazlet@sasktel.net
hazletsk.ca
Municipal Type: Village
Incorporated: Jan. 1, 1963; *Area:* 0.55 sq km
Population in 2016: 106
Provincial Electoral District(s): Cypress Hills
Federal Electoral District(s): Cypress Hills-Grasslands
Next Election: 2022/2024
Terry Bailey, Mayor
Terry Erdelyan, Administrator

Hepburn
P.O. Box 217
311 Main St.
Hepburn, SK S0K 1Z0
Tel: 306-947-2170; *Fax:* 306-947-4202
info@hepburn.ca
hepburn.ca
Municipal Type: Village
Incorporated: July 5, 1919; *Area:* 1.02 sq km
Population in 2016: 688
Provincial Electoral District(s): Martensville
Federal Electoral District(s): Carlton Trail-Eagle Creek
Next Election: 2022/2024
Jeff Peters, Mayor
Brad Wiebe, Administrator

Herbert
P.O. Box 370
503 Herbert Ave.
Herbert, SK S0H 2A0
Tel: 306-784-2400; *Fax:* 306-784-2402
t.o.herbert@sasktel.net
www.townofherbert.com
Municipal Type: Town
Incorporated: June 11, 1907; *Area:* 3.78 sq km
Population in 2016: 856
Provincial Electoral District(s): Thunder Creek
Federal Electoral District(s): Cypress Hills-Grasslands
Next Election: 2022/2024
Note: Proclaimed as a town on Nov. 1, 1912.
Ron Mathies, Mayor
Michelle Mackow, Administrator

Heward
P.O. Box 10
Heward, SK S0G 2G0
Tel: 306-457-2707; *Fax:* 306-457-2888
heward@sasktel.net
Municipal Type: Village
Incorporated: Nov. 21, 1904; *Area:* 0.99 sq km
Population in 2016: 44
Provincial Electoral District(s): Cannington
Federal Electoral District(s): Souris-Moose Mountain
Next Election: 2022/2024
Doug Trowell, Mayor
Zandra Slater, Clerk

Hodgeville
P.O. Box 307
Hodgeville, SK S0H 2B0
Tel: 306-677-2223; *Fax:* 306-677-2466
villageofhodgeville@sasktel.net
Municipal Type: Village
Incorporated: June 22, 1921; *Area:* 1.35 sq km
Population in 2016: 172
Provincial Electoral District(s): Wood River
Federal Electoral District(s): Cypress Hills-Grasslands
Next Election: 2022/2024
Vacant, Mayor
Theresa Mokry, Clerk

Holdfast
P.O. Box 160
Roberts St.
Holdfast, SK S0G 2H0
Tel: 306-488-2000; *Fax:* 306-488-4609
rm.sarnia@sasktel.net
Municipal Type: Village
Incorporated: Oct. 5, 1911; *Area:* 1.29 sq km
Population in 2016: 247
Provincial Electoral District(s): Thunder Creek
Federal Electoral District(s): Moose Jaw-Lake Centre-Lanigan
Next Election: 2022/2024
Chris Thorson, Mayor
Patti Vance, Administrator

Hubbard
P.O. Box 190
Ituna, SK S0A 1N0
Tel: 306-795-2484
Municipal Type: Village
Incorporated: June 11, 1910; *Area:* 1.25 sq km
Population in 2016: 35
Provincial Electoral District(s): Last Mountain-Touchwood
Federal Electoral District(s): Regina-Qu'Appelle
Next Election: 2022/2024
Ron Rokosh, Mayor
Diane M. Olech, Administrator

Hudson Bay
P.O. Box 730
304 Main St.
Hudson Bay, SK S0E 0Y0
Tel: 306-865-2261; *Fax:* 306-865-2800
hudson.bay@sasktel.net
www.townofhudsonbay.com
Municipal Type: Town
Incorporated: Sept. 25, 1907; *Area:* 17.35 sq km
Population in 2016: 1,397
Provincial Electoral District(s): Carrot River Valley
Federal Electoral District(s): Yorkton-Melville
Next Election: 2022/2024
Note: Proclaimed as a town on Nov. 30, 1946.
Glen McCaffery, Mayor
Richard Dolezsar, Administrator

Humboldt

P.O. Box 640
715 Main St.
Humboldt, SK S0K 2A0
Tel: 306-682-2525; *Fax:* 306-682-3144
info@humboldt.ca
www.humboldt.ca
Municipal Type: Town
Incorporated: June 30, 1905; *Area:* 11.72 sq km
Population in 2016: 5,869
Provincial Electoral District(s): Humboldt
Federal Electoral District(s): Carlton Trail-Eagle Creek
Next Election: 2022/2024
Note: Incorporated as a city on Nov. 7, 2000.
Rob Muench, Mayor
Roy Hardy, City Manager, 306-682-2525

Hyas

P.O. Box 40
Hyas, SK S0A 1K0
Tel: 306-594-2817; *Fax:* 306-594-2944
hyas@sasktel.net
villageofhyas.com
Municipal Type: Village
Incorporated: May 23, 1919; *Area:* 1.17 sq km
Population in 2016: 70
Provincial Electoral District(s): Canora-Pelly
Federal Electoral District(s): Yorkton-Melville
Next Election: 2022/2024
Barry Bogucky, Mayor
Sabrina Chernyk, Administrator

Ile-à-la-Crosse

P.O. Box 280
Lajeunesse Ave.
Ile-à-la-Crosse, SK S0M 1C0
Tel: 306-833-2122; *Fax:* 306-833-2132
village.of.ilealacrosse@sasktel.net
www.sakitawak.ca
Municipal Type: Northern Village
Incorporated: Oct. 1, 1983; *Area:* 23.84 sq km
Population in 2016: 1,296
Provincial Electoral District(s): Athabasca
Federal Electoral District(s): Desnethé-Missinippi-Churchill River
Next Election: 2022/2024
Duane Favel, Mayor
Dianne McCallum, Administrator

Imperial

P.O. Box 90
Imperial, SK S0G 2J0
Tel: 306-963-2220; *Fax:* 306-963-2445
town.imperial@sasktel.net
www.imperial.ca
Municipal Type: Town
Incorporated: July 4, 1911; *Area:* 1.23 sq km
Population in 2016: 360
Provincial Electoral District(s): Arm River-Watrous
Federal Electoral District(s): Moose Jaw-Lake Centre-Lanigan
Next Election: 2022/2024
Note: Proclaimed as a town on April 1, 1962.
Edward Abrey, Mayor
Sheila Newlove, Administrator

Indian Head

P.O. Box 460
421 Grand Ave.
Indian Head, SK S0G 2K0
Tel: 306-695-3344
townofindianhead@sasktel.net
www.townofindianhead.com
Municipal Type: Town
Incorporated: April 19, 1902; *Area:* 3.17 sq km
Population in 2016: 1,910
Provincial Electoral District(s): Indian Head-Milestone
Federal Electoral District(s): Regina-Qu'Appelle
Next Election: 2022/2024
Sherry Karpa, Mayor
Cam Thauberger, Administrator

Invermay

P.O. Box 234
Invermay, SK S0A 1M0
Tel: 306-593-2242; *Fax:* 306-593-0004
villageofinvermay@sasktel.net
Municipal Type: Village
Incorporated: Sept. 1, 1908; *Area:* 1.22 sq km
Population in 2016: 273
Provincial Electoral District(s): Kelvington-Wadena
Federal Electoral District(s): Yorkton-Melville
Next Election: 2022/2024
Michael J. Kaminski, Mayor

Joyce M. Palagian, Clerk

Island View

Comp. 3, RR#1
Bulyea, SK S0G 0L0
Tel: 306-725-4521; *Fax:* 306-725-4863
islandview@canwan.com
www.resortvillageofislandview.ca
Municipal Type: Resort Village
Incorporated: 1959; *Area:* 0.43 sq km
Population in 2016: 74
Provincial Electoral District(s): Last Mountain-Touchwood
Federal Electoral District(s): Moose Jaw-Lake Centre-Lanigan
Next Election: 2022/2024
Wade Beattie, Mayor
Mae Stohl, Administrator

Ituna

P.O. Box 580
7 - 1st Ave. NE
Ituna, SK S0A 1N0
Tel: 306-795-2272; *Fax:* 306-795-3330
townofituna@sasktel.net
www.ituna.ca
Municipal Type: Town
Incorporated: May 30, 1910; *Area:* 1.56 sq km
Population in 2016: 701
Provincial Electoral District(s): Last Mountain-Touchwood
Federal Electoral District(s): Regina-Qu'Appelle
Next Election: 2022/2024
Note: Proclaimed as a town on Oct. 1, 1961.
Doug Scully, Mayor
Geri Kreway, Administrator

Jans Bay

Maurice Ave., General Delivery
Canoe Narrows, SK S0M 0K0
Tel: 306-829-4320; *Fax:* 306-829-4424
jansbay@sasktel.net
Municipal Type: Northern Hamlet
Incorporated: Oct. 1, 1983; *Area:* 5.94 sq km
Population in 2016: 152
Provincial Electoral District(s): Athabasca
Federal Electoral District(s): Desnethé-Missinippi-Churchill River
Next Election: 2022/2024
Tony Maurice, Mayor
Roxanne Gamble, Clerk

Jansen

P.O. Box 116
Jansen, SK S0K 2B0
Tel: 306-364-2013; *Fax:* 306-364-2088
jansen@jansen.ca
www.jansen.ca
Municipal Type: Village
Incorporated: Oct. 19, 1908; *Area:* 0.85 sq km
Population in 2016: 96
Provincial Electoral District(s): Arm River-Watrous
Federal Electoral District(s): Moose Jaw-Lake Centre-Lanigan
Next Election: 2022/2024
Albert Cardinal, Mayor, 306-364-2028
Joni Mack, Administrator, 306-364-2013

Kamsack

P.O. Box 729
161 Queen Elizabeth Blvd. West
Kamsack, SK S0A 1S0
Tel: 306-542-2155; *Fax:* 306-542-2975
www.kamsack.ca
Municipal Type: Town
Incorporated: March 14, 1905; *Area:* 5.85 sq km
Population in 2016: 1,898
Provincial Electoral District(s): Canora-Pelly
Federal Electoral District(s): Yorkton-Melville
Next Election: 2022/2024
Note: Proclaimed as a town on Nov. 1, 1911.
Nancy Brunt, Mayor
Laura Lomenda, Administrator, 306-542-3806, Fax: 306-542-2975

Kannata Valley

P.O. Box 166
101 Cowen Rd.
Silton, SK S0G 4L0
Tel: 306-731-2447; *Fax:* 306-731-2415
office@kannatavalley.com
www.kannatavalley.com
Other Information: Toll-Free Phone: 877-731-2447
Municipal Type: Resort Village
Incorporated: 1966; *Area:* 0.63 sq km
Population in 2016: 88
Provincial Electoral District(s): Last Mountain-Touchwood

Federal Electoral District(s): Moose Jaw-Lake Centre-Lanigan
Next Election: 2022/2024
Ken MacDonald, Mayor, 306-533-3936
Jack McHardy, Administrator

Katepwa

P.O. Box 250
41 Elm St.
Lebret, SK S0G 2Y0
Tel: 306-332-6645; *Fax:* 306-332-5808
katepwabeach@sasktel.net
www.katepwabeach.com
Municipal Type: Resort Village
Incorporated: 1914; *Area:* 5.78 sq km
Population in 2016: 312
Provincial Electoral District(s): Last Mountain-Touchwood
Federal Electoral District(s): Regina-Qu'Appelle
Next Election: 2022/2024
Don Jewitt, Mayor
Laurie Rudolph, Chief Administrative Officer

Keeler

P.O. Box 33
Keeler, SK S0H 2E0
Tel: 306-759-2302
Municipal Type: Village
Incorporated: July 5, 1910; *Area:* 1.02 sq km
Population in 2016: 15
Provincial Electoral District(s): Thunder Creek
Federal Electoral District(s): Moose Jaw-Lake Centre-Lanigan
Next Election: 2022/2024
Duncan Keeler, Mayor
Rhonda Purdy, Clerk

Kelliher

P.O. Box 190
406 - 2nd Ave.
Kelliher, SK S0A 1V0
Tel: 306-675-2226; *Fax:* 306-675-2240
villageofkelliher@sasktel.net
Municipal Type: Village
Incorporated: April 27, 1909; *Area:* 2.81 sq km
Population in 2016: 217
Provincial Electoral District(s): Last Mountain-Touchwood
Federal Electoral District(s): Regina-Qu'Appelle
Next Election: 2022/2024
Darcy King, Mayor
Glenda Moxham, Acting Administrator

Kelvington

P.O. Box 10
201 Main St.
Kelvington, SK S0A 1W0
Tel: 306-327-4482; *Fax:* 306-327-4946
info@townofkelvington.com
www.townofkelvington.com
Municipal Type: Town
Incorporated: Nov. 18, 1921; *Area:* 3.89 sq km
Population in 2016: 834
Provincial Electoral District(s): Kelvington-Wadena
Federal Electoral District(s): Yorkton-Melville
Next Election: 2022/2024
Note: Proclaimed as a town on May 1, 1944.
Tracey Sauer, Mayor
Tammy Descalchuk, Administrator

Kenaston

P.O. Box 129
Kenaston, SK S0G 2N0
Tel: 306-252-2211; *Fax:* 306-252-2248
kenaston@sasktel.net
www.kenaston.ca
Municipal Type: Village
Incorporated: July 18, 1910; *Area:* 1.17 sq km
Population in 2016: 282
Provincial Electoral District(s): Arm River-Watrous
Federal Electoral District(s): Moose Jaw-Lake Centre-Lanigan
Next Election: 2022/2024
Michael Menzies, Mayor
Carman Fowler, Administrator

Kendal

P.O. Box 97
115 Main St.
Kendal, SK S0G 2P0
Tel: 306-424-2722; *Fax:* 306-424-2722
villageofkendal@sasktel.net
Municipal Type: Village
Incorporated: Feb. 17, 1919; *Area:* 0.65 sq km
Population in 2016: 83
Provincial Electoral District(s): Indian Head-Milestone

Federal Electoral District(s): Souris-Moose Mountain
Next Election: 2022/2024
Lea Zhoner, Mayor
Donna Bodnar, Administrator

Kennedy
P.O. Box 93
Kennedy, SK S0G 2R0
Tel: 306-538-2194; *Fax:* 306-538-4522
village.kennedy@sasktel.net
www.angelfire.com/ca/kennedysk
Municipal Type: Village
Incorporated: Nov. 5, 1907; *Area:* 1.60 km
Population in 2016: 216
Provincial Electoral District(s): Moosomin
Federal Electoral District(s): Souris-Moose Mountain
Next Election: 2022/2024
Linc Brickley, Mayor
Ward Frazer, Administrator

Kenosee Lake
P.O. Box 30
Kenosee Lake, SK S0C 2S0
Tel: 306-577-2139; *Fax:* 306-577-2261
village.kenosee@sasktel.net
Municipal Type: Village
Incorporated: Oct. 1, 1987; *Area:* 0.35 sq km
Population in 2016: 234
Provincial Electoral District(s): Cannington
Federal Electoral District(s): Souris-Moose Mountain
Next Election: 2022/2024
Mark Doty, Mayor
Andrea Kosior, Administrator

Kerrobert
P.O. Box 558
433 Manitoba Ave.
Kerrobert, SK S0L 1R0
Tel: 306-834-2361; *Fax:* 306-834-2633
kerrobert@sasktel.net
www.kerrobertsk.com
Municipal Type: Town
Incorporated: Nov. 9, 1910; *Area:* 7.49 sq km
Population in 2016: 1,026
Provincial Electoral District(s): Kindersley
Federal Electoral District(s): Battlefords-Lloydminster
Next Election: 2022/2024
Note: Proclaimed as a town on Nov. 1, 1911.
Wayne Mock, Mayor
Monica M. Merkosky, Administrator

Killaly
P.O. Box 69
Railway Ave.
Killaly, SK S0A 1X0
Tel: 306-748-2254
Municipal Type: Village
Incorporated: April 28, 1909; *Area:* 2.59 sq km
Population in 2016: 65
Provincial Electoral District(s): Melville-Saltcoats
Federal Electoral District(s): Yorkton-Melville
Next Election: 2022/2024
Robert Blake, Mayor
Murray Hanowski, Administrator

Kincaid
P.O. Box 177
20 Dominion Ave. West
Kincaid, SK S0H 2J0
Tel: 306-264-3910; *Fax:* 306-264-3903
villageofkincaid@sasktel.net
www.villageofkincaid.ca
Municipal Type: Village
Incorporated: July 19, 1913; *Area:* 0.82 sq km
Population in 2016: 111
Provincial Electoral District(s): Wood River
Federal Electoral District(s): Cypress Hills-Grasslands
Next Election: 2022/2024
Cynthia Gross, Mayor
Kimberly Johnson, Administrator

Kindersley
P.O. Box 1269
106 - 5th Ave. East
Kindersley, SK S0L 1S0
Tel: 306-463-2675; *Fax:* 306-463-4577
office@kindersley.ca
www.kindersley.ca
Municipal Type: Town
Incorporated: Jan. 10, 1910; *Area:* 12.55 sq km
Population in 2016: 4,571
Provincial Electoral District(s): Kindersley

Federal Electoral District(s): Cypress Hills-Grasslands
Next Election: 2022/2024
Note: Proclaimed as a town on Nov. 1, 1910.
Rod Perkins, Mayor
Bernie Morton, Chief Administrative Officer

Kinistino
P.O. Box 10
212 Main St.
Kinistino, SK S0J 1H0
Tel: 306-864-2461; *Fax:* 306-864-2880
townofkinistino@sasktel.net
www.townofkinistino.ca
Municipal Type: Town
Incorporated: July 30, 1905; *Area:* 0.98 sq km
Population in 2016: 654
Provincial Electoral District(s): Batoche
Federal Electoral District(s): Prince Albert
Next Election: 2022/2024
Note: Proclaimed as a town on Feb. 7, 1952.
Leonard Margolis, Mayor
Rhonda Bacon, Administrator

Kinley
P.O. Box 51
Kinley, SK S0K 2E0
Tel: 306-237-4601; *Fax:* 306-237-4605
villageofkinley@sasktel.net
Municipal Type: Village
Incorporated: Jan. 7, 1909; *Area:* 1.18 sq km
Population in 2016: 60
Provincial Electoral District(s): Biggar
Federal Electoral District(s): Carlton Trail-Eagle Creek
Next Election: 2022/2024
Doug Harder, Mayor
Lynne Tolley, Administrator

Kipling
P.O. Box 299
301 - 6th Ave.
Kipling, SK S0G 2S0
Tel: 306-736-2515; *Fax:* 306-736-8448
kiptown@sasktel.net
www.townofkipling.ca
Municipal Type: Town
Incorporated: Sept. 13, 1909; *Area:* 2.15 sq km
Population in 2016: 1,074
Provincial Electoral District(s): Moosomin
Federal Electoral District(s): Souris-Moose Mountain
Next Election: 2022/2024
Note: Proclaimed as a town on Jan. 1, 1954.
Buck Bright, Mayor
Gail Dakue, Administrator

Kisbey
P.O. Box 249
Kisbey, SK S0C 1L0
Tel: 306-462-2212; *Fax:* 306-462-2279
vill.kisbey@signaldirect.ca
Municipal Type: Village
Incorporated: May 8, 1907; *Area:* 2.77 sq km
Population in 2016: 153
Provincial Electoral District(s): Cannington
Federal Electoral District(s): Souris-Moose Mountain
Next Election: 2022/2024
John Houston, Mayor
Judy Graham, Administrator

Kivimaa-Moonlight Bay
P.O. Box 120
Livelong, SK S0M 1J0
Tel: 306-845-3336; *Fax:* 306-845-3686
rvkmb@littleloon.ca
www.rvkmb.com
Municipal Type: Resort Village
Area: 0.55 sq km
Population in 2016: 84
Provincial Electoral District(s): Meadow Lake
Federal Electoral District(s): Battlefords-Lloydminster
Next Election: 2022/2024
Steven Nasby, Mayor
Jackie Helgeton, Administrator

Krydor
P.O. Box 160
Hafford, SK S0J 1A0
Tel: 306-549-2333; *Fax:* 306-549-2435
rm435@littleloon.ca
Municipal Type: Village
Incorporated: Aug. 25, 1914; *Area:* 0.82 sq km
Population in 2016: 15
Provincial Electoral District(s): Rosthern-Shellbrook

Federal Electoral District(s): Carlton Trail-Eagle Creek
Next Election: 2022/2024
Stan Lucko, Mayor
Alan J. Tanchak, Clerk

Kyle
P.O. Box 520
Kyle, SK S0L 1T0
Tel: 306-375-2525; *Fax:* 306-375-2534
townofkyle@sasktel.net
www.townofkyle.ca
Municipal Type: Town
Incorporated: April 13, 1926; *Area:* 1.01 sq km
Population in 2016: 449
Provincial Electoral District(s): Rosetown-Elrose
Federal Electoral District(s): Cypress Hills-Grasslands
Next Election: 2022/2024
Note: Proclaimed as a town on Jan. 1, 1959.
Doug Barker, Mayor
Karla Marshall, Administrator

Lafleche
P.O. Box 250
35 - 2nd Ave. East
Lafleche, SK S0H 2K0
Tel: 306-472-5292; *Fax:* 306-472-3706
town.of.lafleche@sasktel.net
www.town.lafleche.sk.ca
Municipal Type: Town
Incorporated: Sept. 3, 1913; *Area:* 1.51 sq km
Population in 2016: 382
Provincial Electoral District(s): Wood River
Federal Electoral District(s): Cypress Hills-Grasslands
Next Election: 2022/2024
Note: Proclaimed as a town on June 1, 1953.
Carmen Ellis, Mayor
Brekke Masse, Administrator

Laird
P.O. Box 189
220A Main St.
Laird, SK S0K 2H0
Tel: 306-223-4343; *Fax:* 306-223-4349
lairdvillage@sasktel.net
www.lairdvillage.ca
Municipal Type: Village
Incorporated: May 4, 1911; *Area:* 1.29 sq km
Population in 2016: 267
Provincial Electoral District(s): Rosthern-Shellbrook
Federal Electoral District(s): Carlton Trail-Eagle Creek
Next Election: 2022/2024
Chris Harris, Mayor
Michelle Zurakowski, Administrator

Lake Alma
P.O. Box 163
Lake Alma, SK S0C 1M0
Tel: 306-447-2002; *Fax:* 306-447-2023
rmalma@sasktel.net
Municipal Type: Village
Incorporated: Jan. 1, 1949; *Area:* 0.47 sq km
Population in 2016: 30
Provincial Electoral District(s): Estevan
Federal Electoral District(s): Souris-Moose Mountain
Next Election: 2022/2024
Wilfred Jacobson, Mayor
Myrna Lohse, Administrator

Lake Lenore
P.O. Box 148
Lake Lenore, SK S0K 2J0
Tel: 306-368-2344; *Fax:* 306-368-2226
www.lakelenore.ca
Municipal Type: Village
Incorporated: April 28, 1921; *Area:* 0.97 sq km
Population in 2016: 284
Provincial Electoral District(s): Batoche
Federal Electoral District(s): Carlton Trail-Eagle Creek
Next Election: 2022/2024
Travis Thompson, Mayor
Barb Politeski, Administrator

Lampman
P.O. Box 70
Lampman, SK S0C 1N0
Tel: 306-487-2462; *Fax:* 306-487-2285
browning.lampman@sasktel.net
Municipal Type: Town
Incorporated: Aug. 16, 1910; *Area:* 2.23 sq km
Population in 2016: 675
Provincial Electoral District(s): Cannington
Federal Electoral District(s): Souris-Moose Mountain

Next Election: 2022/2024
Note: Proclaimed as a town on June 1, 1963.
Sean Paxman, Mayor
Greg Wallin, Administrator

Lancer
P.O. Box 3
Lancer, SK S0N 1G0
Tel: 306-689-2925; *Fax:* 306-689-2890
Municipal Type: Village
Incorporated: Sept. 11, 1913; *Area:* 1.33 sq km
Population in 2016: 69
Provincial Electoral District(s): Cypress Hills
Federal Electoral District(s): Cypress Hills-Grasslands
Next Election: 2022/2024
Ernest Wagner, Mayor
Karen Hartman, Clerk

Landis
P.O. Box 153
100 Princess St.
Landis, SK S0K 2K0
Tel: 306-658-2155; *Fax:* 306-658-2156
villageoflandis@sasktel.net
www.villageoflandis.com
Municipal Type: Village
Incorporated: May 17, 1909; *Area:* 0.80 sq km
Population in 2016: 152
Provincial Electoral District(s): Biggar
Federal Electoral District(s): Battlefords-Lloydminster
Next Election: 2022/2024
Don Beckett, Mayor
Alicia Leclercq, Administrator

Lang
P.O. Box 97
223 Main St.
Lang, SK S0G 2W0
Tel: 306-464-2024; *Fax:* 306-464-2050
voflang@sasktel.net
www.langsk.com
Municipal Type: Village
Incorporated: July 27, 1906; *Area:* 0.64 sq km
Population in 2016: 189
Provincial Electoral District(s): Indian Head-Milestone
Federal Electoral District(s): Souris-Moose Mountain
Next Election: 2022/2024
Allan Broderick, Mayor
Darlene Wingert, Administrator

Langenburg
P.O. Box 400
Langenburg, SK S0A 2A0
Tel: 306-743-2432; *Fax:* 306-743-2723
langenburgt@sasktel.net
www.langenburg.ca
Municipal Type: Town
Incorporated: March 30, 1903; *Area:* 3.46 sq km
Population in 2016: 1,165
Provincial Electoral District(s): Melville-Saltcoats
Federal Electoral District(s): Yorkton-Melville
Next Election: 2022/2024
Note: Proclaimed as a town on Sept. 15, 1959.
Don Fogg, Mayor
Glenda Hodson, Chief Administrative Officer

Langham
P.O. Box 289
230 Main St. East
Langham, SK S0K 2L0
Tel: 306-283-4842; *Fax:* 306-283-4772
admin@langham.ca
www.langham.ca
Municipal Type: Town
Incorporated: June 8, 1906; *Area:* 3.98 sq km
Population in 2016: 1,496
Provincial Electoral District(s): Biggar
Federal Electoral District(s): Carlton Trail-Eagle Creek
Next Election: 2022/2024
Note: Proclaimed as a town on Aug. 1, 1907.
John Hildebrand, Mayor
Jamie Nagy, Administrator

Lanigan
P.O. Box 280
110 Main St.
Lanigan, SK S0K 2M0
Tel: 306-365-2809; *Fax:* 306-365-2960
town.lanigan@sasktel.net
www.town.lanigan.sk.ca
Municipal Type: Town
Incorporated: Aug. 21, 1907; *Area:* 8.33 sq km

Population in 2016: 1,377
Provincial Electoral District(s): Humboldt
Federal Electoral District(s): Moose Jaw-Lake Centre-Lanigan
Next Election: 2022/2024
Note: Proclaimed as a town on April 15, 1908.
Andrew Cebryk, Mayor
Jennifer Thompson, Administrator

Lashburn
P.O. Box 328
78 Main St.
Lashburn, SK S0M 1H0
Tel: 306-285-3533; *Fax:* 306-285-3358
townoflashburn@sasktel.net
www.lashburn.ca
Municipal Type: Town
Incorporated: Dec. 8, 1906; *Area:* 3.11 sq km
Population in 2016: 983
Provincial Electoral District(s): Cut Knife-Turtleford
Federal Electoral District(s): Battlefords-Lloydminster
Next Election: 2022/2024
Note: Proclaimed as a town on March 1, 1979.
Steven Turnbull, Mayor
Vicki Seabrook, Administrator

Leader
P.O. Box 39
151 - 1st St. West
Leader, SK S0N 1H0
Tel: 306-628-3868; *Fax:* 306-628-4337
town.leader@sasktel.net
www.leader.ca
Other Information: Toll-Free Phone: 800-424-8335
Municipal Type: Town
Incorporated: Sept. 13, 1913; *Area:* 1.70 sq km
Population in 2016: 863
Provincial Electoral District(s): Cypress Hills
Federal Electoral District(s): Cypress Hills-Grasslands
Next Election: 2022/2024
Note: Proclaimed as a town on May 1, 1947.
Craig Tondevold, Mayor
Rochelle Francis, Administrator

Leask
P.O. Box 40
15 Main St.
Leask, SK S0J 1M0
Tel: 306-466-2229; *Fax:* 306-466-2239
village.leask@sasktel.net
www.leask.ca
Municipal Type: Village
Incorporated: Sept. 3, 1912; *Area:* 0.75 sq km
Population in 2016: 399
Provincial Electoral District(s): Rosthern-Shellbrook
Federal Electoral District(s): Carlton Trail-Eagle Creek
Next Election: 2022/2024
Maurice Stieb, Mayor
Brenda Lockhart, Administrator

Lebret
P.O. Box 40
Lebret, SK S0G 2Y0
Tel: 306-332-6545; *Fax:* 306-332-5338
villageoflebret@sasktel.net
Municipal Type: Village
Incorporated: Oct. 14, 1912; *Area:* 1.32 sq km
Population in 2016: 216
Provincial Electoral District(s): Last Mountain-Touchwood
Federal Electoral District(s): Regina-Qu'Appelle
Next Election: 2022/2024
Ralph Blondeau, Mayor
Caroline MacMurphy, Administrator

Lemberg
P.O. Box 399
Lemberg, SK S0A 2B0
Tel: 306-335-2244; *Fax:* 306-335-2257
townoffice.lemberg@sasktel.net
www.lemberg-sk-ca.weebly.com
Municipal Type: Town
Incorporated: July 12, 1904; *Area:* 2.67 sq km
Population in 2016: 313
Provincial Electoral District(s): Last Mountain-Touchwood
Federal Electoral District(s): Yorkton-Melville
Next Election: 2022/2024
Note: Proclaimed as a town on Sept. 1, 1907.
John Kittler, Mayor
Tara Harris, Administrator

Leoville
P.O. Box 280
Leoville, SK S0J 1N0
Tel: 306-984-2140; *Fax:* 306-984-2337
leoville@sasktel.net
Municipal Type: Village
Incorporated: June 26, 1944; *Area:* 1.11 sq km
Population in 2016: 375
Provincial Electoral District(s): Meadow Lake
Federal Electoral District(s): Desnethé-Missinippi-Churchill River
Next Election: 2022/2024
Ron Craswell, Mayor
Mona Chalifour, Clerk

Leross
P.O. Box 68
Leross, SK S0A 2C0
Tel: 306-675-4429; *Fax:* 306-675-0024
villageofleross@sasktel.net
Municipal Type: Village
Incorporated: Dec. 1, 1909; *Area:* 1.21 sq km
Population in 2016: 46
Provincial Electoral District(s): Last Mountain-Touchwood
Federal Electoral District(s): Regina-Qu'Appelle
Next Election: 2022/2024
Francis Klyne, Mayor
Elaine Klyne, Clerk

Leroy
P.O. Box 40
Leroy, SK S0K 2P0
Tel: 306-286-3288; *Fax:* 306-286-3400
leroy@leroy.ca
www.leroy.ca
Municipal Type: Town
Incorporated: Dec. 5, 1922; *Area:* 1.06 sq km
Population in 2016: 450
Provincial Electoral District(s): Melfort
Federal Electoral District(s): Moose Jaw-Lake Centre-Lanigan
Next Election: 2022/2024
Note: Proclaimed as a town on March 1, 1963.
Brian Thoen, Mayor
Glenda Hamilton, Administrator

Leslie Beach
P.O. Box 478
Foam Lake, SK S0A 1A0
Tel: 306-272-4579; *Fax:* 306-272-3960
Municipal Type: Resort Village
Area: 0.56 sq km
Population in 2016: 10
Provincial Electoral District(s): Kelvington-Wadena
Federal Electoral District(s): Yorkton-Melville
Next Election: 2022/2024
Roger Nupdal, Mayor
Brenda Kipling, Clerk

Lestock
P.O. Box 209
320 Touchwood Hills Ave.
Lestock, SK S0A 2G0
Tel: 306-274-2277; *Fax:* 306-274-2275
lestockv@sasktel.net
www.lestock.ca
Municipal Type: Village
Incorporated: April 17, 1912; *Area:* 0.87 sq km
Population in 2016: 95
Provincial Electoral District(s): Last Mountain-Touchwood
Federal Electoral District(s): Regina-Qu'Appelle
Next Election: 2022/2024
Edward Mostad, Mayor
Kristine Marengere, Administrator

Liberty
P.O. Box 59
Stalwart, SK S0G 4R0
Tel: 306-963-2402; *Fax:* 306-963-2405
villageofliberty@sasktel.net
Municipal Type: Village
Incorporated: Jan. 23, 1912; *Area:* 1.37 sq km
Population in 2016: 78
Provincial Electoral District(s): Arm River-Watrous
Federal Electoral District(s): Moose Jaw-Lake Centre-Lanigan
Next Election: 2022/2024
Jennifer Langlois, Mayor
Yvonne (Bonny) Goodsman, Administrator

Limerick
P.O. Box 129
Limerick, SK S0H 2P0
Tel: 306-263-2020; *Fax:* 306-263-2013
rm73@sasktel.net

Municipal Type: Village
Incorporated: July 10, 1913; *Area:* 0.79 sq km
Population in 2016: 115
Provincial Electoral District(s): Wood River
Federal Electoral District(s): Cypress Hills-Grasslands
Next Election: 2022/2024
Robert Smith, Mayor
Tammy Franks, Administrator

Lintlaw
P.O. Box 10
Lintlaw, SK S0A 2H0
Tel: 306-325-2006; *Fax:* 306-325-2006
villageoflintlaw@sasktel.net
Municipal Type: Village
Incorporated: Dec. 14, 1921; *Area:* 1.23 sq km
Population in 2016: 172
Provincial Electoral District(s): Kelvington-Wadena
Federal Electoral District(s): Yorkton-Melville
Next Election: 2022/2024
Ervin Lindholm, Mayor
Kathleen Ambrose, Administrator

Lipton
P.O. Box 219
201 Main St.
Lipton, SK S0G 3B0
Tel: 306-336-2505; *Fax:* 306-336-2505
lipton@sasktel.net
www.villageoflipton.com
Municipal Type: Village
Incorporated: May 15, 1905; *Area:* 0.75 sq km
Population in 2016: 345
Provincial Electoral District(s): Last Mountain-Touchwood
Federal Electoral District(s): Regina-Qu'Appelle
Next Election: 2022/2024
Ron Tomolak, Mayor
Marlene Bausmer, Administrator

La Loche
P.O. Box 310
La Loche Ave.
La Loche, SK S0M 1G0
Tel: 306-822-2032; *Fax:* 306-822-2078
nor.vill.laloche@sasktel.net
Municipal Type: Northern Village
Incorporated: Oct. 1, 1983; *Area:* 15.59 sq km
Population in 2016: 2,372
Provincial Electoral District(s): Athabasca
Federal Electoral District(s): Desnethé-Missinippi-Churchill River
Next Election: 2022/2024
Robert St. Pierre, Mayor
Janine Boucher, Clerk

Loon Lake
P.O. Box 40
204 - 1 St. South
Loon Lake, SK S0M 1L0
Tel: 306-837-2090; *Fax:* 306-837-2282
rm561@sasktel.net
www.loonlakesask.com
Municipal Type: Village
Incorporated: Jan. 1, 1950; *Area:* 0.66 sq km
Population in 2016: 288
Provincial Electoral District(s): Meadow Lake
Federal Electoral District(s): Desnethé-Missinippi-Churchill River
Next Election: 2022/2024
Larry Heon, Mayor, 306-837-7605
Erin Simpson, Administrator

Loreburn
P.O. Box 177
Loreburn, SK S0H 2S0
Tel: 306-644-2097; *Fax:* 306-644-4847
villageofloreburn@sasktel.net
www.villageofloreburn.ca
Municipal Type: Village
Incorporated: May 20, 1909; *Area:* 0.62 sq km
Population in 2016: 107
Provincial Electoral District(s): Arm River-Watrous
Federal Electoral District(s): Moose Jaw-Lake Centre-Lanigan
Next Election: 2022/2024
Steven South, Mayor
Brandy Losie, Clerk

Love
P.O. Box 94
Love, SK S0J 1P0
Tel: 306-276-2525
villageoflove@sasktel.net
Municipal Type: Village
Incorporated: June 2, 1945; *Area:* 1.28 sq km

Population in 2016: 50
Provincial Electoral District(s): Saskatchewan Rivers
Federal Electoral District(s): Prince Albert
Next Election: 2022/2024
Shelley Vallier, Mayor
Amy Dixon, Administrator

Lucky Lake
P.O. Box 99
Lucky Lake, SK S0L 1Z0
Tel: 306-858-2234; *Fax:* 306-858-9134
tourismluckylake@gmail.com
www.luckylake.ca
Municipal Type: Village
Incorporated: Nov. 23, 1920; *Area:* 1.28 sq km
Population in 2016: 289
Provincial Electoral District(s): Rosetown-Elrose
Federal Electoral District(s): Cypress Hills-Grasslands
Next Election: 2022/2024
Note: Formerly known as Devil's Lake.
Blaine Trumbley, Mayor
D.B. (Blair) Cleaveley, Administrator

Lumsden
P.O. Box 160
300 James St. North
Lumsden, SK S0G 3C0
Tel: 306-731-2404; *Fax:* 306-731-3572
town.lumsden@sasktel.net
www.lumsden.ca
Municipal Type: Town
Incorporated: Dec. 29, 1898; *Area:* 3.82 sq km
Population in 2016: 1,824
Provincial Electoral District(s): Thunder Creek
Federal Electoral District(s): Moose Jaw-Lake Centre-Lanigan
Next Election: 2022/2024
Note: Proclaimed as a town on March 15, 1905.
Bryan Matheson, Mayor, 306-731-3603
Darcie Cooper, Chief Administrative Officer

Lumsden Beach
P.O. Box 704
Regina Beach, SK S0G 4C0
Tel: 306-222-0087
lumsdenbeach@sasktel.net
www.lumsdenbeach.com
Municipal Type: Resort Village
Incorporated: 1918; *Area:* 0.47 sq km
Population in 2016: 30
Provincial Electoral District(s): Thunder Creek
Federal Electoral District(s): Moose Jaw-Lake Centre-Lanigan
Next Election: 2022/2024
Ross Wilson, Mayor
Judy Young, Administrator, 306-729-4441

Luseland
P.O. Box 130
Luseland, SK S0L 2A0
Tel: 306-372-4218; *Fax:* 306-347-4700
luseland@sasktel.net
www.townofluseland.com
Municipal Type: Town
Incorporated: Dec. 10, 1910; *Area:* 1.53 sq km
Population in 2016: 623
Provincial Electoral District(s): Kindersley
Federal Electoral District(s): Battlefords-Lloydminster
Next Election: 2022/2024
Note: Proclaimed as a town on Jan. 1, 1954.
Len Schlosser, Mayor
Karyl Richardson, Administrator

Macklin
P.O. Box 69
Macklin, SK S0L 2C0
Tel: 306-753-2256; *Fax:* 306-753-3234
town.macklin@sasktel.net
www.macklin.ca
Municipal Type: Town
Incorporated: Nov. 8, 1909; *Area:* 2.85 sq km
Population in 2016: 1,375
Provincial Electoral District(s): Kindersley
Federal Electoral District(s): Battlefords-Lloydminster
Next Election: 2022/2024
Note: Proclaimed as a town on Nov. 1, 1912.
Patrick Doetzel, Mayor
Kim G. Gartner, Administrator

MacNutt
P.O. Box 10
MacNutt, SK S0A 2K0
Tel: 306-742-4391; *Fax:* 306-742-4391
macnutt2013@hotmail.com
www.macnuttsaskatchewan.com
Municipal Type: Village
Incorporated: Feb. 22, 1913; *Area:* 0.81 sq km
Population in 2016: 65
Provincial Electoral District(s): Melville-Saltcoats
Federal Electoral District(s): Yorkton-Melville
Next Election: 2022/2024
Shayne Wagner, Mayor
Kendra Busch, Clerk

Macoun
P.O. Box 58
Macoun, SK S0C 1P0
Tel: 306-634-9352; *Fax:* 306-634-9377
macoun.sask@gmail.com
Municipal Type: Village
Incorporated: Oct. 16, 1903; *Area:* 1.68 sq km
Population in 2016: 269
Provincial Electoral District(s): Estevan
Federal Electoral District(s): Souris-Moose Mountain
Next Election: 2022/2024
Glenys Bareg, Mayor
Carmen Dodd-Vicary, Administrator

Macrorie
P.O. Box 37
Main St.
Macrorie, SK S0L 2E0
Tel: 306-243-2010; *Fax:* 306-243-2010
vmacro@sasktel.net
Municipal Type: Village
Incorporated: Feb. 8, 1912; *Area:* 0.77 sq km
Population in 2016: 68
Provincial Electoral District(s): Rosetown-Elrose
Federal Electoral District(s): Carlton Trail-Eagle Creek
Next Election: 2022/2024
Mike Perry, Mayor
Darla Fraser, Administrator

Maidstone
P.O. Box 208
112 - 1st Ave. West
Maidstone, SK S0M 1M0
Tel: 306-893-2373; *Fax:* 306-893-4378
townofmaidstone@sasktel.net
www.townofmaidstone.com
Municipal Type: Town
Incorporated: July 19, 1907; *Area:* 4.56 sq km
Population in 2016: 1,185
Provincial Electoral District(s): Cut Knife-Turtleford
Federal Electoral District(s): Battlefords-Lloydminster
Next Election: 2022/2024
Note: Proclaimed as a town on March 1, 1955.
Brennan Becotte, Mayor
Lorne Kachur, Administrator, 306-903-7099

Major
P.O. Box 179
Major, SK S0L 2H0
Tel: 306-834-5493
www.villageofmajor.ca
Municipal Type: Village
Incorporated: Sept. 29, 1914; *Area:* 2.68 sq km
Population in 2016: 35
Provincial Electoral District(s): Kindersley
Federal Electoral District(s): Battlefords-Lloydminster
Next Election: 2022/2024
Veryl Richelhoff, Mayor
Margaret Ostrowski, Clerk, 306-834-5508

Makwa
P.O. Box 159
Makwa, SK S0M 1N0
Tel: 306-236-3919; *Fax:* 306-236-3913
villageofmakwa@sasktel.net
Municipal Type: Village
Incorporated: June 1, 1965; *Area:* 0.66 sq km
Population in 2016: 84
Provincial Electoral District(s): Meadow Lake
Federal Electoral District(s): Desnethé-Missinippi-Churchill River
Next Election: 2022/2024
Jerry Graham, Mayor
Claire Elliott, Administrator

Manitou Beach
701 Lakeview Ave.
Manitou Beach, SK S0K 4T1
Tel: 306-946-2831; *Fax:* 306-946-2017
manbe@sasktel.net
www.manitoubeach.ca
Municipal Type: Resort Village
Incorporated: 1919; *Area:* 3.09 sq km
Population in 2016: 314
Provincial Electoral District(s): Arm River-Watrous
Federal Electoral District(s): Moose Jaw-Lake Centre-Lanigan
Next Election: 2022/2024
Eric Upshall, Mayor
Beverley Laird, Administrator

Mankota
P.O. Box 336
Mankota, SK S0H 2W0
Tel: 306-478-2331; *Fax:* 306-478-2525
village.mankota@sasktel.net
Municipal Type: Village
Incorporated: Feb. 3, 1941; *Area:* 1.55 sq km
Population in 2016: 205
Provincial Electoral District(s): Wood River
Federal Electoral District(s): Cypress Hills-Grasslands
Next Election: 2022/2024
Grant Martin, Mayor
April Williamson, Administrator

Manor
P.O. Box 295
45 Main St.
Manor, SK S0C 1R0
Tel: 306-448-2273; *Fax:* 306-448-2274
admin.manor@sasktel.net
Municipal Type: Village
Incorporated: April 15, 1902; *Area:* 2.79 sq km
Population in 2016: 295
Provincial Electoral District(s): Cannington
Federal Electoral District(s): Souris-Moose Mountain
Next Election: 2022/2024
Don Dionne, Mayor
Ashley Corrigan, Administrator

Maple Creek
P.O. Box 428
205 Jasper St.
Maple Creek, SK S0N 1N0
Tel: 306-662-2244; *Fax:* 306-662-4131
townofmaplecreek@sasktel.net
www.maplecreek.ca
Other Information: After Hours Phone: 306-662-7333
Municipal Type: Town
Incorporated: April 28, 1896; *Area:* 4.42 sq km
Population in 2016: 2,084
Provincial Electoral District(s): Cypress Hills
Federal Electoral District(s): Cypress Hills-Grasslands
Next Election: 2022/2024
Note: Proclaimed as a town on April 30, 1903.
Barry Rudd, Mayor
Don McLeod, Administrator

Marcelin
P.O. Box 39
100 - 1st Ave. North
Marcelin, SK S0J 1R0
Tel: 306-226-2168; *Fax:* 306-226-2171
vmarcelin@sasktel.net
www.marcelin.ca
Municipal Type: Village
Incorporated: Sept. 25, 1911; *Area:* 1.32 sq km
Population in 2016: 153
Provincial Electoral District(s): Rosthern-Shellbrook
Federal Electoral District(s): Carlton Trail-Eagle Creek
Next Election: 2022/2024
Dennis Ferster, Mayor
Leanne McCormick, Administrator

Marengo
P.O. Box 70
Marengo, SK S0L 2K0
Tel: 306-968-2922; *Fax:* 306-968-2278
rm292.rm322@sasktel.net
Municipal Type: Village
Incorporated: Nov. 5, 1910; *Area:* 0.87 sq km
Population in 2016: 166
Provincial Electoral District(s): Kindersley
Federal Electoral District(s): Cypress Hills-Grasslands
Next Election: 2022/2024
Travis McKillop, Mayor
Robin Busby, Administrator

Margo
P.O. Box 28
Margo, SK S0A 2M0
Tel: 306-324-2134; *Fax:* 306-324-4563
villagemargo@sasktel.net
Municipal Type: Village
Incorporated: April 24, 1911; *Area:* 0.80 sq km
Population in 2016: 83
Provincial Electoral District(s): Kelvington-Wadena
Federal Electoral District(s): Yorkton-Melville
Next Election: 2022/2024
George Dawe, Mayor
Gail Selch, Administrator

Markinch
P.O. Box 29
Markinch, SK S0G 3J0
Tel: 306-726-4355; *Fax:* 306-726-4355
vofmarkinch@canwan.com
Municipal Type: Village
Incorporated: Feb. 16, 1911; *Area:* 0.68 sq km
Population in 2016: 58
Provincial Electoral District(s): Last Mountain-Touchwood
Federal Electoral District(s): Regina-Qu'Appelle
Next Election: 2022/2024
Robert Fenwick, Mayor
Rita T. Orb, Clerk

Marquis
P.O. Box 40
Marquis, SK S0H 2X0
Tel: 306-788-2022; *Fax:* 306-788-2168
rm191@sasktel.net
Municipal Type: Village
Incorporated: March 21, 1910; *Area:* 0.63 sq km
Population in 2016: 97
Provincial Electoral District(s): Thunder Creek
Federal Electoral District(s): Moose Jaw-Lake Centre-Lanigan
Next Election: 2022/2024
Ken Marcyniuk, Mayor
Margaret Brown, Administrator

Marsden
P.O. Box 69
Marsden, SK S0M 1P0
Tel: 306-826-5215; *Fax:* 306-826-5512
rm442@sasktel.net
Municipal Type: Village
Incorporated: April 24, 1931; *Area:* 0.94 sq km
Population in 2016: 297
Provincial Electoral District(s): Cut Knife-Turtleford
Federal Electoral District(s): Battlefords-Lloydminster
Next Election: 2022/2024
Craig Watson, Mayor
Joanne Loy, Administrator

Marshall
P.O. Box 125
17 Main St.
Marshall, SK S0M 1R0
Tel: 306-387-6340; *Fax:* 306-387-6161
townofmarshallcao@outlook.com
www.townofmarshall.ca
Municipal Type: Town
Incorporated: Jan. 21, 1914; *Area:* 1.01 sq km
Population in 2016: 561
Provincial Electoral District(s): Lloydminster
Federal Electoral District(s): Battlefords-Lloydminster
Next Election: 2022/2024
Note: Proclaimed as a town on Oct. 26, 2006.
Brian Shiloff, Mayor
Linda E. Row, Acting Administrator

Martensville
P.O. Box 970
37 Centennial Dr. South
Martensville, SK S0K 2T0
Tel: 306-931-2166; *Fax:* 306-933-2468
inquiry@martensville.ca
www.martensville.ca
Municipal Type: Town
Incorporated: Sept. 1, 1966; *Area:* 4.78 sq km
Population in 2016: 9,645
Provincial Electoral District(s): Martensville
Federal Electoral District(s): Carlton Trail-Eagle Creek
Next Election: 2022/2024
Note: Proclaimed as a town on Jan. 1, 1969.
Kent Muench, Mayor
Scott Blevins, City Manager

Maryfield
P.O. Box 58
Maryfield, SK S0G 3K0
Tel: 306-646-2143; *Fax:* 306-646-2193
villageofmaryfield@sasktel.net
www.maryfieldsaskatchewan.com
Municipal Type: Village
Incorporated: Aug. 21, 1907; *Area:* 2.69 sq km
Population in 2016: 348
Provincial Electoral District(s): Cannington
Federal Electoral District(s): Souris-Moose Mountain
Next Election: 2022/2024
David Hill, Mayor
Denine Neufeld, Administrator

Maymont
P.O. Box 160
Maymont, SK S0M 1T0
Tel: 306-389-2077; *Fax:* 306-389-2078
villageofmaymont@sasktel.net
Municipal Type: Village
Incorporated: June 24, 1907; *Area:* 0.66 sq km
Population in 2016: 138
Provincial Electoral District(s): Biggar
Federal Electoral District(s): Carlton Trail-Eagle Creek
Next Election: 2022/2024
Carol Deagnon, Mayor
Denise Bernier, Administrator

McLean
P.O. Box 56
McLean, SK S0G 3E0
Tel: 306-699-7279; *Fax:* 306-699-2347
villageofmclean@sasktel.net
www.mcleansask.com
Other Information: Alt. E-mail: villageofmcleanoffice@sasktel.net
Municipal Type: Village
Incorporated: Jan. 24, 1913; *Area:* 1.33 sq km
Population in 2016: 405
Provincial Electoral District(s): Indian Head-Milestone
Federal Electoral District(s): Regina-Qu'Appelle
Next Election: 2022/2024
Mark Towers, Mayor, 306-699-2303
Nadine Jensen, Administrator

McTaggart
P.O. Box 134
McTaggart, SK S0G 3G0
Tel: 306-861-1886; *Fax:* 306-842-1661
wendycarver@hotmail.com
Municipal Type: Village
Incorporated: Oct. 5, 1909; *Area:* 0.69 sq km
Population in 2016: 121
Provincial Electoral District(s): Weyburn-Big Muddy
Federal Electoral District(s): Souris-Moose Mountain
Next Election: 2022/2024
Kevin Donald, Mayor
Wendy Carver, Administrator

Meacham
P.O. Box 9
Meacham, SK S0K 2V0
Tel: 306-376-2003; *Fax:* 306-376-2006
villageofmeacham@baudoux.ca
www.meacham.ca
Municipal Type: Village
Incorporated: June 19, 1912; *Area:* 1.27 sq km
Population in 2016: 99
Provincial Electoral District(s): Humboldt
Federal Electoral District(s): Moose Jaw-Lake Centre-Lanigan
Next Election: 2022/2024
Marion Carlson, Mayor
Juaneta Bendig, Administrator

Meadow Lake
120 - 1st St. East
Meadow Lake, SK S9X 1Y5
Tel: 306-236-3622; *Fax:* 306-236-4299
cityhall@meadowlake.ca
www.meadowlake.ca
Municipal Type: Town
Incorporated: Aug. 24, 1931; *Area:* 7.95 sq km
Population in 2016: 5,344
Provincial Electoral District(s): Meadow Lake
Federal Electoral District(s): Desnethé-Missinippi-Churchill River
Next Election: 2022/2024
Note: Proclaimed as a town on Feb. 1, 1936.
Gary Vidal, Mayor
Diana Burton, City Manager

Meath Park

P.O. Box 255
Meath Park, SK S0J 1T0
Tel: 306-929-2112; *Fax:* 306-929-2281
villpark@sasktel.net
Municipal Type: Village
Incorporated: May 23, 1938; *Area:* 0.77 sq km
Population in 2016: 175
Provincial Electoral District(s): Saskatchewan Rivers
Federal Electoral District(s): Prince Albert
Next Election: 2022/2024
Michael Hydamacka, Mayor
Brenda Moberg, Administrator

Medstead

P.O. Box 148
209 - 2nd Ave.
Medstead, SK S0M 1W0
Tel: 306-342-4898; *Fax:* 306-342-4422
villageofmedstead@sasktel.net
Municipal Type: Village
Incorporated: April 23, 1931; *Area:* 0.67 sq km
Population in 2016: 130
Provincial Electoral District(s): Rosthern-Shellbrook
Federal Electoral District(s): Battlefords-Lloydminster
Next Election: 2022/2024
Albert Schmirler, Mayor
Coleen Kitching, Administrator

Melfort

City Hall
P.O. Box 2230
202 Burrows Ave. West
Melfort, SK S0E 1A0
Tel: 306-752-5911; *Fax:* 306-752-5556
city@cityofmelfort.ca
www.cityofmelfort.ca
Municipal Type: Town
Incorporated: Nov. 4, 1903; *Area:* 14.78 sq km
Population in 2016: 5,992
Provincial Electoral District(s): Melfort
Federal Electoral District(s): Prince Albert
Next Election: 2022/2024
Note: Incorporated as a city on Sept. 2, 1980.
Rick Lang, Mayor, 306-752-3374
Michael Hotsko, City Manager

Melville

P.O. Box 1240
430 Main St.
Melville, SK S0A 2P0
Tel: 306-728-6840; *Fax:* 306-728-5911
cityhall@melville.ca
www.melville.ca
Municipal Type: Town
Incorporated: Dec. 21, 1908; *Area:* 14.82 sq km
Population in 2016: 4,562
Provincial Electoral District(s): Melville-Saltcoats
Federal Electoral District(s): Yorkton-Melville
Next Election: 2022/2024
Note: Incorporated as a city on Aug. 1, 1960.
Walter Streelasky, Mayor
Kayla Hauser, City Manager, 306-728-6844

Melville Beach

P.O. Box 3250
Melville, SK S0A 2P0
Tel: 306-728-7697; *Fax:* 306-728-3180
rvmelvillebeach@gmail.com
Municipal Type: Resort Village
Area: 48.0 sq km
Population in 2016: 19
Provincial Electoral District(s): Melville-Saltcoats
Federal Electoral District(s): Yorkton-Melville
Next Election: 2022/2024
David Boulding, Mayor
Diane Smith, Administrator

Mendham

P.O. Box 69
Mendham, SK S0N 1P0
Tel: 306-679-2000; *Fax:* 306-679-2275
burstall@sasktel.net
Municipal Type: Village
Incorporated: April 1, 1930; *Area:* 0.5 sq km
Population in 2016: 30
Provincial Electoral District(s): Cypress Hills
Federal Electoral District(s): Cypress Hills-Grasslands
Next Election: 2022/2024
Kevin Angerman, Mayor
Lucein Stuebing, Clerk

Meota

P.O. Box 123
Meota, SK S0M 1X0
Tel: 306-892-2277; *Fax:* 306-892-2275
vmeota@sasktel.net
www.meota.ca
Municipal Type: Village
Incorporated: July 6, 1911; *Area:* 1.55 sq km
Population in 2016: 304
Provincial Electoral District(s): Cut Knife-Turtleford
Federal Electoral District(s): Battlefords-Lloydminster
Next Election: 2022/2024
John R. MacDonald, Mayor, 306-892-2452
Jennifer Fisher, Administrator

Mervin

P.O. Box 35
9 Main St.
Mervin, SK S0M 1Y0
Tel: 306-845-2784; *Fax:* 306-845-3563
villageofmervin@littleloon.ca
www.villageofmervin.com
Municipal Type: Village
Incorporated: March 17, 1920; *Area:* 0.73 sq km
Population in 2016: 159
Provincial Electoral District(s): Cut Knife-Turtleford
Federal Electoral District(s): Battlefords-Lloydminster
Next Election: 2022/2024
George Smith, Mayor
Lora Hundt, Administrator

Metinota

P.O. Box 47
Meota, SK S0M 1X0
Tel: 306-892-2557; *Fax:* 306-892-2250
rvmetinota@sasktel.net
Municipal Type: Resort Village
Area: 170.0 sq km
Population in 2016: 80
Provincial Electoral District(s): Cut Knife-Turtleford
Federal Electoral District(s): Battlefords-Lloydminster
Next Election: 2022/2024
Glen Wouters, Mayor
Carmen Menssa, Administrator

Michel Village

Sylvestre Place
P.O. Box 250
Dillon, SK S0M 0S0
Tel: 306-282-4401; *Fax:* 306-282-2155
michelvillage@sasktel.net
Municipal Type: Northern Hamlet
Incorporated: Nov. 1, 1983; *Area:* 3.73 sq km
Population in 2016: 57
Provincial Electoral District(s): Athabasca
Federal Electoral District(s): Desnethé-Missinippi-Churchill River
Next Election: 2022/2024
Brent Janvier, Mayor
Allison Janvier, Clerk

Midale

P.O. Box 128
233 Main St.
Midale, SK S0C 1S0
Tel: 306-458-2400; *Fax:* 306-458-2209
www.townofmidale.com
Municipal Type: Town
Incorporated: Aug. 10, 1907; *Area:* 1.53 sq km
Population in 2016: 604
Provincial Electoral District(s): Estevan
Federal Electoral District(s): Souris-Moose Mountain
Next Election: 2022/2024
Note: Proclaimed as a town on March 1, 1962.
Allan Hauglum, Mayor, 306-458-2807
Linda M. Dugan, Administrator

Middle Lake

P.O. Box 119
Middle Lake, SK S0K 2X0
Tel: 306-367-2149; *Fax:* 306-367-4963
dhvillage@sasktel.net
www.middlelake.ca
Municipal Type: Village
Incorporated: Jan. 1, 1963; *Area:* 1.26 sq km
Population in 2016: 241
Provincial Electoral District(s): Batoche
Federal Electoral District(s): Carlton Trail-Eagle Creek
Next Election: 2022/2024
Ken Herman, Mayor
Colette Hauser, Administrator

Milden

P.O. Box 70
202 Centre St.
Milden, SK S0L 2L0
Tel: 306-935-2131; *Fax:* 306-935-2020
vmilden@sasktel.net
www.villageofmilden.com
Municipal Type: Village
Incorporated: July 20, 1911; *Area:* 1.19 sq km
Population in 2016: 167
Provincial Electoral District(s): Rosetown-Elrose
Federal Electoral District(s): Carlton Trail-Eagle Creek
Next Election: 2022/2024
Travis Inverarity, Mayor
Heather Maxemniuk, Administrator

Milestone

P.O. Box 74
105 Main St.
Milestone, SK S0G 3L0
Tel: 306-436-2130; *Fax:* 306-436-2051
milcal@sasktel.net
www.milestonesk.ca
Municipal Type: Town
Incorporated: March 14, 1903; *Area:* 2.17 sq km
Population in 2016: 699
Provincial Electoral District(s): Indian Head-Milestone
Federal Electoral District(s): Moose Jaw-Lake Centre-Lanigan
Next Election: 2022/2024
Note: Proclaimed as a town on Aug. 15, 1906.
Jeff Brown, Mayor
Stephen Schury, Administrator

Minton

P.O. Box 52
Minton, SK S0C 1T0
Tel: 306-969-2144; *Fax:* 306-969-2127
rmnine@sasktel.net
Municipal Type: Village
Incorporated: Jan. 1, 1951; *Area:* 0.3 sq km
Population in 2016: 55
Provincial Electoral District(s): Weyburn-Big Muddy
Federal Electoral District(s): Souris-Moose Mountain
Next Election: 2022/2024
Dennis Simpart, Mayor
Loran Tessier, Clerk

Missinipe

c/o Government Relations
P.O. Box 5000
La Ronge, SK S0J 1L0
Tel: 306-425-4321; *Fax:* 306-425-2401
Municipal Type: Northern Hamlet
Incorporated: Feb. 1, 1984; *Area:* 1.87 sq km
Population in 2016: 5
Provincial Electoral District(s): Cumberland
Federal Electoral District(s): Desnethé-Missinippe-Churchill River
Next Election: 2022/2024
Sandra Galambos, Advisor

Mistatim

P.O. Box 145
Mistatim, SK S0E 1B0
Tel: 306-889-2008; *Fax:* 306-889-4439
villageofmistatim@yourlink.ca
Municipal Type: Village
Incorporated: July 1, 1952; *Area:* 0.47 sq km
Population in 2016: 101
Provincial Electoral District(s): Carrot River Valley
Federal Electoral District(s): Yorkton-Melville
Next Election: 2022/2024
Gene Legare, Mayor
Cathy Murray, Administrator

Mistusinne

P.O. Box 160
Elbow, SK S0H 1J0
Tel: 306-854-4637; *Fax:* 306-854-4668
mistusinne@sasktel.net
www.mistusinne.com
Other Information: Maintenance Phone: 306-854-2068
Municipal Type: Resort Village
Area: 1.49 sq km
Population in 2016: 77
Provincial Electoral District(s): Thunder Creek
Federal Electoral District(s): Cypress Hills-Grasslands
Next Election: 2022/2024
Lynne Saas, Mayor, 306-854-4658
Yvonne Jess, Administrator
Leanne Hurlburt, Clerk

Montmartre

P.O. Box 146
Montmartre, SK S0G 3M0
Tel: 306-424-2040; *Fax:* 306-424-2065
rm126@sasktel.net
www.montmartre-sk.com
Municipal Type: Village
Incorporated: Oct. 19, 1908; *Area:* 1.63 sq km
Population in 2016: 490
Provincial Electoral District(s): Moosomin
Federal Electoral District(s): Souris-Moose Mountain
Next Election: 2022/2024
Robert Chittenden, Mayor
Dale Brenner, Administrator

Moosomin

P.O. Box 730
701 Main St.
Moosomin, SK S0G 3N0
Tel: 306-435-2988; *Fax:* 306-435-3343
twn.moosomin@sasktel.net
www.moosomin.com
Municipal Type: Town
Incorporated: March 20, 1889; *Area:* 7.59 sq km
Population in 2016: 2,743
Provincial Electoral District(s): Moosomin
Federal Electoral District(s): Souris-Moose Mountain
Next Election: 2022/2024
Larry Tomlinson, Mayor, 306-435-7943
Paul Listrom, Chief Administrative Officer

Morse

P.O. Box 270
400 Main St.
Morse, SK S0H 3C0
Tel: 306-629-3300; *Fax:* 306-629-3235
morse@sasktel.net
morsesask.com
Municipal Type: Town
Incorporated: March 11, 1910; *Area:* 1.45 sq km
Population in 2016: 242
Provincial Electoral District(s): Thunder Creek
Federal Electoral District(s): Cypress Hills-Grasslands
Next Election: 2022/2024
Note: Proclaimed as a town on Nov. 1, 1912.
George Byklum, Mayor
Tamara Knight, Administrator

Mortlach

P.O. Box 10
116 Rose St.
Mortlach, SK S0H 3E0
Tel: 306-355-2554; *Fax:* 306-355-2557
village.mortlach@sasktel.net
www.mortlach.ca
Municipal Type: Village
Incorporated: April 19, 1906; *Area:* 2.76 sq km
Population in 2016: 261
Provincial Electoral District(s): Thunder Creek
Federal Electoral District(s): Cypress Hills-Grasslands
Next Election: 2022/2024
Dale Domeij, Mayor, 306-355-2370
Faye Campbell, Administrator

Mossbank

P.O. Box 370
311 Main St.
Mossbank, SK S0H 3G0
Tel: 306-354-2294; *Fax:* 306-354-7725
townofmossbank@sasktel.net
www.mossbank.ca
Municipal Type: Town
Incorporated: Dec. 14, 1915; *Area:* 1.75 sq km
Population in 2016: 360
Provincial Electoral District(s): Wood River
Federal Electoral District(s): Cypress Hills-Grasslands
Next Election: 2022/2024
Note: Proclaimed as a town on May 15, 1959.
Gregg Nagel, Mayor
Chris Costley, Chief Administrative Officer

Muenster

P.O. Box 98
Muenster, SK S0K 2Y0
Tel: 306-682-2794; *Fax:* 306-682-4179
muenster@sasktel.net
www.villageofmuenster.ca
Municipal Type: Village
Incorporated: Aug. 18, 1908; *Area:* 1.24 sq km
Population in 2016: 430
Provincial Electoral District(s): Humboldt

Federal Electoral District(s): Carlton Trail-Eagle Creek
Next Election: 2022/2024
Reva Bauer, Mayor
Rose M. Haeusler, Administrator

Naicam

P.O. Box 238
Naicam, SK S0K 2Z0
Tel: 306-874-2280; *Fax:* 306-874-5444
naicam@sasktel.net
www.townofnaicam.ca
Municipal Type: Town
Incorporated: April 28, 1921; *Area:* 1.69 sq km
Population in 2016: 661
Provincial Electoral District(s): Melfort
Federal Electoral District(s): Yorkton-Melville
Next Election: 2022/2024
Note: Proclaimed as a town on Sept. 1, 1954.
Rodger Hayward, Mayor
Janelle Scott, Administrator

Neilburg

P.O. Box 280
39 L.E. Gibbons Centre St.
Neilburg, SK S0M 2C0
Tel: 306-823-4321; *Fax:* 306-823-4477
neilburg@sasktel.net
www.neilburg.ca
Municipal Type: Village
Incorporated: Jan. 1, 1947; *Area:* 1.16 sq km
Population in 2016: 379
Provincial Electoral District(s): Cut Knife-Turtleford
Federal Electoral District(s): Battlefords-Lloydminster
Next Election: 2022/2024
Brent Wiens, Mayor
Joline Houk, Administrator

Netherhill

P.O. Box 4
Netherhill, SK S0L 2M0
Tel: 306-463-2905; *Fax:* 306-463-2905
hendersonl@sasktel.net
Municipal Type: Village
Incorporated: April 28, 1910; *Area:* 0.73 sq km
Population in 2016: 25
Provincial Electoral District(s): Rosetown-Elrose
Federal Electoral District(s): Cypress Hills-Grasslands
Next Election: 2022/2024
Bruce Campbell, Mayor
Melissa Chandler, Administrator

Neudorf

P.O. Box 187
Neudorf, SK S0A 2T0
Tel: 306-748-2551; *Fax:* 306-748-2647
vneudorf@sasktel.net
Municipal Type: Village
Incorporated: April 25, 1905; *Area:* 2.05 sq km
Population in 2016: 263
Provincial Electoral District(s): Last Mountain-Touchwood
Federal Electoral District(s): Yorkton-Melville
Next Election: 2022/2024
Murray J. Hanowski, Mayor
Crystal Campbell, Administrator

Neville

P.O. Box 88
Neville, SK S0N 1T0
Tel: 306-627-3255; *Fax:* 306-627-3546
village.neville@sasktel.net
Municipal Type: Village
Incorporated: July 5, 1912; *Area:* 1.10 sq km
Population in 2016: 87
Provincial Electoral District(s): Wood River
Federal Electoral District(s): Cypress Hills-Grasslands
Next Election: 2022/2024
Carolyn Robichaud, Mayor
Cindy Berry, Clerk

Nipawin

P.O. Box 2134
210 Second Ave. East
Nipawin, SK S0E 1E0
Tel: 306-862-9866; *Fax:* 306-862-3076
info@nipawin.com
www.nipawin.com
Municipal Type: Town
Incorporated: May 7, 1925; *Area:* 8.03 sq km
Population in 2016: 4,401
Provincial Electoral District(s): Carrot River Valley
Federal Electoral District(s): Prince Albert

Next Election: 2022/2024
Note: Proclaimed as a town on May 1, 1937.
Rennie Harper, Mayor, 306-862-3320
Barry Elliott, Chief Administrative Officer

Nokomis

P.O. Box 189
101 - 3rd Ave. West
Nokomis, SK S0G 3R0
Tel: 306-528-2010; *Fax:* 306-528-2024
townofnokomis@sasktel.net
www.nokomisweb.com
Municipal Type: Town
Incorporated: March 5, 1908; *Area:* 2.61 sq km
Population in 2016: 404
Provincial Electoral District(s): Arm River-Watrous
Federal Electoral District(s): Moose Jaw-Lake Centre-Lanigan
Next Election: 2022/2024
Note: Proclaimed as a town on Aug. 15, 1908.
David Mark, Mayor
Tanya Zdunich, Assistant Administrator

Norquay

P.O. Box 327
25 Main St.
Norquay, SK S0A 2V0
Tel: 306-594-2101; *Fax:* 306-594-2347
norquay@sasktel.net
www.norquay.ca
Municipal Type: Town
Incorporated: June 4, 1913; *Area:* 1.69 sq km
Population in 2016: 434
Provincial Electoral District(s): Canora-Pelly
Federal Electoral District(s): Yorkton-Melville
Next Election: 2022/2024
Note: Proclaimed as a town on March 1, 1963.
Don Tower, Mayor
Denise Sorrell, Administrator

North Grove

P.O. Box 473
#5, 1410 Caribou St. W
Moose Jaw, SK S6H 4P1
Tel: 306-694-8300; *Fax:* 306-395-2767
rvnorthgrove@shaw.ca
www.northgrovesk.wordpress.com
Municipal Type: Resort Village
Area: 1.03 sq km
Population in 2016: 132
Provincial Electoral District(s): Thunder Creek
Federal Electoral District(s): Moose Jaw-Lake Centre-Lanigan
Next Election: 2022/2024
Sherry Hetherington, Mayor
Tracy Edwards, Administrator

North Portal

P.O. Box 119
204 Park Ave.
North Portal, SK S0C 1W0
Tel: 306-927-5050; *Fax:* 306-927-2033
villagen@sasktel.net
Municipal Type: Village
Incorporated: Nov. 16, 1903; *Area:* 2.49 sq km
Population in 2016: 115
Provincial Electoral District(s): Estevan
Federal Electoral District(s): Souris-Moose Mountain
Next Election: 2022/2024
Kaylah Turner, Mayor
Lindsay Davis, Administrator

Odessa

P.O. Box 91
Odessa, SK S0G 3S0
Tel: 306-957-2020; *Fax:* 306-957-4502
villageofodessa@sasktel.net
www.odessask.com
Municipal Type: Village
Incorporated: March 14, 1911; *Area:* 1.18 sq km
Population in 2016: 205
Provincial Electoral District(s): Indian Head-Milestone
Federal Electoral District(s): Souris-Moose Mountain
Next Election: 2022/2024
Larry Lockert, Mayor, 306-957-2047
Leticia Gould, Administrator

Sheho
P.O. Box 130
Sheho, SK S0A 3T0
Tel: 306-849-2044
shehovillage@sasktel.net
Municipal Type: Village
Incorporated: June 30, 1905; *Area:* 1.95 sq km
Population in 2016: 105
Provincial Electoral District(s): Kelvington-Wadena
Federal Electoral District(s): Yorkton-Melville
Next Election: 2022/2024
Walter Skiehar, Mayor
Raelyn Knudson, Clerk

Shell Lake
P.O. Box 280
Shell Lake, SK S0J 2G0
Tel: 306-427-2272; *Fax:* 306-427-4800
village.sl@sasktel.net
www.villageofshelllake.ca
Municipal Type: Village
Incorporated: Oct. 18, 1940; *Area:* 1.09 sq km
Population in 2016: 175
Provincial Electoral District(s): Rosthern-Shellbrook
Federal Electoral District(s): Desnethé-Missinippi-Churchill River
Next Election: 2022/2024
Anita Weiers, Mayor
Tara Bueckert, Administrator

Shellbrook
P.O. Box 40
71 Main St.
Shellbrook, SK S0J 2E0
Tel: 306-747-4900; *Fax:* 306-747-3111
townoffice@townofshellbrook.ca
www.shellbrook.net
Municipal Type: Town
Incorporated: Nov. 18, 1909; *Area:* 2.13 sq km
Population in 2016: 1,444
Provincial Electoral District(s): Rosthern-Shellbrook
Federal Electoral District(s): Prince Albert
Next Election: 2022/2024
Note: Proclaimed as a town on April 1, 1948.
George Tomporowski, Mayor
Kelly Hoare, Administrator

Shields
P.O. Box 81
Dundurn, SK S0K 1K0
Tel: 306-492-2259; *Fax:* 306-492-2068
shields@xplornet.ca
www.shields.ca
Municipal Type: Resort Village
Area: 0.72 sq km
Population in 2016: 288
Provincial Electoral District(s): Arm River-Watrous
Federal Electoral District(s): Moose Jaw-Lake Centre-Lanigan
Next Election: 2022/2024
Eldon MacKay, Mayor, 306-492-4639
Jessie Williams, Administrator

Silton
P.O. Box 1
Silton, SK S0G 4L0
Tel: 306-731-3222
villageofsilton@xplornet.ca
Municipal Type: Village
Incorporated: July 2, 1914; *Area:* 1.07 sq km
Population in 2016: 71
Provincial Electoral District(s): Last Mountain-Touchwood
Federal Electoral District(s): Moose Jaw-Lake Centre-Lanigan
Next Election: 2022/2024
Peta Rich, Mayor
Lori Wild, Clerk

Simpson
P.O. Box 10
303 George St.
Simpson, SK S0G 4M0
Tel: 306-836-2020; *Fax:* 306-836-4460
lmattson928@hotmail.com
www.simpsonsask.ca
Municipal Type: Village
Incorporated: July 11, 1911; *Area:* 1.41 sq km
Population in 2016: 127
Provincial Electoral District(s): Arm River-Watrous
Federal Electoral District(s): Moose Jaw-Lake Centre-Lanigan
Next Election: 2022/2024
Jeremy Nimchuk, Mayor
Darlene Mann, Administrator

Sintaluta
P.O. Box 150
Sintaluta, SK S0G 4N0
Tel: 306-727-2100; *Fax:* 306-727-2100
sintaluta@yourlink.ca
Municipal Type: Town
Incorporated: Oct. 27, 1898; *Area:* 2.70 sq km
Population in 2016: 119
Provincial Electoral District(s): Indian Head-Milestone
Federal Electoral District(s): Regina-Qu'Appelle
Next Election: 2022/2024
Note: Proclaimed as a town on June 1, 1907.
Kitt Bank, Mayor
Donna Pitre, Administrator

Sled Lake
P.O. Box 850
Big River, SK S0J 0E0
Tel: 306-832-4442; *Fax:* 306-832-2269
Municipal Type: NS
Population in 2016: 10
Provincial Electoral District(s): Athabasca
Federal Electoral District(s): Desnethé-Missinippi-Churchill River
Next Election: 2022/2024
Howard Fonos, Chair
Bruce Leier, Advisor

Smeaton
P.O. Box 70
Smeaton, SK S0J 2J0
Tel: 306-426-2044; *Fax:* 306-426-2291
smeaton@sasktel.net
Municipal Type: Village
Incorporated: March 7, 1944; *Area:* 1.38 sq km
Population in 2016: 182
Provincial Electoral District(s): Saskatchewan Rivers
Federal Electoral District(s): Prince Albert
Next Election: 2022/2024
Sonia Fidyk, Mayor
Michelle Grunerud, Administrator

Smiley
P.O. Box 90
Smiley, SK S0L 2Z0
Tel: 306-838-2020; *Fax:* 306-838-4343
administrator@rmofprairiedale.ca
Municipal Type: Village
Incorporated: Nov. 26, 1913; *Area:* 0.64 sq km
Population in 2016: 60
Provincial Electoral District(s): Kindersley
Federal Electoral District(s): Battlefords-Lloydminster
Next Election: 2022/2024
William Wasleynchuk, Mayor
Charlotte Helfrich, Administrator

South Lake
#6, 1410 Caribou St. W
Moose Jaw, SK S6H 7S9
Tel: 306-692-7399; *Fax:* 306-692-7380
southlake@sasktel.net
www.southlakeresort.ca
Municipal Type: Resort Village
Area: 1.15 sq km
Population in 2016: 169
Provincial Electoral District(s): Thunder Creek
Federal Electoral District(s): Moose Jaw-Lake Centre-Lanigan
Next Election: 2022/2024
Art Schick, Mayor
Judy Szuch, Clerk

Southend
c/o Government Relations
P.O. Box 5000
La Ronge, SK S0J 2L0
Tel: 306-425-4323; *Fax:* 306-425-2401
Other Information: Toll-Free Phone: 800-663-1555
Municipal Type: Northern Hamlet
Population in 2016: 128
Provincial Electoral District(s): Cumberland
Federal Electoral District(s): Desnethé-Missinippi-Churchill River
Next Election: 2022/2024
Valerie , Antoniuk
Valerie Antoniuk, Advisor, 306-425-4323

Southey
P.O. Box 248
260 Keats St.
Southey, SK S0G 4P0
Tel: 306-726-2202; *Fax:* 306-726-2916
townofsouthey@sasktel.net
www.southey.ca
Other Information: Alt. email: townofsouthey@sasktel.net

Municipal Type: Town
Incorporated: Nov. 9, 1907; *Area:* 1.56 sq km
Population in 2016: 804
Provincial Electoral District(s): Last Mountain-Touchwood
Federal Electoral District(s): Regina-Qu'Appelle
Next Election: 2022/2024
Note: Proclaimed as a town on Nov. 1, 1980.
Martin Lingelbach, Mayor
Ferne Senft, Administrator

Spalding
P.O. Box 280
Spalding, SK S0K 4C0
Tel: 306-872-2276; *Fax:* 306-872-2275
spalding.village@sasktel.net
www.villageofspalding.ca
Municipal Type: Village
Incorporated: March 11, 1924; *Area:* 1.18 sq km
Population in 2016: 244
Provincial Electoral District(s): Melfort
Federal Electoral District(s): Yorkton-Melville
Next Election: 2022/2024
Wes Schultz, Mayor
Cathy Holt, Administrator

Speers
P.O. Box 974
Speers, SK S0M 2V0
Tel: 306-246-2114; *Fax:* 306-246-2173
rm436@littleloon.ca
Municipal Type: Village
Incorporated: Dec. 24, 1915; *Area:* 0.69 sq km
Population in 2016: 60
Provincial Electoral District(s): Rosthern-Shellbrook
Federal Electoral District(s): Carlton Trail-Eagle Creek
Next Election: 2022/2024
Kenneth Rebeyka, Mayor
Dean Nicholson, Clerk

Spiritwood
P.O. Box 460
Spiritwood, SK S0J 2M0
Tel: 306-883-2161; *Fax:* 306-883-3212
tos@sasktel.net
www.townofspiritwood.ca
Municipal Type: Town
Incorporated: Oct. 1, 1935; *Area:* 2.95 sq km
Population in 2016: 786
Provincial Electoral District(s): Rosthern-Shellbrook
Federal Electoral District(s): Desnethé-Missinippi-Churchill River
Next Election: 2022/2024
Note: Proclaimed as a town on Sept. 1, 1965.
Gary Von Holwede, Mayor
Rhonda Saam, Chief Administrative Officer

Springside
P.O. Box 414
Springside, SK S0A 3V0
Tel: 306-792-2022; *Fax:* 306-792-2210
springside@sasktel.net
www.townofspringside.ca
Municipal Type: Town
Incorporated: Nov. 11, 1909; *Area:* 0.64 sq km
Population in 2016: 502
Provincial Electoral District(s): Canora-Pelly
Federal Electoral District(s): Yorkton-Melville
Next Election: 2022/2024
Note: Proclaimed as a town on Nov. 1, 1985.
Al Langley, Mayor
Tracey Werner, Administrator

Spy Hill
P.O. Box 69
Spy Hill, SK S0A 3W0
Tel: 306-534-2255; *Fax:* 306-534-4520
spyhillvillage@sasktel.net
www.villageofspyhill.ca
Municipal Type: Village
Incorporated: April 22, 1910; *Area:* 1.19 sq km
Population in 2016: 168
Provincial Electoral District(s): Melville-Saltcoats
Federal Electoral District(s): Yorkton-Melville
Next Election: 2022/2024
Elgin Clark, Mayor
Susan Gawryluk, Administrator

Stanley Mission
c/o Government Relations
P.O. Box 5000
La Ronge, SK S0J 2P0
Tel: 306-425-4321; *Fax:* 306-425-2401
Other Information: Toll-Free Phone: 800-663-1555

Municipal Type: NS
Population in 2016: 95
Provincial Electoral District(s): Cumberland
Federal Electoral District(s): Desnethé-Missinippi-Churchill River
Next Election: 2022/2024
Annie McLeod, Chair
Sandra Galambos, Advisor, 306-425-4321

Star City
P.O. Box 250
145 - 4th St.
Star City, SK S0E 1P0
Tel: 306-863-2282; Fax: 306-863-2277
town.starcity@sasktel.net
www.townofstarcity.com
Municipal Type: Town
Incorporated: April 6, 1906; Area: 0.7 sq km
Population in 2016: 387
Provincial Electoral District(s): Melfort
Federal Electoral District(s): Prince Albert
Next Election: 2022/2024
Note: Proclaimed as a town on Nov. 1, 1921.
Ron Campbell, Mayor
Anita Tkachuk, Administrator

Stenen
P.O. Box 160
Stenen, SK S0A 3X0
Tel: 306-548-4334; Fax: 306-548-4334
villageofstenen@sasktel.net
www.stenensask.com
Municipal Type: Village
Incorporated: Aug. 14, 1912; Area: 0.58 sq km
Population in 2016: 90
Provincial Electoral District(s): Canora-Pelly
Federal Electoral District(s): Yorkton-Melville
Next Election: 2022/2024
Victor Wasylenchuk, Mayor
Sabrina Chernyk, Administrator

Stewart Valley
P.O. Box 10
Stewart Valley, SK S0N 2P0
Tel: 306-778-2105; Fax: 306-778-2152
vlg.stvalley@sasktel.net
Municipal Type: Village
Incorporated: Jan. 1, 1958; Area: 0.86 sq km
Population in 2016: 91
Provincial Electoral District(s): Swift Current
Federal Electoral District(s): Cypress Hills-Grasslands
Next Election: 2022/2024
Blaine Wellsch, Mayor
Teresa Johnsgaard, Clerk

Stockholm
P.O. Box 265
Stockholm, SK S0A 3Y0
Tel: 306-793-2151; Fax: 306-793-4597
stockholm@sasktel.net
www.stockholmsask.com
Municipal Type: Village
Incorporated: June 30, 1905; Area: 1.64 sq km
Population in 2016: 352
Provincial Electoral District(s): Melville-Saltcoats
Federal Electoral District(s): Yorkton-Melville
Next Election: 2022/2024
K. Jason Nichols, Mayor
Lorie Jackson, Administrator

Stony Rapids
P.O. Box 120
Johnson St.
Stony Rapids, SK S0J 2R0
Tel: 306-439-2173; Fax: 306-439-2098
nhstonyrap@sasktel.net
Municipal Type: Northern Hamlet
Incorporated: April 1, 1992; Area: 3.96 sq km
Population in 2016: 262
Provincial Electoral District(s): Athabasca
Federal Electoral District(s): Desnethé-Missinippi-Churchill River
Next Election: 2022/2024
Mervin MacDonald, Mayor
Shawna Sayazie, Clerk

Storthoaks
P.O. Box 40
Storthoaks, SK S0C 2K0
Tel: 306-449-2262; Fax: 306-449-2210
rm31@sasktel.net
Municipal Type: Village
Incorporated: June 5, 1940; Area: 1.28 sq km
Population in 2016: 108

Provincial Electoral District(s): Cannington
Federal Electoral District(s): Souris-Moose Mountain
Next Election: 2022/2024
Sydney Chicoine, Mayor
Gisele Bouchard, Administrator

Stoughton
P.O. Box 397
232 Main St.
Stoughton, SK S0G 4T0
Tel: 306-457-2413; Fax: 306-457-3162
stoughtontown@sasktel.net
stoughtonsk.ca
Other Information: Alt. E-mail: office@stoughtonsk.ca
Municipal Type: Town
Incorporated: Feb. 26, 1904; Area: 2.13 sq km
Population in 2016: 649
Provincial Electoral District(s): Cannington
Federal Electoral District(s): Souris-Moose Mountain
Next Election: 2022/2024
Note: Proclaimed as a town on June 1, 1960.
Bill Knous, Mayor
Chris Miskolczi, Administrator

Strasbourg
P.O. Box 369
1 - 200 Mountain St.
Strasbourg, SK S0G 4V0
Tel: 306-725-3707; Fax: 306-725-3613
strasbourg@sasktel.net
www.townofstrasbourg.ca
Municipal Type: Town
Incorporated: April 19, 1906; Area: 5.70 sq km
Population in 2016: 800
Provincial Electoral District(s): Last Mountain-Touchwood
Federal Electoral District(s): Moose Jaw-Lake Centre-Lanigan
Next Election: 2022/2024
Note: Proclaimed as a town on July 1, 1907.
Kelvin Schapansky, Mayor, 306-725-4512
Jennifer Josephson, Administrator

Strongfield
P.O. Box 87
Strongfield, SK S0H 3Z0
Tel: 306-857-2200; Fax: 306-857-2201
villageofstrongfield@yourlink.ca
Municipal Type: Village
Incorporated: May 3, 1912; Area: 0.8 sq km
Population in 2016: 40
Provincial Electoral District(s): Arm River-Watrous
Federal Electoral District(s): Moose Jaw-Lake Centre-Lanigan
Next Election: 2022/2024
Jeff Vollmer, Mayor
Brandy Losie, Clerk

Sturgis
P.O. Box 520
209 - 1st Ave. SE
Sturgis, SK S0A 4A0
Tel: 306-548-2108; Fax: 306-548-2948
townofsturgis@sasktel.net
www.townofsturgis.com
Municipal Type: Town
Incorporated: Sept. 3, 1912; Area: 3.31 sq km
Population in 2016: 644
Provincial Electoral District(s): Canora-Pelly
Federal Electoral District(s): Yorkton-Melville
Next Election: 2022/2024
Note: Proclaimed as a town on March 1, 1951.
Alan Holmberg, Mayor
Olivia (Bim) Bartch, Administrator

Success
P.O. Box 40
Success, SK S0N 2R0
Tel: 306-773-7934
success1@yourlink.ca
Municipal Type: Village
Incorporated: Oct. 25, 1912; Area: 1.38 sq km
Population in 2016: 45
Provincial Electoral District(s): Swift Current
Federal Electoral District(s): Cypress Hills-Grasslands
Next Election: 2022/2024
Doodnath Gajadhar, Mayor
Donna Butler, Clerk

Sun Valley
P.O. Box 2260
Moose Jaw, SK S6H 7W6
Tel: 306-694-0055
rvsunvalley@yahoo.com

Municipal Type: Resort Village
Area: 2.33 sq km
Population in 2016: 118
Provincial Electoral District(s): Thunder Creek
Federal Electoral District(s): Moose Jaw-Lake Centre-Lanigan
Next Election: 2022/2024
Barry Gunther, Mayor
Kathy Mealing, Administrator

Sunset Cove
P.O. Box 68
Strasbourg, SK S0G 4V0
Tel: 306-725-3485
rvsunsetcove@sasktel.net
www.rvsunsetcove.ca
Municipal Type: Resort Village
Incorporated: 1959; Area: 0.17 sq km
Population in 2016: 18
Provincial Electoral District(s): Last Mountain-Touchwood
Federal Electoral District(s): Moose Jaw-Lake Centre-Lanigan
Next Election: 2022/2024
Tom Fulcher, Mayor
Barbara Griffin, Administrator

Tantallon
P.O. Box 70
Tantallon, SK S0A 4B0
Tel: 306-643-2112; Fax: 306-643-2113
tantallon@sasktel.net
Municipal Type: Village
Incorporated: June 17, 1904; Area: 0.84 sq km
Population in 2016: 95
Provincial Electoral District(s): Melville-Saltcoats
Federal Electoral District(s): Yorkton-Melville
Next Election: 2022/2024
Jim Johnson, Mayor
Susan Gawryluk, Administrator

Tessier
P.O. Box 34
Tessier, SK S0L 3G0
Tel: 306-656-4580
Municipal Type: Village
Incorporated: Aug. 24, 1909; Area: 1 sq km
Population in 2016: 25
Provincial Electoral District(s): Rosetown-Elrose
Federal Electoral District(s): Carlton Trail-Eagle Creek
Next Election: 2022/2024
Maurice Hanson, Mayor
Barbara Shaw, Clerk

Theodore
P.O. Box 417
102 Main St.
Theodore, SK S0A 4C0
Tel: 306-647-2315; Fax: 306-647-2476
theodore.village@sasktel.net
www.villageoftheodore.com
Municipal Type: Village
Incorporated: July 5, 1907; Area: 1.73 sq km
Population in 2016: 323
Provincial Electoral District(s): Kelvington-Wadena
Federal Electoral District(s): Yorkton-Melville
Next Election: 2022/2024
Vacant, Mayor
Lyndon Stachoski, Administrator

Thode
P.O. Box 202
Dundurn, SK S0K 1K0
Tel: 306-492-2259; Fax: 306-492-2068
admin@resortvillageofthode.ca
www.resortvillageofthode.ca
Municipal Type: Resort Village
Area: 0.73 sq km
Population in 2016: 148
Provincial Electoral District(s): Arm River-Watrous
Federal Electoral District(s): Moose Jaw-Lake Centre-Lanigan
Next Election: 2022/2024
Alan Thomarat, Mayor
Jessie Williams, Administrator

Timber Bay
General Delivery
Timber Bay, SK S0J 2T0
Tel: 306-663-5885; Fax: 306-663-5052
northerntimberbay@sasktel.net
Municipal Type: Northern Hamlet
Incorporated: Oct. 1, 1983; Area: 4.44 sq km
Population in 2016: 82
Provincial Electoral District(s): Cumberland

Federal Electoral District(s): Desnethé-Missinippi-Churchill River
Next Election: 2022/2024
Peggy Hennie, Mayor
Celinda Lavallee, Administrator

Tisdale
P.O. Box 1090
901 - 100 St.
Tisdale, SK S0E 1T0
Tel: 306-873-2681; *Fax:* 306-873-5700
contact@tisdale.ca
www.tisdale.ca
Municipal Type: Town
Incorporated: May 15, 1905; *Area:* 6.47 sq km
Population in 2016: 3,235
Provincial Electoral District(s): Carrot River Valley
Federal Electoral District(s): Prince Albert
Next Election: 2022/2024
Note: Proclaimed as a town on Nov. 1, 1920.
Al Jellicoe, Mayor
Brad Hvidston, Administrator

Tobin Lake
P.O. Box 1479
Nipawin, SK S0E 1E0
Tel: 306-862-2895; *Fax:* 306-862-9320
rvtobinlake@sasktel.net
www.resortvillageoftobinlake.com
Municipal Type: Resort Village
Area: 1.81 sq km
Population in 2016: 89
Provincial Electoral District(s): Carrot River Valley
Federal Electoral District(s): Prince Albert
Next Election: 2022/2024
Robert Taylor, Mayor
Karalee Davis, Administrator

Togo
P.O. Box 100
Togo, SK S0A 4E0
Tel: 306-597-2114; *Fax:* 306-597-4766
villageoftogo@sasktel.net
villageoftogo.com
Municipal Type: Village
Incorporated: Sept. 4, 1906; *Area:* 1.5 sq km
Population in 2016: 86
Provincial Electoral District(s): Canora-Pelly
Federal Electoral District(s): Yorkton-Melville
Next Election: 2022/2024
Loretta Erhardt, Mayor
Rita Brock, Administrator

Tompkins
P.O. Box 247
#5, 2nd St.
Tompkins, SK S0N 2S0
Tel: 306-622-2020; *Fax:* 306-622-2025
villageoftompkins@sasktel.net
www.villageoftompkins.ca
Municipal Type: Village
Incorporated: June 2, 1910; *Area:* 2.65 sq km
Population in 2016: 152
Provincial Electoral District(s): Cypress Hills
Federal Electoral District(s): Cypress Hills-Grasslands
Next Election: 2022/2024
John Woodward, Mayor
Colette Evans, Clerk

Torquay
P.O. Box 6
Torquay, SK S0C 2L0
Tel: 306-923-2172; *Fax:* 306-923-2172
villageoftorquay@sasktel.net
www.villageoftorquay.com
Municipal Type: Village
Incorporated: Dec. 11, 1923; *Area:* 1.35 sq km
Population in 2016: 255
Provincial Electoral District(s): Estevan
Federal Electoral District(s): Souris-Moose Mountain
Next Election: 2022/2024
Michael Strachan, Mayor, 306-421-7827
Thera-Lee Deschner, Administrator

Tramping Lake
P.O. Box 157
Tramping Lake, SK S0K 4H0
Tel: 306-228-2621; *Fax:* 306-228-2303
unity.admin@sasktel.net
Municipal Type: Village
Incorporated: April 10, 1917; *Area:* 1.39 sq km
Population in 2016: 60
Provincial Electoral District(s): Kindersley

Federal Electoral District(s): Battlefords-Lloydminster
Next Election: 2022/2024
Christine Lang, Mayor
Aileen Garrett, Clerk

Tribune
P.O. Box 61
Tribune, SK S0C 2M0
Tel: 306-456-2213; *Fax:* 306-456-2213
Municipal Type: Village
Incorporated: Feb. 18, 1914; *Area:* 1.61 sq km
Population in 2016: 45
Provincial Electoral District(s): Estevan
Federal Electoral District(s): Souris-Moose Mountain
Next Election: 2022/2024
Glenn Walkeden, Mayor
Dallas Locken, Clerk

Tugaske
P.O. Box 159
Tugaske, SK S0H 4B0
Tel: 306-759-2211; *Fax:* 306-759-2249
rm233@sasktel.net
www.tugaske.ca
Municipal Type: Village
Incorporated: May 7, 1909; *Area:* 0.76 sq km
Population in 2016: 75
Provincial Electoral District(s): Thunder Creek
Federal Electoral District(s): Moose Jaw-Lake Centre-Lanigan
Next Election: 2022/2024
Lorne Erickson, Mayor
Daryl Dean, Administrator

Turnor Lake
P.O. Box 130
Turnor St.
Turnor Lake, SK S0M 3E0
Tel: 306-894-2080; *Fax:* 306-894-2138
turnorlakehamlet@sasktel.net
Municipal Type: Northern Hamlet
Incorporated: Oct. 1, 1984; *Area:* 4.62 sq km
Population in 2016: 149
Provincial Electoral District(s): Athabasca
Federal Electoral District(s): Desnethé-Missinippi-Churchill River
Next Election: 2022/2024
Renee Desjarlais, Mayor
Doreen Morin, Clerk

Turtleford
P.O. Box 38
Turtleford, SK S0M 2Y0
Tel: 306-845-2156; *Fax:* 306-845-3320
townofturtleford@sasktel.net
www.townofturtleford.com
Municipal Type: Town
Incorporated: Oct. 9, 1914; *Area:* 1.64 sq km
Population in 2016: 496
Provincial Electoral District(s): Cut Knife-Turtleford
Federal Electoral District(s): Battlefords-Lloydminster
Next Election: 2022/2024
Note: Proclaimed as a town on July 1, 1983.
Doug Ask, Mayor
Deanna M. Kahl Lundberg, Administrator

Tuxford
#5, 1410 Caribou St. West
Moose Jaw, SK S0H 4C0
Tel: 306-972-9987
clerk@villageoftuxford.ca
www.villageoftuxford.ca
Municipal Type: Village
Incorporated: July 19, 1907; *Area:* 0.62 sq km
Population in 2016: 113
Provincial Electoral District(s): Thunder Creek
Federal Electoral District(s): Moose Jaw-Lake Centre-Lanigan
Next Election: 2022/2024
Chad Johnson, Mayor
Tracy Edwards, Administrator

Unity
P.O. Box 1030
#2, 100 First Ave. West
Unity, SK S0K 4L0
Tel: 306-228-2621; *Fax:* 306-228-4221
www.townofunity.com
Municipal Type: Town
Incorporated: May 18, 1909; *Area:* 9.77 sq km
Population in 2016: 2,573
Provincial Electoral District(s): Kindersley
Federal Electoral District(s): Battlefords-Lloydminster
Next Election: 2022/2024
Note: Proclaimed as a town on Nov. 1, 1919.

Ben Weber, Mayor
Aileen Garrett, Administrator

Uranium City
c/o Government Relations
P.O. Box 5000
La Ronge, SK S0J 1L0
Fax: 306-425-2401
Other Information: Toll-Free Phone: 800-663-1555
Municipal Type: Northern Settlement
Population in 2016: 73
Provincial Electoral District(s): Athabasca
Federal Electoral District(s): Desnethé-Missinippi-Churchill River
Next Election: 2022/2024
Dean Classen, Chair
Sandra Galambos, Advisor, 306-425-4321

Val Marie
P.O. Box 178
Val Marie, SK S0N 2T0
Tel: 306-298-2022; *Fax:* 306-298-2224
vovm@sasktel.net
www.valmarie.ca
Municipal Type: Village
Incorporated: Sept. 13, 1926; *Area:* 0.42 sq km
Population in 2016: 126
Provincial Electoral District(s): Wood River
Federal Electoral District(s): Cypress Hills-Grasslands
Next Election: 2022/2024
Roland Facette, Mayor
Cathy Legault, Administrator

Valparaiso
P.O. Box 473
Star City, SK S0E 1P0
Tel: 306-863-2522; *Fax:* 306-863-2255
r.m.starcity@sasktel.net
Municipal Type: Village
Incorporated: July 18, 1924; *Area:* 0.69 sq km
Population in 2016: 15
Provincial Electoral District(s): Melfort
Federal Electoral District(s): Prince Albert
Next Election: 2022/2024
Margaret Emro, Mayor
Ann Campbell, Clerk

Vanguard
P.O. Box 187
601 Dominion St.
Vanguard, SK S0N 2V0
Tel: 306-582-2295; *Fax:* 306-582-2296
vill.vanguard@sasktel.net
www.vanguardsk.ca
Municipal Type: Village
Incorporated: July 8, 1912; *Area:* 1.86 sq km
Population in 2016: 134
Provincial Electoral District(s): Wood River
Federal Electoral District(s): Cypress Hills-Grasslands
Next Election: 2022/2024
Allen Kuhlmann, Mayor
Sandra Krushelniski, Administrator

Vanscoy
P.O. Box 480
109 Main St.
Vanscoy, SK S0L 3J0
Tel: 306-668-2008; *Fax:* 306-978-0237
vanscoy@sasktel.net
www.vanscoyvillage.com
Municipal Type: Village
Incorporated: June 17, 1919; *Area:* 1.49 sq km
Population in 2016: 462
Provincial Electoral District(s): Biggar
Federal Electoral District(s): Carlton Trail-Eagle Creek
Next Election: 2022/2024
Robin Odnokon, Mayor
Dawn Steeves, Administrator

Vibank
Vibank Heritage Centre
P.O. Box 204
101 - 2nd Ave.
Vibank, SK S0G 4Y0
Tel: 306-762-2130; *Fax:* 306-762-4722
www.vibank.ca
Municipal Type: Village
Incorporated: June 23, 1911; *Area:* 0.73 sq km
Population in 2016: 385
Provincial Electoral District(s): Indian Head-Milestone
Federal Electoral District(s): Souris-Moose Mountain
Next Election: 2022/2024
Ryan Reiss, Mayor, 306-530-9405

Provincial Electoral District(s): Arm River-Watrous
Federal Electoral District(s): Moose Jaw-Lake Centre-Lanigan
Next Election: 2022/2024
Robert Clinkard, Mayor
Amber Clinkard, Administrator

Zealandia
P.O. Box 52
Zealandia, SK S0L 3N0
Tel: 306-882-3825; *Fax:* 306-882-4178
townofzealandia@yahoo.com
Municipal Type: Town
Incorporated: May 22, 1909; *Area:* 1.38 sq km
Population in 2016: 80
Provincial Electoral District(s): Rosetown-Elrose
Federal Electoral District(s): Carlton Trail-Eagle Creek
Next Election: 2022/2024
Note: Proclaimed as a town on Nov. 1, 1911.
Darren Haugen, Mayor
Amanda Bors, Clerk

Zelma
Zelma GMB #14
Allan, SK S0K 0C0
Tel: 306-257-3927; *Fax:* 306-257-4125
Municipal Type: Village
Incorporated: Aug. 10, 1910; *Area:* 0.72 sq km
Population in 2016: 35
Provincial Electoral District(s): Humboldt
Federal Electoral District(s): Moose Jaw-Lake Centre-Lanigan
Next Election: 2022/2024
R. Glen Crockett, Mayor
Maxine A. Fischer, Clerk

Zenon Park
P.O. Box 278
Zenon Park, SK S0E 1W0
Tel: 306-767-2233; *Fax:* 306-767-2226
vofzenon@sasktel.net
www.zenonpark.com
Municipal Type: Village
Incorporated: July 28, 1941; *Area:* 0.56 sq km
Population in 2016: 194
Provincial Electoral District(s): Carrot River Valley
Federal Electoral District(s): Prince Albert
Next Election: 2022/2024
Gilbert Ferre, Mayor
Lisa LeBlanc, Administrator

Rural Municipalities in Saskatchewan

Aberdeen No. 373
P.O. Box 40
101 Industrial Dr.
Aberdeen, SK S0K 0A0
Tel: 306-253-4312; *Fax:* 306-253-4445
rm373@sasktel.net
www.rmofaberdeen.ca
Municipal Type: Rural Municipalities
Incorporated: Dec. 13, 1909; *Area:* 673.43 sq km
Population in 2016: 1,379
Federal Electoral District(s): Carlton Trail-Eagle Creek
Next Election: 2022/2024
Martin Bettker, Reeve
Gary Dziadyk, Administrator

Abernethy No. 186
P.O. Box 249
Abernethy, SK S0A 0A0
Tel: 306-333-2044; *Fax:* 306-333-2285
rm186@sasktel.net
Municipal Type: Rural Municipalities
Incorporated: Dec. 11, 1911; *Area:* 779.42 sq km
Population in 2016: 362
Federal Electoral District(s): Regina-Qu'Appelle
Next Election: 2022/2024
John Fishley, Reeve
Karissa Lingelbach, Administrator

Antelope Park No. 322
P.O. Box 70
Marengo, SK S0L 2K0
Tel: 306-968-2922; *Fax:* 306-968-2278
rm292.rm322@sasktel.net
Municipal Type: Rural Municipalities
Incorporated: Dec. 11, 1911; *Area:* 612.66 sq km
Population in 2016: 130
Federal Electoral District(s): Battlefords-Lloydminster
Next Election: 2022/2024
Gordon Dommett, Reeve
Robin Busby, Administrator

Antler No. 61
P.O. Box 70
Redvers, SK S0C 2H0
Tel: 306-452-3263; *Fax:* 306-452-3518
rm61@sasktel.net
Municipal Type: Rural Municipalities
Incorporated: Dec. 13, 1909; *Area:* 832.23 sq km
Population in 2016: 523
Federal Electoral District(s): Souris-Moose Mountain
Next Election: 2022/2024
Ron Henderson, Reeve
Melissa Roberts, Administrator

Arborfield No. 456
P.O. Box 280
Arborfield, SK S0E 0A0
Tel: 306-769-8533; *Fax:* 306-769-8301
arborfieldrm456@sasktel.net
Municipal Type: Rural Municipalities
Incorporated: Jan. 1, 1913; *Area:* 1,416.01 sq km
Population in 2016: 343
Federal Electoral District(s): Prince Albert
Next Election: 2022/2024
Donald Underhill, Reeve
Allan Frisky, Administrator

Argyle No. 1
P.O. Box 120
Gainsborough, SK S0C 0Z0
Tel: 306-685-2010; *Fax:* 306-685-2161
rm.1@sasktel.net
Municipal Type: Rural Municipalities
Incorporated: Dec. 19, 1912; *Area:* 579.99 sq km
Population in 2016: 290
Federal Electoral District(s): Souris-Moose Mountain
Next Election: 2022/2024
Allen Henderson, Reeve
Erin McMillen, Administrator

Arlington No. 79
P.O. Box 1115
264 Centre St.
Shaunavon, SK S0N 2M0
Tel: 306-297-2108; *Fax:* 306-297-2144
rm79@sasktel.net
Municipal Type: Rural Municipalities
Incorporated: Jan. 1, 1913; *Area:* 846.79 sq km
Population in 2016: 366
Federal Electoral District(s): Cypress Hills-Grasslands
Next Election: 2022/2024
Donald Lundberg, Reeve
Richard Goulet, Administrator

Arm River No. 252
P.O. Box 250
Lincoln St.
Davidson, SK S0G 1A0
Tel: 306-567-3103; *Fax:* 306-567-3266
rm252@sasktel.net
www.rmarmriver.com
Municipal Type: Rural Municipalities
Incorporated: Dec. 13, 1909; *Area:* 725.26 sq km
Population in 2016: 250
Federal Electoral District(s): Moose Jaw-Lake Centre-Lanigan
Next Election: 2022/2024
Wayne Obrigewitsch, Reeve
Yvonne (Bonny) Goodsman, Administrator

Auvergne No. 76
P.O. Box 60
Ponteix, SK S0N 1Z0
Tel: 306-625-3210; *Fax:* 306-625-3681
rm76@sasktel.net
myrm.info/076
Municipal Type: Rural Municipalities
Incorporated: Jan. 1, 1913; *Area:* 853.40 sq km
Population in 2016: 412
Federal Electoral District(s): Cypress-Hills-Grasslands
Next Election: 2022/2024
Richard Marleau, Reeve
Melanie Huyghebaert, Administrator

Baildon No. 131
P.O. Box 1902
#1, 1410 Caribou St. West
Moose Jaw, SK S6H 7S9
Tel: 306-693-2166; *Fax:* 306-693-2170
rm131@sasktel.net
Municipal Type: Rural Municipalities
Incorporated: Dec. 9, 1912; *Area:* 846.21 sq km
Population in 2016: 620

Federal Electoral District(s): Moose Jaw-Lake Centre-Lanigan
Next Election: 2022/2024
Charlene Loos, Reeve
Carol Bellefeuille, Administrator

Barrier Valley No. 397
P.O. Box 246
Archerwill, SK S0E 0B0
Tel: 306-323-2101; *Fax:* 306-323-2106
rm397@sasktel.net
Municipal Type: Rural Municipalities
Incorporated: Oct. 29, 1917; *Area:* 819.99 sq km
Population in 2016: 431
Federal Electoral District(s): Yorkton-Melville
Next Election: 2022/2024
Wayne Black, Reeve
Glenda Smith, Administrator

Battle River No. 438
P.O. Box 159
Battleford, SK S0M 0E0
Tel: 306-937-2235; *Fax:* 306-937-2235
rm438@sasktel.net
Municipal Type: Rural Municipalities
Incorporated: Dec. 12, 1910; *Area:* 1,061.40 sq km
Population in 2016: 1,154
Federal Electoral District(s): Battlefords-Lloydminster
Next Election: 2022/2024
Joseph Beckman, Reeve
Betty Johnson, Administrator

Bayne No. 371
P.O. Box 130
Bruno, SK S0K 0S0
Tel: 306-369-2511; *Fax:* 306-369-2528
rm371@sasktel.net
Municipal Type: Rural Municipalities
Incorporated: Dec. 12, 1910; *Area:* 802.93 sq km
Population in 2016: 467
Federal Electoral District(s): Carlton Trail-Eagle Creek
Next Election: 2022/2024
David Leuschen, Reeve
Lonnie Sowa, Administrator

Beaver River No. 622
P.O. Box 129
159 Main St.
Pierceland, SK S0M 2K0
Tel: 306-839-2060; *Fax:* 306-839-2178
rm622@sasktel.net
www.rmofbeaverriver622.ca
Municipal Type: Rural Municipalities
Incorporated: Jan. 1, 1978; *Area:* 2,370.25 sq km
Population in 2016: 1,216
Federal Electoral District(s): Desnethé-Missinippi-Churchill River
Next Election: 2022/2024
Joe Rolfes, Reeve, 780-753-0357
Coral Dale, Administrator, 306-839-2090

Bengough No. 40
P.O. Box 429
Bengough, SK S0C 0K0
Tel: 306-268-2055; *Fax:* 306-268-2054
rm40@sasktel.net
Municipal Type: Rural Municipalities
Incorporated: Jan. 1, 1913; *Area:* 1,036.91 sq km
Population in 2016: 281
Federal Electoral District(s): Souris-Moose Mountain
Next Election: 2022/2024
Eugene Hoffart, Reeve
Lara Hazen, Administrator

Benson No. 35
P.O. Box 69
Benson, SK S0C 0L0
Tel: 306-634-9410; *Fax:* 306-634-8804
rm35@sasktel.net
Municipal Type: Rural Municipalities
Incorporated: Dec. 13, 1909; *Area:* 836.39 sq km
Population in 2016: 472
Federal Electoral District(s): Souris-Moose Mountain
Next Election: 2022/2024
David Hoffort, Reeve
Chantel Walsh, Administrator

Big Arm No. 251
P.O. Box 120
Imperial, SK S0G 2J0
Tel: 306-963-2402; *Fax:* 306-963-2405
rm251@sasktel.net
www.rmbigarm.com
Municipal Type: Rural Municipalities
Incorporated: Dec. 11, 1911; *Area:* 699.47 sq km

Population in 2016: 191
Federal Electoral District(s): Moose Jaw-Lake Centre-Lanigan
Next Election: 2022/2024
Sheldon Vance, Reeve
Yvonne (Bonny) Goodsman, Administrator

Big Quill No. 308
P.O. Box 898
Wynyard, SK S0A 4T0
Tel: 306-554-2533; *Fax:* 306-554-3935
rm308@sasktel.net
Municipal Type: Rural Municipalities
Incorporated: Dec. 13, 1909; *Area:* 739.86 sq km
Population in 2016: 519
Federal Electoral District(s): Regina-Qu'Appelle
Next Election: 2022/2024
Howie Linnen, Reeve
Gail Wolfe, Administrator

Big River No. 555
P.O. Box 219
606 First St. North
Big River, SK S0J 0E0
Tel: 306-469-2323; *Fax:* 306-469-2428
rm555@sasktel.net
www.bigriver.ca/about-big-river/rm-of-big-river
Municipal Type: Rural Municipalities
Incorporated: Oct. 1, 1977; *Area:* 2,488.22 sq km
Population in 2016: 889
Federal Electoral District(s): Desnethé-Missinippi-Churchill River
Next Election: 2022/2024
John Teer, Reeve, 306-469-5671
Donna Tymiak, Administrator

Big Stick No. 141
P.O. Box 9
Golden Prairie, SK S0N 0Y0
Tel: 306-662-2883; *Fax:* 306-662-3954
rm141@sasktel.net
Municipal Type: Rural Municipalities
Incorporated: Dec. 11, 1911; *Area:* 821.40 sq km
Population in 2016: 136
Federal Electoral District(s): Cypress Hills-Grasslands
Next Election: 2022/2024
Edward Feil, Reeve
Melinda Hammer, Administrator

Biggar No. 347
P.O. Box 280
Biggar, SK S0K 0M0
Tel: 306-948-2422; *Fax:* 306-948-2250
rm347@sasktel.net
www.rmofbiggar.ca
Municipal Type: Rural Municipalities
Incorporated: Dec. 11, 1911; *Area:* 1,597.87 sq km
Population in 2016: 798
Federal Electoral District(s): Carlton Trail-Eagle Creek
Next Election: 2022/2024
Kent Dubreuil, Reeve
Cheryl Martens (Forbes), Administrator

Birch Hills No. 460
P.O. Box 369
126 McCallum Ave.
Birch Hills, SK S0J 0G0
Tel: 306-749-2233; *Fax:* 306-749-2220
rm460@sasktel.net
www.rmbirchhills460.ca
Municipal Type: Rural Municipalities
Incorporated: Dec. 11, 1911; *Area:* 554.52 sq km
Population in 2016: 656
Federal Electoral District(s): Prince Albert
Next Election: 2022/2024
Alan Evans, Reeve
Lois Lange, Administrator

Bjorkdale No. 426
P.O. Box 10
Crooked River, SK S0E 0R0
Tel: 306-873-2470; *Fax:* 306-873-2365
rm.426.bjork@xplornet.com
Municipal Type: Rural Municipalities
Incorporated: Jan. 1, 1913; *Area:* 1,458.79 sq km
Population in 2016: 851
Federal Electoral District(s): Yorkton-Melville
Next Election: 2022/2024
Glen Clarke, Reeve
Lise Carpentier, Administrator

Blaine Lake No. 434
P.O. Box 38
Blaine Lake, SK S0J 0J0
Tel: 306-497-2282; *Fax:* 306-497-2511
rm434@sasktel.net
www.blainelake.ca/RM/rm434.html
Municipal Type: Rural Municipalities
Incorporated: Dec. 9, 1912; *Area:* 799.89 sq km
Population in 2016: 291
Federal Electoral District(s): Carlton Trail-Eagle Creek
Next Election: 2022/2024
Allan Sorenson, Mayor
Bertha Buhler, Administrator

Blucher No. 343
P.O. Box 100
Bradwell, SK S0K 0P0
Tel: 306-257-3344; *Fax:* 306-257-3303
rm343@sasktel.net
rm343.com
Municipal Type: Rural Municipalities
Incorporated: Dec. 13, 1909; *Area:* 789.28 sq km
Population in 2016: 2,006
Federal Electoral District(s): Moose Jaw-Lake Centre-Lanigan
Next Election: 2022/2024
Note: Absorbed the former Village of Elstow in 2014.
Daniel Greschuk, Reeve
R. Doran Scott, Administrator

Bone Creek No. 108
P.O. Box 459
Shaunavon, SK S0N 2M0
Tel: 306-297-2570; *Fax:* 306-297-6270
rmbc@sasktel.net
Municipal Type: Rural Municipalities
Incorporated: Dec. 11, 1911; *Area:* 847.16 sq km
Population in 2016: 394
Federal Electoral District(s): Cypress Hills-Grasslands
Next Election: 2022/2024
Mel Larson, Reeve
Lana Bavle, Administrator

Bratt's Lake No. 129
P.O. Box 130
Wilcox, SK S0G 5E0
Tel: 306-732-2030; *Fax:* 306-732-4495
rm129@sasktel.net
Municipal Type: Rural Municipalities
Incorporated: Jan. 1, 1913; *Area:* 844.94 sq km
Population in 2016: 315
Federal Electoral District(s): Moose Jaw-Lake Centre-Lanigan
Next Election: 2022/2024
J. Barry Hamdorf, Reeve
Tammy Ritchie, Administrator

Britannia No. 502
P.O. Box 661
4824 - 47th St.
Lloydminster, SK S9V 0Y7
Tel: 306-825-2610; *Fax:* 306-825-8894
rm502@sasktel.net
www.rmbritannia.com
Municipal Type: Rural Municipalities
Incorporated: Dec. 13, 1909; *Area:* 950.39 sq km
Population in 2016: 2,153
Federal Electoral District(s): Battlefords-Lloydminster
Next Election: 2022/2024
John Light, Reeve
Wanda Boon, Administrator

Brock No. 64
P.O. Box 247
Kisbey, SK S0C 1L0
Tel: 306-462-2010; *Fax:* 306-462-2016
rm64@signaldirect.ca
Municipal Type: Rural Municipalities
Incorporated: Dec. 12, 1910; *Area:* 827.53 sq km
Population in 2016: 267
Federal Electoral District(s): Souris-Moose Mountain
Next Election: 2022/2024
Paul Cameron, Reeve
Treena Heshka, Administrator

Brokenshell No. 68
23 - 6th St. NE
Weyburn, SK S4H 1A7
Tel: 306-842-2314; *Fax:* 306-842-1002
rm.68@sasktel.net
Municipal Type: Rural Municipalities
Incorporated: Dec. 13, 1909; *Area:* 850.01 sq km
Population in 2016: 312

Federal Electoral District(s): Souris-Moose Mountain
Next Election: 2022/2024
Garry Christopherson, Reeve
Pamela Scott, Administrator

Browning No. 34
P.O. Box 40
Lampman, SK S0C 1N0
Tel: 306-487-2444; *Fax:* 306-487-2496
browning.lampman@sasktel.net
www.rmofbrowning.ca
Municipal Type: Rural Municipalities
Incorporated: Dec. 11, 1911; *Area:* 823.39 sq km
Population in 2016: 375
Federal Electoral District(s): Souris-Moose Mountain
Next Election: 2022/2024
Pius Loustel, Reeve, 306-421-0141
Greg Wallin, Administrator

Buchanan No. 304
P.O. Box 10
Buchanan, SK S0A 0J0
Tel: 306-592-2055; *Fax:* 306-592-4436
rm304@sasktel.net
Municipal Type: Rural Municipalities
Incorporated: Jan. 1, 1913; *Area:* 738.80 sq km
Population in 2016: 301
Federal Electoral District(s): Yorkton-Melville
Next Election: 2022/2024
Don Skoretz, Reeve
Twila Hadubiak, Administrator

Buckland No. 491
99 River St. East
Prince Albert, SK S6V 0A1
Tel: 306-763-2585; *Fax:* 306-763-6369
rm491@sasktel.net
www.rmbuckland.ca
Municipal Type: Rural Municipalities
Incorporated: Dec. 11, 1911; *Area:* 791.55 sq km
Population in 2016: 3,375
Federal Electoral District(s): Prince Albert
Next Election: 2022/2024
Don Fyrk, Reeve, 306-922-9174
Tara Kerber, Administrator

Buffalo No. 409
P.O. Box 100
214 - 2nd Ave. East
Wilkie, SK S0K 4W0
Tel: 306-843-2342; *Fax:* 306-843-2455
rm409@sasktel.net
Municipal Type: Rural Municipalities
Incorporated: Dec. 13, 1909; *Area:* 1,222.08 sq km
Population in 2016: 506
Federal Electoral District(s): Battlefords-Lloydminster
Next Election: 2022/2024
Leslie Krochinski, Reeve
Sherry Huber, Administrator

Calder No. 241
P.O. Box 10
Wroxton, SK S0A 4S0
Tel: 306-742-4233; *Fax:* 306-742-4559
calderrm@sasktel.net
Municipal Type: Rural Municipalities
Incorporated: Jan. 1, 1913; *Area:* 807.15 sq km
Population in 2016: 370
Federal Electoral District(s): Yorkton-Melville
Next Election: 2022/2024
Roy Derworiz, Reeve
Linda Napady, Administrator

Caledonia No. 99
P.O. Box 328
Milestone, SK S0G 3L0
Tel: 306-436-2050; *Fax:* 306-436-2051
milcal@sasktel.net
Municipal Type: Rural Municipalities
Incorporated: Dec. 13, 1909; *Area:* 845.68 sq km
Population in 2016: 245
Federal Electoral District(s): Moose Jaw-Lake Centre-Lanigan
Next Election: 2022/2024
Mark Beck, Reeve
Stephen Schury, Administrator

Cambria No. 6
P.O. Box 210
Torquay, SK S0C 2L0
Tel: 306-923-2000; *Fax:* 306-923-2099
rm.cambria@sasktel.net
Municipal Type: Rural Municipalities
Incorporated: Dec. 13, 1909; *Area:* 814.14 sq km

Population in 2016: 309
Federal Electoral District(s): Souris-Moose Mountain
Next Election: 2022/2024
Darwin Daae, Reeve
Monica Kovach, Administrator

Cana No. 214
P.O. Box 550
Melville, SK S0A 2P0
Tel: 306-728-5645; Fax: 306-728-3807
rmcana@sasktel.net
Municipal Type: Rural Municipalities
Incorporated: Dec. 13, 1909; Area: 820.81 sq km
Population in 2016: 867
Federal Electoral District(s): Yorkton-Melville
Next Election: 2022/2024
Robert Almasi, Reeve
Donna Westerhaug, Administrator

Canaan No. 225
P.O. Box 99
Lucky Lake, SK S0L 1Z0
Tel: 306-858-2234; Fax: 306-858-9134
rm225.vll@sasktel.net
Municipal Type: Rural Municipalities
Incorporated: Jan. 1, 1913; Area: 549.09 sq km
Population in 2016: 140
Federal Electoral District(s): Cypress Hills-Grasslands
Next Election: 2022/2024
Lars Bjorgan, Reeve
D.B. (Blair) Cleaveley, Administrator

Canwood No. 494
P.O. Box 10
Canwood, SK S0J 0K0
Tel: 306-468-2014; Fax: 306-468-2666
rm494@sasktel.net
Municipal Type: Rural Municipalities
Incorporated: Jan. 1, 1913; Area: 1,945.20 sq km
Population in 2016: 1,381
Federal Electoral District(s): Desnethé-Missinippi-Churchill River
Next Election: 2022/2024
Lyndon Pease, Reeve
Lorna Benson, Administrator

Carmichael No. 109
P.O. Box 420
Gull Lake, SK S0N 1A0
Tel: 306-672-3501; Fax: 306-672-3295
rm109@sasktel.net
Municipal Type: Rural Municipalities
Incorporated: Dec. 9, 1912; Area: 846.40 sq km
Population in 2016: 444
Federal Electoral District(s): Cypress Hills-Grasslands
Next Election: 2022/2024
Jim Bradley, Reeve
Natasha Brown, Administrator

Caron No. 162
#2, 1410 Caribou St. West
Moose Jaw, SK S6H 7S9
Tel: 306-692-2293; Fax: 306-692-2193
rm162@sasktel.net
Municipal Type: Rural Municipalities
Incorporated: Dec. 9, 1912; Area: 569.87 sq km
Population in 2016: 576
Federal Electoral District(s): Cypress Hills-Grasslands
Next Election: 2022/2024
Gregory McKeown, Reeve
John Morris, Administrator

Chaplin No. 164
P.O. Box 60
Chaplin, SK S0H 0V0
Tel: 306-395-2244; Fax: 306-395-2767
rm164@sasktel.net
Municipal Type: Rural Municipalities
Incorporated: Jan. 1, 1913; Area: 802.74 sq km
Population in 2016: 113
Federal Electoral District(s): Cypress Hills-Grasslands
Next Election: 2022/2024
Duane Doell, Reeve
Tammy Knight, Administrator

Chester No. 125
P.O. Box 180
Glenavon, SK S0G 1Y0
Tel: 306-429-2110; Fax: 306-429-2260
rmchester125@sasktel.net
Municipal Type: Rural Municipalities
Incorporated: Dec. 13, 1909; Area: 837.08 sq km
Population in 2016: 383

Federal Electoral District(s): Souris-Moose Mountain
Next Election: 2022/2024
Merril Wozniak, Reeve
James Hoff, Administrator

Chesterfield No. 261
P.O. Box 70
Eatonia, SK S0L 0Y0
Tel: 306-967-2222; Fax: 306-967-2424
rm261@sasktel.net
www.eatonia.ca/RM/council.html
Municipal Type: Rural Municipalities
Incorporated: Dec. 9, 1912; Area: 1,942.72 sq km
Population in 2016: 481
Federal Electoral District(s): Cypress Hills-Grasslands
Next Election: 2022/2024
Karrie Derouin, Reeve, 306-967-0000
Tosha McCubbing, Administrator

Churchbridge No. 211
P.O. Box 211
Churchbridge, SK S0A 0M0
Tel: 306-896-2522; Fax: 306-896-2743
rmchurchbridge@sasktel.net
Municipal Type: Rural Municipalities
Incorporated: Jan. 1, 1913; Area: 958.98 sq km
Population in 2016: 619
Federal Electoral District(s): Yorkton-Melville
Next Election: 2022/2024
Neil Mehrer, Reeve
Brenda Goulden, Administrator

Clayton No. 333
P.O. Box 220
Hyas, SK S0A 1K0
Tel: 306-594-2832; Fax: 306-594-2944
rm333@sasktel.net
Municipal Type: Rural Municipalities
Incorporated: Jan. 1, 1913; Area: 1,401.69 sq km
Population in 2016: 592
Federal Electoral District(s): Yorkton-Melville
Next Election: 2022/2024
Duane Hicks, Reeve
Kelly Kim Rea, Administrator

Clinworth No. 230
P.O. Box 120
Sceptre, SK S0N 2H0
Tel: 306-623-4229; Fax: 306-623-4229
rm230@yourlink.ca
Municipal Type: Rural Municipalities
Incorporated: Dec. 9, 1912; Area: 1,432.75 sq km
Population in 2016: 154
Federal Electoral District(s): Cypress Hills-Grasslands
Next Election: 2022/2024
Ken Dietz, Reeve
Sherry Egeland, Administrator

Coalfields No. 4
P.O. Box 190
Bienfait, SK S0C 0M0
Tel: 306-388-2323; Fax: 306-388-2330
rm.04@myaccess.ca
Municipal Type: Rural Municipalities
Incorporated: Jan. 1, 1913; Area: 819.76 sq km
Population in 2016: 368
Federal Electoral District(s): Souris-Moose Mountain
Next Election: 2022/2024
Richard Tessier, Reeve
Glenda Johnston, Administrator

Colonsay No. 342
P.O. Box 130
100 Jura St.
Colonsay, SK S0K 0Z0
Tel: 306-255-2233; Fax: 306-255-2291
rm342@sasktel.net
www.colonsay.ca/rm-administration/rm-council
Municipal Type: Rural Municipalities
Incorporated: Dec. 13, 1909; Area: 549.99 sq km
Population in 2016: 269
Federal Electoral District(s): Moose Jaw-Lake Centre-Lanigan
Next Election: 2022/2024
Gerald Yausie, Reeve
Deborah Prosper, Administrator

Connaught No. 457
P.O. Box 25
Tisdale, SK S0E 1T0
Tel: 306-873-2657; Fax: 306-873-4442
rm457@sasktel.net
Municipal Type: Rural Municipalities
Incorporated: Dec. 11, 1911; Area: 853.11 sq km

Population in 2016: 586
Federal Electoral District(s): Prince Albert
Next Election: 2022/2024
Arthur Lalonde, Reeve
Tamie McLean, Administrator

Corman Park No. 344
111 Pinehouse Dr.
Saskatoon, SK S7K 5W1
Tel: 306-242-9303; Fax: 306-242-6965
rm344@rmcormanpark.ca
www.rmcormanpark.ca
Municipal Type: Rural Municipalities
Incorporated: Jan. 1, 1970; Area: 1,978.14 sq km
Population in 2016: 8,568
Federal Electoral District(s): Carlton Trail-Eagle Creek;
Saskatoon West; Saskatoon-Grasswood
Next Election: 2022/2024
Judy Harwood, Reeve
Adam Tittemore, Administrator, 306-975-1651

Cote No. 271
P.O. Box 669
Kamsack, SK S0A 1S0
Tel: 306-542-2121; Fax: 306-542-2428
rm271@sasktel.net
www.rmofcote271.com
Municipal Type: Rural Municipalities
Incorporated: Dec. 12, 1910; Area: 880.23 sq km
Population in 2016: 548
Federal Electoral District(s): Yorkton-Melville
Next Election: 2022/2024
Jim Tomochko, Reeve, 306-590-7111
Sherry Guenther, Administrator

Coteau No. 255
P.O. Box 30
Birsay, SK S0L 0G0
Tel: 306-573-2047; Fax: 306-573-2111
rm255@sasktel.net
Municipal Type: Rural Municipalities
Incorporated: Dec. 12, 1910; Area: 899.27 sq km
Population in 2016: 475
Federal Electoral District(s): Cypress Hills-Grasslands
Next Election: 2022/2024
Clayton Ylioja, Reeve
Lindsay Hargrave, Administrator

Coulee No. 136
1680 Chaplin St. East
Swift Current, SK S9H 1K8
Tel: 306-773-5420; Fax: 306-773-1859
rm136@sasktel.net
Municipal Type: Rural Municipalities
Incorporated: Dec. 12, 1910; Area: 842.95 sq km
Population in 2016: 563
Federal Electoral District(s): Cypress Hills-Grasslands
Next Election: 2022/2024
Greg Targerson, Reeve
Laurel Dyck, Administrator

Craik No. 222
P.O. Box 420
Craik, SK S0G 0V0
Tel: 306-734-2242; Fax: 306-734-2257
rm222@sasktel.net
www.craik.ca/rmofcraik.html
Municipal Type: Rural Municipalities
Incorporated: Dec. 9, 1912; Area: 883.02 sq km
Population in 2016: 259
Federal Electoral District(s): Moose Jaw-Lake Centre-Lanigan
Next Election: 2022/2024
Neil Dolman, Reeve
Shawn McCauley, Administrator

Cupar No. 218
P.O. Box 400
Cupar, SK S0G 0Y0
Tel: 306-723-4726; Fax: 306-723-4726
rm218@sasktel.net
www.rmofcupar.ca
Municipal Type: Rural Municipalities
Incorporated: Dec. 13, 1909; Area: 919.01 sq km
Population in 2016: 503
Federal Electoral District(s): Regina-Qu'Appelle
Next Election: 2022/2024
Raymond Orb, Reeve
Nicole Czemeres, Administrator

Cut Knife No. 439
P.O. Box 70
Cut Knife, SK S0M 0N0
Tel: 306-398-2353; *Fax:* 306-398-2839
rm439@sasktel.net
Municipal Type: Rural Municipalities
Incorporated: Dec. 13, 1909; *Area:* 651.43 sq km
Population in 2016: 364
Federal Electoral District(s): Battlefords-Lloydminster
Next Election: 2022/2024
Lorne Veikle, Reeve
Don McCallum, Administrator

Cymri No. 36
P.O. Box 238
Midale, SK S0C 1S0
Tel: 306-458-2244; *Fax:* 306-458-2699
rmcymri@sasktel.net
Municipal Type: Rural Municipalities
Incorporated: Dec. 13, 1909; *Area:* 832.36 sq km
Population in 2016: 549
Federal Electoral District(s): Souris-Moose Mountain
Next Election: 2022/2024
Joe Vilcu, Reeve
Gwen Johnston, Administrator

Deer Forks No. 232
P.O. Box 250
Burstall, SK S0N 0H0
Tel: 306-679-2000; *Fax:* 306-679-2275
rm232@sasktel.net
Municipal Type: Rural Municipalities
Incorporated: Jan. 1, 1913; *Area:* 735.49 sq km
Population in 2016: 109
Federal Electoral District(s): Cypress Hills-Grasslands
Next Election: 2022/2024
Doug Smith, Reeve
Tim C. Lozinsky, Administrator

Douglas No. 436
P.O. Box 964
Speers, SK S0M 2V0
Tel: 306-246-2171; *Fax:* 306-246-2173
rm436@littleloon.ca
Municipal Type: Rural Municipalities
Incorporated: Dec. 13, 1909; *Area:* 820.37 sq km
Population in 2016: 350
Federal Electoral District(s): Carlton Trail-Eagle Creek
Next Election: 2022/2024
Nick Partyka, Reeve
Charles W. Linnell, Administrator

Duck Lake No. 463
P.O. Box 250
Duck Lake, SK S0K 1J0
Tel: 306-467-2011; *Fax:* 306-476-4423
rm463@sasktel.net
www.rmducklake.com
Municipal Type: Rural Municipalities
Incorporated: Jan. 1, 1913; *Area:* 1,046.57 sq km
Population in 2016: 1,004
Federal Electoral District(s): Carlton Trail-Eagle Creek
Next Election: 2022/2024
Marcel Perrin, Reeve
Karen Baynton, Acting Administrator

Dufferin No. 190
P.O. Box 67
507 Main St.
Bethune, SK S0G 0H0
Tel: 306-638-3112; *Fax:* 306-638-3102
190@sasktel.net
www.rmofdufferin190.com
Municipal Type: Rural Municipalities
Incorporated: Dec. 9, 1912; *Area:* 961.44 sq km
Population in 2016: 559
Federal Electoral District(s): Moose Jaw-Lake Centre-Lanigan
Next Election: 2022/2024
Terry Neugebauer, Reeve
Rodney Audette, Administrator

Dundurn No. 314
P.O. Box 159
314 - 2nd St.
Dundurn, SK S0K 1K0
Tel: 306-492-2132; *Fax:* 306-492-4758
admin.314@sasktel.net
www.myrm.ca/314
Municipal Type: Rural Municipalities
Incorporated: Dec. 13, 1909; *Area:* 800.91 sq km
Population in 2016: 2,404

Federal Electoral District(s): Moose Jaw-Lake Centre-Lanigan
Next Election: 2022/2024
Trevor Reid, Reeve
Donna Goertzen, Administrator

Eagle Creek No. 376
P.O. Box 278
First St.
Arelee, SK S0K 0H0
Tel: 306-237-4424; *Fax:* 306-237-4294
rm376eaglecreek@xplornet.ca
Municipal Type: Rural Municipalities
Incorporated: Dec. 13, 1909; *Area:* 833.08 sq km
Population in 2016: 595
Federal Electoral District(s): Carlton Trail-Eagle Creek
Next Election: 2022/2024
Faith Struhan, Reeve
Lloyd Cross, Administrator

Edenwold No. 158
P.O. Box 10
100 Queen St.
Balgonie, SK S0G 0E0
Tel: 306-771-2522; *Fax:* 306-771-2631
rm158@sasktel.net
www.rmedenwold.ca
Municipal Type: Rural Municipalities
Incorporated: Dec. 9, 1912; *Area:* 882.67 sq km
Population in 2016: 4,490
Federal Electoral District(s): Regina-Qu'Appelle
Next Election: 2022/2024
Mitchell Huber, Reeve
Kim McIvor, Administrator

Elcapo No. 154
P.O. Box 668
Broadview, SK S0G 0K0
Tel: 306-696-2474; *Fax:* 306-696-3573
rm154@sasktel.net
Municipal Type: Rural Municipalities
Incorporated: Dec. 12, 1910; *Area:* 846.54 sq km
Population in 2016: 488
Federal Electoral District(s): Souris-Moose Mountain
Next Election: 2022/2024
Sid Quibell, Reeve
Mervin Schmidt, Administrator

Eldon No. 471
P.O. Box 130
212 Main St.
Maidstone, SK S0M 1M0
Tel: 306-893-2391; *Fax:* 306-893-4644
rm471@sasktel.net
www.rmeldon.ca
Municipal Type: Rural Municipalities
Incorporated: Dec. 13, 1909; *Area:* 1,007.59 sq km
Population in 2016: 750
Federal Electoral District(s): Battlefords-Lloydminster
Next Election: 2022/2024
Garry Taylor, Reeve
Ken E. Reiter, Administrator

Elfros No. 307
P.O. Box 40
Elfros, SK S0A 0V0
Tel: 306-328-2011; *Fax:* 306-328-4490
rm307@sasktel.net
Municipal Type: Rural Municipalities
Incorporated: Dec. 13, 1909; *Area:* 696.71 sq km
Population in 2016: 391
Federal Electoral District(s): Regina-Qu'Appelle
Next Election: 2022/2024
Michael Yaskowich, Reeve
Tina Heistad Douglas, Administrator

Elmsthorpe No. 100
P.O. Box 240
Avonlea, SK S0H 0C0
Tel: 306-868-2221; *Fax:* 306-868-2040
rm.100@sasktel.net
Municipal Type: Rural Municipalities
Incorporated: Dec. 12, 1910; *Area:* 843.12 sq km
Population in 2016: 226
Federal Electoral District(s): Moose Jaw-Lake Centre-Lanigan
Next Election: 2022/2024
Ken Miller, Reeve
Jaimie Paranuik, Administrator

Emerald No. 277
P.O. Box 160
Wishart, SK S0A 4R0
Tel: 306-576-2002; *Fax:* 306-576-2132
rm277@sasktel.net
www.rm277emerald.ca
Municipal Type: Rural Municipalities
Incorporated: Dec. 12, 1910; *Area:* 854.44 sq km
Population in 2016: 405
Federal Electoral District(s): Regina-Qu'Appelle
Next Election: 2022/2024
Morris Karakochuk, Reeve
Sharolyn Prisiak, Administrator

Enfield No. 194
P.O. Box 70
2nd Ave. West
Central Butte, SK S0H 0T0
Tel: 306-796-2025; *Fax:* 306-796-2025
rm194@sasktel.net
Municipal Type: Rural Municipalities
Incorporated: Dec. 13, 1909; *Area:* 1,014.10 sq km
Population in 2016: 226
Federal Electoral District(s): Cypress Hills-Grasslands
Next Election: 2022/2024
Jim Campbell, Reeve
Joe Van Leuken, Administrator

Enniskillen No. 3
P.O. Box 179
307 Main St.
Oxbow, SK S0C 2B0
Tel: 306-483-2277; *Fax:* 306-483-2598
rm3@sasktel.net
Municipal Type: Rural Municipalities
Incorporated: Dec. 13, 1909; *Area:* 834.78 sq km
Population in 2016: 459
Federal Electoral District(s): Souris-Moose Mountain
Next Election: 2022/2024
Trevor Walls, Reeve
Luke Lochart, Administrator

Enterprise No. 142
P.O. Box 150
Richmound, SK S0N 2E0
Tel: 306-669-2000; *Fax:* 306-669-2052
rm142@sasktel.net
Municipal Type: Rural Municipalities
Incorporated: April 18, 1913; *Area:* 988.80 sq km
Population in 2016: 110
Federal Electoral District(s): Cypress Hills-Grasslands
Next Election: 2022/2024
Wayne Freitag, Reeve
Rolande Davis, Administrator

Estevan No. 5
#1, 322 - 4th St.
Estevan, SK S4A 0T8
Tel: 306-634-2222; *Fax:* 306-634-2223
rm5@sasktel.net
rmestevan.ca
Municipal Type: Rural Municipalities
Incorporated: Dec. 12, 1910; *Area:* 774.67 sq km
Population in 2016: 1,370
Federal Electoral District(s): Souris-Moose Mountain
Next Election: 2022/2024
Terry Keating, Reeve
Grace Potter, Administrator

Excel No. 71
P.O. Box 100
Viceroy, SK S0H 4H0
Tel: 306-268-4555; *Fax:* 306-268-4547
rm71.excel@gmail.com
Municipal Type: Rural Municipalities
Incorporated: Jan. 1, 1913; *Area:* 1,122.02 sq km
Population in 2016: 391
Federal Electoral District(s): Souris-Moose Mountain
Next Election: 2022/2024
Arnold Montgomery, Reeve
Sheri-Lyn Simpson, Administrator

Excelsior No. 166
P.O. Box 180
Rush Lake, SK S0H 3S0
Tel: 306-784-3121; *Fax:* 306-784-3479
rm166@sasktel.net
Municipal Type: Rural Municipalities
Incorporated: Dec. 13, 1909; *Area:* 1,198.35 sq km
Population in 2016: 806
Federal Electoral District(s): Cypress Hills-Grasslands
Next Election: 2022/2024

Harold Martens, Reeve
Dianne Hahn, Administrator

Eye Hill No. 382
P.O. Box 39
Macklin, SK S0L 2C0
Tel: 306-753-2075; *Fax:* 306-753-2304
rm382@sasktel.net
Municipal Type: Rural Municipalities
Incorporated: Dec. 12, 1910; *Area:* 797.96 sq km
Population in 2016: 590
Federal Electoral District(s): Battlefords-Lloydminster
Next Election: 2022/2024
Robert Brost, Reeve
Jason Pilat, Administrator

Eyebrow No. 193
P.O. Box 99
Eyebrow, SK S0H 1L0
Tel: 306-759-2101; *Fax:* 306-759-2026
rm193@yourlink.ca
www.rmofeyebrow.ca
Municipal Type: Rural Municipalities
Incorporated: Dec. 13, 1909; *Area:* 835.04 sq km
Population in 2016: 195
Federal Electoral District(s): Moose Jaw-Lake Centre-Lanigan
Next Election: 2022/2024
Michael Cavan, Reeve
Chris Bueckert, Administrator

Fertile Belt No. 183
P.O. Box 190
100 Ohlen St.
Stockholm, SK S0A 3Y0
Tel: 306-793-2061; *Fax:* 306-793-2063
rm183@sasktel.net
Municipal Type: Rural Municipalities
Incorporated: January 1, 1913; *Area:* 1,006.68 sq km
Population in 2016: 781
Federal Electoral District(s): Yorkton-Melville
Next Election: 2022/2024
Arlynn Kurtz, Reeve
Lorie Jackson, Administrator

Fertile Valley No. 285
P.O. Box 70
Conquest, SK S0L 0L0
Tel: 306-856-2037; *Fax:* 306-856-2211
rmfv285@yourlink.ca
Municipal Type: Rural Municipalities
Incorporated: Dec. 13, 1909; *Area:* 1,016.37 sq km
Population in 2016: 539
Federal Electoral District(s): Carlton Trail-Eagle Creek
Next Election: 2022/2024
Barry Friesen, Reeve
L. Jean Jones, Administrator

Fillmore No. 96
P.O. Box 130
Fillmore, SK S0G 1N0
Tel: 306-722-3251; *Fax:* 306-722-3775
rm96@sasktel.net
Municipal Type: Rural Municipalities
Incorporated: Dec. 13, 1909; *Area:* 828.33 sq km
Population in 2016: 223
Federal Electoral District(s): Souris-Moose Mountain
Next Election: 2022/2024
Gerald Nixon, Reeve
Vernna Wiggins, Administrator

Fish Creek No. 402
P.O. Box 160
Wakaw, SK S0K 4P0
Tel: 306-233-4412; *Fax:* 306-233-5234
rm402@sasktel.net
Municipal Type: Rural Municipalities
Incorporated: Jan. 1, 1913; *Area:* 597.90 sq km
Population in 2016: 345
Federal Electoral District(s): Carlton Trail-Eagle Creek
Next Election: 2022/2024
Brian Domotor, Reeve
Lois Gartner, Administrator

Flett's Springs No. 429
P.O. Box 160
Melfort, SK S0E 1A0
Tel: 306-752-3606; *Fax:* 306-752-3882
rm429@sasktel.net
Municipal Type: Rural Municipalities
Incorporated: Dec. 13, 1909; *Area:* 844.61 sq km
Population in 2016: 732
Federal Electoral District(s): Prince Albert
Next Election: 2022/2024

Blaine Forsyth, Reeve
Shelley L. Holmes, Administrator

Foam Lake No. 276
P.O. Box 490
Foam Lake, SK S0A 1A0
Tel: 306-272-3334; *Fax:* 306-272-4722
rm276@sasktel.net
Municipal Type: Rural Municipalities
Incorporated: Dec. 12, 1910; *Area:* 1,345.91 sq km
Population in 2016: 586
Federal Electoral District(s): Yorkton-Melville
Next Election: 2022/2024
Ken Kaban, Reeve
Shanna Loeppky, Administrator

Fox Valley No. 171
P.O. Box 190
100 Centre St.
Fox Valley, SK S0N 0V0
Tel: 306-666-2055; *Fax:* 306-666-2074
rm171@sasktel.net
www.rm171fv.com
Municipal Type: Rural Municipalities
Incorporated: Oct. 29, 1913; *Area:* 1,253.79 sq km
Population in 2016: 330
Federal Electoral District(s): Cypress Hills-Grasslands
Next Election: 2022/2024
Anthony Hoffart, Reeve
Stephanie MacPhail, Administrator

Francis No. 127
P.O. Box 36
Francis, SK S0G 1V0
Tel: 306-245-3256; *Fax:* 306-245-3203
rm127@sasktel.net
www.myrm.ca/127
Municipal Type: Rural Municipalities
Incorporated: Dec. 13, 1909; *Area:* 1,106.80 sq km
Population in 2016: 674
Federal Electoral District(s): Souris-Moose Mountain
Next Election: 2022/2024
Schmidt Clayton, Reeve
Megan Macomber, Administrator

Frenchman Butte No. 501
P.O. Box 180
Paradise Hill, SK S0M 2G0
Tel: 306-344-2034; *Fax:* 306-344-4434
rm501@sasktel.net
www.rmfrenchmanbutte.ca
Municipal Type: Rural Municipalities
Incorporated: Jan. 1, 1954; *Area:* 1,928.32 sq km
Population in 2016: 1,494
Federal Electoral District(s): Battlefords-Lloydminster
Next Election: 2022/2024
B. Bonnie Mills-Midgley, Reeve, 306-344-4978
Rita Rogers, Administrator

Frontier No. 19
P.O. Box 30
Frontier, SK S0N 0W0
Tel: 306-296-2030; *Fax:* 306-296-2175
rm19@sasktel.net
Municipal Type: Rural Municipalities
Incorporated: Jan. 1, 1913; *Area:* 1,675.02 sq km
Population in 2016: 326
Federal Electoral District(s): Cypress Hills-Grasslands
Next Election: 2022/2024
Troy Heggestad, Reeve
Barb Webber, Administrator

The Gap No. 39
P.O. Box 188
Ceylon, SK S0C 0T0
Tel: 306-454-2202; *Fax:* 306-454-2627
rmgap39@sasktel.net
Municipal Type: Rural Municipalities
Incorporated: Dec. 12, 1903; *Area:* 830.92 sq km
Population in 2016: 199
Federal Electoral District(s): Souris-Moose Mountain
Next Election: 2022/2024
Lorne McClarty, Reeve
Yvonne Johnston, Administrator

Garden River No. 490
P.O. Box 70
Meath Park, SK S0J 1T0
Tel: 306-929-2020; *Fax:* 306-929-2281
rm490@sasktel.net
Municipal Type: Rural Municipalities
Incorporated: Jan. 1, 1913; *Area:* 662.90 sq km
Population in 2016: 727

Federal Electoral District(s): Prince Albert
Next Election: 2022/2024
Ryan Scragg, Reeve
Brenda Moberg, Administrator

Garry No. 245
P.O. Box 10
Jedburgh, SK S0A 1R0
Tel: 306-647-2450; *Fax:* 306-647-2452
rm245@yourlink.ca
Municipal Type: Rural Municipalities
Incorporated: Jan. 1, 1913; *Area:* 853.59 sq km
Population in 2016: 364
Federal Electoral District(s): Yorkton-Melville
Next Election: 2022/2024
Allan Polegi, Reeve
Tanis Ferguson, Administrator

Glen Bain No. 105
P.O. Box 39
Glen Bain, SK S0N 0X0
Tel: 306-264-3607; *Fax:* 306-264-3956
rm105@sasktel.net
Municipal Type: Rural Municipalities
Incorporated: Dec. 11, 1911; *Area:* 843.40 sq km
Population in 2016: 180
Federal Electoral District(s): Cypress Hills-Grasslands
Next Election: 2022/2024
Ted Wornath, Reeve
Audrey Rotheisler, Administrator

Glen McPherson No. 46
P.O. Box 277
Mankota, SK S0H 2W0
Tel: 306-478-2323; *Fax:* 306-478-2606
rm45.46@sasktel.net
Municipal Type: Rural Municipalities
Incorporated: Jan. 1, 1913; *Area:* 848.29 sq km
Population in 2016: 72
Federal Electoral District(s): Cypress Hills-Grasslands
Next Election: 2022/2024
Gordon Kruger, Reeve
Michael Sherven, Administrator

Glenside No. 377
P.O. Box 1084
Biggar, SK S0K 0M0
Tel: 306-948-3681; *Fax:* 306-948-3684
rm377@sasktel.net
Municipal Type: Rural Municipalities
Incorporated: Dec. 13, 1909; *Area:* 905.74 sq km
Population in 2016: 248
Federal Electoral District(s): Carlton Trail-Eagle Creek;
Battlefords-Lloydminster
Next Election: 2022/2024
Elmer Dove, Reeve
Joanne Fullerton, Administrator

Golden West No. 95
P.O. Box 70
Corning, SK S0G 0T0
Tel: 306-224-4456; *Fax:* 306-224-2196
goldwest@sasktel.net
Municipal Type: Rural Municipalities
Incorporated: Dec. 13, 1909; *Area:* 790.13 sq km
Population in 2016: 291
Federal Electoral District(s): Souris-Moose Mountain
Next Election: 2022/2024
Kurt Corscadden, Reeve
Edward Mish, Administrator

Good Lake No. 274
P.O. Box 896
401 Main St.
Canora, SK S0A 0L0
Tel: 306-563-5244; *Fax:* 306-563-5005
rm274@sasktel.net
www.goodlakerm.com
Municipal Type: Rural Municipalities
Incorporated: Jan. 1, 1913; *Area:* 800.06 sq km
Population in 2016: 747
Federal Electoral District(s): Yorkton-Melville
Next Election: 2022/2024
David Popowich, Reeve
Joan Popoff, Administrator

Grandview No. 349
P.O. Box 39
Kelfield, SK S0K 2C0
Tel: 306-932-4911; *Fax:* 306-932-4923
rm349@xplornet.com
Municipal Type: Rural Municipalities
Incorporated: Dec. 11, 1911; *Area:* 712.05 sq km

Population in 2016: 348
Federal Electoral District(s): Battlefords-Lloydminster
Next Election: 2022/2024
Note: On Dec. 31st 2013, the village of Ruthilda dissolved into the Rural Municipality of Grandview No. 349.
Steven Suter, Reeve
Shonda Toner, Administrator

Grant No. 372
P.O. Box 190
Vonda, SK S0K 4N0
Tel: 306-258-2022; Fax: 306-258-2011
rm372@baudoux.ca
Municipal Type: Rural Municipalities
Incorporated: Dec. 13, 1909; Area: 666.16 sq km
Population in 2016: 466
Federal Electoral District(s): Carlton Trail-Eagle Creek
Next Election: 2022/2024
Travis Hryniuk, Reeve
Brenda Skakun, Administrator

Grass Lake No. 381
P.O. Box 40
101 Main St.
Reward, SK S0K 3N0
Tel: 306-228-2988; Fax: 306-228-4188
rm381@sasktel.net
Municipal Type: Rural Municipalities
Incorporated: Dec. 13, 1909; Area: 801.29 sq km
Population in 2016: 399
Federal Electoral District(s): Battlefords-Lloydminster
Next Election: 2022/2024
Scott Vetter, Reeve
Brenda M. Kasas, Administrator

Grassy Creek No. 78
P.O. Box 400
Shaunavon, SK S0N 2M0
Tel: 306-297-2520; Fax: 306-297-3162
rm77.78@sasktel.net
Municipal Type: Rural Municipalities
Incorporated: Jan. 1, 1913; Area: 837.40 sq km
Population in 2016: 364
Federal Electoral District(s): Cypress Hills-Grasslands
Next Election: 2022/2024
Wayne Oberle, Reeve
Kathy Collins, Administrator

Gravelbourg No. 104
P.O. Box 510
Gravelbourg, SK S0H 1X0
Tel: 306-648-2412
rm104@sasktel.net
www.rmofgravelbourg.com
Municipal Type: Rural Municipalities
Incorporated: Dec. 9, 1912; Area: 842.08 sq km
Population in 2016: 472
Federal Electoral District(s): Cypress Hills-Grasslands
Next Election: 2022/2024
Guy Lorrain, Reeve
Dara Cowan, Administrator

Grayson No. 184
P.O. Box 69
131 Taylor St.
Grayson, SK S0A 1E0
Tel: 306-794-2044; Fax: 306-794-4655
grayson184@sasktel.net
www.rmofgrayson.ca
Municipal Type: Rural Municipalities
Incorporated: Jan. 1, 1913; Area: 875.22 sq km
Population in 2016: 512
Federal Electoral District(s): Yorkton-Melville
Next Election: 2022/2024
Harvey Mucha, Reeve
Darlene Paquin, Administrator

Great Bend No. 405
P.O. Box 150
200 Shepard St.
Borden, SK S0K 0N0
Tel: 306-997-2101; Fax: 306-997-2201
rm405@sasktel.net
Municipal Type: Rural Municipalities
Incorporated: Dec. 12, 1910; Area: 830.57 sq km
Population in 2016: 509
Federal Electoral District(s): Carlton Trail-Eagle Creek
Next Election: 2022/2024
Ron Saunders, Reeve
Valerie Fendelet, Administrator

Griffin No. 66
P.O. Box 70
Griffin, SK S0C 1G0
Tel: 306-842-6298; Fax: 306-842-6400
rm66@sasktel.net
Municipal Type: Rural Municipalities
Incorporated: Dec. 13, 1909; Area: 816.59 sq km
Population in 2016: 438
Federal Electoral District(s): Souris-Moose Mountain
Next Election: 2022/2024
Stacey Lund, Reeve
Tawnya Moore, Administrator

Gull Lake No. 139
P.O. Box 180
Gull Lake, SK S0N 1A0
Tel: 306-672-4430; Fax: 306-672-3879
rm139@sasktel.net
www.rmgulllake.ca
Municipal Type: Rural Municipalities
Incorporated: Jan. 1, 1913; Area: 836.41 sq km
Population in 2016: 201
Federal Electoral District(s): Cypress Hills-Grasslands
Next Election: 2022/2024
Terry Winter, Reeve
Jeanette Kerr, Administrator

Happy Valley No. 10
P.O. Box 39
Big Beaver, SK S0H 0G0
Tel: 306-267-4540; Fax: 306-267-4540
rm10@sasktel.net
Municipal Type: Rural Municipalities
Incorporated: Jan. 1, 1913; Area: 812.74 sq km
Population in 2016: 139
Federal Electoral District(s): Souris-Moose Mountain
Next Election: 2022/2024
Richard Lapaire, Reeve
Leanne Totton, Administrator

Happyland No. 231
P.O. Box 339
106 - 3rd St. West
Leader, SK S0N 1H0
Tel: 306-628-3800; Fax: 306-628-4228
rm231@sasktel.net
www.rmofhappyland.ca
Municipal Type: Rural Municipalities
Incorporated: Jan. 1, 1913; Area: 1,259 sq km
Population in 2016: 249
Federal Electoral District(s): Cypress Hills-Grasslands
Next Election: 2022/2024
Timothy Geiger, Reeve, 306-628-4335
Tim Lozinsky, Administrator

Harris No. 316
P.O. Box 146
Harris, SK S0L 1K0
Tel: 306-656-2072; Fax: 306-656-2151
rm316@sasktel.net
Municipal Type: Rural Municipalities
Incorporated: Dec. 12, 1910; Area: 805.42 sq km
Population in 2016: 193
Federal Electoral District(s): Carlton Trail-Eagle Creek
Next Election: 2022/2024
David Husband, Reeve
Judy Douglas, Administrator

Hart Butte No. 11
P.O. Box 210
Coronach, SK S0H 0Z0
Tel: 306-267-2005; Fax: 306-267-2391
rm11@sasktel.net
Municipal Type: Rural Municipalities
Incorporated: Jan. 1, 1913; Area: 841.98 sq km
Population in 2016: 252
Federal Electoral District(s): Souris-Moose Mountain
Next Election: 2022/2024
Craig Eger, Reeve
Leanne Totton, Administrator

Hazel Dell No. 335
P.O. Box 87
Okla, SK S0A 2X0
Tel: 306-325-4315; Fax: 306-352-4314
rm335@sasktel.net
Municipal Type: Rural Municipalities
Incorporated: Jan. 1, 1913; Area: 1,394.02 sq km
Population in 2016: 515
Federal Electoral District(s): Yorkton-Melville
Next Election: 2022/2024
Randall Harriman, Reeve

Christina Sorgen, Administrator

Hazelwood No. 94
P.O. Box 270
Kipling, SK S0G 2S0
Tel: 306-736-8121; Fax: 306-736-2496
rm94@sasktel.net
Municipal Type: Rural Municipalities
Incorporated: Jan. 1, 1913; Area: 780.68 sq km
Population in 2016: 230
Federal Electoral District(s): Souris-Moose Mountain
Next Election: 2022/2024
James Husband, Reeve
Gary Vargo, Administrator

Heart's Hill No. 352
P.O. Box 458
Luseland, SK S0L 2A0
Tel: 306-372-4224; Fax: 306-372-4770
Municipal Type: Rural Municipalities
Incorporated: Nov. 15, 1910; Area: 838.20 sq km
Population in 2016: 244
Federal Electoral District(s): Battlefords-Lloydminster
Next Election: 2022/2024
Gordon Stang, Reeve, 306-834-5041
Janet Fisher, Administrator

Hillsborough No. 132
#4, 1410 Caribou St. West
Moose Jaw, SK S6H 7S9
Tel: 306-693-1329; Fax: 306-693-2810
rm.132@sasktel.net
Municipal Type: Rural Municipalities
Incorporated: Jan. 1, 1913; Area: 445.25 sq km
Population in 2016: 101
Federal Electoral District(s): Cypress Hills-Grasslands
Next Election: 2022/2024
Blaine Barnett, Reeve
Charlene Loos, Administrator

Hillsdale No. 440
P.O. Box 280
39 Centre St.
Neilburg, SK S0M 2C0
Tel: 306-823-4321; Fax: 306-823-4477
rm440@sasktel.net
www.rmofhillsdale.com
Municipal Type: Rural Municipalities
Incorporated: Jan. 1, 1913; Area: 1,028.75 sq km
Population in 2016: 553
Federal Electoral District(s): Battlefords-Lloydminster
Next Election: 2022/2024
Glenn Goodfellow, Reeve, 306-823-4560
Janet L. Black, Administrator

Hoodoo No. 401
Cudworth, SK S0K 1B0
Tel: 306-256-3281; Fax: 306-256-7147
rm401@sasktel.net
www.rmofhoodoo.com
Municipal Type: Rural Municipalities
Incorporated: Jan. 1, 1913; Area: 810.61 sq km
Population in 2016: 675
Federal Electoral District(s): Carlton Trail-Eagle Creek
Next Election: 2022/2024
Derreck Kolla, Reeve
David Yorke, Administrator

Hudson Bay No. 394
P.O. Box 520
Hudson Bay, SK S0E 0Y0
Tel: 306-865-2691; Fax: 306-865-2857
rm394@sasktel.net
Municipal Type: Rural Municipalities
Incorporated: May 1, 1977; Area: 12,460.90 sq km
Population in 2016: 1,114
Federal Electoral District(s): Yorkton-Melville
Next Election: 2022/2024
Neal Hardy, Reeve
Tracy Smith, Administrator

Humboldt No. 370
P.O. Box 420
Humboldt, SK S0K 2A0
Tel: 306-682-2242; Fax: 306-682-3239
r.m.humboldt@sasktel.net
Municipal Type: Rural Municipalities
Incorporated: Jan. 1, 1913; Area: 798.51 sq km
Population in 2016: 935
Federal Electoral District(s): Carlton Trail-Eagle Creek
Next Election: 2022/2024
Larry Ries, Reeve
Corinne Richardson, Administrator

Huron No. 223
P.O. Box 159
Tugaske, SK S0H 4B0
Tel: 306-759-2211; Fax: 306-759-2249
rm223@sasktel.net
Municipal Type: Rural Municipalities
Incorporated: Dec. 12, 1910; Area: 842.11 sq km
Population in 2016: 198
Federal Electoral District(s): Moose Jaw-Lake Centre-Lanigan
Next Election: 2022/2024
Corey Doerksen, Reeve
Daryl Dean, Administrator

Indian Head No. 156
P.O. Box 39
Indian Head, SK S0G 2K0
Tel: 306-695-3464; Fax: 306-695-3462
rm156@sasktel.net
Municipal Type: Rural Municipalities
Incorporated: Aug. 6, 1884; Area: 759.98 sq km
Population in 2016: 336
Federal Electoral District(s): Regina-Qu'Appelle
Next Election: 2022/2024
Lorne Scott, Reeve
Lorelei Theaker, Administrator

Insinger No. 275
P.O. Box 179
Insinger, SK S0A 1L0
Tel: 306-647-2422; Fax: 306-647-2740
rm275@yourlink.ca
Municipal Type: Rural Municipalities
Incorporated: Jan. 1, 1913; Area: 849.38 sq km
Population in 2016: 315
Federal Electoral District(s): Yorkton-Melville
Next Election: 2022/2024
Willy Zuchkan, Reeve
Sonya Butuk, Administrator

Invergordon No. 430
P.O. Box 40
Crystal Springs, SK S0K 1A0
Tel: 306-749-2852; Fax: 306-749-2499
rm430@sasktel.net
Municipal Type: Rural Municipalities
Incorporated: Dec. 11, 1911; Area: 853.55 sq km
Population in 2016: 565
Federal Electoral District(s): Prince Albert
Next Election: 2022/2024
Bruce Hunter, Reeve
Trent Smith, Administrator

Invermay No. 305
P.O. Box 130
Invermay, SK S0A 1M0
Tel: 306-593-2152; Fax: 306-593-2132
rm.inv.305@sasktel.net
Municipal Type: Rural Municipalities
Incorporated: Dec. 11, 1911; Area: 728.23 sq km
Population in 2016: 325
Federal Electoral District(s): Yorkton-Melville
Next Election: 2022/2024
Bev Whyatt, Reeve
Dana Jack, Administrator

Ituna Bon Accord No. 246
P.O. Box 190
Ituna, SK S0A 1N0
Tel: 306-795-2202; Fax: 306-795-2202
rmofituna@sasktel.net
Municipal Type: Rural Municipalities
Incorporated: Jan. 1, 1913; Area: 837.23 sq km
Population in 2016: 374
Federal Electoral District(s): Regina-Qu'Appelle
Next Election: 2022/2024
Edward Datchko, Reeve
Wilma Hrenyk, Administrator

Kellross No. 247
P.O. Box 10
222 Main St.
Leross, SK S0A 2C0
Tel: 306-675-4423; Fax: 306-675-2097
rm247@sasktel.net
www.kellross.ca
Municipal Type: Rural Municipalities
Incorporated: Dec. 13, 1909; Area: 834.09 sq km
Population in 2016: 305
Federal Electoral District(s): Regina-Qu'Appelle
Next Election: 2022/2024
John Olinik, Reeve, 306-675-4970
Edith Goddard, Administrator

Kelvington No. 366
P.O. Box 519
201 Main St.
Kelvington, SK S0A 1W0
Tel: 306-327-4222; Fax: 306-327-4222
rm366@sasktel.net
Municipal Type: Rural Municipalities
Incorporated: Jan. 1, 1913; Area: 907.37 sq km
Population in 2016: 398
Federal Electoral District(s): Yorkton-Melville
Next Election: 2022/2024
Maurice Patenaude, Reeve
Heather Elmy, Administrator

Key West No. 70
P.O. Box 159
Ogema, SK S0C 1Y0
Tel: 306-459-2262; Fax: 306-459-2762
rm.70@sasktel.net
Municipal Type: Rural Municipalities
Incorporated: Dec. 12, 1910; Area: 825.26 sq km
Population in 2016: 255
Federal Electoral District(s): Souris-Moose Mountain
Next Election: 2022/2024
Zane McKerricher, Reeve
Peggy Tuchscherer, Administrator

Keys No. 303
P.O. Box 899
203 Main St.
Canora, SK S0A 0L0
Tel: 306-563-5331; Fax: 306-563-6759
rm303@sasktel.net
Municipal Type: Rural Municipalities
Incorporated: Jan. 1, 1913; Area: 661.61 sq km
Population in 2016: 390
Federal Electoral District(s): Yorkton-Melville
Next Election: 2022/2024
Garth Bates, Reeve
Barry Hvidston, Administrator

Kindersley No. 290
P.O. Box 1210
417 Main St.
Kindersley, SK S0L 1S0
Tel: 306-463-2524; Fax: 306-463-4197
rm290@sasktel.net
www.rmofkindersley.ca
Municipal Type: Rural Municipalities
Incorporated: Dec. 12, 1910; Area: 2,113.36 sq km
Population in 2016: 1,049
Federal Electoral District(s): Cypress Hills-Grasslands
Next Election: 2022/2024
Glen Harrison, Reeve, 306-463-3189
Glenda M. Giles, Administrator

King George No. 256
P.O. Box 100
Dinsmore, SK S0L 0T0
Tel: 306-846-2022; Fax: 306-846-2032
rm256@sasktel.net
Municipal Type: Rural Municipalities
Incorporated: Dec. 11, 1911; Area: 831.97 sq km
Population in 2016: 226
Federal Electoral District(s): Cypress Hills-Grasslands
Next Election: 2022/2024
Norm McIntyre, Reeve
Cheryl Joel, Administrator

Kingsley No. 124
P.O. Box 239
Kipling, SK S0G 2S0
Tel: 306-736-2272; Fax: 306-736-2798
rm124@sasktel.net
Municipal Type: Rural Municipalities
Incorporated: Dec. 12, 1910; Area: 844.61 sq km
Population in 2016: 444
Federal Electoral District(s): Souris-Moose Mountain
Next Election: 2022/2024
Clinton Neuls, Reeve
Holly Heikkila, Administrator

Kinistino No. 459
P.O. Box 310
Kinistino, SK S0J 1H0
Tel: 306-864-2474; Fax: 306-864-2880
rm459@sasktel.net
Municipal Type: Rural Municipalities
Incorporated: Dec. 11, 1911; Area: 949.13 sq km
Population in 2016: 554
Federal Electoral District(s): Prince Albert
Next Election: 2022/2024

Vance Shmyr, Reeve
Shelley L. Holmes, Administrator

Lac Pelletier No. 107
P.O. Box 70
Neville, SK S0N 1T0
Tel: 306-627-3226; Fax: 306-627-3641
rm107@sasktel.net
Municipal Type: Rural Municipalities
Incorporated: Jan. 1, 1913; Area: 849.27 sq km
Population in 2016: 546
Federal Electoral District(s): Cypress Hills-Grasslands
Next Election: 2022/2024
Cornie Martens, Reeve
Sandra Krushelniski, Administrator

Lacadena No. 228
P.O. Box 39
Lacadena, SK S0L 1V0
Tel: 306-574-4753; Fax: 306-574-4705
rm228@yourlink.ca
Municipal Type: Rural Municipalities
Incorporated: Dec. 12, 1910; Area: 1,890.08 sq km
Population in 2016: 535
Federal Electoral District(s): Cypress Hills-Grasslands
Next Election: 2022/2024
Bradley Sander, Reeve
Yvonne Nelson, Administrator

Laird No. 404
P.O. Box 160
3025 Central Ave.
Waldheim, SK S0K 4R0
Tel: 306-945-2133; Fax: 306-945-4824
www.rmoflaird.ca
Municipal Type: Rural Municipalities
Incorporated: Dec. 12, 1910; Area: 729.98 sq km
Population in 2016: 1,387
Federal Electoral District(s): Carlton Trail-Eagle Creek
Next Election: 2022/2024
Terry Knippel, Reeve
Paulette Wolkowski, Administrator

Lajord No. 128
P.O. Box 36
Lajord, SK S0G 2V0
Tel: 306-781-2744; Fax: 306-781-1023
www.myrm.ca/128
Municipal Type: Rural Municipalities
Incorporated: Dec. 13, 1909; Area: 943.87 sq km
Population in 2016: 1,232
Federal Electoral District(s): Souris-Moose Mountain
Next Election: 2022/2024
Erwin Beitel, Reeve
Rod Heise, Administrator

Lake Alma No. 8
P.O. Box 100
Lake Alma, SK S0C 1M0
Tel: 306-447-2022; Fax: 306-447-2023
rmalma@sasktel.net
Municipal Type: Rural Municipalities
Incorporated: May 5, 1913; Area: 822.47 sq km
Population in 2016: 242
Federal Electoral District(s): Souris-Moose Mountain
Next Election: 2022/2024
Rodney Robinson, Reeve
Myrna Lohse, Administrator

Lake Johnston No. 102
P.O. Box 160
Mossbank, SK S0H 3G0
Tel: 306-354-2414; Fax: 306-354-7725
rm102.103@sasktel.net
Municipal Type: Rural Municipalities
Incorporated: Dec. 9, 1912; Area: 567.24 sq km
Population in 2016: 170
Federal Electoral District(s): Cypress Hills-Grasslands
Next Election: 2022/2024
Sacha Martens, Reeve
Sherry Green, Administrator

Lake Lenore No. 399
P.O. Box 280
200 Main St.
St Brieux, SK S0K 3V0
Tel: 306-275-2066; Fax: 306-275-4667
brieux@sasktel.net
www.townofstbrieux.com
Municipal Type: Rural Municipalities
Incorporated: Jan. 1, 1913; Area: 724.06 sq km
Population in 2016: 587

Federal Electoral District(s): Yorkton-Melville
Next Election: 2022/2024
Jean Kernaleguen, Reeve
Jolynne Gallays, Administrator

Lake of the Rivers No. 72
P.O. Box 610
Assiniboia, SK S0H 0B0
Tel: 306-642-3533; *Fax:* 306-642-4382
rm72@sasktel.net
Municipal Type: Rural Municipalities
Incorporated: Dec. 11, 1911; *Area:* 677.51 sq km
Population in 2016: 279
Federal Electoral District(s): Cypress Hills-Grasslands
Next Election: 2022/2024
Norm Nordgulen, Reeve
Ellen Klein, Administrator

Lakeland No. 521
P.O. Box 27
Christopher Lake, SK S0J 0N0
Tel: 306-982-2010; *Fax:* 306-982-2589
office@lakeland521.ca
www.lakeland521.ca
Municipal Type: Rural Municipalities
Incorporated: Aug. 1, 1977; *Area:* 494.06 sq km
Population in 2016: 915
Federal Electoral District(s): Desnethé-Missinippi-Churchill River
Next Election: 2022/2024
Cheryl Bauer Hyde, Reeve
Dave Dmytruk, Administrator

Lakeside No. 338
P.O. Box 9
Quill Lake, SK S0A 3E0
Tel: 306-383-2261; *Fax:* 306-383-2255
rm338@sasktel.net
Municipal Type: Rural Municipalities
Incorporated: Dec. 12, 1910; *Area:* 636.80 sq km
Population in 2016: 415
Federal Electoral District(s): Yorkton-Melville
Next Election: 2022/2024
Arnold Boyko, Reeve
Judy Kanak, Administrator

Lakeview No. 337
P.O. Box 220
Wadena, SK S0A 4J0
Tel: 306-338-2341; *Fax:* 306-338-2595
rm337@sasktel.net
www.myrm.ca/337
Municipal Type: Rural Municipalities
Incorporated: Dec. 13, 1909; *Area:* 724.89 sq km
Population in 2016: 368
Federal Electoral District(s): Yorkton-Melville
Next Election: 2022/2024
Mervin Kryzanowski, Reeve
Carrie Turnbull, Administrator

Langenburg No. 181
P.O. Box 489
120 Carl Ave. West
Langenburg, SK S0A 2A0
Tel: 306-743-2341; *Fax:* 306-743-5282
rm181@sasktel.net
www.langenburg.ca/town_office/rm_of_langenburg.html
Municipal Type: Rural Municipalities
Incorporated: Jan. 1, 1913; *Area:* 675.66 sq km
Population in 2016: 557
Federal Electoral District(s): Yorkton-Melville
Next Election: 2022/2024
Terry Hildenbrandt, Reeve
Krystal Johnston, Administrator

Last Mountain Valley No. 250
P.O. Box 160
Govan, SK S0G 1Z0
Tel: 306-484-2011; *Fax:* 306-484-2113
rm250@sasktel.net
Municipal Type: Rural Municipalities
Incorporated: Dec. 13, 1909; *Area:* 871.17 sq km
Population in 2016: 275
Federal Electoral District(s): Moose Jaw-Lake Centre-Lanigan
Next Election: 2022/2024
Allan Magel, Reeve
Kelly Holbrook, Administrator

Laurier No. 38
P.O. Box 219
505 Healy Ave.
Radville, SK S0C 2G0
Tel: 306-869-2255; *Fax:* 306-869-2524
rm.38@sasktel.net
www.radville.ca
Municipal Type: Rural Municipalities
Incorporated: Dec. 13, 1909; *Area:* 840.86 sq km
Population in 2016: 296
Federal Electoral District(s): Souris-Moose Mountain
Next Election: 2022/2024
Todd Labbie, Reeve
Ursula Scott, Administrator

Lawtonia No. 135
P.O. Box 10
Hodgeville, SK S0H 2B0
Tel: 306-677-2266; *Fax:* 306-677-2446
rm135@sasktel.net
myrm.ca/135
Municipal Type: Rural Municipalities
Incorporated: Dec. 12, 1910; *Area:* 845.28 sq km
Population in 2016: 346
Federal Electoral District(s): Cypress Hills-Grasslands
Next Election: 2022/2024
Andrew Hanson, Reeve
Raelee Boehm, Administrator

Leask No. 464
P.O. Box 190
Leask, SK S0J 1M0
Tel: 306-466-2000; *Fax:* 306-466-2091
rmleask.464@sasktel.net
www.leask.ca/RM/rmoffice.html
Municipal Type: Rural Municipalities
Incorporated: Dec. 9, 1912; *Area:* 1,257.36 sq km
Population in 2016: 686
Federal Electoral District(s): Carlton Trail-Eagle Creek
Next Election: 2022/2024
Len Cantin, Reeve
Robert Jorgensen, Administrator

Leroy No. 339
P.O. Box 100
Leroy, SK S0K 2P0
Tel: 306-286-3261; *Fax:* 306-286-3400
rm339@sasktel.net
Municipal Type: Rural Municipalities
Incorporated: Jan. 1, 1913; *Area:* 840.40 sq km
Population in 2016: 502
Federal Electoral District(s): Moose Jaw-Lake Centre-Lanigan
Next Election: 2022/2024
Calvin Buhs, Reeve
Wendy Gowda, Administrator

Lipton No. 217
P.O. Box 40
Lipton, SK S0G 3B0
Tel: 306-336-2244; *Fax:* 306-336-2322
rm.217@sasktel.net
Municipal Type: Rural Municipalities
Incorporated: Dec. 11, 1911; *Area:* 813.69 sq km
Population in 2016: 381
Federal Electoral District(s): Regina-Qu'Appelle
Next Election: 2022/2024
Corey Senft, Reeve
Frank Kosa, Administrator

Livingston No. 331
P.O. Box 40
Arran, SK S0A 0B0
Tel: 306-595-4521; *Fax:* 306-595-4531
rm331@sasktel.net
Municipal Type: Rural Municipalities
Incorporated: Jan. 1, 1913; *Area:* 1,338.64 sq km
Population in 2016: 281
Federal Electoral District(s): Yorkton-Melville
Next Election: 2022/2024
Glen Smith, Reeve
Yvonne Bilsky, Administrator

Lomond No. 37
P.O. Box 280
Weyburn, SK S4H 2K1
Tel: 306-456-2566; *Fax:* 306-456-2440
rm37@sasktel.net
Municipal Type: Rural Municipalities
Incorporated: Dec. 11, 1911; *Area:* 833.95 sq km
Population in 2016: 296
Federal Electoral District(s): Souris-Moose Mountain
Next Election: 2022/2024

Desmond McKenzie, Reeve
Kevin Melle, Administrator

Lone Tree No. 18
P.O. Box 30
Climax, SK S0N 0N0
Tel: 306-293-2124; *Fax:* 306-293-2702
rmltno.18@sasktel.net
Municipal Type: Rural Municipalities
Incorporated: Dec. 8, 1913; *Area:* 838 sq km
Population in 2016: 150
Federal Electoral District(s): Cypress Hills-Grasslands
Next Election: 2022/2024
Larry Jarman, Reeve
Shawna Bertram, Administrator

Longlaketon No. 219
P.O. Box 100
Earl Grey, SK S0G 1J0
Tel: 306-939-2144; *Fax:* 306-939-2036
rm219@sasktel.net
Municipal Type: Rural Municipalities
Incorporated: Dec. 12, 1910; *Area:* 1,024.61 sq km
Population in 2016: 1,016
Federal Electoral District(s): Moose Jaw-Lake Centre-Lanigan;
Regina-Qu'Appelle
Next Election: 2022/2024
Delbert Schmidt, Reeve
Courtney Wiers, Administrator

Loon Lake No. 561
P.O. Box 40
Loon Lake, SK S0M 1L0
Tel: 306-837-2076; *Fax:* 306-837-2282
rm561@sasktel.net
www.rmofloonlake.com
Municipal Type: Rural Municipalities
Incorporated: Jan. 1, 1978; *Area:* 2,802.51 sq km
Population in 2016: 756
Federal Electoral District(s): Desnethé-Missinippi-Churchill River
Next Election: 2022/2024
Greg Cardinal, Reeve, 306-236-3637
Erin Simpson, Administrator

Loreburn No. 254
P.O. Box 40
Loreburn, SK S0H 2S0
Tel: 306-644-2022; *Fax:* 306-644-2064
rm254@sasktel.net
www.rmloreburn.ca
Municipal Type: Rural Municipalities
Incorporated: Dec. 12, 1910; *Area:* 966.78 sq km
Population in 2016: 327
Federal Electoral District(s): Moose Jaw-Lake Centre-Lanigan
Next Election: 2022/2024
Kevin Vollmer, Reeve
Vanessa Tastad, Administrator

Lost River No. 313
P.O. Box 159
Allan, SK S0K 0C0
Tel: 306-257-3272; *Fax:* 306-257-3337
rm313@sasktel.net
Municipal Type: Rural Municipalities
Incorporated: Dec. 11, 1911; *Area:* 549.90 sq km
Population in 2016: 242
Federal Electoral District(s): Moose Jaw-Lake Centre-Lanigan
Next Election: 2022/2024
Charles E. Smith, Reeve
Christine Dyck, Administrator

Lumsden No. 189
P.O. Box 160
300 James St. North
Lumsden, SK S0G 3C0
Tel: 306-731-2404; *Fax:* 306-731-3572
rm189@sasktel.net
www.lumsden.ca
Municipal Type: Rural Municipalities
Incorporated: Dec. 9, 1912; *Area:* 818.66 sq km
Population in 2016: 1,938
Federal Electoral District(s): Moose Jaw-Lake Centre-Lanigan;
Regina-Qu'Appelle
Next Election: 2022/2024
Kent Farago, Reeve, 306-731-3116
Darcie Cooper, Chief Administrative Officer

Manitou Lake No. 442
P.O. Box 69
Marsden, SK S0M 1P0
Tel: 306-826-5215; *Fax:* 306-826-5512
rm442@sasktel.net
www.rmmanitou.ca

Municipal Type: Rural Municipalities
Incorporated: Dec. 12, 1910; *Area:* 850.32 sq km
Population in 2016: 573
Federal Electoral District(s): Battlefords-Lloydminster
Next Election: 2022/2024
Ian Lamb, Reeve
Joanne Loy, Administrator

Mankota No. 45
P.O. Box 148
Mankota, SK S0H 2W0
Tel: 306-478-2323; *Fax:* 306-478-2606
rm45.46@sasktel.net
Municipal Type: Rural Municipalities
Incorporated: Jan. 1, 1913; *Area:* 1,696.22 sq km
Population in 2016: 292
Federal Electoral District(s): Cypress Hills-Grasslands
Next Election: 2022/2024
Vacant, Reeve
Michael E. Sherven, Administrator

Maple Bush No. 224
P.O. Box 160
Riverhurst, SK S0H 3P0
Tel: 306-353-2292; *Fax:* 306-353-2293
rm224@sasktel.net
Municipal Type: Rural Municipalities
Incorporated: Dec. 13, 1909; *Area:* 811.95 sq km
Population in 2016: 192
Federal Electoral District(s): Cypress Hills-Grasslands
Next Election: 2022/2024
Maurice Bartzen, Reeve
JoAnne Wandler, Administrator

Maple Creek No. 111
P.O. Box 188
Maple Creek, SK S0N 1N0
Tel: 306-662-2300; *Fax:* 306-662-3566
rm111@sasktel.net
Municipal Type: Rural Municipalities
Incorporated: Dec. 10, 1917; *Area:* 3,242.96 sq km
Population in 2016: 1,068
Federal Electoral District(s): Cypress Hills-Grasslands
Next Election: 2022/2024
Walter Ehret, Reeve
Christine Hoffman, Administrator

Mariposa No. 350
P.O. Box 228
603 Atlantic Ave.
Kerrobert, SK S0L 1R0
Tel: 306-834-5037; *Fax:* 306-834-5047
rm350@sasktel.net
Municipal Type: Rural Municipalities
Incorporated: Dec. 12, 1910; *Area:* 636.73 sq km
Population in 2016: 205
Federal Electoral District(s): Battlefords-Lloydminster
Next Election: 2022/2024
Dale MacArthur, Reeve
Kathy Wurz, Administrator

Marquis No. 191
P.O. Box 40
Marquis, SK S0H 2X0
Tel: 306-788-2022; *Fax:* 306-788-2168
rm191@sasktel.net
myrm.ca/191
Municipal Type: Rural Municipalities
Incorporated: Dec. 11, 1911; *Area:* 805.48 sq km
Population in 2016: 297
Federal Electoral District(s): Moose Jaw-Lake Centre-Lanigan
Next Election: 2022/2024
Kenneth Waldenberger, Reeve
Margaret Brown, Administrator

Marriott No. 317
P.O. Box 366
Rosetown, SK S0L 2V0
Tel: 306-882-4030; *Fax:* 306-882-4401
rm317@sasktel.net
Municipal Type: Rural Municipalities
Incorporated: Dec. 12, 1910; *Area:* 843.29 sq km
Population in 2016: 366
Federal Electoral District(s): Carlton Trail-Eagle Creek
Next Election: 2022/2024
Orville Minish, Reeve
Jill Omiecinski, Administrator

Martin No. 122
P.O. Box 1109
Moosomin, SK S0G 3N0
Tel: 306-435-3113; *Fax:* 306-435-4313
rm122@sasktel.net
www.myrm.ca/122
Municipal Type: Rural Municipalities
Incorporated: Jan. 1, 1913; *Area:* 556.50 sq km
Population in 2016: 289
Federal Electoral District(s): Souris-Moose Mountain
Next Election: 2022/2024
Gerald Flaman, Reeve
Cheryl Barrett, Administrator

Maryfield No. 91
P.O. Box 70
Maryfield, SK S0G 3K0
Tel: 306-646-2033; *Fax:* 306-646-2033
rm91@sasktel.net
Municipal Type: Rural Municipalities
Incorporated: Dec. 9, 1912; *Area:* 759.63 sq km
Population in 2016: 324
Federal Electoral District(s): Souris-Moose Mountain
Next Election: 2022/2024
Cameron Thompson, Reeve
Daphne Brady, Administrator

Mayfield No. 406
P.O. Box 100
Maymont, SK S0M 1T0
Tel: 306-389-2112; *Fax:* 306-389-2162
rm406@sasktel.net
Municipal Type: Rural Municipalities
Incorporated: Dec. 13, 1909; *Area:* 782.50 sq km
Population in 2016: 377
Federal Electoral District(s): Battlefords-Lloydminster; Carlton
Trail-Eagle Creek
Next Election: 2022/2024
Craig Hamilton, Reeve
Laurie DuBois, Administrator

McCraney No. 282
P.O. Box 129
Kenaston, SK S0G 2N0
Tel: 306-252-2240; *Fax:* 306-252-2248
rm282@sasktel.net
Municipal Type: Rural Municipalities
Incorporated: Dec. 13, 1909; *Area:* 948.36 sq km
Population in 2016: 310
Federal Electoral District(s): Moose Jaw-Lake Centre-Lanigan
Next Election: 2022/2024
Murray Kadlec, Reeve
Mark Zdunich, Administrator

McKillop No. 220
P.O. Box 369
2 - 200 Mountain St.
Strasbourg, SK S0G 4V0
Tel: 306-725-3230; *Fax:* 306-725-3206
rm220@sasktel.net
www.rmofmckillop220.com
Municipal Type: Rural Municipalities
Incorporated: Dec. 13, 1909; *Area:* 668.45 sq km
Population in 2016: 732
Federal Electoral District(s): Moose Jaw-Lake Centre-Lanigan
Next Election: 2022/2024
Vacant, Reeve
Michele Cruise-Pratchler, Administrator

McLeod No. 185
P.O. Box 130
Neudorf, SK S0A 2T0
Tel: 306-748-2233; *Fax:* 306-748-2647
rm185@sasktel.net
Municipal Type: Rural Municipalities
Incorporated: Jan. 1, 1913; *Area:* 886.6 sq km
Population in 2016: 365
Federal Electoral District(s): Regina-Qu'Appelle; Souris-Moose
Mountain; Yorkton-Melville
Next Election: 2022/2024
Allen Clifford, Reeve
Murray J. Hanowski, Administrator

Meadow Lake No. 588
P.O. Box 668
#1, 225 Centre St.
Meadow Lake, SK S9X 1L5
Tel: 306-236-5651; *Fax:* 306-236-3115
rm588@sasktel.net
Municipal Type: Rural Municipalities
Incorporated: Feb. 1, 1976; *Area:* 6,303.31 sq km
Population in 2016: 2,501

Federal Electoral District(s): Desnethé-Missinippi-Churchill River
Next Election: 2022/2024
Timothy McKay, Reeve
Gina Bernier, Administrator

Medstead No. 497
P.O. Box 12
209 - 2nd Avenue
Medstead, SK S0M 1W0
Tel: 306-342-4609; *Fax:* 306-342-2067
rm497@sasktel.net
Municipal Type: Rural Municipalities
Incorporated: Jan. 1, 1913; *Area:* 1,203.22 sq km
Population in 2016: 508
Federal Electoral District(s): Battlefords-Lloydminster;
Desnethé-Missinippi-Churchill River
Next Election: 2022/2024
Ronald Jesse, Reeve
Christin Egeland, Administrator

Meeting Lake No. 466
P.O. Box 26
Mayfair, SK S0M 1S0
Tel: 306-246-4228; *Fax:* 306-246-4974
rm466@sasktel.net
www.myrm.ca/466
Municipal Type: Rural Municipalities
Incorporated: Jan. 1, 1913; *Area:* 1,066.74 sq km
Population in 2016: 319
Federal Electoral District(s): Carlton Trail-Eagle Creek
Next Election: 2022/2024
Randy Aumack, Reeve
Janelle Lavallee, Administrator

Meota No. 468
P.O. Box 80
300 - 1st St. East
Meota, SK S0M 1X0
Tel: 306-892-2061; *Fax:* 306-892-2449
rm.468@sasktel.net
www.rmmeota468.ca
Municipal Type: Rural Municipalities
Incorporated: Dec. 13, 1909; *Area:* 651.09 sq km
Population in 2016: 933
Federal Electoral District(s): Battlefords-Lloydminster
Next Election: 2022/2024
Sherry Jimmy, Reeve
Nicolle Griffith, Administrator

Mervin No. 499
P.O. Box 130
211 Main St.
Turtleford, SK S0M 2Y0
Tel: 306-845-2045; *Fax:* 306-845-2950
rm499@sasktel.net
www.rmofmervin.com
Municipal Type: Rural Municipalities
Incorporated: Jan. 1, 1913; *Area:* 1,594.64 sq km
Population in 2016: 1,256
Federal Electoral District(s): Battlefords-Lloydminster
Next Election: 2022/2024
Tom Brown, Reeve, 306-845-2325
L. Ryan Domotor, Administrator

Milden No. 286
P.O. Box 160
113 Centre St.
Milden, SK S0L 2L0
Tel: 306-935-2181; *Fax:* 306-935-2046
rm286@sasktel.net
Municipal Type: Rural Municipalities
Incorporated: Dec. 12, 1910; *Area:* 735.31 sq km
Population in 2016: 327
Federal Electoral District(s): Carlton Trail-Eagle Creek
Next Election: 2022/2024
Grant Thomson, Reeve
Denise Ward, Administrator

Milton No. 292
P.O. Box 70
Marengo, SK S0L 2K0
Tel: 306-968-2922; *Fax:* 306-968-2278
rm292.rm322@sasktel.net
www.myrm.ca/292
Municipal Type: Rural Municipalities
Incorporated: Dec. 11, 1911; *Area:* 655.76 sq km
Population in 2016: 241
Federal Electoral District(s): Cypress Hills-Grasslands
Next Election: 2022/2024
David Bond, Reeve
Robin Busby, Administrator

Miry Creek No. 229
P.O. Box 210
Abbey, SK S0N 0A0
Tel: 306-689-2281; *Fax:* 306-689-2901
rm229@sasktel.net
www.rm229.com
Municipal Type: Rural Municipalities
Incorporated: Jan. 1, 1913; *Area:* 1,220.38 sq km
Population in 2016: 370
Federal Electoral District(s): Cypress Hills-Grasslands
Next Election: 2022/2024
Note: On December 31st 2013, the village of Shackleton dissolved into the Rural Municipality of Miry Creek No. 229.
Mark Hughes, Reeve
Jan Stern, Administrator

Monet No. 257
P.O. Box 370
210 Railway Ave. East
Elrose, SK S0L 0Z0
Tel: 306-378-2212; *Fax:* 306-378-2212
rm257@sasktel.net
www.elrose.ca/r-m-of-monet-257
Municipal Type: Rural Municipalities
Incorporated: Dec. 13, 1909; *Area:* 1,591.75 sq km
Population in 2016: 445
Federal Electoral District(s): Cypress Hills-Grasslands
Next Election: 2022/2024
Duncan Campbell, Reeve
Lori McDonald, Administrator

Montmartre No. 126
P.O. Box 120
136 Central Ave.
Montmartre, SK S0G 3M0
Tel: 306-424-2040; *Fax:* 306-424-2065
rm126@sasktel.net
Municipal Type: Rural Municipalities
Incorporated: Dec. 13, 1909; *Area:* 853.91 sq km
Population in 2016: 483
Federal Electoral District(s): Souris-Moose Mountain
Next Election: 2022/2024
Kenneth W. Weichel, Reeve
Dale Brenner, Administrator

Montrose No. 315
P.O. Box 129
First Ave. North
Delisle, SK S0L 0P0
Tel: 306-493-2694; *Fax:* 306-493-3057
rm315@sasktel.net
www.rmmontrose.ca
Municipal Type: Rural Municipalities
Incorporated: Dec. 13, 1909; *Area:* 898.38 sq km
Population in 2016: 712
Federal Electoral District(s): Carlton Trail-Eagle Creek
Next Election: 2022/2024
Murray Purcell, Reeve
Desiree Bouvier, Administrator

Moose Creek No. 33
P.O. Box 10
118 - 5th St.
Alameda, SK S0C 0A0
Tel: 306-489-2044; *Fax:* 306-489-2112
rm33@sasktel.net
www.mofmoosecreek.com
Municipal Type: Rural Municipalities
Incorporated: Dec. 12, 1910; *Area:* 842.03 sq km
Population in 2016: 379
Federal Electoral District(s): Souris-Moose Mountain
Next Election: 2022/2024
Howard Sloan, Reeve, 306-483-7576
Sentura Freitag, Administrator

Moose Jaw No. 161
#3, 1410 Caribou St. West
Moose Jaw, SK S6H 7S9
Tel: 306-692-3446; *Fax:* 306-691-0015
rm161@sasktel.net
www.moosejawrm161.ca
Municipal Type: Rural Municipalities
Incorporated: Dec. 11, 1911; *Area:* 797.60 sq km
Population in 2016: 1,163
Federal Electoral District(s): Moose Jaw-Lake Centre-Lanigan
Next Election: 2022/2024
Ron Brumwell, Reeve, 306-694-1956
Mike Wirges, Administrator

Moose Mountain No. 63
P.O. Box 445
105 - 100 Main St.
Carlyle, SK S0C 0R0
Tel: 306-453-6175; *Fax:* 306-453-2430
rm63@sasktel.net
Municipal Type: Rural Municipalities
Incorporated: Dec. 11, 1911; *Area:* 740.91 sq km
Population in 2016: 492
Federal Electoral District(s): Souris-Moose Mountain
Next Election: 2022/2024
Kelly Brimner, Reeve
Lynne Hewitt, Administrator

Moose Range No. 486
P.O. Box 699
40 Railway Dr.
Carrot River, SK S0E 0L0
Tel: 306-768-2212; *Fax:* 306-768-2211
rm486@sasktel.net
www.myrm.ca/486
Municipal Type: Rural Municipalities
Incorporated: Dec. 11, 1916; *Area:* 2,419.06 sq km
Population in 2016: 1,000
Federal Electoral District(s): Prince Albert
Next Election: 2022/2024
Bud Charko, Reeve, 306-768-2297
Beverly Doerksen, Administrator

Moosomin No. 121
P.O. Box 1109
602 Main St.
Moosomin, SK S0G 3N0
Tel: 306-435-3113; *Fax:* 306-435-4313
rm121@sasktel.net
www.rm121.com
Municipal Type: Rural Municipalities
Incorporated: Jan. 1, 1913; *Area:* 566.39 sq km
Population in 2016: 470
Federal Electoral District(s): Souris-Moose Mountain
Next Election: 2022/2024
David Moffatt, Reeve
Kendra Lawrence, Administrator

Morris No. 312
P.O. Box 130
121 Main St.
Young, SK S0K 4Y0
Tel: 306-259-2211; *Fax:* 306-259-2225
rm312@sasktel.net
www.young.ca/rm-morris.htm
Municipal Type: Rural Municipalities
Incorporated: Dec. 13, 1909; *Area:* 847.16 sq km
Population in 2016: 290
Federal Electoral District(s): Moose Jaw-Lake Centre-Lanigan
Next Election: 2022/2024
Robert Penrose, Reeve
Belinda Rowan, Administrator

Morse No. 165
P.O. Box 340
401 Main St.
Morse, SK S0H 3C0
Tel: 306-629-3282; *Fax:* 306-629-3212
rm165@sasktel.net
Municipal Type: Rural Municipalities
Incorporated: Dec. 11, 1911; *Area:* 1,244.38 sq km
Population in 2016: 427
Federal Electoral District(s): Cypress Hills-Grasslands
Next Election: 2022/2024
Bruce Gall, Reeve
Mark Wilson, Administrator

Mount Hope No. 279
P.O. Box 190
Semans, SK S0A 3S0
Tel: 306-524-2055; *Fax:* 306-524-4526
rm279@sasktel.net
www.myrm.ca/279
Municipal Type: Rural Municipalities
Incorporated: Dec. 11, 1911; *Area:* 1,669.29 sq km
Population in 2016: 531
Federal Electoral District(s): Moose Jaw-Lake Centre-Lanigan; Regina-Qu'Appelle
Next Election: 2022/2024
Bob Digney, Reeve
Cal Shaw, Administrator

Mount Pleasant No. 2
P.O. Box 278
1312 Railway Ave.
Carnduff, SK S0C 0S0
Tel: 306-482-3313; *Fax:* 306-482-3422
rm.2@sasktel.net
Municipal Type: Rural Municipalities
Incorporated: Dec. 11, 1911; *Area:* 781.48 sq km
Population in 2016: 414
Federal Electoral District(s): Souris-Moose Mountain
Next Election: 2022/2024
Chad Baglole, Reeve
Valerie A. Olney, Administrator

Mountain View No. 318
P.O. Box 130
Herschel, SK S0L 1L0
Tel: 306-377-2144; *Fax:* 306-377-2023
rm318@sasktel.net
rm318.ca
Municipal Type: Rural Municipalities
Incorporated: Dec. 13, 1909; *Area:* 838.67 sq km
Population in 2016: 337
Federal Electoral District(s): Carlton Trail-Eagle Creek
Next Election: 2022/2024
Rodney G. Wiens, Reeve
Rachel Deobald, Administrator

Newcombe No. 260
P.O. Box 40
Glidden, SK S0L 1H0
Tel: 306-463-3338; *Fax:* 306-463-4748
rm260@yourlink.ca
Municipal Type: Rural Municipalities
Incorporated: Dec. 11, 1911; *Area:* 1,075.6 sq km
Population in 2016: 342
Federal Electoral District(s): Cypress Hills-Grasslands
Next Election: 2022/2024
Ken McBride, Reeve
Monica Buddecke, Administrator

Nipawin No. 487
P.O. Box 250
Codette, SK S0E 0P0
Tel: 306-862-9551; *Fax:* 306-862-2432
rm487@sasktel.net
Municipal Type: Rural Municipalities
Incorporated: Dec. 9, 1912; *Area:* 886.73 sq km
Population in 2016: 1,004
Federal Electoral District(s): Prince Albert
Next Election: 2022/2024
Hoppe Dona, Reeve
Nathalie Hipkins, Administrator

North Battleford No. 437
#4, 1462 - 100th St.
North Battleford, SK S9A 0W2
Tel: 306-445-3604; *Fax:* 306-445-3694
rm437@sasktel.net
rmofnorthbattleford.com
Municipal Type: Rural Municipalities
Incorporated: Dec. 12, 1910; *Area:* 797.20 sq km
Population in 2016: 725
Federal Electoral District(s): Battlefords-Lloydminster
Next Election: 2022/2024
Dan Bartko, Reeve
Debbie Arsenault, Administrator

North Qu'Appelle No. 187
P.O. Box 99
Fort Qu'Appelle, SK S0G 1S0
Tel: 306-332-5202; *Fax:* 306-332-6028
rm187@sasktel.net
Municipal Type: Rural Municipalities
Incorporated: Dec. 12, 1910; *Area:* 494.98 sq km
Population in 2016: 855
Federal Electoral District(s): Regina-Qu'Appelle
Next Election: 2022/2024
Harry McDonald, Reeve
Marcy Johnson, Administrator

Norton No. 69
P.O. Box 189
410 Mergens St.
Pangman, SK S0C 2C0
Tel: 306-442-2131; *Fax:* 306-442-2144
rm.69@sasktel.net
www.myrm.ca/069
Municipal Type: Rural Municipalities
Incorporated: Dec. 13, 1909; *Area:* 844.8 sq km
Population in 2016: 233

Federal Electoral District(s): Souris-Moose Mountain
Next Election: 2022/2024
Tom Webb, Reeve
Patti Gurskey, Administrator

Oakdale No. 320
P.O. Box 249
200 Main St.
Coleville, SK S0L 0K0
Tel: 306-965-2281; *Fax:* 306-965-2466
rm320@sasktel.net
www.rmofoakdale320.ca
Other Information: Alt. Email: rmoakassist@sasktel.net
Municipal Type: Rural Municipalities
Incorporated: Dec. 13, 1909; *Area:* 806.52 sq km
Population in 2016: 253
Federal Electoral District(s): Battlefords-Lloydminster
Next Election: 2022/2024
Darwin Whitfield, Reeve
Gillain Lund, Administrator

Old Post No. 43
P.O. Box 70
Wood Mountain, SK S0H 4L0
Tel: 306-266-2002; *Fax:* 306-266-2020
rm43@sasktel.net
Municipal Type: Rural Municipalities
Incorporated: Jan. 1, 1967; *Area:* 1,757 sq km
Population in 2016: 377
Federal Electoral District(s): Cypress Hills-Grasslands
Next Election: 2022/2024
Vacant, Reeve
Vickie Greffard, Administrator

Orkney No. 244
26 - 5th Ave. North
Yorkton, SK S3N 0Y8
Tel: 306-782-2333; *Fax:* 306-782-5177
orkney@sasktel.net
rmorkney.ca
Municipal Type: Rural Municipalities
Incorporated: Jan. 1, 1913; *Area:* 815.87 sq km
Population in 2016: 1,875
Federal Electoral District(s): Yorkton-Melville
Next Election: 2022/2024
Randy Trost, Reeve
Clint Mauthe, Administrator

Paddockwood No. 520
P.O. Box 187
Paddockwood, SK S0J 1Z0
Tel: 306-989-2124; *Fax:* 306-989-4625
rm520@sasktel.net
www.rmofpaddockwood.com
Municipal Type: Rural Municipalities
Incorporated: Jan. 1, 1978; *Area:* 2,456.51 sq km
Population in 2016: 895
Federal Electoral District(s): Desnethé-Missinippi-Churchill River;
Prince Albert
Next Election: 2022/2024
Leander (Lance) Fehr, Reeve, 306-982-4805
Naomi Hrischuk, Administrator

Parkdale No. 498
P.O. Box 310
Glaslyn, SK S0M 0Y0
Tel: 306-342-2015; *Fax:* 306-342-4442
rm498@sasktel.net
www.rmofparkdale498.com
Municipal Type: Rural Municipalities
Incorporated: Jan. 1, 1913; *Area:* 1,388.91 sq km
Population in 2016: 621
Federal Electoral District(s): Battlefords-Lloydminster
Next Election: 2022/2024
Daniel Hicks, Reeve
Jennifer Ernst, Administrator

Paynton No. 470
P.O. Box 10
Paynton, SK S0M 2J0
Tel: 306-895-2020; *Fax:* 306-895-4800
rm470@sasktel.net
Municipal Type: Rural Municipalities
Incorporated: Jan. 1, 1913; *Area:* 593.95 sq km
Population in 2016: 255
Federal Electoral District(s): Battlefords-Lloydminster
Next Election: 2022/2024
Kevin Garrett, Reeve
Jade Johnson, Administrator

Pense No. 160
P.O. Box 190
324 Elder St.
Pense, SK S0G 3W0
Tel: 306-345-2303; *Fax:* 306-345-2583
rm160@sasktel.net
www.pense160.ca
Municipal Type: Rural Municipalities
Incorporated: Jan. 1, 1913; *Area:* 841.48 sq km
Population in 2016: 508
Federal Electoral District(s): Moose Jaw-Lake Centre-Lanigan
Next Election: 2022/2024
Tom Lemon, Reeve
Cathy Ripplinger, Administrator

Perdue No. 346
P.O. Box 208
Perdue, SK S0K 3C0
Tel: 306-237-4202; *Fax:* 306-237-4202
rm346@sasktel.net
www.myrm.ca/346
Municipal Type: Rural Municipalities
Incorporated: Dec. 13, 1909; *Area:* 826.14 sq km
Population in 2016: 445
Federal Electoral District(s): Carlton Trail-Eagle Creek
Next Election: 2022/2024
John Gray, Reeve
Allan Kirzinger, Administrator

Piapot No. 110
P.O. Box 100
Piapot, SK S0N 1Y0
Tel: 306-558-2011; *Fax:* 306-558-2125
rm110@sasktel.net
www.myrm.ca/110
Municipal Type: Rural Municipalities
Incorporated: Dec. 8, 1913; *Area:* 1,912.81 sq km
Population in 2016: 302
Federal Electoral District(s): Cypress Hills-Grasslands
Next Election: 2022/2024
John Wagner, Reeve
Jenny Robinson, Administrator

Pinto Creek No. 75
P.O. Box 239
Kincaid, SK S0H 2J0
Tel: 306-264-3277; *Fax:* 306-264-3254
rm75@sasktel.net
Municipal Type: Rural Municipalities
Incorporated: Jan. 1, 1913; *Area:* 845.01 sq km
Population in 2016: 283
Federal Electoral District(s): Cypress Hills-Grasslands
Next Election: 2022/2024
Brian Corcoran, Reeve
Roxanne Empey, Administrator

Pittville No. 169
P.O. Box 150
Hazlet, SK S0N 1E0
Tel: 306-678-2131; *Fax:* 306-678-2132
rm169@sasktel.net
Municipal Type: Rural Municipalities
Incorporated: Jan. 1, 1913; *Area:* 1,258.06 sq km
Population in 2016: 208
Federal Electoral District(s): Cypress Hills-Grasslands
Next Election: 2022/2024
Larry Sletten, Reeve
Terry Erdelyan, Administrator

Pleasant Valley No. 288
P.O. Box 2080
Rosetown, SK S0L 2V0
Tel: 306-882-4030; *Fax:* 306-882-4401
rm317@sasktel.net
Municipal Type: Rural Municipalities
Incorporated: Dec. 11, 1911; *Area:* 830.53 sq km
Population in 2016: 302
Federal Electoral District(s): Carlton Trail-Eagle Creek
Next Election: 2022/2024
Blake Jeffries, Reeve
Jill Omiecinski, Administrator

Pleasantdale No. 398
P.O. Box 70
Naicam, SK S0K 2Z0
Tel: 306-874-5732; *Fax:* 306-874-2225
rm398@sasktel.net
Municipal Type: Rural Municipalities
Incorporated: Dec. 11, 1911; *Area:* 757.91 sq km
Population in 2016: 596
Federal Electoral District(s): Yorkton-Melville
Next Election: 2022/2024

Fred Graham, Reeve
Janelle Scott, Administrator

Ponass Lake No. 367
P.O. Box 98
Rose Valley, SK S0E 1M0
Tel: 306-322-2162; *Fax:* 306-322-2168
rm367@sasktel.net
Municipal Type: Rural Municipalities
Incorporated: Jan. 1, 1913; *Area:* 770.21 sq km
Population in 2016: 422
Federal Electoral District(s): Yorkton-Melville
Next Election: 2022/2024
Allan Nelson, Reeve
Loretta Prevost, Administrator

Poplar Valley No. 12
P.O. Box 190
Rockglen, SK S0H 3R0
Tel: 306-476-2062; *Fax:* 306-476-2175
rm12@sasktel.net
Municipal Type: Rural Municipalities
Incorporated: Jan. 1, 1913; *Area:* 769.37 sq km
Population in 2016: 195
Federal Electoral District(s): Cypress Hills-Grasslands
Next Election: 2022/2024
Nairn Nielsen, Reeve
Lynn Fisher, Administrator

Porcupine No. 395
P.O. Box 190
440 McAllister Ave.
Porcupine Plain, SK S0E 1H0
Tel: 306-278-2368; *Fax:* 306-278-3473
rm395@sasktel.net
www.porcupineplain.com
Municipal Type: Rural Municipalities
Incorporated: Feb. 28, 1944; *Area:* 2,339.96 sq km
Population in 2016: 803
Federal Electoral District(s): Yorkton-Melville
Next Election: 2022/2024
Steve Kwiatkowski, Reeve
Nicole Smith, Administrator

Prairie Rose No. 309
P.O. Box 89
Main St.
Jansen, SK S0K 2B0
Tel: 306-364-2013; *Fax:* 306-364-2088
rm309@sasktel.net
www.myrm.ca/309
Municipal Type: Rural Municipalities
Incorporated: Dec. 12, 1910; *Area:* 839.08 sq km
Population in 2016: 220
Federal Electoral District(s): Moose Jaw-Lake Centre-Lanigan;
Regina-Qu'Appelle
Next Election: 2022/2024
Darin Pedersen, Reeve
Joni Mack, Administrator

Prairiedale No. 321
P.O. Box 90
Main St.
Smiley, SK S0L 2Z0
Tel: 306-838-2020; *Fax:* 306-838-4343
administration@rmofprairiedale.ca
www.rmofprairiedale.ca
Municipal Type: Rural Municipalities
Incorporated: Dec. 13, 1909; *Area:* 546.74 sq km
Population in 2016: 247
Federal Electoral District(s): Battlefords-Lloydminster
Next Election: 2022/2024
Tim Richelhoff, Reeve, 306-384-5590
Charlotte Helfrich, Administrator

Preeceville No. 334
P.O. Box 439
33 - 1st Ave. NW
Preeceville, SK S0A 3B0
Tel: 306-547-2029; *Fax:* 306-547-2081
rm334@sasktel.net
www.townofpreeceville.ca
Municipal Type: Rural Municipalities
Incorporated: Jan. 1, 1913; *Area:* 1,394.80 sq km
Population in 2016: 919
Federal Electoral District(s): Yorkton-Melville
Next Election: 2022/2024
Richard Pristie, Reeve
Lisa Peterson, Administrator

Prince Albert No. 461
99 River St. East
Prince Albert, SK S6V 0A1
Tel: 306-763-2469; *Fax:* 306-763-6369
rm461@sasktel.net
www.rmprincealbert.ca
Other Information: Alt. Email: rm461.concerns@sasktel.net
Municipal Type: Rural Municipalities
Incorporated: Dec. 9, 1912; *Area:* 1,019.01 sq km
Population in 2016: 3,562
Federal Electoral District(s): Prince Albert
Next Election: 2022/2024
Paul Rybka, Reeve
Roxanne Roy, Administrator

Progress No. 351
P.O. Box 460
Luseland, SK S0L 2A0
Tel: 306-372-4322; *Fax:* 306-372-4146
rm351@sasktel.net
Municipal Type: Rural Municipalities
Incorporated: Dec. 12, 1910; *Area:* 803.09 sq km
Population in 2016: 268
Federal Electoral District(s): Battlefords-Lloydminster
Next Election: 2022/2024
Gordon Meyer, Reeve
Kim Adams, Administrator

Reciprocity No. 32
P.O. Box 70
302 Highway 361
Alida, SK S0C 0B0
Tel: 306-443-2212; *Fax:* 306-443-2287
rm.of.reciprocity@sasktel.net
www.rmofreciprocity.ca
Municipal Type: Rural Municipalities
Incorporated: Dec. 11, 1911; *Area:* 733.06 sq km
Population in 2016: 344
Federal Electoral District(s): Souris-Moose Mountain
Next Election: 2022/2024
Alan Arthur, Reeve
Marilyn Larsen, Chief Administrative Officer

Redberry No. 435
P.O. Box 160
Hafford, SK S0J 1A0
Tel: 306-549-2333; *Fax:* 306-549-2435
rm435@littleloon.ca
Municipal Type: Rural Municipalities
Incorporated: Jan. 1, 1913; *Area:* 1,015.53 sq km
Population in 2016: 342
Federal Electoral District(s): Carlton Trail-Eagle Creek
Next Election: 2022/2024
Les Welkie, Reeve
Alan Tanchak, Administrator

Redburn No. 130
P.O. Box 250
Rouleau, SK S0G 4H0
Tel: 306-776-2270; *Fax:* 306-776-2482
redrou@sasktel.net
Municipal Type: Rural Municipalities
Incorporated: Jan. 1, 1913; *Area:* 847.91 sq km
Population in 2016: 250
Federal Electoral District(s): Moose Jaw-Lake Centre-Lanigan
Next Election: 2022/2024
Ronald Hughes, Reeve
Guy Lagrandeur, Administrator

Reford No. 379
P.O. Box 100
214 - 2nd Ave. East
Wilkie, SK S0K 4W0
Tel: 306-843-2342; *Fax:* 306-843-2455
rm409@sasktel.net
Municipal Type: Rural Municipalities
Incorporated: Dec. 12, 1910; *Area:* 707.06 sq km
Population in 2016: 257
Federal Electoral District(s): Battlefords-Lloydminster
Next Election: 2022/2024
Gerald Gerlinsky, Reeve
Sherry Huber, Administrator

Reno No. 51
P.O. Box 90
Consul, SK S0N 0P0
Tel: 306-299-2133; *Fax:* 306-299-4433
rm51@sasktel.net
Municipal Type: Rural Municipalities
Incorporated: Dec. 11, 1911; *Area:* 3,460.66 sq km
Population in 2016: 379

Federal Electoral District(s): Cypress Hills-Grasslands
Next Election: 2022/2024
Brian McMillan, Reeve
Kim Lacelle, Administrator

Riverside No. 168
P.O. Box 129
211 Standard St.
Pennant, SK S0N 1X0
Tel: 306-626-3255; *Fax:* 306-626-3661
rm168@sasktel.net
www.rm168.ca
Municipal Type: Rural Municipalities
Incorporated: Jan. 1, 1913; *Area:* 1,295.21 sq km
Population in 2016: 477
Federal Electoral District(s): Cypress Hills-Grasslands
Next Election: 2022/2024
Richard Bye, Reeve
Brandi Prentice, Administrator

Rocanville No. 151
P.O. Box 298
Rocanville, SK S0A 3L0
Tel: 306-645-2055; *Fax:* 306-645-2697
rm151@sasktel.net
www.myrm.ca/151
Municipal Type: Rural Municipalities
Incorporated: Dec. 9, 1912; *Area:* 758.64 sq km
Population in 2016: 507
Federal Electoral District(s): Souris-Moose Mountain
Next Election: 2022/2024
Murray Reid, Reeve
Sylvia Anderson, Administrator

Rodgers No. 133
#4, 1410 Caribou St. West
Moose Jaw, SK S6H 7S9
Tel: 306-693-1329; *Fax:* 306-693-2810
rm133@sasktel.net
Municipal Type: Rural Municipalities
Incorporated: Dec. 9, 1912; *Area:* 719.80 sq km
Population in 2016: 90
Federal Electoral District(s): Cypress Hills-Grasslands
Next Election: 2022/2024
Brent Tremblay, Reeve
Charlene Loos, Administrator

Rosedale No. 283
P.O. Box 150
Hanley, SK S0G 2E0
Tel: 306-544-2202; *Fax:* 306-544-2252
rm283@sasktel.net
Municipal Type: Rural Municipalities
Incorporated: Dec. 13, 1909; *Area:* 921.50 sq km
Population in 2016: 526
Federal Electoral District(s): Moose Jaw-Lake Centre-Lanigan
Next Election: 2022/2024
Sira Wade, Reeve
Danielle Hache, Administrator

Rosemount No. 378
P.O. Box 184
Landis, SK S0K 2K0
Tel: 306-658-2034; *Fax:* 306-658-2028
rm378@sasktel.net
Municipal Type: Rural Municipalities
Incorporated: Dec. 12, 1910; *Area:* 571.35 sq km
Population in 2016: 201
Federal Electoral District(s): Battlefords-Lloydminster
Next Election: 2022/2024
Albert L. Kammer, Reeve
Kara Kirilenko, Administrator

Rosthern No. 403
P.O. Box 126
2022 - 6th St.
Rosthern, SK S0K 3R0
Tel: 306-232-4393; *Fax:* 306-232-5321
rm403@sasktel.net
www.rmofrosthern.ca
Municipal Type: Rural Municipalities
Incorporated: Dec. 9, 1912; *Area:* 954.66 sq km
Population in 2016: 2,003
Federal Electoral District(s): Carlton Trail-Eagle Creek
Next Election: 2022/2024
Martin Penner, Reeve
Amanda McCormick, Administrator

Round Hill No. 467
P.O. Box 9
Rabbit Lake, SK S0M 2L0
Tel: 306-824-2044; *Fax:* 306-824-2044
rm467@yourlink.ca

Municipal Type: Rural Municipalities
Incorporated: Dec. 11, 1911; *Area:* 815.21 sq km
Population in 2016: 361
Federal Electoral District(s): Battlefords-Lloydminster
Next Election: 2022/2024
Note: Absorbed the former Village of Rabbit Lake in 2015.
Alvin Wiebe, Reeve
Christina Moore, Administrator

Round Valley No. 410
P.O. Box 538
Unity, SK S0K 4L0
Tel: 306-228-2248; *Fax:* 306-228-3483
rm410@sasktel.net
www.myrm.ca/410
Municipal Type: Rural Municipalities
Incorporated: Dec. 13, 1909; *Area:* 810.57 sq km
Population in 2016: 423
Federal Electoral District(s): Battlefords-Lloydminster
Next Election: 2022/2024
Jim Powell, Reeve
Mervin Bosch, Administrator

Rudy No. 284
P.O. Box 1010
400 Saskatchewan Ave. West
Outlook, SK S0L 2N0
Tel: 306-867-9349; *Fax:* 306-867-9898
rmrudy@sasktel.net
www.rmrudy.ca
Municipal Type: Rural Municipalities
Incorporated: Dec. 13, 1909; *Area:* 813.86 sq km
Population in 2016: 466
Federal Electoral District(s): Moose Jaw-Lake Centre-Lanigan
Next Election: 2022/2024
Dennis Fuglerud, Reeve, 306-867-8903
Trent Michelman, Administrator

St. Andrews No. 287
P.O. Box 488
Rosetown, SK S0L 2V0
Tel: 306-882-2314; *Fax:* 306-882-3287
rm.287@sasktel.net
www.myrm.ca/287
Municipal Type: Rural Municipalities
Incorporated: Dec. 12, 1910; *Area:* 805.30 sq km
Population in 2016: 522
Federal Electoral District(s): Carlton Trail-Eagle Creek
Next Election: 2022/2024
Geoff Legge, Reeve
Joan Babecy, Administrator

St. Louis No. 431
P.O. Box 28
Hoey, SK S0J 1E0
Tel: 306-422-6170; *Fax:* 306-422-8520
rm431@sasktel.net
Municipal Type: Rural Municipalities
Incorporated: Jan. 1, 1913; *Area:* 790.18 sq km
Population in 2016: 1,086
Federal Electoral District(s): Prince Albert
Next Election: 2022/2024
Emile Boutin, Reeve
Sindy Tait, Administrator

St. Peter No. 369
P.O. Box 70
Annaheim, SK S0K 0G0
Tel: 306-598-2122; *Fax:* 306-598-4526
rm369@sasktel.net
www.myrm.ca/369
Municipal Type: Rural Municipalities
Incorporated: Dec. 11, 1911; *Area:* 823.22 sq km
Population in 2016: 773
Federal Electoral District(s): Carlton Trail-Eagle Creek
Next Election: 2022/2024
Glenn Ehalt, Reeve
Angie Peake, Administrator

St. Philips No. 301
P.O. Box 220
Pelly, SK S0A 2Z0
Tel: 306-595-2050; *Fax:* 306-595-4941
rm301@sasktel.net
Municipal Type: Rural Municipalities
Incorporated: Jan. 1, 1913; *Area:* 655.79 sq km
Population in 2016: 220
Federal Electoral District(s): Yorkton-Melville
Next Election: 2022/2024
Bernard Vogel, Reeve
Frances Olson, Administrator

Saltcoats No. 213
P.O. Box 150
Saltcoats, SK S0A 3R0
Tel: 306-744-2202; *Fax:* 306-744-2455
rm.saltcoats@sasktel.net
www.rmsaltcoats.ca
Municipal Type: Rural Municipalities
Incorporated: Dec. 9, 1912; *Area:* 830.58 sq km
Population in 2016: 712
Federal Electoral District(s): Yorkton-Melville
Next Election: 2022/2024
Don Taylor, Reeve, 306-621-4218
Ronald R. Risling, Administrator, 306-744-2202

Sarnia No. 221
P.O. Box 160
125 Roberts St.
Holdfast, SK S0G 2H0
Tel: 306-488-2033; *Fax:* 306-488-4609
rm.sarnia@sasktel.net
Municipal Type: Rural Municipalities
Incorporated: Dec. 13, 1909; *Area:* 870.11 sq km
Population in 2016: 322
Federal Electoral District(s): Moose Jaw-Lake Centre-Lanigan
Next Election: 2022/2024
Carl Erlandson, Reeve
Patti Vance, Administrator

Saskatchewan Landing No. 167
P.O. Box 40
Stewart Valley, SK S0N 2P0
Tel: 306-778-2105; *Fax:* 306-778-2152
rm167@sasktel.net
www.myrm.ca/167
Municipal Type: Rural Municipalities
Incorporated: Jan. 1, 1913; *Area:* 797.52 sq km
Population in 2016: 415
Federal Electoral District(s): Cypress Hills-Grasslands
Next Election: 2022/2024
Darwin Johnsgaard, Reeve
Kayla Krusky, Administrator

Sasman No. 336
P.O. Box 130
Kuroki, SK S0A 1Y0
Tel: 306-338-2263; *Fax:* 306-338-2048
rm336@yourlink.ca
Municipal Type: Rural Municipalities
Incorporated: Jan. 1, 1913; *Area:* 1,006.49 sq km
Population in 2016: 765
Federal Electoral District(s): Yorkton-Melville
Next Election: 2022/2024
Dwayne Nakrayko, Reeve
Shandy Wegwitz, Administrator

Scott No. 98
P.O. Box 210
Yellow Grass, SK S0G 5J0
Tel: 306-465-2512; *Fax:* 306-465-2802
rm98@sasktel.net
Municipal Type: Rural Municipalities
Incorporated: Dec. 13, 1909; *Area:* 850.08 sq km
Population in 2016: 195
Federal Electoral District(s): Souris-Moose Mountain
Next Election: 2022/2024
Ryley Richards, Reeve
Shelly Robertson, Administrator

Senlac No. 411
P.O. Box 130
Senlac, SK S0L 2Y0
Tel: 306-228-3339; *Fax:* 306-228-2264
rm411@sasktel.net
Municipal Type: Rural Municipalities
Incorporated: Jan. 1, 1913; *Area:* 1,026.25 sq km
Population in 2016: 216
Federal Electoral District(s): Battlefords-Lloydminster
Next Election: 2022/2024
Owen Mawbey, Reeve
Pauline Herle, Administrator

Shamrock No. 134
P.O. Box 40
Shamrock, SK S0H 3W0
Tel: 306-648-3594; *Fax:* 306-648-3687
rm134@sasktel.net
www.shamrockpark.ca
Municipal Type: Rural Municipalities
Incorporated: Dec. 9, 1912; *Area:* 757.52 sq km
Population in 2016: 205
Federal Electoral District(s): Cypress Hills-Grasslands
Next Election: 2022/2024

Wayne Rud, Reeve
Jody Kennedy, Administrator

Shellbrook No. 493
P.O. Box 250
71 Main St.
Shellbrook, SK S0J 2E0
Tel: 306-747-2178; *Fax:* 306-747-4315
rm493@sasktel.net
www.rmofshellbrook.com
Municipal Type: Rural Municipalities
Incorporated: Jan. 1, 1913; *Area:* 1,237.29 sq km
Population in 2016: 1,587
Federal Electoral District(s): Prince Albert;
Desnethé-Missinippi-Churchill River
Next Election: 2022/2024
Robert Ernst, Reeve
Michael Rattray, Administrator

Sherwood No. 159
4400 Campbell St.
Regina, SK S4W 0L3
Tel: 306-525-5237; *Fax:* 306-352-1760
admin@rmofsherwood.ca
www.rmofsherwood.ca
Municipal Type: Rural Municipalities
Incorporated: Dec. 11, 1911; *Area:* 719.32 sq km
Population in 2016: 974
Federal Electoral District(s): Regina-Qu'Appelle
Next Election: 2022/2024
Jeff Poissant, Reeve
Michele Cruise-Pratchler, Administrator

Silverwood No. 123
P.O. Box 700
Whitewood, SK S0G 5C0
Tel: 306-735-2500; *Fax:* 306-735-2524
rm123@sasktel.net
www.myrm.ca/123
Municipal Type: Rural Municipalities
Incorporated: Oct. 31, 1911; *Area:* 844.61 sq km
Population in 2016: 410
Federal Electoral District(s): Souris-Moose Mountain
Next Election: 2022/2024
William MacPherson, Reeve
Jennalee Beutler, Administrator

Sliding Hills No. 273
P.O. Box 70
Mikado, SK S0A 2R0
Tel: 306-563-5285; *Fax:* 306-563-4447
slidinghills_rm273@sasktel.net
Municipal Type: Rural Municipalities
Incorporated: Jan. 1, 1913; *Area:* 853.76 sq km
Population in 2016: 421
Federal Electoral District(s): Yorkton-Melville
Next Election: 2022/2024
Harvey Malanowich, Reeve
Todd Steele, Administrator

Snipe Lake No. 259
P.O. Box 786
213 Main St.
Eston, SK S0L 1A0
Tel: 306-962-3214; *Fax:* 306-962-4330
rm259@sasktel.net
Municipal Type: Rural Municipalities
Incorporated: Dec. 11, 1911; *Area:* 1,573.80 sq km
Population in 2016: 396
Federal Electoral District(s): Cypress Hills-Grasslands
Next Election: 2022/2024
Bill Owens, Reeve
Debbie Shaw, Administrator

Souris Valley No. 7
P.O. Box 40
Oungre, SK S0C 1Z0
Tel: 306-456-2676; *Fax:* 306-456-2480
rm07@sasktel.net
Municipal Type: Rural Municipalities
Incorporated: Dec. 13, 1909; *Area:* 817.52 sq km
Population in 2016: 249
Federal Electoral District(s): Souris-Moose Mountain
Next Election: 2022/2024
Robert Forrester, Reeve
Erica Pederson, Administrator

South Qu'Appelle No. 157
P.O. Box 66
Qu'Appelle, SK S0G 4A0
Tel: 306-699-2257; *Fax:* 306-699-2671
rm157@sasktel.net
www.rm157.ca

Municipal Type: Rural Municipalities
Incorporated: Aug. 6, 1884; *Area:* 889.73 sq km
Population in 2016: 1,275
Federal Electoral District(s): Regina Qu'Appelle
Next Election: 2022/2024
Jeannie DesRochers, Reeve, 306-699-2814
Heidi Berlin, Administrator

Spalding No. 368
P.O. Box 10
Spalding, SK S0K 4C0
Tel: 306-872-2166; *Fax:* 306-872-2275
bob368@sasktel.net
Municipal Type: Rural Municipalities
Incorporated: Dec. 11, 1911; *Area:* 811.47 sq km
Population in 2016: 453
Federal Electoral District(s): Yorkton-Melville
Next Election: 2022/2024
Eugene Eggerman, Reeve
Cathy Holt, Administrator

Spiritwood No. 496
P.O. Box 340
Spiritwood, SK S0J 2M0
Tel: 306-883-2034; *Fax:* 306-883-2557
rm496@sasktel.net
www.rmofspiritwood.ca
Municipal Type: Rural Municipalities
Incorporated: Dec. 9, 1929; *Area:* 2,410.62 sq km
Population in 2016: 1,349
Federal Electoral District(s): Desnethé-Missinippi-Churchill River;
Carlton Trail-Eagle Creek; Battlefords-Lloydminster
Next Election: 2022/2024
Shirley Dauvin, Reeve
Colette Bussiere, Administrator

Spy Hill No. 152
P.O. Box 129
Spy Hill, SK S0A 3W0
Tel: 306-534-2022; *Fax:* 306-534-2230
rm152@sasktel.net
Municipal Type: Rural Municipalities
Incorporated: Dec. 11, 1911; *Area:* 679.28 sq km
Population in 2016: 323
Federal Electoral District(s): Yorkton-Melville
Next Election: 2022/2024
Bob Bruce, Reeve
Carey Nicholauson, Administrator

Stanley No. 215
P.O. Box 70
238 - 3rd Ave. West
Melville, SK S0A 2P0
Tel: 306-728-2818; *Fax:* 306-728-2818
rm.ofstanley@sasktel.net
Municipal Type: Rural Municipalities
Incorporated: Jan. 1, 1913; *Area:* 855.40 sq km
Population in 2016: 505
Federal Electoral District(s): Regina-Qu'Appelle; Yorkton-Melville
Next Election: 2022/2024
Kenneth Petlock, Reeve
Dawn Oehler, Administrator

Star City No. 428
P.O. Box 370
Star City, SK S0E 1P0
Tel: 306-863-2522; *Fax:* 306-863-2255
r.m.starcity@sasktel.ca
www.myrm.ca/428
Municipal Type: Rural Municipalities
Incorporated: Jan. 1, 1913; *Area:* 824.85 sq km
Population in 2016: 918
Federal Electoral District(s): Prince Albert
Next Election: 2022/2024
Kenneth Naber, Reeve
Levina Cronk, Administrator

Stonehenge No. 73
P.O. Box 129
Limerick, SK S0H 2P0
Tel: 306-263-2020; *Fax:* 306-263-2013
rm73@sasktel.net
www.myrm.ca/073
Municipal Type: Rural Municipalities
Incorporated: Dec. 11, 1911; *Area:* 985.74 sq km
Population in 2016: 319
Federal Electoral District(s): Cypress Hills-Grasslands
Next Election: 2022/2024
Chris Sinclair, Reeve
Tammy Franks, Administrator

Storthoaks No. 31
P.O. Box 40
Storthoaks, SK S0C 2K0
Tel: 306-449-2262; *Fax:* 306-449-2210
rm31@sasktel.net
Municipal Type: Rural Municipalities
Incorporated: Dec. 11, 1911; *Area:* 582.57 sq km
Population in 2016: 292
Federal Electoral District(s): Souris-Moose Mountain
Next Election: 2022/2024
Brian Chicoine, Reeve
Elissa Henrion, Administrator

Surprise Valley No. 9
P.O. Box 52
Minton, SK S0C 1T0
Tel: 306-969-2144; *Fax:* 306-969-2127
rmnine@sasktel.net
Municipal Type: Rural Municipalities
Incorporated: Jan. 1, 1913; *Area:* 813.38 sq km
Population in 2016: 217
Federal Electoral District(s): Souris-Moose Mountain
Next Election: 2022/2024
Herb Axten, Reeve
Loran Tessier, Administrator

Sutton No. 103
P.O. Box 100
Mossbank, SK S0H 3G0
Tel: 306-354-2414; *Fax:* 306-354-7725
rm102.103@sasktel.net
www.myrm.ca/103
Municipal Type: Rural Municipalities
Incorporated: Dec. 11, 1911; *Area:* 822.40 sq km
Population in 2016: 240
Federal Electoral District(s): Cypress Hills-Grasslands
Next Election: 2022/2024
Richard Nagel, Reeve
Sherry Green, Administrator

Swift Current No. 137
2024 South Service Rd. West
Swift Current, SK S9H 5J5
Tel: 306-773-7314; *Fax:* 306-773-9538
rmsc137@sasktel.net
www.rmswiftcurrent.ca
Municipal Type: Rural Municipalities
Incorporated: Dec. 12, 1910; *Area:* 1,107.7 sq km
Population in 2016: 1,932
Federal Electoral District(s): Cypress Hills-Grasslands
Next Election: 2022/2024
Robert Neufeld, Reeve, 306-773-4167
Linda Boser, Administrator

Tecumseh No. 65
P.O. Box 300
Stoughton, SK S0G 4T0
Tel: 306-457-2277; *Fax:* 306-457-3149
rm65@sasktel.net
www.myrm.ca/65
Municipal Type: Rural Municipalities
Incorporated: Dec. 13, 1909; *Area:* 826.11 sq km
Population in 2016: 271
Federal Electoral District(s): Souris-Moose Mountain
Next Election: 2022/2024
Zandra Slater, Reeve
Alysson Slater, Administrator

Terrell No. 101
P.O. Box 60
Spring Valley, SK S0H 3X0
Tel: 306-475-2803; *Fax:* 306-475-2805
street101@sasktel.net
www.rmofterrell101.ca
Municipal Type: Rural Municipalities
Incorporated: Jan. 1, 1913; *Area:* 864.06 sq km
Population in 2016: 241
Federal Electoral District(s): Moose Jaw-Lake Centre-Lanigan
Next Election: 2022/2024
Darrell Howe, Reeve, 306-354-2698
Kimberly Sippola, Administrator

Three Lakes No. 400
P.O. Box 100
Middle Lake, SK S0K 2X0
Tel: 306-367-2172; *Fax:* 306-367-2011
rm400@sasktel.net
Municipal Type: Rural Municipalities
Incorporated: Jan. 1, 1913; *Area:* 772.49 sq km
Population in 2016: 598
Federal Electoral District(s): Carlton Trail-Eagle Creek
Next Election: 2022/2024

Allen Baumann, Reeve
Tim Schmidt, Administrator

Tisdale No. 427
P.O. Box 128
Tisdale, SK S0E 1T0
Tel: 306-873-2334; *Fax:* 306-873-4442
rm427@sasktel.net
www.myrm.ca/427
Municipal Type: Rural Municipalities
Incorporated: Dec. 9, 1912; *Area:* 849.24 sq km
Population in 2016: 911
Federal Electoral District(s): Prince Albert
Next Election: 2022/2024
Ian Allan, Reeve
Fern Lucas, Administrator

Torch River No. 488
P.O. Box 40
White Fox, SK S0J 3B0
Tel: 306-276-2066; *Fax:* 306-276-2099
rm488@sasktel.net
www.rmtorchriver.ca
Municipal Type: Rural Municipalities
Incorporated: Jan. 1, 1950; *Area:* 5,179 sq km
Population in 2016: 1,471
Federal Electoral District(s): Prince Albert;
Desnethé-Missinippi-Churchill River
Next Election: 2022/2024
Louise Nicklen, Reeve
Nathalie Hipkins, Administrator

Touchwood No. 248
P.O. Box 160
Punnichy, SK S0A 3C0
Tel: 306-835-2110; *Fax:* 306-835-2100
rm248@aski.ca
Municipal Type: Rural Municipalities
Incorporated: Dec. 12, 1910; *Area:* 706.72 sq km
Population in 2016: 343
Federal Electoral District(s): Regina-Qu'Appelle
Next Election: 2022/2024
Ernest Matai, Reeve
Lorelei Paulsen, Administrator

Tramping Lake No. 380
P.O. Box 129
104 Main St.
Scott, SK S0K 4A0
Tel: 306-247-2033; *Fax:* 306-247-2055
rmtrampinglake@xplornet.com
Municipal Type: Rural Municipalities
Incorporated: Dec. 12, 1910; *Area:* 615.56 sq km
Population in 2016: 375
Federal Electoral District(s): Battlefords-Lloydminster
Next Election: 2022/2024
Peter Volk, Reeve
Stacy Hawkins, Administrator

Tullymet No. 216
P.O. Box 190
Balcarres, SK S0G 0C0
Tel: 306-334-2366; *Fax:* 306-334-2930
rm216@sasktel.net
www.townofbalcarres.ca
Municipal Type: Rural Municipalities
Incorporated: Jan. 1, 1913; *Area:* 562.99 sq km
Population in 2016: 200
Federal Electoral District(s): Regina-Qu'Appelle
Next Election: 2022/2024
Aaron Keisig, Reeve
Sheila Keisig, Administrator

Turtle River No. 469
P.O. Box 128
Edam, SK S0M 0V0
Tel: 306-397-2311; *Fax:* 306-397-2346
rm469@sasktel.net
Municipal Type: Rural Municipalities
Incorporated: Dec. 9, 1912; *Area:* 664.49 sq km
Population in 2016: 344
Federal Electoral District(s): Battlefords-Lloydminster
Next Election: 2022/2024
Louis McCaffrey, Reeve
Nicole Collins, Administrator

Usborne No. 310
P.O. Box 310
220 St Samson St.
Guernsey, SK S0K 2M0
Tel: 306-365-2924; *Fax:* 306-365-2129
rm310@sasktel.net

Municipal Type: Rural Municipalities
Incorporated: Dec. 13, 1909; *Area:* 810.38 sq km
Population in 2016: 529
Federal Electoral District(s): Moose Jaw-Lake Centre-Lanigan
Next Election: 2022/2024
Jack Gibney, Reeve
Anna Rintoul, Administrator

Val Marie No. 17
P.O. Box 59
Val Marie, SK S0N 2T0
Tel: 306-298-2009; *Fax:* 306-298-2224
rm17@sasktel.net
Municipal Type: Rural Municipalities
Incorporated: Jan. 1, 1969; *Area:* 3,105.26 sq km
Population in 2016: 413
Federal Electoral District(s): Cypress Hills-Grasslands
Next Election: 2022/2024
Larry Grant, Reeve
Cathy Legault, Administrator

Vanscoy No. 345
P.O. Box 187
Vanscoy, SK S0L 3J0
Tel: 306-668-2060; *Fax:* 306-668-1338
rm345@sasktel.net
www.rmvanscoy.ca
Municipal Type: Rural Municipalities
Incorporated: Dec. 13, 1909; *Area:* 866.68 sq km
Population in 2016: 2,840
Federal Electoral District(s): Carlton Trail-Eagle Creek
Next Election: 2022/2024
Floyd Chapple, Reeve, 306-329-4697
Tony Obrigewitch, Administrator

Victory No. 226
P.O. Box 100
Beechy, SK S0L 0C0
Tel: 306-859-2270; *Fax:* 306-859-2271
rm226@sasktel.net
Municipal Type: Rural Municipalities
Incorporated: Dec. 8, 1919; *Area:* 1,375.44 sq km
Population in 2016: 380
Federal Electoral District(s): Cypress Hills-Grasslands
Next Election: 2022/2024
Donald Shirtliff, Reeve
Diane Watt, Administrator

Viscount No. 341
P.O. Box 100
215 Bangor Ave.
Viscount, SK S0K 4M0
Tel: 306-944-2044; *Fax:* 306-944-2016
patrm341@sasktel.net
www.myrm.ca/341
Municipal Type: Rural Municipalities
Incorporated: Dec. 13, 1909; *Area:* 831.23 sq km
Population in 2016: 338
Federal Electoral District(s): Moose Jaw-Lake Centre-Lanigan
Next Election: 2022/2024
Gordon Gusikoski, Reeve
Patrick T. Clavelle, Administrator

Wallace No. 243
26 - 5th Ave. North
Yorkton, SK S3N 0Y8
Tel: 306-782-2455; *Fax:* 306-782-5177
wallace@sasktel.net
www.rmwallace.ca
Municipal Type: Rural Municipalities
Incorporated: Dec. 11, 1911; *Area:* 832.01 sq km
Population in 2016: 852
Federal Electoral District(s): Yorkton-Melville
Next Election: 2022/2024
Garry Liebrecht, Reeve, 306-621-1776
Gerry Burym, Administrator

Walpole No. 92
P.O. Box 117
Wawota, SK S0G 5A0
Tel: 306-739-2545; *Fax:* 306-739-2777
rm92@sasktel.net
walpolerm.com
Municipal Type: Rural Municipalities
Incorporated: Dec. 12, 1910; *Area:* 844.66 sq km
Population in 2016: 326
Federal Electoral District(s): Souris-Moose Mountain
Next Election: 2022/2024
Hugh Smyth, Reeve
Deborah C. Saville, Administrator

Waverley No. 44
P.O. Box 70
Glentworth, SK S0H 1V0
Tel: 306-266-4920; *Fax:* 306-266-2077
rm44@yourlink.ca
Municipal Type: Rural Municipalities
Incorporated: Feb. 1, 1913; *Area:* 1,429.30 sq km
Population in 2016: 336
Federal Electoral District(s): Cypress Hills-Grasslands
Next Election: 2022/2024
Lloyd Anderson, Reeve
Deidre Nelson, Administrator

Wawken No. 93
P.O. Box 90
Wawota, SK S0G 5A0
Tel: 306-739-2332; *Fax:* 306-739-2222
rm93@sasktel.net
www.myrm.ca/093
Municipal Type: Rural Municipalities
Incorporated: Jan. 1, 1913; *Area:* 766.53 sq km
Population in 2016: 571
Federal Electoral District(s): Souris-Moose Mountain
Next Election: 2022/2024
Dawn Cameron, Reeve
Linda Klimm, Administrator

Webb No. 138
P.O. Box 100
Webb, SK S0N 2X0
Tel: 306-674-2230; *Fax:* 306-674-2324
rm138@xplornet.com
www.myrm.ca/138
Municipal Type: Rural Municipalities
Incorporated: Dec. 13, 1909; *Area:* 1,098.78 sq km
Population in 2016: 541
Federal Electoral District(s): Cypress Hills-Grasslands
Next Election: 2022/2024
Dennis Fiddler, Reeve
Raylene Packet, Administrator

Wellington No. 97
P.O. Box 1390
2nd Ave.
Weyburn, SK S4H 3J9
Tel: 306-842-5606; *Fax:* 306-842-5601
rm97@sasktel.net
Municipal Type: Rural Municipalities
Incorporated: Dec. 13, 1909; *Area:* 838.68 sq km
Population in 2016: 371
Federal Electoral District(s): Souris-Moose Mountain
Next Election: 2022/2024
Kelly Schneider, Reeve
Heather Wawro, Administrator

Weyburn No. 67
23 - 6th St. NE
Weyburn, SK S4H 1A7
Tel: 306-842-2314; *Fax:* 306-842-1002
rm.67@sasktel.net
www.rmweyburn.ca
Municipal Type: Rural Municipalities
Incorporated: Dec. 13, 1909; *Area:* 811.70 sq km
Population in 2016: 1,064
Federal Electoral District(s): Souris-Moose Mountain
Next Election: 2022/2024
Carmen Sterling, Reeve, 306-842-5409
Pam Scott, Administrator

Wheatlands No. 163
P.O. Box 129
Mortlach, SK S0H 3E0
Tel: 306-355-2233; *Fax:* 306-355-2351
rm163@sasktel.net
Municipal Type: Rural Municipalities
Incorporated: Dec. 13, 1909; *Area:* 827.4 sq km
Population in 2016: 149
Federal Electoral District(s): Cypress Hills-Grasslands
Next Election: 2022/2024
Kim Bokinac, Reeve
Julie Gerbrandt, Administrator

Whiska Creek No. 106
P.O. Box 10
Vanguard, SK S0N 2V0
Tel: 306-582-2133; *Fax:* 306-582-4950
rm106@sasktel.net
Municipal Type: Rural Municipalities
Incorporated: Jan. 1, 1913; *Area:* 851.89 sq km
Population in 2016: 465
Federal Electoral District(s): Cypress Hills-Grasslands
Next Election: 2022/2024

Kelly Williamson, Reeve
Teresa Richards, Administrator

White Valley No. 49
P.O. Box 520
Eastend, SK S0N 0T0
Tel: 306-295-3553; *Fax:* 306-295-3571
rm49@sasktel.net
Municipal Type: Rural Municipalities
Incorporated: Jan. 1, 1913; *Area:* 2,026.88 sq km
Population in 2016: 478
Federal Electoral District(s): Cypress Hills-Grasslands
Next Election: 2022/2024
James Leroy, Reeve
Edna Laturnus, Administrator

Willner No. 253
P.O. Box 250
101 Lincoln St.
Davidson, SK S0G 1A0
Tel: 306-567-3103; *Fax:* 306-567-3266
rm253@sasktel.net
www.rmwillner.com
Municipal Type: Rural Municipalities
Incorporated: Jan. 1, 1913; *Area:* 834.97 sq km
Population in 2016: 255
Federal Electoral District(s): Moose Jaw-Lake Centre-Lanigan
Next Election: 2022/2024
Len Palmer, Reeve, 306-567-7034
Yvonne (Bonny) Goodsman, Administrator

Willow Bunch No. 42
P.O. Box 220
16 Edouard Beaupré St.
Willow Bunch, SK S0H 4K0
Tel: 306-473-2450; *Fax:* 306-473-2312
rm.42@sasktel.net
www.willowbunch.ca
Municipal Type: Rural Municipalities
Incorporated: Nov. 21, 1912; *Area:* 1,047.8 sq km
Population in 2016: 306
Federal Electoral District(s): Cypress Hills-Grasslands
Next Election: 2022/2024
Denis Bellefleur, Reeve
Sharleine Eger, Administrator

Willow Creek No. 458
P.O. Box 5
Brooksby, SK S0E 0H0
Tel: 306-863-4143; *Fax:* 306-863-2366
rm458@staffcomm.com
www.myrm.ca/458
Municipal Type: Rural Municipalities
Incorporated: Dec. 9, 1912; *Area:* 845.18 sq km
Population in 2016: 630
Federal Electoral District(s): Prince Albert
Next Election: 2022/2024
Gordon Garinger, Reeve
Vicki Baptist, Administrator

Willowdale No. 153
P.O. Box 58
Whitewood, SK S0G 5C0
Tel: 306-735-2344; *Fax:* 306-735-4495
rm153@sasktel.net
www.myrm.ca/153
Municipal Type: Rural Municipalities
Incorporated: Jan. 1, 1913; *Area:* 605.06 sq km
Population in 2016: 299
Federal Electoral District(s): Souris-Moose Mountain
Next Election: 2022/2024
Kenneth Aldous, Reeve, 306-735-7634
Robert (Bob) Laing, Administrator

Wilton No. 472
P.O. Box 40
Marshall, SK S0M 1R0
Tel: 306-387-6244; *Fax:* 306-387-6598
info@rmwilton.ca
www.rmwilton.ca
Municipal Type: Rural Municipalities
Incorporated: Dec. 13, 1909; *Area:* 1,042.72 sq km
Population in 2016: 1,629
Federal Electoral District(s): Battlefords-Lloydminster
Next Election: 2022/2024
Glen Dow, Reeve
Darren Elder, Chief Administrative Officer

Winslow No. 319
P.O. Box 310
Dodsland, SK S0L 0V0
Tel: 306-356-2106; *Fax:* 306-356-2085
rm319@sasktel.net
www.myrm.ca/319
Municipal Type: Rural Municipalities
Incorporated: Dec. 13, 1909; *Area:* 798.07 sq km
Population in 2016: 344
Federal Electoral District(s): Battlefords-Lloydminster
Next Election: 2022/2024
Eldon Summach, Reeve
Regan MacDonald, Administrator

Wise Creek No. 77
P.O. Box 400
Shaunavon, SK S0N 2M0
Tel: 306-297-2520; *Fax:* 306-297-3162
rm77.78@sasktel.net
Municipal Type: Rural Municipalities
Incorporated: Jan. 1, 1913; *Area:* 843.85 sq km
Population in 2016: 205
Federal Electoral District(s): Cypress Hills-Grasslands
Next Election: 2022/2024
Denis Chenard, Reeve
Kathy Collins, Administrator

Wolseley No. 155
P.O. Box 370
Wolseley, SK S0G 5H0
Tel: 306-698-2522; *Fax:* 306-698-2664
rm155@sasktel.net
myrm.ca/155
Municipal Type: Rural Municipalities
Incorporated: Dec. 13, 1909; *Area:* 774.26 sq km
Population in 2016: 372
Federal Electoral District(s): Regina-Qu'Appelle; Souris-Moose
Mountain
Next Election: 2022/2024
Bev Kenny, Reeve
Rose Zimmer, Administrator

Wolverine No. 340
P.O. Box 28
Burr, SK S0K 0T0
Tel: 306-682-3640; *Fax:* 306-682-3614
rm340@sasktel.net
www.myrm.ca/340
Municipal Type: Rural Municipalities
Incorporated: Dec. 13, 1909; *Area:* 834.78 sq km
Population in 2016: 480
Federal Electoral District(s): Moose Jaw-Lake Centre-Lanigan
Next Election: 2022/2024
Bryan Gibney, Reeve
Sandi Dunne, Administrator

Wood Creek No. 281
P.O. Box 10
303 George St.
Simpson, SK S0G 4M0
Tel: 306-836-2020; *Fax:* 306-836-4460
rm281@sasktel.net
www.myrm.ca/281
Municipal Type: Rural Municipalities
Incorporated: Dec. 13, 1909; *Area:* 832.34 sq km
Population in 2016: 224
Federal Electoral District(s): Moose Jaw-Lake Centre-Lanigan
Next Election: 2022/2024
Glen Busse, Reeve
Darlene Mann, Administrator

Wood River No. 74
P.O. Box 250
35 - 2nd Ave. East
Lafleche, SK S0H 2K0
Tel: 306-472-5235; *Fax:* 306-472-3706
rm74@sasktel.net
www.myrm.ca/074
Municipal Type: Rural Municipalities
Incorporated: Dec. 9, 1912; *Area:* 838.45 sq km
Population in 2016: 433
Federal Electoral District(s): Cypress Hills-Grasslands
Next Election: 2022/2024
David Sproule, Reeve
Brekke Massé, Administrator

Wreford No. 280
P.O. Box 99
Nokomis, SK S0G 3R0
Tel: 306-528-2202; *Fax:* 306-528-4411
rm280@sasktel.net
www.myrm.ca/280

Municipal Type: Rural Municipalities
Incorporated: Dec. 12, 1910; *Area:* 798.55 sq km
Population in 2016: 135

Federal Electoral District(s): Moose Jaw-Lake Centre-Lanigan
Next Election: 2022/2024
Dean Hobman, Reeve

Melanie Rich, Administrator

YUKON TERRITORY

The Department of Community Services administers the following key legislation regarding municipalities in the territory. Some of these Acts include: Municipal Act, Municipal Finance and Community Grants Act and Assessment and Taxation Act.

Requirements for municipal incorporation in the Yukon are based on population: town 300–2,500, city over 2,500. Any community may become a Local Advisory Area, an advisory body to the minister, as a first step in local governance. A community may also incorporate as a Rural Government with limited powers, as a developmental step in becoming a full municipality. The Yukon Municipal Act does not include provisions for unorganized settlements or First Nation communities.

Municipal elections are held every three years and polling day is the third Thursday of October in each election year. Mayors and councillors are elected for a three-year period (2021, 2024, etc.).

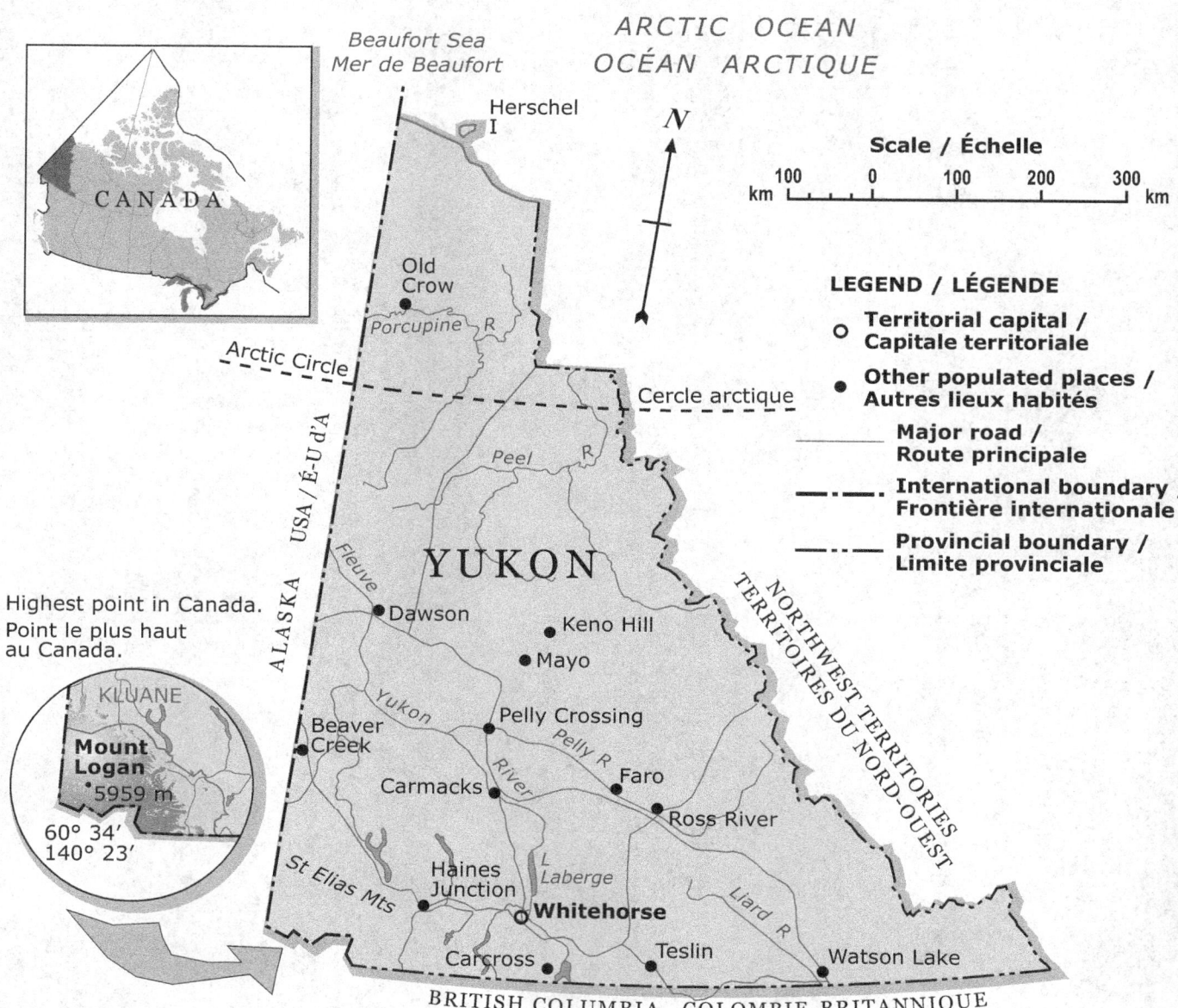

Highest point in Canada.
Point le plus haut
au Canada.

KLUANE
Mount Logan
• 5959 m
60° 34′
140° 23′

LEGEND / LÉGENDE
○ **Territorial capital / Capitale territoriale**
● **Other populated places / Autres lieux habités**
── **Major road / Route principale**
─··─ **International boundary / Frontière internationale**
─·─ **Provincial boundary / Limite provinciale**

Scale / Échelle
100   0   100   200   300

www.atlas.gc.ca

Yukon Territory

Major Municipalities in Yukon Territory

Whitehorse
2121 - 2nd Ave.
Whitehorse, YT Y1A 1C2
Tel: 867-667-6401
mayorandcouncil@whitehorse.ca
www.whitehorse.ca
Municipal Type: City
Incorporated: June 1, 1950; *Area:* 416.54 sq km
Population in 2016: 25,085
Provincial Electoral District(s): Whitehorse Centre; Whitehorse West; Copperbelt North; Copperbelt South; McIntyre-Takhini; Mountainview; Porter Creek Centre; Porter Creek North; Porter Creek South; Riverdale North; Riverdale South
Federal Electoral District(s): Yukon
Next Election: Oct. 17, 2024 (3 year terms)
Laura Cabott, Mayor
Dan Boyd, Councillor
Kirk Cameron, Councillor
Jocelyn Curteanu, Councillor
Michelle Friesen, Councillor
Ted Laking, Councillor
Mellisa Murray, Councillor
Linda Rapp, City Manager, 867-668-8626
Mike Gau, Director, Development Services, 867-335-4455
Peter O'Blenes, Manager, Property Management, 867-689-2970
Richard Graham, Manager, Fleet & Transportation Maintenance, 867-668-8302
Jason Everitt, Fire Chief, 867-668-8383

Other Municipalities in Yukon Territory

Carmacks
P.O. Box 113
Carmacks, YT Y0B 1C0
Tel: 867-863-6271; *Fax:* 867-863-6606
info@carmacks.ca
carmacks.ca
Municipal Type: Village
Incorporated: Nov. 1, 1984; *Area:* 36.95 sq km
Population in 2016: 493
Provincial Electoral District(s): Mayo-Tatchun
Federal Electoral District(s): Yukon
Next Election: Oct. 17, 2024 (3 year terms)
Lee Bodie, Mayor, 867-332-5657
Tracy Thomas, Chief Administrative Officer, 867-863-6271

Dawson City
P.O. Box 308
1336 Front St.
Dawson City, YT Y0B 1G0
Tel: 867-993-7400; *Fax:* 867-993-7434
info@cityofdawson.ca
cityofdawson.ca
Municipal Type: Town
Incorporated: Jan. 9, 1902; *Area:* 32.45 sq km
Population in 2016: 1,375
Provincial Electoral District(s): Klondike
Federal Electoral District(s): Yukon
Next Election: Oct. 17, 2024 (3 year terms)
Bill Kendrick, Mayor
Cory Bellmore, Chief Administrative Officer, 867-993-7400

Deep Creek Development Area
Whitehorse, YT
Other Information: Yukon Land Planning Office Phone: 867-456-3827

Municipal Type: Local Advisory Area
Incorporated: 2001; *Area:* 1.39 sq km
Population in 2016: 25
Provincial Electoral District(s): Lake LaBerge
Federal Electoral District(s): Yukon
Vacant, Chair

Faro
P.O. Box 580
Faro, YT Y0B 1K0
Tel: 867-994-2728; *Fax:* 867-994-3154
admin-faro@faroyukon.ca
faro.ca
Municipal Type: Town
Incorporated: June 13, 1969; *Area:* 203.57 sq km
Population in 2016: 348
Provincial Electoral District(s): Pelly-Nisutlin
Federal Electoral District(s): Yukon
Next Election: Oct. 17, 2024 (3 year terms)
Jack Bowers, Mayor
Vacant, Chief Administrative Officer

Haines Junction
P.O. Box 5339
Haines Junction, YT Y0B 1L0
Tel: 867-634-7100; *Fax:* 867-634-2008
admin@hainesjunction.ca
www.hainesjunctionyukon.com
Municipal Type: Village
Incorporated: Oct. 1, 1984; *Area:* 34.49 sq km
Population in 2016: 613
Provincial Electoral District(s): Kluane
Federal Electoral District(s): Yukon
Next Election: Oct. 17, 2024 (3 year terms)
Thomas Eckervogt, Mayor
Dan Rodin, Chief Administrative Officer

Ibex Valley
P.O. Box 20624
Whitehorse, YT Y1A 7A2

Municipal Type: Local Advisory Area
Area: 209.06 sq km
Population in 2016: 411
Provincial Electoral District(s): Kluane; Lake LaBerge
Federal Electoral District(s): Yukon
David Petkovich, Chair, 867-633-5270
Tracey Andrew, Secretary

Marsh Lake
P.O. Box 1325
Marsh Lake, YT Y0B 1Y1
marshlakelac@mail.com
www.angelfire.com/yt2/marshlakelac
Municipal Type: Local Advisory Area
Area: 821.23 sq km
Population in 2016: 696
Provincial Electoral District(s): Mount Lorne-Southern Lakes
Federal Electoral District(s): Yukon
Jo-Anne Smith, Co-Chair & Councillor, 867-660-4510, Wards: 4. Army Beach
Perry Savoie, Co-Chair & Councillor, 867-660-5116, Wards: 4. Army Beach

Mayo
P.O. Box 160
Mayo, YT Y0B 1M0
Tel: 867-996-2317; *Fax:* 867-996-2907
mayo@northwestel.net
villageofmayo.ca
Municipal Type: Village
Incorporated: June 1, 1984; *Area:* 1.06 sq km
Population in 2016: 200
Provincial Electoral District(s): Mayo/Tatchun

Federal Electoral District(s): Yukon
Next Election: Oct. 17, 2024 (3 year terms)
Trevor Ellis, Mayor
Margrit Wozniak, Chief Administrative Officer, 867-996-4300

Mount Lorne
P.O. Box 10009
Whitehorse, YT Y1A 7A1
Tel: 867-667-7083
mtlorne@northwestel.net
mountlorne.yk.net
Municipal Type: Local Advisory Area
Area: 160.24 sq km
Population in 2016: 437
Provincial Electoral District(s): Mount Lorne-Southern Lakes
Federal Electoral District(s): Yukon
Peter Carr, Chair, Wards: Kookatsoon

South Klondike
P.O. Box 4
Carcross, YT Y0B 1B0
Tel: 867-821-3461
blpringle@northwestel.net
Municipal Type: Local Advisory Area
Incorporated: Aug. 15, 2006; *Area:* 16.14 sq km
Population in 2016: 301
Provincial Electoral District(s): Mount Lorne-Southern Lakes
Federal Electoral District(s): Yukon
Colleen James, Chair, Wards: 3

Tagish
P.O. Box 92
Tagish, YT Y0B 1T0
Tel: 867-399-4002; *Fax:* 867-399-3006
tacadmin@tagishyukon.org
www.tagishyukon.org
Municipal Type: Local Advisory Area
Incorporated: 2005; *Area:* 45.59 sq km
Population in 2016: 249
Provincial Electoral District(s): Mount Lorne-Southern Lakes
Federal Electoral District(s): Yukon
Bonnitta Ritchie, Co-Chair, 867-399-3400
Myron Penner, Co-Chair

Teslin
P.O. Box 32
39 Nisutlin Dr.
Teslin, YT Y0A 1B0
Tel: 867-390-2530; *Fax:* 867-390-2104
admin.teslin@teslin.ca
www.teslin.ca
Municipal Type: Village
Incorporated: Aug. 1, 1984; *Area:* 1.92 sq km
Population in 2016: 124
Provincial Electoral District(s): Pelly-Nisutlin
Federal Electoral District(s): Yukon
Next Election: Oct. 17, 2024 (3 year terms)
Gord Curran, Mayor
Shelley Hassard, Chief Administrative Officer

Watson Lake
P.O. Box 590
Watson Lake, YT Y0A 1C0
Tel: 867-536-8000; *Fax:* 867-536-7522
info@watsonlake.ca
www.watsonlake.ca
Municipal Type: Town
Incorporated: April 1, 1984; *Area:* 6.11 sq km
Population in 2016: 790
Provincial Electoral District(s): Watson Lake
Federal Electoral District(s): Yukon
Next Election: Oct. 17, 2024 (3 year terms)
Chris Irvin, Mayor
Terri Close, Municipal Clerk, 867-536-8000

SECTION 9

GOVERNMENT:

JUDICIAL

Following the federal listings, this section is arranged by province. Within each province, listings are by type of court, then by city.

Federal

Supreme Court of Canada
Cour Suprême du Canada
301 Wellington St., Ottawa, ON K1A 0J1
Tel: 613-995-4330; *Fax:* 613-996-3063
Toll-Free: 888-551-1185
reception@scc-csc.gc.ca
www.scc-csc.gc.ca
Other information: TTY: 613-944-7895; Registry, Email: registry-greffe@scc-csc.gc.ca; Court Library, Email: library-bibliotheque@scc-csc.gc.ca; Tours, Email: tour-visite@scc-csc.gc.ca
In 1875, the Supreme Court of Canada was created by an Act of Parliament. The Court is a general court of appeal, which consists of nine judges. The Governor in Council appoints the judges, who remain in the position until the age of 75. There is a Chief Justice of Canada, plus seven puisne judges. A Registrar is also appointed by the Governor in Council. The Registrar is responsible for all the administrative work in the Court, & answers directly to the Chief Justice. There are approximately 200 employees of the Supreme Court. The Supreme Court sits in Ottawa where, each year, three sessions are held. Approximately 80 appeals are heard by the Court every year. The hearings are open to the public. Cases for review come from the provincial & territorial appellate courts & the Federal Court of Appeal, in criminal, civil, constitutional & administrative law matters. Decisions of the Supreme Court of Canada may be unanimous, or a majority may decide.
In July of 2016, The Rt. Hon. Justin Trudeau announced a new selection process for Supreme Court Justices. A seven-member, independent, non-partisan advisory board will identify suitable candidates. Any qualified Canadian lawyer or judge will be able to put forward their name for consideration by the board.
Chief Justice of Canada:
Richard Wagner
Puisne Judges (The Honourable Mr. / Madam Justice):
Michael J. Moldaver
Andromache Karakatsanis
Suzanne Côté
Russell Brown
Malcolm Rowe
Sheilah L. Martin
Nicholas Kasirer
Mahmud Jamal
Administration:
Acting Registrar: David Poweer, 613-995-4330, Fax: 613-996-9138
Director General: Catherine Laforce, 613-947-0682 catherine.laforce@scc-csc.ca
Director: Information Technology, Philippe Authier
Director: Human Resources, Andrew LeMoine
Director: Library Branch, Alicia Loo

Federal Court of Appeal
Cour d'appel fédérale
Courts Administration Service, Thomas D'Arcy McGee Bldg., 90 Sparks St., Ottawa, ON K1A 0H9
Tel: 613-996-6795 *Toll-Free:* 800-565-0541
information@fca-caf.gc.ca
www.fca-caf.gc.ca
Other information: TTY: 613-995-4640
The Federal Court of Appeal was established by Parliament in accordance with provision of section 101 of the Constitution Act, 1867. The Court is a bilingual tribunal, which sits & hears cases anywhere in Canada. Both common law & civil law are administered by the Federal Court of Appeal. Decisions of the Federal Court of Appeal impact all Canadians. Responsibilities of the Court include enforcing rights & obligations between Canadians & the federal government, & interpreting & implementing Canada's international obligations.
Chief Justice of the Federal Court of Appeal:
The Hon. Marc Noël
Judges (The Hon. Mr. / Madam Justice):
Marc Nadon (Supernumerary)
J.D. Denis Pelletier (Supernumerary)
Johanne Gauthier (Supernumerary)
Judith M. Woods (Supernumerary)
David W. Stratas
Wyman W. Webb
David G. Near
Richard Boivin
Donald J. Rennie
Yves de Montigny
Mary J.L. Gleason
John B. Laskin
Marianne Rivoalen
George R. Locke
Anne Mactavish
René LeBlanc

Court Martial Appeal Court of Canada
Cour d'appel de la cour martiale du Canada
Courts Administration Service, Thomas D'Arcy McGee Bldg., 90 Sparks St., Ottawa, ON K1A 0H9
Tel: 613-996-6795; *Fax:* 613-952-7226
Media Enquiries: media-fca@fca-caf.gc.ca
www.cmac-cacm.ca
Other information: TTY: 613-947-0407
The Court Martial Appeal Court of Canada was established by the Parliament of Canada, pursuant to its authority under section 101 of the Constitution Act, 1867. The Court administers the National Defence Act & the Criminal Code. The Court Martial Appeal Court of Canada hears appeals from military courts. Military courts, known as courts martial, try members of the Canadian Forces, as well as civilians accompanying military personnel abroad, for crimes & offences against the Code of Service Discipline. The Code of Service Discipline is found in Part III & Part VII of the National Defence Act. Military personnel are subjected to military law, except when the offence has little to do with their military role. Offences, such as murder & manslaughter, are tried in civilian courts. There is a right of appeal to the Supreme Court of Canada from the Court Martial Appeal Court of Canada on questions of law.
Chief Justice:
The Hon. Mr. Justice B. Richard Bell
Designated Judges (The Hon. Mr. / Madam Justice):
René LeBlanc
Yvan Roy
Gary T. Trotter
Marc Noël
Sandra J. Simpson
Marc Nadon
Gladys I. Pardu
Lois R. Hoegg
Cecily Y. Strickland
Peter Annis
Elizabeth A. Bennett
J.Derek Green
Louise A. Charbonneau
Elizabeth Heneghan
Luc Martineau
Simon Noël
Johanne Gauthier
James O'Reilly
J. David Watt
Glennys L. McVeigh
Deborah J. McCawley
Peter W.L. Martin
Richard G. Mosley
Michel M.J. Shore
Michael L. Phelan
Anne L. Mactavish
Yves de Montigny
Robert L. Barnes
Russel W. Zinn
Guy Cournoyer
Douglas N. Abra
Richard Boivin
David Near
Robert M. Mainville
David W. Stratas
Paul S. Crampton
Marie-Josée Bédard
Donald J. Rennie
François Doyon
André Vincent
Wyman W. Webb
Mary J.L. Gleason
Jocelyne Gagné
Catherine M. Kane
Michael D. Manson
Martine St-Louis
George R. Locke
Alan Diner
Henry S. Brown
Patrick K. Gleeson
John Edward Scanlan
Marina S. Paperny
Kathleen A. Quigg
Bradley V. Green
Vital O. Ouellette
Administration:
Chief Administrator of the Court: Daniel Gosselin, 613-996-4778
Judicial Administrator: Josée Léger, 613-995-6705

Tax Court of Canada
Cour canadienne de l'impôt
200 Kent St., Ottawa, ON K1A 0M1
Tel: 613-992-0901; *Fax:* 613-957-9034
Toll-Free: 800-927-5499
web@tcc-cci.gc.ca
www.tcc-cci.gc.ca
Other information: TTY: 613-943-0946; Media Contact: 613-996-2700
In 1983, the Tax Court of Canada was established, pursuant to the Tax Court of Canada Act. The Court operates independently of the Canada Revenue Agency & other departments of the Government of Canada. Many of the appeals to the Tax Court of Canada are related to income tax, the goods & services tax, & employment insurance. References are also heard from the Canada Revenue Agency to provide interpretations of the legislation within its jurisdiction.
Chief Justice:
The Hon. Mr. Justice Eugene P. Rossiter
Associate Chief Justice:
The Hon. Madam Justice Lucie Lamarre
Judges in order of seniority (The Honourable Mr./Madam Justice):
Pierre Archambault (Supernumerary)
Diane Campbell (Supernumerary)
Réal Favreau (Supernumerary)
Patrick J. Boyle
Robert James Hogan
Steven K. D'Arcy
Frank J. Pizzitelli
Johanne D'Auray
Randall S. Bocock
David E. Graham
Kathleen T. Lyons
John R. Owen
Dominique Lafleur
Sylvain Ouimet
Don R. Sommerfedlt
Henry A. Visser
Guy R. Smith
Bruce Russell
K.A. Siobhan Monaghan
Susan Wong
Ronald MacPhee
Gabrielle St-Hilaire
David E. Spiro
Administration:
Chief Administrator: Darlene Carreau, 613-944-7758
Registrar of the Court: Donald MacNeil, 613-944-7758

Federal Court
Cour fédérale
Courts Administration Service, Thomas D'Arcy McGee Bldg., 90 Sparks St., Ottawa, ON K1A 0H9
Tel: 613-992-4238; *Fax:* 613-952-3653
Toll-Free: 800-663-2096
media-fct@fct-cf.gc.ca
www.fct-cf.gc.ca
Other information: TTY: 613-995-4640
The Federal Court is a trial court. The jurisdiction of the Federal Court is conferred by the Federal Courts Act, as well as close to one hundred other applicable federal statutes. Its broad federal jurisdiction includes the following: Crown litigation, access to information, admiralty & maritime disputes, citizenship, communications, customs, immigration & refugee matters, intellectual property rights, labour relations, national security, parole & penitentiary proceedings, tax, transportation & aeronautics, war veterans & limited criminal jurisdiction. The Court conducts hearings & renders decisions in disputes anywhere in Canada.
Chief Justice of the Federal Court:
Paul Crampton
Associate Chief Justice of the Federal Court:
Jocelyne Gagné
Judges (The Hon. Mr. / Madam Justice):
Sandra J. Simpson (Supernumerary)
Simon Noël (Supernumerary)
Michel M.J. Shore (Supernumerary)
Michael L. Phelan (Supernumerary)
Elizabeth Heneghan
Luc Martineau (Supernumerary)
James W. O'Reilly (Supernumerary)
Richard Mosley (Supernumerary)
Robert L. Barnes (Supernumerary)
Russel W. Zinn
Catherine M. Kane
Michael D. Manson
Yvan Roy
Cecily Y. Strickland
Peter B. Annis (Supernumerary)
Glennys L. McVeigh

Martine St-Louis
Henry S. Brown
Alan Diner
Simon Fothergill
B. Richard Bell
Denis Gascon
Richard F. Southcottt
Patrick K. Gleeson
E. Susan Elliot
Sylvie E. Roussel
Ann Marie McDonald
Roger Lafrenière (Supernumerary)
William F. Pentney
Shirzad S. Ahmed
Sébastien Grammond
Paul Favel
Elizabeth Walker
John Norris
Peter George Pamel
Nicholas McHaffie
Janet M. Fuhrer
Christine Pallotta
Andrew D. Little
Angela Furlanetto
Lobat Sadrehashemi
Prothonotaries:
Mireille Tabib, 613-947-2453
Martha Milczynski, 416-954-9006
Kevin R. Aalto, 416-954-9009
Mandy Aylen
Kathleen Marie Ring
Alexandra Steele
Sylvie M. Molgat
Administration:
Executive Director & General Counsel: Chantal Proulx
Judicial Administrator: Caroline Perrier, 613-995-0108

Courts Administration Service
Service administratif des tribunaux judiciaires
Thomas D'Arcy McGee Bldg., 90 Sparks St., Ottawa, ON K1A 0H9

Tel: 613-943-4355
media@cas-satj.gc.ca
www.cas-satj.gc.ca
Other information: Website Administration:
reception@cas-satj.gc.ca; Chief, Resourcing Human Resources:
613-947-3561

In 2003, the Courts Administration Service was established by the Courts Administration Service Act, S.C. 2002, c. 8. The Courts Administration Service provides administrative services to the following courts of law: the Federal Court, the Federal Court of Appeal, the Tax Court of Canada, & the Court Martial Appeal Court of Canada. Examples of the duties of the Courts Administration Service are as follows: providing support services, such as library services, to judges, prothonotaries & staff; maintaining courts records; providing facilities & security for judges, prothonotaries & staff; & informing litigants on rules of practice & procedures.
Administration:
Chief Administrator: Darlene Carreau, 613-996-4778
Deputy Chief Administrator & Chief Financial Officer: Corporate Services, Francine Côté, 613-996-1611
Acting Deputy Chief Administrator, Registry Services: Lise Henrie, 613-943-5484
Director, Corporate Secretariat: Communications & Strategic Planning, Yves Leclair, 613-943-4782

Registry of the Courts Administration Service
Principal Office, 90 Sparks St., Ottawa, ON K1A 0H9

Local Offices:
Calgary
Canadian Occidental Tower, 635 - 8th Ave. SW, 3rd Fl., Calgary, AB T2P 3M3

Tel: 403-292-5555; *Fax:* 403-292-5329
Other information: TTY: 403-292-5329

Charlottetown
Sir Louis Henry Davies Law Courts Bldg., 42 Water St., P.O. Box 2000, Charlottetown, PE C1A 8B9

Tel: 800-565-0541; *Fax:* 902-426-5514
Toll-Free: 902-426-9776

Edmonton
Tower 1, Scotia Place, #530, 10060 Jasper Ave., Edmonton, AB T5J 3R8

Tel: 780-495-2502; *Fax:* 780-495-4681
Other information: TTY: 780-495-2428

Fredericton
#100, 82 Westmorland St., Fredericton, NB E3B 3L3

Tel: 506-452-2036; *Fax:* 506-452-3584
Other information: TTY: 506-452-3036

Halifax
#1720, 1801 Hollis St., 17th Fl., Halifax, NS B3J 3N4

Tel: 902-426-5326; *Fax:* 902-426-5514
Other information: TTY: 902-426-9776

Québec
Palais de Justice, #150, 150, boul René-Lévesque est, Québec, QC G1R 2B2

Tel: 418-648-4964; *Fax:* 418-648-4051
Other information: TTY: 418-648-4644

Regina
Court House, 2425 Victoria Ave., Regina, SK S4P 4W6

Toll-Free: 800-565-0541

Iqaluit
Court of Justice, Justice Centre, Bldg. 510, P.O. Box 297, Iqluit, NU X0A 0H0

Fax: 902-426-9776
Toll-Free: 800-565-0541
Other information: TTY: 902-426-9776

Montréal
30, rue McGill, Montréal, QC H2Y 3Z7

Tel: 514-283-5200; *Fax:* 514-283-6004
Toll-Free: 800-565-0541

Saskatoon
Court House, 520 Spadina Cres. East, Saskatoon, SK S7K 2G7

Tel: 800-565-0541

St. John's
#209, 354 Water St., St. John's, NL A1C 1C4

Tel: 709-772-5862; *Fax:* 709-772-5600
Toll-Free: 800-565-0541

Toronto
#200, 180 Queen St. West, Toronto, ON M5V 3L6

Tel: 416-952-8006; *Fax:* 416-973-2154
Toll-Free: 800-565-0541
Other information: TTY: 416-954-4245

Vancouver
Pacific Centre, 701 West Georgia St., P.O. Box 10065, Vancouver, BC V7Y 1B6

Tel: 604-666-2055; *Fax:* 604-666-8181
Toll-Free: 800-565-0541

Whitehorse
Andrew A. Phillipsen Law Centre, 2134 - 2nd Ave., Whitehorse, YT Y1A 5H6

Toll-Free: 800-565-0541
Registry Officer: Edwidge Graham, 867-667-5938
Registry Officer: Lisa Robinson-Fernandes, 867-667-5937

Winnipeg
#400, 363 Broadway, Winnipeg, MB R3C 3N9

Tel: 204-983-2232; *Fax:* 204-983-7636
Other information: TTY: 204-984-4440
Registry Officer: Renée Taillefer, 204-983-2509
Registry Officer: Robert M'vondo, 204-983-2509

Yellowknife
Court House, 4905 - 49th St., P.O. Box 1320, Yellowknife, NT X1A 2L9

Tel: 800-565-0541
Registry Officer: Denise Bertolini, 867-873-2044

Alberta

Alberta Court of Appeal
Law Courts, 1A Sir Winston Churchill Sq., Edmonton, AB T5J 0R2

Fax: 780-422-4127
Toll-Free: 855-738-4747
albertacourts.ca/ca

The Alberta Court of Appeal hears appeals from the following courts: the Provincial Court; the Court of Queen's Bench; & administrative tribunals. The Court of Appeal also provides opinions on questions referred from the Lieutenant Governor under the Judicature Act. Court of Appeal justices are appointed by the federal government. Sittings are held in Edmonton & Calgary.
Chief Justice:
The Hon. Catherine A. Fraser
Justices of the Court of Appeal (The Hon. Mr. / Madam Justice):
Elizabeth A. Hughes
Jolaine Antonio
Peter T. Costigan
Marina S. Paperny
Peter W.L. Martin
Jack Watson
Frans F. Slatter
Patricia A. Rowbotham
Bruce McDonald

Myra Bielby
Brian K. O'Ferrall
Barbara L. Veldhuis
Thomas W. Wakeling
Frederica L. Schutz
Sheila L. Greckol
Michelle G. Crighton
Jo'Anne Strekaf
Ritu Khullar
Elizabeth A. Hughes
Dawn Pentelechuk
Jolaine Antonio
Kevin P. Feehan
Administration:
Registrar: Heidi Schubert
Deputy Registrar: Ileen Moore

Courts:
Calgary: Court of Appeal
TransCanada Pipelines Tower, #2600, 450 - 1st St. SW, Calgary, AB T2P 5H1

Fax: 403-297-5294
Toll-Free: 855-738-4747
albertacourts.ca/ca

Edmonton: Court of Appeal
Law Courts, 1A Sir Winston Churchill Sq., Edmonton, AB T5J 0R2

Fax: 780-422-4127
Toll-Free: 855-738-4747
albertacourts.ca/ca

Alberta Court of Queen's Bench
Calgary Courts Centre, 601 - 5th St. SW, Calgary, AB T2P 5P7

Tel: 403-297-7538; *Fax:* 403-297-8617
albertacourts.ca/qb

In Alberta, the Court of Queen's Bench is the Superior Trial Court. The Court hears trials in both civil & criminal matters, as well as appeals from decisions of the Provincial Court. The Chief Justice & other Justices are also judges of Surrogate Matters. Sittings of the Court of Queen's Bench are held in various areas throughout Alberta.
Chief Justice:
The Hon. Mary T. Moreau
Associate Chief Justice:
The Hon. John D. Rooke
The Hon. Ken G. Nielsen
Justices (The Honourable Mr. / Madam Justice):
S.M. Bensler
Donald Lee
Carolyn S. Philips
W.P. Sullivan
Colleen L. Kenny
R. Paul Belzil
Sterling M. Sanderman
Barbara E.C. Romaine
Doreen A. Sulyama
Rosemary E. Nation
Brian R. Burrows
Terry D. Clackson
Bryan E. Mahoney
Eric F. Macklin
Vital O. Oullette
Karen M. Horner
Steve D. Hillier
A.W. Germain
June M. Ross
John J. Gill
Alan D. Macleod
Robert A. Graesser
Donna L. Shelley
D.K. Miller
Kristine M. Eidsvik
E.C. Wilson
Donald J. Manderscheid
Keith D. Yamauchi
Paul R. Jeffrey
Monica R. Bast
Sandra L. Hunt McDonald
John T. McCarthy
Robert J. Hall
Glen H. Poelman
Rodney A. Jerke
Peter B. Michalyshyn
M. David Gates
Craig M. Jones
Bruce A. Millar
Kim D. Nixon
C.S. Anderson
Eldon J. Simpson
G.A. Campbell
C. Dario

Johanna C. Price
Debbie A. Yungwirth
John S. Little
Larry A. Ackerl
D.B. Nixon
Wayne N. Renke
Richard A. Neufeld
John T. Henderson
Douglas R. Mah
G.D. Marriott
Avril B. Inglis
George R. Fraser
Bonnie L. Bokenfohr
Marilyn D. Slawinsky
Michele H. Hollins
William T. deWitt
Johnna C. Kubik
Janice R. Ashcroft
Steven N. Mandziuk
Michael J. Lema
Marta E. Burns
L. Bernadette Ho
Gaylene D.B. Kendell
David A. Labrenz
James T. Neilson
Nancy Dilts
Anne Kirker
Jane A. Fagnan
April D. Grosse
Michael Kraus
Susan L. Bercov
Alice Woolley
Tamara Friesen
David Vaughan Hartigan
Anna Loparco
Susan E. Richardson
Kevin Feth
Kent H. Davidson
Nicholas E. Devlin
Grant S. Dunlop
J.T. Eamon
Melanie Hayes-Richards
Nathan Whitling
Shaina Leonard
E. Jane Sidnell
Barbara B. Johnston
Denise J. Kiss
Sherry L. Kachur
Thomas G. Rothwell
Ola Malik
Lynn M. Angotti
Robert W. Armstrong
Cheryl Arcand-Kootenay
Lorena K. Harris
Administration:
Director: South Operations, Carol Clark, 403-297-3855
    carol.clark@gov.ab.ca

Courts:
Drumheller: Court of Queen's Bench
Court House, 511 - 3rd Ave. West, P.O. Box 759, Drumheller, AB T0J 0Y0
Tel: 403-820-7300; *Fax:* 403-823-6073
albertacourts.ca

Edmonton: Court of Queen's Bench
Law Courts, 1A Sir Winston Churchill Sq., Edmonton, AB T5J 0R2
Tel: 780-422-2492; *Fax:* 780-427-0629
albertacourts.ca

Administration:
Director: Edmonton & North Operations, Wade Garner, 780-644-5739
    wade.garner@gov.ab.ca

Fort McMurray: Court of Queen's Bench
Court House, 9700 Franklin Ave., Fort McMurray, AB T9H 4W3
Tel: 780-743-7136; *Fax:* 780-743-7135
albertacourts.ca

Grande Prairie: Court of Queen's Bench
Court House, 10260 - 99th St., Grande Prairie, AB T8V 2H4
Tel: 780-538-5240; *Fax:* 780-538-5493
albertacourts.ca

Lethbridge: Court of Queen's Bench
Court House, 320 - 4th St. South, Lethbridge, AB T1J 1Z8
Tel: 403-381-5196; *Fax:* 403-381-5128
albertacourts.ca

Medicine Hat: Court of Queen's Bench
Law Courts, 460 - 1st St. SE, Medicine Hat, AB T1A 0A8
Tel: 403-529-8710; *Fax:* 403-529-8607
albertacourts.ca

Peace River: Court of Queen's Bench
Court House, 9905 - 97th Ave., P.O. Box 900-34, Peace River, AB T8S 1T4
Tel: 780-624-6256; *Fax:* 780-624-6175
albertacourts.ca

Red Deer: Court of Queen's Bench
Court House, 4909 - 48th Ave., Red Deer, AB T4N 3T5
Tel: 403-340-5220; *Fax:* 403-340-7984
albertacourts.ca

St. Paul: Court of Queen's Bench
Court House, 4704 - 50 St., P.O. Box 1900, St. Paul, AB T0A 3A0
Fax: 780-645-6273
Toll-Free: 780-645-6387
albertacourts.ca

Wetaskiwin: Court of Queen's Bench
Law Courts, 4605 - 51 St., Wetaskiwin, AB T9A 1K7
Fax: 780-361-1319
Toll-Free: 780-361-1258
albertacourts.ca

Alberta Provincial Court
Law Courts, 1A Sir Winston Churchill Sq., Edmonton, AB T5J 0R2
Toll-Free: 855-738-4747
albertacourts.ca/pc
The Provincial Court of Alberta serves as the point of entry to the justice system in the following areas of law: civil matters (Small Claims Court), related to damages & debt & pretrial conferences; criminal law; family law, such as Parenting & Contact Orders; traffic offences, under federal statutes, provincial statutes & municipal bylaws; & Criminal Code offences committed by youth from ages 12 to 17. Circuit point courts are situated throughout the province.
Judges (The Hon.):
D.G. Redman (Chief Judge)
M.J. Durant (Deputy Chief Judge)

Courts:
Calgary - Civil, Criminal, Family, Regional, Traffic & Youth
Calgary Courts Centre, 601 - 5th St. SW, Calgary, AB T2P 5P7
Tel: 403-297-3122; *Fax:* 403-297-3179
Toll-Free: 855-738-4747
albertacourts.ca

Judges (The Hon.):
D.G. Redman (Chief Judge)
M.J. Durant (Deputy Chief Judge)

Calgary - Civil
Calgary Courts Centre, #606S, 601 - 5th St. SW, Calgary, AB T2P 5P7
Tel: 403-297-7217; *Fax:* 403-297-7374
albertacourts.ca

Judges (The Hon.):
G.W. Sharek (Assistant Chief Judge)
L.L. Burt
D.B. Higa
M.A. McCorquodale
Administration:
Manager: Marilyn Clisdell

Calgary - Family & Youth
Calgary Courts Centre, #704N, 601 - 5th St. SW, Calgary, AB T2P 5P7
Tel: 403-297-3471; *Fax:* 403-297-3461
albertacourts.ca

Youth Suite: 201N
Judges (The Hon.):
G.H. Cornfield (Assistant Chief Judge)
F. Airth
G.L.M. Benns
T.K.M. Davis
N.W. D'Souza
T. LaRochelle
S.E. Lipton
D. Mah
L. McLellan
R.J. O'Gorman
J.R. Shaw
V.T. Tousignant
Administration:
Manager: Salema Hage
    salema.hage@gov.ab.ca

Calgary - Regional
Calgary Courts Centre, #607S, 601 - 5th St. SW, Calgary, AB T2P 5P7
Tel: 403-297-3010; *Fax:* 403-297-3237
albertacourts.ca
Circuit point courts are located in the following places: Airdrie (#113, 104 - 1st Ave. NW), Canmore (#101, 800 Railway Ave.),

Cochrane (213 - 1st St., West), Didsbury (1611 - 15th Ave.), Okotoks (98 McRae St.) & Tsuu T'ina Nation (9911 Chula Blvd., Sarcee).
Judges (The Hon.):
J.B. Hawkes (Assistant Chief Judge)
P.B. Barley
K.A. Crowshoe
M.V. De Souza
G.J. Gaschler
M.M. Keelaghan
S.E. Pepper
J. Shriar
G.D.M. Stirling
E.J. Tolppanen
Administration:
Manager: L. Blair-Kaye

Calgary - Traffic
Calgary Courts Centre, #203S, 601 - 5th St. SW, Calgary, AB T2P 5P7
Tel: 403-297-2283; *Fax:* 403-297-2220
albertacourts.ca
Administration:
Acting Manager: Lynn Quinton
    lynn.quinton@gov.ab.ca

Camrose
Court House, 5210 - 49th Ave., Camrose, AB T4V 3Y2
Tel: 780-679-1240; *Fax:* 780-679-1253
albertacourts.ca
A circuit point court is located in Killam (4903 - 50th St.).
Judges (The Hon.):
W.A. Andreassen
Administration:
Manager: C. Walker

Drumheller
Court House, 511 - 3rd Ave. West, Drumheller, AB T0J 0Y0
Tel: 403-820-7300; *Fax:* 403-823-6073
albertacourts.ca
Circuit point courts are situated in the following places: Hanna (401 Centre St.), Siksika Nation (Junction of Highways 901 & 547) & Strathmore (226 - 2nd Ave.).
Administration:
Manager: Gurvinder Singh

Edmonton - Civil, Criminal, Family & Youth & Traffic
Law Courts, 1A Sir Winston Churchill Sq., Edmonton, AB T5J 0R2
Toll-Free: 855-738-4747
albertacourts.ca

Judges (The Hon. Mr./Madam):
A. Veylan (Assistant Chief Judge)
G.W. Sharek (Assistant Chief Judge)
R.K. Bodnarek (Assistant Chief Judge)

Edmonton - Civil
Law Courts, 1A Sir Winston Churchill Sq., Edmonton, AB T5J 0R2
Tel: 780-422-2508; *Fax:* 780-427-4348
albertacourts.ca

Judges (The Hon. Mr./Madam):
G.W. Sharek (Assistant Chief Judge)
S.L. Corbett
K. Haymour
J.L. Skitsko
L.D. Young
Administration:
Manager: Edison Cruz

Edmonton - Criminal
Law Courts, 1A Sir Winston Churchill Sq., Edmonton, AB T5J 0R2
Tel: 780-427-7868; *Fax:* 780-422-9736
albertacourts.ca

Judges (The Hon. Mr./Madam):
R.K. Bodnarek (Assistant Chief Judge)
L.G. Anderson
S.M.L. Bilodeau
R.W. Brandt
M.M. Carminati
R.R.M. Cochard
S.R. Creagh
D. DePoe
J.L. Dixon
M.C. Doyle
C.D. Godfrey
D.M. Groves
K.E. Hewitt
E.A. Johnson
G.B. Lepp
F.E. LeReverend
J.L. Lester
F.K. MacDonald
T.J. Matchett

J.J. Moher
F.Y. Roy
C.J. Sharpe
O. Shoyele
L.K. Stevens
R.E. Tibbitt
D.R. Valgardson
Administration:
Manager: Karli Lucas
  karli.lucas@gov.ab.ca

Edmonton - Family & Youth
Law Courts, 1A Sir Winston Churchill Sq., Edmonton, AB T5J 0R2

Tel: 780-427-2743; Fax: 780-427-5797
albertacourts.ca

Judges (The Hon. Mr./Madam):
A. Veylan (Assistant Chief Judge)
W.S. Andrew
M.J. Burch
D. Dalton
J.M. Filice
D.G. Hancock
K.A. Holmstrom
G.B.N. Ho
P.E. Kvill
J.C. Lloyd
M.J. Savaryn
D. Zalmanowitz
Administration:
Acting Manager: Angela Cappellano
  angela.cappellano@gov.ab.ca

Edmonton - Regional
Law Courts, 1A Sir Winston Churchill Sq., Edmonton, AB T5J 0R2

Tel: 780-422-2691; Fax: 780-422-2971
albertacourts.ca

Judges (The Hon.):
J.E. Schaffter (Assistant Chief Judge)

Edmonton - Traffic
Law Courts, 1A Sir Winston Churchill Sq., Edmonton, AB T5J 0R2

Tel: 780-427-5913; Fax: 780-427-5791
albertacourts.ab.ca

Administration:
Manager: Leanne Malcolm
  leanne.malcolm@gov.ab

Fort McMurray
Court House, 9700 Franklin Ave., Fort McMurray, AB T9H 4W3

Tel: 780-743-7195; Fax: 780-743-7395
albertacourts.ca

A circuit point court is located in Fort Chipewyan (Multi-Plex, Flett St.).
Judges (The Hon.):
S.A. Cleary
J.R. Jacques
Administration:
Manager: Michelle Reagen
  michelle.reagen@gov.ab.ca

Fort Saskatchewan
Court House, 10504 - 100th Ave., Fort Saskatchewan, AB T8L 3S9

Tel: 780-998-1200; Fax: 780-998-7222
albertacourts.ca

A circuit point court is located in Boyle (5006 - 3rd St.).
Judges (The Hon.):
T.W. Achtymichuk
K.R. Wilberg
Administration:
Manager: Marilea McMullen
  marilea.mcmullen@gov.ab.ca

Grande Prairie
Court House, 10260 - 99th St., Grande Prairie, AB T8V 2H4

Tel: 780-538-5360; Fax: 780-538-5454
albertacourts.ca

Circuit point courts are located in the following places: Fox Creek (100 - 4th Ave.) & Valleyview (5102 - 50th Ave.).
Judges (The Hon.):
D.R. Shynkar (Assistant Chief Judge)
A.B. Chrenek
M.B. Golden
B.R. Hougestol
J. Sihra

High Level
Court House, 10106 - 100th Ave., P.O. Box 1560, High Level, AB T0H 1Z0

Tel: 780-926-3715; Fax: 780-926-4068
albertacourts.ca

Circuit point courts are located in the following places: Assumption (Court House, Chateh) & Fort Vermilion (4607 River Rd.).
Administration:
Manager: Shelley Shumik
  shelley.shumik@gov.ab.ca

High Prairie
Court House, 4911 - 53rd Ave., P.O. Box 1470, High Prairie, AB T0G 1E0

Tel: 780-523-6600; Fax: 780-523-6643
albertacourts.ca

Circuit point courts are located in the following places: Red Earth Creek (122 Forestry Rd.), Slave Lake (101 - 3rd St. SW) & Wabasca-Desmarais (867 Stony Point Rd.).
Judges (The Hon.):
D.R. Shynkar
Administration:
Manager: Debbie Poirier
  debbie.poirier@gov.ab.ca

Hinton
Court House, 237 Jasper St. West, P.O. Box 6450, Hinton, AB T7V 1X7

Tel: 780-865-8280; Fax: 780-865-8253
albertacourts.ca

Circuit point courts are located in the following places: Edson (111 - 54th St.), Grande Cache (Provincial Building, Hoppe Ave.), & Jasper (629 Patricia St.).
Judges (The Hon.):
J.P. Higgerty
Administration:
Angela Rahall
  angela.rahall@gov.ab.ca

Leduc
Court House, 4612 - 50th St., Leduc, AB T9E 6L1

Tel: 780-986-6911; Fax: 780-986-0345
albertacourts.ca

Circuit point courts are located in the following places: Breton (4911 - 50th Ave.) & Drayton Valley (5136 - 51st Ave.).
Judges (The Hon.):
J.E. Schaffter (Assistant Chief Judge)
J.B. Champion
M.M. Collinson
C.G. Purvis

Lethbridge
Court House, 320 - 4th St. South, Lethbridge, AB T1J 1Z8

Tel: 403-381-5223; Fax: 403-381-5763
albertacourts.ca

Circuit point courts are located in the following places: Cardston (576 Main St.), Pincher Creek (782 Main St.) & Taber (5126 - 49th Ave.).
Judges (The Hon.):
S.L. Oishi (Assistant Chief Judge)
K.R. Ailsby
T.G. Hironaka
J.N. LeGrandeur
G.S. Maxwell
E. Olsen
E.W. Peterson
P.G. Pharo
Administration:
Manager: Maria McCulloch
  marla.mcculloch@gov.ab.ca

Medicine Hat
Law Courts, 460 - 1st St. SE, Medicine Hat, AB T1A 0A8

Tel: 403-529-8644; Fax: 403-529-8606
albertacourts.ca

Judges (The Hon.):
E.D. Brooks
M.C. Christopher
F.C. Fisher
G.K. Krinke

Peace River
Court House, 9905 - 97th Ave., P.O. Box 900-34, Peace River, AB T8S 1T4

Tel: 780-624-6256; Fax: 780-624-6175
albertacourts.ca

Circuit point courts are located in the following places: Fairview (10209 - 109th St.) & Falher (028 Main St. SE).
Judges (The Hon.):
G.R. Ambrose
R.B. Marceau
C.K.W. Thietke
Administration:
Manager: Shelly Rendle
  shelly.rendle@gov.ab.ca

Red Deer
Court House, 4909 - 48th Ave., Red Deer, AB T4N 3T5

Tel: 403-340-5250; Fax: 403-340-7985
albertacourts.ca

Circuit point courts are located in the following places: Coronation (4909 Royal St.), Rimbey (5025 - 55th St.), Rocky Mountain House (4919 - 51st St.) & Stettler (4705 - 49th Ave.).
Judges (The Hon.):
J.A. Hunter (Assistant Chief Judge)
J.A. Glass
G. Hatch
J.D. Holmes
J.B. Mitchell
T.M. Scrase
W.A. Skinner
R.A. Snider
G.A.G. Yake
Administration:
Manager: Heather Bounds
  heather.bounds@gov.ab.ca

St. Albert
Court House, 3 St Anne St., St Albert, AB T8N 2E8

Tel: 780-458-7300; Fax: 780-460-2963
albertacourts.ca

Circuit point courts are located in the following places: Athabasca (4903 - 50th St.), Barrhead (6203 - 49th St.), Morinville (10008 - 107th St.) & Westlock (10003 - 100th St.).
Judges (The Hon.):
B.H. Fraser
B.R. Garriock
V.H. Myers
Administration:
Manager: J. Green

St. Paul
Court House, 4704 - 50th St., P.O. Box 1900, St Paul, AB T0A 3A0

Tel: 780-645-6324; Fax: 780-645-6273
albertacourts.ca

Circuit point courts are located in the following places: Bonnyville (4902 - 50th Ave.) & Lac La Biche (9503 Beaver Hill Rd.).
Judges (The Hon.):
I.M.L. Ladouceur
K.D. Williams
Administration:
Manager: Ruth Westman
  ruth.westman@gov.ab.ca

Sherwood Park
Court House, 190 Chippewa Rd., Sherwood Park, AB T8A 4H5

Tel: 780-464-0114; Fax: 780-449-1490
albertacourts.ca

Judges (The Hon.):
J. Maher
Administration:
Manager: Marilea McMullen
  marilea.mcmullen@gov.ab.ca

Stony Plain
Court House, 4711 - 44th Ave., Stony Plain, AB T7Z 1N5

Tel: 780-963-6205; Fax: 780-963-6402
albertacourts.ca

Circuit point courts are located in the following places: Evansburg (4921 - 50th St.), Glenevis (Administration Office, Alexis Reserve), Mayerthorpe (5013 - 50th St.) & Whitecourt (5020 - 52nd Ave.).
Judges (The Hon.):
C.D. Gardner
R.M. Saccomani
R.C. Shaigec
K.E. Tjosvold
Administration:
Manager: J. Green

Vermilion
Provincial Bldg., 4701 - 52nd St., P.O. Box 30, Vermilion, AB T9X 1J9

Tel: 780-853-8130; Fax: 780-853-8200
albertacourts.ca

Circuit point courts are located in the following places: Lloydminster (5124 - 50th St.), Vegreville (4809 - 50th St.) & Wainwright (738 - 2nd Ave.).
Judges (The Hon.):
G.A. Rice
Administration:
Manager: Ruth Westman
  ruth.westman@gov.ab.ca

Wetaskiwin
Law Courts, 4605 - 51st St., Wetaskiwin, AB T9A 1K7

Tel: 780-361-1204; Fax: 780-361-1338
albertacourts.ca

A circuit point court is located in Ponoka (5110 - 49th Ave.).

Judges (The Hon.):
J. Neustaeter
Administration:
Manager: C. Walker

British Columbia

British Columbia Court of Appeal
The Law Courts, #400, 800 Hornby St., Vancouver, BC V6Z 2C5

Tel: 604-660-2468; *Fax:* 604-660-1951
www.courts.gov.bc.ca/Court_of_Appeal

The Court of Appeal is the highest court in the province. It hears appeals from the Supreme Court & from the Provincial Court on some criminal matters. It also hears reviews & appeals from some administrative boards & tribunals.
Chief Justice:
The Hon. Robert James Bauman
Justices of Appeal (The Hon. Mr./Madam Justice):
Patrice Abrioux *March 7, 2019*
Elizabeth A. Bennett *May 14, 2009*
G. Bruce Butler *August 31, 2018*
Joyce Dewitt-Van Oosten *May 7, 2013*
Gail M. Dickson *July 29, 2015*
Lauri Ann Fenlon *June 15, 2015*
Barbara Fisher *September 14, 2017*
Gregory J. Fitch *September 1, 2015*
S. David Frankel *May 10, 2007*
Richard Goepel *November 7, 2013*
J. Christopher Grauer *December 20, 2019*
Susan Griffin *July 2, 2018*
Harvey M. Groberman *May 8, 2008*
David C. Harris *April 10, 2012*
John J.L. Hunter *December 4, 2017*
Anne W. MacKenzie *December 31, 2011*
Leonard Marchand *March 24, 2021*
Mary V. Newbury *September 26, 1995*
Mary E. Saunders *July 1, 1999*
Sunni Stromberg-Stein *June 7, 2013*
David Franklin Tysoe *May 22, 2007*
Peter G. Voith *September 9, 2020*
Peter M. Willcock *May 7, 2013*
Administration:
Registrar: Timothy Outerbridge, 604-660-2729

British Columbia Supreme Court
The Law Courts, 800 Smithe St., Vancouver, BC V6Z 2E1

Tel: 604-660-2847; *Fax:* 604-660-2420
www.courts.gov.bc.ca/supreme_court

The Supreme Court is a trial court of original jurisdiction for all civil & criminal matters arising in B.C., save & except matters expressly excluded by statute. It hears most appeals from the Provincial Court.
Chief Justice:
Christopher E. Hinkson *November 7, 2013*
Associate Chief Justice:
Heather J. Holmes *June 22, 2018*
Judges (The Hon. Mr./Madam Justice):
Elaine J. Adair *November 28, 2008*
Jasmin Ahmad *September 9, 2020*
Wendy A. Baker *February 22, 2018*
Jasvinder S. Basran *January 9, 2018*
Lauren Blake *April 27, 2021*
Ward K. Branch *June 8, 2017*
Jan Brongers *April 27, 2021*
Michael J. Brundrett *June 21, 2017*
Emily M. Burke *May 13, 2014*
Grace Choi *May 29, 2015*
Simon R. Coval *December 21, 2020*
David A. Crerar *June 25, 2019*
E. David Crossin *September 29, 2017*
Austin F. Cullen (Supernumerary) *May 13, 2014*
Barry M. Davies (Supernumerary) *January 10, 1996*
Karen F. Douglas *March 8, 2019*
Jennifer M.I. Duncan *December 19, 2013*
Peter H. Edelmann *December 20, 2019*
Shelley C. Fitzpatrick *June 18, 2010*
Margot L. Fleming *June 6, 2013*
Carla L. Forth *June 14, 2017*
Amy D. Francis *June 6, 2013*
Gordon S. Funt *October 5, 2012*
Laura B. Gerow (Supernumerary) *October 10, 2002*
Christopher Giaschi *August 31, 2018*
Geoffrey B. Gomery *June 15, 2018*
J. Miriam Gropper (Supernumerary) *April 14, 2005*
Joel R. Groves *May 19, 2005*
Karen Horsman *August 31, 2018*
Nitya Iyer *June 14, 2017*
Veronica Jackson *June 14, 2017*
Nigel P. Kent *December 19, 2013*
Kathleen M. Ker *June 8, 2008*

Matthew Kirchner *March 24, 2021*
Lindsay M. Lyster *July 3, 2020*
George Macintosh *December 19, 2013*
Diane Cheryl MacDonald *February 7, 2018*
Heather MacNaughton *October 20, 2016*
Miriam A. Maisonville *March 19, 2010*
Andrew Majawa *March 16, 2020*
Francesca V. Marzari *December 19, 2017*
David M. Masuhara (Supernumerary) *October 11, 2002*
Sharon Matthews *February 22, 2018*
Andrew P.A. Mayer *April 12, 2017*
Elizabeth McDonald *April 12, 2017*
Warren B. Milman *June 14, 2017*
Maria Morellato *June 17, 2016*
Elliott M. Myers (Supernumerary) *November 22, 2005*
Carol J. Ross (Supernumerary) *March 12, 2001*
Alan M. Ross *March 12, 2001*
Robert J. Sewell (Supernumerary) *January 22, 2009*
Neena Sharma *December 19, 2013*
Arne H. Silverman (Supernumerary) *November 26, 2004*
Ronald A. Skolrood *June 6, 2013*
Harry A. Slade (Supernumerary) *March 27, 2001*
Nathan H. Smith (Supernumerary) *May 19, 2005*
Michael Tammen *June 14, 2017*
H. William Veenstra *June 23, 2020*
Paul W. Walker *June 18, 2008*
Lisa A. Warren *June 6, 2013*
Jeanne E. Watchuk (Supernumerary) *October 28, 2010*
Gordon C. Weatherill *May 31, 2012*
Catherine A. Wedge (Supernumerary) *April 4, 2001*
Sandra Wilkinson *May 1, 2020*
James W. Williams (Supernumerary) *October 10, 2002*
Janet Winteringham *August 17, 2017*

Courts:
Campbell River
500 - 13th Ave., Campbell River, BC V9W 6P1
Tel: 250-286-7510; *Fax:* 250-286-7512
Toll-Free: 877-741-3820
Registry (County): Vancouver Island

Chilliwack
Court House, 46085 Yale Rd., Chilliwack, BC V2P 2L8
Tel: 604-795-8350; *Fax:* 604-795-8393
Registry (County): Westminster
Judges (The Hon. Mr./Madam Justice):
William G.E. Grist (Supernumerary) *May 19, 2005*
Thomas J. Crabtree *May 4, 2018*
Ardith Walkem *December 14, 2020*

Courtenay
Court House, #100, 420 Cumberland Rd., Courtenay, BC V9N 2C4
Tel: 250-334-1115; *Fax:* 250-334-1191
Toll-Free: 877-741-3820
Registry (County): Vancouver Island

Cranbrook
Court House, #147, 102 - 11th Ave. South, Cranbrook, BC V1C 2P3
Tel: 250-426-1234; *Fax:* 250-426-1352
Registry (County): Kootenay

Dawson Creek
Court House, 1201 - 103rd Ave., Dawson Creek, BC V1G 4J2
Tel: 250-784-2278; *Fax:* 250-784-2339
Toll-Free: 866-614-2750
Registry (County): Kootenay

Duncan
Court House, 238 Government St., Duncan, BC V9L 1A5
Tel: 250-746-1258; *Fax:* 250-746-1244
Toll-Free: 877-288-0828
Registry (County): Vancouver Island

Fort Nelson
5431 Airport Dr., P.O. Box 1000, Fort Nelson, BC V0C 1R0
Tel: 250-774-5999; *Fax:* 250-774-6904
Toll-Free: 866-614-2750
Registry (County): Cariboo

Fort St. John
Court House, 10600 - 100th St., Fort St John, BC V1J 4L6
Tel: 250-787-3231; *Fax:* 250-787-3518
Toll-Free: 866-614-2750
Registry (County): Cariboo

Golden
837 Park Dr., P.O. Box 1500, Golden, BC V0A 1H0
Tel: 250-344-7581; *Fax:* 250-344-7715
Registry (County): Kootenay

Kelowna
Court House, 1355 Water St., Kelowna, BC V1Y 9R3
Tel: 250-470-6900; *Fax:* 250-470-6939
Registry (County): Yale
Judges (The Hon. Mr./Madam Justice):

Alison J. Beames (Supernumerary) *August 7, 1996*
Gary P. Weatherill *February 10, 2013*
Steven Wilson *August 17, 2018*

Nanaimo
Court House, 35 Front St., Nanaimo, BC V9R 5J1
Tel: 250-716-5908; *Fax:* 250-716-5911
Registry (County): Vancouver Island
Judges (The Hon. Mr./Madam Justice):
Robin A.M. Baird *October 5, 2012*
Douglas W. Thompson *December 13, 2012*

Nelson
Court House, 320 Ward St., Nelson, BC V1L 1S6
Tel: 250-354-6165; *Fax:* 250-354-6539
Toll-Free: 888-828-4351
Registry (County): Kootenay

New Westminster
Begbie Sq., 651 Carnarvon St., New Westminster, BC V3M 1C9
Tel: 604-660-8522; *Fax:* 604-660-2072
Registry (County): Vancouver
Judges (The Hon. Mr./Madam Justice):
Trevor C. Armstrong *October 1, 2010*
Kenneth W. Ball *November 2, 2012*
Lance W. Bernard *July 24, 2003*
Murray B. Blok *October 28, 2010*
Brenda Brown (Supernumerary) *April 18, 2002*
Martha M. Devlin *December 12, 2014*
John S. Harvey *January 22, 2009*
Julianne K. Lamb *April 27, 2021*
Barbara J. Norell *February 22, 2018*
W. Paul Riley *May 11, 2017*
Terence A. Schultes *May 14, 2009*
Palbinder Kaur Shergill *June 21, 2017*
Matthew Taylor *March 16, 2020*
Sheila Tucker *June 25, 2019*
Frits E. Verhoeven *January 22, 2009*

Penticton
Court House, 100 Main St., Penticton, BC V2A 5A5
Tel: 250-492-1231; *Fax:* 250-492-1378
Toll-Free: 888-526-8555
Registry (County): Yale

Port Alberni
2999 - 4th Ave., Port Alberni, BC V9Y 8A5
Tel: 250-720-2424; *Fax:* 250-720-2426
Toll-Free: 877-741-3820
Registry (County): Vancouver Island

Powell River
#103, 6953 Alberni St., Powell River, BC V8A 2B8
Tel: 604-485-3630; *Fax:* 604-485-3637
Toll-Free: 877-741-3820
Registry (County): Vancouver Island

Prince George
Court House
J.O. Wilson Sq., 250 George St., Prince George, BC V2L 5S2
Tel: 250-614-2700; *Fax:* 250-614-2737
Registry (County): Cariboo
Judges (The Hon. Mr./Madam Justice):
Ronald S. Tindale *October 20, 2011*

Prince Rupert
Court House, 100 Market Pl., Prince Rupert, BC V8J 1B8
Tel: 250-624-7525; *Fax:* 250-624-7538
Registry (County): Prince Rupert
Judges (The Hon. Mr./Madam Justice):
Robert D. Punnett *June 19, 2009*

Quesnel
Court House, #305, 350 Barlow Ave., Quesnel, BC V2J 2C1
Tel: 250-992-4256; *Fax:* 250-992-4171
Toll-Free: 866-614-2750
Registry (County): Cariboo

Kamloops
#223, 455 Columbia St., Kamloops, BC V2C 6K4
Tel: 250-828-4344; *Fax:* 250-828-4332
Registry (County): Yale
Judges (The Hon. Mr./Madam Justice):
Sheri Ann Donegan *June 6, 2013*
Dennis K. Hori *February 8, 2019*

Rossland
Court House, 2288 Columbia Ave., P.O. Box 639, Rossland, BC V0G 1Y0
Tel: 250-362-7368; *Fax:* 250-362-9632
Toll-Free: 888-526-8555
Registry (County): Kootenay

Salmon Arm
Court House, 550 - 2nd Ave. NE, P.O. Box 100 Main, Salmon Arm, BC V1E 4S4
Tel: 250-832-1610; Fax: 250-832-1749
Toll-Free: 888-828-4351

Registry (County): Yale

Smithers
#40, 3793 Alfred Ave., P.O. Box 5000, Smithers, BC V0J 2N0
Tel: 250-847-7376; Fax: 250-847-7710
Registry (County): Prince Rupert

Terrace
Court House, 3408 Kalum St., Terrace, BC V8G 2N6
Tel: 250-638-2111; Fax: 250-638-2123
Registry (County): Prince Rupert

Vernon
Court House, 3001 - 27th St., Vernon, BC V1T 4W5
Tel: 250-549-5422; Fax: 205-549-5621
Toll-Free: 888-526-8555

Registry (County): Yale
Judges (The Hon. Mr./Madam Justice):
D. Allan Betton *June 24, 2011*

Victoria
Court House, 850 Burdett Ave., Victoria, BC V8W 1B4
Tel: 250-356-1478; Fax: 250-356-6669
Registry (County): Vancouver Island
Judges (The Hon. Mr./Madam Justice):
Geoffrey R.J. Gaul *January 31, 2008*
Robert Johnston (Supernumerary) *November 26, 2004*
Brian D. MacKenzie (Supernumerary) *October 23, 2009*
Catherine Murray *October 20, 2016*
Jennifer A. Power *August 6, 2010*
Anthony Saunders *November 26, 2009*
John J. Steeves *October 5, 2012*
Barbara M. Young *June 19, 2015*

Williams Lake
Court House, 540 Borland St., Williams Lake, BC V2G 1R8
Tel: 250-398-4301; Fax: 250-398-4459
Toll-Free: 866-614-2750

Registry (County): Cariboo
Judges (The Hon. Mr./Madam Justice):
Marguerite H. Church *June 17, 2016*

British Columbia Provincial Court
#337, 800 Hornby St., Vancouver, BC V6Z 2C5
Tel: 604-660-2864; Fax: 604-660-1108
info@provincialcourt.bc.ca
www.provincialcourt.bc.ca
The Provincial Court is a statutory, trial court. It hears cases in criminal, family, youth, small claims & traffic matters.
Chief Judge:
Melissa Gillespie *October 19, 2018*
Associate Chief Judges:
Paul Dohm
Susan Wishart
Regional Administrative Judges:
Victor Galbraith
Robert Hamilton
John Milne
Carmen Rogers
Marguerite Shaw
Judges (The Hon.):
Nancy Adams
David Albert
Mariane Armstrong
Therese Alexander
Kimberly Arthur-Leung
James Bahen
Laura Baken
Jennifer Barrett
Wendy Bernt
Evan Blake
Richard Blaskovits
Dawn Boblin
Patricia Bond
Rita Bowry
Michael Brecknell
Adrian Brooks
Anja Brown
Gregory Brown
Robert Brown
Richard Browning
Andrea Brownstone
Ellen Burdett
Elisabeth Burgess
Clarke Burnett
Jeffrey Campbell
Jane Cartwright
Joanne Challenger
Loretta Chaperon

Patrick Chen
Valliammai Chettiar
Christopher Cleaveley
Gary Cohen
Bonnie Craig
Catherine Crockett
Roger Cutler
Brian Daley
Michelle Daneliuk
Andrea Davis
Kathryn Denhoff
Harbans Dhillon
Roy Dickey
Tina Dion
Georgia Docolas
Lynal Doerksen
Patrick Doherty
Diana Dorey
Shehni Dossa
Judith Doulis
Emmet Duncan
Danielle Dunn
Kathryn Ferriss
Oliver Fleck
Barbara Flewelling
Stella Frame
Deanne Gaffar
Joseph Galati
Maria Giardini
Gurmail Gil
Tamera Golinsky
Ellen Gordon
Ted Gouge
Thomas Gove
Jeremy Guild
Robert Gunnell
Jodie Harris
Reginald Harris
Stephen Harrison
Brian Harvey
Cathie Heinrichs
Richard Hewson
Robert Higinbotham
Brent Hoy
Brian Hutcheson
William Jackson
Delaram Jahani
Eugene Jamieson
Patricia Janzen
Mark Jetté
Shannon Keyes
Gregory Koturbash
Peter La Prairie
Ronald Lamperson
Glenn Lee
Lee Wilson
George Leven
Jennifer Lopes
Christine Lowe
Parker MacCarthy
Trudy Macdonald
Malcolm Maclean
Derek Mah
Cassandra Malfair
Peter McDermick
Mayland McKimm
Monica McParland
Robin McQuillan
Susan Mengering
Steven Merrick
Paul Meyers
Richard Miller
Dennis Morgan
Lisa Mrozinski
Kristen Mundstock
Martin Nadon
Andrea Ormistan
Jennifer Oulton
David Patterson
Nancy Philips
Raymond Philips
Rose Raven
Darin Reeves
Gregory Rideout
Edna Ritchie
Jill Routhwaite
Karina Sacca
Justine Saunders
Donna Senniw
Grant Sheard
Craig Sicotte
Satinder Sidhu

David Silverman
Kenneth Skilnick
Garth Smith
Lyndsay Smith
Robin Smith
Jay Solomon
David St. Pierre
Michelle Stanford
Patricia Stark
Daniel Steinberg
Dwight Stewart
Calvin Struyk
Danny Sudeyko
James Sutherland
Andrew Tam
Linda Thomas
Diana Vandor
Daniel Weatherly
Ronald Webb
Jodie Werier
Karen Whonnock
Peter Whyte
James Wingham
Alexander Wolf
Terence Wright
Lisa Wyatt
Wendy Young
Administration:
Gerry Hayes (Administrative Judicial Justice)
Lori Plater (Administrative Judicial Justice)

Courts:
Abbotsford
32203 South Fraser Way, Abbotsford, BC V2T 1W6
Tel: 604-855-3200; Fax: 604-855-7057

Atlin
3rd St., Atlin, BC V0W 1A0
Tel: 250-651-7595

Burns Lake
508 Yellowhead Hwy., Burns Lake, BC V0J 1E0
Tel: 250-692-7711

Campbell River
500 - 13th Ave., Campbell River, BC V9W 6P1
Tel: 250-286-7510

Chilliwack
46085 Yale Rd., Chilliwack, BC V2P 2L8
Tel: 604-795-8350

Penticton
100 Main St., Penticton, BC V2A 5A5
Tel: 250-492-1231

Courtenay
420 Cumberland Rd., Courtenay, BC V9N 2C4
Tel: 250-334-1115

Cranbrook
#147, 102 - 11th Ave. South, Cranbrook, BC V1C 2P3
Tel: 250-426-1234

Dawson Creek
#205, 1201 - 103rd Ave., Dawson Creek, BC V1G 4J2
Tel: 250-784-2278

Duncan
238 Government St., Duncan, BC V9L 1A5
Tel: 250-746-1228

Fort Nelson
5431 Airport Dr., Fort Nelson, BC V0C 1R0
Tel: 250-774-5999

Fort St. John
10600 - 100th St., Fort St John, BC V1J 4L6
Tel: 250-787-3231

Golden
837 Park Dr., Golden, BC V0A 1H0
Tel: 250-344-7581

Kamloops
455 Columbia St., Kamloops, BC V2C 6K4
Tel: 250-828-4344

Kelowna
1355 Water St., Kelowna, BC V1Y 9R3
Tel: 250-470-6900; Fax: 250-470-6810

Mackenzie
64 Centennial Dr., P.O. Box 2050, Mackenzie, BC V0J 2C0
Tel: 250-997-3377

Nanaimo
Court House, 35 Front St., Nanaimo, BC V9R 5J1
Tel: 250-716-5908

Nelson
320 Ward St., Nelson, BC V1L 1S6
Tel: 250-354-6165

New Westminster
651 Carnarvon St., New Westminster, BC V3M 1C9
Tel: 604-660-8522

North Vancouver
200 East 23rd St., North Vancouver, BC V7L 4R4
Tel: 604-981-0200

Pemberton
1366 Aster St., Pemberton, BC V0N 2L0
Tel: 604-894-6122

Port Alberni
2999 - 4th Ave., Port Alberni, BC V9Y 8A5
Tel: 250-720-2424

Port Coquitlam
2620 Mary Hill Rd., Port Coquitlam, BC V3C 3B2
Tel: 604-927-2100

Port Hardy
9300 Trustee Rd., Port Hardy, BC V0N 2P0
Tel: 250-949-6122

Powell River
6953 Alberni St., Powell River, BC V8A 2B8
Tel: 604-485-3630

Prince George
J.O. Wilson Square, 250 George St., Prince George, BC V2L 5S2
Tel: 250-614-2700; Fax: 250-614-2790

Prince Rupert
100 Market Pl., Prince Rupert, BC V8J 1B8
Tel: 250-624-7525

Quesnel
350 Barlow Ave., Quesnel, BC V2J 2C1
Tel: 250-992-4256

Richmond
7577 Elmridge Way, Richmond, BC V6X 4J2
Tel: 604-660-6900

Rossland
Court House, 2288 Columbia Ave., P.O. Box 639, Rossland, BC V0G 1Y0
Tel: 250-362-7368

Salmon Arm
550 - 2nd Ave. NE, P.O. Box 100 Main, Salmon Arm, BC V1E 4S4
Tel: 250-832-1610; Fax: 250-832-1749

Sechelt
5480 Shorncliffe Ave., Sechelt, BC V0N 3A0
Tel: 604-740-8929

Smithers
3793 Alfred Ave., Smithers, BC V0J 2N0
Tel: 250-847-7376

Surrey
14340 - 57th Ave., Surrey, BC V3X 1B2
Tel: 604-572-2200

Terrace
3408 Kalum St., Terrace, BC V8G 2N6
Tel: 250-638-2111

Valemount
1300 - 4th Ave., Valemount, BC V0E 2Z0
Tel: 250-566-4652

Vancouver - Civil (Family, Youth, Small Claims & Traffic) Division
Robson Sq., 800 Hornby St., P.O. Box 21, Vancouver, BC V6Z 2C5
Tel: 604-660-8989

Vancouver - Criminal Division
222 Main St., Vancouver, BC V6A 2S8
Tel: 604-660-4200; Fax: 604-660-4322

Vernon
3001 - 27th St., Vernon, BC V1T 4W5
Tel: 250-549-5422; Fax: 250-549-5621

Victoria
850 Burdett Ave., Victoria, BC V8W 1B4
Tel: 250-356-1478

Victoria - Western Communities
1756 Island Hwy., Victoria, BC V9B 1H8
Tel: 250-391-2888

Williams Lake
540 Borland St., Williams Lake, BC V2G 1R8
Tel: 250-398-4301; Fax: 250-398-4415

Manitoba

Manitoba Court of Appeal
Law Courts Bldg., #100E, 408 York Ave., Winnipeg, MB R3C 0P9
Tel: 204-945-2647; Fax: 204-948-2072
www.manitobacourts.mb.ca
The Court is the senior & final court in the province & has appellate jurisdiction in all civil & criminal cases adjudicated by the Court of Queen's Bench & indictable offences adjudicated by the Provincial Court. The Court hears, in limited circumstances & as mandated by statute, appeals from professional bodies & some government boards & tribunals.
Chief Justice
Richard J.F. Chartier *March 7, 2013*
Justices of Appeal (The Hon. Mr./Madam Justice):
Freda M. Steel (Supernumerary) *February 28, 2000*
Holly C. Beard (Supernumerary) *September 9, 2009*
Marc M. Monnin (Supernumerary) *February 3, 2011*
Diana M. Cameron *November 2, 2012*
William J. Burnett *March 7, 2013*
Christopher J. Mainella *October 1, 2013*
Janice leMaistre *June 19, 2015*
Jennifer A. Pfuetzner *June 19, 2015*
Karen I. Simonsen *August 31, 2018*
Lori T. Spivak *March 26, 2019*

Manitoba Court of Queen's Bench
Law Courts Bldg., 408 York Ave., Winnipeg, MB R3C 0P9
Tel: 204-945-0344; Fax: 204-948-2369
www.manitobacourts.mb.ca
The highest trial court for the province, The Court of Queen's Bench is a court of original jurisdiction & hears all civil & criminal cases arising in Manitoba, except matters expressly excluded by statute. The Court is comprised of the General Division & the Family Division; it also has appellate jurisdiction & hears appeals from decisions of the Provincial Court in less serious criminal & quasi-criminal matters, decisions of the Hearing Officers in small claims matters, & decisions made by Masters of the court.
Chief Justice:
Glenn D. Joyal *February 3, 2011*
Associate Chief Justices:
Shane I. Perlmutter *March 7, 2013*
Gwen B. Hatch *May 14, 2020*
Judges, Family Division (The Hon. Mr./Madam Justice):
Frank Aquila (Supernumerary) *February 28, 2000*
Robert B. Doyle *February 28, 2000*
A. Catherine Everett *November 22, 2006*
Michael A. Thomson *June 1, 2007*
Joan A. MacPhail *January 22, 2009*
William Johnston *July 30, 2009*
Allan D. Dueck *May 9, 2014*
Kaye E. Dunlop *June 19, 2015*
Regan Thatcher *June 19, 2015*
Lore Mirwaldt *October 20, 2016*
Annette Horst *October 9, 2018*
Connie Petersen *October 9, 2018*
L. Kim Antonio *December 11, 2020*
Judges, General Division (The Hon. Mr./Madam Justice):
Brenda L. Keyser (Supernumerary) *October 3, 1995*
Deborah J. McCawley (Supernumerary) *September 16, 1997*
Joan G. McKelvey *September 27, 2001*
Colleen Suche (Supernumerary) *July 16, 2002*
Shawn D. Greenberg *October 28, 2003*
Douglas N. Abra (Supernumerary) *June 22, 2007*
Chris W. Martin *January 22, 2009*
Robert A. Dewar *September 9, 2009*
Richard A. Saull *February 10, 2010*
Gerald L. Chartier *September 30, 2010*
Herbert Rempel *December 1, 2011*
Sheldon W. Lanchbery *June 7, 2013*
James G. Edmond *October 1, 2013*
Victor E. Toews *March 7, 2014*
Sadie Bond *April 11, 2014*
Candace Grammond *October 20, 2016*
David Kroft *October 20, 2016*
Kenneth Champagne *April 4, 2018*
Jeffrey Harris *October 9, 2018*
Shauna McCarthy *June 27, 2019*
Anne Turner *June 27, 2019*
Theodor Bock *February 5, 2020*

Courts:
Brandon
#100, 1104 Princess Ave., Brandon, MB R7A 0P9
Tel: 204-726-6240; Fax: 204-726-6547
Judges (The Hon. Mr./Madam Justice):
John A. Menzies (Supernumerary) *October 6, 1998*
Scott Abel *December 19, 2017*
Elliot H. Leven *December 11, 2020*

Dauphin
114 River Ave. West, Dauphin, MB R7N 0J7
Tel: 204-622-2100; Fax: 204-622-2099
Judges (The Hon. Mr./Madam Justice):
Sandra Zinchuk *February 26, 2015*

Flin Flon
#104, 143 Main St., Flin Flon, MB R8A 1K2
Tel: 204-687-1670; Fax: 204-687-1673

Minnedosa
70 - 3rd Ave. SW, P.O. Box 414, Minnedosa, MB R0J 1E0
Tel: 204-867-4722; Fax: 204-867-4720

Morden
301 Wardrop St., Morden, MB R6M 1X6
Tel: 204-822-2882; Fax: 204-822-2883

Portage la Prairie
20 - 3rd St. SE, Portage la Prairie, MB R1N 1M9
Tel: 204-239-3383; Fax: 204-239-3402

St. Boniface
#100, 614 Desmeurons St., St. Boniface, MB R2H 2P9
Tel: 204-945-8010; Fax: 204-945-5562
Justices (The Hon. Mr./Madam Justice):
D.H. Layh

Selkirk
#101, 235 Eaton Ave., Selkirk, MB R1A 0W7
Tel: 204-785-5122; Fax: 204-785-5125

Swan River
201 - 4th Ave. South, P.O. Box 206, Swan River, MB R0L 1Z0
Tel: 204-734-2252; Fax: 204-734-9544

Virden
232 Wellington St. West, P.O. Box 1478, Virden, MB R0M 2C0
Tel: 204-748-4288; Fax: 204-748-2980

The Pas
300 - 3rd St. East, P.O. Box 1259, The Pas, MB R9A 1L2
Tel: 204-627-8420; Fax: 204-623-6528

Thompson
59 Elizabeth Dr., P.O. Box 34, Thompson, MB R8N 1X4
Tel: 204-677-6757; Fax: 204-677-6686

Manitoba Provincial Court
Law Courts Bldg., 408 York Ave., Main Fl., Winnipeg, MB R3C 0P9
Tel: 204-945-3454; Fax: 204-945-7130
www.manitobacourts.mb.ca
The Provincial Court has jurisdiction in youth, & select family & criminal matters, including summary conviction offences.
Chief Judge:
Margaret I. Wiebe *December 12, 2012*
Associate Chief Judges:
Tracey M. Lord *November 19, 2008*
Anne Krahn *June 5, 2013*
Judges (His/Her Hon.):
Marvin Garfinkel (Senior Judge) *December 5, 1979*
Brian M. Corrin (Senior Judge) *March 4, 1988*
Heather R. Pullan *December 21, 1994*
Brent D. Stewart (Senior Judge) *April 15, 1998*
Raymond E. Wyant (Senior Judge) *May 20, 1998*
Sidney B. Lerner *August 4, 1999*
Lynn A. Stannard (Senior Judge) *August 4, 1999*
Marva J. Smith (Senior Judge) *October 27, 1999*
Judith A. Elliott (Senior Judge) *July 26, 2000*
Mary Kate Harvie *July 26, 2000*
Kathlyn Mary A. Curtis (Senior Judge) *February 28, 2001*
Murray Thompson *March 26, 2003*
Timothy Preston (Senior Judge) *April 30, 2003*
Kelly Moar *April 13, 2005*
Robin A. Finlayson (Senior Judge) *January 31, 2006*
Catherine Carlson *November 22, 2006*
R.L. (Rocky) Pollack (Senior Judge) *December 14, 2006*
Lee Ann Martin *September 17, 2007*
Wanda M. Garreck *November 19, 2008*
Herbert Lawrence Allen *November 19, 2008*
Sandra L. Chapman *August 4, 2009*
Robert M. Heinrichs *September 1, 2009*
Dale C. Schille *May 19, 2010*
Donald R. Slough (Senior Judge) *July 28, 2010*
Cynthia A. Devine *July 23, 2012*
Timothy J.P. Killeen *July 23, 2012*
Dale Harvey *July 10, 2013*
Alain Huberdeau *September 24, 2014*
Ryan Rolston *December 17, 2014*
Lindy Choy *April 29, 2015*
Kael McKenzie *December 17, 2015*
Julie Frederickson *February 13, 2018*
Kusham Sharma *February 13, 2018*
Keith Eyrikson *March 6, 2019*
Victoria Cornick *August 7, 2019*
Tony Celliti *August 7, 2019*

Stacy Cawley *November 21, 2019*
Samuel Raposo *September 30, 2020*
Cindy Sholdice *September 30, 2020*
Dave Mann *October 28, 2020*

Courts:
Brandon
Provincial Court, #100, 1104 Princess Ave., Brandon, MB R7A 0P9
Tel: 204-726-7114; *Fax:* 204-726-6995
Judges (His/Her Hon.):
John Combs (Senior Judge) *March 26, 2003*
Shauna Hewitt-Michta *January 29, 2009*
Donovan Dvorak *February 27, 2013*
Patrick Sullivan *February 4, 2021*

Dauphin
Provincial Court, 114 River Ave. West, Dauphin, MB R7N 0J7
Tel: 204-622-2192; *Fax:* 204-622-2099
Judges (His/Her Hon.):
Geoffrey H. Bayly *February 19, 2020*
Christina L. Cheater *February 19, 2020*

Portage la Prairie
Provincial Court, 25 Tupper St. North, Portage la Prairie, MB R1N 3K1
Tel: 204-239-3337; *Fax:* 204-239-3402
Judges (His/Her Hon.):
Jean McBride *June 18, 2008*

The Pas
300 - 3rd St. East, P.O. Box 1259, The Pas, MB R9A 1L2
Tel: 204-627-8420; *Fax:* 204-623-6528
Associate Chief Judges:
Malcolm W. McDonald *February 3, 2010*
Judges (His/Her Hon.):
Theresa McDonald *October 10, 2018*

Thompson
Provincial Court, 59 Elizabeth Rd., P.O. Box 34, Thompson, MB R8N 1X4
Tel: 204-677-6761; *Fax:* 204-677-6686
Judges (His/Her Hon.):
Brian G. Colli (Senior Judge) *September 21, 1994*
Doreen Redhead *April 4, 2007*
Catherine Hembroff *July 16, 2014*
Todd Allen Rambow *December 7, 2016*

New Brunswick

New Brunswick Court of Appeal
Justice Bldg., #202, 427 Queen St., P.O. Box 6000, Fredericton, NB E3B 5H1
Tel: 506-453-4230; *Fax:* 506-453-7921
www.courtsnb-coursnb.ca
The Court of Appeal has appellate jurisdiction in civil & criminal matters.
Chief Justice:
Marc Richard *January 1, 2002*
Justices of Appeal (The Hon. Mr./Madam Justice):
J. Ernest Drapeau (Supernumerary) *January 1, 1998*
Kathleen A. Quigg *March 3, 2008*
Bradley V. Green *July 29, 2009*
Barbara Baird *December 1, 2014*
Raymond French *June 1, 2015*
Lucie A. LaVigne *June 6, 2018*
Charles A. LeBlond *March 8, 2019*

New Brunswick Court of Queen's Bench
Justice Bldg., 427 Queen St., P.O. Box 6000, Fredericton, NB E3B 5H1
Tel: 506-453-2015; *Fax:* 506-444-5675
www.courtsnb-coursnb.ca
The Court of Queen's Bench is a court of original jurisdiction, having jurisdiction in all civil & criminal matters arising in New Brunswick, except those expressly excluded by statute. The Court is comprised of two divisions: Trial & Family.
Chief Justice:
The Hon. Tracy K. DeWare

Courts:
Bathurst
Court House, 254 St Patrick St., P.O. Box 5001, Bathurst, NB E2A 3Z9
Tel: 506-547-2150; *Fax:* 506-547-2966
Judges (His/Her Hon.):
Réginald Léger (Supernumerary)
Michel A. Robichaud (Supernumerary)
Ivan Robichaud
Michelle Boudreau-Dumas

Campbellton
City Centre Mall, #202, 157 Water St., P.O. Box 5001, Campbellton, NB E3N 3H5
Tel: 506-789-2364; *Fax:* 506-789-2062

Judges (His/Her Hon.)
Larry Landry

Edmundston
Carrefour Assomption, 121, rue de l'Église, P.O. Box 5001, Edmundston, NB E3V 1J9
Tel: 506-735-2029; *Fax:* 506-737-4419
Judges (His/Her Hon.):
Thomas E. Cyr (Supernumerary)
Zoel R. Dionne
Marylène Pilote

Fredericton
Justice Bldg., 427 Queen St., P.O. Box 6000, Fredericton, NB E3B 5H1
Tel: 506-453-2015; *Fax:* 506-444-5675
Judges (His/Her Hon.):
Anne D. Wooder (Supernumerary)
Terrence Morrison
Bruce Noble
E. Thomas Christie
Nathalie L. Godbout

Moncton
Moncton Law Courts, 145 Assumption Blvd., P.O. Box 5001, Moncton, NB E1C 8R3
Tel: 506-856-2304; *Fax:* 506-856-2951
Judges (His/Her Hon.):
Brigitte Robichaud (Supernumerary)
Colette M. d'Entremont (Supernumerary)
Jean-Paul Ouellette
Marie-Claude Blais
Denise A. LeBlanc
Marie-Claude Bélanger-Richard
Christa A. Bourque
Robert Dysart

Miramichi
Court House, 673 King George Hwy., Miramichi, NB E1V 1N6
Tel: 506-627-4023; *Fax:* 506-627-4069
Judges (His/Her Hon.):
Frederick P. Ferguson

Saint John
10 Peel Plaza, P.O. Box 5001, Saint John, NB E2L 3G6
Tel: 506-658-2560; *Fax:* 506-658-2400
Judges (His/Her Hon.):
Hugh H. McLellan (Supernumerary)
William T. Grant (Supernumerary)
Darrell Stephenson
Deobrah Hackett
Chantal Daigle
Arthur Doyle
Krista Colford
Kathryn A. Gregory

Woodstock
Court House, 689 Main St., P.O. Box 5001, Woodstock, NB E7M 5C6
Tel: 506-325-4414; *Fax:* 506-325-4484
Judges (His/Her Hon.):
Richard Petrie

New Brunswick Provincial Court
Justice Bldg., #105, 427 Queen St., P.O. Box 6000, Fredericton, NB E3B 5H1
Tel: 506-453-2120
www.courtsnb-coursnb.ca
The Provincial Court has jurisdiction in select criminal matters as well as youth matters.
Chief Judge:
Jolène Richard *November 13, 2008*
Associate Chief Judge
The Hon. Mary Jane Richards

Courts:
Bathurst
#223, 254 St Patrick St., P.O. Box 5001, Bathurst, NB E2A 3Z9
Tel: 506-547-2155
Judges (His/Her Hon.):
Brigitte Sivret *April 1, 2007*
Joanne Durette *June 1, 2017*

Burton
23 Route #102, Burton, NB E2V 2Y6
Tel: 506-357-4020
Judges (His/Her Hon.):
Pierre F. Dubé *December 11, 2003*
Kenneth Oliver *April 5, 2012*

Campbellton
#202, 157 Water St., P.O. Box 5001, Campbellton, NB E3N 3H5
Tel: 506-789-2337
Judges (His/Her Hon.):

Suzanne C. Bernard *January 27, 2016*

Caraquet
P.O. Box 5559, Caraquet, NB E1W 1B7
Tel: 506-726-2502
The courthouse is located at 23 Route 102 Highway, River Road, in Burton, NB.
Judges (His/Her Hon.):
Johanne-Marguerite Landry *June 1, 2017*

Edmundston
Carrefour Assomption, #235, 121, rue de l'Église, P.O. Box 5001, Edmundston, NB E3V 3L3
Tel: 506-735-2026
Judges (His/Her Hon.):
Nicole Angers *July 16, 2019*

Fredericton
Justice Bldg., #105, 427 Queen St., P.O. Box 6000, Fredericton, NB E3B 5H1
Tel: 506-453-2120
Associate Chief Judge:
Mary Jane Richards *June 3, 2005*
Judges (His/Her Hon.):
Pierre Dubé *December 11, 2003*
Julian Dickson *October 1, 2009*

Miramichi
673 King George Hwy., Miramichi, NB E1V 1N6
Tel: 506-627-4018
Judges (His/Her Hon.):
Natalie H. LeBlanc *June 1, 2017*
Cameron Gunn *February 28, 2019*

Moncton
Moncton Law Courts, 145 Assumption Blvd., P.O. Box 5001, Moncton, NB E1C 8R3
Tel: 506-856-2307
Chief Judge:
Jolène Richard *November 13, 2008*
Judges (His/Her Hon.):
Pierre W. Arseneault (Supernumerary) *October 1, 1988*
J. Camille Vautour (Supernumerary) *June 5, 1989*
Yvette Finn (Supernumerary) *August 5, 1999*
Anne Dugas-Horsman (Supernumerary) *August 22, 2001*
Ronald LeBlanc (Supernumerary) *April 2, 2002*
Paul E. Duffie *June 19, 2008*
D. Troy Sweet *April 5, 2012*
Brigitte Volpé *April 5, 2012*
Lucie N. Mathurin *June 1, 2017*
Luc J. Labonté *February 28, 2019*

Saint John
10 Peel Plaza, P.O. Box 5001, Saint John, NB E2L 3G6
Tel: 506-658-2568
Judges (His/Her Hon.):
Alfred H. Brien (Supernumerary) *August 15, 1988*
Anne Jeffries (Per Diem Judge) *November 7, 1997*
David C. Walker (Supernumerary) *November 7, 1997*
Henrik G. Tonning *July 29, 1999*
W. Andrew LeMesurier *December 11, 2003*
Marco Robert Cloutier *January 30, 2013*
Richard Andrew Palmer *November 7, 2014*
Kelly Ann Winchester *June 1, 2017*

Tracadie-Sheila
Place Tracadie, 3514 Main St., 1st Fl., Tracadie-Sheila, NB E1X 1C9
Tel: 506-394-3700
Judges (His/Her Hon.):
Donald J. LeBlanc (Supernumerary) *April 13, 2000*
Éric P. Sonier *January 27, 2016*

Woodstock
689 Main St., P.O. Box 5001, Woodstock, NB E7M 5C6
Tel: 506-325-4415
Judges (His/Her Hon.):
R. Leslie Jackson (Supernumerary) *November 7, 1997*
Brian McLean *March 24, 2014*

New Brunswick Probate Court
Justice Bldg., 423 Queen St., P.O. Box 6000, Fredericton, NB E3B 5H1
Tel: 506-453-2015
www.courtsnb-coursnb.ca
The Probate Court has jurisdiction in estate matters. Clerks of the Court of Queen's Bench are, ex officio, Clerks of Probate Court. There are court locations throughout New Brunswick.

Newfoundland & Labrador

Supreme Court of Newfoundland & Labrador: General Division
Courthouse, 309 Duckworth St., P.O. Box 937, St. John's, NL A1C 5M3

Tel: 709-729-1137; *Fax:* 709-729-6623
inquiries@supreme.court.nl.ca
court.nl.ca/supreme/general

The Supreme Court of Newfoundland & Labrador is the province's superior trial court. The General Division deals with cases in realtion to civil, family, criminal, estates & guardianship issues, as well as appeals from the provincial court.

Chief Justice:
Raymond P. Whalen *June 19, 2008*
Judges (The Hon.):
Maureen Dunn (Supernumerary) *October 4, 1994*
James P. Adams (Supernumerary) *August 7, 1996*
Richard D. LeBlanc (Supernumerary) *June 20, 2000*
Garrett A. Handrigan (Supernumerary) *March 27, 2001*
Carl R. Thompson (Supernumerary) *December 4, 2001*
Kendra J. Goulding *June 5, 2002*
Alphonsus E. Faour (Supernumerary) *November 5, 2003*
Valerie L. Marshall *April 29, 2009*
Robert P. Stack *November 30, 2009*
Deborah J. Paquette *June 18, 2010*
Donald H. Burrage *April 10, 2012*
Rosalie McGrath *May 31, 2012*
Laura A. Mennie *March 9, 2014*
George L. Murphy *April 10, 2014*
Jane M. Fitzpatrick *March 27, 2015*
Cilian D. Sheahan *June 20, 2015*
Sandra R. Chaytor *May 12, 2017*
Frances J. Knickle *May 12, 2017*
Vikas Khaladkar *October 20, 2017*
Alexander MacDonald *November 9, 2017*
Daniel Boone *November 2, 2018*
Michelle A. Coady *March 26, 2019*
Katherine O'Brien *March 26, 2019*
Glenn L.C Noel *May 21, 2019*

Courts:
Corner Brook
Courthouse, 82 Mt. Bernard Ave., P.O. Box 2006, Corner Brook, NL A2H 6J8

Tel: 709-637-2633; *Fax:* 709-637-8036
inquirycb@supreme.court.nl.ca

Gander
Law Court Bldg., 98 Airport Blvd., P.O. Box 2222, Gander, NL A1V 2N9

Tel: 709-256-1115; *Fax:* 709-256-1120
inquirygander@supreme.court.nl.ca

Grand Bank
T. Alex Hickman Courthouse, 69 Grandview Blvd., P.O. Box 910, Grand Bank, NL A0E 1W0

Tel: 709-832-1720; *Fax:* 709-832-2755
inquirygb@supreme.court.nl.ca

Grand Falls—Windsor
The Law Courts, 3 Cromer Ave., Grand Falls, NL A2A 1W9
Tel: 709-292-4260; *Fax:* 709-292-4224
inquirygfw@supreme.court.nl.ca

Happy Valley—Goose Bay
Courthouse, P.O. Box 3014 B, Happy Valley-Goose Bay, NL A0P 1E0

Tel: 709-896-7892; *Fax:* 709-896-9212
inquiryhvgb@supreme.court.nl.ca

Court of Appeal of Newfoundland & Labrador
287 Duckworth St., P.O. Box 937, St. John's, NL A1C 5M3
Tel: 709-729-0066; *Fax:* 709-729-7909
coaregistry@appeal.court.nl.ca
www.court.nl.ca/appeal

The Court of Appeal has appellate jurisdiction in criminal & civil matters from decisions of the lower courts & designated administrative boards & tribunals. Founded in 1975, the court became an independent institution when it ceased being a division of the Supreme Court of Newfoundland & Labrador in 2018.

Chief Justice:
The Hon. Deborah E. Fry
Justices of Appeal (The Hon. Mr./Madam Justice):
J. Derek Green (Supernumerary) *June 1, 1996*
Gale Welsh *March 1, 2001*
Charles W. White (Supernumerary) *April 29, 2009*
Lois R. Hoegg *June 18, 2010*
Francis P. O'Brien *June 8, 2017*
William H. Goodridge *October 19, 2018*
Gillian D. Butler *May 1, 2019*

Supreme Court of Newfoundland & Labrador: Family Division
68 Portugal Cove Rd., St. John's, NL A1B 2L9
Tel: 709-729-2258; *Fax:* 709-729-0784
familyinquiries@supreme.court.nl.ca
court.nl.ca/supreme/family

Judicial matters regarding families are shared / divided between the Supreme & Provincial Courts along geographical boundaries. The Family Division of the Supreme Court has exclusive jurisdiction for all family matters on the Avalon Peninsula (including Bell Island). In the "expanded service area" of the United Family Court (from Holyrood to Port Blandford & Bonavista Peninsula), however, there is concurrent jurisdiction.There is a second location at 82 Mt. Bernard Ave., Corner Brook, NL, P.O. Box 2006, A2H 6J8.

Provincial Court of Newfoundland & Labrador
215 Water St., P.O. Box 68, St. John's, NL A1C 6C9
Tel: 709-729-1004; *Fax:* 709-729-0796
inquiries@provincial.court.nl.ca
court.nl.ca/provincial

The Provincial Court has jurisdiction in select criminal & family (outside the judicial area of St. John's) matters as well as small claims & youth matters.

Chief Judge:
The Hon. Pamela Goulding
Associate Chief Judge:
Michael Madden *February 3, 2010*
Judges (The Hon.):
Gregory O. Brown (Per Diem Judge) *February 28, 1992*
Kymil Howe *March 11, 1993*
David Orr *August 25, 1994*
Wayne Gorman *November 9, 2000*
Harold Porter *October 12, 2001*
Bruce Short *November 1, 2003*
Wynne Anne Trahey *June 8, 2007*
Jacqueline Jenkins *September 24, 2008*
D. Mark Pike *November 17, 2008*
Jacqueline Brazil *February 3, 2010*
Lois Skanes *February 15, 2010*
Lori A. Marshall *August 13, 2012*
James G. Walsh *September 3, 2012*
Mark T. Linehan *March 4, 2014*
Lynn E. Cole *March 6, 2014*
Phyllis Harris *June 10, 2014*
Paul Noble *September 17, 2015*
Robin Fowler *August 7, 2017*
Kari Ann Pike *August 7, 2017*
Rolf Pritchard *June 13, 2019*
Jennifer Mercer *July 16, 2021*

Courts:
Clarenville
47 Marine Dr., Clarenville, NL A5A 1M5
Tel: 709-466-2635; *Fax:* 709-466-3147

Corner Brook
82 Mt. Bernard Ave., P.O. Box 2006, Corner Brook, NL A2H 6J8
Tel: 709-637-2323; *Fax:* 709-637-2656

Gander
100 Airport Rd., P.O. Box 2222, Gander, NL A1V 2N9
Tel: 709-256-1100; *Fax:* 709-256-1097

Grand Bank
Grand Bank-Fortune Hwy., P.O. Box 339, Grand Bank, NL A0E 1W0
Tel: 709-832-1450; *Fax:* 709-832-1758

Grand Falls—Windsor
Law Courts Bldg., Grand Falls—Windsor, NL A2A 1W9
Tel: 709-292-4212; *Fax:* 709-292-4388

Happy Valley—Goose Bay
P.O. Box 3014 B, Happy Valley-Goose Bay, NL A0P 1E0
Tel: 709-896-7870; *Fax:* 709-896-8767

Harbour Grace
2 Harvey St., P.O. Box 519, Harbour Grace, NL A0A 2M0
Tel: 709-596-6141; *Fax:* 709-596-4304

Stephenville
35 Alabama Dr., Stephenville, NL A2N 3K9
Tel: 709-643-2966; *Fax:* 709-643-4022

Wabush
Whiteway Dr., P.O. Box 1060, Wabush, NL A0R 1B0
Tel: 709-282-6617; *Fax:* 709-282-6905

Northwest Territories

Northwest Territories: Court of Appeal
4903 - 49th St., P.O. Box 550, Yellowknife, NT X1A 2N4
Tel: 866-822-5864
www.nwtcourts.ca/en/courts/court-of-appeal

The Court of Appeal has appellate jurisdiction in criminal & civil matters from the Supreme Court & Territorial Court.
Chief Justice:
The Hon. C.J.A. Fraser
Justices of Appeal (The Hon. Mr./Madam Justice):
P.T. Costigan
M.S. Paperny
P.W.L. Martin
L.A. Charbonneau
J. Watson
F.F. Slatter
P.A. Rowbotham
N.A. Sharkey
J.D.B. McDonald
S. Cooper
M.B. Bielby
B.K. O'Ferrall
K.M. Shaner
S.H. Smallwood
A.M. Mahar
B.M Tulloch
B.L. Veldhuis
T.W. Wakeling
F.L. Schutz
P. Bychok
S.J Greckol
M.G Crighton
J. Strekaf
R. Khullar
E. Campbell
S. Charlesworth
C. Lyons
E. Hughes
D. Pentelechuk
S. Duncan
J. Antonio
K. Feehan
K. Wenckebach

Northwest Territories: Supreme Court
4903 - 49th St., P.O. Box 550, Yellowknife, NT X1A 2N4
Tel: 867-920-8760; *Fax:* 867-873-0291
www.nwtcourts.ca/en/courts/supreme-court

The Supreme Court has jurisdiction in all civil & criminal matters arising in the Northwest Territories, except those expressly excluded by statute.
Chief Justice:
The Hon. L.A. Charbonneau
Judges (The Hon. Mr./Madam Justice):
K.M. Shaner
S.H. Smallwood
A.M. Mahar

Northwest Territories: Territorial Court
4903 - 49th St., P.O. Box 550, Yellowknife, NT X1A 2N4
Tel: 867-767-9289; *Fax:* 867-873-0291
www.nwtcourts.ca/en/courts/territorial-court

The Territorial Court has jurisdiction in small claims, youth, family & select criminal matters.
Chief Judge:
The Hon. R.D. Gorin
Judges (His/Her Hon.):
C. Gagnon
G.E. Malakoe
D.F. Molloy

Northwest Territories: Justice of the Peace Court
4903 - 49th St., P.O. Box 550, Yellowknife, NT X1A 2N4
Tel: 867-920-6439; *Fax:* 867-873-0203
Toll-Free: 844-300-7015
jp_program@nwtcourts.ca
www.nwtcourts.ca/en/courts/justice-of-the-peace-court

The Justices of the Peace have jurisdiction in summary conviction matters arising out of territorial statute, municipal by-law & select criminal matters.

Nova Scotia

Nova Scotia Supreme Court: Family Division
3380 Devonshire Ave., Halifax, NS B3K 5R5
Tel: 902-424-3990; *Fax:* 902-424-0562
www.courts.ns.ca/supreme_court_family/nsscfd_home.htm

The Family Division of the Supreme Court of Nova Scotia was established to deal with all family law matters arising within the Halifax Regional Municipality (HRM) & on Cape Breton Island. Family law matters arising in areas outside of the HRM & Cape Breton are dealt with by the Family Court of Nova Scotia.
Associate Chief Justice:
Lawrence I. O'Neil
Judges (The Hon. Mr./Madam Justice):
Samuel Moreau

C. Lou Ann Chiasson
Cindy G. Cormier
Leslie J. Dellapinna (Supernumerary)
Jean M. Dewolfe (Supernumerary)
Theresa M. Forgeron
Robert M. Gregan
Kenneth Haley
R. Lester Jesudason
Elizabeth Jollimore
Moira C. Legere Sers (Supernumerary)
Pamela J. MacKeigan
Lee Anne MacLeod-Archer
Cindy Murray
R. James Williams (Supernumerary)
Michelle K. Christenson
Pamela Marche
Paul Morris
S. Raymond Morse

Nova Scotia Court of Appeal
The Law Courts Bldg., 1815 Upper Water St., Halifax, NS B3J 1S7

Tel: 902-424-4900; Fax: 902-424-0524
www.courts.ns.ca/appeal_court/nsca_home.htm

The Nova Scotia Court of Appeal is the province's highest court & has appellate jurisdiction in civil & criminal matters. It sits only in Halifax & hears appeals from both the Supreme & Provincial Courts.

Chief Justice:
Michael J. Wood
Justices of Appeal (The Hon. Justice):
M. Jill Hamilton (Supernumerary)
Joel E. Fichaud (Supernumerary)
Duncan R. Beveridge
David P.S. Farrar
Peter M.S. Bryson
J. Edward (Ted) Scanlan (Supernumerary)
Cindy A. Bourgeois
Elizabeth Van den Eynden
Anne S. Derrick
Carole A. Beaton

Nova Scotia Supreme Court
The Law Courts Bldg., 1815 Upper Water St., Halifax, NS B3J 1S7

Tel: 902-424-4900; Fax: 902-424-0524
www.courts.ns.ca/supreme_court/nssc_home.htm

The Supreme Court is the highest trial court in the province with jurisdiction in all civil & criminal matters, except those expressly excluded by statute. It hears appeals on Provincial Court, Small Claims Court & Residential Tenancies Board matters. The Supreme Court has two divisions: Supreme Court (general) & the Family Division.

Chief Justice:
The Hon. Deborah K. Smith
Associate Chief Justice:
The Hon. Patrick J. Duncan
Judges (The Hon. Mr./Madam Justice):
Joshua M. Arnold
John Bodurtha
Denise Boudreau
Christa M. Brothers
Jamie S. Campbell
James L. Chipman
Kevin Coady (Supernumerary)
C. Richard Coughlan (Supernumerary)
D. Timothy Gabriel
Gail L. Gatchalian
Robin C.M. Gogan
Frank P. Hoskins
Jeffrey R. Hunt
Darlene Jamieson
John A. Keith
Mona Lynch (Supernumerary)
Glen P. McDougall (Supernumerary)
Pierre L. Muise
Patrick J. Murray
Scott Norton
Peter Rosinski
Diane Rowe
Nick Scaravelli (Supernumerary)
Ann E. Smith
Gregory M. Warner (Supernumerary)
Robert W. Wright (Supernumerary)

Courts:
Amherst
16 Church St., 3rd Fl., Amherst, NS B4H 3A6
Tel: 902-667-2256; Fax: 902-667-1108
amherstsupreme@courts.ns.ca

Antigonish
11 James St., Antigonish, NS B2G 1R6
Tel: 902-863-3676; Fax: 902-863-7479
antigonishsupreme@courts.ns.ca

Bridgewater
Justice Centre, 141 High St., Bridgewater, NS B4V 1W2
Tel: 902-543-4679; Fax: 902-543-0678
bridgewatersupreme@courts.ns.ca

Digby
Justice Centre, 119 Queen St., P.O. Box 1089, Digby, NS B0V 1A0
Tel: 902-245-7134; Fax: 902-245-6722
supremecourtdigbyjc@courts.ns.ca

Kentville
Justice Centre, 87 Cornwallis St., Kentville, NS B4N 2E5
Tel: 902-679-5540; Fax: 902-679-6178
kentvillesupreme@courts.ns.ca

Pictou
Court House, 69 Water St., P.O. Box 1750, Pictou, NS B0K 1H0
Tel: 902-485-7350; Fax: 902-485-6737
pictousupreme@courts.ns.ca

Port Hawkesbury
Justice Centre, 15 Kennedy St., Port Hawkesbury, NS B9A 2Y1
Tel: 902-625-2665; Fax: 902-625-4084
porthawkesburysupreme@courts.ns.ca

Sydney
Justice Centre, #1 & 2, 136 Charlotte St., Sydney, NS B1P 1C3
Tel: 902-563-3550; Fax: 902-563-2224
sydneysupreme@courts.ns.ca

Truro
Justice Centre, 1 Church St., Truro, NS B2N 3Z5
Tel: 902-893-3953; Fax: 902-893-6114
trurosupreme@courts.ns.ca

Yarmouth
Justice Centre, 164 Main St., Yarmouth, NS B5A 1C2
Tel: 902-742-4142; Fax: 902-742-0678
scyarmouth@courts.ns.ca

Nova Scotia Probate Court
Law Courts Bldg., 1815 Upper Water St., Halifax, NS B3J 1S7
Tel: 902-424-7422; Fax: 902-424-0524
www.courts.ns.ca/probate_court/nspbc_home.htm
The Probate Court has jurisdiction in respect of estate matters.

Courts:
Amherst
Justice Centre, 16 Church St., 3rd Fl., Amherst, NS B4H 3A6
Tel: 902-667-2256; Fax: 902-667-1108

Annapolis Royal
Justice Centre, 377 St George St., P.O. Box 129, Annapolis Royal, NS B0S 1A0
Tel: 902-532-5462; Fax: 902-532-7225

Antigonish
Justice Centre, 11 James St., Antigonish, NS B2G 1R6
Tel: 902-863-7396; Fax: 902-863-7479

Bridgewater
Justice Centre, 141 High St., Bridgewater, NS B4V 1W2
Tel: 902-543-4679; Fax: 902-543-0678

Digby
Court House, 119 Queen St., P.O. Box 1089, Digby, NS B0V 1A0
Tel: 902-245-4567; Fax: 902-245-6722

Halifax
Law Courts Bldg., 1815 Upper Water St., Halifax, NS B3J 1S7
Tel: 902-424-7422; Fax: 902-424-0524

Kentville
Justice Centre, 87 Cornwallis St., Kentville, NS B4N 2E5
Tel: 902-679-5540; Fax: 902-679-6178

Pictou
69 Water St., P.O. Box 1750, Pictou, NS B0K 1H0
Tel: 902-485-7350; Fax: 902-485-6737

Port Hawkesbury
Justice Centre, 15 Kennedy St., Port Hawkesbury, NS B9A 2Y1
Tel: 902-625-2665; Fax: 902-625-4084

Sydney
Justice Centre, #6, 136 Charlotte St., Sydney, NS B1P 1C3
Tel: 902-563-3545; Fax: 902-563-5701

Truro
Justice Centre, 1 Church St., Truro, NS B2N 3Z5
Tel: 902-893-5870; Fax: 902-893-6114

Yarmouth
Justice Centre, 164 Main St., Yarmouth, NS B5A 1C2
Tel: 902-742-5469; Fax: 902-742-0678

Nova Scotia Provincial Court
5250 Spring Garden Rd., Halifax, NS B3J 1E7
Tel: 902-424-8718; Fax: 902-424-0551
www.courts.ns.ca/provincial_court/nspc_home.htm
The Provincial Court has jurisdiction over almost all indictable charges under provincial & federal statutes and regulations. When judges are not available, presiding Justices of the Peace deal with release or detention of those arrested.

Chief Judge:
Pamela S. Williams
Associate Chief Judge:
Vacant
Judges (The Hon.):
Barbara Beach
Perry Borden
Elizabeth A. Buckle
Marc C. Chisholm
John D. Comeau
Aleta Cromwell
William Digby
Gregory E. Lenehan
Claudine MacDonald
Amy Sakalauskas
Michael B. Sherar
Ann Marie Simmons
Alan Tufts
Brian D. Williston
Jim Wilson
Warren Zimmer

Courts:
Amherst
16 Church St., 3rd Fl., Amherst, NS B4H 3A6
Tel: 902-667-2256; Fax: 902-667-1108
amherstprovincialcourt@courts.ns.ca

Judges (The Hon.):
Rosalind Michie

Annapolis Royal
Satellite Court, 377 St George St., P.O. Box 129, Annapolis Royal, NS B0S 1A0
Tel: 902-245-4567

Antigonish
11 James St., Antigonish, NS B2G 1R6
Tel: 902-863-3676; Fax: 902-863-7479
antigonishprovincialcourt@courts.ns.ca

Bridgewater
Justice Centre, 141 High St., Bridgewater, NS B4V 1W2
Tel: 902-543-4679; Fax: 902-543-0678
bridgewaterprovincialcourt@courts.ns.ca

Judges (The Hon.):
Catherine Benton
Marci Lin Melvin
Paul B. Scovil

Dartmouth
277 Pleasant St., Dartmouth, NS B2Y 4B7
Tel: 902-424-2390; Fax: 902-424-0677

Judges (The Hon.):
Rickcola Brinton
Alanna Murphy
Corrine Sparks
Theodore K. Tax
Jean M. Whalen

Kentville
Justice Centre, 87 Cornwallis St., Kentville, NS B4N 2E5
Tel: 902-679-6070; Fax: 902-679-6190
kentvilleprovincialcourt@courts.ns.ca

Judges (The Hon.):
Chris Manning
Rhonda van der Hoek

Digby
119 Queen St., P.O. Box 1089, Digby, NS B0V 1A0
Tel: 902-245-4567; Fax: 902-245-6722
digbyprovincialcourt@courts.ns.ca

Judges (His/Her Hon.):
Timothy D. Landry

Pictou
Justice Centre, 69 Water St., P.O. Box 1750, Pictou, NS B0K 1H0
Tel: 902-485-7350; Fax: 902-485-3552
pictoucourt@courts.ns.ca

Judges (The Hon.):

Del W. Atwood
Timothy Daley

Port Hawkesbury
Justice Centre, 15 Kennedy St., Port Hawkesbury, NS B9A 2Y1
Tel: 902-625-2665; *Fax:* 902-625-4084
porthawkesburyprovincialcourt@courts.ns.ca
Judges (The Hon.):
Laurel J. Halfpenny-MacQuarrie

Sydney
Justice Centre, #4 & 5, 136 Charlotte St., Sydney, NS B1P 1C3
Tel: 902-563-3510; *Fax:* 902-563-3421
sydneyprovincialcourt@courts.ns.ca
Judges (The Hon.):
E. Ann Marie MacInnes
Daniel A. MacRury
Diane L. McGrath
Peter Ross

Truro
Justice Centre, 540 Prince St., Truro, NS B2N 1G1
Tel: 902-893-5840; *Fax:* 902-893-6261
truroprovincialcourt@courts.ns.ca
Judges (The Hon.):
Alain Bégin

Yarmouth
Justice Centre, 164 Main St., Yarmouth, NS B5A 1C2
Tel: 902-742-0500; *Fax:* 902-742-0678
yarmouthprovincialcourt@courts.ns.ca
Judges (The Hon.):
James H. Burrill
Timothy D. Landry

Nova Scotia Family Court
Provincial Court, 5250 Spring Garden Rd., Halifax, NS B3J 1E7
Tel: 902-424-8718; *Fax:* 902-424-0551
www.courts.ns.ca/Family_Court/NSFC_home.htm
The Family Court is available for residents living outside of the Halifax Regional Municipality or outside Cape Breton for family matters. Residents living inside the Halifax Regional Municipalitiy or in Cape Breton that have a family matter are under the jurisdiction of the Supreme Court Family Divison.
Chief Judge:
Pamela S. Williams
Judges (The Hon.):
Perry Borden
Elizabeth A. Buckle
Marc C. Chisholm
John D. Comeau
Aleta Cromwell
William Digby
Gregory E. Lenehan
Ann Marie Simmons
Warren Zimmer

Courts:
Amherst
Justice Centre, 16 Church St., 3rd Fl., Amherst, NS B4H 3A6
Tel: 902-667-2256; *Fax:* 902-667-1108

Antigonish
Justice Centre, 11 James St., Antigonish, NS B2G 1R6
Tel: 902-863-3676; *Fax:* 902-863-7479

Bridgewater
Justice Centre, 141 High St., Bridgewater, NS B4V 1W2
Tel: 902-543-4679; *Fax:* 902-543-0678
bjc.family.court@courts.ns.ca
Judges (The Hon.)
Marci Lin Melvin
Paul B. Scovil

Dartmouth
Provincial Court, 277 Pleasant St., Dartmouth, NS B2Y 4B7
Tel: 902-424-2390; *Fax:* 902-424-0677
Judges (The Hon.)
Corrine Sparks
Theodore K. Tax
Jean M. Whalen

Digby
Justice Centre, 119 Queen St., P.O. Box 1089, Digby, NS B0V 1A0
Tel: 902-245-4567; *Fax:* 902-245-6722
Judges (The Hon.)
Timothy D. Landry

Port Hawkesbury
#201, 15 Kennedy St., Port Hawkesbury, NS B9A 2Y1
Tel: 902-625-2665; *Fax:* 902-625-4084
Judges (The Hon.)
Laurel J. Halfpenny-MacQuarrie

Sydney
Provincial Court, #4 & #5, 136 Charlotte St., Sydney, NS B1P 1C3
Tel: 902-563-3510; *Fax:* 902-563-3421
Judges (The Hon.)
E. Ann Marie MacInnes
Daniel A. MacRury
A. Peter Ross

Kentville
136 Exhibition St., Kentville, NS B4N 4E5
Tel: 902-679-6070; *Fax:* 902-679-6190
Judges (The Hon.)
Chris Manning
Rhonda van der Hoek

Truro
540 Prince St., Truro, NS B2N 1G1
Tel: 902-893-5840; *Fax:* 902-893-6261

Yarmouth
Justice Centre, 164 Main St., Yarmouth, NS B5A 1C2
Tel: 902-742-0550; *Fax:* 902-742-0678
Judges (The Hon.)
James H. Burrill
Timothy D. Landry

Nunavut

Nunavut Court of Appeal
Court Services Division, Dept. of Justice, P.O. Box 297, Iqaluit, NU X0A 0H0
Tel: 867-975-6100; *Fax:* 867-975-6168
Toll-Free: 866-286-0546
www.nunavutcourts.ca/nunavut-court-of-appeal
The Nunavut Court of Appeal consists of judges from the Nunavut Court of Justice & the Courts of Alberta, the NWT & Yukon. The Nunavut Court of Appeal sits two to three times a year.
Chief Justice:
The Hon. Catherine A. Fraser
Justices (The Hon. Mr./Madam Justice):
Peter Thomas Costigan (Supernumerary)
Ronald Stuart Veale
Louise Anne Marie Charbonneau
Frans Felling Slatter
Marina Sarah Paperny (Supernumerary)
Peter W.L. Martin (Supernumerary)
Jack Watson (Supernumerary)
Patricia Adele Rowbotham (Supernumerary)
Neil A. Sharkey
John D.B. McDonald (Supernumerary)
Susan Cooper
Myra Beth Bielby (Supernumerary)
Brian Kenneth O'Ferrall
Karan M. Shaner
Shannon Smallwood
Andrew M. Mahar
Bonnie M. Tulloch
Barbara Lea Veldhuis
Thomas W. Wakeling
Frederica L. Schutz
Paul Bychok
Sheila J. Greckol (Supernumerary)
Michelle G. Crighton
Jo'Anne Strekaf
Ritu Khullar
Edith Campbell
Susan Charlesworth
Christian Lyons
Elizabeth Hughes
Dawn Pentelechuk
Jolaine Antonio
Kevin Feehan

Nunavut Court of Justice
Court Services Division, Dept. of Justice, P.O. Box 297, Iqaluit, NU X0A 0H0
Tel: 867-975-6100; *Fax:* 867-975-6168
Toll-Free: 866-286-0546
www.nunavutcourts.ca/nunavut-court-of-justice
The Nunavut Court of Justice is both the superior court & territorial court of the Nunavut territory.
Chief Justice:
Neil Sharkey *December 1, 2008*
Judges (The Hon. Mr./Madam Justice):
Susan Cooper *December 1, 2009*
Bonnie Tulloch *March 1, 2012*
Paul Bychok *July 1, 2015*
Susan Charlesworth *June 1, 2018*
Christion Lyons *June 1, 2018*

Ontario

Court of Appeal for Ontario
Osgoode Hall, 130 Queen St. West, Toronto, ON M5H 2N5
Tel: 416-327-5020 *Toll-Free:* 855-718-1756
www.ontariocourts.ca/coa/en
The Court of Appeal is the final court of appeal for Ontario. Appeals from the Court of Appeal may be pursued in the Supreme Court of Canada.
Chief Justice:
The Hon. George R. Strathy
Associate Chief Justice:
The Hon. J. Michael Fairburn
Justices (The Hon. Mr./Madam Justice):
Mary Lou Benotto *January 1, 2013*
David M. Brown *December 1, 2014*
Steve A. Coroza *April 1, 2020*
David H. Doherty *September 1, 1990*
Kathryn N. Feldman *June 11, 1998*
Eileen E. Gillese *January 1, 2002*
Allison Harvison Young *August 29, 2018*
C. William Hourigan *August 1, 2013*
Alexandra Hoy *December 1, 2011*
Grant Huscroft *December 1, 2014*
Russell G. Juriansz *March 1, 2004*
Peter D. Lauwers *December 13, 2012*
James MacPherson *January 1, 1999*
Bradley Miller *June 1, 2015*
Ian V.B. Nordheimer *September 15, 2017*
David M. Paciocco *April 7, 2017*
Gladys Pardu *November 7, 2013*
Sarah E. Pepall *April 1, 2012*
Lois B. Roberts *April 30, 2015*
Paul S. Rouleau *April 14, 2005*
Janet M. Simmons *August 1, 2000*
Lorne Sossin *November 1, 2020*
Julie A. Thorburn *June 1, 2019*
Gary T. Trotter *November 23, 2016*
Michael H Tulloch *June 30, 2012*
Katherine van Rensburg *October 1, 2013*
David Watt *October 12, 2007*
Benjamin Zarnett *November 1, 2018*
Administration:
Registrar & Manager: Court Operations, Daniel Marentic
Deputy Registrar & Manager: Judicial Support, Warren Robertson
Deputy Registrar & Manager: Court Operations, Sandra Theroulde

Ontario Superior Court of Justice
Osgoode Hall, 130 Queen St. West, Toronto, ON M5H 2N5
Tel: 905-853-4809
www.ontariocourts.ca/scj
In addition to its regular trial court functions, the Superior Court of Justice has two branches: the Divisional Court, which generally hears appeals from a final order of a Judge of the Superior Court involving disputes of up to $25,000, & the Small Claims Court, which generally hears cases involving claims up to $10,000. The Governor General appoints the Judges to all but the Ontario Court of Justice.
Chief Justice:
The Hon. Geoffrey B. Morawetz
Associate Chief Justice:
The Hon. Frank N. Marrocco, 416-327-5000
Senior Judge of Family Court:
The Hon. Suzanne M. Stevenson

Central East Region
50 Eagle St. West, 4th Fl., Newmarket, ON L3Y 6B1
Tel: 905-853-4809; *Fax:* 905-853-4826
Serving the communities of Barrie, Bracebridge, Cobourg, Durham, Lindsay, Newmarket & Peterborough.
Regional Senior Justice:
The Hon. Mark L. Edwards
Justices (The Hon. Mr./Madam Justice):
Stephen T. Bale
Richard T. Bennett
Laura A. Bird
R. Cary Boswell
Joanne Bruhn
Jill C. Cameron
Annette Casullo
Robert Charney
Vanessa V. Christie
J. Christopher Corkery
Jonathan Dawe
Chris de Sa
Joseph Di Luca
Peter A. Douglas
Margaret Eberhard
John A. Finlayson
Laura E. Fryer

Michelle Fuerst
Fred Graham
Drew S. Gunsolus
Susan E. Healey
Andrea Himel
Jayne E. Hughes
Alan P. Ingram
R. Sonya Jain
David Jarvis
Ronald P. Kaufman
Pamela M. Krause
Myrna L. Lack
Sharon Lavine
Howard Leibovich
Karen M.D. Leef
John R. McCarthy
John P.L. McDermot
Michael K. McKelvey
J. Scott McLeod
George MacPherson
Paul W. Nicholson
Hugh K. O'Connell
Allan R. Rowsell
David Salmers
Margaret A. C. Scott
Clyde Smith
Alexander Sosna
Jocelyn Speyer
Phillip Sutherland
Mary E. Vallee
Catriona Verner
Ramona A. Wildman
Susan Woodley

Central South Region
45 Main St. East, Hamilton, ON L8N 2B7
Tel: 905-645-5253; *Fax:* 905-645-5374
Serving the communities of Brantford, Cayuga, Hamilton, Kitchener, Simcoe, St. Catharines & Welland.
Regional Senior Justice:
The Hon. Paul R. Sweeney
Justices (The Hon. Mr./Madam Justice):
Harrison S. Arrell
Lauren Bale
Catrina Braid
Jennifer Breithaupt-Smith
David A. Broad
Caroline E. Brown
Kim A. Carpenter-Gunn
Deborah L. Chappel
Meredith Donohue
David L. Edwards
Giulia Gambacorta
Michael R. Gibson
Andrew J. Goodman
Donald J. Gordon
Nathalie Gregson
R. John Harper
Joseph R. Henderson
John Krawchenko
Mary Anne Kril
Cheryl Lafrenière
Richard A. Lococo
Robert Macleod
Byrdena MacNeil
Wendy L. MacPherson
Theresa Maddalena
Lene Madsen
Mary Jo McLaren
Robert J. Nightingale
Dale Parayeski
Alex Pazaratz
Diana Piccoli
James A. Ramsay
Robert B. Reid
J. Wilma Scott
Elizabeth C. Sheard
Antonio Skarica
James W. Sloan
Ian Smith
Leanne E. Standryk
Gerald E. Taylor
Jacalyn D. Walters
Linda M. Walters

Central West Region
7755 Hurontario St., Brampton, ON L6W 4T6
Tel: 905-456-4837; *Fax:* 905-456-4836
Serving the communities of Brampton, Guelph, Milton, Orangeville, Owen Sound & Walkerton.
Regional Senior Justice:
The Hon. Leonard Ricchetti
Justices (The Hon. Mr./Madam Justice):

Irving W. André
Deena F. Baltman
Kofi N. Barnes
Thomas A. Bielby
Ivan S. Bloom
Roger Chown
Erika Chozik
Kendra D. Coats
Clayton Conlan
Peter A. Daley
Fletcher Dawson
Nancy L. Dennison
Michael T. Doi
Bruce Durno
Michael G. Emery
Dale F. Fitzpatrick
Judy A. Fowler Byrne
Joseph M. Fragomeni
David E. Harris
Suranganie Kumaranayake
Marvin Kurz
William Le May
Gordon D. Lemon
Renu J. Mandhane
Heather A. McGee
Lucy K. McSweeney
Gisele M. Miller
Nancy M. Mossip
Cynthia Peterson
David Price
M.J. Lucille Shaw
James Stribopoulos
John R. Sproat
Jamie K. Trimble
E. Ria Tzimas
Francine Van Melle
Jennifer Woollcombe

East Region
161 Elgin St., Ottawa, ON K2P 2K1
Tel: 613-239-1054; *Fax:* 613-239-1067
Serving the communities of Belleville, Brockville, Cornwall, Kingston, L'Orignal, Ottawa, Napanee, Pembroke, Perth & Picton.
Regional Senior Justice:
The Hon. Calum U.C. MacLeod
Justices (The Hon. Mr./Madam Justice):
Brian W. Abrams
Catherine D. Aitken
Julie Audet
Robert N. Beaudoin
Jennifer A. Blishen
Nathalie Champagne
Michel Z. Charbonneau
Sylvia Corthorn
Hélène C. Desormeau
Adriana Doyle
Tracy Engelking
Sally A. Gomery
Charles T. Hackland
Patrick Hurley
Martin S. James
John M. Johnston
Stanley J. Kershman
Marc R. Labrosse
Laurie Lacelle
Johanne Lafrance-Cardinal
Ronald M. Laliberté
Rick Leroy
Anne E. London-Weinstein
Pamela MacEachern
V. Jennifer MacKinnon
Wendy B. Malcolm
Robert L. Maranger
Hugh R. McLean
James E. McNamara
Graeme Mew
Timothy Minnema
Kristin Muszynski
Michelle O'Bonsawin
Julianne A. Parfett
Robert Pelletier
Kevin B. Phillips
Robert A. Riopelle
Cheryl Robertson
Pierre E. Roger
Robyn M. Ryan Bell
Robert F. Scott
Mark P. Shelston
Marc E. Smith
Robert J. Smith
Narissa Somji

Darlene L. Summers
Deborah Swartz
Nicole J. Tellier
Gary W. Tranmer
Anne C. Trousdale
Tami Waters
Heather J. Williams

Toronto Region
361 University Ave., Toronto, ON M5G 1T3
Tel: 416-327-5917; *Fax:* 416-327-9931
Serving the region of Toronto.
Regional Senior Justice:
The Hon. Stephen E. Firestone
Justices (The Hon. Mr./Madam Justice):
Jasmine T. Akbarali
Suhail A.Q. Akhtar
Beth A. Allen
Nancy L. Backhouse
Peter Bawden
Edward P. Belobaba
William Black
Susanne Boucher
Carole J. Brown
Michael F. Brown
Kelly P. Byrne
Kenneth L. Campbell
Peter J. Cavanagh
William S. Chalmers
Michael Code
Barbara A. Conway
Jill M. Copeland
David L. Corbett
Katherine B. Corrick
Bonnie L. Croll
George Czutrin
Michael R. Dambrot
Breese Davies
James F. Diamond
Bernadette Dietrich
Grant R. Dow
Todd Ducharme
Sean F. Dunphy
Mario D. Faieta
Lise G. Favreau
Jane Ferguson
Maureen D. Forestell
Nola E. Garton
Cory A. Gilmore
Benjamin T. Glustein
Robert F. Goldstein
Glenn A. Hainey
Susan G. Himel
Kenneth G. Hood
Carolyn J. Horkins
Jane E. Kelly
Jessica Kimmel
Frances P. Kiteley
Markus Koehnen
Melanie Kraft
Freya Kristjanson
Thomas R. Lederer
Janet Leiper
Wailan Low
Ian A. MacDonnell
Wendy M. Matheson
Rita-Jean Maxwell
Heather McArthur
Thomas J. McEwen
John B. McMahon
Anne M. Molloy
Patrick J. Monahan
Edward M. Morgan
Frederick L. Myers
Shaun S. Nakatsuru
E. Llana Nakonechny
Sandra Nishikawa
Shaun O'Brien
Alfred J. O'Marra
Brian P. O'Marra
Eugenia Papageogiou
Laurence A. Pattillo
Michael A. Penny
Paul M. Perell
Andrew Pinto
Andra Pollack
Jill Presser
Michael G. Quigley
Audrey P. Ramsey
Gillian E. Roberts
Harriet E. Sachs
Mary A. Sanderson

Andrew A. Sanfilippo
P. Andras Schreck
Paul B. Schabas
Mohan Sharma
Sharon Shore
Gertrude F. Spiegel
Nancy J. Spies
Jana Steele
Elizabeth M. Stewart
David G. Stinson
P. Tamara Sugunasiri
Katherine E. Swinton
Susan Vella
Marie-Andrée Vermette
Darla A. Wilson
Janet Wilson
Herman J. Wilton-Siegel

Northeast Region
155 Elm St., Sudbury, ON P3C 1T9
Tel: 705-564-7814; *Fax:* 705-564-7902
Serving the communities of Cochrane, Gore Bay, Haileyburt,
North Bay, Parry Sound, Sault Ste. Marie, Sudbury & Timmins.
Regional Senior Justice:
The Hon. M. Gregory Ellies
Justices (The Hon. Mr./Madam Justice):
Patrick Boucher
Victoria R. Chiappetta
R. Dan Cornell
Kathleen E. Cullin
Edward E. Gareau
Louise L. Gauthier
Robbie D. Gordon
Patricia C. Hennessy
Edward J. Koke
Alexander Kurke
Cindy A.M. MacDonald
David J. Nadeau
Annalisa Rasaiah
Paul U. Rivard
Robin Tremblay
Michael N. Varpio
James A.S. Wilcox

Northwest Region
125 Brodie St. North, Thunder Bay, ON P7C 0A3
Tel: 807-626-7083; *Fax:* 807-626-7090
Serving the communities of Fort Frances, Kenora & Thunder
Bay.
Regional Senior Justice:
The Hon. Bonnie R. Warkentin
Justices (The Hon. Mr./Madam Justice):
F. Bruce Fitzpatrick
John S. Fregeau
W. Danial Newton
Tracey Nieckarz
Helen Pierce
Douglas C. Shaw

Southwest Region
80 Dundas St., London, ON N6A 6A2
Tel: 519-660-3000; *Fax:* 519-660-3087
Serving the communities of Chatham, Goderich, London, Sarnia,
St. Thomas, Stratford, Windsor & Woodstock.
Regional Senior Justice:
The Hon. Bruce G. Thomas
Justices (The Hon. Mr./Madam Justice):
David Aston
Christopher Bondy
Scott K. Campbell
Thomas J. Carey
Maria V. Carroccia
John Desotti
Brian Dubé
Marc A. Garson
Jonathon C. George
Kelly A. Gorman
A. Duncan Grace
Pamela L. Hebner
Thomas A. Heeney
Paul J. Henderson
Paul R. Howard
George W. King
Denise M. Korpan
Ian F. Leach
Lynne Leitch
Michael D. McArthur
Alissa K. Mitchell
Victor Mitrow
Kirk W. Munroe
Spencer Nicholson
Renee M. Pomerance
Timothy G. Price

Helen A. Rady
Russell M. Raikes
Kiran Sah
Barry M. Tobin
Kelly C. Tranquilli
Gregory J. Verbeem

Ontario Court of Justice
60 Queen St. West, P.O. Box 91, Toronto, ON M5C 2W5
Tel: 416-327-5614
www.ontariocourts.on.ca/ocj
The Ontario Court of Justice generally performs functions
assigned to it by Acts such as the *Criminal Code* the *Provincial
Offences Act* the *Family Law Act* the *Children's Law Reform Act*
& the *Child & Family Services Act*. It is also a youth court. The
Lieutenant Governor in Council, on the recommendation of the
Attorney General, appoints the justices.
Chief Justice:
The Hon. Lise Maisonneuve
Associate Chief Justices:
The Hon. Aston J. Hall
The Hon. Sharon M. Nicklas
Senior Advisory Family Justice:
The Hon. Lise S. Parent

Central East Region
50 Eagle St. West, Newmarket, ON L3Y 6B1
Tel: 905-853-4801
Regional Senior Justice:
The Hon. Esther Rosenberg
Justices (The Hon.):
John F. Adamson
Cecile Applegate
Simon C. Armstrong
Robert W. Beninger
Jonathan Bliss
Philop J. Brissette
Jennifer Broderick
Paul Burstein
Edward A. Carlton
Paul M. Cooper
Lara A. Crawford
Nancy A. Dawson
Mary Teresa E. Devlin
Jon-Jo Douglas
Nyron Dwyer
Robert Gattrell
Amit A. Ghosh
Victor Giourgas
Brenda M. Green
Marcella Henschel
Ferhan Javed
Cynthia Johnston
Joseph F. Kenkel
Stuart W. Konyer
Susan M. Magotiaux
Angela L. McLeod
Enno J. Meijers
Mary E. Misener
Mark Moorcroft
Anastasia M. Nichols
John N. Olver
John A. Payne
Christine Pirraglia
Edward Prutschi
David S. Rose
Jessica E. Sickinger
Peter Tetley
Jodie-Lynn Waddilove
Peter C. West
Russell Wood

Central West Region
45 Main St. East, Hamilton, ON L8N 2B7
Tel: 905-645-5252
Regional Senior Justice:
The Hon. Paul R. Currie
Justices (The Hon.):
P.H. Marjoh Agro
Hafeez S. Amarshi
Kathleen A. Baker
Lesley M. Baldwin
W. James Blacklock
Stephen D. Brown
Harvey P. Brownstone
Deborah L. Calderwood
Ann-Marie Calsavara
Amanda J. Camara
Sandra Caponecchia
Michelle Cheung
Philip J. Clay
Sarah S. Cleghorn
Alan D. Cooper

Jennifer A. Crawford
Joseph A. De Filippis
Allison Dellandrea
Bruce W. Duncan
Gethin B. Edward
Kathryn A. Fillier
Joe P.P. Fiorucci
Jacqueline Freeman
Robert Gee
Colette D. Good
Kathryn L. Hawke
Aubrey D. Hilliard
Iona M. Jaffe
Khatira (Kathy) J. Jalali
Nancy S. Kastner
Sonia V. Khemani
Tanya M. Kranjc
Scott N. Latimer
Anthony F. Leitch
Alison R. MacKay
Sandra Martins
Kevin K. McCallum
Donald McLeod
Katherine L. McLeod
Shannon B. McPherson
Paul F. Monahan
Fergus C. O'Donnell
Paul T. O'Marra
Lise S. Parent
Bruce E. Pugsley
Mohammed M. Rahman
G. Paul Renwick
Lynn Robinson
Lynda J. Rogers
Richard H. K. Schwarzl
Victoria A. Starr
A. William J. Sullivan
Susan M. Sullivan
Graham Wakefield
R. Cameron B. Watson
Donald L. Wolfe
Bernd E. Zabel
Martha Zivolak

East Region
161 Elgin St., Ottawa, ON K2P 2L1
Tel: 613-239-1153
Regional Senior Justice:
The Hon. W. Vincent Clifford
Justices (The Hon.):
Ann Alder
David Berg
John D. Bonn
Julie Bourgeois
Normand D. Boxall
Trevor A. Brown
Jonathan Brunet
Frank D. Crewe
Marc D'Amours
Elaine Deluzio
Peter K. Doody
Célynne S. Dorval
Marlyse Dumel
Franco Giamberardino
Geoffrey Griffin
Mitch Hoffman
Stephen J. Hunter
Catherine A. Kehoe
Deborah A. Kinsella
Richard T. Knott
Diane M. Lahaie
Jean G. Legault
Allan G. Letourneau
Jacqueline Loignon
Michael G. March
Kimberly Moore
Janet O'Brien
Larry B. O'Brien
Heather E. Perkins-McVey
Gilles Renaud
Jeffery R. Richardson
Robert Wadden
Matthew C. Webber
Alison J. Wheeler

Northeast Region
#201, 159 Cedar St., Sudbury, ON P3E 6A5
Tel: 705-564-7600
Regional Senior Justice:
The Hon. Patrick J. Boucher
Justices (The Hon.):
Pierre Bradley
Andrew Buttazzoni

John P. Condon
Melanie D. Dunn
André L. Guay
Romuald F. Kwolek
Michel R. Labelle
Erin J. Lainevool
Randall W. Lalande
Martin P. Lambert
Joseph G. R. Maille
Catherine Mathias
Heather A. Mendes
Bonnie Oldham
Alain H. Perron
Michelle Rocheleau
Louise Serré
David A. Thomas
Robert P. Villeneuve
Jessica Wolfe

Northwest Region
125 Brodie St. North, Thunder Bay, ON P7C 0A3
Tel: 807-626-7000

Regional Senior Justice:
The Hon. David M. Gibson
Justices (The Hon.):
Evelyn J. Baxter
Claudia C. Belda Perez
Chantal M. Brochu
Elaine A.A. Burton
Jana-Rae Dewson
Joyce Elder
Jennifer R. Hoshizaki
Pieter Joubert
Danalyn J. MacKinnon
Joyce L. Pelletier
Vince Scaramuzza
Francesco Valente

Toronto Region
Old City Hall, #257, 60 Queen St. West, Toronto, ON M5H 2M4
Tel: 416-326-0111

Regional Senior Justice:
The Hon. Sandra Bacchus
Justices (The Hon.):
Patrice F. Band
Maureen H. Bellmore
Feroza Bhabha
Michael Block
Miriam Bloomenfeld
Howard Borenstein
Louise Botham
Joseph W. Bovard
Timotny E. Breen
Carol Brewer
Beverly A. Brown
Kathleen J. Caldwell
Michael Callaghan
James R. Chaffe
André Chamberlain
Leslie A.P. Chapin
Susan M. Chapman
Howard I. Chisvin
Steven R. Clark
Kimberley A. Crosbie
Carole Curtis
Peter J. DeFreitas
Antonio Di Zio
Kate Doorly
Philip Anthony Downes
Karen M. Erlick
Cidalia C. Faria
Lucia Favret
Lawrence T. Feldman
Marquis S.V. Felix
Faith M. Finnestad
Peter Fraser
Mara B. Greene
Rachel Grinberg
Mary L. Hogan
Derek Ishak
Carolyn J. Jones
Edward J. Kelly
Robert Kelly
Ramez Khawly
Neil L. Kozloff
Eric (Rick) N. Libman
David Maylor
John McInnes
Malcolm McLeod
Cathy Mocha
Lori B. Montague
Daniel F. Moore

John C. Moore
Katrina Mulligan
Apple Newton-Smith
John North
Sheilagh O'Connell
Diane I. Oleskiw
Debra A. W. Paulseth
Manjusha Pawagi
M. Samantha G. Peeris
David M. Porter
Heather F. Pringle
Leslie C. Pringle
Sheila Ray
Paul Robertson
Vincenzo Rondinelli
Rebecca Rutherford
Melanie Sager
Richard D. Schneider
Brian M. Scully
Riun Shandler
Stanley B. Sherr
Russell S. Silverstein
Maria N. Sirivar
Robert J. Spence
Maria Speyer
Jennifer D. Strasberg
Lori A. Thomas
Andrea Tuck-Jackson
Brian Weagant
Mavin Wong
Roselyn Zisman

West Region
80 Dundas St. East, London, ON N6A 6K1
Tel: 519-660-3013

Regional Senior Justice:
The Hon. Jeanine E. LeRoy
Justices (The Hon.):
Lorelei M. Amlin
Deborah J. Austin
Pamela Borghesan
Valerie L. Brown
Gregory A. Campbell
Michael B. Carnegie
Jane E. Caspers
Glen S. Donald
M. Edward Graham
Wendy L. Harris Bentley
Steven P. Harrison
Robert Horton
Karey Katzsch
Dominique Kennedy
Paul J. S. Kowalyshyn
Krista Leszcynski
Timothy G. Macdonald
Allan Maclure
Christine E.J Malott
Ronald A. Marion
Anne E.E. McFadyen
Kevin G. McHugh
A. Thomas McKay
Kathryn L. McKerlie
Julia A. Morneau
Sharon Murphy
Katherine S. Neill
George L. Orsini
Craig A. Parry
Stephen E.J. Paull
Douglas W. Phillips
Mark Poland
Shannon Pollock
Scott G. Pratt
Wayne G. Rabley
Nicole E. Redgate
Lynda S. Ross
Kevin Sherwood
Craig Sigurdson
Melanie A. Sopinka
Marnie Vickerd
Michael K. Wendl
Gerri Lynn Wong

Court Services Division
McMurtry-Scott Bldg., #204, 720 Bay St., Toronto, ON M7A 2S9
Tel: 416-326-4263
www.attorneygeneral.jus.gov.on.ca/english/courts
Court Services Division manages the court offices in communities across Ontario: scheduling court cases, maintaining records & files, collecting fines & fees, enforcing civil orders, & providing information to the public. It also provides administrative support to judicial offices in the Superior Court of

Justice & the Ontario Court of Justice: providing clerks, court reporters, registrars & interpreters for court proceedings.

Barrie
45 Cedar Pointe Dr., Barrie, ON L4N 5R7
Tel: 705-739-4291; *Fax:* 705-739-4292
poa.barrie@barrie.ca
www.barrie.ca/Living/Pages/Court-Services.aspx

Belleville - Hastings
235 Pinnacle St, 3rd Fl., Belleville, ON K8P 0C7
Tel: 613-966-0331; *Fax:* 613-966-7045
poa@hastingscounty.com
hastingscounty.com/services/provincial-offences

Bracebridge - Muskoka
76 Pine St., Bracebridge, ON P1L 0C4
Tel: 705-645-1231; *Fax:* 705-645-5319
poa@muskoka.on.ca

Brampton
5 Ray Lawson Blvd., Brampton, ON L6Y 5L7
Tel: 905-450-4770; *Fax:* 905-450-4794
provincialoffencescourt@brampton.ca
www.brantford.ca/en/your-government/provincial-offences-court. aspx
Other information: TTY: 905-874-2130

Brantford
102 Wellington St., P.O. Box 760, Brantford, ON N3T 5R7
Tel: 519-751-9100; *Fax:* 519-751-0404
brantfordpoa@brantford.ca
www.brantford.ca/en/your-government/provincial-offences-court. aspx

Brockville - Leeds & Grenville
#100, 32 Wall St., Brockville, ON K6V 4R9
Tel: 613-342-2357; *Fax:* 613-342-8891
Toll-Free: 800-539-8685
poacourt@uclg.on.ca
www.leedsgrenville.com/en/services/provincial-offences.aspx
Other information: TTY: 613-341-3854

Caledon East
6311 Old Church Rd., Caledon East, ON L7C 1J6
Tel: 905-584-2273; *Fax:* 905-584-2861
www.caledon.ca/en/government/poa.aspx

Cayuga - Haldimand
53 Thorburn St. South, Cayuga, ON N0A 1E0
Tel: 905-772-3327; *Fax:* 905-772-5810
poa@haldimandcounty.on.ca
www.haldimandcounty.ca/provincial-offences

Chatham - Kent
21633 Communication Rd., RR#5, Bleheim, ON N0P 1A0
Tel: 519-352-8484; *Fax:* 519-352-7979
ckpoc@chatham-kent.ca
www.chatham-kent.ca/localgovernment/poc/Pages/Contact-Info-and-Processes.aspx

Cobourg - Northumberland
860 William St., Cobourg, ON K9A 3A9
Tel: 905-372-3329; *Fax:* 905-372-6529
www.northumberlandcounty.ca

Cochrane
#1, 171 - 4th St., Cochrane, ON P0L 1C0
Tel: 705-272-2538; *Fax:* 705-272-3593
www.cochraneontario.com/town-hall/provincial-offences-office

Cornwall - Stormont, Dundas & Glengarry
#308, 26 Pitt St., Cornwall, ON K6J 3P2
Tel: 613-933-4301; *Fax:* 613-933-4161
courtservices@sdgcounties.ca
www.sdgcounties.ca/services/court-services

Dryden
30 Van Horne Ave., P.O. Box 105, Dryden, ON P8N 2A7
Tel: 807-223-1429; *Fax:* 807-223-5839
provincial_offences@dryden.ca
www.dryden.ca/en/city-services/provincial-offences-office.aspx

Durham
605 Rossland Rd. East, Lower Level, P.O. Box 740, Whitby, ON L1N 0B3
Tel: 905-668-3130; *Fax:* 905-668-3166
poa.courts@durham.ca
www.durham.ca

Elliot Lake & Espanola
#4, 100 Tudhope St., Espanola, ON P5E 1S6
Tel: 705-862-7875; *Fax:* 705-862-7876
www.espanola.ca/services/provincial-offences

Fort Frances
320 Portage Ave., Fort Frances, ON P9A 3P9
Tel: 807-274-1676; *Fax:* 807-274-0446
www.fort-frances.com

Goderich - Huron
1 Court House Sq., Goderich, ON N7A 1M2
Tel: 519-524-8394; *Fax:* 519-524-2044
poa@huroncounty.ca
www.huroncounty.ca/poa/provincial-offences-administration

Gore Bay
15 Water St., P.O. Box 500, Gore Bay, ON P0P 1H0
Tel: 705-282-2837; *Fax:* 705-282-3076
gorebaypoa@gorebay.ca
www.gorebay.ca/provincial-offences

Guelph
59 Carden St., Guelph, ON N1H 2Z9
Tel: 519-826-0762; *Fax:* 519-826-6814
courtservices@guelph.ca
guelph.ca/living/provincial-offences-court
Other information: TTY: 519-826-9771

Haileybury - Temiskaming Shores
325 Farr Dr., P.O. Box 2050, Haileybury, ON P0J 1K0
Tel: 705-672-3221; *Fax:* 705-672-2911
poa@temiskamingshores.ca
www.temiskamingshores.ca/en/city-hall/Provincial-Offences.aspx

Halton Region
4085 Palladium Way, Burlington, ON L7M 2A6
Tel: 905-637-1274; *Fax:* 905-637-5919
burlingtoncourt@burlington.ca
www.burlington.ca/en/halton-court-services/Halton-Home.asp

Hamilton
50 Main St. East, Hamilton, ON L8N 1E9
Tel: 905-540-5592; *Fax:* 905-540-5730
www.hamilton.ca

Kenora
1 Main St. South, Kenora, ON P9N 3X2
Tel: 807-467-2984; *Fax:* 807-467-8530
poa@kenora.ca
www.kenora.ca/en/your-government/provincial-offences.aspx

Kingston
362 Montreal St., Kingston, ON K7K 3H5
Tel: 613-547-8557; *Fax:* 613-547-8558
contactus@cityofkingston.ca
www.cityofkingston.ca/city-hall/provincial-offences-court
Other information: TTY: 613-546-4889

Kitchener - Waterloo Region
77 Queen St. North, Kitchener, ON N2H 2H1
Tel: 519-745-9446; *Fax:* 519-742-1112
www.regionofwaterloo.ca
Other information: TTY: 519-575-4607

L'Orignal - Prescott Russell
28 Court St., P.O. Box 347, L'Orignal, ON K0B 1K0
Tel: 613-675-4661; *Fax:* 613-675-4940
Toll-Free: 800-667-6307
lip-poa@prescott-russell.on.ca
en.prescott-russell.on.ca/services/provincial_offences

Lindsay - Kawartha Lakes
440 Kent St. West, Lindsay, ON K9V 5P2
Tel: 705-324-3962; *Fax:* 705-324-7991
poaadmin@kawarthalakes.ca
www.kawarthalakes.ca/en/municipal-services/provincial-offences
-and-tickets.aspx

London
824 Dundas St. East, London, ON N5W 5R1
Tel: 519-661-1882; *Fax:* 519-661-1944
poaadmin@london.ca
london.ca/provincial-offences

Mississauga
950 Burnhamthorpe Rd. West, Mississauga, ON L5C 3B4
Tel: 905-615-4500; *Fax:* 905-615-4038
www.mississauga.ca/services-and-programs/tickets-fines-and-pe
nalties

Napanee - Lennox & Addington
97 Thomas St. East, Napanee, ON K7R 4B9
Tel: 613-354-1672; *Fax:* 613-354-3112
court@lennox-addington.on.ca
www.lennox-addington.on.ca/offences

Newmarket - York Region
17150 Yonge St., 2nd Fl., Newmarket, ON L3Y 8V3
Tel: 905-898-0425; *Fax:* 905-898-5218
www.york.ca

North Bay
200 McIntyre St. East, P.O. Box 360, North Bay, ON P1B 8H8
Tel: 705-474-0626; *Fax:* 705-474-8302
poagroup@cityofnorthbay.ca
www.northbay.ca/services-payments/court-services

Orangeville
55 Zina St., Orangeville, ON L9W 1E5
Tel: 519-941-5808; *Fax:* 519-940-3685
dufferin.poa@caledon.ca
www.caledon.ca/en/government/poa.aspx
Other information: Caledon POA, Email:
caledon.poa@caledon.ca

Orillia
#10, 575 West St. South, Orillia, ON L3V 7N6
Tel: 705-326-2960; *Fax:* 705-326-3613
poa.orillia@barrie.ca
www.barrie.ca/Living/Pages/Court-Services.aspx

Ottawa
100 Constellation Cres., Ottawa, ON K2G 6J8
Tel: 613-580-2665; *Fax:* 613-580-2664
ottawa.ca

Owen Sound - Walkerton - Grey Bruce
595 - 9 Ave. East, Owen Sound, ON N4K 3E3
Tel: 519-376-3470; *Fax:* 519-376-0638
poa@grey.ca
www.grey.ca/traffic-tickets-provincial-offences

Parry Sound
52 Seguin St., Parry Sound, ON P2A 1B4
Tel: 705-746-2553; *Fax:* 705-746-7461
www.parrysound.ca/en/inside-town-hall/provincial-offences.asp

Pembroke - Renfrew
7 International Dr., Pembroke, ON K8A 6W5
Tel: 613-735-3482; *Fax:* 613-735-8484
poaoffice@countyofrenfrew.on.ca
www.countyofrenfrew.on.ca

Perth - Lanark
80 Gore St. East, Perth, ON K7H 1H9
Tel: 613-326-3122; *Fax:* 613-267-5635
poa@perth.ca
www.perth.ca/en/town-hall/Provincial-Offences.aspx

Peterborough
99 Simcoe St., Peterborough, ON K9H 2H3
poacourt@peterborough.ca
www.peterborough.ca/poa
Other information: Toll-Free Phone: 855-738-3755, ext. 2099

Picton - Prince Edward County
332 Main St., Picton, ON K0K 2T0
Tel: 613-476-2148; *Fax:* 613-476-8356

Richmond Hill - York
50 High Tech Rd., 1st Fl., Richmond Hill, ON L4B 4N7
Tel: 905-762-2105; *Fax:* 905-762-2106
www.york.ca

Sarnia - Lambton
Bldg. 1020, Western Sarnia-Lambton Research Park, #200S,
1086 Modeland Rd., Sarnia, ON N7S 6L2
Tel: 519-344-8880; *Fax:* 519-344-9379
poa@lambton-county.on.ca
www.lambtononline.ca/en/county-government/court-services.asp
x

Sault Ste Marie
99 Foster Dr., 1st Fl., P.O. Box 580, Sault Ste Marie, ON P6A
5N1
Tel: 705-541-7334; *Fax:* 705-759-5395
saultstemarie.ca/City-Hall/City-Departments/Legal/Provincial-Off
ences.aspx

Simcoe - Norfolk
#100, 185 Robinson St., Simcoe, ON N3Y 5L6
Tel: 519-426-5870; *Fax:* 519-427-5900
poa@norfolkcounty.ca
www.norfolkcounty.ca/government/provincial-offences-office

St Thomas - Elgin
480 Sunset Dr., St Thomas, ON N5R 0J5
Tel: 519-631-1460; *Fax:* 519-631-5088
poa@elgin-county.on.ca
www.elgincounty.ca/provincial-offences-administration

Stratford - Perth
1 Huron St., Stratford, ON N5A 5S4
Tel: 519-271-0531; *Fax:* 519-271-7993
poa@perthcounty.ca
www.perthcounty.ca

Sudbury
#102, 199 Larch St., Sudbury, ON P3A 5P3
Tel: 705-674-4455; *Fax:* 705-673-9505
poacourt@greatersudbury.ca
www.greatersudbury.ca/city-hall/provincial-offences-office

Thunder Bay
Victoriaville Mall, 101 South Syndicate Ave., P.O. Box 1600,
Thunder Bay, ON P7C 6A9
Tel: 807-625-2999; *Fax:* 807-623-7751
www.thunderbay.ca/en/city-hall/thunder-bay-court-services.aspx

Timmins
220 Algonquin Blvd. East, Timmins, ON P4N 1B3
Tel: 705-360-2620; *Fax:* 705-360-2694
poa@timmins.ca
www.timmins.ca/our_services/provincial_offences_centre

Toronto East
1530 Markham Rd., Main Fl., Toronto, ON M1B 3M4
Tel: 416-338-7320
poacourt@toronto.ca
www.toronto.ca/services-payments/tickets-fines-penalties
Other information: TTY: 416-338-7394

Toronto South
#12W, 60 Queen St. West, Toronto, ON M5H 2M3
Tel: 416-338-7320
poacourt@toronto.ca
www.toronto.ca/services-payments/tickets-fines-penalties
Other information: TTY: 416-338-7394

Toronto West
York Civic Centre, 2700 Eglinton Ave. West, Toronto, ON
M6M 1V1
Tel: 416-338-7320
poacourt@toronto.ca
www.toronto.ca/services-payments/tickets-fines-penalties
Other information: TTY: 416-338-7394

Welland - Niagara Region
445 East Main St., Welland, ON L3B 3X7
Tel: 905-687-6590; *Fax:* 905-687-6614
poainfo@niagararegion.ca
www.niagararegion.ca/living/provincial-offences

Windsor
350 City Hall Sq. West, Windsor, ON N9A 6S1
Tel: 519-255-6555; *Fax:* 519-255-6556
www.citywindsor.ca/cityhall/legal-services-/Provincial-Offences

Woodstock - Oxford
P.O. Box 1614, Woodstock, ON N4S 7Y3
Tel: 519-537-4890; *Fax:* 519-537-3024
poa@oxfordcounty.ca
oxfordcounty.ca/Services-for-You/Fines-Provincial-Offences

Prince Edward Island

Prince Edward Island Supreme Court
Sir Louis Henry Davies Law Courts Bldg., 42 Water St., P.O.
Box 2000, Charlottetown, PE C1A 7N8
Tel: 902-368-6000; *Fax:* 902-368-6123
www.courts.pe.ca/supreme-court
The Supreme Court is a Court of original jurisdiction & has
jurisdiction in all civil (including family, estate & small claims) &
criminal matters arising in Prince Edward Island.
Chief Justice:
Tracey L. Clements
Justices (The Hon. Mr./Madam Justice):
Gregory A. Cann
Gordon Campbell (Supernumerary)
Wayne D. Cheverie (Supernumerary)
James W. Gormley
Nancy L. Key
Terri A. MacPherson
Jacqueline R. Matheson (Supernumerary)
Administration:
Prothonotary: Karen Rose
Manager: Court Services, Kerrilee MacConnell
kdmacconnell@gov.pe.ca

Prince Edward Island Court of Appeal
Sir Louis Henry Davies Law Courts Bldg., 42 Water St., P.O.
Box 2000, Charlottetown, PE C1A 7N8
Tel: 902-368-6000; *Fax:* 902-368-6123
www.courts.pe.ca/court-of-appeal
The Court of Appeal is the highest court in the province. It has
appellate jurisdiction in criminal & civil matters.
Chief Justice:
The Hon. David H. Jenkins
Justices (The Hon. Mr./Madam Justice):
John K. Mitchell
Michele M. Murphy
Administration:
Prothonotary: Karen A. Rose
kjmackay@gov.pe.ca
Deputy Registrar & Docket Clerk: Sheila Gallant
sfgallant@gov.pe.ca
Deputy Registrar: Roxanne Smith
rmsmith@gov.pe.ca

Prince Edward Island Provincial Court
Kelly Bldg., 3 Harbourside Access Rd., P.O. Box 2000, Charlottetown, PE C1N 7N8

Tel: 902-368-6030; Fax: 902-368-6210
www.courts.pe.ca/provincial-court

The Provincial Court has jurisdiction in select criminal matters as well as youth matters.

Chief Judge:
Nancy K. Orr
Judges (The Hon.):
Jeffrey E. Lantz
Krista J. MacKay

Courts:
Georgetown
Kings County Courthouse, 60 Kent St., P.O. Box 70, Georgetown, PE C0A 1L0

Tel: 902-652-8990; Fax: 902-652-8992

Summerside
108 Central St., Summerside, PE C1N 3L4

Tel: 902-888-8190; Fax: 902-888-8222

Québec

Cour Supérieure du Québec
Québec Superior Court
300, boul Jean-Lesage, Québec, QC G1K 8K6

Tél: 418-649-3400; Téléc: 418-528-0932
coursuperieureduquebec.ca

Affaires civiles et commerciales dont l'enjeu est de 70 000$ ou plus; litiges en matières administratives et familiale, faillite, procès devant jury en matière pénale, et appels en matière de poursuites sommaires

Juge en chef:
Jacques R. Fournier October 1, 2002
Juge en chef associée:
Catherine La Rosa October 1, 2019
Juge en chef adjointe:
Eva Petras December 15, 2006
Juges (Les honorables):
Johanne April May 18, 2010
Jacques Babin (Surnuméraire) November 28, 1995
Nancy Bonsaint January 30, 2020
Pierre C. Bellavance November 7, 2013
France Bergeron October 1, 2009
Lise Bergeron October 4, 2012
Jacques Blanchard November 2, 2012
Claude Bouchard (Surnuméraire) October 22, 2004
Jacques G. Bouchard November 2, 2012
Philippe Cantin March 4, 2020
Michel Caron (Surnuméraire) June 20, 2000
Guy De Blois April 10, 2014
Louis Dionne February 7, 2013
Daniel Dumais April 10, 2014
Jean-François Émond May 14, 2009
Marie-Paule Gagnon July 14, 2017
Isabelle Germain May 13, 2020
Bernard Godbout (Surnuméraire) March 1, 2001
Richard Grenier (Surnuméraire) June 23, 1998
Éric Hardy August 29, 2018
Suzanne Hardy-Lemieux (Surnuméraire) July 15, 1998
Simon Hébert May 28, 2015
François Huot July 29, 2009
Denis Jacques (Surnuméraire) April 1, 2004
Michèle Lacroix (Surnuméraire) June 6, 2000
Manon Lavoie December 17, 2013
Alain Michaud May 18, 2010
Marie-Hélène Montminy September 30, 2020
Benoit Moulin March 19, 2002
Pierre Ouellet (Surnuméraire) May 14, 2009
Suzanne Ouellet September 29, 2005
Marc Paradis November 2, 2012
Claudia P. Prémont March 4, 2020
Clément Samson December 15, 2011
Alicia Soldevila September 14, 2006
Damien St-Onge March 7, 2019
Carl Thibault November 29, 2017
Bernard Tremblay June 30, 2015
Marie-France Vincent June 22, 2017

Abitibi—Rouyn-Noranda—Témiscamingue
QC
Juges (Les honorables):
Robert Dufresne December 23, 2006
Isabelle Breton November 29, 2017
Nathalie Pelletier August 29, 2018

Alma
QC
Juges (Les honorables):
Sandra Bouchard November 2, 2012

Baie-Comeau—Mingan
QC
Juges (Les honorables):
Serge Francoeur May 22, 2010

Beauharnois
QC
Juges (Les honorables):
François P. Duprat April 5, 2012

Chicoutimi
QC
Juges (Les honorables):
Martin Dallaire July 29, 2009
Carl Lachance (Surnuméraire) October 22, 2004
Jocelyn Pilote May 13, 2020
Nicole Tremblay December 11, 2014

Drummond
QC
Juges (Les honorables):
Steve J. Reimnitz December 13, 2007

Gatineau—Pontiac—Labelle
QC
Juges (Les honorables):
Marie-Josée Bédard June 20, 2015
Pierre Dallaire (Surnuméraire) July 30, 2008
Jean Faullem June 20, 2019
Dominique Goulet April 27, 2007
Pierre Isabelle (Surnuméraire) February 16, 1999
Catherine Mandeville May 14, 2009
Suzanne Tessier June 5, 2007
Carole Therrien December 2, 2011

Joliette
QC
Juges (Les honorables):
Pierre Labelle May 9, 2014

Laval
QC
Juges (Les honorables):
Christiane Alary May 13, 2003
Chantal Chatelain July 1, 2015
Jean-Yves Lalonde (Surnuméraire) November 5, 2003

Longueuil
QC
Juges (Les honorables):
Pierre-C. Gagnon (Surnuméraire) December 12, 2002
Carole Julien (Surnuméraire) November 1, 1994
Chantal Lamarche April 10, 2014
Chantal Masse November 29, 2006
Sophie Picard April 27, 2007

Montréal
QC
Juges (Les honorables):
Louisa Arcand June 19, 2009
Marie-Claude Armstrong April 10, 2014
Babak Barin July 10, 2015
Guylène Beaugé March 2, 2007
Philippe Bélanger November 18, 2020
Pierre A. Béliveau May 21, 2021
Charles Bienvenu April 26, 2021
Donald Bisson April 10, 2014
Marc-André Blanchard March 2, 2007
Alexandre Boucher June 29, 2015
Sophie Bourque February 25, 2005
Gabrielle Brochu June 29, 2021
Christian J. Brossard October 4, 2012
James I. Brunton (Surnuméraire) February 27, 2003
Patrick Buchholz June 27, 2019
Robert Castiglio (Surnuméraire) December 11, 2008
Martin Castonguay June 22, 2007
France Charbonneau (Surnuméraire) February 26, 2004
Louis Charette June 29, 2021
Carol Cohen (Surnuméraire) November 4, 1997
David R. Collier October 20, 2011
Silvana Conte July 5, 2015
Chantal Corriveau February 25, 2005
Suzanne Courchesne October 9, 2014
François Dadour October 20, 2017
Marc David November 23, 2005
Thomas M. Davis September 29, 2011
Lyne Décarie December 6, 2018
Katheryne Alexandra Desfossés September 30, 2020
Michel Déziel (Surnuméraire) November 5, 2003
Tiziana Di Donato September 30, 2020
Hélène Di Salvo December 13, 2012
Éric Downs June 16, 2016
Jean-Guy Dubois (Surnuméraire) January 29, 1997
Gérard Dugré January 22, 2009
France Dulude October 4, 2012
Guylaine Duplessis December 6, 2018

Jeffrey Edwards June 2, 2019
Benoît Emery (Surnuméraire) December 12, 2002
Jérôme Frappier April 4, 2018
Anne-France Gagnon June 2, 2019
Serge Gaudet May 29, 2015
Marie Gaudreau (Surnuméraire) September 16, 2003
Louis J. Gouin (Surnuméraire) February 3, 2011
Lukasz Granosik December 11, 2014
Carole Hallée (Surnuméraire) November 7, 2001
Judith Harvie June 2, 2019
Marie-Christine Hivon June 27, 2019
Christian Immer March 7, 2019
Anne Jacob July 20, 2015
Bernard Jolin December 11, 2020
Karen Kear Jodoin March 7, 2013
Pierre Labrie February 7, 2013
Myriam Lachance October 26, 2017
Stéphane Lacoste June 27, 2019
Louis Lacoursière (Surnuméraire) December 12, 2002
Marie-Claude Lalande April 5, 2012
Julien Lanctôt (Surnuméraire) June 23, 1998
Mario Longpré July 14, 2017
Florence Lucas June 19, 2015
Sylvain Lussier August 31, 2018
Johanne Mainville November 22, 2006
Paul Mayer June 18, 2008
Danièle Mayrand (Surnuméraire) March 1, 2001
Michèle Monast (Surnuméraire) February 28, 2000
Gregory Moore March 24, 2017
Gary D.D. Morrison April 5, 2012
Geeta Narang December 11, 2020
Pascale Nolin January 18, 2018
Pierre Nollet April 23, 2010
Maire-Anne Paquette August 6, 2010
Daniel W. Payette July 3, 2008
Michel Pennou February 27, 2015
Micheline Perrault June 18, 2010
Catherine Perreault December 11, 2020
Eliane B. Perreault December 17, 2013
Janick Perreault March 7, 2019
Frédéric Pérodeau December 11, 2020
Mark Phillips April 3, 2020
Michel A. Pinsonnault December 7, 2013
David E. Platts April 4, 2018
Alexander Pless September 30, 2020
Yves Poirier June 19, 2009
Dominique Poulin March 7, 2019
Yvan Poulin June 29, 2021
André Prévost (Surnuméraire) December 9, 2004
Aline U.K. Quach June 8, 2017
Marie-Claude Rigaud May 21, 2021
Brian J. Riordan (Surnuméraire) December 9, 2004
Karen M. Rogers May 3, 2017
André Roy (Surnuméraire) November 5, 2003
Daniel Royer May 6, 2017
Martin F. Sheehan March 7, 2019
Johanne St-Gelais September 30, 2010
Marc St-Pierre June 18, 2008
Bernard Synnott August 31, 2018
Chantal Tremblay May 29, 2015
Daniel Urbas June 29, 2021
Sébastien Vaillancourt November 7, 2018
André Vincent (Surnuméraire) May 10, 2007
André Wery (Surnuméraire) November 4, 1997
Michel Yergeau May 31, 2012

Richelieu—St-Hyacinthe
QC
Juges (Les Honorables):
Louis-Paul Cullen November 22, 2006

Rimouski
QC
Juges (Les honorables):
Daniel Beaulieu November 2, 2012
Gilles Blanchet (Surnuméraire) November 28, 1995

St-François—Bedford—Mégantic - Granby
QC
Juges (Les honorables):
Johanne Brodeur December 19, 2017
Claude Dallaire September 9, 2009

St-Maurice
QC
Juges (Les honorables):
Étienne Parent December 15, 2006
Raymond W. Pronovost (Surnuméraire) January 29, 1997

St-François—Bedford—Mégantic - Sherbrooke
QC
Juges (Les honorables):
Martin Bureau (Surnuméraire) September 16, 2003
Gaétan Dumas September 24, 2004

Charles Ouellet *June 24, 2011*
Sylvain Provencher *June 19, 2015*
Line Samoisette *February 20, 2008*
Claude Villeneuve *June 19, 2015*

Terrebonne
QC
Juges (Les honorables):
Claude Auclair (Surnuméraire) *September 24, 2004*
Annie Breault *April 26, 2021*
Jean-François Michaud *February 7, 2013*
Élise Poisson *October 9, 2014*
Danielle Turcotte *September 9, 2009*

Trois-Rivières
QC
Juges (Les honorables):
Alain Bolduc *September 6, 2010*
Danye Daigle *June 19, 2015*
Jocelyn Geoffroy *February 20, 2008*

Cour du Québec
Court of Québec
300, boul Jean-Lesage, Québec, QC G1K 8K6
Tél: 418-643-5140*Ligne sans frais:* 866-536-5140
info@courduquebec.ca
courduquebec.ca
Composée d'au plus 290 juges dont le juge en chef, le juge en chef associé, 4 juges en chef adjoints, et 18 juges coordonnateurs et coordonnateurs adjoints; matières civile, criminelle et pénale; matière de jeunesse; matière administrative ou en appel dans les cas prévus par la loi; cour d'archives.
Juges en chef:
Lucie Rondeau
Chantale Pelletier (Juge en chef adjointe)
Juge coordonnateurs (Les honorables):
Jean-Louis Lemay
Pierre A. Gagnon (Juge coordonnateur adjoint)
José Rhéaume (Juge coordonnateur adjoint)
Palais de Justice de Québec Juges (Les honorables):
Jean Asselin
Pascal Bérubé
Hélène Bouillon
Christian Boulet
Hélène Bourassa
Christian Boutin
Christian Brunelle
Hélène Carrier
Louis Charette
Sarah-Julie Chicoine
Pierre Coderre
Sylvie Côté
Fannie Côtes
René de la Sablonnière
Réna Émond
Rachel Gagnon
Marie-Claude Gilbert
Chantal Gosselin
Thomas Jacques
Judith Landry
Nathalie Lavoie
François LeBel
Louise Lévesque
Steve Magnan
Dominic Pagé
Stéphane Poulin
Sandra Rioux
Dominic Roux
Johanne Roy
Charles Taschereau
Jacques Tremblay
Mario Tremblay
Annie Trudel
Julie Vachon
Nathalie Vaillant
Palais de Justice de Saint-Joseph-de-Beauce Juges (Hon.):
Frank D'Amours

Abitibi-Témiscamingue - Amos
891, 3e rue ouest, Amos, QC J9T 2T4
Tél: 819-444-5577; *Téléc:* 819-444-5204
Juges (Les honorables):
Marie-Chantal Brassard
Lucille Chabot (Juge coordonnatrice)
Marc Ouimette
Thierry Roland Potvin

Abitibi-Témiscamingue - Rouyn-Noranda
2, av du Palais, Rouyn-Noranda, QC J9X 2N9
Tél: 819-763-3058; *Téléc:* 819-763-3389
Juges (Les honorables):
Marie-Claude Bélanger
Marc E. Grimard
Peggy Warolin

Abitibi-Témiscamingue - Val d'Or
900, 7e rue, Val d'Or, QC J9P 3P8
Tél: 819-354-4462; *Téléc:* 819-354-4447
Juges (Les honorables):
Denise Descôteaux
Jean-Pierre Gervais
Jacques Ladouceur
Christian Leblanc
Renée Lemoine

Bas-Saint-Laurent—Côte-Nord—Gaspésie—Iles-de-la-Madeleine - Baie-Comeau
71, av Mance, Baie-Comeau, QC G4Z 1N2
Tél: 418-296-5534; *Téléc:* 418-294-8717
Ligne sans frais: 866-854-4075
Juges (Les honorables):
Sonia Bérubé (Juge coordonnatrice adjointe)
François Boisjoli
Annick Boivin

Bas-Saint-Laurent—Côte-Nord—Gaspésie—Iles-de-la-Madeleine - Matane
382, av Saint-Jérôme, Matane, QC G4W 3B3
Tél: 418-562-2497; *Téléc:* 418-560-8746
Juges (Les honorables):
Jules Berthelot

Bas-Saint-Laurent—Côte-Nord—Gaspésie—Iles-de-la-Madeleine - New Carlisle
#103, 87, boul Gérard-D.-Lévesque, New Carlisle, QC G0C 1Z0
Tél: 418-752-3376; *Téléc:* 418-752-6979
Juges (Les honorables):
Celestina Almeida
Janick Poirier

Bas-Saint-Laurent—Côte-Nord—Gaspésie—Iles-de-la-Madeleine - Percé
124, rte 132, Percé, QC G0C 2L0
Tél: 418-782-2055; *Téléc:* 418-782-2906
Juges (Les honorables):
Denis Paradis

Bas-Saint-Laurent—Côte-Nord—Gaspésie—Iles-de-la-Madeleine - Rimouski
183, av de la Cathédrale, Rimouski, QC G5L 5J1
Tél: 418-727-3852; *Téléc:* 418-727-3635
Juges (Les honorables):
Richard Côté
Lucie Morissette
James Rondeau
Andrée St-Pierre

Bas-Saint-Laurent—Côte-Nord—Gaspésie—Iles-de-la-Madeleine - Rivière-du-Loup
33, rue de la Cour, Rivière-du-Loup, QC G5R 1J1
Tél: 418-862-3579; *Téléc:* 418-867-8794
Ligne sans frais: 800-463-8009
Juges (Les honorables):
Martin Gagnon (Juge coordonnateur)
Luce Kennedy
Hermina Popescu

Bas-Saint-Laurent—Côte-Nord—Gaspésie—Iles-de-la-Madeleine - Sept-Iles
425, boul Laure, Sept-Iles, QC G4R 1X6
Tél: 418-962-3044; *Téléc:* 418-964-8714
Ligne sans frais: 866-405-7951
Juges (Les honorables):
Nathalie Aubry
Louise Gallant
Vicky Lapierre

Estrie - Drummondville
1680, boul Saint-Joseph, Drummondville, QC J2C 2G3
Tél: 819-478-2513; *Téléc:* 819-475-8459
Juges (Les honorables):
Marie-Pierre Jutras
Gilles Lafrenière (Juge coordonnateur)
Marie-Josée Ménard

Estrie - Granby
Édifice Roger-Paré, #1.32, 77, rue Principale, Granby, QC J2G 9B3
Tél: 450-776-7110; *Téléc:* 450-776-4080
Juges (Les honorables):
Julie Beauchesne
Pascale Berardino
Serge Champoux

Estrie - Sherbrooke
375, rue King ouest, Sherbrooke, QC J1H 6B9
Juges (Les honorables):
Madeleline Aubé
Catherine Brousseau
Danielle Côté

Claire Desgens
Paul Dunnigan
Hélène Fabi
Benoit Gagnon
Lise Gagnon
Sophie Lapierre
Monique Lavallée
Martin Tétreault
Patrick Théroux

Laval—Lanaudière—Laurentides—Labelle - Joliette
200, rue Saint-Marc, Joliette, QC J6E 8C2
Juges (Les honorables):
Normand Bonin
Patrick Choquette
Sophie Gravel
Luc Joly
Claude Lachapelle
François Landry
Denis Le Reste
Bruno Leclerc
Jean Roy

Laval—Lanaudière—Laurentides—Labelle - Laval
2800, boul Saint-Martin ouest, Laval, QC H7T 2S9
Tél: 450-686-5006
Juge en chef adjointe:
Claudie Bélanger
Juge coordonnateurs adjoint (Les honorables):
Benoit Sabourin
Juges (Les honorables):
Maria Albanese
Serge Cimon
Marc-André Dagenais
Johanne Gagnon
Gilles Garneau
Yanick Laramée
Dominique Larochelle
Marie-Suzanne Lauzon
Lisa Leroux
Julie Messier
Yvan Nolet
Daniel Villeneuve

Laval—Lanaudière—Laurentides—Labelle - Saint-Jérôme
25, rue de Martigny ouest, Saint-Jérôme, QC J7Y 4Z1
Juge coordonnateurs (Les honorables):
Élaine Bolduc
Michel Bellehumeur (Juge coordonnateur adjoint)
Juges (Les honorables):
Chantale Beaudin
Marie-Pierre Bellemare
Sandra Blanchard
Pierre Cliche
Éric Côté
Kathlyn Gauthier
Pierre Hamel
Denis Lapierre
Francine Lauzé
Sophie Lavergne
Sylvain Lépine
Ginette Maillet
Jean-François Mallette
Nancy McKenna
Dany Pilon
Diane Roux
Michèle Toupin
Jimmy Vallée

Mauricie—Bois-Francs—Centre-du-Québec - Shawinigan
212, 6e rue de la Pointe, Shawinigan, QC G9N 8B6
Tél: 819-536-2571; *Téléc:* 819-536-2992
Juges (Les honorables):
Annie Vanasse

Mauricie—Bois-Francs—Centre-du-Québec - Trois-Rivières
850, rue Hart, Trois-Rivières, QC G9A 1T9
Tél: 819-372-4153
Juge coordonnateurs (Les honorables):
David Bouchard (Juge coordonnateur)
Juges (Les honorables):
Pierre Allen
Maryse Brouillette
Jacques Lacoursière
Daniel Perreault
Simon Ricard
Jacques Rioux
Dominique Slater
Alain Trudel
Jacques Trudel

Mauricie—Bois-Francs—Centre-du-Québec - Victoriaville
800, boul Bois-Francs sud, Victoriaville, QC G6P 5W5
Tél: 819-357-2054; *Téléc:* 819-357-5517
Juges (Les honorables):

Pierre Labbé
Bruno Langelier

Montérégie - Longueuil
1111, boul Jacques-Cartier est, Longueuil, QC J4M 2J6
Tél: 450-646-4010; Téléc: 450-928-7982
Juge en chef adjoint:
Robert Proulx (Juge en chef adjoint)
Juge coordonnateurs (Les honorables):
Mélanie Roy
Julie-Maude Greffe (Juge coordonnatrice adjointe)
Juges (Les honorables):
François Arteau-Gauthier
Jean-Pierre Authier
Ann-Mary Beauchemin
Marc Bisson
Marc-Antoine Carette
Serge Délisle
Nathalie Drouin
Dominique Dudemaine
Monique Dupuis
Francine Gendron
Mario Gervais
Stéphane Godri
Anne-Marie Jacques
Marco LaBrie
Dannie Leblanc
Louise Leduc
Magali Lepage
Daniel Lévesque
Nancy Moreau
Lyne Morin
Chantal Sirois
Luc Hervé Thibaudeau

Montérégie - Saint-Hyacinthe
1550, rue Dessaulles, Saint-Hyacinthe, QC J2S 2S8
Tél: 450-778-6585
Juges (Les honorables):
Annick Bergeron
Gilles Charpentier
Benoît Gariépy
Suzanne Paradis

Montérégie - Saint-Jean-sur-Richelieu
109, rue Saint-Charles, Saint-Jean-sur-Richelieu, QC J3B 2C2
Juges (Les honorables):
Christel d'Auteuil-Jobin
Luc Poirier
Éric Simard

Montérégie - Salaberry-de-Valleyfield
74, rue Académie, Salaberry-de-Valleyfield, QC J6T 0B8
Tél: 450-370-4006; Téléc: 450-370-3022
Ligne sans frais: 866-455-1585
Juge coordonnateurs adjoint (Les honorables):
Céline Gervais
Juges (Les honorables):
Béatrice Clément
Marie-Chantal Doucet
Joey Dubois
Éric Hamel
Gilbert Lanthier
Claude Montpetit
Bernard St-Arnaud

Montréal
1, rue Notre-Dame est, Montréal, QC H2Y 1B6
Tél: 514-393-2721; Téléc: 514-873-4760
Juges en chef:
Scott Hughes (Juge en chef associé)
Martine L. Tremblay (Juge en chef adjointe)
Juge coordonnateurs (Les honorables):
Daniel Bédard
Marie-Julie Croteau (Juge coordonnateur adjoint)
Nathalie Fafard (Juge coordonnatrice adjointe)
Odette Fafard (Juge coordonnatrice adjointe)
Dominique B. Joly (Juge coordonnatrice adjointe)
Palais de Justice de Montréal juges (Les honorables):
Claudine Alcindor
Josée Bélanger
Martin Bergeron
Daniel Bourgeois
Alain Breault
David L. Cameron
Nathalie Chalifour
Patricia Compagnone
Suzanne Costom
Sylvain Coutlée
Éric Couture
Marie-Julie Croteau
Alexandre Dalmau
Stéphane Davignon

Manlio Del Negro
Linda Despots
Marie-Josée Di Lallo
Daniel Dortélus
Nathalie Duchesneau
Éric Dufour
Pierre Dupras
Sylvie Durand
Enrico Forlini
Gatien Fournier
Jean-Jacques Gagné
Dennis Galiatsatos
Dominique Gibbens
Karine Giguère
Geneviève Graton
Mylène Grégoire
Yves Hamel
Mélanie Hébert
Luc Huppé
Ann-Marie Jones (Présidente)
Silvie Kovacevich
Pierre E. Labelle
Sylvie Lachapelle
Anne-Marie Lanctôt
Gilles Lareau
Marie Michelle Lavigne
Magali Lewis
Flavia K. Longo
Robert Marchi (Vice-présidente)
Eliana Marengo
Salvatore Mascia
Sonia Mastro Matteo
Denis Mondor
Hélène V. Morin
Thierry Nadon
Yves Paradis
André Perreault
Julie Philippe
Catherine Pilon
Henri Richard
Julie Riendeau
Louis Riverin
Guylaine Rivest
Jean-François Roberge
Joëlle Roy
Emmanuelle Saucier
Mark Shamie
David Simon
Alexandre St-Onge
Christian M. Tremblay
Érick Vanchestein
Julie Veilleux (Président)
Lori Renée Weitzman
Jo Ann Zaor
Chambre de la jeunesse à Montréal Juges (Les honorables):
Marie Archambault
Line Bachand
Éric Beauparlant
Alain Brillon
Taya di Pietro
Louis Grégoire
Paul Grzela
Robert Hamel
Patrice Hurtubise
Pauline Reinhardt Laforce
Claude Lamoureux
Jacques A. Nadeau
Martine Nolin
Karen Ohayon
Anne-Marie Otis
Anne-Claire Perron
Jacky Roy
Annie Savard
François Ste-Marie

Outaouais - Gatineau
17, rue Laurier, Gatineau, QC J8X 4C1
Juge coordonnateurs (Les honorables):
Richard Laflamme
Juges (Les honorables):
Patsy Bouthillette
Anouk Desaulniers
Karine Dutilly
Steve Guénard
Gaston Paul Langevin
Serge Laurin
Alexandra Marcil
Richard Meredith
Sylvain Meunier
Rosemarie Millar
Jean-François Noël
Mark Philippe

Nadine Piché
Stéphane D. Tremblay

Saguenay—Lac-Saint-Jean - Alma
725, rue Harvey ouest, Alma, QC G8B 1P5
Tél: 418-668-3334; Téléc: 418-662-3697
Juge coordonnateurs (Les honorables):
Jean Hudon

Saguenay—Lac-Saint-Jean - Chicoutimi
227, rue Racine est, 1e étage, Chicoutimi, QC G7H 7B4
Tél: 418-696-9926; Téléc: 418-698-3558
Juges (Les honorables):
Kathy Beaumont
Isabelle Boillat
Michel Boudreault
Richard P. Daoust
Paul Guimond
Pierre Lortie
Sonia Rouleau
Doris Thibault

Saguenay—Lac-Saint-Jean - Roberval
750, boul Saint-Joseph, Roberval, QC G8H 2L5
Tél: 418-275-3666; Téléc: 418-275-6169
Juges (Les honorables):
Jean-François Poirier

Points de service de justice
Judicial Service Centres
QC

Points de service:
Amqui
29, boul Saint-Benoît ouest, Amqui, QC G5J 2E4
Tél: 418-629-4488; Téléc: 418-629-6450

Dolbeau-Mistassini
1420, boul Walberg, 1e étage, Dolbeau-Mistassini, QC G8L 1H4
Tél: 418-276-0683; Téléc: 418-276-6110

Forestville
134, rte 138 est, P.O. Box 400, Forestville, QC G0T 1E0
Tél: 418-587-4471; Téléc: 418-587-6639

Gaspé
#101, 11, rue de la Cathédrale, Gaspé, QC G4X 2V9
Tél: 418-368-5756; Téléc: 416-360-8030

Lachute
#216, 505, av Béthany, Lachute, QC J8H 4A6
Tél: 450-562-3711; Téléc: 450-569-7645

Magog
Hôtel de Ville, #127, 7, rue Principale est, Magog, QC J1X 1Y4
Tél: 819-843-7323; Téléc: 819-843-4533

Matane
382, av Saint-Jérôme, Matane, QC G4W 3B3
Tél: 418-562-2497; Téléc: 418-560-8746

Mont-Joli
40, rue de l'Hôtel-de-ville, Mont-Joli, QC G5H 1W8
Tél: 418-775-8811; Téléc: 418-775-7517

Sainte-Agathe-des-Monts
85, rue Saint-Vincent, Sainte-Agathe-des-Monts, QC J8C 2A8
Tél: 819-326-6462; Téléc: 450-569-7645

Sainte-Anne-des-Monts
10B, boul Sainte-Anne ouest, Sainte-Anne-des-Monts, QC G4V 1P3
Tél: 418-763-2791; Téléc: 418-763-3107

Cour d'Appel du Québec
Québec Court of Appeal
Édifice Ernest-Cormier, 100, rue Notre-Dame est, Montréal, QC H2Y 4B6
Tél: 514-393-2022; Téléc: 514-864-7270
courdappelmtl@judex.qc.ca
courdappelduquebec.ca

Le plus haut tribunal du Québec; la cour est la gardienne de l'intégrité du droit civil de la province; en matière civile, la cour entend les appels des jugements finals de la Cour supérieure et de la Cour du Québec lorsque la valeur de l'objet du litige en appel est à 50 000$ ou plus; outrage, adoption, évaluation psychiatrique, garde en établissement, faillite et divorce.
Juge en chef:
Manon Savard *April 25, 2013*
Juges (Les honorables):
Jacques Chamberland (Surnuméraire) *June 10, 1993*
France Thibault (Surnuméraire) *December 1, 1998*
François Pelletier (Surnuméraire) *June 6, 2000*
Yves-Marie Morissette (Surnuméraire) *November 7, 2002*
Allan Ross Hilton (Surnuméraire) *September 26, 2003*

François Doyon (Surnuméraire) *May 7, 2004*
Marie-France Bich (Surnuméraire) *September 24, 2004*
Julie Dutil (Surnuméraire) *September 24, 2004*
Guy Gagnon *September 27, 2009*
Jean Bouchard (Surnuméraire) *October 1, 2009*
Dominique Bélanger (Surnuméraire) *November 2, 2012*
Jacques J. Levesque (Surnuméraire) *November 2, 2012*
Martin Vauclair *December 17, 2013*
Geneviève Marcotte *April 10, 2014*
Mark Schrager *June 13, 2014*
Robert Mainville *July 1, 2014*
Marie-Josée Hogue *June 19, 2015*
Patrick Healy *October 19, 2016*
Jocelyn F. Rancourt *June 21, 2017*
Simon Ruel *June 21, 2017*
Suzanne Gagné *November 29, 2017*
Geneviève Cotnam *June 26, 2018*
Stephen Hamilton *August 29, 2018*
Stéphane Sansfaçon *January 31, 2019*
Michel Beaupré *March 8, 2019*
Lucie Fournier *June 22, 2019*
Benoît Moore *June 22, 2019*
Guy Cournoyer *September 30, 2020*
Sophie Lavallée *September 30, 2020*
Frédéric Bachand *November 18, 2020*
Christine Baudouin *November 18, 2020*
Peter Kalichman *April 26, 2021*

Québec
Palais de justice de Québec, #4.27, 300, boul Jean-Lesage, Québec, QC G1K 8K6
Tél: 418-649-3401; *Téléc:* 418-646-6961
courdappelmtl@judex.qc.ca

Cours municipales du Québec
Québec Municipal Courts
Édifice Louis-Philippe-Pigeon, 1200, rte de l'Église, 6e étage, Québec, QC G1V 4M1
Tél: 418-643-5140*Ligne sans frais:* 866-536-5140
coursmunicipales.ca
Les cours municipales ont une compétence limitée en matière civile, notamment dans le domaine des réclamations de taxes; en matière pénale en ce qui concerne les infractions aux règlements municipaux et les infractions aux lois québécoises; et pour entendre et juger les infractions visées par la partie XXVII du Code criminel.
Juge responsable:
Claudie Bélanger

Acton Vale
1025, rue Boulay, Acton Vale, QC J0H 1A0
Tél: 450-546-2703; *Téléc:* 450-546-4865
Juges (Les honorables):
Alain Boisvert

Alma
140, rue St-Joseph sud, Alma, QC G8B 3R1
Tél: 418-669-5001; *Téléc:* 418-669-5029
courmunicipale@ville.alma.qc.ca
Juges (Les honorables):
André Lalancette

Baie-Comeau
2, Place Lasalle, Baie-Comeau, QC G4Z 1K3
Tél: 418-296-8172; *Téléc:* 418-296-8151
cour.municipale@ville.baie-comeau.qc.ca
Juges (Les honorables):
Dave Boulianne

Beloeil
Hôtel de ville, 777, rue Laurier, Beloeil, QC J3G 4S9
Tél: 450-467-2835
cour-mun@beloeil.ca
Juges (Les honorables):
Michel Moisan

Blainville
Hôtel de ville, 1000, ch du Plan-Bouchard, Blainville, QC J7C 3S9
Tél: 450-434-5225; *Téléc:* 450-434-8285
courmunicipale@blainville.ca
Juges (Les honorables):
Nathalie Thibeault

Boisbriand
940, boul de la Grande-Allée, Boisbriand, QC J7G 2J7
Tél: 450-435-1954; *Téléc:* 450-435-6398
Juges (Les honorables):
Catherine Haccoun

Candiac
100, boul Montcalm nord, 2e étage, Candiac, QC J5R 3L8
Tél: 450-444-6060; *Téléc:* 450-444-0789
cour@ville.candiac.qc.ca
Juges (Les honorables):
Véronique Beauchamp

Iles de la Madeleine
460, ch Principal, Cap-Aux-Meules, QC G4T 1A1
Tél: 418-986-3100; *Téléc:* 418-986-6962
Juges (Les honorables):
Michel Lalande

Chambly
1, Place de la Mairie, Chambly, QC J3L 4X1
Tél: 450-658-6619; *Téléc:* 450-658-4214
cour@ville.chambly.qc.ca
Juges (Les honorables):
Pierre-Armand Tremblay

Châteauguay
#101, 265, boul d'Anjou, Châteauguay, QC J6J 5J9
Tél: 450-698-3246; *Téléc:* 450-698-3259
cour.municipale@ville.chateauguay.qc.ca
Juges (Les honorables):
Véronique Beauchamp

Chibougamau
650, 3e rue, Chibougamau, QC G8P 1P1
Tél: 418-748-2688; *Téléc:* 418-748-6562
courmunicipale@ville.chibougamau.qc.ca
Juges (Les honorables):
Frédérique Lalancette

Coaticook
150, rue Child, Coaticook, QC J1A 2B3
Tél: 819-849-2721; *Téléc:* 819-849-9669
sec.direction@coaticook.ca
Juges (Les honorables):
Monique Perron

Cowansville
220, Place Municipale, Cowansville, QC J2K 1T4
Tél: 450-263-0141; *Téléc:* 450-263-4332
Juges (Les honorables):
Monique Perron

Deux-Montagnes
1502, ch d'Oka, Deux-Montagnes, QC J7R 1M8
Tél: 450-473-2796; *Téléc:* 450-473-0094
Juges (Les honorables):
Jean-Sébastien Brunet

Dolbeau-Mistassini
1100, boul Walberg, Dolbeau, QC G8L 1G7
Tél: 418-276-0160; *Téléc:* 418-276-9803
courmunicipale@ville.dolbeau-mistassini.qc.ca
Juges (Les honorables):
Frédérique Lalancette

Donnacona
138, av Pleau, Donnacona, QC G3M 1A1
Tél: 418-285-0110; *Téléc:* 418-285-0020
courmunicipale@villededonnacona.com
Juges (Les honorables):
André Lalancette

Drummondville
415, rue Lindsay, P.O. Box 398, Drummondville, QC J2B 6W3
Tél: 819-478-6556; *Téléc:* 819-478-0920
courmunicipale@drummondville.ca
Juges (Les honorables):
Martine St-Yves

East Angus
200, rue Saint-Jean est, East Angus, QC J0B 1R0
Tél: 819-560-8600; *Téléc:* 819-560-8611
courmunicipale.eastangus@hsfqc.ca
Juges (Les honorables):
Alain Boisvert

Gatineau
25, rue Laurier, Gatineau, QC J8X 4C8
Tél: 819-595-7272
Juges (Les honorables):
Joanne Cousineau
Martin Gosselin (Juge responsable)

Granby
735, rue Dufferin, Granby, QC J2H 2H5
Tél: 450-776-8340; *Téléc:* 450-776-8342
cour.municipale@granby.ca
Juges (Les honorables):
Monique Perron

Joliette
614, boul Manseau, Joliette, QC J6E 3E4
Tél: 450-753-8123; *Téléc:* 450-753-8121
cour.municipale@ville.joliette.qc.ca
Juges (Les honorables):
Yves Briand

L'Assomption
399, rue Dorval, L'Assomption, QC J5W 1A1
Tél: 450-589-5671; *Téléc:* 450-589-4512
courmunicipale@ville.lassomption.qc.ca
Juges (Les honorables):
Michel Moisan

La Pocatière
412, 9e rue, La Pocatière, QC G0R 1Z0
Tél: 418-856-3394; *Téléc:* 418-856-5465
Juges (Les honorables):
Dave Boulianne

La Prairie
#400, 170, boul Taschereau, La Prairie, QC J5R 5H6
Tél: 450-444-6626
cour@ville.laprairie.qc.ca

La Tuque
375, rue Saint-Joseph, La Tuque, QC G9X 1L5
Tél: 819-523-8200; *Téléc:* 819-523-5419
courmunicipale@ville.latuque.qc.ca
Juges (Les honorables):
Frédérique Lalancette

Lac-Mégantic
5527, rue Frontenac, Lac-Mégantic, QC G6B 1H6
Tél: 819-583-2815; *Téléc:* 819-583-2841
cour.municipale@ville.lac-megantic.qc.ca
Juges (Les honorables):
Mélanie Trottier

Lachute
380, rue Principale, Lachute, QC J8H 1Y2
Tél: 450-562-3781; *Téléc:* 450-562-1431
Juges (Les honorables):
Michel Lalande

Laval
55, boul des Laurentides, Laval, QC H7G 2T1
Tél: 450-662-4466; *Téléc:* 450-662-8501
Juge-président:
Martine Hébert
Juges (Les honorables):
Aryanne Guérin
Jonathan Meunier
Chantal Paré

Lévis
5333, rue de la Symphonie, Charny, QC G6X 3B6
Tél: 418-832-4695; *Téléc:* 418-832-7743
csaccourmunicipale@ville.levis.qc.ca
Juges (Les honorables):
Marie-Eve Roy

Longueuil
4025, boul Taschereau, Longueuil, QC J4T 2G6
Tél: 450-463-7006; *Téléc:* 450-646-8897
Juges (Les honorables):
Annie Bellemare
Cathy Noseworthy (Juge responsable)

Magog
7, rue Principale est, Magog, QC J1X 1Y4
Tél: 819-843-3333
c.municipale@ville.magog.qc.ca
Juges (Les honorables):
Monique Perron

Mascouche
3038, ch Sainte-Marie, Mascouche, QC J7K 1P4
Tél: 450-474-4133; *Téléc:* 450-474-6401
cour@ville.mascouche.qc.ca
Juges (Les honorables):
Juliana Côté

Mercier
869, boul Saint-Jean-Baptiste, 2e étage, Mercier, QC J6R 2L3
Tél: 450-691-6090; *Téléc:* 450-691-6529
cour.municipale@ville.mercier.qc.ca
Juges (Les honorables):
Sylvain Dorais

Mirabel
17690, rue du Val d'Espoir, P.O. Box 1140, Mirabel, QC J7J 1A1
Tél: 450-475-2009
Juges (Les honorables):
Nathalie Thibeault

Mont-Saint-Hilaire
Hôtel de Ville, 100, rue du Centre-Civique, Mont-Saint-Hilaire, QC J3H 3M8
Tél: 450-467-2854; *Téléc:* 450-467-7459
cour.municipale@villemsh.ca
Juges (Les honorables):
Yves Briand

Montmagny
134, rue Saint-Jean-Baptiste est, Montmagny, QC G5V 1K6
Tél: 418-248-3361; *Téléc:* 418-248-0923
Juges (Les honorables):
Dave Boulianne

Montréal
775, rue Gosford, Montréal, QC H2Y 3B9
Tél: 514-872-2964; *Téléc:* 514-872-8271
cour-municipale@ville.montreal.qc.ca
Juge-présidents:
Bernard Mandeville
Sophie Beauchemin (Juge-présidente adjointe)
Juges (Les honorables):
Marc Alain
Lison Asseraf
Gabriel Boutros
Stéphane Brière
Marie Brouillet
Julie Caumartin
Line Charest
Annie-Claude Chassé
Richard Chassé
José Costa
Gianni Cuffaro
Marie-Josée Dionne
Isabelle Doray
Johanne Duplessis
Sylvie Girard
Isabelle Grondin
Nathalie Haccoun
Josée Hamel
Steeve Larivière
Guylaine Lavigne
Martine Leclerc
Katia Léontieff
Katia Mouscardy
Line Ouellet
Francis Paradis
Gaétan Plouffe
Marc Renaud
Randall Richmond
Alain St-Pierre

Mont-Tremblant
1145, rue de Saint-Jovite, Mont-Tremblant, QC J8E 1V1
Tél: 819-425-8614
cour@villedemont-tremblant.qc.ca
Juges (Les honorables):
Catherine Haccoun

M.R.C. d'Autray
550, rue Montcalm, Berthierville, QC J0K 1A0
Tél: 450-836-7007; *Téléc:* 450-836-5230
Juges (Les honorables):
Michel Moisan

M.R.C. d'Antoine-Labelle
Édifice Émile-Lauzon, 425, rue du Pont, Mont-Laurier, QC J9L 2R6
Tél: 819-623-3485; *Téléc:* 819-623-5052
courmunicipale@mrc-antoine-labelle.qc.ca
Juges (Les honorables):
Catherine Haccoun

M.R.C. de Bellechasse
100, rue Monseigneur-Bilodeau,
Saint-Lazare-de-Bellechasse, QC G0R 3J0
Tél: 418-883-3347; *Téléc:* 418-883-2555
Juges (Les honorables):
Mélanie Trottier

M.R.C. de l'Islet
34A, rue Fortin, Saint-Jean-Port-Joli, QC G0R 3G0
Tél: 418-598-3076; *Téléc:* 418-598-6880
Juges (Les honorables):
Dave Boulianne

M.R.C. de La Côte-de-Beaupré
3, rue de la Seigneurie, Château-Richer, QC G0A 1N0
Tél: 418-583-3444; *Téléc:* 418-824-3917
courmunicipale@mrccotedebeaupre.qc.ca
Juges (Les honorables):
André Lalancette

M.R.C. de La Mitis
300, av du Sanatorium, Mont-Joli, QC G5H 1V7
Tél: 418-775-8445; *Téléc:* 418-775-9303
Juges (Les honorables):
Dave Boulianne

M.R.C. de Lotbinière
121A, rue St-André, Laurier-Station, QC G0S 1N0
Tél: 418-728-2787; *Téléc:* 418-728-2501
cour.municipale@mrclotbiniere.org
Juges (Les honorables):

Mélanie Trottier

M.R.C. de Marguerite-D'Youville
609, rte Marie Victorin, Vercheres, QC J0L 2R0
Tél: 450-583-3435; *Téléc:* 450-583-6575
cour@margueritedyouville.ca
Juges (Les honorables):
Carole Lepage

M.R.C. de Maskinongé
651, boul Saint-Laurent est, Louiseville, QC J5V 1J1
Tél: 819-228-9461; *Téléc:* 819-228-2193
cour.municipale@mrc-maskinonge.qc.ca
Juges (Les honorables):
Martine St-Yves

M.R.C. de Matawinie
3184, 1e av, P.O. Box 1239, Rawdon, QC J0K 1S0
Tél: 450-834-5441; *Téléc:* 450-834-6560
cour@matawinie.org
Juges (Les honorables):
Michel Lalande

M.R.C. de Mékinac
560, rue Notre-Dame, Saint-Tite, QC G0X 3H0
Tél: 418-365-5151; *Téléc:* 418-365-7377
Juges (Les honorables):
Pierre Bordeleau

M.R.C. de Vaudreuil-Soulanges
280, boul Harwood, Vaudreuil-Dorion, QC J7V 1Y5
Tél: 450-455-9480; *Téléc:* 450-455-8856
cmrvs@mrcvs.ca
Juges (Les honorables):
Gilles Chaloux

M.R.C. des Collines-de-l'Outaouais
216, ch Old Chelsea, Chelsea, QC J9B 1J4
Tél: 819-827-0516; *Téléc:* 819-827-5712
Ligne sans frais: 833-477-2687
courmunicipale@mrcdescollines.com
Juges (Les honorables):
Slobodan Delev

M.R.C. du Val-St-François
#101, 3, rue Greenlay sud, Windsor, QC J1S 2J1
Tél: 819-845-2016; *Téléc:* 819-845-3209
cour.municipale@val-saint-francois.qc.ca
Juges (Les honorables):
Alain Boisvert

M.R.C. le Haut-Saint-Laurent
#400, 10, rue King, Huntingdon, QC J0S 1H0
Tél: 450-264-5422; *Téléc:* 450-264-6885
courmunicipale@mrchsl.com
Juges (Les honorables):
Véronique Beauchamp

M.R.C. Montcalm
1530, rue Albert, P.O. Box 308, Sainte-Julienne, QC J0K 2T0
Tél: 450-831-2182; *Téléc:* 450-831-4712
courmunicipale@mrcmontcalm.com
Juges (Les honorables):
Michel Moisan

Nicolet
180, rue de Monseigneur-Panet, Nicolet, QC J3T 1S6
Tél: 819-293-6901; *Téléc:* 819-293-6767
cour.municipale@nicolet.ca
Juges (Les honorables):
Carole Lepage

Plessisville
1700, rue Saint-Calixte, Plessisville, QC G6L 1R3
Tél: 819-362-3284; *Téléc:* 819-362-6421
Juges (Les honorables):
Pierre Bordeleau

Princeville
50, rue Saint-Jacques ouest, Princeville, QC G6L 4Y5
Tél: 819-364-3333
Juges (Les honorables):
Pierre Bordeleau

Québec
1130, rue de l'Église, Québec, QC G1V 4X6
Tél: 418-641-6179
courmunicipale@ville.quebec.qc.ca
Juge-président:
Nathalie Duchesne
Juges (Les honorables):
Nicolas Champoux
Paulin Cloutier
François Dugré
Jean-Claude Gingras
Sabrina Grand
Jacques Ouellet
Patrice Simard

Joanne Tourville

Repentigny
1, Montée des Arsenaux, #E, Repentigny, QC J5Z 2C1
Tél: 450-470-3500; *Téléc:* 450-654-2447
cour-municipale@ville.repentigny.qc.ca
Juges (Les honorables):
Yves Briand

Rimouski
205, av de la Cathédrale, P.O. Box 710, Rimouski, QC G5L 7C7
Tél: 418-724-3181; *Téléc:* 418-724-9795
cour.municipale@ville.rimouski.qc.ca
Juges (Les honorables):
Dave Boulianne

Rivière-du-Loup
75, rue de l'Hôtel-de-ville, Rivière-du-Loup, QC G5R 3Y7
Tél: 418-867-6628; *Téléc:* 418-867-6638
cour.municipale@villerdl.ca
Juges (Les honorables):
Dave Boulianne

Roberval
851, boul Saint-Joseph, Roberval, QC G8H 2L6
Tél: 418-275-0202; *Téléc:* 418-275-5031
Juges (Les honorables):
Frédérique Lalancette

Rosemère
100, rue Charbonneau, Rosemère, QC J7A 3W1
Tél: 450-621-3500; *Téléc:* 450-621-1022
cour@ville.rosemere.qc.ca
Juges (Les honorables):
Jean-Sébastien Brunet

Saguenay
201, rue Racine est, P.O. Box 8060, Chicoutimi, QC G7H 5B8
Tél: 418-698-3160; *Téléc:* 418-541-5961
Juges (Les honorables):
Camille Morin

Saint-Césaire
1111, av Saint-Paul, Saint-Césaire, QC J0L 1T0
Tél: 450-469-3108; *Téléc:* 450-469-5275
Juges (Les honorables):
Monique Perron

Saint-Constant
66, rue du Maçon, Saint-Constant, QC J5A 1T1
Tél: 450-638-2010
Juges (Les honorables):
Sylvain Dorais

Saint-Félicien
1209, boul Sacré-Coeur, P.O. Box 7000, Saint-Félicien, QC G8K 2R5
Tél: 418-679-2100; *Téléc:* 418-679-2178
cour@ville.stfelicien.qc.ca
Juges (Les honorables):
Frédérique Lalancette

Saint-Georges
11700, boul Lacroix, Saint-Georges, QC G5Y 1L3
Tél: 418-228-5555; *Téléc:* 418-226-2282
cour.municipale@saint-georges.ca
Juges (Les honorables):
Mélanie Trottier

Saint-Hyacinthe
700, av de l'Hôtel-de-ville, Saint-Hyacinthe, QC J2S 5B2
Tél: 450-778-8310
Juges (Les honorables):
Carole Lepage

Saint-Jean-sur-Richelieu
855, 1e rue, Saint-Jean-sur-Richelieu, QC J2X 3C7
Tél: 450-357-2087; *Téléc:* 450-357-2750
cour.municipale@sjsr.ca
Juges (Les honorables):
Pierre-Armand Tremblay

Saint-Jérôme
280, rue Labelle, Saint-Jérôme, QC J7Z 5L1
Tél: 450-432-0585; *Téléc:* 450-436-4506
cour@vsj.ca
Juges (Les honorables):
Michel Lalande

Saint-Raymond
375, rue Saint-Joseph, Saint-Raymond, QC G3L 1A1
Tél: 418-337-2202; *Téléc:* 418-337-2203
cour.municipale@villesaintraymond.com
Juges (Les honorables):
André Lalancette

Saint-Rémi
105, rue de la Mairie, Saint-Rémi, QC J0L 2L0
Tél: 450-454-3994; *Téléc:* 450-454-6898
Juges (Les honorables):
Véronique Beauchamp

Sainte-Adèle
1381, boul de Sainte-Adèle, Sainte-Adèle, QC J8B 1A3
Tél: 450-229-2921; *Téléc:* 450-229-5300
adjointecour@ville.sainte-adele.qc.ca
Juges (Les honorables):
Catherine Haccoun

Sainte-Agathe-des-Monts
50, rue Saint-Joseph, Sainte-Agathe-des-Monts, QC J8C 1M9
Tél: 819-326-4595; *Téléc:* 819-326-5784
cour@ville.sainte-agathe-des-monts.qc.ca
Juges (Les honorables):
Catherine Haccoun

Sainte-Marie
270, av Marguerite Bourgeoys, Sainte-Marie, QC G6E 3Z3
Tél: 418-387-2301; *Téléc:* 418-387-2454
cour.municipale@sainte-marie.ca
Juges (Les honorables):
Mélanie Trottier

Sainte-Thérèse
6, rue de l'Église, P.O. Box 100, Sainte-Thérèse, QC J7E 4H7
Tél: 450-434-1440
cour@sainte-therese.ca
Juges (Les honorables):
Nathalie Thibeault

Salaberry-de-Valleyfield
29, rue Fabre, Salaberry-de-Valleyfield, QC J6S 4K5
Tél: 450-370-4810; *Téléc:* 450-370-4868
Juges (Les honorables):
Sylvain Dorais

Sept-Iles
546, av de Quen, Sept-Iles, QC G4R 2R4
Tél: 418-964-3250
greffe@septiles.ca
Juges (Les honorables):
Dave Boulianne

Shawinigan
550, av de l'Hôtel-de-ville, P.O. Box 400, Shawinigan, QC G9N 6V3
Tél: 819-536-7200; *Téléc:* 819-536-2797
Juges (Les honorables):
Pierre Bordeleau

Sherbrooke
191, rue Palais, P.O. Box 610, Sherbrooke, QC J1H 5M4
Tél: 819-821-5600; *Téléc:* 819-822-6064
portail.affaires.juridiques@ville.sherbrooke.qc.ca
Juges (Les honorables):
Alain Boisvert

Sorel-Tracy
3025, boul de Tracy, P.O. Box 368, Sorel-Tracy, QC J3R 1C2
Tél: 450-742-7775; *Téléc:* 450-742-2420
courmunicipale@ville.sorel-tracy.qc.ca
Juges (Les honorables):
Carole Lepage

Terrebonne
3630, rue Émile-Roy, Terrebonne, QC J7M 1A1
Tél: 450-961-8378; *Téléc:* 450-471-9322
Juges (Les honorables):
Juliana Côté

Thetford Mines
144, rue Notre-Dame ouest, P.O. Box 489, Thetford Mines, QC G6G 5T3
Tél: 418-335-2981; *Téléc:* 418-335-7089
courmunicipale@villethetford.ca
Juges (Les honorables):
Mélanie Trottier

Trois-Rivières
#100, 80, rue Paré, Trois-Rivières, QC G8T 9W2
Tél: 819-372-4628; *Téléc:* 819-371-9777
courmunicipale@v3r.net
Juges (Les honorables):
Martine St-Yves

Val-d'Or
#100, 855, 2e av, P.O. Box 400, Val-d'Or, QC J9P 4P4
Tél: 819-824-9613
cour.municipale@ville.valdor.qc.ca
Juges (Les honorables):
Slobodan Delev

Val-des-Sources
341, boul Saint-Luc, Val-des-Sources, QC J1T 2W4
Tél: 819-879-7171; *Téléc:* 819-879-2343
cour@ville.asbestos.qc.ca
Juges (Les honorables):
Pierre Bordeleau

Victoriaville
1, rue Notre-Dame ouest, P.O. Box 370, Victoriaville, QC G6P 6T2
Tél: 819-758-1571; *Téléc:* 819-751-4529
cmcaisse@victoriaville.ca
Juges (Les honorables):
Pierre Bordeleau

Waterloo
#210, 417, rue de la Cour, Waterloo, QC J0E 2N0
Tél: 450-539-2282; *Téléc:* 450-539-3257
Juges (Les honorables):
Monique Perron

Saskatchewan

Saskatchewan Court of Appeal
2425 Victoria Ave., Regina, SK S4P 3W6
Tel: 306-787-5382; *Fax:* 306-787-5815
sasklawcourts.ca/court-of-appeal
The Court of Appeal has appellate jurisdiction with respect to any judgement, order or decree made by the Court of Queen's Bench & any matter granted to it by statute.
Chief Justice:
Robert Richards
Justices of Appeal (The Hon. Mr./Madam Justice):
Brian Barrington-Foote
Neal W. Caldwell
Georgina Jackson (Supernumerary)
Jeffery D. Kalmakoff
Robert W. Leurer
Ralph Ottenbreit
Jacelyn Ryan-Froslie (Supernumerary)
Lian M. Schwann
Jerome Tholl
Administration:
Amy Groothuis (Registrar)
caregistrar@sasklawcourts.ca

Saskatchewan Court of Queen's Bench
2425 Victoria Ave., Regina, SK S4P 4W6
Tel: 306-787-5377; *Fax:* 306-787-7217
www.sasklawcourts.ca
The Court of Queen's Bench is a court of original jurisdiction having jurisdiction in civil & criminal matters arising in Saskatchewan, except those matters expressly excluded by statute.
Chief Justice:
M.D. Popescul
Justices (The Hon. Mr./Madam Justice):
C.L. Dawson (Supernumerary)
B.L. Klatt
F.J. Kovach (Supernumerary)
L.L. Krogan
M.R. McCreary
J.E. McMurtry
G.G. Mitchell
D.N. Robertson
M.D. Tochor
Justices, Family Division (The Hon. Mr./Madam Justice):
D.J. Brown
M.T. Megaw
C.M. Richmond
Courts:
Battleford
Court House, 291 - 23rd St. West, P.O. Box 340, Battleford, SK S0M 0E0
Tel: 306-446-7675; *Fax:* 306-446-7737
Justices (The Hon. Mr./Madam Justice):
B.R. Hildebrandt

Estevan
Court House, 1016 - 4th St., Estevan, SK S4A 0W5
Tel: 306-637-4527; *Fax:* 306-637-4536
Justices (The Hon. Mr./Madam Justice):
K.D. Kilback

Moose Jaw
Court House, 64 Ominica St. West, Moose Jaw, SK S6H 6V2
Tel: 306-694-3602; *Fax:* 306-694-3056
Justices (The Hon. Mr./Madam Justice):
D.C. Chow

Prince Albert
Court House, 1800 Central Ave., Prince Albert, SK S6V 4W7
Tel: 306-953-3200; *Fax:* 306-953-3210

Justices (The Hon. Mr./Madam Justice):
G.A. Meschishnick
Justices, Family Division (The Hon. Mr./Madam Justice):
L.W. Zuk

Saskatoon
520 Spadina Cres. East, Saskatoon, SK S7K 3G7
Tel: 306-933-5135; *Fax:* 306-975-4818
Justices (The Hon. Mr./Madam Justice):
M.D. Acton (Supernumerary)
G.N. Allbright (Supernumerary)
N. Bardai
C.D. Clackson
N.D. Crooks
G.M. Currie
R.W. Danyliuk
M.L. Dovell (Supernumerary)
R.W. Elson
N.G. Gabrielson (Supernumerary)
D.B. Konkin (Supernumerary)
H.D. MacMillan-Brown
R.C. Mills (Supernumerary)
A.R. Rothery (Supernumerary)
L.A. Schatz
B.J. Scherman (Supernumerary)
R.S. Smith (Supernumerary)
K.L. Zerr
Justices, Family Division (The Hon. Mr./Madam Justice):
G.V. Goebel
C.L. Haaf
D.E. Labach
F.N. Turcotte
Y.G.K Wilkinson (Supernumerary)

Swift Current
Court House, 121 Lorne St. West, Swift Current, SK S9H 0J4
Tel: 306-778-8400; *Fax:* 306-778-8581
Justices (The Hon. Mr./Madam Justice):
T.J. Keene

Yorkton
Court House, 29 Darlington St. East, Yorkton, SK S3N 0C2
Tel: 306-786-1515; *Fax:* 306-786-1521

Saskatchewan Provincial Court
1815 Smith St., Regina, SK S4P 2N5
Tel: 306-787-5250; *Fax:* 306-787-7037
sasklawcourts.ca/provincial-court
The Provincial Court has jurisdiction in both civil (including small claims & family) & select criminal (including young offender) matters.
Chief Judge:
The Hon. S. Metivier
Courts:
Estevan
Court House, 1016 - 4th St., Estevan, SK S4A 0W5
Tel: 306-637-4528; *Fax:* 306-637-4536
Judges (The Hon.):
M.R. Brass

La Ronge
1320 La Ronge Ave., P.O. Box 117, La Ronge, SK S0J 1L0
Tel: 306-425-4505; *Fax:* 306-425-4269
Judges (The Hon.):
E. Layton
R. Mackenzie

Lloydminster
4815 - 50th St., Lloydminster, SK S9V 0M8
Tel: 306-825-6420; *Fax:* 306-825-6497

Meadow Lake
207 - 3rd Ave. East, Meadow Lake, SK S9X 1E7
Tel: 306-236-7575; *Fax:* 306-236-7598
Judges (The Hon.):
J.E. McIvor
M.A. Segu
M. Tomka

Melfort
107 Crawford Ave. East, P.O. Box 4480, Melfort, SK S0E 1A0
Tel: 306-752-6230; *Fax:* 306-752-6126
Judges (The Hon.):
I.J. Cardinal
L. Stang

Moose Jaw
#211, 110 Ominica St. West, Moose Jaw, SK S6H 6V2
Tel: 306-694-3612; *Fax:* 306-694-3043
Judges (The Hon.):
B. Hendrickson
D. Rayner

North Battleford
3 Railway Ave. East, North Battleford, SK S9A 2P9
Tel: 306-446-7400; *Fax:* 306-446-7432

Judges (The Hon.):
M. Baldwin
K.D. Hill
D. O'Hanlon
M. Pelletier

Prince Albert
188 - 11th St. West, P.O. Box 3003, Prince Albert, SK S6V 6G1
Tel: 306-953-2640; *Fax:* 306-953-2819

Judges (The Hon.):
F.M.A.L. Daunt
H.W. Harradence (Administrative Judge)
T. Healey
J. Lubyk
M. McAuley
S. Schiefner

Regina
1815 Smith St., Regina, SK S4P 2N5
Tel: 306-787-5250; *Fax:* 306-787-7037

Associate Chief Judge:
L. Wiegers
Judges (The Hon.):
M.T. Beaton (Administrative Judge)
A.M. Crugnale-Reid
P. Demong (Administrative Judge)
N. Evanchuk
M.J. Hinds
D.J. Kovatch
K.A. Lang
P.A. Reis
J.F. Rybchuk

Saskatoon
220 - 19th St. East, Saskatoon, SK S7K 0A2
Tel: 306-933-7052; *Fax:* 306-933-7043

Associate Chief Judge:
S. Anand (Associate Chief Judge)
Judges (The Hon.):
Q.D. Agnew
M.M. Baniak
B. Bauer (Administrative Judge)
L. Gibb
M. Gray
R.D. Jackson
B.M. Klause
M.F. Martinez
V. Monar Enweani
M. Penner
D.C. Scott
B. Wright

Swift Current
Court House, 121 Lorne St. West, Swift Current, SK S9H 0J4
Tel: 306-778-8390; *Fax:* 306-778-8581

Judges (The Hon.):
K.P. Bazin

Wynyard
Court House, 410 Ave. C East, P.O. Box 1449, Wynyard, SK S0A 4T0
Tel: 306-554-5521; *Fax:* 306-554-5531

Judges (The Hon.):
M. Marquette

Yorkton
Court House, 120 Smith St. East, Yorkton, SK S3N 3V3
Tel: 306-786-1400; *Fax:* 306-786-1422

Judges (The Hon.):
R. Green
P.R. Koskie
D. Taylor

Yukon Territory

Yukon Court of Appeal
Court Registry, 2134 - 2nd Ave., Ground Fl., Whitehorse, YT Y1A 5H6
Tel: 867-456-3821; *Fax:* 867-393-6212
Toll-Free: 800-661-0408
courtofappeal@yukon.ca
www.yukoncourts.ca/en/court-appeal
The Court of Appeal has appellate jurisdiction in all civil & criminal matters from decisions by the Territorial Court & Supreme Court. The court is made up of justices from the British Columbia Court of Appeal & the courts of the three territories.

Yukon Supreme Court
2134 - 2nd Ave., Whitehorse, YT Y1A 5H6
Tel: 867-667-5937; *Fax:* 867-393-6212
courtservices@yukon.ca
www.yukoncourts.ca/en/supreme-court
The Supreme Court is a superior court of record having original jurisdiction in all civil & criminal matters arising in the Yukon, unless excluded by statute.
Resident Judges (The Hon. Mr./Madam Justice):
Suzanne Duncan (Chief Justice)
Edith M. Campbell
Karen Wenckebach
Deputy Judges (The Hon. Mr./Madam Justice):
David R. Aston
Mary Lou Benotto
Myra Bielby
Paul Bychok
Louise Charbonneau
Susan Charlesworth
Susan Cooper
David Crerar
Barry Davies
Todd Ducharme
Fred Ferguson
David Gates
Geoffrey Gaul
John Gill
Harvey Groberman
Joel Groves
R.J. Haines
Thomas Heeney
Stephen D. Hillier
Elizabeth A. Hughes
Mary Humphries
Paul B. Kane
Colleen Kenny
Adele Kent
Brenda Keyser
John S. Little
Christian Lyons

Eric F. MacKlin
A.M. Mahar
Bryan E. Mahoney
Miriam A. Maisonville
Deborah J. McCawley
John Menzies
Gisele M. Miller
Mary Moreau
Gregory M. Mulligan
Rosemary Nation
D. Blair Nixon
Vital Ouellette
Paul S. Rouleau
Jacelyn Ryan-Froslie
Virginia A. Schuler
Karan M. Shaner
Neil Sharkey
Shannon Smallwood
Anne C. Trousdale
Bonnie Tulloch
John Z. Vertes
David Watt
James W. Williams

Yukon Territorial Court
2134 - 2nd Ave., Whitehorse, YT Y1A 5H6
Tel: 867-667-5441
courtservices@yukon.ca
www.yukoncourts.ca/en/territorial-court
The Territorial Court has jurisdiction in family, youth & select criminal matters.
Chief Judge:
Michael Cozens
Presiding Judges:
Peter Chisholm
Karen Ruddy
Deputy Judges/Justices (The Hon. Mr./Madam Justice):
Michael S. Block
Michelle R. Brass
Adrian F. Brooks
Kathleen J. Caldwell
Stephen C. Carter
Joseph De Filippis
William Digby
John Faulkner
Gurmail S. Gill
Peter Griffiths
Murray J. Hinds
Timothy J. Killeen
Martin Lambert
Robert Joseph Lane
E. Ann Marie MacInnes
Gerald Morin
Brian M. Neal
Nancy K. Orr
James Plemel
Richard D. Schneider
Herman J. Seidemann III
Carol Ann Snell
Murray P. Thompson
David C. Walker
Raymond E. Wyant

SECTION 10

HOSPITALS & HEALTH CARE FACILITIES

Listings in this section are arranged by province, and then by city. Each provincial section includes the following six categories.

Government Department

Regional Health Authorities

Hospitals

Community Health Centres

Long Term/Retirement Care

Mental Health Facilities

CANADIAN ALMANAC & DIRECTORY
RÉPERTOIRE ET ALMANACH CANADIEN

Alberta

Government Departments in Charge

Edmonton: Alberta Health
PO Box 1360 Stn. Main, Edmonton, AB T5J 2N3
Tel: 780-427-7164 *Fax:* 780-427-1171
TTY: 780-427-9999
www.alberta.ca/health.aspx
Hon. Jason Copping, Minister
780-427-3665, health.minister@gov.ab.ca
Hon. Mike Ellis, Associate Minister, Mental Health & Addictions
780-427-0165, associateminister-mha@gov.ab.ca

Regional Health Authorities

Edmonton: Alberta Health Services (AHS)
Seventh Street Plaza, North Tower, 14th Fl., 10030 - 107 St. NW, Edmonton, AB T5J 3E4
Tel: 780-342-2000 *Fax:* 780-342-2060
Toll-Free: 888-342-2471
ahsinfo@albertahealthservices.ca
www.albertahealthservices.ca
Info Line: 811
www.facebook.com/albertahealthservices;
twitter.com/AHS_media; www.youtube.com/ahschannel
Year Founded: 2009
Number of Beds: 27,163 continuing care beds; 8,483 acute care beds; 249 palliative & hospice beds; 2,772 mental health beds
Population Served: 4300000 *Number of Employees:* 110k+
Note: Provincial governance board, overseeing hospitals, other health facilities, & ground ambulance service in Alberta.
Verna Yiu, President & CEO
Dr. Francois Belanger, Chief Medical Officer & Vice-President, Quality
Deb Gordon, Chief Health Operations Officer, Northern Alberta
Brenda Huband, Chief Health Operations Officer, Central & Southern Alberta

Hospitals - General

Athabasca: Athabasca Healthcare Centre
Affiliated with: Alberta Health Services
Also Known As: Athabasca Hospital
3100 - 48 Ave., Athabasca, AB T9S 1M9
Tel: 780-675-6000 *Fax:* 780-675-7050
www.albertahealthservices.ca
www.facebook.com/albertahealthservices;
twitter.com/AHS_media; www.youtube.com/ahschannel
Number of Beds: 50 beds
Note: Programs & services include: emergency services; diagnostic imaging; laboratory services; acute care; obstetrics; pediatrics; continuing care; rehabilitation; recreation services; palliative care; & x-ray.
Mary Proskie, Site Manager

Banff: Banff - Mineral Springs Hospital
Covenant Health
Affiliated with: Alberta Health Services
PO Box 1050, 305 Lynx St., Banff, AB T1L 1H7
Tel: 403-762-2222
info_banffmineralspringshospital@covenanthealth.ca
www.covenanthealth.ca
www.facebook.com/Banff.MSH
Year Founded: 1930
Number of Beds: 12 acute care beds; 25 continuing care beds; 10 day surgery beds
Number of Employees: 268
Note: Programs & services include: emergency services; surgery; acute care; maternal & child care; physiotherapy; occupational therapy; recreation therapy; music therapy; mental health services; continuing care; outpatient clinics; & palliative care.
Shelley Buchan, Site Administrator

Barrhead: Barrhead Healthcare Centre
Affiliated with: Alberta Health Services
Former Name: Barrhead General and Auxilliary Hospital; Barrhead Nursing Home
4815 - 51 Ave., Barrhead, AB T7N 1M1
Tel: 780-674-2221
www.albertahealthservices.ca
www.facebook.com/albertahealthservices;
twitter.com/AHS_media; www.youtube.com/ahschannel
Number of Beds: 34 beds
Note: Programs & services include: emergency services; diagnostic imaging; laboratory services; obstetrics; community cancer centre; rehabilitation services; social work; diet counselling; education programs; outpatient clinics; & palliative care.

Bassano: Bassano Health Centre
Affiliated with: Alberta Health Services
PO Box 120, 608 - 5 Ave., Bassano, AB T0J 0B0
Tel: 403-641-6100
www.albertahealthservices.ca
www.facebook.com/albertahealthservices;
twitter.com/AHS_media; www.youtube.com/ahschannel
Year Founded: 1914
Number of Beds: 4 acute care beds; 8 continuing care beds; 1 palliative care bed; 1 respite care bed
Note: Programs & services include: emergency services; diagnostic imaging; acute care; physiotherapy; occupational therapy; physiotherapy; mental health services; nutrition services; social work; continuing care; respite care; & palliative care.

Beaverlodge: Beaverlodge Municipal Hospital
Affiliated with: Alberta Health Services
PO Box 480, 422 - 10A St., Beaverlodge, AB T0H 0C0
Tel: 780-354-2136
www.albertahealthservices.ca
www.facebook.com/albertahealthservices;
twitter.com/AHS_media; www.youtube.com/ahschannel
Number of Beds: 18 acute care beds
Note: Programs & services include: emergency services; general radiography; medical laboratory; acute care; obstetrics; physiotherapy; occupational therapy; & palliative care.
Janet Wallace, Site Manager

Black Diamond: Oilfields General Hospital
Affiliated with: Alberta Health Services
717 Government Rd., Black Diamond, AB T0L 0H0
Tel: 403-933-2222
www.albertahealthservices.ca
www.facebook.com/albertahealthservices;
twitter.com/AHS_media; www.youtube.com/ahschannel
Number of Beds: 45 beds
Note: Programs & services include: addiction services; adult day support program; diagnostic imaging; laboratory services; occupational therapy; physical therapy; & speech language pathology.
Carla Ralph, Site Manager

Blairmore: Crowsnest Pass Health Centre
Affiliated with: Alberta Health Services
2001 - 107 St., Blairmore, AB
Tel: 403-562-5011 *Fax:* 403-562-8992
www.albertahealthservices.ca
www.facebook.com/albertahealthservices;
twitter.com/AHS_media; www.youtube.com/AHSChannel
Number of Beds: 58 long-term care beds; 16 acute care beds
Note: Programs & services include: emergency; diagnostic imaging services; laboratory; surgery; neonatal intensive care nursery; pediatrics; critical care services; acute care; rehabilitation services, including occupational therapy & therapeutic recreation; Southern Alberta Renal Program; continuing care; & palliative care.
Liz Cook, Site Manager, Acute Care

Bonnyville: Bonnyville Healthcare Centre
Covenant Health
Affiliated with: Alberta Health Services
PO Box 1008, 5001 Lakeshore Dr., Bonnyville, AB T9N 2J7
Tel: 780-826-3311
www.covenanthealth.ca/hospitals-care-centres/bonnyville-health-centre
www.facebook.com/albertahealthservices;
twitter.com/AHS_media; www.youtube.com/ahschannel
Year Founded: 1986
Number of Beds: 33 acute care beds; 30 continuing care beds
Number of Employees: 358
Note: Programs & services include: emergency services; regional laboratory services; diagnostic imaging; pathology; surgery; acute care; community cancer centre; cardiac stress testing; obstetrics; rehabilitation; medical accupuncture; occupational therapy; respiratory therapy; continuing care; & palliative care.
Mr. James Anderson, Site Administrator

Bow Island: Bow Island Health Centre
Affiliated with: Alberta Health Services
938 Centre St., Bow Island, AB T0K 0G0
Tel: 403-545-3200
www.albertahealthservices.ca
www.facebook.com/albertahealthservices;
twitter.com/AHS_media; www.youtube.com/ahschannel
Number of Beds: 10 acute care beds; 20 continuing care beds
Note: Programs & services include: emergency services; diagnostic imaging & laboratory services; acute care; physiotherapy; occupational therapy; continuing care; & respite services.

Boyle: Boyle Healthcare Centre
Affiliated with: Alberta Health Services
5004 Lakeview Rd., Boyle, AB T0A 0M0
Tel: 780-689-3731
www.albertahealthservices.ca
www.facebook.com/albertahealthservices;
twitter.com/AHS_media; www.youtube.com/ahschannel
Year Founded: 1966
Number of Beds: 19 acute care beds; 1 palliative care bed
Note: Programs & services include: emergency services; diagnostic imaging; laboratory services; acute care services; nutrition services; community health; social work; & palliative care.

Brooks: Brooks Health Centre
Affiliated with: Alberta Health Services
440 - 3rd St. East, Brooks, AB T1R 0E7
Tel: 403-501-3232
www.albertahealthservices.ca
www.facebook.com/albertahealthservices;
twitter.com/AHS_media; www.youtube.com/ahschannel
Number of Beds: 37 acute care beds; 15 long-term beds; 10 emergency beds
Note: Programs & services include: emergency services; ambulatory care; acute care; obstetrics; pediatrics; physiotherapy; occupational therapy; recreational therapy; Healthy Living Program / cardiac rehabilitation; diabetes education; community health; continuing care; & palliative care.

Calgary: Alberta Children's Hospital
Affiliated with: Alberta Health Services
Former Name: Alberta Crippled Children's Hospital; Junior Red Cross Hospital
West Campus, University of Calgary, 28 Oki Dr. NW, Calgary, AB T3B 6A8
Tel: 403-955-7211
www.albertahealthservices.ca/Facilities/ACH
www.facebook.com/albertahealthservices;
twitter.com/AHS_media; www.youtube.com/AHSChannel
Year Founded: 2006
Number of Beds: 141 beds
Note: Programs & services include: Aboriginal services; angiography; pediatrics (birth to age 18); emergency services; surgery; complex pain service; diagnostic imaging; burn treatment; eating disorder program - day treatment; sexual assault response team; child abuse service; child & adolescent mental health inpatient services; community education service; & Infant Headshape Program.
Margaret Fullerton, Senior Operating Officer

Calgary: Foothills Medical Centre
Affiliated with: Alberta Health Services
1403 - 29 St. NW, Calgary, AB T2N 2T9
Tel: 403-944-1110
www.albertahealthservices.ca
www.facebook.com/albertahealthservices;
twitter.com/AHS_media; www.youtube.com/ahschannel
Year Founded: 1966
Number of Beds: 1,079 beds
Note: Programs & services include: emergency services; trauma services; diagnostic imaging; acute care; gynecology; newborn care; cardiology; gastrointestinal services; hematology; adult neuropsychology service; neurology; psychiatry; renal services; Movement Disorders Program; respiratory services; social work; & addiction services.
MacNeil Cornez, Site Manager

Calgary: Peter Lougheed Centre
Affiliated with: Alberta Health Services
Former Name: Calgary Health Region Peter Lougheed Centre
3500 - 26 Ave. NE, Calgary, AB T1Y 6J4
Tel: 403-943-4555
www.albertahealthservices.ca
www.facebook.com/albertahealthservices;
twitter.com/AHS_media; www.youtube.com/AHSChannel
Year Founded: 1988
Number of Beds: 51 intensive care beds; 39 obstetrical beds; 12 pediatric beds; 110 mental health beds; 285 acute care beds
Note: Programs & services include: Aboriginal services; abortion; angiography; anticoagulation management; bronchoscopy; cardiology; clinics; CT imaging; mental health services; surgery; diabetes, hypertension & cholesterol; diagnostic imaging; electroencephalography; emergency; enterostomal therapy; fluoroscopy; gastrointestinal; general medicine; general radiography; hematology; hemodialysis; intensive care; laboratory; magnetic resonance imaging; neurology; nuclear medicine; nutrition; occupational therapy; oncology; palliative care; pharmacy; psychiatry; speech language pathology; social work; & ultrasound.

High Prairie: High Prairie Health Complex
Affiliated with: Alberta Health Services
5101 - 38 St., High Prairie, AB T0G 1E0
Tel: 780-523-6440 Fax: 780-523-6472
www.albertahealthservices.ca
www.facebook.com/albertahealthservices;
twitter.com/AHS_media; www.youtube.com/ahschannel
Number of Beds: 25 beds
Note: Programs & services include: acute care; continuing care; emergency; rehabilitation; palliative care; pediatrics; radiology; recreational therapy; & speech-language pathology.
Bikramjit Jammu, Site Manager

High River: High River General Hospital
Affiliated with: Alberta Health Services
560 - 9 Ave. SW, High River, AB T1V 1B3
Tel: 403-652-2200
www.albertahealthservices.ca
www.facebook.com/albertahealthservices;
twitter.com/AHS_media; www.youtube.com/ahschannel
Year Founded: 1982
Number of Beds: 27 acute care beds; 50 long-term care beds
Note: Programs & services include: cancer treatment & care; cardiology; CT imaging; continuing care; diagnostic imaging; emergency services; gynecological surgery; holter monitoring; laboratory; nutrition; & physical therapy.

Hinton: Hinton Healthcare Centre
Affiliated with: Alberta Health Services
1280 Switzer Dr., Hinton, AB T7V 1V2
Tel: 780-865-3333 Fax: 780-865-3581
www.albertahealthservices.ca
www.facebook.com/albertahealthservices;
twitter.com/AHS_media; www.youtube.com/ahschannel
Number of Beds: 23 beds
Note: Programs & services include: acute care; community cancer centre; diabetic nephropathy; pharmacy; rehabilitation; ultrasound; x-ray, CT scan; & MRI.
Fiona Murray-Galbraith, Site Manager

Innisfail: Innisfail Health Centre
Affiliated with: Alberta Health Services
5023 - 42 St., Innisfail, AB T4G 1A9
Tel: 403-227-7800
www.albertahealthservices.ca
www.facebook.com/albertahealthservices;
twitter.com/AHS_media; www.youtube.com/ahschannel
Number of Beds: 78 long-term care beds; 28 acute beds
Note: Programs & services include: addiction & mental health services; child & adolescent services; community health; continuing care; diagnostic imaging; emergency; general radiography; laboratory services; long-term care; nutrition; occupational & physical therapy; oral health program; palliative care; pharmacy; public health; pulmonary function testing; rehabilitation; respite care; speech language pathology; spiritual care; & tuberculosis testing.

Jasper: Seton - Jasper Healthcare Centre
Affiliated with: Alberta Health Services
PO Box 310, 518 Robson St., Jasper, AB T0E 1E0
Tel: 780-852-3344 Fax: 780-852-3413
www.albertahealthservices.ca
www.facebook.com/albertahealthservices;
twitter.com/AHS_media; www.youtube.com/ahschannel
Number of Beds: 11 beds
Note: Programs & services include: emergency; acute care services; diagnostic imaging; eating disorder services; mental health services; occupational therapy; palliative care; physiotherapy; & social work.
Lorna Chisholm, Site Manager

Killam: Killam Health Care Centre
Covenant Health
Affiliated with: Alberta Health Services
5203 - 49 Ave., Killam, AB T0B 2L0
Tel: 780-385-3741 Fax: 780-385-3901
www.covenanthealth.ca/hospitals-care-centres/killam-health-cent
re
www.facebook.com/albertahealthservices;
twitter.com/AHS_media; www.youtube.com/AHSChannel
Year Founded: 1930
Number of Beds: 5 acute care beds; 45 long-term care beds
Number of Employees: 126
Note: Programs & services include: adult day support; Asthma Education Program; continuing care; diagnostic imaging; emergency; general radiography; laboratory; long-term care; palliative care; respiratory / pulmonary; respite care; & Vital Heart Response / STEMI Program.
Geraldine Clark, Site Administrator

Lac La Biche: William J. Cadzow - Lac La Biche
Healthcare Centre
Affiliated with: Alberta Health Services
9110 - 93 St., Lac La Biche, AB T0A 2C0
Tel: 780-623-4404
www.albertahealthservices.ca
www.facebook.com/albertahealthservices;
twitter.com/AHS_media; www.youtube.com/ahschannel
Number of Beds: 23 acute care beds; 41 continuing care beds
Note: Programs & services include: ambulatory services; clinics; continuing care; day surgery; diagnostic imaging; emergency; environmental; general medicine; general radiography; hemodialysis; laboratory; nutrition; obstetrics; occupational & physical therapy; palliative care; pastoral care; pediatrics; pharmacy; respiratory; respite care; social work; special care unit; stress testing; & therapeutic recreation.

Lacombe: Lacombe Hospital & Care Centre
Affiliated with: Alberta Health Services
5430 - 47 Ave., Lacombe, AB T4L 1G8
Tel: 403-782-3336
www.albertahealthservices.ca
www.facebook.com/albertahealthservices;
twitter.com/AHS_media; www.youtube.com/ahschannel
Number of Beds: 31 acute care beds; 79 long-term care beds
Note: Programs & services include: acute care; continuing care; crisis response team (rural); diagnostic imaging; emergency; general radiography; laboratory; long-term care; nutrition; obstetrics; occupational & physical therapy; palliative care; pharmacy; pulmonary; speech language pathology; spiritual care; surgery; & ultrasound.
Kimberley Sommerville, Site Manager

Lamont: Lamont Health Care Centre
Affiliated with: Alberta Health Services
PO Box 479, 5216 - 53 St., Lamont, AB T0B 2R0
Tel: 780-895-2211 Fax: 780-895-7305
info@lamonthcc.ca
www.lamonthealthcarecentre.com
Year Founded: 1912
Number of Beds: 14 acute care beds; 101 continuing care beds; 2 palliative care beds; 2 respite beds; 6 day surgery beds; 2 surgical suites
Population Served: 10000
Note: Programs & services include: acute & continuing care; emergency; general radiography; occupational therapy; mental health services; rehabilitation; & palliative care. Affiliated with the United Church of Canada.
Shahad Bharmal, CEO & Executive Director

Leduc: Leduc Community Hospital
Affiliated with: Alberta Health Services
Former Name: Leduc Community Hospital & Health Centre
4210 - 48 St., Leduc, AB T9E 5Z3
Tel: 780-986-7711
www.albertahealthservices.ca/leduc
www.facebook.com/albertahealthservices;
twitter.com/AHS_media; www.youtube.com/ahschannel
Number of Beds: 74 acute beds
Note: Programs & services include: inpatient medical & surgical care; general & specialized day surgery; rehabilitation programs; laboratory services; diagnostic imaging; outpatient clinics; emergency; audiology; echocardiography; endoscopy; fluoroscopy; radiography; infectious diseases; nutrition; pediatrics; Pulmonary Rehabilitation Program; Sexual Assault Response Team; social work; & ultrasound.
Korynna Wolfe, Site Director

Lethbridge: Chinook Regional Hospital
Affiliated with: Alberta Health Services
Former Name: Lethbridge Regional Hospital
960 - 19 St. South, Lethbridge, AB T1J 1W5
Tel: 403-388-6111
www.albertahealthservices.ca
www.facebook.com/albertahealthservices;
twitter.com/AHS_media; www.youtube.com/AHSChannel
Year Founded: 1988
Number of Beds: 30 intensive care beds; 25 obstetrical beds; 11 pediatric beds; 41 mental health beds; 25 rehabilitation beds; 156 acute beds
Population Served: 150000
Note: Programs & services include: acute geriatrics; angiography; breast health program; cardiology; CT imaging; surgery; diagnostic imaging; echocardiography; emergency; fluoroscopy; clinics; general radiography; hemodialysis; laboratory; children & adolescent mental health program; labour delivery & maternal child services; magnetic resonance imaging; occupational therapy; palliative care; post partum & gynecology; pediatrics; social work; speech language pathology; therapeutic recreation; & ultrasound.
James Ostoya, Site Manager

Manning: Manning Community Health Centre
Affiliated with: Alberta Health Services
600 - 2 St. NE, Manning, AB T0H 2M0
Tel: 780-836-3391
www.albertahealthservices.ca
www.facebook.com/albertahealthservices;
twitter.com/AHS_media; www.youtube.com/ahschannel
Number of Beds: 11 acute care beds; 16 long-term care beds
Note: Programs & services include: acute care; clinics; cardiology; community health services; continuing care; diabetes prevention & wellness program; diagnostic imaging; early childhood development; eating disorder services; emergency; environmental; general radiography; home care; laboratory; mental health; newborn hearing screening program; nutrition; occupational & physical therapy; oral health; palliative care; pediatrics; pharmacy; prenatal education; P.A.R.T.Y. (Prevent Alcohol & Risk Related Trauma in Youth); respiratory; social work; therapeutic recreation; travel health; tuberculosis testing; & ultrasound.
Jo Kelemen, Director, Health Services

Mayerthorpe: Mayerthorpe Healthcare Centre
Affiliated with: Alberta Health Services
4417 - 45 St., Mayerthorpe, AB T0E 1N0
Tel: 780-786-2261
www.albertahealthservices.ca
www.facebook.com/albertahealthservices;
twitter.com/AHS_media; www.youtube.com/ahschannel
Number of Beds: 24 acute care beds; 30 long-term care beds; 1 palliative care bed
Note: Programs & services include: acute care; continuing care; community health; emergency; pharmacy; rehabilitation; x-ray; & laboratory.

McLennan: Sacred Heart Community Health Centre
Affiliated with: Alberta Health Services
Former Name: McLennan Sacred Heart Community Health Centre
350 - 3 Ave. NW, McLennan, AB T0H 2L0
Tel: 780-324-3730 Fax: 780-324-2267
www.albertahealthservices.ca
www.facebook.com/albertahealthservices;
twitter.com/AHS_media; www.youtube.com/ahschannel
Number of Beds: 20 beds
Note: Programs & services include: acute care; emergency; Indigenous Health Program; intensive care; laboratory; rehabilitation; palliative care; & pediatrics.
Barbara Mader, Site Manager

Medicine Hat: Medicine Hat Regional Hospital
Affiliated with: Alberta Health Services
666 - 5 St. SW, Medicine Hat, AB T1A 4H6
Tel: 403-529-8000 Fax: 403-529-8950
www.albertahealthservices.ca
www.facebook.com/albertahealthservices;
twitter.com/AHS_media; www.youtube.com/ahschannel
Number of Beds: 17 intensive care beds; 14 obstetrical beds; 10 pediatric beds; 31 mental health beds; 52 rehabilitation bed; 156 acute beds
Note: Programs & services include: acute care; supportive rehab; laboratory; surgery; mental health; critical care; pediatrics; emergency; ambulatory care; obstetrics; neonatal intensive care; geriatric services; community health; home care; & x-ray.
Linda Iwasiw, Senior Operating Officer

Olds: Olds Hospital & Care Centre
Affiliated with: Alberta Health Services
3901 - 57 Ave., Olds, AB T4H 1T4
Tel: 403-556-3381
www.albertahealthservices.ca
www.facebook.com/albertahealthservices;
twitter.com/AHS_media; www.youtube.com/ahschannel
Number of Beds: 33 acute care beds; 50 continuing care beds
Note: Programs & services include: clinics; continuing care; crisis response team (rural); diagnostic imaging; emergency; general radiography; hemodialysis; laboratory services; long-term care; nutrition; obstetrics; occupational & physical therapy; palliative care; pharmacy; pulmonary/respiratory; seniors mental health program; speech language pathology; spiritual care; surgical; & Vital Heart Response/STEMI Program.
Wayne Krejci, Site Manager

Oyen: Big Country Hospital
Affiliated with: Alberta Health Services
312 - 3 St. East, Oyen, AB T0J 2J0
Tel: 403-664-4300
www.albertahealthservices.ca
www.facebook.com/albertahealthservices;
twitter.com/AHS_media; www.youtube.com/ahschannel
Number of Beds: 10 acute care beds; 30 continuing care beds
Note: Programs & services include: acute care; continuing care;

diagnostic imaging; emergency; general radiography; laboratory; labour delivery & maternal child services; occupational & physical therapy; respiratory services; respite services; & therapeutic recreation.
Dianne Swantz, Site Manager

Peace River: Peace River Community Health Centre
Affiliated with: Alberta Health Services
10101 - 68 St., Peace River, AB T8S 1T6
Tel: 780-624-7500
www.albertahealthservices.ca
www.facebook.com/albertahealthservices;
twitter.com/AHS_media; www.youtube.com/AHSChannel
Number of Beds: 31 acute care beds; 40 long-term care beds
Note: Programs & services include: acute care; CT; continuing care; diagnostic imaging; early childhood intervention; emergency; environmental public health; fluoroscopy; general radiography; home care; Indigenous health program; laboratory; mammography; nutrition; occupational therapy; oral health; palliative care; pharmacy; physical therapy; respiratory therapy; sexual health; social work; speech language pathology; therapeutic recreation; tuberculosis testing; & ultrasound.

Pincher Creek: Pincher Creek Health Centre
Affiliated with: Alberta Health Services
Former Name: Pincher Creek Hospital
1222 Bev McLachlin Dr., Pincher Creek, AB T0K 1W0
Tel: 403-627-1234
www.albertahealthservices.ca
www.facebook.com/albertahealthservices;
twitter.com/AHS_media; www.youtube.com/ahschannel
Number of Beds: 16 acute care beds; 3 long-term beds
Note: Programs & services include: audiology; diagnostic imaging; emergency; general radiography; laboratory; nutrition; & pediatrics.
Jordan Koch, Site Manager

Ponoka: Ponoka Hospital & Healthcare Centre
Affiliated with: Alberta Health Services
5800 - 57 Ave., Ponoka, AB T4J 1P1
Tel: 403-783-3341
www.albertahealthservices.ca
www.facebook.com/albertahealthservices;
twitter.com/AHS_media; www.youtube.com/ahschannel
Number of Beds: 57 beds
Note: Programs & services include: acute care; continuing care; emergency; general medicine; laboratory; obstetrics; surgery; pediatrics; & radiology.

Provost: Provost Health Centre
Affiliated with: Alberta Health Services
5002 - 54 Ave., Provost, AB T0B 3S0
Tel: 780-753-2291
www.albertahealthservices.ca
www.facebook.com/albertahealthservices;
twitter.com/AHS_media; www.youtube.com/ahschannel
Number of Beds: 15 acute care beds; 47 long-term care beds
Note: Programs & services include: acute care; continuing care; day support; emergency; respite & palliative care; surgery; obstetrics; & x-ray.

Raymond: Raymond Health Centre
Affiliated with: Alberta Health Services
Former Name: Raymond Hospital
150 North 4th St. East, Raymond, AB T0K 2S0
Tel: 403-752-4561 *Fax:* 403-752-3554
www.albertahealthservices.ca
www.facebook.com/albertahealthservices;
twitter.com/AHS_media; www.youtube.com/ahschannel
Number of Beds: 17 beds
Note: Programs & services include: continuing care; diagnostic imaging; emergency; general radiography; laboratory; nutrition; occupational & physical therapy; & therapeutic recreation.

Red Deer: Red Deer Regional Hospital Centre
Affiliated with: Alberta Health Services
3942 - 50A Ave., Red Deer, AB T4N 4E7
Tel: 403-343-4422
www.albertahealthservices.ca/rdrhc
www.facebook.com/albertahealthservices;
twitter.com/AHS_media; www.youtube.com/ahschannel
Number of Beds: 370 beds
Population Served: 453300
Note: Programs & services include: Indigenous health; mental health (adult & child); angiography; laboratory; bronchoscopy; cardiology; clinics; CT scan; crisis response team; diagnostic imaging; echocardiography; electroencephalography; electromyography; emergency; Fibromyalgia group; fluoroscopy; general radiography; hemodialysis; MRI; neonatal intensive care; nuclear medicine; nuclear stress testing; nutrition; obstetrics; palliative care; pediatrics; perinatal bereavement program; pharmacy; physical therapy; pulmonary/respiratory;

rehabilitation; specialized geriatric services; speech language pathology; spiritual care; stress echocardiography; surgery; & ultrasound.

Redwater: Redwater Health Centre
Affiliated with: Alberta Health Services
4812 - 58 St., Redwater, AB T0A 2W0
Tel: 780-942-3932 *Fax:* 780-942-2373
www.albertahealthservices.ca
www.facebook.com/albertahealthservices;
twitter.com/AHS_media; www.youtube.com/AHSChannel
Year Founded: 1973
Number of Beds: 14 acute care beds; 7 long-term care beds
Note: Programs & services include: addiction & mental health; continuing care; diagnostic imaging; emergency; environmental; general radiography; laboratory; nutrition; social work; & spiritual care.

Rimbey: Rimbey Hospital & Care Centre
Affiliated with: Alberta Health Services
PO Box 440, 5228 - 50 Ave., Rimbey, AB T0C 2J0
Tel: 403-843-2271
www.albertahealthservices.ca
www.facebook.com/albertahealthservices;
twitter.com/AHS_media; www.youtube.com/AHSChannel
Number of Beds: 84 long-term care beds; 23 acute care beds; 11 emergency beds
Population Served: 2500
Note: Programs & services include: addiction & mental health; child & adolescent services; continuing care counselling; crisis response team (rural); diagnostic imaging; emergency; general radiography; laboratory; long-term care; nutrition; obstetrics; occupational & physical therapy; palliative care; pharmacy; respite care; speech language pathology; & spiritual care.

Rocky Mountain House: Rocky Mountain House Health Centre
Affiliated with: Alberta Health Services
5016 - 52 Ave., Rocky Mountain House, AB T4T 1T2
Tel: 403-845-3347 *Fax:* 403-845-7030
www.albertahealthservices.ca
www.facebook.com/albertahealthservices;
twitter.com/AHS_media; www.youtube.com/ahschannel
Number of Beds: 31 beds
Note: Programs & services include: Indigenous health; addiction & mental health; child & adolescent services; community health centres; continuing care counselling; crisis response team (rural); diagnostic imaging; emergency; environmental public health; general radiography; hemodialysis; home care; laboratory; long-term care; nutrition; obstetrics; occupational & physical therapy; oral health; palliative care; pharmacy; prenatal education; public health; respiratory; speech language pathology; surgery; tuberculosis testing; ultrasound; & Vital Heart Response/STEMI Program.
Shirley Hope, Site Manager

Sherwood Park: Strathcona Community Hospital
Affiliated with: Alberta Health Services
Former Name: Health First Strathcona
9000 Emerald Dr., Sherwood Park, AB T8H 0J3
Tel: 780-449-5380
www.albertahealthservices.ca/strath
www.facebook.com/albertahealthservices;
twitter.com/AHS_media; www.youtube.com/ahschannel
Year Founded: 2014
Note: Programs & services include: addiction & mental health; CT scans; diabetes program; diagnostic imaging; emergency; laboratory; rehabilitation; radiography; & ultrasound.
Susan Chesney, Site Manager

Slave Lake: Slave Lake Healthcare Centre
Affiliated with: Alberta Health Services
309 - 6 St. NE, Slave Lake, AB T0G 2A2
Tel: 780-805-3500
www.albertahealthservices.ca
www.facebook.com/albertahealthservices;
twitter.com/AHS_media; www.youtube.com/ahschannel
Number of Beds: 24 acute care beds; 20 long-term care beds
Note: Programs & services include: emergency; acute care; continuing care; mental health; pharmacy; renal dialysis; rehabilitation; obstetrics; occupational therapy; pediatrics; respiratory therapy; social work; ultrasound; & x-ray.

Smoky Lake: George McDougall - Smoky Lake Healthcare Centre
Affiliated with: Alberta Health Services
PO Box 340, 4212 - 55 Ave., Smoky Lake, AB T0A 3C0
Tel: 780-656-3034
www.albertahealthservices.ca
www.facebook.com/albertahealthservices;
twitter.com/AHS_media; www.youtube.com/ahschannel

Number of Beds: 12 active beds; 23 auxiliary beds
Note: Programs & services include: emergency services; diagnostic imaging; laboratory services; ambulatory services; acute care; rehabilitation; occupational therapy; physical therapy services; therapeutic recreation; community health services; nutrition services; social work; continuing care; & palliative care.

Spirit River: Central Peace Health Complex
Affiliated with: Alberta Health Services
5010 - 45th Ave., Spirit River, AB T0H 3G0
Tel: 780-864-3993 *Fax:* 780-864-3495
www.albertahealthservices.ca
www.facebook.com/albertahealthservices;
twitter.com/AHS_media; www.youtube.com/ahschannel
Year Founded: 1972
Number of Beds: 12 acute care beds; 16 continuing care beds
Note: Programs & services include: emergency care; laboratory services; acute care; newborn hearing screening program; pediatrics; rehabilitation; physical therapy; nutrition counselling; continuing care; & palliative care.

St. Albert: Sturgeon Community Hospital
Affiliated with: Alberta Health Services
Former Name: Sturgeon Community Hospital & Health Centre
201 Boudreau Rd., St. Albert, AB T8N 6C4
Tel: 780-418-8200 *Fax:* 780-418-8262
www.albertahealthservices.ca
www.facebook.com/albertahealthservices;
twitter.com/AHS_media; www.youtube.com/ahschannel
Year Founded: 1992
Number of Beds: 14 intensive care beds; 22 obstetrical beds; 127 acute care beds
Note: Programs & services include: emergency; cardiac rehabilitation; diagnostic imaging (CT scans, radiology, fluoroscopy); intensive care unit; nutrition counselling; obstetrics; physical therapy/occupational therapy; prenatal program; sexual assault response team; spiritual care; & surgery.
Wendy Tanaka-Collins, Site Director

St. Paul: St. Therese - St. Paul Healthcare Centre
Affiliated with: Alberta Health Services
4713 - 48 Ave., St. Paul, AB T0A 3A3
Tel: 780-645-3331
www.albertahealthservices.ca
www.facebook.com/albertahealthservices;
twitter.com/AHS_media; www.youtube.com/ahschannel
Number of Beds: 70 beds
Note: Programs & services include: emergency; diagnostic imaging (ultrasound, x-ray); eating disorder services; obstetrics; pharmacy; rehabilitation; renal dialysis; & laboratory.

Stettler: Stettler Hospital & Care Centre
Affiliated with: Alberta Health Services
5912 - 47 Ave., Stettler, AB T0C 2L0
Tel: 403-742-7400 *Fax:* 403-742-1244
www.albertahealthservices.ca
www.facebook.com/albertahealthservices;
twitter.com/AHS_media; www.youtube.com/ahschannel
Number of Beds: 46 long-term care beds; 30 acute care beds
Note: Programs & services include: continuing care; diagnostic imaging; mental health; obstetrics; occupational therapy (for acute & continuing care); palliative care; pharmacy; physical therapy; renal dialysis; respiratory therapy; sleep program; & speech language pathology.
Diane Palmer, Site Manager

Stony Plain: WestView Health Centre
Affiliated with: Alberta Health Services
4405 South Park Dr., Stony Plain, AB T7Z 2M7
Tel: 780-968-3600
www.albertahealthservices.ca
www.facebook.com/albertahealthservices;
twitter.com/AHS_media; www.youtube.com/AHSChannel
Number of Beds: 40 long-term care beds; 29 acute care beds
Note: Programs & services include: acute care; continuing care; emergency; diagnostic imaging; laboratory; day surgery; obstetrics; public health; environmental health; community care; rehabilitation; dental; & mental health.
Ellen Elliott, Site Director

Strathmore: Strathmore District Health Services
Affiliated with: Alberta Health Services
200 Brent Blvd., Strathmore, AB T1P 1J9
Tel: 403-361-7000 *Fax:* 403-361-7048
www.albertahealthservices.ca
www.facebook.com/albertahealthservices;
twitter.com/AHS_media; www.youtube.com/ahschannel
Number of Beds: 23 acute care beds
Note: Programs & services include: Adult Day Support Program; diagnostic imaging; cardiology; laboratory; occupational therapy;

palliative care; pharmacy; physical therapy; respiratory services; respite care; & speech language pathology.

Sundre: Sundre Hospital & Care Centre
Affiliated with: Alberta Health Services
709 - 1 St. NE, Sundre, AB T0M 1X0
Tel: 403-638-3033 Fax: 403-636-6284
www.albertahealthservices.ca
www.facebook.com/albertahealthservices;
twitter.com/AHS_media; www.youtube.com/ahschannel
Number of Beds: 14 acute care beds; 9 long-term care beds
Number of Employees: 135
Note: Programs & services include: emergency; nutrition; continuing care counseling; diagnostic imaging; laboratory; obstetrics; occupational therapy; palliative care; pharmacy; physical therapy; & speech language pathology.

Swan Hills: Swan Hills Healthcare Centre
Affiliated with: Alberta Health Services
PO Box 261, 29 Freeman Dr., Swan Hills, AB T0G 2C0
Tel: 780-333-7000 Fax: 780-333-7009
www.albertahealthservices.ca
www.facebook.com/albertahealthservices;
twitter.com/AHS_media; www.youtube.com/AHSChannel
Year Founded: 1985
Number of Beds: 4 beds
Note: Programs & services include: ambulatory services; clinics; community health; diagnostic imaging; early childhood development; eating disorder services; emergency; environmental; general medicine; general radiography; home care; laboratory; mental health; nutrition; oral health; palliative care; pharmacy; P.A.R.T.Y. (Prevent Alcohol & Risk Related Trauma in Youth); sexual health; & social work.

Taber: Taber Health Centre
Affiliated with: Alberta Health Services
Former Name: Taber Hospital
4326 - 50 Ave., Taber, AB T1G 1N9
Tel: 403-223-7211 Fax: 403-223-1703
www.albertahealthservices.ca
www.facebook.com/albertahealthservices;
twitter.com/AHS_media; www.youtube.com/AHSChannel
Number of Beds: 10 long-term care beds; 19 acute care beds
Note: Programs & services include: addiction services; continuing care; emergency; diagnostic imaging; environmental; laboratory; mental health services; nutrition; occupational therapy; pediatrics; radiography; speech language pathology; & therapeutic recreation.

Three Hills: Three Hills Health Centre
Affiliated with: Alberta Health Services
1504 - 2nd St. North, Three Hills, AB T0M 2A0
Tel: 403-443-2444
www.albertahealthservices.ca
www.facebook.com/albertahealthservices;
twitter.com/AHS_media; www.youtube.com/ahschannel
Number of Beds: 24 long-term care beds; 21 acute care beds
Note: Programs & services include: community health; continuing care; diagnostic imaging; early intervention program; emergency; fluoride protection for toddlers; general radiography; home care & Alberta Aids to Daily Living; laboratory; long-term care; nutrition; obstetrics; occupational & physical therapy; oral health; palliative care; pharmacy; prenatal education; public health; pulmonary; rehabilitation; respite care; speech language pathology; surgery; travel health services; tuberculosis testing; & ultrasound.
Ruth Wold, Site Manager

Tofield: Tofield Health Centre
Affiliated with: Alberta Health Services
5543 - 44 St., Tofield, AB T0B 4J0
Tel: 780-662-3263 Fax: 780-662-3835
www.albertahealthservices.ca
www.facebook.com/albertahealthservices;
twitter.com/AHS_media; www.youtube.com/AHSChannel
Number of Beds: 50 long-term care beds; 16 acute care beds
Note: Programs & services include: emergency; acute care; asthma education program; continuing care; home care; laboratory; occupational therapy; palliative care; physiotherapy; postnatal services; radiography; respiratory therapy; respite care; speech language services; & surgery.

Two Hills: Two Hills Health Centre
Affiliated with: Alberta Health Services
Also Known As: Two Hills Hospital
4401 - 53 Ave., Two Hills, AB T0B 4K0
Tel: 780-657-3344 Fax: 780-657-2508
www.albertahealthservices.ca
www.facebook.com/albertahealthservices;
twitter.com/AHS_media; www.youtube.com/AHSChannel
Year Founded: 1986
Number of Beds: 15 acute care beds; 56 long term care beds;

12 rehabilitation beds
Note: Programs & services include: emergency; acute care; community health; nutrition; continuing care; home care; general radiography; laboratory; occupational therapy; oral health; palliative care; pharmacy; prenatal education; respiratory therapy; respite care; & stroke & geriatric empowerment unit.

Valleyview: Valleyview Health Centre
Affiliated with: Alberta Health Services
Former Name: Valleyview Health Complex
4802 Highway St., Valleyview, AB T0H 3N0
Tel: 780-524-3356 Fax: 780-524-2107
www.albertahealthservices.ca
www.facebook.com/albertahealthservices;
twitter.com/AHS_media; www.youtube.com/AHSChannel
Number of Beds: 45 beds
Note: Programs & services include: Indigenous health; cardiology; continuing care; diagnostic imaging; early intervention; emergency; environmental; general radiography; laboratory; newborn hearing screening program; nutrition; occupational & physical therapy; palliative care; pediatrics; pharmacy; respiratory; social work; therapeutic recreation; & tuberculosis testing.

Vegreville: St. Joseph's General Hospital
Covenant Health
Affiliated with: Alberta Health Services
5241 - 43 St., Vegreville, AB T9C 1R5
Tel: 780-632-2811
www.covenanthealth.ca/hospitals-care-centres/st-josephs-gener
al-hospital
www.facebook.com/albertahealthservices;
twitter.com/AHS_media; www.youtube.com/AHSChannel
Year Founded: 1910
Number of Beds: 24 acute care beds
Number of Employees: 157
Note: Programs & services include: emergency; medicine; laboratory; diagnostic imaging (x-ray, ultrasound); dialysis; diabetic education; occupational & physical therapy; respiratory therapy; palliative care; & day support.
Anthony Brannen, Site Administrator

Vermilion: Vermilion Health Centre
Affiliated with: Alberta Health Services
5720 - 50 Ave., Vermilion, AB T9X 1K7
Tel: 780-853-5305 Fax: 780-853-4786
www.albertahealthservices.ca
www.facebook.com/albertahealthservices;
twitter.com/AHS_media; www.youtube.com/AHSChannel
Number of Beds: 25 acute care beds
Note: Programs & services include: acute care; clinics; diagnostic imaging; emergency; general radiography; laboratory; long-term care; nutrition; occupational & physical therapy; palliative care; pharmacy; pulmonary/respiratory; surgery; ultrasound; & Vital Heart Response/STEMI Program.

Viking: Viking Health Centre
Affiliated with: Alberta Health Services
PO Box 60, 5110 - 57 Ave., Viking, AB T0B 4N0
Tel: 780-336-4786 Fax: 780-336-4983
www.albertahealthservices.ca
www.facebook.com/albertahealthservices;
twitter.com/AHS_media; www.youtube.com/AHSChannel
Number of Beds: 16 acute care beds
Note: Programs & services include: emergency; acute care; continuing care; palliative care; surgery; mental health services; nutrition; obstetrics; rehabilitation; respiratory therapy; & x-ray.

Vulcan: Vulcan Community Health Centre
Affiliated with: Alberta Health Services
610 Elizabeth St. South, Vulcan, AB T0L 2B0
Tel: 403-485-3333
www.albertahealthservices.ca
www.facebook.com/albertahealthservices;
twitter.com/AHS_media; www.youtube.com/AHSChannel
Number of Beds: 8 acute care beds; 15 long-term care beds
Note: Programs & services include: adult day program; continuing care; diabetes education; diagnostic imaging; emergency; general medicine; general radiography; surgery; Healthy Moms, Healthy Babies Program; Home Parenteral Therapy Program; laboratory; mental health; nutrition; pharmacy; & respiratory therapy.

Wabasca: Wabasca/Desmarais Healthcare Centre
Affiliated with: Alberta Health Services
Former Name: Wabasca/Desmarais General Hospital
881 Mistassiniy Rd., Wabasca, AB T0G 2K0
Tel: 780-891-3007 Fax: 780-891-3784
www.albertahealthservices.ca
www.facebook.com/albertahealthservices;
twitter.com/AHS_media; www.youtube.com/ahschannel

Number of Beds: 10 beds
Note: Serves the Wabasca, Desmarais, Sandy Lake, Chipewyan Lake & Bigstone Cree Nation area. Programs & services: emergency; laboratory; rehabilitation; & x-ray.

Wainwright: Wainwright Health Centre
Affiliated with: Alberta Health Services
530 - 6 Ave., Wainwright, AB T9W 1R6
Tel: 780-842-3324
www.albertahealthservices.ca
www.facebook.com/albertahealthservices;
twitter.com/AHS_media; www.youtube.com/AHSChannel
Number of Beds: 69 long-term care beds; 25 acute bar beds
Note: Programs & services include: acute care; asthma education program; emergency; continuing care; palliative care; surgery; obstetrics; cardiac education; speech language services; respiratory therapy; physical therapy; ultrasound; & x-ray.
Cheryl Huxley, Site Manager

Westlock: Westlock Healthcare Centre
Affiliated with: Alberta Health Services
10220 - 93 St., Westlock, AB T7P 2G4
Tel: 780-349-3301
www.albertahealthservices.ca
www.facebook.com/albertahealthservices;
twitter.com/AHS_media; www.youtube.com/AHSChannel
Number of Beds: 166 beds
Note: Programs & services include: ambulatory services; day surgery; diagnostic imaging; emergency; environmental; fluoroscopy; general medicine; general radiography; laboratory; MRI; obstetrics; occupational therapy; orthopedic; palliative care; pastoral care; pediatrics; respiratory; special care; & ultrasound.
Sherry Gough, Site Manager

Wetaskiwin: Wetaskiwin Hospital & Care Centre
Affiliated with: Alberta Health Services
Former Name: Crossroads Hospital & Health Centre - Wetaskiwin
6910 - 47 St., Wetaskiwin, AB T9A 3N3
Tel: 780-361-7100 Fax: 780-361-4107
www.albertahealthservices.ca
www.facebook.com/albertahealthservices;
twitter.com/AHS_media; www.youtube.com/AHSChannel
Number of Beds: 97 beds
Note: Programs & services include: Indigenous Health Program; bronchoscopy; cardiology; continuing care; Northern Alberta Renal Program; diagnostic imaging; emergency; fluoroscopy; general radiography; hemodialysis; laboratory; nutrition; obstetrics; occupational therapy; physical therapy; palliative care; pharmacy; respiratory / pulmonary; respite care; sleep program; speech language pathology; surgery; & ultrasound.
Lisa Barrett, Site Manager

Whitecourt: Whitecourt Healthcare Centre
Affiliated with: Alberta Health Services
20 Sunset Blvd., Whitecourt, AB T7S 1M8
Tel: 780-778-2285 Fax: 780-778-8554
www.albertahealthservices.ca
www.facebook.com/albertahealthservices;
twitter.com/AHS_media; www.youtube.com/AHSChannel
Number of Beds: 22 acute care beds
Note: Programs & services include: acute care; special care; palliative care; emergency; pharmacy; rehabilitation; ultrasound; x-ray; ambulatory; audiology; clinics; community health services; day surgery; diagnostic imaging; early childhood development; Early Intervention Program; eating disorder services; environmental services; general medicine; general radiography; home care; laboratory; nutrition; obstetrics; occupational therapy; physical therapy; pastoral care; pediatrics; prenatal education; P.A.R.T.Y. (Prevent Alcohol & Risk Related Trauma in Youth); respiratory; sexual health; social work; stress testing; travel health; tuberculosis testing; & ultrasound.
Allan Shemanko, Site Manager

Auxiliary Hospitals

Breton: Breton Health Centre
Affiliated with: Alberta Health Services
4919 - 49th Ave., Breton, AB T0C 0P0
Tel: 780-696-4713
www.albertahealthservices.ca
Year Founded: 1994
Number of Beds: 23 long-term care beds
Note: Programs & services include: laboratory services; occupational therapy; physical therapy; speech language pathology; nutrition; continuing care; & palliative care.

Cardston: **Cardston Health Centre**
Affiliated with: Alberta Health Services
PO Box 1440, 144 - 2nd St. West, Cardston, AB T0K 0K0
Tel: 403-653-5234
www.albertahealthservices.ca
www.facebook.com/albertahealthservices;
twitter.com/AHS_media; www.youtube.com/AHSChannel
Note: Programs & services include: continuing care; diagnostic imaging; emergency; general radiography; laboratory; occupational therapy; physical therapy; & speech language pathology.
Kerry Roberts, Site Manager

Claresholm: **Willow Creek Continuing Care Centre**
Affiliated with: Alberta Health Services
4221 - 8 St. West, Claresholm, AB T0L 0T0
Tel: 403-625-3361 *Fax:* 403-625-3822
www.albertahealthservices.ca
Number of Beds: 100 beds
Note: Continuing care facility

Edmonton: **St. Joseph's Auxiliary Hospital**
Covenant Health
Affiliated with: Alberta Health Services
10707 - 29 Ave. NW, Edmonton, AB T6J 6W1
Tel: 780-430-9110 *Fax:* 780-430-9777
www.covenanthealth.ca
Year Founded: 1927
Number of Beds: 202 beds
Note: Continuing care hospital

Lacombe: **Lacombe Community Health Centre**
Affiliated with: Alberta Health Services
5010 - 51 St., Lacombe, AB T4L 1W2
Tel: 403-782-3218
www.albertahealthservices.ca
Note: Programs & services include: community health; continuing care; home care; clinics; oral health; prenatal education; public health; rehabilitation; travel health; & tuberculosis testing.

Lethbridge: **St. Michael's Health Centre**
Covenant Health
Affiliated with: Alberta Health Services
1400 - 9 Ave. South, Lethbridge, AB T1J 4V5
Tel: 403-382-6400 *Fax:* 403-382-6413
www.covenanthealth.ca
Year Founded: 1929
Number of Beds: 202 beds
Note: A long-term care (continuing care) facility focusing on assisted living, palliative care, & post-acute rehabilitative program; offers the Bridges program (care for the elderly in their own home).

Mundare: **Mary Immaculate Care Centre**
Covenant Health
Affiliated with: Alberta Health Services
PO Box 349, 165018 Township Rd. 534, Mundare, AB T0B 3H0
Tel: 780-764-3730
www.covenanthealth.ca/hospitals-care-centres/mary-immaculate
-care-centre
www.facebook.com/albertahealthservices;
twitter.com/AHS_media; www.youtube.com/ahschannel
Year Founded: 1929
Number of Beds: 30 continuing care beds
Number of Employees: 57
Note: Programs & services include: ambulatory care; continuing care; occupational therapy; palliative care; & spiritual care.
Anthony Brannen, Site Administrator

Trochu: **St. Mary's Health Care Centre**
Covenant Health
Affiliated with: Alberta Health Services
451 De Chauney Ave., Trochu, AB T0M 2C0
Tel: 403-442-3955
www.covenanthealth.ca
Number of Beds: 56 beds
Number of Employees: 72
Note: Programs & services include: continuing care counselling; diagnostic imaging; general radiography; interpretive services; laboratory; long-term care; occupational therapy; & palliative care.
Kathy Smith, Clinical Manager

Community Health Care Centres

Airdrie: **Airdrie Community Health Centre**
Affiliated with: Alberta Health Services
604 Main St. South, Airdrie, AB T4B 3K7
Tel: 403-912-8400 *Fax:* 403-912-8410
www.albertahealthservices.ca/achc/achc.aspx

Note: Programs & services include: 24-hour urgent care; public health; home care; mental health.

Anzac: **Anzac Community Health Services**
Affiliated with: Alberta Health Services
240 Christina Dr., Anzac, AB T0P 1J0
Tel: 780-334-2023 *Fax:* 780-791-6288
www.albertahealthservices.ca
Note: Services: immunization; public health nursing.

Athabasca: **Athabasca Community Health Services**
Affiliated with: Alberta Health Services
3401 - 48 Ave., Athabasca, AB T9S 1M7
Tel: 780-675-2231 *Fax:* 780-675-3111
www.albertahealthservices.ca
Note: Programs & services include: addiction; environmental public health; home care; general radiography; immunization; palliative care; prenatal classes; respiratory thereapy; postpartum depressin support; nutrition counselling; tuberculosis testing.

Banff: **Banff Community Health Centre**
Affiliated with: Alberta Health Services
Former Name: Banff National Park Health Unit Office
303 Lynx St., Banff, AB T1L 1B3
Tel: 403-762-2990 *Fax:* 403-762-5570
www.albertahealthservices.ca
Note: Programs & services include: diabetes clinic; environmental public health; immunization; mental health.

Barrhead: **Barrhead Community Health Services**
Affiliated with: Alberta Health Services
6203 - 49 St., Barrhead, AB T7N 1A1
Tel: 780-674-3408 *Fax:* 780-674-3941
www.albertahealthservices.ca
Note: Programs & services include: addiction; environmental public health; immunization; physical therapy; prenatal classes; social work; tuberculosis testing.

Bashaw: **Bashaw Community Health Centre**
Affiliated with: Alberta Health Services
5308 - 53 St., Bashaw, AB T0B 0H0
Tel: 780-372-3731 *Fax:* 780-372-4050
www.albertahealthservices.ca
Note: Programs & services include: diagnostic imaging; laboratory; occupational therapy; physical therapy; dietitian; & respiratory services.

Beaumont: **Beaumont Public Health Centre**
Affiliated with: Alberta Health Services
4918 - 50 Ave., Beaumont, AB T4X 1J9
Tel: 780-929-4822
www.albertahealthservices.ca
Note: Services include: addiction & mental health; immunization; public health; & tuberculosis testing.

Beaverlodge: **Beaverlodge Community Health Services**
Affiliated with: Alberta Health Services
Former Name: Beaverlodge Public Health Centre
412 - 10A St., Beaverlodge, AB T0H 0C0
Tel: 780-354-2647 *Fax:* 780-354-8410
www.albertahealthservices.ca
Note: Programs & services include: addiction; mental health; palliative care; speech & language; environmental public health; home care; general radiography; immunization; nutrition counselling; & tuberculosis testing.

Black Diamond: **Black Diamond Public Health Unit at Oilfields General Hospital**
Affiliated with: Alberta Health Services
Also Known As: Black Diamond Community Health Services
717 Government Rd., Black Diamond, AB T0L 0H0
Tel: 403-933-6505 *Fax:* 403-933-2031
www.albertahealthservices.ca
Note: Community health services

Blairmore: **Crowsnest Pass Provincial Building**
Affiliated with: Alberta Health Services
12501 - 20 Ave., Blairmore, AB T0K 0E0
Tel: 403-562-5030
www.albertahealthservices.ca
Note: Programs & services include: addiction; environmental public health; home care; general radiography; immunization; nutrition counselling; & tuberculosis testing; occupational therapy; physiotherapy; prenatal education.

Bonnyville: **Bonnyville Community Health Services**
Affiliated with: Alberta Health Services
4904 - 50 Ave., Bonnyville, AB T9N 2G4
Tel: 780-826-3381 *Fax:* 780-826-6470
www.albertahealthservices.ca

Note: Programs & services include: environmental public health; home care; general radiography; immunization; nutrition counselling; palliative care; prenatal classes; physical therapy; tuberculosis testing.

Bow Island: **Bow Island Provincial Building**
Affiliated with: Alberta Health Services
Former Name: Bow Island Public Health / Home Care
802 - 6 St. East, Bow Island, AB T0K 0G0
Tel: 403-545-2296
www.albertahealthservices.ca
Note: Programs & services include: addiction & mental health; audiology; home care; immunization; public health nurse; tuberculosis testing.

Boyle: **Boyle Healthcare Centre**
Affiliated with: Alberta Health Services
5004 Lakeview Rd., Boyle, AB T0A 0M0
Tel: 780-689-3731 *Fax:* 780-689-3951
www.albertahealthservices.ca
Note: Programs & services include: breastfeeding clinic; emergency; home care; physical therapy; immunization; nutrition counselling; social work; tuberculosis testing.
Mary Proskie, Site Manager

Brooks: **Brooks Community Health Care**
Affiliated with: Alberta Health Services
440 - 3rd St. East, Brooks, AB T1R 1B3
Tel: 403-501-3323
www.albertahealthservices.ca

Buffalo Lake Settlement: **Buffalo Lake Settlement Community Health Services**
Affiliated with: Alberta Health Services
Buffalo Lake Dr., Buffalo Lake Settlement, AB T0A 0R0
Tel: 780-689-4771
www.albertahealthservices.ca

Cadotte Lake: **Woodland Cree Health Centre**
Affiliated with: Alberta Health Services
General Delivery, Cadotte Lake, AB T0H 0N0
Tel: 780-629-8963
www.albertahealthservices.ca
Note: Services: immunization; public health nursing.

Calgary: **Acadia Community Health Centre**
Affiliated with: Alberta Health Services
#132, 151 - 86 Ave. SE, Calgary, AB T2H 3A5
Tel: 403-944-7200 *Fax:* 403-253-5129
www.albertahealthservices.ca

Calgary: **East Calgary Health Centre**
Affiliated with: Alberta Health Services
4715 - 8 Ave. SE, Calgary, AB T2A 3N4
Tel: 403-955-1250 *Fax:* 403-955-1299
www.albertahealthservices.ca
Note: Programs & services include: addiction; prenatal & parenting classes; home care; immunization; nutrition counselling; sexual & reproductive health; mental health; tuberculosis testing.
Sue Ramsden, Site Manager

Calgary: **North Hill Community Health Centre**
Affiliated with: Alberta Health Services
1527 - 19 St. NW, Calgary, AB T2N 2K2
Tel: 403-944-7400
www.albertahealthservices.ca

Calgary: **Ranchlands Village Mall**
Affiliated with: Alberta Health Services
Former Name: High Level General Hospital; Northwest Health Centre
Northwest Community Health Centre, #109, 1829 Ranchlands Blvd. NW, Calgary, AB T3G 2A7
Tel: 403-943-9700 *Fax:* 403-943-9735
www.albertahealthservices.ca
Note: Programs & services include: cardiology; immunization; laboratory; & nutrition counselling.

Calgary: **Shaganappi Complex**
Affiliated with: Alberta Health Services
3415 - 8th Ave. SW, Calgary, AB T3C 0E8
Tel: 403-944-7373 *Fax:* 403-246-0326
www.albertahealthservices.ca
Note: Programs & services include: immunization; school health program; & Well Child services.

Calgary: **Sheldon M. Chumir Health Centre**
Affiliated with: Alberta Health Services
1213 - 4 St. SW, Calgary, AB T2R 0X7
Tel: 403-955-6200
www.albertahealthservices.ca

Note: Programs & services include: addiction & mental health; Community Accessible Rehabilitation; computed tomography; diagnostic imaging; general radiography; hemodialysis; laboratory; public health; sexual & reproductive health; speech language pathology; travel health; tuberculosis testing; & urgent care.

Calgary: South Calgary Health Centre
Affiliated with: Alberta Health Services
31 Sunpark Plaza SE, Calgary, AB T2X 3W5
Tel: 403-943-9300
www.albertahealthservices.ca
Note: Programs & services include: mental health; cardiology; general radiography; environmental public health; home care; general radiography; immunization; tuberculosis testing.
Sue Ramsden, Site Manager

Calgary: Thornhill Community Health Centre
Affiliated with: Alberta Health Services
Former Name: Thornhill District Office
6617 Centre St. North, Calgary, AB T2K 4Y5
Tel: 403-944-7500 *Fax:* 403-275-9064
www.albertahealthservices.ca
Note: Programs & services include: fluoride protection; immunization; school health & oral health; & tuberculosis testing

Calgary: Village Square Community Health Centre
Affiliated with: Alberta Health Services
2623 - 56 St. NE, Calgary, AB T1Y 6E7
Tel: 403-944-7000 *Fax:* 403-285-6304
www.albertahealthservices.ca
Note: Programs & services include: prenatal program; postpartum services; school health; & Well Child services

Calling Lake: Calling Lake Community Health Services
Affiliated with: Alberta Health Services
General Delivery, Calling Lake, AB T0G 0K0
Tel: 780-331-3760 *Fax:* 780-331-2200
www.albertahealthservices.ca

Camrose: Camrose Community Health Centre Briarcrest
Affiliated with: Alberta Health Services
5510 - 46 Ave., Camrose, AB T4V 4P8
Tel: 780-679-2980 *Fax:* 780-679-2999
www.albertahealthservices.ca
Note: Programs & services include: audiology; environmental public health; home care; general radiography; immunization; nutrition counselling; & tuberculosis testing.

Canmore: Canmore Provincial Building
Affiliated with: Alberta Health Services
Former Name: Canmore Public Health Office
800 Railway Ave., Canmore, AB T1W 1P1
Tel: 403-678-5656 *Fax:* 403-678-5068
www.albertahealthservices.ca
Note: Public health programs

Cardston: Cardston Health Unit
Affiliated with: Alberta Health Services
Former Name: Cardston Community Health Centre
Cardston Provincial Building, 576 Main St., Cardston, AB T0K 0K0
Tel: 403-653-5230 *Fax:* 403-653-2926
www.albertahealthservices.ca
Note: Services include: Children's Allied Health Services; prenatal education; public health nursing; & oral health.

Castor: Castor Community Health Centre
Affiliated with: Alberta Health Services
4909 - 50 Ave., Castor, AB T0C 0X0
Tel: 403-882-3404
www.albertahealthservices.ca

Claresholm: Claresholm Community Health Centre
Affiliated with: Alberta Health Services
5221 - 2nd St. West, Claresholm, AB T0L 0T0
Tel: 403-625-4061 *Fax:* 403-625-4062
www.albertahealthservices.ca

Cochrane: Cochrane Community Health Centre
Affiliated with: Alberta Health Services
60 Grande Blvd., Cochrane, AB T4C 0S4
Tel: 403-851-6000
www.albertahealthservices.ca
Note: Programs & services include: addiction; cardiology; environmental public health; home care; general radiography; immunization; urgent care; speech language pathology; nutrition counselling; & tuberculosis testing.

Cold Lake: Cold Lake Community Health Services
Affiliated with: Alberta Health Services
4720 - 55 St., Cold Lake, AB T9M 1V8
Tel: 780-594-4404 *Fax:* 780-594-2404
www.albertahealthservices.ca
Note: Programs & services include: environmental public health; home care; immunization; physical therapy; occupation therapy; social work; speech & language; palliative care; prenatal classes; & tuberculosis testing.

Consort: Consort Community Health Centre
Affiliated with: Alberta Health Services
5410 - 52 Ave., Consort, AB T0C 1B0
Tel: 403-577-3770 *Fax:* 403-577-2235
www.albertahealthservices.ca
Note: Programs & services include: home care; immunization; occupation therapy; physioterapy; prenatal education; public health nurse; tuberculosis testing.

Coronation: Coronation Community Health Centre
Affiliated with: Alberta Health Services
4909 Royal St., Coronation, AB T0C 1C0
Tel: 403-578-3200
www.albertahealthservices.ca

Drayton Valley: Drayton Valley Community Health Centre
Affiliated with: Alberta Health Services
4110 - 50 Ave., Drayton Valley, AB T7A 0B3
Tel: 780-542-4415 *Fax:* 780-621-4998
www.albertahealthservices.ca
Note: Programs & services include: audiology; electrocardiogram; environmental public health; home care; immunization; nutrition counselling; tuberculosis testing.

Drumheller: Drumheller Health Centre
Affiliated with: Alberta Health Services
351 - 9 St. NW, Drumheller, AB T0J 0Y1
Tel: 403-823-6500
www.albertahealthservices.ca
Note: Programs & services include: addiction; general radiography; home care; general radiography; immunization; nutrition counselling; tuberculosis testing.

East Prairie Metis Settle: East Prairie Metis Settlement
Affiliated with: Alberta Health Services
East Prairie Metis Settle, AB T0G 1E0
Tel: 780-523-2594
www.albertahealthservices.ca
Note: Services: immunization; oral health.

Eckville: Eckville Community Health Centre
Affiliated with: Alberta Health Services
PO Box 150, 5120 - 51 Ave., Eckville, AB T0M 0X0
Tel: 403-746-2201 *Fax:* 403-746-2185
www.albertahealthservices.ca
Note: Programs & services include: continuing care counselling; diagnostic imaging; general radiography; home care; immunization; laboratory; occupational therapy; oral health; palliative care; physical therapy; prenatal education; public health; speech language pathology; & tuberculosis testing.

Edmonton: Belvedere Medical Clinic
12720 - 66 St., Edmonton, AB T5C 0A3
Tel: 780-761-8529

Edmonton: Bonnie Doon Public Health Centre
Affiliated with: Alberta Health Services
8314 - 88 Ave. NW, Edmonton, AB T6C 1L1
Tel: 780-342-1520
www.albertahealthservices.ca
Note: Programs & services include: immunization; tuberculosis testing; toddler fluoride protection.
Lisa Sereda, Operations Manager

Edmonton: Boyle McCauley Health Centre
Affiliated with: Alberta Health Services
10628 - 96 St., Edmonton, AB T5H 2J2
Tel: 780-422-7333 *Fax:* 780-422-7343
www.bmhc.net
www.facebook.com/BoyleMcCauleyHealthCentre.BMHC
twitter.com/BMHC_HealthCare
Note: Programs & services include: acupuncture; chiropractic clinic; dental; foot care; medical; mental health; optometry; & women's health clinic.
Cecilia Blasetti, Executive Director
cblasetti@bmhc.net
Karin Frederiksen, Clinic Coordinator
kfrederiksen@bmhc.net

Edmonton: Capilano Medical Centre Medigroup Inc.
Affiliated with: Alberta Health Services
5818 Terrace Rd. NW, Edmonton, AB T6A 3Y8
Tel: 780-761-3330 *Fax:* 780-756-5442
kaihealth.ca

Edmonton: East Edmonton Health Centre
Affiliated with: Alberta Health Services
7910 - 112 Ave. NW, Edmonton, AB T5B 0C2
Tel: 780-342-4700 *Fax:* 780-342-4911
www.albertahealthservices.ca
Note: Programs & services include: addiction & mental health; community prenatal program; diagnostic imaging; family care clinic; general radiography; immunization; laboratory; public health; school dental, health, & oral health services; tuberculosis testing; & urgent care.

Edmonton: Eastwood Medical Clinic
Affiliated with: Alberta Health Services
7919 - 118 Ave., Edmonton, AB T5B 0R5
Tel: 780-756-3666
info@eastwoodmedical.ca
www.eastwoodmedical.ca
Note: Programs & services include: pediatrics; psychiatry; neurology; respiratory therapy; women's health; physioterapy; minor surgery.

Edmonton: Kensington Medical Clinic Medigroup Inc.
Affiliated with: Alberta Health Services
12620A - 132 Ave., Edmonton, AB T5L 3P9
Tel: 780-990-1820 *Fax:* 780-488-0988
kaihealth.ca

Edmonton: Millwoods Public Health Centre
Affiliated with: Alberta Health Services
7525 - 38 Ave. NW, Edmonton, AB T6K 3X9
Tel: 780-342-1660 *Fax:* 780-461-2504
www.albertahealthservices.ca
Note: Programs & services include: immunization; tuberculosis testing; toddler fluoride protection.

Edmonton: Mother Rosalie Health Services Centre Misericordia Community Hospital
Affiliated with: Alberta Health Services
16930 - 87 Ave., Edmonton, AB T5R 4H5
Tel: 780-735-2413
www.albertahealthservices.ca
Note: Programs & services include: diabetes education; urodynamics; child health; outpatient psychiatry; & physiotherapy.

Edmonton: Northeast Community Health Centre
Affiliated with: Alberta Health Services
14007 - 50 St., Edmonton, AB T5A 5E4
Tel: 780-342-4000
www.albertahealthservices.ca

Edmonton: Northgate Centre
Affiliated with: Alberta Health Services
9499 - 137 Ave., Edmonton, AB T5E 5R8
Tel: 780-342-2800
www.albertahealthservices.ca
Note: Programs & services include: immunization; health education; assessments & screenings; referral; & community resources.

Edmonton: Rutherford Health Centre
Affiliated with: Alberta Health Services
11153 Ellerslie Rd. SW, Edmonton, AB T6W 0E9
Tel: 780-342-6800
www.albertahealthservices.ca
Note: Programs & services include: addiction & mental health; immunization; public health; school health & oral health services; & tuberculosis testing.

Edmonton: Seniors' Clinic Good Samaritan Society
Affiliated with: Alberta Health Services
8861 - 75 St., Edmonton, AB T6C 4G8
Tel: 780-440-8274 *Fax:* 780-469-6495
goodsaminfo@gss.org
www.gss.org
Note: Physician's office for seniors
Shawn Terlson, President & CEO, Good Samaritan Society
sterlson@gss.org

Edmonton: Seventh Street Plaza
Affiliated with: Alberta Health Services
10030 - 107 St., Edmonton, AB T5J 3E4
Tel: 780-735-0010
www.albertahealthservices.ca

Note: Programs & services include: birth control centre; immunization; & travel health.

Edmonton: Tipaskan Medical Clinic
#3236, 3206 - 82 St., Edmonton, AB T6K 3Y3
Tel: 780-761-3335

Edmonton: Twin Brooks Public Health Centre
Affiliated with: Alberta Health Services
1110 - 113 St. NW, Edmonton, AB T6J 7J4
Tel: 780-342-1560
www.albertahealthservices.ca
Note: Programs & services include: immunization; health education; assessments & screenings; referral; & community resources.

Edmonton: West Jasper Place Public Health Centre
Affiliated with: Alberta Health Services
9720 - 182 St., Edmonton, AB T5T 3T9
Tel: 780-342-1234
www.albertahealthservices.ca
Note: Programs & services include: fluoride protection; immunization; public health; school dental, nursing, & health services; & tuberculosis testing

Edmonton: Westmount Medical Clinic
Medigroup Inc.
Affiliated with: Alberta Health Services
11035 Groat Rd. NW, Edmonton, AB T5M 3J9
Tel: 780-705-4090 *Fax:* 780-705-4394
kaihealth.ca

Edmonton: Woodcroft Public Health Centre
Affiliated with: Alberta Health Services
Westmount Shopping Centre, #448, 111 Ave. & Groat Rd., Edmonton, AB T5M 4B7
Tel: 780-342-1600 *Fax:* 780-451-5886
www.albertahealthservices.ca

Edson: Edson Community Health Services
Affiliated with: Alberta Health Services
5028 - 3 Ave., Edson, AB T7E 1X4
Tel: 780-723-4421 *Fax:* 780-723-6299
www.albertahealthservices.ca

Elizabeth Metis Settlemen: Elizabeth Settlement
Community Health Services
Affiliated with: Alberta Health Services
Elizabeth Metis Settlemen, AB T9M 1V8
Tel: 780-594-3383 *Fax:* 780-594-3384
www.albertahealthservices.ca
Note: Programs & services include: home care; immunization; Indigenous Health Program; oral health; postpartum support; sexual health; & tuberculosis testing

Elnora: Elnora Community Health Centre
Affiliated with: Alberta Health Services
PO Box 659, 425 - 8 Ave., Elnora, AB T0M 0Y0
Tel: 403-773-3636 *Fax:* 403-773-3949
www.albertahealthservices.ca
Note: Programs & services include: immunization; prenatal education; public health; tuberculosis testing.

Fishing Lake Metis Settle: Fishing Lake Metis
Settlement Community Health Services
Affiliated with: Alberta Health Services
Fishing Lake Metis Settle, AB T0A 1A0
Tel: 780-943-3058 *Fax:* 780-943-2575
www.albertahealthservices.ca
Note: Programs & services include: home care; immunization; Indigenous Health Program; oral health; postpartum support; sexual health; & tuberculosis testing

Fort MacLeod: Fort Macleod Community Health
Affiliated with: Alberta Health Services
744 - 26 St. South, Fort MacLeod, AB T0L 0Z0
Tel: 403-553-5311 *Fax:* 403-553-4567
www.albertahealthservices.ca
Note: Programs & services include: emergency; x-ray; immunization; environmental public health; prenatal education; & public health nursing.

Fort MacLeod: Fort Macleod Health Centre
Affiliated with: Alberta Health Services
744 - 26 St. South, Fort MacLeod, AB T0L 0Z0
Tel: 403-553-5311 *Fax:* 403-553-4567
www.albertahealthservices.ca
Note: Programs & services include: addiction; environmental public health; home care; general radiography; immunization; emergency; hemodialysis; physiotherapy; speech language pathology; respiratory therapy; prenatal education; nutrition counselling; & tuberculosis testing.

Fort McMurray: Fort McMurray Community Health
Services
Affiliated with: Alberta Health Services
113 Thickwood Blvd., Fort McMurray, AB T9H 5E5
Tel: 780-791-6247 *Fax:* 780-641-9185
www.albertahealthservices.ca
Note: Services: immunization; public health nursing.

Fort Vermilion: Fort Vermilion Community Health
Centre
Affiliated with: Alberta Health Services
4804 - 50 St., Fort Vermilion, AB T0H 1N0
Tel: 780-927-3391
www.albertahealthservices.ca
Note: Programs & services include: mental health; home care; STI program; speech & language; travel health; & tuberculosis testing.

Fox Creek: Fox Creek Healthcare Centre
Affiliated with: Alberta Health Services
Former Name: Aspen Health Services
600 - 3rd St., Fox Creek, AB T0H 1P0
Tel: 780-622-3545 *Fax:* 780-622-3474
www.albertahealthservices.ca
Note: Programs & services include: addiction; environmental public health; eating disorder; mental health; palliative care; home care; general radiography; immunization; nutrition counselling; & tuberculosis testing.

Gibbons: Gibbons Health Unit
Affiliated with: Alberta Health Services
4720 - 50 Ave., Gibbons, AB T0A 1N0
Tel: 780-342-2660
www.albertahealthservices.ca
Note: Programs & services include: immunization; new moms network; school health; tuberculosis testing.

Gift Lake: Gift Lake Community Health Services
Affiliated with: Alberta Health Services
Main St., Gift Lake, AB T0G 1B0
Tel: 780-767-2101
www.albertahealthservices.ca
Note: Programs & services include: home care; immunization; oral health; palliative care; & tuberculosis.

Glendon: Glendon Community Health Services
Affiliated with: Alberta Health Services
Former Name: Glendon Community Health Clinic
2 St. Railway Ave., Glendon, AB T0A 1P0
Tel: 780-635-3861 *Fax:* 780-635-4213
www.albertahealthservices.ca
Note: Programs & services include: general medicine; immunization; laboratory; social work; & tuberculosis testing.

Grande Cache: Grande Cache Provincial Building
Affiliated with: Alberta Health Services
10001 Hoppe Ave., Grande Cache, AB T0E 0Y0
Tel: 780-827-3504
www.albertahealthservices.ca
Note: Programs & services include: breastfeeding clinic; immunization; oral health; nutrition counselling; prenatal classes; speech & language services; & tuberculosis testing.

Grande Prairie: Community Village
Affiliated with: Alberta Health Services
10116 - 102 Ave., Grande Prairie, AB T8V 1A1
Tel: 780-532-4494
admin@thecommunityvillage.ca
www.thecommunityvillage.ca
Note: Offers immunization clinics, wellness clinics, nurse practitioner, & other services

Grande Prairie: Grande Prairie College & Community
Health Centre
Affiliated with: Alberta Health Services
10620 - 104 Ave., Grande Prairie, AB T8V 8J8
Tel: 780-814-5800
www.albertahealthservices.ca
Note: Programs & services include: physician; nurse practitioner; dietitian; nutrition; mental health; diagnostic imaging; immunization; laboratory; & sexual health.

Grande Prairie: Grande Prairie Provincial Building
Affiliated with: Alberta Health Services
Former Name: Public Health Centre
10320 - 99 St., Grande Prairie, AB T8V 6J4
Tel: 780-513-7500
www.albertahealthservices.ca
Note: Services include immunization & public health nursing.

Grande Prairie: Grande Prairie Virene Building
Affiliated with: Alberta Health Services
10121 - 97 Ave., Grande Prairie, AB T8V 0N5
Tel: 780-532-4447
www.albertahealthservices.ca
Note: Programs & services include: audiology; home care; occupation therapy; palliative care; physical therapy; nutrition counselling; palliative care; prenatal classes; & tuberculosis testing.

Hanna: Hanna Health Centre
Affiliated with: Alberta Health Services
Former Name: Hanna Health Unit
PO Box 730, 904 Centre St. North, Hanna, AB T0J 1P0
Tel: 403-854-3331
www.albertahealthservices.ca
Note: Programs & services include: addiction; general radiography; palliative care; physioteraphy; speech language pathology; environmental public health; home care; general radiography; immunization; tuberculosis testing.

High River: High River Public Health Centre
Affiliated with: Alberta Health Services
310 Macleod Trail SW, High River, AB T1V 1M7
Tel: 403-652-5450 *Fax:* 403-652-5455
www.albertahealthservices.ca
Note: Programs & services include: diabetes clinic; immunization; lactation; school health; shool oral health; tuberculosis testing.

Jasper: Seton - Jasper Healthcare Centre
Affiliated with: Alberta Health Services
Former Name: Jasper Community Health Services
PO Box 310, 518 Robson St., Jasper, AB T0E 1E0
Tel: 780-852-3344 *Fax:* 780-852-3413
www.albertahealthservices.ca
Note: Programs & services include: addiction; environmental public health; home care; general radiography; immunization; nutrition counselling; pharmacy; palliative care; prenatal classes; social work; tuberculosis testing.

Kikino: Kikino Community Health Services
Affiliated with: Alberta Health Services
Kikino, AB T0A 2B0
Tel: 780-623-7797
www.albertahealthservices.ca
Note: Programs & services include: home care; immunization; palliative care; & tuberculosis testing.

Kinuso: Kinuso Community Health Services
Affiliated with: Alberta Health Services
230 Centre St., Kinuso, AB T0G 1K0
Tel: 780-775-3501 *Fax:* 780-775-3944
www.albertahealthservices.ca
Note: Programs & services include: home care; immunization; oral health; palliative care; & tuberculosis testing.

Kitscoty: Kitscoty Community Health Centre
Affiliated with: Alberta Health Services
4922 - 49 Ave., Kitscoty, AB T0B 2P0
Tel: 780-846-2824 *Fax:* 780-846-2731
www.albertahealthservices.ca
Note: Programs & services include: immunization; infant nutrition classes; occupation therapy; physiotherapy; prenatal education; public health nurse; tuberculosis testing.

La Crete: La Crete Continuing Care Centre
Affiliated with: Alberta Health Services
Former Name: La Crete Health Centre
10601 - 100 Ave., La Crete, AB T0H 2H0
Tel: 780-928-4215 *Fax:* 780-928-4237
www.albertahealthservices.ca
Note: Offers community health services as well as continuing care.

Lac La Biche: Lac La Biche Provincial Building
Affiliated with: Alberta Health Services
Former Name: Lac La Biche Community Health
Services
PO Box 297, 9503 Beaverhill Rd., Lac La Biche, AB T0A 2C0
Tel: 780-623-4471
www.albertahealthservices.ca
Note: Programs & services include: addiction; environmental public health; home care; mental health; immunization; prenatal classes; occupational therapy; tuberculosis testing; speech language pathology.

Leduc: Leduc Public Health Centre
Affiliated with: Alberta Health Services
4219 - 50 St., Leduc, AB T9E 8C9
Tel: 780-980-4644
www.albertahealthservices.ca

Note: Programs & services include: immunization; health education; assessments & screenings; & referral.

Lethbridge: **Lethbridge Health Unit**
Affiliated with: Alberta Health Services
801 - 1 Ave. South, Lethbridge, AB T1J 4L5
Tel: 403-388-6666 *Fax:* 403-328-5934
www.albertahealthservices.ca
Note: Programs & services include: environmental public health; immunization; prenatal education; tuberculosis testing.

Magrath: **Magrath Community Health Centre**
Affiliated with: Alberta Health Services
Former Name: Magrath Hospital
PO Box 550, 37E - 2 Ave. North, Magrath, AB T0K 1J0
Tel: 403-758-6149
www.albertahealthservices.ca
Note: Programs & services include: diagnostic imaging; general radiography; laboratory; occupational therapy; physical therapy; public health nursing; respiratory therapy; & speech language pathology.

Manning: **Manning Community Health Centre**
Affiliated with: Alberta Health Services
Former Name: Peace Country Health Unit
PO Box 1260, 600 - 2 St. NE, Manning, AB T0H 2M0
Tel: 780-836-3391
www.albertahealthservices.ca
Note: Programs & services include: addiction; cardiac diagnostics; environmental public health; home care; general radiography; immunization; mental health; physical therapy; pharmacy; prenatal classes; nutrition counselling; & tuberculosis testing.

Maskwacis: **Maskwacis Health Services**
PO Box 100, Maskwacis, AB T0C 1N0
Tel: 780-585-3830 *Fax:* 780-585-2203
mhs@mymhs.ca
www.mymhs.ca
twitter.com/Maskwacishealth;
www.linkedin.com/company/maskwacis-health-services
Note: Programs & services include: community health; environmental health; HIV / AIDS education; medical clinic; optical; dental; pharmacy; home care; diabetes; counselling & support services; National Native Alcohol & Drug Awareness Program; & Indian Residential School Support Program.

Mayerthorpe: **Mayerthorpe Healthcare Centre**
Affiliated with: Alberta Health Services
4417 - 45 St., Mayerthorpe, AB T0E 1N0
Tel: 780-786-2261
www.albertahealthservices.ca
Note: Programs & services include: mental health; home care; general radiography; pediatrics; physical therapy; nutrition counselling; tuberculosis testing.

McLennan: **Public Health Centre**
Affiliated with: Alberta Health Services
Former Name: Peace Country Health Unit - McLennan
c/o Sacred Heart Community Health Centre, 300 - 3 Ave. NW, McLennan, AB T0H 2L0
Tel: 780-324-3750
www.albertahealthservices.ca

Medicine Hat: **Medicine Hat Community Health Services**
Affiliated with: Alberta Health Services
2948 Dunmore Rd. SE, Medicine Hat, AB T1A 8E3
Tel: 403-502-8200
www.albertahealthservices.ca
Note: Programs & services include: immunization; nutrition; prenatal education; public health nursing; tuberculosis testing.

Milk River: **Milk River Health Centre**
Affiliated with: Alberta Health Services
Former Name: Milk River Hospital
PO Box 90, 517 Centre Ave. East, Milk River, AB T0K 1M0
Tel: 403-647-3500 *Fax:* 403-647-2197
www.albertahealthservices.ca
Note: Programs & services include: diagnostic imaging; emergency; general radiography; laboratory; nutrition counselling; occupational therapy; physical therapy; prenatal education; public health nursing; respiratory therapy; & speech language pathology.

Morinville: **Morinville Provincial Building**
Affiliated with: Alberta Health Services
Former Name: Morinville Public Health Centre; Morinville Health Services
10008 - 107 St., Morinville, AB T8R 1L3
Tel: 780-342-2600 *Fax:* 780-939-7126
www.albertahealthservices.ca

Note: Public health services

Nanton: **Nanton Community Health Centre**
Affiliated with: Alberta Health Services
2214 - 20th St., Nanton, AB T0L 1R0
Tel: 403-646-2218 *Fax:* 403-646-3046
www.albertahealthservices.ca
Note: Programs & services include: adult day support program; electrocardiogram; immunization; laboratory; mental health; occupational therapy; physiotherapy; & tuberculosis testing.

Okotoks: **Okotoks Health & Wellness Centre**
Affiliated with: Alberta Health Services
11 Cimarron Common, Okotoks, AB T1S 2E9
Tel: 403-995-2600 *Fax:* 403-995-2663
www.albertahealthservices.ca
Note: Programs & services include: diabetes clinic; electrocardiogram; environmental public health; general radiography; immunization; nutrition counselling; tuberculosis testing; urgent care.

Olds: **Olds Campus Community Health Centre**
Affiliated with: Alberta Health Services
Ralph Klein Bldg., #2029, 4500 - 50th St., Olds, AB T4H 1R6
Tel: 403-559-2150 *Fax:* 403-559-2151
www.albertahealthservices.ca
Note: Programs & services include: early intervention program; environmental; immunization; oral health; prenatal education; public health; travel health; & tuberculosis testing.

Olds: **Olds Provincial Building**
Affiliated with: Alberta Health Services
Former Name: Olds Community Health Centre
5025 - 50th St., Olds, AB T4H 1R9
Tel: 403-556-8441 *Fax:* 403-556-6842
www.albertahealthservices.ca
Note: Public health programs

Onoway: **Onoway Community Health Services**
Affiliated with: Alberta Health Services
4919 Lac St. Anne Trail, Onoway, AB T0E 1V0
Tel: 780-967-6200 *Fax:* 780-967-4433
www.albertahealthservices.ca
Note: Services include immunization & public health nursing.

Oyen: **Oyen Community Health Services**
Affiliated with: Alberta Health Services
PO Box 296, 315 - 3 Ave. East, Oyen, AB T0J 2J0
Tel: 403-664-3651 *Fax:* 403-664-2934
www.albertahealthservices.ca
Note: Programs & services include: addiction; early hearing detection & intervention; home care; physical therapy; public health nursing; & travel health.

Paddle Prairie: **Paddle Prairie Health Centre**
Affiliated with: Alberta Health Services
PO Box 46, Paddle Prairie, AB T0H 2W0
Tel: 780-841-3342 *Fax:* 780-926-7394
Toll-Free: 855-371-4122
www.albertahealthservices.ca

Peerless Lake: **Trout / Peerless Lake Health Centre**
Affiliated with: Alberta Health Services
PO Box 90, Peerless Lake, AB T0G 2W0
Tel: 780-869-2362 *Fax:* 780-869-2351
www.albertahealthservices.ca
Note: Programs & services include: home care; oral health; social work; palliative care; & tuberculosis testing.

Picture Butte: **Piyami Health Centre**
Affiliated with: Alberta Health Services
Former Name: Picture Butte Hospital
300-A Rogers Ave., Picture Butte, AB T0K 1V0
Tel: 403-388-6751
www.albertahealthservices.ca
Note: Programs & services include: ambulatory care; diagnostic imaging; general radiography; laboratory; occupational therapy; physical therapy; public health nursing; respiratory therapy; & speech language pathology.

Pincher Creek: **Pincher Creek Health Centre**
Affiliated with: Alberta Health Services
1222 Bev McLachlin Dr., Pincher Creek, AB T0K 1W0
Tel: 403-627-1234 *Fax:* 403-627-5275
www.albertahealthservices.ca
Note: Programs & services include: addiction; environmental public health; home care; general radiography; immunization; nutrition counselling; & tuberculosis testing; emergency; spiritual care; speech language pathology; prenatal education; physiotherapy.

Ponoka: **Ponoka Community Health Centre**
Affiliated with: Alberta Health Services
5900 Hwy. 2A, Ponoka, AB T4J 1P5
Tel: 403-783-4491 *Fax:* 403-783-3825
www.albertahealthservices.ca
Note: Programs and services include: immunization; mental health; sexual health; nutrition counselling; & more.

Provost: **Provost Provincial Building**
Affiliated with: Alberta Health Services
Former Name: Hughenden Public Health: Home Care
5419 - 44 St., Provost, AB T0B 3S0
Tel: 780-753-6180 *Fax:* 780-753-2064
www.albertahealthservices.ca
Note: Programs & services include: health promotion; disease prevention; health protection; public health nurse.

Rainbow Lake: **Rainbow Lake Community Health Services**
Affiliated with: Alberta Health Services
Former Name: Rainbow Lake Health Centre
PO Box 177, 6A Commercial Rd., Rainbow Lake, AB T0H 2Y0
Tel: 780-956-3646
www.albertahealthservices.ca
Note: Programs & services include: addiction & mental health; environmental; nutrition counselling; & tuberculosis testing.

Red Deer: **Red Deer - 49th Street Community Health Centre**
Affiliated with: Alberta Health Services
Also Known As: Red Deer Commuinity Health Centre
4755 - 49th St., Red Deer, AB T4N 1T6
Tel: 403-314-5225
www.albertahealthservices.ca
Note: Programs & services include: audiology; occupational therapy; physiotherapy; speech language pathology; & tuberculosis testing.

Red Deer: **Red Deer - Bremner Ave. Community Health Centre**
Affiliated with: Alberta Health Services
2845 Bremner Ave., Red Deer, AB T4R 1S2
Tel: 403-341-2100 *Fax:* 403-346-2610
www.albertahealthservices.ca
Note: Programs & services include: asthma education program; continuing care counselling; enterostomal therapy; home care; mobility clinic; nutrition counselling; & rehabilitation

Red Deer: **Red Deer - Johnstone Crossing Community Health Centre**
Affiliated with: Alberta Health Services
300 Jordan Pkwy., Red Deer, AB T4P 0G8
Tel: 403-356-6300 *Fax:* 403-356-6440
www.albertahealthservices.ca
Note: Programs & services include: early intervention program; environmental; immunization; oral health; prenatal education; dietitian counselling; public health; respiratory therapy; travel health; & tuberculosis testing.

Red Earth Creek: **Red Earth Creek Community Health Services**
Affiliated with: Alberta Health Services
Red Earth Creek, AB T0G 1X0
Tel: 780-649-2242 *Fax:* 780-649-2029
www.albertahealthservices.ca
Note: Services include Alberta Aids to Daily Living Program & tuberculosis testing.

Redwater: **Redwater Health Centre**
Affiliated with: Alberta Health Services
4812 - 58 St., Redwater, AB T0A 2W0
Tel: 780-942-3932 *Fax:* 780-942-2373
www.albertahealthservices.ca
Number of Beds: 14 acute care beds; 7 continuing care beds
Note: Programs & services include: emergency; general radiography; social work; spiritual care.

Rimbey: **Rimbey Community Health Centre**
Affiliated with: Alberta Health Services
4709 - 51 Ave., Rimbey, AB T0C 2J0
Tel: 403-843-2288 *Fax:* 403-843-3050
www.albertahealthservices.ca
Note: Programs & services include: home care; occupational therapy; immunization; prenatal classes; tuberculosis testing.

Rocky Mountain House: Rocky Mountain House
Health Centre
Affiliated with: Alberta Health Services
5016 - 52 Ave., Rocky Mountain House, AB T4T 1T2
Tel: 403-845-3030 *Fax:* 403-845-4975
www.albertahealthservices.ca

Sedgewick: Sedgewick Community Health Centre
Affiliated with: Alberta Health Services
4822 - 50 St., Sedgewick, AB T0B 4C0
Tel: 780-384-3652 *Fax:* 780-384-3699
www.albertahealthservices.ca
Note: Programs & services include: palliative care; respiratory
therapy; environmental public health; home care; general
radiography; immunization; occupational therapy; prenatal
education; & tuberculosis testing.

Sherwood Park: Strathcona County Health Centre
Affiliated with: Alberta Health Services
2 Brower Dr., Sherwood Park, AB T8H 1V4
Tel: 780-342-4600
www.albertahealthservices.ca
Note: Programs & services include: environmental public health;
immunization; school health; & tuberculosis testing.

Smoky Lake: George McDougall - Smoky Lake
Healthcare Centre
Affiliated with: Alberta Health Services
4212 - 55 Ave., Smoky Lake, AB T0A 3C0
Tel: 780-656-3034
www.albertahealthservices.ca
Note: Programs & services include: emergency; breastfeeding
clinic; home care; general radiography; immunization; nutrition
counselling; mental health; tuberculosis testing.

Spirit River: Spirit River Community Health Services
Affiliated with: Alberta Health Services
Former Name: Mistahia Health Unit - Spirit River
5003 - 45 Ave., Spirit River, AB T0H 3G0
Tel: 780-864-3063
www.albertahealthservices.ca
Note: Programs & services include: mental health; home care;
immunization; nutrition counselling; prenatal counselling; speech
& language; palliative care; prenatal classes; & tuberculosis
testing.

Spruce Grove: Spruce Grove Health Unit
Affiliated with: Alberta Health Services
505 Queen St., Spruce Grove, AB T7X 2V2
Tel: 780-342-1300
www.albertahealthservices.ca
Note: Programs & services include: early intervention program;
laboratory; public health; & school dental & health services.

Spruce Grove: Stan Woloshyn Building
Affiliated with: Alberta Health Services
205 Diamond Ave., Spruce Grove, AB T7X 3A8
Tel: 780-342-1380 *Fax:* 780-960-0369
www.albertahealthservices.ca
Note: Primarily provides environmental health services.

St. Albert: St. Albert Public Health Centre
Affiliated with: Alberta Health Services
23 Sir Winston Churchill Ave., St. Albert, AB T8N 2S7
Tel: 780-459-6671 *Fax:* 780-460-7062
www.albertahealthservices.ca
Note: Programs & services include: environmental public health;
immunization; school dental, nursing, & health services; & travel
health

St. Paul: St. Paul Community Health Services
Affiliated with: Alberta Health Services
5610 - 50 Ave., St. Paul, AB T0A 3A1
Tel: 780-645-3396 *Fax:* 780-645-6609
www.albertahealthservices.ca
Note: Programs & services include: audiology; environmental
public health; home care; palliative care; immunization;
tuberculosis testing.

Stettler: Stettler Community Health Centre
Affiliated with: Alberta Health Services
5911 - 50 Ave., Stettler, AB T0C 2L0
Tel: 403-742-3326 *Fax:* 403-742-1353
www.albertahealthservices.ca
Note: Programs & services include: audiology; environmental
public health; home care; mobility clinic; immunization; public
health nurse; tuberculosis testing.

Strathmore: Strathmore Public Health Office
Affiliated with: Alberta Health Services
650 Westchester Rd., Strathmore, AB T1P 1H8
Tel: 403-361-7200 *Fax:* 403-361-7244
www.albertahealthservices.ca

Sundre: Sundre Community Health Centre
Affiliated with: Alberta Health Services
212 - 6 Ave. NE, Sundre, AB T0M 1X0
Tel: 403-638-4063 *Fax:* 403-638-4460
www.albertahealthservices.ca

Swan Hills: Swan Hills Healthcare Centre
Affiliated with: Alberta Health Services
Public Health Centre, PO Box 261, 29 Freeman Dr., Swan
Hills, AB T0G 2C0
Tel: 780-333-7000 *Fax:* 780-333-7009
www.albertahealthservices.ca
Note: Programs & services include: emergency; mental health;
home care; general radiography; immunization; nutrition
counselling; tuberculosis testing.

Sylvan Lake: Sylvan Lake Community Health Centre
Affiliated with: Alberta Health Services
4602 - 49 Ave., Sylvan Lake, AB T4S 1M7
Tel: 403-887-2241 *Fax:* 403-887-2610
www.albertahealthservices.ca
Note: Programs & services include: addiction; cardiac
monitoring; continuing care counselling; environmental public
health; home care; general radiography; immunization; nutrition
counselling; tuberculosis testing.

Thorhild: Thorhild Community Health Services
Affiliated with: Alberta Health Services
302 - 2 Ave., Thorhild, AB T0A 3J0
Tel: 780-398-3879 *Fax:* 780-398-2671
www.albertahealthservices.ca
Note: Programs & services include: early childhood intervention
program; fluoride protection; home care; laboratory; oral health;
postpartum support; sexual health; social work; & tuberculosis
testing

Thorsby: Thorsby Public Health Centre
Affiliated with: Alberta Health Services
4825 Hankin St., Thorsby, AB T0C 2P0
Tel: 780-789-4800
www.albertahealthservices.ca
Note: Programs & services include: immunization; new moms
network; fluoride protection for toddlers; & tuberculosis testing.

Valleyview: Valleyview Community Health Services
Affiliated with: Alberta Health Services
**Former Name: Mistahia Health Unit, Valleyview;
Valleyview District Home Care Office**
5112 - 50 Ave., Valleyview, AB T0H 3N0
Tel: 780-524-3338
www.albertahealthservices.ca
Note: Programs & services include: mental health; breastfeeding
clinic; eating disorder; immunization; prenatal classes; sexual
health; travel health; Well Baby Clinic.

Vauxhall: Vauxhall Community Health
Affiliated with: Alberta Health Services
406 - 1 Ave. North, Vauxhall, AB T0K 2K0
Tel: 403-223-7229 *Fax:* 403-654-2134
www.albertahealthservices.ca
Note: Programs & services include: immunization; public health
nursing; tuberculosis testing.

Vegreville: Vegreville Community Health Centre
Affiliated with: Alberta Health Services
5318 - 50 St., Vegreville, AB T9C 1R1
Tel: 780-632-3331 *Fax:* 780-632-4334
www.albertahealthservices.ca
Note: Programs & services include: addiction; environmental
public health; home care; palliative care; immunization; nutrition
counselling; & tuberculosis testing.

Vermilion: Vermilion Provincial Building
Affiliated with: Alberta Health Services
**Former Name: Vermilion Public Health, Home Care,
Rehab**
4701 - 52 St., Vermilion, AB T9X 1J9
Tel: 780-853-5270
www.albertahealthservices.ca

Viking: Viking Community Health Centre
Affiliated with: Alberta Health Services
Former Name: Viking Health Centre
5224 - 50 St., Viking, AB T0B 4N0
Tel: 780-336-4782
www.albertahealthservices.ca
Note: Programs & services include: continuing care counselling;
home care; immunization; nutrition counselling; occupational
therapy; physiotherapy; palliative care; prenatal classes; &
tuberculosis testing.

Vilna: Vilna Community Health Services
Affiliated with: Alberta Health Services
Former Name: Our Lady's Health Centre
5103 - 48 St., Vilna, AB T0A 3L0
Tel: 780-636-3533 *Fax:* 780-656-2242
www.albertahealthservices.ca
Note: Programs & services include: early childhood intervention
program; environmental; laboratory; social work; & tuberculosis
testing.

Vulcan: Vulcan Health Unit
Affiliated with: Alberta Health Services
Vulcan Community Health Centre, 610 Elizabeth St. South,
Vulcan, AB T0L 2B0
Tel: 403-485-3333
www.albertahealthservices.ca

Wabasca: Wabasca / Desmarais Community Health
Services
Affiliated with: Alberta Health Services
867 Stoney Point Rd., Wabasca, AB T0G 2K0
Tel: 780-891-3931
www.albertahealthservices.ca
Note: Programs & services include: home care; immunization;
postpartum depression support; sexual health; & tuberculosis
testing.

Wainwright: Wainwright Provincial Building
Affiliated with: Alberta Health Services
810 - 14 Ave., Wainwright, AB T9W 1R2
Tel: 780-842-4077 *Fax:* 780-842-3151
www.albertahealthservices.ca
Note: Programs & services include: palliative care;
environmental public health; home care; occupation therapy;
speech language pathology; immunization; tuberculosis testing.

Westlock: Westlock Community Health Services
Affiliated with: Alberta Health Services
10024 - 107 Ave., Westlock, AB T7P 2E3
Tel: 780-349-3316 *Fax:* 780-349-5725
www.albertahealthservices.ca
Note: Programs & services include: mental health; eating
disorder; prenatal classes; social work; environmental public
health; home care; general radiography; immunization; nutrition
counselling; tuberculosis testing.

Wetaskiwin: Wetaskiwin Community Health Centre
Affiliated with: Alberta Health Services
5610 - 40 Ave., Wetaskiwin, AB T9A 3E4
Tel: 780-361-4333 *Fax:* 780-361-4335
www.albertahealthservices.ca

Whitecourt: Whitecourt Community Health Services
Affiliated with: Alberta Health Services
4707 - 50 Ave., Whitecourt, AB T7S 1P1
Tel: 780-706-3173 *Fax:* 780-706-7154
www.albertahealthservices.ca
Note: Programs & services include: mental health; oral health;
speech and language.

Winfield: Winfield Community Health Centre
Affiliated with: Alberta Health Services
Former Name: Crossroads Health Unit - Winfield
PO Box 114, 10 - 2 Ave. West, Winfield, AB T0C 2X0
Tel: 780-682-4755 *Fax:* 780-682-4750
www.albertahealthservices.ca
Note: Programs & services include: home care; general
radiography; immunization; nutrition counselling; tuberculosis
testing.

Worsley: Worsley Community Health Services
Affiliated with: Alberta Health Services
404 Alberta Ave., Worsley, AB T0H 3W0
Tel: 780-685-3752
www.albertahealthservices.ca
Note: Services include immunization & public health nursing.

Nursing Stations

Chateh: Hay Lake Assumption Nursing Station
PO Box 90, Chateh, AB T0H 0X0
Tel: 780-321-3733

Rocky Mountain House: Bighorn Health Station
PO Box 1617, Rocky Mountain House, AB T4T 1B2
Tel: 403-845-3660

Special Treatment Centres

Banff: Cascade Plaza
Affiliated with: Alberta Health Services
#320, 317 Banff Ave., Banff, AB T1L 1B4
Tel: 403-678-3133 Fax: 403-678-3138
www.albertahealthservices.ca
Note: Addiction prevention & adult & youth counselling.

Barrhead: Barrhead - 5143-50 Street
Affiliated with: Alberta Health Services
PO Box 4504, 5143 - 50 St., Barrhead, AB T7N 1A4
Tel: 780-674-8239 Fax: 780-674-8294
Toll-Free: 866-332-2322
www.albertahealthservices.ca
Note: Addiction prevention & adult & youth counselling.

Barrhead: Barrhead Community Cancer Centre
Affiliated with: Alberta Health Services
Barrhead Healthcare Centre, 4815 - 51 Ave., Barrhead, AB T7N 1M1
Tel: 780-305-3304
www.albertahealthservices.ca

Blackfoot: Thorpe Recovery Centre (TRC)
Affiliated with: Alberta Health Services
Also Known As: Walter A. "Slim" Thorpe Recovery Centre
PO Box 291, Blackfoot, AB T0B 0L0
Tel: 780-875-8890 Fax: 780-875-2161
Toll-Free: 877-875-8890
info@thorperecoverycentre.org
www.thorperecoverycentre.org
www.facebook.com/thorperecoverycentre
Year Founded: 1975
Note: Detox, residential & transitional services.
Teressa Krueckl, Executive Director

Bonnyville: Bonnyville Community Cancer Centre
Affiliated with: Alberta Health Services
Bonnyville Healthcare Centre, 5001 Lakeshore Dr., Bonnyville, AB T9N 2J7
Tel: 780-826-3311 Fax: 780-826-6527
www.albertahealthservices.ca

Bonnyville: Bonnyville Provincial Building
Affiliated with: Alberta Health Services
PO Box 7085, #201, 4904 - 50 Ave., Bonnyville, AB T9N 2J6
Tel: 780-826-8054 Fax: 780-826-8057
Toll-Free: 866-332-2322
www.albertahealthservices.ca
Note: Addiction prevention & adult & youth counselling.

Brooks: Brooks - 403-2 Avenue West
Affiliated with: Alberta Health Services
403 - 2nd Ave. West, Brooks, AB T1R 0S3
Tel: 403-362-1265 Fax: 403-362-1248
Toll-Free: 866-332-2322
brooks@albertahealthservices.ca
www.albertahealthservices.ca
Note: Addiction prevention & adult & youth counselling.

Calgary: Alcove Addiction Recovery for Women
Affiliated with: Alberta Health Services
Former Name: Youville Women's Residence
1937 - 42 Ave. SW, Calgary, AB T2T 2M6
Tel: 403-242-0722 Fax: 403-242-3915
www.alcoverecovery.net
www.facebook.com/alcoverecoveryforwomen;
twitter.com/AlcoveRecovery; instagram.com/alcoverecovery
Year Founded: 1977
Note: Provides support & services for women experiencing addiction & mental health issues.

Calgary: Alpha House
Affiliated with: Alberta Health Services
203 - 15 Ave. SE, Calgary, AB T2G 1G4
Tel: 403-234-7388 Fax: 403-234-7391
info@alphahousecalgary.com
www.alphahousecalgary.com
www.facebook.com/AlphaHouseSociety;
twitter.com/alphahouseyyc
Year Founded: 1981
Note: Programs & services include: outreach; shelter; detox; & housing.
Kathy Christiansen, Executive Director
kathy@alphahousecalgary.com

Calgary: Aventa Addiction Treatment For Women
Affiliated with: Alberta Health Services
610 - 25 Ave. SW, Calgary, AB T2S 0L6
Tel: 403-245-9050 Fax: 403-245-9485
info@aventa.org
www.aventa.org
www.facebook.com/AventaAddictionTreatmentForWomen
Note: Provides addiction treatment services for women.
Kim Turgeon, Executive Director
kturgeon@aventa.org
Garth Boak, Financial Manager
gboak@aventa.org
Diane MacPherson, Communications Manager
dmacpherson@aventa.org

Calgary: Calgary - 707-10 Avenue SW
Affiliated with: Alberta Health Services
707 - 10th Ave. SW, 3rd Fl., Calgary, AB T2R 0B3
Tel: 403-367-5000 Fax: 403-367-5010
www.albertahealthservices.ca
Note: Addiction prevention & adult counselling.

Calgary: Calgary Women's Health Centre
Affiliated with: Alberta Health Services
1441 29 St. NW, Calgary, AB T2N 4J8
Tel: 403-944-2270 Fax: 403-944-2271
www.albertahealthservices.ca
Note: Provides breast health & nutrition counselling services.

Calgary: Calgary Youth Addiction Services Centre
Affiliated with: Alberta Health Services
1005 - 17 St. NW, Calgary, AB T2N 2E5
Tel: 403-297-4664 Fax: 403-297-4668
Toll-Free: 866-332-2322
www.albertahealthservices.ca
Note: Services include: recovery, stabalization, & detox; counselling; mobile services; day treatment programs; & community health promotion.

Calgary: Fresh Start Recovery Centre
Affiliated with: Alberta Health Services
411 - 41 Ave. NE, Calgary, AB T2E 2N4
Tel: 403-387-6266 Fax: 403-235-1532
Toll-Free: 844-768-6266
info@freshstartrecovery.ca
www.freshstartrecovery.ca
www.facebook.com/FreshStartRecovery;
twitter.com/FreshStartRC;
www.linkedin.com/company/fresh-start-recovery-centre
Year Founded: 1992
Number of Beds: 50 beds
Note: Residential alcohol & drug addiction treatment centre for men.
Stacey Petersen, Executive Director
Bruce Holstead, Director, Operations
Pat Cole, Financial Administrator

Calgary: Renfrew Recovery Detoxification Centre
Affiliated with: Alberta Health Services
1611 Remington Rd. NE, Calgary, AB T2E 5K6
Tel: 403-297-3337 Fax: 403-297-4592
Toll-Free: 866-332-2322
www.albertahealthservices.ca

Calgary: Sunrise Healing Lodge Society
Affiliated with: Alberta Health Services
Former Name: Sunrise Native Addictions Services Society; Native Addiction Services
Also Known As: SUNRISE
1231 - 34 Ave. NE, Calgary, AB T2E 6N4
Tel: 403-261-7921 Fax: 403-261-7945
nasgeneral@nass.ca
www.nass.ca
Year Founded: 1974
Number of Beds: 36
Area Served: Calgary & area Number of Employees: 32
Note: Offers 12-step & Aboriginal-based addiction programming. Only treatment centre in Calgary that uses Aboriginal Spiritual Teachings as a core part of the program. Serves people 18 & over, of all nationalities.
Leslie Big Bull, Executive Director, Operations
403-261-7921, lbigbull@nass.ca
Bryan Flack, Program Director
403-261-7921, bflack@nass.ca
Deborah Axworthy, Manager, Administration
403-261-7921, daxworthy@nass.ca

Calgary: Tom Baker Cancer Centre (TBCC)
Affiliated with: Alberta Health Services
1331 - 29 St. NW, Calgary, AB T2N 4N2
Tel: 403-521-3723 Fax: 403-355-3206
Toll-Free: 866-238-3735
calgarypsychosocial@albertahealthservices.ca
www.ahs.ca/tbcc
Year Founded: 1958
Note: Programs & services include: medical oncology; surgery (E-mail, Alberta Radiosurgery Centre:
arcinfo@cancerboard.ab.ca); radiation oncology; radiology; chemotherapy treatments; psychosocial resources; pathology; genetics; & research.
Heather Chappell, Acting Executive Director

Canmore: Bow Valley Community Cancer Centre
Affiliated with: Alberta Health Services
Canmore General Hospital, 1100 Hospital Pl., Canmore, AB T1W 1N2
Tel: 403-679-7313
www.albertahealthservices.ca

Canmore: Camrose Community Cancer Centre
Affiliated with: Alberta Health Services
St. Mary's Hospital, 4607 - 53 St., Canmore, AB T4V 1Y5
Tel: 780-679-2822
www.albertahealthservices.ca

Canmore: Canmore Boardwalk Building
Affiliated with: Alberta Health Services
743 Railway Ave., Canmore, AB T1W 1P2
Tel: 403-678-3133 Fax: 403-678-3138
Toll-Free: 866-332-2322
www.albertahealthservices.ca
Note: Addiction prevention & adult & youth counselling.

Clareshom: Lander Treatment Centre
Affiliated with: Alberta Health Services
221 Fairway Dr., Clareshom, AB T0L 0T0
Tel: 403-625-1395 Fax: 403-625-1300
Number of Beds: 48 beds
Note: Adult residential addiction services.

Cold Lake: Cold Lake - 5013-51 Street
Affiliated with: Alberta Health Services
5013 - 51 St., Cold Lake, AB T9M 1P3
Tel: 780-594-7556 Fax: 780-594-2144
Toll-Free: 866-332-2322
www.albertahealthservices.ca
Note: Addiction prevention & adult & youth counselling.

Drayton Valley: Drayton Valley Community Cancer Centre
Affiliated with: Alberta Health Services
Drayton Valley Hospital & Care Centre, 4550 Madsen Ave., Drayton Valley, AB T7A 1N8
Tel: 780-542-5321 Fax: 780-621-4966
www.albertahealthservices.ca

Drumheller: Drumheller Community Cancer Centre
Affiliated with: Alberta Health Services
Drumheller Health Centre, 351 - 9th St. NW, Drumheller, AB T0J 0Y1
Tel: 403-823-6500 Fax: 403-823-5076
www.albertahealthservices.ca

Edmonton: ACCESS Open Minds Clinic
Affiliated with: Alberta Health Services
10211 - 105 St. NW, Edmonton, AB T5J 1E3
Tel: 780-415-0048
www.albertahealthservices.ca
Note: Walk-in clinic for youth seeking addiction and mental health support.

Edmonton: Addiction Recovery Centre
Affiliated with: Alberta Health Services
10302 - 107 St. NW, Edmonton, AB T5J 1K2
Tel: 780-427-4291 Fax: 780-422-2881
www.albertahealthservices.ca
Note: Adult detoxification

Edmonton: Cross Cancer Institute (CCI)
Affiliated with: Alberta Health Services
11560 University Ave., Edmonton, AB T6G 1Z2
Tel: 780-432-8771 Fax: 780-432-8886
www.albertahealthservices.ca
www.facebook.com/179579998746821; twitter.com/AHS_media;
www.youtube.com/AHSChannel
Number of Beds: 56 beds
Specialties: Cancer
Note: Cancer prevention, research & treatment program in northern Alberta.

David Dyer, Executive Director

Edmonton: Glenrose Rehabilitation Hospital
Affiliated with: Alberta Health Services
10230 - 111 Ave. NW, Edmonton, AB T5G 0B7
Tel: 780-735-7999
www.ahs.ca/grh
www.facebook.com/179579998746821; twitter.com/AHS_media;
www.youtube.com/AHSChannel

Year Founded: 1964
Number of Beds: 244 beds
Specialties: Rehabilitation
Note: Rehabilitation centre for both adults & children; research &
training centre for rehabilitation fields.
Lisa Froese, Site Director
Isabel Henderson, Senior Operating Officer
Dr. Gary Faulkner, Director, Rehabilitation Research &
Technology Development

Edmonton: Henwood Treatment Centre
Affiliated with: Alberta Health Services
18750 - 18th St. NW, Edmonton, AB T5Y 6C1
Tel: 780-422-9069 Fax: 780-422-2223
www.albertahealthservices.ca
Note: Adult residential addiction services.

Edmonton: Lois Hole Hospital for Women
Royal Alexandra Hospital
Affiliated with: Alberta Health Services
10405 - 111th Ave. NW, Edmonton, AB T5G 0B6
Tel: 780-735-4111
www.albertahealthservices.ca/lhhw/lhhw.aspx
www.facebook.com/LoisHoleHospitalForWomen
Year Founded: 2010
Note: Programs & services include: clinical care (high-risk
obstetrics, gynecological services & surgery); & innovation,
research, education & prevention in women's health issues.
Located within the Royal Alexandra Hospital.
Janie Clink, Executive Director

Edmonton: Mazankowski Alberta Heart Institute
University of Alberta Hospital
Affiliated with: Alberta Health Services
11220 - 83 Ave., Edmonton, AB T6G 2B7
Tel: 780-407-8407
maz@ahs.ca
www.albertahealthservices.ca/maz/maz.aspx
Year Founded: 2001
Note: Programs & services include: cardiac surgery, cardiology
services, & patient education.
Mishaela Houle, Executive Director, Cardiac Sciences,
Edmonton Zone

Edmonton: McConnell Place North
CapitalCare
Affiliated with: Alberta Health Services
9113 - 144 Ave. NW, Edmonton, AB T5E 6K2
Tel: 780-496-2575 Fax: 780-456-1114
www.capitalcare.net/Page157.aspx
www.facebook.com/capitalcare.edmonton;
twitter.com/CapitalCareYEG
Year Founded: 1995
Number of Beds: 36 beds
Note: Residential care for persons with Alzheimer disease;
Reminiscence therapy.
Francine Drisner, Chief Operating Officer, CapitalCare

Edmonton: Our House Addiction Recovery Centre
Affiliated with: Alberta Health Services
22210 Stony Plain Rd. NW, Edmonton, AB T5S 2C3
Tel: 780-474-8945 Fax: 780 474-8945
ed@ourhouseedmonton.com
www.ourhouseedmonton.com
www.facebook.com/OurHouseAddiction;
twitter.com/OurHouseYEG
Note: Offers a residential program for men over 18 years;
addiction recovery programs for men & women; & education
initiatives.
Mark MacKenzie, Executive Director

Edmonton: Poundmaker's Lodge Treatment Centres
(PMLTC)
Affiliated with: Alberta Health Services
PO Box 34007 Stn. Kingsway Mall, Edmonton, AB T5G 3G4
Tel: 780-458-1884 Fax: 780-459-1876
Toll-Free: 866-458-1884
info@poundmaker.org
www.poundmakerslodge.ca
www.facebook.com/poundmakers.lodge; twitter.com/pmltc14
Year Founded: 1973
Number of Beds: 64 beds
Number of Employees: 58
Specialties: Alcohol & drug treatment

Note: Aboriginal addiction treatment centre near Edmonton,
Alberta. Provides holistic addiction treatment using concepts
based in traditional First Nations, Metis, & Inuit beliefs as well as
12-step, abstinence based recovery. Serves adults aged 18
years & over from all walks of life.

Edmonton: Woman's Health Options
Former Name: Morgentaler Clinic of Edmonton
12409 - 109A Ave., Edmonton, AB T5M 4A7
Tel: 780-484-1124 Fax: 780-489-3379
info@whol.ca
www.womanshealthoptions.com
Note: Provides reproductive health services, primarily abortion.
Kim Cholewa, Director, Operations

Fort McMurray: Fort McMurray Community Cancer
Centre
Affiliated with: Alberta Health Services
Northern Lights Regional Health Centre, 7 Hospital St., Fort
McMurray, AB T9H 1P2
Tel: 780-791-6217
www.albertahealthservices.ca

Fort McMurray: Fort McMurray Recovery Centre
Affiliated with: Alberta Health Services
451 Sakitawaw Trail, Fort McMurray, AB T9H 4P3
Tel: 780-793-8300 Fax: 780-793-8301
www.albertahealthservices.ca
Note: Addiction prevention, day treatment & adult & opioid
depedency program.

Grande Prairie: Grande Prairie Aberdeen Centre
Affiliated with: Alberta Health Services
#300, 9728 Montrose Ave., Grande Prairie, AB T8V 5B6
Tel: 780-538-6330 Fax: 780-538-5256
Toll-Free: 866-332-2322
www.albertahealthservices.ca
Note: Offers addiction & mental health services.

Grande Prairie: Grande Prairie Cancer Centre
Affiliated with: Alberta Health Services
Queen Elizabeth II Hospital, 10409 - 98 St., Grande Prairie,
AB T8V 2E8
Tel: 780-538-7100
www.albertahealthservices.ca
Note: Programs & services include: cancer treatment & care;
chemotherapy; laboratory; nuclear medicine; pastoral care;
pharmacy; social work; & symptom control & palliative care.

Grande Prairie: Northern Addictions Centre
Affiliated with: Alberta Health Services
11333 - 106 St., Grande Prairie, AB T8V 6T7
Tel: 780-538-5210 Fax: 780-538-6359
www.albertahealthservices.ca
Irene Gladue, Site Manager

Hanna: Hanna Provincial Building
Affiliated with: Alberta Health Services
401 Centre St., Hanna, AB T0J 1P0
Tel: 403-854-5276 Fax: 403-854-5280
Toll-Free: 866-332-2322
www.albertahealthservices.ca
Note: Offers addiction prevention services

High Level: Action North Recovery Centre
Affiliated with: Alberta Health Services
PO Box 872, 10502 103rd St., High Level, AB T0H 1Z0
Tel: 780-926-3113 Fax: 780-926-2060
intake@actionnorth.org
www.actionnorth.org
Number of Beds: 18 beds
Note: Residential addictions treatment facility.

High River: High River Community Cancer Centre
Affiliated with: Alberta Health Services
High River General Hospital, 560 - 9th Ave. West, High River,
AB T1V 1B3
Tel: 403-652-0139 Fax: 403-652-0165
www.albertahealthservices.ca

Hinton: Hinton Civic Centre Building
Affiliated with: Alberta Health Services
#102, 131 Civic Centre Rd., Hinton, AB T7V 2E8
Tel: 780-865-8263 Fax: 780-865-8314
Toll-Free: 866-332-2322
www.albertahealthservices.ca
Note: Addiction prevention & adult & youth counselling.

Hinton: Hinton Community Cancer Centre
Affiliated with: Alberta Health Services
Hinton Healthcare Centre, 1280 Switzer Dr., Hinton, AB T7V
1V2
Tel: 780-817-5009 Fax: 780-817-5034
www.albertahealthservices.ca

Killam: Flagstaff Family & Community Services
Affiliated with: Alberta Health Services
PO Box 450, 4809 - 49 Ave., Killam, AB T0B 2L0
Tel: 780-385-3976
Note: Adult & youth addiction counselling services.
Lynne Jenkinson, Executive Director

Lake Louise: Lake Louise - 200 Hector Street
Affiliated with: Alberta Health Services
200 Hector St., Lake Louise, AB T0L 1E0
Tel: 403-678-3133 Fax: 403-678-3138
www.albertahealthservices.ca
Note: Addiction prevention & adult & youth counselling;
ambulatory community physiotherapy.

Lethbridge: Jack Ady Cancer Centre
Affiliated with: Alberta Health Services
960 - 19th St. South, Lethbridge, AB T1J 1W5
Tel: 403-388-6800
www.albertahealthservices.ca
Note: Programs & services include: cancer treatment & care;
chemotherapy; diagnostic imaging; laboratory; palliative care;
radiation therapy; & social work.
Dr. Malcolm Brigden, Medical Director

Lethbridge: Lethbridge Youth Treatment Centre
Affiliated with: Alberta Health Services
402 - 6th Ave. North, Lethbridge, AB T1H 6J9
Tel: 403-388-7600 Fax: 403-388-7619
www.albertahealthservices.ca
Note: Addictions counselling & treatment.

Lethbridge: Sifton Family & Youth Services
528 Stafford Dr. North, Lethbridge, AB T1H 2B2
Tel: 403-381-5411 Fax: 403-382-4565
Note: Provides a treatment program for young people with
behavioural &/or emotional challenges.

Lloydminster: Lloydminster Community Cancer
Centre
Affiliated with: Alberta Health Services
Lloydminster Hospital, 3820 - 43 Ave., Lloydminster, AB S9V
1Y5
Tel: 306-820-6144 Fax: 306-820-6145
www.albertahealthservices.ca

Medicine Hat: Margery E. Yuill Cancer Centre
Affiliated with: Alberta Health Services
Also Known As: Medicine Hat Cancer Centre
Medicine Hat Regional Hospital, 666 - 5th St. SW, Medicine
Hat, AB T1A 4H6
Tel: 403-529-8817
www.albertahealthservices.ca
Year Founded: 1989
Number of Beds: 4 treatment beds
Note: Programs & services include: cancer treatment & care;
chemotherapy; colposcopy; diagnostic imaging; laboratory;
nuclear medicine; & social work.
Jill Forsyth, Manager

Medicine Hat: Medicine Hat Recovery Centre
Affiliated with: Alberta Health Services
370 Kipling St. SE, Medicine Hat, AB T1A 1Y6
Tel: 403-529-9021 Fax: 403-529-9065
www.albertahealthservices.ca
Number of Beds: 18 beds
Note: Adult detoxification & addiction treatment.

Oyen: Oyen Community Health Services
Affiliated with: Alberta Health Services
315 - 3 Ave. East, Oyen, AB T0J 2J0
Tel: 403-529-3582 Fax: 403-529-3130
www.albertahealthservices.ca
Note: Addiction prevention & adult & youth counselling.

Peace River: Peace River Community Cancer Centre
Affiliated with: Alberta Health Services
Peace River Community Health Centre, 10101 - 68 St., Peace
River, AB T8S 1T6
Tel: 780-624-7593 Fax: 780-624-7562
www.albertahealthservices.ca

Peace River: **Peace River Provincial Building**
Affiliated with: Alberta Health Services
9621 - 96 Ave., Peace River, AB T8S 1T4
Tel: 780-624-6151 Fax: 780-624-6579
Toll-Free: 866-332-2322
www.albertahealthservices.ca
Note: Addictions prevention & adult & youth counselling.

Red Deer: **Central Alberta Cancer Centre**
Affiliated with: Alberta Health Services
PO Box 5030, 3942 - 50A Ave., Red Deer, AB T4N 4E7
Tel: 403-343-4526
www.albertahealthservices.ca
Note: Programs & services include: cancer treatment & care;
chemotherapy; clinical breast health program; nutrition;
laboratory; palliative care; pharmacy; radiation therapy; &
spiritual care.

Red Deer: **Red Deer Provincial Building**
Affiliated with: Alberta Health Services
4920 - 51 St., Red Deer, AB T4N 6K8
Tel: 403-340-5274 Fax: 403-340-4804
Toll-Free: 866-332-2322
www.albertahealthservices.ca
Note: Addictions prevention; adult & youth counselling &
treatment.

Red Deer: **Safe Harbour Society for Health &
Housing**
Affiliated with: Alberta Health Services
5246 - 53 Ave., Red Deer, AB T4N 5K2
Tel: 403-347-0181 Fax: 403-347-7275
office@safeharboursociety.org
www.safeharboursociety.org
Year Founded: 2007
Number of Employees: 60
Note: Adult detox & shelter.
Kath Hoffman, Executive Director
kath@safeharboursociety.org

Slave Lake: **Slave Lake - 101-3 Street SW**
Affiliated with: Alberta Health Services
**PO Box 1278, #104, 101 - 3rd St. SW, Slave Lake, AB T0G
2A4**
Tel: 780-849-7127 Fax: 780-849-7394
www.albertahealthservices.ca
Note: Addiction prevention & adult & youth counselling.

St. Paul: **St. Paul Provincial Building**
Affiliated with: Alberta Health Services
#116, 5025 - 49 Ave., St. Paul, AB T0A 3A4
Tel: 780-645-6346 Fax: 780-645-6249
Toll-Free: 866-332-2322
www.albertahealthservices.ca
Note: Addiction prevention & adult & youth counselling.

Strathmore: **Hilton Plaza**
Affiliated with: Alberta Health Services
209 - 3 Ave., Strathmore, AB T1P 1K2
Tel: 403-361-7277 Fax: 403-361-7266
www.albertahealthservices.ca
Note: Addiction prevention & adult & youth counselling.

Vegreville: **Vegreville Provincial Building**
Affiliated with: Alberta Health Services
4809 - 50 St., Vegreville, AB T9C 1R1
Tel: 780-632-6617 Fax: 780-632-6618
www.albertahealthservices.ca
Note: Addiction prevention & adult & youth counselling.

Whitecourt: **Whitecourt Provincial Building**
Affiliated with: Alberta Health Services
5020 - 52 Ave., Whitecourt, AB T7S 1N2
Tel: 780-778-7123 Fax: 780-778-7220
Toll-Free: 866-332-2322
www.albertahealthservices.ca
Note: Addiction prevention & adult & youth counselling.

Long Term Care Facilities

Airdrie: **Bethany Airdrie**
Bethany Care Society
Affiliated with: Alberta Health Services
1736 - 1st Ave. NW, Airdrie, AB T4B 2C4
Tel: 403-948-6022 Fax: 403-948-3897
airdrie@bethanyseniors.com
www.bethanyseniors.com
www.facebook.com/bethanyseniors; twitter.com/BethanyCare;
www.youtube.com/user/BethanyCareSociety;
www.linkedin.com/company/88398
Note: Services include: audiology; foot care; professional
therapy; & recreation.
Jennifer McCue, President & CEO, Bethany Care Society

Athabasca: **Athabasca Healthcare Centre**
Affiliated with: Alberta Health Services
3100 - 48 Ave., Athabasca, AB T9S 1M9
Tel: 780-675-6030 Fax: 780-675-7050
Toll-Free: 855-371-4122
www.albertahealthservices.ca
Number of Beds: 23 beds

Barrhead: **Barrhead Continuing Care Centre**
Affiliated with: Alberta Health Services
Former Name: Keir Care Centre
5336 - 59 Ave., Barrhead, AB T7N 1L2
Tel: 780-674-4506 Fax: 780-674-3003
www.albertahealthservices.ca
Number of Beds: 115 beds
Note: Services include: community care; dementia care; foot
care; nutrition; palliative care; & respite care.

Bentley: **Bentley Care Centre**
Affiliated with: Alberta Health Services
4834 - 52 Ave., Bentley, AB T0C 0J0
Tel: 403-748-4115 Fax: 403-748-2727
www.albertahealthservices.ca
Note: Programs & services include: continuing care services;
physiotherapy; occupational therapy; recreational therapy; &
palliative care.

Calgary: **AgeCare Glenmore**
AgeCare
Affiliated with: Alberta Health Services
Former Name: Beverly Centre - Glenmore
1729 - 90 Ave. SW, Calgary, AB T2V 4S1
Tel: 403-253-8806 Fax: 403-212-3530
glenmore@agecare.ca
www.agecare.ca/glenmore
Year Founded: 1971
Number of Beds: 212 beds
Population Served: 200 Number of Employees: 400
Note: Services include: nursing care; personal care; &
medication management.

Calgary: **Bethany Calgary**
Bethany Care Society
Affiliated with: Alberta Health Services
916 - 18A St. NW, Calgary, AB T2N 1C6
Tel: 403-284-6000 Fax: 403-284-6085
info@bethanyseniors.com
www.bethanyseniors.com
www.facebook.com/bethanyseniors; twitter.com/BethanyCare;
www.youtube.com/user/BethanyCareSociety;
www.linkedin.com/company/88398
Number of Beds: 400 residents
Note: Specialized care, including for younger adults with
disabilities & individuals with complex dementia
Jennifer McCue, President & CEO, Bethany Care Society

Calgary: **Bethany Harvest Hills**
Bethany Care Society
Affiliated with: Alberta Health Services
19 Harvest Gold Manor NE, Calgary, AB T3K 4Y1
Tel: 403-226-8200 Fax: 403-226-7265
info@bethanyseniors.com
www.bethanyseniors.com
www.facebook.com/bethanyseniors; twitter.com/BethanyCare;
www.youtube.com/user/BethanyCareSociety;
www.linkedin.com/company/88398
Number of Beds: 60 long-term care beds
Note: Care centre for persons with Alzheimer disease & other
forms of dementia
Jennifer McCue, President & CEO, Bethany Care Society

Calgary: **Beverly Centre - Lake Midnapore**
AgeCare
Affiliated with: Alberta Health Services
500 Midpark Way SE, Calgary, AB T2X 3S3
Tel: 403-873-2600
bclm@agecare.ca
www.agecare.ca/beverly-centre-lake-midnapore
Number of Beds: 270 residents

Calgary: **Bow-Crest**
Revera Inc.
Affiliated with: Alberta Health Services
5927 Bowness Rd. NW, Calgary, AB T3B 0C7
Tel: 403-288-2373 Fax: 403-288-2403
www.reveraliving.com/bowcrest
www.facebook.com/ReveraInc; twitter.com/Revera_Inc;
www.youtube.com/user/ReveraInc;
www.linkedin.com/company/revera-inc
Number of Beds: 150 beds
Note: Programs & services include: 24 hour nursing care;

dementia care; occupational therapy; pain & symptom
management; rehabilitation; & social work.
Thomas G. Wellner, President & CEO, Revera Living

Calgary: **Carewest Dr. Vernon Fanning Centre**
Affiliated with: Alberta Health Services
722 - 16 Ave. NE, Calgary, AB T2E 6V7
Tel: 403-230-6900 Fax: 403-230-6969
www.carewest.ca
Number of Beds: 289 beds
Note: Services include: adult day support; continuing care;
hemodialysis; & respite care.

Calgary: **Carewest Garrison Green**
Affiliated with: Alberta Health Services
3108 Don Ethell Blvd. SW, Calgary, AB T3E 6Z5
Tel: 403-944-0100 Fax: 403-944-0180
www.carewest.ca

Calgary: **Carewest Glenmore Park**
Affiliated with: Alberta Health Services
6909 - 14 St. SW, Calgary, AB T2V 1P8
Tel: 403-258-7650 Fax: 403-258-7676
www.carewest.ca
Year Founded: 1963
Number of Beds: 147 beds
Note: Programs & services include: Day Hospital;
musculoskeletal program; & geriatric mental health program.

Calgary: **Carewest Rouleau Manor**
Affiliated with: Alberta Health Services
2208 - 2nd St. SW, Calgary, AB T2S 3C1
Tel: 403-943-9850
www.carewest.ca
Number of Beds: 77 beds

Calgary: **Carewest Royal Park**
Affiliated with: Alberta Health Services
4222 Sarcee Rd. SW, Calgary, AB T3E 7J8
Tel: 403-240-7475 Fax: 403-240-7476
www.carewest.ca
Number of Beds: 50 beds

Calgary: **Carewest Signal Pointe**
Affiliated with: Alberta Health Services
6363 Simcoe Rd. SW, Calgary, AB T3H 4M3
Tel: 403-240-7950 Fax: 403-240-7958
www.carewest.ca

Calgary: **Carewest**
Affiliated with: Alberta Health Services
10101 Southport Rd. SW, Calgary, AB T2W 3N2
Tel: 403-943-8140 Fax: 403-943-8188
www.carewest.ca
Year Founded: 1961
Note: Administration location for Carewest.
Dwight Nelson, Chief Operating Officer
dwight.nelson@ahs.ca

Calgary: **Intercare - Brentwood Care Centre**
Intercare Corporate Group Inc.
Affiliated with: Alberta Health Services
2727 - 16 Ave. NW, Calgary, AB T2N 3Y6
Tel: 403-289-2576 Fax: 403-282-7027
www.intercarealberta.com/brentwood-care-centre.html
Number of Beds: 236 private & semi-private rooms
Christopher Kane, Facility Leader

Calgary: **Intercare - Chinook Care Centre**
Intercare Corporate Group Inc.
Affiliated with: Alberta Health Services
1261 Glenmore Trail SW, Calgary, AB T2V 4Y8
Tel: 403-252-0141 Fax: 403-253-0292
www.intercarealberta.com/chinook-care-centre.html
Number of Beds: Long-term care: 214 private & semi-private
rooms; Hospice: 14 private beds
Lorraine Nygard, Facility Leader

Calgary: **Intercare @ Millrise**
Intercare Corporate Group Inc.
Affiliated with: Alberta Health Services
14911 - 5th St. SW, Calgary, AB T2Y 3E2
Tel: 403-451-4211 Fax: 403-451-4223
www.intercarealberta.com/intercare-millrise.html
Number of Beds: 51 private & semi-private rooms
Ali Bezuidenhout, Clinical Team Leader

Calgary: **Mayfair Care Centre**
Affiliated with: Alberta Health Services
Former Name: Mayfair Nursing Home
8240 Collicutt St. SW, Calgary, AB T2V 2X1
Tel: 403-252-4445 Fax: 403-253-6216
admin@mayfaircarecentre.com
www.mayfaircarecentre.com
Number of Beds: 142 private & semi-private rooms
Note: Services include nursing care, physiotherapy, & dietary.

Calgary: **McKenzie Towne Care Centre**
Revera Inc.
Affiliated with: Alberta Health Services
80 Promenade Way SE, Calgary, AB T2Z 4G4
Tel: 403-508-9808 Fax: 403-257-9268
www.reveraliving.com/mckenzie-ccc
www.facebook.com/Reverainc; twitter.com/Revera_Inc;
www.youtube.com/user/Reverainc;
www.linkedin.com/company/revera-inc
Note: Programs & services include 24 hour nursing care;
recreation therapists; spiritual services; palliative and end-of-life
care; foot care; exercise classes; art therapy; meditation; BBQs;
bus excursions; friendly pet visitations.
Thomas G. Wellner, President & CEO, Revera Living

Calgary: **Mount Royal Care Centre**
Revera Inc.
Affiliated with: Alberta Health Services
1813 - 9 St. SW, Calgary, AB T2T 3C2
Tel: 403-244-8994
www.reveraliving.com/mountroyal
www.facebook.com/Reverainc; twitter.com/Revera_Inc;
www.youtube.com/user/Reverainc;
www.linkedin.com/company/revera-inc
Number of Beds: 107 beds
Note: Programs & services include: 24 hour nursing care;
dietician; foot care; pain & symptom management; recreation;
rehabilitation; & sensory therapy.
Thomas G. Wellner, President & CEO, Revera Living

Calgary: **Newport Harbour**
Park Place Seniors Living
Affiliated with: Alberta Health Services
10 Country Village Cove, Calgary, AB T3K 5T9
Tel: 403-567-5100 Fax: 403-567-5105
nhccadmin@parkplaceseniorsliving.com
www.parkplaceseniorsliving.com
Number of Beds: 131 beds

Calgary: **The Salvation Army Agapé Hospice**
1302 - 8 Ave. NW, Calgary, AB T2N 1B8
Tel: 403-282-6588 Fax: 403-284-1778
information@agapehospice.ca
www.agapehospice.ca
www.facebook.com/thesalvationarmyagapehospice
Year Founded: 1992
Number of Beds: 18 beds
Note: Hospice for terminally ill

Camrose: **The Bethany Group**
Affiliated with: Alberta Health Services
Also Known As: Rosehaven Care Centre
4612 - 53 St., Camrose, AB T4V 1Y6
Tel: 780-679-2000 Fax: 780-679-2001
www.thebethanygroup.ca
Number of Beds: 270 beds
Note: Faith-based organization that operates homes & services
for older, disabled & vulnerable people in the Central Alberta
area, serving over 2300 residents through over 900 staff
members.
Denis Beesley, President & CEO
780-679-2010, denis.beesley@bethanygrp.ca

Camrose: **Louise Jensen Care Centre**
The Bethany Group
Affiliated with: Alberta Health Services
5400 - 46 Ave., Camrose, AB T4V 4P8
Tel: 780-679-3097 Fax: 780-679-2001
www.thebethanygroup.ca

Camrose: **Rosehaven Care Centre**
The Bethany Group
Affiliated with: Alberta Health Services
4612 - 53 St., Camrose, AB T4V 1Y6
Tel: 780-679-3000 Fax: 780-679-2001
www.thebethanygroup.ca

Cochrane: **Bethany Cochrane**
Bethany Care Society
Affiliated with: Alberta Health Services
#1000, 32 Quigley Dr., Cochrane, AB T4C 1X9
Tel: 403-932-6422 Fax: 403-932-4617
cochrane@bethanyseniors.com
www.bethanyseniors.com
www.facebook.com/bethanyseniors; twitter.com/BethanyCare;
www.youtube.com/user/BethanyCareSociety;
www.linkedin.com/company/88398
Note: Services include: foot care; recreation; & professional
therapy.
Jennifer McCue, President & CEO, Bethany Care Society

Cold Lake: **Cold Lake Healthcare Centre**
Affiliated with: Alberta Health Services
314 - 25 St., Cold Lake, AB T9M 1G6
Tel: 780-639-6515 Fax: 780-639-2255
Toll-Free: 855-371-4122
www.albertahealthservices.ca

Didsbury: **Bethany Didsbury**
Bethany Care Society
Affiliated with: Alberta Health Services
1201 - 15th Ave., Didsbury, AB T0M 0W0
Tel: 403-335-4775 Fax: 403-335-4233
info@bethanyseniors.com
www.bethanyseniors.com
www.facebook.com/bethanyseniors; twitter.com/BethanyCare;
www.youtube.com/user/BethanyCareSociety;
www.linkedin.com/company/88398
Number of Beds: 100 suites
Jennifer McCue, President & CEO, Bethany Care Society

Edmonton: **Allen Gray Continuing Care Centre**
Affiliated with: Alberta Health Services
5005 - 28 Ave. NW, Edmonton, AB T6L 7G1
Tel: 780-469-2371 Fax: 780-465-2073
www.allengray.ab.ca
Number of Beds: 156 beds
Note: Services include continuing care & adult day support
program.

Edmonton: **CapitalCare Dickinsfield**
Affiliated with: Alberta Health Services
14225 - 94 St. NW, Edmonton, AB T5E 6C6
Tel: 780-371-6500 Fax: 780-371-6583
www.capitalcare.net/Page149.aspx
www.facebook.com/capitalcare.edmonton;
twitter.com/CapitalCareYEG
Year Founded: 1979
Number of Beds: 275 long-term care beds
Note: Programs & services include: continuing care; secure units
for residents with dementia; supportive & comfort units for
residents in middle to later stages of dementia; care for young
adults who are disabled; & young adult day support program.

Edmonton: **CapitalCare Grandview**
Affiliated with: Alberta Health Services
6215 - 124 St. NW, Edmonton, AB T6H 3V1
Tel: 780-496-7100 Fax: 780-496-7150
www.capitalcare.net/Page151.aspx
www.facebook.com/capitalcare.edmonton;
twitter.com/CapitalCareYEG
Year Founded: 1973
Number of Beds: 135 long-term care beds; 45 post-acute care
beds
Note: Programs & services include: continuing care for persons
with dementia & who are chronically disabled; secure unit for
residents with dementia who are at risk of leaving the building;
supportive & comfort units for residents in middle to later stages
of dementia; & orthopedic sub-acute program.

Edmonton: **CapitalCare Lynnwood**
Affiliated with: Alberta Health Services
8740 - 165 St., Edmonton, AB T5R 2R8
Tel: 780-341-2300 Fax: 780-341-2363
www.capitalcare.net/Page139.aspx
www.facebook.com/capitalcare.edmonton;
twitter.com/CapitalCareYEG
Year Founded: 1966
Number of Beds: 282 long-term care beds
Note: Programs & services include: continuing care; behavioural
assessment & stabilization unit; secure unit for residents with
dementia; supportive & comfort care units for residents in middle
to later stages of dementia; & mental health services.

Edmonton: **CapitalCare Norwood**
Affiliated with: Alberta Health Services
10410 - 111 Ave., Edmonton, AB T5G 3A2
Tel: 780-496-3200 Fax: 780-474-9806
www.capitalcare.net/Page150.aspx
www.facebook.com/capitalcare.edmonton;
twitter.com/CapitalCareYEG
Year Founded: 1964
Number of Beds: 205 beds
Note: Programs & services include: continuing care; brain injury
unit; chronic ventilator unit; medical sub-acute program;
transition program; & palliative care.

Edmonton: **Devonshire Care Centre**
Park Place Seniors Living
Affiliated with: Alberta Health Services
1808 Rabbit Hill Rd., Edmonton, AB T6R 3H2
Tel: 780-665-8050 Fax: 780-665-8051
devonshire@parkplaceseniorsliving.com
devonshirecarecentre.com

Edmonton: **Dianne & Irving Kipnes Centre for
Veterans**
CapitalCare
Affiliated with: Alberta Health Services
4470 McCrae Ave., Edmonton, AB T5E 6M8
Tel: 780-442-5700 Fax: 780-442-5711
www.capitalcare.net/centres/kipnes.html
www.facebook.com/capitalcare.edmonton;
twitter.com/CapitalCareYEG
Year Founded: 2005
Number of Beds: 120 residents
Iris Neumann, Chief Operating Officer, CapitalCare

Edmonton: **Dr. Gerald Zetter Care Centre**
Good Samaritan Society
Affiliated with: Alberta Health Services
9649 - 71 Ave., Edmonton, AB T6E 5J2
Tel: 780-431-3634 Fax: 780-431-3699
goodsaminfo@gss.org
www.gss.org
Number of Beds: 198 long-term care beds; 2 respite beds
Specialties: Tracheostomy care
Shawn Terlson, President & CEO, Good Samaritan Society
sterlson@gss.org

Edmonton: **Edmonton Chinatown Care Centre**
Affiliated with: Alberta Health Services
9539 - 102A Ave., Edmonton, AB T5H 0G2
Tel: 780-429-0888 Fax: 780-429-0803
reception@edmccc.net
www.edmccc.net
Severson Truman, Chief Executive Officer
tseverson@edmccc.net

Edmonton: **Edmonton General Continuing Care
Centre**
Covenant Health
Affiliated with: Alberta Health Services
11111 Jasper Ave., Edmonton, AB T5K 0L4
Tel: 780-342-8000
www.covenanthealth.ca/hospitals-care-centres/edmonton-gener
al-continuing-care-centre
Year Founded: 1895
Number of Beds: 14 long-term care units
Note: Houses a continuing care program for seniors

Edmonton: **Extendicare - Eaux Claires**
Extendicare Canada
Affiliated with: Alberta Health Services
Former Name: Extendicare - Somerset
16503 - 95th St., Edmonton, AB T5Z 0G7
Tel: 780-472-1106
cnh_eauxclaires@extendicare.com
www.extendicarecanada.com/eaux_claires
Number of Beds: 180 beds

Edmonton: **Hardisty Care Centre**
Park Place Seniors Living
Affiliated with: Alberta Health Services
Former Name: Hardisty Nursing Home
6420 - 101 Ave. NW, Edmonton, AB T6A 0H5
Tel: 780-466-9267 Fax: 780-450-8046
hardisty@parkplaceseniorsliving.com
www.parkplaceseniorsliving.com
Year Founded: 1958
Number of Beds: 180 beds
Note: Services include: 24 hour nursing care; dietitian; personal
care assistance; pharmacy; & rehabilitation.
Marek Lupicki, Administrator
Cindy Morris, Director, Care

Edmonton: Jasper Place
Revera Inc.
Affiliated with: Alberta Health Services
8903 - 168th St., Edmonton, AB T5R 2V6
Tel: 780-489-4931
www.reveraliving.com/jasper
www.facebook.com/ReveraInc; twitter.com/Revera_Inc;
www.youtube.com/user/ReveraInc;
www.linkedin.com/company/revera-inc
Note: Programs & services include 24 hour nurse on duty;
Montessori-based memory care program; Yoga; art therapy; bus
excursions; backyard BBQs.
Thomas G. Wellner, President & CEO, Revera Living

Edmonton: McConnell Place West
CapitalCare
Affiliated with: Alberta Health Services
8720 - 165 St., Edmonton, AB T5R 5Y8
Tel: 780-413-4770 Fax: 780-413-4773
www.capitalcare.net/centres/mcconnell_west.html
www.facebook.com/capitalcare.edmonton;
twitter.com/CapitalCareYEG
Number of Beds: 36 beds
Iris Neumann, Chief Operating Officer, CapitalCare

Edmonton: Mill Woods Centre
Good Samaritan Society
Affiliated with: Alberta Health Services
101 Youville Dr. East, Edmonton, AB T6L 7A4
Tel: 780-413-3501 Fax: 780-462-8850
goodsaminfo@gss.org
www.gss.org
Number of Beds: 60 beds
Shawn Terlson, President & CEO, Good Samaritan Society
sterlson@gss.org

Edmonton: Miller Crossing Long Term Care
Revera Inc.
Affiliated with: Alberta Health Services
145251 - 50 St., Edmonton, AB T5A 5J4
Tel: 780-478-9212 Fax: 780-478-2894
www.reveraliving.com/miller
www.facebook.com/ReveraInc; twitter.com/Revera_Inc;
www.youtube.com/user/ReveraInc;
www.linkedin.com/company/revera-inc
Note: Programs & services include 24 hour nurse on staff; foot
care; palliative care; Montessori-based memory care; Tai Chi;
music therapy; backyard BBQs.
Thomas G. Wellner, President & CEO, Revera Living

Edmonton: St. Michael's Long Term Care Centre
St. Michael's Health Group
Affiliated with: Alberta Health Services
7404 - 139 Ave., Edmonton, AB T5C 3H7
Tel: 780-473-5621 Fax: 780-472-4506
Toll-Free: 800-472-6169
smeccs@smhg.ca
www.smhg.ca
www.facebook.com/www.smhg.ca; twitter.com/SMHG
Number of Beds: 153 beds
Note: Services include: 24 hour nursing care; medical care;
dental; gerontology; ophthalmology; podiatry; occupational
therapy; physiotherapy; recreational therapy; laboratory;
nutritional assessment; & social work.
Stan C. Fisher, President & CEO

Edmonton: The Salvation Army Edmonton Grace
Manor
Former Name: Sunset Lodge
12510 - 140 Ave., Edmonton, AB T5X 6C4
Tel: 780-454-5484 Fax: 780-455-7196
www.edmontongracemanor.ca
Year Founded: 2002
Number of Beds: 100 beds
Note: Intermediate care

Edmonton: Shepherd's Care - Kensington Campus
Shepherd's Care Foundation
Affiliated with: Alberta Health Services
12603 - 135 Ave., Edmonton, AB T5L 5B1
Tel: 780-447-3840 Fax: 780-452-3794
www.shepherdscare.org/kensington-campus.php
Year Founded: 1998
Number of Beds: 600 residents

Edmonton: Shepherd's Care - Millwoods Campus
Shepherd's Care Foundation
Affiliated with: Alberta Health Services
6620 - 28 Ave., Edmonton, AB T6K 2R1
Tel: 780-463-9810 Fax: 780-462-1643
www.shepherdscare.org/millwoods-campus.php

Edmonton: South Terrace Long Term Care
Revera Inc.
5905 - 112 St., Edmonton, AB T6H 3J4
Tel: 780-434-1451 Fax: 780-436-4300
www.reveraliving.com/southterrace
www.facebook.com/ReveraInc; twitter.com/Revera_Inc;
www.youtube.com/user/ReveraInc;
www.linkedin.com/company/revera-inc
Year Founded: 1961
Note: Programs & services include 24 hour nurse on staff;
memory care; backyard BBQs; spiritual programs; friendly pet
visitations.
Thomas G. Wellner, President & CEO, Revera Living

Edmonton: Southgate Care Centre
Good Samaritan Society
Affiliated with: Alberta Health Services
4225 - 107 St. NW, Edmonton, AB T6J 2P1
Tel: 780-431-3854 Fax: 780-431-3898
goodsaminfo@gss.org
www.gss.org
Year Founded: 1973
Number of Beds: 226 long-term care suites
Note: Services include: 24 hour nursing care; occupational
therapy; physical therapy; recreational therapy; & social work.
Shawn Terlson, President & CEO, Good Samaritan Society
sterlson@gss.org

Edmonton: Touchmark at Wedgewood
Touchmark, LLC
Affiliated with: Alberta Health Services
18333 Lessard Rd. NW, Edmonton, AB T6M 0A1
Tel: 780-800-7189
www.touchmarkedmonton.com
www.facebook.com/TouchmarkAtWedgewood;
www.youtube.com/user/TouchmarkRetirement
Year Founded: 1980
Number of Beds: 66 bungalows; 115-suite complex
Note: Retirement community with long-term care options
Leanne Gugenheimer, Executive Director

Edmonton: Venta Care Centre
Affiliated with: Alberta Health Services
Former Name: Venta Nursing Home
13525 - 102 St. NW, Edmonton, AB T5E 4K3
Tel: 780-476-6633 Fax: 780-476-6943
www.ventacarecentre.com
Year Founded: 1953
Note: Services include: 24 hour nursing care; dental; dietitian;
occupational therapy; oxygen therapy; pharmacy; physical
therapy; podiatry; recreational programs; & social work.
Dr. Peter Birzgalis, Chief Operating Officer

Edson: Edson Healthcare Centre
Affiliated with: Alberta Health Services
4716 - 5 Ave., Edson, AB T7E 1S8
Tel: 780-723-2229 Fax: 780-723-2135
Toll-Free: 855-371-4122
www.albertahealthservices.ca

Evansburg: Pembina Village
Good Samaritan Society
Affiliated with: Alberta Health Services
5225 - 50 St., Evansburg, AB T0E 0T0
Tel: 780-727-2288
goodsaminfo@gss.org
www.gss.org
Number of Beds: 30 supportive living suites; 30 long-term care
suites; 10 bed dementia care cottage
Shawn Terlson, President & CEO, Good Samaritan Society
sterlson@gss.org

Fairview: Fairview Health Complex
Affiliated with: Alberta Health Services
10628 - 110 St., Fairview, AB T0H 1L0
Tel: 780-835-6180 Fax: 855-776-3805
Toll-Free: 855-371-4122
www.albertahealthservices.ca
Number of Beds: 51 continuing care beds (11 dementia beds); 1
respite bed

Fort McMurray: Northern Lights Regional Health
Centre
Affiliated with: Alberta Health Services
7 Hospital St., 4th Fl., Fort McMurray, AB T9H 1P2
Tel: 780-791-6066 Fax: 855-776-3805
Toll-Free: 855-371-4122
www.albertahealthservices.ca
Number of Beds: 30 beds

Fort Saskatchewan: Rivercrest Care Centre
Qualicare Corporation
Affiliated with: Alberta Health Services
Former Name: Rivercrest Lodge Nursing Home
10104 - 101 Ave., Fort Saskatchewan, AB T8L 2A5
Tel: 780-998-2425 Fax: 780-992-9432
reception@rivercrestlodge.com
www.qualicarehealthservices.com/rivercrest
Number of Beds: 85 beds
Note: Services include: 24 hour nursing care; occupational
therapy; oxygen therapy; recreational therapy; & social work.

Fort Vermilion: St. Theresa General Hospital
Affiliated with: Alberta Health Services
4506 - 46 Ave., Fort Vermilion, AB T0H 1N0
Tel: 780-841-3207 Fax: 855-776-3805
Toll-Free: 855-371-4122
www.albertahealthservices.ca
Number of Beds: 8 beds

Grande Prairie: Mackenzie Place Continuing Care
Affiliated with: Alberta Health Services
Queen Elizabeth II Hospital, 10409 - 98 St., Grande Prairie,
AB T8V 2E8
Tel: 780-538-7100 Fax: 855-776-3805
Toll-Free: 855-371-4122
www.albertahealthservices.ca
Number of Beds: 3 respite beds

Grande Prairie: Points West Living Grande Prairie
Affiliated with: Alberta Health Services
11460 - 104 Ave., Grande Prairie, AB T8V 3G9
Tel: 780-357-5700 Fax: 780-357-5710
info.grandeprairie@pointswestliving.com
pointswestliving.com/gp_pwl_home.php
Year Founded: 2011
Number of Beds: 155 units
Note: Long-term care; hospice; supportive living; & independent
living

High Level: Northwest Health Centre
Affiliated with: Alberta Health Services
11202 - 100 St., High Level, AB T0H 1Z0
Tel: 780-841-3207 Fax: 855-776-3805
Toll-Free: 855-371-4122
www.albertahealthservices.ca

High Prairie: High Prairie J.B. Wood Continuing Care
Affiliated with: Alberta Health Services
High Prairie Health Complex, 4620 - 53 Ave., High Prairie,
AB T0G 1E0
Tel: 780-523-6470 Fax: 780-523-6642
Toll-Free: 855-371-4122
www.albertahealthservices.ca
Number of Beds: 35 beds; 2 respite beds

Hythe: Hythe Continuing Care Centre
Affiliated with: Alberta Health Services
10307 - 100 St., Hythe, AB T0H 2C0
Tel: 780-356-3818 Fax: 855-776-3805
Toll-Free: 855-371-4122
www.albertahealthservices.ca
Number of Beds: 30 long-term care beds; 1 respite bed
Note: Services include: continuing care; diagnostic imaging;
general radiography; immunization; laboratory; pharmacy;
physical therapy; respite care; & therapeutic recreation.

Islay: Islay Assisted Living
Affiliated with: Alberta Health Services
5016 - 53 St., Islay, AB T0B 2J0
Tel: 780-744-3795 Fax: 780-744-3922
www.albertahealthservices.ca
Note: Services include: continuing care counselling; home care;
palliative care; & respite care.

La Crete: La Crete Continuing Care Centre
Affiliated with: Alberta Health Services
10601 - 100 Ave., La Crete, AB T0H 2H0
Tel: 780-841-3207 Fax: 855-776-3508
Toll-Free: 855-371-4122
www.albertahealthservices.ca

Lac La Biche: William J. Cadzow - Lac La Biche
Healthcare Centre
Affiliated with: Alberta Health Services
9110 - 93 St., Lac La Biche, AB T0A 2C0
Tel: 780-623-5911 Fax: 855-776-3805
Toll-Free: 855-371-4122
www.albertahealthservices.ca
Number of Beds: 42 long-term care beds; 1 palliative bed; 1
respite bed

Leduc: Extendicare - Leduc
Extendicare Canada
Affiliated with: Alberta Health Services
4309 - 50 St., Leduc, AB T9E 6K6
Tel: 780-986-2245 *Fax:* 780-986-0669
cnh_leduc@extendicare.com
www.extendicarecanada.com/leduc

Lethbridge: Edith Cavell Care Centre
Chantelle Management Ltd.
Affiliated with: Alberta Health Services
1255 - 5 Ave. South, Lethbridge, AB T1J 0V6
Tel: 403-328-6631 *Fax:* 403-320-9061
edithcavell@chantellegroup.com
www.chantellegroup.com/edith_cavell.htm
Year Founded: 2000
Number of Beds: 120 rooms; 30 special care rooms
Note: Services include: 24 hour nursing care; occupational
therapy; physiotherapy; recreation therapy; & counselling.

Mannville: Mannville Care Centre
Affiliated with: Alberta Health Services
5007 - 46 St., Mannville, AB T0B 2W0
Tel: 780-763-3621 *Fax:* 780-763-3678
Toll-Free: 855-371-4122
www.albertahealthservices.ca
Number of Beds: 23 beds
Note: Services include: continuing care; early intervention
program; home care; laboratory; palliative; & respite care.

McLennan: Manoir du Lac
Integrated Life Care Inc.
Affiliated with: Alberta Health Services
164 - 3rd Ave., McLennan, AB T0H 2L0
Tel: 780-324-2513 *Fax:* 780-324-2060
www.integratedlifecare.ca
Lloyd Del Rosario, Manager & Director, Care
mdlnm@integratedlifecare.ca

Medicine Hat: Riverview Long Term Care
Revera Inc.
Affiliated with: Alberta Health Services
603 Prospect Dr. SW, Medicine Hat, AB T1A 4C2
Tel: 403-527-5531 *Fax:* 403-527-5175
www.reveraliving.com
www.facebook.com/ReveraInc; twitter.com/Revera_Inc;
www.youtube.com/user/ReveraInc;
www.linkedin.com/company/revera-inc
Note: Programs & services include: 24 hour nursing care;
dietician; occupational therapy; pain & symptom management;
Montessori-based memory program; Laughter Yoga; Music & Art
therapy.
Thomas G. Wellner, President & CEO, Revera Living

Medicine Hat: South Ridge Village
Good Samaritan Society
Affiliated with: Alberta Health Services
550 Spruce Way SE, Medicine Hat, AB T1B 4P1
Tel: 403-528-5050 *Fax:* 403-504-2520
goodsaminfo@gss.org
www.gss.org
Number of Beds: 70 continuing care suites; 42 supportive living
suites; three 10-bed dementia care cottages
Shawn Terlson, President & CEO, Good Samaritan Society
sterlson@gss.org

Morinville: Aspen House
Affiliated with: Alberta Health Services
9706 - 100 Ave., Morinville, AB T8R 1T2
Tel: 780-939-1416 *Fax:* 780-939-6144
www.albertahealthservices.ca
Note: Supportive living

Olds: Olds Hospital & Care Centre
Affiliated with: Alberta Health Services
3901 - 57 Ave., Olds, AB T4H 1T4
Tel: 403-507-8110
www.albertahealthservices.ca

Peace River: Sutherland Place Continuing Care
Centre
Affiliated with: Alberta Health Services
Peace River Community Health Centre, 10101 - 68 St., Peace
River, AB T8S 1T6
Tel: 780-624-7538 *Fax:* 855-776-3805
Toll-Free: 855-371-4122
www.albertahealthservices.ca
Number of Beds: 27 continuing care beds; 12 dementia beds; 1
respite bed

Ponoka: Northcott Care Centre
Qualicare Corporation
Affiliated with: Alberta Health Services
4209 - 48 Ave., Ponoka, AB T4J 1P4
Tel: 403-783-4764 *Fax:* 403-783-6420
tserle@northcottcarecentre.com
www.qualicarehealthservices.com/northcott
Number of Beds: 73 beds

Radway: Radway Continuing Care Centre
Affiliated with: Alberta Health Services
5002 - 52 St., Radway, AB T0A 2V0
Tel: 780-736-3740 *Fax:* 780-736-2353
Toll-Free: 855-371-4122
www.albertahealthservices.ca

Red Deer: Bethany CollegeSide
Bethany Care Society
Affiliated with: Alberta Health Services
99 College Circle, Red Deer, AB T0M 1R0
Tel: 403-357-3700 *Fax:* 403-341-5613
info@bethanyseniors.com
www.bethanyseniors.com
www.facebook.com/bethanyseniors; twitter.com/BethanyCare;
www.youtube.com/user/BethanyCareSociety;
www.linkedin.com/company/88398
Jennifer McCue, President & CEO, Bethany Care Society

Rimbey: Rimbey Hospital & Care Centre
Affiliated with: Alberta Health Services
5228 - 50 St., Rimbey, AB T0C 2J0
Tel: 403-843-7807
www.albertahealthservices.ca

Rocky Mountain House: Clearwater Centre
Good Samaritan Society
Affiliated with: Alberta Health Services
5615 - 60 St., Rocky Mountain House, AB T4T 1W2
Tel: 403-845-6033 *Fax:* 403-845-6420
goodsaminfo@gss.org
www.gss.org
Number of Beds: 30 long-term care suites; 29 supportive living
suites; 2 dementia care cottages
Shawn Terlson, President & CEO, Good Samaritan Society
sterlson@gss.org

Sherwood Park: CapitalCare Strathcona
Affiliated with: Alberta Health Services
12 Brower Dr., Sherwood Park, AB T8H 1V3
Tel: 780-467-3366 *Fax:* 780-467-4095
www.capitalcare.net/centres/strathcona.html
www.facebook.com/capitalcare.edmonton;
twitter.com/CapitalCareYEG
Year Founded: 1994
Number of Beds: 111 beds
Note: Programs & services include: continuing care; secure
dementia unit; Eden Alternative philosophy of care; recreational
programs; occupational therapy; respite program; & adult
community day support program.

Sherwood Park: Sherwood Care
Affiliated with: Alberta Health Services
Former Name: Sherwood Park Care Center
2020 Brentwood Blvd. North, Sherwood Park, AB T8A 0X1
Tel: 780-467-2281 *Fax:* 780-449-1529
info@sherwoodcare.com
www.sherwoodcare.com
www.facebook.com/sherwoodcare2020;
twitter.com/sherwood_care
Year Founded: 1969
Number of Employees: 200
Note: Services include: 24 hour nursing care; dietitian; physical
support; therapeutic recreation; & social work.

Smoky Lake: George McDougall - Smoky Lake
Healthcare Centre
Affiliated with: Alberta Health Services
4607 - 52 Ave., Smoky Lake, AB T0A 3C0
Tel: 780-656-3818 *Fax:* 855-776-3805
Toll-Free: 855-371-4122
www.albertahealthservices.ca
Number of Beds: 32 beds

St. Albert: Citadel Care Centre
Qualicare Corporation
Affiliated with: Alberta Health Services
25 Erin Ridge Rd., St. Albert, AB T8N 7K8
Tel: 780-458-3044 *Fax:* 780-458-8563
chowatt@citadelcarecentre.com
www.qualicarehealthservices.com/citadel
Number of Beds: 115 continuing care rooms; 7 semi-private
rooms

St. Albert: Youville Home
Covenant Health
Affiliated with: Alberta Health Services
9A St. Vital Ave., St. Albert, AB T8N 1K1
Tel: 780-460-6900 *Fax:* 780-459-4139
www.covenanthealth.ca/hospitals-care-centres/youville-home
Year Founded: 1963
Number of Beds: 227 beds
Number of Employees: 420
Note: Provides long-term care services.

Standoff: Kainai Continuing Care Centre
Blood Tribe Department of Health Inc.
PO Box 380, Standoff, AB T0L 1Y0
Tel: 403-737-3652
btdh.ca/staff/kainai-continuing-care-centre
Number of Beds: 21 extended care beds; 2 respite care beds; 2
palliative care beds
Crystal Day Chief, Director

Stony Plain: Stony Plain Care Centre
Good Samaritan Society
Affiliated with: Alberta Health Services
4800 - 55 Ave., Stony Plain, AB T7Z 1P9
Tel: 780-963-2261 *Fax:* 780-963-5156
goodsaminfo@gss.org
www.gss.org
Number of Beds: 126 long-term care suites; 30-bed dementia
care cottage
Shawn Terlson, President & CEO, Good Samaritan Society
sterlson@gss.org

Stony Plain: WestView Continuing Care Centre
Affiliated with: Alberta Health Services
4405 South Park Dr., Stony Plain, AB T7Z 2M7
Tel: 780-968-3656 *Fax:* 780-968-3657
www.albertahealthservices.ca

Sylvan Lake: Bethany Sylvan Lake
Bethany Care Society
Affiliated with: Alberta Health Services
4700 - 47 Ave., Sylvan Lake, AB T4S 2M3
Tel: 403-887-7741 *Fax:* 403-887-8447
info@bethanyseniors.com
www.bethanyseniors.com
www.facebook.com/bethanyseniors; twitter.com/BethanyCare;
www.youtube.com/user/BethanyCareSociety;
www.linkedin.com/company/88398
Jennifer McCue, President & CEO, Bethany Care Society

Three Hills: Three Hills Health Centre
Affiliated with: Alberta Health Services
1504 - 2nd St. North, Three Hills, AB T0M 2A0
Tel: 403-443-8006
www.albertahealthservices.ca

Vegreville: Vegreville Care Centre
Affiliated with: Alberta Health Services
4525 - 50 St., Vegreville, AB T9C 0A1
Tel: 780-632-2871 *Fax:* 780-632-6680
www.albertahealthservices.ca
Note: Provides continuing care services for individuals with
complex medical needs.

Westlock: Westlock Continuing Care Centre
Affiliated with: Alberta Health Services
Former Name: Westlock Long Term Care Centre
10203 - 96 St., Westlock, AB T7P 2R3
Tel: 780-349-3306 *Fax:* 780-349-5647
Toll-Free: 855-371-4122
www.albertahealthservices.ca
Number of Beds: 120 beds
Note: Services include: continuing care; adult day program; foot
care clinic; occupational therapy; palliative care; physical
therapy; respite care; therapeutic recreation; & social work.

Wetaskiwin: Wetaskiwin Hospital & Care Centre
Affiliated with: Alberta Health Services
Former Name: Crossroads Hospital & Health Centre
- Wetaskiwin
6910 - 47 St., Wetaskiwin, AB T9A 3N3
Tel: 780-312-3628 *Fax:* 780-312-3727
www.albertahealthservices.ca
Number of Beds: 105 long-term care beds

Nursing Homes

Athabasca: **Extendicare - Athabasca**
Extendicare Canada
Affiliated with: Alberta Health Services
PO Box 119, 4517 - 53 St., Athabasca, AB T9S 1K4
Tel: 780-675-2291 *Fax:* 780-675-3833
cnh_athabasca@extendicare.com
www.extendicareathabasca.com

Number of Beds: 50 beds
Note: Offers nursing, medical, therapeutic, & rehabilitative care.
Joan Cody, Administrator
Judy Scherer, Director, Care
Dr. Adrian Mol, Medical Director

Blairmore: **York Creek Lodge**
Crowsnest Pass Senior Housing
Affiliated with: Alberta Health Services
PO Box 1050, 1810 - 112 St., Blairmore, AB T0K 0E0
Tel: 403-562-2102
www.crowsnestpass-seniorhousing.com
www.facebook.com/YorkCreekLodge
Year Founded: 1980
Number of Beds: 20 beds

Bonnyville: **Extendicare - Bonnyville**
Extendicare Canada
Affiliated with: Alberta Health Services
PO Box 1080, 4602 - 47 Ave., Bonnyville, AB T9N 2E8
Tel: 780-826-3341 *Fax:* 780-826-4890
cnh_bonnyville@extendicare.com
www.extendicarebonnyville.com

Number of Beds: 50 beds
Note: Services include: long-term care; nursing; medical; therapeutic care; & rehabilitative care.
Kim Mercier, Administrator
Rachelle Woods, Director, Care
Dr. Edward Ndovi, Medical Director

Calgary: **Bow View Manor**
Brenda Strafford Foundation Ltd.
Affiliated with: Alberta Health Services
4628 Montgomery Blvd. NW, Calgary, AB T3B 0K7
Tel: 403-288-4446 *Fax:* 403-288-8522
www.thebsf.ca

Year Founded: 1961
Number of Beds: 193 beds
Note: Offers long-term care services & an adult day program.
Catherine Kettlewell, Administrator
catherine.kettlewell@theBSF.ca
Bennette Aguirre, Director, Nursing
bennette.aguirre@theBSF.ca

Calgary: **Carewest George Boyack**
Affiliated with: Alberta Health Services
1203 Centre Ave. NE, Calgary, AB T2E 0A5
Tel: 403-267-2750 *Fax:* 403-267-2757
www.carewest.ca

Number of Beds: 221 beds
Note: Services include: nursing care; personal care; physical therapy; occupational therapy; recreational therapy; & pharmacy.

Calgary: **Carewest Sarcee**
Affiliated with: Alberta Health Services
3504 Scarcee Rd. SW, Calgary, AB T3E 4T4
Tel: 403-686-8100 *Fax:* 403-686-8104
www.carewest.ca

Year Founded: 1962
Note: Provides long-term care, rehabilitation, & recovery services.

Calgary: **Clifton Manor**
Brenda Strafford Foundation Ltd.
Affiliated with: Alberta Health Services
Former Name: Forest Grove Care Centre
4726 - 8 Ave. SE, Calgary, AB T2A 0A8
Tel: 403-272-9831 *Fax:* 403-248-5788
www.thebsf.ca

Number of Beds: 258 beds
Note: Services include: nursing care; personal care; physical therapy; occupational therapy; recreational therapy; & pharmacy.
Escandor Leo, Administrator
leojade.escandor@thebsf.ca
Enongene Emile, Director, Nursing
emile.enongene@thebsf.ca

Calgary: **Extendicare - Cedars Villa**
Extendicare Canada
Affiliated with: Alberta Health Services
3330 - 8 Ave. SW, Calgary, AB T3C 0E7
Tel: 403-249-8915 *Fax:* 403-246-7561
cnh_cedarsvilla@extendicare.com
www.extendicarecedarsvilla.com

Number of Beds: 248 beds
Note: Provides nursing, medical, therapeutic, & rehabilitative care.
Betty Dyck, Administrator
Brittany Jones, Director, Care

Calgary: **Extendicare - Hillcrest**
Extendicare Canada
Affiliated with: Alberta Health Services
1512 - 8 Ave. NW, Calgary, AB T2N 1C1
Tel: 403-289-0236 *Fax:* 403-289-2350
www.extendicarehillcrest.com

Number of Beds: 112 beds
Note: Provides long-term care services.
Kathy Trail, Administrator
ktrail@extendicare.com
Annette Meeuwse, Director, Care

Calgary: **Father Lacombe Care Centre**
Affiliated with: Alberta Health Services
270 Providence Blvd. SE, Calgary, AB T2X 0V6
Tel: 403-256-4641 *Fax:* 403-254-6297
info@fatherlacombe.ca
www.flnh.net

Number of Beds: 110 beds
Note: Services include: nursing; health surveillance; medication management; nutritional counselling; personal care; physiotherapy; occupational therapy; recreational therapy; & social work.
Raymond Cormie, Chief Executive Officer

Calgary: **Glamorgan Care Centre**
Affiliated with: Alberta Health Services
105 Galbraith Dr. SW, Calgary, AB T3E 4Z5
Tel: 403-242-5911 *Fax:* 403-242-7613
www.albertahealthservices.ca

Number of Beds: 52 beds
Note: Services include: nursing care; personal care; physical therapy; occupational therapy; recreational therapy; & pharmacy.

Calgary: **Intercare - Southwood Care Centre**
Intercare Corporate Group Inc.
Affiliated with: Alberta Health Services
211 Heritage Dr. SE, Calgary, AB T2H 1M9
Tel: 403-252-1194 *Fax:* 403-253-0393
www.intercarealberta.com/southwood-care-centre.html
Number of Beds: Long term care: 202 private & semi-private rooms; Hospice: 24 private; Special Care Unit (Brain Injury): 23 private rooms
Note: Services include: dietitian; occupational therapy; physical therapy; recreational therapy; & social worker.
Lydia Wright, Facility Leader

Calgary: **Wentworth Manor**
Brenda Strafford Foundation Ltd.
Affiliated with: Alberta Health Services
5717 - 14 Ave. SW, Calgary, AB T3H 3M2
Tel: 403-242-5005 *Fax:* 403-686-8702
www.wentworthmanor.ca

Number of Beds: 214 beds
Carol Heckel, Administrator
carol.henckel@thebsf.ca
Trish Ramstead, Director, Nursing
trish.ramstead@thebsf.ca

Calgary: **Wing Kei Care Centre**
Chinese Christian Wing Kei Nursing Home Association
Affiliated with: Alberta Health Services
1212 Centre St. NE, Calgary, AB T2E 2R4
Tel: 403-277-7433 *Fax:* 403-230-3857
admin@wingkei.org
www.wingkeicarecentre.org
Year Founded: 2005
Number of Beds: 135 beds

Calgary: **Wing Kei Greenview**
Chinese Christian Wing Kei Nursing Home Association
Affiliated with: Alberta Health Services
307 - 35 Ave. NE, Calgary, AB T2E 2K6
Tel: 403-520-0400 *Fax:* 403-520-0418
admin@wingkei.org
www.wingkeicarecentre.org

Year Founded: 2014
Number of Beds: 95 beds

Camrose: **Bethany Meadows**
The Bethany Group
Affiliated with: Alberta Health Services
4209 - 55 St., Camrose, AB T4V 4Y6
Tel: 780-679-1000
www.thebethanygroup.ca

Number of Beds: 130 beds; 78 supportive housing
Note: Provides continuing care, housing, & support services for adults with health issues.

Derwent: **Northern Lights Manor**
Eagle Hill Foundation
Affiliated with: Alberta Health Services
102 - 1 St. West, Derwent, AB T0B 1C0
Tel: 780-657-2061 *Fax:* 780-657-0044
ehfadmin@eaglehillfoundation.ca
www.eaglehillfoundation.ca/dervent_northern_lights.php
Adrienne Kuzio, Foundation Administrator
ehfadmin@eaglehillfoundation.com

Drumheller: **Hillview Lodge**
Drumheller & District Seniors Foundation
Affiliated with: Alberta Health Services
696 - 6th Ave. East, Drumheller, AB T0J 0Y5
Tel: 403-823-3290 *Fax:* 403-823-3777
reception@ddsf.ca
www.ddsf.ca

Note: Supportive living
Janet Senior, Chief Administrative Officer

Drumheller: **Sunshine Lodge**
Drumheller & District Seniors Foundation
Affiliated with: Alberta Health Services
698 - 6th Ave. East, Drumheller, AB T0J 0Y5
Tel: 403-823-3290 *Fax:* 403-823-3777
reception@ddsf.ca
www.ddsf.ca

Note: Supportive living
Janet Senior, Chief Administrative Officer

Edmonton: **Extendicare - Holyrood**
Extendicare Canada
Affiliated with: Alberta Health Services
8008 - 95 Ave., Edmonton, AB T6C 2T1
Tel: 780-469-1307 *Fax:* 780-469-5196
cnh_holyrood@extendicare.com
www.extendicarecanada.com/edmontonholyrood

Edmonton: **Jubilee Lodge Nursing Home**
Qualicare Corporation
Affiliated with: Alberta Health Services
10333 - 76 St., Edmonton, AB T6A 3A8
Tel: 780-469-4456 *Fax:* 780-450-3297
officemanager@jubileelodgenursinghome.com
www.qualicarehealthservices.com/jubilee
Number of Beds: 156 beds

Fort MacLeod: **Extendicare - Fort Macleod**
Extendicare Canada
Affiliated with: Alberta Health Services
PO Box 189, 654 - 29 St., Fort MacLeod, AB T0L 0Z0
Tel: 403-553-3955 *Fax:* 403-553-2812
cnh_fortmacleod@extendicare.com
www.extendicarefortmcleod.com

Number of Beds: 50 beds
Note: Provides long-term care services.
Patricia White, Administrator
Janelle Jubinville, Director, Care
Dr. Steven Beekman, Medical Director

Galahad: **Galahad Care Centre**
Affiliated with: Alberta Health Services
102 Lady Helen Ave., Galahad, AB T0B 1R0
Tel: 780-583-3788 *Fax:* 780-583-2105
www.albertahealthservices.ca

Note: Programs & services include: continuing care; respite care; & palliative care.
Norah Griffiths, Manager

Grande Prairie: **Grande Prairie Care Centre**
Chantelle Management Ltd.
Affiliated with: Alberta Health Services
9705 - 94 Ave., Grande Prairie, AB T8V 3A2
Tel: 780-532-3525 *Fax:* 780-532-6504
grandeprairie@chantellegroup.com
www.chantellegroup.com/grande_prairie.htm
Number of Beds: 120 beds
Note: Services include: 24 hour nursing care; dietary; occupational therapy; physiotherapy; & pharmacy.

Leduc: **Salem Manor Nursing Home**
Affiliated with: Alberta Health Services
4419 - 46 St., Leduc, AB T9E 6L2
Tel: 780-986-8654 Fax: 780-986-4130
www.albertahealthservices.ca
Note: Provides continuing care services.

Lethbridge: **AgeCare Columbia**
AgeCare
Affiliated with: Alberta Health Services
785 Columbia Blvd. West, Lethbridge, AB T1K 4T8
Tel: 403-320-9363 Fax: 403-327-9676
calreception@agecare.ca
www.agecare.ca/columbia
Number of Beds: 50 beds

Lethbridge: **Alberta Rose Lodge**
Green Acres Foundation
2251 - 32 St. South, Lethbridge, AB T1K 4J9
Tel: 403-327-5745
www.greenacres.ab.ca/residence/alberta-rose
Number of Beds: 47 rooms
Note: Independent living; rooms for patients undergoing treatment at the Lethbridge Regional Hospital & the Jack Ady Cancer Treatment Centre.
Adrian Boe, Manager

Lethbridge: **Black Rock Terrace**
Green Acres Foundation
105 - 5th Ave. South, Lethbridge, AB T1J 0Z7
Tel: 403-328-3194
www.greenacres.ab.ca/residence/black-rock-terrace
Number of Beds: 121 rooms
Note: Independent living

Lethbridge: **Blue Sky Lodge**
Green Acres Foundation
1431 - 16 Ave. North, Lethbridge, AB T1H 4B9
Tel: 403-328-9422
www.greenacres.ab.ca/residence/blue-sky
Number of Beds: 81 rooms
Note: Independent living
Yamura Coteron, Manager

Lethbridge: **Extendicare - Fairmont Park**
Extendicare Canada
Affiliated with: Alberta Health Services
115 Fairmont Blvd. South, Lethbridge, AB T1K 5V2
Tel: 403-320-0102 Fax: 403-327-0083
cnhfairmontpark@extendicare.com
www.extendicarecanada.com/fairmont_park
Number of Beds: 140 beds

Lethbridge: **Garden View Lodge**
Green Acres Foundation
751 - 1st Ave. South, Lethbridge, AB T1J 4N7
Tel: 403-327-3387
www.greenacres.ab.ca/residence/garden-view
Note: Independent living
Jackie Gray, Manager

Lethbridge: **Heritage Lodge**
Green Acres Foundation
601 - 6th St. South, Lethbridge, AB T1H 2E4
Tel: 403-327-1116
www.greenacres.ab.ca/residence/heritage-lodge
Number of Beds: 74 rooms
Note: Independent living
Pauline McCran, Manager

Lethbridge: **Martha's House**
Covenant Health
Affiliated with: Alberta Health Services
950 - 14th St. South, Lethbridge, AB T1J 2Y8
Tel: 403-327-7564 Fax: 403-327-3020
www.covenanthealth.ca/hospitals-care-centres/marthas-house

Lethbridge: **Pemmican Lodge West**
Green Acres Foundation
102 - 5th Ave. South, Lethbridge, AB T1J 0S9
Tel: 403-328-4127
www.greenacres.ab.ca/residence/pemmican-west-lodge
Number of Beds: 60 rooms
Note: Independent living
Roger Hacior, Manager

Mayerthorpe: **Extendicare - Mayerthorpe**
Extendicare Canada
Affiliated with: Alberta Health Services
PO Box 569, 4706 - 54 St., Mayerthorpe, AB T0E 1N0
Tel: 780-786-2211 Fax: 780-786-4710
cnh_mayerthorpe@extendicare.com
www.extendicaremayerthorpe.com

Number of Beds: 50 beds
Note: Provides long-term care services.
Rick Hatt, Administrator
Hazel Smelt, Director, Care
Dr. Zahirali Jamal, Medical Director

Okotoks: **Tudor Manor**
Brenda Strafford Foundation Ltd.
Affiliated with: Alberta Health Services
200 Sandstone Dr., Okotoks, AB T1S 1R1
Tel: 403-995-9540
www.thebsf.ca

Year Founded: 2012
Number of Beds: 152 beds
Carroll Brenda, Administrator
brenda.carroll@thebsf.ca

Pincher Creek: **Vista Village**
Good Samaritan Society
Affiliated with: Alberta Health Services
1240 Ken Thornton Blvd., Pincher Creek, AB T0K 1W0
Tel: 403-627-1900 Fax: 403-627-3939
goodsaminfo@gss.org
www.gss.org
Number of Beds: 45 supportive living suites; 20 independent living suites; two 10-bed dementia care cottages; 10 enhanced care; 5 community support beds
Shawn Terlson, President & CEO, Good Samaritan Society
sterlson@gss.org

Red Deer: **Extendicare - Michener Hill**
Extendicare Canada
Affiliated with: Alberta Health Services
12 Michener Blvd., Red Deer, AB T4P 0M1
Tel: 403-348-0340 Fax: 403-348-5970
cnh_michenerhill@extendicare.com
www.extendicarecanada.com/michener
Number of Beds: 220 continuing care beds; 60 supportive living beds

Spruce Grove: **Spruce Grove Centre**
Good Samaritan Society
Affiliated with: Alberta Health Services
415 King St., Spruce Grove, AB T7X 3Y8
Tel: 780-962-3415 Fax: 780-962-3416
goodsaminfo@gss.org
www.gss.org
Number of Beds: 30 supportive living suites
Shawn Terlson, President & CEO, Good Samaritan Society
sterlson@gss.org

St. Paul: **Extendicare - St. Paul**
Extendicare Canada
Affiliated with: Alberta Health Services
4614 - 47 Ave., St. Paul, AB T0A 3A0
Tel: 780-645-3375 Fax: 780-645-4290
cnh_st.paul@extendicare.com
www.extendicarecanada.com/saintpaul
Number of Beds: 76 beds

Stony Plain: **George Hennig Place**
Good Samaritan Society
Affiliated with: Alberta Health Services
4808 - 57 Ave., Stony Plain, AB T7Z 2J9
Tel: 780-963-3403 Fax: 780-963-9808
goodsaminfo@gss.org
www.gss.org
Number of Beds: 30 supportive living suites
Shawn Terlson, President & CEO, Good Samaritan Society
sterlson@gss.org

Taber: **Clearview Lodge**
Taber & District Housing Foundation
4730 - 50th Ave., Taber, AB T1G 1N6
Tel: 780-223-2822 Fax: 866-283-1812
www.taberhsg.ca
Number of Beds: 20 beds
Joan Hart, Lodge Manager
JoanH@taberhsg.ca

Three Hills: **Chateau Three Hills**
inSite Housing, Hospitality & Health Services
Affiliated with: Alberta Health Services
920 Main St. East, Three Hills, AB T0M 2A0
Tel: 403-443-2121 Fax: 403-443-2151
c3hadmin@insiteseniorcare.com
www.insiteseniorcare.com
Kletke Norah, Community Manager
nkletke@vantageliving.ca

Two Hills: **Eventide Homes**
Eagle Hill Foundation
Affiliated with: Alberta Health Services
PO Box 279, 4801 - 53 Ave., Two Hills, AB T0B 4K0
Tel: 780-657-2061 Fax: 780-657-0044
ehfadmin@eaglehillfoundation.ca
www.eaglehillfoundation.ca/two_hills_eventide.php

Viking: **Extendicare - Viking**
Extendicare Canada
Affiliated with: Alberta Health Services
PO Box 430, 5020 - 57 Ave., Viking, AB T0B 4N0
Tel: 780-336-4790 Fax: 780-336-4004
cnh_viking@extendicare.com
www.extendicareviking.com
Number of Beds: 60 beds
Note: Provides long-term care services.
Darlene Thibault, Administrator
Niel Corpuz, Director, Care

Vulcan: **Extendicare - Vulcan**
Extendicare Canada
Affiliated with: Alberta Health Services
PO Box 810, 715 - 2nd Ave. South, Vulcan, AB T0L 2B0
Tel: 403-485-2022 Fax: 403-485-2879
cnh_vulcan@extendicare.com
www.extendicarecanada.com/vulcan
Number of Beds: 46 beds

Retirement Residences

Airdrie: **Luxstone Manor Seniors' Residence**
Integrated Life Care Inc.
Affiliated with: Alberta Health Services
2014 Luxstone Blvd., Airdrie, AB T4B 0L6
Tel: 403-945-4700 Fax: 403-945-4701
Toll-Free: 888-948-0544
info@luxstonemanor.ca
www.luxstonemanor.ca
twitter.com/luxstonemanor
Year Founded: 2009

Calgary: **Carewest Colonel Belcher**
Affiliated with: Alberta Health Services
1939 Veterans Way NW, Calgary, AB T3B 5Y8
Tel: 403-944-7800 Fax: 403-944-7870
www.carewest.ca
Year Founded: 2003
Number of Beds: 175 residents in seniors' residence, most of whom are veterans
Note: Services include: adult day support; continuing care; & respite care.

Devon: **Discovery Place**
Integrated Life Care Inc.
Affiliated with: Alberta Health Services
2 Highwood Blvd., Devon, AB T9G 2G2
Tel: 780-987-6500 Fax: 780-987-6502
info@discoveryplace.ca
www.discoveryplace.ca
Note: Assisted living

Drayton Valley: **Seasons Drayton Valley**
Seasons Retirement Communities
Affiliated with: Alberta Health Services
3902 - 47 St., Drayton Valley, AB T7A 0A2
Tel: 780-542-5572 Fax: 780-542-5548
www.sunrisevillages.com
Number of Beds: 68 suites

Edmonton: **Good Samaritan Place**
Good Samaritan Society
Affiliated with: Alberta Health Services
8425 - 83 St., Edmonton, AB T6C 2Z2
Tel: 780-413-3500 Fax: 780-989-3290
goodsaminfo@gss.org
www.gss.org
Number of Beds: 40 apartments
Shawn Terlson, President & CEO, Good Samaritan Society
sterlson@gss.org

Lethbridge: **Seasons Lethbridge**
Seasons Retirement Communities
Affiliated with: Alberta Health Services
1730 - 10th Ave. South, Lethbridge, AB T1K 0B5
Tel: 403-320-2270 Fax: 403-331-2402
www.seasonsretirement.com
Number of Beds: 58 suites

Red Deer: **Parkvale Lodge**
Piper Creek Foundation
Affiliated with: Alberta Health Services
4277 - 46A Ave., Red Deer, AB T4N 6T6
Tel: 403-343-0688
www.pipercreek.ca
Number of Beds: 61 rooms; 4 couples' suites
Lisa Manning-Eaton, Manager

Red Deer: **Piper Creek Lodge**
Piper Creek Foundation
Affiliated with: Alberta Health Services
4820 - 33 St., Red Deer, AB T4N 0N5
Tel: 403-343-1066
www.pipercreek.ca
Number of Beds: 65 rooms

Wetaskiwin: **Northtown Village**
Good Samaritan Society
Affiliated with: Alberta Health Services
4710 Northmount Dr., Wetaskiwin, AB T9A 3P6
Tel: 780-352-6671
goodsaminfo@gss.org
www.gss.org
Note: Life lease retirement community
Shawn Terlson, President & CEO, Good Samaritan Society
sterlson@gss.org

Personal Care Homes

Airdrie: **Arbor Manor**
Bethany Care Society
Affiliated with: Alberta Health Services
1736 - 1st Ave. NW, Airdrie, AB T4B 2C4
Tel: 403-948-6022 Fax: 403-948-3897
info@bethanyseniors.com
www.bethanyseniors.com
www.facebook.com/bethanyseniors; twitter.com/BethanyCare;
www.youtube.com/user/BethanyCareSociety;
www.linkedin.com/company/88398
Number of Beds: 52 supportive living suites
Note: Located inside Bethany Airdrie
Jennifer McCue, President & CEO, Bethany Care Society

Barrhead: **Shepherd's Care - Barrhead**
Shepherd's Care Foundation
Affiliated with: Alberta Health Services
5236 - 59 Ave., Barrhead, AB T7N 0A3
Tel: 780-674-4249 Fax: 780-674-4204
www.shepherdscare.org/barrhead.php
Year Founded: 2007
Number of Beds: 43 units

Brooks: **Sunrise Gardens**
AgeCare
Affiliated with: Alberta Health Services
1235 - 3rd St. West, Brooks, AB T1R 0P7
Tel: 403-794-2105
sgreception@agecare.ca
www.agecare.ca/sunrise-gardens

Calgary: **Evanston Grand Village**
Golden Life Management
40 Evanston Way NW, Calgary, AB T3P 0B1
Tel: 403-274-6416
goldenlifemanagement.ca
Number of Beds: 1300 residents
Note: Independent & assisted living

Calgary: **Hillside Manor**
Bethany Care Society
Affiliated with: Alberta Health Services
916 - 18A St. NW, Calgary, AB T2N 1C6
Tel: 403-284-6000 Fax: 403-284-6085
info@bethanyseniors.com
www.bethanyseniors.com
www.facebook.com/bethanyseniors; twitter.com/BethanyCare;
www.youtube.com/user/BethanyCareSociety;
www.linkedin.com/company/88398
Number of Beds: 19 supportive living suites
Note: Located inside Bethany Calgary
Jennifer McCue, President & CEO, Bethany Care Society

Calgary: **Walden Heights**
AgeCare
Affiliated with: Alberta Health Services
250 Walden Heights Dr. SE, Calgary, AB T2X 0M7
Tel: 403-873-4700
walden@agecare.ca
www.agecare.ca/walden-heights

Camrose: **Faith House**
The Bethany Group
Affiliated with: Alberta Health Services
4832 - 54 St., Camrose, AB T4V 2A4
Tel: 780-679-5427
www.thebethanygroup.ca

Camrose: **Seasons Camrose**
Seasons Retirement Communities
Affiliated with: Alberta Health Services
6821 - 50 Ave., Camrose, AB T4V 5G5
Tel: 780-672-2746 Fax: 780-672-2985
www.seasonsretirement.com
Number of Beds: 59 private suites; 82 supportive living suites

Cardston: **Lee Crest**
Good Samaritan Society
Affiliated with: Alberta Health Services
PO Box 850, 989 - 1st St. East, Cardston, AB T0K 0K0
Tel: 403-653-2034 Fax: 403-653-1103
goodsaminfo@gss.org
www.gss.org
Year Founded: 2011
Number of Beds: 95 supportive living suites; 5 community support beds
Area Served: Alberta *Number of Employees:* 120
Specialties: Dementia cottages (2 with 12 suites each)
Note: Supportive living care home
Karen Olshaski, Care Home Manager
403-653-2034, kolshaski@gss.org
Melanie Kennard, Care Home Assistant Manager
403-653-2934, mkennard@gss.org

Coaldale: **Sunny South Lodge**
Green Acres Foundation
1122 - 20 Ave., Coaldale, AB T1M 1L4
Tel: 403-345-5955
www.greenacres.ab.ca/residence/sunny-south
Number of Beds: 88 rooms (13 supportive living)
Note: Independent living & enhanced care options
Glen Herbst, Manager

Cochrane: **Quigley Manor**
Bethany Care Society
Affiliated with: Alberta Health Services
302 Quigley Dr., Cochrane, AB T4C 1M2
Tel: 403-932-6422 Fax: 403-932-4617
info@bethanyseniors.com
www.bethanyseniors.com
www.facebook.com/bethanyseniors; twitter.com/BethanyCare;
www.youtube.com/user/BethanyCareSociety;
www.linkedin.com/company/88398
Jennifer McCue, President & CEO, Bethany Care Society

Cold Lake: **Points West Living Cold Lake**
Affiliated with: Alberta Health Services
512 - 25 St., Cold Lake, AB T9M 1G6
Tel: 780-639-1260 Fax: 780-639-0834
reception.coldlake@pointswestliving.com
pointswestliving.com/cold_lake_home.php
Number of Beds: 52 supportive living units

Daysland: **Providence Place**
Affiliated with: Alberta Health Services
6120 - 51 Ave., Daysland, AB T0B 1A0
Tel: 780-374-2527 Fax: 780-374-2529
www.albertahealthservices.ca

Drayton Valley: **Serenity House**
Affiliated with: Alberta Health Services
4552 Madsen Ave., Drayton Valley, AB T7A 1T2
Tel: 780-542-3610
www.albertahealthservices.ca

Eckville: **Eckville Manor House**
Lacombe Foundation
Affiliated with: Alberta Health Services
5111 - 51 Ave., Eckville, AB T0M 0X0
Tel: 403-746-2661 Fax: 403-746-3903
lacombe.foundation@bethanygrp.ca
www.lacombefoundation.ca

Edmonton: **Laurier House Lynnwood**
CapitalCare
Affiliated with: Alberta Health Services
16815 - 88 Ave., Edmonton, AB T5R 5Y7
Tel: 780-413-4712 Fax: 780-413-4736
www.capitalcare.net/centres/lh_lynnwood.html
www.facebook.com/capitalcare.edmonton;
twitter.com/CapitalCareYEG
Year Founded: 1997
Number of Beds: 80 beds
Note: Life-lease supportive care living

Iris Neumann, Chief Operating Officer, CapitalCare

Edmonton: **Shepherd's Care - Greenfield**
Shepherd's Care Foundation
Affiliated with: Alberta Health Services
3820 - 114 St., Edmonton, AB T6J 1M5
Tel: 780-430-3613 Fax: 780-430-0833
www.shepherdscare.org/greenfield.php
Number of Beds: 30 beds

Edmonton: **Shepherd's Care - Southside Manor**
Shepherd's Care Foundation
Affiliated with: Alberta Health Services
10745 - 29 Ave., Edmonton, AB T6J 5H6
Tel: 780-435-3169 Fax: 780-435-3169
www.shepherdscare.org/southside-manor.php

Edmonton: **Shepherd's Care - Vanguard**
Shepherd's Care Foundation
Affiliated with: Alberta Health Services
10311 - 122 Ave., Edmonton, AB T5G 0K8
Tel: 780-474-1798
www.shepherdscare.org/vanguard.php
Year Founded: 2011
Number of Beds: 115 units

Edmonton: **The Waterford of Summerlea**
Chantelle Management Ltd.
Affiliated with: Alberta Health Services
9395 - 172 St., Edmonton, AB T5T 5S6
Tel: 780-444-4545 Fax: 780-487-8443
waterford@chantellegroup.com
www.thewaterford.ca

Edmonton: **Wedman House & Village**
Good Samaritan Society
Affiliated with: Alberta Health Services
10525 - 19 Ave. NW, Edmonton, AB T6J 6X9
Tel: 780-413-3520 Fax: 780-435-8435
goodsaminfo@gss.org
www.gss.org
Number of Beds: 30 supportive living suites; 3 dementia care cottages
Wanda Beaudoin, Site Manager
780-413-3520, wbeaudoin@gss.org

High River: **Seasons High River**
Seasons Retirement Communities
Affiliated with: Alberta Health Services
660 - 7th St., High River, AB T1V 1S7
Tel: 403-652-1581 Fax: 403-652-2287
www.seasonsretirement.com
Number of Beds: 68 private suites; 108 supportive living suites

Hinton: **Mountain View Centre**
Good Samaritan Society
Affiliated with: Alberta Health Services
1290 Switzer Dr., Hinton, AB T7V 2E9
Tel: 780-865-5926 Fax: 780-865-4098
goodsaminfo@gss.org
www.gss.org
Number of Beds: 37 supportive living suites; 10 bed dementia care cottage
Shawn Terlson, President & CEO, Good Samaritan Society
sterlson@gss.org

Innisfail: **Sunset Manor**
Chantelle Management Ltd.
Affiliated with: Alberta Health Services
3312 - 52 Ave., Innisfail, AB T4G 0C3
Tel: 403-227-8200 Fax: 403-227-8201
innisfail@chantellegroup.com
www.chantellegroup.com/sunset_manor.htm
Number of Beds: 102 supportive living suites

Lacombe: **Royal Oak Manor**
Affiliated with: Alberta Health Services
4501 College Ave., Lacombe, AB T4L 2M8
Tel: 403-782-4435
www.albertahealthservices.ca
Number of Beds: 23 supportive living suites; 50 life lease apartments
Note: Provides services, housing, & support for adults with health issues, including dementia.

Lethbridge: **Golden Acres Lodge**
Green Acres Foundation
1615 - 13th St. North, Lethbridge, AB T1H 2V2
Tel: 403-328-5111
www.greenacres.ab.ca/residence/golden-acres
Number of Beds: 45 beds
Note: Independent living & enhanced care options
Yumara Coteron, Manager

Lethbridge: Park Meadows
Good Samaritan Society
Affiliated with: Alberta Health Services
1511 - 15 Ave. North, Lethbridge, AB T1H 1W2
Tel: 403-328-9404 Fax: 403-328-8208
goodsaminfo@gss.org
www.gss.org
Number of Beds: 40 supportive living suites; four 10-bed dementia care cottages; three 12-bed dementia care cottages; 5 community support beds
Shawn Terlson, President & CEO, Good Samaritan Society
sterlson@gss.org

Lethbridge: St. Therese Villa
Covenant Health
Affiliated with: Alberta Health Services
253 Southgate Blvd. South, Lethbridge, AB T1K 2S1
Tel: 403-332-5300
www.covenanthealth.ca/hospitals-care-centres/st-therese-villa
Number of Beds: 124 private studio suites; 16 couple suites; 60 secure dementia suites
Note: Supportive living facility

Lethbridge: West Highland Centre & Estates
Good Samaritan Society
Affiliated with: Alberta Health Services
2867 Gary Dr. West, Lethbridge, AB T1J 5A3
Tel: 403-380-6275 Fax: 403-380-6732
goodsaminfo@gss.org
www.gss.org
Number of Beds: 90 supportive living suites; 49 independent living apartments; 10 bed dementia care cottage
Shawn Terlson, President & CEO, Good Samaritan Society
sterlson@gss.org

Linden: Westview Care Community
Affiliated with: Alberta Health Services
Former Name: Linden Nursing Home
PO Box 220, 700 Nursing Home Rd., Linden, AB T0M 1J0
Tel: 403-546-3966 Fax: 403-546-4061
www.westviewcare.ca
Number of Beds: 37 beds; 18 supportive living suites
Note: Services include: nursing care; medical care; dental; optical care; foot care; occupational therapy; physical therapy; & rehabilitation.
Gideon Berniko, Managing Director

Lloydminster: Points West Living Lloydminster
Affiliated with: Alberta Health Services
4025 - 56 Ave., Lloydminster, AB T9V 1N9
Tel: 780-874-4300 Fax: 780-874-9199
reception.lloydminster@pointswestliving.com
pointswestliving.com/lloydminster_home.php
Number of Beds: 55 studios; 5 couples suites; 5 cottages with 12 one-bedroom suites

Magrath: Garden Vista
Good Samaritan Society
Affiliated with: Alberta Health Services
37 East & 2nd Ave. North, Magrath, AB T0K 1J0
Tel: 403-758-6149 Fax: 403-758-6053
goodsaminfo@gss.org
www.gss.org
Number of Beds: 22 supportive living suites; 10-bed dementia care cottage; 3 community support beds
Shawn Terlson, President & CEO, Good Samaritan Society
sterlson@gss.org

Medicine Hat: AgeCare Valleyview
AgeCare
Affiliated with: Alberta Health Services
65 Valleyview Dr., Medicine Hat, AB T1A 7K5
Tel: 403-526-7000
valleyview@agecare.ca
www.agecare.ca/valleyview

Medicine Hat: St. Joseph's Home
Covenant Health
Affiliated with: Alberta Health Services
156 - 3rd St. NE, Medicine Hat, AB T1A 5M1
Tel: 403-526-3818 Fax: 403-528-8942
www.covenanthealth.ca/hospitals-care-centres/st-therese-villa
Year Founded: 1951
Note: Assisted living program

Medicine Hat: The Wellington Retirement Residence
Affiliated with: Park Place Seniors Living
1595 Southview Dr. SE, Medicine Hat, AB T1B 0A1
Tel: 403-526-5762 Fax: 403-526-9479
www.parkplaceseniorsliving.com/find-a-location/alberta/medicine-hat/the-wellington
www.facebook.com/WellingtonMedicineHat

Year Founded: 2005
Allyson MacArthur, Assistant Manager
amacarthur@parkplaceseniorsliving.com

Myrname: Eagle View Lodge
Eagle Hill Foundation
Affiliated with: Alberta Health Services
PO Box 280, 4802 - 49 Ave., Myrname, AB T0B 3K0
Tel: 780-366-3750 Fax: 780-366-2297
ehfadmin@eaglehillfoundation.ca
www.eaglehillfoundation.ca/myrnam_eagle_view.php
Rayner Krystal, Wellness Team Leader
krayner@eaglehillfoundation.ca

Olds: Seasons Olds
Seasons Retirement Communities
Affiliated with: Alberta Health Services
5600 Sunrise Cres., Olds, AB T4H 1W4
Tel: 403-556-3446 Fax: 403-556-3475
www.seasonsretirement.com
Number of Beds: 40 supportive living suites

Olds: Seasons Olds
Seasons Retirement Communities
Affiliated with: Alberta Health Services
3300 - 57 Ave., Olds, AB T4H 1C4
Tel: 403-556-2232
www.seasonsretirement.com
Number of Beds: 47 private suites; 60 supportive living suites

Peace River: Points West Living Peace River
Affiliated with: Alberta Health Services
11011 - 99 St., Peace River, AB T8S 1B3
Tel: 780-624-0700 Fax: 780-624-0701
reception.peaceriver@pointswestliving.com
pointswestliving.com/peaceriver_home.php
Number of Beds: 53 supportive living units
David Haastrup, General Manager
Bernadette Harris, Office Manager

Picture Butte: Piyami Lodge
Green Acres Foundation
301 Rogers Ave., Picture Butte, AB T0K 1V0
Tel: 403-732-4811 Fax: 403-732-4580
www.greenacres.ab.ca/residence/piyami-lodge
Number of Beds: 32 rooms
Note: Independent living & enhanced care options
Brenda McDonald, Manager

Pincher Creek: Whispering Winds Village
Golden Life Management
PO Box 579, 941 Elizabeth St., Pincher Creek, AB T0K 1W0
Tel: 403-627-1997
wwvmanager@glm.ca
goldenlifemanagement.ca

Note: Independent & assisted living
Eileen Woolf, Community Manager
ewoolf@glm.ca

Ponoka: Seasons Ponoka
Seasons Retirement Communities
Affiliated with: Alberta Health Services
4004 - 40 St., Ponoka, AB T4J 0A3
Tel: 403-783-3373 Fax: 403-783-3324
www.seasonsretirement.com
Number of Beds: 68 suites (20 designated supportive living)

Red Deer: Pines Lodge
Piper Creek Foundation
Affiliated with: Alberta Health Services
52 Pipe Dr., Red Deer, AB T4P 1H8
Tel: 403-343-0656 Fax: 403-343-7789
www.pipercreek.ca
Number of Beds: 64 rooms; 20 supportive living suites; 1 couples' suite
Thea Mawbey, Manager

Red Deer: West Park Lodge
Affiliated with: Alberta Health Services
5715 - 41 St. Crescent, Red Deer, AB T4N 1B3
Tel: 403-343-7471 Fax: 403-343-3424
info@westparklodge.com
www.westparklodge.com
Year Founded: 1996
Number of Beds: 36 suites
Note: Services include personal care & recreation.

Sherwood Park: Laurier House Strathcona
CapitalCare
Affiliated with: Alberta Health Services
12 Brower Dr., Sherwood Park, AB T8V 1V3
Tel: 780-467-3366 Fax: 780-417-4350
www.capitalcare.net/centres/lh_strathcona.html
www.facebook.com/capitalcare.edmonton;
twitter.com/CapitalCareYEG
Year Founded: 2001
Number of Beds: 42 beds
Note: Life-lease supportive care living
Iris Neumann, Chief Operating Officer, CapitalCare

Stettler: Points West Living Stettler
Affiliated with: Alberta Health Services
4501 - 70 St., Stettler, AB T0C 2L3
Tel: 403-740-7700 Fax: 403-742-1514
reception.stettler@pointswestliving.com
pointswestliving.com/stettler_home.php
Number of Beds: 104 supportive living units

Strathmore: AgeCare Sagewood
AgeCare
Affiliated with: Alberta Health Services
140 Cambridge Glen Dr., Strathmore, AB T1P 0E2
Tel: 403-361-8000
swreception@agecare.ca
www.agecare.ca/sagewood

Taber: Linden View
Good Samaritan Society
Affiliated with: Alberta Health Services
4700 - 64 Ave., Taber, AB T1G 0C6
Tel: 403-223-3341 Fax: 403-223-2360
goodsaminfo@gss.org
www.gss.org
Number of Beds: 64 supportive living suites; three 12-bed dementia care cottages; 5 community support beds
Shawn Terlson, President & CEO, Good Samaritan Society
sterlson@gss.org

Two Hills: Hillside Lodge
Eagle Hill Foundation
Affiliated with: Alberta Health Services
PO Box 279, 4801 - 53 Ave., Two Hills, AB T0B 4K0
Tel: 780-657-2061 Fax: 780-657-0044
ehfadmin@eaglehillfoundation.ca
www.eaglehillfoundation.ca/two_hills_hillside.php
Nancy Lawrence, Site Supervisor
nlawrence@eaglehillfoundation.com

Vegreville: Points West Heritage House
Affiliated with: Alberta Health Services
4570 Maple St., Vegreville, AB T9C 1X2
Tel: 780-603-0853 Fax: 780-603-2237
reception.heritagehouse@pointswestliving.com
pointswestliving.com/heritage_house_home.php

Vegreville: Points West Living Century Park
Affiliated with: Alberta Health Services
4613 - 50 St., Vegreville, AB T9C 1L7
Tel: 780-632-3042 Fax: 780-632-2732
reception.centurypark@pointswestliving.com
pointswestliving.com/vegreville_home.php
Number of Beds: 40 supportive living spaces; 40 apartments

Vermilion: Vermilion - Valley Lodge
Affiliated with: Alberta Health Services
4610 - 53 Ave., Vermilion, AB T9X 1G6
Tel: 780-853-5706 Fax: 780-853-1951
www.albertahealthservices.ca

Vilna: Vilna Lodge
Affiliated with: Alberta Health Services
5404 - 50 St., Vilna, AB T0A 3L0
Tel: 780-636-3545 Fax: 780-636-3555
www.albertahealthservices.ca

Wainwright: Points West Living Wainwright
Affiliated with: Alberta Health Services
2710 - 11th Ave., Wainwright, AB T9W 0B1
Tel: 780-845-2080 Fax: 780-845-2090
reception.wainwright@pointswestliving.com
pointswestliving.com/wainwright_home.php
Number of Beds: 59 supportive living spaces; 16 rental suites; 16 life lease apartments

Wetaskiwin: Good Shepherd Home
Good Samaritan Society
Affiliated with: Alberta Health Services
4702 Northmount Dr., Wetaskiwin, AB T9A 3T3
Tel: 403-353-3628 Fax: 403-352-3379
goodsaminfo@gss.org
www.gss.org
Number of Beds: 68 supportive living suites; 1 community
support bed
Shawn Terlson, President & CEO, Good Samaritan Society
sterlson@gss.org

Wetaskiwin: Seasons Wetaskiwin
Seasons Retirement Communities
Affiliated with: Alberta Health Services
5430 - 37A Ave., Wetaskiwin, AB T9A 3A8
Tel: 780-352-4725 Fax: 780-361-1970
www.seasonsretirement.com
Number of Beds: 92 suites (20 designated supportive living)

Willingdon: Eagle Hill Lodge
Eagle Hill Foundation
Affiliated with: Alberta Health Services
PO Box 387, 5303 - 49 St., Willingdon, AB T0B 4R0
Tel: 780-367-2717 Fax: 780-367-2717
ehfadmin@eaglehillfoundation.ca
www.eaglehillfoundation.ca/willingdon_eagle_hill.php
Gowsell Jennifer, Supervisor
jennifer.gowsell@connectingcare.ca

Mental Health Hospitals/Facilities

Airdrie: Airdrie Mental Health Clinic
Affiliated with: Alberta Health Services
Former Name: Airdrie Mental Health Clinic
Airdrie Provincial Building, 117 - 1 Ave. NW, Airdrie, AB T4B
0R2
Tel: 403-948-3878 Fax: 403-592-4228
Toll-Free: 844-943-1500
www.albertahealthservices.ca

Athabasca: Athabasca Community Health Services
Affiliated with: Alberta Health Services
3401 - 48 Ave., Athabasca, AB T9S 1M7
Tel: 780-675-5404 Fax: 780-675-3111
www.albertahealthservices.ca

Banff: Banff - Mineral Springs Hospital
Covenant Health
Affiliated with: Alberta Health Services
303 Lynx St., Banff, AB T1L 1B3
Tel: 403-762-4451 Fax: 403-762-5570
www.albertahealthservices.ca
Note: Provides assessment, treatment, counselling, & referral
services for people experiencing mental health issues.

Barrhead: Barrhead Healthcare Centre
Affiliated with: Alberta Health Services
PO Box 4504, 4815 - 51 Ave., Barrhead, AB T7N 1M1
Tel: 780-674-8243 Fax: 780-674-8352
www.albertahealthservices.ca

Black Diamond: Black Diamond Mental Health
Centre at Oilfields General Hospital
Affiliated with: Alberta Health Services
717 Government Rd., Black Diamond, AB T0L 0H0
Tel: 403-933-3800 Toll-Free: 844-943-1500
www.albertahealthservices.ca
Note: Services include: assessment; treatment; group therapy; &
geriatric services.

Blairmore: Crowsnest Pass Provincial Building
Affiliated with: Alberta Health Services
#206, 12501 - 20 Ave., Blairmore, AB T0K 0E0
Tel: 403-562-5040 Fax: 403-562-3226
www.albertahealthservices.ca

Bon Accord: Oak Hill Boys Ranch
PO Box 97, 56119 - Range Rd. 240, Bon Accord, AB T0A 0K0
Tel: 780-921-2121
info@oakhillranch.ca
www.oakhillboysranch.ca
Number of Beds: 32 beds
Note: Residential treatment facility for young males (11-16)
suffering from issues such as mental health & substance abuse.
Anton Smith, Executive Director

Bonnyville: Bonnyville New Park Place
Affiliated with: Alberta Health Services
Bonnyville Remax Bldg., 5201 - 44 St., Bonnyville, AB T9N
2G5
Tel: 780-826-2404 Fax: 780-826-6114
www.albertahealthservices.ca

Bow Island: Bow Island Provincial Building
Affiliated with: Alberta Health Services
Former Name: Bow Island Mental Health Clinic
802 - 6 St. East, Bow Island, AB T0K 0G0
Tel: 403-529-3500 Fax: 403-529-3562
www.albertahealthservices.ca

Brooks: Brooks Community Mental Health Clinic
Affiliated with: Alberta Health Services
440 - 3rd St. East, Brooks, AB T1R 1C5
Tel: 403-793-6655 Fax: 403-793-6656
www.albertahealthservices.ca

Calgary: Arnika Centre
Affiliated with: Alberta Health Services
3465 - 26 Ave. NE, Calgary, AB T1Y 6L4
Tel: 403-943-8301 Fax: 403-943-8367
www.albertahealthservices.ca
Note: Psychiatric assessment for people 16 years & older.

Calgary: Bridgeland Seniors Health Centre
Affiliated with: Alberta Health Services
1070 Mcdougall Rd. NE, Calgary, AB T2E 7Z2
Tel: 403-955-1555 Fax: 403-955-1564
www.albertahealthservices.ca

Calgary: Carewest Operational Stress Injury Clinic
Affiliated with: Alberta Health Services
Also Known As: Carewest OSI Clinic
Market Mall, #203, 3625 Shaganappi Trail NW, Calgary, AB
T3A 0E2
Tel: 403-216-9860 Fax: 403-216-9861
www.carewest.ca
Note: Provides programs & services to help deal with mental
health problems caused by shock or stress for veterans,
Canadian Forces members, RCMP members, & their families.

Calgary: Distress Centre Calgary (DCC)
Affiliated with: Alberta Health Services
#500, 999 - 8th Ave. SW, Calgary, AB T2R 1J5
Tel: 403-266-1601
info@distresscentre.com
www.distresscentre.com
Info Line: 403-266-4357
www.facebook.com/distresscentre; twitter.com/Distress_Centre;
www.youtube.com/user/DistressCentreYYC
Year Founded: 1970
Note: Offers crisis support, professional counselling, & referrals
to people in distress.
Jerilyn Dressler, Executive Director
Bing Hu, Chief Financial Officer
Jerilyn Dressler, Director, Operations
Diane Jones Konihowski, Director, Fund Development &
Communications

Calgary: East Calgary Health Centre
Affiliated with: Alberta Health Services
4715 - 8 Ave. SE, Calgary, AB T2A 3N4
Tel: 403-955-1010 Fax: 403-955-1013
www.albertahealthservices.ca
Note: Perinatal mental health; child & adolescent addiction &
mental health

Calgary: Foothills Professional Building
Affiliated with: Alberta Health Services
1620 - 29th St. NW, 2nd Fl., Calgary, AB T2N 4L7
Tel: 403-943-1500 Toll-Free: 866-943-1500
www.albertahealthservices.ca

Calgary: Northeast Calgary Mental Health Clinic
Affiliated with: Alberta Health Services
Sunridge Mall, #200, 2580 - 32 St. NE, Calgary, AB T1Y 7M8
Tel: 403-943-1500 Toll-Free: 866-943-1500
www.albertahealthservices.ca
Note: Provides mental health assessment, treatment, & therapy
services.

Calgary: Safe Communities Opportunity and
Resource Centre
Affiliated with: Alberta Health Services
316 - 7 Ave. SE, Calgary, AB T2G 0J2
Tel: 403-608-5559
www.scorce.ca
Info Line: 403-428-3300
Note: A multi-agency collaborative that connects people
experiencing homelessness, or those at imminent risk of
homelessness, to programs and services that can help to
address the barriers to stable housing, including mental health &
addiction.

Calgary: Society for Treatment of Autism (STA)
404 - 94 Ave. SE, Calgary, AB T2J 0E8
Tel: 403-253-2291 Fax: 403-253-6974
Toll-Free: 888-301-2872
consultation@sta-ab.com
www.sta-ab.com
www.facebook.com/SocietyForTreatmentOfAutism;
twitter.com/Autism_STA;
www.linkedin.com/company/society-for-treatment-of-autism
Number of Beds: 20 beds
Note: Programs & services for people with autism & other
pervasive developmental disorders.
Dave Mikkelsen, Executive Director

Calgary: South Calgary Health Centre
Affiliated with: Alberta Health Services
31 Sunpark Plaza SE, 2nd Fl., Calgary, AB T2X 3W5
Tel: 403-943-9374
www.albertahealthservices.ca
Note: Mental health urgent care & walk-in services
Sue Ramsden, Site Manager

Calgary: Sunridge Professional Building
Affiliated with: Alberta Health Services
#201, 2675 - 36 St. NE, Calgary, AB T1Y 6H6
Tel: 403-943-4596 Fax: 403-219-3521
www.albertahealthservices.ca
Note: Mental health forensic assessment services.

Calgary: Wood's Homes - Bowness Campus
Affiliated with: Alberta Health Services
9400 - 48 Ave. NW, Calgary, AB T3B 2B2
Tel: 403-247-6751 Fax: 403-286-0878
askus@woodshomes.ca
www.woodshomes.ca
www.facebook.com/woodshomesnfp;
twitter.com/ChildMntlHealth;
www.youtube.com/user/WoodsHomes1;
www.linkedin.com/company/wood%27s-homes
Number of Beds: 110 beds

Calgary: Wood's Homes - Parkdale Campus
805 - 37 St. NW, Calgary, AB T2N 4N8
Tel: 403-270-4102 Fax: 403-283-9735
askus@woodshomes.ca
www.woodshomes.ca
Info Line: 800-563-6106
www.facebook.com/woodshomesnfp;
twitter.com/ChildMntlHealth;
www.youtube.com/user/WoodsHomes1;
www.linkedin.com/company/wood%27s-homes
Year Founded: 1914
Number of Beds: 150 beds
Area Served: Alberta; Northwest Territories *Population Served:*
20000 *Number of Employees:* 500
Specialties: Crisis counselling & outreach services; residential
treatment
Note: Foster care; homeless youth shelters; specialized learning;
day treatment; residential treatment; outreach services; & child
welfare services.
Sylvia MacIver, Communications Manager
403-270-1768, sylvia.maciver@woodshomes.ca

Camrose: Camrose Addiction & Mental Health Clinic
Affiliated with: Alberta Health Services
4911 - 47 St., Camrose, AB T4V 1J9
Tel: 780-679-1181 Fax: 780-679-1740
www.albertahealthservices.ca

Cardston: Cardston Community Mental Health Clinic
Affiliated with: Alberta Health Services
576 Main St., Cardston, AB T0K 0K0
Tel: 403-653-5240 Fax: 403-653-2926
www.albertahealthservices.ca

Chestermere: Chestermere Community Health
Centre
Affiliated with: Alberta Health Services
#104, 288 Kinniburgh Blvd., Chestermere, AB T1X 0V8
Tel: 403-365-5400 Fax: 403-592-4229
Toll-Free: 844-943-1500
www.albertahealthservices.ca
Note: Provides mental health assessment & treatment as well as
addiction prevention services.

Claresholm: Claresholm Centre for Mental Health &
Addictions
Affiliated with: Alberta Health Services
PO Box 490, 139 - 43 Ave. West, Claresholm, AB T0L 0T0
Tel: 403-682-3563 Fax: 403-625-4318
claresholmcentre@albertahealthservices.ca
www.claresholmcentre.com

Year Founded: 1933
Number of Beds: 108 beds
Note: Programs & services include: active rehabilitation; concurrent disorders; extended treatment; & transitions.

Claresholm: Claresholm Mental Health Clinic
Affiliated with: Alberta Health Services
4901 - 2nd St. West, Claresholm, AB T0L 0T0
Tel: 403-625-4068
Note: Services include: assessment; treatment; information; & referral.

Cochrane: Cochrane Addiction & Mental Health Clinic
Affiliated with: Alberta Health Services
60 Grande Blvd., Cochrane, AB T4C 0S4
Tel: 403-851-6100 *Fax:* 403-851-6101
Toll-Free: 877-652-4700
www.albertahealthservices.ca

Cold Lake: Cold Lake Healthcare Centre
Affiliated with: Alberta Health Services
#208, 314 - 25 St., Cold Lake, AB T9M 1G6
Tel: 780-639-4922 *Fax:* 780-639-4990
www.albertahealthservices.ca

Consort: Consort Community Health Centre
Affiliated with: Alberta Health Services
5410 - 52 Ave., Consort, AB T0C 1B0
Tel: 403-577-3770 *Fax:* 403-577-2235
www.albertahealthservices.ca

Didsbury: Didsbury District Health Services
Affiliated with: Alberta Health Services
1210 - 20 Ave., Didsbury, AB T0M 0W0
Tel: 403-335-7285 *Fax:* 403-592-4769
Toll-Free: 844-943-1500
www.albertahealthservices.ca

Drayton Valley: Drayton Valley Mental Health Clinic
Affiliated with: Alberta Health Services
4110 - 50 Ave., Drayton Valley, AB T7A 0B3
Tel: 780-542-3140 *Fax:* 780-542-4461
www.albertahealthservices.ca

Drumheller: Drumheller Health Centre
Affiliated with: Alberta Health Services
351 - 9 St. NW, Drumheller, AB T0J 0Y1
Tel: 403-820-7863 *Fax:* 403-820-7865
www.albertahealthservices.ca

Edmonton: Addiction Services Edmonton
Affiliated with: Alberta Health Services
10010 - 102A Ave. NW, Edmonton, AB T5J 0G5
Tel: 780-427-2736 *Fax:* 780-427-4180
www.albertahealthservices.ca
Note: Addiction prevention & mental health promotion.

Edmonton: Alberta Hospital Edmonton
Affiliated with: Alberta Health Services
17480 Fort Rd., Edmonton, AB T5J 2J7
Tel: 780-342-5555
www.albertahealthservices.ca
Year Founded: 1923
Number of Beds: 410 beds
Note: Provides assessment, diagnosis, treatment, education, & consultation. Conducts research. Programs & services include: acute inpatient services; early psychosis intervention; group home support; inpatient intensive care; inpatient rehabilitation; & wellness recovery.
Donna Tchida, Site Director

Edmonton: Edmonton 108 Street Building
Affiliated with: Alberta Health Services
9942 - 108th St. NW, Edmonton, AB T5K 2J5
Tel: 780-909-4546
www.albertahealthservices.ca
Note: Specialises in youth & young adult diversion & treatment programs.

Edmonton: Forensic Assessment & Community Services
Affiliated with: Alberta Health Services
10225 - 106 St., Edmonton, AB T5J 1H5
Tel: 780-342-6400
www.albertahealthservices.ca
Note: Offers counselling as well as addiction & mental health treatment.

Edmonton: Villa Caritas
Covenant Health
Affiliated with: Alberta Health Services
16515 - 88 Ave. NW, Edmonton, AB T5R 0A4
Tel: 780-342-6500
www.covenanthealth.ca/hospitals-care-centres/villa-caritas
Number of Beds: 120 acute geriatric psychiatry beds; 30 geriatric psychiatry transitional beds
Note: Acute mental health facility for seniors, located on the Misericordia Community Hospital campus.

Edson: Edson Provincial Building
Affiliated with: Alberta Health Services
Former Name: Edson Mental Health Centre
#100, 111 - 54 St., Edson, AB T7E 1T2
Tel: 780-723-8294 *Fax:* 780-723-8297
www.albertahealthservices.ca

Fairview: Fairview Health Complex
Affiliated with: Alberta Health Services
PO Box 2201, 10628 - 110 St., Fairview, AB T0H 1L0
Tel: 780-835-6149 *Fax:* 780-835-6185
Info Line: 877-303-2642

Fort MacLeod: Fort Macleod Community Health
Affiliated with: Alberta Health Services
744 - 26 St., Fort MacLeod, AB T0L 0Z0
Tel: 403-553-5340 *Fax:* 403-553-4940
www.albertahealthservices.ca

Fort McMurray: Northern Lights Regional Health Centre
Affiliated with: Alberta Health Services
7 Hospital St., Fort McMurray, AB T9H 1P2
Tel: 780-791-6194 *Fax:* 780-791-6219
www.albertahealthservices.ca

Fort Vermilion: St. Theresa General Hospital
Affiliated with: Alberta Health Services
4506 - 46 Ave., Fort Vermilion, AB T0H 1N0
Tel: 780-841-3229 *Fax:* 780-926-3738
Toll-Free: 877-823-6433
www.albertahealthservices.ca
Note: Provides mental health treatment & information services.

Fox Creek: Fox Creek Healthcare Centre
Affiliated with: Alberta Health Services
600 - 3rd St., Fox Creek, AB T0H 1P0
Tel: 780-622-5106
www.albertahealthservices.ca

Grande Cache: Pine Plaza Building
Affiliated with: Alberta Health Services
PO Box 120, 702 Pine Plaza NW, Grande Cache, AB T0E 0Y0
Tel: 780-827-4998 *Fax:* 780-827-7207
www.albertahealthservices.ca
Info Line: 877-303-2642
Note: Addictions & mental health services

Grande Prairie: Grande Prairie Nordic Court
Affiliated with: Alberta Health Services
Former Name: Nordic Court Mental Health Clinic
#600, 10014 - 99th St., Grande Prairie, AB T8V 3N4
Tel: 780-538-5162 *Fax:* 780-538-6279
www.albertahealthservices.ca

Hanna: Hanna Health Centre
Affiliated with: Alberta Health Services
904 Centre St. North, Hanna, AB T0J 1P0
Tel: 403-854-5276 *Fax:* 403-854-5280
www.albertahealthservices.ca

High Level: Northwest Health Centre
Affiliated with: Alberta Health Services
11202 - 100 Ave., High Level, AB T0H 1Z0
Tel: 780-841-3229 *Fax:* 780-926-3738
Toll-Free: 877-823-6433
www.albertahealthservices.ca

High Prairie: High Prairie Health Complex
Affiliated with: Alberta Health Services
4620 - 53 Ave., High Prairie, AB T0G 1E0
Tel: 780-523-6490 *Fax:* 780-523-6491
Toll-Free: 877-823-6433
www.albertahealthservices.ca

High River: High River Addiction & Mental Health Clinic
Affiliated with: Alberta Health Services
#200, 617 - 1 St. West, High River, AB T1V 1M5
Tel: 403-652-8340 *Fax:* 403-601-8016
Toll-Free: 844-943-1500
www.albertahealthservices.ca

Hinton: Hinton Community Health Services
Affiliated with: Alberta Health Services
Former Name: Hinton Mental Health Centre
1280A Switzer Dr., Hinton, AB T7V 1T5
Tel: 780-865-8247 *Fax:* 780-865-8327
www.albertahealthservices.ca

Innisfail: Innisfail Health Centre
Affiliated with: Alberta Health Services
5023 - 42 St., Innisfail, AB T4G 1A9
Tel: 403-227-4601
www.albertahealthservices.ca

Jasper: Seton - Jasper Healthcare Centre
Affiliated with: Alberta Health Services
PO Box 310, 518 Robson St., Jasper, AB T0E 1E0
Tel: 780-852-6640 *Fax:* 780-852-3413
Toll-Free: 877-303-2642
www.albertahealthservices.ca

Killam: Killam 4811 - 49 Avenue
Affiliated with: Alberta Health Services
4811 - 49 Ave., Killam, AB T0B 2L0
Tel: 780-385-7161 *Fax:* 780-385-3329
www.albertahealthservices.ca
Note: Provides assessment, treatment, & rehabilitation services for individuals experiencing mental health issues.

La Crete: La Crete Continuing Care Centre
Affiliated with: Alberta Health Services
10601 - 100 Ave., La Crete, AB T0H 2H0
Tel: 780-928-6821 *Fax:* 877-853-5380
Toll-Free: 877-823-6433
www.albertahealthservices.ca

Lac La Biche: Lac La Biche Provincial Building
Affiliated with: Alberta Health Services
Former Name: Lac La Biche Community Health Services
PO Box 297, 9503 Beaver Hill Rd., Lac La Biche, AB T0A 2C0
Tel: 780-623-5230 *Fax:* 780-623-5232

Lacombe: Lacombe Mental Health Centre
Affiliated with: Alberta Health Services
5033 - 52 St., Lacombe, AB T4L 2A6
Tel: 403-782-3413 *Fax:* 403-782-3878
www.albertahealthservices.ca

Lamont: Lamont Health Care Centre
Affiliated with: Alberta Health Services
PO Box 479, 5216 - 53 St., Lamont, AB T0B 2R0
Tel: 780-895-5817 *Fax:* 780-895-7305
info@lamonthcc.ca
www.lamonthealthcarecentre.com
Note: Affiliated with the United Church of Canada.
Harold James, Executive Director
harold.james@ahs.ca

Leduc: Leduc Addiction & Mental Health Clinic
Affiliated with: Alberta Health Services
Centre Hope Bldg., 4906 - 49 Ave., 2nd Fl., Leduc, AB T9E 6W6
Tel: 780-986-2660 *Fax:* 780-986-9292
www.albertahealthservices.ca

Lethbridge: Chinook Regional Hospital
Affiliated with: Alberta Health Services
Former Name: Lethbridge Regional Hospital
960 - 19 St. South, Lethbridge, AB T1J 1W5
Tel: 403-388-6244 *Fax:* 403-388-6250
www.albertahealthservices.ca
Note: Child & adolescent mental health; day treatment centre

Lethbridge: Lethbridge Provincial Building
Affiliated with: Alberta Health Services
#103, 200 - 5th Ave. South, Lethbridge, AB T1J 4L1
Tel: 403-381-5260 *Fax:* 403-382-4518
www.albertahealthservices.ca
Note: Addictions & mental health services

Mayerthorpe: Mayerthorpe Healthcare Centre
Affiliated with: Alberta Health Services
PO Box 30, 4417 - 45 St., Mayerthorpe, AB T0E 1N0
Tel: 780-786-2279 *Fax:* 780-786-2023
www.albertahealthservices.ca
Note: Provides mental health assessment, diagnosis, treatment, therapy, support, & referral services.

Medicine Hat: Medicine Hat Provincial Building
Affiliated with: Alberta Health Services
Former Name: Medicine Hat Community Mental Health
346 - 3 St. SE, Medicine Hat, AB T1A 0G7
Tel: 403-529-3500 *Fax:* 403-529-3562
www.albertahealthservices.ca

Medicine Hat: Regional Resource Centre
Affiliated with: Alberta Health Services
Mental Health Outreach Depot Clinic, 631 Prospect Dr. SW, Medicine Hat, AB T1A 4C2
Tel: 403-529-8030 *Fax:* 403-502-8618
www.albertahealthservices.ca
Note: Programs & services include: child & adolescent mental health program; mental health diversion services for adults with low risk minor criminal offences; & mental health outreach.

Morinville: Morinville Provincial Building
Affiliated with: Alberta Health Services
10008 - 107 St., Morinville, AB T8R 1L3
Tel: 780-342-2620 *Fax:* 780-939-1216
www.albertahealthservices.ca
Note: Addiction & mental health community clinics

Okotoks: Okotoks Mental Health Centre
Affiliated with: Alberta Health Services
11 Cimarron Common, Okotoks, AB T1S 2E9
Tel: 403-995-2712
www.albertahealthservices.ca
Note: Addiction prevention & mental health assessment & treatment services.

Olds: Olds Provincial Building (South)
Affiliated with: Alberta Health Services
#212, 5025 - 50th St., Olds, AB T4H 1R9
Tel: 403-507-8174 *Fax:* 403-556-1584
www.albertahealthservices.ca
Note: Addictions & mental health services

Onoway: Onoway Community Health Services
Affiliated with: Alberta Health Services
PO Box 1047, 5115 Lac St. Anne Trail, Onoway, AB T0E 1V0
Tel: 780-967-9117 *Fax:* 780-967-2547
www.albertahealthservices.ca
Note: Provides short term adult mental health services, including individual & group therapy.

Peace River: Peace River Mental Health Clinic
Affiliated with: Alberta Health Services
10015 - 98 St., Peace River, AB T8S 1T4
Tel: 780-624-6151 *Fax:* 780-624-6565
www.albertahealthservices.ca

Pincher Creek: Pincher Creek Community Mental Health Clinic
Affiliated with: Alberta Health Services
#212, 782 Main St., Pincher Creek, AB T0K 1W0
Tel: 403-627-1121 *Fax:* 403-627-1145
www.albertahealthservices.ca

Ponoka: Centennial Centre for Mental Health & Brain Injury
Affiliated with: Alberta Health Services
PO Box 1000, 46 St. South, Ponoka, AB T4J 1R8
Tel: 403-783-7600 *Fax:* 403-783-7774
www.albertahealthservices.ca
Note: Specialized mental health & brain injury treatment & care

Ponoka: Ponoka Provincial Building
Affiliated with: Alberta Health Services
#223, 5110 - 49th Ave., Ponoka, AB T4J 1R6
Tel: 403-783-7903 *Fax:* 403-785-7926
www.albertahealthservices.ca
Note: Addictions & mental health services

Provost: Provost Provincial Building
Affiliated with: Alberta Health Services
5419 - 44 St., Provost, AB T0B 3S0
Tel: 780-753-2575 *Fax:* 780-753-8096
www.albertahealthservices.ca

Raymond: Prairie Ridge
Good Samaritan Society
Affiliated with: Alberta Health Services
Former Name: Prairie Ridge Hospital
PO Box 630, 328 Broadway South, Raymond, AB T0K 2S0
Tel: 403-752-3441 *Fax:* 403-752-3250
goodsaminfo@gss.org
www.gss.org
Number of Beds: 30 geriatric mental health care beds; 5 community support beds
Note: Services include assisted living & dementia care.
Julius van Wyk, President & CEO, Good Samaritan Society

Raymond: Raymond Health Centre
Affiliated with: Alberta Health Services
150 North - 4 St. East, Raymond, AB T0K 2S0
Tel: 403-752-5440 *Fax:* 403-752-4147
www.albertahealthservices.ca

Red Deer: Red Deer - 49th Street Community Health Centre
Affiliated with: Alberta Health Services
4733 - 49 St., Red Deer, AB T4N 1T6
Tel: 403-340-5466 *Fax:* 403-340-4874
www.albertahealthservices.ca

Rocky Mountain House: Rocky Mountain House Health Centre
Affiliated with: Alberta Health Services
5016 - 52 Ave., Rocky Mountain House, AB T4T 1T2
Tel: 403-844-5235 *Fax:* 403-844-5236
www.albertahealthservices.ca
Note: Provides assessment, treatment, & rehabilitation services for people with mental health issues.

Slave Lake: Slave Lake Mental Health Services
Affiliated with: Alberta Health Services
PO Box 1278, 101 Main St. SE, Slave Lake, AB T0G 2A4
Tel: 780-849-7127 *Fax:* 780-849-7394
www.albertahealthservices.ca

Smoky Lake: George McDougall - Smoky Lake Healthcare Centre
Affiliated with: Alberta Health Services
Smoky Lake Health Unit, 4212 - 55 Ave., Smoky Lake, AB T0A 3C0
Tel: 780-656-3595 *Fax:* 780-656-2242
www.albertahealthservices.ca

Spirit River: Spirit River Community Health Services
Affiliated with: Alberta Health Services
Former Name: Mistahia Health Unit - Spirit River
5003 - 45 Ave., Spirit River, AB T0H 3G0
Tel: 780-538-5160 *Fax:* 780-538-6279
Toll-Free: 877-823-6433
www.albertahealthservices.ca
Note: Provides assessment, diagnosis, treatment, therapy, support, & referral services for individuals experiencing mental health issues.

St. Paul: St. Therese - St. Paul Healthcare Centre
Affiliated with: Alberta Health Services
4713 - 48 Ave., St. Paul, AB T0A 3A3
Tel: 780-645-1850 *Fax:* 780-645-2788
www.albertahealthservices.ca

Standoff: Kainai Wellness Centre
Blood Tribe Department of Health Inc.
PO Box 229, Standoff, AB T0L 1Y0
Tel: 403-737-3883 *Fax:* 403-737-2036
btdh.ca/staff/kainai-wellness-centre
Year Founded: 1985
Note: Provides programs & services for the Blood Tribe Community, including criss intervention & counseling, mental health, alcohol & drug abuse programs, counselling, stress management, relaxation therapy, mental illness education, grief & loss recovery, & wellness.
Kevin Cowan, Chief Executive Officer, Blood Tribe Department of Health

Stettler: Stettler Hospital & Care Centre
Affiliated with: Alberta Health Services
5912 - 47 Ave., Stettler, AB T0C 2L0
Tel: 403-743-2000 *Fax:* 403-740-8880
www.albertahealthservices.ca

Stony Plain: WestView Health Centre
Affiliated with: Alberta Health Services
4405 South Park Dr., Stony Plain, AB T7Z 2M7
Tel: 780-963-6151 *Fax:* 780-963-7186
Toll-Free: 866-332-2322
www.albertahealthservices.ca
Note: Addiction prevention & mental health promotion services.

Swan Hills: Swan Hills Healthcare Centre
Affiliated with: Alberta Health Services
PO Box 261, 29 Freeman Dr., Swan Hills, AB T0G 2C0
Tel: 780-333-4241 *Fax:* 780-333-7009
www.albertahealthservices.ca

Sylvan Lake: Sylvan Lake Community Health Centre
Affiliated with: Alberta Health Services
4602 - 49 Ave., Sylvan Lake, AB T4S 1M7
Tel: 403-887-6777 *Fax:* 403-887-6721
www.albertahealthservices.ca
Note: Provides mental health assessment, treatment, & rehabilitation programs & services.

Taber: Taber Health Centre
Affiliated with: Alberta Health Services
4326 - 50 Ave., Taber, AB T1G 1N9
Tel: 403-223-7244 *Fax:* 403-223-7236
www.albertahealthservices.ca
Note: Offers assessment, treatment, counselling, & other addiction & mental health services.

Three Hills: Three Hills Provincial Building
Affiliated with: Alberta Health Services
Former Name: Three Hills Mental Health Centre
128 - 3 Ave. SE, Three Hills, AB T0M 2A0
Tel: 403-443-8532 *Fax:* 403-443-8541
www.albertahealthservices.ca
Note: Addictions (403-820-7863) & mental health services.

Tofield: Tofield Health Centre
Affiliated with: Alberta Health Services
5543 - 44 St., Tofield, AB T0B 4J0
Tel: 780-672-1181 *Fax:* 780-679-5088
www.albertahealthservices.ca
Note: Child & adolescent addiction & mental health services.

Vegreville: Vegreville Community Health Centre
Affiliated with: Alberta Health Services
5318 - 50 St., Vegreville, AB T9C 1R1
Tel: 780-632-2714
www.albertahealthservices.ca

Vermilion: Vermilion Provincial Building
Affiliated with: Alberta Health Services
4701 - 52 St., Vermilion, AB T9X 1J9
Tel: 780-581-8000 *Fax:* 780-851-8001
www.albertahealthservices.ca

Vulcan: Vulcan Community Health Centre
Affiliated with: Alberta Health Services
610 Elizabeth St. South, Vulcan, AB T0L 2B0
Tel: 403-485-3356
www.albertahealthservices.ca
Note: Offers mental health assessment, treatment, counselling, & referral services.

Wainwright: Wainwright 905A 3 Avenue
Affiliated with: Alberta Health Services
905A 3 Ave., Wainwright, AB T9W 1C5
Tel: 780-842-7522 *Fax:* 780-842-7520
www.albertahealthservices.ca

Westlock: Westlock Community Health Services
Affiliated with: Alberta Health Services
10024 - 107 Ave., Westlock, AB T7P 2E3
Tel: 780-349-5246 *Fax:* 780-349-5846
www.albertahealthservices.ca
Note: Mental health assessment, diagnosis, treatment, therapy, support, & referral services

Wetaskiwin: Wetaskiwin Provincial Building
Affiliated with: Alberta Health Services
#101, 5201 - 50 Ave., Wetaskiwin, AB T9A 0S7
Tel: 780-361-1245 *Fax:* 780-361-1387
www.albertahealthservices.ca

Whitecourt: Whitecourt Healthcare Centre
Affiliated with: Alberta Health Services
20 Sunset Blvd., Whitecourt, AB T7S 1M8
Tel: 780-706-3281 *Fax:* 780-706-7154
www.albertahealthservices.ca

Special Care Homes

Lloydminster: Dr. Cooke Extended Care Centre
Affiliated with: Saskatchewan Health Authority
3915 - 56 Ave., Lloydminster, AB T9V 1N9
Tel: 780-871-7900 *Fax:* 780-875-3505
www.albertahealthservices.ca
Info Line: 306-820-5970
Number of Beds: 105 beds
Joan Zimmer, Director, Continuing Care

British Columbia

Government Departments in Charge

Victoria: **British Columbia Ministry of Health**
PO Box 9050 Stn. Prov Govt, Victoria, BC V8W 9E2
Toll-Free: 800-663-7867
HLTH.Health@gov.bc.ca
www.gov.bc.ca/health
Hon. Adrian Dix, Minister
250-953-3547, Fax: 250-356-9587, HLTH.Minister@gov.bc.ca

Regional Health Authorities

Kelowna: **Interior Health Authority**
505 Doyle Ave., Kelowna, BC V1Y 0C5
Tel: 250-469-7070 *Fax:* 250-469-7068
www.interiorhealth.ca
Info Line: 811
www.facebook.com/InteriorHealth; twitter.com/Interior_Health;
www.youtube.com/user/InteriorHealthAuth;
www.linkedin.com/company/interior-health-authority
Year Founded: 2001
Number of Beds: 6,584 residential care & assisted living beds;
1,369 hospital beds
Area Served: 215,422 sq km *Population Served:* 750000
Number of Employees: 20000
Note: Serves cities such as Kelowna, Kamloops, Cranbrook,
Trail, Penticton & Vernon, as well as rural & remote
communities. Services include: Acute care, health promotion &
prevention, community care, residential care, mental health &
substance use, & public health.
Dr. Doug Cochrane, Board Chair
Susan Brown, President & CEO
Karen Bloemink, Vice-President, Clinical Operations
Dr. Sue Pollock, Interim Chief Medical Health Officer
Donna Lommer, Chief Financial Officer & Vice-President,
Support Services
Norma Malanowich, Chief Information Officer & Vice-President,
Clinical Support Services
Dr. Mike Ertel, Vice-President, Medicine & Quality
Jenn Goodwin, Vice-President, Communications & Public
Engagement
Mal Griffin, Vice-President, Human Resources

Prince George: **Northern Health Authority**
Former Name: Northern Interior Health Board
Corporate Office, #600, 299 Victoria St., Prince George, BC
V2L 5B8
Tel: 250-565-2649 *Fax:* 250-565-2640
Toll-Free: 866-565-2999
hello@northernhealth.ca
www.northernhealth.ca
Info Line: 811
www.facebook.com/NorthernHealth; twitter.com/northern_health;
www.youtube.com/northernhealthbc;
www.linkedin.com/company/northern-health-authority
Number of Beds: 1,106 HCC residential care beds; 599 hospital
beds
Area Served: 600,000 sq km in northern British Columbia
Population Served: 300000 *Number of Employees:* 7000
Note: Services administered through 3 service delivery areas:
Northwest, Northeast, Northern Interior.
Colleen Nyce, Board Chair
Cathy Ulrich, President & Chief Executive Officer
Penny Anguish, Chief Operating Officer, Northern Interior
Ciro Panessa, Chief Operating Officer, Northwest
Angela De Smit, Chief Operating Officer, Northeast

Surrey: **Fraser Health Authority**
Central City Tower, #400, 13450 - 102nd Ave., Surrey, BC
V3T 0H1
Tel: 604-587-4600 *Fax:* 604-587-4666
Toll-Free: 877-935-5669
feedback@fraserhealth.ca
www.fraserhealth.ca
Info Line: 811
www.facebook.com/FraserHealthAuthority;
twitter.com/Fraserhealth; www.youtube.com/user/Fraserhealth;
www.linkedin.com/company/fraser-health-authority
Number of Beds: 7,760 residential care beds
Area Served: Burnaby to Hope to Boston Bar in British Columbia
Population Served: 1800000 *Number of Employees:* 25000
Note: Communities served include around 38,100 First Nations
people, associated with 32 bands; provides mental health care,
public health, home, & community care services.
Jim Sinclair, Board Chair
Dr. Victoria Lee, President & CEO
Dr. Martin Lavoie, Chief Medical Health Officer & Vice-President,
Population Health
Brenda Liggett, Chief Financial Officer

Brent Kruschel, Vice-President, Informatics, Technology &
Facilities
Cameron Brine, Vice-President, Employee Experience
Linda Dempster, Vice-President, Patient Experience
Dr. Roy Morton, Vice-President, Medicine
Naseem Nuraney, Vice-President, Communications & Public
Affairs

Vancouver: **Provincial Health Services Authority**
(PHSA)
#700, 1380 Burrard St., Vancouver, BC V6Z 2H3
Tel: 604-675-7400 *Fax:* 604-708-2700
phsacomm@phsa.ca
www.phsa.ca
Info Line: 811
www.facebook.com/ProvincialHealthServices;
twitter.com/PHSAofBC; www.youtube.com/ProvHealthServAuth;
www.linkedin.com/company/provincial-health-services-authority
Number of Employees: 19000
Note: PHSA operates provincial agencies including BC
Children's Hospital, BC Transplant, & BC Cancer Agency. It is
also responsible for specialized provincial health services like
chest surgery & trauma services.
Tim Manning, Board Chair
Benoit Morin, President & CEO
Thomas Chan, Chief Financial Officer & Executive
Vice-President, Corporate Services
Linda Lupini, Executive Vice-President, Commercial Services
Kendra McPherson, Vice-President, Transformation &
Sustainability
Dr. Maureen O'Donnell, Executive Vice-President, Clinical
Policy, Planning & Partnerships
Ron Quirk, Executive Vice-President, Digital Information
Services & Innovation
Catherine Syms, Vice-President, Legal, Privacy & Risk
Susan Wannamaker, Executive Vice-President, Clinical Service
Delivery
Donna Wilson, Executive Vice-President, People and Diagnostic
& Treatment Services

Vancouver: **Vancouver Coastal Health (VCH)**
Corporate Office, 601 West Broadway, 11th Fl., Vancouver,
BC V5Z 4C2
Tel: 604-736-2033 *Toll-Free:* 866-884-0888
www.vch.ca
Info Line: 811
www.facebook.com/VCHhealthcare; twitter.com/vchhealthcare;
www.youtube.com/user/VCHhealthcare
Number of Beds: 1,500 acute care beds; 5,600 residential beds;
85 rehabilitation beds; 900 assissted living / respite beds
Area Served: 12 municipalities and 4 regional districts (25% of
BC) *Population Served:* 1250000
Note: Vancouver Coastal Health provides health care services
through a network of hospitals, primary care clinics, community
health centres & residential care homes. Search VCH health
care services in Vancouver, Richmond, North & West Vancouver
& along the Sea-to-Sky Highway, Sunshine Coast & BC's
Central Coast: www.vch.ca/locations-services.

Victoria: **Vancouver Island Health Authority**
Former Name: Capital Health Region
Also Known As: Island Health
1952 Bay St., Victoria, BC V8R 1J8
Tel: 250-370-8699 *Toll-Free:* 877-370-8699
info@viha.ca
www.viha.ca
Info Line: 811
www.facebook.com/VanIslandHealth;
twitter.com/vanislandhealth;
www.instagram.com/vanislandhealth;
www.linkedin.com/company/vancouver-island-health-authority
Number of Beds: 1,728 acute care & rehabilitation beds; 6,593
residential care beds & assisted living units; 1,503 mental health
beds
Area Served: Vancouver Island & the islands of the George
Strait *Population Served:* 800000 *Number of Employees:* 22000
Leah Hollins, Board Chair
Kathy MacNeil, President & CEO
Dr. Richard Stanwick, Chief Medical Health Officer
Catherine Claiter-Larsen, Chief Information Officer &
Vice-President, Innovation & Analytics
Kim Kerrone, Chief Financial Officer & Vice-President, Legal
Services & Risk
Dawn Nedzelski, Chief Professional Practice & Nursing Officer
Dr. Elin Bjarnason, Vice-President, Clinical Service Delivery
Jamie Braman, Vice-President, Communications, Planning &
Partnerships
James Hanson, Vice-President, Operations & Support
Sharon Torgerson, Vice-President, People

West Vancouver: **First Nations Health Authority**
(FNHA)
#501, 100 Park Royal South, West Vancouver, BC V7T 1A2
Tel: 604-693-6500 *Fax:* 604-913-2081
Toll-Free: 866-913-0033
info@fnha.ca
www.fnha.ca
Info Line: 855-550-5454
www.facebook.com/firstnationshealthauthority;
twitter.com/FNHA; www.youtube.com/user/fnhealthcouncil;
www.linkedin.com/company/first-nations-health-authority
Year Founded: 2013
Area Served: 5 regions; 955,186 sq km
Note: Assumed the following responsibilities, formerly handled
by Health Canada's First Nations Inuit Health Branch - Pacific
Region: to plan, design, manage, & fund the delivery of First
Nations health programs & services in BC. Health services
include: primary care services; children, youth & maternal health;
mental health & addictions programming; health & wellness
planning; health infrastructure & human resources;
environmental health & research; First Nations health benefits; &
eHealth technology.
Areas served include the following regions: Fraser Salish;
Interior; North; Vancouver Coastal; & Vancouver Island.
Marion Colleen Erickson, Board Chair
Richard Jock, Interim Chief Executive Officer
Dr. Evan Adams, Chief Medical Officer
Dr. Becky Palmer, Chief Nursing Officer

Hospitals - General

Abbotsford: **Abbotsford Regional Hospital & Cancer**
Centre
Affiliated with: Fraser Health Authority
32900 Marshall Rd., Abbotsford, BC V2S 0C2
Tel: 604-851-4700
www.fraserhealth.ca
www.facebook.com/FraserHealthAuthority;
twitter.com/Fraserhealth; www.youtube.com/user/fraserhealth;
www.linkedin.com/company/fraser-health-authority
Number of Beds: 26 intensive care beds; 48 obstetrical beds; 12
pediatric beds; 27 mental health beds; 168 acute care beds
Note: Programs & services include: acute care; ambulatory care;
angiography; antepartum care; audiology; bone densitometry;
cardiac; clinics; CT scans; echocardiography; emergency;
enterostomal therapy; fluoroscopy; forensic nursing; general
medicine, radiography & surgery; geriatric; hemodialysis;
inpatient psychiatric unit; intensive care; interventional
radiography; MRI; mammography; maternity; medical oncology;
nuclear medicine; outpatient services; pediatrics; pharmacy;
postpartum; pulmonary function lab; sleep lab; spiritual care; &
ultrasound.
Brendan Abbott, Executive Director

Alert Bay: **Cormorant Island Health Centre**
Affiliated with: Vancouver Island Health Authority
49 School Rd., Alert Bay, BC V0N 1A0
Tel: 250-974-5585
www.islandhealth.ca
www.facebook.com/VanIslandHealth;
twitter.com/vanislandhealth;
www.linkedin.com/company/vancouver-island-health-authority
Number of Beds: 14 beds
Note: Programs & services include: emergency; acute care;
residential care; ambulatory outpatient services; laboratory;
medical imaging; palliative care; emergency obstetrics; visiting
specialists; & medical detox.
Sarah Kowalenko, Communications & Public Relations
Assistant, VIHA
250-740-6951, sarah.kowalenko@viha.ca

Ashcroft: **Ashcroft Hospital & Community Health**
Care Centre
Affiliated with: Interior Health Authority
700 Ash-Cache Creek Hwy., Ashcroft, BC V0K 1A0
Tel: 250-453-2211 *Fax:* 250-453-1926
Toll-Free: 877-499-6599
www.interiorhealth.ca
www.facebook.com/InteriorHealth; twitter.com/Interior_Health;
www.linkedin.com/company/interior-health-authority
Year Founded: 1970
Number of Beds: 24 extended care beds; 4 emergency beds; 1
respite bed
Note: Programs & services include: diabetes education program;
laboratory & radiology; urgent care; ambulatory care; community
services; long-term residential care; & on-site doctors' offices.

Burnaby: **Burnaby Hospital**
Affiliated with: Fraser Health Authority
3935 Kincaid St., Burnaby, BC V5G 2X6

Tel: 604-434-4211
feedback@fraserhealth.ca
www.fraserhealth.ca
www.facebook.com/FraserHealthAuthority;
twitter.com/Fraserhealth;
www.linkedin.com/company/fraser-health-authority
Number of Beds: 286 beds
Note: Programs & services include: acute care; ambulatory care;
antepartum care; cardiac; CT scan; concurrent disorders;
echocardiography; emergency; fluoroscopy; general medicine,
radiography & surgery; geriatric; inpatient psychiatry unit;
intensive care; interventional radiography; MRI; mammography;
maternity; medical oncology; neonatal intensive care; nuclear
medicine; ophthalmology services; orthopaedic surgery;
outpatient services; pharmacy; postpartum care; pulmonary
function lab; & ultrasound.
Leanne Appleton, Executive Director

Burns Lake: **Lakes District Hospital & Health Centre**
Affiliated with: Northern Health Authority
PO Box 7500, 741 Centre St., Burns Lake, BC V0J 1E0

Tel: 250-692-2400 *Fax:* 250-692-2403
www.northernhealth.ca
www.facebook.com/NorthernHealth;
twitter.com/Northern_Health;
www.youtube.com/northernhealthBC;
www.linkedin.com/company/northern-health-authority
Number of Beds: 9 beds
Note: Programs & services include: acute care; emergency;
diagnostic imaging; laboratory; public health; mental health &
addictions; home & community care; pharmacy; & rehabilitation.

Campbell River: **North Island Hospital - Campbell
River & District**
Affiliated with: Vancouver Island Health Authority
Also Known As: Campbell River Hospital
375 - 2nd Ave., Campbell River, BC V9W 3V1

Tel: 250-286-7100
www.islandhealth.ca
www.facebook.com/VanIslandHealth;
twitter.com/vanislandhealth;
www.linkedin.com/company/vancouver-island-health-authority
Number of Beds: 13 intensive care beds; 11 obstetrical beds; 3
pediatric beds; 72 acute care beds
Note: Programs & services include: Aboriginal health nurse;
diabetes education; heart function clinic; heart health services;
laboratory; medical imaging; nutrition; pacemaker clinic;
rehabilitation; & surgery.
Christina Rozema, Site Director

Chetwynd: **Chetwynd Hospital & Health Centre**
Affiliated with: Northern Health Authority
PO Box 507, 5500 Hospital Rd., Chetwynd, BC V0C 1J0

Tel: 250-788-2236 *Fax:* 250-788-7247
www.northernhealth.ca
www.facebook.com/NorthernHealth; twitter.com/northern_health;
www.youtube.com/northernhealthbc;
www.linkedin.com/company/northern-health-authority
Number of Beds: 7 long-term care beds; 4 acute care beds
Note: Programs & services include: Aboriginal liaison;
emergency; medical inpatient; palliative; public health nursing;
home & community nursing; home support; & respiratory
therapy.

Chilliwack: **Chilliwack General Hospital**
Affiliated with: Fraser Health Authority
45600 Menholm Rd., Chilliwack, BC V2P 1P7

Tel: 604-795-4141
feedback@fraserhealth.ca
www.fraserhealth.ca
www.facebook.com/FraserHealthAuthority;
twitter.com/Fraserhealth; www.youtube.com/user/fraserhealth;
www.linkedin.com/company/fraser-health-authority
Number of Beds: 101 acute care beds; 90 long-term care beds;
14 mental health beds; 20 obstetrical beds; 6 intensive care
beds
Note: Programs & services include: acute care; ambulatory care;
angiography; antepartum care; cardiac; CT scan; emergency;
enterostomal therapy; fluoroscopy; general medicine,
radiography & surgery; geriatric; home detox; inpatient
psychiatry unit; intensive care; interventional radiography;
mammography; maternity; medical oncology; ophthalmology;
orthopaedic surgery; outpatient services; pantomography;
pharmacy; postpartum; pulmonary function lab; spiritual care;
substance use; & ultrasound.
Petra Pardy, Executive Director

Clearwater: **Dr. Helmcken Memorial Hospital (DHM)**
Affiliated with: Interior Health Authority
640 Park Dr., RR#1, Clearwater, BC V0E 1N0

Tel: 250-674-2244 *Fax:* 250-674-2477
www.interiorhealth.ca
www.facebook.com/InteriorHealth; twitter.com/Interior_Health;
www.youtube.com/InteriorHealthAuth;
www.linkedin.com/company/interior-health-authority
Number of Beds: 6 beds
Note: Programs & services include: community care;
emergency; end of life / palliative care; extended care; general
medicine; general rehabilitation; geriatric medicine; hematology;
hospice; laboratory; nutrition; orthotics; physiotherapy; radiology;
telehealth; & wound care.
John Soles, Chief of Staff

Comox: **St. Joseph's General Hospital**
Affiliated with: Vancouver Island Health Authority
2137 Comox Ave., Comox, BC V9M 1P2

Tel: 250-339-2242
www.islandhealth.ca
www.facebook.com/VanIslandHealth;
twitter.com/vanislandhealth;
www.linkedin.com/company/vancouver-island-health-authority
Year Founded: 1913
Number of Beds: 241 beds
Note: Programs & services include: colposcopy; daycare;
diabetes; diagnostic imaging (mammography, radiology,
ultrasound); emergency; extended care; intensive care;
laboratory; maternity; nursing; nutritional; oncology; paediatrics;
physical medicine; psychiatry; social work; & surgery.
Dr. Paul Herselman, Medical Director

Cranbrook: **East Kootenay Regional Hospital
(EKRH)**
Affiliated with: Interior Health Authority
13 - 24th Ave. North, Cranbrook, BC V1C 3H9

Tel: 250-426-5281 *Fax:* 250-426-5285
Toll-Free: 866-288-8082
www.interiorhealth.ca
www.facebook.com/InteriorHealth; twitter.com/Interior_Health;
www.youtube.com/InteriorHealthAuth;
www.linkedin.com/company/interior-health-authority
Number of Beds: 6 intensive care beds; 8 obstetrical beds; 2
pediatric beds; 10 mental health beds; 55 acute care beds
Note: Programs & services include: antepartum care; bone
density; cardioversion; chemotherapy; chronic obstructive
pulmonary disease services; community care; convalescent
care; CT scan; dental surgery; diagnostic bronchoscopy;
diagnostic cardiology; ear, nose & throat; echocardiogram, ECG
/ EKG; emergency; end of life / palliative care; endoscopy;
enterostomal therapy; fluoroscopy; general medicine; general
rehabilitation; general surgery; hematology; holter monitor;
intensive care; intrapartum care; laboratory; mammography;
maternity; microbiology; MRI; nuclear medicine; nutrition;
oncology; ophthalmology; orthotics; pediatrics; pharmacy;
physiotherapy; postpartum care; pulmonary diagnostics;
radiology; respiratory therapy; speech-language pathology;
spiritual care; telehealth; transfusion; ultrasound; urology;
vasectomy; & wound care. Also hosts the Mary Pack Arthritis
Program, a service of Vancouver Coastal Health.
Erica Phillips, Administrator, Acute Health Service

Creston: **Creston Valley Hospital & Health Care
(CVH)**
Affiliated with: Interior Health Authority
312 - 15th Ave. North, Creston, BC V0B 1G0

Tel: 250-428-2286 *Fax:* 250-428-4860
www.interiorhealth.ca
www.facebook.com/InteriorHealth; twitter.com/Interior_Health;
www.youtube.com/InteriorHealthAuth;
www.linkedin.com/company/interior-health-authority
Number of Beds: 16 beds
Note: Programs & services include: adult day services;
antepartum care; community care; community nursing;
community nutrition; community respiratory therapy;
convalescent care; diabetes education program; dental surgery;
ear, nose & throat; ECG / EKG; emergency; end of life /
palliative care; endoscopy; enterostomal therapy; general
medicine; general rehabilitation; general surgery; hematology;
holter monitor; home support; hospice; intrapartum care;
laboratory; maternity; pharmacy; physiotherapy; postpartum
care; psychiatry; radiology; social work; telehealth; transfusion;
ultrasound; vasectomy; vision; & wound care.
Carolyn Hawton, Site Manager

Dawson Creek: **Dawson Creek & District Hospital**
Affiliated with: Northern Health Authority
11100 - 13th St., Dawson Creek, BC V1G 3W8

Tel: 250-782-8501 *Fax:* 250-784-7301
www.northernhealth.ca
www.facebook.com/NorthernHealth; twitter.com/northern_health;
www.youtube.com/northernhealthbc;
www.linkedin.com/company/northern-health-authority
Number of Beds: 2 intensive care beds; 4 obstetrical beds; 11
mentlah health beds; 25 acute care beds
Note: Programs & services include: emergency; ICU; medical &
surgical inpatient care; day surgery; maternity; respiratory
therapy; rehab therapy; diabetic education; primary care; general
surgery; diagnostics (laboratory & medical imaging); cancer
care; & visiting specialists in urology, dermatology, & pediatrics.

Delta: **Delta Hospital**
Affiliated with: Fraser Health Authority
5800 Mountain View Blvd., Delta, BC V4K 3V6

Tel: 604-946-1121
feedback@fraserhealth.ca
www.fraserhealth.ca
www.facebook.com/FraserHealthAuthority;
twitter.com/Fraserhealth; www.youtube.com/user/fraserhealth;
www.linkedin.com/company/fraser-health-authority
Number of Beds: 58 beds; 92 long-term care beds
Number of Employees: 580
Note: Programs & services include: acute care; cardiac; CT
scan; emergency; electrocardiogram; general medicine,
radiography & surgery; mammography; outpatient services;
pharmacy; pulmonary function testing; palliative care; respiratory
therapy; & ultrasound.
Teresa O'Callaghan, Executive Director

Duncan: **Cowichan District Hospital (CDH)**
Affiliated with: Vancouver Island Health Authority
3045 Gibbins Rd., Duncan, BC V9L 1E5

Tel: 250-737-2030
www.islandhealth.ca
www.facebook.com/VanIslandHealth;
twitter.com/vanislandhealth;
www.linkedin.com/company/vancouver-island-health-authority
Number of Beds: 7 intensive care beds; 20 obstetrical beds; 15
mental health care beds; 98 acute care beds
Population Served: 83000
Note: Programs & services include: Aboriginal health nurse;
acute inpatient psychiatric services; diabetes education; eye
health; heart health; laboratory; medical imaging; mental health;
nutrition; rehabilitation; spiritual care; & surgery.
Sarah Kowalenko, Communications Assistant, VIHA
250-740-6951, sarah.kowalenko@viha.ca
Helen Dunlop, Aboriginal Liaison Nurse, Cowichan & Duncan
250-746-6184, helen.dunlop@cowichantribes.com

Fernie: **Elk Valley Hospital**
Affiliated with: Interior Health Authority
1501 - 5th Ave., Fernie, BC V0B 1M0

Tel: 250-423-4453 *Fax:* 250-423-3732
www.interiorhealth.ca
www.facebook.com/InteriorHealth; twitter.com/Interior_Health;
www.youtube.com/InteriorHealthAuth;
www.linkedin.com/company/interior-health-authority
Number of Beds: 20 beds
Note: Programs & services include: antepartum care; community
care; convalescent care; dental surgery; ear, nose & throat; ECG
/ EKG; emergency; end of life / palliative care; endoscopy;
enterostomal therapy; gastroenterology; general medicine;
general rehabilitation; general surgery; hematology; holter
monitor; hospice; intrapartum care; laboratory; maternity; mental
health & substance abuse; nutrition; pharmacy; physiotherapy;
postpartum care; radiology; telehealth; transfusion; urology;
vasectomy; & wound care.

Fort Nelson: **Fort Nelson Hospital**
Affiliated with: Northern Health Authority
PO Box 1000, 5315 Liard St., Fort Nelson, BC V0C 1R0

Tel: 250-774-8100 *Fax:* 250-774-8110
www.northernhealth.ca
www.facebook.com/NorthernHealth; twitter.com/northern_health;
www.youtube.com/northernhealthbc;
www.linkedin.com/company/northern-health-authority
Number of Beds: 10 beds
Note: Programs & services include: acute care; child & youth
programs; counselling services; dental clinic; drug & alcohol
programs; health unit; laboratory & x-ray; obstetrics; surgeries;
specialists (pediatricians & OB-GYN); & complementary
massage therapy, acupuncture & physiotherapy.

Fort St. James: Stuart Lake Hospital
Affiliated with: Northern Health Authority
600 Stuart Dr. East, Fort St. James, BC V0J 1P0
Tel: 250-996-8201 Fax: 250-996-8777
www.northernhealth.ca
www.facebook.com/NorthernHealth; twitter.com/northern_health;
www.youtube.com/northernhealthbc;
www.linkedin.com/company/northern-health-authority
Number of Beds: 12 beds
Note: Programs & services include: acute care; emergency;
medicine; mental health & addictions counselling; laboratory; &
x-ray.

Fort St. John: Fort St. John Hospital & Peace Villa
Affiliated with: Northern Health Authority
Former Name: Fort St. John Hospital & Health
Centre
8407 - 112 Ave., Fort St. John, BC V1J 0J5
Tel: 250-262-5200 Fax: 250-261-7650
www.northernhealth.ca
www.facebook.com/NorthernHealth; twitter.com/northern_health;
www.youtube.com/northernhealthbc;
www.linkedin.com/company/northern-health-authority
Number of Beds: 3 intensive care beds; 8 obstetrical beds; 123
long-term care beds; 1 respite bed
Population Served: 21000
Note: Programs & services include: Aboriginal liaison; acute
care; diagnostics; surgery; medicine; ICU; maternity; mental
health & addictions; palliative care; community cancer centre;
community hemodialysis; social work; & visiting specialists. Also
connected to the Fort St. John Health Unit, North Peace Villa &
Heritage Manor II.

Golden: Golden & District General Hospital
Affiliated with: Interior Health Authority
835 - 9th Ave. South, Golden, BC V0A 1H0
Tel: 250-344-5271 Fax: 250-344-3907
www.interiorhealth.ca
www.facebook.com/InteriorHealth; twitter.com/Interior_Health;
www.youtube.com/InteriorHealthAuth;
www.linkedin.com/company/interior-health-authority
Number of Beds: 8 beds
Note: Programs & services include: antepartum care; community
care; community respiratory therapy; convalescent care;
diabetes education program; ear, nose & throat; ECG / EKG;
emergency; end of life / palliative care; endoscopy; general
medicine; general rehabilitation; general surgery; hematology;
holter monitor; hospice; intrapartum care; laboratory; maternity;
nutrition; orthopedics; postpartum care; psychiatry; pulmonary
diagnostics; radiology; telehealth; transfusion; ultrasound;
vasectomy; & wound care.

Grand Forks: Boundary District Hospital
Affiliated with: Interior Health Authority
7649 - 22nd St., Grand Forks, BC V0H 1H2
Tel: 250-443-2100 Fax: 250-442-8331
www.interiorhealth.ca
www.facebook.com/InteriorHealth; twitter.com/Interior_Health;
www.youtube.com/InteriorHealthAuth;
www.linkedin.com/company/interior-health-authority
Number of Beds: 12 beds
Note: Programs & services include: chemotherapy; community
care; community respiratory therapy; diabetes education
program; ECG / EKG; emergency; end of life / palliative;
extended care; general medicine; holter monitor; hospice;
laboratory; mental health & substance abuse; nutrition;
oncology; physiotherapy; pulmonary diagnostics; radiology;
telehealth; transfusion; ultrasound; & wound care.

Hazelton: Wrinch Memorial Hospital
Affiliated with: Northern Health Authority
PO Box 999, 2510 Hwy. 62, Hazelton, BC V0J 1Y0
Tel: 250-842-5211 Fax: 250-842-5865
www.northernhealth.ca
www.facebook.com/NorthernHealth; twitter.com/northern_health;
www.youtube.com/northernhealthbc;
www.linkedin.com/company/northern-health-authority
Number of Beds: 10 beds
Population Served: 7000 *Number of Employees:* 70
Note: Programs & services include: acute care; complex care;
diabetes education; doctors clinic; emergency room; home &
community care; laboratory (ultrasound & x-ray); pharmacy;
physiotherapy & occupational therapy; & visiting specialists.

Hope: Fraser Canyon Hospital
Affiliated with: Fraser Health Authority
1275 - 7th Ave., Hope, BC V0X 1L4
Tel: 604-869-5656
feedback@fraserhealth.ca
www.fraserhealth.ca
www.facebook.com/FraserHealthAuthority;
twitter.com/Fraserhealth; www.youtube.com/user/fraserhealth;
www.linkedin.com/company/fraser-health-authority
Number of Beds: 50 long-term care beds; 10 acute care beds
Note: Programs & services include: acute care; ambulatory care;
emergency; general medicine & radiography; hospice residence;
outpatient services; & spiritual care.
Petra Pardy, Executive Director

Invermere: Invermere & District Hospital
Affiliated with: Interior Health Authority
850 - 10th Ave., Invermere, BC V0A 1K0
Tel: 250-342-9201 Fax: 250-342-6303
www.interiorhealth.ca
www.facebook.com/InteriorHealth; twitter.com/Interior_Health;
www.youtube.com/InteriorHealthAuth;
www.linkedin.com/company/interior-health-authority
Number of Beds: 8 beds
Note: Programs & services include: antepartum care; community
care; community respiratory therapy; convalescent care;
diabetes education program; ear, nose & throat; ECG / EKG;
end of life / palliative care; general medicine; general
rehabilitation; hematology; holter monitor; hospice; intrapartum
care; laboratory; maternity; nutrition; postpartum care;
psychiatry; pulmonary diagnostics; radiology; transfusion; &
wound care.

Kamloops: Royal Inland Hospital (RIH)
Affiliated with: Interior Health Authority
311 Columbia St., Kamloops, BC V2C 2T1
Tel: 250-374-5111
www.interiorhealth.ca
www.facebook.com/InteriorHealth; twitter.com/Interior_Health;
www.youtube.com/InteriorHealthAuth;
www.linkedin.com/company/royal-inland-hospital
Year Founded: 1885
Number of Beds: 171 acute care beds; 16 intensive care beds;
12 obstetrical beds; 18 rehabilitation beds; 28 mental health
beds; 9 pediatric beds
Note: Programs & services include: acute neurology; antepartum
care; cardioversion; chemotherapy; chronic obstructive
pulmonary disease services; community care; community
respiratory therapy; convalescent care; CT scan; dental surgery;
diabetes education program; diagnostic bronchoscopy; ear, nose
& throat; echocardiogram; ECG / EKG; emergency; end of life /
palliative; endoscopy; enterostomal therapy; fluoroscopy;
gastroenterology; general medicine, rehabilitation & surgery;
geriatric medicine; hematology; holter monitor; hospice; intensive
care; intrapartum care; laboratory; mammography; maternity;
mental health & substance abuse; microbiology; MRI; neonatal
intensive care; nutrition; oncology; ophthalmology; orthotics;
otolaryngology surgery; pediatrics; pharmacy; physiotherapy;
plastic surgery; postpartum care; pulmonary diagnostics;
radiology; respiratory therapy; sleep disorders; speech-language
pathology; spiritual care; telehealth; transfusion; ultrasound;
urology; vascular & thoracic; vasectomy; & wound care.
Deb Donald, Aboriginal Patient Liaison

Kelowna: Kelowna General Hospital
Affiliated with: Interior Health Authority
2268 Pandosy St., Kelowna, BC V1Y 1T2
Tel: 250-862-4000 Fax: 250-862-4020
Toll-Free: 888-877-4442
www.interiorhealth.ca
www.facebook.com/InteriorHealth; twitter.com/Interior_Health;
www.youtube.com/InteriorHealthAuth;
www.linkedin.com/company/interior-health-authority
Year Founded: 1908
Number of Beds: 271 acute care beds; 38 rehabilitation beds; 44
mental health beds; 10 pediatric beds; 17 obstetrical beds; 25
intensive care beds
Note: Programs & services include: acute neurology; acute
psychiatry; angioplasty; antepartum care; arthritis rehabilitation;
cardiac angiogram; cardioversion; chemotherapy; chronic
obstructive pulmonary disease services; community care;
community respiratory therapy; convalescent care; CT scan;
dental surgery; diabetes education program; diagnostic
bronchoscopy; diagnostic cardiology; ear, nose & throat;
echocardiogram; ECG / EKG; emergency; end of life / palliative;
endocrinology; endoscopy; enterostomal therapy; fluoroscopy;
gastroenterology; general medicine, rehabilitation & surgery;
geriatric medicine; hematology; holter monitor; hospice; intensive
care; intrapartum care; laboratory; mammography; maternity;
mental health & substance abuse; microbiology; MRI; nuclear
medicine; nutrition; oncology; ophthalmology; orthotics;
otolaryngology surgery; pediatrics; pharmacy; physiotherapy;

plastic surgery; postpartum care; psoriasis & phototherapy;
radiology; respiratory therapy; sleep disorders; speech-language
pathology; spiritual care; Telehealth; transfusion; ultrasound;
urology; vascular & thoracic surgery; vasectomy; vision; &
wound care.
John Cabral, Director, Health Services
Dr. Devin Harris, Executive Medical Director
Dr. Neil Hanon, Head of Psychiatry & Clerkship Site Director,
Department of Psychiatry; Southern Medical Program

Kitimat: Kitimat General Hospital & Health Centre
Affiliated with: Northern Health Authority
920 Lahakas Blvd. South, Kitimat, BC V8C 2S3
Tel: 250-632-2121 Fax: 250-632-8726
www.northernhealth.ca
www.facebook.com/NorthernHealth; twitter.com/northern_health;
www.youtube.com/northernhealthbc;
www.linkedin.com/company/northern-health-authority
Number of Beds: 17 beds
Note: Programs & services include: acute care; medicine;
pediatrics; surgery; obstetrics; emergency; physiotherapy;
radiology; laboratory; home support / home nursing; long-term
care case management; orthopedics; & visiting specialists in
urology, ENT surgery, dermatology, neurology, ophthalmology, &
radiology.
Jonathan Cooper, Administrator, Health Services

Langley: Langley Memorial Hospital
Affiliated with: Fraser Health Authority
Former Name: Langley Health Services
22051 Fraser Hwy., Langley, BC V3A 4H4
Tel: 604-514-6000 Fax: 604-534-8283
www.fraserhealth.ca
www.facebook.com/FraserHealthAuthority;
twitter.com/Fraserhealth; www.youtube.com/user/fraserhealth;
www.linkedin.com/company/fraser-health-authority
Number of Beds: 135 acute care beds; 220 long-term care beds;
18 mental health beds; 12 intensive care beds; 9 pediatric beds;
28 obstetrical beds
Note: Programs & services include: acute care; ambulatory care;
antepartum care; CT scan; echocardiography; emergency;
fluoroscopy; general medicine, radiography & surgery; hospice
residence; inpatient psychiatry unit; intensive care; interventional
radiography; maternity; outpatient services; pediatrics;
pharmacy; postpartum care; spiritual care; & ultrasound.
Jason Cook, Executive Director

Lillooet: Lillooet Hospital & Health Centre
Affiliated with: Interior Health Authority
Former Name: Lillooet District Hospital &
Community Health Programs
951 Murray St., Lillooet, BC V0K 1V0
Tel: 250-256-4233 Fax: 250-256-1336
Toll-Free: 855-656-4233
www.interiorhealth.ca
www.facebook.com/InteriorHealth; twitter.com/Interior_Health;
www.youtube.com/InteriorHealthAuth;
www.linkedin.com/company/interior-health-authority
Number of Beds: 6 beds
Note: Programs & services include: antepartum care; community
care; dental surgery; diabetes education program; ECG / EKG;
emergency; end of life / palliative care; endoscopy; general
medicine; general surgery; holter monitor; home support;
hospice; intrapartum care; laboratory; maternity; mental health &
substance issues; nutrition; physiotherapy; postpartum care;
prenatal; radiology; rehabilitation; social work; telehealth;
vasectomy; & wound care.

Mackenzie: Mackenzie & District Hospital & Health
Centre
Affiliated with: Northern Health Authority
Former Name: Mackenzie & District Hospital
PO Box 249, 45 Centennial Dr., Mackenzie, BC V0J 2C0
Tel: 250-997-3263 Fax: 250-997-3940
www.northernhealth.ca
www.facebook.com/NorthernHealth; twitter.com/northern_health;
www.youtube.com/northernhealthbc;
www.linkedin.com/company/northern-health-authority
Number of Beds: 4 beds
Population Served: 4539
Note: Programs & services include: emergency; medicine;
medical imaging; laboratory; home care nursing; public health; &
mental health & addictions.
Barb Crook, Administrator

Maple Ridge: Ridge Meadows Hospital
Affiliated with: Fraser Health Authority
Former Name: Ridge Meadows Hospice Society
11666 Laity St., Maple Ridge, BC V2X 7G5
Tel: 604-463-4111
www.fraserhealth.ca
www.facebook.com/FraserHealthAuthority;
twitter.com/Fraserhealth;
www.linkedin.com/company/fraser-health-authority
Number of Beds: 93 acute care beds; 148 long-term care beds;
25 rehabilitation beds; 20 mental health beds; 7 intensive care
beds; 26 obstetrical beds
Note: Programs & services include: acute care; ambulatory care;
antepartum care; cardiac; CT scan; emergency; fluoroscopy;
general medicine, radiography, rehabilitation & surgery; inpatient
psychiatry; intensive care; interventional radiography;
mammography; maternity; medical daycare; medical oncology;
outpatient services; pediatrics; pharmacy; postpartum;
pulmonary; spiritual care; & ultrasound.
Valerie Spurrell, Executive Director

Masset: Northern Haida Gwaii Hospital & Health
Centre
Affiliated with: Northern Health Authority
2520 Harrison Ave., Masset, BC V0T 1M0
Tel: 250-626-4700 Fax: 250-626-4709
www.northernhealth.ca
www.facebook.com/NorthernHealth;
twitter.com/Northern_Health;
www.youtube.com/northernhealthBC;
www.linkedin.com/company/northern-health-authority
Number of Beds: 4 acute care beds; 4 long-term care beds; 1
respite bed
Note: Programs & services include: acute care; emergency;
general medicine; surgery; community health; public health; &
mental health.

McBride: McBride & District Hospital
Affiliated with: Northern Health Authority
PO Box 669, 1136 - 5th Ave., McBride, BC V0J 2E0
Tel: 250-569-2251 Fax: 250-569-3369
www.northernhealth.ca
www.facebook.com/NorthernHealth; twitter.com/northern_health;
www.youtube.com/northernhealthbc;
www.linkedin.com/company/northern-health-authority
Number of Beds: 3 acute care beds; 8 long-term care beds; 1
respite bed
Note: Programs & services include: acute care; diagnostic
imaging; emergency; laboratory; long-term care; mental health &
addictions counselling; physiotherapy; & public health.

Merritt: Nicola Valley Hospital & Health Centre
Affiliated with: Interior Health Authority
Former Name: Nicola Valley General Hospital
3451 Voght St., Merritt, BC V1K 1C6
Tel: 250-378-2242 Fax: 250-378-3287
www.interiorhealth.ca
www.facebook.com/InteriorHealth; twitter.com/interior_health;
www.youtube.com/InteriorHealthAuth;
www.linkedin.com/company/interior-health-authority
Number of Beds: 8 beds
Note: Programs & services include: diabetes education program;
emergency; rehabilitation & physiotherapy; public health; mental
health; home & community care nursing; home support;
laboratory; & x-ray.

Mission: Mission Memorial Hospital
Affiliated with: Fraser Health Authority
7324 Hurd St., Mission, BC V2V 3H5
Tel: 604-826-6261 Fax: 604-826-9513
feedback@fraserhealth.ca
www.fraserhealth.ca
www.facebook.com/FraserHealthAuthority;
twitter.com/Fraserhealth; www.youtube.com/user/fraserhealth;
www.linkedin.com/company/fraser-health-authority
Number of Beds: 200 long-term care beds; 45 acute care beds
Note: Programs & services include: acute care; ambulatory care;
emergency; general medicine & radiography; hospice residence;
orthopaedic surgery; outpatient laboratory; residential care;
spiritual care; & ultrasound.
Brendan Abbot, Executive Director

Nakusp: Arrow Lakes Hospital
Affiliated with: Interior Health Authority
97 - 1st Ave. NE, Nakusp, BC V0G 1R0
Tel: 250-265-3622 Fax: 250-265-4435
www.interiorhealth.ca
www.facebook.com/InteriorHealth; twitter.com/Interior_Health;
www.youtube.com/InteriorHealthAuth;
www.linkedin.com/company/interior-health-authority
Number of Beds: 6 beds
Note: Programs & services include: community care; community

respiratory therapy; diabetes education program; emergency;
end of life / palliative care; extended care; general medicine;
hospice; laboratory; mental health & substance abuse; nutrition /
dietitian; physiotherapy; pulmonary diagnostics; radiology;
telehealth; transfusion; & wound care.

Nanaimo: Nanaimo Regional General Hospital
(NRGH)
Affiliated with: Vancouver Island Health Authority
1200 Dufferin Cres., Nanaimo, BC V9S 2B7
Tel: 250-755-7691 Toll-Free: 250-947-8214
www.islandhealth.ca
www.facebook.com/VanIslandHealth;
twitter.com/vanislandhealth;
www.linkedin.com/company/vancouver-island-health-authority
Number of Beds: 221 acute care beds; 25 rehabilitation beds; 31
mental health beds; 10 ICU beds; 8 pediatric beds; 19 obstetrical
beds
Note: Programs & services include: Aboriginal health nurse;
acute inpatient psychiatric services; cardiac risk reduction;
diabetes education; eye health; heart function; heart health;
laboratory; medical imaging; neurophysiology; nutrition;
pacemaker; pain program; rehabilitation; spiritual care; &
surgery.
Damian Lange, Director of Clinical Operations
Carol Nelson, Aboriginal Liaison Nurse
carol.nelson@viha.ca

Nelson: Kootenay Lake Hospital
Affiliated with: Interior Health Authority
3 View St., Nelson, BC V1L 2V1
Tel: 250-352-3111 Fax: 250-354-2320
www.interiorhealth.ca
www.facebook.com/InteriorHealth; twitter.com/Interior_Health;
www.youtube.com/InteriorHealthAuth;
www.linkedin.com/company/interior-health-authority
Number of Beds: 30 beds
Note: Services offered include: antepartum care; chemotherapy;
chronic obstructive pulmonary disease services; community
care; community respiratory therapy; convalescent care; CT
scan; dental surgery; diabetes education program;
echocardiogram; ECG / EKG; emergency; end of life / palliative
care; endoscopy; general medicine & rehabilitation; geriatric
medicine; hematology; holter monitor; hospice; intrapartum care;
laboratory; mammography; maternity; microbiology; nutrition;
oncology; ophthalmology; pediatrics; pharmacy; physiotherapy;
postpartum care; pulmonary diagnostics & rehabilitation;
radiology; Telehealth; transfusion; & ultrasound.

New Westminster: Royal Columbian Hospital
Affiliated with: Fraser Health Authority
330 East Columbia St., New Westminster, BC V3L 3W7
Tel: 604-520-4253
feedback@fraserhealth.ca
www.fraserhealth.ca
www.facebook.com/FraserHealthAuthority;
twitter.com/Fraserhealth
Year Founded: 1862
Number of Beds: 75 intensive care beds; 56 obstetrical beds; 12
pediatric beds; 30 mental health beds; 281 acute care beds
Note: Programs & services include: emergency; acute care; care
for the elderly, angiography; antepartum care; bone
densitometry; cardiac; bronchoscopy services; ultrasound;
fluoroscopy; radiography; surgery unit; hemodialysis; psychiatry;
intensive care unit; MRI; mammography; oncology; neonatal
intensive care; neurological services; orthopaedic surgery;
paediatrics; pantomography; physiotherapy; plastc surgery; &
vascular & thoracic surgery.
Sheila Finamore, Executive Director

Oliver: South Okanagan General Hospital
Affiliated with: Interior Health Authority
911 McKinney Rd., Oliver, BC V0H 1T0
Tel: 250-498-5000 Fax: 250-498-5004
www.interiorhealth.ca
www.facebook.com/InteriorHealth; twitter.com/Interior_Health;
www.youtube.com/InteriorHealthAuth;
www.linkedin.com/company/interior-health-authority
Number of Beds: 18 beds
Note: Programs & services include: chronic obstructive
pulmonary disease services; community care; diabetes
education program; ECG / EKG; emergency; end of life /
palliative care; extended care; fluoroscopy; general medicine;
hematology; holter monitor; hospice; laboratory; nutrition;
pharmacy; physiotherapy; radiology; Telehealth; & wound care.
Sara Evans, Manager, Acute Care

Penticton: Penticton Regional Hospital (PRH)
Affiliated with: Interior Health Authority
550 Carmi Ave., Penticton, BC V2A 3G6
Tel: 250-492-4000 Fax: 250-492-9068
www.interiorhealth.ca
www.facebook.com/InteriorHealth; twitter.com/Interior_Health;
www.youtube.com/InteriorHealthAuth;
www.linkedin.com/company/interior-health-authority
Number of Beds: 87 acute care beds; 15 mental health beds; 13
rehabilitation beds; 11 pediatric beds; 7 intensive care beds; 7
obstetrical beds
Note: Programs & services include: acute neurology &
psychiatric services; antepartum care; cardioversion;
chemotherapy; chronic obstructive pulmonary disease services;
community care; community respiratory therapy; CT scan;
diabetes education program; diagnostic bronchoscopy;
diagnostic cardiology; ear, nose & throat; echocardiogram; ECG
/ EKG; emergency; endoscopy; enterostomal therapy; extended
care; fluoroscopy; gastroenterology; general medicine,
rehabilitation & surgery; hematology; holter monitor; hospice;
intensive care; intrapartum care; laboratory; mammography;
maternity; mental health & substance abuse; microbiology; MRI;
nutrition; oncology; ophthalmology; orthotics; otolaryngology
surgery; pediatrics; pharmacy; physiotherapy; postpartum care;
pulmonary diagnostics; radiology; respiratory therapy;
speech-language pathology; spiritual care; telehealth;
transesophageal echocardiogram (TEE); transfusion; ultrasound;
urology; vasectomy; & wound care. Also offers the Mary Pack
Arthritis Program, a service of Vancouver Coastal Health.

Port Alberni: West Coast General Hospital
Affiliated with: Vancouver Island Health Authority
3949 Port Alberni Hwy., Port Alberni, BC V9Y 4S1
Tel: 250-731-1370
www.islandhealth.ca
www.facebook.com/VanIslandHealth;
twitter.com/vanislandhealth;
www.linkedin.com/company/vancouver-island-health-authority
Number of Beds: 3 intensive care beds; 4 obstetrical beds; 11
mental health beds; 25 acute care beds
Note: Programs & services include: Aboriginal health; diabetes
education; laboratory; nutrition; rehabilitation; & surgery.
Sarah Kowalenko, Communications Assistant, VIHA
250-740-6951, sarah.kowalenko@viha.ca
Vanessa Gallic, Aboriginal Liaison Nurse
vanessa.gallic@viha.ca

Port Hardy: Port Hardy Hospital
Affiliated with: Vancouver Island Health Authority
9120 Granville St., Port Hardy, BC V0N 2P0
Tel: 250-902-6011
www.islandhealth.ca
www.facebook.com/VanIslandHealth;
twitter.com/vanislandhealth;
www.linkedin.com/company/vancouver-island-health-authority
Number of Beds: 22 long-term care beds; 12 acute care beds
Note: Programs & services include: Aboriginal health; acute
care; emergency; residential care; ambulatory outpatient
services; laboratory; medical detox; palliative care; emergency
obstetrics; visiting specialists; & x-ray.
Sarah Kowalenko, Communications Assistant, VIHA
sarah.kowalenko@viha.ca

Port McNeill: Port McNeill Hospital
Affiliated with: Vancouver Island Health Authority
2750 Kingcome Pl., Port McNeill, BC V0N 2R0
Tel: 250-956-4461
www.islandhealth.ca
www.facebook.com/VanIslandHealth;
twitter.com/vanislandhealth;
www.linkedin.com/company/vancouver-island-health-authority
Number of Beds: 10 acute care beds
Note: Services include: acute care; ambulatory outpatient
services; diabetes education; emergency; laboratory; medical
detox; medical imaging; nutrition; palliative care; regional
obstetrics; & visiting specialists.
Sarah Kowalenko, Communications Assistant, VIHA
250-740-6951, sarah.kowalenko@viha.ca

Port Moody: Eagle Ridge Hospital (ERH)
Affiliated with: Fraser Health Authority
475 Guildford Way, Port Moody, BC V3H 3W9
Tel: 604-461-9972 Fax: 604-461-9972
www.fraserhealth.ca
www.facebook.com/FraserHealthAuthority;
twitter.com/Fraserhealth; www.youtube.com/user/fraserhealth;
www.linkedin.com/company/fraser-health-authority
Year Founded: 1984
Number of Beds: 147 acute care beds; 75 long-term care beds;
26 rehabilitation beds
Note: Programs & services include: acute care; ambulatory care;
cardiac; CT scan; emergency; fluoroscopy; general medicine,

Victoria: **Glengarry Hospital**
Affiliated with: Vancouver Island Health Authority
Former Name: Glengarry Extended Care Hospital
1780 Fairfield Rd., Victoria, BC V8S 1G7
Tel: 250-370-8699 Toll-Free: 866-995-3299
info@viha.ca
www.viha.ca/hcc/residential/locations/glengarry.htm
Year Founded: 1963
Number of Beds: 135 units
Note: Extended care hospital

Victoria: **Mount Tolmie Extended Care Hospital**
Affiliated with: Vancouver Island Health Authority
3690 Richmond Rd., Victoria, BC V8P 4R6
Tel: 250-370-5757 Toll-Free: 866-995-3299
info@viha.ca
www.viha.ca/hcc/residential/locations/mount_tolmie.htm
Number of Beds: 72 units
Note: Extended care hospital

Victoria: **Priory Hospital**
Affiliated with: Vancouver Island Health Authority
567 Goldstream Ave., Victoria, BC V9B 2W4
Tel: 250-370-5626 Toll-Free: 866-995-3299
info@viha.ca
www.viha.ca/hcc/residential/locations/priory_hiscock_heritage_w
oods.htm
www.facebook.com/VanIslandHealth; twitter.com/vanislandhealth
Number of Beds: 140 units
Note: Extended care hospital

Community Health Care Centres

100 Mile House: **South Cariboo Health Centre**
Affiliated with: Interior Health Authority
555 Cedar Ave. South, 100 Mile House, BC V0K 2E0
Tel: 250-395-7676 Fax: 250-395-7675
www.interiorhealth.ca
Note: Programs & services include: acquired brain injury
services; adult day services; BC Early Hearing Program;
caregiver support; case management; community care clinic;
community nursing; community nutrition; diabetes education;
hearing; home support; immunization; postpartum care; prenatal
services; rehabilitation; social work; speech-language pathology;
& Tuberculin Skin Testing.

Abbotsford: **Abbotsford Health Protection Office**
Affiliated with: Fraser Health Authority
207 - 2776 Bourquin Cres. West, Abbotsford, BC V2S 6A4
Tel: 604-870-7900 Fax: 604-870-7901

Abbotsford: **Abbotsford Home Health Office**
Affiliated with: Fraser Health Authority
103 - 34194 Marshall Rd., Abbotsford, BC V2S 5E4
Tel: 604-556-5000 Fax: 604-556-5010

Abbotsford: **Abbotsford Public Health Unit**
Affiliated with: Fraser Health Authority
104 - 34194 Marshall Rd., Abbotsford, BC V2S 5E4
Tel: 604-864-3400 Fax: 604-864-3410

Agassiz: **Agassiz Health Protection Office**
Affiliated with: Fraser Health Authority
7243 Pioneer Ave., Agassiz, BC V0M 1A0
Tel: 604-793-7160

Agassiz: **Agassiz Home Health Office**
Affiliated with: Fraser Health Authority
7243 Pioneer Ave., Agassiz, BC V0M 1A0
Tel: 604-793-7160 Fax: 604-796-8587

Agassiz: **Agassiz Public Health Unit**
Affiliated with: Fraser Health Authority
7243 Pioneer Ave., Agassiz, BC V0M 1A0
Tel: 604-793-7160 Fax: 604-796-8587

Alexis Creek: **Alexis Creek Health Centre**
Affiliated with: Interior Health Authority
2592 Morton Rd., Alexis Creek, BC V0L 1A0
Tel: 250-394-4313 Fax: 250-394-5179
www.interiorhealth.ca
Note: Services include: adult day services; caregiver support;
case management; community care clinic; nursing; nutrition;
home support; laboratory; rehabilitation; social work; &
Telehealth.

Armstrong: **Armstrong Community Services**
Affiliated with: Interior Health Authority
3800 Patten Dr., Armstrong, BC V0E 1B2
Tel: 250-546-4752 Fax: 250-546-4753
www.interiorhealth.ca

Armstrong: **Pleasant Valley Health Centre**
Affiliated with: Interior Health Authority
3800 Patten Dr., Armstrong, BC V0E 1B2
Tel: 250-546-4700 Fax: 250-546-8834
www.interiorhealth.ca
Note: Programs & services include: acquired brain injury
services; adult community support services; adult day services;
caregiver support; case management; child & youth
immunization program; community care clinic; community
nursing; counselling; diabetes education; early psychosis
intervention; eating disorders; electrocardiogram; general
medicine; home support; immunization; laboratory; nutrition;
oncology; ophthalmology; palliative care; physiotherapy;
postpartum care; prenatal; Publicly Funded Tuberculin Skin
Testing; radiology; rehabilitation; social work; surgical daycare; &
wound care.

Bamfield: **Bamfield Health Centre**
Affiliated with: Vancouver Island Health Authority
PO Box 40, 353 Bamfield Rd., Bamfield, BC V0R 1B0
Tel: 250-728-3312

Barriere: **Barriere Adult Day Centre**
Affiliated with: Interior Health Authority
4431 Barriere Town Rd., Barriere, BC V0E 1E1
Tel: 250-672-0025
www.interiorhealth.ca
Note: Offers adult day services for individuals at risk of losing
their independence

Barriere: **Barriere Health Centre**
Affiliated with: Interior Health Authority
4537 Barriere Town Rd., Barriere, BC V0E 1E0
Tel: 250-672-9731 Fax: 250-672-5144
www.interiorhealth.ca
Note: Services include: emergency; immunization; postpartum
care; radiology; & Telehealth.

Blue River: **Blue River Health Centre**
Affiliated with: Interior Health Authority
Former Name: Red Cross Outpost Hospital
858 Main St., Blue River, BC V0E 1J0
Tel: 250-673-8311 Fax: 250-673-2380
www.interiorhealth.ca
Note: Services include: adult day services; case management;
Choice in Support for Independent Living; community care clinic;
nursing; nutrition; home support; laboratory; Publicly Funded
Tuberculin Skin Testing; rehabilitation; social work; & Telehealth.

Burnaby: **Burnaby Health Protection Office**
Affiliated with: Fraser Health Authority
300 - 4946 Canada Way, Burnaby, BC V5G 4H7
Tel: 604-918-7683 Fax: 604-918-7520

Burnaby: **Burnaby Home Health Office**
Affiliated with: Fraser Health Authority
400 - 4946 Canada Way, Burnaby, BC V5G 4H7
Tel: 604-918-7447 Fax: 604-918-7631

Burnaby: **Burnaby Public Health Unit**
Affiliated with: Fraser Health Authority
300 - 4946 Canada Way, Burnaby, BC V5G 4H7
Tel: 604-918-7605 Fax: 604-918-7630

Castlegar: **Castlegar & District Community Health**
Centre
Castlegar & District Hospital Foundation
Affiliated with: Interior Health Authority
709 - 10th St., Castlegar, BC V1N 2H7
Tel: 250-365-7711 Fax: 250-304-1234
www.interiorhealth.ca
Note: Programs & services include: acquired brain injury
services; addictions treatment programs; adult day services; BC
Early Hearing Program; caregiver support; case management;
community care clinic; community nursing; community nutrition;
community respiratory therapy; diabetes education;
electrocardiogram; emergency; harm reduction services; HIV
testing; Holter monitor; home support; immunization; postpartum
care; prenatal services; Publicly Funded Tuberculin Skin Testing;
pulmonary diagnostics; radiology; rehabilitation; social work;
Telehealth; & ultrasound.

Celista: **Scotch Creek Medical Clinic**
Affiliated with: Interior Health Authority
#2, 3874 Squilax-Anglemont Rd., Celista, BC V2C 2T1
Tel: 250-955-0660
www.interiorhealth.ca
Note: Programs & services include: acquired brain injury
services; adult day services; caregiver support; case
management; community care clinic; community nursing;
community nutrition; home support; rehabilitation; & social work.

Chase: **Chase Health Centre**
Affiliated with: Interior Health Authority
825 Thompson Ave., Chase, BC V0E 1M0
Tel: 250-679-3312 Fax: 250-679-5329
Toll-Free: 855-459-3312
www.interiorhealth.ca
Note: Programs & services include: immunization; home
support; postpartum care; prenatal; rehabilitation; respiratory
therapy; social work; caregiver support; case management; HIV
testing; & Telehealth.

Chase: **Chase Primary Health Care Clinic**
Affiliated with: Interior Health Authority
826 Thompson Ave., Chase, BC V0E 1M0
Tel: 250-679-1400
www.interiorhealth.ca
Note: Programs & services include: acquired brain injury
services; adult day services; caregiver support; community care
clinic; community nursing; community nutrition; emergency
health services; home support; primary health care; pulmonary
rehabilitation; rehabilitation; & social work.

Chemainus: **Chemainus Health Care Centre**
Affiliated with: Vancouver Island Health Authority
9909 Esplanade St., Chemainus, BC V0R 1K1
Tel: 250-737-2040 Fax: 250-246-3844
Number of Beds: 75 beds
Note: Services include: long-term care; laboratory; medical
imaging / radiology; adult day program; & mobile mammogram
clinic.

Chetwynd: **Chetwynd Health Unit**
Affiliated with: Northern Health Authority
PO Box 507, 5500 Hospital Rd., Chetwynd, BC V0C 1J0
Tel: 250-788-7200 Fax: 250-788-7247
www.northernhealth.ca

Chilliwack: **Chilliwack Health Protection Office**
Affiliated with: Fraser Health Authority
101 - 45485B Knight Rd., Chilliwack, BC V2R 3G3
Tel: 604-702-4950 Fax: 604-824-5896

Chilliwack: **Chilliwack Home Health Office**
Affiliated with: Fraser Health Authority
45470 Menholm Rd., Chilliwack, BC V2P 1M2
Tel: 604-702-4800 Fax: 604-702-4801

Chilliwack: **Chilliwack Mental Health Office**
Affiliated with: Fraser Health Authority
45470 Menholm Rd., Chilliwack, BC V2P 1M2
Tel: 604-702-4860 Fax: 604-702-4861

Chilliwack: **Chilliwack Public Health Unit**
Affiliated with: Fraser Health Authority
45470 Menholm Rd., Chilliwack, BC V2P 1M2
Tel: 604-702-4900 Fax: 604-702-4901

Clearwater: **Clearwater Community Health**
Affiliated with: Interior Health Authority
640 Park Dr., Clearwater, BC V0E 1N0
Tel: 250-674-3141
www.interiorhealth.ca
Note: Programs & services include: acquired brain injury
services; adult day services; caregiver support; community care
clinic; community nursing; community nutrition; home support;
immunization; postpartum care; prenatal services; rehabilitation;
& social work.

Clinton: **Clinton Health & Wellness Centre**
Affiliated with: Interior Health Authority
1510 Cariboo Hwy., Clinton, BC V0K 1K0
Tel: 250-459-2080 Fax: 250-459-2083
Toll-Free: 855-459-2080
www.interiorhealth.ca
Note: Programs & services include: caregiver support; case
management; home support; rehabilitation; & social work.

Cranbrook: **Associates Medical Clinic**
Affiliated with: Interior Health Authority
123 - 10th Ave. South, Cranbrook, BC V1C 2N1
Tel: 250-426-4231
www.interiorhealth.ca
Note: Services include: pregnancy options & sexual health
counselling; immunizations; & referrals.

Cranbrook: **Cranbrook Community Dialysis Clinic**
Affiliated with: Interior Health Authority
13 - 24th Ave. North, Cranbrook, BC V1C 3H9
Tel: 250-417-3588 Fax: 250-420-4180
Toll-Free: 866-288-8082
www.interiorhealth.ca
Note: Provides renal programs & hemodialysis services

Cranbrook: Cranbrook Family Connections
Affiliated with: Interior Health Authority
209A - 16th Ave. North, Cranbrook, BC V1V 5S8
Tel: 250-489-5011 *Fax:* 250-489-5905
www.interiorhealth.ca

Cranbrook: Cranbrook Health Centre
Affiliated with: Interior Health Authority
20 - 23rd Ave. South, Cranbrook, BC V1C 5V1
Tel: 250-420-2200 *Fax:* 250-420-2295
www.interiorhealth.ca
Note: Programs & services include: acquired brain injury services; adult day services; asthma education; caregiver support; case management; community care clinic; community nursing; dietitian / nutrition; dental; diabetes education; environmental; harm reduction supplies & services; hearing services; home oxygen program; home support; immunization; postpartum care; prenatal services; Publicly Funded Tuberculin Skin Testing; rehabilitation; respiratory therapy; social work; & speech-language pathology.

Cranbrook: Cranbrook Wellness Centre
Affiliated with: Interior Health Authority
20 - 23rd Ave. South, Cranbrook, BC V1C 5V1
Tel: 250-489-6414 *Fax:* 250-489-6420
www.interiorhealth.ca
Note: Programs & services include: Breathe Well Program; Healthy Heart Program; Heart Function Clinic; pulmonary rehabilitation; & TIA Rapid Access Clinic.

Cranbrook: East Kootenay Area Heart Function Clinic
Affiliated with: Interior Health Authority
20 - 23rd Ave. South, Cranbrook, BC V1C 5V1
Tel: 250-489-6414 *Fax:* 250-489-6420
www.interiorhealth.ca
Note: Support for patients diagnosed with heart failure

Cranbrook: East Kootenay CKD Clinic
Affiliated with: Interior Health Authority
20 - 23rd Ave. South, Cranbrook, BC V1C 5V1
Tel: 250-420-4113 *Fax:* 250-489-6420
www.interiorhealth.ca
Note: Hemodialysis clinic

Crawford Bay: East Shore Community Health Centre
Affiliated with: Interior Health Authority
15985 Hwy. 3A, Crawford Bay, BC V0B 1E0
Tel: 250-227-9006
www.interiorhealth.ca
Note: Programs & services include: caregiver support; case management; home support; immunization; postpartum care; prenatal; rehabilitation; & social work.

Creston: Creston Community Dialysis Clinic
Affiliated with: Interior Health Authority
312 - 15th Ave. North, Creston, BC V0B 1G5
Tel: 250-428-3830 *Fax:* 250-428-3831
www.interiorhealth.ca
Note: Offers renal programs & hemodialysis services

Creston: Creston Health Unit
Affiliated with: Interior Health Authority
312 - 15th Ave. North, Creston, BC V0B 1G0
Tel: 250-428-3873
www.interiorhealth.ca
Note: Programs & services include: acquired brain injury services; adult day services; caregiver support; case management; community care clinic; community nursing; community nutrition; dental; envronmental; home support; immunization; postpartum care; prenatal services; rehabilitation; social work; & Tuberculin Skin Testing.

Dawson Creek: Dawson Creek Health Unit
Affiliated with: Northern Health Authority
1001 - 110th Ave., Dawson Creek, BC V1G 4X3
Tel: 250-719-6500 *Fax:* 250-719-6513
www.northernhealth.ca

Dease Lake: Stikine Health Centre
Affiliated with: Northern Health Authority
PO Box 386, 7171 Hwy. 37, Dease Lake, BC V0C 1L0
Tel: 250-771-4444 *Fax:* 250-771-3911
www.northernhealth.ca

Delta: Delta Health Protection Office
Affiliated with: Fraser Health Authority
201 - 11245 84 Ave., Delta, BC V4C 2L9
Tel: 604-507-5478 *Fax:* 604-507-5492

Delta: Delta South Home Health Office
Affiliated with: Fraser Health Authority
4470 Clarence Taylor Cres., Delta, BC V4K 3W3
Tel: 604-952-3552 *Fax:* 604-946-6953

Edgewood: Edgewood Health Centre
Affiliated with: Interior Health Authority
Former Name: Red Cross Outpost Nursing Station
322 Monashee Ave., Edgewood, BC V0G 1J0
Tel: 250-269-7313 *Fax:* 250-269-7520
www.interiorhealth.ca
Note: Programs & services include: caregiver support; case management; home support; rehabilitation; social work; & Telehealth.

Elkford: Elkford Health Centre
Affiliated with: Interior Health Authority
212 Alpine Way, Elkford, BC V0B 1H0
Tel: 250-865-2247 *Fax:* 250-865-2797
www.interiorhealth.ca
Note: Programs & services include: breastfeeding clinic; caregiver support; case management; home support; immunization; postpartum care; prenatal; radiology; rehabilitation; social work; & Telehealth.

Enderby: Enderby Community Health Centre
Affiliated with: Interior Health Authority
707 - 3rd Ave., Enderby, BC V0E 1V0
Tel: 250-838-2450 *Fax:* 250-838-6005
www.interiorhealth.ca
Note: Programs & services include: breastfeeding clinic; caregiver support; case management; home support; immunization; postpartum care; prenatal; rehabilitation; social work; & Telehealth.

Fernie: Fernie Health Centre
Affiliated with: Interior Health Authority
1501 - 5th Ave., Fernie, BC V0B 1M0
Tel: 250-423-8288 *Fax:* 250-423-8280
www.interiorhealth.ca
Note: Programs & services include: acquired brain injury services; adult day services; caregiver support; case management; community care clinic; community nursing; community nutrition; diabetes education; home support; immunization; postpartum care; prenatal services; Publicly Funded Tuberculin Skin Testing; rehabilitation; & social work.

Fort Nelson: Fort Nelson Health Unit
Affiliated with: Northern Health Authority
PO Box 1000, 5217 Airport Dr., Fort Nelson, BC V0C 1R0
Tel: 250-774-7092 *Fax:* 250-774-7096
www.northernhealth.ca

Fort St. James: Fort St. James Health Unit
Affiliated with: Northern Health Authority
#111, 250 Stuart Dr. NE, Fort St. James, BC V0J 1P0
Tel: 250-996-2700 *Fax:* 250-996-2216
www.northernhealth.ca

Fort St. John: Fort St. John Health Unit
Affiliated with: Northern Health Authority
10115 - 110 Ave., Fort St. John, BC V1J 6M9
Tel: 250-263-6000 *Fax:* 250-263-6086
www.northernhealth.ca

Fort St. John: Fort St. John Unattached Patient Clinic
Affiliated with: Northern Health Authority
10011 - 96th St., Fort St. John, BC V1J 3P3
Tel: 250-262-5210
www.northernhealth.ca

Fraser Lake: Fraser Lake Community Health Centre
Affiliated with: Northern Health Authority
PO Box 1000, 130 Chowsunket St., Fraser Lake, BC V0J 1S0
Tel: 250-699-6225 *Fax:* 250-699-6987
www.northernhealth.ca
Note: Includes 4 doctors, x-ray services, laboratory services, & a public health nurse office.

Gold River: Gold River Health Centre
Affiliated with: Vancouver Island Health Authority
601 Trumpeter Dr., Gold River, BC V0P 1G0
Tel: 250-283-2626 *Fax:* 250-283-7436
Note: Services: medical imaging; physiotherapist; urgent care centre; laboratory; addiction services; child health care; & Telehealth.

Golden: Golden & District Home Support
Affiliated with: Interior Health Authority
835 - 9th Ave. South, Golden, BC V0A 1H0
Tel: 250-344-3005 *Fax:* 250-344-3004
www.interiorhealth.ca

Note: Provides home-based services, including assessment & case management, nursing, rehabilitation, home support, & palliative care.

Golden: Golden Health Centre
Affiliated with: Interior Health Authority
835 - 9th Ave. South, Golden, BC V0A 1H0
Tel: 250-344-3001 *Fax:* 250 344-2817
www.interiorhealth.ca
Note: Programs & services include: adult day services; caregiver support; case management; community care clinic; community nursing; community nutrition; home support; immunization; postpartum care; prenatal services; rehabilitation; social work; speech-language pathology; & Tuberculin Skin Testing.

Grand Forks: Boundary Community Health Centre
Affiliated with: Interior Health Authority
7441 - 2nd St., Grand Forks, BC V0H 1H0
Tel: 250-443-3150 *Fax:* 250-443-3180
www.interiorhealth.ca

Grand Forks: Glanville Family Centre
Boundary Family & Individual Services Society
Affiliated with: Interior Health Authority
PO Box 2498, 1200 Central Ave., Grand Forks, BC V0H 1H0
Tel: 250-442-2267 *Toll-Free:* 877-442-5355
info@bfiss.org
www.boundaryfamily.org
Note: Programs for children, youth, women & families

Grand Forks: Grand Forks Community Dialysis Clinic
Affiliated with: Interior Health Authority
7649 - 22nd St., Grand Forks, BC V0H 1H0
Tel: 250-443-2119 *Fax:* 250-442-2129
www.interiorhealth.ca
Note: Offers hemodialysis services

Grand Forks: Grand Forks Public Health
Affiliated with: Interior Health Authority
7441 2nd St., Grand Forks, BC V0H 1H0
Tel: 250-443-3150
www.interiorhealth.ca
Note: Programs & services include: dental; environmental; food safety; immunization; postpartum care; & prenatal services.

Granisle: Granisle Community Health Centre
Affiliated with: Northern Health Authority
PO Box 219, 1 Hagen St., Granisle, BC V0J 1W0
Tel: 250-697-2251 *Fax:* 250-697-6221
www.northernhealth.ca

Hazelton: Hazelton Community Health
Affiliated with: Northern Health Authority
Bag 999, 2510 Hwy. 62, Hazelton, BC V0J 1Y0
Tel: 250-842-4640 *Fax:* 250-842-4642
www.northernhealth.ca

Houston: Houston Health Centre
Affiliated with: Northern Health Authority
PO Box 538, 3202 - 14 St., Houston, BC V0J 1Z0
Tel: 250-845-2294 *Fax:* 250-845-7884
www.northernhealth.ca

Hudson's Hope: Hudson's Hope Health Centre
Affiliated with: Northern Health Authority
Former Name: Hudson's Hope Gething Diagnostic & Treatment Centre
PO Box 599, 10309 Kyllo St., Hudson's Hope, BC V0C 1V0
Tel: 250-783-9991 *Fax:* 250-783-9125
www.northernhealth.ca
Number of Beds: 2 emergency beds
Population Served: 1000

Invermere: Invermere Health Centre
Affiliated with: Interior Health Authority
PO Box 2069, 850 - 10th Ave., Invermere, BC V0A 1K0
Tel: 250-342-2360 *Fax:* 250-342-2373
www.interiorhealth.ca
Note: Programs & services include: adult day services; caregiver support; case management; community care clinic; community nursing; community nutrition; emergency; environmental health; home support; immunization; postpartum care; prenatal services; rehabilitation; social work; speech language pathology; & Tuberculin Skin Testing.

Kamloops: Kamloops Community Dialysis Clinic
Affiliated with: Interior Health Authority
795 Tranquille Rd., Kamloops, BC V2B 3J3
Tel: 250-314-2100 *Fax:* 250-314-2335
www.interiorhealth.ca
Note: Offers hemodialysis services

Kamloops: Kamloops Home & Community Care
Affiliated with: Interior Health Authority
#37, 450 Lansdowne St., Kamloops, BC V2C 1Y2
Tel: 250-851-7900 Fax: 250-851-7910
www.interiorhealth.ca
Note: Programs & services include: community care clinic;
community nutrition; home support; rehabilitation; & social work.

Kamloops: Kamloops Pacemaker Clinic
Affiliated with: Interior Health Authority
311 Columbia St., 2nd Fl., Kamloops, BC V2C 2T1
Tel: 250-314-2100 Toll-Free: 250-314-2391
www.interiorhealth.ca
Note: Provides support & services for patients with pacemakers,
defibrillators, loop recorders, & other implanted devices.

Kamloops: Kamloops Primary Care Clinic
Affiliated with: Interior Health Authority
#36, 450 Lansdowne St., Kamloops, BC V2C 1Y3
Tel: 250-851-7954
www.interiorhealth.ca
Note: Programs & services include: Breathe Well program;
primary health care; & pulmonary rehabilitation.

Kamloops: Kamloops Public Health Unit
Affiliated with: Interior Health Authority
519 Columbia St., Kamloops, BC V2C 2T8
Tel: 250-851-7300 Fax: 250-851-7301
Toll-Free: 866-847-4372
www.interiorhealth.ca
Note: Programs & services include: adult day services; caregiver
support; case management; community care clinic; community
nursing; community nutrition; dental; environmental; hearing;
home support; immunization; nutrition; postpartum care; prenatal
services; Publicly Funded Tuberculin Skin Testing; recreational
water safety; rehabilitation; social work; & speech-language
pathology.

Kamloops: North Shore X-Ray Clinic
Affiliated with: Interior Health Authority
789 Fortune Dr., #B3, Kamloops, BC V2B 2L3
Tel: 250-314-2420
www.interiorhealth.ca
Note: Services include bone density & radiology.

Kamloops: TCS Chronic Kidney Disease Clinic
Affiliated with: Interior Health Authority
Royal Inland Hospital, 311 Columbia St., Kamloops, BC V2C
2T1
Tel: 250-314-2849
www.interiorhealth.ca
Note: Also the Thompson Cariboo Shuswap Peritoneal
Hemodialysis Clinic (250-314-2100, ext. 3259), Thompson
Cariboo Shuswap Home Hemodialysis Clinic, Thompson
Cariboo Shuswap In-Center Hemodialysis Clinic & Thompson
Cariboo Shuswap Transplant Clinic (250-314-2260).

Kamloops: TCS Heart Function Clinic
Affiliated with: Interior Health Authority
311 Columbia St., Kamloops, BC V2C 2T1
Tel: 250-314-2727 Fax: 250-314-2169
www.interiorhealth.ca
Note: Support for patients with chronic heart failure. Also
includes the Vascular Improvement Clinic.

Kaslo: Kaslo Physiotherapy
Affiliated with: Interior Health Authority
673A Ave., Kaslo, BC V0G 1M0
Tel: 250-353-2742
www.interiorhealth.ca

Kaslo: Kaslo Primary Health Centre
Affiliated with: Interior Health Authority
673A Ave., Lower Level, Kaslo, BC V0G 1M0
Tel: 250-353-2291 Fax: 250-353-2738
www.interiorhealth.ca
Note: Programs & services include: adult day services; caregiver
support; case management; community care clinic; community
nursing; community nutrition; home support; immunization;
postpartum care; prenatal services; primary health care;
rehabilitation; social work; & Tuberculin Skin Testing.

Kaslo: Victorian Community Health Centre of Kaslo
Affiliated with: Interior Health Authority
Former Name: Victoria Hospital of Kaslo
673 A Ave., Kaslo, BC V0G 1M0
Tel: 250-353-2211 Fax: 250-353-2747
www.interiorhealth.ca
Note: Programs & services include: acquired brain injury
services; addictions day treatment program; adult day services;
caregiver support; case management; community care clinic;
community nursing; community nutrition; emergency health;

home support; radiology; rehabilitation; social work; &
Telehealth.

Kelowna: Central Okanagan Heart Function Clinic
Affiliated with: Interior Health Authority
505 Doyle Ave., Kelowna, BC V1Y 0C5
Tel: 250-469-7070
www.interiorhealth.ca
Note: Support for patients diagnosed with heart failure

Kelowna: Kelowna Chronic Kidney Disease Clinic
Affiliated with: Interior Health Authority
2268 Pandosy St., Kelowna, BC V1Y 1T2
Tel: 250-862-4156 Fax: 250-862-4341
www.interiorhealth.ca
Note: Also the Kelowna Peritoneal Dialysis Clinic, Kelowna
Home Hemodialysis Clinic & the Kelowna In-Centre
Hemodialysis Clinic (250-862-4345).

Kelowna: Kelowna Pacemaker Clinic
Affiliated with: Interior Health Authority
2268 Pandosy St., Kelowna, BC V2Y 1T2
Tel: 250-862-4450 Fax: 250-862-4104
www.interiorhealth.ca
Note: Provides support & services for patients with pacemakers,
defibrillators, loop recorders, & other implanted devices.

Kelowna: Kelowna Research Centre
Affiliated with: Interior Health Authority
2309 Abbott St., Kelowna, BC V1Y 1T2
Tel: 250-862-9777 Fax: 250-862-9771
www.interiorhealth.ca
Note: Services include: assessment & case management;
nursing; rehabilitation; home support; & palliative care.

Kelowna: Kelowna TIA Clinic
Affiliated with: Interior Health Authority
2251 Pandosy St., Kelowna, BC V1Y 1T1
Tel: 250-980-1392 Fax: 250-862-4463
www.interiorhealth.ca
Note: Services for identifying & treating transient ischemic attack
(TIA).

Kelowna: Kelowna Transplant Clinic
Affiliated with: Interior Health Authority
2268 Pandosy St., Kelowna, BC V1Y 1T2
Tel: 250-862-4156 Toll-Free: 250-862-4291
www.interiorhealth.ca
Note: Follow-up care for organ transplant recipients, primarily
renal transplant.

Kelowna: May Bennett Wellness Centre
Affiliated with: Interior Health Authority
Former Name: May Bennett Home
135 Davie Rd., Kelowna, BC V1X 1Y8
Tel: 250-980-1400 Fax: 250-712-0847
www.interiorhealth.ca
Note: Services include: adult day services; caregiver support;
case management; Choice in Support for Independent Living;
community care clinic; nursing; nutrition; diabetes education;
home support; rehabilitation; & social work.

Kelowna: Outreach Urban Health Centre
Affiliated with: Interior Health Authority
455 Leon Ave., Kelowna, BC V1V 6J3
Tel: 250-868-2230 Fax: 250-868-2006
www.interiorhealth.ca
Note: Primary health centre

Kelowna: Rutland Aurora Health Centre
Affiliated with: Interior Health Authority
#102, 285 Aurora Cres., Kelowna, BC V1X 7N6
Tel: 250-491-1100
www.interiorhealth.ca

Kelowna: Rutland Community Dialysis
Affiliated with: Interior Health Authority
125 Park Rd., Kelowna, BC V1X 3E3
Tel: 250-491-7613 Fax: 250-491-2719
www.interiorhealth.ca
Note: Offers hemodialysis services

Kelowna: Rutland Health Centre
Affiliated with: Interior Health Authority
155 Gray Rd., Kelowna, BC V1X 1W6
Tel: 250-980-4825 Fax: 250-765-7710
www.interiorhealth.ca
Note: Programs & services include: immunization; postpartum
care; & prenatal services.

Kelowna: Surgical Optimization Clinic (Hip & Knee)
Affiliated with: Interior Health Authority
#118, 1835 Gordon Dr., Kelowna, BC V1Y 3H5
Tel: 250-980-1515 Fax: 250-980-1519
www.interiorhealth.ca

Keremeos: South Similkameen Health Centre
Affiliated with: Interior Health Authority
700 - 3rd St., Keremeos, BC V0X 1N3
Tel: 250-499-3000 Fax: 250-499-3027
www.interiorhealth.ca
Note: Community services (250-499-3029). Programs & services
include: acquired brain injury services; adult day services;
caregiver support; case management; community care clinic;
community nursing; community nutrition; diabetes education;
electrocardiogram; emergency; Holter monitor; home support;
immunization; postpartum care; prenatal services; Publicly
Funded Tuberculin Skin Testing; radiology; rehabilitation; social
work; & Telehealth.

Kimberley: Kidney Care Clinic
Affiliated with: Interior Health Authority
260 - 4th Ave., Kimberley, BC V1A 2R6
www.interiorhealth.ca
Note: Offers services for individuals & families affected by
chronic kidney disease.

Kimberley: Kimberley Health Centre & Home
Support
Affiliated with: Interior Health Authority
260 - 4th Ave., Kimberley, BC V1A 2R6
Tel: 250-427-2215 Fax: 250-427-7389
www.interiorhealth.ca
Note: A primary health care centre also providing home-based
services, such as assessment & case management, nursing,
rehabilitation, home support, & palliative care.

Ladysmith: Ladysmith Community Health Centre
Affiliated with: Vancouver Island Health Authority
Former Name: Ladysmith & District General Hospital
PO Box 10, 1111 - 4 Ave., Ladysmith, BC V9G 1A1
Tel: 250-739-5777 Fax: 250-740-2689
info@viha.ca
www.viha.ca
www.facebook.com/VanIslandHealth; twitter.com/vanislandhealth
Heather Dunne, Site Manager

Lillooet: Lillooet Home & Community Centre
Affiliated with: Interior Health Authority
951 Murray St., Lillooet, BC V0K 1V0
Tel: 250-256-4233 Fax: 250-256-1332
www.interiorhealth.ca

Logan Lake: Logan Lake Primary Health Care
Affiliated with: Interior Health Authority
Former Name: Logan Lake Health Centre
5 Beryl Dr., Logan Lake, BC V0K 1W0
Tel: 250-523-9414 Fax: 250-523-6869
www.interiorhealth.ca
Note: Programs & services include: caregiver support; case
management; home support; postpartum care; prenatal;
radiology; rehabilitation; social work; & Telehealth.

Lumby: Lumby Health Unit
Affiliated with: Interior Health Authority
2135 Norris Ave., Lumby, BC V0E 2G0
Tel: 250-547-9741 Fax: 250-547-9741
www.interiorhealth.ca
Note: Programs & services include: acquired brain injury
services; adult day services; caregiver support; case
management; community care clinic; community nursing;
community nutrition; home support; immunization; postpartum
care; prenatal services; Publicly Funded Tuberculin Skin Testing;
rehabilitation; & social work.

Lumby: Whitevalley Community Resource Centre
Affiliated with: Interior Health Authority
2114 Shuswap Ave., Lumby, BC V0E 2G0
Tel: 250-547-8866 Fax: 250-547-6285
www.interiorhealth.ca

Lytton: St. Bartholomew's Health Centre
Affiliated with: Interior Health Authority
575A Main St., Lytton, BC V0K 1Z0
Tel: 250-455-2221 Fax: 250-455-6621
Toll-Free: 855-955-2221
www.interiorhealth.ca
Note: Programs & services include: acquired brain injury
services; adult day services; caregiver support; case
management; community care clinic; community nursing;
community nutrition; electrocardiogram; emergency health;
home support; Publicly Funded Tuberculin Skin Testing;
radiology; rehabilitation; social work; & Telehealth.

Masset: Masset Community Health
Affiliated with: Northern Health Authority
PO Box 215, 2520 Harrison Ave., Masset, BC V0T 1M0
Tel: 250-626-4702 *Fax:* 250-626-6015
www.northernhealth.ca

McBride: McBride Health Unit
Affiliated with: Northern Health Authority
1126 - 5th Ave., McBride, BC V0J 2E0
Tel: 250-569-2251 *Fax:* 250-569-2232
Info Line: 888-562-1214
Note: Includes after hours & emergency (888-562-1214), mental health & addictions (ext. 2038) & home care nursing (ext. 2034) services.

Merritt: Merritt Adult Day Centre
Affiliated with: Interior Health Authority
2201 Jackson Ave., Merritt, BC V1K 1C6
www.interiorhealth.ca

Merritt: Merritt Public Health
Affiliated with: Interior Health Authority
3451 Voght St., Merritt, BC V1K 1C6
Tel: 250-378-3400
www.interiorhealth.ca
Note: Programs & services include: immunization; postpartum care; prenatal services; & Tuberculin Skin Testing.

Midway: Midway Health Unit
Affiliated with: Interior Health Authority
540 - 7th Ave., Midway, BC V0H 1M0
Tel: 250-449-2887 *Fax:* 250-449-2889
www.interiorhealth.ca
Note: Programs & services include: acquired brain injury services; adult day services; caregiver support; case management; community care clinic; community nursing; community nutrition; home support; immunization; postpartum care; prenatal services; rehabilitation; social work; & Tuberculin Skin Testing.

Nakusp: Arrow & Slocan Lakes Community Services
Affiliated with: Interior Health Authority
205 - 6th Ave., Nakusp, BC V0G 1R0
Tel: 250-265-3674 *Fax:* 250-265-3855
www.interiorhealth.ca
Note: Services: addictions treatment.
Tim Payne, Executive Director

Nakusp: Nakusp Health Unit
Affiliated with: Interior Health Authority
97 - 1st Ave. NE, Nakusp, BC V0G 1R0
Tel: 250-265-3608 *Fax:* 250-265-3104
www.interiorhealth.ca
Note: Programs & services include: acquired brain injury services; adult day services; caregiver support; case management; community care clinic; community nursing; community nutrition; home support; immunization; postpartum clinic; prenatal services; rehabilitation; social work; & Tuberculin Skin Testing.

Nelson: Chronic Disease Management Clinic
Affiliated with: Interior Health Authority
#443, 3 View St., Nelson, BC V1L 2V1
Tel: 250-354-2397 *Fax:* 250-352-6273
www.interiorhealth.ca
Note: Heart function clinic with cardiac rehab

Nelson: Gordon Road Wellness Centre
Affiliated with: Interior Health Authority
905 Gordon Rd., Nelson, BC V1L 3L8
Tel: 250-352-1401 *Fax:* 250-352-1405
www.interiorhealth.ca
Note: Provides an adult day program

Nelson: Nelson Health Centre
Affiliated with: Interior Health Authority
333 Victoria St., Nelson, BC V1L 4K3
Tel: 250-505-7200 *Fax:* 250-505-7211
www.interiorhealth.ca
Note: Programs & services include: acquired brain injury services; addictions treatment programs; caregiver support; case management; community care clinic; community nursing; community nutrition; dental; environmental; home support; immunization; nutrition; postpartum care; prenatal services; Publicly Funded Tuberculin Skin Testing; rehabilitation; social work; & speech-language pathology.

New Denver: Slocan Community Health Centre
Affiliated with: Interior Health Authority
401 Galena Ave., New Denver, BC V0G 1S0
Tel: 250-358-7911 *Fax:* 250-358-7117
www.interiorhealth.ca

Note: Primary health care centre. Services include: caregiver support; community care clinic; electrocardiogram; emergency; home support; radiology; rehabilitation; social work; & therapy.

Oliver: Oliver Cardiac Rehab Clinic
Affiliated with: Interior Health Authority
36003 - 79th St., Oliver, BC V0H 1T0
Tel: 250-770-5507 *Fax:* 250-770-5506
www.interiorhealth.ca
Note: Offers a 5-week supervised exercise program to improve lung & heart health.

Oliver: Oliver Health Centre
Affiliated with: Interior Health Authority
930 Spillway Rd., Oliver, BC V0H 1T0
Tel: 250-498-5080 *Fax:* 250-498-0351
www.interiorhealth.ca
Note: Programs & services include: acquired brain injury services; adult day services; caregiver support; case management; community care clinic; community nursing; community nutrition; home support; immunization; postpartum care; prenatal services; Publicly Funded Tuberculin Skin Testing; rehabilitation; social work; & speech-language pathology.

Osoyoos: Osoyoos Cardiac Rehab Clinic
Affiliated with: Interior Health Authority
8505 - 68th Ave., Osoyoos, BC V0H 1V0
Tel: 250-770-5507 *Fax:* 250-770-5506
www.interiorhealth.ca
Note: Offers a 5-week supervised exercise program to improve lung & heart health.

Osoyoos: Osoyoos Health Centre
Affiliated with: Interior Health Authority
4816 - 89 St., Osoyoos, BC V0H 1V1
Tel: 250-495-6433 *Fax:* 250-495-5142
www.interiorhealth.ca
Note: Programs & services include: breastfeeding clinic; caregiver support; case management; home support; immunization; postpartum care; prenatal; rehabilitation; & social work.

Parksville: Oceanside Health Centre
Affiliated with: Vancouver Island Health Authority
489 Alberni Hwy., Parksville, BC V9P 1J9
Tel: 250-951-9550
www.viha.ca
Note: Services include: urgent care; primary care; medical imaging; laboratory; Telehealth; environmental health; & medical day care.
Nancy Kroes, Coordinator, Integrated Services

Penticton: Heart Function Clinic - Cardiopulmonary Wellness Clinic (HFC)
Affiliated with: Interior Health Authority
Also Known As: Cardiopulmonary Wellness Clinic
740 Carmi Ave., Penticton, BC V2A 8P9
Tel: 250-770-3530 *Fax:* 250-770-3470
www.interiorhealth.ca
Note: For patients with a diagnosis of heart failure

Penticton: Penticton Chronic Kidney Disease Clinic
Affiliated with: Interior Health Authority
Penticton Health Centre, 740 Carmi Ave., Penticton, BC V2A 8P9
Tel: 250-770-3530 *Fax:* 250-770-3410
Toll-Free: 800-707-8550
www.interiorhealth.ca
Note: Offers hemodialysis services

Penticton: Penticton Health Centre
Affiliated with: Interior Health Authority
740 Carmi Ave., Penticton, BC V2A 8P9
Tel: 250-770-3434 *Fax:* 250-770-3410
www.interiorhealth.ca
Note: Programs & services include: acquired brain injury services; adult day services; BC Early Hearing Program; caregiver support; case management; community care clinic; community nursing; community nutrition; dental; diabetes education; harm reduction services; home support; immunization; nutrition; postpartum care; prenatal services; Publicly Funded Tuberculin Skin Testing; pulmonary rehabilitation; rehabilitation; social work; & speech-language pathology.

Penticton: Penticton Home Hemodialysis Clinic
Affiliated with: Interior Health Authority
550 Carmi Ave., Penticton, BC V2A 3G6
Tel: 250-492-4000
www.interiorhealth.ca
Note: Also the Penticton In-Centre Hemodialysis Clinic (250-492-9059), Penticton Peritoneal Dialysis Clinic

(250-492-4000, ext. 2650) & Penticton Transplant Clinic (250-492-4000, ext. 2603).

Penticton: Penticton Pacemaker Clinic
Affiliated with: Interior Health Authority
550 Carmi Ave., Penticton, BC V2A 3G6
Tel: 250-492-4000 *Fax:* 250-770-5526
www.interiorhealth.ca
Note: Offers support & services to patients with implanted cardiac devices.

Port Alice: Port Alice Health Centre
Affiliated with: Vancouver Island Health Authority
Former Name: Port Alice Hospital
1090 Marine Dr., Port Alice, BC V0N 2N0
Tel: 250-284-3555
info@viha.ca
www.viha.ca

Prince George: Centre for Healthy Living
Affiliated with: Northern Health Authority
1788 Diefenbaker Dr., Prince George, BC V2N 4V7
Tel: 250-649-7011
www.northernhealth.ca

Prince George: Northern Interior Health Unit - Prince George
Affiliated with: Northern Health Authority
1444 Edmonton St., Prince George, BC V2M 6W5
Tel: 250-565-7478
www.northernhealth.ca
Note: Programs & services: mental health; public health (250-565-7381).

Prince Rupert: Prince Rupert Community Health
Affiliated with: Northern Health Authority
300 - 3rd Ave. West, Prince Rupert, BC V8J 1L4
Tel: 250-622-6380 *Fax:* 250-622-6391
www.northernhealth.ca

Princeton: Princeton Health Centre
Affiliated with: Interior Health Authority
98 Ridgewood Dr., Princeton, BC V0X 1W0
Tel: 250-295-4442 *Fax:* 250-295-4443
www.interiorhealth.ca
Note: Programs & services include: acquired brain injury services; adult day services; caregiver support; case management; community care clinic; community nursing; community nutrition; diabetes education; home support; immunization; postpartum care; prenatal services; rehabilitation; social work; & Tuberculin Skin Testing.

Quesnel: Quesnel Community Health Services
Affiliated with: Northern Health Authority
523 Front St., Quesnel, BC V2J 2K7
Tel: 250-983-6850 *Fax:* 250-991-7577
www.northernhealth.ca
Debbie Strang, Administrator, Health Services

Revelstoke: Queen Victoria Health Centre
Affiliated with: Interior Health Authority
1200 Newlands Rd., Revelstoke, BC V0E 2S0
Tel: 250-837-2131 *Fax:* 250-814-2285
www.interiorhealth.ca
Note: Programs & services include: acquired brain injury services; adult day services; caregiver support; case management; community care clinic; community nursing; community nutrition; home support; Publicly Funded Tuberculin Skin Testing; rehabilitation; & social work.

Revelstoke: Revelstoke Public Health
Affiliated with: Interior Health Authority
1200 Newlands Rd., Revelstoke, BC V0E 2S0
Tel: 250-814-2244
www.interiorhealth.ca
Note: Programs & services include: acquired brain injury services; adult day services; BC Early Hearing Program; caregiver support; case management; community care clinic; community nursing; community nutrition; home support; immunization; postpartum care; prenatal services; rehabilitation; social work; & Tuberculin Skin Testing.

Rock Creek: Rock Creek Health Centre
Affiliated with: Interior Health Authority
100 Rock Creek Cutoff Rd., Rock Creek, BC V0H 1Y0
Tel: 250-446-2272
www.interiorhealth.ca
Note: Programs & services include: acquired brain injury services; adult day services; caregiver support; case management; community care clinic; community nursing; community nutrition; home support; Publicly Funded Tuberculin Skin Testing; rehabilitation; & social work.

Salmo: Salmo Health & Wellness Centre
Affiliated with: Interior Health Authority
413 Baker Ave., Salmo, BC V0G 1Z0
Tel: 250-357-0104 *Fax:* 250-357-0107
www.interiorhealth.ca

Note: Programs & services include: acquired brain injury services; adult day services; caregiver support; case management; community care clinic; community nursing; community nutrition; home support; immunization; postpartum care; prenatal services; Publicly Funded Tuberculin Skin Testing; rehabilitation; & social work.

Salmon Arm: Salmon Arm Health Centre
Affiliated with: Interior Health Authority
851 - 16th St. NE, Salmon Arm, BC V1E 4N7
Tel: 250-833-4100 *Fax:* 250-833-4117
www.interiorhealth.ca

Note: Programs & services include: acquired brain injury services; BC Early Hearing Program; caregiver support; case management; community care clinic; community nursing; community nutrition; environmental health; harm reduction services; home support; immunization; postpartum care; prenatal services; Publicly Funded Tuberculin Skin Testing; rehabilitation; social work; & speech-language pathology.

Salmon Arm: Salmon Arm Pacemaker Clinic
Affiliated with: Interior Health Authority
601 - 10th St. NE, Salmon Arm, BC V1E 4N6
Tel: 250-833-3636 *Fax:* 250-833-3604
www.interiorhealth.ca

Salmon Arm: Salmon Arm Physiotherapy
Affiliated with: Interior Health Authority
#1, 2770 - 10th Ave., Salmon Arm, BC V1E 2E8
www.interiorhealth.ca

Salmon Arm: Shuswap Home & Community Care
Affiliated with: Interior Health Authority
2770 - 10th Ave. NE, #B, Salmon Arm, BC V1E 4N6
Tel: 250-832-6643 *Fax:* 250-832-8781
www.interiorhealth.ca

Sicamous: Sicamous Health Centre
Affiliated with: Interior Health Authority
1133 Hwy. 97A, Sicamous, BC V0E 2V0
Tel: 250-836-4835 *Fax:* 250-836-3166
www.interiorhealth.ca

Note: Programs & services include: acquired brain injury services; adult day services; caregiver support; case management; community care clinic; community nursing; community nutrition; home support; immunization; Publicly Funded Tuberculin Skin Testing; rehabilitation; & social work.

Smithers: Smithers Community Health
Affiliated with: Northern Health Authority
Bag 5000, 3793 Alfred Ave., Smithers, BC V0J 2N0
Tel: 250-847-6400 *Fax:* 250-847-5908
www.northernhealth.ca

Smithers: Smithers Home & Community Care
Affiliated with: Northern Health Authority
PO Box 370, 3950 - 8th Ave., Smithers, BC V0J 2N0
Tel: 250-847-6234 *Fax:* 250-847-6239
www.northernhealth.ca

Note: Services include: personal care; nursing; respite care; physiotherapy; occupational therapy; adult day care centre; palliative care.

Sorrento: Sorrento & Area Community Health Centre
Affiliated with: Interior Health Authority
1250 TransCanada Hwy., Sorrento, BC V0E 2W0
Tel: 250-803-5251 *Fax:* 250-803-5281
www.interiorhealth.ca

Note: Offers primary health care services
Marilyn Clark, Chair

Sparwood: Sparwood Community Dialysis Clinic
Affiliated with: Interior Health Authority
570 Pine Ave., Sparwood, BC V0B 2G0
Tel: 250-425-4527 *Fax:* 250-425-4529
www.interiorhealth.ca

Note: Offers hemodialysis services

Sparwood: Sparwood Mental Health & Substance Use
Affiliated with: Interior Health Authority
570 Pine Ave., Sparwood, BC V0B 2G0
Tel: 250-425-2064 *Fax:* 250-425-2378
Toll-Free: 800-661-0329
www.interiorhealth.ca

Note: Programs & services include: adult community support; counselling; Early Psychosis Intervention; eating disorders; & seniors mental health.

Sparwood: Sparwood Primary Health Care
Affiliated with: Interior Health Authority
570 Pine Ave., Sparwood, BC V0B 2G0
Tel: 250-425-6212 *Fax:* 250-425-2313
www.interiorhealth.ca

Note: Programs & services include: acquired brain injury services; adult day services; BC Early Hearing program; caregiver support; case management; child & youth immunization program; community care clinic; community nursing; community nutrition; diabetes education; electrocardiogram; emergency health; home support; immunization; postpartum care; prenatal; primary health care; pulmonary diagnostics; radiology; rehabilitation; social work; Telehealth; & Tuberculin Skin Testing.

Summerland: Summerland Health Centre
Affiliated with: Interior Health Authority
12815 Atkinson Rd., Summerland, BC V0H 1Z0
Tel: 250-404-8000 *Fax:* 250-404-8005
www.interiorhealth.ca

Note: Programs & services include: acquired brain injury services; adult day services; caregiver support; case management; community care clinic; community nursing; community nutrition; dental; diabetes education; ear, nose, & throat services; electrocardiogram; extended care unit; general medicine; home support; immunization; laboratory outpatient services; ophthalmology; otolaryngology surgery; post-anaesthetic care; postpartum care; prenatal services; Publicly Funded Tuberculin Skin Testing; radiology; rehabilitation; social work; speech-language pathology; & surgical daycare.

Surrey: Guildford Public Health Unit
Affiliated with: Fraser Health Authority
100 - 10233 153 St., Surrey, BC V3R 0Z7
Tel: 604-587-4750 *Fax:* 604-587-4777

Tahsis: Tahsis Health Centre
Affiliated with: Vancouver Island Health Authority
1085 Maquinna Dr., Tahsis, BC V0P 1X0
Tel: 250-934-6322 *Fax:* 250-934-6404
www.viha.ca

Note: Services include: child health clinic; communicable disease control program; family practice medical care; home care nursing; home support; laboratory; & urgent care.
Enid O'Hara, Manager, Rural Services
250-283-2626, Fax: 250-283-7561, enid.ohara@viha.ca

Tatla Lake: West Chilcotin Health Centre
Affiliated with: Interior Health Authority
16452 Hwy. 20, Tatla Lake, BC V0L 1V0
Tel: 250-476-1114 *Fax:* 250-476-1266
www.interiorhealth.ca

Note: Programs & services include: caregiver support; case management; home support; immunization; postpartum care; prenatal; rehabilitation; social work; & Telehealth.

Terrace: Terrace Health Unit
Affiliated with: Northern Health Authority
3412 Kalum St., Terrace, BC V8G 4T2
Tel: 250-631-4200 *Fax:* 250-638-2264
www.northernhealth.ca

Trail: Kiro Wellness Centre
Affiliated with: Interior Health Authority
1500 Columbia Ave., Trail, BC V1R 1J9
Tel: 250-364-6219 *Fax:* 250-364-6290
www.interiorhealth.ca

Note: Programs & services include: acquired brain injury services; addictions treatment programs; adult day services; caregiver support; case management; community care clinic; community nursing; community nutrition; dental; environmental; home support; immunization; postpartum care; prenatal services; Publicly Funded Tuberculin Skin Testing; pulmonary rehabilitation; rehabilitation; social work; & speech-language pathology.

Trail: Kootenay Boundary Chronic Kidney Disease Clinic
Affiliated with: Interior Health Authority
1200 Hospital Bench, Trail, BC V1R 4M1
Tel: 250-364-6270 *Fax:* 250-364-6290
www.interiorhealth.ca

Note: Also the Kootenay Boundary Home Hemodialysis Clinic, Kootenay Boundary In-Center Hemodialysis Clinic, & Kootenay Boundary Peritoneal Dialysis Clinic (250-364-3450).

Trail: Kootenay Boundary Transplant Clinic
Affiliated with: Interior Health Authority
1200 Hospital Bench, Trail, BC V1R 4M1
Tel: 250-364-3494
www.interiorhealth.ca

Note: Follow-up care for organ transplant recipients, primarily renal transplant.

Trail: Trail Heart Function Clinic
Affiliated with: Interior Health Authority
1500 Columbia Ave., Trail, BC V1R 1J9
Tel: 250-364-6297 *Fax:* 250-352-6273
www.interiorhealth.ca

Note: Offers treatment & services to patients with congestive heart failure.

Trail: Trail Pacemaker Clinic
Affiliated with: Interior Health Authority
1200 Hospital Bench, Trail, BC V1R 4M1
Tel: 250-368-3311 *Fax:* 250-364-3422
www.interiorhealth.ca

Note: Provides support & services for patients with pacemakers, defibrillators, loop recorders, & other implanted devices.

Tumbler Ridge: Tumbler Ridge Community Health Unit
Affiliated with: Northern Health Authority
PO Box 1090, 220 Front St., Tumbler Ridge, BC V0C 2W0
Tel: 250-242-5271 *Fax:* 250-242-3889
www.northernhealth.ca

Tumbler Ridge: Tumbler Ridge Community Health Unit
Affiliated with: Northern Health Authority
PO Box 1090, 220 Front St., Tumbler Ridge, BC V0C 2W0
Tel: 250-242-5271 *Fax:* 250-242-3889
www.northernhealth.ca

Valemount: Valemount Community Health Centre
Affiliated with: Northern Health Authority
PO Box 697, 1445 - 5 Ave., Valemount, BC V0E 2Z0
Tel: 250-566-9138 *Fax:* 250-566-4319
www.northernhealth.ca

Population Served: 1000
Note: Full-service health centre with 3 doctors, support staff, lab technicians and nurses.

Vanderhoof: Vanderhoof Health Unit
Affiliated with: Northern Health Authority
3299 Hospital Rd., Vanderhoof, BC V0J 3A2
Tel: 250-567-6900 *Fax:* 250-567-6170
www.northernhealth.ca

Vernon: Day-Break Adult Day Centre
Affiliated with: Interior Health Authority
Gateby Care Facility, 3000 Gateby Pl., Vernon, BC V1T 1P4
Tel: 250-545-4456 *Fax:* 250-545-4439
www.interiorhealth.ca

Note: Offers adult day services

Vernon: North Okanagan Heart Function Clinic
Affiliated with: Interior Health Authority
2101 - 32nd St., Vernon, BC V1T 5L2
Tel: 250-558-1200 *Fax:* 250-558-4101
www.interiorhealth.ca

Note: Support for patients with chronic heart failure. Secondary phones: 250-306-9700 & 250-503-8805.

Vernon: Vernon - Ortho Clinic
Affiliated with: Interior Health Authority
3210 - 25th Ave., Vernon, BC V1T 2T1
www.interiorhealth.ca

Vernon: Vernon Cardiac Rehab Clinic
Affiliated with: Interior Health Authority
2101 - 32nd St., Vernon, BC V1T 5L2
Tel: 250-503-3712 *Fax:* 250-503-3722
www.interiorhealth.ca

Note: Also includes the Vernon Pacemaker Clinic (250-558-1200).

Vernon: Vernon Community Care Health Services
Affiliated with: Interior Health Authority
4505 - 25th St., Vernon, BC V1T 4S8
Tel: 250-541-2200 *Fax:* 250-541-2244
www.interiorhealth.ca

Note: Programs & services include: acquired brain injury services; adult day services; caregiver support; case management; community care clinic; community nursing; community nutrition; home support; rehabilitation; respiratory therapy; & social work.

Vernon: **Vernon Downtown Primary Care Centre**
Affiliated with: Interior Health Authority
3306A - 32nd Ave., Vernon, BC V1T 2M6
Tel: 250-541-1097 *Fax:* 250-541-1098
www.interiorhealth.ca
Note: Programs & services include: case management; health outreach; needle distribution; primary care mental health; & primary health care.

Vernon: **Vernon Health Centre**
Affiliated with: Interior Health Authority
1440 - 14th Ave., Vernon, BC V1B 2T1
Tel: 250-549-5700 *Fax:* 250-549-5711
www.interiorhealth.ca
Note: Programs & services include: acquired brain injury; breastfeeding clinic; caregiver support; case management; home support; immunization; postpartum care; prenatal; speech-language pathology; rehabilitation; & social work.

Vernon: **Vernon Renal Clinic**
Affiliated with: Interior Health Authority
#700, 3115 - 48th Ave., Vernon, BC V1T 3R5
Tel: 250-503-3320 *Fax:* 250-503-3324
www.interiorhealth.ca
Note: Offers services to patients with chronic kidney disease.

West Kelowna: **West Kelowna Health Centre**
Affiliated with: Interior Health Authority
#106, 2300 Carrington Rd., West Kelowna, BC V4T 2N6
Tel: 250-980-5150 *Fax:* 250-768-9813
www.interiorhealth.ca
Note: Programs & services include: acquired brain injury services; adult day services; caregiver support; case management; community care clinic; community nursing; community nutrition; dental; diabetes education; home support; immunization; postpartum care; prenatal services; Publicly Funded Tuberculin Skin Testing; rehabilitation; & social work.

Williams Lake: **Cariboo Memorial Health Centre**
Affiliated with: Interior Health Authority
517 North 6th Ave., Williams Lake, BC V2G 2G8
Tel: 250-392-4411 *Fax:* 250-392-2157
www.interiorhealth.ca
Note: Programs & services include: adult day services; nursing; nutrition; home support; rehabilitation; & social work.

Williams Lake: **Williams Lake Community Dialysis**
Affiliated with: Interior Health Authority
517 - 6th Ave. North, Williams Lake, BC V2G 2G8
Tel: 250-302-3209 *Fax:* 250-302-3253
www.interiorhealth.ca
Note: Offers hemodialysis services

Nursing Stations

Alexis Creek: **Alexis Creek Outpost**
2591 Morton Rd., Alexis Creek, BC V0L 1A0
Tel: 250-394-4313

Anahim Lake: **Anahim Lake Nursing Station**
Affiliated with: Interior Health Authority
PO Box 207, 6674 Clinic Lane, Anahim Lake, BC V0L 1C0
Tel: 250-742-3305 *Fax:* 250-742-3336
www.interiorhealth.ca
Note: Services include: acquired brain injury; case management; community care clinic; home support; postpartum care; prenatal; rehabilitation; social work; & Telehealth.

Atlin: **Atlin Health Centre**
Affiliated with: Northern Health Authority
Former Name: Red Cross Outpost Hospital
PO Box 330, 164 3rd St., Atlin, BC V0W 1A0
Tel: 250-651-7677 *Fax:* 250-651-7687
www.northernhealth.ca
Note: Non-emergency services on a walk-in basis; two nurses.

Fort James: **Takla Landing Nursing Station**
117 Bah'Lats Rd., Fort James, BC V0J 1P0
Tel: 250-996-7780
Note: Services include: pre- & post-natal care; nutrition care; pregnancy testing and counselling; baby clinics; immunization clinics; & STI testing and counselling.

Hartley Bay: **Hartley Bay Nursing Station**
Hartley Bay, BC V0V 1A0
Tel: 250-841-2556 *Fax:* 250-841-2554

Iskut: **Iskut Valley Health Services (IVHS)**
Iskut, BC V0J 1K0
Tel: 250-234-3511 *Fax:* 250-234-3512
iskut.org/programs-services/health
Terri Nole, Contact, Iskut Valley Health Services
terrilynn.nole@iskut.org

Kitkatla: **Kitkatla Nursing Station**
PO Box 150, Kitkatla, BC V0V 1C0
Tel: 250-848-2254 *Fax:* 250-848-2263

Klemtu: **Klemtu Nursing Station**
General Delivery, Klemtu, BC V0T 1L0
Tel: 250-839-1221 *Fax:* 250-839-1184
klemtu.com/kitasoo-band/programs-2/health-centre

Kyuquot: **Kyuquot Health Centre**
Affiliated with: Vancouver Island Health Authority
100 Okime St., Kyuquot, BC V0P 1J0
Tel: 250-332-5289 *Fax:* 250-332-5215
Note: Programs & services include: urgent care; family medicine; & child health clinics.
Enid O'Hara, Manager
250-283-2626, Fax: 250-283-7561, enid.ohara@viha.ca

Telegraph Creek: **Telegraph Creek Nursing Station**
PO Box 112, Telegraph Creek, BC V0J 2W0
Tel: 250-235-3211 *Fax:* 250-235-3213

Special Treatment Centres

Burnaby: **The Burnaby Centre for Mental Health & Addiction (BCMHA)**
Affiliated with: Interior Health Authority
3405 Willingdon Ave., Burnaby, BC V5G 3H4
Tel: 604-675-3950 *Fax:* 604-675-3955
burnabycentreinfo@interiorhealth.ca
www.interiorhealth.ca
Number of Beds: 100 beds
Note: Six to nine-month residential treatment program for BC residents with concurrent disorders.

Chilliwack: **Cedar Ridge**
Affiliated with: Fraser Health Authority
9090 Newman Rd., Chilliwack, BC V2P 3Z8
Tel: 604-701-3671

Kamloops: **Phoenix Centre**
922 - 3 Ave., Kamloops, BC V2C 6W5
Tel: 250-374-4634 *Fax:* 250-374-4621
Toll-Free: 877-318-1177
www.phoenixcentre.org
Number of Beds: 20 beds
Note: Detoxification centre
Sian Lewis, Executive Director
sian.lewis@phoenixcentre.org

Kelowna: **BC Cancer Agency Sindi Ahluwalia Hawkins Centre for the Southern Interior**
Affiliated with: Interior Health Authority
Also Known As: Cancer Centre for the Southern Interior
399 Royal Ave., Kelowna, BC V1Y 5L3
Tel: 250-712-3900 *Toll-Free:* 888-563-7773
www.bccancer.bc.ca
Number of Employees: 220

Kelowna: **Bridgeway Intensive Residential Treatment**
The Bridge Youth & Family Services
Former Name: Parkside Residence Ltd.
265 Gray Rd., Kelowna, BC V1X 1W8
Tel: 250-763-0456
info@thebridgeservices.ca
www.thebridgeservices.ca
www.facebook.com/TheBridgeServices;
twitter.com/thebridgeserv
Number of Beds: 20 beds
Note: Alcohol/substance abuse treatment centre, registered as an Assisted Living Residence with the Ministry of Health. Offers therapeutic group work, workshops and wellness support meetings; meetings focus on building new skills to better manage life, relationships and stress. A six-week program that operates throughout the year.

Kelowna: **Central Okanagan Hospice House**
Central Okanagan Hospice Association (COHA)
Affiliated with: Interior Health Authority
2035 Ethel St., Kelowna, BC V1Y 2Z6
Tel: 250-862-4126 *Fax:* 250-862-4129
hospicehousekelowna.com
Note: Provides palliative / end of life care.
Marion Henselwood, President, COHA

Penticton: **Moog & Friends Hospice House**
Penticton & District Hospice Society
Affiliated with: Interior Health Authority
1701 Government St., Penticton, BC V2A 8J7
Tel: 250-492-9071 *Fax:* 250-492-9097
www.pentictonhospice.com

Year Founded: 1998
Note: Palliative / end of life care.
Linda Brooks, Contact
linda.brooks@pentictonhospice.com

Port Coquitlam: **Community Integration Services Society**
2175 Mary Hill Rd., Port Coquitlam, BC V3C 3A2
Tel: 604-461-2131 *Fax:* 778-285-5520
humanresources@gociss.org
www.gociss.org
Year Founded: 1990
Note: Helps adults with disabilities gain skills to become more active members of society.
Shari Mahar, Executive Director
604-568-4753, smahar@gociss.org

Vancouver: **British Columbia Cancer Agency Vancouver**
Affiliated with: Provincial Health Services Authority
Also Known As: BC Cancer
600 - 10 Ave. West, Vancouver, BC V5Z 4E6
Tel: 604-877-6000 *Fax:* 604-872-4596
Toll-Free: 800-663-3333
twitter.com/BCCancer_Agency
Note: Cancer prevention, screening, diagnosis, treatment, rehabilitation, & care.
Dr. Kim Nguyen Chi, Vice President & Chief Medical Officer
Heather Findlay, Chief Operating Officer
Dr. François Bénard, Senior Executive Director, Research
Dr. Frances Wong, Senior Executive Director
Dr. Gary Pansegrau, Senior Executive Director, Clinical Programs & Policy
Kevin Hare, Senior Executive Director, Operations

Vancouver: **Sunny Hill Health Centre for Children**
Affiliated with: Provincial Health Services Authority
3644 Slocan St., Vancouver, BC V5M 3E8
Tel: 604-453-8300 *Fax:* 604-453-8301
Toll-Free: 888-300-3088
TTY: 604-453-8315
www.bcchildrens.ca
Number of Beds: 18 beds
Note: Provincial rehabilitation & assessment centre for children with disabilities.

Long Term Care Facilities

100 Mile House: **Mill Site Lodge & Fischer Place**
Affiliated with: Interior Health Authority
555 Cedar Ave. South, 100 Mile House, BC V0K 2E0
Tel: 250-395-7690
www.interiorhealth.ca
Number of Beds: 79 beds

Abbotsford: **Bevan Lodge**
Trillium Care
Affiliated with: Fraser Health Authority
33386 Bevan Ave., Abbotsford, BC V2S 5G6
Tel: 604-850-5416 *Fax:* 604-850-5418
info@bevanvillage.ca
bevanvillage.ca
www.facebook.com/TrilliumCare; twitter.com/TrilliumCare;
www.youtube.com/user/TrilliumCare
Number of Beds: 15 beds
Angelo Boholst, Executive Director

Abbotsford: **M.S.A. Manor**
Maplewood Seniors Care Society
Affiliated with: Fraser Health Authority
2510 Gladwin Rd., Abbotsford, BC V2T 3N9
Tel: 604-853-5831 *Fax:* 604-853-1647
admin@maplewood.bc.ca
www.maplewood.bc.ca
Heidi Mannis, Interim CEO

Abbotsford: **Maplewood House**
Affiliated with: Fraser Health Authority
1919 Jackson St., Abbotsford, BC V2S 2Z8
Tel: 604-853-5585 *Fax:* 604-853-5590
admin@maplewood.bc.ca
www.maplewood.bc.ca
Number of Beds: 77 beds
Heidi Mannis, Interim CEO

Abbotsford: **Menno Hospital**
Affiliated with: Fraser Health Authority
32945 Marshall Rd., Abbotsford, BC V2S 1K1
Tel: 604-859-7631 *Fax:* 604-859-6931
www.mennoplace.ca

Number of Beds: 150 beds
Note: Residential care facility offering 24 hour nursing care, physician, dietitian, occupational therapy, physiotherapy, pharmacy, & recreation services.
Karen Baillie, CEO
Kathrin McMath, Executive Director, Finance & Operations
Hilde Wiebe, Executive Director, Care Services
Jeanette Lee, Director, Human Resources
Sharon Simpson, Director, Communications & Stakeholder Engagement

Abbotsford: Sherwood Crescent Manor Ltd.
Affiliated with: Fraser Health Authority
32073 Sherwood Cres., Abbotsford, BC V2T 1C1
Tel: 604-853-7854 *Fax:* 604-853-9910
sherwoodcrescentmanor@telus.net
tcgcare.com/sherwood.html
Number of Beds: 41 permanent, 10 transitional care, 3 respite beds
Note: intermediate/residential care

Abbotsford: Tabor Manor
Affiliated with: Fraser Health Authority
Former Name: Tabor Home
31950 Sunrise Cres., Abbotsford, BC V2T 1N5
Tel: 604-859-8715 *Fax:* 604-859-6695
info.manor@taborvillage.org
website.taborvillage.org
Year Founded: 1960
Dan Levitt, Executive Director, Tabor Village
Kate Tate, Director, Tabor Village

Abbotsford: Valhaven Home
Affiliated with: Fraser Health Authority
4212 Balmoral St., Abbotsford, BC V4X 2P7
Tel: 604-856-2812 *Fax:* 604-856-3243
www.taborhome.org
Number of Beds: 26
Note: Complex care facility forming part of Tabor Village.

Agassiz: Glenwood Care Centre
Affiliated with: Fraser Health Authority
1458 Glenwood Dr., Agassiz, BC V0M 1A2
Tel: 604-796-9202 *Fax:* 604-796-9186
Note: Glenwood Care Centre provide residential care & day programs for the elderly.

Aldergrove: La Rosa de Matsqui
28711 Huntingdon Rd., Aldergrove, BC V0X 1A0
Tel: 604-856-1555 *Fax:* 604-856-3252
Number of Beds: 15 beds
Ari Jimenez, Manager

Armstrong: Pioneer Square
Kaigo Retirement Communities Ltd.
Affiliated with: Interior Health Authority
2865 Willowdale Dr., Armstrong, BC V0E 1B1
Tel: 250-546-3396 *Fax:* 250-546-9033
www.kaigo.ca
Number of Beds: 17 suites

Armstrong: Pleasant Valley Manor
Affiliated with: Interior Health Authority
3800 Patten Dr., Armstrong, BC V0E 1B2
Tel: 250-546-4707
www.interiorhealth.ca
Number of Beds: 81 permanent beds; 1 respite bed
Note: Complex care facility

Ashcroft: Jackson House
Affiliated with: Interior Health Authority
700 Ash-Cache Creek Hwy., Ashcroft, BC V0K 1A0
Tel: 250-453-1913 *Toll-Free:* 877-499-6599
www.interiorhealth.ca
Number of Beds: 25 beds
Note: Residential care facility

Burnaby: Carlton Gardens Long Term Care
Affiliated with: Chartwell Retirement Residences
4108 Norfolk St., Burnaby, BC V5G 0B4
Tel: 604-419-3000
www.chartwell.com
Number of Beds: 128 beds
Brent Binions, President & CEO, Chartwell Retirement Residences

Burnaby: Dania Home Society
Affiliated with: Fraser Health Authority
4279 Norland Ave., Burnaby, BC V5G 3Z6
Tel: 604-299-2414 *Fax:* 604-299-7775
info@dania.bc.ca
www.dania.bc.ca
Number of Beds: 67 beds

Margaret Douglas-Matthews, Executive Director

Burnaby: Fair Haven United Church Homes
Affiliated with: Fraser Health Authority
7557 Sussex Ave., Burnaby, BC V5J 3V6
Tel: 604-435-0525 *Fax:* 604-435-7031
info@fairhaven.bc.ca
www.fairhaven.bc.ca
Year Founded: 1978
Carol Mathersill, CEO
604-433-2939,

Burnaby: Fellburn Care Centre
Affiliated with: Fraser Health Authority
6050 Hastings St. East, Burnaby, BC V5B 1R6
Tel: 604-412-6510 *Fax:* 604-299-1015
Number of Beds: 110 beds
Note: extended care facility

Burnaby: Finnish Manor
Finnish Canadian Rest Home Association
Affiliated with: Fraser Health Authority
3460 Kalyk Ave., Burnaby, BC V5G 3B2
Tel: 604-434-2666 *Fax:* 604-439-7448
info@finncare.ca
finncare.ca
Year Founded: 1975
Number of Beds: 60 beds
Tanya Rautava, Administrator
604-325-8241

Burnaby: George Derby Centre
Affiliated with: Fraser Health Authority
7550 Cumberland St., Burnaby, BC V3N 3X5
Tel: 604-521-2676 *Fax:* 604-521-0220
info@georgederby.ca
www.georgederbycentre.ca
www.facebook.com/georgederbycentre;
twitter.com/gderbycentre;
www.youtube.com/channel/UCm5d_BAVtyYhU7qJZ_G8zgg
Year Founded: 1988
Note: Care facility for veterans
Ricky Kwan, Executive Director
rkwan@georgederby.ca

Burnaby: New Vista Society
Affiliated with: Fraser Health Authority
Former Name: New Vista Care Home
7550 Rosewood St., Burnaby, BC V5E 3Z3
Tel: 604-521-7764 *Fax:* 604-527-6001
info@newvista.bc.ca
www.newvista.bc.ca
Number of Beds: 236 beds
Number of Employees: 25
Note: The Society operates a complex care home and provides housing for low-income families and seniors.
Carol Finnie, CEO

Burnaby: Normanna Rest Home
Affiliated with: Fraser Health Authority
7725 - 4 St., Burnaby, BC V3N 5B6
Tel: 604-522-5812 *Fax:* 604-522-5803
info@normanna.ca
www.normanna.ca
Number of Beds: 100 beds
Note: multi level care
Margaret Douglas-Matthews, Executive Director

Burns Lake: The Pines
Affiliated with: Northern Health Authority
PO Box 7500, 800 Center St., Burns Lake, BC V0J 1E0
Tel: 250-692-2490 *Fax:* 250-692-2492
www.northernhealth.ca
Number of Beds: 30 beds

Campbell River: Yucalta Lodge
Affiliated with: Vancouver Island Health Authority
555 - 2 Ave., Campbell River, BC V9W 3V1
Tel: 250-850-2900
www.viha.ca
Year Founded: 2001
Number of Beds: 100 beds
Note: Multi-level care facility located next to Campbell River Hospital; building amenities include large bistro area with library; smoking area; gift shop; hair salon; 3 courtyards with gardens.

Castlegar: Castleview Care Centre (CVCC)
Chantelle Management Ltd.
Affiliated with: Interior Health Authority
2300 - 14 Ave., Castlegar, BC V1N 4A6
Tel: 250-365-7277 *Fax:* 250-365-3291
castleview@chantellegroup.com
www.chantellegroup.com

Year Founded: 1991
Number of Beds: 61 beds

Castlegar: Talarico Place
Affiliated with: Interior Health Authority
Castlegar & District Community Health Centre, 709 - 10 St., Castlegar, BC V1N 1A1
Tel: 250-365-7221 *Fax:* 250-304-1238
www.interiorhealth.ca
Number of Beds: 49 rooms

Chilliwack: Bradley Centre
Affiliated with: Fraser Health Authority
45600 Menholm Rd., Chilliwack, BC V2P 1P7
Tel: 604-795-4103 *Fax:* 604-795-4150

Chilliwack: The Cascades
Baltic Properties Group
Affiliated with: Fraser Health Authority
44586 McIntosh Dr., Chilliwack, BC V2P 7W8
Tel: 604-795-2500 *Fax:* 604-795-5693
www.balticproperties.ca
Cheryl Dawes, General Manager
cheryl.dawes@balticproperties.ca

Chilliwack: Heritage Village
Affiliated with: Fraser Health Authority
7525 Topaz Dr., Chilliwack, BC V2R 3C9
Tel: 604-858-1833 *Fax:* 604-793-7130

Chilliwack: Valleyhaven Guest Home
Affiliated with: Fraser Health Authority
45450 Menholm Rd., Chilliwack, BC V2P 1M2
Tel: 604-792-0037 *Fax:* 604-792-6766

Chilliwack: Waverly Seniors Village
Retirement Concepts
8445 Young Rd., Chilliwack, BC V2P 4P2
Tel: 604-792-6340 *Fax:* 604-792-5611
www.retirementconcepts.com
Number of Beds: 119 beds

Clearwater: Forest View Place
Affiliated with: Interior Health Authority
Dr. Helmcken Memorial Hospital, 640 Park Dr., Clearwater, BC V0E 1N1
Tel: 250-674-2244
www.interiorhealth.ca
Number of Beds: 19 permanent residential beds; 2 palliative & respite beds

Coquitlam: Cartier House
Park Place Seniors Living
Affiliated with: Fraser Health Authority
1419 Cartier Ave., Coquitlam, BC V3K 2C6
Tel: 604-939-4654 *Fax:* 604-939-6442
cartierhouse@parkplaceseniorsliving.com
www.parkplaceseniorsliving.com
Number of Beds: 78 beds
Al Jina, Owner

Coquitlam: Dufferin Care Centre
Affiliated with: Fraser Health Authority
1131 Dufferin St., Coquitlam, BC V3B 7X5
Tel: 604-552-1166 *Fax:* 604-552-3116

Coquitlam: Foyer Maillard
Affiliated with: Fraser Health Authority
1010 Alderson Ave., Coquitlam, BC V3K 1W1
Tel: 604-937-5578 *Fax:* 604-937-7133
www.foyermaillard.com
Year Founded: 1969

Courtenay: Glacier View Lodge
2450 Back Rd., Courtenay, BC V9N 9G8
Tel: 250-338-1451 *Fax:* 250-338-1115
www.glacierviewlodge.ca
Number of Beds: 100 beds
Michael Aikins, CEO

Cranbrook: F.W. Green Memorial Home
Affiliated with: Interior Health Authority
1700 - 4th St. South, Cranbrook, BC V1C 6E1
Tel: 250-426-3710 *Fax:* 250-426-3622
www.interiorhealth.ca
Number of Beds: 60 beds (2 tertiary geriatric, 1 rehabilitative)

Cranbrook: Rocky Mountain Lodge
20 - 23rd Ave. South, Cranbrook, BC V1C 5V1
Tel: 250-489-3361 *Fax:* 250-489-3545
Number of Beds: 63 beds
Brianna Hawkins, General Steward
205-489-6414

Creston: **Swan Valley Lodge**
Affiliated with: Interior Health Authority
818 Vancouver St., Creston, BC V0B 1G0
Tel: 250-428-2283 *Fax:* 250-428-9318
www.interiorhealth.ca
Number of Beds: 90 beds; 23-bed dementia unit; 6 respite beds
Note: Residential care

Cumberland: **Cumberland Lodge**
Affiliated with: Vancouver Island Health Authority
PO Box 400, 2696 Windermere Ave., Cumberland, BC V0R 1S0
Tel: 250-331-8505 *Fax:* 250-336-2100
Number of Beds: 66 beds

Dawson Creek: **Rotary Manor**
Affiliated with: Northern Health Authority
1121 - 90 Ave., Dawson Creek, BC V1G 5A3
Tel: 250-719-3480 *Fax:* 250-719-3781
www.northernhealth.ca

Delta: **Delta View Habilitation Centre**
Affiliated with: Fraser Health Authority
9341 Burns Dr., Delta, BC V4K 3N3
Tel: 604-501-6700
goodsaminfo@gss.org
gss.org/locations/good-samaritan-delta-view-care-centre
Number of Beds: 292 beds
Note: cares for peoples with Alzheimer's disease; specializing in caring for people with difficult behaviour

Delta: **KinVillage West Court**
Affiliated with: Fraser Health Authority
5410 - 10 Ave., Delta, BC V4M 3X8
Tel: 604-943-0155 *Fax:* 604-943-0947
kinsmen.vcn.bc.ca
Number of Beds: 100 beds
Donna Ellis, Chief Executive Officer
dellis@kinvillage.org

Delta: **Northcrest Care Centre**
Affiliated with: Fraser Health Authority
6771 - 120 St., Delta, BC V4E 2A7
Tel: 604-597-7878 *Fax:* 604-597-7805
general@northcrestcare.ca

Delta: **West Shore Laylum**
Affiliated with: Fraser Health Authority
4900 Central Ave., Delta, BC V4K 2G7
Tel: 604-946-2822 *Fax:* 604-946-2217
laylumrh@telus.net

Duncan: **Cairnsmore Place**
Affiliated with: Vancouver Island Health Authority
250 Cairnsmore St., Duncan, BC V9L 4H2
Tel: 250-709-3080 *Fax:* 250-746-0351
Number of Beds: 100 beds

Enderby: **Parkview Place**
Affiliated with: Interior Health Authority
707 - 3 Ave., Enderby, BC V0E 1V0
Tel: 250-838-2470
www.interiorhealth.ca
Number of Beds: 31 beds
Note: Complex care facility

Fort Langley: **Fort Langley Seniors Community**
Affiliated with: Fraser Health Authority
Former Name: Simpson Manor
8838 Glover Rd., Fort Langley, BC V1M 2R4
Tel: 604-888-0711 *Fax:* 604-888-1218
www.parkplaceseniorsliving.com
Note: Intermediate & extended care
Terri Ferguson, General Manager
tferguson@parkplaceseniorsliving.com

Fort St. John: **North Peace Care Centre**
9907 - 110 Ave., Fort St. John, BC V1J 2R3
Tel: 250-785-8941 *Fax:* 250-785-2296
Number of Beds: 47 beds
Note: Complex care special care unit

Grand Forks: **Hardy View Lodge**
Affiliated with: Interior Health Authority
7649 - 22 St., RR#2, Grand Forks, BC V0H 1H0
Tel: 250-443-2100
www.interiorhealth.ca
Number of Beds: 80 beds

Invermere: **Columbia House**
Affiliated with: Interior Health Authority
1030 - 10th St., Invermere, BC V0A 1K0
Tel: 250-342-2329
www.interiorhealth.ca
Number of Beds: 20 beds

Kamloops: **The Hamlets at Westsyde**
H&H Total Care Services Inc.
Affiliated with: Interior Health Authority
3255 Overlander Dr., Kamloops, BC V2B 0A5
Tel: 250-579-9061 *Fax:* 250-579-9069
info@thehamletsatwestsyde.com
www.thehamletsatwestsyde.com
Note: Residential care & assisted living

Kamloops: **Hilltop House**
Affiliated with: Interior Health Authority
470 Hilltop Ave., Kamloops, BC V2B 2S3
Tel: 250-376-3788 *Fax:* 250-376-9141
www.interiorhealth.ca
Number of Beds: 6 adult tertiary specialized residential beds

Kamloops: **Ridgeview Lodge**
Baltic Properties Group
Affiliated with: Interior Health Authority
920 Desmond St., Kamloops, BC V2B 5K6
Tel: 250-376-3131 *Fax:* 250-376-3151
www.balticproperties.ca
Number of Beds: 129 units
Note: Complex & respite care
Dana Levere, General Manager
dana.levere@balticproperties.ca

Kaslo: **Victorian Community Residential Care**
Affiliated with: Interior Health Authority
673 A Ave., Kaslo, BC V0G 1M0
Tel: 250-353-2211
www.interiorhealth.ca

Kelowna: **Avonlea House**
1658 Blondeaux Cres., Kelowna, BC V1Y 4J7
Tel: 250-762-4378 *Fax:* 250-762-0167
avonleahouse@avonleacare.com
www.avonleacare.com
Number of Beds: 14 beds
Note: specialized care home for severely brain-injured
Lynda Asselstine, Senior Manager & Director of Care
lyndacaringforpeople@shaw.ca

Kelowna: **Brandt's Creek Mews**
Vantage Living Inc.
Affiliated with: Interior Health Authority
2081 Cross Rd., Kelowna, BC V1V 2G2
Tel: 778-478-8800 *Fax:* 778-478-8801
vantageliving.ca/community/brandts-creek-mews
Number of Beds: 102 complex care beds
Scott Shearer, Regional Director, Long-Term Care & Assisted Living
sshearer@vantageliving.ca

Kelowna: **Cottonwoods Care Centre**
Affiliated with: Interior Health Authority
2255 Ethel St., Kelowna, BC V1Y 2Z9
Tel: 250-862-4100
www.interiorhealth.ca
Number of Beds: 153 residential beds; 60 short-stay beds; 2 respite beds

Kelowna: **David Lloyd Jones Home**
Affiliated with: Interior Health Authority
934 Bernard Ave., Kelowna, BC V1Y 6P8
Tel: 250-762-2706 *Fax:* 250-762-5961
www.interiorhealth.ca
Number of Beds: 64 permanent beds; 3 respite residential beds

Kelowna: **Mountainview Village**
Good Samaritan Society
Affiliated with: Interior Health Authority
1540 KLO Rd., Kelowna, BC V1W 3P6
Tel: 250-717-3918
goodsaminfo@gss.org
www.gss.org
Number of Beds: 89 assisted living suites; 90 complex care suites; 83 life lease apartments
Shawn Terlson, President & CEO, Good Samaritan Society
sterlson@gss.org

Kelowna: **Spring Valley Care Centre**
Park Place Seniors Living
Affiliated with: Interior Health Authority
Former Name: Windsor Manor
355 Terai Ct., Kelowna, BC V1X 5X6
Tel: 250-979-6000 *Fax:* 250-979-6002
springvalley@parkplaceseniorsliving.com
www.parkplaceseniorsliving.com
Number of Beds: 150 beds
Specialties: Residential care
Jody Edwards, Administrator
jedwards@parkplaceseniorsliving.com

Kelowna: **Sun Pointe Village**
Baptist Housing
Affiliated with: Interior Health Authority
700 Rutland Rd. North, Kelowna, BC V1X 7W8
Tel: 250-491-1400
sunpointe@baptisthousing.org
www.baptisthousing.org
www.facebook.com/130827606961613;
twitter.com/BaptistHousing;
www.youtube.com/user/BaptistHousing
Number of Beds: 100 residential care suites; 20 assisted living suites

Kelowna: **Sutherland Hills**
Affiliated with: Interior Health Authority
3081 Hall Rd., Kelowna, BC V1W 2R5
Tel: 250-860-2330 *Fax:* 250-860-2399
www.interiorhealth.ca
Year Founded: 1972
Number of Beds: 99 rooms

Kelowna: **Three Links Manor**
Affiliated with: Interior Health Authority
1449 Kelglen Cres., Kelowna, BC V1Y 8P4
Tel: 250-763-2585 *Fax:* 250-763-6773
www.interiorhealth.ca
Number of Beds: 80 beds

Kelowna: **Village at Mill Creek**
Baptist Housing
Affiliated with: Interior Health Authority
Former Name: Still Waters Private Hospital
1450 Sutherland Ave., Kelowna, BC V1Y 5Y5
Tel: 250-860-2216
millcreek@baptisthousing.org
www.baptisthousing.org
www.facebook.com/130827606961613;
twitter.com/BaptistHousing;
www.youtube.com/user/BaptistHousing
Number of Beds: 96 residential care suites; 38 assisted living suites
Howard Johnson, President & CEO, Baptist Housing

Keremeos: **Orchard Heaven**
Affiliated with: Interior Health Authority
700 - 3rd St., Keremeos, BC V0X 1N0
Tel: 250-499-3030
www.interiorhealth.ca
Number of Beds: 35 rooms; 10-bed dementia care unit

Ladysmith: **Oyster Harbour Seniors Community**
Affiliated with: Vancouver Island Health Authority
Former Name: Lodge on 4th
PO Box 820, 1127 - 4 Ave., Ladysmith, BC V9G 1A6
Tel: 250-245-3318
www.viha.ca
Number of Beds: 22 beds

Lake Country: **Lake Country Lodge Retirement & Care Community**
Sienna Senior Living
Affiliated with: Interior Health Authority
10163 Konschuh Rd., Lake Country, BC V4V 2M2
Tel: 250-766-3007 *Fax:* 250-766-3316
www.siennaliving.ca/retirement/british-columbia/lake-country-lodge-retirement-and-care-community
Number of Beds: 45 residential beds
Note: Supportive housing, complex care, & respite care.
Lois Cormack, President & CEO, Sienna Senior Living

Langley: **Jackman Manor**
Affiliated with: Fraser Health Authority
27447 - 28 Ave., Langley, BC V4W 3L9
Tel: 604-856-4161 *Fax:* 604-856-2562

Langley: **Langley Lodge**
Affiliated with: Fraser Health Authority
5451 - 204 St., Langley, BC V3A 5M9
Tel: 604-530-2305
www.langleylodge.org
www.facebook.com/LangleyLodge; twitter.com/langleylodge
Number of Beds: 139 beds
Note: seniors
Debra Haupman, Chief Executive Officer

Lillooet: **Mountain View Lodge**
Affiliated with: Interior Health Authority
951 Murray St., Lillooet, BC V0K 1V0
Tel: 250-256-1312
www.interiorhealth.ca
Number of Beds: 22 beds

Lytton: **Spintlum Lodge**
Affiliated with: Interior Health Authority
533 Main St., Lytton, BC V0K 1Z0
Tel: 250-455-2221
www.interiorhealth.ca
Number of Beds: 6 suites

Merritt: **Gillis House**
Affiliated with: Interior Health Authority
Former Name: Coquihalla Gillis House
1699 Tutill Crt., Merritt, BC V1K 1B8
Tel: 250-378-3271
www.interiorhealth.ca
Number of Beds: 74 residential care beds
Note: Complex care facility

Midway: **Parkview Manor**
Affiliated with: Interior Health Authority
PO Box 427, 670 - 9th Ave., Midway, BC V0H 1M0
Tel: 250-449-2842
www.interiorhealth.ca
Number of Beds: 15 supportive/independent units; 5 assisted
living units

Mission: **Pleasant View Care Home**
Affiliated with: Fraser Health Authority
7530 Hurd St., Mission, BC V2V 3H9
Tel: 604-826-2154 Fax: 604-826-8672
Number of Beds: 76 beds

Nakusp: **Halcyon House**
Affiliated with: Interior Health Authority
PO Box 910, 83 - 8th Ave. NW, Nakusp, BC V0G 1R0
Tel: 250-265-3692 Fax: 250-265-4141
halcyonhouse@telus.net
www.interiorhealth.ca
Number of Beds: 10 suites
Karolina Moskal, Site Manager

Nakusp: **Minto House**
Affiliated with: Interior Health Authority
**Arrow Lakes Hospital, 97 - 1st Ave. NE, Nakusp, BC V0G
1R0**
Tel: 250-265-3622
www.interiorhealth.ca
Number of Beds: 14 residential beds

Nanaimo: **Chartwell Malaspina Care Residence**
Affiliated with: Chartwell Retirement Residences
Former Name: Malaspina Gardens Inc.
100 - 11th St., Nanaimo, BC V9R 6R6
Tel: 250-754-7711 Fax: 250-754-2175
www.chartwell.com
Number of Beds: 136 beds
Brent Binions, President & CEO, Chartwell Retirement
Residences

Nanaimo: **Eden Gardens Compassionate Dementia
Care**
Affiliated with: Vancouver Island Health Authority
Former Name: Nanaimo Travellers Lodge
1917 Northfield Rd., Nanaimo, BC V9S 3B6
Tel: 250-758-4676 Fax: 250-758-4698
linda.reetham-clayton@edengardens.ca
www.edengardens.ca
Year Founded: 2004
Number of Beds: 90 beds

Nanaimo: **Kiwanis Village Lodge**
Affiliated with: Vancouver Island Health Authority
1233 Kiwanis Cres., Nanaimo, BC V9S 5Y1
Tel: 250-753-6471 Fax: 250-740-2816
info@kiwanisvillage.ca
www.kiwanisvillage.ca
Number of Beds: 102 beds

Melanie Young, Executive Director
melanieyoung@kiwanisvillage.ca

Nelson: **Mountain Lake Seniors Community**
Park Place Seniors Living
Affiliated with: Interior Health Authority
908 - 11th St., Nelson, BC V1L 7A6
Tel: 250-352-2600 Fax: 250-352-2665
mountainlake@parkplaceseniorsliving.com
www.parkplaceseniorsliving.com
Year Founded: 2005
Number of Beds: 135 beds
Note: Complex care & assisted living

Nelson: **Nelson Jubilee Manor**
Affiliated with: Interior Health Authority
500 West Beasley St. West, Nelson, BC V1L 6G9
Tel: 250-352-7011 Fax: 250-352-7044
www.interiorhealth.ca
Number of Beds: 39 beds

New Denver: **Slocan Community Health Centre**
Affiliated with: Interior Health Authority
401 Galena Ave., New Denver, BC V0G 1S0
Tel: 250-358-7911 Fax: 250-358-7117
www.interiorhealth.ca
Number of Beds: 10 rooms

New Westminster: **Buchanan Lodge**
Affiliated with: Fraser Health Authority
409 Blair Ave., New Westminster, BC V3L 4A4
Tel: 604-522-7033 Fax: 604-522-3689
admin@buchanan-lodge.com

New Westminster: **Honour House**
Honour House Society
Former Name: Blue Spruce Cottage
509 St. George St., New Westminster, BC V3L 1L1
Tel: 778-397-4399 Fax: 778-397-4396
admin@honourhouse.ca
www.honourhouse.ca
Year Founded: 2010
Number of Beds: 11 beds
Number of Employees: 2
Note: Honour House provides a free of charge, temporary home
for Canadian Armed Forces, Veterans, Emergency Services
Personnel & their families while they travel to receive medical
care & treatment in the Metro Vancouver Area.
Craig Longstaff, General Manager
craig@honourhouse.ca

New Westminster: **Kiwanis Intermediate Care Centre**
Affiliated with: Fraser Health Authority
35 Clute St., New Westminster, BC V3L 1Z5
Tel: 604-525-6471 Fax: 604-525-8522
reception@kiwaniscarecentre.com
kiwaniscarecentre.com
Year Founded: 1982
Number of Beds: 75 beds
Note: intermediate care
Lorrie Gerrard, Executive Director
lgerrard@kiwaniscarecentre.com

New Westminster: **Queen's Park Care Centre**
Affiliated with: Fraser Health Authority
315 McBride Blvd., New Westminster, BC V3L 5E8
Tel: 604-520-0911 Fax: 604-517-8651
Note: Extended care facility

New Westminster: **Royal City Manor Long Term
Care**
Revera Inc.
77 Jamieson Ct., New Westminster, BC V3L 5P8
Tel: 604-522-6699 Fax: 604-522-1022
www.reveraliving.com
www.facebook.com/Reveralnc; twitter.com/Revera_Inc;
www.youtube.com/user/Reveralnc;
www.linkedin.com/company/revera-inc
Note: Programs & services include 24 hour nurse on staff;
Revera / 3M skin and wound care program; physical activities;
music therapy; pet therapy.
Thomas G. Wellner, President & CEO, Revera Living

New Westminster: **Salvation Army Buchanan Lodge**
Affiliated with: Fraser Health Authority
409 Blair Ave., New Westminster, BC V3L 4A4
Tel: 604-522-7033 Fax: 604-522-3689
admin@buchanan-lodge.com
www.buchanan-lodge.com
Number of Beds: 112 beds
Famella Altejos, Executive Director

Oliver: **McKinney Place Extended Care**
Affiliated with: Interior Health Authority
911 McKinney Rd., Oliver, BC V0H 1T0
Tel: 250-498-5040
www.interiorhealth.ca
Number of Beds: 75 rooms

Oliver: **Sunnybank Retirement Centre**
Affiliated with: Interior Health Authority
6553 Park Dr., Oliver, BC V0H 1T0
Tel: 250-498-4951 Fax: 250-498-2287
www.interiorhealth.ca
Number of Beds: 51 beds; 13-bed dementia unit

Osoyoos: **Country Squire Retirement Villa**
Affiliated with: Interior Health Authority
9707 North 87 St., Osoyoos, BC V0H 1V0
Tel: 250-495-6568 Fax: 250-495-7466
www.interiorhealth.ca
Note: Provides tertiary psychiatric services.

Osoyoos: **Mariposa Gardens**
Baltic Properties Group
Affiliated with: Interior Health Authority
8816 - 97th St., Osoyoos, BC V0H 1V5
Tel: 250-495-8124 Fax: 250-495-8134
www.balticproperties.ca
Number of Beds: 10 units
Note: Assisted living & residential care
Marlese Hutter, General Manager
marlese.hutter@balticproperties.ca

Parksville: **Arrowsmith Lodge & Cokely Manor**
Arrowsmith Rest Home Society
Former Name: Arrowsmith Lodge
266A/B Moilliet St., Parksville, BC V9P 1M9
Tel: 250-248-4331 Fax: 250-248-4813
arrowsmithlodge.ca
Year Founded: 1971
Number of Beds: 75 long term care beds; 30 assisted living
suites
Note: These two facilities are located on the same property
within strolling distance.
Deanna Smith, Secretary/Treasurer

Parksville: **Halliday House**
PO Box 518, 188 McCarter St., Parksville, BC V9P 1A1
Tel: 250-248-2835 Fax: 250-248-2403
Number of Beds: 20 beds

Penticton: **The Hamlets at Penticton**
H&H Total Care Services Inc.
Affiliated with: Interior Health Authority
103 Duncan Ave., Penticton, BC V2A 2Y3
Tel: 250-490-8503 Fax: 250-490-8523
info@thehamletsatpenticton.com
www.thehamletsatpenticton.com
Year Founded: 2008
Number of Beds: 98 beds
Note: Services include: complex care; dementia care; brain
injured/young adult care; & respite care.

Penticton: **Haven Hill Retirement Centre**
Affiliated with: Interior Health Authority
415 Haven Hill Rd., Penticton, BC V2A 4E9
Tel: 250-492-2600
www.havenhill.ca
Number of Beds: 152 beds

Penticton: **Penticton & District Society for
Community Living (PSDCL)**
180 Industrial Ave. West, Penticton, BC V2A 6X9
Tel: 250-493-0312 Fax: 250-493-9113
admin@pdscl.org
www.pdscl.org
Year Founded: 1958
Note: Offers a number of community services including assisted
living and activities for seniors

Penticton: **Trinity Care Centre**
Affiliated with: Interior Health Authority
75 West Green Ave., Penticton, BC V2A 7N6
Tel: 250-493-6601
www.interiorhealth.ca
Number of Beds: 75 rooms

Penticton: **Village by the Station**
Good Samaritan Society
Affiliated with: Interior Health Authority
270 Hastings Ave., Penticton, BC V2A 2V6
Tel: 250-490-4949 Fax: 250-490-9733
goodsaminfo@gss.org
www.gss.org

Number of Beds: 35 assisted living suites; four 10-bed dementia care cottages; 60 residential care suites
Shawn Terlson, President & CEO, Good Samaritan Society
sterlson@gss.org

Penticton: **Westview Place**
Affiliated with: Interior Health Authority
550 Carmi Ave., Penticton, BC V2A 3G6
Tel: 250-492-7174
www.interiorhealth.ca
Number of Beds: 102 rooms

Port Alberni: **Echo Village**
Affiliated with: Vancouver Island Health Authority
4200 - 10 Ave., Port Alberni, BC V9Y 4X3
Tel: 250-724-1090 *Fax:* 250-724-2115
info@acccs.ca
www.albernicontinuingcare.ca/echo-village
Number of Beds: 68 beds
Note: 24-hour nursing care; activities include music therapy; pet therapy; swimming; games such as bingo, bowling, board games; trivia; walking program.

Port Alberni: **Fir Park Village**
Affiliated with: Vancouver Island Health Authority
4411 Wallace St., Port Alberni, BC V9Y 7Y5
Tel: 250-724-6541 *Fax:* 250-724-6543
info@acccs.ca
www.albernicontinuingcare.ca
Year Founded: 1981
Number of Beds: 65 beds
Area Served: Alberni Valley, Central Vancouver Island
Note: 24-hour nursing care; dietitian; music therapy; pet therapy; games; swimming program; crafts & baking programs; outings.

Port Alberni: **Tsawaayuus-Rainbow Gardens**
Affiliated with: Vancouver Island Health Authority
6151 Russell Pl., Port Alberni, BC V9Y 7W3
Tel: 250-724-5655 *Fax:* 250-724-5666
info@rainbowgardens.bc.ca
rainbowgardens.bc.ca
Year Founded: 1992
Shaunee Casavant, Manager

Port Coquitlam: **Hawthorne Seniors Care Community**
Affiliated with: Fraser Health Authority
2111 Hawthorne Ave., Port Coquitlam, BC V3C 1W3
Tel: 604-941-4051 *Fax:* 604-941-5829
hawthornecare.com
Year Founded: 1970
Number of Beds: 271 beds
Lenore Pickering, Executive Director
607-468-5003, lpickering@hawthornecare.com

Port Moody: **Eagle Ridge Manor**
Affiliated with: Fraser Health Authority
475 Guildford Way, Port Moody, BC V3H 3W9
Tel: 604-469-3211 *Fax:* 604-949-8212

Prince George: **AiMHi - Prince George Association for Community Living**
950 Kerry St., Prince George, BC V2M 5A3
Tel: 250-564-6408 *Fax:* 250-564-6801
aimhi@aimhi.ca
www.aimhi.ca
www.facebook.com/AiMHibc; twitter.com/AiMHiBC
Note: Non-profit, supports individuals with developmental disabilities & children with special needs
Melinda Heidsma, Executive Director

Prince George: **Hazelton Street Residence**
Affiliated with: Northern Health Authority
2554 Hazelton St., Prince George, BC V2L 1H1
Tel: 250-960-1499
www.northernhealth.ca
Number of Beds: 6 long-term beds
Note: Programs & services include: assistance with daily activities; medication management; & support & education for clients, families & caregivers. Managed by Western Human Resource Corporation.

Prince George: **Jubilee Lodge**
Affiliated with: Northern Health Authority
1475 Edmonton St., Prince George, BC V2M 1S2
Tel: 250-565-2286 *Fax:* 250-565-2778
www.northernhealth.ca
Note: Local seniors' programs & care services: 250-565-7317 & 250-565-7325.

Prince George: **Parkside Care Facility**
Affiliated with: Northern Health Authority
788 Ospika Blvd., Prince George, BC V2M 6Y2
Tel: 250-563-1916 *Fax:* 250-563-9424
www.northernhealth.ca
Note: Local seniors' programs & care services: 250-565-7317 & 250-565-7325.

Prince George: **Simon Fraser Lodge**
2410 Laurier Cres., Prince George, BC V2M 2B3
Tel: 250-563-3413 *Fax:* 250-563-7209
www.simonfraserlodge.ca
Number of Beds: 130 beds
Note: 24-hour nursing & care; dietitian; occupational therapist & physiotherapist. Exercise program offered; games; socializing; outings.

Princeton: **Ridgewood Lodge**
Affiliated with: Interior Health Authority
95A Ridgewood Dr., Princeton, BC V0X 1W0
Tel: 250-295-3211
www.interiorhealth.ca
Number of Beds: 37 rooms

Qualicum Beach: **Arranglen Gardens**
2300 Fowler Rd., Qualicum Beach, BC V9K 2A5
Tel: 250-752-9277 *Fax:* 250-752-5525
Number of Beds: 85 beds

Qualicum Beach: **Eagle Park Health Care Facility**
Affiliated with: Vancouver Island Health Authority
777 Jones St., Qualicum Beach, BC V9K 2L1
Tel: 250-947-8220
www.viha.ca
Number of Beds: 75 beds
Note: Amenities include 24-hour nursing care; activities & outings.

Revelstoke: **Mt. Cartier Court**
Affiliated with: Interior Health Authority
1200 Newlands Rd., Revelstoke, BC V0E 2S1
Tel: 250-814-2232
www.interiorhealth.ca
Number of Beds: 44 rooms
Note: Residential living for individuals with complex health needs

Salmon Arm: **Hillside Village**
Good Samaritan Society
Affiliated with: Interior Health Authority
2891 - 15 Ave. NE, Salmon Arm, BC V1E 2B6
Tel: 250-833-5877 *Fax:* 250-833-5890
goodsaminfo@gss.org
www.gss.org
Number of Beds: 112 residential care suites (including six 12-bed dementia care cottages)
Shawn Terlson, President & CEO, Good Samaritan Society
sterlson@gss.org

Salmon Arm: **Piccadilly Care Home**
Park Place Seniors Living
Affiliated with: Interior Health Authority
821 - 10th Ave. SW, Salmon Arm, BC V1E 1T2
Tel: 250-804-1676 *Fax:* 250-804-0672
piccadilly@parkplaceseniorsliving.com
www.parkplaceseniorsliving.com
Number of Beds: 56 rooms
Note: Complex care

Salt Spring Island: **Greenwoods Care Facility**
Affiliated with: Greenwoods Elder Care Society
133 Blain Rd., Salt Spring Island, BC V8K 1Z9
Tel: 250-537-5561 *Fax:* 250-537-1124
Toll-Free: 888-533-2273
reception@greenwoodseldercare.org
www.greenwoodseldercare.org
Year Founded: 1979
Number of Beds: 50 beds
Althea Humphreys, Executive Director
250-537-5561, althea.humphreys@greenwoodseldercare.org

Shawnigan Lake: **Acacia Ty Mawr Lodge**
PO Box 100, 2655 Shawnigan Lake Rd., Shawnigan Lake, BC V0R 2W0
Tel: 250-743-2124 *Fax:* 250-743-2130
www.acaciatymawr.ca
Number of Beds: 35 beds
Andrea Henwood, Director, Care

Sidney: **Sidney Intermediate Care Home Ltd.**
9888 - 5 St., Sidney, BC V8L 2X3
Tel: 250-656-0121 *Fax:* 250-656-0189
www.tcgcare.com
Number of Beds: 52 beds

Leah Bergen, Office Manager
sidneycare@tcgcare.com
Alison Marshall, Director of Care
sidneycaredoc@tcgcare.com

Smithers: **Bulkley Lodge**
Affiliated with: Northern Health Authority
PO Box 3640, 3668 - 11th Ave., Smithers, BC V0J 2N0
Tel: 250-847-4443 *Fax:* 250-847-3895
www.northernhealth.ca

Summerland: **Parkdale Place Senior Citizens**
Former Name: Kelly Care Centre
12801 Kelly Ave., Summerland, BC V0H 1Z0
Tel: 250-494-7911 *Fax:* 250-494-4027
Number of Beds: 79 beds

Summerland: **Summerland Extended Care**
Affiliated with: Interior Health Authority
Dr. Andrew Pavillion, 12815 Atkinson Rd., Summerland, BC V0H 1Z0
Tel: 250-404-8020
www.interiorhealth.ca
Number of Beds: 50 rooms

Surrey: **Amenida Seniors' Community**
Affiliated with: Fraser Health Authority
Former Name: Newton Regency Care Home
13855 - 68th Ave., Surrey, BC V3W 2G9
Tel: 604-235-1933 *Fax:* 604-597-8032
www.homecareliving.ca
www.facebook.com/150449131720398
Year Founded: 2010
Note: Independent, assisted living
Teena Love, General Manager
604-597-9333, teena.love@homecareliving.ca
Sandra Prance, Administrative Coordinator
604-597-9333, sandra.prance@homecareliving.ca

Surrey: **Carelife/Fleetwood**
Affiliated with: Fraser Health Authority
8265 - 159 St., Surrey, BC V4N 5T5
Tel: 604-598-7200 *Fax:* 604-598-7229

Surrey: **Chartwell Crescent Gardens**
Affiliated with: Chartwell Retirement Residences
Former Name: Crescent Gardens Retirement Community
1222 King George Blvd., Surrey, BC V4A 9W6
Tel: 778-736-0345
www.chartwell.com
Brent Binions, President & CEO, Chartwell Retirement Residences

Surrey: **Evergreen Hamlets**
Affiliated with: Fraser Health Authority
15660 - 84 Ave., Surrey, BC V4N 0W3
Tel: 604-597-7906 *Fax:* 604-597-9025
info@evergreenhamlets.com

Surrey: **Fleetwood Place**
Affiliated with: Fraser Health Authority
16011 - 83rd Ave., Surrey, BC V3S 8M2
Tel: 604-590-6860
info@fleetwoodplace.ca
www.fleetwoodplace.ca

Surrey: **Guildford Seniors Village**
Retirement Concepts
Affiliated with: Fraser Health Authority
14568 - 104A Ave., Surrey, BC V3R 1R3
Tel: 604-582-0808 *Fax:* 604-582-7011
www.retirementconcepts.com
Year Founded: 2001
Number of Beds: 69 beds
Bianca Goldberg, Contact
604-582-0808, bgoldberg@retirementconcepts.com

Surrey: **H & H Total Care Services**
8382 - 156 St., Surrey, BC V3S 3R7
Tel: 604-597-7931 *Fax:* 604-596-3641
info@hhtotalcare.com
www.hhtotalcare.com
Year Founded: 1989
Note: Parent company operating residential care facilities that focus on helping people with brain injuries and mental health issues.
Hank Van Ryk, CEO

Surrey: Hilton Villa Care Centre
Park Place Seniors Living
13525 Hilton Rd., Surrey, BC V3R 5J3
Tel: 604-588-3424 Fax: 604-588-3433
hiltonvilla@parkplaceseniorsliving.com
www.parkplaceseniorsliving.com
Number of Beds: 124 beds
Al Jina, President
604-266-1436, Fax: 604-266-8557,
ajina@parkplaceseniorsliving.com

Surrey: Kinsmen Lodge
Affiliated with: Fraser Health Authority
Former Name: Kinsmen Place Lodge
9650 - 137A St., Surrey, BC V3T 4H9
Tel: 604-588-0445 Fax: 604-588-7211
info@kinsmenlodge.ca
kinsmenlodge.ca
www.facebook.com/127417500669218
Number of Beds: 157 beds
Note: Intermediate care
Kathleen Strath, Chief Executive Officer
kstrath@kinsmenlodge.ca

Surrey: Morgan Place
Affiliated with: Fraser Health Authority
3288 - 156A St., Surrey, BC V3S 9T1
Tel: 604-535-7328
admin@morganplace.ca
www.morganplace.ca

Surrey: Zion Park Manor
Affiliated with: Fraser Health Authority
5939 - 180th St., Surrey, BC V3S 4L2
Tel: 604-576-2891
www.zionparkmanor.com
www.facebook.com/zionparkmanor
Number of Beds: 99 beds
Erroll Hastings, Executive Director
ehastings@zionparkmanor.com

Terrace: Terraceview Lodge
Affiliated with: Northern Health Authority
4707 Kerby St., Terrace, BC V8G 2W2
Tel: 250-631-4209 Fax: 250-847-3895
www.northernhealth.ca
Number of Beds: 99 beds
Note: Services include: rehabilitation; recreational therapy; food & nutrition; housekeeping; hairdressing & barber.
Doris Mitchell, Administrator

Trail: Columbia View Lodge
Affiliated with: Interior Health Authority
2920 Laburnum Dr., Trail, BC V1R 4N2
Tel: 250-364-1271 Fax: 250-364-0911
www.interiorhealth.ca
Number of Beds: 76 beds
Note: Complex care facility

Trail: Kiro Manor
1500 Columbia Ave., Trail, BC V1R 1J9
Tel: 250-364-6219 Fax: 250-364-6218
Number of Beds: 9 beds

Trail: Poplar Ridge Pavillion
Affiliated with: Interior Health Authority
1200 Hospital Bench, Trail, BC V1R 4M1
Tel: 250-368-3311 Fax: 250-364-3422
www.interiorhealth.ca
Number of Beds: 15 double rooms; 4 single rooms; four 4-bed rooms

Vancouver: Amica at Arbutus Manor
2125 Eddington Dr., Vancouver, BC V6L 3A9
Tel: 604-736-8936 Fax: 604-731-8933
arbutus@amica.ca
www.amica.ca/arbutus
Number of Beds: 125 beds

Vancouver: Crofton Manor
Revera Inc.
2803 West 41 Ave., Vancouver, BC V6N 4B4
Tel: 604-263-0921 Fax: 604-263-7719
www.facebook.com/ReveraInc; twitter.com/Revera_Inc;
www.youtube.com/user/ReveraInc;
www.linkedin.com/company/revera-inc
Year Founded: 1961
Number of Beds: 194 suites
Thomas G. Wellner, President & CEO, Revera Living

Vancouver: Renfrew Care Centre
Retirement Concepts
1880 Renfrew St., Vancouver, BC V5M 3H9
Tel: 604-255-7723 Fax: 604-255-2045
info@retirementconcepts.com
www.retirementconcepts.com
Number of Beds: 88 beds
Loraine Coffin, General Manager
lcoffin@retirementconcepts.com

Vanderhoof: Stuart Nechako Manor
Affiliated with: Northern Health Authority
3277 Hospital Rd., Vanderhoof, BC V0J 3A2
Tel: 250-567-2013 Fax: 250-567-2018
www.northernhealth.ca

Vernon: Creekside Landing Assisted Living
Kaigo Retirement Communities Ltd.
Affiliated with: Interior Health Authority
6190 Okanagan Landing Rd., Vernon, BC V1H 1M3
Tel: 250-549-9550
www.kaigo.ca
Number of Beds: 24 suites
Note: Complex care facility

Vernon: Heritage Square
Kaigo Retirement Communities Ltd.
Affiliated with: Interior Health Authority
3904 - 27 St., Vernon, BC V1T 4X7
Tel: 250-545-2060 Fax: 250-545-4060
www.kaigo.ca
Number of Beds: 50 private care suites; 26 assisted living suites
Note: Combined health care services & assisted living for adults who are not able to live alone.

Vernon: Heron Grove
Good Samaritan Society
Affiliated with: Interior Health Authority
4900 - 20th St., Vernon, BC V1T 9W3
Tel: 250-542-6101 Fax: 250-542-6227
goodsaminfo@gss.org
www.gss.org
Number of Beds: 40 assisted living suites; four 12-bed complex care cottages for dementia; two 14-bed complex care cottages; 15 life lease apartments
Lisa Kelly, Site Manager
250-542-6101, lkelly@gss.org
Aimee Droder, Facility Administration Assistant
250-542-6101, adroder@gss.org

Vernon: Noric House
Affiliated with: Interior Health Authority
1400 Mission Rd., Vernon, BC V1T 9C3
Tel: 250-545-9167 Fax: 250-545-4980
www.interiorhealth.ca
Number of Beds: 85 beds

Victoria: Beacon Hill Villa
Retirement Concepts
635 Superior St., Victoria, BC V8V 1V1
Tel: 250-383-5447 Fax: 753-546-2231
info@retirementconcepts.com
www.retirementconcepts.com
Number of Beds: 80 beds
Note: 24-hour nursing care; activities include exercise & walking groups; knitting, book & gardening groups; music therapy; bowling; bingo; brain fitness.
Dr. Azim Jamal, President & CEO

Victoria: Beckley Farm Lodge
Affiliated with: Vancouver Island Health Authority
530 Simcoe St., Victoria, BC V8V 1V1
Tel: 250-381-4421 Fax: 250-381-0112
www.broadmeadcare.com
Year Founded: 1981
Number of Beds: 65 beds
Note: In addition to being a residential care facility, Beckley Farm Lodge provides an outreach service that offers recreational and meal programs at two off-site locations in the James Bay community.

Victoria: Chinatown Care Centre
555 Herald St., Victoria, BC V8W 1S5
Tel: 250-381-4322 Fax: 250-920-0318
Year Founded: 1982
Number of Beds: 31 beds
Note: Provides services in Chinese and English; Chinese foods, activities, and care are provided in a culturally sensitive way.

Victoria: Craigdarroch Care Home
Affiliated with: Vancouver Island Health Authority
1048 Craigdarroch Rd., Victoria, BC V8S 2A4
Tel: 250-595-3813 Fax: 250-595-3836
info@craigdarrochcarehome.ca
www.craigdarrochcarehome.ca
Number of Beds: 18 beds
Note: Long-term care home neighbouring Victoria's historic landmark Craigdarroch Castle.
Shawn Matyczuk, Resident Care Manager

Victoria: Hart Home Seniors Residence
1961 Fairfield Rd., Victoria, BC V8S 1H5
Tel: 250-598-3542 Fax: 250-598-2594
info@harthousevictoria.ca
www.trilliumcommunities.com
Number of Beds: 20 beds
Note: Originally a heritage home and the private residence of former B.C. Premier, John Hart.
Kimberley Chretien, Director of Care

Victoria: James Bay Long Term Care
Revera Inc.
336 Simcoe St., Victoria, BC V8V 1L2
Tel: 250-388-6457 Fax: 250-381-2969
www.reveraliving.com
www.facebook.com/ReveraInc; twitter.com/Revera_Inc;
www.youtube.com/user/ReveraInc;
www.linkedin.com/company/revera-inc
Number of Beds: 208 beds
Note: Programs & services include 24 hour nurse on site; Revera/3M skin and wound care program; pain and symptom management; friendly pet visitations.
Thomas G. Wellner, President & CEO, Revera Living
Stan Dubas, Administrator

Victoria: The Kensington Retirement Living
3965 Shelbourne St., Victoria, BC V8N 6J4
Tel: 250-477-1232 Fax: 250-472-1271
www.reveraliving.com/kensington-victoria
Number of Beds: 116 suites
Amber Reis, Executive Director

Victoria: Kiwanis Pavilion
Affiliated with: Vancouver Island Health Authority
Former Name: Oak Bay Kiwanis Pavilion
3034 Cedar Hill Rd., Victoria, BC V8T 3J3
Tel: 250-598-2022 Fax: 250-598-0023
admin@obkp.org
www.kiwanispavilion.ca
Year Founded: 1982
Number of Beds: 117 beds
Note: Residential care facility with a focus on caring for people living with dementia.
Barb Ruegg, Director, Administration and Hospitality Services
250-598-2022

Victoria: Lodge at Broadmead
Affiliated with: Broadmead Care
4579 Chatterton Way, Victoria, BC V8X 4Y7
Tel: 250-658-0311 Fax: 250-658-0948
info@broadmeadcare.com
www.broadmeadcare.com
Number of Beds: 229 beds
David Cheperdak, CEO

Victoria: Luther Court
Affiliated with: Luther Court Society
1525 Cedar Hill Cross Rd., Victoria, BC V8P 5M1
Tel: 250-477-7241 Fax: 250-477-5740
www.luthercourt.org
Year Founded: 1979
Number of Beds: 60 beds
Note: Assisted living community offering 60 complex care units & 21 independent apartments.
Karen Johnson-Lefsrud, Executive Director

Victoria: Mount St. Mary Hospital
Affiliated with: Vancouver Island Health Authority
861 Fairfield Rd., Victoria, BC V8V 5A9
Tel: 250-480-3100 Fax: 250-480-3110
vo-clerk@mtstmary.victoria.bc.ca
mountstmary.ca
www.facebook.com/mtstmary;
www.youtube.com/channel/UCcdAxP3qbaZOCkCqyeDEKrw;
www.linkedin.com/company/mount-st.-mary-hospital
Number of Beds: 200 beds
Sara John Fowler, Chief Executive Officer
250-480-3101, sfowler@mountstmary.ca
Sandra Noel, Director, Human Resources
snoel@mountstmary.ca
Neil Johnson, Director, Finance
njohnson@mountstmary.ca

Alastair Myles, Director, Support Services
amyles@mountstmary.ca

Victoria: **Rose Manor**
857 Rupert Terrace, Victoria, BC V8V 3E5
Tel: 250-383-0414 Fax: 250-360-2039
www.rosemanor.ca

Year Founded: 1898
Number of Beds: 128 beds

Victoria: **Sandringham Long Term Care**
Revera Inc.
1650 Fort St., Victoria, BC V8R 1H9
Tel: 250-595-2313 Fax: 250-595-4137
www.reveraliving.com
www.facebook.com/ReveraInc; twitter.com/Revera_Inc;
www.youtube.com/user/ReveraInc;
www.linkedin.com/company/revera-inc
Number of Beds: 85 beds
Note: Programs & services include 24 hour nurse on site; pain and symptom management; multi-sensory therapy program; meditation program; music therapy; friendly pet visitation.
Thomas G. Wellner, President & CEO, Revera Living

Victoria: **Victoria Sunset Lodge**
Affiliated with: Salvation Army
952 Arm Street, Victoria, BC V9A 4G7
Tel: 250-385-3422 Fax: 250-995-3858
www.sunsetlodge.ca

Number of Beds: 41 beds
Note: provides care to residents within a Christian environment.
Randy Randall, Executive Director

West Kelowna: **Village at Smith Creek**
Baptist Housing
Affiliated with: Interior Health Authority
2425 Orlin Rd., West Kelowna, BC V4T 3C7
Tel: 250-768-0488
smithcreek@baptisthousing.org
www.baptisthousing.org
www.facebook.com/130827606961613;
twitter.com/BaptistHousing;
www.youtube.com/user/BaptistHousing
Year Founded: 1992
Number of Beds: 130 residential care rooms; 22 assisted living suites
Howard Johnson, President & CEO, Baptist Housing

West Vancouver: **Capilano Long Term Care**
Revera Inc.
525 Clyde Ave., West Vancouver, BC V7T 1C4
Tel: 604-926-6856 Fax: 604-926-0245
www.reveraliving.com
www.facebook.com/ReveraInc; twitter.com/Revera_Inc;
www.youtube.com/user/ReveraInc;
www.linkedin.com/company/revera-inc
Number of Beds: 217 beds
Note: Programs & services include Revera/3M skin and wound care; pain & symptom management; foot care; Tai chi classes; Aquatics; pet therapy; weekly musical entertainment.
Thomas G. Wellner, President & CEO, Revera Living

West Vancouver: **Hollyburn House**
Revera Inc.
2095 Marine Dr., West Vancouver, BC V7V 4V5
Tel: 604-922-7616 Fax: 604-922-9163
www.reveraliving.com
www.facebook.com/ReveraInc; twitter.com/Revera_Inc;
www.youtube.com/user/ReveraInc;
www.linkedin.com/company/revera-inc
Number of Beds: 102 suites
Thomas G. Wellner, President & CEO, Revera Living

Westbank: **Brookhaven Care Centre**
Affiliated with: Interior Health Authority
1775 Shannon Lake Rd., Westbank, BC V4T 2N7
Tel: 250-862-4040 Fax: 250-862-4048
www.interiorhealth.ca
Number of Beds: 83 residential beds; 20 specialized geriatric CBDU beds; 1 respite bed

Westbank: **Pine Acres Home**
Affiliated with: Interior Health Authority
1902 Pheasant Lane, Westbank, BC V4T 2H4
Tel: 250-768-7676 Fax: 250-768-3234
www.wfn.ca/salmon/pineacreshome.htm
Year Founded: 1983
Number of Beds: 63 complex care beds; 53 private rooms; 5 semi-private rooms; 40 Interior Health beds; 23 Indian Affairs beds; 1 respite room
Note: Intermediate care
Steve Gardner, Administrator
250-768-7676

White Rock: **Evergreen Baptist Home**
Affiliated with: Fraser Health Authority
1550 Oxford St., White Rock, BC V4B 3R5
Tel: 604-536-3344
info@evergreen-home.com
www.evergreen-home.com
www.facebook.com/158535384275255;
twitter.com/EvergreenCare1
Year Founded: 1959
Number of Beds: 249 beds
Stephen Bennett, Executive Director
s.bennett@evergreen-home.com

White Rock: **Ocean View Care Home**
Affiliated with: Fraser Health Authority
15628 Buena Vista Ave., White Rock, BC V4B 1Z4
Tel: 604-531-2273 Fax: 604-531-8782
Number of Beds: 71 beds
Note: Specialty: Residential care for seniors; Secure unit for persons with dementia

White Rock: **Peace Portal Lodge**
15441 - 16 Ave., White Rock, BC V4A 8T8
Tel: 604-535-2273 Fax: 604-535-3051
ppsv.info@retirementconcepts.com
www.retirementconcepts.com
Number of Beds: 27 beds
Note: 24-hour nursing care; features activities such as art therapy; baking; discussion groups; pet therapy; bingo; book club.
Diane Miller, General Manager
dmiller@retirementconcepts.com

Williams Lake: **Cariboo Place**
Vantage Living
Affiliated with: Canadian Mental Health Association
Former Name: Jubilee Care House
185 - 4th Ave. North, Williams Lake, BC V2G 2C8
Tel: 778-417-0275 Fax: 778-417-0276
vantageliving.ca/community/cariboo-place
www.facebook.com/vantageliving
Number of Beds: 72 beds
Note: Mental health group home.

Williams Lake: **Deni House**
Affiliated with: Interior Health Authority
517 North 6th Ave., Williams Lake, BC V2G 2G8
Tel: 250-392-4411
www.interiorhealth.ca
Note: Complex care facility

Williams Lake: **Williams Lake Seniors Village**
Retirement Concepts
Affiliated with: Interior Health Authority
1455 Western Ave., Williams Lake, BC V2G 5N1
Tel: 250-305-1131 Fax: 250-305-3333
www.williamslakeseniorsvillage.com
Number of Beds: 113 residential care rooms; 101 assisted living suites; 17 independent living suites
Nancy Fenner, General Manager
nfenner@retirementconcepts.com

Nursing Homes

Abbotsford: **Hallmark on the Park**
Affiliated with: Fraser Health Authority
3055 Princess St., Abbotsford, BC V2T 4A8
Tel: 604-859-0053 Toll-Free: 866-399-0053
info@hallmarkretirement.ca
hallmarkretirement.ca

Abbotsford: **Menno Home**
Affiliated with: Fraser Health Authority
32945 Marshall Rd., Abbotsford, BC V2S 1K1
Tel: 604-859-7631
info@mennoplace.ca
www.mennoplace.ca
www.facebook.com/mennoplacelife; twitter.com/MennoPlace;
www.youtube.com/mennoplace
Karen L. Baillie, Chief Executive Officer

Abbotsford: **Sunrise Special Care Facility**
2411 Railway St., Abbotsford, BC V2S 2E3
Tel: 604-853-3078

Agassiz: **Cheam Village**
Cheam Village Holdings Ltd.
Affiliated with: Fraser Health Authority
1525 MacKay Cres., Agassiz, BC V0M 1A2
Tel: 604-796-3886 Fax: 604-796-3844
inquiries@valleycare.info
www.valleycare.info/cheam.php

Year Founded: 2008
Number of Beds: 68 beds

Burnaby: **Carlton Gardens Care Centre**
Chartwell Retirement Residences
Affiliated with: Fraser Health Authority
4108 Norfolk St., Burnaby, BC V5G 0B4
Tel: 604-229-1385
chartwell.com

Burnaby: **Dania Manor**
Dania Home Society
Affiliated with: Fraser Health Authority
4155 Norland Ave., Burnaby, BC V5G 3S7
Tel: 604-299-1379 Fax: 604-299-7775
www.dania.bc.ca

Burnaby: **St. Michael's Centre**
Affiliated with: Fraser Health Authority
7451 Sussex Ave., Burnaby, BC V5J 5C2
Tel: 604-434-1323 Fax: 604-434-6469
info@stmichaels.bc.ca
www.stmichaels.bc.ca
Number of Beds: 128 extended care beds
Dianne Doyle, Executive Director
ddoyle@stmichaels.bc.ca
David Thompson, Executive Director
dthompson@stmichaels.bc.ca

Chilliwack: **Eden Care Centre**
Affiliated with: Fraser Health Authority
Former Name: Eden Rest Home
9100 Charles St., Chilliwack, BC V2P 5K6
Tel: 604-792-8166 Fax: 604-792-1111

Coquitlam: **Belvedere Care Centre**
Affiliated with: Fraser Health Authority
Also Known As: Belvedere Care Centre & Residences at Belvedere
739 Alderson Ave., Coquitlam, BC V3K 7B3
Tel: 604-939-5991 Fax: 604-939-5910
belvederecare@telus.net
www.belvederecare.com
Number of Beds: 148 complex care beds at care centre; 114 units for seniors at assisted living centre, including a secure unit for 11 residents
Note: Specialties: Complex care for seniors; Assisted living for residents with mild cognitive impairment; Wellness programs; Diabetes management; Therapy; Rehabilitation; Dementia care; Chronic care; Palliative care
Berton B. Evertt, Chair; Chief Executive Officer
Annamae Clarke, Vice-President

Coquitlam: **Dufferin Care Centre**
Retirement Concepts
1131 Dufferin St., Coquitlam, BC V3B 7X5
Tel: 604-552-1166 Fax: 604-552-3116
duff.info@retirementconcepts.com
www.retirementconcepts.com
Number of Beds: 153 beds
Note: Specialties: Continuing care; Nursing care; Physiotherapy; Recreation therapy; Music therapy
Joyce Halliday, General Manager
jhalliday@retirementconcepts.com
Melissa Palana, Director, Care
mpalana@retirementconcepts.com
Ken Thomson, Coordinator, Administration
kthomson@retirementconcepts.com

Coquitlam: **Dufferin Care Centre**
Retirement Concepts
Affiliated with: Fraser Health Authority
1131 Dufferin St., Coquitlam, BC V3B 7X5
Tel: 604-552-1166 Fax: 604-552-3116
www.retirementconcepts.com
Number of Beds: 153 beds
Melissa Palana, Contact
mpalana@retirementconcepts.com

Delta: **Delta View Life Enrichment Centre**
Affiliated with: Fraser Health Authority
9321 Burns Dr., Delta, BC V4K 3N3
Tel: 604-501-6700 Fax: 604-596-7613
info@deltaview.ca
deltaview.ca
Number of Beds: 212 beds

Duncan: **Cowichan Lodge**
Affiliated with: Vancouver Island Health Authority
2041 Tzouhalem Rd., Duncan, BC V9L 4H2
Tel: 250-709-3098 Fax: 250-709-3335
www.viha.ca
Number of Beds: 51 beds

Laurie Chisholm

Golden: **Henry Durand Manor**
Affiliated with: Interior Health Authority
803 - 9th Ave. South, Golden, BC V0A 1H0
Tel: 250-344-5271 *Fax:* 250-344-2511
www.interiorhealth.ca
Number of Beds: 26 beds
Note: Group home for the elderly mainly who are no longer able to live in the community

Kamloops: **Kamloops Personal Care Home Ltd. - Garden Manor**
63 Nicola St. West, Kamloops, BC V2C 1J5
Tel: 250-374-7612

Number of Beds: 24 beds
John H. Stewart, Administrator

Kamloops: **Overlander Residential Care**
Affiliated with: Interior Health Authority
Former Name: Overlander Extended Care Hospital
953 Southill St., Kamloops, BC V2B 7Z9
Tel: 250-554-2323
www.interiorhealth.ca
Number of Beds: 183 beds

Kamloops: **Pine Grove Care Centre**
Park Place Seniors Living
Affiliated with: Interior Health Authority
313 McGowan Ave., Kamloops, BC V2B 2N8
Tel: 250-376-5701 *Fax:* 250-376-2453
pinegrove@parkplaceseniorsliving.com
www.parkplaceseniorsliving.com
Number of Beds: 75 beds

Kitimat: **Mountainview Lodge Residential Care Kitimat**
Affiliated with: Northern Health Authority
920 Lahakas Blvd. South, Kitimat, BC V8C 2S3
Tel: 250-632-2121
www.northernhealth.ca
Number of Beds: 36 beds

Langley: **Cedar Hill**
Affiliated with: Fraser Health Authority
22051 Fraser Hwy., Langley, BC V3A 4H4
Tel: 604-533-6413 *Fax:* 604-533-6468

Langley: **Murrayville Manor Ltd.**
21616 - 46 Ave., Langley, BC V3A 8M9
Tel: 604-530-9033 *Fax:* 604-530-9023
Number of Beds: 41 beds
Lori Crowley, Manager

Maple Ridge: **Baillie House**
Affiliated with: Fraser Health Authority
11666 Laity St., Maple Ridge, BC V2X 7G5
Tel: 604-476-7888 *Fax:* 604-463-1894
Number of Beds: 148 beds

Nanaimo: **Kiwanis Village Care Home**
1233 Kiwanis Cres., Nanaimo, BC V9S 5Y1
Tel: 250-753-6471 *Fax:* 250-740-2816
info@kiwanisvillage.ca
www.kiwanisvillage.ca
Number of Beds: 75 rooms
Dennis Regnier, Site Manager

Parksville: **Trillium Lodge**
Affiliated with: Vancouver Island Health Authority
401 Moilliet St., Parksville, BC V9P 2G9
Tel: 250-947-8230

Number of Beds: 75 complex care beds
Jane Finerty, Manager, Volunteer Resources
jane.finerty@viha.ca

Port Coquitlam: **Hawthorne Care Centre**
Affiliated with: Fraser Health Authority
2111 Hawthorne Ave., Port Coquitlam, BC V3C 1W3
Tel: 604-941-4051 *Fax:* 604-941-5829

Prince George: **Gateway Residential Care Facility**
Affiliated with: Northern Health Authority
1462 - 20th Ave., Prince George, BC V2L 0B3
Tel: 250-645-6100
www.northernhealth.ca
Note: Local seniors' programs & care services: 250-565-7317 & 250-565-7325.

Prince George: **Legion Wing, Seniors Housing**
Affiliated with: Northern Health Authority
2175 - 9th Ave., Prince George, BC V2M 5E3
Tel: 250-561-1499
www.northernhealth.ca

Note: Semi-independent housing for seniors experiencing dementia, or mental health/substance issues.

Salmon Arm: **Bastion Place**
Affiliated with: Interior Health Authority
700 - 11 St. NE, Salmon Arm, BC V1E 4P9
Tel: 250-833-3616 *Fax:* 250-833-3605
www.interiorhealth.ca
Number of Beds: 101 beds

Sidney: **Rest Haven Lodge**
2281 Mills Rd., Sidney, BC V8L 2C3
Tel: 250-656-0717
Year Founded: 1982
Number of Beds: 73 beds

Surrey: **Argyll Lodge**
14590 - 106A Ave., Surrey, BC V3R 1T4
Tel: 604-581-4174
Number of Beds: 25 beds
Baljit Kandola, Manager

Surrey: **Cherington Place**
Belvedere Seniors Living
Affiliated with: Fraser Health Authority
13453 - 111A Ave., Surrey, BC V3R 2C5
Tel: 604-581-2885 *Fax:* 604-582-9028
belvederecare@telus.net
www.belvederebc.com
Number of Beds: 75 beds
Berton B. Evertt, Chairman & CEO

Surrey: **K & C Care Ltd.**
1504 - 160 St., Surrey, BC V4A 4W9
Tel: 604-531-7900
Number of Beds: 11 beds
Kwan-Ying Jen, Manager

Vancouver: **Ananda House**
1249 - 8 Ave. East, Vancouver, BC V5T 1V3
Tel: 604-872-7134 *Fax:* 604-872-8420
Number of Beds: 20 beds
Darrell Burnham, Executive Director

Vancouver: **Britannia Lodge**
1090 Victoria Dr., Vancouver, BC V5L 4G2
Tel: 604-255-3711

Vancouver: **Gordon Neighbourhood House**
1019 Broughton St., Vancouver, BC V6G 2A7
Tel: 604-683-2554 *Fax:* 604-683-4486
welcome@gordonhouse.org
gordonhouse.org
www.facebook.com/GordonNeighbourhoodHouse
Allen Smith, Executive Director

Vernon: **Polson Residential Care**
Affiliated with: Interior Health Authority
2101 - 32nd St., Vernon, BC V1T 5L2
Tel: 250-558-1200
www.interiorhealth.ca
Number of Beds: 97 beds

Victoria: **Glenwarren Lodge**
1230 Balmoral Rd., Victoria, BC V8T 1B3
Tel: 250-383-2323
www.reveraliving.com/glenwarren
Number of Beds: 131 beds
Note: Registered nurse 24 hours a day; pain & symptom management; occupational therapist; physiotherapist; dietitian; pastoral service; friendly pet visitation.
Norman Carelius, Administrator

White Rock: **Ocean View Care Home**
Former Name: Buena Vista Rest Home
15628 Buena Vista Ave., White Rock, BC V4B 1Z4
Tel: 604-531-2273
Number of Beds: 12 beds

Retirement Residences

Agassiz: **Glenwood Care Centre**
Affiliated with: Fraser Health Authority
1458 Glenwood Dr., Agassiz, BC V0M 1A2
Tel: 604-796-9202 *Fax:* 604-796-9186
Number of Beds: 37 beds

Burnaby: **Chartwell Carlton Care Residence**
Affiliated with: Chartwell Retirement Residences
Former Name: Carlton Gardens Long Term Care Residence
4108 Norfolk St., Burnaby, BC V5G 0B4
Tel: 604-419-3000
www.chartwell.com

Number of Beds: 128 beds

Coquitlam: **Parkwood Manor**
Revera Inc.
1142 Dufferin St., Coquitlam, BC V3B 6V4
Tel: 604-941-7651
www.reveraliving.com/parkwoodmanor
www.facebook.com/ReveraInc; twitter.com/Revera_Inc;
www.youtube.com/user/Reverainc;
www.linkedin.com/company/revera-inc
Number of Beds: 140 suites
Note: Services include: resident-centered care; restorative program; & recreation.
Thomas G. Wellner, President & CEO, Revera Living

Delta: **Augustine House**
Affiliated with: Fraser Health Authority
3820 Arthur Dr., Delta, BC V4K 5E6
Tel: 604-940-6005 *Fax:* 604-940-6015
Toll-Free: 866-940-6005
info@augustinehouse.ca
augustinehouse.ca
twitter.com/AugustineHouse
Year Founded: 2003
Tanya Snow, Executive Director
tsnow@augustinehouse.ca

Fruitvale: **Mountain Side Village**
Golden Life Management
Affiliated with: Interior Health Authority
135 Mountain Side Village, Fruitvale, BC V0G 1L0
Tel: 250-367-9870
mountainside@glm.ca
goldenlifemanagement.ca
Note: Independent living community
John Turco, Community Manager
Sue Turco, Community Manager

Grand Forks: **Silver Kettle Village**
Golden Life Management
Affiliated with: Interior Health Authority
2350 - 72nd Ave., Grand Forks, BC V0H 1H0
Tel: 250-442-0667
goldenlifemanagement.ca
Note: Independent living community

Surrey: **Brookside Lodge**
Affiliated with: Fraser Health Authority
19550 Fraser Hwy., Surrey, BC V3S 6K5
Tel: 604-530-6595 *Fax:* 604-530-6596
www.balticproperties.ca
Number of Beds: 89 beds
Dave Sedore, Proprietor

Surrey: **Fleetwood Villa**
Revera Inc.
Affiliated with: Fraser Health Authority
16028 - 83rd Ave., Surrey, BC V4N 0N2
Tel: 604-590-2889 *Fax:* 604-590-2887
www.reveraliving.com
www.facebook.com/ReveraInc; twitter.com/Revera_Inc;
www.youtube.com/user/Reverainc;
www.linkedin.com/company/revera-inc
Thomas G. Wellner, President & CEO, Revera Living

Surrey: **Freedom Place**
Affiliated with: Fraser Health Authority
10342 - 148 St., Surrey, BC V3R 3X3
Tel: 604-936-9944

Surrey: **Gateway Independent Living for Seniors**
Affiliated with: Fraser Health Authority
13787 - 100 Ave., Surrey, BC V3T 5X7
Tel: 604-585-2906 *Fax:* 604-495-4560
thegateway@shawlink.ca
gatewayassistedliving.ca
Number of Beds: 60 suites
Daljit Gill, Owner/Operator

Surrey: **Guru Nanak Niwas**
Affiliated with: Fraser Health Authority
12075 - 75A Ave., Surrey, BC V3W 1S8
Tel: 604-596-0052 *Fax:* 604-596-7721

Surrey: **Whitecliff**
Revera Inc.
15501 - 16th Ave., Surrey, BC V4A 9M5
Tel: 604-538-7227
www.reveraliving.com/whitecliff
www.facebook.com/Reverainc; twitter.com/Revera_Inc;
www.youtube.com/user/Reverainc;
www.linkedin.com/company/revera-inc

Year Founded: 1961
Number of Beds: 126 suites
Note: Independent living & assisted living.
Thomas G. Wellner, President & CEO, Revera Living

Victoria: Parkwood Court
Revera Inc.
3000 Shelbourne St., Victoria, BC V8R 4M8
Tel: 250-598-1575
www.reveraliving.com/parkwoodcourt
www.facebook.com/ReveraInc; twitter.com/Revera_Inc;
www.youtube.com/user/ReveraInc;
www.linkedin.com/company/revera-inc
Number of Beds: 78 suites
Note: Services include: personalized health care program; recreation program; restorative program; dietitian; & memory care.
Thomas G. Wellner, President & CEO, Revera Living

Victoria: Parkwood Place
Rivera Inc.
3051 Shelbourne St., Victoria, BC V8R 6T2
Tel: 250-598-1565
www.reveraliving.com/parkwoodplace
Number of Beds: 100 suites
Note: Services include: fitness program; recreation; & restorative program.

White Rock: Evergreen Heights
Affiliated with: Fraser Health Authority
1501 Everall St., White Rock, BC V4B 3S8
Tel: 604-541-3832 Fax: 604-541-3803

Personal Care Homes

100 Mile House: Carefree Manor
Affiliated with: Interior Health Authority
812 Cariboo Trail, 100 Mile House, BC V0K 2E0
Tel: 250-395-4807 Fax: 250-395-4847
www.carefreemanor.ca
Number of Beds: 36 assisted & supportive living units
Mel Torgerson, General Manager
mel.carefree@shawcable.com

Ashcroft: Thompson View Lodge
Affiliated with: Interior Health Authority
710 Elm St., Ashcroft, BC V0K 1A0
Tel: 250-453-9223
tvms@telus.net
www.interiorhealth.ca
Number of Beds: 10 suites
Note: Assisted living for seniors & persons with disabilities

Barriere: Yellowhead Pioneer Residence
Affiliated with: Interior Health Authority
PO Box 212, 4557 Barriere Town Rd., Barriere, BC V0E 1E0
Tel: 250-672-0019
www.interiorhealth.ca
Number of Beds: 10 suites

Burnaby: Harmony Court Centre
AgeCare
Affiliated with: Fraser Health Authority
Former Name: Canada Way Care Centre & Lodge
7195 Canada Way, Burnaby, BC V5E 3R7
Tel: 604-527-3300
hcreception@agecare.ca
www.agecare.ca/harmony-court
Year Founded: 1976
Dr. Kabir Jivraj, Managing Director

Burns Lake: Tweedsmuir House
Affiliated with: Northern Health Authority
53 - 9th Ave., Burns Lake, BC V0J 1E0
Tel: 250-692-3781
www.northernhealth.ca
Note: Assisted living

Castlegar: Castle Wood Village
Golden Life Management
Affiliated with: Interior Health Authority
525 Columbia Ave., Castlegar, BC V1N 1G8
Tel: 250-365-6686
castlewood@glm.ca
goldenlifemanagement.ca
Number of Beds: 110 suites
Linda Frew, Community Manager
Jane Phillips, Community Manager

Chase: Parkside Community
Affiliated with: Interior Health Authority
743 Okanagan Ave., Chase, BC V0E 1M0
Fax: 250-679-4496
Toll-Free: 866-930-3572
parksidecommunity.ca
Number of Beds: 20 units
Note: Assisted & independent living
Juergen Mueller, General Manager

Cranbrook: Joseph Creek Village
Golden Life Management
Affiliated with: Interior Health Authority
1901 Willowbrook Dr., Cranbrook, BC V1C 6S4
Tel: 250-417-0666
goldenlifemanagement.ca
Number of Beds: 102 residential care suites; 28 assisted living suites
Allan Brander, Community Manager

Creston: Crest View Care Village
Golden Life Management
Affiliated with: Interior Health Authority
800 Cavell St., Creston, BC V0B 1G0
Tel: 250-428-9986
goldenlifemanagement.ca
Number of Beds: 31 residential care suites; 23 assisted living suites; 51 independent living suites
Kathy Castellarin, Community Manager
kcastellarin@glm.ca

Fernie: Rocky Mountain Village
Golden Life Management
Affiliated with: Interior Health Authority
55 Cokato Rd., Fernie, BC V0B 1M4
Tel: 250-423-4214
goldenlifemanagement.ca
Number of Beds: 12 assisted living suites; 12 independent living suites
Sandra Peterson, Community Manager
speterson@glm.ca

Fort St. James: Pioneer Lodge
Affiliated with: Northern Health Authority
200 School Rd., Fort St. James, BC V0J 1P0
Tel: 250-804-4814 Fax: 250-804-4815
www.northernhealth.ca
Number of Beds: 30 assisted living suites

Fort St. John: Heritage Manor II
Affiliated with: Northern Health Authority
9824 - 106 Ave., Fort St. John, BC V1J 2N9
Tel: 250-263-6000 Fax: 250-263-6086
www.northernhealth.ca
Number of Beds: 24 assisted living units

Golden: Mountain View
Affiliated with: Interior Health Authority
#120, 750 - 8th Ave. South, Golden, BC V0A 1H0
Tel: 250-344-7924
www.interiorhealth.ca
Note: Assisted living

Grand Forks: Boundary Lodge
Affiliated with: Interior Health Authority
7130 - 9 St., Grand Forks, BC V0H 1H4
Tel: 250-443-0006 Fax: 250-443-0015
www.interiorhealth.ca
Number of Beds: 10 living suites

Hazelton: Skeena Place
Affiliated with: Northern Health Authority
4780 Janze Way, Hazelton, BC V0J 1Y0
Tel: 250-842-5217
www.northernhealth.ca
Number of Beds: 6 assisted living units
Note: Independent & assisted living

Houston: Cottonwood Manor
Affiliated with: Northern Health Authority
3322 - 13th St., Houston, BC V0J 1Z0
Tel: 250-845-3770
www.northernhealth.ca
Note: Assisted living

Invermere: Columbia Garden Village
Golden Life Management
Affiliated with: Interior Health Authority
800 - 10th Ave., Invermere, BC V0A 1K0
Tel: 250-341-3350
columbiagarden@glm.ca
goldenlifemanagement.ca
Number of Beds: 63 independent & assisted living suites

Adrienne Turner, Community Manager

Kamloops: Bedford Manor
The John Howard Society of the Thompson Region
Affiliated with: Interior Health Authority
529 Seymour St., Kamloops, BC V2C 0A1
Tel: 250-434-1702 Fax: 250-434-1704
info@jhstr.ca
www.jhstr.ca/housing/bedford-manor
Number of Beds: 76 units

Kamloops: Kamloops Seniors Village
Retirement Concepts
Affiliated with: Interior Health Authority
1220 Hugh Allan Dr., Kamloops, BC V1S 2B3
Tel: 250-571-1800 Fax: 250-571-1799
www.kamloopsseniorsvillage.com
Number of Beds: 101 independent/assisted living suites; 100 funded rooms; 14 private pay residential care rooms
Sean Adams, General Manager
sadams@retirementconcepts.com

Keremeos: Kyalami Place
Lower Similkameen Community Services Society
Affiliated with: Interior Health Authority
720 - 3rd St., Keremeos, BC V0X 1N3
Tel: 250-499-2352
admin@lscss.org
ttpwebhost.com/lscss/kyalami-place
Number of Beds: 13 one-bedroom apartments; 1 two-bedroom apartment
Note: Assisted living
Sarah Martin, Executive Director, Lower Similkameen Community Services Society

Kimberley: Garden View Village
Golden Life Management
Affiliated with: Interior Health Authority
280 - 4th Ave., Kimberley, BC V1A 2R6
Tel: 250-427-4014
goldenlifemanagement.ca
Number of Beds: 74 independent apartments; 13 assisted living suites
LeeAnn McDonald, Community Manager
lmcdonald@glm.ca

Lake Country: Blue Heron Villa
Affiliated with: Interior Health Authority
#100, 9509 Main St., Lake Country, BC V4V 2N3
Tel: 250-766-1660
blueheronvilla.ca
Number of Beds: 25 suites

Langley: Evergreen Timbers
Affiliated with: Fraser Health Authority
5464 - 203 St., Langley, BC V3A 0A4
Tel: 604-530-7171 Fax: 604-530-7104
Note: Evergreen Timbers is an assisted living residence that is owned & operated by the Langley Lions Senior Citizens Housing Society.

Merritt: Nicola Meadows
Affiliated with: Interior Health Authority
2670 Garcia St., Merritt, BC V1K 1B8
Tel: 250-378-4254 Fax: 250-378-4264
www.interiorhealth.ca
Number of Beds: 81 rooms
Note: Assisted living

Nelson: Lake View Village
Golden Life Management
Affiliated with: Interior Health Authority
1020 - 7th St., Nelson, BC V1L 3A3
Tel: 250-352-0051
goldenlifemanagement.ca
Note: Independent & assisted living
Janet Boisvert, Community Manager
jboisvert@glm.ca

Oliver: Heritage House
Benchmark Lifestyles Inc.
Affiliated with: Interior Health Authority
#100, 409 Salamander Ave., Oliver, BC V0H 1T3
Tel: 250-498-0622 Fax: 250-498-8842
heritagehouse@benchlife.com
www.benchlife.com
www.facebook.com/100008183678517; twitter.com/benchlife
Number of Beds: 33 units
Note: Assisted living

Penticton: Chestnut Place
Affiliated with: Interior Health Authority
453 Winnipeg St., Penticton, BC V2A 5M7
Tel: 250-490-0200
www.interiorhealth.ca

Penticton: The Concorde
Diversicare Canada Management Services Inc
Affiliated with: Interior Health Authority
3235 Skaha Lake Rd., Penticton, BC V2A 6G5
Tel: 250-490-8800 *Fax:* 250-490-8810
www.diversicare.ca

Number of Beds: 77 units
Note: Assisted living

Prince George: Alward Place
Affiliated with: Northern Health Authority
2121 - 6th Ave., Prince George, BC V2M 1L9
Tel: 250-646-6100
www.northernhealth.ca

Number of Beds: 120 apartments

Prince George: Gateway Lodge Assisted Living
Affiliated with: Northern Health Authority
1462 - 20th Ave., Prince George, BC V2L 0B3
Tel: 250-645-6100
www.northernhealth.ca
Note: Local seniors' programs & care services: 250-565-7317 &
250-565-7325.

Prince George: Laurier Manor
Affiliated with: Northern Health Authority
2175 - 9th Ave., Prince George, BC V2M 5E3
Tel: 250-561-1499
www.northernhealth.ca
Note: Assisted living

Prince George: Rainbow Adult Day Centre
Affiliated with: Northern Health Authority
1000 Laird Dr., Prince George, BC V2M 3Z3
Tel: 250-649-7290 *Fax:* 250-563-4376
www.northernhealth.ca
Number of Beds: 36 beds
Note: Local seniors' programs & care services: 250-565-7317 &
250-565-7325.

Prince Rupert: Acropolis Manor
Affiliated with: Northern Health Authority
1325 Summit Ave., Prince Rupert, BC V8J 4C1
Tel: 250-622-6400 *Fax:* 250-627-1490
www.northernhealth.ca
Year Founded: 2009
Number of Beds: 15 apartments
Karen Inkpen, Clinical Coordinator

Queen Charlotte: Martin Manor
Affiliated with: Northern Health Authority
306 - 2nd Ave., Queen Charlotte, BC V0T 1S0
Tel: 250-555-1234
www.northernhealth.ca
Note: Assisted living

Quesnel: Dunrovin Park Lodge Care Facility
Affiliated with: Northern Health Authority
900 St. Laurent Ave., Quesnel, BC V2J 3S3
Tel: 250-985-5800
www.northernhealth.ca
Note: Located at the GR Baker Memorial Hospital site. Personal
care residential facilities; programs & services to allow seniors &
adults with disabilities to continue to live in their own homes.

Revelstoke: Moberly Manor
Arrow & Slocan Lakes Community Services
Affiliated with: Interior Health Authority
PO Box 1570, 712 - 2nd St. East, Revelstoke, BC V0E 2S0
Tel: 250-265-3674 *Fax:* 250-837-5720
moberly@rctvonline.net
www.aslcs.com
Number of Beds: 11 units
Note: Assisted living
Tim Payne, Executive Director
tim.payne@aslcs.com
Agata Lofts, Site Manager

Salmon Arm: Pioneer Lodge
Good Samaritan Society
Affiliated with: Interior Health Authority
1051 - 6th Ave. NE, Salmon Arm, BC V1E 0A6
Tel: 250-804-4814 *Fax:* 250-804-4815
goodsaminfo@gss.org
www.gss.org
Number of Beds: 30 assisted living suites

Shawn Terlson, President & CEO, Good Samaritan Society
sterlson@gss.org

Sicamous: Eagle Valley Manor
Eagle Valley Senior Citizen's Housing Society
Affiliated with: Interior Health Authority
319 Gordon Mackie Lane, Sicamous, BC V0E 2V1
Tel: 250-836-2310
www.interiorhealth.ca
Number of Beds: 12 units
Note: Assisted living complex

Summerland: Summerland Seniors Village
Retirement Concepts
Affiliated with: Interior Health Authority
12803 Atkinson Rd., Summerland, BC V0H 1Z4
Tel: 250-404-4400 *Fax:* 250-404-4399
www.retirementconcepts.com
Number of Beds: 120 independent/assisted living suites
Scott Shearer, General Manager
sshearer@retirementconcepts.com

Trail: Rose Wood Village
Golden Life Management
Affiliated with: Interior Health Authority
8125 Devito Dr., Trail, BC V1R 4X9
Tel: 250-364-3150
rosewood@glm.ca
goldenlifemanagement.ca
Number of Beds: 40 independent & assisted living suites
Jane Power, Community Manager
jpower@glm.ca

Vanderhoof: Omineca Lodge
Affiliated with: Northern Health Authority
3255 Hospital Rd., Vanderhoof, BC V0J 3A2
Tel: 250-567-2216
www.northernhealth.ca
Note: Assisted living

Vernon: Gateby Care Facility
Affiliated with: Interior Health Authority
3000 Gateby Pl., Vernon, BC V1T 1P4
Tel: 250-545-4456 *Fax:* 250-545-4439
www.interiorhealth.ca
Number of Beds: 75 beds

Mental Health Hospitals/Facilities

100 Mile House: 100 Mile Mental Health
Affiliated with: Interior Health Authority
555 Cedar Ave. South, 100 Mile House, BC V0K 2E0
Tel: 250-395-7676
www.interiorhealth.ca
Note: Services include: assessment; treatment; crisis
intervention; counselling; & mental health support.

Abbotsford: Abbotsford Mental Health Centre
Affiliated with: Fraser Health Authority
11 - 32700 George Ferguson Way, Abbotsford, BC V2T 4V6
Tel: 604-870-7800 *Fax:* 604-870-7801

Agassiz: Agassiz Mental Health Centre
Affiliated with: Fraser Health Authority
7243 Pioneer Ave., Agassiz, BC V0M 1A0
Tel: 604-793-7160 *Fax:* 604-796-8587

Ashcroft: Ashcroft Mental Health & Substance Use
Affiliated with: Interior Health Authority
700 Ash-Cache Creek Hwy., Ashcroft, BC V0K 1A0
Tel: 250-453-1940 *Toll-Free:* 877-499-6599
www.interiorhealth.ca
Note: Services include: assessment; treatment; crisis
intervention; counselling; & mental health support.

Barriere: Barriere Mental Health & Substance Use
Affiliated with: Interior Health Authority
4936 Barriere Town Rd., Barriere, BC V0E 1A0
Tel: 250-672-9773
www.interiorhealth.ca
Note: Services include: assessment; treatment; crisis
intervention; counselling; & mental health support.

Burnaby: Burnaby Mental Health Centre
Affiliated with: Fraser Health Authority
3935 Kincaid St., Burnaby, BC V5G 2X6
Tel: 604-453-1900 *Fax:* 604-453-1929

Burnaby: Craigend Rest Home
5488 Patterson Ave., Burnaby, BC V5H 2M5
Tel: 604-433-8600
Number of Beds: 10 beds

Castlegar: Castlegar Mental Health & Substance Use
Affiliated with: Interior Health Authority
707 - 10th St., Castlegar, BC V1N 2H7
Tel: 250-304-1846 *Fax:* 250-304-1240
www.interiorhealth.ca
Note: Services include: adult community support; counselling;
early psychosis intervention; eating disorders; intake, urgent
response, & emergency; & seniors mental health.

Chase: Chase Mental Health & Substance Use
Affiliated with: Interior Health Authority
825 Thompson Ave., Chase, BC V0E 1M0
Tel: 250-679-3312
www.interiorhealth.ca
Note: Services include: assessment; treatment; crisis
intervention; counselling; & mental health support.

Clearwater: Clearwater Mental Health & Substance
Use
Affiliated with: Interior Health Authority
612 Park Dr., Clearwater, BC V0E 1N1
Tel: 250-674-2600
www.interiorhealth.ca
Note: Services include: adult community support; counselling;
early psychosis intervention; eating disorders; intake, urgent
response, & emergency services; & seniors mental health.

Coquitlam: BC Mental Health & Substance Use
Services
Forensic Psychiatric Hospital
70 Colony Farm Rd., Coquitlam, BC V3C 5X9
Tel: 604-524-7700 *Fax:* 604-524-7905
feedback@bcmhs.bc.ca
www.bcmhsus.ca
Number of Beds: 190 beds
Note: Facility providing specialized clinical services &
rehabilitative & vocational programs.
Dr. George Wiehahn, Medical Director

Cranbrook: Cranbrook Developmental Disability
Mental Health Services
Affiliated with: Interior Health Authority
1212 - 2nd St. North, Cranbrook, BC V1C 4T6
Tel: 250-417-2534
www.interiorhealth.ca
Note: Provides developmental disability mental health services.

Cranbrook: Cranbrook Mental Health & Substance
Use
Affiliated with: Interior Health Authority
20 - 23rd Ave. South, Cranbrook, BC V1C 5V1
Tel: 250-420-2210 *Fax:* 250-420-2279
Toll-Free: 888-426-7566
www.interiorhealth.ca
Note: Services include: adult community support; assessment;
treatment; crisis intervention; counselling; & mental health
support.

Cranbrook: Kootenay Clover Club House
Affiliated with: Interior Health Authority
400 Victoria Ave. North, Cranbrook, BC V1C 3Y3
Tel: 250-426-0102
www.interiorhealth.ca
Note: Services include: adult community support; assessment;
treatment; crisis intervention; counselling; & mental health
support.

Cranbrook: Tamarack Cottage
Affiliated with: Interior Health Authority
2005 - 5th St. North, Cranbrook, BC V1C 4Y2
Tel: 250-417-0103
www.interiorhealth.ca
Number of Beds: 5 tertiary specialized residential beds; 2 tertiary
rehabilitative beds
Note: Offers tertiary psychiatric services & a tertiary
rehabilitation & recovery program.

Creston: Creston Mental Health & Substance Use
Affiliated with: Interior Health Authority
243 - 16th Ave. North, Creston, BC V0B 1G0
Tel: 250-428-8734 *Fax:* 250-428-8956
www.interiorhealth.ca
Note: Services include: adult community support; counselling;
early psychosis intervention; eating disorders; intake, urgent
response, & emergency; & seniors mental health.

Delta: Delta North Mental Health Centre
Affiliated with: Fraser Health Authority
129 - 6345 120th St., Delta, BC V4E 2A6
Tel: 604-592-3700 *Fax:* 604-591-2302

Delta: Delta South Mental Health Centre
Affiliated with: Fraser Health Authority
15 - 1835 56 St., Delta, BC V4L 2L8
Tel: 604-948-7010 *Fax:* 604-943-0872

Golden: Golden Mental Health & Substance Use
Affiliated with: Interior Health Authority
835 - 9th Ave. South, Golden, BC V0A 1H0
Tel: 250-344-3015 *Fax:* 250-344-2817
www.interiorhealth.ca
Note: Services include: adult community support; assessment; treatment; crisis intervention; counselling; & mental health support.

Grand Forks: Boundary Mental Health & Substance Use Services
Affiliated with: Interior Health Authority
7441 2nd St., Grand Forks, BC V0H 1H0
Tel: 250-442-0330 *Fax:* 250-442-0334
www.interiorhealth.ca
Note: Services include: adult community support; counselling; early psychosis intervention; eating disorders; intake, urgent response, & emergency; & seniors mental health.

Grand Forks: Granby Clubhouse
Affiliated with: Interior Health Authority
8443 Riverside Dr., Grand Forks, BC V0H 1H0
Tel: 250-442-2465
www.interiorhealth.ca
Note: Services include: adult community support; assessment; treatment; crisis intervention; & mental health support.

Hazelton: Hazelton Mental Health & Addictions
Affiliated with: Northern Health Authority
PO Box 999, 2506 Hwy. 62, Hazelton, BC V0J 1Y0
Tel: 250-842-5144 *Fax:* 250-842-2179
www.northernhealth.ca
Info Line: 888-562-1214
Note: Programs & services include: assessment & treatment; life skills training; recreational therapy; observation unit; perinatal depression; supportive recovery; & community response unit.

Invermere: Invermere Mental Health & Substance Use
Affiliated with: Interior Health Authority
850 - 10th Ave., Invermere, BC V0A 1K0
Tel: 250-342-2363 *Fax:* 250-342-2374
www.interiorhealth.ca
Note: Services include: adult community support; assessment; treatment; crisis intervention; counselling; & mental health support.

Kamloops: Apple Lane Tertiary Mental Health Geriatric Unit
Affiliated with: Interior Health Authority
#200, 945 Southill St., Kamloops, BC V2B 7Z9
Tel: 250-554-5590 *Fax:* 250-554-5558
www.interiorhealth.ca
Number of Beds: 6 beds
Note: Provides care for elderly patients who have been diagnosed with a serious mental illness. Offers tertiary psychiatric services & a tertiary rehabilitation & recovery program.

Kamloops: Developmental Disability Mental Health Child, Youth & Children's Assessment Network
Affiliated with: Interior Health Authority
624 Tranquille Rd., Kamloops, BC V2B 3H6
Tel: 250-554-0085
www.interiorhealth.ca
Note: Offers developmental disability mental health services.

Kamloops: Forensic Psychiatric Services Commission
Kamloops Clinic
#5, 1315 Summit Dr., Kamloops, BC V2C 5R9
Tel: 250-377-2660 *Fax:* 250-377-2688
www.bcmhsus.ca/regional-clinics

Kamloops: Hillside Centre
Affiliated with: Interior Health Authority
311 Columbia St., Kamloops, BC V2C 2T1
Tel: 250-314-2700 *Fax:* 250-314-2410
www.interiorhealth.ca
Year Founded: 2006
Number of Beds: 44 beds
Note: Offers services to individuals with acute illness & / or severely dysfunctional behaviours.

Kamloops: Kamloops Developmental Disability Mental Health Services
Affiliated with: Interior Health Authority
#235 Lansdowne St., 1st Fl., Kamloops, BC V2C 1X8
Tel: 250-377-6500
www.interiorhealth.ca
Note: Provides mental health services for people with developmental disabilities.

Kamloops: Kamloops Mental Health & Substance Use
Affiliated with: Interior Health Authority
200 - 235 Lansdowne St., Kamloops, BC V2C 1X8
Tel: 250-377-6500 *Fax:* 250-377-6502
www.interiorhealth.ca
Note: Services include: adult community support; counselling; early psychosis intervention; eating disorders; intake, urgent response, & emergency; & seniors mental health.

Kamloops: South Hills Tertiary Psychiatric Rehabilitation Centre
Affiliated with: Interior Health Authority
#200, 945 Southill St., Kamloops, BC V2B 7Z9
Tel: 250-554-5590 *Fax:* 250-554-5558
www.interiorhealth.ca
Number of Beds: 40 beds
Note: Provides a rehabilitation & recovery program for adults with a serious mental illness.

Kamloops: Youth Forensic Psychiatric Services Kamloops Outpatient Clinic
#8 Tudor Village, 1315 Summit Dr., Kamloops, BC V2C 5R9
Tel: 250-828-4940 *Fax:* 250-828-4946
Note: For young offenders directed by court / probation to assessment / treatment.
Deanna Dewer, Coordinator, Youth Forensic Services
705 474-8600

Kaslo: Kaslo Mental Health & Substance Use
Affiliated with: Interior Health Authority
673 A Ave., Kaslo, BC V0G 1M0
Tel: 250-353-2291
www.interiorhealth.ca
Note: Services include: adult community support; assessment; treatment; crisis intervention; counselling; & mental health support.

Kelowna: Cara Centre
Affiliated with: Interior Health Authority
160 Nickel Rd., Kelowna, BC V1X 4E6
Tel: 250-763-4144 *Fax:* 250-763-4143
www.interiorhealth.ca
Year Founded: 2011
Number of Beds: 11 beds
Note: Provides tertiary psychiatric services & a tertiary rehabilitation & recovery program for individuals who have a mental illness or psychiatric concerns. Admission is by referral only.

Kelowna: Central Okanagan Brain Injury Society
Affiliated with: Interior Health Authority
#11, 368 Industrial Ave., Kelowna, BC V1Y 4N7
Tel: 250-762-3233 *Fax:* 250-861-3008
www.interiorhealth.ca
Note: Services for people affected by brain injury, as well as their families.

Kelowna: Kelowna Developmental Disability Mental Health Services
Affiliated with: Interior Health Authority
505 Doyle Ave., Kelowna, BC V1Y 0C5
Tel: 250-469-7070
www.interiorhealth.ca
Note: Provides mental health services for people with developmental disabilities.

Kelowna: Kelowna Mental Health & Substance Use
Affiliated with: Interior Health Authority
505 Doyle Ave., Kelowna, BC V1Y 0C5
Tel: 250-469-7070
www.interiorhealth.ca
Note: Services include: adult community support; assessment; treatment; crisis intervention; counselling; & mental health support.

Kelowna: Seniors Mental Health & Eating Disorders Program
Affiliated with: Interior Health Authority
Community Health Services Centre, 505 Dolye Ave., 2nd Fl., Kelowna, BC V1Y 6V8
Tel: 250-469-7070
www.interiorhealth.ca

Note: Services include: adult community support; assessment; treatment; crisis intervention; counselling; & mental health support.

Kelowna: White Heather Manor
3728 Casorso Rd., Kelowna, BC V1W 4M8
Tel: 250-763-6554 *Fax:* 250-763-6754
whiteheather@optimaliving.com
whiteheathermanor.ca
www.facebook.com/Cottonwoodclaresholm
Number of Beds: 44 beds
Sean Rathwell, Manager, Care

Keremeos: Keremeos Mental Health & Substance Use
Affiliated with: Interior Health Authority
700 - 3rd St., Keremeos, BC V0X 1N3
Tel: 250-499-3029 *Fax:* 250-499-3027
Toll-Free: 800-663-7867
www.interiorhealth.ca
Note: Services include: adult community support; assessment; treatment; crisis intervention; counselling; & mental health support.

Kimberley: Kimberley Mental Health
Affiliated with: Interior Health Authority
260 - 4th Ave., Kimberley, BC V1A 2R6
Tel: 250-427-2215 *Fax:* 250-427-7389
www.interiorhealth.ca
Note: Services include: adult community support; assessment; treatment; crisis intervention; counselling; & mental health support.

Lillooet: Lillooet Mental Health & Substance Use
Affiliated with: Interior Health Authority
951 Murray St., Lillooet, BC V0K 1V0
Tel: 250-256-1343 *Fax:* 855-656-4233
www.interiorhealth.ca
Note: Services include: adult community support; counselling; early psychosis intervention; eating disorders; intake, urgent response, & emergency; & seniors mental health.

Logan Lake: Logan Lake Mental Health & Substance Use
Affiliated with: Interior Health Authority
5 Beryl Dr., Logan Lake, BC V0K 1W0
Tel: 250-523-9414
www.interiorhealth.ca
Note: Services include: adult community support; assessment; treatment; crisis intervention; counselling; & mental health support.

Lytton: Lytton Mental Health & Substance Use
Affiliated with: Interior Health Authority
575 Main St., Lytton, BC V0K 1Z0
Tel: 250-455-2221
www.interiorhealth.ca
Note: Services include: adult community support; counselling; early psychosis intervention; eating disorders; intake, urgent response, & emergency; & seniors mental health.

Maple Ridge: Trejan Lodge Ltd.
25402 Hilland Ave., Maple Ridge, BC V4R 1G3
Tel: 604-467-3377 *Fax:* 604-467-0705

Merritt: Merritt Mental Health & Substance Use
Affiliated with: Interior Health Authority
3451 Voght St., Merritt, BC V1K 1C6
Tel: 250-378-3401
www.interiorhealth.ca
Note: Services include: adult community support; assessment; treatment; crisis intervention; counselling; & mental health support.

Midway: Boundary Access Centre
Affiliated with: Interior Health Authority
7th Ave., Midway, BC V0H 1M0
Tel: 250-449-2887
www.interiorhealth.ca
Note: Services include: assessment; treatment; crisis intervention; counselling; & mental health support.

Nakusp: Nakusp Mental Health & Substance Use
Affiliated with: Interior Health Authority
97 - 1st Ave. NE, Nakusp, BC V0G 1R0
Tel: 250-265-5253
www.interiorhealth.ca
Note: Services include: adult community support; assessment; treatment; crisis intervention; counselling; & mental health support.

Nakusp: **Terra Pondera Clubhouse**
Affiliated with: Interior Health Authority
97 - 2nd Ave. NW, Nakusp, BC V0G 1R0
Tel: 250-265-0064
www.interiorhealth.ca
Note: Services include: adult community support; assessment; treatment; crisis intervention; counselling; & mental health support.

Nanaimo: **Forensic Psychiatric Services Commission**
Nanaimo Clinic
Former Name: Nanaimo Adult Forensic Psychiatric Community Services
#101, 190 Wallace St., Nanaimo, BC V9R 5B1
Tel: 250-739-5000 *Fax:* 250-739-5001
www.bcmhsus.ca/regional-clinics

Nanaimo: **Vancouver Island Mental Health Society**
Former Name: Columbian Centre Society
2356 Rosstown Rd., Nanaimo, BC V9T 3R7
Tel: 250-758-8711 *Fax:* 250-751-1128
info@vimhs.org
www.vancouverislandmentalhealthsociety.org
Number of Beds: 10 beds
Taryn O'Flanagan, Executive Director
executive.director@vimhs.org

Nanaimo: **Youth Forensic Psychiatric Services**
Nanaimo Outpatient Clinic
1 - 1925 Bowen Rd., Nanaimo, BC V9S 1H1
Tel: 250-760-0409 *Toll-Free:* 800-663-9122
Note: Mental health assessment & treatment services for youth involved in the criminal justice system.
André Picard, Provincial Director
778-452-2202,

Nelson: **McKim Cottage Stabilization Unit**
Affiliated with: Interior Health Authority
916 - 11th St., Nelson, BC V1L 7A6
Tel: 250-352-2022 *Fax:* 250-354-5955
www.interiorhealth.ca
Note: Services include: adult community support; assessment; treatment; crisis intervention; counselling; & mental health support.

Nelson: **Nelson Friendship Outreach Clubhouse**
Affiliated with: Interior Health Authority
818 Vernon Rd., Nelson, BC V1L 4G4
Tel: 250-352-7730 *Fax:* 250-352-7709
www.interiorhealth.ca
Note: Services include: adult community support; assessment; treatment; crisis intervention; counselling; & mental health support.

Nelson: **Nelson Mental Health & Substance Use**
Affiliated with: Interior Health Authority
333 Victoria St., Nelson, BC V1L 4K3
Tel: 250-505-7248
www.interiorhealth.ca
Note: Services include: adult community support; assessment; treatment; crisis intervention; counselling; & mental health support.

Old Masset: **Old Massett Adult Day Program**
Affiliated with: Northern Health Authority
510 Naanii Rd., Old Masset, BC V0T 1M0
Tel: 250-626-5671
www.northernhealth.ca
Note: Offers programs & services designed to help seniors & adults with disabilities to continue to live in their own homes.

Oliver: **Desert Sun Counselling & Resource Centre**
Affiliated with: Interior Health Authority
PO Box 1890, 762 Fairview Rd., Oliver, BC V0X 1C0
Tel: 250-498-2538 *Fax:* 250-498-6088
Toll-Free: 877-723-3911
www.desertsuncounselling.ca
www.facebook.com/desertsuncounselling
www.instagram.com/desertsuncounselling
Year Founded: 1998
Note: Services include: counselling; crisis help; parenting resources; seniors' resources; & community outreach.
Patricia Batchelor, Chair

Oliver: **Robert Bateman House**
Affiliated with: Interior Health Authority
538 Fairview Rd., Oliver, BC V0H 1T0
Tel: 250-485-0043 *Fax:* 250-495-2748
www.interiorhealth.ca
Note: Services include: adult community support; assessment; treatment; crisis intervention; counselling; & mental health support.

Osoyoos: **Osoyoos Mental Health & Substance Use**
Affiliated with: Interior Health Authority
4816 - 89 St., Osoyoos, BC V0H 1V1
Tel: 250-495-6433
www.interiorhealth.ca
Note: Services include: adult community support; assessment; treatment; crisis intervention; counselling; & mental health support.

Penticton: **Braemore Lodge**
Affiliated with: Interior Health Authority
2402 South Main St., Penticton, BC V2A 5H9
Tel: 250-492-2969 *Fax:* 250-492-2901
www.interiorhealth.ca
Number of Beds: 16 beds (4 tertiary specialized residential beds)
Note: Offers tertiary psychiatric & psychosocial rehabilitation services to individuals with a serious mental illness.

Penticton: **Penticton Mental Health & Substance Use**
Affiliated with: Interior Health Authority
#117 - 437 Martin St., Penticton, BC V1L 5L1
Tel: 250-770-3555
www.interiorhealth.ca
Note: Services include: adult community support; assessment; treatment; crisis intervention; counselling; & mental health support.

Prince George: **Forensic Psychiatric Services Commission**
Prince George Clinic
1584 - 7 Ave., 2nd Fl., Prince George, BC V2L 3P4
Tel: 250-561-8060 *Fax:* 250-561-8075
www.bcmhsus.ca/regional-clinics
Note: Outpatient mental health services

Prince George: **Iris House**
Affiliated with: Northern Health Authority
1111 Lethbridge St., Prince George, BC V2M 7E9
Tel: 250-649-7245 *Fax:* 250-563-2706
www.northernhealth.ca
Year Founded: 2002
Number of Beds: 20 beds
Note: Tertiary rehabilitation & residential facility for adults with long-term mental illness. Affiliated with Seven Sisters in Terrace, BC.

Princeton: **Anchorage Drop-In Centre**
Affiliated with: Interior Health Authority
136 Vermillion Ave., Princeton, BC V0X 1W0
Tel: 250-295-6936
www.interiorhealth.ca
Note: Services include: assessment; treatment; crisis intervention; counselling; & mental health support.

Queen Charlotte: **Queen Charlotte City Health Centre**
Affiliated with: Northern Health Authority
302 - 2nd Ave., Queen Charlotte, BC V0T 1S0
Tel: 250-559-8765 *Fax:* 250-559-8765
www.northernhealth.ca
Note: Programs & services include: mental health & addictions; home care nursing; & home support.

Quesnel: **Quesnel Mental Health Team & QUESST Unit**
Affiliated with: Northern Health Authority
543 Front St., Quesnel, BC V2J 2K7
Tel: 250-985-5608 *Fax:* 250-992-2765
www.northernhealth.ca
Number of Beds: 5 beds
Note: Short-term intensive services including assessment, stabilization, consultation, brief treatment, & discharge planning. QUESST stands for Quesnel Unit for Emergency Short Stay Treatment.

Revelstoke: **Revelstoke Mental Health & Substance Use**
Affiliated with: Interior Health Authority
1200 Newlands Rd., Revelstoke, BC V0E 2S0
Tel: 250-814-2241
www.interiorhealth.ca
Note: Services include: adult community support; assessment; treatment; crisis intervention; counselling; & mental health support.

Salmo: **Salmo Mental Health & Substance Use**
Affiliated with: Interior Health Authority
311 Railway Ave., Salmo, BC V0G 1Z0
Tel: 250-357-2277
www.interiorhealth.ca
Note: Services include: adult community support; counselling; early psychosis intervention; eating disorders; intake, urgent response, & emergency; & seniors mental health.

Salmon Arm: **Salmon Arm Mental Health Services**
Affiliated with: Interior Health Authority
851 - 16th St. NE, Salmon Arm, BC V1E 4N7
Tel: 250-833-4100 *Fax:* 250-833-4117
www.interiorhealth.ca
Note: Services include: adult community support; assessment; treatment; crisis intervention; counselling; & mental health support.

Surrey: **Timber Creek Tertiary Care Facility**
Affiliated with: Fraser Health Authority
13646 - 94A Ave., Surrey, BC V3V 1N1
Tel: 604-580-6500 *Fax:* 604-580-6516
Note: Specializes in psychological rehabilitation

Terrace: **Birchwood Place**
Affiliated with: Northern Health Authority
3183 Kofoed Dr., Terrace, BC V8G 3P8
Tel: 250-635-2171 *Fax:* 250-635-7057
www.northernhealth.ca
Number of Beds: 8 beds
Note: Supported living residential care.

Terrace: **Terrace Community Mental Health Services**
Affiliated with: Northern Health Authority
#34, 3412 Kalum St., Terrace, BC V8G 0G5
Tel: 250-631-4202 *Fax:* 250-631-4282
www.northernhealth.ca
Info Line: 250-638-4082
Note: Programs & services include: intake; crisis response; counselling; case management; life skills support; medication management; education; & psychiatric consultation.

Trail: **Friend of Friends Clubhouse**
Affiliated with: Interior Health Authority
1454 - 2nd Ave., Trail, BC V1R 1M2
Tel: 250-368-6343 *Fax:* 250-368-6343
www.interiorhealth.ca
Note: Services include: adult community support; assessment; treatment; crisis intervention; counselling; & mental health support.

Trail: **Harbour House**
Affiliated with: Interior Health Authority
1100 Hospital Bench, Trail, BC V1R 4M1
Tel: 250-364-9995 *Fax:* 250-364-9909
www.interiorhealth.ca
Number of Beds: 6 tertiary specialized residential beds; 3 tertiary rehabilitative beds
Note: Provides services for clients in need of longer-term residential psychosocial rehabilitation.

Trail: **Trail Mental Health & Substance Use**
Affiliated with: Interior Health Authority
#3, 1500 Columbia Ave., Trail, BC V1R 1J9
Tel: 250-364-6262
www.interiorhealth.ca
Note: Services include: adult community support; assessment; treatment; crisis intervention; counselling; & mental health support.

Tumbler Ridge: **Tumbler Ridge Mental Health & Addictions**
Affiliated with: Northern Health Authority
PO Box 1205, 220 Front St., Tumbler Ridge, BC V0C 2W0
Tel: 250-242-5505 *Fax:* 250-242-3595
www.northernhealth.ca
Note: Services include: case management; counselling; crisis response; education; intake; life skills support; medication management; & psychiatric consultation.

Vanderhoof: **Vanderhoof Health Unit**
Affiliated with: Northern Health Authority
3299 Hospital Rd., Vanderhoof, BC V0J 3A2
Tel: 250-567-6900 *Fax:* 250-567-6171
www.northernhealth.ca

Vernon: **Aberdeen House**
Affiliated with: Interior Health Authority
9604 Shamanski Dr., Vernon, BC V1B 2L7
Tel: 250-542-9350
aberdeenhouse@shawbiz.ca
www.interiorhealth.ca
Number of Beds: 14 beds (7 tertiary specialized residential)
Note: Provides specialized mental health services

Vernon: **Okanagan House**
Affiliated with: Interior Health Authority
4007 - 24th Ave., Vernon, BC V1T 4N7
Tel: 250-549-5737
www.interiorhealth.ca

Note: Services include: adult community support; assessment; treatment; crisis intervention; counselling; & mental health support.

Vernon: Vernon Mental Health & Substance Use
Affiliated with: Interior Health Authority
1440 - 14th Ave., Vernon, BC V1B 2T1
Tel: 250-549-5737
www.interiorhealth.ca
Note: Services include: adult community support; assessment; treatment; group therapy; crisis intervention; counselling; & mental health support.

Vernon: Willowview Stabilization Unit
Affiliated with: Interior Health Authority
1808 - 30th St., Vernon, BC V1T 5C5
Tel: 250-542-4890 Fax: 250-260-2836
www.interiorhealth.ca
Note: Services include: adult community support; assessment; treatment; crisis intervention; counselling; community residential programs; geriatric programs; group therapy; & mental health support.

Victoria: Pacific Operational Trauma & Stress Support Centre (OTSSC)
Canadian Forces Health Services
1200 Colville Rd., Victoria, BC V9A 7N2
Tel: 250-363-4411
Year Founded: 1999
Note: Specialties: Assistance to serving members of the Canadian Forces & their families, who are dealing with psychological, emotional, spiritual, & social problems stemming from military operations, especially deployments abroad; Psychiatry; Psychology; Social work; Community health nursing; Educational programs; Chaplain services

Victoria: Youth Forensic Psychiatric Services
Victoria Outpatient Clinic
1515 Quadra St., Victoria, BC V8V 3P4
Tel: 250-387-2830 Fax: 250 387-3217

Williams Lake: Gateway Crisis Stabilization Unit
Affiliated with: Interior Health Authority
517 North 6th Ave., 3rd Fl., Williams Lake, BC V2G 2P3
Tel: 250-302-3261 Fax: 250-302-3262
www.interiorhealth.ca
Number of Beds: 5 beds
Note: Services include: adult community support; assessment; treatment; crisis intervention; counselling; & mental health support.

Williams Lake: Williams Lake Mental Health & Substance Use
Affiliated with: Interior Health Authority
487 Borland St., Williams Lake, BC V2G 1R9
Tel: 250-392-1483 Fax: 250-392-1484
www.interiorhealth.ca
Note: Services include: adult community support; counselling; early psychosis intervention; eating disorders; intake; urgent response, & emergency; & seniors mental health.

Special Care Homes

Kamloops: Ponderosa Lodge
Affiliated with: Interior Health Authority
425 Columbia St., Kamloops, BC V2C 2T4
Tel: 250-374-5671 Fax: 250-374-8873
www.interiorhealth.ca
Number of Beds: 68 First Appropriate beds; 68 Pathway to Home beds
Note: Short-term beds for residents waiting for a permanent bed in a residential care facility; convalescent care & respite care beds.

Kimberley: Kimberley Special Care Home
Affiliated with: Interior Health Authority
386 - 2nd Ave., Kimberley, BC V1A 2Z8
Tel: 250-427-4807 Fax: 250-427-5377
www.interiorhealth.ca
Number of Beds: 53 residential beds; 2 flexible short-stay beds
Specialties: Residential care

Langley: Arbutus Place
Affiliated with: Fraser Health Authority
20619 Eastleigh Cres., Langley, BC V3A 4C3
Tel: 604-539-7800 Fax: 604-539-7805
Note: Specialties: geriatric psychiatrics

Vernon: Polson Special Care
Affiliated with: Interior Health Authority
2101 - 32nd St., Vernon, BC V1T 5L2
Tel: 250-558-1318
www.interiorhealth.ca

Number of Beds: 5 tertiary specialized residential beds
Note: For geriatric patients

Manitoba

Government Departments in Charge

Winnipeg: Manitoba Health & Seniors Care
300 Carlton St., Winnipeg, MB R3B 3M9
Tel: 204-786-7101 Fax: 204-783-2171
Toll-Free: 800-392-1207
TTY: 204-774-8618
www.gov.mb.ca/health

Hon. Audrey Gordon, Minister
204-945-3731, Fax: 204-945-0441, minhsc@leg.gov.mb.ca

Regional Health Authorities

Flin Flon: Northern Regional Health Authority
Also Known As: Northern Health Region
84 Church St., Flin Flon, MB R8A 1L8
Tel: 204-687-1300 Fax: 204-687-6405
Toll-Free: 888-340-6742
www.northernhealthregion.ca
www.facebook.com/248714775264934;
twitter.com/NorthHealthMB

Year Founded: 2012
Area Served: 396,000 sq km Population Served: 74175
Note: Northern Regional Health Authority is an amalgamation of NOR-MAN Regional Health Authority & Burntwood Regional Health Authority.
Cal Huntley, Board Chair
Helga Bryant, Chief Executive Officer
Dr. Deborah Mabin, Chief Medical Officer & Vice-President, Medical Services
Shawn Hnidy, Chief Financial Officer & Vice-President, Corporate Services
Charlene Lafreniere, Chief Indigenous Officer
Wanda Reader, Chief Human Resources Officer & Vice-President
Joy Tetlock, Vice-President, Planning & Innovation

La Broquerie: Southern Health-Santé Sud
La Broquerie Regional Office, PO Box 470, 94 Principale St., La Broquerie, MB R0A 0W0
www.southernhealth.ca
Area Served: 27,025 sq km Population Served: 204274 Number of Employees: 6000
Note: Regional offices are located in La Broquerie, Morden, Notre Dame de Lourdes & Southport. For a complete list of health sites overseen by Southern Health-Santé Sud, please visit www.southernhealth.ca.

Norway House: Norway House Cree Nation Health Division (NHHS)
PO Box 250, Norway House, MB R0B 1B0
Tel: 204-359-6704 Fax: 204-359-6161
www.nhcn.ca/health_division/
Year Founded: 2003
Area Served: 19,435 acre reserve
Note: Provides health services to the community of the Norway House Cree Nation. Oversees Pinaow Wachi Personal Care Home, Kinosao Sipi Dental Centre, Norway House Community Clinic & Norway House Hospital / Norway House Nursing Station (with Northern Regional Health Authority).

Selkirk: Interlake-Eastern Regional Health Authority
Former Name: Interlake Regional Health Authority, North Eastman Regional Health Authority
Corporate Office, 233A Main St., Selkirk, MB R1A 1S1
Tel: 204-785-4700 Fax: 204-482-4300
Toll-Free: 855-347-8500
info@ierha.ca
www.ierha.ca
twitter.com/IERHA_MB
Area Served: 61,000 sq km Population Served: 124000 Number of Employees: 3100
Note: Interlake-Eastern RHA is an amalgamation of Interlake Regional Health Authority & North Eastman Regional Health Authority.
Margaret Mills, Board Chair
Ron Van Denakker, Chief Executive Officer
Marion Ellis, Chief Nursing Officer & Vice-President, Acute Care
Dorothy Forbes, Chief Financial Officer & Vice-President, Finance
Karen Stevens-Chambers, Chief Allied Health Officer & Vice-President, Community Services
Dr. Myron Thiessen, Chief Medical Officer & Vice-President, Primary Health Care
Randy Dallinger, Vice-President, Human Resources
Ron Janzen, Vice-President, Corporate Services

Souris: Prairie Mountain Health/Santé Prairie Mountain
PO Box 579, 192 - 1st Ave. West, Souris, MB R0K 2C0
Tel: 204-483-5000 Fax: 204-483-5005
Toll-Free: 888-682-2253
www.prairiemountainhealth.ca
www.facebook.com/prairiemountainhealth;
twitter.com/prairiemhealth

Year Founded: 2012
Number of Beds: 2,003 long term care beds; 795 acute care beds; 91 transitional care beds
Area Served: 67,000 sq km (55 municipalities) Population Served: 170899 Number of Employees: 8746
Note: Prairie Mountain Health is an amalgamation of Brandon Regional Health Authority, Assiniboine Regional Health Authority & Parkland Regional Health Authority. Services include: public health, home care, long term care, mental health services, comprehensive health services (cancer care, cardiac, birthing & neonatal, rehabilitation, & surgery).
Lee Jebb, Board Chair
Penny Gilson, Chief Executive Officer

Winnipeg: Winnipeg Regional Health Authority (WRHA)
650 Main St., 4th Fl., Winnipeg, MB R3B 1E2
Tel: 204-926-7000 Fax: 204-926-7007
www.wrha.mb.ca
www.facebook.com/winnipegregionalhealthauthority;
twitter.com/WinnipegRHA;
www.youtube.com/user/WinnipegHealthRegion
Population Served: 700000 Number of Employees: 28000
Note: The WRHA provides services to residents of the City of Winnipeg as well as the surrounding Rural Municipalities of East & West St. Paul, & the Town of Churchill in northern Manitoba. The authority also provides support & referral services to Manitobans who live outside its boundaries, as well as to residents of northwestern Ontario & Nunavut.
Vickie Kaminski, President & CEO
vkaminski@wrha.mb.ca
Krista Allan, Chief Nursing Officer & Chief Operations Officer
kallan3@wrha.mb.ca
Dr. Nancy Dixon, Interim Chief Medical Officer
ndixon@wrha.mb.ca
Gina Trinidad, Chief Health Operations Officer
gtrinidad@wrha.mb.ca
Shelley Hopkins, Chief Financial Officer
shopkins@wrha.mb.ca
Gary Williment, Chief Human Resources Officer
Scott Sime, Regional Director, Communications & Public Relations
ssime@wrha.mb.ca

Hospitals - General

Arborg: Arborg & District Hospital
Affiliated with: Interlake-Eastern Regional Health Authority
Former Name: Arborg & District Health Centre
PO Box 10, 234 Gislason Dr., Arborg, MB R0C 0A0
Tel: 204-376-5247 Fax: 204-376-5669
www.ierha.ca
Number of Beds: 14 acute care beds
Note: Services offered include: acute care; diagnostic imaging; emergency; laboratory; occupational therapy; palliative care; physiotherapy; rehabilitation; medical clinic; spiritual care.

Ashern: Ashern - Lakeshore General Hospital
Affiliated with: Interlake-Eastern Regional Health Authority
PO Box 110, 1 Steenson Dr., Ashern, MB R0C 0E0
Tel: 204-768-2461 Fax: 204-768-2337
www.ierha.ca
Number of Beds: 14 acute care beds
Note: Programs & services include: acute care; dental clinic; diagnostic imaging; laboratory; hemodialysis; emergency / out patient; EMS / ambulance; palliative care; rehabilitation; spiritual care; dietitian; First Nations liaison worker

Beausejour: Beausejour Hospital in Beausejour Health Centre
Affiliated with: Interlake-Eastern Regional Health Authority
PO Box 1178, 151 First St. South, Beausejour, MB R0E 0C0
Tel: 204-268-1076 Fax: 204-268-1207
www.ierha.ca
Number of Beds: 30 acute care beds
Note: Programs & services include: acute care; diagnostic imaging; laboratory; emergency / out patient; occupational therapy; physiotherapy; palliative care; regional staff educator; regional staff pharmacist; rehabilitation; & spiritual care.

Boissevain: **Boissevain Health Centre**
Affiliated with: Prairie Mountain Health
PO Box 889, 305 Mill Rd., Boissevain, MB R0K 0E0
Tel: 204-534-2451 *Fax:* 204-534-6487
www.pmh-mb.ca
Number of Beds: 11 acute care beds
Note: Programs & services include: acute care; diagnostic;
emergency; public health; mental health; home care; physicians
clinic; palliative care; occupational & physiotherapy; dietitian; &
respite care.

Brandon: **Brandon Regional Health Centre**
Affiliated with: Prairie Mountain Health
Former Name: Brandon General Hospital
150 McTavish Ave. East, Brandon, MB R7A 2B3
Tel: 204-578-4000
www.pmh-mb.ca
Number of Beds: 300 beds
Note: Services include: inpatient & outpatient care; psychiatry;
intensive care unit; surgery; palliative care; pediatrics; GI unit;
hemodialysis; cancer program; rehabilitation; diagnostics; &
clinics.
Penny Gilson, CEO, Prairie Mountain Health
Dr. Shaun Gauthier, Vice-President, Medical & Diagnostic
Services

Dauphin: **Dauphin Regional Health Centre (DRHC)**
Affiliated with: Prairie Mountain Health
625 - 3rd St. SW, Dauphin, MB R7N 1R7
Tel: 204-638-3010 *Fax:* 204-629-3418
www.pmh-mb.ca
Number of Beds: 90 beds
Note: Programs & services include: cancer care; dialysis;
emergency; inpatient rehab; maternity; outpatient therapy;
palliative care; surgery.
Curt Gullett, Director

Deloraine: **Deloraine Health Centre**
Affiliated with: Prairie Mountain Health
PO Box 447, 109 Kellett St. South, Deloraine, MB R0M 0M0
Tel: 204-747-2745
www.pmh-mb.ca
Number of Beds: 14 acute care beds; 16 personal care beds
(Delwynda Court PCH); 30 personal care beds (Bren-del-Win
Lodge)
Note: Programs & services include: acute care; diagnostic;
emergency; public health; mental health; home care; Manitoba
Telehealth; community bath program; adult day program; Meals
on Wheels; physicians clinic; palliative care; occupational &
physiotherapy; dietitian; & community cancer program.

Eriksdale: **Eriksdale - E.M. Crowe Memorial Hospital**
Affiliated with: Interlake-Eastern Regional Health
Authority
PO Box 130, 40 Railway Ave., Eriksdale, MB R0C 0W0
Tel: 204-739-2611 *Fax:* 204-739-2065
www.ierha.ca
Number of Beds: 13 acute care beds
Note: Programs & services include: acute care; diagnostic
imaging; laboratory; emergency / out patient; palliative care;
physiotherapy; rehabilitation; & spiritual care.

Flin Flon: **Flin Flon General Hospital**
Affiliated with: Northern Regional Health Authority
Third Ave. & Church St., Flin Flon, MB R8A 1N2
Tel: 204-687-7591 *Fax:* 204-687-8494
www.northernhealthregion.ca
Number of Beds: 42 beds
Note: Programs & services: acute care; palliative care; minor
surgery; emergency; x-ray; EKG; ultrasound; Meals on Wheels
(204-687-9315); MB Telehealth.

Gillam: **Gillam Hospital Inc.**
Affiliated with: Northern Regional Health Authority
PO Box 2000, 115 Gillam Dr., Gillam, MB R0B 0L0
Tel: 204-652-2600 *Fax:* 204-652-2536
www.northernhealthregion.ca
Number of Beds: 7 acute care beds; 3 long-term care beds
Note: Programs & services include: emergency services;
laboratory services; acute care; public health; long term care;
x-ray; medical clinic; visiting specialists (optometry, chiropractic
& pediatrics); full-time Public Health Nurse; Mental Health
Worker; Probation Officer; Employment & Income Assistance
Counsellor; & Addictions Foundation Rehabilitation Counsellor.

Gimli: **Gimli Community Health Centre (GCHC)**
Affiliated with: Interlake-Eastern Regional Health
Authority
PO Box 250, 120 - 6th Ave., Gimli, MB R0C 1B0
Tel: 204-642-5116 *Fax:* 204-642-5860
www.ierha.ca

Year Founded: 2004
Number of Beds: 26 acute care beds
Note: The centre contains the following: Johnson Memorial
Hospital; Community Health Office; & Gimli Clinic.
Programs & services include: acute care; adult day program;
chemotherapy; community cancer program; diagnostic imaging;
laboratory; emergency / out patient; EMS / ambulance;
hemodialysis; occupational therapy; palliative care;
physiotherapy; medical clinic; & spiritual care.

Grandview: **Grandview Health Centre**
Affiliated with: Prairie Mountain Health
PO Box 339, 644 Mill St., Grandview, MB R0L 0Y0
Tel: 204-546-2425 *Fax:* 204-629-3442
www.prairiemountainhealth.ca
Number of Beds: 18 beds
Note: Programs & services include: acute medicine; EKG;
laboratory testing; outpatient services; palliative care; telehealth;
x-ray; & 24-hour emergency services.

Hodgson: **Percy E. Moore Hospital**
Affiliated with: Interlake-Eastern Regional Health
Authority
Former Name: Fisher River Indian Hospital
PO Box 190, Hodgson, MB R0C 1N0
Tel: 204-372-6052 *Fax:* 204-372-6103
www.ierha.ca
Year Founded: 1973
Number of Beds: 16 beds
Area Served: RM of Fisher, Peguis, Fisher River, &
Kinonjeoshtegon *Population Served:* 10000
Note: The hospital is operated by First Nations & Inuit Health of
Health Canada.

Lynn Lake: **Lynn Lake Hospital**
Affiliated with: Northern Regional Health Authority
PO Box 2030, 2040 Camp St., Lynn Lake, MB R0B 0W0
Tel: 204-356-2474 *Fax:* 204-356-8023
www.northernhealthregion.ca
Number of Beds: 11 acute care beds; 8 long-term care beds

McCreary: **McCreary/Alonsa Health Centre**
Affiliated with: Prairie Mountain Health
PO Box 250, 613 Provincial Trunk Hwy. 50, McCreary, MB
R0J 1B0
Tel: 204-835-2482 *Fax:* 204-835-2713
www.pmh-mb.ca
Number of Beds: 12 beds
Note: Programs & services include: diagnostic; home care;
outpatient; palliative care; & clinics.

Melita: **Melita Health Centre**
Affiliated with: Prairie Mountain Health
PO Box 459, 147 Summit Ave., Melita, MB R0M 1L0
Tel: 204-522-3403
www.pmh-mb.ca
Number of Beds: 11 beds
Note: Programs & services include: acute care; EMS /
ambulance; diagnostic; emergency; public health; mental health;
home care; physicians clinic; palliative care; occupational &
physiotherapy; dietitian; & Meals on Wheels.

Neepawa: **Neepawa Health Centre**
Affiliated with: Prairie Mountain Health
Former Name: Neepawa District Memorial Hospital
PO Box 1240, 500 Hospital St., Neepawa, MB R0J 1H0
Tel: 204-476-2394 *Fax:* 204-476-5007
www.pmh-mb.ca
Number of Beds: 38 beds
Note: Programs & services include: acute care; general surgery;
obstetrics; diagnostic; ultrasound; EMS / ambulance; home care;
palliative care; occupational & physiotherapy; dietitian; & Meals
on Wheels.

Pinawa: **Pinawa Hospital**
Affiliated with: Interlake-Eastern Regional Health
Authority
PO Box 220, 30 Vanier Dr., Pinawa, MB R0E 1L0
Tel: 204-753-2334 *Fax:* 204-753-2219
www.ierha.ca
Year Founded: 1964
Number of Beds: 17 acute care beds
Note: Programs & services include: acute care; community
cancer care; dietitians; diagnostics; EMS / ambulance; medical
clinic; occupational therapy; physiotherapy; palliative care;
rehabilitation; & spiritual care.

Pine Falls: **Pine Falls Hospital in Pine Falls Health**
Complex
Affiliated with: Interlake-Eastern Regional Health
Authority
PO Box 2000, 37 Maple St., Pine Falls, MB R0E 1M0
Tel: 204-367-4441 *Fax:* 204-367-8981
www.ierha.ca
Number of Beds: 23 acute care beds
Note: Programs & services include: dietitians; diagnostic
imaging; laboratory; hemodialysis; occupational therapy;
palliative care; physiotherapy; rehabilitation; & spiritual care.

Roblin: **Roblin Health Centre**
Affiliated with: Prairie Mountain Health
PO Box 940, 15 Hospital St., Roblin, MB R0L 1P0
Tel: 204-937-2142 *Fax:* 204-629-3453
www.pmh-mb.ca
Number of Beds: 25 acute care beds
Note: Programs & services include: acute care; diagnostic; EKG;
emergency; laboratory; outpatient services; palliative care;
Manitoba Telehealth; & x-ray.

Russell: **Russell Health Centre**
Affiliated with: Prairie Mountain Health
426 Alexandria Ave., Russell, MB R0J 1W0
Tel: 204-773-2125
www.pmh-mb.ca
Number of Beds: 30 beds
Note: Programs & services include: acute care; community
cancer program; diagnostic; EMS / ambulance; public health;
mental health; home care; Manitoba Telehealth; physicians
clinic; palliative care; occupational & physiotherapy; dietitian;
Meals on Wheels; & pharmacy.

Selkirk: **Selkirk Regional Health Centre**
Affiliated with: Interlake-Eastern Regional Health
Authority
PO Box 5000, 120 Easton Dr., Selkirk, MB R1A 2M2
Tel: 204-482-5800 *Fax:* 204-785-9113
www.ierha.ca
Year Founded: 1907
Number of Beds: 65 beds
Note: Programs & services include: acute care; chemotherapy;
community cancer care; diagnostic imaging & ultrasound;
dialysis; emergency / out patient; EMS / ambulance; obstetrical
program; occupational therapy; palliative care; physiotherapy;
regional surgical services; & spiritual care.

Shoal Lake: **Shoal Lake/Strathclair Health Centre**
Affiliated with: Prairie Mountain Health
PO Box 490, 526 Mary St., Shoal Lake, MB R0J 1Z0
Tel: 204-759-2336
www.pmh-mb.ca
Number of Beds: 12 beds
Note: Programs & services include: acute care; diagnostic; EMS
/ ambulance; public health; mental health; home care; physicians
clinic; palliative care; occupational & physiotherapy; dietitian;
Meals on Wheels; & Elderly Persons Housing.

Souris: **Souris Health Centre**
Affiliated with: Prairie Mountain Health
PO Box 10, 155 Brindle Ave., Souris, MB R0K 2C0
Tel: 204-483-2121 *Fax:* 204-483-2310
www.pmh-mb.ca
Number of Beds: 25 beds
Note: Programs & services include: acute care; EMS; general
surgery; diagnostic; public health; mental health; home care;
physicians clinic; palliative care; occupational & physiotherapy;
dietitian; & Meals on Wheels.

Ste Rose du Lac: **Ste. Rose General Hospital**
Affiliated with: Prairie Mountain Health
Also Known As: Ste Rose Health Centre
PO Box 149, 480 - 3rd Ave. SE, Ste Rose du Lac, MB R0L
1S0
Tel: 204-447-2131 *Fax:* 204-629-3462
www.pmh-mb.ca
Number of Beds: 25 beds
Note: Programs & services include: acute care; EKG;
emergency; laboratory; outpatient services; palliative care; x-ray;
rehabilitation; & public health.

Stonewall: **Stonewall & District Health Centre**
Affiliated with: Interlake-Eastern Regional Health
Authority
589 - 3rd Ave., Stonewall, MB R0C 2Z0
Tel: 204-467-5514 *Fax:* 204-467-8101
www.ierha.ca
Number of Beds: 15 acute care beds
Note: Centre contains: hospital; community health office; &
clinic.
Programs & services include: diagnostic imaging; laboratory;

emergency / out patient; EMS / ambulance; occupational therapy; palliative care; physiotherapy; rehabilitation; & spiritual care.

Swan River: Swan Valley Health Centre
Affiliated with: Prairie Mountain Health
PO Box 1450, 1011 Main St., Swan River, MB R0L 1Z0
Tel: 204-734-3441
www.pmh-mb.ca

Year Founded: 2005
Number of Beds: 52 beds
Note: Programs & services include: public health; home care; diagnostics; dialysis; physiotherapy; speech therapy; surgery; mental health; emergency; chemotherapy; Manitoba Telehealth; occupational therapy; respiratory therapy; rehabilitation; long term care; & Meals on Wheels.

Teulon: Teulon - Hunter Memorial Hospital
Affiliated with: Interlake-Eastern Regional Health Authority
PO Box 89, 162 - 3rd Ave. SE, Teulon, MB R0C 3B0
Tel: 204-886-2433 *Fax:* 204-886-2653
www.ierha.ca

Number of Beds: 20 acute care beds
Note: Programs & services include: acute care; diagnostic imaging; laboratory; emergency / out patient; EMS / ambulance; physiotherapy / occupational therapy; dietary; palliative care; & rehabilitation.

The Pas: St. Anthony's General Hospital
Affiliated with: Northern Regional Health Authority
Also Known As: The Pas Health Complex
PO Box 240, 67 - 1 St. West, The Pas, MB R9A 1K4
Tel: 204-623-6431 *Fax:* 204-623-9263
www.northernhealthregion.ca

Year Founded: 1969
Number of Beds: 40 acute care beds (including 8 in-patient acute care adult psychiatric beds)

Thompson: Thompson General Hospital
Affiliated with: Northern Regional Health Authority
871 Thompson Dr. South, Thompson, MB R8N 0C8
Tel: 204-677-2381 *Fax:* 204-778-1413
www.northernhealthregion.ca

Number of Beds: 79 acute care beds (including 10 in-patient acute care adult psychiatric beds)
Note: Programs & services include: emergency; community mental health; cancer services / chemotherapy; consultation clinic; diagnostic (lab & radiology); general medicine; Northern Patient Transportation Program (NPTP); nutritional services; obstetrics; pediatrics; physiotherapy; surgery & telehealth.

Winnipeg: Concordia Hospital
Affiliated with: Winnipeg Regional Health Authority
1095 Concordia Ave., Winnipeg, MB R2K 3S8
Tel: 204-667-1560 *Fax:* 204-667-1049
www.concordiahospital.mb.ca

Year Founded: 1928
Number of Beds: 185 beds
Number of Employees: 1100
Specialties: Orthopaedics - lower & upper joint replacement
Note: Programs & services include: diagnostic imaging; laboratory services (204-661-7174); surgery (a major centre for hip & knee replacements); intensive care; A.M.I. (Acute Myocardial Infarcation) Program; occupational therapy (204-661-7216); physiotherapy (204-661-7354); respiratory therapy (204-661-7346); oncology haematology service; social work (204-661-7185); cardiac teaching program (nurse home visit); urgent care; & lifeline personal response & support services.
Valerie Wiebe, President & COO

Winnipeg: Grace Hospital
Affiliated with: Winnipeg Regional Health Authority
Former Name: The Salvation Army Grace General Hospital
300 Booth Dr., Winnipeg, MB R3J 3M7
Tel: 204-837-0111
pr@ggh.mb.ca
www.gracehospital.ca

Year Founded: 1904
Number of Beds: 262 beds
Note: Programs & services include: emergency & critical care; surgery; mental health; Aboriginal health services; & hospice care.
Kellie O'Rourke, Chief Operating Officer
Dr. Ramin Hamedani, Chief Medical Officer

Winnipeg: Health Sciences Centre (HSC)
Affiliated with: Winnipeg Regional Health Authority
820 Sherbrook St., Winnipeg, MB R3A 1R9
Tel: 204-787-3661 *Toll-Free:* 877-499-8774
info@hsc.mb.ca
www.hsc.mb.ca
www.facebook.com/HealthSciencesCentreWinnipeg;
twitter.com/hsc_winnipeg

Year Founded: 1973
Number of Beds: 950 beds
Area Served: Manitoba, northwestern Ontario & Nunavut
Number of Employees: 8000
Specialties: Transplants, burns, neurosciences & pediatric care
Note: Includes HSC Women's Hospital. A teaching hospital & the designated Trauma Centre for Manitoba. Programs & services include: Aboriginal health services; adult mental health; anesthesia; child & adolescent mental health; child health; clinical health psychology; critical care; diagnostic imaging; dialysis; emergency; medicine; oncology; rehab; geriatrics; surgery; & women's health.
Ronan Segrave, Chief Operating Officer
Dr. Perry Gray, Vice-President & Chief Medical Officer
Carrie Fruehm, Chief Allied Health Officer
Jane MacKay, Chief Human Resources Officer
Jennifer Bjarnarson, Chief Administrative Officer
Craig Doerksen, Divisional Director of Facility Management
Katherine Fox, Director of Communications

Winnipeg: Hôpital St-Boniface Hospital
Affiliated with: Winnipeg Regional Health Authority
Former Name: St. Boniface General Hospital
Also Known As: St. Boniface Hospital
409 Taché Ave., Winnipeg, MB R2H 2A6
Tel: 204-233-8563
sbghweb@sbgh.mb.ca
www.sbgh.mb.ca
twitter.com/sbh_winnipeg; www.youtube.com/stbonifacehosp

Year Founded: 1871
Number of Beds: 510 beds
Number of Employees: 4000
Note: Catholic tertiary care facility & teaching hospital affiliated with the University of Manitoba & dedicated to the values of care of the Sisters of Charity of Montreal (Grey Nuns). Programs & services include: Aboriginal health services; emergency services; family medicine; mental health; geriatrics & rehabilitation; surgery; women's health; & paediatrics.
Martine Bouchard, President & CEO
204-237-2340
Dr. Scott Brudney, Executive Director, Chief Medical Officer
204-235-3021
Rhonda Cairns, Executive Director, Chief Nursing Officer
204-235-3021
Doug Chervinski, Chief Human Resources Officer, Human Resources
204-237-2735
Nicole Aminot, Executive Director, Chief Financial Officer
204-237-2632
Dr. Grant Pierce, Exective Director, Research
204-235-3206
Micheline St-Hilaire, Director, Corporate Affairs & Communications
204-235-3557

Winnipeg: Seven Oaks General Hospital
Affiliated with: Winnipeg Regional Health Authority
Also Known As: Seven Oaks
2300 McPhillips St., Winnipeg, MB R2V 3M3
Tel: 204-632-7133
www.sogh.ca
www.facebook.com/SevenOaksGeneralHospital;
twitter.com/sevenoakswpg

Year Founded: 1981
Number of Beds: 304 beds
Note: Programs & services include: Aboriginal health; core rehabilitation; day hospital; diagnostic; family medicine; geriatric mental health; geriatric rehabilitation; health library; intensive care; kidney health; Koldonan Medical Centre; laboratory; mental health; oncology clinic; orthopedic clinic; pharmacy; Prairie Trail at the Oaks; respiratory therapy; surgery; Surgery Centre; Urology Centre; urgent care; & Wellness Institute.
Brenda Badiuk, President & Chief Operating Officer
Shauna Boitson, Chief Nursing Officer
Dr. Ricardo Lobato de Faria, Chief Medical Officer
Donna Kenny, Chief Administrative Officer
Rose Schwarz, Director, Human Resources, Human Resources

Winnipeg: Victoria General Hospital (VGH)
Affiliated with: Winnipeg Regional Health Authority
2340 Pembina Hwy., Winnipeg, MB R3T 2E8
Tel: 204-269-3570
info@vgh.mb.ca
www.vgh.mb.ca

Year Founded: 1971
Number of Beds: 298 beds
Number of Employees: 1200
Note: Programs & services include: allied health services; audiology; mental health; surgery; critical care; oncology; medicine / family medicine; & urgent care.
Rachel Ferguson, Chief Operating Officer

Winnipegosis: Winnipegosis Health Centre
Affiliated with: Prairie Mountain Health
Former Name: Winnipegosis General Hospital
Also Known As: Winnipegosis & District Health Centre
PO Box 280, 230 Bridge St., Winnipegosis, MB R0L 2G0
Tel: 204-656-4881
www.pmh-mb.ca

Number of Beds: 15 beds
Note: Programs & services include: acute medicine; outpatient; palliative care; & 24-hour emergency services.
Michelle Quennelle, CEO

Community Health Care Centres

Alonsa: Alonsa Community Health Services
Affiliated with: Prairie Mountain Health
General Delivery, 27 Railway Ave. South, Alonsa, MB R0H 0A0
Tel: 204-767-3000 *Fax:* 204-767-3001
www.prairiemountainhealth.ca
Note: Services include: home care; mental health; primary health care; & public health.

Arborg: Arborg Community Health Office
Affiliated with: Interlake-Eastern Regional Health Authority
317 River Rd., Arborg, MB R0C 0A0
Tel: 204-376-5559 *Fax:* 204-376-5970
www.ierha.ca

Baldur: Baldur Health Centre
Affiliated with: Prairie Mountain Health
PO Box 128, 531 Elizabeth St., Baldur, MB R0K 0B0
Tel: 204-535-2373 *Fax:* 204-535-2116
www.prairiemountainhealth.ca
Number of Beds: 14 long-term care beds
Note: Programs & services include: transitional care; laboratory; public health; mental health; home care; physicians clinic; adult day program; palliative care; occupational & physiotherapy; dietitian; & Meals on Wheels.

Beausejour: Beausejour HEW Primary Health Care Centre
Affiliated with: Interlake-Eastern Regional Health Authority
31 - 1st St., Beausejour, MB R0E 0C0
Tel: 204-268-2288
www.ierha.ca

Beausejour: Beausejour Primary Health Care Centre
Affiliated with: Interlake-Eastern Regional Health Authority
151 - 1st St. South, Beausejour, MB R0E 0C0
Tel: 204-268-4966
www.ierha.ca

Benito: Benito Health Centre
Affiliated with: Prairie Mountain Health
PO Box 490, 200 - 1st St. SE, Benito, MB R0L 0C0
Tel: 204-539-2815
www.prairiemountainhealth.ca
Note: Includes home care services (204-539-2075)

Birtle: Birtle Health Centre
Affiliated with: Prairie Mountain Health
PO Box 2000, 843 Gertrude St., Birtle, MB R0M 0C0
Tel: 204-842-3317 *Fax:* 204-842-3375
www.prairiemountainhealth.ca
Number of Beds: 14 personal care beds
Note: Programs & services include: transitional care; diagnostic; EMS / ambulance; public health; mental health; home care; physicians clinic; palliative care; occupational & physiotherapy; dietitian; & elderly persons housing unit.

Brandon: 7th Street Health Access Centre
Affiliated with: Prairie Mountain Health
Also Known As: ACCESS Brandon
20 - 7th St., Brandon, MB R7A 6M8
Tel: 204-578-4800 *Fax:* 204-578-4950
www.prairiemountainhealth.ca
Note: ACCESS Centres offer health & social services. Programs & services at this location include: nurse practitioner; community health nurse; adult community mental health worker; community

social worker; addictions services; housing resource worker; cultural facilitators; consumer peer support educator; & Community Volunteer Income Tax Program.

Camperville: **Camperville Health Centre**
Affiliated with: Prairie Mountain Health
PO Box 177, Camperville, MB R0L 0J0
Tel: 204-524-2169
www.prairiemountainhealth.ca
Note: Services include: diabetes / heart / chronic disease program (877-509-7852); home care; mental health; Telehealth; & public health.

Carberry: **Carberry Plains Health Centre**
Affiliated with: Prairie Mountain Health
PO Box 2000, 340 Toronto St., Carberry, MB R0K 0H0
Tel: 204-834-2144 Fax: 204-834-3333
www.prairiemountainhealth.ca
Number of Beds: 10 acute care beds
Note: Programs & service include: acute care; diagnostic; emergency; EMS / ambulance; public health; mental health; home care; physicians clinic; primary care nurse; dietitian; Meals on Wheels; palliative care; & occupational & physiotherapy. Also has Personal Care Home on site.

Cartwright: **Davidson Memorial Health Centre**
Affiliated with: Prairie Mountain Health
Former Name: Cartwright & District Hospital
PO Box 118, 345 Davidson St., Cartwright, MB R0K 0L0
Tel: 204-529-2483 Fax: 204-529-2562
www.prairiemountainhealth.ca
Number of Beds: 10 beds
Note: Programs & services include: transitional care; home care; mental health; public health; & Meals on Wheels.

Churchill: **Churchill Health Centre**
Affiliated with: Winnipeg Regional Health Authority
162 La Vérendrye Ave., Churchill, MB R0B 0E0
Tel: 204-675-8881
www.churchillhealthcentre.com
www.facebook.com/ChurchillHealthCentre
Number of Beds: 21 acute care beds
Area Served: Churchill; Kivalliq Region of Nunavut *Population Served:* 831 *Number of Employees:* 129
Note: Health & social services include: acute care; primary care clinic; diagnostic; dental clinic / oral surgery; clinical & retail pharmacy; optometry; physiotherapy; chiropractic; massage therapy; mental health; public health; probation; addictions; children & family; child & youth receiving home; home care; Children's Centre; & Telehealth.
Services provided through the J.A. Hildes Northern Medical Unit, Department of Community Medicine, University of Manitoba, include: anaesthesia; orthopedics; surgery; geriatrics; internal medicine; gynaecology; ophthalmology; otolaryngology; paediatrics; colposcopy; psychiatry; pediatric dental surgery; & urology.
Patti Macewan, Acting Chief Operating Officer
Charlene Cornwallis-Bate, Director, Integrated Health & Integrated Services
ccharlene@wrha-ch.ca
Bobbi Sigurdson, Director, Corporate Services
bsigurdson2@wrha-ch.ca

Cormorant: **Cormorant Health Care Centre**
Affiliated with: Northern Regional Health Authority
PO Box 42, 103 Clark St., Cormorant, MB R0B 0G0
Tel: 204-357-2161 Fax: 204-357-2259
www.northernhealthregion.ca

Cranberry Portage: **Cranberry Portage Wellness Centre**
Affiliated with: Northern Regional Health Authority
PO Box 186, Cranberry Portage, MB R0B 0H0
Tel: 204-472-3338 Fax: 204-472-3389
www.northernhealthregion.ca

Crane River: **Crane River Health Services**
Affiliated with: Prairie Mountain Health
PO Box 156, Crane River, MB R0L 0M0
Tel: 204-732-2286
www.prairiemountainhealth.ca
Note: Programs & services include: home care; mental health; primary health care; public health; & diabetes / heart / chronic disease program (877-509-7852).

Dauphin: **Dauphin Community Health Services**
Affiliated with: Prairie Mountain Health
625 - 3rd St. SW, Dauphin, MB R7N 1R7
Tel: 204-638-2118 Fax: 204-629-3406
www.prairiemountainhealth.ca
Note: Includes home care services (204-638-2105). Other services include: mental health; child health; immunization;

infection prevention & control; prenatal; sexual health; & school health programs.

Duck Bay: **Duck Bay Community Health**
Affiliated with: Prairie Mountain Health
PO Box 133, Duck Bay, MB R0L 0N0
Tel: 204-524-2176
www.prairiemountainhealth.ca
Note: Programs & services include: diabetes / heart / chronic disease program (877-509-7852); home care; mental health; primary health care; & public health

Ebb & Flow: **Bacon Ridge Community Health Services**
Affiliated with: Prairie Mountain Health
General Delivery, Post Office Bldg., Ebb & Flow, MB R0L 0R0
Tel: 204-448-2229
www.prairiemountainhealth.ca
Note: Services include: home care; mental health; primary health care; & public health.

Erickson: **Erickson Health Centre**
Affiliated with: Prairie Mountain Health
PO Box 25, 60 Queen Elizabeth Rd., Erickson, MB R0J 0P0
Tel: 204-636-7777 Fax: 204-636-2471
www.prairiemountainhealth.ca
Number of Beds: 9 transitional care beds
Note: Programs & services include: transitional care; diagnostic; EMS / ambulance; public health; mental health; home care; physicians; primary care nurse; Meals on Wheels; & community bath program.

Ethelbert: **Ethelbert Community Health Services**
Affiliated with: Prairie Mountain Health
PO Box 156, 31 Railway Ave., Ethelbert, MB R0L 0T0
Tel: 204-742-4400
www.prairiemountainhealth.ca
Note: Services include: diabetes / heart / chronic disease program (877-509-7852); family physician; home care; cancer navigation (855-346-3710); mental health; primary health care; & public health

Gilbert Plains: **Gilbert Plains Health Centre**
Affiliated with: Prairie Mountain Health
PO Box 368, 100 Cutforth St. North, Gilbert Plains, MB R0L 0X0
Tel: 204-548-2161
www.prairiemountainhealth.ca
Note: Physician clinic attached to Gilbert Plains Personal Care Home. Services include: emergency / ambulance; home care; mental health; primary health care; & public health.

Glenboro: **Glenboro Health Centre**
Affiliated with: Prairie Mountain Health
Former Name: Glenboro Health District Hospital
PO Box 310, 219 Murray Ave., Glenboro, MB R0K 0X0
Tel: 204-827-2438 Fax: 204-827-2199
www.prairiemountainhealth.ca
Number of Beds: 20 long-term care beds; 11 acute care beds
Note: Programs & services include: acute care; diagnostic; EMS / ambulance; public health; mental health; home care; physicians clinic; palliative care; occupational & physiotherapy; dietitian; & Meals on Wheels. Also includes a Personal Care Home on site.

Hamiota: **Hamiota Health Centre**
Affiliated with: Prairie Mountain Health
177 Birch Ave., Hamiota, MB R0M 0T0
Tel: 204-764-2412 Fax: 204-764-2049
www.prairiemountainhealth.ca
Number of Beds: 30 personal care home beds
Note: Programs & services include: acute care; community cancer program; diagnostic; EMS / ambulance; public health; mental health; home care; Manitoba Telehealth; physicians clinic; primary care nurse; palliative care; occupational & physiotherapy; dietitian; Meals on Wheels; Lilac Elderly Person Housing (30 units); & congregate meal program.

Hartney: **Hartney Health Centre**
Affiliated with: Prairie Mountain Health
Former Name: Hartney Medical Nursing Unit
PO Box 280, 617 River Ave., Hartney, MB R0M 0X0
Tel: 204-858-2054 Fax: 204-858-2303
www.prairiemountainhealth.ca
Number of Beds: 20 personal care beds
Note: Programs & services include: rehabilitation; long-term care; public health; mental health; & home care. Also includes a Personal Care Home on site.

Ilford: **Ilford Community Health Centre**
Affiliated with: Northern Regional Health Authority
53 First St., Ilford, MB R0B 0S0
Tel: 204-288-4348 Fax: 204-288-4248
www.northernhealthregion.ca

Killarney: **Tri-Lake Health Centre**
Affiliated with: Prairie Mountain Health
PO Box 5000, 86 Ellis Dr., Killarney, MB R0K 1G0
Tel: 204-523-4661
www.prairiemountainhealth.ca
Number of Beds: 60 personal care beds
Note: Programs & services include: acute care; diagnostic; EMS / ambulance; public health; mental health; home care; Manitoba Telehealth; physicians clinic; palliative care; occupational & physiotherapy; dietitian; & Meals on Wheels.

Lac du Bonnet: **Lac du Bonnet Primary Health Care Centre**
Affiliated with: Interlake-Eastern Regional Health Authority
89 McIntosh St., Lac du Bonnet, MB R0E 1A0
Tel: 204-345-8647 Fax: 204-345-8609
www.ierha.ca
Note: Diagnostics; physiotherapy; counselling; clinic.
Lorri Beer, Regional Manager, Physician Services

Leaf Rapids: **Leaf Rapids Health Centre**
Affiliated with: Northern Regional Health Authority
PO Box 370, 1 Mooswu Rd., Leaf Rapids, MB R0B 1W0
Tel: 204-473-2441 Fax: 204-473-8273
www.northernhealthregion.ca
Year Founded: 1973

Lundar: **Lundar Health Centre**
Affiliated with: Interlake-Eastern Regional Health Authority
97 - 1st St. South, Lundar, MB R0C 1Y0
Tel: 204-762-6076
www.ierha.ca
Note: Nurse Practitioner Clinic (one day a week)

Lundar: **Lundar Medical Clinic**
38 Main St., Lundar, MB R0C 1Y0
Tel: 204-762-5609
Note: Private clinic

McCreary: **McCreary Community Health Services**
Affiliated with: Prairie Mountain Health
PO Box 208, 613 Provincial Trunk Hwy. 50, McCreary, MB R0J 1B0
Tel: 204-835-5010 Fax: 204-835-5011
www.prairiemountainhealth.ca
Note: Offers public health services

Minnedosa: **Minnedosa Health Centre**
Affiliated with: Prairie Mountain Health
PO Box 960, 334 1st St. SW, Minnedosa, MB R0J 1E0
Tel: 204-867-2701 Fax: 204-867-2239
www.prairiemountainhealth.ca
Number of Beds: 27 acute care beds
Note: Programs & services include: acute care; general surgery; diagnostic; EMS / ambulance; public health; mental health; home care; physicians clinic; occupational & physiotherapy; dietitian; & Meals on Wheels.

Opaskwayak: **Beatrice Wilson Health Centre**
Affiliated with: Northern Regional Health Authority
245 Waller Rd., Opaskwayak, MB R0B 2J0
Tel: 204-627-7410 Fax: 204-623-1491
www.northernhealthregion.ca

Pikwitonei: **Pikwitonei Community Health Centre**
Affiliated with: Northern Regional Health Authority
General Delivery, Pikwitonei, MB R0B 1E0
Tel: 204-458-2402 Fax: 204-458-2468
www.northernhealthregion.ca

Pinawa: **Pinawa Primary Health Care Centre**
Affiliated with: Interlake-Eastern Regional Health Authority
30 Vanier Dr., Pinawa, MB R0E 1L0
Tel: 204-753-2351
www.ierha.ca

Pine Falls: **Pine Falls Primary Health Care Centre Complex**
Affiliated with: Interlake-Eastern Regional Health Authority
37 Maple St., Pine Falls, MB R0E 1M0
Tel: 204-367-2278
www.ierha.ca

Reston: Reston Health Centre
Affiliated with: Prairie Mountain Health
PO Box 250, 523 1st St. North, Reston, MB R0M 1X0
Tel: 204-877-3925
www.prairiemountainhealth.ca
Number of Beds: 20 personal care beds
Note: Programs & services include: transitional care; public health; mental health; home care; long-term care; occupational & physiotherapy; primary health care; & Meals on Wheels.

Rivers: Riverdale Health Centre
Affiliated with: Prairie Mountain Health
PO Box 428, 512 Quebec St., Rivers, MB R0K 1X0
Tel: 204-328-5321 *Fax:* 204-328-7130
www.prairiemountainhealth.ca
Number of Beds: 20 personal care beds
Note: Programs & services include: rehabilitation unit; diagnostic; public health; mental health; home care; physicians clinics; palliative care; occupational & physiotherapy; dietitian; Meals on Wheels & elderly persons housing (12 units).
Greg Paddock, Area Manager

Riverton: Riverton Community Health Office
Affiliated with: Interlake-Eastern Regional Health Authority
68 Main St., Riverton, MB R0C 2R0
Tel: 204-378-2460
www.ierha.ca

Roblin: Roblin Community Health Service
Affiliated with: Prairie Mountain Health
PO Box 940, 15 Hospital St., Roblin, MB R0L 1P0
Tel: 204-937-2151
www.prairiemountainhealth.ca
Note: Includes home care (204-937-6271), community rehabilitation, & mental health services.

Rossburn: Rossburn District Health Centre
Affiliated with: Prairie Mountain Health
PO Box 40, 166 Parkview Dr., Rossburn, MB R0J 1V0
Tel: 204-859-2413
www.prairiemountainhealth.ca
Number of Beds: 20 personal care beds
Note: Programs & services include: transitional care; diagnostic; public health; mental health; home care; physician clinic; primary care nurse; palliative care; occupational & physiotherapy; & dietitian.

Selkirk: Clandeboye Medical Clinic & Interlake Surgical Associates
210 Clandeboye Ave., Selkirk, MB R1A 0X1
Tel: 204-785-2555 *Fax:* 204-482-4525
www.clandeboyeclinic.ca
Note: Interlake Surgical Associates Phone: 204-785-5507.
Clandeboye Medical Clinic specializes in general & family practice.
Interlake Surgical Associates specializes in general, endoscopic, & laparoscopic surgery.

Selkirk: Eveline Street Clinic
Affiliated with: Interlake-Eastern Regional Health Authority
62-Eveline St., Selkirk, MB R1A 1K6
Tel: 204-785-5550 *Fax:* 204-785-5555
evelinestreetclinic.ca
Note: Alternate phone: 204-785-5552

Selkirk: Selkirk Medical Centre
Affiliated with: Interlake-Eastern Regional Health Authority
353 Eveline St., Selkirk, MB R1A 1N1
contact@selkirkmedicalassociates.ca
www.selkirkmedicalassociates.ca
Note: Physicians at this location should be contacted directly

Selkirk: Selkirk QuickCare Clinic
Affiliated with: Interlake-Eastern Regional Health Authority
#3, 1020 Manitoba Ave., Selkirk, MB R1A 4M2
Tel: 204-482-4399
www.ierha.ca
Note: Part of Manitoba's QuickCare Clinic initiative; for diagnosing & treating minor health issues.

Selkirk: Selkirk Travel Health Clinic
Affiliated with: Interlake-Eastern Regional Health Authority
#202, 237 Manitoba Ave., Selkirk, MB R1A 0Y4
Tel: 204-785-4891
www.ierha.ca
Note: Appointments available only on Wednesdays

Sherridon: Sherridon Health Centre
Affiliated with: Northern Regional Health Authority
General Delivery, Sherridon, MB R0B 1L0
Tel: 204-468-2012 *Fax:* 204-468-2167
www.northernhealthregion.ca

Snow Lake: Snow Lake Health Centre
Affiliated with: Northern Regional Health Authority
100 Lakeshore Dr., Snow Lake, MB R0B 1M0
Tel: 204-358-2300 *Fax:* 204-358-7310
www.northernhealthregion.ca
Number of Beds: 3 long-term care beds
Kelly Wiwcharuk, Nurse Manager

St. Laurent: St. Laurent Health Centre
Affiliated with: Interlake-Eastern Regional Health Authority
51 Parish Lane, St. Laurent, MB R0C 2S0
Tel: 204-646-2504
www.ierha.ca
Note: Nurse Practitioner Clinic (one day a week)

Ste Rose: Ste Rose Community Health Services
Affiliated with: Prairie Mountain Health
PO Box 149, 603 - 1st Ave. East, Ste Rose, MB R0L 1S0
Tel: 204-447-4080
www.prairiemountainhealth.ca
Note: Services include: home care; mental health; public health; occupational therapy; speech therapy; physiotherapy; & Telehealth.

Stonewall: Interlake Medicentre - Stonewall
Affiliated with: Interlake-Eastern Regional Health Authority
#2, 330 - 3 Ave. South, Stonewall, MB R0C 2Z0
Tel: 204-467-5717 *Fax:* 204-272-6775
www.ierha.ca

Stonewall: Stonewall Medical Group
Affiliated with: Interlake-Eastern Regional Health Authority
583 - 3rd Ave. South, Stonewall, MB R0C 2Z0
Tel: 204-467-5509
www.ierha.ca

Swan River: Swan River Community Health Services
Affiliated with: Prairie Mountain Health
PO Box 1028, 1013 Main St., Swan River, MB R0L 1Z0
Tel: 204-734-6660
www.prairiemountainhealth.ca
Note: Services include: acute care; outpatient; diagnostic; emergency / ambulance; rehabilitation; home care; mental health; long-term care; primary health care; public health; & Telehealth.

Teulon: Teulon - Private Clinic
34 Main St., Teulon, MB R0C 3B0
Tel: 204-886-3039

Thicket Portage: Thicket Portage Health Centre
Affiliated with: Northern Regional Health Authority
398 Evens Ave., Thicket Portage, MB R0B 1R0
Tel: 204-286-3254 *Fax:* 204-286-3216
www.northernhealthregion.ca

Thompson: Burntwood Community Health Resource Centre
Affiliated with: Northern Regional Health Authority
50 Selkirk Ave., Thompson, MB R8N 0M7
Tel: 204-677-1777 *Fax:* 204-677-1755
Note: Family doctor.

Treherne: Tiger Hills Health Centre
Affiliated with: Prairie Mountain Health
PO Box 130, 64 Clark St., Treherne, MB R0G 2V0
Tel: 204-723-2133 *Fax:* 204-723-2869
www.prairiemountainhealth.ca
Number of Beds: 22 personal care beds; 13 acute care beds
Note: Programs & services include: acute care; diagnostic; emergency; public health; mental health; home care; physician clinic; palliative care; occupation & physiotherapy; dietitian; Meals on Wheels; & Elderly Persons Housing (21 units).

Virden: Virden Health Centre
Affiliated with: Prairie Mountain Health
PO Box 400, 480 King St., Virden, MB R0M 2C0
Tel: 204-748-1230 *Fax:* 204-748-2053
www.prairiemountainhealth.ca
Number of Beds: 25 acute care beds
Note: Programs & services include: acute care; diagnostic; EMS / ambulance; laboratory; Manitoba Telehealth; physician clinic; palliative care; occupational & physiotherapy; & dietitian

Wabowden: Wabowden Community Health Centre
Affiliated with: Northern Regional Health Authority
88 Lakeside Dr., Wabowden, MB R0B 1S0
Tel: 204-689-2600 *Fax:* 204-689-2180
www.northernhealthregion.ca

Waterhen: Waterhen Health Centre
Affiliated with: Prairie Mountain Health
PO Box 10, 104 North Mallard Rd., Waterhen, MB R0L 2C0
Tel: 204-628-3329
www.prairiemountainhealth.ca
Note: Services include: emergency / ambulance; home care; mental health; primary health care; & public health.

Wawanesa: Wawanesa Health Centre
Affiliated with: Prairie Mountain Health
Former Name: Wawanesa & District Memorial Health Centre
PO Box 309, 506 George St., Wawanesa, MB R0K 2G0
Tel: 204-824-2335 *Fax:* 204-824-2148
www.prairiemountainhealth.ca
Number of Beds: 20 personal care beds; 6 transitional care beds
Note: Programs & services include: transitional care; diagnostic; public health; mental health; home care; physician clinic; primary care nurse; occupational & physiotherapy; dietitian; & Meals on Wheels.

Whitemouth: Whitemouth Primary Health Care Centre
Affiliated with: Interlake-Eastern Regional Health Authority
75 Hospital St., Whitemouth, MB R0E 2G0
Tel: 204-348-2291
www.ierha.ca

Winnipeg: Aboriginal Health & Wellness Centre
Affiliated with: Winnipeg Regional Health Authority
#215, 181 Higgins Ave., Winnipeg, MB R3B 3G1
Tel: 204-925-3700 *Fax:* 204-925-3709
www.wrha.mb.ca
Note: Programs & services include: traditional medicine; diabetes education; children's health; & health promotion.
Darlene Hall, Executive Director

Winnipeg: ACCESS Downtown
Affiliated with: Winnipeg Regional Health Authority
#2, 640 Main St., Winnipeg, MB R3B 0L8
Tel: 204-940-3638
www.wrha.mb.ca
Note: ACCESS Centres offer health & social services; programs & services vary by community.

Winnipeg: ACCESS Fort Garry
Affiliated with: Winnipeg Regional Health Authority
135 Plaza Dr., Winnipeg, MB R3T 6E8
Tel: 204-940-7100
www.wrha.mb.ca
Note: ACCESS Centres offer health & social services; programs & services vary by community.

Winnipeg: ACCESS NorWest
Affiliated with: Winnipeg Regional Health Authority
785 Keewatin St., Winnipeg, MB R2X 3B9
Tel: 204-938-5900
www.wrha.mb.ca
Note: ACCESS Centres offer health & social services; programs & services vary by community. This branch is in the same location as NorWest Co-op Community Health.

Winnipeg: ACCESS River East
Affiliated with: Winnipeg Regional Health Authority
975 Henderson Hwy., Winnipeg, MB R2K 4L7
Tel: 204-938-5000
www.wrha.mb.ca
Note: ACCESS Centres offer health & social services; programs & services vary by community.

Winnipeg: ACCESS St. Boniface
Affiliated with: Winnipeg Regional Health Authority
170 Goulet St., Winnipeg, MB R2H 0R7
Tel: 204-940-1692
www.wrha.mb.ca
Note: ACCESS Centres offer health & social services; programs & services vary by community.

Winnipeg: ACCESS Transcona
Affiliated with: Winnipeg Regional Health Authority
845 Regent Ave. West, Winnipeg, MB R2C 3A9
Tel: 204-938-5555
www.wrha.mb.ca
Note: ACCESS Centres offer health & social services; programs & services vary by community.

Winnipeg: ACCESS Winnipeg West
Affiliated with: Winnipeg Regional Health Authority
280 Booth Dr., Winnipeg, MB R3J 3R5
Tel: 204-940-2040
www.wrha.mb.ca
Note: ACCESS Centres offer health & social services; programs
& services vary by community. St. James clients
(204-940-2397); Assiniboine South clients (204-940-2453).

Winnipeg: Centre de santé Saint-Boniface/St.
Boniface Health Centre
Affiliated with: Winnipeg Regional Health Authority
170 Goulet St., Winnipeg, MB R2H 0R7
Tel: 204-940-1155 Fax: 204-237-9057
access@centresante.mb.ca
www.centredesante.mb.ca
www.facebook.com/centredesantesaintboniface
Note: Bilingual primary health centre. Programs & services
include: medical; nutrition; mental health; community support; &
Health Links - Info Santé.
Monique Constant, Executive Director

Winnipeg: Community Health and Social Services
Centre
Affiliated with: Winnipeg Regional Health Authority
755 Portage Ave., Winnipeg, MB R3G 0N2
Tel: 204-940-2236
www.wrha.mb.ca

Winnipeg: Hope Centre Health Care Inc.
Affiliated with: Winnipeg Regional Health Authority
240 Powers St., Winnipeg, MB R2W 5L1
Tel: 204-589-8354 Fax: 204-586-4260
hopece@mymts.net
hopecentrehealthcare.com
Year Founded: 1982
Note: Programs & services include primary care, outreach and
counselling.

Winnipeg: Klinic Community Health Centre
Affiliated with: Winnipeg Regional Health Authority
870 Portage Ave., Winnipeg, MB R3G 0P1
Tel: 204-784-4090 Fax: 204-772-7998
info@klinic.mb.ca
www.klinic.mb.ca
Nicole Chammartin, Executive Director
204-784-4075, nchammartin@klinic.mb.ca

Winnipeg: MFL Occupational Health Centre, Inc.
Affiliated with: Winnipeg Regional Health Authority
#102, 275 Broadway, Winnipeg, MB R3C 4M6
Tel: 204-949-0811 Fax: 204-956-0848
Toll-Free: 888-843-1229
mflohc@mflohc.mb.ca
www.mflohc.mb.ca
www.facebook.com/OccupationalHealthCentre;
www.linkedin.com/company/mfl-occupational-health-centre
Year Founded: 1983
Note: Specializes in occupational health (health issues related to
work experiences), improvement of workplace health & safety
conditions, & elimination of hazards.
Carly Nicholson, Executive Director
204-926-7900, cnicholson@mflohc.mb.ca

Winnipeg: Misericordia Health Centre (MHC)
Affiliated with: Winnipeg Regional Health Authority
99 Cornish Ave., Winnipeg, MB R3C 1A2
Tel: 204-774-6581 Fax: 204-783-6052
info@misericordia.mb.ca
www.misericordia.mb.ca
www.facebook.com/MisericordiaMB; twitter.com/MisericordiaMB;
instagram.com/misericordiamb
Year Founded: 1898
Number of Beds: 250 beds; 100 personal care home beds
Note: Research & teaching health centre, with programs &
services including: ambulatory care; Buhler Eye Care Centre;
Community IV Program; diagnostics; Easy Street rehabilitation
program; eye bank; interim care; laboratory; long-term care
(through Misericordia Place); Health Care for Lungs;
occupational therapy; ophthalmology; pediatric dental surgery;
Provincial Health Contact Centre; physiotherapy; recreation
therapy; rehabilitation services; respiratory therapy; Sleep
Disorder Centre; social work; spiritual & religious care; & support
services.
Raymond Cadieux, Chair of the Board, Misericordia Corporation
Caroline DeKeyster, President & CEO

Winnipeg: Mount Carmel Clinic
Affiliated with: Winnipeg Regional Health Authority
886 Main St., Winnipeg, MB R2W 5L4
Tel: 204-582-2311 Fax: 204-582-6006
info@mountcarmel.ca
www.mountcarmel.ca
Year Founded: 1926
Note: Health services include: Aboriginal health & wellness;
child; dental; general health; Hepatitis C clinic; homeless / harm
reduction; immigrant / refugee; LGBT; mental health; pregnancy /
parenting; reproductive / sexual health; & youth.
Bobbette Shoffner, Executive Director
204-582-0311, bshoffner@mountcarmel.ca
Al Shpeller, Director, Operations
204-589-9476, ashpeller@mountcarmel.ca

Winnipeg: Nine Circles Community Health Centre
Affiliated with: Winnipeg Regional Health Authority
705 Broadway, Winnipeg, MB R3G 0X2
Tel: 204-940-6000 Fax: 204-940-6003
Toll-Free: 888-305-8647
ninecircles@ninecircles.ca
www.ninecircles.ca
www.facebook.com/NineCirclesCommunityHealthCentre;
twitter.com/ninecircleschc; instagram.com/ninecircleschc
Note: Non-profit centre specializing in STI / HIV prevention &
care services.
Michael Payne, Executive Director

Winnipeg: NorWest Co-op Community Health
Affiliated with: Winnipeg Regional Health Authority
Also Known As: Inkster/Nor'west Co-op Community
Health Centre
785 Keewatin St., Winnipeg, MB R2X 3B9
Tel: 204-938-5900 Fax: 204-938-5994
www.norwestcoop.ca
www.facebook.com/193978229794; twitter.com/NorWestCoop;
www.instagram.com/norwestcoop
Note: Programs & services include: primary health care;
community development; counselling & support services; & early
learning & childcare. This health centre is in the same location
as ACCESS NorWest.
Ivan Sabesky, President & Board Chair

Winnipeg: Street Connections
Affiliated with: Winnipeg Regional Health Authority
496 Hargrave St., Winnipeg, MB R3A 0X7
Tel: 204-981-0742
outreach@wrha.mb.ca
www.streetconnections.ca
Note: Mobile harm reduction program specializing in harm
reduction & free services to those in need. Programs & services
include: general assistance (housing, addictions, food, legal, &
more); counselling; nursing services; prenatal services; clean
drug use supplies; needle exchange; & safe sex supplies.

Winnipeg: Win Gardner Place
Affiliated with: Winnipeg Regional Health Authority
Former Name: North End Wellness Centre
363 McGregor St., Winnipeg, MB R2W 4X4
Tel: 204-925-4486
www.wingardnerplace.ca
www.facebook.com/WinGardnerPlace;
twitter.com/WinGardnerPlace
Note: A collaborative effort among the following organizations:
Ma Mawi Wi Chi Itata Centre, the YMCA-YWCA of Winnipeg,
North End Community Renewal Corp., SPLASH Child
Enrichment Centre & the Winnipeg Regional Health Authority.

Winnipeg: Winnipeg West Integrated Health & Social
Services
Affiliated with: Winnipeg Regional Health Authority
280 Booth Dr., Winnipeg, MB R3J 3R5
Tel: 204-940-2040
www.wrha.mb.ca
Note: This office is in the same location as ACCESS Winnipeg
West.

Winnipeg: Women's Health Clinic Inc. (WHC)
Affiliated with: Winnipeg Regional Health Authority
419 Graham Ave., #A, Winnipeg, MB R3C 0M3
Tel: 204-947-1517 Fax: 204-943-3844
Toll-Free: 866-947-1517
TTY: 204-956-0385
whc@womenshealthclinic.org
www.womenshealthclinic.org
www.facebook.com/WHCwpg; twitter.com/whcwpg;
www.instagram.com/WHCwpg
Year Founded: 1981
Note: Services include: parenting support; mental health; eating
disorder workshops & support groups; reproductive & sexual
health; nutrition counselling; primary care; & health promotion.

Amy Tuckett, Specialist, Communications
atuckett@womenshealthclinic.org

Winnipeg: WRHA Point Douglas
Affiliated with: Winnipeg Regional Health Authority
601 Aikins St., Winnipeg, MB R2W 4J5
Tel: 204-940-2025
www.wrha.mb.ca
Note: Provides services related to: healthy parenting & early
childhood development; healthy children & youth; nutrition
promotion; communicable disease prevention & management;
immunization; & more.

Winnipeg: WRHA Seven Oaks
Affiliated with: Winnipeg Regional Health Authority
#3, 1050 Leila Ave., Winnipeg, MB R2P 1W6
Tel: 204-938-5600
www.wrha.mb.ca
Note: Provides services related to: healthy parenting & early
childhood development; healthy children & youth; nutrition
promotion; communicable disease prevention & management;
immunization; & more.

Winnipeg: Youville - St. Vital Community Health
Centre
Affiliated with: Winnipeg Regional Health Authority
Also Known As: Youville Community Health Centre
St. Vital Square, #6, 845 Dakota St., Winnipeg, MB R2M 5M3
Tel: 204-255-4840 Fax: 204-255-4903
www.youville.ca
Year Founded: 1984
Note: Programs & services include: health care & wellness
education; counselling; & support. This Centre is in the same
location as the WRHA St. Vital Community Office.
Patrick Griffith, Executive Director

Winnipegosis: Winnipegosis Community Health
Services
Affiliated with: Prairie Mountain Health
PO Box 280, 230 Bridge St., Winnipegosis, MB R0L 2G0
Tel: 204-656-4881
www.prairiemountainhealth.ca
Note: Services include: transitional care; palliative care;
rehabilitation; diagnostic; laboratory; emergency / ambulance;
occupational therapy; home care; mental health; long-term care;
primary health care; public health; Telehealth; & Meals on
Wheels.

Woodlands: Woodlands Clinic
Affiliated with: Interlake-Eastern Regional Health
Authority
78 Porteous Ave., Woodlands, MB R0C 3H0
Tel: 204-383-5970
www.ierha.ca

Nursing Stations

Berens River: Berens River Nursing Station
First Nations Health Group
Affiliated with: Interlake-Eastern Regional Health
Authority
General Delivery, Berens River, MB R0B 0A0
Tel: 204-382-2285
Population Served: 3310 Number of Employees: 5

Bloodvein: Bloodvein Nursing Station
First Nations Health Group
Affiliated with: Interlake-Eastern Regional Health
Authority
General Delivery, Bloodvein, MB R0C 0J0
Tel: 204-395-2161 Fax: 204-395-2087
Population Served: 1760 Number of Employees: 2

Brochet: Brochet/Barren Lands Nursing Station
Affiliated with: Northern Regional Health Authority
General Delivery, Brochet, MB R0B 0B0
Tel: 204-323-2120 Fax: 204-323-2650
www.northernhealthregion.ca
Number of Beds: 6 beds
Number of Employees: 3

Cross Lake: Cross Lake Nursing Station
First Nations Health Group
Affiliated with: Northern Regional Health Authority
PO Box 160, Cross Lake, MB R0B 0J0
Tel: 204-676-2011 Fax: 204-676-3179
www.northernhealthregion.ca
Population Served: 5000 Number of Employees: 15

Easterville: Easterville/Chemawawin Nursing Station
Affiliated with: Northern Regional Health Authority
PO Box 122, Easterville, MB R0C 0V0
Tel: 204-329-2212 *Fax:* 204-329-2337
www.northernhealthregion.ca
Number of Employees: 6

Garden Hill: Garden Hill Nursing Station
First Nations Health Group
Affiliated with: Northern Regional Health Authority
PO Box 264, Garden Hill, MB R0B 0T0
Tel: 204-456-2615 *Fax:* 204-456-2866
www.northernhealthregion.ca
Population Served: 3200 *Number of Employees:* 4

God's Lake: God's Lake Nursing Station
First Nations Health Group
Affiliated with: Northern Regional Health Authority
Former Name: God's Lake Narrows Nursing Station
General Delivery, God's Lake, MB R0B 0M0
Tel: 204-335-2557 *Fax:* 204-335-2043
www.northernhealthregion.ca
Population Served: 2170 *Number of Employees:* 3

God's River: God's River/Manto Sipi Nursing Station
First Nations Health Group
Affiliated with: Northern Regional Health Authority
Also Known As: God's River Health Station
PO Box 100, God's River, MB R0B 0N0
Tel: 204-366-2355 *Fax:* 204-366-2474
www.northernhealthregion.ca
Population Served: 620 *Number of Employees:* 2

Grand Rapids: Grand Rapids/Misipawistik Nursing Station
Affiliated with: Northern Regional Health Authority
PO Box 53, Grand Rapids, MB R0C 1E0
Tel: 204-639-2215 *Fax:* 204-639-2448
www.northernhealthregion.ca

Lac Brochet: Lac Brochet/Northlands Nursing Station
First Nations Health Group
Affiliated with: Northern Regional Health Authority
PO Box 90, Lac Brochet, MB R0B 2E0
Tel: 204-337-2161 *Fax:* 204-337-2143
www.northernhealthregion.ca
Population Served: 630 *Number of Employees:* 2

Little Grand Rapids: Little Grand Rapids Nursing Station
First Nations Health Group
Affiliated with: Interlake-Eastern Regional Health Authority
General Delivery, Little Grand Rapids, MB R0B 0V0
Tel: 204-397-2115
Population Served: 1555 *Number of Employees:* 2

Moose Lake: Moose Lake/Mosakahiken Nursing Station
Affiliated with: Northern Regional Health Authority
General Delivery, Moose Lake, MB R0B 0Y0
Tel: 204-678-2252 *Fax:* 204-678-2343
www.northernhealthregion.ca

Negginan: Poplar River Nursing Station
First Nations Health Group
Affiliated with: Interlake-Eastern Regional Health Authority
General Delivery, Negginan, MB R0B 0Z0
Tel: 204-244-2102 *Fax:* 204-244-2001
Population Served: 1843 *Number of Employees:* 2

Nelson House: Nelson House/Nisichawayasihk Nursing Station
First Nations Health Group
Affiliated with: Northern Regional Health Authority
General Delivery, Nelson House, MB R0B 1A0
Tel: 204-484-2031 *Fax:* 204-484-2284
www.northernhealthregion.ca
Population Served: 2500 *Number of Employees:* 5

Norway House: Norway House Nursing Station
Norway House Health Services Inc.
Affiliated with: Northern Regional Health Authority
Also Known As: Norway House Hospital
PO Box 730, Norway House, MB R0B 1B0
Tel: 204-359-8230 *Fax:* 204-359-6599
www.northernhealthregion.ca
Number of Employees: 20
Note: Programs & services include: dialysis; laboratory; x-ray; & dietary.

Oxford House: Oxford House/Bunibonibee Nursing Station
First Nations Health Group
Affiliated with: Northern Regional Health Authority
General Delivery, Oxford House, MB R0B 1C0
Tel: 204-538-2347 *Fax:* 204-538-2445
www.northernhealthregion.ca
Year Founded: 2011
Population Served: 2325 *Number of Employees:* 4

Pauingassi: Pauingassi Nursing Station
First Nations Health Group
Affiliated with: Interlake-Eastern Regional Health Authority
Pauingassi, MB R0B 2G0
Tel: 204-397-2395
Population Served: 612 *Number of Employees:* 2

Pukatawagan: Pukatawagan/Mathias Colomb Nursing Station
First Nations Health Group
Affiliated with: Northern Regional Health Authority
Also Known As: Nikawiy Nursing Station
General Delivery, Pukatawagan, MB R0B 1G0
Tel: 204-553-2271 *Fax:* 204-553-2241
www.northernhealthregion.ca
Population Served: 1464 *Number of Employees:* 5

Red Sucker Lake: Red Sucker Lake Nursing Station
First Nations Health Group
Affiliated with: Northern Regional Health Authority
General Delivery, Red Sucker Lake, MB R0B 1H0
Tel: 204-469-5321 *Fax:* 204-469-5769
www.northernhealthregion.ca
Population Served: 814 *Number of Employees:* 3

Shamattawa: Shamattawa Nursing Station
First Nations Health Group
Affiliated with: Northern Regional Health Authority
General Delivery, Shamattawa, MB R0B 1K0
Tel: 204-565-2370 *Fax:* 204-565-2519
www.northernhealthregion.ca
Population Served: 1426 *Number of Employees:* 4

South Indian Lake: South Indian Lake/O-Pipon-Na-Piwin Nursing Station
First Nations Health Group
Affiliated with: Northern Regional Health Authority
PO Box 22, South Indian Lake, MB R0B 1N0
Tel: 204-374-2013 *Fax:* 204-374-2039
www.northernhealthregion.ca
Number of Beds: 5 beds
Population Served: 1452 *Number of Employees:* 3

Split Lake: Split Lake/Tataskweyak Nursing Station
First Nations Health Group
Affiliated with: Northern Regional Health Authority
General Delivery, Split Lake, MB R0B 1P0
Tel: 204-342-2033 *Fax:* 204-342-2319
www.northernhealthregion.ca
Year Founded: 2009
Population Served: 1500 *Number of Employees:* 5

St. Theresa Point: St Theresa Point Nursing Station
First Nations Health Group
Affiliated with: Northern Regional Health Authority
General Delivery, St. Theresa Point, MB R0B 1J0
Tel: 204-462-2264 *Fax:* 204-462-2642
www.northernhealthregion.ca
Year Founded: 2010
Population Served: 2630 *Number of Employees:* 5

Tadoule Lake: Tadoule Lake/Sayisi Nursing Station
First Nations Health Group
Affiliated with: Northern Regional Health Authority
General Delivery, Tadoule Lake, MB R0B 2C0
Tel: 204-684-2031 *Fax:* 204-684-2049
www.northernhealthregion.ca
Population Served: 330 *Number of Employees:* 2

Waasagamach: Wasagamack Nursing Station
First Nations Health Group
Affiliated with: Northern Regional Health Authority
General Delivery, Waasagamach, MB R0B 1Z0
Tel: 204-457-2189 *Fax:* 204-457-2348
www.northernhealthregion.ca
Population Served: 1400 *Number of Employees:* 4

Winnipeg: First North Health Group
#1, 1700 Ness Ave., Winnipeg, MB R3J 3Y1
Tel: 204-943-5160 *Fax:* 866-985-4060

Year Founded: 1997
Number of Employees: 100
Specialties: Helping 22 First Nations communities

York Landing: York Landing Nursing Station
First Nations Health Group
Affiliated with: Northern Regional Health Authority
General Delivery, York Landing, MB R0B 2B0
Tel: 204-341-2325 *Fax:* 204-341-2179
www.northernhealthregion.ca
Year Founded: 2010
Population Served: 464 *Number of Employees:* 2

Special Treatment Centres

Brandon: Western Manitoba Cancer Centre (WMCC)
Brandon Regional Health Centre
Affiliated with: Prairie Mountain Health
300 McTavish Ave. East, Brandon, MB R7A 2B3
Tel: 204-578-2222 *Fax:* 204-578-4991
www.prairiemountainhealth.ca
Year Founded: 2011

St. Norbert: The Behavioural Health Foundation, Inc. (BHF)
Affiliated with: Winnipeg Regional Health Authority
PO Box 250, 35, av de la Digue, St. Norbert, MB R3V 1L6
Tel: 204-269-3430 *Fax:* 204-269-8049
Toll-Free: 855-447-9212
info@bhf.ca
www.bhf.ca
www.facebook.com/BehaviouralHealthFoundation
Note: Long-term residential addictions treatment for adults, teens & families.
Jean Doucha, Executive Director
jeand@bhf.ca

Winnipeg: Addictions Recovery Inc. (ARI)
Affiliated with: Winnipeg Regional Health Authority
93 Cathedral Ave., Winnipeg, MB R2W 0W7
Tel: 204-586-2550
info@addictionsrecovery.ca
www.addictionsrecovery.ca
Year Founded: 1979
Note: Provides an alcohol & drug addiction treatment program; runs two recovery homes in Winnipeg.

Winnipeg: CancerCare Manitoba
Affiliated with: Winnipeg Regional Health Authority
675 McDermot Ave., Winnipeg, MB R3E 0V9
Tel: 204-787-2197 *Fax:* 204-787-1184
Toll-Free: 866-561-1026
www.cancercare.mb.ca
twitter.com/cancercaremb
www.youtube.com/user/CancerCareMB/videos
Number of Employees: 800
Note: Provides cancer treatment in all areas: prevention, early detection, diagnosis, treatment & care, & end of life care.
Dr. Sri Navaratnam, President & CEO
Dr. Piotr Czaykowski, Chief Medical Officer

Winnipeg: Esther House
Affiliated with: Winnipeg Regional Health Authority
PO Box 68022 Stn. Osborne Vill., Winnipeg, MB R3L 2V9
Tel: 204-582-4043
estherhs@mymts.net
www.estherhousewinnipeg.ca
Year Founded: 1997
Number of Beds: 6 beds
Note: Provides second-stage addiction recovery treatment for women. Works in cooperation with the Addictions Foundation of Manitoba.

Winnipeg: The Laurel Centre
Affiliated with: Winnipeg Regional Health Authority
104 Roslyn Rd., Winnipeg, MB R3L 0G6
Tel: 204-783-5460 *Fax:* 204-774-2912
info@thelaurelcentre.com
thelaurelcentre.com
Note: Provides dual treatment for women with substance addictions & who are experiencing the traumatic effects of childhood / adolescent sexual abuse.
Heather Leeman, Executive Director

Winnipeg: Main Street Project (MSP)
Affiliated with: Winnipeg Regional Health Authority
661 Main St., 2nd Fl., Winnipeg, MB R3B 1E3
Tel: 204-982-8245 *Fax:* 204-943-9474
admin@mainstreetproject.ca
www.mainstreetproject.ca
www.facebook.com/mainstreetprojectinc;
twitter.com/mainstreetwpg;
www.instagram.com/mainstreetproject;
www.linkedin.com/company/main-street-project-inc
Year Founded: 1972
Note: Programs & services include: emergency shelter & food;
drug & alcohol detoxification unit; on-site counselling; transitional
housing; & other critical services.
Rick Lees, Executive Director
204-982-8244,

Winnipeg: Native Addictions Council of Manitoba
(NACM)
Affiliated with: Winnipeg Regional Health Authority
160 Salter St., Winnipeg, MB R2W 4K1
Tel: 204-586-8395 *Fax:* 204-589-3921
www.nacm.ca
Year Founded: 1971
Note: Provides holistic treatment of addictions.
Bertha Fontaine, Executive Director

Winnipeg: New Directions for Children, Youth,
Adults & Families
Former Name: Children's Home of Winnipeg
#500, 717 Portage Ave., Winnipeg, MB R3G 0M8
Tel: 204-786-7051 *Fax:* 204-774-6468
TTY: 204-774-8541
www.newdirections.mb.ca
Year Founded: 1885
Note: Programs & services in the following categories:
Counselling, Assessment, Support & Prevention Programs;
Training & Education Programs; & Residential & Support
Programs.
Dr. Jennifer Frain, Chief Executive Officer

Winnipeg: Rehabilitation Centre for Children (RCC)
Affiliated with: Winnipeg Regional Health Authority
1155 Notre Dame Ave., Winnipeg, MB R3E 3G1
Tel: 204-452-4311 *Fax:* 204-477-5547
www.rccinc.ca
Note: Offers services to children with physical & developmental
challenges.
Cheryl Susinski, Executive Director

Winnipeg: Reh-Fit Centre
Affiliated with: Winnipeg Regional Health Authority
Former Name: Manitoba Cardiac Institute
1390 Taylor Ave., Winnipeg, MB R3M 3V8
Tel: 204-488-8023 *Fax:* 204-488-4819
reh-fit@reh-fit.com
www.reh-fit.com
www.facebook.com/RehFit; twitter.com/RehFit
Year Founded: 1979
Note: A certified medical fitness facility specializing in cardiac
rehabilitation.
Pat Kloepfer, Board Chair
Sue Boreskie, Chief Executive Officer
204-488-5850

Winnipeg: Tamarack Recovery Centre Inc.
Affiliated with: Winnipeg Regional Health Authority
Former Name: Kia Zan Inc.
60 Balmoral St., Winnipeg, MB R3C 1X4
Tel: 204-775-3546 *Fax:* 204-772-9908
info@tamarackrecovery.org
www.tamarackrehab.org
Year Founded: 1974
Note: Provides abstinence-based addictions treatment &
recovery services.
Lisa Cowan, Executive Director
204-772-9836

Long Term Care Facilities

Arborg: Riverdale Place Homes Inc.
PO Box 968, 332 Ingolfs St., Arborg, MB R0C 0A0
Tel: 204-376-2940 *Fax:* 204-376-5051
riverdale@mts.net
Year Founded: 1977
Number of Beds: 19 beds
Note: Provides residential services to adults with intellectual
disabilities.

St-Malo: Chalet Malouin Inc.
PO Box 1010, 14 St. Hilaire St., St-Malo, MB R0A 1T0
Tel: 204-347-5753 *Fax:* 204-347-5107
chaletmalouin@mts.net
www.chaletmalouin.ca
www.facebook.com/chaletmalouin
Year Founded: 1971
Number of Beds: 47 independent living apartments; 38 assisted
living / supportive housing suites
Note: Chalet Malouin is a bilingual housing complex for seniors.
Louise Maynard, Administrator

Winnipeg: Deer Lodge Centre
Affiliated with: Winnipeg Regional Health Authority
2109 Portage Ave., Winnipeg, MB R3J 0L3
Tel: 204-837-1301 *Fax:* 204-889-0430
info@deerlodge.mb.ca
www.deerlodge.mb.ca
Year Founded: 1916
Number of Beds: 429 beds, including 140 personal care beds for
veterans
Note: Provides rehabilitation services, including physiotherapy,
occupational therapy, respiratory therapy, & therapeutic
recreation services. Inpatient programs include: assessment &
rehabilitation; chronic care; personal care; peritoneal dialysis; &
respite care. Outpatient programs include: PRIME health care
for seniors program; day hospital; diagnostics; geriatric mental
health team; speech & language pathology for personal care
home; physiotherapy; & Get-Away Club adult day programming.
Services for advanced care & communications devices are also
available.
Gina Trinidad, Chief Operating Officer
Dr. Nancy Dixon, Chief Medical Officer

Winnipeg: Riverview Health Centre
Affiliated with: Winnipeg Regional Health Authority
1 Morley Ave., Winnipeg, MB R3L 2P4
Tel: 204-478-6203 *Fax:* 204-284-9446
rhcinfo@rhc.mb.ca
www.riverviewhealthcentre.com
Number of Beds: 387 beds
Note: Provides long-term care, catering to the needs of the
elderly & rehabilitation patients
Norman Kasian, President & CEO
Dr. Daryl Perry, Chief Medical Officer

Winnipeg: St. Amant Inc.
Affiliated with: Winnipeg Regional Health Authority
440 River Rd., Winnipeg, MB R2M 3Z9
Tel: 204-256-4301 *Fax:* 204-257-4349
inquiries@stamant.mb.ca
www.stamant.ca
www.facebook.com/StAmantMB; twitter.com/StAmantMB;
www.youtube.com/user/StAmantMB;
www.linkedin.com/company/st-amant
Year Founded: 1931
Number of Beds: 212 beds
Note: Developmental disability resource centre
John Leggat, President & CEO

Retirement Residences

Selkirk: Cambridge House
Affiliated with: Interlake-Eastern Regional Health
Authority
c/o Woodland Courts, 387 Annie St., Selkirk, MB R1A 3Y8
Tel: 204-785-1066 *Fax:* 204-482-4369
www.geriatricare.ca/cambridgehouse
Number of Beds: 34 rental & assisted living suites
Joyce Lloyd, Residence Manager
204-785-1066, jlloyd@geriatricare.ca

Selkirk: Woodland Courts
Affiliated with: Interlake-Eastern Regional Health
Authority
387 Annie St., Selkirk, MB R1A 3Y8
Tel: 204-785-1066 *Fax:* 204-482-4369
www.geriatricare.ca/woodlandcourts
Number of Beds: 53 one- & two-bedroom suites
Note: An assisted-living retirement community.
Joyce Lloyd, Residence Manager
204-785-1066, jlloyd@geriatricare.ca

Shoal Lake: Lakeshore Lodge
Shoal Lake/Strathclair Health Centre
Affiliated with: Prairie Mountain Health
c/o Shoal Lake/Strathclair Health Centre, PO Box 490, Shoal
Lake, MB 0J 1Z0
Tel: 204-759-2118
www.assiniboine-rha.ca
Number of Beds: 9 units
Note: Elderly Person's Housing

Kim Manuliak, Contact

Shoal Lake: Morley House
Shoal Lake/Strathclair Health Centre
Affiliated with: Prairie Mountain Health
PO Box 459, Shoal Lake, MB R0J 1Z0
Tel: 204-759-2118
www.assiniboine-rha.ca
Number of Beds: 18 units
Note: Elderly Person's Housing with on-call medical services
Susan Richardson, Contact

Winnipeg: Portsmouth
Revera Inc.
125 Portsmouth Blvd., Winnipeg, MB R3P 2M3
Tel: 204-284-5432
www.reveraliving.com/portsmouth
www.facebook.com/Reveralnc; twitter.com/Revera_Inc;
www.youtube.com/user/Reveralnc;
www.linkedin.com/company/revera-inc
Thomas G. Wellner, President & CEO, Revera Living

Winnipeg: Rosewood
Revera Inc.
857 Wilkes Ave., Winnipeg, MB R3P 2M2
Tel: 204-487-9600
www.reveraliving.com/rosewood
www.facebook.com/Reveralnc; twitter.com/Revera_Inc;
www.youtube.com/user/Reveralnc;
www.linkedin.com/company/revera-inc
Thomas G. Wellner, President & CEO, Revera Living

Winnipeg: St. James Kiwanis Village
Kiwanis Club of St. James
90 Sinawik Bay, Winnipeg, MB R3J 1J4
Tel: 204-837-2305 *Fax:* 204-889-6476
www.stjameskiwanisvillage.ca
Year Founded: 1958
Note: Five separate seniors' housing projects surrounding a
central recreation centre.

Winnipeg: The Waverley
Revera Inc.
857 Wilkes Ave., Winnipeg, MB R3P 2M2
Tel: 204-487-9600
www.reveraliving.com/waverley
www.facebook.com/Reveralnc; twitter.com/Revera_Inc;
www.youtube.com/user/Reveralnc;
www.linkedin.com/company/revera-inc
Thomas G. Wellner, President & CEO, Revera Living

Winnipeg: The Wellington
Revera Inc.
3161 Grant Ave., Winnipeg, MB R3R 3R1
Tel: 204-831-0788
www.reveraliving.com/wellington
www.facebook.com/Reveralnc; twitter.com/Revera_Inc;
www.youtube.com/user/Reveralnc;
www.linkedin.com/company/revera-inc
Note: Services include: blood pressure clinics; foot care clinics;
home care; private care; & recreation.
Thomas G. Wellner, President & CEO, Revera Living

Personal Care Homes

Arborg: Arborg Personal Care Home
Affiliated with: Interlake-Eastern Regional Health
Authority
Former Name: Pioneer Health Services Inc
PO Box 10, 233 St. Phillips Dr., Arborg, MB R0C 0A0
Tel: 204-376-5226 *Fax:* 204-376-3691
www.ierha.ca
Number of Beds: 40 beds
Note: Offers long-term care services.

Ashern: Ashern Personal Care Home
Affiliated with: Interlake-Eastern Regional Health
Authority
PO Box 110, 1 Steenson Dr., Ashern, MB R0C 0E0
Tel: 204-768-5216 *Fax:* 204-768-2337
info@ierha.ca
www.ierha.ca
Number of Beds: 20 beds

Baldur: Baldur Personal Care Home
Baldur Health Centre
Affiliated with: Prairie Mountain Health
PO Box 128, Baldur, MB R0K 0B0
Tel: 204-535-2373 *Fax:* 204-535-2116
www.assiniboine-rha.ca
Number of Beds: 20 beds
D. Rea, Area Manager
drea@arha.ca

Number of Beds: 42 long-term care beds; 1 respite care bed
Note: Programs & services include: adult day program; community bath program; palliative care; occupational & physiotherapy; dietitian; & meals on wheels.
G. Paddock, Area Manager
gpaddock@arha.ca

Ste Rose: Dr. Gendreau Personal Care Home
Affiliated with: Prairie Mountain Health
PO Box 420, 515 Mission St., Ste Rose, MB R0L 1S0
Tel: 204-447-2019
www.prairiemountainhealth.ca
Number of Beds: 65 beds; 1 respite bed
Note: Services include: long-term care; home care; community rehabilitation; therapy; & mental health.

Stonewall: Rosewood Lodge Personal Care Home
Affiliated with: Interlake-Eastern Regional Health Authority
513 - 1 Ave. North, Stonewall, MB R0C 2Z0
Tel: 204-467-5257 Fax: 204-467-4750
info@ierha.ca
www.ierha.ca
Number of Beds: 50 beds

Swan River: Swan River Valley Personal Care Home Inc.
Affiliated with: Prairie Mountain Health
PO Box 1390, 334 - 8th St., Swan River, MB R0L 1Z0
Tel: 204-734-4521
www.prairiemountainhealth.ca
Number of Beds: 45 beds; 2 respite beds
Note: Includes home care services.

Swan River: Swan Valley Lodge
Affiliated with: Prairie Mountain Health
PO Box 1450, 1013 Main St., Swan River, MB R0L 1Z0
Tel: 204-734-3441
www.prha.mb.ca
Number of Beds: 70 beds
Note: Offers an adult day program.

Teulon: Goodwin Lodge Personal Care Home
Affiliated with: Interlake-Eastern Regional Health Authority
PO Box 89, 162 - 3rd Ave. SE, Teulon, MB R0C 3B0
Tel: 204-886-2108 Fax: 204-886-2653
info@ierha.ca
www.ierha.ca
Number of Beds: 20 beds

The Pas: St. Paul's Personal Care Home
Affiliated with: Northern Regional Health Authority
PO Box 240, 34 - 2nd St., The Pas, MB R9A 1K4
Tel: 204-623-9226 Fax: 204-623-9605
www.northernhealthregion.ca
Number of Beds: 60 beds

Thompson: Northern Spirit Manor
Affiliated with: Northern Regional Health Authority
879 Thompson Dr., Thompson, MB R8N 0A9
Tel: 204-778-3805 Fax: 204-778-1563
www.northernhealthregion.ca
Number of Beds: 35 beds

Treherne: Tiger Hills Manor Personal Care Home
Affiliated with: Prairie Mountain Health
Former Name: Tiger Hills Manor Inc.
PO Box 130, 64 Clark St., Treherne, MB R0G 2V0
Tel: 204-723-3407 Fax: 204-723-2869
www.pmh-mb.ca
Number of Beds: 22 beds
Note: Programs & services include: long-term care; facility respite; home care; community bath program; & mental health.

Virden: Virden Sherwood Personal Care Home
Affiliated with: Prairie Mountain Health
PO Box 2000, 223 Hargrave St. East, Virden, MB R0M 2C0
Tel: 204-748-1546 Fax: 204-748-2822
www.prairiemountainhealth.ca
Number of Beds: 46 long-term care beds; 1 respite care bed
Note: Programs & services include: long-term care; facility respite; dietitian; home care; & community bath program.

Virden: West-Man Personal Care Home
Affiliated with: Prairie Mountain Health
PO Box 1630, 427 Frame St. East, Virden, MB R0M 2C0
Tel: 204-748-4335 Fax: 204-748-2053
www.prairiemountainhealth.ca
Number of Beds: 50 personal care beds; 1 respite care bed
Note: Programs & services include: long-term care; facility respite; dietitian; home care; community bath program; adult day program; & Meals on Wheels.

Wawanesa: Wawanesa Personal Care Home
Wawanesa Health Centre
Affiliated with: Prairie Mountain Health
PO Box 309, 506 George St., Wawanesa, MB R0K 2G0
Tel: 204-824-2335 Fax: 204-824-2148
www.assiniboine-rha.ca
Number of Beds: 20 beds
Note: Programs & services include: community bath program; palliative care; occupational & physiotherapy; dietitian; & meals on wheels.
D. Obach, Area Manager
dobach@arha.ca

West St. Paul: Middlechurch Home of Winnipeg Inc.
Affiliated with: Winnipeg Regional Health Authority
280 Balderstone Rd., West St. Paul, MB R4A 4A6
Tel: 204-339-1947 Fax: 204-334-2503
www.middlechurchhome.mb.ca
Year Founded: 1884
Number of Beds: 197 beds
Number of Employees: 320
Note: Programs & services include: activity centre; physiotherapy; occupational therapy; speech therapy; pet therapy; dentist; foot care; adult day program; physicians; & respite care.
Lynda Braccio, Director, Operations
lynda@middlechurchhome.mb.ca

Whitemouth: Whitemouth District Health Centre PCH
Affiliated with: Interlake-Eastern Regional Health Authority
PO Box 160, 75 Hospital St., Whitemouth, MB R0E 2G0
Tel: 204-348-7191 Fax: 204-348-7911
info@ierha.ca
www.ierha.ca
Number of Beds: 26 beds

Winnipeg: 285 Pembina Inc.
Bethania Group
Affiliated with: Winnipeg Regional Health Authority
Also Known As: Deaf Centre
285 Pembina Hwy., Winnipeg, MB R3L 2E1
Tel: 204-284-0802 Fax: 204-474-0073
www.bethania.ca
Number of Beds: 57 beds
Note: Independent living residence for adults who are deaf or hard of hearing, & students enrolled in the Deaf Studies Program.

Winnipeg: Actionmarguerite (Saint-Boniface)
Affiliated with: Winnipeg Regional Health Authority
Former Name: Taché Centre
Also Known As: Actionmarguerite - Taché
185 Despins St., Winnipeg, MB R2H 2B3
Tel: 204-233-3692 Fax: 204-233-6803
www.actionmarguerite.ca
Year Founded: 1935
Number of Beds: 309 beds
Number of Employees: 470
Note: Programs & service include: personal care; dementia care; adults with complex health needs; & day program.
Charles Gagné, Chief Executive Officer, Actionmarguerite

Winnipeg: Actionmarguerite (Saint-Vital)
Affiliated with: Winnipeg Regional Health Authority
Former Name: Foyer Valade
Also Known As: Actionmarguerite - Valade
450 River Rd., Winnipeg, MB R2M 5M4
Tel: 204-254-3332 Fax: 204-254-0329
www.actionmarguerite.ca
Year Founded: 1988
Number of Beds: 154 beds; 39-bed dementia care unit
Number of Employees: 220
Note: Owned by the Catholic Health Corporation of Manitoba.
Charles Gagné, Chief Executive Officer, Actionmarguerite

Winnipeg: Beacon Hill Lodge
Revera Inc.
Affiliated with: Winnipeg Regional Health Authority
190 Fort St., Winnipeg, MB R3C 1C9
Tel: 204-942-7541 Fax: 204-944-0135
www.reveraliving.com/beaconhill
www.facebook.com/ReveraInc; twitter.com/Revera_Inc;
www.youtube.com/user/ReveraInc;
www.linkedin.com/company/revera-inc
Number of Beds: 175 beds
Note: Programs & services include: 24 hour nursing care; physician; rehabilitation; physical activities; foot care; pain & symptom management; occupational therapy; dental; & dietitian.
Thomas G. Wellner, President & CEO, Revera Living

Winnipeg: Bethania Mennonite Personal Care Home Inc.
Bethania Group
Affiliated with: Winnipeg Regional Health Authority
1045 Concordia Ave., Winnipeg, MB R2K 3S7
Tel: 204-667-0795 Fax: 204-667-7078
www.bethania.ca
Number of Beds: 148 beds; 1 respite care bed
Note: Offers nursing, dietitian, & rehabilitation services.
Gary Ledoux, Chief Executive Officer, Bethania Group

Winnipeg: Calvary Place Personal Care Home
Affiliated with: Winnipeg Regional Health Authority
1325 Erin St., Winnipeg, MB R3E 3R6
Tel: 204-943-4424 Fax: 204-783-7524
calvaryplacepch.ca
Number of Beds: 100 beds
Note: Sponsored by the Heritage Benevolent Association of Manitoba, Inc.
Kevin Friesen, CEO/DOC
kfriesen@calvaryplace.mb.ca

Winnipeg: Charleswood Care Centre
Revera Inc.
Affiliated with: Winnipeg Regional Health Authority
5501 Roblin Blvd., Winnipeg, MB R3R 0G8
Tel: 204-888-3363 Fax: 204-896-4763
www.reveraliving.com/charleswood
www.facebook.com/ReveraInc; twitter.com/Revera_Inc;
www.youtube.com/user/ReveraInc;
www.linkedin.com/company/revera-inc
Number of Beds: 155 beds
Note: Programs & services include 24 hour nurse on duty; dietitian; sensory and Montessori programs; musical entertainment; music therapy; art classes; friendly pet visitations.
Thomas G. Wellner, President & CEO, Revera Living

Winnipeg: Concordia Place Personal Care Home
Concordia Hospital
Affiliated with: Winnipeg Regional Health Authority
1000 Molson St., Winnipeg, MB R2K 4L5
Tel: 204-661-7372 Fax: 204-661-7297
www.concordiahospital.mb.ca/cp.html
Year Founded: 2000
Number of Beds: 140 beds
Les W. Janzen, Chief Operating Officer

Winnipeg: Convalescent Home of Winnipeg
Affiliated with: Winnipeg Regional Health Authority
276 Hugo St. North, Winnipeg, MB R3M 2N6
Tel: 204-453-4663 Fax: 204-453-7140
www.tchw.com
Number of Beds: 84 residents
Note: Services include: dental; dietitian; eye care; laboratory; medical aids & equipment; nursing; occupational therapy; physical therapy; pharmacy; physician; podiatry; radiology; & social work.
Sharon Wilms, Administrator

Winnipeg: Donwood Manor Personal Care Home
Affiliated with: Winnipeg Regional Health Authority
171 Donwood Dr., Winnipeg, MB R2G 0V9
Tel: 204-668-4410 Fax: 204-663-5429
info@donwoodmanor.org
www.donwoodmanor.org
Year Founded: 1970
Number of Beds: 121 beds
Note: Faith-based facility supported by eight Winnipeg-based Mennonite Brethren Churches.
James Heinrichs, Chief Executive Officer

Winnipeg: Extendicare - Oakview Place
Extendicare Canada
Affiliated with: Winnipeg Regional Health Authority
2395 Ness Ave., Winnipeg, MB R3J 1A5
Tel: 204-888-3005 Fax: 204-831-8101
cnh_oakviewplace@extendicare.com
www.extendicareoakviewplace.com
Number of Beds: 245 beds; 1 respite bed
Note: Programs & services include: nursing & supportive care; rehabilitation & rehabilitative services; optometry services; dental services; social & therapeutic programs; adult day program; care for persons with Alzheimer's disease & related dementias; & palliative care.
Ronald Parent, Administrator

Winnipeg: **Extendicare - Tuxedo Villa**
Extendicare Canada
Affiliated with: Winnipeg Regional Health Authority
2060 Corydon Ave., Winnipeg, MB R3P 0N3
Tel: 204-889-2650 *Fax:* 204-896-0258
cnh_tuxedovilla@extendicare.com
www.extendicaretuxedovilla.com

Number of Beds: 213 beds
Note: Programs & services include: professional nursing & supportive care; rehabilitation services; care for persons with Alzheimer's disease & related dementias; & social & therapeutic programs.
Claude Lachance, Administrator

Winnipeg: **Extendicare - Vista Park Lodge**
Extendicare Canada
Affiliated with: Winnipeg Regional Health Authority
144 Nova Vista Dr., Winnipeg, MB R2N 1P8
Tel: 204-257-6688 *Fax:* 204-257-0446
www.extendicarevistaparklodge.com

Number of Beds: 100 beds
Note: Services include: nursing; medical; therapeutic care; rehabilitative care; & long-term care.
Gwen Johnston, Administrator

Winnipeg: **Fred Douglas Lodge**
Fred Douglas Society Inc.
Affiliated with: Winnipeg Regional Health Authority
1275 Burrows Ave., Winnipeg, MB R2X 0B8
Tel: 204-586-8541 *Fax:* 204-586-5510
admin@fdl.mb.ca
www.freddouglassociety.com

Number of Beds: 136 beds; 11 beds for behaviorally challenged
Note: Owned by the United Church of Canada. Programs & services include: life-lease housing; independent living apartments; supportive housing suites; respite; & an adult day program.
Roslyn Garofalo, Chief Executive Officer
204-586-8541, rgarofalo@fdl.mb.ca
Deb Corner, Director of Care
204-586-8541, dcorner@fdl.mb.ca

Winnipeg: **Golden Door Geriatric Centre**
Affiliated with: Winnipeg Regional Health Authority
1679 Pembina Hwy., Winnipeg, MB R3T 2G6
Tel: 204-269-6308 *Fax:* 204-269-5626
info@goldendoor.ca
www.goldendoor.ca

Number of Beds: 78 beds
Scarlet Pollock, Administrator

Winnipeg: **Golden Links Lodge**
Affiliated with: Winnipeg Regional Health Authority
2280 St. Mary's Rd., Winnipeg, MB R2N 3Z6
Tel: 204-257-9947 *Fax:* 204-257-2405
info@goldenlinks.mb.ca
www.goldenlinks.mb.ca

Number of Beds: 88 beds; 2 respite beds; 17-bed unit for dementia care
Note: Owned by the Oddfellows & Rebekahs. Services include: 24 hour nursing care; dietary; medications & pharmacy; nutrition; personal care; physician; & recreation.

Winnipeg: **Heritage Lodge Personal Care Home**
Revera Inc.
Affiliated with: Winnipeg Regional Health Authority
3555 Portage Ave., Winnipeg, MB R3K 0X2
Tel: 204-888-7940 *Fax:* 204-832-6544
www.reveraliving.com/heritage-pch
www.facebook.com/Reverainc; twitter.com/Revera_Inc;
www.youtube.com/user/Reverainc;
www.linkedin.com/company/revera-inc

Number of Beds: 86 beds
Note: Programs & services include: 24 hour nursing care; dietitian; pain & symptom management; & rehabilitation.
Thomas G. Wellner, President & CEO, Revera Living
Joanne Sigfusson, Administrator

Winnipeg: **Holy Family Home**
Affiliated with: Winnipeg Regional Health Authority
165 Aberdeen Ave., Winnipeg, MB R2W 1T9
Tel: 204-589-7381 *Fax:* 204-589-8605
info@holyfamilyhome.mb.ca
www.holyfamilyhome.mb.ca

Number of Beds: 276 beds
Note: Personal care home for the elderly within the Ukrainian & Slavic communities. Includes programs such as respite care & an adult day program.
Jean R. Piché, Chief Executive Officer

Winnipeg: **Kildonan Personal Care Centre**
Revera Inc.
Affiliated with: Winnipeg Regional Health Authority
Former Name: Kildonan Long Term Care
1970 Henderson Hwy., Winnipeg, MB R2G 1P2
Tel: 204-334-4633 *Fax:* 204-334-4632
www.reveraliving.com/kildonan
www.facebook.com/Reverainc; twitter.com/Revera_Inc;
www.youtube.com/user/Reverainc;
www.linkedin.com/company/revera-inc

Number of Beds: 120 beds
Note: Programs & services include 24 hour nurse on staff; arts & crafts; movies; BBQ; friendly pet visitations.
Thomas G. Wellner, President & CEO, Revera Living
Nina Labun, Administrator

Winnipeg: **Lions Personal Care Centre**
Affiliated with: Winnipeg Regional Health Authority
320 Sherbrook St., Winnipeg, MB R3B 2W6
Tel: 204-784-1240 *Fax:* 204-784-2723
www.wrha.mb.ca

Number of Beds: 116 rooms
Note: Programs & services include a supportive housing program & an adult day program.
Laurel Ann Kalupar, Executive Director

Winnipeg: **Luther Home**
Affiliated with: Winnipeg Regional Health Authority
1081 Andrews St., Winnipeg, MB R2V 2G9
Tel: 204-338-4641 *Fax:* 204-338-4643
www.lutherhome.com

Year Founded: 1969
Number of Beds: 80 beds
Note: Offers adult day & home care programs.
Keith Bytheway, Chief Executive Officer

Winnipeg: **Maples Care Centre**
Revera Inc.
Affiliated with: Winnipeg Regional Health Authority
Also Known As: Maples Personal Care Home
500 Mandalay Dr., Winnipeg, MB R2P 1V4
Tel: 204-632-8570 *Fax:* 204-697-0249
www.reveraliving.com/maples
www.facebook.com/Reverainc; twitter.com/Revera_Inc;
www.youtube.com/user/Reverainc;
www.linkedin.com/company/revera-inc

Year Founded: 1982
Number of Beds: 200 beds
Note: Programs & services include: 24 hour nursing care; dietitian; foot care; optometry; occupational therapy; pain & symptom management; rehabilitation; restorative; & recreation.
Thomas G. Wellner, President & CEO, Revera Living
Jason Chester, Administrator

Winnipeg: **Meadowood Manor**
Affiliated with: Winnipeg Regional Health Authority
577 St. Anne's Rd., Winnipeg, MB R2M 5B2
Tel: 204-257-2394 *Fax:* 204-254-5402
info@meadowood.ca
www.meadowood.ca

Number of Beds: 88 beds; 1 respite care bed; 89 suite apartment complex
Note: Faith-based facility for seniors affiliated with the North American Baptist Conference. Programs & services include: long-term care; rehabilitation services; foot care services; social work; recreation programs; respite care; & palliative care.
Laurie Cerqueti, Administrator

Winnipeg: **Misericordia Place**
Misericordia Health Centre
Affiliated with: Winnipeg Regional Health Authority
99 Cornish Ave., Winnipeg, MB R3C 1A2
Tel: 204-774-6581 *Fax:* 204-783-6052
info@misericordia.mb.ca
www.misericordia.mb.ca/Programs/LTCare.html
www.facebook.com/263816864499; twitter.com/MisericordiaMB;
instagram.com/misericordiamb

Number of Beds: 100 beds
Note: Misericordia Health Centre also provides interim care for up to 145 residents waiting for placement in the personal care home of their choice.
Rosie Jacuzzi, President & CEO
Patty Johnson, Director, Long-Term Care Program
204-788-8451, pjohnson@misericordia.mb.ca

Winnipeg: **Park Manor Personal Care Home Inc.**
Affiliated with: Winnipeg Regional Health Authority
301 Redonda St., Winnipeg, MB R2C 1L7
Tel: 204-222-3251 *Fax:* 204-222-3237
info@parkmanor.ca
www.parkmanor.ca

Number of Beds: 100 beds
Note: Owned by the Seventh-day Adventist Church. Services include: 24 hour nursing care; personal care; family care; & palliative care.
Collin Akre, Executive Director
cakre@parkmanor.ca

Winnipeg: **Parkview Place Long Term Care**
Revera Inc.
Affiliated with: Winnipeg Regional Health Authority
440 Edmonton St., Winnipeg, MB R3B 2M4
Tel: 204-942-5291 *Fax:* 204-947-1969
www.reveraliving.com/parkviewplace
www.facebook.com/Reverainc; twitter.com/Revera_Inc;
www.youtube.com/user/Reverainc;
www.linkedin.com/company/revera-inc

Number of Beds: 277 beds
Note: Programs & services include: 24 hour nursing care; dental; dietitian; foot care; occupational therapy; ophthalmology; pain & symptom management; rehabilitation; social work; & wound care.
Thomas G. Wellner, President & CEO, Revera Living
Donald Solar, Administrator

Winnipeg: **Pembina Place Mennonite Personal Care Home**
Bethania Group
Affiliated with: Winnipeg Regional Health Authority
1045 Concordia Ave., Winnipeg, MB R2K 3S7
Tel: 204-667-0795 *Fax:* 204-667-7078
general.inquiries@bethania.ca
www.bethania.ca/pembina-place-pch

Year Founded: 1998
Number of Beds: 57 beds
Specialties: Accommodating language & cultural needs of Deaf persons
Gary Ledoux, Chief Executive Officer
Andrea Grozli, Manager, Resident Care

Winnipeg: **Poseidon Care Centre**
Rivera Inc.
Affiliated with: Winnipeg Regional Health Authority
70 Poseidon Bay, Winnipeg, MB R3M 3E5
Tel: 204-452-6204 *Fax:* 204-474-2173
www.reveraliving.com/poseidon

Number of Beds: 218 beds
Note: Programs & services include: 24 hour nursing care; dental; dietitian; occupational therapy; optometry; palliative care; & rehabilitation.
Thomas G. Wellner, President & CEO, Revera Living
Wendy Gilmour, Senior Vice-President, Long Term Care
Wanda Metro, Administrator

Winnipeg: **River East Personal Care Home Ltd.**
Affiliated with: Winnipeg Regional Health Authority
1375 Molson St., Winnipeg, MB R2K 4K8
Tel: 204-668-7460 *Fax:* 204-668-7459
dsaunders@extendicare.com
www.rivereast.ca

Year Founded: 1993
Number of Beds: 120 beds

Winnipeg: **River Park Gardens**
Affiliated with: Winnipeg Regional Health Authority
735 St. Annes Rd., Winnipeg, MB R2N 0C4
Tel: 204-255-9073 *Fax:* 204-257-6467
www.wrha.mb.ca

Number of Beds: 80 beds
Mary Baranski, Administrator

Winnipeg: **St. Joseph's Residence Inc.**
Affiliated with: Winnipeg Regional Health Authority
1149 Leila Ave., Winnipeg, MB R2P 1S6
Tel: 204-697-8031 *Fax:* 204-697-8075
www.sjri.ca

Number of Beds: 100 beds
Note: Owned by The Catholic Health Corporation of Manitoba.
Charles Gagné, Chief Executive Officer
cgagne@actionmarguerite.ca

Winnipeg: **St. Norbert Personal Care Home**
Affiliated with: Winnipeg Regional Health Authority
50 St. Pierre St., Winnipeg, MB R3V 1J6
Tel: 204-269-4538 *Fax:* 204-269-6374
www.wrha.mb.ca

Year Founded: 1971
Number of Beds: 91 beds

Winnipeg: **The Salvation Army Golden West Centennial Lodge**
Affiliated with: Winnipeg Regional Health Authority
811 School Rd., Winnipeg, MB R2Y 0S8
Tel: 204-888-3311 Fax: 204-831-0544
www.goldenwestlodge.ca
Number of Beds: 116 beds
Note: Programs & services include: nursing; medical; dentistry; dietary; foot care; laboratory; pharmacy; recreation; rehabilitation; & respite care.
Joyce Kristjansson, Executive Director
jkristjansson@goldenwestlodge.ca

Winnipeg: **The Saul & Claribel Simkin Centre**
The Sharon Home Inc.
Affiliated with: Winnipeg Regional Health Authority
Also Known As: The Simkin Centre
1 Falconridge Dr., Winnipeg, MB R3Y 1V9
Tel: 204-586-9781 Fax: 204-589-9760
info@simkincentre.ca
www.simkincentre.ca
Year Founded: 2002
Number of Beds: 200 beds
Note: Provides care for elders of Jewish community; therapeutic recreation; walking track for residents recovering from hip surgery or a stroke; tracking program for resident safety; & an adult day program.
Alanna Kull, Director of Care
Alanna.Kull@sharonhome.mb.ca

Winnipeg: **Southeast Personal Care Home Inc. (SEPCH)**
Southeast Resource Development Council Corp.
Affiliated with: Winnipeg Regional Health Authority
1265 Lee Blvd., Winnipeg, MB R3T 2M3
Tel: 204-269-7111 Fax: 204-269-8819
www.serdc.mb.ca/programs-and-services/sepersonalcarehome
Year Founded: 2011
Number of Beds: 80 beds
Note: Personal care home for Aboriginal elders
Jean Foster, Executive Director

Winnipeg: **West Park Manor Personal Care Home Inc.**
Affiliated with: Winnipeg Regional Health Authority
3199 Grant Ave., Winnipeg, MB R3R 1X2
Tel: 204-889-3330 Fax: 204-832-9555
www.wrha.mb.ca
Number of Beds: 150 beds; 1 respite care bed
Note: Faith-based facility sponsored by the Seventh-day Adventist Church.
Ruben Wollmann, Administrator

Winnipegosis: **Winnipegosis & District Personal Care Home**
Affiliated with: Prairie Mountain Health
PO Box 280, 230 Bridge St., Winnipegosis, MB R0L 2G0
Tel: 204-656-4881
www.prha.mb.ca
Number of Beds: 20 beds
Note: Includes home care services (204-656-4721)

Mental Health Hospitals/Facilities

Altona: **Blue Sky Opportunities Inc.**
PO Box 330, 122 - 10th Ave. NW, Altona, MB R0G 0B0
Tel: 204-324-5401 Fax: 204-324-5094
office@blueskyop.com
www.blueskyop.com
Note: Employment & training opportunities as well as non-vocational services for adults with intellectual disabilities.
Richard Neufeld, General Manager
204-324-5401, bsogm@mymts.net

Boissevain: **Prairie Partners Inc.**
298 South Railway St., Boissevain, MB R0K 0E0
Tel: 204-534-2956
residential@prairiepartners.ca
www.prairiepartners.ca
www.facebook.com/theSAWMILL
Note: Residential & employment services for adults with intellectual disabilities.
Misheyla Iwasiuk, Executive Director

Brandon: **Brandon Community Options Inc.**
136 - 11th St., Brandon, MB R7A 4J4
Tel: 204-571-5770 Fax: 204-571-5780
bdnco@mts.net
www.brandoncommunityoptionsinc.com
Note: Residential & day programs for adults with mental disabilities.

Brandon: **Brandon Support Services**
1540 Rosser Ave., Brandon, MB R7A 0M6
Tel: 204-728-2025 Fax: 204-728-2052
admin@bssmb.ca
Area Served: Brandon, Portage La Prairie, MacGregor & Carberry
Note: Community-based agency providing supportive services to individuals with intellectual &/or physical disabilities.

Brandon: **Centre for Adult Psychiatry (CAP)**
Affiliated with: Prairie Mountain Health
Brandon Regional Health Centre, 150 McTavish Ave. East, Brandon, MB R7A 2B3
Tel: 204-578-4555
www.prairiemountainhealth.ca
Number of Beds: 25 beds
Note: Acute services for adults 18-64 experiencing a psychiatric illness (DSM IV diagnosis) &/or severe psychosocial crisis.

Brandon: **Centre for Geriatric Psychiatry**
Affiliated with: Prairie Mountain Health
150 McTavish Ave. East, Brandon, MB R7A 2B3
Tel: 204-578-4560 Fax: 204-578-4948
www.prairiemountainhealth.ca
Number of Beds: 22 beds
Area Served: Parkland, Assiniboine, Brandon
Note: Provides assessment & short-term treatment for adults 65 years & over experiencing difficulties with day to day functioning due to mental health issues.
Pamela Gulay, Manager

Brandon: **Child & Adolescent Treatment Centre (CATC)**
Affiliated with: Prairie Mountain Health
1240 - 10 St., Brandon, MB R7A 7L6
Tel: 204-578-2700 Fax: 204-578-2850
Toll-Free: 866-403-5459
www.prairiemountainhealth.ca
Note: Programs & services include: mental health assessments & treatment; crisis stabilization; individualized treatment plans; individual, group, & family therapy; & mental health education/promotion.

Brandon: **Family Visions Inc.**
2705 Victoria Ave., Brandon, MB R7B 0N1
Tel: 204-726-5602 Fax: 204-571-0907
reception@familyvisions.ca
www.familyvisions.ca
Year Founded: 2000
Note: Residential & day services for adults with intellectual disabilities.
Kim Longstreet, Executive Director

Brandon: **Mental Health Services - Brandon**
Affiliated with: Prairie Mountain Health
800 Rosser Ave., #B13, Brandon, MB R7A 6N5
Tel: 204-578-2400 Fax: 204-578-2822
www.prairiemountainhealth.ca
Note: Services include counselling, resource coordination, & group programming.

Brandon: **Westman Crisis Services**
Affiliated with: Prairie Mountain Health
Brandon, MB
Tel: 204-725-4411 Fax: 204-726-4665
Toll-Free: 888-379-7699
www.prairiemountainhealth.ca
Area Served: Brandon & Assiniboine regions
Note: Services include Mobile Crisis Unit (assessment, screening, & intervention) & Crisis Stabilization Unit (residential unit providing short-term intensive care for individuals experiencing a mental health crisis)

Ninette: **Southwest Community Options Inc. (SWCO)**
PO Box 46, 210 Queen St. North, Ninette, MB R0K 1R0
Tel: 204-528-5060 Fax: 877-919-8681
www.swco.ca
Year Founded: 2000
Note: Residential & day services for adults with intellectual disabilities.
Linda Stephenson, Executive Director
Valerie Tripp, Financial Officer

Notre Dame de Lourdes: **Mountain Industries**
Also Known As: Atelier la Montagne
65 Notre-Dame Ave., Notre Dame de Lourdes, MB R0G 1M0
Tel: 204-248-2154
www.mountainindustries.ca
Year Founded: 1978
Note: Provides a day program for over 25 individuals with special needs.

Pine Falls: **Wings of Power Inc.**
PO Box 66, 39 Pine St., Pine Falls, MB R0E 1M0
Tel: 204-367-9641 Fax: 204-367-9784
reception@wingsofpower.org
www.wingsofpower.org
Note: Community & family resource centre. Programs & services include: prenatal / postnatal; children's; summer; school; & programs for adults with disabilities.
Guy Borlase, Executive Director
gbwingsdirector@mymts.net

Portage la Prairie: **Manitoba Developmental Centre**
#840, 3rd St. NE, Portage la Prairie, MB R1N 3C6
Tel: 204-856-4200 Fax: 204-856-4258
www.gov.mb.ca/fs/mdc/index.html
Number of Beds: 180 resident capacity
Note: Developmental centre for residents with an intellectual disability. Programs & services include: Extended Care Program & Habilitation / Specialty Program.

Portage la Prairie: **Portage ARC Industries Inc.**
1675 Saskatchewan Ave. West, Portage la Prairie, MB R1N 0R4
Tel: 204-857-7752 Fax: 204-239-0968
portagearc@mymts.net
Year Founded: 1975
Note: Activities for individuals with special needs.
Tara Ryzner, Executive Director

Selkirk: **Hearthstone Community Group**
209 Superior Ave., Selkirk, MB R1A 0Z7
Tel: 204-817-1996 Fax: 204-817-1997
www.hearthstone-community-group.ca
Note: Community living homes & day programs for people with developmental disabilities
Lori Zdebiak, General Manager
204-817-1996
Karen Fraser, Office Manager

Selkirk: **Selkirk Mental Health Centre**
Affiliated with: Interlake-Eastern Regional Health Authority
PO Box 9600, 825 Manitoba Ave., Selkirk, MB R1A 2B5
Tel: 204-482-3810 Fax: 204-785-8936
Toll-Free: 800-881-3073
smhc@gov.mb.ca
www.gov.mb.ca/health/smhc
Number of Beds: 252 beds
Note: Long-term mental health inpatient care & rehabilitation; also provides mental health services to people from the Territory of Nunavut.
D. Bellehumeur, Chief Executive Officer
Dr. M. Teillet, Medical Director
R. Cromarty, Chief Nursing Officer & Director, Programs
B. Wynnobel, Director, Operations

St. Malo: **Smile of St. Malo Inc./Epic de St. Malo Inc.**
112 St. Malo Ave., St. Malo, MB R0A 1T0
Tel: 204-347-5418
www.epicsmile.ca
Note: Provides residential & day programs for adults with intellectual disabilities.
Helene Lariviere, Executive Director
helene@epicsmile.ca

Steinbach: **enVision Community Living**
84 Brandt St., Steinbach, MB R5G 0E1
Tel: 204-326-7539 Fax: 204-346-3639
info@envisioncl.com
www.envisioncl.com
www.facebook.com/envisioncl; twitter.com/enVisioncl
Note: Offers residential & daytime support services to adults with intellectual disabilities.
Jeannette Delong, Executive Director
203-326-7539, jdelong@envisioncl.com

Winkler: **Gateway Resources Inc.**
PO Box 1448, 1582 Pembina Ave. West, Winkler, MB R6W 4B4
Tel: 204-325-7304 Fax: 204-325-1958
gradmin@gatewayresourcesinc.com
www.gatewayresourcesinc.com
www.facebook.com/575874922554789
Area Served: Winkler / Morden area of South Central Manitoba
Note: Operates 13 group homes that provide services & programs for individuals with an intellectual disability.
Kimberly Nelson, Chief Executive Officer
kim@gatewayresourcesinc.com
Loni Derksen, Director, Operations
loni@gatewayresourcesinc.com
Dianne Hildebrand, Director, Housing
dianne@gatewayresourcesinc.com

PattyAnne LePage, Director, Human Resources
pattyanne@gatewayresourcesinc.com
Brenda Pohl, Director, Programs
brenda@gatewayresourcesinc.com

Winnipeg: Arcane Horizon Inc. (AHI)
#62, 1313 Border St., Winnipeg, MB R3H 0X4
Tel: 204-897-5482
www.arcanehorizon.org
www.facebook.com/arcanehorizon
Note: Support services for adults living with developmental disabilities.
Jason Dyck, Executive Director

Winnipeg: L'Avenir Cooperative Inc.
80 Sherbrook St., Winnipeg, MB R3C 2B3
Tel: 204-789-9777 *Fax:* 204-837-8614
www.lavenircoop.ca
Year Founded: 1983
Note: Provides support services to people with intellectual &/or physical disabilities.
Marc Piché, Executive Director
204-789-9777, mpiche@lavenircoop.ca
Mariano Bautista, Finance & Administration Head
204-772-9503, mbautista@lavenircoop.ca
Tess De Jesus, Manager, Finance
204-772-9503, tdjesus@lavenircoop.ca

Winnipeg: Changes
200 - 395 Stafford St., Winnipeg, MB R3M 2X4
Tel: 204-953-5300 *Fax:* 204-953-5305
info@changeswinnipeg.ca
changeswinnipeg.ca
Note: Services for adults who need support in their homes & communities.

Winnipeg: Clubhouse of Winnipeg, Inc.
Affiliated with: Winnipeg Regional Health Authority
172 Sherbrook St., Winnipeg, MB R3C 2B6
Tel: 204-783-9400 *Fax:* 204-783-9890
clubhousewinnipeg@shaw.ca
www.clubhousewinnipeg.ca
Note: Employment & educational opportunities to people coping with mental illness.
Mark Elie, Director

Winnipeg: Community Respite Service Inc.
1155 Notre Dame Ave., Winnipeg, MB R3E 3G1
Tel: 204-953-2400 *Fax:* 204-775-6214
www.communityrespiteservice.ca
Year Founded: 1984
Note: Respite care for families & individuals with intellectual & physical disabilities.
Michelle Hammond, Executive Director

Winnipeg: Crisis Response Centre (CRC)
Affiliated with: Winnipeg Regional Health Authority
Also Known As: Adult Mental Health Crisis Response Centre
817 Bannatyne Ave., Winnipeg, MB R3E 0Y1
Tel: 204-940-1781
TTY: 204-779-8902
Year Founded: 2013
Note: Provides 24/7 walk-in & schedules urgent care services; acts as a base for a Mobile Crisis Team.
James Bolton, Medical Director

Winnipeg: DASCH Inc.
Also Known As: Direct Action in Support of Community Homes
#1, 117 Victor Lewis Dr., Winnipeg, MB R3P 1J6
Tel: 204-987-1550 *Fax:* 204-987-1552
www.dasch.mb.ca
twitter.com/dasch_inc
Year Founded: 1974
Note: Provides residential, day program, respite & foster care programs & services for people with developmental disabilities.
Karen Fonseth, Chief Executive Officer
Nadeen Haverstock, Chief Operating Officer

Winnipeg: Friends Housing Inc.
Affiliated with: Winnipeg Regional Health Authority
#100, 890 Sturgeon Rd., Winnipeg, MB R2Y 0L2
Tel: 204-953-1160 *Fax:* 204-953-1162
fhousing@shaw.ca
www.friendshousinginc.ca
Note: Provides housing & daily living support for people with mental illnesses, or people in need of subsidized housing.

Winnipeg: Innovative LIFE Options Inc. (LIFE)
Also Known As: Living in Friendship Everyday
#4, 120 Maryland St., Winnipeg, MB R3G 1L1
Tel: 204-772-3557 *Fax:* 204-784-4816
Toll-Free: 866-516-5445
info@icof-life.ca
www.innovativelifeoptions.ca
www.facebook.com/LifeIsGoodInTheCompanyOfFriendsicof;
twitter.com/lifeisgoodicof
Year Founded: 2000
Note: Provides guidance, resources, training, & information to individuals receiving funding through Manitoba Family Service's program In the Company of Friends (ICOF).
Patti Chiappetta, Executive Director
204-784-4814, patti@icof-life.ca
Laureen Spitzke, Office Manager
204-784-4810
Liz Allen, Financial Coordinator
204-414-6398, liz@icof-life.ca

Winnipeg: Manitoba Adolescent Treatment Centre Inc. (MATC)
Affiliated with: Winnipeg Regional Health Authority
120 Tecumseh St., Winnipeg, MB R3E 2A9
Tel: 204-477-6391
info@matc.ca
www.matc.ca
Number of Beds: 14 beds
Note: Mental health services for children, youth, & families.
Marcia Thomson, Chief Executive Officer

Winnipeg: Norshel Inc.
Also Known As: Norshel Centre
890 Nairn Ave., Winnipeg, MB R2L 0X8
Tel: 204-654-6117
www.norshel.mb.ca
Note: Provides support for adults with physical & developmental disabilities.
Colin Rivers, Executive Director
colinrivers@norshel.mb.ca

Winnipeg: Opportunities For Independence, Inc.
1070 Portage Ave., Winnipeg, MB R3G 0S3
Tel: 204-786-0100 *Fax:* 204-786-0109
www.ofii.ca
Year Founded: 1983
Number of Employees: 100
Note: Programs & services for adults with intellectual disabilities who engage in high-risk behaviour, including: residential; alternative vocational programming; living skills training; & therapeutic programs.

Winnipeg: Pulford Community Living Services Inc. (PCLS)
#5, 1146 Waverley St., Winnipeg, MB R3T 0P4
Tel: 204-284-2255 *Fax:* 204-453-5657
www.pulford.ca
Year Founded: 1986
Note: Provides housing & support services for people with developmental disabilities.
Rod Retelback, Executive Director

Winnipeg: The Salvation Army Community Venture
1350 Church Ave., Winnipeg, MB R2X 1G4
Tel: 204-946-9418 *Fax:* 204-946-5347
www.communityventure.mb.ca
Note: Programs & services for adults living with developmental disabilities include: day programs; residential services; transportation; outreach; & respite.
Kim Park, Executive Director
204-946-9418, Fax: 204-946-5347,
director@communityventure.mb.ca

Winnipeg: Sara Riel Inc.
Affiliated with: Winnipeg Regional Health Authority
#101, 66 Moore Ave., Winnipeg, MB R2M 2C4
Tel: 204-237-9263 *Fax:* 204-233-2564
info@sararielinc.com
www.sararielinc.com
Year Founded: 1977
Note: Provides housing support, rehabilitation, & employment counselling to individuals with mental health issues.
Diane Lau, Executive Director

Winnipeg: Shalom Residences Inc.
1033 McGregor St., Winnipeg, MB R2V 3H4
Tel: 204-582-7064 *Fax:* 204-582-7162
shalom@mts.net
www.shalomresidences.com
Note: Community-based care homes for adults with intellectual disabilities; Judaic-oriented programs.
Nancy Hughes, Executive Director
Maureen Baskin, Coordinator

Shelley Nagle, Coordinator
Meaghan Spenchuk, Office Manager

Winnipeg: Special People in Kildonan East Inc. (SPIKE)
Also Known As: SPIKE House
1303 Dugald Rd., #B, Winnipeg, MB R2J 0H3
Tel: 204-338-0773 *Fax:* 204-338-1129
www.spikeinc.org
Year Founded: 1978
Note: Permanent & respite care for mentally &/or physically disabled individuals.
Peter Court, Executive Director
204-339-2990, Fax: 204-338-1129, pcourt@spikeinc.org

Winnipeg: Turning Leaf Community Support Services Inc.
Also Known As: Turning Leaf Inc.
2585 Portage Ave., 2nd Fl., Winnipeg, MB R3J 0P5
Tel: 204-221-5594 *Fax:* 204-219-1821
Toll-Free: 855-221-5594
info@turningleafservices.com
www.turningleafservices.com
www.facebook.com/TurningLeafWpg; twitter.com/turningleafwpg;
instagram.com/turningleafwpg;
www.linkedin.com/company-beta/3634827
Note: Provides treatment & support for youth & adults with intellectual challenges & mental illnesses.
Barkley Engel, Founder & CEO
204-221-5594, bjengel@turningleafservices.com
Jennifer Biggs, Director, Supported Independent Living
jbiggs@turningleafservices.com
Renee Voss, Director, Residential Services
reneevoss@turningleafservices.com
Samneek Sandhu, Director, Finance

Winnipeg: Visions of Independence Inc.
#211, 530 Century St., Winnipeg, MB R3H 0Y4
Tel: 204-453-5982 *Fax:* 204-452-0714
www.visionsofindependence.org
www.facebook.com/visionsofindependenceMB;
twitter.com/VofIndependence;
www.instagram.com/visionsofindependence_mb;
www.linkedin.com/in/voi
Note: Provides housing & programs to people with intellectual disabilities. Programs & services include: residential; day programs; & supported independent living / respite.
Jennifer Hagedorn, Executive Director
jhagedorn@visionsofindependence.org
Ven Block, Director, Operations
vblock@visionsofindependence.org
Shannon Harley, Director, Advocacy, Training and Development
sharley@visionsofindependence.org

New Brunswick

Government Departments in Charge

Fredericton: New Brunswick Department of Health
Former Name: Dept. of Health & Community Services
HSBC Place, PO Box 5100, Fredericton, NB E3B 5G8
Tel: 506-457-4800 *Fax:* 506-453-5243
www.gnb.ca/health
twitter.com/NBHealth
Hon. Dorothy Shephard, Minister

Regional Health Authorities

Bathurst: Vitalité Health Network/Réseau de santé Vitalité
Former Name: Restigouche Health Authority / Régie de la santé du Restigouche
#600, 275 Main St., Bathurst, NB E2A 1A9
Tel: 506-544-2133 *Fax:* 506-544-2145
Toll-Free: 888-472-2220
info@vitalitenb.ca
www.vitalitenb.ca
www.facebook.com/vitalitenb; twitter.com/vitalitenb;
www.instagram.com/vitalitenb
Year Founded: 2008
Number of Beds: 1,173 hospital beds
Population Served: 239600 *Number of Employees:* 7200
Note: The Vitalité Health Network amalgamates Regional Health Authority 4, the Restigouche Health Authority, the Acadie-Bathurst Health Authority, & the Beauséjour Health Authority. The network is comprised of 11 hospitals, 9 health centres, 5 clinics, 10 community mental health centres, 4 addiction service centres, 2 veterans' centres, & 11 public & sexual health offices.
Michelyne Paulin, Board Chair

Gilles Lanteigne, President & CEO
Dr. France Desrosiers, Vice-President, Medical Services,
Training & Research
Gisèle Beaulieu, Vice-President, Performance, Quality &
Corporate Services
Jacques Duclos, Vice-President, Community Services & Mental
Health
Stéphane Legacy, Vice-President, Outpatient & Professional
Services
Johanne Roy, Vice-President, Clinical Services

Fredericton: **Horizon Health Network/Réseau de
santé Horizon**
Former Name: Regional Health Authority B
180 Woodbridge St., Fredericton, NB E3B 4R3
Tel: 506-623-5500 *Fax:* 506-452-5624
horizon@horizonnb.ca
www.horizonnb.ca
www.facebook.com/HorizonNB; twitter.com/HorizonHealthNB;
www.linkedin.com/company/horizon-health-network
Year Founded: 2008
Number of Beds: 1,650 beds
Area Served: Provinces of New Brunswick, PEI, & northern
Nova Scotia *Number of Employees:* 12600
Note: Along with the Vitalité Health Network, the Horizon Health
Network amalgamates the 8 former regional health authorities in
New Brunswick. Horizon Health Network serves the Moncton,
Saint John, Fredericton & Miramichi areas, as well as
communities in Nova Scotia & Prince Edward Island.
Karen McGrath, President & CEO
Jean Daigle, Vice-President, Community
Dr. John Dornan, Chief of Staff
Gary Foley, Vice-President, Professional Services
Geri Geldart, Vice-President, Clinical
Dr. Édouard Hendriks, Vice-President, Medical, Academic &
Research Affairs
Margaret Melanson, Vice-President, Quality & Patient Centred
Care

Hospitals - General

Bathurst: **Hôpital régional Chaleur**
Affiliée à: Vitalité Health Network
Ancien nom: Centre hospitalier régional
1750, promenade Sunset, Bathurst, NB E2A 4L7
Tél: 506-544-3000
info@vitalitenb.ca
www.vitalitenb.ca
www.facebook.com/vitalitenb; twitter.com/vitalitenb;
www.instagram.com/vitalitenb
Nombre de lits: 215 lits
Note: Services: diagnostiques; chirurgie; cliniques de soins
ambulatoires; mère et à l'enfant; specialises; spécialisés de
réadaptation; thérapeutiques; programme de suivi des porteurs
d'implants cochléaires du Nouveau-Brunswick; et Pavillon UCT.

Campbellton: **Campbellton Regional
Hospital/Hôpital régional de Campbellton**
Affiliated with: Vitalité Health Network
PO Box 880, 189 Lily Lake Rd., Campbellton, NB E3N 3H3
Tel: 506-789-5000
info@vitalitenb.ca
www.vitalitenb.ca
www.facebook.com/vitalitenb; twitter.com/vitalitenb;
www.instagram.com/vitalitenb
Year Founded: 1991
Number of Beds: 163 beds
Number of Employees: 900
Note: Programs & services include: acute psychiatry; ambulatory
care; audiology; care for veterans; clinical nutrition; diagnostic
imaging & laboratory; emergency; ENT; geriatrics; general
surgery; intensive care; medical; obstetrics / gynecology;
occupational therapy; orthopedics; palliative care; pediatrics;
psychology; recreology; rehabilitation; social work;
speech-language pathology; & urology.

Caraquet: **Hôpital de l'Enfant-Jésus (RHSJT)**
Affiliée à: Vitalité Health Network
Ancien nom: Hôpital de l'Enfant-Jésus RHSJ
1, boul St-Pierre ouest, Caraquet, NB E1W 1B6
Tél: 506-726-2100 *Téléc:* 506-726-2188
info@vitalitenb.ca
www.vitalitenb.ca
www.facebook.com/vitalitenb; twitter.com/vitalitenb;
www.instagram.com/vitalitenb
Nombre de lits: 12 lits
Note: Services: clinique avec un infirmier praticien; clinique de
phénylcétonurie (PCU); clinique de tests de Pap; clinique
mère-enfant; cliniques et programmes multidisciplinaires;
Lifeline; médecine / soins palliatifs; programme de réadaptation
cardiaque; services diagnostiques; services thérapeutiques;

soins ambulatoires; soins spirituels et religieux; télésanté; unité
de formation médicale; et urgence.
Judy Butler, Facilitiy Manager

Edmundston: **Hôpital régional
d'Edmundston/Edmundston Regional Hospital**
Affiliée à: Vitalité Health Network
275, boul Hébert, Edmundston, NB E3V 4E4
Tél: 506-739-2200 *Téléc:* 506-739-2248
info@vitalitenb.ca
www.vitalitenb.ca
www.facebook.com/vitalitenb; twitter.com/vitalitenb;
www.instagram.com/vitalitenb
Fondée en: 1991
Nombre de lits: 169 lits
Personnel: 1000
Note: Services: audiologie; bénévoles et soins spirituels et
religieux; clinique de réadaptation cardiaque; clinique sur les
maladies pulmonaires; dialyse rénale; électrodiagnostic;
ergothérapie; imagerie médicale; médecine; nutrition clinique;
obstétrique; oncologie; orthophonie; pédiatrie; pharmacie;
psychiatrie; psychologie; services diagnostiques; soins
ambulatoires; soins intensifs; soins prolongés et soins palliatifs;
thérapie respiratoire; travailleurs sociaux en milieu hospitalier;
unités de chirurgie; et urgence.

Fredericton: **Dr. Everett Chalmers Regional Hospital
(DECH)**
Affiliated with: Horizon Health Network
PO Box 9000, 700 Priestman St., Fredericton, NB E3B 5N5
Tel: 506-452-5400
www.horizonnb.ca
www.facebook.com/HorizonNB; twitter.com/HorizonHealthNB;
www.linkedin.com/company/horizon-health-network
Year Founded: 1976
Number of Beds: 314 beds
Note: Programs & services include: Addictions & Mental Health
(community forensics, children & youth treatment programs);
Clinical Services (day surgery, dermatology, dialysis, ear, nose &
throat, emergency, family medicine, gastroenterology, general
surgery, geriatrics, gynecology surgery, intensive care, internal
medicine, minor surgery, neonatal intensive care, opthalmology
surgery, orthopedic surgery, pediatrics, palliative care, plastic
surgery, physiatry, psychiatry, obstetrics, thoracic surgery,
urology surgery, vascular surgery & oncology); Diagnostics &
Testing (blood & specimen, bone marrow, breathing function,
bronchoscopy, CT scan, cystoscopy, endoscopy, ECG,
fluoroscopy, holter monitoring, EEG, pathology, MRI,
mammography, nuclear medicine, spirometry, ultrasound &
x-ray); Public Health Programs (health emergency, health
promotion, healthy learners, children & adolescents,
immunization, communicable disease prevention, HIV testing &
sexual health program); & Support & Therapy (audiology, clinical
nutrition, occupational, physiotherapy, psychology, recreational,
respiratory, speech-language pathology, spiritual care, social
work & telehealth).
Nicole Tupper, Executive Director
506-452-5667, Fax: 506-452-5670, nicole.tupper@horizonnb.ca

Grand Manan: **Grand Manan Hospital**
Affiliated with: Horizon Health Network
196 Rte. 776, Grand Manan, NB E5G 1A3
Tel: 506-662-4060
horizon@horizonnb.ca
www.horizonnb.ca
www.facebook.com/HorizonNB; twitter.com/HorizonHealthNB;
www.linkedin.com/company/horizon-health-network
Number of Beds: 10 beds
Population Served: 5000
Specialties: Chronic diseases & women's health issues
Note: Programs & services include: clinical services (emergency,
family medicine & palliative care); diagnostics & testing (blood &
specimen collection, ECG & x-ray); & support & therapy
(physiotherapy & Telehealth).

Grand-Sault: **Hôpital général de Grand-Sault
inc./Grand Falls General Hospital Inc.**
Affiliée à: Vitalité Health Network
**CP 7061, 625, boul Evérard H. Daigle, Grand-Sault, NB E3Z
2R9**
Tél: 506-473-7555 *Téléc:* 506-473-7530
info@vitalitenb.ca
www.vitalitenb.ca
www.facebook.com/vitalitenb; twitter.com/vitalitenb;
www.instagram.com/vitalitenb
Fondée en: 1962
Nombre de lits: 20 lits
Population desservi: 15000 *Personnel:* 160
Note: Services: chirurgie mineure; clinique du diabète; clinique
sur l'hypertension; dermatologie; électrocardiographie;
endocrinologie; gastro-entérologie; gynécologie/obstétrique;
imagerie médicale; inhalothérapie; laboratoire; médecine interne;

nutrition; oncologie; ophtalmologie; orthopédie;
oto-rhino-laryngologie; pédiatrie; physiothérapie; programme
mère / enfant; réadaptation cardiaque; rhumatologie; services de
traitement des dépendances; soins préanesthésiques; soins
médicaux d'un jour; traitement anticoagulant; traitements
mineurs; et urologie.

Lamèque: **Hôpital de Lamèque/Centre de santé
communautaire de Lamèque**
Affiliée à: Vitalité Health Network
**Également connu sous le nom de: Hôpital et CSC de
Lamèque**
29, rue de l'Hôpital, Lamèque, NB E8T 1C5
Tél: 506-344-2261 *Téléc:* 506-344-3403
info@vitalitenb.ca
www.vitalitenb.ca
www.facebook.com/vitalitenb; twitter.com/vitalitenb;
www.instagram.com/vitalitenb
Nombre de lits: 12 lits
Note: Services: clinique de dépistage du cancer du col de
l'utérus (test Pap); clinique de gériatrie; clinique de vaccination
contre la grippe; clinique pour femmes enceintes; clinique pour
les patients sans médecin de famille (suivi par les infirmières
praticiennes); développement communautaire; électrodiagnostic
cardiaque; ergothérapie; imagerie médicale; laboratoire;
médecine; nutrition clinique; pharmacie; physiothérapie;
programme d'abandon du tabac; programme Santé active;
programme Mes choix, Ma santé; programme pour les
endeuillés; soins des problèmes de santé chroniques; soutien à
l'allaitement; télésanté; thérapie respiratoire (inhalothérapie);
travail social; et unité de médecine familiale.

Miramichi: **Miramichi Regional Hospital**
Affiliated with: Horizon Health Network
500 Water St., Miramichi, NB E1V 3G5
Tel: 506-623-3000 *Fax:* 506-623-3465
horizon@horizonnb.ca
www.horizonnb.ca
www.facebook.com/HorizonNB; twitter.com/HorizonHealthNB;
www.linkedin.com/company/horizon-health-network
Number of Beds: 150 beds
Note: Programs & services include: Addictions & Mental Health
(children & youth, gambling, inpatient acute care psychiatric unit,
inpatient addictions, individual family & group counseling,
community care, methadone treatment, substance abuse,
smoking cessation program & youth outpatient); Clinical
Services (day surgery, dermatology, ear, nose & throat,
emergency, family medicine, general surgery, gynecology
surgery, geriatrics, intensive care, internal medicine, minor
surgery, obstetrics, pediatrics, palliative care, psychiatry,
oncology, ophthalmology surgery, orthopedic surgery,
rehabilitation & urology surgery); Diagnostics & Testing (blood &
specimen collection, breathing function lab, CT scan,
cystoscopy, endoscopy, ECG, fluoroscopy, holter monitoring,
pathology, MRI, mammography, ultrasound, x-rays &
spirometry); Public Health Programs (early childhood, health
emergency & promotion, healthy learners, immunization,
communicable disease, HIV testing & sexual health); & Support
& Therapy (audiology, clinical nutrition, occupational,
physiotherapy, recreational, respiratory, speech-language
pathology, spiritual care, social work & telehealth).
Marilyn Underhill, Executive Director
Dr. Camille Haddad, Medical Director

Moncton: **Le Centre hospitalier universitaire
Dr-Georges-L.-Dumont (CHUDGLD)**
Affiliée à: Vitalité Health Network
330, av Université, Moncton, NB E1C 2Z3
Tél: 506-862-4000
info@vitalitenb.ca
www.vitalitenb.ca
www.facebook.com/vitalitenb; twitter.com/vitalitenb;
www.instagram.com/vitalitenb
Nombre de lits: 302 lits
Personnel: 2000
Note: Services: Appel Dumont Response; Auberge
Mgr-Henri-Cormier; audiologie; chirurgie; clinique d'obstétrique;
clinique de gynéco-oncologie; clinique de santé du sein; clinique
de traitement; clinique d'oncologie médicale et clinique de
radio-oncologie; clinique d'oncologie palliative; curiethérapie de
la prostate; imagerie médicale; laboratoire et prises de sang;
médecine générale et médecine interne; néphrologie; nutrition
clinique; physiothérapie; physique médicale; programme
provincial de PCU et centre de coordination du dépistage des
troubles métaboliques; psychologie; service de travail social;
service d'ergothérapie; service d'orthophonie; soins
ambulatoires; soins spirituels et religieux; thérapie respiratoire;
travail social; urgence; service de radiothérapie; soins palliatifs;
thérapie systémique communautaire; unité 4D (unité
d'oncologie); unité des naissances (3B); et unité de pédiatrie
(3D).
Gilles Lanteigne, Président-directeur général

Moncton: **The Moncton Hospital/L'Hôpital de Moncton**
Affiliated with: Horizon Health Network
135 MacBeath Ave., Moncton, NB E1C 6Z8
Tel: 506-857-5111 *Fax:* 506-857-5545
horizon@horizonnb.ca
www.horizonnb.ca
www.facebook.com/HorizonNB; twitter.com/HorizonHealthNB;
www.linkedin.com/company/horizon-health-network
Number of Beds: 381 beds
Specialties: Critical care & trauma cases
Note: Programs & services include: Addictions & Mental Health (inpatient acute care psychiatric unit, inpatient addictions, individual family & group counseling, community care, methadone treatment & smoking cessation program); Clinical Services (day surgery, dermatology, ear, nose & throat, emergency, family medicine, general surgery, gynecology surgery, gastroenterology, geriatrics, intensive care, internal medicine, neurology, neurosurgery, neonatal intensive care, minor surgery, obstetrics, oncology, ophthalmology surgery, orthopedic surgery, palliative care, plastic surgery, rehabilitation, rheumatology, thoracic surgery, urology surgery & vascular surgery); Diagnostics & Testing (blood & specimen, bone marrow, breathing function, bronchoscopy, CT scan, cystoscopy, endoscopy, ECG, fluoroscopy, holter monitoring, neuro electrodiagnostics, pathology, MRI, mammography, nuclear medicine, spirometry, ultrasound & x-ray); & Support & Therapy (audiology, clinical nutrition, occupational, physiotherapy, psychology, recreational, respiratory, speech-language pathology, spiritual care, social work & Telehealth).
Nancy Parker, Executive Director

Oromocto: **Oromocto Public Hospital**
Affiliated with: Horizon Health Network
103 Winnebago St., Oromocto, NB E2V 1C6
Tel: 506-357-4700
horizon@horizonnb.ca
www.horizonnb.ca
www.facebook.com/HorizonNB; twitter.com/HorizonHealthNB;
www.linkedin.com/company/horizon-health-network
Number of Beds: 45 beds
Note: Programs & services include: Clinical Services (day surgery, ear, nose & throat, emergency, family medicine, general surgery, gynecology surgery, gastroenterology, geriatrics, minor surgery, opthalmology surgery, plastic surgery, palliative care, rehabilitation & urology surgery); Diagnostics & Testing (blood & specimen collection, bronchoscopy, cystoscopy, endoscopy, ECG, fluoroscopy, holter monitoring, mammography, spirometry, ultrasound & x-ray); & Support & Therapy (clinical nutrition, occupational therapy, physiotherapy, recreational therapy, respiratory therapy, speech-language pathology, spiritual care & social work).

Perth-Andover: **Hotel-Dieu of St. Joseph/Hôtel-Dieu Saint-Joseph**
Affiliated with: Horizon Health Network
10 Woodland Hill, Perth-Andover, NB E7H 5H5
Tel: 506-273-7100 *Fax:* 506-273-7200
horizon@horizonnb.ca
www.horizonnb.ca
www.facebook.com/HorizonNB; twitter.com/HorizonHealthNB;
www.linkedin.com/company/horizon-health-network
Number of Beds: 22 beds
Population Served: 10000
Note: Programs & services include: Addictions & Mental Health (smoking cessation program); Clinical Services (day surgery, emergency, general surgery, family medicine, minor surgery, pediatrics, palliative care, oncology, rehabilitation); Diagnostics & Testing (blood & specimen collection, endoscopy, ECG, fluoroscopy, Holter monitoring, mammography, spirometry, x-rays & ultrasound); & Support & Therapy (clinical nutrition, occupational therapy, physiotherapy, respiratory therapy, speech-language pathology, spiritual care, social work & Telehealth).
Karen O'Regan, Facility Manager

Plaster Rock: **Tobique Valley Community Health Centre (TVCHC)**
Affiliated with: Horizon Health Network
Former Name: Tobique Valley Hospital Inc.
120 Main St., Plaster Rock, NB E7G 2E5
Tel: 506-356-6600 *Fax:* 506-356-6618
horizon@horizonnb.ca
www.horizonnb.ca
www.facebook.com/HorizonNB; twitter.com/HorizonHealthNB;
www.linkedin.com/company/horizon-health-network
Year Founded: 1957
Note: Services include: addictions & mental health (smoking cessation program); clinical services (family medicine); diagnostics & testing (blood & specimen collection, ECG, Holter monitoring, x-ray, & spirometry); & support & therapy (clinical

nutrition, occupational therapy, physiotherapy, respiratory therapy, speech language pathology, social work, & Telehealth).

Sackville: **Sackville Memorial Hospital/L'Hôpital mémorial de Sackville**
Affiliated with: Horizon Health Network
8 Main St., Sackville, NB E4L 4A3
Tel: 506-364-4100 *Fax:* 506-536-1983
www.horizonnb.ca
www.facebook.com/HorizonNB; twitter.com/HorizonHealthNB;
www.linkedin.com/company/horizon-health-network
Number of Beds: 21 beds
Number of Employees: 105
Note: Programs & services include: Addictions & Mental Health (geriatrics, smoking cessation program); Clinical Services (day surgery, emergency, family medicine & geriatrics); Diagnostics & Testing (ECG, Holter monitoring & x-ray); & Support & Therapy (clinical nutrition, occupational therapy, physiotherapy, respiratory, speech-language pathology, spiritual care, social work & Telehealth).

Saint John: **Saint John Regional Hospital**
Affiliated with: Horizon Health Network
PO Box 2100, 400 University Ave., Saint John, NB E2L 4L4
Tel: 506-648-6000
horizon@horizonnb.ca
www.horizonnb.ca
www.facebook.com/HorizonNB; twitter.com/HorizonHealthNB;
www.linkedin.com/company/horizon-health-network
Number of Beds: 445 beds
Note: Teaching hospital affiliated with Dalhousie University, New Brunswick Community College, University of New Brunswick & Memorial University in St. John's Newfoundland.
Programs & services include: Addictions & Mental Health (emergency & inpatient acute care psychiatry); Clinical Services (cardiac surgery, day surgery, dermatology, dialysis, ear, nose & throat, emergency, family medicine, general surgery, gynecology surgery, gastroenterology, geriatrics, intensive care, internal medicine, neonatal intensive care, minor surgery, pediatrics, palliative care, physiatry, plastic & burns, psychiatry, neurology, neurosurgery, obstetrics, oncology, ophthalmology surgery, orthopedic surgery, plastic surgery, rehabilitation, rheumatology, sleep centre, thoracic surgery, urology surgery, & vascular surgery); Diagnostics & Testing (blood & specimen collection, bone marrow, breathing function, bronchoscopy, CT scan, cystoscopy, endoscopy, ECG, fluoroscopy, holter monitoring, neuro electrodiagnostics, pathology, MRI, mammography, positron emissions tomography, nuclear medicine, spirometry, ultrasound & x-ray); & Support & Therapy (audiology, clinical nutrition, occupational therapy, physiotherapy, psychology, recreational therapy, respiratory therapy, speech-language pathology, spiritual care, social work & Telehealth).

Saint John: **St. Joseph's Hospital**
Affiliated with: Horizon Health Network
130 Bayard Dr., Saint John, NB E2L 3L6
Tel: 506-632-5555 *Fax:* 506-632-5551
horizon@horizonnb.ca
www.horizonnb.ca
www.facebook.com/HorizonNB; twitter.com/HorizonHealthNB;
www.linkedin.com/company/horizon-health-network
Number of Beds: 103 beds
Note: Programs & services include: Addictions & Mental Health (methadone treatment program); Clinical Services (surgery, ENT, emergency, gastroenterology, geriatrics, oncology, palliative care); Diagnostics & Testing (blood & specimen collection, CT scan, cystoscopy, endoscopy, ECG, fluoroscopy, holter monitoring, neuro electrodiagnostics, mammography, spirometry, ultrasound & x-ray); & Support & Therapy (clinical nutrition, occupational therapy, physiotherapy, recreational therapy, respiratory therapy, speech-language pathology, spiritual care, social work & Telehealth).
Heather Oakley, Facility Administrator

Saint-Quentin: **Hôtel-Dieu St-Joseph de Saint-Quentin**
Affiliée à: Vitalité Health Network
21, rue Canada, Saint-Quentin, NB E8A 2P6
Tél: 506-235-2300 *Téléc:* 506-235-7201
info@vitalitenb.ca
www.vitalitenb.ca
www.facebook.com/vitalitenb; twitter.com/vitalitenb;
www.instagram.com/vitalitenb
Fondée en: 1636
Nombre de lits: 6 lits
Population desservi: 6000 *Personnel:* 80
Note: Services: anticoagulant; clinique du prédiabète; clinique pulmonaire; diabète; gastroentérologie; hypertension artérielle; imagerie médicale; laboratoire; médecine interne; mère-enfant; nutrition; obstétrique; oncologie; ophtalmologie; pédiatrie; physiothérapie; préanesthésie; santé mentale; soins médicaux

d'un jour; traitement des dépendances; traitements mineurs; urologie; et urgence.
Dr. Isabelle-Anne Girouard, Directrice médicale

St. Stephen: **Charlotte County Hospital**
Affiliated with: Horizon Health Network
4 Garden St., St. Stephen, NB E3L 2L9
Tel: 506-465-4444 *Fax:* 506-465-4418
horizon@horizonnb.ca
www.horizonnb.ca
www.facebook.com/HorizonNB; twitter.com/HorizonHealthNB;
www.linkedin.com/company/horizon-health-network
Number of Beds: 44 beds
Note: Programs & services include: Addictions & Mental Health (methadone treatment program); Clinical Services (dialysis, emergency, family medicine, geriatrics, intensive care, minor surgery & palliative care); Diagnostics & Testing (blood & specimen collection, endoscopy, ECG, holter monitoring, mammography, ultrasound, spirometry & x-ray); & Support & Therapy (clinical nutrition, occupational therapy, physiotherapy, respiratory therapy & speech-language pathology).

Ste-Anne-de-Kent: **Hôpital Stella-Maris-de-Kent**
Affiliée à: Vitalité Health Network
7714 Rte. 134, Ste-Anne-de-Kent, NB E4S 1H5
Tél: 506-743-7800
info@vitalitenb.ca
www.vitalitenb.ca
www.facebook.com/vitalitenb; twitter.com/vitalitenb;
www.instagram.com/vitalitenb
Nombre de lits: 20 lits
Note: Services: alimentation et nutrition / clinique de nutrition; clinique de santé; clinique de soins de la femme; clinique du diabète; cliniques externes avec spécialistes; électrocardiogramme; ergothérapie; imagerie diagnostique; laboratoire; liaison autochtone; orthophonie; pharmacie; physiothérapie; service de l'environnement; services spirituels et religieux; thérapie respiratoire; unité de médecine; et urgence.

Sussex: **Sussex Health Centre**
Affiliated with: Horizon Health Network
75 Leonard Dr., Sussex, NB E4E 2P7
Tel: 506-432-3100 *Fax:* 506-432-3106
horizon@horizonnb.ca
www.horizonnb.ca
www.facebook.com/HorizonNB; twitter.com/HorizonHealthNB;
www.linkedin.com/company/horizon-health-network
Number of Beds: 25 beds
Population Served: 30000
Note: Programs & services include: Clinical Services (day surgery, emergency, family medicine, general surgery, palliative care & rehabilitation); Diagnostics & Testing (blood & specimen collection, ECG, holter monitoring, mammography, spirometry, ultrasound & x-ray); & Support & Therapy (audiology, clinical nutrition, occupational therapy, physiotherapy, respiratory therapy, speech-language pathology & spiritual care).

Tracadie: **Hôpital de Tracadie-Sheila**
Affiliée à: Vitalité Health Network
CP 3180 Stn. Main, 400, rue des Hospitalières, Tracadie, NB E1X 1G5
Tél: 506-394-3000
info@vitalitenb.ca
www.vitalitenb.ca
www.facebook.com/vitalitenb; twitter.com/vitalitenb;
www.instagram.com/vitalitenb
Fondée en: 1991
Nombre de lits: 59 lits
Note: Services: 2e nord et soins concentres; diététique; électrodiagnostic; ergothérapie; imagerie médicale; laboratoire; médecine et pédiatrie; orthophonie; physiothérapie; service alimentaire; service de psychologie; soins ambulatoires; travail social; services spirituels et religieux; thérapie respiratoire; traitement des dépendances; unité satellite de dialyse; et urgence.

Waterville: **Upper River Valley Hospital**
Affiliated with: Horizon Health Network
11300 Rte. 130, Waterville, NB E7P 0A4
Tel: 506-375-5900
horizon@horizonnb.ca
www.horizonnb.ca
www.facebook.com/HorizonNB; twitter.com/HorizonHealthNB;
www.linkedin.com/company/horizon-health-network
Number of Beds: 52 beds
Population Served: 45000 *Number of Employees:* 800
Note: Programs & services include: Addictions & Mental Health (smoking cessation program); Clinical Services (day surgery, dialysis, emergency, family medicine, general surgery, gastroenterology, geriatrics, intensive care, internal medicine, minor surgery, pediatrics, palliative care, obstetrics, oncology, ophthalmology surgery, rehabilitation & urology surgery);

Diagnostics & Testing (blood & specimen collection, bone marrow biopsies, breathing function lab, CT scan, endoscopy, ECG, fluoroscopy, Holter monitoring, MRI, mammography, spirometry, ultrasound & x-ray); Public Health Programs (health emergency & promotion, healthy learners program, children & adolescents, immunization, communicable disease prevention, HIV testing & sexual health); & Support & Therapy (audiology, clinical nutrition, occupational, physiotherapy, psychology, respiratory therapy, speech-language pathology, spiritual care, social work & Telehealth).
Joy VanTassel, Facility Manager

Auxiliary Hospitals

Saint John: Saint John Regional Hospital -
Ridgewood Veterans Wing (RVW)
Affiliated with: Horizon Health Network
PO Box 2100, 422 Bay St., Saint John, NB E2L 4L2
Tel: 506-635-2420 *Fax:* 506-635-2425
horizon@horizonnb.ca
www.horizonnb.ca
www.facebook.com/HorizonNB; twitter.com/HorizonHealthNB;
www.linkedin.com/company/horizon-health-network
Year Founded: 1976
Number of Beds: 80 beds
Note: A facility for veterans who require long-term care; works with Veteran Affairs Canada & the Royal Canadian Legion.

Community Health Care Centres

Baie-Sainte-Anne: Baie Ste-Anne Health
Centre/Centre de santé Baie-Ste-Anne
Affiliated with: Horizon Health Network
13, rue de l'Église, Baie-Sainte-Anne, NB E9A 1A9
Tel: 506-228-2004 *Fax:* 506-228-2008
horizonnb.ca
Note: Patients may access the services of a physician who works 2 days per week, & a full time nurse on site; monthly public health clinic; laboratory clinic twice a week.

Belledune: Jacquet River Health Centre/Centre de
santé de Jacquet River
Affiliated with: Vitalité Health Network
41 Mack St., Belledune, NB E8G 2R3
Tel: 506-237-3222
www.vitalitenb.ca
Note: Services: medical consultation; blood pressure clinic; smoking cessation clinic; social work; public health; mental health; addiction; & ambulatory care.

Blacks Harbour: Fundy Health Centre
Affiliated with: Horizon Health Network
PO Box 1298, 34 Hospital St., Blacks Harbour, NB E5H 1K2
Tel: 506-456-4200 *Fax:* 506-456-4222
horizon@horizonnb.ca
www.horizonnb.ca

Blackville: Blackville Health Centre
Affiliated with: Horizon Health Network
2 Shaffer Lane, Blackville, NB E9B 1P4
Tel: 506-843-2910 *Fax:* 506-843-2911
horizonnb.ca
Year Founded: 1989
Note: Services include: addictions & mental health; clinical; diagnostics; & therapy.

Boiestown: Boiestown Health Centre
Affiliated with: Horizon Health Network
#2, 6154 rte 8, Boiestown, NB E6A 1M4
Tel: 506-369-2700 *Fax:* 506-369-2702
horizonnb.ca
Note: Services include: addictions & mental health; clinical; support & therapy; & diagnostics & testing.

Chipman: Chipman Health Centre
Affiliated with: Horizon Health Network
9 Civic Ct., Chipman, NB E4A 2H8
Tel: 506-339-7650 *Fax:* 506-339-7652
horizonnb.ca
Note: Offers clinical, diagnostics, mental health, & therapy services.

Dalhousie: Centre de santé communautaire St.
Joseph/St. Joseph Community Health Centre
Affiliated with: Vitalité Health Network
#1, 280, rue Victoria, Dalhousie, NB E8C 2R6
Tel: 506-684-7000
www.vitalitenb.ca
Note: Le Réseau de santé Vitalité regroupe les huit anciennes régies régionales dans la province. Le Centre a pour mission d'améliorer l'accès aux soins de santé primaires, et l'état de santé des collectivités; promotion de la santé, prévention des

maladies et blessures, et traitement des maladies chroniques; services diagnostiques; soins ambulatoires.

Doaktown: Central Miramichi Community Health
Centre (CMCHC)
Affiliated with: Horizon Health Network
Former Name: Upper Miramichi Health Services
Centre - Doaktown
11 Prospect St., Doaktown, NB E9C 1C3
Tel: 506-365-6100 *Fax:* 506-365-6104
horizonnb.ca
Note: Services include: addictions & mental health; clinical; support & therapy; & diagnostics & testing.
Lorri Amos, Nurse Manager

Fairhaven: Deer Island Health Centre
Affiliated with: Horizon Health Network
999 Rte. 772, Fairhaven, NB E5V 1P2
Tel: 506-747-4150 *Fax:* 506-747-4151
horizonnb.ca
Note: Patients may access the services of a physician who works 1 day per week & a nurse practitioner who works 3 days per week. Services include: addictions & mental health; clinical; support & therapy; & diagnostics & testing.

Fredericton Junction: Fredericton Junction Health
Centre
Affiliated with: Horizon Health Network
233 Sunbury Dr., Fredericton Junction, NB E5L 1S1
Tel: 506-368-6501 *Fax:* 506-368-6502
horizonnb.ca
Note: Services include: addictions & mental health; clinical; diagnostics; & therapy.

Harvey Station: Harvey Health Centre
Affiliated with: Horizon Health Network
Former Name: Harvey Community Hospital Ltd.
2019 Rte. 3, Harvey Station, NB E6K 3E9
Tel: 506-366-6400 *Fax:* 506-366-6403
horizon@horizonnb.ca
www.horizonnb.ca

McAdam: McAdam Health Centre
Affiliated with: Horizon Health Network
15 Saunders Rd., McAdam, NB E6J 1K9
Tel: 506-784-6300 *Fax:* 506-784-6306
horizonnb.ca
Note: Services include: clinical; support & therapy; & diagnostics & testing.

Minto: Queens North Community Health Centre
Affiliated with: Horizon Health Network
Also Known As: Queens North Health Centre
1100 Pleasant Dr., Minto, NB E4B 2V6
Tel: 506-327-7800 *Fax:* 506-327-7899
horizonnb.ca
Note: Services include: primary health care; addiction & mental health; support & therapy; illness & injury prevention; chronic disease management; & community development.
Isabel Camp, Manager

Moncton: NB Extra-Mural Program
Medavie Health Services New Brunswick
Affiliated with: Horizon Health Network
#101, 210 John St., Moncton, NB E1C 0B8
Tel: 506-872-6500 *Toll-Free:* 888-862-2111
extramuralnb.ca
www.facebook.com/ANBEMP; twitter.com/ANB_EMP
Number of Employees: 900
Note: Brings care to the home working out of 29 office locations with a fleet of 515 vehicles. The team includes: registered nurses; licensed practical nurses; social workers; respiratory therapists; registered dietians; physiotherapists; occupational therapists; speech-language pathologists; & rehabilitation assisstants.
René Boudreau, Chair, EM / ANB Inc. Board of Directors
Richard Losier, Chief Executive Officer

Nackawic: Nackawic Community Health Centre
Affiliated with: Horizon Health Network
Nackawic Shopping Centre, Upper Floor, #201, 135 Otis Dr.,
Nackawic, NB E6G 1H1
Tel: 506-575-6600 *Fax:* 506-575-6603
horizonnb.ca
Note: Services include: clinical; support & therapy; & diagnostics & testing.

Néguac: Neguac Health Centre
Affiliated with: Horizon Health Network
38 Otho St., Néguac, NB E9G 4H3
Tel: 506-776-3876 *Fax:* 506-776-3877
horizonnb.ca

Note: Provides clinical, diagnostics, & support & therapy services.

Paquetville: Centre de santé de Paquetville
Affiliée à: Vitalité Health Network
1096, rue du Parc, Paquetville, NB E8R 1J4
Tél: 506-764-2424 *Téléc:* 506-764-2425
www.vitalitenb.ca
Note: Services: injections; monitorage de la tension artérielle; suivi pour pansements; clinique de tests de Pap; clinique de vaccination antigrippale.

Petitcodiac: Petitcodiac Health Centre/Centre de
santé de Petitcodiac
Affiliated with: Horizon Health Network
32 Railway Ave., Petitcodiac, NB E4Z 6H4
Tel: 506-756-3400 *Fax:* 506-756-3406
horizonnb.ca
Note: Number of staff: 2 physicians. Offers clinical, mental health, diagnostics & drop-in nursing services.

Pointe-Verte: Centre de santé de Chaleur/Chaleur
Health Centre
Affiliée à: Vitalité Health Network
Ancien nom: Centre de santé Pointe Verte
415, rue Principale, Pointe-Verte, NB E8J 2S5
Tél: 506-542-2434 *Téléc:* 506-542-2436
Note: Services: injections; vaccins; pansents; retrait de points de suture; clinique de test de Pap.

Rexton: Rexton Health Centre/Centre de santé de
Rexton
Affiliated with: Horizon Health Network
33 Main St., Rexton, NB E4W 0E5
Tel: 506-523-7940 *Fax:* 506-523-7949
horizonnb.ca
Year Founded: 1974
Note: Drop-in services, clinics, immunization, nutrition & diabetes education.

Riverside-Albert: Albert County Community Health
Centre/Centre de santé communautaire du comté
d'Albert
Affiliated with: Horizon Health Network
8 Forestdale Rd., Riverside-Albert, NB E4H 3Y7
Tel: 506-882-3100 *Fax:* 506-882-3101
horizonnb.ca
Year Founded: 1961
Note: Multidisciplinary, primary health care services, including clinical services, support, therapy, diagnostics & testing, & addictions & mental health programs.

Rogersville: Rogersville Health Centre
Affiliated with: Horizon Health Network
9, rue des Ormes, Rogersville, NB E4Y 1S6
Tel: 506-775-2030 *Fax:* 506-775-2025
horizonnb.ca
Note: Provides daily nursing services, physician services by appointment four days per week, & laboratory services one day per week.

Saint John: Hospice Greater Saint John
Affiliated with: Horizon Health Network
Former Name: Hospice Saint John & Sussex
385 Dufferin Row, Saint John, NB E2M 2J9
Tel: 506-632-5593 *Fax:* 506-632-5592
info@hospicesj.ca
www.hospicesj.ca
www.facebook.com/hospicesj
Year Founded: 1983
Number of Beds: 10 beds
Number of Employees: 7
Sandy Maxwell, CEO

Saint John: St. Joseph's Community Health Centre
Affiliated with: Horizon Health Network
116 Coburg St., Saint John, NB E2L 3K1
Tel: 506-632-5537 *Fax:* 506-632-5539
horizonnb.ca
Note: Services include: addictions & mental health; clinical; support & therapy; & diagnostics & testing,

Saint John: Senior Watch Inc.
Affiliated with: Horizon Health Network
Prince Edward Square Mall, #111, 100 Prince Edward St.,
Saint John, NB E2L 4M5
Tel: 506-634-8906 *Fax:* 506-633-2992
Toll-Free: 800-561-2463
services@seniorwatch.com
www.seniorwatch.com
www.facebook.com/SeniorWatch

Year Founded: 1987
Note: New Brunswick-based firm specializing in developing & managing home care services for seniors.
Jean E. Porter Mowatt, President & CEO
jean@seniorwatch.com
Sharon A. O'Brien, Chief Learning Officer & Executive Vice-President
sharon@seniorwatch.com
Mary-Ellen Morin, Finance Officer
financeac@seniorwatch.com

Sainte-Anne-de-Madawaska: **Dr.-Chanel-Dupuis Health Centre/Centre de santé Dr-Chanel-Dupuis**
Affiliated with: Vitalité Health Network
1, rue de la Clinique, Sainte-Anne-de-Madawaska, NB E7E 1B9
Tel: 506-445-6200 *Fax:* 506-445-6201
www.vitalitenb.ca
Note: Staff includes 2 physicians, 2 nurse practioners & 1 nurse.

Shediac: **Shediac Regional Medical Centre/Centre médical régional de Shédiac**
Affiliated with: Vitalité Health Network
PO Box 1477, 419 Main St., Shediac, NB E4P 2B8
Tel: 506-533-2700
www.vitalitenb.ca
Note: Services: blood pressure clinic; diabetes clinic; flu immunization clinic; pap test clinic; smoking cessation clinic; & physical activity program for those suffer from diabetes, high blood pressure & obesity.

Stanley: **Stanley Health Centre**
Affiliated with: Horizon Health Network
PO Box 340, Stanley, NB E6B 2K5
Tel: 506-367-7730 *Fax:* 506-367-7738
horizonnb.ca
Note: Services (by appointment) include: addictions & mental health; clinical; & diagnostices & testing.

Special Treatment Centres

Campbellton: **Notre-Dame House Inc./Maison Notre-Dame**
PO Box 158, Campbellton, NB E3N 3G4
Tel: 506-753-4703 *Fax:* 506-753-3718
maisonnotredame@nb.aibn.com
Note: Maison Notre-Dame is a shelter for women who have experienced violence or abuse.
Stefanie Savoie, Executive Director

Edmundston: **Services de toxicomanie**
Affiliée à: Vitalité Health Network
345, boul Hébert, Edmundston, NB E3V 0E7
Tél: 506-735-2092
www.vitalitenb.ca
Nombre de lits: 10 lits

Fredericton: **Fredericton Addiction Services**
Affiliated with: Horizon Health Network
c/o Victoria Health Centre, 65 Brunswick St., Fredericton, NB E3B 1G5
Tel: 506-453-2132 *Fax:* 506-452-5533
horizonnb.ca

Fredericton: **Stan Cassidy Centre for Rehabilitation**
Affiliated with: Horizon Health Network
800 Priestman St., Fredericton, NB E3B 0C7
Tel: 506-452-5225 *Fax:* 506-452-5190
www.stancassidy.ca
Number of Beds: 20 beds
Note: Rehabilitation centre specializing in the treatment of complex neurological conditions, including brain injury, stroke, spinal cord injury, & neuromuscular disorders, as well as complex forms of autism spectrum disorder.
Robert Leckey, Medical Director

Moncton: **Moncton Addiction Services/Services de traitement des dépendances**
Affiliated with: Horizon Health Network
125 Mapleton Rd., Moncton, NB E1C 9G3
Tel: 506-856-2333 *Fax:* 506-856-2796
horizonnb.ca
Number of Beds: 20 beds
Note: Detoxification unit, methadone maintenance treatment program, addiction prevention & education, counselling, assessments.

Saint John: **Ridgewood Addiction Services**
Affiliated with: Horizon Health Network
416 Bay St., Saint John, NB E2M 7L4
Tel: 506-674-4300 *Fax:* 506-674-4374
horizonnb.ca

Number of Beds: 90 beds
Note: Comprehensive addiction treatment programs, detoxification, outpatient & short term residential services, addiction prevention & education, community reintegration.

Saint John: **WorkSafeNB Rehabilitation Centre**
Affiliated with: Horizon Health Network
PO Box 160, 1 Portland St., Saint John, NB E2L 3X9
Tel: 506-632-2200 *Toll-Free:* 800-222-9775
www.worksafenb.ca
Year Founded: 1965
Note: Occupational rehabilitation
Douglas Jones, President & CEO
Shelly Dauphinee, Vice-President, WorkSafe Services

Long Term Care Facilities

Acadieville: **Villa Acadie Ltée**
4057, rte. 480, Acadieville, NB E4Y 1Z3
Tél: 506-775-6088
Nombre de lits: 13 lits

Baker Brook: **Résidence Notre Dame**
CP 38, 3741, rue Principale, Baker Brook, NB E7A 2A5
Tél: 506-258-3322
Nombre de lits: 18 lits

Fredericton: **Women's Institute Home**
681 Union St., Fredericton, NB E3A 3N8
Tel: 506-454-0798
nbwi@nb.aibn.com
www.nbwi.ca
www.facebook.com/pages/Womens-Institute-Home/2842958017
81170
Year Founded: 1911
Number of Beds: 21 rooms

Miramichi: **Howard Henderson House Inc.**
Affiliated with: Horizon Health Network
225 Wellington St., Miramichi, NB E1N 1N1
Tel: 506-773-6522
Note: Residential care is provided for adults who are mentally or physically challenged.

Moncton: **Alternative Residences Alternatives (ARA)**
Affiliated with: Horizon Health Network
100 Botsford St., Moncton, NB E1C 4W9
Tel: 506-854-7229 *Fax:* 506-853-6051
altres@rogers.com
www.alternativeresidences.org
Year Founded: 1984
Number of Beds: 32
Area Served: South East New Brunswick *Number of Employees:* 50
Specialties: Mental health support
Note: Alternative Residences provides supervision & support to persons with a mental illness. Services include assistance with medication intake, the development of social & personal skills, dietary guidance, assistance with budgets, & searches for housing.
Alternative Residences' subsidized shared housing complexes accommodate 28, with minimal staff support. The organization's affordable community apartments house 16 clients.
George Murray, Executive Director
506-854-7229, exdirara@rogers.com
Chantal Ricker, Manager, Operations
Susan McLure, Accounting Officer

Moncton: **Birchmount Lodge**
Affiliated with: Horizon Health Network
144 Birchmount Dr., Moncton, NB E1C 8E7
Tel: 506-384-7573
Number of Beds: 32 beds
Donald Vossburgh, Administrator

Moncton: **Moncton Community Residences Inc.**
Affiliated with: Horizon Health Network
Former Name: Reade House
11 Brandon St., Moncton, NB E1C 9Z6
Tel: 506-858-0550 *Fax:* 506-858-0271
mcri@nb.aibn.com
www.monctoncommunityresidences.com
Number of Beds: 5 beds
Note: Provides residential services to people with developmental challenges, ranging from group homes to assistance with independent living.

Pennfield: **Collingwood Special Care Home**
249 Rte. 176, Pennfield, NB E5H 1R9
Tel: 506-456-3533
Number of Beds: 20 beds
Nancy Drost, Administrator

Riverview: **Grass Home**
Former Name: N-Joy Homes Ltd.
774 Coverdale Rd., Riverview, NB E1B 3L5
Tel: 506-386-1740 *Fax:* 506-386-7040
www.thegrasshome.com
Year Founded: 1983
Number of Beds: 24 beds
Michael Aikins, Chief Executive Officer

Robertville: **La Villa Sormany Inc.**
1289, ch Robertville, Robertville, NB E8K 2V9
Tél: 506-542-2731 *Téléc:* 506-542-2733
Nombre de lits: 60 lits

Sackville: **Drew Nursing Home**
165 Main St., Sackville, NB E4L 4S2
Tel: 506-364-4900 *Fax:* 506-364-4921
office@drewnursinghome.ca
www.drewnursinghome.ca
Number of Beds: 118 beds
Note: Offers health, therapy, & rehabilitation services.
Linda Shannon, Executive Director

Saint John: **Westport Residential Facility**
Affiliated with: Horizon Health Network
427 Prince St., Saint John, NB E2M 1R2
Tel: 506-674-2069 *Fax:* 506-832-0808
Number of Beds: 15 beds

Sainte-Anne-de-Madawaska: **Foyer Mont St-Joseph**
8, rue St-Joseph, Sainte-Anne-de-Madawaska, NB E7E 1L1
Tél: 506-445-2755

Tabusintac: **Foyer Prime Breau**
14 Covedell Rd., Tabusintac, NB E9H 1E6
Tél: 506-779-4445
Nombre de lits: 2 lits
Roséanna Breau, Propriétrice

Nursing Homes

Bath: **River View Manor Inc.**
96 Hospital St., Bath, NB E7J 1B9
Tel: 506-278-6030 *Fax:* 506-278-5962
rvmadministrator@nb.aibn.com
www.riverviewmanor.ca
Year Founded: 1981
Number of Beds: 40 beds
Note: Nursing home offering medical, nursing, rehabilitation, & nutrition services.
Guildo Cyr, Administrator
Gloria Crain, Director, Nursing

Bathurst: **Le Foyer Notre-Dame de Lourdes Inc.**
2055, Vallée-Lourdes Dr., Bathurst, NB E2A 4P8
Tél: 506-549-5085 *Téléc:* 506-549-5052
www.fndl.org
Nombre de lits: 130 lits
Personnel: 190
Note: Les services de soutien; le personnel des soins; soins palliatifs; la réadaptation
Léo-Paul Sonier, Directeur général
506-549-5085, dg.fndl@nb.aibn.com

Bathurst: **Robert L. Knowles Veterans Unit, Villa Chaleur**
795, rue Champlain, Bathurst, NB E2A 4M8
Tel: 506-549-5582 *Fax:* 506-545-6424
www.atlanticbaptisthousing.com
Year Founded: 1994
Number of Beds: 13 beds

Blacks Harbour: **Fundy Nursing Home**
34 Hospital St., Blacks Harbour, NB E5H 1C2
Tel: 506-456-4218 *Fax:* 506-456-4259
Number of Beds: 26 beds

Boiestown: **Central New Brunswick Nursing Home Inc.**
3458 rte 625, Boiestown, NB E6A 1C8
Tel: 506-369-7262 *Fax:* 506-369-2331
Number of Beds: 30 beds

Bouctouche: **Manoir Saint-Jean Baptiste**
5, av Richard, Bouctouche, NB E4S 3T2
Tél: 506-743-7344 *Téléc:* 506-743-7343
Nombre de lits: 50 lits
Ian Drapeau, Directeur général

Campbellton: **Campbellton Nursing Home Inc.**
PO Box 850, 101 Dover St., Campbellton, NB E3N 3K6
Tel: 506-789-7350 *Fax:* 506-789-7360
Number of Beds: 100 beds

Caraquet: **Villa Beauséjour Inc.**
CP 5608, 274, boul St-Pierre ouest, Caraquet, NB E1W 1B7
Tél: 506-726-2744 *Téléc:* 506-726-2745
Nombre de lits: 80 lits

Dalhousie: **Dalhousie Nursing Home Inc.**
#1, 296 Victoria St., Dalhousie, NB E8C 2R8
Tel: 506-684-7800 *Fax:* 506-684-7832
Number of Beds: 105 beds
Diane Léger, Administrator

Fredericton: **Pine Grove**
521 Woodstock Rd., Fredericton, NB E3B 2J2
Tel: 506-444-3400 *Fax:* 506-444-3407
adminclerk@pinegrovenh.com
www.pinegrovenh.com
Number of Beds: 70 beds
Note: Nursing home offering various services, including medical, nursing, dietary, medications, & activities.
Cheryl Wiggins, Administrator

Fredericton: **York Care Centre**
Former Name: York Manor Inc.
100 Sunset Dr., Fredericton, NB E3A 1A3
Tel: 506-444-3880 *Fax:* 506-444-3544
info@yorkcarecentre.ca
www.yorkcarecentre.ca
Number of Beds: 214 beds
Note: Services include: dental; laboratory & diagnostic; medical; nursing; nutrition; pharmacy; rehabilitation; & therapeutic recreation.
Kevin Harter, President & CEO
506-444-3880, kharter@yorkcarecentre.ca
Erin MacDonald, Director, Care Services
emacdonald@yorkcarecentre.ca
Robin Rickard, Director, Operations
rrickard@yorkcarecentre.ca
Byard Smith, Director, Finance
byard.smith@yorkcarecentre.ca

Fredericton Junction: **White Rapids Manor Inc.**
Affiliated with: Horizon Health Network
233 Sunbury Dr., Fredericton Junction, NB E5L 1S1
Tel: 613-368-6508 *Fax:* 613-368-6512
office@whiterapidsmanor.nb.ca
www.whiterapidsmanor.nb.ca
Year Founded: 1978
Number of Beds: 40 beds
Note: Activities include morning coffee; bingo; bus trips for shopping & sight-seeing.

Gagetown: **Orchard View Long Term Care Facility**
Former Name: Gagetown Nursing Home Ltd.
2230 Rte 102, Gagetown, NB E5M 1J6
Tel: 506-488-3544 *Fax:* 506-488-3551
www.orchardviewcare.ca
Year Founded: 1972
Number of Beds: 40 beds
Note: Services include: 24 hour nursing care; attending physician; nutritional assessment & therapy; recreational therapy; rehabilitation therapy; & pharmacy.
Steve Little, Administrator
506-488-3586, slittle@orchardviewltc.ca
Hollie Keddy, Director, Care

Grand Falls: **Villa Des Chutes**
433, rue Evangeline, Grand Falls, NB E3Z 1G5
Tel: 506-473-7726 *Fax:* 506-473-7849
www.fallsvilladeschutes.com
Number of Beds: 69 beds
Note: Services include: nursing; medical; pharmacy; rehabilitation (occupational therapy & physiotherapy); & activities.
Maurice Richard, Executive Director
506-473-7727, richardmaurice@rogers.com

Grand Manan: **Grand Manan Nursing Home Inc.**
266, Rte. 776, Grand Manan, NB E5G 1A5
Tel: 506-662-7111 *Fax:* 506-662-7117
Number of Beds: 30 beds

Hampton: **Dr. V.A. Snow Centre Inc.**
54 Demille Ct., Hampton, NB E5N 5S7
Tel: 506-832-6210 *Fax:* 506-832-7674
info@snownursing.com
snownursing.com
Number of Beds: 50 beds
Note: Services include: clinical; nursing care; nutrition; palliative care; pharmacy; & therapeutic recreation.
Terry O'Neill, Administrator
506-832-6210
Janice Robinson, Director, Care
Lynne MacNeil, Manager, Support Services

Hartland: **Central Carleton Nursing Home Inc.**
139 Rockland Rd., Hartland, NB E7P 1E9
Tel: 506-375-3033 *Fax:* 506-375-3035
www.ccnh.ca
Number of Beds: 30 beds
Note: Programs & services include: audiology; dental; foot care; medical; nursing; nutrition; pharmacy; recreation; rehabilitation; & vision care.
Florin Allen, Chair

Inkerman: **Résidences Inkerman Inc.**
1171, ch Pallot, Inkerman, NB E8P 1C2
Tel: 506-336-3909 *Fax:* 506-336-3912
Number of Beds: 30 lits

Lamèque: **Les Résidences Lucien Saindon Inc.**
26, rue de l'Hôpital, Lamèque, NB E8T 1C3
Tél: 506-344-3232 *Téléc:* 506-344-3240
Nombre de lits: 54 lits

Memramcook: **Foyer St. Thomas de la Vallée de Memramcook Inc.**
100, rue Notre-Dame, Memramcook, NB E4K 3W3
Tél: 506-758-2110 *Téléc:* 506-758-9489
Nombre de lits: 30 lits

Mill Cove: **Mill Cove Nursing Home Inc.**
12 Lakeview Lane, Mill Cove, NB E4C 3E3
Tel: 506-488-3033 *Fax:* 506-488-3037
Note: Specialties: Nursing care for persons with special needs; Podiatry; Psychology; Rehabilitation; Snoezelen rooms
Daniel Gilman, CEO

Minto: **W.G. Bishop Nursing Home**
PO Box 1004, 1100 Pleasant Dr., Minto, NB E4B 3Y6
Tel: 506-327-7853 *Fax:* 506-327-7812
www.wgbishopnursinghome.org
Number of Beds: 30 beds
Area Served: Minto, Chipman, & the surrounding area
Kathy Donaldson, Administrator
506-327-7809

Miramichi: **Miramichi Senior Citizens Home Inc.**
1400 Water St., Miramichi, NB E1N 1A4
Tel: 506-778-6810 *Fax:* 506-778-6860
Number of Beds: 81 beds

Miramichi: **Mount Saint Joseph Nursing Home**
51 Lobban Ave., Miramichi, NB E1N 2W8
Tel: 506-778-6550 *Fax:* 506-778-0193
www.mountsj.ca
www.facebook.com/mountsj
Number of Beds: 133 beds
Note: Services include: medical; rehabilitation; pharmacy; dental; vision care; nursing; recreation; food & nutrition; support; & pain management.
Angus Lamont, Chair
Ellen Cook, Vice-Chair

Moncton: **Kenneth E. Spencer Memorial Home Inc.**
35 Atlantic Baptist Ave., Moncton, NB E1E 4N3
Tel: 506-858-7870 *Fax:* 506-858-9674
Year Founded: 1973
Number of Beds: 200 beds
Note: Services include: 24 hour nursing care; medical care; dietitian; recreation; & rehabilitation.

Moncton: **Villa du Repos Inc.**
125 Ave. Murphy, Moncton, NB E1A 8V2
Tél: 506-857-3560 *Téléc:* 506-859-1619
www.villadurepos.ca
Nombre de lits: 126 lits
Personnel: 160

Paquetville: **Manoir Édith B. Pinet Inc.**
1189, rue des Fondateurs, Paquetville, NB E8R 1A9
Tél: 506-764-2444 *Téléc:* 506-764-2451
Nombre de lits: 30 lits

Perth-Andover: **Victoria Glen Manor Inc.**
20 Tepper Lane, Perth-Andover, NB E7H 0B8
Tel: 506-273-4885 *Fax:* 506-273-4975
office@vgm.ca
www.vgm.ca
Number of Beds: 60 beds
Note: Long-term care home offering a range of services, including relief care, dietary, & activities.
Donna Miller-Wallace, Executive Director
millerwallace@vgm.ca
Erica McCrea, Director, Nursing
don@vgm.ca
Michelle Jamer, Director, Finance
michelle@vgm.ca

Mark McCarthy, Manager, Maintenance
office@vgm.ca

Port Elgin: **Westford Nursing Home**
57 West Main St., Port Elgin, NB E4M 1L7
Tel: 506-538-1302
www.westfordnursinghome.com
Year Founded: 1986
Number of Beds: 30 beds
Note: Home for seniors & adults with physical & mental challenges.
Nancy Burridge, Director, Nursing
n.burridge@nb.aibn.com
Karen Hurley, Administrative Secretary
k.hurley@nb.aibn.com

Rexton: **Rexton Lions Nursing Home Inc.**
23 Main St., Rexton, NB E4W 0E4
Tel: 506-523-7720 *Fax:* 506-523-7703
rex_general@nb.aibn.com
Number of Beds: 30 beds
Number of Employees: 43

Riverview: **The Salvation Army Lakeview Manor**
50 Suffolk St., Riverview, NB E1B 4K6
Tel: 506-387-2012 *Fax:* 506-387-7200
www.salvationarmy.ca
Number of Beds: 50 beds
Note: Specialties: Geriatric care; Care for persons with dementia
Kym Elder, Executive Director
kym_elder@can.salvationarmy.org

Rogersville: **Foyer Assomption**
62, rue Assomption, Rogersville, NB E4Y 1S5
Tél: 506-775-2040 *Téléc:* 506-775-2053
dg.fa@nb.aibn.com
Fondée en: 1981
Nombre de lits: 50 lits
Anne Cormier, Directrice générale

Saint John: **Carleton-Kirk Lodge**
2 Carleton Kirk Pl., Saint John, NB E2M 5B8
Tel: 506-635-7040 *Fax:* 506-635-7038
Number of Beds: 70 beds
Tim Stevens, Administrator
506-643-7043, tstev1@nb.aibn.com

Saint John: **Church of St. John & St. Stephen Home Inc.**
130 University Ave., Saint John, NB E2K 4K3
Tel: 506-643-6001 *Fax:* 506-643-6126
Number of Beds: 80 beds
Note: Specialty: Long-term care

Saint John: **Kennebec Manor Inc.**
475 Woodward Ave., Saint John, NB E2K 4N1
Tel: 506-632-9628 *Fax:* 506-658-9376
Number of Beds: 70 beds
Judy Lane, Administrator

Saint John: **Loch Lomond Villa, Inc.**
185 Loch Lomond Rd., Saint John, NB E2J 3S3
Tel: 506-643-7175 *Fax:* 506-643-7198
www.lochlomondvilla.com
Year Founded: 1973
Number of Beds: 190 beds
Note: Specialties: Specialized units for Alzheimers & Psychogeriatric needs
Cindy Donovan, CEO
cdonovan@lochlomondvilla.com
Shelley Shillington, Director, Operations
sshillington@lochlomondvilla.com
Gordon Burnett, Director, Finance
gburnett@lochlomondvilla.com

Saint John: **Rocmaura Inc.**
10 Parks St., Saint John, NB E2K 4P1
Tel: 506-643-7050 *Fax:* 506-643-7053
reception@rocmaura.com
www.rocmaura.com
www.facebook.com/RocmauraNursingHome
Year Founded: 1972
Number of Beds: 150 beds
Note: Christian nursing home; affiliated with the Sisters of Charity of the Immaculate Conception (SCIC)
Sheana Mohra, Executive Director
506-643-7060, smohra@rocmaura.com
Kim Roberts, Director, Nursing
kim.roberts@rocmaura.com
Theresa Mercer, Director, Finance
theresa.mercer@rocmaura.com
Harry Searle, Manager, Maintenance
harry.searle@rocmaura.com

Saint John: **Turnbull Nursing Home Inc.**
Former Name: Turnbull Home
231 Britain St., Saint John, NB E2L 0A4
Tel: 506-643-7200 *Fax:* 506-648-9786
Number of Beds: 50 beds
Note: Long-term care
Patti Alcorn, Administrator

Saint-Antoine: **Foyer Saint-Antoine**
7, av de l'Église, Saint-Antoine, NB E4V 1L6
Tél: 506-525-4040 *Téléc:* 506-525-4090
Nombre de lits: 30 lits
Gilles Ouellette, Directeur

Saint-Basile: **Foyer Saint-Joseph de Saint-Basile Inc.**
475, rue Principale, Saint-Basile, NB E7C 1J2
Tél: 506-263-3462 *Téléc:* 506-263-3467
Nombre de lits: 126 lits

Saint-Léonard: **Foyer Notre-Dame de Saint-Léonard Inc.**
604, rue Principale, Saint-Léonard, NB E7E 2H5
Tél: 506-423-3100 *Téléc:* 506-423-3152
Nombre de lits: 45 lits
Roger Levesque, Administrateur

Saint-Louis-de-Kent: **Villa Maria Inc.**
45, rue Vue de la Rivière, Saint-Louis-de-Kent, NB E4X 0C6
Tél: 506-876-3488 *Téléc:* 506-876-3466
Nombre de lits: 73 lits

Saint-Quentin: **Résidence Mgr. Melanson Inc.**
11, rue Levesque, Saint-Quentin, NB E8A 1T1
Tél: 506-235-6030 *Téléc:* 506-235-6075
Nombre de lits: 42 lits
André Savoie, Directeur

Shediac: **Villa Providence Shédiac Inc.**
403, rue Main, Shediac, NB E4P 2B9
Tél: 506-532-4484 *Téléc:* 506-532-5909
Nombre de lits: 190 lits
Yvon Belliveau, Président
Ronald Leblanc, Directeur général

Shippagan: **Les Résidences Mgr. Chiasson Inc.**
130, boul J.D.-Gauthier, Shippagan, NB E8S 1N8
Tél: 506-336-3266 *Fax:* 506-336-3099
recreologue.rmc@nb.aibn.com
Nombre de lits: 85 lits
Anselme Albert

St. Andrews: **Passamaquoddy Lodge Inc.**
230 Sophia St., St. Andrews, NB E5B 2C2
Tel: 506-529-5240 *Fax:* 506-529-5258
www.passamaquoddylodge.ca
Number of Beds: 60 beds
Note: Nursing home for seniors & disabled people.
Lezlie LeBlanc, Administrator
506-529-5240, lezlie.leblanc@passamaquoddylodge.ca
Patricia Bartlett, Director, Nursing
pat.bartlett@passamaquoddylodge.ca
Paul Sullivan, Manager, Facility Services
paul.sullivan@passamaquoddylodge.ca

St. Stephen: **Lincourt Manor Inc.**
PO Box 116, 1 Chipman St., St. Stephen, NB E3L 2W9
Tel: 506-466-7855 *Fax:* 506-466-7853
www.lincourtmanorinc.com
Number of Beds: 60 beds
Note: Specialty: Long term care
Stacy Butler, Administrator
sbutler.lincourt@nb.aibn.com
Diane Beaulieu, Director, Nursing
don.lincourt@nb.aibn.com
Ron Gardiner, Manager, Maintenance
rgardiner.lincourt@nb.aibn.com

St. Stephen: **Maria F. Ganong Seniors Residence**
Former Name: Maria F. Ganong Old Folks Home
Also Known As: Lonicera Hall
28 Union St., St. Stephen, NB E3L 1T1
Tel: 506-466-1471
hello@lonicerahall.com
www.lonicerahall.com
Pat Stevens, Administrator

Stanley: **Nashwaak Villa Inc.**
67 Limekiln Rd., Stanley, NB E6B 1E9
Tel: 506-367-7731
info@nashwaakvilla.ca
www.nashwaakvilla.ca

Number of Beds: 30 beds
Note: Services include: medical; nursing; rehabilitation; dietary; & pharmacy.
Daphne Noonan, Executive Director
506-367-7734, ed@nashwaakvilla.ca
Sherry Holder, Director, Nursing
don@nashwaakvilla.ca

Sussex: **Kiwanis Nursing Home Inc.**
11 Bryant Dr., Sussex, NB E4E 2P3
Tel: 506-432-3118 *Fax:* 506-432-3104
knhi@nb.aibn.com
www.kiwanisnursinghome.com
Number of Beds: 70 beds
Note: Provides nursing care & support services for seniors.
Keri Marr, CA, Administrator
506-432-3118
Holly Jones, Director, Nursing

Tabusintac: **Tabusintac Nursing Home**
10 Old Manse Rd., Tabusintac, NB E9H 1G4
Tel: 506-779-4100 *Fax:* 506-779-8149
www.tabusintacnursinghome.ca
Number of Beds: 30 beds
Note: Services include nursing care, dietary, & recreation, as well as physiotherapy, occupational therapy, speech pathology, & respiratory therapy (provided on a referral basis).
Robert Stewart, Executive Director
Linda O'Shea, Director, Nursing

Tracadie-Sheila: **Villa Saint-Joseph Inc.**
3400, rue Albert, Tracadie-Sheila, NB E1X 1C8
Tél: 506-394-4800
Nombre de lits: 74 lits
Paul Arseneau, Directeur général

Welshpool: **Campobello Lodge**
#2, 640 Rte. 774, Welshpool, NB E5E 1A5
Tel: 506-752-7101 *Fax:* 506-752-7105
Number of Beds: 30 beds
Population Served: 925
Sherry Johnston, Administrator
506-752-7101, admin_cmplodge@nb.aibn.com

Mental Health Hospitals/Facilities

Campbellton: **Centre Hospitalier Restigouche/Restigouche Hospital Centre**
Affiliée à: Vitalité Health Network
CP 10, 63, promenade Gallant, Campbellton, NB E3N 3G2
Tél: 506-760-4000 *Téléc:* 506-760-4035
info@vitalitenb.ca
www.vitalitenb.ca
Nombre de lits: 140 lits

Saint John: **Centracare Saint John Inc.**
Affiliated with: Horizon Health Network
PO Box 3220 Stn. B, 414 Bay St., Saint John, NB E2M 7L4
Tel: 506-649-2550 *Fax:* 506-649-2520
horizonnb.ca
Number of Beds: 50 beds

Shippagan: **Pavillon St-Jérôme Inc.**
150, 17e rue, Shippagan, NB E8S 1G4
Tel: 506-336-8609 *Fax:* 506-336-8652
pavillon.stj@nb.aibn.com
Number of Beds: 12 lits
Note: Résidence pour adultes handicapés intellectuels.
Marie-Reine Hébert, Directrice

Special Care Homes

Campbellton: **Duguay's Special Care Home**
20 Dover St., Campbellton, NB E3N 1P3
Tel: 506-789-1208
Note: Duguay's is a licensed special care home in New Brunswick.
Susan Duguay, Administrator

Harvey Station: **Swanhaven Adult Residential Facility**
1915, Rte. 3, Harvey Station, NB E6K 3K1
Tel: 506-366-2950
Number of Beds: 28 beds
Note: Specialty: Long-term care
Malcolm Cairns, Contact

Moncton: **Autumn Lee Retirement Home**
Affiliated with: Horizon Health Network
Former Name: Ritchie V Manor II
2031 Mountain Rd., Moncton, NB E1G 1B1
Tel: 506-384-7658 *Fax:* 506-855-8994
www.autumnleeretirement.com

Number of Beds: 20 beds

Moncton: **Smith Special Care Home Ltd.**
Affiliated with: Horizon Health Network
56 Dorchester St., Moncton, NB E1E 3A7
Tel: 506-874-0757
Number of Beds: 10 beds
Connie Whitman, Contact

Ratters Corner: **Wilson Special Care Home**
510 Drury's Cove Rd., Ratters Corner, NB E4E 3L4
Tel: 506-433-5532
Number of Beds: 2 beds
Sharon Wilson, Proprietor

Saint John: **Forest Hills Special Care Home**
Affiliated with: Horizon Health Network
Former Name: Burnside Special Care Home
30 Mountain Rd., Saint John, NB E2J 2W8
Tel: 506-633-0743
Number of Beds: 10 beds
Janet Hebert, Proprietor

Titusville: **Yvonne's Special Care Home**
1773 Rte. 860, Titusville, NB E5N 3W2
Tel: 506-832-7186
Number of Beds: 18 units
Note: Yvonne's is a special care home for the elderly.
Yvonne Clark, Proprietor

Newfoundland & Labrador

Government Departments in Charge

St. John's: **Newfoundland & Labrador Department of Health & Community Services**
1st Floor, West Block, Confederation Bldg., PO Box 8700, 100 Prince Philip Dr., St. John's, NL A1B 4J6
Tel: 709-729-4984
healthinfo@gov.nl.ca
www.gov.nl.ca/hcs
Hon. Dr. John Haggie, Minister
709-729-3124, hcsminister@gov.nl.ca

Regional Health Authorities

Corner Brook: **Western Regional Health Authority**
Former Name: Western Regional Integrated Health Authority
Also Known As: Western Health
Western Memorial Hospital, PO Box 2005, 1 Brookfield Ave., Corner Brook, NL A2H 6J7
Tel: 709-637-5245
www.westernhealth.nl.ca
twitter.com/WesternHealthNL;
www.youtube.com/WesternHealthNL
Number of Beds: 293 acute care beds; 434 long-term care beds; 40 enhanced assisted living beds; 14 restorative care beds
Population Served: 77980 *Number of Employees:* 3100
Note: Health facilities include two hospitals: Sir Thomas Roddick Hospital (Stephenville) & Western Memorial Regional Hospital (Corner Brook); four health centres: Dr. Charles L. LeGrow Health Centre (Port aux Basques), Bonne Bay Health Centre (Norris Point), Calder Health Centre (Burgeo) & Rufus Guinchard Health Centre (Port Saunders); & four long-term care centres: Corner Brook Long Term Care Centre (Corner Brook), Bay St. George Long Term Care Centre (Stephenville Crossing), Protective Community Residences (Corner Brook), & Emile Benoit House (Stephenville Crossing).
Bryson Webb, Board Chair
Cynthia Davis, President & CEO
Christopher Squire, Chief Financial Officer & Vice-President, Corporate Services
Kelli O'Brien, Vice-President, Population Health & Human Resources
Dennis Rashleigh, Vice-President, Medical Services
Tara J. Pye, Regional Director, Communications

Grand Falls-Windsor: **Central Regional Health Authority**
Also Known As: Central Health
Regional Office, 21 Carmelite Rd., Grand Falls-Windsor, NL A2A 1Y4
Tel: 709-292-2138 *Fax:* 709-292-2249
www.centralhealth.nl.ca
www.facebook.com/CentralHealthNL;
twitter.com/CentralHealthNL
Number of Beds: 517 long-term care; 268 acute care; 32 residential units; 28 bassinets
Area Served: 177 communities; half the landmass of the island
Population Served: 94000 *Number of Employees:* 3100
Donald Sturge, Board Chair

Andrée Robichaud, President & CEO
Vanessa Mercer-Oldford, Vice-President, People &
Transformation
John Kattenbusch, Vice-President, Corporate Services &
Provincial Shared Services Sup
709-292-3014, Fax: 709-256-7800, dale.hull@centralhealth.nl.ca
Joanne Pelley, Vice-President & Chief Nursing Executive,
Integrated Health
joanne.pelley@centralhealth.nl.ca

Happy Valley-Goose Bay: **Labrador-Grenfell
Regional Health Authority**
**Former Name: Grenfell Regional Health Services;
Health Labrador Corporation**
Also Known As: Labrador-Grenfell Health
**Administration Bldg., Labrador-Grenfell Health, PO Box
7000 Stn. C, Happy Valley-Goose Bay, NL A0P 1C0**
Fax: 709-896-4032
Toll-Free: 855-897-2267
www.lghealth.ca
twitter.com/LGHealthNL; www.linkedin.com/company/lghealth
Year Founded: 2005
Area Served: North of Bartlett's Harbour on the Northern
Peninsula, Labrador *Population Served:* 37000 *Number of
Employees:* 1500
Note: Labrador-Grenfell Health partners with the following to
deliver services to Aboriginal communities: Nunatsiavut
Department of Health & Social Development; 2 Innu Band
Councils; NunatuKavut (formerly the Labrador Métis Nation);
Health Canada; & private practitioners.
Heather Brown, Chief Executive Officer
Peter Deegan, Chief Financial Officer & Vice-President,
Corporate Services
Donnie Sampson, Chief Nursing Officer & Vice-President
Sam Mansfield, Senior Director, People
Dr. Gabe Woollam, Vice-President
Paula March, Executive Director, Patient Safety & Quality
Amanda MacNeil, Regional Director, Communications
Dr. Thomas Plggott, Medical Officer of Health

St. John's: **Eastern Regional Health Authority**
Also Known As: Eastern Health
**Health Sciences Centre, Prince Philip Dr., St. John's, NL
A1B 3V6**
Tel: 709-777-6500 *Toll-Free:* 877-444-1399
client.relations@easternhealth.ca
www.easternhealth.ca
Info Line: 811
www.facebook.com/EasternHealthNL;
twitter.com/EasternHealthNL;
www.youtube.com/user/CommunicationsEH;
www.linkedin.com/company/eastern-health_2
Number of Beds: 1,696 long term care beds; 987 acute care
beds; 9 observation beds
Area Served: Avalon, Burin & Bonavista Peninsulas; 21,000 sq
km *Population Served:* 300000 *Number of Employees:* 13000
Note: Area served includes 111 incorporated municipalities, 69
local service districts, & 66 unincorporated municipal units.
Leslie O'Reilly, Board Chair
David S. Diamond, President & CEO
Ron Johnson, Chief Information Officer & Vice-President
Collette Smith, Chief Nursing Officer & Vice President
Larry Alteen, Vice-President
Ken Baird, Vice-President
Debbie Molloy, Vice-President
Judy O'Keefe, Vice-President
Elaine Warren, Vice-President

Hospitals - General

Carbonear: **Carbonear General Hospital**
Affiliated with: Eastern Regional Health Authority
86 Highroad South, Carbonear, NL A1Y 1A4
Tel: 709-945-5111 *Fax:* 709-945-5511
client.relations@easternhealth.ca
www.easternhealth.ca
www.facebook.com/EasternHealthNL;
twitter.com/EasternHealthNL
Number of Beds: 80 beds
Note: Programs & services include: blood collection; diagnostic
imaging; dialysis; emergency; inpatient services; laboratory;
outpatient services; & surgery.

Clarenville: **Dr. G.B. Cross Memorial Hospital**
Affiliated with: Eastern Regional Health Authority
67 Manitoba Dr., Clarenville, NL A5A 1K3
Tel: 709-466-3411
client.relations@easternhealth.ca
www.easternhealth.ca
www.facebook.com/EasternHealthNL;
twitter.com/EasternHealthNL;
www.linkedin.com/company/eastern-health_2

Number of Beds: 4 intensive care beds; 9 obstetrical beds; 44
long-term care beds; 28 acute care beds
Note: Programs & services include: blood collection; diagnostic
imaging; emergency; inpatient services; outpatient services;
surgery; & x-ray.

Corner Brook: **Western Memorial Regional Hospital**
Affiliated with: Western Regional Health Authority
PO Box 2005, 1 Brookfield Ave., Corner Brook, NL A2H 6J7
Tel: 709-637-5000
www.westernhealth.nl.ca
twitter.com/WesternHealthNL;
www.youtube.com/WesternHealthNL
Number of Beds: 217 beds
Population Served: 77980
Note: Programs & services include: cardiology; emergency;
geriatrics; internal medicine & surgery; intensive care;
laboratory; medical imaging; medical; nephrology; neurology;
nursing; obstetrics / gynecology; ophthalmology; orthopedics;
pediatrics; pharmacy; psychiatry; renal care; surgical services; &
urology.
Cynthia Davis, President & CEO, WRHA

Fogo: **Fogo Island Health Centre**
Affiliated with: Central Regional Health Authority
PO Box 9, Main St., Fogo, NL A0G 2B0
Tel: 709-266-2221
www.centralhealth.nl.ca
Year Founded: 2004
Number of Beds: 14 beds
Note: Programs & services include: acute care; long-term care;
emergency; laboratory; community health services; & x-ray.
Natasha Decker, Manager, Client Care Services
natasha.decker@centralhealth.nl.ca

Gander: **James Paton Memorial Regional Health
Centre**
Affiliated with: Central Regional Health Authority
125 Trans Canada Hwy., Gander, NL A1V 1P7
Tel: 709-256-2500 *Fax:* 709-256-7800
www.centralhealth.nl.ca
Number of Beds: 85 beds
Note: Programs & services include: acute care; emergency; &
specialized medical services.
Kathy Winsor, Director, Site Operations
kathy.winsor@centralhealth.nl.ca

Grand Falls-Windsor: **Central Newfoundland
Regional Health Centre (CNRHC)**
Affiliated with: Central Regional Health Authority
50 Union St., Grand Falls-Windsor, NL A2A 2E1
Tel: 709-292-2500 *Fax:* 709-292-2645
www.centralhealth.nl.ca
Number of Beds: 117 beds
Number of Employees: 600
Note: Programs & services include: emergency; acute care; &
specialized medical services.
Tanya Letto, Director, Site Operations
tanya.letto@centralhealth.nl.ca

Happy Valley—Goose Bay: **Labrador Health Centre**
**Affiliated with: Labrador-Grenfell Regional Health
Authority**
Former Name: Melville Hospital
PO Box 7000 Stn. C, Happy Valley—Goose Bay, NL A0P 1C0
Tel: 709-897-2000
www.lghealth.ca
Number of Beds: 25 beds
Note: Programs & services include: emergency; satellite dialysis;
laboratory & diagnostic imaging; physiotherapy; occupational
therapy; speech-language pathology; oncology / chemotherapy;
respiratory therapy; dietitian; community health & home care
nursing; mental health & addictions; & obstetrics / gynecology.
Roland Hewitt, Nursing Site Manager
roland.hewitt@lghealth.ca

Labrador City: **Labrador West Health Centre**
**Affiliated with: Labrador-Grenfell Regional Health
Authority**
**Former Name: Captain William Jackman Memorial
Hospital**
1700 Nichols-Adam Hwy., Labrador City, NL A2V 0B2
Tel: 709-285-8100
www.lghealth.ca
Number of Beds: 28 beds
Note: Programs & services include: emergency; outpatient;
surgery; satellite dialysis; maternity care; obstetrics /
gynecology; laboratory & diagnostic imaging; physiotherapy;
occupational therapy; speech-language pathology; audiology;
respiratory therapy; EEG; EKG; oncology / chemotherapy;
dietary; diabetes education; mental health & addictions; &
population health.

St. Anthony: **Charles S. Curtis Memorial Hospital**
**Affiliated with: Labrador-Grenfell Regional Health
Authority**
Also Known As: Curtis Hospital
#178, 200 West St., St. Anthony, NL A0K 4S0
Tel: 709-454-3333
www.lghealth.ca
Number of Beds: 50 beds
Note: Programs & services include: acute care; anaesthesia;
dentistry; family practice; general surgery; internal medicine;
obstetrics / gynecology; ophthalmology; orthopedics; pathology;
pediatrics; emergency; intensive care; oncology / chemotherapy;
day surgery; satellite dialysis; laboratory & diagnostic imaging;
physiotherapy; occupational therapy; speech-language
pathology; respiratory therapy; EEG / ECG; pharmacy;
audiology; clinical nutrition; diabetes education; social work;
mental health & addictions; & psychology.

St. John's: **Health Sciences Centre - General
Hospital**
Affiliated with: Eastern Regional Health Authority
300 Prince Phillip Dr., St. John's, NL A1B 3V6
Tel: 709-777-6300
client.relations@easternhealth.ca
www.easternhealth.ca
www.facebook.com/EasternHealthNL;
twitter.com/EasternHealthNL;
www.linkedin.com/company/eastern-health_2
Number of Beds: 348 beds
Note: A tertiary acute care facility & teaching hospital affiliated
with Memorial University Schools of Medicine, Nursing, &
Pharmacy. Programs & services include: blood collection;
diagnostic imaging; dialysis; emergency; inpatient services;
laboratory; outpatient services; radiography; & surgery.

St. John's: **Janeway Children's Health &
Rehabilitation Centre**
Affiliated with: Eastern Regional Health Authority
300 Prince Philip Dr., St. John's, NL A1B 3V6
Tel: 709-777-6300
client.relations@easternhealth.ca
www.easternhealth.ca
www.facebook.com/EasternHealthNL;
twitter.com/EasternHealthNL
Number of Beds: 42 acute cared beds; 8 mental health beds; 28
neonatal intensive care beds; 6 pediatric intensive care beds
Note: Teaching hospital for the Memorial University of
Newfoundland Faculty of Medicine. Programs & services
include: children & women's health; diagnostic services; dialysis;
emergency services; inpatient services; laboratory; outpatient
services; radiography; & surgery.

St. John's: **St. Clare's Mercy Hospital**
Affiliated with: Eastern Regional Health Authority
154 LeMarchant Rd., St. John's, NL A1C 5B8
Tel: 709-777-5000
client.relations@easternhealth.ca
www.easternhealth.ca
www.facebook.com/EasternHealthNL;
twitter.com/EasternHealthNL
Year Founded: 1922
Number of Beds: 192 beds
Note: Tertiary hospital. Programs & services include: blood
collection; diagnostic imaging; dialysis; emergency; inpatient
services; laboratory; outpatient services; radiography; & surgery.

Stephenville: **Sir Thomas Roddick Hospital**
Affiliated with: Western Regional Health Authority
142 Minnesota Dr., Stephenville, NL A2N 2V6
Tel: 709-643-5111
www.westernhealth.nl.ca
twitter.com/WesternHealthNL;
www.youtube.com/WesternHealthNL
Year Founded: 2003
Number of Beds: 44 beds
Population Served: 24000
Note: Programs & services include: emergency; medical;
nursing; obstetric / gynecaelogical; outpatient; pharmacy; renal
care; specialty clinics; & surgical.

Community Health Care Centres

Baie Verte: **Baie Verte Peninsula Health Centre**
Affiliated with: Central Regional Health Authority
PO Box 190, 7 Hospital Dr., Baie Verte, NL A0K 1B0
Tel: 709-532-4281 *Fax:* 709-532-5251
www.centralhealth.nl.ca/baie-verte-buchans
Number of Beds: 18 long-term care beds; 1 respite bed; 6 acute
care beds; 1 palliative care bed
Note: Acute & long term care; dental clinic; addiction treatment;
rehabilitation services.

Craig Davis, Site Director
709-532-5234, craig.davis@centralhealth.nl.ca

Bell Island: Dr. Walter Templeman Health Care
Centre
Affiliated with: Eastern Regional Health Authority
PO Box 580, Wabana, Bell Island, NL A0A 4H0
Tel: 709-488-2821 *Fax:* 709-488-2600
www.easternhealth.ca

Number of Beds: 20 beds
Note: Services include: addictions; blood collection; community
health; diagnostic imaging; emergency; inpatient; long-term care;
minor procedures; outpatient clinics; palliative care; public
health; & social work.

Black Tickle: Black Tickle Community Clinic
Affiliated with: Labrador-Grenfell Regional Health
Authority
General Delivery, Black Tickle, NL A0K 1N0
Tel: 709-471-8872
www.lghealth.ca

Number of Beds: 1 holding bed
Note: Primary health care services

Bonavista: Bonavista Peninsula Health Centre
Affiliated with: Eastern Regional Health Authority
Former Name: Bonavista Community Health Centre
20-24 Hospital Rd., Bonavista, NL A0C 1B0
Tel: 709-468-7881
www.easternhealth.ca

Number of Beds: 10 beds
Note: Services include: blood collection; diagnostic imaging;
emergency; inpatient; laboratory; radiography; & outpatient
clinics.

Burgeo: Calder Health Care Centre
Affiliated with: Western Regional Health Authority
PO Box 190, Burgeo, NL A0N 2H0
Tel: 709-886-2898
westernhealth.nl.ca

Number of Beds: 3 acute care beds; 18 continuing care beds
Population Served: 1900
Note: Services include: diagnostic & laboratory services;
recreational therapy; occupational & physiotherapy; Telehealth;
& chemotherapy.

Burin: Burin Peninsula Health Care Centre
Affiliated with: Eastern Regional Health Authority
PO Box 340, #51, 85 Main St., Burin, NL A0E 1E0
Tel: 709-891-1040
www.easternhealth.ca

Note: Features an interim clinic staffed with three hospital
physicians

Churchill Falls: Churchill Falls Community Health
Centre
Affiliated with: Labrador-Grenfell Regional Health
Authority
General Delivery, Churchill Falls, NL A0R 1A0
Tel: 709-925-3381
www.lghealth.ca

Number of Beds: 2 holding beds
Note: Offers primary health care.

Flowers Cove: Strait of Belle Isle Health Centre
Affiliated with: Labrador-Grenfell Regional Health
Authority
PO Box 59, Flowers Cove, NL A0K 2N0
Tel: 709-456-2401
www.lghealth.ca

Number of Beds: 3 beds
Note: Specialties: Ambulatory care; Family medicine; Public
health services; Pre-natal classes; Post-natal visiting; Preschool
& baby assessments; Dental services; Rehabilitation services;
Home care.

Grand Bank: Grand Bank Community Health Centre
Affiliated with: Eastern Regional Health Authority
PO Box 310, 3 Grandview Blvd., Grand Bank, NL A0E 1W0
Tel: 709-832-2500

Note: Services include: 24-hour ambulance; dental clinic; home
care; optometrist; & public health.

Harbour Breton: Connaigre Peninsula Health Centre
Affiliated with: Central Regional Health Authority
Former Name: Harbour Breton Health Centre
PO Box 70, 1 Alexander Ave., Harbour Breton, NL A0H 1P0
Tel: 709-885-2043 *Fax:* 709-885-2358
Toll-Free: 844-885-2359
www.centralhealth.nl.ca/lewisporte-exploits-coast-of-bays
Number of Beds: 6 acute beds; 12 continuing care beds; 1
palliative bed; 1 respite bed

Note: Services include: 24-hour emergency; lab & x-ray;
Telehealth; social work; physiotherapy; & more.
Wendy Pierce, Manager, Client Care Services
wendy.pierce@centralhealth.nl.ca

Hopedale: Hopedale Community Clinic
Affiliated with: Labrador-Grenfell Regional Health
Authority
General Delivery, Hopedale, NL A0P 1G0
Tel: 709-933-3857
www.lghealth.ca

Number of Beds: 3 beds
Number of Employees: 7
Note: Provides primary health care services.

Nain: Nain Community Clinic
Affiliated with: Labrador-Grenfell Regional Health
Authority
General Delivery, Nain, NL A0P 1L0
Tel: 709-922-2912
www.lghealth.ca

Number of Beds: 4 holding beds
Number of Employees: 16
Note: Offers primary health care services.

New-Wes-Valley: Dr. Y. K. Jeon Kittiwake Health
Centre (DYKJKHC)
Affiliated with: Central Regional Health Authority
Hwy. 26, New-Wes-Valley, NL A0G 1J0
Tel: 709-536-2405 *Fax:* 709-536-2433
www.centralhealth.nl.ca/isles-of-notre-dame-kittiwake-coast
Year Founded: 1944
Number of Beds: 12 beds
Population Served: 3000
Note: Services inlude: 24-hour emergency; Telehealth; diabetes
education; clinical dietician; mental health; social work; public
health; physiotherapy; occupational therapy; & speech language.

Norris Point: Bonne Bay Health Centre
Affiliated with: Western Regional Health Authority
PO Box 70, Norris Point, NL A0K 3V0
Tel: 709-458-2211 *Fax:* 709-458-2074
westernhealth.nl.ca
Number of Beds: 8 acute care beds; 14 continuing care beds
Note: Services include: clinical dietitian; diagnostic; emergency
care; laboratory; medical; nursing; occupational therapy;
outpatient; palliative care; physiotherapy; recreation therapy;
social work; & specialty clinics.

Old Perlican: Dr. A.A. Wilkinson Memorial Health
Centre
Affiliated with: Eastern Regional Health Authority
PO Box 70, Old Perlican, NL A0A 3G0
Tel: 709-587-2200

Number of Beds: 4 beds
Note: Offers laboratory, diagnostic imaging, x-ray, & blood
collection services.

Port Saunders: Rufus Guinchard Health Care Centre
Affiliated with: Western Regional Health Authority
PO Box 40, Port Saunders, NL A0K 4H0
Tel: 709-861-3139 *Fax:* 709-861-3772
westernhealth.nl.ca
Number of Beds: 1 palliative care bed; 6 acute care beds; 22
long-term care beds
Note: Services include laboratory, diagnostics, therapy,
pharmacy, dietitian, & social work.

Port aux Basques: Dr. Charles L. LeGrow Health
Centre
Affiliated with: Western Regional Health Authority
PO Box 250, Port aux Basques, NL A0M 1C0
Tel: 709-695-2175
westernhealth.nl.ca
Number of Beds: 14 acute care beds; 30 long-term care beds
Population Served: 9000
Note: Services include pharmacy, dietitian, physiotherapy,
laboratory, & diagnostics.

Sheshatshiu: North West River / Sheshatshiu
Community Clinic
Affiliated with: Labrador-Grenfell Regional Health
Authority
Also Known As: Mani Ashini Community Clinic
Sheshatshiu, NL A0P 1M0
Tel: 709-497-8202
www.lghealth.ca

Note: Offers primary health care services.

Springdale: Green Bay Community Health Centre
Affiliated with: Central Regional Health Authority
Community College Building, PO Box 280, 275 Main St.,
Springdale, NL A0J 1T0
Tel: 709-673-4974
www.centralhealth.nl.ca/baie-verte-buchans
Note: Services include: addictions counsellor; behaviour
management sepcialist; child management specialist; & early
youth outreach worker.

Twillingate: Notre Dame Bay Memorial Health Centre
Affiliated with: Central Regional Health Authority
General Delivery, Twillingate, NL A0G 4M0
Tel: 709-884-2131 *Fax:* 709-884-2586
www.centralhealth.nl.ca/isles-of-notre-dame-kittiwake-coast
Number of Beds: 31 long-term care beds; 19 acute care beds
Note: Specialties: Outpatient services; Social work;
Physiotherapy; Recreation therapy; Dietetics; Diabetes
education; Health promotion & protection; Respite care, for
children with special needs.

Whitbourne: Dr. W. H. Newhook Community Health
Centre
Affiliated with: Eastern Regional Health Authority
PO Box 449, 7 Whitbourne Ave., Whitbourne, NL A0B 3K0
Tel: 709-759-2300

Note: Emergency centre; family physicians; laboratory &
diagnostic services
Dr. Stephanie A. Squibb, Contact
stephanie.squibb@easternhealth.ca

Nursing Stations

Cartwright: Cartwright Community Clinic
Affiliated with: Labrador-Grenfell Regional Health
Authority
General Delivery, Cartwright, NL A0K 1V0
Tel: 709-938-7285
www.lghealth.ca/facilities/community-clinics/cartwright
Number of Beds: 1 bed
Number of Employees: 9

Charlottetown: Charlottetown Community Clinic
Affiliated with: Labrador-Grenfell Regional Health
Authority
Former Name: Charlottetown Nursing Station
General Delivery, Charlottetown, NL A0K 5Y0
Tel: 709-949-0259
www.lghealth.ca/facilities/community-clinics/charlottetown
Number of Beds: 3 beds
Number of Employees: 4
Note: Programs & services include: ambulatory care; family
medicine; emergency; palliative care; public health, mental
health, & home care nursing; dental; diagnostic; & child, youth, &
family services.

Forteau: Labrador South Health Centre
Affiliated with: Labrador-Grenfell Regional Health
Authority
Forteau, NL A0K 2P0
Tel: 709-931-2450
www.lghealth.ca/facilities/health-centres/labrador-south-health-c
entre
Number of Beds: 5 in-patient beds

Makkovik: Makkovik Community Health Clinic
Affiliated with: Labrador-Grenfell Regional Health
Authority
General Delivery, Makkovik, NL A0P 1J0
Tel: 709-923-2229 *Fax:* 709-923-2428
www.lghealth.ca/facilities/community-clinics/makkovik
Number of Beds: 3 beds
Note: Specialties: pharmaceutical services; social work. Number
of Employees: 2 nurses + 1 part time physician.

Mary's Harbour: Mary's Harbour Community Clinic
Affiliated with: Labrador-Grenfell Regional Health
Authority
Mary's Harbour, NL A0K 3P0
Tel: 709-921-6228 *Fax:* 709-921-6975
www.lghealth.ca/facilities/community-clinics/marys-harbour
Number of Beds: 1 holding bed; 1 crib
Note: Number of Employees: 3 nurses + 1 personal care
attendant + 1 maintenance person.

Natuashish: Natuashish Nursing Station
Affiliated with: Labrador-Grenfell Regional Health
Authority
Former Name: Davis Inlet Nursing Station
General Delivery, Natuashish, NL A0P 1A0
Tel: 709-478-8842
www.lghealth.ca/facilities/community-clinics/natuashish

Port Hope Simpson: Port Hope Simpson Community Clinic
Affiliated with: Labrador-Grenfell Regional Health Authority
General Delivery, Port Hope Simpson, NL A0K 4E0
Tel: 709-960-0271
www.lghealth.ca/facilities/community-clinics/port-hope-simpson
Year Founded: 1975
Note: Specialties: Emergency room, basic trauma, cardiac monitoring & resuscitation, dental suite. Number of staff: 8.

Postville: Postville Community Clinic
Affiliated with: Labrador-Grenfell Regional Health Authority
General Delivery, Postville, NL A0P 1N0
Tel: 709-479-9851
www.lghealth.ca/facilities/community-clinics/postville
Number of Beds: 1 bed, 1 crib
Number of Employees: 3

Rigolet: Rigolet Nursing Station
Affiliated with: Labrador-Grenfell Regional Health Authority
General Delivery, Rigolet, NL A0P 1P0
Tel: 709-947-3386
www.lghealth.ca/facilities/community-clinics/rigolet
Note: Number of staff: 2 Registered Nurses & personal care attendant

Roddickton: White Bay Central Health Centre
Affiliated with: Labrador-Grenfell Regional Health Authority
General Delivery, Roddickton, NL A0K 4P0
Tel: 709-457-2215
www.lghealth.ca/facilities/health-centres/white-bay-central
Note: Programs & services include: ambulatory care; family medicine; emergency; palliative care; public health, mental health, & home care nursing; dental; diagnostic; & child, youth, & family services.

St. Lewis: St. Lewis Community Clinic
Affiliated with: Labrador-Grenfell Regional Health Authority
General Delivery, St. Lewis, NL A0K 4W0
Tel: 709-939-2230
www.lghealth.ca/facilities/community-clinics/st-lewis
Note: Programs & services include: ambulatory care; family medicine; emergency; palliative care; public health, mental health, & home care nursing; dental; diagnostic; & child, youth, & family services.

Special Treatment Centres

St. John's: Dr. H. Bliss Murphy Cancer Centre
Affiliated with: Eastern Regional Health Authority
Dr. H. Bliss Murphy Cancer Care Foundation, 300 Prince Philip Dr., St. John's, NL A1B 3V6
Tel: 709-777-6480
www.easternhealth.ca

St. John's: St. John's Morgentaler Clinic
The Morgentaler Clinic
#408, Unit 50 Hamlyn Rd. Plaza, St. John's, NL A1E 5X7
Tel: 709-754-3572 *Fax:* 709-754-6626
Toll-Free: 800-755-2044
sjmc@nf.aibn.com
www.morgentaler.ca
Year Founded: 1990
Note: Specialties: Abortion services; Counselling.

Long Term Care Facilities

Badger's Quay: Bonnews Lodge
Affiliated with: Central Regional Health Authority
Badger's Quay, NL
Tel: 709-536-2160
www.centralhealth.nl.ca/isles-of-notre-dame-kittiwake-coast
Number of Beds: 45 long-term care beds
Note: Services inlude: nuursing; clinical dietician; recreational therapy; Meals on Wheels; beautician; physician; & occupational therapy & speech-language pathology.

Bonavista: Golden Heights Manor
Affiliated with: Eastern Regional Health Authority
27 - 43 Campbell St., Bonavista, NL A0C 1B0
Tel: 709-468-2043
www.easternhealth.ca
Year Founded: 1986
Number of Beds: 70 beds
Pauline Pardy

Placentia: Placentia Health Centre
Affiliated with: Eastern Regional Health Authority
PO Box 480, 1 Corrigan Pl., Placentia, NL A0B 2Y0
Tel: 709-227-2061 *Fax:* 709-227-5476
www.easternhealth.ca
Number of Beds: 10 inpatient beds; 75 long-term care beds
Note: Acute care & long term care (Lions Manor Nursing Home) on an in-patient & out-patient basis; services include chemotherapy, diabetes education, emergency care, & pastoral care.
Dr. Sandeep Mangat, Contact

St. John's: Dr. Leonard A. Miller Centre
Affiliated with: Eastern Regional Health Authority
Former Name: Quidi Vidi Hospital
Also Known As: The Miller Centre
100 Forest Rd., St. John's, NL A1A 1E5
Tel: 709-777-6555
www.easternhealth.ca
Year Founded: 1851
Note: Provides continuing care, rehabilitation, residential care for veterans of Newfoundland & Labrador, & includes a centre for Nursing Studies.

St. Lawrence: U.S. Memorial Health Centre
Affiliated with: Eastern Regional Health Authority
PO Box 398, 1 Memorial Dr., St. Lawrence, NL A0E 2V0
Tel: 709-873-2330 *Fax:* 709-873-2390
www.easternhealth.ca
Number of Beds: 40 beds
Note: Long term & protective care units, ambulatory care clinic, nutritional services, pharmacy, visiting specialty clinics

Nursing Homes

Botwood: Dr. Hugh Twomey Health Care Centre
Affiliated with: Central Regional Health Authority
PO Box 250, Botwood, NL A0H 1E0
Tel: 709-257-5250
www.centralhealth.nl.ca/dr-hugh-twomey-health-centre
Number of Beds: 77 long-term care beds; 2 respite beds; 1 palliative care bed
Note: Services include: diagnostic imaging; dietitian; emergency; laboratory; long-term care; outpatient; palliative care; rehabilitation; & respite care.
Allison Champion, Manager, Client Care Services
allison.champion@centralhealth.nl.ca

Buchans: A.M. Guy Memorial Health Centre
Affiliated with: Central Regional Health Authority
PO Box 39, Buchans, NL A0H 1G0
Tel: 709-672-3304
Number of Beds: 18 long-term beds; 2 acute care beds; 1 holding bed; 1 palliative bed
Note: Services include: chemotherapy; diagnostic imaging; laboratory; outpatient & 24 hour emergency; physician & nurse practitioner clinics; public health; recreation; & rehabilitation.

Corner Brook: Corner Brook Long Term Care Home (CBLTC)
Affiliated with: Western Regional Health Authority
40 University Dr., Corner Brook, NL A2H 5G4
Tel: 709-637-3999
Year Founded: 2010
Number of Beds: 250 long-term care beds

Gander: Lakeside Homes
Affiliated with: Central Regional Health Authority
95 Airport Blvd., Gander, NL A1V 2L7
Tel: 709-256-8850 *Fax:* 709-256-4259
www.centralhealth.nl.ca/lakeside-homes
Number of Beds: 102 beds; 1 respite bed
Note: Services include: medical care; nursing; nutrition; pharmacy; physiotherapy; social work; & therapeutic recreation.
Cynthia Bursey, Regional Director, Long Term Care
cynthia.bursey@centralhealth.nl.ca

Gander Bay South: Riverview Retirement Home Ltd.
Also Known As: Gander Bay Retirement Home
9 Main St., Gander Bay South, NL A0G 2H0
Tel: 709-676-2773

Grand Bank: Blue Crest Nursing Home
Affiliated with: Eastern Regional Health Authority
PO Box 160, 1 Senior Citizens Pl., Grand Bank, NL A0E 1W0
Tel: 709-832-1660
www.easternhealth.ca
Year Founded: 1974
Number of Beds: 58 LTC beds; 1 palliative bed; 1 respite bed; 1 convalescent/assessment bed

Grand Falls-Windsor: Carmelite House
Affiliated with: Central Regional Health Authority
21 Carmelite Rd., Grand Falls-Windsor, NL A2A 1Y4
Tel: 709-292-2528 *Fax:* 709-292-2593
Number of Beds: 60 longterm care beds
Krista Toms, Facility Director
krista.toms@centralhealth.nl.ca

Happy Valley-Goose Bay: Happy Valley-Goose Bay Long Term Care Home
Affiliated with: Labrador-Grenfell Regional Health Authority
PO Box 766 Stn. B, Happy Valley-Goose Bay, NL A0P 1E0
Tel: 709-896-2469
www.lghealth.ca
Number of Beds: 70 beds

Lewisporte: North Haven Manor Senior Citizens' Home
Affiliated with: Central Regional Health Authority
Lewisporte Health Centre, PO Box 880, Lewisporte, NL A0G 3A0
Tel: 709-535-6767
Number of Beds: 59 long-term care beds; 1 palliative bed; 2 respite beds
Note: Services include: occupational therapy; palliative care; physiotherapy; social work; & therapeutic recreation.
Cheryl Peckford, Manager, Client Care Services
cheryl.peckford@centralhealth.nl.ca

Springdale: Valley Vista Senior Citizens' Home
Affiliated with: Central Regional Health Authority
PO Box 130, Springdale, NL A0J 1T0
Tel: 709-673-3936 *Fax:* 709-673-2832

St. Anthony: John M. Gray Centre
Affiliated with: Labrador-Grenfell Regional Health Authority
Former Name: St. Anthony Interfaith Home
PO Box 69, St. Anthony, NL A0K 4S0
Tel: 709-454-0371
Year Founded: 1998
Number of Beds: 46 beds; 1 respite bed
Note: Services include: day care; palliative care; & respite care.
Heather Bromley, Specialist, Recreation Development

St. John's: Agnes Pratt Nursing Home
Affiliated with: Eastern Regional Health Authority
239 Topsail Rd., St. John's, NL A1E 2B4
Tel: 709-752-8950 *Fax:* 709-752-8937
www.easternhealth.ca
Year Founded: 1958
Number of Beds: 134 long-term care beds; 2 respite beds
Annette Morgan, Administrator

St. John's: Pleasant View Towers
Affiliated with: Eastern Regional Health Authority
65 Newfoundland Dr., St. John's, NL A1A 0L7
Tel: 709-752-8800
www.easternhealth.ca
Number of Beds: 460 beds

St. John's: Saint Luke's Home
Affiliated with: Eastern Regional Health Authority
24 Rd. Deluxe, St. John's, NL A1E 5Z3
Tel: 709-752-8900 *Fax:* 709-752-8924
www.saintlukeshomes.com
Year Founded: 1965
Number of Beds: 117 beds
Note: Nursing home also owns & operates 54 independent living cottages & the 76-unit Bishop John Meaden Manor Complex. Services include: adult day care; ambulatory care; nursing care; physiotherapy; & respite care.
Kelly Manning, Administrator

St. John's: St. Patrick's Mercy Home
Affiliated with: Eastern Regional Health Authority
146 Elizabeth Ave., St. John's, NL A1B 1S5
Tel: 709-726-2687
www.easternhealth.ca
Number of Beds: 210 long-term care beds
Note: Long-term care facility affiliated with the Roman Catholic Diocese of St. John's. Services include: dietitian; nursing; occupational therapy; pharmacy; physiotherapy; physician care; recreation therapy; & social work.
Joan Marie Aylward, Executive Director

Stephenville Crossing: Bay St. George Long Term Care Centre
Affiliated with: Western Regional Health Authority
Former Name: Bay St. George Senior Citizens Home
PO Box 250, Stephenville Crossing, NL A0N 2C0
Tel: 709-646-5800 *Fax:* 709-646-2375
Number of Beds: 114 beds
Note: Services include: medical; nursing care; nutrition; occupational therapy; physiotherapy; pharmacy; recreation therapy; & social work.
Anne Doyle, Regional Director, Long Term Care

Personal Care Homes

Arnolds Cove: Hilltop Manor
PO Box 430, 96 Spencers Cove Rd., Arnolds Cove, NL A1A 4Y6
Tel: 709-463-5000
hollismetcalge@hotmail.com
Number of Beds: 32 beds
Trey Metcalfe

Baie Verte: H. Pardy Manor
PO Box 1, Baie Verte, NL A0K 1B0
Tel: 709-532-4603
Number of Beds: 22 beds
Kim Sacrey, Manager

Bay Bulls: Walsh's Personal Care Home
PO Box 42, Rte. 10, Bay Bulls, NL A0A 1C0
Tel: 709-334-2619
Number of Beds: 10 beds
Delores Walsh, Proprietor

Bishops Falls: Exploits Manor
26 Exploits Lane, Bishops Falls, NL A0H 1C0
Tel: 709-258-6446

Cape Anguille: Hilliard's Personal Care Home
PO Box 18, Cape Anguille, NL A0N 1H0
Tel: 709-955-2339
Number of Beds: 14 beds
Minnie Hilliard, Owner/Administrator

Carmanville: Carmanville Manor
PO Box 42, Carmanville, NL A0G 1N0
Tel: 709-534-2244
www.centralhealth.nl.ca/carmanville-manor
Number of Beds: 21 beds
Jeanne Clarke

Catalina: Shirley's Haven
PO Box 29, Catalina, NL A0C 1J0
Tel: 709-469-3160 *Fax:* 709-469-3161
facebook.com/pages/Shirleys-Haven-Personal-Care-Home/7799
4615307
Number of Beds: 50 beds
Shirley Barney

Clarenville: Cozy Quarters Personal Care Home
13 Whiteway Pl., Clarenville, NL A5A 2B5
Tel: 709-466-2447 *Fax:* 709-466-4447
cozyquarters@nf.aibn.com
www.cozyquartersnl.ca
Number of Beds: 34 beds

Conception Bay South: Woodford's Golden Care Home
Con Bay Hwy., Conception Bay South, NL A0A 2R0
Tel: 709-229-3343
Number of Beds: 10 beds
Josephine Woodford, Contact

Corner Brook: Brake's Personal Care Home
292 Curling St., Corner Brook, NL A2H 3J7
Tel: 709-785-5092
Number of Beds: 6 beds
Vera Brake
Vivian Brake

Corner Brook: Mountain View House
PO Box 3850, RR#2, Corner Brook, NL A2H 6B9
Tel: 709-783-2019 *Fax:* 709-783-2292
mountainviewhousenl@gmail.com
www.mountainviewhouse.ca
Number of Beds: 30 beds
Jessica Brake, Manager

Corner Brook: Mountain View Retirement Centre
161 Premier Dr., Corner Brook, NL A2H 7M6
Tel: 709-637-7960 *Fax:* 709-634-0235
www.mountainviewretirementcentre.com
Note: Nursing home
Barbara Baker, Contact

Corner Brook: Xavier House Inc.
19 Mount Bernard Ave., Corner Brook, NL A2H 6K7
Tel: 709-634-2787
www.presentationsisters.ca
Year Founded: 1985
Number of Beds: 20 beds
Note: Care home for adults with mental illness seeking a supervised setting & support.
Sr. Rosalie Carey, Administrator

Deer Lake: Deer Lake Manor
#119, 123 Nicholsville Rd., Deer Lake, NL A8A 1W6
Tel: 709-635-2868
Number of Beds: 31 Beds
Dwight Ball, Contact

Embree: Twilight Manor
19 Main St., Embree, NL A0G 2A0
Tel: 709-535-6094

Flowers Cove: Ivey Durley Place
Former Name: Straits-St Barbe Chronic Care
PO Box 157, Flowers Cove, NL A0K 2N0
Tel: 709-456-9104
Number of Beds: 20 beds
Judy Way, Contact
709-456-2022
Dennis Coates, Contact
704-456-2022

Fogo: Riverhead Manor
PO Box 375, Fogo, NL A0G 2B0
Tel: 709-266-2336

Gander: Nightingale Manor
11 Hadfield Pl., Gander, NL A1V 2V6
Tel: 709-256-3711 *Fax:* 709-256-3712
info@nightingalemanor.com
nightingalemanor.com
Number of Beds: 60 beds
Lawrence Guy

Glovertown: Baywatch Manor
PO Box 120, Glovertown, NL A0G 2M0
Tel: 709-533-6999 *Fax:* 709-533-6994
baywatchmanor@nf.aibn.com
www.baywatchmanor.ca
Number of Beds: 38 beds
Denise Button

Glovertown: Oram's Birchview Manor
PO Box 10, 200 Station Rd., Glovertown, NL A0G 2L0
Tel: 709-533-2600
www.centralhealth.nl.ca
www.facebook.com/OramsBirchviewManor
Number of Beds: 50 beds
Paul Oram

Goulds: Kelly's Personal Care Home
Former Name: Kelly Boarding Home
478 Main Road, Goulds, NL A1S 1G3
Tel: 709-745-5343
Number of Beds: 19 beds

Goulds: Lawlor's Personal Care Home
PO Box 419, Goulds, NL A1S 1G5
Tel: 709-745-1956
Number of Beds: 14 beds
Albert Lawlor

Goulds: Maloney's Personal Care Home
PO Box 568, Barton's Rd., Goulds, NL A1S 1G3
Tel: 709-745-4986
Number of Beds: 10 beds
Note: Nursing Home
Mary Maloney, Contact

Grand Falls-Windsor: Golden Years Estate
348 Grenfell Heights, Grand Falls-Windsor, NL A2A 2J2
Tel: 709-489-7363 *Fax:* 709-489-7306
tgyestate.com
Info Line: 709-489-7263
Number of Beds: 67 beds
Zetta Lane, Owner

Grand Falls-Windsor: Islandside Manor
PO Box 814, Grand Falls-Windsor, NL A2A 2P7
Tel: 709-483-2121
Number of Beds: 24 beds
Max Arnold

Grand Falls-Windsor: Twin Town Manor
15 King St., Grand Falls-Windsor, NL A2B 1J6
Tel: 709-489-0988
twintownmanor@bellaliant.com
www.twintownretirement.ca
Number of Beds: 96 beds

Holyrood: Kennedy's Riverside Boarding Home Ltd.
PO Box 114, Holyrood, NL A0A 2R0
Tel: 709-229-6886
Number of Beds: 33 beds
Geneviève Kennedy

Holyrood: Tobin's Guest Home Inc.
PO Box 95, Holyrood, NL A0A 2R0
Tel: 709-229-7464
Number of Beds: 30 beds
Betty Tobin
Walter Tobin

Holyrood: Woodford's Golden Care
PO Box 158, Holyrood, NL A0A 2R0
Tel: 709-229-3343

Kelligrews: Gully Pond Manor
39 Gully Pond Rd., Kelligrews, NL A1X 6Z2
Tel: 709-834-8083

Kilbride: Hennessey's Personal Care Home
222 Old Bay Bulls Rd., Kilbride, NL A1G 1E1
Tel: 709-368-5558 *Fax:* 709-368-4910

Lark Harbour: Blow Me Down Retirement Centre
Former Name: Guardian Angel Seniors Home
PO Box 91, 195A Main St., Lark Harbour, NL A0L 1H0
Tel: 709-681-2288
info@blowmedownretirement.ca
www.blowmedownretirement.ca
Number of Beds: 16 beds
Note: Home overlooking the ocean in Lark Harbour, at the foothills of the Blow Me Down Mountains from which it gets its name.
Michelle Bennett, Owner/Operator

Lewisporte: Pleasantville Manor
PO Box 207, 14 Pleasant St., Lewisporte, NL A0G 3A0
Tel: 709-535-0941 *Fax:* 709-535-0943
pleasantview@nfld.net
www.centralhealth.nl.ca
Number of Beds: 60 beds

Manuels: Greenslade's Personal Care Home
Former Name: Greenslade Special Care Home
PO Box 84, Manuels, NL A1W 2K1
Tel: 709-834-3047

Mary's Harbour: Harbourview Manor
186 Main St., Mary's Harbour, NL A0K 3P0
Tel: 709-921-6440

Mount Pearl: Pearl House
163 Park Ave., Mount Pearl, NL A1N 1K6
Tel: 709-368-3850
Number of Beds: 44 beds
Lawrence Guy

Musgrave Harbour: Hillcrest Manor
PO Box 100, Musgrave Harbour, NL A0G 3J0
Tel: 709-655-2777

Musgravetown: Greenwood Rest Home Ltd.
PO Box 9, Bunyan's Cove Rd., Musgravetown, NL A0C 1Z0
Tel: 709-467-5243

New Harbour: Jackson's Country Manor
New Harbour Barrens, New Harbour, NL A0B 2P0
Tel: 709-588-2382
Number of Beds: 39 Beds
Wallace Jackson, Contact
709-582-2888

Pollards Point: Main River Manor Ltd.
Former Name: Golden Crest Haven
General Delivery, Pollards Point, NL A0K 4B0
Tel: 709-482-2334
Number of Beds: 20 beds

Port aux Basques: Mountain Hope Manor
PO Box 957, 2 Barhaven Dr., Port aux Basques, NL A0M 1C0
Tel: 709-695-3458
Number of Beds: 32 beds

Porterville: Bayside Manor
PO Box 134, RR#1, Porterville, NL A0G 3A0
Tel: 709-654-3171 *Fax:* 709-654-2176

Number of Beds: 50 beds

Roddickton: Roddickton House
Former Name: Claudelle Manor
PO Box 40, Roddickton, NL A0K 4P0
Tel: 709-457-2166 *Fax:* 709-457-2079
Number of Beds: 22 beds
Chris Decker

Shearstown: Pondview Manor
100 Shearstown Rd., Shearstown, NL A0A 3V0
Tel: 709-786-7051
Note: Nursing home

St. Albans: K.M. Homes Limited
8 Meadow Pl, St. Albans, NL A0H 2E0
Tel: 709-538-3162
www.centralhealth.nl.ca/k-m-homes-ltd
Number of Beds: 30 beds
Shirley Ingram

St. Anthony: Shirley's Haven Personal Care Home
PO Box 74, St. Anthony, NL A0K 4S0
Tel: 709-454-1070
www.facebook.com/144461468186
Note: Personal care home

St. John's: Katherine House
90 Lemarchant Rd., St. John's, NL A1C 2H1
Tel: 709-754-3864

St. John's: Margaret's Manor
57 Bonaventure Ave., St. John's, NL A1C 3Z3
Tel: 709-722-4040
Note: Nursing home

St. John's: North Pond Home
34 Virginia Place, St. John's, NL A1A 3G6
Tel: 709-437-1415
Number of Beds: 35 beds
Maxine Isaacs
Barry Isaacs

St. Lawrence: Mount Margaret Manor
PO Box 278, St. Lawrence, NL A0E 2V0
Tel: 709-873-3199
Number of Beds: 31 beds
Mildred Marsden

St. Marys: Lewis' Personal Care Home, Inc.
PO Box 219, St. Marys, NL A0B 3B0
Tel: 709-525-2244
Number of Beds: 20 beds
Carolann Lewis, Proprietor

St. Marys: Neville's Special Care Home
General Delivery, St. Marys, NL A0B 3B0
Tel: 709-525-2098
Number of Beds: 21 beds
Paul Neville

Stephenville: Silverwood Manor
42 Kippens Rd., Stephenville, NL A2N 1A7
Tel: 709-643-6550
westernhealth.nl.ca
Number of Beds: 30 beds
Judy Gallant

Trepassey: Ocean View Rest Home
PO Box 5, Trepassey, NL A0A 4B0
Tel: 709-438-2227

Twillingate: Sunset Manor
PO Box 638, Twillingate, NL A0G 4M0
Tel: 709-884-5301
Number of Beds: 23 beds
Note: Rest home

Wesleyville: Otterbury Manor
PO Box 42, 428 Main St., Wesleyville, NL A0G 4R0
Tel: 709-536-3383
Number of Beds: 30 beds

Witless Bay: Alderwood Estates
Encore Living
Former Name: Dunn's Personal Care Home
PO Box 10, 112 Harbour Rd., Witless Bay, NL A0A 4K0
Tel: 709-334-2183
Info@EncoreLiving.ca
encoreliving.ca
Number of Beds: 35 suites
Debbie Dunne, Manager

Mental Health Hospitals/Facilities

St. John's: Waterford Hospital
Affiliated with: Eastern Regional Health Authority
306 Waterford Bridge Rd., St. John's, NL A1E 4J8
Tel: 709-777-3300
www.easternhealth.ca
Note: Programs & services include: mental health program; acute & outpatient care; dialysis services; blood collection; & x-ray.

Northwest Territories

Government Departments in Charge

Yellowknife: Department of Health & Social Services
PO Box 1320, Yellowknife, NT X1A 2L9
Tel: 867-767-9052
www.hss.gov.nt.ca
Hon. Julie Green, Minister
867-767-9141, Julie_green@gov.nt.ca

Regional Health Authorities

Behchoko: Tlicho Community Services Agency
PO Box 5, Behchoko, NT X0E 0Y0
Tel: 867-392-3000 *Fax:* 867-392-3001
www.tlicho.ca
Note: A person can contact a member of the primary community care team in their home community & receive access to healthcare services in their own community, in the region &, as necessary, outside the NWT.
Shannon Barnett-Aikman, Chief Executive Officer
867-392-3002, Fax: 867-392-3001, shannon_aikman@tlicho.net

Hay River: Hay River Health & Social Services Authority (HRHSSA)
37911 Mackenzie Hwy., Hay River, NT X0E 0R6
Tel: 867-874-8000 *Fax:* 867-874-8016
www.hrhssa.org
www.youtube.com/user/HSSCommunications
Number of Beds: 29 hospital beds; 15 long-term care beds
Area Served: Southern shore of Great Slave Lake, NWT, Enterprise & Hay River *Population Served:* 3800 *Number of Employees:* 185
Note: Facilities: Hay River Emergency Group Home; Hay River Public Health Unit; Hay River Social Services Office; H.H. Williams Memorial Hospital; Hay River Medical Clinic; Woodland Manor; Hay River Reserve Health Station; Hay River Reserve Social Services; Enterprise Social Services. Area served includes six outlying communities with a total population of more than 6,000 people.
Erin Griffiths, Chief Executive Officer
867-874-8160, erin_griffiths@gov.nt.ca
Frances Aylward, Director, Client Services
867-874-8020, frances_aylward@gov.nt.ca
Doug Maclennan, Director, Finance
867-874-7119, doug_maclennan@gov.nt.ca

Yellowknife: Northwest Territories Health & Social Services Authority (NTHSSA)
Government of the Northwest Territories, PO Box 1320, Yellowknife, NT X1A 2L9
Tel: 867-767-9090
www.nthssa.ca
Year Founded: 2016
Area Served: Beaufort-Delta, Sahtu, Dehcho, Yellowknife, & Fort Smith regions
Note: Formed in Aug. 2016 as a result of the amalgamation of six regional health authorities: Beaufort-Delta Health & Social Services Authority, Dehcho Health & Social Services Authority, Fort Smith Health & Social Services Authority, Sahtu Health & Social Services Authority, Stanton Territorial Health Authority, & Yellowknife Health & Social Services Authority.
Sue Cullen, Chief Executive Officer
Sheila Silva, Chief Financial Officer
Sarah Cook, Territorial Medical Director

Hospitals - General

Hay River: H.H. Williams Memorial Hospital
Affiliated with: Hay River Health & Social Service Authority
3 Gaetz Dr., Hay River, NT X0E 0R8
Tel: 867-874-7169 *Fax:* 867-874-2926
www.hrhssa.org
Number of Beds: 10 beds
Note: Provides physician & emergency services; also includes a long-term care facility.

Inuvik: Inuvik Regional Hospital
Affiliated with: Northwest Territories Health & Social Services Authority
PO Box Bag 2, #285, 289 Mackenzie Rd., Inuvik, NT X0E T0T
Tel: 867-777-8000 *Fax:* 867-777-8054
www.nthssa.ca/en/beaufort-delta-region
www.youtube.com/HSSCommunications
Number of Beds: 51 beds
Note: Programs & services include: acute care; dermatology; diagnostic imaging; ENT; emergency; gynecology; health promotion; internal medicine; laboratory; long term care; medical social work; neurology; nutrition; obstetrical care; ophthalmology; orthopedics; pediatrics; pharmacy; physician family clinics; psychiatry; regional mental health & addictions program; regional; social services; rehabilitation; surgery; telehealth; & visiting specialist clinics.

Yellowknife: Stanton Territorial Hospital
Affiliated with: Northwest Territories Health & Social Services Authority
PO Box 10, 550 Byrne Rd., Yellowknife, NT X1A 2N1
Tel: 867-669-4111
sthainfo@gov.nt.ca
www.nthssa.ca/en/stanton-territorial-hospital
www.youtube.com/user/HSSCommunications
Year Founded: 1967
Number of Beds: 105
Note: Programs & services include: diagnostic imaging; emergency; intensive care; medical day care; medicine; obstetrics; pediatrics; psychiatry; surgery; & surgical day care.
Les Harrison, Interim Chief Operating Officer
Dr. Shireen Mansouri, Medical Director, Central Area
Brianne Timpson, Patient Representative
brianne_timpson@gov.nt.ca

Community Health Care Centres

Aklavik: Susie Husky Health & Social Services Centre
Affiliated with: Northwest Territories Health & Social Services Authority
Former Name: Susie Husky Health Centre
PO Box 114, 2 Airport Rd., Aklavik, NT X0E 0A0
Tel: 867-978-2516 *Fax:* 867-978-2160
www.nthssa.ca/en/beaufort-delta-region
Note: Specialties: Clinics, such as chronic disease & well child, woman, & man clinics; School health program; Health promotion; Dental therapy; Home care; Immunization programs; Rehabilitative services; Child protection; Child & family services; Palliative care. Number of Employees: 1 nurse in charge + 3 community health nurses + 2 community social service workers; 1 dental therapist + 1 community health representative + 1 home support worker + 1 clerk + 1 caretaker

Behchoko: Behchoko Health Centre
Affiliated with: Tlicho Community Services Agency
Former Name: Rae Health Centre
PO Box 5, Behchoko, NT X0E 0Y0
Tel: 867-392-6075 *Fax:* 867-392-6612
www.tlicho.ca
Rebecca Nash, Nurse-in-Charge
rebecca_nash@tlicho.net

Colville Lake: Colville Lake Health Station
Affiliated with: Northwest Territories Health & Social Services Authority
PO Box 50, Colville Lake, NT X0E 1L0
Tel: 867-709-2409 *Fax:* 867-709-2504
Note: Services include: chronic disease clinic; emergency; diagnostics; rehabilitation; palliative care; home care; immunization; pre- & post-natal programs; & school health program.

Deline: Deline Health Centre
Affiliated with: Northwest Territories Health & Social Services Authority
PO Box 199, Deline, NT X0E 0G0
Tel: 867-589-3111

Fort Good Hope: Cassien Edgi Health Centre
Affiliated with: Northwest Territories Health & Social Services Authority
PO Box 9, Fort Good Hope, NT X0E 0N0
Tel: 867-598-3333 *Fax:* 867-598-2605
www.nthssa.ca/en/sahtu-region
Population Served: 585

Fort Liard: Fort Liard Health Centre
Affiliated with: Northwest Territories Health & Social Services Authority
General Delivery, Fort Liard, NT X0E 0A0
Tel: 867-770-4301

Fort McPherson: Fort McPherson Health Services
Affiliated with: Northwest Territories Health & Social Services Authority
PO Box 56, 439 Tetlit Gwich'in Rd., Fort McPherson, NT X0E 0J0
Tel: 867-952-2586 *Fax:* 867-952-2620
www.nthssa.ca/en/beaufort-delta-region

Fort Providence: Fort Providence Health Centre
Affiliated with: Northwest Territories Health & Social Services Authority
PO Box 260, Fort Providence, NT X0E 0L0
Tel: 867-699-4311 *Fax:* 867-699-3811

Fort Simpson: Fort Simpson Health Centre
Affiliated with: Northwest Territories Health & Social Services Authority
PO Box 246, Fort Simpson, NT X0E 0N0
Tel: 867-695-7000 *Fax:* 867-695-7017

Fort Smith: Fort Smith Health Centre
Affiliated with: Northwest Territories Health & Social Services Authority
PO Box 1080, 41 Breynet St., Fort Smith, NT X0E 0P0
Tel: 867-872-6203 *Fax:* 867-872-6260
www.nthssa.ca/en/fort-smith-region
Number of Beds: 25 beds

Fort Smith: Fort Smith Public Health Unit
Affiliated with: Northwest Territories Health & Social Services Authority
PO Box 1080, 41 Breynet St., Fort Smith, NT X0E 0P0
Tel: 867-872-6203 *Fax:* 867-872-6260

Gameti: Gamètì Health Centre
Affiliated with: Tlicho Community Services Agency
General Delivery, Gameti, NT X0E 1R0
Tel: 867-997-3141 *Fax:* 867-997-3045
www.tlicho.ca
Linda Thomas, Nurse-in-Charge
linda_thomas@tlicho.net

Hay River: Hay River Public Health Unit
Affiliated with: Hay River Health & Social Service Authority
3 Gaetz Dr., Hay River, NT X0E 0R8
Tel: 867-874-7201 *Fax:* 867-874-7109
www.hrhssa.org

Inuvik: Inuvik Public Health Unit
Affiliated with: Northwest Territories Health & Social Services Authority
Bag 2, Inuvik, NT X0E 0T0
Tel: 867-777-7246 *Fax:* 867-777-3255
www.nthssa.ca/en/beaufort-delta-region
Note: Services include: maternal wellness; therapeutic abortion counselling; immunization; medical injections; & school health program.
Barb Lennie, Nurse-in-Charge

Jean Marie River: Jean Marie River Health Centre
Affiliated with: Northwest Territories Health & Social Services Authority
General Delivery, Jean Marie River, NT X0E 0N0
Tel: 867-809-2900
www.nthssa.ca/en/deh-cho-region
Note: Services include: chronic disease clinic; diagnostics; rehabilitation; palliative care; home care; immunization; pre- & post-natal programs; & school health program.

Lutselk'e: Lutsel K'e Health Centre
Affiliated with: Northwest Territories Health & Social Services Authority
PO Box 56, Lutselk'e, NT X0E 1A0
Tel: 867-370-3111 *Fax:* 867-370-3022
www.nthssa.ca/en/yellowknife-region-0
Note: Specialties: Public health programs; Counselling & crisis intervention & referrals.

Nahanni Butte: Nahanni Butte Health Centre
Affiliated with: Northwest Territories Health & Social Services Authority
General Delivery, Nahanni Butte, NT X0E 0N0
Tel: 867-602-2203 *Fax:* 867-602-2021
www.nthssa.ca/en/deh-cho-region

Note: Services include: chronic disease clinic; diagnostics; rehabilitation; palliative care; home care; immunization; pre- & post-natal programs; & school health program.

Norman Wells: Norman Wells Health Centre
Affiliated with: Northwest Territories Health & Social Services Authority
PO Box 340, 26 Woodland Ave., Norman Wells, NT X0E 0V0
Tel: 867-587-3333 *Fax:* 867-587-2934
www.nthssa.ca/en/sahtu-region

Paulatuk: Paulatuk Health Services
Affiliated with: Northwest Territories Health & Social Services Authority
PO Box 114, 91353 Main St., Paulatuk, NT X0E 1N0
Tel: 867-580-3231 *Fax:* 867-580-3300
www.nthssa.ca/en/beaufort-delta-region
Number of Beds: 1 bed
Note: Services include: chronic disease clinic; emergency; diagnostics; rehabilitation; palliative care; home care; immunization; pre- & post-natal programs; & school health program.

Sachs Harbour: Sachs Harbour Health Centre
Affiliated with: Northwest Territories Health & Social Services Authority
PO Box 14, Sachs Harbour, NT X0E 0Z0
Tel: 867-690-4181 *Fax:* 867-690-3802
www.nthssa.ca/en/beaufort-delta-region
Note: Services include: chronic disease clinic; emergency; diagnostic; home care; health promotion; disease prevention; & immunization.

Sambaa K'e: Sambaa K'e (Trout Lake) Health Centre
Affiliated with: Northwest Territories Health & Social Services Authority
Sambaa K'e, NT X0E 1Z0
Tel: 867-206-2838
Note: Services include: chronic disease clinic; diagnostics; rehabilitation; palliative care; home care; immunization; pre- & post-natal programs; & school health program.

Tuktoyaktuk: Tuktoyaktuk Health Services
Affiliated with: Northwest Territories Health & Social Services Authority
PO Box 1000, Tuktoyaktuk, NT X0E 1C0
Tel: 867-977-2321 *Fax:* 867-977-2535
www.nthssa.ca/en/beaufort-delta-region
Note: Services include: chronic disease clinic; emergency; diagnostics; rehabilitation; palliative care; home care; immunization; pre- & post-natal programs; & school health program.

Tulita: Tulita Wellness Centre
Affiliated with: Northwest Territories Health & Social Services Authority
PO Box 135, Tulita, NT X0E 0K0
Tel: 867-588-3222 *Fax:* 867-588-4017
www.nthssa.ca/en/sahtu-region
Note: Services include: chronic disease clinic; emergency; diagnostics; rehabilitation; palliative care; home care; immunization; pre- & post-natal programs; & school health program.

Ulukhaktok: Emegak Health & Social Services Centre
Affiliated with: Northwest Territories Health & Social Services Authority
PO Box 160, Ulukhaktok, NT X0E 0S0
Tel: 867-396-3111 *Fax:* 867-396-3221
www.nthssa.ca/en/beaufort-delta-region
Note: Services include: chronic disease clinic; emergency; diagnostics; rehabilitation; palliative care; home care; immunization; pre- & post-natal programs; & school health program.

Ulukhaktok: Ulukhaktok Health Services
Affiliated with: Northwest Territories Health & Social Services Authority
PO Box 160, Ulukhaktok, NT X0E 0S0
Tel: 867-396-3111 *Fax:* 867-396-3221
www.nthssa.ca/en/beaufort-delta-region
Note: Services include: chronic disease clinic; diagnostics; rehabilitation; palliative care; home care; immunization; pre- & post-natal programs; & school health program.

Wekweèti: Wekweèti Health Centre
Affiliated with: Tlicho Community Services Agency
General Delivery, Wekweèti, NT X0E 1W0
Tel: 867-713-2904 *Fax:* 867-713-2903

Whati: Whati Health Centre
Affiliated with: Tlicho Community Services Agency
General Delivery, Whati, NT X0E 1P0
Tel: 867-573-3261 *Fax:* 867-573-3701
www.tlicho.ca
Carolyn Coey-Simpson, Nurse-in-Charge
carolyn_coey@tlicho.net

Wrigley: Wrigley Health Centre
Affiliated with: Northwest Territories Health & Social Services Authority
General Delivery, Wrigley, NT X0E 1E0
Tel: 867-581-3441 *Fax:* 867-581-3200
www.nthssa.ca/en/deh-cho-region
Note: Services include: child & family services; emergency; palliative care; health promotion; disease prevention; home care; immunization; mental health; & rehabilitation.

Yellowknife: Yellowknife Public Health Clinic
Affiliated with: Northwest Territories Health & Social Services Authority
Jan Stirling Bldg., 4702 Franklin Ave., 1st Fl., Yellowknife, NT X1A 1N2
Tel: 867-920-6570 *Fax:* 867-873-0158
www.nthssa.ca/en/yellowknife-region-0
Note: Services include: immunization; family services; services for children & adults.

Nursing Stations

Fort Resolution: Fort Resolution Health Centre
Affiliated with: Northwest Territories Health & Social Services Authority
PO Box 1997, General Delivery, Fort Resolution, NT X0E 0M0
Tel: 867-394-4511 *Fax:* 867-394-3117
www.nthssa.ca/en/yellowknife-region-0
Note: Services include: emergency; acute; diagnostic; public health; continuing care; & addiction referrals.

Inuvik: Beaufort-Delta Health & Social Services
Affiliated with: Northwest Territories Health & Social Services Authority
285 - 289 Mackenzie Rd., Inuvik, NT X0E 0T0
Tel: 867-777-8000
www.nthssa.ca/en/health-services-beaufort-delta-region

Special Treatment Centres

Fort Liard: Fort Liard Mental Health & Addictions Program
Affiliated with: Northwest Territories Health & Social Services Authority
General Delivery, Fort Liard, NT X0G 0A0
Tel: 867-770-4770 *Fax:* 867-770-4813

Fort Simpson: Fort Simpson Mental Health & Addictions Program
Affiliated with: Northwest Territories Health & Social Services Authority
PO Box 246, Fort Simpson, NT X0E 0N0
Tel: 867-695-2293 *Fax:* 867-695-2364

Hay River Reserve: Anne Buggins Wellness Centre
Affiliated with: Northwest Territories Health & Social Services Authority
Hay River Reserve, NT X0E 1G4
Fax: 867-874-3005
Toll-Free: 867-874-3560
www.nthssa.ca/en/deh-cho-region

Long Term Care Facilities

Behchoko: Jimmy Erasmus Seniors Home
Affiliated with: Tlicho Community Services Agency
General Delivery, Behchoko, NT X0E 0Y0
Tel: 867-392-3018 *Fax:* 867-392-3001
www.tlicho.ca
Number of Beds: 7 beds; 1 respite bed

Fort Simpson: Fort Simpson Long Term Care Home
Affiliated with: Northwest Territories Health & Social Services Authority
PO Box 246, Fort Simpson, NT X0E 0N0
Tel: 867-695-7080 *Fax:* 867-695-7083
Number of Beds: 17

Fort Simpson: **Stanley Isaiah Supportive Independent Living Home**
Affiliated with: Northwest Territories Health & Social Services Authority
PO Box 240, Fort Simpson, NT X0E 0N0
Tel: 867-695-2365 *Fax:* 867-695-2364

Hay River: **Woodland Manor**
Affiliated with: Hay River Health & Social Services Authority
52A Woodland Dr., Hay River, NT X0E 0R8
Tel: 867-874-7226 *Fax:* 867-874-7234
Number of Beds: 15 beds
Note: Services include: 24 hour nursing care; dental; dietary; medication administration; occupational therapy; physical therapy; physician; recreational programming; speech language pathology; & vision care.

Inuvik: **Billy Moore Home**
Affiliated with: Northwest Territories Health & Social Services Authority
PO Box 1078, Inuvik, NT X0E 0T0
Tel: 867-777-3204 *Fax:* 867-777-2472
Number of Beds: 5
Note: Provides accommodation combined with integrated case management & program offerings to individuals with physical/cognitive impairments.

Inuvik: **Charlotte Vehus Home**
Affiliated with: Northwest Territories Health & Social Services Authority
PO Box 1800, Inuvik, NT X0E 0T0
Tel: 867-777-4780 *Fax:* 867-777-4687
Number of Beds: 8
Note: Provides accommodation & personal support staffing to individuals with physical/cognitive impairments.

Yellowknife: **Aven Manor**
Affiliated with: AVENS - A Community for Seniors
Also Known As: Aven Cottage
#1-5710, 50th Ave., Yellowknife, NT X1A 1G1
Tel: 867-920-2443 *Fax:* 867-873-9915
www.avensseniors.com
www.facebook.com/avensseniors
Year Founded: 1987
Number of Beds: 29 beds
Note: Services include: dementia care; dental; foot care; long-term care; nursing; occupational therapy; physiotherapy; recreation therapy; respite care; & Snoezelen therapy.
Morgan Gebauer, Acting CEO

Nursing Homes

Fort Smith: **Northern Lights Special Care Home**
Affiliated with: Northwest Territories Health & Social Services Authority
PO Box 1319, Fort Smith, NT X0E 0P0
Tel: 867-872-5403 *Fax:* 867-872-5404
Number of Beds: 28 beds
Note: Services include: nursing; occupational therapy; physiotherapy; palliative care; & recreational programming.

Nova Scotia

Government Departments in Charge

Halifax: **Nova Scotia Department of Health & Wellness**
Barrington Tower, PO Box 488, 1894 Barrington St., Halifax, NS B3J 2R8
Tel: 902-424-5818 *Toll-Free:* 800-387-6665
TTY: 800-670-8888
novascotia.ca/dhw
twitter.com/nshealth
Hon. Zach Churchill, Minister
902-424-5818, Fax: 902-424-0559,
Health.Minister@novascotia.ca

Regional Health Authorities

Bridgewater: **Nova Scotia Health Authority - Western Zone**
Affiliated with: Nova Scotia Health Authority
#109, 215 Dominion St., Bridgewater, NS B4V 2K7
Tel: 902-543-0850 *Fax:* 902-543-8024
Dr. Cheryl Pugh, Executive Medical Director
cheryl.pugh@nshealth.ca
Wanda Matthews, Operations Executive Director
wanda.matthews@nshealth.ca

Dartmouth: **Nova Scotia Health Authority - Central Zone**
Affiliated with: Nova Scotia Health Authority
#5, 7 Mellor Ave., Dartmouth, NS B3B 0E6
Tel: 902-481-5800 *Fax:* 902-481-5803
Dr. Todd Howlett, Interim Executive Medical Director
todd.howlett@nshealth.ca
Brent Powers, Director, Medical Affairs
brent.powers@nshealth.ca
Vickie Sullivan, Operations Executive Director
vickie.sullivan@health.ca

Halifax: **Nova Scotia Health Authority**
#201, 90 Lovett Lake Ct., Halifax, NS B3S 0H6
Toll-Free: 844-491-5890
wearelistening@nshealth.ca
www.nshealth.ca
Info Line: 811
www.facebook.com/NovaScotiaHealthAuthority;
twitter.com/healthns
Year Founded: 2015
Number of Beds: 3,503
Area Served: Province of Nova Scotia *Number of Employees:* 23400
Note: All former Nova Scotia health districts merged in 2015, forming the Nova Scotia Health Authority. The organization oversees 10 hospitals, 33 auxiliaries, & 37 community health boards.
Brendan Carr, President & CEO
ceo@nshealth.ca
Nicole Boutilier, Vice-President, Medicine
John McGarry, Chief Financial Officer & Vice-President, Corporate Services
Paula Bond, Vice-President, Integrated Health Services Program
Madonna MacDonald, Vice-President, Health Services
Gail Tomblin Murphy, Vice-President, Research & Innovation
Colin Stevenson, Vice-President, Quality & System Performance

Sydney: **Nova Scotia Health Authority - Eastern Zone**
Affiliated with: Nova Scotia Health Authority
235 Townsend St., 2nd Fl., Sydney, NS B1P 5E7
Tel: 902-563-2400
Dr. Dale Miller, Interim Executive Medical Director
dale.miller@nshealth.ca
Brett MacDougall, Operations Executive Director
brett.macdougall@nshealth.ca

Truro: **Nova Scotia Health Authority - Northern Zone**
Affiliated with: Nova Scotia Health Authority
600 Abenaki Rd., Truro, NS B2N 5A1
Tel: 902-893-5820 *Fax:* 902-893-5839
Dr. Ryan Sommers, Interim Executive Medical Director
ryan.sommers@nshealth.ca
Cheryl Northcott, Operations Executive Director
cheryl.northcott@nshealth.ca

Hospitals - General

Amherst: **Cumberland Regional Health Care Centre (CRHCC)**
Affiliated with: Nova Scotia Health Authority
19428 Hwy 2, RR #6, Amherst, NS B4H 1N6
Tel: 902-667-3361 *Fax:* 902-667-6306
www.nshealth.ca
Year Founded: 2002
Number of Beds: 72 beds
Note: Programs & services include: ambulatory care; cancer patient navigation; diabetes education; diagnostic imaging; dietary / nutrition; emergency; intensive care unit; laboratory; maternal / child unit; medical inpatient unit; palliative care; pharmacy; rehabilitative services; respiratory therapy; social work; & surgery.
Norah Doucet, Site Manger & Director, Health Services

Antigonish: **St. Martha's Regional Hospital**
Affiliated with: Nova Scotia Health Authority
25 Bay St., Antigonish, NS B2G 2G4
Tel: 902-867-4500
www.nshealth.ca
Year Founded: 1906
Number of Beds: 89 beds
Note: Programs & services include: anesthesia; bone densitometry; cancer & supportive care; cardio-respiratory; chemotherapy; chronic pain clinic; clinical nutrition; colposcopy clinic; cystometry clinic; diabetes education; diagnostic imaging; emergency; foot clinic; general medical / surgical; geriatric assessment & rehabilitation / clinic; gynecology/obstetrics/midwifery; heart health clinic; hospice & palliative care; internal medicine; laboratory services; mental health inpatient / outpatient; obstetrics; occupational therapy; Open Arms Clinic; ophthalmology; orthoptics clinic; ostomy

clinic; otolaryngology; pediatrics; physiotherapy; plastic surgery; pre-surgical assessment clinic; social work; spiritual & religious care; & wound care clinic.
Martha Cooper, Site Lead
Neil McKenna, Manager, Spiritual and Religious Care

Baddeck: **Victoria County Memorial Hospital (VCMH)**
Affiliated with: Nova Scotia Health Authority
PO Box 220, 30 Old Margaree Rd., Baddeck, NS B0E 1B0
Tel: 902-295-2112
www.nshealth.ca
Year Founded: 1949
Number of Beds: 12 beds
Note: Services include: ambulatory care; diabetes education; diagnostic imaging; emergency care; general medicine; general & specialized clinical support services; laboratory; mental health & addiction; & palliative care.
Christine Hines, Facility Manager

Bridgewater: **South Shore Regional Hospital (SSRH)**
Affiliated with: Nova Scotia Health Authority
Former Name: Health Services Association of the South Shore
90 Glen Allan Dr., Bridgewater, NS B4V 3S6
Tel: 902-543-4603
www.nshealth.ca
Year Founded: 1988
Number of Beds: 85 beds
Population Served: 60000
Specialties: Trauma care
Note: Programs & services include: 24 hour emergency; ambulatory care; anesthesiology; cardiology; diagnostic imaging; EKG; gastroenterology; general medicine; intensive care; internal medicine; laboratory; mental health; obstetrics; pathology; pediatrics; radiology; rehabilitation; respiratory therapy; rheumatology; & surgery.

Canso: **Eastern Memorial Hospital**
Affiliated with: Nova Scotia Health Authority
PO Box 10, 1746 Union St., Canso, NS B0H 1H0
Tel: 902-366-2794
www.nshealth.ca
Year Founded: 1948
Number of Beds: 6 beds
Note: Programs & services include: acute care; adult day clinic; adult mental health & addiction prevention & treatment services; ambulatory care; clinical nutrition; continuing care; diagnostic imaging; laboratory; Meals on Wheels; nurse practitioner; occupational therapy; outpatient / emergency; palliative care; physiotherapy; public health; respite care; seniors mental health; social work; spiritual care; & Telehealth.

Cheticamp: **Sacred Heart Community Health Centre**
Affiliated with: Nova Scotia Health Authority
Former Name: Sacred Heart Hospital
PO Box 129, 15102 Cabot Trail, Cheticamp, NS B0E 1H0
Tel: 902-224-4000
www.nshealth.ca
Year Founded: 1999
Number of Beds: 10 beds
Note: Programs & services include: ambulatory care; emergency care; general diagnostic imaging; general medicine; laboratory; mental health & addiction; & palliative care.

Dartmouth: **Dartmouth General Hospital (DGH)**
Affiliated with: Nova Scotia Health Authority
325 Pleasant St., Dartmouth, NS B2Y 4G8
Tel: 902-465-8300
www.nshealth.ca
Year Founded: 1976
Number of Beds: 116 beds
Population Served: 120000
Note: Programs & services include: CT scanning; dentistry; ear, nose, & throat surgery; general surgery; gynaecology; inpatient medical, surgical care, & critical care; laboratory; mammography; oral maxillofacial surgery; orthopedic surgery; outpatient; plastic surgery; radiography; renal dialysis; & urology.
Dr. Ravi Parkash, Site Chief
Heather Francis, Director, Health Services

Digby: **Digby General Hospital**
Affiliated with: Nova Scotia Health Authority
75 Warwick St., Digby, NS B0V 1A0
Tel: 902-245-2501
www.nshealth.ca
Number of Beds: 33 beds
Population Served: 18992
Note: Programs & services include: cardiac / respiratory; continuing care; day surgery; diabetes education; diagnostic imaging; dietitian; emergency; laboratory; mental health & addiction; Nova Scotia Hearing & Speech Centre; nurse

practitioner; nutrition; palliative care; pharmacy; public health; rehabilitation; restorative care; social work; & Telehealth.
Hubert d'Entremont, Site Manager
902-245-2502

Evanston: Strait Richmond Hospital
Affiliated with: Nova Scotia Health Authority
138 Hospital Rd., Evanston, NS B0E 1J0
Tel: 902-625-3100
www.nshealth.ca

Year Founded: 1980
Number of Beds: 31 beds
Note: Programs & services include: chemotherapy; diabetes education; diagnostic imaging; dialysis (QEII Satellite Clinic); EKG; emergency; foot care; Holter monitors; internal medicine; laboratory; loop monitors; mental health outpatient services; nutrition & dietetic counselling; occupational therapy; palliative care; pediatrics; physiotherapy; Renal Clinic; rheumatology; social work; & Surgical Service Clinic.
Kathy Chisholm, Facility Manager

Guysborough: Guysborough Memorial Hospital
Affiliated with: Nova Scotia Health Authority
PO Box 170, 10560 Rte. 16, Guysborough, NS B0H 1H0
Tel: 902-533-3702
www.nshealth.ca

Number of Beds: 10 beds
Note: Programs & services include: diabetes education; diagnostic imaging; EKG; emergency; foot care clinic; laboratory; mental health outpatient; nutrition & dietetic counseling; physiotherapy; social work; & Well Men's Clinic (urology).

Halifax: IWK Health Centre
PO Box 9700, 5850/5980 University Ave., Halifax, NS B3K 6R8
Tel: 902-470-8888 Toll-Free: 888-470-5888
feedback@iwk.nshealth.ca
www.iwk.nshealth.ca
www.facebook.com/iwkhealthcentre; twitter.com/iwkhealthcentre; www.youtube.com/iwkhealthcentre

Year Founded: 1909
Number of Beds: 132 beds
Number of Employees: 3600
Note: The IWK Health Centre provides care to women, children, youth and families in the Maritime provinces and beyond. In addition to providing highly specialized (tertiary) care, the IWK also provides primary care services.
Dr. Krista Jangaard, President & CEO
Ronald Smith, Chair, Board of Directors

Halifax: Queen Elizabeth II Health Sciences Centre (QEII)
Affiliated with: Nova Scotia Health Authority
1796 Summer St., Halifax, NS B3H 3A7
Tel: 902-473-2700
www.nshealth.ca

Year Founded: 1997
Number of Beds: 968 beds
Note: The largest teaching hospital in Atlantic Canada, made up of 10 buildings on 2 sites (the Halifax Infirmary site & the Victoria General site). The QEII provides general & specialized medical care, including mental health programs; cancer care; long-term care; geriatric assessment & restorative care.

Inverness: Inverness Consolidated Memorial Hospital
Affiliated with: Nova Scotia Health Authority
Former Name: Inverness Consolidated Hospital
PO Box 610, 39 James St., Inverness, NS B0E 1N0
Tel: 902-258-2100
www.nshealth.ca

Number of Beds: 33 beds
Note: Services include: ambulatory care; continuing care; diabetes education; emergency care; general medicine; general surgery; laboratory; mental health & addiction; palliative care; & renal dialysis.

Kentville: Valley Regional Hospital
Affiliated with: Nova Scotia Health Authority
150 Exhibition St., Kentville, NS B4N 5E3
Tel: 902-678-7381
www.nshealth.ca

Year Founded: 1992
Number of Beds: 137 beds
Number of Employees: 700
Note: Programs & services include: addiction services; anaesthesia; asthma care; chronic pain; diabetes; diagnostic imaging; emergency; laboratory; mental health; Nova Scotia Hearing & Speech Centre; organ & tissue donation; palliative care; pastoral care; pharmacy; residential mental health; seniors mental health; & surgery.

Liverpool: Queens General Hospital
Affiliated with: Nova Scotia Health Authority
175 School St., Liverpool, NS B0T 1K0
Tel: 902-354-3436
www.nshealth.ca

Number of Beds: 22 beds
Note: Programs & services include: 24-hour outpatients / emergency; asthma; blood collection; diabetes education; diagnostic imaging; day surgery / ambulatory care; EKG; endoscopy; family medicine; geriatrics; gynecology; internal medicine; palliative care; pediatrics; psychiatry; rehabilitation; & renal dialysis.

Lunenburg: Fishermen's Memorial Hospital
Affiliated with: Nova Scotia Health Authority
PO Box 1180, 14 High St., Lunenburg, NS B0J 2C0
Tel: 902-634-8801
www.nshealth.ca

Number of Beds: 53 beds
Note: Services include: 16-hour emergency; addiction; ambulatory care; blood collection; diagnostic imaging; EKG; general medicine; palliative care; rehabilitation; restorative care; & veterans long term care.

Middle Musquodoboit: Musquodoboit Valley Memorial Hospital
Affiliated with: Nova Scotia Health Authority
492 Archibald Brook Rd., Middle Musquodoboit, NS B0N 1X0
Tel: 902-384-2220
www.nshealth.ca

Number of Beds: 6 inpatient beds; palliative care room
Note: Programs & services include: acute home nursing care; clinical nutrition; diabetic clinic & Meals-on-Wheels; diagnostic services (including laboratory, EKG & radiology); emergency services; occupational therapy; outpatient services; palliative services; physiotherapy; public health; Shared Care Mental Health; social work; & The Musquodoboit Valley Family Practice.

Middleton: Soldiers Memorial Hospital
Affiliated with: Nova Scotia Health Authority
PO Box 730, 462 Main St., Middleton, NS B0S 1P0
Tel: 902-825-3411
www.nshealth.ca

Year Founded: 1916
Number of Beds: 82 beds
Population Served: 40000
Note: Programs & services include: adult mental health & addiction; cardiac investigation; continuing care; diabetes education; diagnostic imaging; emergency; enterostomal therapy; laboratory; Nova Scotia Hearing & Speech Centre; occupational therapy; palliative care; pharmacy; physiotherapy; public health; social work; ophthalmology day surgery; & transitional care.

Musquodoboit Harbour: Twin Oaks Memorial Hospital
Affiliated with: Nova Scotia Health Authority
7704 - 7 Hwy., Musquodoboit Harbour, NS B0J 2L0
Tel: 902-889-2200
www.nshealth.ca

Year Founded: 1976
Number of Beds: 14 beds
Note: Programs & services include: acute care; addiction; diabetic & foot care clinics; diagnostic imaging; emergency; family practice; Home Care Nova Scotia; laboratory; Meals on Wheels; Nova Scotia Hearing & Speech Clinic; nutrition counselling; occupational therapy; outpatient care; palliative & respite services; physiotherapy; & social services.

Neils Harbour: Buchanan Memorial Community Health Centre
Affiliated with: Nova Scotia Health Authority
32610 Cabot Trail, Neils Harbour, NS B0C 1N0
Tel: 902-336-2200
www.nshealth.ca

Year Founded: 1943
Number of Beds: 10 beds
Population Served: 4200
Note: Programs & services include: ambulatory care; ECG; emergency care; general & specialized clinical support services; general diagnostic imaging; general medicine; medical laboratory; mental health & addiction; palliative care; & public health.

New Glasgow: Aberdeen Hospital
Affiliated with: Nova Scotia Health Authority
835 East River Rd., New Glasgow, NS B2H 3S6
Tel: 902-752-7600
www.nshealth.ca

Number of Beds: 113 beds
Population Served: 48000

Note: Services include: diagnostic imaging; emergency; general surgery; internal medicine; laboratory; obstetrics & gynecology; ophthalmology; orthopedics; pediatrics; psychiatry; & rehabilitation.

North Sydney: Northside General Hospital
Affiliated with: Nova Scotia Health Authority
PO Box 399, 520 Purves St., North Sydney, NS B2A 3M4
Tel: 902-794-8521
www.nshealth.ca

Number of Beds: 45 acute care beds; 36 long-term care beds
Number of Employees: 271
Note: Programs & services include: ambulatory care; clinical support; continuing care; diabetes education; diagnostic imaging; emergency; general medicine; laboratory; mental health & addiction; orthoptics; pain clinic; palliative care; renal dialysis; surgery; Telehealth; & Well Women's Clinic.

Parrsboro: South Cumberland Community Care Centre
Affiliated with: Nova Scotia Health Authority
50 Jenks Ave., Parrsboro, NS B0M 1S0
Tel: 902-254-2540
www.nshealth.ca

Year Founded: 1975
Number of Beds: 16 beds (14 long-term care; 2 acute care beds)
Note: Programs & services include: adult day care; Collaborative Emergency Centre; diagnostic imaging; long term care; outpatient; palliative care; primary health care clinic; & rehabilitation.
Ron McCormick, Site Manager

Pictou: Sutherland Harris Memorial Hospital
Affiliated with: Nova Scotia Health Authority
PO Box 1059, 222 Haliburton Rd., Pictou, NS B0K 1H0
Tel: 902-485-4324
www.nshealth.ca

Year Founded: 1966
Number of Beds: 38 beds
Note: Programs & services include: Diabetes Education Clinic; geriatric consultation service; Northumberland Veterans Unit; occupational therapy; physiotherapy; recreation; Restorative Care Unit; Satellite Hemodialysis Clinic; social work; & speech-language therapy.

Pugwash: North Cumberland Memorial Hospital
Affiliated with: Nova Scotia Health Authority
260 Gulf Shore Rd., Pugwash, NS B0K 1L0
Tel: 902-243-2521
www.nshealth.ca

Year Founded: 1966
Number of Beds: 4 beds
Note: Services include: Collaborative Emergency Centre; diagnostic imaging; laboratory collection; outpatient; primary health care clinic; rehabilitative services; & short stay & palliative care.

Sheet Harbour: Eastern Shore Memorial Hospital
Affiliated with: Nova Scotia Health Authority
22637 Hwy. #7, Sheet Harbour, NS B0J 3B0
Tel: 902-885-2554
www.nshealth.ca

Year Founded: 1976
Number of Beds: 5 beds
Note: Programs & services include: acute care; Adult Day Clinic; adult mental health & addiction prevention & treatment; clinical nutrition; community blood collection; continuing care; diabetes management; diagnostic imaging; Home Care Nova Scotia; laboratory; Meals on Wheels; NS Hearing & Speech; nurse practitioner; occupational therapy; outpatient / emergency; palliative care; physiotherapy; primary care physicians; public health; respite care; Sexual Health Center; social services; social work; spiritual care; & Telehealth.

Shelburne: Roseway Hospital
Affiliated with: Nova Scotia Health Authority
PO Box 610, 1606 Lake Rd., Shelburne, NS B0T 1W0
Tel: 902-875-3011
www.nshealth.ca

Number of Beds: 19 beds
Population Served: 15000
Note: Programs & services include: 24 hour emergency; addiction; audiology; cardiac stress testing; continuing care; diabetes education; diagnostic; internal medicine; mental health centre; nutrition counselling; obstetrics & gynecology; occupational therapy; otolaryngology; palliative care; physiotherapy; speech therapy; & surgery.
Jodi Ybarra, Site Manager

Sherbrooke: St. Mary's Memorial Hospital
Affiliated with: Nova Scotia Health Authority
PO Box 299, 91 Hospital Rd., Sherbrooke, NS B0J 3C0
Tel: 902-522-2882
www.nshealth.ca

Year Founded: 1949
Number of Beds: 6 beds
Note: Programs & services include: diabetes education; diagnostic imaging; EKG; emergency; foot care clinic; hospice & palliative care; laboratory; nutrition & dietetic counselling; physiotherapy; social work; & Telehealth.

Springhill: All Saints Springhill Hospital (ASSH)
Affiliated with: Nova Scotia Health Authority
Also Known As: All Saints Hospital
10 Princess St., Springhill, NS B0M 1X0
Tel: 902-597-3773
www.nshealth.ca

Year Founded: 1963
Number of Beds: 30 beds
Note: Programs & services include: Addiction Services In-Patient Unit; Collaborative Emergency Centre; diagnostic imaging; dialysis; laboratory; outpatient; palliative care; Primary Health Care Clinic; rehabilitative services; & restorative care.

Sydney: Cape Breton Regional Hospital
Affiliated with: Nova Scotia Health Authority
1482 George St., Sydney, NS B1P 1P3
Tel: 902-567-8000
www.nshealth.ca

Year Founded: 1995
Number of Beds: 162 acute care beds; 36 emergency beds; 23 intensive care beds; 40 obstetrical beds; 52 mental health beds; 9 palliative care beds
Note: Programs & services include: Addictions Primary Unit; ambulatory care; bone densitometer; Cape Breton Cancer Centre; cardio / pulmonary / neuro services; clinical support; diabetes education; diagnostic imaging; emergency trauma care; laboratory; medicine; mental health & addiction; MRI; obstetrics; palliative care; pediatrics; renal dialysis; specialized intensive care; & surgery.

Tatamagouche: Lillian Fraser Memorial Hospital
Affiliated with: Nova Scotia Health Authority
PO Box 40, 110 Blair Ave., Tatamagouche, NS B0K 1V0
Tel: 902-657-2382
www.nshealth.ca

Number of Beds: 10 beds
Note: Programs & services include: diabetes clinic; diagnostic imaging; emergency; food services; inpatient medical unit; laboratory; medical day unit; nutrition counselling; outpatient clinics; palliative care; perinatal & gynecology clinic; physiotherapy; primary care; rehabilitation; surgical clinic; & Telehealth.
Barbara Cook, Site Manager

Truro: Colchester East Hants Health Centre
Affiliated with: Nova Scotia Health Authority
Former Name: Colchester Regional Hospital
600 Abenaki Rd., Truro, NS B2N 5A1
Tel: 902-893-5554
www.nshealth.ca

Number of Beds: 106 beds
Note: Programs & services include: asthma care; blood / specimen collection; breast screening; cardiovascular; colpolscopy; coronary care; CT scan; dermatology; diabetes; diagnostic imaging; dialysis; dietary / nutrition; ECG; emergency; enterostomal therapy; general medicine; hearing & speech; intensive care; laboratory; medical day unit; mental health & addiction; occupational therapy; oncology; ophthalmology; ostomy clinic; outpatients; palliative care; perinatal; pharmacy; physiotherapy; pre-operative clinic; rehabilitation; respiratory; social work; surgery; Telehealth; water testing; women & children's health; & wound management.

Windsor: Hants Community Hospital
Affiliated with: Nova Scotia Health Authority
89 Payzant Dr., Windsor, NS B0N 2T0
Tel: 902-792-2000
www.nshealth.ca

Number of Beds: 28 acute care beds; 32 long-term care beds
Note: Programs & services include: acute medical; ambulatory day surgical care; ambulatory specialty consultation clinics; cardiac investigation; chronic pain clinic; community mental health & addictions; diagnostic imaging; laboratory; Nova Scotia Hearing & Speech Clinic; occupational therapy; physiotherapy; public health; respiratory; social work; & Well Womens Clinics.
Dr. Mike Clory, Site Chief
Sherri Parker, Director, Health Services

Yarmouth: Yarmouth Regional Hospital
Affiliated with: Nova Scotia Health Authority
60 Vancouver St., Yarmouth, NS B5A 2P5
Tel: 902-742-3541
www.nshealth.ca

Number of Beds: 124 beds
Population Served: 58000
Note: Programs & services include: addictions & withdrawal management services; ambulatory care; breast screening; Cancer Care Centre; cardiovascular program; chronic pain clinic; continuing care; diabetes education; diagnostic imaging; emergency; falls prevention; family wellness; kidney clinic; intensive care unit; laboratory; mental health; obstetrics; occupational therapy; palliative care; physiotherapy; pre-natal clinic; public health; recreational therapy; renal dialysis; respiratory therapy; stroke program; surgery; & Veterans Place.

Auxiliary Hospitals

Advocate Harbour: Bayview Memorial Health Centre
Affiliated with: Nova Scotia Health Authority
3375 Hwy. 209, Advocate Harbour, NS B0M 1A0
Tel: 902-392-2859
www.nshealth.ca

Year Founded: 1989
Number of Beds: 10 beds
Note: Provides community health services & long-term care.

Community Health Care Centres

Annapolis Royal: Annapolis Community Health Centre
Affiliated with: Nova Scotia Health Authority
PO Box 426, 821 St. George St., Annapolis Royal, NS B0S 1A0
Tel: 902-532-2381 Fax: 902-532-2113
www.nshealth.ca
Note: Programs & services include: diagnostic imaging; emergency; laboratory; mental health & addictions; occupational therapy; palliative care; physiotherapy; & public health.

Berwick: Western Kings Memorial Health Centre
Affiliated with: Nova Scotia Health Authority
PO Box 490, 121 Orchard St., Berwick, NS B0P 1E0
Tel: 902-538-3111 Fax: 902-538-9590
www.nshealth.ca
Note: Services include outpatient department, laboratory, diagnostic imaging, physiotherapy, nutritional counselling, dialysis, mental health clinic, & Victorian Order of Nurses Adult Day Care program.

Lower Sackville: Cobequid Community Health Centre (CCHC)
Affiliated with: Nova Scotia Health Authority
40 Freer Lane, Lower Sackville, NS B4C 0A2
Tel: 902-869-6100
www.nshealth.ca
Note: Ambulatory care facility
Dr. Mike Clory, Site Chief
Margaret Merlin-Wilson, Director, Health Services

Wolfville: Eastern Kings Memorial Community Health Centre
Affiliated with: Nova Scotia Health Authority
Former Name: Eastern Kings Community Health Centre
23 Earnscliffe Ave., Wolfville, NS B4P 1X4
Tel: 902-542-2266 Fax: 902-542-4619
www.nshealth.ca
Note: Services include laboratory services and x-ray.

Special Treatment Centres

Halifax: IWK Health Centre
Halifax Community Mental Health & Central Referral Service
Former Name: Atlantic Child Guidance Center
#1001, 6080 Young St., Halifax, NS B3K 5L2
Tel: 902-464-4110 Fax: 902-464-3008
Toll-Free: 855-635-4110
www.iwk.nshealth.ca
Dr. Krista Jangaard, President & CEO

Halifax: Nova Scotia Hearing & Speech Centres
Provincial Centre, Park Lane Terraces, PO Box 120, #401, 5657 Spring Garden Rd., Halifax, NS B3J 3R4
Tel: 902-492-8289 Fax: 902-423-0532
Toll-Free: 888-780-3330
info@nshsc.nshealth.ca
www.nshsc.nshealth.ca
Note: Specialties: Speech-language pathology services; Audiology services; Augmentative communication program;

Cochlear implant program; Industrial & community audiology; Newborn hearing screening program.
Anne Mason-Browne, President & CEO

Waterville: Kings Regional Rehabilitation Centre
PO Box 128, 1349 County Home Rd., Waterville, NS B0P 1V0
Tel: 902-538-3103 Fax: 902-538-7022
info@krrc.ns.ca
www.krrc.ns.ca

Number of Beds: 199 beds
Number of Employees: 600
Note: Residential rehabilitation centre for clients with mental illness, brain injury, & physical & intellectual disabilities; offers medical, dental, social work, psychiatry, & therapy services.
Judy Heffern, Chief Executive Officer

Yarmouth: Addiction Services
Affiliated with: Nova Scotia Health Authority
Former Name: Western Drug Dependency Program
c/o Yarmouth Regional Hospital, 60 Vancouver St., Yarmouth, NS B5A 2P5
Tel: 902-742-2406 Fax: 902-742-0684

Long Term Care Facilities

Advocate Harbour: Chignecto Manor Co-op Ltd.
24 Bayview Manor Rd., Advocate Harbour, NS B0M 1A0
Tel: 902-392-2028

Antigonish: Highland Crest Home
Affiliated with: Nova Scotia Health Authority
44 Hillcrest St., Antigonish, NS B2G 1Z3
Tel: 902-863-3855 Fax: 902-863-1833
caringforseniors@high-crest.com
www.high-crest.com

Year Founded: 1981
Number of Beds: 40 beds
Mary Beaver, Administrator
mbeaver@high-crest.com

Barrington: Bayside Home Adult Residential Centre
96 Bayside Dr., Barrington, NS
Tel: 902-637-2098
www.baysidehome.ca

Number of Beds: 62 beds
Note: Adult residential centre
Paula Hatfield, Administrator

Berwick: New Visions Home for Seniors
PO Box 566, 4507 Hwy. 1, Berwick, NS B0P 1E0
Tel: 902-538-9579 Fax: 902-538-0390
newvision2@ns.sympatico.ca
www.newvision2.ca

Year Founded: 1993
Number of Beds: 25 beds + 1 respite
Helen B. Walsh, Administrator

Bridgetown: Grace Haven Enterprises Ltd.
9791 Hwy 1, Bridgetown, NS B0S 1C0
Tel: 902-665-4224

Note: residential care facility

Bridgetown: Meadow Adult Residential Centre
Annapolis County Municipal Housing Corporation
200 Church St., Bridgetown, NS B0S 1C0
Tel: 902-665-4566 Fax: 902-665-5265
homesforcare.com

Year Founded: 1987
Note: Adult residential centre

Bridgetown: Saunders Rest Home
PO Box 114, 9 Freeman St., Bridgetown, NS B0S 1C0
Tel: 902-665-4331 Fax: 902-665-4768

Number of Beds: 8 beds
Shaun Saunders, Administrator

Bridgewater: La Have House
Riverview Enhanced Living
PO Box 270, Bridgewater, NS B4V 2W9
Tel: 902-543-7851 Fax: 902-543-8332
www.ourriverview.com

Number of Beds: 66 beds
Note: Adult residential centre.
Joanne Wentzell, Chief Executive Officer, Riverview Enhanced Living
jwentzell@ourriverview.com

Chelsea: Hillsview Acres
PO Box 4, 14 Middlefield Rd., RR#1, Chelsea, NS B0T 1E0
Tel: 902-685-2966 Fax: 902-685-2446
hillsview.acres@ns.sympatico.ca

Number of Beds: 28 beds + 1 respite
Janie Ryan, Administrator

Chester: Bonny Lea Farm
PO Box 560, Chester, NS B0J 1J0
Tel: 902-275-5622 Fax: 902-275-2567
www.bonnyleafarm.ca

Year Founded: 1973
Number of Beds: 35 beds
Note: Adult residential centre; small option units & apartments
David Outhouse, Managing Director
davidouthouse@sswap.ca

Dartmouth: Clarmar Residential Care
Affiliated with: Nova Scotia Health Authority
Former Name: Hilltop Villa
200 Main St., Dartmouth, NS B2X 1S3
Tel: 902-435-6186 Fax: 902-435-9354
Number of Beds: 24 beds

Dartmouth: Harbour Glen Manor Ltd.
229 Pleasant St., Dartmouth, NS B2Y 3R5
Tel: 902-465-5770
Note: Residential care facility

Dartmouth: Regional Residential Services Society (RRSS)
#LKD1, 202 Brownlow Ave., Dartmouth, NS B3B 1T5
Tel: 902-465-4022 Fax: 902-465-3124
www.rrss.ns.ca
Number of Beds: 185 beds
Note: Developmental residences & group homes, supported apartments, short & long term respite services, personal support planning, counseling, assessment. Number of staff: 400+
Carol Ann Brennan, Executive Director
902-465-2702, carolann.brennan@rrss.ns.ca

Dayspring: LaHave Manor
Riverview Enhanced Living Society
Also Known As: LaHave House
171 Leary Fraser Rd., Dayspring, NS B4V 5S7
Tel: 902-543-7851 Fax: 902-543-8332
www.ourriverview.com
Note: group home for mentally challenged adults
Joanne Wentzell, CEO

Enfield: Corridor Community Options Society
Former Name: Lantz Residential Programs
21 Convent Rd., Enfield, NS B2T 1C9
Tel: 902-883-9404 Fax: 902-883-1251
Number of Beds: 11 beds
Note: Group home/small options home; vocational training/social enterprise; runs the Lantz Residential Programs & Corridor Community Options for Adults
Robin C. Strickland, Executive Director
ccosdirector@gmail.com

Glace Bay: Terrace Manor
208 South St., Glace Bay, NS B1A 1W1
Tel: 902-849-2849 Fax: 902-842-0359

Halifax: Basinview Drive Developmental Residence
3838 Basinview Dr., Halifax, NS B3K 5A2
Tel: 902-455-7421
Number of Beds: 8 beds

Halifax: Haven Manor
Affiliated with: GEM Health Care
6411 Cobourg Rd., Halifax, NS B3H 2A6
Tel: 902-421-1167
www.gemhealth.com
Number of Beds: 17 beds
Hilda Stevens, Administrator

Halifax: Homes for Independent Living
2505 Oxford St., Halifax, NS B3L 2T5
Tel: 902-422-9591 Fax: 902-425-3151
hil@hfx.eastlink.ca
www.nsraa.ca
Year Founded: 1980
Number of Beds: 6 group home beds, with 1 respite bed
Note: Specialty: Programs & accommodation for young adults with physical disabilities; Community outreach programs
Lee-Anne Penny, Executive Director

Halifax: Lynden Rest Home
1019 Lucknow St., Halifax, NS B3H 2T2
Tel: 902-420-0697 Fax: 902-492-3936

Halifax: Melville Gardens Residential & Level 2 Nursing Care Facility
11 Ramsgate Lane, Halifax, NS B3P 2S9
Tel: 902-477-3135 Fax: 902-477-2718
www.gemhealth.com
Year Founded: 1991
Number of Beds: 91 beds

Cecile Adair, Administrator
cecile.adair@gemhealth.com

Halifax: Point Pleasant Lodge
1121 South Park St., Halifax, NS B3H 2W6
Tel: 902-421-1599 Fax: 902-429-9722
guestservices@pointpleasantlodge.com
www.pointpleasantlodge.com
Number of Beds: 100 guest rooms
Note: A specialty hotel, with guest rooms for people directly or indirectly associated with medical attention in the Halifax area

Halifax: Robert Allen Drive Development Residence
31 Robert Allen Dr., Halifax, NS B3M 3G9
Tel: 902-443-6804
Number of Beds: 7 beds

Halifax: Vernon St. Group Home
1648 Vernon St., Halifax, NS B3H 3N1
Tel: 902-422-6742
Number of Beds: 8 beds

Kentville: Wedgewood House
19 Leverett Ave., Kentville, NS B4N 2K5
Tel: 902-678-1242 Fax: 902-679-2808
info@thewedgewood.ca
www.thewedgewood.ca
Year Founded: 1960
Number of Beds: 15 beds
Note: 24-hour nursing care; dietitian; weekly visits from a medical advisor.

Lower West Pubnico: Pont du Marais Home Ltd.
Affiliated with: Nova Scotia Health Authority
PO Box 236, Lower West Pubnico, NS B0W 2C0
Tel: 902-762-3099 Fax: 902-762-2072
pdm@auracom.com
Number of Beds: 23 beds + 2 respite

Margaree Valley: Brookside Residential Care Facility
843 East Big Intervale Rd., Margaree Valley, NS B0E 2C0
Tel: 902-248-2181
Note: Residential care facility

Meteghan: Au Logis Meteghan Ltd.
Affiliated with: Nova Scotia Health Authority
PO Box 128, Meteghan, NS B0W 2J0
Tel: 902-645-3594 Fax: 902-645-2429
Number of Beds: 20 beds, 2 respite
Note: Residential care

Meteghan: Cottage Celeste
Affiliated with: Nova Scotia Health Authority
PO Box 314, 8064 Hwy. 1, Meteghan, NS B0W 2J0
Tel: 902-645-2248
Number of Beds: 19 beds
Kathy MacDonald, Administrator

Musquodoboit Harbour: Braeside Nursing Home
126 Higginsville Rd., Musquodoboit Harbour, NS B0N 1X0
Tel: 902-384-3007 Fax: 902-384-3310
www.facebook.com/169178906442

New Glasgow: High-Crest Home New Glasgow
Affiliated with: Nova Scotia Health Authority
Former Name: Sunset Haven Home
253 Forbes St., New Glasgow, NS B2H 4P5
Tel: 902-752-3461 Fax: 902-752-2672
www.high-crest.com
Number of Beds: 36 beds
Note: Specialties: Medication monitoring; Recreational program.
Robert MacDonald, Administrator
rmacdonald@high-crest.com

Oxford: Four Seasons Manor Special Care
63 Water St., Oxford, NS B0M 1P0
Tel: 902-447-2819
Note: Residential care facility

Oxford: Shady Rest Ltd.
237 Water St., Oxford, NS B0M 1P0
Tel: 902-447-2786
Year Founded: 1900

Pugwash: Sunset Residential & Rehabilitation Services Inc.
140 Sunset Ln., Pugwash, NS B0K 1L0
Tel: 902-243-2571 Fax: 902-243-3222
sunsetcommunity.ca
Note: Specialties: Residential care & support services for persons who are mentally challenged & disabled; Day programs; Life & vocational skills programs; Social development programs; Advocacy services
Julie Matheson, CEO

Saulnierville: La Maison au Coucher du Soleil Ltd.
RR#1, Saulnierville, NS B0W 2Z0
Tél: 902-769-2270
info@maisonaucoucher.com
www.maisonaucoucher.com
Fondée en: 1972
Nombre de lits: 25 lits
Note: Residential care facility

Shelburne: Mary's Abide-A-While Home Ltd.
Affiliated with: Nova Scotia Health Authority
PO Box 609, 188 Water St., Shelburne, NS B0T 1W0
Tel: 902-875-4384 Fax: 902-875-4384
Number of Beds: 14 beds
Mary Davis, Administrator

Stellarton: Highland Community Residential Services (HCRS)
PO Box 2140, 276 Foord St., Stellarton, NS B0K 1S0
Tel: 902-752-1755 Fax: 902-752-4256
info@hcrsweb.ca
hcrsweb.ca
Year Founded: 1977
Note: Residential care facility

Stellarton: Riverview Home Corp.
6105 Trafalgar Rd., RR#1, Stellarton, NS B0K 1S0
Tel: 902-755-4884 Fax: 902-755-3207
info@riverviewhome.ca
riverviewhome.ca
Number of Beds: 106 beds + 3 community homes & supervised depts.
Note: Residential care facility for mentally and/or physically challenged adults, group homes, & developmental residence. Number of staff: 150
Patricia Bland, CEO

Stewiacke: Elmwood Manor Limited
98 Riverside Ave., Stewiacke, NS B0N 2J0
Tel: 902-639-9003
Note: Residential care facility

Sydney: Cape Breton Community Housing Association
PO Box 1292, 50 Dorchester St., 2nd Fl., Sydney, NS B1P 6K3
Tel: 902-539-0025 Fax: 902-562-5476
communityhousing@cbcha.ca
www.cbcha.ca
Year Founded: 1977
Note: The organization helps clients develop skills so they may live independently in the community. Information sessions are held on a regular basis.

Sydney: Mayfair Guest Home
1038 Upper Prince St., Sydney, NS B1P 5P6
Tel: 902-539-5611

Sydney: My Cape Breton Home for Seniors
Affiliated with: Nova Scotia Health Authority
137 Riverdale Dr., Sydney, NS B1R 0A9
Tel: 902-564-4461 Fax: 902-564-4247
www.mycbhome.ca
Number of Beds: 16 beds
Sherry MacNeil, Owner/Operator
sherry@mycbhome.ca

Sydney: Resi-Care (Cape Breton) Association
146 Vulcan Ave., Sydney, NS B1P 5W5
Tel: 902-539-0935 Fax: 902-562-0717
Number of Beds: 60 beds
Note: Group home
Judy Ryan, Executive Director
judyryan@resi-care.ca

Sydney River: Breton Ability Centre
Former Name: Braemore Home
1300 Kings Rd., Sydney River, NS B1S 0H3
Tel: 902-539-7640 Fax: 902-539-5340
www.bretonabilitycentre.ca
Number of Beds: 124 beds
Millie Colbourne, CEO
mcolbourne@cb-bac.ca

Tatamagouche: Maplewood Manor
Affiliated with: Nova Scotia Health Authority
150 Blair Ave., Tatamagouche, NS B0K 1V0
Tel: 902-657-2876 Fax: 902-657-1022
maplewood.manor@ns.aliantzinc.ca
Number of Beds: 6 beds
Jeff Williams, Owner & Administrator

Truro: **Karlaine Place Ltd.**
Affiliated with: Nova Scotia Health Authority
PO Box 691, 104 Pictou Rd., Truro, NS B2N 5E5
Tel: 902-895-5111 *Fax:* 902-893-1513
Number of Beds: 8 beds

Truro: **Townsview Estates**
Affiliated with: Nova Scotia Health Authority
PO Box 1825, 310 Abenaki Rd., Truro, NS B2N 5Z5
Tel: 902-895-9559 *Fax:* 902-893-8094
Number of Beds: 85 beds

Truro: **Wynn Park Villa**
32 Windsor Way, Truro, NS B2N 0B4
Tel: 902-893-3939 *Fax:* 902-893-3936
contact@wynnparkvilla.ca
wynnparkvilla.ca
Year Founded: 2008
Number of Beds: 60 beds
Sheila Peck, Administrator
speck@wynnparkvilla.ca

Windsor: **Kendall Lane Housing Society**
Victoria Park Guest House Inc.
PO Box 556, Windsor, NS B0N 2T0
Tel: 902-798-4375 *Fax:* 902-798-4378
vpghinc@gmail.com
www.vpgh.ca
Year Founded: 1993
Number of Beds: 6 beds
Note: Provides residential & support services for individuals with physical challenges.

Windsor: **Kings Meadows Residence Society**
5466 Hwy. 14, Windsor, NS B0N 2T0
Tel: 902-798-4657
www.kingsmeadow.wixsite.com/kmrs
Year Founded: 1969
Number of Beds: 10 beds
Barbara Campbell, Administrator

Windsor: **Victoria Park Guest House**
Affiliated with: Nova Scotia Health Authority
PO Box 556, 350 King St., Windsor, NS B0N 2T0
Tel: 902-798-4375 *Fax:* 902-798-4378
vpghinc@gmail.com
www.vpgh.ca
Year Founded: 1989
Number of Beds: 15 beds
Note: Adult residential care facility; 24-hour staff; foot care.
Dorothy Blakely, Administrator

Wolfville: **Wolfville Elms (The Elms Rest Home)**
701 Main St., Wolfville, NS B4P 2N4
Tel: 902-542-2420 *Fax:* 902-542-1048
Number of Beds: 23 beds

Yarmouth: **Sunset Terrace**
Former Name: Old Ladies Home Society
8 James St., Yarmouth, NS B5A 2V1
Tel: 902-742-3322
Year Founded: 1890
Number of Beds: 21
Barb Rodney, President, Board of Directors

Nursing Homes

Annapolis Royal: **Annapolis Royal Nursing Home**
9745 Hwy. 8, RR#2, Annapolis Royal, NS B0S 1A0
Tel: 902-532-2240 *Fax:* 902-532-7151
Number of Beds: 53 nursing home beds; 1 respite bed
Teresa Andrews, Director, Facility & Resident Care

Antigonish: **R.K. MacDonald Nursing Home**
Affiliated with: Nova Scotia Health Authority
64 Pleasant St., Antigonish, NS B2G 1W7
Tel: 902-863-2578
www.rkmacdonald.ca
Number of Beds: 137 beds

Arichat: **St. Anne Community & Nursing Care Centre**
PO Box 30, 2313 Hwy. 206, Arichat, NS B0E 1A0
Tel: 902-226-2826 *Fax:* 902-226-1529
www.stannecentre.ca
Number of Beds: 29 beds
Note: Provides long-term care.
Annette Fougere, Chief Executive Officer
annette.fougere@sacentre.nshealth.ca
Renette Sampson, Financial Officer
renette.sampson@sacentre.nshealth.ca
Connie Pierce, Director, Recreation
connie.pierce@sacentre.nshealth.ca

Trinia George, Supervisor, Environmental Services
trinia.george@sacentre.nshealth.ca

Beaverbank: **Scotia Nursing Homes Ltd.**
Affiliated with: Nova Scotia Health Authority
Former Name: Scotia Nursing Homes Ltd.
125 Knowles Cres., Beaverbank, NS B4G 1E7
Tel: 902-865-6364 *Fax:* 902-865-3582
Number of Beds: 49 beds + 1 respite

Berwick: **Grand View Manor**
110A Commercial St., Berwick, NS B0P 1E0
Tel: 902-538-3118 *Fax:* 902-538-3998
inquiries@grandviewmanor.org
www.grandviewmanor.org
Number of Beds: 142 beds
Note: Services include: dietary; nursing; occupational therapy; physiotherapy; & recreation.
Jorge VanSlyke, CEO & Administrator
Beth Hakkert, Director, Care
Carol Breckon, Director, Finance & Organizational Development
John Bigelow, Director, Environmental & Support Services

Bridgetown: **Mountain Lea Lodge**
170 Church St., Bridgetown, NS B0S 1C0
Tel: 902-665-4489 *Fax:* 902-665-2900
www.homesforcare.com
www.facebook.com/acmhc
Number of Beds: 106 long-term care beds; 1 respite bed
Note: Services include: dental care; dietary; foot care; nursing care; nutrition; palliative care; personal care; pharmacy; recreation; & rehabilitation.
Joyce d'Entremont, CEO & Administrator
jdentremont@homesforcare.com
Mark Muise, Finance Officer
Kathy Wilson, Director, Resident Care
kwilson@homesforcare.com
Julie Hannam, Director, Support Services
jhannam@homesforcare.com

Bridgewater: **Hillside Pines**
77 Exhibition Dr., Bridgewater, NS B4V 3K6
Tel: 902-543-1525 *Fax:* 902-543-8083
info@hillsidepines.com
www.hillsidepines.com
Number of Beds: 50 beds
Note: Services include: recreation; occupational therapy; & physiotherapy.
Marisa Eisner, Administrator
m.eisner@hillsidepines.com
Tracy Cousins, Director, Elder Care
t.cousins@hillsidepines.com
Gina Steadman, Director, Therapeutic & Recreation
g.steadman@hillsidepines.com
Hiedi Turner, Director, Finance
h.turner@hillsidepines.com
Cecil Haughn, Director, Environmental Services
cecil.haughn@hillsidepines.com

Caledonia: **North Queens Nursing Home**
9565 Hwy. #8, Caledonia, NS B0T 1B0
Tel: 902-682-2553
www.nqnh.ca
Number of Beds: 43 beds
Note: Adult residential centre
Ashley Surette, Director, Care

Canso: **Canso Seaside Manor**
1748 Union St., Canso, NS B0H 1H0
Tel: 902-366-3030
Number of Beds: 15 beds
Susan Bouchie, Administrator

Cheticamp: **Foyer Père Fiset**
Affiliée à: Nova Scotia Health Authority
CP 219, 15092 Cabot Trail, Cheticamp, NS B0E 1H0
Tél: 902-224-2087 *Téléc:* 902-224-1188
foyer.fiset@ns.sympatico.ca
Nombre de lits: 60 lits
Mona Poirier, Administrator

Conway: **Tideview Terrace**
Affiliated with: Nova Scotia Health Authority
PO Box 1120, 74 Pleasant St., Conway, NS B0V 1A0
Tel: 902-245-4718 *Fax:* 902-245-6674
www.tideviewterrace.ca
www.facebook.com/tideviewterrace
Year Founded: 1973
Number of Beds: 89 beds; 1 respite bed
Note: Specialties: Long-term care (level II); Dementia care; Adult day programs; Respite care; Palliative care
Debra Boudreau, Administrator
debra.boudreau@nshealth.ca

Darlene Cook, Director, Care
darlene.cook@nshealth.ca
Kara Gilliatt, Manager, Finance
kara.gilliatt@nshealth.ca
Kimberly Nichols, Manager, Building
kimberly.nichols@nshealth.ca

Dartmouth: **Oakwood Terrace**
Affiliated with: Nova Scotia Health Authority
10 Mount Hope Ave., Dartmouth, NS B2Y 4K1
Tel: 902-469-3702 *Fax:* 902-469-3824
nurturinglife@oakwoodterrace.ns.ca
www.oakwoodterrace.ns.ca
www.facebook.com/oakwoodterrace
Year Founded: 1982
Number of Beds: 111 beds
Number of Employees: 160
Note: Specialties: Physiotherapy; Adult Day Program; Medical services; Palliative care
Anthony Taylor, Administrator
Gary Comeau, Director, Recreation Therapy & Volunteer Services

Dartmouth: **Woodside Manor**
351 Pleasant St., Dartmouth, NS B2Y 3S4
Tel: 902-463-5845
Number of Beds: 29 beds

Eastern Passage: **Ocean View Manor**
Affiliated with: Nova Scotia Health Authority
PO Box 130, 1909 Caldwell Rd., Eastern Passage, NS B3G 1M4
Tel: 902-465-6020 *Fax:* 902-465-4929
oceanv.ca
Year Founded: 1967
Number of Beds: 176 beds
Note: Specialties: Physiotherapy; Occupational therapy; Recreation therapy; Social work; Respite care; Palliative care
Dion Mouland, President & CEO
Jacob D. Hillier, Senior Director, Facility & Resident Supports
Steve Vincent, Director, Finance

Falmouth: **Windsor Elms Village for Continuing Care Society**
Affiliated with: Nova Scotia Health Authority
174 Dyke Rd., Falmouth, NS B0P 1L0
Tel: 902-798-2251 *Fax:* 902-798-3302
www.windsorelms.com
Number of Beds: 107 beds; 1 respite bed
Note: Long-term care home offering physician services, nursing care, respite services, & therapeutic services.
Sherry Keen, Chief Executive Officer
sherry.keen@winelms.ca
Donald van Nostrand, Director, Financial Services
donald.vannostrand@winelms.ca
Judy Hayes, Director, Care
judy.hayes@winelms.ca

Glace Bay: **Seaview Manor**
Affiliated with: Nova Scotia Health Authority
275 South St., Glace Bay, NS B1A 1W6
Tel: 902-849-7300 *Fax:* 902-849-2354
www.seaviewmanor.ca
Number of Beds: 101 beds; 2 respite beds
Note: Services include: dietary; nursing; physiotherapy; & recreation.
Eric Doucette, CEO & Director, Resident Care
ericdoucette@seaside.ns.ca
Janet Chenhall, Director, Finance
janetchenhall@seaside.ns.ca
Wayne MacAulay, Director, Environmental Services
wayne@seaside.ns.ca

Glace Bay: **Taigh Na Mara**
Affiliated with: Nova Scotia Health Authority
974 Main St., Glace Bay, NS B1A 4L8
Tel: 902-842-3900 *Fax:* 902-842-3926
Number of Beds: 67 beds
Note: Continuing care for residents & veterans
Sharon Sheppard, Administrator

Glace Bay: **Victoria Haven Nursing Home**
PO Box 219, 5 Third St., Glace Bay, NS B1A 5V2
Tel: 902-849-4127 *Fax:* 902-849-8826
Number of Beds: 52 beds; 2 respite beds
Penney Campbell, Administrator

Glenwood: Nakile Home for Special Care
Affiliated with: Nova Scotia Health Authority
Former Name: Nakile Home for the Aged
35 Nakile Dr., Glenwood, NS B0W 1W0
Tel: 902-643-2707 Fax: 902-643-2862
www.nakilehome.ca
www.facebook.com/NakileHomeforSpecialCare
Number of Beds: 48 beds
Gail Kaiser, Administrator
gail@nakile.ns.ca

Halifax: Maplestone Enhanced Care
Shannex
Affiliated with: Nova Scotia Health Authority
245 Main Ave., Halifax, NS B3M 1B7
Tel: 902-443-1971 Fax: 902-443-9037
care@shannex.com
www.shannex.com
Number of Beds: 87 beds
Gavin Slade, Director, Client Care

Halifax: Melville Lodge Long Term Care Centre
50 Shoreham Lane, Halifax, NS B3P 2R3
Tel: 902-479-1030 Fax: 902-477-1663
www.gemhealth.com
Year Founded: 1984
Number of Beds: 122 beds
Note: Services include occupational therapy & physiotherapy.
Shelley Noonan, Administrator

Halifax: Northwoodcare Inc.
Affiliated with: Nova Scotia Health Authority
2615 Northwood Terrace, Halifax, NS B3K 3S5
Tel: 902-454-8311
information@nwood.ns.ca
www.nwood.ns.ca
Number of Beds: 406 beds
Note: Adult residental centre
Janet Simm, President & CEO
John Verlinden, Corporate Director, Communications &
Community Engagement
jverlinden@nwood.ns.ca

Halifax: Parkstone Enhanced Care
Shannex
Affiliated with: Nova Scotia Health Authority
156 Parkland Dr., Halifax, NS B3S 1N9
Tel: 902-446-8501 Fax: 902-446-4044
care@shannex.com
shannex.com
Number of Beds: 194 beds

Halifax: Saint Vincent's Nursing Home
Affiliated with: Nova Scotia Health Authority
Former Name: Saint Vincent Guest Home
2080 Windsor St., Halifax, NS B3K 5B2
Tel: 902-429-0550 Fax: 902-492-3703
info@svnh.ca
www.svnh.ca
Number of Beds: 149 beds
Note: Nursing home affiliated with the Roman Catholic
Archdiocese of Halifax.
Angela Berrette, Executive Director
Scott Bell, Director, Finance
Ken Rehman, Director, Resident Care
Kim Wright, Manager, Quality & Education
Scott Muzzerall, Manager, Facility & Maintenance

Inverness: Aite Curam
Affiliated with: Nova Scotia Health Authority
PO Box 610, 39 James St., Inverness, NS B0E 1N0
Tel: 902-258-2100
Note: Part of Inverness Consolidated Memorial Hospital

Kentville: Evergreen Home for Special Care
655 Park St., Kentville, NS B4N 3V7
Tel: 902-678-7355 Fax: 902-678-5996
evergreen@evergreenhome.ns.ca
www.evergreenhome.ns.ca
Number of Beds: 97 beds; 19 children's beds; 2 respite beds
Note: Seniors' Centre; Childrens' Centre
Fred Houghton, Administrator
Dr. Jim Seaman, Medical Director

Liverpool: Queens Manor
PO Box 1283, 20 Hollands Dr., Liverpool, NS B0T 1K0
Tel: 902-354-3451 Fax: 902-354-5383
www.queensmanor.ca
www.facebook.com/queenscountyrocks
Number of Beds: 60 beds; 1 respite bed
Note: Provides palliative care services.

Lockeport: Surf Lodge Nursing Home
Affiliated with: Nova Scotia Health Authority
PO Box 160, 73 Howe St., Lockeport, NS B0T 1L0
Tel: 902-656-2014 Fax: 902-656-2026
www.surflodge.ca
Note: Specialties: Long-term care; Massage therapy; Activity
program; Physiotherapy
Karla Swansburg, Administrator
doug@macleodgroup.ca

Lunenburg: Harbour View Haven
PO Box 1480, 25 Blockhouse Hill Rd., Lunenburg, NS B0J
2C0
Tel: 902-634-8836 Fax: 902-634-8792
www.hvh.ca
Number of Beds: 143 long-term care beds; 1 respite bed
Note: Long-term care home providing medical care, nursing
care, recreation therapy, dementia care, pharmacare, & physical
therapy services.
Tim McAuley, Administrator
tmcauley@hvh.ca
Shirley O'Donnell, Director, Finance & Human Resources
sodonnell@hvh.ca
Marie McIntyre, Director, Resident Care
mmcintyre@hvh.ca
Wellesley Eisnor, Director, Operations
weisnor@hvh.ca
Janet DeLong, Office Manager
jdelong@hvh.ca

Mahone Bay: Mahone Nursing Home
PO Box 320, 640 Main St., Mahone Bay, NS B0J 2E0
Tel: 902-624-8341 Fax: 902-624-6338
Year Founded: 1965
Number of Beds: 60 beds
Note: Specialties: Long-term care Physiotherapy & occupational
therapy; Palliative care
Tracey Cousins, Administrator

Meteghan: Villa Acadienne
Affiliée à: Nova Scotia Health Authority
CP 248, 8403 Hwy. 1, Meteghan, NS B0W 2K0
Tél: 902-645-2065 Téléc: 902-645-3899
www.villaacadienne.com
www.facebook.com/VillaAcadienne
Fondée en: 1975
Nombre de lits: 85 beds; 1 respite bed
Lucille Maillet, Administrator
lucillemaillet@villaacadienne.ca

Middle Musquodoboit: Musquodoboit Valley Home
for Special Care (Braeside)
Affiliated with: Nova Scotia Health Authority
126 Higginsville Rd., Middle Musquodoboit, NS B0N 1X0
Tel: 902-384-3007 Fax: 902-384-3310
Number of Beds: 28 beds + 1 respite
Diana Graham-Lentz, Site Manager

Musquodoboit Harbour: Twin Oaks/Birches
Health Care Charitable Foundation, PO Box 186,
Musquodoboit Harbour, NS B0J 2L0
Tel: 902-889-3475
www.twinoaksbirches.ca
Number of Beds: 40 nursing home beds; 2 respite care beds; 14
beds
Note: Specialties: Long-term care for older adults; Community
outreach adult day programs
Marny Warner, Manager, Therapeutic Services

New Germany: Rosedale Home for Special Care
Former Name: Rosedale Home
4927 Hwy. 10, New Germany, NS B0R 1E0
Tel: 902-644-2008 Fax: 902-644-3260
Year Founded: 1984
Number of Beds: 39 beds
Valerie Veinot, Administrator

New Glasgow: Glen Haven Manor
Affiliated with: Nova Scotia Health Authority
739 East River Rd., New Glasgow, NS B2H 5E9
Tel: 902-752-2585 Fax: 902-752-0053
info@glenhavenmanor.ca
www.glenhavenmanor.ca
Number of Beds: 202 beds
Note: Adult residential centre
Lisa M. Smith, CEO
902-752-2588

New Waterford: Maple Hill Manor
Affiliated with: Nova Scotia Health Authority
700 King St., New Waterford, NS B1H 3Z5
Tel: 902-862-6495
www.maplehillmanor.ca

Number of Beds: 50 beds
Number of Employees: 80
Note: Long term & secured care
Cathy MacPhee, Administrator
Arla Tomiczek, Director, Resident Care
Wil van Hal, Director, Programs

North Sydney: Northside Community Guest Home
Affiliated with: Nova Scotia Health Authority
11 Queen St., North Sydney, NS B2A 1A2
Tel: 902-794-4733
www.northsideguesthome.com
Number of Beds: 144 beds
Note: Services include: dietary; nursing care; physiotherapy;
recreation; & social work.
Joanne MacNeil, Administrator

Pictou: Maritime Odd Fellows Home
Affiliated with: Nova Scotia Health Authority
143 Norway Point Rd., Pictou, NS B0K 1H0
Tel: 902-485-5492 Fax: 902-485-9233
adminioof@eastlink.ca
maritimeoddfellowshome.ca
Number of Beds: 47 beds
Note: Specialty: Long-term care; Therapeutic recreation
Rhonda Richards, Director, Nursing

Pictou: Shiretown Nursing Home
Affiliated with: Nova Scotia Health Authority
280 Haliburton Rd., Pictou, NS B0K 1H0
Tel: 902-485-4341 Fax: 902-485-9203
www.shiretown.ca
Number of Beds: 36 nursing home beds; 17 RCF beds
Note: Nursing & residential care
Tammy MacKenzie, Director, Facility & Resident Care
tammymackenzie@macleodgroup.ca

Port Hawkesbury: Port Hawkesbury Nursing Home
Affiliated with: Nova Scotia Health Authority
2 MacQuarrie Dr. Extension, Port Hawkesbury, NS B9A 3A2
Tel: 902-625-1460 Fax: 902-625-3232
Number of Beds: 50 beds; 4 respite beds
Note: Adult residential centre
Erin Hawley, Director, Facility & Resident Care

Sheet Harbour: Harbourview Lodge
Affiliated with: Nova Scotia Health Authority
Former Name: Duncan MacMillan Nursing Home;
Duncan MacMillan Home for the Aged
PO Box 68, 22651 7 Hwy., Sheet Harbour, NS B0J 3B0
Tel: 902-885-3668
www.harbourviewlodge.ca
Year Founded: 1948
Number of Beds: 28 nursing home beds
Roberta Duchesne, Manager, Health Services
roberta.duchesne@nshealth.ca
Sandra Hatch, Clinical Supervisor
sandra.hatch@nshealth.ca
Cathy Logan, Quality Coordinator
cathy.logan@nshealth.ca
Ronda Faulkner, Business Coordinator
ronda.faulkner@nshealth.ca

Shelburne: Roseway Manor Inc.
Affiliated with: Nova Scotia Health Authority
PO Box 518, 1604 Lake Rd., Shelburne, NS B0T 1W0
Tel: 902-875-4707 Fax: 902-875-4105
admin@rosewaymanor.com
www.rosewaymanor.com
Number of Beds: 66 beds; 1 respite bed
Note: Services include: dietary; environmental; nursing; &
recreational therapy.
Cathy Hambleton, Administrator
admin@rosewaymanor.com
Deborah Atwood, Director, Care
doc@rosewaymanor.com
Patsy Jones, Director, Recreation
rec@rosewaymanor.com

Sherbrooke: High-Crest Sherbrooke Home for
Special Care
Affiliated with: Nova Scotia Health Authority
PO Box 284, 53 Court St., Sherbrooke, NS B0J 3C0
Tel: 902-522-2147 Fax: 902-522-2628
GGrant@high-crest.com
www.high-crest.com
Number of Beds: 39 beds
Marion Carroll, Administrator

St. Peters: **Richmond Villa**
Affiliated with: Nova Scotia Health Authority
PO Box 250, 9361 Pepperell St., St. Peters, NS B0E 3B0
Tel: 902-535-3030 *Fax:* 902-535-2256
www.richmondvilla.ca
Number of Beds: 59 nursing home beds; 8 resident care beds
Note: Nursing & residential care centre
Carson Samson, Chief Executive Officer
carson.samson@richmondvilla.ca
Gail Mackeigan, Director, Care
gail.mackeigan@richmondvilla.ca
Janelle Fougere, Director, Support Services
janelle.fougere@richmondvilla.ca
Karen Budden, Lead, Recreation
karen.budden@richmondvilla.ca
Sharon Hall, Manager, Business
sharon.hall@richmondvilla.ca

Stellarton: **Valley View Villa**
Affiliated with: Nova Scotia Health Authority
6125 Trafalgar Rd., RR#1, Stellarton, NS B0K 1S0
Tel: 902-755-5780 *Fax:* 902-755-3104
www.valleyviewvilla.com
Year Founded: 1978
Number of Beds: 112 long-term beds; 1 respite care bed
Note: Home for special care
Denise Budgen, Director, Care
dbudgen@vvvilla.ca
Heidi Meyer, Business Office Manager
hmeyer@vvvilla.ca

Sydney: **Celtic Court**
Shannex
Affiliated with: Nova Scotia Health Authority
16 St. Anthony Dr., Sydney, NS B1S 2R5
Tel: 902-270-4700 *Fax:* 902-270-4701
care@shannex.com
shannex.com
Number of Beds: 12 beds

Sydney: **Cove Guest Home**
Affiliated with: Nova Scotia Health Authority
320 Alexandra St., Sydney, NS B1S 2G1
Tel: 902-539-5267 *Fax:* 902-539-7565
www.coveguesthome.com
Year Founded: 1944
Number of Beds: 110 beds
Note: Services include: medical; nursing; dietary; occupational
therapy; & physiotherapy.
Cheryl Deveaux, Administrator
Sandy MacPherson, Director, Finance
Michelle MacIsaac, Director, Resident Care
Donald Goguen, Director, Support Services
Jennifer White, Director, Activities
Derrick MacNamara, Director, Maintenance
Sheri McPhee, Assistant Director, Resident Care

Sydney: **Harbourstone Enhanced Care**
Shannex
Affiliated with: Nova Scotia Health Authority
84 Kenwood Dr., Sydney, NS B1S 3V7
Tel: 902-539-4560 *Fax:* 902-567-6234
care@shannex.com
www.shannex.com
Year Founded: 2002
Number of Beds: 268 beds + 4 respite

Sydney: **New Dawn Guest Home**
75 Prince St., Sydney, NS B1P 5J9
Tel: 902-539-9560 *Fax:* 902-539-7210
newdawn@newdawn.ca
newdawn.ca
Number of Beds: 30 beds + 1 respite
Janet Gillis-Hussey, Administrator

Sydney: **R.C. MacGillivray Guest Home Society**
Affiliated with: Nova Scotia Health Authority
25 Xavier Dr., Sydney, NS B1S 2R9
Tel: 902-539-6110 *Fax:* 902-567-0437
www.mggh.org
Number of Beds: 82 long-term care beds; 1 respite bed
Note: Services include: nursing; dietary; & recreation.
Jody Gentile, CEO
jody.gentile@mggh.org
Gwen MacKenzie, Director, Resident Care
gwen.mackenzie@mggh.org
Kendra Baldwin, Director, Recreation Services
kendra.baldwin@mggh.org
Sandy MacPherson, Director, Finance
sandy.macpherson@mggh.org
Donna Rose, Director, Support Services
donna.rose@mggh.org

Sydney Mines: **Miner's Memorial Manor**
Affiliated with: Nova Scotia Health Authority
15 Lorne St., Sydney Mines, NS B1V 3B9
Tel: 902-736-1992 *Fax:* 902-736-0667
Number of Beds: 36 nursing home beds; 1 respite bed
Carole MacLean, Administrator
carol-maclean@ns.sympatico.ca

Tatamagouche: **Willow Lodge**
Affiliated with: Nova Scotia Health Authority
PO Box 249, 100 Blair Ave., Tatamagouche, NS B0K 1V0
Tel: 902-657-3101 *Fax:* 902-657-3859
www.willowlodge.ca
Number of Beds: 61 beds
Note: Nursing home offering various services, including foot
care, palliative care, wellness monitoring, occupational therapy,
& physical therapy.
Janine Jaconelli, Executive Director
Lisa Hodder, Director, Care
Shelley LeFresne, Director, Community Life
Peggy Weatherby, Director, Finance
John Sellers, Director, Operations
Daphne Mertin, Office Administrator

Truro: **The Mira Long Term Care Centre**
426 Young St., Truro, NS B2N 7B1
Tel: 902-895-8715 *Fax:* 902-897-1903
themira@gemhealth.com
www.gemhealth.com
Year Founded: 1999
Number of Beds: 90 beds
Note: Specialty: Long-term care for seniors; Medication
administration; Peritoneal dialysis unit; Seniors' dental clinic;
Palliative care
Lynn Smith, Administrator

Truro: **Parkland Truro**
Shannex/Parkland Retirement Living
Affiliated with: Nova Scotia Health Authority
Former Name: Cedarstone Enhanced Care
356-378 Young St., Truro, NS B2N 7H2
Tel: 902-843-7275
www.parklandretirementliving.com
Number of Beds: 57 active lifestyle suites; 49 assisted living &
dementia care
Population Served: 126
Darlene Walsh, General Manager

Windsor: **Avonview Rest Home**
Former Name: Windsor House
PO Box 938, 16 Wentworth St., Windsor, NS B0N 2T0
Tel: 902-798-2115
Number of Beds: 16 beds
Carole Stewart, General Manager

Windsor: **Hants County Residence for Senior
Citizens**
Affiliated with: Nova Scotia Health Authority
Also Known As: Dykeland Lodge
124 Cottage St., Windsor, NS B0N 2T0
Tel: 902-798-8346 *Fax:* 902-798-8312
www.dykelandlodge.ca
Year Founded: 1974
Number of Beds: 111 beds
Note: Services include: medical; nursing; foot care;
physiotherapy; recreation; & environmental.
Emily Samson, Administrator
administrator@dykelandlodge.ca
Chris Ivany, Director, Resident Care
Brenda Ennis, Director, Finance
Victoria Gagne, Director, Recreation

Wolfville: **Wolfville Nursing Home**
601 Main St., Wolfville, NS B4P 1E9
Tel: 902-542-2429 *Fax:* 902-542-1048
Number of Beds: 67 beds
Paul MacDonald, Administrator

Yarmouth: **Harbourside Lodge**
62 Vancouver St., Yarmouth, NS B5A 2P5
Tel: 902-742-3542 *Fax:* 902-749-0622
pthibodeau@swndha.nshealth.ca
harboursidelodge.ca
Number of Beds: 32 beds
Paulette Dugas, Director of Care

Yarmouth: **Villa Saint Joseph-du-Lac**
Affiliated with: Nova Scotia Health Authority
PO Box 810, RR1, Yarmouth, NS B5A 4A5
Tel: 902-742-7128 *Fax:* 902-742-4230
rickatkinson@eastlink.ca
www.villasaintjoseph.com
Number of Beds: 79 beds

Barry Granter, Administrator

Mental Health Hospitals/Facilities

Dartmouth: **East Coast Forensic Psychiatric
Hospital (ECFH)**
Affiliated with: Nova Scotia Health Authority
88 Gloria McCluskey Ave., Dartmouth, NS B3B 2B8
Tel: 902-460-7300
www.nshealth.ca
Number of Beds: 30 rehabilitation beds; 24 inpatient beds
Note: The hospital and correctional facility are co-located.
Includes a mentally ill offender unit where court ordered
assessments are performed.

Dartmouth: **The Nova Scotia Hospital**
Affiliated with: Nova Scotia Health Authority
PO Box 1004, 300 Pleasant St., Dartmouth, NS B2Y 3S3
Tel: 902-464-3111 *Fax:* 902-464-6032
www.nshealth.ca
Note: Specialties: Mental health programs. Affiliated with
Dalhousie University.
John McCarthy, Board Development Officer
john.mccarthy@cdha.nshealth.ca

Halifax: **Metro Community Housing Association**
#280, 7071 Bayers Rd., Halifax, NS B3L 2C2
Tel: 902-453-6444 *Fax:* 902-453-1188
info@mcha.ns.ca
www.mcha.ns.ca
www.facebook.com/metrocommunityhousingassociation
Number of Beds: 86 residential capacity & 79 supported
apartments
Note: Specialties: Support & residential services to persons who
have experienced mental health difficulties.
Cathy Crouse, Executive Director

Special Care Homes

Glace Bay: **Jones Manor**
Affiliated with: Nova Scotia Health Authority
1 Minto St., Glace Bay, NS B1Z 5B2
Tel: 902-849-1605
Number of Beds: 7 beds

Wilmot: **Tibbetts Home Wilmot**
15074 Hwy. 1, Wilmot, NS B0P 1W0
Tel: 902-765-6614 *Fax:* 902-765-0687
tibbetts_home@bellaliant.com
www.facebook.com/tibbettshome
Number of Beds: 25 beds
C. Jennifer Millett, Administrator

Nunavut

Government Departments in Charge

Iqaluit: **Nunavut Department of Health**
PO Box 1000 Stn. 1000, Iqaluit, NU X0A 0H0
Tel: 867-975-5700 *Fax:* 867-975-5705
www.gov.nu.ca/health
Hon. Lorne Kusugak, Minister

Hospitals - General

Iqaluit: **Qikiqtani General Hospital**
Ring Rd., Iqaluit, NU X0A 0H0
Tel: 867-975-8600
www.gov.nu.ca/health/information/qikiqtani-general-hospital
Number of Beds: 35 beds
Population Served: 16000
Note: Programs & services include: allergist; cardiology;
dermatology; ENT; internal medicine; gynaecology; neurology;
ophthalmology; orthopaedics; paediatric cardiology, orthopedics,
neurology; respirology; rheumatology; & urology.

Community Health Care Centres

Arctic Bay: **Arctic Bay Health Centre**
PO Box 60, Arctic Bay, NU X0A 0A0
Tel: 867-439-8816 *Fax:* 867-439-8315

Arviat: **Arviat Health Centre**
PO Box 510, Arviat, NU X0C 0E0
Tel: 867-857-3100 *Fax:* 867-857-3149

Baker Lake: **Baker Lake Health Centre**
PO Box 120, Baker Lake, NU X0C 0A0
Tel: 867-793-2816 *Fax:* 867-793-2812

Cambridge Bay: **Cambridge Bay Health Centre**
PO Box 83, Cambridge Bay, NU X0B 0C0
Tel: 867-983-4500 *Fax:* 867-983-4509
www.cambridgebay.ca
Number of Beds: 2 beds

Cape Dorset: **Cape Dorset Health Centre**
PO Box 180, Cape Dorset, NU X0A 0C0
Tel: 867-897-8820

Chesterfield Inlet: **Chesterfield Inlet Health Centre**
PO Box 9, Chesterfield Inlet, NU X0C 0B0
Tel: 867-898-9968 *Fax:* 867-898-9122

Clyde River: **Clyde River Health Centre**
PO Box 40, Clyde River, NU X0A 0E0
Tel: 867-924-6377 *Fax:* 867-924-6244

Coral Harbour: **Coral Harbour Health Centre**
PO Box 120, Coral Harbour, NU X0C 0C0
Tel: 867-925-9916 *Fax:* 867-925-8380

Gjoa Haven: **Gjoa Haven Kativik Health Centre**
General Delivery, Gjoa Haven, NU X0B 1J0
Tel: 867-360-7441 *Fax:* 867-360-6110

Grise Fjord: **Grise Fjord Health Centre**
PO Box 81, Grise Fjord, NU X0A 0J0
Tel: 867-980-9923 *Fax:* 867-980-9067

Hall Beach: **Hall Beach Health Centre**
General Delivery, Hall Beach, NU X0A 0K0
Tel: 867-928-8827 *Fax:* 867-928-8847

Igloolik: **Igloolik Health Centre**
PO Box 240, Igloolik, NU X0A 0L0
Tel: 867-934-2100 *Fax:* 867-934-2149

Iqaluit: **Iqaluit Public Health Centre**
Iqaluit, NU X0A 0H0
Tel: 867-975-4800 *Fax:* 867-975-4830

Kimmirut: **Kimmirut Health Centre**
PO Box 30, Kimmirut, NU X0A 0N0
Tel: 867-939-2217 *Fax:* 867-939-2068

Kugaaruk: **St. Theresa Kugaaruk Health Centre**
General Delivery, Kugaaruk, NU X0B 1K0
Tel: 867-769-6441 *Fax:* 867-769-6059

Kugluktuk: **Kugluktuk Health Centre**
PO Box 288, Kugluktuk, NU X0E 0E0
Tel: 867-982-4531 *Fax:* 867-982-3115

Naujaat: **Naujaat Health Centre**
General Delivery, Naujaat, NU X0C 0H0
Tel: 867-462-9916 *Fax:* 867-462-4212
Number of Beds: 2 beds
Population Served: 1082

Pangnirtung: **Pangnirtung Health Centre**
PO Box 454, Pangnirtung, NU X0A 0R0
Tel: 867-473-8977 *Fax:* 867-473-8519
Note: Specialty: general health care by registered nurses; individual counseling & referral; massage therapy; workshops for stress relief.

Pond Inlet: **Pond Inlet Health Centre**
PO Box 280, Pond Inlet, NU X0A 0S0
Tel: 867-899-7500 *Fax:* 867-899-7538
Year Founded: 2004
Population Served: 1290
Note: Comprehensive health care. Number of employees: 20
Sherry Parks, Supervisor, Health Programs

Qikiqtarjuaq: **Qikiqtarjuaq Health Centre**
PO Box 911, Qikiqtarjuaq, NU X0A 0B0
Tel: 867-927-8916 *Fax:* 867-927-8217
www.gov.nu.ca/health-centre/qikiqtarjuaq

Rankin Inlet: **Rankin Inlet Health Centre**
Rankin Inlet, NU X0C 0G0
Tel: 867-645-8300 *Fax:* 867-645-8304

Resolute: **Resolute Bay Health Centre**
PO Box 180, Resolute, NU X0A 0V0
Tel: 867-252-3844 *Fax:* 867-252-3601

Sanikiluaq: **Sanikiluaq Health Centre**
PO Box 157, Sanikiluaq, NU X0A 0W0
Tel: 867-266-8965 *Fax:* 867-266-8802
Note: Provides general health care, counseling & referral.
Services in Inuktitut & English.

Taloyoak: **Taloyoak Judy Hill Memorial Health Centre**
General Delivery, Taloyoak, NU X0E 1B0
Tel: 867-561-5111 *Fax:* 867-561-6906
Number of Employees: 5

Whale Cove: **Whale Cove Health Centre**
PO Box 45, Whale Cove, NU X0C 1J0
Tel: 867-896-9916 *Fax:* 867-896-9115

Long Term Care Facilities

Arviat: **Andy Aulatjut Elders' Centre**
PO Box 147, Arviat, NU X0C 0E0
Tel: 867-857-4351

Chesterfield Inlet: **Naja Isabelle Home**
PO Box 1, Chesterfield Inlet, NU X0C 0B0
Tel: 867-898-5600 *Fax:* 867-898-9288
Year Founded: 2005
Note: Homecare facility for disabled persons.

Iqaluit: **Iqaluit Elders' Facility**
Pairijait Tigumivik Society, PO Box 640, Iqaluit, NU X0A 0H0
Tel: 867-979-2733 *Fax:* 867-979-3413

Mental Health Hospitals/Facilities

Iqaluit: **Akausisarvik Mental Health Facility**
PO Box 1000, Iqaluit, NU X0A 0H0
Tel: 867-979-7631
Number of Beds: 13 beds

Ontario

Government Departments in Charge

Toronto: **Ministry of Health & Long-Term Care**
Hepburn Block, Queen's Park, 80 Grosvenor St., 10th Fl.,
Toronto, ON M7A 2C4
Tel: 416-314-5518 *Toll-Free:* 866-532-3161
TTY: 800-387-5559
www.health.gov.on.ca
www.facebook.com/ONThealth; twitter.com/ONThealth
Note: In February 2019, the Ontario government announced plans to absorb the existing Local Health Integration Networks (LHINs) in the province, as well as other health organizations, into one super agency.
Hon. Christine Elliott, Minister, Health
416-327-4300
Hon. Merrilee Fullerton, Minister, Long-Term Care

Regional Health Authorities

Ontario Health/Santé Ontario
ON
Toll-Free: 877-280-8538
TTY: 800-855-0511
info@ontariohealth.ca
www.ontariohealth.ca
Year Founded: 2019
Note: In 2019, Ontario began assuming control of Ontario's health care services, beginning with five agencies (Cancer Care Ontario; HealthHealth Quality Ontario; eHealth Ontario; Health Shared Services Ontario; HealthForceOntario Marketing & Recruitment Agency), all 14 LHIN's, & Trillium Gift of Life Network. There are changes yet to come.
Bill Hatanaka, Chair, Board of Directors
Matthew Anderson, President & Ceo

Ajax: **Central East Local Health Integration Network/RLISS du Centre-Est**
Affiliated with: Ontario Health
Also Known As: Central East LHIN
Harwood Plaza, #204A, 314 Harwood Ave. South, Ajax, ON L1S 2J1
Tel: 905-427-5497 *Fax:* 905-427-9659
Toll-Free: 866-804-5446
centraleast@lhins.on.ca
www.centraleastlhin.on.ca
twitter.com/CentralEastLHIN
Year Founded: 2005
Area Served: From Victoria Park to Algonquin Park; 16,673 sq km *Population Served:* 1400000
Renato Discenza, Chief Executive Officer & Transitional Regional Lead, Ontario Health
Stewart Sutley, Vice-President, Health System Strategy
Lisa Burden, Vice-President, Home & Community Care
Marco Aguila, Vice-President, Human Resources & Organizational Development

Arnprior: **Arnprior Regional Health (ARH)**
350 John St. North, Arnprior, ON K7S 2P6
Tel: 613-623-3166
www.arnpriorregionalhealth.ca
Year Founded: 2005
Note: Acute, long-term & other healthcare services.
Barbara Darlow, Board Chair
Eric Hanna, President & CEO
613-623-3166, eric.hanna@arnpriorhealth.ca
Brad Hilker, Chief Financial Officer & Vice-President, Finance & Support Services
613-623-3166, bhilker@arnpriorhealth.ca
Susan Leach, Chief Nursing Executive & Vice-President, Patient / Resident Services
613-623-3166, sleach@arnpriorhealth.ca
Angie Heinz, Vice-President, People & Community Programs
613-623-3166, aheinz@arnpriorhealth.ca

Belleville: **South East Local Health Integration Network/Réseau local d'intégration des services de santé (RLISS) du**
Affiliated with: Ontario Health
Also Known As: South East LHIN
71 Adam St., Belleville, ON K8N 5K3
Tel: 613-967-0196 *Fax:* 613-967-1341
Toll-Free: 866-831-5446
southeast.communications@lhins.on.ca
www.southeastlhin.on.ca
twitter.com/SouthEastLHIN;
www.youtube.com/user/SouthEastLHIN
Year Founded: 2005
Area Served: South East region of Ontario *Population Served:* 495000
Note: The South East Local Health Integration Network plans, manages, & funds the health care system at the local & regional levels. Includes 7 hospitals, 37 long-term care homes, 1 Community Care Access Centre, 5 Community Health Centres, 4 Addictions & Mental Health Agencies, & 22 Community Support Agencies. The South East region extends from Brighton on the west to Prescott & Cardinal on the east, north to Perth & Smith Falls, & back to Bancroft.
Renato Discenza, Chief Executive Officer & Transitional Regional Lead, Ontario Health
renato.discenza@lhins.on.ca
Cynthia Martineau, Vice-President, Strategy, Planning & Integration, Home & Community
Dr. Davod Zelt, Vice-President, Clinical
Lisa Tweedy, Acting Vice-President, Human Resources & Organizational Development
Amber Gooding, Director, Communications & Engagement

Brampton: **Central West Local Health Integration Network/RLISS du Centre-Ouest**
Affiliated with: Ontario Health
Also Known As: Central West LHIN
199 Court Blvd., Brampton, ON L6W 4P3
Tel: 905-796-0040 *Toll-Free:* 888-733-1177
centralwest@lhins.on.ca
www.centralwestlhin.on.ca
www.facebook.com/CentralWestLHIN;
twitter.com/CentralWestLHIN
Year Founded: 2005
Area Served: From northern Dufferin County to northern Peel Region *Population Served:* 922000
Note: Health service providers include 15 community support services & 8 mental health & addictions agencies.
Scott McLeod, Chief Executive Officer & Transitional Regional Lead, Ontario Health
scott.mcleod@lhins.on.ca
Kimberley Floyd, Vice-President, Home & Community Care
kimberley.floyd@lhins.on.ca
Brock Hovey, Vice-President, Corporate Services, Accountability & Quality
brock.hovey@lhins.on.ca
Marla Krakower, Vice-President, People Services & Public Relations
marla.krakower@lhins.on.ca

Chatham: **Erie St. Clair Local Health Integration Network (ESC LHIN)/RLISS d'Érié St. Clair**
Affiliated with: Ontario Health
Also Known As: Erie St. Clair LHIN
180 Riverview Dr., Chatham, ON N7M 5Z8
Tel: 519-351-5677 *Fax:* 519-351-9672
Toll-Free: 866-231-5446
www.eriestclairlhin.on.ca
www.facebook.com/esclhin1; twitter.com/ESCLHIN;
www.youtube.com/user/esclhin
Year Founded: 2006
Area Served: 7,234 sq km *Population Served:* 636020
Note: Serves the counties of Chatham-Kent, Sarnia / Lambton & Windsor / Essex.

Bruce Lauckner, Chief Executive Officer
bruce.lauckner@lhins.on.ca
Cathy Kelly, Vice-President, Home & Community Care
cathy.kelly@lhins.on.ca
Jean-Francois Harvey, Vice-President, HR & Organizational
Development
jean-francois.harvey@lhins.on.ca
Nicole Robinson, Vice-President, Integrated Delivery Systems
nicole.robinson@lhins.on.ca
Dr. Martin Lees, Vice-President, Clinical
martin.lees@lhins.on.ca

Grimsby: **Hamilton Niagara Haldimand Brant Local
Health Integration Network (HNHB LHI)/RLISS de
Hamilton Niagara Haldimand Brant
Affiliated with: Ontario Health
Also Known As: Hamilton Niagara Haldimand Brant
LHIN**
264 Main St. East, Grimsby, ON L3M 1P8
Tel: 905-945-4930 *Fax:* 905-945-1992
Toll-Free: 866-363-5446
hamiltonniagarahaldimandbrant@lhins.on.ca
www.hnhblhin.on.ca
twitter.com/HNHB_LHINgage; www.youtube.com/user/hnhblhin
Year Founded: 2005
Area Served: Brant, Burlington, Haldimand, Hamilton, Niagara,
Norfolk *Population Served:* 1400000
Note: Funds 90 community support services, including 56
community support services programs, 3 acquired brain injury
programs, 17 assisted living services supportive housing
programs, & 43 community mental health & addictions
programs.
Bruce Lauckner, Chief Executive Officer & Transitional Regional
Lead, Ontario Health
Emily Christoffersen, Vice-President, Commissioning,
Performance & Accountability
Dr. Jennifer Everson, Vice-President, Clinical
Miranda Ingribelli, Vice-President, Talent & People Management
Martina Rozsa, Vice-President, Home & Community Care
Rosalind Tarrant, Vice-President, Health System Strategy &
Integration
Cindy Ward, Vice-President, Resource Stewardship
Trish Nelson, Director, Communications & Community
Engagement

London: **South West Local Health Integration
Network/RLISS du Sud-Ouest
Affiliated with: Ontario Health
Also Known As: South West LHIN**
356 Oxford St. West, London, ON N6H 1T3
Fax: 519-472-4045
Toll-Free: 800-811-5146
TTY: 519-473-9626
southwest@lhins.on.ca
www.southwestlhin.on.ca
www.facebook.com/SouthWestLHIN;
twitter.com/SouthWestLHIN;
www.youtube.com/user/SouthWestLHIN;
linkedin.com/company/south-west-local-health-integration-netwo
rk
Year Founded: 2005
Area Served: Area from Lake Erie to the Bruce Peninsula;
21,639 sq km *Population Served:* 962539 *Number of
Employees:* 700
Note: The South West Local Health Integration Network (LHIN)
is a crown agency responsible for the planning, integration &
funding of nearly 200 health service providers including
hospitals, long-term care homes, mental health & addictions
agencies, community support services, community health
centres, & the South West Community Care Access Centre.
Bruce Lauckner, Chief Executive Officer & Transitional Regional
Lead, Ontario Health
Hilary Anderson, Vice-President, Corporate Services
Lynn Hinds, Interim Vice-President, Strategy System Design &
Integration
Daryl Nancekivell, Vice-President, Home & Community Care
Dan Brennan, Director, Communications

Markham: **Central Local Health Integration
Network/RLISS du Centre
Affiliated with: Ontario Health
Also Known As: Central LHIN**
#500, 11 Allstate Pkwy., Markham, ON L3R 9T8
Tel: 905-948-1872 *Fax:* 905-948-8011
Toll-Free: 866-392-5446
central.lhin@lhins.on.ca
www.centrallhin.on.ca
twitter.com/Central_LHIN;
www.youtube.com/user/TheCentralLHIN;
www.linkedin.com/company/centrallhin
Year Founded: 2005
Area Served: 2,730 sq km *Population Served:* 1900000

Note: Areas served include parts of northern Toronto &
Etobicoke, most of York Region, & South Simcoe County.
Scott McLeod, Chief Executive Officer & Transitional Regional
Lead, Ontario Health
Barbara Bell, Vice-President, Quality & Safety, Ontario Health
Karin Dschankilic, Chief Financial Officer & Vice-President,
Performance & Corporate Services
Tini Le, Vice-President, Home & Community Care & System
Planning

North Bay: **North East Local Health Integration
Network
Affiliated with: Ontario Health
Also Known As: North East LHIN**
555 Oak St. East, 3rd Fl., North Bay, ON P1B 8E3
Tel: 705-840-2872 *Fax:* 705-840-0142
Toll-Free: 866-906-5446
www.nelhin.on.ca
www.facebook.com/NorthEastLHIN; twitter.com/NorthEastLHIN;
www.youtube.com/user/LHIN101;
linkedin.com/company/north-east-local-health-integration-networ
k
Year Founded: 2005
Area Served: 400,000 sq km *Population Served:* 565000
Note: The North East LHIN brings 150 of the region's health care
partners together - hospitals, community support services,
mental health & addictions, community health centres, long-term
care homes, & the Community Care Access Centre.
Dr. Rhonda Crocker Ellacott, Chief Executive Officer &
Transitional Regional Lead, Ontario Health
Kate Fyfe, Vice-President, Business Solutions & Human
Resources
kate.fyfe@lhins.on.ca
Kerby Audet, Vice-President, Home & Community Care
Dr. Paul Preston, Vice-President, Clinical
paul.preston@lhins.on.ca
Cynthia Stables, Senior Director, Communications & Patient
Experience
cynthia.stables@lhins.on.ca
Terry Tilleczek, Vice-President, Strategy & System Planning
terry.tilleczek@lhins.on.ca

Oakville: **Mississauga Halton Local Health
Integration Network (MH LHIN)/RLISS Mississauga
Halton
Affiliated with: Ontario Health
Also Known As: Mississauga Halton LHIN**
#500, 700 Dorval Dr., Oakville, ON L6K 3V3
Tel: 905-337-7131 *Fax:* 905-337-8330
Toll-Free: 866-371-5446
mississaugahalton@lhins.on.ca
www.mississaugahaltonlhin.on.ca
www.facebook.com/Miss.HaltonLHIN; twitter.com/MH_LHIN;
www.youtube.com/user/mhlhin
Year Founded: 2005
Area Served: 900 sq km *Population Served:* 1200000
Note: Includes the south-west portion of the City of Toronto, the
south part of Peel Region, & all of Halton Region except for
Burlington, which is part of the Hamilton Niagara Haldimand
Brant LHIN; includes the municipalities of South Etobicoke,
Mississauga, Halton Hills, Oakville, & Milton.
Scott McLeod, Chief Executive Officer & Transitional Regional
Lead, Ontario Health
Dr. Mira Backo-Shannon, Vice-President, Ontario, Clinical
Angela Burden, Vice-President, Home & Community Care
Liane Fernandes, Vice-President, Transition Support, Ontario
Health
Dale McGregor, Vice-President, Finance, Performance &
Corporate Services
Jutta Schafler Argao, Vice-President, Quality & People, Ontario
Health

Orillia: **North Simcoe Muskoka Local Health
Integration Network/RLISS de Simcoe Nord
Muskoka
Affiliated with: Ontario Health
Also Known As: North Simcoe Muskoka LHIN**
#128, 210 Memorial Ave., Orillia, ON L3V 7V1
Tel: 705-326-7750 *Fax:* 705-326-1392
Toll-Free: 866-903-5446
northsimcoemuskoka@lhins.on.ca
www.nsmlhin.on.ca
twitter.com/NSMLHIN
Year Founded: 2005
Population Served: 479471
Note: Encompasses the District of Muskoka, most of the County
of Simcoe & a portion of Grey County. North Simcoe Muskoka
is home to four First Nations. Health service providers include: 7
hospitals, 26 long-term care homes, 3 community health centres,
27 community support services, & 7 community mental health
providers.

Scott McLeod, Chief Executive Officer & Transitional Regional
Lead, Ontario Health
Jeff Kwan, Vice-President, Financial Health & Accountability
Debbie Roberts, Vice-President, Quality & Performance, Ontario
Health
Karen Taillefer, Vice-President, Home & Community Care
Neil Walker, Vice-President, System Transformation, Ontario
Health
Kathleen Bain, Director, Communications

Ottawa: **Champlain Local Health Integration
Network/RLISS de Champlain
Affiliated with: Ontario Health
Also Known As: Champlain LHIN**
#204, 1900 City Park Dr., Ottawa, ON K1J 1A3
Tel: 613-747-6784 *Fax:* 613-747-6519
Toll-Free: 866-902-5446
champlain@lhin.on.ca
www.champlainlhin.on.ca
twitter.com/champlainlhin
www.youtube.com/user/ChamplainLHIN
Year Founded: 2005
Population Served: 1300000
Note: Area Served: Renfrew County; City of Ottawa; Prescott &
Russell; Stormont; Dundas & Glengarry; North Grenville; four
parts of North Lanark
Renato Discenza, Chief Executive Officer & Transitional
Regional Lead, Ontario Health
Catherine Butler, Vice-President, Home & Community Care
James Fahey, Interim Vice-President, Ontario Health

Thunder Bay: **North West Local Health Integration
Network
Affiliated with: Ontario Health
Also Known As: North West LHIN**
#201, 975 Alloy Dr., Thunder Bay, ON P7B 5Z8
Tel: 807-684-9425 *Fax:* 866-684-9533
Toll-Free: 866-907-5446
northwest@lhins.on.ca
www.northwestlhin.on.ca
www.facebook.com/nwlhin; twitter.com/NorthWestLHIN
Year Founded: 2005
Population Served: 235900
Note: The North West LHIN is responsible for planning,
integrating & funding local health services, including hospitals,
the Community Care Access Centre, community health centres,
long-term care homes, community support service agencies &
community mental health & addiction services. The North West
LHIN extends from just west of White River to the Manitoba
border & from Hudson Bay in the north down to the United
States border.
Dr. Rhonda Crocker Ellacott, Chief Executive Officer &
Transitional Regional Lead, Ontario Health
Brian Ktytor, Vice-President, Corporate Services
Dr. Sarah Newbery, Vice-President, Clinical
Dr. Gordon Porter, Interim Vice-President, System
Transformation, Integration & Quality
Adam Vinet, Interim Vice-President, Home & Community Care

Toronto: **Toronto Central Local Health Integration
Network (TC LHIN)/RLISS du Centre-Toronto
Affiliated with: Ontario Health
Also Known As: Toronto Central LHIN**
#201, 425 Bloor St. East, Toronto, ON M4W 3R4
Tel: 416-921-7453 *Fax:* 416-921-0117
Toll-Free: 866-383-5446
torontocentral@lhins.on.ca
www.torontocentrallhin.on.ca
twitter.com/tc_lhin; www.youtube.com/user/TorontoCentralLHIN
Year Founded: 2005
Area Served: City of Toronto, Scarborough, North York &
Etobicoke *Population Served:* 1200000
Note: 170 health service providers including hospitals, the
Toronto Central Community Care Access Centre, community
support services, community health centres, mental health &
addictions agencies & long-term care homes are funded through
the TC LHIN.
Tess Romain, Chief Executive Officer & Transitional Regional
Lead, Ontario Health
Raj Krishnapillai, Chief Financial Officer & Vice-President,
Finance & IT
Joel Borgida, Interim Vice-President, Human Resources &
Communications
Wilfred Cheung, Interim Vice-President, Health System Strategy,
Integration & Planning
Lindsay Wingham-Smith, Vice-President, Home & Community
Care
Dr. Matthew Morgan, Vice-President, Clinical

Waterloo: Waterloo Wellington Local Health Integration Network (WWLHIN)/RLISS de Waterloo Wellington
Affiliated with: Ontario Health
Also Known As: Waterloo Wellington LHIN
141 Weber St. South, Waterloo, ON N2J 2A9
Tel: 519-748-2222 *Toll-Free:* 888-883-3313
www.waterloowellingtonlhin.on.ca
www.facebook.com/WWLHIN; twitter.com/WW_LHIN;
www.youtube.com/user/TheWWLHIN
Year Founded: 2005
Area Served: Waterloo, Wellington, Guelph & southern Grey County; 4,800 sq km *Population Served:* 778676
Note: A crown agency of Ontario that works to plan, integrate, & fund local health services.
Bruce Lauckner, Chief Executive Officer & Transitional Regional Lead, Ontario Health
Dr. Mohamed Alarakhia, Chief Clinical Information Officer, Digital Health & Innovation
Zeynep Danis, Vice-President, Finance & Corporate Services
Andrew Davidson, Vice-President, People Culture & Organizational Development
Elliot Fung, Vice-President, Innovation & Strategic Partnerships
Karyn Lumsden, Vice-President, Home & Community Care

Hospitals - General

Ajax: Ajax Pickering Hospital
Lakeridge Health
Affiliated with: Central East Local Health Integration Network
Former Name: Rouge Valley Ajax & Pickering
580 Harwood Ave. South, Ajax, ON L1S 2J4
Tel: 905-683-2320
www.lakeridgehealth.on.ca
www.linkedin.com/company/lakeridge-health
Number of Beds: 208 beds
Note: Programs & services include: clinical nutrition; diabetes education; emergency; mental health; obstetrics; Ontario Breast Screening Program; paediatrics; physiotherapy; regional cardiac care; speech-language pathology; & surgery.

Alexandria: Glengarry Memorial Hospital (HGMH)/Hôpital Glengarry Memorial
Affiliated with: Champlain Local Health Integration Network
20260 County Rd. 43, Alexandria, ON K0C 1A0
Tel: 613-525-2222
www.hgmh.on.ca
Year Founded: 1965
Number of Beds: 37 beds
Number of Employees: 150
Note: Programs & services include: chronic care; dermatology; diabetes; dietary; foot care; gastroenterology; internal medicine; laboratory; neurology; obstetrics / gynecology; orthopedic medicine / surgery; orthotics; physiotherapy; psychiatry; pulmonary function; radiology; rehabilitation; surgery; & urology.
Michael Cohen, Chief Executive Officer
Dr. N. Kucherepa, Chief of Staff
Kim Woods, Chief Nursing Officer & Vice-President, Clinical Services
Linda Ramsay, Chief Financial Officer & Vice-President, Support Services

Alliston: Stevenson Memorial Hospital (SMH)
Affiliated with: Central Local Health Integration Network
PO Box 4000, 200 Fletcher Cres., Alliston, ON L9R 1W7
Tel: 705-435-3377
www.stevensonhospital.ca
www.facebook.com/stevensonhospital;
twitter.com/StevensonHosp;
www.instagram.com/stevensonhospital
Year Founded: 1928
Number of Beds: 38 beds
Note: Programs & services include: acute care; day surgery; diagnostic imaging; dialysis; emergency; laboratory; mental health; obstetrics & gynecology; outpatient clinics; pharmacy; & physiotherapy / occupational therapy.
Jody Joseph Levac, President & CEO
Carrie Jeffreys, Chief Nursing Executive & Vice-President, Patient Services
Dr. Barry Nathanson, Chief of Staff
William Bye, Chief Financial & Chief Information Officer

Almonte: Almonte General Hospital (AGH)
Affiliated with: Champlain Local Health Integration Network
75 Spring St., Almonte, ON K0A 1A0
Tel: 613-256-2500 *Fax:* 613-256-8549
info@agh-fvm.com
www.almontegeneral.com
Number of Beds: 52 beds (21 medical & surgical, 5 obstetrical, & 26 chronic care)
Population Served: 11000
Note: Programs & services include: acute care; cardiology; complex continuing care; day hospital; dental surgery; diabetic education; emergency; geriatric assessment; long-term care program; obstetrics; occupational therapy; outpatient service clinics; physiotherapy; rehabilitation; respite care / convalescent care; & sexual assault support / treatment.
Mary Wilson Trider, President & CEO
613-256-2514, mwilsontrider@agh-fvm.com
Kimberley Harbord, Integrated Vice President & Chief Financial Officer
613-256-2514, Fax: 613-256-8549
Randy Shaw, Integrated Vice President, Corporate Support Services
613-256-2514

Arnprior: Arnprior & District Memorial Hospital (ADMH)
Affiliated with: Arnprior Regional Health
350 John St. North, Arnprior, ON K7S 2P6
Tel: 613-623-3166 *Fax:* 613-623-4844
www.arnpriorregionalhealth.ca
Number of Beds: 44 beds
Population Served: 30000 *Number of Employees:* 300
Note: Hospital Specialties: Emergency services; Diagnostic imaging; Acute care; Ontario Breast Screening Program; Diabetes clinic; Physiotherapy; Speech therapy; Urotherapy; Palliative care; & Telemedicine.
Eric Hanna, President & CEO
eric.hanna@arnpriorhealth.ca
Susan Leach, Vice-President & Chief Nursing Executive, Patient and Resident Services
sleach@arnpriorhealth.ca

Atikokan: Atikokan General Hospital (AGH)
Affiliated with: North West Local Health Integration Network
PO Box 2490, 120 Dorothy St., Atikokan, ON P0T 1C0
Tel: 807-597-4215 *Fax:* 807-597-4305
www.aghospital.on.ca
twitter.com/AtikokanHosp;
www.linkedin.com/company/atikokan-general-hospital
Number of Beds: 41 acute care beds; 26 long-term care beds
Number of Employees: 100
Note: Programs & services include: emergency services; diagnostic services; acute care; cardiac care; rehabilitation services; counselling & addictions program; diabetic counselling; complex continuing care; & long-term care.
Jorge VanSlyke, Chief Executive Officer
Jennifer Learning, Chief Nursing Officer
learningj@aghospital.on.ca
Dr. Sara Van Der Loo, Chief of Staff

Bancroft: QHC North Hastings Hospital
Quinte Health Care
Affiliated with: South East Local Health Integration Network
Former Name: North Hastings District Hospital
PO Box 157, 1-H Manor Lane, Bancroft, ON K0L 1C0
Tel: 613-332-2825 *Fax:* 613-332-3847
www.qhc.on.ca
www.facebook.com/173689537296; twitter.com/QuinteHealth;
www.youtube.com/QuinteHealthCare
Year Founded: 1927
Number of Beds: 6 beds
Note: Part of the North Hastings Health Centre Campus, which includes: six-chair dialysis unit; 110-bed long-term care facility; Family Health Team; public health; Community Care Access Centre; & Community Care North Hastings.
Mary Clare Egberts, President & CEO, Quinte Health Care
Dr. Colin MacPherson, Chief of Staff, Quinte Health Care
Carol Smith Romeril, Chief Nursing Officer, Quinte Health Care

Barrie: Royal Victoria Regional Health Centre (RVH)
Affiliated with: North Simcoe Muskoka Local Health Integration Network
Former Name: Royal Victoria Hospital
201 Georgian Dr., Barrie, ON L4M 6M2
Tel: 705-728-9802 *Fax:* 705-792-3324
TTY: 705-739-5618
www.rvh.on.ca
Year Founded: 1897
Number of Beds: 328 beds

Number of Employees: 2500
Note: Programs & services include: cardiac; cardio-respiratory; intensive care; chronic disease management; renal services; education; emergency; Home First; imaging; laboratory; medicine; mental health & addictions; internal medicine; pharmacy; rehabilitation & acute geriatrics; stroke program; surgery; telemedicine; & women's & children's program. Has 380+ physicians on staff.
Janice Skot, President & CEO
skotj@rvh.on.ca
Nancy Savage, Executive Vice-President, Patient & Family Experience
savagen@rvh.on.ca
Dr. Chris Tebbutt, Vice-President, Academic & Medical Affairs
tebbuttc@rvh.on.ca
Dr. Jeffrey Tyberg, Chief of Staff
ybergj@rvh.on.ca
Ben Petersen, Executive Vice President & Chief Financial Officer, Corporate Services
petersenb@rvh.on.ca

Barry's Bay: St. Francis Memorial Hospital (SFMH)
Affiliated with: Champlain Local Health Integration Network
PO Box 129, 7 St. Francis Memorial Dr., Barry's Bay, ON K0J 1B0
Tel: 613-756-3044 *Fax:* 613-756-0168
www.sfmhosp.com
Year Founded: 1960
Number of Beds: 20 beds
Population Served: 10000
Note: Programs & services include: active care unit; addictions treatment; bone density; complex continuing care; diabetic clinic; diagnostic imaging; discharge planning; ear, nose & throat; emergency; foot care clinic; general surgery; hemodialysis & nephrology; holter monitor; internal medicine; Meals on Wheels; medical laboratories; OBSP / mammography; Ontario Breast Screening Program; orthotist; palliative care; pastoral care; physiotherapy; pre-op clinics; recreation; respiratory therapy; St. Francis Health Centre; Telemedicine; x-ray; & ultrasound.
Randy Penney, Chief Executive Officer
613-432-4851, Fax: 613-432-0711
Gregory McLeod, Chief Operating Officer
613-756-3044, Fax: 613-756-0106, mcleodg@sfmhosp.com
Mary-Ellen Harris, CNO & Director, Patient Care Services
613-756-3044, Fax: 613-756-0106, harrism@sfmhosp.com
Tim Sonnenburg, Vice President, Financial Services
613-432-4851, Fax: 613-432-8649

Belleville: QHC Belleville General Hospital
Quinte Health Care
Affiliated with: South East Local Health Integration Network
265 Dundas St. East, Belleville, ON K8N 5A9
Tel: 613-969-7400 *Fax:* 613-968-8234
Toll-Free: 800-483-2811
www.qhc.on.ca
www.facebook.com/173689537296; twitter.com/QuinteHealth;
www.youtube.com/QuinteHealthCare
Year Founded: 1886
Number of Beds: 192 beds
Note: Programs & services include: cardiology; complex continuing care; children's treatment centre; clinical nutrition; diabetes education; emergency; intensive care; laboratory; maternal / child service; medical day clinic; medical service; oncology; outpatient clinics; orthopaedics; pharmacy; psychiatry / mental health; radiology / diagnostic services; rehabilitation; stroke (District Stroke Centre & stroke prevention clinic); surgery; & symptom management / palliative care.
Mary Clare Egberts, President & CEO, Quinte Health Care
Dr. Colin MacPherson, Chief of Staff, Quinte Health Care
Carol Smith Romeril, Chief Nursing Officer & Vice-President, Quinte Health Care

Blind River: North Shore Health Network - Blind River Site (BRDHC)/Pavillion Santé du District de Blind River
Affiliated with: North East Local Health Integration Network
Former Name: Blind River District Health Centre; Robb Hospital; St. Joseph's General Hospital
PO Box 970, 525 Causley St., Blind River, ON P0R 1B0
Tel: 705-356-2265 *Fax:* 705-356-1220
www.nshn.care
Year Founded: 1928
Number of Beds: 16 acute care beds; 10 complex care beds; 32 long-term care beds
Number of Employees: 200
Note: Programs & services include: acute care; community support services; diabetes; diagnostic imaging; dietitian; emergency & ambulatory care; exercise & falls prevention;

laboratory; long-term care; oncology; & pharmacy. Has 50 physicians on staff.
Ralph Barker, Chief Executive Officer
Mary-Ellen Luukkonen, Interim Chief Nursing Executive & Director, Clinical Services
Jennifer Stanton Smith, Chief Financial Officer
Dr. Lenka Snajdrova, Chief of Staff
Dan Lewis, Director, Environmental Services

Bowmanville: Lakeridge Health Bowmanville
Affiliated with: Central East Local Health Integration Network
Also Known As: Bowmanville Hospital
47 Liberty St. South, Bowmanville, ON L1C 2N4
Tel: 905-623-3331
patientrelations@lakeridgehealth.on.ca
www.lakeridgehealth.on.ca
www.facebook.com/LakeridgeHealth;
twitter.com/lakeridgehealth; www.youtube.com/lakeridgehealth;
www.linkedin.com/company/lakeridge-health
Note: Programs & services include: surgery; continuing care; diabetes education; rehabilitation; palliative care; diagnostic imaging; emergency.

Bracebridge: South Muskoka Memorial Hospital Site
Muskoka Algonquin Healthcare (MAHC)
Affiliated with: North Simcoe Muskoka Local Health Integration Network
75 Ann St., Bracebridge, ON P1L 2E4
Tel: 705-645-4404 Fax: 705-645-4594
www.mahc.ca
Year Founded: 1949
Number of Beds: 43 acute care beds; 16 complex continuing care beds
Number of Employees: 650
Note: Programs & services include: cardio-respiratory; cancer supportive care & infusion clinic; clinical nutrition; complex continuing care; diabetes education; diagnostic imaging; discharge planning; emergency; fracture clinic; general surgery / endoscopy; gynaecological surgery; intensive care; laboratory; obstetrics; palliative care; paediatric clinic; pharmacy; rehabilitation; seniors assessment; speech-language pathology; spiritual care; telemedicine; & urology. Muskoka Algonquin Healthcare employs around 85 physicians.
Natalie Bubela, Chief Executive Officer, MAHC
705-789-2311
Dr. Khaled Abdel-Razek, Chief of Medical Staff, MAHC
705-789-2311
Carol Anderson, Chief Nursing Executive, MAHC
705-645-4404

Brampton: Brampton Civic Hospital
William Osler Health System
Affiliated with: Central West Local Health Integration Network
Also Known As: William Osler Health Centre
2100 Bovaird Dr. East, Brampton, ON L6R 3J7
Tel: 905-494-2120
www.williamoslerhs.ca
www.facebook.com/WilliamOslerHealth; twitter.com/OslerHealth;
www.youtube.com/WilliamOslerTV;
www.linkedin.com/company/william-osler-health-system
Year Founded: 2007
Number of Beds: 608 beds
Note: Programs & services include: cancer care; cardiac care; complex continuing care; critical care; diabetes care; diagnostic imaging; emergency; general & internal medicine; kidney care; laboratories; mental health & addictions; naturopathic care; palliative care; rehabilitation services; respirology; seniors' care; surgical services; & women's & children's services.
Dr. Frank Martino, Interim President & CEO, William Osler Health System

Brantford: Brantford General Hospital
Brant Community Healthcare System
Affiliated with: Hamilton Niagara Haldimand Brant Local Health Integration Network
Also Known As: The Brantford General
200 Terrace Hill St., Brantford, ON N3R 1G9
Tel: 519-751-5544
www.bchsys.org
www.facebook.com/bchsys; twitter.com/BCHSYS;
www.youtube.com/user/bchsys2011;
www.linkedin.com/company/brantford-general-hospital
Year Founded: 1885
Number of Beds: 260+ beds
Number of Employees: 1200
Note: Programs & services include: acute care; Brant Community Cancer Clinic; critical care; CT scan; emergency; gynaecology; mental health; obstetrics; paediatrics; S.C. Johnson Dialysis Clinic; & surgery. Has 175 physicians on staff.

Brant Community Healthcare System is affiliated with the Michael G. DeGroote School of Medicine, McMaster University.
Dr. David McNeil, President & CEO, Brant Community Healthcare System
Dr. Eugene Jarrell, Chief of Staff & Vice-President, Brant Community Healthcare System
Martin Ruaux, Chief Nursing Executive & Vice-President, Brant Community Healthcare System

Brockville: Brockville General Hospital (BGH)
Affiliated with: South East Local Health Integration Network
75 Charles St., Brockville, ON K6V 1S8
Tel: 613-345-5649
www.brockvillegeneralhospital.ca
www.facebook.com/brockvillegeneralhospital;
twitter.com/BrockvilleGener;
www.linkedin.com/company/brockville-general-hospital
Year Founded: 1885
Number of Beds: 148 beds
Population Served: 66000 Number of Employees: 830
Note: Programs & services include: cardiology diagnostics; children's speech & language therapy; diagnostic imaging; early language; emergency; gynecology; inpatient rehabilitation; infant & child development program; mental health; Ontario Breast Screening Program; Ontario Telehealth Network; outpatient paediatric physiotherapy; pain management; & stroke prevention. BGH's Garden Street Site provides palliative care services.
Nicholas Vlacholias, President & Chief Executive Officer
613-345-5649
Dr. Robert Malone, Chief of Staff
613-345-5649
Julie Caffin, Chief Nursing Officer & Vice-President
613-345-5649

Burlington: Joseph Brant Hospital
Affiliated with: Hamilton Niagara Haldimand Brant Local Health Integration Network
Former Name: Joseph Brant Memorial Hospital
1245 Lakeshore Rd., Burlington, ON L7S 0A2
Tel: 905-632-3737 Fax: 905-336-6480
www.josephbranthospital.ca
www.facebook.com/JosephBrantHospital; twitter.com/Jo_Brant;
www.linkedin.com/company/joseph-brant-hospital
Number of Beds: 253 beds
Number of Employees: 1650
Note: Programs & services include: community mental health; emergency; maternal & child; outpatient clinics; paediatric & gestational diabetes clinic; palliative care (outpatient); & Wellness House. Has 198 physicians on staff.
Eric J. Vandewall, President & CEO
Ian Preyra, Chief of Staff

Cambridge: Cambridge Memorial Hospital
Affiliated with: Waterloo Wellington Local Health Integration Network
Former Name: South Waterloo Memorial Hospital
700 Coronation Blvd., Cambridge, ON N1R 3G2
Tel: 519-621-2330 Fax: 519-740-4938
TTY: 519-621-9180
information@cmh.org
www.cmh.org
Year Founded: 1953
Number of Beds: 197 beds
Number of Employees: 1100
Note: Programs & services include: clinical nutrition & diabetes education; diagnostic imaging; emergency; infection control; inpatient surgery & ambulatory surgical services; laboratory & CRU; medicine / medical day care; mental health (inpatient & outpatient); perioperative; pharmacy; rehabilitation, Allied Health, seniors & COPD; & women's & children's health.
Patrick Gaskin, Chief Executive Officer
519-621-2330
Dr. Kunuk Rhee, Chief of Staff
519-621-2330,
Sandra Hett, Chief Nursing Executive & Vice-President, Clinical Programs
519-621-2330

Campbellford: Campbellford Memorial Hospital (CMH)
Affiliated with: Central East Local Health Integration Network
146 Oliver Rd., Campbellford, ON K0L 1L0
Tel: 705-653-1140 Fax: 705-653-4371
wellness@cmh.ca
www.cmh.ca
www.facebook.com/cmhospitalfoundation;
twitter.com/cmhfoundation; www.youtube.com/cmhfoundation;
www.linkedin.com/company/lakeridge-health

Number of Beds: 34 beds
Population Served: 30000
Note: Programs & services include: cardiac / diabetes education; emergency; laboratory; mammography; mental health; nursing care; palliative care; physiotherapy (inpatient); surgery; & x-ray, bone mineral density & ultrasound.
Varouj Eskedjian, President & CEO
705-653-1140, veskedjian@cmh.ca
Paul Nichols, Board Chair

Carleton Place: Carleton Place & District Memorial Hospital (CPDMH)
Affiliated with: Champlain Local Health Integration Network
211 Lake Ave. East, Carleton Place, ON K7C 1J4
Tel: 613-257-2200
info@carletonplacehosp.com
www.carletonplacehospital.ca
Year Founded: 1955
Number of Beds: 22 beds
Population Served: 25000
Note: Programs & services include: inpatient services (pastoral care & palliative care); outpatient services (dietitian, laboratory, physiotherapy, sleep lab, speech & language therapy, surgery, & Telemedicine); diagnostic (cardiac diagnostics, loop monitoring, radiography, & ultrasound); & emergency.
Mary Wilson Trider, President & CEO
613-253-3825, mwilsontrider@cpdmh.ca
Randy Shaw, Integrated Vice President, Corporate Support Services
613-257-2200, rshaw@cpdmh.ca
Kimberley Harbord, Vice President & Chief Financial Officer
613-253-3826, kharbord@cpdmh.ca

Chapleau: Chapleau Health Services (SSCHS)/Services de sante de Chapleau
Affiliated with: North East Local Health Integration Network
6 Broomhead Rd., Chapleau, ON P0M 1K0
Tel: 705-864-1520 Fax: 705-864-0449
chapleauhr@sschs.ca
www.sschs.ca
Number of Beds: 13 acute care beds; 25 long-term care beds; 4 chronic care beds; 2 respite beds
Note: Programs & services include: emergency services; acute care; occupational therapy; rehabilitation services; adult mental health services; counselling; services for the for the developmentally disabled; diabetes education; community services, such as Meals on Wheels, home support services & lifeline; operation of a nursing station in Foleyet; long term care; chronic care; & respite care.
Tim Gehrke, Chief Executive Officer
Dr. Kendra Saari, Chief of Medical Staff

Chatham: Chatham-Kent Health Alliance (CKHA)
Affiliated with: Erie St. Clair Local Health Integration Network
PO Box 2030, 80 Grand Ave. West, Chatham, ON N7M 5L9
Tel: 519-352-6400
info@ckha.on.ca
www.ckha.on.ca
www.facebook.com/ckhamedia; twitter.com/ckhamedia;
www.youtube.com/ckhamedia
Year Founded: 1998
Number of Beds: 200+ beds (total for both CKHA sites)
Population Served: 102000 Number of Employees: 1360
Note: Programs & services include: adult & pediatric day surgery; ambulatory care; arthritis & stroke aquatic program; bone mineral densitometry; cardiac; chemotherapy / oncology; chiropody clinic; chronic disease management; continence clinic; coronary artery disease clinic; CT scan; diabetes education; dialysis; district stroke centre; echocardiography; emergency; EMG; endoscopy; fluoroscopy; general radiography; general surgery; gynaecology; health education; inpatient family medicine; inpatient surgical unit; integrated acute stroke unit; intensive care; mammography; mental health & addictions; MRI; nuclear medicine; nurse practitioner clinic; occupational therapy; Ontario Breast Screening Program; ophthalmology; oral surgery / dentistry; orthopedic surgery; orthotist/prosthetist; otolaryngology; outpatient hand clinic; parkinson's class; physiatry consultations / clinic; physiotherapy; progressive care; rehabilitation / complex continuing care; respiratory health; secondary stroke prevention clinic; sexual assault treatment centre; social work; speech-language pathology; supportive care & palliative care; therapeutic recreation; transitional stroke program; ultrasound; urology; women & children's health; & wound, skin & ostomy consultations. Affiliated with the Schulich School of Medicine - University of Western Ontario.
Lori Marshall, President & CEO
519-352-6401, lmarshall@ckha.on.ca

Aaron Ryan, Chief Financial Officer & Vice-President, Performance
519-352-6401, amryan@ckha.on.ca
Lisa Northcott, Chief Nursing Executive & Vice-President, People
519-352-6401, lnorthcott@ckha.on.ca

Chesley: South Bruce Grey Health Centre - Chesley Site
South Bruce Grey Health Centre
Affiliated with: South West Local Health Integration Network
Former Name: Chesley & District Memorial Hospital
39 - 2nd St. SE, Chesley, ON N0G 1L0
Tel: 519-363-2340 Fax: 519-363-9871
info@sbghc.on.ca
www.sbghc.on.ca
www.facebook.com/sbghc; twitter.com/SBG_HC
Year Founded: 1944
Number of Beds: 8 acute care beds; 10 restorative care beds
Note: Programs & services include: cardio-respiratory; diagnostic imaging; emergency department; emergency response system; inpatient medical beds; laboratory; nutrition services; outpatient clinics; palliative care; & restorative care.
Michael Barrett, President & CEO, SBGHC
519-370-2400, mbarrett@sbghc.on.ca
Anegla Stanley, Chief Nursing Officer & Vice-President, SBGHC
519-370-2400, astanley@sbghc.on.ca

Clinton: Clinton Public Hospital
Huron Perth Healthcare Alliance
Affiliated with: South West Local Health Integration Network
98 Shipley St., Clinton, ON N0M 1L0
Tel: 519-482-3440 Toll-Free: 888-275-1102
administration@hpha.ca
www.hpha.ca
Number of Beds: 20 acute care beds
Note: Programs & services include: ambulatory clinics; bone density; dietitian; emergency; laboratory; social work; speech language pathology; surgical daycare; ultrasound; & x-ray.
Andrew Williams, President & CEO, HPHA
519-272-8202, andrew.williams@hpha.ca
Dr. Kevin Lefebvre, Interim Chief of Staff, HPHA
dr.kevin.lefebvre@hpha.ca
Mary Cardinal, Vice-President & Chief Quality Officer, HPHA
519-272-8206, mary.cardinal@hpha.ca

Cobourg: Northumberland Hills Hospital
Affiliated with: Central East Local Health Integration Network
Former Name: Northumberland Health Care Corp.
1000 DePalma Dr., Cobourg, ON K9A 5W6
Tel: 905-372-6811 Fax: 905-372-4243
info@nhh.ca
www.nhh.ca
twitter.com/NorHillsHosp
www.linkedin.com/company/northumberland-hills-hospital
Number of Beds: 112 beds
Population Served: 60000 *Number of Employees:* 600
Note: Programs & services include: emergency; intensive care; obstetric; surgery; diagnostic imaging; women's health; ambulatory care; cancer & supportive care clinic; community mental health services; dialysis; Telemedicine; rehabilitation; restorative care; & palliative care.
Linda Davis, President & CEO
905-377-7755, ldavis@nhh.ca
Susan Walsh, Chief Nursing Executive & Vice-President, Patient Services
905-377-7756, sbwalsh@nhh.ca
Abhi Mukherjee, Vice President & Chief Financial Officer
905-372-6811
Jennifer Gillard, Senior Director, Public Affairs & Strategic Partnerships
905-377-7757, jgillard@nhh.ca

Cochrane: Lady Minto Hospital
MICs Group of Health Services
Affiliated with: North East Local Health Integration Network
PO Box 4000, 241 - 8 St., Cochrane, ON P0L 1C0
Tel: 705-272-7200 Fax: 705-272-2624
www.micsgroup.com
Year Founded: 1915
Number of Beds: 25 acute care beds; 8 complex continuing care beds; 37 long-term care beds
Note: Programs & services include: clinical nutrition; complex continuing care; diabetes; diagnostic imaging; emergency; general surgery; laboratory; oncology; physiotherapy; respiratory therapy; telemedicine; & visiting specialty clinics. The Villa Minto chronic care wing houses a long-term care unit.

Paul Chatelain, Chief Executive Officer, MICs Group of Health Services
705-272-7200, paul.chatelain@micsgroup.com
Isabelle Boucher, Chief Nursing Officer, MICs Group of Health Services
705-272-7200, isabelle.boucher@micsgroup.com

Collingwood: Collingwood G&M Hospital (CGMH)
Affiliated with: North Simcoe Muskoka Local Health Integration Network
Former Name: Collingwood General & Marine Hospital
459 Hume St., Collingwood, ON L9Y 1W9
Tel: 705-445-2550
www.cgmh.on.ca
www.facebook.com/CollingwoodGMHospital;
twitter.com/CollingwoodHosp;
www.youtube.com/user/CollingwoodGMHosp;
www.linkedin.com/company/collingwood-general-and-marine-hospital
Year Founded: 1887
Number of Beds: 74 beds
Population Served: 60000
Note: Programs & services include: ambulatory care; cardio-respiratory; community mental health; diagnostic imaging; dialysis; emergency; general medicine; general surgery; intensive care; laboratory services; obstetrics / gynaecology; orthopaedic surgery; rehabilitation; & Telemedicine.
Norah Holder, President & CEO
Dr. Michael Lisi, Chief of Staff
Michael Lacroix, CFO & Vice-President, Corporate Services

Cornwall: Cornwall Community Hospital/Hôpital communautaire de Cornwall
Affiliated with: Champlain Local Health Integration Network
840 McConnell Ave., Cornwall, ON K6H 5S5
Tel: 613-938-4240 Fax: 613-930-4502
communications@cornwallhospital.ca
www.cornwallhospital.ca
Number of Beds: 145 beds
Note: Programs & services include: addiction services; adult counselling & treatment; Arterial Blood Gas (ABG); assault & sexual abuse program; Assertive Community Treatment Team (ACTT); cardiac stress test; cardio-respiratory therapy; children's mental health; critical care; CT scan; day hospital; dentistry; diabetes education; dialysis; ECG / EEG; emergency; geriatrics; gynecology / obstetrics; inpatient psychiatric care unit; internal medicine; laboratory; MRI; mammography; mental health & addictions; neurology; nuclear medicine; ophthalmology; orthopedics; palliative care; pediatrics; psychiatry; psychogeriatric service; radiology; regional hip & knee replacement program; rehabilitation; sleep clinic; spiritual care; spirometry; stroke prevention; surgery; thrombosis; ultrasound; urology; women & children's health; & x-ray.
Jeanette Despatie, President & Chief Executive Officer
Dr. Lorne Scharf, Chief of Staff
Ginette Ferguson, Chief Nursing Officer & Vice-President, Patient Services
Christine Penney, Vice-President, Community Program
Mohammed Shaheen, Chief Information Officer
Karin Hagen, Chief Finance Officer
Lennie Lejasisaks, Chief Privacy and Human Resource Officer

Deep River: Deep River & District Hospital (DRDH)
Affiliated with: Champlain Local Health Integration Network
117 Banting Dr., Deep River, ON K0J 1P0
Tel: 613-584-3333 Fax: 613-584-4920
Toll-Free: 866-571-8168
www.drdh.org
Year Founded: 1974
Number of Beds: 14 beds
Note: Programs & services include: acute inpatient care; children's speech-language program; diabetes; diagnostic imaging; DRDH physiotherapy centre; emergency; laboratory; mental health; nutritional counselling; & Ontario Telemedicine.
Richard Bedard, Chief Executive Officer
richard.bedard@drdh.org
Janna Hotson, Chief Nursing Officer
janna.hotson@drdh.org
William Willard, Vice-President & Chief Financial Officer, Operations
Michelle Robertson, Human Resources Officer

Dryden: Dryden Regional Health Centre (DRHC)
Affiliated with: North West Local Health Integration Network
PO Box 3003, 58 Goodall St., Dryden, ON P8N 2Z6
Tel: 807-223-8201 Fax: 807-223-2370
TTY: 807-223-8295
patientrelations@drhc.on.ca
www.drhc.on.ca
Year Founded: 1952
Number of Beds: 41 beds (31 acute care beds & 10 continuing complex care beds)
Number of Employees: 300
Note: Programs & services include: crisis response (807-223-8884); diabetes education (807-223-8208); diagnostic imaging; dietary; laboratory; mental health & addiction (807-223-6678); occupational therapy; oncology; physiotherapy; & sexual assault/domestic violence services (807-223-7427).
Doreen Armstrong-Ross, President & Chief Executive Officer
Dr. George Rabbat, President of Staff

Dunnville: Haldimand War Memorial Hospital
Affiliated with: Hamilton Niagara Haldimand Brant Local Health Integration Network
206 John St., Dunnville, ON N1A 2P7
Tel: 905-774-7431 Fax: 905-774-6776
www.hwmh.ca
Year Founded: 1920
Number of Beds: 22 acute care beds; 2 transitional beds; 4 assess & restore beds; 13 chronic care beds
Note: Specializes in diagnostic imaging for acute life-threatening injuries or severe illnesses, as well as treatment for non-life-threatening injuries or illnesses such as broken bones, cuts, earaches, eye injuries, fever, infections, minor burns, nose & throat issues & sprains & strains.
David Montgomery, President & CEO
Sharon Moore, Vice-President & Chief Nursing Officer

Durham: South Bruce Grey Health Centre - Durham Site
South Bruce Grey Health Centre
Affiliated with: South West Local Health Integration Network
Former Name: Durham Memorial Hospital
PO Box 638, 320 College St., Durham, ON N0G 1R0
Tel: 519-369-2340 Fax: 519-369-6180
info@sbghc.on.ca
www.sbghc.on.ca
www.facebook.com/sbghc; twitter.com/SBG_HC
Year Founded: 1946
Number of Beds: 10 beds
Note: Programs & services include: cardio-respiratory; diagnostic imaging; emergency department; emergency response system; inpatient medical beds; laboratory; nutrition services; outpatient clinics; palliative care; & spiritual care.
Michael Barrett, President & CEO, SBGHC
519-370-2400, mbarrett@sbghc.on.ca
Angela Stanley, Chief Nursing Officer & Vice-President, SBGHC
519-370-2400, astanley@sbghc.on.ca

Elliot Lake: St. Joseph's General Hospital
Affiliated with: North East Local Health Integration Network
70 Spine Rd., Elliot Lake, ON P5A 1X2
Tel: 705-848-7182
www.sjghel.ca
Year Founded: 1958
Number of Beds: 57 beds
Note: Programs & services include: emergency; bone density; cardiology; chemotherapy; chiropody; clinical nutrition; diabetes education; ears, nose, & throat; electrocardiogram; endoscopy; gastroenterology; gerontology; intensive care; mental health; nephrology; obstetrics; ophthalmology; orthopedics; paediatrics; palliative care; pastoral care; physiotherapy; radiology; renal dialysis (as a satellite of Sudbury Regional Hospital); speech therapy; social work; surgery; urology; & ultrasound. The hospital corporation also manages St. Joseph's Manor long term care facility, & the Oaks Substance Abuse Treatment Centre.
Pierre Ozolins, Chief Executive Officer
Connie Free, Chief Nursing Executive & Director, Clinical Services

Englehart: Englehart & District Hospital Inc.
Affiliated with: Blanche River Health
PO Box 69, 61 - 5th St., Englehart, ON P0J 1H0
Tel: 705-544-2301 Fax: 705-544-5222
www.blancheriverhealth.ca
Number of Beds: 30 beds
Note: Programs & services include: acute care; cancer care; complex continuing care; diabetes; diagnostic imaging; emergency; foot care; laboratory; occupational therapy; palliative care; physiotherapy; respiratory therapy; & Telemedicine.

Sean Conroy, Interim President & CEO, CFO, Blanche River Health
Monika Schallenberger, Chief Nursing Officer, Blanche River Health

---

Espanola: **Espanola Regional Hospital & Health Centre (ERHHC)/Hôpital régional et centre de santé d'espanola**
Affiliated with: North East Local Health Integration Network
Former Name: Espanola General Hospital
825 McKinnon Dr., Espanola, ON P5E 1R4
Tel: 705-869-1420 *Fax:* 705-869-3091
info@esphosp.on.ca
www.espanolaregionalhospital.ca
www.facebook.com/1400019880221710

Year Founded: 1949
Number of Beds: 47 beds
Note: Programs & services include: diagnostic imaging; emergency / acute care; Espanola Nursing Home; family health team; laboratory; pharmacy; physiotherapy; Queensway Place; & sleep lab.
Nicole Haley, Chief Executive Officer
Jane Battistelli, Chief Nursing Officer
Kim Roy, Chief Financial Officer

Exeter: **South Huron Hospital Association (SHHA)**
Affiliated with: South West Local Health Integration Network
24 Huron St. West, Exeter, ON N0M 1S2
Tel: 519-235-2700 *Fax:* 519-235-3405
shha.administration@shha.on.ca
www.shha.on.ca

Year Founded: 1953
Number of Beds: 19 beds
Note: Programs & services include: clinical nutrition & counselling; diabetes education; diagnostic imaging; emergency; inpatient services; laboratory; nursing; palliative care; physiotherapy; social work; speech language pathology; & Telemedicine.
Bruce Quigly, President & CEO
Jennifer Peckitt, Site Director & Chief Nursing Executive

Fergus: **Groves Memorial Community Hospital (GMCH)**
Affiliated with: Waterloo Wellington Local Health Integration Network
235 Union St. East, Fergus, ON N1M 1W3
Tel: 519-843-2010
info@gmch.fergus.net
www.gmch.ca

Number of Beds: 44 beds
Population Served: 34500 *Number of Employees:* 277
Note: Programs & services include: ambulatory care; chiropody; diabetes education; diagnostic imaging; emergency; geriatric emergency management; Hospital Elder Life Care Program; inpatient medicine; infection prevention & control; laboratory; nutritional services; obstetrics; Ontario Breast Screening Program; outpatient oncology unit; pastoral services; pharmacy; physiotherapy; respiratory therapy; speech-language pathology; & surgery.
Stephen Street, President & CEO
Dr. Doug Roach, Chief of Staff

Fort Erie: **Douglas Memorial Hospital Site**
Niagara Health System / Système de santé de Niagara
Affiliated with: Hamilton Niagara Haldimand Brant Local Health Integration Network
230 Bertie St., Fort Erie, ON L2A 1Z2
Tel: 905-378-4647
www.niagarahealth.on.ca
twitter.com/niagarahealth;
www.youtube.com/niagarahealthsystem

Year Founded: 1931
Number of Beds: 55 beds
Note: Programs & services include: complex care; diagnostic imaging; laboratory; Ontario Breast Screening Clinic; outpatient mental health; & urgent care.
Laura Morrison, Site Director
laura.morrison@niagarahealth.on.ca

Fort Frances: **Riverside Health Care Facilities Inc.**
Affiliated with: North West Local Health Integration Network
110 Victoria Ave., Fort Frances, ON P9A 2B7
Tel: 807-274-3266 *Fax:* 807-274-2898
riverside@rhcf.on.ca
www.riversidehealthcare.ca

Year Founded: 1989
Number of Beds: 55 beds (La Verendrye); 15 beds (Emo); 24 beds (Rainy River)

Note: Operates the La Verendrye General Hospital (Fort Frances - acute care, continuing care, obstetrics & surgery); the Emo Health Centre (Emo - acute care, urgent care, long tern care, diagnostic imaging, physiotherapy, dental clinic); & Rainy River Health Centre (Rainy River - acute care, long term care, diagnostic imaging, dental clinic).
Henry Gauthier, President & CEO
Julie Loveday, Vice-President & Chief Nursing Executive, Clinical Services
Dr. Melanie Kowal, Chief of Staff

Fort Frances: **La Verendrye General Hospital**
Riverside Health Care Facilities Inc.
Affiliated with: North West Local Health Integration Network
110 Victoria Ave., Fort Frances, ON P9A 2B7
Tel: 807-274-3261 *Fax:* 807-274-2898
Number of Beds: 30 acute care beds; 25 medical & surgical beds
Note: Programs & services include: acute care; intermediate care. The hospital hosts visiting specialists each year.

Georgetown: **Georgetown Hospital**
Halton Healthcare Services
Affiliated with: Mississauga Halton Local Health Integration Network
Former Name: Georgetown & District Memorial Hospital
1 Princess Anne Dr., Georgetown, ON L7G 2B8
Tel: 905-873-0111
pr@haltonhealthcare.on.ca
www.haltonhealthcare.on.ca
www.facebook.com/HaltonHealthcare;
twitter.com/haltonhlthcare;
www.linkedin.com/company/halton-healthcare-services
Year Founded: 1961
Number of Beds: 33 acute care beds; 20 continuing care beds
Population Served: 59000 *Number of Employees:* 326
Note: Programs & services include: complex continuing care; diagnostic imaging; emergency; general medicine; mammography; medical & surgical services; outpatient clinics & community programs; rehabilitation & geriatrics; smoking cessation program; & supportive housing program.
Denise Hardenne, President & CEO, Halton Healthcare
Dr. David McConachie, Chief of Staff, Halton Healthcare
Cindy McDonell, Chief Operating Officer & Program Director, Georgetown Hospital
Judy Linton, Chief Nursing Executive & Senior Vice-President, Georgetown Hospital

---

Geraldton: **Geraldton District Hospital/L'Hopital du District de Geraldton**
Affiliated with: North West Local Health Integration Network
PO Box 4, 500 Hogarth Ave., Geraldton, ON P0T 1M0
Tel: 807-854-1862 *Fax:* 807-854-1568
www.geraldtondh.com

Year Founded: 1963
Number of Beds: 23 acute care beds; 26 long term care beds
Number of Employees: 5700
Note: Programs & services include: 24-hour emergency services; clinical nutrition; chemotherapy; diagnostic imaging; laboratory; nursing; nutrition; rehabilitation; social work; & Telemedicine.
Lucy Bonanno, Chief Executive Officer
lbonanno@geraldtondh.com
Brigitte Ouellet, Chief of Clinical Services
Laurie Heerema, Chief Nursing Executive
lheerema@geraldtondh.com

Goderich: **Alexandra Marine & General Hospital (AMGH)**
Affiliated with: South West Local Health Integration Network
120 Napier St., Goderich, ON N7A 1W5
Tel: 519-524-8323 *Fax:* 519-524-8504
amgh.administration@amgh.ca
www.amgh.ca

Year Founded: 1901
Number of Beds: 42 beds
Note: Programs & services include: ambulatory care clinics; Diabetes Education Centre; diagnostic; dialysis; emergency; medicine; mental health; obstetrics; palliative care; pharmacy; physiotherapy; speech language therapy; support services; & surgery.
Bruce Quigley, President & CEO
519-524-8689, bruce.quigley@amgh.ca
Samantha Marsh, Chief Nursing Executive
519-524-8689, samantha.marsh@amgh.ca
Jimmy Trieu, Chief Information Officer
519-524-8689, jimmy.trieu@amgh.ca

Grimsby: **West Lincoln Memorial Hospital**
Hamilton Health Sciences
Affiliated with: Hamilton Niagara Haldimand Brant Local Health Integration Network
169 Main St. East, Grimsby, ON L3M 1P3
Tel: 905-945-2253 *Fax:* 905-945-5016
wlmhcomments@hhsc.ca
www.wlmh.on.ca
www.vimeo.com/hamiltonhealthsciences
Number of Beds: 60 beds
Population Served: 65000 *Number of Employees:* 391
Note: Programs & services include: complex continuing care; diagnostic imaging; emergency; general medical; geriatric assessment (inpatient & outpatient); intensive care; mental health; obstetrics; outpatient diagnostic & treatment services; palliative care; & surgery. Has 124 medical staff. Affiliated with Michael G. DeGroote School of Medicine, McMaster University.
Rob MacIsaac, President & CEO, Hamilton Health Sciences
Kirsten Krull, Vice-President & Chief Nursing Executive, Hamilton Health Sciences

---

Guelph: **Guelph General Hospital**
Affiliated with: Waterloo Wellington Local Health Integration Network
115 Delhi St., Guelph, ON N1E 4J4
Tel: 519-822-5350
TTY: 519-837-6437
info@gghorg.ca
www.gghorg.ca
www.facebook.com/FdnGGH; twitter.com/FdnofGGH
Year Founded: 1875
Number of Beds: 182 beds (including 22 intensive care, 62 surgery, 8 paediatric, 68 medicine & 22 obstetric)
Population Served: 200000 *Number of Employees:* 1400
Note: Programs & services include: ambulatory care; bariatric surgery; bariatric medical program; cardio respiratory; critical care unit; diagnostic imaging; dietetics / nutritional counselling; emergency; family birthing unit; laboratory; medical unit; paediatric care; pharmacy; rehabilitation therapies; sexual assault & domestic violence; sleep lab; support services; & surgical suite. Employs 300 professional staff.
Marianne Walker, President & CEO
Dr. Jennifer Caspers, Chief of Staff
Melissa Skinner, Vice-President & Chief Nursing Executive, Patient Services

---

Guelph: **St. Joseph's Health Centre Guelph**
St. Joseph's Health System
100 Westmount Rd., Guelph, ON N1H 5H8
Tel: 519-824-6000 *Fax:* 519-763-0264
info@sjhcg.ca
www.sjhcg.ca
twitter.com/STJOESGUELPH
Year Founded: 1861
Number of Beds: 240 long-term care beds; 86 specialty beds
Area Served: Waterloo Wellington
Note: Programs & services include: clinics & medical services; community outreach; complex care; long-term care; nutrition; palliative care; recreation therapy; rehabilitation; social work; speech-language pathology; & spiritual & religious care.
David Wormald, President
519-824-6000, president@sjhcg.ca

Hagersville: **West Haldimand General Hospital**
Affiliated with: Hamilton Niagara Haldimand Brant Local Health Integration Network
75 Parkview Rd., Hagersville, ON N0A 1H0
Tel: 905-768-3311
www.whgh.ca
Year Founded: 1964
Number of Beds: 23 inpatient beds
Note: Programs & services include: acute care; day surgery; diagnostic imaging; emergency; Haldimand Norfolk diabetes services; laboratory; nutrition; outpatient clinics & laboratory services; pastoral care; & physiotherapy.
Kelly Isfan, President & CEO
905-768-3311, kelly.isfan@whgh.ca
Nancy Gabel, Chief of Staff
905-768-3311

Haliburton: **Haliburton Highlands Health Services - Haliburton Site (HHHS)**
Affiliated with: Central East Local Health Integration Network
PO Box 115, 7199 Gelert Rd., Haliburton, ON K0M 1S0
Tel: 705-457-1392 *Fax:* 705-457-2398
www.hhhs.ca
www.linkedin.com/company/lakeridge-health
Year Founded: 2000
Number of Beds: 14 acute care beds; 30 long-term care beds
Note: Programs & services include: acute care / emergency;

diabetes education; diagnostic imaging; infection control; mental health; physiotherapy; & Telemedicine.
Carolyn Plummer, President & CEO
705-457-2527, cplummer@hhhs.ca
Keith Hay, Interim Chief of Staff
Norm Bottum, President of Medical Staff
Diane Duff, Vice-President & Chief Nurse Executive, Clinical Services

Hamilton: Hamilton General Hospital
Hamilton Health Sciences
Affiliated with: Hamilton Niagara Haldimand Brant Local Health Integration Network
237 Barton St. East, Hamilton, ON L8L 2X2
Tel: 905-521-2100
www.hamiltonhealthsciences.ca
www.facebook.com/HamHealthSci;
www.vimeo.com/hamiltonhealthsciences
Year Founded: 1848
Number of Beds: 304 beds (91 inpatient beds)
Specialties: Cardiovascular care, neuosciences, trauma & burn treatment
Note: Major programs & services include: cardiac & vascular; neurosciences & trauma; & Population Health Institute. Others include: addictions & mental health; emergency; Hospital Elder Life Program; pain management centre; palliative care consultation; Regional Rehabilitation Centre; rehabilitation & seniors health program; seniors health; sexual assault & domestic violence care; & STD clinic.
Rob MacIsaac, President & CEO, Hamilton Health Sciences
Kirsten Krull, Vice-President & Chief Nursing Executive, Hamilton Health Sciences

Hamilton: Juravinski Hospital
Hamilton Health Sciences
Affiliated with: Hamilton Niagara Haldimand Brant Local Health Integration Network
Former Name: Mount Hamilton Hospital
711 Concession St., Hamilton, ON L8V 1C3
Tel: 905-521-2100
www.hamiltonhealthsciences.ca
www.facebook.com/HamHealthSci;
www.vimeo.com/hamiltonhealthsciences
Year Founded: 1917
Number of Beds: 228 beds
Note: Programs & services include: diagnostic services & medical diagnostic unit; emergency hematology oncology medicine & JCC Ambulance Care; perioperative services; rehabilitation; & surgical oncology, orthopedics & critical care program.
Dr. Barry Lumb, Site Director
905-527-4322, blumb@mcmaster.ca

Hamilton: McMaster Children's Hospital
Hamilton Health Sciences
Affiliated with: Hamilton Niagara Haldimand Brant Local Health Integration Network
1200 Main St. West, Hamilton, ON L8N 3Z5
Tel: 905-521-2100
www.hamiltonhealthsciences.ca/mcmaster-childrens-hospital
www.facebook.com/HamHealthSci;
www.vimeo.com/hamiltonhealthsciences
Year Founded: 1988
Number of Beds: 120 acute care beds
Specialties: Acute pediatrics
Note: Provides tertiary health care services for children in Hamilton & the surrounding region. Programs & services include: 2G, 2Q & 3E child & youth clinic; audiology; Child Advocacy & Assessment Program (CAAP); child & youth mental health program; children's exercise & nutrition centre; emergency; outpatient clinical services for children with diabetes; pediatric eating disorders program; pharmacy; & sexual assault & domestic violence care centre.
Rob MacIsaac, President & CEO, Hamilton Health Sciences
Bruce Squires, President, McMaster Children's Hospital

Hamilton: McMaster Children's Hospital - Chedoke Site
Hamilton Health Sciences
Affiliated with: Hamilton Niagara Haldimand Brant Local Health Integration Network
PO Box 2000, 559 Sanitorium Rd., Hamilton, ON L8N 3Z5
Tel: 905-521-2100
www.hamiltonhealthsciences.ca
www.facebook.com/HamHealthSci;
www.vimeo.com/hamiltonhealthsciences
Year Founded: 1906
Note: Programs & services include: autism spectrum disorder service (Hamilton Autism Intervention Program); child & youth mental health programs; cleft lip & palate program; developmental pediatrics & rehabilitation; family resource centre;

pediatric lipid clinic; specialized developmental & behavioural services; & technology access clinic.
Rob MacIsaac, President & CEO, Hamilton Health Sciences
Kirsten Krull, Vice-President & Chief Nursing Executive, Hamilton Health Sciences

Hamilton: St. Joseph's Healthcare Hamilton - Charlton Campus
St. Joseph's Health System
Affiliated with: Hamilton Niagara Haldimand Brant Local Health Integration Network
50 Charlton Ave. East, Hamilton, ON L8N 4A6
Tel: 905-522-1155
www.stjoes.ca
twitter.com/STJOESHAMILTON;
www.youtube.com/Stjoesfoundation;
Number of Beds: 443 acute care beds; 298 non-acute care beds; 36 bassinets
Note: Programs & services include: Best Foot Forward; Brant seniors mental health outreach program; audiology; Brant Assertive Community Treatment Team (ACTT); continence care clinic; cleghorn early psychosis intervention program; community schizophrenia service; east region mental health services; geriatric assessment clinic; Niagara seniors mental health outreach program; relaxation group; & spiritual care. Affiliated with the Faculty of Health Sciences at McMaster University & Mohawk College.
Vacant, CEO, St. Joseph's Healthcare
Melissa Farrell, President, St. Joseph's Healthcare
Winnie Doyle, Vice-President & Chief Nursing Executive, St. Joseph's Healthcare

Hamilton: St. Joseph's Healthcare Hamilton - King Campus
St. Joseph's Health System
Affiliated with: Hamilton Niagara Haldimand Brant Local Health Integration Network
2757 King St. East, Hamilton, ON L8G 5E4
Tel: 905-522-1155
www.stjoes.ca
twitter.com/STJOESHAMILTON;
www.youtube.com/Stjoesfoundation
Note: Programs & services include: diabetes; east region mental health services; family practice; chiropody clinic; Health for Older Adults; women's health centre; continence care; family asthma education; & urgent care. Affiliated with the Faculty of Health Sciences at McMaster University & Mohawk College.
Dr. Thomas Stewart, CEO
Melissa Farrell, President
Winnie Doyle, Executive Vice-President & Chief Nursing Executive, Clinical Operations

Hamilton: St. Peter's Hospital
Hamilton Health Sciences
Affiliated with: Hamilton Niagara Haldimand Brant Local Health Integration Network
88 Maplewood Ave., Hamilton, ON L8M 1W9
Tel: 905-777-3837
www.hamiltonhealthsciences.ca
www.facebook.com/HamHealthSci;
www.vimeo.com/hamiltonhealthsciences
Year Founded: 1890
Number of Beds: 250 beds
Specialties: Care for seniors, aged 65 & over
Note: Programs & services include: behavioural health; Centre for Healthy Aging; complex continuing care; palliative care; & rehabilitation. Affiliated with McMaster University & Mohawk College.
Rob MacIsaac, President & CEO, Hamilton Health Sciences
Kirsten Krull, Vice-President & Chief Nursing Executive, Hamilton Health Sciences

Hanover: Hanover & District Hospital (HDH)
Affiliated with: South West Local Health Integration Network
90 - 7 Ave., Hanover, ON N4N 1N1
Tel: 519-364-2340 *Fax:* 519-364-3984
info@hdhospital.ca
www.hanoverhospital.on.ca
www.facebook.com/HDHospital; twitter.com/HDHospital;
www.linkedin.com/company/hanover-&-district-hospital
Year Founded: 1923
Number of Beds: 28 beds
Note: Programs & services include: auxiliary services; chaplaincy services; diagnostic imaging; diabetes education program; emergency; Family Care Suites; Family Centered Birthing Unit; hemodialysis; infection control; intensive care unit; laboratory; medical / surgical; pet therapy; pharmacy; rehabilitation; restorative care; & specialty clinics.
Dana Howes, President & CEO
519-364-2341

Michelle Scime-Summers, Chief Nursing Officer & Vice-President, Patient Care Services
519-364-2341
Kim Mighton, Vice-President, Finance & Operations
519-364-2341, kmighton@hdhospital.ca
Stacy Hogg, Vice-President, Human Resources
519-364-2341, shogg@hdhospital.ca

Hawkesbury: Hawkesbury & District General Hospital/Hôpital général de Hawkesbury et district
Affiliated with: Champlain Local Health Integration Network
1111 Ghislain St., Hawkesbury, ON K6A 3G5
Tel: 613-632-1111
info@hgh.ca
www.hgh.ca
www.linkedin.com/company/2779119
Year Founded: 1984
Number of Beds: 71 beds
Note: Programs & services include: diagnostic imaging; emergency; Ontario Breast Screening Program; mental health & addictions; geriatric psychiatry; & physiotherapy.
Marc LeBoutillier, Chief Executive Officer
Dr. Julie Maranda, Chief of Staff
Marcel Leclair, Vice-President, Finance & Corporate Services
Imrana Jeoffrey, Vice-President, Ambulatory Care, Quality and Performance
Gisèle Larocque, Vice-President, Human Resources and Community Relations
Dr. Suzanne Filion, Vice-President, Development and Integration

Hearst: Hôpital Nôtre-Dame Hospital
PO Box 8000, 1405 Edward St., Hearst, ON P0L 1N0
Tel: 705-362-4291 *Fax:* 705-372-2923
info@ndh.on.ca
www.ndh.on.ca
www.facebook.com/HopitalNotreDameHospitalHearst
Number of Beds: 44 beds
Population Served: 10000
Lynda G. Morin, Chief Executive Officer
Dr. Richard Claveau, Chief of Medical Staff

Hornepayne: Hornepayne Community Hospital
PO Box 190, 278 Front St., Hornepayne, ON P0M 1Z0
Tel: 807-868-2442 *Fax:* 807-868-2697
www.hornepaynecommunityhospital.ca
Number of Beds: 8 acute care beds; 12 long-term care beds
Note: Provides medical, inpatient, & outpatient care services.
Heather Jaremy-Berube, Chief Executive Officer
807-868-2442, heather.jaremyberube@hpch.ca
Alison Morrison, Chief Nursing Officer
807-868-2442, alison.morrison@hpch.ca

Huntsville: Huntsville District Memorial Hospital Site
Muskoka Algonquin Healthcare (MAHC)
Affiliated with: North Simcoe Muskoka Local Health Integration Network
100 Frank Miller Dr., Huntsville, ON P1H 1H7
Tel: 705-789-2311 *Fax:* 705-789-0557
www.mahc.ca
Number of Beds: 37 acute care beds
Number of Employees: 650
Note: Programs & services include: cardio respiratory; clinical nutrition; complex continuing care; diabetes education; diagnostic imaging; District Stroke Centre; emergency; food & nutrition; fracture clinic; general surgery; intensive care unit; laboratory; obstetrics; oncology; paediatric clinic; prenatal clinic; palliative care; rehabilitation; social work; & Telemedicine. Muskoka Algonquin Healthcare employs around 85 physicians.
Natalie Bubela, Chief Executive Officer, MAHC
705-789-2311
Dr. Khaled Abdel-Razek, Chief of Medical Staff, MAHC
705-789-2311
Carol Anderson, Chief Nursing Executive, MAHC
705-645-4404

Ingersoll: Alexandra Hospital
Affiliated with: South West Local Health Integration Network
29 Noxon St., Ingersoll, ON N5C 3V6
Tel: 519-485-1700 *Fax:* 519-485-9606
feedback@ahi.ca
www.alexandrahospital.on.ca
Year Founded: 1909
Number of Beds: 26 beds
Number of Employees: 500
Note: Programs & services include: ambulatory clinics; complex continuing care; day surgery; Diabetes Education Centre; diagnostics; emergency department; inpatient unit; intensive care; nutrition; occupational therapy; Oxford County Cardiac Rehabilitation & Secondary Prevention Program; palliative care program; & physiotherapy.

Sandy Jansen, President & Chief Executive Officer
519-842-3611, sandy.jansen@tdmh.on.ca
Mike Bastow, Chief Operating Officer & Vice-President, Finance
Cheryl Pfaff, Chief Nursing Executive & Vice-President, Clinical Services

Iroquois Falls: Anson General Hospital
MICs Group of Health Services
Affiliated with: North East Local Health Integration Network
58 Anson Dr., Iroquois Falls, ON P0K 1E0
Tel: 705-258-3911 *Fax:* 705-258-3221
www.micsgroup.com

Year Founded: 1955
Number of Beds: 19 acute care beds; 15 complex continuing care beds; 69 long-term care beds
Note: Programs & services include: clinical nutrition; complex continuing care; diabetes; diagnostic imaging; emergency; laboratory; physiotherapy; respiratory therapy; visiting specialty clinics; & Telemedicine.
Paul Chatelain, Chief Executive Officer, MICs Group of Health Services
705-258-3911, paul.chatelain@micsgroup.com

Kapuskasing: Sensenbrenner Hospital
Affiliated with: North East Local Health Integration Network
101 Progress Cres., Kapuskasing, ON P5N 3H5
Tel: 705-337-6111 *Fax:* 705-337-4021
info@senhosp.ca
www.senhosp.ca

Number of Beds: 53 beds
Note: Programs & services include: active care; continuing care; diabetes education; diagnostic imaging; dietitian; ECG / respiratory therapy; emergency; infection control; laboratory; occupational therapy; physiotherapy; pharmacy; special care unit; specialty clinics; spiritual care; & surgical suite.
France Dallaire, Chief Executive Officer
Chantal Boyer-Brochu, Chief Financial Officer
Jeanette Vaillancourt, Chief Information Officer
Jessica Allarie, Chief Human Resources Officer

Kemptville: Kemptville District Hospital
Affiliated with: Champlain Local Health Integration Network
PO Box 2007, 2675 Concession Rd., Kemptville, ON K0G 1J0
Tel: 613-258-6133 *Fax:* 613-258-4997
info@kdh.on.ca
www.kdh.on.ca
www.facebook.com/KemptvilleDistrictHospital;
twitter.com/KDHonline;
www.youtube.com/user/KemptvilleHospital

Number of Beds: 18 inpatient beds; 4 interim long-term care beds; 8 convalescent care beds; 10 surgical beds
Note: Programs & services include: 24 hour emergency; convalescent care; diabetes education; diagnostic imaging; education; in-hospital care; long-term care; outpatient care; & surgery.
Frank Vassallo, Chief Executive Officer
Dr. Penny McGregor, Chief of Staff
Cathy Burke, Chief Nursing Executive
Zahra Saleh, President of Medical Staff

Kenora: Lake of the Woods District Hospital (LWDH)
Affiliated with: North West Local Health Integration Network
21 Sylvan St. West, Kenora, ON P9N 3W7
Tel: 807-468-9861 *Fax:* 807-468-3939
admin@lwdh.on.ca
www.lwdh.on.ca

Year Founded: 1897
Number of Beds: 74 beds
Note: Programs & services include: emergency & ambulatory care; mental health programs; acute care; intensive & surgical care services; diagnostic imaging; mammography; sexual assult centre; physiotherapy; & palliative care.
Ray Racette, President & CEO
807-468-9861
Dr. J.K. MacDonald, Chief of Staff

Kincardine: South Bruce Grey Health Centre - Kincardine Site
South Bruce Grey Health Centre
Affiliated with: South West Local Health Integration Network
Former Name: Kincardine & District General Hospital
1199 Queen St., Kincardine, ON N2Z 1G6
Tel: 519-396-3331 *Fax:* 519-396-3699
www.sbghc.on.ca
www.facebook.com/sbghc; twitter.com/SBG_HC

Year Founded: 1908
Number of Beds: 17 beds
Note: Programs & services include: cardio-respiratory; family birthing centre; diagnostic imaging; emergency department; emergency response system; inpatient medical beds; laboratory; nutrition services; palliative care; & pastoral care.
Michael Barrett, President & CEO, SBGHC
519-370-2400, mbarrett@sbghc.on.ca
Angela Stanley, Chief Nursing Officer & Vice-President, SBGHC
519-370-2400, astanley@sbghc.on.ca

Kingston: Hotel Dieu Hospital (HDH)
Kingston Health Sciences Centre
Affiliated with: South East Local Health Integration Network
Former Name: The Religious Hospitaliers of Saint-Joseph of the Hotel Dieu of Kingston
166 Brock St., Kingston, ON K7L 5G2
Tel: 613-544-3310 *Fax:* 613-544-9948
Toll-Free: 855-554-3400
www.hoteldieu.com
www.facebook.com/HotelDieuHospital;
www.youtube.com/user/HDHKingston

Year Founded: 1845
Note: An ambulatory care teaching facility with programs & services including: audiology; cardiac rehabilitation; child development; Children's Outpatient Centre (COPC); day surgery; detox centre; diabetes education; ENT; eating disorders; eye clinic; Geaganano Residence; infant development; infection & immunology; mental health; & urgent care. It is affiliated with Queen's University & is partnered with Kingston's university hospitals.
Dr. David Pichora, President & CEO, Kingston Health Sciences Centre
khscceo@kingstonhsc.ca
Dr. Michael Fitzpatrick, Chief of Staff, Kingston Health Sciences Centre
mike.fitzpatrick@Kingstonhsc.ca
Mike McDonald, Chief Nursing Executive & Executive Vice-President, Kingston Health Sciences Centre
mike.mcdonald@kingstonhsc.ca

Kingston: Kingston General Hospital (KGH)
Kingston Health Sciences Centre
Affiliated with: South East Local Health Integration Network
76 Stuart St., Kingston, ON K7L 2V7
Tel: 613-548-3232 *Toll-Free:* 800-567-5722
www.kgh.on.ca
Info Line: 613-549-6666

Year Founded: 1838
Number of Beds: 440 beds
Population Served: 500000
Note: Teaching & research hospital affiliated with Queen's University. Programs & services include: cancer; cardiac; critical care; emergency; endocrinology & metabolism; gastroenterology; imaging; infectious diseases; internal medicine; medical genetics; mental health; nephrology & dialysis; neurology; obstetrics & gynecology; pathology & molecular medicine; pediatrics; pharmacy; respirology; rheumatology; sexual assault & domestic violence; & surgical, perioperative & anesthesiology.
Dr. David Pichora, President & CEO, Kingston Health Sciences Centre
khscceo@kingstonhsc.ca
Dr. Michael Fitzpatrick, Chief of Staff, Kingston Health Sciences Centre
mike.fitzpatrick@kingstonhsc.ca
Mike McDonald, Chief Nursing Executive & Executive Vice-President, Kingston Health Sciences Centre
mike.mcdonald@kingstonhsc.ca

Kirkland Lake: Kirkland & District Hospital
Affiliated with: Blanche River Health
145 Government Rd. East, Kirkland Lake, ON P2N 3P4
Tel: 705-567-5251 *Fax:* 705-568-2102
administration@kdhospital.com
www.blancheriverhealth.ca

Year Founded: 1976
Number of Beds: 41 acute care beds; 15 continuing complex care beds; 6 intensive care beds
Number of Employees: 250
Note: Services include diagnostic imaging, respiratory therapy, diabetic clinic, physiotherapy, pastoral care, telemedicine, & renal dialysis.
Sean Conroy, Interim President & CEO, CFO, Blanche River Health
Monika Schallengerger, Chief Nursing Officer, Blanche River Health

Kitchener: Grand River Hospital - Freeport Health Centre
Affiliated with: Waterloo Wellington Local Health Integration Network
PO Box 9056, 3570 King St. East, Kitchener, ON N2A 2W1
Tel: 519-742-3611
info@grhosp.on.ca
www.grhosp.on.ca

Number of Beds: 574 beds (including Kitchener-Waterloo Site)
Note: Programs & services offered across both hospital sites include: cancer care; childbirth; children (including neonatal intensive care); complex continuing care; critical care; emergency; laboratory; medical imaging; medical program & stroke centre; mental health & addictions; renal care; pharmacy; rehabilitation; & surgery.
Ron Gagnon, President & CEO
Dr. Peter Potts, Joint Chief of Staff

Kitchener: Grand River Hospital - Kitchener-Waterloo Site
Affiliated with: Waterloo Wellington Local Health Integration Network
PO Box 9056, 835 King St. West, Kitchener, ON N2G 1G3
Tel: 519-742-3611
info@grhosp.on.ca
www.grhosp.on.ca

Number of Beds: 574 beds
Number of Employees: 3390
Note: Programs & services offered across both hospital sites include: cancer care; childbirth; children (including neonatal intensive care); complex continuing care; critical care; emergency; laboratory; medical imaging; medical program & stroke centre; mental health & addictions; renal care; pharmacy; rehabilitation; & surgery.
Ron Gagnon, President & CEO
Dr. Peter Potts, Joint Chief of Staff
Robinne Hauck, Chief Nursing Executive

Kitchener: St. Mary's General Hospital
St. Joseph's Health System
Affiliated with: Waterloo Wellington Local Health Integration Network
911 Queen's Blvd., Kitchener, ON N2M 1B2
Tel: 519-744-3311 *Fax:* 519-749-6426
info@smgh.ca
www.smgh.ca
www.facebook.com/StMarysGeneralHospital;
twitter.com/StMarysGenHosp;
www.youtube.com/channel/UCMdDvrpTcVtQxPqN162z9Pw;
www.linkedin.com/company/st—mary's-general-hospital

Year Founded: 1924
Number of Beds: 147 acute care beds
Number of Employees: 1500
Note: Catholic hospital, home to the Regional Cardiac Care Centre. Other programs & services include respiratory care, day surgery, general medicine, & emergency care.
Lee Fairclough, President
lfairclough@smgh.ca
Dr. Peter Potts, Chief of Staff
peter.potts@grhosp.on.ca
Leisa Faulkner, Acting Chief Nursing Executive & Vice-President, Patient Services
lfaulkner@smgh.ca
Jui Datta, Acting Chief Financial Officer & Vice-President, Corporate Services
jdatta@smgh.ca

Leamington: Erie Shores HealthCare (LDMH)
Affiliated with: Erie St. Clair Local Health Integration Network
194 Talbot St. West, Leamington, ON N8H 1N9
Tel: 519-326-2373
www.erieshoreshealthcare.ca
www.linkedin.com/company/leamington-district-memorial-hospita
l

Number of Beds: 58 beds
Note: Programs & services include: 24 hour emergency; ambulatory care; diagnostic services; gynecology; intensive care; medicine; obstetrics; palliative care; rehabilitation; & surgery.
Janice Dawson, Chief Executive Officer
Kristin Kennedy, Chief Nursing Executive & Vice-President
Dr. Ross Moncur, Chief of Staff

Lindsay: Ross Memorial Hospital (RMH)
Affiliated with: Central East Local Health Integration Network
10 Angeline St. North, Lindsay, ON K9V 4M8
Tel: 705-324-6111 *Fax:* 705-328-6087
Toll-Free: 800-510-7365
publicrelations@rmh.org
www.rmh.org
twitter.com/RossMemorial;
www.linkedin.com/company/lakeridge-health
Year Founded: 1902
Number of Beds: 175 beds
Population Served: 80000 *Number of Employees:* 820
Note: Programs & services include: continuing care; critical care; diagnostic imaging; dialysis; Health First (disease management); infection prevention & control; laboratory; medical program; mental health; radiation oncology consulation; spiritual; Ontario Telemedicine Network (OTN); pharmacy; surgery; therapy; & woman & child.
Kelly Isfan, President & CEO
Anne Overhoff, Chief Nursing Executive

Lions Head: Lion's Head Hospital
Grey Bruce Health Services
Affiliated with: South West Local Health Integration Network
22 Moore St., Lions Head, ON N0H 1W0
Tel: 519-793-3424 *Fax:* 519-793-4407
web@gbhs.on.ca
www.gbhs.on.ca
twitter.com/greybrucehealth
Number of Beds: 4 acute care beds
Note: Programs & services include: acute care; ambulatory care; diagnostic imaging (general radiography); emergency; laboratory; physiotherapy; & spiritual care.
Gary Sims, President & CEO, Grey Bruce Health Services
519-376-2121

Listowel: Listowel Memorial Hospital
Listowel Wingham Hospitals Alliance
Affiliated with: South West Local Health Integration Network
255 Elizabeth St. East, Listowel, ON N4W 2P5
Tel: 519-291-3120 *Fax:* 519-291-5440
www.lwha.ca
Year Founded: 1919
Number of Beds: 50 beds
Note: Programs & services include: breast health centre; complex continuing care; diabetes education; diagnostic imaging; emergency; laboratory; maternal / newborn; medical unit; occupational therapy; outpatient clinics; palliative care; pastoral care; physiotherapy; speech-language pathology; & surgery.
Karl Ellis, President & CEO
519-291-3120, karl.ellis@lwha.ca

Little Current: Manitoulin Health Centre
PO Box 640, 11 Meredith St. East, Little Current, ON P0P 1K0
Tel: 705-368-2300 *Fax:* 705-368-3566
www.mhc.on.ca
Number of Beds: 32 beds
Note: Services include: chemotherapy; chiropody clinic; day surgery; dialysis; emergency care; laboratory; medical / surgical; mental health; nutrition counselling; obstetrics; paediatrics; physiotherapy; radiology; & ultrasound. Includes Little Current & Mindemoya sites.
Lynn Foster, President & CEO
Paula Fields, Vice-President & Chief Nursing Officer, Clinical Services

London: London Health Sciences Centre - Children's Hospital
Affiliated with: South West Local Health Integration Network
PO Box 5010 Stn. B, 800 Commissioners Rd. East, London, ON N6A 5W9
Tel: 519-685-8500
www.lhsc.on.ca
Info Line: 519-685-8380
www.facebook.com/LHSCCanada; twitter.com/LHSCCanada;
www.youtube.com/LHSCCanada
Year Founded: 1917
Number of Beds: 12 critical care beds; 58 acute care beds; 43 neonatal intensive care beds
Note: Provides specialized paediatric inpatient & outpatient services, including liver & bowel transplants; oncology; infectious disease programs; trauma; & intensive care.
Vacant, President & CEO
Jackie Schleifer Taylor, Vice-President, Children's Hospital & Women's Care

London: London Health Sciences Centre - University Hospital Site
Affiliated with: South West Local Health Integration Network
Also Known As: University Hospital
PO Box 5339 Stn. B, 339 Windermere Rd., London, ON N6A 5A5
Tel: 519-685-8500
www.lhsc.on.ca
Info Line: 519-685-8380
www.facebook.com/LHSCCanada; twitter.com/LHSCCanada;
www.youtube.com/LHSCCanada
Number of Beds: 424 beds
Note: Programs & services include: carpal tunnel syndrome & mononeuropathy clinic; Clinical Neurological Sciences (CNS); cochlear implant program; Critical Care Outreach Team (CCOT); dentistry; diagnostic imaging; EEG; emergency; family medicine & palliative care; general surgery; general cardiology & cardiovascular surgery; intensive care; motor neuron disease clinic; movement disorder clinic; multi-organ transplant; multiple sclerosis clinic; occupational therapy; orthopaedics; pathology & laboratory medicine; physiotherapy; prescription centre pharmacy; psychological; renal care; social work; speech-language pathology; & surgery.
Vacant, President & CEO

London: London Health Sciences Centre - Victoria Hospital Site
Affiliated with: South West Local Health Integration Network
PO Box 5010 Stn. B, 800 Commissioners Rd. East, London, ON N6A 5W9
Tel: 519-685-8500
www.lhsc.on.ca
Info Line: 519-685-8380
www.facebook.com/LHSCCanada; twitter.com/LHSCCanada;
www.youtube.com/LHSCCanada
Year Founded: 1995
Number of Beds: 588 beds
Note: Programs & services include: adult mental health care; bleeding disorders; blood conservation; cardiac care; Cardiac Fitness Institute of Southwestern Ontario; Critical Care Trauma Centre (CCTC); emergency; family medicine & palliative care; fertility clinic; maternal newborn care; medical genetics program of Southwestern Ontario; occupational therapy; pathology & laboratory medicine; pharmacy services; physiotherapy; renal care; sleep & apnea assessment unit; sleep medicine clinic; social work; speech-language pathology; surgical services; trauma program; urology; & women's health care.
Vacant, President & CEO

London: St. Joseph's Health Care, London
Affiliated with: South West Local Health Integration Network
268 Grosvenor St., London, ON N6A 4V2
Tel: 519-646-6100
comdept@sjhc.london.on.ca
www.sjhc.london.on.ca
www.facebook.com/stjosephslondon;
twitter.com/stjosephslondon; www.youtube.com/stjosephslondon
Number of Beds: 1,014 beds
Note: Includes St. Joseph's Hospital; Parkwood Institute; St. Joseph's Family Medical & Dental Centre; Mount Hope Centre for Long Term Care; & Southwest Centre for Forensic Mental Health Care. Affiliated with Western University & Fanshawe College.
Dr. Gillian Kernaghan, President & CEO
askgillian@sjhc.london.on.ca

London: St. Joseph's Hospital
Affiliated with: St. Joseph's Health Care, London
PO Box 5777 Stn. B, 268 Grosvenor St., London, ON N6A 4V2
Tel: 519-646-6100
www.sjhc.london.on.ca
Number of Beds: 21 beds
Note: Programs & services include: arthritis; bone disease & osteoporosis; diabetes education; diagnostic imaging; gastroenterology; otolaryngology; respirology; rheumatology; & ultrasound.
Dr. Gillian Kernaghan, President & CEO, St. Joseph's Health Care London
askgillian@sjhc.london.on.ca

Manitouwadge: Manitouwadge General Hospital
Affiliated with: North West Local Health Integration Network
1 Health Care Cres., Manitouwadge, ON P0T 2C0
Tel: 807-826-3251 *Fax:* 807-826-4216
infoserv@mh.on.ca
www.mh.on.ca

Number of Beds: 18 beds
Note: Programs & services include: chemotherapy; diabetes education; laboratory; physiotherapy; & diagnostic imaging.
Debbie Hardy, Chief Executive Officer
807-826-3251, dhardy@mh.on.ca
Annie Janveau, Director & CNO, Clinical and Rehabilitation Services
807-826-3251, ajanveau@mh.on.ca
Megan Estarte, Director, Community Prgrams & Services
807-826-3251, mestarte@mh.on.ca

Marathon: Wilson Memorial General Hospital
North of Superior Healthcare Group
Affiliated with: North West Local Health Integration Network
PO Box 780, 26 Peninsula Rd., Marathon, ON P0T 2E0
Tel: 807-229-1740 *Fax:* 807-229-1721
wilson@nosh.ca
www.nosh.ca
Year Founded: 1971
Number of Beds: 21 beds
Population Served: 7500
Note: Programs & services include: chemotherapy; rehabilitation; diabetes education; & eye & foot specialty treatment.
Adam Brown, Chief Executive Officer
807-229-1740
Janet Gobeil, Chief Nursing Officer
807-229-1740

Markdale: Markdale Hospital
Grey Bruce Health Services
Affiliated with: South West Local Health Integration Network
Also Known As: Centre Grey Hospital
PO Box 406, 55 Isla St., Markdale, ON N0C 1H0
Tel: 519-986-3040
web@gbhs.on.ca
www.gbhs.on.ca
twitter.com/greybrucehealth
Number of Beds: 14 acute care beds
Note: Programs & services include: acute care; ambulatory care; Diabetes Grey Bruce; diagnostic imaging; emergency; laboratory; physiotherapy; spiritual care; & surgery.
Gary Sims, President & CEO, Grey Bruce Health Services
519-376-2121

Markham: Markham Stouffville Hospital - Markham Site (MSH)
Affiliated with: Central Local Health Integration Network
PO Box 1800, 381 Church St., Markham, ON L3P 7P3
Tel: 905-472-7373
TTY: 905-472-7585
myhospital@msh.on.ca
Info Line: 905-472-7100
www.facebook.com/MarkhamStouffvilleHospital;
twitter.com/MSHospital; www.youtube.com/MSHospital;
www.linkedin.com/company/markham-stouffville-hospital
Year Founded: 1990
Number of Beds: 329 beds
Note: Programs & services include: diabetes education; diagnostic & respiratory; emergency; ICU / NICU; laboratory; maternal child; medical; mental health; oncology; outpatient ambulatory care; palliative care; rehabilitation & transitional care; speech & language program; & surgery.
Jo-anne Marr, President & CEO
Dr. Caroline Geenen, Chief of Staff

Matheson: Bingham Memorial Hospital
MICs Group of Health Services
Affiliated with: North East Local Health Integration Network
PO Box 70, 507 - 8th Ave., Matheson, ON P0K 1N0
Tel: 705-273-2424 *Fax:* 705-273-2515
www.micsgroup.com
Year Founded: 1955
Number of Beds: 11 acute care beds; 6 complex continuing care beds; 20 long-term care beds
Note: Programs & services include: clinical nutrition; diabetes; diagnostic imaging; emergency; laboratory; respiratory therapy; Telemedicine; & visiting specialty clinics.
Paul Chatelain, Chief Executive Officer, MICs Group of Health Services
705-273-2424, paul.chatelain@micsgroup.com

Mattawa: Mattawa Hospital/Hôpital de Mattawa
PO Box 70, 217 Turcotte Park Rd., Mattawa, ON P0H 1V0
Tel: 705-744-5511 *Fax:* 705-744-6020
admin@mattawahospital.ca
www.mattawahealth.ca

Year Founded: 1878
Number of Beds: 19 beds
Note: Specialties: Primary care; Acute care; Ambulatory programs; Diabetic resource centre; Adult & children's mental health services; Paediatric, urology, psychiatry, & women's clinic; Physiotherapy services; Palliative care
Pierre Noel, President & CEO
Kayla Michaud, Director of Care

Meaford: Meaford Hospital
Grey Bruce Health Services
Affiliated with: South West Local Health Integration Network
229 Nelson St. West, Meaford, ON N4L 1A3
Tel: 519-538-1311 *Fax:* 519-538-5500
web@gbhs.on.ca
www.gbhs.on.ca
twitter.com/greybrucehealth
Number of Beds: 15 acute care beds
Note: Programs & services include: acute care; ambulatory care; Diabetes Grey Bruce; diagnostic imaging; emergency; laboratory; physiotherapy; spiritual care; & surgery.
Gary Sims, President & CEO, Grey Bruce Health Services
519-376-2121

Midland: Georgian Bay General Hospital - Midland Site/Hôpital général de la baie Georgienne
Affiliated with: North Simcoe Muskoka Local Health Integration Network
PO Box 760, 1112 St. Andrews Dr., Midland, ON L4R 4P4
Tel: 705-526-1300 *Fax:* 705-526-4491
www.gbgh.on.ca
Number of Beds: 69 acute care beds; 6 ICU beds
Note: Programs & services include: acute & intensive care; emergency; inpatient & ambulatory care; obstetrics; regional complex continuing care; regional rehabilitation; & surgery.
Gail Hunt, President & CEO
705-526-1300, huntg@gbgh.on.ca
Dr. Vikram Ralhan, Chief of Staff
705-526-1300, ralhanv@gbgh.on.ca
Lucille Perreault, Vice President & Nursing Executive, Patient Services
705-526-1300, perreaultl@gbgh.on.ca

Milton: Milton District Hospital
Halton Healthcare Services
Affiliated with: Mississauga Halton Local Health Integration Network
725 Bronte St. South, Milton, ON L9T 9K1
Tel: 905-878-2383
TTY: 905-878-7202
mdhinfodesk@haltonhealthcare.on.ca
www.haltonhealthcare.on.ca
www.facebook.com/HaltonHealthcare
twitter.com/haltonhlthcare;
www.linkedin.com/company/halton-healthcare-services
Year Founded: 1959
Number of Beds: 129 beds
Population Served: 100000 *Number of Employees:* 379
Note: Programs & services include: acute hand program; asthma education; audiology & hearing aid services; breastfeeding clinics, drop-ins & prenatal classes; cardiac rehabilitation program; complex continuing care; ConnectCARE; diagnostic imaging; emergency; Falls Prevention Clinic; Halton Diabetes Centre; inpatient rehabilitation; mammography; medical & surgical services; mental health urgent care clinic; obstetrics; outpatient rehabilitation; respiratory rehabilitation program; smoking cessation program; speech-language pathology; & Work-Fit Total Therapy Centre.
Denise Hardenne, President & CEO, Halton Healthcare
Dr. David McConachie, Chief of Staff, Halton Healthcare
Cindy McDonell, Chief Operating Officer & Program Director, Halton Healthcare
Judy Linton, Chief Nursing Executive & Senior Vice-President, Halton Healthcare

Mindemoya: Manitoulin Health Centre
Mindemoya Medical Clinic
PO Box 150, Mindemoya, ON P0P 1S0
Tel: 705-377-5371 *Fax:* 705-377-5372
www.manitoulinhealthcentre.com
Number of Beds: 14 beds
Note: Provides physician, nursing, social work, & dietitian services.
Lynn Foster, President & CEO
Paula Fields, Vice-President & Chief Nursing Officer, Clinical Services

Minden: Haliburton Highlands Health Services - Minden Site (HHHS)
Affiliated with: Central East Local Health Integration Network
PO Box 30, 6 McPherson St., Minden, ON K0M 2K0
Tel: 705-286-2140 *Fax:* 705-286-6384
www.hhhs.ca
www.linkedin.com/company/lakeridge-health
Note: Programs & services include: community programs; diabetes education; long-term care; mental health; physiotherapy; primary care; & ultrasound.

Mississauga: The Credit Valley Hospital
Trillium Health Partners
Affiliated with: Mississauga Halton Local Health Integration Network
2200 Eglinton Ave. West, Mississauga, ON L5M 2N1
Tel: 905-813-2200 *Fax:* 905-813-4444
Toll-Free: 877-292-4284
patient.relationscvh@trilliumhealthpartners.ca
trilliumhealthpartners.ca
twitter.com/Trillium_Health;
www.youtube.com/user/TrilliumHealth;
www.linkedin.com/company/trillium-health-partners
Year Founded: 1985
Number of Beds: 382 beds
Number of Employees: 3125
Note: Programs & services include: ambulatory care; asthma education; cardiac; diabetes education; diagnostic imaging; emergency; geriatric emergency; gynaecology; maternity; mental health; obstetrics; oncology; paediatrics; & renal services.
Michelle E. DiEmanuele, President & CEO, Trillium Health Partners
Dr. Dante Morra, Chief of Staff, Trillium Health Partners
Kathryn Hayward-Murray, Chief Nursing Executive & Senior Vice-President, Patient Care Services, Trillium Health Partners

Mississauga: Mississauga Hospital
Trillium Health Partners
Affiliated with: Mississauga Halton Local Health Integration Network
Former Name: Queensway General Hospital
100 Queensway West, Mississauga, ON L5B 1B8
Tel: 905-848-7100 *Fax:* 905-848-7140
patient.relationsmh@trilliumhealthpartners.ca
trilliumhealthpartners.ca
twitter.com/Trillium_Health;
www.youtube.com/user/TrilliumHealth;
www.linkedin.com/company/trillium-health-partners
Number of Beds: 748 beds
Note: Programs & services include: emergency care centre; birthing centre; critical care; neurosurgery; stroke & cardiac care; sexual assault & domestic violence services; & women's & children's health (Colonel Harland Sanders Family Care Centre).
Michelle E. DiEmanuele, President & CEO, Trillium Health Partners
Dr. Dante Morra, Chief of Staff, Trillium Health Partners
Kathryn Hayward-Murray, Chief Nursing Executive & Senior Vice-President, Patient Care Services, Trillium Health Partners

Moose Factory: Weeneebayko Area Health Authority/Weeneebayko General Hospital (WAHA)
Affiliated with: North East Local Health Integration Network
PO Box 664, 19 Hospital Dr., Moose Factory, ON P0L 1W0
Tel: 705-658-4544 *Fax:* 705-658-4917
www.waha.ca
Number of Beds: 69 beds
Note: Programs & services include: emergency room; operating room; in-patient; & out-patient.
Lynne Innes, President & CEO
Elaine Innes, Chief of Staff
Sandra Kioke, Chief Nursing Executive

Mount Forest: Louise Marshall Hospital
North Wellington Health Care Corporation
Affiliated with: Waterloo Wellington Local Health Integration Network
630 Dublin St., Mount Forest, ON N0G 2L3
Tel: 519-323-2210 *Fax:* 519-323-3741
www.nwhealthcare.ca
Year Founded: 1923
Number of Beds: 15 inpatient beds
Population Served: 15000
Note: Programs & services include: anesthesiology; emergency; ENT; general surgery; gynecology; inpatient & outpatient care; internal medicine; neurology; obstetrics; pathology; pediatrics; radiology; specialist clinics; supportive diagnostic services; & urology.
Stephen Street, President & CEO, North Wellington Health Care
Chris Rowley, Chief Of Staff, North Wellington Health Care

Napanee: Lennox & Addington County General Hospital
Affiliated with: South East Local Health Integration Network
8 Richmond Park Dr., Napanee, ON K7R 2Z4
Tel: 613-354-3301 *Fax:* 613-354-7157
web.lacgh.napanee.on.ca
Number of Beds: 52 beds (24 active care, 2 palliative care, 4 special care, 22 long-term care)
Number of Employees: 270
Note: Programs & services include: bone mineral densitometry; cardiopulmonary; chemotherapy; day surgery; diabetes education; diagnostic imaging; emergency; inpatient; laboratory; mammography; nutrition; occupational therapy; pharmacy; physiotherapy; & respiratory therapy.
Wayne Coveyduck, President & CEO
Dr. Kimberley Morrison, Chief of Staff
Tracy Kent-Hills, Chief Nursing Officer & Director of Care

New Liskeard: Temiskaming Hospital
Affiliated with: North East Local Health Integration Network
421 Shepherdson Rd., New Liskeard, ON P0J 1P0
Tel: 705-647-8121 *Fax:* 705-647-5800
www.temiskaming-hospital.com
Year Founded: 1980
Number of Beds: 59 beds (40 acute, 11 chronic, 5 obstetric & 3 special care unit beds)
Population Served: 30000 *Number of Employees:* 257
Note: Programs & services include: emergency; cardiac rehabilitation; diagnostic imaging (CT scans); laboratory; nutrition services; occupational therapy; pastoral care; pharmacy; physiotherapy; respiratory therapy; speech language pathology; & telestroke program. Visiting specialists conduct services in neurology, nephrology, obstetrics & gynecology, orthotics, rehab / physical medicine, psychiatry, ophthalmology, & pediatrics.
Mike Baker, President & CEO
705-647-1088, mbaker@temiskaming-hospital.com
Andrew Brown, Chief Financial Officer & Director, Corporate Services
705-647-1088, abrown@temiskaming-hospital.com
Erin Montgomery, Chief Nursing Executive & Director, Patient Services
705-647-1088, emontgomery@temiskaming-hospital.com

Newbury: Four Counties Health Services (FCHS)
Middlesex Hospital Alliance
Affiliated with: South West Local Health Integration Network
1824 Concession Dr., RR#3, Newbury, ON N0L 1Z0
Tel: 519-693-4441
www.mhalliance.on.ca
Number of Beds: 12 acute care beds
Population Served: 23000
Note: Programs & services include: ambulatory care; community support; diabetes education; diagnostic imaging; emergency; medical surgical day services; & physiotherapy.
Todd Stepanuik, President & CEO, Middlesex Hospital Alliance
519-245-1550
Kim Jenkins, Site Director
519-245-1550,

Newmarket: Southlake Regional Health Centre
Affiliated with: Central Local Health Integration Network
Former Name: York County Hospital
596 Davis Dr., Newmarket, ON L3Y 2P9
Tel: 905-895-4521
TTY: 905-952-3062
www.southlakeregional.org
www.facebook.com/southlakeregionalhealthcentre;
twitter.com/southlake_news; www.youtube.com/SouthlakeRHC;
www.linkedin.com/company/southlake-regional-health-centre
Year Founded: 1922
Number of Beds: 426 beds
Note: Programs & services include: chronic diseases clinics & programs; emergency; ethics; health information; maternal child; medicine; mental health; musculoskelatal; regional cancer program; regional cardiac care program; rehabilitation; surgery; & spiritual care.
Arden Krystal, President & CEO
Dr. Steven Beatty, Chief of Staff
Helena Hutton, Chief Operating Officer
Annette Jones, Chief Nursing Officer & Vice-President, Patient Experience

Niagara Falls: **Greater Niagara General Site**
Niagara Health System / Système de santé de
Niagara
Affiliated with: Hamilton Niagara Haldimand Brant
Local Health Integration Network
5546 Portage Rd., Niagara Falls, ON L2E 6X2
Tel: 905-378-4647
patientrelations@niagarahealth.on.ca
www.niagarahealth.on.ca
twitter.com/niagarahealth;
www.youtube.com/niagarahealthsystem
Year Founded: 1907
Number of Beds: 180+ beds
Note: Programs & services include: cardiology; complex care;
critical care; diagnostic imaging; emergency; laboratory;
medicine; off-site dialysis centre; Ontario Breast Screening
Clinic; outpatient clinics; outpatient mental health; regional
geriatric assessment; regional stroke services; surgery; &
pharmacy.
Laura Morrison, Site Director

Niagara-on-the-Lake: **Niagara-on-the-Lake Site**
Niagara Health System / Système de santé de
Niagara
Affiliated with: Hamilton Niagara Haldimand Brant
Local Health Integration Network
176 Wellington St., Niagara-on-the-Lake, ON L0S 1J0
Tel: 905-378-4647
patientrelations@niagarahealth.on.ca
www.niagarahealth.on.ca
twitter.com/niagarahealth;
www.youtube.com/niagarahealthsystem
Year Founded: 1921
Note: Programs & services include: complex care; diagnostic
imaging; & laboratory.
Dr. Thomas Stewart, Chief Executive Officer, Niagara Health
System
Lynn Guerriero, President, Niagara Health System
905-378-4647, lynn.guerriero@niagarahealth.on.ca
Dr. Johan Viljoen, Chief of Staff & Executive Vice-President,
Niagara Health System
905-378-4647, johan.viljoen@niagarahealth.on.ca

Nipigon: **Nipigon District Memorial Hospital**
Affiliated with: North West Local Health Integration
Network
PO Box 37, 125 Hogan Rd., Nipigon, ON P0T 2J0
Tel: 807-887-3026 *Fax:* 807-887-2800
admin@ndmh.ca
www.ndmh.ca
Number of Beds: 37 beds
Note: Services include: acute & complex continuing care;
emergency services; diagnostic imaging; physiotherapy; respite
care; & Telehealth.
David Murray, Chief Executive Officer
Cathy Covino, Chief Nursing Executive & Chief Operating Officer

North Bay: **North Bay Regional Health Centre**
(NBRHC)/Centre régional de santé de North Bay
Former Name: North Bay General Hospital;
Northeast Mental Health Centre
PO Box 2500, 50 College Dr., North Bay, ON P1B 5A4
Tel: 705-474-8600
pr@nbrhc.on.ca
www.nbrhc.on.ca
www.facebook.com/nbrhc; twitter.com/nbrhc;
www.youtube.com/thenbrhc
Number of Beds: 389 beds
Note: The North Bay Regional Health Centre is the result of an
amalgamation of the North Bay General Hospital & the
Northeast Mental Health Centre, which occurred in 2010. The
facility now offers acute, specialist & mental health services to
North Bay & the surrounding communities.
Paul Heinrich, President & CEO
Dr. Donald Fung, Vice-President & Chief of Staff, Quality

Oakville: **Oakville-Trafalgar Memorial Hospital**
Halton Healthcare Services
Affiliated with: Mississauga Halton Local Health
Integration Network
3001 Hospital Gate, Oakville, ON L6M 0L8
Tel: 905-845-2571 *Fax:* 905-338-4636
TTY: 905-815-5111
infodesk@haltonhealthcare.on.ca
www.haltonhealthcare.on.ca
www.facebook.com/HaltonHealthcare;
twitter.com/haltonhlthcare; www.linkedin.com/company/3186579
Number of Beds: 457 beds
Population Served: 182500
Note: Programs & services include: ambulatory care; complex

continuing care; critical care; diagnostics; emergency care;
maternal & child care; mental health; rehabilitation; & surgery.
Denise Hardenne, President & CEO, Halton Healthcare
Dr. David McConachie, Chief of Staff, Halton Healthcare
Carole Moore, Chief Operating Officer, Oakville-Trafalgar
Memorial Hospital

Orangeville: **Headwaters Health Care Centre**
Affiliated with: Central West Local Health Integration
Network
Former Name: Headwaters Orangeville
100 Rolling Hills Dr., Orangeville, ON L9W 4X9
Tel: 519-941-2410 *Fax:* 519-942-0483
www.headwatershealth.ca
www.facebook.com/HeadwatersHCC;
twitter.com/HeadwatersHCC;
www.instagram.com/headwatershcc
www.linkedin.com/company/headwaters-health-care-centre
Year Founded: 1997
Number of Beds: 73 beds
Population Served: 135000
Note: Programs & services include: ambulatory care; cardiac
care; chemotherapy; complex continuing care; diabetes care;
diagnostic imaging; dialysis; domestic & sexual assault program;
emergency; intensive care unit; laboratory; mental health;
nutrition; obstetrics; occupational therapy; ophthalmology;
paediatrics; palliative care; pharmacy; physiotherapy; respiratory
therapy; speech-language pathology; spiritual care; surgery; &
Telemedicine.
Kim Delahunt, President & CEO
519-941-2702, kdelahunt@headwatershealth.ca
Dr. Peter Cino, Chief of Staff & Vice-President, Medical Affairs
519-941-2702, pcino@headwatershealth.ca
Peter Varga, Chief Nursing Executive & Vice-President, Patient
Services
519-941-2702, pvarga@headwatershealth.ca
Cathy van Leipsig, Chief Financial Officer & Vice-President,
Coporate Services
519-941-2702

Orillia: **Orillia Soldiers' Memorial Hospital (OSMH)**
Affiliated with: North Simcoe Muskoka Local Health
Integration Network
170 Colborne St. West, Orillia, ON L3V 2Z3
Tel: 705-325-2201 *Fax:* 705-325-7394
TTY: 705-325-1231
info@osmh.on.ca
www.osmh.on.ca
www.facebook.com/TheOrilliaSoldiersMemorialHospital;
twitter.com/OSMH_News; www.youtube.com/OSMHVideos;
www.linkedin.com/company/orillia-soldiers-memorial-hospital
Number of Beds: 230 beds
Number of Employees: 1200
Note: Programs & services include: cancer care; chronic disease
management; clinical nutrition services; critical care; diagnostic
imaging; emergency; infection prevention & control; laboratory;
maternal, child & youth; mental health services; rehabilitation;
regional kidney care program; surgical services; & Telemedicine.
Has 300 physicians on staff.
Carmine Stumpo, President & CEO
705-325-2201, ceo@osmh.on.ca
Dr. Nancy Merrow, Chief of Staff & Vice-President, Medical
Affairs
Cheryl Harrison, Vice-President, Regional Patient Programs

Oshawa: **Lakeridge Health Oshawa**
Affiliated with: Central East Local Health Integration
Network
Former Name: Oshawa General Hospital
Also Known As: Oshawa Hospital
1 Hospital Ct., Oshawa, ON L1G 2B9
Tel: 905-576-8711
www.lakeridgehealth.on.ca
www.facebook.com/LakeridgeHealth;
twitter.com/lakeridgehealth; www.youtube.com/lakeridgehealth;
www.linkedin.com/company/lakeridge-health
Note: Programs & services include: ambulatory & rehabilitation
centre; Central East Regional Cardiac Care Program; child,
youth & family program; community respiratory services; dialysis
unit; eating disorders program; emergency department; GAIN
geriatric clinic; interact treatment program; mental health day
treatment program; Ontario Breast Screening Program;
paediatric feeding / swallowing clinic; pain clinic; palliative care;
Pinewood Centre (alcohol & addictions); & positive care clinic.

Ottawa: **Children's Hospital of Eastern Ontario**
(CHEO)/Centre hospitalier pour enfants de l'est de
l'Ontario
Affiliated with: Champlain Local Health Integration
Network
401 Smyth Rd., Ottawa, ON K1H 8L1
Tel: 613-737-7600 *Toll-Free:* 866-736-2436
www.cheo.on.ca
www.facebook.com/CHEOkids; twitter.com/cheohospital;
www.youtube.com/user/CHEOvideos
Year Founded: 1974
Number of Beds: 133 beds
Number of Employees: 1966
Note: Programs & services include: Autism Program of Eastern
Ontario; Centre for Healthy Active Living; child & youth
protection service; cleft lip & palate craniofacial clinic; diabetes
clinic; Eastern Ontario Regional Genetics Program; inpatient
psychiatric units; Kaitlin Atkinson Family Resource Library;
mental health outpatient regional eating disorders program;
regional psychiatric emergency service for children & youth;
sexually assaulted youth counselling; social work; teen health
centre; & Youth Net / Réseau Ado. Has 307 physicians on staff.
Alex Munter, President & CEO
amunter@cheo.on.ca
Dr. Lindy Samson, Chief of Staff
Ann Lynch, Chief Nursing Executive

Ottawa: **Hôpital Montfort**
Affiliée à: Champlain Local Health Integration
Network
713, ch Montréal, Ottawa, ON K1K 0T2
Tél: 613-746-4621 *Ligne sans frais:* 866-670-4621
montfort@montfort.on.ca
www.hopitalmontfort.com
www.facebook.com/hopital.montfort; twitter.com/hopitalmontfort;
www.youtube.com/user/telehopitalmontfort;
www.linkedin.com/company/hopital-montfort
Nombre de lits: 276 lits
Note: Services: centre familiale de naissance; medicine;
programme de cancérologie; programme de santé mentale;
services diagnostiques incluant imagerie diagnostique et
laboratoire du sommeil; services de santé cardiovasculaire et
pulmonaire; services thérapeutiques y inclus la physiothérapie et
clinique pour les troubles de la communication; soins
ambulatoires; soins aux malades en phase critique y inclus les
soins intensive et soins d'urgence; et soins palliatifs.
Dr. Bernard Leduc, Président-directeur général
Dr. Stéphane Roux, Médecin-chef
Suzanne Robichaud, Chef de la pratique infirmière et
vice-présidente, Direction des services cliniques

Ottawa: **The Ottawa Hospital - Civic**
Campus/L'Hôpital d'Ottawa
Affiliated with: Champlain Local Health Integration
Network
1053 Carling Ave., Ottawa, ON K1Y 4E9
Tel: 613-722-7000
TTY: 613-761-4024
www.ottawahospital.on.ca
www.facebook.com/OttawaHospital; twitter.com/OttawaHospital;
www.youtube.com/user/TheOttawaHospital
Year Founded: 1845
Number of Beds: 1,122 beds across the system
Note: Programs & services include: cardiology; emergency;
family health team; Mohs Surgery Clinic; neurosciences;
Regional Geriatric Program for Eastern Ontario; spinal surgery;
trauma services; University of Ottawa Skills & Simulation Centre
(uOSSC); vascular surgery; weight management clinic - Bariatric
Centre of Excellence; & women's breast health centre.
Dr. Jack Kitts, President & CEO
613-761-4800, jbkitts@toh.ca
Dr. Virginia Roth, Chief of Staff
613-737-8899, vroth@toh.ca
Dr. Debra A. Bournes, Chief Nursing Executive &
Vice-President, Clinical Programs
613-737-8749, dbournes@toh.ca

Ottawa: **The Ottawa Hospital - General**
Campus/L'Hôpital d'Ottawa
Affiliated with: Champlain Local Health Integration
Network
501 Smyth Rd., Ottawa, ON K1H 8L6
Tel: 613-722-7000
TTY: 613-761-4024
www.ottawahospital.on.ca
www.facebook.com/OttawaHospital; twitter.com/OttawaHospital;
www.youtube.com/user/TheOttawaHospital
Year Founded: 1845
Number of Beds: 1,122 beds across the system
Specialties: Cardiovascular
Note: Programs & services include: bone marrow transplant;

chest diseases centre; emergency; regional cancer program; rehabilitation centre; robotic surgery; thoracic surgery; total joint replacement; & the University of Ottawa Eye Institute.
Dr. Jack Kitts, President & CEO
613-761-4800, jbkitts@toh.ca
Dr. Virginia Roth, Chief of Staff
613-737-8899, vroth@toh.ca
Dr. Debra A. Bournes, Chief Nursing Executive & Vice-President, Clinical Programs
613-737-8749, dbournes@toh.ca

Ottawa: The Ottawa Hospital - Riverside Campus/L'Hôpital d'Ottawa
Affiliated with: Champlain Local Health Integration Network
1967 Riverside Dr., Ottawa, ON K1H 7W9
Tel: 613-722-7000
TTY: 613-761-4024
www.ottawahospital.on.ca
www.facebook.com/OttawaHospital; twitter.com/OttawaHospital; www.youtube.com/user/TheOttawaHospital
Year Founded: 1845
Number of Beds: 1,122 beds across the system
Note: Programs & services include: arthritis centre; eye care centre; family health team; Foustanellas Endocrine & Diabetes Centre; nephrology; & Shirley E. Greenberg Women's Health Centre. Affiliated with the University of Ottawa.
Dr. Jack Kitts, President & CEO
613-761-4800, jbkitts@toh.ca
Dr. Virginia Roth, Chief of Staff
613-737-8899, vroth@toh.ca
Dr. Debra A. Bournes, Chief Nursing Executive & Vice-President, Clinical Programs
613-737-8749, dbournes@toh.ca

Ottawa: Queensway Carleton Hospital (QCH)
Affiliated with: Champlain Local Health Integration Network
3045 Baseline Rd., Ottawa, ON K2H 8P4
Tel: 613-721-2000 *Toll-Free:* 888-824-9111
www.qch.on.ca
Year Founded: 1976
Number of Beds: 264 beds
Population Served: 400000 *Number of Employees:* 1900
Note: Programs & services include: childbirth centre; emergency; geriatric services; medical & surgical services; mental health; & rehabilitation.
Dr. Andrew Falconer, President & CEO
Sanjay Acharya, Chief of Staff
Leah Levesque, Chief Nurse Executive & Vice-President, Patient Care
Cameron Best, Chief Financial Officer & Vice-President, Corporate Services

Owen Sound: Owen Sound Hospital
Grey Bruce Health Services
Affiliated with: South West Local Health Integration Network
1800 - 8th St. East, Owen Sound, ON N4K 6M9
Tel: 519-376-2121
web@gbhs.on.ca
www.gbhs.on.ca
twitter.com/greybrucehealth
Number of Beds: 18 inpatient beds; 4 restorative care beds
Note: Regional referral centre for Grey & Bruce counties. Programs & services include: acute care; acute inpatient rehabilitation; ambulatory care; cardiac rehabilitation program; critical care; Diabetes Grey Bruce; diagnostic imaging; dialysis; electro diagnostics; emergency; Grey Bruce District Stroke Centre; health centre pharmacy; mental health; occupational therapy; physiotherapy; respiratory therapy; restorative care unit; sleep lab; social work; spiritual care; surgery; & women & child care.
Gary Sims, President & CEO, Grey Bruce Health Services
519-376-2121
Dr. Michael Marriott, Chief of Medical Staff, Grey Bruce Health Services
519-376-2121

Palmerston: Palmerston & District Hospital
North Wellington Health Care Corporation
Affiliated with: Waterloo Wellington Local Health Integration Network
500 Whites Rd., Palmerston, ON N0G 2P0
Tel: 519-343-2030 *Fax:* 519-343-3821
www.nwhealthcare.ca
Year Founded: 1908
Number of Beds: 15 inpatient beds
Population Served: 15000
Note: Programs & services include: anesthesiology; emergency; ENT; general surgery; gynecology; inpatient & outpatient care;

internal medicine; obstetrics; pathology; radiology; specialist clinics; & supportive diagnostic services.
Stephen Street, President & CEO, North Wellington Health Care
Dr. Chris Rowley, Chief of Staff, North Wellington Health Care

Paris: Willett Hospital
Brant Community Healthcare System
Affiliated with: Hamilton Niagara Haldimand Brant Local Health Integration Network
Also Known As: The Willett
238 Grand River St. North, Paris, ON N3L 2N7
Tel: 519-442-2251
www.bchsys.org
www.facebook.com/bchsys; twitter.com/BCHSYS; www.youtube.com/user/bchsys2011; www.linkedin.com/company/brantford-general-hospital
Year Founded: 1922
Number of Beds: 262 beds (including Brantford General Hospital)
Specialties: Urgent care
Note: Programs & services include: diagnostic imaging; fitness centres & programs; rehabilitation (outpatient); walk-in medical clinics & urgent care. Brant Community Healthcare System is affiliated with the Michael G. DeGroote School of Medicine, McMaster University.
Dr. David McNeil, President & CEO, Brant Community Healthcare System
Dr. Gene Jarrell, Chief of Staff & Vice-President, Brant Community Healthcare System
eugene.jarrell@bchsys.org
Luara Doherty, Chief Financial Officer & Vice-President, Brant Community Healthcare System
Martin Roux, Chief Nurse Executive & Vice-President, Brant Community Healthcare System

Pembroke: Pembroke Regional Hospital (PRH)
Affiliated with: Champlain Local Health Integration Network
Former Name: Pembroke General Hospital
705 MacKay St., Pembroke, ON K8A 1G8
Tel: 613-732-2811 *Fax:* 613-732-9986
pr@prh.email
www.pemreghos.org
Info Line: 866-996-0991
www.facebook.com/pembrokeregionalhospital; twitter.com/PRHospital; www.youtube.com/user/pembrokeregionalhosp
Number of Beds: 138 beds
Population Served: 55000 *Number of Employees:* 750
Note: Programs & services include: acute mental health; ambulatory clinics; clinical ethics; community mental health; diabetes education & nutrition; diagnostic imaging; dialysis; emergency / ICU; infection prevention & control; laboratory; maternal & child care; medical; rehabilitation (inpatient & outpatient); respiratory therapy; social work; spiritual care; & surgery.
Pierre Noel, President & CEO
pierre.noel@prh.email
Dr. Tom Hurley, Chief of Staff
thomas.hurley@prh.email
Francois Lemaire, Chief Nursing Executive & Vice-President, Patient Services - Acute Care
francois.lemaire@prh.email

Penetanguishene: Georgian Bay General Hospital - Penetanguishene Site/Hôpital général de la baie Georgienne
Affiliated with: North Simcoe Muskoka Local Health Integration Network
25 Jeffery St., Penetanguishene, ON L9M 1K6
Tel: 705-526-1300 *Fax:* 705-526-4491
www.gbgh.on.ca
Number of Beds: 105 beds between both sites
Note: Programs & services include: dialysis unit; Georgian Bay Cancer Support Centre; & Hospice Huronia. There is no emergency service at this location.
Gail Hunt, President & CEO
705-526-1300, huntg@gbgh.on.ca
Dr. Vikram Ralhan, Chief of Staff
705-526-1300, ralhanv@gbgh.on.ca
Lucille Perreault, Chief Nursing Executive & Vice-President, Patient Services
705-526-1300, perreaultl@gbgh.on.ca

Perth: Perth & Smiths Falls District Hospital - Perth Site
Also Known As: Great War Memorial Site
33 Drummond St. West, Perth, ON K7H 2K1
Tel: 613-267-1500 *Fax:* 613-264-0365
webinquiry@psfdh.on.ca
www.psfdh.on.ca
www.facebook.com/PSFDH

Number of Beds: 85 beds
Note: Programs & services include: assistive devices program; breast screening centre; clinics (obstetrical, pain, pediatric, respirology, orthopedics, general surgery & internal medicine); day hospital; diagnostic imaging; early language; emergency; general medicine; internal medicine; laboratory; sexual assault support & domestic violence program; oncology / palliative care; orthopedics; pharmacy; rehabilitation program; stroke prevention; & urology.
Dr. Barry Guppy, President & CEO
Dr. Kate Stolee, Chief of Staff

Peterborough: Peterborough Regional Health Centre (PRHC)
Affiliated with: Central East Local Health Integration Network
1 Hospital Dr., Peterborough, ON K9J 7C6
Tel: 705-743-2121 *Fax:* 705-876-5120
TTY: 705-876-5141
info@prhc.on.ca
www.prhc.on.ca
www.facebook.com/prhc1; twitter.com/PRHC1; www.youtube.com/user/PRHChospital; www.linkedin.com/company/prhc
Number of Beds: 494 beds
Population Served: 300000 *Number of Employees:* 2200
Note: Programs & services include: diagnostic imaging; emergency; laboratory; medicine; mental health; nutrition; outpatient; rehabilitation; pharmacy; social work; surgery; & woman & child.
Dr. Peter McLaughlin, President & CEO
Dr. Nancy Martin-Ronson, Chief Nursing Executive & CIO

Petrolia: Charlotte Eleanor Englehart Hospital (CEEH)
Bluewater Health
Affiliated with: Erie St. Clair Local Health Integration Network
Former Name: Charlotte Eleanor Englehart Hospital
450 Blanche St., Petrolia, ON N0N 1R0
Tel: 519-882-4325 *Fax:* 519-882-3711
www.bluewaterhealth.ca
www.facebook.com/bluewaterhealth; twitter.com/bluewaterhealth; www.youtube.com/bluewaterhealth; www.linkedin.com/company/bluewater-health
Year Founded: 1911
Number of Beds: 326 beds (total for both Bluewater sites)
Note: Programs & services include: acute care; ambulatory care; continuing care; diagnostic imaging; emergency; inpatient medicine; laboratory services; & primary care.
Mike Lapaine, President & CEO, Bluewater Health
519-464-4400, mlapaine@bluewaterhealth.ca

Picton: QHC Prince Edward County Memorial Hospital (PECMH)
Quinte Health Care
Affiliated with: South East Local Health Integration Network
PO Box 1900, 403 Main St. East, Picton, ON K0K 2T0
Tel: 613-476-1008 *Fax:* 613-476-8600
www.qhc.on.ca
www.facebook.com/173689537296; twitter.com/QuinteHealth; www.youtube.com/QuinteHealthCare
Year Founded: 1959
Number of Beds: 12 beds
Note: Programs & services include: emergency; endoscopy; hospice; laboratory; outpatient clinics; pharmacy; primary care medical inpatients; Prince Edward Family Health Team; & radiology.
Mary Clare Egberts, President & CEO, Quinte Health Care
Dr. Colin MacPherson, Chief of Staff, Quinte Health Care
Carol Smith Romeril, Chief Nursing Officer & Vice-President, Quinte Health Care

Port Colborne: Port Colborne Site
Niagara Health System / Système de santé de Niagara
Affiliated with: Hamilton Niagara Haldimand Brant Local Health Integration Network
260 Sugarloaf St., Port Colborne, ON L3K 2N7
Tel: 905-378-4647
patientrelations@niagarahealth.on.ca
www.niagarahealth.on.ca
twitter.com/niagarahealth; www.youtube.com/niagarahealthsystem
Year Founded: 1951
Number of Beds: 46 beds inpatient beds for complex continuing care; 35 beds at the New Port Centre for addiction recovery
Note: Programs & services include: addictions services; complex care; diagnostic imaging; laboratory; Ontario Breast Screening Clinic; outpatient clinics; & urgent care.

Jaelynne Sonke, Site Director
905-378-4647, jaelynne.sonke@niagarahealth.on.ca
Patty Welychka, Chief Nursing Officer
905-378-4647, patty.welychka@niagarahealth.on.ca

Port Perry: Lakeridge Health Port Perry
Affiliated with: Central East Local Health Integration Network
Also Known As: Port Perry Hospital
451 Paxton St., Port Perry, ON L9L 1L9
Tel: 905-985-7321
www.lakeridgehealth.on.ca
www.facebook.com/LakeridgeHealth;
twitter.com/lakeridgehealth; www.youtube.com/lakeridgehealth;
www.linkedin.com/company/lakeridge-health
Year Founded: 1946
Number of Employees: 180
Note: Programs & services include: palliative care; ultrasound; ambulatory rehabilitation centres / musculoskeletal physiotherapy clinics; diabetes education; & emergency.

Rainy River: Rainy River Health Centre
Riverside Health Care Facilities Inc.
Affiliated with: North West Local Health Integration Network
115 - 4th St., Rainy River, ON P0W 1L0
Tel: 807-274-3261
riverside@rhcf.on.ca
www.riversidehealthcare.ca

Number of Beds: 24 beds
Note: Programs & services include: emergency; diagnostic imaging; acute care; & long term care.
Tammy McNally, Manager
t.mcnally@rhcf.on.ca

Red Lake: Red Lake Margaret Cochenour Memorial Hospital
Affiliated with: North West Local Health Integration Network
Also Known As: Red Lake Hospital
PO Box 5005, 51 Hwy. 105, Red Lake, ON P0V 2M0
Tel: 807-727-2066 *Fax:* 807-727-2923
www.redlakehospital.ca
Year Founded: 1973
Number of Beds: 18 beds
Note: Services include: emergency; laboratory; nursing; diagnostic imaging; physiotherapy; support services; & Family Health Team.
Sue LeBeau, President & CEO
807-727-3800, ceo4rlh@redlakehospital.ca
Meghan Gilbert, Chief Nursing Executive
Alex McAuley, Chief Financial Officer

Renfrew: Renfrew Victoria Hospital
Affiliated with: Champlain Local Health Integration Network
Also Known As: RVH
499 Raglan St. North, Renfrew, ON K7V 1P6
Tel: 613-432-4851 *Fax:* 613-432-8649
www.renfrewhosp.com
www.facebook.com/renfrewvictoriahospital
Year Founded: 1897
Number of Beds: 55 beds
Number of Employees: 450
Note: Programs & services include: ambulatory; counselling; diagnostic; emergency; inpatient; outreach programs; & rehabilitation. Affiliated with Algonquin College & Cambrian College.
Randy Penney, President & CEO
613-432-4851
Christine Ferguson, Vice-President, Patient Care Services
613-432-4851, Fax: 613-432-8649

Richards Landing: North Shore Health Network - Richards Landing Site
Affiliated with: North East Local Health Integration Network
PO Box 188, 1180 Richards St., Richards Landing, ON P0R 1J0
Tel: 705-246-2570 *Fax:* 705-246-2569
www.nshn.care
Note: Services include emergency & diagnostics.
Ralph Barker, Chief Executive Officer
rbarker@nshn.care
Connie Lee, Chief Nursing Officer & Director, Clinical Services
Dr. Lenka Snajdrova, Chief of Staff

Richmond Hill: Mackenzie Richmond Hill Hospital
Mackenzie Health
Affiliated with: Central Local Health Integration Network
Former Name: York Central Hospital
10 Trench St., Richmond Hill, ON L4C 4Z3
Tel: 905-883-1212 *Fax:* 905-883-2455
www.mackenziehealth.ca
www.facebook.com/MackenzieHealth;
twitter.com/mackenziehealth;
www.youtube.com/user/MackenzieHealthVideo;
www.linkedin.com/company/mackenzie-health
Number of Beds: 241 acute care beds; 168 long-term care beds; 84 complex continuing care beds; 22 integrated stroke beds (all Mackenzie Health sites)
Number of Employees: 2641
Note: Has 465 physicians on staff. Programs & Services: stroke centre; kidney disease program; domestic abuse and sexual assault care centre; brain injury.
Altaf Stationwala, President & CEO, Mackenzie Health
Dr. Steven Jackson, Chief of Staff & Vice-President, Mackenzie Health
Mary-Agnes Wilson, Chief of Operating Officer & Chief Nursing Executive, Mackenzie Health

Sarnia: Bluewater Health
Affiliated with: Erie St. Clair Local Health Integration Network
Former Name: Charlotte Eleanor Englehart Hospital; Sarnia General Hospital; St. Joseph's Health
Norman Site, 89 Norman St., Sarnia, ON N7T 6S3
Tel: 519-464-4400 *Fax:* 519-464-4407
www.bluewaterhealth.ca
www.facebook.com/bluewaterhealth;
www.youtube.com/bluewaterhealth
Year Founded: 2002
Number of Beds: 326 beds (total for both Bluewater sites)
Number of Employees: 2500
Note: Programs & services include: ambulatory care; bone density; Cancer Care Assessment & Treatment Centre; cancer clinic; cardiology; communication disorders; CT scan; day hospital; day surgery; diabetes & clinical nutrition; diagnostic imaging; dialysis; district stroke centre; eating disorders; emergency; endoscopy; infection prevention & control; inpatient medicine, rehabilitation, & surgery; intensive care; laboratory; mammography; maternal / infant / child; mental health & addiction; MRI; nuclear medicine; nutrition & food services; occupational therapy; outpatient rehabilitation; palliative care; Pat Mailloux Eye Centre; physiotherapy; prostate cancer clinic; respiratory therapy; rural health; sexual / domestic assault treatment centre; social work; spiritual care; surgery; Telemedicine; ultrasound; withdrawal management; & x-ray.
Mike Lapaine, President & CEO
519-464-4400, mlapaine@bluewaterhealth.ca
Dr. Michel Haddad, Chief of Staff
519-464-4400, mhaddad@bluewaterhealth.ca
Shannon Landry, Chief Nursing Executive
519-464-4400, slandry@bluewaterhealth.ca
Julia Oosterman, Chief, Communications & Public Affairs
519-464-4400, joosterman@bluewaterhealth.ca
Samer Abou-Sweid, Vice-President, Operations
519-464-4400, sabousweid@bluewaterhealth.ca
Laurie Zimmer, Vice-President, Operations
519-464-4400, lzimmer@bluewaterhealth.ca

Sault Ste Marie: Sault Area Hospital (SAH)
Affiliated with: North East Local Health Integration Network
750 Great Northern Rd., Sault Ste Marie, ON P6B 0A8
Tel: 705-759-3434 *Fax:* 705-541-7810
publicaffairs@sah.on.ca
www.sah.on.ca
www.facebook.com/SaultAreaHospital;
twitter.com/SaultAreaHosp
Number of Beds: 293 beds
Population Served: 115000 *Number of Employees:* 1700
Note: Programs & services include: emergency & critical care; medicine; surgery; obstetrics, maternity & pediatrics; mental health & addiction; complex continuing care; & rehabilitation.
Wendy Hansson, President & CEO
Dr. Silvana Spadafora, Chief of Staff
Sue Roger, Interim Chief Nursing Officer & Vice-President, Clinical Operations

Seaforth: Seaforth Community Hospital
Huron Perth Healthcare Alliance
Affiliated with: South West Local Health Integration Network
24 Centennial Dr., Seaforth, ON N0K 1W0
Tel: 519-527-1650 *Fax:* 519-527-8414
Toll-Free: 888-275-1102
www.hpha.ca
Year Founded: 1965
Number of Beds: 20 beds
Note: Programs & services include: adult speech therapy services; ambulatory clinics; community stroke rehabilitation team; complex continuing care; emergency; imaging; Huron Perth Diabetes Education Program; laboratory; medicine; occupational therapy; physiotherapy; & social work.
Andrew Williams, President & CEO, HPHA
519-272-8202, andrew.williams@hpha.ca
Dr. Kevin Lefebvre, Interim Chief of Staff, HPHA
dr.kevin.lefebvre@hpha.ca
Anne Campbell, Vice-President & Chief Nursing Executive, HPHA
519-272-8210, anne.campbell@hpha.ca

Simcoe: Norfolk General Hospital
Affiliated with: Hamilton Niagara Haldimand Brant Local Health Integration Network
365 West St., Simcoe, ON N3Y 1T7
Tel: 519-426-0130 *Fax:* 519-429-6998
www.ngh.on.ca
www.facebook.com/NGHSimcoe; twitter.com/NorfolkGeneralH
Number of Beds: 106 beds (including 45 chronic beds)
Note: Programs & services include: breast screening; complex care; continence care; detox (Holmes House); diabetes; diagnostic imaging; emergency; ICU; infection control; laboratory; obesity & metabolic surgery; obstetrics; palliative care; rehabilitation; respiratory; social work; stroke clinic; surgery; & surgical day care & endoscopy.
Kelly Isfan, President & CEO
519-426-0130, Fax: 519-429-6998
Dr. Mohammad Amir Sheik-Yousouf, Chief of Staff

Sioux Lookout: Sioux Lookout Meno Ya Win Health Centre (SLMHC)
Affiliated with: North West Local Health Integration Network
PO Box 909, 1 Meno Ya Win Way, Sioux Lookout, ON P8T 1B4
Tel: 807-737-3030
info@slmhc.on.ca
www.slmhc.on.ca
Number of Beds: 60 acute care beds; 20 long-term care beds
Note: Primary health care services including a broad range of basic & some specialist hospital services, specialized community based programs & services responding to population health needs (withdrawal management, suicide, TB, etc.), long term care, & integrated traditional & modern medicine. Serves Nishnawbe-Aski communities north of Sioux Lookout, the Treaty #3 community of Lac Seul First Nation, as well as residents of Hudson, Pickle Lake & Savant Lake.
Heather Lee, President & CEO
Dr. Barbara Russell-Mahoney, Chief of Staff
Dean Osmond, Chief Operating Officer & Executive Vice-President

Smiths Falls: Perth & Smiths Falls District Hospital - Smiths Falls Site
Affiliated with: South East Local Health Integration Network
60 Cornelia St. West, Smiths Falls, ON K7A 2H9
Tel: 613-283-2330 *Fax:* 613-283-8990
webinquiry@psfdh.on.ca
www.psfdh.on.ca
Year Founded: 1995
Number of Beds: 85 beds
Population Served: 44000
Note: Programs & services include: assistive devices program; clinics; dialysis; diagnostic imaging; emergency; general medicine; general surgery; internal medicine; laboratory; obstetrics / gynaecology; oncology / palliative care; orthopedics; pharmacy; sexual assault support & domestic violence program; & urology.
Barry Guppy, President & CEO
613-283-2330, bmcfarlane@psfdh.on.ca
Dr. Kate Stolee, Chief of Staff

Smooth Rock Falls: Hôpital de Smooth Rock Falls Hospital (HSRFH)
Affiliated with: North East Local Health Integration Network
Also Known As: SRF Hospital
107 Kelly Rd., 219, Smooth Rock Falls, ON P0L 2B0
Tel: 705-338-2781 *Fax:* 705-338-4410
info@srfhosp.ca
www.srfhosp.ca
Number of Beds: 16 acute care beds; 23 long term care beds
Number of Employees: 85
Note: Programs & services include: acute care; long term care; emergency services; laboratory; physiotherapy; & diagnostic imaging.
Samantha Hiebert, Chief Executive Officer
705-338-3212, shiebert@srfhosp.ca
Maryse Gauvin, Chief Financial Officer
705-372-2906, gauvinm@ndh.on.ca
Eliane Labonte-Bernier, Chief Nursing Officer
705-338-3213, ebernier@srfhosp.ca

Southampton: **Southampton Hospital**
Grey Bruce Health Services
Affiliated with: South West Local Health Integration Network
340 High St., Southampton, ON N0H 2L0
Tel: 519-797-3230
web@gbhs.on.ca
www.gbhs.on.ca
twitter.com/greybrucehealth
Number of Beds: 16 acute care beds
Note: Programs & services include: acute care; ambulatory care; Diabetes Grey Bruce; diagnostic imaging; emergency; laboratory; physiotherapy; spiritual care; & surgery.
Gary Sims, President & CEO, Grey Bruce Health Services
519-376-2121,

St. Catharines: **St. Catharines General Site**
Niagara Health System / Système de santé de Niagara
Affiliated with: Hamilton Niagara Haldimand Brant Local Health Integration Network
1200 Fourth Ave., St. Catharines, ON L2S 0A9
Tel: 905-378-4647
patientrelations@niagarahealth.on.ca
www.niagarahealth.on.ca
twitter.com/niagarahealth;
www.youtube.com/niagarahealthsystem
Year Founded: 1865
Number of Beds: 375 beds
Note: Programs & services include: cardiology; children's health; critical care; diagnostic imaging; emergency & urgent care; kidney care; laboratory; medicine; mental health & addictions; Ontario Breast Screening Clinic; outpatient services; pharmacy; surgery; Walker Family Cancer Centre; women's & babies health.
Jill Randall, Site Director
905-378-4647, jill.randall@niagarahealth.on.ca
Heather Paterson, Chief Nursing Officer
905-378-4647, heather.paterson@niagarahealth.on.ca

St. Marys: **St. Marys Memorial Hospital**
Huron Perth Healthcare Alliance
Affiliated with: South West Local Health Integration Network
267 Queen St. West, St. Marys, ON N4X 1B6
Tel: 519-284-1332 *Fax:* 519-284-8324
Toll-Free: 888-275-1102
administration@hpha.ca
www.hpha.ca
Year Founded: 1950
Number of Beds: 20 beds
Note: Programs & services include: ambulatory clinics; complex continuing care; emergency; Huron Perth Diabetes Education Program; laboratory; medicine unit; occupational therapy; physiotherapy; social work; & spiritual care.
Andrew Williams, President & CEO, HPHA
519-272-8202, andrew.williams@hpha.ca
Dr. Kevin Lefebvre, Interim Chief of Staff, HPHA
dr.kevin.lefebvre@hpha.ca
Mary Cardinal, Vice-President & Chief Quality Executive, HPHA
519-272-8206, mary.cardinal@hpha.ca

St. Thomas: **St. Thomas-Elgin General Hospital**
Affiliated with: South West Local Health Integration Network
189 Elm St., St. Thomas, ON N5R 5C4
Tel: 519-631-2030
TTY: 519-631-7789
publicrelations@stegh.on.ca
www.stegh.on.ca
www.facebook.com/St.ThomasElginGeneralHospital;
twitter.com/stegh_cares
Year Founded: 1954
Number of Beds: 157 beds
Number of Employees: 860
Note: Programs & services include: acute medical unit; cardiac intensive care; clinical nutrition; continuing care; diagnostic imaging; education programs; emergency; laboratory; mental health care; pastoral care; surgery; & women & children's program.
Robert Biron, President & CEO
Karen Davies, Chief Nursing Executive
Mary Stewart, Vice-President

Stratford: **Stratford General Hospital**
Huron Perth Healthcare Alliance
Affiliated with: South West Local Health Integration Network
46 General Hospital Dr., Stratford, ON N5A 2Y6
Tel: 519-272-8210 *Fax:* 519-271-7137
Toll-Free: 888-275-1102
administration@hpha.ca
www.hpha.ca
Year Founded: 1896
Number of Beds: 118 beds
Note: Programs & services include: ambulatory clinics; cardio respiratory; chemotherapy; complex continuing care & rehabilitation; critical care (ICU & telemetry); dialysis; emergency; Huron Perth Diabetes Education Program; Huron Perth District Stroke Centre; imaging; inpatient mental health services; laboratory services; maternal child unit; medicine; social work; spiritual care; & surgery.
Andrew Williams, President & CEO, HPHA
519-272-8202, andrew.williams@hpha.ca
Dr. Kevin Lefebvre, Interim Chief of Staff, HPHA
dr.kevin.lefebvre@hpha.ca
Ken Haworth, Vice-President & Chief Financial Executive, HPHA
519-272-8210, ken.haworth@hpha.ca

Strathroy: **Strathroy Middlesex General Hospital**
Middlesex Hospital Alliance
Affiliated with: South West Local Health Integration Network
395 Carrie St., Strathroy, ON N7G 3J4
Tel: 519-245-5295 *Fax:* 519-245-0366
admin@mha.tvh.ca
www.mhalliance.on.ca
Year Founded: 1914
Number of Beds: 54 beds
Population Served: 35000 *Number of Employees:* 300
Note: Programs & services include: ambulatory care clinics; diabetes education program; diagnostic imaging; emergency; intensive care; medical inpatient unit; medical surgical inpatient unit; obstetrics inpatient unit; occupational therapy; physiotherapy; speech-language pathology; & surgery.
Todd Stepanuik, President & CEO, Middlesex Hospital Alliance
519-245-5295

Sturgeon Falls: **The West Nipissing General Hospital (WNGH)/L'Hôpital général de Nipissing Ouest**
Affiliated with: North East Local Health Integration Network
725 Coursol Rd., Sturgeon Falls, ON P2B 2Y6
Tel: 705-753-3110 *Fax:* 705-753-0210
administration@wngh.ca
www.wngh.ca
Year Founded: 1977
Number of Beds: 50 acute care beds; 48 intermin long-term beds
Note: Programs & services include: diagnostic & therapeutic; dietitian; emergency; inpatient services; outpatient services; pharmacy; physiotherapy; & Telemedicine.
Cynthia Désormiers, President & Chief Executive Officer
Jo-Ann Labelle, Chief Nursing Officer

Sudbury: **Health Sciences North (HSN)**
Affiliated with: North East Local Health Integration Network
41 Ramsey Lake Rd., Sudbury, ON P3E 5J1
Tel: 705-523-7100 *Toll-Free:* 866-469-0822
communications@hsnsudbury.ca
www.hsnsudbury.ca
www.facebook.com/HSNSudbury; twitter.com/HSN_Sudbury;
www.youtube.com/user/healthsciencesnorth;
www.linkedin.com/company/health-sciences-north
Number of Beds: 462 beds
Number of Employees: 3907
Note: Programs & services include: cancer care; domestic violence & sexual assault treatment; mental health & addiction services; & transitional & rehabilitative care.
Dominic Giroux, President & CEO
Dr. John Fenton, Chief of Staff
Lorraine Carrington, Vice-President & Chief Nursing Executive

Sudbury: **Ramsey Lake Health Centre**
Affiliated with: Health Sciences North
Former Name: Sudbury Regional Hospital - Laurentian Site
41 Ramsey Lake Rd., Sudbury, ON P3E 5J1
Tel: 705-523-7100 *Toll-Free:* 866-469-0822
www.hsnsudbury.ca
Note: Programs & services include critical care, palliative care, emergency care, medical imaging, rehabilitation, & mental health services.
Dominic Giroux, President & CEO, Health Sciences North

Sudbury: **Sudbury Outpatient Centre**
Affiliated with: Health Sciences North
865 Regent St. South, Sudbury, ON P3E 3Y9
Tel: 705-523-7100 *Toll-Free:* 866-469-0822
www.hsnsudbury.ca
Note: Provides the following programs & services: Ontario Breast Screening Program; genetic counselling; nutrition counselling; HAVEN; hemophilia; Regional Bariatric Assessment and Treatment Centre.
Dominic Giroux, President & CEO, Health Sciences North

Terrace Bay: **The McCausland Hospital**
North of Superior Healthcare Group
Affiliated with: North West Local Health Integration Network
PO Box 370, 20B Cartier Rd., Terrace Bay, ON P0T 2W0
Tel: 807-825-3273 *Fax:* 807-825-9623
www.nosh.ca
Year Founded: 1980
Number of Beds: 45 beds
Population Served: 4000
Note: Services include: emergency; cancer care; diabetes program; diagnostic imaging (ECG, Holter monitors, radiology, ultrasound); laboratory; obstetrics & gynecology; physiotherapy; seniors drop-in program; & surgery.
Adam Brown, Chief Executive Officer
807-825-3273
Carol Huard, Chief Nursing Officer

Thessalon: **North Shore Health Network - Thessalon Site**
Affiliated with: North East Local Health Integration Network
135 Dawson St., Thessalon, ON P0R 1L0
Tel: 705-842-2014
www.nshn.care
Number of Beds: 4 acute care beds; 2 short-term observation beds
Note: Programs & services include: diagnostic imaging; emergency; & surgery.
Ralph Barker, Chief Executive Officer
rbarker@nshn.care
Connie Lee, Chief Nursing Officer & Director, Clinical Services
Dr. Lenka Snajdrova, Chief of Staff

Thunder Bay: **St. Joseph's Hospital**
St. Joseph's Care Group
Affiliated with: North West Local Health Integration Network
PO Box 3251, 35 Algoma St. North, Thunder Bay, ON P7B 5G7
Tel: 807-343-2431 *Fax:* 807-343-0144
contact.sjcg@tbh.net
www.sjcg.net
Year Founded: 1884
Number of Beds: 269 beds (across divison)
Note: Programs & services include: ambulatory care clinics; chiropody & foot care; day hospital; general rehabilitation; geriatric assessment & rehabilitative care; hospice / palliative care; orthopedic physiotherapy & occupational therapy;

outpatient neurology rehabilitation; pulmonary rehabilitation; rheumatic disease; & transition.
Tracy Buckler, President & CEO, St. Joseph's Care Group
bucklert@tbh.net

Thunder Bay: Thunder Bay Regional Health Sciences Centre/Centre régional des sciences de la santé de Thunder Bay
Affiliated with: North West Local Health Integration Network
980 Oliver Rd., Thunder Bay, ON P7B 6V4

Tel: 807-684-6000
tbrhsc@tbh.net
www.tbrhsc.net

Year Founded: 2004
Number of Beds: 375 acute care beds
Population Served: 250000 *Number of Employees:* 2800
Note: A comprehensive, multi-disciplinary, acute care facility with services incuding ambulatory care, cardio respiratory services, critical care, diagnostic assessment, diagnostic imaging, emergency, laboratory services, palliative care, prevention & screening, rehabilitation, supportive care, surgery, & Telemedicine. The TBRHSC amalgamates the former Port Arthur & McKellar sites of the Thunder Bay Regional Hospital.
Jean Bartkowiak, President & CEO
Dr. Gordon Porter, Chief of Staff
Dr. Rhonda Crocker Ellacott, Chief Nursing Executive

Tillsonburg: Tillsonburg District Memorial Hospital (TDMH)
Affiliated with: South West Local Health Integration Network
167 Rolph St., Tillsonburg, ON N4G 3Y9

Tel: 519-842-3611 *Fax:* 519-688-1031
info@tdmh.on.ca
www.tillsonburghospital.on.ca

Number of Beds: 45 beds
Note: Programs & services include: ambulatory; complex continuing care; diabetes education; diagnostic & treatment; dialysis; emergency; intensive coronary care; medical/surgical unit; palliative care; rehabilitation; & surgery.
Sandy Jansen, President & CEO
sandy.jansen@tdmh.on.ca
Cheryl Pfaff, Chief Nursing Executive & Vice-President, Clinical Services, Quality & Safety

Timmins: Timmins & District Hospital (TADH)/L'Hôpital de Timmins et du district
Affiliated with: North East Local Health Integration Network
700 Ross Ave. East, Timmins, ON P4N 8P2

Tel: 705-267-2131 *Fax:* 705-267-6311
generalinquiries@tadh.com
www.tadh.com

Year Founded: 1993
Number of Beds: 134 beds
Number of Employees: 850
Note: Programs & services include: cardiopulmonary; complex continuing care; critical care; emergency; maternal child; medical; medical imaging; mental health; nephrology; oncology; palliative care; rehabilitation; sleep centre; surgery; & Telemedicine.
Blaise MacNeil, President & CEO
Dr. Harry Voogjarv, Chief of Staff
Joan Ludwig, Chief Nursing Executive & Vice-President, Clinical Services

Toronto: Etobicoke General Hospital (EGH)
William Osler Health System
Affiliated with: Central West Local Health Integration Network
Also Known As: William Osler Health Centre
101 Humber College Blvd., Toronto, ON M9V 1R8

Tel: 416-494-2120
www.williamoslerhs.ca
www.facebook.com/WilliamOslerHealth; twitter.com/OslerHealth;
www.youtube.com/WilliamOslerTV;
www.linkedin.com/company/william-osler-health-system

Number of Beds: 330 beds
Note: Programs & services include: cancer care; cardiac care; complex continuing care; critical care; diabetes care; diagnostic imaging; emergency; general & internal medicine; joint assessment centre; kidney care; laboratories; mental health & addictions; naturopathic care; palliative care; rehabilitation services; respirology; seniors' care; surgical services; & women's & children's services.
Dr. Frank Martino, Interim President & CEO, William Osler Health System

Toronto: The Hospital for Sick Children
Affiliated with: Toronto Central Local Health Integration Network
Also Known As: SickKids
555 University Ave., Toronto, ON M5G 1X8

Tel: 416-813-1500
www.sickkids.ca
Info Line: 416-813-6621
www.facebook.com/sickkidsfoundation;
twitter.com/SickKidsNews;
www.youtube.com/SickKidsInteractive;
www.linkedin.com/company/the-hospital-for-sick-children

Year Founded: 1875
Number of Beds: 300 beds
Note: Paediatric acute care hospital, with programs & services including: adolescent medicine; allergy; anxiety disorders; audiology; blood & marrow transplant; burns; cancer detection & treatment; cardiology; cleft lip & palate; dental clinic; diabetes clinic; dialysis; eating disorders; emergency; genetic counselling; gynecology; hand clinic; hematology; infectious diseases (including HIV); International Patient Office; Motherisk program; ophthalmology; otolaryngology; pain clinic; psychiatry; psychiatric emergency crisis service; respiratory illnesses; SCAN (Suspected Child Abuse & Neglect) program; sleep disorders; social work; speech language clinic; substance abuse outreach & day treatment; Tay Sachs testing; trauma unit; & Young Families Program (Tots of Teens).
Dr. Ronald Cohn, President & CEO
Dr. Lennox Huang, Chief Medical Officer
Laurie Harrison, Chief Financial Officer
Dr. Sarah Muttitt, Chief Information Officer
Judy Van Clieaf, Chief of Professional Practice & Nursing

Toronto: Humber River Regional Hospital
Affiliated with: Toronto Central Local Health Integration Network
1235 Wilson Ave., Toronto, ON M3M 0B2

Tel: 416-242-1000
www.hrh.ca
www.facebook.com/HRHospital; twitter.com/HRHospital;
www.youtube.com/humberriverhospital;
www.linkedin.com/company/humber-river-hospital

Year Founded: 2015
Number of Beds: 656 beds
Number of Employees: 3300
Note: Programs & services include: acute care; adult day treatment; assessment program; child & adolescent mental health inpatient unit; child & adolescent outpatient services; community treatment program; early intervention in psychosis program; elective inpatient withdrawal management program; general psychiatry unit; geriatric psychiatry outpatient clinic services; geriatric psychiatry outreach team; Humber River Hospital funded clinic; Humber River Rehabilitation Centre; intensive day treatment; internal geriatric psychiatry consultation teams; outpatient services; psychogeriatric outreach & consultation team; & transition child & adolescent program.
Affiliated with the University of Toronto & Queen's University.
Barb Collins, President & CEO
Vacant, Chief of Staff
Peter Bak, Chief Information Officer
Dr. Vanessa Burkoski, Chief Nursing Executive

Toronto: Michael Garron Hospital - Toronto East Health Network
Affiliated with: Toronto Central Local Health Integration Network
Former Name: Toronto East General Hospital
825 Coxwell Ave., Toronto, ON M4C 3E7

Tel: 416-461-8272 *Fax:* 416-469-6106
community@tegh.on.ca
www.tegh.on.ca
Info Line: 416-469-6487
twitter.com/MGHToronto;
www.youtube.com/user/TorontoEastGeneral;
www.linkedin.com/company/toronto-east-general-hospital

Year Founded: 1929
Number of Beds: 515 beds
Population Served: 400000 *Number of Employees:* 2500
Note: Affiliated with the University of Toronto. Programs & services include: acute care; breastfeeding centre for families; complex continuing care; inpatient rehabilitation; alternate level of care; cancer care; cardiology; child development centre; DEC NET (Diabetes Education Community Network of East Toronto); diabetes care; diagnostic imaging; East Toronto postpartum adjustment program; emergency; family health centre; geriatric assessment; hematology; mental health outpatient programs; neonatal care; nephrology; obstetrics; palliative care; pediatrics; prolonged-ventilation weaning centre; psychiatry; respiratory diseases; & surgery.
Sarah Downey, President & CEO
Dr. Ian Fraser, Chief of Staff

Irene Andress, Chief Nursing Executive

Toronto: Mount Sinai Hospital
Affiliated with: Toronto Central Local Health Integration Network
600 University Ave., Toronto, ON M5G 1X5

Tel: 416-596-4200
TTY: 416-586-8275
communicationsandmarketing@mtsinai.on.ca
www.mountsinai.on.ca
www.facebook.com/MountSinaiHospital; twitter.com/MountSinai;
www.youtube.com/user/MountSinaiHospital;
www.linkedin.com/company/mount-sinai-hospital-toronto

Year Founded: 1923
Number of Beds: 442 beds
Number of Employees: 4544
Note: Teaching & research Hospital, affiliated with the University of Toronto. Home to six Centres of Excellence: Frances Bloomberg Centre for Women's & Infants' Health; Christopher Sharp Centre for Surgical Oncology; The Daryl A. Katz Centre for Urgent & Critical Care; The Centre for Inflammatory Bowel Disease; Centre for Musculoskeletal Disease; & The Samuel Lunenfeld Research Institute.
Hospital programs & services include: acute care; Alzheimer's support & training centre; arthritis & autoimmune diseases; asthma; audiology; cancer (breast, colon & sarcoma); cardiology; Chinese outreach program; clinic for HIV related concerns; day surgery; dental clinic; diabetes education; digestive diseases; eye clinic; family medicine centre; geriatric psychiatry; nutrition counselling; Ontario Breast Screening Program; orthopedics; pain management; palliative care; psychiatric unit; rehabilitation; speech disorders; sports medicine; urology; & women's & infants' health programs.
Dr. Gary Newton, President & CEO
Jane Merkley, Executive Vice-President, Chief Nurse Executive, & COO

Toronto: North York General Hospital - Branson Ambulatory Care Centre
Affiliated with: Toronto Central Local Health Integration Network
555 Finch Ave. West, Toronto, ON M2R 1N5

Tel: 416-633-9420
www.nygh.on.ca
www.facebook.com/NorthYorkGeneralHospital;
twitter.com/NYGH_News; www.youtube.com/user/NYGHNews

Number of Beds: 431 acute beds (all sites); 192 long-term care beds (all sites)
Note: Programs & services include: adolescent eating disorder program; cataract high volume centre; diabetes education centre; Gale & Graham Wright Prostate Centre; laboratory medicine; medical imaging; mental health; pharmacy.
Dr. Joshua Tepper, President & CEO
Dr. Stan Feinberg, Chief of Staff
Susan Woollard, Vice-President & Chief Nursing Executive, Clinical Services

Toronto: North York General Hospital - General Site
Affiliated with: Toronto Central Local Health Integration Network
4001 Leslie St., Toronto, ON M2K 1E1

Tel: 416-756-6000
www.nygh.on.ca
www.facebook.com/NorthYorkGeneralHospital;
twitter.com/NYGH_News; www.youtube.com/user/NYGHNews

Number of Beds: 410 acute beds (all sites); 192 long-term care beds (all sites)
Note: Community teaching hospital affiliated with the University of Toronto. Programs & services include: cancer care; child & teen; diagnostic imaging; emergency & urgent care; genetics; family & community medicine; laboratory; maternal newborn care; medicine & elder care; mental health; pharmacy; & surgery.
Dr. Joshua Tepper, President & CEO
Dr. Stan Feinberg, Chief of Staff
Susan Woollard, Vice-President & Chief Nursing Executive, Clinical Services

Toronto: Princess Margaret Cancer Centre
University Health Network
Affiliated with: Toronto Central Local Health Integration Network
Former Name: Princess Margaret Hospital
Also Known As: The Princess Margaret
610 University Ave., Toronto, ON M5G 2M9

Tel: 416-946-2000
www.uhn.ca/PrincessMargaret
www.facebook.com/UniversityHealthNetwork; twitter.com/UHN;
www.youtube.com/UHNToronto;
www.linkedin.com/company/university-health-network

Year Founded: 1952
Number of Beds: 202 inpatient beds

Number of Employees: 3000
Specialties: Cancer research
Note: A teaching hospital of the University of Toronto, & a top cancer treatment & research centre. Programs & services include: allied health; dental oncology, ocular & maxillofacial prosthetics; laboratory medicine; medical imaging; medical oncology & hematology; oncology nursing; patient education & survivorship; pharmacy; psychosocial oncology & palliative care; radiation medicine; & surgical oncology. The Ontario Institute for Cancer Research comprises the research wing of the hospital.

Toronto: Queensway Health Centre
Trillium Health Partners
Affiliated with: Mississauga Halton Local Health Integration Network
150 Sherway Dr., Toronto, ON M9C 1A5

Tel: 416-259-6671
patient.relationsmh@trilliumhealthpartners.ca
trilliumhealthpartners.ca
twitter.com/Trillium_Health;
www.youtube.com/user/TrilliumHealth;
www.linkedin.com/company/2949012

Year Founded: 1956
Note: An ambulatory care facility with services including urgent care centre, day surgery, diabetes management centre, cardiac wellness & rehabilitation, Kingsway Financial Spine Centre, & The Betty Wallace Women's Health Centre (focusing on osteoporosis & breast disease). There is no emergency centre here; it is located at the Mississauga branch.
Vacant, President & CEO, Trillium Health Partners
Dr. Dante Morra, Chief of Staff, Trillium Health Partners
Kathryn Haywood-Murray, Chief Nursing Executive & Senior Vice-President, Patient Care Services, Trillium Health Partners

Toronto: St. Joseph's Health Centre Toronto
Unity Health Toronto
Affiliated with: Toronto Central Local Health Integration Network
30 The Queensway, Toronto, ON M6R 1B5

Tel: 416-530-6000
TTY: 416-530-6820
stjoestoronto.ca
www.facebook.com/UnityHealthToronto;
twitter.com/UnityHealthTO;
www.youtube.com/user/StJoesHealthCentre

Year Founded: 1921
Number of Beds: 426 beds
Number of Employees: 2600
Note: Programs & services include: acute care; cardiology; cancer care; diabetes; diagnostic imaging; dialysis; ear, nose & throat (ENT); elderly community health services; family medicine centre; geriatric emergency & outpatient services; gynecology; Lifeline; mental health programs; obstetrics; ophthalmology; orthopedics; pediatrics; pre & postnatal care; psychiatric unit; respiratory care; sleep lab; speech disorders; surgery; & urology. This teaching hospital was founded by the Sisters of St. Joseph. Has 488 physicians on staff.
Dr. Tim Rutledge, President & CEO
Sonya Canzian, Executive Vice-President & Chief Nursing Officer, Clinical Programs

Toronto: St. Michael's Hospital
Unity Health Toronto
Affiliated with: Toronto Central Local Health Integration Network
30 Bond St., Toronto, ON M5B 1W8

Tel: 416-360-4000
www.stmichaelshospital.com
www.facebook.com/UnityHealthToronto;
twitter.com/UnityHealthTO;
www.youtube.com/user/StMichaelsHospital;
www.linkedin.com/company/st.-michael's-hospital

Number of Beds: 455 inpatient beds
Number of Employees: 6140
Note: Catholic hospital with a focus on teaching & research, affiliated with the University of Toronto. Programs & services include: acute care; addiction; arthritis; breast centre; cancer care; cardiology; chiropody; critical care; diabetes clinic; dialysis; fracture clinic; general internal medicine; geriatrics; gynecology; hemophilia; HIV / AIDS; inner city health program; inpatient oncology; mental health; mobility; multiple sclerosis; neo-natal intensive care; neurosurgery; obstetrics; Ontario Breast Screening Program; ophthalmology; osteoporosis; outpatient services; palliative care; pediatrics; services for seniors; stroke centre; respirology; sleep laboratory; specialized complex care; trauma centre; urology; & vascular disease.
Dr. Tim Rutledge, President & CEO
Sonya Canzian, Executive Vice-President & Chief Nursing Officer, Clinical Programs

Toronto: Scarborough Health Network - Birchmount Hospital
Scarborough Health Network
Affiliated with: Central East Local Health Integration Network
Former Name: Scarborough Grace Hospital
3030 Birchmount Rd., Toronto, ON M1W 3W3

Tel: 416-495-2400
www.shn.ca
www.facebook.com/SHNcares; twitter.com/SHNcares;
www.linkedin.com/company/scarborough-health-network

Number of Beds: 213 beds
Number of Employees: 1106
Note: A health facility with emphasis on emergency outpatient psychiatric concerns, notably its Regional Crisis Program, an emergency response team to acute psychiatric crises. Affiliated with the University of Toronto.
Elizabeth Buller, President & CEO, Scarborough & Rouge Hospital
Dr. Dick Zoutman, Chief of Staff, Scarborough & Rouge Hospital

Toronto: Scarborough Health Network - Centenary Hospital
Scarborough Health Network
Affiliated with: Central East Local Health Integration Network
Former Name: Rouge Valley Centenary
Also Known As: Centenary Hospital
2867 Ellesmere Rd., Toronto, ON M1E 4B9

Tel: 416-284-8131
www.shn.ca
www.facebook.com/SHNcares; twitter.com/SHNcares;
www.linkedin.com/company/scarborough-health-network

Year Founded: 1967
Number of Beds: 318 beds
Number of Employees: 1956
Note: Programs & services include: acute care; cancer care; cardiac care; continuing care; critical care; diabetes education; diagnostic imaging; emergency; geriatric assessment; maternal newborn care; mental health; paediatrics; palliative care; respiratory therapy; & surgical care.
Elizabeth Buller, President & CEO, Scarborough & Rouge Hospital
Dr. Dick Zoutman, Chief of Staff, Scarborough & Rouge Hospital
David Graham, Chief Administrative Officer, Scarborough & Rouge Hospital
Linda Calhoun, Chief Nursing Executive, Scarborough & Rouge Hospital

Toronto: Scarborough Health Network - General Campus
Scarborough Health Network
Affiliated with: Central East Local Health Integration Network
Also Known As: Scarborough General Hospital
3050 Lawrence Ave. East, Toronto, ON M1P 2V5

Tel: 416-438-2911
www.shn.ca
www.facebook.com/SHNcares; twitter.com/SHNcares;
www.linkedin.com/company/scarborough-health-network

Year Founded: 1956
Number of Beds: 297 beds
Number of Employees: 2067
Note: Programs & services include: adult mental health; diabetes education; Dorif Lawrence Breast Clinic; emergency; family & community medicine; maternal / newborn; medical; Ontario Breast Screening Program; outpatient services; paediatrics; prenatal classes; & surgery. Affiliated with the University of Toronto.
Elizabeth Buller, President & CEO

Toronto: Sunnybrook Health Sciences Centre - Bayview Campus
Affiliated with: Toronto Central Local Health Integration Network
2075 Bayview Ave., Toronto, ON M4N 3M5

Tel: 416-480-6100
www.sunnybrook.ca
www.facebook.com/SunnybrookHSC; twitter.com/Sunnybrook;
www.youtube.com/SunnybrookMedia;
www.linkedin.com/company/sunnybrook-health-sciences-centre

Year Founded: 1948
Number of Beds: 1,355 beds (including bassinet beds)
Note: A comprehensive health facility with a focus on cancer care (Odette Cancer Centre), cardiac care (Schulich Heart Centre), musculoskeletal care (Holland Musculoskeletal Program), brain science program (stroke, dementias, mood disorders), women's health, infertility, perinatal care, pediatrics, emergency services, trauma & critical care, veterans' care & residence, research & education.
Dr. Andy Smith, President & CEO

Toronto: Toronto General Hospital (TGH)
University Health Network
Affiliated with: Toronto Central Local Health Integration Network
200 Elizabeth St., Toronto, ON M5G 2C4

Tel: 416-340-3111
www.uhn.ca/corporate/AboutUHN/OurHospitals/TGH
www.facebook.com/UniversityHealthNetwork; twitter.com/UHN;
www.youtube.com/UHNToronto;
www.linkedin.com/company/university-health-network

Year Founded: 1829
Number of Beds: 433 beds
Note: A comprehensive health care & teaching facility, its specialties include cardiac care (Peter Munk Cardiac Centre), transplantation, kidney diseases & care, tropical disease, eating disorders, nephrology, psychiatry, HIV / AIDS care, & telemedicine. It is home to the MaRS Discovery District, a not-for-profit research corporation with funding from both private & public sectors. Affiliated with the University of Toronto.

Toronto: Toronto Western Hospital
University Health Network
Affiliated with: Toronto Central Local Health Integration Network
399 Bathurst St., Toronto, ON M5T 2S8

Tel: 416-603-2581
www.uhn.ca/corporate/AboutUHN/OurHospitals/TWH
www.facebook.com/UniversityHealthNetwork; twitter.com/UHN;
www.youtube.com/UHNToronto;
www.linkedin.com/company/university-health-network

Year Founded: 1905
Number of Beds: 281 beds
Note: Primary areas of focus are neural & sensory sciences, community & population health & musculoskeletal health & arthritis. Programs & services include: acquired brain injury clinic; aneurysm clinic; artists health centre; asthma; cardiac & pulmonary rehab; diabetes education; eye clinic; memory clinic; mental health & addictions; movement disorders clinic; sleep clinic; stroke clinic; Tourette's Clinic; & tuberculosis clinic. Affiliated with the University of Toronto.

Toronto: University Health Network (UHN)
Affiliated with: Toronto Central Local Health Integration Network
R. Fraser Elliot Building, 1st Fl., 190 Elizabeth St., Toronto, ON M5G 2C4

Tel: 416-340-4800
www.uhn.ca
www.facebook.com/UniversityHealthNetwork; twitter.com/UHN;
www.youtube.com/UHNToronto;
www.linkedin.com/company/university-health-network

Number of Beds: 1,272 beds (total, all sites)
Number of Employees: 14986
Note: Comprised of Princess Margaret Hospital, Toronto General Hospital, Toronto Western Hospital & Toronto Rehab, UHN is a comprehensive health care, research & teaching facility with fields of focus including cancer care, cardiac care, musculoskeletal health & arthritis, neuroscience, ophthalmology, surgical & critical care, transplantation. The network is affiliated with the University of Toronto, Faculty of Medicine.
Dr. Kevin Smith, President & CEO
Brian Hodges, Executive Vice-President & Chief Medical Officer, Education
Shaf Keshavjee, Surgeon-in-Chief

Toronto: Women's College Hospital (WCH)
Affiliated with: Toronto Central Local Health Integration Network
76 Grenville St., Toronto, ON M5S 1B2

Tel: 416-323-6400
info@wchospital.ca
www.womenscollegehospital.ca
www.facebook.com/wchospital; twitter.com/wchospital;
www.youtube.com/wchospital;
www.linkedin.com/company/women%27s-college-hospital

Year Founded: 1928
Note: Programs & services include: asthma; breastfeeding support; breast screening; cardiac rehabilitation for women; child & family psychiatry; chronic pain; complex care; Crossroads Refugee Health Clinic; day surgery; diabetes education (TRIDEC); environmental health; gynecology; headache clinic; infertility; mental health programs; osteoporosis; prenatal & postnatal support; Ricky Kanee Schacter Dermatology Centre; sexual assault & domestic violence care centre; WISE program; & Women's Health Matters (online resource). The hospital was renovated in 2016, offering updated access to diagnostic imaging services & additional operating rooms.
Heather McPherson, President & CEO
Dr. Danielle Martin, Vice-President, Medical Affairs & Health System Solutions

Trenton: QHC Trenton Memorial Hospital
Quinte Health Care
Affiliated with: South East Local Health Integration Network
242 King St., Trenton, ON K8V 5S6
Tel: 613-392-2540 *Fax:* 613-392-3749
www.qhc.on.ca
www.facebook.com/173689537296; twitter.com/QuinteHealth;
www.youtube.com/QuinteHealthCare
Year Founded: 1951
Number of Beds: 26 beds
Note: Programs & services include: cardiology; clinical nutrition; diabetes education; emergency services; laboratory; medical services; Nursing Home Ready Unit; outpatient clinics; pharmacy; psychiatry / mental health crisis clinic; radiology / diagnostic services; surgery; & symptom management / palliative care.
Mary Clare Egberts, President & CEO, Quinte Health Care
Dr. Colin MacPherson, Chief of Staff, Quinte Health Care
Carol Smith Romeril, Chief Nursing Officer & Vice-President, Quinte Health Care

Uxbridge: Markham Stouffville Hospital - Uxbridge Site (MSH)
Affiliated with: Central Local Health Integration Network
Also Known As: Uxbridge Cottage Hospital
PO Box 5003, 4 Campbell Dr., Uxbridge, ON L9P 1S4
Tel: 905-852-9771
myhospital@msh.on.ca
www.msh.on.ca
www.facebook.com/MarkhamStouffvilleHospital;
twitter.com/MSHospital; www.youtube.com/MSHospital
Year Founded: 1959
Number of Beds: 20 beds
Note: Programs & services include: day surgery; diagnostic imaging; emergency; laboratory; & physiotherapy.
Jo-anne Marr Marr, President & CEO
Dr. Caroline Green, Chief of Staff

Walkerton: South Bruce Grey Health Centre - Walkerton Site
South Bruce Grey Health Centre
Affiliated with: South West Local Health Integration Network
Former Name: County of Bruce General Hospital
PO Box 1300, 21 McGivern St. West, Walkerton, ON N0G 2V0
Tel: 519-881-1220 *Fax:* 519-881-0452
info@sbghc.on.ca
www.sbghc.on.ca
www.facebook.com/sbghc; twitter.com/SBG_HC
Year Founded: 1900
Number of Beds: 15 acute care beds; 6 obstetrical beds
Note: Programs & services include: cardio-respiratory; family birthing centre; diagnostic imaging; emergency department; emergency; inpatient medical beds; laboratory; nutrition services; outpatient clinics; palliative care; & pastoral care.
Michael Barrett, President & CEO, SBGHC
519-379-2400, mbarrett@sbghc.on.ca
Angela Stanley, Chief Nursing Officer & Vice-President, SBGHC
519-370-2400, astanley@sbghc.on.ca

Wallaceburg: Chatham-Kent Health Alliance - Wallaceburg Site (CKHA)
Affiliated with: Erie St. Clair Local Health Integration Network
325 Margaret Ave., Wallaceburg, ON N8A 2A7
Tel: 519-352-6400
www.ckha.on.ca
www.facebook.com/ckhamedia; twitter.com/ckhamedia;
www.youtube.com/ckhamedia
Year Founded: 1952
Number of Beds: 200+ beds (total for both CKHA sites)
Note: Programs & services include: ambulatory care; diagnostic imaging; emergency; inpatient medicine unit; laboratory; rehabilitation therapy; & respiratory services.
Lori Marshall, President & CEO, CKHA
519-352-6400, lmarshall@ckha.on.ca

Wawa: Lady Dunn Health Centre
PO Box 179, 17 Government Rd., Wawa, ON P0S 1K0
Tel: 705-856-2335 *Fax:* 705-856-7533
Toll-Free: 866-832-3321
www.ldhc.com
Number of Beds: 28 beds
Population Served: 4300
Note: Programs & services include: 24 hour emergency; acute care; diagnostic; long-term care; obstetrics; oncology; & physiotherapy.

Kadean Ogilvie-Pinter, Chief Executive Officer & Director, Patient Care Services
kogilvie@ldhc.com
Gigi Dumont, Chief Financial Officer
gdumont@ldhc.com
Dr. Anjali Oberai, Chief of Staff

Welland: Welland Hospital Site
Niagara Health System / Système de santé de Niagara
Affiliated with: Hamilton Niagara Haldimand Brant Local Health Integration Network
65 - 3rd St., Welland, ON L3B 4W6
Tel: 905-378-4647
patientrelations@niagarahealth.on.ca
www.niagarahealth.on.ca
twitter.com/niagarahealth;
www.youtube.com/niagarahealthsystem
Year Founded: 1908
Number of Beds: 155 beds (including 15 nephrology beds)
Note: Programs & services include: ambulatory clinics; complex care; critical care; diabetes education; diagnostic imaging; emergency; laboratory; long-term care; medicine; Ontario Breast Screening Clinic; ophthalmology; satellite dialysis centre; & surgery.
Jaelynne Sonke, Site Director
905-378-4647, jaelynne.sonke@niagarahealth.on.ca
Patty Welychka, Chief Nursing Officer
905-378-4647, patty.welychka@niagarahealth.on.ca
Debbie Smith, Director, Extended Care Unit
905-378-4647, dsmith@niagarahealth.on.ca

Whitby: Lakeridge Health Whitby
Affiliated with: Central East Local Health Integration Network
Also Known As: Whitby Hospital
300 Gordon St., Whitby, ON L1N 2T5
Tel: 905-668-6831
www.lakeridgehealth.on.ca
www.facebook.com/LakeridgeHealth;
twitter.com/lakeridgehealth; www.youtube.com/lakeridgehealth
Number of Beds: 42+ beds
Note: Programs & services include: ambulatory rehabilitation centres / musculoskeletal physiotherapy clinics; diabetes education; & respiratory rehabilitation.
Matthew Anderson, President & CEO, Lakeridge Health
905-576-8711
Dr. Tony Stone, Chief of Staff, Lakeridge Health
905-576-8711
Leslie Motz, Chief Nursing Executive, Lakeridge Health
905-576-8711

Wiarton: Wiarton Hospital
Grey Bruce Health Services
Affiliated with: South West Local Health Integration Network
369 Mary St., Wiarton, ON N0H 2T0
Tel: 519-534-1260 *Fax:* 519-534-5159
web@gbhs.on.ca
www.gbhs.on.ca
twitter.com/greybrucehealth
Number of Beds: 22 beds
Note: Programs & services include: acute care; ambulatory care; complex continuing care; Diabetes Grey Bruce; diagnostic imaging; emergency; laboratory; North Bruce Community Mental Health Team; physiotherapy; spiritual care; & surgery.
Gary Sims, President & CEO, Grey Bruce Health Services
519-376-2121

Winchester: Winchester District Memorial Hospital (WDMH)
Affiliated with: Champlain Local Health Integration Network
566 Louise St., Winchester, ON K0C 2K0
Tel: 613-774-2420 *Fax:* 613-774-0453
info@wdmh.on.ca
www.wdmh.on.ca
www.facebook.com/WinchesterDistrictMemorialHospital;
twitter.com/WDMHPride;
www.linkedin.com/company/winchester-district-memorial-hospita l
Number of Beds: 55 beds
Number of Employees: 320
Note: Programs & services include: clinics; complex continuing care; diabetes education; diagnostic imaging; emergency; enhanced care; inpatient laboratory; maternity; medical day care; medical / surgical; occupational therapy; Ontario breast screening program; physiotherapy; Robillard Hearing Centre; sleep lab; & surgical day care. Has 135 physicians, dentists & midwives on staff. Affiliated with approximately 20 college & university programs.

Cholly Boland, Chief Executive Officer
613-774-1049, cboland@wdmh.on.ca
Nathalie Boudreau, Chief Nursing Executive & Vice-President, Clinical Services
613-774-2420, nboudreau@wdmh.on.ca
Michelle Blouin, Chief Financial Officer & Vice-President, Corporate Services
613-774-2420, mblouin@wdmh.on.ca
Brian Devin, Chief of Staff
613-774-2420, bdevin@wdmh.on.ca

Windsor: Hôtel-Dieu Grace Healthcare
Affiliated with: Erie St. Clair Local Health Integration Network
1453 Prince Rd., Windsor, ON N9C 3Z4
Tel: 519-257-5111
www.hdgh.org
www.facebook.com/HDGHF; twitter.com/HDGHWindsor;
www.youtube.com/user/HOTELDIEUGRACE
Number of Beds: 259 beds
Note: Programs & services include: acquired brain injury; addiction & mental health; adult day program; bariatric assessment & treatment; cardiac; chiropody; community crisis centre; complex continuing care; concurrent disorder program; dual diagnosis; stabilization; geriatrics; mood & anxiety treatment; palliative program; pharmacy; Regional Children's Centre; rehabilitation; remedial measures; residential rehabilitation; wellness program for extended psychosis; & withdrawal management services.
Janice Kaffer, President & CEO
Marie Campagna, Chief Financial Officer & Vice-President, Corporate Services & New Business Development
Dr. Andrea Steen, Chief of Staff & Vice-President, Medical Affairs & Quality

Windsor: Windsor Regional Hospital - Metropolitan Campus
Affiliated with: Erie St. Clair Local Health Integration Network
1995 Lens Ave., Windsor, ON N8W 1L9
Tel: 519-254-5577 *Fax:* 519-254-2317
www.wrh.on.ca
www.facebook.com/WindsorRegionalHospital;
twitter.com/WRHospital; www.youtube.com/user/WRHWeCare
Year Founded: 1928
Number of Beds: 549 beds (total of all WRH sites)
Population Served: 400000
Note: Programs & services on both campuses include: cardiac care; complex trauma; emergency services; intensive care; medicine; neonatal intensive care; paediatric services; regional cancer services; renal dialysis; stroke & neurosurgery; & surgery.
David Musyj, President & CEO
519-254-5577, david.musyj@wrh.on.ca
Karen McCullough, Chief Operating Officer & Chief Nursing Executive
karen.mccullough@wrh.on.ca

Windsor: Windsor Regional Hospital - Ouellette Campus
Affiliated with: Erie St. Clair Local Health Integration Network
1030 Ouellette Ave., Windsor, ON N9A 1E1
Tel: 519-254-5577
www.wrh.on.ca
www.facebook.com/WindsorRegionalHospital;
twitter.com/WRHospital; www.youtube.com/user/WRHWeCare
Year Founded: 1888
Number of Beds: 549 beds (total of all WRH sites)
Population Served: 400000
Note: Acquired by Windsor Regional Hospital in 2013; renovations in 2008 expanded emergency services, operating rooms & diagnostic imaging departments. Programs & services on both campuses include: cardiac care; complex trauma; emergency services; family birthing centre; intensive care; medicine; neonatal intensive care; paediatric services; regional cancer services; renal dialysis; stroke & neurosurgery; & surgery.
David Musyj, President & CEO

Wingham: Wingham & District Hospital
Listowel Wingham Hospitals Alliance
Affiliated with: South West Local Health Integration Network
270 Carling Terrace, Wingham, ON N0G 2W0
Tel: 519-357-3210 *Fax:* 519-357-2931
www.lwha.ca
Number of Beds: 36 beds
Note: Programs & services include: breast health; diabetes education; diagnostic imaging; emergency; inpatient / medical; laboratory; maternal / newborn; nutrition; oncology; outpatient clinics; surgical; & therapy.

Karl Ellis, President & CEO
519-357-3711, karl.ellis@lwha.ca

Woodstock: Woodstock General Hospital
Affiliated with: South West Local Health Integration Network
310 Juliana Dr., Woodstock, ON N4V 0A4
Tel: 519-421-4211 *Fax:* 519-421-4247
info@wgh.on.ca
www.wgh.on.ca

Number of Beds: 178 beds
Note: Programs & services include: ambulatory care; complex continuing care; critical care; diagnostic imaging; inpatient rehabilitation; intensive rehabilitation outpatient program; maternal child services; medical / surgical unit; mental health; surgery; & urology.
Perry Lang, President & CEO
plang@wgh.on.ca
Dr. Malcolm MacLeod, Chief of Staff
Jayne Menard, Chief Nursing Officer & Vice-President, Patient Care
jmenard@wgh.on.ca

Federal Hospitals

Ottawa: Canadian Forces Health Care Centre Ottawa
Affiliated with: Champlain Local Health Integration Network
713 Montreal Rd., Ottawa, ON K1K 0T1
Tel: 613-945-1111
www.canada.ca/en/department-national-defence/services/bases-support-units/cf-health-services-centre
Note: Hospital Specialties: Primary health care services to the military community in the National Capital Region (613-945-1502); Laboratory services; Surgery; Cardio Pulmonary Unit; Operational Trauma & Stress Support Centre (613-945-1060); Mental health (613-945-1060); Addiction counselling (613-945-1060); Ophthalmology (613-945-1550); & Physiotherapy (613-945-1585).
BGen A.M.T. Downes, Commander, Canadian Forces Health Services Group

Private Hospitals

Penetanguishene: Hôpital Privé Beechwood Private Hospital
58 Church St., Penetanguishene, ON L9M 1B3
Tel: 705-549-7473 *Fax:* 705-549-7194
bph@rogers.com

Number of Beds: 20 beds
Larry Bellisle, CEO

Thornhill: Shouldice Hospital Ltd.
Affiliated with: Central Local Health Integration Network
7750 Bayview Ave., Thornhill, ON L3T 4A3
Tel: 905-889-1125 *Fax:* 905-889-4216
Toll-Free: 800-291-7750
postoffice@shouldice.com
www.shouldice.com

Year Founded: 1945
Number of Beds: 89 beds
Specialties: Hernia repair
Note: Has 10 surgeons on staff.
John Hughes, Managing Director

Toronto: Don Mills Surgical Unit Inc. (DMSU)
Centric Health Surgical
Affiliated with: Central Local Health Integration Network
#103, 20 Wynford Dr., Toronto, ON M3C 1J4
Tel: 647-556-1554 *Fax:* 416-441-2114
Toll-Free: 877-804-1677
www.centrichealthsurgical.com/location/toronto
Year Founded: 1960
Note: Surgical services & procedures offered include: general, orthopaedic, ophthalmology, plastic surgery, upper & lower extremity, cosmetics, dental & ENT.

Woodstock: Woodstock Private Hospital
Affiliated with: South West Local Health Integration Network
369 Huron St., Woodstock, ON N4S 7A5
Tel: 519-537-8162 *Fax:* 519-537-7204

Number of Beds: 16 beds
Note: Chronic care hospital
Lisa Figg, Administrator

Auxiliary Hospitals

Ottawa: Bruyère Continuing Care/Soins continus Bruyère
Affiliated with: Champlain Local Health Integration Network
Former Name: Sisters of Charity of Ottawa Health Service
43 Bruyère St., Ottawa, ON K1N 5C8
Tel: 613-562-6262
communications@bruyere.org
www.bruyere.org
www.facebook.com/bruyerecare; twitter.com/bruyerecare; www.linkedin.com/company/bruyerecare
Year Founded: 1993
Number of Beds: 731 beds
Number of Employees: 2087
Note: Specializes in complex continuing care, rehabilitation, palliative care, long-term care, & seniors housing; includes Saint-Vincent Hospital, Élisabeth Bruyère Hospital, Élisabeth Bruyère Residence, Saint-Louis Residence, & Bruyère Village.
Guy Chartrand, President & CEO
Dr. Shaun McGuire, Chief of Staff
Debbie Gravelle, Chief Nursing Executive & Senior Vice-President, Clinical Programs
Carolyn Brennan, Chief Financial Officer & Vice-President, Corporate Services
Rob Jones, Vice-President, Human Resources & Organizational Development
Amy Porteous, Vice-President, Public Affairs & Planning
Dr. Carol Wiebe, Vice-President, Medical Affairs
Heidi Sveistrup, Vice-President, Research & Academic Affairs
Melissa Donskov, Executive Director, Long-Term Care

Toronto: Baycrest Hospital
Affiliated with: Toronto Central Local Health Integration Network
Also Known As: Baycrest Health Sciences
3560 Bathurst St., Toronto, ON M6A 4A6
Tel: 416-785-2500 *Fax:* 416-785-2378
www.baycrest.org
www.facebook.com/baycrestcentre; twitter.com/baycrest; www.youtube.com/thebaycrestchannel; www.linkedin.com/company/baycrest
Year Founded: 1986
Number of Beds: 300 hospital beds
Note: Programs & services include: acute geriatric care; rehabilitation; psychiatry; behavioural neurology; complex continuing care for the elderly; & palliative care.
William Reichman, President & CEO
Dr. Gary Naglie, Chief of Staff & Vice-President, Medical Services
Margot DaCosta, Chief Nursing Executive

Toronto: Bridgepoint Active Healthcare
Sinai Health System
Affiliated with: Toronto Central Local Health Integration Network
Former Name: The Riverdale Hospital
Also Known As: Bridgepoint Hospital
1 Bridgepoint Dr., Toronto, ON M4M 2B5
Tel: 416-461-8252 *Fax:* 416-461-5696
www.bridgepointhealth.ca
www.facebook.com/BridgepointHealth; twitter.com/BridgepointTO; www.youtube.com/bridgepointhospital; www.linkedin.com/company/bridgepoint-health
Number of Beds: 404 beds
Specialties: Complex continuing care & rehabilitation
Note: Programs & services include: ambulatory care; diabetes education; dialysis; endocrinology; general internal medicine; geriatric psychiatry; neurological care; orthopedic care; pain management; palliative care; physiatry; therapeutic recreation; & urgent care.
Dr. Gary Newton, President & CEO, Sinai Health System
Jane Merkley, Chief Nurse Executive & Chief Operating Officer
Dr. Maureen Shandling, Executive Vice-President, Academic & Medical Affairs

Toronto: Providence Healthcare
Affiliated with: Toronto Central Local Health Integration Network
Former Name: Providence Centre Home for the Aged, Chronic Care & Rehabilitation Hospital
3276 St. Clair Ave. East, Toronto, ON M1L 1W1
Tel: 416-285-3666 *Fax:* 416-285-3758
info@providence.on.ca
www.providence.on.ca
www.facebook.com/ProvidenceHealthcareTO; twitter.com/Providence3276; www.youtube.com/ProvHealthcare

Number of Beds: 288 long-term care beds; 245 hospital beds
Note: Comprised of Providence Hospital, the Cardinal Ambrozic Houses of Providence, & Providence Community Centre; long-term care, rehabilitation, & complex continuing care, community clinics, Alzheimer Day Program, caregiver support services, Tamil Caregiver Project. Focus is on the mission & values of the founding Sisters of St. Joseph.
Maggie Bruneau, Site Lead

Toronto: Runnymede Healthcare Centre
Affiliated with: Toronto Central Local Health Integration Network
625 Runnymede Rd., Toronto, ON M6S 3A3
Tel: 416-762-7316 *Fax:* 416-762-3836
communications@runnymedehc.ca
www.runnymedehc.ca
www.facebook.com/RunnymedeHC; twitter.com/RunnymedeHC; www.youtube.com/RunnymedeHC; www.linkedin.com/company/runnymedehc
Year Founded: 1945
Note: Complex continuing care hospital with rehabilitation, speech therapy, dental care, & foot care services.
Connie Dejak, President & CEO
Raj Sewda, Chief Nursing Executive & Chief Privacy Officer
Daniel Germain, Chief Financial Officer & Vice-President, Finance
Sharleen Ahmed, Vice-President, Strategy, Quality & Clinical Programs
Richard Mendonca, Vice-President, Human Resources & Organizational Development

Toronto: The Salvation Army Toronto Grace Health Centre (TGHC)
Affiliated with: Toronto Central Local Health Integration Network
Also Known As: Toronto Grace Hospital
650 Church St., Toronto, ON M4Y 2G5
Tel: 416-925-2251 *Fax:* 416-925-3211
www.torontograce.org
www.facebook.com/torontogracehealthcentre; twitter.com/torontogracehc; www.linkedin.com/company/toronto-grace-health-centre
Year Founded: 1905
Number of Beds: 119 beds
Note: Complex continuing care facility providing services such as foot clinic/chiropody, palliative care & slow-paced rehabilitation.
Dr. John Ruth, Medical Director
Ralph Anstey, Chief Financial Officer

Community Health Care Centres

Ajax: Carea Community Health Centre - Ajax Office
Former Name: The Youth Centre; Barbara Black Centre for Youth Resources
#5, 360 Bayly St., Ajax, ON L1S 1P1
Tel: 905-428-1212 *Fax:* 905-428-9151
Toll-Free: 877-227-3217
info@careachc.ca
www.careachc.ca
www.facebook.com/CareaCHC; twitter.com/careachc
Note: Offers community health & wellness programs, as well as primary care, counselling, & chronic disease management services.
Francis Garwe, Chief Executive Officer

Armstrong: NorWest Community Health Centre - Armstrong Site
Affiliated with: North West Local Health Integration Network
PO Box 104, Armstrong, ON P0T 1A0
Tel: 807-583-1145 *Fax:* 807-583-1147
www.norwestchc.org/armstrong.htm
www.facebook.com/NorWestCHC

Juanita Lawson, CEO

Barrie: Barrie Community Health Centre
490 Huronia Rd., Barrie, ON L4N 6M2
Tel: 705-734-9690 *Fax:* 705-734-0239
www.bchc.ca

Note: Provides community-focused health promotion, illness prevention, & primary care services. Services provided by physicians, registered nurses, social workers, physiotherapists, & dietitians. North Innisfil office located at: 902 Lockhart Rd., 705-431-9245.
Christine Colcy, Executive Director

Barrie: **Home & Community Care North Simcoe Muskoka**
Affiliated with: North Simcoe Muskoka Local Health Integration Network
#100, 15 Sperling Dr., Barrie, ON L4M 6K9
Tel: 705-721-8010 *Toll-Free:* 888-721-2222
healthcareathome.ca/nsm
twitter.com/NSMCCAC; www.youtube.com/ccacnsm
Note: With offices in Orillia, Barrie & Huntsville, provides health & personal support services for individuals living independently at home or making the transition to alternative care settings; information & referral, advocacy.

Belleville: **Home & Community Care - Belleville Branch**
Affiliated with: South East Local Health Integration Network
Bayview Mall, 470 Dundas St. East, Belleville, ON K8N 1G1
Tel: 613-966-3530 *Fax:* 613-966-0996
Toll-Free: 800-668-0901
healthcareathome.ca/southeast
Note: Services include: nursing; personal support; physiotherapy & occupational therapy; speech & language therapy; social work; & dietitians.

Brampton: **Home & Community Care - Brampton Branch**
Affiliated with: Central West Local Health Integration Network
199 County Court Blvd., Brampton, ON L6W 4P3
Tel: 905-796-0040 *Fax:* 905-796-4671
Toll-Free: 888-733-1177
healthcareathome.ca/centralwest
Note: Services include: nursing; personal support; physiotherapy & occupational therapy; speech & language therapy; social work; dietitians; & palliative care.

Brantford: **Home & Community Care - Brant Branch**
Affiliated with: Hamilton Niagara Haldimand Brant Local Health Integration Network
Building 4, #4, 195 Henry St., Brantford, ON N3S 5C9
Tel: 519-759-7752 *Fax:* 519-759-7130
Toll-Free: 800-810-0000
access@lhins.on.ca
healthcareathome.ca/hnhb
Note: Services include: nursing; personal support; physiotherapy & occupational therapy; speech & language therapy; social work; dietitians; & palliative care.

Burlington: **Home & Community Care - Burlington Branch**
Affiliated with: Hamilton Niagara Haldimand Brant Local Health Integration Network
440 Elizabeth St., 4th Fl., Burlington, ON L7R 2M1
Tel: 905-639-5228 *Fax:* 905-639-8704
Toll-Free: 800-810-0000
access@lhins.on.ca
healthcareathome.ca/hnhb
Note: Services include: nursing; personal support; physiotherapy & occupational therapy; speech & language therapy; social work; dietitians; & palliative care.

Cambridge: **Langs Community Health Centre**
1145 Concession Rd., Cambridge, ON N3H 4L5
Tel: 519-653-1470 *Fax:* 519-653-1285
info@langs.org
www.langs.org
www.facebook.com/LangsCommunity;
twitter.com/langscommunity
William Davidson, Executive Director
519-653-1470, billd@langs.org
Kerry-Lynn Wilkie, Director, Health Link
519-653-1470, kerrylynnw@langs.org

Chatham: **Home & Community Care - Erie St. Clair Branch**
Affiliated with: Erie St. Clair Local Health Integration Network
PO Box 306, 712 Richmond St., Chatham, ON N7M 5K4
Fax: 519-351-5842
Toll-Free: 888-447-4468
TTY: 519-258-8092
esc-engagement@lhins.on.ca
healthcareathome.ca/eriestclair
Note: Services include: nursing; personal support; physiotherapy & occupational therapy; speech & language therapy; social work; care connector; in-home; mental health & addiction; school health support; dietitians; & palliative care.

Cornwall: **Centre de santé communautaire de l'Estrie**
#6, 841, rue Sydney, Cornwall, ON K6H 3J7
Tél: 613-937-2683 *Téléc:* 613-937-2698
info@cscestrie.on.ca
www.cscestrie.on.ca
www.facebook.com/179209222111118; twitter.com/CSCE_
Note: Programmes: santé physique; santé mentale; santé communautaire; nutrition; programme d'éducation sur le diabète.
Marc Bisson, Directeur général
m.bisson@cscestrie.on.ca

Cornwall: **Home & Community Care Champlain - Cornwall Branch Office**
Affiliated with: Champlain Local Health Integration Network
709 Cotton Mill St., Cornwall, ON K6H 7K7
Tel: 310-2222 *Toll-Free:* 800-538-0520
healthcareathome.ca/champlain

Ear Falls: **Ear Falls Community Health Centre**
Affiliated with: North West Local Health Integration Network
PO Box 250, 25 Spruce St., Ear Falls, ON P0V 1T0
Tel: 807-222-3728 *Fax:* 807-222-2053
earfallsfht@live.com
Note: Programs & services include: blood & lab work; Ministry of Transportation medical reviews; Northern Ontario Travel Grant Application.

Emo: **Emo Health Centre**
Riverside Health Care Facilities Inc.
Affiliated with: North West Local Health Integration Network
PO Box 390, 170 Front St., Emo, ON P0W 1E0
Tel: 807-274-3261 *Fax:* 807-482-2493
www.riversidehealthcare.ca
Number of Beds: 12 long-term care beds; 3 acute care beds
Note: Programs & services include: physiotherapy; dietician; diagnostics; urgent care.
Ted Scholten, President & CEO

Forest: **North Lambton Community Health Centre**
Affiliated with: Erie St. Clair Local Health Integration Network
PO Box 1120, 3 - 59 King St. West, Forest, ON N0N 1J0
Tel: 519-786-4545 *Fax:* 519-786-3023
nlinfo@nlchc.com
www.nlchc.com
www.facebook.com/NorthLambtonCHC
Note: Programs for children, seniors, healthy living, excercise & diabetes education.
Kathy Bresett, Executive Director
kbresett@nlchc.com

Fort Frances: **Fort Frances Tribal Area Health Services**
Affiliated with: North West Local Health Integration Network
PO Box 608, Fort Frances, ON P9A 3M9
Tel: 807-274-2042 *Fax:* 807-274-2050
www.fftahs.com
Note: Programs & services include: behavioural health services; chiropody & foot care services; diabetes education; home & community care.
Calvin Morrisseau, Executive Director

Fort Frances: **Gizhewaadiziwin Health Access Centre**
Affiliated with: North West Local Health Integration Network
PO Box 686, Fort Frances, ON P9A 3M9
Tel: 807-274-3131 *Fax:* 807-274-6280
www.gizhac.com
Note: Programs & services include: primary care; nutrition; traditional healing; mental health; diabetes education.
Shanna Weir, Executive Director

Grand Bend: **Grand Bend Area Community Health Centre**
PO Box 1269, 69 Main St. East, Grand Bend, ON N0M 1T0
Tel: 519-238-2362 *Fax:* 519-238-6478
www.gbachc.ca
www.facebook.com/GBACHC; twitter.com/gbachc
Area Served: Grand Bend, Hensall, Thedford
Note: Programs & services include: diabetes education; dietitian; occupational therapy; physiotherapy; primary care; & social work.
Cate Melito, Executive Director

Guelph: **Home & Community Care Waterloo Wellington - Guelph Branch**
Affiliated with: Waterloo Wellington Local Health Integration Network
Also Known As: WWCCAC
#201, 450 Speedvale Ave. West, Guelph, ON N1H 7G7
Tel: 519-823-2550
healthcareathome.ca/ww
Note: Long-term care placement services; information & referral to other community services; in-home health services; school health support services; access to long-term care facilities; access to adult day programs; mental health & palliative care services

Hamilton: **Centre de santé communautaire Hamilton / Niagara**
1320, rue Barton est, Hamilton, ON L8H 2W1
Tél: 905-528-0163 *Téléc:* 905-528-9196
Ligne sans frais: 866-437-7606
cschn@cschn.ca
www.cschn.ca
www.facebook.com/cschn
Marcel Castonguay, Directeur général

Hamilton: **Hamilton Urban Core Community Health Centre**
71 Rebecca St., Hamilton, ON L8R 1B6
Tel: 905-522-3233 *Fax:* 905-522-3433
administration@hucchc.com
www.hucchc.com
www.facebook.com/HamiltonUrbanCoreCommunityHealthCentre
; twitter.com/hucchc
Denise Brooks, Executive Director
905-522-3233, Fax: 905-522-5374, dbrooks@hucchc.com

Hamilton: **Home & Community Care - Hamilton Branch**
Affiliated with: Hamilton Niagara Haldimand Brant Local Health Integration Network
#1, 211 Pritchard Rd., Hamilton, ON L8J 0G5
Tel: 905-523-8600 *Fax:* 905-528-1883
Toll-Free: 800-810-0000
access@lhins.on.ca
healthcareathome.ca/hnhb
Note: Services include: nursing; personal support; physiotherapy & occupational therapy; speech & language therapy; social work; dietitians; & palliative care.

Hamilton: **North Hamilton Community Health Centre**
438 Hughson St. North, Hamilton, ON L8L 4N5
Tel: 905-523-6611 *Fax:* 905-523-5173
www.nhchc.ca
Year Founded: 1987
Note: Offers a variety of services & programs, including programs for men & women living with HIV / AIDS & programs for new immigrants / refugees.
Kathy Allan-Fleet, Chief Executive Officer
kallanfleet@compassch.org

Huntsville: **Muskoka Algonquin Healthcare**
Huntsville District Memorial Hospital, 100 Frank Miller Dr., Huntsville, ON P1H 1H7
Tel: 705-789-2311 *Fax:* 705-789-0557
www.mahc.ca
Number of Beds: 96 beds
Number of Employees: 650
Note: Provides emergency health services & acute care.
Natalie Bubela, CEO
Esther Millar, Chief Nursing Executive

Ignace: **Mary Berglund Community Health Centre (MBCHC)**
PO Box 450, 1100 Main St., Ignace, ON P0T 1T0
Tel: 807-934-2251 *Fax:* 807-934-6552
www.facebook.com/867609549975894
Note: Specialties: primary care; public health nursing; physiotherapy; chronic disease follow-up; health promotion; men's & women's wellness clinics; blood sugar & blood pressure screening programs; chiropractic services; massage therapy.
Heidi West, Executive Director

Kenora: **Home & Community Care - Kenora Branch**
Affiliated with: North West Local Health Integration Network
#3, 35 Wolsley St., Kenora, ON P9N 0H8
Tel: 807-467-4757 *Fax:* 807-468-1437
Toll-Free: 877-661-6621
healthcareathome.ca/northwest
Note: Services include: nursing; personal support; physiotherapy & occupational therapy; speech & language therapy; social work; dietitians; & palliative care.

Kingston: Home & Community Care - Kingston Branch
Affiliated with: South East Local Health Integration Network
City Place, #200, 1471 John Counter Blvd., Kingston, ON K7M 8S8
Tel: 613-544-7090 *Fax:* 613-544-1494
Toll-Free: 800-869-8828
healthcareathome.ca/southeast
Note: Services include: nursing; personal support; physiotherapy & occupational therapy; speech & language therapy; social work; dietitians; & palliative care.

Kingston: Kingston Community Health Centres (KCHC)
263 Weller Ave., Kingston, ON K7K 2V4
Tel: 613-542-2949 *Fax:* 613-542-7657
info@kchc.ca
www.kchc.ca
www.facebook.com/KingstonCHC; twitter.com/kingstonchc
Year Founded: 1988
Lisa Lund, Program Manager
lisal@kchc.ca

Kirkland Lake: Home & Community Care North East - Kirkland Lake Branch Office
Affiliated with: North East Local Health Integration Network
53 Government Rd. West, Kirkland Lake, ON P2N 2E5
Tel: 705-567-2222 *Fax:* 705-567-9407
Toll-Free: 888-602-2222
healthcareathome.ca/northeast

Kitchener: Kitchener Downtown Community Health Centre
44 Francis St. South, Kitchener, ON N2G 2A2
Tel: 519-745-4404 *Fax:* 519-745-3709
mail@kdchc.org
www.kdchc.org
www.facebook.com/KDCHC
Elizabeth Beader, Executive Director
519-745-4404, ebeader@kdchc.org

Lanark: North Lanark County Community Health Centre
207 Robertson Dr., Lanark, ON K0G 1K0
Tel: 613-259-2182 *Fax:* 613-259-5235
Toll-Free: 866-762-0496
info@nlchc.on.ca
www.northlanarkchc.on.ca
Year Founded: 1992
John Jordan, Executive Director, Lanark Renfrew Health & Community Services

Lindsay: Home & Community Care - Lindsay Branch
Affiliated with: Central East Local Health Integration Network
370 Kent St. West, Lindsay, ON K9V 6G8
Tel: 705-324-9165 *Fax:* 855-352-2555
Toll-Free: 800-263-3877
healthcareathome.ca/centraleast
Note: Services include: nursing; personal support; physiotherapy & occupational therapy; speech & language therapy; social work; dietitians; & palliative care.

London: Home & Community Care - London & Middlesex Branch
Affiliated with: South West Local Health Integration Network
Former Name: South West Community Care Access Centre
356 Oxford St. West, London, ON N6H 1T3
Fax: 519-472-4045
Toll-Free: 800-811-5146
TTY: 519-473-9626
southwest@lhins.on.ca
healthcareathome.ca/southwest
Note: Services include: nursing; personal support; physiotherapy & occupational therapy; speech & language therapy; social work; dietitians; & palliative care.

London: London InterCommunity Health Centre
659 Dundas St., London, ON N5W 2Z1
Tel: 519-660-0874 *Fax:* 519-642-1532
mail@lihc.on.ca
www.lihc.on.ca
www.facebook.com/LondonInterCommunityHealthCentre; twitter.com/HealthCentre
Year Founded: 1989
Number of Employees: 70
Note: Specialties: Inclusive & equitable health & social services to persons who experience barriers to care; Mental health care;

Diabetes program; Options clinic HIV anonymous testing; Health & youth outreach services.
Scott Courtice, Executive Director
519-660-0875, scourtice@lihc.on.ca

Longlac: NorWest Community Health Centre - Longlac Site
Affiliated with: North West Local Health Integration Network
PO Box 910, 99 Skinner Ave., Longlac, ON P0T 2A0
Tel: 807-876-2271 *Fax:* 807-876-2473
Toll-Free: 888-876-2271
www.norwestchc.org/longlac.htm
www.facebook.com/NorWestCHC
Note: Primary care services; programs for children & seniors.
Juanita Lawson, CEO

Markham: Home & Community Care - Markham
Affiliated with: Central Local Health Integration Network
Former Name: Etobicoke & York CCAC
#500, 11 Allstate Pkwy., Markham, ON L3R 9T8
Tel: 905-895-1240 *Fax:* 905-952-2404
Toll-Free: 888-470-2222
TTY: 416-222-0876
central.lhin@lhins.on.ca
healthcareathome.ca/central
Note: Services include: chronic disease clinic; diagnostics; rehabilitation; palliative care; home care; immunization; pre- & post-natal programs; & school health program.

Merrickville: Merrickville District Community Health Centre
PO Box 550, 354 Read St., Merrickville, ON K0G 1N0
Tel: 613-269-3400 *Fax:* 613-269-4958
info@rideauchs.ca
www.rideauchs.ca
Note: Services include: social work; dietitian; health education; individual & family counselling; case management; foot care; flu clinics; immunization.
Michele Bellows, Chief Executive Officer, Rideau Community Health Services
613-269-3400, mbellows@rideauchs.ca

Mount Brydges: Southwest Middlesex Health Centre
22262 Mill Rd., RR#5, Mount Brydges, ON N0L 1W0
Tel: 519-264-2800 *Fax:* 519-264-2742
www.smhc.net
Year Founded: 1974
Area Served: Mount Brydges & the surrounding area
Note: Appointments are necessary.
Barbara Spratley, Administrator

New Liskeard: Centre de santé communautaire du Témiskaming
CP 38, 20 May St. South, New Liskeard, ON P0J 1P0
Tél: 705-647-5775 *Téléc:* 833-696-9426
Ligne sans frais: 800-835-2728
www.csctim.on.ca
Jocelyne Maxwell, Directrice générale

North Bay: Home & Community Care - North Bay Branch
Affiliated with: North East Local Health Integration Network
1164 Devonshire Ave., North Bay, ON P1B 6X7
Tel: 705-476-2222 *Fax:* 705-474-0080
Toll-Free: 888-533-2222
TTY: 888-533-2222
healthcareathome.ca/northeast
Note: Services include: nursing; personal support; physiotherapy & occupational therapy; speech & language therapy; social work; dietitians; & palliative care.

Oshawa: Carea Community Health Centre - Oshawa Office
Former Name: Oshawa Community Health Centre
115 Grassmere Ave., Oshawa, ON L1H 3X7
Tel: 905-723-0036 *Fax:* 905-723-3391
Toll-Free: 877-227-3217
info@careachc.ca
www.careachc.ca
www.facebook.com/CareaCHC; twitter.com/careachc
Note: Services: child development; youth recreation; women's wellness; health promotion; family community outreach; education services, such as the diabetes education program; counselling; parenting groups; regular check-ups; rehabilitation.
Lee Kierstead, CEO

Ottawa: Carlington Community Health Centre
900 Merivale Rd., Ottawa, ON K1Z 5Z8
Tel: 613-722-4000 *Fax:* 613-761-1805
info@carlington.ochc.org
www.carlington.ochc.org
Note: Services include: immunization; management of chronic & short-term health problems; Telehealth; counselling; & health promotion.
Cameron MacLeod, Executive Director
613-722-4000, cammacleod@carlington.ochc.org

Ottawa: Centretown Community Health Centre
420 Cooper St., Ottawa, ON K2P 2N6
Tel: 613-233-4443 *Fax:* 613-233-3987
TTY: 613-233-0651
info@centretownchc.org
www.centretownchc.org
www.facebook.com/CentretownCHC; twitter.com/centretownchc
Note: Services include: counselling; child & family programs; community inniatives; health education & LGBTQ+ support; & homeless iniative.
Simone Thibault, Executive Director
sthibault@centretownchc.org

Ottawa: Champlain Local Health Integration Network - Gloucester
Affiliated with: Champlain Local Health Integration Network
#100, 4200 Labelle St., Ottawa, ON K1J 1J8
Tel: 613-310-2222 *Toll-Free:* 800-538-0520
healthcareathome.ca/champlain
Note: Specialties: Home care; Coordination of community care; Information about long-term care options.

Ottawa: Pinecrest-Queensway Health & Community Services (PQCHC)
1365 Richmond Rd., 2nd Fl., Ottawa, ON K2B 6R7
Tel: 613-820-4922 *Fax:* 613-288-3407
info@pqchc.com
www.pqchc.com
www.facebook.com/PQCHC; twitter.com/PQCHC
Year Founded: 1979
Note: Services include: primary health care; mental health & housing; children & family; & community health.
Christopher McIntosh, Chief Executive Officer
613-820-4922, c.mcintosh@pqchc.com

Ottawa: Sandy Hill Community Health Centre
221 Nelson St., Ottawa, ON K1N 1C7
Tel: 613-789-1500 *Fax:* 613-789-7962
www.shchc.ca
www.facebook.com/sandyhillchc; twitter.com/sandyhillchc
www.linkedin.com/company/sandy-hill-community-health-centre
Year Founded: 1973
Note: Provides a variety of health & social services in the Eastern Ottawa region.
David Gibson, Executive Director
613-789-1500, dgibson@sandyhillchc.on.ca

Ottawa: Somerset West Community Health Centre
55 Eccles St., Ottawa, ON K1R 6S3
Tel: 613-238-8210 *Fax:* 613-238-7595
info@swchc.on.ca
www.swchc.on.ca
www.facebook.com/somersetwestchc; twitter.com/swchc
Note: Programs & services include: pulmonary rehabilitation; asthma program; mental health; obstetrical care; HIV testing; dental screening; foot care; primary care; & services for seniors.
Naini Cloutier, Executive Director

Ottawa: South-East Ottawa Community Health Centre
#600, 1355 Bank St., Ottawa, ON K1H 8K7
Tel: 613-737-5115 *Fax:* 613-739-3723
office@seochc.on.ca
www.seochc.on.ca
www.facebook.com/142007129166107; twitter.com/SEOCHC
Note: Programs & services include: diabetes education; dental screening; HIV testing; foot care; & mental health.
Kelli Tonner, Executive Director
613-737-7195, kellit@seochc.on.ca

Owen Sound: Home & Community Care - Owen Sound Branch
Affiliated with: South West Local Health Integration Network
Former Name: South West Community Care Access Centre
#3009, 1415 - 1 Ave. West, Owen Sound, ON N4K 4K8
Tel: 519-371-2112 *Fax:* 519-371-5612
Toll-Free: 888-371-2112
TTY: 800-811-5147
southwest@lhins.on.ca
healthcareathome.ca/southwest
Note: Services include: nursing; personal support; physiotherapy & occupational therapy; speech & language therapy; social work; dietitians; & palliative care.

Parry Sound: West Parry Sound Health Centre (WPSHC)
Affiliated with: North East Local Health Integration Network
6 Albert St., Parry Sound, ON P2A 3A4
Tel: 705-746-9321 *Fax:* 705-746-7364
www.wpshc.com
Year Founded: 1995
Number of Beds: 180 beds
Note: Programs & services include: acute & complex continuing care; rehabilitation; on-site Lakeland Long Term Care Facility; Community Care Access Centre; emergency services; surgery; diagnostic imaging; chemotherapy; sleep disorder clinic; lab; telehealth; Base Hospital Program & nursing stations in Britt, Pointe au Baril, Rosseau, Whitestone, Argyle & Moosedeer; specialist clinics
Donald Sanderson, CEO

Peterborough: Home & Community Care - Peterborough Branch
Affiliated with: Central East Local Health Integration Network
#202, 700 Clonsilla Ave., Peterborough, ON K9J 5Y3
Tel: 705-743-2212 *Fax:* 855-352-2555
Toll-Free: 800-263-3877
TTY: 877-743-7939
healthcareathome.ca/centraleast
Note: Services include: nursing; personal support; physiotherapy & occupational therapy; speech & language therapy; social work; dietitians; & palliative care.

Pickle Lake: Pickle Lake Health Centre
Affiliated with: North West Local Health Integration Network
PO Box 302, 3 Anne St., Pickle Lake, ON P0V 3A0
Tel: 807-928-2047 *Fax:* 807-928-2584
picklelake.healthclinic@picklelake.org
Note: Programs & services include: chronic disease management; disease prevention; nutritional counselling.

Portland: Country Roads Community Health Centre
PO Box 58, 4319 Cove Rd., Portland, ON K0G 1V0
Tel: 613-272-3302 *Fax:* 613-272-3024
Toll-Free: 888-998-9927
info@crchc.on.ca
www.crchc.on.ca
www.facebook.com/CRCHC
Note: Programs & services include: immunization; pre-natal care, post-natal care, & early childhood development programs; lung health; pharmacy; nutrition counselling; dental; & diabetes prevention.
Marty Crapper, Executive Director
mcrapper@crchc.on.ca

Sault Ste Marie: Group Health Centre Sault Ste. Marie
240 McNabb St., Sault Ste Marie, ON P6B 1Y5
Tel: 705-759-1234 *Fax:* 705-759-7469
Toll-Free: 800-461-2407
inquiries@ghc.on.ca
www.ghc.on.ca
Year Founded: 1963
Population Served: 80000
Note: GHC is a consumer-sponsored health care facility, built by private funds donated by local union members. A partnership of the Sault Ste. Marie & District Group Health Association & the Algoma District Medical Group. Number of staff: 300+
Alex Lambert, President & CEO
705-759-5606

Sault Ste Marie: Home & Community Care - Sault Ste Marie Branch
Affiliated with: North East Local Health Integration Network
390 Bay St., Sault Ste Marie, ON P6A 1X2
Tel: 705-949-1808 *Fax:* 705-949-1663
Toll-Free: 800-668-7705
healthcareathome.ca/northeast
Note: Services include: nursing; personal support; physiotherapy & occupational therapy; speech & language therapy; social work; dietitians; & palliative care.

Seaforth: Home & Community Care - Seaforth Branch
Affiliated with: South West Local Health Integration Network
PO Box 580, 32 Centennial Dr., Seaforth, ON N0K 1W0
Tel: 519-527-0000 *Fax:* 519-527-1255
Toll-Free: 800-267-0535
TTY: 519-473-9626
southwest@lhins.on.ca
healthcareathome.ca/southwest
Note: Services include: nursing; personal support; physiotherapy & occupational therapy; speech & language therapy; social work; dietitians; & palliative care.

Simcoe: Home & Community Care - Haldimand Norfolk Branch
Affiliated with: Hamilton Niagara Haldimand Brant Local Health Integration Network
76 Victoria St., Simcoe, ON N3Y 1L5
Tel: 519-426-7400 *Fax:* 519-426-4384
Toll-Free: 800-810-0000
access@lhins.on.ca
healthcareathome.ca/hnhb
Note: Services include: nursing; personal support; physiotherapy & occupational therapy; speech & language therapy; social work; dietitians; & palliative care.

Smiths Falls: Home & Community Care - Smiths Falls Branch
Affiliated with: South East Local Health Integration Network
#1, 52 Abbott St. North, Smiths Falls, ON K7A 1W3
Tel: 613-283-8012 *Fax:* 613-283-0308
Toll-Free: 800-267-6041
healthcareathome.ca/southeast
Note: Services include: nursing; personal support; physiotherapy & occupational therapy; speech & language therapy; social work; dietitians; & palliative care.

St. Catharines: Home & Community Care - Niagara Branch
Affiliated with: Hamilton Niagara Haldimand Brant Local Health Integration Network
149 Hartzel Rd., St. Catharines, ON L2P 1N6
Tel: 905-684-9441 *Fax:* 905-684-8463
Toll-Free: 800-810-0000
access@lhins.on.ca
healthcareathome.ca/hnhb
Note: Services include: nursing; personal support; physiotherapy & occupational therapy; speech & language therapy; social work; dietitians; & palliative care.

St. Jacobs: Woolwich Community Health Centre
PO Box 370, 10 Parkside Dr., St. Jacobs, ON N0B 2N0
Tel: 519-664-3794 *Fax:* 519-664-2182
genmail@wchc.on.ca
www.wchc.on.ca
Year Founded: 1985
Note: Focuses on primary health care, illness prevention, & health promotion services.
Rosslyn Bentley, Executive Director
519-664-3794, rbentley@wchc.on.ca

St. Thomas: Home & Community Care - St. Thomas Branch
Affiliated with: South West Local Health Integration Network
#70, 1063 Talbot St., St. Thomas, ON N5P 1G4
Tel: 519-631-9907 *Fax:* 519-631-2236
Toll-Free: 800-811-5146
TTY: 519-473-9626
southwest@lhins.on.ca
healthcareathome.ca/southwest
Note: Services include: nursing; personal support; physiotherapy & occupational therapy; speech & language therapy; social work; dietitians; & palliative care.

Stratford: Home & Community Care - Stratford Branch
Affiliated with: South West Local Health Integration Network
Former Name: South West Community Care Access Centre
65 Lorne Ave. East, Stratford, ON N5A 6S4
Tel: 519-273-2222 *Fax:* 519-273-2847
Toll-Free: 800-269-3683
TTY: 519-473-9626
southwest@lhins.on.ca
healthcareathome.ca/southwest
Note: Services include: chronic disease clinic; diagnostics; rehabilitation; palliative care; home care; immunization; pre- & post-natal programs; & school health program.

Sudbury: Centre de santé communautaire du Grand Sudbury
19, ch Frood, Sudbury, ON P3C 4Y9
Tél: 705-670-2274 *Téléc:* 705-670-2277
www.santesudbury.ca
www.facebook.com/CSCGrandSudbury;
twitter.com/CSCGrandSudbury
Denis Constantineau, Directeur exécutif

Sudbury: Home & Community Care - Sudbury Branch
Affiliated with: North East Local Health Integration Network
Rainbow Centre, #41-C, 40 Elm St., Sudbury, ON P3C 1S8
Tel: 705-522-3461 *Fax:* 705-522-3855
Toll-Free: 800-461-2919
healthcareathome.ca/northeast
Note: Services include: nursing; personal support; physiotherapy & occupational therapy; speech & language therapy; social work; dietitians; & palliative care.

Sudbury: Sudbury & District Health Unit
Also Known As: Public Health Sudbury & Districts
1300 Paris St., Sudbury, ON P3E 3A3
Tel: 705-522-9200 *Fax:* 705-522-5182
Toll-Free: 866-522-9200
www.phsd.ca
www.facebook.com/PublicHealthSD;
twitter.com/PublicHealthSD; www.youtube.com/PublicHealthSD
Number of Employees: 250+
Dr. Penny Sutcliffe, Medical Officer of Health & CEO

Thunder Bay: Anishnawbe Mushkiki
Affiliated with: North West Local Health Integration Network
#2B, 101 North Syndicate Ave., Thunder Bay, ON P7C 3V4
Tel: 807-623-0383
info@mushkiki.com
mushkiki.com
Note: Programs & services include: clinic care; culture; education; intervention; prevention.

Thunder Bay: NorWest Community Health Centre - Thunder Bay Site
Affiliated with: North West Local Health Integration Network
525 Simpson St., Thunder Bay, ON P7C 3J6
Tel: 807-622-8235 *Fax:* 807-622-3548
Toll-Free: 866-357-5454
www.norwestchc.org/thunder_bay.htm
www.facebook.com/NorWestCHC
Juanita Lawson, CEO

Timmins: Home & Community Care North East - Timmins Branch Office
Affiliated with: North East Local Health Integration Network
#101, 330 - 2nd Ave., Timmins, ON P4N 8A4
Tel: 705-267-2334 *Fax:* 705-267-7795
Toll-Free: 888-668-2222
healthcareathome.ca/northeast
Richard Joly, Vice-President, Home & Community Care
richard.joly@lhins.on.ca

Timmins: Misiway Milopemahtesewin Community Health Centre
130 Wilson Ave., Timmins, ON P4N 2S9
Tel: 705-264-2200 *Fax:* 705-264-2243
www.misiway.ca
Note: Clinic services; traditional healing services; diabetes education program.
Rachel Cull, Executive Director
rcull@misiway.ca

Tobermory: **Tobermory Clinic**
Affiliated with: Peninsula Family Health Team
PO Box 220, 7275 Hwy. 6, Tobermory, ON N0H 2R0
Tel: 519-596-2305 *Fax:* 519-596-2979
Note: Specialties: family health; community care; minor day surgery; mental health counselling. Number of Employees: 4 physicians + 1 nurse practitioner + 1 social worker + several clinic nurses.
Pamela Loughlean, Executive Director

Toronto: **Access Alliance Multicultural Community Health Centre**
#500, 340 College St., Toronto, ON M5T 3A9
Tel: 416-324-8677 *Fax:* 416-324-9074
mail@accessalliance.ca
www.accessalliance.ca
www.facebook.com/AccessAlliance; twitter.com/accessalliance
Note: Provides community health services to refugees & immigrants.
Axelle Janczur, Executive Director

Toronto: **Anishnawbe Health Toronto**
225 Queen St. East, Toronto, ON M5A 1S4
Tel: 416-360-0486 *Fax:* 416-365-1083
info@aht.ca
www.aht.ca

Year Founded: 1984
Note: Utilizes traditional healing approaches. A range of services is available, including fetal alcohol spectrum disorder services, diabetic care, HIV testing, mental health services & psychiatry, counselling, naturopathy, chiropody, women's services, massage therapy, & dental services. Other centres located at: 179 Gerrard St. East, 416-920-2605; & 22 Vaughan Rd., 416-657-0379. Mental Health Crisis Management Service: 416-891-8606.
Joe Hester, Executive Director

Toronto: **Bernard Betel Centre for Creative Living**
1003 Steeles Ave. West, Toronto, ON M2R 3T6
Tel: 416-225-2112 *Fax:* 416-225-2097
reception@betelcentre.org
www.betelcentre.org
www.facebook.com/betelcentre; twitter.com/betelcentre
Note: Provides education, recreation, arts, fitness & health services.
Gail Gould, Executive Director
416-225-2112, gailg@betelcentre.org

Toronto: **Black Creek Community Health Centre**
#5, 2202 Jane St., Toronto, ON M3M 1A4
Tel: 416-249-8000 *Fax:* 416-249-4594
info@bcchc.com
www.bcchc.com
twitter.com/BlackCreekCHC
Note: Programs & services include: clinical services; counselling; dietitian; & diabetes education.
Cheryl Prescod, Executive Director

Toronto: **Centre francophone de Toronto**
Ancien nom: Centre médico-social communautaire
#303, 555, rue Richmond ouest, Toronto, ON M5V 3B1
Tél: 416-922-2672 *Téléc:* 416-922-6624
Ligne sans frais: 800-268-1697
infos@centrefranco.org
www.centrefranco.org
www.facebook.com/Centre.francophone.de.Toronto;
twitter.com/CentrefrancoT;
www.linkedin.com/company/centre-francophone-de-toronto
Florence Ngenzebuhoro, Directrice générale

Toronto: **Davenport Perth Neighbourhood Centre (DPNCHC)**
1900 Davenport Rd., Toronto, ON M6N 1B7
Tel: 416-656-8025 *Fax:* 416-656-1264
info@dpnchc.ca
www.dpnchc.ca
twitter.com/DPNCHC
Note: Offers primary health care, health promotion, disease prevention, & mental health services.
Kim Fraser, Executive Director
kfraser@dpnchc.ca

Toronto: **East End Community Health Centre**
1619 Queen St. East, Toronto, ON M4L 1G4
Tel: 416-778-5858 *Fax:* 416-778-5855
www.eastendchc.on.ca
Note: Services include counselling, physiotherapy, nutrition, & medical.
Joyce Kalsen, Executive Director

Toronto: **Flemingdon Health Centre**
10 Gateway Blvd., Toronto, ON M3C 3A1
Tel: 416-429-4991 *Fax:* 416-422-3573
fhcinfo@fhc-chc.com
www.fhc-chc.com
Note: Programs & services include: medical care; health education; immunization; obstetrical care; nutrition counselling; chiropody; social services; health promotion; & diabetes prevention programs.
John Elliott, Executive Director

Toronto: **Four Villages Community Health Centre**
1700 Bloor St. West, Toronto, ON M6P 4C3
Tel: 416-604-0640 *Fax:* 416-604-3367
info@4villages.on.ca
www.4villageschc.ca
Note: Programs & services include: chronic disease & pain management; nutrition; & mental health.
Tariq Asmi, Chief Operating Officer

Toronto: **Home & Community Care - Scarborough Branch**
Affiliated with: Toronto Central Local Health Integration Network
#801, 100 Consilium Pl., Toronto, ON M1H 3E3
Tel: 416-750-2444 *Fax:* 855-352-2555
Toll-Free: 800-263-3877
TTY: 877-743-7939
healthcareathome.ca/torontocentral
Note: Chinese Line: 416-701-4806. Services include: nursing; personal support; physiotherapy & occupational therapy; speech & language therapy; social work; dietitians; & palliative care.

Toronto: **Home & Community Care - Toronto Central Branch**
Affiliated with: Toronto Central Local Health Integration Network
#305, 250 Dundas St. West, Toronto, ON M5T 2Z5
Tel: 416-506-9888 *Fax:* 416-506-0374
Toll-Free: 866-383-5446
feedback@tc.lhins.on.ca
healthcareathome.ca/torontocentral
Note: Services include: nursing; personal support; physiotherapy & occupational therapy; speech & language therapy; social work; dietitians; & palliative care.

Toronto: **Lawrence Heights Community Health Centre**
12 Flemington Rd., Toronto, ON M6A 2N4
Tel: 416-787-1661 *Fax:* 416-787-3761
www.unisonhcs.org
www.facebook.com/UnisonHCS; twitter.com/unisonhcs
Note: Programs & services include: medical care; counselling; diabetes management; dietitian; dental; footcare; & seniors health care.
Michelle Joseph, Chief Executive Officer

Toronto: **Parkdale Community Health Centre - Parkdale Site**
1229 Queen St. West, Toronto, ON M6K 1L2
Tel: 416-537-2455 *Fax:* 416-537-5133
pqwchc.org
Year Founded: 1984
Note: Specialties: Service in several languages; Primary care; Educational programs, such as pre- & post-natal classes; Support groups; Counselling; Mental health support; HIV testing.
Angela Robertson, Executive Director
arobertson@ctchc.com

Toronto: **Parkdale Queen West Community Health Centre - Queen West Site**
168 Bathurst St., Toronto, ON M5V 2R4
Tel: 416-703-8482 *Fax:* 416-703-7832
pqwchc.org
Note: Medical services (with specialized services for the homeless), psychiatric & mental health services, individual & group counselling, harm reduction program (safer sex, safer drug use, Hepatitis C & HIV prevention), needle exchange, diabetes education program, chiropody, perinatal nursing, dental clinic.
Angela Robertson, Executive Director
arobertson@ctchc.com

Toronto: **Regent Park Community Health Centre**
465 Dundas St. East, Toronto, ON M5A 2B2
Tel: 416-364-2261 *Fax:* 416-364-0822
www.regentparkchc.org
Year Founded: 1973
Note: Emphasis on an integrated approach: health promotion, disease prevention, social services. A community-founded & operated facility, with a focus on comprehensive, accessible care. Services in English, Cantonese, Mandarin, Vietnamese, Somali & Spanish. The Pathways to Education Program for youth at risk, created & first implemented in Regent Park, has been adopted by communities across Canada.
Paulos Gebreyesus, Executive Director
paulosg@regentparkchc.org

Toronto: **Scarborough Centre for Healthy Communities**
Former Name: West Hill Community Services
2660 Eglinton Ave. East, Toronto, ON M1K 2S3
Tel: 416-642-9445
ask@schcontario.ca
www.schcontario.ca
Info Line: 416-847-4173
www.facebook.com/ScarboroughCentreforHealthyCommunities;
twitter.com/schcont; www.instagram.com/schcontario
Year Founded: 1977
Number of Employees: 130
Note: Offers 38 integrated services across 11 sites. They provide medical assistance through their clinics, are involved in a youth program, & have other social support programs including a food bank..
Jeanie Joaquin, CEO
416-847-4091, jjoaquin@schcontario.ca

Toronto: **South East Toronto Family Health Team - Coxwell Site**
#105, 840 Coxwell Ave., Toronto, ON M4C 5T2
Tel: 416-469-6464 *Fax:* 416-469-6164
setfht.on.ca
Year Founded: 2002
Note: Specialties: Low-risk obstetrics; Psychotherapy; Telephone health advisory service.

Toronto: **South Riverdale Community Health Centre**
955 Queen St. East, Toronto, ON M4M 3P3
Tel: 416-461-1925 *Fax:* 416-469-3442
www.srchc.ca
www.facebook.com/445944888819281;
twitter.com/SRiverdaleCHC
Note: Programs & services include: counselling; diabetes education; environmental health; nutrition; chiropody; health care clinic; physiotherapy; & Teleophthalmology.
Lynne Raskin, Chief Executive Officer

Toronto: **Stonegate Community Health Centre**
150 Berry Rd., Toronto, ON M8Y 1W3
Tel: 416-231-7070 *Fax:* 416-231-6903
info@stonegatechc.org
www.stonegatechc.org
www.facebook.com/318730301566322;
twitter.com/StonegateCHC
Note: Services: asthma education; chiropody; counselling; dental; diabetes education; dietitian; medical; & smoking cessation.
Bev Leaver, Executive Director

Toronto: **Vibrant Healthcare Alliance**
Former Name: Anne Johnston Health Station
2398 Yonge St., Toronto, ON M4P 2H4
Tel: 416-486-8666 *Fax:* 416-486-8660
info@vibranthealthcare.ca
www.vibranthealthcare.ca
Note: Programs & services include: chiropody; counselling; occupational therapy; nutrition; physiotherapy; Seniors Home Health Program; & youth health clinic.
Simone Atungo, Chief Executive Officer

Toronto: **Women's Health in Women's Hands**
#500, 2 Carlton St., Toronto, ON M5B 1J3
Tel: 416-593-7655 *Fax:* 416-593-5867
info@whiwh.com
www.whiwh.com
www.facebook.com/whiwhchc; twitter.com/whiwhchc;
www.youtube.com/user/TorontoWHIWHCHC
Year Founded: 1993
Number of Employees: 33
Note: Provides mental & physical health services for women ages 16 & above.
Lori-Ann Green-Walker, Executive Director
lori-ann@whiwh.com

Tweed: **Gateway Community Health Centre**
PO Box 99, 41 McClellan St., Tweed, ON K0K 3J0
Tel: 613-478-1211 *Fax:* 613-478-6692
Toll-Free: 855-478-1211
www.gatewaychc.org
Year Founded: 1991
Note: Programs & services include: primary care; chronic disease management; nutritional counselling; mental health; & health promotion.
Lyn Linton, Executive Director
613-478-1211

Waterloo: **Home & Community Care - Waterloo Branch**
Affiliated with: Waterloo Wellington Local Health Integration Network
141 Weber St. South, Waterloo, ON N2J 2A9
Tel: 519-748-2222 *Fax:* 519-883-5555
Toll-Free: 888-883-3313
TTY: 519-883-5589
healthcareathome.ca/ww
Note: Services include: nursing; personal support; physiotherapy & occupational therapy; speech & language therapy; social work; dietitians; & palliative care.

West Lorne: **West Elgin Community Health Centre**
153 Main St., West Lorne, ON N0L 2P0
Tel: 519-768-1715 *Fax:* 519-768-2548
info@wechc.on.ca
www.wechc.on.ca
Note: Provides health services & community programs to residents of the western Elgin area.
Andy Kroeker, Executive Director
akroeker@wechc.on.ca

Whitby: **Home & Community Care - Whitby Branch**
Affiliated with: Central East Local Health Integration Network
Former Name: Durham Access to Care
920 Champlain Ct., Whitby, ON L1N 6K9
Tel: 905-430-3308 *Fax:* 855-352-2555
Toll-Free: 800-263-3877
healthcareathome/centraleast
Note: Services include: nursing; personal support; physiotherapy & occupational therapy; speech & language therapy; social work; dietitians; & palliative care.

Windsor: **Home & Community Care Erie St. Clair - Windsor Branch**
Affiliated with: Erie St. Clair Local Health Integration Network
5415 Tecumseh Rd. East, 2nd Fl., Windsor, ON N8T 1C5
Tel: 519-436-2222 *Fax:* 519-351-5842
Toll-Free: 888-447-4468
healthcareathome.ca/eriestclair

Windsor: **Sandwich Community Health Centre**
Affiliated with: Windsor Essex Community Health Centre
3325 College Ave., Windsor, ON N9C 0E1
Tel: 519-258-6002 *Fax:* 519-258-3693
www.wechc.org
www.facebook.com/weCHC519; twitter.com/wechc_
Year Founded: 1982
Note: Focuses on providing primary health care & counselling.
Rita Taillefer, Executive Director
519-253-8481, rtaillefer@wechc

Windsor: **Teen Health Centre**
Affiliated with: Windsor Essex Community Health Centre
#101, 1361 Ouellette Ave., Windsor, ON N8X 1J6
Tel: 519-253-8481 *Fax:* 519-253-4362
www.wechc.org
www.facebook.com/weCHC519; twitter.com/wechc_
Note: Specialties: counselling; primary care; Special Additions, a prenatal program; Diabetes In Action, a community based diabetes program; Street Health Homeless Initiative Program, a program to serve homeless or at-risk persons in Windsor & Essex County.
Rita Taillefer, Executive Director
519-253-8481, rtaillefer@wechc.org

Woodstock: **Home & Community Care - Woodstock Branch**
Affiliated with: South West Local Health Integration Network
Former Name: South West Community Care Access Centre
1147 Dundas St., Woodstock, ON N4S 8W3
Tel: 519-539-1284 *Fax:* 519-539-0065
Toll-Free: 800-561-5490
TTY: 519-473-9626
southwest@lhins.on.ca
healthcareathome.ca/southwest
Note: Services include: nursing; personal support; physiotherapy & occupational therapy; speech & language therapy; social work; dietitians; & palliative care.

Bearskin Lake: **Bearskin Lake Nursing Station**
Affiliated with: North West Local Health Integration Network
c/o Bearskin Lake Nursing Station, PO Box 56, Bearskin Lake, ON P0V 1E0
Tel: 807-363-2582 *Fax:* 807-363-1021
Note: Programs & services include: diabetes clinic; health awareness workshop; alcohol / drug abuse workshop; communicable diseases clinic.
Wesley Nothing, Director, Health
807-738-0127, wesn@michikan.ca

Big Trout Lake: **Kitchenuhmaykoosib Inninuwug Nursing Station**
Affiliated with: North West Local Health Integration Network
c/o Nursing Station, PO Box 329, Big Trout Lake, ON P0V 1G0
Tel: 807-537-2262 *Fax:* 807-537-2283
Note: Programs & services include: emergency; mental health; & immunization clinic.
Shane Cutfeet, Acting Director
807-537-2265

Cat Lake: **Margaret Gray Nursing Station**
Affiliated with: North West Local Health Integration Network
c/o Nursing Station, PO Box 75, Cat Lake, ON P0V 1J0
Tel: 807-347-2110 *Fax:* 807-347-2140
Note: Programs & services include: diabetes clinic; health awareness workshop; alcohol / drug abuse workshop; communicable diseases clinic.

Deer Lake: **Deer Lake Nursing Station**
Deer Lake Health Centre
Affiliated with: North West Local Health Integration Network
PO Box 10, Deer Lake, ON P0V 1N0
Tel: 807-775-2054 *Fax:* 807-775-2309
Note: Programs & services include: diabetes clinic; health awareness workshop; alcohol / drug abuse workshop; communicable diseases clinic.
Garylene Meekis, Director, Health
807-775-2226, garylenemeekis@knet.ca

Eabamet Lake: **Eabametoong Nursing Station**
Affiliated with: North West Local Health Integration Network
c/o Nursing Station, PO Box 70, Eabamet Lake, ON P0T 1L0
Tel: 807-242-7401 *Fax:* 807-242-1344
Note: Programs & services include: emergency; X-ray; & immunization clinic.
John Louie Oskineegish, Supervisor, Health Clinic
807-242-7401

Keewaywin: **Keewaywin Nursing Station**
Affiliated with: North West Local Health Integration Network
PO Box 59, 204 Band Offfice Rd., Keewaywin, ON P0V 3G0
Tel: 807-771-1407 *Fax:* 866-437-9505
Toll-Free: 807-771-1078
Note: Programs & services include: emergency; mental health; & immunization clinic.
James Kakepetum, Director
jameskakepetum@knet.ca

Sandy Lake: **Sandy Lake Nursing Station**
Sandy Lake Health Authority
Affiliated with: North West Local Health Integration Network
PO Box 20, Sandy Lake, ON P0V 1V0
Tel: 807-774-3461 *Fax:* 807-774-1585
www.sandylake.firstnation.ca/?q=sandy-lake-health-authority
Note: Programs & services include: emergency; mental health; & immunization clinic.
Joan Rae, Director, Health
807-774-1133, joanrae@knet.ca

Summer Beaver: **Nibinamik Nursing Station**
Affiliated with: North West Local Health Integration Network
PO Box 116, Summer Beaver, ON P0T 3B0
Tel: 807-593-2211 *Fax:* 807-593-2253
Note: Programs & services include: emergency; mental health; & immunization clinic.
Annie Oskineegish

Barrie: **Royal Victoria Hospital - Barrie Community Care Centre for Substance Abuse**
70 Wellington St. West, Barrie, ON L4N 1K4
Tel: 705-728-4226 *Fax:* 705-728-7308
Toll-Free: 866-850-7034
www.rvh.on.ca
Number of Beds: 41 beds
Note: Intoxification management, withdrawal management, assessments, family education, discharge planning.
Brian Irving, Interim Manager, Addictions Services

Brantford: **Lansdowne Children's Centre**
39 Mount Pleasant St., Brantford, ON N3T 1S7
Tel: 519-753-3153 *Fax:* 519-753-5927
Toll-Free: 800-454-7186
info@lansdownecc.com
www.lansdownecentre.ca
www.facebook.com/127644350608842;
twitter.com/LansdowneBrant;
www.youtube.com/user/LansdowneCC
Note: The centre provides services for children & youth with physical, communication & developmental challenges.
Rita-Marie Hadley, Executive Director

Cambridge: **KidsAbility Centre for Child Development**
Cambridge
Former Name: Rotary Children's Centre
887 Langs Dr., Cambridge, ON N3H 5K4
Tel: 519-886-8886 *Fax:* 519-886-7292
info@kidsability.ca
www.kidsability.ca
Year Founded: 1957
Note: Specialty: Services for children & young adults with physical, developmental, & communication disabilities.
Paola Zimmer, Client Services Manager, Cambridge
pzimmer@kidsability.ca

Chatham: **Children's Treatment Centre of Chatham-Kent**
Former Name: Prism Centre for Audiology & Children's Rehabilitation
355 Lark St., Chatham, ON N7L 5B2
Tel: 519-354-0520 *Fax:* 519-354-7355
Toll-Free: 833-241-0628
TTY: 226-996-9967
info@ctc-ck.com
www.ctc-ck.com
www.facebook.com/CTCCK; twitter.com/CTC_CK
Year Founded: 1948
Note: Services include: music therapy; occupational therapy; physiotherapy; respite services; & speech therapy.

Cornwall: **Cornwall Withdrawal Management Services**
Cornwall Community Hospital
850 McConnell Ave., Cornwall, ON K6H 4M3
Tel: 613-938-8506 *Fax:* 613-938-2867
www.cornwallhospital.ca/en/WithdrawalManagement
Note: Cornwall's Withdrawal Management Services hosts AA & NA meetings & group therapy for men & women sixteen years of age & over. Strategies & information are provided to prevent substance misuse. The organization is bilingual.
Angel Quesnel, Manager
angel.quesnel@cornwallhospital.ca

Fergus: **KidsAbility Centre for Child Development**
Fergus
Former Name: Rotary Children's Centre
c/o Community Resource Centre, 160 St. David St. South, Fergus, ON N1M 2L3
Fax: 519-886-7292
Toll-Free: 888-372-2259
wellingtonreception@kidsability.ca
www.kidsability.ca
Year Founded: 1957
Note: Specialty: Services for children & young adults with physical, developmental, & communication disabilities
Mary Ellen McIlroy, Client Services Manager, Guelph & Fergus
memcilroy@kidsability.ca

Guelph: **KidsAbility Centre for Child Development**
Guelph
Former Name: Rotary Children's Centre
c/o West End Community Centre, 21 Imperial Rd. South, Guelph, ON N1K 1X3
Fax: 519-780-0470
Toll-Free: 888-372-2259
info@kidsability.ca
www.kidsability.ca

Year Founded: 1957
Note: Specialty: Services for children & young adults with physical, developmental, & communication disabilities.
Mary Ellen McIlroy, Client Services Manager, Guelph & Fergus
memcilroy@kidsability.ca

Hamilton: **Juravinski Cancer Centre**
Hamilton Health Sciences
Affiliated with: Hamilton Niagara Haldimand Brant Local Health Integration Network
Former Name: Hamilton Regional Cancer Centre
699 Concession St., Hamilton, ON L8V 5C2
Tel: 905-387-9495
www.jcc.hhsc.ca

Dr. Ralph Meyer, President

Kingston: **Cancer Centre of Southeastern Ontario**
Kingston General Hospital
25 King St. West, Kingston, ON K7L 5P9
Tel: 613-549-6666   *Toll-Free:* 800-567-5722
kingstonhsc.ca/cancer-care
Brenda Carter, Regional Vice-President

Kingston: **KidsInclusive Centre for Child & Youth Development/Le Centre de développement de l'enfant**
Hotel Dieu Hospital
Former Name: Child Development Centre
c/o Hotel Dieu Hospital, 166 Brock St., Kingston, ON K7L 5G2
Tel: 613-544-3400 *Fax:* 613-545-3557
www.kidsinclusive.ca
Area Served: Kingston & the surrounding area *Number of Employees:* 50
Note: Most services require physician referral. The Infant & Child Development Program accepts referrals from parents, physicians, therapists, or community service providers.

Kingston: **Kingston Detoxification Centre**
Hotel Dieu Hospital
240 Brock St., Kingston, ON K7L 5G2
Tel: 613-549-6461
www.hoteldieu.com
Note: The Detoxification Centre provides counselling, self-help groups, & referral to community services

Kitchener: **Waterloo Regional Withdrawal Management Centre**
Grand River Hospital
52 Glasgow St., Kitchener, ON N2G 1N6
Tel: 519-749-4318
info@grhosp.on.ca
www.grhosp.on.ca
Number of Beds: 28 beds

London: **London Regional Cancer Program**
London Health Sciences Centre
PO Box 5165, 790 Commissioners Rd. East, London, ON N6A 4L6
Tel: 519-685-8600 *Fax:* 519-685-8808
www.lhsc.on.ca
Note: Services include: inpatient & outpatient cancer care; radiation therapy; chemotherapy; syooirt services, such as social work & diet & nutrition counselling.
Brenda Fleming, Program Director, Cancer Services

London: **Thames Valley Children's Centre**
779 Baseline Rd. East, London, ON N6C 5Y6
Tel: 519-685-8700 *Fax:* 519-685-8689
Toll-Free: 866-590-8822
info@tvcc.on.ca
www.tvcc.on.ca
Year Founded: 1949
Note: Specialties: Rehabilitation services for children with physical disabilities, developmental delays, & communication disorders; Assessment & diagnosis services; Autism intervention program; Intensive behavioural intervention; Physiotherapy; Occupational therapy; Research; School support program.
Number of Employees: 350+ + 500 volunteers + 55 students.
John A. LaPorta, CEO

Mississauga: **Erinoak Kids**
2277 South Millway, Mississauga, ON L5L 2M5
Tel: 905-855-2690 *Toll-Free:* 877-374-6625
www.erinoakkids.ca
www.facebook.com/ErinoakKids; twitter.com/ErinoakKids; www.youtube.com/ErinoakKidsCentre
Year Founded: 1978
Number of Employees: 650
Note: Offers autism, communication, hearing, medical, occupational therapy, physiotherapy, & vision services to children & families.
Bridget Fewtrell, President & CEO

Pauline Eaton, Vice-President, Autism Services
Chris Hartley, Vice-President, Clinical Services
Kathy Swaile, Vice-President, Human Resources & Facilities
Christina Djokoto, Vice-President, Quality, Improvement & Operational Readiness

Oshawa: **Grandview Children's Centre**
Former Name: Grandview Rehabilitation & Treatment Centre of Durham Region
600 Townline Rd. South, Oshawa, ON L1H 7K6
Tel: 905-728-1673 *Fax:* 905-728-2961
Toll-Free: 800-304-6180
www.grandviewkids.ca
www.facebook.com/GrandviewKids; twitter.com/grandviewkids
Note: A treatment centre for children with physical, developmental & communication disabilities.
Lorraine Sunstrum-Mann, Chief Executive Officer
905-728-1673, lorraine.sunstrum-mann@grandviewkids.ca

Ottawa: **The Ottawa Children's Treatment Centre (OCTC)/Le Centre de traitement pour enfants d'Ottawa**
395 Smyth Rd., Ottawa, ON K1H 8L2
Tel: 613-737-0871 *Fax:* 613-523-5167
Toll-Free: 800-565-4839
www.cheo.on.ca
www.facebook.com/CHEOkids; twitter.com/CHEO; www.instagram.com/cheohospital
Year Founded: 1951
Note: From several locations in Ottawa & area, The Centre provides specialized care for children with multiple physical, developmental & behavioural needs. Services in English & French. Amalgamated with the Children's Hospital of Eastern Ontario in October 2016.
Alex Munter, Chief Executive Director
Dr. Lindsay Sampson, Chief of Staff
Ann Lynch, Chief Nurse Executive & Vice-President Acute Care

Ottawa: **Ottawa Hospital Cancer Program**
General Campus, 501 Smyth Rd., Ottawa, ON K1H 8L6
Tel: 613-737-7700
Note: Services include: screening; early detection; diagnosis; treatment; supportive care; palliative care; & research.
Debra A. Bournes, Regional Vice-President, Cancer Care Ontario
613-737-8749, debra.bournes@toh.ca

Ottawa: **The Ottawa Morgentaler Clinic**
The Morgentaler Clinic
65 Bank St., Ottawa, ON K1P 5N2
Tel: 613-567-8300 *Fax:* 613-567-9128
www.morgentaler.ca
Note: Specialty: Abortion services; Counselling.

Ottawa: **Rehabilitation Centre (TRC)**
The Ottawa Hospital
505 Smyth Rd., Ottawa, ON K1H 8M2
Tel: 613-737-7350
TTY: 613-526-1132
feedback@toh.ca
www.ottawahospital.on.ca
Note: Specialties: Rehabilitation of persons with a disabling physical illness or injury; Prosthetics & orthotics; Physiotherapy; Occupational therapy; Respiratory therapy; Speech-language pathology; Psychological services; Vocational rehabilitation counselling; Social work; Research.
Dr. Jack Kitts, President & CEO
613-761-4800, jbkitts@toh.ca

Peterborough: **Five Counties Children's Centre**
872 Dutton Rd., Peterborough, ON K9H 7G1
Tel: 705-748-2221 *Fax:* 705-748-3526
Toll-Free: 888-779-9916
www.fivecounties.on.ca
www.facebook.com/FiveCountiesChildrensCentre; twitter.com/5CountiesKids; www.youtube.com/user/FiveCountiesChildren
Note: Helps children with special needs 0-19 years of age. Services include speech & language therapy, occupational therapy, physiotherapy, therapautic recreation, & augmentative communication.
Diane Pick, Chief Executive Officer
705-748-2337, dpick@fivecounties.on.ca
Darlene Callan, Director, Clinical Services
705-748-2337, dcallan@fivecounties.on.ca

Sarnia: **Pathways Health Centre for Children**
1240 Murphy Rd., Sarnia, ON N7S 2Y6
Tel: 519-542-3471 *Fax:* 519-542-4115
Toll-Free: 855-542-3471
info@pathwayscentre.org
www.pathwayscentre.org
www.facebook.com/PathwaysHealthCentreforChildren; twitter.com/PathwaysSarnia
Year Founded: 1975
Alison Morrison, Executive Director

Sault Ste Marie: **Sault Ste. Marie Withdrawal Management Services**
Sault Area Hospital
911 Queen St. East, Sault Ste Marie, ON P6A 2B6
Tel: 705-942-1872 *Fax:* 705-759-6369
www.sah.on.ca
Number of Beds: 15 beds
Note: Detox centre
Wendy Hansson, President & CEO, Sault Area Hospital

Sault Ste Marie: **THRIVE Child Development Centre/Centre de développement de l'enfant**
Former Name: Children's Rehabilitation Centre Algoma
74 Johnson Ave., Sault Ste Marie, ON P6C 2V5
Tel: 705-759-1131 *Fax:* 705-759-0783
Toll-Free: 855-759-1131
info@kidsthrive.ca
www.kidsthrive.ca
Year Founded: 1952
Note: Programs & services include therapy, respite care, & resource support.
Susan Vanagas-Cote, Interim CEO
Mirja Keranen, Business Director
Kate Lawrence, Professional Services Manager, Early Childhood Education
Maxine Orr, Professional Services Manager, Occupational Therapy
Scott Nieson, Professional Services Manager, Physiotherapy

St. Agatha: **Carizon Family & Community Services**
Former Name: kidsLINK
PO Box 190, 1855 Notre Dame Dr., St. Agatha, ON N0B 2L0
Tel: 519-746-5437
info@carizon.ca
www.carizon.ca
www.facebook.com/carizonupdates; twitter.com/carizon; www.linkedin.com/company/carizon-family-and-community-servi ces
Note: Mental health & counselling services for children, youth, & families.
Tracy Elop, CEO

St. Catharines: **Hôtel Dieu Shaver Health & Rehabilitation Centre**
Affiliated with: Hamilton Niagara Haldimand Brant Local Health Integration Network
Former Name: Hôtel-Dieu Health Sciences Hospital - Niagara
541 Glenridge Ave., St. Catharines, ON L2T 4C2
Tel: 905-685-1381 *Fax:* 905-687-4871
www.hoteldieushaver.org
www.facebook.com/HotelDieuShaver; twitter.com/HotelDieuShaver; www.instagram.com/hoteldieushaver
Number of Beds: 134 beds
Number of Employees: 400
Note: Complex continuing care, rehabilitation, & palliative care.
Lynne Pay, Interim CEO & Vice-President, Corporate Services
lynne.pay@hoteldieushaver.org
Dr. Jack Luce, Chief of Staff
dr.johnthomas.luce@hoteldieushaver.org
Jennifer Hansen, Chief Nursing Officer & Director, Nursing
jennifer.hansen@hoteldieushaver.org
David Ceglie, Vice-President, Clinical Services
david.ceglie@hoteldieushaver.org

St. Catharines: **Niagara Children's Centre**
Former Name: Niagara Peninsula Children's Centre
567 Glenridge Ave., St. Catharines, ON L2T 4C2
Tel: 905-688-3550 *Fax:* 905-688-1055
Toll-Free: 800-896-5496
info@niagarachildrenscentre.com
www.niagarachildrenscentre.com
Note: Children's rehabilitation centre.
Oksana Fisher, Chief Executive Officer
905-688-1890
Marla Smith, Director, Development
Dorothy Harvey, Director, Clinical Services & Coporate Services & Finance

St. Catharines: **Niagara Regional Men's Withdrawal Management Service**
Niagara Health System / Système de santé de Niagara
Affiliated with: Hamilton Niagara Haldimand Brant Local Health Integration Network
10 Adams St., St. Catharines, ON L2R 2V8
Tel: 905-682-7211 *Fax:* 905-687-9768
Number of Beds: 18 beds
Note: The withdrawal management service offers crisis intervention, assessments, counselling, self-help groups, & treatment referrals for inpatients & outpatients.

St. Catharines: **St Catharines Detoxification (Women's) Centre**
6 Adams St., St. Catharines, ON L2R 2V8
Tel: 905-687-9721 *Fax:* 905-687-9768
Number of Beds: 14 beds

Sudbury: **Children's Treatment Centre**
Affiliated with: Health Sciences North
41 Ramsey Lake Rd., Sudbury, ON P3E 5J1
Tel: 705-523-7337 *Fax:* 705-523-7157
www.hsnsudbury.ca
www.facebook.com/HSNSudbury; twitter.com/HSN_Sudbury;
www.youtube.com/user/healthsciencesnorth;
www.linkedin.com/company/health-sciences-north
Note: Outpatient, community-based rehabilitation centre for children & young adults with motor & communication challenges.
Dr. Sean Murray, Medical Director
Joanne Tramontini, Clinical Manager

Sudbury: **Withdrawal Management Services**
Health Sciences North
336 Pine St., Sudbury, ON P3C 1X8
Tel: 705-671-7366 *Fax:* 705-675-7962
www.hsnsudbury.ca
Note: Offers detox services & short-term crisis safe bed program.

Thunder Bay: **George Jeffrey Children's Centre (GJCC)**
Former Name: George Jeffrey Children's Treatment Centre
200 Brock St. East, Thunder Bay, ON P7E 0A2
Tel: 807-623-4381 *Fax:* 807-623-7161
Toll-Free: 888-818-7330
info@georgejeffrey.com
www.georgejeffrey.com
www.facebook.com/132052553534644
Year Founded: 1948
Note: Services include occupational therapy, physiotherapy, speech & language therapy & social work.
Tina Bennett, Chief Executive Officer

Timmins: **Cochrane Temiskaming Children's Treatment Centre/Centre de traitement pour enfants Cochrane Temiskaming**
#1, 733 Ross Ave. East, Timmins, ON P4N 8S8
Tel: 705-264-4700 *Fax:* 705-268-3585
Toll-Free: 800-575-3210
Year Founded: 1980
Area Served: Districts of Cochrane and Temiskaming *Number of Employees:* 30
Note: Services include consultation, assessment, treatment and education.
Marie Rouleau, Executive Director
marie.rouleau@ctctc.org

Toronto: **Bob Rumball Centre for the Deaf**
2395 Bayview Ave., Toronto, ON M2L 1A2
Tel: 416-449-9651 *Fax:* 416-449-8881
TTY: 416-449-2728
info@bobrumball.org
www.bobrumball.org
Number of Beds: 56 beds
Note: Long-term care facility for the deaf.
Derek Rumball, President

Toronto: **Cabbagetown Women's Clinic**
302 Gerrard St. East, Toronto, ON M5A 2G7
Tel: 416-323-0642 *Fax:* 416-323-3099
Toll-Free: 800-399-1592
www.cabbagetownwomensclinic.com
Year Founded: 1989
Note: Licensed as an Independent Health facility funded by the Ontario Min. of Health & Long Term Care, the clinic provides safe & legal abortion services.
Dr. M. Buruiana, Medical Director

Toronto: **Casey House**
119 Isabella St., Toronto, ON M4Y 1P2
Tel: 416-962-7600
heart@caseyhouse.ca
www.caseyhouse.com
www.facebook.com/CaseyHouseTO; twitter.com/caseyhouseTO;
www.youtube.com/caseyhousetv;
www.linkedin.com/company/casey-house-foundation
Year Founded: 1988
Number of Beds: 13 beds
Note: Hospice; home care office
Joanne Simons, CEO

Toronto: **Centre for Addiction & Mental Health ARF Site**
Former Name: Addiction Research Foundation
33 Russell St., Toronto, ON M5S 2S1
Tel: 416-595-6000 *Fax:* 416-595-9997
Toll-Free: 800-463-2338
info@camh.ca
www.camh.ca
www.facebook.com/CentreforAddictionandMentalHealth;
twitter.com/CAMHnews; www.youtube.com/camhtv;
www.linkedin.com/company/camh
Note: Drug rehabilitation centre
David Cunic, Vice-President, Redevelopment & Support Services

Toronto: **Centre for Addiction & Mental Health (Corporate Office)**
1001 Queen St. West, Toronto, ON M6J 1H4
Tel: 416-535-8501 *Toll-Free:* 800-463-2338
info@camh.ca
www.camh.ca
www.facebook.com/CentreforAddictionandMentalHealth;
twitter.com/CAMHnews; www.youtube.com/user/CAMHTV;
www.linkedin.com/company/camh
Number of Beds: 530 inpatient beds
Dr. Catherine Zahn, President & CEO

Toronto: **Child Development Institute**
Former Name: West End Creche Child & Family Clinic
197 Euclid Ave., Toronto, ON M6J 2J8
Tel: 416-603-1827 *Fax:* 416-603-6655
info@childdevelop.ca
www.childdevelop.ca
www.facebook.com/childdevelop; twitter.com/officialcdi;
www.youtube.com/user/CDICanada;
www.linkedin.com/company/child-development-institute
Year Founded: 1909
Note: Provides mental health programs & services for children & youth.
Dr. Lynn Ryan MacKenzie, Chief Executive Officer
lrmackenzie@childdevelop.ca
Steve Blake, Chief Operating Officer
sblake@childdevelop.ca
Dr. Leena Augimeri, Director, Scientific & Program Development
laugimeri@childdevelop.ca

Toronto: **Choice in Health Clinic**
#301, 1678 Bloor St. West, Toronto, ON M6P 1A9
Tel: 416-975-9300 *Fax:* 416-975-0314
Toll-Free: 866-565-9300
www.choiceinhealth.ca
Note: Abortion clinic

Toronto: **Eye Bank of Canada**
Ontario Division
Affiliated with: Kensington Health
340 College St., #B100, Toronto, ON M5T 3A9
Tel: 416-978-7355 *Fax:* 416-978-1522
eyebank@kensingtonhealth.org
www.kensingtonhealth.org/eye-bank
Year Founded: 1955
Christine Humphreys, Director

Toronto: **Holland Bloorview Kids Rehabilitation Hospital**
Affiliated with: Toronto Central Local Health Integration Network
Former Name: Bloorview Children's Hospital
150 Kilgour Road, Toronto, ON M4G 1R8
Tel: 416-425-6220 *Fax:* 416-425-6591
Toll-Free: 800-363-2440
www.hollandbloorview.ca
www.facebook.com/HBKRH; twitter.com/HBKidsHospital;
www.youtube.com/user/PRBloorview
Year Founded: 1899
Number of Beds: 75 beds
Note: Pediatric rehabilitation & continuing care complex.
Julia Hanigsberg, President & CEO

Marilyn Ballantyne, Chief Nursing Executive
Dr. Golda Milo-Manson, Vice-President, Medicine & Academic Affairs
Stewart Wong, Vice-President, Communications, Marketing & Advocacy

Toronto: **Marvelle Koffler Breast Centre**
J. & W. Lebovic Health Complex, Mount Sinai Hospit, 600 University Ave., 12th Fl., Toronto, ON M5G 1X5
Tel: 416-586-8799
www.mountsinai.on.ca/care/mkbc
Year Founded: 1995
Note: Specialties: Outpatient facility for breast health & disease; mammography / breast imaging; pathology; surgery; psychiatry; nutrition; boutique addressing the needs of women who have experienced breast cancer; palliative medicine.
Dr. Christine Elser, Head, Familial Breast Cancer Clinic

Toronto: **The Morgentaler Clinic**
727 Hillsdale Ave. East, Toronto, ON M4S 1V4
Tel: 416-932-0446 *Fax:* 416-932-0837
Toll-Free: 800-556-6835
mclinic@passport.ca
www.morgentaler.ca
Note: Services include: abortion; counselling; contraceptive education; & STI testing.

Toronto: **Neurology Centre of Toronto (NCT)**
#100, 491 Eglinton Ave., Toronto, ON M5N 1A7
Tel: 416-860-7554 *Fax:* 416-860-7559
admin@neurologycentretoronto.com
neurologycentretoronto.com
www.facebook.com/neurologycentretoronto;
twitter.com/NCTtweets;
www.instagram.com/neurologycentretoronto
Specialties: Autism; concussions; epilepsy; neurodevelopmental disorders
Note: NCT offers expertise care in a variety of areas in neurology, including autism, cognitive behavioural therapy, concussions, developmental delay, epilepsy & seizures, headache & migraine, & neurodevelopmental disorders. NCT offers patient patient consultations via telemedicine. NCT also offers CBD as a form of treatment pertaining to epilepsy.
Dr. Evan Cole Lewis, MD, FRCPC, Director
Nicole Karpinski, Operations Manager
Caitlin Nolan, Clinic Coordinator

Toronto: **Pine Villa**
1035 Eglinton Ave. West, Toronto, ON M6C 2C8
Tel: 416-787-4538
www.pinevilla.ca
Year Founded: 1961
Number of Beds: 69 units
Note: Transitional care site providing short-term services for older adults who no longer require care in a hospital and are waiting to move home with community supports or awaiting placement in a long-term care facility or another care setting. Site of a former retirement home by the same name.
Sharon Rosenblum, Executive Director

Toronto: **St. Michael's Hospital Withdrawal Management Services**
135 Sherbourne St., Toronto, ON M5A 2R5
Fax: 416-864-5146
Toll-Free: 866-366-9513
www.stmichaelshospital.com
Number of Beds: 17 beds
Note: Detoxification centre

Toronto: **Sunnybrook Health Sciences Centre - Holland Orthopaedic & Arthritic Centre**
Affiliated with: Toronto Central Local Health Integration Network
43 Wellesley St. East, Toronto, ON M4Y 1H1
Tel: 416-967-8500 *Fax:* 416-967-8521
www.sunnybrook.ca
Note: Care for complex injuries of the musculoskeletal system, with a focus on traumatic injury management, joint reconstruction & replacement, surgery, sports & activity-related injury management, rehabilitation, & rheumatology. The Clinic has a second location at the main Sunnybrook site, 2075 Bayview Ave., Toronto.
Dr. Andy Smith, President & CEO

Toronto: **Sunnybrook Health Sciences Centre - St. John's Rehab**
Affiliated with: Toronto Central Local Health Integration Network
285 Cummer Ave., Toronto, ON M2M 2G1
Tel: 416-226-6780 *Fax:* 416-226-6265
www.sunnybrook.ca
Number of Beds: 160 beds
Note: Provides specialized rehabilitation services & care in burn

injuries, organ transplant rehabilitation, cancer, cardiovascular surgery, strokes & other neurological conditions, traumatic injuries & complex medical conditions. Teaching site for the University of Toronto & a research facility. A multicultural & multifaith environment dedicated to the values of care of the Sisters of St. John the Divine.
Dr. Andy Smith, President & CEO

Toronto: Sunnybrook Health Sciences Centre - The Odette Cancer Centre
Affiliated with: Toronto Central Local Health Integration Network
2075 Bayview Ave., Toronto, ON M4N 3M5
Tel: 416-480-5000
TTY: 416-480-5342
questions@sunnybrook.ca
sunnybrook.ca/content/?page=odette-cancer-centre
Note: Comprehensive cancer care, multidisciplinary, evidence-based approach; research, education & community outreach.
Dr. Andy Smith, President & CEO

Toronto: Toronto Rehabilitation Institute
University Health Network
Affiliated with: Toronto Central Local Health Integration Network
Also Known As: Toronto Rehab
550 University Ave., Toronto, ON M5G 2A2
Tel: 416-597-3422 *Fax:* 416-597-1977
www.uhn.ca/torontorehab
www.facebook.com/UniversityHealthNetwork;
twitter.com/UHN_News; www.youtube.com/UHNToronto;
www.linkedin.com/company/university-health-network
Note: Rehabilitation & complex continuing care; includes Lakeside Long-Term Care Centre; Lyndhurst Centre; E.W. Bickle Centre; Rumsey Centre, & University Centre.
Dr. Kevin Smith, President & CEO

Toronto: Toronto Western Hospital - Addiction Outpatient/Aftercare Clinic
University Health Network
Affiliated with: Toronto Central Local Health Integration Network
399 Bathurst St., Toronto, ON M5T 2S8
Tel: 416-603-5800 *Fax:* 416-603-5490
www.uhn.ca
Note: Assessment & referral, individual & group therapy, counseling, psychiatric consultation, education. Services in English, French, Portuguese, Polish.

Toronto: West Park Healthcare Centre
Affiliated with: Toronto Central Local Health Integration Network
Former Name: West Park Hospital
82 Buttonwood Ave., Toronto, ON M6M 2J5
Tel: 416-243-3600 *Fax:* 416-243-8947
feedback@westpark.org
www.westpark.org
www.facebook.com/WestParkHealthcareCentre;
twitter.com/westparkhcc;
www.youtube.com/WestParkhealthcare;
www.linkedin.com/company/218953
Year Founded: 1904
Number of Beds: 200 long-term care beds; 140 complex continung care beds; 130 rehab beds
Number of Employees: 932
Note: Rehabilitation & chronic care facility.
Anne-Marie Malek, President & CEO
Dr. Nora Cullen, Chief of Staff
Jay Cooper, CFO & Vice-President, Corporate Services
Jan Walker, CIO & Vice-President, Strategy & Innovation

Toronto: Withdrawal Management Centre
Michael Garron Hospital
985 Danforth Ave., Toronto, ON M4J 1M1
Tel: 416-461-2189 *Fax:* 416-461-1164
Toll-Free: 866-366-9513
www.tehn.ca
Number of Beds: 30 beds
Note: Specialties: Crisis intervention for adult males; Physical care for males in acute states of intoxication; Withdrawal from alcohol & other addictive substances; Addictions assessments; Counselling; Rehabilitation services; Education on substance abuse to family members.

Waterloo: KidsAbility - Centre for Child Development
Former Name: Rotary Children's Centre
500 Hallmark Dr., Waterloo, ON N2K 3P5
Tel: 519-886-8886 *Fax:* 519-886-7292
Toll-Free: 888-372-2259
info@kidsability.ca
www.kidsability.ca
www.facebook.com/KidsAbility; twitter.com/KidsAbility
Year Founded: 1957
Note: Specialties: Services for children & young adults with physical, developmental, & communication disabilities; Autism intervention; Occupational therapy; Physiotherapy; Speech-language therapy; Augmentative communication; Therapeutic recreation; Social work. Number of Employees: 200 + 300 volunteers.
Linda Kenny, Chief Executive Officer
lkenny@kidsability.ca
Nancy Buchanan, CFO
nbuchanan@kidsability.ca

Windsor: The John McGivney Children's Centre
Former Name: Children's Rehabilitation Centre of Essex County
3945 Matchette Rd., Windsor, ON N9C 4C2
Tel: 519-252-7281 *Fax:* 519-252-5873
Toll-Free: 800-976-5622
info@jmccentre.ca
www.jmccentre.ca
www.facebook.com/243715438993933; twitter.com/JMCCentre
Note: Services include augmentative communication, autism services, & speech, occupational, & physiotherapy.
Jessica Sartori, Chief Executive Officer

Windsor: Windsor Withdrawal Management Residential Service
Hôtel-Dieu Grace Healthcare
1453 Prince Rd., Windsor, ON N9C 3Z4
Tel: 519-257-5225
www.hdgh.org/withdrawalmanagement
Number of Beds: 20 beds
Area Served: Counties of Essex, Kent, & Lambton, Ontario
Note: The agency assists men & women who are 16 years of age or older to access treatment for addiction. The service is funded by the Ministry of Health & Long-term Care.
Leslie Davis, Program Manager
leslie.davis@hdgh.org

Long Term Care Facilities

Alliston: Good Samaritan Seniors Complex
481 Victoria St. East, Alliston, ON L9R 1J8
Tel: 705-435-5722 *Fax:* 705-435-0235
www.goodsamseniors.com
Number of Beds: 64 beds
Note: Services include: 24 hour nursing care; medication administration; pharmacist consulting; recreation; respite care; & wound care
Lynda Weaver, Administrator & Director, Care

Amherstburg: Richmond Terrace
89 Rankin Ave., Amherstburg, ON N9V 1E7
Tel: 519-736-5571
www.richmondterrace.ca
Number of Beds: 126 long-term care beds; 2 respite beds
Note: Long-term care home offering nursing, foot care, dietary care, personal care, & rehabilitation services.
Laura Scott, Administrator
lscott@richmondterrace.ca

Ancaster: The Willowgrove Long Term Care Residence
Affiliated with: Chartwell Retirement Residences
1217 Old Mohawk Rd., Ancaster, ON L9K 1P6
Tel: 905-304-6781
www.chartwell.com
Number of Beds: 169 units
Brent Binions, President & CEO, Chartwell Retirement Residences

Aurora: Chartwell Aurora Long Term Care Residence
Affiliated with: Chartwell Retirement Residences
32 Mill St., Aurora, ON L4G 2R9
Tel: 905-727-1939 *Fax:* 905-727-6299
www.chartwell.com
Number of Beds: 235 beds
Note: Services include: 24 hour nursing care; Alzheimer & dementia care; pain & symptom management; palliative care; personal care; occupational therapy; physiotherapy; restorative care; & skin & wound care
Greg Boudreau, Administrator

Barrie: Heritage Place
Affiliated with: IOOF Seniors Homes Inc.
20 Brooks St., Barrie, ON L4N 7X2
Tel: 705-728-2389 *Fax:* 705-728-8149
www.ioof.com
Number of Beds: 90 beds
Garry C. Hopkins, CEO
ghopkins@ioof.com

Barrie: Owen Hill Care Community
Sienna Senior Living
130 Owen St., Barrie, ON L4M 3H7
Tel: 705-726-8621
www.siennaliving.ca
Number of Beds: 57 beds
Note: Services include: 24 hour nursing & personal care; medical care; rehabilitation; & restorative care.
Lois Cormack, President & CEO, Sienna Senior Living

Barrie: Roberta Place Long-Term Care
Affiliated with: Jarlette Health Services
503 Essa Rd., Barrie, ON L4N 9E4
Tel: 705-733-3231 *Fax:* 705-733-2592
www.jarlette.com
Number of Beds: 139 long term care beds
Megan Merz, Administrator

Barrie: Victoria Village Manor
78 Ross St., Barrie, ON L4N 1G3
Tel: 705-728-3456 *Fax:* 705-728-4057
info@victoriavillage.ca
www.victoriavillage.ca
Year Founded: 2003
Number of Beds: 128 long-term care beds, 57 life-lease housing units

Beaverton: Lakeview Manor
133 Main St., Beaverton, ON L0K 1A0
Tel: 705-426-7388 *Fax:* 705-426-4218
Number of Beds: 149 beds
Note: Services include: 24 hour nursing care; medical; dietitian; physical therapy; recreation; & social work
Mike MacDonald, Administrator
Barb Surge, Director of Care

Belleville: Welcome to Community Living Belleville & Area
Former Name: Plainfield Community Homes; Plainfield Children's Home
91 Millennium Pkwy., Belleville, ON K8N 4Z5
Tel: 613-969-7407 *Fax:* 613-969-7775
www.communitylivingbelleville.org
www.facebook.com/communitylivingbellevilleandarea;
twitter.com/CLBelleville
Year Founded: 1951
Note: Community Living Belleville & Area works toward the full inclusion in community life of persons with intellectual disabilities.
John B. Klassen, Executive Director
Stephen Ollerenshaw, Director, Finance
Katherine Potts, Director, Human Resources
Christine Semark, Director, Services
Jim Burgess, Manager, Buildings & Property
Sharon Wright, Manager, Community Development & Volunteer Services

Blind River: Golden Birches Terrace
525 Causley St., Blind River, ON P0R 1B0
Tel: 705-356-2265 *Fax:* 705-356-1220
www.nshn.care
Number of Beds: 32 beds
Note: Services include: medication administration; IV therapy; physiotherapy; & occupational therapy
Gaston Lavigne, CEO

Bracebridge: The Pines Long Term Care Home
Also Known As: The Pines
98 Pine St., Bracebridge, ON P1L 1N5
Tel: 705-645-4488 *Fax:* 705-645-6857
www.muskoka.on.ca
Year Founded: 1961
Number of Beds: 160 beds
Note: Long term care residence
Katharine Rannie, Administrator
705-645-4488, krannie@muskoka.on.ca
Charmaine Kaye, Director of Care
705-645-4488, ckaye@muskoka.on.ca

Bradford: Bradford Valley
Affiliated with: Sienna Senior Living
2656 - 6 Line, Bradford, ON L3Z 3H5
Tel: 905-952-2270 *Fax:* 905-775-0263
www.siennaliving.ca

Brampton: **Leisureworld Caregiving Centre**
Sienna Senior Living
133 Kennedy Rd. South, Brampton, ON L6W 3G3
Tel: 905-459-2324
www.siennaliving.ca

Year Founded: 1965
Number of Beds: 159 beds
Note: Specialties: Long-term care; Restorative care;
Occupational therapy; Physiotherapy; Care for persons with
Alzheimer's disease; Respite care; Pet therapy; Palliative care.

Brampton: **Rosedale Retirement Residence**
12 William St., Brampton, ON L6V 1L2
Tel: 905-454-3788 *Fax:* 905-846-0447
www.rosedaleretirement.ca
Number of Beds: 12 beds

Brampton: **Woodhall Park**
Affiliated with: Sienna Senior Living
10260 Kennedy Rd. North, Brampton, ON L6T 3S1
Tel: 905-495-4695 *Fax:* 905-495-4693
www.siennaliving.ca

Number of Beds: 147 beds

Brantford: **Brantwood Residential Development**
Centre
Former Name: Brant Sanatorium
Also Known As: Brantwood Centre
25 Bell Lane, Brantford, ON N3T 1E1
Tel: 519-753-2658
www.brantwood.ca

Year Founded: 1913
Number of Employees: 220
Note: Brantwood provides services to persons who live in twelve
group homes located in the city of Brantford & Brant County. A
community day program is available for individuals who live in
the community.
Jo-Anne Link, Executive Director
Ellen Brocklebank, Director, Support Services
Lori Broughton, Director, Support Services
Steve Wood, Director, Finance
Audrey Casey, Nurse Manager

Brantford: **John Noble Home**
97 Mount Pleasant Rd., Brantford, ON N3T 1T5
Tel: 519-756-2920 *Fax:* 519-756-7942
info@jnh.ca
www.jnh.ca

Number of Beds: 156 beds
Note: Services include: nursing; medical; personal care; &
physiotherapy
Jennifer Miller, Administrator

Brantford: **St. Joseph's Lifecare Centre**
Former Name: St. Joseph's Hospital
99 Wayne Gretzky Pkwy., Brantford, ON N3S 6T6
Tel: 519-751-7096 *Fax:* 519-753-7996
www.sjlc.ca

Number of Beds: 205 beds
Note: Programs & services include: dialysis; palliative care;
laboratory; dietitian; pharmacy; & therapy.
Derrick Bernardo, President
Jacqueline Pitt-Bjerno, Deputy Chief Financial Officer
Mieke Ewen, Director, Care
Thelma Constantino, Director, Dietary & Support Services
Phil Ciapanna, Manager, Quality & Performance & Projects

Brighton: **Maplewood**
Omni Health Care
PO Box 249, 12 Maplewood Ave., Brighton, ON K0K 1H0
Tel: 613-475-2442 *Fax:* 613-475-4445
www.omniway.ca

Number of Beds: 49 beds
Note: Long-term care residence
Rachel Corkery, Administrator
rcorkery@omniway.ca
Carolyn Adams, Office Manager
cadams@omniway.ca

Burlington: **Billings Court Manor**
Affiliated with: Conmed Health Care Group
3700 Billings Crt, Burlington, ON L7N 3N6
Tel: 905-333-4006 *Fax:* 905-333-4416
Toll-Free: 888-274-6445
info@billingscourtmanor.com
www.conmedhealth.com

Number of Beds: 160 units

Burlington: **Brant Centre Long Term Care Residence**
Affiliated with: Chartwell Retirement Residences
1182 Northshore Blvd. East, Burlington, ON L7S 1C5
Tel: 905-639-2848
www.chartwell.com

Year Founded: 2003
Number of Beds: 175 beds
Lorianne Ledwez, Administrator
Barbara Carey, Director of Care

Burlington: **Mount Nemo Christian Nursing Home**
4486 Guelph Line, Burlington, ON L7P 0N2
Tel: 905-335-3636 *Fax:* 905-335-3699
mountnemonursinghome@cogeco.net
www.mountnemochristiannh.on.ca

Number of Beds: 60 beds
Note: Long term care home offering nursing care, dental,
laboratory, occupational therapy, pharmaceutical, podiatry,
radiology, speech language pathology, & social services.
Lynette Royeppen, Administrator
lroyeppen@mountnemochristiannh.on.ca
Jackie Malda, Director, Care
jmalda@mountnemochristiannh.on.ca

Burlington: **Wellington Park Care Centre**
802 Hager Ave., Burlington, ON L7S 1X2
Tel: 905-637-3481 *Fax:* 905-637-7514
www.wellingtonparkcarecentre.ca

Number of Beds: 132 beds
Note: Services include: 24 hour nursing care; diagnostic
imaging; laboratory; pharmacy; occupational therapy;
physiotherapy; restorative therapy; & social work
Charlotte Nevills, Administrator
Dale Bamforth, Director, Nursing & Personal Care

Cambridge: **Fairview Mennonite Home**
515 Langs Dr., Cambridge, ON N3H 5E4
Tel: 519-653-5719 *Fax:* 519-650-1242
info@fairviewmh.com
www.fairviewmh.com

Number of Beds: 84 beds
Note: Long-term care home offering recreation, activation, &
restoration care programs.
Pawelko Steve, Executive Director
spawelko@fairviewmh.com
Michelle Rak, Director, Care
mrak@fairviewmh.com

Chatham: **Copper Terrace Long Term Care Facility**
91 Tecumseh Rd., Chatham, ON N7M 1B3
Tel: 519-354-5442 *Fax:* 519-354-0362
www.copperterrace.ca

Number of Beds: 151 beds
Note: Services include: nursing; dietary care; foot care;
laboratory; occupational therapy; palliative care; personal care;
pharmacy; rehabilitation; & wound care.
Susan Petahtegoose, Administrator
spetahtegoose@copperterrace.ca

Chatham: **Meadow Park Care Centre**
Affiliated with: Jarlette Health Services
110 Sandys St., Chatham, ON N7L 4X3
Tel: 519-351-1330 *Fax:* 519-351-7933
www.jarlette.com
Number of Beds: 98 long-term beds; 1 short stay bed; 1 interim
bed
Note: Services include: 24 hour nursing care; laboratory;
pharmacy consultation; & restorative care.
Anne Marie Rumble, Administrator
amrumble@jarlette.com
Susan Vanek, Director of Care
svanek@jarlette.com

Chatham: **Riverview Gardens**
Former Name: Thamesview Lodge
519 King St. West, Chatham, ON N7M 1G8
Tel: 519-352-4823 *Fax:* 519-352-2891
ckseniors@chatham-kent.ca
www.chatham-kent.ca

Number of Beds: 320 beds
Note: Offers medical, personal, dietary, & recreational services.

Chatsworth: **Country Lane Long Term Care**
Residence
Southbridge Care Homes
RR#3, 317079 Hwy 6 & 10, Chatsworth, ON N0H 1G0
Tel: 519-794-2244 *Fax:* 519-794-2597
country-lane.ca

Number of Beds: 34 beds
Jake Presseault, Executive Director
jpresseault@southbridgecare.ca

Chesley: **Parkview Manor**
Extendicare Assist
98 - 3rd St. SE, Chesley, ON N0G 1L0
Tel: 519-363-2416 *Fax:* 519-363-2171
www.parkview-manor.ca

Number of Beds: 34 beds
Note: Services include: 24 hour nursing care; medical; dietitian;
kinesiology; physiotherapy; rehabilitation; & restorative care.
Carole Woods, Administrator
cwoods2@extendicare.com

Clarence Creek: **Centre d'accueil Roger-Séguin**
435 Lemay St., Clarence Creek, ON K0A 1N0
Tel: 613-488-2053 *Fax:* 613-488-2274
www.centrerogerseguin.org

Number of Beds: 115 beds
Joanne Henrie, Administrator
jhenrie@centrerogerseguin.org

Cobourg: **Golden Plough Lodge**
983 Burnham St., Cobourg, ON K9A 5J6
Tel: 905-372-8759 *Fax:* 905-372-8525
www.northumberlandcounty.ca

Number of Beds: 151 beds
Note: Services include: nursing; dental care; diagnostic imaging;
dietary; foot care; physician; physiotherapy; & vision care.
Clare Dawson, Administrator
dawsonc@northumberlandcounty.ca

Cochrane: **Villa Minto**
PO Box 280, 241 - 8 St., Cochrane, ON P0L 1C0
Tel: 705-272-7200 *Fax:* 705-258-2624
www.micsgroup.com

Number of Beds: 33 beds
Note: Villa Minto is an independent LTC facility housed in the
chronic care wing of The Lady Minto Hospital.
Paul Chatelain, Chief Executive Officer

Cornwall: **Sandfield Place**
Also Known As: 458422 Ontario Limited
220 Emma Ave., Cornwall, ON K6J 5V8
Tel: 613-933-6972 *Fax:* 613-938-2261
www.sandfieldplace.com
Number of Beds: 53 long term care beds; 34 retirement beds
Note: Long term care & retirement living
Stephanie Kinnear, Administrator

Delaware: **Middlesex Terrace**
2094 Gideon Dr., RR#1, Delaware, ON N0L 1E0
Tel: 519-652-3483 *Fax:* 519-652-6915
www.middlesexterrace.ca

Number of Beds: 104 beds
Note: Services include: medical care; nursing; foot care;
laboratory; palliative care; personal care; & rehabilitation.
Jan Shkilnyk, Administrator
jshkilnyk@middlesexterrace.ca
Rachel Dent, RN, Director of Nursing
rdent@middlesexterrace.ca

Dundas: **St. Joseph's Villa (Dundas)**
Affiliated with: Hamilton Niagara Haldimand Brant
Local Health Integration Network
56 Governor's Rd., Dundas, ON L9H 5G7
Tel: 905-627-3541 *Fax:* 905-628-0825
www.sjv.on.ca

Year Founded: 1879
Number of Beds: 390 beds
Note: Services include: nursing; dental; dermatology; ear, nose,
& throat; end of life care; foot care; restorative care; social work;
therapeutic recreation; therapy; & wound care. Personal services
include: housekeeping; hair salon; maintenance; & a cafe.
Derrick Bernardo, President

Dundas: **Wentworth Lodge**
41 South St. West, Dundas, ON L9H 4C4
Tel: 905-546-2618 *Fax:* 905-546-2854
wentworthlodge@hamilton.ca
www.hamilton.ca/social-services

Number of Beds: 160 beds

Dunnville: **Grandview Lodge**
657 Lock St. West, Dunnville, ON N1A 1V9
Tel: 905-774-7547 *Fax:* 905-774-1440
www.haldimandcounty.on.ca

Number of Beds: 128 beds
Note: Services include: medical; physiotherapy; recreation; &
Snoezelen rooms.
Joanne Jackson, Administrator
905-774-7547 ext 224, jjackson@haldimandcounty.on.ca

Durham: **Rockwood Terrace**
PO Box 660, 575 Saddler St. East, Durham, ON N0G 1R0
Tel: 519-369-6035 *Fax:* 519-369-6736
www.grey.ca

Number of Beds: 100 beds
Note: Services include: 24 hour nursing care; medical; dental;
foot care; physiotherapy; & therapeutic programs.
Karen Kraus, Administrator
karen.kraus@grey.ca

Elmira: Chartwell Elmira Long Term Care Residence
Affiliated with: Chartwell Retirement Residences
11 Herbert St., Elmira, ON N3B 2B8
Tel: 519-669-2921 *Fax:* 519-669-3027
www.chartwell.com

Number of Beds: 48 beds
Note: Services include 24 hour nursing & personal care.
Brent Binions, President & CEO, Chartwell Retirement
Residences

Elmvale: Sara-Vista Long Term Care Facility
Rivera Inc.
27 Simcoe St., Elmvale, ON L0L 1P0
Tel: 705-322-2182
www.facebook.com/Reveralnc; twitter.com/Revera_Inc;
www.youtube.com/ReveraInc;
www.linkedin.com/company/revera-inc
Year Founded: 1961
Number of Beds: 60 beds
Note: Programs & services include music therapy; art & creative
classes; garden & horticulture activities; Montessori-based
dementia program; rehabilitation programs; 24 hour nursing
care; therapy; dietitian; & pain & symptom management.
Karen Jones, Executive Director

Fergus: Wellington Terrace Long Term Care Home
Former Name: Wellington Terrace Home for the Aged
474 Wellington Rd. 18, Fergus, ON N1M 0A1
Tel: 519-846-5359 *Fax:* 519-846-9192
www.wellington.ca

Number of Beds: 176 beds
Number of Employees: 242

Fort Erie: Gilmore Lodge
50 Gilmore Rd., Fort Erie, ON L2A 2M1
Tel: 905-871-6160 *Fax:* 905-871-0435
www.niagararegion.ca

Number of Beds: 79 beds

Fort Erie: Maple Park Lodge
Affiliated with: Conmed Health Care Group
6 Hagey Ave., Fort Erie, ON L2A 5M5
Tel: 905-994-0224 *Fax:* 905-994-8628
info@mapleparklodge.com
www.conmedhealth.com

Year Founded: 2003
Number of Beds: 96 units
Carole Jukosky, Administrator
carolej@conmedhealth.com

Fort Frances: Rainycrest Long Term Care
Riverside Health Care Facilities Inc.
Affiliated with: North West Local Health Integration Network
550 Osborne St., Fort Frances, ON P9A 3T2
Tel: 807-274-3261 *Fax:* 807-274-7368
Note: Home for the aged

Glenburnie: Fairmount Home
2069 Battersea Rd., Glenburnie, ON K0H 1S0
Tel: 613-546-4264 *Fax:* 613-546-0489
www.frontenaccounty.ca
Number of Beds: 128 beds

Gore Bay: Manitoulin Lodge
Affiliated with: Jarlette Health Services
3 Main St., Gore Bay, ON P0P 1H0
Tel: 705-282-2007 *Fax:* 705-282-3422
www.jarlette.com

Number of Beds: 61 beds
Susan Farren, Administrator
Amanda Gibbons, Resident & Family Services Coordinator

Grimsby: Deer Park Villa
150 Central Ave., Grimsby, ON L3M 4Z3
Tel: 905-945-4164
www.niagararegion.ca

Number of Beds: 40 beds

Guelph: The Elliott Community
170 Metcalfe St., Guelph, ON N1E 4Y3
Tel: 519-822-0491 *Fax:* 519-822-5658
info@elliottcommunity.org
www.elliottcommunity.org

Number of Beds: 270 beds
Note: Retirement suites & long term care.
Michelle Karker, CEO

Haileybury: Temiskaming Lodge
Affiliated with: Jarlette Health Services
100 Bruce St., Haileybury, ON P0J 1K0
Tel: 705-672-2123 *Fax:* 705-672-5734
www.jarlette.com

Number of Beds: 82 beds
Francine Gosselin, Administrator
fgosselin@jarlette.com
Sarah Davis, Resident & Family Services Coordinator

Hamilton: AbleLiving Services Inc.
Thrive Group
Former Name: Participation House - Hamilton & District
125 Redfern Ave., Hamilton, ON L9C 7W9
Tel: 905-383-0448 *Fax:* 905-383-1099
info@ableliving.org
www.ableliving.org

Year Founded: 1975
Area Served: Hamilton through to Mississauga *Number of Employees:* 325
Note: Provides support services designed to enhance the quality
of life & independence of adults with disabilities & seniors.
Lucy Sheehan, Director, Operations
905-692-4465, lsheehan@ableliving.org

Hamilton: Baywoods Place
Revera Inc.
330 Main St. East, Hamilton, ON L8N 3T9
Tel: 905-523-7134
www.reveraliving.com/baywoods
www.facebook.com/Reveralnc; twitter.com/Revera_Inc;
www.youtube.com/user/ReveraInc;
www.linkedin.com/company/revera-inc
Note: Programs provided at Baywoods Place include the
following: rehabilitation, recreation, music therapy, skin & wound
care, Snoezelen multi-sensory therapy, pet therapy, & safety
programs.
Thomas G. Wellner, President & CEO, Revera Living

Hamilton: Grace Villa Long Term Care Home
Affiliated with: APANS Health Services
45 Lockton Cres., Hamilton, ON L8V 4V5
Tel: 905-387-4812 *Fax:* 905-387-4814
www.gracevilla.ca

Number of Beds: 184 beds
Wendy Hall, Administrator
whall@gracevilla.ca

Hamilton: Idlewyld Manor
449 Sanatorium Rd., Hamilton, ON L9C 2A7
Tel: 905-574-2000 *Fax:* 905-574-0482
office@idlewyldmanor.com
www.idlewyldmanor.com

Number of Beds: 192 beds
Maureen Goodram, Executive Director

Hamilton: St. Peter's Residence at Chedoke
Affiliated with: Thrive Group
125 Redfern Ave., Hamilton, ON L9C 7W9
Tel: 905-383-0448 *Fax:* 905-383-1099
reception@stpeterscc.ca
www.stpeterscc.ca

Number of Beds: 210 beds
Donna Cripps, President/CEO

Hamilton: Shalom Village
Former Name: The Hamilton Jewish Home for the Aged
70 Macklin St. North, Hamilton, ON L8S 3S1
Tel: 905-529-1613 *Fax:* 905-529-7542
info@shalomvillage.ca
https://www.shalomvillage.ca/
www.facebook.com/ShalomVillage; twitter.com/ShalomVillage;
www.youtube.com/user/shalomvillage
Year Founded: 1974
Number of Beds: 60 beds
Note: Long term care & assisted living, day program; kosher
meals provided; Jewish & ecumenical services. Shalom Village
Too with 64 beds & 30 apartments is located adjacent.
Jeanette O'Leary, CEO
jeanette@shalomvillage.ca
Kathleen Thomas, Director
kathleen@shalomvillage.ca

Hamilton: Townsview Lifecare Centre
39 Mary St., Hamilton, ON L8R 3L8
Tel: 905-523-6427 *Fax:* 905-528-0610

Number of Beds: 219 beds

Hamilton: The Village at St. Elizabeth Mills
Affiliated with: ZEST Communities Inc.
393 Rymal Rd. West, Hamilton, ON L9B 1V2
Tel: 905-389-4777 *Fax:* 905-389-6956
Toll-Free: 855-875-8178
www.stelizabethmills.com
Year Founded: 1981

Hamilton: The Wellington Retirement Community
1430 Upper Wellington St., Hamilton, ON L9A 5H3
Tel: 905-385-2111 *Fax:* 905-385-2110
Toll-Free: 866-385-2111
www.thewellington.ca
www.facebook.com/271440946270671;
twitter.com/TheWellingtonCa;
www.youtube.com/user/thewellingtonca
Number of Beds: 102 long term care beds, 80 retirement beds
Doretta DeRosa, Residence Contact
dderosa@thewellington.ca

Huntsville: Muskoka Landing
Affiliated with: Jarlette Health Services
65 Rogers Cove Dr., Huntsville, ON P1H 2L9
Tel: 705-788-7713 *Fax:* 705-788-1424
www.jarlette.com

Number of Beds: 94 long-term care beds
David Jarlette, President
705-549-4889, Fax: 705-549-2494, djarlette@jarlette.com

Jacksons Point: Cedar Lane Lodge
895 Lake Dr., RR#1, Jacksons Point, ON L0E 1L0
Tel: 905-722-8928
Note: Housing is provided for adults who require support for daily
living.

Jasper: Rosebridge Manor
Omni Health Care
131 Roses Bridge Rd., RR#2, Jasper, ON K0G 1G0
Tel: 613-283-5471 *Fax:* 613-283-9012
www.omniway.ca

Number of Beds: 78 beds
Tracy Foster, Administrator
613-283-5471, tfoster@omniway.ca
Krikit Craig, Office Manager
613-283-5471, kcraig@omniway.ca

Kemptville: Bayfield Manor Long Term Care Home
PO Box 3000, 100 Elvira St., Kemptville, ON K0G 1J0
Tel: 613-258-1611 *Fax:* 613-258-3838
www.bayfieldmanorltc.com
Number of Beds: 66 bed long-term care home & 57 suite
retirement home
Gerry Miller, Executive Director
gemiller@southbridgecare.ca

Kincardine: Trillium Court Retirement Living
Revera Inc.
550 Phillip Pl., Kincardine, ON N2Z 3A6
Tel: 519-396-4400 *Fax:* 519-366-9092
trillium@reveraliving.com
www.reveraliving.com
www.facebook.com/Reveralnc; twitter.com/Revera_Inc;
www.youtube.com/user/ReveraInc;
www.linkedin.com/company/revera-inc
Number of Beds: 40 beds, 60 retirement suites
Note: Independent & assisted living, retirement lodge, long-term
care, respite & convalescent options.
Thomas G. Wellner, President & CEO, Revera Living
M. Furnvale, Supervisor, Environmental Services

Kingston: Providence Manor
Affiliated with: Providence Care
275 Sydenham St., Kingston, ON K7K 1G7
Tel: 613-549-4164 *Fax:* 613-549-7472
www.providencecare.ca
www.facebook.com/ProvidenceCareCA;
twitter.com/providence_care;
www.youtube.com/user/ProvidenceCareCA
Number of Beds: 243 beds
Note: For both residential and long-term care patients; has a
secure Dementia home-area, two short stay respite beds and
five designated veterans' beds.
Shelagh Nowlan, Vice-President, Long-Term Care
613-548-7222, nowlans@providencecare.ca

Kingston: St. Mary's of the Lake Hospital
Affiliated with: Providence Care
340 Union St., Kingston, ON K7L 5A2
Tel: 613-544-5220 *Fax:* 613-544-8558
www.providencecare.ca

Year Founded: 1946
Number of Beds: 144 inpatient beds
Note: Offers acute care, complex continuing care, geriatric

medicine, rehabilitation, palliative care, & respite care services. Serves as a teaching hospital with Queen's University.
Shelagh Nowlan, Vice-President, Long-Term Care
nowlans@providencecare.ca

Kingston: **Trillium Retirement & Care Community**
Former Name: Specialty Care Trillium Centre
800 Edgar St., Kingston, ON K7M 8S4
Tel: 613-547-0040 Fax: 613-547-3734
www.siennaliving.ca
www.facebook.com/siennaliving;
www.linkedin.com/company/sienna-senior-living
Number of Beds: 186 units
Note: 24-hour nursing; dental services; medication & pharmacy services; daily activities.
Dawn Black, Administrator
dawn.black@specialty-care.com

Kitchener: **Chartwell Westmount Long Term Care**
Residence
Affiliated with: Chartwell Retirement Residences
200 David Bergey Dr., Kitchener, ON N2E 3Y4
Tel: 519-570-2115 Fax: 519-579-9770
www.chartwell.com
Number of Beds: 160 units
Brent Binions, President & CEO, Chartwell Retirement Residences

Kitchener: **Lanark Heights Long-Term Care**
Affiliated with: S & R Nursing Homes Ltd.
46 Lanark Cres., Kitchener, ON N2N 2Z8
Tel: 519-743-4200 Fax: 519-743-4225
lanarkheights@srgroup.ca
srgroup.ca
Number of Beds: 160 units

Kitchener: **PeopleCare AR Goudie**
369 Frederick St., Kitchener, ON N2H 2P1
Tel: 519-744-5182 Fax: 519-744-3887
www.peoplecare.ca/long-term-care/ar-goudie
Number of Beds: 80 beds
Paul Rektor, Executive Director

Kitchener: **Sunnyside Home**
247 Franklin St. North, Kitchener, ON N2A 1Y5
Tel: 519-893-8482 Fax: 519-893-4450
www.region.waterloo.on.ca
Number of Beds: 263 residential capacity

Kitchener: **Village of Winston Park**
Schlegel Villages
695 Block Line Rd., Kitchener, ON N2E 3K1
Tel: 519-576-2430 Fax: 519-576-8990
www.schlegelvillages.com
Number of Beds: 95 beds
Brad Lawrence, General Manager

Komoka: **Country Terrace Long Term Care Home**
Omni Health Care
Former Name: Country Terrace Nursing Home
10072 Oxbow Dr., Komoka, ON N0L 1R0
Tel: 519-657-2955 Fax: 519-657-8516
www.omniway.ca
Number of Beds: 120 beds
Karen Dann, Administrator
kdann@omniway.ca
Heather Davidson, Resident Services Coordinator
hdavidson@omniway.ca

L'Orignal: **Résidence Champlain**
Affiliated with: Chartwell Retirement Residences
428 Front Rd. West, L'Orignal, ON K0B 1K0
Tel: 613-675-4617
www.chartwell.com
Number of Beds: 60 beds
Brent Binions, President & CEO, Chartwell Retirement Residences

Lancaster: **Chartwell Lancaster Long Term Care**
Residence
Affiliated with: Chartwell Retirement Residences
Former Name: Chateau Gardens Lancaster
PO Box 429, 105 Military Rd. North, Lancaster, ON K0C 1N0
Tel: 613-347-3016 Fax: 613-347-1680
www.chartwell.com
Number of Beds: 60 beds
Brent Binions, President & CEO, Chartwell Retirement Residences

Limoges: **Résidence Limoges**
131-133 Ottawa St., Limoges, ON K0A 2M0
Tél: 613-443-5303 Téléc: 613-443-1943

Nombre de lits: 25 lits

Limoges: **St. Viateur Nursing Home**
Affiliated with: Genesis Gardens
1003 Limoges Rd. South, Limoges, ON K0A 2M0
Tel: 613-443-5751 Fax: 613-443-9940
info@genesisgardens.ca
www.genesisgardens.ca
Number of Beds: 64 beds
Richard R. Marleau, CEO
613-443-5751, Fax: 613-443-9940, richardmarleau@rogers.com

Lindsay: **Frost Manor**
Omni Health Care
225 Mary St. West, Lindsay, ON K9V 5K3
Tel: 705-324-8333 Fax: 705-878-5840
www.omniway.ca
Number of Beds: 62 beds
Note: Activities: shopping excursions; picnics; scenic boat trips along the Trent Canal; and fall bus tours to Haliburton. Residents participate in local fall fairs, selling their crafts and baked goods.
Doneath Stewart, Administrator
dstewart@omniway.ca

London: **Anago Resources Inc.**
371 Princess Ave., London, ON N6B 2A7
Tel: 519-435-1099 Fax: 519-435-0062
info@anago.on.ca
www.anago.on.ca
www.facebook.com/AnagoResources
Number of Beds: 63 beds
Note: young offenders; developmental handicap group home; child & family intervention treatment
Mandy L. Bennett, Executive Director

London: **Chartwell London Long Term Care**
Residence
Former Name: Chateau Gardens London
2000 Blackwater Rd., London, ON N5X 4K6
Tel: 519-434-2727
www.chartwell.com
Number of Beds: 95 beds

London: **Chelsey Park Retirement Community**
310 Oxford St. West, London, ON N6H 4N6
Tel: 519-432-1855 Fax: 516-432-7548
adm.cpo@diversicare.ca
www.chelseypark.com
Number of Beds: 247 beds
Diane Pope, Customer Relations Manager
519-432-1845, info.cprc@diversicare.ca
Suzi Holster, Administrator
519-432-1855

London: **Dearness Long-Term Care Services**
710 Southdale Rd. East, London, ON N6E 1R8
Tel: 519-661-0400 Fax: 519-661-0446
www.london.ca
Number of Beds: 348 beds

London: **Longworth Retirement Residence**
600 Longworth Rd., London, ON N6K 4X9
Tel: 519-472-1115 Fax: 519-472-1132
info@longworth.sifton.com
www.sifton.com
Number of Beds: 160 beds
Note: Specialties: Long term care; Restorative care program; Massage therapy; Physiotherapy; Family & personal counseling services

London: **Meadow Park Care Centre & Retirement**
Lodge
London
Affiliated with: Jarlette Health Services
1210 Southdale Rd. East, London, ON N6E 1B4
Tel: 519-686-0484 Fax: 519-686-9932
www.jarlette.com
twitter.com/Jarlette
Number of Beds: 119 long term care beds; 3 short stay beds; 4 interim beds; 1 palliative bed
Note: Long term care facility & retirement lodge
David Jarlette, President
705-549-4889, djarlette@jarlette.com
Judy Maltais, Director, Long Term Care
Michelle Priester, Acting Administrator, Meadow Park London

London: **Mount Hope Centre for Long Term Care**
Affiliated with: St. Joseph's Health Care, London
21 Grosvenor St., London, ON N6A 1Y1
Tel: 519-646-6100 Fax: 519-646-6054
www.sjhc.london.on.ca
Year Founded: 1869
Number of Beds: 394 beds

Note: Facility boasts a library; beauty shop; cafe; chapel. Activities include bingo; bowling; fitness classes; gardening.

Markdale: **Grey Gables Home for the Aged**
Former Name: Grey Owen Lodge
PO Box 380, 206 Toronto St. South, Markdale, ON N0C 1H0
Tel: 519-986-3010 Fax: 519-986-4644
www.grey.ca
Number of Beds: 66 beds
Jennifer Cornell, Administrator
jennifer.cornell@grey.ca

Markham: **The Woodhaven Long Term Care**
Residence
Affiliated with: Chartwell Retirement Residences
380 Church St., Markham, ON L6B 1E1
Tel: 905-472-3320
www.chartwell.com
Number of Beds: 192 units
Brent Binions, President & CEO, Chartwell Retirement Residences

Matheson: **Rosedale Centre**
Affiliated with: Bingham Memorial Hospital
507 - 8th Ave., Matheson, ON P0K 1N0
Tel: 705-273-2424 Fax: 705-273-2515
www.micsgroup.com
Year Founded: 1989
Number of Beds: 20 beds
Note: Specialty: Long term nursing & supportive care; Foot care; Therapy

Maxville: **Maxville Manor**
80 Mechanic St. West, Maxville, ON K0C 1T0
Tel: 613-527-2170 Fax: 613-527-3103
info@maxvillemanor.ca
www.maxvillemanor.ca
Year Founded: 1968
Number of Beds: 120 beds + 2 respite beds
Number of Employees: 130
Note: Specialties: Long-term care services; Therapy services; The Seniors' Centre, providing outreach services to persons in the community with physical disabilities & special needs; Adult day program; Seniors' clinics, such as hearing, optometry, & foot care.
Ivan Coleman, Board Chair

Midland: **Hillcrest Village Care Centre**
Former Name: St. Andrew's Centennial Manor
255 Russell St., Midland, ON L4R 5L6
Tel: 705-526-3781 Fax: 705-526-5656
www.hillcrestvillage.com
Year Founded: 1978
Number of Beds: 164 beds

Milton: **Allendale**
185 Ontario St. South, Milton, ON L9T 2M4
Tel: 905-825-6000 Fax: 905-825-9833
Toll-Free: 866-442-5866
TTY: 905-827-9833
accesshalton@halton.ca
www.halton.ca
Year Founded: 1993
Number of Beds: 200 beds

Minden: **Hyland Crest**
6 McPherson St., Minden, ON K0M 2K0
Tel: 705-286-2140 Fax: 705-286-6384
www.hhhs.ca
Year Founded: 2000
Number of Beds: 62 beds

Mississauga: **Camilla Care Community**
Sienna Senior Living
Former Name: Chelsey Park Mississauga
Long-Term Care Facility
2250 Hurontario St., Mississauga, ON L5B 1M8
Tel: 905-270-0411
Year Founded: 1970
Number of Beds: 237 beds
Note: Programs include restorative care & physiotherapy, pet therapy, cultural cooking, & a palliative care program. Spiritual services, including mass, are provided regularly for residents.

Mississauga: **Cawthra Gardens**
590 Lolita Gardens, Mississauga, ON L5A 4N8
Tel: 905-306-9984
www.delcare.com
Number of Beds: 192 beds

Seaforth: Seaforth Long Term Care Home
PO Box 280, 100 James St., Seaforth, ON N0K 1W0
Tel: 519-527-0030 Fax: 855-226-9214
www.seaforthltc.ca
www.facebook.com/SeaforthLTCRC
Number of Beds: 63 beds
Cathy Stewart, Executive Director
castewart@southbridgecare.ca

Shelburne: Dufferin Oaks Long Term Care Home
151 Centre St., Shelburne, ON L9V 3R7
Tel: 519-925-2140 Fax: 519-925-5067
dufferinoaks@dufferincounty.ca
www.dufferincounty.ca
Year Founded: 1962
Number of Beds: 160 beds

Shelburne: Shelburne Long Term Care Home
200 Robert St., Shelburne, ON L9V 3S1
Tel: 519-925-3746 Fax: 888-207-0031
shelburneltc.ca
Number of Beds: 60 beds
Jason Gay, Executive Director
jgay@southbridgecare.ca

Simcoe: Norview Lodge
PO Box 604, 44 Rob Blake Way, Simcoe, ON N3Y 0E3
Tel: 519-426-0902 Fax: 519-426-9867
www.norfolkcounty.on.ca
Number of Beds: 179 beds

St. Catharines: Heidehof Long Term Care Home
600 Lake St., St. Catharines, ON L2N 4J4
Tel: 905-935-3344 Fax: 905-935-0081
www.heidehof.com
Number of Beds: 106 beds
Elena Caddis, Administrator
ecaddis@heidehof.com
Erika Ledwez, Manager, Resident & Community Relations
eledwez@heidehof.com

St. Catharines: Henley House
Affiliated with: Primacare Living Solutions
20 Earnest St., St. Catharines, ON L2N 7T2
Tel: 905-937-9703 Fax: 905-937-9723
henley@primacareliving.com
www.primacareliving.com
Number of Beds: 160 beds
Note: Specialties: Long-term nursing & personal care;
Therapeutic programs; Physiotherapy; Restorative care;
Palliative care
Matthew Melchior, President, Primacare Living Solutions

St. Catharines: Linhaven
403 Ontario St., St. Catharines, ON L2N 1L5
Tel: 905-934-3364 Fax: 905-934-6975
www.niagararegion.ca
Number of Beds: 248 beds
Note: Specialties: Long term care; Alzheimer's disease, memory
loss, & related dementias; Respite services; Adult day service.

St. Catharines: Niagara Ina Grafton Gage Home
413 Linwell Rd., St. Catharines, ON L2M 7Y2
Tel: 905-935-6822 Fax: 905-935-6847
www.niggv.on.ca
Year Founded: 1959
Number of Beds: 40 long term care beds
Note: A mix of long-term care units and rentals for more active
seniors, Ina Grafton is affiliated with Stone Road Village, a
retirement community located in Niagara-on-the-Lake.
Bob Tanouye, Executive Chair

St. Thomas: Elgin Manor Home
Affiliated with: County of Elgin Homes and Seniors
Services
39262 Fingal Line RR #1, St. Thomas, ON N5P 3S5
Tel: 519-631-0620 Fax: 519-631-2307
www.elgincounty.ca
Number of Beds: 90 beds
Area Served: Southwold Township
Terri Benwell, Adminstrator
519-631-0620, tbenwell@elgin.ca
Michele Harris, Director, Homes & Seniors Services
519-631-1460, mharris@elgin.ca

St. Thomas: St. George Residence
Former Name: Kettle Creek Residence
58 St. George St., St. Thomas, ON N5P 2L1
Tel: 519-633-7647 Fax: 519-633-9312
stgeorge.laura@outlook.com
Note: for adults with a mental health diagnosis
Laura Westra, Housing Manager

St. Thomas: Valleyview Home for the Aged
350 Burwell Rd., St. Thomas, ON N5P 0A3
Tel: 519-631-1030 Fax: 519-631-3462
www.stthomas.ca
Year Founded: 1969
Number of Beds: 136 beds

Stayner: Stayner Care Centre
Affiliated with: Jarlette Health Services
Former Name: Stayner Nursing Home
PO Box 350, 7308 Hwy. 26, Stayner, ON L0M 1S0
Tel: 705-428-3614
www.jarlette.com/long-term-care/stayner-care-centre
Year Founded: 1984
Number of Beds: 49 beds

Stittsville: Granite Ridge Care Community
Sienna Senior Living
5501 Abbott St. East, Stittsville, ON K2S 2C5
Tel: 613-836-0331 Fax: 613-836-0643
www.siennaliving.ca
Number of Beds: 224 beds
Norm Slatter, Administrator
norm.slatter@specialty-care.com

Stoney Creek: Clarion Nursing Home
337 Hwy. 8, Stoney Creek, ON L8G 1E7
Tel: 905-664-2281 Fax: 905-664-2966
info@clarionnursinghome.on.ca
www.clarionnursinghome.on.ca
Year Founded: 1960
Number of Beds: 100 beds

Stoney Creek: Heritage Green Long Term Care
Centre
353 Isaac Brock Dr., Stoney Creek, ON L8J 2J3
Tel: 905-573-7177 Fax: 905-573-7151
info@hgseniorcare.ca
hgseniorcare.com
Number of Beds: 167 beds
Rosemary Okimi, Administrator

Stoney Creek: Orchard Terrace Care Centre
Former Name: Stoney Creek Lifecare Centre
199 Glover Rd., Stoney Creek, ON L8E 5J2
Tel: 905-643-1795
info@orchardterracecarecentre.ca
orchardterracecarecentre.ca
Number of Beds: 45 beds

Stouffville: Parkview Home
123 Weldon Rd., Stouffville, ON L4A 0G8
Tel: 905-640-1911 Fax: 905-640-4051
admin@parkviewhome.ca
www.parkviewhome.ca
Number of Beds: 128 beds
Note: Long-term care facility
Terry Collins, Administrator
905-640-1911, tcollins@parkviewhome.ca

Stouffville: Specialty Care Bloomington Cove
Sienna Senior Living
13621 - 9 Line, Stouffville, ON L4A 7X3
Tel: 905-640-1310 Fax: 905-640-0995
www.siennaliving.ca
Number of Beds: 112 beds
Janet Iwaszczenko, Administrator
janet.iwaszczenko@specialty-care.com

Stratford: Greenwood Court
90 Greenwood Dr., Stratford, ON N5A 7W5
Tel: 519-273-4662 Fax: 519-273-1458
www.tcmhomes.com
Number of Beds: 45 beds
Note: In addition to its 45 long term care beds, Greenwood has
85 Independent Living apartments & 18 retirement units.
Joyce Penney, Executive Director
519-273-4662, jpenney@greenwoodcourt.com

Thornbury: Errinrung Long Term Care Home
Former Name: Errinrung Nursing & Retirement
Home
PO Box 69, 67 Bruce St., Thornbury, ON N0H 2P0
Tel: 519-599-2737 Fax: 855-226-9213
errinrungltc.ca
www.facebook.com/ErrinrungLTCRC
Number of Beds: 60 beds
Jenny Allison, Executive Director
jallison@southbridgecare.ca

Thunder Bay: Hogarth Riverview Manor
St. Joseph's Care Group
300 Lillie St. North, Thunder Bay, ON P7C 4Y7
Tel: 807-625-1110 Fax: 807-623-4520
www.sjcg.net
Number of Beds: 96 beds
Note: Long-term care home
Tracy Buckler, President & CEO, St. Joseph's Care Group

Thunder Bay: OPTIONS Northwest Personal Support
Services
95 Cumberland St. North, Thunder Bay, ON P7A 4M1
Tel: 807-344-4994 Fax: 807-346-5811
general@optionsnorthwest.com
www.optionsnorthwest.com
Year Founded: 1965
Note: Specialty: Personal & residential support for persons with
developmental challenges, physical disabilities, chronic
behaviour problems, & mental health challenges; Counselling;
Support groups

Thunder Bay: Southbridge Roseview
Southbridge Care Homes
Former Name: Roseview Manor; Central Park Lodge
99 Shuniah St., Thunder Bay, ON P7A 2Z2
Tel: 807-344-6929 Fax: 807-344-7132
www.southbridgeroseview.ca
Number of Beds: 157 beds
Note: Programs include community outings; physical activities;
live music; art & creative classes; friendly pet visits.
Joanne Lent, Executive Director
jlent@southbridgecare.ca

Tilbury: Tilbury Manor Long-Term Care Home
Diversicare Canada Management Services Inc
PO Box 160, 16 Fort St., Tilbury, ON N0P 2L0
Tel: 519-682-0243 Fax: 519-682-2358
adm.tilbury@vervesenorliving.com
www.vervesenorliving.com/tilbury-manor
Number of Beds: 75 beds
Note: Services include 24-hour nursing care; foot care; dental
care; palliative care.
John Carnella, President & CEO, Diversicare

Toronto: Baycrest Centre for Geriatric Care
3560 Bathurst St., Toronto, ON M6A 2E1
Tel: 416-785-2500 Fax: 416-785-2378
www.baycrest.org
www.facebook.com/baycrestcentre; twitter.com/baycrest;
www.youtube.com/thebaycrestchannel;
www.linkedin.com/company/baycrest
Year Founded: 1918
Number of Beds: 300 beds
Note: A research facility as well as a care centre for seniors.
William E. Reichman, President & CEO
Dr. Paul Katz, Vice-President, Medical Services & Chief of Staff
Carol Anderson, Vice-President, Programs & Chief Nursing
Executive

Toronto: Cheltenham Long-Term Care Facility
Sienna Senior Living
5935 Bathurst St., Toronto, ON M2R 1Y8
Tel: 416-223-4050
www.siennaliving.ca
plus.google.com/+CheltenhamCareCommunityToronto
Year Founded: 1966
Number of Beds: 170 beds
Note: Situated in the heart of Toronto's Jewish community; offers
programs that tend to the physical, intellectual, emotional, social,
and spiritual needs of residents.

Toronto: Copernicus Lodge
66 Roncesvalles Ave., Toronto, ON M6R 3A7
Tel: 416-536-7122 Fax: 416-536-8242
www.copernicuslodge.com
Number of Beds: 108 beds
Note: Specialities: service to residents of Toronto's Polish
community.
Catharine Kowalenko, CEO

Toronto: Dom Lipa Nursing Home & Seniors Centre
52 Neilson Dr., Toronto, ON M9C 1V7
Tel: 416-621-3820 Fax: 416-621-9336
info@domlipa.ca
www.domlipa.ca
Number of Beds: 66 nursing home, 30 retirement beds
Note: A long-term care facility and retirement community geared
towards the city's Slovenian Catholic community.
Jolanta Linde, Executive Director
416-621-3820

Toronto: Downsview Long Term Care Centre
Former Name: Casa Verde Nursing Home
3595 Keele St., Toronto, ON M3J 1M7
Tel: 416-633-3431 *Fax:* 416-633-6736
www.downsviewretirement.com
Number of Beds: 252 beds
Christiane Burns, Administrator

Toronto: The Gibson Long Term Care Centre
Affiliated with: Chartwell Retirement Residences
Former Name: Extendicare - North York
1925 Steeles Ave. East, Toronto, ON M2H 2H3
Tel: 416-493-4666 *Fax:* 416-493-4886
www.chartwell.com
Number of Beds: 202 beds
Brent Binions, President & CEO, Chartwell Retirement
Residences

Toronto: Ina Grafton Gage Home
40 Bell Estate Rd., Toronto, ON M1L 0E2
Tel: 416-422-4890 *Fax:* 416-422-1613
info@iggh.org
www.iggh.org
Number of Beds: 128 beds
Note: Recreation programs include exercise sessions; religious
services; arts & crafts; baking; bingo; sensory stimulation.
Rob Bissonnette, Executive Director
Dr. Bharat Kalra, Medical Director

Toronto: Lakeside Long-Term Care Centre
Affiliated with: Extendicare
150 Dunn Ave., Toronto, ON M6K 2R6
Tel: 416-533-2828 *Fax:* 406-533-1984
Number of Beds: 128 Beds

Toronto: Maynard Nursing Home
Schlegel Villages
28 Halton St., Toronto, ON M6J 1R3
Tel: 416-533-5198 *Fax:* 416-533-3492
www.schlegelvillages.com/maynard-toronto
Year Founded: 1961
Number of Beds: 77 beds
Note: Specialties: Service to residents of Portuguese origin;
Recreational & social activities.

Toronto: McCowan Retirement Residence
2881 Eglinton Ave. East, Toronto, ON M1J 0A2
Tel: 416-266-4445 *Fax:* 416-264-8377
info@mccowanRR.com
www.mccowanrr.com
www.facebook.com/132492233505515
Year Founded: 2004
Gina Cook, Executive Director
Tim Valyear, Director, Marketing
marketingoffice.kams@rogers.com

Toronto: Midland Gardens Care Community
Sienna Senior Living
130 Midland Ave., Toronto, ON M1N 4B2
Tel: 416-264-2301
www.siennaliving.ca
Number of Beds: 299 beds

Toronto: Nisbet Lodge
740 Pape Ave., Toronto, ON M4K 3S7
Tel: 416-469-1105 *Fax:* 416-469-2996
info@nisbetlodge.com
www.nisbetlodge.com
www.facebook.com/NisbetLodge
Number of Beds: 103 beds
Note: Christian long-term care home.
Glen Moorhouse, CEO
416-469-1105, g.moorhouse@nisbetlodge.com

Toronto: North York General Hospital - Seniors'
Health Centre
Affiliated with: Toronto Central Local Health
Integration Network
2 Buchan Ct., Toronto, ON M2J 5A3
Tel: 416-756-6050 *Fax:* 416-756-3144
www.nygh.on.ca
Number of Beds: 192 long-term care beds
Note: Long term care facility, ambulatory geriatric services.
Karyn Popovich, Interim CEO, North York General Hospital

Toronto: The O'Neill Centre
33 Christie St., Toronto, ON M6G 3B1
Tel: 416-536-1116 *Fax:* 416-536-6941
www.oneillcentre.ca
Number of Beds: 162 beds
Note: Programs include fitness activities; pet visitations;
multi-faith spiritual services; Chinese fan dance; horticultural

activities; music club. Physiotherapy; rehabilitation services;
alternative treatments available.
Deslyn Jack, Executive Director
Amy Gorr, Director of Care

Toronto: Oakdale Child & Family Service Ltd.
291 Chisholm Ave., Toronto, ON M4C 4W5
Tel: 416-699-5600 *Fax:* 416-699-6547
tor-oakdale@bellnet.ca
www.oakdaleservices.com
Note: Specialties: Long & short term care for children with
special needs; Teaching independence in life skills, social &
community awareness, & appropriate communication methods

Toronto: Rockcliffe Care Community
Sienna Senior Living
Former Name: Rockcliffe Long Term Care Facility
3015 Lawrence Ave. East, Toronto, ON M1P 2V7
Tel: 416-264-3201
www.siennaliving.ca
Year Founded: 1972
Number of Beds: 204 beds

Toronto: St. George Care Community
Sienna Senior Living
225 St. George St., Toronto, ON M5R 2M2
Tel: 416-967-3985
Number of Beds: 238 beds

Toronto: La Salle Manor
61 Fairfax Cres., Toronto, ON M1L 1Z7
Tel: 416-752-3932
Note: The manor is a private retirement home for De La Salle
Brothers & Sisters of Service.

Toronto: Seven Oaks
9 Neilson Rd., Toronto, ON M1E 5E1
Tel: 416-392-3500
ltc-so@toronto.ca
Year Founded: 1989
Number of Beds: 249 beds
Note: Services for long term care, including adult day programs,
services to the Armenian & Tamil communities, & an on-site child
care centre
Peter Puiatti, Administrator

Toronto: Shepherd Lodge
3760 Sheppard Ave. East, Toronto, ON M1T 3K9
Tel: 416-609-5700 *Fax:* 416-609-8329
info@shepherdvillage.org
www.shepherdvillage.org
Year Founded: 1961
Number of Beds: 252 beds
Note: Provides long-term care for seniors

Toronto: Suomi-Koti Toronto
Also Known As: Toronto Finnish Cdn Srs Centre &
Nursing Home
795 Eglinton Ave. East, Toronto, ON M4G 4E4
Tel: 416-425-4134 *Fax:* 416-425-6319
seniorscentre@suomikoti.ca
www.suomikoti.ca
Number of Beds: 88 apartment units, 34 nursing beds
Note: Suomi-Koti serves Toronto's Finnish community.
Juha Mynttinen, Executive Director
416-425-4134, mynttinen@suomikoti.ca
Leila Carnegie, Nursing Home Administrator
416-421-6719, carnegie@suomikoti.ca

Toronto: Tendercare Living Centre
1020 McNicoll Ave., Toronto, ON M1W 2J6
Tel: 416-499-2020 *Fax:* 416-499-3379
www.tendercare.ca
www.facebook.com/1020McNicoll
Number of Beds: 254 beds
Note: Nursing home & retirement community
Francis Martis, Executive Director
fmartis@tendercare.ca

Toronto: Villa Colombo Homes for the Aged Inc.
Affiliated with: Villa Charities
40 Playfair Ave., Toronto, ON M6B 2P9
Tel: 416-789-2113 *Fax:* 416-789-5986
www.villacharities.com
www.facebook.com/villa.charities; ww.youtube.com/VillaChannel;
www.linkedin.com/company/villa-charities-foundation
Year Founded: 1976
Number of Beds: 391 beds
Note: Specialties: service to residents of Italian origin.
Tracey Comeau, Executive Director
tcomeau@villacolombo.on.ca
Cinzia Scacchi, Admissions Office
416-789-2113

Toronto: West Park Healthcare Centre
82 Buttonwood Ave., Toronto, ON M6M 2J5
Tel: 416-243-3600 *Fax:* 416-243-8947
feedback@westpark.org
www.westpark.org
www.facebook.com/WestParkHealthcareCentre;
twitter.com/westparkhcc;
www.youtube.com/WestParkhealthcare;
www.linkedin.com/company/218953
Year Founded: 1904
Number of Beds: 130 rehab beds; 140 complex continuing care
beds; 200 long term care beds
Number of Employees: 885
Note: Rehabilitation, complex continuing care, and long-term
care facility
Anne-Marie Malek, President & CEO
Nora Cullen, Chief of Staff
Barbara Bell, Chief Nurse

Toronto: The Westbury Long Term Care Centre
Affiliated with: Chartwell Retirement Residences
495 The West Mall, Toronto, ON M9C 5S3
Tel: 416-622-7094
www.chartwell.com
Note: Specialties: Nursing & personal care; Restorative care;
Social, recreational, & physical activity programs; Specialized
neighbourhood for persons with dementia; Palliative care
Brent Binions, Chartwell Retirement Residences

Toronto: Westside Long-Term Care
Former Name: Central Park Lodge West Side
1145 Albion Rd., Toronto, ON M9V 4J7
Tel: 416-745-4800 *Fax:* 416-745-0445
Toll-Free: 877-929-9222
www.reveraliving.com/westside
www.facebook.com/Reveranc; twitter.com/Revera_Inc;
www.youtube.com/Reveranc;
www.linkedin.com/company/Revera-Inc
Number of Beds: 218 beds
Area Served: Etobicoke North; Greater Toronto Area; Peel
Region
Note: Programs include art and creative classes; 3M skin and
wound care; gardening and horicultural activties; snoezelen
multi-sensory therapy.
Vaishali Thorat, Resident Services Coordinator
416-745-4800

Toronto: The Wexford Residence Inc.
1860 Lawrence Ave. East, Toronto, ON M1R 5B1
Tel: 416-701-2503 *Fax:* 416-701-2530
Toll-Free: 877-807-0810
information@thewexford.org
www.thewexford.org
Year Founded: 1978
Number of Beds: 166 beds
Note: Specialties: Long-term care & apartment accommodation
for seniors; Secure units for persons with cognitive impairments;
Physiotherapy; Podiatry; Life enrichment therapy
Sandra Bassett, Executive Director
416-752-8879

Toronto: White Eagle Long Term Care Residence
Affiliated with: Chartwell Retirement Residences
138 Dowling Ave., Toronto, ON M6K 3A6
Tel: 416-533-7935 *Fax:* 416-533-5154
www.chartwell.com
Number of Beds: 56 beds
Brent Binions, President & CEO, Chartwell Retirement
Residences

Trenton: Crown Ridge Place Nursing Home
106 Crown St., Trenton, ON K8V 6R3
Tel: 613-392-1289 *Fax:* 613-394-8672
admin@crownridgeplace.ca
www.crownridgeplace.ca
Number of Beds: 116 beds

Unionville: Union Villa
Affiliated with: Unionville Home Society
**Unionville Home Society, 4300 Hwy. #7 East, Unionville, ON
L3R 1L8**
Tel: 905-477-2822
customerservice@uhs.on.ca
www.uhs.on.ca/union-villa
www.facebook.com/172141492820772;
twitter.com/UHSUnionVilla
Year Founded: 1970
Number of Beds: 160
Note: Services include 24-hour nurse care; dental clinic; library;
chapel.
John Carruthers, Chair

Val Caron: **Elizabeth Centre/Centre Elizabeth**
Affiliated with: Jarlette Health Services
2100 Main St., Val Caron, ON P3N 1S7
Tel: 705-897-7695 Fax: 705-897-0181
www.jarlette.com

Number of Beds: 128 beds
Stephanie Zakrocki, Administrator

Vanier: **Centre d'accueil Champlain**
275 Perrier Ave., Vanier, ON K1L 5C6
Tel: 613-746-3543 Fax: 613-746-5572
ottawa.ca

Year Founded: 1969
Number of Beds: 160 beds
Note: French language living environment. Families may access information in English by contacting the administration office.

Wallaceburg: **Fairfield Park**
1934 Dufferin Ave., Wallaceburg, ON N8A 4M2
Tel: 519-627-1663 Fax: 519-627-9920
www.fairfieldpark.ca

Year Founded: 2000
Number of Beds: 103 beds
Note: Therapeutic & holistic programs; recreational activities include cooking; gardening; crafts; group & individual exercise programs; sporting games such as bowling, shuffle board; spiritual services; live music programs; Montessori programming.

Watford: **Watford Quality Care Centre**
PO Box 400, 344 Victoria St., Watford, ON N0M 2S0
Tel: 519-876-2520 Fax: 519-876-3930
www.watfordqualitycare.ca

Number of Beds: 62 beds
Note: Services include recreation program; library; spiritual care.
Lynne-Anne Gallaway, Administrator
lgallaway@watfordqualitycare.ca

West Hill: **Altmaont Care Community**
Sienna Senior Living
92 Island Rd., West Hill, ON M1C 2P5
Tel: 416-284-4781 Fax: 416-284-3634
www.siennaliving.ca
plus.google.com/118187577645349984064
Year Founded: 1968
Number of Beds: 159 beds
Lois Cormack, CEO, Leisureworld Senior Care Corporation

Willowdale: **Carefree Lodge**
306 Finch Ave. East, Willowdale, ON M2N 4S5
Tel: 416-397-1500 Fax: 416-397-1501
ltc-cfl@toronto.ca
www.toronto.ca

Year Founded: 1991
Number of Beds: 127 beds
Bambo Oluwadimu, Administrator

Winchester: **Dundas Manor Long-Term Care Home**
533 Clarence St., Winchester, ON K0C 2K0
Tel: 613-774-2293 Fax: 613-774-4015
info@dundasmanor.ca
www.dundasmanor.ca

Number of Beds: 98 beds
Cholly Boland, CEO
cboland@wdmh.on.ca
Susan Poirier, Administrator
susan.poirier@dundasmanor.ca

Windsor: **Chateau Park Long Term Care Home**
Affiliated with: Meritas Care Corporation
2990B Riverside Dr. West, Windsor, ON N9C 1A2
Tel: 519-254-4341 Fax: 519-254-7931
chateau@meritascare.ca
www.meritascare.ca

Number of Beds: 59 beds
Annemarie Meloche, Administrator

Windsor: **Huron Lodge**
1881 Cabana Rd. West, Windsor, ON N9G 1C7
Tel: 519-253-6060 Fax: 519-977-8027
www.citywindsor.ca

Number of Beds: 256 beds
Note: Activities include bingo; bowling; euchre; pet visitations.
Alina Sirbu, Administrator & Executive Director
519-253-6060, asirbu@city.windsor.on.ca

Windsor: **Regency Park Nursing Home**
Affiliated with: Meritas Care Corporation
567 Victoria Ave., Windsor, ON N9A 4N1
Tel: 519-254-1141 Fax: 519-254-3759
regency@meritascare.ca
www.meritascare.ca

Number of Beds: 72 beds
Note: Offers: nurse on-call 24 hours a day; skin & wound care; mental health; palliative care; pain management; foot care; music/art therapy; exercise.
Norbert Warnke, President & CEO, Meritas Care Corporation

Woodbridge: **Kristus Darzs Latvian Home**
11290 Pine Valley Dr., Woodbridge, ON L4L 1A6
Tel: 905-832-3300 Fax: 905-832-2029
kristusdarzs@kdlatvianhome.com
www.kdlatvianhome.com
www.facebook.com/kristusdarzs.latvianhome
Year Founded: 1985
Number of Beds: 100 beds
Note: A long term care home dedicated to serving those of Latvian heritage.

Woodstock: **Woodingford Lodge**
300 Juliana Dr., Woodstock, ON N4V 0A1
Tel: 519-421-5556 Fax: 519-533-0781
www.county.oxford.on.ca

Number of Beds: 160 beds
Corrie Fransen, Administrator

Nursing Homes

Ailsa Craig: **Craigwiel Gardens**
221 Main St., RR#1, Ailsa Craig, ON N0M 1A0
Tel: 519-293-3215 Fax: 519-293-3941
info@craigwielgardens.on.ca
www.craigwielgardens.on.ca

Number of Beds: 83 beds
Gemma Nott, Administrator

Ajax: **Ballycliffe Lodge Ltd.**
70 Station Rd., Ajax, ON L1S 1R9
Tel: 905-683-7321 Fax: 905-427-5846
www.chartwell.com
Number of Beds: 100 beds; 65 retirement lodge beds

Akwesasne: **Tsi ion kwa nonh so:te**
Former Name: Akwesasne Adult Care Facility
70 Kawehnoke Apartment Rd., Akwesasne, ON K6H 5R7
Tel: 613-932-1409 Fax: 613-932-8845
Number of Beds: 30 beds
Note: Specialties: Geriatric residential health care; Water therapy; Palliative care

Alexandria: **Community Nursing Home Alexandria**
92 Centre St., Alexandria, ON K0C 1A0
Tel: 613-525-2022 Fax: 613-525-2023
Number of Beds: 70 beds
Terry Dubé, Administrator

Almonte: **Almonte Country Haven**
Omni Health Care
333 Country St., Almonte, ON K0A 1A0
Tel: 613-256-3095 Fax: 613-256-3096
www.omniway.ca

Number of Beds: 82 beds
Note: Long-term care home offering a number of specialized health care services, including individualized care of residents with dementia or Alzheimer's disease.
Carolyn Della Foresta, Administrator
613-256-3095, cdellaforesta@omniway.ca

Almonte: **Fairview Manor**
75 Spring St., Almonte, ON K0A 1A0
Tel: 613-256-3113 Fax: 613-256-5780
www.almontegeneral.com

Number of Beds: 111 beds; 1 respite bed
Note: Long-term care facility with a special care unit for residents with memory loss. Services include physiotherapy, occupational therapy, & therapeutic recreation.
Mary Wilson Trider, President & Chief Executive Officer
613-256-2514, mwilsontrider@agh-fvm.com
Brian Burns, Vice-President & Chief Financial Officer
bburns@agh-fvm.com
Randy Shaw, Vice-President, Corporate Support Services
rshaw@agh-fvm.com

Amherstview: **Helen Henderson Care Centre**
343 Amherst Dr., Amherstview, ON K7N 1X3
Tel: 613-384-4585 Fax: 613-384-9407
www.gibsonfamilyhealthcare.com

Number of Beds: 66 beds
Note: Services include: 24 hour nursing care; pharmacy; physiotherapy; & medication supervision
Lisa Gibson, Administrator
lisagibson@gibsonfamilyhealthcare.com

Arnprior: **The Grove Nursing Home**
Affiliated with: Arnprior Regional Health
275 Ida St. North, Arnprior, ON K7S 3M7
Tel: 613-623-6547 Fax: 613-623-4554
Joan Hughes, Director of Care

Arthur: **Caressant Care Arthur**
Affiliated with: Caressant Care Nursing and Retirement Homes Limited
PO Box 700, 215 Eliza St., Arthur, ON N0G 1A0
Tel: 519-848-3795 Fax: 519-848-2273
www.caressantcare.com
Number of Beds: 80 beds
Note: Programs & services include physiotherapy, restorative care, & wound care

Aurora: **Willows Estate**
Omni Health Care
13837 Yonge St., Aurora, ON L4G 0N9
Tel: 905-727-0128 Fax: 905-841-0454
www.omniway.ca

Number of Beds: 84 beds
Note: Specialties: Long-term care; Care for persons with Alzheimer's disease & dementia; Life enrichment program
Linda Burr, Administrator
lburr@omniway.ca
Alisa Duva, Office Manager
aduva@omniway.ca

Aylmer: **Chartwell Aylmer Long Term Care Residence**
Affiliated with: Chartwell Retirement Residences
465 Talbot St. West, Aylmer, ON N5H 1K8
Tel: 519-773-3423
www.chartwell.com
Number of Beds: 59 beds
Note: Provides 24 hour nursing support & long-term care services
Brent Binions, President & CEO, Chartwell Retirement Residences

Aylmer: **Terrace Lodge**
475 Talbot St. East, Aylmer, ON N5H 3A5
Tel: 519-773-9205 Fax: 519-765-2627
tl@elgin.ca
www.elgincounty.ca
Number of Beds: 100 beds
Note: Programs & serivces include: long-term care; secure unit; physiotherapy; activity program; adult day program, including a specialized program for alzheimer's patients; respite care; palliative care.
Lisa Penner, Administrator
519-773-9205, lpenner@elgin.ca
Annemarie Atkinson, Manager, Support Services
aatkinson@elgin.ca

Bancroft: **Centennial Manor**
PO Box 758, 1 Manor Lane, Bancroft, ON K0L 1C0
Tel: 613-332-2070 Fax: 613-332-2837
www.hastingscounty.com
Number of Beds: 110 beds
Note: Services include: palliative care; dietary; & nursing
Kathy Plunkett, Administrator
613-332-2070
Cheryl Marks, Director, Nursing
613-332-2070
Debbie Rollins, Director, Long Term Care
613-332-2070
Colin Rushlow, Manager, Environmental Services
613-332-2070

Barrie: **Coleman Care Centre**
Schlegel Villages
140 Cundles Rd. West, Barrie, ON L4N 9X8
Tel: 705-726-8691 Fax: 705-726-5085
coleman.admin@schlegelvillages.com
www.schlegelvillages.com
Number of Beds: 112 beds
Note: Long-term care home with specialized care suites for residents with physical, behavioural, or Alzheimer's/dementia-related care needs.
Pam Wiebe, General Manager
pam.wiebe@schlegelvillages.com

Barrie: **Grove Park Home for Senior Citizens**
234 Cook St., Barrie, ON L4M 4H5
Tel: 705-726-1003 Fax: 705-726-1076
business.office@groveparkhome.on.ca
www.groveparkhome.on.ca
twitter.com/GroveParkHome
Number of Beds: 143 beds
Note: Offers retirement living & nurse practitioner services, as well as an Adult Day Program

Barry's Bay: Valley Manor Inc.
PO Box 880, 88 Mintha St., Barry's Bay, ON K0J 1B0
Tel: 613-756-2643 Fax: 613-756-7601
www.valleymanor.org

Number of Beds: 90 beds
Note: Regulated under the Ministry of Health & Long Term Care
Trisha Sammon, CEO
Gail Yantha, Director, Care
Mila Pereira, Manager, Financial Services
Martin Yaraskavitch, Manager, Maintenance
Amanda Pinto, Manager, Support Services

Beamsville: Albright Manor
5050 Hillside Dr., Beamsville, ON L0R 1B2
Tel: 905-563-8252 Fax: 905-563-5223

Number of Beds: 231 beds
William ter Harmsel, CEO

Beeton: Simcoe Manor Home for the Aged
PO Box 100, 5988 Main St. East, Beeton, ON L0G 1A0
Tel: 905-729-2267 Fax: 905-729-4350

Number of Beds: 126 beds
Note: Services include: 24 hour nursing care; medical; dental; foot care; occupational therapy; physiotherapy; & speech therapy
Susan Fagan, Administrator
Janina Grabowski, Director, Care

Belleville: Bellmont Long-Term Care Facility
Former Name: Montgomery Lodge Nursing Home
250 Bridge St. West, Belleville, ON K8P 5N3
Tel: 613-968-4434 Fax: 613-968-5443
www.belmontltcf.ca

Number of Beds: 128 beds
Note: Services include: 24 hour nursing care; medical care; dental; dietary; foot care; occupational therapy; physiotherapy; & restorative care
Denise Mackey, Administrator

Belleville: Hastings Manor
PO Box 458, 476 Dundas St. West, Belleville, ON K8N 5B2
Tel: 613-968-6467 Fax: 613-771-2409
ltcinquiries@hastingscounty.com
www.hastingscounty.com

Year Founded: 1908
Number of Beds: 253 beds
Note: Services include: palliative care; dietary; & nursing
Jim Pine, Chief Administrative Officer
613-966-1319, Fax: 613-966-2574, pinej@hastingscounty.com
Debbie Rollins, Site Manager

Belleville: Westgate Lodge
37 Wilkie St., Belleville, ON K8P 4E4
Tel: 613-966-1323 Fax: 613-968-5644
admin@westgatelodge.ca
www.westgatelodge.ca

Number of Beds: 88 beds
Note: Services include: medical care; respite care; & supportive care

Blenheim: Blenheim Community Village
Revera Inc.
PO Box 220, 10 Mary Ave., Blenheim, ON N0P 1A0
Tel: 519-676-8119 Fax: 519-676-0610
www.reveraliving.com/blenheim
www.facebook.com/Reveralnc; twitter.com/Revera_Inc;
www.youtube.com/user/Reveralnc;
www.linkedin.com/company/revera-inc

Number of Beds: 65 beds
Note: Retirement lodge; also long-term care facility with programs & services including: 24 hour nursing; music therapy; pet visitations; spiritual services.
Thomas G. Wellner, President & CEO, Revera Living

Bobcaygeon: Case Manor Care Community
28 Boyd St., Bobcaygeon, ON K0M 1A0
Tel: 705-738-2374 Fax: 705-738-3821
www.siennaliving.ca

Number of Beds: 96 beds
Note: Services include physiotherapy & restorative care
Monica Cara, Administrator

Bobcaygeon: Pinecrest Nursing Home
3418 County Rd. 36, RR#2, Bobcaygeon, ON K0M 1A0
Tel: 705-738-2366 Fax: 705-738-9414

Number of Beds: 65 beds
Note: Specialties: Activation program
Mary Carr, Administrator
mcarr@pinecrestnh.ca

Bolton: King Nursing Home
49 Sterne St., Bolton, ON L7E 1B9
Tel: 905-857-4117 Fax: 905-857-5181

Year Founded: 1966
Number of Beds: 86 beds
Janice L. King, Administrator
janice.king@kingnursinghome.com

Bolton: Vera M. Davis Community Care Centre
80 Allan Dr., Bolton, ON L7E 1P7
Tel: 905-857-0975 Fax: 905-857-7872
www.peelregion.ca/ltc/davis

Number of Beds: 64 beds
Liezle Trinidad, Administrator

Bourget: Caressant Care Bourget
Affiliated with: Caressant Care Nursing and
Retirement Homes Limited
PO Box 99, 2279 Laval St., Bourget, ON K0A 1E0
Tel: 613-487-2331 Fax: 613-487-3464
www.caressantcare.com

Number of Beds: 56 beds
Note: Offers physiotherapy & recreational services
James Lavelle, President, Caressant Care Nursing and Retirement Homes Ltd.

Bowmanville: Glen Hill Marnwood
Affiliated with: Durham Christian Homes
26 Elgin St., Bowmanville, ON L1C 3C8
Tel: 905-623-5731 Fax: 905-623-4497
www.dchomes.ca

Year Founded: 1983
Number of Beds: 60 beds
Note: Specialties: Social work; Physiotherapy
Vanda Cozier, Administrator
vcozier@dchomes.ca

Bowmanville: Glen Hill Strathaven
Affiliated with: Durham Christian Homes
264 King St. East, Bowmanville, ON L1C 1P9
Tel: 905-623-2553 Fax: 905-623-1374
www.dchomes.ca

Number of Beds: 199 beds
Note: Long-term care & convalescent care
Michelle Stroud, Administrator
mstroud@dchomes.ca

Bradford: Bradford Valley Care Community
Former Name: Bradford Valley Specialty Care;
Bradford Place Nursing Home
2656 - 6 Line, Bradford, ON L3Z 2A4
Tel: 905-952-2270 Fax: 905-775-0263
www.siennaliving.ca

Number of Beds: 246 beds
Note: Services include physiotherapy & restorative care
Barbara Renton, Director, Care
barbara.renton@siennaliving.ca

Brampton: Extendicare - Brampton
Extendicare Canada
7891 McLaughlin Rd., Brampton, ON L6Y 5H8
Tel: 905-459-4904 Fax: 905-459-5625
www.extendicarebrampton.com

Number of Beds: 150 beds

Brampton: Hawthorn Woods Care Community
Former Name: Leisureworld Caregiving Centre -
Brampton Woods
9257 Goreway Dr., Brampton, ON L6T 3Y7
Tel: 905-799-7502
www.siennaliving.ca

Number of Beds: 160 beds

Brampton: Holland Christian Homes Inc.
Former Name: Faith Manor Nursing Home
7900 McLaughlin Rd. South, Brampton, ON L6Y 5A7
Tel: 905-459-3333 Fax: 905-459-8667
www.hch.ca

Number of Beds: 120 beds
Note: Home for seniors of Dutch heritage
Ken Rawlins, CEO
ken.rawlins@hch.ca
Peter Dykstra, Administrator, Grace Manor
petedy@hch.ca
Anthony Faul, Contact, Human Resources
anthfa@hch.ca

Brampton: Maple Grove Care Community
Former Name: Leisureworld Caregiving Centre -
Brampton Meadows
215 Sunny Meadows Blvd., Brampton, ON L6R 3B5
Tel: 905-458-7604
www.siennaliving.ca

Number of Beds: 160 beds
Angie Heinze, Administrator

Brampton: Peel Manor
525 Main St. North, Brampton, ON L6X 1N9
Tel: 905-453-4140
www.peelregion.ca/ltc/peel

Number of Beds: 177 beds
Note: Long-term care centre
Susan Griffin Thomas, Administrator

Brantford: Brierwood Gardens Long Term Care
Revera Inc.
425 Park Rd. North, Brantford, ON N3R 7G5
Tel: 519-759-1040 Fax: 519-759-5343
www.reveraliving.com
www.facebook.com/Reveralnc; twitter.com/Revera_Inc;
www.youtube.com/user/Reveralnc;
www.linkedin.com/company/revera-inc

Number of Beds: 79 beds
Note: Services include: 24 hour nursing care; 24 hour on-call medical care; foot care; physiotherapy; restorative care; & skin & wound care
Thomas G. Wellner, President & CEO, Revera Living
Debbie Boakes, Administrator

Brantford: Fox Ridge Care Community
Former Name: Leisureworld Caregiving Centre -
Brantford
389 West St., Brantford, ON N3R 3V9
Tel: 519-759-4666 Fax: 519-759-0200
www.siennaliving.ca

Number of Beds: 122 beds
Note: Long-term care home offering nursing care, personal care, medical care, rehabilitation, & restorative care services
Susan Hastings, Executive Director
susan.hastings@siennaliving.ca

Brantford: Hardy Terrace Long Term Care
612 Mount Pleasant Rd., RR#2, Brantford, ON N3T 5L5
Tel: 519-484-2431 Fax: 519-484-2590
adm.hterrace@verveseniorliving.com
www.verveseniorliving.com/hardy-terrace

Number of Beds: 101 beds
Paul Rooyakker, Administrator

Brockville: St. Lawrence Lodge
PO Box 1130, 1803 Country Rd. East, Brockville, ON K6V 5T1
Tel: 613-345-0255 Fax: 613-345-1029
info@stll.org
www.stll.org

Number of Beds: 224 beds
Note: Long-term care home
Tom Harrington, Administrator
tharrington@stll.org
Tracey Davidson, Director, Care
Bradley Morton, Director, Support Services
bmorton@stll.org

Brockville: Sherwood Park Manor
1814 County Rd. 2 East, Brockville, ON K6V 5T1
Tel: 613-342-5531 Fax: 613-342-3767
www.sherwoodparkmanor.com

Number of Beds: 107 beds
Note: Services include: nursing; personal care; dental; dietary; & palliative care
Alfred O'Rourke, Administrator
aorourke@sherwoodparkmanor.com
Anne Rodger, Director, Care
Nicole Smith, Manager, Corporate Services
Nancy Nesbitt-Boucher, Manager, Resident & Family Services

Brunner: Country Meadows Retirement Residence
6124 Ana St., Brunner, ON N0K 1C0
Tel: 519-595-8903 Fax: 519-595-8272
rv@countrymeadowsrr.com
www.countrymeadowsrr.com
www.facebook.com/455549397831324

Number of Beds: 59 beds
Note: Retirement home offering 24 hour nursing care
Rick Veleke, Administrator
rv@countrymeadowsrr.com

Brussels: Huronlea Home for the Aged
820 Turnberry St. South, Brussels, ON N0G 1H0
Tel: 519-887-9267 Fax: 519-887-9143
contactseniors@huroncounty.ca
www.huroncounty.ca

Number of Beds: 64 beds
Angela Steadman, Administrator

Burlington: Cama Woodlands Nursing Home
159 Panin Rd., Burlington, ON L7P 5A6
Tel: 905-681-6441 Fax: 905-681-2678
www.camawoodlands.com

Number of Beds: 128 beds
Note: Services include: 24 hour nursing care; medical; physiotherapy; & recreation
Pat Cervoni, Administrator
p.cervoni@camawoodlands.ca

Burlington: Maple Villa Long Term Care Centre
441 Maple Ave., Burlington, ON L7S 1L8
Tel: 905-639-2264 *Fax:* 905-639-3034
maplevilla@maplevilla.ca
www.maplevilla.ca
instagram.com/maplevillalifeenrichment
Year Founded: 1971
Number of Beds: 93 beds
Note: Services include: 24 hour nursing care; in-house physicians; audiology; chiropody; dental; optometry; oxygen therapy; palliative care; pharmacy; podiatry; physiotherapy; radiology; respiratory; & restorative care
Barb Goetz, Administrator

Cambridge: Cambridge Country Manor
Caressant Care Nursing and Retirement Homes Limited
3680 Speedsville Rd., Cambridge, ON N3H 4R6
Tel: 519-650-0100
www.caressantcare.com
Number of Beds: 79 beds
Heather Richardson, Administrator

Cambridge: Golden Years Nursing Home
704 Eagle St. North, Cambridge, ON N3H 4T3
Tel: 519-653-5493 *Fax:* 519-650-1495
Number of Beds: 88 beds
Note: Services include 24 hour nursing & personal care.
Lynn Hopkins, Executive Director

Cambridge: Riverbend Place Retirement Community
Revera Inc.
650 Coronation Blvd., Cambridge, ON N1R 7S6
Tel: 519-740-3820 *Fax:* 519-740-0961
www.reveraliving.com
www.facebook.com/ReveraInc; twitter.com/Revera_Inc;
www.youtube.com/user/ReveraInc;
www.linkedin.com/company/revera-inc
Number of Beds: 53 beds
Note: Programs & services include: 24 hour nursing & medical care; dental; foot care; physiotherapy; & restorative care; community includes nursing home, retirement lodge, & apartments.
Thomas G. Wellner, President & CEO, Revera Living

Cambridge: Saint Luke's Place
1624 Franklin Blvd., Cambridge, ON N3C 3P4
Tel: 519-658-5183 *Fax:* 519-658-2991
www.saintlukesplace.ca
Number of Beds: 150 beds
Note: Home for the aged; provides long term care, retirement home & apartments.
Brian Swainson, CEO

Campbellford: Burnbrae Gardens
Omni Health Care
320 - 6 Line East, Campbellford, ON K0L 1L0
Tel: 705-653-4100 *Fax:* 705-653-2598
www.omniway.ca
Number of Beds: 43 beds
Kathy Deline, Office Manager
kdeline@omniway.ca
April Faux, Administrator
afaux@omniway.ca

Cannifton: E.J. McQuigge Lodge
PO Box 68, 38 Black Diamond Rd., Cannifton, ON K0K 1K0
Tel: 613-966-7717 *Fax:* 613-966-7646
www.mcquiggelodge.com
Number of Beds: 57 beds
Note: Services include: 24 hour nursing & personal care; activity programs; foot care; nutrition; physiotherapy; & pharmacy.
Anita Garland, Administrator
agarland@mcquiggelodge.com

Cannington: Bon-Air Residence
Affiliated with: Chartwell Retirement Residences
PO Box 400, 131 Laidlaw St. South, Cannington, ON L0E 1E0
Tel: 705-432-2385 *Fax:* 705-432-3331
www.chartwell.com
Number of Beds: 55 units
Note: Services include nursing & personal care.
Brent Binions, President & CEO, Chartwell Retirement Residences

Carleton Place: Stoneridge Manor
Revera Inc.
256 High St., Carleton Place, ON K7C 1X1
Tel: 613-257-4355 *Fax:* 613-253-2190
www.reveraliving.com/stoneridge
www.facebook.com/ReveraInc; twitter.com/Revera_Inc;
www.youtube.com/user/ReveraInc;
www.linkedin.com/company/revera-inc
Number of Beds: 60 beds
Note: Programs & services include: 24 hour nursing; music therapy; shuffleboard; puzzle activities; pain & symptom management; palliative care; physical activity; rehabilitation; therapy; & wound care.
Thomas G. Wellner, President & CEO, Revera Living

Chapleau: Bignucolo Residence
Chapleau Health Services
PO Box 757, 6 Broomhead Rd., Chapleau, ON P0M 1K0
Tel: 705-864-1520 *Fax:* 705-864-0449
Year Founded: 1998
Number of Beds: 25 beds
Note: Specialties: Long-term care; Chronic care; Respite care; Pet therapy

Chatham: St. Andrew's Residence
99 Park St., Chatham, ON N7M 3R5
Tel: 519-354-8103 *Fax:* 519-351-2407
info@standrewsresidence.com
www.standrewsresidence.com
www.facebook.com/staresidence
Number of Beds: 95 beds
Carolynn Barko, CEO
519-354-8103, cbarko@standrewsresidence.com

Chesley: Elgin Abbey Continuing Care Residence for Seniors
PO Box 7, 380 1st Ave. North, Chesley, ON N0G 1L0
Tel: 519-363-3195 *Fax:* 519-363-0375
elginabbey@xplornet.ca
Number of Beds: 41 beds; 27 long-term-care, 14 retirement home
Note: Services include 24 hour nursing care & personal care.
Leanne Haynes, Administrator

Clinton: Huronview Home for the Aged
77722A London Rd., Hwy 4 South, RR#5, Clinton, ON N0M 1L0
Tel: 519-482-3451 *Fax:* 519-482-5263
www.huroncounty.ca/homes-for-the-aged
Number of Beds: 120 beds
Connie Townsend, Administrator

Cobden: Caressant Care Cobden
Affiliated with: Caressant Care Nursing and Retirement Homes Limited
12 Wren Dr., Cobden, ON K0J 1K0
Tel: 613-646-2109
www.caressantcare.com
Year Founded: 2000
Number of Beds: 64 beds
James Lavelle, President, Caressant Care Nursing and Retirement Homes Ltd.

Cobourg: Extendicare - Cobourg
Extendicare Canada
130 Densmore Rd., Cobourg, ON K9A 5W2
Tel: 905-372-0377 *Fax:* 905-372-0477
www.extendicarecobourg.com
Number of Beds: 69 beds

Cobourg: Streamway Villa Nursing Home
Omni Health Care
19 James St. West, Cobourg, ON K9A 2J8
Tel: 905-372-0163 *Fax:* 905-372-0581
www.omniway.ca
Number of Beds: 59 beds
Note: Services include physiotherapy & social & recreation programs.
Kylie Szczebonski, Administrator & Director of Care
kszczebonski@omniway.ca

Collingwood: Bay Haven Senior Care Community
Former Name: Bay Haven Nursing Home Inc.
499 Hume St., Collingwood, ON L9Y 4H8
Tel: 705-445-6501 *Fax:* 705-445-6506
info@bayhaven.com
www.bayhaven.com
Number of Beds: 60 beds
Note: Services include: 24 hour nursing care; medication administration; & recreation.

Collingwood: Collingwood Nursing Home Limited
250 Campbell St., Collingwood, ON L9Y 4J9
Tel: 705-445-3991 *Fax:* 705-445-5060
cnh@collingwoodnursinghome.com
www.collingwoodnursinghome.ca
Number of Beds: 60 beds
Note: Services include: convalescent care; dietitian; foot care; occupational therapy; physiotherapy; & restorative care.
Peter Zober, President & Administrator
peter@collingwoodnursinghome.com

Collingwood: Sunset Manor & Village
49 Raglan St., Collingwood, ON L9Y 4X1
Tel: 705-445-4499 *Fax:* 705-445-9742
www.simcoe.ca
Year Founded: 1968
Number of Beds: 148 beds
Note: Sunset Manor is a municipal long-term care facility.

Corbeil: Nipissing Manor Nursing Care Centre
1202 Hwy. 94, Corbeil, ON P0H 1K0
Tel: 705-752-1100 *Fax:* 705-752-2570
admin@nipissingmanor.ca
www.nipissingmanor.ca
Number of Beds: 120 beds
Note: Services include: medical care; nursing & personal care; occupational therapy; physiotherapy; restorative care; & speech language pathology.
Wentworth Graham, Administrator

Cornwall: Glen-Stor-Dun Lodge
1900 Montréal Rd., Cornwall, ON K6H 7L1
Tel: 613-933-3384 *Fax:* 613-933-7214
www.cornwall.ca
Year Founded: 1912
Number of Beds: 132 beds
Note: Serves as a municipal home for older people. Provides a variety of services including dietary, house cleaning, recreation & leisure activities, & more.
Norm Quenneville, Administrator
Sally Munroe, Director of Care

Cornwall: Heartwood Long Term Care
Revera Inc.
201 - 11 St. East, Cornwall, ON K6H 2Y6
Tel: 613-933-7420
www.reveraliving.com
www.facebook.com/ReveraInc; twitter.com/Revera_Inc;
www.youtube.com/user/ReveraInc;
www.linkedin.com/company/revera-inc
Number of Beds: 118 beds
Note: Programs & services include: 24 hour nursing care; dietitian; pain & symptom management; physical activity; rehabilitation; therapy; & wound care.
Thomas G. Wellner, President & CEO, Revera Living

Cornwall: Parisien Manor
439 Second St. East, Cornwall, ON K6H 1Z2
Tel: 613-933-2592 *Fax:* 613-933-3839
www.parisienmanor.ca
Year Founded: 1982
Number of Beds: 65 beds
Note: Services include: nursing care; dispensing of medications; foot care; laboratory & other off-site medical services; & physiotherapy.
Andrew Lauzon, Administrator
alauzon@extendicare.com

Cornwall: St. Joseph's Continuing Care Centre
14 York St., Cornwall, ON K6J 5T2
Tel: 613-933-6040 *Fax:* 613-933-0163
executiveoffices@stjosephscentre.ca
www.stjosephscentre.ca
Number of Beds: 150 long-term care beds; 58 restorative care beds
Gizanne Lafrance-Allaire, Executive Director
Ann Surch, Coordinator, Administration Services

Courtland: Caressant Care Courtland
Affiliated with: Caressant Care Nursing and Retirement Homes Limited
Former Name: Sacred Heart Villa
PO Box 279, 4850 County Rd. 59, Courtland, ON N0J 1E0
Tel: 519-688-0710 *Fax:* 519-688-0052
www.caressantcare.com
Number of Beds: 54 beds
Note: Long-term care home offering a range of services, including 24 hour nursing & personal care.
Michele Hough, Administrator

Creemore: **Creedan Valley Care Community**
Sienna Senior Living
143 Mary St., Creemore, ON L0M 1G0
Tel: 705-466-3437 *Fax:* 705-466-3063
www.siennaliving.ca
Number of Beds: 95 beds
Note: Offers a rehabilitation program, respite care, & other services.
Lois Cormack, President & CEO, Sienna Senior Living

Creemore: **Creedan Valley Care Community**
Former Name: Leisureworld Caregiving Centre -
Creedan Valley
143 Mary St., Creemore, ON L0M 1G0
Tel: 705-466-3437
www.siennaliving.ca
Number of Beds: 95 beds

Deep River: **North Renfrew Long-Term Care Centre**
PO Box 1988, 47 Ridge Rd., Deep River, ON K0J 1P0
Tel: 613-584-1900 *Fax:* 613-584-9183
nrltc@nrltc.ca
www.nrltc.ca
Year Founded: 1994
Number of Beds: 20 long-term care beds; 1 respite bed
Kim Rodgers, Administrator
kim.rodgers@nrltc.ca

Delhi: **Delhi Long Term Care Centre**
Affiliated with: peopleCare
750 Gibralter St., Delhi, ON N4B 3B3
Tel: 519-582-3400 *Fax:* 519-582-0300
www.peoplecare.ca
Year Founded: 1972
Number of Beds: 60 beds
Note: Services include 24 hour nursing & personal care.
Jeremy Zinger, Executive Director

Embrun: **St. Jacques Nursing Home/Foyer**
St-Jacques
PO Box 870, 915 Notre Dame St., Embrun, ON K0A 1W0
Tel: 613-443-3442 *Fax:* 613-443-1716
www.stjacques.ca
Number of Beds: 60 beds
Note: Medical services include: 24 hour nursing care; laboratory; physiotherapy; occupational therapy; podiatry; pharmaceutical; & visits from an optometrist & a dentist.
Yvon Brisson, President

Englehart: **Northview Nursing Home**
Affiliated with: Conmed Health Care Group
PO Box 1139, 77 River Rd., Englehart, ON P0J 1H0
Tel: 705-544-8191 *Fax:* 705-544-8255
administrator@northviewnursinghome.com
www.northviewnursinghome.com
Number of Beds: 47 beds
Note: Services include: 24 hour nursing care; dietitian; physiotherapy; & recreation.
Tracey Gemmill, Administrator & Director of Care
tgemmill@conmedhealth.com

Espanola: **Espanola Nursing Home**
825 McKinnon Dr., Espanola, ON P5E 1R4
Tel: 705-869-1420 *Fax:* 705-869-3091
www.espanolaregionalhospital.ca
Number of Beds: 62 beds
Nicole Haley, Administrator

Essex: **Iler Lodge**
Former Name: Essex Health Care Centre
111 Iler Ave., Essex, ON N8M 1T6
Tel: 519-776-9482
www.reveraliving.com
www.facebook.com/ReveraInc; www.twitter.com/Revera_Inc;
www.youtube.com/ReveraInc;
www.linkedin.com/company/revera-inc
Number of Beds: 104 beds
Note: Programs include physiotherapy; 3M skin and wound care; ALIVE program
Cheryl Labute, Administrator

Exeter: **Exeter Villa Nursing & Retirement Home**
Affiliated with: ATK Care Inc.
155 John St. East, Exeter, ON N0M 1S1
Tel: 519-235-1581 *Fax:* 519-235-3219
atkcare.com/exetervilla.html
Number of Beds: 57 nursing care beds, 66 retirement beds
Erika King, Administrator
erika.k@exetervilla.ca

Fergus: **Caressant Care Fergus**
Affiliated with: Caressant Care Nursing and
Retirement Homes Limited
450 Queen St. East, Fergus, ON N1M 2Y7
Tel: 519-843-2400
www.caressantcare.com
Year Founded: 1986
Number of Beds: 87 beds
James Lavelle, President, Caressant Care Nursing and Retirement Homes Ltd.

Fordwich: **Fordwich Village Nursing Home**
Affiliated with: ATK Care Inc.
3063 Adelaide St., Fordwich, ON N0G 1V0
Tel: 519-335-3168 *Fax:* 519-335-3825
atkcare.com/fordvichvillage.html
Number of Beds: 33 beds
Susan Jaunzemis, Administrator, Director of Care

Forest: **North Lambton Lodge**
PO Box 640, 39 Morris St., Forest, ON N0N 1J0
Tel: 519-786-2151 *Fax:* 519-786-2156
www.lambtoncares.ca
Number of Beds: 88 beds
Jane Joris, General Manager
Janet Groen, Administrator

Fort Erie: **Crescent Park Lodge**
Affiliated with: Conmed Health Care Group
4 Hagey Ave., Fort Erie, ON L2A 5M5
Tel: 905-871-8330 *Fax:* 905-991-1456
info@crescentparklodge.com
www.crescentparklodge.com
Number of Beds: 68 beds

Gananoque: **Carveth Care Centre**
375 James St., Gananoque, ON K7G 2Z1
Tel: 613-382-4752 *Fax:* 613-382-8514
www.gibsonfamilyhealthcare.com
Number of Beds: 104 beds
Brett Gibson, Administrator

Georgetown: **Bennett Health Care Centre**
1 Princess Anne Dr., Georgetown, ON L7G 2B8
Tel: 905-873-0115 *Fax:* 905-873-1403
info@bennettvillage.ca
www.bennetthealthcarecentre.ca
Number of Beds: 66 beds
Brian Jackson, Chief Executive Officer

Georgetown: **Extendicare - Halton Hills**
Extendicare Canada
9 Lindsay Court, Georgetown, ON L7G 6G9
Tel: 905-702-8760 *Fax:* 905-702-7430
www.extendicarehaltonhills.com
Number of Beds: 130 beds

Gloucester: **Extendicare - Laurier Manor**
Extendicare Canada
1715 Montréal Rd., Gloucester, ON K1J 6N4
Tel: 613-741-5122 *Fax:* 613-741-8432
cnh_lauriermanor@extendicare.com
www.extendicarelauriermanor.com
Number of Beds: 240 beds
Jennifer Cummins, Administrator

Goderich: **Maitland Manor**
290 South St., Goderich, ON N7A 4G6
Tel: 519-524-7324 *Fax:* 519-524-8739
maitlandmanor.ca
Number of Beds: 90 beds
Note: Specialties: Long-term care; Restorative care programs; Foot care; Specialized skin & wound care program; Physiotherapy; Music therapy; Respite care
Tanya Adams, Executive Director
taadams@southbridgecare.ca

Gravenhurst: **Muskoka Shores Care Community**
Former Name: Leisureworld Caregiving Centre -
Muskoka
200 Kelly Dr., Gravenhurst, ON P1P 1P3
Tel: 705-687-3444 *Fax:* 705-687-9094
www.siennaliving.ca
Year Founded: 1999
Number of Beds: 180 long-term care, 2 short term beds, 28 retirement suites
Note: 24-hour nursing care; rehabilitation & restorative care; regular daily activities & special events such as Fall Fair Day.
Lois Cormack, CEO

Grimsby: **Kilean Lodge**
Revera Inc.
83 Main St. East, Grimsby, ON L3M 1N6
Tel: 905-945-9243 *Fax:* 905-945-1126
Kilean@reveraliving.com
www.reveraliving.com
www.facebook.com/ReveraInc; twitter.com/Revera_Inc;
www.youtube.com/user/ReveraInc;
www.linkedin.com/company/revera-inc
Number of Beds: 50 beds
Note: Programs & services include 24 hour nurse on site; dietitian; memory care program; friendly pet visitations.
Thomas G. Wellner, President & CEO, Revera Living

Grimsby: **Shalom Manor**
12 Bartlett Ave., Grimsby, ON L3M 4N5
Tel: 905-945-9631 *Fax:* 905-945-1211
info@shalommanor.ca
www.shalommanor.ca
Year Founded: 1966
Number of Beds: 144 beds
Note: Home for the aged affiliated with the Christian Reformed Church
Peet Konnie, CEO

Guelph: **Eden House Nursing Home**
Affiliated with: Waterloo Wellington Local Health
Integration Network
5016 Wellington Rd. 29, Guelph, ON N1H 6H8
Tel: 519-856-4622 *Fax:* 519-856-1274
admin@edenhousecarehome.ca
www.edenhousecarehome.ca
Number of Beds: 58 nursing home, 21 retirement home

Guelph: **Lapointe-Fisher Nursing Home**
271 Metcalfe St., Guelph, ON N1E 4Y8
Tel: 519-821-9030 *Fax:* 519-821-6021
guelph@lapointefisher.ca
www.lapointefisher.ca
Number of Beds: 92 beds

Hagersville: **Anson Place Care Centre**
Former Name: Norcliffe LifeCare Centre
85 Main St. North, Hagersville, ON N0A 1H0
Tel: 905-768-1641 *Fax:* 905-768-1685
www.ansonplacecarecentre.ca
Year Founded: 1991
Number of Beds: 61 long-term care units; 40 retirement units

Haileybury: **Extendicare - Tri-Town**
Extendicare Canada
PO Box 999, 143 Bruce St., Haileybury, ON P0J 1K0
Tel: 705-672-2151 *Fax:* 705-672-5348
www.extendicaretritown.com
Number of Beds: 60 beds

Hamilton: **Arbour Creek Long Term Care Centre**
2717 King St. East, Hamilton, ON L8G 1J3
Tel: 905-573-4900 *Fax:* 905-573-4340
thomashealthcare.com
Number of Beds: 128 beds
Shirley Thomas Weir
sthomasweir@thomashealthcare.com

Hamilton: **Baywoods Place**
Revera Inc.
Former Name: Versa-Care Centre - Hamilton
330 Main St. East, Hamilton, ON L8N 3T9
Tel: 905-523-7134
www.reveraliving.com
www.facebook.com/ReveraInc; twitter.com/Revera_Inc;
www.youtube.com/user/ReveraInc;
www.linkedin.com/company/revera-inc
Number of Beds: 128 beds
Note: Programs & services include a 24 hour nurse on staff; dietitian; music therapy; pet therapy; art classes; casino outings & other day trips.
Thomas G. Wellner, President & CEO, Revera Living

Hamilton: **Extendicare - Hamilton**
Extendicare Canada
90 Chedmac Dr., Hamilton, ON L9C 7S6
Tel: 905-318-4472 *Fax:* 905-318-1162
www.extendicarehamilton.com
Number of Beds: 160 beds

Hamilton: **Hamilton Continuing Care**
125 Wentworth St. South, Hamilton, ON L8N 2Z1
Tel: 905-527-1482 *Fax:* 905-527-0679
www.schlegelvillages.com
Number of Beds: 64 beds
Ron Schlegel, Director

Hamilton: Macassa Lodge
701 Upper Sherman Ave., Hamilton, ON L8V 3M7
Tel: 905-546-2800 Fax: 905-546-4989
macassalodge@hamilton.ca
www.hamilton.ca
Number of Beds: 270 beds
Note: Specialties: Long term care; Adult day program; Social work

Hamilton: Parkview Nursing Centre
545 King St. West, Hamilton, ON L8P 1C1
Tel: 905-525-5903 Fax: 905-525-8717
parkviewnursingcentre.ca
Number of Beds: 126 beds

Hamilton: Victoria Gardens
176 Victoria Ave. North, Hamilton, ON L8L 5G1
Tel: 905-527-9111 Fax: 905-526-1871
www.victoriagardens.ca
Number of Beds: 76 beds
Ranka Stipancic, Administrator
ranka@victoriagardens.ca

Hanover: Hanover Care Centre
700 - 19 Ave., Hanover, ON N4N 3S6
Tel: 519-364-3700 Fax: 519-364-7194
cancarecentres.ca
Number of Beds: 41 beds
Brenda Weppler, Administrator

Harriston: Caressant Care Harriston
Affiliated with: Caressant Care Nursing And Retirement Homes Limited
PO Box 520, 24 Louise St., Harriston, ON N0G 1Z0
Tel: 519-338-3700 Fax: 519-338-2744
www.caressantcare.com
Number of Beds: 89 beds
Note: Long term care facility, with secure unit for residents with dementia, & adjacent retirement home.
James Lavelle, President, Caressant Care Nursing and Retirement Homes

Hawkesbury: Résidence Prescott et Russell/Prescott & Russell Residence
1020, boul Cartier, Hawkesbury, ON K6A 1W7
Tél: 613-632-2755 Téléc: 613-632-4056
www.prescott-russell.on.ca
Fondée en: 1906
Nombre de lits: 146 lits
Note: Maison de soins de longue durée. Employés: 171

Hearst: Foyer des Pionniers
PO Box 1538, 67 - 15 St., Hearst, ON P0L 1N0
Tel: 705-372-2978 Fax: 705-372-2996
Number of Beds: 61 beds
Joëlle Lacroix, Director of Care, Administrator
jlacroix@hearst.ca

Huntsville: Fairvern Nursing Home Inc.
Affiliated with: Huntsville District Nursing Home Inc.
14 Mill St., Huntsville, ON P1H 2A4
Tel: 705-789-6011 Fax: 705-789-1371
info@fairvern.ca
www.fairvernnursinghome.ca
Number of Beds: 76 beds
Bev MacWilliams, Chair

Ingersoll: Secord Trails Care Community
Former Name: Leisureworld Caregiving Centre - Oxford
263 Wonham St. South, Ingersoll, ON N5C 3P6
Tel: 519-485-3920
www.siennaliving.ca
Year Founded: 1975
Number of Beds: 80 long-term care beds
Note: Programs & entertainment include: clay art therapy with a local artist; exotic animal shows; Family Fun Fest Day; Ingersoll Cheese Museum visits; John Deere Museum visits; camp fires.
Specialities: palliative care program; pet therapy.
Lois Cormack, CEO, Leisureworld Senior Care Corporation

Iroquois Falls: South Centennial Manor
240 Fyfe St., Iroquois Falls, ON P0K 1E0
Tel: 705-258-3836 Fax: 705-258-3694
www.micsgroup.com
Number of Beds: 69 beds
Note: Services include pastoral care; foot care; nursing and personal care services; assisting with activities of daily living.
Dan O'Mara, CEO
Richard Hadley, Director, Physical Plant

Kapuskasing: Extendicare - Kapuskasing
Extendicare Canada
PO Box 460, 45 Ontario St., Kapuskasing, ON P5N 2Y5
Tel: 705-335-8337 Fax: 705-337-6051
cnh_kapuskasing@extendicare.com
www.extendicarekapuskasing.com
Number of Beds: 60 beds

Kapuskasing: North Centennial Manor
2 Kimberly Dr., Kapuskasing, ON P5N 1L5
Tel: 705-335-6125 Fax: 705-337-1091
info@ncmanor.com
www.ncmanor.com
Number of Beds: 78 beds
Note: Non-profit charitable home for the aged.
Claude Tremblay, Administrator

Kenora: Birchwood Terrace Nursing Home
237 Lakeview Dr., Kenora, ON P9N 4J7
Tel: 807-468-8625 Fax: 807-468-4060
birchwoodterrace.ca
Number of Beds: 96 beds
Alecia DiMario, Executive Director
birchwoodltc@southbridgecare.ca

Kenora: Pinecrest Home for the Aged
1220 Valley Dr., Kenora, ON P9N 2W7
Tel: 807-468-3165 Fax: 807-468-6346
Number of Beds: 116 beds
Kevin Queen, Chief Executive Officer
kevin.queen@kenoradistricthomes.ca

Keswick: Cedarvale Lodge Care Community
Sienna Senior Living
121 Morton Ave., Keswick, ON L4P 3T5
Tel: 905-476-2656
www.siennaliving.ca
Number of Beds: 60 beds

King City: King City Lodge Nursing Home
146 Fog Rd., King City, ON L7B 1A3
Tel: 905-833-5037 Fax: 905-833-5925
Number of Beds: 36 beds

Kingston: Extendicare - Kingston
Extendicare Canada
309 Queen Mary Rd., Kingston, ON K7M 6P4
Tel: 613-549-5010 Fax: 613-549-7347
cnh_kingston@extendicare.com
www.extendicarekingston.com
Number of Beds: 150 beds
Tawnia Pilgrim, Administrator

Kingston: Rideaucrest Home
175 Rideau St., Kingston, ON K7K 3H6
Tel: 613-530-2818
Number of Beds: 256 beds

Kirkland Lake: Extendicare - Kirkland Lake
Extendicare Canada
PO Box 3900, 155 Government Rd. East, Kirkland Lake, ON P2N 3P4
Tel: 705-567-3268 Fax: 705-567-4638
cnh_kirklandlake@extendicare.com
www.extendicarekirklandlake.com
Number of Beds: 100 beds

Kirkland Lake: Teck Pioneer Residence
145A Government Rd. East, Kirkland Lake, ON P2N 3P4
Tel: 705-567-3257 Fax: 705-567-3737
kltpr.com
Year Founded: 1965
Note: Specialties: Nursing services for long-term care residents; Dementia care; Activity program; Restorative care
Nancy Theriault, Administrator

Kitchener: Forest Heights Long Term Care Centre
Revera Inc.
60 Westheights Dr., Kitchener, ON N2N 2A8
Tel: 519-576-3320 Fax: 519-745-3227
generalforestheights@reveraliving.com
www.reveraliving.com
www.facebook.com/Reverainc; twitter.com/Revera_Inc;
www.youtube.com/user/Reverainc;
www.linkedin.com/company/revera-inc
Number of Beds: 240 beds
Note: Programs & services include 24 hour nurse on site; dietitian; pain & symptom management; physical activities; music therapy; multi-sensory therapy.
Thomas G. Wellner, President & CEO, Revera Living

Kitchener: Trinity Village Care Centre (TVCC)
2727 Kingsway Dr., Kitchener, ON N2C 1A7
Tel: 519-893-6320 Fax: 519-893-3432
www.trinityvillage.com
Number of Beds: 150 beds
Note: Specialties: Eden Alternative Philosophy of Care;
Long-term care; Therapeutic services; Recreation programming;
Palliative care
Debby Riepert, Chief Operating Officer
519-893-6320, driepert@trinityvillage.com

Lakefield: Extendicare - Lakefield
Extendicare Canada
19 Fraser St., Lakefield, ON K0L 2H0
Tel: 705-652-7112 Fax: 705-652-7733
www.extendicarelakefield.com
Number of Beds: 100 beds

Leamington: Leamington United Mennonite Home
35 Pickwick Dr., Leamington, ON N8H 4T5
Tel: 519-326-6109 Fax: 519-326-3595
www.mennonitehome.ca
Year Founded: 1964
Number of Beds: 84 beds
Jeff Konrad, Administrator
jeffkonrad@mennonitehome.ca

Leamington: Sun Parlor Home
175 Talbot St. East, Leamington, ON N8H 1L9
Tel: 519-326-5731 Fax: 519-326-8952
TTY: 877-624-4832
www.countyofessex.on.ca
Year Founded: 1900
Number of Beds: 206 beds
Note: Specialties: Long-term care; Mental health services;
Physiotherapy; Restorative care programs; Speech therapy;
Occupational therapy; Audiology screening; Life enrichment services

Lindsay: Extendicare - Kawartha Lakes
Extendicare Canada
125 Colborne St. East, Lindsay, ON K9V 4R3
Tel: 705-878-5392 Fax: 705-878-7910
www.extendicarekawarthalakes.com
Number of Beds: 64 beds

Lion's Head: Golden Dawn Senior Citizen Home
PO Box 129, 80 Main St., Lion's Head, ON N0H 1W0
Tel: 519-793-3433 Fax: 519-793-4503
office@goldendawn.ca
www.goldendawn.ca
Number of Beds: 45 beds
Kevin Jones, Administrator

Listowel: Caressant Care Listowel
Affiliated with: Caressant Care Nursing and Retirement Homes Limited
710 Reserve Ave., Listowel, ON N4W 2L1
Tel: 519-291-1041 Fax: 519-291-5420
www.caressantcare.com
Number of Beds: 52 beds
James Lavelle, President, Caressant Care Nursing and Retirement Homes Ltd.

Little Current: Manitoulin Centennial Manor
70 Robinson St. West, Little Current, ON P0P 1K0
Tel: 705-368-2710 Fax: 705-368-2694
manitoulincentennial.ca
Number of Beds: 60 beds
Michelle Bond, Administrator
mbond@extendicare.com

London: Chelsey Park Long Term Care
310 Oxford St. West, London, ON N6H 4N6
Tel: 519-432-1855 Fax: 519-679-7324
www.chelseyparkltc.ca
Number of Beds: 243 beds
Suzi Holster, Executive Director
519-432-1855, sholster@southbridgecare.ca

London: Elmwood Place Long Term Care
Revera Inc.
Former Name: Elmwood Place
46 Elmwood Pl. West, London, ON N6J 1J2
Tel: 519-433-7259 Fax: 519-660-0158
www.reveraliving.com
www.facebook.com/Reverainc; twitter.com/Revera_Inc;
www.youtube.com/user/Reverainc;
www.linkedin.com/company/revera-inc
Number of Beds: 97 beds
Note: Programs & services include 24 hour nurse on site;
dietitian; pain & symptom management; multi-sensory therapy;
friendly pet visitations.

Thomas G. Wellner, President & CEO, Revera Living

London: Extendicare - London
Extendicare Canada
860 Waterloo St., London, ON N6A 3W6
Tel: 519-433-6658 Fax: 519-642-1711
cnh_london@extendicare.com
www.extendicarelondon.com

Number of Beds: 170 beds
Abe Moharram, Administrator

London: McCormick Home
2022 Kains Rd., London, ON N6K 0A8
Tel: 519-432-2648 Fax: 519-645-6982
www.mccormickcaregroup.ca

Number of Beds: 158 beds
Note: Specialties: Long-term care; Ddementia care; Alzheimer outreach services day program; Social work

Long Sault: Woodland Villa
Omni Health Care
30 Mille Roches Rd., Long Sault, ON K0C 1P0
Tel: 613-534-2276 Fax: 613-534-8559
www.omniway.ca

Number of Beds: 112 beds
Michael Rasenberg, Administrator
mrasenberg@omniway.ca

Markham: Markhaven Home for Seniors
54 Parkway Ave., Markham, ON L3P 2G4
Tel: 905-294-2233 Fax: 905-294-6521
markhaven@markhaven.ca
www.markhaven.ca

Number of Beds: 96 beds
Note: Specialties: Medical care; Nursing care; Physiotherapy; Special needs activities
Mike Bakewell, Executive Director
905-294-2233, mike.bakewell@markhaven.ca

Marmora: Caressant Care Marmora
Affiliated with: Caressant Care Nursing and Retirement Homes Limited
58 Bursthall St., Marmora, ON K0K 2M0
Tel: 613-472-3130 Fax: 613-472-5388
www.caressantcare.com

Number of Beds: 84 beds
James Lavelle, President, Caressant Care Nursing and Retirement Homes Ltd.

Maryhill: Twin Oaks of Maryhill Inc.
1360 Maryhill Rd., Maryhill, ON N0B 2B0
Tel: 519-648-2117
www.twinoaksmaryhill.com

Number of Beds: 31 beds
Note: Specialties: Secured area
Ralph Link, Administrator

Mattawa: Algonquin Nursing Home
PO Box 270, 231 - 10 St., Mattawa, ON P0H 1V0
Tel: 705-744-2202 Fax: 705-744-2787
Toll-Free: 800-579-4284
www.mattawahealth.ca

Number of Beds: 73 beds

Meaford: Meaford Long Term Care Centre
135 William St., Meaford, ON N4L 1T4
Tel: 519-538-1010 Fax: 519-538-5699
businessoffice@meafordlongtermcare.com
www.meafordlongtermcare.com

Number of Beds: 77 beds
Note: Specialties: Restorative care program; Psychogeriatric outreach; Life enrichment programs; Services of a wound care specialist; Services of a pain specialist; Palliative care

Merrickville: Hilltop Manor Nursing Home Ltd.
PO Box 430, 1005 St. Lawrence St., Merrickville, ON K0G 1N0
Tel: 613-269-4707 Fax: 613-269-3534
www.hilltopmanor.ca

Number of Beds: 89 beds

Metcalfe: Osgoode Care Centre
7650 Snake Island Rd., Metcalfe, ON K0A 2P0
Tel: 613-821-1034 Fax: 613-821-0070
www.osgoodecare.ca

Number of Beds: 100 beds
Note: Specialties: Long-term nursing care; Organized leisure activities
Lori Norris-Dudley, Executive Director
lnorris@osgoodecare.com

Milverton: Knollcrest Lodge
PO Box 453, 50 William St., Milverton, ON N0K 1M0
Tel: 519-595-8121 Fax: 519-595-8199
info@knollcrestlodge.com
www.knollcrestlodge.com

Number of Beds: 78 beds
Susan Rae, Chief Executive Officer
srae@knollcrestlodge.com

Mississauga: Cooksville Care Centre
Former Name: Mississauga Lifecare Centre
55 Queensway West, Mississauga, ON L5B 1B5
Tel: 905-270-0170 Fax: 905-270-8465
www.cooksvillecarecentre.ca

Number of Beds: 26 restore unit beds; 166 long-term care beds
Nicole Powell, Executive Director

Mississauga: Extendicare - Mississauga
Extendicare Canada
855 John Watt Blvd., Mississauga, ON L5W 1G2
Tel: 905-696-0719 Fax: 905-696-8875
www.extendicaremississauga.com

Number of Beds: 140 beds

Mississauga: Mississauga Long Term Care Facility
Former Name: Mississauga Nursing Home Inc.
26 Peter St. North, Mississauga, ON L5H 2G7
Tel: 905-278-2213 Fax: 905-278-0962
feedback@mltcfacility.com
www.mltcfacility.com

Number of Beds: 55 beds
Novak Bajin, Administrator
novak@mltcfacility.com

Mississauga: Tyndall Seniors Village
Sharon Village Care Homes
1060 Eglinton Ave. East, Mississauga, ON L4W 1K3
Tel: 905-624-1511 Fax: 905-629-9346
www.svch.ca

Number of Beds: 151 beds
Note: Specialties: Long-term care; Restorative feeding program
Pat Bedford, Administrator

Mitchell: Mitchell Nursing Home Ltd.
Affiliated with: Ritz Lutheran Villa
184 Napier St., Mitchell, ON N0K 1N0
Tel: 519-348-8861 Fax: 519-348-8300
www.ritzlutheranvilla.com

Year Founded: 1969
Number of Beds: 48 beds
Jeff Renaud, Administrator
jrenaud@ritzlutheranvilla.com

Mount Forest: Saugeen Valley Nursing Centre Ltd.
Sharon Village Care Homes
465 Dublin St., Mount Forest, ON N0G 2L3
Tel: 519-323-2140 Fax: 519-323-3540
www.svch.ca

Number of Beds: 87 beds
Note: Nursing & respite care
Cate MacLean, Administrator
519-323-2140

New Hamburg: Nithview Community
Affiliated with: Tri-County Mennonite Homes
200 Boullee St., New Hamburg, ON N3A 2K4
Tel: 519-662-2280 Fax: 519-662-1090
www.tcmhomes.com

Year Founded: 1972
Number of Beds: 97 beds
Note: Mennonite nursing home
Nancy Eros, Executive Director
neros@tcmhomes.com

Newcastle: Fosterbrooke Long Term Care Facility
Revera Inc.
330 King St. West, Newcastle, ON L1B 1G9
Tel: 905-987-4703 Fax: 905-987-3621
www.reveraliving.com/fosterbrooke
www.facebook.com/Reveralnc; twitter.com/Revera_Inc;
www.youtube.com/user/Reveralnc;
www.linkedin.com/company/revera-inc

Number of Beds: 88 beds
Note: Programs & services include 24 hour nurse; dietitian; Revera/3M skin and wound care; art and music therapy; friendly pet visitations.
Thomas G. Wellner, President & CEO, Revera Living

Newmarket: Eagle Terrace
Revera Inc.
329 Eagle St., Newmarket, ON L3Y 1K3
Tel: 905-895-5187 Fax: 905-895-2645
EagleTerrace@reveraliving.com
www.reveraliving.com
www.facebook.com/Reveralnc; twitter.com/Revera_Inc;
www.youtube.com/user/Reveralnc;
www.linkedin.com/company/revera-inc

Number of Beds: 70 beds
Note: Programs & services include 24 hour nurse on site; dietitian; hospice palliative care; foot care; vision care; alternative therapy; friendly pet visitation.
Thomas G. Wellner, President & CEO, Revera Living

Newmarket: Mackenzie Place
Revera Inc.
52 George St., Newmarket, ON L3Y 4V3
Tel: 905-853-3242 Fax: 905-895-5139
www.reveraliving.com/mackenzieplace

Number of Beds: 93 beds
Yvonne Carvalho, Executive Director
yvonne.carvalho@reveraliving.com

Newmarket: Newmarket Health Centre - Long-Term Care Home
194 Eagle St., Newmarket, ON L3Y 1J6
Tel: 905-895-3628 Fax: 905-895-5368
Toll-Free: 877-464-9675
www.york.ca

Lisa Salonen MacKay, Administrator

Niagara Falls: Oakwood Park Lodge
Affiliated with: Conmed Health Care Group
6747 Oakwood Dr., Niagara Falls, ON L2G 0J3
Tel: 905-356-8732 Fax: 905-356-2122
info@oakwoodparklodge.com
www.oakwoodparklodge.com

Year Founded: 1975
Number of Beds: 153 beds
Stephen G. Moran, Administrator

Niagara Falls: The Salvation Army Honorable Ray & Helen Lawson Eventide Home
5050 Jepson St., Niagara Falls, ON L2E 1K5
Tel: 905-356-1221 Fax: 905-356-9609
www.niagaraeventide.ca
Note: Specialties: Long-term care for senior; Activity program

Niagara Falls: Valley Park Lodge
Affiliated with: Conmed Health Care Group
6400 Valley Way, Niagara Falls, ON L2E 7E3
Tel: 905-358-3277 Fax: 905-358-3012
info@valleyparklodge.com
www.valleyparklodge.com

Year Founded: 1985
Number of Beds: 65 beds

Northbrook: Pine Meadow Nursing Home
PO Box 100, 124 Lloyd St., Northbrook, ON K0H 2G0
Tel: 613-336-9120 Fax: 613-336-9144
www.pinemeadownursinghome.com

Year Founded: 1993
Number of Beds: 64 beds
Note: Specialties: Residential nursing care for seniors
Margaret Palimaka, Administrator
mpalimaka@extendicare.com

Norwood: Pleasant Meadow Manor
Omni Health Care
99 Alma St., Norwood, ON K0L 2V0
Tel: 705-639-5308 Fax: 705-639-5309
www.omniway.ca

Number of Beds: 61 beds
Note: Long term care
Sandra Tucker, Administrator
sbrow@omniway.ca
Sylvia Sanders, Officer Manager
705-639-5308, ssanders@omniway.ca

Ohsweken: Iroquois Lodge
PO Box 309, 1755 Chiefswood Rd., Ohsweken, ON N0A 1M0
Tel: 519-445-2224 Fax: 519-445-4180

Number of Beds: 50 beds
Susanne Mt. Pleasant, Manager
smtpleasant@sixnations.ca

Orangeville: Avalon Care Centre
355 Broadway Ave., Orangeville, ON L9W 3Y3
Tel: 519-941-5161 Fax: 519-941-9532
www.jarlette.com

Number of Beds: 135 long term care beds; 2 short stay beds

Klara Hamvas, Administrator
519-941-5161,

Orillia: Oak Terrace Long Term Care
Revera Inc.
291 Mississauga St. West, Orillia, ON L3V 3B9
Tel: 705-325-2289 Fax: 705-325-7178
oakterrace@reveraliving.com
www.reveraliving.com
www.facebook.com/ReveraInc; twitter.com/Revera_Inc;
www.youtube.com/user/ReveraInc;
www.linkedin.com/company/revera-inc
Note: Specialties: Foot care; Physiotherapy programs;
Restorative care programs; Dental services; Music therapy; Pet
therapy.
Thomas G. Wellner, President & CEO, Revera Living

Orillia: Trillium Manor Home for the Aged
12 Grace Ave., Orillia, ON L3V 2K2
Tel: 705-325-1504 Fax: 705-325-7661
www.simcoe.ca
Year Founded: 1969
Number of Beds: 122 beds
Janice McCuaig, Administrator

Oshawa: Extendicare - Oshawa
Extendicare Canada
82 Park Rd. North, Oshawa, ON L1J 4L1
Tel: 905-579-0011 Fax: 905-579-1733
cnh_oshawa@extendicare.com
www.extendicareoshawa.com
Number of Beds: 175 beds
Deborah Woods, Administrator

Ottawa: Elisabeth Bruyère Residence
75 Bruyère St., Ottawa, ON K1N 5C8
Tel: 613-562-6262 Fax: 613-562-4223
elisabethbruyereresidence@bruyere.org
www.bruyere.org
Number of Beds: 71 beds
Note: Long-term care

Ottawa: Extendicare - Medex
Extendicare Canada
1865 Baseline Rd., Ottawa, ON K2C 3K6
Tel: 613-225-5650 Fax: 613-225-0960
cnh_medex@extendicare.com
www.extendicaremedex.com
Number of Beds: 193 beds
Tina Nault, Administrator

Ottawa: Extendicare - New Orchard Lodge
Extendicare Canada
99 New Orchard Ave., Ottawa, ON K2B 5E6
Tel: 613-820-2110 Fax: 613-820-6380
cnh_neworchardlodge@extendicare.com
www.extendicareneworchardlodge.com
Number of Beds: 111 beds
Clayton Donnelly, Administrator

Ottawa: Extendicare - Starwood
Extendicare Canada
114 Starwood Rd., Ottawa, ON K2G 3N5
Tel: 613-224-3960 Fax: 613-224-9309
www.extendicarestarwood.com
Number of Beds: 192 beds

Ottawa: Extendicare - West End Villa
Extendicare Canada
2179 Elmira Dr., Ottawa, ON K2C 3S1
Tel: 613-829-3501 Fax: 613-829-3504
cnh_westendvilla@extendicare.com
www.extendicarewestendvilla.com
Number of Beds: 240 beds

Ottawa: Garry J Armstrong House
200 Island Lodge Rd., Ottawa, ON K1N 5M2
Tel: 613-789-5100 Fax: 613-789-3704
Number of Beds: 180 beds

Ottawa: The Glebe Centre
77 Monk St., Ottawa, ON K1S 5A7
Tel: 613-238-2727 Fax: 613-238-4759
www.glebecentre.ca
Number of Beds: 254 beds
Lawrence Grant, Executive Director
lgrant@glebecentre.ca

Ottawa: Perley & Rideau Veterans' Health Centre
1750 Russell Rd., Ottawa, ON K1G 5Z6
Tel: 613-526-7170 Fax: 613-526-7172
www.perleyrideau.ca
www.facebook.com/perleyrideau

Year Founded: 1995
Number of Beds: 250 beds
Note: Specialties: Geriatric care; Recreation services; Dementia
programming; Respite care for people in the mid-stages of
dementia; Convalescent care
Akos Hoffer, Chief Executive Officer
Mary Boutette, Chief Operating Officer
Ross Quane, Chief Financial Officer
Dr. Benoit Robert, Medical Director
Carolyn Vollicks, Director, Community Outreach & Programming
Jay Innes, Director, Communications
Russ Tattersall, Director, Human Resources
Jennifer Plant, Director, Clinical Practice
Lorie Stuckless, Director, Support Services
Doris Jenkins, Director, Nursing Operations

Ottawa: Villa Marconi
1026 Baseline Rd., Ottawa, ON K2C 0A6
Tel: 613-727-6201 Fax: 613-727-5045
administrator@villamarconi.com
www.villamarconi.com
Number of Beds: 128 beds
Gaetan Grondin, Administrator

Owen Sound: Lee Manor
875 - 6 St. East, Owen Sound, ON N4K 5W5
Tel: 519-376-4420 Fax: 519-371-5406
www.grey.ca
Number of Beds: 150 beds
Note: Municipal home for aged
Renate Cowan, Administrator
renate.cowan@grey.ca

Paris: Telfer Place Retirement Residence
Revera Inc.
245 Grand River St. North, Paris, ON N3L 3V8
Tel: 519-442-4411 Fax: 519-442-6724
telferplaceretirementresidence@reveraliving.com
www.reveraliving.com
www.facebook.com/ReveraInc; twitter.com/Revera_Inc;
www.youtube.com/user/ReveraInc;
www.linkedin.com/company/revera-inc
Number of Beds: 45 LTC beds; 65 assisted living beds; 115
retirement apartments
Note: Independent living program; retirement lodge, apartments;
long-term care; convalescent & respite options
Thomas G. Wellner, President & CEO, Revera Living

Parry Sound: Belvedere Heights
21 Belvedere Ave., Parry Sound, ON P2A 2A2
Tel: 705-746-5871 Fax: 705-774-7300
www.belvedereheights.com
Year Founded: 1965
Number of Beds: 101 beds
Marsha Rivers, Administrator

Perth: Perth Community Care Centre
101 Christie Lake Rd., RR#4, Perth, ON K7H 3C6
Tel: 613-267-2506 Fax: 613-267-7060
www.diversicare.ca
Number of Beds: 121 residential capacity
Note: Specialties: Long-term care; Activity program; Restorative
care program; Physiotherapy

Peterborough: Extendicare - Peterborough
Extendicare Canada
860 Alexander Ct., Peterborough, ON K9J 6B4
Tel: 705-743-7552 Fax: 705-742-9664
cnh_peterborough@extendicare.com
extendicarepeterborough.com
Number of Beds: 174 beds
Bill Thurlow, Administrator

Peterborough: St. Joseph's at Fleming
Former Name: Marycrest Home of the Aged; Anson
House
659 Brealey Dr., Peterborough, ON K9K 2R8
Tel: 705-743-4744 Fax: 705-743-7532
www.sjfltc.com
Year Founded: 2004
Carolyn Rodd, CEO

Petrolia: Fiddick's Nursing Home
PO Box 340, 437 First Ave., Petrolia, ON N0N 1R0
Tel: 519-882-0370 Fax: 519-882-0375
www.fiddicksnursinghome.com
Number of Beds: 92 beds
Michael Fiddick, Administrator

Picton: H.J. MacFarland Memorial Home
603 Hwy 49, RR#2, Picton, ON K0K 2T0
Tel: 613-476-2138 Fax: 613-476-6952
hjm.info@pecounty.on.ca
www.thecounty.ca
Number of Beds: 84 beds
Kyle Cotton, Administrator
613-476-2138, kcotton@pecounty.on.ca

Picton: Hallowell House Long Term Care
Revera Inc.
PO Box 800, 13628 Loyalist Pkwy., Picton, ON K0K 2T0
Tel: 613-476-4444 Fax: 613-476-1566
www.reveraliving.com
www.facebook.com/ReveraInc; twitter.com/Revera_Inc;
www.youtube.com/user/ReveraInc;
www.linkedin.com/company/revera-inc
Number of Beds: 97 beds
Area Served: Prince Edward County, South East
Note: Programs & services include 24 nurse on staff; Revera/3M
skin and wound care program; pain & symptom management;
dietitian; multi-sensory therapy; music therapy; pet visitation.
Thomas G. Wellner, President & CEO, Revera Living

Picton: Kentwood Park
Omni Health Care
PO Box 1298, 2 Ontario St., Picton, ON K0K 2T0
Tel: 613-476-5671 Fax: 613-476-3986
www.omniway.ca
Number of Beds: 48 beds
Tina Cole, Administrator
tcole@omniway.ca

Picton: West Lake Terrace
Omni Health Care
PO Box 2229, R.R. #1, 1673 County Rd. #12, Picton, ON K0K
2T0
Tel: 613-393-2055 Fax: 613-393-2592
www.omniway.ca
Number of Beds: 47 beds
Jackie Maxwell, Administrator
jmaxwell@omniway.ca
Lynda Mitchell, Office Manager
lmitchell@omniway.ca

Plantagenet: Pinecrest Nursing Home Ltd.
PO Box 250, 101 Parent St., Plantagenet, ON K0B 1L0
Tel: 613-673-4835 Fax: 613-673-2675
www.pinecrestnursinghome.ca
Note: Specialties: Long-term care; Activity program
Diane Pelletier, Executive Director
dpelletier@southbridgecare.ca

Port Dover: Dover Cliffs Long Term Care
Revera Inc.
Former Name: Versa-Care Centre, Port Dover
PO Box 430, 501 St. George St., Port Dover, ON N0A 1N0
Tel: 519-583-1422 Fax: 519-583-3197
www.reveraliving.com
www.facebook.com/ReveraInc; twitter.com/Revera_Inc;
www.youtube.com/user/ReveraInc;
www.linkedin.com/company/revera-inc
Number of Beds: 70 beds
Note: Programs & services include 24 hour nurse on site; pain &
symptom management; dietitian; art & creative classes; physicial
activities.
Thomas G. Wellner, President & CEO, Revera Living

Port Hope: Extendicare - Port Hope
Extendicare Canada
360 Croft St., Port Hope, ON L1A 4K8
Tel: 905-885-1266 Fax: 905-885-5328
cnh_porthope@extendicare.com
www.extendicareporthope.com
Number of Beds: 128 beds

Powassan: Eastholme Home for the Aged
PO Box 400, 62 Big Bend Ave., Powassan, ON P0H 1Z0
Tel: 705-724-2005 Fax: 705-724-5429
info@eastholme.ca
www.eastholme.ca
Number of Beds: 128 beds
Natalie Bellehumeur, Administrator

Prescott: Wellington House
990 Edward St. North, Prescott, ON K0E 1T0
Tel: 613-925-2834 Fax: 613-925-5425
Number of Beds: 60 beds

Puslinch: Morriston Park Nursing Home Inc.
7363 Calfass Rd., RR#2, Puslinch, ON N0B 2J0
Tel: 519-822-9179 Fax: 519-822-4459
www.morristonpark.com
www.facebook.com/MorristonParkNursingHome
Number of Beds: 28 beds
Karen Bolger, Chief Operating Officer

Red Lake: Northwood Lodge
Affiliated with: District of Kenora Home for the Aged
PO Box 1335, Hwy 105, Red Lake, ON P0V 2M0
Tel: 807-727-2323 Fax: 807-727-3546
northwood.lodge@kenoradistricthomes.ca
www.kenoradistricthomes.ca
Number of Beds: 32 beds

Renfrew: Bonnechere Manor
470 Albert St., Renfrew, ON K7V 4L5
Tel: 613-432-4873 Fax: 613-432-7138
bonncheremanor@countyofrenfrew.on.ca
www.countyofrenfrew.on.ca
Year Founded: 1958
Number of Beds: 180 beds

Richmond Hill: Langstaff Square Care Community
Former Name: Leisureworld Caregiving Centre -
Richmond Hill
170 Red Maple Rd., Richmond Hill, ON L4B 4T8
Tel: 905-731-2273
www.siennaliving.ca
Number of Beds: 160 beds

Sarnia: Trillium Villa
Affiliated with: S & R Nursing Homes Ltd.
1221 Michigan Ave., Sarnia, ON N7S 3Y3
Tel: 519-542-5529 Fax: 519-542-5953
trilliumvilla@srgroup.ca
ltc.srgroup.ca
Year Founded: 1970
Number of Beds: 152 beds
Kim Van Dam, Administrator
kim_vandam@srgroup.ca

Sarnia: Vision Nursing Home
229 Wellington St., Sarnia, ON N7T 1G9
Tel: 519-336-6551 Fax: 519-336-5878
www.vision74.com
Number of Beds: 146 beds

Sault Ste Marie: F.J. Davey Home
733 Third Line East, Sault Ste Marie, ON P6A 7C1
Tel: 705-942-2204 Fax: 705-942-2234
www.fjdaveyhome.org
Number of Beds: 374 beds
Specialties: Provides services for people with dementia
Barbara Harten, Administrator
bharten@fjdaveyhome.org

Sault Ste Marie: Mauno Kaihla Koti
Affiliated with: Ontario Finnish Rest Home
Association
725 North St., Sault Ste Marie, ON P6B 5Z3
Tel: 705-945-5262 Fax: 705-945-1217
www.ontariofinnishresthome.ca
Number of Beds: 63 beds

Sault Ste Marie: Van Daele Manor
Affiliated with: Extendicare Canada
39 Van Daele St., Sault Ste Marie, ON P6B 4V3
Tel: 705-949-7934 Fax: 705-945-0968
cnh_vandaele@extendicare.com
www.extendicarevandaele.com
Number of Beds: 100 beds
Diana Stenlund, Administrator

Selby: Village Green Long Term Care Facility
Omni Health Care
160 Pleasant Dr., Selby, ON K0K 2Z0
Tel: 613-388-2693 Fax: 613-388-2694
www.omniway.ca
Number of Beds: 66 beds
Note: Activities include: annual boat cruise to the Thousand
Islands; hockey games in Napanee; van outings; visits to local
fairs; shopping excursions.
Linda Pierce, Administrator
lpierce@omniway.ca

Simcoe: Cedarwood Village
500 Queensway West, Simcoe, ON N3Y 4R4
Tel: 519-426-8305 Fax: 519-426-2511
Number of Beds: 91 beds

Simcoe: Norfolk Hospital Nursing Home (NHNH)
Affiliated with: Hamilton Niagara Haldimand Brant
Local Health Integration Network
365 West St., Simcoe, ON N3Y 1T7
Tel: 519-426-0130 Fax: 519-429-6988
www.ngh.on.ca/norfolk-hospital-nursing-home.html
Year Founded: 1975
Number of Beds: 80 beds
Note: Programs & services include: long-term nursing care;
activation program; wound care; physiotherapy; occupational
therapy; speech Therapy; restorative care; pet therapy; social
work; psychogeriatics; & palliative care.
Vicki Florio, Director, Care
519-429-6973, vflorio@ngh.on.ca

Sioux Lookout: William A. (Bill) George Extended
Care Facility
75 - 5 Ave., Sioux Lookout, ON P8T 1K9
Tel: 807-737-3030 Fax: 807-737-2449
www.slmhc.on.ca
Number of Beds: 20 beds

Smiths Falls: Broadview Nursing Centre
210 Brockville St., Smiths Falls, ON K7A 3Z4
Tel: 613-283-1845 Fax: 613-283-7073
www.broadviewnc.ca
Number of Beds: 75 beds
Alaina Parsons, Administrator

St. Catharines: Extendicare - St. Catharines
Extendicare Canada
283 Pelham Rd., St. Catharines, ON L2S 1X7
Tel: 905-688-3311 Fax: 905-688-5774
cnh_stcatharines@extendicare.com
www.extendicarestcatharines.com
Number of Beds: 153 beds

St. Catharines: Garden City Manor Long Term Care
Revera Inc.
168 Scott St., St. Catharines, ON L2N 1H2
Tel: 905-934-3321 Fax: 905-934-9011
www.reveraliving.com
www.facebook.com/ReveraInc; twitter.com/Revera_Inc;
www.youtube.com/user/ReveraInc;
www.linkedin.com/company/revera-inc
Number of Beds: 200 beds
Note: Programs & services include 24 hour nurse on site;
Revera/3M skin and wound care program; pain and symptom
management; dietitian; various recreational activities.
Thomas G. Wellner, President & CEO, Revera Living

St. Catharines: Tabor Manor
Radiant Care
1 Tabor Dr., St. Catharines, ON L2N 1V9
Tel: 905-934-2548 Fax: 905-934-6467
radiantcare.net
Number of Beds: 128 beds
Note: Specialties: Accommodation & nursing care to senior
citizens, especially those of the Mennonite constituency in
Niagara; Activity program; Foot care
Tim Siemens, Chief Executive Officer, Radiant Care
905-934-3414, tims@radiantcare.net

St. Catharines: Tufford Manor Retirement Home
Affiliated with: Hampton Trufford
312 Queenston St., St. Catharines, ON L2P 2X4
Tel: 905-682-0411 Fax: 905-682-2770
info@tufford.ca
www.tufford.ca
Info Line: 905-682-0411
Year Founded: 1960
Number of Beds: 50 retirement residents; 64 long-term care
beds
Note: This facility is a combined long-term care home (first floor)
& retirement home (second floor). Specialties: Long-term nursing
care; Social work; Physiotherapy; Podiatry; Activation program;
Palliative care.

St. Catharines: West Park Health Centre
103 Pelham Rd., St. Catharines, ON L2S 1S9
Tel: 905-688-1031 Fax: 905-688-4495
westparkhealthcentre.ca
Number of Beds: 93 beds
Sharon Darby, Executive Director
sdarby@southbridgecare.ca

St. Jacobs: Derbecker's Heritage House Ltd.
54 Eby St., St. Jacobs, ON N0B 2N0
Tel: 519-664-2921 Fax: 519-664-2380
Year Founded: 1964
Number of Beds: 72 beds

St. Marys: Kingsway Lodge
310 Queen St. East, St. Marys, ON N4X 1C8
Tel: 519-284-2921 Fax: 519-284-4468
info@kingswaylodge.com
www.kingswaylodge.com
twitter.com/Kingsway_Lodge
Number of Beds: 61 beds

St. Marys: Wildwood Care Centre Inc.
Omni Health Care
PO Box 2200, 100 Ann St., St. Marys, ON N4X 1A1
Tel: 519-284-3628 Fax: 519-284-0575
omniway.ca/homes/wildwood
www.facebook.com/261059940770; twitter.com/WildwoodCC
Number of Beds: 60 long-term beds; 24 retirement units
Scott Walsh, Administrator
swalsh@omniway.ca

St. Thomas: Caressant Care on Bonnie Place
Affiliated with: Caressant Care Nursing and
Retirement Homes Ltd
15 Bonnie Pl., St. Thomas, ON N5R 5T8
Tel: 519-633-6493 Fax: 519-633-4247
retirementbp@caressantcare.com
www.caressantcare.com
Number of Beds: 116 beds
Suzanne Mezenberg, Executive Director

St. Thomas: Caressant Care St. Thomas - Mary
Bucke
Caressant Care Nursing and Retirement Homes
Limited
4 Mary Bucke St., St. Thomas, ON N5R 5J6
Tel: 519-633-3164 Fax: 519-631-8362
www.caressantcare.com
Number of Beds: 60 beds
Kori Amon, Executive Director

Stirling: Stirling Manor Nursing Home
PO Box 220, 218 Edward St., Stirling, ON K0K 3E0
Tel: 613-395-2596 Fax: 613-395-0930
www.stirlingmanor.com
Number of Beds: 75 beds

Stoney Creek: Pine Villa Nursing Home
490 Hwy. #8, Stoney Creek, ON L8G 1G6
Tel: 905-573-4900 Fax: 905-662-0833
www.thomashealthcare.com
Year Founded: 1967
Number of Beds: 41 beds
Note: Specialties: Nursing care; Enhanced restorative care
program; Physiotherapy; Foot care; Massage therapy; Activity
program

Stratford: Hillside Manor
Revera Inc.
5066 Line 34, RR#5, Stratford, ON N5A 6S6
Tel: 519-393-5132 Fax: 519-393-5130
reveraliving.com/en/live-with-us/ontario/stratford/hillside-manor
Number of Beds: 90 beds
Trudy Gibson, Executive Director
trudy.gibson@reveraliving.com
Paula Leland, Director, Care
paula.leland@reveraliving.com

Stratford: PeopleCare Stratford
198 Mornington St., Stratford, ON N5A 5G3
Tel: 519-271-4440 Fax: 519-271-4446
www.peoplecare.ca
Year Founded: 1980
Number of Beds: 60 beds
Note: Specialties: Long-term care; Activity program; Restorative
care
Jennifer Killing, Executive Director

Stratford: Spruce Lodge Senior Citizens Residence
643 West Gore St., Stratford, ON N5A 1L4
Tel: 519-271-4090 Fax: 519-271-5862
www.sprucelodge.on.ca
Number of Beds: 128 beds
Peter Bolland, Administrator
peterb@sprucelodge.on.ca

Strathroy: Sprucedale Care Centre Inc.
96 Kittridge Ave. East, Strathroy, ON N7G 2A8
Tel: 519-245-2808 Fax: 519-245-1767
info@sprucedale.ca
www.sprucedale.ca
Number of Beds: 96 beds
Darren Micallef, Director, Operations
darren@sprucedale.ca

Strathroy: Strathmere Lodge
PO Box 5000, 599 Albert St., Strathroy, ON N7G 3J3
Tel: 519-245-2520 *Fax:* 519-245-5711
www.middlesex.ca
Year Founded: 1880
Note: Specialties: Special care area for Alzheimer residents;
Respite care & short stays
Brent Kerwin, Administrator
519-245-2520

Sturgeon Falls: Au Château Home for the Aged
100 Michaud St., Sturgeon Falls, ON P2B 2Z4
Tel: 705-753-1550 *Fax:* 705-753-3135
Number of Beds: 160 beds
Jacques Dupuis, Administrator

Sudbury: Extendicare - Falconbridge
Extendicare Canada
281 Falconbridge Rd., Sudbury, ON P3A 5K4
Tel: 705-566-7980 *Fax:* 705-566-2997
cnh_falconbridge@extendicare.com
www.extendicarefalconbridge.com
Number of Beds: 234 beds

Sudbury: Extendicare - York
Extendicare Canada
333 York St., Sudbury, ON P3E 5J3
Tel: 705-674-4221 *Fax:* 705-674-4281
cnh_york@extendicare.com
www.extendicareyork.com
Number of Beds: 264 beds
Tracy Lamirande, Administrator

Sudbury: St. Joseph's Continuing Care Centre of Sudbury
Affiliated with: North East Local Health Integration Network
1140 South Bay Rd., Sudbury, ON P3E 0B6
Tel: 705-674-2846 *Fax:* 705-673-1009
info@sjsudbury.com
www.stjosephccc.ca
Note: A long term care facility whose staff works to care for
people with disabilities or long term illnesses
Jo-Anne Palkovits, President & CEO
Jacqueline Squarzolo, Director of Care

Sutton: River Glen Haven Nursing Home
Affiliated with: ATK Care Inc.
160 High St., Sutton, ON L0E 1R0
Tel: 905-722-3631 *Fax:* 905-722-8638
atkcare.com
Number of Beds: 119 beds
Note: Long term & secured care
Delphine Gay, Director, Care

Tavistock: The Maples Home for Seniors
Affiliated with: Caressant Care Nursing and Retirement Homes Ltd
94 William St. South, Tavistock, ON N0B 2R0
Tel: 519-655-2344 *Fax:* 519-655-2162
www.caressantcare.com
Number of Beds: 43 beds
Joan Hergott, Executive Director

Tecumseh: Brouillette Manor
11900 Brouillette Ct., Tecumseh, ON N8N 4X8
Tel: 519-735-9810 *Fax:* 519-735-8569
Number of Beds: 60 beds
Nancy Comiskey, Administrator

Tecumseh: Extendicare - Tecumseh
Extendicare Canada
2475 St. Alphonse St., Tecumseh, ON N8N 2X2
Tel: 519-739-2998 *Fax:* 519-739-2815
www.extendicaretecumseh.com
Number of Beds: 128 beds

Thessalon: Algoma Manor Nursing Home
145 Dawson St., Thessalon, ON P0R 1L0
Tel: 705-842-2840 *Fax:* 705-842-2650
Number of Beds: 95 beds
Pamela Ficociello, Administrator

Thunder Bay: Bethammi Nursing Home
Affiliated with: St. Joseph's Care Group
63 Carrie St., Thunder Bay, ON P7A 4J2
Tel: 807-768-4430 *Fax:* 807-768-7793
www.sjcg.net
Number of Beds: 112 beds
Tracy Buckler, President & CEO, St. Joseph's Care Group

Thunder Bay: Pioneer Ridge
750 Tungsten St., Thunder Bay, ON P7B 6R1
Tel: 807-684-3910 *Fax:* 807-684-3916
www.thunderbay.ca
Number of Beds: 150 beds
Note: Specialties: Long-term nursing care for older persons;
Restorative care; Rehabilitation; Units for persons with cognitive
challenges, Alzheimer's disease, & other dementias; Secure
therapeutic parks; Life enrichment program
Lee Mesic, Administrator
807-684-3917, lmesic@thunderbay.ca

Thunder Bay: Southbridge Lakehead
Southbridge Care Homes
Former Name: Revera Lakehead Manor Long Term Care
135 South Vickers St., Thunder Bay, ON P7E 1J2
Tel: 807-623-9511 *Fax:* 807-623-6992
www.southbridgelakehead.ca
Number of Beds: 131 beds
Note: Programs & services include fitness activities; music
therapy; outings; friendly pet visitations.
Brittany Dumont, Executive Director
bdumont@southbridgecare.ca

Thunder Bay: Southbridge Pinewood
Southbridge Care Homes
Former Name: Revera Pinewood Court Long Term Care
2625 East Walsh St., Thunder Bay, ON P7E 2E5
Tel: 807-577-1127 *Fax:* 807-475-9455
www.southbridgepinewood.ca
Number of Beds: 128 beds
Note: Programs include exercise and weight classes; music
therapy; baking; friendly pet visitations.
Jonathon Riabov, Executive Director
jriabov@southbridgecare.ca

Tillsonburg: Maple Manor Nursing Home
73 Bidwell St., Tillsonburg, ON N4G 3T8
Tel: 519-842-3563 *Fax:* 519-842-3038
Number of Beds: 103 beds
Marlene Van Ham, Administrator

Timmins: Extendicare - Timmins
Extendicare Canada
62 St. Jean Ave., Timmins, ON P4R 0A6
Tel: 705-531-3322 *Fax:* 705-264-3500
cnh_timmins@extendicare.com
www.extendicaretimmins.com
Number of Beds: 180 beds
Kelly Roy, Administrator

Timmins: Golden Manor Home for the Aged
481 Melrose Blvd., Timmins, ON P4N 5H3
Tel: 705-360-2664 *Fax:* 705-360-2683
golden_manor@timmins.ca
www.timmins.ca
Number of Beds: 177 beds
Carol Halt, Administrator
carol.halt@timmins.ca

Toronto: Apotex Centre, Jewish Home for the Aged & The Louis & Leah Posluns Centre for Stroke & Cognition
3560 Bathurst St., Toronto, ON M6A 2E1
Tel: 416-785-2500
www.baycrest.org
Number of Beds: 472 beds
Note: Care is offered to adults 65 years of age & older within the
context of orthodox Jewish traditions.

Toronto: Bendale Acres
2920 Lawrence Ave. East, Toronto, ON M1P 2T8
Tel: 416-397-7000 *Fax:* 416-397-7067
ltc-ba@toronto.ca
Number of Beds: 302 beds
Margaret Aerola, Administrator

Toronto: Castleview Wychwood Towers
351 Christie St., Toronto, ON M6G 3C3
Tel: 416-392-5700
ltc-cwt@toronto.ca
Number of Beds: 456 beds
Nelson Ribeiro, Administrator

Toronto: Cedarvale Terrace Long Term Care Home
429 Walmer Rd., Toronto, ON M5P 2X9
Tel: 416-967-6949 *Fax:* 416-928-1965
www.cedarvaleterrace.ca
Number of Beds: 217 beds
Adele Lopes, Executive Director

Toronto: Christie Gardens
600 Melita Cres., Toronto, ON M6G 3Z4
Tel: 416-530-1330 *Fax:* 416-530-1686
www.christiegardens.org
www.facebook.com/ChristieGardens; twitter.com/christiegardens
Number of Beds: 88 beds
Grace Sweatman, CEO

Toronto: Craiglee Nursing Home
102 Craiglee Dr., Toronto, ON M1N 2M7
Tel: 416-264-2000 *Fax:* 416-267-8176
craigleenursinghome.ca
Number of Beds: 169 beds
Patrick Brown, Executive Director
pjbrown@southbridgecare.ca

Toronto: Cummer Lodge
205 Cummer Ave., Toronto, ON M2M 2E8
Tel: 416-392-9500
ltc-cl@toronto.ca
Number of Beds: 391 beds
Tim Burns, Administrator

Toronto: Deerwood Creek Care Community
Former Name: Leisureworld Caregiving Centre - Etobicoke
70 Humberline Dr., Toronto, ON M9W 7H3
Tel: 416-213-7300
www.siennaliving.ca
Number of Beds: 160 beds

Toronto: Eatonville Care Centre
420 The East Mall, Toronto, ON M9B 3Z9
Tel: 416-621-8000
eatonvillecarecentre.ca
Number of Beds: 247 beds
Evelyn MacDonald, Executive Director

Toronto: Ehatare Nursing Home
40 Old Kingston Rd., Toronto, ON M1E 3J5
Tel: 416-284-0813 *Fax:* 416-284-9916
www.ehatare.ca
Number of Beds: 32 beds
Einar Medri, Chief Executive Officer

Toronto: Extendicare - Bayview
Extendicare Canada
550 Cummer Ave., Toronto, ON M2K 2M2
Tel: 416-226-1331 *Fax:* 416-226-2745
cnh_bayview@extendicare.com
www.extendicarebayview.com
Number of Beds: 205 beds
Danielle Zhang, Administrator

Toronto: Extendicare - Guildwood
Extendicare Canada
60 Guildwood Pkwy., Toronto, ON M1E 1N9
Tel: 416-266-7711 *Fax:* 416-269-5123
cnh_guildwood@extendicare.com
www.extendicareguildwood.com
Number of Beds: 169 beds

Toronto: Extendicare - Rouge Valley
Extendicare Canada
551 Conlins Rd., Toronto, ON M1B 5S1
Tel: 416-282-6768 *Fax:* 416-282-6766
www.extendicarerougevalley.com
Number of Beds: 192 beds

Toronto: Extendicare - Scarborough
Extendicare Canada
3830 Lawrence Ave. East, Toronto, ON M1G 1R6
Tel: 416-439-1243 *Fax:* 416-439-4818
cnh_scarborough@extendicare.com
www.extendicarescarborough.com
Number of Beds: 150 beds
Specialties: Nursing care for seniors; Care for persons with
Alzheimer's or other dementias; Physiotherapy; Optometry
services; Social & therapeutic programs
Pinky Virdi, Administrator

Toronto: Fairview Nursing Home
Schlegel Villages
14 Cross St., Toronto, ON M6J 1S8
Tel: 416-534-8829 *Fax:* 416-534-7243
schlegelvillages.com/fairview-toronto
Number of Beds: 108 beds

Toronto: **Fieldstone Commons Care Community**
Former Name: Leisureworld Caregiving Centre -
Ellesmere
1000 Ellesmere Rd., Toronto, ON M1P 5G2
Tel: 416-291-0222
www.siennaliving.ca

Number of Beds: 224 beds

Toronto: **Fudger House**
439 Sherbourne St., Toronto, ON M4X 1K6
Tel: 416-392-5252 *Fax:* 416-392-4174

Number of Beds: 250 beds
Nancy Lew, Administrator

Toronto: **Garden Court Nursing Home**
1 Sand Beach Rd., Toronto, ON M6M 2J7
Tel: 416-259-6172

Number of Beds: 45 beds
Deana Bennett, Administrator

Toronto: **Harmony Hills Care Community**
Former Name: Leisureworld Caregiving Centre -
O'Connor
1800 O'Connor Dr., Toronto, ON M4A 1W7
Tel: 416-285-2000
www.siennaliving.ca

Year Founded: 2001
Number of Beds: 318 beds

Toronto: **Hawthorne Place Care Centre**
2045 Finch Ave. West, Toronto, ON M3N 1M9
Tel: 416-745-0811
www.hawthorneplacecarecentre.ca
Year Founded: 1973
Number of Beds: 215 beds
Linda Joseph-Massiah, Executive Director

Toronto: **Hellenic Care for Seniors**
33 Winona Dr., Toronto, ON M6G 3Z7
Tel: 416-654-7700 *Fax:* 416-654-0943
hcare@hellenichome.org
www.hellenichome.org

Number of Beds: 82 beds

Toronto: **Heritage Nursing Home**
1195 Queen St. East, Toronto, ON M4M 1L6
Tel: 416-461-8185 *Fax:* 416-461-5472
www.heritagenursinghome.com

Number of Beds: 201 beds
Note: Specialties: Long-term nursing care; Supervision &
security for residents with Alzheimer's Disease or dementia;
Restorative care, including physiotherapy; Activation &
recreation program; Chinese programs
Jordan Glick, Administrator

Toronto: **Humber Valley Terrace Long Term Care**
Revera Inc.
95 Humber College Blvd., Toronto, ON M9V 5B5
Tel: 416-746-7466 *Fax:* 416-740-5812
www.reveraliving.com
www.facebook.com/Reveralnc; twitter.com/Revera_Inc;
www.youtube.com/user/Reveralnc;
www.linkedin.com/company/revera-inc
Number of Beds: 158 beds
Note: Programs & services include 24 hour nurse on staff; music
therapy; dietitian; friendly pet visitations.
Thomas G. Wellner, President & CEO, Revera Living

Toronto: **Ivan Franko Ukrainian Home (Etobicoke)**
767 Royal York Rd., Toronto, ON M8Y 2T3
Tel: 416-239-7364 *Fax:* 416-239-5102
www.ivanfrankohomes.com

Number of Beds: 85 beds

Toronto: **Kennedy Lodge Long Term Care**
Revera Inc.
1400 Kennedy Rd., Toronto, ON M1P 4V6
Tel: 416-752-8282 *Fax:* 416-752-0645
kennedylodge@reveraliving.com
www.reveraliving.com
www.facebook.com/Reveralnc; twitter.com/Revera_Inc;
www.youtube.com/user/Reveralnc;
www.linkedin.com/company/revera-inc
Number of Beds: 289 beds
Note: Programs & services include 24 hour nurse on site; pain &
symptom management; palliative care; spiritual services; art &
creative classes; friendly pet visitations.
Thomas G. Wellner, President & CEO, Revera Living

Toronto: **Kipling Acres**
2233 Kipling Ave., Toronto, ON M9W 4L3
Tel: 416-392-2300

Year Founded: 1959
Number of Beds: 337 beds
Robert Petrushewsky, Administrator

Toronto: **Lakeshore Lodge**
3197 Lakeshore Blvd. West, Toronto, ON M8V 3X5
Tel: 416-392-9400
www.toronto.ca/ltc/lakeshore.htm

Number of Beds: 150 beds
Ranjit Caley, Administrator

Toronto: **Mon Sheong Home for the Aged**
36 D'Arcy St., Toronto, ON M5T 1J7
Tel: 416-977-3762 *Fax:* 416-977-3231
msf@monsheong.org
www.monsheong.org
Number of Beds: 105 beds
Grace Lo, Administrator
gracelo@monsheong.org

Toronto: **Norfinch Care Community**
Former Name: Leisureworld Caregiving Centre -
Norfinch
22 Norfinch Dr., Toronto, ON M3N 1X1
Tel: 416-623-1120 *Fax:* 416-623-1121
www.siennaliving.ca
Year Founded: 2003
Number of Beds: 160 beds

Toronto: **North Park Nursing Home**
450 Rustic Rd., Toronto, ON M6L 1W9
Tel: 416-247-0531 *Fax:* 416-247-6159
northparknursinghome@rogers.com
Number of Beds: 75 beds

Toronto: **Norwood Nursing Home Ltd.**
122 Tyndall Ave., Toronto, ON M6K 2E2
Tel: 416-535-3011 *Fax:* 416-535-6439
www.norwoodcare.ca
Year Founded: 1957
Number of Beds: 60 beds
Note: Specialties: Long-term care; Rehabilitative care; Palliative
care room
Martha Acuna-Galeano, Administrator
416-535-3011, Fax: 416-535-6439, macuna@norwoodcare.ca

Toronto: **The Rekai Centre**
345 Sherbourne St., Toronto, ON M5A 2S3
Tel: 416-964-1599 *Fax:* 416-964-3907
reception@rekaicentres.com
www.rekaicentre.com
Number of Beds: 126 beds
Colette Cameron, Executive Director
colette@rekaicentres.com

Toronto: **St. Clair O'Connor Community Nursing**
Home
2701 St. Clair Ave. East, Toronto, ON M4B 1M5
Tel: 416-757-8757 *Fax:* 416-751-7315
Number of Beds: 25 beds
Russell Borden, Executive Director
r.borden@scoc.ca

Toronto: **Thompson House**
1 Overland Dr., Toronto, ON M3C 2C3
Tel: 416-447-7244 *Fax:* 416-447-6364
info@betterlivinghealth.org
www.betterlivinghealth.org
Number of Beds: 136 beds
Note: Specialties: Long-term care; Nursing care; Physiotherapy;
Rehabilitative services; Recreation program; Restorative care;
Social work; Palliative care
William Krever, President & CEO, Better Living Health &
Community Services

Toronto: **Tony Stacey Centre for Veterans Care**
59 Lawson Rd., Toronto, ON M1C 2J1
Tel: 416-284-9235 *Fax:* 416-284-7169
info@tonystaceycentre.ca
www.tonystaceycentre.ca
www.facebook.com/TonyStaceyCentreForVeteransCare;
twitter.com/tonystaceyctr
Year Founded: 1977
Number of Beds: 100 beds

Toronto: **True Davidson Acres**
200 Dawes Rd., Toronto, ON M4C 5M8
Tel: 416-397-0400
ltc-tda@toronto.ca
Year Founded: 1973
Number of Beds: 187 beds
Note: Specialties: Nursing care; Rehabilitation; Recreation
program; Music & art therapy
Hao Chau, Administrator

Toronto: **Ukrainian Canadian Care Centre**
60 Richview Rd., Toronto, ON M9A 5E4
Tel: 416-243-7653 *Fax:* 416-243-7452
uccc@stdemetrius.ca
www.stdemetrius.ca
Number of Beds: 152 beds
Note: Specialties: Long-term care; Therapeutic recreation; Social
work
Sandy Lomaszewycz, Executive Director

Toronto: **Vermont Square Long Term Care Home**
914 Bathurst St., Toronto, ON M5R 3G5
Tel: 416-533-9473 *Fax:* 416-538-2685
www.vermontsquare.ca
Number of Beds: 130 beds
Gale Coburn, Executive Director

Toronto: **Wesburn Manor**
400 The West Mall, Toronto, ON M9C 5S1
Tel: 416-394-3600 *Fax:* 416-394-3606
ltc-wm@toronto.ca
Year Founded: 2003
Number of Beds: 192 beds
Susan Schendel, Administrator

Toronto: **Weston Terrace Care Community**
Former Name: Leisureworld Caregiving Centre -
Lawrence
2005 Lawrence Ave. West, Toronto, ON M9N 3V4
Tel: 416-243-8879
www.siennaliving.ca
Year Founded: 2002
Number of Beds: 224 beds; 2 respite

Toronto: **Yee Hong Centre for Geriatric Care**
2311 McNicoll Ave., Toronto, ON M1V 5L3
Tel: 416-321-6333 *Fax:* 416-321-6313
centre@yeehong.com
www.yeehong.com
Number of Beds: 250 beds
Kaiyan Fu, CEO

Trenton: **Trent Valley Lodge**
195 Bay St., Trenton, ON K8V 1H9
Tel: 613-392-9235 *Fax:* 613-392-0688
info@tvlodge.ca
www.tvlodge.ca
Year Founded: 1970
Number of Beds: 102 beds
Note: Specialties: Restorative care; Activation services;
Long-term stroke care

Unionville: **Bethany Lodge**
23 Second St., Unionville, ON L3R 2C2
Tel: 905-477-3838 *Fax:* 905-477-2888
info@bethanylodge.org
www.bethanylodge.org
Number of Beds: 128 beds

Uxbridge: **ReachView Village**
Revera Inc.
Former Name: Versa-Care Centre, Uxbridge
130 Reach St., Uxbridge, ON L9P 1L3
Tel: 905-852-5191 *Fax:* 905-852-0117
reachviewvillage@reveraliving.com
www.reveraliving.com
www.facebook.com/Reveralnc; twitter.com/Revera_Inc;
www.youtube.com/user/Reveralnc;
www.linkedin.com/company/revera-inc
Number of Beds: 100 beds
Note: Programs & services include 24 hour nurse on staff;
Revera/3M skin and wound care program; pain & symptom
management; palliative care; music therapy; friendly pet
visitation.
Thomas G. Wellner, President & CEO, Revera Living

Vineland: **United Mennonite Home (UMH)**
Former Name: United Mennonite Home for the Aged
4024 - 23 St., Vineland, ON L0R 2C0
Tel: 905-562-7385 *Fax:* 905-562-3711
thehome@umh.ca
www.umh.ca
Year Founded: 1955
Number of Beds: 128 beds
Note: Specialties: Activity program; Physiotherapy; Pet therapy
Walter Sguazzin, Executive Director
wsguazzin@umh.ca

Virgil: **Heritage Place**
1743 Four Mile Creek Rd., Virgil, ON L0S 1T0
Tel: 905-684-9441
radiantcare.net/live-here/pleasant-manor
Number of Beds: 36 beds

Tim Siemens, Chief Executive Officer, Radiant Care
905-934-2548, tims@radiantcare.net

Walkerton: Brucelea Haven
PO Box 1600, 41 McGivern St. West, Walkerton, ON N0G 2V0
Tel: 519-881-1570 *Fax:* 519-881-0231
www.brucecounty.on.ca

Year Founded: 1898
Number of Beds: 144 beds
Willy Van Klooster, Administrator
519-881-1570

Wardsville: Babcock Community Care Centre
Former Name: Babcock Nursing Home
196 Wellington St., Wardsville, ON N0L 2N0
Tel: 519-693-4415 *Fax:* 519-693-4876
www.babcockonline.com
www.facebook.com/BabcockCommunityCareCentre
Number of Beds: 60 beds
Area Served: Elgin, Kent, Lambton, Middlesex

Warkworth: Warkworth Place
97 Mill St., Warkworth, ON K0K 3K0
Tel: 705-924-2311 *Fax:* 705-924-1711
warkworthplace.ca

Number of Beds: 60 beds
Lisa Allanson, Executive Director
lallanson@southbridgecare.ca

Waterdown: Alexander Place
329 Parkside Dr., Waterdown, ON L0K 2H0
Tel: 905-689-2662 *Fax:* 905-689-2625
www.jarlette.com

Number of Beds: 128 beds

Waterloo: Parkwood Mennonite Home Inc.
726 New Hampshire St., Waterloo, ON N2K 4M1
Tel: 519-885-4810 *Fax:* 519-885-6720
office@parkwoodmh.com
parkwoodmh.com
Number of Beds: 96 beds
Elaine Shantz, Chief Executive Officer

Waterloo: Pinehaven Nursing Home
Schlegel Villages
229 Lexington Rd., Waterloo, ON N2K 2E1
Tel: 519-885-0255 *Fax:* 519-885-4216
www.schlegelvillages.com/pinehaven-waterloo
Number of Beds: 84 beds

Welland: Foyer Richelieu Welland Inc.
655 Tanguay Ave., Welland, ON L3B 6A1
Tel: 905-734-1400 *Fax:* 905-734-1386
www.foyerrichelieuwelland.com

Year Founded: 1989
Number of Beds: 65 beds
Sean Keays, CEO
sean.keays@foyerrichelieu.com

Welland: Woodlands of Sunset
Affiliated with: Hamilton Niagara Haldimand Brant
Local Health Integration Network
920 Pelham St., Welland, ON L3C 1Y5
Tel: 905-892-3845 *Fax:* 905-892-5882
www.niagararegion.ca
Number of Beds: 121 beds
Tracey Tait, Administrator

Whitby: Fairview Lodge
PO Box 300, 632 Dundas St. West, Whitby, ON L1N 5S3
Tel: 905-668-5851 *Fax:* 905-668-8934
www.durham.ca

Number of Beds: 198 beds
Marcey Wilson, Administrator
marcey.wilson@durham.ca

Whitby: Sunnycrest Nursing Home
1635 Dundas St. East, Whitby, ON L1N 2K9
Tel: 905-576-0111 *Fax:* 905-576-4712
info@sunnycrest.ca
www.sunnycrest.ca
Number of Beds: 136 beds

Wiarton: Gateway Haven
PO Box 10, 671 Frank St., Wiarton, ON N0H 2T0
Tel: 519-534-1113 *Fax:* 519-534-4733
gatewayhavenreception@brucecounty.on.ca
www.brucecounty.on.ca
Number of Beds: 100 beds
Heather Penny, Administrator
hpenny@brucecounty.on.ca

Wikwemikong: Wikwemikong Nursing Home
PO Box 114, 2281 Wikwemikong Way, Wikwemikong, ON P0P 2J0
Tel: 705-859-3107 *Fax:* 705-859-2057
www.wikwemikongnursinghome.com
Number of Beds: 59 beds
Cheryl Osawabine-Peltier, Administrator

Windsor: Banwell Gardens Care Centre
3000 Banwell Rd., Windsor, ON N8N 2M4
Tel: 519-735-3204 *Fax:* 519-735-1836
www.banwellgardenscarecentre.ca
Number of Beds: 142 beds
Note: Bilingual; offers music therapy; pet therapy.
Tanya Adams, Executive Director

Windsor: Berkshire Care Centre
Former Name: Revera Rose Garden Villa Long Term
Care
350 Dougall Ave., Windsor, ON N9A 4P4
Tel: 519-256-7868 *Fax:* 519-256-1991
www.berkshirecarecentre.ca
Number of Beds: 214 beds
Note: Services include 24 hour nurse on staff; infection prevention & control program; Daily housekeeping; Physiotherapy; Foot care.
Bidarekere Swamy, Executive Director
Bonnie Spry, Administrator

Windsor: Extendicare - Southwood Lakes
Extendicare Canada
1255 North Talbot Rd., Windsor, ON N9G 3A4
Tel: 519-945-7249 *Fax:* 519-945-7816
www.extendicaresouthwoodlakes.com
Number of Beds: 150 beds

Windsor: Riverside Place
Revera Inc.
3181 Meadowbrook Lane, Windsor, ON N8T 0A4
Tel: 519-974-0148 *Fax:* 519-974-7305
riversideplace@reveraliving.com
www.reveraliving.com
www.facebook.com/ReveraInc; twitter.com/Revera_Inc;
www.youtube.com/user/ReveraInc;
www.linkedin.com/company/revera-inc
Note: Programs & services include 24 hour nurse on site; pain & symptom management; music therapy; spiritual services.
Thomas G. Wellner, President & CEO, Revera Living

Windsor: Villa Maria Home for the Aged
2856 Riverside Dr. West, Windsor, ON N9C 1A2
Tel: 519-254-3763 *Fax:* 519-254-7657
Note: Home for the aged

Woodbridge: Pine Grove Long Term Care &
Retirement Resident
Affiliated with: Chartwell Retirement Residences
Former Name: Devonshire Pine Grove Inc.
8403 Islington Ave. North, Woodbridge, ON L4L 1X3
Tel: 905-850-3605
www.chartwellreit.ca

Woodslee: Country Village Homes - Woodslee
440 County Rd. 8, RR#2, Woodslee, ON N0R 1V0
Tel: 519-839-4812 *Fax:* 519-839-4813
country-village.ca
Number of Beds: 104 beds
Lenna Rombout, Executive Director
lrombout@southbridgecare.ca

Woodstock: Caressant Care Woodstock
Affiliated with: Caressant Care Nursing and
Retirement Homes Ltd
81 Fyfe Ave., Woodstock, ON N4S 8Y2
Tel: 519-539-6461 *Fax:* 519-539-7467
www.caressantcare.com
Number of Beds: 163 beds
Ann Wouters, Executive Director

Zurich: Blue Water Rest Home
37792 Zurich-Hensall Rd., RR#3, Zurich, ON N0M 2T0
Tel: 519-236-4373 *Fax:* 519-236-7685
bwrh.info@bluewaterresthome.com
www.bwrh.ca
Number of Beds: 65 beds
Angie Dunn, Administrator

Retirement Residences

Amherstview: Briargate Retirement Living Centre
Revera Inc.
4567 Bath Rd., Amherstview, ON K7N 1A8
Tel: 613-384-9333 *Fax:* 613-384-4443
www.reveraliving.com/briargate
www.facebook.com/ReveraInc; twitter.com/Revera_Inc;
www.youtube.com/user/ReveraInc;
www.linkedin.com/company/revera-inc
Number of Beds: 65 beds
Note: Services include: 24 hour nursing care; foot care; recreation program; & restorative program.
Thomas G. Wellner, President & CEO, Revera Living

Ancaster: Carrington Place Retirement Home
75 Dunham Dr., Ancaster, ON L9G 1X7
Tel: 905-648-0343
info@carringtonplace.com
www.carringtonplaceretirement.ca
Note: Services include respite care for seniors, physiotherapy, an exercise program, & social activities.
Elyse Latimer, Administrator
Lynn Gledhill, Director, Activity
Jeanine Lavallee, Director, Community Resources

Ancaster: Highgate Retirement Residence
325 Fiddlers Green Rd., Ancaster, ON L9G 1W9
Tel: 905-648-8399
www.highgateresidence.com
Year Founded: 1989
Number of Beds: 40 rooms
Note: Services include: 24 hour nursing care; medication administration; oxygen therapy supervision; personal care; recreation programs; & wound care.
Paula Wiggins, Administrator

Arnprior: Arnprior Villa Retirement Residence
Revera Inc.
15 Arthur St., Arnprior, ON K7S 1A1
Tel: 613-623-0414
www.reveraliving.com/arnprior
www.facebook.com/ReveraInc; twitter.com/Revera_Inc;
www.youtube.com/user/ReveraInc;
www.linkedin.com/company/revera-inc
Number of Beds: 81 suites
Note: Services include: 24 hour emergency response; 24 hour nursing supervision; pharmacy; recreation; & restorative program.
Thomas G. Wellner, President & CEO, Revera Living

Aurora: Aurora Retirement Centre
145 Murray Dr., Aurora, ON L4G 2C7
Tel: 905-841-2777 *Fax:* 905-841-1562
www.kingswayarms.com
Number of Beds: 54 units
Maret Cox, Executive Director

Aurora: Park Place Manor
15055 Yonge St., Aurora, ON L4G 6T4
Tel: 905-727-2952
www.chartwell.com/locations/park-place-manor
Number of Beds: 94 beds
Note: Services include: 24 hour medical attention; medication administration; oxygen service; physiotherapy; & recreational therapy.
Marie Gagnon, General Manager

Barrie: Barrie Manor Retirement Residence
340 Blake St., Barrie, ON L4M 1L3
Tel: 705-722-3611 *Fax:* 705-722-4530
www.barriemanor.ca
www.facebook.com/barriemanor
Note: Services include nursing care, senior's day away program, overnight post-op, respite care, physiotherapy, massage therapy, foot care, & recreation.

Barrie: Mulcaster Mews
130 Mulcaster St., Barrie, ON L4M 3M9
Tel: 705-725-9119 *Fax:* 705-725-8848
www.mulcastermews.ca
Year Founded: 1998
Number of Beds: 44 rooms
Area Served: Simcoe County *Number of Employees:* 20
Specialties: Home style living
Note: Services include: physical therapy; rehabilitation; & respite care.
Maggie Rae, Administrator
maggierae@mulcastermews.ca

Barrie: Roberta Place Retirement Lodge
503 Essa Rd., Barrie, ON L4N 9E4
Tel: 705-733-3231
www.jarlette.com
Number of Beds: 138 bed retirement lodge

Barrie: Simcoe Terrace Retirement Community
Affiliated with: Specialty Care Retirement
Communities
44 Donald St., Barrie, ON L4N 1E3
Tel: 705-722-5750 *Fax:* 705-722-7041
info@simcoeterrace.com
www.simcoeterrace.com
Note: Simcoe Terrace offers nursing services, physiotherapy, rest & recuperation stays, leisure activities, & spa services.

Barrie: Woods Park Care Centre
Sienna Senior Living
110 Lillian Cres., Barrie, ON L4N 5H7
Tel: 705-739-6881 *Fax:* 705-739-0638
Toll-Free: 888-982-8667
www.siennaliving.ca
Number of Beds: 123 beds
Note: Services include: nursing care; personal care; & convalescent care.
Cathy Cotton, Administrator

Barry's Bay: Water Tower Lodge
9 Stafford St., Barry's Bay, ON K0J 1B0
Tel: 613-756-9086 *Fax:* 613-756-9369
info@watertowerlodge.com
www.watertowerlodge.com
Number of Beds: 44 units

Beachburg: Country Haven Retirement Home
1387 Beachburg Rd., RR#1, Beachburg, ON K0J 1C0
Tel: 613-582-7021 *Fax:* 613-582-7075
info@countryhavenretirementhome.com
www.countryhavenretirementhome.com
Number of Beds: 75 beds
Anil Verma, M.A., M.B.A., General Manager

Belleville: Bayview Retirement Home
435 Dundas St. West, Belleville, ON K8P 1B6
Tel: 613-966-6268 *Fax:* 613-966-6675
www.chartwell.com
Number of Beds: 60 beds
Patricia Tooze, Administrator

Belleville: The Richmond Retirement Residence
175 North Front St., Belleville, ON K8P 4Y8
Tel: 613-966-4407
www.verveseniorliving.com/the-richmond
Number of Beds: 82 beds
Note: Services include: medication management; personal care assistance; physiotherapy; post-surgical care; & respite care.
Monique Quackenbush, General Manager

Bracebridge: James Street Retirement Residence
148 James St., Bracebridge, ON P1L 1S7
Tel: 705-645-1431
www.chartwell.com/retirement-homes/chartwell-james-street-retirement-residence
Number of Beds: 73 suites
Note: Services include: convalescent care; medication administration; palliative care; & respite care.
Rosalind Marshall, General Manager

Bracebridge: Muskoka Hills Retirement Villa
690 Hwy. 118 West, Bracebridge, ON P1L 1W8
Tel: 705-645-6364
www.bracebridgevilla.ca

Brampton: Woodhall Park Retirement Village
10250 Kennedy Rd., Brampton, ON L6Z 4N7
Tel: 905-846-1441 *Fax:* 905-846-1451
postmaster@woodhallpark.ca
www.woodhallpark.ca
Number of Beds: 80 suites
Note: Services include: audiology; dementia care; hospice care; medical care; medication administration; nursing care; memory care; personal care assistance; & physiotherapy.
Andrew Post, Administrator

Brantford: Amber Lea Place
Affiliated with: Mundi Holdings Ltd.
384 St. Paul Ave., Brantford, ON N3R 4N4
Tel: 519-754-0000 *Fax:* 519-752-2338
info@amberleaplace.com
www.amberleaplace.com
Number of Beds: 50 beds
Note: Services include: 24 hour care; medication administration; nursing & dietary assessments; recreation; & wellness program.
Ruby Toor, Administrator

Brantford: Charlotte Villa Retirement Residence
Revera Inc.
120 Darling St., Brantford, ON N3T 5W6
Tel: 519-759-5250
www.reveraliving.com/charlotte
www.facebook.com/Reverainc; twitter.com/Revera_Inc;
www.youtube.com/user/Reverainc;
www.linkedin.com/company/revera-inc
Number of Beds: 54 independent living suites; 19 assisted living suites
Note: Services include: assisted living; falls prevention; fitness program; laboratory; physiotherapy; recreation; & restorative program.
Matthew Osborn, Executive Director

Brantford: Tranquility Place
436 Powerline Rd., Brantford, ON N3T 6G5
Tel: 519-759-2222
www.chartwell.com/locations/tranquility-place
Year Founded: 1988
Note: Services include: 24 hour care; medication administration; & personal care.
Darem Murray, General Manager

Brighton: Applefest Lodge
120 Elizabeth St., Brighton, ON K0K 1H0
Tel: 613-475-3510
applefestlodge@cogeco.net
www.applefestlodge.ca
www.facebook.com/applefestlodge; twitter.com/applefestlodge
Number of Beds: 66 beds
Note: Services include: convalescent care; foot care; medication administration; physiotherapy; recreation; & respite care.
Charlotte Irvine, Administrator

Brockville: Bridlewood Manor
Rivera Inc.
1026 Bridlewood Dr., Brockville, ON K6V 7J8
Tel: 613-345-2477
www.reveraliving.com/bridlewood
Number of Beds: 69 beds
Note: Services include: 24 hour nursing care; foot care; recreation; & restorative program.
Diana Dodge, Administrator

Brockville: Rosedale Retirement Centre
Affiliated with: Chartwell Seniors Housing REIT
1813 County Rd. 2E, RR#1, Brockville, ON K6V 5T1
Tel: 613-342-0200
www.chartwell.com
Number of Beds: 69 suites
Stephen Suske, CEO, Chartwell Seniors Housing REIT

Burlington: Appleby Place
Revera Inc.
500 Appleby Line, Burlington, ON L7L 5Z6
Tel: 905-333-1611
www.reveraliving.com/appleby
www.facebook.com/Reverainc; twitter.com/Revera_Inc;
www.youtube.com/user/Reverainc;
www.linkedin.com/company/revera-inc
Number of Beds: 90 units
Note: Services include: cardio-exercise program; foot care; nursing station; physiotherapy; recreation; & restorative program.
Greg Fortier, Executive Director

Burlington: Bethany Residence
2387 Industrial St., Burlington, ON L7P 3A1
Tel: 905-335-3463 *Fax:* 905-335-1202
info@bethanyresidence.ca
www.bethanyresidence.ca
Number of Beds: 127 beds
Sheri Levy-Abraham, Manager

Burlington: Christopher Terrace Retirement Home
3131 New St., Burlington, ON L7N 3P8
Tel: 905-632-5072 *Fax:* 905-632-5074
www.chartwell.com
Number of Beds: 80 beds
Laurie Johnston, Manager

Burlington: Lakeshore Place Retirement Residence
Affiliated with: Chartwell Retirement Residences
5314 Lakeshore Rd., Burlington, ON L7L 6L8
Tel: 905-333-0009 *Fax:* 905-333-3103
www.chartwell.com
Number of Beds: 156 beds (residential care, assisted & daily living)
Note: both long term care & retirement services.
Nancy Fischer, Administrator

Burlington: Park Avenue Manor
924 Park Ave. West, Burlington, ON L7T 1N7
Tel: 905-333-3323
www.parkavenuemanor.ca
www.facebook.com/1989412214625773
Number of Beds: 69 suites
Note: Specialties: Recreational activities; Medication administration; Wellness monitoring; Respite care; Convalescent, seasonal, & trial stays.
Carrie T. Campbell, General Manager

Cambridge: Avonlea Place
611 Dunbar Rd., Cambridge, ON N3H 2T4
Tel: 519-650-1102

Cambridge: Queen's Square Terrace
Affiliated with: Chartwell Retirement Residences
10 Melville St. North, Cambridge, ON N1S 1H5
Tel: 519-621-2777
www.chartwell.com
Number of Beds: 80 suites
Stephen Suske, CEO, Chartwell Seniors Housing REIT

Carleton Place: Carleton Place Manor
Symphony Senior Living
6 Arthur St., Carleton Place, ON K7C 4S4
Tel: 613-253-7360 *Fax:* 613-253-5048
www.symphonyseniorliving.com
www.facebook.com/Symphonyseniorliving;
twitter.com/SymphonySL
Number of Beds: 115 rooms
Lisa Brush, CEO

Chatham: Maple City Retirement Residence
97 McFarlane Ave., Chatham, ON N7L 4V6
Tel: 519-354-7111 *Fax:* 519-351-5780
Number of Beds: 75 beds
Hilda Michielsen, Administrator

Chatham: Residence on The Thames
Affiliated with: Steeves & Rozema Group
850 Grand Ave. West, Chatham, ON N7L 5H5
Tel: 519-351-7220 *Fax:* 519-436-0360
residenceonthethames@srgroup.ca
chatham.ontarioretirementcommunity.com
Note: Independent living
Ian Murray, Executive Director
Crystal Houle, Office Manager

Codrington: Golden Pond House Retirement
Residence
387 Goodrich Rd., Codrington, ON K0K 1R0
Tel: 613-475-4846 *Fax:* 613-475-4961
Toll-Free: 866-575-4846
gandrmgt@sympatico.ca
www.goldenpondretirement.ca
Number of Beds: 28 beds
Note: Services include: independent living & assisted living; medication assistance; nursing; & palliative care.
Ralph Villman, Owner
Laurie Bieber, Owner

Cornwall: Chateau Cornwall
Affiliated with: Chartwell Retirement Residences
41 Amelia St., Cornwall, ON K6H 7E5
Tel: 613-937-4700 *Fax:* 613-932-6407
www.chartwell.com
Number of Beds: 105 suites
Denis Carr, Manager

Delhi: Delrose Retirement Residence
725 Gibraltar St., Delhi, ON N4B 3C7
Tel: 519-582-4072 *Fax:* 519-582-0005
delrose@nor-del.com
www.delroseretirement.ca
Bonnie Guthrie, Administrator
bonnieguthrie@nor-del.com

Dresden: Park Street Place Retirement Residence
650 Park St., Dresden, ON N0P 1M0
Tel: 519-683-4474 *Fax:* 519-683-4555
www.comfortofliving.com/dresden.php
Year Founded: 1987
Note: Specialties: Foot care; Physiotherapy; Medication management; Recreational activities; Respite & convalescent stays

Dundas: The Georgian Retirement Residence
Affiliated with: Chartwell Retirement Residences
255 Governor's Rd., Dundas, ON L9H 3K4
Tel: 905-627-8444
www.chartwell.com
Number of Beds: 64 suites

Stephen Suske, CEO, Chartwell Seniors Housing REIT

Elliot Lake: Huron Lodge
100 Manitoba Rd., Elliot Lake, ON P5A 3T1
Tel: 705-848-2019 *Fax:* 705-848-1306
mail@huronlodge.ca
www.huronlodge.ca
Note: Huron Lodge is a residence for 36 older adults. Respite service is available.
Norman Mann, Chief Executive Officer
norman.mann@huronlodge.ca

Fort Erie: Garrison Place Retirement Residence
Rivera Inc.
373 Garrison Rd., Fort Erie, ON L2A 1N1
Tel: 905-871-6410
reveraliving.com/Retirement-Living/Locations/Garrison-Place
www.facebook.com/ReveraInc; twitter.com/Revera_Inc;
www.youtube.com/user/ReveraInc;
www.linkedin.com/company/revera-inc
Number of Beds: 74 suites
Note: Secured living for dementia care residents; respite & convalescent options
Thomas G. Wellner, President & CEO, Revera Living

Georgetown: Mountainview Residence
222 Mountainview Rd. North, Georgetown, ON L7G 3R2
Tel: 905-877-1800
info@mountainviewterrace.ca
www.mountainviewterrace.ca
Number of Beds: 82 suites
Christopher Summer, Manager

Gloucester: Blackburn Lodge Seniors Residence
2412 Cléroux Cres., Gloucester, ON K1W 1A3
Tel: 613-837-7467 *Fax:* 613-837-0250
info@blackburnseniorsresidence.ca
www.blackburnseniorsresidence.ca
Note: Health services are provided, as well as personal services & activities.
David Porter, BA, BComm, CA, Executive Director & President
porterd@blackburnseniorsresidence.ca
Sanjee Mendis, Director, Care
smendis@blackburnseniorsresidence.ca
Shawna Melanson, Manager, Dining Room
smelanson@blackburnseniorsresidence.ca
Katrina Doy-yat, Activity Coordinator
katrina@blackburnseniorsresidence.ca

Gloucester: Camilla Gardens Retirement Residence
1119 Bathgate Dr., Gloucester, ON K1J 9N4
Tel: 613-747-7000 *Fax:* 613-747-1804
info@camillagardensretirementhome.com
www.camillagardensretirementhome.com
Note: Nursing supervision & assistance with person needs are available. Camilla Gardens also offers short term convalescent, respite, or trial stays.

Gloucester: Elmsmere Villa Retirement Residence
Former Name: Elmsmere Retirement Residence
889 Elmsmere St., Gloucester, ON K1J 8G4
Tel: 613-745-2409
www.villaelmsmere.ca
Number of Beds: 57 units
Pierre Lefebvre, Manager

Gloucester: Ogilvie Villa
1345 Ogilvie Rd., Gloucester, ON K1J 7P5
Tel: 613-742-6524
www.reveraliving.com/ogilvie
Year Founded: 1995
Number of Beds: 64 residential capacity
Note: Specialties: Recreation program; Short term stays; pet friendly.

Goderich: Goderich Place Retirement Residence
30 Balvina Dr. East, Goderich, ON N7A 4L5
Tel: 519-524-4243
www.goderichplace.com
www.facebook.com/GoderichPlace; twitter.com/GoderichPlace;
www.youtube.com/user/TheRetirementLife
Note: Goderich Place is a residence for seniors that offers bachelor, one, & two bedroom suites.
Sue Lebeau, Contact
salesgp@hurontel.on.ca

Gravenhurst: Gravenhurst Manor
300 Muskoka Rd. North, Gravenhurst, ON P1P 1N8
Tel: 705-687-3356
themanoratgravenhurst.ca
Number of Beds: 42 beds
Note: Services include: falls prevention; mobility assistance; personal support; & specialized care.

Stephanie Bolger, Executive Director
stephanie.bolger@themanoratgravenhurst.ca

Grimsby: Maplecrest Village Retirement Residence
Rivera Inc.
85 Main St., Grimsby, ON L3M 1N6
Tel: 905-945-7044
www.reveraliving.com/maplecrest
Number of Beds: 70 suites
Note: Services include: fitness program; laboratory; physiotherapy; & restorative program.

Guelph: College Place Retirement Residence
Former Name: Meadowcroft Place Retirement Centre
166 College Ave. West, Guelph, ON N1G 1S4
Tel: 519-822-0090 *Fax:* 519-822-2310
www.collegeplace.ca
Note: Specialties: Assisted living program; Podiatry services; Recreation program; Short term stays
Colleen Brosseau, Manager

Guelph: Norfolk Manor
128 Norfolk St., Guelph, ON N1H 4J8
Tel: 519-837-1100 *Fax:* 519-836-4003
david@norfolkmanor.ca
www.norfolkmanor.ca
Number of Beds: 67 beds
David Ing, Manager

Guelph: Stone Lodge Retirement Residence
Rivera Inc.
165 Cole Rd., Guelph, ON N1G 4N9
Tel: 519-767-0880
www.reveraliving.com/stonelodge
Number of Beds: 102 units
Note: Services include: physiotherapy; recreation; & restorative program.
Sasha Pepper, Executive Director

Guelph: Village of Riverside Glen
60 Woodlawn Rd. East, Guelph, ON N1H 8M8
Tel: 519-822-5272
riverside.retadmin@schlegelvillages.com
www.schlegelvillages.com/guelph1
Number of Beds: 196 beds
Michell Vermeeren, Manager

Hamilton: The Carlisle Retirement Residence
Former Name: Atrium Villa
467 Main St. East, Hamilton, ON L8M 1K1
Tel: 905-521-4442
www.thecarlisle.ca
Number of Beds: 67 units

Hamilton: Deerview Crossing Retirement Residence
Affiliated with: Chartwell Retirement Residences
460 Rymal Rd. W, Hamilton, ON L9B 0B2
Tel: 289-309-7436
www.chartwell.com
Note: Amenities include gardens; a games room; library; craft/activity room; elevator; fitness room; air conditioning.

Hamilton: Proctor Manor Retirement Home
Former Name: Proctor Manor Nursing Home
81 Proctor Blvd., Hamilton, ON L8M 2M5
Tel: 905-545-2427

Hamilton: Stinson Manor
112 Stinson St., Hamilton, ON L8N 1S5
Tel: 905-521-9112 *Fax:* 905-521-9106

Hanover: The Village Seniors Community
Revera Inc.
101 10th St., Hanover, ON N4N 1M9
Tel: 519-364-4320
www.reveraliving.com
www.facebook.com/ReveraInc; twitter.com/Revera_Inc;
www.youtube.com/user/ReveraInc;
www.linkedin.com/company/revera-inc
Year Founded: 1961
Note: Services include: fitness program; foot care; phlebotomy; physiotherapy; & wellness monitoring.
Thomas G. Wellner, President & CEO, Revera Living

Harrow: Harrowood Seniors Community
Former Name: Harrowood Rest Home
1 Pollard Dr., Harrow, ON N0R 1G0
Tel: 519-738-2286 *Fax:* 519-738-2700
harrowoodseniorscommunity@bellnet.ca
www.harrowood.ca
Note: Seniors community
Carol Chisholm, Administrator

Hawkesbury: Place Mont Roc
100 Industrial Blvd., Hawkesbury, ON K6A 3M8
Tel: 613-632-2900 *Fax:* 613-632-9790
Frank Zambito, President

Hensall: Queensway Retirement Living and Long Term Care
PO Box 369, 100 Queen St. East, Hensall, ON N0M 1X0
Tel: 519-262-2830 *Fax:* 519-226-9215
queensway.gm@pltchomes.com
www.facebook.com/147704828612916
Number of Beds: 60 long-term care beds; 35 retirement suites; 2 respite beds
Note: Provides retirement living & long term care services.
Donna McLeod, General Manager

Huntsville: Rogers Cove Retirement Residence
Affiliated with: Chartwell Retirement Residences
4 Coveside Dr., Huntsville, ON P1H 2J9
Tel: 705-789-1600
www.chartwell.com
Number of Beds: 55 suites
Stephen Suske, CEO, Chartwell Seniors Housing REIT

Ingersoll: Oxford Manor Retirement Residence
276 Oxford St., Ingersoll, ON N5G 2W1
Tel: 519-485-0350
www.oxfordmanorretirement.ca
Number of Beds: 46 units

Kanata: Fairfield Manor Retirement Home
17 Lombardo Dr., Kanata, ON K2L 4E8
Tel: 613-592-5772 *Fax:* 613-592-8928
info@fairfieldmanor.ca
www.fairfieldmanor.ca

Kanata: Kanata Retirement Residence
Affiliated with: Chartwell Retirement Residences
20 Shirley's Brook Dr., Kanata, ON K2K 2W8
Tel: 613-591-8939 *Fax:* 613-591-1933
www.chartwell.com
Number of Beds: 81 beds

Kanata: Symphony Senior Living Kanata
Affiliated with: Symphony Senior Living
Former Name: Walden Village
27 Weaver Cres., Kanata, ON K2K 2Z8
Tel: 613-591-3991 *Fax:* 613-591-9647
www.symphonyseniorliving.com
www.facebook.com/Symphonyseniorliving;
twitter.com/SymphonySL
Number of Beds: 96

Kincardine: Malcolm Place
255 Durham St., Kincardine, ON N2Z 2X9
Tel: 519-396-5800 *Fax:* 866-615-7773
Toll-Free: 877-669-7760
malcolmplace@tnt21.com
www.malcolmplace.ca
www.facebook.com/183752401675548
Number of Beds: 41 beds
Note: Services include: 24 hour nursing care; convalescent care; fitness & recreation; personal care; & respite care.
John Piper, Owner

Kingston: The Rosewood
833 Sutton Mills Ct., Kingston, ON K7P 2N9
Tel: 613-384-7131 *Fax:* 613-634-3247
www.specialty-care.com
Number of Beds: 66 units
Note: Independent living
Rhonda Jarvis, Sales & Marketing Manager
rhonda.jarvis@specialty-care.com

Kingston: St. Lawrence Place
181 Ontario St., Kingston, ON K7L 5M1
Tel: 613-544-5900
www.reveraliving.com
Year Founded: 1983
Number of Beds: 71 units

Kingston: Trillium Retirement Residence
Sienna Senior Living
800 Edgar St., Kingston, ON K7M 8S4
Tel: 613-547-0040
www.siennaliving.ca
Note: Independent living. Specialty Care Trillium Centre long-term care residence located adjacent
Lois Cormack, President & CEO, Sienna Senior Living

Kingsville: Kings Manor Residence
54 Spruce St. North, Kingsville, ON N9Y 3J1
Tel: 519-733-8376
augustinevillas@yahoo.ca
www.kingsmanorresidence.com

Kitchener: Bankside Terrace
Affiliated with: Chartwell Retirement Residences
71 Bankside Dr., Kitchener, ON N2N 3L1
Tel: 519-749-9999 *Fax:* 519-749-1947
www.chartwell.com
Number of Beds: 89 units
Brad Lawrence, Manager

Kitchener: Conestoga Lodge Retirement Residence
55 Hugo Cres., Kitchener, ON N2M 5J1
Tel: 519-576-2140
admin@conestogalodge.com
www.conestogalodge.com
Number of Beds: 88 beds
Note: Activities include exercise classes; shopping trips; brain games; walks; films.

Kitchener: Fergus Place Retirement Residence
Rivera Inc.
Former Name: Meadowcroft Place
164 Fergus Ave., Kitchener, ON N2A 2H2
Tel: 519-894-9600
www.reveraliving.com/fergus
Number of Beds: 61 suites
Note: Services include: personal care; physiotherapy; recreation; & restorative program.
Jennifer Vickers, Director

Kitchener: Lanark Place Retirement Residence
44 Lanark Cres., Kitchener, ON N2N 2Z8
Tel: 519-743-0121 *Fax:* 519-743-8901
administrator_lanarkplace@srgroup.ca
kitchener.ontarioretirementcommunity.com
Note: Services include: foot care; nursing; physiotherapy; & wellness services.
Bradley Lukas, General Manager
bradley_lukas@srgroup.ca

Kitchener: Victoria Place Retirement Residence
Rivera Inc.
290 Queen St. South, Kitchener, ON N2G 1W3
Tel: 519-576-1300
www.reveraliving.com/victoria
Number of Beds: 53 independent living suites; 35 assisted living suites
Note: Services include: foot care; laboratory; personal care; physiotherapy; recreation; & restorative program.
Lindsay Hounsell, Executive Director

Leamington: Erie Glen Manor Retirement Residence
119 Robson Rd., Leamington, ON N8H 3V4
Tel: 519-322-2384 *Fax:* 519-322-1411
Number of Beds: 81 beds
Note: Services include: chiropody; laboratory; massage therapy; medication administration; & physiotherapy.
Heather Fontaine, General Manager

Leamington: Leamington Lodge Residential Care
Centre Ltd.
PO Box 353, 24 Russell St., Leamington, ON N8H 3W3
Tel: 519-326-3591 *Fax:* 519-326-8787
Number of Beds: 43 beds

London: Ashwood Manor Ltd.
79 David St., London, ON N6P 1B4
Tel: 519-652-9006 *Fax:* 519-652-2592
info@ashwoodmanor.com
www.ashwoodmanor.com
Number of Beds: 72 beds
Note: Services include: 24 hour nursing care; foot care; laboratory; medication administration; & pharmacy.
Wilma DeVries, Assistant Administrator

London: Horizon Place Retirement Residence
760 Horizon Dr., London, ON N6H 5G3
Tel: 519-641-6330 *Fax:* 519-641-0570
www.reveraliving.com/horizon
Number of Beds: 84 residential capacity
Note: Specialties: Assisted living program; Recreation therapy; Podiatry; Short term stays
Marilyn Weekley, Manager

London: Kensington Village
1340 Huron St., London, ON N5V 3R3
Tel: 519-455-3910 *Fax:* 519-455-1570
www.svch.ca

Year Founded: 1984
Number of Beds: 138 beds
Note: Services include: 24 hour nursing staff; foot care; medication administration; physiotherapy; & recreational programs.
Tracie Klisht, Administrator
tklisht@svch.ca

London: Longworth Retirement Residence
Sifton Properties
600 Longworth Rd., London, ON N6A 4M8
Tel: 519-472-1115
sifton.com/retirement-living/longworth.html
Number of Beds: 126 suites
Note: Specialty: Retirement / assisted living; Physiotherapy; Massage therapy; Reiki; Reflexology.

London: Maple View Terrace
Trillium Retirement Living
279 Horton St., London, ON N6B 1L3
Tel: 519-434-4544
mapleview@trilliumretirementliving.com
www.trilliumretirementliving.com/london
Number of Beds: 90 units

London: The Waverley
10 Grand Ave., London, ON N5C 1K9
Tel: 519-667-1381 *Fax:* 519-667-9601
Year Founded: 1987
Number of Beds: 65 beds

Midland: King Place Midland
Affiliated with: Trillium Retirement Living
750 King St., Midland, ON L4R 4K5
Tel: 705-526-0514
kingplace@trilliumretirementliving.com
www.trilliumretirementliving.com/midland
Number of Beds: 80 beds
Note: Independent & assisted living; secured living for dementia care residents; respite & convalescent options.

Midland: The Villa Care Centre
Affiliated with: Jarlette Health Services
689 Young St., Midland, ON L4R 2E1
Tel: 705-526-4238 *Fax:* 705-526-5080
www.jarlette.com
Number of Beds: 114 long term care beds
Note: Services include: 24 hour nursing care; laboratory; restorative care; & spiritual care.
Sadie Friesner, Administrator

Mississauga: Beechwood Place
Revera Inc.
1500 Rathburn Rd. East, Mississauga, ON L4W 4L7
Tel: 905-238-0800 *Fax:* 905-238-4926
www.reveraliving.com
www.facebook.com/Reveralnc; twitter.com/Revera_Inc;
www.youtube.com/user/Reveralnc;
www.linkedin.com/company/revera-inc
Number of Beds: 202 units
Note: Services include: 24 hour nursing care; medication administration; personal care; & restorative program.
Thomas G. Wellner, President & CEO, Revera Living

Mississauga: Bough Beeches Place Retirement
Residence
Former Name: Meadowcroft Place
1130 Bough Beeches Blvd., Mississauga, ON L4W 4G3
Tel: 905-625-2022
reveraliving.com/Retirement-Living/Locations/Bough-Beeches
Year Founded: 1984
Number of Beds: 98 suites
Note: Specialties: Assisted living program; Secured living program, for persons with dementia & Alzheimers disease; Short term stays; Fitness program; Podiatry services

Mississauga: Erin Mills Lodge
Schlegel Villages
2132 Dundas St. West, Mississauga, ON L5K 2K7
Tel: 905-823-7273
www.schlegelvillages.com
Number of Beds: 86 long-term care beds
Note: Services include: nursing care; personal care; physiotherapy; restorative care; & recreation.
Mary Whalen, General Manager

Mississauga: King Gardens Retirement Residence
Revera Inc.
85 King St. East, Mississauga, ON L5A 4G6
Tel: 905-566-4545
www.reveraliving.com
www.facebook.com/Reveralnc; twitter.com/Revera_Inc;
www.youtube.com/user/Reveralnc;
www.linkedin.com/company/revera-inc
Year Founded: 1989
Number of Beds: 79 Independent Living suites; 47 Assisted Living suites; 15 Memory Care suites
Thomas G. Wellner, President & CEO, Revera Living

Morrisburg: Chartwell Hartford Retirement
Residence
Former Name: Hartford Retirement Centre
3 - 5th St. West, Morrisburg, ON K0C 1X0
Tel: 613-937-7273
chartwell.com/retirement-homes/chartwell-hartford-retirement-re
sidence

Mount Forest: Birmingham Retirement Community
356A Birmingham St. East, Mount Forest, ON N0G 2L2
Tel: 519-323-4019 *Fax:* 519-323-3005
www.birminghamretirement.ca
Number of Beds: 95 units
Note: Services include: daily care & nurse call system; hearing aid clinic; & wellness program.

Napanee: The Riverine Independent & Retirement
Living
328 Dundas St. West, Napanee, ON K7R 4B5
Tel: 613-354-8188 *Fax:* 613-354-8186
Toll-Free: 866-387-2217
admin@riverine.ca
www.riverine.ca
Number of Beds: 42 beds
Note: Amenities include a solarium; piano; workshop & craft area; card games & billiards.
Greg Freeman, Manager

Nepean: Chartwell Riverpark Retirement Community
Chartwell Master Care LP
1 Corkstown Rd., Nepean, ON K2H 1B6
Tel: 613-366-6187
chartwell.com/en/continuum-of-care/chartwell-riverpark-retireme
nt-community
Number of Beds: 172 beds (residential care, assisted & daily living)
Note: Services include: medical care; nursing care; memory care; & recreation.

Nepean: Chartwell Stillwater Creek Retirement
Community
Chartwell Master Care LP
2018 Robertson Rd., Nepean, ON K2H 1C6
Tel: 613-366-6161
chartwell.com/continuum-of-care/chartwell-stillwater-creek-retire
ment-community
Year Founded: 2001
Number of Beds: 200 units
Area Served: West Ottawa; Kanata; Bells Comers
Specialties: Independent apartments; residential care; assisted living; memory care; palliative care
Note: For seniors over the age of 65.

Newmarket: Alexander Muir Retirement Residence
Chartwell Retirement Residences
197 Prospect St., Newmarket, ON L3Y 3T7
Tel: 289-366-3690
chartwell.com/retirement-homes/chartwell-alexander-muir-retire
ment-residence

Niagara Falls: Cavendish Manor Retirement Living
5781 Dunn St., Niagara Falls, ON L2G 2N9
Tel: 905-354-2733 *Fax:* 905-354-4164
www.cavendishmanor.com
Number of Beds: 69 units
Note: Residential & assisted residential living, with 24 hour care available. Activities include shopping trips; knitting group; exotic animals visit; movie night; bingo; card games.
Janice Amos, Manager

Niagara Falls: Chippawa Place
Supportive Living
4118 Main St., Niagara Falls, ON L2G 6C2
Tel: 905-714-9517 *Fax:* 905-714-4558
admin@supportiveliving.ca
www.chippawaplace.com
Year Founded: 1994
Number of Beds: 25 beds

Niagara Falls: **Lundy Manor Retirement Residence**
7860 Lundy's Lane, Niagara Falls, ON L2H 1H1
Tel: 905-356-1511
www.reveraliving.com/lundy
Number of Beds: 95 capacity
Note: Specialties: Assisted living program; Short term stays;
Podiatry services
Art Derbernardi, Manager

Niagara Falls: **Willoughby Manor**
3584 Bridgewater St., Niagara Falls, ON L2G 6H1
Tel: 905-295-6288
www.willoughbymanor.ca
Number of Beds: 51 suites
Note: Services: 24 hour nursing care; medication administration;
personal care; recreation; & specialized care.
Eddie Stark, Executive Director

North Bay: **Barclay House Retirement Residence**
Affiliated with: Chartwell Retirement Residences
600 Chippewa St. West, North Bay, ON P1B 9E7
Tel: 705-476-6585
www.chartwell.com
Number of Beds: 64 suites
Note: Services include: care & wellness services; medication
administration; & personal support.
Elizabeth Evans, General Manager

Norwood: **Maple View Retirement Centre**
2281 County Rd. 45, RR#2, Norwood, ON K0L 2V0
Tel: 705-639-5374 *Fax:* 705-639-1793
info@mapleviewretirement.com
www.mapleviewretirement.com
Number of Beds: 60 beds
Note: Services include: nursing assessments; medication
administration; palliative care; physiotherapy; & recreation.
Cindy McGriskin, Administrator

Oakville: **Churchill Place**
345 Church St., Oakville, ON L6J 7G4
Tel: 905-338-3311
www.reveraliving.com/churchillplace
Number of Beds: 69 suites
Rick Halford, Executive Director

Oakville: **The Kensington**
Rivera Inc.
25 Lakeshore Rd. West, Oakville, ON L6K 1C6
Tel: 905-844-4000 *Fax:* 905-842-9229
www.reveraliving.com/kensington-oakville
Number of Beds: 117 suites
Note: Independent living & assisted living.

Oakville: **Oakville Senior Citizens Residence**
#2220, 2222 Lakeshore Rd. West, Oakville, ON L6L 5G5
Tel: 905-827-4139 *Fax:* 905-827-8047
oscr@oscrservices.ca
www.oscrservices.ca
Number of Beds: 164 apartment tower units; 172 residential
tower rooms
Note: Services include: chiropody; fitness & wellness programs;
& pharmacy.
Angela Katunas, CEO
akatunas@oakvilleseniors.com

Oakville: **Trafalgar Lodge Retirement Residence**
Revera Inc.
299 Randall St., Oakville, ON L6J 6B4
Tel: 905-842-8408 *Fax:* 905-842-8410
www.reveraliving.com/trafalgar
www.facebook.com/ReveraInc; twitter.com/Revera_Inc;
www.youtube.com/user/ReveraInc;
www.linkedin.com/company/revera-inc
Number of Beds: 69 units
Note: Services include: 24 hour nursing care; audiology;
chiropody; chiropractor; laboratory; medication administration;
personal care; physician clinic; physiotherapy; & recreation.
Thomas G. Wellner, President & CEO, Revera Living

Orangeville: **Lord Dufferin Centre**
32 First St., Orangeville, ON L9W 2E1
Tel: 519-941-8433 *Fax:* 519-941-2615
tabendroth@lorddufferincentre.ca
www.lorddufferincentre.ca
Year Founded: 1998
Number of Beds: 78 private suites
Note: Short term & trial stays available.

Orillia: **Atrium Retirement Residence**
230 Coldwater Rd. West, Orillia, ON L3V 3M2
Tel: 705-325-7300
www.atriumretirement.ca

Number of Beds: 50
Note: Retirement home offering residential, independent, &
assisted living care to seniors; 24 hour care available.
Linda Thompson, Executive Director

Orillia: **Birchmere Retirement Residence**
234 Bay St., Orillia, ON L3V 3W8
Tel: 705-326-8520 *Fax:* 705-326-5273
retire-orillia.com/bm-home
Year Founded: 1981
Note: Services include: nursing care; foot care; & activity
programs.
Jackie Payne, Administrator

Orillia: **Champlain Manor**
65 Fittons Rd. West, Orillia, ON L3V 3V2
Tel: 705-326-8597 *Fax:* 705-326-9831
champlainmanor@gmail.com
www.retireorillia.com
Year Founded: 1997
Number of Beds: 65 beds
Jackie Payne, Administrator

Orillia: **Spencer House**
Sienna Senior Living
835 West Ridge Blvd., Orillia, ON L3V 8B3
Tel: 705-326-6609
www.siennaliving.ca
Number of Beds: 160 beds
Note: Services include: nursing care; personal care; medical
care; rehabilitation; & restorative care.
Lois Cormack, President & CEO, Sienna Senior Living

Oshawa: **Cedarcroft Place**
649 King St. East, Oshawa, ON L1H 8P9
Tel: 905-723-9490
www.reveraliving.com/cedarcroft
Year Founded: 1990
Number of Beds: 76 units
Brad Meekin, Executive Director

Ottawa: **Amica at Bearbrook**
Former Name: Bearbrook Court
2645 Innes Rd., Ottawa, ON K1B 3J7
Tel: 613-837-8720 *Fax:* 613-837-8107
amica.ca/bearbrook
Number of Beds: 101 suites
Area Served: Blackburn; Orleans; Gloucester
Specialties: Independent living & assisted living
Note: Offers independent living & assisted living services,
including professional care & support (24 hour nursing care,
physician, massage therapy, physiotherapy, podiatry, audiology,
& dental), personalized wellness plans, activities, & on-site
amenities.
Bruno Gamache, Director, Community Relations
613-853-6219, b.gamache@amica.ca
Adam DeVries, General Manager
a.devries@amica.ca
Carmen Penney, Manager, Community Operations
c.penney@amica.ca

Ottawa: **Billings Lodge**
1180 Bélanger Ave., Ottawa, ON K1H 8A2
Tel: 613-737-7877
www.billingslodge.ca
Year Founded: 1984

Ottawa: **Chartwell Rideau Place Retirement**
Residence
Affiliated with: Chartwell Retirement Residences
Former Name: Rideau Place On-The-River
550 Wilbrod St., Ottawa, ON K1N 9M3
Tel: 343-882-4760
www.chartwell.com
Number of Beds: 98 suites

Ottawa: **Colonel By Retirement Residence**
43 Aylmer St., Ottawa, ON K1S 4R5
Tel: 613-730-2002
www.reveraliving.com/colonelby
Number of Beds: 135 units

Ottawa: **The Edinburgh Retirement Residence**
Revera Inc.
10 Vaughan St., Ottawa, ON K1M 2H6
Tel: 613-747-2233 *Fax:* 613-747-6741
www.reveraliving.com/edinburgh
www.facebook.com/ReveraInc; twitter.com/Revera_Inc;
www.youtube.com/user/ReveraInc;
www.linkedin.com/company/revera-inc
Number of Beds: 65 suites
Note: Services include: 24 hour nursing care; dental care; foot
care; physiotherapy; & recreation.

Thomas G. Wellner, President & CEO, Revera Living

Ottawa: **Hunt Club Manor**
1351 Hunt Club Rd., Ottawa, ON K1V 1A6
Tel: 613-733-4776
www.reveraliving.com/huntclub
Number of Beds: 78 beds
Tracy Fowers, General Manager

Ottawa: **New Edinburgh Square**
420 MacKay St., Ottawa, ON K1M 2C4
Tel: 613-744-0901
www.chartwell.com
Number of Beds: 121 beds

Ottawa: **Parklane Residence**
1095 Merivale Rd., Ottawa, ON K1Z 6A9
Tel: 613-725-1064 *Fax:* 613-728-3533
parlane@on.aibn.com
Number of Beds: 107 beds

Ottawa: **Presland Residence**
198 Presland Rd., Ottawa, ON K1K 2B8
Tel: 613-745-0089 *Fax:* 613-745-6060
Number of Beds: 78 beds
Nathalie Grégoire, Administrator
613-745-0089

Ottawa: **Rothwell Heights Retirement Residence**
1735 Montréal Rd., Ottawa, ON K1J 6N4
Tel: 613-744-2322 *Fax:* 613-745-2320
Number of Beds: 150 beds
Dorothy Vlaming, Owner
Linda Vlaming, Owner

Ottawa: **Stittsville Retirement Community**
1354 Stittsville Main St., Ottawa, ON K2S 1V4
Tel: 613-836-2216
www.reveraliving.com/stittsville
Number of Beds: 71 independent living suites; 31 seniors'
apartments
Note: Independent lifestyle community featuring 24-hour staff;
pet-friendly.
Pat Leishman, Manager

Ottawa: **Thorncliffe Place Retirement Home**
1 Thorncliffe Pl., Ottawa, ON K2H 9N9
Tel: 613-596-3853 *Fax:* 613-596-6225
info@thorncliffeplace.com
www.thorncliffeplace.com
Year Founded: 1989
Number of Beds: 62 units
Note: Services include: activity program; convalescent care;
medication supervision; & physiotherapy.
Michael Francis, Owner

Ottawa: **Watford House Residence**
75 Powell Ave., Ottawa, ON K1S 1Z9
Tel: 613-230-9194
www.watfordhouse.ca
Info Line: 613-230-7423
Number of Beds: 22 beds
Note: Residence for women.
Valentina Mammadova, Manager

Ottawa: **The Westwood**
Revera Inc.
Former Name: Central Park Lodges - Ottawa 1
2374 Carling Ave., Ottawa, ON K2B 7G5
Tel: 613-820-7333
reveraliving.com/Retirement-Living/Locations/the-westwood
www.facebook.com/ReveraInc; twitter.com/Revera_Inc;
www.youtube.com/user/ReveraInc;
www.linkedin.com/company/revera-inc
Year Founded: 1969
Number of Beds: 93 Independent Living suites; 134 Assisted
Living suites; 19 Memory Care suites
Note: Independent & assisted living, respite & convalescent
options.
Thomas G. Wellner, President & CEO, Revera Living

Ottawa: **Windsor Park Manor Retirement Living**
990 Hunt Club Rd., Ottawa, ON K1V 8S8
Tel: 613-249-0722 *Fax:* 613-249-0575
windsorpark@regallc.com
www.windsorparkmanor.com
Note: Convalescence, respite, & short term stays are available.

Owen Sound: **Central Place**
855 - 3 Ave. East, Owen Sound, ON N4K 2K6
Tel: 519-371-1968 *Fax:* 519-371-5357
info@cpretirement.ca
www.cpretirement.ca
Year Founded: 1998

Owen Sound: Hannah Walker Place
832 - 2 Ave. West, Owen Sound, ON N4K 4M5
Tel: 519-371-1664 *Fax:* 519-371-5286
www.owensoundretirement.com

Owen Sound: John Joseph Place
854 - 2 Ave. West, Owen Sound, ON N4K 4M5
Tel: 519-371-1664 *Fax:* 519-371-5286
www.owensoundretirement.com

Pakenham: Country View Lodge
4676 Dark's Side Rd., Pakenham, ON K0A 2X0
Tel: 613-624-5714 *Fax:* 888-960-0247
Toll-Free: 855-932-2739
info@countryviewlodge.com
www.countryviewlodge.com
Note: Retirement home with assisted living / nursing service
Ali Abbas, General Manager

Paris: Penmarvian Retirement Home
185 Grand River St. North, Paris, ON N3L 2N2
Tel: 519-442-7140 *Fax:* 519-442-7156
www.penmarvian.com

Year Founded: 1980
Number of Beds: 40 beds
Note: Services include 24 hour nursing care & activities.
Maria Toncic, Administrator

Perth: Rideau Ferry Country Home
1333 Rideau Ferry Rd., Perth, ON K7H 3C7
Tel: 613-267-6213 *Fax:* 613-267-6261
www.rideauferrycountryhome.com

Year Founded: 1980
Number of Beds: 35 units
Number of Employees: 16
Note: Offers full service retirement & assisted living.
Clare McCartney, General Manager
ken.mccartney@sympatico.ca
Sheena Miller, Administrator & Director of Care

Peterborough: Empress Gardens Retirement Residence
131 Charlotte St., Peterborough, ON K9J 2T6
Tel: 705-876-1314 *Fax:* 705-876-1908
www.empressgardens.ca

Peterborough: Peterborough Retirement Residence
Former Name: Peterborough Manor
1039 Water St., Peterborough, ON K9H 3P5
Tel: 705-748-5343
www.peterboroughretirement.ca

Year Founded: 1982
Number of Beds: 101 suites
Note: 24-hour care available; Permanent, short stay, vacation stays or respite programs.
Martha Creally, Administrator

Peterborough: Princess Gardens Retirement Residence
100 Charlotte St., Peterborough, ON K9J 7L4
Tel: 705-750-1234 *Fax:* 705-750-0711
Toll-Free: 877-742-9779
www.princessgardens.ca

Number of Beds: 132 beds
Note: Independent retirement amenities; assisted living/enriched care options; respite & convalescent care
Juris Taurins, Manager

Pickering: Orchard Villa Retirement
Southbridge Care Homes
Former Name: Community Nursing Home
1955 Valley Farm Rd., Pickering, ON L1V 3R6
Tel: 905-831-2522 *Fax:* 905-420-5030
www.orchardvilla.ca
Number of Beds: 233 long-term care beds, 61 retirement suites
Lesreen Thomas, Executive Director
lethomas@southbridgecare.ca

Port Hope: The Tower of Port Hope Retirement Residence
164 Peter St., Port Hope, ON L1A 1C6
Tel: 905-885-7261
www.towerofporthope.ca

Number of Beds: 43 beds
Note: Services include: 24 hour emergency response; convalescent care; medication administration; & recreation.
Diana Armstrong, General Manager

Port Perry: West Shore Village
293 Perry St., Port Perry, ON L9L 1S6
Tel: 905-985-8660 *Toll-Free:* 800-248-0848
info@westshorevillage.ca
www.westshorevillage.ca

Number of Beds: 71 suites
Note: Specialties: Supported living for seniors; Foot care; Reflexology; Massage therapy; Recreational program; Respite care
Tammy Brandenburg, Director

Renfrew: Quail Creek Retirement Residence
Affiliated with: Chartwell Retirement Residences
450 Albert St., Renfrew, ON K7V 4K4
Tel: 613-432-9502
www.chartwell.com

Number of Beds: 92 suites
Bev Powell, General Manager

Richmond: Richmond Lodge Ltd.
PO Box 1030, 6197 Perth St., Richmond, ON K0A 2Z0
Tel: 613-838-5016 *Fax:* 613-838-5017
info@richmondlodge.ca
richmondlodge.ca

Number of Beds: 40 beds
Note: 24-hour nursing staff; medication supervision; organized leisure activities.
Shelly Ahrens, Director of Care
directorofcare@richmondlodge.ca

Richmond Hill: Brookside Court/Hilltop Retirement Residence
Rivera Inc.
980 Elgin Mills Rd. East, Richmond Hill, ON L4S 1M4
Tel: 905-884-9248 *Fax:* 905-884-9745
www.reveraliving.com/brookside
Year Founded: 1961
Number of Beds: 88 beds
Note: Independent living & assisted living.
Jai Sukhai, Executive Director

Rockland: Résidence Jardins Bellerive
2950 rue Laurier, Rockland, ON K4K 1T3
Tel: 613-446-7122 *Fax:* 613-446-7343
lesjardinsbellerive@gmail.com
www.jardinsbellerive.ca
Number of Beds: 80 Units

Rockland: Résidence Simon Inc.
CP 400, 845, rue St-Jean, Rockland, ON K4K 1K5
Tél: 613-446-7023 *Téléc:* 613-446-4867
info@residencesimon.ca
www.residencesimon.ca

Fondée en: 1989
Nombre de lits: 46 lits
Albert Bourdeau, Propriétaire

Sarnia: Marshall Gowland Manor
749 Devine St., Sarnia, ON N7T 1X3
Tel: 519-336-3720 *Fax:* 519-336-3734
www.lambtoncares.ca

Year Founded: 2004
Number of Beds: 126 beds
Note: Services include: behaviour support; medication management; pain management; palliative care; physiotherapy; recreation; Snoezelen therapy; social work; & spiritual care.
Jennifer Allison, Administrator

Sarnia: Residence on the St. Clair
Affiliated with: Steeves & Rozema Group
#22 - 265 North Front St., Sarnia, ON N7T 7X1
Tel: 519-344-8829 *Fax:* 519-344-8518
general_inquiries@srgroup.ca
www.srgroup.ca

Number of Beds: 73 beds
Cathy McIntosh, Managing Director

Sarnia: Rosewood Manor
Affiliated with: Steeves & Rozema Group
711 Indian Rd. North, Sarnia, ON N7T 7Z5
Tel: 519-332-8877 *Fax:* 519-332-5047
rosewoodmanor@srgroup.ca
sarnia.ontarioretirementcommunity.com
Note: Independent & assisted living
Janice Horley, Executive Director

Sault Ste Marie: Great Northern Retirement Home
760 Great Northern Rd., Sault Ste Marie, ON P6A 5K7
Tel: 705-945-9405 *Fax:* 705-942-2063
greatnorthern@shaw.ca
www.greatnorthernretirement.com
Number of Beds: 120 retirement, 34 interim nursing home beds
Nadia Longo, Administrator

Sault Ste Marie: Pathways Retirement Residence
Former Name: Pathways Seniors Residence
375 Trunk Rd., Sault Ste Marie, ON P6A 6T5
Tel: 705-759-1079 *Fax:* 705-759-1211
www.pathwaysretirement.com

Number of Beds: 133 suites
Note: Services include 24 hour medical assistance, convalescent care, & daily activities.

Seaforth: Maplewood Manor
Comfort of Living
13 Church St., Seaforth, ON N0K 1W0
Tel: 519-441-2722
info@comfortofliving.com
www.comfortofliving.com

Simcoe: Simcoe Heritage Retirement Home
182 Norfolk St. South, Simcoe, ON N3Y 2W4
Tel: 519-428-0930
www.simcoeheritage.ca
Number of Beds: 31 rooms

Smiths Falls: Willowdale Retirement Centre
Affiliated with: Chartwell Retirement Residences
9 Armstrong Dr., Smiths Falls, ON K7A 5H7
Tel: 613-283-0691
Number of Beds: 63 beds
Note: Services include: convalescent care; respite care; nursing care; & medication administration.

St. Catharines: The Loyalist Retirement Residence
190 King St., St. Catharines, ON L2R 3J7
Tel: 905-641-4422 *Fax:* 905-641-4989
info@loyalist-retirement.com
www.loyalist-retirement.com
Number of Beds: 118 residential capacity
Note: Specialties: Assisted living; Nursing supervision; Medication administration; Podiatry services; Recreation & fitness program; Respite care; Convalescent stays
Nicole Cairns, Executive Director

St. Catharines: Mount Carmel Home
78 Yates St., St. Catharines, ON L2R 5R9
Tel: 905-685-9155 *Fax:* 905-682-3922
carmel@bellnet.ca
www.mountcarmelretirement.ca
Year Founded: 1920
Note: Seniors residence
Sr. M. Rosario, Administrator

St. Catharines: Tufford Manor Retirement Home
312 Queenston St., St. Catharines, ON L2P 2X4
Tel: 905-682-0411 *Fax:* 905-682-2770
info@tufford.ca
www.tufford.ca
Number of Beds: 50 beds
Note: Offers long & short-term stays; on-site physiotherapy; medication administration; & maintenance, laundry, & housekeeping.
Amy Matwijow, Contact
amatwijow@tufford.ca

St. Joachim: St. Joachim Manor
2718 County Rd. 42, St. Joachim, ON N0R 1S0
Tel: 519-728-1215 *Fax:* 519-728-0113
Number of Beds: 24 beds
Note: Services include: medical care; adult respite & daycare services; dental care; foot care; massage therapy; occupational therapy; pharmacy; physiotherapy; recreational therapy; rehabilitation; & vision care.
Nada Horvat, Director, Care

St. Thomas: Metcalfe Gardens Retirement Residence
45 Metcalfe St., St. Thomas, ON N5R 5Y1
Tel: 519-631-9393 *Fax:* 519-631-2563
Year Founded: 1988
Number of Beds: 94 suites
Note: Services include: 24 hour nursing care; foot care; medication management; & personal care assistance.
Lori Lackey, General Manager

Stoney Creek: Orchard Terrace Care Centre
199 Glover Rd., Stoney Creek, ON L8E 5J2
Tel: 905-643-1795 *Fax:* 905-643-1085
www.orchardterracecarecentre.ca
Year Founded: 1994
Number of Beds: 38 units
Note: Services include: 24 hour nursing care; medication administration; personal care; & recreation programs.
Linda Calabrese, Interim Administrator

Stratford: Anne Hathaway Residence
480 Downie St., Stratford, ON N5A 7Y5
Tel: 519-275-2125 *Fax:* 519-275-2126
www.chartwell.com
Number of Beds: 67 beds
Dianne Roth, Administrator

Stratford: Cedarcroft Place Retirement Residence
Affiliated with: All Seniors Care Living Centres
260 Church St., Stratford, ON N5A 2R6
Tel: 519-273-0030
www.allseniorscare.com/residence/cedarcroft-place-retirement-r
esidence
Number of Beds: 100 beds
Note: Services include: nursing supervision; medications;
physiotherapy; & audiology.
Dan Vito, Director
danvito@allseniorscare.com

Sudbury: Westmount on William Retirement Residence
Affiliated with: Chartwell Retirement Residences
599 William Ave., Sudbury, ON P3A 5W3
Tel: 705-566-6221
www.chartwell.com
Number of Beds: 84 suites
Lisa Brule, General Manager

Temiskaming Shores: Northdale Manor
142-130 Lakeshore Rd. North, Temiskaming Shores, ON P0J
1P0
Tel: 705-647-6541 Fax: 705-647-5284
nordale@ntl.sympatico.ca
www.northdalemanor.ca
Number of Beds: 70 suites
Note: Services include: 24 hour nursing care; activity program; &
medication administration.
Trisha Hopkins, Administrator

Thornhill: Glynnwood Retirement Residence
Revera Inc.
7700 Bayview Ave., Thornhill, ON L3T 5W1
Tel: 905-881-9475 Fax: 905-881-9490
www.reveraliving.com/glynnwood
www.facebook.com/Reveralnc; twitter.com/Revera_Inc;
www.youtube.com/user/Reveralnc;
www.linkedin.com/company/revera-inc
Number of Beds: 134 independent living suites; 42 assisted
living suites
Note: Services include: personal care; house physician;
physiotherapy; & recreation.
Thomas G. Wellner, President & CEO, Revera Living

Thorold: Cobblestone Gardens Retirement Residence
Affiliated with: Mundi Holdings Ltd.
Former Name: Chestnut Court
10 Ormond St. North, Thorold, ON L2V 1Y7
Tel: 905-227-5550 Fax: 905-227-5575
info@cobblestonegardens.ca
www.cobblestonegardens.ca
Year Founded: 1984
Note: Services include: 24 hour care staff; 24 hour emergency
response system; dietary assessments; nursing assessments;
medication administration; recreation; & wellness program.
Jeannie Redekop, Administrator
Ronda Pereira, Assistant Administrator

Tilbury: Hudson Manor
36 Lawson St., Tilbury, ON N0P 2L0
Tel: 519-682-3366 Fax: 519-682-0688
Number of Beds: 50 beds
Note: Services include: 24 hour health & wellness office;
medication monitoring; & convalescent & respite care.
Andrea Sullivan, General Manager

Tillsonburg: Tillsonburg Retirement Residence
183 Rolph St., Tillsonburg, ON N4G 3Y9
Tel: 519-688-0347 Fax: 519-688-0245
www.tillsonburgretirement.ca
Number of Beds: 51 beds
Note: Services include: 24 hour nursing care; medication
administration; mobility assistance; & personal support.
Rhonda Wilton, Executive Director

Timmins: Chateau Georgian Retirement Residence
Affiliated with: Chartwell Retirement Residences
455 Cedar St. North, Timmins, ON P4N 8K4
Tel: 705-267-7935
www.chartwell.com
Number of Beds: 63 suites
Note: Services include: 24 hour medical attention; medication
administration; & physiotherapy.
Terri Scott, Contact

Toronto: The Annex Retirement Residence
Revera Inc.
123 Spadina Rd., Toronto, ON M5R 2T1
Tel: 416-961-6446 Fax: 416-961-3299
www.reveraliving.com/annex

Year Founded: 1961
Number of Beds: 98 suites
Note: Services include: 24 hour nursing care; foot care;
recreation; & restorative program.

Toronto: The Balmoral Club
155 Balmoral Ave., Toronto, ON M4V 1J5
Tel: 416-927-0055 Fax: 416-927-0925
www.amica.ca/balmoral
Number of Beds: 66 beds
Note: Services include 24 hour nursing care & physical fitness
programs.
Monica Byrne, Administrator

**Toronto: Baycrest Centre for Geriatric Care -
Terraces of Baycrest**
55 Ameer Ave., Toronto, ON M6A 2Z1
Tel: 416-785-2500 Fax: 416-785-2496
mjacobson@baycrest.org
www.baycrest.org
Info Line: 416-785-2379
www.facebook.com/baycrestcentre; twitter.com/baycrest;
www.youtube.com/thebaycrestchannel;
www.linkedin.com/company/baycrest
Number of Beds: 199 Apartments
William E. Reichman, CEO

Toronto: Beach Arms Retirement Residence
505 Kingston Rd., Toronto, ON M4L 1V5
Tel: 416-698-0414 Fax: 416-698-9839
info@beacharms.com
www.beacharms.com
Number of Beds: 73 suites
Note: Services include: 24 hour nursing care; foot care; house
physician; laboratory; personal care; pharmacy; & physiotherapy.
Susan Turner, Administrator

Toronto: Belmont House
55 Belmont St., Toronto, ON M5R 1R1
Tel: 416-964-9231 Fax: 416-964-1448
information@belmonthouse.com
www.belmonthouse.com
Number of Beds: 55 apartments, 26 retirement suites; 140
long-term care beds
Number of Employees: 28
Note: Services include: dietitian consultation; physiotherapy;
recreation; & social support.
Maria Elias, CEO
melias@belmonthouse.com

**Toronto: Centennial Park Place Retirement
Residence**
Former Name: Meadowcroft Place Retirement
Residence
25 Centennial Park Rd., Toronto, ON M9C 5H1
Tel: 416-621-2139
www.reveraliving.com/centennial
Number of Beds: 48 residential capacity
Note: Specialty: Podiatry services; Fitness program
Naida McKechnie, Manager

**Toronto: Chartwell Guildwood Retirement
Residence**
65 Livingston Rd., Toronto, ON M1E 1L1
Tel: 647-846-7004
chartwell.com/retirement-homes/chartwell-guildwood-retirement-
residence
Note: Specialities: Physiotherapy; Foot care

Toronto: Don Mills Seniors' Apartments
Revera Inc.
1055-1057 Don Mills Rd., Toronto, ON M3C 1W9
Tel: 416-445-5532
www.reveraliving.com/donmills
www.facebook.com/Reveralnc; twitter.com/Revera_Inc;
www.youtube.com/user/Reveralnc;
www.linkedin.com/company/revera-inc
Number of Beds: 143 suites
Thomas G. Wellner, President & CEO, Revera Living

Toronto: Donway Place
Revera Inc.
8 The Donway East, Toronto, ON M3C 3R7
Tel: 416-445-7555
www.reveraliving.com
www.facebook.com/Reveralnc; twitter.com/Revera_Inc;
www.youtube.com/user/Reveralnc;
www.linkedin.com/company/revera-inc
Number of Beds: 145 independant living suites; 90 assisted
living suites
Thomas G. Wellner, President & CEO, Revera Living

Toronto: Forest Hill Place
645 Castlefield Ave., Toronto, ON M5N 3A5
Tel: 416-785-1511 Fax: 416-785-6228
www.reveraliving.com/foresthill
Number of Beds: 125 suites

Toronto: Grenadier Retirement Residence
2100 Bloor St. West, Toronto, ON M6S 1M7
Tel: 416-769-2885 Fax: 416-769-7238
www.chartwell.com
Note: various activities offered, such as book club, brain gym,
fitness classes, gardening, art classes & day trips.

Toronto: Harold & Grace Baker Centre
Revera Inc.
1 Northwestern Ave., Toronto, ON M6M 2J7
Tel: 416-654-2889 Fax: 416-654-0217
www.bakercentre.com
www.facebook.com/Reveralnc; twitter.com/Revera_Inc;
www.youtube.com/user/Reveralnc;
www.linkedin.com/company/revera-inc
Number of Beds: 120 long term care beds; 91 retirement care
beds
Note: Services include: 24 hour nursing care; 24 hour on-call
physician services; foot care; physiotherapy; & therapeutic
recreation.
Thomas G. Wellner, President & CEO, Revera Living
Susan Michalchuk, Director, Retirement Residence

Toronto: Hazelton Place
111 Avenue Rd., Toronto, ON M5R 3J8
Tel: 416-928-0111
mkg.mgr.hazleton@vervesseniorliving.com
www.vervesseniorliving.com/hazelton-place
Number of Beds: 130 units
Note: 24-hour care; medication management; daily & specialized
weekly exercise; arts & crafts; discussion groups including book
club; outings including movies & shopping.
Ron Khan, General Manager

Toronto: Lansing Retirement Residence
10 Senlac Rd., Toronto, ON M2N 6P8
Tel: 416-250-7029 Fax: 416-250-7853
www.chartwell.com
Number of Beds: 108 beds
Note: Services include: care & wellness services; nursing; &
medication administration.
Lauren Shoom, General Manager

Toronto: Leaside Retirement Residence
Revera Inc.
10/14 William Morgan Dr., Toronto, ON M4H 1E7
Tel: 416-425-3722 Fax: 416-425-3946
www.reveraliving.com/leaside
www.facebook.com/Reveralnc; twitter.com/Revera_Inc;
www.youtube.com/user/Reveralnc;
www.linkedin.com/company/revera-inc
Year Founded: 1961
Number of Beds: 72 independent living suites; 97 assisted living
suites; 62 memory care suites
Note: Services include: 24 hour nursing care; physiotherapy; &
recreation.
Thomas G. Wellner, President & CEO, Revera Living

Toronto: McNicoll Manor
Affiliated with: Tendercare
1020 McNicoll Ave., Toronto, ON M1W 2J6
Tel: 416-499-3313
www.tendercare.ca
Year Founded: 1976
Number of Beds: 254
Note: A community consisting of Long Term Care, Convalescent
Care, & Retirement Living, focusing on culturally sensitive care;
Specialties: Physiotherapy
Amy Leong, Manager, Retirement Residences
416-499-3313, aleong@tendercare.ca

Toronto: New Horizons Tower
1140 Bloor St. West, Toronto, ON M6H 4E6
Tel: 416-536-6111 Fax: 416-536-6748
info@newhorizonstower.com
www.newhorizonstower.com
Number of Beds: 197 beds
Note: Christian nursing home
Ian C. Logan, Administrator

Toronto: Rayoak Place Retirement Residence
1340 York Mills Rd., Toronto, ON M3A 3R1
Tel: 416-391-0633
www.reveraliving.com/rayoak
Number of Beds: 66 beds
Note: Offers both independent & assisted living options.

Toronto: **Shepherd Terrace Retirement Suites**
3758 Sheppard Ave. East, Toronto, ON M1T 3K9
Tel: 416-609-5700 *Fax:* 416-609-8329
www.shepherdvillage.org
Number of Beds: 150 beds
Note: Retirement living & assisted living.

Toronto: **Terrace Gardens Retirement Residence**
3705 Bathurst St., Toronto, ON M6A 2E8
Tel: 416-789-7670
www.reveraliving.com/terracegardens
Note: Jewish retirement residence; independent & assisted living, secured living for dementia care, convalescent & respite options; COR supervised, mashgiach on site

Toronto: **Weston Gardens Retirement Residence**
303 Queens Dr., Toronto, ON M6L 3C1
Tel: 416-241-1113
www.westongardens.ca
Note: Independent & assisted living, respite & convalescent options.

Toronto: **Weston Gardens Retirement Residence**
Former Name: **Central Park Lodges - Queens Drive 2**
303 Queens Dr., Toronto, ON M6L 3C1
Tel: 416-241-1113 *Fax:* 416-241-1801
www.westongardens.ca
Number of Beds: 156 units

Trenton: **The Carrington Retirement Residence**
114 Whites Rd., RR#2, Trenton, ON K8V 5P5
Tel: 613-392-1615 *Fax:* 613-392-3879
Toll-Free: 877-392-1615
www.thecarringtonretirement.com
Number of Beds: 37 units
Note: The Carrington is an approved member of the Ontario Retirement Communities Association. Services include the availability of nuses & health care aides, assistance with daily living activities & outside agency services, plus social, cultural, & recreational programming.

Utterson: **Rowanwood Retirement Lodge**
81 Rowanwood Rd., RR#3, Utterson, ON P0B 1M0
Tel: 705-789-6424 *Fax:* 705-789-1821
Number of Beds: 86 beds
Gail Sargeant, Manager

Vankleek Hill: **Heritage Lodge Retirement Residence**
Former Name: **Vankleek Residence**
48 Wall St., Vankleek Hill, ON K0B 1R0
Tel: 613-678-2690 *Toll-Free:* 877-929-9222
Number of Beds: 72 beds

Vineland: **Chartwell Orchards Retirement Residence**
Chartwell Master Care LP
Heritage Village, 3421 Frederick Ave., Vineland, ON L0R 2C0
Tel: 289-438-2542
chartwell.com/en/retirement-residences/chartwell-orchards-retirement-residence
Year Founded: 1999
Note: Programs & services include: medication management; personal care assistance; activities; physiotherapy; respite & convalescence care.
Dustin Gibson, General Manager

Walkerton: **Maple Court Retirement Residence**
Former Name: **Maple Court Villa**
PO Box 879, 5 Fourth St., Walkerton, ON N0G 2V0
Tel: 519-881-2233 *Fax:* 519-881-0336
www.maplecourtretirement.ca
Number of Beds: 47 Suites
Note: Nursing home
JoAnn Todd, Administrator

Waterloo: **Luther Village on the Park**
Luthewood
139 Father David Bauer Dr., Waterloo, ON N2L 6L1
Tel: 519-747-4413
www.luthervillage.org
Note: This retirement community has 154 Atrium Suites & 72 Garden Villa townhomes; The adjacent Sunshine Centre offers assisted living services with 148 suites & a special memory care/dementia wing.

Waterloo: **Oak Park Terrace**
Affiliated with: **Chartwell Retirement Residences**
1750 North Service Rd., Waterloo, ON N8E 1Y3
Tel: 519-972-3330
www.chartwell.com
Number of Beds: 112
Stephen Suske, CEO, Chartwell Seniors Housing REIT

Windsor: **Devonshire Riverside House**
Former Name: **Devonshire Seniors' Residence**
901 Riverside Dr. West, Windsor, ON N9A 7J6
Tel: 519-252-2273
www.devonshireretirement.ca
Number of Beds: 195 beds

Windsor: **Lifetimes on Riverside Retirement Residence**
Former Name: **The Grandview Retirement Living by Revera Inc.**
3387 Riverside Dr. East, Windsor, ON N8Y 1A8
Tel: 519-946-1800 *Fax:* 519-948-4525
www.lifetimesonriverside.ca
Number of Beds: 141 units
Note: Services include recreation & activity programs; 24 hour a day snacks; exercise & wellness programs.

Wingham: **Braemar Retirement Centre**
719 Josephine St., Wingham, ON N0G 2W0
Tel: 519-357-3430 *Fax:* 519-357-2303
Toll-Free: 888-817-5828
www.braemar-rc.com
Number of Beds: 18 beds
Note: Services include: 24 hour nursing care; medication administration; personal care; physiotherapy; & recreational programs.
Archie MacGowan, Administrator
519-357-3430, macgowana@hurontel.on.ca

Personal Care Homes

Ottawa: **Governor's Walk**
AgeCare
150 Stanley Ave., Ottawa, ON K1M 2J7
Tel: 613-564-9255
www.governorswalkresidence.com
www.facebook.com/GovernorsWalk
Note: Services include personal care, dementia care & temporary care

Mental Health Hospitals/Facilities

Brockville: **Brockville Mental Health Centre**
Royal Ottawa Health Care Group
Former Name: **Brockville Psychiatric Hospital**
PO Box 1050, 1804 Hwy. 2 East, Brockville, ON K6V 5W7
Tel: 613-345-1461 *Fax:* 613-342-6194
Toll-Free: 800-433-7371
www.theroyal.ca
Number of Beds: 163 inpatient beds
Specialties: Mental Health
Note: Affiliated with the University of Ottawa.
Joanne Bezzubetz, President & CEO
Dr. Raj Bhatla, Psychiatrist-in-Chief & Chief of Staff

Fergus: **Canadian Mental Health Association - Waterloo Wellington**
Fergus
Former Name: **Trellis Mental Health & Developmental Services**
234 St. Patrick St. East, Fergus, ON N1M 1M6
Fax: 519-843-7608
Toll-Free: 844-264-2993
www.cmhaww.ca
Note: Services include counselling & treatment, psychiatry assessment, developmental services, support groups, education & training, family support, crisis support, geriatric services, respite services, & mental health & justice services.
Helen Fishburn, Executive Director, Canadian Mental Health Association

Guelph: **Homewood Health Centre**
150 Delhi St., Guelph, ON N1E 6K9
Tel: 519-824-1010 *Fax:* 519-824-8751
healthcentre@homewoodhealth.com
www.homewoodhealth.com
www.facebook.com/HomewoodHealth; twitter.com/homewoodhc;
www.linkedin.com/company/homewood-health-centre
Year Founded: 1883
Number of Beds: 300 beds
Number of Employees: 650
Specialties: Mental Health
Note: Specialty: Behavioural, addiction & psychiatric services.
Jagoda Pike, President & CEO
Marg Bellman, Executive Vice-President, Return to Work Services
Francine Bolduc, Executive Vice-President, Human Resources
Jared Landry, Executive Vice-President, Growth & Strategy
Al Van Leeuwen, Executive Vice-President, Operations
Dr. Ann Malain, Executive Vice-President, Stay at Work Services

Kimberly Mirotta, Executive Vice-President, Finance & Administration
Sean Slater, Executive Vice-President, Sales & Marketing

Hamilton: **St. Joseph's Healthcare Hamilton - Mental Health & Addiction Services**
St. Joseph's Health System
PO Box 585, 100 - 5 St. West, Hamilton, ON L8N 3K7
Tel: 905-522-1155
www.stjoes.ca
www.facebook.com/stjosephshealthcarefoundation;
twitter.com/STJOESHAMILTON;
www.youtube.com/Stjoesfoundation
Specialties: Mental Health
Note: Offers a full suite of mental health & addiction services.

Hamilton: **St. Joseph's Healthcare Hamilton - West 5th Campus**
St. Joseph's Health System
Affiliated with: **Hamilton Niagara Haldimand Brant Local Health Integration Network**
100 West 5th St., Hamilton, ON L9C 0E3
Tel: 905-522-1155
twitter.com/STJOESHAMILTON;
www.youtube.com/Stjoesfoundation
Note: Offers mental health & medical services, as well as teaching & research facilities. Affiliated with the Faculty of Health Sciences at McMaster University & Mohawk College.
Dr. Peter Bieling, Acting Vice-President, Mental Health & Addiction Services

Holland Landing: **Southdown Institute**
18798 Old Yonge St., Holland Landing, ON L9N 0L1
Tel: 905-727-4214 *Fax:* 905-895-6296
www.southdown.on.ca
Number of Beds: 44 beds
Note: Specialties: Residential & outpatient psychological treatment to clergy & religious; Psychodynamic group therapy; Individual & group addiction counselling; 12-step groups; Specialized group treatment for persons who have violated sexual boundaries; Art therapy; Health education.
Rev. Stephan Kappler, President & Chief Psychologist

Kingston: **Ongwanada Hospital**
191 Portsmouth Ave., Kingston, ON K7M 8A6
Tel: 613-548-4417 *Fax:* 613-548-8135
www.ongwanada.com
www.facebook.com/Ongwanada1; twitter.com/ongwanada
Year Founded: 1948
Number of Beds: 227 beds
Number of Employees: 494
Note: Specialties: Support for persons with developmental disabilities; Day support; Vocational & life skills training; Occupational therapy; Physiotherapy; Hydrotherapy; Snoezelen Room; Community behavioural services; Research.
Wade Durling, Chief Executive Officer

Kingston: **Providence Care - Mental Health Services**
Affiliated with: **Providence Care**
Former Name: **Kingston Psychiatric Hospital**
752 King St. West, Kingston, ON K7L 4X3
Tel: 613-546-1101 *Fax:* 613-548-5588
www.providencecare.ca
www.facebook.com/ProvidenceCareCA;
twitter.com/providence_care;
www.instagram.com/providence_care
Number of Beds: 198 beds
Note: Adult Treatment & Rehabilitation, Geriatric Psychiatry, Forensic Psychiatry. Affilated with Queen's University.
Cathy Szabo, President & CEO

Lindsay: **Chimo Youth & Family Services**
107 Lindsay St. South, Lindsay, ON K9V 2M5
Tel: 705-324-3300 *Toll-Free:* 877-661-2973
info@chimoyouth.ca
www.chimoyouth.ca
Note: Chimo Youth & Family Services is accredited under Children's Mental Health Ontario. Programs include clinical & crisis care, group meetings, day treatment, & residential & respite care.

London: **Child & Parent Resource Institute (CPRI)**
600 Sanatorium Rd., London, ON N6H 3W7
Tel: 519-858-2774 *Fax:* 519-858-3913
Toll-Free: 877-494-2774
www.cpri.ca
Number of Beds: 75 beds
Note: Provides outpatient, intensive / residential, support, & referral services for children & youth with developmental disabilities or mental health needs.

London: **Parkwood Institute**
Affiliated with: St. Joseph's Health Care, London
Former Name: Parkwood Hospital; Regional Mental
Healthcare London
550 Wellington Rd. South, London, ON N6C 0A7
Tel: 519-646-6100
www.sjhc.london.on.ca
Number of Beds: 403 beds
Note: Programs & services include: geriatric services; Veterans
Care program; mental health care programs; & rehabilitation
programs & assessments. Mental Health Building opened in
2014 with 156 beds and over 700 staff.
Dr. Gillian Kernaghan, President & CEO, St. Joseph's Health
Care London
askgillian@sjhc.london.on.ca

North Bay: **North Bay Regional Health Centre -
Mental Health Clinic**
Former Name: North Bay Psychiatric Hospital
120 King St. West, North Bay, ON P1B 5Z7
Tel: 705-494-3050
www.nbrhc.on.ca
Tanya Nixon, Vice-President, Mental Health

North Bay: **North Bay Regional Health Centre -
Mental Health Clinic**
Former Name: North Bay Psychiatric Hospital
120 King St. West, North Bay, ON P1B 5Z7
Tel: 705-494-3050 *Fax:* 705-494-3092
www.nbrhc.on.ca

Oakville: **Central West Specialized Developmental
Services**
Former Name: Oaklands Regional Centre
53 Bond St., Oakville, ON L6K 1L8
Tel: 905-844-7864 *Fax:* 905-844-3545
info@cwsds.ca
www.cwsds.ca
Year Founded: 1975
Note: Specialties: care & support to persons with multiple
developmental disabilities; basic life skill development;
psychiatry; behaviour therapy; occupational therapy; speech
therapy; respite care.
James Duncan, Executive Director

Ottawa: **Royal Ottawa Mental Health Centre**
1145 Carling Ave., Ottawa, ON K1Z 7K4
Tel: 613-722-6521 *Toll-Free:* 800-987-6424
www.theroyal.ca
www.facebook.com/TheRoyalMHC; twitter.com/TheRoyalMHC
Year Founded: 1910
Number of Beds: 190
Note: Affiliated with the University of Ottawa.
George Weber, President & CEO
Dr. Raj Bhatla, Psychiatrist-in-Chief & Chief of Staff
Dr. A.G. Ahmed, Associate Chief, Integrated Forensic Program
Cal Crocker, Chief Financial Officer
Joanne Bezzubetz, Vice-President, Patient Care Services
Nicole Loreto, Vice-President, Communications & Partnerships
Susan Engels, Chief Nursing Executive & Vice-President,
Quality & Professional Practice

Penetanguishene: **Waypoint Centre for Mental
Health Care**
Former Name: Penetanguishene Mental Health
Centre
500 Church St., Penetanguishene, ON L9M 1G3
Tel: 705-549-3181 *Fax:* 705-549-3778
Toll-Free: 877-341-4729
info@waypointcentre.ca
www.waypointcentre.ca
Year Founded: 1859
Number of Beds: 301 beds
Number of Employees: 1200
Specialties: Mental Health
Note: Offers psychiatric services to Simcoe County, Muskoka, &
parts of Dufferin County & Parry Sound.
Carol Lambie, President & CEO
Linda Adams, Chief Nursing Executive & Vice-President, Quality
& Professional Practice
Rob Desroches, Vice-President, Clinical Services
Lorraine Smith, Vice-President, Corporate Services
Terry McMahon, Vice-President, Human Resources &
Organizational Development
Bob Savage, Vice-President, Redevelopment
Deborah Duncan, Vice-President, Clinical Support Services
Dr. Jeff Van Impe, Psychiatrist-in-Chief

St. Thomas: **Southwest Centre for Forensic Mental
Health Care**
Affiliated with: St. Joseph's Health Care, London
401 Sunset Dr., St. Thomas, ON N5R 3C6
Tel: 519-646-6100
www.sjhc.london.on.ca
Dr. Gillian Kernaghan, President & CEO
askgillian@sjhc.london.on.ca

Sudbury: **North Bay Regional Health Centre
(NBRHC)/Centre régional de santé de North Bay
Kirkwood Place**
Former Name: Northeast Mental Health Centre,
Sudbury Campus
680 Kirkwood Dr., Sudbury, ON P3E 1X3
Tel: 705-675-9193 *Fax:* 705-675-6817
pr@nbrhc.on.ca
www.nbrhc.on.ca
www.facebook.com/nbrhc; twitter.com/nbrhc;
www.youtube.com/thenbrhc
Ann Loyst, Interim Vice-President, Mental Health

Sudbury: **Sudbury Mental Health and Addictions
Centre**
Kirkwood Place
Affiliated with: Health Sciences North
680 Kirkwood Dr., Sudbury, ON P3E 1X3
Tel: 705-675-5900
www.hsnsudbury.ca
Note: Acute inpatient psychiatry services.
Dominic Giroux, President & CEO, Health Sciences North

Toronto: **Bellwood Health Services**
Edgewood Health Network Inc.
Affiliated with: Toronto Central Local Health
Integration Network
175 Brentcliffe Rd., Toronto, ON M4G 0C5
Tel: 416-495-0926 *Fax:* 416-495-7943
Toll-Free: 800-387-6198
info@bellwood.ca
www.bellwood.ca
www.facebook.com/bellwoodhealthservices;
twitter.com/BellwoodHealth;
www.youtube.com/user/BellwoodHealth
Year Founded: 1984
Number of Beds: 88
Specialties: Addiction & eating disorders
Note: Serves men & women aged 19 years & over. Programs &
services include: treatment & education for individuals & families
struggling with addictions, including alcohol & drugs, gambling,
sex, eating disorders, workplace trauma with or without
concurrent addiction; assessments; detox services; funded
residential treatment program for alcohol addiction of Ontario
residents with valid OHIP card; continuing care programs; family
services; & outpatient individual & group counselling services.
Cara Vaccarino, Chief Operating Officer
cvaccarino@bellwood.ca
Kristen Cleary, Clinical Director
kcleary@bellwood.ca
Joshua Montgomery, Operations Director
jmontgomery@bellwood.ca

Toronto: **Community Outreach Services (COS)**
Michael Garron Hospital
671 Danforth Ave., 2nd Fl., Toronto, ON M4J 1L3
Tel: 416-461-2000
community@tegh.on.ca
www.tegh.on.ca
Note: Specialties: community based mental health services;
counselling to adults; supported housing; psychiatric treatment;
psycho-social rehabilitation; family support program; community
& school outreach program.

Toronto: **Youthdale Treatment Centres**
227 Victoria St., Toronto, ON M5B 1T8
Tel: 416-368-4896
www.youthdale.ca
Year Founded: 1969
Note: Youthdale provides mental health services to
approximately 5,000 children & their families each year. A crisis
service line is available (416-363-9990). The non-profit,
charitable community agency also offers clinical services,
including psychiatric crisis response, residential treatment, &
outpatient consultation.

Waterloo: **Children's Mental Health Services
Lutherwood**
285 Benjamin Rd., Waterloo, ON N2J 3Z4
Tel: 519-884-1470
www.lutherwood.ca
Note: Specialties: Day treatment program; Residential treatment
program; Group & individual skills training; Individual & family

counselling; Home support; Community integration; Crisis
support

Waterloo: **Lutherwood**
285 Benjamin Rd., Waterloo, ON N2J 3Z4
Tel: 519-884-7755 *Fax:* 519-884-9071
www.lutherwood.ca
www.facebook.com/lutherwoodjobs; twitter.com/lutherwood;
www.youtube.com/user/LutherwoodCanada;
www.linkedin.com/company/lutherwood
Year Founded: 1970
Number of Employees: 500
Note: Specialties: Mental health services for children & families,
including assessment, a youth shelter, housing support services,
residential treatment, family crisis & prevention counselling, a
community services program, & school-based interventions;
Senior services, including independent & supported living
resources
John Colangeli, CEO

Whitby: **Ontario Shores Centre for Mental Health
Sciences**
Former Name: Whitby Mental Health Centre
700 Gordon St., Whitby, ON L1N 5S9
Tel: 905-430-4055 *Toll-Free:* 800-341-6323
centralizedreferral@ontarioshores.ca
www.ontarioshores.ca
Year Founded: 1919
Number of Employees: 1200
Specialties: Mental Health
Note: Specialized, tertiary mental health care on an inpatient /
outpatient basis. Community service sites in Newmarket,
Lindsay, Peterborough, & Whitby.
Karim Mamdani, President & CEO

Special Care Homes

Aurora: **Kerry's Place Autism Services**
34 Berczy St., Aurora, ON L4G 1W9
Tel: 905-841-6611
info@kerrysplace.org
www.kerrysplace.org
Year Founded: 1974
Note: Autistic adults home.
Dr. Sue Vandevelde-Coke, President and CEO

Aurora: **York Hills Centre for Children, Youth &
Families**
402 Bloomington Rd., Aurora, ON L4G 0L9
Tel: 905-503-9560 *Fax:* 905-773-8133
Toll-Free: 866-536-7608
yorkhills@yorkhills.ca
www.yorkhills.ca
Note: Children's mental health centre; special care home;
outpatient services; family therapy
Dean Rokos, Executive Director

Belleville: **Cheshire Homes (Hastings - Prince
Edward) Inc.**
41 Pinnacle St. South, Belleville, ON K8N 3A1
Tel: 613-966-2941 *Fax:* 613-966-2461
receptionist@cheshirehpe.ca
www.cheshirehpe.ca
Year Founded: 1973
Note: Cheshire Homes offers support housing & an outreach
program to physically disabled adults.

Brantford: **Participation Support Services**
Former Name: Participation House Brantford
PO Box 2048, 10 Bell Lane, Brantford, ON N3T 5W5
Tel: 519-756-1430
www.pssbrantford.org
Number of Beds: 30 beds
Note: Non-for-profit organization serving the needs of adults with
physical disabilities
Sherry Kerr, Executive Director
519-756-1430, skerr@pssbrantford.org

Cochrane: **Cochrane Community Living**
PO Box 2330, 18 - 2nd Ave., Cochrane, ON P0L 1C0
Tel: 705-272-2999
www.communitylivingontario.ca
Number of Beds: 12 beds in 3 facilities
Mac Hiltz, Interim Executive Director

Cornwall: **Open Hands Residential Services**
17383 South Branch Rd., Cornwall, ON K6K 1T3
Tel: 613-933-0012 *Fax:* 613-932-5134
www.ocapdd.on.ca
Note: The non-profit agency offers both residential & daytime
community support services to persons with development
disabilities. Open Hands is operated by the Ottawa Carleton

Association for Persons with Developmental Disabilities (OCAPDD).
David A. Ferguson, Executive Director
dferguson@ocapdd.on.ca

Dryden: Patricia Gardens Care Home
35 Van Horne Ave., Dryden, ON P8N 3B4
Tel: 807-223-5278 *Fax:* 807-223-5273
info@drydenseniorservices.ca
www.drydenseniorservices.ca
Penney Bradley, Program Coordinator
penney.bradley@drytel.net

East Garafraxa: Dufferin Association for Community Living
065371 County Rd. 3, East Garafraxa, ON L9W 7J8
Tel: 519-941-8971 *Fax:* 519-941-9121
info@communitylivingdufferin.ca
www.communitylivingdufferin.ca
www.facebook.com/communitylivingdufferin;
twitter.com/cldufferin; www.youtube.com/user/CLDufferin/videos
Note: Dufferin Association for Community Living assists children & adults with developmental disabilities.
Residential services include supported independent living, the operation of group homes & a home for adults with Prader Willi Syndrome, a family home program, a transitional living co-operative, & respite care. The association's group homes provide accommodations for 56 adults with developmental disablties.
Sheryl Chandler, Executive Director
sheryl@communitylivingdufferin.ca
Diane Slater, Director, Adult Services
diane@communitylivingdufferin.ca
Ann Somerville, Director, Business & Finance
ann@communitylivingdufferin.ca
Karen Bowen, Manager, Preschool Resource Program
karen@communitylivingdufferin.ca
Nadene Buck, Manager, Residential
nadene@communitylivingdufferin.ca
Joyce Cook, Manager, Options
joyce@communitylivingdufferin.ca
Teresa Donaldson, Manager, Systems
teresa@communitylivingdufferin.ca
Darlene Morrow, Manager, Residential
darlene@communitylivingdufferin.ca
Lindsay Pendleton, Manager, Residential
lindsay@communitylivingdufferin.ca
Catherine Ryan, Manager, Residential
cryan@communitylivingdufferin.ca
Denyse Small, Manager, Employment Services
denyse@communitylivingdufferin.ca

Gravenhurst: Doe Lake Residence
1750 Gravenhurst Pkwy., Gravenhurst, ON P1P 1R3
Tel: 705-687-6285 *Fax:* 705-687-0100
doelakeresidence@hotmail.com
Angie Joseph, Manager

Hamilton: Good Shepherd Centre
PO Box 1003, 10 Delaware Ave., Hamilton, ON L8N 3R1
Tel: 905-528-9109 *Fax:* 905-528-6967
info@goodshepherdcentres.ca
www.goodshepherdcentres.ca
Year Founded: 1961
Richard MacPhee, Executive Director

Hamilton: Lynwood Charlton Centre
Former Name: Lynwood Hall Child & Family Centre
526 Upper Paradise Rd., Hamilton, ON L9C 5E3
Tel: 905-389-1361 *Fax:* 905-389-8765
info@lynwoodcharlton.ca
www.lynwoodcharlton.ca
Note: Specialties: Mental health services, including day treatment, home-based services, & residential services

Hanover: Community Living Hanover
521 - 11th Ave., Hanover, ON N4N 2J3
Tel: 519-364-6100 *Fax:* 519-364-7488
www.clhanover.com
Number of Beds: 15 beds
Jeff Pilkington, Executive Director

Holland Landing: Cedar Lane Residential Home
19704 Holland Landing Rd., Holland Landing, ON L9N 1M8
Tel: 905-836-4272 *Fax:* 905-836-8277
Cathy Dowling, Contact

Holland Landing: Porter Place, Men's Shelter
18838 Hwy. 11, Holland Landing, ON L9N 0C5
Tel: 905-898-1015 *Fax:* 905-898-6414
Toll-Free: 888-554-5525
www.bluedoorshelters.ca
Number of Beds: 19 beds

Monica Auerbach, Executive Director

Keswick: Pipe & Slipper Home
2926 Old Homestead Rd., Keswick, ON L4P 3E9
Tel: 905-989-0907
Note: Residential care is provided for adults. Referral is necessary.

Kitchener: Sunbeam Lodge
389 Pinnacle Dr., Kitchener, ON N2G 3W5
Tel: 519-896-6718 *Fax:* 519-748-5537
www.sunbeamlodge.com
Number of Beds: 22 beds
Note: Specialties: Lont-term residential care & treatment for children with special needs; Day program; Physiotherapy treatment; Kinesiology; Communications programs; Independent living skills program. Number of Employees: 9 Registered Nurses & Registered Practical Nurses + 2 Kinessiologists + 1 Program Coordinator + 21 Child Care Attendants + 1 Dietician + 2 Housekeepers + 1 Executive Secretary
John Vos, Administrator
jvos@sunbeamlodge.com
Shabnam Vos, Administrator

Kitchener: Sunbeam Residential Development Centre
2749 Kingsway Dr., Kitchener, ON N2C 1A7
Tel: 519-893-6200 *Fax:* 519-893-9034
www.sunbeamcentre.com
Year Founded: 1956
Note: Specialties: Care for individuals with diverse & complex developmental challenges; Long-term & short-term support; Activation; Sensory stimulation

Lucan: Crest Support Services
13570 Elginfield Rd., RR#1, Lucan, ON N0M 2J0
Tel: 519-227-6766 *Fax:* 519-227-6768
www.crestsupportservices.ca
Note: Specialties: Services for adults with mental health or developmental disabilities; Accommodation services; Operation of three small businesses to provide training & employment opportunities
Agnieszka Ciszewska, Executive Director
agnieszka@crestsupportservices.ca

Markham: Kinark Child & Family Services
Corporate Office, #200, 500 Hood Rd., Markham, ON L3R 9Z3
Tel: 905-474-9595 *Fax:* 905-474-1448
Toll-Free: 800-230-8533
info@kinark.on.ca
www.kinark.on.ca
www.facebook.com/kinark; twitter.com/mykinark;
www.youtube.com/user/mykinark
Year Founded: 1916
Number of Employees: 800
Note: Services include crisis services, therapeutic family programs, child care, day treatment, residential treatment, adventure-based programming, autism services, & youth justice services.
Cathy Paul, President & CEO

Markham: Participation House
#402, 379 Church St., Markham, ON L6B 0T1
Tel: 905-294-1008 *Fax:* 905-294-4471
postmaster@participationhouse.net
www.participationhouse.net
Number of Beds: 52 beds
Note: Provides services designed to enhance the qualify of life of people with disabilities
Shelley Brillinger, Executive Director
shelley.brilinger@participationhouse.net

Nepean: Total Communication Environment (TCE)
#5, 203 Colonnade Rd. South, Nepean, ON K2E 7K3
Tel: 613-228-0999 *Fax:* 613-228-1402
TTY: 613-228-8669
tceadmin@tceottawa.org
www.tceottawa.org
Year Founded: 1979
Note: Specialties: Services for adults with multiple disabilities & special communication needs; Respite care; Day services; Outreach to long-term care homes
Karen Anderson, Executive Director

Newmarket: Brigitta's Residential Home Inc.
128 Arden Ave., Newmarket, ON L3Y 4H6
Tel: 905-895-5890
Number of Beds: 22 beds
Note: A home for women with mental health concerns; no nursing care provdied.
Brigitta Miller, Administrator

Newmarket: Brown's Residential Home
399 Queen St., Newmarket, ON L3Y 2G9
Tel: 905-898-1955 *Fax:* 905-898-1955
Note: Supportive residential care is provided for adults.

Newmarket: Heritage Lodge
508 College St., Newmarket, ON L3Y 1C6
Tel: 905-853-1587 *Fax:* 905-853-1587
Note: Heritage Lodge is a home for special care to assist persons with a mental health disability.

North Bay: Community Living North Bay
161 Main St. East, North Bay, ON P1B 1A9
Tel: 705-476-3288 *Fax:* 705-476-4788
info@communitylivingnorthbay.org
www.communitylivingnorthbay.org
Year Founded: 1954
Jennifer Valenti, Executive Director

Ottawa: Roberts/Smart Centre
1199 Carling Ave., Ottawa, ON K1Z 8N8
Tel: 613-728-1946 *Fax:* 613-728-4986
Toll-Free: 800-279-9941
info@rsc-crs.com
www.robertssmartcentre.com
Number of Beds: 47 beds

Owen Sound: Kent Residential Home
Former Name: Tucker's Residential Home
1065 - 9th Ave. West, Owen Sound, ON N4K 2G5
Tel: 519-371-5029 *Fax:* 519-371-3237
Number of Beds: 18 beds
Note: Residential home for people with mental illness.
Yvonne Kent

Peterborough: Community Living Peterborough
223 Aylmer St., Peterborough, ON K9J 3K3
Tel: 705-743-2411 *Fax:* 705-743-3722
www.communitylivingpeterborough.ca
www.facebook.com/CommunityLivingPtbo;
twitter.com/CLPeterborough;
www.youtube.com/user/CommunityLivingPtbo
Year Founded: 1953
Note: The following services are provided: supported housing for adults over the age of 21; family support; community access; & employment options.
Jack Gillan, Chief Executive Officer
Barb Hiland, Director, Operations
Cindy Hobbins, Manager, Community Development, Communications, & Quality Enhancement
Pat McNamara, Manager
Edna O'Toole, General Manager, Supportive Housing

Petrolia: Lambton County Developmental Services
Former Name: Lambton County Association for Mentally Handicapped
PO Box 1210, 339 Centre St., Petrolia, ON N0N 1R0
Tel: 519-882-0933 *Fax:* 519-882-3386
administration@lcds.on.ca
www.lcds.on.ca
Number of Beds: 68 beds
Note: Provides services to persons with intellectual disabilities
Tom McCallum, Executive Director
tmccallum@lcds.on.ca

Powassan: Eide's Residential Home
PO Box 459, 532 Main St., Powassan, ON P0H 1Z0
Tel: 705-724-2748 *Fax:* 705-724-5721

Saint-Pascal-Baylon: St. Pascal Residential Home
2454 du Lac Rd., RR#1, Saint-Pascal-Baylon, ON K0A 3N0
Tel: 613-488-2626 *Fax:* 613-488-2626
admin@stpascalresidence.com
www.stpascalresidence.com
Note: Long-term or short-term support for adults over the age of 18 who are suffering from mental health or developmental disabilities.Individualized care plans include nursing, medication management, assistance with activities of daily life.

Severn Bridge: Trentview House
1647 Kilworthy Rd., RR#1, Severn Bridge, ON L0K 2B0
Tel: 705-689-5685
Year Founded: 1979
Number of Beds: 25 beds
Note: Specialties: Services for adults with mental health disabilities

St. Catharines: Montebello Place
Former Name: Horvath Residence
1 Montebello St., St. Catharines, ON L2R 6B5
Tel: 905-984-6506
Year Founded: 1973
Number of Beds: 15 beds

Note: Housing care & residential treatment supports for adults with a mental illness; nursing care available 24/7.
John Gaspar, Co-Owner
johngas@gmail.com
Lindsay Gaspar, Co-Owner

St. Thomas: **New Beginnings Residence**
Former Name: Tara Hall Residential Care Home
38 Chester St., St. Thomas, ON N5R 1V2
Tel: 519-631-4937 Fax: 519-631-1526
newbeginningsresidence@gmail.com
Year Founded: 1988
Number of Beds: 36 beds
Note: Specialties: Assisted living for adults with an intellectual disability, brain injury, or mental illness
Sandra Ferguson, Owner
Trudy Marchand, Manager

Thorold: **Bethesda Home for the Mentally Handicapped Inc.**
3280 Schmon Pkwy., Thorold, ON L2V 4Y6
Tel: 905-684-6918 Fax: 905-684-6918
info@bethesdaservices.com
www.bethesdaservices.com
Donald Boese, Executive Director

Thunder Bay: **Marcinowsky Residential Home**
601 Alice Ave., RR#14, Thunder Bay, ON P7G 1X1
Tel: 807-767-6199

Toronto: **Community Head Injury Resource Services (CHIRS)**
Former Name: Ashby House
62 Finch Ave. West, Toronto, ON M2N 7G1
Tel: 416-240-8000 Fax: 416-240-1149
Chirs@chirs.com
www.chirs.com
www.facebook.com/chirstoronto
Year Founded: 1974
Number of Employees: 160
Note: A range of residential services are offered for persons living with the effects of acquired brain injury. Community Head Injury Resource Services serves the Greater Toronto Area.
Hedy Chandler, Contact
hedyc@rogers.com

Toronto: **Griffin Centre**
24 Silverview Dr., Toronto, ON M2M 2B3
Tel: 416-222-1153 Fax: 416-222-1321
contact@griffin-centre.org
www.griffin-centre.org
Number of Beds: 10 beds
Note: Dedicated to promoting positive change for vulnerable youth & adults with mental health challenges; focused on creating an atmosphere of respect, inclusion, diversity.

Toronto: **Salvation Army Broadview Village**
1132 Broadview Ave., Toronto, ON M4K 2S5
Tel: 416-425-1052 Toll-Free: 888-333-1229
www.salvationarmy.ca
Number of Beds: 61 beds
Note: Facility for adults with developmental disabilities

Toronto: **The SickKids Centre for Community Mental Health**
Former Name: Hincks-Dellcrest Treatment Centre
440 Jarvis St., Toronto, ON M4Y 2H4
Tel: 416-924-1164 Fax: 416-924-8208
info@sickkidscmh.ca
www.sickkidscmh.ca
www.facebook.com/gailappelinstitute; twitter.com/hdcinstitute
Note: Children's mental health services.
Christina Bartha, Executive Director

Vars: **Pine Rest Residence**
PO Box 109, 5876 Bearbrook Rd., Vars, ON K0A 3H0
Tel: 613-835-2849 Fax: 613-835-9335
Number of Beds: 33 residential capacity
Note: Specialties: Residential care for persons with developmental disabilities, psychiatric disabilities, or those who suffer from alcoholism; Medication supervision; Respite care

Vars: **Résidence Ste-Marie/Ste-Marie Residence**
5855, rue Buckland RR#2, Vars, ON K0H 3H0
Tel: 613-835-2525
Number of Beds: 40 lits
Note: Spécialisée à la prestation des soins aux personnes atteintes de maladie mentale grave; soins infirmiers, activités hebdomadaires
Gaétan Brisson, Propriétaire
Suzanne Brisson, Propriétaire

Waterloo: **Underhill Residential Home**
127 Erb St. West, Waterloo, ON N2L 1T7
Tel: 519-884-7160 Fax: 519-884-5936
Note: Specialties: Residential & personal care services for seniors & persons with mental health concerns
Tanya Tompkins, Administrator
tompkins4@sympatico.ca

Prince Edward Island

Government Departments in Charge

Charlottetown: **Prince Edward Island Department of Health & Wellness**
4th Fl. North, Shaw Bldg., 105 Rochford St., Charlottetown, PE C1A 7N8
Tel: 902-368-6414 Fax: 902-368-4121
DeptHW@gov.pe.ca
www.princeedwardisland.ca/en/topic/health-and-wellness
Hon. Ernie Hudson, Minister, Health & Wellness
902-368-5250, Fax: 902-368-4121,
ehhudsonminister@gov.pe.ca

Regional Health Authorities

Charlottetown: **Health PEI**
PO Box 2000, 16 Garfield St., Charlottetown, PE C1A 7N8
Tel: 902-368-6130 Fax: 902-368-6136
healthpei@gov.pe.ca
www.healthpei.ca
Info Line: 811
twitter.com/health_pei
Year Founded: 2010
Number of Beds: 598 long-term care beds
Area Served: Province-wide *Population Served:* 152021 *Number of Employees:* 4724
Note: Health PEI is responsible for the operation & delivery of publicly funded health services & long term care in Prince Edward Island.
Derek Key, Chair, Board of Directors
Dr. Michael Gardam, Chief Executive Officer

Hospitals - General

Alberton: **Western Hospital**
Affiliated with: Health PEI
PO Box 10, 148 Poplar St., Alberton, PE C0B 1B0
Tel: 902-853-8650 Fax: 902-853-8658
www.healthpei.ca/westernhospital
twitter.com/Health_PEI
Number of Beds: 27 beds (25 medical, 2 palliative)
Population Served: 8000
Note: Services include: addiction; diagnostic imaging; dialysis; laboratory; pharmacy; physiotherapy; & nutrition counselling.

Charlottetown: **Queen Elizabeth Hospital Inc. (QEH)**
Affiliated with: Health PEI
PO Box 6600, 60 Riverside Dr., Charlottetown, PE C1A 8T5
Tel: 902-894-2111
www.healthpei.ca/qeh
twitter.com/Health_PEI
Year Founded: 1982
Number of Beds: 243 beds
Note: Acute care hospital, with burn care services; coronary care; psychiatry; physiotherapy; occupational therapy; orthpedic & specialized gynecological surgery; eye surgery; plastic surgery; neonatal intensive care; cancer care; diagnostic imaging.
Denise Lewis Fleming, CEO, Health PEI

Montague: **King's County Memorial Hospital**
Affiliated with: Health PEI
PO Box 490, 409 MacIntyre Ave., Montague, PE C0A 1R0
Tel: 902-838-0777 Fax: 902-838-0770
www.healthpei.ca/kcmh
twitter.com/Health_PEI
Number of Beds: 30 beds
Note: Services include: emergency; inpatient; & ambulatory care.

O'Leary: **Community Hospital O'Leary**
Affiliated with: Health PEI
PO Box 160, 14 MacKinnon Dr., O'Leary, PE C0B 1V0
Tel: 902-859-8700 Fax: 902-859-8774
www.healthpei.ca/cho
twitter.com/Health_PEI
Year Founded: 1957
Number of Beds: 13 extended care beds
Note: Services include: diagnostic imaging; laboratory; pharmacy; physiotherapy; & nutrition counselling.

Souris: **Souris Hospital**
Affiliated with: Health PEI
PO Box 640, 17 Knights Ave., Souris, PE C0A 2B0
Tel: 902-687-7150 Fax: 902-687-7175
www.healthpei.ca
twitter.com/Health_PEI
Number of Beds: 17 beds
Population Served: 7000
Note: Acute care rural facility. Services include: addiction; ambulatory; diabetes program; diagnostic imaging; extended care; home care; mental health; palliative care; renal program; & public health nursing.

Summerside: **Prince County Hospital (PCH)**
Affiliated with: Health PEI
PO Box 3000, 65 Roy Boates Ave., Summerside, PE C1N 2A9
Tel: 902-438-4200 Fax: 902-438-4511
www.healthpei.ca/pch
twitter.com/Health_PEI
Number of Beds: 110 beds
Note: Services include: ambulatory care; emergency; hemodialysis; inpatient mental health; intensive care; obstetrics; & pediatrics.
Arlene Gallant-Bernard, Chief Administrative Officer
902-438-4514, algallant-bernard@gov.pe.ca

Tyne Valley: **Stewart Memorial Hospital**
Affiliated with: Health PEI
PO Box 10, 6926 rte 12, Tyne Valley, PE C0B 2C0
Tel: 902-831-7900 Fax: 902-831-7901
www.healthpei.ca
twitter.com/Health_PEI
Number of Beds: 23 beds
Note: Services include: nursing; medical; dental care; nutrition; podiatry; occupational therapy; & physiotherapy.

Community Health Care Centres

Montague: **Home Care Support - Health PEI Montague**
Affiliated with: Health PEI
6 Harmony Lane, Montague, PE C0A 1R0
Tel: 902-838-0786

O'Leary: **Home Care Support - Community Hospital**
Affiliated with: Health PEI
14 MacKinnon Dr., O'Leary, PE C0B 1V0
Tel: 902-859-8730

Special Treatment Centres

Charlottetown: **Euston Street Group Home**
Affiliated with: Health PEI
190 Euston St., Charlottetown, PE C1A 1W8
Tel: 902-566-2964
Note: Respite care is available for adolescents who are in the care of the Director of Child Welfare.

Charlottetown: **Provincial Addictions Treatment Facility**
PO Box 2000, 2814 rte 215, Mt. Herbert, Charlottetown, PE C1A 7N8
Tel: 902-368-4120 Fax: 902-368-6229
Toll-Free: 888-299-8399
www.healthpei.ca
Number of Beds: 24 withdrawal management beds; 16 rehab beds
Specialties: Medically supervised detoxification

Tracadie Cross: **Provincial Adolescent Group Home**
171 Station Rd., Tracadie Cross, PE C1A 7N8
Tel: 902-676-3242 Fax: 902-676-3241
Number of Beds: 9 beds; 1 emergency 72-hour bed
Note: Adolescent residential treatment

Long Term Care Facilities

Alberton: **Partners in Action**
Affiliated with: Health PEI
120 Dufferin St., Alberton, PE C0B 1B0
Tel: 902-853-3109
Note: community care & beds

Belfast: **Dr. John Gillis Memorial Lodge**
3134 Garfield Rd., Belfast, PE C0A 1A0
Tel: 902-659-2337 Fax: 902-659-2865
www.gillislodge.com
Number of Beds: 68 nursing care beds; 13 community care beds
Note: Library updated monthly; a pet bird lives on-site.
Douglas MacKenzie
douglas@gillislodge.com

Charlottetown: Andrews of Charlottetown
Affiliated with: Health PEI
73 Malpeque Rd., Charlottetown, PE C1A 7J9
Tel: 902-368-2790 *Fax:* 902-894-3464
andrewsseniorcare.com/charlottetown
Number of Beds: 72 beds
Note: Community care beds

Charlottetown: Champion Lodge
Affiliated with: Health PEI
48 Green St., Charlottetown, PE C1A 2E8
Tel: 902-894-8968

Charlottetown: Charlotte Residence
Affiliated with: Health PEI
39 All Souls Lane, Charlottetown, PE C1A 1P9
Tel: 902-894-8134

Charlottetown: Corrigan Lodge
Affiliated with: Health PEI
8 Ellis Rd., Charlottetown, PE C1A 8N4
Tel: 902-894-7837
Note: community care beds
Noreen Corrigan, Contact

Charlottetown: Langille House
Affiliated with: Health PEI
#212, 214 Kent St., Charlottetown, PE C1A 1P2
Tel: 902-628-8228
Note: community care beds

Charlottetown: McQuaid Lodge
Affiliated with: Health PEI
36 Kent St., Charlottetown, PE C1A 1M8
Tel: 902-892-0791

Charlottetown: Old Rose Lodge
Affiliated with: Health PEI
319 Queen St., Charlottetown, PE C1A 4C4
Tel: 902-368-8313 *Fax:* 902-368-8313

Charlottetown: Stamper Residence
Affiliated with: Health PEI
29 Fitzroy St., Charlottetown, PE C1A 1R2
Tel: 902-894-3815
Joyce Pickles, Administrator

Charlottetown: Tenderwood Lodge Inc.
Affiliated with: Health PEI
15 Hawthorne Ave., Charlottetown, PE C1A 5X8
Tel: 902-566-5174

Crapaud: South Shore Villa
Affiliated with: Health PEI
PO Box 111, Sherwood Forest Dr., RR#2, Crapaud, PE C0A 1J0
Tel: 902-658-2228 *Fax:* 902-658-2576
info@southshorevilla.ca
www.southshorevilla.ca

Georgetown: Carroll's Lodge
Affiliated with: Health PEI
PO Box 133, 110 Gordon St., Georgetown, PE C0A 1L0
Tel: 902-652-2369

Hunter River: Rosewood Residence
Affiliated with: Health PEI
PO Box 97, 4260 Hopedale Rd., Route 13, Hunter River, PE C0A 1N0
Tel: 902-964-2436 *Fax:* 902-964-2436
www.rosewoodresidence.ca
Note: community care beds

Kensington: MacEwen Mews Seniors Residence
Affiliated with: Health PEI
RR#6, Kensington, PE C0B 1M0
Tel: 902-836-4678

Miscouche: Miscouche Community Care Villa
Affiliated with: Health PEI
PO Box 40, 20 Lady Slipper Dr. North, Miscouche, PE C0B 1T0
Tel: 902-436-1946 *Fax:* 902-436-3215
Note: community care beds

Montague: MacKinnon Pines Lodge
Affiliated with: Health PEI
PO Box 847, Montague, PE C0A 1R0
Tel: 902-838-2656 *Fax:* 902-838-3542

O'Leary: Lady Slipper Villa
Affiliated with: Health PEI
490 Main St., O'Leary, PE C0B 1V0
Tel: 902-859-3544 *Fax:* 902-859-3255
ladyslippervilla@peiseniorshomes.com
ladyslippervilla.peiseniorshomes.com/ladyslippervilla
Note: community care beds
Karen Cook, Administrator

Souris: Bayview Lodge Community Care Facility
Affiliated with: Health PEI
22 Washington St., Souris, PE C0A 2R0
Tel: 902-687-3122 *Fax:* 902-687-3512
Note: community care beds
Gerard Arsenault, Contact

Summerside: Andrews of Summerside
Affiliated with: Health PEI
317 Pope Rd., Summerside, PE C1N 6G4
Tel: 902-436-0859 *Fax:* 902-436-1565
info@andrewsofpei.com
www.andrewsofpei.com/andrews-of-summerside.php
Note: community care facility

Summerside: MacDonald's Community Care Home Inc.
Affiliated with: Health PEI
197 Cambridge St., Summerside, PE C1N 1N1
Tel: 902-436-7359 *Fax:* 902-436-7359
Gail MacDonald, Contact

Tignish: Tignish Seniors Home Care Cooperative Limited
Affiliated with: Health PEI
116 MacLeod Lane, Tignish, PE C0B 2B0
Tel: 902-882-4663
Year Founded: 2002
Note: Specialty: Assisted living

Nursing Homes

Alberton: Maplewood Manor
Affiliated with: Health PEI
PO Box 400, 405 Church St., Alberton, PE C0B 1B0
Tel: 902-853-8610 *Fax:* 902-853-8616
Number of Beds: 48 beds

Charlottetown: Beach Grove Home
Affiliated with: Health PEI
200 Beach Grove Rd., Charlottetown, PE C1E 1L3
Tel: 902-368-6750 *Fax:* 902-368-6764
Number of Beds: 131 beds

Charlottetown: Garden Home
Affiliated with: Health PEI
310 North River Rd., Charlottetown, PE C1A 3M4
Tel: 902-892-4131 *Fax:* 902-892-7326
office@peiseniorshomes.com
gardenhome.peiseniorshomes.com/gardenhome
Note: private
Phyllis Johnson, General Manager, Director of Care
generalmanager@peiseniorshomes.com

Charlottetown: Lennox Nursing Home
140 Water St., Charlottetown, PE C1A 1A7
Tel: 902-894-4968 *Fax:* 902-368-2004
Note: private

Charlottetown: MacMillan Lodge Ltd.
Affiliated with: Health PEI
215 Sydney St., Charlottetown, PE C1A 1J5
Tel: 902-894-7173 *Fax:* 902-894-3818
mlnursing@peiseniorshomes.com
Year Founded: 1999
Ann MacNeill, Director, Care

Charlottetown: Park West Lodge
Affiliated with: Health PEI
22 Richmond St., Charlottetown, PE C1A 1H4
Tel: 902-566-2260 *Fax:* 902-894-7818
Gerry MacPhee, Contact

Charlottetown: PEI Atlantic Baptist Homes Inc.
Affiliated with: Health PEI
16 Centennial Dr., Charlottetown, PE C1A 5C5
Tel: 902-566-5975
www.abschi.com
Note: Specialty: Long-term care by an interdisciplinary team

Charlottetown: The Prince Edward Home
Affiliated with: Health PEI
75 Maypoint Rd., Charlottetown, PE C1E 3H1
Tel: 902-368-4607 *Fax:* 902-368-5646
www.healthpei.ca/pehome
Number of Beds: 120 beds
Note: Palliative care, convalescent, respite care; long-term care; day program for seniors; meals-on-wheels program

Montague: Riverview Manor
Affiliated with: Health PEI
PO Box 820, 14 Rosedale Rd., Montague, PE C0A 1R0
Tel: 902-838-0772 *Fax:* 902-838-5294
www.healthpei.ca/riverviewmanor
Number of Beds: 49 beds
Note: Long-term & palliative care

Souris: Colville Manor
Affiliated with: Health PEI
PO Box 640, 20 MacPhee Ave., Souris, PE C0A 2B0
Tel: 902-687-7090 *Fax:* 902-687-7103
www.healthpei.ca/colvillemanor
Number of Beds: 52 beds; 4 households, each with 13 residents in this facility

Summerside: Summerset Manor
Affiliated with: Health PEI
15 Frank Mellish St., Summerside, PE C1N 0H3
Tel: 902-888-8310 *Fax:* 902-888-8338
Number of Beds: 82 beds
Note: Specialties: Long-term care; Operation of the Chapman Centre, a day program that provides therapeutic services to seniors who live in their own home; Physiotherapy; Occupational therapy; Foot care; Respite care

Summerside: Wedgewood Manor
Affiliated with: Health PEI
310 Brophy St., Summerside, PE C1N 5N4
Tel: 902-888-8340 *Fax:* 902-888-8369
www.healthpei.ca/wedgewoodmanor
Number of Beds: 76 beds

Personal Care Homes

Charlottetown: Corrigan Lodge / Corrigan Home Inc.
Affiliated with: Health PEI
8 Ellis Rd., Charlottetown, PE C1A 8N4
Tel: 902-894-7837
Note: The licensed community care facility is privately owned & operated.
Noreen Corrigan, Contact

Charlottetown: Elm Crest Lodge
Affiliated with: Health PEI
267 Richmond St., Charlottetown, PE C1A 1J7
Tel: 902-566-5996
Note: Elm Crest Lodge is a privately owned community care facility, licensed in Prince Edward Island.

Kensington: Clinton View Lodge
PO Box 8, Kensington, PE C0B 1M0
Tel: 902-866-2276 *Fax:* 902-886-2073
Note: The community care facility is privately owned. It is located at 30 Clinton View Court in Clinton.
Sherry Cole, Contact

Wellington: La Coopérative Le Chez-Nous Ltée
Affiliated with: Health PEI
PO Box 40, 64 Sunset Dr., Wellington, PE C0B 2E0
Tel: 902-854-3426 *Fax:* 902-854-3055
cheznous@pei.aibn.com
Year Founded: 1993
Area Served: Évangéline region
Note: The community care facility is privately owned & operated. French is spoken at the housing complex.
Edgar Arsenault, Director

Mental Health Hospitals/Facilities

Charlottetown: Hillsborough Hospital & Special Care Centre
Affiliated with: Health PEI
PO Box 1929, 115 Deacon Grove Lane, Charlottetown, PE C1A 7N5
Tel: 902-368-5400 *Fax:* 902-368-5467
Number of Beds: 69 beds
Note: Specialties: Psychiatry; Medical services for persons with acute or long-term mental illnesses or mental handicaps, & psychogeriatric patients; Day services for former patients; Assessment; Behavioural management

Charlottetown: Sherwood Home
Affiliated with: Health PEI
75 Murchison Lane, Charlottetown, PE C1A 7N5
Tel: 902-368-4141 *Fax:* 902-368-4931
Number of Beds: 14 beds
Note: Sherwood Home is a provincial residential service for persons with physical and/or developmental disabilities. The home offers residential, respite and day program services.

Québec

Département gouvernemental responsable

Québec: Ministère de la Santé et des services sociaux/Ministry of Health & Social Services
1075, ch Sainte-Foy, Québec, QC G1S 2M1
Tél: 418-266-7171 *Téléc:* 418-266-7197
ministre@msss.gouv.qc.ca
www.msss.gouv.qc.ca

Hon. Christian Dubé, Ministre
Hon. Lionel Carmant, Ministre délégué
Hon. Marguerite Blais, Ministre responsable, Aînés et des Proches aidants

Agences de la santé et de services sociaux

Baie-Comeau: Centre intégré de santé et de services sociaux de la Côte-Nord
Également connu sous le nom de: CISSS de la Côte-Nord
835, boul Jolliet, Baie-Comeau, QC G5C 1P5
Tél: 418-589-9845 *Téléc:* 418-589-8574
Ligne sans frais: 800-463-5142
www.cisss-cotenord.gouv.qc.ca
Info Line: 811
www.facebook.com/cisss.cotenord;
www.linkedin.com/company/cisss-cotenord
Région desservi: Tadoussac à Blanc-Sablon, 1,300 km
Population desservi: 95000
Marc Fortin, Président-directeur général

Cap-aux-Meules: Centre intégré de santé et de services sociaux des Iles
Également connu sous le nom de: CISSS des Iles
430, ch Principal, Cap-aux-Meules, QC G4T 1R9
Tél: 418-986-2121 *Téléc:* 418-986-6845
www.cisssdesiles.com
www.facebook.com/cisssdesiles
Population desservi: 12475
Jasmine Martineau, Présidente-directrice générale

Châteauguay: Centre intégré de santé et de services sociaux de la Montérégie-Ouest
Également connu sous le nom de: CISSS de la Montérégie-Ouest
200, boul Brisebois, Châteauguay, QC J6K 4W8
Tél: 450-699-2425
www.santemo.quebec
Info Line: 811
www.facebook.com/cisssmo;
www.linkedin.com/company/cisss-monteregie-ouest
Fondée en: 2015
Région desservi: 3,727 sq km *Population desservi:* 460000
Personnel: 10000
Yves Masse, Président-directeur général
Claude Jolin, Président, Conseil d'administration

Chibougamau: Centre régional de santé et services sociaux de la Baie-James (CRSSSBJ)
Également connu sous le nom de: CRSSS de la Baie-James
312, 3e rue, Chibougamau, QC G8P 1N5
Tél: 418-748-3575 *Téléc:* 418-748-6391
Ligne sans frais: 866-748-2676
info.crsssbj@ssss.gouv.qc.ca
www.crsssbaiejames.gouv.qc.ca
www.facebook.com/CRSSSBJ
Fondée en: 1996
Région desservi: Nord-du-Québec (350,000 sq km)
Note: Centres de santé (CS): Centre de santé René-Ricard; Centre de santé de Chibougamau; Centre de santé Lebel; Centre de santé Isle-Dieu; Centre de santé de Radisson
Nathalie Boisvert, Présidente-directrice générale
Dr. Éric Goyer, Directeur, Santé publique
Jean-Luc Imbeault, Directeur, ressources financières, techniques et informationnelles
Jean Lemoyne, Directeur, services professionnels, et des services multidisciplinaires
Luc Néron, Directeur, soins infirmiers
Jean-Pierre Savary, Directeur, Ressources humaines

Chicoutimi: Centre intégré universitaire de santé et de services sociaux du Saguenay-Lac-St-Jean
Également connu sous le nom de: CIUSSS Saguenay-Lac-St-Jean
930, rue Jacques-Cartier est, Chicoutimi, QC G7H 7K9
Tél: 418-545-4980 *Téléc:* 418-545-8791
Ligne sans frais: 800-370-4980
info@santesaglac.gouv.qc.ca
santesaglac.gouv.qc.ca
Info Line: 811
www.facebook.com/SanteSagLac; twitter.com/CIUSSS_SLSJ;
www.linkedin.com/company/ciusss-saguenay-lac-saint-jean
Fondée en: 2015
Région desservi: 95,762 sq km *Population desservi:* 277406
Personnel: 10500
Julie Labbé, Présidente-directrice générale

Chisasibi: Conseil Cri de la santé et des services sociaux de la Baie James (CCSSSBJ)/Cree Board of Health & Social Services of James Bay
PO Box 250, Chisasibi, QC J0M 1E0
Tel: 819-855-2844 *Fax:* 819-855-2098
ccsssbj-cbhssjb@ssss.gouv.qc.ca
www.creehealth.org
www.facebook.com/creehealth; twitter.com/creehealth;
www.youtube.com/creehealth
Year Founded: 1978
Area Served: Terres-Cries-de-la-Baie-James *Population Served:* 18563
Bella M. Petawabano, Présidente

Gaspé: Centre intégré de santé et de services sociaux de la Gaspésie
Également connu sous le nom de: CISSS de la Gaspésie
215, boul de York ouest, Gaspé, QC G4X 2W2
Tél: 418-368-3301 *Téléc:* 418-368-6850
cisssgaspesie@ssss.gouv.qc.ca
www.cisss-gaspesie.gouv.qc.ca
Info Line: 811
www.facebook.com/cisssgaspesie; twitter.com/cisssgaspesie;
www.linkedin.com/company/cisssgaspésie
Fondée en: 2015
Région desservi: Gaspésie *Population desservi:* 92727
Chantal Duguay, Présidente-directrice générale

Gatineau: Centre intégré de santé et de services sociaux de l'Outaouais
Également connu sous le nom de: CISSS de l'Outaouais
80, av Gatineau, Gatineau, QC J8T 4J3
Tél: 819-966-6000 *Ligne sans frais:* 800-267-2325
relationaveclacommunauteagence07@ssss.gouv.qc.ca
cisss-outaouais.gouv.qc.ca
Info Line: 811
www.facebook.com/CISSSOUTAOUAIS;
www.linkedin.com/company/cissso
Fondée en: 2015
Population desservi: 389496
Josée Filion, Présidente-directeur général
Michel Roy, Président du conseil d'administration

Greenfield Park: Centre intégré de santé et de services sociaux de la Montérégie-Centre
Également connu sous le nom de: CISSS de la Montérégie-Centre
3120, boul Taschereau, Greenfield Park, QC J4V 2H1
Tél: 450-466-5000 *Téléc:* 450-466-8887
santemonteregie.qc.ca/fr/center
www.facebook.com/cisssmc; twitter.com/cisssmc;
www.linkedin.com/company/cisssmc
Population desservi: 408715 *Personnel:* 11000
Richard Deschamps, Président-directeur général

Joliette: Centre intégré de santé et de services sociaux de Lanaudière
Également connu sous le nom de: CISSS de Lanaudière
260, rue Lavaltrie sud, Joliette, QC J6E 5X7
Tél: 450-759-1157 *Ligne sans frais:* 800-668-9229
santelanaudiere@ssss.gouv.qc.ca
www.santelanaudiere.qc.ca
Info Line: 811
www.facebook.com/CISSSdeLanaudiere
Fondée en: 2015
Région desservi: Lanaudière *Population desservi:* 502846
Daniel Castonguay, Président-directeur général
Jacques Perreault, Président, Conseil d'administration

Kuujjuaq: Régie régionale de la santé et des services sociaux du Nunavik (RRSSSN)/Nunavik Regional Board of Health & Social Services
CP 900, Kuujjuaq, QC J0M 1C0
Tél: 819-964-2222 *Téléc:* 819-964-2888
Ligne sans frais: 844-964-2244
info@sante-services-sociaux.ca
www.nrbhss.ca
www.facebook.com/NunavikHealthBoard;
vimeo.com/user21609307; www.linkedin.com/company/nrbhss
Fondée en: 1995
Nombre de lits: 50 lits; 12 lits (personnes en perte d'autonomie); 14 lits (direction régionale de la réadaptation)
Région desservi: Nunavik; 14 communautés; sous-régions: Hudson et Ungava *Personnel:* 89
Minnie Grey, Executive Director
minnie.grey@ssss.gouv.qc.ca

Laval: Centre intégré de santé et de services sociaux de Laval
Également connu sous le nom de: CISSS de Laval
1755, boul René-Laennec, Laval, QC H7M 3L9
Tél: 450-668-1010
communications.cissslaval@ssss.gouv.qc.ca
www.lavalensante.com
Info Line: 811
www.facebook.com/cissslaval; twitter.com/cissslaval;
www.youtube.com/cisssdelaval;
www.linkedin.com/company/cisssdelaval
Fondée en: 2015
Population desservi: 437413
Christian Gagné, Président-directeur général
Yves Carignan, Président, Conseil d'administration

Montréal: Centre intégré universitaire de santé et de services sociaux de l'Ouest-de-l'Ile-de-Montréal
Également connu sous le nom de: CIUSS de l'Ouest-de-l'Ile-de-Montréal
Les Centres de la jeunesse et de la famille Batsha, 410, rue De Bellechasse est, Montréal, QC H2S 1X3
Tél: 514-630-2123 *Téléc:* 514-762-3856
informations.comtl@ssss.gouv.qc.ca
www.ciusss-ouestmtl.gouv.qc.ca
Info Line: 811
www.facebook.com/ciusss.ouestmtl; twitter.com/ciusss_ouestmtl
Fondée en: 2015
Région desservi: 184,000 sq km *Population desservi:* 368740
Lynne McVey, Présidente-directrice générale

Montréal: Centre intégré universitaire de santé et de services sociaux du Centre-Ouest-de-l'Ile-de-Montréal
Également connu sous le nom de: CIUSSS du Centre-Ouest-de-l'Ile-de-Montréal
Hôpital Général Juif, 3755, ch de la Côte-Sainte-Catherine, Montréal, QC H3T 1E2
Tél: 514-340-8222
www.ciusscentreouest.ca
Info Line: 811
www.facebook.com/CIUSSSCentreOuest;
twitter.com/CIUSSS_COMTL; www.instagram.com/ciusss_comtl
Fondée en: 2015
Population desservi: 362000
Lawrence Rosenberg, Président-directeur général

Montréal: Centre intégré universitaire de santé et de services sociaux du Centre-Sud-de-l'Ile-de-Montréal
Également connu sous le nom de: CIUSSS du Centre-Sud-de-l'Ile-de-Montréal
4675, rue Bélanger, Montréal, QC H1T 1C2
Tél: 514-593-2118
www.ciusss-centresudmtl.gouv.qc.ca
www.facebook.com/ciusss.csmtl; twitter.com/ciusss_csmtl;
www.linkedin.com/company/ciusss-centre-sud-de-l'île-de-montré al
Population desservi: 300000 *Personnel:* 14343
Sonia Bélanger, Présidente-directrice générale

Montréal: Centre intégré universitaire de santé et de services sociaux du Nord-de-l'Ile-de-Montréal
Également connu sous le nom de: CIUSSS du Nord-de-l'Ile-de-Montréal
555, boul Gouin ouest, Montréal, QC H3L 1K5
Tél: 514-336-6673
ciusss-nordmtl.gouv.qc.ca
www.facebook.com/CIUSSSnmtl; twitter.com/CIUSSSnmtl;
www.linkedin.com/company/ciusssnmtl
Population desservi: 411000
Frédéric Abergel, Président-directeur général

Montréal: Centre intégré universitaire de santé et de services sociaux de l'Est-de-l'Île-de-Montréal
Également connu sous le nom de: CIUSSS de l'est-de-l'île-de-Montréal
5415, boul de l'Assomption, Montréal, QC H1T 2M4
Tél: 514-252-3400
www.ciusss-estmtl.gouv.qc.ca
Nombre de lits: 1,279 lits de courte durée; 2,502 lits d'hébergement de longue durée
Population desservi: 527000 *Personnel:* 15000
Sylvain Lemieux, Président-directeur général

Québec: Centre intégré universitaire de santé et de services sociaux de la Capitale-Nationale
Également connu sous le nom de: CIUSSS de la Capitale-Nationale
2915, av du Bourg-Royal, Québec, QC G1C 3S2
Tél: 418-266-1019 *Téléc:* 418-661-2845
www.ciusss-capitalenationale.gouv.qc.ca
Info Line: 811
www.facebook.com/538181276359816; twitter.com/CIUSSS_CN
Fondée en: 2015
Région desservi: Les territoires de Charlevoix et de Portneuf (69 municipalités) *Population desservi:* 737787
Note: Le CIUSSS de la Capitale-Nationale est la fusion des Agence de la santé et des services sociaux de la Capitale-Nationale, Centre de réadaptation en déficience intellectuelle de Québec (CDRIQ), Centre de réadaptation en dépendance de Québec, CSSS de Charlevoix, CSSS de la Vieille-Capitale, CSSS de Portneuf, CSSS de Québec-Nord, Centre jeunesse de Québec-Institut universitaire, Institut de réadaptation en déficience physique de Québec (IRDPQ), Institut universitaire en santé mentale de Québec (IUSMQ) et Hôpital Jeffrey Hale-Saint Brigid's (établissement regroupé).
Michel Delamarre, Président-directeur général
Simon Lemay, Président, Conseil d'administration

Rimouski: Centre intégré de santé et de services sociaux du Bas-St-Laurent
Également connu sous le nom de: CISSS Bas-St-Laurent
355, boul Saint-Germain ouest, Rimouski, QC G5L 3N2
Tél: 418-724-5231
www.cisss-bsl.gouv.qc.ca
Info Line: 811
Fondée en: 2015
Nombre de lits: 471 lits de courte durée
Population desservi: 200880 *Personnel:* 7492
Isabelle Malo, Présidente-directrice générale
418-724-3000

Rouyn-Noranda: Centre intégré de santé et de services sociaux de l'Abitibi-Témiscamingue
Également connu sous le nom de: CISSS de l'Abitibi-Témiscamingue
1, 9e rue, Rouyn-Noranda, QC J9X 2A9
Tél: 819-764-3264 *Téléc:* 819-764-2948
info_sante-abitibi-temiscamingue@ssss.gouv.qc.ca
www.cisss-at.gouv.qc.ca
Info Line: 811
www.facebook.com/CISSSAT;
www.linkedin.com/company/cisss-abitibi-témiscamingue
Fondée en: 2015
Région desservi: La région de l'Abitibi-Témiscamingue (65 municipalités) *Population desservi:* 147982 *Personnel:* 6000
Caroline Roy, Président-directeur général
Claude Morin, Président, Conseil d'administration

Saint-Hyacinthe: Centre intégré de santé et de services sociaux de la Montérégie-Est
2750, boul Laframboise, Saint-Hyacinthe, QC J2S 4Y8
Tél: 450-771-3333
santemonteregie.qc.ca/fr/est
www.facebook.com/CISSSME;
www.linkedin.com/company/cisss-de-la-montérégie-est
Fondée en: 2015
Région desservi: 3,845 sq km *Population desservi:* 527000
Personnel: 13483
Louise Potvin, Présidente-directrice générale

Saint-Jérôme: Centre intégré de santé et de services sociaux des Laurentides
Également connu sous le nom de: CISSS des Laurentides
290, rue Montigny, Saint-Jérôme, QC J7Z 5T3
Tél: 450-432-2777 *Ligne sans frais:* 866-963-2777
www.santelaurentides.gouv.qc.ca
Info Line: 811
www.facebook.com/171472830204004; twitter.com/CisssL
Fondée en: 2015
Région desservi: Plus de 80 installations *Population desservi:* 595000 *Personnel:* 14000

Rosemonde Landry, Président-directeur général
André Poirier, Président, Conseil d'administration

Sainte-Marie: Centre intégré de santé et de services sociaux de Chaudière-Appalaches
Également connu sous le nom de: CISSS de Chaudière-Appalaches
363, rte Cameron, Sainte-Marie, QC G6E 3E2
Tél: 418-386-3363 *Téléc:* 418-386-3361
reception.cisss-ca@ssss.gouv.qc.ca
www.cisssca.com
Info Line: 811
www.facebook.com/cisssca12; twitter.com/cisssca12;
www.instagram.com/cisss_de_chaudiere_appalaches;
www.linkedin.com/company/cisss-de-chaudiere-appalaches
Région desservi: 136 municipalités *Population desservi:* 426791
Personnel: 12000
Daniel Paré, Président-directeur général
Brigitte Busque, Présidente, Conseil d'administration

Sherbrooke: Centre intégré universitaire de santé et de services sociaux de l'Estrie
Également connu sous le nom de: CIUSSS de l'Estrie - CHUS
375, rue Argyll, Sherbrooke, QC J1J 3H5
Tél: 819-780-2222
www.santeestrie.qc.ca
Info Line: 811
www.facebook.com/SanteEstrie; twitter.com/CIUSSE_CHUS;
www.linkedin.com/company/ciusss-de-lestrie-chus
Nombre de lits: 3,200 lits
Région desservi: Lac-Mégantic à Granby, environ 13,000 km2
Population desservi: 500000 *Personnel:* 19000
Patricia Gauthier, Présidente-directrice générale

Trois-Rivières: Centre intégré universitaire de santé et de services sociaux de la Mauricie-et-du-Centre-du-Québec
Également connu sous le nom de: CIUSSS MCQ
858, terrasse Turcotte, Trois-Rivières, QC G9A 5C5
Tél: 819-375-3111
www.ciusssmcq.ca
Info Line: 811
www.facebook.com/ciusssmauriciecentreduquebec;
vimeo.com/ciusssmcq
Fondée en: 2015
Population desservi: 512274
Note: Fournit des services dans les domaines suivants: Arthabaska-et-de-l'Érable, Bécancour-Nicolet-Yamaska, Drummond, De l'Énergie (Shawinigan et les environs), Haut-Saint-Maurice, Maskinongé, Trois-Rivières et Vallée-de-la-Batiscan.
Carol Fillion, Président-directeur général
Marcel Dubois, Président du conseil d'administration

Centres hospitaliers

Amos: Hôpital Hôtel-Dieu d'Amos
Affiliée à: CISSS de l'Abitibi-Témiscamingue
622, 4e rue ouest, Amos, QC J9T 2S2
Tél: 819-732-3341
www.cisss-at.gouv.qc.ca
www.facebook.com/CISSSAT;
www.linkedin.com/company/cisss-abitibi-témiscamingue
Nombre de lits: 90 lits
Note: Services diagnostiques; urgence et traumatologie; othopédie; rhumatologie; ophtalmologie; chirurgie plastique / reconstructive / maxillo-faciale; gynécologie; obstétrique; gériatrie; physiotherapie; réadaptation cardio-respiratoire.

Amqui: Hôpital d'Amqui
Affiliée à: CISSS du Bas-St-Laurent
135, av Gaétan-Archambault, Amqui, QC G5J 2K5
Tél: 418-629-2211
www.facebook.com/CISSSBSL; twitter.com/CISSSBSL
Population desservi: 21000
Note: Services: imagerie médicale; inhalothérapie; mammographie; réadaptation.

Baie-Comeau: Hôpital Le Royer
Affiliée à: CISSS de la Côte-Nord
635, boul Jolliet, Baie-Comeau, QC G5C 1P1
Tél: 418-589-3701 *Téléc:* 418-589-9654
www.cisss-cotenord.gouv.qc.ca
www.facebook.com/cisss.cotenord;
www.linkedin.com/company/cisss-cotenord
Fondée en: 1951
Nombre de lits: 85 lits de santé physique; 21 lits de psychiatrie
Note: Programmes et services comprennent: chirurgie; médecine nucléaire; pédopsychiatrie; radiologie; urologie.

Baie-Saint-Paul: Hôpital de Baie-Saint-Paul
Affiliée à: CIUSSS de la Capitale-Nationale
74, rue Ambroise-Fafard, Baie-Saint-Paul, QC G3Z 2J6
Tél: 418-435-5150
Nombre de lits: 40 lits hospitaliers; 56 lits de soins de longue durée
Note: Services: anesthésiologie, chirurgie gériatrie, psychiatrie, radiologie, ophtalmologie, urologie; soins généraux et spécialisés; urgence.

Cap-aux-Meules: Hôpital de l'Archipel
Affiliée à: CISSS des Iles
430, ch Principal, Cap-aux-Meules, QC G4T 1R9
Tél: 418-986-2121
www.cisssdesiles.com
www.facebook.com/cisssdesiles
Nombre de lits: 105 lits

Chandler: Hôpital de Chandler
Affiliée à: CISSS de la Gaspésie
451, rue Mgr Ross est, Chandler, QC G0C 1K0
Tél: 418-689-2261
cisssgaspesie@ssss.gouv.qc.ca
www.cisss-gaspesie.gouv.qc.ca
Nombre de lits: 155 lits
Note: Soins hospitaliers; soins de longue durée; a fusionné avec le CLSC-CHSLD Pabok en 2004.

Châteauguay: Hôpital Anna-Laberge
Affiliée à: CISSS de la Montérégie-Ouest
200, boul Brisebois, Châteauguay, QC J6K 4W8
Tél: 450-699-2425
www.santemonteregie.qc.ca/ouest
www.facebook.com/cisssmo;
www.linkedin.com/company/cisss-monteregie-ouest
Fondée en: 1988
Nombre de lits: 226 lits hospitaliers
Note: Services: radiologie et imagerie médicale; chirurgie; diabète; endoscopie; cancer; urgence; santé mentale; soins palliatifs; gériatrie; pédiatrie; suivi de grossesse; déficience physique.
Patrick Murphy-Lavallée, Président-directeur général adjoint, CISSS de la Montérégie-Ouest

Chicoutimi: Hôpital de Chicoutimi
Affiliée à: CIUSSS du Saguenay-Lac-St-Jean
305, rue Saint-Vallier, Chicoutimi, QC G7H 5H6
Tél: 418-541-1000
santesaglac.gouv.qc.ca
www.facebook.com/SanteSagLac; twitter.com/CIUSSS_SLSJ;
www.youtube.com/channel/UCp-otUKvKshivZJ-xJbViNA;
www.linkedin.com/company/ciusss-saguenay-lac-saint-jean
Nombre de lits: 626
Personnel: 3300
Note: Services: chirurgie mineure; contraception; contraception orale d'urgence; désintoxication; livraison; récupération des seringues et des aiguilles usagées; soins en fin de vie; vaccination.

Chisasibi: Hôpital de Chisasibi
Affiliée à: Conseil Cri de la santé et des services sociaux de la Baie James
21, rue Maamuu, Chisasibi, QC J0M 1E0
Tél: 819-855-2844 *Téléc:* 819-855-9060
ccsssbj-cbhssjb@ssss.gouv.qc.ca
www.creehealth.org
www.facebook.com/creehealth; twitter.com/creehealth;
www.instagram.com/creehealth
Nombre de lits: 17 servent aux soins actifs (5 en pédiatrie); 9 aux malades chroniques; 3 aux soins respiratoires
Personnel: 34

Coaticook: Centre hospitalier de Coaticook
Affiliée à: CIUSSS de l'Estrie
138, rue Jeanne-Mance, Coaticook, QC J1A 1W3
Tél: 819-849-9102
www.santeestrie.qc.ca
www.facebook.com/SanteEstrie; twitter.com/CIUSSSE_CHUS;
www.youtube.com/channel/UCecOsAu7inOjWek_gpJDRtg
Note: Services: chirurgie mineure; contraception; contraception orale d'urgence; désintoxication; vaccination; médecine familiale.

Dolbeau-Mistassini: Hôpital de Dolbeau-Mistassini
Affiliée à: CIUSSS du Saguenay-Lac-Saint-Jean
2000, boul Sacré-Coeur, Dolbeau-Mistassini, QC G8L 2R5
Tél: 418-276-1234
santesaglac.gouv.qc.ca
www.facebook.com/SanteSagLac; twitter.com/CIUSSS_SLSJ;
www.youtube.com/channel/UCp-otUKvKshivZJ-xJbViNA;
www.linkedin.com/company/ciusss-saguenay-lac-saint-jean
Note: Services: chirurgie mineure; contraception; contraception orale d'urgence; récupération des seringues et des aiguilles usagées; vaccination; médecine familiale.

Drummondville: **Hôpital Sainte-Croix**
Affiliée à: CIUSSS de la santé
Mauricie-et-du-Centre-du-Québec
570, rue Heriot, Drummondville, QC J2B 1C1
Tél: 819-478-6464
ciusssmcq.ca
www.facebook.com/ciusssmauriciecentreduquebec;
vimeo.com/ciusssmcq
Note: Anatomopathologie, chirurgie générale, gynécologie-obstétrique, pédiatrie, médecine familiale / interne / nucléaire, ophtalmologie, orthopédie, psychiatrie, radiologie, urologie.

Gaspé: **Hôpital de Gaspé**
Affiliée à: CISSS de la Gaspésie
215, boul de York ouest, Gaspé, QC G4X 2W2
Tél: 418-368-3301
cisssgaspesie@ssss.gouv.qc.ca
www.cisss-gaspesie.gouv.qc.ca
Note: Services: centre désigné, services spécialisés pour les victimes d'agression sexuelle; chirurgie mineure; contraception; contraception orale d'urgence; doppler; ECG / EMG; endoscopie; mammographie; récupération des seringues et des aiguilles usagées; angiographie; coloscopie; radiologie; résonance magnétique.

Gatineau: **Hôpital de Gatineau**
Affiliée à: CISSS de l'Outaouais
909, boul La Vérendrye ouest, Gatineau, QC J8P 7H2
Tél: 819-966-6100

Gatineau: **Hôpital de Hull**
Affiliée à: CISSS de l'Outaouais
116, boul Lionel-Émond, Gatineau, QC J8Y 1W7
Tél: 819-966-6200
Note: Services: chirurgie mineure; ECG / EEG / EMG; récupération des seringues et des aiguilles usagées; coloscopie; médecine familiale; radiologie.

Gatineau: **Hôpital de Papineau**
Affiliée à: CISSS de l'Outaouais
155, rue Maclaren est, Gatineau, QC J8L 0C2
Tél: 819-986-3341
Nombre de lits: 63 lits hospitaliers
Note: Services: chirurgie mineure; contraception; contraception orale d'urgence; mammographie; récupération des seringues et des aiguilles usagées; radiologie.

Granby: **Hôpital de Granby**
Affiliée à: CIUSSS de l'Estrie
205, boul Leclerc ouest, Granby, QC J2G 1T7
Tél: 450-375-8000
www.santeestrie.qc.ca
www.facebook.com/SanteEstrie; twitter.com/CIUSSSE_CHUS;
www.youtube.com/channel/UCecOsAu7inOjWek_gpJDRtg
Note: Services: doppler; ECG / EMG; récupération des seringues et des aiguilles usagées.

Greenfield Park: **Hôpital Charles-LeMoyne**
Affiliée à: CISSS de la Montérégie-Centre
3120, boul Taschereau, Greenfield Park, QC J4V 2H1
Tél: 450-466-5000
santemonteregie.qc.ca
Nombre de lits: 515 lits
Personnel: 3500
Note: L'Hôpital est le centre hospitalier régional et universitaire de la Montérégie; affilié à l'Université de Sherbrooke; soins et services de court durée en santé physique, santé mentale, réadaptation; recherche; enseignement universitaire.

Jonquière: **Hôpital de Jonquière**
Affiliée à: CIUSSS du Saguenay-Lac-St-Jean
2230, rue de l'Hôpital, Jonquière, QC G7X 7X2
Tél: 418-695-7700
santesaglac.gouv.qc.ca
www.facebook.com/SanteSagLac; twitter.com/CIUSSS_SLSJ;
www.youtube.com/channel/UCp-otUKvKshivZJ-xJbViNA;
www.linkedin.com/company/ciusss-saguenay-lac-saint-jean
Note: Services: centre désigné, services spécialisés pour les victimes d'agression sexuelle; contraception; contraception orale d'urgence; mammographie; récupération des seringues et des aiguilles usagées; vaccination; radiologie.

La Baie: **Hôpital de La Baie**
Affiliée à: CIUSSS du Saguenay-Lac-St-Jean
1000, rue Docteur-Desgagné, La Baie, QC G7B 3M9
Tél: 418-544-3381
santesaglac.gouv.qc.ca
www.facebook.com/SanteSagLac; twitter.com/CIUSSS_SLSJ;
www.youtube.com/channel/UCp-otUKvKshivZJ-xJbViNA;
www.linkedin.com/company/ciusss-saguenay-lac-saint-jean

Note: Services: contraception; contraception orale d'urgence; récupération des seringues et des aiguilles usagées; vaccination.

La Malbaie: **Hôpital de La Malbaie**
Affiliée à: CIUSSS de la Capitale-Nationale
303, rue Saint-Étienne, La Malbaie, QC G5A 1T1
Tél: 418-665-1700
Note: Services: allergie, immunologie, physiologie respiratoire; anesthésiologie; cardiologie; chimiothérapie; chirurgie dentaire; chirurgie générale; chirurgie mineure; endocrinologie; gastroentérologie; gynécologie; médecine de jour; médecine interne; neurologie; obstétrique; oncologie; orthopédie; ORL (oreilles, nez, larynx); physiatrie; pneumologie; psychiatrie; radiologie diagnostique.

La Pocatière: **L'Hôpital Notre-Dame-de-Fatima**
Affiliée à: CISSS du Bas-St-Laurent
1201, 6e av Pilote, La Pocatière, QC G0R 1Z0
Tél: 418-856-7000 *Téléc:* 418-856-4737
www.cisss-bsl.gouv.qc.ca
www.facebook.com/CISSSBSL; twitter.com/CISSSBSL
Nombre de lits: 49 lits
Note: Services: récupération des seringues et des aiguilles usagées; radiologie; réadaptation; inhalothérapie; imagerie médicale.

La Sarre: **Centre hospitalier de La Sarre**
Affiliée à: CISSS de l'Abitibi-Témiscamingue
679, 2e rue est, La Sarre, QC J9Z 2X7
Tél: 819-333-2311
www.cisss-at.gouv.qc.ca
www.facebook.com/CISSSAT;
www.linkedin.com/company/cisss-abitibi-témiscamingue
Note: Services: centre désigné, services spécialisés pour les victimes d'agression sexuelle; chirurgie mineure; contraception; cours prénataux; dépistage; récupération des seringues et des aiguilles usagées; vaccination; radiologie.

LaSalle: **Hôpital de LaSalle**
Affiliée à: CIUSSS de l'Ouest-de-l'Ile-de-Montréal
8585, Terrasse Champlain, LaSalle, QC H8P 1C1
Tél: 514-362-8000
ciusss-ouestmtl.gouv.qc.ca
www.facebook.com/ciusss.ouestmtl; twitter.com/ciusss_ouestmtl
Nombre de lits: 110 lits
Note: Services: urgence; obstétrique; soins de longue durée; petites procédures.

Lachine: **Hôpital de Lachine/Lachine Hospital**
Centre universitaire de santé McGill
Affiliée à: RUISSS McGill
650, 16e Avenue, Lachine, QC H8S 3N5
Tél: 514-934-1934
cusm.ca/lachine
www.facebook.com/CUSM.MUHC; twitter.com/cusm_muhc;
www.instagram.com/cusm_muhc;
www.linkedin.com/company/muhc
Fondée en: 1913
Note: Spécialisés en médecine gériatrique, médecine bariatrique et en ophtalmologie, l'Hôpital de Lachine inclut le pavillon d'hébergement de soins de longue durée Camille Lefebvre.

Laval: **Hôpital de la Cité-de-la-Santé**
Affiliée à: CISSS de Laval
1755, boul René-Laennec, Laval, QC H7M 3L9
Tél: 450-668-1010
www.lavalensante.com
www.facebook.com/cissslaval; twitter.com/cissslaval;
www.linkedin.com/company/cisssdelaval
Nombre de lits: 489 lits

Laval: **Hôpital juif de réadaptation (JRH)/Jewish Rehabilitation Hospital**
Affiliée à: CISSS de Laval
3205, Place Alton-Goldbloom, Laval, QC H7V 1R2
Tél: 450-688-9550
www.lavalensante.com/hjr-jrh
www.facebook.com/cissslaval; twitter.com/cissslaval;
www.linkedin.com/company/cisssdelaval
Fondée en: 1962
Nombre de lits: 132 lits
Personnel: 550

Lévis: **Hôtel-Dieu de Lévis**
Affiliée à: CISSS de Chaudière-Appalaches
143, rue Wolfe, Lévis, QC G6V 3Z1
Tél: 418-835-7121 *Ligne sans frais:* 888-835-7105
www.cisssca.com
www.facebook.com/cisssca12; twitter.com/cisssca12;
www.instagram.com/cisss_de_chaudiere_appalaches;
www.linkedin.com/company/cisss-de-chaudiere-appalaches
Note: Associé à l'Université Laval.

Longueuil: **Hôpital Pierre-Boucher**
Affiliée à: CISSS de la Montérégie-Est
1333, boul Jacques-Cartier est, Longueuil, QC J4M 2A5
Tél: 450-468-8111
santemonteregie.qc.ca
Nombre de lits: 329 lits
Note: Services comprennent: urgence; soins intensifs; soins palliatifs; services médicaux; chirurgie; psychiatrie.

Maniwaki: **Hôpital de Maniwaki**
Affiliée à: CISSS de l'Outaouais
309, boul Desjardins, Maniwaki, QC J9E 2E7
Tél: 819-449-4690
Fondée en: 1998
Nombre de lits: 36 lits de courte durée; 4 lits soins intermédiaires
Note: Services: salle d'allaitement; contraception; contraception orale d'urgence; mammographie; récupération des seringues et des aiguilles usagées; soins en fin de vie; vaccination; traitement des verrues plantaires; radiologie.

Maria: **Hôpital de Maria**
Affiliée à: CISSS de la Gaspésie
419, boul Perron, Maria, QC G0C 1Y0
Tél: 418-759-3443
www.cisss-gaspesie.gouv.qc.ca
Nombre de lits: 77 lits
Chantal Duguay, Présidente-directrice générale, CISSS de la Gaspésie

Matane: **Hôpital de Matane**
Affiliée à: CISSS du Bas-St-Laurent
333, rue Thibault, Matane, QC G4W 2W5
Tél: 418-562-3135
www.cisss-bsl.gouv.qc.ca
www.facebook.com/CISSSBSL; twitter.com/CISSSBSL
Population desservi: 21000
Note: Services: centre désigné, services spécialisés pour les victimes d'agression sexuelle; chirurgie mineure; récupération des seringues et des aiguilles usagées; soins en fin de vie; Radiologie.

Mont-Laurier: **Hôpital de Mont-Laurier**
Affiliée à: CISSS des Laurentides
2561, ch de la Lièvre sud, Mont-Laurier, QC J9L 3G3
Tél: 819-623-1234
www.santelaurentides.gouv.qc.ca
www.facebook.com/171472830204004; twitter.com/CisssL
Nombre de lits: 62 lits
Note: Services: salle d'allaitement; chirurgie mineure; contraception; contraception orale d'urgence; désintoxication; avortement; livraison; récupération des seringues et des aiguilles usagées; soins en fin de vie; vaccination; médecine familiale.

Montmagny: **Hôpital de Montmagny**
Affiliée à: CISSS de Chaudière-Appalaches
350, boul Taché ouest, Montmagny, QC G5V 3R8
Tél: 418-248-0630
www.cisssca.com
www.facebook.com/cisssca12; twitter.com/cisssca12;
www.instagram.com/cisss_de_chaudiere_appalaches;
www.linkedin.com/company/cisss-de-chaudiere-appalaches
Nombre de lits: 101 lits
Note: Services: anesthésiologie; chirurgie; ergothérapie; gériatrie; gynécologie-obstétrique; hémodialyse; inhalothérapie; laboratoires; médecine d'urgence; nutrition; oncologie; orthopédie; oto-rhino-laryngologie et ophtalmologie; pédiatrie; pédopsychiatrie et psychiatrie; pharmacie; physiothérapie; radiologie.

Montréal: **Centre hospitalier de l'Université de Montréal (CHUM)**
Affiliée à: CIUSSS du
Centre-Sud-de-l'Ile-de-Montréal
1000, rue Saint-Denis, Montréal, QC H2X 0C1
Tél: 514-890-8000
www.chumontreal.qc.ca
www.facebook.com/chum.montreal; twitter.com/chumontreal;
www.youtube.com/user/chumontreal
Nombre de lits: 1217 lits hospitaliers, 170 lits longue durée
Personnel: 13136
Fabrice Brunet, Président-directeur général

Montréal: **Centre hospitalier de St. Mary/St. Mary's Hospital Center**
Affiliée à: CIUSSS de l'Ouest-de-l'Ile-de-Montréal
3830, av Lacombe, Montréal, QC H3T 1M5
Tél: 514-345-3511
www.smhc.qc.ca
Nombre de lits: 271 lits hospitaliers
Note: Affilié à l'Université McGill.

Montréal: Centre universitaire de santé McGill - Site Glen
Centre universitaire de santé McGill
Affiliée à: RUISSS McGill
1001, boul Décarie, Montréal, QC H4A 3J1
Tél: 514-934-1934
cusm.ca/glen
www.facebook.com/CUSM.MUHC; twitter.com/cusm_muhc;
www.instagram.com/cusm_muhc;
www.linkedin.com/company/muhc
Fondée en: 1913
Note: Inclut cinq établissements.

Montréal: **Hôpital Catherine Booth de l'Armée du Salut**
Affiliée à: CIUSSS du
Centre-Ouest-de-l'Ile-de-Montréal
4375, av Montclair, Montréal, QC H4B 2J5
Tél: 514-484-7878
www.ciusscentreouest.ca
www.facebook.com/CIUSSSCentreOuest;
twitter.com/CIUSSS_COMTL; www.instagram.com/ciusss_comtl
Note: Services: réadaptation; orthopédie; neurologie.

Montréal: **Hôpital de Montréal pour enfants (HME /MCH)/Montreal Children's Hospital**
Centre universitaire de santé McGill - Site Glen
Affiliée à: RUISSS McGill
1001, boul Décarie, Montréal, QC H4A 3J1
Tél: 514-412-4400
mchpr@muhc.mcgill.ca
www.hopitalpourenfants.com
www.facebook.com/lechildren; twitter.com/HopitalChildren;
www.instagram.com/lechildren
Fondée en: 1904
Dr. Bruce Mazer, Directeur exécutif

Montréal: **Hôpital de réadaptation Lindsay**
Affiliée à: CIUSSS du
Centre-Ouest-de-l'Ile-de-Montréal
6363, ch Hudson, Montréal, QC H3S 1M9
Tél: 514-737-3661
ciusss-centresudmtl.gouv.qc.ca
www.facebook.com/ciusss.csmtl; twitter.com/ciusss_csmtl
Fondée en: 1914
Note: Hôpital spécialisé de courte-durée.

Montréal: **Hôpital de Verdun**
Affiliée à: CIUSSS du
Centre-Sud-de-l'Ile-de-Montréal
4000, boul LaSalle, Montréal, QC H4G 2A3
Tél: 514-362-1000
www.ciusss-centresudmtl.gouv.qc.ca
www.facebook.com/ciusss.csmtl; twitter.com/ciusss_csmtl
Nombre de lits: 258 lits
Personnel: 1600
Note: Affilié à l'Université de Montréal. Services: chirurgie mineure; doppler; endoscopie; soins en fin de vie; vaccination; coloscopie; radiologie; résonance magnétique; tomodensitométrie; tomographie.

Montréal: **Hôpital du Sacré-Coeur de Montréal**
Affiliée à: CIUSSS du Nord-de-l'Ile-de-Montréal
5400, boul Gouin ouest, Montréal, QC H4J 1C5
Tél: 514-338-2222
www.ciusssnordmtl.ca
www.facebook.com/CIUSSSnmtl; twitter.com/CIUSSSnmtl;
www.linkedin.com/company/ciusssnmtl
Nombre de lits: 540 lits
Personnel: 4000
Note: Services: caisson hyperbare; chirurgie mineure; test de cholestérol; contraception; contraception orale d'urgence; soins en fin de vie; vaccination; coloscopie; médecine familiale; radiologie.

Montréal: **Hôpital Fleury**
Affiliée à: CIUSSS du Nord-de-l'Ile-de-Montréal
2180, rue Fleury est, Montréal, QC H2B 1K3
Tél: 514-384-2000
www.ciusssnordmtl.ca
www.facebook.com/CIUSSSnmtl; twitter.com/CIUSSSnmtl;
www.linkedin.com/company/ciusssnmtl
Nombre de lits: 174 lits
Région desservi: Le territoire d'Ahuntsic et de Montréal-Nord, QC
Spécialités: Prélèvements; Urgence psychiatrique
Note: Services: chirurgie mineure; coloscopie; médecine familiale; radiologie.

Montréal: **Hôpital général de Montréal/The Montréal General Hospital**
Centre universitaire de santé McGill
Affiliée à: RUISSS McGill
Également connu sous le nom de: HGM / MGH
1650, av Cedar, Montréal, QC H3G 1A4
Tél: 514-934-1934
cusm.ca/mgh
www.facebook.com/CUSM.MUHC; twitter.com/cusm_muhc;
www.instagram.com/cusm_muhc;
www.linkedin.com/company/muhc
Fondée en: 1821
Nombre de lits: 533 lits
Note: Centre de traumatologie désigné par la province. Services: endoscopie; coloscopie; radiologie; résonance magnétique; tomodensitométrie; tomographie.
Dr. Pierre Gfeller, Président et directeur général, CUSM

Montréal: **Hôpital général juif/Jewish General Hospital**
Affiliée à: CIUSSS du
Centre-Ouest-de-l'Ile-de-Montréal
3755, ch de la Côte-Sainte-Catherine, Montréal, QC H3T 1E2
Tél: 514-340-8222
www.hgj.ca
www.facebook.com/CIUSSSCentreOuest;
twitter.com/CIUSSS_COMTL; www.instagram.com/ciusss_comtl
Fondée en: 1934
Nombre de lits: 637 lits hospitaliers
Personnel: 4869
Note: Services: Chirurgie mineure; contraception; dépistage; ECG; soins en fin de vie; vaccination; coloscopie; médecine familiale; radiologie.
Lawrence Rosenberg, Président-directeur général

Montréal: **Hôpital Jean-Talon**
Affiliée à: CIUSSS du Nord-de-l'Ile-de-Montréal
1385, rue Jean-Talon est, Montréal, QC H2E 1S6
Tél: 514-495-6767
www.ciusssnordmtl.ca
www.facebook.com/CIUSSSnmtl; twitter.com/CIUSSSnmtl;
www.linkedin.com/company/ciusssnmtl
Note: Services: dépistage; soins en fin de vie.

Montréal: **Hôpital Maisonneuve-Rosemont**
Affiliée à: CIUSSS de l'Est-de-l'Ile-de-Montréal
5415, boul de l'Assomption, Montréal, QC H1T 2M4
Tél: 514-252-3400 *Ligne sans frais:* 844-634-3400
ciusss-estmtl.gouv.qc.ca
www.facebook.com/ciusss.estmtl.hmr; twitter.com/ciusss_estmtl;
www.linkedin.com/company/ciusss-de-l'est-de-l'île-de-montréal
Fondée en: 1971

Montréal: **Hôpital Mont-Sinai**
Affiliée à: CIUSSS du
Centre-Ouest-de-l'Ile-de-Montréal
5690, boul Cavendish, Montréal, QC H4W 1S7
Tél: 514-369-2222 *Téléc:* 514-369-2225
www.sinaimontreal.ca
Fondée en: 1909
Nombre de lits: 107 lits
Note: Services comprennent: soins respiratoires; soins palliatifs; soins long-terme; services de soutien. Affilié avec McGill University.

Montréal: **Hôpital Richardson**
Affiliée à: CIUSSS du
Centre-Ouest-de-l'Ile-de-Montréal
5425, rue Bessborough, Montréal, QC H4V 2S7
Tél: 514-484-7878
www.hopitalrichardson.ca
www.facebook.com/CIUSSSCentreOuest;
twitter.com/CIUSSS_COMTL; www.instagram.com/ciusss_comtl
Note: Hôpital de réadaptation.
Felicia Guarna, Directrice de la Réadaptation

Montréal: **Hôpital Royal Victoria (HME /MCH)/Royal Victoria Hospital**
Centre universitaire de santé McGill - Site Glen
Affiliée à: RUISSS McGill
1001, boul Décarie, Montréal, QC H4A 3J1
Tél: 514-934-1934
www.cusm.ca
www.facebook.com/CUSM.MUHC; twitter.com/cusm_muhc;
www.instagram.com/cusm_muhc;
www.linkedin.com/company/muhc
Note: Services: mammographie; coloscopie; & radiologie.

Montréal: **Hôpital Santa Cabrini**
Affiliée à: CIUSSS de l'Est-de-l'Ile-de-Montréal
5655, rue Saint-Zotique est, Montréal, QC H1T 1P7
Tél: 514-252-6000
ciusss-estmtl.gouv.qc.ca
www.facebook.com/ciusss.estmtl; twitter.com/ciusss_estmtl
www.linkedin.com/company/ciusss-de-l'est-de-l'île-de-montréal
Nombre de lits: 369 de soins actifs; 103 lits longue durée
Note: Services: chirurgie mineure; désintoxication; mammographie; soins en fin de vie; vaccination; médecine familiale; radiologie.

Montréal: **Hôpital Shriners pour enfants (Quebec) inc.**
1003, boul Decarie, Montréal, QC H4A 0A9
Tél: 514-842-4464 *Ligne sans frais:* 800-361-7256
fr.shrinershospitalsforchildren.org/-a4db/montréal
www.facebook.com/ShrinersHospitalsforChildren;
twitter.com/shrinershosp;
www.youtube.com/user/shrinershospitals;
www.linkedin.com/company/shriners-hospitals-for-children
Jacques Boissonneault, Directeur général

Montréal: **Institut de cardiologie de Montréal**
Affiliée à: CIUSSS de l'Est-de-l'Ile-de-Montréal
5000, rue Bélanger, Montréal, QC H1T 1C8
Tél: 514-376-3330 *Ligne sans frais:* 855-922-6387
www.icm-mhi.org
www.facebook.com/institutcardiologiemontreal;
twitter.com/ICMtl; www.youtube.com/user/InstitutdeCardioMtl;
www.linkedin.com/company/institut-cardiologie-de-montr-al
Nombre de lits: 153 lits
Personnel: 1900
Note: Services: soins en fin de vie; résonance magnétique; tomodensitométrie; tomographie.
Mélanie La Couture, Présidente-directrice générale

Montréal: **Institut et hôpital neurologiques de Montréal/Montréal Neurological Institute & Hospital**
Centre universitaire de santé McGill
Affiliée à: RUISSS McGill
Également connu sous le nom de: Le Neuro
3801, rue University, Montréal, QC H3A 2B4
Tél: 514-398-6644
www.mcgill.ca/neuro
www.facebook.com/TheNeuroMNI; twitter.com/TheNeuro_MNI;
www.youtube.com/user/MontrealNeuro;
www.linkedin.com/company/the-montreal-neurological-institute
Nombre de lits: 85 lits
Spécialités: Neurologie
Guy Rouleau, Directeur général

Montréal: **Institut Philippe Pinel de Montréal**
10905, boul Henri-Bourassa est, Montréal, QC H1C 1H1
Tél: 514-648-8461
www.pinel.qc.ca
www.facebook.com/InstitutPinel; twitter.com/InstitutPinel;
www.instagram.com/institutpinel
Fondée en: 1927
Nombre de lits: 292 lits
Personnel: 700
Annie Côté, Directrice, Services techniques

Montréal: **Institut universitaire de gériatrie de Montréal (IUGM)**
Affiliée à: CIUSSS du
Centre-Sud-de-l'Ile-de-Montréal
Pavillon Côte-des-Neiges, 4565, ch Queen-Mary, Montréal, QC H3W 1W5
Tél: 514-340-2800 *Téléc:* 514-340-2802
www.iugm.qc.ca
www.facebook.com/ciusss.csmtl; twitter.com/ciusss_csmtl;
www.youtube.com/user/criugmqcca
Nombre de lits: 446 lits
Note: Affilié à l'Université de Montréal.

Montréal: **Réseau Universitaire Intégré de Santé et Services Sociaux McGill/McGill University Health Centre**
Également connu sous le nom de: RUISSS McGill
3605 de la Montagne, Montréal, QC H3G 2M1
Tél: 514-398-2705
ruismed_coord@mcgill.ca
www.mcgill.ca/ruisss
www.facebook.com/McGillFacultyofMedicine;
twitter.com/mcgillmed; www.instagram.com/mcgillmed
Population desservi: 1900000 *Personnel:* 12000
Dr. Pierre Gfeller, President

Ormstown: **Hôpital Barrie Memorial**
Affiliée à: CISSS de la Montérégie-Ouest
28, rue Gale, Ormstown, QC J0S 1K0
Tél: 450-829-2321 Téléc: 450 829-3582
www.santemonteregie.qc.ca/ouest
www.facebook.com/cisssmo;
www.linkedin.com/company/cisss-monteregie-ouest
Fondée en: 2006
Note: Affilié à l'université McGill. Services: radiologie et imagerie médicale; chirurgie; diabète; médecine générale et spécialisée; cliniques externes; endoscopie; pneumologie et laboratoire du sommeil; urgence; soins palliatifs; déficience physique.

Pointe-Claire: **Hôpital général du Lakeshore**
Affiliée à: CIUSSS de l'Ouest-de-l'Île-de-Montréal
160, av Stillview, Pointe-Claire, QC H9R 2Y2
Tél: 514-630-2225
ciusss-ouestmtl.gouv.qc.ca
Nombre de lits: 265 lits
Population desservi: 300000 *Personnel:* 1599
Note: Services: chirurgie mineure; ECG; soins en fin de vie; vaccination; coloscopie; radiologie; résonance magnétique; tomodensitométrie; tomographie.

Québec: **Centre hospitalier de l'Université Laval (CHUL)**
Centre hospitalier universitaire de Québec
Affiliée à: CIUSSS de la Capitale-Nationale
2705, boul Laurier, Québec, QC G1V 4G2
Tél: 418-525-4444
www.chudequebec.ca
www.facebook.com/chudequebec; twitter.com/chudequebec;
www.youtube.com/user/chudequebec
Note: Affilié à l'Université Laval.
Gertrude Bourdon, Présidente-directrice générale

Québec: **Centre hospitalier universitaire de Québec (CHUQ)**
11, côte du Palais, Québec, QC G1R 2J6
Tél: 418-525-4444
www.chudequebec.ca
www.facebook.com/chudequebec; twitter.com/chudequebec;
www.youtube.com/user/chudequebec;
linkedin.com/company/centre-hospitalier-universitaire-de-qu-bec
Personnel: 13500
Martin Beaumont, Président-directeur général

Québec: **Hôpital Chauveau**
Affiliée à: CIUSSS de la Capitale-Nationale
11999, rue de l'Hôpital, Québec, QC G2A 2T7
Tél: 418-842-3651 Téléc: 418-842-8660
www.ciusss-capitalenationale.gouv.qc.ca
Note: Services: anesthésie, chirurgie, gériatrie, psychiatrie, radiologie, ophtalmologie, urologie; soins généraux et spécialisés; urgence.

Québec: **Hôpital de l'Enfant-Jésus**
Affiliée à: CIUSSS de la Capitale-Nationale
1401, 18e rue, Québec, QC G1J 1Z4
Tél: 418-525-4444
info@chudequebec.ca
www.chudequebec.ca
Fondée en: 1923
Note: Affilié à l'Université Laval et Université de Québec.

Québec: **Hôpital du Saint-Sacrement**
Centre hospitalier affilié universitaire de Québec
Affiliée à: CIUSSS de la Capitale-Nationale
1050, ch Sainte-Foy, Québec, QC G1S 4L8
Tél: 418-525-4444
www.chudequebec.ca
www.facebook.com/chudequebec; twitter.com/chudequebec;
www.youtube.com/user/chudequebec
Note: Affilié à l'Université Laval et Université de Québec.

Québec: **Hôpital Jeffery Hale**
Affiliée à: CIUSSS de la Capitale-Nationale
1250, ch Sainte-Foy, Québec, QC G1S 2M6
Tél: 418-684-5333 Téléc: 418-684-2290
Ligne sans frais: 888-984-5333
www.jhsb.ca
Nombre de lits: 99 lits de soins de longue durée
Note: Services: imagerie médicale et prélèvements; clinique externe; urgence mineure.

Québec: **Hôpital Sainte-Anne-de-Beaupré**
Affiliée à: CIUSSS de la Capitale-Nationale
11000, rue des Montagnards, Québec, QC G0A 1E0
Tél: 418-827-3726
Nombre de lits: 158 lits d'hébergement et de soins de longue durée; 9 lits UTRF; 3 lits de soins palliatifs; 2 lits de transition
Note: Services infirmiers, médicaux, et psychosociaux.

Québec: **Hôpital Saint-François d'Assise**
Centre hospitalier universitaire de Québec
Affiliée à: CIUSSS de la Capitale-Nationale
10, rue de l'Espinay, Québec, QC G1L 3L5
Tél: 418-525-4444
www.chudequebec.ca
www.facebook.com/chudequebec; twitter.com/chudequebec;
www.youtube.com/user/chudequebec
Note: Affilié à l'Université Laval.

Québec: **L'Hôtel-Dieu de Québec**
Centre hospitalier universitaire de Québec
Affiliée à: CIUSSS de la Capitale-Nationale
11, côte du Palais, Québec, QC G1R 2J6
Tél: 418-525-4444
www.chudequebec.ca
www.facebook.com/chudequebec; twitter.com/chudequebec;
www.youtube.com/user/chudequebec
Note: Affilié à l'Université Laval.

Québec: **Institut universitaire de cardiologie et de pneumologie de Québec (IUCPQ)**
Affiliée à: CIUSSS de la Capitale-Nationale
Ancien nom: Hôpital Laval
2725, ch Sainte-Foy, Québec, QC G1V 4G5
Tél: 418-656-8711
iucpq.qc.ca
twitter.com/IUCPQ; www.youtube.com/IUCPQ;
www.linkedin.com/company/iucpq
Fondée en: 1918
Nombre de lits: 326 lits
Personnel: 3000
Spécialités: Cardiologie et de pneumologie
Note: Spécialisé dans la santé des personnes souffrant de maladies cardio-pulmonaires et dans le traitement des troubles liés à l'obésité. Affilié à l'Université Laval.

Rimouski: **Hôpital régional de Rimouski**
Affiliée à: CISSS du Bas-St-Laurent
150, av Rouleau, Rimouski, QC G5L 5T1
Tél: 418-724-3000
www.cisss-bsl.gouv.qc.ca
www.facebook.com/CISSSBSL; twitter.com/CISSSBSL
Nombre de lits: 255 lits
Note: Services: audiologie; cardiologie; chirurgie générale; dermatologie; endocrinologie; gastro-entérologie; inhalothérapie; mammographie; microbiologie-infectiologie; néphrologie; neurologie; nutrition clinique; ophtalmologie; orthopédie; Oto-rhino-laryngologie; pédiatrie; pneumologie; psychiatrie; radiologie; réadaptation; rhumatologie; urologie.

Rivière-Rouge: **Centre de services de Rivière-Rouge**
Affiliée à: CISSS des Laurentides
1525, rue L'Annonciation nord, Rivière-Rouge, QC J0T 1T0
Tél: 819-275-2118
www.santelaurentides.gouv.qc.ca
www.facebook.com/171472830204004; twitter.com/CisssL
Note: Services: centre désigné, services spécialisés pour les victimes d'agression sexuelle; chirurgie mineure; vaccination.

Rivière-du-Loup: **Le Centre hospitalier régional du Grand-Portage (CHRGP)**
Affiliée à: CISSS du Bas-St-Laurent
75, rue Saint-Henri, Rivière-du-Loup, QC G5R 2A4
Tél: 418-868-1000 Téléc: 418-868-1032
www.cisss-bsl.gouv.qc.ca
www.facebook.com/CISSSBSL; twitter.com/CISSSBSL
Nombre de lits: 145 lits
Population desservi: 85400
Note: Services: urgence; périnatalité; pédiatrie; psychiatrie ambulatoire; gériatrie ambulatoire; locomoteur.

Roberval: **Hôpital de Roberval**
Affiliée à: CIUSSS du Saguenay-Lac-Saint-Jean
450, rue Brassard, Roberval, QC G8H 1B9
Tél: 418-275-0110
santesaglac.gouv.qc.ca
www.facebook.com/SanteSagLac; twitter/CIUSSS_SLSJ;
www.youtube.com/channel/UCp-otUKvKshivZJ-xJbViNA;
www.linkedin.com/company/ciusss-saguenay-lac-saint-jean
Note: L'hôpital offre service d'urgence, médecine générale / interne / nucléaire, ophtalmologie, obstétrique, orthopédie, pédiatrie, chirurgie, psychiatrie, urologie, réadaptation physique.

Rouyn-Noranda: **Hôpital de Rouyn-Noranda**
Affiliée à: CISSS de l'Abitibi-Témiscamingue
4, 9e rue, Rouyn-Noranda, QC J9X 2B2
Tél: 819-764-5131
www.cisss-at.gouv.qc.ca
www.facebook.com/CISSSAT;
www.linkedin.com/company/cisss-abitibi-témiscamingue

Note: Services: centre désigné, services spécialisés pour les victimes d'agression sexuelle; dépistage; récupération des seringues et des aiguilles usagées.

Saint-Charles-Borromée: **Centre hospitalier régional de Lanaudière (CHRDL)**
Affiliée à: CISSS de Lanaudière
1000, boul Sainte-Anne, Saint-Charles-Borromée, QC J6E 6J2
Tél: 450-759-8222
www.cisss-lanaudiere.gouv.qc.ca
www.facebook.com/CISSSdeLanaudiere

Saint-Eustache: **Hôpital de Saint-Eustache**
Affiliée à: CISSS des Laurentides
520, boul Arthur-Sauvé, Saint-Eustache, QC J7R 5B1
Tél: 450-473-6811 Téléc: 450-473-6966
www.santelaurentides.gouv.qc.ca
www.facebook.com/171472830204004; twitter.com/CisssL
Nombre de lits: 261 lits
Note: Services: contraception; avortment; radiologie.

Saint-Georges: **Hôpital de Saint-Georges**
Affiliée à: CISSS de Chaudière-Appalaches
1515, 17e rue ouest, Saint-Georges, QC G5Y 4T8
Tél: 418-228-2031 Téléc: 418-227-3825
www.cisssca
www.facebook.com/cisssca12; twitter.com/cisssca12;
www.instagram.com/cisss_de_chaudiere_appalaches;
www.linkedin.com/company/cisss-de-chaudiere-appalaches
Nombre de lits: 142 lits
Note: Services: chirurgie générale; gynécologie-obstétrique; psychiatrie; radiologie.

Saint-Hyacinthe: **Hôpital Honoré-Mercier**
Affiliée à: CISSS de la Montérégie-Est
2750, boul Laframboise, Saint-Hyacinthe, QC J2S 4Y8
Tél: 450-771-3333
santemonteregie.qc.ca
Nombre de lits: 213 lits en soins aigus; 35 lits de psychiatrie courte durée; 25 lits en hébergement santé mentale
Note: Services comprennent: centre mère-enfant-famille; Pédiatrie; Soins intensifs; Chirurgie.

Saint-Jean-sur-Richelieu: **Hôpital du Haut-Richelieu**
Affiliée à: CISSS de la Montérégie-Centre
920, boul du Séminaire nord, Saint-Jean-sur-Richelieu, QC J3A 1B7
Tél: 450-359-5000 Téléc: 450-359-5251
Ligne sans frais: 866-967-4825
santemonteregie.qc.ca
Nombre de lits: 295 lits
Personnel: 1500
Note: Services: hémato-oncologie; chirurgie; chimiothérapie; imagerie médicale; Services sociaux, de psychologie, de nutrition, d'ergothérapie et de physiothérapie.

Saint-Jérôme: **Hôpital régional de Saint-Jérôme**
Affiliée à: CISSS des Laurentides
290, rue de Montigny, Saint-Jérôme, QC J7Z 5T3
Tél: 450-432-2777 Ligne sans frais: 866-963-2777
www.santelaurentides.gouv.qc.ca
www.facebook.com/171472830204004; twitter.com/CisssL
Nombre de lits: 405 lits de courte durée (76 en psychiatrie); 305 lits répartis
Population desservi: 600000 *Personnel:* 3900
Note: Services: chirurgie mineure; ECG / EEK / EMG; endoscopie; avortement; soins en fin de vie; coloscopie; radiologie.

Saint-Raymond: **Hôpital régional de Portneuf**
Affiliée à: CIUSSS de la Capitale-Nationale
700, rue Saint-Cyrille, Saint-Raymond, QC G3L 1W1
Tél: 418-337-4611
Nombre de lits: 30 lits
Note: Services: cardiologie; chirurgie mineure; fonction respiratoire; gériatrie; gynécologie; obstétrique; pédopsychiatrie; radiologie diagnostique.

Sainte-Agathe-des-Monts: **Hôpital Laurentien**
Affiliée à: CISSS des Laurentides
234, rue Saint-Vincent, Sainte-Agathe-des-Monts, QC J8C 2B8
Tél: 819-324-4000
www.santelaurentides.gouv.qc.ca
www.facebook.com/171472830204004; twitter.com/CisssL
Note: Services: salle d'allaitement; chirurgie mineure; mammographie; récupération des seringues et des aiguilles usagées; soins en fin de vie; coloscopie; radiologie.

Sainte-Anne-de-Bellevue: Hôpital Sainte-Anne
Affiliée à: CIUSSS de l'Ouest-de-l'Île-de-Montréal
305, boul des Anciens-Combattants,
Sainte-Anne-de-Bellevue, QC H9X 1Y9
Tél: 514-457-3440 *Ligne sans frais:* 800-361-9287
informations.comtl@ssss.gouv.qc.ca
www.ciusss-ouestmtl.gouv.qc.ca
Nombre de lits: 446 lits
Note: Services: gériatrie; gérontopsychiatrie; psychogériatrie;
spécialistes en réadaptation; diététistes; pharmaciens.

Salaberry-de-Valleyfield: Hôpital du Suroît
Affiliée à: CISSS de la Montérégie-Ouest
150, rue Saint-Thomas, Salaberry-de-Valleyfield, QC J6T
6C1
Tél: 450-371-9920 *Téléc:* 450 377-1372
www.santemonteregie.qc.ca/ouest
www.facebook.com/cisssmo
www.linkedin.com/company/cisss-monteregie-ouest
Note: Services: maladies rénales et hémodialyse;
accouchement; radiologie et imagerie médicale; chirurgie;
diabète; hôpital de jour; endoscopie; médecine générale et
spécialisée; pneumologie et laboratoire du sommeil; cancer;
déficience physique.

Sept-Îles: Hôpital de Sept-Îles
Affiliée à: CISSS de la Côte-Nord
45, rue du Père-Divet, Sept-Îles, QC G4R 3N7
Tél: 418-962-9761 *Téléc:* 418-962-2701
www.cisss-cotenord.gouv.qc.ca
www.facebook.com/cisss.cotenord
www.linkedin.com/company/cisss-cotenord
Note: Services: cardiologie; chirurgie générale; médecine
nucléaire; obstétrique gynécologie; radiologie diagnostique.

Shawinigan: Hôpital du Centre-de-la-Mauricie
Affiliée à: CIUSSS de la
Mauricie-et-du-Centre-du-Québec
50, 119e rue, Shawinigan, QC G9P 5K1
Tél: 819-536-7500
ciusssmcq.ca
www.facebook.com/ciusssmauriciecentreduquebec;
vimeo.com/ciusssmcq

Shawville: Hôpital du Pontiac
Affiliée à: CISSS de l'Outaouais
200, rue Argue, Shawville, QC J0X 2Y0
Tél: 819-647-2211
Note: Serivces: mammographie; récupération des seringues et
des aiguilles usagées; médecine familiale; radiologie.

Sherbrooke: Centre hospitalier universitaire de
Sherbrooke - Édifice Murray (CHUS)
Affiliée à: CIUSSS de l'Estrie
500, rue Murray, Sherbrooke, QC J1G 2K6
Tél: 819-346-1110 *Ligne sans frais:* 866-638-2601
www.santeestrie.qc.ca
www.facebook.com/SanteEstrie; twitter.com/CIUSSSE_CHUS;
www.youtube.com/channel/UCecOsAu7inOjWek_gpJDRtg
Fondée en: 1995
Nombre de lits: 677 lits
Région desservi: Sherbrooke; Haut-St-François; Val-St-François;
MRC de Coaticook *Personnel:* 6244
Note: Programmes et services comprennent: chimiothérapie
cérébrale; neurochirurgie par scalpel-gamma; neurochirurgie
assistée par IRM 3D avancé; dépistage du cancer colorectal;
production de radioisotopes par cyclotron (au Centre de
recherche). Associé à l'Université de Sherbrooke.

Sherbrooke: Centre hospitalier universitaire de
Sherbrooke - Fleurimont (CHUS)
Affiliée à: CIUSSS de l'Estrie
3001, 12e av nord, Sherbrooke, QC J1H 5N4
Tél: 819-346-1110 *Ligne sans frais:* 866-638-2601
www.santeestrie.qc.ca
www.facebook.com/SanteEstrie; twitter.com/CIUSSSE_CHUS;
www.youtube.com/channel/UCecOsAu7inOjWek_gpJDRtg
Fondée en: 1995
Nombre de lits: 677 lits
Région desservi: Sherbrooke; Haut-St-François; Val-St-François;
MRC de Coaticook *Personnel:* 6244
Note: Programmes et services comprennent: chimiothérapie
cérébrale; neurochirurgie par scalpel-gamma; neurochirurgie
assistée par IRM 3D avancé; dépistage du cancer colorectal;
production de radioisotopes par cyclotron (au Centre de
recherche). Associé à l'Université de Sherbrooke.

Sherbrooke: Centre hospitalier universitaire de
Sherbrooke - Hôtel-Dieu (CHUS)
Affiliée à: CIUSSS de l'Estrie
580, rue Bowen sud, Sherbrooke, QC J1G 2E8
Tél: 819-346-1110 *Ligne sans frais:* 866-638-2601
www.santeestrie.qc.ca
www.facebook.com/SanteEstrie; twitter.com/CIUSSSE_CHUS;
www.youtube.com/channel/UCecOsAu7inOjWek_gpJDRtg
Fondée en: 1995
Nombre de lits: 677 lits
Région desservi: Sherbrooke; Haut-St-François; Val-St-François;
MRC de Coaticook *Personnel:* 6244
Note: Programmes et services comprennent: chimiothérapie
cérébrale; neurochirurgie par scalpel-gamma; neurochirurgie
assistée par IRM 3D avancé; dépistage du cancer colorectal;
production de radioisotopes par cyclotron (au Centre de
recherche). Associé à l'Université de Sherbrooke.

Sherbrooke: Hôpital et centre d'hébergement Argyll
Affiliée à: CIUSSS de l'Estrie
375, rue Argyll, Sherbrooke, QC J1J 3H5
Tél: 819-780-2222
www.facebook.com/SanteEstrie; twitter.com/CIUSSSE_CHUS;
www.youtube.com/channel/UCecOsAu7inOjWek_gpJDRtg
Note: Programmes et services comprennent: centre
d'hébergement; centre de prélèvements; cliniques ambulatoires
gériatriques; unité de courte durée gériatrique.

Sherbrooke: Hôpital et centre d'hébergement
D'Youville
Affiliée à: CIUSSS de l'Estrie
1036, rue Belvédère sud, Sherbrooke, QC J1H 4C4
Tél: 819-780-2222
www.facebook.com/SanteEstrie; twitter.com/CIUSSSE_CHUS;
www.youtube.com/channel/UCecOsAu7inOjWek_gpJDRtg
Note: Programmes et services comprennent: centre
d'hébergement; hôpital de jour; unité de réadaptation; centre de
recherche sur le vieillissement.

Sorel-Tracy: Hôtel-Dieu de Sorel
Affiliée à: CISSS de la Montérégie-Est
400, av de l'Hôtel-Dieu, Sorel-Tracy, QC J3P 1N5
Tél: 450-746-6000
santemonteregie.qc.ca
Note: Services: ECP: récupération des seringues et des aiguilles
usagées; médecine familiale; radiologie.

Témiscouata-sur-le-Lac: Hôpital de
Notre-Dame-du-Lac
Affiliée à: CISSS du Bas-St-Laurent
58, rue de l'Église, Témiscouata-sur-le-Lac, QC G0L 1X0
Tél: 418-899-6751 *Téléc:* 418-899-2809
www.cisss-bsl.gouv.qc.ca
www.facebook.com/CISSSBSL; twitter.com/CISSSBSL
Nombre de lits: 35 lits
Note: Services: vaccination; inhalothérapie; mammographie;
réadaptation.

Terrebonne: Hôpital Pierre-Le Gardeur
Affiliée à: CISSS de Lanaudière
911, montée des Pionniers, Terrebonne, QC J6V 2H2
Tél: 450-654-7525 *Ligne sans frais:* 888-654-7525
www.cisss-lanaudiere.gouv.qc.ca
www.facebook.com/CISSSdeLanaudiere
Nombre de lits: 272 lits
Note: Programmes et services comprennent chirurgies, cliniques
spécialisées, suppléance rénale, centre d'oncologie et soins en
santé psychiatrique.

Thetford Mines: Hôpital de Thetford Mines
Affiliée à: CISSS de Chaudière-Appalaches
1717, rue Notre-Dame est, Thetford Mines, QC G6G 2V4
Tél: 418-338-7777
www.cisssca.com
www.facebook.com/cisssca12; twitter.com/cisssca12;
www.instagram.com/cisss_de_chaudiere_appalaches;
www.linkedin.com/company/cisss-de-chaudiere-appalaches
Nombre de lits: 130 lits
Note: Services: chirurgie générale; gynécologie-obstétrique;
médecine nucléaire; pédiatrie; psychiatrie; radiologie; urologie.

Trois-Pistoles: Centre hospitalier Trois-Pistoles
Affiliée à: CISSS du Bas-St-Laurent
550, rue Notre-Dame est, Trois-Pistoles, QC G0L 4K0
Tél: 418-851-1111 *Téléc:* 418-851-2944
www.cisss-bsl.gouv.qc.ca
www.facebook.com/CISSSBSL; twitter.com/CISSSBSL
Population desservi: 9000
Note: Services: imagerie médicale et électrophysiologie;
inhalothérapie; mammographie; réadaptation.

Trois-Rivières: Centre hospitalier affilié universitaire
régional
Affiliée à: CIUSSS de la
Mauricie-et-du-Centre-du-Québec
1991, boul du Carmel, Trois-Rivières, QC G8Z 3R9
Tél: 819-697-3333
ciusssmcq.ca
www.facebook.com/ciusssmauriciecentreduquebec;
vimeo.com/ciusssmcq
Note: Affilié à l'Université de Montréal en Mauricie.

Trois-Rivières: Centre St-Joseph
Affiliée à: CIUSSS de la
Mauricie-et-du-Centre-du-Québec
731, rue Sainte-Julie, Trois-Rivières, QC G9A 1Y1
Tél: 819-370-2100
ciusssmcq.ca
www.facebook.com/ciusssmauriciecentreduquebec;
vimeo.com/ciusssmcq
Nombre de lits: 198 lits hospitaliers; 100 lits de soins de longue
durée
Note: Centre St-Joseph: services hospitaliers; Centre
d'hébergement pour personnes âgées

Val-d'Or: Hôpital de Val-d'Or
Affiliée à: CISSS de l'Abitibi-Témiscamingue
725, 6e rue, Val-d'Or, QC J9P 3Y1
Tél: 819-825-5858
www.cisss-at.gouv.qc.ca
www.facebook.com/CISSSAT;
www.linkedin.com/company/cisss-abitibi-témiscamingue
Nombre de lits: 88 lits
Note: Programmes et services comprennent: audiologie;
biochimie; chirurgie générale; gastro-entérologie; médecine
nucléaire; néphrologie; pneumologie; réadaptation physique;
santé mentale

Verdun: Centre d'hébergement du Manoir-de-Verdun
Affiliée à: CIUSSS du
Centre-Sud-de-l'Île-de-Montréal
Ancien nom: CHSLD Champlain - Manoir de Verdun
5500, boul Lasalle, Verdun, QC H4H 1N9
Tél: 514-769-8801
www.ciusss-centresudmtl.gouv.qc.ca
www.facebook.com/ciusss.csmtl; twitter.com/ciusss_csmtl;
www.linkedin.com/company/ciusss-centre-sud-de-l%27île-de-mo
ntréal
Nombre de lits: 220 lits
Note: Services: denturologie; ergothérapie; hémodyalise;
médecine générale; nutrition clinique; pharmacie;
physiothérapie; podiatrie; psychologie; soins adaptés en fin de
vie.

Victoriaville: Hôtel-Dieu d'Arthabaska
Affiliée à: CIUSSS de la
Mauricie-et-du-Centre-du-Québec
5, rue des Hospitalières, Victoriaville, QC G6P 6N2
Tél: 819-357-2030
ciusssmcq.ca
www.facebook.com/ciusssmauriciecentreduquebec;
vimeo.com/ciusssmcq
Fondée en: 1884
Nombre de lits: 199 lits
Population desservi: 95000 *Personnel:* 2331
Note: Services diagnostiques et des soins médicaux généraux et
spécialisés.

Ville-Marie: Hôpital de Ville-Marie
Affiliée à: CISSS de l'Abitibi-Témiscamingue
22, rue Notre-Dame nord, Ville-Marie, QC J9V 1W8
Tél: 819-629-2420
www.cisss-at.gouv.qc.ca
www.facebook.com/CISSSAT;
www.linkedin.com/company/cisss-abitibi-témiscamingue
Nombre de lits: 31 lits courte durée; 69 lits longue durée
Note: Services: urgence; unité de soins intensifs; soins de
longue durée; petites procédures; obstétriques; soins prénatal et
postnatal; chirurgie mineure; oncologie.

Wakefield: Hôpital Mémorial de Wakefield
Affiliée à: CISSS de l'Outaouais
101, ch Burnside, Wakefield, QC J0X 3G0
Tél: 819-459-1112 *Téléc:* 819-459-1894
Ligne sans frais: 877-459-1112
Nombre de lits: 16 lits
Note: Services: récupération des seringues et des aiguilles
usagées; médecine familiale.

Hôpitaux privés

Kahnawake: Kateri Memorial Hospital Centre/Centre hospitalier Kateri Memorial
Affiliated with: CISSS de la Montérégie-Ouest
Also Known As: Tehsakotitsén:tha
PO Box 10, Kahnawake, QC J0L 1B0
Tel: 450-638-3930 *Fax:* 450-638-4634
www.kmhc.ca
www.facebook.com/kmhckahnawake
Number of Beds: 43 beds
Note: Services include family medicine, home care, community health, infection prevention & control, nutrition services, occupational therapy, physiotherapy, speech therapy, & social services.
Lisa Westaway, Executive Director
Lynda Delisle, Director, Support Services
Dr. Suzanne Jones, Director, Professional Services
Valerie Diabo, Director, Nursing

Montréal: Brassard Plasticien
Ancien nom: Centre métropolitain de Chirurgie Plastique Inc.
995, rue de Salaberry est, Montréal, QC H3L 1L2
Tél: 514-288-2097 *Téléc:* 514-288-3547
www.drbrassard.com
Nombre de lits: 17 lits
Dr. Pierre Brassard, Directeur général

Montréal: Hôpital Marie-Clarac
3530, boul Gouin est, Montréal, QC H1H 1B7
Tél: 514-321-8800 *Téléc:* 514-321-9626
ressourceshumaines.macl@ssss.gouv.qc.ca
www.hopitalmarie-clarac.qc.ca
Nombre de lits: 184 lits
Sr. Pierre-Anne Mandato, Directrice générale

Québec: La Maison Michel Sarrazin
Affiliée à: CIUSSS de la Capitale-Nationale
2101, ch Saint-Louis, Québec, QC G1T 1P5
Tél: 418-688-0878 *Téléc:* 418-681-8636
info@michel-sarrazin.ca
www.michel-sarrazin.ca
Nombre de lits: 15 lits
Alain-Philippe Lemieux, Directeur général
aplemieux@michel-sarrazin.ca

Centres locaux des services communautaires (CLSC)

Aupaluk: Dispensaire d'Aupaluk
Aupaluk, QC J0M 1X0
Tél: 819-491-9090
Nombre de lits: 1 lit

Bedford: CLSC de Bedford
Affiliée à: CIUSSS de l'Estrie
34, rue Saint-Joseph, Bedford, QC J0J 1A0
Tél: 450-248-4321
www.santeestrie.qc.ca

Beloeil: CLSC des Patriotes
Affiliée à: CISSS de la Montérégie-Est
300, rue Serge-Pepin, Beloeil, QC J3G 0B8
Tél: 450-536-2572 *Téléc:* 450-536-6367
www.santemonteregie.qc.ca/richelieu-yamaska
Fondée en: 1985
Région desservi: MRC de la Vallée-du-Richelieu
Spécialités: Cliniques de vaccination; Clinique du diabète; Programmes en périnatalité; Services à domicile aux personnes en perte d'autonomie

Boucherville: CLSC des Seigneuries de Boucherville
Affiliée à: CISSS de la Montérégie-Est
160, boul de Montarville, Boucherville, QC J4B 6S2
Tél: 450-468-3530 *Téléc:* 450-468-8530
santemonteregie.qc.ca

Candiac: CLSC Kateri
Affiliée à: CISSS de la Montérégie-Ouest
90, boul Marie-Victorin, Candiac, QC J5R 1C1
Tél: 450-659-7661 *Téléc:* 450-444-6260
santemonteregie.qc.ca/installations/clsc-kateri
Nombre de lits: 340 lits
Note: Services: abandon du tabagisme; cancer; clinique jeunesse; rencontres prénatales; soins de fin de vie; & vaccination.

Cantley: CLSC de Cantley
Affiliated with: CISSS de l'Outaouais
850, Montée de la Source, Cantley, QC J8V 3H4
Toll-Free: 844-966-6631
cisss-outaouais.gouv.qc.ca/clsc/cantley

Note: Services: santé sexuelle et infections transmises sexuellement ou par le sang (ITSS); problèmes de dépendance; soutien à domicile; & vaccination.

Cap-Chat: CLSC de Cap-Chat
Affiliée à: CISSS de la Gaspésie
CP 415, 49, rue Notre-Dame, Cap-Chat, QC G0J 1E0
Tél: 418-786-5594 *Téléc:* 418-786-2638
www.cisss-gaspesie.gouv.qc.ca
Note: Services: récupération des seringues et des aiguilles usagées; & vaccination.

Caplan: CLSC de Caplan
Affiliée à: CISSS de la Gaspésie
96, boul Perron ouest, Caplan, QC G0C 1H0
Tél: 418-388-2572
www.cisss-gaspesie.gouv.qc.ca

Carleton-sur-Mer: CLSC de Saint-Omer
Affiliée à: CISSS de la Gaspésie
CP 10, 107, rte 132 Ouest, Carleton-sur-Mer, QC G0C 2Z0
Tél: 418-364-7064 *Téléc:* 418-364-7119
www.cisss-gaspesie.gouv.qc.ca
Note: Services: prélèvements; récupération des seringues et aiguilles usagées; & vaccination.

Chandler: CLSC de Chandler
Affiliée à: CISSS de la Gaspésie
CP 1090, 633, av Daigneault, Chandler, QC G0C 1K0
Tél: 418-689-2572 *Téléc:* 418-689-4707
Nombre de lits: 62 lits

Châteauguay: CLSC Châteauguay
Affiliée à: CISSS de la Montérégie-Ouest
95, ave de la Verdure, Châteauguay, QC J6K 0E8
Tél: 450-699-3333 *Téléc:* 450-691-6202
santemonteregie.qc.ca/installations/clsc-chateauguay
Note: Services: abandon du tabagisme; clinique jeunesse; cancer; rencontres prénatales; soins de fin de vie; & vaccination.

Chertsey: CLSC de Chertsey
Affiliée à: CISSS de Lanaudière
485, rue Dupuis, Chertsey, QC J0K 3K0
Tél: 450-882-2488
www.cisss-lanaudiere.gouv.qc.ca

Côte Saint-Luc: CLSC René-Cassin
Affiliée à: CIUSSS du Centre-Ouest-de-l'Île-de-Montréal
5800, boul Cavendish, Côte Saint-Luc, QC H4W 2T5
Tél: 514-484-7878
www.ciusss-centreouestmtl.gouv.qc.ca
Spécialités: Services médicaux; Services psychosociaux; Centre d'éducation pour la santé; Clinique enfance - jeunesse; Services de nutrition; Vaccination

Drummondville: CLSC Drummond
Affiliée à: CIUSSS de la Mauricie-et-du-Centre-du-Québec
350, rue Saint-Jean, Drummondville, QC J2B 5L4
Tél: 819-478-6464
www.ciusssmcq.ca

Forestville: Pavillon Forestville
Affiliée à: CISSS de la Côte-Nord
CP 790, 2, 7e rue, Forestville, QC G0T 1E0
Tél: 418-587-2212 *Téléc:* 418-587-2865
Nombre de lits: 20 lits

Gaspé: CLSC de Gaspé
Affiliée à: CISSS de la Gaspésie
CP 2275, 205, boul de York ouest, 2e étage, Gaspé, QC G4X 2V7
Tél: 418-368-2572
www.cisss-gaspesie.gouv.qc.ca
Note: CSSS Côte-de-Gaspé.

Gaspé: CLSC de Rivière-au-Renard
Affiliée à: CISSS de la Gaspésie
154, boul Renard est, Gaspé, QC G4X 5R5
Tél: 418-269-2572
www.cisss-gaspesie.gouv.qc.ca
Nombre de lits: 3 lits
Note: Services: test de cholestérol; changement et suivi de pansement; récupération des seringues et des aiguilles usagées; & vaccination.

Gatineau: Centre multiservices de santé et de services sociaux de Gatineau
Affiliée à: CISSS de l'Outaouais
777, boul de la Gappe, Gatineau, QC J8T 8R2
Tél: 819-966-6550
cisss-outaouais.gouv.qc.ca/clsc/gatineau

Note: Services généraux santé; soins infirmiers et ambulatoires; consulation médicale pour les clientèles vulnérables.

Gatineau: CLSC LeGuerrier
Affiliée à: CISSS de l'Outaouais
425, rue LeGuerrier, Gatineau, QC J9H 6N8
Tél: 819-966-6540 *Téléc:* 819-966-6541
cisss-outaouais.gouv.qc.ca/clsc/leguerrier
Note: Services: santé sexuelle et infections transmises sexuellement ou par le sang (ITSS); problèmes de dépendance; soutien à domicile; & vaccination.

Gatineau: CLSC Saint-Rédempteur
Affiliée à: CISSS de l'Outaouais
85, rue Saint-Rédempteur, Gatineau, QC J8X 4E6
Tél: 819 966-6510
cisss-outaouais.gouv.qc.ca/clsc/saint-redempteur
Note: Services: santé sexuelle et infections transmises sexuellement ou par le sang (ITSS); problèmes de dépendance; soutien à domicile; & vaccination.

Gatineau: CLSC Vallée-de-la-Lièvre
Affiliée à: CISSS de l'Outaouais
578, rue Maclaren est, Gatineau, QC J8L 2W1
Tél: 819-986-3359 *Téléc:* 819-986-5671
cisss-outaouais.gouv.qc.ca/clsc/vallee-de-la-lievre
Note: Services: santé sexuelle et infections transmises sexuellement ou par le sang (ITSS); problèmes de dépendance; soutien à domicile; & vaccination.

Grande-Vallée: CLSC de Grande-Vallée
Affiliée à: CISSS de la Gaspésie
CP 190, 71, rue Saint-François-Xavier ouest, Grande-Vallée, QC G0E 1K0
Tél: 418-393-2001 *Ligne sans frais:* 866-393-2572
www.cisss-gaspesie.gouv.qc.ca
Note: Services: chirurgie mineure; changement et suivi de pansement; récupération des seringues et des aiguilles usagées; & vaccination.

Grosse-Ile: CLSC de l'Est
Affiliée à: CISSS des Iles
773, ch Principal, Grosse-Ile, QC G4T 6B5
Tél: 418-985-2572 *Téléc:* 418-985-2862
www.cisssdesiles.com

Huntingdon: CLSC Huntingdon
Affiliée à: CISSS de la Montérégie-Ouest
10, rue King, Huntingdon, QC J0S 1H0
Tél: 450-829-2321 *Téléc:* 450-264-6801
www.santemonteregie.qc.ca/haut-saint-laurent
Spécialités: Services médicaux; Santé mentale adulte et jeunesse; Santé publique; Clinique de vaccination; Soutien à domicile

Joliette: CLSC de Joliette
Affiliée à: CISSS de Lanaudière
380, boul Base-de-Roc, Joliette, QC J6E 9J6
Tél: 450-755-2111
www.cisss-lanaudiere.gouv.qc.ca
Spécialités: Clinique santé; Centre d'enseignement sur l'asthme; Clinique d'enseignement sur le diabète; Services de santé mentale; Cessation tabagique

Jonquière: CLSC de Jonquière
Affiliée à: CIUSSS du Saguenay-Lac-St-Jean
3667, boul Harvey, Jonquière, QC G7X 3A9
Tél: 418-695-7700

Kawawachikamach: CLSC Naskapi
Affiliée à: CISSS de la Côte-Nord
CP 5154, Kawawachikamach, QC G0G 2Z0
Tél: 418-585-2897 *Téléc:* 418-585-3126
Région desservi: La communauté autochtone de Kawawachikamach

Kebaowek: Kebaowek Health Centre
Ancien nom: Health Centre of Eagle Village
Kebaowek, QC J0Z 3R1
Tél: 819-627-9060 *Téléc:* 819-627-1885
kebaowek.ca/HC.html

Kuujjuaq: Centre de santé Tulattavik de l'Ungava
Affiliée à: Régie régionale de la santé et des services sociaux Nunavik
CP 149, Kuujjuaq, QC J0M 1C0
Tél: 819-964-2905
Nombre de lits: 15 lits hospitaliers; 10 lits de soins de longue durée
Note: Urgence; soins médicaux; soins infirmiers; maternité; radiologie; pharmacie; électrocardiographie; laboratoire; physiothérapie.

La Malbaie: CLSC de La Malbaie
Affiliée à: CIUSSS de la Capitale-Nationale
535, boul de Comporté, La Malbaie, QC G5A 1S8
Tél: 418-665-6413
www.ciusss-capitalenationale.gouv.qc.ca

La Pêche: CLSC de la Pêche
Affiliée à: CISSS de l'Outaouais
9, ch Passe-Partout, La Pêche, QC J0X 2W0
Tél: 819-459-1112 *Téléc:* 819-456-4531
Ligne sans frais: 877-459-1112
cisss-outaouais.gouv.qc.ca
André Désilets, Directeur général

LaSalle: CLSC de LaSalle
Affiliée à: CIUSSS de l'Ouest-de-l'Ile-de-Montréal
8550, boul Newman, LaSalle, QC H8N 1Y5
Tél: 514-364-2572 *Téléc:* 514-364-6365
ciusss-ouestmtl.gouv.qc.ca

Lachine: CLSC de Dorval-Lachine
Affiliée à: CIUSSS de l'Ouest-de-l'Ile-de-Montréal
1900, rue Notre-Dame, Lachine, QC H8S 2G2
Tél: 514-639-0650 *Téléc:* 514-639-0666
ciusss-ouestmtl.gouv.qc.ca
Note: Services de santé; services sociaux curatifs et préventifs.

Laval: CLSC des Mille-Iles
Affiliée à: CISSS de Laval
4731, boul Levesque est, Laval, QC H7C 1M9
Tél: 450-661-2572 *Téléc:* 450-661-6177
www.lavalensante.com
Note: Services: contraception; dépistage; ECG; changement et suivi de pansement; & vaccination.

Les Iles-de-la-Madeleine: CLSC de Bassin
Affiliée à: CISSS des Iles
599, ch du Bassin, Les Iles-de-la-Madeleine, QC G4T 0C6
Tél: 418-937-2572 *Téléc:* 418-937-5381
www.cisssdesiles.com

Les Iles-de-la-Madeleine: CLSC de Cap-aux-Meules
Affiliée à: CISSS des Iles
420, ch Principal, Les Iles-de-la-Madeleine, QC G4T 1R9
Tél: 418-986-2572 *Téléc:* 418-986-4911
www.cisssdesiles.com

Longueuil: CLSC de Longueuil-Ouest
Affiliée à: CISSS de la Montérégie-Est
201, boul Curé-Poirier ouest, Longueuil, QC J4J 2G4
Tél: 450-651-9830 *Téléc:* 450-651-4606
santemonteregie.qc.ca

Longueuil: CLSC Simonne-Monet-Chartrand
Affiliée à: CISSS de la Montérégie-Est
1303, boul Jacques-Cartier est, Longueuil, QC J4M 2Y8
Tél: 450-463-2850 *Téléc:* 450-646-7552
santemonteregie.qc.ca

Low: CLSC de Low
Affiliée à: CISSS de l'Outaouais
334, rte 105, Low, QC J0X 2C0
Tél: 819-422-3548 *Téléc:* 819-422-3568

Marsoui: CLSC de Marsoui
Affiliée à: CISSS de la Gaspésie
CP 415, 8, rte Principale est, Marsoui, QC G0E 1S0
Tél: 418-763-2261
www.cisss-gaspesie.gouv.qc.ca

Matapédia: CLSC Malauze de Matapédia
Affiliée à: CISSS de la Gaspésie
CP 190, 14, boul Perron, Matapédia, QC G0J 1V0
Tél: 418-865-2221 *Téléc:* 418-865-2317
www.cisss-gaspesie.gouv.qc.ca
Note: Services sociaux; programme petite enfance; clinique de vaccination et dépistage; programme de santé mentale; services aux personnes handicapées; soutien à domicile; service dentaire. Le centre d'hébergement est situé au deuxième étage du CLSC.

Métabetchouan-Lac-a-la-Cr: CLSC Secteur-Sud
Affiliée à: CIUSSS du Saguenay-Lac-Saint-Jean
1895, rte 169, Métabetchouan-Lac-a-la-Cr, QC G8G 1B4
Tél: 418-669-2000
santesaglac.gouv.qc.ca

Mont-Louis: CLSC de Mont-Louis
Affiliée à: CISSS de la Gaspésie
CP 100, 19, 1e av ouest, Mont-Louis, QC G0E 1T0
Tél: 418-797-2744 *Téléc:* 418-797-5173
www.cisss-gaspesie.gouv.qc.ca

Montréal: Clinique communautaire de Pointe-Saint-Charles
500, av Ash, Montréal, QC H3K 2R4
Tél: 514-937-9251 *Téléc:* 514-937-3492
ccpsc.qc.ca
Luc Leblanc, Coordonnateur général

Montréal: CLSC d'Ahuntsic
Affiliée à: CIUSSS du Nord-de-l'Ile-de-Montréal
1165, boul Henri-Bourassa est, Montréal, QC H2C 3K2
Tél: 514-384-2000
ciusss-nordmtl.gouv.qc.ca
Spécialités: Prélèvements; Services sociaux courants; Réadaptation; Information sur les vaccins

Montréal: CLSC de Benny Farm
Affiliée à: CIUSSS du Centre-Ouest-de-l'Ile-de-Montréal
6484, av de Monkland, Montréal, QC H4B 1H3
Tél: 514-484-7878 *Téléc:* 514-485-6406

Montréal: CLSC de Bordeaux-Cartierville
Affiliée à: CIUSSS du Nord-de-l'Ile-de-Montréal
11822, av du Bois-de-Boulogne, Montréal, QC H3M 2X6
Tél: 514-331-2572
ciusss-nordmtl.gouv.qc.ca

Montréal: CLSC de Côte-des-Neiges
Affiliée à: CIUSSS du Centre-Ouest-de-l'Ile-de-Montréal
5700, ch de la Côte-des-Neiges, Montréal, QC H3T 2A8
Tél: 514-731-8531 *Téléc:* 514-731-9600
www.csssdelamontagne.qc.ca

Montréal: CLSC de Hochelaga-Maisonneuve
Affiliée à: CIUSSS de l'Est-de-l'Ile-de-Montréal
4201, rue Ontario est, Montréal, QC H1V 1K2
Tél: 514-253-2181
www.cssslucilleteasdale.qc.ca
Spécialités: Les services de santé; Les services sociaux

Montréal: CLSC de l'Est-de-Montréal
Affiliée à: CIUSSS de l'Est-de-l'Ile-de-Montréal
13926, rue Notre-Dame est, Montréal, QC H1A 1T5
Tél: 514-642-4050
www.cssspointe.ca
Spécialités: Services sociaux; Réadaptation; Aide domestique; Vaccination

Montréal: CLSC de La Petite Patrie
Affiliée à: CIUSSS du Nord-de-l'Ile-de-Montréal
6520, rue de Saint-Vallier, Montréal, QC H2S 2P7
Tél: 514-273-4508
ciusss-nordmtl.gouv.qc.ca
Spécialités: Service de santé; Services sociaux; Services de psychogériatrie; Services d'aide à domicile; Réadaptation; Services d'information

Montréal: CLSC de Mercier-Est
Affiliée à: CIUSSS de l'Est-de-l'Ile-de-Montréal
9503, rue Sherbrooke est, Montréal, QC H1L 6P2
Tél: 514-356-2572
www.cssspointe.ca
Note: Les Services: Sevices de prélèvement; Services pour les futurs parents, nourrissons, enfant âgés de moins de 5 ans et leurs parents; Clinique des jeunes (jeunes âgés de 12 à 18 ans); Santé mentale; Radiologie

Montréal: CLSC de Montréal-Nord
Affiliée à: CIUSSS du Nord-de-l'Ile-de-Montréal
11441, boul Lacordaire, Montréal, QC H1G 4J9
Tél: 514-384-2000
ciusss-nordmtl.gouv.qc.ca
Spécialités: Clinique des adultes; Clinique des jeunes; Informations et counselling; Clinique d'avortement; Pose de dispositifs intra-utérins (DIU)

Montréal: CLSC de Parc Extension
Affiliée à: CIUSSS du Centre-Ouest-de-l'Ile-de-Montréal
7085, rue Hutchison, Montréal, QC H3N 1Y9
Tél: 514-273-9591
www.csssdelamontagne.qc.ca
Spécialités: Soins infirmiers et médicaux; Services psychosociaux; Réadaptation; Aide domestique; Assistance personnelle

Montréal: CLSC de Rivière-des-Prairies
Affiliée à: CIUSSS de l'Est-de-l'Ile-de-Montréal
8655, boul Perras, Montréal, QC H1E 4M7
Tél: 514-494-4924
Spécialités: Les services de santé; Les services sociaux

Montréal: CLSC de Rosemont
Affiliée à: CIUSSS de l'Est-de-l'Ile-de-Montréal
Centre administratif, 2909, rue Rachel est, Montréal, QC H1W 0A9
Tél: 514-524-3541
www.cssslucilleteasdale.qc.ca
Spécialités: Services de santé; Services psychosociaux; Services sociaux scolaires; Services de maintien à domicile; Service de santé dentaire

Montréal: CLSC de Saint-Henri
Affiliée à: CIUSSS du Centre-Sud-de-l'Ile-de-Montréal
3833, rue Notre-Dame ouest, Montréal, QC H4C 1P8
Tél: 514-933-7541
ciusss-centresudmtl.gouv.qc.ca

Montréal: CLSC de Saint-Michel
Affiliée à: CIUSSS de l'Est-de-l'Ile-de-Montréal
3355, rue Jarry est, Montréal, QC H1Z 2E5
Tél: 514-722-3000
Spécialités: Clinique médicale; Prélèvements; Vaccination; Soutien à domicile

Montréal: CLSC de Villeray
Affiliée à: CIUSSS du Nord-de-l'Ile-de-Montréal
1425, rue Jarry est, Montréal, QC H2E 1A7
Tél: 514-376-4141
ciusss-nordmtl.gouv.qc.ca
Fondée en: 1985
Spécialités: Promotion de la santé; Intervention psychosociale; Services thérapeutiques; Vaccination des enfants; Support à l'allaitement; Soutien à domicile

Montréal: CLSC des Faubourgs - Visitation
Affiliée à: CIUSSS du Centre-Sud-de-l'Ile-de-Montréal
1705, rue de la Visitation, Montréal, QC H2L 3C3
Tél: 514-527-2361 *Téléc:* 514-598-7754
www.ciusss-centresudmtl.gouv.qc.ca

Montréal: CLSC du Lac-Saint-Louis
Affiliée à: CIUSSS de l'Ouest-de-l'Ile-de-Montréal
180, av Cartier, Montréal, QC H9S 4S1
Tél: 514-697-4110
ciusss-ouestmtl.gouv.qc.ca
Note: Les Services: Santé sexuelle (514-697-4110, poste 1313); Suivis post-natals (514-697-4110, poste 1346); Soutien à l'allaitement (514-697-4110, poste 1346); Suivi diététique (514-697-4110, poste 1346); Vaccination (514-697-4110); Suivis intensifs et continus pour la clientèle vulnérable (514-697-4110, poste 1346); Clinique des jeunes (514-697-4110, poste 1313); Services psychosociaux (514-697-4110, poste 1334); Santé dentaire (514-697-4110).

Montréal: CLSC du Lac-Saint-Louis
Affiliée à: CIUSSS de l'Ouest-de-l'Ile-de-Montréal
13800, bou Gouin ouest, Montréal, QC H8Z 3H6
Tél: 514-626-2572
ciusss-ouestmtl.gouv.qc.ca

Montréal: CLSC du Plateau Mont-Royal
Affiliée à: CIUSSS du Centre-Sud-de-l'Ile-de-Montréal
4625, av de Lorimier, Montréal, QC H2H 2B4
Tél: 514-521-7663
ciusss-centresudmtl.gouv.qc.ca
Spécialités: Services psychosociaux; Services médicaux courants; Service en nutrition; Service d'échange de seringues pour personnes toxicomanes; Réadaptation

Montréal: CLSC Métro
Affiliée à: CIUSSS du Centre-Ouest-de-l'Ile-de-Montréal
1801, boul de Maisonneuve ouest, Montréal, QC H3H 1J9
Tél: 514-934-0354
www.csssdelamontagne.qc.ca
Spécialités: Clinique médicale; Services sociaux; Programmes de santé pour les écoles et les garderies; Thérapie familiale et de couple

Montréal: CLSC Olivier-Guimond
Affiliée à: CIUSSS de l'Est-de-l'Ile-de-Montréal
5810, rue Sherbrooke est, Montréal, QC H1N 1B2
Tél: 514-255-2365
www.cssslucilleteasdale.qc.ca
Spécialités: Maladies infectieuses; Santé mentale; Violence conjugale et familiale; Santé dentaire; Nutrition; Réadaptation

Montréal: CLSC Saint-Louis-du-Parc
**Affiliée à: CIUSSS du
Centre-Sud-de-l'Île-de-Montréal**
#100, 15, av du Mont-Royal ouest, Montréal, QC H2T 2R9
Tél: 514-286-9657 *Téléc:* 514-286-9706
www.ciusss-centresudmtl.gouv.qc.ca

Murdochville: CLSC de Murdochville
Affiliée à: CISSS de la Gaspésie
600, rue William-May, Murdochville, QC G0E 1W0
Tél: 418-784-2572 *Téléc:* 418-784-3629
www.cisss-gaspesie.gouv.qc.ca
Note: Services: centre désigné, services spécialisés pour les
victimes d'agression sexuelle; chirurgie mineure; changement et
suivi de pansement; récupération des seringues et des aiguilles
usagées.; & vaccination.

Paspébiac: CLSC de Paspébiac
Affiliée à: CISSS de la Gaspésie
CP 7000, 273, boul Gérard-D.-Lévesque, Paspébiac, QC G0C
2K0
Tél: 418-752-2572
www.cisss-gaspesie.gouv.qc.ca

Percé: CLSC de Barachois
Affiliée à: CISSS de la Gaspésie
1070, rte 132 est, Percé, QC G0C 1A0
Tél: 418-645-2572 *Téléc:* 418-645-2106
www.cisss-gaspesie.gouv.qc.ca
Note: CSSS Côte-de-Gaspé.

Percé: CLSC de Percé
Affiliée à: CISSS de la Gaspésie
CP 269, 98, rte 132 ouest, Percé, QC G0C 2L0
Tél: 418-782-2572
www.cisss-gaspesie.gouv.qc.ca
Note: CSSS du Rocher-Percé.

Plessisville: CLSC de l'Érable
**Affiliée à: CIUSSS de la
Mauricie-et-du-Centre-du-Québec**
1331, rue Saint-Calixte, Plessisville, QC G6L 1P4
Tél: 819-362-6301 *Téléc:* 819-362-6812
ciusssmcq.ca
Nombre de lits: 40 lits de soins de longue durée
Note: CLSC de l'Érable, et l'Unité de soins longue durée de
l'Érable.

Pohénégamook: CLSC de Pohénégamook
Affiliée à: CISSS du Bas-St-Laurent
1922, rue Saint-Vallier, Pohénégamook, QC G0L 1J0
Tél: 418-859-2450 *Téléc:* 418-859-1285
www.cisss-bsl.gouv.qc.ca

Pointe-à-la-Croix: CLSC de Pointe-à-la-Croix
Affiliée à: CISSS de la Gaspésie
CP 389, 48, boul Interprovincial, Pointe-à-la-Croix, QC G0C
1L0
Tél: 418-788-5454 *Téléc:* 418-788-2510
www.cisss-gaspesie.gouv.qc.ca

Port-Daniel-Gascons: CLSC Gascons
Affiliée à: CISSS de la Gaspésie
CP 28, 63, rte 132, Port-Daniel-Gascons, QC G0C 1P0
Tél: 418-396-2572 *Téléc:* 418-396-2367
www.cisss-gaspesie.gouv.qc.ca
Note: Services: prélèvements; récupération des seringues et des
aiguilles usagées.; & vaccination.

Puvirnituq: Centre de santé Inuulitsivik
**Affiliated with: Régie régionale de la santé et des
services sociaux Nunavik**
ch Baie D'Hudson, Puvirnituq, QC J0M 1P0
Tél: 819-988-2957
recruitment.csi@ssss.gouv.qc.ca
www.inuulitsivik.ca
Number of Beds: 17 lits hospitaliers; 8 lits de soins de longue
durée
Note: Soins médicaux, soins dentaires; sages-femmes; services
en santé mentale; télémedicine; laboratoire; points de service:
Akulivik, Inukjuak, Ivujivik, Kuujjuarapik, Puvirnituq, Salluit et
Umiujuaq.

Quaqtaq: Dispensaire de Quaqtaq
General Delivery, Quaqtaq, QC J0M 1J0
Tél: 819-492-9090
Région desservi: Nunavik (région sociosanitaire)
Spécialités: Services intégrés de dépistage et de prévention des
infections transmissibles sexuellement et par le sang (SIDEP)

Québec: CLSC de la Basse-Ville
Affiliée à: CIUSSS de la Capitale-National
50, rue Saint-Joseph, Québec, QC G1K 3A5
Tél: 418-529-2572 *Téléc:* 418-524-3234
www.ciusss-capitalenationale.gouv.qc.ca

Québec: CLSC de la Haute-Ville
Affiliée à: CIUSSS de la Capitale-Nationale
55, ch Sainte-Foy, Québec, QC G1R 1S9
Tél: 418-641-2572
www.ciusss-capitalenationale.gouv.qc.ca
Note: Services: Consultations médicales; Consultations
psychosociales; Clinique jeunesse; Contraception orale
d'urgence; Cours prénataux; Vaccination; Soutien à domicile

Québec: CLSC de la Jacques-Cartier (Loretteville)
Affiliée à: CIUSSS de la Capitale-Nationale
11999A, rue de l'Hôpital, Québec, QC G2A 2T7
Tél: 418-843-2572 *Téléc:* 418-843-3880
www.ciusss-capitalenationale.gouv.qc.ca
Spécialités: Clinique prénatale; Soutien à domicile; Services
infirmiers

Richelieu: CLSC du Richelieu
Affiliée à: CISSS de la Montérégie-Centre
300, ch de Marieville, Richelieu, QC J3L 3V8
Tél: 450-658-7561 *Téléc:* 450-658-4390
www.santemonteregie.qc.ca/haut-richelieu-rouville
Spécialités: Rencontres prénatales; Clinique de la petite enfance
(450-658-7561, poste 4164)

Richmond: CLSC de Richmond
Affiliée à: CIUSSS de l'Estrie
110, rue Barlow, Richmond, QC J0B 2H0
Tél: 819-542-2777
www.santeestrie.qc.ca

Rimouski: CLSC Rimouski
Affiliée à: CISSS du Bas-St-Laurent
165, rue des Gouverneurs, Rimouski, QC G5L 7R2
Tél: 418-724-7204
www.cisss-bsl.gouv.qc.ca
Note: 3 autres points de service: Saint-Fabien, Saint-Marcellin,
et Saint-Narcisse

Rivière-du-Loup: CLSC de Rivière-du-Loup
Affiliée à: CISSS du Bas-St-Laurent
22, rue Saint-Laurent, Rivière-du-Loup, QC G5R 4W5
Tél: 418 868-1000 *Téléc:* 418-867-4713
www.cisss-bsl.gouv.qc.ca

Rouyn-Noranda: CLSC de Rouyn-Noranda
Affiliée à: CISSS de l'Abitibi-Témiscamingue
1, 9e rue, Rouyn-Noranda, QC J9X 2A9
Tél: 819-762-5599
www.cisss-at.gouv.qc.ca
Note: Point de service CLSC, et consultations externes CHSGS.

Saint-Félicien: CLSC Saint-Félicien - Édifice
Bon-Conseil
Affiliée à: CIUSSS du Saguenay-Lac-St-Jean
1228, boul Sacré-Coeur, Saint-Félicien, QC G8K 2P8
Tél: 418-679-5270

Saint-Félicien: CLSC Saint-Félicien - Édifice Hôtel de
Ville
Affiliée à: CIUSSS du Saguenay-Lac-St-Jean
1209, boul Sacré-Coeur, Saint-Félicien, QC G8K 2R5
Tél: 418-679-5270

Saint-Hubert: CLSC Saint-Hubert
Affiliée à: CISSS de la Montérégie-Centre
6800, boul Cousineau, Saint-Hubert, QC J3Y 8Z4
Tél: 450-443-7400
www.santemonteregie.qc.ca/champlain
Région desservi: L'arrondissement Saint-Hubert de la Ville de
Longueuil
Spécialités: Rencontres prénatales; Consultations
psychosociales

Saint-Jean-sur-Richelieu: CLSC de la
Vallée-des-Forts
Affiliée à: CISSS de la Montérégie-Centre
978, boul du Séminaire nord, Saint-Jean-sur-Richelieu, QC
J3A 1E5
Tél: 450-358-2572 *Téléc:* 450-349-0724

Saint-Léonard: CLSC de Saint-Léonard
Affiliée à: CIUSSS de l'Est-de-l'Île-de-Montréal
5540, rue Jarry est, Saint-Léonard, QC H1P 1T9
Tél: 514-722-3000
ciusss-estmtl.gouv.qc.ca

Note: Services: abandon du tabagisme; soutien psychosocial;
clinique jeunesse; soins de fin de vie; & vaccination.

Saint-Ludger: CLSC Saint-Ludger
Affiliée à: CIUSSS de l'Estrie
210-A, rue La Salle, Saint-Ludger, QC G0M 1W0
Tél: 819-583-0330 *Ligne sans frais:* 800-827-2572
www.santeestrie.qc.ca

Saint-Paulin: CLSC de St-Paulin
**Affiliée à: CIUSSS de la
Mauricie-et-du-Centre-du-Québec**
2841, rue Laflèche, Saint-Paulin, QC J0K 3G0
Tél: 819-268-2572
www.csssm.qc.ca
Spécialités: Services infirmiers courants; Vaccination

Saint-Rémi: CLSC Jardin-du-Québec
Affiliée à: CISSS de la Montérégie-Ouest
2, rue Sainte-Famille, Saint-Rémi, QC J0L 2L0
Tél: 450-454-4671 *Téléc:* 450-454-4538
santemonteregie.qc.ca/installations/clsc-jardin-du-quebec-saint-r
emi
Note: Services: abandon du tabagisme; cancer; clinique
jeunesse; rencontres prénatales; soins de fin de vie; &
vaccination.

Saint-Siméon: CLSC de Saint-Siméon
Affiliée à: CIUSSS de la Capitale-Nationale
371, rue Saint-Laurent, Saint-Siméon, QC G0T 1X0
Tél: 418-638-2369
www.ciusss-capitalenationale.gouv.qc.ca
Nombre de lits: 18 lits
Note: Centre local de services communautaires (418-638-2369);
centre d'hébergement et centre de jour.

Sherbrooke: CLSC Camirand
Affiliée à: CIUSSS de l'Estrie
50, rue Camirand, Sherbrooke, QC J1H 4J5
Tél: 819-780-2220
www.santeestrie.qc.ca
Note: Services: dépistage; désintoxication; récupération des
seringues et des aiguilles usagées.; & vaccination.

Sorel-Tracy: CLSC Gaston-Bélanger
Affiliée à: CISSS de la Montérégie-Est
Également connu sous le nom de: CLSC du Havre
30, rue Ferland, Sorel-Tracy, QC J3P 3C7
Tél: 450-746-4545
santemonteregie.qc.ca
Nombre de lits: 18 lits

Ste-Anne-des-Monts: CLSC de
Sainte-Anne-des-Monts
Affiliée à: CISSS de la Gaspésie
50, rue Belvédère, Ste-Anne-des-Monts, QC G4V 1X4
Tél: 418-763-7771 *Téléc:* 418-763-7176
www.cisss-gaspesie.gouv.qc.ca

Ste-Catherine-de-la-J-Car: CLSC de la
**Jacques-Cartier
(Sainte-Catherine-de-la-Jacques-Cartier)**
Affiliée à: CIUSSS de la Capitale-Nationale
4570, rte de Fossambault, Ste-Catherine-de-la-J-Car, QC
G3N 2T5
Tél: 418-843-2572 *Téléc:* 418-843-3880
www.ciusss-capitalenationale.gouv.qc.ca
Spécialités: Soutien à domicile; Services infirmiers

Terrebonne: CLSC Lamater - boul des Seigneurs
Affiliée à: CISSS de Lanaudière
2099, boul des Seigneurs, Terrebonne, QC J6X 4A7
Tél: 450-471-2881
www.cisss-lanaudiere.gouv.qc.ca
Spécialités: Clinique médicale; Services sociaux scolaires;
Service en santé mentale; Services dentaires préventifs;
Clinique des jeunes; Vaccination

Trois-Rivières: CLSC Laviolette
**Affiliée à: CIUSSS de la
Mauricie-et-du-Centre-du-Québec**
1274, rue Laviolette, Trois-Rivières, QC G9A 1W4
Tél: 819-379-5650
ciusssmcq.ca
Spécialités: Soutien à domicile

Victoriaville: CLSC Suzor-Côté
**Affiliée à: CIUSSS de la
Mauricie-et-du-Centre-du-Québec**
100, rue de l'Ermitage, Victoriaville, QC G6P 9N2
Tél: 819-758-7281
ciusssmcq.ca
Fondée en: 1981

Ile d'Entrée: CLSC de l'Ile d'Entrée
Affiliée à: CISSS des Iles
124, ch Big Isle, Ile d'Entrée, QC G4T 1Z1
Tél: 418-986-4299 *Téléc:* 418-986-4094
www.cisssdesiles.com

Centres de traitements spécialisés

Amos: Centre Normand
Affiliée à: CISSS de l'Abitibi-Témiscamingue
621, rue de l'Harricana, Amos, QC J9T 2P9
Tél: 819-732-8241 *Téléc:* 819-727-2210
www.cisss-at.gouv.qc.ca

Fondée en: 1981
Nombre de lits: 10 lits
Note: Offre des services de réadaptation aux personnes qui présentent une dépendance - à l'alcool, drogues illicites, médicaments, jeu; services de support psychosocial.

Amos: CRDI Abitibi-Témiscamingue Clair-Foyer
Affiliée à: CISSS de l'Abitibi-Témiscamingue
841, 3e rue ouest, Amos, QC J9T 2T4
Tél: 819-732-6511 *Téléc:* 819-732-0922
www.cisss-at.gouv.qc.ca

Nombre de lits: 31 lits
Note: Centre de réadaptation (déficience intellectuelle); services de support.

Baie-Comeau: Centre de protection et de réadaptation de la Côte-Nord
Affiliée à: CISSS de la Côte-Nord
835, boul Joliet, Baie-Comeau, QC G5C 1P5
Tél: 418-589-9927 *Téléc:* 418-589-4304
www.cisss-cotenord.gouv.qc.ca
Nombre de lits: 225 lits

Beauceville: Centre de réadaptation en alcoolisme et toxicomanie de Beauceville
Affiliée à: CISSS de Chaudière-Appalaches
Ancien nom: Centre de réadaptation en alcoolisme et toxicomanie de Chaudière-Appalaches
253, rte 108, 3e étage, Beauceville, QC G5X 2Z3
Tél: 418-774-3329 *Téléc:* 418-774-4423
Ligne sans frais: 888-774-3329
www.cisss-ca.gouv.qc.ca

Nombre de lits: 14 lits

Bonaventure: Centre de réadaptation pour les jeunes en difficulté d'adaptation de Bonaventure
Affiliée à: CISSS de la Gaspésie
Ancien nom: Centre jeunesse Gaspésie/Les Iles - Unité La Balise
238, av de Port Royal, Bonaventure, QC G0C 1E0
Tél: 418-534-3283
www.cisss-gaspesie.gouv.qc.ca/ou-obtenir-ces-services/par-site/centres-et-points-de-service-en-jeune

Nombre de lits: 12 lits

Bonaventure: Point de service Réadaptation et Jeunesse de Bonaventure
Affiliée à: CISSS de la Gaspésie
238, av Port-Royal, Bonaventure, QC G0C 1E0
Tél: 418-534-4243 *Téléc:* 418-534-2411
www.cisss-gaspesie.gouv.qc.ca

Chandler: Point de service Jeunesse du Rocher-Percé
Affiliée à: CISSS de la Gaspésie
Ancien nom: Centre jeunesse Gaspésie/Les Iles - Succursale Rocher-Percé
#102, 105, rue Commerciale ouest, Chandler, QC G0C 1K0
Tél: 418-689-2286
www.cisss-gaspesie.gouv.qc.ca

Chicoutimi: Centre de protection et de réadaptation pour les jeunes en difficulté d'adaptation de Chicoutimi
Affiliée à: CIUSSS du Saguenay-Lac-Saint-Jean
1109, rue Bégin, Chicoutimi, QC G7H 4P1
Tél: 418-549-4853
santesaglac.gouv.qc.ca

Fatima: Centre de réadaptation en déficience intellectuelle et troubles du spectre de l'autisme (CRDITSA)
Affiliée à: CISSS des Iles
695, ch des Caps, Fatima, QC G4T 2S9
Tél: 418-986-3590
www.cssssdesiles.qc.ca

Gaspé: Centre de réadaptation pour les jeunes en difficulté d'adaptation de Gaspé
Affiliée à: CISSS de la Gaspésie
Ancien nom: Centre jeunesse Gaspésie/Les Iles - Unité La Vigie
418, montée de Wakeham, Gaspé, QC G4X 2P4
Tél: 418-368-5344
www.cisss-gaspesie.gouv.qc.ca/ou-obtenir-ces-services/par-site/centres-et-points-de-service-en-jeune

Gaspé: Centre jeunesse Gaspésie/Les Iles - Unité La Rade
Affiliée à: CISSS de la Gaspésie
#100, 205, boul de York ouest, Gaspé, QC G4X 2V7
Tél: 418-368-1803
www.cisss-gaspesie.gouv.qc.ca

Gaspé: Point de service - Réadaptation Gaspé
Affiliée à: CISSS de la Gaspésie
150, rue Mgr Ross, Gaspé, QC G4X 2S7
Tél: 418-368-2306
www.cisss-gaspesie.gouv.qc.ca

Gaspé: Programme Jeunesse
Affiliée à: CISSS de la Gaspésie
Ancien nom: Centre jeunesse Gaspésie/Les Iles
#100, 205, boul de York ouest, Gaspé, QC G4X 2V7
Tél: 418-368-1803
Nombre de lits: 55 lits

Gatineau: Centre de réadaptation en dépendance de l'Outaouais
Affiliée à: CISSS de l'Outaouais
Ancien nom: Centre Jellinek; Pavillon Jelinek
25, rue Saint-François, Gatineau, QC J9A 1B1
Tél: 819-776-5584 *Téléc:* 819-776-0255
www.cisss-outaouais.gouv.qc.ca
Nombre de lits: 33 places
Note: Centre de réadaptation des drogues, de l'alcool ou du jeu.

Gatineau: Les Centres jeunesse de l'Outaouais
Affiliée à: CISSS de l'Outaouais
105, boul Sacré-Coeur, Gatineau, QC J8X 1C5
Tél: 819-771-6631
cisss-outaouais.gouv.qc.ca
Nombre de lits: 149 lits
Note: Centre jeunesse, protection

Gatineau: Pavillon du Parc inc.
Affiliée à: CISSS de l'Outaouais
124, rue Lois, Gatineau, QC J8Y 3R7
Tél: 819-770-1022 *Téléc:* 819-770-1023
www.cisss-outaouais.gouv.qc.ca
Nombre de lits: 92 lits
Note: Centre de réadaptation.
Jean Dansereau, Directeur général

Joliette: Centre de réadaptation La Myriade
Affiliée à: CISSS de Lanaudière
339, boul Base-de-Roc, Joliette, QC J6E 5P3
Tél: 450-753-9600 *Téléc:* 450-753-1930
www.cisss-lanaudiere.gouv.qc.ca
Nombre de lits: 38 lits

Joliette: Les Centres jeunesse de Lanaudière (CJL)
Affiliée à: CISSS de Lanaudière
260, rue Lavaltrie sud, Joliette, QC J6E 5X7
Tél: 450-759-1157 *Ligne sans frais:* 800-668-9229
www.cisss-lanaudiere.gouv.qc.ca
Maryse Olivier, Directrice, Protection de la jeunesse

Lachine: Centre de réadaptation de l'Ouest de Montréal (CROM/WMR)/West Montreal Readaptation Centre
Affiliée à: CIUSSS de l'Ouest-de-l'Ile-de-Montréal
8000, rue Notre-Dame, Lachine, QC H8R 1H2
Tél: 514-363-3025 *Téléc:* 514-364-0608
crom.ca
Région desservi: CSSS de l'Ouest de l'Ile; CSSS Cavendish; CSSS de la Montagne
Spécialités: Services spécialisés pour des adultes et enfants présentant une déficience intellectuelle ou un trouble du spectre autistique
Dre. Katherine Moxness, Directrice générale

Laval: Centre de protection de l'enfance et de la jeunesse de Laval
Affiliée à: CISSS de Laval
308, boul Cartier ouest, Laval, QC H7N 2J2
Tél: 450-975-4150
www.lavalensante.com

Laval: CRDI Normand-Laramée
304, boul Cartier ouest, Laval, QC H7N 2J2
Tél: 450-972-2099
www.lavalensante.com

Les Iles-de-la-Madeleine: Centre de protection et de réadaptation pour les jeunes des Iles-de-la-Madeleine
Affiliée à: CISSS de la Gaspésie
Ancien nom: Centre jeunesse Gaspésie/Les Iles - Succursale des Iles
539-2, ch Principal, Les Iles-de-la-Madeleine, QC G4T 1E7
Tél: 418-986-2230
www.cisss-gaspesie.gouv.qc.ca

Les Iles-de-la-Madeleine: Centre de réadapation en déficience physique des Iles-de-la-Madeleine
Affiliée à: CISSS de la Gaspésie
695, ch des Caps, Les Iles-de-la-Madeleine, QC G4T 2S9
Tél: 418-986-4870 *Téléc:* 418-986-2623
www.cisss-gaspesie.gouv.qc.ca

Lévis: Centre de protection et de réadaptation pour les jeunes en difficulté d'adaptation
Affiliée à: CISSS de Chaudière-Appalaches
100, rue Mgr Ignace-Bourget, Lévis, QC G6V 2Y9
Tél: 418 837-9331
www.cisss-ca.gouv.qc.ca
Nombre de lits: 146 lits
Note: Services de la protection de la jeunesse; service aux jeunes contrevenants; service d'adoption; services de réadaptation. Installations: Lévis, Saint-Romuald, Montmagny, Sainte-Marie, Saint-Joseph, Saint-Georges & Thetford Mines.

Lévis: Centre de réadaptation en déficience intellectuelle de Chaudière-Appalaches
Affiliée à: CISSS de Chaudière-Appalaches
55, rue du Mont-Marie, Lévis, QC G6V 0B8
Tél: 418-833-3218 *Téléc:* 418-833-9849
Ligne sans frais: 866-333-3218
www.cisss-ca.gouv.qc.ca
Nombre de lits: 674 lits

Lévis: Centre de réadaptation en déficience physique de Charny
Affiliée à: CISSS de Chaudière-Appalaches
9500, boul du Centre-Hospitalier, Lévis, QC G6X 0A1
Tél: 418-380-2064 *Téléc:* 418-380-2096
www.cisss-ca.gouv.qc.ca
Nombre de lits: 48 lits
Note: Programmes: Déficience auditive, Déficience du langage, Déficience motrice (enfant, adulte), Clinique de sclérose en plaques, Programme d'évaluation & de réadaptation en conduite automobile, Neurotraumatisme, Dépistage du traumatisme craniocérébral léger, Programme intensif de gestion autonome de la douleur, et Programme de suppléance à la communication.

Listuguj: Centre de réadaptation pour les jeunes en difficulté d'adaptation de Listuguj
Affiliée à: CISSS de la Gaspésie
Ancien nom: Centre jeunesse Gaspésie/Les Iles - Unité Gignu
CP 193, 4, rue Pacific, Listuguj, QC G0C 2R0
Tél: 418-788-5605
www.cisss-gaspesie.gouv.qc.ca

Longueuil: Centre de réadaptation en déficience intellectuelle Montérégie-est (CRDITED)
Affiliée à: CISSS de la Montérégie-Est
1255, rue Beauregard, Longueuil, QC J4K 2M3
Tél: 450-679-6511 *Téléc:* 450-928-3315
santemonteregie.qc.ca
Nombre de lits: 1157 lits
Yves Masse, Président-directeur général

Longueuil: Centre jeunesse de la Montérégie (CJM)
Affiliée à: CISSS de la Montérégie-Est
575, rue Adoncour, Longueuil, QC J4G 2M6
Tél: 450-928-5125 *Ligne sans frais:* 800-641-4315
www.centrejeunessemonteregie.qc.ca
Fondée en: 1992
Personnel: 1906
Louise Potvin, Présidente-directrice générale

Montréal: Atelier le Fil d'Ariane inc.
#100, 4837, rue Boyer, Montréal, QC H2J 3E6
Tél: 514-842-5592 *Téléc:* 514-842-8343
atelier.bureau.ariane@ssss.gouv.qc.ca
atelier@atelierlefildariane.org
www.atelierlefildariane.org
www.facebook.com/www.atelierlefildariane.org
Nombre de lits: 20 places
Note: Un atelier de travail pour des adultes ayant des limitations

fonctionnelles sur le plan intellectuel; l'atelier favorise l'intégration sociale & communautaire & l'autonomie personnelle & professionnelle des artisans.
Gaétan Gagné, Directeur général

Montréal: Centre d'accueil le programme de Portage inc.
Also Known As: Portage
885, carré Richmond, Montréal, QC H3J 1V8
Tel: 514-939-0202
www.portage.ca
www.facebook.com/PortageCanada;
twitter.com/PortageCanada; www.linkedin.com/company/portage
Year Founded: 1970
Note: Portage operates drug addiction treatment centres in the Québec cities of Montréal, Québec, Prévost, & Saint-Malachie. Centres in Atlantic Canada & Ontario assist adolescents.

Montréal: Centre de réadaptation Constance-Lethbridge
Affiliée à: CIUSSS du Centre-Ouest-de-l'Ile-de-Montréal
7005, boul de Maisonneuve ouest, Montréal, QC H4B 1T3
Tél: 514-487-1770 Ligne sans frais: 866-487-1891
www.constance-lethbridge.qc.ca
www.facebook.com/CIUSSSCentreOuest
Note: Déficience motrice

Montréal: Centre de réadaptation en déficience intellectuelle et trouble du spectre de l'autisme
Affiliée à: CIUSSS du Centre-Sud-de-l'Ile-de-Montréal
Ancien nom: Centre de réadaptation en déficience intellectuelle et en troubles envahissants
Fondation DI-TSA de Montréal, #110, 75, rue de Port-Royal est, Montréal, QC H3L 3T1
Tél: 514-387-1234
www.ciusss-centresudmtl.gouv.qc.ca

Montréal: Centre de réadaptation physique Lucie-Bruneau
Affiliée à: CIUSSS du Centre-Sud-de-l'Ile-de-Montréal
2275, av Laurier est, Montréal, QC H2H 2N8
Tél: 514-527-4527 Téléc: 514-527-0979
www.ciusss-centresudmtl.gouv.qc.ca
Nombre de lits: 50 lits
Note: Centre de réadaptation (déficience motrice).
Pierre-Paul Milette, Directeur général adjoint santé physique générale, CIUSSS du Centre-Sud-de-l'Ile-de-Montréal

Montréal: Centre de réadaptation en dépendance de Montréal - Institut universitaire
Affiliée à: CIUSSS du Centre-Sud-de-l'Ile-de-Montréal
Ancien nom: Centre Dollard-Cormier
CP 3109, 950, rue de Louvain est, Montréal, QC H2M 2E8
Tél: 514-385-1232
www.ciusss-centresudmtl.gouv.qc.ca
Nombre de lits: 55 lits

Montréal: Centre de réadaptation Mab-Mackay (CRMM)
7000, rue Sherbrooke ouest, Montréal, QC H4B 1R3
Tél: 514-488-5552 Téléc: 514-489-3477
info@mabmackay.ca
www.mabmackay.ca
Fondée en: 2006
Note: Fournit des services de réadaptation pour les personnes ayant une déficience visuelle & déficience auditive afin qu'ils puissent vivre de façon autonome. Le centre de réadaptation a été formé à la suite d'une fusion entre l'Association montréalaise pour les aveugles et le Centre de réadaptation Mackay.

Montréal: Centre hospitalier universitaire Sainte-Justine
Affiliée à: CIUSSS du Centre-Ouest-de-l'Ile-de-Montréal
3175, ch de la Côte-Sainte-Catherine, Montréal, QC H3T 1C5
Tél: 514-345-4931
www.chusj.org
www.facebook.com/ChuSteJustine; twitter.com/ChuSteJustine
Nombre de lits: 55 lits
Caroline Barbir, Présidente-directrice générale

Montréal: Centre Miriam/Miriam Home
Affiliée à: CIUSSS du Centre-Ouest-de-l'Ile-de-Montréal
8160, ch Royden, Montréal, QC H4P 2T2
Tél: 514-345-0210 Téléc: 514-345-8965
mircea.bruj.miriam@ssss.gouv.qc.ca
www.centremiriam.ca

Fondée en: 1960
Note: Soutient les personnes ayant une déficience intellectuelle.
Dr. Abraham Fuks, M.D., Président, Conseil d'administration
Daniel Amar, Directeur général

Montréal: Hôpital de réadaptation Villa Medica
225, rue Sherbrooke est, Montréal, QC H2X 1C9
Tél: 514-288-8201
info@villamedica.ca
www.villamedica.ca
Nombre de lits: 150 lits
Anne Beauchamp, Directrice générale

Montréal: Institut de réadaptation Gingras-Lindsay-de-Montréal
Affiliée à: CIUSSS du Centre-Sud-de-l'Ile-de-Montréal
Ancien nom: Institut de réadaptation de Montréal
6300, av Darlington, Montréal, QC H3S 2J4
Tél: 514-340-2085 Téléc: 514-340-2091
ciusss-centresudmtl.gouv.qc.ca
Fondée en: 1949
Nombre de lits: 200 lits

Montréal: Institut Raymond-Dewar (IRD)
Affiliée à: CIUSSS du Centre-Sud-de-l'Ile-de-Montréal
3600, rue Berri, Montréal, QC H2L 4G9
Tél: 514-284-2581 Téléc: 514-284-5086
www.ciusss-centresudmtl.gouv.qc.ca
Note: Centre de réadaptation (déficience auditive et de la parole et du language).

Montréal: Maison Elisabeth
2131, av de Marlowe, Montréal, QC H4A 3L4
Tél: 514-482-2488 Téléc: 514-482-9467
info@maisonelizabeth.ca
www.maisonelizabethhouse.com
www.facebook.com/elizabethhousemontreal;
www.linkedin.com/company/maison-elizabeth-house
Nombre de lits: 18 lits
Christine Christine, Directrice générale
christine.jagiello.elizabeth@ssss.gouv.qc.ca

Montréal: The Montréal Morgentaler Clinic/Clinique Morgentaler
The Morgentaler Clinic
#900, 1259 rue Berri, Montréal, QC H2L 4C7
Tél: 514-844-4844 Fax: 514-844-7883
Toll-Free: 888-401-4844
infos@montrealmorgentaler.ca
www.morgentalermontreal.ca
Year Founded: 1968
Note: Specialties: Pregnancy termination services; Post-abortion service.
France Desilets, General Manager

Québec: Centre de réadaptation en déficience intellectuelle de Québec (CRDIQ)
Affiliée à: CIUSSS de la Capitale-Nationale
7843, rue des Santolines, Québec, QC G1G 0G3
Tél: 418-683-2511 Téléc: 418-683-9735
www.ciusss-capitalenationale.gouv.qc.ca
Fondée en: 2001
Nombre de lits: 530 lits

Québec: Centre de réadaptation en dépendance de Québec
Affiliée à: CIUSSS de la Capitale-Nationale
Ancien nom: Centre de réadaptation Ubald-Villeneuve
2525, ch de la Canardière, Québec, QC G1J 2G3
Tél: 418-663-5008
www.ciusss-capitalenationale.gouv.qc.ca

Québec: Institut de réadaptation en déficience physique de Québec
Affiliée à: CIUSSS de la Capitale-Nationale
Également connu sous le nom de: IRDPQ
525, boul Wilfrid Hamel, Québec, QC G1M 2S8
Tél: 418-529-9141 Téléc: 418-529-7318
TTY: 418-649-3733
www.ciusss-capitalenationale.gouv.qc.ca
Nombre de lits: 165 lits
Note: Centre de réadaptation (déficience physique).

Rimouski: Centre de protection de l'enfance et de la jeunesse Pierre-Saindon
Affiliée à: CISSS du Bas-St-Laurent
CP 3500, 287, rue Pierre-Saindon, 3e étage, Rimouski, QC G5L 8V5
Tél: 418-723-1255 Téléc: 418-722-0620
www.cisss-bsl.gouv.qc.ca
Nombre de lits: 73 lits

Rimouski: Centre de réadaptation en déficience intellectuelle du Bas St-Laurent (CRDITED)
Affiliée à: CISSS du Bas-St-Laurent
Ancien nom: Centre de réadaptation intellectuelle du Bas St-Laurent
325, rue Saint-Jean-Baptiste est, Rimouski, QC G5L 1Y8
Tél: 418-723-4425 Téléc: 418-723-3196
www.cisss-bsl.gouv.qc.ca

Rouyn-Noranda: Centre de réadaptation La Maison
Affiliée à: CISSS de l'Abitibi-Témiscamingue
100, ch Docteur-Lemay, Rouyn-Noranda, QC J9X 5T2
Tél: 819-762-6592 Téléc: 819-762-2049
www.cisss-at.gouv.qc.ca
Nombre de lits: 55 lits
Note: Centre de réadaptation (déficience physique, troubles envahissants du développement).

Saint-Jean-sur-Richelieu: Les services de réadaptation du Sud-Ouest et du Renfort
Affiliée à: CISSS de la Montérégie-Ouest
#105, 315, rue MacDonald, Saint-Jean-sur-Richelieu, QC J3B 8J3
Tél: 450-348-6121 Téléc: 450-348-8440
santemonteregie.ca
Nombre de lits: 581 lits

Saint-Jérôme: Centre du Florès
Affiliée à: CISSS de Laurentides
500, boulevard des Laurentides, #255, Saint-Jérôme, QC J7Z 4M2
Tél: 450 436-5984
www.santelaurentides.gouv.qc.ca

Saint-Jérôme: Centre jeunesse des Laurentides
Affiliée à: CISSS des Laurentides
500, boul des Laurentides, Saint-Jérôme, QC J7Z 5M2
Tél: 450-436-7607 Téléc: 450-436-4811
Ligne sans frais: 866-492-3263
www.santelaurentides.gouv.qc.ca
Nombre de lits: 160 lits

Sainte-Anne-des-Monts: Point de service - Réadaptation de la Haute-Gaspésie
Affiliée à: CISSS de la Gaspésie
230, rte du Parc, Sainte-Anne-des-Monts, QC G4V 2C4
Tél: 418-763-3325
www.cisss-gaspesie.gouv.qc.ca

Sherbrooke: Centre de réadaptation Estrie (CRE)
Affiliée à: CIUSSS de l'Estrie
#200, 300, rue King est, Sherbrooke, QC J1G 1B1
Tél: 819-346-8411 Téléc: 819-346-4580
www.santeestrie.qc.ca
Spécialités: Réadaptation fonctionnelle intensive; Ressources résidentielles et d'hébergement

Sherbrooke: Centre Jean-Patrice Chiasson/Maison St-Georges
1930, rue King ouest, Sherbrooke, QC J1J 2E2
Tél: 819-821-2500
Nombre de lits: 40 places
Note: Centre de réadaptation des drogues

Sherbrooke: Centre jeunesse de l'Estrie (CJE)
Affiliée à: CIUSSS de l'Estrie
594, boul Queen Victoria, Sherbrooke, QC J1H 3R7
Tél: 819-564-7100 Téléc: 819-564-7109
Ligne sans frais: 800-567-3495
www.santeestrie.qc.ca
Personnel: 620
Alain Trudel, Directeur, Protection de la jeunesse

Sherbrooke: CRDITED Estrie
Affiliée à: CIUSSS de l'Estrie
1621, rue Prospect, Sherbrooke, QC J1J 1K4
Tél: 819-346-8471 Ligne sans frais: 800-750-0551
www.santeestrie.qc.ca
Fondée en: 1958

Sherbrooke: Villa Marie-Claire inc.
Affiliée à: CIUSSS de l'Estrie
470, rue Victoria, Sherbrooke, QC J1H 3J2
Tél: 819-563-1622 Téléc: 819-563-6990

St-Philippe: **Foster Addiction Rehabilitation Centre**
Affiliated with: CISSS de la Montérégie-Ouest
Former Name: Pavillon Foster
6, rue Foucreault, St-Philippe, QC J0L 2K0
Tél: 450-659-8911 *Fax:* 450-659-7173
santemonteregie.qc.ca/services/dependances
Year Founded: 1964
Number of Beds: 20 lits
Note: Quebec's only English alcohol / drug rehabilitation centre.

Ste-Anne-des-Monts: **Centre de réadaptation en dépendance de la Gaspésie et des Iles-de-la-Madeleine**
Affiliée à: CISSS de la Gaspésie
Ancien nom: Centre de réadaptation L'Escale
50, rue Belvédère, Ste-Anne-des-Monts, QC G4V 1X4
Tél: 418-763-5000 *Téléc:* 418-763-9024
www.cisss-gaspesie.gouv.qc.ca

Ste-Anne-des-Monts: **Point de service jeunesse de La Haute-Gaspésie**
Affiliée à: CISSS de la Gaspésie
230, rte du Parc, Ste-Anne-des-Monts, QC G4V 2C4
Tél: 418 763-5000
www.cisss-gaspesie.gouv.qc.ca

Ste-Anne-des-Monts: **Programme Jeunesse - Succursale Haute-Gaspésie**
Affiliée à: CISSS de la Gaspésie
230, rte du Parc, #EB-132, Ste-Anne-des-Monts, QC G4V 2C4
Tél: 418-763-2251
www.cisss-gaspesie.gouv.qc.ca

Trois-Rivières: **Centre de réadaptation en déficience physique Vachon**
Affiliée à: CIUSSS de la Mauricie-et-du-Centre-du-Québec
375, rue Vachon, Trois-Rivières, QC G8T 8P6
Tél: 819-378-4083
ciusssmcq.ca

Trois-Rivières: **Centre jeunesse de la Mauricie et Centre-du-Québec**
Affiliée à: CIUSSS de la Mauricie-et-du-Centre-du-Québec
Centre administratif, 1455, boul du Carmel, Trois-Rivières, QC G8Z 3R7
Ligne sans frais: 855-378-5481
ciusssmcq.ca
Robert Levasseur, Directeur, Protection de la jeunesse

Trois-Rivières: **CRDITED de la Mauricie et du Centre-du-Québec**
3255, rue Foucher, Trois-Rivières, QC G8Z 1M6
Tél: 819-379-7732 *Téléc:* 819-379-5155
Ligne sans frais: 888-379-7732
www.crditedmcq.qc.ca
Région desservi: La région sociosanitaire de la Mauricie et du Centre-du-Québec
Note: Le Centre de réadaptation en déficience intellectuelle et en troubles envahissants du développement de la Mauricie et du Centre-du-Québec (CRDITED MCQ) est affilié à l'Université du Québec à Trois-Rivières (UQTR).

Trois-Rivières: **Domremy Mauricie-Centre-du-Québec**
440, rue des Forges, Trois-Rivières, QC G9A 2H5
Tél: 819-374-4744 *Téléc:* 819-374-4502
Fondée en: 1958
Note: Centre de réadaptation des drogues

Val-d'Or: **Centre jeunesse de l'Abitibi-Témiscamingue**
Affiliée à: CISSS de l'Abitibi-Témiscamingue
700, boul Forest, Val-d'Or, QC J9P 2L3
Tél: 819-825-0002 *Téléc:* 819-825-5132
www.cisss-at.gouv.qc.ca
Fondée en: 1996
Nombre de lits: 57 lits
Personnel: 450

Verdun: **Teen Haven/Hâvre Jeunesse**
4360, boul Lasalle, Verdun, QC H4G 2A8
Tél: 514-769-1441
administration@thaven.ca
www.teenhaven.ca
Number of Beds: 15 lits
Wendy Wendy, Executive Director
wlavier@thaven.ca

Wemotaci: **Conseil de la Nation Atikamekw**
Wemotaci, QC G0X 3R0
Tél: 819-523-6153 *Téléc:* 819-523-8706
Ligne sans frais: 866-523-6153
Nombre de lits: 9
Constant Awashish, Président

Westmount: **Les centres de la jeunesse et de la famille Batshaw**
Affiliée à: CIUSSS de l'Ouest-de-l'Ile-de-Montréal
Ancien nom: Les centres de la jeunesse et de la famille Saint-Georges
5, rue Weredale Park, Westmount, QC H3Z 1Y5
Tél: 514-989-1885
www.batshaw.qc.ca
Nombre de lits: 243 lits
Note: Centre de réadaptation (déficience motrice) et déficience sensorielle.

Centres d'hébergement et des soins de longue durée (CHSLD)

Acton Vale: **Centre d'hébergement de la MRC-d'Acton**
Affiliée à: CISSS de la Montérégie-Est
1268, rue Ricard, Acton Vale, QC J0H 1A0
Tél: 450-546-3234 *Téléc:* 450-546-4811
communication.csssry16@ssss.gouv.qc.ca
www.santemonteregie.qc.ca
Nombre de lits: 77 lits

Akwesasne: **Conseil Mohawk d'Akwesasne**
CP 40, Akwesasne, QC H0M 1A0
Tél: 613-575-2507
Nombre de lits: 30 lits
Patti Jocko-Adia Conieti, Directrice générale

Amos: **Centre d'hébergement Harricana**
Affiliée à: CISSS de l'Abitibi-Témiscamingue
612, 5e av Ouest, Amos, QC J9T 4L3
Tél: 819-732-6521 *Téléc:* 819-732-7526
www.csssea.ca

Anjou: **Centre Le Royer**
7351, rue Jean-Desprez, Anjou, QC H1K 5A6
Tél: 514-493-9397 *Téléc:* 514-493-9103
Fondée en: 1989
Nombre de lits: 66 lits
Suzanne Larin
514-493-9397, suzanne.larin.groys@ssss.gouv.qc.ca

Baie-Saint-Paul: **Centre d'hébergement Pierre-Dupré**
Affiliée à: CIUSSS de la Capitale-Nationale
10, rue Boivin, Baie-Saint-Paul, QC G3Z 1S8
Tél: 418-435-5150
Nombre de lits: 46 lits

Beaconsfield: **Manoir Beaconsfield**
34, av Woodland, Beaconsfield, QC H9W 4V9
Tél: 514-694-2000 *Téléc:* 514-694-5000
info@manoirbeaconsfield.ca
www.manoirbeaconsfield.ca
Nombre de lits: 21 lits

Beauharnois: **Centre d'accueil le Vaisseau d'Or**
55, rue Saint-André, Beauharnois, QC J6N 3G7
Tél: 450-429-6403 *Téléc:* 450-429-6602
Nombre de lits: 88 lits

Beauport: **Centre d'hébergement du Fargy**
Affiliée à: CIUSSS de la Capitale-Nationale
700, boul des Chutes, Beauport, QC G1E 2B7
Tél: 418-663-9934
Nombre de lits: 60 lits; 4 lits d'hébergement temporaires

Beloeil: **Centre d'hébergement Champlain-des-Pommetiers Groupe Champlain**
Affiliée à: CIUSSS de la Mauricie-et-du-Centre-du-Québec
350, rue Serge Pepin, Beloeil, QC J3G 0C3
Tél: 450-464-7666 *Téléc:* 450-464-4144
www.groupechamplain.qc.ca
Nombre de lits: 132 lits

Beloeil: **Centre d'hébergement Marguerite-Adam**
Affiliée à: CISSS de la Montérégie-Est
425, rue Hubert, Beloeil, QC J3G 2T1
Tél: 450-467-1631 *Téléc:* 450-467-4210
communication.csssry16@ssss.gouv.qc.ca
www.santemonteregie.qc.ca
Nombre de lits: 70 lits

Berthierville: **Centre d'hébergement Champlain Le Château**
1231, rue Dr Olivier M. Gendron, Berthierville, QC J0K 1A0
Tél: 450-836-6241 *Téléc:* 450-836-4013
Nombre de lits: 64 lits
Christine Lessard, Directrice générale

Boucherville: **Centre d'hébergement Jeanne-Crevier**
Affiliée à: CISSS de la Montérégie-Est
151, rue De Muy, Boucherville, QC J4B 4W7
Tél: 450-641-0595 *Téléc:* 450-641-3082
www.santemonteregie.qc.ca/cssspierreboucher
Nombre de lits: 93 lits

Brossard: **Centre d'accueil Marcelle Ferron inc.**
8600, boul Marie Victorin, Brossard, QC J4X 1A1
Tél: 450-923-1430 *Téléc:* 450-923-1805
www.chsldmarcelleferron.com
Fondée en: 1989
Nombre de lits: 249 lits

Brossard: **CHSLD Vigi Brossard**
Affiliée à: Vigi Santé Ltée
5955, boul Grande-Allée, Brossard, QC J4Z 3G4
Tél: 450-656-8500 *Téléc:* 450-656-8586
www.vigisante.com
Nombre de lits: 66 lits
Note: Agence/région administrative: Agence de la santé et des services sociaux de Montérégie.

Chambly: **Manoir Soleil inc.**
Affiliée à: CISSS de la Montérégie-Centre
125, rue Daigneault, Chambly, QC J3L 1G7
Tél: 450-658-4441 *Téléc:* 450-658-6521
Fondée en: 1983
Nombre de lits: 68 lits

Chandler: **CHSLD Villa Pabos**
Affiliée à: CISSS de la Gaspésie
CP 1088, 75, rue des Cèdres, Chandler, QC G0C 1K0
Tél: 418-689-6621 *Téléc:* 418-689-4860

Charlesbourg: **Centre d'hébergement de Charlesbourg**
Affiliée à: CIUSSS de la Capitale-Nationale
7150, boul Cloutier, Charlesbourg, QC G1H 5V5
Tél: 418-628-0456 *Téléc:* 418-622-8676
Nombre de lits: 64 lits
Note: Hébergement permanent, centre de jour

Châteauguay: **Centre d'hébergement Champlain Châteauguay Groupe Champlain Soins de Longue Durée**
Affiliée à: CISSS de la Montérégie-Ouest
210, rue Salaberry sud, Châteauguay, QC J6K 3M9
Tél: 450-699-1694 *Téléc:* 450-699-1696
www.groupechamplain.qc.ca
Nombre de lits: 96 lits
Christine Lessard, Directrice générale, Groupe Champlain Soins de Longue Durée

Chicoutimi: **Centre d'hébergement Mgr-Victor-Tremblay**
Affiliée à: CIUSSS du Saguenay-Lac-St-Jean
1236, rue D'Angoulême, Chicoutimi, QC G7H 6P9
Tél: 418-698-3907 *Téléc:* 418-549-5850
www.csss-chicoutimi.qc.ca
Nombre de lits: 50 lits

Chicoutimi: **Centre d'hébergement Saint-François**
Affiliée à: CIUSSS du Saguenay-Lac-Saint-Jean
912, rue Jacques-Cartier est, Chicoutimi, QC G7H 2A9
Tél: 418-549-3727 *Téléc:* 418-543-2038
centrestfrancois.ca
Nombre de lits: 64 lits
Sonia Bergeron, Présidente et directrice générale

Chicoutimi: **CHSLD de Chicoutimi**
904, rue Jacques-Cartier est, Chicoutimi, QC G7H 2A9
Tél: 418-698-3900 *Téléc:* 418-543-6285
Nombre de lits: 104 lits

Clermont: **Centre d'hébergement de Clermont**
Affiliée à: CIUSSS de la Capitale-Nationale
6, rue du Foyer, Clermont, QC G4A 1G8
Tél: 418-665-1712
Nombre de lits: 42 lits

Cleveland: **Foyer Wales**
506, rte 243, Cleveland, QC J0B 2H0
Tél: 819-826-3266 *Téléc:* 819-826-2549
info@waleshome.ca
waleshome.ca

Nombre de lits: 222 lits
Simms Stuart, Directeur général

Cleveland: Wales Home/Foyer Wales
506, rte 243 nord, Cleveland, QC J0B 2H0
Tél: 819-826-3266 Téléc: 819-826-3910
Ligne sans frais: 877-826-3266
info@waleshome.ca
www.waleshome.ca

Nombre de lits: 190 lits
Brendalee Piironen, Directrice générale
819-826-3266, bpiironen@waleshome.ca

Contrecoeur: CLSC des Seigneuries de Contrecoeur
/ Centre d'hébergement De Contrecoeur
Affiliée à: CISSS de la Montérégie-Est
4700, boul Marie-Victorin, Contrecoeur, QC J0L 1C0
Tél: 450-468-8413

Nombre de lits: 52 lits
Note: Centre d'hébergement, et le point de service CLSC des Seigneuries de Contrecoeur (450-652-2917).

Côte Saint-Luc: Centre d'hébergement Waldorf inc.
Revera Inc.
7400, ch Côte Saint-Luc, Côte Saint-Luc, QC H4W 3J4
Tél: 514-369-1000 Téléc: 514-489-3968
lewaldorf@reveraliving.com
www.reveraliving.com
www.facebook.com/Reveralnc; twitter.com/Revera_Inc;
www.youtube.com/user/Reveralnc;
www.linkedin.com/company/revera-inc
Fondée en: 1991
Nombre de lits: 20 lits
Thomas G. Wellner, President & CEO, Revera Living

Coteau-du-Lac: Pavillon Laura Ferguson
CP 909, 60, ch du Fleuve, Coteau-du-Lac, QC J0P 1B0
Tél: 450-267-3379

Cowansville: Résidence Manoir Beaumont (1988)
Inc.
430, rue Beaumont, Cowansville, QC J2K 1W1
Tél: 514-263-6235 Téléc: 514-263-8598
Nombre de lits: 36 lits
Note: Hébergement et soins de longue durée

Deux-Montagnes: CHSLD Vigi Deux-Montagnes inc.
580, 20e av, Deux-Montagnes, QC J7R 7E9
Tél: 450-473-5111 Téléc: 450-491-4309
www.vigisante.com

Nombre de lits: 76 lits
Note: Agence/région administrative: Agence de la santé et des services sociaux des Laurentides.

Disraéli: Centre d'hébergement René-Lavoie
Affiliée à: CISSS de Chaudière-Appalaches
CP 698, 260, av Champlain, Disraéli, QC G0N 1E0
Tél: 418-449-2020 Téléc: 418-449-4006
csssrt@ssss.gouv.qc.ca
www.centresantethetford.ca/sante-quebec/
Nombre de lits: 47 lits

Dolbeau: Maison du Bel Age
2020, rue Provencher, Dolbeau, QC G8L 3E6
Tél: 418-276-1866 Téléc: 418-276-1866
Nombre de lits: 53 lits
Note: Maison d'hébergement pour personnes agées autonomes

Dollard-des-Ormeaux: Vigi Santé Ltée
197, rue Thornhill, Dollard-des-Ormeaux, QC H9B 3H8
Tél: 514-684-0930 Téléc: 514-684-0179
www.vigisante.com

Nombre de lits: 1,500 lits
Note: Propriétaire et administrateur de 15 centres d'hébergement, présente dans plusieurs régions du Québec. Le siège du CHSLD Vigi Dollard-des-Ormeaux, avec 160 lits.

Dorval: Chartwell Maison Herron
Affiliée à: Chartwell Retirement Residence
2400, ch Herron, Dorval, QC H9S 5W3
Tél: 438-819-8468
chartwell.com

Drummondville: Centre d'hébergement et CLSC
Frederick-George-Heriot
Affiliée à: CIUSSS de la
Mauricie-et-du-Centre-du-Québec
75, rue Saint-Georges, Drummondville, QC J2C 4G6
Tél: 819-478-6464
ciusssmcq.ca

Nombre de lits: 354 lits

Farnham: Les Foyers Farnham
Affiliée à: CISSS de la Montérégie-Ouest
800, rue Saint-Paul, Farnham, QC J2N 2K6
Tél: 450-293-3167 Téléc: 450-293-7878
Nombre de lits: 61 lits

Gaspé: Centre d'hébergement Mgr-Ross
Affiliée à: CISSS de la Gaspésie
150, rue Mgr Ross, Gaspé, QC G4X 2S7
Tél: 418-368-3301 Téléc: 418-368-6730
Nombre de lits: 129 lits
Note: CSSS Côte-de-Gaspé.

Gatineau: Centre d'hébergement - Bon Séjour
Affiliée à: CISSS de l'Outaouais
134, rue Jean-René Monette, Gatineau, QC J8P 7C3
Tél: 819-966-6450 Téléc: 819-966-6453
Nombre de lits: 100 lits

Gatineau: Centre d'hébergement - Foyer du Bonheur
Affiliée à: CISSS de l'Outaouais
125, boul Lionel-Émond, Gatineau, QC J8Y 5S8
Tél: 819-966-6410 Téléc: 819-966-6414
Nombre de lits: 263 lits

Gatineau: Centre d'hébergement - La Pietà
Affiliée à: CISSS de l'Outaouais
273, rue Laurier, Gatineau, QC J8X 3W8
Tél: 819-966-6420 Téléc: 819-966-6427
www.csssgatineau.qc.ca
Nombre de lits: 158 lits
Denis Beaudoin, Directeur Général, CSSS Gatineau
819-966-6560

Gatineau: Centre d'hébergement Vallée-de-la-Lièvre
Affiliée à: CISSS de l'Outaouais
111, rue Gérard-Gauthier, Gatineau, QC J8L 3C9
Tél: 819-986-4115 Téléc: 819-986-9602
Nombre de lits: 79 lits

Gracefield: Le Foyer d'accueil de Gracefield
Affiliée à: CISSS de l'Outaouais
CP 317, 1, rue du Foyer, Gracefield, QC J0X 1W0
Tél: 819-463-2100 Téléc: 819-463-4721
Nombre de lits: 31 lits

Granby: Centre d'hébergement Villa Bonheur
Affiliée à: CISSS de la Montérégie-Ouest
71, rue Court, Granby, QC J2G 4Y7
Tél: 450-776-5222 Téléc: 450-372-7617
Nombre de lits: 108 lits

Grand-Mère: Centre d'hébergement Laflèche
Affiliée à: CIUSSS de la
Mauricie-et-du-Centre-du-Québec
1650, 6e av, Grand-Mère, QC G9T 2K4
Tél: 819-533-2500
ciusssmcq.ca
Nombre de lits: 319 places

Huntingdon: Centre d'hébergement du comté de
Huntingdon
Affiliée à: CISSS de la Montérégie-Ouest
198, rue Châteauguay, Huntingdon, QC J0S 1H0
Tél: 450-829-2321 Téléc: 450-264-4923
www.santemonteregie.qc.ca/haut-saint-laurent
Nombre de lits: 60 lits

Joliette: Centre d'hébergement de Saint-Eusèbe
Affiliée à: CISSS de Lanaudière
585, boul Manseau, Joliette, QC J6E 3E5
Tél: 450-759-1662
www.csssnl.qc.ca
Nombre de lits: 159 lits

Jonquière: Centre d'hébergement Des Chênes
Affiliée à: CIUSSS du Saguenay-Lac-St-Jean
CP 1200, 1841, rue Deschênes, Jonquière, QC G7S 4K6
Tél: 418-695-7727
www.csssjonquiere.qc.ca

Jonquière: Centre d'hébergement Georges-Hébert
Affiliée à: CIUSSS du Saguenay-Lac-St-Jean
2841, rue Faraday, Jonquière, QC G7S 5C8
Tél: 418-695-7727 Téléc: 418-695-7737
Nombre de lits: 75 lits

Jonquière: Centre d'hébergement Sainte-Marie
Affiliée à: CIUSSS du Saguenay-Lac-St-Jean
2184, rue Perrier, Jonquière, QC G7X 9C9
Tél: 418-695-7727
Nombre de lits: 66 lits
Note: Hébergement permanent et temporaire

La Baie: Centre d'hébergement Bagotville
Affiliée à: CIUSSS Saguenay-Lac-St-Jean
562, rue Victoria, La Baie, QC G7B 3M6
Tél: 418-544-3381 Téléc: 418-544-6407

La Baie: Foyer St-Joseph de La Baie inc.
Affiliée à: CIUSSS du Saguenay-Lac-St-Jean
1893, rue Alexis-Simard, La Baie, QC G7B 2K9
Tél: 418-544-2673 Téléc: 418-544-8936
Nombre de lits: 48 lits

La Guadeloupe: Résidence La Guadeloupe
435, 15e rue ouest, La Guadeloupe, QC G0M 1G0
Tél: 418-459-3476
www.facebook.com/reslaguadeloupe
Nombre de lits: 49 lits

La Sarre: CHSLD de La Sarre
Affiliée à: CISSS de l'Abitibi-Témiscamingue
22, 1e av est, La Sarre, QC J9Z 1C4
Tél: 819-333-5525
www.csssab.qc.ca
Nombre de lits: 25 chambres privées
Spécialités: Les services d'hébergement; Physiothéapie; Ergothérapie; Le service psychosocial

LaSalle: Centre d'hébergement de LaSalle
Affiliée à: CIUSSS de l'Ouest-de-l'Île-de-Montréal
8686, rue Centrale, LaSalle, QC H8P 3N4
Tél: 514-364-6700 Téléc: 514-364-0484
www.csssdll.qc.ca
Nombre de lits: 202 lits

Labelle: Centre d'hébergement de Labelle
Affiliée à: CISSS des Laurentides
CP 38, 50, rue de l'Église, Labelle, QC J0T 1H0
Tél: 819-686-2372 Téléc: 819-686-1950
Nombre de lits: 46 lits

Lac-Bouchette: Centre d'hébergement de
Lac-Bouchette
Édifice Foyer de Lac-Bouchette, CP 39, 99, rte de l'Ermitage, Lac-Bouchette, QC G0W 1V0
Tél: 418-348-6313 Téléc: 418-348-6342
Nombre de lits: 14 lits

Lac-Mégantic: CHSLD / Centre de jour Lac-Mégantic
Affiliée à: CIUSSS de l'Estrie
3675, rue du Foyer, Lac-Mégantic, QC G6B 2K2
Tél: 819-583-0330 Téléc: 819-583-0900
www.bonjourresidences.com
Nombre de lits: 200 lits
Pierre Latulippe, Directeur général, CSSS du Granit

Lac-au-Saumon: Centre d'hébergement Marie-Anne
Ouellet
Affiliée à: CISSS du Bas-St-Laurent
6, rue Turbide, Lac-au-Saumon, QC G0J 1M0
Tél: 418-778-5816
Nombre de lits: 96 lits

Lachine: Centre d'hébergemen Nazaire-Piché
Affiliée à: CIUSSS de l'Ouest-de-l'Île-de-Montréal
150, 15e av, Lachine, QC H8S 3L9
Tél: 514-637-2326
www.csssdll.qc.ca
Nombre de lits: 100 lits
Personnel: 113

Lachine: Centre d'hébergement de Lachine
Affiliée à: CIUSSS de l'Ouest-de-l'Île-de-Montréal
650, place d'Accueil, Lachine, QC H8S 3Z5
Tél: 514-634-7161
www.csssdll.qc.ca
Nombre de lits: 187 lits
Personnel: 261

Lambton: CLSC / CHSLD de Lambton
Affiliée à: CIUSSS de l'Estrie
310, rue Principale, Lambton, QC G0M 1H0
Tél: 418-486-7417

Nombre de lits: 32 lits
Note: Le point de service Lambton regroupe un centre local de services communautaire (CLSC), un centre d'hébergement, et un centre de jour.

Lanoraie: Centre d'hébergement Alphonse-Rondeau
Affiliée à: CISSS de Lanaudière
419, rue Faust, Lanoraie, QC J0K 1E0
Tél: 450-887-2343
www.csssnl.qc.ca

Laval: **Centre d'hébergement de la Rive Prodimax inc.**
4605, boul Sainte-Rose, Laval, QC H7R 5S9
Tél: 450-627-5599 *Téléc:* 450-627-5107
Nombre de lits: 79 lits
Note: Centre privé non-conventionné.

Laval: **Centre d'hébergement de la Villa-des-Tilleuls inc.**
5590, boul des Laurentides, Laval, QC H7K 2K2
Tél: 450-628-0322 *Téléc:* 450-622-3674
Nombre de lits: 68 lits
Note: Centre privé non-conventioné.

Laval: **Centre d'hébergement de Sainte-Dorothée**
Affiliée à: CISSS de Laval
350, boul Samson ouest, Laval, QC H7X 1J4
Tél: 514-689-0933 *Téléc:* 514-689-3147
cucssslaval.ca
Nombre de lits: 277 lits
Note: Les autres centres d'hébergement: Fernand-Larocque, Idola-Saint-Jean, La Pinière, et Rose-de-Lima.

Laval: **Centre d'hébergement l'Eden de Laval inc**
8528, boul Lévesque est, Laval, QC H7A 1W6
Tél: 450-665-6283 *Téléc:* 450-665-7127
Nombre de lits: 43 lits
Note: Centre privé non-conventioné.

Laval: **Centre d'hébergement St-François inc.**
Affiliée à: Groupe Champlain Soins de Longue Durée
4105, Montée Masson, Laval, QC H7B 1B6
Tél: 450-666-6541 *Téléc:* 450-666-1601
www.groupechamplain.qc.ca
Nombre de lits: 53 lits
Christine Lessard, Directrice générale, Groupe Champlain

Laval: **CHSLD Saint-Jude inc.**
Affiliée à: Siège social Age3
4410, boul Saint-Martin ouest, Laval, QC H7T 1C3
Tél: 450-687-7714 *Téléc:* 450-682-0330
info@age-3.com
www.age-3.com
Fondée en: 1957
Nombre de lits: 204 lits
Daniel Leclair, Directeur général

Laval: **Manoir St-Patrice inc.**
3615, boul Perron, Laval, QC H7V 1P4
Tél: 450-681-1621 *Téléc:* 450-681-6120
www.chsldmanoirstpatrice.com
Nombre de lits: 132 lits

Laval: **La Résidence du Bonheur**
5855, rue Boulard, Laval, QC H7B 1A3
Tél: 450-666-1567 *Téléc:* 450-666-6387
info@residencedubonheur.com
www.residencedubonheur.com
Nombre de lits: 50 lits
Note: Centre privé non-conventionné.

Laval: **Résidence Riviera inc.**
2999, boul Notre-Dame, Laval, QC H7V 4C4
Tél: 450-682-0111 *Téléc:* 450-682-0154
info@chsldresidenceriviera.com
www.chsldresidenceriviera.com
Fondée en: 1959
Nombre de lits: 128 lits
Jean Nadon, Directeur général
450-682-0111, jnadon_riviera@ssss.gouv.qc.ca

Laval: **Santé Courville inc.**
5200, 80e rue, Laval, QC H7R 5T6
Tél: 450-627-7990 *Téléc:* 450-627-7993
www.santecourville.com
Fondée en: 1935
Nombre de lits: 120 lits
Christine Durocher, Directrice générale

Lévis: **CLSC-CHSLD de la MRC Desjardins**
15, rue de l'Arsenal, Lévis, QC G6V 4P6
Tél: 418-835-3400 *Téléc:* 418-835-1978
Nombre de lits: 95 lits
Renée Lachance-Auger, Directrice générale

Lévis: **Pavillon Bellevue inc.**
99, rue Monseigneur-Bourget, Lévis, QC G6V 9V2
Tél: 418-833-3490 *Téléc:* 418-833-6874
Nombre de lits: 50 lits

Lévis: **Villa Mon Domaine inc.**
109, rue du Mont-Marie, Lévis, QC G6V 8B4
Tél: 418-837-6408 *Téléc:* 418-837-2626

Nombre de lits: 57 lits

Longueuil: **Centre d'accueil St-Laurent inc.**
Affiliée à: CISSS de la Montérégie-Est
480, rue LeMoyne ouest, Longueuil, QC J4H 1X1
Tél: 450-670-5480 *Téléc:* 450-670-9874
Nombre de lits: 32 lits
Note: CHSLD privé non conventionné

Longueuil: **Centre d'hébergement de Mgr-Coderre**
Affiliée à: CISSS de la Montérégie-Est
2761, rue Beauvais, Longueuil, QC J4M 2A4
Tél: 450-448-3111 *Téléc:* 450-448-4322
www.santemonteregie.qc.ca
Nombre de lits: 154 lits

Longueuil: **Centre d'hébergement du Chevalier-De Lévis**
Affiliée à: CISSS de la Montérégie-Est
40, rue Lévis, Longueuil, QC J4H 1S5
Tél: 450-670-5110 *Téléc:* 450-670-7292
www.santemonteregie.qc.ca/cssspierreboucher
Nombre de lits: 142 lits

Longueuil: **Centre d'hébergement du Manoir-Trinité**
Affiliée à: CISSS de la Montérégie-Est
1275, boul Jacques-Cartier est, Longueuil, QC J4M 2Y8
Tél: 450-674-4948 *Téléc:* 450-674-8571
www.santemonteregie.qc.ca/cssspierreboucher
Spécialités: Un centre de jour offrant des services à des adultes en perte d'autonomie demeurant à domicile; Services de réadaptation

Longueuil: **Centre d'hébergement René-Lévesque**
Affiliée à: CISSS de la Montérégie-Est
1901, rue Claude, Longueuil, QC J4G 1Y5
Tél: 450-651-2210 *Téléc:* 450-670-7731
www.santemonteregie.qc.ca
Nombre de lits: 224 lits

Loretteville: **Centre d'hébergement Loretteville**
Affiliée à: CIUSSS de la Capitale-Nationale
165, rue Lessard, Loretteville, QC G2B 2V9
Tél: 418-842-9191
Nombre de lits: 74 lits

Lyster: **Centre d'hébergement de Lyster**
Affiliée à: CIUSSS de la Mauricie-et-du-Centre-du-Québec
Ancien nom: Centre d'hébergement des Quatre-Vents; Le Foyer de Lyster
2180, rue Bécancour, Lyster, QC G0S 1V0
Tél: 819-389-5923
www.ciusssmcq.ca
Fondée en: 1969
Nombre de lits: 26 lits

Magog: **Résidence Ste-Marguerite Marie**
64, rue Saint-Pierre, Magog, QC J1X 3A2
Tél: 819-843-0202
info@residencesmagog.ca
www.residencesmagog.ca

Malartic: **Centre d'hébergement Saint-Martin de Malartic**
Affiliée à: CISSS de l'Abitibi-Témiscamingue
CP 639, 987, rue des Pins, Malartic, QC J0Y 1Z0
Tél: 819-825-5858 *Téléc:* 819-825-7753
agence.abitibi.santelaurentides.qc.ca
Nombre de lits: 62 lits
Note: Centre d'hébergement/centre de jour.

Maria: **Centre d'hébergement de Maria**
Affiliée à: CISSS de la Gaspésie
491, boul Perron, Maria, QC G0C 1Y0
Tél: 418-759-3458 *Téléc:* 418-759-5103
www.csssbc.qc.ca
Nombre de lits: 91 lits

Marieville: **Centre d'hébergement Sainte-Croix**
Affiliée à: CISSS de la Montérégie-Centre
300, rue Docteur-Poulin, Marieville, QC J3M 1L7
Tél: 450-460-4475 *Téléc:* 450-460-4104
Nombre de lits: 174 lits

Matane: **Centre d'hébergement de Matane**
Affiliée à: CISSS du Bas-St-Laurent
150, av Saint-Jérôme, Matane, QC G4W 3A2
Tél: 418-562-4154 *Téléc:* 418-562-9281
www.cisss-bsl.gouv.qc.ca
Nombre de lits: 106 lits

Matapédia: **Centre d'hébergement de Matapédia**
Affiliée à: CISSS de la Gaspésie
14, boul Perron est, Matapédia, QC G0J 1V0
Tél: 418-865-2221 *Téléc:* 418-865-2317
www.csssbc.qc.ca
Spécialités: Services d'hébergement; Réadaptation

Mont-Joli: **CLSC de La Mitis**
Affiliée à: CISSS du Bas-St-Laurent
800, av du Sanatorium, Mont-Joli, QC G5H 3L6
Tél: 418-775-7261
www.cisss-bsl.gouv.qc.ca
Nombre de lits: 136 lits

Mont-Laurier: **Centre d'Hébergement Sainte-Anne**
Affiliée à: CISSS de Laurentides
411, rue de la Madone, Mont-Laurier, QC J9L 1S1
Tél: 819-623-5940
www.santelaurentides.gouv.qc.ca
Nombre de lits: 128 lits

Mont-Royal: **CHSLD Vigi Mont-Royal**
Affiliée à: Vigi Santé Ltée
275, av Brittany, Mont-Royal, QC H3P 3C2
Tél: 514-739-5593 *Téléc:* 514-733-7973
www.vigisante.com
Nombre de lits: 273 lits
Note: Agence/région administrative: Agence de la santé et des services sociaux de Montréal.

Mont-Tremblant: **Centre d'hébergement de Mont-Tremblant**
Affiliée à: CISSS des Laurentides
925, rue de Saint-Jovite, Mont-Tremblant, QC J8E 3J8
Tél: 819-425-2793 *Ligne sans frais:* 855-766-6387

Montmagny: **CLSC et Centre d'hébergement de Montmagny**
Affiliée à: CISSS de Chaudière-Appalaches
168, rue Saint-Joseph, Montmagny, QC G5V 1H8
Tél: 418-248-1572 *Téléc:* 418-248-3374
www.csssml.qc.ca
Nombre de lits: 65 lits
Région desservi: Le territoire de Montmagny-L'Islet

Montréal: **Les Cèdres - Le Centre d'accueil pour personnes âgées**
#200, 1275, boul de la Côte-Vertu, Montréal, QC H4L 4V2
Tél: 514-389-1023 *Téléc:* 514-389-0581
info@centrelescedres.ca
www.centrelescedres.ca
Fondée en: 1960
Fadia El Khoury, Directrice générale

Montréal: **Centre d'hébergement Armand-Lavergne**
Affiliée à: CIUSSS du Centre-Sud-de-l'Ile-de-Montréal
3500, rue Chapleau, Montréal, QC H2K 4N3
Tél: 514-527-8921
www.csssjeannemance.ca
Nombre de lits: 182 lits
Note: Centre de jour; centre d'hébergement permanent.

Montréal: **Centre d'hébergement Biermans**
Affiliée à: CIUSSS de l'Est-de-l'Ile-de-Montréal
7905, rue Sherbrooke est, Montréal, QC H1L 1A4
Tél: 514-351-9891
Fondée en: 1936

Montréal: **Centre d'hébergement Champlain-de-Gouin**
Affiliée à: Groupe Champlain inc.
4445, boul Henri-Bourassa est, Montréal, QC H1H 5M4
Tél: 514-327-6209 *Téléc:* 514-327-9912
www.groupechamplain.qc.ca
Nombre de lits: 93 lits
Note: Agence/région administrative: Agence de la santé et des services sociaux de Montréal.

Montréal: **Centre D'Hébergement de la Maison-Saint-Joseph**
5605, rue Beaubien est, Montréal, QC H1T 1X4
Tél: 514-254-4991 *Téléc:* 514-257-1742
www.ch-maison-saint-joseph.com
Nombre de lits: 80 lits

Montréal: **Centre d'hébergement de Louvain**
Affiliée à: CIUSSS du Nord-de-l'Ile-de-Montréal
9600, rue Saint-Denis, Montréal, QC H2M 1P2
Tél: 514-381-7256 *Téléc:* 514-381-6486
www.csssamn.ca
Nombre de lits: 155 lits

Montréal: **Centre d'hébergement de Saint-Michel**
Affiliée à: CIUSSS de l'Est-de-l'Île-de-Montréal
3130, rue Jarry est, Montréal, QC H1Z 4N8
Tél: 514-722-3000 *Téléc:* 514-593-7400
dotation.slsm@ssss.gouv.qc.ca
csss-stleonardstmichel.qc.ca
Nombre de lits: 192 lits
Note: Centre administratif du CSSS, et centre d'hébergement.
Denis Blanchard, Directeur général, CSSS de Saint-Léonard et
Saint-Michel

Montréal: **Centre d'hébergement des Quatre-Temps**
Affiliée à: CIUSSS de l'Est-de-l'Île-de-Montréal
7400, boul Saint-Michel, Montréal, QC H2A 2Z8
Tél: 514-722-3000
Nombre de lits: 192 lits

Montréal: **Centre d'hébergement des Seigneurs**
Affiliée à: CIUSSS du
Centre-Sud-de-l'Île-de-Montréal
1800, rue Saint-Jacques, Montréal, QC H3J 2R5
Tél: 514-935-4681 *Téléc:* 514-935-6189
www.sov.qc.ca

Montréal: **Centre d'hébergement du
Centre-Ville-de-Montréal**
Affiliée à: CIUSSS du
Centre-Sud-de-l'Île-de-Montréal
66, boul René-Lévesque est, Montréal, QC H2X 1N3
Tél: 514-861-9331 *Téléc:* 514-861-8385
www.csssjeannemance.ca
Nombre de lits: 196 lits

Montréal: **Centre d'hébergement du
Manoir-de-l'Age-d'Or**
Affiliée à: CIUSSS du
Centre-Sud-de-l'Île-de-Montréal
3430, rue Jeanne-Mance, Montréal, QC H2X 2J9
Tél: 514-842-1147 *Téléc:* 514-842-1146
www.csssjeannemance.ca
Nombre de lits: 189 lits

Montréal: **Centre d'hébergement Émilie-Gamelin**
Affiliée à: CIUSSS du
Centre-Sud-de-l'Île-de-Montréal
1440, rue Dufresne, Montréal, QC H2K 3J3
Tél: 514-527-8921
jeannemance.ciusss-centresudmtl.gouv.qc.ca
Nombre de lits: 184 lits

Montréal: **Centre d'hébergement
Father-Dowd/Father Dowd Home**
6565, ch Hudson, Montréal, QC H3S 2T7
Tél: 514-932-3630
Nombre de lits: 134 lits

Montréal: **Centre D'hebergement Jeanne-le Ber**
Affiliée à: CIUSSS de l'Est-de-l'Île-de-Montréal
Ancien nom: Centre d'accueil Gouin-Rosemont;
CHSLD Jeanne-Leber
7445, rue Hochelaga, Montréal, QC H1N 3V2
Tél: 514-251-6000
Nombre de lits: 344 lits

Montréal: **Centre d'hébergement Jeanne-Le Ber**
Affiliée à: CIUSSS de l'Est-de-l'Île-de-Montréal
7445, rue Hochelaga, Montréal, QC H1N 3V2
Tél: 514-251-6000
www.cssslucilleteasdale.qc.ca
Nombre de lits: 351 lits

Montréal: **Centre d'hébergement Louis Riel**
Affiliée à: CIUSSS du
Centre-Sud-de-l'Île-de-Montréal
2120, rue Augustin-Cantin, Montréal, QC H3K 3G3
Tél: 514-931-2263
ciusss-centresudmtl.gouv.qc.ca
Nombre de lits: 100 lits
Sonia Bélanger, Présidente-directrice générale

Montréal: **Centre d'hébergement Paul-Gouin**
Affiliée à: CIUSSS du Nord-de-l'Île-de-Montréal
5900, rue de Saint-Vallier, Montréal, QC H2S 2P3
Tél: 514-273-3681
Nombre de lits: 100 lits

Montréal: **Centre d'hébergement St-Andrew**
Affiliée à: CIUSSS du
Centre-Ouest-de-l'Île-de-Montréal
3350, boul Cavendish, Montréal, QC H4B 2M7
Tél: 514-932-3630
www.cssscavendish.qc.ca

Nombre de lits: 300 lits

Montréal: **Centre d'hébergement St-Margaret/St.
Margaret Residence**
Affiliée à: CIUSSS du
Centre-Ouest-de-l'Île-de-Montréal
50, av Hillside, Montréal, QC H3Z 1V9
Tél: 514-932-3630

Montréal: **Centre d'hébergement Yvon-Brunet**
Affiliée à: CIUSSS du
Centre-Sud-de-l'Île-de-Montréal
6250, av Newman, Montréal, QC H4E 4K4
Tél: 514-765-8000
ciusss-centresudmtl.gouv.qc.ca
Fondée en: 1982
Nombre de lits: 185 lits

Montréal: **Centre de soins prolongés Grace Dart**
Affiliée à: CIUSSS de l'Ouest-de-l'Île-de-Montréal
5155, rue Sainte-Catherine est, Montréal, QC H1V 2A5
Tél: 514-255-2833 *Téléc:* 514-255-0650
www.gracedart.ca
Nombre de lits: 357 lits
M. Benoit Morin, Président-directeur général

Montréal: **Centre Le Cardinal inc.**
12900, rue Notre-Dame est, Montréal, QC H1A 1R9
Tél: 514-645-2766 *Téléc:* 514-640-6267
Nombre de lits: 174 lits
Personnel: 230

Montréal: **CHSLD Benjamin-Victor-Rousselot**
Affiliée à: CIUSSS de l'Est-de-l'Île-de-Montréal
5655, rue Sherbrooke est, Montréal, QC H1N 1A4
Tél: 514-254-9421
www.cssslucilleteasdale.qc.ca
Nombre de lits: 171 lits
Yvan Gendron, Président-directeur général

Montréal: **CHSLD Bourget inc.**
11570, rue Notre-Dame est, Montréal, QC H1B 2X4
Tél: 514-645-1673 *Téléc:* 514-645-8451
Nombre de lits: 112 lits
Note: Un établissement privé.
Diane Girard, Directrice générale
diane_girard@ssss.gouv.qc.ca

Montréal: **CHSLD de Cartierville**
Affiliée à: CIUSSS du Nord-de-l'Île-de-Montréal
12235, rue Grenet, Montréal, QC H4J 2N9
Tél: 514-337-7300
ciusss-nordmtl.gouv.qc.ca
Nombre de lits: 285 lits

Montréal: **CHSLD juif de Montréal**
Affiliée à: CIUSSS du
Centre-Ouest-de-l'Île-de-Montréal
5725, av Victoria, Montréal, QC H3W 3H6
Tél: 514-738-4500 *Téléc:* 514-738-2611
www.chsldjuif.ca
Nombre de lits: 160 beds
Barbra Gold, Directrice, Programme soutien à l'autonomie des
personnes âgées

Montréal: **CHSLD Légaré**
Affiliée à: CIUSSS du Nord-de-l'Île-de-Montréal
1615, rue Émile-Journault, Montréal, QC H2M 2G3
Tél: 514-384-2000
ciusss-nordmtl.gouv.qc.ca
Nombre de lits: 105 lits

Montréal: **CHSLD Manoir Fleury inc.**
2145, rue Fleury est, Montréal, QC H2B 1J8
Tél: 514-388-1553 *Téléc:* 514-388-4161
Nombre de lits: 25 lits

Montréal: **CHSLD Marie-Claret inc.**
Affiliée à: Vigi Santé Ltée
3345, boul Henri-Bourassa est, Montréal, QC H1H 1H6
Tél: 514-322-4380 *Téléc:* 514-326-8811
www.vigisante.com
Nombre de lits: 78 lits
Note: Agence/région administrative: Agence de la santé et des
services sociaux de Montréal.

Montréal: **CHSLD Marie-Rollet**
Affiliée à: CIUSSS de l'Est-de-l'Île-de-Montréal
5003, rue Saint-Zotique est, Montréal, QC H1T 1N6
Tél: 514-729-5281
www.cssslucilleteasdale.qc.ca
Nombre de lits: 110 lits
Note: Hébergement et soins de longue durée
Yvan Gendron, Président-directeur général

Montréal: **CHSLD Providence
Notre-Dame-de-Lourdes**
1870, boul Pie-IX, Montréal, QC H1V 2C6
Tél: 514-527-4595 *Téléc:* 514-527-4475
communication.nddl@ssss.gouv.qc.ca
www.chsld-providence-notre-dame-lourdes.com
Fondée en: 1934
Nombre de lits: 162 lits

Montréal: **Groupe Champlain Soins de Longue
Durée**
Affiliée à: Groupe Santé Sedna inc.
7150, rue Marie-Victorin, Montréal, QC H1G 2J5
Tél: 514-324-2044 *Téléc:* 514-324-5900
www.groupechamplain.qc.ca
Fondée en: 1966
Nombre de lits: 1443 lits
Note: 15 établissements
Marie-Claude Ouellet, Présidente & Directrice Générale

Montréal: **L'Hôpital Chinois de Montréal**
Affiliée à: CIUSSS du
Centre-Sud-de-l'Île-de-Montréal
189, av Viger est, Montréal, QC H2X 3Y9
Tél: 514-871-0961 *Téléc:* 514-871-0966
www.montrealchinesehospital.ca
Fondée en: 1963
Nombre de lits: 128 lits
Vincent Tam, Directeur général

Montréal: **Institut Canadien-Polonais du Bien-Etre
inc.**
Affiliée à: CIUSSS de l'Est-de-l'Île-de-Montréal
5655, rue Bélanger, Montréal, QC H1T 1G2
Tél: 514-259-2551 *Téléc:* 514-259-9948
Nombre de lits: 126 lits

Montréal: **Résidence Berthiaume-du Tremblay**
1635, boul Gouin est, Montréal, QC H2C 1C2
Tél: 514-381-1841 *Téléc:* 514-381-1090
www.residence-berthiaume-du-tremblay.com
Nombre de lits: 246 lits
Chantal Bernatchez, Directrice générale
chantal_bernatchez@ssss.gouv.qc.ca

Montréal: **La Résidence Fulford**
1221, rue Guy, Montréal, QC H3H 2K8
Tél: 514-933-7975 *Téléc:* 514-933-3773
fulford@fulfordresidence.com
www.fulfordresidence.com
Nombre de lits: 6 lits
Note: Réservée exclusivement aux femmes
Marie-France Lacoste, Directrice

Montréal: **Résidence Rive Soleil inc.**
15150, rue Notre-Dame est, Montréal, QC H1A 1W6
Tél: 514-642-5509
Nombre de lits: 30 chambres

Montréal: **Résidence Sainte-Claire inc.**
8950, rue Sainte-Claire est, Montréal, QC H1L 1Z1
Tél: 514-351-3877 *Téléc:* 514-352-5956
Nombre de lits: 38 lits

Montréal: **Résidence St-Jacques**
8712, rue Saint-Hubert, Montréal, QC H2M 1Y5
Tél: 514-389-5880
Fondée en: 1989
Nombre de lits: 25 lits

Montréal-Nord: **CHSLD Villa Belle Rive**
5320, boul Gouin est, Montréal-Nord, QC H1G 1B4
Tél: 514-321-1367 *Téléc:* 514-322-4211
info@chsldvillabellerive.com
www.chsldvillabellerive.com
Nombre de lits: 31 lits

Montréal-Nord: **Résidence Angelica inc.**
3435, boul Gouin est, Montréal-Nord, QC H1H 1B1
Tél: 514-324-6110 *Téléc:* 514-324-4005
www.angelica-residence.com
Nombre de lits: 400 lits

New Carlisle: **Centre d'hébergement de New Carlisle**
Affiliée à: CISSS de la Gaspésie
108, rue Principale, New Carlisle, QC G0C 1Z0
Tél: 418-752-3386 *Téléc:* 418-752-6483
Nombre de lits: 75 lits

Normandin: **Centre de Normandin**
Affiliée à: Centre de santé et de services sociaux
Maria-Chapdelaine
1205, rue Saint-Cyrille, Normandin, QC G8M 4K1
Tél: 418-274-1234 *Téléc:* 418-274-6970
www.csssmariachapdelaine.com
Nombre de lits: 35 lits de soins de longue durée
Note: Centre d'hébergement; point de service CLSC; centre de jour.
Normand Brassard, Directeur général, CSSS Maria Chapdelaine

North Hatley: **Connaught Home**
Affiliée à: Massawippi Retirement Communities
77, rue Main, North Hatley, QC J0B 2C0
Tél: 819-842-2164 *Téléc:* 819-842-2667
www.masscom.ca
Nombre de lits: 41 lits
Donna Barker, Adjointe administrative
dbarker@masscom.ca

Notre-Dame-du-Bon-Conseil: **Centre d'hébergement**
et CLSC Notre-Dame-du-Bon-Conseil
Affiliée à: CIUSSS de la
Mauricie-et-du-Centre-du-Québec
91, rue Saint-Thomas, Notre-Dame-du-Bon-Conseil, QC J0C 1A0
Tél: 819-336-2122
ciusssmcq.ca
Nombre de lits: 52 lits
Note: Centre d'hébergement; le point de service CLSC: 819-474-2572.
Yves Martin, Directeur général, CSSS Drummond 819-478-6401

Notre-Dame-du-Nord: **CHSLD des premières nations**
du Timiskaming
20, av Algonquin, Notre-Dame-du-Nord, QC J0Z 3B0
Tél: 819-723-2225 *Téléc:* 819-723-2112
wpp01.mss.gouv.qc.ca
Nombre de lits: 20 lits
Note: Établissement privé non conventionné

Oka: **Manoir Oka inc.**
2083, ch Oka, Oka, QC J0N 1E0
Tél: 450-479-6447
manoiroka@videotron.ca
manoiroka.com
Nombre de lits: 34 lits
Cody Boisvert, Directeur général

Ormstown: **Centre d'hébergement d'Ormstown**
Affiliée à: CISSS de la Montérégie-Ouest
65, rue Hector, Ormstown, QC J0S 1K0
Tél: 450-829-2321 *Téléc:* 450-829-3110
Fondée en: 1978
Nombre de lits: 74 lits

Palmarolle: **CHSLD de Palmarolle**
Affiliée à: CISSS de l'Abitibi-Témiscamingue
136, rue Principale, Palmarolle, QC J0Z 3C0
Tél: 819-787-2612 *Téléc:* 819-787-3293
www.csssab.qc.ca
Nombre de lits: 22 chambres privées
Spécialités: Les services d'hébergement; Physiothérapie; Ergothéapie; Optométrie

Pierrefonds: **Le Manoir Pierrefonds**
Affiliée à: Chartwell Résidences Pour Retraités
18465, boul Gouin ouest, Pierrefonds, QC H9K 1A6
Tél: 514-626-6651 *Téléc:* 514-626-6415
www.chartwell.com
Nombre de lits: 183 unités

Pierreville: **Centre d'hébergement Lucien Shooner**
Affiliée à: CIUSSS de la
Mauricie-et-du-Centre-du-Québec
50, rue du Lt-Gouv.-Paul-Comtois, Pierreville, QC J0G 1J0
Tél: 450-568-2712
ciusssmcq.ca
Nombre de lits: 36 lits

Plessisville: **CLSC et Centre de services externes**
pour les aînés de Plessisville
Affiliée à: CIUSSS de la
Mauricie-et-du-Centre-du-Québec
1450, av Trudelle, Plessisville, QC G6L 3K4
Tél: 819-362-3558 *Téléc:* 819-362-9266
ciusssmcq.ca
Nombre de lits: 40 lits
Claude Charland, Directeur général, CSSS d'Arthabaska-et-de-L'Érable

Pointe-Claire: **CHSLD Bayview inc.**
Également connu sous le nom de: Centre Bayview
27, ch du Bord-du-Lac, Pointe-Claire, QC H9S 4H1
Tél: 514-695-9384 *Téléc:* 514-695-5723
contact@chsldbayview.com
www.chsld-bayview.com
Nombre de lits: 128 lits
Note: Un établissement privé de soins de longue durée.
George Guillon, Directeur général
admin@chsldbayview.com
Michel Larose, Directeur, Finances
mlarose@chsldbayview.com

Princeville: **Centre d'hébergement de Saint-Eusèbe**
Affiliée à: CIUSSS de la
Mauricie-et-du-Centre-du-Québec
Également connu sous le nom de: Foyer St-Eusèbe
CP 610, 435, rue Saint-Jacques est, Princeville, QC G6L 5C5
Tél: 819-364-2355
www.ciusssmcq.ca
Nombre de lits: 26 lits

Québec: **Centre d'accueil Nazareth inc.**
715, rue des Glacis, Québec, QC G1R 3P8
Tél: 418-694-0492 *Téléc:* 418-694-9452
Nombre de lits: 75 lits

Québec: **Centre d'hébergement Christ-Roi**
Affiliée à: CIUSSS de la Capitale-Nationale
900, boul Wilfrid-Hamel, Québec, QC G1M 2R9
Tél: 418-682-1711
Nombre de lits: 142 lits
Note: Hébergement permanent/soins de longue durée, hôpital de jour, hébergement temporaire, consultations externes

Québec: **Centre d'hébergement Henri-Bradet**
Affiliée à: CIUSSS du
Centre-Ouest-de-l'Ile-de-Montréal
6465, av Chester, Québec, QC H4V 2Z8
Tél: 514-484-7878 *Téléc:* 514-483-4596
www.cssscavendish.qc.ca

Québec: **Centre d'hébergement Louis-Hebert**
Affiliée à: CIUSSS de la Capitale-Nationale
1550, rue de la Pointe-aux-Lièvres nord, Québec, QC G1L 4M8
Tél: 418-529-5511 *Téléc:* 418-524-1143
www.ciusss-capitalenationale.gouv.qc.ca
Nombre de lits: 52 lits

Québec: **Centre d'hébergement Saint-Antoine**
Affiliée à: CIUSSS de la Capitale-Nationale
1451, boul Père-Lelièvre, Québec, QC G1M 1N8
Tél: 418-683-2516
www.ciusss-capitalenationale.gouv.qc.ca
Nombre de lits: 284 lits
Note: Hébergement et soins de longue durée

Québec: **Centre d'hébergement Saint-Augustin**
Affiliée à: CIUSSS de la Capitale-Nationale
2135, rue de la Terrasse-Cadieux, Québec, QC G1C 1Z2
Tél: 418-667-3910
www.ciusss-capitalenationale.gouv.qc.ca
Nombre de lits: 34 lits de gériatrie

Québec: **Centre d'hébergement St-Jean-Eudes**
(CHSJE)
Affiliée à: CIUSSS de la Capitale-Nationale
6000, 3e av ouest, Québec, QC G1H 7J5
Tél: 418-627-1124 *Téléc:* 418-781-2604
www.chsje.qc.ca
Nombre de lits: 150 lits
Note: Le Centre d'hébergement St-Jean-Eudes est un établissement privé conventionné.

Québec: **La Corporation Notre-Dame de**
Bon-Secours
990, rue Gérard-Morisset, Québec, QC G1S 1X6
Tél: 418-681-4637
Nombre de lits: 20 lits
Michel Bilodrau, Directeur général

Québec: **Foyer Ste-Marie-des-Anges Résidence**
2340, boul Masson, Québec, QC G1P 1J4
Tél: 418-871-5365 *Téléc:* 418-667-7537
www.cmafhaiti.org/foyer.htm
Nombre de lits: 14 chambres
Note: Pour personnes retraitées autonomes et en perte d'autonomie

Québec: **Hôpital Ste-Monique inc.**
Affiliée à: CIUSSS de la Capitale-Nationale
4805, boul Wilfrid-Hamel, Québec, QC G1P 2J7
Tél: 418-871-8701 *Téléc:* 418-871-0105
www.chsld-ste-monique.com
Nombre de lits: 58 lits
Note: Centre d'hébergement de soins de longue durée.

Québec: **Maison Paul-Triquet**
Affiliée à: CIUSSS de la Capitale-Nationale
Également connu sous le nom de: La Maison
Paul-Triquet
789, rue de Belmont, Québec, QC G1V 4V2
Tél: 418-657-6890
www.ciusss-capitalenationale.gouv.qc.ca
Fondée en: 1987
Nombre de lits: 64 lits
Note: Centre d'hébergement de soins de longue durée pour anciens combattants

Rawdon: **CHSLD Bouleaux Argentés**
3567, rue Church, Rawdon, QC J0K 1S0
Tél: 450-834-2794 *Téléc:* 450-834-8286
Nombre de lits: 16 lits

Rawdon: **Manoir Heather/Heather Lodge**
3462, 3e av, Rawdon, QC J0K 1S0
Tél: 450-834-2512 *Téléc:* 450-834-5805
www.manoirheather.com
Nombre de lits: 76 lits
Note: CHSLD Heather II: 3462, 3e av, Rawdon, QC J0K 1S0, 450-834-2512.
Paul Arbec, Directeur général
paul_arbec@ssss.gouv.qc.ca

Richmond: **Centre d'hébergement de Richmond**
Affiliée à: CIUSSS de l'Estrie
110, rue Barlow, Richmond, QC J0B 2H0
Tél: 819-542-2777 *Téléc:* 819-826-3867
vsf.santeestrie.qc.ca
Nombre de lits: 54 lits
Pierre Lalande, Directeur général, CSSS du Val-Saint-François

Rimouski: **Centre d'hébergement de Rimouski**
Affiliée à: CISSS du Bas-St-Laurent
645, boul Saint-Germain, Rimouski, QC G5L 3S2
Tél: 418-724-4111
www.cisss-bsl.gouv.qc.ca
Nombre de lits: 246 lits

Rimouski: **Manoir Les Generations**
Ancien nom: Foyer Ste-Bernadette inc.
280, av Belzile, Rimouski, QC G5L 8K7
Tél: 418-723-0040 *Téléc:* 418-723-0615
Nombre de lits: 24 lits

Rivière-Bleue: **Centre d'hébergement de**
Rivière-Bleue
Affiliée à: CISSS du Bas-St-Laurent
45, rue du Foyer, Rivière-Bleue, QC G0L 2B0
Tél: 418-893-5511 *Téléc:* 418-893-7151
www.cisss-bsl.gouv.qc.ca
Nombre de lits: 44 lits

Rivière-Ouelle: **Centre d'hébergement**
Thérèse-Martin
Affiliée à: CISSS du Bas-St-Laurent
100, ch Petite-Anse, Rivière-Ouelle, QC G0L 2C0
Tél: 418-856-7000 *Téléc:* 418-856-4381
www.agencessbsl.gouv.qc.ca

Rivière-du-Loup: **Centre d'hébergement**
Saint-Joseph
28, rue Joly, Rivière-du-Loup, QC G5R 3H2
Tél: 418-862-6385 *Téléc:* 418-862-1986
www.csssriviereduloup.qc.ca
Nombre de lits: 121 lits

Rouyn-Noranda: **Centre d'hébergement de**
Rouyn-Noranda
Affiliée à: CISSS de l'Abitibi-Témiscamingue
512, av Richard, Rouyn-Noranda, QC J9X 4M1
Tél: 819-762-0908 *Téléc:* 819-764-5036
www.csssrn.qc.ca
Nombre de lits: 157 lits
Note: Centre d'hébergement, centre de jour, hôpital de jour.
Jean-Pierre Lemire, Directrice générale, CSSS de Rouyn-Noranda
Annie Audet, Directrice, Programme des personnes en perte d'autonomie

Saint-Alexandre: Centre d'hébergement Villa Maria
Affiliée à: CISSS du Bas-St-Laurent
404, av du Foyer, Saint-Alexandre, QC G0L 2G0
Tél: 418-856-7000 Téléc: 418-492-1951
www.cisss-bsl.gouv.qc.ca

Saint-André-Avellin: CLSC et Centre d'hébergement Petite-Nation
Affiliée à: CISSS de l'Outaouais
14, rue Saint-André, Saint-André-Avellin, QC J0V 1W0
Tél: 819-983-7341
cisss-outaouais.gouv.qc.ca

Saint-Antoine-sur-Richeli: Accueil du Rivage inc.
Affiliée à: CISSS de la Montérégie-Est
1008, ch du Rivage, Saint-Antoine-sur-Richeli, QC J0L 1R0
Tél: 450-787-3436 Téléc: 450-787-1156
www.accueildurivage.com
Nombre de lits: 32 lits
Linda Williamson, Adminstrator
linda.williamson.accrivage16@ssss.gouv.qc.ca

Saint-Antonin: Centre d'hébergement de Saint-Antonin
Affiliée à: CISSS du Bas-St-Laurent
286, rue Principale, Saint-Antonin, QC G0L 2J0
Tél: 418-868-1000
www.cisss-bsl.gouv.qc.ca
Nombre de lits: 42 lits

Saint-Augustin-de-Desmaur: Jardins du Haut Saint-Laurent
Affiliée à: CIUSSS de la Capitale-Nationale
4770, rue Saint-Felix, Saint-Augustin-de-Desmaur, QC G3A 1B1
Tél: 418-872-4936 Téléc: 418-872-4245
info@jardins-hsl.com
www.jardins-hsl.com
Nombre de lits: 140 lits

Saint-Bernard-de-Lacolle: Florence Groulx inc.
7, rue Saint-Louis RR#2, Saint-Bernard-de-Lacolle, QC J0J 1V0
Tél: 450-246-3879 Téléc: 450-246-4111
Nombre de lits: 50 lits
Daniel Gaudette, Directeur général

Saint-Bruno-de-Montarvill: Centre d'hébergement de Montarville
Affiliée à: CISSS de la Montérégie-Est
265, boul Seigneurial ouest, Saint-Bruno-de-Montarvill, QC J3V 2H4
Tél: 450-461-2650 Téléc: 450-461-2968
communication.csssry16@ssss.gouv.ac.ca
www.santemonteregie.qc.ca/richelieu-yamaska
Nombre de lits: 155 lits

Saint-Casimir: Centre d'hébergement Saint-Casimir
Affiliée à: CIUSSS de la Capitale-Nationale
605, rue Fleury, Saint-Casimir, QC G0A 3L0
Tél: 418-339-2861 Téléc: 418-339-2875
www.ciusss-capitalenationale.gouv.qc.ca
Nombre de lits: 64 lits

Saint-Célestin: Centre d'hébergement Saint-Célestin
Affiliée à: CIUSSS de la Mauricie-et-du-Centre-du-Québec
CP 90, 475, rue Houde, Saint-Célestin, QC J0C 1G0
Tél: 819-229-3617
ciusssmcq.ca
Nombre de lits: 52 lits

Saint-Constant: Centre d'hébergement Champlain Jean-Louis Lapierre
Groupe Champlain Soins de Longue Durée
Affiliée à: CISSS de la Montérégie-Ouest
199, rue Saint-Pierre, Saint-Constant, QC J5A 2N8
Tél: 450-632-4451 Téléc: 450-632-2004
www.santemonteregie.qc.ca/jardins-roussillon
Nombre de lits: 76 lits
Marie-Claude Ouellet, Directrice générale, Groupe Champlain Soins de Longue Durée

Saint-Cyprien: Centre d'hébergement de Saint-Cyprien
Affiliée à: CISSS du Bas-St-Laurent
101-C, rue Collin, Saint-Cyprien, QC G0L 2P0
Tél: 418-868-1000
www.cisss-bsl.gouv.qc.ca
Nombre de lits: 20 lits

Saint-Eustache: Centre d'hébergement de Saint-Eustache
Affiliée à: CISSS des Laurentides
CP 850, 55, rue Chenier, Saint-Eustache, QC J7R 4Y8
Tél: 450-472-0013 Téléc: 450-472-3104
Nombre de lits: 194 lits

Saint-Eustache: Société en commandite centre d'accueil l'Ermitage
112, 25e av, Saint-Eustache, QC J7P 2V2
Tél: 450-473-5961 Téléc: 450-491-1847

Saint-Félicien: Centre d'hébergement de Saint-Félicien
Affiliée à: Centre de santé et de services sociaux Domaine-du-Roy
Édifice Foyer de la Paix, 1229, boul Sacré-Coeur, Saint-Félicien, QC G8K 1A5
Tél: 418-679-1585 Téléc: 418-679-2376
www.cssdomaineduroy.com
Nombre de lits: 46 lits
Note: Hébergement permanent et temporaire; centre de jour.
Jacques Dubois, Directeur général, CSSS Domaine-du-Roy

Saint-Ferdinand: Pavillon Morisset-Huppé Inc.
Ancien nom: Ressource Intermédiaire
CP 2060, 290, rte 165, Saint-Ferdinand, QC G0N 1N0
Tél: 418-428-3568
Fondée en: 1980
Note: Hébergement pour adultes en déficience intellectuells et handicapés physiques.

Saint-Gabriel-de-Brandon: Centre d'hébergement Desy
Affiliée à: CISSS de Lanaudière
CP 840, 90, rue Maskinonge, Saint-Gabriel-de-Brandon, QC J0K 2N0
Tél: 450-835-4712 Téléc: 450-835-7606
www.csssnl.qc.ca
Nombre de lits: 54 lits
Martin Beaumont, Directeur Général

Saint-Georges: Centre hospitalier de l'Assomption
16750, boul Lacroix, Saint-Georges, QC G5Y 2G4
Tél: 416-228-2041

Saint-Georges-de-Beauce: CHSLD L'Assomption
Affiliée à: Groupe Champlain Soins de Longue Durée
16750, boul Lacroix, Saint-Georges-de-Beauce, QC G5Y 2G4
Tél: 418-228-2041
www.groupechamplain.qc.ca
Note: Agence/région administrative: Agence de la santé et des services sociaux de Lanaudière.

Saint-Hubert: Centre d'hébergement Henriette Céré
Affiliée à: CISSS de la Montérégie-Centre
6435, ch de Chambly, Saint-Hubert, QC J3Y 3R6
Tél: 450-672-3320

Saint-Hubert: Pavillon St-Hubert
3823, rue Grand Boulevard, Saint-Hubert, QC J4T 2M3
Tél: 450-445-3598 Téléc: 450-462-3767

Saint-Hyacinthe: Centre d'hébergement Andrée-Perrault
Affiliée à: CISSS de la Montérégie-Est
1955, av Pratte, Saint-Hyacinthe, QC J2S 7W5
Tél: 514-771-4536 Téléc: 450-771-5499
info@lesommetavotreportee.qc.ca
www.santemonteregie.qc.ca/richelieu-yamaska
Nombre de lits: 70 lits
Lise Pouliot, Directrice générale, CSSS Richelieu-Yamaska

Saint-Hyacinthe: CHSLD Résidence Bourg-Joli inc.
2915, boul Laframboise, Saint-Hyacinthe, QC J2S 4Z3
Tél: 450-773-4197 Téléc: 450-773-6545
wpp01.msss.gouv.qc.ca
Nombre de lits: 24 lits

Saint-Jean-sur-Richelieu: Centre d'hébergement Georges-Phaneuf
Affiliée à: CISSS de la Montérégie-Centre
230, rue Jacques-Cartier nord, Saint-Jean-sur-Richelieu, QC J3B 6T4
Tél: 450-346-1133 Téléc: 450-346-2199
www.santemonteregie.qc.ca
Nombre de lits: 124 lits

Saint-Jean-sur-Richelieu: Centre d'hébergement Gertrude-Lafrance
Affiliée à: CISSS de la Montérégie-Centre
150, boul Saint-Luc, Saint-Jean-sur-Richelieu, QC J3A 1G2
Tél: 450-359-5555 Téléc: 450-348-7693
www.santemonteregie.qc.ca/haut-richelieu-rouville
Nombre de lits: 174 lits

Saint-Jérome: Centre d'hébergement L'Auberge
Affiliée à: CISSS des Laurentides
66, rue Danis, Saint-Jérome, QC J7Y 2R3
Tél: 450-432-2777
Nombre de lits: 92 lits

Saint-Jérome: CHSLD de la Rivière du Nord
531, rue Laviolette, Saint-Jérome, QC J7Y 2T8
Tél: 450-432-2777
Nombre de lits: 305 lits
Note: Centres d'hébergement: Youville, l'Auberge, et Lucien G. Rolland.

Saint-Lambert: CHSLD de la MRC de Champlain
831, av Notre-Dame, Saint-Lambert, QC J4R 1S1
Tél: 450-672-3320 Téléc: 450-672-3370
Nombre de lits: 313 lits

Saint-Laurent: Centre d'hébergement de Saint-Laurent
Affiliée à: CIUSSS du Nord-de-l'Ile-de-Montréal
1055, av Ste-Croix, Saint-Laurent, QC H4L 3Z2
Tél: 514-744-4981 Téléc: 514-744-0895
Nombre de lits: 154 lits

Saint-Liguori: Centre d'hébergement Saint-Liguori
Affiliée à: CISSS de Lanaudière
771, rue Principale, Saint-Liguori, QC J0K 2X0
Tél: 450-753-7062 Téléc: 450-753-3208
Nombre de lits: 48 lits
Paul-Yvon de Billy, Directeur général

Saint-Louis-du-Ha!-Ha!: Centre d'hébergement St-Louis
Affiliée à: CISSS du Bas-St-Laurent
25, rue Saint-Philippe, Saint-Louis-du-Ha!-Ha!, QC G0L 3S0
Tél: 418-854-2631 Téléc: 418-854-0430
www.cssstemiscouata.com
Nombre de lits: 43 lits

Saint-Michel-de-Bellechas: CHSLD Vigi Notre-Dame de Lourdes
80, rue Principale, Saint-Michel-de-Bellechas, QC G0R 3S0
Tél: 418-884-2811 Téléc: 418-884-3714
www.vigisante.com
Nombre de lits: 40 lits
Note: Agence/région administrative: Agence de la santé et des services sociaux de Chaudière-Appalaches.

Saint-Michel-des-Saints: Centre d'hébergement Brassard
Affiliée à: CISSS de Lanaudière
CP 309, 390, rue Brassard, Saint-Michel-des-Saints, QC J0K 3B0
Tél: 514-833-6331 Téléc: 514-833-6093
Nombre de lits: 35 lits
Jean-Jacques Lamarche, Directeur général par intérim

Saint-Michel-du-Squatec: Centre d'hébergement de Squatec
Affiliée à: CISSS du Bas-St-Laurent
Ancien nom: Domaine du Sommet
10, rue Saint-André, Saint-Michel-du-Squatec, QC G0L 4H0
Tél: 418-855-2442 Téléc: 418-855-2357
www.cisss-bsl.gouv.qc.ca

Saint-Pacôme: Centre d'hébergement D'Anjou
127, rue Galarneau, Saint-Pacôme, QC G0L 3X0
Tél: 418-856-7000 Téléc: 418-856-3948
www.cssskamouraska.ca
Nombre de lits: 53 lits d'hébergement permanents

Saint-Pierre-les-Becquets: Centre d'hébergement Romain-Becquet
Affiliée à: CIUSSS de la Mauricie-et-du-Centre-du-Québec
255, rte Marie-Victorin, Saint-Pierre-les-Becquets, QC G0Z 2Z0
Tél: 819-263-2245
Nombre de lits: 35 lits
Note: Hébergement permanent et temporaire

Saint-Raymond: Centre d'hébergement Saint-Raymond
Affiliée à: CISS de la Capitale-Nationale
324, rue Saint-Joseph, Saint-Raymond, QC G3L 1J7
Tél: 418-337-4611 *Téléc:* 418-337-4662
www.ciusss-capitalenationale.gouv.qc.ca

Saint-Rémi: Centre d'hébergement de Saint-Rémi
Affiliée à: CISS de la Montérégie-Ouest
110, rue du Collège, Saint-Rémi, QC J0L 2L0
Tél: 450-454-4694 *Téléc:* 450-454-3614
Nombre de lits: 58 lits

Saint-Romuald: CHSLD Chanoine-Audet inc.
Affiliée à: Groupe Champlain inc.
2155, ch du Sault, Saint-Romuald, QC G6W 2K7
Tél: 418-834-5322 *Téléc:* 418-834-5754
www.groupechamplain.qc.ca
Nombre de lits: 96 lits
Note: Agence/région administrative: Agence de la santé et des services sociaux de Chaudière-Appalaches.

Saint-Timothée: La Maison des Aîné(e)s
1, rue des Aînes, Saint-Timothée, QC J6S 6M8
Tél: 450-377-3925 *Téléc:* 450-377-3490
Nombre de lits: 65 lits

Saint-Tite: Centre d'hébergement et CLSC Mgr Paquin
Affiliée à: CIUSSS de la Mauricie-et-du-Centre-du-Québec
CP 400, 580, rue du Couvent, Saint-Tite, QC G0X 3H0
Tél: 418-365-5107
ciusssmcq.ca
Nombre de lits: 55 lits

Sainte-Adèle: Centre d'hébergement des Hauteurs
707, boul Sainte-Adèle, Sainte-Adèle, QC J8B 2N1
Tél: 450-229-6601
Nombre de lits: 112 lits

Sainte-Anne-de-la-Pérade: Centre multiservice Foyer de la Pérade
CP 217, 60, rue de la Fabrique, Sainte-Anne-de-la-Pérade, QC G0X 2J0
Tél: 418-325-2313 *Téléc:* 418-325-3233
Nombre de lits: 42 lits

Sainte-Cécile: Pavillon Ste-Cécile
4581, rue Principale, Sainte-Cécile, QC G0Y 1J0
Tél: 819-583-0400 *Téléc:* 819-583-0983
Nombre de lits: 15 lits

Sainte-Sophie: Villa du Nord
2319, rang Sainte-Marie, Sainte-Sophie, QC J5J 1M8
Tél: 450-436-5627

Sainte-Thérèse: Centre d'hébergement Drapeau-Deschambault
Affiliée à: CISS des Laurentides
100, rue du Chanoine Lionel-Groulx, Sainte-Thérèse, QC J7E 5E1
Tél: 450-433-2777 *Téléc:* 450-437-0788
www.cssstheresedeblainville.qc.ca
Nombre de lits: 203 lits

Sainte-Thérèse: CHSLD Boise Ste-Thérèse Inc.
179, Place Fabien-Drapeau, Sainte-Thérèse, QC J7E 5W6
Tél: 450-430-6767 *Téléc:* 450-430-6965
info@le-boise.com
www.le-boise.com
Nombre de lits: 41 CHSLD privé; 60 autonomes

Saint-Éphrem-de-Beauce: Résidence St-Éphrem inc.
CP 310, 1, rue Plante, Saint-Éphrem-de-Beauce, QC G0M 1R0
Tél: 418-484-2121 *Téléc:* 418-484-2144
info@residencestephrem.com
www.residencestephrem.com
Nombre de lits: 40 lits
Lynda Roy, Directrice Générale

Salaberry-de-Valleyfield: Centre d'hébergement Docteur-Aimé-Leduc
Affiliée à: CISS de la Montérégie-Ouest
80, rue de Marche, Salaberry-de-Valleyfield, QC J6T 1P5
Tél: 450-373-4818 *Téléc:* 450-373-0325
santemonteregie.qc.ca/en/installations/centre-dhebergement-docteur-aime-leduc
Nombre de lits: 177 lits

Shawinigan: CHSLD Vigi Les Chutes
Affiliée à: Vigi Santé Ltée
5000, av Albert-Tessier, Shawinigan, QC G9N 8P9
Tél: 819-539-5408 *Téléc:* 819-539-5400
www.vigisante.com
Nombre de lits: 64 lits
Note: Agence/région administrative: Agence de la santé et des services sociaux de la Mauricie.

Shawville: Pavillon Centre d'accueil Pontiac
Affiliée à: CISS de l'Outaouais
CP 2001, 290, rue Marion, Shawville, QC J0X 2Y0
Tél: 819-647-5755 *Téléc:* 819-647-2453
Nombre de lits: 50 lits

Sherbrooke: Centre d'hébergement St-Joseph
Affiliée à: CIUSSS de l'Estrie
611, boul Queen-Victoria, Sherbrooke, QC J1H 3R6
Tél: 819-780-2222
www.csss-iugs.ca
Nombre de lits: 144 lits
Carol Fillion, Directeur général, CSSS-Institut universitaire de gériatrie de Sherbro

Sherbrooke: CHSLD Vigi Shermont inc.
Affiliée à: Vigi Santé Ltée
3220, 12e av nord, Sherbrooke, QC J1H 5H3
Tél: 819-820-8900 *Téléc:* 819-820-8902
www.vigisante.com
Nombre de lits: 52 lits
Note: Agence/région administrative: Agence de la santé et des services sociaux de l'Estrie.

Sherbrooke: Les Dominicaines des saints anges gardiens
Ancien nom: Mont St-Dominique
361, rue Moore, Sherbrooke, QC J1H 1C1
Tél: 819-346-5512

Sillery: Pavillon Saint-Dominique
1045, boul René-Lévesque ouest, Sillery, QC G1S 1V3
Tél: 418-681-3561 *Téléc:* 418-687-9196
info@domaine-saint-dominique.com
www.domaine-saint-dominique.com
Nombre de lits: 152 lits

Sillery: Saint Brigid's Home Inc.
Affiliée à: CIUSSS de la Capitale-Nationale
1645, ch Saint-Louis, Sillery, QC G1S 4M3
Tél: 418-681-4687 *Téléc:* 418-527-6862
www.jhsb.ca/fr/chsld-saint-brigids
Fondée en: 1856
Nombre de lits: 142 lits

Sorel-Tracy: Centre d'hébergement de Tracy
Affiliée à: CISS de la Montérégie-Est
4025, rue Frontenac, Sorel-Tracy, QC J3R 4G8
Tél: 450-742-9427 *Téléc:* 450-742-9668
Nombre de lits: 64 lits

Sorel-Tracy: Centre d'hébergement J.-Arsène-Parenteau
Affiliée à: CISS de la Montérégie-Est
Également connu sous le nom de: Foyer Richelieu
40, rue de Ramezay, Sorel-Tracy, QC J3P 3Y7
Tél: 514-742-5936 *Téléc:* 514-742-1613
Nombre de lits: 60 lits
Jacques Blais, Directeur général

Sorel-Tracy: CHSLD du Bas-Richelieu
151, rue George, Sorel-Tracy, QC J3P 1C8
Tél: 450-746-5555 *Téléc:* 450-746-4897
Nombre de lits: 145 lits

St-Charles-de-Bellechasse: Résidence Charles Couillard Inc.
20, av Saint-Georges, St-Charles-de-Bellechasse, QC G0R 2T0
Tél: 418-887-6455 *Téléc:* 418-887-1316
rcouillard1@hotmail.com
www.saint-charles.ca
Nombre de lits: 35 lits

St-Pierre-de-l'Ile-d'Orlé: Centre d'hébergement Alphonse-Bonenfant
Affiliée à: CIUSSS de la Capitale-Nationale
1395, ch Royal, St-Pierre-de-l'Ile-d'Orlé, QC G0A 4E0
Tél: 418-828-9114 *Téléc:* 418-828-1127
www.ciusss-capitalenationale.gouv.qc.ca
Nombre de lits: 50 lits

Sutton: Foyer Sutton
Affiliée à: CISS de la Montérégie-Ouest
50, rue Western, Sutton, QC J0E 2K0
Tél: 514-538-3332 *Téléc:* 514-538-0514
Nombre de lits: 71 lits
Spécialités: Centre d'hébergement

Terrebonne: CHSLD de La Côte Boisée inc.
4300, rue d'Angora, Terrebonne, QC J6X 4P1
Tél: 450-471-5877 *Téléc:* 450-471-7511
www.chslddelacoteboisee.org
Nombre de lits: 140 lits
Gerald Asselin, Directeur général

Thetford Mines: Résidence La Rosée d'Or
736, boul Ouellet, Thetford Mines, QC G6G 4X5
Tél: 418-338-3774
Nombre de lits: 9 lits

Trois-Rivières: Centre d'hébergement Cooke
Affiliée à: CIUSSS de la Mauricie-et-du-Centre-du-Québec
3450, rue Sainte-Marguerite, Trois-Rivières, QC G8Z 1X3
Tél: 819-370-2100
www.cssstr.qc.ca
Nombre de lits: 190 lits

Trois-Rivières: Centre d'hébergement Louis-Denoncourt
Affiliée à: CIUSSS de la Mauricie-et-du-Centre-du-Québec
435, rue Saint-Roch, Trois-Rivières, QC G9A 2L9
Tél: 819-376-2566 *Téléc:* 819-376-5620
ciusssmcq.ca
Nombre de lits: 75 lits
Note: Hébergement permanent.

Trois-Rivières: Centre d'hébergement Roland-Leclerc
Affiliée à: CIUSSS de la Mauricie-et-du-Centre-du-Québec
3500, rue Sainte-Marguerite, Trois-Rivières, QC G8Z 1X3
Tél: 819-370-2100
ciusssmcq.ca
Note: Hébergement permanent et temporaire.

Upton: Domaine du Bel Age
CP 89, 906, rue Lanoie, Upton, QC J0H 2E0
Tél: 514-549-4404
Nombre de lits: 9 lits
Jacqueline Gosslin, Directrice générale

Varennes: Centre d'hébergement de Lajemmerais
Affiliée à: CISS de la Montérégie-Est
60, rue D'Youville, Varennes, QC J3X 1R1
Tél: 450-463-2995 *Téléc:* 450-468-8329
www.santemonteregie.qc.ca/cssspierreboucher
Fondée en: 1971
Spécialités: Un centre de jour pour la clientèle en perte d'autonomie vivant à domicile; Une unité prothétique; éadaptation

Vaudreuil-Dorion: CHSLD Manoir Harwood
Affiliée à: CISS de la Montérégie-Ouest
Ancien nom: Le Manoir Harwood
170, rue Boileau, Vaudreuil-Dorion, QC J7V 8A3
Tél: 450-424-6458 *Téléc:* 450-424-2074
info@chsldmanoirharwood.com
www.chsldmanoirharwood.com

Verdun: Centre d'hébergement Réal Morel
Affiliée à: CIUSSS du Centre-Sud-de-l'Ile-de-Montréal
3500, rue Wellington, Verdun, QC H4G 1T3
Tél: 514-761-5874 *Téléc:* 514-761-7264
www.sov.qc.ca
Nombre de lits: 148 lits

Victoriaville: Centre d'hébergement du Chêne
Affiliée à: CIUSSS de la Mauricie-et-du-Centre-du-Québec
61, rue de l'Ermitage, Victoriaville, QC G6P 6X4
Tél: 819-758-7511 *Téléc:* 819-758-7967
ciusssmcq.ca
Fondée en: 1971
Nombre de lits: 122 lits
Note: Les autres centres d'hébergement: Quatre-Vents, Saint-Eusèbe, Sacré-Coeur, Étoiles-d'Or, et Roseau.

Victoriaville: Centre d'hébergement du Roseau
Affiliée à: CIUSSS de la
Mauricie-et-du-Centre-du-Québec
Ancien nom: La Résidence le Roseau
45, rue de l'Ermitage, Victoriaville, QC G6P 6X4
Tél: 819-758-7511
ciusssmcq.ca

Fondée en: 1952
Nombre de lits: 88 lits d'hébergement permanent; 12 lits à
l'URFI; 5 lits en soins posthospitaliers

Waterloo: Santé Courville Waterloo
CP 580, 5305, av Courville, Waterloo, QC J0E 2N0
Tél: 450-539-1821 Téléc: 450-539-1937
santecourville.com
www.facebook.com/SanteCourvilledeWaterloo
Nombre de lits: 52 lits
Kenneth Courville, Président
Christine Durocher, Directrice générale

Weedon: Centre d'hébergement de Weedon
Affiliée à: CIUSSS de l'Estrie
Également connu sous le nom de: CHSLD de
Weedon
245, rue Saint-Janvier, Weedon, QC J0B 3J0
Tél: 819-877-2500 Téléc: 819-877-3089
www.csshsf.com

Westmount: Chateau Westmount inc.
4860, boul de Maisonneuve ouest, Westmount, QC H3Z 3G2
Tél: 514-369-3000 Téléc: 514-369-0014
www.chateauwestmount.ca
Nombre de lits: 112 lits
Nancy Fournier, Contact, Ressources humaines
nancy.fournier@chateauwestmount.ca
Zara Pilian, Contact
zara.pilian@chateauwestmount.ca

Ile Bizard: Centre d'hébergement Denis-Benjamin
Viger
Affiliée à: CIUSSS de l'Ouest-de-l'Ile-de-Montréal
3292, rue Cherrier, Ile Bizard, QC H9C 1E4
Tél: 514-620-6310
ciusss-ouestmtl.gouv.qc.ca
Nombre de lits: 125 lits

Ile-Perrot: Centre d'hébergement Laurent-Bergevin
Affiliée à: CISSS de la Montérégie-Ouest
Également connu sous le nom de: Centre d'accueil
Laurent-Bergevin
200, boul Perrot, Ile-Perrot, QC J7V 7M7
Tél: 514-453-5860
Nombre de lits: 82 lits

Centres d'accueil et d'hébergement

Gatineau: Manoir Ste-Marie
156, boul Lorrain, Gatineau, QC J8P 2G2
Tél: 819-663-5736 Téléc: 819-643-1358
info@manoirstemarie.com
manoirstemarie.com
Nombre de lits: 40 lits

Grandes-Bergeronnes: Pavillon Bergeronnes
Affiliée à: CISSS de la Côte-Nord
450, rue de la Mer, Grandes-Bergeronnes, QC G0T 1G0
Tél: 418-232-6224 Téléc: 418-232-6771
Nombre de lits: 32 lits

Ham-Nord: Foyer Saints-Anges de Ham-Nord inc.
CP 269, 493, rue Principale, Ham-Nord, QC G0P 1A0
Tél: 819-344-2940
www.chsldstsanges.ca
Nombre de lits: 38 lits
Alain Lavertu, Directeur général
alain_lavertu@ssss.gouv.qc.ca

La Doré: Ressource intermédiaire de La Doré
Également connu sous le nom de: Résidence La
Doré
CP 190, 4921, rue des Peupliers, La Doré, QC G0W 2J0
Tél: 418-256-3851 Téléc: 418-256-3608
santesaglac.com
Nombre de lits: 21 lits

Montréal: Centre d'hebergement Judith Jasmin
Affiliée à: CIUSSS de l'Est-de-l'Ile-de-Montréal
8850, rue Bisaillon, Montréal, QC H1K 4N2
Tél: 514-354-5990
www.csspointe.ca
Nombre de lits: 75 lits

Montréal: Centre hospitalier gériatrique
Maimonides/Donald Berman Maimonides Geriatric
Centre
Affiliée à: CIUSSS du
Centre-Ouest-de-l'Ile-de-Montréal
5795, av Caldwell, Montréal, QC H4W 1W3
Tél: 514-483-2121 Téléc: 514-483-1561
www.donaldbermanmaimonides.net
twitter.com/MaimonidesGC;
www.youtube.com/user/MaimonidesGeriatric
Nombre de lits: 387 lits
Barbara Gold, Directrice générale
barbra.gold@ssss.gouv.qc.ca

Montréal: Résidence Pie IX
4090, rue Martial, Montréal, QC H1H 1X4
Tél: 514-327-2333 Téléc: 514-327-3276
Nombre de lits: 42 lits
Note: Centre de réadaptation

Montréal-Nord: Château Beaurivage
Affiliée à: Résidences Azur
6880, boul Gouin est, Montréal-Nord, QC H1G 6L8
Tél: 514-687-6259
chateaubeaurivage.com
www.facebook.com/chateaubeaurivage
Julie Dagenais, Directrice générale
jacques@chateaubeaurivage.com

Pierrefonds: CHSLD Manoir Ile de l'Ouest
17725, boul Pierrefonds, Pierrefonds, QC H9J 3L1
Tél: 514-620-9850 Téléc: 514-620-3196
admin@westislandmanor.com
www.westislandmanor.com
Nombre de lits: 63 lits
Heather Karakas, Directrice générale

Roberval: Résidence des Érables
992, boul Saint-Joseph, Roberval, QC G8H 2L9
Tél: 418-275-4376
Nombre de lits: 23 lits
Note: déficience intellectuelle

Saint-Benoît-Labre: Pavillon Baillargeon inc.
#357, 271 Rte 1, Saint-Benoît-Labre, QC G0M 1P0
Tél: 418-228-9141 Téléc: 418-226-3772
Nombre de lits: 35 places

Saint-Eustache: Domaine des Trois Pignons
112, 25e av, Saint-Eustache, QC J7P 2V2
Tél: 450-473-5961

Saint-Fabien: Foyer St-Fabien
CP 520, 142, 1e rue, Saint-Fabien, QC G0L 2Z0
Tél: 418-869-2709

Saint-Zacharie: Résidence l'Eden
668, 12e av, Saint-Zacharie, QC G0M 2C0
Tél: 418-593-5200 Téléc: 418-593-5200
Fondée en: 1964
Nombre de lits: 30 lits

Sainte-Geneviève: Château sur le Lac
16289, boul Gouin ouest, Sainte-Geneviève, QC H9H 1E2
Tél: 514-620-9794 Téléc: 514-696-3196
info@chateausurlelac.com
chateausurlelac.com
Nombre de lits: 50 lits

Verdun: Manoir des Floralies Verdun
1050, av Gordon, Verdun, QC H4G 2S2
Tél: 514-766-2858 Téléc: 514-766-8701
www.floraliesverdun.com
Nombre de lits: 103 lits

Maisons de retraite

Baie-d'Urfé: Maxwell Residence
678, rue Surrey, Baie-d'Urfé, QC H9X 3S1
Tél: 514-457-3111 Fax: 514-457-7909
www.maxwellresidence.com
Note: Services include: fitness center & health programs;
medication management; & pharmacy.
Linda Sedlak, Contact
linda@maxwellresidence.com

Laval: Les Loggias et Villa Val des Arbres
3245, boul Saint-Martin est, Laval, QC H7E 4T6
Tél: 450-661-0911
info@vvda.ca
www.vvda.ca
Number of Beds: 163
Note: Centre privé non-conventionné; 163 unités, 48
appartements, 115 chambres.

Denis Lagueux, Président, Chartwell-Québec

Rimouski: Manoir Les Générations
280, av Belzile, Rimouski, QC G5L 8K7
Tél: 418-723-0611 Téléc: 418-723-0615
www.manoirlesgenerations.com
Nombre de lits: 85 lits

Hôpitaux psychiatriques et assistance communautaire

Gatineau: Hôpital Pierre-Janet
Affiliée à: CISSS de l'Outaouais
20, rue Pharand, Gatineau, QC J9A 1K7
Tél: 819-771-7761 Téléc: 819-771-2908
www.chpj.ca
Fondée en: 1965
Nombre de lits: 87 lits
Alain Godmaire, Directeur, Programmes en santé mentale et
dépendance

Malartic: Hôpital en santé mentale et CLSC de
Malartic
Affiliée à: CISSS de l'Abitibi-Témiscamingue
1141, rue Royale, Malartic, QC J0Y 1Z0
Tél: 819-825-5858
Nombre de lits: 34 lits
Note: Services de santé mentale et psychiatrie; soins aigus;
soins de longue durée.

Montréal: Hôpital Rivière-des-Prairies
Affiliée à: CIUSSS du Nord-de-l'Ile-de-Montréal
7070, boul Perras, Montréal, QC H1E 1A4
Tél: 514-323-7260 Téléc: 514-323-8622
www.ciusssnordmtl.ca
Nombre de lits: 125 lits

Montréal: L'Institut universitaire en santé mentale de
Montréal
Affiliée à: CIUSSS de l'Est-de-l'Ile-de-Montréal
Ancien nom: Hôpital Louis-H. Lafontaine
7401, rue Hochelaga, Montréal, QC H1N 3M5
Tél: 514-251-4000
ciusss-estmtl.gouv.qc.ca/etablissement/institut-universitaire-en-s
ante-mentale-de-montreal
Nombre de lits: 389 lits

Montréal: Institut universitaire en santé mentale
Douglas
Affiliée à: CIUSSS de l'Ouest-de-l'Ile-de-Montréal
Ancien nom: Hôpital Douglas
6875, boul LaSalle, Montréal, QC H4H 1R3
Tél: 514-761-6131
www.douglas.qc.ca
www.facebook.com/institutdouglas; twitter.com/institutdouglas;
www.youtube.com/douglasinstitute
Nombre de lits: 266 lits
Note: Affilié à l'Université McGill. Services: pédopsychiatrie;
gérontopsychiatrie; troubles de l'humeur; troubles psychotiques;
PEPP-Montréal; troubles de l'alimentation; déficience
intellectuelle; & réadaptation

Québec: Centre de réadaptation en santé mentale
Également connu sous le nom de: La Maisonnée
855, boul Louis XIV, Québec, QC G1H 1A6
Tél: 418-628-0662
www.ciusss-capitalenationale.gouv.qc.ca
Région desservi: Région de la Capitale-Nationale

Québec: L'Institut universitaire en santé mentale de
Québec/The Mental Health University Institute of
Québec
Affiliée à: CIUSSS de la Capitale-Nationale
Ancien nom: Centre hospitalier Robert Giffard
2601, ch de la Canardière, Québec, QC G1J 2G3
Tél: 418-663-5000
www.ciusss-capitalenationale.gouv.qc.ca
Fondée en: 1976
Nombre de lits: 513 lits
Note: Affilié à l'Université Laval.
Rodrigue Côté, Directeur adjoint, Santé mentale et dépendance

Rimouski: L'hôpital de jour psychiatrie
95, rue de l'Évêché ouest, Rimouski, QC G5L 4H4
Tél: 418-725-0544
Population desservi: 21000

Saskatchewan

Government Departments in Charge

Regina: Saskatchewan Health
T.C. Douglas Building, 3475 Albert St., Regina, SK S4S 6X6
Fax: 306-787-4533
Toll-Free: 800-667-7766
info@health.gov.sk.ca
www.saskatchewan.ca/health
Hon. Paul Merriman, Minister
306-787-7345, Fax: 306-787-0237, he.minister@gov.sk.ca
Hon. Everett Hindley, Minister, Mental Health &
Addictions/Seniors/Rural & Remote
306-798-9014, Fax: 306-798-9013, minister.rrhe@gov.sk.ca

Regional Health Authorities

Black Lake: Athabasca Health Authority (AHA)
PO Box 124, Black Lake, SK S0J 0H0
Tel: 306-439-2200 *Fax:* 306-439-2212
www.athabascahealth.ca
Population Served: 3038 *Number of Employees:* 72
Note: Provides health care services to the First Nations
communities of Black Lake, Fond du Lac, Stony Rapids,
Uranium City, & Camsell Portage.
Darryl Galusha, Chief Executive Officer
dgalusha@athabascahealth.ca

Saskatoon: Saskatchewan Health Authority (SHA)
Saskatoon City Hospital, 701 Queen St., Saskatoon, SK S7K
0M7
Tel: 306-655-0080 *Toll-Free:* 833-445-0080
info@saskhealthauthority.ca
www.saskhealthauthority.ca
www.facebook.com/saskhealthauthority; twitter.com/saskhealth
Year Founded: 2017
Population Served: 1169752 *Number of Employees:* 40000
Note: Saskatchewan Health Authority was launched on
December 4, 2017, following the amalgamation of 12 of the
province's former regional health authorities: Cypress Health
Region, Five Hills Health Region, Heartland Health Region,
Keewatin Yatthé Health Region, Kelsey Trail Health Region,
Mamawetan Churchill River Health Region, Prairie North Health
Region, Prince Albert Parkland Health Region, Regina
Qu'Appelle Health Region, Saskatoon Health Region, Sun
Country Health Region, & Sunrise Health Region. During the
transition period, the websites of the former regional health
authorities will continue to provide up-to-date information about
facilities & services.
Scott Livingstone, Chief Executive Officer
Suann Laurent, Chief Operating Officer
Mike Northcott, Chief Human Resources Officer
Robbie Peters, Chief Financial Officer
Dr. Susan Shaw, Chief Medical Officer
Beth Vachon, Vice-President, Quality, Safety & Strategy
Andrew Will, Vice-President, Infrastructure, Information &
Support
Lori Frank, Executive Director, Governance & Policy
Kim McKechney, Executive Director, Community Engagement &
Communications

Hospitals - General

Arcola: Arcola Health Centre
Sun Country Health Region
Affiliated with: Saskatchewan Health Authority
PO Box 419, 607 Prairie Ave., Arcola, SK S0C 0G0
Tel: 306-455-2771
www.suncountry.sk.ca
Number of Beds: 12 acute care beds
Note: Programs & services include: Telehealth; palliative care;
mental health services; & acute care services.
Enoch Pambour, Contact

Assiniboia: Assiniboia Union Hospital
Five Hills Health Region
Affiliated with: Saskatchewan Health Authority
501 - 6 Ave., Assiniboia, SK S0H 0B0
Tel: 306-642-9400
www.fhhr.ca/AssiniboiaHospital.htm
Info Line: 306-642-9444
Number of Beds: 22 long term care beds; 12 acute care beds; 4
respite / palliative care beds
Note: Programs & services include: emergency services; acute
care; laboratory; respite care; & palliative care.

Balcarres: Balcarres Integrated Care Centre
Regina Qu'Appelle Health Region
Affiliated with: Saskatchewan Health Authority
PO Box 340, 100 South Elgin St., Balcarres, SK S0G 0C0
Tel: 306-334-6260 *Fax:* 306-334-2865
www.rqhealth.ca/facilities/balcarres-integrated-care-centre
Year Founded: 1999
Number of Beds: 44 beds
Note: Programs & services include: addictions counselling;
dietitian; electrocardiogram; laboratory; long-term care; mental
health therapist; outpatient / ambulatory care; physical therapy;
physician & nurse practitioner; & x-ray.

Big River: Big River Health Centre
Prince Albert Parkland Health Region
Affiliated with: Saskatchewan Health Authority
220 - 1st Ave. North, Big River, SK S0J 0E0
Tel: 306-469-2220 *Fax:* 303-469-2193
paphr.ca
Number of Beds: 34 long-term care beds; 1 interim bed
Note: Programs & services include: chronic disease
management; home care; laboratory; mental health; primary
health care clinic; public health nursing; special care home; &
x-ray.

Biggar: Biggar & District Health Centre
Heartland Health Region
Affiliated with: Saskatchewan Health Authority
PO Box 130, 501 - 1 Ave. West, Biggar, SK S0K 0M0
Tel: 306-948-3323
www.hrha.sk.ca
Number of Beds: 53 long term care beds; 13 acute care beds; 3
alternate level of care beds
Note: Services include: acute care; diagnostics; emergency;
home care; laboratory; long term care; outpatient; physicians;
Telehealth; & x-ray.

Broadview: Broadview Hospital
Regina Qu'Appelle Health Region
Affiliated with: Saskatchewan Health Authority
PO Box 100, 901 Nina St., Broadview, SK S0G 0K0
Tel: 306-696-5500 *Fax:* 306-696-2611
www.rqhealth.ca/facilities/the-broadview-hospital
Number of Beds: 16 beds
Note: Programs & services include: ambulatory care; inpatient;
laboratory; Native liaison worker; outpatient; palliative care;
perinatal/delivery; & x-ray.

Canora: Canora Hospital
Sunrise Health Region
Affiliated with: Saskatchewan Health Authority
PO Box 749, 1219 Main St., Canora, SK S0A 0L0
Tel: 306-563-5621 *Fax:* 306-563-1257
www.sunrisehealthregion.sk.ca
Year Founded: 1968
Number of Beds: 16 acute care beds
Note: Programs & services include: emergency; cardiac;
laboratory; medicine; occupational therapy; outpatient;
pharmacy; physical therapy; & x-ray.

Central Butte: Central Butte Regency Hospital
Five Hills Health Region
Affiliated with: Saskatchewan Health Authority
PO Box 40, 601 Canada St., Central Butte, SK S0H 0T0
Tel: 306-796-2190
www.fhhr.ca/CentralButte.htm
Number of Beds: 22 long term care beds; 5 alternate level of
care beds
Note: Programs & services include acute care & special care
home.

Davidson: Davidson Health Centre
Heartland Health Region
Affiliated with: Saskatchewan Health Authority
PO Box 758, 900 Government Rd., Davidson, SK S0G 1A0
Tel: 306-567-2300
www.hrha.sk.ca/health-facilities/Pages/Davidson.aspx
Number of Beds: 2 acute care beds; 30 long-term care beds; 6
alternate level of care beds
Number of Employees: 70
Note: Services include: acute care; diagnostics; emergency;
home care; laboratory; long-term care; outpatient; physicians;
public health nurse; Telehealth; & x-ray.

Esterhazy: St. Anthony's Hospital
Sunrise Health Region
Affiliated with: Saskatchewan Health Authority
PO Box 280, 216 Ancona St., Esterhazy, SK S0A 0X0
Tel: 306-745-3973 *Fax:* 306-745-3245
www.sunrisehealthregion.sk.ca
Year Founded: 1940
Number of Beds: 14 acute care beds

Note: Services include: 24 hour emergency; dietitian; laboratory;
medicine; outpatient; pastoral care; & x-ray.

Estevan: St. Joseph's Hospital
Emmanuel Care
Affiliated with: Saskatchewan Health Authority
1176 Nicholson Rd., Estevan, SK S4A 0H3
Tel: 306-637-2400
stjosephsestevan.ca
Number of Beds: 53 beds
Note: Programs & services include: adult day program;
diagnostic; dialysis; emergency; endoscopy; intensive care;
laboratory; long term care; medical unit; & pharmacy.
Greg Hoffort, Executive Director
greg.hoffort@schr.sk.ca

**Fort Qu'Appelle: All Nations' Healing Hospital
(ANHH)**
Regina Qu'Appelle Health Region
Affiliated with: Saskatchewan Health Authority
PO Box 300, 450 - 8th St., Fort Qu'Appelle, SK S0G 1S0
Tel: 306-332-5611 *Fax:* 306-332-5033
www.rqhealth.ca/facilities/all-nations-healing-hospital
Number of Beds: 14 beds
Population Served: 2500
Note: Hospital Specialties: First Nations health services; acute
care; emergency services; women's health; palliative care;
laboratory; & radiology.
Lorna Breitkreuz, Director, Client Services

Gravelbourg: St. Joseph's Hospital/Foyer d'Youville
Five Hills Health Region
Affiliated with: Saskatchewan Health Authority
PO Box 810, 216 Bettez St., Gravelbourg, SK S0H 1X0
Tel: 306-648-3185 *Fax:* 306-648-3440
www.fhhr.ca/Gravelbourg.htm
Number of Beds: 9 acute care beds; 49 long-term care beds; 1
respite / palliative / convalescent bed
Number of Employees: 110
Note: Services include: acute care; diagnostics; emergency; long
term care; palliative / respite care; occupational therapy; &
physiotherapy.
Patricia MacEwan, CEO

Herbert: Herbert & District Integrated Health Facility
Cypress Health Region
Affiliated with: Saskatchewan Health Authority
PO Box 520, 405 Herbert Ave., Herbert, SK S0H 2A0
Tel: 306-784-2466
cypresshealth.ca/health-facilities/herbert
Number of Beds: 36 long term care beds; 6 acute care beds; 2
multipurpose beds
Note: Programs & services include: acute care; addictions; child
& youth counsellor; dietitian; emergency; home care; laboratory;
long-term care; mental health; outpatient procedures; palliative
care; physiotherapy; public health nurse; respite care; speech
language pathology; & x-ray.

Hudson Bay: Hudson Bay Health Care Facility
Kelsey Trail Health Region
Affiliated with: Saskatchewan Health Authority
PO Box 940, 614 Prince St., Hudson Bay, SK S0E 0Y0
Tel: 306-865-5600 *Fax:* 306-865-2429
www.kelseytrailhealth.ca
Number of Beds: 20 long term care beds; 2 respite care beds
Note: Programs & services include: 24 hour emergency
outpatient care; ambulance; acute care; day care; laboratory;
mental health; palliative care; primary health care; radiology; &
Telehealth.

**Humboldt: Humboldt District Health Complex
(HDHC)**
Saskatoon Health Region
Affiliated with: Saskatchewan Health Authority
Former Name: St. Elizabeth's Hospital
PO Box 10, 515 - 14th Ave., Humboldt, SK S0K 2A0
Tel: 306-682-2603
www.saskatoonhealthregion.ca
Year Founded: 2011
Number of Beds: 38 beds
Note: Programs & services include: home care; mental health;
addiction services; laboratory / x-ray; & therapy.
Yvonne Berscheid, Site Manager

Ile-à-la-Crosse: St. Joseph's Hospital
Keewatin Yatthé Region
Affiliated with: Saskatchewan Health Authority
PO Box 630, La Jeunesse Ave., Ile-à-la-Crosse, SK S0M 1C0
Tel: 306-833-2016 *Fax:* 306-833-2556
kyrha.ca
Number of Beds: 13 beds
Note: Services include: acute care; dental therapy; emergency

care; home care; inpatient social detox; laboratory; long-term health; physical therapy; physician; public health clinic; & x-ray.

Indian Head: Indian Head Union Hospital
Regina Qu'Appelle Health Region
Affiliated with: Saskatchewan Health Authority
PO Box 340, 300 Hospital St., Indian Head, SK S0G 2K0
Tel: 306-695-4000 *Fax:* 306-695-4002
www.rqhealth.ca

Number of Beds: 15 beds
Note: Services include: ambulatory care; emergency; inpatient services; & outpatient services.

Kamsack: Kamsack Hospital / Kamsack Nursing Home
Sunrise Health Region
Affiliated with: Saskatchewan Health Authority
PO Box 429, 341 Stewart St., Kamsack, SK S0A 1S0
Tel: 306-542-2635 *Fax:* 306-542-4360
www.sunrisehealthregion.sk.ca

Number of Beds: 20 acute care beds; 61 long-term care beds; 2 respite beds
Note: Services include: 24 hour emergency; cardiac services; intensive care; laboratory; medicine; outpatient services; pediatrics; pharmacy; physiotherapy; & x-ray.

Kelvington: Kelvington & Area Hospital
Kelsey Trail Health Region
Affiliated with: Saskatchewan Health Authority
PO Box 70, 701 - 6th Ave. West, Kelvington, SK S0A 1W0
Tel: 306-327-5500 *Fax:* 306-327-5115
www.kelseytrailhealth.ca

Number of Beds: 7 beds
Note: Services include: 24 hour emergency outpatient care; inpatient acute care; laboratory; palliative care; radiology; & Telehealth.

Kindersley: Kindersley & District Health Centre
Heartland Health Region
Affiliated with: Saskatchewan Health Authority
1003 - 1 St. West, Kindersley, SK S0L 1S2
Tel: 306-463-1000
www.hrha.sk.ca

Number of Beds: 21 acute care beds; 77 long-term care beds; 7 alternate level of care beds
Note: Programs & services: child & youth counselor; addictions; obstetrics; occupational therapy; 24 / 7 emergency room; X-ray; Telehealth; ultrasound; foot care; podiatry; long term care; acute care.

Kipling: Kipling Integrated Health Centre
Sun Country Health Region
Affiliated with: Saskatchewan Health Authority
PO Box 420, 906 Industrial Dr., Kipling, SK S0G 2S0
Tel: 306-736-2552
www.suncountry.sk.ca

Number of Beds: 32 long-term care beds; 12 acute care beds; 1 respite bed
Note: Programs & services include: diabetes program; dietitian services; respite care; rehabilitation; palliative care; & Telehealth.
Kelly Beattie, Contact

La Loche: La Loche Health Centre
Keewatin Yatthe Regional Health Authority
Affiliated with: Saskatchewan Health Authority
Bag Service 1, La Loche, SK S0M 1G0
Tel: 306-822-3200 *Fax:* 306-822-2274
Toll-Free: 888-688-7087
kyrha.ca

Number of Beds: 19 beds
Note: Services include: acute care; dental therapy; emergency; home care; inpatient social detox; laboratory; long-term care; medical health clinic; mental health & addictions; physical therapy; physician; public health clinic; & x-ray.

Lanigan: Lanigan Hospital
Saskatoon Health Region
Affiliated with: Saskatchewan Health Authority
PO Box 609, 36 Downing St. East, Lanigan, SK S0K 2M0
Tel: 306-365-1400 *Fax:* 306-365-3354
www.saskatoonhealthregion.ca

Year Founded: 1968
Number of Beds: 4 acute care beds; 6 long-term care beds
Number of Employees: 88
Note: Services include: acute care; home care; laboratory; long-term care; mental health & addiction; occupational therapy; physiotherapy; public health; & x-ray.

Leader: Leader Hospital
Cypress Health Region
Affiliated with: Saskatchewan Health Authority
PO Box 129, 423 Main St., Leader, SK S0N 1H0
Tel: 306-628-3845
cypresshealth.ca

Number of Beds: 10 acute / multipurpose beds
Note: Services include: acute care; addictions; dietitian; emergency; home care; laboratory; mental health; outpatient; pharmacy; physiotherapy; podiatry; psychiatry; public health nurse; & x-ray.

Lestock: St. Joseph's Integrated Care Centre
Regina Qu'Appelle Health Region
Affiliated with: Saskatchewan Health Authority
PO Box 280, 508 Westmoor St., Lestock, SK S0A 2G0
Tel: 306-274-2300 *Fax:* 306-274-2301
www.rqhealth.ca

Number of Beds: 10 beds
Note: Services include: adult day care; long-term care; & respite care.

Lloydminster: Lloydminster Hospital
Affiliated with: Saskatchewan Health Authority
3820 - 43 Ave., Lloydminster, SK S9V 1Y5
Tel: 306-820-6000 *Fax:* 306-825-6516

Number of Beds: 15 obstetrical beds; 39 acute care beds
Note: Services include: community cancer centre; emergency; hemodialysis; magnetic resonance imaging; obstetrics; occupational therapy; palliative care; & physical therapy.

Loon Lake: Loon Lake Health Centre & Special Care Home
Prairie North Health Region
Affiliated with: Saskatchewan Health Authority
PO Box 69, 510 - 2nd St., Loon Lake, SK S0M 1L0
Tel: 306-837-2114 *Fax:* 306-837-2268
www.pnrha.ca

Number of Beds: 12 long-term care beds; 4 short-term beds; 1 respite bed; 1 palliative bed
Note: Services include: addictions; diagnostic imaging; dietitian; home care; laboratory; medical clinic; occupational therapy; & public health.

Maidstone: Maidstone Health Complex
Prairie North Health Region
Affiliated with: Saskatchewan Health Authority
PO Box 160, 214 - 5th Ave. East, Maidstone, SK S0M 1M0
Tel: 306-893-2622 *Fax:* 306-893-2922
www.pnrha.ca

Number of Beds: 11 acute care beds; 24 long-term care beds; 2 respite beds
Note: Services include: addictions; ambulance; Collaborative Emergency Centre; diagnostic imaging; dietitian; home care; laboratory; medical clinic; occupational therapy; physiotherapy; & public health.

Meadow Lake: Meadow Lake Hospital
Prairie North Health Region
Affiliated with: Saskatchewan Health Authority
#2, 711 Centre St., Meadow Lake, SK S9X 1E6
Tel: 306-236-1500 *Fax:* 306-236-3244
www.pnrha.ca

Number of Beds: 32 beds
Note: Services include: acute care; home care; mental health; palliative care; & therapy.

Melfort: Melfort Hospital
Kelsey Trail Health Region
Affiliated with: Saskatchewan Health Authority
PO Box 1480, 510 Broadway Ave., Melfort, SK S0E 1A0
Tel: 306-752-8700 *Fax:* 306-752-8711
www.kelseytrailhealth.ca

Number of Beds: 24 beds
Note: Programs & services include: 24 hour emergency outpatient care; chemotherapy; endoscopy; general surgery; inpatient acute care; laboratory; labour & delivery; palliative care; radiology; & Telehealth.
Nadine Mevel-Degerness, Facility Administrator

Melville: St. Peter's Hospital
Sunrise Health Region
Affiliated with: Saskatchewan Health Authority
PO Box 1810, 200 Heritage Dr., Melville, SK S0A 2P0
Tel: 306-728-5407 *Fax:* 306-728-1859
www.sunrisehealthregion.sk.ca

Year Founded: 1942
Number of Beds: 30 acute care beds
Number of Employees: 87
Note: Programs & services include: 24 hour emergency; chemotherapy outreach program; dietitian; endoscopy;

Moose Jaw: Dr. F.H. Wigmore Regional Hospital
Five Hills Health Region
Affiliated with: Saskatchewan Health Authority
55 Diefenbaker Dr., Moose Jaw, SK S6J 0C2
Tel: 306-694-0200
www.fhhr.ca/MooseJawHospital.htm

Number of Beds: 73 beds
Note: Services include: emergency; diagnostics; dialysis; laboratory; mental health outpatient services; patient education; surgery; & therapy.

Moosomin: Southeast Integrated Care Centre - Moosomin
Regina Qu'Appelle Health Region
Affiliated with: Saskatchewan Health Authority
Former Name: Moosomin Union Hospital
601 Wright Rd., Moosomin, SK S0G 3N0
Tel: 306-435-3303 *Fax:* 306-435-3211
www.rqhealth.ca

Number of Beds: 27 acute care beds; 58 long-term care beds
Note: Services include: acute care; diagnostics; emergency; home care; laboratory; long-term care; mental health; outpatient; physiotherapy; & public health.

Nipawin: Nipawin Hospital
Kelsey Trail Health Region
Affiliated with: Saskatchewan Health Authority
PO Box 389, 800 - 6 St. East, Nipawin, SK S0E 1E0
Tel: 306-862-6100 *Fax:* 306-862-9310
www.kelseytrailhealth.ca

Number of Beds: 24 beds
Note: Programs & services include: 24 hour emergency outpatient care; chemotherapy; endoscopy; general surgery; inpatient acute care; laboratory; labour & delivery; palliative care; pediatrician; radiology; & Telehealth.
Linda Brothwell, Facility Administrator

North Battleford: Battlefords Union Hospital
Affiliated with: Saskatchewan Health Authority
1092 - 107 St., North Battleford, SK S9A 1Z1
Tel: 306-446-6600 *Fax:* 306-446-6561
www.pnrha.ca

Number of Beds: 66 beds
Note: Services include: acute care; diagnostic imaging; dialysis; & laboratory.

Outlook: Outlook & District Health Centre
Heartland Health Region
Affiliated with: Saskatchewan Health Authority
PO Box 369, 500 Semple St., Outlook, SK S0L 2N0
Tel: 306-867-5020 *Fax:* 306-867-5021
www.hrha.sk.ca

Year Founded: 2008
Number of Beds: 10 acute care beds; 42 long-term care beds; 6 alternate level of care beds
Note: Programs & services include: acute care; diagnostics; dietitian; emergency; foot care; home care; laboratory; long term care; mental health counselling; occupational therapy; outpatient; physicians; physiotherapy; public health; & Telehealth.

Porcupine Plain: Porcupine Carragana Hospital
Kelsey Trail Health Region
Affiliated with: Saskatchewan Health Authority
PO Box 70, Windsor Ave., Porcupine Plain, SK S0E 1H0
Tel: 306-278-6262 *Fax:* 306-278-3088
www.kelseytrailhealth.ca

Number of Beds: 7 acute care beds
Note: Programs & services include: 24 hour emergency outpatient care; ambulance; home care; inpatient acute care; laboratory; palliative care; radiology; & Telehealth.

Preeceville: Preeceville & District Health Centre
Sunrise Health Region
Affiliated with: Saskatchewan Health Authority
Former Name: Preeceville Hospital; Preeceville & District Integrated Health Care Facility
PO Box 469, 712 - 7 St. NE, Preeceville, SK S0A 3B0
Tel: 306-547-2102 *Fax:* 306-547-2223
www.sunrisehealthregion.sk.ca

Number of Beds: 10 acute care beds; 38 long-term care beds; 2 respite beds
Note: Programs & services include: dietitian; emergency; laboratory; mental health & addictions; outpatient; pharmacy; physician; physiotherapy; primary health care; Telehealth; & x-ray.
Monica Dutchak, Manager

Prince Albert: **Victoria Hospital**
Prince Albert Parkland Health Region
Affiliated with: Saskatchewan Health Authority
1200 - 24 St. West, Prince Albert, SK S6V 4B2
Tel: 306-765-6000 *Fax:* 306-763-2871
paphr.ca

Number of Beds: 173 beds
Note: Services include: ambulatory care; anesthesiology; diagnostic imaging; dialysis; emergency; day surgery; general surgery; inpatient; intensive care; internal medicine; laboratory; obstetrics & gynecology; orthopedics; pediatrics; & psychiatry.

Redvers: **Redvers Health Centre**
Sun Country Health Region
Affiliated with: Saskatchewan Health Authority
PO Box 30, 18 Eichhorst St., Redvers, SK S0C 2H0
Tel: 306-452-3553
www.suncountry.sk.ca

Year Founded: 1948
Number of Beds: 7 acute care beds; 23 long-term care beds; 1 respite/multipurpose bed
Number of Employees: 92
Note: Programs & services include: inpatient care; long-term care; & emergency outpatient services.
Polly Godenir, Contact

Regina: **Pasqua Hospital**
Regina Qu'Appelle Health Region
Affiliated with: Saskatchewan Health Authority
4101 Dewdney Ave., Regina, SK S4T 1A5
Tel: 306-766-2222
www.rqhealth.ca/facilities/pasqua-hospital

Year Founded: 1907
Number of Beds: 24 long-term care beds; 243 acute care beds
Note: Programs & services include: a cancer centre; radiology; 24 hour emergency services; intensive care; respiratory therapy; physical therapy; surgery; eye care; palliative care.

Regina: **Regina General Hospital**
Regina Qu'Appelle Health Region
Affiliated with: Saskatchewan Health Authority
Former Name: Victoria Hospital
1440 - 14 Ave., Regina, SK S4P 0W5
Tel: 306-766-4444
www.rqhealth.ca/facilities/regina-general-hospital
Year Founded: 1901
Number of Beds: 31 intensive care beds; 36 obstetrical beds; 25 pediatric beds; 60 mental health beds; 315 acute care beds
Note: Offers full-range acute care services; home to the Wasakaw Pisim Native Health Centre, Sleep Disorders Centre, and 50-bed mental health facility

Rosthern: **Rosthern Hospital**
Saskatoon Health Region
Affiliated with: Saskatchewan Health Authority
2016 - 2 St., Rosthern, SK S0K 3R0
Tel: 306-232-4811
www.saskatoonhealthregion.ca

Year Founded: 1950
Number of Beds: 30 beds
Number of Employees: 60
Note: Acute care facility with six physicians on-staff.

Saskatoon: **Jim Pattison Children's Hospital**
Affiliated with: Saskatchewan Health Authority
Former Name: Children's Hospital of Saskatchewan
c/o Royal University Hospital, 103 Hospital Dr., 3rd Fl., Saskatoon, SK S7N 0W8
Tel: 306-655-2293
www.saskatoonhealthregion.ca
Note: Programs & services include: maternal services; children's sleep lab; children's hemodialysis

Saskatoon: **Royal University Hospital**
Saskatoon Health Region
Affiliated with: Saskatchewan Health Authority
103 Hospital Dr., Saskatoon, SK S7N 0W8
Tel: 306-655-1000
www.saskatoonhealthregion.ca

Year Founded: 1955
Number of Beds: 455 beds
Note: Affiliated with the University of Saskatchewan.

Saskatoon: **St. Paul's Hospital**
Emmanuel Care
Affiliated with: Saskatchewan Health Authority
1702 - 20 St. West, Saskatoon, SK S7M 0Z9
Tel: 306-655-5000 *Fax:* 306-655-5900
info@stpaulshospital.org
www.stpaulshospital.org

Year Founded: 1907
Number of Beds: 9 intensive care beds; 219 acute care beds

Note: Programs & services include: chronic disease management; ambulatory services; kidney health and provincial transport; mental health and addictions; palliative care and hospice.
Jean Morrison, President & CEO

Saskatoon: **Saskatoon City Hospital**
Saskatoon Health Region
Affiliated with: Saskatchewan Health Authority
701 Queen St., Saskatoon, SK S7K 0M7
Tel: 306-655-8000
www.saskatoonhealthregion.ca

Year Founded: 1909
Number of Beds: 176 beds

Shaunavon: **Shaunavon Hospital & Care Centre**
Cypress Health Region
Affiliated with: Saskatchewan Health Authority
PO Box 789, 660 - 4 St. East, Shaunavon, SK S0N 2M0
Tel: 306-297-2644
cypresshealth.ca/health-facilities/shaunavon
Number of Beds: 41 long term care beds; 10 acute / multidisciplinary beds; 3 multipurpose beds
Note: Programs & services include: acute care; addictions program; child & youth counsellor; day program; dietitian; emergency; home care; laboratory; long-term care; mental health; physiotherapy; podiatry; public health nurse; respite care; speech language pathology; & x-ray.
Crystal Elliott, Manager, Health Services

Shellbrook: **Parkland Integrated Health Centre**
Prince Albert Parkland Health Region
Affiliated with: Saskatchewan Health Authority
#100, Dr. J.L. Spencer Dr., Shellbrook, SK S0J 2E0
Tel: 306-747-2603 *Fax:* 306-747-3004
paphr.ca
Number of Beds: 20 acute care beds; 34 long-term care beds
Note: Services include: home care; laboratory; mental health; public health; therapy; & x-ray.

Swift Current: **Cypress Regional Hospital**
Cypress Health Region
Affiliated with: Saskatchewan Health Authority
Former Name: Swift Current Regional Hospital
2004 Saskatchewan Dr., Swift Current, SK S9H 5M8
Tel: 306-778-9400
cypresshealth.ca

Year Founded: 1951
Number of Beds: 91 acute care beds
Note: Programs & services include: emergency; general surgery; intensive care; internal medicine; obstetrics & gynecology; pathology; pediatrics; psychiatry; & radiology.

Tisdale: **Tisdale Hospital**
Kelsey Trail Health Region
Affiliated with: Saskatchewan Health Authority
PO Box 1630, 2010 - 110th Ave. West, Tisdale, SK S0E 1T0
Tel: 306-873-6500 *Fax:* 306-873-5994
www.kelseytrailhealth.ca
Number of Beds: 15 beds
Note: Services include: 24 hour emergency outpatient care; chemotherapy; inpatient acute care; laboratory; labour & delivery; palliative care; radiology; sigmiodoscopy; & Telehealth.
Tracy Farber, Administrator

Wadena: **Wadena Hospital**
Saskatoon Health Region
Affiliated with: Saskatchewan Health Authority
PO Box 10, 533 - 5 St. NE, Wadena, SK S0A 4J0
Tel: 306-338-2515
www.saskatoonhealthregion.ca
Year Founded: 1967
Number of Beds: 52 beds
Number of Employees: 107
Note: Provides acute, respite, & long-term care services.

Watrous: **Watrous Hospital**
Saskatoon Health Region
Affiliated with: Saskatchewan Health Authority
PO Box 130, 702 - 4 St. East, Watrous, SK S0K 4T0
Tel: 306-946-1200
www.saskatoonhealthregion.ca
Number of Beds: 8 beds
Note: Services include: acute care; diagnostic imaging; laboratory; public health; & therapy.

Wawota: **Wawota Memorial Health Centre**
Sun Country Health Region
Affiliated with: Saskatchewan Health Authority
PO Box 60, 609 Choo Foo Cres., Wawota, SK S0G 5A0
Tel: 306-739-5200
www.suncountry.sk.ca

Number of Beds: 29 long-term care beds; 3 respite / multipurpose beds
Note: Programs & services include: child speech language pathology; diabetes program; dietitian; emergency medical services; mental health; occupational therapy; palliative care; & Telehealth.
Holly Hodgson, Contact

Weyburn: **Weyburn General Hospital**
Sun Country Health Region
Affiliated with: Saskatchewan Health Authority
201 - 1 Ave. NE, Weyburn, SK S4H 0N1
Tel: 306-842-8428
www.suncountry.sk.ca
Number of Beds: 40 acute care beds
Note: Programs & services include: acute care; addiction services; diabetes education program; mental health services; occupational therapy; palliative care; rehabilitation; & spiritual care.
James Anderson, Contact

Wolseley: **Wolseley Memorial Integrated Health Centre**
Regina Qu'Appelle Health Region
Affiliated with: Saskatchewan Health Authority
PO Box 458, 801 Ouimet St., Wolseley, SK S0G 5H0
Tel: 306-698-4440 *Fax:* 306-698-4434
www.rqhealth.ca/facilities/wolseley-memorial-integrated-care-centre
Number of Beds: 10 beds
Note: Services include: ambulatory care; laboratory; outpatient; palliative care; & x-ray.

Wynyard: **Wynyard Integrated Facility**
Saskatoon Health Region
Affiliated with: Saskatchewan Health Authority
PO Box 670, 300 - 10 St. East, Wynyard, SK S0A 4T0
Tel: 306-554-2586
www.saskatoonhealthregion.ca
Number of Beds: 8 hospital beds; 59 long-term care beds
Number of Employees: 100
Note: Acute care; long-term care; respite care.

Yorkton: **Yorkton Regional Health Centre**
Sunrise Health Region
Affiliated with: Saskatchewan Health Authority
270 Bradbrooke Dr., Yorkton, SK S3N 2K6
Tel: 306-782-2401 *Fax:* 306-786-6295
www.sunrisehealthregion.sk.ca
Number of Beds: 87 acute care beds
Note: Services include: 24 hour emergency; diagnostic laboratory; hemodialysis; intensive care; medical imaging; obstetrics; outpatient; pediatrics; pharmacy; respiratory therapy; & social work.

Federal Hospitals

Saskatoon: **Regional Psychiatric Centre (Prairies)**
PO Box 9243, 2520 Central Ave. North, Saskatoon, SK S7K 3X5
Tel: 306-975-5400 *Fax:* 306-975-6024
www.csc-scc.gc.ca/institutions/001002-4009-eng.shtml
Year Founded: 1978
Number of Beds: 204 beds
Tim Krause, Assistant Warden, Management Services

Community Health Care Centres

Arborfield: **Arborfield & District Health Care Centre**
Affiliated with: Saskatchewan Health Authority
PO Box 160, 509 - 5 Ave., Arborfield, SK S0E 0A0
Tel: 306-769-4200 *Fax:* 306-769-8759
Number of Beds: 36 beds
Note: Programs & services include: clinic; laboratory; day care; health care.

Beauval: **Beauval Health Centre**
Affiliated with: Saskatchewan Health Authority
PO Box 68, Beauval, SK S0M 0G0
Tel: 306-288-4800 *Fax:* 306-288-2225
Toll-Free: 866-848-8022
Note: Addiction treatments; mental health; dentistry; ambulance.

Beechy: **Beechy Health Centre**
Affiliated with: Saskatchewan Health Authority
PO Box 68, 226 - 1st Ave. North, Beechy, SK S0L 0C0
Tel: 306-859-2118 *Fax:* 306-859-2206
Note: Programs & services include: primary health care; lab/radiology services; visiting community health services: public health, counselling, occupational health, nutrition.

Moose Jaw: Crescent View Clinic
Affiliated with: Saskatchewan Health Authority
131 - 1st Ave. NE, Moose Jaw, SK S6H 0Y9
Tel: 306-691-2040

Mossbank: Mossbank Primary Health Care Centre
Affiliated with: Saskatchewan Health Authority
PO Box 322, Mossbank, SK S0H 3G0
Tel: 306-354-2300 Fax: 306-354-2819
www.fhhr.ca/Mossbank.htm

Muskoday: Muskoday Health Centre
Affiliated with: Saskatchewan Health Authority
PO Box 40, Muskoday, SK S0J 3H0
Tel: 306-764-6737 Fax: 306-764-4664

Naicam: Naicam Home Care Office
Affiliated with: Saskatchewan Health Authority
305 - 1 St. South, Naicam, SK S0K 2Z0
Tel: 306-874-2276

Neilburg: Manitou Health Centre
Affiliated with: Saskatchewan Health Authority
PO Box 190, 105 - 2nd Ave. West, Neilburg, SK S0M 2C0
Tel: 306-823-4262 Fax: 306-823-4590
Note: Programs & services include: laboratory/diagnostic imaging; home care; public health; addictions

Neudorf: Neudorf Health & Social Centre
410 Main St., Neudorf, SK S0A 2T0
Tel: 306-748-2878

Nipawin: Nipawin Public Health Office
Affiliated with: Saskatchewan Health Authority
PO Box 389, 210 - 2 St. West, Nipawin, SK S0E 1E0
Tel: 306-862-7230 Fax: 306-862-0763

Nokomis: Nokomis Health Centre
Affiliated with: Saskatchewan Health Authority
PO Box 98, 103 - 2 Ave. East, Nokomis, SK S0G 3R0
Tel: 306-528-2114 Fax: 306-528-4445
Number of Beds: 14 beds

Norquay: Norquay Health Centre
Affiliated with: Saskatchewan Health Authority
PO Box 190, Norquay, SK S0A 2V0
Tel: 306-594-2133 Fax: 306-594-2488
Number of Beds: 32 long term care beds; 1 respite bed
Note: Programs & services include: laboratory/diagnostic imaging; home care; public health; addictions. Palliative care beds provided as needed.

Norquay: Norquay Home Care Office
Affiliated with: Saskatchewan Health Authority
PO Box 535, 355 East Rd. Allowance South, Norquay, SK S0A 2V0
Tel: 306-594-2277 Fax: 306-594-2220

Outlook: Outlook Home Care Office
Affiliated with: Saskatchewan Health Authority
PO Box 1100, Outlook, SK S0L 2N0
Tel: 306-867-8676

Oxbow: Galloway Health Centre
Affiliated with: Saskatchewan Health Authority
PO Box 268, 917 Tupper St., Oxbow, SK S0C 2B0
Tel: 306-483-2956
Note: Programs & services include: convalescent care; respite care; telehealth.
Caroline Hill, Contact

Pangman: Pangman Health Centre
Affiliated with: Saskatchewan Health Authority
PO Box 90, 211 Keeler St., Pangman, SK S0C 2C0
Tel: 306-442-2044
Note: Programs & services include: rehabilitation services; public health inspection; mental health services; diabetes program; ambulance services; home care; palliative care

Paradise Hill: Paradise Hill Health Centre
Affiliated with: Saskatchewan Health Authority
PO Box 179, 1st Ave., Paradise Hill, SK S0M 2G0
Tel: 306-344-2255 Fax: 306-344-2277
Number of Beds: No patient/resident care beds
Note: Programs & services include: laboratory; clinic; dietician; addiction treatment.

Patuanak: English River Health Services
Affiliated with: Saskatchewan Health Authority
PO Box 60, Patuanak, SK S0M 2H0
Tel: 306-396-2072 Fax: 306-396-2177

Pinehouse: Pinehouse Health Centre
Affiliated with: Saskatchewan Health Authority
PO Box 70, Pinehouse, SK S0J 2B0
Tel: 306-884-5670 Fax: 306-884-5699
Note: Programs & services include: public health; health education; primary care; addiction services; mental health services; home care services

Ponteix: Ponteix Health Centre
Affiliated with: Saskatchewan Health Authority
PO Box 600, 428 - 2 Ave., Ponteix, SK S0N 1Z0
Tel: 306-625-3382 Fax: 306-625-3764
Note: Programs & services include: Radiology, Laboratory Services, Home Care, Nutrition, Mental Health, Baby Clinic, Public Health, Foyer St. Joseph Nursing Home, Ambulance Service.

Preeceville: Preeceville Home Care Office
Affiliated with: Saskatchewan Health Authority
PO Box 407, 712 - 7 Ave. NW, Preeceville, SK S0A 3B0
Tel: 306-547-4441 Fax: 306-547-5514

Preeceville: Preeceville Public Health & Physiotherapy Office
Affiliated with: Saskatchewan Health Authority
PO Box 466, 239 Highway Ave. East, Preeceville, SK S0A 3B0
Tel: 306-547-2815 Fax: 306-547-2092

Prince Albert: Associate Medical Clinic
Affiliated with: Saskatchewan Health Authority
Bldg. 20, #400, 14 St. West, Prince Albert, SK S6V 3K8
Tel: 306-764-1513 Fax: 306-764-3091

Prince Albert: Crescent Heights Family Medical Centre
Affiliated with: Saskatchewan Health Authority
2805 - 6 Ave. East, Prince Albert, SK S6V 3K7
Tel: 306-763-2681

Prince Albert: First Nations & Inuit Health North Service Centre
Affiliated with: Saskatchewan Health Authority
PO Box 5000, 3601 - 5 Ave. East, Prince Albert, SK S6V 7V6
Tel: 306-953-8600 Fax: 306-953-8566

Prince Albert: Prince Albert Co-Operative Health Centre
Affiliated with: Saskatchewan Health Authority
110 - 8th St. East, Prince Albert, SK S6V 0V7
Tel: 306-763-6464 Fax: 306-763-2101
www.coophealth.com
Year Founded: 1962
Renee Danylczuk, Executive Director

Prince Albert: Prince Albert Medical Clinic
Affiliated with: Saskatchewan Health Authority
681 - 15th St. West, Prince Albert, SK S6V 7H9
Tel: 306-764-1505

Prince Albert: South Hill Family Practice
Affiliated with: Saskatchewan Health Authority
2685 - 2nd Ave. West, Prince Albert, SK S6V 5E3
Tel: 306-922-9570 Fax: 306-922-2464

Prince Albert: West Hill Medical Clinic
Affiliated with: Saskatchewan Health Authority
#1A, 2995 - 2nd Ave. West, Prince Albert, SK S6V 5V5
Tel: 306-765-8500 Fax: 306-765-8501

Quill Lake: Quill Lake Community Health & Social Centre
Affiliated with: Saskatchewan Health Authority
PO Box 126, Quill Lake, SK S0A 3E0
Tel: 306-383-2266

Radville: Radville Marian Health Centre Emmanuel Care
Affiliated with: Saskatchewan Health Authority
PO Box 310, 840 Conrad Ave., Radville, SK S0C 0G0
Tel: 306-869-2224 Fax: 306-869-2653
Number of Beds: 30 beds
Note: Programs & services include: palliative care; home care; diabetes program; acute care services.
Debbie Donald, Executive Director

Radville: Radville Public Health Office
Affiliated with: Saskatchewan Health Authority
PO Box 683, 840 Conrad Ave., Radville, SK S0C 2G0
Tel: 306-869-2555 Fax: 306-369-3118
Judy DeRoose, Contact

Raymore: Raymore Community Health & Social Centre
Affiliated with: Saskatchewan Health Authority
PO Box 134, 806 - 2 Ave., Raymore, SK S0A 3J0
Tel: 306-746-2231 Fax: 306-746-4639
Year Founded: 1981

Regina: Al Ritchie Health Action Centre
Affiliated with: Saskatchewan Health Authority
325 Victoria Ave., Regina, SK S4N 0P5
Tel: 306-766-7660
Note: Programs & services include: GED exam support services; skills registry; job search support; prenatal nutrition advice; community computer; Dad's Group; family crafts; quit smoking program; seniors' potluck lunch; community kitchen; foot care; primary care nurse (by appt); food bank referrals; video lending library.

Regina: Four Directions Community Health Centre
Affiliated with: Saskatchewan Health Authority
3510 - 5 Ave., Regina, SK S4T 0M2
Tel: 306-766-7540 Fax: 306-766-7534

Regina: Meadow Primary Health Care Centre
Affiliated with: Saskatchewan Health Authority
4006 Dewdney Ave., Regina, SK S4T 1A2
Tel: 306-766-6399 Toll-Free: 855-766-6399

Regina Beach: Regina Beach Primary Health Care Centre
Affiliated with: Saskatchewan Health Authority
410 Centre St., Regina Beach, SK S0G 4C0
Toll-Free: 855-766-6399

Rockglen: Grasslands Health Centre
Affiliated with: Saskatchewan Health Authority
PO Box 219, 1006 Hwy. 2, Rockglen, SK S0H 3R0
Tel: 306-476-2030 Fax: 306-476-2534
www.fhhr.ca
Number of Beds: 17 beds

Rose Valley: Rose Valley Health Centre
Affiliated with: Saskatchewan Health Authority
PO Box 310, McCallum St., Rose Valley, SK S0E 1M0
Tel: 306-322-2115 Fax: 306-322-2037

Rosetown: Rosetown & District Health Centre
Affiliated with: Saskatchewan Health Authority
PO Box 850, 409 - Hwy. 4 North, Rosetown, SK S0L 2V0
Tel: 306-882-2672
Year Founded: 1964
Number of Beds: 75 beds

Rosetown: Rosetown Home Care Office
Affiliated with: Saskatchewan Health Authority
PO Box 850, Rosetown, SK S0L 2V0
Tel: 306-882-2672

Rosthern: Rosthern Public Health Office
Affiliated with: Saskatchewan Health Authority
PO Box 216, 2014 - 6th St., Rosthern, SK S0K 3R0
Tel: 306-232-6001 Toll-Free: 888-301-4636

Sandy Bay: Sandy Bay Health Centre
Affiliated with: Saskatchewan Health Authority
PO Box 210, Sandy Bay, SK S0P 0G0
Tel: 306-754-5400 Fax: 306-754-5429
Note: Programs & services include: primary care; public health; health education; telehealth; home care services

Saskatoon: 20th & Q Family Walk-In
Affiliated with: Saskatchewan Health Authority
1631 - 20th St. West, Saskatoon, SK S7M 0Z7
Tel: 306-384-9888

Saskatoon: Blairmore Medical Clinic
Affiliated with: Saskatchewan Health Authority
225 Betts Ave., Saskatoon, SK S7M 1L2
Tel: 306-652-6400

Saskatoon: Idylwyld Centre Public Health Office
Affiliated with: Saskatchewan Health Authority
#101, 310 Idylwyld Dr. North, Saskatoon, SK S7L 0Z2
Tel: 306-655-4620

Saskatoon: Lakeside Medical Clinic
Affiliated with: Saskatchewan Health Authority
3919 - 8th St. East, Saskatoon, SK S7H 5M7
Tel: 306-374-6884 Fax: 306-374-2552
www.lakeside.ca
www.facebook.com/404868042884244;
twitter.com/LMCSaskatoon

Maple Creek: Cypress Lodge Nursing Home
Affiliated with: Saskatchewan Health Authority
PO Box 1330, 510 Hwy. 21 South, Maple Creek, SK S0N 1N0
Tel: 306-662-2671

Number of Beds: 48 beds
Specialties: Long term care services; Exercise maintenance programs

Melfort: Nirvana Pioneer Villa
300 Burns Ave. East, Melfort, SK S0E 1A0
Tel: 306-752-2116 *Fax:* 306-752-4099

Melfort: Parkland Place
Affiliated with: Saskatchewan Health Authority
Former Name: Parkland Care Centre
PO Box 2260, 402 Bemister Ave. East, Melfort, SK S0E 1A0
Tel: 306-752-1777 *Fax:* 306-752-3170

Number of Beds: 103 long-term care beds; 2 respite beds
Specialties: Acquired brain injury program

Melville: St. Paul Lutheran Home
Affiliated with: Saskatchewan Health Authority
PO Box 1390, 100 Heritage Dr., Melville, SK S0A 2P0
Tel: 306-728-7340 *Fax:* 306-728-5471

Number of Beds: 128 long term care beds; 1 respite bed
Note: Long-term care facility affiliated with the Evangelical Lutheran Church in Canada

Moose Jaw: Extendicare - Moose Jaw
Extendicare Canada
1151 Coteau St. West, Moose Jaw, SK S6H 5G5
Tel: 306-693-5191 *Fax:* 306-692-1770
cnh_moosejaw@extendicare.com
www.extendicarecanada.com/moosejaw/index.aspx
Number of Beds: 127 beds
Specialties: Nursing & supportive care; Rehabilitation services; Therapeutic & social programs

Moose Jaw: Pioneer Housing Lodge & Village
Affiliated with: Saskatchewan Health Authority
1000 Albert St., Moose Jaw, SK S6H 2Y2
Tel: 306-693-4616 *Fax:* 306-692-0771
Number of Beds: Long Term Care: 60; Convalescent, Palliate, Respite Care: 14; Seniors Housing Units: 24 Married, 37 Single

Moose Jaw: Providence Place
Affiliated with: Saskatchewan Health Authority
100 - 2nd Ave. NE, Moose Jaw, SK S6H 1B8
Tel: 306-694-8081 *Fax:* 306-694-8804
www.provplace.ca
Number of Beds: 174 beds
Note: Geriatric long-term care, assessment & rehabilitation

Nipawin: Pineview Lodge
Affiliated with: Saskatchewan Health Authority
PO Box 2105, 400 - 6th Ave. East, Nipawin, SK S0E 1E0
Tel: 306-862-9828 *Fax:* 306-862-2400
Number of Beds: 95 long term care beds; 1 respite bed
Note: Program & services include: long-term care; dementia care unit; day care services; respite care

North Battleford: River Heights Lodge
Affiliated with: Saskatchewan Health Authority
2001 - 99 St., North Battleford, SK S9A 0S3
Tel: 306-446-6950 *Fax:* 306-445-6032
Note: Special care home

Ponteix: Foyer St. Joseph Nursing Home
Affiliated with: Saskatchewan Health Authority
428 - 2 Ave., Ponteix, SK S0N 1Z0
Tel: 306-625-3366 *Fax:* 306-625-3764
Year Founded: 1958
Number of Beds: 32 beds
Number of Employees: 50

Porcupine Plain: Red Deer Nursing Home
Affiliated with: Saskatchewan Health Authority
PO Box 70, 330 Oak St., Porcupine Plain, SK S0E 1H0
Tel: 306-278-2469 *Fax:* 306-278-3088
Number of Beds: 38 long-term care beds

Preeceville: Preeceville & District Health Centre - Long Term Care Facility
Affiliated with: Saskatchewan Health Authority
PO Box 348, 712 - 7 St. NE, Preeceville, SK S0A 3B0
Tel: 306-547-3112 *Fax:* 306-547-3215
Number of Beds: 38 long term care beds; 10 acute care beds; 2 respite beds

Redvers: Redvers Centennial Haven
Affiliated with: Saskatchewan Health Authority
PO Box 30, 18 Eichhorst St., Redvers, SK S0C 2H0
Tel: 306-452-3553 *Fax:* 306-452-3556

Number of Beds: 24 beds

Regina: Extendicare - Elmview
Extendicare Canada
Affiliated with: Saskatchewan Health Authority
4125 Rae St., Regina, SK S4S 3A5
Tel: 306-586-1787 *Fax:* 306-585-0255
www.extendicarecanada.com/reginaelmview
Number of Beds: 62 beds

Regina: Extendicare - Parkside
Extendicare Canada
Affiliated with: Saskatchewan Health Authority
4540 Rae St., Regina, SK S4S 3B4
Tel: 306-586-0220 *Fax:* 306-585-0622
www.extendicarecanada.com/reginaparkside
Number of Beds: 228 beds

Regina: Extendicare - Sunset
Extendicare Canada
Affiliated with: Saskatchewan Health Authority
260 Sunset Dr., Regina, SK S4S 2S3
Tel: 306-586-3355 *Fax:* 306-584-8082
www.extendicarecanada.com/reginasunset

Regina: Qu'Appelle House
Affiliated with: Saskatchewan Health Authority
1425 College Ave., Regina, SK S4P 1B4
Tel: 306-522-0335 *Fax:* 306-522-4800

Regina: Regina Lutheran Home
Affiliated with: Eden Care Communities
1925 - 5 Ave. North, Regina, SK S4R 7W1
Tel: 306-543-4055 *Fax:* 306-543-4094
info@edencare.ca
www.edencare.ca

Number of Beds: 62 beds

Regina: Regina Pioneer Village Ltd.
Affiliated with: Saskatchewan Health Authority
430 Pioneer Dr., Regina, SK S4T 6L8
Tel: 306-757-5646 *Fax:* 306-757-5001
Year Founded: 1955
Number of Beds: 390 beds

Regina: Santa Maria Senior Citizens Home
Affiliated with: Saskatchewan Health Authority
4215 Regina Ave., Regina, SK S4S 4J5
Tel: 306-766-7100 *Fax:* 306-766-7115
SantaMariaGeneral@rqhealth.ca
santamariaregina.ca
Number of Beds: 147 beds
John Kelly, Executive Director

Rosetown: Wheatbelt Centennial Lodge
Affiliated with: Saskatchewan Health Authority
PO Box 250, Rosetown, SK S0L 2V0
Tel: 306-882-2672 *Fax:* 306-882-3335

Rosthern: Mennonite Nursing Home Inc.
Affiliated with: Saskatchewan Health Authority
PO Box 370, Hwy. 11 South, Rosthern, SK S0K 3R0
Tel: 306-232-4861 *Fax:* 306-232-5611
www.saskatoonhealthregion.ca
Year Founded: 1963
Number of Beds: 68
Note: Specialties: Long-term care; Adult Day Program
Joan Lemauviel, Administrator

Saltcoats: Lakeside Manor Care Home Inc.
Affiliated with: Saskatchewan Health Authority
PO Box 340, 101 Crescent Lake Rd., Saltcoats, SK S0A 3R0
Tel: 306-744-2353 *Fax:* 306-744-2414
Number of Beds: 29 beds, 1 respite

Saskatoon: Central Haven Special Care Home
Affiliated with: Saskatchewan Health Authority
1020 Ave. I North, Saskatoon, SK S7L 2H7
Tel: 306-665-6180 *Fax:* 306-665-5540
www.sherbrookecommunitycentre.ca
Number of Beds: 60 beds

Saskatoon: Jubilee Residences
Affiliated with: Saskatchewan Health Authority
#25, 2602 Taylor St. East, Saskatoon, SK S7H 1X2
Tel: 306-955-0234 *Fax:* 306-373-8828
www.jubileeresidences.ca
Year Founded: 1955
Specialties: Nursing & personal care; Physical & occupational therapy
Note: Long term care is provided to 200 older adults at Stensrud & Porteous Lodges. Independent living suites are available for

approximately 300 older adults at the Cosmopolitan, Eamer, & Mount Royal facilities.
Yvonne Morgan, CEO
Bob Cowan, Chair

Saskatoon: Oliver Lodge
Affiliated with: Saskatchewan Health Authority
1405 Faulkner Cres., Saskatoon, SK S7L 3R5
Tel: 306-986-5462 *Fax:* 306-382-9822
www.oliverlodge.ca
Year Founded: 1949
Number of Beds: 139 beds
Note: Specialties: Specialized services for persons with dementia; Day program for seniors; Respite care
Brandon Little, Executive Director
306-986-5462

Saskatoon: Parkridge Centre
Affiliated with: Saskatchewan Health Authority
110 Gropper Cres., Saskatoon, SK S7M 5N9
Tel: 306-655-3800 *Fax:* 306-655-3801
Number of Beds: 237 beds

Saskatoon: Porteous Lodge
Jubilee Residences
Affiliated with: Saskatchewan Health Authority
833 Ave. PN, Saskatoon, SK S7L 2W5
Tel: 306-382-2626 *Fax:* 306-382-2633
www.jubileeresidences.ca
Number of Beds: 95 beds

Saskatoon: St. Ann's Senior Citizens Village Corporation
Emmanuel Care
Affiliated with: Saskatchewan Health Authority
Former Name: St. Ann's Home
2910 Louise St., Saskatoon, SK S7J 3L8
Tel: 306-374-8900 *Fax:* 306-477-2623
stannsvillage.ca
Year Founded: 1953
Number of Beds: 80 long-term care beds; 60 independent living beds; 61 enriched living beds
Number of Employees: 155
Rae Sveinbjornson, Executive Director
rae.sveinbjornson@saskhealthauthority.ca
Deb Lesyk, Director, Care
deb.lesyk@saskhealthauthority.ca

Saskatoon: St. Joseph's Home
Affiliated with: Saskatchewan Health Authority
33 Valens Dr., Saskatoon, SK S7L 3S2
Tel: 306-382-6306 *Fax:* 306-384-0140
Number of Beds: 85 beds

Saskatoon: Samaritan Place
Affiliated with: Saskatchewan Health Authority
375 Cornish Rd., Saskatoon, SK S7T 0P3
Tel: 306-986-1460 *Fax:* 306-986-1464
reception@samaritanplace.ca
www.samaritanplace.ca
www.facebook.com/181815878562092
Number of Beds: 100 beds
Lynn Kohle, Executive Director
Sharon Koop, Administrative Coordinator

Saskatoon: Saskatoon Convalescent Home
Affiliated with: Saskatchewan Health Authority
101 - 31 St. West, Saskatoon, SK S7L 0P6
Tel: 306-244-7155 *Fax:* 306-244-2066
www.saskatoonconvalescenthome.com
Number of Beds: 60 beds
Jill Beatty, Chair

Saskatoon: Sherbrooke Community Centre
Affiliated with: Saskatchewan Health Authority
401 Acadia Dr., Saskatoon, SK S7H 2E7
Tel: 306-655-3600 *Fax:* 306-655-3727
www.sherbrookecommunitycentre.ca
www.facebook.com/SherbrookeCommunityCentre;
twitter.com/SherbrookeCC
Year Founded: 1966
Number of Beds: 263 beds
Number of Employees: 500
Note: Long-term care home. Also provides a Community Day Program for 100 local residents
Suellen Beatty, CEO

Saskatoon: Stensrud Lodge
Jubilee Residences
Affiliated with: Saskatchewan Health Authority
2202 McEown Ave., Saskatoon, SK S7J 3L6
Tel: 306-373-5580 *Fax:* 306-477-0308
www.jubileeresidences.ca

Number of Beds: 100 beds

Saskatoon: Sunnyside Adventist Care Centre
Affiliated with: Saskatchewan Health Authority
Former Name: Sunnyside Nursing Home
2200 St. Henry Ave., Saskatoon, SK S7M 0P5
Tel: 306-653-1267 *Fax:* 306-653-7223
www.sunnysidecare.ca

Year Founded: 1964
Note: Specialties: Nursing care; Physiotherapy; Activity program; Palliative care
Randy Kurtz, Adminstrator
Randy.Kurtz@saskatoonhealthregion.ca

Spiritwood: Idylwild Lodge
PO Box 159, 416 Main St., Spiritwood, SK S0J 2M0
Tel: 306-883-2267

Number of Beds: 35 beds
Carroll Joyes, Director, Care
Louis Willick, Director, Maintenance

Stoughton: New Hope Pioneer Lodge Inc.
Affiliated with: Saskatchewan Health Authority
PO Box 38, 123 Government Rd. North, Stoughton, SK S0G 4T0
Tel: 306-457-2552
Linda Wilson, Contact

Swift Current: Palliser Regional Care Centre
Affiliated with: Saskatchewan Health Authority
440 Central Ave. South, Swift Current, SK S9H 3G6
Tel: 306-778-5160
Number of Beds: 94 beds

Swift Current: Prairie Pioneers Lodge
Affiliated with: Saskatchewan Health Authority
302 Central Ave. South, Swift Current, SK S9H 3G3
Tel: 306-778-5192
Number of Beds: 41 beds

Swift Current: Swift Current Care Centre (SCCC)
Affiliated with: Saskatchewan Health Authority
700 Aberdeen St. SE, Swift Current, SK S9H 3E3
Tel: 306-778-9371
Number of Beds: 63 beds
Note: Programs & services include: Nursing care from Registered Nurses, Registered Psychiatric Nurses, & Licensed Practical Nurses; Social work; Activity program; Respite care program

Tisdale: Newmarket Manor
Affiliated with: Saskatchewan Health Authority
PO Box 2620, 2001 Newmarket Dr., Tisdale, SK S0E 1T0
Tel: 306-873-6550 *Fax:* 306-873-4822
Number of Beds: 40 beds

Tisdale: Sasko Park Lodge
Affiliated with: Saskatchewan Health Authority
806 - 97 Ave., Tisdale, SK S0E 1T0
Tel: 306-873-4585 *Fax:* 306-873-2404
Number of Beds: 33 beds

Watrous: Manitou Lodge
Affiliated with: Saskatchewan Health Authority
PO Box 130, Watrous, SK S0K 4T0
Tel: 306-946-1200 *Fax:* 306-946-2396
Number of Beds: 43 beds

Wawota: Deer View Lodge
Affiliated with: Saskatchewan Health Authority
PO Box 240, 201 Wilfred St., Wawota, SK S0G 5A0
Tel: 306-739-2400
Number of Beds: 30 beds
Note: Area Served: Regional Municipality of Walpole; Regional Municipality of Wawken; Regional Municipality of Maryfield; Wawota; Maryfield; Fairlight; half the villages of Kennedy & Kenosee, & half the Regional Municipality of Moose Mountain

Wolseley: Lakeside Home
Affiliated with: Saskatchewan Health Authority
PO Box 10, 710 Quimet St., Wolseley, SK S0G 5H0
Tel: 306-698-4400 *Fax:* 306-698-4401
Number of Beds: 80 beds
Area Served: Wolseley, SK
Specialties: Long term care
Note: Lakeside Home is linked to Wolseley Memorial Hospital.

Wynyard: Golden Acres
Affiliated with: Saskatchewan Health Authority
300 - 10 St. East, Wynyard, SK S0A 4V0
Tel: 306-554-2586 *Fax:* 306-554-2247
Number of Beds: 59 beds
Population Served: 1800

Yorkton: Yorkton & District Nursing Home Corporation
Affiliated with: Saskatchewan Health Authority
200 Bradbrooke Dr., Yorkton, SK S3N 2K5
Tel: 306-786-0801 *Fax:* 306-786-0808
Number of Beds: 211 long term care beds; 5 respite beds; 5 program beds; 3 stroke beds; 4 transition beds

Personal Care Homes

Avonlea: Coteau Range Manor
Affiliated with: Saskatchewan Health Authority
PO Box 60, 210 New Warren Pl., Avonlea, SK S0H 0C0
Tel: 306-868-2033 *Fax:* 306-868-4790
avonleamanor@sasktel.net
Number of Beds: 30 beds
Note: Respite care is available at the personal care home.
Jeannine Cote

Bangor: Morris Lodge Society Inc.
PO Box 54, Lots 4-12, Block 6, Main St., Bangor, SK S0A 0E0
Tel: 306-728-5322 *Fax:* 306-728-2048
www.morris-lodge.ca
www.facebook.com/personalcarehomebangorsk2015
Year Founded: 1974
Number of Beds: 20 beds
Cherylynn Walters, Executive Director
306-794-2051

Codette: Serenity Lane
Affiliated with: Saskatchewan Health Authority
PO Box 152, Codette, SK S0E 0P0
Tel: 306-862-2579
Number of Beds: 10 beds
Debbie Karlee

Eatonia: Eatonia Oasis Living Inc.
Former Name: Eatonia Personal Care Home
PO Box 217, 205, 2nd Ave. W, Eatonia, SK S0L 0Y0
Tel: 306-967-2447 *Fax:* 306-967-2373
eol@sasktel.net
eatoniaoasisliving.com
Number of Beds: 16 single rooms; 4 double rooms

Estevan: Creighton Lodge
1028 Hillcrest Dr., Estevan, SK S4A 1Y7
Tel: 306-634-4154 *Fax:* 306-634-2396
Number of Beds: 44 suites
Number of Employees: 11

Herbert: Herbert Heritage Manor
Former Name: Herbert Senior Citizens Home
PO Box 10, Herbert, SK S0H 2A0
Tel: 306-784-3167 *Fax:* 306-784-3456
Year Founded: 1962
Note: Personal care home level 1 & 2

Kamsack: Eaglestone Lodge Personal Care Home Inc.
PO Box 1330, 346 Miles St., Kamsack, SK S0A 1S0
Tel: 306-542-2620 *Fax:* 306-542-4342
eaglestone@sasktel.net
Number of Beds: 42 beds

Moose Jaw: Capilano Court
Affiliated with: Saskatchewan Health Authority
1236 - 3rd Ave. NW, Moose Jaw, SK S6H 3V3
Tel: 306-693-4518

Moose Jaw: Chez Nous Senior Citizens Home
Affiliated with: Saskatchewan Health Authority
1101 Grafton Ave., Moose Jaw, SK S6H 3S4
Tel: 306-693-4371
chez.nous@sasktel.net
www.cheznoushome.ca

Moose Jaw: Oxford Place Inc.
1007 Main St. North, Moose Jaw, SK S6H 0X1
Tel: 306-692-2837

Oxbow: Bow Valley Villa Corp.
319 Wylie Ave., Oxbow, SK S0C 2B0
Tel: 306-483-2744 *Fax:* 306-483-2915
www.facebook.com/BowValleyVilla

Pangman: Deep South Personal Care Home
PO Box 150, 211 Keeler St., Pangman, SK S0C 2C0
Tel: 306-442-2043 *Fax:* 306-442-4261
Number of Beds: 25 beds
Note: Deep South Care Home is a private personal care home for 25 residents.
Gail Santon, Administrator

Prince Albert: Nelson Care Home Ltd.
Affiliated with: Saskatchewan Health Authority
1336 - 7th St. East, Prince Albert, SK S6V 0V1
Tel: 306-922-9506

Rosthern: Prairie Meadow Place Inc.
Former Name: Rosthern Mennonite Home for the Aged
PO Box 790, 510 4th Ave., Rosthern, SK S0K 3R0
Tel: 306-232-4822
hfta@sasktel.net
www.prairiemeadowplace.com
www.facebook.com/PrairieMeadowPlace
Number of Beds: 20 beds
Art Klaassen, Chair

Saskatoon: Arbor Villa Care Home Inc.
202 Lewis Cres., Saskatoon, SK S7L 7H5
Tel: 306-384-1419
yourcarehome@shaw.ca
www.arborvillacarehomeinc.ca
Note: The personal care home offers respite care.
Agnes Lopez, Operator

Saskatoon: Ashton Care Home Inc.
Affiliated with: Saskatoon Health Region
438 Ave. Y North, Saskatoon, SK S7L 3L2
Tel: 306-382-8975
Number of Beds: 7 single bedrooms; 2 double bedrooms

Saskatoon: Balicanta Personal Care Home
Affiliated with: Saskatoon Health Region
Also Known As: Balicanta Holdings Ltd.
510 Spencer Cres., Saskatoon, SK S7K 7T4
Tel: 306-934-5903 *Fax:* 306-934-5903
Number of Beds: 6 single bedrooms; 3 double bedrooms
I. Balicanta, Contact

Saskatoon: Betty Sandulak Personal Care Home
122 Adilman Dr., Saskatoon, SK S7K 7S5
Tel: 306-931-7859
Note: Respite care is available.

Saskatoon: Cabello Personal Care Home
518/520 Russell Rd., Saskatoon, SK S7K 6L6
Tel: 306-242-6501
Note: Specialties: Diabetic care; Respite care
Marionela Cabello, Contact

Saskatoon: Fairhaven Care Home Inc.
Affiliated with: Saskatoon Health Region
139 Olmstead Rd., Saskatoon, SK S7M 4L9
Tel: 306-974-1156
Number of Beds: 6 single rooms; 3 double rooms

Saskatoon: Healthy Life Care Home
Affiliated with: Saskatchewan Health Authority
Former Name: Bergman's Private Home Care
333 LaRonge Rd., Saskatoon, SK S7K 4S1
Tel: 306-934-2031 *Fax:* 306-934-2031

Saskatoon: Miel's Private Care Home
Affiliated with: Saskatchewan Health Authority
Former Name: Marg's Care Home Ltd.
310 Adilman Dr., Saskatoon, SK S7K 7K5
Tel: 306-491-6912
miel_marial@icloud.com
www.mielsprivatecarehome.com

Shellbrook: T.L.C. Personal Care Home
308 - 3rd Ave. East, Shellbrook, SK S0J 2E0
Tel: 306-747-3123
Year Founded: 1997

St. Louis: McDougall Wings Care Home
457 River Rd., St. Louis, SK S0J 2C0
Tel: 306-422-8223
Lynn Regnier

Theodore: Theodore Health Centre
Affiliated with: Saskatchewan Health Authority
PO Box 70, 615 Anderson Ave., Theodore, SK S0A 4C0
Tel: 306-647-2115 *Fax:* 306-647-2238
Number of Beds: 19 beds (18 long term care beds, 1 respite/palliative care bed)
Note: Specialties: Long-term care; Nursing services; Phlebotomy service; Respite care; Palliative care

Watson: Quill Plains Centennial Lodge
Affiliated with: Saskatchewan Health Authority
PO Box 459, Watson, SK S0K 4V0
Tel: 306-287-3791 *Fax:* 306-287-4444
Number of Beds: 53 beds

Weyburn: **Crocus Plains Villa Ltd.**
Affiliated with: Saskatchewan Health Authority
1135 Park Ave., Weyburn, SK S4H 0K6
Tel: 306-842-0616 Fax: 306-842-2361
nickturanich@sasktel.net
www.crocusplainsvilla.com
Note: Care planning is provided by a multidisciplinary team.
Crocus Plains Villa features a secured area for persons with a
cognitive impairment. The personal care home also offers respite
care.
Nick Turanich, President
nickturanich@sasktel.net

Weyburn: **Parkway Lodge Personal Care Home**
Affiliated with: Saskatchewan Health Authority
420 - 8 Ave. SE, Weyburn, SK S4H 3N2
Tel: 306-842-7868 Fax: 306-842-6808
parkwaylodge@gmail.com
www.parkwaylodge.ca
www.facebook.com/1541385692555494
Number of Beds: 23 suites

Weyburn: **Tatagwa View**
Affiliated with: Saskatchewan Health Authority
Former Name: Souris Valley Extended Care Centre
PO Box 2003, 808 Souris Valley Rd., Weyburn, SK S4H 2Z9
Tel: 306-842-8398
Year Founded: 2005
Note: Programs & services include: long-term care; mental
health services (10 beds); acquired brain injury services;
diabetes program; rehabilitation services; day care centre;
palliative care
Marnell Cornish, Administrator

Mental Health Hospitals/Facilities

Arcola: **Arcola Mental Health Clinic**
Affiliated with: Saskatchewan Health Authority
PO Box 419, Arcola, SK S0C 0G0
Tel: 306-455-2159
Note: Programs & services include: children's mental health.

Cumberland House: **Cumberland House Addiction
Services**
Affiliated with: Saskatchewan Health Authority
PO Box 218, Cumberland House, SK S0E 0S0
Tel: 306-888-2155 Fax: 306-888-4633

Estevan: **Estevan Mental Health Clinic**
Affiliated with: Saskatchewan Health Authority
PO Box 5000-202, 1174 Nicholson Rd., Estevan, SK S4A 2V6
Tel: 306-637-3610
Note: Programs & services include: children's mental health.

Kipling: **Kipling Mental Health Clinic**
Affiliated with: Saskatchewan Health Authority
PO Box 420, Kipling, SK S0G 2S0
Tel: 306-736-2638
Note: Programs & services include: children's mental health.

Lloydminster: **Lloydminster Mental Health &
Addictions Services**
Affiliated with: Saskatchewan Health Authority
3830 - 43 Ave., Lloydminster, SK S9V 1Y3
Tel: 306-820-6250 Fax: 306-820-6256
Info Line: 811

Melfort: **Sakwatamo Lodge**
Affiliated with: Saskatchewan Health Authority
PO Box 3917, Melfort, SK S0E 1A0
Tel: 306-864-3631 Fax: 306-864-2204
Note: Programs & services include: addiction services; family
support; suicide prevention.

Prince Albert: **Addiction Services Prince Albert**
Affiliated with: Saskatchewan Health Authority
101 - 15th St. East, Prince Albert, SK S6V 1G1
Tel: 306-765-6550 Fax: 306-765-6554
Toll-Free: 855-765-6550

Weyburn: **Weyburn Mental Health Clinic**
Affiliated with: Saskatchewan Health Authority
PO Box 2003, 900 Saskatchewan Dr., Weyburn, SK S4H 2Z9
Tel: 306-842-8665
Note: Programs & services include: children's mental health.

Yorkton: **Yorkton Mental Health & Addiction
Services**
Affiliated with: Saskatchewan Health Authority
270 Bradbrooke Dr., Yorkton, SK S3N 2K6
Tel: 306-786-0558 Fax: 306-786-0556

Number of Beds: 18 inpatient and assessment beds
Note: Programs & services include: adult community services;
rehabilitation services; child & youth services.

Special Care Homes

Arborfield: **Arborfield Special Care Lodge**
Affiliated with: Saskatchewan Health Authority
PO Box 160, 509 - 5th Ave., Arborfield, SK S0E 0A0
Tel: 306-769-8757 Fax: 306-769-8759
www.kelseytrailhealth.ca
Number of Beds: 36 beds
Sharon Frisky, Community Coordinator

Battleford: **Battlefords District Care Centre**
Affiliated with: Saskatchewan Health Authority
PO Box 69, Battleford, SK S0M 0E0
Tel: 306-446-6900 Fax: 306-937-2258

Canora: **Canora Gateway Lodge**
Affiliated with: Saskatchewan Health Authority
PO Box 1387, 212 Centre Ave. East, Canora, SK S0A 0L0
Tel: 306-563-5685 Fax: 306-563-5711
Number of Beds: 63 long-term beds; 1 respite

Carrot River: **Pasquia Special Care Home**
Affiliated with: Saskatchewan Health Authority
PO Box 250, 4101 - 1st Ave West, Carrot River, SK S0E 0L0
Tel: 306-768-2725 Fax: 306-768-3233
Number of Beds: 35 long-term care beds

Dalmeny: **Spruce Manor Special Care Home**
Affiliated with: Saskatchewan Health Authority
PO Box 190, 701 - 1st St., Dalmeny, SK S0K 1E0
Tel: 306-254-2101 Fax: 306-254-2178
sprucemanor.mennonite.net
Year Founded: 1950
Number of Beds: 36 beds

Esterhazy: **Centennial Special Care Home**
Affiliated with: Saskatchewan Health Authority
PO Box 310, 300 James St., Esterhazy, SK S0A 0X0
Tel: 306-745-6444 Fax: 306-745-2741
Number of Beds: 52 long term care beds; 1 respite bed

Fort Qu'appelle: **Echo Lodge Special Care Home**
Affiliated with: Saskatchewan Health Authority
PO Box 1790, 560 Broadway St. West, Fort Qu'appelle, SK
S0G 1S0
Tel: 306-332-4300 Fax: 306-332-5708
Number of Beds: 50 beds
Note: Adult day care & respite care are available.

Herbert: **Herbert Nursing Home Inc.**
Affiliated with: Saskatchewan Health Authority
PO Box 520, 405 Herbert Ave., Herbert, SK S0H 2A0
Tel: 306-784-2466
Year Founded: 1951
Number of Beds: 48 beds

Humboldt: **St. Mary's Villa**
Affiliated with: Saskatchewan Health Authority
PO Box 1360, 1109 - 13 St. North, Humboldt, SK S0K 2A0
Tel: 306-682-2628 Fax: 306-682-3211
Number of Beds: 85 beds

Langenburg: **Centennial Special Care Home**
Affiliated with: Saskatchewan Health Authority
PO Box 370, 407 - 2 St. South, Langenburg, SK S0A 2A0
Tel: 306-743-2232 Fax: 306-743-5025
Number of Beds: 44 long-term care beds; 2 respite beds; 1
palliative care bed

Mankota: **Prairie View Health Centre**
Affiliated with: Saskatchewan Health Authority
PO Box 390, 241 - 1 Ave., Mankota, SK S0H 2W0
Tel: 306-478-2200
Number of Beds: 20 beds

Meadow Lake: **Northland Pioneers Lodge Inc.**
Affiliated with: Saskatchewan Health Authority
515 - 3 St. West, Meadow Lake, SK S9X 1L1
Tel: 306-236-5812

North Battleford: **Villa Pascal**
Affiliated with: Saskatchewan Health Authority
Also Known As: Société Joseph Breton Inc.
1301 - 113 St., North Battleford, SK S9A 3K1
Tel: 306-445-8465 Fax: 306-445-5117

Prince Albert: **Herb Bassett Home**
Affiliated with: Saskatchewan Health Authority
PO Box 3000, 1220 - 25 St. West, Prince Albert, SK S6V 5T4
Tel: 306-765-6000 Fax: 306-765-6207

Note: Herb Basset Home hosts an adult day program.

Prince Albert: **Mont St. Joseph Home Inc.**
Affiliated with: Saskatchewan Health Authority
777 - 28 St. East, Prince Albert, SK S6V 8C2
Tel: 306-953-4500 Fax: 306-953-4550
montstjoseph.org
www.facebook.com/montstjosephhome
Year Founded: 1956
Number of Beds: 120 beds
Note: Special care home
Brian Martin, Executive Director

Raymore: **Silver Heights Special Care Home**
Affiliated with: Saskatchewan Health Authority
PO Box 549, 402 McLean St., Raymore, SK S0A 3J0
Tel: 306-746-5744 Fax: 306-746-5747
Number of Beds: 29 beds
Population Served: 600

Regina: **Salvation Army William Booth Special Care
Home**
Affiliated with: Saskatchewan Health Authority
50 Angus Rd., Regina, SK S4R 8P6
Tel: 306-543-0655 Fax: 306-543-1292
www.williamboothregina.ca
Number of Beds: 53 beds
Ivy Scobie, Executive Director

Saskatoon: **Circle Drive Special Care Home Inc.**
Affiliated with: Saskatchewan Health Authority
3055 Preston Ave. South, Saskatoon, SK S7T 1C3
Tel: 306-955-4800 Fax: 306-955-2376
circlecare@saskatoonhealthregion.ca
circledrivespecialcarehome.ca
Number of Beds: 53 beds
Diane Martin, Director of Care
Clint Kinchen, Administrator
Brad Traill, Board Chair

Saskatoon: **Extendicare - Preston
Extendicare Canada**
Affiliated with: Saskatchewan Health Authority
2225 Preston Ave., Saskatoon, SK S7J 2E7
Tel: 306-374-2242 Fax: 306-373-2203
cnh_preston@extendicare.com
www.extendicarecanada.com/saskatoon/index.aspx
Number of Beds: 82 beds

Saskatoon: **Luther Seniors Centre
LutherCare Communities**
1800 Alexandra Ave., Saskatoon, SK S7K 3C7
Tel: 306-664-0366 Fax: 306-664-0395
info@luthercare.com
luthercare.com/our-services/luther-seniors-centre
Year Founded: 1985
Note: Specialties: Day program for adults with irreversible
dementia; Social services; Nursing; Personal care; Sensory
stimulation.

Saskatoon: **Luther Special Care Home
LutherCare Communities**
Affiliated with: Saskatchewan Health Authority
1212 Osler St., Saskatoon, SK S7N 0T9
Tel: 306-664-0300 Fax: 306-664-0311
www.luthercare.com
Year Founded: 1955
Number of Beds: 129 beds, including 49 special needs beds & 2
respite beds
Note: Specialties: Secure special needs unit for residents with
cognitive impairment; Nursing care; Physio, occupational, &
recreational therapy; Community day program for seniors at risk;
Respite care

Saskatoon: **LutherCare Communities**
Affiliated with: Saskatchewan Health Authority
Former Name: Lutheran Sunset Home
Main Corporate Office, 1212 Osler St., Saskatoon, SK S7N
0T9
Tel: 306-664-0300 Fax: 306-664-0311
info@luthercare.com
www.luthercare.com
www.youtube.com/user/LutherCareSask
Year Founded: 1955
Population Served: 1,000 *Number of Employees:* 400
Specialties: Group living for young adults; Community day
programs for adults; Home support; Intermediate care; Seniors'
housing; Long-term nursing care
Vivienne Hauck, Chief Executive Officer
306-664-0301, vivienne.hauck@luthercare.com

Strasbourg: **Last Mountain Pioneer Home**
Affiliated with: Saskatchewan Health Authority
PO Box 459, 700 Prospect Ave., Strasbourg, SK S0G 4V0
Tel: 306-725-3342 Fax: 306-725-3404
www.saskatoonhealthregion.ca
Number of Beds: 39 beds
Connie Fuessel, Manager

Tisdale: **Nipawin District Nursing Home**
Affiliated with: Saskatchewan Health Authority
PO Box 1780, Tisdale, SK S0E 1T0
Tel: 306-873-6600 Fax: 306-873-6605
tdemarsh@kthr.sk.ca
www.kelseytrailhealth.ca
Number of Beds: 96 beds

Warman: **Warman Mennonite Special Care Home**
Affiliated with: Saskatchewan Health Authority
PO Box 100, 201 Centennial Blvd., Warman, SK S0K 4S0
Tel: 306-933-2011 Fax: 306-933-2782
Number of Beds: 31 beds

Weyburn: **Weyburn Special Care Home**
Affiliated with: Saskatchewan Health Authority
PO Box 2003, 704 - 5th St. NE, Weyburn, SK S4H 2Z9
Tel: 306-842-4455
Note: Programs & services include: dietician; home care; palliative care; respite care.
Debbie Obst, Contact

Yukon Territory

Government Departments in Charge

Whitehorse: **Yukon Health & Social Services**
PO Box 2703, Whitehorse, YT Y1A 2C6
Tel: 867-393-7048
hssweb@yukon.ca
yukon.ca/en/department-health-social-services
www.facebook.com/yukonhss; twitter.com/HSSYukon;
www.youtube.com/user/hssyukongovernment
Hon. Tracy-Anne McPhee, Minister
867-393-7488, Fax: 867-393-7135, tracy.mcphee@yukon.ca

Hospitals - General

Dawson: **Dawson City Community Hospital**
Yukon Hospital Corporation
Former Name: Dawson City Health Centre
PO Box 870, 501 - 6th Ave., Dawson, YT Y0B 1G0
Tel: 867-993-4444 Fax: 867-993-4317
yukonhospitals.ca
www.facebook.com/yukonhospitals; twitter.com/YukonHospitals;
www.instagram.com/yukonhospitals;
www.linkedin.com/company/yukon-hospital-corporation
Number of Beds: 6 beds
Number of Employees: 28
Note: Services offered by the Dawson Community Health Centre & Dawson Medical Clinic are now located within this facility. Programs & services include: ambulatory care; basic diagnostic & lab tests; communicable disease screening; diagnostic imaging; emergency; healthy lifestyle support; hearing services; house calls; immunizations; infant & preschool health exams; inpatient care; mental health services; palliative care; pharmacy; physiotherapy; pre & post-natal education; school health program; third party medical assessments; & travel health education & immunizations.
Jason Bilsky, Chief Executive Officer, Yukon Hospital Corporation
Jorge Van Slyke, Director, Community Patient Experience

Watson Lake: **Watson Lake Hospital**
Yukon Hospital Corporation
817 Ravenhill Dr., Watson Lake, YT Y0A 1C0
Tel: 867-536-4444
yukonhospitals.ca/yukonhospitalsfacilities/watsonlake
www.facebook.com/yukonhospitals; twitter.com/YukonHospitals;
www.instagram.com/yukonhospitals;
www.linkedin.com/company/yukon-hospital-corporation
Number of Beds: 6 beds
Number of Employees: 29
Note: Programs & services include: ambulatory care; convalescent care; diagnostic services (laboratory & medical imaging); emergency; First Nations health program; inpatient care; respite care; & stabilization, observation & monitoring.
Jason Bilsky, Chief Executive Officer, Yukon Hospital Corporation
Carol Chiasson, Director, Community Patient Experience

Whitehorse: **Whitehorse General Hospital (WGH)**
Yukon Hospital Corporation
5 Hospital Rd., Whitehorse, YT Y1A 3H7
Tel: 867-393-8700 Fax: 867-393-8771
Toll-Free: 877-307-9042
yukonhospitals.ca
www.facebook.com/yukonhospitals; twitter.com/YukonHospitals;
www.instagram.com/yukonhospitals
Year Founded: 1902
Number of Beds: 55 beds
Number of Employees: 503
Specialties: Medical imaging services; Laboratory services; Diabetes Education Centre; Nutrition services; First Nations health programs; Therapy services
Note: Programs & services include: First Nations health programs; cancer care; cardiac stress testing; diabetes education; emergency; environmental; intensive care; laboratory; maternity; medical; medical imaging (CT scanning, digital mammography, MRI & ultrasound); nutrition; pediatrics; pharmacy; social work; specialists clinic; surgery; therapy; & pastoral care.
Jason Bilsky, Chief Executive Officer, Yukon Hospital Corporation
Lara Murphy, Director, Patient Care & Experience
Dr. Huy Chau, Associate Chief of Staff

Community Health Care Centres

Beaver Creek: **Beaver Creek Health Centre**
PO Box 3, Beaver Creek, YT Y0B 1A0
Tel: 867-862-4444 Fax: 867-862-7909

Carmacks: **Carmacks Health Centre**
PO Box 230, Carmacks, YT Y0B 1C0
Tel: 867-863-4444 Fax: 867-863-6612
Number of Beds: 2 beds

Destruction Bay: **Destruction Bay Health Centre**
General Delivery, Destruction Bay, YT Y0B 1H0
Tel: 867-841-4444 Fax: 867-841-5274

Faro: **Faro Health Centre**
PO Box 99, Faro, YT Y0B 1K0
Tel: 867-994-4444 Fax: 867-994-3457
Note: Services include: primary health care; acute care; chronic disease management; basic lab & x-ray; immunization; public health; wellness clinics; & 24-hour emergency.

Haines Junction: **Haines Junction Health Centre**
PO Box 5369, Haines Junction, YT Y0B 1L0
Tel: 867-634-4444 Fax: 867-634-2733
Note: Services include: primary health care; public health care; emergency; & physician (by appointment).

Mayo: **Mayo Health Centre**
PO Box 98, 21 Centre St., Mayo, YT Y0B 1M0
Tel: 867-996-4444 Fax: 867-996-2018
Note: Specialties: Public health services; Health promotion services; Home care services. Number of Employees: 1 doctor + 3 community nurse practitioners.

Old Crow: **Old Crow Health Centre**
PO Box 92, Old Crow, YT Y0B 1N0
Tel: 867-996-4444 Fax: 867-966-3614
www.oldcrow.ca/nursing
Year Founded: 1960
Number of Employees: 4
Note: Specialties: Nursing care; Health promotion; Home & community care.

Pelly Crossing: **Pelly Crossing Health Centre**
PO Box 20, Pelly Crossing, YT Y0B 1P0
Tel: 867-537-4444 Fax: 867-537-3611

Ross River: **Ross River Health Centre**
5 Kulan St., Ross River, YT Y0B 1S0
Tel: 867-969-4444 Fax: 867-969-2014

Teslin: **Teslin Health Centre**
27 Dawson Ave., Teslin, YT Y0B 1B0
Tel: 867-390-4444 Fax: 867-390-2217
Note: Specialties: Public health services; Health promotion; Clinical care by community nurses; Home care.

Watson Lake: **Watson Lake Health Centre**
PO Box 500, 817 Raven Hill Dr., Watson Lake, YT Y0A 1C0
Tel: 867-536-5255 Fax: 867-536-5258
Note: Services include: community health programs; immunization; prenatal classes; postnatal care; & school health clinics.

Long Term Care Facilities

Dawson City: **Alexander McDonald Home for Seniors**
PO Box 310, 636 - 5th Ave., Dawson City, YT Y0B 1G0
Tel: 867-993-5345 Fax: 867-993-5849
Toll-Free: 800-661-0408
Number of Beds: 11 residential beds, including 2 respite beds
Note: Specialties: Residential care for seniors & physically challenged persons who require moderate assistance; Recreational & therapeutic activities; Respite care; Home support services; Palliative care

Whitehorse: **Copper Ridge Place**
60 Lazulite Dr., Whitehorse, YT Y1A 6S9
Tel: 867-393-7500 Fax: 867-393-7510
www.hss.gov.yk.ca
Number of Beds: 96 beds

Whitehorse: **Norman D. Macaulay Lodge**
2 Klondike Rd., Whitehorse, YT Y1A 3L5
Tel: 867-667-5955 Fax: 867-393-6237
Number of Beds: 44 beds

Retirement Residences

Whitehorse: **Front Street Senior's Residence**
1190 Front St., Whitehorse, YT Y1A 0P4

Year Founded: 2016
Number of Beds: 48 unites

SECTION 11
LAW FIRMS

Major Law Firms

Aird & Berlis LLP - Toronto
Former Name: Aird, Zimmerman & Berlis
#1800, Brookfield Place, 181 Bay St., Toronto, ON M5J 2T9
Tel: 416-863-1500; Fax: 416-863-1515
Toll-Free: 800-375-3480
airdberlis@airdberlis.com
www.airdberlis.com
www.facebook.com/AirdBerlis, twitter.com/AirdBerlis,
www.linkedin.com/company/aird-&-berlis-llp
Profile: 1 Offices, 190 Lawyers, Founded in: 1919
Legal services in the areas of Banking Law, Corporate &
Commercial Law, Corporate Finance, Insolvency &
Restructuring, Litigation, Real Estate Law & Tax Law.
Senior and Managing Partners:
Steven Zakem, Managing Partner
416-865-3440
szakem@airdberlis.com

BCF LLP - Montréal
1100, boul René-Lévesque ouest, 25e étage, Montréal, QC
H3B 5C9
Tel: 514-397-8500; Fax: 514-397-8515
info@bcf.ca
www.bcf.ca
twitter.com/bcf_avocats_law, www.linkedin.com/company/bcf
Profile: 2 Offices, 272 Lawyers, Founded in: 1995
Financial areas of expertise include: banking; business;
corporate & commercial; labour & employment; intellectual
property; real estate; securities; tax.
Senior and Managing Partners:
Pierre T. Allard, Managing Partner
514-397-6932
pierre.allard@bcf.ca
Mario Charpentier, Founding Partner
514-397-6950
mario.charpentier@bcf.ca
André Morrissette, Firm Chair & Partner
514-397-6915
andre.morrissette@bcf.ca

BCF LLP - Québec
Complexe Jules-Dallaire, T1, 2828, boul Laurier, 12e étage,
Québec, QC G1V 0B9
Tel: 418-266-4500; Fax: 418-266-4515
info@bcf.ca
www.bcf.ca
Profile: 81 Lawyers
Senior and Managing Partners:
Mario Welsh, Québec Office Managing Partner
418-649-5473
mario.welsh@bcf.ca

Bennett Jones LLP - Calgary
#4500, Bankers Hall East Tower, 855 - 2nd St. SW, Calgary,
AB T2P 4K7
Tel: 403-298-3100; Fax: 403-265-7219
www.bennettjones.ca
twitter.com/BennettJonesLaw,
www.linkedin.com/company/bennett-jones
Profile: 7 Offices, 392 Lawyers, Founded in: 1922
The firm specializes in many aspects of financial law that
include: corporate & commercial law; class action litigation;
financial services; fraud law; mergers & acquisitions; pensions &
benefits; tax; venture capital; wills & estates; real estate &
project finance.
Senior and Managing Partners:
Patrick T. Maguire, Calgary Managing Partner
403-298-3184
maguirep@bennettjones.com
John M. Mercury, Vice-Chair & Partner
403-298-4493
mercuryj@bennettjones.com
Perry Spitznagel, Q.C., Firm Vice-Chair & Partner
403-298-3153
spitznagelp@bennettjones.com
Blair C. Yorke-Slader, Q.C., Vice-Chair & Partner
403-298-3291
yorkesladerb@bennettjones.com

Bennett Jones LLP - Edmonton
#3200, TELUS House, South Tower, 10020 - 100th St.,
Edmonton, AB T5J 0N3
Tel: 780-421-8133; Fax: 780-421-7951
www.bennettjones.ca
Profile: 38 Lawyers
Senior and Managing Partners:
David M. Hawreluk, Edmonton Managing Partner
780-917-5238
hawrelukd@bennettjones.com

Bennett Jones LLP - Ottawa
#1900, World Exchange Plaza, 45 O'Connor St., Ottawa, ON
K1P 1A4
Tel: 613-683-2300; Fax: 613-683-2323
www.bennettjones.ca
Profile: 1 Lawyers

Bennett Jones LLP - Toronto
#3400, One First Canadian Place, P.O. Box 130, Toronto, ON
M5X 1A4
Tel: 416-863-1200; Fax: 416-863-1716
www.bennettjones.ca
Profile: 175 Lawyers
Senior and Managing Partners:
Stephen W. Bowman, Toronto Managing Partner
416-777-4624
bowmans@bennettjones.com
Hugh L. MacKinnon, Firm Chair & CEO
416-777-4810
mackinnonh@bennettjones.com

Bennett Jones LLP - Vancouver
#2500, 666 Burrard St., Vancouver, BC V6C 2X8
Tel: 604-891-7500; Fax: 604-891-5100
www.bennettjones.ca
Profile: 17 Lawyers
Senior and Managing Partners:
Radha D. Curpen, Vancouver Managing Partner
604-891-5158
curpenr@bennettjones.com

Blake, Cassels & Graydon LLP - Toronto
Also Known As: Blakes
#4000, Commerce Court West, 199 Bay St., Toronto, ON M5L
1A9
Tel: 416-863-2400; Fax: 416-863-2653
toronto@blakes.com
www.blakes.com
www.facebook.com/blakes, twitter.com/blakeslaw,
www.linkedin.com/blake-cassels-&-graydon-llp
Profile: 7 Offices, 659 Lawyers, Founded in: 1856
The firm provides services in structuring, negotiating &
documenting a wide variety of domestic & cross-border financing
transactions. These include syndications, project finance,
asset-based lending, trade finance, high-yield offerings, debt &
debtor-in-possession financing, warehouse facilities credit
arrangements, private placements, securitizations & structured
financing, subordinated debt arrangements, as well as aircraft &
other equipment finance & capital markets debt offerings.
Senior and Managing Partners:
Brock W. Gibson, Q.C., Firm Chair
416-863-2150
brock.gibson@blakes.com
Bryson A. Stokes, Firm Managing Partner
416-863-2179
bryson.stokes@blakes.com

Blake, Cassels & Graydon LLP - Calgary
#3500, Bankers Hall East Tower, 855 - 2nd St. SW, Calgary,
AB T2P 4J8
Tel: 403-260-9600; Fax: 403-260-9700
calgary@blakes.com
www.blakes.com
Profile: 109 Lawyers
Senior and Managing Partners:
Ben Rogers, Calgary Managing Partner
403-260-9702
ben.rogers@blakes.com

Blake, Cassels & Graydon LLP - Montréal
#3000, 1, Place Ville Marie, Montréal, QC H3B 4N8
Tél: 514-982-4000; Téléc: 514-982-4099
montreal@blakes.com
www.blakes.com
Profile: 86 Lawyers
Senior and Managing Partners:
Robert Torralbo, Montréal Managing Partner
514-982-4014
robert.torralbo@blakes.com

Blake, Cassels & Graydon LLP - Ottawa
#1750, Tower 3, Constitution Square, 340 Albert St., Ottawa,
ON K1R 7Y6
Tel: 613-788-2200; Fax: 613-788-2247
ottawa@blakes.com
www.blakes.com
Profile: 8 Lawyers

Blake, Cassels & Graydon LLP - Vancouver
#2600, Three Bentall Centre, P.O. Box 49314, 595 Burrard
St., Vancouver, BC V7X 1L3
Tel: 604-631-3300; Fax: 604-631-3309
vancouver@blakes.com
www.blakes.com

Profile: 107 Lawyers
Senior and Managing Partners:
Peter J. O'Callaghan, Vancouver Managing Partner
604-631-3345
peter.ocallaghan@blakes.com

Blaney McMurtry LLP
#1500, 2 Queen St. East, Toronto, ON M5C 3G5
Tel: 416-593-1221; Fax: 416-593-5437
www.blaney.com
www.facebook.com/blaneymcmurtry,
twitter.com/blaneymcmurtry,
www.linkedin.com/company/blaney-mcmurtry-llp
Profile: 1 Offices, 118 Lawyers, Founded in: 1954
Blaney McMurtry LLP is a regional law firm recognized for their
expertise in litigation, real estate & business law. Financial areas
of expertise include: class actions; corporate & commercial;
corporate finance & securities; insurance; employment;
international trade & real estate.
Senior and Managing Partners:
Maria Scarfo, Firm Managing Partner
416-593-3955

Borden Ladner Gervais LLP - Toronto
Also Known As: BLG
#3400, East Tower, Bay Adelaide Centre, 22 Adelaide St.
West, Toronto, ON M5H 4E3
Tel: 416-367-6000; Fax: 416-367-6749
Toll-Free: 855-660-6003
info@blg.com
www.blg.com
www.facebook.com/bordenladnergervaisllp, twitter.com/blglaw,
www.linkedin.com/company/blglaw
Profile: 5 Offices, 790 Lawyers, Founded in: 1936
Borden Ladner Gervais LLP has the following financial practice
areas: banking & financial services; class actions; corporate &
commercial; competition & antitrust; insurance; labour &
employment; mergers & acquisitions; real estate; securities &
tax. Financial industries served include the financial services
sector; insurance firms; charities & not-for-profits; private equity
& venture capital.
Senior and Managing Partners:
Rebecca Bush, Partner & National Leader
416-367-6162
rburhs@blg.com
Kate A. Crawford, National Leader, Health
416-367-6729
kcrawford@blg.com
Shane Freitag, National Leader, Electricity
416-367-6137
sfreitag@blg.com
Andrew Harrison, Toronto Managing Partner
416-367-6046
ahrrison@blg.com
J. Pitman Patterson, National Business Leader
416-367-6109
ppatterson@blg.com
Victoria Prince, National Leader, Charities
416-367-6648
vprince@blg.com

Borden Ladner Gervais LLP - Calgary
#1900, Centennial Place, East Tower, 520 - 3rd Ave. SW,
Calgary, AB T2P 0R3
Tel: 403-232-9500; Fax: 403-266-1395
Toll-Free: 855-660-6003
info@blg.com
www.blg.com
Profile: 130 Lawyers
Senior and Managing Partners:
Jason Howg, National Business Leader, IP
403-232-9415
jhowg@blg.com
Patricia L. Morrison, National Business Leader
403-232-9472
pmorrison@blg.com
Alan Ross, Calgary Managing Partner
403-232-9656
aross@blg.com

Borden Ladner Gervais LLP - Montréal
#900, 1000, rue de la Gauchetière ouest, Montréal, QC H3B
5H4
Tel: 514-879-1212; Fax: 514-954-1905
Toll-Free: 855-660-6003
info@blg.com
www.blg.com
Profile: 149 Lawyers
Senior and Managing Partners:
Curtis Behmann, Partner & National Leader
514-954-2596
cbehmann@blg.com

André Dufour, Montréal Managing Partner
514-954-2526
adufour@blg.com
Claudine Millette, National Business Leader
514-954-3174
cmillette@blg.com
John G. Murphy, National Managing Partner/CEO
514-954-3155
jmurphy@blg.com
Mathieu Piché-Messier, National Business Leader
514-954-3136
mpmessier@blg.com

Borden Ladner Gervais LLP - Ottawa
#1300, World Exchange Plaza, 100 Queen St., Ottawa, ON K1P 1J9
Tel: 613-237-5160; Fax: 613-230-8842
Toll-Free: 855-660-6003
info@blg.com
www.blg.com

Profile: 90 Lawyers
Senior and Managing Partners:
Larry A. Elliot, Ottawa Managing Partner
613-787-3537
lelliot@blg.com

Borden Ladner Gervais LLP - Vancouver
#1200, Waterfront Centre, P.O. Box 48600, 200 Burrard St., Vancouver, BC V7X 1T2
Tel: 604-687-5744; Fax: 604-687-1415
Toll-Free: 855-660-6003
info@blg.com
www.blg.com

Profile: 138 Lawyers, Founded in: 1911
Senior and Managing Partners:
Kent D. Kufeldt, National Business Leader
604-640-4195
kkufeldt@blg.com
David C.S. Longcroft, National Business Leader
604-640-4211
dlongcroft@blg.com
Graham Walker, Group Head & Business Leader
604-640-4045
gwalker@blg.com
Steve M. Winder, Regional Managing Vancouver
604-640-4118
swinder@blg.com

Burnet, Duckworth & Palmer LLP
Also Known As: BD&P
#2400, 525 - 8th Ave. SW, Calgary, AB T2P 1G1
Tel: 403-260-0100; Fax: 403-260-0332
www.bdplaw.com
Profile: 1 Offices, 100 Lawyers, Founded in: 1905
Financial practices include: Banking & Finance; Commercial; Restructuring & Insolvency; Securities, Mergers & Acquisitions; Taxation; & Wills & Estates.
Senior and Managing Partners:
John A. Brussa, Partner & Chair
403-260-0131
jab@bdplaw.com
Grant A. Zawalsky, Managing Partner
403-260-0376
gaz@bdplaw.com
Harry S. Campbell, Q.C., Partner & Chair Emeritus
403-260-0281
hsc@bdplaw.com

Cain Lamarre - Val-d'Or
Former Name: Cain Lamarre Casgrain Wells
865, 3e av, Val-d'Or, QC J9P 1T2
Tél: 819-825-4153; Téléc: 819-825-9769
www.cainlamarre.ca
www.facebook.com/CainLamarre
www.linkedin.com/company/cain-lamarre
Profile: 18 Offices, 153 Lawyers, Founded in: 1999
Cain Lamarre est spécialisé dans le droit bancaire et financier, la faillite et l'insolvabilité; Affaires commerciales et commerciales; propriété intellectuelle; Travail et emploi; immobilier; Titres et impôts.
Senior and Managing Partners:
Jean-François Brouillard, Associé directeur du CDQ
819-477-2544
jean.francois.brouillard@cainlamarre.ca
Michel Claveau, Associé directeur, Côte-Nord
michel.claveau@cainlamarre.ca
Gaston Desrosiers, Président du cabinet
418-522-4580
gaston.desrosiers@cainlamarre.ca
Gina Doucet, Associé directrice du cabinet
418-522-4580
gina.doucet@cainlamarre.ca

Stéphan Ferron, Associé directeur, Abitibi
stephan.ferron@cainlamarre.ca
Jean-François Hudon, Associé directeur, Montréal
514-393-4580
jean.francois.hudon@cainlamarre.ca
Eric Monfette, Associé directeur, BSL
eric.monfette@cainlamarre.ca
Louis Ste-Marie, Associé directeur, CN
louis.ste.marie@cainlamarre.ca
Guillaume Daigneault, Associé directeur, Estrie
guillaume.daigneault@cainlamarre.ca

Cain Lamarre - Alma
95, rue St-Joseph, Alma, QC G8B 3E5
Tél: 418-669-4580; Téléc: 418-669-0088
www.cainlamarre.ca

Profile: 3 Lawyers

Cain Lamarre - Saguenay
#300, 190, rue Racine est, Saguenay, QC G7H 1R9
Tél: 418-545-4580; Téléc: 418-549-9590
www.cainlamarre.ca

Profile: 35 Lawyers

Cain Lamarre - Drummondville
#201, 330, rue Cormier, Drummondville, QC J2C 8B3
Tél: 819-477-2544; Téléc: 819-477-4343
www.cainlamarre.ca

Profile: 12 Lawyers

Cain Lamarre - Lac-Mégantic
#202, 4050, rue Laval, Lac-Mégantic, QC G6B 1B1
Tél: 819-554-6666; Téléc: 819-780-2280
www.cainlamarre.ca

Profile: 1 Lawyers

Cain Lamarre - Montréal
#2780, 630, boul René-Lévesque ouest, Montréal, QC H3B 1S6
Tél: 514-393-4580; Téléc: 514-393-9590
www.cainlamarre.ca

Profile: 54 Lawyers

Cain Lamarre - Plessisville
2284, rue de la Coopérative, Plessisville, QC G6L 1X2
Tél: 819-362-6699; Téléc: 418-529-9590
www.cainlamarre.ca

Profile: 1 Lawyers

Cain Lamarre - Québec
#1, 500, Grande Allée est, Québec, QC G1R 2J7
Tél: 418-522-4580; Téléc: 418-529-9590
www.cainlamarre.ca

Profile: 47 Lawyers

Cain Lamarre - Rimouski
#400, 2, rue St-Germain est, Rimouski, QC G5L 8T7
Tél: 418-723-3302; Téléc: 418-722-6939
www.cainlamarre.ca

Profile: 9 Lawyers

Cain Lamarre - Rivière-du-Loup
#201, 299, rue Lafontaine, Rivière-du-Loup, QC G5R 3A9
Tél: 418-860-4580; Téléc: 418-860-4588
www.cainlamarre.ca

Profile: 4 Lawyers

Cain Lamarre - Roberval
814, boul Saint-Joseph, Roberval, QC G8H 2L5
Tél: 418-275-2472; Téléc: 418-275-6878
www.cainlamarre.ca

Profile: 3 Lawyers

Cain Lamarre - Rouyn-Noranda
#200, 33, av Horne, Rouyn-Noranda, QC J9X 4S1
Tél: 819-797-5222; Téléc: 819-762-6810
www.cainlamarre.ca

Profile: 10 Lawyers

Cain Lamarre - Saint-Félicien
1067, boul du Sacré-Coeur, Saint-Félicien, QC G8K 1R3
Tél: 418-679-1331; Téléc: 418-679-9344
www.cainlamarre.ca

Profile: 2 Lawyers

Cain Lamarre - Saint-Raymond
423B, rue Saint-Cyrille, Saint-Raymond, QC G3L 4S6
Tél: 418-337-6971; Téléc: 418-529-9590
www.cainlamarre.ca

Profile: 3 Lawyers

Cain Lamarre - Sept-Îles
#200, 440, av Brochu, Sept-Îles, QC G4R 2W8
Tél: 418-962-6572; Téléc: 418-968-8576
www.cainlamarre.ca

Profile: 7 Lawyers

Cain Lamarre - Sherbrooke
#300, 455, rue King ouest, Sherbrooke, QC J1H 6E9
Tél: 819-780-1515; Téléc: 819-780-1341
www.cainlamarre.ca

Profile: 15 Lawyers

Cassels Brock & Blackwell LLP - Toronto
Also Known As: Cassels
#2100, Scotia Plaza, 40 King St. West, Toronto, ON M5H 3C2
Tel: 416-869-5300; Fax: 416-360-8877
cassels.com
twitter.com/cassels,
www.linkedin.com/company/cassels-brock-&-blackwell-llp
Profile: 3 Offices, 252 Lawyers, Founded in: 1888
Full-service law firm, with an emphasis on tax & business law, both domestic & international.
Senior and Managing Partners:
Mark T. Bennett, Partner & Firm Executive Chair
416-869-5407
mbennett@cassels.com
Noble C. Chummar, Deputy Managing Partner
416-869-5454
nchummar@cassels.com
Kristin Taylor, Managing Partner
416-860-2973
ktaylor@cassels.com

Cassels Brock & Blackwell LLP - Calgary
#3810, Bankers Hall West, 888 - 3rd St. SW, Calgary, AB T2P 5C5
Tel: 403-351-2920; Fax: 403-648-1151
cassels.com
Profile: 21 Lawyers

Cassels Brock & Blackwell LLP - Vancouver
#2200, HSBC Bldg., 885 West Georgia St., Vancouver, BC V6C 3E8
Tel: 604-691-6100; Fax: 604-691-6120
cassels.com
Profile: 42 Lawyers
Senior and Managing Partners:
David Budd, Deputy Managing Partner
604-691-6111
dbudd@cassels.com

Cox & Palmer - St. John's
#1100, Scotia Centre, 235 Water St., St. John's, NL A1C 1B6
Tel: 709-738-7800; Fax: 709-738-7999
stjohns@coxandpalmer.com
coxandpalmerlaw.com
www.facebook.com/CoxandPalmerLaw,
twitter.com/CoxandPalmer,
www.linkedin.com/company/cox-&-palmer
Profile: 10 Offices, 203 Lawyers, Founded in: 1995
Financial areas of practice include: corporate & commercial; employment; estates; intellectual property & restructuring & insolvency.
Senior and Managing Partners:
Leanne M. O'Leary, Office Managing Partner
709-570-5516
loleary@coxandpalmer.com

Cox & Palmer - Alberton
P.O. Box 40, 347 Church St., Alberton, PE C0B 1B0
Tel: 902-853-3313; Fax: 902-853-3753
alberton@coxandpalmer.com
coxandpalmerlaw.com
Profile: 3 Lawyers

Cox & Palmer - Charlottetown
#600, 97 Queen St., Charlottetown, PE C1A 4A9
Tel: 902-628-1033; Fax: 902-566-2639
charlottetown@coxandpalmer.com
coxandpalmerlaw.com
Profile: 18 Lawyers
Senior and Managing Partners:
Robin K. Aitken, Charlottetown Managing Partner
902-629-3910
raitken@coxandpalmer.com

Cox & Palmer - Fredericton
#300, TD Tower, Stn. A, 77 Westmorland St., Fredericton, NB E3B 6Z3
Tel: 506-453-7771; Fax: 506-453-9600
fredericton@coxandpalmer.com
coxandpalmerlaw.com
Profile: 24 Lawyers
Senior and Managing Partners:
Daniel L. Stevenson, Fredericton Managing Partner
506-462-4754
dstevenson@coxandpalmer.com

Cox & Palmer - Halifax
#1100, Tower One, Purdy's Wharf, 1959 Upper Water St., Halifax, NS B3J 3N2

Tel: 902-421-6262; *Fax:* 902-421-3130
halifax@coxandpalmer.com
coxandpalmerlaw.com

Profile: 63 Lawyers
Senior and Managing Partners:
Daniel W. Ingersoll, Q.C., Halifax Managing Partner
902-491-4211
ingersoll@coxandpalmer.com

Cox & Palmer - Moncton
#500, Blue Cross Centre, 644 Main St., Moncton, NB E1C 1E2

Tel: 506-856-9800; *Fax:* 506-856-8150
moncton@coxandpalmer.com
coxandpalmerlaw.com

Profile: 19 Lawyers
Senior and Managing Partners:
George L. Cooper, Q.C., Firm CEO & Partner
506-863-0793
gcooper@coxandpalmer.com
Tracy L. Wong, Moncton Managing Partner
506-863-1137
twong@coxandpalmer.com

Cox & Palmer - Montague
P.O. Box 516, 4A Riverside Dr., Montague, PE C0A 1R0

Tel: 902-838-1033; *Fax:* 902-838-3440
montague@coxandpalmer.com
coxandpalmerlaw.com

Profile: 3 Lawyers

Cox & Palmer - Morell
29 Park St., Morell, PE C0A 1S0

Tel: 902-961-9300
coxandpalmerlaw.com

Profile: 1 Lawyers

Cox & Palmer - Saint John
#1500, Brunswick Square, 1 Germain St., Saint John, NB E2L 4V1

Tel: 506-632-8900; *Fax:* 506-632-8809
saintjohn@coxandpalmer.com
coxandpalmerlaw.com

Profile: 31 Lawyers
Senior and Managing Partners:
Edward W. Keyes, Q.C., Saint John Managing Partner
506-633-2706
ekeyes@coxandpalmer.com

Cox & Palmer - Summerside
#401, South Tower, Holman Centre, 250 Water St., Summerside, PE C1N 1B6

Tel: 902-888-1033; *Fax:* 902-436-7131
summerside@coxandpalmer.com
coxandpalmerlaw.com

Profile: 6 Lawyers

Davies Ward Phillips & Vineberg LLP - Toronto
Former Name: Davies Ward & Beck
155 Wellington St. West, Toronto, ON M5V 3J7

Tel: 416-863-0900
www.dwpv.com
twitter.com/_davies_,
www.linkedin.com/company/davies-ward-phillips-&-vineberg-llp
Profile: 3 Offices, 265 Lawyers, Founded in: 1961
Financial specialties include: capital markets; securities; competition & antitrust; corporate & commercial; financing; white collar crime; insolvency; mergers & acquisitions; pensions & employment; private equity & tax. The firm also has an office in New York, USA.
Senior and Managing Partners:
Sarbjit S. Basra, Managing Partner
416-367-6926
sbasra@dwpv.com
Melanie M. Koszegi, Dep. Toronto Managing Partner
416-863-5563
mkoszegi@dwpv.com

Davies Ward Phillips & Vineberg LLP - Montréal
Former Name: Phillips & Vineberg
1501, av McGill College, Montréal, QC H3A 3N9

Tel: 514-841-6400
www.dwpv.com

Profile: 95 Lawyers
Senior and Managing Partners:
Philippe Johnson, Montréal Managing Partner
514-841-6501
pjohnson@dwpv.com

Dentons Canada LLP - Toronto
Former Name: Fraser Milner Casgrain LLP
#400, 77 King St. West, Toronto, ON M5K 0A1

Tel: 416-863-4511; *Fax:* 416-863-4592
www.dentons.com
twitter.com/dentons, www.linkedin.com/company/dentons
Profile: 6 Offices, 573 Lawyers,
Dentons is a global law firm with more than 140 locations in 57 countries; the firm has 6 offices in Canada. The firm has over 7,000 lawyers globally & over 500 lawyers in Canada alone. Financial specialties include banking & finance; capital markets; competition & antitrust; corporate; employment & labour; franchising; insurance; mergers & acquisitions; pensions & benefits; restructuring & insolvency; private equity; real estate; tax; securities; trusts & estates; venture capital & project development.
Senior and Managing Partners:
Blair W. McCreadie, Toronto Managing Partner
416-863-4532
Beth Wilson, Firm Chief Executive Officer
416-863-4715
Richard Scott, Global Vice-Chair & Partner
416-863-4370

Dentons Canada LLP - Calgary
Bankers Court, 850 - 2nd St. SW, 15th Fl., Calgary, AB T2P 0R8

Tel: 403-268-7000; *Fax:* 403-268-3100
www.dentons.com

Profile: 101 Lawyers
Senior and Managing Partners:
Tim Haney, Calgary Managing Partner
403-268-3014

Dentons Canada LLP - Edmonton
#2500, Stantec Tower, 10220 - 103rd Ave. NW, Edmonton, AB T5J 0K4

Tel: 780-423-7100; *Fax:* 780-423-7276
www.dentons.com

Profile: 93 Lawyers
Senior and Managing Partners:
Fausto Franceschi, Edmonton Managing Partner
780-423-7348

Dentons Canada LLP - Montréal
1, Place Ville-Marie, 39e étage, Montréal, QC H3B 4M7

Tel: 514-878-8800; *Fax:* 514-866-2241
www.dentons.com

Profile: 100 Lawyers
Senior and Managing Partners:
Claude Morency, Montréal Managing Partner
514-878-8870

Dentons Canada LLP - Ottawa
#1420, 99 Bank St., Ottawa, ON K1P 1H4

Tel: 613-783-9600; *Fax:* 613-783-9690
www.dentons.com

Profile: 36 Lawyers
Senior and Managing Partners:
David Little, Ottawa Managing Partner
613-783-9639

Dentons Canada LLP - Vancouver
250 Howe St., 20th Fl., Vancouver, BC V6C 3R8

Tel: 604-687-4460; *Fax:* 604-683-5214
www.dentons.com

Profile: 80 Lawyers, Founded in: 1980
Senior and Managing Partners:
John Sandrelli, Vancouver Managing Partner
604-443-7132

DLA Piper (Canada) LLP - Vancouver
Former Name: Davis LLP; Davis & Company LLP
#2800, Park Place, 666 Burrard St., Vancouver, BC V6C 2Z7

Tel: 604-687-9444; *Fax:* 604-687-1612
www.dlapiper.com/en/canada
www.facebook.com/dlapiperglobal, twitter.com/dla_pipercanada, www.linkedin.com/company/dla-piper
Profile: 6 Offices, 251 Lawyers, Founded in: 1892
DLA Piper (Canada) LLP was established in April 2015, with the merger of Davis LLP & DLA Piper LLP (US). The firm works in more than 50 practice areas, with an emphasis on corporate & finance areas related to energy, natural resources, infrastructure, development, litigation & transportation. Globally, DLA Piper has over 4,000 lawyers.
Senior and Managing Partners:
Franco Trasolini, Vancouver Managing Partner
franco.trasolini@dlapiper.com

DLA Piper (Canada) LLP - Calgary
Former Name: Davis LLP
#1000, Livingston Place West, 250 - 2nd St. SW, Calgary, AB T2P 0C1

Tel: 403-296-4470; *Fax:* 403-296-4474
www.dlapiper.com/en/canada

Profile: 46 Lawyers, Founded in: 2002
Senior and Managing Partners:
Jarrod Isfeld, Calgary Managing Partner
403-776-8821
jarrod.isfeld@dlapiper.com

DLA Piper (Canada) LLP - Edmonton
Former Name: Davis LLP
#2700, 10220 - 103rd Ave. NW, Edmonton, AB T5J 0K4

Tel: 780-426-5330; *Fax:* 780-428-1066
www.dlapiper.com/en/canada

Profile: 23 Lawyers, Founded in: 2002
Senior and Managing Partners:
Veronica Monteiro, Edmonton Managing Partner
veronica.monteiro@dlapiper.com
Robert Seidel, Q.C., Canada Managing Partner
780-429-6814
robert.seidel@dlapiper.com

DLA Piper (Canada) S.E.N.C.R.L. - Montréal
Former Name: Davis LLP
#1400, Tour McGill College, 1501, av McGill College, Montréal, QC H3A 3M8

Tel: 514-392-1991; *Fax:* 514-392-1999
www.dlapiper.com/fr/canada

Profile: 15 Lawyers
Senior and Managing Partners:
Marc Philibert, Montréal Managing Partner
514-392-8442
marc.philibert@dlapiper.com

DLA Piper (Canada) LLP - Toronto
Former Name: Davis LLP
#6000, 1 First Canadian Place, P.O. Box 367, 100 King St. West, Toronto, ON M5X 1E2

Tel: 416-365-3500; *Fax:* 416-365-7886
www.dlapiper.com/en/canada

Profile: 88 Lawyers
Senior and Managing Partners:
Michael Richards, Toronto Managing Partner
416-941-5395
michael.richards@dlapiper.com

Farris LLP - Vancouver
Former Name: Farris, Vaughan, Wills & Murphy LLP
Pacific Centre South, P.O. Box 10026, 700 West Georgia St., 25th Fl., Vancouver, BC V7Y 1B3

Tel: 604-684-9151; *Fax:* 604-661-9349
Toll-Free: 877-684-9151
info@farris.com
farris.com

www.facebook.com/farrisllp, www.linkedin.com/company/farrisllp
Profile: 3 Offices, 100 Lawyers, Founded in: 1903
The firm has experience in the areas of acquisitions, reorganizations, mergers, joint ventures, public securities issues, private placements & banking transactions; also European & U.S. / Canada financings; counsel in real estate financings for both borrower & lender; acquisitions financings & privatization transactions.
Senior and Managing Partners:
Jeffrey J. Kay, Q.C., Firm Managing Partner
604-661-9321
jkay@farris.com

Farris LLP - Kelowna
#1800, 1631 Dickson Ave., Kelowna, BC V1Y 0B5

Tel: 250-861-5332; *Fax:* 250-861-8772
info@farris.com
farris.com

Profile: 13 Lawyers
Senior and Managing Partners:
Peter C.T. MacPherson, Office Managing Partner
250-869-3881
pmacpherson@farris.com

Farris LLP - Victoria
1005 Langley St., 3rd Fl., Victoria, BC V8W 1V7

Tel: 250-382-1100; *Fax:* 250-405-1984
info@farris.com
farris.com

Profile: 8 Lawyers, Founded in: 2005

Fasken Martineau DuMoulin LLP - Toronto
Former Name: Fasken
#2400, Bay Adelaide Centre, P.O. Box 20, 333 Bay St., Toronto, ON M5H 2T6
Tel: 416-366-8381; *Fax:* 416-364-7813
Toll-Free: 800-268-8424
toronto@fasken.com
www.fasken.com
www.facebook.com/FaskenMartineau, twitter.com/faskenlaw,
www.linkedin.com/company/fasken
Profile: 7 Offices, 786 Lawyers, Founded in: 1863
Fasken is primarily a business law & litigation firm with ten offices worldwide. Financial areas of expertise include banking & finance; corporate & commercial; estate planning; insolvency & restructuring; investment products; mergers & acquisitions; private equity & venture capital; real estate; start-ups & emerging companies & tax.
Senior and Managing Partners:
Martin K. Denyes, Ontario Managing Partner
416-868-3489
mdenyes@fasken.com
Peter Feldberg, Firm Managing Partner
416-865-4563
pfeldberg@fasken.com

Fasken Martineau DuMoulin LLP - Calgary
#3400, First Canadian Centre, 350 - 7th Ave. SW, Calgary, AB T2P 3N9
Tel: 403-261-5350; *Fax:* 403-261-5351
Toll-Free: 877-336-5350
calgary@fasken.com
www.fasken.com/en/calgary
Profile: 51 Lawyers
Senior and Managing Partners:
Clarke Barnes, Calgary Managing Partner
403-261-5374
clbarnes@fasken.com

Fasken Martineau DuMoulin LLP - Montréal
#3500, P.O. Box 242, 800, rue du Square-Victoria, Montréal, QC H4Z 1E9
Tel: 514-397-7400; *Fax:* 514-397-7600
Toll-Free: 800-361-6266
montreal@fasken.com
www.fasken.com
Profile: 234 Lawyers
Senior and Managing Partners:
Éric Bédard, Québec Managing Partner
514-397-4314
ebedard@fasken.com

Fasken Martineau DuMoulin LLP - Ottawa
#1300, 55 Metcalfe St., Ottawa, ON K1P 6L5
Tel: 613-236-3882; *Fax:* 613-230-6423
Toll-Free: 877-609-5685
ottawa@fasken.com
www.fasken.com
Profile: 35 Lawyers
Senior and Managing Partners:
Scott M. Prescott, Co-Managing Partner
613-236-3882
sprescott@fasken.com
Virginia K. Schweitzer, Co-Managing Partner
613-696-6889
vschweitzer@fasken.com

Fasken Martineau DuMoulin LLP - Québec
#800, 140, Grande Allée est, Québec, QC G1R 5M8
Tel: 418-640-2000; *Fax:* 418-647-2455
Toll-Free: 800-463-2827
quebec@fasken.com
www.fasken.com
Profile: 59 Lawyers
Senior and Managing Partners:
Carl Tremblay, Québec Managing Partner
418-640-2055
ctremblay@fasken.com

Fasken Martineau DuMoulin LLP - Surrey
#1800, 13401 - 108th Ave., Surrey, BC V3T 5T3
Tel: 604-631-3131; *Fax:* 604-631-3232
Toll-Free: 866-635-3131
surrey@fasken.com
www.fasken.com
Profile: 10 Lawyers

Fasken Martineau DuMoulin LLP - Vancouver
#2900, 550 Burrard St., Vancouver, BC V6C 0A3
Tel: 604-631-3131; *Fax:* 604-631-3232
Toll-Free: 866-635-3131
vancouver@fasken.com
www.fasken.com
Profile: 148 Lawyers
Senior and Managing Partners:

William Westeringh, Q.C., BC Managing Partner
604-631-3155
wwesteringh@fasken.com

Field LLP - Edmonton
Also Known As: Field Law
#2500, 10175 - 101st St. NW, Edmonton, AB T5J 0H3
Tel: 780-423-3003; *Fax:* 780-428-9329
Toll-Free: 800-222-6479
info@fieldlaw.com
www.fieldlaw.com
www.facebook.com/fieldlaw, twitter.com/FieldLaw,
www.linkedin.com/companies/field-law
Profile: 3 Offices, 120 Lawyers, Founded in: 1915
Field Law offers the following financial services: negotiation; preparation & registration of security; foreclosures & collections; security realization; negotiation & finalization of loan agreements; regulatory compliance matters; financing agreements; security enforcement matters; loan restructuring; reorganizations & work-outs; bankruptcy; & insolvency & receivership.
Senior and Managing Partners:
Ayla Akgungor, Partner & Practice Group Lead
780-423-9595
aakgungor@fieldlaw.com
Brian Futoransky, Partner & Practice Group Lead
780-643-8758
bfutoransky@fieldlaw.com
Gregory Sim, Partner & Practice Group Lead
780-423-7673
gsim@fieldlaw.com
Peter Gibson, Partner & Practice Group Lead
780-423-7631
pgibson@fieldlaw.com
Jay Guthrie, Partner & Practice Group Lead
780-423-7634
jguthrie@fieldlaw.com
Jeremy Taylor, Partner & Practice Group Lead
780-423-7624
jtaylor@fieldlaw.com
Jeremiah Kowalchuk, Firm Managing Partner
780-643-8768
jkowalchuk@fieldlaw.com

Field LLP - Calgary
Also Known As: Field Law
#400, 444 - 7th Ave. SW, Calgary, AB T2P 0X8
Tel: 403-260-8500; *Fax:* 403-264-7084
Toll-Free: 877-260-6515
info@fieldlaw.com
fieldlaw.com
Profile: 61 Lawyers
Senior and Managing Partners:
Robert Rakochey, Partner & Practice Group Lead
403-232-1767
rrakochey@fieldlaw.com
Kevin Schouten, Partner & Practice Group Lead
403-260-8552
kschouten@fieldlaw.com
Laura MacFarlane, Partner & Practice Group Lead
403-260-8577
lmacfarlane@fieldlaw.com

Field LLP - Yellowknife
Also Known As: Field Law
#601, 4920 - 52nd St., Yellowknife, NT X1A 3T1
Tel: 867-920-4542; *Fax:* 867-873-4790
Toll-Free: 800-753-1294
info@fieldlaw.com
fieldlaw.com
Profile: 1 Lawyers

Fogler, Rubinoff LLP - Toronto
#3000, TD Centre, North Tower, P.O. Box 95, 77 King St. West, Toronto, ON M5K 1G8
Tel: 416-864-9700; *Fax:* 416-941-8852
Toll-Free: 866-861-9700
info@foglers.com
www.foglers.com
twitter.com/foglerrubinoff,
www.linkedin.com/company/fogler-rubinoff-llp
Profile: 2 Offices, 113 Lawyers, Founded in: 1982
Practice areas include: Banking & Financial; Capital Markets & Securities; Commercial Real Estate; Corporate Commercial; Employment & Labour; Insolvency & Restructuring; Intellectual Property; Tax; & Wills & Estates.
Senior and Managing Partners:
Lloyd S.D. Fogler, Q.C., Firm Founding Partner
416-941-8810
lsdf@foglers.com
Michael S. Slan, FirmManaging Partner
416-941-8857
mslan@foglers.com

Michael H. Appleton, Q.C., Managing Partner Emeritus
416-941-8801
mha@foglers.com

Fogler, Rubinoff LLP - Ottawa
#701, 116 Albert St., Ottawa, ON K1P 5G3
Fax: 613-842-7445
Toll-Free: 866-363-8386
info@foglers.com
www.foglers.com
Profile: 2 Lawyers

Goodmans LLP - Toronto
Former Name: Goodman Phillips & Vineberg
#3400, Bay Adelaide Centre, West Tower, 333 Bay St., Toronto, ON M5H 2S7
Tel: 416-979-2211; *Fax:* 416-979-1234
info@goodmans.ca
www.goodmans.ca
twitter.com/GoodmansLLP
Profile: 1 Offices, 184 Lawyers, Founded in: 1917
Goodmans is a full-service business law firm that offers clients a wide range of services & expertise in all of the major business law areas, including: Broadcasting, Telecommunications & New Media; Commercial Real Estate; Corporate & Commercial Law; Corporate Restructuring; Corporate Finance & Securities; Litigation; Mergers & Acquisitions; Municipal, Planning & Property Tax Law; Pensions; Trusts & Estates & Tax.
Senior and Managing Partners:
Dale Lastman, C.M., Partner & Firm Chair
416-597-4129
dlastman@goodmans.ca

Gowling WLG (Canada) LLP - Toronto
Former Name: Gowling Lafleur Henderson LLP
#1600, 1 First Canadian Place, 100 King St. West, Toronto, ON M5X 1G5
Tel: 416-862-7525; *Fax:* 416-862-7661
gowlingwlg.com
www.facebook.com/gowlingwlgcanada,
twitter.com/gowlingwlg_ca,
www.linkedin.com/company/gowlingwlg
Profile: 8 Offices, 727 Lawyers, Founded in: 2015
In 2015, Gowling Lafleur Henderson LLP merged with UK firm Wragge Lawrence Graham & Co to create the international firm Gowling WLG International Limited. The firm offers legal services & solutions in many areas of business & corporate law. In addition, the firm's practice groups include the areas of intellectual property law, advocacy, international trade law, technology law, administrative law, & government affairs. Both Gowling WLG (Canada) LLP & Gowling WLG (UK) LLP operate as independent & autonomous entities.
Senior and Managing Partners:
James H. Buchan, Firm Managing Partner
416-862-4426
james.buchan@gowlingwlg.com
Mark Ledwell, Toronto ManagingPartner
416-862-4652
mark.ledwell@gowlingwlg.com
Peter J. Lukasiewicz, Chief Executive Officer
416-862-4328
peter.lukasiewicz@gowlingwlg.com
Tina M. Woodside, Firm Managing Partner
416-369-4584
tina.woodside@gowlingwlg.com

Gowling WLG (Canada) LLP - Calgary
Former Name: Code Hunter; Ballem MacInnes
#1600, 421 - 7th Ave. SW, Calgary, AB T2P 4K9
Tel: 403-298-1000; *Fax:* 403-263-9193
gowlingwlg.com
Profile: 90 Lawyers
Senior and Managing Partners:
Regina M. Corrigan, Calgary Managing Partner
403-298-1964
regina.corrigan@gowlingwlg.com
Dan Polonenko, Firm Principal
403-298-1950
dan.polonenko@gowlingwlg.com

Gowling WLG (Canada) LLP - Hamilton
1 Main St. West, Hamilton, ON L8P 4Z5
Tel: 905-540-8208; *Fax:* 905-528-5833
gowlingwlg.com
Profile: 42 Lawyers
Senior and Managing Partners:
Pam Vermeersch, Hamilton Managing Partner
905-540-3247
pam.vermeersch@gowlingwlg.com

Gowling WLG (Canada) LLP - Hamilton - King St.
#1500, 1 King St. West, Hamilton, ON L8P 1A4
Tel: 905-540-8208; *Fax:* 905-528-5833
gowlingwlg.com

Gowling WLG (Canada) LLP - Kitchener
#1020, P.O. Box 2248, 50 Queen St. North, Kitchener, ON
N2H 6M2
Tel: 519-576-6910; Fax: 519-576-6030
gowlingwlg.com
Profile: 55 Lawyers
Senior and Managing Partners:
Bryce Kraeker, Waterloo Reg. Managing Partner
519-575-7545
bryce.kraeker@gowlingwlg.com

Gowling WLG (Canada) S.E.N.C.R.L./LLP - Montréal
#3700, 1, Place Ville Marie, Montréal, QC H3B 3P4
Tel: 514-878-9641; Fax: 514-878-1450
gowlingwlg.com
Profile: 93 Lawyers
Senior and Managing Partners:
Pierre Pilote, Montréal Managing Partner
514-392-9536
pierre.pilote@gowlingwlg.com

Gowling WLG (Canada) LLP - Ottawa
#2600, 160 Elgin St., Ottawa, ON K1P 1C3
Tel: 613-233-1781; Fax: 613-563-9869
gowlingwlg.com
Profile: 207 Lawyers
Senior and Managing Partners:
Wayne B. Warren, Ottawa Managing Partner
613-786-0191
wayne.warren@gowlingwlg.com

Gowling WLG (Canada) LLP - Vancouver
#2300, Bentall V, 550 Burrard St., Vancouver, BC V6C 2B5
Tel: 604-683-6498; Fax: 604-683-3558
gowlingwlg.com
Profile: 67 Lawyers
Senior and Managing Partners:
A. Brent Kerr, Q.C., Vancouver Managing Partner
604-891-2788
brent.kerr@gowlingwlg.com

Hicks Morley Hamilton Stewart Storie LLP - Toronto
Also Known As: Hicks Morley
TD Centre, P.O. Box 371, 77 King St. West, 39th Fl., Toronto,
ON M5K 1K8
Tel: 416-362-1011; Fax: 416-362-9680
hicksmorley.com
Profile: 5 Offices, 122 Lawyers,
The firm is exclusively devoted to representing employers on
human resources law & advocacy issues. Financial practice
areas include pensions & benefits & workplace safety &
insurance
Senior and Managing Partners:
Craig S. Rix, Toronto Managing Partner
416-864-7284
craig-rix@hicksmorley.com

Hicks Morley Hamilton Stewart Storie LLP - Kingston
#310, 366 King St. East, Kingston, ON K7K 6Y3
Tel: 613-549-6353; Fax: 613-549-4068
hicksmorley.com
Profile: 3 Lawyers

Hicks Morley Hamilton Stewart Storie LLP - London
#1608, 148 Fullerton St., London, ON N6A 5P3
Tel: 519-433-7515; Fax: 519-433-8827
hicksmorley.com
Profile: 5 Lawyers

Hicks Morley Hamilton Stewart Storie LLP - Ottawa
#2000, 150 Metcalfe St., Ottawa, ON K2P 1P1
Tel: 613-234-0386; Fax: 613-234-0418
hicksmorley.com
Profile: 8 Lawyers

Hicks Morley Hamilton Stewart Storie LLP - Waterloo
#404, 150 Caroline St. South, Waterloo, ON N2L 0A5
Tel: 519-746-0411; Fax: 519-746-4037
hicksmorley.com
Profile: 7 Lawyers

Langlois Avocats - Québec
Former Name: Langlois Kronström Desjardins
Complexe Jules-Dallaire, T3, 2820, boul Laurier, 13e étage,
Québec, QC G1V 0C1
Tél: 418-650-7000; Téléc: 418-650-7075
Ligne sans frais: 888-650-7001
info@langlois.ca
langlois.ca
www.facebook.com/LangloisAvocats,
twitter.com/LangloisAvocats,
www.linkedin.com/company/langloisavocats
Profile: 2 Offices, 128 Lawyers,
The firm is one of the largest in Québec. Financial areas of

practice include Bankruptcy, Insolvency & Restructuring;
Business; Financial Services & Insurance.

Langlois Avocats - Montréal
1250, boul René-Lévesque ouest, 20e étage, Montréal, QC
H3B 4W8
Tel: 514-842-9512; Fax: 514-845-6573
Toll-Free: 888-650-7001
info@langlois.ca
langlois.ca
Senior and Managing Partners:
Jean-François Gagnon, CEO & Partner
514-842-7801
jean-francois.gagnon@langlois.ca

Lavery, de Billy - Montréal
#4000, 1, Place Ville-Marie, Montréal, QC H3B 4M4
Tel: 514-871-1522; Fax: 514-871-8977
info@lavery.ca
www.facebook.com/laveryavocats, twitter.com/Laveryavocats,
www.linkedin.com/company/lavery-avocats
Profile: 4 Offices, 175 Lawyers, Founded in: 1913
The firm practices in financial areas such as corporate &
commercial law; business succession; debt financing; financial
products & services; class actions; pension & benefits; private
equity; real estate; securities & franchises.
Senior and Managing Partners:
Anik Trudel, Firm Chief Executive Officer
514-878-5555
atrudel@lavery.ca

Lavery, de Billy - Sherbrooke
#200, Cité du Parc, 95, boul Jacques Cartier sud,
Sherbrooke, QC J1J 2Z3
Tel: 819-346-5058; Fax: 819-346-5007
www.lavery.ca
Profile: 19 Lawyers, Founded in: 1913
Senior and Managing Partners:
Christian Dumoulin, Sherbrooke Managing Partner
819-346-4430
cdumoulin@lavery.ca

Lavery, de Billy - Québec
#500, 925, Grande Allée ouest, Québec, QC G1S 1C1
Tel: 418-688-5000; Fax: 418-688-3458
www.lavery.ca
Profile: 24 Lawyers, Founded in: 1913
Senior and Managing Partners:
Simon Clément, Québec Managing Partner
418-266-3087
sclement@lavery.ca

Lavery, de Billy - Trois-Rivières
#360, 1500, rue Royale, Trois-Rivières, QC G9A 6E6
Tel: 819-373-7000; Fax: 819-373-0943
www.lavery.ca
Profile: 7 Lawyers
Senior and Managing Partners:
Marie-Josée Hétu, Managing Partner
819-373-4274
mjhetu@lavery.ca

Lawson Lundell LLP - Vancouver
Former Name: Lawson, Lundell, Lawson & McIntosh
#1600, Cathedral Place, 925 West Georgia St., Vancouver,
BC V6C 3L2
Tel: 604-685-3456; Fax: 604-669-1620
inquiries@lawsonlundell.com
www.lawsonlundell.com
twitter.com/LawsonLundell,
www.linkedin.com/company/lawsonlundell
Profile: 4 Offices, 170 Lawyers, Founded in: 1886
The firm's range of practice includes: corporate finance, mergers
& acquisitions, general business & commercial matters,
pensions, tax, labour & employment, real estate, Aboriginal
issues, mining, energy, public utility, oil & gas, regulatory &
resolution of disputes through negotiations, mediation arbitration
or litigation.
Senior and Managing Partners:
Clifford Proudfoot, Q.C., Firm Managing Partner
604-631-9217
cproudfoot@lawsonlundell.com

Lawson Lundell LLP - Calgary
#1100, Brookfield Place, 225 - 6th Ave. SW, Calgary, AB T2P
1N2
Tel: 403-269-6900; Fax: 403-269-9494
www.lawsonlundell.com
Profile: 40 Lawyers

Lawson Lundell LLP - Kelowna
#403, 460 Doyle Ave., Kelowna, BC V1Y 0B5
Tel: 778-738-2610
www.lawsonlundell.com

Profile: 2 Lawyers

Lawson Lundell LLP - Yellowknife
Former Name: Gullberg, Weist, MacPherson & Kay
#200, P.O. Box 818, 4915 - 48th St., Yellowknife, NT X1A 2N6
Tel: 867-669-5500; Fax: 867-920-2206
Toll-Free: 888-465-7608
www.lawsonlundell.com
Profile: 8 Lawyers

McCarthy Tétrault LLP - Toronto
#5300, TD Bank Tower, Box 48, 66 Wellington St. West,
Toronto, ON M5K 1E6
Tel: 416-362-1812; Fax: 416-868-0673
Toll-Free: 877-244-7711
info@mccarthy.ca
www.facebook.com/McCarthyTetrault, twitter.com/McCarthy_ca,
www.linkedin.com/company/mccarthy-tetrault
Profile: 5 Offices, 1034 Lawyers, Founded in: 1855
McCarthy Tétrault is a Canadian integrated business law firm
that also has international offices in London, UK & New York,
NY. Financial areas of expertise include: bankruptcy &
restructuring; business; competition & antitrust; foreign
investment; labour & employment; business litigation; real
estate; tax; FinTech & retail.
Senior and Managing Partners:
Godyne N.L. Sibay, Ontario Managing Partner
416-601-7748
gsibay@mccarthy.ca

McCarthy Tétrault LLP - Calgary
#4000, 421 - 7th Ave. SW, Calgary, AB T2P 4K9
Tel: 403-260-3500; Fax: 403-260-3501
Toll-Free: 877-244-7711
info@mccarthy.ca
www.mccarthy.ca
Profile: 110 Lawyers
Senior and Managing Partners:
Olivia Colic, AB Region Managing Partner
403-260-3661
ocolic@mccarthy.ca

McCarthy Tétrault LLP - Montréal
#2500, 1000, rue de la Gauchetière ouest, Montréal, QC H3B
0A2
Tel: 514-397-4100; Fax: 514-875-6246
Toll-Free: 877-244-7711
info@mccarthy.ca
www.mccarthy.ca
Profile: 251 Lawyers
Senior and Managing Partners:
Karl Tabbakh, Québec Region Managing Partner
514-397-2326
ktabbakh@mccarthy.ca

McCarthy Tétrault LLP - Québec
500, Grande Allée est, 9e étage, Québec, QC G1R 2J7
Tel: 418-521-3000; Fax: 418-521-3099
Toll-Free: 877-244-7711
info@mccarthy.ca
www.mccarthy.ca
Profile: 42 Lawyers
Senior and Managing Partners:
Mathieu Laflamme, Québec Office Lead Partner
418-521-3018
mlaflamme@mccarthy.ca

McCarthy Tétrault LLP - Vancouver
#2400, 745 Thurlow St., Vancouver, BC V6E 0C5
Tel: 604-643-7100; Fax: 604-643-7900
Toll-Free: 877-244-7711
info@mccarthy.ca
www.mccarthy.ca
Profile: 140 Lawyers
Senior and Managing Partners:
Sven O. Milelli, BC Region Managing Partner
604-643-7125
smilelli@mccarthy.ca

McInnes Cooper - Halifax
#1300, McInnes Cooper Tower, Purdy's Wharf, 1969 Upper
Water St., Halifax, NS B3J 3R7
Tel: 902-425-6500; Fax: 902-425-6350
www.mcinnescooper.com
www.facebook.com/mcinnescooperlaw,
twitter.com/mcinnescooper,
www.linkedin.com/company/mcinnescooper
Profile: 6 Offices, 178 Lawyers, Founded in: 1859
Financial law services include: Banking & Financial Services;
Bankruptcy & Insolvency; Business Disputes; Corporate &
Business; Corporate Finance & Securities; Corporate
Governance; Estates & Trusts; Pensions & Benefits; & Tax,
among others.

Senior and Managing Partners:
Basia Dzierzanowska, Office Lead Partner
902-444-8485
basia.dzierzanowska@mcinnescooper.com
Brad Proctor, Office Lead Partner
902-444-8595
brad.proctor@mcinnescooper.com
Wendy J. Johnston, Q.C., Counsel; Practice Group Leader
902-444-8433
wendy.johnston@mcinnescooper.com
Jeff Blucher, T.E.P., Practice Group Leader
902-444-8514
jeffrey.blucher@mcinnescooper.com

McInnes Cooper - Charlottetown
#300, McInnes Cooper Bldg., 141 Kent St., Charlottetown, PE C1A 1N3
Tel: 902-368-8473; *Fax:* 902-368-8346
www.mcinnescooper.com
Profile: 13 Lawyers
Senior and Managing Partners:
Gary Scales, Office Lead Partner
902-629-6271
gary.scales@mcinnescooper.com
Kevin J. Kiley, Firm Managing Partner
902-629-6262
kevin.kiley@mcinnescooper.com

McInnes Cooper - Fredericton
#600, Barker House, P.O. Box 610, Stn. A, 570 Queen St., Fredericton, NB E3B 5A6
Tel: 506-458-8572; *Fax:* 506-458-9903
www.mcinnescooper.com
Profile: 15 Lawyers
Senior and Managing Partners:
Leonard T. Hoyt, Q.C., Office Lead Partner
506-458-1622
len.hoyt@mcinnescooper.com

McInnes Cooper - Moncton
#400, South Tower, Blue Cross Bldg., 644 Main St., Moncton, NB E1C 1E2
Tel: 506-857-8970; *Fax:* 506-857-4095
www.mcinnescooper.com
Profile: 15 Lawyers
Senior and Managing Partners:
Chris Borden, Office Lead Partner
506-877-0878
christopher.borden@mcinnescooper.com

McInnes Cooper - Saint John
#1700, Brunswick Square, Stn. A, 1 Germain St., Saint John, NB E2L 4V1
Tel: 506-643-6500; *Fax:* 506-643-6505
www.mcinnescooper.com
Profile: 12 Lawyers
Senior and Managing Partners:
James C. Mosher, Office Lead Partner
506-633-3803
james.mosher@mcinnescooper.com
Matthew T. Hayes, Practice Group Leader
506-643-6509
matt.hayes@mcinnescooper.com

McInnes Cooper - St. John's
Baine Johnston Centre, 10 Fort William Place, 5th Fl., St. John's, NL A1C 1K4
Tel: 709-722-8735; *Fax:* 709-722-1763
www.mcinnescooper.com
Profile: 36 Lawyers, Founded in: 1859
Senior and Managing Partners:
Geoffrey Spencer, Regional Lead Partner
709-724-5675
geoffrey.spencer@mcinnescooper.com
Darren Stratton, Practice Group Leader
709-724-8236
darren.stratton@mcinnescooper.com
Beth McGrath, Practice Group Leader
709-570-7342
beth.mcgrath@mcinnescooper.com

McLennan Ross LLP - Edmonton
#600, McLennan Ross Bldg., 12220 Stony Plain Rd., Edmonton, AB T5N 3Y4
Tel: 780-482-9200; *Fax:* 780-482-9100
Toll-Free: 800-567-9200
www.mross.com
twitter.com/mclennanrosslaw,
www.linkedin.com/company/mclennan-ross-llp
Profile: 3 Offices, 110 Lawyers, Founded in: 1903
Senior and Managing Partners:
Steve Livingstone, Firm Managing Partner
780-482-9242
slivingstone@mross.com

McLennan Ross LLP - Calgary
#1900, Eau Claire Tower, 600 - 3rd Ave. SW, Calgary, AB T2P 0G5
Tel: 403-543-9120; *Fax:* 403-543-9150
Toll-Free: 888-543-9120
www.mross.com
Profile: 46 Lawyers, Founded in: 1903

McLennan Ross LLP - Yellowknife
#301, Nunasi Bldg., 5109 - 48th St., Yellowknife, NT X1A 1N5
Tel: 867-766-7677; *Fax:* 867-766-7678
Toll-Free: 888-836-6684
www.mross.com
Profile: 6 Lawyers

McMillan LLP - Toronto
Former Name: McMillan Binch LLP/Mendelsohn GP; McMillan Binch Mendelsohn
#4400, Brookfield Place, 181 Bay St., Toronto, ON M5J 2T3
Tel: 416-865-7000; *Fax:* 416-865-7048
Toll-Free: 888-622-4624
info@mcmillan.ca
mcmillan.ca
twitter.com/mcmillanllp, www.linkedin.com/company/mcmillanllp
Profile: 6 Offices, 274 Lawyers, Founded in: 1903
McMillan LLP is a Canadian business law firm, which also has one office in Hong Kong. Financial areas of expertise include: business; capital markets; competition & antitrust; employment & labour; financial services; international trade; mergers & acquisitions; restructuring & insolvency; tax & intellectual property.
Senior and Managing Partners:
Teresa Dufort, Partner & Firm CEO
416-865-7145
teresa.dufort@mcmillan.ca
Eric B. Friedman, Toronto Managing Partner
416-307-4030
eric.friedman@mcmillan.ca

McMillan LLP - Calgary
Former Name: Lang Michener LLP
#1700, TD Canada Trust Tower, 421 - 7th Ave. SW, Calgary, AB T2P 4K9
Tel: 403-531-4700; *Fax:* 403-531-4720
info@mcmillan.ca
mcmillan.ca
Profile: 22 Lawyers, Founded in: 1951
Senior and Managing Partners:
Adam C. Maerov, Calgary Managing Partner
403-215-2752
adam.maerov@mcmillan.ca

McMillan S.E.N.C.R.L., s.r.l. - Montréal
Former Name: Lang Michener LLP
#2700, 1000, rue Sherbrooke ouest, Montréal, QC H3A 3G4
Tel: 514-987-5000; *Fax:* 514-987-1213
info@mcmillan.ca
mcmillan.ca
Profile: 34 Lawyers, Founded in: 1951
Senior and Managing Partners:
Shari Munk-Manel, Montréal Managing Partner
514-987-5004
shari.munk-manel@mcmillan.ca

McMillan LLP - Ottawa
Former Name: Lang Michener LLP
#2000, World Exchange Plaza, 45 O'Connor St., Ottawa, ON K1P 1A4
Tel: 613-232-7171; *Fax:* 613-231-3191
info@mcmillan.ca
mcmillan.ca
Profile: 14 Lawyers, Founded in: 1984
Senior and Managing Partners:
Martin J. Thompson, Ottawa Managing Partner
613-691-6104
martin.thompson@mcmillan.ca

McMillan LLP - Vancouver
Former Name: Lang Michener LLP
#1500, Royal Centre, P.O. Box 11117, 1055 West Georgia St., Vancouver, BC V6E 4N7
Tel: 604-689-9111; *Fax:* 604-685-7084
info@mcmillan.ca
mcmillan.ca
Profile: 67 Lawyers, Founded in: 1926
Senior and Managing Partners:
Cory Kent, Vancouver Managing Partner
604-691-7446
cory.kent@mcmillan.ca

Miller Thomson LLP - Toronto
#5800, Scotia Plaza, P.O. Box 1011, 40 King St. West, Toronto, ON M5H 3S1
Tel: 416-595-8500; *Fax:* 416-595-8695
Toll-Free: 888-762-5559
toronto@millerthomson.com
www.millerthomson.com
twitter.com/millerthomson,
www.linkedin.com/company/miller-thomson-llp
Profile: 12 Offices, 502 Lawyers, Founded in: 1957
Miller Thomson LLP is a full-service national law firm. Financial areas of expertise include: capital markets & securities; competition & antitrust; corporate & commercial; financial services; insolvency; mergers & acquisitions; private equity; labour & employment; pensions & benefits; class actions; estates; insurance; real estate & tax.
Senior and Managing Partners:
Nora F. Osbaldeston, Office Managing Partner
416-595-8680
nosbaldeston@millerthomson.com

Miller Thomson LLP - Calgary
#3000, 700 - 9th Ave. SW, Calgary, AB T2P 3V4
Tel: 403-298-2400; *Fax:* 403-262-0007
Toll-Free: 888-298-2400
calgary@millerthomson.com
www.millerthomson.com
Profile: 41 Lawyers, Founded in: 1987
Senior and Managing Partners:
Michael J. Morcom, Office Managing Partner
403-298-2414
mmorcom@millerthomson.com

Miller Thomson LLP - Edmonton
10155 - 102nd St., Edmonton, AB T5J 4G8
Tel: 780-429-1751; *Fax:* 780-424-5866
Toll-Free: 800-215-1016
edmonton@millerthomson.com
www.millerthomson.com
Profile: 53 Lawyers, Founded in: 1953
Senior and Managing Partners:
Sandra L. Hawes, Q.C., Office Managing Partner
780-429-9787
hawes@millerthomson.com

Miller Thomson LLP - Guelph
#301, 100 Stone Rd. West, Guelph, ON N1G 5L3
Tel: 519-822-4680; *Fax:* 519-822-1583
Toll-Free: 866-658-0092
guelph@millerthompson.com
www.millerthomson.com
Profile: 17 Lawyers, Founded in: 1906

Miller Thomson LLP - London
#2010, 255 Queens Ave., London, ON N6A 5R8
Tel: 519-931-3500; *Fax:* 519-858-8511
Toll-Free: 877-319-3500
london@millerthomson.com
www.millerthomson.com
Profile: 15 Lawyers

Miller Thomson LLP - Markham
#600, 60 Columbia Way, Markham, ON L3R 0C9
Tel: 905-415-6700; *Fax:* 905-415-6777
Toll-Free: 866-348-2432
markham@millerthomson.com
www.millerthomson.com
Profile: 9 Lawyers, Founded in: 1957
Senior and Managing Partners:
Andy Chan, Office Managing Partner
905-532-6612
achan@millerthomson.com

Miller Thomson LLP - Montréal
#3700, 1000, rue de la Gauchetière ouest, Montréal, QC H3B 4W5
Tél: 514-875-5210; *Téléc:* 514-875-4308
Ligne sans frais: 888-875-5210
montreal@millerthomson.com
www.millerthomson.com
Profile: 72 Lawyers, Founded in: 1952
Senior and Managing Partners:
Philipp Park, Office Managing Partner
514-871-5446
ppark@millerthomson.com

Miller Thomson LLP - Regina
Former Name: Balfour Moss
#600, 2103 - 11th Ave., Regina, SK S4P 3Z8
Tel: 306-347-8300; *Fax:* 306-347-8350
Toll-Free: 855-347-8300
regina@millerthomson.com
www.millerthomson.com
Profile: 20 Lawyers

Miller Thomson LLP - Saskatoon
Former Name: Balfour Moss
#300, 15 - 23rd St. East, Saskatoon, SK S7K 0H6
Tel: 306-665-7844; *Fax:* 306-652-1586
Toll-Free: 855-665-7844
saskatoon@millerthomson.com
www.millerthomson.com
Profile: 11 Lawyers, Founded in: 2010
Senior and Managing Partners:
David G. Gerecke, Saskatchewan Managing Partner
306-667-5615
dgerecke@millerthomson.com

Miller Thomson LLP - Vancouver
#400, Pacific Centre, 725 Granville St., Vancouver, BC V7Y 1G5
Tel: 604-687-2242; *Fax:* 604-643-1200
Toll-Free: 800-794-6866
vancouver@millerthomson.com
www.millerthomson.com
Profile: 59 Lawyers, Founded in: 2000
Senior and Managing Partners:
Rory Godinho, Office Managing Partner
604-643-1282
rgodinho@millerthomson.com

Miller Thomson LLP - Vaughan
#700, 100 New Park Pl., Vaughan, ON L4K 0H9
Tel: 905-532-6600; *Fax:* 905-660-0139
Toll-Free: 866-591-5778
vaughan@millerthomson.com
www.millerthomson.com
Profile: 30 Lawyers, Founded in: 2017
Senior and Managing Partners:
Andy Chan, Office Managing Partner
905-532-6612
achan@millerthomson.com

Miller Thomson LLP - Waterloo
#300, 295 Hagey Blvd., Waterloo, ON N2L 6R5
Tel: 519-579-3660; *Fax:* 519-743-2540
Toll-Free: 866-658-0091
waterloo@millerthomson.com
www.millerthomson.com
Profile: 30 Lawyers, Founded in: 1876
Senior and Managing Partners:
Steven Lubczuk, SW Ontario Managing Partner
519-593-2434
slubczuk@millerthomson.com

MLT Aikins LLP - Winnipeg
Former Name: MacPherson Leslie & Tyerman LLP
360 Main St., 30th Fl., Winnipeg, MB R3C 4G1
Tel: 204-957-0050; *Fax:* 204-957-0840
www.mltaikins.com
twitter.com/mltaikins, www.linkedin.com/company/mlt-aikins
Profile: 6 Offices, 266 Lawyers,
MLT Aikins LLP, the result of a 2016 merger between
MacPherson Leslie & Tyerman LLP & Aikins, MacAulay &
Thorvaldson LLP, is a business-oriented law firm. Financial
areas of expertise include class actions; corporate &
commercial; debt collection; insolvency & restructuring;
insurance; litigation; pensions & benefits; real estate & taxation.

MLT Aikins LLP - Calgary
#2100, Livingston Place, 222 - 3rd Ave. SW, Calgary, AB T2P 0B4
Tel: 403-693-4300; *Fax:* 403-508-4349
www.mltaikins.com
Profile: 41 Lawyers

MLT Aikins LLP - Edmonton
#2200, 10235 - 101st St., Edmonton, AB T5J 3G1
Tel: 780-969-3500; *Fax:* 780-969-3549
www.mltaikins.com
Profile: 26 Lawyers
Senior and Managing Partners:

MLT Aikins LLP - Regina
#1500, Hill Center I, 1874 Scarth St., Regina, SK S4P 4E9
Tel: 306-347-8000; *Fax:* 306-352-5250
www.mltaikins.com
Profile: 46 Lawyers
Senior and Managing Partners:
Aaron Runge, Managing Partner
306-347-8490
arunge@mltaikins.com

MLT Aikins LLP - Saskatoon
#1201, 409 - 3rd Ave. South, Saskatoon, SK S7K 5R5
Tel: 306-975-7100; *Fax:* 306-975-7145
www.mltaikins.com
Profile: 42 Lawyers

MLT Aikins LLP - Vancouver
#2600, 1066 West Hastings St., Vancouver, BC V6E 3X1
Tel: 604-682-7737; *Fax:* 604-682-7131
www.mltaikins.com
Profile: 25 Lawyers

Norton Rose Fulbright Canada LLP - Montréal
Former Name: Ogilvy Renault LLP/S.E.N.C.R.L., s.r.l. -
Montréal
#2500, 1, Place Ville Marie, Montréal, QC H3B 1R1
Tél: 514-847-4747
www.nortonrosefulbright.com/ca
www.facebook.com/NortonRoseFulbright,
twitter.com/NLawGlobal,
www.linkedin.com/company/nortonrosefulbright
Profile: 6 Offices, 641 Lawyers, Founded in: 1879
Financial areas of expertise include: acquisition finance &
corporate lending; antitrust; banking & finance; insolvency;
capital markets; class actions; corporate & commercial;
intellectual property; insurance; labour & employment; mergers
& acquisitions; patents & trademarks; pensions; real estate;
security; tax.
Senior and Managing Partners:
Solomon Sananes, Montréal Managing Partner
514-847-4411
solomon.sananes@nortonrosefulbright.com

Norton Rose Fulbright Canada LLP - Calgary
Also Known As: Norton Rose
Former Name: Ogilvy Renault LLP; Macleod Dixon LLP
#3700, 400 - 3rd Ave. SW, Calgary, AB T2P 4H2
Tel: 403-267-8222
www.nortonrosefulbright.com/ca
Profile: 119 Lawyers
Senior and Managing Partners:
Roger F. Smith, Managing Partner
403-257-9409
roger.smith@nortonrosefulbright.com

Norton Rose Fulbright Canada LLP - Ottawa
Also Known As: Norton Rose
Former Name: Ogilvy Renault LLP
#1500, 45 O'Connor St., Ottawa, ON K1P 1A4
Tel: 613-780-8661
www.nortonrosefulbright.com/ca
Profile: 44 Lawyers
Senior and Managing Partners:
Pierre-Paul Henrie, Ottawa Managing Partner
613-780-3777
pierre-paul.henrie@nortonrosefulbright.com
Charles E. Hurdon, Canada Managing Partner
613-780-8653
charles.hurdon@nortonrosefulbright.com

Norton Rose Fulbright Canada LLP - Québec
Also Known As: Norton Rose
Former Name: Ogilvy Renault LLP
**#1500, Complexe Jules-Dallaire / Tour Norton Rose
Fulbright, 2828, boul Laurier, Québec, QC G1V 0B9**
Tel: 418-640-5000
www.nortonrosefulbright.com/ca
Profile: 56 Lawyers
Senior and Managing Partners:
Olga Farman, Québec Managing Partner
418-640-5852
olga.farman@nortonrosefulbright.com

Norton Rose Fulbright Canada LLP - Toronto
Also Known As: Norton Rose
Former Name: Ogilvy Renault LLP
#3000, P.O. Box 53, 222 Bay St., Toronto, ON M5K 1E7
Tel: 416-216-4000
www.nortonrosefulbright.com/ca
Profile: 171 Lawyers
Senior and Managing Partners:
Terence S. Dobbin, Toronto Managing Partner
416-216-3935
terence.dobbin@nortonrosefulbright.com
Walied Soliman, Firm Chair
416-216-4820
walied.soliman@nortonrosefulbright.com

Norton Rose Fulbright Canada LLP - Vancouver
Also Known As: Norton Rose
Former Name: Ogilvy Renault LLP
#1800, 510 West Georgia St., Vancouver, BC V6B 0M3
Tel: 604-687-6575
www.nortonrosefulbright.com/ca
Profile: 95 Lawyers
Senior and Managing Partners:
Kieran Siddall, Vancouver Managing Partner
604-641-4868
kieran.siddall@nortonrosefulbright.com

Osler, Hoskin & Harcourt LLP - Toronto
Also Known As: Osler
**#6200, One First Canadian Place, P.O. Box 50, 100 King St.
West, Toronto, ON M5X 1B8**
Tel: 416-362-2111; *Fax:* 416-862-6666
www.osler.com
twitter.com/osler_law,
www.linkedin.com/company/osler-hoskin-&-harcourt-llp
Profile: 6 Offices, 507 Lawyers, Founded in: 1862
The firm specializes in mergers & acquisitions, tax, competition
& litigation, commercial property & infrastructure projects, IP &
IT, & more It also has one American office in New York, NY.
Senior and Managing Partners:
Douglas Bryce, National Managing Partner
416-862-6465
dbryce@osler.com
Dale R. Ponder, National Firm Co-Chair
416-862-6500
dponder@osler.com

Osler, Hoskin & Harcourt LLP - Calgary
#2700, Brookfield Place, 225 - 6th Ave. SW, Calgary, AB T2P 1N2
Tel: 403-260-7000; *Fax:* 403-260-7024
www.osler.com
Profile: 71 Lawyers
Senior and Managing Partners:
Shawn Denstedt, Q.C., Vice-Chair, Western Canada
403-260-7088
sdenstedt@osler.com
Brian Thiessen, Q.C., Calgary Managing Partner
403-260-7018
bthiessen@osler.com

Osler, Hoskin & Harcourt S.E.N.C.R.L./LLP - Montréal
#2100, 1000, rue de la Gauchetière ouest, Montréal, QC H3B 4W5
Tel: 514-904-8100; *Fax:* 514-904-8101
www.osler.com
Profile: 67 Lawyers
Senior and Managing Partners:
Sandra Abitan, Montréal Managing Partner
514-904-5648
sabitan@osler.com
Shahir Guindi, National Firm Co-Chair
514-904-8126
sguindi@osler.com

Osler, Hoskin & Harcourt LLP - Ottawa
#1900, 340 Albert St., Ottawa, ON K1R 7Y6
Tel: 613-235-7234; *Fax:* 613-235-2867
www.osler.com
Profile: 27 Lawyers
Senior and Managing Partners:
Donna White, Ottawa Managing Partner
613-787-1061
dwhite@osler.com

Osler, Hoskin & Harcourt LLP - Vancouver
#1700, Guinness Tower, 1055 West Hastings St., Vancouver, BC V6E 2E9
Tel: 778-785-3000; *Fax:* 778-785-2745
www.osler.com
Profile: 39 Lawyers
Senior and Managing Partners:
Mark Longo, Vancouver Managing Partner
778-785-2746
mlongo@osler.com

Stewart McKelvey - Halifax
Former Name: Stewart McKelvey Stirling Scales
#600, Queen's Marque, 1741 Lower Water St., Halifax, NS B3J 0J2
Tel: 902-420-3200; *Fax:* 902-420-1417
halifax@stewartmckelvey.com
www.stewartmckelvey.com
www.facebook.com/StewartMcKelveyLaw, twitter.com/SM_Law,
www.linkedin.com/company/stewart-mckelvey
Profile: 6 Offices, 225 Lawyers, Founded in: 1867
Financial areas of expertise include: business; commercial;
competition; corporate; estates; insurance; real estate; labour;
securities & tax.
Senior and Managing Partners:
Lydia Bugden, Firm Managing Partner & CEO
902-420-3372
lbugen@stewartmckelvey.com
Rebecca Saturley, Halifax Managing Partner
902-420-3333
rsaturley@stewartmckelvey.com

Stewart McKelvey - Charlottetown
65 Grafton St., Charlottetown, PE C1A 1K8
Tel: 902-892-2485; *Fax:* 902-566-5283
charlottetown@stewartmckelvey.com
www.stewartmckelvey.com
Profile: 24 Lawyers
Senior and Managing Partners:
Murray L. Murphy, Charlottetown Managing Partner
902-629-4558
mmurphy@stewartmckelvey.com

Stewart McKelvey - Fredericton
#501, 140 Carleton St., Fredericton, NB E3B 3T4
Tel: 506-458-1970; *Fax:* 506-444-8974
fredericton@stewartmckelvey.com
www.stewartmckelvey.com
Profile: 19 Lawyers
Senior and Managing Partners:
Nicholas Russon, Fredericton Managing Partner
506-443-0128
nrusson@stewartmckelvey.com

Stewart McKelvey - Moncton
#601, Blue Cross Centre, 644 Main St., Moncton, NB E1C 1E2
Tel: 506-853-1970; *Fax:* 506-858-8454
moncton@stewartmckelvey.com
www.stewartmckelvey.com
Profile: 17 Lawyers
Senior and Managing Partners:
Mathieu Poirier, Moncton ManagingPartner
506-853-1949
mpoirier@stewartmckelvey.com

Stewart McKelvey - Saint John
#1000, Brunswick House, 44 Chipman Hill, Saint John, NB E2L 2A9
Tel: 506-632-1970; *Fax:* 506-652-1989
saint-john@stewartmckelvey.com
www.stewartmckelvey.com
Profile: 28 Lawyers
Senior and Managing Partners:
Clarence Bennett, Saint John Managing Partner
506-634-6414
cbennett@stewartmckelvey.com

Stewart McKelvey - St. John's
#1100, Cabot Place, 100 New Gower St., St. John's, NL A1C 6K3
Tel: 709-722-4270; *Fax:* 709-722-4565
st-johns@stewartmckelvey.com
www.stewartmckelvey.com
Profile: 35 Lawyers
Senior and Managing Partners:
Tauna Staniland, St. John's Managing Partner
709-570-8842
tstaniland@stewartmckelvey.com

Stikeman Elliott LLP - Montréal
1155, boul René-Lévesque ouest, 41e étage, Montréal, QC H3B 3V2
Tel: 514-397-3000; *Fax:* 514-397-3222
www.stikeman.com
twitter.com/stikemanelliott,
www.linkedin.com/company/stikeman-elliott-llp
Profile: 8 Offices, 490 Lawyers, Founded in: 1952
Les spécialités du bureau de Montréal sont les fusions et les acquisitions, les restructurations financières transfrontalières, l'impartition, les valeurs mobilières, le droit bancaire, la fiscalité et les opérations sur les marchandises à l'échelle internationale, la technologie de l'information et le commerce électronique, le transport, le droit des assurances et le droit du travail. Le savoir-faire de Stikeman Elliott en droit civil et dans les opérations commerciales. La majorité du travail effectué par le bureau de Montréal porte principalement sur des activités internationales.
Senior and Managing Partners:
Warren M. Katz, Montréal Managing Partner
514-397-3260
wkatz@stikeman.com

Stikeman Elliott LLP - Calgary
#4300, Bankers Hall West, 888 - 3rd St. SW, Calgary, AB T2P 5C5
Tel: 403-266-9000; *Fax:* 403-266-9034
www.stikeman.com
Profile: 57 Lawyers, Founded in: 1992
Stikeman Elliott's Calgary office maintains a business law practice that is focused on mergers & acquisitions; securities; real estate; project finance; joint ventures; employment & tax.
Senior and Managing Partners:
Chrysten E. Perry, Calgary Managing Partner
403-266-9010
cperry@stikeman.com

Stikeman Elliott LLP - Ottawa
#1600, 50 O'Connor St., Ottawa, ON K1P 6L2
Tel: 613-234-4555; *Fax:* 613-230-8877
Toll-Free: 877-776-2263
www.stikeman.com
Profile: 9 Lawyers, Founded in: 1981
Stikeman Elliott's Ottawa office focuses on administrative law, with an emphasis on competition law & international trade.
Senior and Managing Partners:
Susan M. Hutton, Senior Partner
613-566-0530
shutton@stikeman.com
Justine M. Whitehead, Ottawa Managing Partner
613-566-0541
jwhitehead@stikeman.com

Stikeman Elliott LLP - Toronto
#5300, Commerce Court West, 199 Bay St., Toronto, ON M5L 1B9
Tel: 416-869-5500; *Fax:* 416-947-0866
Toll-Free: 877-973-5500
www.stikeman.com
Profile: 229 Lawyers,
Stikeman Elliott's Toronto office is a broad corporate & commercial law practice, with a strong focus on transactions. Financial specialties include: mergers & acquisitions; securities; banking; insolvency; taxation; real estate; employment & pensions. The office is renowned for its expertise in cross border transactional & litigation work.
Senior and Managing Partners:
John Ciardullo, Toronto Managing Partner
416-869-5235
jciardullo@stikeman.com
Jeffrey M. Singer, Firm Chair
416-869-5656
jsinger@stikeman.com
Anne Ristic, Toronto Co-Managing Partner
416-869-5682
aristic@stikeman.com

Stikeman Elliott LLP - Vancouver
#1700, Park Place, 666 Burrard St., Vancouver, BC V6C 2X8
Tel: 604-631-1300; *Fax:* 604-681-1825
www.stikeman.com
Profile: 45 Lawyers, Founded in: 1988
Stikeman Elliott's Vancouver practice includes lawyers that focus in mergers & acquisitions; securities; banking; real estate & litigation.
Senior and Managing Partners:
Richard J. Jackson, Vancouver Managing Partner
604-631-1357
rjackson@stikeman.com

Torkin Manes LLP
#1500, 151 Yonge St., Toronto, ON M5C 2W7
Tel: 416-863-1188; *Fax:* 416-863-0305
info@torkinmanes.com
www.torkinmanes.com
twitter.com/TorkinManesLLP,
www.linkedin.com/company/torkin-manes
Profile: 1 Offices, 107 Lawyers, Founded in: 1974
Services includes banking & financial services, business law, commercial real estate, corporate finance & securities, employment & labour law, insolvency & restructuring, insurance defence, international & cross-border business, mergers & acquisitions, private equity, tax law, & wills, trusts & estates
Senior and Managing Partners:
Barry S. Arbus, Q.C., Senior Partner
416-777-5423
barbus@torkinmanes.com
David M. Golden, Chair, Health Care Group
416-777-5408
dgolden@torkinmanes.com
Jeffrey I. Cohen, Managing Partner
416-777-5422
jcohen@torkinmanes.com
S. Fay Sulley, Partner & Head, Banking Group
416-777-5419
fsulley@torkinmanes.com
Neil M. Abramson, Chair, Litigation & Health
416-777-5454
nabramson@torkinmanes.com
Mark B. Harrington, Head, Insurance Defence
416-777-5358
mharrington@torkinmanes.com
Gregory D. Hersen, Chair, Construction Law
416-777-5400
ghersen@torkinmanes.com
Leonard D. Rodness, Chair, Commercial Real Estate
416-777-5409
lrodness@torkinmanes.com

Aaron M. English, Chair, Commercial Real Estate
416-643-8811
aenglish@torkinmanes.com
Linda J. Godel, Chair, Charities & NFP Group
416-643-8809
lgodel@torkinmanes.com
Andrew J. Wilder, Chair, Finance & Cannabis
416-777-5402
awilder@torkinmanes.com
Matt Maurer, Chair, Cannabis & Franchise
416-777-5452
mmaurer@torkinmanes.com

Torys LLP - Toronto
Former Name: Tory Tory DesLauriers & Binnington
TD South Tower, P.O. Box 270, 79 Wellington St. West, 30th Fl., Toronto, ON M5K 1N2
Tel: 416-865-0040; *Fax:* 416-865-7380
www.torys.com
www.facebook.com/TorysLLP, twitter.com/torysllp,
www.linkedin.com/company/torys-llp
Profile: 5 Offices, 370 Lawyers, Founded in: 1941
Torys LLP is an international business law firm providing services that include the following: mergers & acquisitions; corporate & capital markets; litigation & dispute resolution; restructuring & insolvency; taxation; competition & antitrust; environmental, health & safety; debt finance & lending; project development & finance; managed assets; private equity & venture capital; financial institutions; pension & employment; intellectual property; technology, media & telecom; life sciences; real estate; infrastructure & energy; climate change & emissions trading; & personal client services. It also has an office in New York, NY.
Senior and Managing Partners:
Matthew W. Cockburn, Firm Managing Partner
416-865-7662
mcockburn@torys.com

Torys LLP - Calgary
Eighth Avenue Place East, 525 - 8th Ave. SW, 46th Fl., Calgary, AB T2P 1G1
Tel: 403-776-3700; *Fax:* 403-776-3800
www.torys.com
Profile: 33 Lawyers, Founded in: 2011
Senior and Managing Partners:
Luigi A. Cusano, Office Managing Partner
403-776-3797
lcusano@torys.com

Torys LLP - Halifax
Also Known As: Torys Legal Services Centre (LSC)
#200, Torys Legal Services Centre, 1871 Hollis St., Halifax, NS B3J 0C3
Tel: 902-720-3500
www.torys.com
Profile: 19 Lawyers, Founded in: 2015
The Legal Services Centre (LSC) supports Torys lawyers across all offices with the following services: drafting of documents; corporate reorganization implementation; due diligence; banking & security documentation; & more
Senior and Managing Partners:
Christopher J. Fowles, Office Managing Partner
902-720-3501
cfowles@torys.com

Torys LLP - Montréal
Also Known As: Torys Law Firm LLP
#2880, 1, Place Ville Marie, Montréal, QC H3B 4R4
Tél: 514-868-5600; *Téléc:* 514-868-5700
www.torys.com
Profile: 13 Lawyers, Founded in: 2013
Senior and Managing Partners:
Sylvie Rodrigue, Ad. E., Office Managing Partner
514-868-5601
srodrigue@torys.com

WeirFoulds LLP - Toronto
#4100, TD Bank Tower, P.O. Box 35, 66 Wellington St. West, Toronto, ON M5K 1B7
Tel: 416-365-1110; *Fax:* 416-365-1876
www.weirfoulds.com
twitter.com/WeirFoulds
www.linkedin.com/company/weirfoulds-llp
Profile: 2 Offices, 117 Lawyers, Founded in: 1860
Excels in planning & experience with complex & sophisticated legal problems; focus is on commercial litigation; corporate/securities; commercial real estate
Senior and Managing Partners:
Lisa A. Borsook, Executive Partner
416-947-5003
lborsook@weirfoulds.com

* indicates number of lawyers

Wayne T. Egan, Managing Partner
416-947-5086
wegan@weirfoulds.com

WeirFoulds LLP - Oakville
#10, 1525 Cornwall Rd., Oakville, ON L6J 0B2
Tel: 905-829-8600; *Fax:* 905-829-2035
www.weirfoulds.com

Law Firms/By Province

Alberta

Airdrie: **Warnock, Rathgeber & Company - *2**
Also Known As: Warnock Rathgeber & Company
Former Name: Warnock, Rathgeber & Hassett
225 First Ave. NW, Airdrie, AB T4B 2M8
Tel: 403-948-0009; *Fax:* 403-948-6740
office@wrlawyers.ca
www.wrlawyers.ca

Banff: **Eric Harvie - *1**
#202, P.O. Box 3220, 216 Banff Ave., Banff, AB T1L 1C8
Tel: 403-762-3438; *Fax:* 403-762-8101
www.ericharvielaw.ca

Barrhead: **Driessen De Rudder LLP - *2**
Former Name: Driessen Law Office
P.O. Box 4220, 5017 - 50 Ave., Barrhead, AB T7N 1A2
Fax: 780-674-4592
Toll-Free: 888-517-3798
www.driessenlaw.ca

Blairmore: **Valerie J. Danielson Law Office - *1**
P.O. Box 1620, 13143 - 20th Ave., Blairmore, AB T0K 0E0
Tel: 403-562-2132; *Fax:* 403-562-2700
valeriejdanielson@shaw.ca

Bonnyville: **Wood & Wiebe - *2**
#101, P.O. Box 8060, Stn. Main, 4811 - 50 Ave., Bonnyville, AB T9N 2J3
Tel: 780-826-5767; *Fax:* 780-826-4654
woodwieb@telusplanet.net

Brooks: **Douglas H. Bell Law Office - *1**
P.O. Box 670, Stn. Main, 103 - 2nd Ave. West, Brooks, AB T1R 1B6
Tel: 403-362-3447; *Fax:* 403-362-4379

Brooks: **Susan E. Robertson - *1**
411B Third Ave. West, Brooks, AB T1R 0B2
Tel: 403-362-4064; *Fax:* 403-362-4024
www.susanrobertsonlawoffice.ca

Calgary: **Allen Hryniuk - *2**
Former Name: Laurie Allen & Associates
#403, 888 - 4 Ave. SW, Calgary, AB T2P 0V2
Tel: 403-266-5556; *Fax:* 403-266-5427
mail@allenhryniuk.com
allenhryniuk.com

Calgary: **Robert J.E. Allen Law Office - *1**
1817 Crowchild Trail NW, Calgary, AB T3A 2L6
Tel: 403-216-5522; *Fax:* 403-216-5524
admin@calgarylawyer.net

Calgary: **Linda A. Anderson - *1**
#16, 2439 - 54 Ave. SW, Calgary, AB T3E 1M4
Tel: 403-243-6400; *Fax:* 403-243-0126
linda@lindaandersonlaw.com

Calgary: **Armstrong & Partners - *4**
#800, 736 - 6 Ave. SW, Calgary, AB T2P 3T7
Tel: 403-537-9950; *Fax:* 403-537-9951
lawyers@aplaw.com
www.aplaw.com

Calgary: **Deborah L. Barron - *1**
Macleod Place II, 5940 Macleod Trail SW, 5th Fl., Calgary, AB T2H 2G4
Tel: 403-238-0000; *Fax:* 403-238-2255
dbarron@deborahbarronlaw.com
www.deborahbarronlaw.com
www.facebook.com/CalgaryInjuryLawyer,
twitter.com/DeborahLBarron1

Calgary: **Batting, Wyman - *2**
#2650, 645 - 7 Ave. SW, Calgary, AB T2P 4G8
Tel: 403-814-0910
www.criminallawyercalgary.ca

Calgary: **Alan V.M. Beattie, Q.C. - *1**
3621 - 1A St. SW, Calgary, AB T2S 1R4
Tel: 403-245-5255; *Fax:* 403-228-0254
beattiea@shaw.ca

Calgary: **Gary E. Bilyk Professional Corporation - *1**
#602, 706 - 7 Ave. SW, Calgary, AB T2P 0Z1
Tel: 403-266-2810; *Fax:* 403-264-1151
gebilyklawyer@shaw.ca

Calgary: **Blake, Nichol Law Office - *1**
Former Name: Reich Nichol
#100, 4603 Varsity Dr. NW, Calgary, AB T3A 2V7
Tel: 403-288-6500; *Fax:* 403-288-6510
blake@blakenichol.ca
www.blakenichol.ca

Calgary: **Blumell & Hartney - *2**
#203, 2411 - 4 St. NW, Calgary, AB T2M 2Z8
Tel: 403-282-4544; *Fax:* 403-284-4503

Calgary: **Michael J. Bondar, Professional Corporation - *1**
#1840, 801 - 6 Ave. SW, Calgary, AB T2P 3W2
Tel: 403-266-5511; *Fax:* 403-237-6620
mjbondar@shaw.ca

Calgary: **Burstall Winger Zammit LLP - *17**
Former Name: Burstall Winger LLP
#1600, Dome Tower, 333 - 7th Ave. SW, Calgary, AB T2P 2Z1
Tel: 403-264-1915; *Fax:* 403-266-6016
www.burstall.com
www.linkedin.com/company/burstall-winger-zammit-llp

Calgary: **Richard Cairns, Q.C. - *1**
#1210, 630 - 6th Ave. SW, Calgary, AB T2P 0S8
Tel: 403-205-3155; *Fax:* 403-546-0034
thegcvcard.wixsite.com/echambers

Calgary: **Calgary Legal Guidance - *5**
#100, 840 - 7th Ave. SW, Calgary, AB T2P 3G2
Tel: 403-234-9266; *Fax:* 403-234-9299
clg@clg.ab.ca
www.clg.ab.ca
www.facebook.com/calgarylegalguidance,
twitter.com/calgarylegal,
www.linkedin.com/company/calgary-legal-guidance

Calgary: **Cameron Horne Law Office LLP - *2**
Former Name: A.B. Cameron
#820, 10201 Southport Rd. SW, Calgary, AB T2W 4X9
Tel: 403-531-2700; *Fax:* 403-531-2707
www.cameronhorne.ca

Calgary: **Campbell O'Hara - *4**
Former Name: Campbell Taylor O'Hara
#920, 734 - 7th Ave. SW, Calgary, AB T2P 3P8
Tel: 403-294-0030; *Fax:* 403-229-2977
assistant@campbellohara.com
info@campbellohara.com
www.facebook.com/150802634953217

Calgary: **Carbert Waite LLP - *21**
Former Name: Stones Carbert Waite LLP
#2300, Encor Place, 645 - 7th Ave. SW, Calgary, AB T2P 4G8
Tel: 403-263-5656; *Fax:* 403-263-5553
info@carbertwaite.com
www.carbertwaite.com
www.facebook.com/carbertwaitellp, twitter.com/calgary_lawyers,
www.linkedin.com/company/carbert-waite-llp

Calgary: **Caron & Partners LLP - *16**
#2100, Scotia Centre, 700 - 2 St. SW, Calgary, AB T2P 2W1
Tel: 403-262-3000; *Fax:* 403-237-0111
www.caronpartners.com
twitter.com/CaronPartners,
www.linkedin.com/company/caron-&-partners-llp

Calgary: **Carscallen LLP - *24**
#1500, 407 - 2 St. SW, Calgary, AB T2P 2Y3
Tel: 403-262-3775; *Fax:* 403-262-2952
info@carscallen.com
www.carscallen.com

Calgary: **Cassidy Hea - *1**
Former Name: Chadi & Company
1832 - 19th Ave. SW, Calgary, AB T2T 0J6
Tel: 403-777-1099
info@cassidyhea.ca
www.cassidyhea.ca

Calgary: **Castle & Associates - *5**
#302, 221 - 10th Ave. SE, Calgary, AB T2G 0V9
Tel: 587-326-0128; *Fax:* 403-269-3217
Toll-Free: 800-655-9680
www.castleandassociates.ca

Calgary: **Clark & Associates - *2**
Also Known As: Brian N. Clark Professional Corporation
#203, 136 - 17 Ave. NE, Calgary, AB T2E 1L6
Tel: 403-520-2011; *Fax:* 403-230-3509
bclark@clarkandassociates.ca
www.clarkandassociates.ca

Calgary: **James K. Conley - *1**
#210, The Burns Bldg., 237 - 8th Ave. SE, Calgary, AB T2G 5C3
Tel: 403-290-0994; *Fax:* 403-265-7680
jkconley@telus.net

Calgary: **Timothy J. Corcoran - *1**
#701, 4656 Westwinds Dr. NE, Calgary, AB T3J 3Z5
Tel: 403-263-6000; *Fax:* 403-280-7666
alberta@lawyer.com
albertalaw.wordpress.com

Calgary: **Cornerstone Law Group LLP - *2**
Former Name: Keeler Law Firm; Milne & Company
#225, 10655 Southport Rd. SW, Calgary, AB T2W 4Y1
Tel: 403-296-1700; *Fax:* 403-258-0020
www.cornerstonelaw.ca

Calgary: **Cougle + Company**
2nd Fl., 1612 17th Ave. SW, Calgary, AB T2T 0E3
Tel: 403-249-9000
info@cougle.co
www.cougle.co

Calgary: **Craig Law LLP - *3**
Former Name: Mullen Craig
3408 - 114 Ave. SE, Calgary, AB T2Z 3V6
Tel: 403-297-0130; *Fax:* 403-297-0133

Calgary: **Cuming & Gillespie - *6**
Former Name: McNally Cuming Raymaker; McNally Cuming
#4050, 525 - 8 Ave. SW, Calgary, AB T2P 1G1
Tel: 403-571-0555; *Fax:* 403-232-8818
Toll-Free: 800-682-2480
info@cglaw.ca
www.cuminggillespie.com
www.facebook.com/cuminggillespie, twitter.com/cginjurylawyers

Calgary: **Damen Hoffman LLP - *2**
Former Name: Arkell Damen Hoffman
109 - 14 Ave. SE, Calgary, AB T2G 1C6
Tel: 403-531-4151; *Fax:* 403-531-4153
info@damenhoffman.com

Calgary: **Daniel J. Aberle, Barrister & Solicitor - *1**
Former Name: Stirling, Aberle & Row
#416, 602 - 11 Ave. SW, Calgary, AB T2R 1J8
Tel: 403-229-1129; *Fax:* 403-245-9660
www.danieljaberle.com

Calgary: **Gary A. Daniels - *1**
#200, 209 - 19 St. NW, Calgary, AB T2N 2H9
Tel: 403-297-0800; *Fax:* 403-283-7000
garyadaniels@shaw.ca

Calgary: **Dartnell & Lutz - *2**
Former Name: Dartnell, Wenngatz & Lutz
#607, 888 - 4th Ave. SW, Calgary, AB T2P 0V2
Tel: 403-264-8484; *Fax:* 403-263-9110
info@dartnell-lutz.com

Calgary: **Daunais McKay Harms + Jones - *12**
#2050, 645 - 7th Ave. SW, Calgary, AB T2P 4G8
Tel: 403-218-6275; *Fax:* 403-218-6299
contact@dmhjfamilylaw.com
www.dhjfamilylaw.com

Calgary: **Dawe Law Office - *2**
#200, 1409 Edmonton Trail NE, Calgary, AB T2E 3K8
Tel: 403-277-3100; *Fax:* 403-230-5855
terry@dawelawoffice.ca

* indicates number of lawyers

Calgary: Demiantschuk Burke & Hoffinger LLP - *10
Also Known As: DBH Law
Former Name: Demiantschuk Lequier Burke & Hoffinger LLP
#1200, 1015 - 4th St. SW, Calgary, AB T2R 1J4
Tel: 403-252-9937; *Fax:* 403-263-8529
reception@dbhllp.com
www.dbhllp.com
www.linkedin.com/company/dlbh-law

Calgary: Derburgis - *2
#2410, 645 - 7 Ave. SW, Calgary, AB T2P 4G8
Tel: 403-213-2999; *Fax:* 403-261-8977
lburgis@telus.net
www.derburgis.com

Calgary: Dixon Law Firm - *2
#501, 888 - 4 Ave. SW, Calgary, AB T2P 0V2
Tel: 403-297-9480; *Fax:* 403-266-1487

Calgary: Dunphy Best Blocksom LLP - *25
Also Known As: DBB LLP
#800, 517 - 10th Ave. SW, Calgary, AB T2R 0A8
Tel: 403-265-7777; *Fax:* 403-269-8911
info@dbblaw.com
www.dbblaw.com
www.linkedin.com/company/dunphy-best-blocksom-llp

Calgary: Ellert Law - *2
#510, 706 - 7 Ave. SW, Calgary, AB T2P 0Z1
Tel: 403-269-3315; *Fax:* 403-269-3329

Calgary: P. Robert Enns - *1
#222, 1100 - 8 Ave. SW, Calgary, AB T2P 3T8
Tel: 403-262-6588; *Fax:* 403-262-6590
prenns@shaw.ca

Calgary: Patrick Fagan, Q.C. - *2
#304, 1117 - 1st St. SW, Calgary, AB T2R 0T9
Tel: 403-517-1777; *Fax:* 403-517-1776
www.patrickfagan.com

Calgary: Felesky Flynn LLP - Calgary - *37
#5000, Suncor Energy Centre, 150 - 6th Ave. SW, Calgary, AB T2P 3Y7
Tel: 403-260-3300; *Fax:* 403-263-9649
felesky@felesky.com
www.felesky.com

Calgary: Philip L. Fiess - *1
#312, 602 - 11 Ave. SW, Calgary, AB T2R 1J8
Tel: 403-266-0033; *Fax:* 403-261-4958
phillfeiss@hotmail.com

Calgary: Findlay McQuaid Law Firm - *2
Former Name: Findlay Smith LLP; Millar Smith & Associates
#300, 1550 - 8th St. SW, Calgary, AB T2R 1K1
Tel: 403-244-0116; *Fax:* 403-244-0178
www.findlaylawfirm.com

Calgary: First West Law LLP - *6
Former Name: Butlin Oke Roberts Nobles Braun; Butlin Oke Roberts & Nobles; Butlin Oke & Roberts
#100, 1501 - 1 St. SW, Calgary, AB T2R 0W1
Tel: 403-543-7750; *Fax:* 403-543-7759
reception@firstwest.com
www.firstwest.com

Calgary: Foster Iovinelli Beyak - *6
#201, 224 - 11 Ave. SW, Calgary, AB T2R 0C3
Tel: 403-269-3655; *Fax:* 403-237-5109
Toll-Free: 800-884-4780
info@fiblaw.com
www.fiblaw.ca

Calgary: Fric, Lowenstein & Co. LLP - *4
#420, 1925 - 18 Ave. NE, Calgary, AB T2E 7T8
Tel: 403-291-2594; *Fax:* 403-291-2668
friclow@telusplanet.net
www.fl-legal.ca

Calgary: Goodfellow Law - *3
#715, 999 - 8th St. SW, Calgary, AB T2R 1J5
Tel: 403-228-7102; *Fax:* 403-228-7199
reception@goodfellowqc.com
www.goodfellowqc.com

Calgary: Gorman, Gorman, Burns & Watson - *2
#500, 1135 - 17 Ave. SW, Calgary, AB T2T 0B6
Tel: 403-244-5515; *Fax:* 403-244-5605

Calgary: Hadley & Davis - *2
#311, 1711 - 4 St. SW, Calgary, AB T2S 1V8
Tel: 403-264-1234; *Fax:* 403-264-0999
info@hadleydavis.com
www.hadleydavis.com

Calgary: Hansen & Company - *8
558 - 9th Ave. SE, Calgary, AB T2G 0S1
Tel: 403-261-6890
info@hansen-company.com
www.hansen-company.com
www.linkedin.com/in/hansencompany

Calgary: Larry S. Heald - *1
#300, 840 - 6 Ave. SW, Calgary, AB T2P 3E5
Tel: 403-266-2131; *Fax:* 403-261-6862
heald@shaw.ca

Calgary: Stephen Graham Heinz - *1
#2900, 350 - 7 Ave. SW, Calgary, AB T2P 3N9
Tel: 403-262-4462; *Fax:* 403-265-4496

Calgary: Hendrix Law - *3
Former Name: Vickers Hendrix LLP
#500, 707 - 7th Ave. SW, Calgary, AB T2P 3H6
Tel: 403-269-9400; *Fax:* 403-266-2447
www.hendrixlaw.com

Calgary: Alain Hepner - *4
Former Name: Ross, Hepner
921 - 18 Ave. SW, Calgary, AB T2T 0H2
Tel: 403-244-6800; *Fax:* 403-265-2455

Calgary: Horne Wytrychowski - *5
#14, 620 - 1st Ave. NW, Calgary, AB T4B 2R3
Tel: 403-912-3565
www.airdrielawyers.com

Calgary: Jensen Shawa Solomon Duguid Hawkes LLP - *31
Also Known As: JSS Barristers
Former Name: May Jensen Shawa Solomon LLP
#800, 304 - 8 Ave. SW, Calgary, AB T2P 1C2
Tel: 403-571-1520; *Fax:* 403-571-1528
inquiries@jssbarristers.ca
www.jssbarristers.ca

Calgary: Jivraj Knight & Pritchett, Barristers & Solicitors - *3
Also Known As: JKP Barristers & Solicitors
#1000, 444 - 5 Ave. SW, Calgary, AB T2P 2T8
Tel: 403-261-0017; *Fax:* 403-266-6030
mailbox@jkp-law.com

Calgary: Kelly & Kelly - *4
#220, 3505 - 32nd St. NE, Calgary, AB T1Y 5Y9
Tel: 403-266-6296; *Fax:* 403-264-2954

Calgary: Robert D. Kerr - *1
#300, 840 - 6 Ave. SW, Calgary, AB T2P 3E5
Tel: 403-265-1331; *Fax:* 403-265-1332

Calgary: George R. Klatt - *1
#400, Centre 70, 7015 Macleod Trail SW, Calgary, AB T2H 2K6
Tel: 403-255-3033; *Fax:* 403-255-0403

Calgary: John Kong - *2
#330, 1324 - 17 Ave. SW, Calgary, AB T2T 5S8
Tel: 403-233-9432; *Fax:* 403-237-9614
johnkong@shaw.ca

Calgary: Kubitz & Company - *3
Former Name: Everard & Kubitz
1716 - 10th Ave. SW, Calgary, AB T3C 0J8
Tel: 403-250-7100
www.kubitzlaw.com

Calgary: Kuefler & Company - *3
#12, 601 - 10th Ave. SW, Calgary, AB T2R 0B2
Tel: 403-237-0123; *Fax:* 403-237-0128
quinn.kuefler@kueflerlaw.com

Calgary: Catherine G. Langlois - *1
#222, 1100 - 8 Ave. SW, Calgary, AB T2P 3T8
Tel: 403-531-9300
www.langloislegal.com

Calgary: Lauzon Law Office - *1
#218, 5403 Crowchild Trail NW, Calgary, AB T3B 4Z1
Tel: 403-288-7601; *Fax:* 403-288-3689

Calgary: Laven & Company - *2
#310, McFarlane Tower, 700 - 4th Ave. SW, Calgary, AB T2P 3J4
Tel: 403-263-2444; *Fax:* 403-263-3235
www.lavenco.com

Calgary: Corinna Lee - *1
509 - 20th Ave. SW, Calgary, AB T2S 0E7
Tel: 403-228-2238; *Fax:* 403-228-5550

Calgary: Lenhardt Law Office - *1
#301, 888 - 7 Ave. SW, Calgary, AB T2P 3J3
Tel: 403-237-6970; *Fax:* 403-237-6974

Calgary: Leon Brener Law - *4
Former Name: Leon Bickman Brener; Faber Gurevitch Bickman
#100, 522 - 11th Ave. SW, Calgary, AB T2R 0C8
Tel: 403-263-1540; *Fax:* 403-269-2653
www.leonbrenerlaw.com

Calgary: Low, Glenn & Card LLP - *5
#120, 3636 - 23 St. NE, Calgary, AB T2E 8Z5
Tel: 403-291-2532; *Fax:* 403-291-2534
lawyer@lgclaw.ca
www.lgclaw.ca

Calgary: Birjinder P.S. Mangat
#217, 3825 - 34 St. NE, Calgary, AB T1Y 6Z8
Tel: 403-735-6088; *Fax:* 403-735-6089
bmangat@cadvision.com

Calgary: MasuchLaw LLP - Calgary - *18
Former Name: Masuch Albert LLP
#125, 8838 Blackfoot Trail SE, Calgary, AB T2J 3J1
Tel: 403-543-1100; *Fax:* 403-543-1111
www.masuchlaw.com

Calgary: McCaffery Mudry Pritchard LLP - *3
#1510, 736 - 6 Ave. SW, Calgary, AB T2P 3T7
Tel: 587-331-7304
www.lawfirmscalgaryab.ca

Calgary: McConnell MacInnes - *7
Former Name: McConnell, MacInnes, Graham
#4, 12110 - 40 St. SE, Calgary, AB T2Z 4K6
Tel: 403-278-7001; *Fax:* 403-271-2826
info@mcmaclaw.ca
mcmaclaw.ca

Calgary: McGown Cook - *5
Former Name: McGown Johnson
#120, 7260 - 12th St. SE, Calgary, AB T2H 2S5
Tel: 403-255-5114; *Fax:* 403-258-3840
www.mcgowncook.com

Calgary: McKinnon Carstairs - *2
#525, First Alberta Place, 777 - 8 Ave. SW, Calgary, AB T2P 3R5
Tel: 403-261-8822; *Fax:* 403-261-4892
rlmckinnon@mckinnoncarstairs.com

Calgary: McLeod Law LLP - Calgary - Bannister Rd. SE - *47
Former Name: McLeod & Company LLP
#300, 14505 Bannister Rd. SE, Calgary, AB T2X 3J3
Tel: 403-278-9411; *Fax:* 403-271-1769
www.mcleod-law.com
www.facebook.com/McLeodLawLLP, twitter.com/mcleodlawllp,
www.linkedin.com/company/326750

Calgary: McManus & Hubler - *2
63 Rockcliff Landing NW, Calgary, AB T3G 5Z5
Tel: 403-208-6099; *Fax:* 403-208-6018
Toll-Free: 877-423-6054
sean@mcmanus-hubler.ca
www.mcmanus-hubler.ca

Calgary: Anne E. McTavish - *1
7410E - 5th St. SE, Calgary, AB T2H 2L9
Tel: 403-252-4965; *Fax:* 403-253-7743

Calgary: Meyers Davis LLP - *1
Former Name: Milne, Davis & Young
#200, 1518 - 7th St. SW, Calgary, AB T2R 1A7
Tel: 403-229-3000; *Fax:* 403-800-9227
pm@mdmlaw.ca
mdmlaw.ca

Calgary: **Miles Davison LLP - *19**
Former Name: Miles, Davison, McCarthy; McNiven Kelly
#900, 517 - 10th Ave. SW, Calgary, AB T2R 0A8
Tel: 403-298-0333; *Fax:* 403-263-6840
thefirm@milesdavison.com
www.milesdavison.com

Calgary: **Moore Wittman Phillips - *6**
#307, 1228 Kensington Rd. NW, Calgary, AB T2N 3P7
Tel: 403-269-8500; *Fax:* 403-269-8515

Calgary: **Maureen Morgan - *1**
#206, P.O. Box 73001, Stn. RPO Woodbine, 2525 Woodview
Dr. SW, Calgary, AB T2W 6E4
Tel: 403-233-2215; *Fax:* 403-264-1328
maureenmorgan96@hotmail.com

Calgary: **Rick Muenz - *1**
#2410, 645 - 7 Ave. SW, Calgary, AB T2P 4G8
Tel: 403-543-6666; *Fax:* 403-261-8977
info@rickmuenz.ca
www.rickmuenz.ca

Calgary: **Mullen & Company - *2**
Former Name: Peterson, Shields, Milne, Mullen &
Galbraith
#120, 11012 Macleod Trail SE, Calgary, AB T2J 6A5
Tel: 587-331-8259; *Fax:* 403-271-3942
Toll-Free: 800-607-5676
www.mullenco.ca

Calgary: **Munro & Wood - *2**
#720, 2424 - 4 St. SW, Calgary, AB T2S 2T4
Tel: 403-299-9283; *Fax:* 403-228-1389
www.munrowood.ca

Calgary: **Murray & Company - *1**
Also Known As: Murray & Company Law Office
#104, 2003 - 14 St. NW, Calgary, AB T2M 3N4
Tel: 403-297-9850; *Fax:* 403-297-9855
www.murraylaw.ca

Calgary: **O'Brien, Devlin, MacLeod - *3**
Former Name: O'Brien, Devlin, Markey & MacLeod
#1310, 530 - 8th Ave. SW, Calgary, AB T2P 3S8
Tel: 403-265-5616; *Fax:* 403-264-8146
www.obriendevlin.com

Calgary: **Osuji & Smith Lawyers - *2**
Former Name: Smith Law Office
348 - 14 St. NW, Calgary, AB T2N 1Z7
Tel: 403-283-8018; *Fax:* 403-270-3065
www.osujismith.ca
www.facebook.com/OsujiandSmith, twitter.com/OsujiandSmith

Calgary: **Parlee McLaws LLP - *15**
#3300, TD Canada Trust Tower, 421 - 7 Ave. SW, Calgary, AB
T2P 4K7
Tel: 403-294-7000; *Fax:* 403-265-8263
www.parlee.com

Calgary: **Peacock Linder Halt & Mack LLP - *19**
Former Name: Mack Meagher LLP; Machida Mack
Shewchuk Meagher LLP
#4050, 400 - 3rd Ave. SW, Calgary, AB T2P 4H2
Tel: 403-296-2280; *Fax:* 403-296-2299
info@plhlaw.ca
www.plhlaw.ca

Calgary: **Phipps Law Office - *1**
#303, 8180 MacLeod Trail SE, Calgary, AB T2H 2B8
Tel: 403-531-0182; *Fax:* 403-531-0180

Calgary: **Pittman MacIsaac & Roy - *5**
Also Known As: PMR Law
#1400, North Tower, Sun Life Plaza, 140 - 4th Ave. SW,
Calgary, AB T2P 3N3
Tel: 403-237-6566; *Fax:* 403-237-6594
www.pmrlaw.ca

Calgary: **Lawrence S. Portigal - *1**
6638 Bow Cres. NW, Calgary, AB T3B 2B9
Tel: 403-286-6380; *Fax:* 403-286-6821
lportig@yahoo.com

Calgary: **ProVenture Law LLP - *4**
#310, 525 - 11th Ave. SW, Calgary, AB T2R OC9
Tel: 403-294-5710; *Fax:* 403-262-4860
www.proventurelaw.com

Calgary: **Quarry Park Law - *5**
#2, 11410 - 27th St. SE, Calgary, AB T2Z 3R6
Tel: 403-775-1719; *Fax:* 403-648-1890
info@quarryparklaw.com
quarryparklaw.com
www.facebook.com/quarryparklaw,
www.linkedin.com/company/quarry-park-law

Calgary: **Radke & Associates - *1**
#205, 5917 - 1A St. SW, Calgary, AB T2H 0G4
Tel: 403-252-4466; *Fax:* 403-258-0695
info@radkeandassociates.com
www.radkeandassociates.com

Calgary: **Rae & Company - *4**
#900, 1000 - 5th Ave. SW, Calgary, AB T2P 4V1
Tel: 403-264-8389; *Fax:* 403-264-8399
reception@raeandcompany.com
www.raeandcompany.com
www.linkedin.com/company/rae-and-company

Calgary: **Clayton Rice, Q.C. - *1**
Former Name: Ouellette, Rice
#310, 1117 - 1st St. SW, Calgary, AB T2R 0T9
Tel: 403-861-4211; *Fax:* 403-517-1776
claytonrice@claytonrice.com
www.claytonrice.com

Calgary: **Ridout Barron, Barristers & Solicitors - *4**
1827 - 14th St. SW, Calgary, AB T2T 3T1
Tel: 403-278-3730; *Fax:* 403-271-8016
info@ridoutbarron.com
www.ridoutbarron.com

Calgary: **Rogers & Company, Barristers & Solicitors
- *3**
#200, 815 - 10th Ave. SW, Calgary, AB T2R 0B4
Tel: 403-263-6805; *Fax:* 403-263-6800
reception@rogcolaw.com
rogcolaw.com

Calgary: **Salmon & Company - *1**
#577, 717 - 7 Ave. SW, Calgary, AB T2P 0Z3
Tel: 403-231-2705; *Fax:* 403-705-1214

Calgary: **Sara Anand Law - *2**
Former Name: Zinner & Sara
#145, 1935 - 32 Ave. NE, Calgary, AB T2E 7C8
Tel: 403-262-7363; *Fax:* 403-233-0392

Calgary: **Schwartzberg Law Office - *1**
#214, 222 - 16th Ave. NE, Calgary, AB T2E 1J8
Tel: 403-232-1302; *Fax:* 403-249-6655

Calgary: **Scott Venturo LLP - *30**
#203, 200 Barclay Parade SW, Calgary, AB T2P 4R5
Tel: 403-261-9043; *Fax:* 403-265-4632
Toll-Free: 877-505-5651
www.scottventuro.com

Calgary: **Sefcik & Company - *1**
Former Name: Douglas M. Sefcik
#212, 20 Sunpark Plaza SE, Calgary, AB T2X 3T2
Tel: 403-258-1124; *Fax:* 403-640-1220

Calgary: **William J. Shachnowich - *1**
1700 Varsity Estates Dr. NW, Calgary, AB T3B 2W9
Tel: 403-269-1313; *Fax:* 403-210-0106

Calgary: **Shea Nerland LLP - *16**
Former Name: Shea Nerland Calnan LLP
#2800, 715 - 5th Ave. SW, Calgary, AB T2P 2X6
Tel: 403-299-9600; *Fax:* 403-299-9601
info@sheanerland.com
sheanerland.com

Calgary: **Singh & Partner LLP - *7**
#1101, 3961 - 52 Ave. NE, Calgary, AB T3J 0J7
Tel: 403-285-7070; *Fax:* 403-590-7800
splaw.ca

Calgary: **Smith Mack Lamarsh - *3**
#450, United Place, 808 - 4 Ave. SW, Calgary, AB T2P 3E8
Tel: 403-234-7779; *Fax:* 403-263-7897
slamarsh@telusplanet.net

Calgary: **W. Murray Smith - *1**
348 - 14 St. NW, Calgary, AB T2N 1Z7
Tel: 403-283-8018; *Fax:* 403-270-3065

Calgary: **Sparrow Law Office - *1**
#10, 628 - 12 Ave. SW, Calgary, AB T2R 0H6
Tel: 403-234-9722; *Fax:* 403-237-8748
sparrow@nucleus.com

Calgary: **Spier Harben - *9**
#1400, 707 - 7th St. SW, Calgary, AB T2P 3H6
Tel: 403-263-5130; *Fax:* 403-264-9600
www.spierharben.com

Calgary: **Stephens Holman Devraj - *2**
Former Name: Stephens & Holman
412 - 16th Ave. NE, Calgary, AB T2E 1K2
Tel: 403-265-6400; *Fax:* 403-262-9294
www.shdlawyers.ca
www.facebook.com/126283444109348

Calgary: **Peter A. Stone - *1**
Former Name: Paterson Foster
1923 - 5th St. SW, Calgary, AB T2S 2B2
Tel: 403-283-8460; *Fax:* 403-283-8461
peter@pastonelaw.com

Calgary: **Story Law Office - *1**
#115, 1925 - 18th Ave. NE, Calgary, AB T2E 7T8
Tel: 403-250-1918; *Fax:* 866-404-1476
www.storylawoffice.ca

Calgary: **Sugimoto & Company - *9**
#204, 2635 - 37 Ave. NE, Calgary, AB T1Y 5Z6
Tel: 403-291-4650; *Fax:* 403-291-4099
sugimoto@sugimotolaw.com
sugimotolaw.com

Calgary: **Nancy A. Swanby - *1**
#700, One Executive Place, 1816 Crowchild Trail NW,
Calgary, AB T2M 3Y7
Tel: 403-520-5455; *Fax:* 403-220-1389
info@swanbylaw.com
www.swanbylaw.com

Calgary: **Szabo & Company, Barristers & Solicitors**
#200, 1115 - 11th Ave. SW, Calgary, AB T2R 0G5
Tel: 403-229-1111; *Fax:* 403-245-0569
info@szaboco.com
www.szaboco.com

Calgary: **Michael J. Tadman - *1**
#10, 628 - 12 Ave. SW, Calgary, AB T2R 0H6
Tel: 403-234-9722; *Fax:* 403-237-8748
tadman@nucleus.com

Calgary: **Mark S. Takada - *1**
#200, 604 - 1 St. SW, Calgary, AB T2P 1M7
Tel: 403-234-9477; *Fax:* 403-261-1839
www.mycalgarycriminallawyer.ca

Calgary: **Taylor Conway - *3**
Former Name: Taylor, Zinkhofer & Conway
#240, 550 - 71st Ave. SE, Calgary, AB T2H 0S6
Tel: 403-640-1009; *Fax:* 403-640-0103
info@taylorconway.ca
www.taylorconway.ca
www.facebook.com/289786387802529,
twitter.com/taylorconwaybs

Calgary: **Thompson Laughlin - *2**
Former Name: Thompson, Ball & Associates
#390, 11012 Macleod Trail SE, Calgary, AB T2J 6A5
Tel: 403-271-5050
info@thompsonlaughlin.ca
www.thompsonlaughlin.ca

Calgary: **Thornborough Smeltz LLP - *8**
Former Name: Thornborough, Smeltz, Gillis & Mebs
11650 Elbow Drive SW, Calgary, AB T2W 1S8
Tel: 403-271-3221; *Fax:* 403-271-6684
info@thornsmeltz.com
www.thornsmeltz.com
www.linkedin.com/company/thornborough-smeltz-llp

Calgary: **TingleMerrett LLP - *12**
#1250, Standard Life Bldg., 639 - 5th Ave. SW, Calgary, AB
T2P 0M9
Tel: 403-571-8000; *Fax:* 403-571-8008
www.tinglemerrett.com

Calgary: **Richard T. Tumanon - *1**
#301, 5555 Falsbridge Dr. NE, Calgary, AB T3J 3E8
Tel: 403-262-3841; *Fax:* 403-269-7173

Calgary: **Vinci, Phillips - *2**
1509 - 26 Ave. SW, Calgary, AB T2T 1C4
Tel: 403-265-4323; *Fax:* 403-262-8087

* indicates number of lawyers

Calgary: **Walsh LLP - *24**
#2800, 801 - 6 Ave. SW, Calgary, AB T2P 4A3
Tel: 403-879-1502; *Fax:* 403-264-9400
Toll-Free: 800-682-4052
info@walshlaw.ca
walshlaw.ca

Calgary: **Samuel D.C. Wan - *1**
191 Edgepark Way NW, Calgary, AB T3A 4T2
Tel: 403-973-0678

Calgary: **Peter M. Ward - *1**
#300, 840 - 6th Ave. SW, Calgary, AB T2P 3E5
Tel: 403-263-1158; *Fax:* 403-265-3783

Calgary: **Warren Benson Amantea LLP - *11**
Former Name: Warren Tettensor Amantea LLP
1413 - 2nd St. SW, Calgary, AB T2R 0W7
Tel: 403-228-7007; *Fax:* 403-244-1948
info@wbalaw.ca
www.facebook.com/1571312086502551

Calgary: **Peggy A. Wedderburn - *1**
#16, 2439 - 54th Ave. SW, Calgary, AB T3E 1M4
Tel: 403-242-8081; *Fax:* 403-246-2055
pwedderburn@shaw.ca

Calgary: **Weeks Law - *1**
#403, Willow Park Centre, 10325 Bonaventure Dr. SE,
Calgary, AB T2J 7E4
Tel: 403-209-4988; *Fax:* 403-444-6827
info@weekslaw.com
www.weekslaw.com

Calgary: **West End Legal Centre - *2**
1705 - 10th Ave. SW, Calgary, AB T3C 0K1
Tel: 403-249-5297; *Fax:* 403-249-5001
info@westendlegalcentre.com
westendlegalcentre.com

Calgary: **Wilson Laycraft - *10**
#1601, 333 - 11th Ave. SW, Calgary, AB T2R 1L9
Tel: 403-290-1601; *Fax:* 403-290-0828
www.wilcraft.com

Calgary: **Dawn M. Wilson - *1**
44 Bow Village Cres. NW, Calgary, AB T3B 4X2
Tel: 403-247-9090; *Fax:* 403-247-9090

Calgary: **Wise Scheible Barkauskas - *7**
Former Name: Wise Walden Barkauskas
#750, 700 - 4 Ave. SW, Calgary, AB T2P 3J4
Tel: 587-331-7550; *Fax:* 403-269-6785
www.wisedivorce.com

Calgary: **Stephen R. Wojcik - *1**
#200, The Lougheed Bldg., 604 - 1 St. SW, Calgary, AB T2P
1M7
Tel: 403-547-4415; *Fax:* 403-208-0717
wojicks@shaw.ca

Calgary: **Wolch deWit Silverberg & Watts - *7**
Former Name: Wolch, Ogle, Wilson, Hursh & deWit
#1500, 633 - 6 Ave. SW, Calgary, AB T2P 2Y5
Tel: 403-265-6500; *Fax:* 403-263-1111
msmale@calgarycriminaldefence.ca
calgarycriminaldefence.ca

Calgary: **David I. Wolfman - *1**
Former Name: Wolfman Ryder Barristers & Solicitors
328 Pumphill Gardens SW, Calgary, AB T2V 4M7
Tel: 403-266-4433; *Fax:* 403-266-4433
thewolfmans@telus.net

Calgary: **Yanko & Popovic Law Firm - *7**
Former Name: Yanko & Company
#301, 300 Manning Rd. NE, Calgary, AB T2A 7H8
Tel: 403-262-0262; *Fax:* 403-204-0284
www.yankopopovic.com

Calgary: **Your Lawyer LLP - *6**
Former Name: Lehan, Menzies, Walters & Abdi
#305, 602 - 11th Ave. SE, Calgary, AB T2R 1J8
Tel: 403-261-4010; *Fax:* 403-261-4040
reception@yourlawyeralberta.ca

Calgary: **Youth Criminal Defence Office - Calgary - *9**
#600, 444 - 5 Ave. SW, Calgary, AB T2P 2T8
Tel: 403-297-4400; *Fax:* 403-297-4201
sfellger@ycdo.ca
www.ycdo.ca

Camrose: **Andreassen Borth - Camrose - *5**
Former Name: Andreassen Olson Borth
#200, 4870 - 51 St., Camrose, AB T4V 1S1
Tel: 780-672-3181; *Fax:* 780-672-0682
aob@telusplanet.net
www.andreassenborth.com

Camrose: **Farnham West Stolee Kambeitz LLP - *6**
Former Name: Farnham West Stolee LLP
5016 - 52 St., Camrose, AB T4V 1V7
Tel: 780-679-0444; *Fax:* 780-679-0958
camlaw@telusplanet.net
www.fwsllp.ca

Camrose: **Fielding & Company LLP - *4**
#100, 4918 - 51 St., Camrose, AB T4V 1S3
Tel: 780-672-8851; *Fax:* 844-677-9689
lawyers@fieldingco.com
www.fielding-and-company.com

Camrose: **Knaut Johnson Francoeur LLP - *4**
Former Name: Knaut Johnson
4925 - 51 St., Camrose, AB T4V 1S4
Tel: 780-672-5561; *Fax:* 780-672-5565
info@kjf-law.ca
www.kjf-law.ca
www.facebook.com/KnautJohnsonFrancoeurLLP

Canmore: **Canmore Legal Services - *1**
Also Known As: Schneider Law Office
909A Railway Ave., Canmore, AB T1W 1P3
Tel: 403-678-9818; *Fax:* 403-609-2333
johnschneider@shaw.ca

Canmore: **Tannis J. Naylor - *1**
826B - 10th St., Canmore, AB T1W 2A7
Tel: 403-678-5777; *Fax:* 403-678-5679
t_naylor@telus.net

Canmore: **Peter Perren - *1**
726 - 10 St., Canmore, AB T1W 2A6
Tel: 403-678-6988; *Fax:* 403-678-5952
pperren@telusplanet.net

Carstairs: **Stiles Law Office - *1**
Former Name: Stiles & Naqi
P.O. Box 790, 209 - 10th Ave. South, Carstairs, AB T0M 0N0
Tel: 403-337-3357; *Fax:* 403-337-3359

Coaldale: **Leonard D. Fast - *1**
P.O. Box 1360, Stn. Main, 1709 - 20 Ave., Coaldale, AB T1M
1N2
Tel: 403-345-4415; *Fax:* 403-345-2719
lfastlaw@telusplanet.net

Coaldale: **Vincent A. Lammi - *1**
Also Known As: Lammi Law
P.O. Box 1329, Stn. Main, 1910 - 18 St., Coaldale, AB T1M
1N1
Tel: 403-345-3922; *Fax:* 403-345-2172

Cochrane: **Fercho Law Offices - *1**
#14, 205 - 1 St. East, Cochrane, AB T4C 1X6
Tel: 403-932-4477; *Fax:* 403-932-4084
rfercho@fercholaw.com

Cochrane: **Mabbott & Company - *6**
Also Known As: M&C Law
#5, 201 Grand Blvd., Cochrane, AB T4C 2G4
Tel: 403-932-3066; *Fax:* 403-932-3076
info@mabbott.ca
www.mabbott.ca
www.facebook.com/mabbottandcompany
www.linkedin.com/company/mabbott-&-company

Cochrane: **Rask Law Office - *1**
216 Sunterra Views, Cochrane, AB T4C 1W8
Tel: 403-981-7275; *Fax:* 403-981-7277
info@rasklaw.com
www.rasklaw.com

Cold Lake: **Todd & Drake LLP - *6**
Former Name: Todd, Drake, Williams, Findlater LLP
P.O. Box 908, 4807 - 51 St., Cold Lake, AB T9M 1P2
Tel: 780-594-7151 *Toll-Free:* 877-594-7151
reception@tdlaw.ca
www.tdlaw.ca
www.facebook.com/168339593224163

Coronation: **E. Roger Spady - *1**
P.O. Box 328, 5015 Victoria Ave., Coronation, AB T0C 1C0
Tel: 403-578-3131; *Fax:* 403-578-2660

Didsbury: **Brian M. Forestell - *1**
P.O. Box 625, 1701 - 20th Ave., Didsbury, AB T0M 0W0
Tel: 403-335-8491; *Fax:* 403-335-8589
briandid@telusplanet.net
brianforestelllaw.com

Didsbury: **Roy D. Shellnutt - *1**
P.O. Box 898, 2021 - 19th Ave., Didsbury, AB T0M 0W0
Tel: 403-335-2145; *Fax:* 403-335-3185
shellnutlaw@hotmail.com

Drumheller: **Herman, Kloot & Company - *5**
P.O. Box 970, 98 - 3 Ave. West, Drumheller, AB T0J 0Y0
Tel: 403-823-4000; *Fax:* 403-823-6407
reception@drumhellerlaw.com
www.drumhellerlaw.com

Drumheller: **Schumacher, Gough & Company - *2**
Former Name: Schumacher, Gough & Pedersen
P.O. Box 2800, 196 - 3rd Ave. West, Drumheller, AB T0J 0Y0
Tel: 403-823-2424; *Fax:* 403-823-6984
enquiries@schumachergough.com
www.schumachergough.com

Edmonton: **Abbey Hunter Davison Lieslar Luchak -
*5**
Former Name: Abbey Hunter Davison; Abbey Hunter
Davison Spencer
9636 - 102A Ave. NW, Edmonton, AB T5H 0G5
Tel: 780-421-8585
www.ahdll.ca

Edmonton: **Abells Regan - *2**
Former Name: Elizabeth M. Regan
#2500, 10303 Jasper Ave. NW, Edmonton, AB T5J 3N6
Tel: 780-442-4420; *Fax:* 780-424-9370

Edmonton: **Ackroyd LLP Barristers & Solicitors - *17**
#1500, First Edmonton Place, 10665 Jasper Ave., Edmonton,
AB T5J 3S9
Tel: 780-423-8905; *Fax:* 780-423-8946
info@ackroydlaw.com
www.ackroydlaw.com

Edmonton: **Anderson Haak & Engels - *2**
#102, 9811 - 34 Ave., Edmonton, AB T6E 5X9
Tel: 780-413-1763; *Fax:* 780-413-1734
info@ahelaw.com
www.albertarealestatelawyers.com

Edmonton: **Andrew, March & Oake - *9**
#300, 10020 - 101A Ave. NW, Edmonton, AB T5J 3G2
Tel: 780-429-3391; *Fax:* 780-424-8483

Edmonton: **Attia, Reeves, Tensfeldt, Snow - *9**
Former Name: Attia, Reeves
#200, 10525 Jasper Ave. NW, Edmonton, AB T5J 1Z4
Tel: 780-424-3334; *Fax:* 780-424-4252
attia-reeves-tensfeldt-snow.alberta.canadab.com

Edmonton: **Barr Picard - *12**
#1100, 10020 - 101A Ave. NW, Edmonton, AB T5J 3G2
Tel: 780-414-5400; *Fax:* 780-414-5509
info@barrpicard.com
www.barrpicard.com

Edmonton: **Dennis E. Bayrak - *1**
#800, 10310 Jasper Ave. NW, Edmonton, AB T5J 2W4
Tel: 780-426-4884; *Fax:* 780-425-9358
bayrak@telus.net

Edmonton: **Beresh Aloneissi O'Neill Hurley O'Keefe
Millsap - Edmonton - *12**
Former Name: Beresh Cunningham Aloneissi O'Neill
Hurley; Beresh DePoe Cunningham
#300, MacLean Block, 10110 - 107 St., Edmonton, AB T5J
1J4
Tel: 780-421-4766; *Fax:* 780-429-0346
Toll-Free: 877-277-4766
info@libertylaw.ca
libertylaw.ca

Edmonton: **Helmut Berndt - *1**
Former Name: Berndt & Associates
#1780, 10020 - 101A Ave. NW, Edmonton, AB T5J 3G2
Tel: 780-439-6643; *Fax:* 780-439-6696

Edmonton: **Bhalla Law Offices - *2**
9360 - 34 Ave., Edmonton, AB T6E 5X8
Tel: 780-450-6155; *Fax:* 780-490-0116
www.bhallalawoffice.com

---

* indicates number of lawyers

Edmonton: Biamonte LLP - Edmonton - *15
Former Name: Biamonte Cairo & Shortreed LLP
#1600, 10025 - 102A Ave., Edmonton, AB T5J 2Z2
Tel: 780-425-5800; Fax: 780-426-1600
Toll-Free: 888-425-2620
biamonte.com
www.facebook.com/biamontepersonalinjury

Edmonton: Bishop & McKenzie LLP - Edmonton - *45
#2300, 10180 - 101st St. NW, Edmonton, AB T5J 1V3
Tel: 780-426-5550; Fax: 780-426-1305
www.bmllp.ca

Edmonton: Bitner & Associates Law Offices - *1
6932 Roper Rd. NW, Edmonton, AB T6B 3H9
Tel: 780-461-6633; Fax: 780-461-9239
www.bitnerlaw.ca

Edmonton: Kerry A. Bjarnason - *1
#600, 9707 - 110 St., Edmonton, AB T5K 2L9
Tel: 780-433-4547; Fax: 780-482-6613
kbjarnason@telusplanet.net

Edmonton: Bosecke & Associates - *6
Former Name: Bosecke Song LLP
#102, 9333 - 47 St. NW, Edmonton, AB T6B 2R7
Tel: 780-469-0494; Fax: 780-469-4181
www.edmontonlaw.ca
www.facebook.com/edmontonlaw

Edmonton: Braithwaite Boyle - Edmonton - *12
11816 - 124 St. NW, Edmonton, AB T5L 0M3
Tel: 780-451-9191 Toll-Free: 800-661-4902
help@accidentinjurylawyer.com
www.accidentinjurylawyer.com

Edmonton: Braul McEvoy & Gee - *2
#1920, 10123 - 99 St., Edmonton, AB T5J 3H1
Tel: 780-423-2481; Fax: 780-423-2474

Edmonton: Brownlee LLP - Edmonton - *69
#2200, Commerce Place, 10155 - 102 St., Edmonton, AB T5J 4G8
Tel: 780-497-4800; Fax: 780-424-3254
Toll-Free: 800-661-9069
contactus@brownleelaw.com
www.brownleelaw.com

Edmonton: Bryan & Company LLP - Edmonton - *36
#2600, Manulife Place, 10180 - 101 St., Edmonton, AB T5J 3Y2
Tel: 780-423-5730; Fax: 780-428-6324
Toll-Free: 800-357-9265
info@bryanco.com
www.bryanco.com

Edmonton: J.K.J. Campbell - *1
Also Known As: Whitemud Law
#311, Whitemud Business Park, 9622 - 42 Ave., Edmonton, AB T6E 5Y4
Tel: 780-434-8777; Fax: 780-436-6357
johncam@telusplanet.net
www.whitemudlaw.ca

Edmonton: Chatwin LLP - *6
Former Name: Chatwin Cox & Michalyshyn
#1630, Phipps-McKinnon Building, 10020 - 101A Ave. NW, Edmonton, AB T5J 3G2
Tel: 780-421-7667
www.chatwinllp.com

Edmonton: Chomicki Baril Mah LLP - *28
Also Known As: CBM Lawyers
#e201, TD Tower, 10088 - 102 Ave., Edmonton, AB T5J 4K2
Tel: 780-423-3441; Fax: 780-420-1763
www.cbmllp.com

Edmonton: Shirish P. Chotalia, Q.C. - *2
Also Known As: Pundit & Chotalia
#3400, Manulife Place, 10080 - 101 St., Edmonton, AB T5J 3S4
Tel: 780-421-0861
info@shirishchotalia.com
www.shirishchotalia.com

Edmonton: Michael H. Clancy - *1
9844 - 106 St. NW, Edmonton, AB T5K 1B8
Tel: 780-424-9014; Fax: 780-424-9023
Toll-Free: 800-647-7723

Edmonton: Coley Hennessy Cassis Ewasko - *2
#212, 3132 Parsons Rd., Edmonton, AB T6N 1L6
Tel: 780-468-2551; Fax: 780-466-8006
Toll-Free: 877-460-2551
info@chclaw.ca
www.chclaw.ca

Edmonton: Combe & Kent - *2
10614-124 St. NW, Edmonton, AB T5N 1S3
Tel: 780-425-4666; Fax: 780-425-9358

Edmonton: Coulter & Power - *2
9452 - 51 Ave. NW, Edmonton, AB T6E 5A6
Tel: 780-413-2300

Edmonton: Charles D. Cousineau - *1
#215, 11098 - 156 St. SW, Edmonton, AB T5P 4M8
Tel: 780-455-0485; Fax: 780-447-5853

Edmonton: Cox Trofimuk Campbell - *4
#311, 9622 - 42 Ave. NW, Edmonton, AB T6E 5Y4
Tel: 780-437-6600; Fax: 780-436-6357
Toll-Free: 866-282-4340
www.coxtrofimukcampbell.com

Edmonton: Ted R. Croll - *1
#1300, 10665 Jasper Ave., Edmonton, AB T5J 3S9
Tel: 780-420-9903; Fax: 780-424-3631

Edmonton: Cummings Andrews Mackay LLP - *7
Also Known As: CAM LLP
#600, 10150 - 100 St. NW, Edmonton, AB T5J 0P6
Tel: 780-428-8222; Fax: 780-424-0643
Toll-Free: 800-565-5745
www.camllp.com
www.facebook.com/CAMLLP, twitter.com/camllp,
www.linkedin.com/company/cummings-andrews-mackay-llp

Edmonton: Brock I. Dagenais - *1
#1405, TD Tower, 10088 - 102 Ave., Edmonton, AB T5J 2Z1
Tel: 780-424-8519; Fax: 780-425-0931
brockd@bidlaw.ca

Edmonton: Davidson Gregory Danyliuk - *1
Also Known As: Rod Gregory
10008 - 110 St., Edmonton, AB T5K 1J6
Tel: 780-993-6999 Toll-Free: 855-321-4111
rod.gregory@davidsongregory.com
www.thedefencelawyer.com
www.facebook.com/TheDefenceLawyer,
twitter.com/rodgregory12

Edmonton: Dawson, Duckett, Shaigec & Garcia - Edmonton - *8
Former Name: Dawson; Stevens, Duckett & Shaigec;
Anderson, Dawson, Knisely, Stevens & Shaigec
#300, Anderson Dawson Bldg., 9924 - 106 St., Edmonton, AB T5K 1C4
Tel: 780-424-9058; Fax: 780-425-0172
Toll-Free: 800-661-3176
www.dsscrimlaw.com
www.facebook.com/dsscrimlaw, twitter.com/dsscrimlaw

Edmonton: de Villars Jones - *6
#300, Noble Bldg., 8540 - 109 St., Edmonton, AB T6G 1E6
Tel: 780-433-9000; Fax: 780-433-9780
sagecounsel.com

Edmonton: Dean Duckett Carlson LLP - *13
#700, Bell Tower, 10104 - 103 Ave. NW, Edmonton, AB T5J 0H8
Tel: 780-423-3366; Fax: 780-423-0505
www.deanduckett.com

Edmonton: Gary A. Dlin - *1
7904 Gateway Blvd., Edmonton, AB T6E 6C3
Tel: 780-438-4972; Fax: 780-435-1037

Edmonton: Doherty Schuldhaus - *2
#219, 6203 - 28 Ave., Edmonton, AB T6L 6K3
Tel: 780-450-1106; Fax: 780-461-8612

Edmonton: Duncan Craig LLP - Edmonton - *44
Former Name: Duncan & Craig LLP, Lawyers & Mediators
#2800, 10060 Jasper Ave., Edmonton, AB T5J 3V9
Tel: 780-428-6036; Fax: 780-428-9683
Toll-Free: 800-782-9409
edmonton@dcllp.com
www.dcllp.com
www.facebook.com/DuncanCraigLLP, twitter.com/dcllp,
www.linkedin.com/company/duncan-craig-llp

Edmonton: Durocher Simpson Koehli & Erler - *6
Former Name: Durocher Simpson
7904 Gateway Blvd., Edmonton, AB T6E 6C3
Tel: 780-420-6850; Fax: 780-425-9185
mail@dursim.com
www.dursim.com

Edmonton: Edmonton Community Legal Centre
#200, 10115 - 100A St., Edmonton, AB T5J 2W2
Tel: 780-702-1725; Fax: 780-702-1726
Intake@eclc.ca
www.eclc.ca

Edmonton: Embury & McFayden - *1
#602, Centre 104, 5241 Calgary Trail NW, Edmonton, AB T6H 5G8
Tel: 780-439-7302; Fax: 780-433-6510

Edmonton: Emery Jamieson LLP - *31
#1700, 10235 - 101st St. NW, Edmonton, AB T5J 3G1
Tel: 780-426-5220; Fax: 780-420-6277
Toll-Free: 866-212-5220
general@emeryjamieson.com
www.emeryjamieson.com

Edmonton: Environmental Law Centre (ELC) - *5
#410, 10115 - 100A St., Edmonton, AB T5J 2W2
Tel: 780-424-5099; Fax: 780-424-5133
Toll-Free: 800-661-4238
elc@elc.ab.ca
www.elc.ab.ca
www.facebook.com/environmentallawcentre,
twitter.com/elc_alberta

Edmonton: Feehan Law Office - *2
Former Name: Mark E. Feehan
10160 - 118 St., Edmonton, AB T5K 1Y4
Tel: 780-424-6425
feehanlaw.ca

Edmonton: Finlay Maxston Law - *6
Former Name: Hansma Bristow Finlay LLP
13815 - 127 St. NW, 2nd Fl., Edmonton, AB T6V 1A8
Tel: 780-456-3661; Fax: 780-457-9381
www.fm-law.ca

Edmonton: Fix & Smith - *3
10277 - 97 St. NW, Edmonton, AB T5J 0L9
Tel: 780-424-2245; Fax: 780-423-0425
www.fixandsmith.com

Edmonton: Fleming & Gubbins - *2
9636 - 102A Ave. NW, Edmonton, AB T5H 0G5
Tel: 780-424-9505; Fax: 780-425-0472

Edmonton: Galbraith Empson - *2
#180, 10123 - 99 St., Edmonton, AB T5J 3H1
Tel: 780-424-9558; Fax: 780-424-5852
galson@shaw.ca

Edmonton: Galbraith Law - *2
17318 - 106 Ave., Edmonton, AB T5S 1H9
Tel: 780-483-6111; Fax: 780-483-6411
Toll-Free: 866-483-6111
www.galbraith.ab.ca

Edmonton: Blair M. Geiger - *1
7904 Gateway Blvd. NW, Edmonton, AB T6E 6C3
Tel: 780-438-4972; Fax: 780-436-7771
bgeiger@telusplanet.net

Edmonton: Dale Gibson Consulting Barrister - *1
11018 - 125 St., Edmonton, AB T5M 0M1
Tel: 780-454-5081; Fax: 780-454-5081
giblaw@shaw.ca

Edmonton: Gledhill Larocque - *5
#300, Wentworth Bldg., 10209 - 97 St., Edmonton, AB T5J 0L6
Tel: 780-425-3511; Fax: 780-426-5919
www.gledhill-larocque.com

Edmonton: Goldford Law Office - *2
#200, 10735 - 107th St., Edmonton, AB T5H 0W6
Tel: 780-482-1000; Fax: 780-482-0963
Toll-Free: 877-438-2667
hgoldford@goldfordlaw.com

Edmonton: Gunn & Prithipaul - *4
Also Known As: Gunn Law Group
Former Name: Gunn Prithipaul & Hatch
11210 - 142 St., Edmonton, AB T5M 1T9
Tel: 780-488-4460; Fax: 780-488-4783
www.gunnlawgroup.ca
www.facebook.com/GunnLaw

indicates number of lawyers

Edmonton: Hajduk Gibbs LLP
#202, Platinum Place Bldg., 10120 - 118 St. NW, Edmonton, AB T5K 1Y4
Tel: 780-428-4258; *Fax:* 780-425-9439
Toll-Free: 800-749-9989
www.hajdukandgibbs.com

Edmonton: Hall, Van Campenhout & Pidde - *2
Former Name: Hall & Van Campenhout
12026 - 102 Ave. NW, Edmonton, AB T5K 0R9
Tel: 780-482-5732; *Fax:* 780-482-5736
info@hallvancamp.com
www.hallvancamp.com

Edmonton: Hardman Law Office - *1
18067 - 107 Ave., Edmonton, AB T5S 1K3
Tel: 780-484-2041; *Fax:* 780-484-8950
hardman@compusmart.ab.ca

Edmonton: R. Allan Harris Professional Corp. - *1
#10109, 502 Energy Square, 106 St. NW, Edmonton, AB T5J 3L7
Tel: 780-421-1641; *Fax:* 780-421-1936

Edmonton: Haymour Kalil - *1
#2031, 10060 Jasper Ave. NW, Edmonton, AB T5J 3R8
Tel: 780-429-4573

Edmonton: Christopher R. Head - *1
#300, 10209 - 97 St. NW, Edmonton, AB T5J 0L6
Tel: 780-441-4758; *Fax:* 780-702-1552
chead@shawbiz.ca

Edmonton: Henning Byrne - *5
Former Name: Henning Byrne Whitmore & McKall
#1450, Standard Life Centre, 10405 Jasper Ave. NW, Edmonton, AB T5J 3N4
Tel: 780-421-1707; *Fax:* 780-425-9438
Toll-Free: 888-702-1707
www.henningbyrne.com

Edmonton: Heritage Law Offices - *3
#410, 316 Windermere Rd. NW, Edmonton, AB T6W 2Z8
Tel: 780-436-0011; *Fax:* 780-436-7000
lawyers@heritagelaw.com
heritagelaw.com
www.facebook.com/1299861596725027

Edmonton: Leroy N. Hiller - *1
#1720, Sun Life Place, 10123 - 99th St., Edmonton, AB T5J 3H1
Tel: 780-424-6660; *Fax:* 780-426-2980
lhiller@leroyhiller.com
www.leroyhiller.com

Edmonton: John Hinton - *1
5508 - 141 St. NW, Edmonton, AB T6H 4A2
Tel: 780-434-4710; *Fax:* 780-437-4281

Edmonton: Hladun & Company - *1
#300, 10711 - 102 St., Edmonton, AB T5H 2T8
Tel: 780-423-1888; *Fax:* 780-424-0934
inquiries@hladun.com
www.hladun.com

Edmonton: Terry E. Hofmann - *1
P.O. Box 51070, Stn. Highlands, 6525 - 118 Ave., Edmonton, AB T5W 5G5
Tel: 780-448-3885; *Fax:* 780-448-5840

Edmonton: Holman & Tilleard - *2
Former Name: Michael J. Tilleard
#720, 10150 - 100 St. NW, Edmonton, AB T5J 0P6
Tel: 780-429-3644; *Fax:* 780-429-3685

Edmonton: Douglas B. Holman - *1
#720, 10150 - 100 St. NW, Edmonton, AB T5J 0P6
Tel: 780-429-3644; *Fax:* 780-429-3685

Edmonton: William K. Horwitz - *1
#220, 8702 Meadowlark Rd. NW, Edmonton, AB T5R 5W5
Tel: 780-486-3100; *Fax:* 780-489-9671

Edmonton: Stanley V.T. Hum - *1
#1003, 10010 - 106 St. SW, Edmonton, AB T5J 3L8
Tel: 780-453-8988; *Fax:* 780-424-7379
stan_hum@hotmail.com

Edmonton: Hustwick Payne - *5
#600, 9707 - 110 St. NW, Edmonton, AB T5K 2L9
Tel: 780-482-6555; *Fax:* 780-482-6613
reception@hplegal.com
www.hplegal.com

Edmonton: Johnson Turner Lefaivre - *3
Former Name: Cochard Johnson
#607, 10117 Jasper Ave., Edmonton, AB T5J 1W8
Tel: 780-429-9929; *Fax:* 780-429-9981
www.johnsonturnerlefaivre.com

Edmonton: Jomha, Skrobot LLP
10621 - 124 St. NW, Edmonton, AB T5N 1S5
Tel: 780-424-0688; *Fax:* 780-424-0695
www.jomhalaw.com

Edmonton: KBL Law LLP - *4
Also Known As: Kolthammer, Batchelor & Laidlaw LLP
17318 - 106 Ave. NW, Edmonton, AB T5S 1H9
Tel: 780-489-5003; *Fax:* 780-486-2107
office@kbllaw.com
www.kbllaw.com

Edmonton: Kennedy Agrios LLP - *4
#1325, 10180 - 101 St. NW, Edmonton, AB T5J 3S4
Tel: 780-969-6900; *Fax:* 780-969-6901
www.kennedyagrios.com

Edmonton: Kirwin LLP - *9
Former Name: Kirwin & Kirwin
#100, Business Park, 12420 - 104th St., Edmonton, AB T5N 3Z9
Tel: 780-448-7401; *Fax:* 780-453-3281
www.kirwinllp.com

Edmonton: K. June Koska Professional Corporation - *1
#10209, 97 St. NW, Edmonton, AB T5J 0L6
Tel: 780-448-9137

Edmonton: I. Samuel Kravinchuk - *1
#800, 10310 Jasper Ave. NW, Edmonton, AB T5J 2W4
Tel: 780-426-4884; *Fax:* 780-428-8259

Edmonton: Katherine A. Kubica Professional Corporation - *1
10530 - 110 St., Edmonton, AB T5H 3C5
Tel: 780-425-8000; *Fax:* 780-425-8488

Edmonton: Kuckertz Law Office - *1
#202, 8003 - 102 St., Edmonton, AB T6E 4A2
Tel: 780-432-9308; *Fax:* 780-439-9950
www.facebook.com/kuckertzlaw
www.linkedin.com/company/kuckertzlaw

Edmonton: Kulasa Campbell - *3
#100, 10703 - 181 St. NW, Edmonton, AB T5S 1N3
Tel: 780-484-0665; *Fax:* 780-486-7282

Edmonton: Laurier Law Office - *3
8623 - 149 St., Edmonton, AB T5R 1B3
Tel: 780-486-0207; *Fax:* 780-483-0848

Edmonton: Liddell Law Office - Edmonton - *2
Former Name: Polack, Meindersma, Liddell
#320, Circle Square, 11808 St Albert Trail, Edmonton, AB T5L 4G4
Tel: 780-486-0926; *Fax:* 780-444-1393
www.liddelllaw.ca

Edmonton: Linton Law Office - *1
Former Name: Kathleen S.V. Linton
#52, Commonwealth Bldg., 9912-106 St. NW, Edmonton, AB T5K 1C5
Tel: 780-415-5540; *Fax:* 780-415-5541
info@lintonlawoffice.com

Edmonton: Philip G. Lister Law Office - *1
Former Name: Lister & Associate
#302, 10080 Jasper Ave. NW, Edmonton, AB T5J 1V9
Tel: 780-422-6114; *Fax:* 780-421-0818

Edmonton: Julie C. Lloyd - *1
#950, 10303 Jasper Ave. NW, Edmonton, AB T5J 3N6
Tel: 780-442-4417; *Fax:* 780-424-9370
jclloyd@telusplanet.net

Edmonton: Peter T.K. Loong - *1
11440 Kingsway Ave. NW, Edmonton, AB T5G 0X4
Tel: 780-424-3200; *Fax:* 780-424-2369
peterloonglaw@telusplanet.net

Edmonton: Lyons Albert & Cook - *2
#306, 10328 - 81 Ave. NW, Edmonton, AB T6E 1X2
Tel: 780-437-0743; *Fax:* 780-438-6695
laclaw@telusplanet.net
www.lyonsalbertcook.com

Edmonton: Machida Mack Shewchuk Meagher LLP - *1
#1300, 710-7 Ave. SW, Edmonton, AB T2P 3H6
Tel: 403-221-8322; *Fax:* 403-221-8339

Edmonton: Mah & Company - *2
#1013, TD Tower, 10088 - 102 Ave., Edmonton, AB T5J 2Z1
Tel: 780-428-3888; *Fax:* 780-425-8383

Edmonton: Rajiv Malhotram - *1
#315, 10909 Jasper Ave., Edmonton, AB T5J 3L9
Tel: 780-423-5792; *Fax:* 780-426-0081

Edmonton: James W. Mandick Professional Corporation - *1
#1850, 10123 - 99 St. NW, Edmonton, AB T5J 3H1
Tel: 780-423-3311; *Fax:* 780-423-3321
jmandick@wmlaw.ca

Edmonton: Michael B. Marcovitch - *1
#1300, 10665 Jasper Ave. NW, Edmonton, AB T5J 3S9
Tel: 780-453-4390; *Fax:* 780-424-3631

Edmonton: McAllister LLP - *12
Former Name: Cleall Barrsiters Solicitors; Cleall Pahl
#2500, Commerce Place, 10155 - 102nd St., Edmonton, AB T5J 4G8
Tel: 780-425-2500; *Fax:* 780-425-1222
main@mcallisterllp.com
www.mcallisterllp.com

Edmonton: McGee Richard Toogood LLP - *6
Former Name: McGee Richard
#1155, Weber Centre, 5555 Calgary Trail NW, Edmonton, AB T6H 5P9
Tel: 780-437-2240; *Fax:* 780-438-5788
www.mcgeerichard.com

Edmonton: McKay-Carey & Company - *1
200-6928 Roper Rd., Edmonton, AB T6B 3H9
Tel: 780-424-0222; *Fax:* 780-421-0834

Edmonton: McKee & Company - *2
#213, 14065 Victoria Trail, Edmonton, AB T5Y 2B6
Tel: 780-471-1100; *Fax:* 780-471-1150
www.mckeeandcompany.ca

Edmonton: Mckenzie House Law Group - *2
Former Name: G.D. Honey
#8603, 104 St. NW, Edmonton, AB T6E 4G6
Tel: 780-428-4531

Edmonton: Ingrid E. Meier - *1
2406 Tegler Green NW, Edmonton, AB T6R 3K2
Tel: 780-436-5954; *Fax:* 780-401-3204
lawyer@meier.ca

Edmonton: Ron J. Meleshko - *1
15412 - 55 St. NW, Edmonton, AB T5Y 2S4
Tel: 780-414-0298

Edmonton: Miller Boileau - *3
11835 - 102nd Ave. NW, Edmonton, AB T5K 0R6
Tel: 780-482-2888; *Fax:* 780-482-4600
mail@millerboileau.com
www.millerboileau.com

Edmonton: Minsos Stewart Masson - *3
#220, 8723 - 82 Ave., Edmonton, AB T6C 0Y9
Tel: 780-466-1175; *Fax:* 780-465-6717
www.realestatelawedmonton.com

Edmonton: Mintz Law - *4
#400, 10357 - 109 St. NW, Edmonton, AB T5J 1N3
Tel: 780-425-2041; *Fax:* 780-425-2195
www.mintzlaw.ca

Edmonton: Moustarah & Company - *3
#400, 10150 - 100 St., Edmonton, AB T5J 0P6
Tel: 780-428-5565; *Fax:* 780-428-6564
firm@moustarah.com
moustarah.com

Edmonton: Murray, Chilibeck & Horne - *3
10605 - 172nd St. NW, Edmonton, AB T5S 1P1
Tel: 780-484-2323; *Fax:* 780-486-4289
mchlaw@telusplanet.net
www.murraychilibeckandhorne.ca

Edmonton: Alann J. Nazarevich - *1
#201, 9035 - 51 Ave., Edmonton, AB T6E 5X4
Tel: 780-430-0363; *Fax:* 780-435-9279

* indicates number of lawyers

Edmonton: Neuman Thompson - *11
#301, 550 - 91 St. SW, Edmonton, AB T6X 0V1
Tel: 780-482-7645; Fax: 780-488-0026
www.neumanthompson.com

Edmonton: Kenneth Ng - *1
3234 Parsons Rd. NW, Edmonton, AB T6N 1M2
Tel: 780-988-9188; Fax: 780-496-9717

Edmonton: Nicholl & Akers - *8
#200, 10187 - 104 St., Edmonton, AB T5J 0Z9
Tel: 780-429-2771; Fax: 780-425-1665
info@nalawyers.ca
www.nalawyers.ca

Edmonton: Nickerson Roberts Holinski & Mercer - Edmonton - *11
Former Name: Nickerson, Roberts
#100, 7712 - 104 St., Edmonton, AB T6E 4C5
Tel: 780-428-0041; Fax: 780-425-0272
www.nrhmlaw.com

Edmonton: Gregory O'Laughlin - *1
#300, 10209 - 97 St. NW, Edmonton, AB T5J 0L6
Tel: 780-424-9059; Fax: 780-429-2615

Edmonton: Ronald J. Obirek - *1
#240, 6005 Gateway Blvd. NW, Edmonton, AB T6H 2H3
Tel: 780-496-9046; Fax: 780-436-9669
rjobirek@telusplanet.net

Edmonton: Ogilvie LLP - *33
#1400, Canadian Western Bank Place, 10303 Jasper Ave., Edmonton, AB T5J 3N6
Tel: 780-421-1818; Fax: 780-429-4453
info@ogilvielaw.com
www.ogilvielaw.com

Edmonton: Kelly R. Palmer - *1
#1800, 10250 - 101 St. NW, Edmonton, AB T5J 3P4
Tel: 780-448-9275; Fax: 780-423-0163

Edmonton: Phillip G. Parker - *1
#12, 11440 Kingsway NW, Edmonton, AB T5G 0X4
Tel: 780-471-2244

Edmonton: Patrick & Patrick - *1
#800, 10310 Jasper Ave. NW, Edmonton, AB T5J 2W4
Tel: 780-426-4884; Fax: 780-425-9358

Edmonton: Patrick Dolphin Professional Corporation - *1
Former Name: Edney, Hattersley & Dolphin
10621 - 124 St. NW, Edmonton, AB T5N 1S5
Tel: 780-423-4081; Fax: 780-425-5247

Edmonton: Penonzek Murray - *2
Former Name: Kenneth W. Penonzek Professional Corp
#147, 10403 - 122 St. NW, Edmonton, AB T5N 4C1
Tel: 780-482-1199; Fax: 780-482-1883
k.penonzek@shawbiz.ca

Edmonton: Patrick J. Phelan - *1
#1550, Sun Life Pl., 10123 - 99 St., Edmonton, AB T5J 3H1
Tel: 780-424-7730; Fax: 780-428-4484
patrick.phelan@telus.net

Edmonton: Ronald W. Poitras - *1
#300, 10209 - 97 St., Edmonton, AB T5J 0L6
Tel: 780-424-3270; Fax: 780-429-2615

Edmonton: Pringle Chivers Sparks Teskey - *7
Former Name: Pringle Chivers Sparks
#300, 10150 - 100 St. NW, Edmonton, AB T5J 0P6
Tel: 587-400-2049; Fax: 780-426-1470
Toll-Free: 877-424-8866
lawyers@pringlelaw.ca
www.pringlelaw.ca

Edmonton: Purdon Lintz - *3
Former Name: Purdon Caskenette; Baker & Purdon
10263 - 178 St. NW, Edmonton, AB T5S 1M3
Tel: 780-489-5566; Fax: 780-486-7735
www.purdonlaw.ca

Edmonton: Rackel Belzil LLP - *4
#100, Westgrove Professional Building, 10230 - 142 St. NW, Edmonton, AB T5N 3Y6
Tel: 780-424-2929; Fax: 780-451-8460
rackelbelzil.ca

Edmonton: Rand Kiss Turner LLP - *4
Former Name: Frohlich Rand Kiss
#1600, 10316 - 124th St., Edmonton, AB T5J 3G2
Tel: 780-423-1984; Fax: 780-423-1969
randkissturner.com

Edmonton: Raponi Rideout Tarrabain - Edmonton - *7
Former Name: Tarrabain & Company
#520, Manulife Place, 10180 - 101 St., Edmonton, AB T5J 3S4
Tel: 780-429-1010; Fax: 780-429-0101
lawyers@raponirideout.com
www.raponirideout.com

Edmonton: M. Naeem Rauf
#300, 10209 - 97 St. NW, Edmonton, AB T5J 0L6
Tel: 780-453-4399; Fax: 780-429-2615

Edmonton: Peter E. Recto - *1
6423 - 154th Avenue, Edmonton, AB T5Y 2N7
Tel: 780-423-1283; Fax: 780-473-8324
recto2001@hotmail.com

Edmonton: James E. Redmond - *1
P.O. Box 67306, Edmonton, AB T6M 0J5
Tel: 780-444-3035; Fax: 780-481-9124
info@jimeredmond.com
www.jimeredmond.com

Edmonton: Hans Reich - *1
#207, 10110 - 124 St. NW, Edmonton, AB T5N 1P6
Tel: 780-424-7732; Fax: 780-428-4484
reichlaw@telus.net

Edmonton: Richard S. Rennick - *1
Former Name: Rennick & Di Pinto
2320 Sun Life Pl., Edmonton, AB T5J 3H1
Tel: 780-426-5510; Fax: 780-420-1645

Edmonton: Reynolds Mirth Richards & Farmer LLP - *50
#3200, Manulife Place, 10180 - 101 St., Edmonton, AB T5J 3W8
Tel: 780-425-9510; Fax: 780-429-3044
Toll-Free: 800-661-7673
www.rmrf.com

Edmonton: Richards + Company - *4
Former Name: Richards Hunter Toogood; Worton Hunter & Callaghan; Richard Wood Toogood
#302, 1524 - 91 St. SW, Edmonton, AB T6X 1M5
Tel: 780-436-8554; Fax: 780-436-8566
www.richardslaw.ca
www.facebook.com/richardslawedmonton

Edmonton: Ritchie Mill Law Office - *3
Also Known As: RMLO
#101, 10301 - 109 St. NW, Edmonton, AB T5J 1N4
Tel: 780-431-1444; Fax: 780-431-1499
Toll-Free: 888-333-8818
lawyers@rmlo.com
rmlo.com

Edmonton: James A. Robertson - *1
10735-42 Ave. NW, Edmonton, AB T6J 2P5
Tel: 780-423-1680; Fax: 780-421-7304
jamesrob@shaw.ca

Edmonton: Robinson LLP - *6
Former Name: Frieser Robinson MacKay
#101, 10410 - 81 Ave., Edmonton, AB T6E 1X5
Tel: 780-429-1717; Fax: 780-421-8335
Toll-Free: 877-302-1717
inquiries@robinsonllp.com
www.robinsonllp.com

Edmonton: Terry J. Romaniuk - *1
9743 - 89 Ave. NW, Edmonton, AB T6E 2S1
Tel: 780-433-8127

Edmonton: David W. Ross - *1
8623 - 149 St. NW, Edmonton, AB T5R 1B3
Tel: 780-425-1965; Fax: 780-483-0848
dwross@bigfoot.com

Edmonton: James D. Ross - *1
#1003, Highfield Place, 10010 - 106 St., Edmonton, AB T5J 3L8
Tel: 780-482-3144; Fax: 780-424-7379

Edmonton: Samy F. Salloum - *1
1341 Carter Crest Rd. NW, Edmonton, AB T6R 2L6
Tel: 780-426-7777; Fax: 780-426-7778

Edmonton: David L. Schwartz - *1
11210 - 142 St. NW, Edmonton, AB T5M 1T9
Tel: 780-424-0259; Fax: 780-424-0299
thebigkahuna@interbaun.com

Edmonton: Sharek Logan & van Leenen LLP - *7
Also Known As: Sharek&Co.
Former Name: Sharek Logan Collingwood van Leenen LLP
#701, Tower 2, Scotia Place, 10060 Jasper Ave. NW, Edmonton, AB T5J 3R8
Tel: 780-413-3100; Fax: 780-413-3152
www.yeglaw.ca

Edmonton: William Shim
#2000, 10123 - 99 St. NW, Edmonton, AB T5J 3H1
Tel: 780-423-8060; Fax: 780-425-4201

Edmonton: Shores Jardine LLP - *8
#2250, Bell Tower, 10104 - 103 Ave., Edmonton, AB T5J 0H8
Tel: 780-448-9275; Fax: 780-423-0163
info@shoresjardine.com
www.shoresjardine.com

Edmonton: William J. Shymko - *1
#200, 9602 - 111 Ave. NW, Edmonton, AB T5G 0A8
Tel: 780-425-6414; Fax: 780-425-6416

Edmonton: Simons & Stephens - *3
#750, First Edmonton Pl., 10665 Jasper Ave. NW, Edmonton, AB T5J 3S9
Tel: 780-482-1536; Fax: 780-488-1914
nsimons@lawsimons.com

Edmonton: Snyder & Associates LLP - *16
#2500, Sun Life Pl., 10123 - 99 St., Edmonton, AB T5J 3H1
Tel: 780-426-4133; Fax: 780-424-1588
Toll-Free: 877-426-4148
inquiries@snyder.ca
www.snyder.ca

Edmonton: Stadnyk Law - Edmonton - 91 St. - *2
Former Name: Kobewka Stadnyk
#202, 1289 - 91 St. SW, Edmonton, AB T6X 1H1
Tel: 780-414-0222; Fax: 780-414-0002
Toll-Free: 877-414-0222
www.stadnyklaw.com

Edmonton: Stewart Law Offices - *2
11724 - 103 Ave. NW, Edmonton, AB T5K 0S7
Tel: 780-482-3800; Fax: 780-482-5600
stwlaw@telusplanet.net

Edmonton: Stillman LLP - *13
#300, 10335 - 172 St., Edmonton, AB T5S 1K9
Tel: 780-484-4445; Fax: 780-484-4184
Toll-Free: 888-258-2529
lawyers@stillmanllp.com
www.stillmanllp.com

Edmonton: André A. Szaszkiewicz - *1
#202, 1289 - 91 St., Edmonton, AB T6X 1H1
Tel: 780-452-2000; Fax: 780-455-7229
andresz@telusplanet.net

Edmonton: Christopher G. Taskey - *1
16404-100 Ave, NW, Edmonton, AB T5P 4Y2
Tel: 780-424-3558; Fax: 780-423-5515

Edmonton: Taylor & Jewell - *2
#215, Tower One, Millbourne Market Mall, 38 Ave. NW, Edmonton, AB T6K 3L6
Tel: 780-450-5761; Fax: 780-468-4524

Edmonton: Sylvia O. Tensfeldt - *1
#200, 10525 Jasper Ave. NW, Edmonton, AB T5J 1Z4
Tel: 780-424-3334; Fax: 780-424-4252

Edmonton: Thom Law Office - *1
8506 - 104 St., Edmonton, AB T6E 4G4
Tel: 780-434-5870; Fax: 780-756-8008
www.thomlaw.com

Edmonton: Tkachuk & Patterson - *2
#201, 17815 - 106 Ave. NW, Edmonton, AB T5S 2H1
Tel: 780-428-1593; Fax: 780-426-6679
www.tkachuklaw.ca

Edmonton: Helen S. Tymoczko - *1
#106, 10108 - 125 St., Edmonton, AB T5N 4B6
Tel: 780-472-1758; Fax: 780-476-4085

indicates number of lawyers

Edmonton: Tyson Law - *1
#300, 10209 - 97th St. NW, Edmonton, AB T5J 0L6
Tel: 780-488-3333; *Fax:* 780-429-2615
brent@tysonlaw.ca
www.tysonlaw.ca

Edmonton: Van Doesburg Law - *2
10060 - 164 St., Edmonton, AB T5P 4Y3
Tel: 780-451-2661; *Fax:* 780-452-1051
info@jvdlaw.ca
www.vandoesburglaw.com

Edmonton: Vantage Point Law Office - *4
Former Name: Venkatraman Purewal & Pillay
#303, 9811 - 34 Ave., Edmonton, AB T6E 5X9
Tel: 780-436-7060
info@vantagepointlawoffice.ca
www.vantagepointlawoffice.ca

Edmonton: Wachowich & Company
#410, 10113 - 104 St. NW, Edmonton, AB T5J 1A1
Tel: 780-429-0555; *Fax:* 780-425-4795
mail@wachowich.com
www.wachowich.com

Edmonton: Weir Bowen LLP - *14
#500, The Revillon Building, 10320 - 102 Ave. NW,
Edmonton, AB T5J 4A1
Tel: 780-424-2030; *Fax:* 780-424-2323
weirbowen.com

Edmonton: Uwe Welz - *1
7904 - 103 St. NW, Edmonton, AB T6E 6C3
Tel: 780-432-7711; *Fax:* 780-439-1177
uwpc@telusplanet.net

Edmonton: Wheatley Sadownik - Edmonton - *2
#2000, Sun Life Place, 10123 - 99 St., Edmonton, AB T5J
3H1
Tel: 780-423-6671; *Fax:* 780-420-6327
mail@wheatleysadownik.com
www.wheatleysadownik.com

Edmonton: Willis Bokenfohr Thorsrud - *3
Former Name: Willis & Bokenfohr
#410, ATB Place, 9888 Jasper Ave., Edmonton, AB T5J 5C6
Tel: 780-452-2764; *Fax:* 780-452-3247

Edmonton: Witten LLP - Edmonton - *54
#2500, Canadian Western Bank Place, 10303 Jasper Ave.,
Edmonton, AB T5J 3N6
Tel: 780-428-0501; *Fax:* 780-429-2559
Toll-Free: 888-429-9900
lawyers@wittenlaw.com
www.wittenlaw.com

Edmonton: Collin Wong - *1
10704 - 108 St., Edmonton, AB T5H 3A3
Tel: 780-488-7003; *Fax:* 780-488-1593
cwongpf@compusmart.ab.ca

Edmonton: Peter S. Wong - *1
#204, Kingsdale Professional Centre, 9644 - 54 Ave. NW,
Edmonton, AB T6E 5V1
Tel: 780-430-1070; *Fax:* 780-430-1773
pwong@sequiter.com

Edmonton: Worobec Law Offices - *4
Heritage Crt., 268-150 Chippewa Rd., Edmonton, AB T8A
6A2
Tel: 780-467-6325; *Fax:* 780-467-6326

Edmonton: Hu Eliot Young Law Office - *1
#440, Hong Kong Bank, 10055-106 St. NW, Edmonton, AB
T5J 2Y2
Tel: 780-425-8400; *Fax:* 780-424-3777
heyoung@telusplanet.net

Edmonton: Ronald J. Young - *1
#204, 10265 - 107 St., Edmonton, AB T5J 5G2
Tel: 780-424-3311; *Fax:* 780-425-9609

Edmonton: Zariwny Law Office - *1
9211-96 St. NW, Edmonton, AB T6C 3Y5
Tel: 780-433-5999; *Fax:* 780-439-6456
zlo@oanet.com

Edson: Dennis C. Calvert - *1
P.O. Box 6658, Stn. Main, 107 - 50 St., Edson, AB T7E 1V1
Tel: 780-723-6047; *Fax:* 780-723-3602

Fort McMurray: Cooper & Company - *8
Former Name: Campbell & Cooper; Campbell, Germain,
Cooper & Jean
#212, 9714 Main St., Fort McMurray, AB T9H 1T6
Tel: 780-791-7787; *Fax:* 780-791-0750
lawyers@ctwlaw.ca
mcmurraylaw.com

Fort McMurray: Evelyn J Roblee - *1
#202A, Plaza Shopping Centre, 8706 Franklin Ave., Fort
McMurray, AB T9H 2J6
Tel: 780-743-2860; *Fax:* 780-790-1618
frontdeskmiel@shaw.ca
www.evelynroblee.com

Fort Saskatchewan: Jenkins & Jenkins - *4
#200, 9906 - 102 St., Fort Saskatchewan, AB T8L 2C3
Tel: 780-998-4200; *Fax:* 780-998-4370
www.jenkinslaw.ca

Grande Cache: Harry Arnesen - *1
P.O. Box 385, 2502 Pine Plaza, Grande Cache, AB T0E 0Y0
Tel: 780-827-2458; *Fax:* 780-827-3734

Grande Prairie: Dobko & Wheaton - *6
10022 - 102 Ave., Grande Prairie, AB T8V 0Z7
Tel: 780-539-6200; *Fax:* 780-532-9052
Toll-Free: 866-539-6200
receptionist@dwlaw.ca
www.dwlaw.ca
www.facebook.com/dobkowheaton

**Grande Prairie: Gurevitch Burnham Law Office -
Grande Prairie - *3**
Former Name: Burgess & Gurevitch
9931 - 106th Ave., Grande Prairie, AB T8V 1J4
Tel: 780-539-3710; *Fax:* 780-532-2788
info@grandeprairielaw.ca
www.grandeprairielaw.ca

Grande Prairie: Howey Law Office - *1
#201, Professional Bldg., 9905 - 101 Ave., Grande Prairie,
AB T8V 0X7
Tel: 780-539-0690; *Fax:* 780-539-3813

Grande Prairie: KMSC Law - Grande Prairie - *16
Former Name: Kay McVey Smith & Carlstrom LLP
#401, 10514 - 67 Ave., Grande Prairie, AB T8W 0K8
Tel: 780-532-7771; *Fax:* 780-532-1158
Toll-Free: 888-531-7771
www.kmsc.ca
www.facebook.com/kmsclaw, twitter.com/KMSCLaw,
www.linkedin.com/company/kmsc-law-llp

Grande Prairie: Lewis & Chrenek LLP - *5
#108, 9824 - 97 Ave., Grande Prairie, AB T8V 7K2
Tel: 780-539-6800; *Fax:* 780-539-7975
contact@lewischrenek.com
www.lewischrenek.com

Grande Prairie: Walisser Shavers LLP - *2
#202, 10027 - 101 Ave., Grande Prairie, AB T8V 0X9
Tel: 780-532-0315; *Fax:* 780-532-3369

Hanna: Ross, Todd & Company - *3
P.O. Box 1330, 124 - 2 Ave. West, Hanna, AB T0J 1P0
Tel: 403-854-4431; *Fax:* 403-854-2561
reception@drumhellerlaw.com

High Prairie: Harry J. Jong - *2
P.O. Box 1379, 5119 - 50 St., High Prairie, AB T0G 1E0
Tel: 780-523-4554; *Fax:* 780-523-5550
hjlaw@cablecomet.com

**High River: A. George Dearing Professional Corp. -
*1**
#103, 14 - 2 Ave. SE, High River, AB T1V 2B8
Tel: 403-652-2771; *Fax:* 403-652-2699
info@ageorgedearing.ca
www.ageorgedearing.ca

Hinton: Johnson McClelland Murdoch - *4
213 Pembina Ave., Hinton, AB T7V 2B3
Tel: 780-865-2222; *Fax:* 780-865-8857
lawyer@jmmlaw.ca

Hinton: Woods & Robson - *2
110 Brewster Dr., Hinton, AB T7V 1B4
Tel: 780-865-3086; *Fax:* 780-865-7149
woodsrob@telusplanet.net

Innisfail: Tulloch Law Office - *1
P.O. Box 6099, Stn. Main, 5030 - 50 St., Innisfail, AB T4G 1S7
Tel: 403-227-5591; *Fax:* 403-227-1230
carolyntulloch@gmail.com
* indicates number of lawyers

Lac La Biche: John W. Kozina - *1
Also Known As: Kozina Law Office
Former Name: Kozina & Gregory
P.O. Box 1439, 10130 Alberta Ave., Lac La Biche, AB T0A
2C0
Tel: 780-623-4818; *Fax:* 780-623-2933
jwklaw@telus.net

Leduc: Arends Law Office - *1
4915-48 Ave., Leduc, AB T9E 7H9
Tel: 780-986-1443; *Fax:* 780-980-5385
arendslaw@shaw.ca

Leduc: Elgert & Company - *1
5206 - 50 St., Leduc, AB T9E 6Z6
Tel: 780-986-3487; *Fax:* 780-986-2040
herbelgert@shaw.ca

**Leduc: Jackie, Handerek & Forester, Barristers &
Solicitors - Leduc - *8**
4710 - 50th St., Leduc, AB T9E 6W2
Tel: 780-986-5081; *Fax:* 780-986-8807
www.leduclawyers.ab.ca

Leduc: Pahl Howard Rowland LLP - *4
#1, 5304 - 50 St., Leduc, AB T9E 6Z6
Tel: 780-986-8428; *Fax:* 780-986-2552

Lethbridge: Douglas N. Alger - *1
#230, 719 - 4 Ave. South, Lethbridge, AB T1J 0O1
Tel: 403-380-6005; *Fax:* 403-380-6088

Lethbridge: Connolly & Associates - *2
#203, P.O. Box 1207, Stn. Main, 506 - 7 St. South,
Lethbridge, AB T1J 4A4
Tel: 403-329-8188; *Fax:* 403-328-7079

Lethbridge: Davidson & Williams LLP - *7
P.O. Box 518, 501 - 4 St. South, Lethbridge, AB T1J 3Z4
Tel: 403-328-1766; *Fax:* 403-320-5434
info@dwlaw.pro
dwlaw.pro

Lethbridge: Frank de Walle - *1
323 - 7 St. South, Lethbridge, AB T1J 2G4
Tel: 403-328-8800; *Fax:* 403-328-8502
dewalle@telusplanet.net

Lethbridge: Dimnik & Company - *3
334 - 12 St. South, Lethbridge, AB T1J 2R1
Tel: 403-320-9800; *Fax:* 403-320-9124
info@lethbridgelawyers.com
www.lethbridgelawyers.com

Lethbridge: Huckvale LLP - Lethbridge - *10
Former Name: Huckvale Wilde Harvie MacLennan LLP
410 - 6th St. South, Lethbridge, AB T1J 2C9
Tel: 403-328-8856; *Fax:* 403-380-4050
www.huckvale.ca

Lethbridge: MacLachlan McNab Hembroff LLP - *10
1003 - 4th Ave. South, Lethbridge, AB T1J 0P7
Tel: 403-381-4966; *Fax:* 403-329-9300
mmh@mmhlawyers.com
www.mmhlawyers.com

Lethbridge: Millar & Keith LLP - *2
Former Name: Millar, Thiessen & Keith
200 - 3rd St. South, Lethbridge, AB T1J 1Y7
Tel: 403-327-5716; *Fax:* 403-329-4063
mtklaw@telusplanet.net

Lethbridge: Milne Pritchard Law Office - *3
#807, 400 - 4 Ave. South, Lethbridge, AB T1J 4E1
Tel: 403-329-1133; *Fax:* 403-329-0395
www.milnepritchard.com

Lethbridge: Harold N. Moodie Law Office - *1
424 - 7th St. South, Lethbridge, AB T1J 2G6
Tel: 403-328-0005; *Fax:* 403-329-0945
Toll-Free: 800-207-8482
hmoodie@moodielaw.ca
www.moodielaw.ca

Lethbridge: North & Company LLP - *19
#600, Chancery Court, 220 - 4th St., Lethbridge, AB T1J 4J7
Tel: 403-328-7781; *Fax:* 403-320-8958
Toll-Free: 800-552-8022
www.north-co.com

Lethbridge: Peterson & Purvis LLP - *6
P.O. Box 1165, 537 - 7th St. South, Lethbridge, AB T1J 4A4
Tel: 403-328-9667; *Fax:* 403-320-1393
p-plaw@telusplanet.net
www.petersonpurvislaw.ca

Lethbridge: Pollock & Company - Lethbridge - *3
Former Name: Fletcher, Norton & Pollock
#200, P.O. Box 1386, 434 - 7th St. South, Lethbridge, AB T1J
4K1

Tel: 403-329-6900
dlplaw@lawpollock.com
www.lawpollock.com

Lethbridge: RMcD Law Offices - *1
243-12B St. N, Lethbridge, AB T1H 2K8
Tel: 403-328-9125; Fax: 403-328-9143
wfmlaw@telus.net

Lethbridge: Shapiro & Company - *1
#200, 427 - 5 St. South., Lethbridge, AB T1J 2B6
Tel: 403-328-9300; Fax: 403-328-9307
shapco@telusplanet.net

Lethbridge: Stringam LLP - Lethbridge - *19
Former Name: Stringam Denecky Law Office
150 - 4 St. South, Lethbridge, AB T1J 5G4
Tel: 403-328-5577; Fax: 403-327-1141
www.stringam.ca
www.facebook.com/stringam, twitter.com/StringamLLP,
www.linkedin.com/company/stringam-denecky-llp

Lethbridge: Thiessen Law Group - *3
1412 - 3rd Ave. South, Lethbridge, AB T1J 0K6
Tel: 403-381-7343; Fax: 403-381-7350
thiessenlaw@thiessenlaw.ca
www.thiessenlaw.ca
www.facebook.com/171450492908177, twitter.com/ThiessenLaw

Lethbridge: Torry Lewis Abells LLP - *7
#110, Chancery Court, 220 - 4 St. South, Lethbridge, AB T1J
4J7

Tel: 403-327-4406; Fax: 403-328-4597
Toll-Free: 888-327-4406
ken.torry@tlalaw.com
www.tlalaw.com

Lloydminster: Clements & Smith - *3
#212, 5704 - 44 St., Lloydminster, AB T9V 2A1
Tel: 750-875-7999

Lloydminster: Kindrachuk Dobson - *2
Former Name: Kindrachuk Law Office
Stafford Building, 5014 - 48 St., 2nd fl., Lloydminster, AB
T9V 0H8

Tel: 780-875-6600; Fax: 780-875-6601
info@kindrachukdobson.com
www.linkedin.com/company/2269686

Lloydminster: Kirzinger, Wells Law Office - *2
#203, 5101 - 48 St., Lloydminster, AB T9V 0H9
Tel: 780-875-8400; Fax: 780-875-8499

Lloydminster: Knight Law Office - *1
P.O. Box 1500, Stn. Main, 4912 - 50th Ave., Lloydminster, AB
S9V 1K5

Tel: 780-875-9555; Fax: 780-875-9557
bknight@silvercrest.ca

Medicine Hat: Haynes, William L., Law Office - *1
#108, 1235 Southview Dr. SE, Medicine Hat, AB T1B 4K3
Tel: 403-528-8883; Fax: 403-526-7698
bill@hayneslaw.net

Medicine Hat: Hill & Hill - *2
#6, 3151 Dunmore Rd. SE, Medicine Hat, AB T1B 2H2
Tel: 403-527-1544; Fax: 403-526-2551

Medicine Hat: Leis, Wiese & Company - *3
#35, 7 St. SE, Medicine Hat, AB T1A 1J2
Tel: 403-527-7766; Fax: 403-527-7788

Medicine Hat: MacLean Wiedemann Lawyers LLP -
*4
422 - 6th St. SE, Medicine Hat, AB T1A 1H5
Tel: 403-527-3343; Fax: 403-526-0473
www.mwllp.ca/mmllp

Medicine Hat: Niblock & Company LLP - *7
P.O. Box 609, Stn. Main, 420 Macleaod Trail SE, Medicine
Hat, AB T1A 7G5

Tel: 403-526-2806; Fax: 403-526-2356
Toll-Free: 800-245-9411
reception@Niblock.com
www.niblock.ca

Medicine Hat: Pritchard & Co. Law Firm, LLP - *4
#204, P.O. Box 100, 430 - 6th Ave. SE, Medicine Hat, AB T1A
7E8

Tel: 403-527-4411; Fax: 403-527-9806
lawyers@pritchardandco.com
www.pritchardandcompany.ca
www.facebook.com/PritchardCompanyLlp, twitter.com/PCo_LLP

Medicine Hat: Schindel Law Office - *1
#1, 3295 Dunmore Rd. SE, Medicine Hat, AB T1B 3R2
Tel: 403-529-5548; Fax: 403-529-2694
schindellaw.com

Medicine Hat: Sihvon Carter Fisher & Berger LLP -
*4
499 - 1st St. SE, Medicine Hat, AB T1A 0A7
Tel: 403-526-2600; Fax: 403-526-3217
info@scfb.ca

Medicine Hat: Smith & Hersey Law Firm - Medicine
Hat - *4
Former Name: Gordon, Smith & Company
#104, Westside Common, 2201 Box Springs Blvd. NW,
Medicine Hat, AB T1C 0C8
Tel: 403-527-5506; Fax: 403-527-0577
Toll-Free: 800-598-7626
smithhersey.com

Nanton: Laurie M. Gordon - *1
P.O. Box 586, 2213 - 20th St., Nanton, AB T0L 1R0
Tel: 403-646-6111; Fax: 403-646-6112
lmgordon@telusplanet.net

Nanton: Roddie Law Office - *1
P.O. Box 100, 2117 - 20 St., Nanton, AB T0L 1R0
Tel: 403-646-2211; Fax: 403-646-3159
rodmclaw@telusplanet.net

Okotoks: Brandi Aymount - *1
Also Known As: Okotoks Law
P.O. Box 669, 84 Elizabeth St., Okotoks, AB T1S 1A8
Tel: 403-938-2101; Fax: 403-938-6020
aymontb@okotokslaw.com
okotokslaw.com

Okotoks: Diane Luttmer Professional Corporation -
*1
Former Name: Diane Dolsen
P.O. Box 267, Okotoks, AB T1S 1A5
Tel: 403-938-8296; Fax: 403-938-8286

Okotoks: Charles A. Dixon - *1
P.O. Box 1169, Stn. Main, 51 Riverside Gate, Okotoks, AB
T1S 1B2

Tel: 403-938-8131; Fax: 403-938-6365

Olds: R. Brent Carlyle
P.O. Box 3755, Stn. Main, 4911 - 51 Ave., Olds, AB T4H 1P5
Tel: 866-279-2110; Fax: 866-619-2904
brentc@reveal.ca

Olds: Alvin F. Ganser - *1
P.O. Box 4040, Stn. Main, 4834 - 50 St., Olds, AB T4H 1P7
Tel: 403-556-8481; Fax: 403-556-3830
aganser@oldsnet.ca

Olds: Martinson & Harder - *3
#1, 5401 - 49 Ave., Olds, AB T4H 1G3
Tel: 403-556-8955; Fax: 403-556-8895
contact@martinsonharder.com
martinsonharder.com

Peace River: Mathieu Hryniuk LLP - Peace River - *6
P.O. Box 6210, 10012 - 101 St., Peace River, AB T8S 1S2
Tel: 780-624-2565; Fax: 780-624-5766
Toll-Free: 800-661-1962
mh@mhllp.ca
mhllp.ca

Ponoka: Noble & Kidd - *1
P.O. Box 4278, Stn. Main, Ponoka, AB T4J 1R7
Tel: 403-783-3325; Fax: 403-783-5080
noblekid@telus.net

Ponoka: Paterson & Company - *2
#4550, 5016 - 51 Ave., Ponoka, AB T4J 1S1
Tel: 403-783-5521; Fax: 403-783-2012
office@craigpatersonlaw.com
www.craigpatersonlaw.com

Priddis: Rath & Company - *3
P.O. Box 44, RR#1, Site 8, Priddis, AB T0L 1W0
Tel: 403-931-4047; Fax: 403-931-4048
rathco@rathandcompany.com
www.rathandcompany.com

* indicates number of lawyers

Red Deer: Brian Adair - *1
#B, 4921 - 47 St., Red Deer, AB T4N 1R4
Tel: 403-342-1777; Fax: 403-341-4775
www.brianadair.ca

Red Deer: Susan K. Allison - *1
4919 - 48 St., 2nd Floor, Red Deer, AB T4N 1S8
Tel: 403-340-3136; Fax: 403-343-7016
sallison@reddeerlaw.com

Red Deer: Altalaw LLP - *12
Former Name: Duhamel Manning Feehan Warrender
Glass LLP
5233 - 49 Ave., Red Deer, AB T4N 6G5
Tel: 403-343-0812; Fax: 403-340-3545
altalaw@altalaw.ca
www.altalaw.ca

Red Deer: Dunkle McBeath - *2
5004 - 48 Ave., Red Deer, AB T4N 3T6
Tel: 403-347-5522; Fax: 403-347-5632
dkm_law@telusplanet.net

Red Deer: C.E. Forgues - *1
#103, 4310-49 Ave., Red Deer, AB T4N 6M5
Tel: 403-342-7044; Fax: 403-342-7055

Red Deer: Gerig Hamilton Neeland LLP - *6
#501, 4901 - 48 St., Red Deer, AB T4N 6M4
Tel: 403-343-2444; Fax: 403-343-6522
info@ghnlawyers.ca
www.ghnlawyers.ca

Red Deer: Donald A. Gross - *1
#274, 4919 - 59 St., Red Deer, AB T4N 6C9
Tel: 403-343-3715; Fax: 403-343-7435

Red Deer: Johnston Ming Manning LLP - Red Deer -
*12
Royal Bank Bldg., 4943 - 50th St., 3rd & 4th Fl., Red Deer,
AB T4N 1Y1

Tel: 403-346-5591; Fax: 403-346-5599
info@jmmlawrd.ca
www.johnstonmingmanning.com

Red Deer: Gayle A. Langford - *1
#303, 5008 - 50th St., Red Deer, AB T4N 1Y3
Tel: 403-358-3559; Fax: 403-356-0397
gayle@galangford.ca
www.galangford.ca

Red Deer: Brian S. MacNairn - *1
#201, 5008 Ross St., Red Deer, AB T4N 1Y3
Tel: 403-347-2700; Fax: 403-346-5825
macnairn@telusplanet.net

Red Deer: P.E.B. MacSween - *1
4824 - 51 St., Red Deer, AB T4N 2A5
Tel: 403-342-5595; Fax: 403-342-7519

Red Deer: Peter C. McElhaney - *1
#5, 4801 - 51 Ave., Red Deer, AB T4N 4H2
Tel: 403-346-2026; Fax: 403-309-1969

Red Deer: Gerald W. Neufeld - *1
#504, 4909-49 St., Red Deer, AB T4N 1V1
Tel: 403-343-2202; Fax: 403-343-2203
gneufeld@telusplanet.net

Red Deer: Patrick A. Penny - *1
10 Reeves Cres., Red Deer, AB T4P 2Y4
Tel: 403-342-9595; Fax: 403-346-9778
pmanpenny@telus.net
red-deer-criminal-lawyer.ca

Red Deer: Schnell Hardy Jones LLP - Red Deer - *9
Former Name: Schnell, MacSween & Hardy
#504, 4909 - 49th St., Red Deer, AB T4N 1V1
Tel: 403-342-7400; Fax: 403-340-0520
Toll-Free: 800-342-7405
lawyers@schnell-law.com
www.schnell-law.com

Red Deer: Sully Chapman Beattie LLP - *2
Former Name: Flanagan, Sully, Surkan
#202, Park Place, 4825 - 47th St., Red Deer, AB T4N 1R3
Tel: 403-342-7715; Fax: 403-347-5955
info@scblaw.ca
www.scblaw.ca

Red Deer: **Warren Sinclair LLP - *16**
Former Name: Sisson Warren Sinclair
#600, First Red Deer Place, 4911 - 51 St., Red Deer, AB T4N 6V4
Tel: 403-343-3320; Fax: 403-343-6069
email@warrensinclair.com
www.warrensinclair.com

Red Deer: **William D. Weiswasser - *1**
#300, 4808-50 St., Red Deer, AB T4N 1X5
Tel: 403-343-0317; Fax: 403-343-0318
mediate@agt.net

Redwater: **D. Lawrence McCallum - *1**
4816-50 Ave., Redwater, AB T0A 2W0
Tel: 780-942-3040; Fax: 780-942-2003
Toll-Free: 800-390-2257

Rimbey: **David R. Pfau - *1**
P.O. Box 1009, 5001 - 50th Ave., Rimbey, AB T0C 2J0
Tel: 403-843-2296; Fax: 403-843-2344

Rocky Mountain House: **Peter Crossley Law Office - *1**
P.O. Box 1108, 4616 - 47 Ave., Rocky Mountain House, AB T4T 1A8
Tel: 403-845-2828; Fax: 403-845-4630
crossleylaw@shawbiz.ca

Rocky Mountain House: **Dunsford & Scott - *2**
5135 - 48 Ave., Rocky Mountain House, AB T4T 1A3
Tel: 403-845-7112; Fax: 403-845-4670
reception@dunsfordandscott.com
www.dunsfordandscott.com

Sherwood Park: **Ahlstrom Wright - Sherwood Park - *12**
#200, 80 Chippewa Rd., Sherwood Park, AB T8A 4W6
Tel: 780-464-7477; Fax: 780-467-6428
lawyers@ahlstromwright.ca
www.ahlstromwright.ca

Sherwood Park: **Stanley H. King - *1**
241 Kaska Rd., 2nd Fl., Sherwood Park, AB T8A 4E8
Tel: 780-449-1404; Fax: 780-449-1409
stan@westana.com

Sherwood Park: **Wayne LeDrew - *1**
#16, 140 Athabascan Ave., Sherwood Park, AB T8A 4E3
Tel: 780-467-3014; Fax: 780-464-8504
wledrew@telusplanet.net

Sherwood Park: **Nigro & Company - *2**
282 Kaska Rd., Sherwood Park, AB T8A 4G7
Tel: 780-467-9559; Fax: 780-467-0720
nigroco@shaw.ca

Sherwood Park: **Thomas E. Spratlin - *1**
Former Name: Spratlin Tonnellier
#120, 363 Sioux Rd., Sherwood Park, AB T8A 4W7
Tel: 780-464-5404; Fax: 780-417-1759
spratlinlaw.petrasite.com

Sherwood Park: **Strathcona Law Group - *4**
#132, Heritage Court, 150 Chippewa Rd., Sherwood Park, AB T8A 6A2
Tel: 780-417-9222; Fax: 780-449-1222
info@strathconalawgroup.com
www.strathconalawgroup.com

Slave Lake: **Allan G. McMillan - *1**
#107, P.O. Box 533, 201 - 2 St. NE, Slave Lake, AB T0G 2A0
Tel: 780-849-2227; Fax: 780-849-2143
mcmillan@telusplanet.net

Slave Lake: **Twinn Barristers & Solicitors - *1**
Former Name: Catherine M. Twinn
P.O. Box 1460, 810 Caribou Trail NE, Slave Lake, AB T0G 2A0
Tel: 780-849-4319; Fax: 780-805-3274
ctwinn@twinnlaw.com

Spruce Grove: **Larry D. Ayers - *2**
#210, P.O. Box 4372, Stn. Main, 215 McLeod Ave., Spruce Grove, AB T7X 3B5
Tel: 780-962-9500; Fax: 780-962-9535
ayers@ayerslawco.com
www.ayerslawco.com

Spruce Grove: **Loretta (Lori) Edlund - *1**
#35, 54023 SH 779, Spruce Grove, AB T7X 3V5
Tel: 780-968-1668; Fax: 780-968-1667
nlaedlund@gmail.com
sprucegrovelaywer.ca

Spruce Grove: **Randall C. Heil - *1**
#201, 93 McLeod Ave., Spruce Grove, AB T7X 2Z9
Tel: 780-962-9700; Fax: 780-962-9329
www.rcheillaw.com

Spruce Grove: **Robert A. Joly - *1**
#4, 20 McLeod Ave., Spruce Grove, AB T7X 3Y1
Tel: 780-962-4447; Fax: 780-962-3638
bbjoly@shaw.ca

Spruce Grove: **Mainstreet Law Offices - *7**
115 Main St., Spruce Grove, AB T7X 3A7
Tel: 780-960-8100
www.mainstreetlaw.ca

Spruce Grove: **Robinson & Company - *2**
P.O. Box 4113, 16 Westgrove Dr., Spruce Grove, AB T7X 3B3
Tel: 780-962-0660; Fax: 780-962-0622
office@sprucegrovelaw.com
www.sprucegrovelaw.com

St Albert: **Cody Law Office - *1**
#407, 22 Sir Winston Churchill Ave., St Albert, AB T8N 1B4
Tel: 780-470-0500; Fax: 780-670-0501
www.codylawoffice.com

St Albert: **Oddleifson & Kaup - *2**
#200, 39 St Thomas St., St Albert, AB T8N 6N8
Tel: 780-459-2220; Fax: 780-459-0621

St Albert: **Quantz Law Group - *3**
Former Name: Stonhouse & Downie
#220, 8 Perron St., St Albert, AB T8N 1E4
Tel: 780-458-7690; Fax: 780-458-5510
info@quantzlaw.com
www.quantzlaw.com

St Albert: **Thomas A. Rowand Professional Corp. - *1**
22 Perron St., St Albert, AB T8N 6B9
Tel: 780-458-9440; Fax: 780-458-9442
trowand@telusplanet.net

St Albert: **Wallace Law Office - *1**
#3, 30 Rayborn Cres., St Albert, AB T8N 5B7
Tel: 780-458-7717; Fax: 780-460-1818

St Albert: **Weary & Company - *3**
#400, 30 Green Grove Dr., St Albert, AB T8N 5H6
Tel: 780-459-5596; Fax: 780-459-6572
info@wearyandco.com
www.wearyandco.com

St Paul: **Lamoureux Culham LLP - *3**
Former Name: Lamoureux & Lawrence
4713 - 50th St., St Paul, AB T0A 3A4
Tel: 780-645-5202; Fax: 780-645-6507
www.stpaul-law.ca

Stony Plain: **Birdsell Grant LLP - Stony Plain - *10**
Former Name: Birdsell Grant Gardner Morck
#102, 5300 - 50 St., Stony Plain, AB T7Z 1T8
Tel: 780-963-8181; Fax: 780-963-9618
info@birdsell.ca
www.birdsell.ca

Stony Plain: **Deborah A. Kay - *1**
#104, 4310 - 33 St., Stony Plain, AB T7Z 0A8
Tel: 780-591-0225; Fax: 780-591-0223
info@kaylawandmediation.com
www.kaylawandmediation.com

Stony Plain: **Glen G. McAllister - *1**
#128, 5211 - 50 St., Stony Plain, AB T7Z 0C1
Tel: 780-968-2900; Fax: 780-968-2224
contact@mcallisterlawfirm.ca
www.mcallisterlawfirm.ca/en/

Strathmore: **Getz & Associates - *2**
P.O. Box 2370, Stn. Main, 225A Wheatland Trail, Strathmore, AB T1P 1K3
Tel: 403-934-2500; Fax: 403-934-2794
getzlaw@getzlaw.ca

Strathmore: **Jarvis, Randal E.J. - *2**
#110, 304 Third Ave., Strathmore, AB T1P 1Z1
Tel: 403-934-5000; Fax: 403-934-4853
rejarvis@shaw.ca

Sylvan Lake: **Brian C. Flanagan - *1**
#203, 5043 - 50A St., Sylvan Lake, AB T4S 1R1
Tel: 403-887-5441; Fax: 403-887-3010
burflan@telusplanet.net

Sylvan Lake: **Vanden Brink Law Office - *1**
Former Name: Vanden Brink & Madden
P.O. Box 9613, Stn. Main, Sylvan Lake, AB T4S 1S8
Tel: 403-885-2222; Fax: 403-885-2226
benbrink@hughes.net

Taber: **Baldry Sugden LLP - *3**
5401 - 50 Ave., Taber, AB T1G 1V2
Tel: 403-223-3585; Fax: 403-223-1732
balsug@telusplanet.net
baldrysugden.ca

Three Hills: **Norman L. Tainsh, Q.C. Professional Corporation - *1**
P.O. Box 1234, 205 Main St., Three Hills, AB T0M 2A0
Tel: 403-443-2200 Toll-Free: 888-939-2200
info@tainsh.ca
www.tainsh.ca
www.facebook.com/normanl.tainshpc,
www.linkedin.com/in/norman-tainsh-5811036

Turner Valley: **Beverly A.B. Broadhurst - *1**
#2, P.O. Box 501, 101 Sunset Blvd. SW, Turner Valley, AB T0L 2A0
Tel: 403-933-3255; Fax: 403-933-4104

Vermilion: **Reynolds & Flemke - *2**
#11, Vermilion Prof. Bldg., 5125 - 50 Ave., Vermilion, AB T9X 1A8
Tel: 780-853-5339; Fax: 780-853-4200
rfverm@telusplanet.net

Vermilion: **Wheat Law Office - *2**
5042 - 49 Ave., Vermilion, AB T9X 1B7
Tel: 780-853-4707; Fax: 780-853-4499
wheatlaw@telusplanet.net

Wainwright: **Peter Van Winssen - *1**
1013 - 5 Ave., Wainwright, AB T9W 1L6
Tel: 780-842-5140; Fax: 780-842-3830

Westlock: **ProperziTims - *5**
#2, P.O. Box 490, 9831 - 107th St., Westlock, AB T7P 1R9
Tel: 780-349-5366; Fax: 780-349-6510
candice@properzitims.com
properzitims.com

Wetaskiwin: **McDonald Street Law Office - *1**
4408 - 51 St., Wetaskiwin, AB T9A 1K5
Tel: 780-352-0369; Fax: 780-352-0393

Wetaskiwin: **SIRRS LLP - Wetaskiwin - *7**
Former Name: Deckert Allen Cymbaluk Genest
5220 - 51st Ave., Wetaskiwin, AB T9A 2G3
Tel: 780-352-3301; Fax: 780-352-5976
wetaskiwin@sirrsllp.com
www.sirrsllp.com

Wetaskiwin: **Sockett Law - *4**
5118 - 50th Ave., Wetaskiwin, AB T9A 0S6
Tel: 780-352-6691; Fax: 780-352-0599
sockett@sockettlaw.com

Whitecourt: **McConnell Law Office - *1**
P.O. Box 1795, Stn. Main, 5115 Highway St., Whitecourt, AB T7S 1P5
Tel: 780-778-4945; Fax: 780-778-3851

British Columbia

100 Mile House: **Centennial Law Corporation - *2**
#1, P.O. Box 2169, 241 Birch Ave., 100 Mile House, BC V0K 2E0
Tel: 250-395-1080; Fax: 250-395-1088
centenniallaw@bcinternet.net
centenniallaw.com

Abbotsford: **Balakshin Hargrave Law Corporation - *2**
#202, 2955 Gladwin Rd., Abbotsford, BC V2T 5T4
Tel: 604-859-1220
info@bhlawyers.ca
www.bhlawyers.ca
www.facebook.com/BalakshinHargraveLawCorporation

Abbotsford: **Kenneth R. Beatch - *1**
2459 Pauline St., Abbotsford, BC V2S 3S1
Tel: 604-853-9555; Fax: 604-859-3361
ken@drugdefence.com
www.drugdefence.com

* indicates number of lawyers

Abbotsford: Conroy & Company - *3
2459 Pauline St., Abbotsford, BC V2S 3S1
Tel: 604-852-5110; Fax: 604-859-3361
Toll-Free: 877-852-5110
office@johnconroy.com
www.johnconroy.com

Abbotsford: Stanley T. Cope - *1
#205, 2692 Clearbrook Rd., Abbotsford, BC V2T 2Y8
Tel: 604-855-2089
stan@copeinjuryclaimlawyers.ca
www.copeinjuryclaimlawyers.ca/en/

Abbotsford: Dhami Narang & Company - *4
#301, 2975 Gladwin Rd., Abbotsford, BC V2T 5T4
Tel: 604-864-6131; Fax: 604-864-6116
Toll-Free: 877-864-6131
www.dnclaw.ca
www.facebook.com/dnclaw, twitter.com/injurylawyersbc

Abbotsford: Donald R. Gardner - *1
Abbotsford Registry & Judges' Chambers, 32203 South
Fraset Way, Abbotsford, BC V2T 1W6
Tel: 604-855-3200; Fax: 604-855-3232

Abbotsford: Integra Law Group - *1
#101, 2776 Bourquin Cres. West, Abbotsford, BC V2S 6A4
Tel: 604-859-7187; Fax: 604-859-7185
josh@integralaw.ca

Abbotsford: Just Law Corpoartion - *1
#10, 2151 McCallum Rd., Abbotsford, BC V2S 3N8
Tel: 604-854-6689; Fax: 604-852-4789
mv.law@telus.net
www.justlawinc.com

Abbotsford: Kuhn LLP - *12
#100, 2160 South Fraser Way, Abbotsford, BC V2T 1W5
Tel: 604-864-8877; Fax: 604-864-8867
Toll-Free: 888-704-8877
www.kuhnco.net

Abbotsford: Linley Welwood LLP - *10
Former Name: Linley, Duignan & Company; Welwood
Wiens Warkentin; Fast Welwood & Wiens; Linley
Duignan
#305, 2692 Clearbrook Rd., Abbotsford, BC V2T 2Y8
Tel: 604-425-0588; Fax: 604-850-6616
info@linleywelwood.com
www.linleywelwood.com
www.facebook.com/LinleyWelwoodLLP,
twitter.com/linleywelwood,
www.linkedin.com/company/linley-welwood-llp

Abbotsford: MacAdams Law Firm - *3
#205, Gladwin Centre, 2955 Gladwin Rd., Abbotsford, BC
V2T 5T4
Fax: 604-850-1937
Toll-Free: 800-800-2967
www.macadamslaw.com
www.linkedin.com/company/macadams-law-firm

Abbotsford: Palmer Gillen - *2
#1, 33775 Essendene Ave., Abbotsford, BC V2S 2H1
Tel: 604-859-3887; Fax: 604-859-3883
www.abbotsfordlawyers.com

Abbotsford: Robertson, Downe & Mullally - *20
Also Known As: RDM Lawyers LLP
33695 South Fraser Way, Abbotsford, BC V2S 2C1
Tel: 604-853-0774; Fax: 604-852-3829
Toll-Free: 888-853-0774
info@rdmlawyers.com
www.rdmlawyers.com
www.facebook.com/RDMLawyers,
www.linkedin.com/company/rdm-lawyers

Abbotsford: Rosborough & Company - *3
#201, 33832 Fraser Way South, Abbotsford, BC V2S 2C5
Tel: 604-859-7171
MBurke@Rosborough.com
www.rosborough.com

Abbotsford: Valley Law Group LLP - *4
Former Name: Kuzminski & Haraldsen
#301, 2031 McCallum Rd., Abbotsford, BC V2S 3N5
Tel: 604-853-5401; Fax: 604-853-8358
info@vlgllp.com
www.valleylawgroup.com

Armstrong: Culos & Company - *1
Former Name: Clarke & Company
#1, P.O. Box 70, 2516 Patterson Ave., Armstrong, BC V0E
1B0
Tel: 250-546-2448; Fax: 250-546-2621
robculos@telus.net

Brentwood Bay: Sandra E. Jenko - *1
#112, P.O. Box 425, Stn. Main, 7088 West Saanich Rd.,
Brentwood Bay, BC V8M 1R3
Tel: 250-652-5151; Fax: 250-652-9687
jenkolaw@shaw.ca

Burnaby: Baily McLean, Barristers & Solicitors - *2
Former Name: Greenbank Murdoch & Company; Baily,
McLean, Greenbank & Murdoch
#900, Metrotower II, 4720 Kingsway, Burnaby, BC V5H 4M2
Tel: 604-437-6611; Fax: 604-437-3065
info@bmgm.com
www.bmgm.com

Burnaby: Cobbett & Cotton - *8
#300, 410 Carleton Ave., Burnaby, BC V5C 6P6
Tel: 604-299-6251; Fax: 604-299-6627
mail@cobbett-cotton.com
cobbett-cotton.com

Burnaby: Eder Birgit - *2
#216, 3989 Henning Dr., Burnaby, BC V5C 6P8
Tel: 604-687-0134; Fax: 604-687-5176
Toll-Free: 800-461-3455

Burnaby: Edwards & Co. - *2
Former Name: Edwards, Edwards & Edwards
#510, 4885 Kingsway, Burnaby, BC V5H 4T2
Tel: 604-433-2445; Fax: 604-433-8209
eee@bcpersonalinjurylaw.com
www.bcpersonalinjurylaw.com

Burnaby: James K. Fitzsimmons - *1
#200, 6960 Royal Oak Ave., Burnaby, BC V5J 4J2
Tel: 604-298-8939; Fax: 604-298-8956

Burnaby: James K. Fraser Law Corporation - *1
#200, 4603 Kingsway, Burnaby, BC V5H 4M4
Tel: 604-433-0010
jkf@jkf.ca
www.jkf.ca

Burnaby: Hawthorne, Piggott & Company - *5
Also Known As: HP Law
#208, 1899 Willingdon Ave., Burnaby, BC V5C 5T1
Tel: 604-299-8371; Fax: 604-299-1523
info@hplaw.ca
www.hplaw.ca

Burnaby: O'Neill Rozenberg - *2
#201, 4547 Hastings St., Burnaby, BC V5C 2K3
Tel: 604-294-8311

Burnaby: Sellens & Associates - *3
#320, 9940 Lougheed Hwy., Burnaby, BC V3J 1N3
Tel: 604-421-0716; Fax: 604-421-7692

Burnaby: Maureen J. Wesley - *1
4270 McGill St., Burnaby, BC V5C 1M9
Tel: 604-298-6555; Fax: 604-298-6540

Burnaby: Patricia Yaremovich - *1
#105, 6540 East Hastings St., Burnaby, BC V5B 4Z5
Tel: 604-320-0688; Fax: 604-320-0007
pyaremovich@shaw.ca

Burns Lake: Warren Chapman - *1
#17, P.O. Box 258, 343 16 Hwy. East, Burns Lake, BC V0J
1E0
Tel: 250-692-3339; Fax: 250-692-3342
chapmanlaw@telus.net
www.warrenchapmanlaw.com/en/

Campbell River: Frame & Co. Injury Law - *2
#301, 1100 Island Hwy., Campbell River, BC V9W 8C6
Tel: 250-286-6691; Fax: 250-286-1191
Toll-Free: 800-661-0238
www.frameandcolaw.com

Campbell River: Claire I. Moglove - *1
#201, 909 Island Hwy., Campbell River, BC V9W 2C2
Tel: 250-286-9946; Fax: 250-287-3592
cmoglove@shaw.ca

Campbell River: Shook, Wickham, Bishop & Field -
*9
Also Known As: CR Lawyers
Former Name: McVea, Shook, Wickham & Bishop
906 Island Hwy., Campbell River, BC V9W 2C3
Tel: 250-287-8355; Fax: 250-287-8112
info@crlawyers.ca
www.crlawyers.ca

Campbell River: Karen D. Stevan - *1
748 Galerno Rd., Campbell River, BC V9W 5J3
Tel: 250-926-0120; Fax: 250-926-0121
kdstevan@yahoo.ca

Campbell River: Tees Kiddle Spencer - *7
#200, 1260 Shoppers Row, Campbell River, BC V9W 2C8
Tel: 250-287-7755; Fax: 250-287-3999
info@tkslaw.com
www.tkslaw.com

Castlegar: Polonicoff & Perehudoff - *2
1115 - 3 St., Castlegar, BC V1N 2A1
Tel: 250-365-3343; Fax: 250-365-6307

Chemainus: Mary Lynn Bancroft - *1
Box 168, 9834 Croft St., Chemainus, BC V0R 1K0
Tel: 250-246-4771; Fax: 250-246-2547
mbancroft@shaw.ca

Chilliwack: Baker Newby LLP - Chilliwack - *17
P.O. Box 390, 9259 Main St., Chilliwack, BC V2P 6K2
Tel: 604-792-1376; Fax: 604-792-8711
www.bakernewby.com
www.facebook.com/BakerNewbyLLP,
www.linkedin.com/company-beta/1312992

Chilliwack: Clearpath Law Group
#101, 9123 Mary St., Chilliwack, BC V2P 4H7
Tel: 604-795-4522; Fax: 604-795-4522
info@clearpathlaw.com
clearpathlaw.com

Chilliwack: Fraserwest Law Group LLP - *4
Former Name: Kaye Thome Toews & Hansford
P.O. Box 372, 9202 Young Rd., Chilliwack, BC V2P 6J4
Tel: 604-792-1977 Toll-Free: 888-792-1977
www.fraserwestlaw.com

Chilliwack: Patten Thornton - *4
P.O. Box 379, 9245 Main St., Chilliwack, BC V2P 6J4
Tel: 604-795-9188; Fax: 604-795-6340
Toll-Free: 877-529-9799
info@pattenthornton.com
www.pattenthornton.com

Chilliwack: Stander & Company - *1
#108, 7491 Vedder Rd., Chilliwack, BC V2R 4E7
Tel: 604-847-9777; Fax: 604-847-9779
info@standerandcompany.ca
www.standerandcompany.com

Clearwater: John Kurta - *1
P.O. Box 5171, 32 East Old North Thompson Hwy.,
Clearwater, BC V0E 1N0
Tel: 250-674-2126; Fax: 250-674-3493

Comox: Schaffrick & Sutton - *2
1984 Comox Ave., Comox, BC V9M 3M7
Tel: 250-339-3363; Fax: 250-339-3315
Toll-Free: 877-778-8866

Coquitlam: David Boulding - *1
2126 Elspeth, Coquitlam, BC V3C 1G3
Tel: 604-942-5301; Fax: 604-942-5302
dmboulding@shaw.ca
www.davidboulding.com

Coquitlam: Drysdale Bacon McStravick LLP -
Coquitlam - *10
Former Name: Feller Bacon McStravick
#211, 1015 Austin Ave., Coquitlam, BC V3K 3N9
Tel: 604-939-8321; Fax: 604-939-7584
inquiries@dbmlaw.ca
www.dbmlaw.ca
www.facebook.com/DrysdaleBaconMcStravick,
www.linkedin.com/company/drysdale-bacon-mcstravick-llp

Coquitlam: Spraggs & Company - *9
#202, 1030 Westwood St., Coquitlam, BC V3C 4E4
Tel: 604-464-3333 Toll-Free: 866-939-3339
spraggslaw.ca
www.facebook.com/123830580985035, twitter.com/spraggslaw,
www.linkedin.com/company/spraggs-&-co-

indicates number of lawyers

Coquitlam: Taylor Bardal - *3
#220, 1024 Ridgeway Ave., Coquitlam, BC V3J 1S5
Tel: 604-931-3477; *Fax:* 604-931-1277

Coquitlam: Judy Wong - *1
#205, 3030 Lincoln Ave., Coquitlam, BC V3B 6B4
Tel: 604-945-6982; *Fax:* 604-945-6819
www.judywonglawcorp.ca

Courtenay: Ansley & Company - *3
#306, 576 England Ave., Courtenay, BC V9N 2N3
Tel: 250-338-0202; *Fax:* 250-338-0902
www.ansleyandcompany.com

Courtenay: Bush & Company - *5
#101, 1350 England Ave., Courtenay, BC V9N 8X6
Tel: 250-338-6741; *Fax:* 250-338-6780
Toll-Free: 877-338-6741
info@bushandcompany.ca
bushandcompany.ca

Courtenay: Crispin Morris Law Corporation - *1
Former Name: Morris, C.H.L.
5463 Headquarters Rd., Courtenay, BC V9J 1M3
Tel: 250-338-5311; *Fax:* 250-338-1818

Courtenay: Ives Burger - *4
Former Name: Gibson Kelly & Ives
505 - 5 St., Courtenay, BC V9N 1K2
Tel: 250-334-2416; *Fax:* 250-334-3198
info@ivesburgerlaw.com
www.ivesburgerlaw.com

Courtenay: Swift Datoo Law Corporation - *9
#201, 467 Cumberland Rd., Courtenay, BC V9N 2C5
Tel: 250-334-4461; *Fax:* 250-334-2335
www.swiftdatoo.com

Cranbrook: Patrick J. Dearden - *1
#201, 129 - 10th Ave. South, Cranbrook, BC V1C 2N1
Tel: 250-426-7431; *Fax:* 250-426-3746

Cranbrook: Kelle M. Maag Law Corporation - *1
1808-8th Ave. South, Cranbrook, BC V1C 7E7
Tel: 250-426-5508
kmaag@cyberlink.ca

Cranbrook: Murielle A. Matthews - *1
801B Baker St., Cranbrook, BC V1C 1A3
Tel: 250-426-0601; *Fax:* 250-426-0642

Cranbrook: Miles, Daroux, Zimmer & Sheard - *4
45 - 8th Ave. South, Cranbrook, BC V1C 2K4
Tel: 250-489-3350; *Fax:* 250-489-2235
mdza.ca

Cranbrook: Rella Paolini Rogers - *5
Former Name: Rella & Paolini
#6, 10 Ave. South, 2nd Fl., Cranbrook, BC V1C 2M8
Tel: 250-426-8981; *Fax:* 250-426-8987
Toll-Free: 866-426-8981
info@rellapaolini.com
www.rellapaolini.com

Cranbrook: Robertson & Company - *1
#200, 135 - 10 Ave. South, Cranbrook, BC V1C 2N1
Tel: 250-489-4346; *Fax:* 250-489-1899
robertson@cranbrooklaw.com
www.cranbrooklaw.com

Cranbrook: Darrel C. Symington - *1
123 - 12th Ave. South, Cranbrook, BC V1C 2S2
Tel: 250-489-2800; *Fax:* 250-489-1173
dsymington@cyberllink.ca

Dawson Creek: Allen & Associates - *2
#2, 933 - 103 Ave., Dawson Creek, BC V1G 2G4
Tel: 250-782-8155; *Fax:* 250-782-4525

Dawson Creek: Higson Apps - *3
Former Name: Plenert Higson
#201, 1136 - 103 Ave., Dawson Creek, BC V1G 2G7
Tel: 250-782-9134; *Fax:* 250-782-9135
Toll-Free: 888-782-9134

Delta: James M. Antifay Law Corporation - *1
#212, 7313 - 120 St., Delta, BC V4C 6P5
Tel: 604-572-8333; *Fax:* 604-572-6744
jantifay@dccnet.com

Delta: James Broad - *1
9337 - Scott Rd., Delta, BC V4C 6R8
Tel: 604-585-3422; *Fax:* 604-585-3613

Delta: Delta Legal Office - *3
4873 Delta St., Delta, BC V4C 6P5
Tel: 604-946-2199; *Fax:* 604-946-8818
Toll-Free: 877-203-1100
info@deltalawoffice.com
deltalawoffice.com

Delta: Lehal & Company - *1
#200, 6905 - 120th St., Delta, BC V4E 2A8
Tel: 604-596-1321; *Fax:* 604-596-1320
info@lehallaw.ca
www.lehallaw.com

Delta: Millichamp & Company - *1
#210, 1530 - 56 St., Delta, BC V4L 2A8
Tel: 604-943-7401; *Fax:* 604-943-7402
millichamplawco@gmail.com

Delta: Severide Law Group - *5
#201, 5027 - 47A Ave., Delta, BC V4K 1T9
Tel: 604-940-8182; *Fax:* 604-940-9892
info@severide.com
www.severidelawgroup.com

Duncan: Donald S. Allan - *1
1500 Kingsview Rd., Duncan, BC V9L 5P1
Tel: 250-748-2340; *Fax:* 250-748-2343
d.s.allan@shaw.ca

Duncan: Hugh J. Armstrong - *1
157 Trunk Rd., Duncan, BC V9L 2P1
Tel: 250-746-4354; *Fax:* 250-746-8101
hugh@hugharmstronglaw.ca
www.hugharmstronglaw.ca

Duncan: Coleman Fraser Whittome Lehan - *4
Former Name: Coleman Parceus Fraser Whittome
#202, 58 Station St., Duncan, BC V9L 1M4
Tel: 250-748-1013; *Fax:* 250-748-2733
Toll-Free: 888-748-1013
www.cowichanlaw.com

Duncan: Molnar Desjardins Arndt - *3
Former Name: Molnar, Desjardins & Arndt
435 Trunk Rd., Duncan, BC V9L 2P5
Tel: 250-748-5253

Duncan: Robert W. Nelford - *1
2340 Trillium Terrace, Duncan, BC V9L 3Z6
Tel: 250-478-5805; *Fax:* 250-748-1957
rnelford@shaw.ca

Duncan: Orchard & Company - *6
321 St. Julian St., Duncan, BC V9L 3S5
Tel: 250-746-5899; *Fax:* 250-746-7182
admin@orchardandco.ca
www.orchardandco.ca

Duncan: Ridgway & Company - *5
#200, 44 Queens Rd., Duncan, BC V9L 2W4
Tel: 250-746-7121; *Fax:* 250-746-4070
info@ridgco.com
www.ridgco.com

Duncan: Taylor Granitto Inc. - *3
466 Trans Canada Hwy., Duncan, BC V9L 3R6
Tel: 250-748-4444; *Fax:* 250-748-5920
Toll-Free: 800-665-5414
dtaylor@taylor-co.com
www.taylor-co.com

Fernie: Etheridge Law - *1
P.O. Box 9, 401 - 2nd Ave., 2nd Fl., Fernie, BC V0B 1M0
Tel: 250-430-0007; *Fax:* 866-462-3992
angela@eastkootenaylaw.com
www.eastkootenaylaw.com

Fernie: Leffler Law Office - *2
862 - 3rd Ave., Fernie, BC V0B 1M0
Tel: 250-423-3904; *Fax:* 250-423-7417
info@fernielaw.com
www.fernielaw.com

Fernie: Majic, Purdy Law Corpoartion - *3
P.O. Box 369, 592 - 2nd Ave., Fernie, BC V0B 1M0
Tel: 250-423-4497; *Fax:* 250-423-6714
www.majicpurdy.com

Fernie: Rockies Law Corporation - Fernie - *7
Former Name: Sliva & Summers
#202, P.O. Box 490, 502 - 3rd Ave., Fernie, BC V0B 1M0
Tel: 250-423-4446; *Fax:* 250-423-4065
Toll-Free: 866-427-0111
fernie@rockieslaw.com
rockieslaw.com

Fort St John: Giesbrecht Law Corporation - *2
Former Name: Earmme & Associates; Daley & Earmme
10740 - 101st Ave., Fort St John, BC V1J 2B4
Tel: 250-785-6961; *Fax:* 250-785-6967
info@delaw.ca
www.earmme.com

Fort St John: Rodney J. Strandberg Law Corp. - *1
#320, 9900 - 100 Ave., Fort St John, BC V1J 5S7
Tel: 250-787-7760; *Fax:* 250-787-7752
strandberglaw@telus.net

Garibaldi Highlands: Brian N. Hughes - *1
#201, P.O. Box 557, 1364 Pemberton Ave., Garibaldi
Highlands, BC V0N 1T0
Tel: 604-892-5114; *Fax:* 604-892-0114

Gibsons: Peter J. Holden - *1
995 Grandview Rd., Gibsons, BC V0N 1V3
Tel: 604-630-3913
pholden@dccnet.com

Gibsons: J. Wayne Rowe - *2
P.O. Box 1880, 758 School Rd., Gibsons, BC V0N 1V0
Tel: 604-886-2029; *Fax:* 604-886-9191

Gibsons: Leanne L. Turnbull - *1
523 Central Ave., RR#1, Gibsons, BC V0N 1V1
Tel: 604-886-7666; *Fax:* 604-886-7636
leeturnbull@dccnet.com

Golden: William J. Alexander Law Corporation - *1
#102, 509-9th Ave. North, Golden, BC V0A 1H0
Tel: 250-344-1472; *Fax:* 250-344-1543
alextax@shaw.ca

Hope: Kennedy, Jensen - *2
#101, P.O. Box 1719, 400 Park St., Hope, BC V0X 1L0
Tel: 604-869-9981; *Fax:* 604-869-7640

Hornby Island: Sue M. Kelly - *1
6165 Anderson Dr., Hornby Island, BC V0R 1Z0
Tel: 250-335-0735; *Fax:* 250-335-0732
smkelly@telus.net

Invermere: Kluge, Boyd - *2
P.O. Box 2647, 906 - 8 Ave., Invermere, BC V0A 1K0
Tel: 250-342-4447; *Fax:* 250-342-3298
barnim@telus.net

Invermere: MacDonald Thomas Barristers &
Solicitors - *2
10188-7th Ave., Invermere, BC V0A 1K0
Tel: 250-342-6921; *Fax:* 250-342-3237
reception@macdonaldthomas.com
www.macdonaldthomas.com

Kamloops: Bilkey Law Corporation - *7
Former Name: Bilkey Law LLP
#301, 186 Victoria St., Kamloops, BC V2C 5R3
Tel: 778-471-4350; *Fax:* 778-471-4351
admin@bilkeylaw.ca
www.bilkeylaw.ca

Kamloops: Cates Ford Oien Epp - *9
Former Name: Epp Cates Oien; Taylor Epp & Dolder;
Cates Carroll Watt
#300, 125 - Fourth Ave., Kamloops, BC V2C 3N3
Tel: 250-372-8811; *Fax:* 250-828-6697
Toll-Free: 800-949-3362
info@cfoelaw.ca
cfoelaw.ca

Kamloops: George Coutlee & Co. - *1
1270 Salish Rd., Kamloops, BC V2H 1K1
Tel: 250-372-9922; *Fax:* 250-372-1114

Kamloops: Cundari Seibel LLP - *5
Former Name: Cundari & Company Law Corporation
#810, 175 - 2 Ave., Kamloops, BC V2C 5W1
Tel: 250-372-3368; *Fax:* 250-372-5554
www.cundariseibel.com

Kamloops: Fulton & Company LLP, Lawyers &
Trade-Mark Agents - *28
#300, 350 Lansdowne St., Kamloops, BC V2C 1Y1
Tel: 250-372-5542; *Fax:* 250-851-2300
law@fultonco.com
www.fultonco.com

Kamloops: Gibraltar Law Group - *2
#202, 444 Victoria St., Kamloops, BC V2C 2A7
Tel: 250-374-3737; *Fax:* 250-374-0035
Toll-Free: 877-374-3737
www.gibraltarlawgroup.com

* indicates number of lawyers

Kamloops: Gillespie & Company LLP - *10
Former Name: Gillespie Renkema Barnett Broadway LLP
#200, 121 St. Paul St., Kamloops, BC V2C 3K8
Tel: 250-374-4463 Toll-Free: 855-374-4463
info@kamloopslawyers.com
www.gillespieco.ca

Kamloops: Kahle & Co. Law Corporation - *1
172 Battle St., Kamloops, BC V2C 2L2
Tel: 250-372-1234
kahleco@telus.net

Kamloops: Mary MacGregor - *1
975 Victoria St., Kamloops, BC V2C 2C1
Tel: 250-828-0282; Fax: 250-828-0287
mary.macgregor@mmlc.ca
www.marymacgregor.ca

Kamloops: Mair Jensen Blair LLP - Kamloops - *18
Also Known As: MJB Lawyers
#700, 275 Lansdowne St., Kamloops, BC V2C 6H6
Tel: 250-374-3161; Fax: 250-374-6992
Toll-Free: 888-374-3161
info@mjblaw.com
www.mjblaw.com

Kamloops: David A. McMillan - *1
#401, 286 St. Paul St., Kamloops, BC V2C 6G4
Tel: 250-828-0702; Fax: 250-828-0703
dmlawoff@telus.net

Kamloops: Morelli Chertkow LLP, Lawyers - Kamloops - *14
#300, 180 Seymour St., Kamloops, BC V2C 2E3
Tel: 250-374-3344; Fax: 250-374-1144
info@morellichertkow.com
www.morellichertkow.com
www.facebook.com/MorelliChertkow, twitter.com/morellichertkow

Kamloops: Craig Nixon Law Corp. - *1
#880, 175 Second Ave., Kamloops, BC V2C 5W1
Tel: 250-374-1555; Fax: 250-374-9992
cnlc@direct.ca

Kamloops: Wozniak & Walker - *2
533 Nicola St., Kamloops, BC V2C 2P9
Tel: 250-374-6226; Fax: 250-374-4485

Kamloops: Zal & Decker - *5
Former Name: HMZ Law; Horne Marr Zak
#600, 175 Second Ave., Kamloops, BC V2C 5W1
Tel: 250-372-1221; Fax: 250-372-8339
Toll-Free: 800-558-1933
info@zakanddeckerlaw.com
www.zakanddeckerlaw.com

Kaslo: T.R. Humphries - *1
P.O. Box 636, Kaslo, BC V0G 1M0
Tel: 250-353-2292; Fax: 250-353-7430
trhlaw@telus.net

Kelowna: Benson Law LLP - *7
270 Hwy. 33 West, Kelowna, BC V1X 1X7
Tel: 250-491-0206; Fax: 250-491-0266
www.bensonlawllp.com

Kelowna: Burgess & Company - *2
#202, 3528 Scott Rd., Kelowna, BC V1W 3H6
Tel: 250-861-5533; Fax: 250-861-4442
dblaw@live.ca
www.burgessandcompany.com/en/

Kelowna: Bev Churchill - *1
Former Name: Tinker, Churchill, Wallis
#210, 347 Leon Ave., Kelowna, BC V1Y 8C7
Tel: 250-763-7333; Fax: 250-763-5507
bev@bevchurchillfamilylawyer.com
www.bevchurchillfamilylawyer.com

Kelowna: Doak Shirreff Lawyers LLP - *16
#200, 537 Leon Ave., Kelowna, BC V1Y 2A9
Tel: 250-763-4323; Fax: 250-763-4780
Toll-Free: 800-661-4959
thefirm@doakshirreff.com
www.doakshirreff.com

Kelowna: FH&P Lawyers LLP - *14
215 Lawrence Ave., 2nd Fl., Kelowna, BC V1Y 6L2
Tel: 250-762-4222; Fax: 250-762-8616
Toll-Free: 888-320-4488
info@fhplawyers.com
www.fhplawyers.com

Kelowna: Fischer & Company Law Corporation - *1
#202, 1447 Ellis St., Kelowna, BC V1Y 2A3
Tel: 250-712-0066; Fax: 250-712-0061
matthew@fischerandcompany.ca
www.fischerandcompany.ca

Kelowna: Fraser Chris - *2
#200, 1449 St Paul St., Kelowna, BC V1Y 7S5
Tel: 250-868-8306; Fax: 250-868-8301

Kelowna: Glazier Polley - *3
Former Name: Wageman Glazier & Polley
1674 Bertram St., 2nd Fl., Kelowna, BC V1Y 9G4
Tel: 250-763-3343; Fax: 250-763-9524

Kelowna: Gordon & Company - *2
#102, 1433 St. Paul St., Kelowna, BC V1Y 2E4
Tel: 250-860-9997; Fax: 250-860-9937
info@gordoncolaw.com
www.gordoncolaw.com/en/

Kelowna: Laura J. Gosset - *1
#214, 440 Cascia Dr., Kelowna, BC V1W 4Y4
Tel: 250-717-1677; Fax: 250-862-5292
lauragosset@shaw.ca

Kelowna: Jenson & Co. - *1
Also Known As: Wade D. Jenson
#200, 1460 Pandosy St., Kelowna, BC V1Y 1P3
Tel: 250-868-2239; Fax: 250-861-5079
www.jensonlaw.com
www.facebook.com/JensonandCo

Kelowna: Martin Johnson Law Corporation - *2
Also Known As: The Heritage Law Group
830 Bernard Ave., Kelowna, BC V1Y 6P5
Tel: 250-868-2848; Fax: 250-868-3080
Toll-Free: 877-868-2848
office@heritagelawgroup.com
www.heritagelawgroup.com
www.facebook.com/HeritageLawyers

Kelowna: Roberta L. Jordan - *1
#16, 4524 Eldorado Ct., Kelowna, BC V1W 1G3
Tel: 250-764-0888; Fax: 250-764-0680

Kelowna: Kelly Christiansen & Company - *2
Former Name: Christiansen, Newcombe
#208, 1470 St Paul St., Kelowna, BC V1Y 2E6
Tel: 250-862-2327

Kelowna: Kimmitt Wrzesniewski - *2
#202, 1433 St. Paul St., Kelowna, BC V1Y 2E4
Tel: 250-763-6441; Fax: 250-763-1633
info@kimmitt.ca
www.kimmitt.ca

Kelowna: Robert O. Levin - *2
#607, 1708 Dolphin Ave., Kelowna, BC V1Y 9S4
Tel: 250-868-2101; Fax: 250-868-2414
robert@rlevin.com
www.rlevin.com

Kelowna: M. Gail Miller - *1
#904, 1708 Dolphin Ave., Kelowna, BC V1Y 9S4
Tel: 250-763-6767; Fax: 250-763-0980

Kelowna: Mission Law Group - *1
#212, 2900 Pandosy St., Kelowna, BC V1Y 1V9
Tel: 250-868-8803; Fax: 250-868-8876
law@missionlawgroup.com
www.missionlawgroup.com

Kelowna: Oland & Company - *2
803 Bernard Ave., Kelowna, BC V1Y 6P6
Tel: 250-762-8092; Fax: 250-762-2857
shiplaw@aboland.com
www.aboland.com

Kelowna: Pihl & Associates Law Corporation - *8
#100, 1465 Ellis St., Kelowna, BC V1Y 2A3
Tel: 250-762-5434; Fax: 250-762-5450
lawyers@pihl.ca
www.pihl.ca
www.facebook.com/367055590059343, twitter.com/pihllawcorp,
www.linkedin.com/company/pihl-law-corporation

Kelowna: Pihl Law Corporation - *8
Former Name: Pihl & Company
#300, 1465 Ellis St., Kelowna, BC V1Y 2A3
Tel: 604-437-8837; Fax: 604-437-3529
lawyers@pihl.ca
www.pihl.ca
www.facebook.com/367055590059343, twitter.com/pihllawcorp,
www.linkedin.com/company/pihl-law-corporation

* indicates number of lawyers

Kelowna: Porter Ramsay LLP - *8
#200, 1465 Ellis St., Kelowna, BC V1Y 2A3
Tel: 250-763-7646; Fax: 250-762-9960
www.porterramsay.com

Kelowna: Pushor Mitchell LLP - *35
#301, 1665 Ellis St., Kelowna, BC V1Y 2B3
Tel: 250-762-2108; Fax: 250-762-9115
Toll-Free: 800-558-1155
www.pushormitchell.com
twitter.com/pushormitchell,
www.linkedin.com/company/pushor-mitchell-llp

Kelowna: Rush Ihas Hardwick LLP - *5
1368 St. Paul St., Kelowna, BC V1Y 2E1
Tel: 250-868-2313; Fax: 250-868-2659
info@rihlaw.com
www.rihlaw.com

Kelowna: Sabey Rule LLP - *6
#201, 401 Glenmore Rd., Kelowna, BC V1V 1Z6
Tel: 250-762-6111; Fax: 250-762-6480
Toll-Free: 866-268-6383
lawyers@sabeyrule.ca
www.sabeyrule.ca

Kelowna: Smith Peacock - *2
#201, 1180 Sunset Dr., Kelowna, BC V1Y 9W6
Tel: 250-860-7868; Fax: 250-860-7527
Toll-Free: 888-757-6484
www.smithpeacock.ca

Kelowna: Smithson Employment Law Corporation - *1
#204, 1630 Pandosy St., Kelowna, BC V1Y 1P7
Tel: 778-478-0150; Fax: 778-478-0155
robert@smithsonlaw.ca
www.smithsonlaw.ca
www.facebook.com/146651752055816,
twitter.com/youworkhere,
www.linkedin.com/in/robert-smithson-3b144328

Kelowna: Daniel E. Spelliscy - *1
#1, 715 Sutherland Ave., Kelowna, BC V1Y 5X4
Tel: 250-862-9586; Fax: 250-862-2677
dspelliscy@yahoo.com

Kelowna: Tessmer Law Offices - *4
272 Bernard Ave., Kelowna, BC V1Y 6N4
Tel: 250-762-6747; Fax: 250-762-3163
info@tessmerlaw.com
tessmerlaw.com
twitter.com/TessmerLaw

Kelowna: Thomas Butler LLP - *3
#700, Landmark II, 1708 Dolphin Ave., Kelowna, BC V1Y 9S4
Tel: 250-763-0200; Fax: 250-762-8848
admin@thomasbutlerllp.com
www.thomasbutlerllp.com

Kelowna: Touchstone Law Group LLP - *2
#208, 1664 Richter St., Kelowna, BC V1Y 8N3
Tel: 250-448-2637; Fax: 250-484-7101
Toll-Free: 855-889-2637
info@touchstonelawgroup.com
touchstonelawgroup.com
www.facebook.com/TouchstoneLawGroupLlp,
twitter.com/touchstonelaw,

Kelowna: Douglas W. Welder - *1
#200, 586 Leon Ave., Kelowna, BC V1Y 6J6
Tel: 250-868-8228; Fax: 250-868-8232
welder@okanagan.net

Kelowna: Marc R.B. Whittemore - *4
830 Bernard Ave., Kelowna, BC V1V 6P5
Tel: 250-868-2202; Fax: 250-868-2270
whittemorelawcorporation.com

Kimberley: Robert E.C. Apps - *1
230 Spokane St., Kimberley, BC V1A 2E4
Tel: 250-427-2235; Fax: 250-427-5168
bobapps@shaw.ca

Kitimat: Wozney & Company - *1
46 Clifford St., Kitimat, BC V8C 1B4
Tel: 250-632-7151; Fax: 250-632-7100
rwozney@telus.net

Ladysmith: Robson, O'Connor - Ladysmith - *2
P.O. Box 1890, 22 High St., Ladysmith, BC V9G 1B4
Tel: 250-245-7141; Fax: 250-245-2921
www.robsonoconnor.ca

Langley: Campbell, Burton & McMullan LLP - Langley - *18
#200, 4769 - 222 St., Langley, BC V2Z 3C1
Tel: 604-533-3821; Fax: 604-533-5521
info@cbmlawyers.com
www.cbmlawyers.com

Langley: Darnell & Company Lawyers - *3
#202, 6351 - 197 St., Langley, BC V2Y 1X8
Tel: 604-532-9119; Fax: 604-532-9127
www.langleylaw.ca

Langley: Fleming Olson Taneda & MacDougall - *3
Former Name: Fleming, Olson & Taneda
4038 - 200B St., Langley, BC V3A 1N9
Tel: 604-533-3411; Fax: 604-533-8749
fotlawyers@aol.com

Langley: Carl D. Holm - *1
#102, 20475 Douglas Cres., Langley, BC V3A 4B6
Tel: 604-533-4101; Fax: 604-533-2024

Langley: Bryce Jeffrey LLB - *1
20450 Fraser Hwy., 2nd Fl., Langley, BC V3A 4G2
Tel: 604-530-3141; Fax: 604-530-9573
info@jefferymediation.com
www.jefferymediation.com

Langley: J. Michael Le Dressay & Associates - *13
20689 - 56 Ave., Langley, BC V3A 7G9
Tel: 604-530-2191; Fax: 604-530-6282
michael@jmldlaw.com

Langley: Stephen G. Price Law Corp. - *1
#300, 20644 Eastleigh Cres., Langley, BC V3A 4C4
Tel: 604-530-2191
info@stephengprice.com
stephengprice.com

Langley: Waterstone Law Group LLP - Langley - *6
#304, 20338 - 65th Ave., Langley, BC V2Y 2X3
Tel: 604-533-2300; Fax: 604-533-2387
Toll-Free: 800-880-1667
www.waterstonelaw.com

Lantzville: Kristin Rongve - *1
Former Name: Loy & Rongve
7180 Lantzville Rd., Lantzville, BC V0R 2H0
Tel: 250-390-3157; Fax: 250-390-4857
info@kristinrongve.ca
www.kristinrongve.ca

Lillooet: R. Kendel Kaser - *1
P.O. Box 1449, 416 Main St., Lillooet, BC V0K 1V0
Tel: 250-256-7519; Fax: 250-256-7554

Madeira Park: Michael C. Crowe - *1
12874 Madeira Park Rd., Madeira Park, BC V0N 2H0
Tel: 604-883-9875; Fax: 604-883-9873
m_crowe@sunshine.net

Maple Ridge: Fowle & Company - *1
#650, 22470 Dewdney Trunk Rd., Maple Ridge, BC V2X 5Z6
Tel: 604-476-2130; Fax: 604-476-2135
Toll-Free: 800-663-8996
www.fowleandcompany.com

Maple Ridge: Vernon & Thompson Law Group - Maple Ridge - *3
22311 - 119 Ave., Maple Ridge, BC V2X 2Z2
Tel: 604-463-6281; Fax: 604-463-7497
vernon-thompson.com

Mill Bay: Hicks & Co. - *2
#24, Mill Bay Shopping Centre, P.O. Box 83, 2720 Mill Bay Rd., Mill Bay, BC V0R 2P0
Tel: 250-743-3756; Fax: 250-743-3756

Mission: Jarrett & Company - *1
9701 Dewdney Trunk Rd., Mission, BC V2V 7G5
Tel: 604-826-5582

Mission: Taylor, Tait, Ruley & Company - *7
33066 First Ave., Mission, BC V2V 1G3
Tel: 604-826-1266; Fax: 604-826-4288
info@taylortait.com
www.taylortait.com

Mission: Taylor, Tait, Ruley & Company - *6
33066 First Ave., Mission, BC V2V 1G3
Tel: 604-826-1266; Fax: 604-826-4288
info@taylortait.com
www.taylortait.com

Nanaimo: Carlson & Company - *3
669 Terminal Ave. North, Nanaimo, BC V9S 4K1
Tel: 250-753-7582; Fax: 250-753-7583

Nanaimo: Fabris McIver Hornquist & Radcliffe - *4
Former Name: Fabris McIver Hornquist
P.O. Box 778, 40 Cavan St., Nanaimo, BC V9R 5M2
Tel: 250-753-6661; Fax: 250-753-6648
Toll-Free: 800-811-3555
reception@fabris-law.com
www.fabris-law.com

Nanaimo: Geselbracht Brown - *2
#3, 4488 Wellington Rd., Nanaimo, BC V9T 2H3
Tel: 250-758-2825; Fax: 250-758-7412
inquiry@gblaw.bc.ca
www.gblaw.bc.ca

Nanaimo: Heath Law LLP - *16
#200, 1808 Bowen Rd., Nanaimo, BC V9S 5W4
Tel: 250-753-2202; Fax: 250-753-3949
Toll-Free: 866-753-2202
consult@nanaimolaw.com
www.nanaimolaw.com
www.linkedin.com/company/heath-law-llp

Nanaimo: A. Peter Hertzberg - *1
1687 Princess Royal Ave., Nanaimo, BC V9S 4A3
Tel: 250-753-1891

Nanaimo: Johnston Franklin - *7
Former Name: Johnston, Lewis & Franklin
#210, 3260 Norwell Dr., Nanaimo, BC V9T 1X5
Tel: 250-756-3823; Fax: 250-756-6188
Toll-Free: 888-343-0782
lawyers@johnstonfranklin.com
www.johnstonfranklin.ca
www.facebook.com/johnstonfranklin, twitter.com/jflaw_ca,
www.linkedin.com/company/johnston-franklin

Nanaimo: Gary R. Korpan - *1
3598 Hammond Bay Rd., Nanaimo, BC V9T 1E9
Tel: 250-758-9445; Fax: 250-754-8263
gkorpan@island.net

Nanaimo: Manning & Kirkhope - *2
430 Wentworth St., Nanaimo, BC V9R 3E1
Tel: 250-753-6766; Fax: 250-753-0080
office@mannkirk.com
www.mannkirk.com

Nanaimo: Merrill, Long & Co. - *4
201 Milton St., Nanaimo, BC V9R 2K5
Tel: 250-754-4441; Fax: 250-754-4286
ranlaw@telus.net
www.merrill-long.com
www.facebook.com/10150148290075641

Nanaimo: Mont & Walker Law Corporation - *6
Former Name: Allin Anderson Mont & Walker Law Corp
201 Selby St., Nanaimo, BC V9R 2R2
Tel: 250-753-6435; Fax: 250-753-5285
www.islandlaw.ca

Nanaimo: Park Place Law - *3
#100, 2124 Bowen Rd., Nanaimo, BC V9S 1H7
Tel: 250-758-7758; Fax: 250-758-7756
reception@parkplacelaw.ca
parkplacelaw.ca

Nanaimo: Petley-Jones & Co. Law Corp. - *1
5732 Hammond Bay Rd., Nanaimo, BC V9T 5N2
Tel: 250-758-7370; Fax: 250-758-8703
info@petley-jones.net
www.petley-jones.net

Nanaimo: Ramsay Lampman Rhodes - Nanaimo - *19
Former Name: Ramsay Thompson Lampman
111 Wallace St., Nanaimo, BC V9R 5B2
Tel: 250-754-3321; Fax: 250-754-1148
Toll-Free: 800-263-3321
info@rlr-law.com
www.rlr-law.com

Nanaimo: Robert N. Stacey Law Corp. - *1
Former Name: Old City Quarter Law Office
#10, 321 Wesley St., Nanaimo, BC V9R 2T5
Tel: 250-753-0844; Fax: 250-753-0877
rnstacey@telus.net
www.bcdivorceonline.com

Nanaimo: Strain & Company - *2
#103, 360 Selby St., Nanaimo, BC V9R 2R5
Tel: 250-753-0860; Fax: 250-753-0861
reception@strain.ca
www.nanaimofamilylaw.com

Nanaimo: Victor Svacek - *1
155 Commercial St., Nanaimo, BC V9R 5G5
Tel: 250-756-4765

Nanaimo: Vining, Senini
P.O. Box 190, Stn. Main, 30 Front St., Nanaimo, BC V9R 5K9
Tel: 250-754-1234; Fax: 250-754-8080

Nanaimo: Eric L. Williams - *1
#302, 240 Milton St., Nanaimo, BC V9R 2K6
Tel: 250-741-1100; Fax: 250-741-1094
Toll-Free: 888-959-1100
eric.williams@telus.net

Nanaimo: C.D. Wilson & Associates - *1
630 Terminal Ave. North, Nanaimo, BC V9S 4K2
Tel: 250-741-1400; Fax: 250-741-1441
nanaimo@cdwilson.bc.ca
www.cdwilson.bc.ca

Nelson: Susan Kurtz - *1
Sound Legal Solutions, 407 Nelson Ave., Nelson, BC V1L 2N1
Tel: 250-354-1881; Fax: 250-354-1808
Toll-Free: 866-926-1881
susan@resolutionplace.ca
www.resolutionplace.ca
www.facebook.com/resolutionplace,
www.linkedin.com/in/susan-kurtz-560b6425

Nelson: Nasmyth, Morrow & Bogusz - *2
#105, 465 Ward St., Nelson, BC V1L 1S7
Tel: 250-352-3171; Fax: 250-352-1777
info@nbclegal.com

Nelson: Stacey, Trillo & Company - *2
#1, 405 Baker St., Nelson, BC V1L 4H7
Tel: 250-352-3125; Fax: 250-352-3145
greg@stacey-trillo.com
www.stacey-trillo.com

Nelson: Terry Napora Law Offices - *1
Former Name: Napora Underwood & Co.
608 Baker St., Nelson, BC V1L 4J4
Tel: 250-352-3321; Fax: 250-354-4547
Toll-Free: 800-579-5338
terry@naporalaw.ca

Nelson: Susan E. Wallach - *1
#4, 577 Baker St., Nelson, BC V1L 4J1
Tel: 250-352-6124; Fax: 250-352-3460

New Westminster: Amicus Lawyers - *4
Former Name: Hwang, Pollock & Company
Westminster Bldg., 711 Columbia St., New Westminster, BC V3M 1B2
Tel: 604-889-7000; Fax: 604-526-7033
info@amicuslawyers.com
www.amicuslawyers.com
twitter.com/amicuslawyers

New Westminster: Begbie Court Law - *4
Former Name: Browning Ray Soga Dunne & Mirsky
#303, 668 Carnarvon St., New Westminster, BC V3M 5Y6
Tel: 604-526-4525; Fax: 604-526-8595
info@begbiecourtlaw.com
www.begbiecourtlaw.com

New Westminster: Gordon J. Bondoreff - *1
#202, 713 Columbia St., New Westminster, BC V3M 1B2
Tel: 604-526-4491; Fax: 604-526-5979
gbondoreff@telus.net

New Westminster: Darychuk Law - *2
Former Name: Darychuk Deane-Cloutier; Macleod Thorson Darychuk
#206, 26 Lorne Mews, New Westminster, BC V3M 3L7
Tel: 604-256-3405; Fax: 604-464-2533
www.darychuklaw.com
www.facebook.com/Darychuklaw, twitter.com/darychuk,
www.linkedin.com/in/dale-darychuk-q-c-674a067

New Westminster: Raymond E. Drabik Law Corp. - *1
#217, 713 Columbia St., New Westminster, BC V3M 1B2
Tel: 604-526-4875; Fax: 604-526-4879
red_law@telus.net

New Westminster: Goodwin & Mark - *5
#217, 713 Columbia St., New Westminster, BC V3M 1B2
Tel: 778-727-0128; *Fax:* 604-526-8044
Toll-Free: 800-414-5097
www.goodmark.ca

New Westminster: Angela S. Kerslake - *1
131 - 8th St., New Westminster, BC V3M 3P6
Tel: 604-520-6276; *Fax:* 604-520-5765
angela@angelakerslakelaw.com

New Westminster: Stan N. Lanyon - *1
#217, 713 Columbia St., New Westminster, BC V3M 1B2
Tel: 604-522-5002; *Fax:* 604-522-5055
stan.lanyon@arboffices.com

New Westminster: Scarborough, Herman, Harvey & Bluekens - *4
900 Quayside Dr., 10th Fl., New Westminster, BC V3M 6G1
Tel: 604-521-2223; *Fax:* 604-521-7772

North Saanich: Barbara J. Yates - *1
430 Wain Rd., North Saanich, BC V8L 5P9
Tel: 250-656-5536; *Fax:* 250-656-4333

North Vancouver: Ardagh Hunter - *2
#300, 1401 Lonsdale Ave., North Vancouver, BC V7M 2H9
Tel: 604-986-4366; *Fax:* 604-986-9286
account@ahtlaw.com

North Vancouver: Trevors R. Bjurman - *1
#205, 1433 Lonsdale Ave., North Vancouver, BC V7M 2H9
Tel: 604-983-3728; *Fax:* 604-983-0148
bjurman@smartt.com

North Vancouver: Oren E. Breitman - *1
1503 Dovercourt Rd., North Vancouver, BC V7K 1K6
Tel: 604-218-9480; *Fax:* 604-984-0502
orenb@shaw.ca

North Vancouver: Charlotte C. Gregory - *1
205 St. Patrick's Ave., North Vancouver, BC V7L 3N3
Tel: 604-983-2886; *Fax:* 604-983-2886
cgregory@istar.ca

North Vancouver: Hollander Plazzer & Co. LLP - *3
#300, 145 - West 17th St., North Vancouver, BC V7M 3G4
Tel: 778-340-3353; *Fax:* 778-340-2848
reception@hollanderplazzer.ca
www.hollanderplazzer.ca

North Vancouver: Jabour Sudeyko Lucky - North Vancouver - *3
Former Name: Jabour, Sudeyko
#200, 92 Lonsdale Ave., North Vancouver, BC V7M 2E6
Tel: 604-986-8600; *Fax:* 604-986-4872
Toll-Free: 877-860-7575
www.luckylaw.ca
www.facebook.com/jaboursudeykolucky, twitter.com/jsslawfirm

North Vancouver: Robert W. Johnson - *1
#300, 1401 Lonsdale Ave., North Vancouver, BC V7M 2H9
Tel: 604-984-0305; *Fax:* 604-984-0304
robert.johnson@ahtlaw.com

North Vancouver: Lakes, Whyte LLP - *8
#200, 879 Marine Dr., North Vancouver, BC V7P 1R7
Tel: 604-984-3646; *Fax:* 604-984-8573
Toll-Free: 800-488-7788
info@lakeswhyte.com
www.lakeswhyte.com
www.facebook.com/lakeswhyte, twitter.com/lakeswhytellp

North Vancouver: Lee T. Lau Law Corp. - *1
315 Mt. Hwy Ave., North Vancouver, BC V7J 2K7
Tel: 604-603-4907; *Fax:* 604-909-1699
www.leelau.net

North Vancouver: Judith C. Lee - *1
#110, 223 Mountain Hwy., North Vancouver, BC V7J 3V5
Tel: 604-971-5107; *Fax:* 604-971-5109
www.judithleelaw.com

North Vancouver: Lonsdale Law Office - *5
#304, 1200 Lonsdale Ave., North Vancouver, BC V7M 2H6
Tel: 604-980-5089; *Fax:* 604-980-5079
info@lonsdalelaw.ca
www.lonsdalelaw.ca
www.linkedin.com/in/lonsdale-law-7514a2125

North Vancouver: Lynn Valley Law - *1
#40, 1199 Lynn Valley Rd., North Vancouver, BC V7J 3H2
Tel: 604-985-8000; *Fax:* 604-985-5999
admin@lynnlaw.ca
www.lynnlaw.ca

North Vancouver: North Shore Law LLP - *19
Former Name: Bradbrooke Crawford Green
171 West Esplanade, 6th Fl., North Vancouver, BC V7M 3J9
Tel: 604-980-8571; *Fax:* 604-980-4019
Toll-Free: 877-980-8571
inquiries@northshorelaw.com
www.northshorelaw.com
www.facebook.com/NorthShoreLaw, twitter.com/northshorelaw,
www.linkedin.com/company/north-shore-law-llp

North Vancouver: Ron Perrick Law Corp. - *2
#913, 1641 Lonsdale Ave., North Vancouver, BC V7M 1V5
Tel: 604-984-9521; *Fax:* 604-984-9104

North Vancouver: Ratcliff & Company LLP - *29
#500, 221 West Esplanade, North Vancouver, BC V7M 3J3
Tel: 604-988-5201; *Fax:* 604-988-1452
admin@ratcliff.com
www.ratcliff.com

North Vancouver: Robert C. Reid - *1
#233, 1433 Lonsdale Ave., North Vancouver, BC V7M 2H9
Tel: 604-984-4357; *Fax:* 604-984-4326
robertcreid@hotmail.com

North Vancouver: D.A. Roper - *1
334 - West 15th St., North Vancouver, BC V7M 1S5
Tel: 604-986-0488; *Fax:* 604-984-3463
roperlaw@shawbiz.ca

North Vancouver: Thomas Immigration Law Group - *2
Former Name: David L. Thomas Law Corporation
#8, 728 - 14th St. West, North Vancouver, BC V7M 0A8
Tel: 604-988-0795; *Fax:* 604-988-0718
info@executive-visa.com
www.executive-visa.com

North Vancouver: Yeager Employment Law - *4
Former Name: Yeager & Company Law Corporation
#400, 111 Lonsdale Ave., North Vancouver, BC V7M 2E7
Tel: 604-988-1000; *Fax:* 604-988-1200
Toll-Free: 855-921-1295
info@dismissal.ca
www.dismissal.ca
www.linkedin.com/company/yeager-&-company

Okotoks: James C. Lozinsky - *1
#208, P.O. Box 509, 11 Elizabeth St., Okotoks, BC T1S 1A7
Tel: 403-995-7744; *Fax:* 403-995-7045
jclozinsky@jcl-law.ca
www.jcl-law.ca

Oliver: Alan P. Czepil - *1
P.O. Box 1800, 6313 Main St., Oliver, BC V0H 1T0
Tel: 250-498-4901; *Fax:* 250-498-1400
aczepil@gordonandyoung.com

Oliver: Gordon & Young - *3
P.O. Box 1800, 6313 Main St., Oliver, BC V0H 1T0
Tel: 250-498-4941; *Fax:* 250-498-4100
aczepil@gordonandyoung.com

One Hundred Mile House: George J. Wool - *1
5741 Simon Lake Rd., One Hundred Mile House, BC V0K 2E1
Tel: 250-791-9295; *Fax:* 250-791-9228
gjwool@xplornet.ca

Parksville: Davis Avis Randall - *4
Former Name: Davis & Avis
#201, P.O. Box 1600, 156 Morison Ave., Parksville, BC V9P 2H5
Tel: 250-248-5731; *Fax:* 250-248-5730
law@davis-avis.com
www.davis-avis.com

Parksville: John A. Hossack & Associates - *1
P.O. Box 1486, 311 McKinnon St., Parksville, BC V9P 2H4
Tel: 250-248-9241; *Fax:* 250-248-8375
john@hossack-law.com
www.hossack-law.com

Peachland: John E. Humphries Law Corporation - *1
5848B Beach Ave., Peachland, BC V0H 1X7
Tel: 250-767-2221; *Fax:* 250-767-3477
johnehumprieslaw@hotmail.com

Penticton: Boyle & Company - *5
#201, 100 Front St., Penticton, BC V2A 1H1
Tel: 250-492-6100; *Fax:* 250-492-4877
www.boyleco.bc.ca

Penticton: Gilchrist & Company - *4
#101, 123 Martin St., Penticton, BC V2A 7X6
Tel: 250-492-3033; *Fax:* 250-492-6162
info@gilchristlaw.com
www.gilchristlaw.com

Penticton: Kathryn J. Ginther - *1
#301, 301 Main St., Penticton, BC V2A 5B7
Tel: 250-487-4355; *Fax:* 250-487-4356

Penticton: Halbauer & Company - *1
Former Name: Halbauer & McAndrews
#104, 2504 Skana Lake Road, Penticton, BC V2A 6G1
Tel: 250-492-7225; *Fax:* 250-492-7395
www.pentictonlawyers.com

Penticton: Thomas A. Kampman - *1
409 Ellis St., Penticton, BC V2A 4M1
Tel: 250-493-6786; *Fax:* 250-493-3964
tom@kokm.ca

Penticton: Zaseybida, Bonga - *2
#101, 100 Nanaimo Ave. East, Penticton, BC V2A 1M4
Tel: 250-492-2244; *Fax:* 250-492-0090
zaseybida-bonga@telus.net

Pitt Meadows: Becker & Company Law Offices - Pitt Meadows - *6
#230, 19150 Lougheed Hwy., Pitt Meadows, BC V3Y 2H6
Tel: 604-465-9993; *Fax:* 604-465-0066
www.beckerlawyers.ca
www.facebook.com/beckerlawyers, twitter.com/beckerlawyers,
www.linkedin.com/company/becker-&-company

Port Alberni: Beckingham & Co. - *2
5029 Argyle St., Port Alberni, BC V9Y 1V5
Tel: 250-724-0111; *Fax:* 250-724-4422
info@beckinghamandcompany.ca
www.beckinghamandcompany.ca

Port Coquitlam: John K. Bledsoe - *1
2239B McAllister Ave., Port Coquitlam, BC V3C 2A9
Tel: 604-941-6162; *Fax:* 604-941-4369

Port Coquitlam: David Greenbank - *1
Former Name: Greenbank Murdoch & Company
#2300, 2850 Shaughnessy St., Port Coquitlam, BC V3C 6K5
Tel: 604-941-6215; *Fax:* 604-941-6207
dgreenbank@dgreenbank.com
dgreenbank.com

Port Coquitlam: Payne & Associates - *1
#105, 1465 Salisbury Ave., Port Coquitlam, BC V3B 6J3
Tel: 604-944-4115; *Fax:* 604-944-4120

Port Coquitlam: Larry W. Pippard - *1
#2, 3397 Hastings St., Port Coquitlam, BC V3B 4M8
Tel: 604-464-5615; *Fax:* 604-464-5615
larrywpippard@shaw.ca

Port Coquitlam: Smyth & Co. - *4
#330, 2755 Lougheed Hwy., Port Coquitlam, BC V3B 5Y9
Tel: 604-942-6560; *Fax:* 604-942-1347
smythandcompany.ca

Port Hardy: Nowosad & Company - *1
P.O. Box 1289, 8700 Market St., Port Hardy, BC V0N 2P0
Tel: 250-949-6031; *Fax:* 250-949-2633
nowosad1@telus.net
macisaacgroup.com/office/port-hardy/

Port Moody: Burke Tomchenko Morrison LLP - *11
Also Known As: BTM Lawyers LLP
Former Name: Burke Tomchenko & Fraser
#530, 130 Brew St., Port Moody, BC V3H 0E3
Tel: 604-937-1166; *Fax:* 604-937-5577
firm@btmlawyers.com
www.btmlawyers.com

Port Moody: Judy S. Voss Law Corporation - *1
2225 Clarke St., Port Moody, BC V3H 1Y6
Tel: 604-937-4757; *Fax:* 604-937-4714
Toll-Free: 866-944-8888
jsvoss@jsvlc.com

Port Moody: Maryn & Associates - *4
2613 St. Johns St., Port Moody, BC V3H 2B5
Tel: 604-936-9600; *Fax:* 604-936-9800
info@marynlaw.com
www.marynlaw.com

Powell River: Garling Ostensen - *1
4581 Marine Ave., Powell River, BC V8A 2K7
Tel: 604-485-2818; *Fax:* 604-485-7161
garost@powellriverlawyers.com

* indicates number of lawyers

Powell River: James Garrett-Rempel - *1
4766 Michigan Ave., Powell River, BC V8A 2S9
Tel: 604-485-9898; Fax: 604-485-9850
jgrlaw@shaw.ca
www.garrett-rempel.com

Powell River: F. Gregory Reif - *1
#201, 4801 Joyce Ave., Powell River, BC V8A 3B7
Tel: 604-485-2056; Fax: 604-485-2196
gregreif@telus.net

Powell River: Villani & Company - *4
Former Name: Whyard Villani
#103, 7020 Duncan St., Powell River, BC V8A 1V9
Tel: 604-485-6188; Fax: 604-485-6923
info@villaniandco.com
villaniandco.com

Prince George: G.R. Brown Law Corporation
Former Name: Hope Heinrich, Barristers & Solicitors
#330, 500 Victoria St., Prince George, BC V2L 2J9
Tel: 250-563-0681; Fax: 250-562-3761
grb@grblaw.ca

Prince George: Dick Byl Law Corporation - *2
#900, 550 Victoria St., Prince George, BC V2L 2K1
Tel: 250-564-3400; Fax: 250-564-7873
Toll-Free: 800-835-0088
dbyl@dbylaw.com
www.dbylaw.com

Prince George: Richard C. Gibbs - *1
1134 - 3rd Ave., Prince George, BC V2L 3E5
Tel: 250-564-6460; Fax: 250-562-0671
rcgibbs@telus.net

Prince George: Heather Sadler Jenkins LLP - Prince George - *18
#204, 1302 Seventh Ave., Prince George, BC V2L 3P1
Tel: 250-565-8000; Fax: 250-565-8001
Toll-Free: 866-565-8777
hsj@hsjlawyers.com
www.hsjlawyers.com

Prince George: Andrew Kemp, Lawyer & Mediator - *1
#204, 411 Quebec St., Prince George, BC V2L 1W5
Tel: 250-564-5544; Fax: 250-562-4104
Toll-Free: 877-964-5544
www.andrewkemp.ca

Prince George: Richard B. Krehbiel - *1
1415 Douglas St., Prince George, BC V2M 2N1
Tel: 250-562-8935
rkrehbiel@shaw.ca

Prince George: Benjamin D. Levine - *2
Former Name: Bill A. Coller.
1140 - 3rd Ave., Prince George, BC V2L 3E5
Tel: 250-960-2169; Fax: 250-960-2196
coller@collerlevine.ca
www.collerlevine.ca

Prince George: Ronald W. Madill - *1
1033 - 3rd Ave., Prince George, BC V2L 3E3
Tel: 250-562-5000; Fax: 250-562-5105

Prince George: Marcotte Kerrigan - *2
440 Brunswick St., Prince George, BC V2L 2B6
Tel: 250-564-0052; Fax: 250-564-0053
marcottekerrigan.ca

Prince George: Irene G. Peters Law Corp. - *2
Former Name: Peters & O'Byrne
P.O. Box 23050, Stn. College Heights, 5240 Domano Blvd.,
Prince George, BC V2N 6Z2
Tel: 250-964-7844; Fax: 888-219-8502
Toll-Free: 877-365-4093
admin@igpeters.com

Prince George: Traxler Haines - *7
Former Name: Ramsay Nosè Traxler Haines
#614, 1488 - 4 Ave., Prince George, BC V2L 4Y2
Tel: 250-563-7741; Fax: 250-563-2953
info@thlawyers.com
www.traxlerhaines.com

Prince George: Tyo Law Corp. - *1
P.O. Box 10130, Stn. Hart, Prince George, BC V2K 5Y1
Tel: 250-962-5755; Fax: 888-922-6010
tyolaw@shaw.ca

Prince George: Wilson King LLP - *6
Former Name: Wilson, King & Company
#1000, 299 Victoria St., Prince George, BC V2L 5B8
Tel: 250-960-3200; Fax: 250-562-7777
Toll-Free: 800-365-4566
info@wilsonking.bc.ca
www.wilsonking.bc.ca

Prince George: Garth A. Wright Law Corporation - *1
#204, 411 Quebec St., Prince George, BC V2L 1W5
Tel: 250-564-5544 Toll-Free: 877-964-5544
garthwright@shaw.ca
www.garthwrightlaw.ca

Prince Rupert: Johnston Law Office - *1
Former Name: Punnett & Johnston
#7, 222 - 3rd Ave. West, Prince Rupert, BC V8J 1L1
Tel: 250-624-2106; Fax: 250-627-8805
gmjohnston@citytel.net

Prince Rupert: Marina C-K Kan - *1
P.O. Box 722, Prince Rupert, BC V8J 3S1
Tel: 250-624-6060; Fax: 250-624-6451

Prince Rupert: Silversides, Merrick & McLean - *4
Former Name: Silversides, Seidemann & Kucher
P.O. Box 188, Stn. Prince Rupert, 217 - 3rd Ave. West, Prince
Rupert, BC V8J 3P7
Tel: 250-624-2116; Fax: 250-627-7786

Qualicum Beach: Marshall & Lamperson - Qualicum Beach - *4
P.O. Box 879, 710 Memorial Ave., Qualicum Beach, BC V9K 1T2
Tel: 250-752-5615; Fax: 250-752-2055
reception@mllawcorp.ca
mllawcorp.ca

Qualicum Beach: Rodway & Perry - *2
#1, P.O. Box 138, 699 Beach Rd., Qualicum Beach, BC V9K 1S7
Tel: 250-752-9526; Fax: 250-752-9521
rodwayandperry@shaw.ca

Qualicum Beach: Walker Hubbard - *4
#2, 707 Primrose St., Qualicum Beach, BC V9K 2K1
Tel: 250-752-6951; Fax: 250-752-6022
www.qblaw.ca

Quesnel: John B. Schmitz - *1
633 Clark St., Quesnel, BC V2J 1L3
Tel: 250-992-6793; Fax: 250-992-6795

Revelstoke: Bernard C. Lavallée - *1
Former Name: Lavallée, Rackel
#203B, 244, 555 Victoria Rd., Revelstoke, BC V0E 2S0
Tel: 250-837-5168; Fax: 250-837-5178
bcl59lawyer@rctvonline.net

Revelstoke: Robert A. Lundberg Law Corporation - *1
P.O. Box 2490, 119 Campbell Ave., Revelstoke, BC V0E 2S0
Tel: 250-837-5196; Fax: 250-837-4746
robertlundberg@rctvonline.net

Richmond: David G. Baker, Barrister - *1
#210, 7340 Westminster Hwy., Richmond, BC V6X 1A1
Tel: 604-244-7587; Fax: 604-303-6922
davegbaker@yahoo.com
www.davidgbaker.ca

Richmond: Berger & Company - *1
#130, 8400 Granville Ave., Richmond, BC V6Y 1P6
Tel: 604-273-9959; Fax: 604-273-9910
eberger@telus.net
www.berger-and-company.com

Richmond: David W. Blinkhorn - *1
#430, 5900 No. 3 Rd., Richmond, BC V6X 3P7
Tel: 604-244-7880; Fax: 604-244-9611

Richmond: Campbell Froh May & Rice LLP - *13
#200, 5611 Cooney Rd., Richmond, BC V6X 3J6
Tel: 604-273-8481; Fax: 604-273-4729
Toll-Free: 800-883-8288
contact@cfmrlaw.com
richmondbclawyers.com

Richmond: V.N. Carvalho - *1
13811 Gilbert Rd., Richmond, BC V7E 2H8
Tel: 604-274-5636; Fax: 604-275-5694
vncarvalho@shaw.ca

Richmond: Robert J. Charlton - *1
Also Known As: Robert J. Charlton Personal Law
Corporation
#816, 6081 No. 3 Rd., Richmond, BC V6Y 2B2
Tel: 604-214-7818; Fax: 604-214-7819
rjc@rjcharlton.com
www.rjcharlton.com

Richmond: Chouinard & Company - *2
#816, 6081 No. 3 Rd., Richmond, BC V6Y 2B2
Tel: 604-284-5633; Fax: 604-284-5632
Toll-Free: 877-685-8999
ray@chouinardlaw.com
www.chouinardlaw.com

Richmond: Cohen Buchan Edwards LLP - *7
#290, 13777 Commerce Pkwy., Richmond, BC V6V 2X3
Tel: 604-273-6411; Fax: 604-273-4512
info@cbelaw.com
www.cbelaw.com

Richmond: John C. Fairburn
#305, 5811 Cooney Rd., Richmond, BC V6X 3M1
Tel: 604-279-8283; Fax: 604-279-8243
fairburnlaw@execcentre.com

Richmond: Fast & Company, Barristers & Solicitors - *2
#5080, 8171 Ackroyd Rd., Richmond, BC V6X 3K1
Tel: 604-273-6424; Fax: 604-273-2290
Toll-Free: 877-552-2323
mlfast@fastandco.ca
www.fastandco.ca

Richmond: Forbes & Boyle - *2
#215, 8171 Cook Rd., Richmond, BC V6Y 3T8
Tel: 604-273-7575; Fax: 604-273-8475
info@forbesboyle.ca
www.forbesboyle.ca

Richmond: Kojo Frempong
Former Name: Ash O'Donnell Hibbert Law Corporation
#305, South Tower, 5811 Cooney Rd., Richmond, BC V6X 3M1
Tel: 604-273-9111; Fax: 604-273-1117
kojo@kojofrempong.com
www.linkedin.com/in/kojo-frempong-a27b092b

Richmond: Douglas B. Graves - *1
#218, 8055 Anderson Rd., Richmond, BC V6Y 1S2
Tel: 604-276-0069

Richmond: Guo Law Corporation - *1
#120, 6068 - #3 Rd., Richmond, BC V6Y 4M7
Tel: 778-297-6560; Fax: 778-297-6561
office@guolaw.ca
www.guolaw.ca

Richmond: Henderson Law Group - *2
Former Name: Henderson Livingston Stewart LLP
#280, Riverside Professional Centre, 11331 Coppersmith
Way, Richmond, BC V7A 5J9
Tel: 604-639-5175; Fax: 604-639-5176
office@hlglaw.ca
hlglaw.ca

Richmond: Bernard Hoodekoff - *1
#206, 5811 Cooney Rd., Richmond, BC V6X 3M1
Tel: 604-278-8451; Fax: 604-278-8453

Richmond: Humphry Paterson - *2
#205, 8171 Park Rd., Richmond, BC V6Y 1S9
Tel: 604-278-3031; Fax: 604-278-3021

Richmond: INC Business Lawyers - *2
Former Name: Moir & Moir
#1103, 11871 Horseshoe Way, Richmond, BC V7A 5H5
Tel: 604-272-6960; Fax: 604-272-6959
Toll-Free: 888-272-7771
info@incorporate.ca
www.incorporate.ca

Richmond: Jang Cheung Lee Chu Law Corporation - *3
Former Name: Jang, Cheung, Lee
#700, 5951 No. 3 Rd., Richmond, BC V6X 2E3
Tel: 604-276-8300; Fax: 604-276-8309
www.jclclawcorp.com

Richmond: Kahn Zack Ehrlich Lithwick LLP - *17
#300, 10991 Shellbridge Way, Richmond, BC V6X 3C6
Tel: 604-270-9571; Fax: 604-270-8282
www.kzellaw.com

indicates number of lawyers

Richmond: Nancy L. Kinsman - *1
#315, 8171 Cook Rd., Richmond, BC V6Y 3T8
Tel: 604-273-4664; *Fax*: 604-273-7442
nkinsman@familylawbc.ca
www.familylawbc.ca

Richmond: Kenneth B. Krag - *1
#228, 8055 Anderson Rd., Richmond, BC V6Y 1S2
Tel: 604-270-8702; *Fax*: 604-270-6708

Richmond: Susan Label - *1
#280, 11331 Coppersmith Way, Richmond, BC V7A 5J9
Tel: 604-273-6448; *Fax*: 604-273-6998
susan.label@shawcable.com
www.susanlabel.com

Richmond: Levitt Law Office - *1
Also Known As: Morley A. Levitt
#120, 11181 Voyageur Way, Richmond, BC V6X 3N9
Tel: 604-270-9611; *Fax*: 604-270-4588
morley@levittlaw.ca
www.protectmyestate.ca

Richmond: Lim & Company - *5
#320, 7480 Westminster Hwy., Richmond, BC V6X 1A1
Tel: 604-303-0788; *Fax*: 604-303-0789
info@limcolawyers.com
www.limcolawyers.com

Richmond: V. Brent Louie, Personal Law
Corporation - *1
#203, 2680 Shell Rd., Richmond, BC V6X 4C9
Tel: 604-270-8708; *Fax*: 604-270-8735
vblouie@shaw.ca

Richmond: Peter Li & Company - *3
Former Name: Peter S.K. Li
#110, 4400 Hazelbridge Way, Richmond, BC V6X 3R8
Tel: 604-273-6308; *Fax*: 604-273-6393
office@peterliandcompany.com
www.peterliandcompany.com

Richmond: Phillips Paul
#215, 4800 No. 3 Rd., Richmond, BC V6X 3A6
Tel: 604-273-5297; *Fax*: 604-273-1643
inquiries@phillipspaul.com
www.phillipspaul.com

Richmond: Susan L. Polsky Shamash - *1
#150, 4600 Jacombs Rd., Richmond, BC V6V 3B1
Tel: 604-664-7800; *Fax*: 604-664-7898
Toll-Free: 800-663-2782

Richmond: Pryke Lambert Leathley Russell LLP -
*19
#500, North Tower, 5811 Cooney Rd., Richmond, BC V6X
3M1
Tel: 604-243-8912; *Fax*: 604-276-8045
Toll-Free: 800-733-8716
www.pllr.com

Richmond: Rees-Thomas & Company - *3
#5080, 8171 Ackroyd Rd., Richmond, BC V6X 3K1
Tel: 604-279-9300; *Fax*: 604-273-2290
info@reesthomas.com
www.reesthomas.com

Richmond: Scardina & Co. - *1
#215, 4800 No. 3 Rd., Richmond, BC V6X 3A6
Tel: 604-273-5558; *Fax*: 604-273-5550

Richmond: Spry Hawkins Micner - *6
#440, VanCity Tower, 5900 No. 3 Rd., Richmond, BC V6X 3P7
Tel: 604-233-7001; *Fax*: 604-233-7017
www.willpowerlaw.com

Richmond: Bruce Allan Thompson Law Corporation
- *1
#215, Churchill Centre, 2nd Fl., 8171 Cook Rd., Richmond,
BC V6Y 3T8
Tel: 604-270-7773; *Fax*: 604-273-8475

Richmond: Tsang & Company - *2
Former Name: Wong & Tsang
#320, 8171 Cook Rd., Richmond, BC V6Y 3T8
Tel: 604-279-9023; *Fax*: 604-279-9025
www.tsangco.com

Richmond: Webster & Associates - *4
#550, 5900 No. 3 Rd., Richmond, BC V6X 3P7
Tel: 604-713-8030; *Fax*: 604-713-8038
info@braininjurylaw.ca
www.braininjurylaw.ca

Richmond: Mary E.B. Wood - *1
#724, 6081 - No. 3 Rd., Richmond, BC V6Y 2B2
Tel: 604-273-5547; *Fax*: 604-273-3044
mebwood@telus.net
www.marywoodlawyer.com

Roberts Creek: Lynn Chapman - *1
1947 Crystal Cr., Roberts Creek, BC V0N 2W1
Tel: 604-886-0382; *Fax*: 604-886-0366
lchapman@dccnet.com

Saanichton: C.J. (Kip) Wilson - *1
#6, 7855 East Saanich Rd., Saanichton, BC V8M 2B4
Tel: 250-544-0727; *Fax*: 250-544-0728
admin@saanichtonlaw.com
www.saanichtonlaw.com

Salmon Arm: Brooke Downs Vennard LLP - *5
Former Name: Brooke, Jackson, Downs LLP
Centennial Building, P.O. Box 67, 51 - 3rd St. NE, Salmon
Arm, BC V1E 4N2
Tel: 250-832-9311; *Fax*: 250-832-3801
www.bdvlaw.ca

Salmon Arm: Derek McManus Law Corporation - *1
P.O. Box 57, 450 Lakeshore Dr. NE, Salmon Arm, BC V1E
4N2
Tel: 250-833-4720; *Fax*: 250-832-4787
corp@salmonarmlaw.com
www.salmonarmlaw.com

Salmon Arm: Seale Law Corp. - *1
#302, P.O. Box 3248, Stn. Main, 370 Kaleshore Dr. NE,
Salmon Arm, BC V1E 4S1
Tel: 250-832-9301; *Fax*: 250-832-9300

Salmon Arm: Sivertz Kiehlbauch - *3
Former Name: Sivertz, Kiehlbauch & Zachernuk
P.O. Box 190, Stn. Main, 351 Hudson Ave. NE, Salmon Arm,
BC V1E 4N3
Tel: 250-832-8031; *Fax*: 250-832-6177

Salmon Arm: Verdurmen & Company - *1
Former Name: Verdurmen & Lee
P.O. Box 826, 450 Lakeshore Dr. NE, Salmon Arm, BC V1E
4N9
Tel: 250-833-0914; *Fax*: 250-833-0924
Toll-Free: 855-833-0914
vlex@telus.net
www.verdurmenlaw.com

Salt Spring Island: Fisher, Murphy & Woodward - *1
Also Known As: Orca Law Corp.
Former Name: Ian H. Clement Law Corporation
#1, 105 Rainbow Rd., Salt Spring Island, BC V8K 2V5
Tel: 250-537-5505; *Fax*: 250-537-5099
ianhclement@gmail.com
saltspringlawfirm.com

Salt Spring Island: James Pasuta - *1
P.O. Box 414, Stn. Ganges, 560 Fulford-Ganges Rd., Salt
Spring Island, BC V8K 2W1
Tel: 250-537-9995; *Fax*: 250-537-9975

Sechelt: Narbonne Law Office - *1
P.O. Box 762, Sechelt, BC V0N 3A0
Tel: 604-886-7972; *Fax*: 604-886-7147
www.narbonnelawoffice.com

Sechelt: William C. Prowse - *1
6866 Island View Rd., Sechelt, BC V0N 3A8
Tel: 604-740-0303; *Fax*: 604-740-0306
transmed@telus.net

Sechelt: Robinson & Co. Law Office - *1
P.O. Box 920, Sechelt, BC V0N 3A0
Tel: 604-885-7541; *Fax*: 604-885-7561
robco@telus.net

Sidney: Henley & Straub LLP - *3
Former Name: Henley & Walden LLP
#201, 2377 Bevan Ave., Sidney, BC V8L 4M9
Tel: 250-656-7231; *Fax*: 250-656-0937
Toll-Free: 800-656-7231
inquiries@henleystraub.com
www.henleystraub.com

Sidney: McKimm & Lott - Sidney - *8
#7, 9843 - 2nd St., Sidney, BC V8L 2Z3
Tel: 250-656-3961; *Fax*: 250-655-3329
reception@mclott.com
www.mclott.com

Smithers: Perry & Company - *3
P.O. Box 790, 3875 Broadway Ave., Smithers, BC V0J 2N0
Tel: 250-847-4341; *Fax*: 250-847-5634
reception@perryco.ca
www.perryco.ca

Smithers: G. Ronald Toews, Q.C. - *1
P.O. Box 970, 3835 - 10th Ave., Smithers, BC V0J 2N0
Tel: 250-847-2187; *Fax*: 250-847-2183
grt@buckley.net

Sooke: Hallgren & Faulkner - *2
P.O. Box 939, #104, 6739 West Coast Rd., Sooke, BC V9Z
1H9
Tel: 250-642-5271 *Toll-Free*: 877-358-5271
info@hallgrenfaulkner.ca
www.hallgrenfaulkner.ca

Sorrento: Begin & Company - *1
P.O. Box 122, Sorrento, BC V0E 2W0
Tel: 250-835-4857; *Fax*: 250-835-2298
rb@zipitlaw.com

Squamish: Race & Company LLP - Squamish - *13
#301, 37989 Cleveland Ave., Squamish, BC V8B 0B3
Tel: 604-892-5254
info@raceandco.com
www.raceandcompany.com

Summerland: Bell, Jacoe & Company - *2
P.O. Box 520, 13211 Victoria Rd. North, Summerland, BC
V0H 1Z0
Tel: 250-494-6621; *Fax*: 250-494-8055
Toll-Free: 800-663-0392
belljacoe@shaw.ca
www.bell-jacoe.com

Surrey: Alan J. Benson - *1
#106, 15585 - 24 Ave., Surrey, BC V4A 2J4
Tel: 604-538-4911; *Fax*: 604-538-5754
info@alanbensonlaw.com
www.alanbensonlaw.com

Surrey: Roger S. Bhatti - *1
#203, 8556 - 120th St., Surrey, BC V3W 3N5
Tel: 604-590-1177; *Fax*: 604-596-8800
rblaw@intergate.ca

Surrey: Spencer A. Bowers - *1
8893 - 160 St., Surrey, BC V4N 2X8
Tel: 604-951-9224; *Fax*: 604-951-9224
sabowers@axionet.com

Surrey: Brawn, Karras & Sanderson - *4
#309, 1688 - 152nd St., Surrey, BC V4A 4N2
Tel: 604-259-1620; *Fax*: 604-542-5341
Toll-Free: 877-470-7535
www.bkslaw.com

Surrey: Buckley Hogan - *5
Former Name: Buckley & Buckley
#200, 8120 - 128th St., Surrey, BC V3W 1R1
Tel: 604-635-3000; *Fax*: 604-635-3311
lawyers@buckleyhogan.com
www.buckleyhogan.com

Surrey: Caissie & Company - *1
#205, 15127 - 100 Ave., Surrey, BC V3R 0N9
Tel: 604-586-7200; *Fax*: 604-583-5870
info@calaw.bc.ca
www.calaw.bc.ca

Surrey: Chris Temple Law - Surrey - 120 St.
Former Name: TNT Lawyers
7164 - 120 St., Surrey, BC V3W 3M8
Tel: 604-970-2440 *Toll-Free*: 877-536-4520
info@icbcinjurylawyers.ca
www.icbcinjurylawyers.ca
www.linkedin.com/company/chris-temple-law

Surrey: James L. Davidson & Company - *2
#403, 16033 - 108 Ave., Surrey, BC V4N 1P2
Tel: 604-951-2990; *Fax*: 604-951-2991
www.jldlawyers.com

Surrey: De Jager Volkenant & Company - *6
#5, 15243 - 91 Ave., Surrey, BC V3R 8P8
Tel: 604-953-1500; *Fax*: 604-953-1501
Toll-Free: 866-953-1500
dvc@dvclawyers.com
www.dvclawyers.com

Surrey: Paul E. Del Rossi - *1
#1012, 7445 - 132nd St., Surrey, BC V3W 1J8
Tel: 604-590-5600; Fax: 604-590-5626
pdelrossi@sternandalbert.com

Surrey: Fritz Shirreff & Vickers - *4
Former Name: Fritz Lail Shirreff & Vickers
#201, 15127 - 100th Ave., Surrey, BC V3R 0N9
Tel: 604-582-5157; Fax: 604-582-5167

Surrey: Gabbrel & Company - *1
#202, 15388 - 24 Ave., Surrey, BC V4A 2J2
Tel: 604-583-5776
gambrelandcompany.ca

Surrey: Hamilton Duncan Armstrong & Stewart Law Corporation - *20
#1450, Station Tower Gateway, 13401 - 108th Ave., Surrey, BC V3T 5T3
Tel: 604-581-4677; Fax: 604-581-5947
www.hdas.com
www.facebook.com/HamiltonDuncanLaw,
www.linkedin.com/company/812865

Surrey: Hittrich Family Law Group - *2
#300, 15230 - #10 Hwy., Surrey, BC V3S 5K7
Tel: 604-575-2274; Fax: 604-575-2357
info@hittrichlaw.com
www.hzfamilylaw.com

Surrey: Howard Smith & Company - *3
#111, 15272 Croydon Dr., Surrey, BC V3S 0Z5
Tel: 604-535-7688; Fax: 604-535-7699
info@howardsmithlawyers.com
www.howardsmithlawyers.com

Surrey: Sharen Janeson - *1
#456, 15355 - 24 Ave., Surrey, BC V4A 2H9
Tel: 604-536-6884; Fax: 604-618-9500
sjaneson@shaw.ca

Surrey: Kaminsky & Company - *4
#205, 15240 - 56 Ave., Surrey, BC V3S 5K7
Tel: 604-591-7877; Fax: 604-591-1978
inbox@kaminskyco.com
www.kaminskyco.com

Surrey: Kane, Shannon & Weiler LLP - Surrey - *26
#220, 7565 - 132nd St., Surrey, BC V3W 1K5
Tel: 604-635-1780; Fax: 604-591-7149
Toll-Free: 800-497-3069
www.ksw.bc.ca
www.facebook.com/kswlaw

Surrey: Kereluk & Company - *1
#125, 15225 - 104 Ave., Surrey, BC V3R 6Y8
Tel: 604-589-3278; Fax: 604-589-8473
mail@kereluklaw.com
www.kereluklaw.com

Surrey: James R. Kitsul - *1
19395 Langley Bypass, Surrey, BC V3S 6K1
Tel: 604-539-2610; Fax: 604-534-3811
kitsul@supersave.ca

Surrey: Leung, Arthur-Leung - *1
14340-57th Ave., Surrey, BC V3X 1B2
Tel: 604-572-2300

Surrey: MacMillan, Tucker & Mackay - *6
5690 - 176A St., Surrey, BC V3S 4H1
Tel: 604-574-7431; Fax: 604-574-3021
Toll-Free: 800-922-7431
www.mactuc.com
www.facebook.com/macmillantuckermackay,
twitter.com/mactuc1,
www.linkedin.com/company/macmillan-tucker-&-mackay

Surrey: Maier & Co. - *1
#310, 10524 King George Hwy., Surrey, BC V3S 2X2
Tel: 604-582-5951; Fax: 604-588-0779
maier@telus.net

Surrey: Malik Law Corporation - *2
Former Name: Unterman & Associates; South Fraser Law Group
#206, Khalsa Business Center, 8388 - 128th St., Surrey, BC V3W 4G2
Tel: 604-543-9111; Fax: 604-543-9112
info@maliklaw.ca
www.maliklaw.ca

Surrey: Manthorpe Law Offices - *3
#200, 10233 - 153 St., Surrey, BC V3R 0Z7
Tel: 604-582-7743; Fax: 604-582-7753
info@manthorpelaw.com
www.manthorpelaw.com

Surrey: Alistair L. McAndrew - *1
#240, 13711 - 72 Ave., Surrey, BC V3W 2P2
Tel: 604-591-2288; Fax: 604-591-7366

Surrey: Cameron C. McLeod - *1
#310, 10524 King George Hwy, Surrey, BC V3T 2X2
Tel: 604-583-6318; Fax: 604-588-0779
mcleodlaw@dccnet.com

Surrey: David C. McPhillips - *1
#199-800, 15355-24 Ave., Surrey, BC V4A 2H9
Tel: 604-535-7266; Fax: 604-535-6658
dmcphillips@shaw.ca

Surrey: McQuarrie Hunter LLP - *27
#1500, Central City Tower, 13450 - 102nd Ave., 15th Fl., Surrey, BC V3T 5X3
Tel: 604-581-7001; Fax: 604-581-7110
Toll-Free: 877-581-7001
www.mcquarrie.com
www.facebook.com/mcquarrielaw, twitter.com/mcquarrie_law,
www.linkedin.com/company/2365673

Surrey: Morrison & Co. - *1
#303, 15225 - 104th Ave., Surrey, BC V3R 6Y8
Tel: 604-930-9013; Fax: 604-930-9014
admin@morrocolaw.ca
morrocolaw.ca

Surrey: Murchison Thomson & Clarke LLP - *24
#101, Surrey Central Business Park, 7565 - 132 St., Surrey, BC V3W 1K5
Tel: 604-590-8855; Fax: 604-590-2000
info@mtclaw.ca
www.murchisonthomson.com

Surrey: Larry Nelson - *1
#309, 1656 Martin Dr., Surrey, BC V4A 6E7
Tel: 604-538-1511; Fax: 604-535-5344

Surrey: Nyack & Persad - *2
#201, 9380 - 120 St., Surrey, BC V3V 4B9
Tel: 604-588-9933; Fax: 604-588-2731

Surrey: Michael G. Parent, Law Corporation - *1
#203, 15225 - 104 Ave., Surrey, BC V3R 6Y8
Tel: 604-589-6437; Fax: 604-589-7238

Surrey: Peterson Stark Scott - Surrey - *9
#300, 10366 - 136A St., Surrey, BC V3T 5R3
Tel: 604-634-2308; Fax: 604-589-5391
Toll-Free: 800-675-2419
sry@psslaw.ca
www.psslaw.ca
www.facebook.com/1586647948230609, twitter.com/psslaw,
www.linkedin.com/company/peterson-stark-scott

Surrey: Donald F. Porter - *1
#149, 6350 - 120 St., Surrey, BC V3X 3K1
Tel: 604-594-5155; Fax: 604-594-1304
dfporter@uniserve.com

Surrey: Richards & Richards
10325 - 150 St., Surrey, BC V3R 4B1
Tel: 604-588-6844; Fax: 604-588-8800
Toll-Free: 800-790-6844
www.richardslaw.com

Surrey: Roxwal Lawyers LLP - *4
#212, 5455 - 152nd St., Surrey, BC V3S 5A5
Tel: 604-575-3718; Fax: 604-575-3719
info@roxwal.com
www.roxwal.com

Surrey: Sanghera Law Group - *3
#203, 7134 King George Blvd., Surrey, BC V3W 5A3
Tel: 604-543-8484; Fax: 604-543-8584
Toll-Free: 877-778-8484
info@slglawyers.com
www.slglawyers.com

Surrey: Sedai Law Office - *1
#110, 10768 Whalley Blvd., Surrey, BC V3T 0G1
Tel: 778-395-7810; Fax: 604-909-4859
msedai@immigrationcitizenshiplaw.com
www.immigrationcitizenshiplaw.com
www.facebook.com/immigrationcitizenshiplaw,
twitter.com/MarinaSedai, www.linkedin.com/in/marinasedai

Surrey: Shergill & Company, Trial Lawyers - *3
#286, Payal Business Center, 8128 - 128th St., Surrey, BC V3W 1R1
Tel: 604-597-8111; Fax: 604-597-8133
Toll-Free: 855-597-8111
main@shergilllaw.com
www.shergilllaw.com
twitter.com/Shergill_law

Surrey: Sicotte & Henry Criminal Defence Lawyers - *3
#200, 10706 King George Blvd., Surrey, BC V3T 2X3
Tel: 604-585-8898; Fax: 604-585-8964
www.surreycriminallawyer.com/en/

Surrey: Siebenga & King Law Offices - *3
#288, 12899 - 76th Ave., Surrey, BC V3W 1E6
Tel: 604-592-3550; Fax: 604-592-3551
info@sklawoffices.com
www.sklawoffices.com

Surrey: South Coast Law Group - *3
#6, 15243 - 91st Ave., Surrey, BC V3R 8P8
Tel: 604-496-5096; Fax: 604-496-5196
info@southcoastlaw.ca
www.southcoastlaw.ca

Surrey: Starr & Company - *2
#203, 2383 King George Hwy., Surrey, BC V4A 5A4
Tel: 604-536-3393; Fax: 604-536-3115

Surrey: Swedahl & Company - *1
#11, 15243 - 91 Ave., Surrey, BC V3R 8P8
Tel: 604-581-3232; Fax: 604-589-3741

Surrey: Taylor, Bjorge & Company - *2
#205, 1676 Martin Dr., Surrey, BC V4A 6E7
Tel: 604-536-1117; Fax: 604-536-0445

Surrey: Trial Lawyers Advocacy Group - *4
Former Name: Guildford Law Group
#200, 8459 - 160 St., Surrey, BC V4N 0V6
Tel: 604-635-1330; Fax: 604-635-1340
www.tlag.ca

Surrey: Virk Law Group
#1005, 7495 - 132 St., Surrey, BC V3W 1J8
Tel: 604-596-4342; Fax: 604-596-4312
psv@virklawgroup.com
www.virklawgroup.com

Surrey: Gordon G. Walters - *1
12321 Beecher St., Surrey, BC V4A 3A7
Tel: 604-596-3300; Fax: 604-596-9111

Surrey: Wilson & Rasmussen LLP - *3
Former Name: Greig, Wilson & Brajovic
#300, Guildford Landmark Bldg., 15127 - 100th Ave., Surrey, BC V3R 0N9
Tel: 604-583-7917; Fax: 604-583-7139
info@wilsonrasmussen.com
www.wilsonrasmussen.com
www.linkedin.com/company/wilson-rasmussen-llp

Surrey: Yearwood & Company - *2
#2, 9613 - 192nd St., Surrey, BC V4N 4C7
Tel: 604-513-2333; Fax: 604-513-0211
pyearwood@bclaw.bc.ca
www.bclaw.bc.ca

Terrace: Crampton Personal Law Corporation - *2
4623 Park Ave., Terrace, BC V8G 1V5
Tel: 250-635-6330; Fax: 250-635-4795
Toll-Free: 800-667-0080
bryan_crampton@telus.net

Terrace: Talstra Law Corporation - *6
#101, 3219 Eby St., Terrace, BC V8G 4R3
Tel: 250-638-1137; Fax: 250-638-1306
www.talstralaw.ca

Terrace: Warner Bandstra Brown - *3
#200, Nash Building, 4630 Lazelle Ave., Terrace, BC V8G 1S6
Tel: 250-635-2622; Fax: 250-635-4998
Toll-Free: 800-665-5120
www.warnerbandstra.com

Trail: Ghilarducci & Cromarty - *2
1309 Bay Ave., Trail, BC V1R 4A7
Tel: 250-368-6455; Fax: 250-368-6107

* indicates number of lawyers

Trail: McEwan & Company - Trail - *7
Also Known As: McEwan Law
Former Name: McEwan Harrison & Co.
1432 Bay Ave., Trail, BC V1R 4B1
Tel: 250-368-8211; Fax: 250-368-9401
Toll-Free: 888-354-4844
www.mcewanlawco.com

Trail: Thompson LeRose & Brown - *6 1
1199 Cedar St., Trail, BC V1R 4B8
Tel: 250-368-3327; Fax: 250-368-4494

Vancouver: Aaron Gordon Daykin Nordlinger LLP - *9
Former Name: Aaron, MacGregor, Gordon & Daykin
#1100, 777 Hornby St., Vancouver, BC V6Z 1S4
Tel: 604-689-7571; Fax: 604-685-8563
reception@agdnlaw.ca
www.agdnlaw.ca

Vancouver: Access Law Group - *6
#1700, 1185 West Georgia St., Vancouver, BC V6E 4E6
Tel: 604-689-8000; Fax: 604-689-8835
reception@accesslaw.ca
www.accesslaw.ca

Vancouver: Jack A. Adelaar - *1
#1700, P.O. Box 12148, 808 Nelson St., Vancouver, BC V6Z 2H2
Tel: 604-687-8840; Fax: 604-687-8370
jadelaar@telus.net

Vancouver: Adrian & Company - *2
5660 Yew St., Vancouver, BC V6M 3Y3
Tel: 604-266-7811; Fax: 604-266-5869

Vancouver: Alexander Holburn Beaudin & Lang, LLP - *72
#2700, P.O. Box 10057, 700 West Georgia St., Vancouver, BC V7Y 1B8
Tel: 604-484-1700; Fax: 604-484-9700
Toll-Free: 877-688-1351
www.ahbl.ca
www.facebook.com/ahbllawyers,
www.linkedin.com/company/alexander-holburn-beaudin-lang-llp

Vancouver: Allan & Lougheed - *2
1622 - 7th Ave. W, 2nd Fl., Vancouver, BC V6J 1S5
Tel: 604-733-2411; Fax: 604-736-6225
aandllaw@telus.net

Vancouver: Alvin Hui Law Corp. - *1
1606 Hornby St., Vancouver, BC V6Z 2T4
Tel: 604-732-3898; Fax: 604-739-2821

Vancouver: Andersen Paul - Vancouver - *2
1662 - West 8th Ave., Vancouver, BC V6J 1V4
Tel: 604-734-8411; Fax: 604-734-8511
info@andersenpaullaw.com
andersenpaullaw.com

Vancouver: Brian W. Anderson Law Corporation - *1
835 Granville St., 2nd Fl., Vancouver, BC V6Z 1K7
Tel: 604-684-5367

Vancouver: Jane Anderson - *1
#1782, 808 Nelson St., Vancouver, BC V6Z 2H2
Tel: 604-488-1162; Fax: 604-488-0666
janeanderso@telus.net

Vancouver: Armstrong Simpson - *4
Former Name: Armstrong & Company
#2080, 777 Hornby St., Vancouver, BC V6Z 1S4
Tel: 604-683-7361; Fax: 604-662-3231
www.armlaw.ca

Vancouver: Aydin Bird - *6
Former Name: Aydin & Co
#530, Oakridge Centre, North Office Tower, 650 - 41 Ave. West, Vancouver, BC V5Z 2M9
Tel: 604-266-5828; Fax: 604-266-3929
aydin@aydinco.com
www.aydinco.com

Vancouver: Baker & Baker - *2
808 Nelson St., 17th Fl., Vancouver, BC V6Z 2H2
Tel: 604-642-0107; Fax: 604-681-3504

Vancouver: Barbeau, Evans & Goldstein, Barristers & Solicitors - *3
#280, Park Place, 666 Burrard St., Vancouver, BC V6C 2X8
Tel: 604-688-4900; Fax: 604-688-0649
info@beg-law.com
www.beg-law.com

Vancouver: Gail Barnes - *1
195 Alexander St., 2nd Fl., Vancouver, BC V6A 1B8
Tel: 604-684-1124; Fax: 604-684-1122
www.gailbarneslawyer.ca

Vancouver: Beach Avenue Barristers, A Law Corporation - *3
Former Name: Epstein Wood
#150, 1008 Beach Avenue, Vancouver, BC V6E 1T7
Tel: 604-629-0429; Fax: 604-689-4451
beachavenuebarristers.com

Vancouver: Beck, Robinson & Company - *6
#700, 686 West Broadway, Vancouver, BC V5Z 1G1
Tel: 604-874-0204; Fax: 604-874-0820
www.beckrobinson.com
www.facebook.com/beckrobinsonlaw

Vancouver: Patrick J. Beirne - *1
157 Alexander St., 3rd Fl., Vancouver, BC V6A 1B8
Tel: 604-683-4311; Fax: 604-683-4317

Vancouver: David R. Bellamy - *1
#101, 1012 Beach Ave., Vancouver, BC V6E 1T7
Tel: 604-800-5352; Fax: 604-662-8902
Toll-Free: 877-713-8239
www.bellamy.bc.ca

Vancouver: Benchmark Law Corpoartion - *1
#600, 1285 Broadway West, Vancouver, BC V6H 3X8
Tel: 778-371-3446; Fax: 604-757-9904
info@benchmarklaw.ca
www.benchmarklaw.ca
www.facebook.com/benchmarklaw,
twitter.com/BenchmarkLawCo,
www.linkedin.com/in/dana-gordon-a55ab346

Vancouver: Bennett Mounteer LLP - *4
Former Name: Hordo Bennett Mounteer LLP
#400, 856 Homer St., Vancouver, BC V6B 2W5
Tel: 604-639-3680; Fax: 604-639-3681
info@hbmlaw.com
www.bennettmounteer.com
www.linkedin.com/company/hordo-bennett-mounteer-llp

Vancouver: Bernard LLP - *14
#1500, 570 Granville St., Vancouver, BC V6C 3P1
Tel: 604-681-1700; Fax: 604-681-1788
info@bernardllp.ca
www.bernardllp.ca

Vancouver: Anthony Beruschi - *2
#605, 889 West Pender St., Vancouver, BC V6C 3B2
Tel: 604-669-3116; Fax: 604-669-5886

Vancouver: Raymond J. Bianchin - *1
#1410, 1130 West Pender St., Vancouver, BC V6E 4A4
Tel: 604-683-8111; Fax: 604-685-0194
rjblawcorp@telus.net
www.icbcclaimslawyer.com

Vancouver: Birnie & Company
#3334, Four Bentall Centre, P.O. Box 49116, Stn. Bentall, 1055 Dunsmuir St., Vancouver, BC V7X 1G4
Tel: 604-688-4511; Fax: 604-688-0511
www.linkedin.com/company/birnie-&-company

Vancouver: Pamela S. Boles - *1
#210, 970 Burrard St., Vancouver, BC V6Z 2R4
Tel: 604-688-5001; Fax: 604-685-5006

Vancouver: Bolton Law
Former Name: Bolton Hatcher Dance Barristers and Solicitors
#335, 1122 Mainland St., Vancouver, BC V6B 5L1
Tel: 604-687-7078; Fax: 604-687-3022
www.bolton-law.ca

Vancouver: Bond Ellen - *2
#200, 157 Alexander St., Vancouver, BC V6A 1B8
Tel: 604-682-3621; Fax: 604-682-3919

Vancouver: Boughton Law Corporation - *47
Also Known As: Boughton
Former Name: Boughton Peterson Yang Anderson
#700, P.O. Box 49290, 595 Burrard St., Vancouver, BC V7X 1S8
Tel: 604-687-6789; Fax: 604-683-5317
info@boughtonlaw.com
www.boughtonlaw.com
www.facebook.com/boughtonlaw, twitter.com/boughtonlaw/,
www.linkedin.com/company/boughton-law-corporation

Vancouver: Joyce W. Bradley - *1
P.O. Box 45565, Stn. Westside, Vancouver, BC V6S 2N5
Tel: 604-732-3886; Fax: 604-732-3781
jwbmediate@telus.net

Vancouver: W. Anita Braha - *1
#300, Stn. F, 1275 West 6th Ave., Vancouver, BC V6H 1A6
Tel: 604-839-5594
wabraha@telus.net
www.wanitabraha.com

Vancouver: Bronson, Jones & Company - Vancouver - Broadway - *10
Former Name: Bronson & Company
#720, 999 West Broadway, Vancouver, BC V5Z 1K3
Tel: 604-681-9666 Toll-Free: 855-852-5100
www.bronsonco.com

Vancouver: Brown Henry Keith - *3
#1504, 100 West Pender St., 15th Fl., Vancouver, BC V6B 1R8
Tel: 604-684-1021; Fax: 604-688-6243
henrykbrownlawcorporation@telus.net

Vancouver: Peter W. Brown Law Corp. - *2
#402, 1525 Robson St., Vancouver, BC V6G 1C3
Tel: 604-915-7075
peterwbrown@owblawcorp.com

Vancouver: John Buchanan - *1
#788, 601 West Broadway, Vancouver, BC V5Z 4C2
Tel: 604-876-0343; Fax: 604-876-9035

Vancouver: Susan P. Burak - *1
1628 - 7th Ave West, 2nd Fl., Vancouver, BC V6J 1S5
Tel: 604-733-2411; Fax: 604-736-6225
ajzburak@shaw.ca

Vancouver: Burke & Jones - *2
687 - 20th Ave. East, Vancouver, BC V5V 1M9
Tel: 604-879-6365; Fax: 604-879-6367
acb@burkeandjones.com
www.burkeandjones.com

Vancouver: Burns Fitzpatrick LLP - *12
Former Name: Burns, Fitzpatrick, Rogers, Schwartz & Turner LLP
#1400, 510 Burrard St., Vancouver, BC V6C 3A8
Tel: 604-602-5000; Fax: 604-685-2104
www.burnsfitz.com

Vancouver: Bradley M. Caldwell - *1
#401, 815 Hornby St., Vancouver, BC V6Z 2E6
Tel: 604-689-8894; Fax: 604-689-5739
bcaldwell@admiraltylaw.com

Vancouver: Cawkell Brodie Glaister LLP - *4
Former Name: Cawkell, Brodie
439 Helmcken St., Vancouver, BC V6B 2E6
Tel: 604-684-3323; Fax: 604-684-3350
www.cawkell.com

Vancouver: Chan Yue & Lee - *1
#212, 475 Main St., Vancouver, BC V6A 2T7
Tel: 604-687-4576; Fax: 604-683-3258
chanyue@telus.net

Vancouver: Chen & Leung - *3
#728, North Tower, Oakridge Centre, 650 - 41st Ave. West, Vancouver, BC V5Z 2M9
Tel: 604-264-8331; Fax: 604-264-8387
info@cllawyers.ca
www.cllawyers.ca

Vancouver: Chow & Company - *1
378 Smithe St., Vancouver, BC V6B 1T7
Tel: 604-669-0268; Fax: 604-669-9863
n-chow@telus.net

Vancouver: Gregory T. Chu - *1
#650, 1188 Georgia St. West, Vancouver, BC V6E 4A2
Tel: 604-628-5005; Fax: 604-987-9939
gtchu@telus.net

Vancouver: Clark Wilson LLP - *76
#900, 885 West Georgia St., Vancouver, BC V6C 3H1
Tel: 604-687-5700; Fax: 604-687-6314
www.cwilson.com
www.facebook.com/137224656347970,
twitter.com/ClarkWilsonLLP,
www.linkedin.com/company/clark-wilson-llp

indicates number of lawyers

Vancouver: Cobb St. Pierre Lewis - *3
#330, 233 West 1st St., Vancouver, BC V7M 1B3
Tel: 604-770-3311; Fax: 604-770-3389
info@acquit.ca
acquit.ca

Vancouver: Cochran Bradshaw - *3
439 Helmcken St., Vancouver, BC V6B 2E6
Tel: 604-681-9200; Fax: 604-681-8339
cochranlaw@telus.net

Vancouver: Morley E. Cofman Law Corporation - *1
#1500, 701 West Georgia St., Vancouver, BC V7Y 1C6
Tel: 604-696-6674; Fax: 604-801-5911
mcofman@shaw.ca

Vancouver: Leonard M. Cohen - *1
#570, 999 West Broadway, Vancouver, BC V5Z 1K5
Tel: 604-731-8118; Fax: 604-731-5274
www.vancouvernotary.ca

Vancouver: Brian Coleman Q.C. - *1
#320, 425 Carrall St., Vancouver, BC V6B 6E3
Tel: 604-683-5821; Fax: 604-683-9354
coleman@telus.net

Vancouver: Collette Parsons Harris - *8
#1750, P.O. Box 10090, 700 Georgia St. West, Vancouver, BC V7Y 1B6
Tel: 604-662-7777; Fax: 604-669-4053
Toll-Free: 800-999-4991
info@colletteparsons.com
www.colletteparsons.com
twitter.com/bcinjurylawyers

Vancouver: Collins & Cullen - *3
#680, 999 West Broadway, Vancouver, BC V5Z 1K5
Tel: 604-259-2897; Fax: 604-730-2628
Toll-Free: 800-594-4252
www.collinscullen.com

Vancouver: Coric Adler Wener - *3
Former Name: Simon Wener
#620, 1385 - 8 Ave. West, Vancouver, BC V6H 3V9
Tel: 604-736-5500
reception@cawlaw.ca
cawlaw.ca

Vancouver: Coristine Woodall - *2
#540, 220 Cambie St., Vancouver, BC V6B 2M9
Tel: 604-689-3242; Fax: 604-689-3292

Vancouver: Carla Courtenay Law Office - *1
#1160, 777 Hornby St., Vancouver, BC V6Z 1S4
Tel: 604-682-2200; Fax: 604-682-2246
lilias@cclaw.bc.ca
www.cclaw.bc.ca

Vancouver: Coutts Pulver LLP - *6
Former Name: Schiller, Coutts, Weiler & Gibson
#1710, One Bentall Center, 505 Burrard St., Vancouver, BC V7X 1M6
Tel: 604-682-1866; Fax: 604-682-6947
reception@cplaw.ca
www.cplaw.ca

Vancouver: Raffaele Crescenzo - *1
#206, 1651 Commercial Dr., Vancouver, BC V5L 3Y3
Tel: 604-255-9030; Fax: 604-255-9075

Vancouver: Flavio Crestani - *1
5052 Victoria Dr., Vancouver, BC V5P 3T8
Tel: 604-251-1168; Fax: 604-253-7726

Vancouver: Kenneth Cristall Law Corporation - *1
#610, 808 Nelson St., Vancouver, BC V6Z 2H2
Tel: 604-654-2250
www.personalinjurybc.com

Vancouver: Harry Crosby - *1
5052 Victoria Dr., Vancouver, BC V5P 3T8
Tel: 604-321-6922; Fax: 604-323-0093

Vancouver: Cruickshank Huinink Zukerman - *3
#250, 1122 Mainland St., Vancouver, BC V6B 5L1
Tel: 604-688-3933; Fax: 604-681-6677
Toll-Free: 888-553-2450
www.chzlaw.ca

Vancouver: Cummings Law Corporation - *1
#320, North Tower, 650 West 41st Ave., Vancouver, BC V5Z 2M9
Tel: 604-264-7038; Fax: 604-264-7039
info@cummingslawcorp.com

Vancouver: Barbara J. Curran
#407, 825 Granville St., Vancouver, BC V6Z 1K9
Tel: 604-689-4501; Fax: 604-689-5572
bjcurran@telus.net

Vancouver: Cuttler & Company - *1
#1801, Nelson Sq., P.O. Box 12184, Stn. Nelson Square, 808 Nelson St., Vancouver, BC V6Z 2H2
Tel: 604-673-4225
info@cuttlerlegal.com
cuttlerlegal.com

Vancouver: Aspha J. Dada & Co. - *2
2479 Kingsway, Vancouver, BC V5R 5G8
Tel: 604-433-3300; Fax: 604-436-3937
info-ajd@telus.net

Vancouver: Arthur DeMeulemeester - *1
#411, 119 Pender St. West, Vancouver, BC V6B 1S5
Tel: 604-685-6610; Fax: 604-682-5687

Vancouver: Derpak White Spencer LLP - *5
#901, 1788 West Broadway, Vancouver, BC V6J 1Y1
Tel: 604-736-9791; Fax: 604-736-7197
www.dwslaw.ca

Vancouver: David H. Doig & Associates - *2
#1450, 1188 Georgia St. West, Vancouver, BC V6E 4A2
Tel: 604-687-8874; Fax: 604-687-8134
Toll-Free: 877-687-8844
www.daviddoig.com

Vancouver: Dolden Wallace Folick LLP - Vancouver - *34
609 Granville St., 18th Fl., Vancouver, BC V7Y 1G5
Tel: 604-689-3222; Fax: 604-689-3777
reception@dolden.com
www.dolden.com
twitter.com/DWFinsurancelaw
www.linkedin.com/company/dolden-wallace-folick-llp

Vancouver: Donovan & Company - *10
73 Water St., 6th Fl., Vancouver, BC V6B 1A1
Tel: 604-688-4272; Fax: 604-688-4282
www.aboriginal-law.com

Vancouver: Emil M. Doricic - *1
195 Alexander St., 2nd Fl., Vancouver, BC V6A 1B8
Tel: 604-688-8338; Fax: 604-688-8356

Vancouver: Le Dressay & Company - *1
#103, 1525 - 8th Ave. West, Vancouver, BC V6J 1T5
Tel: 604-739-0017; Fax: 604-739-0041
dan@ledressay.com
www.ledressay.com

Vancouver: DuMoulin Boskovich LLP - *15
#1800, Manulife Place, P.O. Box 52, 1095 West Pender St., Vancouver, BC V6E 2M6
Tel: 604-669-5500; Fax: 604-688-8491
Toll-Free: 800-288-9893
info@dubo.com
www.dubo.com
www.linkedin.com/company/2293070

Vancouver: Dunnaway Marnie - *2
Former Name: Dunnaway, Jackson & Hamilton
#1205, 808 Nelson St., Vancouver, BC V6Z 2H2
Tel: 604-682-0007; Fax: 604-682-8711

Vancouver: Edwards, Kenny & Bray LLP - *18
#1900, 1040 West Georgia St., Vancouver, BC V6E 4H3
Tel: 604-689-1811; Fax: 604-689-5177
www.ekb.com
www.facebook.com/295369907165262, twitter.com/EKBlawBC,
www.linkedin.com/company-beta/773304

Vancouver: Ellis Business Lawyers - *3
#440, 319 West Pender St., Vancouver, BC V6B 1T3
Tel: 604-688-7374; Fax: 604-688-7385
info@ellislawyers.com
www.ellislawyers.com

Vancouver: Ellis, Nauss & Jones - *2
#600, 1665 West Broadway, Vancouver, BC V6J 1X1
Tel: 604-731-9276; Fax: 604-734-0206

Vancouver: Ellis, Roadburg - *2
#200, 853 Richards St., Vancouver, BC V6B 3B4
Tel: 604-669-7131; Fax: 604-669-7684

Vancouver: Embarkation Law Group - *5
Also Known As: Larson Sohn
#600, Princess Building, P.O. Box 26, 609 West Hastings St., 6th Fl., Vancouver, BC V6B 4W4
Tel: 604-628-6375; Fax: 604-662-7466
Toll-Free: 877-804-3230
info@elgcanada.com
www.elgcanada.com
www.facebook.com/163198040402130

Vancouver: Dick W. Eng Law Corp. - *1
#701, 601 Broadway West, Vancouver, BC V5Z 4C2
Tel: 604-877-2689; Fax: 604-877-0330
dick_eng@telus.net

Vancouver: English Bay Law Corporation - *2
Former Name: Bennett, Parkes
#510, 2695 Granville St., Vancouver, BC V6H 3H4
Tel: 604-734-6838 Toll-Free: 888-488-0203
www.englishbaylaw.ca

Vancouver: Epstein Law - *1
Former Name: Epstein Wood
#1900, 1177 West Hastings St., Vancouver, BC V6E 2K3
Tel: 604-283-1012 Toll-Free: 800-836-9323
www.epsteinlawcorp.com

Vancouver: Robert J. Falconer, Q.C. - *1
#400, 409 Granville St., Vancouver, BC V6C 1T2
Tel: 604-683-5674; Fax: 604-682-8417
robert.falconer@axion.net

Vancouver: Fayers & Company - *2
#380, 5740 Cambie St., Vancouver, BC V5Z 3A6
Tel: 604-325-1246; Fax: 604-325-1261

Vancouver: Robert S. Fleming - *1
#915, 925 West Georgia, Vancouver, BC V6C 3L2
Tel: 604-682-1659; Fax: 604-568-8548
robbie@fleminglawyer.com
www.robertfleminglawyer.com

Vancouver: Constance C. Fogal - *1
3570 Hull St., Vancouver, BC V5N 4R9
Tel: 604-872-2128

Vancouver: Forrester & Company - *4
#300, Randall Building, 555 West Georgia St., Vancouver, BC V6B 1Z6
Tel: 604-682-1066; Fax: 604-682-8036
info@forresterbarristers.ca
www.forresterbarristers.ca

Vancouver: Fowler & Smith - *3
#502, 602 West Hastings St., Vancouver, BC V6B 1P2
Tel: 604-684-1311; Fax: 604-681-9797
rfowler@fowlersmithlaw.com
fowlersmithlaw.com

Vancouver: Fraser & Company
#1200, 999 Hastings St. West, Vancouver, BC V6C 2W2
Tel: 604-669-5244; Fax: 604-669-5791

Vancouver: Gordon J. Fretwell Law Corp. - *1
#1780, 400 Burrard St., Vancouver, BC V6C 3A6
Tel: 604-689-1280; Fax: 604-689-1288

Vancouver: Friesen & Epp, Barristers & Solicitors - *3
5660 Yew St., Vancouver, BC V6M 3Y3
Tel: 604-264-8386; Fax: 604-264-8815
www.friesenandepp.com

Vancouver: Gall Legge Grant & Munroe LLP - *22
#1000, 1199 West Hastings St., Vancouver, BC V6E 3T5
Tel: 604-669-0011; Fax: 604-669-5101
info@glgmlaw.com
www.glgmlaw.com

Vancouver: Ganapathi Law Group - *2
Former Name: Ganapathi & Company
#501, 1155 Robson St., Vancouver, BC V6E 1B5
Tel: 778-653-7592; Fax: 604-689-4888
www.ganapathico.com
www.facebook.com/ganapathilaw

Vancouver: Alnoor R.S. Gangji - *1
#788, 601 West Broadway, Vancouver, BC V5Z 4C2
Tel: 604-708-3783; Fax: 604-876-9035
aglawyer@smartt.com

Vancouver: Robert G. Gateman - *1
#202, 1112 Brougton St., Vancouver, BC V6G 2A8
Tel: 604-687-4911
robert.gateman@ubc.ca

indicates number of lawyers

Vancouver: Te Hennepe Gerrit - *1
#203, 4545 West 10th Ave., Vancouver, BC V6R 4N2
Tel: 604-228-1433; Fax: 604-228-9822
tehennepe@telus.net

Vancouver: Getz Prince Wells LLP - *5
#530, 355 Burrard St., Vancouver, BC V6C 2G8
Tel: 604-685-6367; Fax: 604-685-9798
www.getzpw.com

Vancouver: Kenneth Glasner Q.C. Law Corp. - *1
#318, 1275 West 6th Ave., Vancouver, BC V6H 1A6
Tel: 604-683-4181; Fax: 604-683-0226
glasnerqc@telus.net
glasnerqc.tripod.com

Vancouver: Paul D. Gornall - *1
#1820, 355 Burrard St., Vancouver, BC V6C 2G8
Tel: 604-681-7932; Fax: 604-775-8555
pdg@telus.net

Vancouver: Granger & Co. - *2
#1400, 777 Hornby St., Vancouver, BC V6Z 1S4
Tel: 604-685-1900; Fax: 604-685-2034

Vancouver: Granville Law Group - *2
Former Name: Vertlieb Anderson
#200, 835 Granville St., Vancouver, BC V6Z 1K7
Tel: 604-669-6580; Fax: 604-688-7291

Vancouver: Grossman & Stanley - *3
#800, Box 55, 1090 West Georgia St., Vancouver, BC V6E 3V7
Tel: 604-683-7454; Fax: 604-683-8602
info@grossmanstanley.com
www.grossmanstanley.com

Vancouver: Gudmundseth Mickelson LLP - *12
#2525, 1075 West Georgia St., Vancouver, BC V6E 3C9
Tel: 604-685-6272; Fax: 604-685-8434
info@lawgm.com
www.lawgm.com

Vancouver: Wayne F. Guinn - *1
671G Market Hill, Vancouver, BC V5Z 4B5
Tel: 604-872-6658; Fax: 604-876-3304

Vancouver: Guy & Company - *1
#100, 190 Alexander St., Vancouver, BC V6A 1B5
Tel: 604-681-6164; Fax: 604-681-7420
guy_and_company@telus.net

Vancouver: Hammerberg Lawyers LLP - *17
#1220, Airport Square, 1200 West 73rd Ave., Vancouver, BC V6P 6G5
Tel: 604-269-8500; Fax: 604-269-8511
Toll-Free: 888-529-5544
www.hammerco.net

Vancouver: Hara & Company - *2
#301, 460 Nanaimo St., Vancouver, BC V5L 4W3
Tel: 604-255-4800; Fax: 604-255-8111
haraco@telus.net

Vancouver: Harper Grey LLP - *55
Former Name: Harper Grey Easton
#3200, Vancouver Centre, 650 West Georgia St., Vancouver, BC V6B 4P7
Tel: 604-687-0411; Fax: 604-669-9385
info@harpergrey.com
www.harpergrey.com
twitter.com/harpergreyllp, www.linkedin.com/company/143149

Vancouver: Harris & Brun - *14
#500, 555 West Georgia St., Vancouver, BC V6B 1Z5
Tel: 604-683-2466; Fax: 604-683-4541
www.harrisbrun.com

Vancouver: Harris & Company LLP - *45
Bentall 5, 550 Burrard St., 14th Floor, Vancouver, BC V6C 2B5
Tel: 604-684-6633; Fax: 604-684-6632
info@harrisco.com
www.harrisco.com
twitter.com/harriscollp,
www.linkedin.com/company/harris-&-company-llp

Vancouver: John E. Helsing - *1
#347, 1275 West 6th Ave., Vancouver, BC V6H 1A6
Tel: 604-739-7731; Fax: 604-738-7134

Vancouver: D. Brad Henry Law Corporation - *1
Former Name: Epstein Wood
#1900, 1177 West Hastings St., Vancouver, BC V6E 2K3
Tel: 604-718-6891; Fax: 604-718-6873
bhenry@dbhlaw.ca

Vancouver: Hobbs Giroday - *4
#908, 938 Howe St., Vancouver, BC V6Z 1N9
Tel: 604-669-6609; Fax: 604-669-6612
info@hobbsgiroday.com
www.hobbsgiroday.com
www.linkedin.com/company/2954352

Vancouver: Hogan & Company - *1
#1730, 355 Burrard St., Vancouver, BC V6C 2G8
Tel: 604-687-8806; Fax: 604-687-7089

Vancouver: Holmes & Company - *2
Former Name: Holmes & Greenslade
#1880, Oceanic Plaza, 1066 Hastings St. West, Vancouver, BC V6E 3X1
Tel: 604-688-7861; Fax: 604-688-0426
www.holmescompany.com
www.linkedin.com/company/holmes-and-company

Vancouver: Holmes & King - *4
#1300, 1111 West Georgia St., Vancouver, BC V6E 4M3
Tel: 604-681-1310; Fax: 604-681-1307
info@holmesandking.com
www.holmesandking.com
www.facebook.com/262297667115077,
twitter.com/HolmesandKing

Vancouver: Hoogbruin & Company - *6
#650, 1188 West Georgia St., Vancouver, BC V6E 4A2
Tel: 604-609-3783; Fax: 604-682-8348
www.hoogbruin.com

Vancouver: Wayne Hum & Co. - *1
#1608, 1166 Alberni St., Vancouver, BC V6E 3Z3
Tel: 604-687-6806; Fax: 604-687-6809

Vancouver: Hunter Litigation Chambers - *24
Former Name: Hunter Voith
#2100, 1040 West Georgia St., Vancouver, BC V6E 4H1
Tel: 604-891-2400; Fax: 604-647-4554
www.litigationchambers.com

Vancouver: Irwin, White & Jennings - *3
Also Known As: Irwin, White & Jennings
Former Name: Alex Irwin Law Corp.
#2020, 1055 West Georgia St., Vancouver, BC V6E 3R5
Tel: 604-664-3723; Fax: 604-689-2806
www.iwjlaw.com

Vancouver: Vahan A. Ishkanian - *1
#1100, 1200 West 73rd Ave., Vancouver, BC V6P 6G5
Tel: 604-267-3033
www.wcbbclawyer.com

Vancouver: Law Offices of Jonathan J. Israels - *1
#760, 475 West Georgia St., Vancouver, BC V6B 4M9
Tel: 604-488-1313
info@CriminalLawyerVancouver.ca
www.criminallawyervancouver.ca

Vancouver: Donald Jang - *1
#701, 601 West Broadway, Vancouver, BC V5Z 4C2
Tel: 604-877-0880; Fax: 604-877-0330

Vancouver: Jeffery & Calder - *4
#601, 815 Hornby St., Vancouver, BC V6Z 2E6
Tel: 604-669-5534; Fax: 604-669-7563
contact@jefferycalder.com
www.jefferycalder.com

Vancouver: Jenkins Marzban Logan LLP - *19
#900, Nelson Square, 808 Nelson St., Vancouver, BC V6Z 2H2
Tel: 604-681-6564; Fax: 604-681-0766
info@jml.ca
www.jml.ca

Vancouver: J. Douglas Jevning - *1
#420, The Standard Bldg., 625 Howe St., Vancouver, BC V6C 2T6
Tel: 604-688-7414; Fax: 604-688-6243
doug_jevning@telus.net

Vancouver: Josephson Litigation Counsel - *1
Former Name: Josephson Associates Barristers;
Josephson & Company
#906, Cathedral Pl., 925 West Georgia St., Vancouver, BC V6C 3L2
Tel: 604-684-9887; Fax: 604-684-3221
info@josephlitigation.ca
www.josephlitigation.ca
twitter.com/jabarristers

Vancouver: Steven B. Jung - *1
#701, 601 Broadway West, Vancouver, BC V5Z 4C2
Tel: 604-877-2684; Fax: 604-877-0330
stevenjung@telus.net

Vancouver: Ramzan N. Jussa - *1
#204, 4676 Main St., Vancouver, BC V5V 3R7
Tel: 604-872-8191; Fax: 604-872-8217

Vancouver: Kaplan & Waddell - *2
#102, 2590 Granville St., Vancouver, BC V6H 3H1
Tel: 604-736-8021; Fax: 604-736-3845
kaplanwaddell.com

Vancouver: David J. Karp Law Corporation - *1
Former Name: Myers, Waddell, McMurdo & Karp
#610, 1111 Melville St., Vancouver, BC V6E 3V6
Tel: 604-688-8331; Fax: 604-688-8350
www.vancouverdefencelawyer.com

Vancouver: Katz & Company - *1
#1018, Nelson Square, P.O. Box 12135, 808 Nelson St., Vancouver, BC V6Z 2H2
Tel: 604-669-6226; Fax: 604-669-6752

Vancouver: Peter M. Kendall - *1
#850, 475 Georgia St. West, Vancouver, BC V6B 4M9
Tel: 604-685-3512; Fax: 604-681-9142

Vancouver: C. Robert Kennedy - *1
#206, 190 Alexander St., Vancouver, BC V6A 1B5
Tel: 604-684-3927; Fax: 604-684-3228

Vancouver: Kerfoot Burroughs LLP - *7
#300, 5687 Yew St., Vancouver, BC V6M 3Y2
Tel: 604-263-2565; Fax: 604-263-2737
www.kblawllp.com

Vancouver: Kestrel Workplace Legal Counsel LLP - *3
#702, 2695 Granville St., Vancouver, BC V6H 3H4
Tel: 604-736-6010; Fax: 604-736-6069
info@kwlc.ca
www.kwlc.ca

Vancouver: Khanna & Co. - *3
#1540, 1100 Melville St., Vancouver, BC V6E 4A6
Tel: 604-605-5500; Fax: 604-689-5596
khanna-law.com

Vancouver: Killam Cordell - *5
#2000, 401 Georgia St. West, Vancouver, BC V6B 5A1
Tel: 604-622-5252; Fax: 604-622-5244

Vancouver: William N. King - *1
5650 Kullahun Dr., Vancouver, BC V6N 2E5
Tel: 604-682-1245; Fax: 604-682-8417

Vancouver: Klein Lyons - Vancouver - *13
#400, 1385 - 8th Ave. West, Vancouver, BC V6H 3V9
Tel: 604-874-7171; Fax: 604-874-7180
info@kleinlyons.com
www.kleinlyons.com
www.facebook.com/kleinlawyersllp, twitter.com/kleinlawyersllp

Vancouver: Koffman Kalef LLP - *23
885 West Georgia St., 19th Fl., Vancouver, BC V6C 3H4
Tel: 604-891-3688; Fax: 604-891-3788
info@kkbl.com
www.kkbl.com

Vancouver: Dimitri A. Kontou - *1
#1550, 355 Burrard St., Vancouver, BC V6G 2C8
Tel: 604-662-7244; Fax: 604-687-3097

Vancouver: Gordon Kopelow Law Offices - *2
#208, 2475 Bayswater St., Vancouver, BC V6K 4N3
Tel: 604-684-0096; Fax: 604-734-0057
www.gordonjkopelow.com

Vancouver: Kornfeld & Company - *2
#640, 943 West Broadway, Vancouver, BC V5Z 4E1
Tel: 604-689-3838; Fax: 604-689-0526

* indicates number of lawyers

Vancouver: Kornfeld LLP - *15
Former Name: Kornfeld Mackoff Silber LLP
#1100, Bentall Centre, P.O. Box 11, 505 Burrard St.,
Vancouver, BC V7X 1M5
Tel: 604-331-8300; Fax: 604-683-0570
info@kornfeldllp.com
www.kornfeldllp.com

Vancouver: Ron Y. Kornfeld - *1
#630, Broadway Medical Bldg., 943 Broadway West,
Vancouver, BC V5Z 4E1
Tel: 604-733-2448; Fax: 604-736-5131
rykornfeld@telus.net

Vancouver: Yoke Lam - *1
#328, 88 East Pender St., Vancouver, BC V6A 1T1
Tel: 604-689-1123; Fax: 604-689-2003

Vancouver: Lando & Company LLP - *8
#2010, Royal Centre, P.O. Box 11140, 1055 West Georgia St.,
Vancouver, BC V6E 3P3
Tel: 604-682-6821; Fax: 604-662-8293
www.lando.ca

Vancouver: Georgialee A. Lee & Associates - *4
#1201, P.O. Box 12163, 808 Nelson St., Vancouver, BC V6Z
2H2
Tel: 604-669-2030; Fax: 604-669-2038
glang@georgialeelang.com

Vancouver: Laughton & Company - *2
#1090, 1090 Georgia St. West, Vancouver, BC V6E 3V7
Tel: 604-683-6665; Fax: 604-683-6622

Vancouver: Laxton Gibbens + Company - *2
Former Name: Laxton & Company
#1119, 808 Nelson St., Vancouver, BC V6Z 2H2
Tel: 604-682-3871; Fax: 604-682-3704
www.laxtongibbens.com

Vancouver: Valmon J. LeBlanc - *1
#1400, 1125 Howe St., Vancouver, BC V6Z 2K8
Tel: 604-687-0909; Fax: 604-688-0933
vleblanc@domuslegis.com

Vancouver: Ledding Richard Law - *2
#415, 1788 - 5th Ave. West, Vancouver, BC V6J 1P2
Tel: 604-731-1161; Fax: 604-731-6527

Vancouver: Lesperance Mendes Lawyers - *10
#550, 900 Howe St., Vancouver, BC V6Z 2M4
Tel: 604-685-3567; Fax: 604-685-7505
admin@lmlaw.ca
www.lmlaw.ca

Vancouver: Lew & Lee - *2
#108, 329 Main St., Vancouver, BC V6A 2S9
Tel: 604-685-8331; Fax: 604-685-8334

Vancouver: Chuck Lew - *1
#1010, 207 Hastings St. West, Vancouver, BC V6B 1H7
Tel: 604-688-3601; Fax: 604-688-7866
lewlaw@uniserve.com

Vancouver: Lex Pacifica Law Corporation - *3
Former Name: John H. Shevchuk, Law Corporation
#1000, 543 Granville St., Vancouver, BC V6C 1X8
Tel: 604-689-1024; Fax: 604-689-1028
johnshevchuk@lexpacifica.com
www.lexpacifica.com

**Vancouver: Carey Linde Personal Law Corporation -
*2**
Also Known As: Divorce for Men
#605, 1080 Howe St., Vancouver, BC V6Z 2T1
Tel: 604-684-7794; Fax: 604-682-1243
lawyer@divorce-for-men.com
www.divorce-for-men.com
twitter.com/Divorce_For_Men

Vancouver: Lindsay Kenney LLP - Vancouver - *35
Also Known As: LK Law
#1800, 401 West Georgia St., Vancouver, BC V6B 5A1
Tel: 604-687-1323; Fax: 604-687-2347
Toll-Free: 866-687-1323
info@lklaw.ca
www.lklaw.ca

Vancouver: Lipetz & Company - *1
#202, 2902 West Broadway, Vancouver, BC V6K 2G8
Tel: 604-733-5611; Fax: 604-738-5611

Vancouver: Keith A. Lo - *2
#338, 237 Keefer St., Vancouver, BC V6A 1X6
Tel: 604-687-4315; Fax: 604-681-2289

Vancouver: Logan & Company
#1119, 808 Nelson St., Vancouver, BC V6Z 2H2
Tel: 604-682-8521; Fax: 604-682-8753

Vancouver: Loh & Company - *4
#802, 1788 West Broadway, Vancouver, BC V6J 1Y1
Tel: 604-261-1234; Fax: 604-261-1222
general@lohandco.com
lohandco.com

Vancouver: Ralph H. Long - *1
865 - 46th Ave. West, Vancouver, BC V5Z 2R4
Tel: 604-876-0492; Fax: 604-876-3219
rhlong@shaw.ca

Vancouver: Lowe & Company - *5
#900, 777 West Broadway, Vancouver, BC V5Z 4J7
Tel: 604-875-9338; Fax: 604-875-1325
info@canadavisalaw.com
www.canadavisalaw.com

Vancouver: Phillip R. Lundrie - *2
#3, 2597 Hastings St. East, Vancouver, BC V5K 1Z2
Tel: 604-257-3588; Fax: 604-257-3511
www.lundrielaw.com

Vancouver: Lyons Hamilton - *4
#404, 815 Hornby St., Vancouver, BC V6Z 2E6
Tel: 604-684-6718; Fax: 604-684-2501

Vancouver: Macaulay McColl LLP - *9
#600, 840 Howe St., Vancouver, BC V6Z 2L2
Tel: 604-687-9811; Fax: 604-687-8716
Toll-Free: 800-233-4405

Vancouver: Macdonald Law Group - *2
Former Name: Macdonald Fahey
#1900, 1177 West Hastings St., Vancouver, BC V6E 2K3
Tel: 604-718-6895; Fax: 604-608-5741
info@mlg.lawyer
www.mlg.lawyer

Vancouver: MacKenzie Fujisawa LLP - *19
#1600, 1095 West Pender St., Vancouver, BC V6E 2M6
Tel: 604-689-3281; Fax: 604-685-6494
lawyers@macfuj.com
macfuj.com

Vancouver: MacKinlay Woodson Diebel - *2
#1170, 1040 West Georgia St., Vancouver, BC V6E 4H1
Tel: 604-669-1511; Fax: 604-669-1566
corp@woodsonlaw.bc.ca

Vancouver: M. Diane MacKinnon - *1
2077 - 37th Ave. West, Vancouver, BC V6M 1N7
Tel: 604-263-7891; Fax: 604-263-5781

Vancouver: MacLean Family Law - Vancouver - *18
Former Name: MacLean Nicol
#2900, 1021 West Hastings St., Vancouver, BC V6E 0C3
Tel: 604-602-9000; Fax: 604-682-0556
info@macleanlaw.ca
www.macleanfamilylaw.ca
www.facebook.com/macleanlawgroup, twitter.com/bcfamilylaw,
www.linkedin.com/company/maclean-family-law-group

Vancouver: MacLeod & Company - *4
#1900, 777 Hornby St., Vancouver, BC V6Z 1S4
Tel: 604-687-7287; Fax: 604-682-2534
Toll-Free: 866-997-7287
info@macleodlaw.com
www.macleodlaw.com

Vancouver: Morag M.J. MacLeod - *1
#800, The Randall Building, 555 West Georgia St. West,
Vancouver, BC V6B 1Z6
Tel: 604-430-8444; Fax: 604-430-1164
mmacleod@celtlaw.com

**Vancouver: Martland & Saulnier Criminal Defence
Counsel - *4**
Former Name: Smart & Williams
#506, 815 Hornby St., Vancouver, BC V6Z 2E6
Tel: 604-687-6278; Fax: 604-687-6298
vancrimlaw.com

Vancouver: Matthew Nathanson Law - *2
Former Name: MN Law
#1000, Marine Building, 355 Burrard St., Vancouver, BC V6C
7G8
Tel: 604-608-6185; Fax: 604-677-5560
www.mnlaw.ca

Vancouver: Maxwell Bulmer Hopman - *4
#310, 1152 Mainland St., Vancouver, BC V6B 4X2
Tel: 604-669-1106

Vancouver: Joanne S. McClusky - *1
#810, 675 Hastings St. West, Vancouver, BC V6B 1N2
Tel: 604-689-4010; Fax: 604-684-2349
jmcclusky@telus.net

Vancouver: McComb Witten - Vancouver - *8
#210, 2730 Commercial Dr., Vancouver, BC V5N 5P4
Tel: 604-255-9018; Fax: 604-255-8588
info@mmw.bc.ca
www.mccombwitten.com
www.facebook.com/McCombWitten,
twitter.com/McComb_Witten,

Vancouver: McCrea Immigration Law
Former Name: McCrea & Associates
#101, 440 Cambie St., Vancouver, BC V6B 2N5
Tel: 604-662-8200
www.mccrealaw.ca
twitter.com/mccreaimmlaw,
www.linkedin.com/company/mccrea-&-associates

Vancouver: McCullough O'Connor Irwin LLP - *15
Also Known As: MOI Solicitors
#2600, Oceanic Plaza, 1066 West Hastings St., Vancouver,
BC V6E 3X1
Tel: 604-687-7077; Fax: 604-687-7099
moimail@moisolicitors.com
www.moisolicitors.com

Vancouver: Ruth E. McIntyre - *1
#1520, 355 Burrard St., Vancouver, BC V6C 2G8
Tel: 604-688-5185; Fax: 604-688-5186
www.rmcintyre.ca

Vancouver: McKenzie & Company - *2
891 Helmcken St., Vancouver, BC V6Z 1B1
Tel: 604-687-7811; Fax: 604-685-4358
lawfirm@mckenzie-co.com

Vancouver: McLachlan Brown Anderson - *7
938 Howe St., 10th Fl., Vancouver, BC V6Z 1N9
Tel: 604-331-6000; Fax: 604-331-6008
mbalawyers.ca

Vancouver: Bruce E. McLeod - *1
#1120, 1040 Georgia St. West, Vancouver, BC V6E 4H1
Tel: 604-682-3133; Fax: 604-682-3161
bmcleod1@telus.net

Vancouver: McNeney McNeney Spieker LLP - *7
Former Name: McNeney & McNeney
#605, 1080 Howe St., Vancouver, BC V6Z 2T1
Tel: 604-867-1766 Toll-Free: 800-535-6565
www.mcneneymcneney.com

Vancouver: Megan Ellis & Company - *2
Former Name: Stowe Ellis
#700, 555 Georgia St. West, Vancouver, BC V6B 1Z6
Tel: 604-683-7144; Fax: 604-683-0207
info@ellisandcompany.ca
www.ellisandcompany.ca

Vancouver: MetroWest Law Corporation - *3
#801, 938 Howe St., Vancouver, BC V6Z 1N9
Tel: 604-428-2211; Fax: 604-428-2212
www.vancouver-realestate-lawyer.com
www.facebook.com/metrowest.law, twitter.com/metrowestlaw,
www.linkedin.com/in/metrowestlaw

Vancouver: Mickelson & Whysall - *4
Former Name: Mickelson & Company Law Corporation
#1005, Sun Tower, 128 West Pender St., Vancouver, BC V6B
1R8
Tel: 604-688-8588; Fax: 604-637-1617
info@mwcrimlaw.com
www.criminallawyervancouver.com

Vancouver: Miller Titerle LLP - *8
#215, 209 Carrall St., Vancouver, BC V6B 2J2
Tel: 604-681-4112; Fax: 604-681-4113
info@millertiterle.com
www.millertiterle.com

Vancouver: Michael Mines - *2
#1550, 355 Burrard St., Vancouver, BC V6C 2G8
Tel: 604-484-1940; Fax: 604-687-3097
Toll-Free: 877-467-1804
www.mineslaw.com

indicates number of lawyers

Vancouver: Morris & Co. - *2
#460, 850 West Hastings St., Vancouver, BC V6C 1E1
Tel: 604-685-5175; Fax: 604-669-2744
info@vancouvermorrismen.org
www.vancouvermorrismen.org

Vancouver: Edward M. Mortimer, QC - *2
#920, 777 Hornby St., Vancouver, BC V6Z 1S4
Tel: 604-669-0440; Fax: 604-669-0228

Vancouver: Murdy & McAllister - *6
#1155, Two Bentall Centre, P.O. Box 49059, 555 Burrard St.,
Vancouver, BC V7X 1C4
Tel: 604-689-5263; Fax: 604-689-9029
www.murdymcallister.com

Vancouver: Murphy Battista LLP - Vancouver - *24
#2020, 650 West Georgia St., Vancouver, BC V6B 4N7
Tel: 604-683-9621; Fax: 604-683-5084
Toll-Free: 888-683-9621
www.murphybattista.com
www.facebook.com/murphybattistallp, twitter.com/mb_llp,
www.linkedin.com/company/murphy-battista-llp

Vancouver: Murray Jamieson Barristers & Solicitors - *4
#200, 1152 Mainland St., Vancouver, BC V6B 4X2
Tel: 604-688-0777; Fax: 604-688-9700
www.murrayjamieson.com

Vancouver: James B. Myers Law Corporation - *1
#619, 610 Granville St., Vancouver, BC V6C 3T3
Tel: 604-682-8670; Fax: 604-682-2348
myerslaw@telus.net

Vancouver: Nathanson, Schachter & Thompson LLP - *8
#750, 900 Howe St., Vancouver, BC V6Z 2M4
Tel: 604-662-8840; Fax: 604-684-1598
info@nst.bc.ca
www.nst.bc.ca

Vancouver: Nexus Law Group LLP - *4
777 Hornby St., Vancouver, BC V6Z 1S4
Tel: 604-689-1622; Fax: 604-689-8300
info@nexuslaw.ca
www.nexuslaw.ca

Vancouver: Ng Ariss Fong - *5
Former Name: Ng & Ariss
#210, P.O. Box 160, 900 Howe St., Vancouver, BC V6Z 2M4
Tel: 604-331-1155; Fax: 604-677-5410
general@ngariss.com
www.ngariss.com

Vancouver: Kimball R. Nichols - *1
1591 Bowser Ave., Vancouver, BC V7P 2Y4
Tel: 604-682-0541; Fax: 604-924-5541

Vancouver: Northwest Law Group
Former Name: O'Neill & Company
#704, 595 Howe St., Vancouver, BC V6C 2T5
Tel: 604-687-5792; Fax: 604-687-6650

Vancouver: Norton Stewart Business Lawyers - *3
#1850, Manulife Place, 1095 West Pender St., Vancouver, BC
V6E 2M6
Tel: 604-687-0555; Fax: 604-689-1248
info@nortonstewart.com
www.nortonstewart.com

Vancouver: Glen Orris Q.C. Law Corporation - *1
#500, 815 Hornby St., Vancouver, BC V6Z 2E6
Tel: 604-669-6711; Fax: 604-669-5180
glen@orrislawcorp.com
www.orrislawcorp.com

Vancouver: Osten & Osten
#356, P.O. Box 11113, 5740 Cambie St., Vancouver, BC V6E
3A6
Tel: 604-683-9104; Fax: 604-688-0034

Vancouver: Owen Bird Law Corporation - *38
Three Bentall Centre, P.O. Box 49130, 595 Burrard St., 29th
Fl., Vancouver, BC V7X 1J5
Tel: 604-688-0401; Fax: 604-688-2827
inquiries@owenbird.com
www.owenbird.com

Vancouver: Oyen Wiggs Green & Mutala LLP - *14
#480, The Station, 601 West Cordova St., Vancouver, BC
V6B 1G1
Tel: 604-669-3432; Fax: 604-681-4081
Toll-Free: 866-475-2922
mail@patentable.com
www.patentable.com

Vancouver: Paine Edmonds LLP - *14
#1100, 510 Burrard St., Vancouver, BC V6C 3A8
Tel: 604-683-1211; Fax: 604-681-5084
Toll-Free: 800-669-8599
info@pelawyers.com
www.pelawyers.com

Vancouver: Pape Salter Teillet LLP - Vancouver - *13
#404, World Trade Centre, 999 Canada Place, Vancouver, BC
V6C 3E2
Tel: 604-681-3002; Fax: 604-681-3050
www.pstlaw.ca

Vancouver: Peck & Company - *9
#610, 744 Hastings St. West, Vancouver, BC V6C 1A5
Tel: 604-669-0208; Fax: 604-669-0616
hmoore@peckandcompany.ca
www.peckandcompany.ca

Vancouver: Peter Altridge Mediation Services - *1
Former Name: Altridge & Company
#741, 1489 Marine Dr., Vancouver, BC V7T 1B8
Tel: 604-688-3557; Fax: 604-688-0535
pga@altridge.com
www.altridge.com

Vancouver: Donald B. Phelps - *1
#1200, 805 Broadway West, Vancouver, BC V5Z 1K1
Tel: 604-736-3722; Fax: 604-736-3725
www.donphelpsfamilylawvancouver.ca

Vancouver: Pierce Law Group - *2
#850, 475 Georgia St. West, Vancouver, BC V6B 4M9
Tel: 604-681-4434; Fax: 604-681-9142
contact@bcdisabilitylaw.com
www.bcdisabilitylaw.com

Vancouver: Vincent E. Pigeon - *1
#410, 688 Hastings St. West, Vancouver, BC V6B 1P1
Tel: 604-684-2889; Fax: 604-685-2900
vpigeon@telus.net
www.vincentpigeonlawyer.com

Vancouver: Sarah B. Pollard - *1
#400, 1681 Chestnut St., Vancouver, BC V6J 4M6
Tel: 604-732-5667; Fax: 604-732-1262
lawoffice@sprint.ca

Vancouver: Lianne Potter Law Corporation - *1
#218, 470 Granville St., Vancouver, BC V6C 1V5
Tel: 604-662-8373; Fax: 604-662-8321
lpotter@lwp-lawcorp.com

Vancouver: Poulsen & Co. - *3
#1800, 999 West Hastings St., Vancouver, BC V6C 2W2
Tel: 604-681-0123; Fax: 604-683-1375
info@poulsenlaw.com
www.poulsenlaw.com

Vancouver: Quinlan Abrioux - *12
Also Known As: QA Law
#1510, TD Tower, P.O. Box 10031, Stn. Pacific Centre, 700
West Georgia St., Vancouver, BC V7Y 1A1
Tel: 604-687-3711; Fax: 604-687-3741
Toll-Free: 877-545-9486
www.qalaw.com

Vancouver: Radelet & Company - *2
#1625, 1075 Georgia St. West, Vancouver, BC V6E 3C9
Tel: 604-689-0878; Fax: 604-689-1386
james@radelet.com

Vancouver: Richard Raibmon - *1
#560, 1125 Howe St., Vancouver, BC V6Z 2K8
Tel: 604-688-8551; Fax: 604-687-1799
rlrlaw@uniserve.com
richardraibmon.com

Vancouver: Rao McKercher & Co. - *2
#908, 510 Burrard St., Vancouver, BC V6C 3A8
Tel: 604-664-7474; Fax: 604-664-7477

Vancouver: Raphanel & Courtenay - *2
Former Name: Gayle M. Raphanel
#1160, 777 Hornby St., Vancouver, BC V6Z 1S4
Tel: 604-682-2200; Fax: 604-682-2246

Vancouver: Resolution Law - *1
Former Name: Chalke & Company
#220, Waterfront Business Centre, 145 Chadwick Ct.,
Vancouver, BC V7M 3K1
Tel: 604-980-4855; Fax: 604-980-6469
www.resolution-law.ca

Vancouver: Rice Harbut Elliott - Vancouver - *9
Former Name: Jarvis McGee Rice LLP
#820, 980 Howe St., Vancouver, BC V6Z 0C8
Tel: 604-682-3771; Fax: 604-682-0587
www.rhelaw.com
www.facebook.com/200219480010862, twitter.com/icbccases,
www.linkedin.com/company/jarvis-mcgee-rice

Vancouver: Richards Buell Sutton LLP - *43
#700, 401 West Georgia St., Vancouver, BC V6B 5A1
Tel: 604-682-3664; Fax: 604-688-3830
info@rbs.ca
www.rbs.ca

Vancouver: Ritchie Sandford - *2
#502, 602 Hastings St. West, Vancouver, BC V6B 1P2
Tel: 604-684-0778; Fax: 604-684-0799

Vancouver: Roberts & Stahl - *4
#500, 220 Cambie St., Vancouver, BC V6B 2M9
Tel: 604-684-6377; Fax: 604-684-6387

Vancouver: Roper Greyell LLP, Employment & Labour Lawyers - *31
Former Name: Greyell MacPhail
#1850, 745 Thurlow St., Vancouver, BC V6E 0C5
Tel: 604-806-0922; Fax: 604-806-0933
www.ropergreyell.com
twitter.com/RoperGreyell,
www.linkedin.com/company/roper-greyell-llp

Vancouver: Rosenberg Law - *4
Former Name: Rosenberg & Rosenberg
671D Market Hill, Vancouver, BC V5Z 4B5
Tel: 604-879-4505; Fax: 604-879-4934
reception@rosenberglaw.ca
www.rosenberglaw.ca

Vancouver: J. Herbert Rosner - *1
#770, 475 Georgia St. West, Vancouver, BC V6B 4M9
Tel: 604-687-6638; Fax: 604-682-2481
roslaw@telus.net

Vancouver: Robert D. Ross Q.C. - *1
4741 West 2 Ave., Vancouver, BC V6T 1C1
Tel: 604-228-9701; Fax: 604-228-9055

Vancouver: Howard Rubin Law Corp. - *1
405E - 4 St., Vancouver, BC V7L 1J4
Tel: 604-984-2030; Fax: 604-988-0068
howard@howard-rubin.com

Vancouver: RWE Law Corporation - *3
Also Known As: Robert W. Evans Law Corpoartion
#1700, 808 Nelson St., Vancouver, BC V6Z 2H2
Tel: 778-899-7028; Fax: 604-608-5385
info@rwelaw.ca
www.rwelaw.ca

Vancouver: Morrie Sacks Law Corporation - *1
#207, 1525 - 8th Ave. West, Vancouver, BC V6T 1T5
Tel: 604-685-7629; Fax: 604-685-7630

Vancouver: Salley Bowes Harwardt Law Corp. - *4
#1750, 1185 Georgia St. West, Vancouver, BC V6E 4E6
Tel: 604-688-0788; Fax: 604-688-0778
www.sbh.bc.ca

Vancouver: Gary M. Salloum - *1
286 - 21st Ave. West, Vancouver, BC V5Y 2E5

Vancouver: Gregory L. Samuels - *1
#204, 1730 - 2nd Ave. West, Vancouver, BC V6J 1H6
Tel: 604-636-9157
gls@borderlaw.com

Vancouver: Charles A. Sandberg - *1
#108, 2786 - 16 Ave. West, Vancouver, BC V6K 4M1
Tel: 604-734-7768; Fax: 604-733-1229

Vancouver: Michael D. Sanders - *1
811 Drake St., Vancouver, BC V6Z 1C1
Tel: 604-669-5005; Fax: 604-669-1334
Toll-Free: 888-778-8803
www.sanderscriminallaw.com

indicates number of lawyers

Vancouver: Sangra Moller LLP - *12
#1000, Cathedral Pl., 925 Georgia St. West, Vancouver, BC V6C 3L2
Tel: 604-662-8808; Fax: 604-669-8803
www.sangramoller.com

Vancouver: Scarlett Manson Angus - *4
#1200, 777 Hornby St., Vancouver, BC V6Z 1S4
Tel: 604-684-4777; Fax: 604-684-7773
lawfirm@smalaw.com

Vancouver: Antya Schrack - *1
#116, 970 Burrard St., Vancouver, BC V6Z 2R4
Tel: 604-682-2078; Fax: 604-682-6697
aschrack@immigrate-to-canada.ca
www.immigrate-to-canada.ca

Vancouver: Schuman Daltrop Basran & Robin - *8
#1200, 777 Hornby St., Vancouver, BC V6Z 1S4
Tel: 604-669-4912; Fax: 604-669-4911
www.sdbrlaw.com

Vancouver: Shandro Dixon Edgson
#400, 999 Hastings St. West, Vancouver, BC V6C 2W2
Tel: 604-689-0400; Fax: 604-685-2009

Vancouver: Shapiro Hankinson & Knutson Law Corporation - *14
#700, Two Bental Centre, 555 Burrard St., Vancouver, BC V7X 1M8
Tel: 604-684-0727; Fax: 604-684-7094
info@shk.ca
www.shk.ca
www.facebook.com/SHKlaw, twitter.com/SHKLaw

Vancouver: Murray H. Shapiro - *1
694 West 19th Ave., Vancouver, BC V5Z 1X1
Tel: 604-879-6777; Fax: 604-879-6728

Vancouver: Shapray Cramer LLP - *5
#670, World Trade Centre, 999 Canada Pl., Vancouver, BC V6C 3E1
Tel: 604-681-0900; Fax: 604-681-0920
enquiries@shapraycramer.com
shapraycramer.com

Vancouver: Sylvia S. Shelton - *1
3469 Commercial St., Vancouver, BC V5N 4E8
Tel: 604-251-2144; Fax: 604-251-2781

Vancouver: George Shimizu - *1
#718, P.O. Box 50959, 808 Nelson St., Vancouver, BC V6Z 2H2
Tel: 604-685-4467; Fax: 604-685-4408
geoshimizu@telus.net

Vancouver: Silbernagel & Company
#700, 595 Howe St., Vancouver, BC V6C 2T5
Tel: 604-687-9621; Fax: 604-687-5960

Vancouver: Singleton Urquhart LLP - *46
#1200, 925 West Georgia St., Vancouver, BC V6C 3L2
Tel: 604-682-7474; Fax: 604-682-1283
su@singleton.com
www.singleton.com

Vancouver: Skorah Doyle - *2
#2100, 200 Granville St., Vancouver, BC V6C 1S4
Tel: 604-602-8502; Fax: 604-608-1660

Vancouver: Michael P.S. Spearing - *1
#501, 1949 Beach Ave., Vancouver, BC V6G 1Z2
Tel: 604-681-0699
michaelspearing@telus.net

Vancouver: Specht & Pryer - *1
#612, 475 Howe St., Vancouver, BC V6C 2B3
Tel: 604-681-2500; Fax: 604-736-0118
staff@spechtandpryer.com
www.spechtandpryer.com
www.facebook.com/bc.lawyer

Vancouver: Stephens & Holman - Vancouver - *13
#500, 1200 - West 73 Ave., Vancouver, BC V6P 6Z6
Tel: 604-730-4120; Fax: 604-736-2867
Toll-Free: 866-200-3575
www.stephensandholman.com

Vancouver: John S. Stowe - *1
#1109, 207 Hastings St. West, Vancouver, BC V6B 1H7
Tel: 604-684-1665; Fax: 604-687-3097
john_stowe@bc.sympatico.ca

Vancouver: Sugden, McFee & Roos LLP - *10
#700, The Landing, 375 Water St., Vancouver, BC V6B 5N3
Tel: 604-687-7700; Fax: 604-687-5596
info@smrlaw.ca
www.smrlaw.ca

Vancouver: Sutherland & Company - *1
Former Name: Sutherland Johnston
#1620, 401 Georgia St. West, Vancouver, BC V6B 5A1
Tel: 604-688-0047; Fax: 604-688-8880

Vancouver: Sutherland Jetté - *1
#201, 128 West Pender St., Vancouver, BC V6B 1R8
Tel: 604-669-6699; Fax: 604-681-0652

Vancouver: David F. Sutherland & Associates - *1
#1700, 1185 West Georgia St., Vancouver, BC V6E 4E6
Tel: 604-737-8711; Fax: 604-737-8655
www.djslaw.ca

Vancouver: Tao & Company
#860, 999 West Broadway, Vancouver, BC V5Z 1K5
Tel: 604-730-8219; Fax: 604-730-2553

Vancouver: Taylor & Blair - Vancouver - *3
#1607, 805 West Broadway, Vancouver, BC V5Z 1K1
Tel: 604-737-6900; Fax: 604-737-6901
graham@taylorandblair.com
taylorandblair.com

Vancouver: Taylor & Company - *2
Former Name: Taylor Wray
#218, 470 Granville St., Vancouver, BC V6C 1V5
Tel: 604-662-8373; Fax: 604-662-8321
wtaylor@twlaw.ca

Vancouver: Taylor Jordan Chafetz - *8
#1010, 777 Hornby St., Vancouver, BC V6Z 1S4
Tel: 604-683-2223; Fax: 604-683-2798
tsaumure@tjclaw.com
www.tjclaw.com

Vancouver: Colin Taylor Professional Corp.
#203, 1275 - 6th Ave. West, Vancouver, BC V6H 1A6
Tel: 604-798-8775; Fax: 604-608-6117
colintaylor@telus.net
colintaylor.ca

Vancouver: Isaac Thau - *1
#101, 1012 Beach Ave., Vancouver, BC V6E 1T7
Tel: 604-685-4220; Fax: 604-685-0400
lthau@orbitinc.net

Vancouver: Eric P. Thiessen - *1
#702, 756 Great Northern Way, Vancouver, BC V5T 1E4
Tel: 604-876-6220; Fax: 604-876-6253

Vancouver: Thomas, Rondeau - *6
#1780, 400 Burrard St., Vancouver, BC V6C 3A6
Tel: 604-688-6775; Fax: 604-688-6995
www.thomasrondeau.com

Vancouver: Tiffany & Company Law Corporation
#304, 68 Water St., Vancouver, BC V6B 1A4
Tel: 604-628-1126
tiffany@tiffanylaw.ca
tiffanylaw.ca
www.facebook.com/TiffanyCompanyLawCorp,
twitter.com/TiffanyLawCorp,
www.linkedin.com/in/tiffany-walsh-79985a47

Vancouver: Tim Louis & Company - *1
Also Known As: TL & Co.
#208, 175 East Broadway, Vancouver, BC V5T 1W2
Tel: 604-732-7678; Fax: 604-732-7579
timlouis@timlouislaw.com
www.timlouislaw.com

Vancouver: Timothy J. Vondette Law Corporation - *1
#506, 1128 Hornby St., Vancouver, BC V6Z 2L4
Tel: 604-669-6990; Fax: 604-669-6944
tvondette@aol.com

Vancouver: Tobin & Associates - *1
#816, 938 Howe St., Vancouver, BC V6Z 1N9
Tel: 604-331-1591; Fax: 604-688-8120
enquiries@endisputes.com
www.endisputes.com

Vancouver: Tupper, Jonsson & Yeadon - *6
#1710, 1177 Hastings St. West, Vancouver, BC V6E 2L3
Tel: 604-683-9262; Fax: 604-681-0139
tupjon@globalserve.net

Vancouver: Winfred A. van der Sande - *1
2774 Granville St., Vancouver, BC V6H 3J3
Tel: 604-739-7989; Fax: 604-909-4798

Vancouver: Varty & Company - *2
#300, 1055 West Hastings St., Vancouver, BC V6E 2E9
Tel: 604-684-5356; Fax: 604-608-3526
www.vartylaw.ca

Vancouver: Vector Corporate Finance Lawyers - *4
Former Name: Scott, Bissett
#1040, 999 West Hastings St., Vancouver, BC V6C 2W2
Tel: 604-683-1102; Fax: 604-683-2643
www.vectorlaw.com

Vancouver: Von Dehn & Company - *3
#700, 595 Howe St., Vancouver, BC V6C 2T5
Tel: 604-688-4541; Fax: 604-687-5960
vondehnco@telus.net

Vancouver: T. Wing Wai - *1
#205, 475 Main St., Vancouver, BC V6A 2T7
Tel: 604-688-2291; Fax: 604-688-8983

Vancouver: Walker & Company - *1
#304, 1230 Haro St., Vancouver, BC V6E 4J9
Tel: 604-682-1147; Fax: 604-681-7705
agwalker@telus.net

Vancouver: Watson Goepel LLP - *31
#1700, 1075 West Georgia St., Vancouver, BC V6E 3C9
Tel: 604-688-1301; Fax: 604-688-8193
info@watsongoepel.com
www.watsongoepel.com
www.facebook.com/WatsonGoepel, twitter.com/WatsonGoepel,
www.linkedin.com/company-beta/200752

Vancouver: Elizabeth E. Watson - *1
#4412, 349 Georgia St. West, Vancouver, BC V6B 3Z8
Tel: 604-877-1412; Fax: 604-877-0134
ewatson@telus.net

Vancouver: Webster Hudson & Coombe LLP - *14
Former Name: Webster Hudson & Akerly LLP
#510, 1040 West Georgia St., Vancouver, BC V6E 4H1
Tel: 604-682-3488; Fax: 604-682-3438
www.wha.bc.ca

Vancouver: Westpoint Law Group - *4
Former Name: Epstein Wood
#1900, 1177 West Hastings St., Vancouver, BC V6E 2K3
Tel: 604-718-6886; Fax: 604-629-1882
www.westpointlawgroup.com

Vancouver: Whitelaw Twining Law Corporation - Vancouver - *52
#2400, 200 Granville St., Vancouver, BC V6C 1S4
Tel: 604-682-5466; Fax: 604-682-5217
Toll-Free: 866-982-9898
contact@wt.ca
www.whitelawtwining.com

Vancouver: Wilcox & Company Law Corporation - *3
Former Name: Dale W. Wilcox Law Corporation
#1910, 777 Hornby St., Vancouver, BC V6Z 1S4
Tel: 604-687-1374; Fax: 604-687-2731
dwilcox@wilcoxlawcorp.com

Vancouver: Williamson Giesen Murray - *3
Former Name: Williamson Giesen
#200, 1290 Homer St., Vancouver, BC V6B 2Y5
Tel: 604-681-1004; Fax: 604-684-1199
agiesen@wgmlaw.ca
www.laurieharrisdesign.com/wgm/

Vancouver: Wilson Butcher - *4
#400, 744 West Hastings St., Vancouver, BC V6C 1A5
Tel: 604-684-4751; Fax: 604-684-8319
info@wbbslaw.com
wbbslaw.com

Vancouver: Andrew J. Winstanley - *1
#410, 688 Hastings St. West, Vancouver, BC V6B 1P1
Tel: 604-682-2939; Fax: 604-682-2241
ajwinstanley@teleus.net

Vancouver: George Wong & Company - *1
4423 Boundary Rd., Vancouver, BC V5R 2N3
Tel: 604-687-6166; Fax: 604-687-8002

Vancouver: Patrick L. Wong - *1
#407, 1541 West Broadway, Vancouver, BC V6J 1W7
Tel: 604-731-5301; Fax: 604-731-1266

* indicates number of lawyers

Vancouver: Robert Wood & Company - *2
Former Name: Dawson, Wood & Company
#100, 2501 Spruce St., Vancouver, BC V6H 2P8
Tel: 604-731-1200; *Fax:* 604-266-0119
rwood@dawsonwood.com

Vancouver: Anthony K. Wooster - *1
#570, 999 West Broadway, Vancouver, BC V5Z 1K5
Tel: 604-684-1204; *Fax:* 604-684-1206
akwoods@aol.com

Vancouver: Donlad W.H. Yerxa - *1
#1200, 805 West Broadway, Vancouver, BC V5Z 1K1
Tel: 604-873-5225

Vancouver: Young & Noble - *1
#1119, 808 Nelson St., Vancouver, BC V6Z 2H2
Tel: 604-669-9755; *Fax:* 604-921-4817
john.noble@youngnoble.com

Vancouver: Young Anderson Barristers & Solicitors - Vancouver - *18
#1616, Nelson Square, P.O. Box 12147, 808 Nelson St., Vancouver, BC V6Z 2H2
Tel: 604-689-7400; *Fax:* 604-689-3444
Toll-Free: 800-665-3540
www.younganderson.ca
www.facebook.com/youngandersonbc,
twitter.com/youngandersonbc

Vancouver: David L. Youngson - *1
#10, 1656 - 11th Ave. West, Vancouver, BC V6J 2B9
Tel: 604-266-6588; *Fax:* 604-266-6393
saluspopuli@shaw.ca

Vancouver: Xiao Zheng - *1
#248, 515 Pender St. West, Vancouver, BC V6B 6H5
Tel: 604-608-0387; *Fax:* 604-608-0385
zheng@axionet.com

Vancouver: Zimmer & Associates - *2
Former Name: Goldman Zimmer Bray
#950, 1111 Melville St., Vancouver, BC V6E 3V6
Tel: 604-682-6181; *Fax:* 604-683-5723
www.zimmers.ca
www.facebook.com/zimmerandassociates

Vancouver: Deborah Lynn Zutter - *1
609 West Hastings, 6th Fl., Vancouver, BC V6B 4W4
Tel: 604-219-2259; *Fax:* 604-662-7466
deb@debzutter.com
www.debzutter.com

Vanderhoof: Steven F. Peleshok - *1
P.O. Box 1128, 2608 Burrard Ave., Vanderhoof, BC V0J 3A0
Tel: 250-567-9277; *Fax:* 250-567-2657

Vernon: Allan Francis Pringle LLP - *6
3009B - 28 St., Vernon, BC V1T 4Z7
Tel: 250-542-1177; *Fax:* 250-542-1105
info@afp-law.ca
www.afp-law.ca

Vernon: Crosby Lawyers
3406 - 32nd Ave., Vernon, BC V1T 2N1
Tel: 250-558-5790; *Fax:* 250-558-3910
crosby@crosbylaw.ca

Vernon: Kenneth R. Fiddes - *1
#2, 2908 - 31 Ave., Vernon, BC V1T 2G4
Tel: 250-542-5391; *Fax:* 250-542-4199
fiddes@shaw.ca

Vernon: Alan M. Gaudette - *1
#9, 11341 Kidston Rd., Vernon, BC V1B 1Z4
Tel: 250-545-3132; *Fax:* 250-545-1617
amgaudette@shaw.ca

Vernon: Jamie MacArthur Barrister & Solicitor - *1
2801 - 28th St., Vernon, BC V1T 4Z5
Tel: 250-549-6030
jamie@macarthurlaw.ca
www.jamiemacarthurlaw.ca

Vernon: Kern & Company Law Corp.
#3, 2908 - 32 St., Vernon, BC V1T 5M1
Tel: 250-549-2184; *Fax:* 250-549-2207

Vernon: Kidston & Company LLP - Vernon - *6
#200, 3005 - 30th St., Vernon, BC V1T 2M1
Fax: 250-545-4776
Toll-Free: 800-262-2678
info@kidston.ca
www.kidston.ca
www.facebook.com/KidstonandCo, twitter.com/kidstonandco,
www.linkedin.com/company/davidson-lawyers-llp

Vernon: John S. Maguire - *1
Former Name: Sigalet, Maguire & Cole
3018 - 29 St., Vernon, BC V1T 5A7
Tel: 250-545-6054; *Fax:* 250-545-7227
jsmag@sigmag.com

Vernon: Nixon Wenger - *21
#301, 2706 - 30th Ave., Vernon, BC V1T 2B6
Tel: 250-542-5353; *Fax:* 250-542-7273
Toll-Free: 800-243-5353
nw@nixonwenger.com
www.nixonwenger.com
twitter.com/NixonWengerLLP

Vernon: Robert Moffat Law Corp. - *1
2912 - 29th St., Vernon, BC V1T 5A6
Tel: 250-542-1312; *Fax:* 250-542-2788
Toll-Free: 800-371-0181

Vernon: Steiner & Company - *1
3107A - 31 Ave., Vernon, BC V1T 2G9
Tel: 250-545-1371; *Fax:* 250-542-5630
Toll-Free: 800-661-2600

Victoria: Acheson Sweeney Foley Sahota - Victoria - *7
Former Name: Acheson Whitley Sweeney Foley
#400, 535 Yates St., Victoria, BC V8W 2Z6
Tel: 250-384-6262; *Fax:* 250-384-5353
Toll-Free: 877-275-8766
www.achesonlaw.ca
www.facebook.com/achesonlaw

Victoria: Robert D. Adair - *1
#201, 4430 Chatterton Way, Victoria, BC V8X 5J2
Tel: 250-479-9367; *Fax:* 250-479-8316
adair@adairlaw.ca

Victoria: Anniko, Hunter - *1
#201, 300 Gorge Rd. West, Victoria, BC V9A 1M8
Tel: 250-385-1233; *Fax:* 250-385-4078
ah@annikohunter-law.com
www.annikohunter-law.ca

Victoria: Jacqueline Beltgens - *1
3929 Woodhaven Terrace, Victoria, BC V8N 1S7
Tel: 250-385-3909
jbeltgens@pinc.com

Victoria: Christopher Brennan - *1
1027 Pandora Ave., Victoria, BC V8V 3P6
Tel: 250-388-9024; *Fax:* 250-388-9060
chrisbrennan@shaw.ca

Victoria: Browne & Associates - *1
1633 Hillside Ave., Victoria, BC V8T 2C4
Tel: 250-598-1888; *Fax:* 250-598-9880
info@browneassociates.ca
www.browneassociates.ca

Victoria: Butterfield Law - *1
#402, 2020 Richmond Rd., Victoria, BC V8R 6R5
Tel: 250-382-4529; *Fax:* 250-480-1896
reception@butterfieldlaw.ca
www.butterfieldlaw.ca

Victoria: Carfra & Lawton - *16
395 Waterfront Cres., 6th Fl., Victoria, BC V8T 5K7
Tel: 250-381-7188; *Fax:* 250-381-7804
info@carlaw.ca
www.carlaw.ca
www.linkedin.com/company/carfra-&-lawton

Victoria: Carr Buchan & Co. - *3
Former Name: Carr Buchan & Co.
#103, 771 Vernon Ave., Victoria, BC V8X 5A7
Tel: 250-388-7571; *Fax:* 250-388-7327
Toll-Free: 888-313-7571
reception@jcarrlawyers.com
www.esquimaltlaw.com

Victoria: Clapp & Company - *1
4599 Chatterton Way, Victoria, BC V8X 4Y7
Tel: 250-479-1422; *Fax:* 250-479-1667

Victoria: Clay & Company - *6
837 Burdett Ave., Main Fl., Victoria, BC V8W 1B3
Tel: 250-386-2261; *Fax:* 250-389-1336
Toll-Free: 877-688-9634
www.clay.bc.ca

Victoria: Coad & Davidson - *2
3200 Quadra St., Victoria, BC V8X 1G2
Tel: 250-388-9003; *Fax:* 250-388-3577
reception@coadlawcorp.com
www.coadlawcorp.com

Victoria: Donald R. Colborne - *1
1125 Fort St., Victoria, BC V8V 3K9
Tel: 807-344-6628; *Fax:* 807-983-3079
drcolborne@shaw.ca

Victoria: Considine & Company, Barristers & Solicitors - *1
30 Dallas Rd., Victoria, BC V8V 0A2
Tel: 250-381-7788; *Fax:* 250-381-1042
www.considinelaw.com

Victoria: Cook Roberts LLP - *14
1175 Douglas St., 7th Fl., Victoria, BC V8W 2E1
Tel: 250-385-1411; *Fax:* 250-413-3300
www.cookroberts.bc.ca

Victoria: Cox Taylor - *12
Burnes House, 26 Bastion Sq., 3rd Fl., Victoria, BC V8W 1H9
Tel: 250-388-4457; *Fax:* 250-382-4236
reception@coxtaylor.ca
www.coxtaylor.bc.ca

Victoria: Crease Harman LLP - *13
#800, 1070 Douglas St., Victoria, BC V8W 2S8
Tel: 250-388-5421; *Fax:* 250-388-4294
www.creaseharman.com

Victoria: Dinning Hunter Jackson Law - Victoria - Fort St. - *17
Former Name: Dinning Hunter Lambert & Jackson; Dinning Crawford; Dinning Hunter
1202 Fort St., Victoria, BC V8V 3L2
Tel: 250-381-2151; *Fax:* 250-386-2123
info@dinninghunter.com
www.dinninghunter.com

Victoria: Jeremy S.G. Donaldson - *1
2555 Sinclair Rd., Victoria, BC V8N 1B8
Tel: 250-721-5759; *Fax:* 250-721-5455

Victoria: Dwyer Tax Lawyers - *2
#900, CIBC Tower, 1175 Douglas St., Victoria, BC V8W 2E1
Tel: 250-360-2110; *Fax:* 250-360-0440
inquiries@dwyertaxlaw.com
www.dwyertaxlaw.com

Victoria: Michael W. Egan - *1
#101, 288 Eltham Rd., Victoria, BC V9B 1J9
Tel: 250-382-3426; *Fax:* 250-382-3427

Victoria: Frank A.V. Falzon Law Corporation - *1
#200, 3561 Shelbourne St., Victoria, BC V8P 4G8
Tel: 250-384-3995; *Fax:* 250-384-4924
favf@islandnet.com

Victoria: Patrick S. Finnegan - *1
#6, 1140 Fort St., Victoria, BC V8V 3K8
Tel: 250-384-4252; *Fax:* 250-384-4252
psfinnegan@shaw.ca

Victoria: Firestone & Tyhurst - *2
#301, 919 Fort St., Victoria, BC V8V 3K3
Tel: 250-386-1112; *Fax:* 250-386-1124
firestone.tyhurst@shawbiz.ca

Victoria: Joseph Gereluk Law Office - *1
#401, 1011 Fort St., Victoria, BC V8V 3K5
Tel: 250-380-1423; *Fax:* 250-380-0920

Victoria: Larry P. Gilbert - *1
275 Pallisier Ave., Victoria, BC V9A 1C5
Tel: 250-478-8881; *Fax:* 250-478-8801

Victoria: Peter Golden - *1
#218, 852 Fort St., Victoria, BC V8W 1H8
Tel: 250-361-3131
www.petergolden.ca

Victoria: Goult & Company - *1
2185 Theatre Lane, Victoria, BC V8R 6T1
Tel: 250-595-1621; *Fax:* 250-595-5888
goultco@shaw.ca

indicates number of lawyers

Victoria: Green & Helme - *4
Former Name: Green & Claus
1161 Fort St., Victoria, BC V8V 3K9
Tel: 250-361-9600; Fax: 250-361-9181
greenandhelme@greenclaus.com

Victoria: Lenore B. Harlton - *1
215 Superior St., Victoria, BC V8V 2G7
Tel: 250-382-5161; Fax: 250-382-5160

Victoria: Hart Legal - *10
Also Known As: Berge Hart Cassels LLP
Former Name: Berge, Hart & Cassels
#300, 1001 Wharf St., Victoria, BC V8W 1T6
Tel: 250-388-9477; Fax: 250-388-9470
hart-legal.com
www.facebook.com/HART.Legal, twitter.com/Hart_Legal,
www.linkedin.com/company/2560603

Victoria: Hatter, Thompson, Shumka & McDonagh - *4
#201, 919 Fort St., Victoria, BC V8V 3K3
Tel: 250-388-4931; Fax: 250-386-8088
Toll-Free: 800-667-0705

Victoria: James I. Heller - *1
2090 Chauchher St., Victoria, BC V8R 1H7
Tel: 250-984-7037
www.jamesheller.ca

Victoria: Helm Legal - *1
1027 Pandora Ave., Victoria, BC V8V 3P6
Tel: 250-588-4356; Fax: 250-483-1952
jordan@helmlegal.ca
helmlegal.ca

Victoria: Hemminger Schmid - *6
#204, 388 Harbour Rd., Victoria, BC V9A 3S1
Tel: 250-220-8686; Fax: 250-385-8686
www.lawyersandmediators.ca
twitter.com/viclawyers

Victoria: Holmes & Isherwood - *1
1190 Fort St., Victoria, BC V8V 3K8
Tel: 250-383-7157; Fax: 250-383-1535

Victoria: Horne Coupar LLP - Victoria - *11
Union Bank Building, 612 View St., 3rd Fl., Victoria, BC V8W 1J5
Tel: 250-388-6631; Fax: 250-388-5974
Toll-Free: 866-467-2490
www.hornecoupar.com

Victoria: Raymond T. Horne - *1
#46, 530 Marsett Pl., Victoria, BC V8Z 7J2
Tel: 250-658-8387

Victoria: Hutchison Oss-Cech Marlatt, Barristers & Solicitors - *7
Former Name: The Seigel Law Group
#1, 505 Fisgard St., Victoria, BC V8W 1R3
Tel: 250-360-2500
info@hom-law.com
www.hom-law.com

Victoria: Jawl Bundon LLP - *7
1007 Fort St., 4th Fl., Victoria, BC V8V 3K5
Tel: 250-385-5787; Fax: 250-385-4364
info@jawlbundon.com
www.jawlbundon.com

Victoria: Johns Southward Glazier Walton & Margetts - *9
#204, 655 Tyee Rd., Victoria, BC V9A 6X5
Tel: 250-381-7321; Fax: 250-381-1181
Toll-Free: 888-442-4042
johnssouthward.com

Victoria: William S. Johnson Law Corp. - *1
Former Name: W.S. Johnson
#309, 895 Fort St., Victoria, BC V8W 1H7
Tel: 250-382-2404; Fax: 250-382-2426

Victoria: Jones Emery Hargreaves Swan LLP - *13
#1212, 1175 Douglas St., Victoria, BC V8W 2E1
Tel: 250-382-7222; Fax: 250-382-5436
www.jonesemery.com

Victoria: Kinar Curry Lawyers - *2
#200, 852 Fort St., Victoria, BC V8W 1B9
Tel: 250-383-8685; Fax: 250-383-7973
gwk@kinarlaw.com
www.kinarlaw.com

Victoria: Lampion Pacific Law Corporation - *2
Victoria, BC
Tel: 250-477-0129
cmorris@lampion.bc.ca
www.lampion.bc.ca

Victoria: Alice Shun Yee Lo - *1
#401, 1011 Fort St., Victoria, BC V8V 3K5
Tel: 250-380-1423; Fax: 250-380-0920
alicelo@telus.net

Victoria: Susan J. Loney Law Office - *1
1006 Russell St., Victoria, BC V9A 3X9
Tel: 250-384-1804; Fax: 250-384-1805
susan@vicwestlaw.com

Victoria: Lovett Westmacott - *3
Former Name: Lovett Westmacott & Clancy
#417, 645 Fort St., Victoria, BC V8W 1G2
Tel: 250-480-7481; Fax: 250-480-7455
www.lw-law.com

Victoria: MacIsaac & Company - Victoria - *11
#400, 777 Broughton St., Victoria, BC V8W 1E3
Tel: 250-381-5353; Fax: 250-380-7272
Toll-Free: 800-663-6299
victoria@macisaacandcompany.com
www.macisaacandcompany.com

Victoria: MacIsaac & MacIsaac - *4
2227 Sooke Rd., Victoria, BC V9B 1W8
Tel: 250-478-1131; Fax: 250-478-3106
mac@macisaaclaw.ca
macisaaclaw.ca

Victoria: Marshall Allen & Massey - *3
Former Name: Brooks & Marshall
1519 Amelia St., Victoria, BC V8W 2K1
Tel: 250-920-0144; Fax: 250-920-0177
claudia@ameliastreetlawyers.com
www.ameliastreetlawyers.com

Victoria: McConnan, Bion, O'Connor & Peterson - *11
#420, 880 Douglas St., Victoria, BC V8W 2B7
Tel: 250-385-1383; Fax: 250-385-2841
Toll-Free: 888-385-1383
info@mcbop.com
www.mcbop.com

Victoria: McCullough Blazina Dieno Gustafson & Watt - *10
#200, 1011 Fort St., Victoria, BC V8V 3K5
Tel: 250-480-1529; Fax: 250-480-4910
Toll-Free: 800-360-6488
info@mbdglaw.com
www.mbdglaw.com

Victoria: McMicken & Bennett - *2
303 - 1111 Blanshard St., Victoria, BC V8W 2H7
Tel: 250-385-9555; Fax: 250-385-9841
lawyer@mcmickenbennett.bc.ca

Victoria: Milton, Johnson - *2
#204, 947 Fort St., Victoria, BC V8V 3K3
Tel: 250-385-5523; Fax: 250-385-7420
miltjohn@pacificcoast.net

Victoria: Robert Moore-Stewart - *1
#616, 620 View St., Victoria, BC V8W 1J6
Tel: 250-380-1887; Fax: 250-380-9134
rmoorest@telus.net

Victoria: Jane B. Morley - *1
Former Name: Morley & Ross
#7, 356 Simcoe St., Victoria, BC V8V 1L1
Tel: 250-480-7487; Fax: 250-480-7488
jbmorley@mrlaw.ca

Victoria: Mulroney & Company - *3
#301, 852 Fort St., Victoria, BC V8W 1H8
Tel: 250-389-6022; Fax: 250-389-6033
Toll-Free: 855-245-6355
www.mulroneyco.com

Victoria: John M. Orr Law Office - *1
2368 The Esplanade, Victoria, BC V8R 2W2
Tel: 250-595-8675; Fax: 250-595-7421
orrlaw@shaw.ca
www.adrweb.ca/john-orr

Victoria: Pearlman Lindholm - *15
#201, 19 Dallas Rd., Victoria, BC V8V 5A6
Tel: 250-388-4433; Fax: 250-388-5856
www.pearlmanlindholm.com

* indicates number of lawyers

Victoria: Purves, Clark
Former Name: Purves, Hickford, Horne & Curry
#203, 919 Fort St., Victoria, BC V8W 1H6
Tel: 250-388-7188

Victoria: Quadra Legal Centre - *6
#101, 2750 Quadra St., Victoria, BC V8T 4E8
Tel: 250-380-1566; Fax: 250-380-3090
info@quadralegal.com
www.quadralegal.com

Victoria: Randall & Murrell LLP - *2
Former Name: Randall & Company
#201, 1006 Fort St., Victoria, BC V8V 3K4
Tel: 250-382-9282; Fax: 250-382-0366
reception@viclawfirm.ca
www.viclawfirm.ca

Victoria: Reed Pope LLP - *6
#202, 1007 Fort St., Victoria, BC V8V 3K5
Tel: 250-383-3838; Fax: 250-385-4324
rkreed@reedpope.ca
www.reedpope.ca

Victoria: Nichola Reid & Company - *2
#214, 284 Helmcken Rd., Victoria, BC V9B 1T2
Tel: 250-744-1844; Fax: 250-744-1890

Victoria: Ross, Johnson & Associates - *2
888 Fort St., 4th Fl., Victoria, BC V8W 1H8
Tel: 250-381-7677; Fax: 250-381-7657
kjohnson@rjalawyers.com
www.kimejohnson.com

Victoria: Marlene Russo - *1
#110, 1175 Cook St., Victoria, BC V8V 4A1
Tel: 250-380-0076; Fax: 250-380-0092
marlenerusso@shaw.ca

Victoria: Sihota & Starkey - *1
1248 Esquimalt Rd., Victoria, BC V9A 3N8
Tel: 250-381-5111; Fax: 250-381-3947

Victoria: Sitka Law Group - *10
#202, 3750 Shelbourne St., Victoria, BC V8P 4H4
Tel: 778-265-2677; Fax: 778-265-5563
www.sitkalaw.ca

Victoria: Smith Hutchison Law Corporation - *1
#108, 1218 Wharf St., Victoria, BC V8W 1T8
Tel: 250-388-6666; Fax: 250-389-0400
www.bclawfirm.com

Victoria: Spier & Company Law - *1
#208, 852 Fort St., Victoria, BC V8W 1H8
Tel: 250-590-1539; Fax: 250-590-2539
info@spierlaw.ca
www.spierlaw.ca
twitter.com/SpierLaw

Victoria: Stevenson, Doell Law Corporation - *4
999 Fort St., Victoria, BC V8V 3K3
Tel: 250-388-7881; Fax: 250-388-7324
Toll-Free: 888-633-5567
stevensondoell@shawcable.com
www.stevensondoell.com

Victoria: Stevenson, Luchies & Legh - *15
#300, 848 Courtney St., Victoria, BC V8W 1C4
Tel: 250-381-4040; Fax: 250-388-9406
Toll-Free: 888-381-8555
lawyers@sll.ca
www.sll.ca
www.facebook.com/VictoriaLawFirms,
twitter.com/LawyersVictoria

Victoria: Stewart Johnston Law Corpoartion - *1
1521 Amelia St., Victoria, BC V8W 2K1
Tel: 250-385-2975; Fax: 250-385-2977
goodadvice@sjlaw.ca
www.sjlaw.ca

Victoria: Christine A. Stretton - *1
#202, 895 Fort St., Victoria, BC V8W 1H7
Tel: 250-388-5333; Fax: 250-382-8644
castretton@pacificcoast.net

Victoria: Thompson Cooper LLP - *2
Also Known As: Barrigar Intellectual Property Law
#201, 1007 Fort St., Victoria, BC V8V 3K5
Tel: 250-389-0387; Fax: 250-389-2659
www.tcllp.ca
www.facebook.com/thompsoncooperllp,
twitter.com/thompsoncooper,
www.linkedin.com/company/316566

Victoria: Deborah Todd Law - *1
Former Name: MacMinn & Company
729 Humboldt St., Victoria, BC V8W 1B1
Tel: 250-590-6226
info@toddlaw.ca
www.deborahtoddlaw.com

Victoria: Diane E. Tourell - *1
#500, 645 Fort St., Victoria, BC V8W 1G2
Tel: 250-384-1443; Fax: 250-380-7299

Victoria: Tousaw Law Corporation
Victoria, BC
Tel: 604-836-1420; Fax: 866-310-3342
info@tousawlaw.ca
www.tousawlaw.ca
www.facebook.com/kirk.tousaw, twitter.com/KirkTousaw,
www.linkedin.com/in/kirk-tousaw-5022a226

Victoria: Dalmar F. Tracy - *1
#206, 1005 Cook St., Victoria, BC V8V 3Z6
Tel: 250-384-5331; Fax: 250-384-5206
dalmartracy@shaw.ca
www.dalmartracy.com

Victoria: Jill K. Turner - *1
#101, 4475 Viewmount Ave., Victoria, BC V8Z 6L8
Tel: 250-360-0983; Fax: 250-658-1949
jill@turnerlegal.com

Victoria: Turnham Woodland, Barristers & Solicitors - *4
1002 Wharf St., Victoria, BC V8W 1T4
Tel: 250-385-1122; Fax: 250-385-6522
www.turnhamwoodland.ca

Victoria: Vangenne & Company
Former Name: Skillings & Company
#B, 777 Blanshard St., Victoria, BC V8W 2G9
Tel: 250-388-5136; Fax: 250-388-5195
vangenne.com

Victoria: Velletta & Company - *11
Former Name: Gordon & Velletta
931 Fort St., 4th Fl., Victoria, BC V8V 3K3
Tel: 250-383-9104; Fax: 250-383-1922
Toll-Free: 866-383-9104
www.victorialaw.ca
www.facebook.com/vellettalawyers, twitter.com/vellettalawyers

Victoria: Waddell Raponi LLP - *5
Former Name: Waddell Raponi, Lawyers
1002 Wharf St., Victoria, BC V8W 1T4
Tel: 250-385-4311; Fax: 250-385-2012
www.waddellraponi.com

Victoria: Peter I. Waldmann - *1
2582 Beach Dr., Victoria, BC V8R 6K4
Tel: 250-381-3113; Fax: 250-381-3122

Victoria: Wilson Marshall Law Corporation - Victoria - *6
#200, 911 Yates St., Victoria, BC V8V 4X3
Tel: 250-385-8741; Fax: 250-385-0433
Toll-Free: 877-385-8741
reception@wilsonmarshall.com
www.wilsonmarshall.com

Victoria: Wong & Doerksen - *2
1618 Government St., Victoria, BC V8W 1Z3
Tel: 250-381-7799; Fax: 250-386-7799
info@wongdoerksen.com
www.wongdoerksen.com

Victoria: Woodward & Company - Victoria - *21
1022 Government St., 2nd Fl., Victoria, BC V8W 1X7
Tel: 250-383-2356; Fax: 250-380-6560
reception@woodwardandcompany.com
www.woodwardandcompany.com

Victoria: Wendy K. Zimmerman - *1
1006 Russell St., Victoria, BC V9A 3X9
Tel: 250-384-1804; Fax: 250-384-1805
Toll-Free: 800-313-9581
wendy@vicwestlaw.ca

West Vancouver: Christopher B. Chu - *1
#200, 100 Park Royal South, West Vancouver, BC V7T 1A2
Tel: 604-925-5898; Fax: 604-648-8361
cbchu@mail.com

West Vancouver: David T. Forsyth - *1
#1110, 100 Park Royal South, West Vancouver, BC V7T 1A2
Tel: 604-925-0045; Fax: 604-926-7782
dforsyth33@shaw.ca

West Vancouver: Goluboff & Mazzei, Barristers & Solicitors - *4
#201, 585 - 16th St., West Vancouver, BC V7V 3R8
Tel: 604-229-4470; Fax: 604-926-7817
Toll-Free: 800-815-5894
info@goluboffmazzei.com
www.goluboffmazzei.com

West Vancouver: James C. Hutchinson - *1
#200, 100 Park Royal South, West Vancouver, BC V7T 1A2
Tel: 604-926-2876; Fax: 604-926-2937
jch@jameschutchinson.com
www.jameschutchinson.ca

West Vancouver: Myrle L. Lawrence, Law Corporation - *1
#203, 815 Main St., West Vancouver, BC V7T 2Z3
Tel: 604-925-9260; Fax: 604-925-9261
mlawrence@veritaslaw.ca

West Vancouver: McLean Armstrong LLP - *9
#300, 1497 Marine Dr., West Vancouver, BC V7T 1B8
Tel: 604-925-0672; Fax: 604-925-8984
www.mcleanarmstrong.com

West Vancouver: David H. Stoller - *1
#801, 100 Park Royal S., West Vancouver, BC V7T 1A2
Tel: 604-922-4702; Fax: 604-922-0374
stoller@stoller.ca
www.stoller.ca

West Vancouver: Ann Marie Sweeney - *1
#201, 1590 Bellevue Ave., West Vancouver, BC V7V 1A7
Tel: 604-922-0131; Fax: 604-922-0171

Whistler: Tom Docking - *1
#338A, 4370 Lorimer Rd., Whistler, BC V0N 1B4
Tel: 604-905-5180; Fax: 866-974-7729
tom@whistlerlawyer.ca
whistlerrealestatelawyer.ca

Whistler: Mountain Law Corporation - Whistler
Former Name: Shrimpton & Company
#200, 1410 Alpha Lake Rd., Whistler, BC V0N 1B1
Tel: 604-938-4947; Fax: 604-938-0471
info@mountainlaw.com
www.mountainlaw.com

Whistler: Ian D. Reith - *1
#14, 4227 Village Stroll, RR#4, Whistler, BC V0N 1B4
Tel: 604-932-6501; Fax: 604-932-5615

Whistler: Whistler Law Offices - *1
Former Name: Davies & McLean
#201A, P.O. Box 449, 4230 Gateway Drl, Whistler, BC V0N 1B0
Tel: 604-938-1763; Fax: 604-938-1764
Toll-Free: 877-938-1763
nick@whistlerlawoffices.com
www.whistlerlawoffices.com

White Rock: Cleveland Doan LLP - *3
1321 Johnston Rd., White Rock, BC V4B 3Z3
Tel: 604-536-5002; Fax: 604-536-7002
lawyers@clevelanddoan.com
www.cleveland-doan.com

White Rock: Dawn Wattie Law Corporation - *1
#2, 15621 Marine Dr., White Rock, BC V4B 1E1
Tel: 604-385-3952; Fax: 604-224-4068
info@dwlc.ca
www.dawnwattielawcorp.ca

White Rock: Medland & Company - *1
14582 - 18th Ave., White Rock, BC V4A 5V5
Tel: 604-230-8476; Fax: 604-535-4145
medlandco@shaw.ca

White Rock: Joseph M. Prodor - *1
15260 Thrift Ave., White Rock, BC V4B 2L2
Tel: 604-536-4676; Fax: 604-535-8981
Toll-Free: 877-577-6367
jprodor@axionet.com

Williams Lake: Vanderburgh & Company - *3
#5, 123 Borland St., Williams Lake, BC V2G 1R1
Tel: 250-392-7161; Fax: 250-392-7060
aev@cariboolaw.com
www.cariboolaw.com

Manitoba

Beausejour: Middleton & Middleton - *1
527 Park Ave., Beausejour, MB R0E 0C0
Tel: 204-268-4566; Fax: 204-268-4572
Toll-Free: 866-222-3259

Birtle: Sims & Company - Birtle
Pratt Building, P.O. Box 190, 7th & Main St., Birtle, MB R0M 0C0
Tel: 204-842-3355; Fax: 204-842-3446
simsco2@mts.net
www.simsco.mb.ca

Brandon: Terri E. Deller Law Office - *1
801 Princess Ave., Brandon, MB R7A 0P5
Tel: 204-726-0128
questions@dellerlaw.com
www.dellerlaw.com

Brandon: Donald & Kehler Law Office - *3
Former Name: Donald Legal Services
22 - Sixth St., Brandon, MB R7A 3N1
Tel: 204-729-4900; Fax: 204-728-4477
www.dklegal.ca

Brandon: Meighen Haddad LLP - Brandon - *17
110 - 11 St., Brandon, MB R7A 4J4
Tel: 204-727-8461; Fax: 204-726-1948
Toll-Free: 800-628-7960
mail@mhlaw.ca
www.mhlaw.ca

Brandon: Paterson Patterson Wyman & Abel - Brandon - *7
Also Known As: Patersons
#1, Carriage House, 1040 Princess Ave., Brandon, MB R7A 0P8
Tel: 204-727-2424; Fax: 204-728-4670
info@patersons.ca
www.patersons.ca

Brandon: James W. Potter - *1
1337 Princess Ave., Brandon, MB R7A 0R4
Tel: 204-727-6431; Fax: 204-727-2818

Brandon: Westman Community Law Centre
236 - 11th St., Brandon, MB R7A 4J6
Tel: 204-729-3484; Fax: 204-726-1732
Toll-Free: 800-876-7326

Carman: Brown & Associates - *4
P.O. Box 1240, 71 Main St. South, Carman, MB R0G 0J0
Tel: 204-745-2028; Fax: 204-745-3513
lawyers@brownlawoffice.org
www.brownlawoffice.org
www.facebook.com/brownlawofficecarman

Carman: Lee & Lee
P.O. Box 656, 5 Centre Ave. West, Carman, MB R0G 0J0
Tel: 204-745-6751; Fax: 204-745-3481
bullsandbears@leeandlee.mb.ca

Dauphin: Amisk Community Law Centre
202 Main St. South, Dauphin, MB R7N 1K6
Tel: 204-622-4660; Fax: 204-622-4679
Toll-Free: 877-622-4660

Dauphin: Irwin Law Office - *2
122 Main St. North, Dauphin, MB R7N 1C2
Tel: 204-638-9249; Fax: 204-638-3647
irwinlaw@mymts.net
www.irwinlawoffice.ca

Dauphin: Johnston & Company - *5
P.O. Box 551, 18 - 3rd Ave. NW, Dauphin, MB R7N 2V4
Tel: 204-638-3211; Fax: 204-638-9646
www.johnstonlawoffice.ca

Dauphin: Johnston & Company - Dauphin - *5
P.O. Box 551, 18 - 3 Ave. NW, Dauphin, MB R7N 2V4
Tel: 204-638-3211; Fax: 204-638-9646
www.johnstonlawoffice.ca

Dauphin: Parklands Community Law Centre - *4
31 - 3rd Ave. NE, Dauphin, MB R7N 0Y5
Tel: 204-622-7000; Fax: 204-622-7029
Toll-Free: 800-810-6977

* indicates number of lawyers

Erickson: **Platt Law Office - *1**
Erickson Professional Centre, P.O. Box 70, 36 Main St.,
Erickson, MB R0J 1P0
Tel: 204-636-7838; Fax: 204-636-7861
ajp@plattlegal.ca
www.plattlegal.ca

Killarney: **Val Duke Law Office - *1**
514 Broadway Ave., Killarney, MB R0K 1G0
Tel: 204-523-4464; Fax: 204-523-5676

Manitou: **Selby Law Office - *3**
P.O. Box 279, 351 Main St., Manitou, MB R0G 1G0
Tel: 204-242-2801; Fax: 204-242-2723
selbylaw@mts.net

Neepawa: **Taylor Law Office - *2**
P.O. Box 309, 269 Hamilton St, Neepawa, MB R0J 1H0
Tel: 204-476-2336; Fax: 204-476-5783
admin@taylorlawoffice.ca

Portage la Prairie: **Miller Pressey Selinger - *1**
P.O. Box 368, 103 Saskatchewan Ave. East, Portage la
Prairie, MB R1N 3B7
Tel: 204-857-3436; Fax: 204-857-9238
mpslaw@mts.net
millerpresseyselingerlawyer.com

Roblin: **Marcel J.J.R. Gregoire - *1**
P.O. Box 1630, 158 Main St., Roblin, MB R0L 1P0
Tel: 204-937-2117; Fax: 204-937-4576
mgreg@mb.sympatico.ca

Russell: **Mason D. Jardine - *1**
P.O. Box 1270, 346 Main St., Russell, MB R0J 1W0
Tel: 204-773-2165; Fax: 204-773-2920
mjardine@escape.ca

Selkirk: **W. Douglas Kitchen - *1**
1202 River Rd., Selkirk, MB R1A 2E1
Tel: 204-482-8929

Selkirk: **Kohaykewych & Associates - *1**
413 Main St., Selkirk, MB R1A 1V2
Tel: 204-482-7925; Fax: 204-482-7099
kohaykewych@mts.net

Selkirk: **David L. Moore & Assoc. - *2**
407 Main St., Selkirk, MB R1A 1T9
Tel: 204-482-3921; Fax: 204-482-5564
Toll-Free: 877-482-3921
david@davidmoorelaw.ca

Steinbach: **Loewen Henderson Banman Legault LLP
- *4**
Former Name: Loewen Henderson Banman; Plett
Goossen & Associates
#200, 250 Main St., Steinbach, MB R5G 1Y8
Tel: 204-326-6454; Fax: 204-326-6917

Steinbach: **Smith Neufeld Jodoin LLP - Steinbach -
*13**
P.O. Box 1267, 85 PTH 12 North, Steinbach, MB R5G 1M9
Tel: 204-326-3442
www.snj.ca
www.facebook.com/snjllp

Stonewall: **Grantham Law Offices - *1**
#1, P.O. Box 1400, 333 Main St., Stonewall, MB R0C 2Z0
Tel: 204-467-5527; Fax: 204-467-5550

Swan River: **Burnside & Ferriss - *2**
P.O. Box 340, 509 Main St. East, Swan River, MB R0L 1Z0
Tel: 204-734-3485; Fax: 204-734-2872
ggb@burnsideferris.com

Swan River: **Palsson & Holmes Law Office - *2**
114 - 5th Ave. North, Swan River, MB R0L 1Z0
Tel: 204-734-4528; Fax: 204-734-5085

Teulon: **Steven R. Shinnie - *1**
P.O. Box 149, 70 Main St., Teulon, MB R0C 3B0
Tel: 204-886-3959; Fax: 204-886-3962

The Pas: **Bjornsson & Wight Law Office - *2**
#3, P.O. Box 1769, 314 Edwards Ave., The Pas, MB R9A 1L5
Tel: 204-627-1200; Fax: 204-627-1210
frontdeskbwlaw@mailme.ca

The Pas: **Kelsey Community Law Centre**
P.O. Box 1770, 130 - 3rd St. West, The Pas, MB R9A 1L5
Tel: 204-627-4833; Fax: 204-627-4840
Toll-Free: 800-839-7946

The Pas: **Northlands Community Law Centre**
P.O. Box 2429, 236 Edwards Ave., The Pas, MB R9A 1M2
Tel: 204-627-4820; Fax: 204-627-4838
Toll-Free: 800-268-9790

Thompson: **Law North Law Corporation - *3**
Former Name: McDonald, Huberdeau; McDonald,
Thompson, Huberdeau
436 Thompson Dr. North, Thompson, MB R8N 0C6
Tel: 204-677-2366; Fax: 204-677-3249

Thompson: **Mayer Dearman & Pellizzaro - *3**
#101, 83 Churchill Dr., Thompson, MB R8N 0L6
Tel: 204-677-2393
www.mdplaw.ca

Thompson: **Ronald J. Nadeau Law Office - *1**
76 Severn Cres., Thompson, MB R8N 1M6
Tel: 204-774-8009; Fax: 204-778-6559
jrnadeau@mts.net

Thompson: **Thompson Community Law Centre**
3 Station Rd., Thompson, MB R8N 0N3
Tel: 204-677-1211; Fax: 204-677-1220
Toll-Free: 800-665-0656

Virden: **McNeill Harasymchuk McConnell - *4**
P.O. Box 520, Virden, MB R0M 2C0
Tel: 204-748-1220; Fax: 204-748-3007
ene@mhmlaw.ca

Winnipeg: **Alexander Law Office - *1**
387 Broadway Ave., Winnipeg, MB R3C 0V5
Tel: 204-957-1717; Fax: 204-949-9232
dalaw_101@hotmail.com

Winnipeg: **Antymniuk & Antymniuk**
Also Known As: Antymniuk van der Krabben
#200, 600 St. Anne's Rd., Winnipeg, MB R2M 2S2
Tel: 204-254-3511; Fax: 204-257-5139

Winnipeg: **Scott Armstrong Law Office - *1**
64 Silver Springs Bay, Winnipeg, MB R2K 4L4
Tel: 204-667-3137; Fax: 204-667-1118
armstrong.scott@shaw.ca

Winnipeg: **Assiniboia Law Office - *1**
Former Name: Barber Law Office
3651 Roblin Blvd., Winnipeg, MB R3R 0E2
Tel: 204-949-3240; Fax: 204-949-3249
algonline.ca

Winnipeg: **Bernstein & Hirsch - *3**
883 Corydon Ave., Winnipeg, MB R3M 0W7
Tel: 204-942-0706; Fax: 204-957-1345

Winnipeg: **Booth Dennehy LLP - *12**
387 Broadway Ave., Winnipeg, MB R3C 0V5
Tel: 204-957-1717; Fax: 204-943-6199
www.boothdennehy.com

Winnipeg: **Broadway Law Group - *5**
#300, 326 Broadway Ave., Winnipeg, MB R3C 0S5
Tel: 204-984-9420; Fax: 204-947-2757

Winnipeg: **Brodsky & Company - *5**
#1212, 363 Broadway Ave., Winnipeg, MB R3C 3N9
Tel: 204-940-4433; Fax: 204-940-4435
www.gregbrodsky.ca

Winnipeg: **Bradley J. Brooks - *1**
P.O. Box 2461, Stn. Main, 360 Main St., Winnipeg, MB R6M
1C2
Tel: 204-992-4700; Fax: 866-744-2579
bbrooks@cite-on-site.ca

Winnipeg: **Campbell, Marr LLP - *12**
10 Donald St., Winnipeg, MB R3C 1L5
Tel: 204-942-3311; Fax: 204-943-7997
www.campbellmarr.com

Winnipeg: **Michael Capozzi - *1**
45 Wharton Blvd., Winnipeg, MB R2Y 0S9
Tel: 204-832-4807; Fax: 204-895-2336

Winnipeg: **Cassidy Ramsay - *6**
#210, 200 Waterfront Dr., Winnipeg, MB R3B 3P1
Tel: 204-943-7454; Fax: 204-943-9563
info@cassidyramsay.com
www.cassidyramsay.com

Winnipeg: **Champagne Law Office - *1**
390 Provencher Blvd., Unit F, Winnipeg, MB R2H 0H1
Tel: 204-956-1199; Fax: 204-956-5333

Winnipeg: **Chapman Goddard Kagan - *9**
1864 Portage Ave., Winnipeg, MB R3J 0H2
Tel: 204-888-7973; Fax: 204-832-3461
info@cgklaw.ca
www.cgklaw.ca

Winnipeg: **Jack M. Chapman & Associates - *1**
#2250, 360 Main St., Winnipeg, MB R3C 3Z3
Tel: 204-942-9994; Fax: 204-885-7420

Winnipeg: **Cherniack Smith - *7**
#200, 100 Osborne St., Winnipeg, MB R3L 1Y5
Tel: 204-452-4000; Fax: 204-477-1856

Winnipeg: **S. Cohan - *1**
#607, 386 Broadway, Winnipeg, MB R3C 3R6
Tel: 204-944-1413; Fax: 204-943-5102

Winnipeg: **Phillip F.B. Cramer Law Office - *1**
390 York St., Winnipeg, MB R3C 0P3
Tel: 204-987-0070; Fax: 204-987-0076

Winnipeg: **D'Arcy & Deacon LLP - Winnipeg - *49**
Former Name: Swift, MacLeod, Deacon; D'Arcy, Irving,
Haig & Smethurst
#2200, 1 Lombard Pl., Winnipeg, MB R3B 0X7
Tel: 204-942-2271; Fax: 204-943-4242
inquiries@darcydeacon.com
www.darcydeacon.com
www.facebook.com/DarcyDeaconLegal,
twitter.com/DarcyDeaconLLP

Winnipeg: **Deeley, Fabbri, Sellen - *15**
#903, 386 Broadway, Winnipeg, MB R3C 3R6
Tel: 204-949-1710; Fax: 204-956-4457
info@dfslaw.com
www.dfslaw.com

Winnipeg: **Dowhan & Dowhan - *2**
#600, 63 Albert St., Winnipeg, MB R3B 1G4
Tel: 204-942-4235; Fax: 204-956-4560

Winnipeg: **Duboff Edwards Haight & Schachter - *10**
#1900, 155 Carlton St., Winnipeg, MB R3C 3H8
Tel: 204-942-3361; Fax: 204-942-3362
duboff@dehslaw.com

Winnipeg: **Edmond & Associates - *4**
#204, 1120 Grant Ave., Winnipeg, MB R3M 2A6
Tel: 204-452-5314; Fax: 204-452-5989
gedmond@edmond.ca

Winnipeg: **Fillmore Riley LLP - *69**
#1700, 360 Main St., Winnipeg, MB R3C 3Z3
Tel: 204-956-2970; Fax: 204-957-0516
frinfo@fillmoreriley.com
www.fillmoreriley.com
twitter.com/fillmore_riley, www.linkedin.com/company/142469

Winnipeg: **Funk & Strell - *2**
#1400, 1 Lombard Pl., Winnipeg, MB R3B 0X3
Tel: 204-957-5600; Fax: 204-949-1043
funk@mts.net

Winnipeg: **George & Tweed Law Corporation - *3**
Former Name: Abrams & Tweed
#4, 549 Regent Ave. West, Winnipeg, MB R2C 1R9
Tel: 204-949-3080; Fax: 204-949-3089
btweed@george-tweed.com

Winnipeg: **J. David George & Associates - *2**
108 Regent Ave. East, Winnipeg, MB R2C 0C1
Tel: 204-982-7503; Fax: 204-222-4761
david-dg@shaw.ca

Winnipeg: **Martin D. Glazer - *1**
#1210, 363 Broadway, Winnipeg, MB R3C 3N9
Tel: 204-942-6560; Fax: 204-942-2696
mglazlaw@mymts.net
members.shaw.ca/Martinglazerlaw

Winnipeg: **Martin R. Gutnik - *1**
201 Portage Ave., 18th Fl., Winnipeg, MB R3B 3K6
Tel: 204-786-8924
martin@gutnik.com
www.gutnik.com

Winnipeg: **Habing Laviolette - *4**
2643 Portage Ave., Winnipeg, MB R3J 0P9
Tel: 204-832-8322; Fax: 204-832-3906
www.habinglaw.com

---

* indicates number of lawyers

Winnipeg: Harrison Law Office - *6
#200, 99 Scurfield Blvd., Winnipeg, MB R3Y 1Y1
Tel: 204-989-8760; *Fax:* 204-989-8765
info@harrisonlaw.ca
www.harrisonlaw.ca

Winnipeg: Hill Sokalski Walsh Trippier LLP - *13
Former Name: Hill & Walsh
#2670, 360 Main St., Winnipeg, MB R3C 3Z3
Tel: 204-943-6740; *Fax:* 204-943-3934
lawyers@hillco.mb.ca
www.hillco.mb.ca

Winnipeg: Alain J. Hogue Law Office - *1
194 Provencher Blvd., Winnipeg, MB R2H 0G3
Tél: 204-237-9600; *Téléc:* 204-233-2689

Winnipeg: Hook & Smith - *4
#201, 3111 Portage Ave., Winnipeg, MB R3K 0W4
Tel: 204-885-4520; *Fax:* 204-837-9846
general@hookandsmith.com
hookandsmith.com

Winnipeg: D.R. Knight Law Office - *5
#202, 900 Harrow St. East, Winnipeg, MB R3M 3Y7
Tel: 204-948-0400; *Fax:* 204-948-0401
www.knightlawoffice.ca

Winnipeg: Krawchuk & Company - *2
#2250, 360 Main St., Winnipeg, MB R3C 3Z3
Tel: 204-943-4561; *Fax:* 204-947-5724
krawchukandco@mts.net

Winnipeg: Frank Lawrence - *1
#202, 1382 Henderson Hwy., Winnipeg, MB R2G 1M8
Tel: 204-338-9705

Winnipeg: Victoria E. Lehman Law Offices - *1
412 Wardlaw Ave., Winnipeg, MB R3L 0L7
Tel: 204-453-6416; *Fax:* 204-477-1379
www.vlehmanlawoffices.com

Winnipeg: Levene Tadman Golub Corporation - *17
#700, 330 St. Mary Ave., Winnipeg, MB R3C 3Z5
Tel: 204-957-0520; *Fax:* 204-957-1696
inquiries@ltglc.ca
www.ltgg.ca

Winnipeg: Liffman Soronow - *2
#210, 400 St. Mary Ave., Winnipeg, MB R3C 4K5
Tel: 204-925-6070; *Fax:* 204-944-0513
hal@escape.ca

Winnipeg: MacInnes, Burbidge - *1
Also Known As: Frank L. Cvitkovitch, Q.C.
#500, 177 Lombard Ave., Winnipeg, MB R3B 0W5
Tel: 204-942-5256; *Fax:* 204-942-5259
macinnesburbidge@gmail.com

Winnipeg: Hilary C. Maxim - *1
212B Regent Ave. West, Winnipeg, MB R2C 1R2
Tel: 204-224-2600; *Fax:* 204-222-2824

Winnipeg: McDonald Law Office - *1
258 Tache Ave., Winnipeg, MB R2H 1Z9
Tel: 204-927-3900; *Fax:* 204-927-3909
Toll-Free: 800-393-1110
info@mcdonaldlaw.ca
www.mcdonaldlaw.ca

Winnipeg: McJannet Rich - *6
#1308, Royal Bank Building, 220 Portage Ave., Winnipeg,
MB R3C 0A5
Tel: 204-957-0951; *Fax:* 204-989-0688
www.mcjannetrich.com

Winnipeg: McRoberts Law Office LLP - *14
#200, Madison Square, 1630 Ness Ave., Winnipeg, MB R3J
3X1
Tel: 204-944-7907; *Fax:* 204-772-1684
www.mcrobertslawoffice.com

Winnipeg: Michaels & Stern - *2
#300, 326 Broadway Ave., Winnipeg, MB R3C 0S5
Tel: 204-989-5500; *Fax:* 204-989-5508
michaelsandstern@mts.net

Winnipeg: Mirwaldt & Gray - *2
#403, 171 Donald St., Winnipeg, MB R3C 1M4
Tel: 204-943-3040; *Fax:* 204-943-5135
Toll-Free: 866-630-4892
info@mirwaldtandgray.com
www.mirwaldtandgray.com

Winnipeg: Peter J. Moss - *5
1002 Pembina Hwy., Winnipeg, MB R3T 1Z5
Tel: 204-284-3221; *Fax:* 204-284-7960
mosslaw@shaw.ca

Winnipeg: Murray & Kovnats - *2
#100, 1600 Ness Ave., Winnipeg, MB R3J 3W7
Tel: 204-957-1700; *Fax:* 204-942-2325

Winnipeg: Myers Weinberg LLP - *30
#724, 240 Graham Ave., Winnipeg, MB R3C 0J7
Tel: 204-942-0501; *Fax:* 204-956-0625
info@myersfirm.com
www.myersfirm.com

Winnipeg: Stanley S. Nozick - *1
Former Name: Nozick, Sinder & Associates
#1130, 386 Broadway, Winnipeg, MB R3C 3R6
Tel: 204-944-8227; *Fax:* 204-944-9246
snozick@escape.ca

Winnipeg: Orle, Bargen, Davidson LLP - *7
280 Stradbrook Ave., Winnipeg, MB R3L 0J6
Tel: 204-989-2760; *Fax:* 204-989-2774
reception@odgb.mb.ca
www.odgb.mb.ca

Winnipeg: Overall Grimes - *3
Former Name: Mutchmor, Violago, Overall, Grimes
390 York Ave., Winnipeg, MB R3C 0P3
Tel: 204-989-1300; *Fax:* 204-989-1301

Winnipeg: Murray S. Palay - *1
#703, 161 Portage Ave. East, Winnipeg, MB R3B 0Y4
Tel: 204-944-2491; *Fax:* 204-944-8046
mpalay@quadasset.com

Winnipeg: Parashin Law Office - *1
404 McGregor St., Winnipeg, MB R2W 4X5
Tel: 204-582-3558

Winnipeg: Phillips, Aiello - *14
668 Corydon Ave., Winnipeg, MB R3M 0X7
Tel: 204-949-7700; *Fax:* 204-452-0922
Toll-Free: 866-949-7701

Winnipeg: Pitblado LLP - Winnipeg - *60
#2500, 360 Main St., Winnipeg, MB R3C 4H6
Tel: 204-956-0560; *Fax:* 204-957-0227
firm@pitblado.com
www.pitblado.com
twitter.com/PitbladoLaw,
www.linkedin.com/company/pitblado-law

Winnipeg: Pollock & Company - *5
#1120, 363 Broadway, Winnipeg, MB R3C 3N9
Tel: 204-956-0450; *Fax:* 204-947-0109
mail@pollockandcompany.com
www.pollockandcompany.com

Winnipeg: Prober Law Offices - *1
#208, 387 Broadway Ave., Winnipeg, MB R3C 0V5
Tel: 204-957-1205; *Fax:* 204-943-6199

**Winnipeg: Pullan Kammerloch Frohlinger -
Winnipeg - *18**
#300, 240 Kennedy St., Winnipeg, MB R3C 1T1
Tel: 204-956-0490; *Fax:* 204-947-3747
www.pkflawyers.com

Winnipeg: Radchuk & Company - *1
10 Salvia Bay, Winnipeg, MB R2V 2L8
Tel: 204-338-8880; *Fax:* 204-334-5241

Winnipeg: Edward Rice - *1
#301, 63 Albert St., Winnipeg, MB R3B 1G4
Tel: 204-944-1905; *Fax:* 204-947-5895
ricelaw@mts.net

Winnipeg: Russell Ridd - *1
#6, 405 Broadway, Winnipeg, MB R3C 3L6
Tel: 204-945-2852; *Fax:* 204-945-1260
russ.ridd@gov.mb.ca

Winnipeg: Robertson Shypit Soble Wood - *7
#202, 1555 St. Mary's Rd., Winnipeg, MB R2M 5L9
Tel: 204-257-6061; *Fax:* 204-254-7183
info@rsswlawyers.com
www.rsswlawyers.com

Winnipeg: Rosenbaum & Company - *1
#201, 2211 McPhillips St., Winnipeg, MB R2V 3M5
Tel: 204-338-4663; *Fax:* 204-338-4667
Toll-Free: 866-772-7526
racplan@mts.net
www.rosenbaumandco.ca

Winnipeg: Sheldon Rosenstock - *1
848 Waterloo St., Winnipeg, MB R3N 0T6
Tel: 204-488-4121; *Fax:* 204-488-1869
sheldon@mymts.net

Winnipeg: St. Mary's Law LLP - *1
Former Name: Inkster Christie Hughes LLP
619 St. Mary Rd., Winnipeg, MB R2M 3L8
Tel: 204-942-1799; *Fax:* 204-947-6800
pbruckshaw@stmaryslaw.com
www.divorcelawyerwinnipeg.com

Winnipeg: Mario J. Santos - *1
#202, 1080 Wall St., Winnipeg, MB R3E 2R9
Tel: 204-783-0554; *Fax:* 204-772-4231
mjsantos@mts.net
www.mariosantoslawoffice.com

Winnipeg: Shewchuk & Associates - *2
2645 Portage Ave., Winnipeg, MB R3J 0P9
Tel: 204-889-4595

Winnipeg: Sinclair & Associates - *2
#231, 1120 Grant Ave., Winnipeg, MB R3M 2A6
Tel: 204-474-2468; *Fax:* 204-474-2535

Winnipeg: Sidney Soronow - *1
Former Name: Liffman Soronow
#210, 400 St. Mary Ave., Winnipeg, MB R3C 4K5
Tel: 204-925-6074; *Fax:* 204-944-0513

Winnipeg: J.S. Sukhan - *1
1158 Clarence Ave., Winnipeg, MB R3T 1S9
Tel: 204-284-0728

Winnipeg: Tacium, Vincent, Orlikow - *1
#200, 99A Scurfield Blvd., Winnipeg, MB R3Y 1G4
Tel: 204-989-4220; *Fax:* 204-254-7744
taciumvincentorlikow.com

Winnipeg: Tapper Cuddy LLP - *30
Former Name: Scufield Tupper Cuddy
#1000, 330 St. Mary Ave., Winnipeg, MB R3C 3Z5
Tel: 204-944-8777; *Fax:* 204-947-2593
tc@tappercuddy.com
www.tappercuddy.com

Winnipeg: Taylor McCaffrey LLP - *64
400 St. Mary Ave., 9th Fl., Winnipeg, MB R3C 4K5
Tel: 204-949-1312; *Fax:* 204-957-0945
www.tmlawyers.com
twitter.com/TM_Lawyers,
www.linkedin.com/company/taylor-mccaffrey-llp

Winnipeg: Tepley Law Office - *1
#401, 460 Main St., Winnipeg, MB R3B 1B6
Tel: 204-942-7218

Winnipeg: Teskey Legal & ADR Services - *1
1905 One Evergreen Pl., Winnipeg, MB R3L 0E9
Tel: 204-943-8395; *Fax:* 204-943-1288
teskey@mb.sympatico.ca

**Winnipeg: Thompson Dorfman Sweatman LLP -
Winnipeg - *82**
Also Known As: TDS
#2200, 201 Portage Ave., Winnipeg, MB R3B 3L3
Tel: 204-957-1930; *Fax:* 204-934-0570
tds@tdslaw.com
www.tdslaw.com
www.facebook.com/tdslaw, twitter.com/tdslaw,
www.linkedin.com/company/thompson-dorfman-sweatman-llp

Winnipeg: John F. Thullner - *1
#102, 2200 McPhillips St., Winnipeg, MB R2V 3P4
Tel: 204-694-0161

Winnipeg: Tradition Law LLP - *4
#200, 207 Donald St., Winnipeg, MB R3C 1M5
Tel: 204-947-6806; *Fax:* 204-947-3705
info@traditionlaw.ca
www.traditionlaw.ca

Winnipeg: Troniak Law - *2
#1000, 444 St Mary Ave., Winnipeg, MB R3C 3T1
Tel: 204-947-1743; *Fax:* 204-947-0101
info@troniaklaw.com
www.troniaklaw.com

* indicates number of lawyers

Winnipeg: **Tupper & Adams** - *3
#201, 90 Garry St., Winnipeg, MB R3C 4H1
Tel: 204-942-0161; *Fax:* 204-943-2385

Winnipeg: **W.R. Van Walleghem** - *1
#206, 1120 Grant Ave., Winnipeg, MB R3M 2A6
Tel: 204-477-0210; *Fax:* 204-452-9746

Winnipeg: **Walsh & Company** - *3
426 Portage Ave., 2nd Fl., Winnipeg, MB R3C 0C9
Tel: 204-947-2282; *Fax:* 204-943-0211
paulwalsh@walshandco.com
www.walshandco.com

Winnipeg: **Warkentin & Calver** - *1
3651 Roblin Blvd., Winnipeg, MB R3R 0E2
Tel: 204-949-3230; *Fax:* 204-949-3249

Winnipeg: **Eugene Waskiw** - *1
441 Perth Ave., Winnipeg, MB R2V 0T9
Tel: 204-334-7372

Winnipeg: **Arthur M. Werier** - *1
905 Corydon Ave., Winnipeg, MB R3M 0W8
Tel: 204-475-7923

Winnipeg: **Wilder Wilder & Langtry** - *6
#1500, Richardson Bldg., 1 Lombard Pl., Winnipeg, MB R3B 0X3
Tel: 204-947-1456; *Fax:* 204-957-1368
www.wilderwilder.com

Winnipeg: **Zaifman Associates** - *4
#500, 191 Lombard Ave., 5th Fl., Winnipeg, MB R3B 0X1
Tel: 204-944-8888; *Fax:* 204-956-2909
zaifman@zaifmanlaw.com
www.zaifmanlaw.com

Winnipeg: **Saheel, Zaman Law Corporation** - *4
#1130, 363 Broadway, Winnipeg, MB R3C 3N9
Tel: 204-943-9922; *Fax:* 204-975-1802
szaman@szamanlaw.com

Winnipeg: **Daria Zyla** - *1
1230 Hector Bay West, Winnipeg, MB R3M 3R9
Tel: 204-452-5626; *Fax:* 204-475-7979

New Brunswick

Atholville: **Roger G. Gauvin** - *1
65 Fairview St., Atholville, NB E3N 4N3
Tel: 506-753-4545; *Fax:* 506-753-2006

Bathurst: **Robert M. Boudreau** - *1
#100, 1154 St. Peter Ave., Bathurst, NB E2A 2Z9
Tél: 506-545-2099; *Tel:* 506-546-4765
rboudro@nbnet.nb.ca

Bathurst: **Chiasson & Roy** - *4
#203, Stn. Main, 216 Main St., Bathurst, NB E2A 3Z2
Tel: 506-548-3375; *Fax:* 506-548-4264
www.chiassonroy.ca

Bathurst: **Riordon & Theriault** - *3
Former Name: Riordon, Arseneault & Theriault
#300, 270 Douglas Ave., Bathurst, NB E2A 1M9
Tel: 506-548-8822; *Fax:* 506-548-5297

Bouctouche: **Yvon J.G. LeBlanc** - *2
P.O. Box 310, 25, boul Irving, Bouctouche, NB E0A 1G0
Tel: 506-743-2427; *Tel:* 506-743-8314
lebbell@nbnet.nb.ca

Bouctouche: **Mark Robere** - *1
#2, 6, rue Station, Bouctouche, NB E4S 3X1
Tel: 506-743-2262; *Fax:* 506-743-9014
roberem@nb.aibn.com

Campbellton: **J.Yvon Arseneau C.P. Inc.** - *3
Former Name: Arseneau & Associés
114 Water St., Campbellton, NB E3N 1B3
Tel: 506-753-3000; *Fax:* 506-753-2393

Campbellton: **Terrance H. Delaney, Q.C.** - *2
#206, P.O. Box 490, Stn. Main, 123 Water St., Campbellton, NB E3N 3G9
Tel: 506-753-7618; *Fax:* 506-759-7315

Chipman: **Nicholas D. DiCarlo**
P.O. Box 489, Stn. Main, 131 Main St., Chipman, NB E4A 3N6
Tel: 506-339-6688; *Fax:* 506-339-5598
ndicarlo@nb.aibn.com

Chipman: **Sharon R. Lockwood** - *1
28 Northrup Dr., Chipman, NB E4A 2P7
Tel: 506-339-6632; *Fax:* 506-339-5130
sharon.lockwood@nb.aibn.com

Dieppe: **Martin J. Aubin** - *1
250 Acadie Ave., Dieppe, NB E1A 1G5
Tel: 506-856-6083; *Fax:* 506-853-0110

Dieppe: **Jacques Gauthier** - *1
157 Lakeburn Ave., Dieppe, NB E1A 8N5
Tél: 506-383-4564
acadian22@hotmail.com

Dieppe: **Alan Schelew** - *1
#4, 299 Champlain St., Dieppe, NB E1A 1P2
Tel: 506-857-2272; *Fax:* 506-857-2276
schelew@nb.aibn.com
www.monctonlawyer.com
www.linkedin.com/in/alan-schelew-a3055837

Dieppe: **Thompson & Thompson** - *2
379 Champlain St., Dieppe, NB E1A 1P2
Tel: 506-859-7794; *Fax:* 506-859-1297
ttlaw@nbnet.nb.ca
www.thompsonandthompson.ca

Edmundston: **Pilote Morin & Moreau** - *3
#304, 121, rue de l'Église, Edmundston, NB E3V 1J9
Tél: 506-739-7311
pmm@nb.aibn.com
www.pilotemorinmoreau.ca

Fredericton: **Athey Gregory & Dickson** - *2
Former Name: Athey & Gregory
206 Rockwood Ave., Fredericton, NB E3B 2M2
Tel: 506-458-8060; *Fax:* 506-459-8288

Fredericton: **Carol H.Y. Boxill** - *1
57 Carleton St., Fredericton, NB E3B 6Y8
Tel: 506-454-5108; *Fax:* 506-450-3880

Fredericton: **Le Cabinet Bertrand Law** - *1
Former Name: Bertrand & Bertrand
700 Mcleod Ave., Fredericton, NB E3B 1V5
Tel: 506-450-3325; *Fax:* 506-450-6333

Fredericton: **Campbell Hughes Law Office** - *1
Former Name: Barbara Hughes Campbell
186 Waterloo Row, Fredericton, NB E3B 1Z2
Tel: 506-458-8140; *Fax:* 506-450-6186
bhclaw@nb.aibn.com
www.barbarahughescampbell.com

Fredericton: **Collingwood Stephen Law Office** - *1
336, Rte. 10, Richibucto Rd., Fredericton, NB E3A 7E1
Tel: 506-458-1880; *Fax:* 506-458-9868

Fredericton: **Eddy & Downs**
#210, P.O. Box 1205, Stn. A, 65 Regent St., Fredericton, NB E3B 5C8
Tel: 506-443-9700; *Fax:* 506-443-9710

Fredericton: **Elliott McCrea Hill** - *6
Former Name: Matthews McCrea Elliott; Matthews Teriault
197 Main St., Fredericton, NB E3A 1E1
Tel: 506-458-5959; *Fax:* 506-460-5934
office@emhlaw.com
emhlaw.com

Fredericton: **Foster & Company** - *9
#200, 919 Prospect St., Fredericton, NB E3B 2T7
Tel: 506-462-4000; *Fax:* 506-462-4001
info@fandclaw.com
www.fandclaw.com

Fredericton: **Glencross Ashford** - *2
288 Union St., Fredericton, NB E3A 1E5
Tel: 506-454-1256; *Fax:* 506-454-2365
www.glencrossashford.com

Fredericton: **Daniel W. McCormack** - *1
P.O. Box 1356, Stn. A, 259 Brunswick St., Fredericton, NB E3B 5S3
Tel: 506-459-3331; *Fax:* 506-457-6332

Fredericton: **McMath Law** - *4
Former Name: Dean & McMath
406 Regent St., Fredericton, NB E3B 3X7
Tel: 506-458-8555; *Fax:* 506-444-0920
info@mcmathlaw.ca
www.mcmathlaw.ca
www.facebook.com/mcmathlaw,
www.linkedin.com/company-beta/11027634

Fredericton: **McNally & Smart** - *2
P.O. Box 3152, Stn. LCD 1, 819 Union St., Fredericton, NB E3A 5G9
Tel: 506-472-4872; *Fax:* 506-472-9844

Fredericton: **E.J. Mockler** - *1
495C Prospect St., Fredericton, NB E3B 9M4
Tel: 506-454-8200; *Fax:* 506-454-7300
pete@ejmockler.ca
www.ejmockler.com/en/

Fredericton: **Murray Digdon & Donovan** - *3
#102, 401 Bishop Dr., Fredericton, NB E3C 2M6
Tel: 506-458-1108; *Fax:* 506-458-2645
www.mddlaw.ca

Fredericton: **J. Shawn O'Toole** - *1
#201, 346 Queen St., Fredericton, NB E3B 1B2
Tel: 506-458-8833; *Fax:* 506-454-1999

Fredericton: **Peters Rouse** - *3
Former Name: Mockler, Peters, Oley, Rouse & Williams
P.O. Box 547, Stn. A., 839 Aberdeen St., Fredericton, NB E3B 5A6
Tel: 506-444-6589; *Fax:* 506-444-6550
www.porlaw.com

Fredericton: **Pink Larkin** - *4
Former Name: Pink Breen Larkin
#210, 1133 Regent St., Fredericton, NB E3B 3Z2
Tel: 506-458-1989; *Fax:* 506-458-1127
Toll-Free: 888-280-2777
jbartlett@pinklarkin.com
www.pinklarkin.com

Fredericton: **Gerald R. Pugh** - *1
57 Carleton St., 4th Fl., Fredericton, NB E3B 3T2
Tel: 506-450-2666; *Fax:* 506-457-4295
info@easternlegal.ca
www.easternlegal.ca

Fredericton: **Rowan McGrath Lawyers** - *2
#206, 403 Regent St., Fredericton, NB E3B 3X6
Tel: 506-451-0657; *Fax:* 506-451-8011
drowan@rowanmcgrath.ca
www.rowanmcgrath.ca

Fredericton: **Michael J.F. Scully** - *1
9 Amanda St., Fredericton, NB E3G 0N5
Tel: 506-999-5035; *Fax:* 506-472-0240
scullylaw@gmail.com
scullylaw.ca

Fredericton: **P. Lorrie Yerxa** - *3
Former Name: Yerxa, Stephenson
#102, 403 Regent St., Fredericton, NB E3B 4Y9
Tel: 506-459-1450; *Fax:* 506-459-2301

Grand Falls: **Godbout, Ouellette** - *2
698 E.H. Daigle Blvd., Grand Falls, NB E3Z 2S1
Tel: 506-473-6272; *Fax:* 506-473-6065
godouel@nbnet.nb.ca

Grand Falls: **Peter Seheult** - *1
275A Sheriff St., Grand Falls, NB E3Z 3A1
Tel: 506-473-2164; *Fax:* 506-473-5543
pdseheult@rogers.com

Hampton: **Veniot Law Office** - *1
Former Name: Veniot Loughery Levine
71 Randall Dr., Hampton, NB E5N 6A4
Tel: 506-832-3418; *Fax:* 506-832-3755
vll@nb.aibn.com

Lamèque: **Roger A. Noël** - *3
Place de la Baie, Stn. Main, 5120E, rte 113, Lamèque, NB E8T 3N4
Tél: 506-344-2217; *Téléc:* 506-344-5380
www.etudelegalenoel.com

Minto: **Mario DiCarlo Law Office** - *1
255 Main St., Minto, NB E4B 3R8
Tel: 506-327-3777; *Fax:* 506-327-6080
maricdicarlo@bellaliant.net

Minto: **Sheila R. Thorne** - *1
29 Queen St., Minto, NB E4B 3P2
Tel: 506-327-6120

Miramichi: **Rosemary Losier** - *1
P.O. Box 112, Stn. Main, 173 Wellington St., Miramichi, NB E1N 3A5
Tel: 506-773-6817

* indicates number of lawyers

Miramichi: **Maynes Law - *4**
P.O. Box 518, 1723 Water St., Miramichi, NB E1N 3A8
Tel: 506-778-8336; Fax: 506-778-2103

Moncton: **Michel C. Arsenault - *1**
1255 Main St., Moncton, NB E1C 1H9
Tel: 506-857-8008; Fax: 506-857-8885
mcalaw@nb.aibn.com

Moncton: **Bingham Law - *19**
Former Name: Bingham Robinson McLennan Ehrhardt
& Teed
#300, Heritage Court, 95 Foundry St., Moncton, NB E1C 5H7
Tel: 506-857-8856; Fax: 506-857-2017
info@bingham.ca
www.bingham.ca
twitter.com/binghamlawdroit
www.linkedin.com/company/bingham-law-droit

Moncton: **Robert N. Charman - *1**
170 Highfield St., Moncton, NB E1C 5P2
Tel: 506-854-8656; Fax: 506-854-8684
rcharman@nbnet.nb.ca
www.robertncharman.com

Moncton: **Delehanty Rinzler Druckman - *2**
Former Name: Tedford Delehanty Rinzler
720 Main St., Moncton, NB E1C 1E4
www.drdlaw.ca

Moncton: **Forbes Roth Basque - *6**
#300, P.O. Box 480, 814 Main St., Moncton, NB E1C 8L9
Tel: 506-857-4880; Fax: 506-857-0151
www.forbesrothbasque.nb.ca

Moncton: **Fowler Law Professional Corporation - *2**
Former Name: Fowler & Fowler
69 Waterloo St., Moncton, NB E1C 0E1
Tel: 506-857-8811
www.fowlerandfowler.ca

Moncton: **groupe Murphy group - *4**
128 Highfield St., Moncton, NB E1C 5N7
Tel: 506-877-0077; Fax: 506-877-0079
info@murphygroup.ca
www.murphygroup.ca

Moncton: **LeBlanc Boucher Rodger Bourque - *3**
740 Main St., Moncton, NB E1C 1E6
Tel: 506-858-0110; Fax: 506-858-9497

Moncton: **LeBlanc Boudreau Maillet**
Former Name: LeBlanc Boudreau Desjardins Maillet
#200, 735 Main St., Moncton, NB E1C 1E5
Tel: 506-858-5666; Fax: 506-858-5570

Moncton: **Susan D. LeBlanc - *1**
76 Albert St., Moncton, NB E1C 1B1
Tel: 506-859-4402; Fax: 506-859-9195

Moncton: **Letcher & Murray - *3**
76 Albert St., Moncton, NB E1C 1B1
Tel: 506-857-2070; Fax: 506-859-9195

Moncton: **Lise Lorrain - *1**
40 Edgett Ave., Moncton, NB E1C 7B2
Tel: 506-855-6084; Fax: 506-389-3867

Moncton: **Kenneth Martin - *1**
51 Highfield St., Moncton, NB E1C 5N2
Tel: 506-867-2522
kennethmartinlaw.yolasite.com

Moncton: **Mitchell Law Office - *1**
Former Name: MacPherson Mitchell
89 Church St., Moncton, NB E1C 4Z4
Tel: 506-853-1105; Fax: 506-857-9129

Moncton: **Murphy Collette Murphy - *6**
250 Lutz St., Moncton, NB E1C 5G3
Tel: 506-856-8560; Fax: 506-856-8579
manager@murco.nb.ca
www.murco.nb.ca

Moncton: **Murphy, Murphy & Mollins - *3**
89 Church St., Moncton, NB E1C 4Z4
Tel: 506-857-9120; Fax: 506-857-9129
mmmlaw@nb.aibn.com

Moncton: **Sheehan Law - *1**
76 Albert St., Moncton, NB E1C 1B1
Tel: 506-387-7400; Fax: 506-859-9588

Oromocto: **Blair W. McKay - *1**
#3, 291 Restigouche Rd., Oromocto, NB E2V 2H2
Tel: 506-446-3000; Fax: 506-446-9010

Perth-Andover: **Mark C. Johnson - *1**
Former Name: Crocco, Hunter, Purvis, Johnson
P.O. Box 3066, 14A Beech Glen Rd., Perth-Andover, NB E7H 1J8
Tel: 506-273-6818; Fax: 506-273-6590
mjlaw@nb.aibn.com

Riverview: **Grew MacDonald - *3**
Former Name: McAllister & Grew
704A Coverdale Rd., Riverview, NB E1B 3L1
Tel: 506-856-8870; Fax: 506-856-8879
hgrew@nbnet.nb.ca

Riverview: **Wilbur Law Offices - *1**
Former Name: Wilbur & Wilbur
706B Coverdale Rd., Riverview, NB E1B 3L1
Tel: 506-387-7715; Fax: 506-387-5875
info@willburlaw.ca
www.wilburlaw.ca
www.linkedin.com/in/stephen-wilbur-8b6864136

Sackville: **Meldrum Law - *2**
7 Bridge St., Sackville, NB E4L 3N6
Tel: 506-536-3870; Fax: 506-536-2131
Toll-Free: 866-792-1416
meldrumk@nbnet.nb.ca

Sackville: **Ove B. Samuelsen - *1**
1 Squire St., Sackville, NB E4L 4K8
Tel: 506-536-0511; Fax: 506-536-1169
www.ovesamuelsen.com

Saint John: **Michael D. Bamford**
#420, 40 Charlotte St., Saint John, NB E2L 2H6
Tel: 506-634-8132; Fax: 506-633-0389

Saint John: **Boyle, Dennis - *1**
345 Lancaster Ave. W, Saint John, NB E2M 2L3
Tel: 506-634-7575

Saint John: **BretonKean Lawyers - *7**
Former Name: Barry Spalding
P.O. Box 6907, 75 Prince William St., 4th Fl., Saint John, NB E2L 4S3
Tel: 506-633-2556; Fax: 506-633-5902
info@brentonkean.com
www.brentonkean.com

Saint John: **Carleton Law Group - *2**
Former Name: Sherwood & Flanagan
117 Carleton St., Saint John, NB E2L 2Z6
Tel: 506-634-0001; Fax: 506-634-0456
info@carletonlawgroup.com
www.carletonlawgroup.com

Saint John: **Correia & Collins - *3**
#D302, One Market Square, 3rd Level Dockside, Saint John, NB E2L 4S4
Tel: 506-648-1700; Fax: 506-648-1701
www.correiaandcollins.com

Saint John: **Allen G. Doyle Law Office - *1**
45 Canterbury St., Saint John, NB E2L 2C6
Tel: 506-633-4198; Fax: 506-633-1645

Saint John: **Lynda D. Farrell - *4**
P.O. Box 1971, Stn. Main, 15 Market Sq., 8th Fl., Saint John, NB E2L 4L1
Tel: 506-658-2860; Fax: 506-649-7939

Saint John: **Gilbert McGloan Gillis - *7**
Also Known As: GMC
#L150, P.O. Box 7174, 90 King St., 2nd Fl., Saint John, NB E2L 1G3
Tel: 506-634-3600; Fax: 506-634-3612
Toll-Free: 888-246-4529
gmg@gmglaw.com
www.gmglaw.com

Saint John: **Gorman Nason Lawyers - *10**
Former Name: Gorman & Gorman; Nason, Farrell, Ljungstrom; Baker & Poley
P.O. Box 7286, Stn. A, 121 Germain St., Saint John, NB E2L 4S6
Tel: 506-634-8600; Fax: 506-634-8685
rec@gormannason.com
www.gormannason.com

Saint John: **John M. Henderson - *1**
#410, 40 Charlotte St., Saint John, NB E2L 2H6
Tel: 506-652-5502; Fax: 506-634-1795
jmhlaw@nbnet.nb.ca

Saint John: **Frank J. Hogan - *1**
491 Bay St. West, Saint John, NB E2M 7L3
Tel: 506-333-4646

Saint John: **Mary Ann G. Holland - *1**
#2B, P.O. Box 7041, Stn. Brunswick Sq., 28 King St., Saint John, NB E2L 4S4
Tel: 506-652-3774; Fax: 506-633-0581
lawyer@nbnet.nb.ca

Saint John: **Lisa A. Keenan - *1**
108 Prince William St., Saint John, NB E2L 2B3
Tel: 506-632-8999

Saint John: **W. Rodney Macdonald - *1**
108 Prince William St., Saint John, NB E2L 3J5
Tel: 506-632-8999; Fax: 506-634-1532

Saint John: **Elizabeth T. McLeod, QC - *1**
#5C, Brunswick Sq., P.O. Box 20045, 28 King St., Saint John, NB E2L 5B2
Tel: 506-632-4048; Fax: 506-652-6594

Saint John: **Mosher Chedore - *9**
885 Danells Dr., Saint John, NB E2M 5A9
Tel: 506-634-1600; Fax: 506-634-0740
info@mosherchedore.ca
www.mosherchedore.ca

Saint John: **Richard A. Northrup - *1**
#420, 40 Charlotte St., Saint John, NB E2L 2H6
Tel: 506-634-8134; Fax: 506-693-3473
nbrick@nb.aibn.com

Saint John: **Riley, John G. - *1**
#410, 40 Charlotte St., Saint John, NB E2L 2H6
Tel: 506-634-1188; Fax: 506-634-1795

Saint John: **Teed & Teed - *1**
107 Charlotte St., Saint John, NB E2L 2J2
Tel: 506-634-7320; Fax: 506-634-7423
info@teedandteed.com
www.teedandteed.com

Saint John: **Whelly & Kelly - *4**
122 Carleton St., Saint John, NB E2L 2Z7
Tel: 506-634-1193; Fax: 506-693-9040

Saint John: **Patrick R. Wilbur - *1**
15 Market Sq., 4th Fl., Saint John, NB E2L 1E8
Tel: 506-658-2580; Fax: 506-658-3061
patrick.wilbur@gnb.ca

Saint John: **Theodore E. Wilson - *1**
#A-112, Prince Edward St., Saint John, NB E2L 4M5
Tel: 506-633-8788; Fax: 506-632-2023
theowil@nb.aibn.com

Shediac: **Michel C. Leger - *2**
Also Known As: Hebert Leger
5, rue Mill, Shediac, NB E4P 2H8
Tel: 506-532-0100; Téléc: 506-532-6332

Shippagan: **Godin, Lizotte, Robichaud, Guignard - *4**
239A J.D Gauthier Blvd., Shippagan, NB E8S 1N2
Tél: 506-336-0400; Téléc: 506-336-0409

Shippagan: **Theriault, Larocque, Boudreau - *3**
Former Name: Theriault, Larocque & Associés
283 J.D. Gauthier Blvd., Shippagan, NB E8S 1N6
Tel: 506-336-4726; Fax: 506-336-1159
tla@nbnet.nb.ca

St Andrews: **David A. Bartlett - *1**
Also Known As: Bartlett & Harrison
Former Name: Larsen & Bartlett
64 King St., St Andrews, NB E5B 1Y3
Tel: 506-529-9000; Fax: 506-529-9003
bartllaw@nb.aibn.com

St George: **Peter A. Johnston Law Office - *2**
4 Main St., St George, NB E5C 3J1
Tel: 506-755-3376; Fax: 506-755-8044
larjon@nbnet.nb.ca

Sussex: **Gary M. Fulton - *1**
30 Church Ave., Sussex, NB E4E 1Y7
Tel: 506-433-4215; Fax: 506-433-4216
lawyers@nbnet.nb.ca

* indicates number of lawyers

Sussex: D. James Garrish - *1
19 Maxwell Dr., Sussex, NB E4S 2S4
Tel: 506-433-8678; Fax: 506-433-6994
jgerrish1@rogers.com

Tracadie-Sheila: Doiron, Lebouthillier, Boudreau, Allain - *4
CP 3010, Stn. Bureau, 3674, rue Principale, Tracadie-Sheila, NB E1X 1G5
Tél: 506-395-0044; Téléc: 506-395-0050
dllb@nbnet.nb.ca

Woodstock: McCue Brewer Dickinson - *3
179 Broadway St., Woodstock, NB E7M 1B7
Tel: 506-325-2835; Fax: 506-328-6248
mblaw@nbnet.nb.ca

Woodstock: Stephen L. Wilson - *1
Former Name: Wilson & Kinney
#1, 733 Main St., Woodstock, NB E7M 2E6
Tel: 506-325-1100; Fax: 506-328-4873
stepwil@nbnet.nb.ca

Newfoundland & Labrador

Bay Roberts: Moores & Collins - *2
Former Name: Moores, Andrews, Collins
P.O. Box 806, 268 Conception Bay Hwy., Bay Roberts, NL A0A 1G0
Fax: 709-786-6952
Toll-Free: 855-786-7114
mac@mac-law.ca
www.mac-law.ca

Bay Roberts: Morrow & Morrow - Bay Roberts - *4
344 Conception Bay Hwy., Bay Roberts, NL A0A 1G0
Tel: 709-786-9207; Fax: 709-786-9507
Toll-Free: 888-786-9207
morrow@nf.aibn.com
www.morrow-law.ca

Carbonear: J. William Finn, Q.C. - *1
66 Powell Dr., Carbonear, NL A1Y 1A5
Tel: 709-596-5143; Fax: 709-596-3208
www.legalservicescbn.com

Channel-Port-aux-Basques: Marks & Parsons - *4
174 Caribou Rd., Channel-Port-aux-Basques, NL A0M 1C0
Tel: 709-695-7341; Fax: 709-695-3944

Clarenville: Hughes & Brannan Law Offices - *2
357 Memorial Dr., Clarenville, NL A5A 1R8
Tel: 709-466-3106; Fax: 709-466-3107
hughes.brannan@nfld.net

Conception Bay South: Robert R. Regular - *2
P.O. Box 14002, Stn. Manuels, 131 Conception Bay Hwy., Conception Bay South, NL A1W 3J1
Tel: 709-834-2132; Fax: 709-834-3025
general@robertregularlaw.com
www.robertregularlaw.com

Corner Brook: Poole Althouse, Barristers & Solicitors - Corner Brook - *9
Former Name: Poole, Althouse, Thompson & Thomas
49 - 51 Park St., Corner Brook, NL A2H 2X1
Tel: 709-634-3136; Fax: 709-634-8247
Toll-Free: 877-634-3136
info@poolealthouse.ca
www.poolealthouse.ca

Corner Brook: Graham Watton - *1
Noton Bldg., P.O. Box 188, 133 Riverside Dr., Corner Brook, NL A2H 6C7
Tel: 709-639-7490; Fax: 709-634-7229

Gander: Easton Hillier Lawrence Preston - *9
Former Name: Easton Facey Hillier Lawrence
Polaris Bldg., 61 Elizabeth Dr., Gander, NL A1V 1G4
Tel: 709-256-4006; Fax: 709-651-2850
Toll-Free: 800-256-4006
info@ganderlawyers.com
www.ganderlawyers.com

Labrador City: Miller & Hearn - *2
P.O. Box 129, Stn. Main, Labrador City, NL A2V 2K3
Tel: 709-944-3666; Fax: 709-944-5494
miller&hearn@crrstv.net

Mount Pearl: Budden, Morris - *4
184 Park Ave., Mount Pearl, NL A1N 1K8
Tel: 709-747-0077; Fax: 709-747-0104
lawyers@buddenmorris.com
www.buddenmorris.com

Paradise: Aylward, Chislett & Whitten - *5
#200, 1655 Topsail Road, Paradise, NL A1L 1V1
Tel: 709-722-6000; Fax: 709-726-1225
contact@acwlaw.ca
www.acwlaw.ca

Paradise: Susan L. Fisher - *1
31 Deborah Lynn Hts., Paradise, NL A1L 3E6
Tel: 709-773-1806; Fax: 709-773-1807

Springdale: Shawn C.A. Colbourne Law Office - *1
8 Juniper Rd., Springdale, NL A0J 1T0
Tel: 709-673-3693; Fax: 709-673-3991
colbourne.5@nf.sympatico.ca

St. John's: Benson Buffett PLC - *17
Former Name: Benson Myles
#900, Atlantic Place, P.O. Box 1538, 200 Water St., St. John's, NL A1C 6C9
Tel: 709-579-2081; Fax: 709-579-2647
Toll-Free: 888-325-3425
info@bensonbuffett.com
www.bensonbuffett.com
www.facebook.com/BensonBuffettLawyers,
www.linkedin.com/company/benson-buffett

St. John's: Browne, Fitzgerald, Morgan & Avis - *4
Former Name: Benson Myles
Terrace on the Square, Level II, P.O. Box 23135, RPO Churchill Sq., St. John's, NL A1B 4J9
Tel: 709-724-3800; Fax: 709-754-3800
info@bfma-law.com
www.bfma-law.com

St. John's: Bussey Horwood - *2
Former Name: Rogers Bussey
#222, Haymarket Square, 233 Duckworth Sq., St. John's, NL A1C 1G8
Tel: 709-753-3557; Fax: 709-753-3525
www.busseyhorwood.ca

St. John's: Curtis Dawe Lawyers - *17
Fortis Building, 139 Water St., 11th Fl., St. John's, NL A1C 5J9
Tel: 709-722-5181; Fax: 709-722-7521
curtisdawe@curtisdawe.com
www.curtisdawe.nf.ca

St. John's: Duffy & Associates
640 Torbay Rd., St. John's, NL A1A 5G9
Tel: 709-726-5298; Fax: 709-726-8883
www.duffylawyers.com

St. John's: Fraize Law Offices - *2
P.O. Box 5217, Stn. C, 268 Duckworth St., St. John's, NL A1C 5W1
Tel: 709-726-7978; Fax: 709-726-8201
tfraize@fraizelawoffices.nf.net

St. John's: French & Associates - *4
Former Name: French, Noseworthy & Associates; French, Dunne & Associates
#122, Elizabeth Towers, 100 Elizabeth Ave., St. John's, NL A1B 1S1
Tel: 709-754-1800
info@french-associates.com
french-associates.com

St. John's: Lewis, Day - *2
#A, 84 Airport Rd., 1st Fl., St. John's, NL A1A 4Y3
Tel: 709-753-2545; Fax: 709-753-2266
Toll-Free: 877-553-2545
admin@lewisday.ca
www.lewisday.ca

St. John's: Lewis, Sinnott, Fitzgerald - *2
Former Name: Lewis, Sinnott, Shortall
#300, TD Place, P.O. Box 884, Stn. C, 140 Water St., St. John's, NL A1C 5L7
Tel: 709-753-7810; Fax: 709-738-2965
www.lssh.ca

St. John's: Martin Whalen Hennebury Stamp - *12
Also Known As: MWHS Law
P.O. Box 5910, 15 Church Hill, St. John's, NL A1C 5X4
Tel: 709-754-1400; Fax: 709-754-0915
info@mwhslaw.com
www.mwhslaw.com

St. John's: John W. Mcgrath - *2
18 Argyle St., St. John's, NL A1A 1V3
Tel: 709-738-2190
jwmcgrath@nf.aibn.com

St. John's: Noonan Piercey - *3
Former Name: Noonan Law
P.O. Box 5303, 339 Duckworth St., St. John's, NL A1C 5W1
Tel: 709-726-9598; Fax: 709-726-9614
www.noonanpiercey.ca

St. John's: O'Brien Anthony White - *3
#300, 53 Bond St., St. John's, NL A1C 1S9
Tel: 709-722-0637; Fax: 709-722-6780
Toll-Free: 888-722-0638
info@obaw.ca
www.obaw.ca

St. John's: O'Dea Earle - *15
P.O. Box 5955, 323 Duckworth St., St. John's, NL A1C 5X4
Tel: 709-726-3524; Fax: 709-726-9600
injury@odeaearle.ca
www.odeaearle.ca
www.facebook.com/odeaearleinjurylawyers

St. John's: Ottenheimer Boone - *2
8 Albany St., St. John's, NL A1E 3C5
Tel: 709-579-7180; Fax: 709-579-1647

St. John's: Roebothan McKay & Marshall - *18
Former Name: Williams, Roebothan, McKay & Marshall
Paramount Building, 34 Harvey Rd., 5th Fl., St. John's, NL A1C 3Y7
Toll-Free: 800-576-2255
www.makethecall.ca

St. John's: Russell Accident Law - *4
Former Name: Ches Crosbie Barristers
169 Water St., St. John's, NL A1C 1B1
Tel: 709-579-4000 Toll-Free: 888-579-3262
info@russellaccidentlaw.com
www.russellaccidentlaw.com

St. John's: Wells & Company - *1
10 Freshwater Rd., St. John's, NL A1E 0A5
Tel: 709-739-7768; Fax: 709-739-4434
www.wellsandcompanynl.com

Stephenville: Fred R. Stagg, Barrister & Solicitor - *1
28 Main St., Stephenville, NL A2N 2Z4
Tel: 709-643-5651; Fax: 709-643-5369
fstagg@frs-law.com

Northwest Territories

Fort Simpson: Rock Matte - *1
P.O. Box 124, 10010 Duplex A, 99A Ave., Fort Simpson, NT X0E 0N0
Tel: 867-695-2000; Fax: 867-695-2000
rockmatte@gmail.com

Hay River: MacDonald & Associates - *2
6 Courtoreille St., Hay River, NT X0E 1G2
Tel: 867-874-6727

Hay River: Stephen M. Shabala - *1
Former Name: Stephen Simpson
#205, 31 Capital Dr., Hay River, NT X0E 1G2
Tel: 867-874-3365; Fax: 867-874-6955

Yellowknife: Kenneth Allison - *1
P.O. Box 2187, Stn. Main, Yellowknife, NT X1A 2P6
Tel: 867-446-8181

Yellowknife: Thomas Boyd - *1
P.O. Box 2788, Stn. Main, Yellowknife, NT XIA 2R1
Tel: 867-873-3904

Yellowknife: Jay Bran - *1
P.O. Box 20034, Yellowknife, NT X1A 3X8
Tel: 867-447-2729
jaybranlaw@gmail.com

Yellowknife: Denroche & Associates - *3
P.O. Box 2910, Stn. Main, 5107 - 53rd. St., Yellowknife, NT X1A 2R2
Tel: 867-920-4151; Fax: 867-920-4252
reception@denrochelaw.ca
www.denrochelaw.ca

Yellowknife: Paul Falvo - *1
P.O. Box 933, Yellowknife, NT X1A 2N7
Tel: 867-669-7285
lawyer@falvo.ca
www.yellowknifedefencelawyer.com
twitter.com/paulfalvo

* indicates number of lawyers

Yellowknife: **Peter C. Fuglsang & Associates - *1**
#104, P.O. Box 2459, Stn. Main, 5103 - 48th St., Yellowknife,
NT XIA 2P8
Tel: 867-444-3641

Yellowknife: **Shannon Gullberg - *1**
#403, 5018 - 49th St., Yellowknife, NT XIA 3R6
Tel: 867-873-6370

Yellowknife: **Keenan Bengts Law Office - *1**
P.O. Box 262, Stn. Main, 5018 - 47th St., Yellowknife, NT X1A
2N2
Tel: 867-873-8631; Fax: 867-920-2511
kbengtslaw@theedge.ca

Yellowknife: **Marshall & Company - *1**
5125 - 48 St., Yellowknife, NT X1A 2N9
Tel: 867-873-4969; Fax: 867-873-6567
amarshall@marshallyk.com
www.marshallyk.com

Yellowknife: **Betty-Lou McIlmoyle - *1**
P.O. Box 11030, 5107 - 53rd St., Lower Floor, Yellowknife, NT
X1A 3X7
Tel: 867-669-0123 Toll-Free: 888-577-2299
www.mcilmoyle.ca

Yellowknife: **Margo L. Nightingale - *1**
P.O. Box 20029, Yellowknife, NT X1A 3X8
Tel: 867-920-2922; Fax: 867-920-2924

Yellowknife: **R. Clark Rehn - *1**
P.O. Box 12, Stn. Main, Yellowknife, NT X1A 2N1
Tel: 867-873-3634

Yellowknife: **Wallbridge Law Office - *1**
P.O. Box 383, 5016 - 47th St., Yellowknife, NT X1A 2N3
Tel: 867-920-4000; Fax: 867-920-7389
www.garthwallbridge.com

Nova Scotia

Amherst: **Beaton Blaikie - *3**
P.O. Box 295, 141 Victoria St. East, Amherst, NS B4H 3Z2
Tel: 902-667-0515; Fax: 902-667-6161
info@bbnflaw.com
www.bbnflaw.com

Amherst: **Hicks LeMoine Law - Amherst - *5**
P.O. Box 279, 15 Princess St., Amherst, NS B4H 3Z2
Tel: 902-667-7214; Fax: 902-667-5886
info@hickslemoine.ca
www.hickslemoine.ca

Annapolis Royal: **Armstrong & Armstrong - *1**
P.O. Box 575, 240 St. George St., Annapolis Royal, NS B0S
1A0
Tel: 902-532-2155; Fax: 902-532-7211

Annapolis Royal: **Patricia L. Reardon - *1**
P.O. Box 366, 234 St. George St., Annapolis Royal, NS B0S
1A0
Tel: 902-532-7904; Fax: 902-532-7775
preardon@ns.aliantzinc.ca

Antigonish: **MacPherson MacNeil Macdonald - *2**
188 Main St., Antigonish, NS B2G 2B9
Tel: 902-863-2925; Fax: 902-863-2925

Antigonish: **William F. Meehan, Q.C. - *1**
P.O. Box 1803, Stn. Main, 195 Main St., Antigonish, NS B2G
2M5
Tel: 902-863-3136; Fax: 902-863-6270

Arichat: **Ivo R. Winter - *1**
P.O. Box 180, 14 Bay St., Arichat, NS B0E 1A0
Tel: 902-226-3711; Fax: 902-226-1837
ivowinter@ns.sympatico.ca

Baddeck: **Daniel T.L. Chiasson - *1**
P.O. Box 567, 137 Upper Twinning St., Baddeck, NS B0E 1B0
Tel: 902-295-1245; Fax: 902-295-2610
dan.baddeck@ns.aliantzinc.ca

Barrington: **G. David Eldridge - *1**
P.O. Box 157, 381 River Rd., Barrington, NS B0W 1E0
Tel: 902-637-2878; Fax: 902-637-2025
eldridgeqc@eastlink.ca

Bedford: **Atlantica Law Group - *22**
Also Known As: ALG Law Group
Atlantic Acres Industrial Park, 2 Bluewater Rd., Bedford, NS
B4B 1G7
Tel: 902-835-6647; Fax: 902-835-3029
Toll-Free: 877-343-9894
halifax@algvip.com
www.algvip.com

Bedford: **Bedford Law - *3**
#100, 1496 Bedford Hwy., Bedford, NS B4A 1E5
Tel: 902-832-2100; Fax: 902-832-2323
bedfordlawreception@gmail.com
www.bedfordlaw.com

Bedford: **Blackburn Law - *6**
Former Name: Blackburn English
#231, Bedford House, Sunnyside Mall, 1595 Bedford Hwy.,
Bedford, NS B4A 3Y4
Tel: 902-883-2264; Fax: 902-835-4310
info@blackburnlaw.ca
www.blackburnlaw.ca

Bedford: **Cameron Rhindress - *1**
Former Name: Rusk & McCay
1394 Bedford Hwy., Bedford, NS B4A 1E2
Tel: 902-835-7444; Fax: 902-835-3819

Bedford: **David G. Barrett Law Inc. - *1**
#404, Sun Tower, 1550 Bedford Hwy., Bedford, NS B4A 1E6
Tel: 902-835-6375; Fax: 902-835-4565
dgbarrett@eastlink.ca
www.barrett-law-inc.com

Bedford: **Gillis & Associates - *2**
Former Name: Gillis & Walden
#310, 1550 Bedford Hwy., Bedford, NS B4A 1E6
Tel: 902-835-6174; Fax: 902-835-1486
Toll-Free: 866-277-3863
www.gillisassociates.ca

Bedford: **Melnick, Doll, Condran - *3**
#302, 1160 Bedford Hwy., Bedford, NS B4A 1C1
Tel: 902-835-2300; Fax: 902-835-2303

Bedford: **Pressé Mason, Barristers & Solicitors - *4**
1254 Bedford Hwy., Bedford, NS B4A 1C6
Tel: 902-832-1175; Fax: 902-832-1856
Toll-Free: 800-630-2254
lawyers@pressemason.ns.ca
www.pressemasonlaw.ca

Bedford: **Resolute Legal - *1**
#204, Southgate Village Professional Centre, 540 Southgate
Dr., Bedford, NS B4A 0C9
Fax: 888-694-7086
Toll-Free: 888-480-9050
resolutelegal.ca
www.facebook.com/ResoluteLegal, twitter.com/Resolute_Legal,
www.linkedin.com/in/davidbrannen

Berwick: **Stewart & Turner - *2**
P.O. Box 208, 196 Cottage St., Berwick, NS B0P 1E0
Tel: 902-538-3123; Fax: 902-538-7933
stewart.turner@ns.sympatico.ca

Berwick: **Waterbury Newton - Berwick - *12**
P.O. Box 475, 188 Commercial St., Berwick, NS B0P 1E0
Tel: 902-538-3168; Fax: 902-538-8680
Toll-Free: 877-559-8585
reception@wnns.ca
www.wnns.ca

Bridgewater: **Power, Leefe, Reddy & Rafuse - *5**
Former Name: Power, Dempsey, Power, Dempsey,
Leefe & Reddy
84 Dufferin St., Bridgewater, NS B4V 2G3
Tel: 902-543-7815; Fax: 902-543-3196
reception@lawpower.ca
lawpower.ca

Bridgewater: **The Law Offices of Timothy A. Reid - *1**
Also Known As: Reid Law Office
176 Aberdeen Rd., Bridgewater, NS B4V 2S9
Tel: 902-543-1303; Fax: 902-543-3243
tareid@ns.sympatico.ca

Bridgewater: **Romneylaw Inc. - *2**
Former Name: Romney & Romney
P.O. Box 368, Stn. Main, 136 Aberdeen Rd., Bridgewater, NS
B4V 2W9
Tel: 902-543-4444; Fax: 902-543-0232
romneylaw1@eastlink.ca

Canning: **Cornwallis Legal Services - *1**
P.O. Box 69, 765 Canard St., Lower Canard, Canning, NS
B0P 1H0
Tel: 902-582-3372; Fax: 902-582-3201

Cheticamp: **Réjean Aucoin - *1**
P.O. Box 328, 15957 Cabot Trail, Cheticamp, NS B0E 1H0
Tel: 902-224-1450; Fax: 902-224-2224
rejean.aucoin@ns.sympatico.ca

Cheticamp: **Carmel A. Lavigne - *1**
P.O. Box 579, 15595 Cabot Trail, Cheticamp, NS B0E 1H0
Tel: 902-224-2551; Fax: 902-224-2555
clavigne@ns.sympatico.ca

Dartmouth: **Bailey & Associates - *3**
#800, 46 Portland St., Dartmouth, NS B2Y 1H4
Tel: 902-465-4888; Fax: 902-465-4844
appointments@baileylawyers.com
www.baileylawyers.com

Dartmouth: **BoyneClarke LLP - *52**
#600, Box Main, P.O. Box 876, 99 Wuse Rd., Dartmouth, NS
B3A 4S5
Tel: 902-469-9500; Fax: 902-463-7500
Toll-Free: 866-339-3400
info@boyneclarke.ca
boyneclarke.com

Dartmouth: **Casey Rodgers Chisholm Penny
Duggan - *10**
Former Name: Casey Rodgers Chisholm Penny
#201, 219 Waverley Rd., Dartmouth, NS B2X 2C3
Tel: 902-434-6181; Fax: 902-434-7737
www.crcplawyers.com
www.facebook.com/caseyrodgerschisholmpennyduggan,
twitter.com/crcplawyers

Dartmouth: **Heritage House Law Office - *7**
92 Ochterloney St., Dartmouth, NS B2Y 1C5
Tel: 902-465-6669; Fax: 902-466-4412
www.heritagelaw.ca

Dartmouth: **Landry McGillivray - *10**
#300, Quaker Landing, P.O. Box 1200, 33 Ochterloney St.,
Dartmouth, NS B2Y 4P5
Tel: 902-463-8800; Fax: 902-463-0590
slg@landrymcgillivray.ca
www.landrymcgillivraylaw.ca

Dartmouth: **Langille & Associates - *1**
#201, P.O. Box 767, Stn. Main, 56 Portland St., Dartmouth,
NS B2Y 3Z3
Tel: 902-463-5200; Fax: 902-465-5200
ken.langille@ns.aliantzinc.ca

Dartmouth: **Donald C. Murray - *1**
#102, 277 Pleasant St., Dartmouth, NS B2Y 4B7
Tel: 902-466-7378; Fax: 902-466-7379
dcmurray@norestdefence.com
www.norestdefence.com

Dartmouth: **Lester Pyne - *1**
194 Caledonia Rd., Dartmouth, NS B2X 1L4
Tel: 902-434-6167; Fax: 902-434-5448

Dartmouth: **Sealy Cornish Coulthard - *4**
#200, 56 Portland St., Dartmouth, NS B2Y 1H2
Tel: 902-466-2500; Fax: 902-463-0500
info@scclaw.ca
scclaw.ca

Dartmouth: **Serbu & Lumsden - *3**
945 Cole Harbour Rd., Dartmouth, NS B2V 1E5
Tel: 902-434-7755; Fax: 902-434-7813
info@serbulumsden.com
www.serbulumsden.com

Dartmouth: **Smith Evans - *3**
Former Name: Owen & Morrison
#604, Queen Sq., 45 Alderney Dr., Dartmouth, NS B2Y 2N6
Tel: 902-463-8100; Fax: 902-465-2581
info@smithevans.ns.ca
www.smithevans.ns.ca

Dartmouth: **Weldon McInnis - *9**
118 Ochterloney St., Dartmouth, NS B2Y 1C7
Tel: 902-469-2421; Fax: 902-463-4452
info@weldonmcinnis.ca
www.weldonmcinnis.ca
www.facebook.com/WM.Barristers.Solicitors,
twitter.com/WeldonMcInnis

* indicates number of lawyers

Digby: Brian E. McConnell - *1
P.O. Box 1239, 3 Birch St., Digby, NS B0V 1A0
Tel: 902-245-5856; *Fax:* 902-245-6800
bmcconnell@ns.aliantzinc.ca

Digby: James L. Outhouse Q.C. - *1
P.O. Box 1567, 78 Water St., Digby, NS B0V 1A0
Tel: 902-245-2551; *Fax:* 902-245-6622
jamesouthouse@ns.aliantzinc.ca

Elmsdale: Quigley's Law Office - *1
P.O. Box 653, 214 Hwy. 214, Elmsdale, NS B2S 1J7
Tel: 902-883-2757; *Fax:* 902-883-4401
kquigleylaw@aol.com

Fall River: Fall River Law Office - *1
3161 Hwy. #2, Fall River, NS B2T 1K6
Tel: 902-886-0151; *Fax:* 902-860-1718
www.fallriverlawoffice.ca

Glace Bay: Crosby, Burke & Macrury
38 Union St., Glace Bay, NS B1A 2P5
Tel: 902-849-3971; *Fax:* 902-849-7009

Glace Bay: McIntyre, Gillis & O'Leary - *1
P.O. Box 187, Stn. Main, 65 Minto St., Glace Bay, NS B1A 5V2
Tel: 902-849-6507; *Fax:* 902-849-0555

Glace Bay: David H. Raniseth - *1
P.O. Box 249, 34 McKeen St., Glace Bay, NS B1A 5B9
Tel: 902-849-0960; *Fax:* 902-849-6512

Greenwood: Proudfoot Law Office Inc. - *1
Former Name: AndersonSinclair
P.O. Box 100, 811 Central Ave., Greenwood, NS B0P 1N0
Tel: 902-765-3301; *Fax:* 902-765-6493
amplaw2@ns.sympatico.ca
dap@davidproudfoot.com

Guysborough: Campbell & MacKeen - *2
P.O. Box 200, 146 Main St., Guysborough, NS B0H 1N0
Tel: 902-533-2644; *Fax:* 902-533-3526

Halifax: Frederick Angus - *1
#435, 5991 Spring Garden Rd., Halifax, NS B3H 1Y6
Tel: 902-420-9595; *Fax:* 902-423-8040

Halifax: Richard G. Arab - *1
Assessment Services, 5151 Terminal Rd., 4th Fl., Halifax, NS B3J 2L6
Tel: 902-424-6091; *Fax:* 902-424-0587
arabg@gov.ns.ca

Halifax: Auld Allen - *3
1452 Dresden Row, Halifax, NS B3J 3T5
Tel: 902-492-3633; *Fax:* 902-492-3655
info@auldallen.com
www.auldallen.com

Halifax: Barss, Hare & Turner - *1
#137, 1657 Barrington St., Halifax, NS B3J 2A1
Tel: 902-423-1249

Halifax: Barteaux Durnford - *6
Former Name: Ritch Durnford, Lawyers
#L106, 1701 Hollis St., Halifax, NS B3J 3M8
Tel: 902-377-2233; *Fax:* 902-377-2234
www.barteauxdurnford.com
www.linkedin.com/company-beta/9330516

Halifax: Blois, Nickerson & Bryson LLP - *14
#1100, P.O. Box 2147, 1645 Granville St., Halifax, NS B3J 3B7
Tel: 902-425-6000; *Fax:* 902-429-7347
www.bloisnickerson.com

Halifax: Burchells LLP - *27
#1800, 1801 Hollis St., Halifax, NS B3J 3N4
Tel: 902-423-6361; *Fax:* 902-420-9326
firm@burchells.ca
www.burchells.ca

Halifax: Burke Thompson - *5
#200, P.O. Box 307, 5162 Duke St., Halifax, NS B3J 2N7
Tel: 902-429-8590; *Fax:* 902-423-2968
www.bmtlaw.ns.ca

Halifax: Evangeline Cain-Grant - *1
6156 Quinpool Rd., Halifax, NS B3L 1A3
Tel: 902-422-3500; *Fax:* 902-422-9660

Halifax: Cantini Law Group
#1700, Purdy's Wharf Tower One, 1959 Upper Water St., Halifax, NS B3J 3N2
Tel: 902-420-9577; *Fax:* 902-482-5210
Toll-Free: 800-606-2529
contact@cantinilaw.com
www.atlanticcanadainjurylawyers.com

Halifax: Cassidy Nearing Berryman - *5
#401, 1741 Brunswick St., Halifax, NS B3J 3X8
Tel: 902-492-1770; *Fax:* 902-423-2485
Toll-Free: 800-792-1770
alexa@cnb.ca
cnb.ca

Halifax: Christie Cuffari Law Office - *1
Former Name: Clare Christie's Law Office
#310, 1657 Barrington St., Halifax, NS B3J 2A1
Tel: 902-422-2297; *Fax:* 902-422-2162

Halifax: Claman Legal Services Limited
#4004, 7071 Bayers Rd., Halifax, NS B3L 2C2
Tel: 902-492-4000; *Fax:* 902-492-4001

Halifax: Crowe Dillon Robinson - *11
#2000, 7075 Bayers Rd., Halifax, NS B3L 2C1
Tel: 902-453-1732; *Fax:* 902-454-9948
www.cdr.ns.ca

Halifax: Gilles J. Deveau - *1
5336 Young St., Halifax, NS B3K 1Z4
Tel: 902-454-4551; *Fax:* 902-454-9154
gilles.deveau@ns.sympatico.ca

Halifax: Kevin P. Downie, Barrister & Solicitor - *1
#402, P.O. Box 580, Stn. Central, 5121 Sackville St., Halifax, NS B3J 2R7
Tel: 902-425-7233; *Fax:* 902-425-2252
kpdownie@accesswave.ca

Halifax: Sally B. Faught - *1
#601, Duke Tower, 5251 Duke St., Halifax, NS B3J 1P3
Tel: 902-423-8200; *Fax:* 902-423-3100
s.faught@ns.sympatico.ca

Halifax: Michael F. Feindel - *1
Nolan Davis Bldg., P.O. Box 22162, Stn. Bayers, 7020 Mumford Rd., Halifax, NS B3L 4T7
Tel: 902-455-7730; *Fax:* 902-455-7739

Halifax: Garson Pink - *1
P.O. Box 1, 1741 Brunswick St., Halifax, NS B3J 3X8
Tel: 902-425-0222; *Fax:* 902-423-4690

Halifax: Gavras & Associates - *2
Former Name: Pavey Gavras Associates
#201, The Maitland Terrace, 2085 Maitland St., Halifax, NS B3K 2Z8
Tel: 902-423-5711; *Fax:* 902-431-9444
jgavras@gavrasassociates.com
gavrasassociates.com

Halifax: Harvey Hebert & Manthorne - *5
Former Name: Harvey & Hebert Affiliated Law Practices
1492 Lower Water St., Halifax, NS B3J 1R9
Tel: 902-492-0614; *Fax:* 902-492-0634
Toll-Free: 877-492-0614
general@harveyhebert.com

Halifax: MacDonald Elliott Legal Services - *2
7071 Bayers Rd., Halifax, NS B3L 2C2
Tel: 902-454-9827; *Fax:* 902-454-7630
macdonaldlegal@hfx.eastlink.ca

Halifax: MacDonald Law Office, Paton & Paton - *1
12 Robert Allen Dr., Halifax, NS B3M 3G8
Tel: 902-457-5111; *Fax:* 902-457-5113
act1@eastlink.ca

Halifax: MacKinnon Buckle Stevenson - *4
Former Name: Beveridge, MacPherson & Buckle
1684 Barrington St., 4th Fl., Halifax, NS B3J 2R7
Tel: 902-423-9143; *Fax:* 902-422-7837

Halifax: McGinty Doucet Walker - *4
Former Name: McGinty Law
#705, Park Lane, Box 227, 5657 Spring Garden Rd., Halifax, NS B3J 3R4
Tel: 902-422-5881; *Fax:* 902-422-5882
info@mdwlaw.ca
mdwlaw.ca

Halifax: McKiggan Hebert Lawyer - *3
#502, Purdy's Wharf, Tower I, 1959 Upper Water St., Halifax, NS B3J 3N2
Tel: 902-423-2050; *Fax:* 902-423-6707
Toll-Free: 888-510-3577
www.mckigganhebert.com
www.facebook.com/136578493034227,
twitter.com/nsinjurylawyers
www.linkedin.com/company/mckiggan-hebert

Halifax: Merrick Jamieson Sterns Washington & Mahody - *8
#503, 5475 Spring Garden Rd., Halifax, NS B3J 3T2
Tel: 902-429-3123; *Fax:* 902-429-3522
www.mjswm.com

Halifax: Metcalf & Company - *5
Benjamin Wier House, 1459 Hollis St., Halifax, NS B3J 1V1
Tel: 902-420-1990; *Fax:* 902-429-1171
www.metcalf.ns.ca

Halifax: Morris Bureau - *3
#307, 6080 Young St., Halifax, NS B3K 5L2
Tel: 902-454-8070; *Fax:* 902-454-7070
www.morrisbureau.com

Halifax: John P. Nisbet - *1
142 Main Ave., Halifax, NS B3M 1B2
Tel: 902-445-3736

Halifax: North Star Immigration Law Inc. - *2
Former Name: Elizabeth Wozniak Inc.
P.O. Box 272, 1684 Barrington St., 5th Fl., Halifax, NS B3J 2N7
Tel: 902-446-4747; *Fax:* 902-446-4745
nsimmigration.ca

Halifax: Noseworthy, Di Costanzo, Diab - *3
Former Name: Thomson, Noseworthy, Di Costanzo
6470 Chebucto Rd., Halifax, NS B3L 1L4
Tel: 902-444-4747; *Fax:* 902-444-4301

Halifax: Patterson Law - Halifax - *43
#2100, 1801 Hollis St., Halifax, NS B3J 3N4
Tel: 902-405-8000; *Fax:* 902-405-8001
Toll-Free: 888-897-2001
contactus@pattersonlaw.ca
www.pattersonlaw.ca
www.facebook.com/PattersonLawNovaScotia,
twitter.com/PattersonLawNS,
www.linkedin.com/company/patterson-law

Halifax: Clyde A. Paul & Associates - *4
349 Herring Cove Rd., Halifax, NS B3R 1V9
Tel: 902-477-2518; *Fax:* 902-479-1482
www.clydepaul.ca

Halifax: Price Havlovic - *2
Former Name: Beatrice A. Havlovic
Halifax, NS
info@pricehavlovic.com
www.pricehavlovic.com

Halifax: Quackenbush Thomson Law - *7
Former Name: Quackenbush, Thomson & Robbins
2571 Windsor St., Halifax, NS B3K 5C4
Tel: 902-492-1655; *Fax:* 902-492-1697
www.qtrlaw.com
twitter.com/QTRLawyer

Halifax: Ritch Williams & Richards Insurance & Marine Law - *11
Former Name: Ritch Durnford, Lawyers; Huestis Ritch
#1200, CIBC Bldg., 1809 Barrington St., Halifax, NS B3J 3K8
Tel: 902-429-3400; *Fax:* 902-422-4713
Toll-Free: 877-896-0706
info@rwrlawyers.com
www.rwrlawyers.ca

Halifax: Joseph S. Roza - *1
#210, 6021 Young St., Halifax, NS B3K 2A1
Tel: 902-425-5111; *Fax:* 902-425-5112
j.roza@ns.sympatico.ca
www.josephroza.com

Halifax: Scaravelli & Associates - *5
#2030, 1801 Hollis St., Halifax, NS B3J 3N4
Tel: 902-429-4104; *Fax:* 902-423-4009
lancescaravelli@eastlink.ca

---

* indicates number of lawyers

Halifax: **Singleton & Associates - *2**
Former Name: Singleton Morrison
#204, 2000 Barrington St., Halifax, NS B3J 3K1
Tel: 902-492-7000; *Fax:* 902-492-4309
tsingleton@singleton.ns.ca
singleton.ns.ca

Halifax: **Stockton, Maxwell & Elliott - *3**
#402, 7020 Mumford Rd., Halifax, NS B3L 4S9
Tel: 902-422-6055; *Fax:* 902-429-7655
stockton@smelaw.ca
www.smelaw.ca

Halifax: **Wagnes Law Firm - *6**
#PH301, Pontac House, P.O. Box 756, Stn. RPO Central,
1869 Upper Water St., 3rd Fl., Halifax, NS B3J 1S9
Tel: 902-425-7330; *Fax:* 902-422-1233
Toll-Free: 800-465-8794
www.wagners.co

Halifax: **Walker Dunlop - *6**
1477 South Park St., Halifax, NS B3J 2L1
Tel: 902-423-8121; *Fax:* 902-429-0621
reception@walkerdunlop.ca
www.walkerdunlop.ca
www.facebook.com/walkerdunloplaw

Halifax: **Walker Law Office Inc. - *1**
Former Name: Walker & Associates
#200, 2742 Robie St., Halifax, NS B3K 4P2
Tel: 902-425-5297; *Fax:* 902-425-5095
reception@walkerlaw.ca
www.walkerlaw.ca

Halifax: **Wickwire Holm - *16**
#300, P.O. Box 1054, 1801 Hollis St., Halifax, NS B3J 2X6
Tel: 902-429-4111; *Fax:* 902-429-8215
Toll-Free: 866-429-4111
wh@wickwireholm.com
www.wickwireholm.com
twitter.com/WickwireHolm

Halifax: **Diane K. Zwicker - *1**
1561 Vernon St., Halifax, NS B3H 3M8
Tel: 902-425-2193
dzwicker@sprint.ca

Kentville: **Astek Legal Services - *1**
P.O. Box 441, Stn. Main, Kentville, NS B4N 3X3
Tel: 902-679-0101; *Fax:* 902-679-0066

Kentville: **Donald C. Fraser - *1**
P.O. Box 668, Stn. Main, 35R Webster St., Kentville, NS B4N 3X9
Tel: 902-678-4006; *Fax:* 902-678-2999
fraser.law@ns.aliantzinc.ca

Kentville: **Manning & Associates - *1**
27 Cornwallis St., Kentville, NS B4N 2E2
Tel: 902-679-1600; *Fax:* 902-679-5122
chris.manning@manningassociates.ca

Kentville: **Muttarts Law Firm - *3**
Also Known As: Muttart Tufts Dewolfe & Coyle
P.O. Box 515, 20 Cornwallis St., Kentville, NS B4N 3X3
Tel: 902-678-2157; *Fax:* 902-678-9455
www.muttartslaw.com

Kentville: **Nathanson Seaman Watts - *7**
Former Name: Forse, Nathanson
24 Webster Crt., Kentville, NS B4N 2E3
Tel: 902-678-1616; *Fax:* 902-678-1615
info@24webster.com
24webster.com

Kentville: **Tayllor MacLellan Cochrane - *12**
Also Known As: TMC Law
50 Cornwallis St., Kentville, NS B4N 2E4
Tel: 902-678-6156; *Fax:* 902-678-6010
Toll-Free: 888-486-2529
lawfirm@tmclaw.com
www.tmclaw.com

Liverpool: **Fownes Law Offices Inc. - Liverpool - *3**
#C, P.O. Box 1739, 190 Main St., Liverpool, NS B0T 1K0
Tel: 902-354-2744; *Fax:* 902-354-2746
www.novascotialaw.com

Lower Sackville: **David F. Farwell - *1**
Former Name: Farwell & Hines
#206, Vogue Optical Plaza, 405 Sackville Dr., Lower Sackville, NS B4C 2R9
Tel: 902-865-5537; *Fax:* 902-865-4354
davidfarwell@ns.sympatico.ca

Lower Sackville: **Robert W. Newman & Associates - *1**
85 Sackville Cross Rd., Lower Sackville, NS B4C 2M2
Tel: 902-864-2722; *Fax:* 902-864-3164

Lower Sackville: **Richardson's Law Office - *2**
#100A, 800 Sackville Dr., Lower Sackville, NS B4E 1R8
Tel: 902-864-2300; *Fax:* 902-864-4410
Toll-Free: 877-304-2300
kim@novalawyer.com
www.novalawyer.com

Lunenburg: **Burke, Macdonald & Luczak - *2**
P.O. Box 549, 28 King St., Lunenburg, NS B0J 2C0
Tel: 902-634-8354
burkelaw@wolffhaus.com
wolffhaus.com

Middleton: **Cole Sawler - *2**
P.O. Box 400, 264 Main St., Middleton, NS B0S 1P0
Tel: 902-825-6288; *Fax:* 902-825-4340
officemanager@colesawlerlaw.ca
www.colesawlerlaw.ca

Middleton: **Durland, Gillis & Schumacher, Associates - *2**
Also Known As: Durland, Gillis
Former Name: Durland Gillis Parker & Richter
P.O. Box 700, 74 Commercial St., Middleton, NS B0S 1P0
Tel: 902-825-3415; *Fax:* 902-825-2522

Musquodoboit Harbour: **Eastern Shore Law Centre - *1**
1653 Ostrea Lake Rd., Musquodoboit Harbour, NS B0J 2L0
Tel: 902-889-2860
easternshorelaw@aol.com
easternshorelawcentre.ca

New Glasgow: **R.A. Balmanoukian - *1**
137 McColl St., New Glasgow, NS B2H 4Z6
Tel: 902-755-3393; *Fax:* 902-755-6373
blackacre@north.nsis.com

New Glasgow: **Goodman MacDonald - *2**
Former Name: Goodman MacDonald Daley
P.O. Box 697, 47 Riverside St., New Glasgow, NS B2H 5G2
Tel: 902-752-5090; *Fax:* 902-755-3545
Toll-Free: 888-253-5455
info@goodmanmacdonald.ca
www.goodmanmacdonald.ca

New Glasgow: **Mac, Mac & Mac - *15**
Former Name: MacIntosh, MacDonnell & MacDonald
#260, Aberdeen Business Centre, Stn. Main, 610 East River Rd., 2nd Fl., New Glasgow, NS B2H 3S2
Tel: 902-752-8441; *Fax:* 902-752-7810
Toll-Free: 888-752-8441
office@macmacmac.ns.ca
macmacmac.ns.ca

New Waterford: **M. Sweeney Hinchey - *1**
3383 Plummer Ave., New Waterford, NS B1H 1Z1
Tel: 902-862-2368; *Fax:* 902-862-9581
hinchems@yahoo.com

North Sydney: **M. Mora B. Maclennan - *1**
33 Archibald Ave., North Sydney, NS B2A 2W6
Tel: 902-794-2060; *Fax:* 902-794-3558
moramaclennan@eastlink.ca

North Sydney: **Michael A. Tobin - *1**
P.O. Box 1925, Stn. Main, 254 Commercial St., North Sydney, NS B2A 3S9
Tel: 902-794-8803; *Fax:* 902-794-9869
miketobinlaw@syd.eastlink.ca

Pictou: **MacLean & MacDonald - *2**
P.O. Box 730, 90 Coleraine St., Pictou, NS B0K 1H0
Tel: 902-485-4347; *Fax:* 902-485-8887
law@macleanmacdonald.com

Pictou: **Scanlan Graham Scanlan - *2**
P.O. Box 1720, 94 Water St., Pictou, NS B0K 1H0
Tel: 902-485-4313; *Fax:* 902-485-5083
sgslaw@ns.sympatico.ca

Port Hawkesbury: **Pickup & MacDowell - *2**
302 Pitt St., Port Hawkesbury, NS B9A 2T8
Tel: 902-625-2500; *Fax:* 902-625-0500
pickupmacdowell@pkpmd.ca
www.pkpmd.ca

Port Hawkesbury: **Robin W. Archibald - *1**
202-15 Kennedy St., Port Hawkesbury, NS B9A 2Y1
Tel: 902-625-2294; *Fax:* 902-625-3060
archibrw@gov.ns.ca

Port Hood: **Francis X. Moloney - *1**
P.O. Box 122, 351 Main St., Port Hood, NS B0E 2W0
Tel: 902-787-3113; *Fax:* 902-787-3105

Pubnico: **d'Entremont & Boudreau - *2**
P.O. Box 118, Pubnico, NS B0W 2W0
Tel: 902-762-3119; *Fax:* 902-762-3124

Shelburne: **Celia J. Melanson, Barristor & Solicitor, Inc. - *1**
P.O. Box 562, 171 Water St., Shelburne, NS B0T 1W0
Tel: 902-875-4188; *Fax:* 902-875-1316
celia.melanson@ns.sympatico.ca
www.celiamelanson.com

Shelburne: **Donald R. Miller - *1**
6767 Shore Rd. RR#3, Shelburne, NS B0T 1W0
Tel: 902-637-2527; *Fax:* 902-637-2165

Shelburne: **Johanne L. Tournier - *1**
Shelburne Industrial Park, 9 Hero Rd., RR#2, Shelburne, NS B0T 1W0
Tel: 902-875-4365; *Fax:* 902-875-4365

Shubenacadie: **Carruthers & MacDonell Law Office Inc. - *3**
#204, Chubenacadie Professional Centre, P.O. Box 280, 5 Mill Village Rd., Shubenacadie, NS B0N 2H0
Tel: 902-758-2591; *Fax:* 902-758-4022
office@carmaclaw.com
easthants.com/law/

Stellarton: **Hector J. MacIsaac - *1**
P.O. Box 849, 195 Foord St., Stellarton, NS B0K 1S0
Tel: 902-752-5143; *Fax:* 902-928-1299

Sydney: **The Breton Law Group - *8**
#300, 292 Charlotte St., Sydney, NS B1P 1C7
Tel: 902-563-1000; *Fax:* 902-563-1113
www.bretonlawgroup.com

Sydney: **Vincent A. Gillis - *1**
P.O. Box 847, Stn. A, 321 Townsend St., Sydney, NS B1P 6J1
Tel: 902-562-3222; *Fax:* 902-539-4199
vagillislaw@ns.sympatico.ca

Sydney: **Khattar & Khattar - *4**
378 Charlotte St., Sydney, NS B1P 1E2
Tel: 902-539-9696; *Fax:* 902-562-7147
Toll-Free: 888-542-8827
law@khattar.ca
www.khattarandkhattarlaw.ca

Sydney: **John G. Khattar - *1**
463 Prince St., Sydney, NS B1P 5L6
Tel: 902-564-6611; *Fax:* 902-564-8805
jkhatter@syd.eastlink.ca

Sydney: **LaFosse MacLeod - *5**
P.O. Box 297, 50 Dorchester St., Sydney, NS B1P 6H1
Tel: 902-563-0025; *Fax:* 902-563-0026
inquiries@lafossemacleod.ca
www.lafossemacleod.ca

Sydney: **Lorway MacEachern - *2**
112 Charlotte St., Sydney, NS B1P 1B9
Tel: 902-539-4447; *Fax:* 902-564-9844
northlaw@eastlink.ca
www.northlawcan.com

Sydney: **MacDonald & MacLennan - *1**
P.O. Box 1148, Stn. A, 205 Charlotte St., 2nd Fl., Sydney, NS B1P 6J7
Tel: 902-564-4429; *Fax:* 902-539-2303

Sydney: **H.F. MacIntyre & Associates - *2**
P.O. Box 788, Stn. A, 245 Charlotte St., Sydney, NS B1P 6J1
Tel: 902-562-4224; *Fax:* 902-562-0606
macintyre.assoc@ns.sympatico.ca

Sydney: **Hugh R. McLeod - *1**
P.O. Box 306, 275 Charlotte St., Sydney, NS B1P 6H2
Tel: 902-539-2261; *Fax:* 902-539-3386
hugh.mcleod@ns.sympatico.ca

Sydney: **John W. Morgan - *1**
#4, 29 Riverdale Dr., Sydney, NS B1R 1P2
Tel: 902-539-2800; *Fax:* 902-562-2554

* indicates number of lawyers

Sydney: Portside Law Office - *4
Former Name: Cusack Law Office
90 Esplanade, Sydney, NS B1P 1A1
Tel: 902-564-5744; Fax: 902-562-0622
www.portsidelawoffice.com

Sydney: Ralph W. Ripley Barrister & Solicitor Inc. - *1
#202, P.O. Box 7, Stn. A, 295 Charlotte St., Sydney, NS B1P 6G9
Tel: 902-564-4446; Fax: 902-539-7765
rripley@ns.aliantzinc.ca

Sydney: M. Joseph Rizzetto - *1
#206, 275 Charlotte St., Sydney, NS B1P 1C6
Tel: 902-562-6262; Fax: 902-539-3567
info@rizzetto.ns.ca

Sydney: Sampson McPhee - *11
Former Name: Sampson McDougall
#200, 66 Wentworth St., Sydney, NS B1P 6T4
Tel: 902-539-2425; Fax: 902-564-0954
mail@sampsonmcphee.com
sampsonmcphee.com

Sydney: Sheldon Nathanson Barristers & Solicitors - *5
P.O. Box 79, Stn. Pier Post., 797 Victoria Rd., Sydney, NS B1N 3B1
Tel: 902-562-1929 Toll-Free: 800-868-1929
sheldonlaw@sheldonnathanson.ca
www.sheldonnathanson.com

Tantallon: Smith-Camp Law - *1
104 Whynacht's Point Rd., Tantallon, NS B3Z 2K9
Tel: 902-826-2193; Fax: 902-826-1043
smithcamplaw@hotmail.com

Truro: Archibald Lederman Barristers - *2
43 Walker St., Truro, NS B2N 4A8
Tel: 902-895-0524; Fax: 902-893-7608
www.archibaldlederman.ca

Truro: Burchell MacDougall Lawyers - Truro - *25
P.O. Box 1128, 710 Prince St., Truro, NS B2N 5H1
Tel: 902-895-1561; Fax: 902-895-7709
Toll-Free: 800-565-1200
truro@burchellmacdougall.com
www.burchellmacdougall.com
www.facebook.com/burmaclawyers, twitter.com/burmaclawyers,
www.linkedin.com/company/burchell-macdougall-lawyers

Truro: David F. Curtis Q.C. - *1
#202, 640 Prince St., Truro, NS B2N 1G4
Tel: 902-895-0528; Fax: 902-893-1158
dcurtislaw@ns.aliantzinc.ca

Truro: Melinda J. MacLean, Q.C. - *1
779 Prince St., Truro, NS B2N 5B6
Tel: 902-895-2866; Fax: 902-897-9890

Truro: McLellan, Richards & Bégin - *3
P.O. Box 1064, 779 Prince St., Truro, NS B2N 5G9
Tel: 902-895-4417; Fax: 902-897-9890
Toll-Free: 866-600-0011
www.truro-law.com

Truro: Gerard P. Scanlan - *1
P.O. Box 1228, Stn. Main, 640 Prince St., Truro, NS B2N 5N2
Tel: 902-895-9249; Fax: 902-893-3078
scanpayn@eastlink.ca

Truro: Yuill Chisholm Killawee - *2
541 Prince St., Truro, NS B2N 1E8
Tel: 902-893-0243; Fax: 902-897-0282

Westville: S. Charles Facey, Q.C. - *1
P.O. Box 610, 1912 Drummond Rd., Westville, NS B0K 2A0
Tel: 902-396-4191; Fax: 902-396-3606
charles.facey@ns.sympatico.ca

Windsor: How Lawrence White Bowes - *3
P.O. Box 3177, 98 Gerrish St., Windsor, NS B0N 2T0
Tel: 902-798-5997; Fax: 902-798-8925
jjwhite@scotialaw.com
www.scotialaw.com

Windsor: Nelson Law - *2
Former Name: Nelson Gardiner
P.O. Box 2018, 258 King St., Windsor, NS B0N 2T0
Tel: 902-798-5797; Fax: 902-798-2332
office@nelson-law.ca

Wolfville: Kimball Law - Wolfville - *4
Former Name: Kimball Brogan Law Office
121 Front St., Wolfville, NS B4P 1A6
Tel: 902-542-5757; Fax: 902-542-5759
Toll-Free: 800-294-7851
info@kimballlaw.ca
www.kimballlaw.ca

Wolfville: LJM Environmental Law & Consulting - *1
P.O. Box 2279, Wolfville, NS B4P 2N5
Tel: 902-670-1113; Fax: 902-542-7315
info@ljmenvironmental.ca
www.ljmenvironmental.ca

Yarmouth: R.K. Murray Judge - *1
#201, 164 Main St., Yarmouth, NS B5A 1C2
Tel: 902-742-7827; Fax: 902-742-0676
murray.judge@nslegalaid.ca

Nunavut

Cambridge Bay: Legal Services Board of Nunavut - Cambridge Bay
Kitikmeot Law Centre, 25 Mitik St., Cambridge Bay, NU X0B 0C0
Tel: 867-983-2906 Toll-Free: 866-240-4006
www.nulas.ca

Iqaluit: Nunavut Tunngavik Inc. - *1
P.O. Box 638, Iqaluit, NU X0A 0H0
Tel: 867-975-4952; Fax: 867-975-4949
mbelleau@tunngavik.com

Iqaluit: Michael Chandler - *1
P.O. Box 2021, Iqaluit, NU X0A 0H0
Tel: 867-979-3505; Fax: 867-979-3506

Iqaluit: Crawford Law Office
Bulding 691B, P.O. Box 747, Iqaluit, NU X0A 0H0
Tel: 867-979-0678; Fax: 800-886-6590
administration@nunavutlegal.com
www.nunavutlegal.com

Iqaluit: Violet Ford - *1
Iqaluit, NU
www.linkedin.com/in/violet-ford-5562953a

Iqaluit: Michael H. Penner - *1
P.O. Box 11032, 2475 Kalla St., Iqaluit, NU X0A 1H0
Tel: 888-979-5777; Fax: 866-387-9580
www.linkedin.com/in/michael-penner-4b1a5939

Iqaluit: Sara R. Siebert - *1
P.O. Box 685, Iqaluit, NU X0A 0H0
Tel: 867-222-9264
sara@siebertlaw.com

Ontario

Ajax: Ajax Law Chambers - *2
#206, 158 Harwood Ave. South, Ajax, ON L1S 2H6
Tel: 905-683-1042; Fax: 905-683-7794
Toll-Free: 800-801-4602
johntlaw@rogers.com
alclaw.ca

Ajax: Daniel J. Balena - *1
Hunt Street Professional Building, 110 Hunt St., Ajax, ON L1S 1P5
Tel: 905-897-4321; Fax: 905-683-4610
info@danielbalena.com
www.danielbalena.com

Ajax: Foden & Doucette - *4
575 Kingston Rd. West, Ajax, ON L1S 6M1
Tel: 905-428-8200; Fax: 905-428-8666
info@fodenanddoucette.com
www.fodenanddoucette.com

Ajax: Glover & Associates - Ajax - *3
Former Name: Glover, Darryl T.G
562 Kingston Rd. West, Ajax, ON L1T 3A2
Tel: 905-619-3700; Fax: 905-619-0022
info@gloverlaw.ca
www.gloverlaw.ca

Ajax: Greening & Bucknam - *1
#202, 50 Commercial Ave., Ajax, ON L1S 2H5
Tel: 905-683-7037; Fax: 905-683-7627
bucknam@rogers.com

Ajax: Jennifer Hirlehey & Associates - *1
7 Mill St., Ajax, ON L1Z 6J8
Tel: 905-427-8082; Fax: 905-427-8084
info@hirleheylaw.ca
www.hirleheylaw.ca

Ajax: Reilly & Partners - *4
Former Name: Reilly D'Heureux Lanzi LLP
555 Kingston Rd. West, 2nd Fl., Ajax, ON L1S 6M1
Tel: 905-427-4077; Fax: 905-427-4042
www.reillyandpartners.com
www.facebook.com/reillyandpartners

Ajax: Juanita Wislesky - *1
#202, 15 Harwood Rd. Ave. South, Ajax, ON L1S 2B9
Tel: 905-686-1686
juanita_wislesky@yahoo.com

Ajax: George D. Wright - *1
543 Kingston Rd. West, Ajax, ON L1S 6M1
Tel: 905-427-7200; Fax: 905-427-2999

Alexandria: Jean-Marc Lefebvre, Q.C. - *2
32 Main St. North, Alexandria, ON K0C 1A0
Tel: 613-525-1358; Fax: 613-525-3411
lefebvre@bellnet.ca
www.lefebvrelaw.com

Allenford: Richard R. Evans - *1
P.O. Box 14, 7771 Hwy. 21, Allenford, ON N0H 1A0
Tel: 519-934-2875; Fax: 519-934-1460
rrevans@bmts.com

Alliston: John W. Clarke - *1
#3, P.O. Box 408, Stn. Main, 103 Victoria St. West, Alliston, ON L9R 1V6
Tel: 705-435-4301; Fax: 705-435-3407

Alliston: Feehely, Gastaldi - *4
P.O. Box 399, 2 Victoria St. East, Alliston, ON L9R 1V6
Tel: 705-435-4386; Fax: 705-435-9256
gastaldi@feehelygastaldi.com

Alliston: Mary L. Galbraith - *1
Former Name: Darling, Smith, McLean
22 Church St. South, Alliston, ON L9R 1V9
Tel: 705-435-4324; Fax: 705-435-2628

Alliston: Gilmore & Gilmore - *2
P.O. Box 250, 458 Victoria St. East, Alliston, ON L9R 1V5
Tel: 705-435-4339; Fax: 705-435-6520
Toll-Free: 877-855-3425
info@gilmoreandgilmore.com
www.gilmoreandgilmore.com
twitter.com/JamieMGilmore

Alliston: James W. Smith - *1
P.O. Box 730, Stn. Main, 8 Victoria St. East, Alliston, ON L9R 1T4
Tel: 705-435-0160; Fax: 705-435-5049
jsmith@bellnet.ca

Almonte: Canadian Hydro Components Ltd. - *1
P.O. Box 640, 16 Main St., Almonte, ON K0A 1A0
Tel: 613-256-1983; Fax: 613-256-4235
plemay@canadianhydro.com

Almonte: Elizabeth A. Swarbrick - *4
#107, P.O. Box 639, 83 Little Bridge St., Almonte, ON K0A 1A0
Tel: 613-256-9811; Fax: 613-256-9814
elizabeth@familyfocusedlaw.com
www.familyfocusedlaw.com

Almonte: Evelyn Wheeler - *1
P.O. Box 1540, 38 Mill St., Almonte, ON K0A 1A0
Tel: 613-256-4148; Fax: 613-256-4708
info@evelynwheeler.com
www.evelynwheeler.com

Amherstburg: Baker Busch - Amherstburg - *2
41 Sandwich St. South, Amherstburg, ON N9V 1Z5
Tel: 519-736-2154; Fax: 519-736-2466
info@bakerbusch.ca
www.bakerbusch.ca

Amherstview: William E.M. Vince - *1
6 Speers Blvd., #G, Amherstview, ON K7N 1Z6
Tel: 613-389-6727; Fax: 613-389-6256
vincelaw@cogeco.net

Ancaster: G. Kevin Eggleton - *1
#S110, 911 Golf Links Rd., Ancaster, ON L9K 1H9
Tel: 905-304-5297; Fax: 905-304-7711

* indicates number of lawyers

Ancaster: Randy L. Levinson - *1
58 Cumming Ct., Ancaster, ON L9G 1V3
Tel: 905-648-7239; Fax: 905-648-4437
randy@randylevinson.com
www.randylevinson.com

Ancaster: Wynne, Dingwall, Pringle & Kovacs - *4
Former Name: Wynne, Dingwall & Pringle; Wynne &
Dingwall
231 Wilson St. East, #B, Ancaster, ON L9G 2B8
Tel: 905-648-1851; Fax: 905-648-1715
www.anclaw.com

Angus: Gordon R. MacKenzie Professional
Corporation - *1
Former Name: MacKenzie, Greenfield
#A, P.O. Box 600, 189 Mill St., Angus, ON L0M 1B2
Tel: 705-424-1331; Fax: 705-424-6441
info@yourlocallawyer.com
www.yourlocallawyer.com

Annan: Alan E. Marsh - *1
RR #2, Annan, ON N0H 1B0
Tel: 519-371-8373; Fax: 519-371-8971
alanmarsh@gbtel.ca

Arnprior: C.P. Merla - *1
#4, 75 Elgin St. West, Arnprior, ON K7S 3T9
Tel: 613-623-6593; Fax: 613-623-8947

Aurora: Allan Law - *2
15393 Yonge St., Aurora, ON L4G 1P1
Tel: 905-895-3425; Fax: 905-726-3098
www.allanlaw.ca

Aurora: Boland Howe LLP - Aurora - *4
222 Edward St., Aurora, ON L4G 1W6
Fax: 905-841-7128
Toll-Free: 844-837-6583
info@bolandhowe.com
www.bolandhowe.com
www.facebook.com/bolandhowellp, twitter.com/bolandhowe

Aurora: Di Cecco Law - *1
Former Name: Di Cecco, Jones
#205, 15171 Yonge St., Aurora, ON L4G 1M1
Tel: 905-751-1517; Fax: 905-751-1518
info@diceccolaw.com
www.diceccolaw.com

Aurora: Michelle E. Hubert - *1
10 Mosley St., Aurora, ON L4G 1G6
Tel: 905-727-3127
Michelle.E.Hubert@gmail.com
www.facebook.com/MichelleEHubert,

Aurora: Laurion Law Office - *1
41 Wellington St. East, Aurora, ON L4G 1H6
Tel: 905-841-2222; Fax: 905-841-3388
jlaurion@laurionlaw.com

Aurora: McPherson & Lewis - *2
Former Name: McPherson, Thomas & Associates
P.O. Box 338, 15220 Yonge St., Aurora, ON L4G 3H4
Tel: 905-727-3151; Fax: 905-841-2164

Aurora: Peddle & Pollard LLP - *2
#102, 15449 Yonge St., Aurora, ON L4G 1P3
Tel: 905-727-1361; Fax: 905-727-9395
info@peddlepollard.ca
www.peddlepollard.ca

Aurora: Sorley & Still - *5
15064 Yonge St., Aurora, ON L4G 1M2
Tel: 905-726-9956; Fax: 905-726-9957
www.sorleyandstill.com

Aurora: Barry W. Switzer - *1
15187 Yonge St., Aurora, ON L4G 1L8
Tel: 905-727-9488; Fax: 905-841-8647
www.barrywswitzer.ca

Aylmer: Doyle & Prendergast - *2
10 Sydenham St. East, Aylmer, ON N5H 1L2
Tel: 519-773-3105; Fax: 519-765-1728

Aylmer: Gloin, Hall & Shields - *2
139 Talbot St. East, Aylmer, ON N5H 1H3
Tel: 519-773-9221; Fax: 519-765-1885
ghsaylaw@amtelecom.net

Bancroft: Lorne C. Plater - *1
P.O. Box 1150, 129 Hastings St. North, Bancroft, ON K0L
1C0
Tel: 613-332-1605; Fax: 613-332-2619
www.bancroftlawyer.ca

Barrie: Nancy Lee Allison - *1
285 Grove St. East, Barrie, ON L4M 2R2
Tel: 705-737-5702

Barrie: John G. Alousis - *1
76 Mulcaster St., Barrie, ON L4M 3M4
Tel: 705-735-0065; Fax: 705-735-0277
contact@alousislaw.com
www.alousislaw.com

Barrie: Peter D. Archibald - *1
P.O. Box 907, 59 Collier St., Barrie, ON L4M 4Y6
Tel: 705-726-4511; Fax: 705-726-0613
pda@bconnex.net

Barrie: Barriston LLP - Barrie - Mulcaster St. - *24
Former Name: Barriston Law
90 Mulcaster St., Barrie, ON L4M 4Y5
Tel: 705-792-9200; Fax: 705-721-4025
www.barristonlaw.com
www.facebook.com/barristonlaw, twitter.com/BarristonLLP,
www.linkedin.com/company/barriston-llp

Barrie: Boswell Chapman - *2
#301, 135 Bayfield St., Barrie, ON L4M 3B3
Tel: 705-719-2200; Fax: 705-719-2265
boswellchapman.com

Barrie: Thomas Bryson - *1
11 Sophia St. West, Barrie, ON L4N 1H9
Tel: 705-728-2232; Fax: 705-728-7525
info@brysonlaw.ca
www.brysonlaw.ca

Barrie: Peter C. Card - *1
#621, 80 Bradford St., Barrie, ON L4N 6S7
Tel: 705-737-9179; Fax: 705-737-1380

Barrie: Carroll Heyd Chown LLP - *11
P.O. Box 5481, 109 Ferris Lane, Barrie, ON L4M 4T7
Tel: 705-722-4400; Fax: 705-722-0704
admin@chcbarristers.com
www.chcbarristers.com
www.facebook.com/CarrollHeydChownLLP,
twitter.com/CHCBarristers,
www.linkedin.com/company/carroll-heyd-chown-llp

Barrie: Cowan & Carter - *1
P.O. Box 722, 107 Collier St., Barrie, ON L4M 4Y5
Tel: 705-728-4521; Fax: 705-728-8744

Barrie: Cugelman & Eisen - *2
#100, 89 Collier St., Barrie, ON L4M 1H2
Tel: 705-721-1888; Fax: 705-721-7755
help@celaw.ca
celaw.ca

Barrie: Alfred W.J. Dick - *1
P.O. Box 758, 90 Mulcaster St., Barrie, ON L4M 4Y5
Tel: 705-725-4900; Fax: 705-721-4025
adick@barristonlaw.com

Barrie: Julianne Ecclestone - *1
80 Worsley St., Barrie, ON L4M 1L8
Tel: 705-725-8050; Fax: 705-722-0189
sandra@jecclestone.ca

Barrie: Galbraith Family Law - *4
Former Name: Brian G. Galbraith
124 Dunlop St. West, Barrie, ON L4N 1B1
Tel: 705-727-4242; Fax: 705-727-4240
Brian@GalbraithFamilyLaw.com
www.galbraithfamilylaw.com
www.facebook.com/GalbraithFamilyLaw,
twitter.com/GalbraithFamLaw,

Barrie: Jacoby & Jacoby - *2
34 Clapperton St., Barrie, ON L4M 4T5
Tel: 705-726-0238; Fax: 705-726-9197
info@jacobylaw.ca
jacobylaw.ca

Barrie: Mark A. Kelly - *1
43 Worsley St., Barrie, ON L4M 1L7
Tel: 705-739-6955; Fax: 705-739-6956
www.markkellylaw.com

Barrie: Peter Lamprey - *1
#204, 85 Bayfield St., Barrie, ON L4M 3A7
Tel: 705-722-1114; Fax: 705-720-1155
www.plamprey.com

Barrie: R. John Mitchell - *1
40 Clapperton St., Barrie, ON L4M 3E7
Tel: 705-726-8855
www.johnmitchelllaw.ca

Barrie: Murray Ralston Lawyers - *3
Also Known As: Murray Ralston Professional
Corporation
576 Bryne Dr., #O, Barrie, ON L4N 9P6
Tel: 705-737-3229; Fax: 705-737-5380
admin@murrayralston.com
www.murrayralston.com
www.facebook.com/MurrayRalstonLawyers,
twitter.com/MurrayRalston

Barrie: Gerald E. Norman - *1
P.O. Box 732, 99 Bayfield St., Barrie, ON L4M 4Y5
Tel: 705-726-2772; Fax: 705-734-1942

Barrie: Owen & Associates Law - *4
Former Name: Owen, Harris-Lowe
26 Owen St., Barrie, ON L4M 4Y6
Tel: 705-726-1181; Fax: 705-726-1463
odlaw@owendickey.com
www.owendickey.com
twitter.com/OAL_Barrie

Barrie: Michael E. Reed - *1
Also Known As: Michael Reed Law
105 Collier St., Barrie, ON L4M 1H2
Tel: 705-726-4300; Fax: 705-725-7910
michael@michaelreedlaw.com
www.michaelreedlaw.com

Barrie: Catherine A. Rogers - *1
78 Mulcaster St., Barrie, ON L4M 3M4
Tel: 705-734-2800; Fax: 705-734-2807

Barrie: Charles F. Ruttan - *1
23 Owen St., Barrie, ON L4M 3G8
Tel: 705-737-0688; Fax: 705-722-4749
chuckruttan@ruttanlaw.ca

Barrie: Mark Scharf - *1
103 Collier St., Barrie, ON L4M 1H2
Tel: 705-728-0555; Fax: 705-722-3741
mscharf@bellnet.ca

Barrie: Eric C. Taves - *1
P.O. Box 295, 86 Worsley St., Barrie, ON L4M 4T2
Tel: 705-728-4770; Fax: 705-728-7642
etaves@etaves-law.com

Barrie: Wall, Armstrong & Green - *3
#B, 375 Yonge St., Barrie, ON L4N 4C9
Tel: 705-722-7272; Fax: 705-722-3568
info@wall-arm.ca
www.wall-arm.ca
www.facebook.com/wallarmstrongandgreen

Beamsville: Monty G. Vandeyar - *1
#7, Lincoln Kingsway Plaza, P.O. Box 489, 5041 King St.,
Beamsville, ON L0R 1B0
Tel: 905-563-8818; Fax: 905-563-7750

Beaverton: Woodcock & Tomlinson - Beaverton - *1
P.O. Box 512, 402 Simcoe St., Beaverton, ON L0K 1A0
Tel: 705-426-7317; Fax: 705-426-5740
stephenwoodcock@rogers.com
www.woodcockandtomlinson.com

Belle River: John L. Deziel - *1
531 Notre Dame St., Belle River, ON N0R 1A0
Tel: 519-728-2000; Fax: 519-728-4599
Toll-Free: 800-501-3494

Belleville: Wendy J. Elliott - *1
187B North Front St., Belleville, ON K8P 3C1
Tel: 613-966-0394; Fax: 613-966-1307
wjelliott@hotmail.com

Belleville: Hurley & Williams - *2
112 Front St., Belleville, ON K8N 2Y7
Tel: 613-966-4614; Fax: 613-966-6182
www.hwlaw.ca

indicates number of lawyers

Belleville: Kafka, Kort Barristers - *3
309 Front St., Belleville, ON K8N 5A2
Tel: 613-968-3416; Fax: 613-968-3417
Toll-Free: 888-355-2352
contactus@kafkakort.com
www.kafkakort.com

Belleville: Richard R. Ketcheson - *1
#200, 199 Front St., Belleville, ON K8N 5H5
Tel: 613-966-1123; Fax: 613-966-0478

Belleville: O'Flynn Weese LLP - *11
Former Name: O'Flynn, Weese & Tausendfreund LLP
65 Bridge St. East, Belleville, ON K8N 1L8
Tel: 613-966-5222; Fax: 613-966-7991
info@owtlaw.com
www.owtlaw.com

Belleville: Procter Professional Corporation - *4
Former Name: Procter, Cameron
#204, P.O. Box 700, 365 Front St. North, Belleville, ON K8N 5B3
Tel: 613-962-2584; Fax: 613-962-0968
wprocter@procterlaw.ca

Belleville: Reynolds O'Brien LLP - *5
183 Front St., Belleville, ON K8N 2Y9
Tel: 613-966-3031; Fax: 613-966-2390
info@reynoldsobrien.com
www.reynoldsobrien.com

Belleville: Peter A. Robertson - *1
#101, 3 Applewood Dr., Belleville, ON K8P 4E3
Tel: 613-969-9611; Fax: 613-969-9775
Toll-Free: 800-561-6385

Belleville: C. Roderick Rolston - *1
#202, 175 Front St., Belleville, ON K8N 2Y9
Tel: 613-962-9154; Fax: 613-962-8109
Toll-Free: 800-361-4437

Belleville: Templeman Menninga LLP - Belleville - *32
#200, P.O. Box 234, 205 Dundas St. East, Belleville, ON K8N 5A2
Tel: 613-966-2620; Fax: 613-966-2866
info@tmlegal.ca
www.tmlegal.ca

Belleville: Berend Van Huizen - *1
210 Church St., Belleville, ON K8N 3C3
Tel: 613-962-8645; Fax: 613-962-7689
berend@berendvanhuizenlaw.com
www.berendvanhuizenlaw.com

Blenheim: Kerr Wood & Mallory - *2
Former Name: Kerr & Wood
P.O. Box 1150, 15 George St., Blenheim, ON N0P 1A0
Tel: 519-676-5465; Fax: 519-676-3918
info@kwmlaw.ca
www.kwmlaw.ca
www.facebook.com/kwmlawblenheim

Bobcaygeon: Robert J. Walker - *1
P.O. Box 243, 4 King St. West, Bobcaygeon, ON K0M 1A0
Tel: 705-738-3588; Fax: 705-738-4252
rwalker@llf.ca

Bolton: Jean P. Carberry - *1
34 Queen St., Bolton, ON L4E 1B3
Tel: 905-857-2332; Fax: 905-857-2367
jpclaw@jpclaw.ca

Bolton: W. Ross Milliken - *1
P.O. Box 225, 49 Queen St. North, Bolton, ON L7E 5T2
Tel: 905-857-2835; Fax: 905-857-0097
ross.milliken@boltonlaw.ca
www.rossmilliken.com

Bolton: Neiman, Callegari - *2
#H3, 18 King St. East, Bolton, ON L7E 1E8
Tel: 905-857-0095; Fax: 905-857-0488
neimancallegari@gmail.com
www.neimancallegari.ca

Bolton: Mark E. Penfold - *1
49 Queen St. North, Bolton, ON L7E 5T2
Tel: 905-857-2835
mark.penfold@boltonlaw.ca
www.boltonlaw.ca

Bowmanville: William Brown - *1
P.O. Box 1, 71 Mearns Court, Bowmanville, ON L1C 4N4
Tel: 905-623-3305; Fax: 905-623-3287

Bracebridge: Ronald G. Burk - *1
32 Wharf Rd., Bracebridge, ON P1L 2A7
Tel: 705-645-3007; Fax: 705-645-3998
rgburklaw@on.aibn.com

Bracebridge: Brian G. Jacques - *1
P.O. Box 1227, 14 Ontario St., Bracebridge, ON P1L 1V4
Tel: 705-645-8743; Fax: 705-645-8895
brianjacqueslaw@bellnet.ca

Bracebridge: Lee Roche & Kerr - *2
Former Name: Lee, Roche & Kelly
P.O. Box 990, 6 Dominion St., Bracebridge, ON P1L 1V2
Tel: 705-645-2286; Fax: 705-645-5541
www.lrklaw.ca

Bracebridge: Penelope A. Lithgow - *1
58 Ontario St., Bracebridge, ON P1L 1S5
Tel: 705-645-8118

Bracebridge: Brian E. Slocum - *1
63 Quebec St., Bracebridge, ON P1L 2A4
Tel: 705-645-2900; Fax: 705-645-2549
slocum@slocumlaw.com

Bracebridge: Bruce McLeod Thompson - *1
3 Dominion St., Bracebridge, ON P1L 1T5
Tel: 705-646-1000; Fax: 705-646-9510
Toll-Free: 800-661-8080

Bracebridge: Wylaw Professional Corporation - Bracebridge - *2
Former Name: Wyjad Fleming Associates
P.O. Box 177, 39 Dominion St., Bracebridge, ON P1L 1T6
Tel: 705-645-8787; Fax: 705-645-3390
bracebridge@wylaw.ca
www.wylaw.ca

Bradford: Evans deVries Higgins LLP - *3
Former Name: Evans & Evans
P.O. Box 190, 21 Holland St. West, Bradford, ON L3Z 2A8
Tel: 905-775-3381; Fax: 905-775-8835
info@edhlaw.ca
www.edhlaw.ca

Bradford: Gaska & Ballantyne-Gaska - *2
P.O. Box 1677, Stn. Main, 60 Barrie St., Bradford, ON L3Z 2B9
Tel: 905-775-0015; Fax: 905-775-7772
ballantyne.gaska@rogers.com

Bradford: E. Pauline Taylor - *1
76 Holland St. West, Bradford, ON L3Z 2B6
Tel: 905-775-9606; Fax: 905-775-0692

Brampton: Linda B. Alexander - *1
#201, 197 County Court Blvd., Brampton, ON L6W 4P6
Tel: 905-450-7757; Fax: 905-455-9190
lba@lindaalexander.com
lindaalexander.com

Brampton: Bowyer, Greenslade, Webster, Allison LLP, Barristers, Solicitors - *3
#600, 24 Queen St. East, Brampton, ON L6V 1A3
Tel: 905-451-1300; Fax: 905-451-4451

Brampton: Edmond O. Brown - *1
#602, 205 County Court Blvd., Brampton, ON L6W 4L2
Tel: 905-454-4141; Fax: 905-866-5575
edmondbrown@rogers.com
www.edmondbrown.com

Brampton: Connon & Iacobelli - *2
21 John St., Brampton, ON L6W 1Z1
Tel: 905-454-3070; Fax: 905-454-2964
connon-iacobelli@on.aibn.com
www.connoniacobelli.com/en/

Brampton: Crawford Chondon & Partners LLP - *11
#500, 24 Queen St. East, Brampton, ON L6V 1A3
Tel: 905-874-9343; Fax: 905-874-1384
Toll-Free: 877-874-9343
info@ccpartners.ca
www.ccpartners.ca
twitter.com/CrawfordChondon,
www.linkedin.com/company/crawford-chondon-&-partners-llp

Brampton: Dale Streiman Law LLP - *8
Former Name: Dale, Streiman & Kurz
480 Main St. North, Brampton, ON L6V 1P8
Tel: 905-455-7300; Fax: 905-455-5848
Toll-Free: 866-219-8109
www.dalestreimanlaw.com
www.facebook.com/dalestreimanlaw,
twitter.com/DaleStreimanLaw,
www.linkedin.com/company/1139736

Brampton: Dalzell & Waite - *2
Former Name: Dalzell, Inglis, Waite
#19, 1 Bartley Bull Pkwy., Brampton, ON L6W 3T7
Tel: 905-454-2288; Fax: 905-454-2297

Brampton: Davis Webb LLP - Brampton - *8
Former Name: Davis Webb Schulze & Moon LLP
#800, 24 Queen St. East, Brampton, ON L6V 1A3
Tel: 905-451-6714; Fax: 905-454-1876
www.daviswebb.com

Brampton: Fader Furlan Moss LLP - *6
#101, 197 County Court Blvd., Brampton, ON L6W 4P6
Tel: 905-459-6160; Fax: 905-459-4606
Toll-Free: 877-468-8494
www.faderfurlanmoss.com

Brampton: Folkes Law Legal Professional Corporation - Brampton - *1
Former Name: Folites Legal Professional Corporation; Ron E. Folkes
#900, 21 Queen St. East, Brampton, ON L6W 3P1
Tel: 905-457-2118; Fax: 905-457-3707
Toll-Free: 877-457-2118
ronefolkes@folkeslaw.ca
www.folkeslaw.ca
www.facebook.com/Folkes-Law-434236576667100,
twitter.com/FolkesLaw, www.linkedin.com/in/ronefolkes

Brampton: Pina Grella - *1
#101, 8501 Mississauga Rd., Brampton, ON L6Y 5G8
Tel: 905-453-6000; Fax: 905-453-6016
pina@grellalaw.com

Brampton: Hillier & Hillier Personal Injury Lawyers - *2
165 Main St. North, Brampton, ON L6X 1N1
Tel: 905-453-8636; Fax: 905-453-6267
www.avahillier.ca

Brampton: Stephen A. Holmes - *1
180 Queen St. West, 2nd Fl., Brampton, ON L6X 1A8
Tel: 905-796-3030; Fax: 905-796-2157
sholmes@on.aibn.com
www.stephenholmeslawoffice.com

Brampton: Hope & Henderson Law Office - *2
Former Name: Henderson Law Office
253 Main St. North, Brampton, ON L6X 1N3
Tel: 905-451-7700; Fax: 905-451-6620

Brampton: Vincent V. Houvardas - *1
#1802, 83 Kennedy Rd. South, Brampton, ON L3W 3P3
Tel: 905-455-9970; Fax: 905-455-6148
vhlaw@rogers.com
www.vhlegal.ca

Brampton: Kania Lawyers
223 Main St. North, Brampton, ON L6X 1N2
Tel: 905-451-3222; Fax: 905-451-1267
Toll-Free: 877-485-2642
www.kanialawyers.com

Brampton: Lawrence, Lawrence, Stevenson LLP - *11
Also Known As: Lawrences Lawyers
43 Queen St. West, Brampton, ON L6Y 1L9
Tel: 905-451-3040; Fax: 905-451-5058
lls@lawrences.com
www.lawrences.com
www.linkedin.com/company/lawrence-lawrence-stevenson-llp

Brampton: Douglas R. Lent - *1
38 Queen St. West, Brampton, ON L6X 1A1
Tel: 905-457-4215; Fax: 905-457-6454

Brampton: Ritchie J. Linton - *1
182 Queen St. West, Brampton, ON L6X 1A8
Tel: 905-453-3145; Fax: 905-454-2270

Brampton: June A. Maresca - *1
#100, Central West Region-Peel Regional Municipality, 7755 Hurontario St., Brampton, ON L6W 4T6
Tel: 905-456-4833; Fax: 905-456-4829

indicates number of lawyers

Brampton: McCabe, Filkin & Garvie - *5
Former Name: James A. Garvie
#320, Plaza II, 350 Rutherford Rd. South, Brampton, ON L6W 4P7
Tel: 905-452-7400; *Fax:* 905-452-6444
mfa@mccabefilkin.com

Brampton: W. John McCulligh - *1
#301, 197 County Court Blvd., Brampton, ON L6W 4P6
Tel: 905-459-1545; *Fax:* 905-459-2826
wjmcculligh@idirect.com
www.peelbarristers.com/mcculligh

Brampton: North Peel & Dufferin Community Legal Services - *4
#601, 24 Queen St. East, Brampton, ON L6V 1A3
Tel: 905-455-0160; *Fax:* 905-455-0832
Toll-Free: 866-455-0160
www.legalclinicsinpeel.ca

Brampton: Laszlo Pandy - *1
#6, 279 Queen St. East, Brampton, ON L6W 2C2
Tel: 905-457-0977; *Fax:* 905-457-8108

Brampton: Prouse Dash & Crouch LLP - *13
50 Queen St. West, Brampton, ON L6X 4H3
Tel: 905-451-6610; *Fax:* 905-451-1549
Toll-Free: 877-217-4732
pdc@pdclawyers.ca
www.pdclawyers.ca
www.linkedin.com/company/prouse-dash-&-crouch-llp

Brampton: Simmons da Silva LLP - *13
Former Name: Simmons, Da Silva & Sinton
#200, 201 County Court Blvd., Brampton, ON L6W 4L2
Tel: 905-457-1660; *Fax:* 905-457-5641
info@sdslawfirm.com
www.sdslawfirm.com
www.facebook.com/SimmonsDaSilva,
www.linkedin.com/company/2356553

Brampton: Mark E. Skursky - *1
#101, 380 Bovaird Dr., Brampton, ON L6Z 2S8
Tel: 905-840-0001; *Fax:* 905-840-0002
skurskylawoffice@on.aibn.com

Brampton: Victor E. Szumlanski - *1
9610 McLaughlin Rd. North, Brampton, ON L6X 0B8
Tel: 905-456-1673; *Fax:* 905-456-1201

Brampton: Cynthia K. Waite - *3
Former Name: Waite and Associates
#102, 197 County Court Blvd., Brampton, ON L6W 4P6
Tel: 905-450-3800; *Fax:* 905-450-8376
cyndy@wjfamilylaw.com

Brampton: Michael J. Walsh - *1
250 Main St. North, Brampton, ON L6V 1P4
Tel: 905-453-4105
www.michaeljwalsh.ca

Brantford: Douglas C. Ainsworth - *1
Stn. Main, 120B Market St., Brantford, ON N3T 3A1
Tel: 519-756-4220; *Fax:* 519-756-3462

Brantford: Donald A. Archi - *1
80 Brant Ave., Brantford, ON N3T 3G7
Tel: 519-751-3101; *Fax:* 519-751-0347
info@archilaw.ca
www.archilaw.ca

Brantford: Boddy Ryerson LLP - *5
#101, P.O. Box 1265, 172 Dalhousie St., Brantford, ON N3T 2J7
Tel: 519-753-8417; *Fax:* 519-753-7421
www.boddy-ryerson.com

Brantford: DeLong Law - *2
16 Darling St., Brantford, ON N3T 2K2
Tel: 519-720-6700; *Fax:* 519-720-6757
www.delonglaw.ca

Brantford: Gerry Smits Law Firm - *1
#4, 45 Dalkeith Dr., Brantford, ON N3P 1M1
Tel: 519-720-6733; *Fax:* 519-720-0933
contact@smitslawfirm.com
www.smitslawfirm.com

Brantford: Sandra J. Harris - *1
#102, 99 Chatham St., Brantford, ON N3T 2P3
Tel: 519-756-0350; *Fax:* 519-756-6611
sjharrison@on.aibn.com

Brantford: Hospodar Davies & Goold - *3
120 Market St., Brantford, ON N3T 3A1
Tel: 519-759-0082; *Fax:* 519-759-8490
www.hospodardaviesandgoold.ca

Brantford: John Jakub - *1
45 Peel St., Brantford, ON N3S 5L7
Tel: 519-754-0495; *Fax:* 519-754-1882
johnjakub@rogers.com

Brantford: Lefebvre & Lefebvre LLP - *8
P.O. Box 488, 75 Chatham St., Brantford, ON N3T 5N9
Tel: 519-756-3350; *Fax:* 519-756-4727
info@lefebvrelawyers.ca
www.lefebvrelawyers.ca

Brantford: McIntosh & Pease - *2
442 Grey St., #D, Brantford, ON N3S 7N3
Tel: 519-752-7733; *Fax:* 519-751-7526
Toll-Free: 800-601-6801
www.mcintosh-pease.com

Brantford: Melanie A. Peters - *1
#109, Royal Victoria Place, 136 Dalhousie St., Brantford, ON N3T 2J3
Tel: 519-900-6055; *Fax:* 519-900-6058
mpeters@melaniepeterslaw.ca
www.melaniepeterslaw.ca

Brantford: Pipe Law Professional Corporation - *1
387 Wellington St., Brantford, ON N3S 4A8
Tel: 226-400-0797; *Fax:* 815-572-0950
Brian@PipeLaw.Com
www.parisontariolawyer.com

Brantford: Staats Law - *2
Former Name: Staats, Newton
P.O. Box 1417, 188 Mohawk St., Brantford, ON N3T 5T6
Tel: 519-756-5217; *Fax:* 519-756-4783
www.staatslaw.ca

Brantford: Shelley M. Stanzlik - *1
P.O. Box 691, 119 Brant Ave., Brantford, ON N3T 3H5
Tel: 519-756-7566; *Fax:* 519-756-7558
shelley.stanzlik@bellnet.ca

Brantford: Thomas H. Buck Law Office - *1
Former Name: Reeves & Buck LLP
442 Grey St., #G, Brantford, ON N3S 7N3
Tel: 226-381-0900
info@thomasbuck.ca
www.thomasbuck.ca

Brantford: Trepanier Verity LLP - *6
P.O. Box 144, Stn. Main, 63 Charlotte St., Brantford, ON N3T 2W6
Tel: 519-756-8700; *Fax:* 519-756-5454
info@trepanierverity.com

Brantford: Underwood, Ion & Johnson LLP - *2
Former Name: Underwood & Ion
P.O. Box 1536, 442 Grey St., #B, Brantford, ON N3T 5V6
Tel: 519-759-0920; *Fax:* 519-759-2122

Brantford: Paul Vandervet - *1
P.O. Box 1495, 107 Wellington St., Brantford, ON N3T 5V6
Tel: 519-759-4240; *Fax:* 519-759-4863

Brantford: Wayne P. Vipond - *1
99 Chatham St., Brantford, ON N3T 2P3
Tel: 519-751-0240; *Fax:* 519-751-0251
wvipond@bellnet.ca

Brantford: Waterous Holden Amey Hitchon LLP - Brantford - *19
P.O. Box 1510, 20 Wellington St., Brantford, ON N3T 5V6
Tel: 519-759-6220; *Fax:* 519-759-8360
law@waterousholden.com
www.waterousholden.com

Brantford: Michael R. White - *1
#103, North Brantford Professional Centre, 525 Park Rd. North, Brantford, ON N3R 7K8
Tel: 519-752-9004; *Fax:* 519-752-0449
mrw@michaelrwhite.com

Brockville: Barr & O'Brien - *2
#206, 9 Broad St., Brockville, ON K6V 6Z4
Tel: 613-498-0800; *Fax:* 613-498-0001
Toll-Free: 800-673-3429
rabarr@barrobrien.com
www.barrobrien.com

Brockville: Angus F. Bickerton, Family Lawyer - *1
Former Name: Fraser & Bickerton
#100, 36 Broad St., Brockville, ON K6V 5V8
Tel: 613-345-3377; *Fax:* 613-345-3372
brockvillefamilylawyer.com
www.facebook.com/angus.bickerton.family.law.and.mediation

Brockville: Michael P. Bird - *1
#304, The Boardwalk, 9 Broad St., Brockville, ON K6V 6Z4
Tel: 613-342-1183; *Fax:* 613-342-0887
mpbird@ripnet.com

Brockville: Fitzpatrick & Culic - *1
21 Pine St., Brockville, ON K6V 1E9
Tel: 613-342-6693; *Fax:* 613-342-8449
www.culiclaw.com

Brockville: Robert W. Flood - *1
13 Hartley St., Brockville, ON K6V 3N2
Tel: 613-345-0087; *Fax:* 613-342-5294

Brockville: David A. Hain - *1
58 King St. Eest, Brockville, ON K6V 1B1
Tel: 613-342-5577; *Fax:* 613-342-1773

Brockville: Hammond Osborne - *3
#207, 9 Broad St., Brockville, ON K6V 6Z4
Tel: 613-498-0944; *Fax:* 613-498-0946
Toll-Free: 877-498-0944
rob@hammondosborne.ca
www.hammondosborne.ca / www.hammondmediation.ca

Brockville: Henderson Johnston Fournier - *3
Eastwood Law Offices, 6 Court Terrace, Brockville, ON K6V 4T4
Tel: 613-345-5613; *Fax:* 613-345-6473
www.hendersonjohnstonfournier.com

Brockville: John M. Johnston - *1
41 Court House Sq., Brockville, ON K6V 7N3
Tel: 613-341-2821; *Fax:* 613-341-2818
john.m.johnston@scj-csj.ca

Brockville: Michael J. O'Shaughnessy - *1
P.O. Box 2121, Stn. Main, 21 Court House Ave., Brockville, ON K6V 6N5
Tel: 613-342-2010; *Fax:* 613-342-6405
mike@courthouse.ca
www.michaeloshaughnessy.ca

Brockville: Preston Lawyers - *2
#201, P.O. Box 1814, Stn. Main, 68 King St. West, Brockville, ON K6V 3P9
Tel: 613-342-1866; *Fax:* 613-342-1634

Brockville: Wilson Evely - *1
P.O. Box 1, 3 Court Terrace, Brockville, ON K6V 4T4
Tel: 613-345-1907; *Fax:* 613-345-4604
wilson-evely@bellnet.ca

Brooklin: Mason Bennett Johncox - *5
79 Baldwin St. North, Brooklin, ON L1M 1A4
Tel: 905-620-4499; *Fax:* 905-620-7738
www.whitbylawyers.com
twitter.com/whitbylawyers

Brooklin: Mason Bennett Johncox - Brooklin - *6
Former Name: Siksay & Fraser
79 Baldwin St. North, Brooklin, ON L1M 1A4
Tel: 905-620-4499; *Fax:* 905-620-7738
www.mbjlawyers.com

Bruce Mines: Peterson & Peterson - Bruce Mines - *1
2 Taylor St., Bruce Mines, ON P0R 1C0
Tel: 705-785-3491; *Fax:* 705-785-3768
www.petersonandpetersonlawfirm.com

Burlington: Christopher C. Breen - *1
3400 Fairview St., Burlington, ON L7N 3G5
Tel: 905-634-1828; *Fax:* 905-634-9630
breenlaw@lawtel.ca
www.lawtel.ca

Burlington: Burgess Law Office - *1
#27, 460 Brant St., Burlington, ON L7R 4B6
Tel: 905-632-9474; *Fax:* 905-632-3035
info@burgesslawoffice.com
burgesslawoffice.com

Burlington: Dunlop & Associates - *1
3556 Commerce Ct., Burlington, ON L7N 3L7
Tel: 905-681-3311; *Fax:* 905-681-3565
info@dunloplaw.com
www.dunloplaw.com

Burlington: **Feltmate Delibato Heagle LLP - *15**
#200, 3600 Billings Ct., Burlington, ON L7N 3N6
Tel: 905-639-8881; *Fax:* 905-639-8017
Toll-Free: 800-636-6927
www.fdhlawyers.com

Burlington: **Forbes Law Office - *1**
Former Name: Forbes, Conant, Barristers & Solicitors
#2, 3455 Harvester Rd., Burlington, ON L7N 3P2
Tel: 905-333-1622; *Fax:* 905-333-1624
robf@forbeslaw.ca

Burlington: **Green Germann Sakran - *5**
411 Guelph Line, 2nd Fl., Burlington, ON L7R 3Y3
Tel: 905-639-1222; *Fax:* 905-632-6977
Toll-Free: 855-512-8002
www.ggslaw.ca
www.facebook.com/ggslaw

Burlington: **Gross, Shuman, Brizdle & Gilfillan, P.C. - *23**
#300, Hoover Business Park, 1100 Burloak Dr., Burlington, ON L7L 6B2
Tel: 416-221-5600
www.gross-shuman.com

Burlington: **Haber & Associates - Burlington - *7**
3370 South Service Rd., 2nd Fl., Burlington, ON L7N 3M6
Tel: 905-639-8894; *Fax:* 905-639-0459
www.haber-lawyer.com
www.facebook.com/HaberAssociates, twitter.com/HaberLawyers

Burlington: **Catherine A. Haber - *1**
3370 South Service Rd., 2nd Fl., Burlington, ON L7N 3M6
Tel: 905-333-4421; *Fax:* 905-333-0575
catherine@catherineahaber.com
www.catherineahaber.com

Burlington: **Charlebois Hastings - *2**
3513 Mainway Dr., Burlington, ON L7M 1A9
Tel: 905-332-1888; *Fax:* 905-332-0021

Burlington: **John Hicks Law Office - *1**
#7, 541 Brant St., Burlington, ON L7R 2G6
Tel: 905-681-3131; *Fax:* 905-333-6688
www.johnhickslaw.ca/en

Burlington: **Hofbauer Professional Corporation - *1**
#3-166, 3350 Fairview St., Burlington, ON L7N 3L5
Tel: 905-319-9168; *Fax:* 905-349-0809
info@capatents.com
www.capatents.com

Burlington: **Eldon Hunt - *3**
Also Known As: Hunt Legal Professional Corporation
Former Name: Cleaver Crawford LLP
562 Maple Ave., Burlington, ON L7S 1M6
Tel: 905-634-5581; *Fax:* 905-634-1563
www.cleavercrawford.ca

Burlington: **Jaskot Family Law - *3**
#203, 3310 South Service Rd., Burlington, ON L7N 3M6
Tel: 905-634-3155; *Fax:* 905-634-3555
Toll-Free: 888-522-3517
www.jaskotfamilylaw.ca

Burlington: **Richard R. Kosterski - *1**
394 Guelph Line, Burlington, ON L7R 3L4
Tel: 905-637-8249; *Fax:* 905-637-6015

Burlington: **Martin & Hillyer Associates - *9**
Former Name: Lakeshore Law Chambers
2122 Old Lakeshore Rd., Burlington, ON L7R 1A3
Tel: 905-637-5641; *Fax:* 905-637-5404
info@mhalaw.ca
www.mhalaw.ca

Burlington: **Gary Rich - *1**
#12, 460 Brant St., Burlington, ON L7R 4B6
Tel: 905-681-1521; *Fax:* 905-333-5075

Burlington: **Snelius Family Law - *2**
Former Name: Snelius, Redfearn LLP
#105, 3410 South Service Rd., Burlington, ON L7N 3T2
Tel: 905-333-5322
info@familylawassociates.ca
www.familylawassociates.ca

Burlington: **Harold Kim Taylor - *1**
3380 South Service Road, Burlington, ON L7N 3J5
Tel: 905-681-6400; *Fax:* 905-681-6510

Burlington: **Thatcher & Wands - *1**
1457 Ontario St., Burlington, ON L7S 1G6
Tel: 905-681-0444; *Fax:* 905-681-2937
www.thatcherandwands.com

Burlington: **Elizabeth A. Urban - *2**
Also Known As: Urban Family Law
#111, 3380 South Service Rd., Burlington, ON L7N 3J3
Tel: 905-333-6640; *Fax:* 905-681-6510
www.urbanfamilylaw.ca
www.facebook.com/urbanfamilylaw,
www.linkedin.com/in/urbanfamilylaw

Caledon East: **George W. Jenney - *1**
P.O. Box 340, 15891 Airport Rd., Caledon East, ON L0N 1E0
Tel: 905-584-9300; *Fax:* 905-584-9233

Caledon East: **Lockyer Law Professional Corporation - Caledon East - *1**
Former Name: Matheson, Holmes A.
#201, 15955 Airport Rd., Caledon East, ON L7C 1H9
Tel: 905-584-4545; *Fax:* 905-584-6565

Caledonia: **Arrell Law LLP - *3**
Former Name: Arrell, Brown, Osier, Murray & Rosewell
2 Caithness St. West, Caledonia, ON N3W 1C1
Tel: 905-765-5414; *Fax:* 905-765-5144
reception@arrelllaw.com
www.arrelllaw.com

Caledonia: **Benedict & Ferguson - *2**
322 Argyle St. South, Caledonia, ON N3W 1K8
Tel: 905-765-4004; *Fax:* 905-765-3001
www.benedictandferguson.com

Caledonia: **Larry S. Humenik - *1**
19 Argyle St. North, Caledonia, ON N3W 1B6
Tel: 905-765-3162; *Fax:* 905-765-4313
www.humeniklaw.com

Callander: **George D. Olah - *1**
492 Main St., Callander, ON P0H 1H0
Tel: 705-752-1323; *Fax:* 705-752-1283
georgeolah@bellnet.ca

Cambridge: **Brownell & Reier - *2**
Former Name: Bond & Brownell
32 Grand Ave. South, Cambridge, ON N2S 2L6
Tel: 519-623-2311; *Fax:* 519-623-6957
info@brownellandreier.ca
www.brownellandreier.ca

Cambridge: **Copp & Cosman - *2**
#409, Cambridge Place, P.O. Box 1729, Stn. Galt, 73 Water St. North, Cambridge, ON N1R 7G8
Tel: 519-623-4799; *Fax:* 519-623-7154
cosman@coppcosman.com

Cambridge: **Teresa L. Fairborn - *1**
285 Fountain St. South, 2nd Fl., Cambridge, ON N3H 1J2
Tel: 519-653-1460; *Fax:* 519-653-4169

Cambridge: **George R. Ingram - *1**
#206, P.O. Box 1447, Stn. Galt, 99 Main St., Cambridge, ON N1R 7G7
Tel: 519-621-9000; *Fax:* 519-621-9009
gringram@sentex.net

Cambridge: **Rein Kao - *1**
#102, 24 Queens Square, Cambridge, ON N1S 1H6
Tel: 519-624-8722; *Fax:* 519-624-3589
r.kao@kaolawoffices.net

Cambridge: **David A. Kinder - *1**
61 Cambridge St., Cambridge, ON N1R 3R8
Tel: 519-740-6676; *Fax:* 519-623-8545
Toll-Free: 888-779-9954
klo@Kinder.ca
www.kinder.ca

Cambridge: **William Korz, Q.C. - *1**
Former Name: Korz & Associates
927 King St. East, Cambridge, ON N3H 3P4
Tel: 519-653-7174; *Fax:* 519-653-5222
wmkorz@execulink.com

Cambridge: **George E. Loker - *1**
P.O. Box 1723, Stn. Galt, 108 Myers Rd., Cambridge, ON N1R 2Z8
Tel: 519-621-4300; *Fax:* 519-621-4300

Cambridge: **Paul M. Mann Professional Corp. - *1**
25 George St. South, Cambridge, ON N1S 2N3
Tel: 519-623-0700; *Fax:* 519-622-4091
info@paulmann.ca
www.paulmann.ca

Cambridge: **McDonald Ross - *2**
9 Brant Rd. South, Cambridge, ON N1S 2W4
Tel: 519-622-0499; *Fax:* 519-740-6368
jwm@mcdonaldross.com

Cambridge: **McSevney Ebben LLP - *2**
Former Name: McSevney Law Offices; Onorato Law Offices
708 Duke St., Cambridge, ON N3H 3T6
Tel: 519-653-3217; *Fax:* 866-891-7016
www.mcsevneylaw.com

Cambridge: **Pavey, Law & Witteveen LLP - *7**
Also Known As: Pavey Law
Former Name: Pavey, Law & Wannop LLP
P.O. Box 1707, Stn. Galt, 19 Cambridge St., Cambridge, ON N1R 3R8
Tel: 519-621-7260; *Fax:* 519-621-1304
info@paveylaw.com
www.paveylaw.com

Cambridge: **Pettitt Pass Schwarz Hills - *3**
Also Known As: PSH Lawyers
Former Name: Pettitt Schwarz Hills
#403, 73 Water St. North, Cambridge, ON N1R 7L6
Tel: 519-621-2450; *Fax:* 519-621-5750
www.pettittschwarz.com
www.facebook.com/136696276391017

Cambridge: **Henry R. Shields - *1**
2 Water St. North, Cambridge, ON N1R 3B1
Tel: 519-622-2150; *Fax:* 519-623-0997
henryshields@on.aibn.com

Cambridge: **J. Craig Wilson - *1**
P.O. Box 1297, 2 Water St. North, Cambridge, ON N1R 3B1
Tel: 519-622-0192

Cambridge: **William C. Wraight - *1**
15 Main St., Cambridge, ON N1R 7G9
Tel: 519-623-3330
www.wraightlaw.com

Campbellford: **Paul D.H. Burgess - *1**
P.O. Box 1540, 64 Front St. North, Campbellford, ON K0L 1L0
Tel: 705-653-5555; *Fax:* 705-653-5557
pdhburgess@xplornet.com

Campbellville: **Robert B. Burgess - *1**
P.O. Box 86, 8220 MacArthur Dr., Campbellville, ON L0P 1B0
Tel: 905-854-2790; *Fax:* 905-854-1968
rbburgess@sympatico.ca

Carleton Place: **Kenneth J. Bennett - *1**
32 Beckwith St., Carleton Place, ON K7C 2T2
Tel: 613-257-1655; *Fax:* 613-257-8837

Carleton Place: **N. Alan Jones - *1**
92 Bridge St., Carleton Place, ON K7C 2V3
Tel: 613-257-3811; *Fax:* 613-253-0479

Casselman: **Mireille C. LaViolette - *1**
CP 179, 719, rue Principale, Casselman, ON K0A 1M0
Tél: 613-764-3747; *Téléc:* 613-764-1000
info@mireillelaviolette.com
www.mireillelaviolette.com

Chatham: **James E.S. Allin - *1**
128 Queen St., Chatham, ON N7M 2G6
Tel: 519-352-6540; *Fax:* 519-352-9097
www.allinlaw.ca

Chatham: **Mark M. MacKew - *1**
Also Known As: The MacKew Law Firm
237 Wellington St. West, Chatham, ON N7M 1J9
Tel: 519-354-0407; *Fax:* 519-354-3250
mark@mackewlaw.com
www.mackewlaw.com

Chatham: **Mayes Law Firm - *1**
Also Known As: Stanley G. Mayes
16 Victoria Ave., Chatham, ON N7L 2Z6
Tel: 519-436-1040; *Fax:* 519-436-2442
sgmayes@mayeslawfirm.ca
www.mayeslawfirm.ca

* indicates number of lawyers

Chatham: Gudrun Mueller-Wilm - *1
P.O. Box 554, Stn. C, 6 Harvey St., Chatham, ON N7M 1L6
Tel: 519-358-1822; Fax: 519-358-7406

Chatham: F. Vaughn Pugh - *1
190 Wellington St. West, Chatham, ON N7M 1J6
Tel: 519-354-4360

Chatham: J. Quaglia Law Office - *1
Former Name: Benoit, Van Raay, Spisani, Fuerth &
Quaglia
P.O. Box 1087, 193 Queen St., Chatham, ON N7M 5L6
Tel: 519-352-8580; Fax: 519-352-4114
www.jquaglialaw.ca
www.facebook.com/QuagliaLaw

Chatham: John B. Trinca - *1
P.O. Box 428, 75 Thames St., Chatham, ON N7L 1S4
Tel: 519-352-7750; Fax: 519-352-4159
jtrinca@mnsi.net

Chatham: Paul D. Watson - *1
84 Dover St., Chatham, ON N7M 5K8
Tel: 519-351-7721; Fax: 519-351-7726
pwatson@cogeco.net

Chelmsford: Gerard E. Guimond
3527 Errington Ave. North, Chelmsford, ON P0M 1L0
Tel: 705-855-4511; Fax: 705-855-5631
guimond12@bellnet.ca

Chesley: McClelland Law Office - *1
159 - 1st Ave. South, Chesley, ON N0G 1L0
Tel: 519-363-3293; Fax: 519-363-2315

Chesley: McLean Lawyers - Chesley - *2
P.O. Box 118, 27 First Ave. South, Chesley, ON N0G 1L0
Tel: 519-363-3190; Fax: 519-363-2213
www.mcleanlawyers.ca

Clinton: Philip B. Cornish - *1
35 Ontario St., Clinton, ON N0M 1L0
Tel: 519-482-1434; Fax: 519-482-1481

Clinton: D. Gerald Hiltz - *1
P.O. Box 1087, 52 Huron St., Clinton, ON N0M 1L0
Tel: 519-482-3414; Fax: 519-482-7525

Coboconk: Tyler P. Higgins
P.O. Box 219, 6654 Hwy. 35, Coboconk, ON K0M 1K0
Tel: 705-454-2625

Cobourg: Ember Leigh Hamilton - *1
289 Lakeview Crt., Cobourg, ON K9A 5C3
Tel: 905-373-0589; Fax: 905-373-0928

Cobourg: Hustler & Kay - *2
301 Division St., Cobourg, ON K9A 3R2
Tel: 905-372-1991; Fax: 905-372-1995

Cobourg: Irvine & Irvine - *1
24 Covert St., Cobourg, ON K9A 2L6
Tel: 905-372-5449; Fax: 905-372-1707
rirvine@eagle.ca

Cobourg: SMM Law Professional Corp. - *3
Former Name: Stewart, Mitchell & Macklin.
#205, 1005 Elgin St. West, Cobourg, ON K9A 5J4
Tel: 905-372-3395; Fax: 905-372-1695
hello@smmlaw.com
www.smmlaw.com

Cobourg: William J. Taggart - *1
#124, 148 Third St., Cobourg, ON K9A 5X2
Tel: 905-372-8700; Fax: 905-372-1943
info@taggartlaw.ca
www.taggartlaw.ca

Cochrane: Beaudoin Boucher
P.O. Box 1898, 174 - 4th Ave., Cochrane, ON P0L 1C0
Tel: 705-272-4346; Fax: 705-272-2991
bblaw@puc.net

Colborne: Carter Thompson Law Office - *1
Former Name: Carter, J.A.
P.O. Box 699, 26 King St. East, Colborne, ON K9A 1K7
Tel: 905-355-3322; Fax: 905-355-3104

Collingwood: Baulke Stahr McNabb LLP - *4
Former Name: Baulke Augaitis Stahr LLP; Baulke &
Augaitis LLP
150 Hurontario St., Collingwood, ON L9Y 3Z4
Tel: 705-445-4930; Fax: 705-445-1871
info@collingwoodlaw.com
www.collingwoodlaw.com

Collingwood: Besse, Merrifield & Cowan LLP - *3
47 Hurontario St., Collingwood, ON L9Y 2L7
Tel: 705-446-2000; Fax: 705-446-1044
Toll-Free: 888-879-3052
besse@blclawoffices.com
www.bmclawoffices.com

Collingwood: Christie/Cummings - Collingwood - *5
325 Hume St., Collingwood, ON L9Y 1W4
Tel: 705-444-3650; Fax: 705-444-0024
www.christiecummings.com
www.facebook.com/cclawfirm
www.linkedin.com/company/christie-cummings

Collingwood: Elstons - *2
#224, The Admiral Building, 1 First St., Collingwood, ON
L9Y 1A1
Tel: 705-445-1200; Fax: 705-445-1209
Harold@Elstons.ca
elstons.ca

Collingwood: Mumford Law Office - *1
Former Name: Neathery & Mumford
150 St. Paul St., Collingwood, ON L9Y 3P2
Tel: 705-444-6051; Fax: 705-444-0969
gailmumfordlaw@hotmail.com
www.mumfordlaw.ca

Concord: Bisceglia & Associates - *4
#200, 7941 Jane St., Concord, ON L4K 4L6
Tel: 905-695-5200; Fax: 905-695-5201
www.lawtoronto.com

Concord: John G. Chris - *1
8700 Dufferin St., Concord, ON L4K 4S6
Tel: 416-661-5989; Fax: 905-669-0444
www.jgc-law.com

Concord: D'Ambrosio Law Office - *1
#204, 3300 Steeles Ave. West, Concord, ON L4K 3R1
Tel: 905-761-7400; Fax: 905-738-4901
romeo36@cromeo@ontariowills.ca
ontariowills.ca

Concord: Gianfranco John De Matteis - *1
#204, 3300 Steeles Ave. West, Concord, ON L4K 2Y4
Tel: 905-738-4900; Fax: 905-738-4901
john@dematteis.ca

Concord: Di Monte & Di Monte LLP - *2
Former Name: Di Monte, Patrick
#211, 3100 Steeles Ave. West, Concord, ON L4K 3R1
Tel: 905-738-2101; Fax: 905-738-1168
patdimonte@on.aibn.com

Concord: Louis M. Fried - *1
#212, 2180 Steeles Ave. West, Concord, ON L4K 2Z5
Tel: 905-738-0180; Fax: 905-738-6203
Toll-Free: 866-306-3286
info@louismfried.com
louismfried.com

Concord: Okell & Weisman - *2
#218, 1600 Steeles Ave. West, Concord, ON L4K 4M2
Tel: 905-761-8711; Fax: 905-761-8633

Concord: Norman S. Panzica - *1
A, 9100 Jane St., 3rd Fl., Concord, ON L4K 4L8
Tel: 905-738-1078; Fax: 905-738-0528
npanzica@rogers.com
www.normanpanzica.com

Concord: Piersanti & Company - *2
#10, 445 Edgeley Blvd., Concord, ON L4K 4G1
Tel: 905-738-2176; Fax: 905-738-5182
piersanti@look.com
piersantico.com

Concord: Enzo Salvatori - *1
#4, 161 Pennsylvania Ave., Concord, ON L4K 1C3
Tel: 416-745-1777; Fax: 905-760-9503

Concord: Vito S. Scalisi - *1
#204, 3300 Steeles Ave. West, Concord, ON L4K 2Y4
Tel: 905-760-5588; Fax: 905-738-4901
vito@scalisilaw.ca
www.scalisilaw.ca

Cornwall: Bergeron Filion - *2
103 Sydney St., Cornwall, ON K6H 3H1
Tel: 613-932-2911; Fax: 613-932-2356

Cornwall: Giovanniello, Bellefeuille - *2
340 - 2nd St. East, Cornwall, ON K6H 1Y9
Tel: 613-938-0294; Fax: 613-932-2374
law@gblawfirm.ca
www.gblawfirm.ca

Cornwall: Guindon, MacLean & Castle - *3
254 Pitt St., Cornwall, ON K6J 3P6
Tel: 613-933-3931; Fax: 613-933-6123
info@g-m-c.on.ca

Cornwall: Law Office of Diane M. Lahaie - *1
132 Second East, Cornwall, ON K6H 1Y4
Tel: 613-936-8833; Fax: 613-936-6717

Cornwall: Levesque, Grenkie - *2
233 Augustus St., Cornwall, ON K6J 3W2
Tel: 613-932-7654; Fax: 613-938-1692
info@levesquegrenkielaw.ca
www.levesquegrenkielaw.ca

Cornwall: Ian D. Paul - *1
5 - 3rd St. East, Cornwall, ON K2H 2L6
Tel: 613-933-9455; Fax: 613-933-7566
ipaul@on.aibn.com
www.ianpaul.ca/lawyer

Cornwall: D. Randolph Ross - *1
120 Sydney St., Cornwall, ON K6H 3H2
Tel: 613-932-2044; Fax: 613-937-0993
drandolphross@bellnet.ca

Cornwall: Wilson, Poirier, Byrne - *2
132 - 2nd St. West, Cornwall, ON K6J 1G5
Tel: 613-938-2224; Fax: 613-938-8005

Deep River: George W. LeConte - *1
P.O. Box 340, 8 Glendale Ave., Deep River, ON K0J 1P0
Tel: 613-584-3154; Fax: 613-584-4877
gleconte@bellnet.ca
www.georgewleconte.com

Deep River: Thomas E. Roche - *1
Former Name: Roche & Dakin
P.O. Box 1240, 27 Champlain St., Deep River, ON K0J 1P0
Tel: 613-584-3392; Fax: 613-584-4922

Delhi: John R. Hanselman - *1
138 Eagle St., Delhi, ON N4B 1S5
Tel: 519-582-0770; Fax: 519-582-1876

Dresden: Timothy D. Mathany - *1
P.O. Box 568, 423 St. George St. South, Dresden, ON N0P
1M0
Tel: 519-683-6219; Fax: 519-683-6548
www.timothymathany.com

Dryden: McAuley & Partners - *4
#w, P.O. Box 159, 4 Whyte Ave., Dryden, ON P8N 2Y8
Tel: 807-223-2254; Fax: 807-223-3794
www.mcauleylaw.com

Dryden: Vermeer & VanWalleghem - *2
P.O. Box 938, 65 King St., 2nd Fl., Dryden, ON P8N 2Z5
Tel: 807-223-3311; Fax: 807-223-4133
lawweb@vermeerlaw.com
www.vermeerlaw.com

Dundas: Lesperance & Associates - *1
Former Name: Lesperance, David S.
#202, 84 King St. West, Dundas, ON L9H 1T9
Tel: 905-627-3037; Fax: 905-627-9868
info@lesperanceassociates.com
lesperanceassociates.com

Dundas: William J. Wilkins - *2
63 King St. West, Dundas, ON L9H 1T5
Tel: 905-628-6321; Fax: 905-628-2767
Toll-Free: 888-556-3368
www.dundaslaw.ca

Dunrobin: Alan Pratt Law Firm - *2
Former Name: Pratt, Alan
P.O. Box 100, 3550 Torwood Dr., Dunrobin, ON K0A 1T0
Tel: 613-832-1261; Fax: 613-832-0856
Shirley@prattlaw.ca
www.prattlaw.ca

Dutton: Martin Joldersma - *1
P.O. Box 279, 159 Main St., Dutton, ON N0L 1J0
Tel: 519-762-2882; Fax: 519-762-2880
martinjoldersmalawoffice@yahoo.ca

Elliot Lake: Kearns Law Office - *1
13 Manitoba Rd., Elliot Lake, ON P5A 2A6
Tel: 705-848-3601; Fax: 705-848-8416
Toll-Free: 800-268-7733
kearn1@bellnet.ca

Elmira: Cynthia M. Rudavsky - *1
9 Church St. West, Elmira, ON N3B 1M2
Tel: 519-669-2200; Fax: 519-669-4349
rudavsky@sentex.net

Elmira: Woods, Clemens & Fletcher Professional
Corporation - *1
Former Name: Woods & Clemens
P.O. Box 216, 9 Memorial Ave., Elmira, ON N3B 2R1
Tel: 519-669-5101; Fax: 519-669-5618

Elora: Morris & Shannon LLP - *2
Former Name: J.E. Morris
149 Geddes St., Elora, ON N0B 1S0
Tel: 519-846-5366; Fax: 519-846-8170
johnmorrislaw.ca

Elora: Gregory A. Oakes - *1
155 Geddes St., Elora, ON N0B 1S0
Tel: 519-846-5555; Fax: 519-846-5554

Embrun: Campbell & Sabourin LLP/S.R.L. - *4
#1, 165 Bay St., Embrun, ON K0A 1W1
Tel: 613-443-5683; Fax: 613-443-3285
info@campbellaw.on.ca
www.campbellaw.on.ca

Embrun: Jean G. Martel - *1
800, rue Notre Dame, Embrun, ON K0A 1W1
Tel: 613-443-3267; Fax: 613-443-3857
jeanmartel@rogers.com

Essex: Jim Renick & Associates - *1
Former Name: Walstedt Renick
78 Talbot St. North, Essex, ON N8M 1A2
Tel: 519-776-9020
info@jamesrenick.com
www.jamesrenick.com

Exeter: Little, Masson & Reid - *3
71 Main St. North, Exeter, ON N0M 1S0
Tel: 519-235-0670; Fax: 519-235-1603
www.littlemassonreid.com

Exeter: Raymond & McLean - *1
P.O. Box 100, 387 Main St. South, Exeter, ON N0M 1S6
Tel: 519-235-2234; Fax: 519-235-2671
www.raymondmclean.com

Fenelon Falls: David J. Gowanlock - *1
P.O. Box 607, 16 May St., Fenelon Falls, ON K0M 1N0
Tel: 705-887-2582; Fax: 705-887-1871

Fenelon Falls: John D. Walden - *1
57 Lindsay St., Fenelon Falls, ON K0M 1N0
Tel: 705-887-2941
walden-nagel@nexicom.net
johndwaldenlaw.ca

Fergus: Leigh G. Fishleigh - *1
169 St. Andrew St. West, Fergus, ON N1M 1N6
Tel: 519-843-7100; Fax: 519-843-3038
leigh.fishleigh@bellnet.ca
leighfishleighlaw.com

Flesherton: John L. Ferris Law Offices - *2
P.O. Box 100, 15 Durham St., Flesherton, ON N0C 1E0
Tel: 519-923-2031; Fax: 519-924-3198
www.ferrislaw.ca

Fonthill: Jill Anthony - *1
10 Hwy. 20 East, Fonthill, ON L0S 1E0
Tel: 905-892-2621; Fax: 905-892-1022
janthony@jillanthony.com

Fort Frances: Clare Allan Brunetta Law Office - Fort
Frances - *1
P.O. Box 656, 420 Victoria Ave., Fort Frances, ON P9A 3M9
Tel: 807-274-9809; Fax: 807-274-8760
info@brunettalaw.com
www.brunettalaw.com

Fort Frances: Lawrence A. Eustace - *1
510 Portage Ave., Fort Frances, ON P9A 2A3
Tel: 807-274-3247; Fax: 807-274-6447
www.eustace-law.com

Fort Frances: Lawrence G. Phillips - *1
406 Church St., Fort Frances, ON P9A 1E2
Tel: 807-274-8525; Fax: 807-274-5758
phillaw19@hotmail.com

Fort Frances: Donald A. Taylor - *1
504 Armit Ave., Fort Frances, ON P9A 2H7
Tel: 807-274-7811; Fax: 807-274-8485
dalaw@shaw.ca

Gananoque: Michael R. Eyolfson - *1
#5, 140 Garden St., Gananoque, ON K7G 1H9
Tel: 613-382-7772; Fax: 613-382-3030
eyolfso1@bellnet.ca

Gananoque: Steacy & Delaney - *1
77 Pine St. South, Gananoque, ON K7G 2W3
Tel: 613-382-2137; Fax: 613-382-7794
www.gananoque.com/steacyanddelaney

Georgetown: Banbury Law Office - *1
#2, 211 Guelph St., Georgetown, ON L7G 5B5
Tel: 905-877-5252; Fax: 905-877-4100
cbanbury@banburylaw.com

Georgetown: Jeffrey L. Eason - *1
116 Guelph St., Georgetown, ON L7G 4A3
Tel: 905-846-1557
jeffreyleason@bellnet.ca
www.jeffreyleason.com

Georgetown: Helson Kogon Ashbee Schaljo &
Associates LLP - *9
132 Mill St., Georgetown, ON L7G 2C6
Tel: 905-877-5200; Fax: 905-877-3948
info@helsons.ca
helsons.ca

Georgetown: W. Glen How & Associates - *7
P.O. Box 40, Stn. Main, Georgetown, ON L7G 4T1
Tel: 905-873-4545; Fax: 905-873-4522
wghow@wghow.ca
www.wghow.ca

Georgetown: William H. Manderson - *1
#1004, 83 Mill St., Georgetown, ON L7G 5E9
Tel: 905-873-0121; Fax: 905-873-4114

Georgetown: R. Paul Millman - *1
116 Guelph St., Georgetown, ON L7G 4A3
Tel: 905-873-9481; Fax: 905-873-9483

Georgetown: Sopinka & Kort LLP - *2
145 Mill St., Georgetown, ON L7G 2C2
Tel: 905-877-0196; Fax: 905-877-0604
www.sopinka-kort.ca

Glencoe: Gary R. Merritt - *1
P.O. Box 309, 213 Main St., Glencoe, ON N0L 1M0
Tel: 519-287-3432; Fax: 519-287-2498
merritt@bellnet.ca

Gloucester: MacQuarrie Whyte - *2
Former Name: MacQuarrie Whyte Killoran
#208, 1980 Ogilvie Rd., Gloucester, ON K1J 9L3
Tel: 613-748-1600; Fax: 613-748-0800
info@mwklaw.ca
www.ottawaorleanslawyers.com

Goderich: Mary E. Cull - *1
1 East St., Goderich, ON N7A 1N3
Tel: 519-524-1115
maryecull@hurontel.on.ca
marycull.com

Goderich: Donnelly & Murphy Lawyers - Goderich -
*6
18 The Square, Goderich, ON N7A 3Y7
Tel: 519-524-2154; Fax: 519-524-8550
Toll-Free: 800-332-7160
admin@dmlaw.ca
www.donnellymurphy.com

Goderich: Timothy G. Macdonald - *1
1 Nelson St. East, Goderich, ON N7A 1R7
Tel: 519-524-1120; Fax: 519-524-2576

Goderich: Norman B. Pickell - *1
58 South St., Goderich, ON N7A 3L5
Tel: 519-524-8335; Fax: 519-524-1530
pickell@normanpickell.com
www.normanpickell.com

Goderich: Troyan & Fincher - *2
44 North St., Goderich, ON N7A 2T4
Tel: 519-524-2115; 519-524-4481
enquiries@troyanfincher.on.ca

Gore Bay: Terence E. Land, Barrister & Solicitor - *1
Former Name: Armstrong & Land
P.O. Box 90, 4 Eleanor St., Gore Bay, ON P0P 1H0
Tel: 705-282-2710; Fax: 705-282-2205
landlaw@gorebaycable.com

Gore Bay: James E. Weppler - *1
P.O. Box 222, 65 Meredith St., Gore Bay, ON P0P 1H0
Tel: 705-282-3354; Fax: 705-282-3211
jamesweppler@bellnet.ca

Grand Bend: Forrester Law - *1
Former Name: Forrester, Michael G.
82 Ontario St. South, Grand Bend, ON N0M 1T0
Tel: 519-238-5297; Fax: 519-238-5234
www.forresterlaw.ca

Gravenhurst: Cruickshank & MacLennan - *2
Former Name: Stuart & Cruickshank
195 Church St., Gravenhurst, ON P1P 1H3
Tel: 705-687-3441; Fax: 705-687-5405
www.maclennanlaw.ca

Grimsby: George Krusell - *1
260 Main St. East, Grimsby, ON L3M 1P8
Tel: 905-945-2300; Fax: 905-945-8529

Grimsby: Donald C. Loney - *1
Former Name: Sinclair, Murakami, Loney & Van Velzen
55 Main St. East, Grimsby, ON L3M 1R3
Tel: 905-945-9271; Fax: 905-945-3066
Toll-Free: 800-363-5073

Grimsby: Paul A. MacLeod - *1
32 Elm St., Grimsby, ON L3M 1H3
Tel: 905-945-9659; Fax: 905-945-0838

Guelph: Lynn Archbold - *1
27 Cork St. West, Guelph, ON N1H 2W9
Tel: 519-763-4748; Fax: 519-763-4207
info@archboldlaw.com
www.archboldlaw.com

Guelph: Andrea S. Clarke - *2
258 Woolwich St., Guelph, ON N1H 3W1
Tel: 519-763-3999; Fax: 519-763-5116
bgjorgieva@andreasclarke.com
andreasclarke.com

Guelph: Dason Law Office - *1
Former Name: Hugh Guthrie Q.C. Professional
Corporation
367 Woolwich St., Guelph, ON N1H 3W4
Tel: 519-824-2020; Fax: 519-824-2023
www.dasonlaw.com

Guelph: David Doney Law Office - *1
20 Douglas St., Guelph, ON N1H 2S9
Tel: 519-804-9829; Fax: 519-837-1758
guelphcriminallawyer.com

Guelph: Charles R. Davidson
172 Woolwich St., Guelph, ON N1H 3V5
Tel: 519-767-6637; Fax: 519-826-5212
charles@crdavidson.ca

Guelph: Guy D.E. Farb - *1
22 Paisley St., Guelph, ON N1H 2N6
Tel: 519-763-6644; Fax: 519-763-8091
lawguy@execulink.com
www.linkedin.com/pub/guy-farb/18/559/986

Guelph: Siobhan Ann Hanley - *1
98 Surrey St. East, Guelph, ON N1H 3P9
Tel: 519-824-2586; Fax: 519-827-1715
Toll-Free: 888-262-6333
shanley@bellnet.ca

Guelph: Jackman & Rowles - *2
Former Name: Moyer Malak Jackman & Rowles
17 Cork St. West, Guelph, ON N1H 2W9
Tel: 519-824-4883
info@jackmanandrowles.ca
www.jackmanandrowles.ca

Guelph: Maiocco & DiGravio - *2
230 Speedvale Ave. West, Guelph, ON N1H 1C4
Tel: 519-836-2710; Fax: 519-836-7312

indicates number of lawyers

Guelph: McElderry & Morris - *5
P.O. Box 875, 84 Woolwich St., Guelph, ON N1H 6M6
Tel: 519-822-8150; *Fax:* 519-822-1921
www.mcelderrymorris.com
www.linkedin.com/company/3500637

Guelph: Bryna D. McLeod - *1
221 Woolwich St., Guelph, ON N1H 3V4
Tel: 519-767-2141; *Fax:* 519-763-2204
www.brynamcleod.com

Guelph: Peter A. McSherry - *1
343 Waterloo Ave., Guelph, ON N1H 3K1
Tel: 519-821-5465; *Fax:* 519-822-2867
www.petermcsherry.ca
www.facebook.com/PeterAMcSherryLawOffice,
twitter.com/PeterMcSherry, www.linkedin.com/company/2853921

Guelph: Nelson, Watson LLP - *6
183 Norfolk St., Guelph, ON N1H 4K1
Tel: 519-821-9610; *Fax:* 519-821-8550
www.nelwat.com

Guelph: Kenneth H. Richardson - *1
#5, 340 Edinburgh Rd. North, Guelph, ON N1H 7Y4
Tel: 519-821-6036; *Fax:* 519-821-3317
richlaw@rogers.com
www.richlaw.ca

Guelph: Judith C. Sidlofsky Stoffman - *1
15 Wyndham St. South, Guelph, ON N1H 4C6
Tel: 519-824-1212; *Fax:* 519-822-0949
judith.stoffman@police.guelph.on.ca

Guelph: Smith Valeriote LLP - *23
#100, P.O. Box 1240, Stn. Main, 105 Silvercreek Pkwy. North,
Guelph, ON N1H 6N6
Tel: 519-837-2100; *Fax:* 519-837-1617
Toll-Free: 800-746-0685
info@smithvaleriote.com
www.smithvaleriote.com

Guelph: Teresa Tummillo-Goy - *1
Also Known As: TTG Law
#101, 75 Farquar St., Guelph, ON N1H 3N4
Tel: 226-251-3008; *Fax:* 226-251-3009
teresa@ttglaw.ca
www.ttglaw.ca

Guelph: Vorvis, Anderson, Gray, Armstrong LLP - *4
353 Elizabeth St., Guelph, ON N1H 2X9
Tel: 519-824-7400; *Fax:* 519-824-7521
www.vaga.ca

Hagersville: James R. Baxter - *1
19 King St. West, Hagersville, ON N0A 1H0
Tel: 905-768-3363; *Fax:* 905-768-1550
jrbaxter@mountaincable.net

Haileybury: Byck Law Office - Haileybury - *4
Former Name: Smith, Wowk
573 Lakeshore St., Haileybury, ON P0J 1K0
Tel: 705-647-8167; *Fax:* 705-647-8575
temlaw@nt.net
www.temlaw.com

Haliburton: Raymond G. Selbie - *1
P.O. Box 699, 34 Maple Ave., Haliburton, ON K0M 1S0
Tel: 705-457-2435; *Fax:* 705-457-3074
rselbie@on.aibn.com
www.selbielaw.com

Halton Hills: Steven C. Foster - *2
#201, 232A Guelph St., Halton Hills, ON L7G 4B1
Tel: 905-873-0204; *Fax:* 905-873-4962
sfoster@arnold-foster.com

Hamilton: John S. Abrams - *1
#300, 69 John St. South, Hamilton, ON L8N 2B9
Tel: 905-522-3600; *Fax:* 905-529-1570
jabrams@bellnet.ca
www.johnabrams.ca

Hamilton: Agro Zaffiro LLP - *24
1 James St. South, 4th Fl., Hamilton, ON L8P 4R5
Tel: 905-527-6877; *Fax:* 905-527-6843
mail@agrozaffiro.com
www.agrozaffiro.com

Hamilton: Ballagh & Edward LLP - *2
#102, McMaster Innovation Park, 175 Longwood Rd. South,
Hamilton, ON L8P 0A1
Tel: 905-572-9300; *Fax:* 905-572-9301
info@ballaghedward.ca
www.ballaghedward.ca

Hamilton: Deborah Lee Barfknecht - *1
#601, 25 Main St. West, Hamilton, ON L8P 1H1
Tel: 905-521-1898; *Fax:* 905-521-0486

Hamilton: Bartolini, Berlingieri, Barrafato, Fortino,
LLP - Hamilton - Main St. - *7
#101, 154 Main St. East, Hamilton, ON L8N 1G9
Tel: 905-577-6833; *Fax:* 905-577-6839
lawfirm@bbb-lawyers.on.ca
bbbflawyershamilton.ca

Hamilton: Bedford Brock Howard - *1
46 Forest Ave., Hamilton, ON L8N 1X1
Tel: 905-527-3867; *Fax:* 905-527-3860

Hamilton: John A. Bland - *1
#801, Union Gas Bldg., 20 Hughson St. South, Hamilton, ON
L8N 2A1
Tel: 905-524-3533; *Fax:* 905-524-5142

Hamilton: Burns Associates - *2
Former Name: Burns, Vasan, Limberis, Vitulli LLP
#305, 21 King St. West, Hamilton, ON L8P 4W9
Tel: 905-522-1381; *Fax:* 905-522-0855
www.adburnslaw.com

Hamilton: Camporese Sullivan Di Gregorio - *12
Former Name: Camporese & Associates
#1700, Commerce Place, 1 King St. West, Hamilton, ON L8P
1A4
Tel: 905-522-7068; *Fax:* 905-522-5734
contactus@csdlawyers.ca
www.csdlawyers.ca

Hamilton: Jerry J. Chaimovitz - *2
#250, 100 Main St. East, Hamilton, ON L8N 3W4
Tel: 905-526-7030; *Fax:* 905-526-0682
info@jjcfamilylaw.com
www.jjcfamilylaw.com

Hamilton: Michael P. Clarke - *1
#1221, 25 Main St. West, Hamilton, ON L8P 1H1
Tel: 905-527-4399; *Fax:* 905-521-0210
michaelpclarke@bellnet.ca

Hamilton: Confente, Garcea - *2
#340, 69 John St. South, Hamilton, ON L8N 2B9
Tel: 905-529-9999; *Fax:* 905-529-1160
confentegarcea.com

Hamilton: Connor, Connor, Guyer & Araiche - *1
#210, 1104 Fennell Ave. East, Hamilton, ON L8T 1R9
Tel: 905-385-3229; *Fax:* 905-385-6182
ccga@araiche.ca

Hamilton: Rory J. Cornale - *2
Also Known As: Cornale & Associates
#201, 4 Hughson St. South, Hamilton, ON L8N 3Z1
Tel: 905-637-8337
www.rorycornalelaw.ca

Hamilton: Earl R. Cranfield Q.C. - *1
#608, 20 Hughson St. South, Hamilton, ON L8N 2A1
Tel: 905-528-0089; *Fax:* 905-528-7692
ecranfield@nas.net

Hamilton: Janis P. Criger - *1
#700, 25 Main St. West, Hamilton, ON L8P 1H1
Tel: 905-525-4639; *Fax:* 905-525-2103
jpcriger@crigerlaw.com
www.crigerlaw.ca

Hamilton: Stephen F. De Wetter - *1
#1215, 25 Main St. West, Hamilton, ON L8P 1H1
Tel: 905-521-8878; *Fax:* 905-577-0229
dewetterlaw@gmail.com

Hamilton: Dermody Law - *3
550 Concession St., Hamilton, ON L8V 1A9
Tel: 905-383-3331; *Fax:* 905-574-3299
info@dermody.ca
dermodylaw.com

Hamilton: DiCenzo & Associates
#41, 1070 Stone Church Rd. East, Hamilton, ON L8W 3K8
Tel: 905-574-3300; *Fax:* 905-574-1766
www.dcalawyers.com

Hamilton: Peter J. Dudzic - *2
#312, 883 Upper Wentworth St., Hamilton, ON L9A 4Y6
Tel: 905-318-4441; *Fax:* 905-318-7775
www.dudziclaw.ca

Hamilton: Duxbury Law Professional Corporation -
*2
Former Name: Duxbury, Brian
#1500, 1 King St. West, Hamilton, ON L8P 1A4
Tel: 905-570-1242; *Fax:* 905-570-1955
brian@duxburylaw.ca

Hamilton: Paul H. Ennis, Q.C - *1
#203, P.O. Box 101, Stn. Main, 58 Jarvis St., Hamilton, ON
L8N 1G6
Tel: 905-871-1888; *Fax:* 905-871-1881

Hamilton: Evans Philp LLP - *18
Commerce Place, 1 King St. West, 16th Fl., Hamilton, ON
L8P 1A4
Tel: 905-525-1200; *Fax:* 905-525-7897
www.evansphilp.com

Hamilton: Evans Sweeny Bordin LLP - *7
Former Name: Evans-Lawyers/Advocates
#1201, 1 King St. West, Hamilton, ON L8P 1A4
Tel: 905-523-5666; *Fax:* 905-523-8098
jfe@esblawyers.com
www.esblawyers.com

Hamilton: Foreman, Rosenblatt & Lewis - *3
425 York Blvd., Hamilton, ON L8R 3M3
Tel: 905-525-3570; *Fax:* 905-523-0363
www.yorklawcentre.com

Hamilton: Frankel Law Offices - Hamilton - Main St.
East - *1
#1001, 105 Main St. East, Hamilton, ON L8N 1G6
Tel: 905-522-3972; *Fax:* 905-528-2767
www.frankelaw.ca

Hamilton: Fyshe McMahon LLP - *5
207 Locke St. South, Hamilton, ON L8P 2V3
Tel: 905-522-0600; *Fax:* 905-522-9101
info@lockelaw.net
www.lockelaw.net

Hamilton: Genesee Martin - *2
Former Name: Genesee & Clarke
#2225, 25 Main St. West, Hamilton, ON L8P 1H1
Tel: 905-522-7066; *Fax:* 905-522-7085
www.geneseemartin.com

Hamilton: Malcolm E. Graham - *1
Former Name: Robinson, McCallum, McKerracher,
Graham
#300, 69 John St. South, Hamilton, ON L8N 2B9
Tel: 905-528-1435; *Fax:* 905-529-1570
www.malcolmgrahamlaw.com

Hamilton: Guyatt, Gaasenbeek & Millikin - *3
#250, 69 John St. South, Hamilton, ON L8N 2B9
Tel: 905-528-8369; *Fax:* 905-528-8066
keith@ggmlaw.ca

Hamilton: Harvey Katz Law Office - *4
14 Hess St. South, Hamilton, ON L8P 3M9
Tel: 905-523-1442; *Fax:* 905-525-3817
www.harveykatzlaw.ca

Hamilton: Michael E. Hinchey - *1
203 MacNab St. South, Hamilton, ON L8P 3C8
Tel: 905-525-1630; *Fax:* 905-527-3686

Hamilton: Inch Hammond Business Lawyers - *15
Former Name: Inch Hammond Professional
Corporation; Inch, Easterbrook & Shaker
#500, 1 King St. West, Hamilton, ON L8P 4X8
Fax: 905-525-0031
Toll-Free: 800-339-6086
www.inchlaw.com

Hamilton: Brian J. Inglis - *1
#803, 20 Hughson St. South, Hamilton, ON L8N 2A1
Tel: 905-527-6727; *Fax:* 905-527-6310
inglislaw@interlynx.net

Hamilton: Jaskula, Sherk - *1
#915, 25 Main St. West, Hamilton, ON L8P 1H1
Tel: 905-577-1040; *Fax:* 905-577-7775
csherk@jaskulasherk.com
jaskulasherk.com

Hamilton: George E. Johnson - *1
19 Augusta St., Hamilton, ON L8N 1P6
Tel: 905-523-7333; *Fax:* 905-523-1311

Hamilton: Kathryn A. Junger - *1
19 Augusta St., Hamilton, ON L8N 1P6
Tel: 905-523-7333; *Fax:* 905-523-1311

indicates number of lawyers

Hamilton: Michael W. Kelly - *1
#101, 154 Main St. East, Hamilton, ON L8N 1G9
Tel: 905-546-1920; Fax: 905-546-8471
mikelly@bellnet.ca

Hamilton: Mary Elizabeth Kneeland Barrister & Solicitor - *1
75 Young St., Hamilton, ON L8N 1V4
Tel: 905-572-7737; Fax: 905-529-8819
maryl@netscape.ca

Hamilton: John O. Krawchenko - *1
#111, 175 Hunter St. East, Hamilton, ON L8N 4E7
Tel: 905-546-0525; Fax: 905-546-0596
j.o.krawchenko@on.aibn.com

Hamilton: Landeg, Spitale - *2
#806, Union Gas Building, 20 Hughson St. South, Hamilton,
ON L8N 2A1
Tel: 905-529-7462; Fax: 905-528-6787

Hamilton: Lees & Lees
#2225, 25 Main St. West, Hamilton, ON L8P 1H1
Tel: 905-523-7830; Fax: 905-523-4677
leeslaw@leesandlees.ca

Hamilton: Mackesy Smye - *11
2 Haymarket St., Hamilton, ON L8N 1G7
Tel: 905-525-2341; Fax: 905-525-6300
maclaw@mackesysmye.com
www.mackesysmye.com

Hamilton: W.J.I. Malcolm - *1
#709, 20 Hughson St. South, Hamilton, ON L8N 2A1
Tel: 905-528-4291; Fax: 905-528-4292
wjimalcolm@bellnet.ca

Hamilton: Nicole Matthews - *1
#908, 20 Hughson St. South, Hamilton, ON L8N 2A1
Tel: 905-523-0017
nicoleblake@hotmail.com
www.nicolematthews.ca

Hamilton: McArthur, Vereschagin & Brown LLP - *4
195 James St. South, Hamilton, ON L8P 3A8
Tel: 905-527-6900; Fax: 905-527-5177
www.labourlaw.com

Hamilton: Anthony E. McCusker - *1
#1, 200 Aberdeen Avenue, Hamilton, ON L8P 2P9
Tel: 905-523-0593; Fax: 905-522-0988

Hamilton: McLelland & Dean
1 King St. West, 7th Fl., Hamilton, ON L8P 1A4
Tel: 905-546-0393; Fax: 905-527-6286

Hamilton: Millar, Alexander - *1
Plaza Level, 120 King St. West, Hamilton, ON L8P 4V2
Tel: 905-528-1186; Fax: 905-529-7073

Hamilton: Milligan Gresko Limberis LLP - *2
Former Name: Milligan Gresko Brown Vitulli Limberis
LLP
#1060, Standard Life Building, 120 King St. West, Hamilton,
ON L8P 4V2
Tel: 905-522-7700; Fax: 905-522-7794
contactus@mgllawyers.com
www.mgllawyers.com

Hamilton: Morris Law Group - *6
125 Main St. East, Hamilton, ON L8N 3Z3
Tel: 905-526-8080; Fax: 905-521-1927
Toll-Free: 877-464-4466
www.morrislawyers.com

Hamilton: Gordon F. Morton Q.C. - *1
#701, Commerce Place, 1 King St. West, Hamilton, ON L8P
1A4
Tel: 905-522-8147; Fax: 905-522-9548
info@gordmortonlaw.com
www.gordmortonlaw.com

Hamilton: Nolan Ciarlo LLP - *5
Former Name: Nolan Law Offices
#700, 1 King St. West, Hamilton, ON L8P 1A4
Tel: 905-522-9261; Fax: 905-525-5836
contact@nolanlaw.ca
www.nolanlaw.ca

Hamilton: Pelech Otto & Powell Barristers & Solicitors - *3
#100, 12 Walnut St. South, Hamilton, ON L8N 2K7
Tel: 905-522-4696; Fax: 905-528-6608
dmorrison@poplaw.ca
www.poplaw.ca

Hamilton: Michael S. Puskas - *1
46 Jackson St. East, Hamilton, ON L8N 1L1
Tel: 905-527-4495; Fax: 905-527-4496
michael.puskas@bellnet.ca

Hamilton: Daniel P. Randazzo - *1
44 Hughson St. South, Hamilton, ON L8N 2A7
Tel: 905-777-1773; Fax: 905-777-1774
randazzo@liuna.ca

Hamilton: Geoffrey M. Read - *1
172 Main St. East, Hamilton, ON L8N 1G9
Tel: 905-529-2028; Fax: 905-522-6677

Hamilton: Ross & McBride - *40
1 King St. West, 10th Fl., Hamilton, ON L8N 3P6
Tel: 905-526-9800; Fax: 905-526-0732
contact@rossmcbride.com
www.rossmcbride.com
twitter.com/rossmcbridellp

Hamilton: Ross & McBride LLP - *42
Former Name: Martin, Martin, Evans, Husband
1 King St. West, 10th Fl., Hamilton, ON L8P 1A4
Tel: 905-526-9800; Fax: 905-526-0732
contact@rossmcbride.com
www.rossmcbride.com
twitter.com/rossmcbridellp,

Hamilton: Michael N. Rubenstein - *1
#200, 242 James St. South, Hamilton, ON L8P 3B3
Tel: 905-525-9636; Fax: 905-521-0690
smerz@primus.ca

Hamilton: Linda Irvine Sapiano - *1
#1115, 25 Main St. West, Hamilton, ON L8P 1H1
Tel: 905-522-2040
linda@sapianolaw.com
sapianolaw.com

Hamilton: Scarfone Hawkins LLP - *22
P.O. Box 926, Stn. Depot 1, 1 James St. South, 14th Fl.,
Hamilton, ON L8N 3P9
Tel: 905-523-1333; Fax: 905-523-5878
info@shlaw.ca
shlaw.ca

Hamilton: Monica U.M. Scholz - *1
184 Jackson St. East, Hamilton, ON L8N 1L4
Tel: 905-577-6070; Fax: 905-577-6051
monica@scholzlaw.ca

Hamilton: Schreiber & Smurlick - *1
1219 Main St. East, Hamilton, ON L8K 1A5
Tel: 905-545-1107

Hamilton: SimpsonWigle LAW LLP - Hamilton - *31
#200, 1 Hunter St. East, Hamilton, ON L8N 3W1
Tel: 905-528-8411; Fax: 905-528-9008
Toll-Free: 800-464-4414
info@simpsonwigle.com
www.simpsonwigle.com

Hamilton: Smith & Smith - *1
1416 King St. East, Hamilton, ON L8M 1H8
Tel: 905-544-6034

Hamilton: Frank P. Sondola - *1
#105, 124 James St. South, Hamilton, ON L8P 2Z4
Tel: 905-523-1970; Fax: 905-523-1971

Hamilton: Sullivan Festeryga LLP - *22
1 James St. South, 11th Fl., Hamilton, ON L8P 4R5
Tel: 905-528-7963; Fax: 905-577-0077
lawyers@sfllp.ca
www.sfllp.ca
www.facebook.com/SullivanFesterygaLLP, twitter.com/SF_LLP

Hamilton: Swaye Crannie Boyd LLP - *4
Former Name: Gerald A. Swaye & Associates
Professional Corporation
#901, 105 Main St. East, Hamilton, ON L8N 1G6
Tel: 905-524-2861; Fax: 905-524-2313
Toll-Free: 855-524-2861
contactus@swaye.ca
www.swaye.ca

Hamilton: Szpiech, Ellis, Skibinski, Shipton - Hamilton - *3
414 Main St. East, Hamilton, ON L8N 1J9
Tel: 905-524-2454; Fax: 905-523-1733
contact@sesslaw.ca
www.sesslaw.ca

Hamilton: Stanley M. Tick & Associates - *3
108 John St. North, Hamilton, ON L8R 1H6
Tel: 905-523-6464; Fax: 905-523-8080
tickinfo@smtick.com
www.smtick.com

Hamilton: Donna Tiqui-Shebib - *1
#601, 20 Hughson St. South, Hamilton, ON L8N 2A1
Tel: 905-523-8049; Fax: 905-523-9368
Toll-Free: 888-523-8049
info@donnatiquishebiblaw.com
www.donnatiquishebiblaw.com
www.facebook.com/DonnaTiquiShebibLaw,
twitter.com/dtiquishebib,
www.linkedin.com/in/donna-tiqui-shebib-6b789029

Hamilton: Tkach & Tokiwa - *1
651 Upper James St., Hamilton, ON L9C 5R8
Tel: 905-383-3545; Fax: 905-574-3020

Hamilton: Turkstra Mazza Lawyers - Hamilton - *11
Former Name: Turkstra Mazza Shinehoft Mihailovich
Associates
15 Bold St., Hamilton, ON L8P 1T3
Tel: 905-529-3476; Fax: 905-529-3663
reception@tmalaw.ca
www.tmalaw.ca

Hamilton: Jennifer M. Vandenberg - *1
172 Main St. East, Hamilton, ON L8N 1G9
Tel: 905-572-6611; Fax: 905-572-9440
jvandenberg@cogeco.ca

Hamilton: Wallace Law - *1
14 Mornington Dr., Hamilton, ON L9B 1Z3
Tel: 905-575-0732; Fax: 905-574-3406
info@wallacelaw.ca
www.wallacelaw.ca

Hamilton: Gary Leonard Waxman - *1
#234, 845 Upper James St., Hamilton, ON L9C 3A3
Tel: 905-388-0585; Fax: 905-575-1613
gary.waxman@shaw.ca
garywaxman.ca

Hamilton: Weisz, Rocchi & Scholes - *3
#200, 242 Main St. East, Hamilton, ON L8N 1H5
Tel: 905-523-1842; Fax: 905-523-4011

Hamilton: Wellenreiter & Wellenreiter - *3
Rastrick House, 46 Forest Ave., Hamilton, ON L8N 1X2
Tel: 905-525-4520; Fax: 905-525-7943
www.wellenreiter.ca

Hamilton: Westdale Law - *2
Former Name: Simpson & Watson
950 King St. West, Hamilton, ON L8S 1K8
Tel: 905-527-1174; Fax: 905-577-0661
www.simpsonwatson.com

Hamilton: Nicholas R. White - *1
120 Jackson St. East, Hamilton, ON L8N 1L3
Tel: 905-521-8901; Fax: 905-521-9564
nwhite@netaccess.on.ca

Hamilton: Wissenz Law - *2
183 James St. South, Hamilton, ON L8P 3A8
Tel: 905-522-1102; Fax: 905-522-1122
reception@wissenzlaw.com
www.wissenzlaw.com

Hamilton: Yachetti Lanza LLP - *5
Former Name: Yachetti, Lanza & Restivo
#100, 154 Main St. East, Hamilton, ON L8N 1G9
Tel: 905-528-7534; Fax: 905-528-5275
info@ylrlawyers.com
www.ylrlawyers.com

Hanover: Garcia & Donnelly Law Office - *2
325 - 10th St., Hanover, ON N4N 1P1
Tel: 519-364-3643; Fax: 519-364-6594

Hanover: Halpin & McMeeken - *1
Former Name: Kevin W. McMeeken Law Office
478 - 10 St., Hanover, ON N4N 1R1
Tel: 519-364-5505; Fax: 519-364-0165
www.hanoverlaw.ca

Harrow: Karl G. Melinz - *1
P.O. Box 880, 41A Centre St. West, Harrow, ON N0R 1G0
Tel: 519-738-2232; Fax: 519-738-9080
kgmelinz@mmsi.net

Hawkesbury: Lachapelle Professional Corporation -
***1**
Former Name: Lachapelle Law Office
444 McGill St., Hawkesbury, ON K6A 1R2
Tel: 613-632-7032; *Fax:* 613-632-5472
lachapellelawoffice@bellnet.ca

Hawkesbury: Pilon Professional Corporation - *1
Former Name: Smith Lacombe Marcotte
280 Main St. West, Hawkesbury, ON K6A 2H7
Tel: 613-632-0103; *Fax:* 613-632-2800
pilons@bellnet.ca

Hawkesbury: Woods Parisien - *1
#200, 115 Main St. East, Hawkesbury, ON K6A 1A1
Tel: 613-632-8557; *Fax:* 613-632-8559
parisien@on.aibn.com

Hillsburgh: Robert P. Harper - *1
P.O. Box 10, 115 Trafalgar Rd., Hillsburgh, ON N0B 1Z0
Tel: 519-855-4961; *Fax:* 519-855-4029
robertharper@bellnet.ca

Huntsville: James S. Anderson
#5, 133 Hwy. 60, Huntsville, ON P1H 1C2
Tel: 705-789-8823; *Fax:* 705-789-1272
jamesanderson@sympatico.ca

Huntsville: Andrew B. Cochran - *1
#5, 133 Hwy. 60, Huntsville, ON P1H 1C2
Tel: 705-789-5538; *Fax:* 705-789-1272
acochran@vianet.ca

Huntsville: Ryan and Lewis Professional
Corporation - *2
#301, 395 Centre St. North, Huntsville, ON P1H 2P5
Tel: 705-788-7077; *Fax:* 705-789-6309
david.ryan@ryanandlewis.com
www.ryanandlewis.com

Huntsville: G.A. Smith - *1
Also Known As: Glen A. Smith
#1, 3 Fairy Ave., Huntsville, ON P1H 1G7
Tel: 705-789-8829; *Fax:* 705-789-2984
glensmith@bellnet.ca

Huntsville: Thoms & Currie - *7
#1, 6 Main St. West, Huntsville, ON P1H 2E1
Tel: 705-789-8844; *Fax:* 705-789-6547
info@thomsandcurrie.com
thomsandcurrie.com

Huntsville: Peter N. Ward - *1
46 West Rd., Huntsville, ON P1H 1L2
Tel: 705-788-0018; *Fax:* 705-788-2944

Ingersoll: Nesbitt Coulter LLP - Ingersoll - *7
183 Thames St. South, Ingersoll, ON N5C 2T6
Tel: 519-485-5651; *Fax:* 519-485-6582
www.nesbittlaw.com

Innisfil: Anderson Adams - *4
Former Name: Gibson & Adams LLP
8034 Yonge St., Innisfil, ON L9S 1L6
Tel: 705-436-1701; *Fax:* 705-436-1710
www.andersonadams.ca

Innisfil: D. Anne Cheney - *1
P.O. Box 7074, 1984 Wilkinson St., Innisfil, ON L9S 1A8
Tel: 705-734-9644; *Fax:* 705-734-0333

Innisfil: Duco & Duco LLP - *2
2093 Lilac Dr., #B, Innisfil, ON L9S 1Z1
Tel: 705-436-1020; *Fax:* 705-436-1027
www.ducolaw.com

Iroquois Falls: J. Kenneth Alexander - *1
P.O. Box 290, Stn. A, 283 Main St., Iroquois Falls, ON P0K
1G0
Tel: 705-232-4309; *Fax:* 705-232-5274

Iroquois Falls: Susan T. McGrath - *1
97 Ambridge Dr., Iroquois Falls, ON P0K 1E0
Tel: 705-232-4055; *Fax:* 705-232-6301
mcgrath@nt.net

Jarvis: William E. Kelly - *1
P.O. Box 430, 32 Main St. North, Jarvis, ON N0A 1J0
Tel: 519-587-4561; *Fax:* 519-587-5052

Kapuskasing: Bourgeault Brunelle Dumais Boucher
- *5
P.O. Box 446, 7 Cain Ave., Kapuskasing, ON P5N 1S8
Tel: 705-335-6121; *Fax:* 705-335-8127

Kapuskasing: J.M. Michel Majerovich - *1
28 Kolb Ave., Kapuskasing, ON P5N 1G1
Tel: 705-335-5051; *Fax:* 705-337-5051

Kapuskasing: Perras Mongenais
Former Name: Perras et Associés
10B Circle St., Kapuskasing, ON P5N 1T3
Tel: 705-335-3939; *Fax:* 705-335-3960

Kapuskasing: Guy A. Wainwright - *1
19 Cain Ave., Kapuskasing, ON P5N 1T2
Tel: 705-335-8501; *Fax:* 705-337-1474
gwainrt@ntl.sympatico.ca

Kenora: Beamish & Associates - *1
P.O. Box 1600, 50 Queen St., Kenora, ON P8T 1C3
Tel: 807-737-2809; *Fax:* 807-737-1211
cathyb@beamishlaw.ca

Kenora: Carten Law Office - *2
#13, 208, 2nd St. South, Kenora, ON P9N 1G4
Tel: 807-468-3036; *Fax:* 807-468-7576

Kenora: David James Elliott - *1
Stone House, 225 Main St. South, Kenora, ON P9N 1T3
Tel: 807-468-3355; *Fax:* 807-468-7858

Kenora: Gibson & Wexler - *2
P.O. Box 2450, 111 Main St. South, Kenora, ON P9N 3X8
Tel: 807-468-3061; *Fax:* 807-468-7940

Kenora: Hook Seller Lundin LLP - *6
#204, 301 - 1st Ave. South, Kenora, ON P9N 1W2
Tel: 807-468-9831; *Fax:* 807-468-8384
www.hsllaw.ca

Kenora: Shewchuk, Ormiston, Richardt & Johnson
LLP - *7
Former Name: Shewchuk, MacDonell, Ormiston &
Richardt LLP
214 Main St. South, Kenora, ON P9N 1T2
Tel: 807-468-5559; *Fax:* 807-468-5504
info@kenoralaw.com
www.kenoralaw.com
www.facebook.com/kenoralaw

Keswick: Altwerger Law - *2
Former Name: Altwerger, Baker, Weinberg
187 Simcoe Ave., Keswick, ON L4P 2H6
Tel: 905-476-2555; *Fax:* 905-476-2560
stevea@lexpertor.com
www.altwergerlaw.com

Keswick: Donnell Law Group - *4
183 Simcoe Ave., Keswick, ON L4P 2H6
Tel: 905-476-9100; *Fax:* 905-476-2027
Toll-Free: 888-307-9991
info@donnellgroup.ca
www.donnellandassociates.com

Keswick: Robert E. Pollock - *1
#300, 449 The Queensway South, Keswick, ON L4P 2C9
Tel: 905-476-0021; *Fax:* 905-476-0134

Kincardine: Marshall & Mahood - *2
Former Name: Mahood & Darcy
313 Lambton St., Kincardine, ON N2Z 2Y8
Tel: 519-396-8144; *Fax:* 519-396-9446
reception@marshallmahood.com
www.marshallmahood.com

Kincardine: William S. Mathers - *1
226 Queen St., Kincardine, ON N2Z 2S5
Tel: 519-396-4147; *Fax:* 519-396-1872
wwmlawyer@bmts.com

King City: Black & Hahn LLP - *2
Former Name: Margaret Black & Associates
2175 King Rd., King City, ON L7B 1G3
Tel: 905-833-9090; *Fax:* 905-833-9091
info@blackandhahn.ca
www.blackandassociates.ca

Kingston: Bédard, Barrister & Solicitor Business
Law - *1
#2, P.O. Box 695, 159 Wellington St., Kingston, ON K7L 4X1
Tel: 613-542-3552; *Fax:* 613-542-1034
jb@bedardlegal.com
www.bedardlegal.com

Kingston: Bergeron Clifford LLP - *13
1 Hyperion Ct., Kingston, ON K7K 7G3
Tel: 613-384-5886; *Fax:* 613-384-0501
Toll-Free: 877-485-3054
info@BergeronClifford.com
www.bergeronclifford.com
www.facebook.com/bergeron.clifford, twitter.com/bclawyers

Kingston: Caldwell & Moore - *1
260 Barrie St., Kingston, ON K7L 3K7
Tel: 613-545-1860; *Fax:* 613-545-1862
caldwell-moore@cogeco.ca

Kingston: Jack W. Chong - *1
Former Name: Chong & O'Neill
P.O. Box 1382, Stn. Main, 273 King St. East, Kingston, ON
K7L 5C6
Tel: 613-549-1225; *Fax:* 613-549-3882
jackchong@chongoneill.ca

Kingston: Robert K. Cooper - *1
11 Carruthers St., Kingston, ON K7L 1L9
Tel: 613-544-3634

Kingston: Cunningham Swan Carty Little & Bonham
LLP - *29
#300, Smith Robinson Bldg., 27 Princess St., Kingston, ON
K7L 1A3
Tel: 613-544-0211; *Fax:* 613-542-9814
info@cswan.com
www.cswan.com

Kingston: Ecclestone Law - *4
Former Name: Ecclestone & Ecclestone LLP
#100, 1480 Bath Rd., Kingston, ON K7M 4X6
Tel: 613-384-0735; *Fax:* 613-384-0731
email@ecclaw.net
www.ecclaw.net

Kingston: John R. Gale - *1
2263 Princess St., Kingston, ON K7M 3G4
Tel: 613-546-4283; *Fax:* 613-546-9861

Kingston: Wayne C. Gay & Associate - *2
P.O. Box 370, Stn. Main, 275 Ontario St., Kingston, ON K7L
4W2
Tel: 613-549-4300; *Fax:* 613-549-6948
waynegay@waynegay.com

Kingston: Good Elliott Hawkins LLP - *3
Former Name: Good & Elliott
153 Brock St., Kingston, ON K7L 4Y8
Tel: 613-544-1330; *Fax:* 613-547-4538
www.geh.ca/mambo/

Kingston: Hickey & Hickey - *2
P.O. Box 110, 93 Clarence St., Kingston, ON K7L 4V6
Tel: 613-548-3191; *Fax:* 613-548-8195
hickeym@on.aibn.com

Kingston: Mary Ann Higgs - *1
#206, P.O. Box 700, 275 Ontario St., Kingston, ON K7L 4X1
Tel: 613-548-7399; *Fax:* 613-548-1862
maryannhiggs@on.aibn.com

Kingston: R. Wayne Keeler - *1
23 Jane Ave., Kingston, ON K7M 3G6
Tel: 613-531-4600; *Fax:* 613-547-4577
keelerw@kos.net

Kingston: J. Bruce MacNaughton - *1
P.O. Box 1621, 45 Johnson St., Kingston, ON K7L 5C8
Tel: 613-546-9990; *Fax:* 613-546-6176
bruce@macnaughtonlaw.com
www.macnaughtonlaw.com

Kingston: Mary-Jo Maur - *1
#3, 159 Wellington St., Kingston, ON K7L 3E1
Tel: 613-530-2665; *Fax:* 613-530-2241
mary-jo.maur@bellnet.ca

Kingston: M.A. McCue - *1
#201A, 837 Princess St., Kingston, ON K7L 1G8
Tel: 613-542-3700; *Fax:* 613-542-5700
mamccue@kingston.net

Kingston: Gordon Y. McDiarmid - *1
P.O. Box 1010, Stn. Main, 3 Rideau St., Kingston, ON K7L
4X8
Tel: 613-546-3274; *Fax:* 613-546-1493
gmcdiarmid@on.aibn.com

* indicates number of lawyers

Kingston: Morley Law Office - *1
211 Division St., Kingston, ON K7K 3Z2
Tel: 613-542-2192; *Fax:* 613-542-2393
www.lesmorley.com
www.facebook.com/MorleyLawOffice, twitter.com/LesMorley
www.linkedin.com/in/lesmorley

Kingston: Fergus J. (Chip) O'Connor - *1
P.O. Box 1959, 104 Johnson St., Kingston, ON K7L 5J7
Tel: 613-546-5581; *Fax:* 613-546-5540
oconnor@kos.net

Kingston: Elizabeth I. Ollson - *1
1770 Bath Rd., Kingston, ON K7M 4Y2
Tel: 613-384-8122; *Fax:* 613-384-7056
eollson@kos.net

Kingston: Philip M. Osanic - *1
819 Blackburn Mews, Kingston, ON K7P 2N6
Tel: 613-634-4440; *Fax:* 613-634-4443

Kingston: J. Yvonne Pelley - *1
819 Blackburn Mews, Kingston, ON K7P 2N6
Tel: 613-634-4440; *Fax:* 613-634-4443
jypelley@on.aibn.com

Kingston: RZCD Law Firm LLP - Kingston - *24
Also Known As: Racioppo Zuber Coetzee Dionne LLP
#210, 650 Dalton Ave., Kingston, ON K7M 8N7
Tel: 613-544-1482; *Fax:* 613-546-3633
www.rzcdlaw.com

Kingston: Jennifer L. Sims - *1
#207, 275 Ontario St., Kingston, ON K7K 2X5
Tel: 613-507-7467; *Fax:* 613-507-7468
jennifer@jennifersims.ca
www.jennifersims.ca

Kingston: Douglas M. Slack - *1
366 King East, Kingston, ON K7K 6Y3
Tel: 613-384-7260; *Fax:* 613-384-7262
dm.slack@utoronto.ca

Kingston: Britton C. Smith - *1
P.O. Box 1376, Stn. Main, 74 Johnson St., Kingston, ON K7L 5C6
Tel: 613-547-3798; *Fax:* 613-547-6814

Kingston: Letitia M. Steele - *1
P.O. Box 29013, Stn. Portsmouth, Kingston, ON K7M 8W6
Tel: 613-542-1795; *Fax:* 613-542-2471

Kingston: Tepper Law Office - *1
461 Princess St., Kingston, ON K7L 1C3
Tel: 613-546-1169; *Fax:* 613-546-6992
gtepper@kingston.net

Kingston: Thomson & Gowsell LLP - *2
232 Brock St., Kingston, ON K7L 1S4
Tel: 613-549-5111; *Fax:* 613-549-4074
thomson@kingston.net
www.thomsonlaw.com

Kingston: Thomas W. Troughton - *1
#103, P.O. Box 668, Stn. Main, 780 Midpark Dr., Kingston, ON K7L 4X1
Tel: 613-634-0302; *Fax:* 613-384-8777
troughton@frontenaclaw.on.ca

Kingston: Viner, Kennedy, Frederick, Allan & Tobias LLP - *8
Also Known As: Viner Kennedy
#300, The Royal Block, 366 King St. East, Kingston, ON K7K 6Y3
Tel: 613-542-7867; *Fax:* 613-542-1279
www.vinerkennedy.com

Kingsville: Dunnion, Dunmore & Schippel LLP - *1
59 Main St. East, Kingsville, ON N9Y 1A1
Tel: 519-733-6573; *Fax:* 519-733-3172
pdunmore@cogeco.net

Kirkland Lake: Richard & Chamaillard Law - *2
Former Name: Gorman & Richard-Gorman
6 Government Rd. West, Kirkland Lake, ON P2N 2E1
Tel: 705-567-9500; *Fax:* 705-567-5014
reception@rclawfirm.ca
www.rclawfirn.ca

Kirkland Lake: Gavin Shorrock - *1
15 Gov't Rd. East, Kirkland Lake, ON P2N 2E6
Tel: 705-567-5213; *Fax:* 705-567-3987
shorlaw@ntl.sympatico.ca

Kitchener: Derek K. Babcock - *1
28 Weber St. West, Kitchener, ON N2H 3Z2
Tel: 519-742-3570; *Fax:* 519-576-7451
dbabcock@on.aibn.com

Kitchener: Thomas L. Brock - *1
17 Irvin St., Kitchener, ON N2H 1K6
Tel: 519-742-1270; *Fax:* 519-742-6973

Kitchener: J. Mark Coffey - *1
#705, 30 Duke St. West, Kitchener, ON N2H 3W5
Tel: 519-742-5100; *Fax:* 519-742-5229

Kitchener: Harold J. Cox - *1
#610, 50 Queen St. North, Kitchener, ON N2H 6M1
Tel: 519-744-6551; *Fax:* 519-744-9885
harold@hjcox.ca

Kitchener: N.A. Crawford - *1
1444 King St. East, Kitchener, ON N2G 2N7
Tel: 519-743-3615; *Fax:* 519-743-2212

Kitchener: Dietrich Law Office - *2
Former Name: G.B. Dietrich
141 Duke St. East, Kitchener, ON N2H 1A6
Tel: 519-749-0770; *Fax:* 519-749-0288
www.dietrichlaw.ca
www.facebook.com/dietrichlaw

Kitchener: Timothy C. Flannery - *1
82 Weber St. East, Kitchener, ON N2P 1K3
Tel: 519-578-8017; *Fax:* 519-578-8327
flannery@flannerylaw.com
www.flannerylaw.ca

Kitchener: George C. Amos - *1
276 Frederick St., Kitchener, ON N2H 2N4
Tel: 519-576-8480; *Fax:* 519-579-3042
george@amoslaw.ca

Kitchener: Gerry V. Schaffer Law Office - *1
Former Name: Roetsch & Schaffer
284 Frederick St., Kitchener, ON N2H 2N4
Tel: 519-576-5310; *Fax:* 519-576-2797

Kitchener: Giesbrecht, Griffin, Funk and Irvine LLP - *7
60 College St., Kitchener, ON N2H 5A1
Tel: 519-579-4300; *Fax:* 519-579-8745
ggfi@ggfilaw.com
www.ggfilaw.com

Kitchener: Giffen LLP - Kitchener - *13
Former Name: Giffen Lee LLP
#500, Commerce House, P.O. Box 2396, 50 Queen St. North, Kitchener, ON N2H 6M3
Tel: 519-578-4150; *Fax:* 519-578-8740
info@giffenlawyers.com
www.giffenlawyers.com

Kitchener: R. Haalboom, Q.C. - *1
#304, 7 Duke St. West, Kitchener, ON N2H 6N7
Tel: 519-579-2920; *Fax:* 519-576-0471
richard@haalboom.ca

Kitchener: Robert J. Hare - *1
741 King St. West, Kitchener, ON N2G 1E3
Tel: 519-576-6710; *Fax:* 519-576-0258
harelawoffice@on.aibn.com

Kitchener: Richard H.F. Herold - *1
53 Roy St., Kitchener, ON N2H 4B4
Tel: 519-749-0555; *Fax:* 519-741-9041
herold.legal@gmail.com

Kitchener: Timothy Jansen - *1
46 Brembel St., Kitchener, ON N2B 3T8
Tel: 519-741-1911; *Fax:* 519-741-5945
timjansen@bellnet.ca

Kitchener: Jennifer Roggemann Law Office - *1
1135 King St. East, Kitchener, ON N2G 2N3
Tel: 519-744-3570; *Fax:* 519-744-3571
www.jrlawoffice.com

Kitchener: Kay Professional Corporation - *4
Former Name: Kay, Bogdon
Legal Innovation Centre, 370 Frederick St., Kitchener, ON N2H 2P3
Tel: 519-579-1220; *Fax:* 519-743-8063
law@kaylaw.ca
www.kaylaw.ca

Kitchener: Kelly & Co. - *2
#903, 50 Queen St. North, Kitchener, ON N2H 6P4
Tel: 519-579-3360; *Fax:* 519-579-2556
www.kellylaw.com

Kitchener: Kokila D. Khanna
#101, 10 Duke St. West, Kitchener, ON N2H 3W4
Tel: 516-571-1542; *Fax:* 516-571-0945
kdkhanna@khannalaw.ca

Kitchener: Sheldon Kosky - *1
P.O. Box 2307, 71 Weber St. East, Kitchener, ON N2H 1C6
Tel: 519-578-1480; *Fax:* 519-579-2537
skosky@kosky.com

Kitchener: Stephanie A. Krug - *1
17 Irvin St., Kitchener, ON N2H 1K6
Tel: 519-743-1603; *Fax:* 519-742-6973
stephaniekrug@aol.com

Kitchener: Madorin, Snyder LLP - *17
P.O. Box 1234, 55 King St. West, 6th Fl., Kitchener, ON N2G 4G9
Tel: 519-744-4491; *Fax:* 519-741-8060
www.kw-law.com
twitter.com/MadorinSnyder
www.linkedin.com/company/madorin-snyder-llp

Kitchener: Richard V. Marchak - *1
245 Frederick St., Kitchener, ON N2H 2M7
Tel: 519-570-3635; *Fax:* 519-570-4427
richardmarchak@hotmail.com

Kitchener: McCarter Grespan Beynon Weir - *14
Also Known As: McCarter Grespan
675 Riverbend Dr., Kitchener, ON N2K 3S3
Tel: 519-571-8800; *Fax:* 519-742-1841
jweir@mgbwlaw.com
www.mgbwlaw.com

Kitchener: Jane A. McKenzie - *1
55 King St. West, 7th Fl., Kitchener, ON N2G 4W1
Tel: 519-745-7614; *Fax:* 519-745-9778
jane.mckenzie@execulink.com
www.janemckenziefamilylawyer.com

Kitchener: McLeod Green Dewar LLP & Associates - *4
#605, 30 Duke St. West, Kitchener, ON N2H 3W6
Tel: 519-742-4297; *Fax:* 519-744-5526
reception@mgdlawyers.ca
www.mgdlawyers.ca
www.facebook.com/mgdlawyers
www.linkedin.com/in/amy-a-green-688a4816

Kitchener: Mollison, McCormick - *7
P.O. Box 2307, Stn. C, 71 Weber St. East, Kitchener, ON N2H 6L2
Tel: 519-579-1040; *Fax:* 519-579-2537

Kitchener: Morrison Reist - *3
279 Queen St. South, Kitchener, ON N2G 1W4
Tel: 519-576-5351; *Fax:* 519-576-5411
Toll-Free: 800-354-5723
law@morrisonreist.com
www.morrisonreist.com

Kitchener: Morscher & Morscher - *1
85 Margaret Ave. N, Kitchener, ON N2J 3R2
Tel: 519-749-8100; *Fax:* 519-749-8141

Kitchener: Jacqueline Mulvey - *1
293 Frederick St., Kitchener, ON N2H 2N6
Tel: 519-744-3704; *Fax:* 519-744-3662
jmulvey@rogers.com

Kitchener: Mark T. Nowak - *1
370 Frederick St., Kitchener, ON N2H 2P3
Tel: 519-746-8340; *Fax:* 519-746-8144

Kitchener: John E. Opolko - *1
372 Queen St. South, Kitchener, ON N2G 1W7
Tel: 519-743-2670; *Fax:* 519-743-2670

Kitchener: Bruce H. Ritter - *1
17 Irvin St., Kitchener, ON N2H 1K6
Tel: 519-744-1169; *Fax:* 519-742-6973
britter1@aol.com

Kitchener: Schmidt Law Office Professional Corporation
#1100, 305 King St. West, Kitchener, ON N2G 1B9
Tel: 519-578-1448; *Fax:* 519-578-1168
admin@schmidtlawoffices.net
www.schmidtlawoffices.net

Kitchener: John D. E. Shannon - *1
30 Spetz St., Kitchener, ON N2H 1K1
Tel: 519-743-3654; *Fax:* 519-578-9521
jdeslaw@bellnet.ca

Kitchener: Sloane & Pinchen - *2
#301, 824 King St. North, Kitchener, ON N2G 1G1
Tel: 519-578-3094; *Fax:* 519-578-3682
david@sloanepinchen.com

Kitchener: Smith, Hunt, Buck - *2
53 Roy St., Kitchener, ON N2H 4B4
Tel: 519-579-3400; *Fax:* 519-741-9041

Kitchener: Smyth, Hobson - *1
#206, 7 Duke St. West, Kitchener, ON N2H 6N7
Tel: 519-578-9400; *Fax:* 519-578-7482

Kitchener: Sorbara, Schumacher, McCann LLP - Kitchener - *33
Also Known As: Sorbara Law
300 Victoria St. North, Kitchener, ON N2H 6R9
Tel: 519-576-0460
www.sorbaralaw.com
www.facebook.com/SorbaraLaw
www.linkedin.com/company/sorbara-schumacher-mccann-llp

Kitchener: Sutherland Mark Flemming Snyder-Penner Professional Corporation - *6
#100, 675 Queen St. South, Kitchener, ON N2M 1A1
Tel: 519-725-2500; *Fax:* 519-725-2525
info@sutherlandmark.com
www.sutherlandmark.com

Kitchener: Carolyn R. Thomas & Associate - *1
#900, 50 Queen St. North, Kitchener, ON N2H 6P4
Tel: 519-576-4459; *Fax:* 519-576-9349

Kitchener: Voll & Santos - *2
30 Spetz St., Kitchener, ON N2H 1K1
Tel: 519-578-3400; *Fax:* 519-578-9521

Kitchener: Colleen J. Winn - *1
604 Charles St. East, Kitchener, ON N2G 2R5
Tel: 519-743-3981; *Fax:* 519-743-3647

Kitchener: Stephen C. Woodworth - *1
#9, 300 Victoria St. North, Kitchener, ON N2H 6R9
Tel: 519-570-0033; *Fax:* 519-570-0104

Kitchener: Wilfrid R. Zalman - *1
#102, 684 Belmont Ave. West, Kitchener, ON N2M 1N6
Tel: 519-579-6170; *Fax:* 519-579-6171

L'Orignal: Tolhurst & Miller - *4
1030 King St., L'Orignal, ON K0B 1K0
Tel: 613-675-4512; *Fax:* 613-675-1103
Toll-Free: 866-752-8277

Lakefield: Baker & Cole - Lakefield - *1
Former Name: T.E. Cole
P.O. Box 658, 8 Bridge St., Lakefield, ON K0L 2H0
Tel: 705-652-8161; *Fax:* 705-652-7088
www.bakerandcole.com

Lancaster: Paul D. Syrduk - *1
P.O. Box 9, 10 Oak St., Lancaster, ON K0C 1N0
Tel: 613-347-2423; *Fax:* 613-347-7118
syryduk@glen-net.ca

Leamington: Ricci, Enns, Rollier & Setterington LLP - *5
Former Name: Ricci, Enns & Rollier LLP; Reid, Reynolds, Collins, Ricci & Enns
60 Talbot St. West, Leamington, ON N8H 1M4
Tel: 519-326-3237; *Fax:* 519-326-8139
www.rers.ca

Lindsay: Brent Walmsley - *1
223 Kent St. West, Lindsay, ON K9V 2Z1
Tel: 705-878-8131; *Fax:* 705-878-4642

Lindsay: J.W. Evans - *1
P.O. Box 427, Stn. Main, 219 Kent St. West, Lindsay, ON K9V 4S5
Tel: 705-324-3207; *Fax:* 705-328-1128

Lindsay: Frost, Frost & Gorwill - *1
#217, 189 Kent St. West, Lindsay, ON K9V 5G6
Tel: 705-324-2193; *Fax:* 705-324-9879

Lindsay: Carol E. Jamieson - *1
18 Cambridge St. North, Lindsay, ON K9V 4C3
Tel: 705-878-8864; *Fax:* 705-878-1813
caroljamieson@cogeco.ca

Lindsay: Timothy W. Johnston - *2
#218, The Kent Place Mall, 189 Kent St. West, Lindsay, ON K9V 5G6
Tel: 705-328-2393; *Fax:* 705-328-2428
twj@nexicom.net

Lindsay: J. Scott McLeod - *1
16 Russell St. West, Lindsay, ON K9V 2W7
Tel: 705-324-6711; *Fax:* 705-324-5723

Lindsay: Leonard S. Siegel - *1
P.O. Box 997, 11 Adelaide St. North, Lindsay, ON K9V 5N4
Tel: 705-878-7990; *Fax:* 705-878-7992
lsiegel@kawarthalaw.ca

London: Ambrogio & Ambrogio - *2
200 Queens Ave., London, ON N6A 1J3
Tel: 519-438-7219; *Fax:* 519-438-5919

London: Anissimoff Mann Professional Corporation - *4
#101, Talbot Centre, 140 Fullarton St., London, ON N6A 5P2
Tel: 519-673-5591; *Fax:* 519-673-6784
info@anissimoff.on.ca
www.anissimoff.on.ca

London: Daniel S.J. Bangarth - *1
562 Waterloo St., London, ON N6B 2P9
Tel: 519-672-2340; *Fax:* 519-657-8173
darlene.howard@sympatico.ca

London: Bates Law Office - *1
Also Known As: Bates, Thomas A.
#1, 151 Pine Valley Blvd., London, ON N6K 3T6
Tel: 519-472-0330; *Fax:* 519-472-1814
tabates@rogers.com

London: Joanne G. Beasley & Associates - *2
Former Name: Joanne G. Beasley & Associates
525 South St., London, ON N6B 1C4
Tel: 519-642-1520; *Fax:* 519-673-3868
info@beasleylawoffice.com
www.beasleylawoffice.com

London: Behr Law Professional Corporation - *3
Former Name: Behr & Rady
472 Ridout St. North, London, ON N6A 2P7
Tel: 519-438-4530
behrlawfirm@gmail.com
www.londoncriminallaw.com

London: Belanger, Cassino, Coulston & Gallagher - *4
#153, 759 Hyde Park Rd., London, ON N6H 3S2
Tel: 226-271-4372; *Fax:* 519-657-5189

London: Belecky & Belecky - *3
#104, 235 North Centre Rd., London, ON N5X 4E7
Tel: 519-673-5630
www.belecky.ca

London: Brown Beattie O'Donovan LLP - *18
380 Wellington St., 16th Fl., London, ON N6A 5B5
Tel: 519-679-0400; *Fax:* 519-679-6350
Toll-Free: 888-363-6045
www.bbo.on.ca

London: Mervin F. Burgard, Q.C. - *1
#203, 219 Oxford St. West, London, ON N6H 1S5
Tel: 519-679-9900; *Fax:* 519-679-8546

London: Carlyle Peterson Lawyers LLP - *6
#7, 717 Richmond St., London, ON N6A 1S2
Tel: 519-432-0632; *Fax:* 519-432-0634
www.cplaw.com

London: Luigi E. Circelli - *1
557 Talbot St., London, ON N6A 2S9
Tel: 519-673-1850; *Fax:* 519-673-4966
lcircelli@bellnet.ca

London: Cohen Highley LLP - London - *33
One London Place, 255 Queens Ave., 11th Fl., London, ON N6A 5R8
Tel: 519-672-9330; *Fax:* 519-672-5960
www.cohenhighley.com

London: Cram & Associates - *5
#514, 200 Queens Ave., London, ON N6A 1J3
Tel: 519-673-1670; *Fax:* 519-439-5011
www.cramassociates.com
twitter.com/CramAssociates

London: William L. Dewar - *1
479 Talbot St., London, ON N6A 2S4
Tel: 519-672-1830; *Fax:* 519-661-0095
wildew@on.aibn.com

London: Kenneth Duggan - *1
#203, 111 Waterloo St., London, ON N6B 2M4
Tel: 519-672-5360; *Fax:* 519-433-6975
kvduggan@bellnet.ca

London: Family Law Group - *3
Also Known As: Brenda Barr, Barrister & Solicitor
Former Name: Barr Family Law
521 Colborne St., London, ON N6B 2T6
Tel: 519-672-5953; *Fax:* 519-672-8736
www.familylawgroup.ca
www.facebook.com/155767857939309

London: Foster Townsend LLP - London - *18
Former Name: Foster, Townsend, Graham & Associates LLP
#900, 150 Dufferin Ave., London, ON N6A 5N6
Tel: 519-672-5272; *Fax:* 519-672-9313
Toll-Free: 888-354-0448
www.fostertownsend.com

London: Frauts, Dobbie - *3
Former Name: Dobson & Dobbie
585 Talbot St., London, ON N6A 2T2
Tel: 519-679-4000; *Fax:* 519-679-7700
info@frautsdobbie.com
www.frautsdobbie.ca

London: David G. Fysh - *1
520 Springbank Dr., London, ON N6J 1G8
Tel: 519-472-3974; *Fax:* 519-472-3756
david@davidfysh.com
www.davidfysh.com

London: Giffen & Partners - *4
465 Waterloo St., London, ON N6B 2P4
Tel: 519-679-4700; *Fax:* 519-432-8003

London: Gordon B. Good - *1
255 Queens Ave., London, ON N6A 5R8
Tel: 519-672-9330
gordongood@goodlawoffice.com

London: Gregory Willoughby Law - *1
Also Known As: Only Immigration
Former Name: Willoughby, MacLeod
100 Fullarton St., London, ON N6A 1K1
Tel: 519-645-1500; *Fax:* 519-645-1503
www.londonimmigrationlawyers.ca

London: Harrison Pensa LLP - London - *58
P.O. Box 3237, 450 Talbot St., London, ON N6A 4K3
Tel: 519-679-9660; *Fax:* 519-667-3362
Toll-Free: 800-263-0489
reception@harrisonpensa.com
www.harrisonpensa.com
www.facebook.com/HarrisonPensa, twitter.com/harrisonpensa,
www.linkedin.com/company/harrison-pensa-llp

London: Antin Jaremchuk - *1
Also Known As: Jaremchuk Law Offices
100 Fullarton St., London, ON N6A 1K1
Tel: 519-432-2417; *Fax:* 519-663-1165
antin@jaremchuklaw.com
www.jaremchuklaw.com

London: Michael J. Lamb - *1
#102, 101 Cherryhill Blvd., London, ON N6H 4S4
Tel: 519-645-1104; *Fax:* 519-645-1107
lamblaw@on.aibn.com

London: Therese D.P. Landry Law Office - *1
#319, 148 York St., London, ON N6A 1A9
Tel: 519-438-4111; *Fax:* 519-438-4113

London: The Lawhouse - Kirwin Fryday Medcalf Lawyers - London - *3
Former Name: Fryday, Murphy, Brown
#104, 140 Fullarton St., London, ON N6A 5P2
Tel: 519-679-8800; *Fax:* 519-518-2362
Toll-Free: 877-633-6878
www.lawhouse.ca

indicates number of lawyers

London: Lerners LLP - London - *70
P.O. Box 2335, 80 Dufferin Ave., London, ON N6A 4G4
Tel: 519-672-4510; *Fax*: 519-672-2044
Toll-Free: 800-263-5583
lerner.london@lerners.ca
www.lerners.ca
www.facebook.com/LernersLLP, twitter.com/LernersLLP,
www.linkedin.com/company/lerners-llp

London: Lexcor Business Lawyers LLP - *6
629 Wellington St., London, ON N6A 3R8
Tel: 519-858-2222; *Fax*: 519-858-2323
Toll-Free: 877-772-2424
lexcor.ca
www.facebook.com/lexcor, www.linkedin.com/company/2455421

London: V. Libis - *1
93 Dufferin Ave., London, ON N6A 1K3
Tel: 519-434-6821
valdis.libis@odyssey.on.ca

London: John R. Lisowski - *1
607 Queens Ave., London, ON N6B 1Y9
Tel: 519-679-5000; *Fax*: 519-673-1717

London: Anthony Little, Q.C. - *1
Former Name: Little & Jarrett
#304, 200 Queens Ave., London, ON N6A 1J3
Tel: 519-672-8121; *Fax*: 519-432-0784
little@litjar.on.ca
www.litjar.on.ca

London: Little, Inglis, Price & Ewer LLP - *4
Former Name: Little, Inglis & Price
148 Wortley Rd., London, ON N6C 3P5
Tel: 519-672-5415; *Fax*: 519-672-3906
www.lipelaw.com

London: Michael F. Loebach - *3
#508, 171 Queens Ave., London, ON N6A 5J7
Tel: 519-439-3031; *Fax*: 519-439-3540
info@mloebachlaw.com

London: MacKewn, Winder LLP - *2
#300, P.O. Box 96, 376 Richmond St., London, ON N6A 3C7
Tel: 519-672-2040; *Fax*: 519-672-6583
mwk@mwk.on.ca

London: Nancy Z. Magguilli - *1
PO Box 29002, RPO Westmount Mall, London, ON N6K 4L9
Tel: 519-641-6255; *Fax*: 519-641-6255

London: Edward J. Mann - *1
#605, 137 Dundas St., London, ON N6A 1E9
Tel: 519-672-8707; *Fax*: 519-660-4678
ejmann@on.aibn.com

London: McKenzie Lake Lawyers LLP - London - *44
#1800, 140 Fullarton St., London, ON N6A 5P2
Tel: 519-672-5666; *Fax*: 519-672-2674
www.mckenzielake.com
www.facebook.com/mckenzielakelawyers,
www.linkedin.com/company/mckenzielake

London: McNamara, Pizzale - *3
#220, 200 Queens Ave., London, ON N6A 1J3
Tel: 519-434-2174; *Fax*: 519-642-7654
mcpizz@execulink.com

London: Menear Worrad & Associates - *5
478 Waterloo St., London, ON N6B 2P6
Tel: 519-672-7370; *Fax*: 519-663-1165
www.menearlaw.com

London: Armand Morrow - *1
42 Hampton Cres., London, ON N6H 2N8
Tel: 519-471-7607; *Fax*: 519-471-9121

London: Frederick A. Mueller - *1
Former Name: Mueller & Reich
141 Wortley Rd., London, ON N6C 3P4
Tel: 519-673-1300; *Fax*: 519-673-1728
fred_mueller@rogers.com

London: Barry F. Nelligan - *1
#202, 145 Wharncliffe Rd. South, London, ON N6J 2K4
Tel: 519-438-1709; *Fax*: 519-438-1700
www.barrynelliganlaw.com

London: Nicholson, Smith & Partners LLP - *6
295 Central Ave., London, ON N6B 2C9
Tel: 519-679-3366; *Fax*: 519-679-0958
reception@nicholsonsmith.com
nicholsonsmith.com

London: Suhas T. Nimkar - *1
151 York St., London, ON N6A 1A8
Fax: 519-474-9578
Toll-Free: 866-551-5255
suhasnimkar@aol.com

London: Michael R. Nyhof
380 Queens Ave., London, ON N6B 1X6
Tel: 519-642-4015; *Fax*: 519-642-4034
michaelnyhof@on.aibn.com

London: Patton Cormier Lawyers - *2
Former Name: Patton Cormier & Associates
#1512, 140 Fullarton St., London, ON N6A 5P2
Tel: 519-432-8282; *Fax*: 519-432-7285
www.pattoncormier.ca

London: Paul Lépine Law Office - *1
100 Fullerton St., London, ON N6A 1K1
Tel: 519-432-4155; *Fax*: 519-432-6861
www.paullepine.ca

London: Judith M. Potter - *1
54 Hunt Club Dr., London, ON N6H 3Y3
Tel: 519-432-8811; *Fax*: 519-663-1165
jpotter@start.ca

London: Peter J. Quigley - *1
924 Oxford East, London, ON N5Y 3J9
Tel: 519-453-3393
PeterQuigley@londonlawyer.ca
www.london-lawyer.ca

London: Wayne G. Rabley - *1
#Unit E., 80 Dundas St., 2nd Fl., London, ON N6A 6A5
Tel: 519-660-3014; *Fax*: 519-660-3024

London: Michael Robertson - *1
#105, 186 Albert St., London, ON N6A 1M1
Tel: 226-289-2119; *Fax*: 519-660-0840
Toll-Free: 800-813-9702
www.londonlitigation.com
www.facebook.com/595358407240498

London: Siskinds LLP - London - *84
Former Name: Siskind, Cromarty, Ivey & Dowler LLP
P.O. Box 2520, 680 Waterloo St., London, ON N6A 3V8
Tel: 519-672-2121; *Fax*: 519-672-6065
Toll-Free: 877-672-2121
hello@siskinds.com
www.siskinds.com
www.facebook.com/siskinds, twitter.com/SiskindsLLP

London: Stambler & Mills - *1
#111, 142 Fullarton St., London, ON N6A 0A4
Tel: 519-672-6240; *Fax*: 519-433-9593
rmills@bellnet.ca

London: Szemenyei Mackenzie Group - London - *7
Also Known As: SMG Law Firm
Former Name: Szemenyei Kerwin MacKenzie LLP; Bitz,
Szemenyei, Ferguson & MacKenzie
376 Richmond St., London, ON N6A 3C7
Tel: 519-433-8155; *Fax*: 519-660-4857
www.smglaw.ca

London: L. Kent Thomas - *1
11 Stanley St., London, ON N6C 1A9
Tel: 519-438-4181; *Fax*: 519-433-5557

London: Thomson Mahoney Delorey LLP - *7
Former Name: Thomson Mahoney Dobson Delorey;
Thomson Mahoney Elliott Delorey
#200, 145 Wharncliffe Rd. South, London, ON N6J 2K4
Tel: 519-673-1151; *Fax*: 519-673-3632
tmd@londonlawyers.com
www.londonlawyers.com

London: Underhill Joles - *1
607 Princess Ave., London, ON N6B 2C1
Tel: 519-432-4644; *Fax*: 519-438-3936
cjoles@bellnet.ca

London: Despina S. Valassis - *1
579 Talbot St., London, ON N6A 2T2
Tel: 519-439-2768

London: Watson Jacobs McCreary LLP - London - *8
Former Name: Jesin, Watson & McCreary
507 Talbot St., London, ON N6A 2S5
Tel: 519-663-2296; *Fax*: 519-663-1034
www.wjm-law.ca

London: Holly A. Watson - *1
380 Queens Ave., London, ON N6B 1X6
Tel: 519-642-4015; *Fax*: 519-642-4034
hollywatson@on.aibn.com

London: Kenneth J. Williams - *1
902 Adelaide St. North, London, ON N6J 1H3
Tel: 519-641-2200; *Fax*: 519-641-7995
kwilliams@kenwlaw.ca

London: David Winninger - *1
557 Talbot St., London, ON N6A 2S9
Tel: 519-858-3152; *Fax*: 519-858-3182

Madoc: Karen J. Yarrow - *1
P.O. Box 340, 246 St. Lawrence St. East, Madoc, ON K0K
2K0
Tel: 613-473-2802; *Fax*: 613-473-4472
kyarrow@lks.net

Manotick: Wilson Law Partners LLP - *2
Also Known As: Wilson & Associates
P.O. Box 429, 5542 Main St., Manotick, ON K4M 1A4
Tel: 613-692-3547; *Fax*: 613-692-0826
www.wilsonlawpartners.com

Maple: Judith Holzman Law Offices - *1
2126 Major Mackenzie Dr., Maple, ON L6A 1P7
Tel: 905-303-1070; *Fax*: 905-303-4364
Toll-Free: 866-233-0945
judith@jhlawoffices.com
www.jhlawoffices.com

Maple: M.D. Newman - *1
62 Lancer Dr., Maple, ON L6A 1C9
Tel: 905-832-5602; *Fax*: 905-832-5446

Maple: Walsh & Associates - *1
Former Name: Walsh McLuskie Doyle
#215, 2535 Major Mackenzie Dr., Maple, ON L6A 1C6
Tel: 905-832-2611; *Fax*: 905-832-2611
www.wmdlawmaple.com

Markdale: McMeeken Law Office - *1
Former Name: Harris, Willis
P.O. Box 466, 45 Main St. West, Markdale, ON N0C 1H0
Tel: 519-986-2740; *Fax*: 519-986-4205
kevin@mcmeeken-law.ca

Markdale: Rodney T. O'Halloran - *1
P.O. Box 522, RR#7, Markdale, ON N0C 1H0
Tel: 519-986-1428; *Fax*: 519-986-1471

Markham: Akai Seto & Friend - *1
Former Name: David G. Friend, Q.C.
#602, 7130 Warden Ave., Markham, ON L3R 1S2
Tel: 905-604-3015; *Fax*: 905-604-3095
akai_seto@lawyer.com

Markham: Elliot Berlin - *1
#101, 16 Esna Park Dr., Markham, ON L3R 5X1
Tel: 905-470-9444; *Fax*: 905-470-9449
eberlin@elliotberlin.com

Markham: Bigioni Barristers & Solicitors - *2
#201, 6060 Hwy. 7 East, Markham, ON L3P 3A9
Tel: 905-294-5222; *Fax*: 905-294-1607

Markham: Marvin B. Bongard - *1
Former Name: Bongard & Associate
P.O. Box 509, 10 Washington St., Markham, ON L3P 3R2
Tel: 905-294-7555; *Fax*: 905-294-8360
marvin@mbongard.com

Markham: Burstein & Greenglass LLP - *4
#200, Royal Bank Bldg., 7481 Woodbine Ave., Markham, ON
L3R 2W1
Tel: 905-475-1266; *Fax*: 905-475-7851
office@bglaw.ca
www.bglaw.ca

Markham: Cattanach Hindson Sutton - *6
Former Name: Cattanach Hindson Sutton
VanVeldhuizen
52 Main St. North, Markham, ON L3P 1X5
Tel: 905-294-0666; *Fax*: 905-294-5688
Toll-Free: 888-258-9798
www.cattanach.ca

Markham: Annie A. Cheng - *1
2919 Bur Oak Ave., Markham, ON L6B 1E6
Tel: 905-294-2289; *Fax*: 905-294-7836
aacheng@solutionsinlaw.ca

indicates number of lawyers

Markham: Anna Chung - *2
#209, 80 Acadia Ave., Markham, ON L3R 9V1
Tel: 905-940-6802; *Fax:* 905-940-6804
Toll-Free: 877-213-2284

Markham: Crupi Law - *3
Former Name: D'Andrea, Crupi
#302, 305 Renfrew Dr., Markham, ON L3R 9S7
Tel: 905-415-8900; *Fax:* 905-415-8902
www.crupilaw.ca

Markham: Marie Davison - *1
182 Town Centre Blvd., Markham, ON L3R 5H9
Tel: 905-940-9701; *Fax:* 905-944-1397

Markham: Sydney Gangbar, Q.C. - *1
#303, 80 Tiverton Ct., Markham, ON L3R 0G4
Tel: 905-470-0272; *Fax:* 905-470-8365
sydneygangbar@rogers.com

Markham: E. Alan Garbe - *1
7507 Kennedy Rd., Markham, ON L3R 0L8
Tel: 905-415-9100; *Fax:* 905-479-3625
www.garbe-law.com

Markham: Paul Gollom - *1
7507 Kennedy Rd., Markham, ON L3R 0L8
Tel: 905-881-6200; *Fax:* 905-881-6200
pgollom@rogers.com

Markham: Jozefacki, Fielding
#200, 4961 Hwy. 7 East, Markham, ON L3R 1N1
Tel: 905-940-3141; *Fax:* 905-940-3139

Markham: Barry M. Kaufman - *1
#308, 3950 - 14th Ave., Markham, ON L3R 0A9
Tel: 905-477-8848; *Fax:* 905-477-8489
barrykaufman@rogers.com

Markham: Anthea Koon - *1
#232, Commerce Gate, 505 Highway 7 East, Markham, ON L3T 7T1
Tel: 905-889-0698; *Fax:* 905-889-8390
antheakoon@rogers.com

Markham: Irene L. Matthews - *1
#104, 7225 Woodbine Ave., Markham, ON L3R 1A3
Tel: 905-475-9716; *Fax:* 905-475-9142

Markham: Mingay & Vereshchak - *3
81 Main St. North, Markham, ON L3P 1X7
Tel: 905-294-0550; *Fax:* 905-294-9141
www.mvlaw.net

Markham: G. Arthur Moad - *1
#206, 5762 Hwy. 7, Markham, ON L3P 1A8
Tel: 905-294-6446; *Fax:* 905-294-4436
gamoad@on.aibn.com

Markham: PW Lawyers - *4
Former Name: Pazuki Wilkins LLP
#301, 3190 Steeles Ave. East, Markham, ON L3R 1G9
Tel: 647-560-0856; *Fax:* 905-479-5551
Toll-Free: 888-431-8368
info@pwlawyers.ca
pwlawyers.ca
www.facebook.com/pwlawyers, twitter.com/PWlawyers

Markham: Theodore B. Rotenberg Barrister - *1
#303, 7461 Woodbine Ave., Markham, ON L3R 2W1
Tel: 905-475-1266
general@rogerlaw.com

Markham: Alan R. Smith - *1
#207, 2800 - 14th Ave., Markham, ON L3R 0E4
Tel: 905-415-8858; *Fax:* 905-940-1285
alansmithlaw@on.aibn.com

Markham: Paul F. Smith - *1
#202, 5762 Hwy. 7, Markham, ON L3P 1A8
Tel: 905-294-9955; *Fax:* 905-294-4004

Markham: A. Melvin Sokolsky - *1
#3, 200 Riviera Dr., Markham, ON L3R 5M1
Tel: 905-944-9427; *Fax:* 905-479-7025
amelvinsokolsky@rogers.com

Markham: E. Bruce Solomon - *1
7507 Kennedy Rd., Markham, ON L3R 0L8
Tel: 905-479-1900; *Fax:* 905-479-9793
ebs@markhamlaw.ca
www.markhamlaw.ca

Markham: Dennis M. Starzynski, Q.C. - *1
20 Main St. North, Markham, ON L3P 1Y2
Tel: 905-294-3891; *Fax:* 905-471-2550
starzynski@sympatico.ca

Markham: Howard J. Stern - *1
#308, 3621 Hwy. 7 East, Markham, ON L2R 0G6
Tel: 416-410-7880; *Fax:* 416-410-7880

Markham: Tenenbaum & Solomon - *2
Former Name: Alan J. Luftspring
#117, 7181 Woodbine Ave., Markham, ON L3R 1A3
Tel: 905-479-1200; *Fax:* 905-479-9769
tenenbaumsolomon.ca
www.linkedin.com/in/sheldon-tenenbaum-97406a22

Markham: Williams HR Law - *4
#100, 11 Allstate Pkwy., Markham, ON L3R 9T8
Tel: 905-205-0496; *Fax:* 905-418-0147
info@williamshrlaw.com
www.williamshrlaw.com
www.facebook.com/248693148539051,
twitter.com/williamshrlaw, www.linkedin.com/company/1661854

Markham: Wilson Vukelich LLP - *18
#710, Valleywood Corporate Centre, 60 Columbia Way, Markham, ON L3R 0C9
Tel: 905-940-8700; *Fax:* 905-940-8785
Toll-Free: 866-508-8700
information@wvllp.ca
www.wvllp.ca

Markham: Judith M. Wolf - *1
#500, 7030 Woodbine Ave., Markham, ON L3R 6G2
Tel: 905-313-0568; *Fax:* 905-313-0569

Markham: Shirley Yee
#200, 80 Acadia Ave., Markham, ON L3R 9V1
Tel: 905-940-6800; *Fax:* 905-305-7630
shirleyyeelaw@hotmail.com

Markham: Zwicker Dispute Resolution Inc. - *1
#306, 7100 Woodbine Ave., Markham, ON L3R 5J2
Tel: 905-470-2544; *Fax:* 905-470-2571
jackzwicker@on.aibn.com
www.zwickerdisputeresolutions.com

Matheson: J.A. Barber - *1
P.O. Box 189, 362 MacDougall St., Matheson, ON P0K 1N0
Tel: 705-273-2151; *Fax:* 705-273-2144

Meaford: Carol A. Allen - *1
P.O. Box 3272, 54 Sykes St. South, Meaford, ON N4L 1A5
Tel: 519-538-9929; *Fax:* 519-538-9931
Toll-Free: 877-538-9929
contact@carolallen.ca

Meaford: Kopperud Hamilton LLP - Meaford - *2
Former Name: Norman A. Kopperud Law Office
#1, 68 Sykes St. North, Meaford, ON N4L 1R2
Tel: 519-538-2044; *Fax:* 519-538-5323
info@kohalaw.com
www.bluemountainlawyers.com

Meaford: Scheifele Erskine & Renken - Meaford - *3
P.O. Box 3395, 39 Nelson St. West, Meaford, ON N4L 1N2
Tel: 519-538-2510; *Fax:* 519-538-1843
info@meafordlawyers.com
www.meafordlawyers.com

Metcalfe: Gary M. Chayko - *1
P.O. Box 579, Metcalfe, ON K2P 1L5
Tel: 613-230-7260; *Fax:* 613-230-2163
gchayko@netscape.net

Midland: Chin & Orr Lawyers - *2
#15, 9225 County Rd. #93, Midland, ON L4R 4K4
Tel: 705-526-5529; *Fax:* 705-526-3071
Toll-Free: 877-526-5529
sonyam@chinandorrlawyers.ca

Midland: Deacon Taws - *2
476 Elizabeth St., Midland, ON L4R 1Z8
Tel: 705-526-3791; *Fax:* 705-526-2688
admin@deacontaws.com
www.deacontaws.com

Midland: Ferguson Barristers LLP - Midland - *5
531 King St., Midland, ON L4R 3N6
Tel: 705-526-1471; *Fax:* 705-526-1067
Toll-Free: 800-563-6348
www.fergusonbarristers.ca
www.facebook.com/fdtlaw, twitter.com/fergusonlaw,
www.linkedin.com/company/1712523

Midland: HGR Graham Partners LLP - Midland - *26
Former Name: Hacker Gignac Rice LLP
518 Yonge St., Midland, ON L4R 2C5
Tel: 705-526-2231; *Fax:* 705-526-0313
info@hgrgp.ca
www.hgrgp.ca

Midland: Mark Kowalsky - *1
P.O. Box 280, 8970 County Rd. #93, Midland, ON L4R 4K8
Tel: 705-526-1336; *Fax:* 705-526-8499

Midland: Prost Associates - *2
P.O. Box 96, 323 Midland Ave., Midland, ON L4R 4K6
Tel: 705-526-9328; *Fax:* 705-526-1209
info@prostlaw.com
www.prostlaw.com

Midland: John F.L. Rose - *1
476 Elizabeth St., Midland, ON L4R 1Z8
Tel: 705-527-1235; *Fax:* 705-527-0066
john@johnroselaw.com
www.johnroselaw.com

Milton: Ingrid Hibbard - *1
440 Harrop Dr., Milton, ON L9T 3H2
Tel: 905-875-3828; *Fax:* 905-875-3829
ihibbard@pelangio.com

Milton: Hutchinson, Thompson, Henderson & Mott - *3
264 Main St. East, Milton, ON L9T 1P2
Tel: 905-878-2841; *Fax:* 905-878-3937
lawmilton.com

Minden: Donald J. Lange - *1
Comp. 50, RR#2, Minden, ON K0M 2K0
Tel: 705-489-4974; *Fax:* 705-489-4975
donaldlange@donaldlange.com
www.donaldlange.com

Mississauga: Esther O. Abraham Law Office - *1
#110A, 377 Burnhamthorpe Rd. East, Mississauga, ON L5A 3Y1
Tel: 905-270-3755; *Fax:* 905-270-3844
esther@dlaw.ca
www.dlaw.ca

Mississauga: David A. Aiken - *1
#200, 39 Lake Shore Rd. East, Mississauga, ON L5G 1C9
Tel: 905-602-5230; *Fax:* 905-871-8507
d.aiken.law@davidaaiken.com

Mississauga: J. Paul Bannon - *1
Former Name: Bannon & Falkeisen
#360, 33 City Centre Dr., Mississauga, ON L5B 2N5
Tel: 905-272-3412; *Fax:* 905-272-0142
paul@bannonlaw.ca

Mississauga: Richard S. Barrett - *1
1498 Lewisham Dr., Mississauga, ON L5J 3R4
Tel: 905-823-1487; *Fax:* 905-823-2529
lawyer@rogers.com
www.the-friendly-lawyer.com

Mississauga: N. Bartels - *1
#304, 470 Hensall Circle, Mississauga, ON L5A 1X7
Tel: 905-276-8286; *Fax:* 905-270-0130
nbartels@sympatico.ca
www.nbartels.com

Mississauga: Paula L. Bateman, Barrister & Solicitor - *2
#C, 6505 Mississauga Rd., Mississauga, ON L5N 1A6
Tel: 905-567-4440; *Fax:* 905-821-1572

Mississauga: Stephen I. Beck - *1
295 Matheson Blvd. E, Mississauga, ON L4Z 1X8
Tel: 905-568-8351
stephen@becklaw.ca

Mississauga: Richard T. Bennett - *2
82 Queen St. South., Mississauga, ON L5M 1K6
Tel: 905-826-1453; *Fax:* 905-826-7185
richard.rtb@sympatico.ca

Mississauga: Bhangal & Virk - *2
295 Derry Rd. West, Mississauga, ON L5W 1G3
Tel: 905-565-0655; *Fax:* 905-565-0649
asb@criminalcases.ca
www.criminalcases.ca

Mississauga: Eugene J. Bhattacharya - *1
295 Matheson Blvd. East, Mississauga, ON L4Z 1X8
Tel: 905-507-3796; *Fax:* 905-507-6011

* indicates number of lawyers

Mississauga: **Binsky Whittle - *2**
Former Name: The Law Office of Howard Binsky
#300, 5660 McAdam Rd., Mississauga, ON L4Z 1T2
Tel: 905-270-8811; *Fax:* 905-270-2977
www.binskywhittle.com

Mississauga: **George F. Brant - *1**
#B2, 223 Queen St. South, Mississauga, ON L5M 1L6
Tel: 905-826-2511; *Fax:* 905-286-1335
www.georgebrant.com

Mississauga: **Brian Chan Barrister, Solicitor &
Notary Public - *1**
#42, 145 Traders Blvd. East, Mississauga, ON L4Z 3L3
Tel: 905-712-2888; *Fax:* 905-712-3838

Mississauga: **Burych Lawyers - *2**
#204, 89 Queensway West, Mississauga, ON L5B 2V2
Tel: 905-896-8600; *Fax:* 905-896-9757
info@burychlawyers.com

Mississauga: **Campbell Partners LLP - *6**
2624 Dunwin Dr., Mississauga, ON L5L 3T5
Tel: 905-828-2247; *Fax:* 905-828-4311
info@campbelllawyers.net
www.campbelllawyers.net

Mississauga: **Carey McCallum & Nimjee - *1**
1325 Burnhamthorpe Rd. East, Mississauga, ON L4Y 3V8
Tel: 905-624-1149

Mississauga: **J.C. Chapman - *1**
2572 Stanfield Rd., Mississauga, ON L4Y 1S2
Tel: 905-270-7034; *Fax:* 905-270-1001
jcchapman@on.aibn.com

Mississauga: **Laurence R. Cutler - *1**
Former Name: Cutler/Goldberg LLP
#1201, 90 Burnhamthorpe Rd. West, Mississauga, ON L5B
3C3
Tel: 905-275-6132; *Fax:* 905-276-2193

Mississauga: **Wieslawa Dabrowska - *1**
#405, 4310 Sherwoodtowne Blvd., Mississauga, ON L4Z 4C4
Tel: 905-281-0308; *Fax:* 905-281-3552
viesiad@istar.ca

Mississauga: **Douglas M. Davidson - *1**
#200, 1552 Dundas St. West, Mississauga, ON L5C 1E4
Tel: 905-279-3330; *Fax:* 905-279-2735

Mississauga: **Day + Borg LLP - *3**
Former Name: Day, Michael J.
93 Queen St. South, Mississauga, ON L5M 1K7
Tel: 905-826-5670
www.dayborg.com

Mississauga: **DeRusha Law Firm - *5**
#1, 1015 Matheson Blvd. East, Mississauga, ON L4W 3A4
Tel: 905-625-2874; *Fax:* 905-625-0614
contact@derushalawfirm.com
www.derushalawfirm.com

Mississauga: **DH Professional Corporation,
Barristers & Solicitors - *3**
Also Known As: Daigle & Hancock
51 Village Centre Pl., Mississauga, ON L4Z 1V9
Tel: 905-273-3339; *Fax:* 905-273-5672
Toll-Free: 877-273-3339
lawyers@daiglehancock.com
www.mississaugalawyer.com

Mississauga: **Eades Law Office - *1**
7229 Pacific Circle, Mississauga, ON L5T 1S9
Tel: 905-795-4040; *Fax:* 905-564-2315

Mississauga: **Richard Alan Fellman - *1**
#100, 46 Village Centre Pl., Mississauga, ON L4Z 1V9
Tel: 905-275-2231; *Fax:* 905-275-8323
rfellman@on.aibn.com

Mississauga: **Michael J. Fisher - *1**
#4, 265 Queen St. South, Mississauga, ON L5M 1L9
Tel: 905-812-9700; *Fax:* 905-812-0770
mjfisher@globalserve.net

Mississauga: **David A. Fram - *1**
810 Meadow Wood Rd., Mississauga, ON L5J 2S6
Tel: 905-916-0130; *Fax:* 905-916-1600

Mississauga: **Garvey & Garvey LLP - *3**
972 Clarkson Rd. South, Mississauga, ON L5J 2V7
Tel: 905-823-4400; *Fax:* 905-823-5153

Mississauga: **Jean Moenis P. Ghalioungui - *1**
#11, 4040 Creditview Rd.., Mississauga, ON L5C 3Y8
Tel: 905-820-4442; *Fax:* 905-820-4442

Mississauga: **Goodman & Griffin - *1**
44 Village Centre Place, 3rd Fl., Mississauga, ON L4Z 1V9
Tel: 905-276-5050; *Fax:* 905-276-8917
Toll-Free: 888-333-3675
realestate@goodgriff.com
www.goodmangriffin.com
twitter.com/goodmangriffin

Mississauga: **John L.Z. Gora - *1**
893 Beechwood Ave., Mississauga, ON L5G 4E3
Tel: 905-278-7678; *Fax:* 905-271-5568

Mississauga: **Harris & Harris LLP - *8**
#300, 2355 Skymark Ave., Mississauga, ON L4W 4Y6
Tel: 905-629-7800; *Fax:* 905-629-4350
info@harrisandharris.com
www.harrisandharris.com

Mississauga: **David L. Hynes - *1**
#30, 1100 Central Pkwy. West, Mississauga, ON L5C 4E5
Tel: 905-361-2020; *Fax:* 905-361-2011
david@davidlhynes.com

Mississauga: **William G., Jeffery Law Office - *1**
#301, 8 Stavebank Rd. North, Mississauga, ON L5G 2T4
Tel: 905-278-7362; *Fax:* 905-278-7514

Mississauga: **Kain & Ball - *7**
#402, 1290 Central Pkwy. West, Mississauga, ON L5C 4R3
Tel: 905-855-4888 *Toll-Free:* 855-773-4588
contact@kainfamilylaw.com
www.kainfamilylaw.com

Mississauga: **John H. Kalina - *1**
#210, 1325 Eglinton Ave. East, Mississauga, ON L4W 4L9
Tel: 416-900-6999; *Fax:* 416-410-5482
hjkalina@lawyer4u.ca
www.lawyer4u.ca

Mississauga: **Julian B. Keller - *1**
#301, 25 Watline Ave., Mississauga, ON L4Z 2Z1
Tel: 905-890-2211; *Fax:* 905-890-2246
juliankeller@rogers.com

Mississauga: **Sami N. Kerba - *1**
1093 Lakeshore Rd. East, Mississauga, ON L5E 1E8
Tel: 905-274-6073; *Fax:* 905-274-9876
samikerba@nskerba.ca

Mississauga: **Keyser Mason Ball LLP - *18**
Also Known As: KMB Law
#1600, 4 Robert Speck Pkwy., Mississauga, ON L4Z 1S1
Tel: 905-276-9111; *Fax:* 905-276-2298
info@kmblaw.com
www.kmblaw.com
twitter.com/KeyserMasonBall,
www.linkedin.com/company/349986

Mississauga: **Klein Law - *1**
4632 Dunedin Cres., Mississauga, ON L5R 1M2
Tel: 905-272-2540; *Fax:* 905-272-2100
contact@kleinlaw.ca
www.kleinlaw.ca

Mississauga: **Kostyniuk & Bruggeman - *3**
#213, 1515 Matheson Blvd. East, Mississauga, ON L4W 2P5
Tel: 905-602-5551; *Fax:* 905-602-9775
rkostyniuk@rogers.com

Mississauga: **Kozlowski & Company - *1**
5065 Foresthill Dr., Mississauga, ON L5M 5A7
Tel: 905-569-9400; *Fax:* 905-608-9400
Toll-Free: 877-569-9499
info@kozlowskiandcompany.com
www.kozlowskiandcompany.com

Mississauga: **Barbara E. LaVieille - *1**
#2A, 1325 Burnhamthorpe Rd. East, Mississauga, ON L4Y
2X3
Tel: 905-238-1411; *Fax:* 905-629-9277
www.lavieillelaw.com

Mississauga: **Law Office of Janusz Puzniak - *1**
295 Matheson Blvd. East, Mississauga, ON L4Z 1X8
Tel: 905-890-2112; *Fax:* 905-502-6982
janusz@polskiprawnik.com
www.polskiprawnik.com

Mississauga: **Malicki Sanchez - *5**
Former Name: Malicki & Malicki
650 Lakeshore Rd. East, Mississauga, ON L5G 1J6
Tel: 905-274-1650; *Fax:* 905-274-1652
info@malickisanchezlaw.com
www.malickisanchezlaw.com
twitter.com/MalickiLaw,
www.linkedin.com/company/malicki-&-malicki-law-firm

Mississauga: **Marks & Ciraco - *2**
#205, 120 Traders Blvd. East, Mississauga, ON L4Z 2H7
Tel: 905-712-8300; *Fax:* 905-712-8559
www.marksandciraco.com

Mississauga: **Cindy McGoldrick - *1**
#102, 6850 Millcreek Dr., Mississauga, ON L5N 4J9
Tel: 905-608-9967; *Fax:* 905-608-8206
cindy@cindymcgoldrick.com
www.cindymcgoldrick.com
www.facebook.com/cindymcgoldrickprocorp

Mississauga: **Ronald F. Mossman - *1**
#300, 34 Village Centre Pl., Mississauga, ON L4Z 1V9
Tel: 905-848-4020; *Fax:* 905-848-4026

Mississauga: **Kotak Nainesh - *1**
#120, 120 Traders Blvd. East, Mississauga, ON L4Z 2H7
Tel: 905-755-8900; *Fax:* 905-755-8901
Toll-Free: 877-945-6825
info@kotaklaw.com
www.mississaugapersonalinjurylawyers.ca

Mississauga: **D.M. Nathwani - *1**
#129, 1250 Mississauga Valley Blvd., Mississauga, ON L5A
3R6
Tel: 905-273-7887

Mississauga: **R. Geoffrey Newbury - *1**
#106, 150 Lakeshore Rd. West, Mississauga, ON L5H 3R2
Tel: 905-271-9600; *Fax:* 905-271-1638
newbury@mandamus.org

Mississauga: **Niebler Law Offices - Mississauga - *1**
Former Name: Niebler, Liebeck
1462 Hurontario St., Mississauga, ON L5G 3H4
Tel: 905-271-3232; *Fax:* 905-271-3677
dniebler@nieblerlaw.com
www.nieblerlaw.com

Mississauga: **O'Connor Zanardo - *2**
#300, 4230 Sherwoodtowne Blvd., Mississauga, ON L4Z 2G6
Tel: 905-896-4370; *Fax:* 905-896-4926
ozlaw.ca

Mississauga: **O'Marra & Elliott - *2**
#203, 125 Lakeshore Rd. East, Mississauga, ON L5G 1E5
Tel: 905-278-7277; *Fax:* 905-278-5805
omarraelliott.com

Mississauga: **Ovenden & Ovenden - *2**
#204, 130 Dundas St. East, Mississauga, ON L5A 3V8
Tel: 905-270-8544; *Fax:* 905-273-7386
ovenden.ca

Mississauga: **Pallett Valo LLP - *80**
#300, West Tower, 77 City Centre Dr., Mississauga, ON L5B
1M5
Tel: 905-273-3300; *Fax:* 905-273-6920
Toll-Free: 800-323-3781
www.pallettvalo.com
twitter.com/pallett_valo
www.linkedin.com/company/pallett-valo-llp

Mississauga: **Petrillo Law - *2**
#201, 2600 Skymark Ave., Unit 1, Mississauga, ON L4W 5B2
Tel: 905-949-9433; *Fax:* 905-949-1153
info@petrillolaw.com
www.petrillolaw.com
www.facebook.com/135489526520149, twitter.com/petrillolaw

Mississauga: **Larry Plenner - *1**
Also Known As: Will Smart
Former Name: Campbell, Plener
#300, 2 Robert Speck Pkwy., Mississauga, ON L4Z 1S1
Tel: 905-897-8611; *Fax:* 905-897-8807
www.willsmart.ca

Mississauga: **Terry D. Richardson - *1**
18 Mississauga Rd. North, Mississauga, ON L5H 2H4
Tel: 905-891-0011; *Fax:* 905-891-1410

* indicates number of lawyers

Mississauga: Ridout & Maybee LLP - *35
#301, Plaza I, 2000 Argentia Rd., Mississauga, ON L5N 1P7
Tel: 905-363-3054; *Fax:* 905-363-0248
mail@ridoutmaybee.com
www.ridoutmaybee.com
twitter.com/RidoutMaybee, www.linkedin.com/company/45189

Mississauga: Roger Foisy Professional Corp. - *1
#295, Plaza 4, Meadowvale Corporate Centre, 2000 Argentia
Rd., Mississauga, ON L5N 1W1
Tel: 905-286-1110; *Fax:* 905-286-4381
Toll-Free: 877-286-0050
info@injurylawyercanada.com
www.injurylawyercanada.com
www.facebook.com/InjuryLawyerCanada,
twitter.com/InjuryLawyerRRF,
www.linkedin.com/company/2260920

Mississauga: Jerry Saltzman
#15, 7205 Goreway Dr., Mississauga, ON L4T 2T9
Tel: 905-671-1178; *Fax:* 905-671-8030
jerry_westwood@hotmail.com

Mississauga: Edgar R. Schink - *1
#405, 130 Dundas St. E, Mississauga, ON L5A 3V8
Tel: 905-270-8882; *Fax:* 905-270-7665
edgarrichards2002@yahoo.ca
www.edgarschink.yp.ca

Mississauga: Allan Shulman - *1
#4, P.O. Box 204, 2225 Erin Mills Pkwy., Mississauga, ON
L5K 1T9
Tel: 905-822-3563; *Fax:* 905-822-6342
ashulman@on.aibn.com

Mississauga: John F. Silvester - *1
#544, 33 City Centre Dr., Mississauga, ON L5B 2N5
Tel: 905-275-2588; *Fax:* 905-275-0714
www.johnsilvesterlaw.ca

Mississauga: Speigel Nichols Fox LLP - *10
#400, 30 Eglinton Ave. West, Mississauga, ON L5R 3E7
Tel: 905-366-9700; *Fax:* 905-366-9707
info@ontlaw.com
www.ontlaw.com
www.linkedin.com/company/speigel-nichols-fox-llp

Mississauga: Harvey A. Swartz - *1
37 Wanita Rd., Mississauga, ON L5G 1B3
Tel: 416-665-0600; *Fax:* 416-665-2848
harvey@haslawfirm.com

Mississauga: Tannahill, Lockhart & Clark - *4
#10, 5805 Whittle Rd., Mississauga, ON L4Z 2J1
Tel: 905-502-5770; *Fax:* 905-502-5009
www.tlcl.ca

Mississauga: Thompson, MacColl & Stacy LLP - *8
#5, 1020 Matheson Blvd. East, Mississauga, ON L4W 4J9
Tel: 905-625-5591; *Fax:* 905-238-3313
www.tmslaw.ca

Mississauga: Brian M. Watson - *1
#105, 3034 Palston Rd., Mississauga, ON L4Y 2Z6
Tel: 905-272-0942; *Fax:* 905-272-1682
watsonlaw@sympatico.ca

Mississauga: Annette Wilson - *1
#203, 1325 Eglinton Ave. East, Mississauga, ON L4W 4L9
Tel: 905-602-1989; *Fax:* 905-602-8491

Mississauga: Michael Woods - *1
#203, 120 Traders Blvd. E, Mississauga, ON L4Z 2H7
Tel: 905-568-3810; *Fax:* 905-568-1206
michaelwoods@on.aibn.com

Mississauga: Richard M. Woodside - *1
2479 Burnford Trail, Mississauga, ON L5M 5E4
Tel: 905-567-4562; *Fax:* 905-564-5534
rwoodside@rogers.com

Mississauga: Janice E. Younker
1370 Hurontario St., Mississauga, ON L5G 3H4
Tel: 905-271-2784; *Fax:* 905-271-5960
younkerlaw@rogers.com

Monotick: Alan C. Macleod - *1
P.O. Box 1158, Stn. Main, 5576 Dickinson St., Monotick, ON
K4M 1A9
Tel: 613-692-4180; *Fax:* 613-692-0073

Moosonee: Keewaytinok Native Legal Services - *2
P.O. Box 218, 40 Revillon Rd. North, Moosonee, ON P0L 1Y0
Tel: 705-336-2981; *Fax:* 705-336-2577
www.facebook.com/193595124668

Morrisburg: Gorrell, Grenkie & Remillard -
Morrisburg - *3
Former Name: Gorrell, Grenkie, Leroy & Rémillard
P.O. Box 820, Stn. Morrisburg, 67 Main St., Morrisburg, ON
K0C 1X0
Tel: 613-543-2922; *Fax:* 613-543-4228
info@yourlawfirm.ca
www.yourlawfirm.ca

Morrisburg: Horner & Pietersma - *3
Former Name: McInnis, MacEwen & Horner
P.O. Box 733, 777 Main St., Morrisburg, ON K0C 1X0
Tel: 613-543-2946; *Fax:* 613-543-3867

Mount Albert: Urquhart, Urquhart, Aiken & Medcof -
*1
P.O. Box 285, Mount Albert, ON L0G 1M0
Tel: 416-595-1111; *Fax:* 416-595-7312
tommax99@yahoo.com

Mount Forest: Deverell & Lemaich - Mount Forest -
*3
Former Name: Grant, Deverell & Lemaich; Grant
Deverell Lemaich & Barclay
P.O. Box 460, 166 Main St. South, Mount Forest, ON N0G
2L0
Tel: 519-323-1600; *Fax:* 519-323-3877
info@northwellington-law.ca
www.northwellington-law.ca

Mount Forest: Fallis, Fallis & McMillan - Mount
Forest - *3
150 Main St. South, Mount Forest, ON N0G 2L0
Tel: 519-323-2800; *Fax:* 519-323-4115
ffmlaw@wightman.ca
www.ffmlaw.ca

Napanee: Chris F. Doreleyers - *2
P.O. Box 398, Stn. Main, 35 Dundas St. East, Napanee, ON
K7R 3P5
Tel: 613-354-3375; *Fax:* 613-354-5641

Nepean: Michael G. Carey - *1
84 Centrepointe Dr., Nepean, ON K2G 6B1
Tel: 613-723-4774; *Fax:* 613-723-2377
careylawoffice@bellnet.ca

Nepean: Chiarelli Cramer Witteveen - *3
92 Centrepointe Dr., Nepean, ON K2G 6B1
Tel: 613-723-9100; *Fax:* 613-723-9105
www.centrepointelaw.com

Nepean: E. Max Cohen, Q.C. - *1
24 Kitimat Cres., Nepean, ON K2H 7G5
Tel: 613-828-5855; *Fax:* 613-237-0510

Nepean: Kathryn d'Artois - *1
#100, 104 Centrepointe Dr., Nepean, ON K2G 1B6
Tel: 613-228-9292; *Fax:* 613-228-0005
dartois@dartoismediation.ca
www.dartoismediation.ca

Nepean: Pablo Fernandez-Davila - *1
Also Known As: HC Law
Former Name: Raymond A. Baumgarten
#215, 35 Auriga Dr., Nepean, ON K2E 8B7
Tel: 613-565-8686; *Fax:* 613-565-8989
huntclublaw.com

Nepean: Rod A. Vanier - *1
90 Centrepointe Dr., Nepean, ON K2G 6B1
Tel: 613-226-3336; *Fax:* 613-226-8767
vanier@vanierlaw.on.ca
www.vanierlaw.on.ca

Nepean: Stephen A. Ritchie - *1
92 Centrepointe Dr., Nepean, ON K2G 6B1
Tel: 613-224-6674; *Fax:* 613-723-9105
stephen.ritchie@centrepointelaw.com

New Liskeard: Ramsay Law Office - *2
P.O. Box 160, 18 Armstrong St., New Liskeard, ON P0J 1P0
Tel: 705-647-4010; *Fax:* 705-647-4341
Toll-Free: 800-837-6648
ramsaypr@nt.net
www.nt.net/~ramsaypr

Newcastle: Michael F. Boland - *1
P.O. Box 20051, 78 George St. West, Newcastle, ON L1B 1M3
Tel: 905-987-1288; *Fax:* 905-987-1416
mfboland@on.aibn.com

Newcastle: Richard J. Mazar Professional Corp. - *2
115 King Ave. West, Newcastle, ON L1B 1L3
Tel: 905-987-1550; *Fax:* 905-987-1552
mazar@mazarlaw.com
www.mazarlaw.com

Newcastle: Valentine Lovekin - *1
Former Name: Cureatz & Lovekin Law Office
35 King St. West, Newcastle, ON L1B 1H2
Tel: 905-987-3500; *Fax:* 905-987-3503
lovekin@lovekinlaw.com

Newmarket: Brown Law Firm - *3
#21-22, 1228 Gorham St., Newmarket, ON L3Y 8Z1
Tel: 905-853-2529; *Fax:* 905-853-3539
cartwright@brownlawfirm.ca
brownlawfirm.ca

Newmarket: Paul H. Caroline - *1
#300, 16775 Yonge St., Newmarket, ON L3Y 8J4
Tel: 905-836-4018; *Fax:* 905-836-4020

Newmarket: Criminal Law Associates - *4
105 Eagle St., Newmarket, ON L3Y 1J2
Tel: 905-898-2686; *Fax:* 905-898-3957
general@criminallawassociates.ca
www.criminallawassociates.ca

Newmarket: Epstein & Associates - *8
71 Main St. South, Newmarket, ON L3Y 3Y5
Tel: 905-898-2266; *Fax:* 905-898-2216
www.epsteinlawyers.com

Newmarket: GPS Law
#217, 16775 Yonge St., Newmarket, ON L3Y 8J4
Tel: 905-952-0002; *Fax:* 905-952-0687
Toll-Free: 855-952-0002
admin@gpslaw.ca
www.gpslaw.ca
www.facebook.com/268397999865931, twitter.com/gpslaw

Newmarket: Hill Hunter Losell Law Firm LLP - *7
#200, P.O. Box 324, 17360 Yonge St., Newmarket, ON L3Y
4X7
Tel: 905-895-1007; *Fax:* 905-895-4064
www.hillhunterlosell.com

Newmarket: Neal J. Kearney - *1
#3, 320 Harry Walker Pkwy. North, Newmarket, ON L3Y 7B4
Tel: 905-898-3012; *Fax:* 905-853-9894
nkearney@kearneylaw.ca

Newmarket: David Lakie - *1
105 Eagle St., Newmarket, ON L3Y 1J2
Tel: 905-898-2686; *Fax:* 905-898-3957
davidlakie@rogers.com
www.davidlakie.com

Newmarket: Debra L. McNairn - *1
78 Main St. South, Newmarket, ON L3Y 3Y6
Tel: 905-836-1371; *Fax:* 905-898-2050
dmcnairn@mcnairnllb.ca

Newmarket: Derrick McNamara - *1
433 Eagle St. E, Newmarket, ON L3Y 1K5
Tel: 905-954-0593; *Fax:* 905-954-1827
dermcnamara@bellnet.ca

Newmarket: Monteith Baker Johnston & Doodnauth
- Professional Corporation - *5
227 Eagle St. East, Newmarket, ON L3Y 4X1
Tel: 905-895-8600; *Fax:* 905-895-8269
info@monteithbaker.com
www.monteithbaker.com

Newmarket: Paul E. Montgomery - *1
#305, 16600 Bayview Ave., Newmarket, ON L3X 1Z9
Tel: 905-836-4018; *Fax:* 905-836-4020
paulmontgomery@rogers.com

Newmarket: Murphy Law Chambers - *2
#300, 390 Davis Dr., Newmarket, ON L3Y 7T8
Tel: 905-836-4750; *Fax:* 905-836-6691
info@murphylawchambers.ca
www.murphylawchambers.ca

Newmarket: Alexander Schneider - *1
291 Davis Dr., Newmarket, ON L3Y 2N6
Tel: 905-898-1342; *Fax:* 905-898-1344

Newmarket: Steinberg, Bruce & Paterson - *3
1091 Gorham St., Newmarket, ON L3Y 8X7
Tel: 905-830-9940; *Fax:* 905-830-9246

---

* indicates number of lawyers

Newmarket: Stiver Vale Barristers and Solicitor
195 Main St. South, Newmarket, ON L3Y 3Y9
Tel: 905-895-4571; *Fax:* 905-853-2958

Niagara Falls: Bev Hodgson Law - *1
6057 Drummond Rd., Niagara Falls, ON L2G 4M1
Tel: 905-354-1600; *Fax:* 905-354-0171
bevh@bevhodgson.com

Niagara Falls: Broderick & Partners LLP - *4
4625 Ontario Ave., Niagara Falls, ON L2E 6V6
Tel: 905-356-2621; *Fax:* 905-356-6904
www.broderickpartners.com

Niagara Falls: David P. Czifra - *1
P.O. Box 868, Stn. Main, 4786 Queen St., Niagara Falls, ON
L2E 6V6
Tel: 905-357-6633; *Fax:* 905-357-0736
czifra@vaxxine.com

Niagara Falls: Charles A. Galloway - *1
5146 Victoria Ave., Niagara Falls, ON L2E 4E3
Tel: 905-356-2512; *Fax:* 905-356-2513

Niagara Falls: Margaret A. Hoy - *1
6617 Drummond Rd., Niagara Falls, ON L2G 4N4
Tel: 905-354-4414; *Fax:* 905-356-7772
hoy@bellnet.ca

Niagara Falls: D. Ceri Hugill - *1
6304 Stonefield Park, Niagara Falls, ON L2J 4K1
Tel: 905-353-1790; *Fax:* 905-353-1790
resolver@cogeco.ca

Niagara Falls: Jaluvka & Sauer Lawyers - *2
#101, 4701 St. Clair Ave., Niagara Falls, ON L2E 3S9
Tel: 905-356-6484; *Fax:* 905-356-3004
Toll-Free: 877-223-5071
www.jaluvka-sauer-niagara-lawyers.com

Niagara Falls: Paul N. Krowchuk - *1
3848 Main St., #A, Niagara Falls, ON L2G 6B2
Tel: 905-295-9995; *Fax:* 905-295-2037
pklaw@bellnet.ca
www.paulkrowchuk.com

Niagara Falls: Patricia Lucas - *1
4056 Dorchester Rd., Niagara Falls, ON L2E 6M9
Tel: 905-357-4510; *Fax:* 905-357-9757

Niagara Falls: Martin Sheppard Fraser LLP - Niagara
Falls - *12
P.O. Box 900, 4701 St. Clair Ave., 2nd Fl., Niagara Falls, ON
L2E 6V7
Tel: 289-271-0005; *Fax:* 905-354-5540
Toll-Free: 800-491-0147
www.msflawyers.com

Niagara Falls: McBurney Durdan Henderson &
Corbett - *4
P.O. Box 177, 4759 Queen St., Niagara Falls, ON L2E 2M1
Tel: 905-356-4511
info@mdhclaw.com
www.mdhclaw.com/en/

Niagara Falls: Daniel J. McDonald - *1
Former Name: Knight, S. James, Q.C.
P.O. Box 726, 4683 Queen St., Niagara Falls, ON L2E 2L9
Tel: 905-356-1524; *Fax:* 905-357-9686

Niagara Falls: Daniel J. McDonald - *1
P.O. Box 726, Stn. Main, 4683 Queen St., Niagara Falls, ON
L2E 6V5
Tel: 905-356-1524; *Fax:* 905-357-9686
danielmcdonald@bellnet.ca

Niagara Falls: McKay & Heath - *2
#102, 4701 St. Clair Ave., Niagara Falls, ON L2E 3S9
Tel: 905-357-0660; *Fax:* 905-357-5680
mckayandheathlaw.yolasite.com

Niagara Falls: Gordon F. McNab, Q.C. - *1
4056 Dorchester Rd., Niagara Falls, ON L2E 6M9
Tel: 905-357-4510; *Fax:* 905-357-9757
mcnablucas@on.aibn.com

Niagara Falls: Sharpe, Beresh & Gnys - *1
Elgin Block, 4673 Ontario Ave., 3rd Fl., Niagara Falls, ON
L2E 3R1
Tel: 289-438-2127; *Fax:* 905-357-5760
Toll-Free: 877-288-5550
sharpe@sbglawfirm.com
www.sbglawfirm.com
www.facebook.com/sbglawfirm, twitter.com/sbglaw

Niagara Falls: Brian N. Sinclair, Q.C. - *3
6617 Drummond Rd., Niagara Falls, ON L2G 4N4
Tel: 905-356-7755
brian@briansinclair.com
www.briansinclair.com

Niagara Falls: William Slovak, Q.C. - *1
5627 Main St., Niagara Falls, ON L2G 5Z3
Tel: 905-374-6000; *Fax:* 905-374-9410
Toll-Free: 877-231-0011
mjs5627@hotmail.com

Niagara Falls: Malcolm A.F. Stockton - *1
P.O. Box 868, Stn. Main, 4786 Queen St., Niagara Falls, ON
L2E 6V6
Tel: 905-357-3500; *Fax:* 905-356-3635
stockton@iaw.com

Niagara Falls: Brian C. Wilcox - *1
#118, 6150 Valley Way, Niagara Falls, ON L2E 1Y3
Tel: 905-358-0782; *Fax:* 905-356-0783
office@bcwlawoffice.com
www.bcwlawoffice.com

Niagara South: Wilson, Opatovsky - *2
P.O. Box 99, Stn. Main, 190 Elm St., Niagara South, ON L3K
5V7
Tel: 905-835-1163; *Fax:* 905-835-2171
Toll-Free: 888-288-8338
cwilson@wilsonop.com

Niagara on the Lake: Richard J.W. Andrews - *1
#202, 111B Garrison Village Dr., Niagara on the Lake, ON
L0S 1J0
Tel: 905-468-0081; *Fax:* 905-468-0087
rjwandrews@bellnet.ca
rjwandrews.ca

North Bay: Bowness & Murray - *2
P.O. Box 327, 348 Fraser St., North Bay, ON P1B 3W7
Tel: 705-474-9680; *Fax:* 705-474-4218
info@bownessandmurray.ca
bownessandmurray.ca

North Bay: Clements Eggerts Professional
Corporation - *1
Former Name: Tafel, Trussler & Eggert
477 Sherbrooke St., North Bay, ON P1B 2C2
Tel: 705-472-4890; *Fax:* 705-472-9612
info@northbaylaw.com
www.c-eggert.com

North Bay: Colvin & Colvin Professional
Corporation - *2
P.O. Box 657, Stn. Main, 577 Main St. West, North Bay, ON
P1B 8J5
Tel: 705-476-5161; *Fax:* 705-476-9902
Toll-Free: 877-268-8566
colvinlaw@cogeco.net

North Bay: M. Lucie Laperriere - *1
325 Ski Club Rd., North Bay, ON P1B 7R3
Tel: 705-495-8554; *Fax:* 705-495-6274
advice@northbaylawyer.ca

North Bay: Larmer Stickland - *2
Former Name: Larmer & Larmer Barristers
#401, 101 Worthington St. East, North Bay, ON P1B 1G5
Tel: 705-478-8200; *Fax:* 705-478-8100
Toll-Free: 888-947-2746
info@larmerstickland.com
www.larmerstickland.com

North Bay: Lucenti, Orlando & Ellies Professional
Corporation - *4
#2nd Fl., 373 Main St. West, North Bay, ON P1B 2T9
Tel: 705-472-9500; *Fax:* 705-472-4814

North Bay: James R. McIntosh - *1
325 Main St. West, North Bay, ON P1B 2T9
Tel: 705-476-2500; *Fax:* 705-476-9347
maclaw@efni.com

North Bay: McLachlan Froud & Rochon LLP - North
Bay - *3
#202, 373 Main St. West, North Bay, ON P1B 2T9
Tel: 705-476-6333; *Fax:* 705-476-4397

North Bay: Joe Sinicrope - *1
495 Main St. West, North Bay, ON P1B 2V3
Tel: 705-495-1334; *Fax:* 705-495-7990
joesinicrope@neilnet.com

North Bay: Wallace Klein Partners in Law LLP - *4
P.O. Box 37, 225 McIntyre St. West, North Bay, ON P1B 8G8
Tel: 705-474-2920; *Fax:* 705-474-1758
info@partnersinlaw.net
www.partnersinlaw.net

Nottawa: Robert Bailey - *1
P.O. Box 73, 11 Donald Ave., Nottawa, ON L0M 1P0
Tel: 705-994-6981; *Fax:* 706-242-7620
bob@iqaluitlaw.ca
www.iqaluitlaw.ca

Oakville: John G. Cox - *1
297 Church St., Oakville, ON L6J 1N9
Tel: 905-844-5600; *Fax:* 905-844-9100
www.jgcoxfamilylaw.com

Oakville: Diane Daly - *1
#301, 165 Cross Ave., Oakville, ON L6J 0A9
Tel: 905-844-5883; *Fax:* 905-844-9765
dianedaly@dalylaw.ca
www.oakvillelaw.com
www.linkedin.com/in/diane-daly-34837b24

Oakville: Fabio Gazzola, Barrister, Solicitor & Notary
- *1
233 Robinson St., Oakville, ON L6J 1G5
Tel: 905-842-8600; *Fax:* 905-842-4774
gazzolaf@bellnet.ca
www.fabiogazzola.com

Oakville: Harrington LLP - *3
#101, 2275 Upper Middle Rd. East, Oakville, ON L6H OC3
Fax: 888-829-5396
Toll-Free: 888-492-0336
help@harringtonllp.com
www.harringtonllp.com

Oakville: Stuart W. Henderson - *1
228 Lakeshore Rd. East, Oakville, ON L6J 1H8
Tel: 905-844-3218; *Fax:* 905-844-3699
swhenderson@on.aibn.com

Oakville: Stuart W. Henderson - *1
P.O. Box 249, 228 Lakeshore Rd. East, Oakville, ON L6J 5A2
Tel: 905-844-3218; *Fax:* 905-844-3699
jbg@quixnet.net

Oakville: Law Offices of Charles W. Pley - *1
#102, 2660 Sherwood Heights Dr., Oakville, ON L6J 7Y8
Tel: 905-829-3888; *Fax:* 905-829-2100
info@pleylaw.com
www.pleylaw.com

Oakville: Lush, Bowker, Aird - *1
P.O. Box 734, 261 Lakeshore Rd. East, Oakville, ON L6J 1H9
Tel: 905-844-0381; *Fax:* 905-849-4540
Toll-Free: 877-844-0381
www.scottaird.com

Oakville: Thomas H. Marshall, Q.C. - *2
#205, 1540 Cornwall Rd., Oakville, ON L6J 7W5
Tel: 905-844-0464; *Fax:* 905-844-3983
www.oakvillefamilylawyer.ca

Oakville: Terri L. McCarthy - *1
#3A, 418 North Service Rd. East, Oakville, ON L6H 5R2
Tel: 905-842-4223; *Fax:* 905-842-7401
tlm.law@on.aibn.com

Oakville: David L. McKenzie - *1
P.O. Box 906, Stn. Main, Oakville, ON L6J 5E8
Tel: 905-845-7591; *Fax:* 905-845-8876

Oakville: Keith D. Nelson - *1
#205, North (Rear) Entrance, 243 North Service Rd. West,
Oakville, ON L6M 3E5
Tel: 905-338-8481; *Fax:* 905-338-0748
kdnelson@nelsonlawyer.com
www.nelsonlawyer.com

Oakville: O'Connor MacLeod Hanna LLP - *17
#300, 700 Kerr St., Oakville, ON L6K 3W5
Tel: 905-842-8030; *Fax:* 905-842-2460
info@omh.ca
www.omh.ca

Oakville: P. William Perras, Jr. - *2
#210, 1540 Cornwall Rd., Oakville, ON L6J 7W5
Tel: 905-827-2700; *Fax:* 905-827-2766
billperras@on.aibn.com

* indicates number of lawyers

Oakville: David J. Pilo - *1
#301, 88 Dunn St., Oakville, ON L6J 3C7
Tel: 905-338-2002; *Fax:* 905-338-3810
dpilo@on.aibn.com

Oakville: Richard Day Law - *1
Beauly Place, 164 Trafalgar Rd., Oakville, ON L6J 3G6
Tel: 905-844-2550; *Fax:* 905-842-6166
rick@daylaw.ca
www.daylaw.ca

Oakville: Martin A. Shanahan - *1
#200, 2620 Bristol Circle, Oakville, ON L6H 6Z7
Tel: 905-829-2700

Oakville: Sweatman Law Firm - *3
#11, 1400 Cornwall Rd., Oakville, ON L6J 7W5
Fax: 905-337-3309
Toll-Free: 888-389-2165
www.sweatmanlaw.com
www.facebook.com/SweatmanLawFirm,
www.linkedin.com/company/3192424

Oakville: Helen M. Thomson - *1
#1160, 1011 Upper Middle Rd. East, Oakville, ON L6H 5Z9
Tel: 416-410-8895; *Fax:* 416-410-8895

Oakville: Townsend & Associates - *3
Also Known As: Lynn Townend
Former Name: Townsend Renaud, Lynda J.
#10, 1525 Cornwall Rd., Oakville, ON L6J 0B2
Tel: 905-829-8600; *Fax:* 905-829-2035
lyn.townsend@ltownsend.ca

Oakville: William B. Kerr, Barrister & Solicitor - *1
Former Name: Ryrie, Kerr, Davidson
233 Robinson St., Oakville, ON L6J 1G5
Tel: 905-842-8600; *Fax:* 905-842-4774

Ohsweken: Bucci Law Office - *2
P.O. Box 819, 1721 Chiefswood Rd., Ohsweken, ON N0A 1M0
Tel: 519-751-0494; *Fax:* 519-751-1342
timbucci@buccilawoffice.net
www.buccilawoffice.net

Orangeville: Parkinson & Parkinson Associates - *1
145 Broadway St., Orangeville, ON L9W 1K2
Toll-Free: 800-831-8106
parkinson@parkinsonparkinson.ca
www.parkinsonparkinson.ca

Orangeville: Patricia L. Sproule Ward Law Office - *1
Former Name: Mullin, Thwaites, Ward LLP
P.O. Box 67, 30 Mill St., Orangeville, ON L9W 2M3
Tel: 519-941-4559; *Fax:* 519-941-4806
www.pswardlawoffice.ca

Orangeville: Anne Welwood - *1
14 Zina St., Orangeville, ON L9W 1E1
Tel: 519-941-9710; *Fax:* 519-941-9244
Toll-Free: 800-919-4919
info@welwoodlaw.com
www.annewelwood.com

Orangeville: White Law Professional Corporation - *2
30 Mill St., Orangeville, ON L9W 2M3
Tel: 519-941-9440; *Fax:* 519-941-3803
www.whitelaw.pro

Orillia: Crawford McLean Anderson LLP - *2
P.O. Box 520, 40 Coldwater St. East, Orillia, ON L3V 6K4
Tel: 705-325-2753; *Fax:* 705-325-4913
wmclean@mclaw.ca
www.mclaw.ca

Orillia: Brian D. Kinnear - *1
#108, P.O. Box 656, 17 Colborne St. East, Orillia, ON L3V 6K7
Tel: 705-323-9386; *Fax:* 705-323-9388
www.briankinnearlaw.ca

Orillia: Lisa Welch Madden Law Firm - *1
Former Name: Bourne, Jenkins & Mulligan
#102, 32 Matchedash St. N, Orillia, ON L3V 4T5
Tel: 705-325-6439; *Fax:* 705-325-7058
madden@lwmlaw.com

Orillia: Allan C. Parslow - *1
212 John St., Orillia, ON L3V 3H7
Tel: 705-329-2223; *Fax:* 705-329-0433

Orillia: Russell, Christie LLP - *7
P.O. Box 158, 505 Memorial Ave., Orillia, ON L3V 6J3
Tel: 705-325-1326; *Fax:* 705-327-1811
rcmkw@russellchristie.com
www.russellchristie.com

Orleans: Galarneau & Associates Professional Corp. - *4
2831 St. Joseph Blvd., Orleans, ON K1C 1G6
Tel: 613-830-7111; *Fax:* 613-830-7108
bjg@galarneauassoc.com
www.galarneauassoc.com

Orleans: Grandmaitre Virgo Evans Professional Corporation - *5
Former Name: Dust Evans Grandmaitre Professional Corporation
2628 St. Joseph Blvd., Orleans, ON K1C 1G3
Tel: 613-837-1010; *Fax:* 613-837-9670
Toll-Free: 800-379-6668
info@gvelaw.ca
gvelaw.ca

Orleans: Jacques Robert - *2
2788, boul St-Joseph, Orleans, ON K1C 1G5
Tel: 613-837-7880; *Fax:* 613-837-7664
mail@jacquesrobert.com
www.jacquesrobert.com

Orleans: Marc Nadon - *1
#101, 3009 St. Joseph Blvd., Orleans, ON K1E 1E1
Tel: 613-837-4437; *Fax:* 613-837-4204
info@marcnadon.ca

Orleans: Sicotte Guilbault LLP - *12
Former Name: Sicotte & Associates
4275 Innes Rd., 2nd Fl., Orleans, ON K1C 1T1
Tel: 613-837-7408; *Fax:* 613-837-8015
info@sicotte.ca
www.sicotte.ca

Orono: W. Kay Lycett, Q.C. - *1
P.O. Box 87, 5301 Main St., Orono, ON L0B 1M0
Tel: 905-983-5007; *Fax:* 905-983-9022
wklycett@look.ca

Oshawa: Affleck & Barrison LLP - *3
Former Name: Farquharson, Adamson & Affleck LLP
201 Bond St. East, Oshawa, ON L1G 1B4
Tel: 905-404-1947; *Fax:* 905-404-9050
www.criminallawoshawa.com

Oshawa: Aleksandr G. Bolotenko - *2
P.O. Box 978, 225 King St. East, Oshawa, ON L1H 7H2
Tel: 905-433-1176; *Fax:* 905-433-0283
abolotenko@agblaw.com
www.agblaw.com

Oshawa: Boychyn & Boychyn - *1
#1E, 57 Simcoe St. South, Oshawa, ON L1H 4G4
Tel: 905-576-2670; *Fax:* 905-576-0915

Oshawa: Julie Clark - *1
P.O. Box 365, Stn. A, 32 Elgin St. East, Oshawa, ON L1H 7L5
Tel: 905-434-6411; *Fax:* 905-571-6114

Oshawa: Catherine Cornwall-Taylor - *1
32 Elgin St. East, Oshawa, ON L1J 1T1
Tel: 905-434-6411; *Fax:* 905-571-6114

Oshawa: Creighton Law LLP - *5
Former Name: Creighton Victor Alexander Hayward Morison & Hall LLP
235 King St. East, Oshawa, ON L1H 1C5
Fax: 905-432-2323
Toll-Free: 800-216-4970
www.durhamlawyers.ca
www.facebook.com/creighton.law.94

Oshawa: Diamond Fischman & Pushman - *2
179 King St. East, Oshawa, ON L1H 1C2
Tel: 905-723-5243; *Fax:* 905-436-6041
www.dfplaw.com

Oshawa: Elliott & Hills - *2
106 Stevenson Rd. South, Oshawa, ON L1J 5M1
Tel: 905-571-1774; *Fax:* 905-571-7706
Toll-Free: 877-272-5220
www.elliottandhills.com
www.facebook.com/elliottandhills, twitter.com/elliottandhills

Oshawa: Diane M. England - *1
167 Simcoe St. North, Oshawa, ON L1G 4S8
Tel: 905-721-1277; *Fax:* 905-721-1217
mail@dianeengland.com
www.dianeengland.com

Oshawa: Shan K. Jain, Q.C. - *1
#2, 215 Simcoe St. North, Oshawa, ON L1G 4T1
Tel: 905-432-7787; *Fax:* 905-432-2343
jainc@sprint.ca

Oshawa: Kelly Greenway Bruce - Oshawa - *8
Former Name: Kelly, Greenway, Bruce, Korb
114 King St. East, Oshawa, ON L1H 7N1
Tel: 905-723-2278; *Fax:* 905-432-2663
mail@oshawalawyers.com
www.oshawalawyers.com

Oshawa: Kitchen Legal - *1
P.O. Box 82, 95 Simcoe St. South, Oshawa, ON L1H 7K8
Tel: 905-436-8787; *Fax:* 905-721-0868
rkitchen@kitchenlegal.ca
www.kitchenlegal.ca

Oshawa: Kitchen Simeson Belliveau LLP - *3
Former Name: Kitchen Simeson LLP
86 Simcoe St. South, Oshawa, ON L1H 4G6
Tel: 905-579-5302; *Fax:* 905-579-6073
Toll-Free: 888-669-6446
kslawfirm.ca
www.facebook.com/KitchenSimesonBelliveauLLP

Oshawa: Laskowsky & Laskowsky - *1
73 Centre St. South, Oshawa, ON L1H 4A1
Tel: 905-579-0777; *Fax:* 905-576-9918

Oshawa: Mack Lawyers - Oshawa - *3
Former Name: Mack, Kisbee & Greer
146 Simcoe St. North, Oshawa, ON L1G 4S7
Tel: 905-571-1405
info@macklawyers.ca
www.macklawyers.ca

Oshawa: Elaine M. Forbes McCallum - *1
174 Athol St. East, Oshawa, ON L1H 1K1
Tel: 905-579-8866; *Fax:* 905-579-8913
Toll-Free: 888-579-5252
elainemfmccallum@on.aibn.com

Oshawa: Sharon A. Moote - *1
Former Name: Moote & Cocchetto
#210, 200 Bond St. West, Oshawa, ON L1J 2L7
Tel: 905-432-7880; *Fax:* 905-432-7674

Oshawa: Neal & Mara Barristers & Solicitors - *2
142 Simcoe St. North, Oshawa, ON L1G 4S7
Tel: 905-436-9015; *Fax:* 905-436-6098

Oshawa: Josef Neubauer - *2
106 Stevenson Rd. South, Oshawa, ON L1J 5M1
Tel: 905-433-1991; *Fax:* 905-433-7038
www.neubauerlawyer.ca

Oshawa: O'Brien, Balka, Elrick & Khehra - *6
Former Name: O'Brien, Balka & Elrick, Barristers & Solicitors
219 King St. East, Oshawa, ON L1H 1C5
Tel: 905-576-3402; *Fax:* 905-576-3915
Toll-Free: 866-245-5063
obek@oshawalaw.com
www.oshawalaw.com

Oshawa: Margot Poepjes - *1
#217, 650 King St. East, Oshawa, ON L1H 1G5
Tel: 905-433-4020; *Fax:* 905-433-7028
mpoepjeslawoffice@rogers.com

Oshawa: Catherine L. Salmers - *1
#101, McLaughlin Square, 55 William St. East, Oshawa, ON L1G 7C9
Tel: 905-723-1101; *Fax:* 905-723-1157
csalmers@ssf-oshawa.com
www.salmerslawoffices.com

Oshawa: Scott & Olver LLP - *3
Former Name: Scott, Kimball, Olver
39 Bond St. East, Oshawa, ON L1G 1B2
Tel: 905-579-9400; *Fax:* 905-579-7400
scottolver@scottandolver.ca
scottandolver.ca

* indicates number of lawyers

Oshawa: Sosna & Burch - *3
#8, 500 King St. West, Oshawa, ON L1J 2K9
Tel: 905-668-6811; *Fax:* 905-668-6899
sosna-burch@sosnaburch.com

Oshawa: Frank H.M. Stolwyk - *1
57 Simcoe St. South, Unit 1-F, Oshawa, ON L1H 4G4
Tel: 905-576-8100; *Fax:* 905-579-6762
franks4950@aol.com

Oshawa: Strike Furlong Ford - *6
Former Name: Salmers, Strike & Furlong
P.O. Box 486, Stn. A, 282 King St. East, Oshawa, ON L1H 1C8
Tel: 905-448-4800; *Fax:* 905-448-4801
sff-law.ca

Oshawa: David B. Thomas - *1
28B Albert St., Oshawa, ON L1H 8S5
Tel: 905-576-5666; *Fax:* 905-576-5289

Oshawa: The Law Office of Martin Tweyman - *3
170 Athol St. East, Oshawa, ON L1H 1K1
Tel: 905-571-1500; *Fax:* 905-571-7528
www.tweymanlaw.com

Oshawa: Walters, Dizenbach, Ferguson - *3
P.O. Box 2307, 218 Centre St. N, Oshawa, ON L1B 1H3
Tel: 905-579-1066

Oshawa: Ronald F. Worboy - *1
153 Simcoe St. North, Oshawa, ON L1G 4S6
Tel: 905-723-2288; *Fax:* 905-576-1355

Oshawa: Yanch & Yanch - *1
#1D, P.O. Box 154, 57 Simcoe St. South, Oshawa, ON L1H 7L1
Tel: 905-728-9495; *Fax:* 905-721-8044
yanchfirm@hotmail.com
yanchlawoffice.com

Ottawa: Douglas R. Adams - *1
#1502, 222 Queen St., Ottawa, ON K1P 5V9
Tel: 613-238-8076; *Fax:* 613-238-5519

Ottawa: Addelman, Baum & Gilbert LLP - *4
Former Name: Baum, Douglas M.
#800, 85 Albert St., Ottawa, ON K1P 6A4
Tel: 613-237-2673; *Fax:* 613-237-8146
Richard.Addelman@addelmanbaumgilbert.com
www.addelmanbaumgilbert.com

Ottawa: Ahmad-Yousuf & Assoc. - *3
Former Name: Moore & Ahmad-Yousuf
#100, 180 Metcalfe St., Ottawa, ON K2P 1P5
Tel: 613-236-1111; *Fax:* 613-232-7763

Ottawa: Aitken Klee LLP - Ottawa - *13
#300, 100 Queen St., Ottawa, ON K1P 1J9
Tel: 613-695-5858; *Fax:* 613-695-5854
info@aitkenklee.com
www.aitkenklee.com

Ottawa: Allan & Snelling LLP, Barristers & Solicitors - *7
#104, Stealth Building, 303 Terry Fox Dr., Ottawa, ON K2K 3J1
Tel: 613-270-8600; *Fax:* 613-270-0900
info@compellingcounsel.com
www.compellingcounsel.com

Ottawa: Anders, Young, Strong & Jonah - *5
Former Name: Anders, Young & Jonah
#401, 1580 Merivale Rd., Ottawa, ON K2G 4B5
Tel: 613-224-1621; *Fax:* 613-224-8827
info@aysj-law.com
www.aysj-law.com

Ottawa: Andrews Robichaud - *7
#500, 1306 Wellington St., Ottawa, ON K1Y 3B2
Tel: 613-237-1512; *Fax:* 613-237-9580
info@andrewsrobichaud.com
www.andrewsrobichaud.com

Ottawa: Arbique & Ahde - *2
Former Name: Fortey & Arbique
#210, 1335 Carling Ave., Ottawa, ON K1Z 8N8
Tel: 613-725-0303; *Fax:* 613-725-1292
info@forteyarbique.com
www.arbiqueahde.com
twitter.com/ArbiqueAhde

Ottawa: Augustine Bater Binks LLP - *8
#1100, 141 Laurier Ave. West, Ottawa, ON K1P 5J3
Tel: 613-569-9500; *Fax:* 613-569-9522
info@abblaw.ca
www.abblaw.ca
twitter.com/abblaw
www.linkedin.com/company/augustine-bater-binks-llp

Ottawa: Robert G. Bales - *1
1041 Harkness Ave., Ottawa, ON K1V 6N9
Tel: 613-731-2129; *Fax:* 613-248-5151
rob.bales@adjudicate.ca

Ottawa: Barnes Sammon LLP - *14
Former Name: Barnes Barristers
#400, 200 Elgin St., Ottawa, ON K2P 1L5
Tel: 613-594-8000; *Fax:* 613-235-7578
www.barnessammon.ca

Ottawa: Barnes, Sammon LLP - *15
#400, 200 Elgin St., Ottawa, ON K2P 1L5
Tel: 613-594-8000; *Fax:* 613-235-7578
www.barnessammon.ca

Ottawa: Beament Hebert Nicholson LLP - *6
Former Name: Beament Green
979 Wellington St. West, Ottawa, ON K1Y 2X7
Tel: 613-241-3400; *Fax:* 613-241-8555
info@beament.com
www.beament.com
www.facebook.com/BeamentHebertNicholsonEnvironmentalEmp
loymentLaw, twitter.com/BHN_LLP,
www.linkedin.com/company-beta/3164030

Ottawa: Bell Baker LLP - *15
#700, 116 Lisgar St., Ottawa, ON K2P 0C2
Tel: 613-237-3444; *Fax:* 613-237-1413
info@bellbaker.com
www.bellbaker.com
www.facebook.com/bellbakerllp

Ottawa: Bell, Unger, Riley, Morris - *4
24 Bayswater Ave., Ottawa, ON K1Y 2E4
Tel: 613-235-1266; *Fax:* 613-230-2727

Ottawa: John E. Bogue - *1
#802, 200 Elgin St., Ottawa, ON K2P 1L5
Tel: 613-234-4901; *Fax:* 613-236-8906

Ottawa: Bosada & Associates - *1
#222, 280 Metcalfe St., Ottawa, ON K2P 1R7
Tel: 613-563-1001; *Fax:* 613-563-1031
richard@bosada.ca

Ottawa: Bradley, Hiscock, McCracken - *5
Former Name: Bradley, Hiscock
1581 Greenbank Rd., Ottawa, ON K2J 4Y6
Tel: 613-825-4585; *Fax:* 613-825-5101
infow@bhlaw.ca
www.bhmlaw.ca

Ottawa: Alan Brass - *1
#1002, 200 Elgin St., Ottawa, ON K2P 1L5
Tel: 613-238-5757; *Fax:* 613-688-1212
abrass@alanbrass.ca
www.alanbrass.ca

Ottawa: BrazeauSeller LLP - *18
#750, 55 Metcalfe St., Ottawa, ON K1P 6L5
Tel: 613-237-4000; *Fax:* 613-237-4001
www.brazeauseller.com
www.facebook.com/BrazeauSeller, twitter.com/BrazeauSeller,
www.linkedin.com/company/brazeauseller.llp

Ottawa: C.P. Brett - *1
70 Gloucester St., Ottawa, ON K2P 0A2
Tel: 613-230-2907; *Fax:* 613-235-4430
cpbrett@attglobal.net

Ottawa: Thomas W. Brooker - *1
#208, 1400 Clyde Ave., Ottawa, ON K2G 3J2
Tel: 613-226-3265; *Fax:* 613-224-8943
tom@brookerlawoffice.ca
www.brookerlawoffice.ca

Ottawa: Bulger, Young - *3
1493 Merivale Rd., Lower Level, Ottawa, ON K2E 5P3
Tel: 613-728-5881; *Fax:* 613-728-6158

Ottawa: Donald J. Byrne - *1
#204, 1568 Carling Ave., Ottawa, ON K1Z 7M4
Tel: 613-722-5292; *Fax:* 613-729-6732
dbyrne@primus.ca

Ottawa: Campbell Clark Yemensky - *4
Former Name: Mount Clark Yemensky
#208, 1400 Clyde Ave., Ottawa, ON K2G 3J2
Tel: 613-727-9698; *Fax:* 613-224-8943
gyemensky@familylaw-ottawa.ca
familylaw-ottawa.ca

Ottawa: Capelle Kane Professional Corporation - *3
#300, 311 Richmond Rd., Ottawa, ON K1Z 6X3
Tel: 613-230-7070; *Fax:* 613-230-9444
contact@capellekane.com
www.capellekane.com

Ottawa: Carroll & Wallace - *3
#502, 66 Slater St., Ottawa, ON K1P 5H1
Tel: 613-236-5494; *Fax:* 613-232-7322

Ottawa: Edward Y.W. Cheung - *1
#22, 5340 Canotek Rd., Ottawa, ON K1J 9C8
Tel: 613-748-9898; *Fax:* 613-748-1114
yw61@aol.com

Ottawa: Paul-Emile Chiasson - *1
18 Nepean St., Ottawa, ON K2P 2L2
Tel: 613-230-8800; *Fax:* 613-236-3136
pechiasson@sympatico.ca

Ottawa: Clermont Clausi Gardiner & Associates - *4
1447 Woodroffe Ave., Ottawa, ON K2G 1W1
Tel: 613-225-0037; *Fax:* 613-225-0921
www.ccglawoffice.com

Ottawa: Connolly Obagi LLP - *7
Former Name: Cooligan/Ryan LLP
#1100, 200 Elgin St., Ottawa, ON K2P 1L5
Tel: 613-567-4412; *Fax:* 613-567-9751
Toll-Free: 855-683-2240
info@connollyobagi.com
www.connollyobagi.com

Ottawa: Law Office of Rosalind E. Conway - *2
#320, 185 Somerset St. West, Ottawa, ON K2P 0J2
Tel: 613-594-0300; *Fax:* 613-594-8111
rosalind.conway@gmail.com
www.rosalindconway.com

Ottawa: Delaney's Law Firm - *4
352 Elgin St., 2nd Fl., Ottawa, ON K2P 1M8
Tel: 613-233-7000; *Fax:* 866-846-4191
info@delaneys.ca
www.delaneys.ca
www.facebook.com/delaneyslawfirm

Ottawa: Donald R. Good & Associates - *3
#207, 43 Roydon Pl., Ottawa, ON K2E 1A3
Tel: 613-228-9676; *Fax:* 613-228-7404
farmlaw@on.aibn.com

Ottawa: Drache Aptowitzer LLP - *5
226 Maclaren St., Ottawa, ON K2P 0L6
Tel: 613-237-3300; *Fax:* 613-237-2786
adamapt@drache.ca
www.drache.ca
twitter.com/charitytax

Ottawa: Dubuc-Osland - *4
#204, Fitzsimmons Building, 265 Carling Ave., Ottawa, ON K1S 2E1
Tel: 613-236-3360; *Fax:* 613-236-3771
dubucosland.com

Ottawa: Daniel F. Dunlap - *1
Stn. B, 111 Sherwood Dr,, Ottawa, ON K1Y 3V1
Tel: 613-722-7788; *Fax:* 613-722-8909
ddunlap@dunlaplaw.ca

Ottawa: Edelson & Friedman LLP - *7
Former Name: Edelson Clifford D'Angelo Barristers LLP
#600, 200 Elgin St., Ottawa, ON K2P 1L5
Tel: 613-237-2290; *Fax:* 613-237-0071
www.edelsonlaw.ca

Ottawa: Emond Harnden SRL/LLP - Ottawa - *29
Glebe Chambers, 707 Bank St., Ottawa, ON K1S 3V1
Tel: 613-563-7660; *Fax:* 613-563-8001
Toll-Free: 888-563-7660
www.ehlaw.ca

Ottawa: Engel & Associates - *2
#210, 116 Lisgar St., Ottawa, ON K2P 0C2
Tel: 613-909-8152; *Fax:* 613-235-3159
www.bruceengel.com

---

* indicates number of lawyers

Ottawa: Fanaian Law Office - *1
30 Staten Way, Ottawa, ON K2C 4E5
Tel: 613-567-0833; *Fax:* 613-567-9549
fanaian@hotmail.com
fan.shojaei.us

Ottawa: Farber Robillard Leith LLP - *5
Former Name: Farber & Robillard
330 Churchill Ave. North, Ottawa, ON K1Z 5B9
Tel: 613-722-9418; *Fax:* 613-722-5981
www.frl-law.ca
www.facebook.com/FarberRobillardLeith, twitter.com/frllaw

Ottawa: Finlayson & Singlehurst - *6
#700, 225 Metcalfe St., Ottawa, ON K2P 1P9
Tel: 613-232-0227; *Fax:* 613-232-0542
mail@fs.ca
www.fs.ca

Ottawa: Ann L. Flint - *1
#203, 190 Somerset St. West, Ottawa, ON K2P 0J4
Tel: 613-594-5461; *Fax:* 613-594-5468

Ottawa: George Flumian - *1
222 Argyle Ave., Ottawa, ON K2P 1B9
Tel: 613-236-8321; *Fax:* 613-230-6597

Ottawa: Steven A. Fried - *1
303 Waverly St., Ottawa, ON K2P 0V9
Tel: 613-233-4420; *Fax:* 613-288-1554
sfried@stevenfried.com

Ottawa: Susan Gahrns Law Office - *1
#401, 1580 Merivale Rd., Ottawa, ON K2G 4B5
Tel: 613-235-6299; *Fax:* 613-224-8827
susan@gahrns.com
www.gahrns.com

Ottawa: Goldberg Stroud LLP Barristers & Solicitors - *3
Also Known As: Goldberg Wiseman Stroud & Hollingsworth
Former Name: Goldberg Stroud LLP; Goldberg, Kronick & Stroud LLP
176 Bronsons Ave., Ottawa, ON K1R 6K9
Tel: 613-237-4922; *Fax:* 613-237-2920
info@gwshlaw.com
gwshlaw.wordpress.com

Ottawa: Donald J. Gormley - *1
#204, 190 Somerset St. West, Ottawa, ON K2P 0J4
Tel: 613-237-7726; *Fax:* 613-237-1977
donald.gormley@sympatico.ca

Ottawa: Goss, McCorriston, Stel - *2
#203, 2430 Bank St., Ottawa, ON K1V 0T7
Tel: 613-738-0023; *Fax:* 613-738-1294
www.gms-law.com

Ottawa: Grant & Dawn - *3
226 MacLaren St., Ottawa, ON K2P 0L6
Tel: 613-235-2212; *Fax:* 613-235-5294
dawn@lexfix.ca

Ottawa: Greenspon, Brown & Associates - *4
Former Name: Karam Greenspon
331 Somerset St. West, Ottawa, ON K2P 0J8
Tel: 613-288-2890; *Fax:* 613-288-2896
info@greensponbrown.ca
greensponbrown.ca

Ottawa: David R. Habib - *1
18 Honeyood Ct., Ottawa, ON K1V 1Y4
Tel: 613-822-4100; *Fax:* 613-691-0656
david@habiblaw.ca
www.habiblaw.ca

Ottawa: Hale Criminal Law Office - *1
#101, 116 Lisgar St., Ottawa, ON K2P 0C2
Tel: 613-230-4253; *Fax:* 613-230-6996
john.hclo@me.com
www.facebook.com/hclo

Ottawa: Hewitt, Hewitt, Nesbitt, Reid LLP - *5
#604, Fuller Bldg., 75 Albert St., Ottawa, ON K1P 5E7
Tel: 613-563-0202; *Fax:* 613-563-0445
info@hewitts-law.com
hewittslaw.com

Ottawa: Susan Hodgson - *1
#307, 150 Isabella St., Ottawa, ON K1S 1V7
Tel: 613-237-0505; *Fax:* 613-567-3559
susan@hodgsonlaw.ca

Ottawa: Honey/MacMillan - *3
146 Richmond Rd., Ottawa, ON K1Z 6W2
Tel: 613-722-2493; *Fax:* 613-722-2773
honeymac@rogers.com

Ottawa: Honeywell Law - *1
Former Name: Callan Honeywell LLP
418 Preston St., Ottawa, ON K1S 4N2
Tel: 613-729-2460; *Fax:* 613-729-1710
www.honeywelllaw.ca

Ottawa: Jay C. Humphrey Professional Corporation - *1
2821 Riverside Dr., Ottawa, ON K1V 8N4
Tel: 613-733-3393; *Fax:* 613-733-3393
jay@humphreylaw.ca
humphreylaw.ca

Ottawa: Katsepontes Law - *2
Former Name: Burton Katsepontes
#200, 283 Dalhousie St., Ottawa, ON K1N 7E5
Tel: 613-239-3064; *Fax:* 613-237-9181
nicholas@katseponteslaw.com
www.katseponteslaw.com

Ottawa: Kelly Santini LLP - Ottawa - *34
#2401, 160 Elgin St., Ottawa, ON K2P 2P7
Tel: 613-238-6321; *Fax:* 613-233-4553
www.kellysantini.com
www.facebook.com/kellysantinilaw, twitter.com/kellysantinilaw,
www.linkedin.com/company/kelly-santini-llp

Ottawa: Kerr & Kerr - *1
#607, 1755 Riverside Dr., Ottawa, ON K1G 3T6
Tel: 613-293-0852; *Fax:* 613-526-3511
akerr@kerr-kerr.com
www.kerr-kerr.com

Ottawa: LaBarge Weinstein LLP - Ottawa - *21
#800, 515 Legget Dr., Ottawa, ON K2K 3G4
Tel: 613-599-9600; *Fax:* 613-599-0018
info@lwlaw.com
www.lwlaw.com
twitter.com/LWConnect,
www.linkedin.com/company/labarge-weinstein

Ottawa: Lafleur & Associes/Associates - *1
237 King Edward Ave., Ottawa, ON K1N 7L8
Tel: 613-241-7335; *Fax:* 613-241-5012
www.mjlafleurlaw.ca

Ottawa: Laird Family & Estate Law - *1
10 Bedale Dr., Ottawa, ON K2H 5M1
Tel: 613-232-3575; *Fax:* 613-232-6622
www.lairdfamilylaw.ca

Ottawa: Langevin Morris Smith LLP - Ottawa - *15
Former Name: Lewis Langevin LLP
190 O'Connor St., 9th Fl., Ottawa, ON K2P 2R3
Tel: 613-230-5787; *Fax:* 613-230-8563
www.lmslawyers.com
www.facebook.com/langevinmorrissmith, twitter.com/310lawyer

Ottawa: Laveaux, Frank
Also Known As: Cabinet Laveaux Law Office
#210, 1725 St-Laurent Blvd., Ottawa, ON K1G 3V4
Tel: 613-523-0307; *Fax:* 613-523-0377

Ottawa: Low Murchison Radnoff LLP - *77
1565 Carling Ave., 4th Fl., Ottawa, ON K1Z 8R1
Tel: 613-236-9442; *Fax:* 613-236-7942
Toll-Free: 888-909-9442
lawyer@lmrlawyers.com
lmrlawyers.com

Ottawa: Macdonald, Affleck - *2
#1100, 200 Elgin St., Ottawa, ON K2P 1L5
Tel: 613-236-8712; *Fax:* 613-236-5145

Ottawa: MacKay & Asangarani LLP - *3
Former Name: Robin D. MacKay & Associates; MacKay & Sanderson
#201, 1580 Merivale Rd., Ottawa, ON K2G 4B5
Tel: 613-238-6180; *Fax:* 613-238-3288
reception@malegal.ca
melegal.ca

Ottawa: MacKinnon & Phillips - *7
#802, 200 Elgin St., Ottawa, ON K2P 1L5
Tel: 613-236-0662; *Fax:* 613-236-8906
www.mackinnonphillips.com

Ottawa: Maclaren Corlett LLP - Ottawa - *5
#1424, 50 O'Connor St., Ottawa, ON K1P 6L2
Tel: 613-233-1146; *Fax:* 613-233-7190
mail@macorlaw.com
www.macorlaw.com
www.facebook.com/MaclarenCorlett, twitter.com/maclarencorlett,
www.linkedin.com/company/maclaren-corlett-llp

Ottawa: Mann Lawyers - Ottawa - Scott St. - *18
Former Name: Mann & Partners LLP
#710, Tower B, 1600 Scott St., Ottawa, ON K1Y 4N7
Tel: 613-722-1500; *Fax:* 613-722-7677
Toll-Free: 800-420-0577
info@mannlawyers.com
www.mannlawyers.com
twitter.com/MannLawyers,
www.linkedin.com/company/mann-&-partners-l-l-p-

Ottawa: Howard Mann - *1
578 O'Connor St., Ottawa, ON K1S 3R3
Tél: 613-729-0621; *Téléc:* 613-729-0306
howard@howardmann.ca
www.howardmann.ca

Ottawa: Marks & Marks LLP - *2
#201, 190 Somerset St. West, Ottawa, ON K2P 0J4
Tel: 613-230-2123; *Fax:* 613-230-5707
bdm@marks-marks.com
www.marks-marks.com

Ottawa: Leonard Max, Q.C.
428 Kent St., Ottawa, ON K2P 2B3
Tel: 613-269-3872

Ottawa: May & Konyer - *5
#305, 185 Somerset St. West, Ottawa, ON K2P 0J2
Tel: 613-230-6524; *Fax:* 613-230-2705
jmccausland@mayandkonyer.com
www.seanmaylaw.ca

Ottawa: Mazerolle & Lemay - *5
#202, 1173 Cyrville Rd., Ottawa, ON K1J 7S6
Tel: 613-746-5700; *Fax:* 613-746-1783
www.mazerollelemay.com

Ottawa: MBM Intellectual Property Law LLP - *8
Former Name: Marusyk Miller & Swain
270 Albert St., 14th Fl., Ottawa, ON K1P 5G8
Tel: 613-567-0762; *Fax:* 613-563-7671
MBMGeneral@mbm.com
www.mbm.com
www.facebook.com/mbmiplaw, twitter.com/mbmiplaw,
www.linkedin.com/company/mbm-intellectual-property-law-llp

Ottawa: McBride Bond Christian LLP - *11
Former Name: Doucet McBride LLP
#500, 265 Caeling Ave., Ottawa, ON K1S 2E1
Tel: 613-233-4474; *Fax:* 613-233-8868
Toll-Free: 888-288-2033
reception@mbclaw.ca
mbclaw.ca

Ottawa: McCann & Lyttle - *2
#800, 200 Elgin St., Ottawa, ON K2P 1L5
Tel: 613-236-1410; *Fax:* 613-563-1367
pmccann@mccannandlyttle.com
mccannandlyttle.com

Ottawa: Ronald McCloskey - *1
Former Name: McCloskey McCloskey
#37, 1010 Polytek St., Ottawa, ON K1J 9J2
Tel: 613-745-0395; *Fax:* 613-745-8007
www.mccloskey.ca

Ottawa: McDonald & Quinn - *1
#1, 1480 Woodward Ave., Ottawa, ON K1Z 7W6
Tel: 613-729-1005; *Fax:* 613-729-1176

Ottawa: McFadden, Fincham - *7
#606, 225 Metcalfe St., Ottawa, ON K2P 1P9
Tel: 613-234-1907; *Fax:* 613-234-5233
mail@mcfaddenfincham.com
www.mcfaddenfincham.com

Ottawa: McGuinty Law Offices Professional Corporation - *4
Former Name: McGuinty & McGuinty
1192 Rockingham Ave., Ottawa, ON K1H 8A7
Tel: 613-526-3858; *Fax:* 613-526-3187
inquiry@mcguintylaw.ca
www.mcguintylaw.com

* indicates number of lawyers

Ottawa: Robert F. Meagher - *1
#502, 66 Slater St., Ottawa, ON K1P 5H1
Tel: 613-563-4278; *Fax:* 613-232-7322
rmeagher@bellnet.ca

Ottawa: Menzies Lawyers - *5
Former Name: Menzies & Coulson
176 Gloucester St., 4th Fl., Ottawa, ON K2P 0A6
Tel: 613-722-1313; *Fax:* 613-722-4712
Toll-Free: 888-722-1313
info@menzieslawyers.com
www.menzieslawyers.com
www.facebook.com/269135529875143,
www.linkedin.com/company/2830426

Ottawa: John E. Merner - *3
Former Name: Merner Burton Massie
136 Lewis St., Ottawa, ON K2P 0S7
Tel: 613-567-6093; *Fax:* 613-567-7164

Ottawa: Merovitz Potechin LLP - *11
#300, 1565 Carling Ave., Ottawa, ON K1Z 8R1
Tel: 613-563-7544; *Fax:* 613-563-4577
www.merovitzpotechin.com
www.facebook.com/merovitz.potechin

Ottawa: Eric A. Milligan - *1
#108, 55 Murray St., Ottawa, ON K1N 5M3
Tel: 613-562-4077; *Fax:* 613-562-4102
milligan@delsysresearch.com

Ottawa: Miltons IP Professional Corporation - *4
Former Name: Milton, Geller LLP
#200, 15 Fitzgerald Rd., Ottawa, ON K2H 9C1
Tel: 613-567-7824 *Toll-Free:* 866-297-1179
info@miltonsip.com
www.miltonsip.com

Ottawa: Richard Minard - *1
58 Clegg St., Ottawa, ON K1S 0H8
Tel: 613-237-6874; *Fax:* 613-234-1728
rminard@on.aibn.com

Ottawa: Moffat & Co., Macera & Jarzyna LLP - *16
#715, P.O. Box 2088, Stn. D, 11 Holland Ave., Ottawa, ON K1Y 4S1
Tel: 613-232-7302; *Fax:* 613-235-2508
mail@moffatco.com
www.moffatco.com

Ottawa: Momentum Business Law - *9
#201, 320 March Rd., Ottawa, ON K2K 2E3
Tel: 613-592-3939 *Toll-Free:* 833-333-1088
info@momentum.legal
momentum.law
www.facebook.com/momentumlaw.ottawa,
twitter.com/momentum_law

Ottawa: Christopher A. Moore - *1
63 Robert St., Ottawa, ON K2P 1G5
Tel: 613-230-9448; *Fax:* 613-230-3624
chalmo@istar.ca

Ottawa: More & McLeod - *1
#212, 2249 Carling Ave., Ottawa, ON K2B 7E9
Tel: 613-820-7888; *Fax:* 613-820-3044
morelaw@bellnet.ca
moreandmcleod.ca

Ottawa: Kevin Murphy - *1
112 Lisgar St., Ottawa, ON K2P 0C2
Tel: 613-238-1333

Ottawa: Robert Elmo Murray - *1
#307, 150 Isabella St., Ottawa, ON K1S 1V7
Tel: 613-237-0505; *Fax:* 613-567-3559

Ottawa: Kenneth J. Naftel - *1
#307, 150 Isabella St., Ottawa, ON K1S 1V7
Tel: 613-237-0505; *Fax:* 613-567-3559
ken@kennaftel.ca

Ottawa: Nelligan O'Brien Payne LLP
#300, 50 O'Connor St., Ottawa, ON K1P 6L2
Tel: 613-238-8080; *Fax:* 613-238-2098
Toll-Free: 833-892-3331
info@nelliganlaw.ca
nelliganlaw.ca

Ottawa: Nelligan O'Brien Payne LLP - Ottawa - *46
#1500, 50 O'Connor St., Ottawa, ON K1P 6L2
Tel: 613-238-8080; *Fax:* 613-238-2098
Toll-Free: 888-565-9912
info@nelligan.ca
www.nelligan.ca
www.facebook.com/nelliganobrienpayne,
twitter.com/NelliganLaw,
www.linkedin.com/company/nelligan-o%27brien-payne-llp_2

Ottawa: Nicol & Lazier - *3
237 Somerset St. West, Ottawa, ON K2P 0J3
Tel: 613-232-4241; *Fax:* 613-236-9325

Ottawa: Paul Niebergall - *1
34 Halldorson Cres., Ottawa, ON K2K 2C7
Tel: 613-232-8508; *Fax:* 613-232-9654
paulniebergall@rogers.com
www.kanata-lawyer.ca
www.facebook.com/paulniebergalllawyer,
www.linkedin.com/in/paul-niebergall-03727920

Ottawa: Wanda Noel Barrister & Solicitor - *1
5496 Whitewood Ave., Ottawa, ON K4M 1C7
Tel: 613-794-1171; *Fax:* 613-692-1735
wanda.noel@bell.net

Ottawa: Michael B. Oliveira - *1
#402, 280 Metcalfe St., Ottawa, ON K2P 1R7
Tel: 613-567-1016; *Fax:* 613-567-9126
moliveira@sprint.ca

Ottawa: Eugene L. Oscapella - *1
70 MacDonald St., Ottawa, ON K2P 1H6
Tel: 613-238-5909; *Fax:* 613-238-2891
eugene@oscapella.ca

Ottawa: Overtveld & Associates - *1
284 Wellington St., Ottawa, ON K1A 0H8
Tel: 613-941-6805; *Fax:* 613-957-4019
Overtveld@magma.ca
www.magma.ca/~overtvel/

Ottawa: Paradis, Jones, Horwitz, Bowles Associates - *4
#900, 200 Elgin St., Ottawa, ON K2P 1L5
Tel: 613-238-5074; *Fax:* 613-230-3250

Ottawa: Diana Carr - *2
#601, 225 Metcalfe St., Ottawa, ON K2P 1P9
Tel: 613-567-1431
info@dianacarrlawyer.com
www.parentcarrlawyers.com

Ottawa: Lawrence S. Pascoe - *1
Former Name: Mirsky, Pascoe
#300, 2039 Robertson Rd., Ottawa, ON K2H 8R2
Tel: 613-828-2120; *Fax:* 613-596-0881
lspascoe@thepascoedifference.com
www.thepascoedifference.com

Ottawa: Francis K. Peddle - *1
168 Henderson Ave., Ottawa, ON K1N 7P6
Tel: 613-232-1740; *Fax:* 613-232-0407
ftpeddle@bellnet.ca

Ottawa: Kimberley A. Pegg - *3
#1, 200 Cooper St., Ottawa, ON K2P 0G1
Tel: 613-232-9331; *Fax:* 613-230-3551
kimberley.pegg@bellnet.ca
www.kimberleypeggbarristers.com

Ottawa: Pender & Leef - *2
#1608, 130 Alber St., Ottawa, ON K1P 5G4
Tel: 613-569-0104; *Fax:* 613-569-6235
stephen@pender-leef.com

Ottawa: Perley-Robertson, Hill & McDougall LLP / s.r.l. - *51
#1400, Constitution Square, 340 Albert St., Ottawa, ON K1R 0A5
Tel: 613-238-2022; *Fax:* 613-238-8775
Toll-Free: 800-268-8292
lawyers@perlaw.ca
www.perlaw.ca

Ottawa: Pfeiffer & Associates - *1
157 McLeod St., Ottawa, ON K2P 0Z6
Tel: 613-238-4115; *Fax:* 613-563-8273
byron.pfeiffer@gmail.com

Ottawa: Piazza Tanner LLP - *3
Former Name: Piazza, Brooks
#600, 225 Metcalfe St., Ottawa, ON K2P 1P9
Tel: 613-238-2244; *Fax:* 613-238-3382
www.piazzalaw.com

Ottawa: Plaskacz & Associates
64 Glen Ave., Ottawa, ON K1S 2Z9
Tel: 613-299-0200
plaskacz@plaskacz.com
www.plaskacz.com

Ottawa: Hugo Prud'homme Professional Law Corporation - *1
Former Name: Legal Opinion North
Ottawa, ON
hprudhomme@legalopinionnorth.ca
www.legalopinionnorth.ca

Ottawa: Prystupa Law Office - *2
#400, 303 Moodie Dr., Ottawa, ON K2H 9R4
Tel: 613-729-4669; *Fax:* 613-729-4669
admin@prystupalaw.ca

Ottawa: Helene Bruce Puccini - *1
247 Fourth Ave., Ottawa, ON K1S 2L9
Tel: 613-230-6295
helenebruce@gmail.com

Ottawa: Ranger & Associés - *1
#1000, 141 Laurier Ave. West, Ottawa, ON K1P 5J3
Tel: 613-234-2255; *Fax:* 613-234-2301

Ottawa: Rasmussen Starr Ruddy LLP - *12
#660, 660 Carling Ave., Ottawa, ON K1Z 1G3
Tel: 613-232-1830; *Fax:* 613-232-2499
mail@rsrlaw.ca
www.rsrlaw.ca

Ottawa: Raven Law - Ottawa - *13
Former Name: Raven, Cameron, Ballantyne, Yazbeck LLP
#1600, 220 Laurier Ave. West, Ottawa, ON K1P 5Z9
Tel: 613-567-2901; *Fax:* 613-567-2921
info@ravenlaw.com
www.ravenlaw.com

Ottawa: Karen Ann Reid - *1
#202, 200 Elgin St., Ottawa, ON K2P 1L5
Tel: 613-238-8777; *Fax:* 613-238-4824
kareid@istop.com

Ottawa: Frank I. Ritchie - *1
2253 Alta Vista Dr., Ottawa, ON K1H 7L9
Tel: 613-731-8288

Ottawa: Terrence M. Romanow - *1
2038 Black Friars Rd., Ottawa, ON K2A 3K8
Tel: 613-722-8224; *Fax:* 613-722-0908
terryromanow@rogers.com

Ottawa: Ross Talarico & Schwisberg Law Offices LLP - *4
406 Queen St., Ottawa, ON K1R 5A7
Tel: 613-236-8000; *Fax:* 613-820-8818
info@talberglaw.com
www.talberglaw.com

Ottawa: Glen F. Schruder - *1
#505, 200 Elgin St., Ottawa, ON K2P 1L5
Tel: 613-235-9924; *Fax:* 613-235-1343
glenshruder@on.aibn.com

Ottawa: Scott Coulson & Scott - *4
Former Name: Scott & Coulson
#300, 1335 Carling Ave., Ottawa, ON K1Z 8N8
Tel: 613-725-3723; *Fax:* 613-729-8613
info@scottcoulsonscott.com
www.scottcoulsonscott.com

Ottawa: Sevigny Westdal - *4
#300, 190 O'Connor St., Ottawa, ON K2P 2R3
Tel: 613-751-4459; *Fax:* 613-751-4471
info@sevignywestdal.com
www.sevignylaw.com

Ottawa: Shapiro Cohen LLP - *4
#850, Tower B, 555 Legget Dr., Ottawa, ON K2K 0E2
Tel: 613-232-5300; *Fax:* 613-563-9231
Toll-Free: 800-563-9390
protectmyIP@shapirocohen.com
www.shapirocohen.com

indicates number of lawyers

Ottawa: Sheppard & Claude - *2
#200, 745A Montreal Rd., Ottawa, ON K1K 0T1
Tel: 613-748-3333; *Fax:* 613-748-1599
www.sheppardclaude.ca

Ottawa: Shields Hunt Duff - *4
Former Name: Shields & Hunt
68 Chamberlain Ave., Ottawa, ON K1S 1V9
Tel: 613-230-3232; *Fax:* 613-230-1664
info@shd.legal
www.shd.legal

Ottawa: Smart & Biggar/Fetherstonhaugh - Ottawa - *87
#900, P.O. Box 2999, Stn. D, 55 Metcalfe St., Ottawa, ON K1P 5Y6
Tel: 613-232-2486; *Fax:* 613-232-8440
ottawa@smart-biggar.ca
www.smart-biggar.ca
twitter.com/smartbiggar,
www.linkedin.com/company/smart-&-biggar

Ottawa: Paula M. Smith - *1
450 Laurier Ave. East, Ottawa, ON K1N 6R3
Tel: 613-565-0490

Ottawa: Soloway, Wright LLP - Ottawa - *32
#900, 427 Laurier Ave. West, Ottawa, ON K1R 7Y2
Tel: 613-236-0111; *Fax:* 613-238-8507
Toll-Free: 800-207-5880
info@solowaywright.com
www.soloways.com
twitter.com/solowaywright

Ottawa: Stewart/Associates - *2
#402, 200 Elgin St., Ottawa, ON K2P 1L5
Tel: 613-235-0453; *Fax:* 613-235-3304

Ottawa: Jennifer A. Stiell - *1
#307, 150 Isabella St., Ottawa, ON K1S 1V7
Tel: 613-237-0505; *Fax:* 613-567-3559
jstiell@cyberus.ca

Ottawa: Christopher C.C. Tan - *1
70 Gloucester St., Ottawa, ON K2P 0A2
Tel: 613-235-2308; *Fax:* 613-235-6933

Ottawa: Thompson Summers - *2
Former Name: Steinberg Thompson d'Artois Rockman Summers
#730, 220 Laurier Ave. West, Ottawa, ON K1P 5Z9
Tel: 613-688-0433; *Fax:* 613-688-0437
www.thompsonsummers.com

Ottawa: Tierney Stauffer LLP - Ottawa - *13
#510, 1600 Carling Ave., Ottawa, ON K1Z 0A1
Tel: 613-728-8057; *Fax:* 613-728-9866
Toll-Free: 888-799-8057
info@tslawyers.ca
www.tierneystauffer.com
www.facebook.com/tierneystauffer, twitter.com/tslawyers,
www.linkedin.com/company/tierney-stauffer

Ottawa: Tom Curran Law - *2
1704 Carling Ave., Ottawa, ON K2A 1C7
Tel: 613-596-2804; *Fax:* 613-596-2013
info@tomcurranlaw.com
www.tomcurranlaw.com
www.facebook.com/TomCurranLaw

Ottawa: Trudel Law Office - *1
Also Known As: Roger P. Trudel
#103, 2828 St. Joseph Blvd., Ottawa, ON K1C 6E7
Tel: 613-837-2641; *Fax:* 613-830-5613
www.trudellawoffice.com

Ottawa: Tunney, McMurray - *2
#806, 200 Elgin St., Ottawa, ON K2P 1L5
Tel: 613-235-5660; *Fax:* 613-235-0805

Ottawa: Gilad Vered - *1
1801 Woodward Dr., Ottawa, ON K2C 0R3
Tel: 613-226-2000; *Fax:* 613-225-0391
gvered@arnon.ca

Ottawa: Victor Vallance Blais LLP - *8
Former Name: Victor Ages Vallance LLP; Kimmel, Victor & Ages
112 Lisgar St., Ottawa, ON K2P 0C2
Tel: 613-238-1333; *Fax:* 613-238-8949
info@vvblawyers.com
vvblawyers.com

Ottawa: Vincent Dagenais Gibson LLP/s.r.l. - *15
#400, 260 Dalhousie St., Ottawa, ON K1N 7E4
Tel: 613-241-2701; *Fax:* 613-241-2599
info@vdg.ca
www.vdg.ca

Ottawa: Ian H. Warren - *1
#2000, 150 Metcalfe St., Ottawa, ON K2P 1P1
Tel: 613-565-3813; *Fax:* 613-234-0418
jacklaw@storm.ca

Ottawa: Robert A. Whillans - *1
540 Courtenay Ave., Ottawa, ON K2A 3B3
Tel: 613-238-1515; *Fax:* 613-238-1323

Ottawa: Williams Litigation Lawyers - *9
Former Name: Williams McEnery
169 Gilmour St., Ottawa, ON K2P 0N8
Tel: 613-237-0520; *Fax:* 613-237-3163
www.williamsmcenery.com
twitter.com/wllmslitigation

Ottawa: David M. Wray - *1
#310, P.O. Box 2760, Stn. D, 151 Slater St., Ottawa, ON K1P 5W8
Tel: 613-233-1322; *Fax:* 613-230-5168
dwray@wray-canada.com

Owen Sound: Arnold & Arnold, LLP - *2
Former Name: Arnold, Neil J.
935 - 2nd Ave. West, Owen Sound, ON N4K 4M8
Tel: 519-372-2218; *Fax:* 519-372-2599
arnoldlaw.os@gmail.com

Owen Sound: Ian C. Boddy - *1
195 - 9th St. West, Owen Sound, ON N4K 3N5
Tel: 519-372-9886; *Fax:* 519-372-1091
ianboddy@bellnet.ca

Owen Sound: Herbert E. Boyce - *1
#103, Dominion Place, P.O. Box 968, 887 Third Ave. East, Owen Sound, ON N4K 6H6
Tel: 519-371-4160; *Fax:* 519-371-1604

Owen Sound: Chander G. Chaddah - *1
P.O. Box 965, 712 - 2 Ave. East, Owen Sound, ON N4K 6H6
Tel: 519-376-4343; *Fax:* 519-376-2547

Owen Sound: Andrew E. Drury - *1
#5B, 945 - 3 Ave. East, Owen Sound, ON N4K 2K8
Tel: 519-372-1850; *Fax:* 519-372-1602

Owen Sound: Douglas A. Grace - *1
P.O. Box 952, Stn. Main, 949 - 2 Ave. West, Owen Sound, ON N4K 4M8
Tel: 519-371-9370; *Fax:* 519-371-5747
dougrace@bmts.com

Owen Sound: Greenfield & Barrie - *2
142 - 10 St. West, Owen Sound, ON N4K 3P9
Tel: 519-376-4930; *Fax:* 519-376-4010
gblaw@btms.com

Owen Sound: Kirby Robinson Treslan Professional Corporation - *7
Former Name: Kirby, Gordon & Robinson
P.O. Box 730, 930 - 1 Ave. West, Owen Sound, ON N4K 5W9
Tel: 519-376-7450; *Fax:* 519-376-8288
Toll-Free: 800-513-5559
info@owensoundlawyers.com
owensoundlawyers.com

Owen Sound: Middlebro' & Stevens LLP - Owen Sound - *5
P.O. Box 100, 1030 - 2 Ave. East, Owen Sound, ON N4K 5P1
Tel: 519-376-8730; *Fax:* 519-376-7135
ms@mslaw.ca
www.mslaw.ca

Owen Sound: Murray & Thomson - *3
P.O. Box 1060, 912 - 2 Ave. West, Owen Sound, ON N4K 6K6
Tel: 519-376-6350; *Fax:* 519-376-0835
message@mtlaw.ca
www.mtlaw.ca

Owen Sound: Scott C. Vining - *1
1199 - 1st Ave. East, Owen Sound, ON N4K 2E2
Tel: 519-371-6210
www.vininglaw.ca

Paris: Tarrison & Hunter - *2
19 William St., Paris, ON N3L 1K9
Tel: 519-442-2287
ghunter@tarrisonandhunter.com
www.tarrisonandhunter.ca/en/

* indicates number of lawyers

Parry Sound: Larry W. Douglas - *1
22 Miller St., Parry Sound, ON P2A 1S8
Tel: 705-746-9471; *Fax:* 705-746-9606

Parry Sound: David A. Holmes - *1
2 William St., Parry Sound, ON P2A 1V1
Tel: 705-746-4223; *Fax:* 705-746-6368
daholmes@cogeco.ca

Parry Sound: Oldham Law Firm - *3
88 James St., Parry Sound, ON P2A 1T9
Tel: 705-746-8852; *Fax:* 705-746-6188
howard@oldhamlaw.ca
www.oldhamlaw.ca

Parry Sound: Powell, Cunningham, Grandy - *1
88 James St., Parry Sound, ON P2A 1T9
Tel: 705-746-4207; *Fax:* 705-746-2945

Parry Sound: D. Andrew Thomson - *1
10 William St., Parry Sound, ON P2A 1V1
Tel: 705-746-5838; *Fax:* 705-746-4351
athomson@dathomsonbarrister.ca

Pembroke: Blair Jones Professional Corporation - *1
Former Name: Kelly Kelly & Jones
1064 Pembroke St. West, Pembroke, ON K8A 5R4
Tel: 613-735-8226; *Fax:* 613-735-8474
blair@jones-law.ca
www.jones-law.ca

Pembroke: Adrian R. Cleaver - *1
P.O. Box 1147, Stn. Main, 595 Pembroke St. East, Pembroke, ON K8A 6Y6
Tel: 613-732-1377; *Fax:* 613-732-3889
acleaver@nrtco.net

Pembroke: Glen Price, Lawyers - *2
Former Name: Garretto & Price
P.O. Box 697, Stn. Main, 141A Lake St., Pembroke, ON K8A 6X9
Tel: 613-732-2883; *Fax:* 613-732-3436
Toll-Free: 877-732-2884
glenpricelawyer.com

Pembroke: Huckabone O'Brien Instance Bradley LLP - *5
Former Name: Huckabone, O'Brien, Instance, Bradley, Lyle; Huckabone, Shaw, O'Brien, Radley-Walters & Reimer
P.O. Box 487, 284 Pembroke St. East, Pembroke, ON K8A 6X7
Tel: 613-735-2341; *Fax:* 613-735-0920
admin@hsolawyers.com
www.hsolawyers.com

Pembroke: Johnson, Fraser & March - *3
259 Pembroke St. East, Pembroke, ON K8A 6X6
Tel: 613-735-0624; *Fax:* 613-735-0625
www.jfmlawyers.ca

Pembroke: Roy C. Reiche - *1
203 Nelson St., Pembroke, ON K8A 3N1
Tel: 613-735-2313; *Fax:* 613-735-2013

Penetanguishene: Wanda L. Warren - *2
P.O. Box 5252, Stn. Main, Penetanguishene, ON L9M 2G4
Tel: 705-549-0287; *Fax:* 705-549-8467

Perth: Anderson Foss - *2
10 Market Sq., Perth, ON K7H 1V7
Tel: 613-267-9898; *Fax:* 613-267-2741
www.andersonfoss.ca

Perth: Bond & Hughes Barristers & Solicitors - *2
Former Name: James M. Bond
10 Market Sq., Perth, ON K7H 1V7
Tel: 613-267-1212; *Fax:* 613-267-7059
www.bondhughes.ca

Perth: John J.S. Chalmers - *1
P.O. Box 2, Stn. Main, RR#3, Perth, ON K7H 3C5
Tel: 613-264-1505; *Fax:* 613-264-9259

Perth: Rubino & Chaplin - *1
P.O. Box 338, 10A Gore St. West, Perth, ON K7H 3E4
Tel: 613-267-5227; *Fax:* 613-267-3951
admin@rubinoandchaplin.ca

Perth: Woodwark Stevens Ireton - *3
Former Name: Woodwark & Stevens
8 Gore St. West, Perth, ON K7H 2L6
Tel: 613-264-8080; *Fax:* 613-264-8084
info@woodwarkstevens.com
www.woodwarkstevens.com

Peterborough: Gary E. Ainsworth - *1
#101, P.O. Box 1358, Stn. Main, 294 Rink St., Peterborough, ON K9J 7H6
Tel: 705-749-0628; Fax: 705-749-0633
gea@ainslaw.com
www.ainslaw.com

Peterborough: Robert W. Beninger - *1
70 Simcoe St., Peterborough, ON K9H 7G9
Tel: 705-876-3834; Fax: 705-876-3847

Peterborough: W. Jelle Bosch - *1
#203, P.O. Box 2364, 130 Hunter St. West, Peterborough, ON K9J 7Y8
Tel: 705-741-3630; Fax: 705-741-6339
wj_bosch@on.aibn.com
www.linkedin.com/in/w-jelle-bosch-52b14133

Peterborough: John S. Crook - *1
Former Name: Crook & Collins
#5, P.O. Box 1539, Stn. Main, 261 George St. North, Peterborough, ON K9J 7H7
Tel: 705-742-5415; Fax: 705-742-1867

Peterborough: H. Girvin Devitt - *1
P.O. Box 1449, Stn. Main, 858 Chemong Rd., Peterborough, ON K9J 7H6
Tel: 705-742-5471
devitt@nexicom.net

Peterborough: Dunn & Dunn - *1
469 Water St., Peterborough, ON K9H 3M2
Tel: 705-743-6460; Fax: 705-748-2675
info@dunnlaw.ca
www.dunnlaw.ca

Peterborough: Michael J. Dwyer - *1
P.O. Box 958, 359 Aylmer St. North, Peterborough, ON K9J 7A5
Tel: 705-743-4221; Fax: 705-743-2187
mdwyer@bellnet.ca

Peterborough: Farquharson Daly - *2
161 Hunter St. West, Peterborough, ON K9H 2L1
Tel: 705-742-9241; Fax: 705-741-1601

Peterborough: Gowland, Boriss - *4
P.O. Box 1629, 371 Reid St., Peterborough, ON K9H 4G4
Tel: 705-743-7252; Fax: 705-743-1850
Toll-Free: 800-808-1850
www.gowlandboriss.ca

Peterborough: Joan M. Guerin - *1
#4, P.O. Box 1420, Stn. Main, 193 Simcoe St., Peterborough, ON K9J 7H6
Tel: 705-743-9087; Fax: 705-743-8528

Peterborough: Harrison Law Office - *1
469 Water St., Peterborough, ON K9H 3M2
Tel: 705-741-5233; Fax: 705-741-2463

Peterborough: James S. Hauraney - *2
305 Reid St., Peterborough, ON K9J 3R2
Tel: 705-748-2333; Fax: 705-748-2618
jameshauraney.com

Peterborough: A. John Hodgins - *1
677 Brown Line, Peterborough, ON M8W 3V7
Tel: 416-251-9390; Fax: 416-251-0449
ajhodgins@hodginslaw.net

Peterborough: Rod E. Johnston - *1
P.O. Box 29, 521 George St. North, Peterborough, ON K9J 6Y5
Tel: 705-748-2244; Fax: 705-748-2540
info@rodjohnstonlaw.com

Peterborough: E.J. Jordan - *1
P.O. Box 958, 359 Aylmer St. North, Peterborough, ON K9J 7A5
Tel: 705-743-4221; Fax: 705-743-2187
jjordan@bellnet.ca

Peterborough: Lech, Lightbody & O'Brien - *2
116 Hunter St. West, Peterborough, ON K9H 2K6
Tel: 705-742-3844; Fax: 705-742-0121

Peterborough: Lillico Bazuk Galloway Halka - *5
Former Name: Lillico Bazuk Kent Galloway
163 Hunter St. West, Peterborough, ON K9J 6Z6
Tel: 705-743-3577; Fax: 705-743-0013
www.lbghlaw.com

Peterborough: LLF Lawyers LLP - Peterborough - *17
P.O. Box 1146, 332 Aylmer St. North, Peterborough, ON K9J 7H4
Tel: 705-742-1674; Fax: 705-742-4677
info@llf.ca
www.llf.ca

Peterborough: J.M. Longworth - *1
P.O. Box 1747, Stn. Main, 310 Rubidge St., Peterborough, ON K9J 7X6
Tel: 705-749-0100; Fax: 705-742-8718

Peterborough: John E. McGarrity - *1
Stn. Main, 343 Stewart St., Peterborough, ON K9H 4A7
Tel: 705-743-1822; Fax: 705-743-4870
mcgarrity@trytel.net

Peterborough: McGillen Keay Cooper - *4
Former Name: McGillen Keay; McGillen, Ayotte, Dupuis
#202, P.O. Box 1718, 140 King St., Peterborough, ON K9J 7X6
Tel: 705-748-2241; Fax: 705-748-9125
www.mkclaw.ca

Peterborough: McMichael, Davidson - *1
223 Aylmer St. North, Peterborough, ON K9J 3K3
Tel: 705-745-0571; Fax: 705-745-0411
lawoffice@mcmichaeldavidson.com

Peterborough: Moldaver & McFadden - *3
Market Plaza, P.O. Box 1387, 121 George St. North, Peterborough, ON K9J 7H6
Tel: 705-743-1801
info@moldavermcfadden.ca
www.moldavermcfadden.ca

Peterborough: Christopher M. Spear - *1
430 Sheridan St., Peterborough, ON K9H 3J9
Tel: 705-741-2144; Fax: 705-741-2712

Peterborough: Richard J. Taylor - *1
P.O. Box 1963, Stn. Main, 193 Dalhousie St., Peterborough, ON K9J 7X7
Tel: 705-876-7791; Fax: 705-876-9280
richardtaylorlaw@cogeco.net

Peterborough: Gordon H. Usher - *1
P.O. Box 327, 359 Aylmer St. North, Peterborough, ON K9J 6Z3
Tel: 705-743-4221; Fax: 705-743-8692

Peterborough: Walker Geale-Barker - *3
243 Hunter St. West, Peterborough, ON K9H 2L4
Tel: 705-748-3012; Fax: 705-748-2746
www.walker-gealebarker.ca

Peterborough: J. Ross Whittington - *1
P.O. Box 327, Stn. Main, 359 Aylmer St. North, Peterborough, ON K9J 6Z3
Tel: 705-743-4221; Fax: 705-743-8692

Petrolia: Robert B. Gray - *1
#3, 4495 Petrolia Line, Petrolia, ON N0N 1R0
Tel: 519-882-0132; Fax: 519-336-3289

Petrolia: Wallace B. Lang - *1
Former Name: Kilby & Lang
4245 Petrolia Lane, Petrolia, ON N0N 1R0
Tel: 519-882-0770; Fax: 519-882-3144

Pickering: G.W. Edmiston - *1
1281 Commerce St., Pickering, ON L1W 1C7
Tel: 905-839-8270

Pickering: Brian R. Hawke - *1
1 Evelyn Ave., Pickering, ON L1V 1N3
Tel: 905-509-5267; Fax: 905-509-5270
bhawke@on.aibn.com
www.brianhawke.com

Pickering: John G. Howes - *1
#800, 1315 Pickering Pkwy., Pickering, ON L1V 7G5
Tel: 905-420-8628; Fax: 905-420-1073
john@howeslaw.com
howeslaw.com

Pickering: Murray Stroud Law Office - *2
356 Kingston Rd., Pickering, ON L1V 1A2
Tel: 905-509-1353; Fax: 905-509-2370

Pickering: Sherwood, Hunt - *2
364 Kingston Rd., Pickering, ON L1V 1A2
Tel: 905-509-5500; Fax: 905-509-0070

Pickering: Tim Vanular Lawyers Professional Corporation - *2
Former Name: Vanular, Timothy C.R.
#C10-C11, Brock North Plaza, 2200 Brock Rd. North, Pickering, ON L1X 2R2
Tel: 905-427-4886; Fax: 905-427-5542
Toll-Free: 800-243-4151
vanular@vanulaw.com
www.vanulaw.com
www.facebook.com/vanulaw, twitter.com/Vanulaw, www.linkedin.com/in/timvanular

Pickering: Walker, Head - *11
#800, 1315 Pickering Pkwy., Pickering, ON L1V 7G5
Tel: 905-839-4484; Fax: 905-420-1073
Toll-Free: 877-839-4484
info@walkerhead.com
www.walkerhead.com
www.facebook.com/walkerheadlawyers,
twitter.com/walkerheadlaw, www.linkedin.com/company/4862129

Picton: Bruce F. Campbell - *1
194 Main St., Picton, ON K0K 2T0
Tel: 613-476-2366; Fax: 613-476-9821
bcampbl@kos.net

Picton: Mathers, Shelagh M. - *1
#4, 6 Talbot St., Picton, ON K0K 2T0
Tel: 613-476-2733; Fax: 613-476-6064
matherslaw@kos.net
www.matherslaw.com

Picton: Donald T. Mowat - *1
P.O. Box 2290, 165 Main St., Picton, ON K0K 2T0
Tel: 613-476-3261; Fax: 613-476-4417

Point Edward: Fleck Law - *5
Former Name: Fleck & Daigneault
131 Kendall St., Point Edward, ON N7V 4G6
Tel: 519-337-5288; Fax: 519-337-5674
info@flecklaw.ca
flecklaw.ca
www.facebook.com/FleckDaigneault, twitter.com/flecklaw, www.linkedin.com/in/carl-e-fleck-q-c-0a27282b

Point Edward: C. Ed Gresham
P.O. Box 84, 611 St. Clair St., Point Edward, ON N7V 1P2
Tel: 519-337-5007; Fax: 519-337-7440

Port Colborne: Brian N. Lambie - *1
151 Charlotte St., Port Colborne, ON L3K 4N6
Tel: 905-835-0404; Fax: 905-835-5966
blambie1@cogeco.ca

Port Dover: Lee Gaunt Law Office - *1
Also Known As: Grant Law Office
Former Name: Driscoll & Gaunt
P.O. Box 580, Stn. Port Dover, Port Dover, ON N0A 1N0
Tel: 519-583-1411; Fax: 519-583-1110

Port Elgin: George D. Gruetzner - *1
P.O. Box 10, 667 Goderich St., Port Elgin, ON N0H 2C0
Tel: 519-832-2482; Fax: 519-389-4617

Port Hope: Mann McCracken Bebee Ross & Schmidt - *6
114 Walton St., Port Hope, ON L1A 1N5
Tel: 905-885-2451; Fax: 905-885-7474
Toll-Free: 866-964-4529
info@northumberlandlaw.com
northumberlandlaw.com

Port Perry: Michael L. Fowler Professional Corporation - *2
175 North St., Port Perry, ON L9L 1B7
Tel: 905-985-8411; Fax: 905-985-0029
www.fowlerlaw.ca

Prescott: Doris Law Office - Prescott - *2
Also Known As: DLO Lawyers
P.O. Box 2019, 257 King St. West, Prescott, ON K0E 1T0
Tel: 613-925-9018; Fax: 613-925-1089
www.dorislaw.com

Rama: Nahwegahbow Corbiere - *9
Former Name: Nahwegahbow, Nadjiwan, Corbiere
#109, 5884 Rama Rd., Rama, ON L3V 6H6
Tel: 705-325-0520; Fax: 705-325-7204
mail@nncfirm.ca
www.nncfirm.ca

* indicates number of lawyers

Renfrew: Sharon L. Anderson-Olmstead - *1
117 Raglan St. South, Renfrew, ON K7V 1P8
Tel: 613-432-5898; Fax: 613-432-5899
sharon_anderson@bellnet.ca

Renfrew: Chown & Smith - *2
#25, 1035 O'Brien Rd., Renfrew, ON K7V 0B3
Tel: 613-432-3669; Fax: 613-432-2874
admin@chownandsmith.com
www.chownandsmith.com

Renfrew: Lawrence E. Gallagher - *1
33 Renfrew Ave. East, Renfrew, ON K7V 2W6
Tel: 613-432-8537; Fax: 613-432-8538
legallagher@nrtco.net

Renfrew: Joseph D. Legris Professional Corp. - *1
248 Argyle St. South, Renfrew, ON K7V 1T7
Tel: 613-432-3689; Fax: 613-432-3936
legris@legrislaw.com
www.legrislaw.com

Renfrew: McNab, Stewart & Prince - *2
117 Raglan St. South, Renfrew, ON K7V 1P8
Tel: 613-432-5844; Fax: 613-432-7832
dstewart@mcnablaw.com
www.mcnablaw.com

Richmond Hill: Ronald A. Balinsky - *1
96 Arnold Cres., Richmond Hill, ON L4C 3R8
Tel: 905-884-8161; Fax: 905-884-3155
info@balinskylawfirm.com
www.balinskylawfirm.com

Richmond Hill: Peter D. Bouroukis - *1
#411, 15 Wertheim Ct., Richmond Hill, ON L4B 3H7
Tel: 905-771-7030; Fax: 905-771-7027
pbouroukis@rogers.com
www.bouroukis.com

Richmond Hill: Jay Chauhan - *1
#309, 330 Hwy. 7, Richmond Hill, ON L4B 3P8
Tel: 905-771-1235; Fax: 905-771-1237
www.jaychauhan.com
twitter.com/jaylawyer,
www.linkedin.com/in/jay-chauhan-41134513

Richmond Hill: James H. Chow - *1
#512, 330 Hwy. 7 East, Richmond Hill, ON L4B 3P8
Tel: 905-881-3363

Richmond Hill: Corinne M. Rivers - *1
#104, 13311 Yonge St., Richmond Hill, ON L4E 3L6
Tel: 905-773-9911; Fax: 905-773-9927
corrine@cmrlaw.ca
cmrlaw.tel
www.linkedin.com/pub/corinne-rivers/4/b44/65

Richmond Hill: CNK Law
Former Name: Chehab & Khan
#179, 10520 Yonge St., Richmond Hill, ON L4C 3C7
Tel: 416-876-6009
info@cnklaw.ca
www.cnklaw.ca

Richmond Hill: Perry H. Gruenberger - *1
#7, 30 Wertheim Crt., Richmond Hill, ON L4B 1B9
Tel: 905-764-6411; Fax: 905-764-5616

Richmond Hill: Harte Law - *3
Former Name: Paul Harte Professional Corporation
#30, 16 Sims Cres., Richmond Hill, ON L4B 2P1
Tel: 289-695-2450; Fax: 289-695-2445
Toll-Free: 855-663-3800
www.hartelaw.com
www.facebook.com/paulhartepc, twitter.com/pharte,
www.linkedin.com/company/paul-harte-professional-corporation

Richmond Hill: Alla Koren - *1
489 Worthington Ave., Richmond Hill, ON L4E 4R6
Tel: 905-780-1500; Fax: 905-773-7906
Toll-Free: 888-622-7673
alla@allakoren.com
www.allakoren.com

Richmond Hill: Shirley K.T. Lo - *1
#PH 10, 330 Hwy. 7 East, Richmond Hill, ON L4B 3P8
Tel: 905-707-5707; Fax: 905-707-5752
kshirleylo@hotmail.com

Richmond Hill: Malach Fidler Sugar + Luxenberg
LLP - *14
#6, 30 Wertheim Ct., Richmond Hill, ON L4B 1B9
Tel: 905-889-1667; Fax: 905-889-1139
info@malach-fidler.com
www.malach-fidler.com

Richmond Hill: Roselyn Pecus - *1
2126 Major Mackenzie Dr., Richmond Hill, ON L6A 1P7
Tel: 905-303-1494; Fax: 905-303-1465
roselyn@pecus.ca

Richmond Hill: Rohmer & Fenn - *5
#503, Park Place Corporate Centre, 15 Wertheim Ct.,
Richmond Hill, ON L4B 3H7
Tel: 905-763-6690; Fax: 905-763-6699
firm@rohmerfenn.com
www.rohmerfenn.com

Richmond Hill: Barry Seltzer - *1
#204, 9140 Leslie St., Richmond Hill, ON L4B 0A9
Tel: 905-475-9001; Fax: 905-475-9004

Richmond Hill: Virgilio Law - *1
#500, 1 West Pearce St., Richmond Hill, ON L4B 3K3
Tel: 905-882-8666; Fax: 905-882-1082
jvirgilio@virgiliolaw.com
virgiliolaw.com

Richmond Hill: Gordon E. Watkin - *1
#212A, 9350 Yonge St., Richmond Hill, ON L4C 5G2
Tel: 905-884-3778; Fax: 905-884-2655

Ridgetown: Edward T. Little - *1
P.O. Box 700, 64 Main St. East, Ridgetown, ON N0P 2C0
Tel: 519-674-5436; Fax: 519-674-3352
etlittle@bellnet.ca

Ridgetown: Daniel B. Nicol - *1
P.O. Box 700, 64 Main St. East, Ridgetown, ON N0P 2C0
Tel: 519-674-3372; Fax: 519-674-3352
dbnicol@bellnet.ca

Ridgeway: Community Legal Services of Niagara
South - *1
P.O. Box 430, 266 Ridge Rd. S, Ridgeway, ON L0S 1N0
Tel: 905-894-4775; Fax: 905-894-6101

Rockwood: Douglas S. Black - *1
P.O. Box 95, 118 Main St. South, Rockwood, ON N0B 2K0
Tel: 519-856-4555; Fax: 519-856-4680
dblacklaw@cogeco.net

Rockwood: Judith P. Ryan - *1
P.O. Box 550, Rockwood, ON N0B 2K0
Tel: 519-856-2223; Fax: 519-856-2047
jpmryan@aol.com

Russell: Anna Sundin - *1
27 Craig St., Russell, ON K4R 1A6
Tel: 613-445-3183; Fax: 613-691-1428
www.sundinlaw.com
www.facebook.com/697818233646093,
www.linkedin.com/in/annaesundin

Sarnia: Paul R. Beaudet - *1
251 Exmouth St., Sarnia, ON N7T 7M7
Tel: 519-337-1529; Fax: 519-336-2569
beaudet@ebtech.net

Sarnia: Terry L. Brandon - *1
1069 London Rd., Sarnia, ON N7S 1P2
Tel: 519-337-4634; Fax: 519-337-5586
terrybrandon@sympatico.ca

Sarnia: Roderick Brown, Q.C. - *1
555 Exmouth St., Sarnia, ON N7T 5P6
Tel: 519-336-7880; Fax: 519-336-6584
re_brown2927@hotmail.com

Sarnia: James J. Carpeneto - *1
316 Christina St. North, Sarnia, ON N7T 5V5
Tel: 519-336-6955; Fax: 519-336-8401

Sarnia: Francis De Sena - *1
422 East St. North, Sarnia, ON N7T 6Y4
Tel: 519-336-9999; Fax: 519-336-9131
francis@desenalaw.com
www.desenalaw.com

Sarnia: David A. Elliott - *2
Former Name: Elliott, Porter, McFadyen & McFadyen
#101, St. Clair Corporate Centre, 265 Front St. North, Sarnia,
ON N7T 7X1
Tel: 519-336-4600; Fax: 519-336-4640

Sarnia: George Murray Shipley Bell, LLP - *11
P.O. Box 2196, 2 Ferry Dock Hill, Sarnia, ON N7T 7L8
Tel: 519-336-8770; Fax: 519-336-1811
www.sarnialaw.com

Sarnia: Gray, Bruce, Cimetta (Carlo Cimetta
Professional Corporation) - *4
P.O. Box 2259, 1166 London Rd., Sarnia, ON N7T 7L7
Tel: 519-336-9700; Fax: 519-336-3289

Sarnia: David G. Hockin - *1
#101, 265 Front St. North, Sarnia, ON N7T 7X1
Tel: 519-336-4357; Fax: 519-336-4367
lawyer@ebtech.net

Sarnia: Pamela J. McLeod - *1
1350 L'Heritage Dr., Sarnia, ON N7S 6H8
Tel: 519-542-7714; Fax: 519-542-5577
mcleodlaw@ebtech.net

Sarnia: Raymond A. Whitnall - *1
#112, 560 Exmouth St., Sarnia, ON N7T 5P5
Tel: 519-336-9460; Fax: 519-336-8366

Sarnia: Wyrzykowski & Robb - *2
P.O. Box 2200, Stn. Main, Sarnia, ON N7T 7L7
Tel: 519-336-6118; Fax: 519-336-9550
mars@ebtech.net

Sault Ste Marie: Aiello, Pawelek - *2
#102, 123 March St., Sault Ste Marie, ON P6A 2Z5
Tel: 705-946-8590; Fax: 705-946-8589

Sault Ste Marie: Allemano & FitzGerald - *2
#103, McCarda Bldg., P.O. Box 10, 139 Queen St. East, Sault
Ste Marie, ON P6A 1Z4
Tel: 705-942-0142; Fax: 705-942-7188

Sault Ste Marie: Kenneth R. Davies - *1
#201, 111 Elgin St., Sault Ste Marie, ON P6A 6L6
Tel: 705-256-7839; Fax: 705-256-7837
kendavies@saultlawyer.com
www.saultlawyer.com

Sault Ste Marie: Laidlaw Paciocco Dumanski
Spadafora & Johnson LLP
Former Name: Bisceglia Dumanski Romano & Johnson
LLP
#202, 747 Queen St. East, Sault Ste Marie, ON P6A 2A8
Tel: 705-942-5856; Fax: 705-942-6493
info@ssmlawfirm.com
www.ssmlawfirm.com

Sault Ste Marie: Laidlaw, Paciocco, Melville - *3
Former Name: Kelleher, Laidlaw, Paciocco, Melville
#604, 421 Bay St., Sault Ste Marie, ON P6A 1X3
Tel: 705-949-7790; Fax: 705-949-5816

Sault Ste Marie: O. Kennedy Lawson - *1
#104, 473 Queen St. East, Sault Ste Marie, ON P6A 1Z5
Tel: 705-759-5030; Fax: 705-942-5309
oklawson@bellnet.ca

Sault Ste Marie: Eric D. McCooeye - *1
348 Albert St. East, Sault Ste Marie, ON P6A 2J6
Tel: 705-945-8868; Fax: 705-945-9051

Sault Ste Marie: O'Neill DeLorenzi Mendes Nanne -
*7
Former Name: O'Neill DeLorenzi & Mendes
116 Spring St., Sault Ste Marie, ON P6A 3A1
Tel: 705-949-6901; Fax: 705-949-0618
info@saultlawyers.com
www.saultlawyers.com
www.facebook.com/saultlawyers, twitter.com/saultlawyers

Sault Ste Marie: Orazietti, Kwolek, Walz - *4
#200, 477 Queen St. East, Sault Ste Marie, ON P6A 1Z5
Tel: 705-256-5601; Fax: 705-945-9427

Sault Ste Marie: Rudolph C. Peres, Q.C. - *1
#104, 212 Queen St. East, Sault Ste Marie, ON P6A 5X8
Tel: 705-949-9411; Fax: 705-949-3759

Sault Ste Marie: William R. Scott - *1
#1, 224B Queen St. East, Sault Ste Marie, ON P6A 1Y7
Tel: 705-949-4333; Fax: 705-945-0958
wmrscottlaw@yahoo.com

Sault Ste Marie: Carol A. Shamess - *1
#3, 553 Queen St. East, Sault Ste Marie, ON P6A 2A3
Tel: 705-942-2580; Fax: 705-942-5048
carola.shamess@shaw.ca

* indicates number of lawyers

Sault Ste Marie: Jack Squire - *1
191 Northern Ave. East, Sault Ste Marie, ON P6B 4H8
Tel: 705-949-0162; Fax: 705-541-9616

Sault Ste Marie: T. Frederick Baxter, Barrister & Solicitor - *1
494 Albert St. East, Sault Ste Marie, ON P6A 2K2
Tel: 705-759-0948; Fax: 705-759-2042
kerriadmin@shaw.ca

Sault Ste Marie: Walker, Thompson - *1
#506, 123 March St., Sault Ste Marie, ON P6A 2Z5
Tel: 705-949-7806; Fax: 705-759-0457
walkerlaw@shaw.ca

Sault Ste Marie: Willson, Carter - *3
494 Albert St. East, Sault Ste Marie, ON P6A 2K2
Tel: 705-942-2000; Fax: 705-942-6511
willsoncarter.com

Sault Ste Marie: Wishart Law Firm LLP - *6
#500, 390 Bay St., Sault Ste Marie, ON P6A 1X2
Tel: 705-949-6700; Fax: 705-949-2465
wishart@wishartlaw.com
www.wishartlaw.com

Seaforth: Devereaux Murray Professional Corporation - *3
P.O. Box 220, 77 Main St. South, Seaforth, ON N0K 1W0
Tel: 519-527-0850; Fax: 519-527-2324
c4thlaw@devereauxmurray.ca
www.devereauxmurray.ca

Seeleys Bay: David J. Atkinson - *1
RR#1, Seeleys Bay, ON K0H 2N0
Tel: 613-382-2692

Shelburne: Timmerman, Haskell & Mills LLP - *2
P.O. Box 216, 305 Owen Sound St., Shelburne, ON L0N 1S0
Tel: 519-925-2608; Fax: 519-925-2268
lhaskell@shelburnelaw.ca
shelburnelaw.ca

Simcoe: Bachmann Personal Injury Law - *1
P.O. Box 156, 39 Kent St. North, Simcoe, ON N3Y 4L1
Tel: 519-428-8090
www.bachmannlaw.ca
www.facebook.com/BachmannLaw

Simcoe: Brimage Law Group LLP - Simcoe - *9
Former Name: Brimage, Tyrrell, Van Severen & Homeniuk
21 Norfolk St. North, Simcoe, ON N3Y 4L1
Tel: 519-426-5840; Fax: 519-426-7515
www.brimage.ca
www.facebook.com/brimagelawgroup
twitter.com/brimagelawgroup,
www.linkedin.com/company/2576968

Simcoe: Cobb & Jones LLP - Simcoe - *8
P.O. Box 548, 23 Argyle St., Simcoe, ON N3Y 4N5
Tel: 519-428-0170; Fax: 519-428-3105
cobblaw@cobbjones.ca
www.cobbjones.ca

Simcoe: MacLeod Hosack Nunn Pereira Kinkel LLP - *7
Also Known As: MHN Lawyers
Former Name: Cline Backus LLP; Sheppard, MacIntosh, Lados & Nunn LLP
P.O. Box 528, 39 Colborne St. North, Simcoe, ON N3Y 3T8
Tel: 519-426-6763; Fax: 519-426-2055
www.mhnlawyers.com
www.facebook.com/mhnlawyers

Simcoe: MacLeod Hosack Nunn Pereria Kinkel LLP - *9
Also Known As: MHN Lawyers
Former Name: Cline Backus LLP; Cline Backus Nightingale McArthur
P.O. Box 528, 39 Colborne St. North, Simcoe, ON N3Y 4N5
Tel: 519-426-6763; Fax: 519-426-2055
www.mhnlawyers.com
www.facebook.com/mhnlawyers

Simcoe: Smelko Law Office - *1
25 Norfolk St. North, Simcoe, ON N3Y 3N6
Tel: 519-426-1711; Fax: 519-426-7863
Toll-Free: 866-684-8527
smelkolaw@on.aibn.com

Sioux Lookout: Kevin W. Romyn - *1
P.O. Box 99, 69 Queen St., Sioux Lookout, ON P8T 1A1
Tel: 807-737-2562; Fax: 807-737-2571
romynlaw@gosiouxlookout.com

Smiths Falls: G.W. Fournier - *1
P.O. Box 752, 35 Daniel St., Smiths Falls, ON K7A 4W6
Tel: 613-283-8818; Fax: 613-283-8951
gwfournier@cogeco.ca

Smiths Falls: Howard Kelford & Dixon - Smiths Falls - *5
Former Name: Howard Ryan Kelford Knott & Dixon
2 Main St. East, Smiths Falls, ON K7A 1A2
Tel: 613-283-6772; Fax: 613-283-8840
www.smithsfallslaw.ca

Smiths Falls: Ross Cliffen & Associates - Smiths Falls - *3
Former Name: Ross Cliffen & Morrison
P.O. Box 804, 30 Russell St. East, Smiths Falls, ON K7A 4W6
Tel: 613-283-7331; Fax: 613-283-6792
rosslaw@ripnet.com
www.rossandcliffen.com

Southampton: Robert E. Forsyth - *1
P.O. Box 430, 243 High St., Southampton, ON N0H 2L0
Tel: 519-797-3223; Fax: 519-797-3192
forsyth3@bmts.com

St Albert: Ritzen Olivieri LLP - *3
#302, 7 St Anne St., St Albert, ON T8N 2X4
Tel: 780-460-2900; Fax: 780-460-2466
dougr@rolaw.ca
www.rolaw.ca

St Catharines: Richard H. Barch - *1
46 Ontario St., St Catharines, ON L2R 5J4
Tel: 905-641-1146; Fax: 905-641-1148

St Catharines: Beresh Smith - St Catharines - *2
#1003, 1 St. Paul St., St Catharines, ON L2R 7L2
Tel: 905-688-9550
www.calvinberesh.com

St Catharines: Jolanta B. Bula - *1
#704, 1 St. Paul St., St Catharines, ON L2R 7L2
Tel: 905-938-5480; Fax: 905-938-5488
jbb@jolantabula.com
www.jolantabula.com

St Catharines: L. Jane Burbage - *1
55 King St., 4th Fl., St Catharines, ON L2R 3H5
Tel: 289-362-1322; Fax: 289-362-2487
ljb@burbagebarristers.com
www.burbagebarristers.com

St Catharines: Chown Cairns Lawyers LLP - *11
#900, P.O. Box 760, 80 King St., St Catharines, ON L2R 6Y8
Tel: 905-346-0775; Fax: 905-688-0015
lawyers@chownlaw.com
www.chownlaw.com
www.facebook.com/chownlaw, twitter.com/chowncairnslaw,
www.linkedin.com/company/chown-cairns-lawyers-llp

St Catharines: Crossingham, Brady - *2
P.O. Box 307, 63 Ontario St., St Catharines, ON L2R 6V2
Tel: 905-641-1621; Fax: 905-685-1461
cbo@crossinghambrady.com

St Catharines: Daniel & Partners LLP - *12
P.O. Box 24022, 39 Queen St., St Catharines, ON L2R 7P7
Tel: 905-688-9411; Fax: 905-688-5747
Toll-Free: 800-263-3650
info@niagaralaw.ca
www.niagaralaw.ca
www.facebook.com/niagaralaw, twitter.com/niagaralaw

St Catharines: Ralph H. Frayne - *1
Former Name: Freeman, Frayne & Hummell
9 Raymond St., St Catharines, ON L2R 2S9
Tel: 905-684-1147; Fax: 905-684-7147

St Catharines: Graves & Richard Professional Corporation - *2
#800, 55 King St., St Catharines, ON L2R 7P7
Tel: 905-641-2020; Fax: 905-641-0484
www.gravesandrichard.com
www.facebook.com/gravesandrichard,
twitter.com/gravesrichardpc,
www.linkedin.com/company/graves-&-richard-personal-injury-lawyers

St Catharines: Erik Grinbergs
37 Church St., St Catharines, ON L2R 3B7
Tel: 905-688-9800; Fax: 905-684-0009
grinberg@vaxxine.com

St Catharines: Heelis Little & Almas LLP, Barristers & Solicitors - *4
Also Known As: HWL&A
Former Name: Heelis, Williams, Little & Almas LLP, Barristers & Solicitors
P.O. Box 1056, 14 Church St., St Catharines, ON L2R 7A3
Tel: 905-581-4242; Fax: 905-684-4844
www.14churchstlawoffice.com

St Catharines: David R. House - *1
31 Church St., St Catharines, ON L2R 3B7
Tel: 905-688-4650; Fax: 905-984-6314
dhouse@houselaw.ca
www.houselaw.ca
www.linkedin.com/pub/david-house/17/874/b13

St Catharines: Lancaster, Brooks & Welch LLP - St Catharines - *19
Former Name: Lancaster, Mix & Welch
#800, P.O. Box 790, 80 King St., St Catharines, ON L2R 6Z1
Tel: 905-641-1551; Fax: 905-641-1830
www.lbwlawyers.com
www.facebook.com/LBWlawyers,
www.linkedin.com/company/lancaster-brooks-&-welch-llp

St Catharines: Leon & Fazari LLP - St Catharines
33 Maywood Ave., St Catharines, ON L2R 1C5
Tel: 905-658-0057
www.leonlaw.ca

St Catharines: Frank M. Marotta - *1
21 Duke St., St Catharines, ON L2R 5W1
Tel: 905-688-5401; Fax: 905-688-6204
fmarotta@vaxxine.com

St Catharines: Martens Lingard LLP - *6
Former Name: Martens, Lingard, Maddalena, Robinson & Koke
#700, 43 Church St., St Catharines, ON L2R 7E1
Tel: 905-687-6551; Fax: 905-687-6553
www.martenslingard.ca

St Catharines: Joseph C. McCallum - *1
#100, 205 King St., St Catharines, ON L2R 3J5
Tel: 289-362-5666; Fax: 289-434-0561
www.joemlaw.com

St Catharines: Paula McPherson - *1
51 Hillcrest Ave., St Catharines, ON L2R 4Y3
Tel: 905-641-3457
resolve@sympatico.ca

St Catharines: Tracy J. Middleton Collini - *1
123 Niagara St., St Catharines, ON L2R 4L6
Tel: 905-937-9229; Fax: 905-937-9228
collinilaw@msn.com
collinilaw.vpweb.com

St Catharines: Morgan, Dilts & Toppari Law - *2
Box 216, 281 St Paul St., St Catharines, ON L2R 6S4
Tel: 905-685-7391; Fax: 905-685-9102
mdt@bellnet.ca
www.mdtlaw.ca

St Catharines: O'Neill & Radford - *1
154 James St., St Catharines, ON L2R 7A3
Tel: 905-641-2633; Fax: 905-682-0264
bmradford@bellnet.ca

St Catharines: Ian G. Pearson - *1
154 James St., 2nd Fl., St Catharines, ON L2R 5C5
Tel: 905-682-7882; Fax: 905-682-0264
ipearson@bellnet.ca

St Catharines: Sullivan, Mahoney LLP - St Catharines - *31
P.O. Box 1360, 40 Queen St., St Catharines, ON L2R 6Z2
Tel: 905-688-6655; Fax: 905-688-5814
www.sullivan-mahoney.com

St Catharines: Wilson Spurr LLP - *3
#168, 261 Martindale Rd., St Catharines, ON L2W 1A2
Tel: 905-682-2775; Fax: 905-682-2357
Toll-Free: 888-722-4193
contactus@wilsonspurrlaw.ca
www.wilsonspurrlaw.ca

indicates number of lawyers

St Catharines: Virginia L. Workman - *1
#1004, 1 St. Paul, St Catharines, ON L2R 7L2
Tel: 905-704-0804; *Fax:* 905-704-4464
lawoffice@virginiaworkman.ca
www.virginiaworkman.ca

St Marys: William J. Galloway - *1
P.O. Box 897, Stn. Main, 172 Queen St. East, St Marys, ON
N4X 1B6
Tel: 519-284-2112; *Fax:* 519-284-3081

St Marys: McCotter Law Office - St Marys - *6
50 Water St. South, St Marys, ON N4X 1C3
Tel: 519-284-2840
stmarys@lawtter.com
lawtter.com
twitter.com/MLOconnect,
www.linkedin.com/company/mccotter-law-office-p-c-

St Thomas: Bowsher & Bowsher - *3
112 Centre St., St Thomas, ON N5R 2Z9
Tel: 519-633-3301; *Fax:* 519-633-5995
sandyb@bowsherandbowsher.ca
www.bowsherandbowsher.com

St Thomas: Jerome A. Collins - *1
36 Hincks St., St Thomas, ON N5R 3N6
Tel: 519-633-3973; *Fax:* 519-633-7916

St Thomas: Ferguson DiMeo Lawyers - *2
#211, Canada Southern Railway Station, 750 Talbot St., St
Thomas, ON N5P 1E2
Tel: 519-633-8838; *Fax:* 519-633-9361
www.fergusondimeolaw.com

St Thomas: William Glover - *1
P.O. Box 575, Stn. Main, 458 Talbot St., St Thomas, ON N5P
3V6
Tel: 519-633-2300; *Fax:* 519-633-0964
gloverlawyer@aol.com

St Thomas: Gunn & Associates - *3
108 Centre St., St Thomas, ON N5R 2Z7
Tel: 519-631-0700; *Fax:* 519-631-1468
lawyers@gunn.on.ca
www.gunn.on.ca

St Thomas: Sanders, Cline - *3
P.O. Box 70, 14 Southwick St., St Thomas, ON N5P 3T5
Tel: 519-633-0800; *Fax:* 519-633-9259
sanderscline@sandlawyers.ca
www.sandlawyers.ca

St Thomas: Arnold B. Walker - *1
P.O. Box 20022, Stn. Centre, 4 Elgin St., St Thomas, ON N5R
4H4
Tel: 519-633-3273; *Fax:* 519-633-8585

Stoney Creek: Cicchi & Giangregorio - *2
1-99 Hwy. 8, Stoney Creek, ON L8G 1C1
Tel: 905-664-6645; *Fax:* 905-664-6952

Stoney Creek: Coombs & Lutz - *1
6 Lake Ave. South, Stoney Creek, ON L8G 1P3
Tel: 905-664-6341; *Fax:* 905-664-8966
info@coombsandlutz.ca
www.coombsandlutz.ca

Stoney Creek: MacKinnon Law Associates - *2
Former Name: MacKinnon, Mary J.
#10, 44 King St. East, Stoney Creek, ON L8G 1K1
Tel: 905-662-0046; *Fax:* 905-662-3339
info@mackinnonlaw.com
www.mackinnonlaw.com

Stoney Creek: Murray Mazza - *1
#1, 426 Hwy. 8, Stoney Creek, ON L8G 1G2
Tel: 905-561-1444; *Fax:* 905-664-2873
www.murraymazza.ca

Stoney Creek: McHugh Whitmore LLP - *9
Former Name: McHugh Mowat Whitmore Ionico
MacPherson LLP
914 Queenston Rd., Stoney Creek, ON L8G 1B7
Tel: 905-662-6001; *Fax:* 905-662-6004
mchughwhitmore.ca

Stoney Creek: O'Brien & Skrtich - *1
26 King St. East, Stoney Creek, ON L8G 1J8
Tel: 905-662-2855; *Fax:* 905-662-8881

Stoney Creek: Mari-Anne Saunders - *1
#303, 800 Queenston Rd., Stoney Creek, ON L8G 1A7
Tel: 905-664-6683; *Fax:* 905-664-4876

Stouffville: Paul J. Crowe - *1
#28, 86 Ringwood Dr., Stouffville, ON L4A 1C3
Tel: 905-640-8100; *Fax:* 905-640-6064
info@pauljcrowe.com
www.pauljcrowe.com

Stouffville: Monica Farrell - *1
6349 Main St., Stouffville, ON L4A 1G5
Tel: 905-591-5510
monica@stouffvillefamilylaw.com
www.monicafarrell.com

**Stouffville: Thomas & Pelman Professional
Corporation - *1**
P.O. Box 940, 6131 Main St., Stouffville, ON L4A 3R6
Tel: 905-640-2211; *Fax:* 905-640-8161
thomasandpelman@thomasandpelman.com

**Stratford: Barenberg & Roth Professional
Corporation - *3**
Former Name: Barenberg, McDonald
160 Erie St., Stratford, ON N5A 2M7
Tel: 519-271-6360; *Fax:* 519-271-3074
Toll-Free: 800-709-3849
info@barenbergandroth.com
www.barenbergandroth.com

Stratford: John W. Buechler - *1
488 Erie St., Stratford, ON N5A 2N6
Tel: 519-271-3520; *Fax:* 519-271-0097
wjblaw@wightman.ca

Stratford: Michael F. Fair - *1
10 Downie St., 2nd Fl., Stratford, ON N5A 7K4
Tel: 519-271-2912; *Fax:* 519-271-2732

Stratford: W. Stirling Kenny Law Office - *1
19 Ontario St., Stratford, ON N5A 3G7
Tel: 519-271-1005

**Stratford: Monteith Ritsma Phillips LLP - Stratford -
*9**
P.O. Box 846, 56 Albert St., Stratford, ON N5A 6W3
Tel: 519-271-6770; *Fax:* 519-271-9261
www.stratfordlawyers.com

**Stratford: Skinner, Dunphy, Burdett & O'Rourke LLP
- *4**
Former Name: Skinner, Dunphy & Bantle LLP
P.O. Box 542, 1 Ontario St., Stratford, ON N5A 6T7
Tel: 519-271-7330; *Fax:* 519-271-1762
thefirm@stratfordlaw.com
www.stratfordlaw.com

Strathroy: Robert J. Dack - *1
16 Front St. East, Strathroy, ON N7G 1Y4
Tel: 519-245-0370; *Fax:* 519-245-0523
robertdack@bam.on.ca

Strathroy: Jones, Gibbons & Reis - *2
39 Front St. W, Strathroy, ON N7G 1X5
Tel: 519-245-0110

Strathroy: Quinlan & Somerville - *2
18 Front St. East, Strathroy, ON N7G 1Y4
Tel: 519-245-0342; *Fax:* 519-245-0108
cquinlan@quinlansomerville.com

Strathroy: George E. Sinker - *2
53 Front St. West, Strathroy, ON N7G 1X6
Tel: 519-245-1144; *Fax:* 519-245-6090
gsinker@bellnet.ca

Sudbury: Michael G. Barnett - *1
264 Elm St., Sudbury, ON P3C 1V4
Tel: 705-674-3210; *Fax:* 705-674-1265

Sudbury: William G. Beach - *1
224 Applegrove St., Sudbury, ON P3C 1N3
Tel: 705-675-5685; *Fax:* 705-675-6601

Sudbury: D. Peter Best - *1
125 Durham St., 2nd Fl., Sudbury, ON P3E 3M9
Tel: 705-674-9292; *Fax:* 705-674-8912
peterbest@peterbestlawoffices.com
www.peterbestlawoffices.com

Sudbury: Gerald D. Brouillette - *1
235 Elm St., Sudbury, ON P3C 1T8
Tel: 705-674-2822; *Fax:* 705-674-2975
gerry.brouillette@sympatico.ca

Sudbury: Conroy Scott LLP - *7
Former Name: Conroy Trebb Scott Hurtubise LLP
164 Elm St., Sudbury, ON P3C 1T7
Tel: 705-674-6441; *Fax:* 705-673-9567
Toll-Free: 800-627-1825
ctsh.ca

Sudbury: DeDiana, Eloranta & Longstreet - *1
219 Pine St., Sudbury, ON P3C 1X4
Tel: 705-674-4289; *Fax:* 705-671-1047

Sudbury: Desmarais, Keenan LLP - *11
#201, 62 Frood Rd., Sudbury, ON P3C 4Z3
Tel: 705-675-7521; *Fax:* 705-675-7390
Toll-Free: 800-290-5465
www.desmaraiskeenan.com

Sudbury: Hugh A. Doig, Q.C. - *1
296 Larc296 Regional Rd. 51, Sudbury, ON P3B 1M1
Tel: 705-674-4213; *Fax:* 705-671-1652
doig@on.aibn.com

Sudbury: Brian N. Howe - *1
235 Elm St. West, Sudbury, ON P3C 1T8
Tel: 705-674-8317; *Fax:* 705-674-2952

Sudbury: Elizabeth Kari - *1
293 Elm St., 2nd Fl., Sudbury, ON P3C 1V6
Tel: 705-670-2770; *Fax:* 705-670-9172
ekari@cyberbeach.net

Sudbury: Donald Kuyek - *1
229 Elm St. West, Sudbury, ON P3C 1T8
Tel: 705-675-1227; *Fax:* 705-675-5350
kuyek@vianet.ca

Sudbury: Lacroix Lawyers | Avocats - *2
#100, 161 Larch St., Sudbury, ON P3E 1C4
Tel: 705-674-1976; *Fax:* 705-674-6978
www.sudburylaw.com

Sudbury: Patricia L. Meehan - *1
293 Elm St. West, Sudbury, ON P3C 1V6
Tel: 705-674-2272; *Fax:* 705-674-5238
meehanlawoffice@bellnet.ca

Sudbury: Mensour & Mensour - *2
#101, 238 Elm St., Sudbury, ON P3C 1V3
Tel: 705-673-6787; *Fax:* 705-673-1418

Sudbury: Miller Maki LLP - *7
176 Elm St., Sudbury, ON P3C 1T7
Tel: 705-675-7503; *Fax:* 705-675-8669
email@millermaki.com
www.millermaki.com

**Sudbury: Paquette-Renzini, Barristers, Solicitors &
Notaries - *2**
#202, 40 Larch St., Sudbury, ON P3E 5M7
Tel: 705-805-0403
www.paquette-renzini.ca

Sudbury: Parisé Law Office - *2
#200, 58 Lisgar St., 2nd Fl., Sudbury, ON P3E 3L7
Tel: 705-674-4042; *Fax:* 705-674-4242
pariselaw@unitz.ca

Sudbury: Stanley J. Thomas - *1
111 Durham St., Sudbury, ON P3E 3M9
Tel: 705-674-8306; *Fax:* 705-675-8466

Sudbury: Law Office of Serge F. Treherne - *1
P.O. Box 1269, 144 Elm St. West, Sudbury, ON P3C 1T7
Tel: 705-670-9689; *Fax:* 705-670-9141
Toll-Free: 877-550-5616

Sudbury: Violette Law Offices - *1
#1, 11 Elgin St., Sudbury, ON P3C 5B6
Tel: 705-674-1300; *Fax:* 705-671-1044
Toll-Free: 866-991-1300
office@violettelaw.com
violettelaw.com

Sudbury: Weaver Simmons LLP - Sudbury - *25
#400, 233 Brady St., Sudbury, ON P3B 4H5
Tel: 705-674-6421; *Fax:* 705-674-9948
thefirm@weaversimmons.com
www.weaversimmons.com

* indicates number of lawyers

Sutton West: Fahey Crate Law Professional Corporation - *4
Former Name: Patrick J. Fahey Law Office
P.O. Box 487, 100 High St., Sutton West, ON L0E 1R0
Tel: 905-722-3771; Fax: 905-722-9852
info@faheycratelaw.ca
www.faheycratelaw.ca
www.facebook.com/faheycratelaw, twitter.com/faheycratelaw

Thornhill: Arrigo Bros Ltd. - *1
Former Name: Augustine M. Arrigo, Q.C.
48 Guardsman Rd., Thornhill, ON L3T 6L4
Tel: 905-889-6131

Thornhill: Leslie (Masood) Brown - *1
#225B, Commerce Gate, 505 Hwy. 7 East, Thornhill, ON L3T 7T1
Tel: 905-731-5083; Fax: 905-731-4078
Toll-Free: 800-268-0314
info@torontolegalservices.ca
www.torontolegalservices.ca

Thornhill: Edward L. Burlew - *1
16 John St., Thornhill, ON L3T 1X8
Tel: 905-882-2422; Fax: 905-882-2431
Toll-Free: 888-486-5677

Thornhill: Iain Stewart Cunningham - *1
20 Cypress Point Ct., Thornhill, ON L3T 1V7
Tel: 905-764-7376; Fax: 905-707-5818

Thornhill: Stephen R. Dyment - *1
#216, 2900 Steeles Ave. E, Thornhill, ON L3T 4X1
Tel: 905-882-1277; Fax: 905-882-8536

Thornhill: Fish & Associates Professional Corporation - *2
7951 Yonge St., Thornhill, ON L3T 2C4
Tel: 905-881-1500 Toll-Free: 877-439-3999
www.familyfight.com

Thornhill: A.M. Flisfeder - *1
45 Janesville Rd., Thornhill, ON L4J 6Z9
Tel: 416-469-0375; Fax: 416-469-0375
sgt_lafourse@sympatico.ca

Thornhill: Gregory J. Gaglione - *1
#202, 7368 Yonge St., Thornhill, ON L4J 8H9
Tel: 905-882-0066; Fax: 905-882-2550

Thornhill: Elana P. Glass - *1
149 Langtry Pl., Thornhill, ON L4J 8L6
Tel: 416-587-5680

Thornhill: Seymour Iseman - *1
Former Name: Iseman & Associate
#216, 2900 Steeles Ave. East, Thornhill, ON L3T 4X1
Tel: 905-881-8800; Fax: 905-881-7391
siseman@allstream.net

Thornhill: Arthur Lundy - *1
#402, 300 John St., Thornhill, ON L3T 5W4
Tel: 905-886-3110; Fax: 905-886-0989

Thornhill: Carolyn L. MacDonald - *1
14 Morgan Ave., Thornhill, ON L3T 1R1
Tel: 905-707-7723; Fax: 905-707-5818

Thornhill: D. Todd Morganstein - *1
#110, 8111 Yonge St., Thornhill, ON L3T 4V9
Tel: 905-881-8289; Fax: 905-881-2696

Thornhill: Newton HR Law - *1
8 Waterloo Ct., Thornhill, ON L3T 6L9
Tel: 416-846-6855
www.newtonhrlaw.com

Thornhill: Tania Perlin - *1
P.O. Box 137, Stn. B10, 800 Steeles Ave. W, Thornhill, ON L4J 7L2
Tel: 416-225-5424; Fax: 416-225-3611
www.taniaperlin.com

Thornhill: Thomas H. Riesz - *1
#218, 180 Steeles Ave. W, Thornhill, ON L4J 2L1
Tel: 905-881-5609; Fax: 905-881-9859

Thornhill: Alan G. Silverstein - *1
14 Windhaven Terrace, Thornhill, ON L4J 7N9
Tel: 905-886-0300; Fax: 647-795-9207

Thornhill: Ben Weinstein - *1
#203, 1 Clark Ave. West, Thornhill, ON L4J 7Y6
Tel: 905-889-5364; Fax: 905-889-3231

Thornhill: Lawrence C. Wesson, Barrister & Solicitor - *1
300 John, Thornhill, ON L3T 5W4
Tel: 905-695-0290

Thornhill: Sheldon Wisener - *1
Former Name: Greenberg, Barry S.
7626A Yonge St., Thornhill, ON L4J 1V9
Tel: 905-886-9535; Fax: 905-886-9540
sheldon@wisenerlaw.com

Thorold: Jurmain Law Office
8A Clairmont St., Thorold, ON L2V 1R1
Tel: 905-227-2829; Fax: 905-227-9206
info@jurmainlaw.com
www.jurmainlaw.com

Thorold: John J. Simon - *1
P.O. Box 505, Stn. Thorold, 7 Front St. North, Thorold, ON L2V 4W1
Tel: 905-227-9191; Fax: 905-227-7234
john_smith@hotmail.com

Thorold: Young McNamara - *1
18 Albert St. East, Thorold, ON L2V 1P1
Tel: 905-227-3777; Fax: 905-227-5988
youngmcnamara@hotmail.com
www.youngmcnamara.com

Thunder Bay: Atwood Labine LLP - *8
Former Name: Atwood Labine Arnone McCartney LLP
501 Donald St. East, Thunder Bay, ON P7E 6N6
Tel: 807-623-4342; Fax: 807-623-2098
info@atwoodlaw.ca
www.atwoodlaw.ca

Thunder Bay: David S. Bruzzese - *1
#320, Marina Park Centre, 180 Park Ave., Thunder Bay, ON P7B 6J4
Tel: 807-344-1020; Fax: 807-344-1433
dsb.law@shawlink.ca

Thunder Bay: Buset & Partners LLP - *15
1121 Barton St., Thunder Bay, ON P7B 5N3
Tel: 807-623-2500; Fax: 807-622-7808
Toll-Free: 866-532-8738
www.buset-partners.com

Thunder Bay: Carrel + Partners LLP - *9
#1, 1100 Roland St., Thunder Bay, ON P7B 5M4
Tel: 807-346-3000; Fax: 807-346-3600
Toll-Free: 800-263-0578
www.carrel.com

Thunder Bay: Cheadles LLP - *9
Former Name: Cheadle Johnson Shanks MacIvor
#2000, P.O. Box 10429, 715 Hewitson St., Thunder Bay, ON P7B 6T8
Tel: 807-622-6821; Fax: 807-623-3892
info@cheadles.com
www.cheadles.com
www.facebook.com/CheadlesLawyers,
www.linkedin.com/company/cheadles-llp

Thunder Bay: Richard W. Courtis - *3
#300, 1119 Victoria Ave. East, Thunder Bay, ON P7C 3B7
Tel: 807-623-3000; Fax: 807-623-1251
Toll-Free: 877-266-6646

Thunder Bay: Cupello & Company - *4
#104, 105 South May St., Thunder Bay, ON P7E 1B1
Tel: 807-622-8201; Fax: 807-622-3755
info.cupellolaw@shaw.ca

Thunder Bay: Erickson & Partners - Thunder Bay - *10
Former Name: Erickson Larson
291 Court St. South, Thunder Bay, ON P7B 2Y1
Tel: 807-345-1213; Fax: 807-345-2526
Toll-Free: 800-465-3912
www.erickson-law.com

Thunder Bay: Filipovic, Conway & Associates - Thunder Bay - *3
1020 East Victoria Ave., Thunder Bay, ON P7C 1B6
Tel: 807-343-9090; Fax: 807-345-1397
Toll-Free: 800-760-8694
www.filipovic.ca

Thunder Bay: Peter Heerema - *1
44 Algoma St. South, Thunder Bay, ON P7B 3A9
Tel: 807-346-4053; Fax: 807-346-8714
peter.heerema@tbaytel.net

Thunder Bay: Illingworth & Illingworth - *2
#201, 1151 Barton St., Thunder Bay, ON P7B 5N3
Tel: 807-623-7222; Fax: 807-622-5297
lawyers@tbaytel.net

Thunder Bay: Rick E. Lauder - *1
217 Van Norman St., Thunder Bay, ON P7A 4B6
Tel: 807-683-4444; Fax: 807-345-0337

Thunder Bay: Martin Scrimshaw Scott LLP - *4
Cumberland Park, 1 Cumberland St. South, Thunder Bay, ON P7B 2T1
Tel: 807-345-3600; Fax: 807-344-8152
msslaw@tbaytel.net

Thunder Bay: Thomas C. Mitton - *1
123 Brodie St. South, Thunder Bay, ON P7E 1B8
Tel: 807-623-4320; Fax: 807-622-8038
tcmitton@tbaytel.net

Thunder Bay: Peter Mrowiec - *1
#816, 34 Cumberland St. North, Thunder Bay, ON P7A 4L3
Tel: 807-344-0099 Toll-Free: 800-634-0660
www.pmlawoffice.ca

Thunder Bay: Robert D. Mullen - *1
Former Name: Macgillivray-Poirier & Mullen In Association
395 Fort William Rd., Thunder Bay, ON P7B 2Z3
Tel: 807-344-5848; Fax: 807-344-5877
rmullen@shawbiz.ca

Thunder Bay: Seppo K. Paivalainen - *1
275 Bay St., Thunder Bay, ON P7B 1R7
Tel: 807-343-9394; Fax: 807-344-1562

Thunder Bay: Petrone & Partners - *10
Former Name: Petrone Hornak Garofalo Mauro
76 Algoma St. North, Thunder Bay, ON P7A 4Z4
Tel: 807-344-9191; Fax: 807-345-8391
Toll-Free: 800-465-3988
info@petronelaw.ca
www.petronelaw.ca

Thunder Bay: Potestio Law - Thunder Bay - *3
Former Name: Christie Potestio Freitag
#102, 1113 Jade Ct., Thunder Bay, ON P7B 6M7
Tel: 807-344-3333; Fax: 807-344-3344
www.potestiolaw.com

Thunder Bay: Kenneth A. Stewart - *1
#112, 105 May St. North, Thunder Bay, ON P7C 3N9
Tel: 807-623-7852; Fax: 807-623-0014
astewart@807-city.on.ca

Thunder Bay: Thomas G. Watkinson - *1
123 Brodie St. South, Thunder Bay, ON P7E 1B8
Tel: 807-624-5605; Fax: 807-623-6096

Thunder Bay: Weiler, Maloney, Nelson - *14
Also Known As: Weilers Law
#201, 1001 William St., Thunder Bay, ON P7B 6M1
Tel: 807-623-1111; Fax: 807-623-4947
Toll-Free: 866-934-5377
weilers@wmnlaw.com
www.weilers.ca

Tilbury: Taylor & Delrue - *3
P.O. Box 459, 40 Queen St. South, Tilbury, ON N0P 2L0
Tel: 519-682-0164; Fax: 519-682-2777
taydel@cogeco.net

Tillsonburg: James G. Battin - *1
25 Bidwell St., Tillsonburg, ON N4G 3T4
Tel: 519-688-9033; Fax: 519-688-9036
jbattinlawoffice@gmail.com

Tillsonburg: Gibson Bennett Groom & Szorenyi - *2
Former Name: Gibson, Linton, Toth, Campbell & Bennett
P.O. Box 5, Stn. Main, 36 Broadway, Tillsonburg, ON N4G 4H3
Tel: 519-842-3658; Fax: 519-842-5001
bbennett@gbgs.ca
tillsonburglawyers.com

Tillsonburg: Gibson Bennett Groom & Szorenyi - *2
36 Broadway, Tillsonburg, ON N4G 4H3
Tel: 519-842-4205; Fax: 519-842-4261
tillsonburglawyers.com

* indicates number of lawyers

Tillsonburg: Jenkins & Gilvesy - *3
Former Name: Morris, Jenkins & Gilvesy
P.O. Box 280, Stn. Main, 107 Broadway St., Tillsonburg, ON
N4G 4H5
Tel: 519-842-9017; Fax: 519-842-3394
info@jenkins-gilvesy.com
www.linkedin.com/pub/lisa-gilvesy/9/622/65a

Tillsonburg: Mandryk, Morgan & Vervaeke
Associates at Law - *4
Former Name: Mandryk, Stewart & Morgan
40 Brock St. West, Tillsonburg, ON N4G 3T8
Tel: 519-842-4228; Fax: 519-842-7659
mhlaw@oxford.net
www.mandrykmorganandvervaeke.ca

Timmins: Barazzutti Strybos - *2
Former Name: Barazzutti, Lisa F.
167 - 3rd Ave., Timmins, ON P4N 1C7
Tel: 705-531-3200; Fax: 705-531-3202
www.barazzuttilaw.ca

Timmins: Sydney Brooks - *1
Also Known As: Brooks & Associates
81 Balsam St. South, Timmins, ON P4N 2C9
Tel: 705-264-5341; Fax: 705-264-2550
www.sydbrookslaw.ca

Timmins: Suzanne Desrosiers Professional
Corporation - *1
92 Spruce St. North, Timmins, ON P4N 6M8
Tel: 705-268-6492; Fax: 705-264-1940
sd@suzannedesrosierslaw.com
suzannedesrosierslaw.com

Timmins: Evans, Bragagnolo & Sullivan LLP -
Timmins - *14
120 Pine St. South, Timmins, ON P4N 2K4
Tel: 705-264-1285; Fax: 705-264-7424
www.ebslawyers.com
www.facebook.com/EvansBragagnoloSullivanLLP,
www.linkedin.com/company/1072215

Timmins: Maisonneuve Dawkins - *3
Former Name: Maisonneuve Labelle LLP
15 Balsam St. South, Timmins, ON P4N 2C7
Tel: 705-264-2385; Fax: 705-268-3949
info@ml-law.ca
www.15balsam.com

Timmins: Riopelle Group Professional Corporation -
Timmins - *8
#202, 85 Pine St. South, Timmins, ON P4N 2K1
Tel: 705-264-9591; Fax: 705-264-1393
Toll-Free: 866-624-1614
www.rglaw.ca
www.facebook.com/RiopelleGriener

Toronto: Aaron & Aaron - *1
#1400, 10 King St. East, Toronto, ON M5C 1C3
Tel: 416-364-9366; Fax: 416-364-3818
bob@aaron.ca
www.aaron.ca

Toronto: G.J. Abols - *1
#2105, 700 Bay St., Toronto, ON M5G 1Z6
Tel: 416-598-8866; Fax: 416-971-7656
abolsgj@on.aibn.com

Toronto: Abrams & Krochak - Canadian Immigration
Lawyers - *2
#402, 250 Merton St., Toronto, ON M4S 1B1
Tel: 416-482-3387; Fax: 416-482-0647
www.abramsandkrochak.com

Toronto: Adair Morse LLP - *12
#1800, 1 Queen St. East, Toronto, ON M5C 2W5
Tel: 416-863-1230; Fax: 416-863-1241
info@adairmorse.com
www.adairmorse.com

Toronto: G. Chalmers Adams - *1
#245, 55 St. Clair Ave. West, Toronto, ON M4V 2Y7
Tel: 416-929-7232; Fax: 416-929-7225
info@gcadams.on.ca

Toronto: Adler Bytensky - *6
#1708, 5000 Yonge St., Toronto, ON M2N 7E9
Tel: 416-365-3151; Fax: 416-365-0866
info@CrimLawCanada.com
www.crimlawcanada.com
www.facebook.com/CrimLawCanada, twitter.com/Prutschi,
www.linkedin.com/in/edward-prutschi-a602894

Toronto: Advocacy Centre for the Elderly - *6
#701, 2 Carlton St., Toronto, ON M5B 1J3
Tel: 416-598-2656; Fax: 416-598-7924
www.advocacycentreelderly.org

Toronto: Affleck Greene McMurtry LLP - *13
Former Name: Kelly Affleck Greene
#200, 365 Bay St., Toronto, ON M5H 2V1
Tel: 416-360-2800; Fax: 416-360-5960
info@agmlawyers.com
www.agmlawyers.com

Toronto: Claudio R. Aiello - *1
#506, 330 University Ave., Toronto, ON M5G 1R7
Tel: 416-969-9900; Fax: 416-969-9060
claudio@aiellolaw.ca

Toronto: Irving J. Aiken - *1
44 Charles St. West, Toronto, ON M4Y 1R7
Tel: 416-947-0199; Fax: 416-947-0379

Toronto: Alloway & Associates - *4
64 Prince Andrew Place, Toronto, ON M3C 2H4
Tel: 416-971-9293; Fax: 416-971-9349
email@alloway.net
www.alloway.net

Toronto: Alpert Law Firm - *1
#900, 1 St. Clair Ave. East, Toronto, ON M4T 2V7
Tel: 416-923-0809; Fax: 416-923-1549
halpert@alpertlawfirm.ca
www.alpertlawfirm.ca

Toronto: Harriet Altman - *1
68 Garnier Court, Toronto, ON M2M 4C9
Tel: 416-224-5240; Fax: 416-224-0360
Toll-Free: 877-224-5229
haltman1@hotmail.com

Toronto: Altmid Roll & Associates - *3
#600, 1120 Finch Ave. West, Toronto, ON M3J 3H7
Tel: 416-663-6888; Fax: 416-663-3442
www.altmidroll.com

Toronto: Jaikrishin R. Ambwani - *1
#330, 100 Cowdray Ct., Toronto, ON M1S 5C8
Tel: 416-754-4404; Fax: 416-754-7746
jack@jackambwani.com
www.jackambwani.com

Toronto: Amnon Kestelman - *2
245 Coxwell Ave., Toronto, ON M4L 3B4
Tel: 416-465-3561; Fax: 416-465-3563

Toronto: Julie Evelyn Amourgis - *1
#2000, 393 University Ave., Toronto, ON M5G 1E6
Tel: 416-504-5844; Fax: 416-593-1352

Toronto: Anderson Bourdon Burgess
454 Brown's Line, Toronto, ON M8W 3T9
Tel: 416-621-9644; Fax: 416-621-9668
www.andersonbb.com

Toronto: Dwight Anderson - *1
1709 Bloor St. West, Toronto, ON M6P 4E5
Tel: 416-769-3522; Fax: 416-769-2302
dwightanderson@rogers.com

Toronto: Andriessen & Associates - *2
#101, 703 Evans Ave., Toronto, ON M9C 5E9
Tel: 416-620-7020; Fax: 416-620-1398
info@andriessen.ca
www.andriessen.ca
twitter.com/andriessenlaw

Toronto: Philip Anisman Barrister & Solicitor - *1
#1704, 80 Richmond St. West, Toronto, ON M5H 2A4
Tel: 416-363-4200; Fax: 416-363-6200

Toronto: Antflyck & Aulis LLP - *2
Former Name: Antflyck & Aulis LLP
#407, 1100 Sheppard Ave. East, Toronto, ON M2K 2W2
Tel: 416-431-1500; Fax: 416-431-1912
www.aulislawfirm.com

Toronto: Dennis Apostolides - *1
#201, 505 Danforth Ave., Toronto, ON M4K 1P5
Tel: 416-463-1147; Fax: 416-463-1762
apostolides@rogers.com

Toronto: Aronovitch Macaulay Rollo LLP - *24
Also Known As: AMR LLP
#300, 145 Wellington St. West, Toronto, ON M5J 1H8
Tel: 416-369-9393; Fax: 416-369-0665
info@amrlaw.ca
www.amrlaw.ca

Toronto: Harvey Ash - *1
#900, 5799 Yonge St., Toronto, ON M2M 3V3
Tel: 416-250-0080; Fax: 416-225-1124
harveyash@yorklegal.ca

Toronto: William Ash - *1
#801, 55 Eglinton Ave. East, Toronto, ON M4P 1G8
Tel: 416-486-8751; Fax: 416-486-8789
willash@bellnet.ca

Toronto: Ashbourne & Caskey - *1
2077 Lawrence Ave. West, Toronto, ON M9N 1H7
Tel: 416-247-6677; Fax: 416-247-3519

Toronto: Atherton Barristers - *1
#703, 357 Bay St., Toronto, ON M5H 2T7
Tel: 416-365-1030; Fax: 416-946-1619
Toll-Free: 866-237-1030
bcatherton@ablaw.com
www.athertonbarristers.com

Toronto: ATX Law - *1
Former Name: Aprile Law
#100, 174 Bedford Rd., Toronto, ON M5R 2K9
Tel: 416-218-5263
info@atxlaw.ca
atxlaw.ca
twitter.com/atxlaw,
www.linkedin.com/pub/peter-aprile/1b/678/a14

Toronto: S.J. AvRuskin - *1
66 Charles St. East., Toronto, ON M4Y 2R3
Tel: 416-922-4147; Fax: 416-922-8022

Toronto: Azevedo & Nelson - *4
892 College St., Toronto, ON M6H 1A4
Tel: 416-533-7133; Fax: 416-533-3114
aazevedo@azevedonelson.com
www.azevedonelson.com

Toronto: Babits, Wappel & Toome - *3
#802, 480 University Ave., Toronto, ON M5G 1V2
Tel: 416-598-1333; Fax: 416-598-5024

Toronto: Denise Badley - *1
#2, 2069 Danforth Ave., 2nd Fl., Toronto, ON M4C 1J8
Tel: 416-690-6195; Fax: 416-690-6271
dbadleylaw@rogers.com

Toronto: J. Waldo Baerg - *1
#506, 372 Bay St., Toronto, ON M5H 2W9
Tel: 416-366-3705; Fax: 416-366-0157
waldobaerg@on.aibn.com

Toronto: Baker & Company - *6
#3300, 130 Adelaide St. West, Toronto, ON M5H 3P5
Tel: 416-777-0100; Fax: 416-366-3992
info@bakerlawyers.com
www.bakerlawyers.com

Toronto: Baker & McKenzie LLP - *57
#2100, Brookfield Place, P.O. Box 874, 181 Bay St., Toronto,
ON M5J 2T3
Tel: 416-863-1221; Fax: 416-863-6275
www.bakermckenzie.com
www.facebook.com/officialbakermckenzie,
twitter.com/bakermckenzie,
www.linkedin.com/company-beta/3957

Toronto: Gordon R. Baker, Q.C. - *1
#200, 2 Lombard St., Toronto, ON M5C 1M1
Tel: 416-365-7203; Fax: 416-365-7204
gord@gordbaker.com
www.gordbaker.com

Toronto: Stanley Baker - *1
#700, 55 Town Centre Ct., Toronto, ON M1P 4X4
Tel: 416-296-1794; Fax: 416-296-1259
stanleybaker@rogers.com

Toronto: Tony Baker - *1
500 Danforth Ave., Toronto, ON M4K 1P6
Tel: 416-463-4411; Fax: 416-463-4562
tbaker1952@aol.com
www.tonybakerlaw.com

* indicates number of lawyers

Toronto: Ahmad N. Baksh - *1
#307, 1280 Finch Ave. West, Toronto, ON M3J 3K6
Tel: 416-667-1922; Fax: 416-667-0304
anbaksh@rogers.com

Toronto: Baldwin Sennecke Halman LLP - *6
Former Name: Brans, Lehun, Baldwin
#1320, Victoria Tower, 25 Adelaide St. East, Toronto, ON M5C 3A1
Tel: 416-601-1040; Fax: 416-601-0655
info@bashllp.com
www.bashllp.com

Toronto: Banks & Starkman - *2
#310, 200 Ronson Dr., Toronto, ON M9W 5Z9
Tel: 416-243-3394; Fax: 416-243-9692
www.banksandstarkman.com

Toronto: Charles N. Barhydt - *1
1199 The Queensway, Toronto, ON M8Z 1R7
Tel: 416-960-0049
info@barhydtcriminallaw.com
www.barhydtcriminallaw.com

Toronto: J.R. Barrs - *1
23 Bedford Rd., Toronto, ON M5R 2J9
Tel: 416-366-6466; Fax: 416-964-8067
randallbarrs.com

Toronto: BartLaw Canadian Immigration Barristers & Solicitors - *7
Former Name: Jacqueline Bart & Associates
#200, 8 Wellington St. East, Toronto, ON M5E 1C5
Tel: 416-601-1346; Fax: 416-601-1357
info@bartlaw.ca
www.bartlaw.ca

Toronto: Batcher, Wasserman
Former Name: Batcher, Wasserman & Associates
#500, 718 Wilson Ave., Toronto, ON M3K 1E2
Tel: 416-635-6300; Fax: 416-635-6376
Toll-Free: 877-813-0820

Toronto: Batcher, Wasserman & Associates
Former Name: Robert G. Wasserman
#500, 718 Wilson Ave., Toronto, ON M3K 1E2
Tel: 416-635-6300; Fax: 416-635-6376

Toronto: Bates Barristers - *1
34 King St. East, 12th Fl., Toronto, ON M5C 2X8
Tel: 416-869-9898; Fax: 416-869-9405
info@batesbarristers.com
www.batesbarristers.com

Toronto: Battista Smith Migration Law Group - *3
#1000, 160 Bloor St. East, Toronto, ON M4W 1B9
Tel: 416-849-5501; Fax: 437-266-2599
reception@migrationlawgroup.com
www.migrationlawgroup.com
www.facebook.com/migrationlawgroup

Toronto: Beard Winter LLP - *64
#701, 130 Adelaide St. West, Toronto, ON M5H 2K4
Tel: 416-593-5555; Fax: 416-593-7760
info@beardwinter.com
www.beardwinter.com

Toronto: Beber & Associates - *7
#2900, 390 Bay St., Toronto, ON M5H 2Y2
Tel: 416-867-2280; Fax: 416-869-0321
www.beber.ca

Toronto: Sandra Bebris - *1
#300, 1370 Don Mills Rd., Toronto, ON M3B 3N7
Tel: 416-510-1324
bebris@pathcom.com

Toronto: Steven Bellissimo - *1
#802, 390 Bay St., Toronto, ON M5H 2Y2
Tel: 416-362-6437; Fax: 416-972-9940
steve@sblaw.ca

Toronto: Belmont, Fine & Associates - *2
#601, 1120 Finch Ave. West, Toronto, ON M3J 3H7
Tel: 416-661-2066; Fax: 416-661-2116
www.belmontfine.com

Toronto: Belmore Neidrauer LLP - *10
#2401, TD South Tower, P.O. Box 16, 79 Wellington St. West, Toronto, ON M5K 1A1
Tel: 416-863-1771; Fax: 416-863-9171
info@belmorelaw.com
www.belmorelaw.com

Toronto: Bennett Bankruptcy Legal Counsel - *2
Former Name: Bennett & Company
#900, 25 Adelaide St. East, Toronto, ON M5C 3A1
Tel: 416-363-8688; Fax: 416-363-8083
bennett@ican.net
www.bennettonbankruptcy.ca

Toronto: Bennett Best Burn LLP - *12
#1700, 150 York St., Toronto, ON M5H 3S5
Tel: 416-362-3400; Fax: 416-362-2211
info@bbburn.com
www.bbburn.com

Toronto: Benson Percival Brown LLP - *19
#800, 250 Dundas St. West, Toronto, ON M5T 2Z6
Tel: 416-977-9777; Fax: 416-977-1241
www.bensonpercival.com

Toronto: Bereskin & Parr LLP - Toronto - *75
Scotia Plaza, 40 King St. West, 40th Fl., Toronto, ON M5H 3Y2
Tel: 416-364-7311; Fax: 416-361-1398
Toll-Free: 888-364-7311
info@bereskinparr.com
www.bereskinparr.com
twitter.com/bereskinparr,
www.linkedin.com/company/bereskin-&-parr

Toronto: Bergel, Magence LLP - *4
#501, 1018 Finch Ave. West, Toronto, ON M3J 3L5
Tel: 416-665-2000; Fax: 416-663-2348
Toll-Free: 866-492-3743
bergellaw.com

Toronto: Max Berger Professional Law Corporation - *2
#207, 1033 Bay St., Toronto, ON M5S 3A5
Tel: 416-969-9263; Fax: 416-969-9098
max@maxberger.ca
www.maxberger.ca

Toronto: Berkow, Cohen LLP - *8
#400, 141 Adelaide St. West, Toronto, ON M5H 3L5
Tel: 416-364-4900; Fax: 416-364-3865
reception@berkowcohen.com
www.berkowcohen.com

Toronto: Bradley F. Berns - *1
554 Annette St., Toronto, ON M6S 2C6
Tel: 416-490-6456; Fax: 416-490-6439

Toronto: Bersenas Jacobsen Chouest Thomson Blackburn LLP - *11
#201, 33 Yonge St., Toronto, ON M5E 1G4
Tel: 416-982-3800; Fax: 416-982-3801
info@lexcanada.com
www.lexcanada.com

Toronto: Myer Betel - *1
7 Farrington Dr., Toronto, ON M2L 2B4
Tel: 416-447-4333; Fax: 416-447-3773
mbetel@rogers.com

Toronto: Lynn Bevan Professional Corporation - *1
1 Coulson Ave., Toronto, ON M4V 1Y3
Tel: 416-955-0400; Fax: 416-955-0410
lbevan@lynnbevan.com
www.lynnbevan.com

Toronto: Bhatia, Minipreet - *1
#405, 3601 Victoria Park Ave., Toronto, ON M1W 3Y3
Tel: 416-493-1727; Fax: 416-756-3663

Toronto: Bigelow Hendy LLP
789 Don Mills Rd., Toronto, ON M3C 1T5
Tel: 416-429-3110; Fax: 416-429-3057
bigelowhendy@bigelowhendy.com
www.bigelowhendy.com

Toronto: Peter Bird - *1
31 Prince Arthur Dr., Toronto, ON M5R 1B2
Tel: 416-929-9408; Fax: 416-960-5456
peterbird@on.aibn.com

Toronto: Birenbaum Gottlieb Professional Corporation - *2
Also Known As: B&G Law
Former Name: Birenbaum & Bernstein
#21, 951 Wilson Ave., Toronto, ON M3K 2A7
Tel: 416-633-3720; Fax: 416-633-4546
www.bgtorontolaw.com

Toronto: Birenbaum Steinberg Landau Savin & Colraine LLP - *11
#1000, 33 Bloor St. East, Toronto, ON M4W 3H1
Tel: 416-961-4100; Fax: 416-961-2531
info@bslsc.com
www.bslsc.com
www.linkedin.com/pub/bslsc-llp/69/987/586

Toronto: Birks, Langdon & Elliott - *2
#329, 4195 Dundas St. West, Toronto, ON M8X 1Y4
Tel: 416-239-3431; Fax: 416-239-8259

Toronto: Donald H. Bitter, Q.C. - *1
#607, 71 Charles St. East, Toronto, ON M4Y 2T3
Tel: 416-360-4357; Fax: 416-463-8259
notguilty@rogers.com

Toronto: Black, Sutherland LLP - *19
Former Name: Black, Sutherland & Crabbe
#3425, P.O. Box 34, 130 Adelaide St. West, Toronto, ON M5H 3P5
Tel: 416-361-1500; Fax: 416-361-1674
Toll-Free: 866-902-7557
info@blacksutherland.com
www.blacksutherland.com

Toronto: Edith M. Blake - *1
75 The Donway West, Toronto, ON M3C 2E9
Tel: 416-445-0310; Fax: 416-445-0316

Toronto: Jonathan A. Bliss - *1
370 Bloor St. East, Toronto, ON M4W 3M6
Tel: 416-927-9000; Fax: 416-927-9069
jonbliss@sympatico.ca

Toronto: Bloom Lanys Professional Corporation - *2
#200, 2171 Avenue Rd., Toronto, ON M5M 4B4
Tel: 416-486-9913; Fax: 416-485-6054
Toll-Free: 877-835-7658
barb@bloom-lanys.com; jessie@bloom-lanys.com

Toronto: Joseph L. Bloomenfeld - *1
#2110, 120 Adelaide St. West, Toronto, ON M5H 1T1
Tel: 416-363-7315; Fax: 416-363-7697

Toronto: Blouin, Dunn LLP - *19
#4805, P.O. Box 207, Stn. Commerce Court, 199 Bay St., Toronto, ON M5L 1E8
Tel: 416-365-7888; Fax: 416-365-7988
info@blouindunn.com
www.blouindunn.com

Toronto: Blumberg Segal LLP - *9
#1202, 390 Bay St., Toronto, ON M5H 2Y2
Tel: 416-361-1982; Fax: 416-363-8451
Toll-Free: 866-961-1982
business@blumbergs.ca
www.blumbergs.ca
twitter.com/BlumbergSegal,
www.linkedin.com/company/blumberg-segal-llp

Toronto: Bobila Walker Law LLP
#5600, First Canadian Place, 100 King St. West, Toronto, ON M5X 1C9
Tel: 416-847-1859; Fax: 416-644-8801
info@bobilawalkerlaw.com
www.cannabis-regulations.ca

Toronto: Carla L. Bocci - *1
#1917, 25 Adelaide St. East, Toronto, ON M5C 3A1
Tel: 416-365-2961; Fax: 416-365-1859

Toronto: Bodnaruk & Capone - *2
53 Yonge St., 3rd Fl., Toronto, ON M5E 1J3
Tel: 416-593-7000; Fax: 416-593-5359

Toronto: Bogart Robertson & Chu - *5
#303, 20 Adelaide St. East, Toronto, ON M5C 2T6
Tel: 416-601-1991; Fax: 416-601-0006
contact@brclaw.com
brclaw.com

Toronto: G.H. Bomza - *1
#2303, 180 Dundas St. West, Toronto, ON M5G 1Z8
Tel: 416-598-2244; Fax: 416-598-3830
rosehallmgmt@bellnet.ca

Toronto: Sharon G.H. Bond - *1
#1501, 5001 Yonge St., Toronto, ON M2N 6P6
Tel: 416-630-5600; Fax: 416-630-5906
sbond@rblawyers.ca

indicates number of lawyers

Toronto: Ira E. Book - *1
#200, 85 Scarsdale Rd., Toronto, ON M3B 2R2
Tel: 416-447-2665; *Fax:* 416-447-0066
ira@irabook.com

Toronto: Norman H.R. Borski, Q.C. - *1
34 Rivercres Rd., Toronto, ON M6S 4H3
Tel: 416-766-2441

Toronto: Y.R. Botiuk - *2
#212, 2323 Bloor St. West, Toronto, ON M6S 4W1
Tel: 416-763-4333; *Fax:* 416-763-0613

Toronto: Bougadis, Chang LLP - *4
#300, 555 Adelaide St. East, Toronto, ON M5C 1K6
Tel: 416-703-2402; *Fax:* 416-703-2406
office@bcbarristers.com
www.bcbarristers.com

Toronto: T. Sam Boutzouvis - *1
#603, 1/2 Parliament St., Toronto, ON M4X 1P9
Tel: 416-591-0111; *Fax:* 416-591-0778
samboutzouvis@yahoo.ca

Toronto: Mary E.E. Boyce - *1
69 Elm St., Toronto, ON M5G 1H2
Tel: 416-591-7588; *Fax:* 416-971-9092

Toronto: Boyle & Co. LLP - *2
#1900, 25 Adelaide St. East, Toronto, ON M5C 3A1
Tel: 416-867-8800; *Fax:* 416-867-8833
www.boyleco.ca

Toronto: Brannan Meiklejohn Barristers - *2
#200, Rosedale Sq., 1055 Yonge St., Toronto, ON M4W 2L2
Tel: 416-926-3797; *Fax:* 416-926-3712

Toronto: Brauti Thorning Zibarras LLP - *17
#1800, 151 Yonge St., Toronto, ON M5C 2W7
Tel: 416-362-4567; *Fax:* 416-362-8410
www.btlegal.ca

Toronto: Philip E. Brent - *1
#210, 4800 Dundas St. West, Toronto, ON M9A 1B1
Tel: 416-203-1449; *Fax:* 416-203-1772
philip@brentayt.com

Toronto: Bresver Grossman Chapman & Habas LLP
- *5
Former Name: Bresver, Grossman, Scheininger & Chapman
390 Bay St., Toronto, ON M5H 2Y2
Tel: 416-869-0366
www.bgchlaw.com

Toronto: Daniel J. Brodsky - *1
Barristers Chambers, 11 Prince Arthur Ave., Toronto, ON M5R 1B2
Tel: 416-964-2618; *Fax:* 416-964-8305
dbrodsky@daniel-brodsky.com

Toronto: Brown & Burnes - *15
#1400, 390 Bay St., Toronto, ON M5H 2Y2
Tel: 416-366-7927; *Fax:* 416-363-9602
info@brownburnes.com
www.brownburnes.com

Toronto: Brown, Peck & Lubelsky - *4
5287 Yonge St., Toronto, ON M2N 5R3
Tel: 416-223-8811; *Fax:* 416-223-8485

Toronto: Anthony G. Bryant - *2
#601, 1280 Finch Ave. West, Toronto, ON M3J 3K6
Tel: 416-927-7441; *Fax:* 416-488-9802
www.bryantcriminallaw.ca

Toronto: Buie Cohen LLP - *2
Former Name: McPhail Buie & Cohen
#205, 250 Merton St., Toronto, ON M4S 1B1
Tel: 416-869-3400; *Fax:* 416-703-6522
cmbuie@buiecohen.com
www.buiecohen.com

Toronto: Harry R. Burkman - *1
#5600, P.O. Box 129, 1 First Canadian Place, Toronto, ON M5X 1A4
Tel: 416-364-3831; *Fax:* 416-364-3832
info@burkman.com
www.burkman.com

Toronto: Burnett & Jacobson - *2
44 St. Clair Ave. West, Toronto, ON M4V 3C9
Tel: 416-922-8710; *Fax:* 416-964-5840

Toronto: Burstein, Unger - *2
Former Name: Paul Burstein & Associate
P.O. Box 180, 127 John St., Toronto, ON M5V 2E2
Tel: 416-204-1825; *Fax:* 416-204-1849
paul@127john.com

Toronto: Bernard Burton - *1
#301, 120 Carlton St., Toronto, ON M5A 4K2
Tel: 416-922-1263; *Fax:* 416-922-1963
bburton@carltonlaw.ca

Toronto: Bussin & Bussin - *3
#1410, 181 University Ave., Toronto, ON M5H 3M7
Tel: 416-364-4925; *Fax:* 416-868-1818
bruce@bussinlaw.com

Toronto: Paul Calarco - *1
#405, 700 Bay St., Toronto, ON M5G 1Z6
Tel: 416-598-1948; *Fax:* 416-596-7629

Toronto: CaleyWray - *14
#1600, 65 Queen St. West, Toronto, ON M5H 2M5
Tel: 416-366-3763; *Fax:* 416-366-3293
mail@caleywray.com
www.caleywray.com

Toronto: John Cannings, Barristers - *2
#400, 425 University Ave., Toronto, ON M5G 1T6
Tel: 416-591-0703; *Fax:* 416-591-0710

Toronto: Ruth Canton - *1
#302, 2489 Bloor St. West, Toronto, ON M6S 1R5
Tel: 416-769-5759; *Fax:* 416-769-3132

Toronto: Rochelle F. Cantor - *1
180 Spadina Rd., Toronto, ON M5R 2T8
Tel: 416-861-1625; *Fax:* 416-861-1466
rochelle.cantor@bellnet.ca

Toronto: Capp, Shupak - *5
#1703, 2 St. Clair Ave. West, Toronto, ON M4V 1L5
Tel: 416-944-2313; *Fax:* 416-323-0697
Toll-Free: 877-308-4878
info@cappshupak.com
www.marilynshupak.com

Toronto: Cappellacci DaRoza LLP - *3
#500, 462 Wellington St. West, Toronto, ON M5V 1E3
Tel: 416-955-9500; *Fax:* 416-955-9503
www.capplaw.ca

Toronto: Caramanna, Friedberg LLP - *6
#405, Lucliff Place, P.O. Box 144, 700 Bay St., Toronto, ON M5G 1Z6
Tel: 416-924-5969; *Fax:* 416-924-9973
info@cflaw.ca
www.cflaw.ca

Toronto: Michael W. Caroline - *2
#2, 374 Bering Ave., Toronto, ON M8Z 3A9
Tel: 416-203-2250; *Fax:* 416-203-2280
www.michaelcaroline.com

Toronto: John S.H. Carriere - *1
#600, 330 Bay St., Toronto, ON M5H 2S8
Tel: 416-363-5594; *Fax:* 416-363-8492
johncarriere@bellnet.ca

Toronto: C. Anthony Carroll - *1
#1807, 8 King St. East, Toronto, ON M5C 1B5
Tel: 416-361-0522; *Fax:* 416-361-0248
carrolltt@istar.ca
tonycarroll-lawyer.com

Toronto: Gary M. Cass - *1
Also Known As: Garry Cass
#305, 23 Lesmill Rd., Toronto, ON M3B 3P6
Tel: 416-767-2277; *Fax:* 416-491-0273
www.garrycass.com

Toronto: Ceresney, Weisberg Associates - *2
#202, 4651 Sheppard Ave. East, Toronto, ON M1S 3V4
Tel: 416-291-7701; *Fax:* 416-291-1766

Toronto: Chaitons LLP - *20
Former Name: Chaiton & Chaiton
5000 Yonge St., 10th Fl., Toronto, ON M2N 7E9
Tel: 416-222-8888; *Fax:* 416-222-8402
info@chaitons.com
www.chaiton.com
www.linkedin.com/company/chaitons-llp

Toronto: Chand Snider LLP - *2
#901, 357 Bay St., Toronto, ON M5H 2T7
Tel: 416-639-3033
www.chandsnider.com

Toronto: Evan Chang - *1
#203, 1315 Lawrence Ave. East, Toronto, ON M3A 3R3
Tel: 416-449-1214
ww.evanchang.ca
www.evanchang.ca

Toronto: Peter P. Chang - *3
#607, 220 Duncan Mill Rd., Toronto, ON M3B 3J5
Tel: 416-497-1575; *Fax:* 416-497-2261
peterchang@rogers.com

Toronto: Chapnick & Associates - *4
228 Carlton St., Toronto, ON M5A 2L1
Tel: 416-968-2160; *Fax:* 416-975-9338
www.chapnick.ca
twitter.com/chapnicklaw

Toronto: Chappell Partners LLP - *7
Former Name: Chappell, Bushell, Stewart LLP
#3310, 20 Queen St. West, Toronto, ON M5H 3R3
Tel: 416-351-0005; *Fax:* 416-351-0002
info@chappellpartners.ca
www.chappellpartners.ca
www.facebook.com/cppulse, twitter.com/cp_llp,
www.linkedin.com/company/chappell-partners-llp

Toronto: Chiarotto Law PC - *1
#5700, First Canadian Place, 100 King St. West, Toronto, ON M5X 1C7
Tel: 416-915-1265; *Fax:* 416-915-1266
www.chiarottolaw.com

Toronto: Ronald W. Chisholm, Q.C. - *1
85 Lonsdale Rd., Toronto, ON M4V 1W4
Tel: 416-586-0777; *Fax:* 416-586-0267

Toronto: Chitiz Pathak LLP - *14
#1600, 320 Bay St. Ave., Toronto, ON M5H 4A6
Tel: 416-368-6200; *Fax:* 416-368-0300
info@chitizpathak.com
www.chitizpathak.com

Toronto: Christopher E. Chop - *1
#2000, 1 Queen St. East, Toronto, ON M5C 2W5
Tel: 416-860-8015; *Fax:* 416-601-0206
choplaw@gmail.com

Toronto: John Christie - *4
750 Scarlett Rd., Toronto, ON M9P 2V1
Tel: 416-249-8300; *Fax:* 416-249-1480
www.christielaw.ca

Toronto: Andrea E.K. Chun - *1
#700, One Corporate Plaza, 2075 Kennedy Rd., Toronto, ON M1T 3V3
Tel: 416-754-3060; *Fax:* 416-754-3321
andreachun@bellnet.ca

Toronto: Cipollone & Cipollone Barristers - *1
#2100, 130 Adelaide St. West, Toronto, ON M5H 3P5
Tel: 416-368-5366; *Fax:* 416-368-5361

Toronto: Dino J. Cirone - *1
#2, 2084 Danforth Ave., Toronto, ON M4C 1J9
Tel: 416-423-8515; *Fax:* 416-423-4971

Toronto: S.G. Clapp - *1
802 Eglinton Ave. East, Toronto, ON M4G 2L1
Tel: 416-484-4840; *Fax:* 416-484-0821
stanleyclapp@on.aibn.com

Toronto: Clark Farb Fiksel LLP - *6
188 Avenue Rd., Toronto, ON M5J 2J1
Tel: 416-599-7761 *Toll-Free:* 888-664-3779
www.cfflaw.com

Toronto: Deta J. Clark - *1
#402, 5075 Yonge St., Toronto, ON M2N 6C6
Tel: 416-733-3135; *Fax:* 416-733-1081

Toronto: Clarke, Freeman, Miller & Ryan - *1
1863 Danforth Ave., Toronto, ON M4C 1J3
Tel: 416-698-9323; *Fax:* 416-698-9110

Toronto: L. Peter Clyne - *1
#207, Xerox Tower, 5650 Yonge St., Toronto, ON M2M 4G3
Tel: 416-922-0864; *Fax:* 416-922-6856

Toronto: Robert G. Coates - *1
#307, 120 Carlton St., Toronto, ON M5A 4K2
Tel: 416-925-6490; *Fax:* 416-925-4492

* indicates number of lawyers

Toronto: Cognition LLP - *31
#503, 263 Adelaide St. West, Toronto, ON M5H 1Y2
Tel: 416-348-0313; Fax: 416-479-0244
info@cognitionllp.com
www.cognitionllp.com
www.facebook.com/cognitionllp, twitter.com/cognitionllp,
www.linkedin.com/company/cognition-llp

Toronto: Cohen & Associate - *1
#800, Yong-Norton Centre, 5255 Yonge St., Toronto, ON M2N 6P4
Tel: 416-323-0907; Fax: 416-324-8053
cohen@bellnet.ca

Toronto: David Cohn - *1
#506, 330 University Ave., Toronto, ON M5G 1R7
Tel: 416-777-1100; Fax: 416-204-1849
david@davidcohn.ca
www.davidcohn.ca

Toronto: John Collins - *1
#400, 357 Bay St., Toronto, ON M5H 2R7
Tel: 416-364-9006; Fax: 416-862-7911
john.collins@on.aibn.com

Toronto: Conway Davis Gryski - *6
#601, 130 Adelaide St. West, Toronto, ON M5H 3P5
Tel: 416-214-4554; Fax: 416-214-9915
Toll-Free: 877-559-4554
contactus@cdglaw.net
www.conwaydavisgryski.com

Toronto: Conway Kleinman Kornhauser LLP - *3
Former Name: Conway Kornhauser & Gotlieb
#1102, 390 Bay St., Toronto, ON M5H 2Y2
Tel: 416-368-5400; Fax: 416-368-5454

Toronto: Allen M. Cooper - *1
#101, 15A Elm St., Toronto, ON M5G 1H1
Tel: 416-977-8070; Fax: 416-977-8151

Toronto: Kirk J. Cooper - *1
207 Queen St. East, Toronto, ON M5A 1S2
Tel: 416-923-4277; Fax: 416-923-4144
kirkcooperlaw@rogers.com
www.kirkcooperlaw.com

Toronto: Cooper, Kleinman - *2
3 Rowanwood Ave., Toronto, ON M4W 1Y5
Tel: 416-867-1400; Fax: 416-867-1873
gwcooper@cooperkleinman.ca

Toronto: Morris Cooper - *1
99 Yorkville Ave., Toronto, ON M5R 3K5
Tel: 416-961-2626; Fax: 416-961-4000
cooper@cooperlaw.ca

Toronto: Robert A. Cooper - *1
#208, 4211 Yonge St., Toronto, ON M2P 2A9
Tel: 416-222-8115; Fax: 416-222-8505

Toronto: Cooper, Sandler, Shime & Bergman LLP - *5
#1900, 439 University Ave., Toronto, ON M5G 1Y8
Tel: 416-585-9191; Fax: 416-408-2372
www.criminal-lawyers.ca

Toronto: Copeland Duncan - *1
31 Prince Arthur Ave., Toronto, ON M5R 1B2
Tel: 416-964-8126; Fax: 416-960-5456
paulcope9@yahoo.com

Toronto: Jack Copelovici - *1
Former Name: Copelovici & Hanuk
#204, 1220 Sheppard Ave. East, Toronto, ON M2K 2S5
Tel: 416-494-0910; Fax: 416-494-5480
jack@copel-law.com

Toronto: Barry S. Corbin - *1
#2000, 393 University Ave., Toronto, ON M5G 1E6
Tel: 416-593-4200; Fax: 416-593-1352
barry.corbin@corbinestateslaw.com
www.corbinestateslaw.com

Toronto: Cornerstone Group
#1800, The Exchange Tower, P.O. Box 427, 130 King St. West, Toronto, ON M5X 1J8
Tel: 416-862-8000; Fax: 416-862-8001
Toll-Free: 888-268-6735
md@cornerstonegroup.com
www.cornerstonegroup.com

Toronto: Costa Law Firm - *4
Former Name: David Costa & Associate
1015 Bloor St. West, Toronto, ON M6H 1M1
Tel: 416-535-6329; Fax: 416-535-4735
www.costalawfirm.ca
twitter.com/costalawfirm

Toronto: Fernando D. Costa - *1
#200, 1112 Dundas St. West, Toronto, ON M6J 1X2
Tel: 416-534-6357; Fax: 416-534-6219
fd.costa@bellnet.ca

Toronto: Coutts Crane - *6
#700, 480 University Ave., Toronto, ON M5G 1V2
Tel: 416-977-0956; Fax: 416-977-5331
info@couttscrane.com
www.couttscrane.com
www.facebook.com/CouttsCrane

Toronto: Ronald Cowitz - *1
#308, 344 Bloor St. West, Toronto, ON M5S 3A7
Tel: 416-944-9594

Toronto: Christopher G. Cox - *1
#209, 1711 McCowan Rd., Toronto, ON M1S 2Y3
Tel: 416-447-4274; Fax: 416-823-3215
cgcoxlaw@hotmail.com

Toronto: Cozen O'Connor - *7
Former Name: Poss & Halfnight
#2730, Bay Adelaide Centre - East Tower, 22 Adelaide St. West, Toronto, ON M5H 4E3
Tel: 416-361-3200; Fax: 416-361-1405
Toll-Free: 888-727-9948
www.cozen.com
www.facebook.com/cozenoconnor, twitter.com/cozen_oconnor,
www.linkedin.com/company/cozen-o%27connor

Toronto: Crawley MacKewn Brush LLP - *12
#800, 179 John St., Toronto, ON M5T 1X4
Tel: 416-217-0110; Fax: 416-217-0220
reception@cmblaw.ca
www.cmblaw.ca

Toronto: Cremer Barristers - *2
Former Name: Cowan & Cremer
#216, 214 King St. West, Toronto, ON M5H 3S6
Tel: 416-322-3671; Fax: 416-971-5520
cremer@cremerbarristers.com
www.cremerbarristers.com

Toronto: F.H. Cremer - *1
#201, 1593 Wilson Ave., Toronto, ON M3L 1A5
Tel: 416-244-5575; Fax: 416-247-3844

Toronto: Crewe & Marks - *2
74 Riverdale Ave., Toronto, ON M4K 1C3
Tel: 416-967-9933; Fax: 416-967-9933
nsc@riv.com

Toronto: Frank D. Crewe - *2
#500, 70 Bond St., Toronto, ON M5B 1X3
Tel: 416-362-2202; Fax: 416-363-9135
fcrewe@bondlaw.net

Toronto: Howard Crosner - *1
309 Cherry St., Toronto, ON M5A 3L3
Tel: 416-947-0455; Fax: 416-947-0553
crosner77@gmail.com
www.crosner.com

Toronto: Leroy A. Crosse - *1
#203, 705 Lawrence Ave. West, Toronto, ON M6A 1B4
Tel: 416-785-8338; Fax: 416-785-9369

Toronto: Crum-Ewing & Poliacik - *3
#412, 245 Fairview Mall Dr., Toronto, ON M2J 4T1
Tel: 416-733-9292; Fax: 416-733-9654
poliacik@ceplaw.ca

Toronto: Cummings Cooper Schusheim & Berliner LLP - *7
#408, 4110 Yonge St., Toronto, ON M2P 2B5
Tel: 416-512-9500; Fax: 416-512-9501
info@ccsb-law.com
www.ccsb-law.com

Toronto: Gino A.J. Cundari - *1
1179 St. Clair Ave. West, Toronto, ON M6E 1B5
Tel: 416-654-9000; Fax: 416-654-6688

Toronto: Peter Cusimano, Barrister & Solicitor - *1
Former Name: Cusimano & Cusimano
#116, 185 Bridgeland Ave., Toronto, ON M6A 1Y7
Tel: 416-222-0588; Fax: 416-222-0239
peter@cusimano.com
www.cusimano.com/lawyer/
twitter.com/petercusimano

Toronto: J. Jerome Cusmariu - *1
1310 Dundas St. West, Toronto, ON M6J 1Y1
Tel: 416-533-1173; Fax: 416-533-0761
jerry@cusmariulaw.com

Toronto: Andrew M. Czernik - *1
#605, 920 Yonge St., Toronto, ON M4W 3C7
Tel: 416-920-4994; Fax: 416-920-5885
aczernik@on.aibn.com

Toronto: Czuma, Ritter - *2
410 - 120 Carlton St., Toronto, ON M5A 4K2
Tel: 416-599-5799; Fax: 416-599-9981
czumamichael@gmail.com
www.michaelczuma.com

Toronto: Anthony D'Avella - *1
#306, 4920 Dundas St. West, Toronto, ON M9A 1B7
Tel: 416-234-2198; Fax: 416-234-5142
anton.davella@on.aibn.com

Toronto: Dale & Lessmann LLP - *26
#2100, 181 University Ave., Toronto, ON M5H 3M7
Tel: 416-863-1010; Fax: 416-863-1009
info@dalelessmann.com
www.dalelessmann.com

Toronto: Damien R. Frost & Associates - *4
#103, 30 St. Clair Ave. West, Toronto, ON M4V 3A1
Tel: 647-800-6744; Fax: 866-235-6191
Toll-Free: 888-853-6010
www.damienfrost.ca
www.linkedin.com/company/2633197

Toronto: Danson Recht LLP - *5
Former Name: Danson, Recht & Freedman
#2000, 700 Bay St., Toronto, ON M5G 1Z6
Tel: 416-929-2200; Fax: 416-929-2192
info@drlitigators.com
drlitigators.com

Toronto: Danson, Zucker & Connelly - *3
#500, 70 Bond St., Toronto, ON M5B 1X3
Tel: 416-863-9955; Fax: 416-863-4896

Toronto: Daoust Vukovich LLP - *13
#3000, 20 Queen St. West, Toronto, ON M5H 3R3
Tel: 416-597-6888; Fax: 416-597-8897
www.dv-law.com

Toronto: James Daris - *1
#101, 8 Irwin Ave., Toronto, ON M4Y 1K9
Tel: 416-461-0395; Fax: 416-465-6042

Toronto: Darren S. Sederoff & Associates PC
#805, Hullmark Corporate Center, 4789 Yonge St., Toronto, ON M2N 0G3
Tel: 647-492-9305
darrensederoff.com

Toronto: David Midanik & Associates - *1
#1100, 55 University Ave., Toronto, ON M5J 2H7
Tel: 416-967-1603; Fax: 416-967-1604
www.midaniklawoffice.com

Toronto: Davies Howe Partners LLP - *20
99 Spadina Ave., 5th Fl., Toronto, ON M5V 3P8
Tel: 416-977-7088; Fax: 416-977-8931
www.davieshowe.com

Toronto: Davies McLean Zweig Associates - *3
1035 McNicoll Ave., Toronto, ON M1W 3W6
Tel: 416-756-7500; Fax: 416-512-1212

Toronto: Davies Spina Falquez LLP - *3
Former Name: Crane Davies Spina LLP
80 Kincort St., 2nd Fl., Toronto, ON M6M 5G1
Tel: 416-787-6529
info@kincortlaw.com
www.kincortlaw.com

Toronto: Davis & Turk - *2
#404, 3910 Bathurst St., Toronto, ON M3H 5Z3
Tel: 416-630-5541; Fax: 416-630-7724

indicates number of lawyers

Toronto: De Faria & De Faria - *2
872 Dundas St. West, Toronto, ON M6J 1V7
Tel: 416-603-4440; *Fax:* 416-603-4441

Toronto: J.N. De Sommer - *1
112 Adelaide St. East, Toronto, ON M5C 1K9
Tel: 416-341-7077; *Fax:* 416-368-2918
jndesommer@rbs.rogers.com

Toronto: Tilaka de Zoysa - *1
#207, 2131 Lawrence Ave. East, Toronto, ON M1R 5G4
Tel: 416-752-2253; *Fax:* 416-752-6356

Toronto: DSFM - *7
#2900, P.O. Box 2384, 2300 Yonge St., Toronto, ON M4P 1E4
Tel: 416-489-5677; *Fax:* 416-489-7794
info@condolaw.to
www.condolaw.to

Toronto: Deeth Williams Wall LLP - *16
#400, 150 York St., Toronto, ON M5H 3S5
Tel: 416-941-9440; *Fax:* 416-941-9443
info@dww.com
www.dww.com
www.facebook.com/deethwilliamswall,
www.linkedin.com/companies/deeth-williams-wall-llp

Toronto: DelZotto, Zorzi LLP - *14
4810 Dufferin St., #D, Toronto, ON M3H 5S8
Tel: 416-665-5555; *Fax:* 416-665-9653
info@dzlaw.com
www.dzlaw.com

Toronto: Richard G.J. Desrocher - *1
20 Leamington Ave., Toronto, ON M8Z 2W4
Tel: 416-236-5679; *Fax:* 416-236-7370

Toronto: Deverett Law Offices
163 Willowdale Ave., Toronto, ON M2N 4Y7
Tel: 416-222-6789; *Fax:* 416-222-7605
info@deverettlaw.com
www.deverettlaw.com

Toronto: Jane H. Devlin - *1
#502, 121 Richmond St. West, Toronto, ON M5H 2K1
Tel: 416-366-3091; *Fax:* 416-366-0879
arbserv@istar.ca

Toronto: Devry Smith Frank LLP - Toronto - *51
#100, 95 Barber Greene Rd., Toronto, ON M3C 3E9
Tel: 416-449-1400; *Fax:* 416-449-7071
Toll-Free: 866-474-1700
info@devrylaw.ca
www.devrylaw.ca
www.facebook.com/devrysmithfrank,
twitter.com/devrysmithfrank,
www.linkedin.com/companies/346809

Toronto: Diamond & Diamond - *8
255 Consumers Rd., 5th Fl., Toronto, ON M2J 1R4
Tel: 416-850-7246; *Fax:* 416-256-0100
Toll-Free: 800-567-4878
jeremy@diamondlaw.ca
www.diamondlaw.ca
www.facebook.com/diamondanddiamondinjurylaw,
twitter.com/diamondlawtor

Toronto: Michael R. Diamond - *1
#706, 55 Eglinton Ave. East, Toronto, ON M4P 1G8
Tel: 416-482-2666; *Fax:* 416-482-4165
syndicator@sympatico.ca

Toronto: Dickinson Wright (Canada) - Toronto - *33
Former Name: Aylesworth LLP
#2200, Commerce Court West, 199 Bay St., Toronto, ON M5L 1G4
Tel: 416-777-0101; *Fax:* 416-865-1398
www.dickinson-wright.com
www.facebook.com/Dickinson-Wright-374489695906146,
twitter.com/dickinsonwright,
www.linkedin.com/company/dickinson-wright-pllc

Toronto: Dickson Appell LLP - *9
Former Name: Dickson MacGregor Appell LLP;
Dickson, MacGregor, Appell & Burton
#306, 10 Alcorn Ave., Toronto, ON M4V 3A9
Tel: 416-927-0891; *Fax:* 416-927-0385
www.dicksonlawyers.com

Toronto: Dimock Stratton LLP - *17
P.O. Box 102, 20 Queen St. West, 32nd Fl., Toronto, ON M5H 3R3
Tel: 416-971-7202; *Fax:* 416-971-6638
firm@dimock.com
www.dimock.com

Toronto: Dion, Durrell & Associates - *2
#2900, 250 Yonge St., Toronto, ON M5B 2L7
Tel: 416-408-2626; *Fax:* 416-408-3721
information@dion-durrell.com
www.dion-durrell.com

Toronto: Chris Dockrill - *1
#2200, DBRS Tower, 181 University Ave., Toronto, ON M5H 3M7
Tel: 416-366-1881; *Fax:* 416-366-0608
chris@chris-dockrill.com
www.chris-dockrill.com

Toronto: Brian P. Donnelly - *1
#2000, 393 University Ave., Toronto, ON M5G 1E6
Tel: 416-597-2191; *Fax:* 416-597-9808

Toronto: J. Brian Donnelly - *1
#201, 1165A St. Clair Ave. West, Toronto, ON M6E 1B2
Tel: 416-653-0311; *Fax:* 416-653-6653
jbd@jbdonnelly.com

Toronto: Dorsey & Whitney LLP - Toronto - *6
#4310, Brookfield Place, 161 Bay St., Toronto, ON M5J 2S1
Tel: 416-367-7370; *Fax:* 416-367-7371
www.dorsey.com
www.facebook.com/DorseyWhitneyLLP,
twitter.com/DorseyWhitney,
www.linkedin.com/company/dorsey-&-whitney-llp

Toronto: Downtown Legal Services - *5
Fasken Martineau Building, 655 Spadina Ave., Toronto, ON M5S 2H9
Tel: 416-934-4535; *Fax:* 416-934-4536
law.dls@utoronto.ca
dls.sa.utoronto.ca

Toronto: William C. Draimin - *1
#101, 45 St. Clair Ave. West, Toronto, ON M4V 1K9
Tel: 416-920-4605; *Fax:* 416-960-0698
wdraimin@draiminlaw.com

Toronto: Dranoff & Huddart - *2
#314, 1033 Bay St., Toronto, ON M5S 3A5
Tel: 416-925-4500; *Fax:* 416-925-5197
info@dranoffhuddart.com
www.dranoffhuddart.com

Toronto: J. Blair Drummie - *1
603 1/2 Parliament St., Toronto, ON M4X 1P9
Tel: 416-921-0915
www.criminallawyer.to
www.facebook.com/criminatorontollawyer,
www.linkedin.com/in/j-blair-drummie-01145615

Toronto: Du Markowitz LLP - *2
#2000, Madison Centre, 4950 Yonge St., Toronto, ON M2N 6K1
Tel: 416-590-1900; *Fax:* 416-590-1600
info@dumarkowitz.com
www.dumarkowitz.com

Toronto: Duncan Morin LLP - *6
#200, 60 Atlantic Ave., Toronto, ON M6K 1X9
Tel: 416-593-2513; *Fax:* 416-593-2514
www.duncanmorin.com

Toronto: Thomas S. Dungey - *1
46 Fairview Blvd., Toronto, ON M4K 1L9
Tel: 416-469-3088; *Fax:* 416-469-6739
tsdungey@rogers.com

Toronto: Lloyd T. Duong - *1
2377 Dundas St. West, Toronto, ON M6P 1W7
Tel: 416-535-3463; *Fax:* 416-536-8279

Toronto: Norman L. Durbin - *1
Wycliffe-Jane Plaza, 2530 Jane St., Toronto, ON M3L 1S1
Tel: 416-743-2345; *Fax:* 416-743-0645

Toronto: Dutton Brock LLP - *43
Former Name: Dutton, Brock, MacIntyre & Collier
#1700, 438 University Ave., Toronto, ON M5G 2L9
Tel: 416-593-4411; *Fax:* 416-593-5922
info@duttonbrock.com
www.duttonbrock.com

Toronto: Diana C. Dzwiekowski - *1
260 Willard Ave., Toronto, ON M6S 3R2
Tel: 416-762-7251; *Fax:* 416-762-7252

Toronto: East Toronto Community Legal Services - *4
1320 Gerrard St. East, Toronto, ON M4L 3X1
Tel: 416-461-8102; *Fax:* 416-461-7497
www.etcls.ca

Toronto: Eccleston LLP - *3
#4020, Toronto-Dominion Bank Tower, P.O. Box 230, 66 Wellington St. West, Toronto, ON M5K 1J3
Tel: 416-504-2722; *Fax:* 416-504-2686
info@ecclestonllp.com
www.ecclestonllp.com

Toronto: Ecclestone, Hamer, Poisson, Neuwald & Freeman - *5
#900, The Sterling Tower, 372 Bay St., Toronto, ON M5C 1J3
Tel: 416-365-7135; *Fax:* 416-365-2189
www.ehpnf.com

Toronto: Ryan Edmonds Workplace Counsel - *1
#1600, 401 Bay St., Toronto, ON M5H 2Y4
Tel: 647-361-8228; *Fax:* 647-361-8229
torontoworkplacecounsel.com
twitter.com/ryanedmondslaw

Toronto: Elliott Law Firm - *1
#1901, 5000 Yonge St., Toronto, ON M2N 7E9
Tel: 416-628-5598; *Fax:* 416-628-5597
elliottlawfirm@gmail.com
www.elliottlawfirm.ca

Toronto: Ellyn Law LLP - *5
#3000, 20 Queen St. West, Toronto, ON M5H 3R3
Tel: 416-365-3700; *Fax:* 416-368-2982
iellyn@ellynlaw.com
www.ellynlaw.com

Toronto: Mitch Engel - *1
#502, 1235 Bay St., Toronto, ON M5R 3K4
Tel: 416-944-8882; *Fax:* 416-925-4571
Toll-Free: 866-761-6904

Toronto: Epstein Cole LLP - *25
#2200, 393 University Ave., Toronto, ON M5G 1E6
Tel: 416-862-9888; *Fax:* 416-862-2142
www.epsteincole.com

Toronto: Norman Epstein - *1
#202, 745 Mount Pleasant Rd., Toronto, ON M4S 2N4
Tel: 416-225-5577; *Fax:* 416-483-5541

Toronto: Eric Lewis & Associates
164 Queen St. East, Toronto, ON M5A 1T9
Tel: 416-367-1918; *Fax:* 416-362-1918
lewis_smyth@hotmail.com

Toronto: EY Law LLP - Toronto - *44
Former Name: Egan LLP; Couzin Taylor LLP; Donahue LLP
#2100, EY Tower, 222 Bay St., Toronto, ON M5K 1H6
Tel: 416-943-2400; *Fax:* 416-943-2735
www.eylaw.ca

Toronto: Charles A. Eyton-Jones - *3
1238 Kingston Rd., Toronto, ON M1N 1P3
Tel: 416-691-4529; *Fax:* 416-691-2563
info@eyton-jones.ca
www.eyton-jones.ca

Toronto: Fair & Siegel
#1002, 250 Heath St. West, Toronto, ON M5P 3L4
Tel: 416-948-1652; *Fax:* 416-483-9228
msiegel@rogers.com

Toronto: Falconer Charney - *7
8 Prince Arthur Ave., Toronto, ON M5R 1A9
Tel: 416-964-3408; *Fax:* 416-929-8179
falconercharney@fcbarristers.com
www.fcbarristers.com

Toronto: Federico Barristers - Toronto - *2
#2001, 400 University Ave., Toronto, ON M5G 1S5
www.federicobarristers.com

Toronto: Frederick S. Fedorsen - *2
551 Gerrard St. East, Toronto, ON M4M 1X7
Tel: 416-463-6666; *Fax:* 416-463-8259
fred@fedorsennorth.com

Toronto: Jodi L. Feldman - *1
#205, 250 Merton St., Toronto, ON M4S 1B1
Tel: 416-922-3233
jfeldman@jfeldmanlaw.com

* indicates number of lawyers

Toronto: Jane L. Ferguson - *1
41 Rosedale Rd., Toronto, ON M4W 2P5
Tel: 416-920-7533; *Fax*: 416-923-5576
jlferg@bellnet.ca

Toronto: Fernandes Hearn LLP - *11
Also Known As: Fernandes, Hearn, Theall
#700, 155 University Ave., Toronto, ON M5H 3B7
Tel: 416-203-9500; *Fax*: 416-203-9444
info@fernandeshearn.com
www.fernandeshearn.com
twitter.com/fernandeshearn,
www.linkedin.com/company/fernandes-hearn-llp

Toronto: Filion Wakely Thorup Angeletti LLP -
Toronto - *42
#2500, P.O. Box 44, 333 Bay St., Toronto, ON M5H 2R2
Tel: 416-408-3221; *Fax*: 416-408-4814
toronto@filion.on.ca
www.filion.on.ca

Toronto: Filmlegals Entertainment Law Service - *1
7 Langley Ave., Toronto, ON M4K 1B4
Tel: 416-466-1487; *Fax*: 416-466-3094
mkrys@filmlegals.com
www.filmlegals.com

Toronto: Andrew Fine - *1
#306, 1000 Finch Ave. West, Toronto, ON M3J 2V5
Tel: 416-785-9499

Toronto: Fireman Steinmetz - *11
Former Name: Fireman Wolfe LLP
#415, P.O. Box 19, 55 St. Clair Ave. West, Toronto, ON M4V
2Y7
Tel: 416-967-9100; *Fax*: 416-967-1200
info@firemanlawyers.com
www.firemanlawyers.com

Toronto: Fisch & Antonette - *2
Former Name: S.J. Antonette
419 College St., 2nd Fl., Toronto, ON M5T 1T1
Tel: 416-920-6312; *Fax*: 416-920-1780
fa@torontorealestatelawyer.co
torontorealestatelawyer.co

Toronto: Steven M. Fishbayn - *1
#318, 100 Richmond St. West, Toronto, ON M5H 3K6
Tel: 416-361-9555; *Fax*: 416-862-7602
steven.fishbayn@sympatico.ca

Toronto: Barry B. Fisher - *1
#2000, Law Chambers, 393 University Ave., Toronto, ON
M5G 1E6
Tel: 416-585-2330; *Fax*: 416-585-2105
barryfisher@rogers.com
barryfisher.ca

Toronto: Flancman & Frisch - *2
1286 Kennedy Rd., Toronto, ON M1P 2L5
Tel: 416-752-2221; *Fax*: 416-752-8434
Toll-Free: 877-468-1120
miskflan@hotmail.com & iifrisch@hotmail.com

Toronto: Fleischer & Kochberg - *1
#201, 1000 Finch Ave. West, Toronto, ON M3J 2V5
Tel: 416-223-8102; *Fax*: 416-223-9502
www.fklawtorontolawyers.ca

Toronto: Fleming, Breen - *2
370 Bloor St. East, Toronto, ON M4W 3M6
Tel: 416-927-9000; *Fax*: 416-927-9069

Toronto: Fleming, White & Burgess - *2
#1002, 60 St. Clair Ave. East, Toronto, ON M4T 1N5
Tel: 416-961-2868; *Fax*: 416-961-2964
flemingwhite@bellnet.ca

Toronto: Fleury, Comery LLP - *5
#104, 215 Morrish Rd., Toronto, ON M1C 1E9
Tel: 416-282-5754; *Fax*: 416-282-9906
www.fleurcom.on.ca

Toronto: Ronald Flom - *2
#712, 2345 Yonge St., Toronto, ON M4P 2E5
Tel: 416-482-2777; *Fax*: 416-482-2599

Toronto: Forget Smith Morel - Toronto - *15
Former Name: Forget & Matthews LLP
#2802, P.O. Box 82, 401 Bay St., Toronto, ON M5H 2Y4
Tel: 416-368-4434; *Fax*: 416-368-7865
toronto@forgetsmith.com
www.forgetsmith.com

Toronto: Fournie Mickleborough LLP - *4
Former Name: Rogers, Campbell, Mickleborough
#701, 90 Adelaide St. West, Toronto, ON M5H 3V9
Tel: 416-366-3999; *Fax*: 416-366-2860
www.companylawyers.com

Toronto: Kevin Fox, Barrister & Solicitor - *1
Former Name: Fox Rovos
174 Davenport Rd., Toronto, ON M5R 1J2
Tel: 416-323-3252; *Fax*: 416-929-6885
kfox@davenportlaw.ca
www.kevinfoxlaw.ca
www.linkedin.com/pub/kevinfoxlaw

Toronto: Walter Fox - *3
#312, 100 Richmond St. West, Toronto, ON M5H 3K6
Tel: 416-363-9238; *Fax*: 416-363-9230
foxoffice@justlaw.ca

Toronto: Fraser Simms Reid & Spyrolpoulos LLP -
*1
#4, 2011 Lawrence Ave. West, Toronto, ON M9N 3V3
Tel: 416-241-0111; *Fax*: 416-241-1911
vassili.fsrs@bellnet.ca
fsrslaw.ca

Toronto: Harvey Freedman - *3
#100, 79 Shuter St., Toronto, ON M5B 1B3
Tel: 416-363-1737; *Fax*: 416-861-9919
hfreedman@freedmans.ca

Toronto: Joel P. Freedman - *1
#200, 3200 Dufferin St., Toronto, ON M6A 2T3
Tel: 416-248-6231; *Fax*: 416-241-0080
www.freedmanlaw.ca

Toronto: Norman J. Freedman, Q.C.
#2150, 121 King St. West, Toronto, ON M5H 3T9
Tel: 416-815-7767; *Fax*: 416-815-7722
elaine.freedman@sympatico.ca

Toronto: Randall R. Friedland - *1
#1301, 2200 Yonge St., Toronto, ON M4S 2C6
Tel: 416-932-4969; *Fax*: 416-932-0541
friedland@jodlaw.ca

Toronto: Fryer Levitt - *1
#2, 421 Eglinton Ave. West, Toronto, ON M5N 1A4
Tel: 416-323-1377; *Fax*: 416-323-9355
jelevitt@fryerlevitt.com
www.fryerlevitt.com
www.facebook.com/fryerlevittlaw, twitter.com/jelevitt,
www.linkedin.com/pub/joel-levitt/1b/845/247

Toronto: Harry Frymer - *1
#320, 100 Richmond St. West, Toronto, ON M5H 3K6
Tel: 416-869-1075; *Fax*: 416-869-1840

Toronto: Laurie A. Galway - *1
712 Logan Ave., Toronto, ON M4K 3C6
Tel: 416-413-9466; *Fax*: 416-778-8364
laurie@lauriegalway.com

Toronto: Gardiner Miller Arnold LLP - *7
#1202, 390 Bay St., Toronto, ON M5H 2Y2
Tel: 416-363-2614; *Fax*: 416-363-8451
gmainfo@gmalaw.ca
www.gmalaw.ca
www.facebook.com/gmalaw, twitter.com/gmalaw,
www.linkedin.com/company/gardiner-miller-arnold-llp

Toronto: Gardiner Roberts LLP - *67
#3600, Bay Adelaide Centre, East Tower, 22 Adelaide St.
West, Toronto, ON M5H 4E3
Tel: 416-865-6600; *Fax*: 416-865-6636
contactGR@grllp.com
www.grllp.com

Toronto: Garfin Zeidenberg LLP - *13
#800, Yonge Norton Centre, 5255 Yonge St., Toronto, ON
M2N 6P4
Tel: 416-512-8000; *Fax*: 416-512-9992
Toll-Free: 877-529-9910
gzinfo@gzlegal.com
www.gzlegal.com

Toronto: Susan W. Garfin - *1
#2000, 393 University Ave., Toronto, ON M5G 1E6
Tel: 416-599-9933; *Fax*: 416-599-5497
garfin@rogers.com

Toronto: Garfinkle Biderman LLP Barristers &
Solicitors - *19
#801, 1 Adelaide St. East, Toronto, ON M5C 2V9
Tel: 416-869-1234; *Fax*: 416-869-0547
www.garfinkle.com

Toronto: Gasee, Cohen & Youngman - *6
#200, 65 Queen St. West, Toronto, ON M5H 2M5
Tel: 416-363-3351; *Fax*: 416-363-0252
www.gcylaw.com
www.facebook.com/GCYLaw

Toronto: Leon Gavendo - *1
#2000, Law Chambers, University Centre, 393 University
Ave., Toronto, ON M5G 1E6
Tel: 416-585-3109; *Fax*: 416-585-9668
lgavendo@on.aibn.com

Toronto: Geller & Minster - *2
2 Keewatin Ave., Toronto, ON M4P 1Z8
Tel: 416-480-2200; *Fax*: 416-480-2693
inquiry@gellerandminster.ca
gellerandminster.ca

Toronto: Genest Murray LLP - *7
#1300, P.O. Box 45, 200 King St. West, Toronto, ON M5H 3T4
Tel: 416-368-8600; *Fax*: 416-360-2625
www.genestmurray.ca

Toronto: Basil L. Georgieff - *1
3543A St. Clair Ave. East, Toronto, ON M1K 1L6
Tel: 416-464-6888; *Fax*: 416-267-1452
basgeo@msn.com

Toronto: Lorne Gershuny - *1
1577 Bloor St. West, Toronto, ON M6P 1A6
Tel: 416-539-0989; *Fax*: 416-536-3618
lgershuny@hotmail.com

Toronto: Gertler Law Office - *1
Former Name: Gertler & Associates
#4, 906 Sheppard Ave. West, Toronto, ON M3H 2T5
Tel: 416-231-9188; *Fax*: 416-231-9492
robert@gertler.ca
www.gertlerlawoffice.com
www.facebook.com/gertlerlawoffice, twitter.com/gertlerlaw,
www.linkedin.com/in/robertgertler

Toronto: Bassanio Ghose - *1
Former Name: Ghose & Malhotra
1620 Albion Rd., Toronto, ON M9V 4B4
Tel: 416-744-1480
www.linkedin.com/in/bassanio-ghose-8b42b940

Toronto: Gilbert & Yallen - *3
Former Name: Howard Gilbert
204 St. George St., 3rd Fl., Toronto, ON M5R 2N5
Tel: 416-927-0001; *Fax*: 416-927-0930

Toronto: Gilbert Kirby Stringer LLP - *11
Former Name: Gilbert, Wright & Kirby LLP
#1920, 145 King St. West, Toronto, ON M5H 1J8
Tel: 416-363-3100; *Fax*: 416-363-1379
www.gkslawyers.com

Toronto: Gilbert's LLP - *17
#2010, Toronto Dominion Centre, P.O. Box 301, 77 King st.
West, Toronto, ON M5K 1K2
Tel: 416-703-1100; *Fax*: 416-703-7422
www.gilbertslaw.ca
www.facebook.com/GilbertsLLP, twitter.com/GilbertsLLP

Toronto: Gilbertson Davis Emerson LLP - *8
#800, The Lumsden Bldg., 6 Adelaide St. East, Toronto, ON
M5C 1H6
Tel: 416-979-2020; *Fax*: 416-979-1285
www.gilbertsondavis.com

Toronto: John D. Gilfillan, Q.C. - *1
#1200, 20 Toronto St., Toronto, ON M5C 2B8
Tel: 416-861-1881; *Fax*: 416-861-1737
gilfillan@interware.net

Toronto: Leslie M. Giroday - *1
190 Sixth St., Toronto, ON M8V 3A5
Tel: 416-255-1063; *Fax*: 416-251-8699
leslie.giroday@girodaylaw.ca

Toronto: Martin Gladstone LL.B. - *1
#111, 579 Kingston Rd., Toronto, ON M4E 1R3
Tel: 416-693-9000; *Fax*: 416-693-9194
contact@gladstonelaw.ca
www.gladstonelaw.ca

* indicates number of lawyers

Toronto: Glaholt LLP - *13
#800, 141 Adelaide St. West, Toronto, ON M5H 3L5
Tel: 416-368-8280; *Fax:* 416-368-3467
Toll-Free: 866-452-4658
www.glaholt.com
twitter.com/GlaholtLLP

Toronto: Earl Glasner - *1
#320, 100 Richmond St. West, Toronto, ON M5H 3K6
Tel: 416-869-1076; *Fax:* 416-869-1840
earlglasner@rogers.com

Toronto: Glass & Associates - *4
50 Richmond St. East, 5th Fl., Toronto, ON M5C 1N7
Tel: 416-363-9295; *Fax:* 416-363-7659
lglass@glassassoc.com

Toronto: Alan A. Glass - *1
#711, 505 Cummer Ave., Toronto, ON M2K 2L8
Tel: 416-222-0904; *Fax:* 416-222-0417
alanglass01@yahoo.ca

Toronto: Global Resolutions Inc. - *7
45 St. Nicholas St., Toronto, ON M4Y 1W6
Tel: 416-964-7497; *Fax:* 416-925-8122
info@globalresolutions.com
globalresolutions.com

Toronto: Saul I. Glober - *3
Former Name: Glober & Cohen, Associates
114 Scollard St., Toronto, ON M5R 1G2
Tel: 416-324-9994; *Fax:* 416-324-0966

Toronto: Gluckstein Personal Injury Lawyers -
Toronto - *8
Former Name: Gluckstein & Associates LLP
#301, P.O. Box 53, 595 Bay St., Toronto, ON M5G 2C2
Toll-Free: 800-320-7773
www.gluckstein.com
www.facebook.com/glucksteinlaw, twitter.com/glucksteinlaw,
www.linkedin.com/company/gluckstein-personal-injury-lawyers

Toronto: Godfrey & Corcoran - *1
#702, 55 Queen St. East, Toronto, ON M5C 1R6
Tel: 416-363-0484; *Fax:* 416-363-0485
ccorcoran@idirect.com

Toronto: Goldblatt Partners LLP - *47
Former Name: Sack Goldblatt Mitchell LLP; Engelmann
Gottheil
#1039, 20 Dundas St. West, Toronto, ON M5G 2C2
Tel: 416-977-6070; *Fax:* 416-591-7333
Toll-Free: 800-387-5422
goldblattpartners.com
twitter.com/GPLLP

Toronto: Sydney L. Goldenberg - *1
125 Highbourne Rd., Toronto, ON M5P 2J5
Tel: 416-482-3206; *Fax:* 416-482-8619
slgoldenberg@sympatico.ca

Toronto: Goldhar & Nemoy - *1
#214, 120 Carlton St., Toronto, ON M5A 4K2
Tel: 416-928-1488; *Fax:* 416-924-7166

Toronto: Avra Goldhar - *1
27 Abbeywood Trail, Toronto, ON M3B 3B4
Tel: 416-444-4378; *Fax:* 416-444-5721
agoldhar@rogers.com

Toronto: H.A. Goldkind - *1
#320, 100 Richmond St. West, Toronto, ON M5H 3K6
Tel: 416-366-5280

Toronto: Goldman Sloan Nash & Haber LLP - *34
#1600, 480 University Ave., Toronto, ON M5G 1V6
Tel: 416-597-9922; *Fax:* 416-597-3370
Toll-Free: 877-597-9922
www.gsnh.com
www.facebook.com/332939780108997, twitter.com/GSNH_Law,
www.linkedin.com/company/143882

Toronto: Goldman Sloan Nash & Haber LLP -
Toronto - *5
Former Name: Willson Lewis LLP
#1600, 480 University Ave., Toronto, ON M5G 1V2
Tel: 416-597-9922; *Fax:* 416-597-3370
Toll-Free: 877-597-9922
urrego@gsnh.com
www.gsnh.com
www.facebook.com/Goldman-Sloan-Nash-Haber-LLP-33293978
0108997, twitter.com/GSNH_Law,
www.linkedin.com/company/143882

Toronto: Jeffrey L. Goldman - *1
#1600, 401 Bay St., Toronto, ON M5H 2Y4
Tel: 416-646-5164; *Fax:* 416-363-0406
jeffgoldmanlaw@gmail.com
jeffreygoldmanlaw.com

Toronto: Jeffrey W. Goldman - *1
#400, 4580 Dufferin St., Toronto, ON M3K 5Y2
Tel: 416-787-1818; *Fax:* 416-661-4858
jeffreygoldmanlaw@gmail.com

Toronto: Goldman, Spring, Kichler & Sanders - *7
#700, 40 Sheppard Ave. West, Toronto, ON M2N 6K9
Tel: 416-225-9400; *Fax:* 416-225-4805

Toronto: Goldstein & Grubner LLP - *2
#100, 100 Cowdray Ct., Toronto, ON M1S 5C8
Tel: 416-292-0414
info@gglawyers.ca
www.gglawyers.ca

Toronto: Goldstein, Rosen & Rassos LLP - *1
#316, 18 Wynford Dr., Toronto, ON M3C 3S2
Tel: 416-757-4156; *Fax:* 416-757-9318
www.grrlaw.ca

Toronto: David Gomes - *1
112 Adelaide St. East, Toronto, ON M5C 1K9
Tel: 416-361-0906; *Fax:* 416-368-2918
dgomes0604@rogers.com

Toronto: Goodman, Solomon & Gold - *2
#1500, 439 University Ave., Toronto, ON M5G 1Y8
Tel: 416-595-5555; *Fax:* 416-595-7020

Toronto: Stanley Goodman, Q.C. - *1
#1800, 4950 Yonge St., Toronto, ON M2N 6K1
Tel: 416-224-0224; *Fax:* 416-224-0758
stangoodman@torlaw.com

Toronto: Martin Z. Goose - *1
#504, 555 Burnhamthorpe Rd., Toronto, ON M9C 2Y3
Tel: 416-239-4811; *Fax:* 416-239-1707
martingoose@bellnet.ca

Toronto: Nathan Gotlieb - *1
#1800, Madison Centre, 4950 Yonge St., Toronto, ON M2N
6K1
Tel: 416-224-0200; *Fax:* 416-224-0758
ngotlieb@torlaw.com

Toronto: G.L. Gottlieb, Q.C. - *1
#309, 600 Bay St., Toronto, ON M5G 1M6
Tel: 416-977-3835; *Fax:* 416-977-3807
glgqc@interlog.com
www.glgqc.com

Toronto: Max A. Gould - *1
#1000, 30 St. Clair Ave. West, Toronto, ON M4V 3A1
Tel: 416-964-0290; *Fax:* 416-964-7102

Toronto: Deryk A. Gravesande - *1
2 Carlton St., Toronto, ON M5B 1J3
Tel: 416-206-1110

Toronto: Green & Spiegel - *18
150 York St., 5th Fl., Toronto, ON M5H 3S5
Tel: 416-862-7880; *Fax:* 416-862-1698
www.gands.com
www.facebook.com/174903892529319,
twitter.com/GreenAndSpiegel,
www.linkedin.com/company/green-&-spiegel

Toronto: David J. Green - *1
#1, 399 Spadina Ave., Toronto, ON M5T 2G6
Tel: 416-979-2333; *Fax:* 416-597-8966

Toronto: Donald M. Greenbaum, Q.C. - *1
#205, 265 Rimrock Rd., Toronto, ON M3J 3C6
Tel: 416-631-7504; *Fax:* 416-631-9895
baum@globility.com

Toronto: Greenberg & Levine - *2
2223 Kennedy Rd., Toronto, ON M1T 3G5
Tel: 416-292-6500; *Fax:* 416-292-6559
reception@greenbergandlevine.com
www.greenbergandlevine.com

Toronto: Greenberg, Jack - *1
#204, 181 Eglinton Ave. East, Toronto, ON M4P 1J4
Tel: 416-485-8833; *Fax:* 416-485-3246
jackgreenberg@greenberglawyers.ca

Toronto: Greenspan Partners LLP - *6
Former Name: Greenspan, White
144 King St. East, Toronto, ON M5C 1G8
Tel: 416-366-3961; *Fax:* 416-366-7994
info@144king.com
www.greenspanpartners.com
twitter.com/GreenspanLLP

Toronto: Greenwood Lam LLP - *3
Former Name: Greenwood Defense Law
#1240, 65 Queen St. West, Toronto, ON M5H 2M5
Tel: 416-686-4612; *Fax:* 416-362-3612
www.greenwooddefence.com

Toronto: E.J. Gresik - *1
101 Scollard St., Toronto, ON M5R 1G4
Tel: 416-924-0781; *Fax:* 416-960-9650

Toronto: Jonathan G. Griffiths
Also Known As: Griffiths Law
#710, 18 Wynford Dr., Toronto, ON M3C 1W1
Tel: 416-441-1253; *Fax:* 416-441-9757
Toll-Free: 866-412-2943
info@griffithslaw.com
griffithslaw.com

Toronto: Groia & Company Professional
Corporation - *6
#1100, 365 Bay St., Toronto, ON M5H 2V1
Tel: 416-203-2115; *Fax:* 416-203-9231
postmaster@groiaco.com
www.groiaco.com

Toronto: Bernard Gropper - *1
#300, 261 Davenport Rd., Toronto, ON M5R 1K3
Tel: 416-962-3000; *Fax:* 416-487-3002

Toronto: Derek T. Ground - *1
16 Oakview Avenue, Toronto, ON M6P 3J2
Tel: 416-604-3434; *Fax:* 416-604-3596
derek.ground@sympatico.ca

Toronto: Grundy, Cass & Campbell Professional
Corporation - *2
Former Name: Cass & Cass
#3150, Canadian Pacific Tower, P.O. Box 11, 100 Wellington
St. West, Toronto, ON M5K 1H1
Tel: 416-849-8003; *Fax:* 416-849-8004
www.grundycass.com

Toronto: Guberman Garson Immigration Lawyers -
Toronto
Former Name: Guberman Garson
8 Adelaide St. West, 9th Fl., Toronto, ON M5H 4E3
Tel: 416-363-1234; *Fax:* 416-363-8760
immlaw@ggilaw.com
www.ggilaw.com

Toronto: H. David Locke & Associates - *3
#200, 37 Prince Arthur Ave., Toronto, ON M5R 1B2
Tel: 416-601-1525; *Fax:* 416-601-0392
www.lockeandassociates.ca

Toronto: Lawrence Hadbavny - *1
Law Society of Upper Canada, 130 Queen St. West, Toronto,
ON M5H 2N6
Tel: 416-947-3394; *Fax:* 416-974-3924
Toll-Free: 800-668-7380
lhadbavn@lsuc.on.ca

Toronto: Michael P. Haddad - *1
548 Parliament St., Toronto, ON M4X 1P6
Tel: 416-926-8151; *Fax:* 416-927-9005

Toronto: Hahn & Maian - *2
664 Mount Pleasant Rd., Toronto, ON M4S 2N3
Tel: 416-486-9445; *Fax:* 416-486-1174
johnhahn@idirect.com

Toronto: Miles M. Halberstadt, Q.C. - *1
120 Carlton St., Toronto, ON M5A 4K2
Tel: 416-944-0441; *Fax:* 416-944-8330
mileshalberstadt@hotmail.com

Toronto: Halfnight & McKinlay - *4
#201, 65 Front St. East, Toronto, ON M5E 1B5
Tel: 416-361-3082; *Fax:* 416-361-0230
jhalfnight@halfnightlaw.com
www.halfnightlaw.com

* indicates number of lawyers

Toronto: **Hall Webber LLP - *3**
#400, 1200 Bay St., Toronto, ON M5R 2A5
Tel: 416-920-3849; *Fax:* 416-920-8373
info@hallwebber.com
www.ent-law.com

Toronto: **David F. Halpenny - *1**
#403, 111 Peter St., Toronto, ON M5V 2H1
Tel: 416-867-9208; *Fax:* 416-867-9139
davetex@pathcom.com

Toronto: **Allan S. Halpert - *1**
37 Maitland St., Toronto, ON M4Y 1C8
Tel: 416-968-7733; *Fax:* 416-968-7192
allan@halpertlaw.com

Toronto: **Harvey L. Hamburg - *1**
#215, 120 Carlton St., Toronto, ON M5A 4K2
Tel: 416-968-9054; *Fax:* 416-968-9023
hhamburg@sympatico.ca

Toronto: **Harasymowycz Law - *2**
#200, 2311 Bloor St. West, Toronto, ON M6S 1P1
Tel: 416-766-2472; *Fax:* 416-766-3297

Toronto: **Murray P. Harrington - *1**
285 Pitfield Rd., Toronto, ON M1S 1Z2
Tel: 416-299-0477; *Fax:* 416-299-7570

Toronto: **David E. Harris - *1**
#1900, 439 University Ave., Toronto, ON M5G 1Y8
Tel: 416-585-9329; *Fax:* 416-408-2372
delih@ca.inter.net

Toronto: **Ricki D. Harris - *2**
#1800, 4950 Yonge St., Toronto, ON M2N 6K1
Tel: 416-224-0200; *Fax:* 416-224-0758
rdharris@torlaw.com

Toronto: **Harris, Sheaffer LLP - *10**
#610, 4100 Yonge St., Toronto, ON M2P 2B5
Tel: 416-250-5800; *Fax:* 416-250-5300
www.harris-sheaffer.com

Toronto: **Harrison Jordan Law**
#402, 197 Spadina Ave., Toronto, ON M5T 2C8
Tel: 647-868-2267 *Toll-Free:* 855-542-0529
harrisonjordanlaw.com

Toronto: **Klaus Hartmann - *1**
391 Willowdale Ave., Toronto, ON M2N 5A8
Tel: 416-590-0311; *Fax:* 416-590-0312

Toronto: **Peter L. Hatch - *1**
31 Prince Arthur Ave., Toronto, ON M5R 1B2
Tel: 416-972-6962; *Fax:* 416-960-5456

Toronto: **Hazzard & Hore - *2**
#1220, 141 Adelaide St. West, Toronto, ON M5H 3L5
Tel: 416-868-0074; *Fax:* 416-868-1468
info@hazzardandhore.com
www.hazzardandhore.com

Toronto: **Marian D. Hebb - *2**
6 Humewood Dr., Toronto, ON M6C 2W2
Tel: 416-971-6618; *Fax:* 866-513-5660
marian@hebbsheffer.ca

Toronto: **Stephen H. Hebscher - *1**
#1800, 4950 Yonge St., Toronto, ON M2N 6K1
Tel: 416-224-0200; *Fax:* 416-224-0758
crimlaw@torlaw.com

Toronto: **E.S. Heiber - *1**
#1, 197 Church St., Toronto, ON M5B 1Y7
Tel: 416-362-2768; *Fax:* 416-865-5328
esheiber@heiberlaw.com

Toronto: **Heifetz, Crozier, Law Barristers & Solicitors - *3**
#601, 110 Yonge St., Toronto, ON M5C 1T4
Tel: 416-863-1717; *Fax:* 416-368-3133
www.hclaw.com

Toronto: **Julian Heller & Associates - *4**
#1905, 120 Adelaide St. West, Toronto, ON M5H 1T1
Tel: 416-364-2404; *Fax:* 416-364-0793

Toronto: **Heller, Rubel - *8**
#1902, 120 Adelaide St. West, Toronto, ON M5H 1T1
Tel: 416-863-9311; *Fax:* 416-863-9465
bheller@hellerrubel.com
hellerrubel.com

Toronto: **John L. Hill - *1**
127 Bishop Ave., Toronto, ON M2M 1Z6
Tel: 416-226-3221; *Fax:* 416-226-3222
conlaw@pathcom.com

Toronto: **Himelfarb Proszanski LLP - *16**
#1400, 480 University Ave., Toronto, ON M5G 1V2
Fax: 416-599-3131
Toll-Free: 877-820-1210
info@himprolaw.com
www.himprolaw.com

Toronto: **Hinkson Sachak Mcleod**
Former Name: Steven M. Hinkson
#301, 366 Bay St., Toronto, ON M5H 4B2
Tel: 416-368-3476; *Fax:* 416-363-9917
shinkson@hinksonlaw.com

Toronto: **Hodder, Wang LLP - Toronto - *5**
Former Name: Hodder Barristers
#2200, 181 University Ave., Toronto, ON M5H 3M7
Tel: 416-601-4818; *Fax:* 416-947-0909
hwlawyers.ca

Toronto: **Hoffer Adler LLP - *5**
#300, 425 University Ave., Toronto, ON M5G 1T6
Tel: 416-977-6666; *Fax:* 416-977-3332
www.hofferadler.com

Toronto: **Hoffman, Sillery, Buckstein & Chuback - *3**
#200, 1810 Avenue Rd., Toronto, ON M5M 3Z2
Tel: 416-787-1161; *Fax:* 416-787-3894

Toronto: **Gerri C. Holder - *1**
#101, 703 Evans Ave., Toronto, ON M9C 5E9
Tel: 416-626-3069; *Fax:* 416-622-8952
gholder@rogers.com

Toronto: **Christopher Holoboff - *1**
#407, 1200 Sheppard Ave. East, Toronto, ON M2K 3C5
Tel: 416-868-0878; *Fax:* 416-868-0879
choloboff@aol.com

Toronto: **Hooey Remus LLP - *4**
#1410, 120 Adelaide St. West, 14th Fl., Toronto, ON M5H 1T1
Tel: 416-362-4000; *Fax:* 416-362-3646
asingh@hooeyremus.com
www.hooeyremus.com

Toronto: **Houser Henry & Syron LLP - *5**
#2701, 145 King St. West, Toronto, ON M5H 1J8
Tel: 416-362-3411; *Fax:* 416-362-3757
inquiries@houserhenry.com
www.houserhenry.com
twitter.com/houserhenry,
www.linkedin.com/company/houser-henry-&-syron-llp

Toronto: **Howard C. Cohen & Associates - *2**
Former Name: Cohen, Sabsay LLP
#901, 350 Bay St., Toronto, ON M5H 2T7
Toll-Free: 800-318-1553
reception@hcohen.law
www.hcohen.law

Toronto: **Howie, Sacks & Henry LLP - Toronto - *17**
#3500, 20 Queen St. West, Toronto, ON M5H 2R3
Tel: 416-361-5990; *Fax:* 416-361-0083
Toll-Free: 877-474-5997
www.hshlawyers.com
www.facebook.com/HSHPersonalInjuryLawyers,
twitter.com/hshlawyers,
www.linkedin.com/company/howie-sacks-&-henry-llp---personal-injury-law

Toronto: **John A. Howlett - *1**
#850, 36 Toronto St., Toronto, ON M5C 2C5
Tel: 416-941-9444; *Fax:* 416-913-1444
jhowlett@bellnet.ca

Toronto: **John P. Howorun - *1**
1199 The Queensway, Toronto, ON M8Z 1R7
Tel: 416-363-9355; *Fax:* 416-363-6371

Toronto: **Hrycyna Pothemont Hunter - *2**
#200, 1081 Bloor St. West, Toronto, ON M6H 1M5
Tel: 416-532-8006; *Fax:* 416-532-2666
taras.hycyna@bellnet.ca

Toronto: **Hughes, Amys LLP - Toronto - *45**
#200, 48 Yonge St., Toronto, ON M5E 1G6
Tel: 416-367-1608; *Fax:* 416-367-8821
Toll-Free: 800-565-1713
www.hughesamys.com

Toronto: **Peter D. Hutcheon - *1**
#300, 55 Adelaide St. East, Toronto, ON M5C 1K6
Tel: 416-515-2049; *Fax:* 416-929-3204

Toronto: **Nick Iannazzo - *1**
Former Name: Iannazzo Onizuka Associates
#500, 425 University Ave., Toronto, ON M5G 1T6
Tel: 416-598-2002; *Fax:* 416-598-8183
niannazzo@on.aibn.com

Toronto: **Iler Campbell LLP - *9**
150 John St., 7th Fl., Toronto, ON M5V 3E3
Tel: 416-598-0103; *Fax:* 416-598-3484
www.ilercampbell.com

Toronto: **Innovate LLP - *6**
#120-E, MaRS Centre, 101 College St., Toronto, ON M5G 1L7
Toll-Free: 888-433-2030
info@innovatellp.com
www.innovatellp.com

Toronto: **Joan M. Irwin - *1**
#2200, P.O. Box 154, 4950 Yonge St., Toronto, ON M2N 6K1
Tel: 416-733-1990; *Fax:* 416-733-1992

Toronto: **Isenberg & Shuman - *2**
#804, 5075 Yonge St., Toronto, ON M2N 6C6
Tel: 416-225-5136; *Fax:* 416-225-6877
info@shumanlaw.ca
www.shumanlaw.ca
www.facebook.com/181620301889035,
twitter.com/isenbergshuman

Toronto: **Israel Foulon LLP - *6**
#200, 65 St. Clair Ave. East, Toronto, ON M4T 2Y8
Tel: 416-640-1550; *Fax:* 416-640-1555
inquiries@israelfoulon.com
israelfoulon.com

Toronto: **Cydney G. Israel - *1**
61 Saint Nicholas St., Toronto, ON M4Y 1W6
Tel: 416-962-6188; *Fax:* 416-925-0162
cydisrael@rogers.com

Toronto: **Carol E.F. Jackson - *1**
#900, 60 Yonge St., Toronto, ON M5E 1H5
Tel: 416-363-3292; *Fax:* 416-868-6381

Toronto: **Jacobson & Jacobson - *2**
#222, 3089 Bathurst St., Toronto, ON M6A 2A4
Tel: 416-787-0611; *Fax:* 416-787-4873

Toronto: **James, Siddall & Derzko - *4**
#1305, 55 Queen St. East, Toronto, ON M5C 1R6
Tel: 416-860-0166; *Fax:* 416-860-0041

Toronto: **Elham Jamshidi - *1**
#920, 6 Adelaide St. East, Toronto, ON M5C 1H6
Tel: 416-363-7172; *Fax:* 416-363-9917
eej@criminallawlitigation.com
criminallawlitigation.com

Toronto: **Jane Finch Community Legal Services - *3**
#409, 1315 Finch Ave. West, Toronto, ON M3J 2G6
Tel: 416-398-0677; *Fax:* 416-398-7172
www.janefinchcommunitylegalservices.ca

Toronto: **Janssen & Associates - *5**
89 Scollard St., Toronto, ON M5R 1G4
Tel: 416-929-1103
enquiry@janssen-law.com
www.janssenlaw.ca

Toronto: **Dale F. Jean-Pierre - *1**
#700, 55 Town Centre Crt., Toronto, ON M1P 4X4
Tel: 416-290-0560; *Fax:* 416-290-1259

Toronto: **Jellinek Law - *2**
62A George St., Toronto, ON M5A 4K8
Tel: 416-955-4800; *Fax:* 416-972-1499
Info@JellinekLaw.com
www.jellineklaw.com

Toronto: **Daphne Johnston - *1**
#2000, 393 University Ave., Toronto, ON M5G 1E6
Tel: 416-599-9635; *Fax:* 416-599-6043
Toll-Free: 800-364-5793
daphnejohnston@rogers.com

Toronto: **Kelly D. Jordan Family Law Firm - *1**
#1000, 160 Bloor St. East, Toronto, ON M4W 1B9
Tel: 416-849-5501; *Fax:* 437-266-2599
info@kellyjordanfamilylaw.com
www.kellyjordanfamilylaw.com

---

* indicates number of lawyers

Toronto: Mary K.E. Joseph - *1
Also Known As: Family Legal Services
Hudson Bay Centre, 2 Bloor St. East, Toronto, ON M4W 1A8
Tel: 416-363-8048
mary@familylegalservices.ca
www.familylegalservices.ca

Toronto: Ron Jourard - *1
#504, 3200 Dufferin St., Toronto, ON M6A 3B2
Tel: 416-398-6685; Fax: 416-398-7396
Toll-Free: 888-257-0002
jourard@defencelaw.com
www.defencelaw.com
www.facebook.com/ronjourardcriminallawyer,
twitter.com/ronjourardlaw,
www.linkedin.com/in/ron-jourard-a976566

Toronto: Robert W. Judge - *1
44 Fairview Blvd., Toronto, ON M4K 1L9
Tel: 416-466-7007; Fax: 416-466-7050

Toronto: Steven W. Junger - *1
#14, 620 Supertest Rd., Toronto, ON M3J 2M8
Tel: 416-787-7247; Fax: 416-787-3021
s.junger@sympatico.ca

Toronto: Juriansz & Li - *6
#1100, 5700 Yonge St., Toronto, ON M2M 4K2
Tel: 416-226-2342; Fax: 416-222-6874
www.jurianszli.com

Toronto: Justice for Children & Youth - *8
55 University Ave., 15th Fl., Toronto, ON M5J 2H7
Tel: 416-920-1633; Fax: 416-920-5855
Toll-Free: 866-999-5329
info@jfcy.org
www.jfcy.org

Toronto: JYJ Law - *1
Former Name: Swanick & Associates
#101, 225 Duncan Mill Rd., Toronto, ON M3B 3K9
Tel: 416-510-1888; Fax: 416-510-1945
info@jyjlaw.com
www.jyjlaw.com

Toronto: Kacaba & Associates - *2
#440, 100 Richmond St. West, Toronto, ON M5H 3K6
Tel: 416-361-1777; Fax: 416-361-1776

Toronto: Kagan Shastri LLP - *6
Former Name: Kagan, Zucker, Feldbloom, Shastri
188 Avenue Rd., Toronto, ON M5R 2J1
Tel: 416-368-2100; Fax: 416-368-8206
info@ksllp.ca
www.ksllp.ca

Toronto: The Kalen Group - *1
262 Avenue Rd., Toronto, ON M4V 2G7
Tel: 416-929-7781; Fax: 416-929-7784
kalen@mrgeenjeans.ca

Toronto: Kalfa Law
#1600, Yonge Eglinton Centre, 2300 Yonge St., Toronto, ON M4P 1E4
Tel: 416-631-7227; Fax: 647-849-3974
Toll-Free: 800-631-7923
reception@kalfalaw.com
www.kalfalaw.com
www.facebook.com/KalfaLaw, twitter.com/KalfaLaw,
www.linkedin.com/company/kalfa-law

Toronto: Speros Kanellos - *1
#202, 211 Consumers Rd., Toronto, ON M2J 4G8
Tel: 416-493-3100; Fax: 416-493-4377

Toronto: Chan Yeung Kang - *1
105 Sheppard Ave. East, Toronto, ON M2N 3A3
Tel: 416-221-1417; Fax: 416-221-1732
kang@cykanglaw.com

Toronto: William Kaplan - *1
#200, 70 Bond St., Toronto, ON M5B 1X3
Tel: 416-865-5341; Fax: 416-360-5746
www.williamkaplan.com

Toronto: Kapoor Barristers - *3
235 King St. East, 2nd Fl., Toronto, ON M5A 1J9
Tel: 416-363-2700
info@kapoorbarristers.com
www.kapoorbarristers.com

Toronto: Joseph H. Kary - *1
90A Isabella St., Toronto, ON M4Y 1N4
Tel: 416-929-9656

Toronto: Sheldon L. Kasman & Associate - *2
#201, 1622 Eglinton Ave. West, Toronto, ON M6E 2G8
Tel: 416-789-1888; Fax: 416-789-5928
law@kasman.com
www.kasman.com

Toronto: Garen Kassabian - *1
#203, 8 Sampson Mews, Toronto, ON M3C 0H5
Tel: 416-443-9494; Fax: 416-443-0575
garen@bellnet.ca

Toronto: J.M. Kavanagh, Q.C. - *1
#340, 100 Cowdray Ct., Toronto, ON M1S 5C8
Tel: 416-265-3560; Fax: 416-265-1944

Toronto: Robert C. Kay - *1
#1108, 8 King St. East, Toronto, ON M5C 1B5
Tel: 416-362-9999

Toronto: Keel Cottrelle LLP - Toronto - *14
#920, 36 Toronto St., Toronto, ON M5C 2C5
Tel: 416-367-2900; Fax: 416-367-2791
www.keelcottrelle.com

Toronto: Kelly, Jennings & Lacy - *4
144 King St. East, 3rd Fl., Toronto, ON M5C 1G8
Tel: 416-366-1758; Fax: 416-366-1762
jennings@144king.com
www.144king.com/kjl/lawyers.htm

Toronto: Evan N. Kenley - *1
#301, 1352 Bathurst St., Toronto, ON M5K 3H7
Tel: 416-932-1148; Fax: 416-932-1108
evan@kenleylaw.com
www.kenleylaw.com

Toronto: Shayne G. Kert - *1
#1902, 120 Adelaide St. West, Toronto, ON M5H 1T1
Tel: 416-863-0141; Fax: 416-863-9465

Toronto: Kestenberg Siegal Lipkus LLP - *10
65 Granby St., Toronto, ON M5B 1H8
Tel: 416-597-0000; Fax: 416-597-6567
www.ksllaw.com
twitter.com/ksllaw,
www.linkedin.com/company/kestenberg-siegal-lipkus-llp

Toronto: El-Farouk A. Khaki - *1
315 Mutual St., Toronto, ON M4Y 1X6
Tel: 416-925-7227; Fax: 416-925-2450
elfin925@rogers.com

Toronto: King & King - *1
#2, 823 Millwood Rd., Toronto, ON M4G 1W3
Tel: 416-368-4678; Fax: 416-368-7234
aek@kingandking.net
www.kingandking.net

Toronto: Don P. Kirsh - *1
#207, 3500 Dufferin St., Toronto, ON M3K 1N2
Tel: 416-630-6136; Fax: 416-630-6135
dkirsh@bellnet.ca
www.donkirsh.ca

Toronto: Sheila Kirsh - *1
#3310, 20 Queen St. West, Toronto, ON M5H 3R3
Tel: 416-367-1765
sheila@kirsh-law.com
www.kirsh-law.com

Toronto: Howard Joshua Kirshenbaum - *1
#17, 1140 Sheppard Ave. West, Toronto, ON M3K 2A2
Tel: 416-865-5339; Fax: 416-777-9255
kirshenbaum@msn.com

Toronto: Klaiman, Edmonds - *3
#1000, 60 Yonge St., Toronto, ON M5E 1H5
Tel: 416-867-9600; Fax: 416-867-9783
www.klaimanedmonds.com
www.linkedin.com/company/klaiman-edmonds-llp

Toronto: Judi E. Klein - *1
#104, 2552 Finch Ave. West, Toronto, ON M9M 2G3
Tel: 416-749-7747; Fax: 416-749-9190
info@jkleinfamilylaw.com
www.judieklein.supersites.ca

Toronto: Paula Knopf Arbitrations Ltd. - *1
4 Biggar Ave., Toronto, ON M6H 2N4
Tel: 416-652-1516; Fax: 416-232-1175
paulaknopf@bellnet.ca
www.paulaknopf.ca

Toronto: Marc Koplowitz Associates - *2
#2900, 390 Bay St., Toronto, ON M5H 2Y2
Tel: 416-368-1100; Fax: 416-368-1998
marc@koplaw.com
www.koplaw.com

Toronto: Kopolovic, Strigberger - *1
#300, 69 Elm St., Toronto, ON M5G 1H2
Tel: 416-971-7272; Fax: 416-971-9092

Toronto: Korman & Company - *6
721 Queen St. East, Toronto, ON M4M 1H1
Tel: 416-465-4232; Fax: 416-465-6912
info@kormancompany.com
www.kormancompany.com

Toronto: Kornblum Law Professional Corporation - *1
#215, 3130 Bathurst St., Toronto, ON M6A 2A1
Tel: 647-496-2570
www.kornblumlawcorp.ca

Toronto: Koroloff & Huckins - *2
#304, 1110 Sheppard Ave. East, Toronto, ON M2K 2W2
Tel: 416-229-6226; Fax: 416-229-6517

Toronto: Koskie Minsky LLP - *52
#900, P.O. Box 52, 20 Queen St. West, Toronto, ON M5H 3R3
Tel: 416-977-8353; Fax: 416-977-3316
www.kmlaw.com
twitter.com/kmlawllp,
www.linkedin.com/company/koskie-minsky-llp

Toronto: Kostyniuk & Greenside - *15
#300, 5468 Dundas St. West, Toronto, ON M9B 6E3
Tel: 416-762-8238; Fax: 416-762-5042
www.kostyniukandgreenside.com

Toronto: Kotler Law Firm - *1
#617, 1 Eglinton Ave. East, Toronto, ON M4P 3A1
Tel: 416-932-4949; Fax: 416-487-2992
hgk@koterlaw.ca

Toronto: S. Lenard Kotylo - *2
#300, 66 Gerrard St. East, Toronto, ON M5B 1G3
Tel: 416-585-9373; Fax: 416-585-9376

Toronto: Neil L. Kozloff - *1
#1900, 439 University Ave., Toronto, ON M5G 1Y8
Tel: 416-414-7031

Toronto: Alex Krakowitz - *1
#3101, P.O. Box 3, 250 Yonge St., Toronto, ON M5B 2L7
Tel: 416-596-4606; Fax: 416-599-8341
alex.krakowitz@lawpro.ca

Toronto: Kramer Simaan Dhillon LLP - *6
Former Name: Kramer Henderson Sidlofsky LLP
#2100, 120 Adelaide St. West, Toronto, ON M5H 1T1
Tel: 416-601-6820; Fax: 416-601-0712
info@kramersimaan.com
kramersimaan.com

Toronto: Krauss, Weinryb - *2
#502, 100 Shepard Ave. East, Toronto, ON M2N 6N5
Tel: 416-222-4446; Fax: 416-222-9788

Toronto: Gerald Kroll, Q.C. - *1
#1800, 4950 Yonge St., Toronto, ON M2N 6K1
Tel: 416-224-0200; Fax: 416-224-0758

Toronto: Grace F. Kwan - *1
90A Isabella St., 3rd Fl., Toronto, ON M4Y 1N4
Tel: 416-968-2014; Fax: 416-968-2054
gkwan@295.ca

Toronto: Stephen M. Labow - *1
#610, 480 University Ave., Toronto, ON M5G 1V2
Tel: 416-947-1172; Fax: 416-596-0808
stephen@labow.ca

Toronto: Lafontaine & Associates - *3
Former Name: Gregory L. Lafontaine
#506, 330 University Ave., Toronto, ON M5G 1R7
Tel: 416-204-1835; Fax: 416-204-1849
greg@127john.com

Toronto: Tikam K. Lalla - *1
1203 Bloor St. West, Toronto, ON M6H 1N4
Tel: 416-532-2801; Fax: 416-532-4942

Toronto: Mary L.F. Lam - *2
40 Binscarth Road, Toronto, ON M4W 1Y1
Tel: 416-383-0266; Fax: 416-383-0299
mary.lam@rogers.com

* indicates number of lawyers

Toronto: Jack S. Lambert - *1
105 Sultana, Toronto, ON M6A 1T4
Tel: 416-226-6343; *Fax:* 416-226-6344
jacklamlaw@rogers.com

Toronto: Garry Lamourie - *1
#2000, 393 University Ave., Toronto, ON M5G 1E6
Tel: 416-597-9828; *Fax:* 416-597-9808
info@lamourie.ca

Toronto: Landy Marr Kats LLP - *6
#900, 2 Sheppard Ave. East, Toronto, ON M2N 5Y7
Tel: 416-221-9343; *Fax:* 416-221-8928
Toll-Free: 855-556-5529
www.thetorontolawyers.ca

Toronto: Wayne S. Laski - *1
197 Byng Ave., Toronto, ON M2N 4K8
Tel: 416-229-1166
wlaski@wlaski.com

Toronto: Law Office of T. Edgar Reilly - *2
701 Coxwell Ave., Toronto, ON M4C 3C1
Tel: 416-461-7553; *Fax:* 416-461-2679
lawoffice@tedgarreilly.ca
www.reilly-lawoffice.ca

Toronto: John V. Lawer, Q.C. - *1
#306, 40 St. Clair Ave. East, Toronto, ON M4T 1M9
Tel: 416-922-0737; *Fax:* 416-922-1896
johnv@johnvlawer.on.ca

Toronto: L.B. Geffen - *1
#205, 2907 Kennedy Rd., Toronto, ON M1V 1S8
Tel: 416-292-6688; *Fax:* 416-292-6649
geffen02@bellnet.ca
lawrencebgeffen.com

Toronto: Lax O'Sullivan Lisus Gottlieb - *20
Former Name: Lax O'Sullivan Scott Lisus LLP
#2750, 145 King St. West, Toronto, ON M5H 1J8
Tel: 416-598-1744; *Fax:* 416-598-3730
info@counsel-toronto.com
www.counsel-toronto.com

Toronto: Laxton Glass LLP - *28
#200, 390 Bay St., Toronto, ON M5H 2Y2
Tel: 416-363-2353; *Fax:* 416-363-7112
info@laxtonglass.com
laxtonglass.com

Toronto: Sheldon S. Lazarovitz - *1
31 Westgate Blvd., Toronto, ON M3H 1N8
Tel: 416-638-6080; *Fax:* 416-638-6246
lazarovitz@rogers.com

Toronto: Timothy J. Leach - *1
#309, 658 Danforth Ave., Toronto, ON M4J 5B9
Tel: 416-868-0265; *Fax:* 416-868-0478

Toronto: Lee & Company - Toronto - *1
#3F, Hullmark Centre, 4773 Yonge St., Toronto, ON M2N 0G2
Tel: 416-321-0100
inquiry@leecompany.ca
www.leecompany.ca
www.facebook.com/leeandcompany,
twitter.com/leeandcompany, www.linkedin.com/company/447694

Toronto: John Y.C. Lee - *1
#418, 4002 Sheppard Ave. East, Toronto, ON M1S 1S6
Tel: 416-299-8900; *Fax:* 416-299-8232

Toronto: Paul Lee & Associates - *4
20 Maitland St., Toronto, ON M4Y 1C5
Tel: 416-961-2707; *Fax:* 416-961-5575
office@paullee.ca
paullee.ca

Toronto: Legal Aid Ontario
#200, Atrium on Bay, 40 Dundas St. West, Toronto, ON M5G 2H1
Tel: 416-979-1446; *Fax:* 416-979-8669
Toll-Free: 800-668-8258
info@lao.on.ca
www.legalaid.on.ca

Toronto: Legge & Legge - *5
#800, 65 St. Clair Ave. East, Toronto, ON M4T 2Y3
Tel: 416-923-1776; *Fax:* 416-925-5344
leggeandlegge.com

Toronto: Joseph C. Lemire - *1
#500, 70 Bond St., Toronto, ON M5B 1X3
Tel: 416-363-1097; *Fax:* 416-863-4896

Toronto: Lenczner Slaght LLP - *49
Former Name: Lenczner Slaght Royce Smith Griffin LLP
#2600, 130 Adelaide St., West, Toronto, ON M5H 3P5
Tel: 416-865-9500; *Fax:* 416-865-9010
Toll-Free: 877-805-7774
info@litigate.com
www.litigate.com

Toronto: Frank Lento - *1
Former Name: Franco, Lento, D'Alimonte
#504, 3200 Dufferin St., Toronto, ON M3K 2A7
Tel: 416-398-4044; *Fax:* 416-398-7396
franklento@lentolaw.com
lentolaw.com

Toronto: George J. Leon - *1
29 Berwick Ave., Toronto, ON M5P 1G9
Tel: 416-487-1385; *Fax:* 647-348-1512
gleon@idirect.com

Toronto: Gérard Lévesque - *1
184 Lake Promenade, Toronto, ON M8W 1A8
Tel: 416-253-0129; *Fax:* 416-253-4737
levesque.gerard@sympatico.ca

Toronto: Levine Associates - *5
#1400, 10 King St. East, Toronto, ON M5C 1C3
Tel: 416-364-2345; *Fax:* 416-364-3818
www.levlaw.com
www.facebook.com/levineassociates, twitter.com/levlaw,
www.linkedin.com/company/levine-associates

Toronto: Levine Sherkin Boussidan Professional Corporation - *7
#300, 23 Lesmill Rd., Toronto, ON M3B 3P6
Tel: 416-224-2400; *Fax:* 416-224-2408
www.lsblaw.com

Toronto: Lorne Levine - *1
401-55 Eglington Ave. E, Toronto, ON M4P 1G8
Tel: 416-483-1251; *Fax:* 416-483-1257
lornelevinelaw@bellnet.ca

Toronto: Levinson & Associates
#2000, 393 University Ave., Toronto, ON M5G 1E6
Tel: 416-591-8484; *Fax:* 416-593-1352
www.levadvocate.net

Toronto: Levitan Lawyers - *1
22 Soho St., Toronto, ON M5T 1Z7
Tel: 416-368-4600; *Fax:* 416-368-1166
jerrylevitan@rogers.com

Toronto: Sherry Levitan - *1
#403, 1 Yorkdale Rd., Toronto, ON M6A 3A1
Tel: 416-784-1222
www.fertilitylaw.ca
www.facebook.com/175217252568557,
twitter.com/sherrylevitan,
www.linkedin.com/in/sherry-levitan-35755643

Toronto: Levitt, Lightman, Dewar & Graham LLP - *4
#1, 16 Four Seasons Pl., Toronto, ON M9B 6E5
Tel: 416-620-0362; *Fax:* 416-620-5158
Toll-Free: 866-730-4919
www.lldg.ca
www.facebook.com/127863840638504, twitter.com/lldg_law,
www.linkedin.com/in/lldgrichard

Toronto: Alan D. Levy - *1
75 Robert St., Toronto, ON M5S 2K4
Tel: 416-929-8282; *Fax:* 416-929-9895

Toronto: Earl J. Levy, Q.C. - *1
#400, 100 Richmond St. West, Toronto, ON M5H 3K6
Tel: 416-364-7292; *Fax:* 416-364-7473

Toronto: Lewin & Sagara LLP - *2
2173 Danforth Ave., Toronto, ON M4C 1K4
Tel: 416-499-7945; *Fax:* 877-459-9747
newclient@lewinsagara.com
www.lewinsagara.ca
www.facebook.com/LewinSagara, twitter.com/Paullewinlawyer

Toronto: Lewis & Associates - *5
41 Madison Ave., Toronto, ON M5R 2S2
Tel: 416-924-2227; *Fax:* 416-924-9993
lewisassociates@eol.ca

Toronto: Andrew C. Lewis - *1
#508, 1 Eglinton Ave. East, Toronto, ON M4P 3A1
Tel: 416-322-7010; *Fax:* 416-483-2737
andrew@andrewclewislaw.com
www.andrewclewislaw.ca

Toronto: Joseph E. Lewis - *1
#202, 327 Eglinton Ave. E, Toronto, ON M4P 1L7
Tel: 416-486-0084; *Fax:* 416-486-7363

Toronto: Susan M.C. Libanio - *1
#617, 1 Summerhill Rd., Toronto, ON M8V 1R9
Tel: 416-533-6002; *Fax:* 416-533-6097
smel@rogers.com

Toronto: Yoel Lichtblau - *1
499 Wilson Heights Blvd., Toronto, ON M3H 2V7
Tel: 416-633-2465
yoel@yichtblaulaw.com
lichtblaulaw.com
www.linkedin.com/in/yoel-lichtblau-58914113

Toronto: Linden & Associates - *4
#2010, Royal Bank Plaza, North Tower, 200 Bay St., Toronto, ON M5J 2J1
Tel: 416-861-9338; *Fax:* 416-861-9973
www.lindenlex.com

Toronto: John Liss - *1
207 Brunswick Ave., Toronto, ON M5S 2M4
Tel: 416-968-2558; *Fax:* 416-961-7906

Toronto: John A.G. Lister - *1
167 Danforth Ave., Toronto, ON M4K 1N2
Tel: 416-461-0983; *Fax:* 416-462-3347
jaglister@on.aibn.com

Toronto: Littler Mendelson Professional Corporation - *11
#3210, 181 Bay St., Toronto, ON M5J 2T3
Tel: 647-256-4509
www.littler.com
www.facebook.com/littlerlaw, twitter.com/littler,
www.linkedin.com/company/littler-mendelson

Toronto: Nadia Liva - *1
#201, Courtyard Chambers, 258 Adelaide St. East, Toronto, ON M5A 1N1
Tel: 416-598-0106; *Fax:* 416-868-0273
nliva@courtyardchambers.ca
www.nadialiva.com

Toronto: Lockyer Campbell Posner Barristers & Solicitors - *11
#103, 30 St. Clair Ave. West, Toronto, ON M4V 3A1
Tel: 416-847-2560; *Fax:* 416-847-2564
www.lcp-law.com

Toronto: Lofranco Corriero LLC - Toronto - *14
Former Name: Rocco C. Lofranco, Barristers & Solicitors
#600, 4950 Yonge St., Toronto, ON M2N 6K1
Toll-Free: 866-563-7262
www.lofrancolawyers.com

Toronto: Gerald P. Logan - *1
317 Grace St., Toronto, ON M6G 3A7
Tel: 416-535-8920; *Fax:* 416-537-6550

Toronto: Joachim M. Loh - *1
#10 b, 3880 Midland Ave., Toronto, ON M1V 5K4
Tel: 416-609-8289; *Fax:* 416-609-8857
jmloh@jmlohlaw.com

Toronto: Loopstra Nixon LLP Barristers & Solicitors - *23
#600, Woodbine Place, 135 Queen's Plate Dr., Toronto, ON M9W 6V7
Tel: 416-746-4710; *Fax:* 416-746-8319
www.loopstranixon.com

Toronto: Lopresti Law - *1
#1510, 5140 Yonge St., Toronto, ON M2N 6L7
Tel: 416-218-5271; *Fax:* 416-250-7008
joseph@loprestilaw.ca
www.loprestilaw.ca

Toronto: Francisco B. Luna - *1
1919 Lawrence Ave. East, Toronto, ON M1R 2Y6
Tel: 416-977-3249

Toronto: Karen D. Lundy - *1
#2400, P.O. Box 22, 1 Dundas St. West, Toronto, ON M5G 1Z3
Tel: 416-866-8858; *Fax:* 416-364-3866
karenlundy@waldin.ca

Toronto: Lawrence M. Lychowyd - *1
236A Bain Ave., Toronto, ON M4K 1G3
Tel: 416-466-8063; *Fax:* 416-694-3367
www.larrythelawyer.ca

* indicates number of lawyers

Toronto: Bryan A. MacBride - *1
#612, 55 Lombard St., Toronto, ON M5C 2R7
Tel: 416-601-9222; Fax: 416-601-9223
bamc@rogers.com

Toronto: MacDonald & Partners LLP - *14
#1700, 155 University Ave., Toronto, ON M5H 3B7
Tel: 416-971-4802; Fax: 416-971-9584
famlaw@mpllp.com
www.macdonaldpartners.com

Toronto: MacDonald Geraldine - *1
80 Richmond St. West, Toronto, ON M5H 2A4
Tel: 416-366-7985; Fax: 416-366-4670

Toronto: Macdonald Sager Manis LLP - *26
#800, 150 York St., Toronto, ON M5H 3S5
Tel: 416-364-1553; Fax: 416-364-1453
www.msmlaw.ca
twitter.com/MSM_law,
www.linkedin.com/company/macdonald-sager-manis-llp

Toronto: Mary-Douglass MacDonald - *1
122 Prince George Dr., Toronto, ON M9B 2Y2
Tel: 416-231-4899; Fax: 647-438-4494
mdmacdonald@rogers.com

Toronto: Carolyn A. MacLean - *1
#102, 40 Isabella St., Toronto, ON M4Y 1N1
Tel: 416-925-4008; Fax: 416-920-0367
camaclean@hotmail.com

Toronto: Theresa M. MacLean - *1
#202, 40 Isabella St., Toronto, ON M4Y 1N1
Tel: 416-964-9224; Fax: 416-920-0367
theresa.m.maclean@gmail.com

Toronto: Thmoas J. MacLennan - *1
#201, 27 Yorkville Ave., Toronto, ON M4W 1L1
Tel: 416-591-1354; Fax: 416-925-3514
maclennanlaw.com

Toronto: MacLeod Law Firm - Toronto - *3
#702, 2 Bloor St. West, Toronto, ON M4W 3E2
Tel: 647-204-8107 Toll-Free: 866-883-8445
inquiry@macleodlawfirm.ca
www.macleodlawfirm.ca
twitter.com/MLFemployeelaw

Toronto: S.G.R. MacMillan
#2110, 120 Adelaide St. West, Toronto, ON M5H 1T1
Tel: 416-363-0100

Toronto: Dan Malamet - *1
10 Audubon Ct., Toronto, ON M2N 1T9
Tel: 416-865-6952; Fax: 416-863-6275
dan.malamet@bakernet.com

Toronto: Malo Pilley Lehman - *3
#302, 1678 Bloor St. West, Toronto, ON M6P 1A9
Tel: 416-534-3555; Fax: 416-534-7625
www.mpllaw.ca
www.facebook.com/544952985564591,
www.linkedin.com/company/malo-pilley-&-lehman

Toronto: Harvey Mandel - *1
#203, 55 Queen St. East, Toronto, ON M5C 1R6
Tel: 416-364-7717; Fax: 416-364-4813
harvey-mandel.com

Toronto: Mantas Bouwer & Rosen
10 King St. East, Toronto, ON M5C 1C3
Tel: 416-777-1400

Toronto: Pierre F. Marchildon - *1
#308, Dundas-Lambton Centre, 4195 Dundas St. West,
Toronto, ON M8X 1Y4
Tel: 416-236-0686; Fax: 416-236-0650
Toll-Free: 866-236-0686
pfmlaw@on.aibn.com

Toronto: Marcos Associates - *2
1718 Dundas St. West, Toronto, ON M6K 1V5
Tel: 416-537-3151; Fax: 416-537-3153
eamarcos.office@gmail.com

Toronto: Marin, Evans & Bell - *2
#500, 200 Adelaide St. West, Toronto, ON M5H 1W7
Tel: 416-408-2177; Fax: 416-408-1718

Toronto: Charles C. Mark, Q.C. - *1
#2010, 401 Bay St., Toronto, ON M5H 2Y4
Tel: 416-869-0929; Fax: 416-869-9118
ccmark@on.aibn.com

Toronto: Markes Lawyers - *3
Former Name: Beach, Hepburn
#506, 1090 Don Mills Rd., Toronto, ON M3C 3R6
Tel: 416-350-3500; Fax: 416-350-3510
www.markeslawyers.com

Toronto: H. David Marks, Q.C. - *1
#1600, 480 University Ave., Toronto, ON M5G 1V2
Tel: 416-863-1550; Fax: 416-863-9670
marks@gsnh.com

Toronto: Larry M. Marshall - *1
#1017, 250 Consumers Rd., Toronto, ON M2J 4V6
Tel: 416-497-2526; Fax: 416-497-3143
lmarshal@idirect.com

Toronto: Malcolm M. Martin - *1
#209, 29 Gervaid Dr., Toronto, ON M3C 1Z1
Tel: 416-449-4111; Fax: 416-449-7879
mmartin@malcolmmartin.com

Toronto: Martinello & Associates
#208, 255 Duncan Mill Rd., Toronto, ON M3B 3H9
Tel: 416-800-1377

Toronto: Ville K. Masalin - *1
#309, 191 Eglinton Ave. East, Toronto, ON M4P 1K1
Tel: 416-484-9347; Fax: 416-484-9027

Toronto: Masters & Masters
#440, 65 Queen St. West, Toronto, ON M5H 2M5
Tel: 416-361-1399; Fax: 416-361-6181

Toronto: Mathews, Dinsdale & Clark LLP - Toronto -
*53
Also Known As: Mathews Dinsdale
#3600, RBC Centre, 155 Wellington St. West, Toronto, ON
M5V 3H1
Tel: 416-862-8280; Fax: 416-862-8247
Toll-Free: 800-411-2900
www.mathewsdinsdale.com
twitter.com/mdclaw, www.linkedin.com/company-beta/2348513

Toronto: Gaetano P. Matteazzi - *1
#400, 340 College St., Toronto, ON M5T 3A9
Tel: 416-534-8881; Fax: 416-972-1885

Toronto: Matthew Wilton & Associates - *3
#1503, 65 Queen St. West, Toronto, ON M5H 2M5
Tel: 416-860-9889; Fax: 416-860-1034
reception@wiltonlaw.com
wiltonlaw.com

Toronto: McBride Wallace Laurent & Cord LLP - *10
#200, 5464 Dundas St. West, Toronto, ON M9B 1B4
Tel: 416-231-6555; Fax: 416-231-6630
www.mwlclaw.com

Toronto: McCague Borlack LLP - Toronto - *49
#2700, The Exchange Tower, P.O. Box 136, Stn. 1st, 130
King St. West, Toronto, ON M5X 1C7
Tel: 416-860-0001; Fax: 416-860-0003
Toll-Free: 888-960-0010
mccagueborlack.com

Toronto: Robert L. McClelland - *1
#313, 2498 Yonge St., Toronto, ON M4P 2H8
Tel: 416-481-7360
robmcc@ca.inter.net

Toronto: John D. McCrie - *1
#9, 15 Belfield Rd., Toronto, ON M9W 1E8
Tel: 416-243-9501; Fax: 416-243-2990
johndmccrie@rogers.com

Toronto: David J. McGhee - *1
390 Bay St., 30th Fl., Toronto, ON M5H 2Y2
Tel: 416-362-9736; Fax: 416-362-9435
djmcghee@on.aibn.com

Toronto: McGregor & Martin Associates - *1
Former Name: McGregor, David R.
#316, 18 Wynford Dr., Toronto, ON M3C 3S2
Tel: 416-485-1123; Fax: 416-485-8742

Toronto: McInnis, Nicoll - *2
#507, 330 Bay St., Toronto, ON M5H 2S8
Tel: 416-362-1354; Fax: 416-362-1465

Toronto: McIver & McIver - *2
#700, 1 Richmond St. West, Toronto, ON M5H 3W4
Tel: 416-864-9000; Fax: 416-864-9190

Toronto: Michael A. McKee - *1
53 Widdicombe Hill Blvd., Toronto, ON M9R 1Y3
Tel: 416-928-6619; Fax: 416-928-9515
mckeelawoffice@yahoo.ca
www.torontooncriminallawyer.ca

Toronto: Michael G. McLachlan - *1
Former Name: McLachlan Winter Freeman
#103, 30 St. Clair Ave. West, Toronto, ON M4V 3A1
Tel: 416-596-7077; Fax: 416-596-7629
info@mgmlaw.org
www.mgmlaw.org

Toronto: McLean & Kerr LLP - *26
#2800, 130 Adelaide St. West, Toronto, ON M5H 3P5
Tel: 416-364-5371; Fax: 416-366-8571
mail@mcleankerr.com
www.mcleankerr.com

Toronto: McMaster, McIntyre & Smyth, LLP - *6
2777 Dundas St. West, Toronto, ON M6P 1Y4
Tel: 647-547-9865; Fax: 416-769-4147
Toll-Free: 800-530-7597
www.mmslawyers.com

Toronto: McPhadden Samac Tuovi Haté LLP - *4
Former Name: McPhadden Samac Tuovi LLP;
McPhadden, Samac, Merner, Darling
161 Bay St., 27th Fl., Toronto, ON M5J 2S1
www.mcst.ca

Toronto: Deborah L. Meldazy - *1
426 Davenport Rd., Toronto, ON M4V 1B5
Tel: 416-929-8524; Fax: 416-929-4042
dmeldazy@sympatico.ca

Toronto: Menzies, von Bogen - *1
Former Name: J. Alexander Menzies, Q.C.
1071B Bloor St. West, Toronto, ON M6H 1M5
Tel: 416-532-2833; Fax: 416-532-6553
Toll-Free: 877-218-0084
vonbogen@bellnet.ca

Toronto: Paul Mergler - *1
1199 The Queensway, Toronto, ON M8Z 1R7
Tel: 416-232-9589; Fax: 416-232-9522
pabkon@interlog.com

Toronto: Clarke A. Merritt - *2
#3300, Box 33, 20 Queen St. West, Toronto, ON M5H 3R3
Tel: 416-971-3306; Fax: 416-971-4849
cmerrittl@aol.com
twitter.com/clarkemerritt

Toronto: Jack A. Mikolajko - *1
#506, P.O. Box 31, 2333 Dundas St. West, Toronto, ON M9R
3A6
Tel: 416-538-8493; Fax: 416-538-2274
jmikolajko@bellnet.ca

Toronto: Millar Kreklewetz LLP - *2
Former Name: Millar Wyslobicky Kreklewetz LLP
24 Duncan St., 3rd Fl., Toronto, ON M5V 2B8
Tel: 416-864-6200; Fax: 416-864-6201
www.taxandtradelaw.com

Toronto: Miller & Miller - *2
1577 Bloor St. West, Toronto, ON M6P 1A6
Tel: 416-536-1159; Fax: 416-536-3618
info@millerandmiller.ca
www.millerandmiller.ca

Toronto: Mills & Mills LLP - *26
#700, 2 St. Clair Ave. West, Toronto, ON M4V 1L5
Tel: 416-863-0125; Fax: 416-863-3997
www.millsandmills.ca

Toronto: Douglas J. Millstone - *1
#309, 2100 Ellesmere Rd., Toronto, ON M1H 3B7
Tel: 416-289-7996; Fax: 416-289-7998
Toll-Free: 888-437-7996
dmilldtone@millstonelaw.com
www.dmillstonelaw.com

Toronto: Minden Gross LLP - *61
Also Known As: Minden Gross Grafstein & Greenstein
LLP
#2200, 145 King St. West, Toronto, ON M5H 4G2
Tel: 416-362-3711; Fax: 416-864-9223
info@mindengross.com
www.mindengross.com
twitter.com/mindengross
www.linkedin.com/company/minden-gross-llp

* indicates number of lawyers

Toronto: **Iqbal I. Dewji - *1**
#201, 161 Frederick St., Toronto, ON M5A 4P3
Tel: 416-848-0704
dewlaw@gmail.com

Toronto: **Paul Minz - *1**
#1, 3520 Pharmacy Ave., Toronto, ON M1W 2T8
Tel: 416-499-9350; *Fax:* 416-499-1463

Toronto: **Mircheff & Mircheff - *1**
#2B, 3030 Midland Ave., Toronto, ON M1S 5C9
Tel: 416-321-2885; *Fax:* 416-321-3345
nick@mircheff-law.com
mircheff-law.com

Toronto: **Misir & Company - *6**
880 St. Clair Ave. West, Toronto, ON M6C 1C5
Tel: 416-653-8600; *Fax:* 416-653-9639
www.misirandcompany.com

Toronto: **Mitchell, Bardyn & Zalucky LLP - *13**
Also Known As: MBZ Law
#200, 3029 Bloor St. West, Toronto, ON M8X 1C5
Tel: 416-234-9111; *Fax:* 416-234-9114
info@mbzlaw.com
www.mbzlaw.com

Toronto: **Heather Mitchell - *1**
#300, 165 Avenue Rd., Toronto, ON M5R 3S4
Tel: 416-927-6565; *Fax:* 416-975-3999
hhmitchell@heathermitchelllaw.com

Toronto: **Said Mohammedally - *1**
#2, 45 Overlea Blvd., Toronto, ON M4H 1C3
Tel: 416-425-7695; *Fax:* 416-425-7596
saidmoha@bellnet.ca

Toronto: **Bernard J. Monaghan - *1**
#4084, 3080 Yonge St., Toronto, ON M4N 3N1
Tel: 416-486-9919; *Fax:* 416-486-1885

Toronto: **Moore Barristers - *5**
Former Name: Bellmore & Moore
#1600, 393 University Ave., Toronto, ON M5G 1E6
Tel: 416-581-1818; *Fax:* 416-581-1279
www.bellmoreandmoore.com

Toronto: **Barbara Morgan - *1**
#216, 4195 Dundas St. West, Toronto, ON M8X 1Y4
Tel: 416-234-8248; *Fax:* 416-234-8252
barbara.morgan@sympatico.ca
www.barbaramorganlaw.com

Toronto: **Morris & Morris LLP - *4**
#203, 425 University Ave., Toronto, ON M5G 1T6
Tel: 416-366-2277; *Fax:* 416-366-5988
www.mmlaw.ca

Toronto: **Dennis S. Morris - *1**
129 John St., Toronto, ON M5V 2E2
Tel: 416-977-4799; *Fax:* 416-977-4472

Toronto: **Leslie J. Morris - *1**
101 Scollard St., Toronto, ON M5R 1G4
Tel: 416-924-0711; *Fax:* 416-960-9650

Toronto: **Morrison Brown Sosnovitch LLP - *14**
#910, P.O. Box 28, 1 Toronto St., Toronto, ON M5C 2V6
Tel: 416-368-0600; *Fax:* 416-368-6068
bizlaw@businesslawyers.com
www.businesslawyers.com

Toronto: **Sam Moskowitz - *1**
60 Bloor West, Toronto, ON M5S 1X1
Tel: 416-961-8864; *Fax:* 416-961-7654

Toronto: **Mostyn & Mostyn - *3**
845 St. Clair Ave. West, 4th Fl., Toronto, ON M6C 1C3
Tel: 416-653-3819; *Fax:* 416-653-3891
info@mostyn.ca
www.mostyn.ca

Toronto: **Anthony Moustacalis - *1**
#1000, 121 Richmond St. West, Toronto, ON M5H 2K1
Tel: 416-363-2656; *Fax:* 416-363-4920

Toronto: **Moyal & Moyal - *2**
North American Centre, 8 Finch Ave. West, Toronto, ON M2N 6L1
Tel: 416-733-3193; *Fax:* 416-250-1818
Toll-Free: 888-847-2078
canada@moyal.com
www.moyal.com

Toronto: **Matthew Moyal - *1**
Also Known As: Moyal & Moyal
8 Finch Ave. West, Toronto, ON M2N 6L1
Tel: 416-733-0330; *Fax:* 416-250-1818
matthew@moyalandassociates.com

Toronto: **J. Naumovich**
#101, 813 Broadview Ave., Toronto, ON M4K 2P8
Tel: 416-466-2119; *Fax:* 416-466-2581

Toronto: **William E. Naylor - *1**
#203, 637 College St., Toronto, ON M6G 1B5
Tel: 416-532-9940; *Fax:* 416-532-9983
naylor-william@on.aibn.com

Toronto: **Neal and Smith - *2**
#300, 3443 Finch Ave. East, Toronto, ON M1W 2S1
Tel: 416-494-4545; *Fax:* 416-494-4660
nealsmith@bellnet.ca
www.nealandsmith.com

Toronto: **Neinstein & Associates LLP - *13**
#700, 1200 Bay St., Toronto, ON M5R 2A5
Tel: 416-920-4242; *Fax:* 416-923-8358
Toll-Free: 866-920-4242
info@neinstein.com
www.neinstein.com
www.facebook.com/NeinsteinPersonalInjuryLawyers,
twitter.com/neinsteinlaw

Toronto: **C. Ann Nelson - *1**
#400, 2490 Bloor St. West, Toronto, ON M6S 1R4
Tel: 416-760-7076; *Fax:* 416-760-7338

Toronto: **Theodore Nemetz - *1**
#801, 1 St. Clair Ave. E, Toronto, ON M4T 2V7
Tel: 416-961-6560; *Fax:* 416-964-2494
nemetz@bellnet.ca

Toronto: **Newman Weinstock - *1**
#201, 3625 Dufferin St., Toronto, ON M3K 1Z2
Tel: 416-630-3220; *Fax:* 416-630-7632
rawein@on.aibn.com

Toronto: **Alexandra Ngan - *1**
#306, 1033 Bay St., Toronto, ON M5S 3A5
Tel: 416-925-3333; *Fax:* 416-925-3339

Toronto: **Metz L. Ngan - *1**
#209, 155 Gordon Baker Rd., Toronto, ON M2H 3N7
Tel: 416-502-9232; *Fax:* 416-502-3061
metznga@ipoline.com

Toronto: **Peter J. Ngan - *1**
#300, 25 Sheppard Ave. West, Toronto, ON M2N 6S6
Tel: 416-298-1828; *Fax:* 416-298-2186
Toll-Free: 855-575-5557
pjngan@yahoo.ca
www.peterngan.com

Toronto: **Trang T. Nguyen - *1**
#12, 3585 Keele St., Toronto, ON M3J 3H5
Tel: 416-638-9422; *Fax:* 416-398-8358

Toronto: **Cynthia A. Nicholas - *1**
17 Annis Rd., Toronto, ON M1M 2Y8
Tel: 416-264-2875; *Fax:* 416-264-2330

Toronto: **Nigel P. Watson Law Firm - *2**
#1518, 2 Carlton St., Toronto, ON M5B 1J3
Tel: 416-977-7700; *Fax:* 416-977-8570
nigel@nigelwatsonlaw.com
www.nigelwatsonlaw.com

Toronto: **Howard Nightingale - *1**
#302, 4580 Dufferin St., Toronto, ON M3H 5Y2
Tel: 416-663-4423; *Fax:* 416-663-4424
Toll-Free: 877-224-8225
www.howardnightingale.com
www.facebook.com-howardnightingaleprofessionalcorporation,
twitter.com-HNPC&Lawyer,
www.linkedin.com/pub/howard-nightingale/3/882/87b

Toronto: **Niman Zemans Gelgoot Barristers LLP - *16**
#300, 10 Price St., Toronto, ON M4W 1Z4
Tel: 416-921-1700; *Fax:* 416-921-8936
niman@nzgfamlaw.com
www.nzgfamlaw.com

Toronto: **Nixon Fleet & Poole LLP - *5**
Former Name: Walker Poole Nixon LLP
#1505, 2 Bloor St. West, Toronto, ON M4W 3E2
Tel: 416-225-5160; *Fax:* 416-225-0072
www.nfplaw.ca

Toronto: **Noik & Associates - *4**
#400, 3410 Sheppard Ave. E, Toronto, ON M1T 3K4
Tel: 416-754-1020; *Fax:* 416-754-1784

Toronto: **O'Neill, Browning, Pineau - *2**
#302, 372 Bay St., Toronto, ON M5H 2W9
Tel: 416-868-0544; *Fax:* 416-868-0724
browninglaw@rigers

Toronto: **O'Sullivan Estate Lawyers Professional Corporation - *3**
Also Known As: O'Sullivan Estate Lawyers
#1410, P.O. Box 68, 222 Bay St., Toronto, ON M5K 1E7
Tel: 416-363-3336; *Fax:* 416-363-9570
Toll-Free: 888-365-6235
www.osullivanlaw.com

Toronto: **Oatley Vigmond Personal Injury Lawyers LLP - Toronto - Wellington St. - *18**
#1052, 66 Wellington St. West, Toronto, ON M5K 1P2
Tel: 416-651-2421; *Fax:* 416-225-8935
Toll-Free: 888-662-2481
info@oatleyvigmond.com
www.oatleyvigmond.com
www.facebook.com/oatleyvigmond, twitter.com/OatleyVigmond,
www.linkedin.com/company/oatley-vigmond-personal-injury-lawyers

Toronto: **Office of the Children's Lawyer - *23**
c/o MGS Mail Delivery Services, 2B-88 Macdonald Block, 77 Wellesley St. West, Toronto, ON M7A 1N3
Tel: 416-314-8000; *Fax:* 416-314-8050
www.attorneygeneral.jus.gov.on.ca/english/family/ocl/

Toronto: **Oiye, Henderson - *2**
#1805 & 1812, 2 Carlton St., Toronto, ON M5B 1J3
Tel: 416-977-7700; *Fax:* 416-977-8570

Toronto: **Olch, Torgov, Cohen LLP - *2**
#901, 111 Richmond St. West, Toronto, ON M5H 2G4
Tel: 416-363-8366; *Fax:* 416-363-0783
otc@otclaw.ca

Toronto: **Olthuis Kleer Townshend LLP - *27**
Former Name: Olthuis Kleer Townshend
250 University Ave.,8th Fl., Toronto, ON M5H 3E5
Tel: 416-981-9330; *Fax:* 416-981-9350
info@oktlaw.com
www.oktlaw.com

Toronto: **Orbach, Katzman & Herschorn - *2**
#1001, 317 Adelaide St. West, Toronto, ON M5V 1P9
Tel: 416-967-6777; *Fax:* 416-967-1506
sender@okhlaw.ca

Toronto: **Mark M. Orkin, Q.C. - *1**
1 Dundas St. West, Toronto, ON M5G 1Z3
Tel: 416-363-4108; *Fax:* 416-365-9276
mmorkin@look.ca

Toronto: **Ormston, Bellissimo, Younan - *3**
#900, 1000 Finch Ave. West, Toronto, ON M3J 2V5
Tel: 416-787-6505; *Fax:* 416-787-0455

Toronto: **Samuel Osak - *1**
6 Bitteroot Rd., Toronto, ON M3H 4J4
Tel: 416-630-1041; *Fax:* 416-630-1043
sosak@sympatico.ca

Toronto: **Oster Wolfman LLP - *4**
Former Name: Kerr, Oster & Wolfman
#200, 133 Berkeley St., Toronto, ON M5A 2X1
Tel: 416-365-7163; *Fax:* 416-365-1270
kow@kow.on.ca

Toronto: **Otis & Korman - *4**
41 Madison Ave., Toronto, ON M5R 2S2
Tel: 416-979-0670; *Fax:* 416-979-3778
info@otisandkorman.com
www.liveincanada.com
twitter.com/OtisandKorman

Toronto: **Samy Ouanounou - *1**
#352, 1111 Finch Ave. West, Toronto, ON M3J 2E5
Tel: 416-222-3434; *Fax:* 416-222-3629
solaw@on.aibn.com

Toronto: **Owens, Wright LLP - *20**
#300, 20 Holly St., Toronto, ON M4S 3B1
Tel: 416-486-9800; *Fax:* 416-486-3309
www.owenswright.com

* indicates number of lawyers

Toronto: Pace Law Firm - *17
300 The East Mall, 5th Fl., Toronto, ON M9B 6B7
Tel: 416-236-3060; *Fax:* 416-236-1809
Toll-Free: 877-236-3060
lawyers@pacelawfirm.com
www.pacelawfirm.com
www.facebook.com/pacelawfirm, twitter.com/pacelawfirm,
www.linkedin.com/company/pace-law-firm

Toronto: Demetrius Pantazis - *1
#204, 1315 Lawrence Ave. East, Toronto, ON M3A 3R3
Tel: 416-469-5355; *Fax:* 416-469-8136
dpantazis@on.aibn.com

Toronto: Pape Barristers Professional Corporation - *3
#1910, P.O. Box 69, 1 Queen St. East, Toronto, ON M5C 2W5
Tel: 416-364-8765; *Fax:* 416-364-8855
www.papebarristers.com

Toronto: Ado Park Q.C. - *1
#604, 357 Bay St., Toronto, ON M5H 2T7
Tel: 416-363-4451; *Fax:* 416-363-9256

Toronto: Parkdale Community Legal Services
1266 Queen St. West, Toronto, ON M6K 1L3
Tel: 416-531-2411; *Fax:* 416-531-0885
www.parkdalelegal.org
www.facebook.com/parkdalelegal, twitter.com/parkdalelegal

Toronto: Mary Lou Parker - *1
#800, 2 St. Clair Ave. East, Toronto, ON M4T 2T5
Tel: 416-920-4708; *Fax:* 416-920-3819

Toronto: Paterson MacDougall LLP - *10
#900, P.O. Box 100, 1 Queen St. East, Toronto, ON M5C 2W5
Tel: 416-366-9607; *Fax:* 416-366-3743
info@pmlaw.com
www.pmlaw.com
twitter.com/pmlawcanada

Toronto: Philip Patterson - *1
#305, 1033 Bay St., Toronto, ON M5S 3A5
Tel: 416-968-9188; *Fax:* 416-925-2860
ppaterson@on.aibn.com

Toronto: Paul & Paul - *2
Former Name: Paul & Kanellos
39 Hayden St., Toronto, ON M4Y 2P2
Tel: 416-968-1777; *Fax:* 416-968-1211
npaul@bellnet.ca

Toronto: Murray E. Payne - *1
3329 Bloor St. West, Toronto, ON M8X 1E7
Tel: 416-232-1242; *Fax:* 416-231-1280

Toronto: Peace, Burns, Halkiw & Manning LLP - *2
#100, 25 Morrow Ave., Toronto, ON M6R 2H9
Tel: 416-533-1025; *Fax:* 416-516-5305

Toronto: Peirce, McNeely Associates - *3
25 Lesmill Rd., Toronto, ON M3B 2T3
Tel: 416-449-2060; *Fax:* 416-449-2068

Toronto: Michael Pelensky - *1
#300, 2 Toronto St., Toronto, ON M5C 2B6
Tel: 416-863-1300; *Fax:* 416-863-4942

Toronto: Penman Vona Professional Corporation, Barristers & Solicitors - *2
Former Name: Penmam & Penman
#307A, 4195 Dundas St. West, Toronto, ON M8X 1Y4
Tel: 416-231-5696; *Fax:* 416-231-5697
gvona@penman-vona.ca
www.penman-vona.ca

Toronto: Peterson Law - *5
#806, 390 Bay St., Toronto, ON M5H 2Y2
Tel: 647-259-1790; *Fax:* 647-259-1785
dhp@petelaw.com
petelaw.com

Toronto: Petropoulos & Rapos - *1
#305, 1920 Ellesmere Rd., Toronto, ON M1H 2V6
Tel: 416-431-5870; *Fax:* 416-289-4144

Toronto: V. Walter Petryshyn - *1
1247 Dundas St. West, Toronto, ON M6J 1X6
Tel: 416-534-8431; *Fax:* 416-531-2455

Toronto: Philip Horgan Law Office - *3
#301, 120 Carlton St., Toronto, ON M5A 4K2
Tel: 416-777-9994; *Fax:* 416-777-9921

Toronto: Phillips Gill LLP - *7
Former Name: Doane Phillips Yonge LLP
#200, 33 Jarvis St., Toronto, ON M5E 1N3
Tel: 416-703-1900; *Fax:* 416-703-1955
www.phillipsgill.com

Toronto: Douglas N. Phillips - *1
13 Reno Dr., Toronto, ON M1K 2V5
Tel: 416-757-3445; *Fax:* 416-759-8036
dnplaw@rogers.com

Toronto: Piasetzki Nenniger Kvas LLP - *9
#2308, 120 Adelaide St. West, Toronto, ON M5H 1T1
Tel: 416-955-0050; *Fax:* 416-955-0053
office@pnklaw.ca
www.pnklaw.ca

Toronto: Picov & Kleinberg Barristers & Solicitors - *2
#100, 110 Eglinton Ave. West, Toronto, ON M4R 1A3
Tel: 416-488-2100
www.picovkleinberg.com

Toronto: Piller & Ross - *2
#2200, 181 University Ave., Toronto, ON M5H 3M7
Tel: 416-601-1622; *Fax:* 416-363-7239

Toronto: Pinto Wray James LLP - *7
#1155, 65 Queen St. West, Toronto, ON M5H 2M5
Tel: 416-642-0460; *Fax:* 416-593-4923
info@pintowrayjames.com
www.pintowrayjames.com

Toronto: Jillian M. Pivnick - *1
#410, 350 Lonsdale Rd., Toronto, ON M5P 1R6
Tel: 416-484-6306

Toronto: Donna V. Pledge - *1
#203, 1013 Wilson Ave., Toronto, ON M3K 1G1
Tel: 416-630-8702; *Fax:* 416-630-8714
donnav.pledge@bellnet.ca
www.dvpledgecriminallawyer.ca

Toronto: Harry Poch - *1
20 Beaverhall Dr., Toronto, ON M2L 2C7
Tel: 416-444-7971; *Fax:* 416-444-8971
harrypoch@rogers.com

Toronto: Podrebarac Barristers Professional Corporation - *3
#701, 151 Bloor St. West, Toronto, ON M5S 1S4
Tel: 416-348-7500; *Fax:* 416-348-7505
podrebaracbarristers.com

Toronto: Stephen P. Ponesse - *1
#3000, 390 Bay St., Toronto, ON M5H 2Y2
Tel: 416-361-3582; *Fax:* 416-368-7217
stephenponesse@on.aibn.com

Toronto: Porjes Employment Law - *2
Former Name: M. Dawn McConnell; Porjes Walsh
#200, 30A Hazelton Ave., Toronto, ON M5R 2E2
Tel: 416-601-0500
mary@porjeslaw.com
www.porjeslaw.com

Toronto: Don Poscente - *1
683 Mt. Pleasant Rd., Toronto, ON M4S 2N2
Tel: 416-410-3333; *Fax:* 416-410-3333

Toronto: Gary M. Posesorski - *1
5 Wembley Rd., Toronto, ON M6C 2E8
Tel: 416-780-9655

Toronto: Wietse G. Posthumus - *1
#2700, West Tower, 55 Avenue Rd., Toronto, ON M5R 3L2
Tel: 416-929-3030; *Fax:* 416-961-9898

Toronto: Potts, Weisberg & Musil - *3
#206, 90 Eglinton Ave. East, Toronto, ON M4P 2Y3
Tel: 416-485-7366; *Fax:* 416-485-7368
pwmlaw@interlog.com

Toronto: Powell Weir, Barristers & Solicitors - *2
#505, 50 Gervais Dr., Toronto, ON M3C 1Z3
Tel: 416-441-6840; *Fax:* 416-441-0330
www.powellweir.com

Toronto: Harry Preisman - *2
#307, 885 Progress Ave., Toronto, ON M1H 3G3
Tel: 416-439-9559; *Fax:* 416-439-9553
pklaw@on.aibn.com
henrypreisman.synthasite.com

Toronto: Preobrazenski & Associates - *2
#414, Sherman Centre, 100 Richmond St. West, Toronto, ON M5H 3K6
Tel: 416-964-1717; *Fax:* 416-964-0823
marie@interware.com

Toronto: Price Altman Barristers - *3
Former Name: Sheldon Altman
#1708, 5000 Yonge St., Toronto, ON M2N 7E9
Tel: 416-365-0766; *Fax:* 416-365-0866
contact@over80law.com
over80law.com

Toronto: Stephen Price & Associates - *3
Former Name: Price, Stephen & Associates
#1708, 5000 Yonge St., Toronto, ON M2N 7E9
Tel: 416-365-0766; *Fax:* 416-365-0866
contact@over80law.com
over80law.com

Toronto: David R. Proctor, Q.C. - *1
#8A, 1921 Eglinton Ave. East, Toronto, ON M1L 2L6
Tel: 416-751-3958; *Fax:* 416-751-3770

Toronto: Richard G. Pyne - *1
3329 Bloor St. West, Toronto, ON M8X 1E7
Tel: 416-231-3339; *Fax:* 416-231-1280

Toronto: Quirk, McGillicuddy & Sutton - *1
1604 Dufferin St., Toronto, ON M6H 3L7
Tel: 416-652-3543; *Fax:* 416-652-2730
fran@qmsutton.ca

Toronto: R.L. & J.H. Webster
2600 Danforth Ave., Toronto, ON M4C 1L3
Tel: 416-699-9644; *Fax:* 416-699-8905

Toronto: Rachlin & Wolfson LLP - *12
#1500, 390 Bay St., Toronto, ON M5H 2Y2
Tel: 416-367-0202; *Fax:* 416-367-1820
enquiry@rachlinlaw.com
www.rachlinlaw.com

Toronto: Danuta H. Radomski - *1
351 Castlefield Ave., Toronto, ON M5N 1L4
Tel: 416-322-6134; *Fax:* 416-489-1462
dradomski@on.aibn.com

Toronto: R. Sam Ramlall - *1
#700, 5799 Yonge St., Toronto, ON M2M 3V3
Tel: 416-512-6465; *Fax:* 416-512-6042
rsamramlall@bellnet.ca

Toronto: Raphael Barristers - *5
#1503, 889 Bay St., Toronto, ON M5S 3K5
Tel: 416-594-1812; *Fax:* 416-594-0868
info@raphaelbar.com
www.raphaelbarristers.com

Toronto: Rawana & Rawana Barristers & Solicitors - *2
11721 Sheppard Ave. East, 2nd Fl., Toronto, ON M1B 1G3
Tel: 416-281-8505; *Fax:* 416-286-4353

Toronto: Rayson & Associates - *4
#302, 3845 Bathurst St., Toronto, ON M3H 3N2
Tel: 416-630-5600; *Fax:* 416-630-5906

Toronto: John L. Razulis - *1
362 Glengarry Ave., Toronto, ON M5M 1E6
Tel: 416-787-1918; *Fax:* 416-787-7161
counsel@lawfulwork.ca
www.lawfulwork.ca

Toronto: Refugee Law Office - *4
#202, 20 Dundas St. West, Toronto, ON M5G 2H1
Tel: 416-977-8111; *Fax:* 416-977-5567
rlo@lao.on.ca
www.legalaid.on.ca

Toronto: Regan Desjardins LLP - *9
Former Name: Regan Kram Desjardins LLP
#1502, P.O. Box 2069, 20 Eglinton Ave. West, Toronto, ON M4R 1K8
Tel: 416-601-1000; *Fax:* 416-601-9255
reception@rkdlaw.com
www.regandesjardins.com

Toronto: Terrence S. Reiber - *1
#211, 1110 Sheppard Ave. East, Toronto, ON M2K 2W2
Tel: 416-927-9841; *Fax:* 416-975-1531

* indicates number of lawyers

Toronto: Reingold & Reingold - *1
#3028, P.O. Box 17, 3080 Yonge St., Toronto, ON M4N 3N1
Tel: 416-483-3364; Fax: 416-440-1942
jrqc58@bellnet.ca

Toronto: Arn C.J. Reisler - *1
161 Bridgeland Ave., Toronto, ON M6A 1Z1
Tel: 416-781-4002; Fax: 416-781-7797
areisler@wastecogroup.com

Toronto: Stanley Reisman - *1
#308, 360 Bloor St. West, Toronto, ON M5S 1X1
Tel: 416-961-8864; Fax: 416-961-7654

Toronto: Reiter-Nemetz - *2
#100, 298 Sheppard Ave. West, Toronto, ON M2N 1N5
Tel: 416-665-1458; Fax: 416-665-0895
www.reiternemetz.com

Toronto: Rekai LLP - *3
Former Name: Rekai Somerleigh Berezowski
#1605, 33 Bloor St. East, 16th Fl., Toronto, ON M4W 3H1
Tel: 416-960-8876; Fax: 416-924-2371
www.mobilitylaw.com
twitter.com/rekaillp

Toronto: David J.M. Rendeiro - *2
#200, 1201 Dundas St. West, Toronto, ON M6J 1X3
Tel: 416-588-8000; Fax: 416-588-8002

Toronto: Reznick, Parsons - *2
#1917, 25 Adelaide St. E, Toronto, ON M5C 3A1
Tel: 416-863-6026; Fax: 416-863-9334

Toronto: Richardson, Schnall & Sanderson - *1
14 Colwood Rd., Toronto, ON M9A 4E3
Tel: 416-233-9671; Fax: 416-233-9671

Toronto: Richman & Richman - *1
#404, 255 Duncan Mill Rd., Toronto, ON M3B 3H9
Tel: 416-510-8866

Toronto: Nina S. Richmond - *1
148 Brookdale Ave., Toronto, ON M5M 1P5
Tel: 416-489-4191; Fax: 416-489-5822
nina.richmond@rogers.com

Toronto: Ricketts, Harris LLP - *18
#800, 181 University Ave., Toronto, ON M5H 2X7
Tel: 416-364-6211; Fax: 416-364-1697
info@rickettsharris.com
www.rickettsharris.com

Toronto: Gerald Rifkin - *1
#500, 1000 Finch Ave. West, Toronto, ON M3J 2V5
Tel: 416-667-9796; Fax: 416-667-8048

Toronto: Riley Aikins - *4
#1509, 180 Dundas St. West, Toronto, ON M5G 1Z8
Tel: 416-364-7611; Fax: 866-820-8360
info@rileyaikins.ca
www.rileyaikins.ca

Toronto: Riverdale Law Group - *3
167 Danforth Ave., Toronto, ON M4K 1N2
Tel: 416-466-6264; Fax: 416-466-8465

Toronto: Riverdale Mediation - *3
#2000, 393 University Ave., Toronto, ON M5G 1E6
Tel: 416-593-0210; Fax: 416-593-1352
hello@riverdalemediation.com
www.riverdalemediation.com
www.facebook.com/RiverdaleMediation,
twitter.com/riverdaleADR, www.linkedin.com/company/875109

Toronto: William H. Roberts - *1
#201, 34 Southport St., Toronto, ON M6S 3N3
Tel: 416-769-3162; Fax: 416-762-8972

Toronto: Robertson & Keith - *1
2481 Kingston Rd., Toronto, ON M1N 1V4
Tel: 416-261-1220; Fax: 416-261-1716

Toronto: Robins Appleby - *26
Former Name: Robins, Appleby & Taub LLP
#2600, 120 Adelaide St. West, Toronto, ON M5H 1T1
Tel: 416-868-1080; Fax: 416-868-0306
info@robapp.com
www.robinsappleby.com

Toronto: Rogers & Rowland - *1
#400, 1235 Bay St., Toronto, ON M5R 3K4
Tel: 416-364-2333; Fax: 416-864-0271
mail@rogersrowland.com

Toronto: Rogers Law Office - *1
Also Known As: RLO
#3B, 4 Deer Park Cres., Toronto, ON M4V 2C3
Tel: 416-363-6626; Fax: 416-363-6628
file@rlo.ca
www.rlo.ca

Toronto: Rogers Partners LLP - *23
#1900, P.O. Box 255, 100 Wellington St. West, Toronto, ON M5K 1J5
Tel: 416-594-4500; Fax: 416-594-9100
info@rogerspartners.com
www.rogersmoore.com

Toronto: Nelson Roland - *1
333 Adelaide St. West, 3rd Fl., Toronto, ON M5V 1R5
Tel: 416-351-1591; Fax: 416-340-9250
nroland@allstream.net

Toronto: Norman W. Ronka - *1
946 College St., Toronto, ON M6H 1A5
Tel: 416-969-0917; Fax: 416-905-8221

Toronto: Law Office of Christopher J. Roper - *1
#3300, The Cadillac Fairview Tower, 20 Queen St. W, Toronto, ON M5H 3R3
Tel: 416-368-6788; Fax: 416-368-5705
cjroper@interhop.net
www.cjroperlaw.com

Toronto: Rose, Persiko, Rakowsky, Melvin LLP - *2
#600, 390 Bay St., Toronto, ON M5H 2Y2
Tel: 416-868-1900; Fax: 416-868-1708

Toronto: Rosen Nastor LLP - *3
Former Name: Rosen & Company
#504, 330 University Ave., Toronto, ON M5G 1R7
Tel: 416-205-9700; Fax: 416-205-9970
reception@rosenlaw.ca
www.rosennaster.com

Toronto: Elliot F. Rosenberg - *1
#201, 4949 Bathurst St., Toronto, ON M2R 2T4
Tel: 416-512-7373; Fax: 416-512-7374
tlpress@patncom.com

Toronto: Irving Rosenberg - *1
#507, 1000 Finch Ave. West, Toronto, ON M3J 2V5
Tel: 416-398-0102; Fax: 416-398-0103
irose@on.aibn.com

Toronto: Rosenblatt Immigration Law - *2
#201, 645 King St. West, Toronto, ON M5V 1M5
Tel: 416-644-4000; Fax: 416-861-1215
contact@rosenblatt.net
www.immigrate.net

Toronto: Stanley Rosenfarb - *1
#800, 2001 Sheppard Ave. East, Toronto, ON M2J 4Z8
Tel: 416-494-4899; Fax: 416-494-3024
stan@srlaw.com

Toronto: Ross & Bank - *2
#300, 123 John St., Toronto, ON M5V 2E2
Tel: 416-572-4910; Fax: 416-551-8808
info@rossandbank.com
www.rossandbank.com

Toronto: Larry H. Ross - *1
#200, 609 Bloor St. West, Toronto, ON M6G 1K5
Tel: 416-535-6211; Fax: 416-535-7698

Toronto: Aubrey M. Rossman - *1
124 Laird Dr. East, Toronto, ON M4G 3V3
Tel: 416-444-2201; Fax: 416-444-0571

Toronto: Cecil L. Rotenberg - *3
#308, 245 Fairveiw Dr., Toronto, ON M2J 4T1
Tel: 416-449-8866; Fax: 416-510-9090
cclrqc@yahoo.com
www.cecilrotenberg.org

Toronto: Frank L. Roth - *1
#500, 70 Bond St., Toronto, ON M5B 1X3
Tel: 416-963-8776; Fax: 416-863-4896
flr@bondlaw.net

Toronto: Neal H. Roth - *1
#401, 60 St. Clair Ave. East, Toronto, ON M4T 1N5
Tel: 416-351-7706; Fax: 416-351-7684
www.nealhroth.com

Toronto: Rothman & Rothman - *1
#638, 121 Richmond St. W, Toronto, ON M5H 2K1
Tel: 416-367-9901; Fax: 416-367-9979
rothman@sympatico.ca

Toronto: Nancy-Gay Rotstein - *1
#202, 40 Holly St., Toronto, ON M4S 3C3
Tel: 416-488-0800; Fax: 416-488-8350
nrotstein@municipal.ca

Toronto: ROUTE Transport & Trade Law - *2
Former Name: William M. Sharpe Barrister & Solicitor
#305, 40 Wynford Dr., Toronto, ON M3C 1J5
Tel: 416-482-5321; Fax: 416-322-2083
info@shippinglaw.ca
www.shipping-law.ca
www.linkedin.com/company-beta/3528586

Toronto: Roy O'Connor LLP - *7
#2300, 200 Front St. West, Toronto, ON M5V 3K2
Tel: 416-362-1989; Fax: 416-362-6204
info@royoconnor.ca
royoconnor.ca

Toronto: Rubenstein, Siegel - *2
#402, 1200 Sheppard Ave. E, Toronto, ON M2K 2S5
Tel: 416-499-5252; Fax: 416-499-2290

Toronto: Rubin Thomlinson LLP - *7
#1104, 20 Adelaide St. East, Toronto, ON M5C 2T6
Tel: 416-847-1814; Fax: 416-847-1815
info@rubinthomlinson.com
www.rubinthomlinson.com
twitter.com/RubinThomlinson,

Toronto: Barry Rubinoff - *1
488 Huron St., Toronto, ON M5R 2R3
Tel: 416-966-4884; Fax: 416-966-6768

Toronto: Ruby Shiller & Enenajor, Barristers - *4
Former Name: Ruby Shiller Chan Hasan Barristers
92 Isabella St., Toronto, ON M4Y 1N4
Tel: 416-964-9664; Fax: 416-964-8305
lawyers@rubyshiller.com
www.rubyshiller.com

Toronto: Ruderman Shaw - *2
#1820, P.O. Box 2037, 20 Eglinton Ave. West, Toronto, ON M4R 1K8
Tel: 416-484-8558; Fax: 416-484-6918
info@rudermanshaw.com

Toronto: Victor E. Rudinskas - *1
27 John St., 2nd Fl., Toronto, ON M9N 1J4
Tel: 416-240-0594; Fax: 416-248-5922
Toll-Free: 877-888-8390
vrudinskas@trebnet.com

Toronto: George A. Rudnik - *1
#1901, 260 Queens Quay West, Toronto, ON M5J 2N3
Tel: 416-927-7788; Fax: 416-925-9963

Toronto: Rueters LLP - *9
Former Name: Rueter Scargall Bennett LLP
#2200, P.O. Box 4, 250 Yonge St., Toronto, ON M5B 2L7
Tel: 416-869-9090; Fax: 416-869-3411
info@ruetersllp.com
www.ruetersllp.com

Toronto: Martin K.I. Rumack - *1
#202, 2 St. Clair Ave. East, Toronto, ON M4T 2T5
Tel: 416-961-3441; Fax: 416-961-1045
martin@martinrumack.com
www.martinrumack.com
twitter.com/MKIRumack, www.linkedin.com/company/3548583

Toronto: Brian A. Rumanek - *1
#201, 200 Evans Ave., Toronto, ON M8Z 1J7
Tel: 416-252-9115; Fax: 416-253-0494
thelawman@rogers.com

Toronto: Richard E. Rusek - *1
1623 Bloor St. West, Toronto, ON M6P 1A6
Tel: 416-533-8563

Toronto: Rusonik, O'Connor, Robbins, Ross, Gorham & Angelini, LLP - *28
#100, 36 Lombard St., Toronto, ON M5C 2X3
Tel: 416-598-1811; Fax: 416-598-3384
www.criminaltriallawyers.ca

Toronto: Rebecca J. Rutherford - *1
Ontario Court of Justice, 444 Yonge St., 2nd Fl., Toronto, ON M5B 2H4
Tel: 416-325-8972; Fax: 416-325-8944

indicates number of lawyers

Toronto: Ryder Wright Blair and Holmes LLP - *1
Also Known As: RWBH
333 Adelaide St. West, 3rd Fl., Toronto, ON M5V 1R5
Tel: 416-340-9070; Fax: 416-340-9250
www.rwbh.ca

Toronto: Lawrence D. Ryder - *1
#502, 1235 Bay St., Toronto, ON MR5 3K4
Tel: 416-862-5557; Fax: 416-862-5551
www.ryderlitigationlawyer.com

Toronto: Nadir Sachak - *1
#920, 6 Adelaide St. East, Toronto, ON M5C 1H6
Tel: 416-363-7172; Fax: 416-363-9917
Toll-Free: 877-878-7206
baylawoffice@gmail.com

Toronto: Howard Saginur - *1
#1300, 5255 Yonge St., Toronto, ON M2N 6P4
Tel: 416-512-1912; Fax: 416-512-1989
howard@saginur.com
www.saginur.com

Toronto: Firoz G. Salehmohamed - *1
#202, 747 Don Mills Rd., Toronto, ON M3C 1T2
Tel: 416-421-7000; Fax: 416-421-5388

Toronto: Maureen K. Saltman Arbitrations Ltd. - *1
#502, 121 Richmond St. West, Toronto, ON M5H 2K1
Tel: 416-366-3091; Fax: 416-366-0879
mksaltman@bellnet.ca

Toronto: Samis & Company - *15
#1600, 400 University Ave., Toronto, ON M5G 1S5
Tel: 416-365-0000; Fax: 416-365-9993
info@samislaw.com
www.samislaw.com

Toronto: Sanderson Entertainment Law - *4
#303, 577 Kingston Rd., Toronto, ON M4E 1R3
Tel: 416-971-6616; Fax: 416-971-4144
info@sandersonlaw.ca
www.sandersonlaw.ca
www.facebook.com/551812878234395

Toronto: Shil K. Sanwalka, Q.C. - *1
#602, 18 Wynford Dr., Toronto, ON M3C 3S2
Tel: 416-449-7755; Fax: 416-449-6969
skslaw@sanwalka.org

Toronto: Umberto Sapone - *1
#201, 3200 Dufferin St., Toronto, ON M6A 2T3
Tel: 416-789-2689; Fax: 416-789-0454

Toronto: Peter M. Scandiffio, Q.C. - *1
#308, 344 Bloor St. West, Toronto, ON M5S 3A7
Tel: 416-515-1660; Fax: 416-515-1526

Toronto: Scher Law Professional Corporation - Toronto - *2
175 Bloor St. East, Toronto, ON M4W 3R8
Tel: 416-515-9686 Toll-Free: 855-246-0243
info@lostjobs.ca
www.lostjobs.ca

Toronto: Schneider Ruggiero LLP - *8
#1000, 120 Adelaide St. West, Toronto, ON M5H 3V1
Tel: 416-363-2211; Fax: 416-363-0645
Toll-Free: 800-268-2111
info@srlawpractice.com
srlawpractice.com

Toronto: Schnurr Kirsh Schnurr Oelbaum Tator LLP - *7
Former Name: Schnurr Kirsh Stephens
#1700, Thomson Building, 65 Queen St., Toronto, ON M5H 2M5
Tel: 416-860-1057; Fax: 416-367-2502
www.estatelitigation.net

Toronto: Cecil Schwartz - *1
#2108, Madison Centre, 4950 Yonge St., Toronto, ON M2N 6K1
Tel: 416-250-0083; Fax: 416-512-8275
cecil@cecilschwartz.com

Toronto: Scott & Oleskiw - *2
Former Name: Diane Oleskiw
#235, 215 Spadina Ave., Toronto, ON M5T 2C7
Tel: 416-591-1261
admin@scottoleskiw.com

Toronto: Peter B. Scully - *1
56 Tranby St., Toronto, ON M5R 1N5
Tel: 416-929-2909; Fax: 416-929-2909
scullylaw@sympatico.ca

Toronto: Alexander Sennecke - *1
#900, Victoria Tower, 25 Adelaide St. East, Toronto, ON M5C 3A1
Tel: 416-410-2113; Fax: 416-410-9423
asennecke@sennecke.com
www.sennecke.com

Toronto: Seon Gutstadt Lash LLP - *6
#1800, 4950 Yonge St., Toronto, ON M2N 6K1
Tel: 416-224-0224; Fax: 416-224-0758
info@torlaw.com
www.torlaw.com/sgl

Toronto: Sera Associates - *2
Former Name: Sera, Harrison Associates
#1800, 4950 Yonge St., Toronto, ON M2N 6K1
Tel: 416-224-0200; Fax: 416-224-0758

Toronto: Frederick J. Shanahan - *1
#414, 100 Richmond St. West, Toronto, ON M5H 3K6
Tel: 416-972-6449; Fax: 416-964-0823
f_shanny@hotmail.com

Toronto: Share Lawyers - *12
Former Name: David Share Associates
3442 Yonge St., Toronto, ON M4N 2M9
Tel: 416-488-9000; Fax: 416-488-9004
Toll-Free: 877-777-1109
www.sharelawyers.com
www.facebook.com/281913208534425, twitter.com/sharelaw,
www.linkedin.com/company/share-lawyers

Toronto: Chet Sharma - *1
#7, 1658 Victoria Park Ave., Toronto, ON M1R 1P7
Tel: 416-285-1550; Fax: 416-285-1698
chetsharma@aol.com

Toronto: Roop N. Sharma - *2
942 Gerrard St. East, Toronto, ON M4M 1Z2
Tel: 416-461-0467; Fax: 416-461-5817

Toronto: Shearman & Sterling LLP - *8
#4405, Commerce Court West, P.O. Box 247, 199 Bay St., Toronto, ON M5L 1E8
Tel: 416-360-8484
www.shearman.com
www.facebook.com/shearmanandsterlingllp,
twitter.com/ShearmanLaw,
www.linkedin.com/company/shearman-&-sterling-llp

Toronto: Shekter, Dychtenberg LLP - *4
#2900, 390 Bay St., Toronto, ON M5H 2Y2
Tel: 416-941-9995; Fax: 416-869-0321
Toll-Free: 855-347-8177
richard@shekter.com
www.shekter.com

Toronto: Shell Lawyers - *1
Former Name: Shell Jacobs Lawyers
615 Lonsdale Rd., Toronto, ON M5P 1R8
Tel: 416-539-0226; Fax: 416-539-0565
inquiry@shelllawyers.ca
www.shelllawyers.ca
twitter.com/shelllawyers,
www.linkedin.com/company/shell-lawyers

Toronto: Shelton Associates - *2
#810, 439 University Ave., Toronto, ON M5G 1Y8
Tel: 416-977-8888; Fax: 416-977-1964

Toronto: Sheppard Shalinksy Brown - *3
488 Huron St., Toronto, ON M5R 2R3
Tel: 416-966-6885; Fax: 416-966-6837
Ysheppard@sfmlaw.com

Toronto: Sheridan, Ippolito Family & Estate Lawyers - *2
#506, 2 Jane St., Toronto, ON M6S 4W3
Tel: 416-763-3399; Fax: 416-763-3443
info@sheridanippolito.com
www.sheridanippolito.com

Toronto: Sherman, Brown, Dryer, Karol, Gold, Lebow - *9
Also Known As: Sherman Brown Barristers & Solicitors
#900, 5075 Yonge St., Toronto, ON M2N 6C6
Tel: 416-224-9800; Fax: 416-222-3091
www.shermanbrown.com

Toronto: Sheldon L. Sherman - *1
2645 Eglinton Ave. East, Toronto, ON M1K 2S2
Tel: 416-261-7161; Fax: 416-261-7163

Toronto: Sherrard Kuzz LLP, Employment & Labour Lawyers - *28
#3300, 250 Yonge St., Toronto, ON M5B 2L7
Tel: 416-603-0700; Fax: 416-603-6035
info@sherrardkuzz.com
www.sherrardkuzz.com
twitter.com/sherrardkuzz

Toronto: Shibley Righton LLP - Toronto
#700, 250 University Ave., Toronto, ON M5H 3E5
Tel: 416-214-5200; Fax: 416-214-5400
Toll-Free: 877-214-5200
admin@shibleyrighton.com
www.shibleyrighton.com

Toronto: Shields O'Donnell MacKillop LLP - *9
Also Known As: Shields O'Donnell MacKillop LLP
Former Name: Hodgson Shields DesBrisay O'Donnell MacKillop Squire LLP
#1800, 65 Queen St. West, Toronto, ON M5H 2M5
Tel: 416-304-6400; Fax: 416-304-6406
info@somlaw.ca
www.somlaw.ca
twitter.com/Som_Law_, www.linkedin.com/company/1175232

Toronto: Bernard S. Shier - *1
219 Carlton St., Toronto, ON M5A 2L2
Tel: 416-923-8997; Fax: 416-923-8380

Toronto: Stanley I. Shier, Q.C. - *1
65 Queen St. West, 17th Fl., Toronto, ON M5H 2M5
Tel: 416-366-9591; Fax: 416-366-2107
stanleyshier@shierlaw.com

Toronto: Shoihet Earle Israel - *1
100 Adelaide St. West, Toronto, ON M5H 1S3
Tel: 416-863-9594

Toronto: Geary B. Shorser Law - *1
#2000, 393 University Ave., Toronto, ON M5G 1E6
Tel: 416-977-7749; Fax: 416-593-1352
shorserlaw.petrasite.com

Toronto: Ian C. Shoub - *1
1000 Finch Ave. West, 4th Fl., Toronto, ON M3J 2V5
Tel: 416-661-0990; Fax: 416-663-3236
ishoub@on.aibn.com

Toronto: Robert Shour - *1
#2000, 393 University Ave., Toronto, ON M5G 1E6
Tel: 416-977-4492; Fax: 416-977-4971
ralshour@on.aibn.com

Toronto: Louis D. Silver, Q.C. - *1
15 Silvergrove Rd., Toronto, ON M2L 2N5
Tel: 416-445-2795; Fax: 416-445-7243
louisdsilverqc@rogers.com

Toronto: Sheldon N. Silverman - *1
#638, 121 Richmond St. West, Toronto, ON M5H 2K1
Tel: 416-363-6295; Fax: 416-363-3047
ssilverman@sympatico.ca
www.sheldonsilverman.com

Toronto: Sim & McBurney - *17
330 University Ave., 6th Fl., Toronto, ON M5G 1R7
Tel: 416-595-1155; Fax: 416-595-1163
simip.com

Toronto: Sim, Lowman, Ashton & McKay LLP - *17
330 University Ave., 6th Fl., Toronto, ON M5G 1R7
Tel: 416-595-1155; Fax: 416-595-1163
simip.com

Toronto: Michael S. Simrod - *1
#500, 1000 Finch Ave. West, Toronto, ON M3J 2V5
Tel: 416-667-0980; Fax: 416-487-1091
fireblade4.8.11@gmail.com

Toronto: Isaac Singer - *1
2424 Bloor St. West, Toronto, ON M6S 1P9
Tel: 416-766-1135; Fax: 416-769-5365
isinger@bellnet.ca

Toronto: Singer, Keyfetz, Crackower & Saltzman - *2
532 Eglinton Ave. East, Toronto, ON M4P 1N6
Tel: 416-488-6900; Fax: 416-488-7530

* indicates number of lawyers

Toronto: Singer, Kwinter LLP - *6
#214, 1033 Bay St., Toronto, ON M5S 3A5
Tel: 416-961-2882; Fax: 416-961-6760
Toll-Free: 866-285-6927
info@singerkwinter.com
www.singerkwinter.com
www.facebook.com/342779048517, twitter.com/Singer_Kwinter,
www.linkedin.com/company/singer-kwinter

Toronto: Yaso Sinnadurai - *1
#202, 2100 Ellesmere Rd., Toronto, ON M1H 3B7
Tel: 416-265-3456; Fax: 416-265-2770

Toronto: Regina Sinukoff - *1
#507, 1000 Finch Ave. West, Toronto, ON M3J 2V5
Tel: 416-739-7272; Fax: 416-739-7770
rsinukoff@on.aibn.com

Toronto: Steven H. Sinukoff - *1
127 Orchard View Blvd., Toronto, ON M4R 1C1
Tel: 416-489-7997; Fax: 416-256-9244
stevensinukoff@bellnet.ca

Toronto: Skadden, Arps, Slate, Meagher & Flom LLP - Toronto - *11
Also Known As: Skadden
#1750, P.O. Box 258, 222 Bay St., Toronto, ON M5K 1J5
Tel: 416-777-4700; Fax: 416-777-4747
www.skadden.com
www.facebook.com/skadden, twitter.com/SkaddenArps,
www.linkedin.com/company/4862

Toronto: Joel Skapinker - *2
P.O. Box 54027, Stn. Lawrence Plaza, Toronto, ON M6A 1A0
Tel: 416-783-1379; Fax: 416-352-0191
joel@skapinker.com
sites.google.com/a/skapinker.com/law

Toronto: Steven H. Skolnik - *1
#318, 4002 Sheppard Ave. East, Toronto, ON M1S 4R5
Tel: 416-297-7300; Fax: 416-298-7142

Toronto: Slater & Wells - *2
Sherway Executive Centre, 300 North Queen St., Toronto,
ON M9C 5K4
Tel: 416-259-4293; Fax: 416-259-1286

Toronto: Andrea M. Smart - *1
8 Rolston Ave., Toronto, ON M5A 3Z2
Tel: 416-961-8829; Fax: 416-961-8829

Toronto: Cindy L. Smith
P.O. Box 43514, Stn. Leaside, 1531 Bayview Ave., Toronto,
ON M4G 4G8
Tel: 416-408-0008

Toronto: Kenneth D. Smith - *1
#500, 70 Bond St., Toronto, ON M5B 1X3
Tel: 416-361-0232; Fax: 416-863-4896

Toronto: Raymond I. Smith - *1
#1507, 8 King St. East., Toronto, ON M5C 1B5
Tel: 416-861-8695; Fax: 416-861-9074
raylaw@on.aibn.com

Toronto: Smitiuch Injury Law - *3
#600, 21 Four Seasons Place, Toronto, ON M9B 6J8
Tel: 647-799-2735; Fax: 416-621-1558
Toll-Free: 800-528-6489
www.smitiuchinjurylaw.com
www.facebook.com/SmitiuchLaw, twitter.com/SmitiuchLaw,
www.linkedin.com/company/smitiuch-injury-law

Toronto: Snider & Digregorio - *2
Former Name: Snider, D.B.
978 Kingston Rd., Toronto, ON M4E 1S9
Tel: 416-699-0424; Fax: 416-699-0285
info@sdlegal.ca
www.sdlegal.ca

Toronto: Kenneth E. Snider - *1
#309, 2100 Ellesmere Rd., Toronto, ON M1H 3B7
Tel: 416-800-2579
www.kennethsnider.ca

Toronto: Irving Snitman - *1
554 Annette St., Toronto, ON M6S 2C2
Tel: 416-767-0805; Fax: 416-767-4619
www.irvingsnitman.com

Toronto: Solnik & Solnik Professional Corp.
2991 Dundas St. West, Toronto, ON M6P 1Z4
Tel: 416-767-7506; Fax: 416-767-4738
info@solnikandsolnik.com
www.solnikandsolnik.com

Toronto: Solomon, Grosberg LLP - *2
#410, 20 Toronto St., Toronto, ON M5C 2B8
Tel: 416-366-7828; Fax: 416-366-3513
lawyers@solgro.com
www.solgro.com

Toronto: Somjen & Peterson - *1
#810, 1240 Bay St., Toronto, ON M5R 2A7
Tel: 416-922-8083; Fax: 416-922-4234
info@somjen.com
www.somjen.com

Toronto: Sommers & Roth - *4
268 Avenue Rd., Toronto, ON M4V 2G7
Tel: 416-961-1212; Fax: 416-961-2827
Toll-Free: 866-802-3789
www.sommersandroth.com

Toronto: Larry S. Sonenberg - *1
1123 Albion Rd., Toronto, ON M9V 1A9
Tel: 416-749-6000; Fax: 416-749-6004
Toll-Free: 877-388-5962

Toronto: Sosa & Associates - *1
#600, 161 Eglinton Ave. East, Toronto, ON M4P 1J5
Tel: 416-480-2324; Fax: 416-480-2923

Toronto: Sotos LLP - *22
#1200, 180 Dundas St. West, Toronto, ON M5G 1Z8
Tel: 416-977-0007; Fax: 416-977-0717
Toll-Free: 888-977-9806
info@sotosllp.com
www.sotosllp.com
www.facebook.com/sotosllp, twitter.com/sotosllp,
www.linkedin.com/company/sotos-llp

Toronto: Spencer Law Firm - *1
Former Name: Spencer Romberg Associates
#300, 162 Cumberland St., Toronto, ON M5R 3N5
Tel: 416-967-1571; Fax: 416-966-1161

Toronto: Spiegel Rosenthal - *1
#2410, P.O. Box 24, 401 Bay St., Toronto, ON M5H 2Y4
Tel: 416-865-9677; Fax: 416-363-7781
david@drlaw.ca
www.drlaw.ca

Toronto: Belva Spiel - *1
#12, 245 Eglington Ave., Toronto, ON M4P 3B7
Tel: 416-486-1688; Fax: 416-486-2274
spiel@on.aibn.com

Toronto: Michael Spiro - *1
#207, 3625 Dufferin St., Toronto, ON M3K 1Z2
Tel: 416-630-1370; Fax: 416-633-2229

Toronto: Sprigings Intellectual Property Law - *6
Former Name: Hitchman & Sprigings
#715, Sun Life Financial Centre, East Tower, 3250 Bloor St.
West, Toronto, ON M8X 2X9
Tel: 416-777-0888; Fax: 416-777-0881
info@sprigings.com
www.sprigings.com

Toronto: Harvey Spring - *1
#488, 22 College St., Toronto, ON M5G 1K2
Tel: 416-967-0800; Fax: 416-967-2783
harveyspring@bellnet.ca

Toronto: Jerome Stanleigh - *1
#800, 5255 Yonge St., Toronto, ON M2N 6P4
Tel: 416-924-0151; Fax: 416-924-2887
jerome@stanleigh.com
www.stanleigh.com

Toronto: James Stefoff - *1
#1505, 80 Richmond St. W, Toronto, ON M5H 2A4
Tel: 416-366-7984

Toronto: Maxwell Steidman, Q.C. - *1
#201, 1013 Wilson Ave., Toronto, ON M3K 1G1
Tel: 416-366-7661; Fax: 416-360-6868

Toronto: Larry C. Stein - *1
#625, 4211 Yonge St., Toronto, ON M2P 2A9
Tel: 416-636-8100; Fax: 416-636-6545

Toronto: Lorisa Stein - *1
#800, 150 York St., Toronto, ON M5H 3S5
Tel: 416-596-8081
lorisa@idirect.com
www.lorisastein.com

Toronto: Steinberg Title Hope & Israel LLP - *15
Former Name: Steinberg Morton Hope & Israel LLP
#1100, 5255 Yonge St., Toronto, ON M2N 6P4
Tel: 416-225-2777; Fax: 416-225-7112
www.sthilaw.com

Toronto: Steinecke Maciura LeBlanc, Barristers & Solicitors - *9
#2308, P.O. Box 23, 401 Bay St., Toronto, ON M5H 2Y4
Tel: 416-599-2200; Fax: 416-593-7867
Toll-Free: 877-498-1630
rsteinecke@sml-law.com
www.sml-law.com

Toronto: Stern Landesman Clark LLP - *3
#1724, 390 Bay St., Toronto, ON M5H 2Y2
Tel: 416-869-3422; Fax: 416-869-3449
Toll-Free: 800-882-9635
www.sternlaw.ca

Toronto: Gary A. Stern - *1
1938 Avenue Rd., Toronto, ON M5M 4A2
Tel: 416-780-0199; Fax: 416-780-0155
Toll-Free: 800-678-6705
gastern@torlaw.com

Toronto: Stevenson Whelton MacDonald & Swan LLP - *8
Former Name: Stevensons LLP
#202, 15 Toronto St., Toronto, ON M5C 2E3
Tel: 416-599-7900; Fax: 416-599-7910
www.stevensonlaw.net

Toronto: Deborah L. Stewart - *1
106 Glencairn Ave., Toronto, ON M4R 1M9
Tel: 416-226-9340; Fax: 416-226-5341

Toronto: Stikeman Keeley Spiegel LLP - *4
Also Known As: SKS
Former Name: Stikeman Keeley Spiegel Pasternack
LLP
#2300, 200 Front St. West, Toronto, ON M5V 3K2
Tel: 416-367-1930; Fax: 416-365-1813
www.stikeman.to

Toronto: Stockwoods LLP - *19
#4130, TD North Tower, P.O. Box 140, 77 King St. West,
Toronto, ON M5K 1H1
Tel: 416-593-7200; Fax: 416-593-9345
reception@stockwoods.ca
www.stockwoods.ca
twitter.com/stockwoodsllp,
www.linkedin.com/company-beta/1182782

Toronto: Stone & Osborne - *2
#201, 100 Sheppard Ave. West, Toronto, ON M2N 1M6
Tel: 416-225-1145; Fax: 416-225-0832

Toronto: David S. Strashin - *1
#702, 55 Eglinton Ave. East, Toronto, ON M4P 1G8
Tel: 416-482-8171; Fax: 416-485-4174

Toronto: Michael Strathman - *1
219 Carlton St., Toronto, ON M5A 2L2
Tel: 416-922-2424; Fax: 416-923-8380
michael@strathmanlaw.ca
www.strathmanlaw.ca

Toronto: Stringer LLP - *8
#800, 390 Bay St., Toronto, ON M5H 2Y2
Tel: 416-862-1616; Fax: 416-363-7358
Toll-Free: 866-821-7306
info@stringerllp.com
www.stringerllp.com
twitter.com/stringerLLP,

Toronto: John F. Stroz, Q.C. - *1
2275 Dundas St. West, Toronto, ON M6R 1X6
Tel: 416-536-2131; Fax: 416-536-5451

Toronto: Robert P. Sullivan - *1
#1807, 8 King St. East, Toronto, ON M5C 1B5
Tel: 416-361-0390; Fax: 416-361-0248
rpsullivan@on.aibn.com

Toronto: Sultan Lawyers PC - *3
#300, 212 Adelaide St. West, Toronto, ON M5H 1W7
Tel: 416-214-5111; Fax: 416-214-5666
www.sultanlawyers.com
www.facebook.com/sultanlawyers, twitter.com/sultanlawyers

Toronto: Suter Law
102 Annette St., Toronto, ON M6P 1N6
Tel: 416-760-0529; Fax: 416-760-9967

indicates number of lawyers

Toronto: Ian Sutherland Barrister & Solicitor - *1
#203, 3415 Dundas St. West, Toronto, ON M6S 2S1
Tel: 416-763-0787; *Fax:* 416-763-0563
ian@sutherland.com
www.iansutherland.com

Toronto: Swadron Associates - *5
115 Berkeley St., Toronto, ON M5A 2W8
Tel: 416-362-1234; *Fax:* 416-362-1232
www.swadron.com

Toronto: Kenneth P. Swan - *1
P.O. Box 1284, Stn. K, 2384 Yonge St., Toronto, ON M4P 3E5
Tel: 416-368-5279; *Fax:* 888-547-0595
kpswan@bondlaw.net

Toronto: Eric J. Swetsky - *1
25 Sylvan Valley Way, Toronto, ON M5M 4M4
Tel: 416-787-4376; *Fax:* 416-787-3538
www.advertisinglawyer.ca

Toronto: Mimi Tang - *1
#202, 1210 Sheppard Ave. East, Toronto, ON M2K 1E3
Tel: 416-491-2929; *Fax:* 416-491-0990

Toronto: Tatham, Pearson LLP - *3
Former Name: Tatham, Pearson & Malcolm LLP
5524 Lawrence Ave. East, Toronto, ON M1C 3B2
Tel: 416-284-4749; *Fax:* 416-284-3086
info@tathampearson.com
www.tathampearson.com

Toronto: Stanley Taube - *1
#503, 33 Jackes Ave., Toronto, ON M4T 1E2
Tel: 416-513-1233

Toronto: Taveroff & Associates - *2
#900, 2 Sheppard Ave. E, Toronto, ON M2N 5Y7
Tel: 416-221-9343; *Fax:* 416-221-8928

Toronto: Fred Tayar & Associates, Professional Corporation
#1200, 65 Queen St. West, Toronto, ON M5H 2M5
Tel: 416-363-1800; *Fax:* 416-363-3356
fred@fredtayar.com

Toronto: Ted Yoannou & Associates - Toronto - *8
#600, 1000 Finch Ave. West, Toronto, ON M3J 2V5
Tel: 416-650-1011; *Fax:* 416-650-1980
info@torontocriminallawyers.com
www.torontocriminallawyers.com

Toronto: Stephen Thom - *1
#300, 19 Yorkville Ave., Toronto, ON M4W 1L1
Tel: 416-364-3371; *Fax:* 416-863-4896

Toronto: Thomson, Rogers - *28
#3100, 390 Bay St., Toronto, ON M5H 1W2
Tel: 416-868-3100; *Fax:* 416-868-3134
Toll-Free: 888-223-0448
info@thomsonrogers.com
www.thomsonrogers.com
www.facebook.com/thomsonrogerslawyers,
twitter.com/thomsonrogers,
www.linkedin.com/company-beta/1121502

Toronto: Ian Thornhill - *1
#406, 255 Duncan Mill Rd., Toronto, ON M3B 3H9
Tel: 416-224-2004; *Fax:* 416-224-2101
ithornhilllaw@rogers.com

Toronto: Thornton Grout Finnigan LLP - *18
#3200, Toronto-Dominion Centre, P.O. Box 329, 100 Wellington St. West, Toronto, ON M5K 1K7
Tel: 416-304-1616; *Fax:* 416-304-1313
info@tgf.ca
www.tgf.ca

Toronto: Thorsteinssons LLP - Toronto - *46
Brookfield Place, P.O. Box 786, 181 Bay St., 33rd Fl., Toronto, ON M5J 2T3
Tel: 416-864-0829; *Fax:* 416-864-1106
www.thor.ca

Toronto: Lorne B. Tick - *1
54 Misty Cres., Toronto, ON M3B 1T2
Tel: 416-444-9146; *Fax:* 416-444-9146
ltick@rogers.com

Toronto: Philip Tinianov - *1
#1800, 4950 Yonge St., Toronto, ON M2N 6K1
Tel: 416-363-0866; *Fax:* 416-224-0758
ptinianov@torlaw.com

Toronto: Michael K. Titherington - *1
#635, 60 Heintzman St., Toronto, ON M6P 5A1
Tel: 416-656-6465; *Fax:* 416-551-0488

Toronto: Tkatch & Associates - Toronto - *5
49 Gloucester St., Toronto, ON M4Y 1L8
Tel: 416-968-0333
www.tkatchlaw.ca

Toronto: Norman W. Tomas - *1
954A Royal York Rd., Toronto, ON M8X 2E5
Tel: 416-233-5567; *Fax:* 416-233-9779
ntomas@bellnet.ca

Toronto: James Tomlinson - *1
#234A, 85 Ellesmere Rd., Toronto, ON M1R 4B9
Tel: 416-447-0476; *Fax:* 416-447-8611
tomlin09@bellnet.ca
www.jtomlinsonlaw.com

Toronto: Toomath & Associates - *1
Also Known As: Toomath, E.H.
100 Richmond St. West, Toronto, ON M5H 3K6
Tel: 416-869-0900; *Fax:* 416-366-4711

Toronto: Traub Moldaver
#1801, 4 King St. West, Toronto, ON M5H 1B6
Tel: 416-214-6500; *Fax:* 416-214-7275

Toronto: Philip J. Traversy - *1
20 Flaming Roseway, Toronto, ON M2N 5W8
Tel: 647-271-4741
p.traversy@rogers.com

Toronto: Quoc Toan Trinh - *1
1577 Bloor St. W, Toronto, ON M6P 1A6
Tel: 416-533-8987; *Fax:* 416-536-3618

Toronto: William M. Trudell - *2
#100, 116 Simcoe St., Toronto, ON M5H 4E2
Tel: 416-598-2019; *Fax:* 416-596-2599
wtrudell@simcoechambers.com

Toronto: Constantine Tsantis - *1
69 Elm St., Toronto, ON M5G 1H2
Tel: 416-599-6689; *Fax:* 416-971-9092

Toronto: Howard Ungerman - *1
37 Maitland St., Toronto, ON M4Y 1C8
Tel: 416-924-4111; *Fax:* 416-924-4112

Toronto: Ursel Phillips Fellows Hopkinson LLP - *25
Former Name: Green & Chercover
#1200, 555 Richmond St. West, Toronto, ON M5V 3B1
Tel: 416-968-3333; *Fax:* 416-968-0325
www.upfhlaw.ca

Toronto: S. Van Duffelen - *1
188 Coxwell Ave., Toronto, ON M4L 3B2
Tel: 416-598-5667; *Fax:* 416-971-7721
vanduffelenlaw@on.aibn.com

Toronto: Michael B. Vaughan Q.C.
#3100, 130 Adelaide St. West, Toronto, ON M5H 3P5
Tel: 416-363-9611; *Fax:* 416-363-9672
michaelbvaughan@yahoo.ca

Toronto: David R. Vine, QC - *1
#1604, 80 Richmond St. West, Toronto, ON M5H 2A4
Tel: 416-863-9341; *Fax:* 416-863-9342

Toronto: Mark H. Viner - *1
70 Bowring Walk, Toronto, ON M3H 5Z6
Tel: 416-785-7469; *Fax:* 416-785-1581
vinerlaw@gmail.com

Toronto: Julia M. Viva - *1
58 Plymbridge Rd., Toronto, ON M2P 1A3
Tel: 416-488-7222; *Fax:* 416-489-6258

Toronto: James D. Vlasis - *1
Crown Attorney's Office, 1911 Eglinton Ave. E, Toronto, ON M1L 4P4
Tel: 416-325-0342; *Fax:* 416-325-0353

Toronto: Wagman, Sherkin - *2
#200, 756A Queen St. East, Toronto, ON M4M 1H4
Tel: 416-465-1102; *Fax:* 416-465-3941
charles_wagman@wagmansherkin.ca

Toronto: Waldin, de Kenedy - *3
1 Dundas St. West, Toronto, ON M5G 1Z3
Tel: 416-364-6761; *Fax:* 416-364-3866
waldin@waldin.ca

Toronto: Waldman & Associates - *14
281 Eglinton Ave. East, Toronto, ON M4P 1L3
Tel: 416-482-6501; *Fax:* 416-489-9618
info@waldmanlaw.ca
www.waldmanlaw.ca

Toronto: Walker & Wood - *1
#1800, 181 University Ave., Toronto, ON M5H 3M7
Tel: 416-591-6832; *Fax:* 416-591-7513

Toronto: Walker, Ellis - *2
390 Bay St., 30th Fl., Toronto, ON M5H 1W2
Tel: 416-363-2144; *Fax:* 416-363-1541

Toronto: James H.G. Wallace - *1
551 Gerrard St. East, Toronto, ON M4M 1X7
Tel: 416-463-6666; *Fax:* 416-463-8259

Toronto: The Rose & Thistle Group Ltd. - *5
30 Hazelton Ave., Toronto, ON M5R 2E2
Tel: 416-489-9790; *Fax:* 416-489-9973
info@roseandthistle.ca
www.roseandthistlegroup.com

Toronto: Walton, Brigham & Kelly - *2
301 Donlands Ave., Toronto, ON M4J 3R8
Tel: 416-425-4300; *Fax:* 416-425-4310
tkelly@bellnet.ca

Toronto: Warren Bergman Associates - *2
Former Name: Farb, Warren LLP
2925 Bathrust St., Toronto, ON M6S 3B1
Tel: 416-763-4183; *Fax:* 416-763-1310
dwarren@warrenbergman.com

Toronto: Warren Mediation Group Inc. - *1
#802, 5255 Yonge St., Toronto, ON M2N 6P4
Tel: 647-890-3384; *Fax:* 416-598-4316
howard@warrenmediationgroup.com
www.warrenmediationgroup.com

Toronto: Robert D. Warren
15 Bedford Rd., Toronto, ON M5R 2J7
Tel: 416-368-5393; *Fax:* 416-905-7736

Toronto: Weatherhead, Weatherhead - *2
#500, 27 Queen St. East, Toronto, ON M5C 2M6
Tel: 416-362-1369; *Fax:* 416-362-5013
weatherhead@bellnet.ca

Toronto: John Weingust, Q.C. - *1
Penthouse, 481 University Ave., 10th Fl., Toronto, ON M5G 2E9
Tel: 416-977-7786; *Fax:* 416-340-0064

Toronto: F. Sheldon Weinles - *1
104 Caribou Rd., Toronto, ON M5N 2A9
Tel: 416-780-1330; *Fax:* 416-780-1331
sheldonweinles@rogers.com

Toronto: Joyce R. Weinman - *1
51 Cardiff Rd., Toronto, ON M4P 2P1
Tel: 416-848-1019; *Fax:* 416-486-3309
joyce@jwdental.com
www.jwdental.com

Toronto: Gilbert Weinstock - *1
#401, 1850 Victoria Park Ave., Toronto, ON M1R 1T1
Tel: 416-759-1354; *Fax:* 416-759-3256
gilbertweinstock@gmail.com

Toronto: Weisdorf McCallum & Tatsiou: Associates - *2
#1000, 121 Richmond St. West, Toronto, ON M5H 2K1
Tel: 416-861-1000; *Fax:* 416-861-8166

Toronto: Wells Criminal Law - *2
#202, 559 College St. 2nd Fl., Toronto, ON M6G 1A9
Tel: 416-944-1485
www.torontocriminallawyer.ca

Toronto: John Wenus Law Office - *2
Former Name: Stone & Wenus
330 Broadview Ave., Toronto, ON M4M 2G9
Tel: 416-469-4125; *Fax:* 416-469-2877
info@johnwenus.com
www.johnwenuslaw.com

Toronto: Stephen Werbowyj Professional Corporation - *1
1199 The Queensway, Toronto, ON M8Z 1R2
Tel: 416-233-9461; *Fax:* 416-233-1524
werbowyj@bellnet.ca
www.werbowyj.com

* indicates number of lawyers

Toronto: Ian D. Werker - *1
#2000, 393 University Ave., Toronto, ON M5G 1E6
Tel: 416-593-7552; Fax: 416-593-0668
ian@werkerlaw.com
www.werkerlaw.com

Toronto: West Scarborough Community Legal Services - *4
#201, 2425 Eglinton Ave. E., Toronto, ON M1K 5G8
Tel: 416-285-4460; Fax: 416-285-1070

Toronto: Lionel B. White, Q.C. - *1
65 Duggan Ave., Toronto, ON M4V 1Y1
Tel: 416-364-1127; Fax: 416-364-6903
lex.white@rogers.com

Toronto: Robin J. Wigdor - *1
#901, 159 Frederick St., Toronto, ON M5A 4P1
Tel: 416-504-7237; Fax: 647-723-0197
robin@wigdor.com
www.wigdor.com/robin

Toronto: Wildeboer Dellelce LLP - *33
Former Name: Wildeboer Rand Thomson Apps & Dellelce LLP
#800, Wildeboer Dellelce Place, 365 Bay St., Toronto, ON M5H 2V1
Tel: 416-361-3121; Fax: 416-361-1790
Toll-Free: 866-645-3529
www.wildlaw.ca
www.facebook.com/wildlawLLP, twitter.com/wildlaw,
www.linkedin.com/company/wildeboer-dellelce-llp

Toronto: Will Davidson LLP - Toronto
Former Name: MacMillan Rooke Boeckle
#1400, 220 Bay St., Toronto, ON M5H 2Y4
Tel: 416-360-1194; Fax: 416-360-8469
Toll-Free: 800-661-7606
www.willdavidson.ca
www.facebook.com/WillDavidsonLLP,
twitter.com/WillDavidsonLLP,
www.linkedin.com/company/will-davidson-llp

Toronto: Willard & Devitt - *1
155 Roncesvalles Ave., Toronto, ON M6R 2L3
Tel: 416-531-1136; Fax: 416-531-4096
robert@robertbeaumont.ca

Toronto: Willms & Shier Environmental Lawyers LLP - Toronto - *15
#900, 4 King St. West, Toronto, ON M5H 1B6
Tel: 416-863-0711; Fax: 416-863-1938
info@willmsshier.com
www.willmsshier.com
www.linkedin.com/company-beta/150500

Toronto: Willowdale Community Legal Services - *2
#106, 245 Fairview Mall Dr., Toronto, ON M2J 4T1
Tel: 416-492-2437; Fax: 416-492-6281
willowdalelegal.com

Toronto: Norman H. Winter - *1
#801, 1 St. Clair Ave. East, Toronto, ON M4T 2V7
Tel: 416-964-0325; Fax: 416-964-2494
nw@nwinlaw.com

Toronto: Wise & Associates Professional Corporation - *3
Former Name: Wise, Roy
#602, 80 Bloor St. West, Toronto, ON M5S 2V1
Tel: 416-866-4144; Fax: 416-866-7946
roy.wise@wiseandassociates.com

Toronto: Gerald R. Wise - *1
3329 Bloor St. West, Toronto, ON M8X 1E7
Tel: 416-231-7399; Fax: 416-231-1280

Toronto: Gary L. Wiseman - *1
#1800, Madison Centre, 4950 Yonge St., Toronto, ON M2N 6K1
Tel: 416-224-0200; Fax: 416-224-0758
gwiseman@idirect.com

Toronto: Newton Wong & Associates - *2
#307, 1033 Bay St., Toronto, ON M5S 3A5
Tel: 416-971-9118; Fax: 416-971-7210

Toronto: Wing H. Wong - *1
#202, 4433 Sheppard Ave. East, Toronto, ON M1S 1V3
Tel: 416-298-6767; Fax: 416-298-3844

Toronto: Cynthia J. Woods - *1
#8, 1 Chestnut Hills Cres., Toronto, ON M9A 2W3
Tel: 416-763-3065; Fax: 866-607-2510
info@woodslaw.ca
www.woodslaw.ca

Toronto: Woolgar VanWiechen Ketcheson Ducoffe LLP - *10
Former Name: Ducoffe, Stuart M.
#401, 70 The Esplanade, Toronto, ON M5E 1R2
Tel: 416-867-1666; Fax: 416-867-1434
info@woolvan.com
www.woolvan.com

Toronto: George A. Wootten, Q.C. - *1
1199 The Queensway, Toronto, ON M8Z 1R7
Tel: 416-621-7470; Fax: 416-621-6838
queenswaylaw@yahoo.ca

Toronto: Keith E. Wright - *1
370 Bloor St. East, Toronto, ON M4W 3M6
Tel: 416-364-1157; Fax: 416-363-4978
keith.wright@rogers.com

Toronto: Peter J. Wuebbolt - *1
1554A Bloor St. West, Toronto, ON M6P 1A4
Tel: 416-516-4621; Fax: 416-516-1679

Toronto: Sara Wunch - *1
#1102, 1166 Bay St., Toronto, ON M5S 2X8
Tel: 416-595-7001; Fax: 416-595-5663

Toronto: Nicholas A. Xynnis - *1
#318, 100 Richmond St. West, Toronto, ON M5H 3K6
Tel: 416-862-1010; Fax: 416-862-7602
naxynnis@istar.ca

Toronto: Arthur Yallen - *1
204 St. George St., Toronto, ON M5R 2N5
Tel: 416-927-0001; Fax: 416-927-0930

Toronto: Gerald B. Yasskin - *1
#402, 1183 Finch Ave. West, Toronto, ON M3J 2G2
Tel: 416-667-0982; Fax: 416-665-4291

Toronto: Yee & Lee - *2
#109, 40 Wynford Dr., Toronto, ON M3C 1J5
Tel: 416-977-0091; Fax: 416-977-6335

Toronto: David P. Yerzy - *1
#108, 14 Prince Arthur Ave., Toronto, ON M5R 1A9
Tel: 416-972-6957; Fax: 416-972-6427
werzy@planeteer.com

Toronto: Yeti Law Professional Corporation - *4
Former Name: Agnew, Gladstone LLP
215 Carlton St., Toronto, ON M5A 2K9
Tel: 416-964-0021; Fax: 416-964-0744
info@yetilaw.com
www.yetilaw.com
www.facebook.com/yetilaw1, twitter.com/legalsherpa,
www.linkedin.com/company/yeti-law

Toronto: Hyun Soo Yi - *1
#204, 640 Bloor St. West, Toronto, ON M6G 1K9
Tel: 416-534-7711; Fax: 416-534-7714

Toronto: Joseph R. Young - *1
#200, 20 Cumberland St., Toronto, ON M4W 1J5
Tel: 416-969-8887; Fax: 416-969-8866
www.globalmigration.com

Toronto: D.R. Zadorozny - *1
#216, 4195 Dundas St. West, Toronto, ON M8X 1Y4
Tel: 416-239-2333; Fax: 416-239-1752
Toll-Free: 866-396-7251
drz@drzlaw.com

Toronto: Silvie Zakuta - *1
#850, 36 Toronto St., Toronto, ON M5C 2C5
Tel: 416-923-1656; Fax: 416-368-2918
szakuta@aol.com

Toronto: Zaldin & Fine LLP - *3
#900, 60 Yonge St., Toronto, ON M5E 1H5
Tel: 416-868-1431; Fax: 416-868-6381
sueking@zaldinandfine.ca

Toronto: Zammit Semple LLP - *2
#200, 129 Yorkville Ave., Toronto, ON M5R 1C4
Tel: 416-923-2601
info@zds.on.ca
www.zds.on.ca

Toronto: Zarek Taylor Grossman Hanrahan LLP - *45
#1301, 20 Adelaide St. East, Toronto, ON M5C 2T6
Tel: 416-777-2811; Fax: 416-777-2050
reception@ztgh.com
www.ztgh.com

Toronto: Zarnett Law Professional Corporation - *2
Former Name: Sandler, Gordon
#101, 275 Macpherson Ave., Toronto, ON M4V 1A4
Tel: 416-971-5102; Fax: 416-971-5305
www.zarnettlaw.com

Toronto: M. David Zbarsky - *1
#1001, 85 Thorncliffe Park Dr., Toronto, ON M4H 1L6
Tel: 416-421-6252; Fax: 416-467-6780

Toronto: Zeldin, Collin - *1
23 Bedford Rd., Toronto, ON M5R 2J9
Tel: 416-964-7914; Fax: 416-964-8067
collin@zecol.com

Toronto: David L. Zifkin - *1
90A Isabella St., 1st Fl., Toronto, ON M4Y 1N4
Tel: 416-927-7720; Fax: 416-964-9348
dzifkin@zifkin.com
www.zifkin.com

Trenton: Bonn Law Office - Trenton - *5
Former Name: G.W. Bonn
80 Division St., Trenton, ON K8V 5S5
Tel: 613-392-9207; Fax: 613-392-6367
Toll-Free: 888-266-6529
www.bonnlaw.ca
www.facebook.com/bonnlawoffice, twitter.com/bonnlawoffice,
www.linkedin.com/company/bonn-law-office

Trenton: Sioui Mitts Law - *5
Former Name: Fleming Garrett Sioui
P.O. Box 397, 21 Quinte St., Trenton, ON K8V 5R6
Tel: 613-965-6430; Fax: 613-965-6400
Toll-Free: 800-616-1294
info@siouimittslaw.com
www.siouimittslaw.com

Tweed: Bart F. Lackie - *1
2718 Mallbank Rd., RR#4, Tweed, ON K0K 3J0
Tel: 613-478-9940; Fax: 613-478-6061
bart@linesat.com

Unionville: Janet L. Gillespie - *1
178 Main St., Unionville, ON L3R 2G9
Tel: 905-479-6352; Fax: 905-479-1991
jlgillespie@rogers.com

Unionville: Minken Employment Lawyers - *4
Former Name: Minken & Associates Professional Corporation
145 Main St., Unionville, ON L3R 2G7
Tel: 905-477-7011; Fax: 905-477-7010
contact@minken.com
www.minkenemploymentlawyers.com
www.facebook.com/employmentlawexperts,
twitter.com/minkenlaw,
www.linkedin.com/company/minken-employment-lawyers

Uxbridge: Bailey & Sedore - *1
11 Brock St. East, Uxbridge, ON L9P 1M4
Tel: 905-852-3363; Fax: 905-852-3480
www.baileyandsedore.ca

Uxbridge: Paul D. Fox - *1
6749 Concession 6, RR#1, Uxbridge, ON L9P 1R1
Tel: 905-852-4560; Fax: 905-852-4435
paulfox@bellnet.ca

Uxbridge: Randall B. Hoban - *2
20 Bascom St., Uxbridge, ON L9P 1J3
Tel: 905-852-3900; Fax: 905-852-3666
www.stadamdesign.com/hobanweb

Uxbridge: P. Douglas Turner, Q.C. - *1
P.O. Box 760, 63 Albert St., Uxbridge, ON L9P 1E5
Tel: 905-852-6196; Fax: 905-852-6197
doug@pdturner.com

Uxbridge: Wilson Associates - *2
22 Brock St. East, Uxbridge, ON L9P 1P1
Tel: 905-852-3353; Fax: 905-852-5120
dwilson@uxbridgelaw.com
www.uxbridgelaw.com

indicates number of lawyers

Vaughan: Bianchi Presta LLP - *9
Bldg. A, 9100 Jane St., 3rd Fl., Vaughan, ON L4K 0A4
Tel: 905-738-1078; *Fax:* 905-738-0528
contact@bianchipresta.com
www.bianchipresta.com

Vaughan: Bortolussi Family Law - *6
#210, 3300 Hwy. 7 West, Vaughan, ON L4K 4M3
Tel: 416-987-3300; *Fax:* 905-907-0707
www.bortolussifamilylaw.com

Vaughan: Brattys LLP - *17
Former Name: Bratty & Partners, LLP Barristers &
Solicitors
#200, 7501 Keele St., Vaughan, ON L4K 1Y2
Tel: 905-760-2600; *Fax:* 905-760-2900
www.bratty.com

Vaughan: Corsianos Lee - *3
#203W, 3800 Steeles Ave. West, Vaughan, ON L4L 4G9
Tel: 905-370-1091; *Fax:* 905-370-1095
info@cl-law.ca
www.cl-law.ca

Vaughan: Drudi, Alexiou, Kuchar LLP - *8
#307, 7050 Weston Rd., Vaughan, ON L4L 8G7
Tel: 905-850-6116; *Fax:* 905-850-9146
www.dakllp.com

Vaughan: Fine & Deo - *12
#300, 3100 Steeles Ave. West, Vaughan, ON L4K 3R1
Tel: 905-760-1800; *Fax:* 905-760-0050
Toll-Free: 888-346-3336
info@finedeo.com
finedeo.com

Vaughan: RQ Partners LLP - *5
Also Known As: Rotundo Dilorio Quaglietta LLP
Former Name: RDQ Law; Gambin RDQ LLP
#400, 3901 Hwy. 7, Vaughan, ON L4L 8L5
Tel: 905-264-7800; *Fax:* 905-264-7808
reception@rqpartners.ca
rqpartners.ca

Vaughan: P.M. Valenti - *1
#300, West Bldg., 3800 Steeles Ave., Vaughan, ON L4L 4G9
Tel: 905-850-8550; *Fax:* 905-850-9998

Vermilion Bay: Shirley D. Gauthier - *1
P.O. Box 490, Stn. Main, Vermilion Bay, ON P0V 2V0
Tel: 807-227-2445; *Fax:* 807-227-2902
sdg@mail.drytel.net

Walkerton: Van De Vyvere & Grove-McClement LLP
Former Name: Magwood, Van De Vyvere, Thompson, &
Grove-McClement LLP
P.O. Box 880, 215 Durham St. East, Walkerton, ON N0G 2V0
Tel: 519-881-3230; *Fax:* 519-881-3595

Wallaceburg: Carscallen, Reinhart, Mathany, Maslak
- *3
P.O. Box 409, Stn. Main, 619 James St., Wallaceburg, ON
N8A 4X1
Tel: 519-627-2261; *Fax:* 519-627-1030

Wallaceburg: Hyde, Hyde & McGregor - *2
233 Creek St., Wallaceburg, ON N8A 4C3
Tel: 519-627-2081; *Fax:* 519-627-1615
hhmlaw.ca

Wasaga Beach: Maurice Loton - *1
P.O. Box 500, 802 Mosley St., Wasaga Beach, ON L9Z 2H4
Tel: 705-429-4332; *Fax:* 705-429-4683

Waterdown: Jansen Personal Injury Law - *1
#3, P.O. Box 1436, 20 Main St. North, Waterdown, ON L0R
2H0
Tel: 905-690-2929; *Fax:* 905-690-2920
info@jansenlaw.ca
jansenlaw.ca

Waterford: Birnie & Gaunt - *2
P.O. Box 429, 70 Alice St., Waterford, ON N0E 1Y0
Tel: 519-443-8676; *Fax:* 519-443-5596

Waterford: Cornelius A. Brennan - *1
P.O. Box 1229, 19 Main St. South, Waterford, ON N0E 1Y0
Tel: 519-443-8643; *Fax:* 905-443-4489

Waterloo: Amy, Appleby & Brennan - *3
Former Name: William R. Appleby, Amy Appleby
Brennan
372 Erb St. West, Waterloo, ON N2L 1W6
Tel: 519-884-7330; *Fax:* 519-884-7390
www.aab-lawoffice.com

Waterloo: Biggs & Gadbois - *2
Former Name: Biggs, Richard C.
500 Dutton Dr., Waterloo, ON N2L 4C6
Tel: 519-886-1678; *Fax:* 519-886-1791
biggslaw@bellnet.ca

Waterloo: Blair L. Botsford - *1
92 Erb St. East, Waterloo, ON N2J 1L9
Tel: 519-594-0936; *Fax:* 519-594-0937
blair@botsfordlaw.ca
botsfordlaw.webs.com

Waterloo: Chris & Volpini - *2
375 University Ave. East, Waterloo, ON N2K 3M7
Tel: 519-888-0999; *Fax:* 519-888-0995
cvlaw@chrisvolpinilawyers.com

Waterloo: Dueck, Sauer, Jutzi & Noll LLP - *8
Former Name: Dueck, Sauer, Jutzi & Noll
403 Albert St., Waterloo, ON N2L 3V2
Tel: 519-884-2620; *Fax:* 519-884-0254
info@dsjnlaw.com
www.dsjnlaw.com

Waterloo: Duncan, Linton LLP - *10
Former Name: White, Duncan & Linton LLP
P.O. Box 457, 45 Erb St. East, Waterloo, ON N2J 4B5
Tel: 519-886-3340; *Fax:* 519-886-8651
www.kwlaw.net

Waterloo: Farhood Boehler Winny LLP - *4
#510, 20 Erb St. West, Waterloo, ON N2L 1T2
Tel: 519-744-9949; *Fax:* 519-744-7974
www.fblaw.ca

Waterloo: W. Marlene Fitzpatrick - *1
420 Weber St. North, Waterloo, ON N2L 4E7
Tel: 519-725-9500; *Fax:* 519-725-2379
marlenefitzpatrick@on.aibn.com

Waterloo: Haney, Haney & Kendall - *3
P.O. Box 185, 41 Erb St. East, Waterloo, ON N2J 3Z9
Tel: 519-747-1010
reception@haneylaw.com
www.haneylaw.com

Waterloo: Fred J. Heimbecker - *1
295 Weber St. North, Waterloo, ON N2J 3H8
Tel: 519-886-1750; *Fax:* 519-886-0503
heim@bellnet.ca

Waterloo: William C. Hoskinson - *1
234 Westcourt Place, Waterloo, ON N2L 2R7
Tel: 519-571-1022; *Fax:* 519-743-0490
whoskinson@rogers.com

Waterloo: John E. Lang - *1
21 Post Horn Place, Waterloo, ON N2L 5E8
Tel: 519-578-3330; *Fax:* 519-578-3337
johnelang@rogers.com

Waterloo: Kominek, Gladstone - *1
28 Weber St. West, Waterloo, ON N2H 3Z2
Tel: 519-886-1050; *Fax:* 519-747-9565
glynne.gladstone2@sympatico.ca

Waterloo: Eric M. Kraushaar - *1
#5, 620 Davenport Rd., Waterloo, ON N2V 2C2
Tel: 519-886-0088; *Fax:* 519-746-1122
eric@churchill-homes.com

Waterloo: Levesque & Deane - *2
#5B, 490 Dutton Dr., Waterloo, ON N2L 6H7
Tel: 519-725-2929; *Fax:* 519-725-2920

Waterloo: Lowes, Salmon & Gadbois - *3
500 Dutton Dr., Waterloo, ON N2L 4C6
Tel: 519-884-0800; *Fax:* 519-884-1026
Toll-Free: 877-258-2575
tlowes@watlaw.ca
www.watlaw.ca

Waterloo: Joe Mattes - *1
#200, 24 Dupont St. East, Waterloo, ON N2J 2G9
Tel: 519-884-5600; *Fax:* 519-884-9963
joe@matteslaw.com
www.mattesevans.com

Waterloo: Peter M. Miller - *1
15 Westmount Rd. South, Waterloo, ON N2L 2K2
Tel: 519-884-1332; *Fax:* 519-884-1161
pmillerlaw@rogers.com
www.petermillerlaw.ca

Waterloo: Oldfield, Greaves, D'Agostino & Scriven -
*5
Former Name: Oldfield, Greaves, D'Agostino, Billo &
Nowak
172 King St. South, Waterloo, ON N2J 1P8
Tel: 519-576-7200; *Fax:* 519-576-0131
info@watlaw.com
www.watlaw.com

Waterloo: Paquette Travers & Deutschmann - *5
295 Weber St. North, Waterloo, ON N2J 3H8
Tel: 519-744-2281; *Fax:* 519-744-8008
Toll-Free: 877-744-2281
info@paquettetravers.com
www.paquettetravers.com

Waterloo: Petker & Associates - *3
295 Weber St. North, Waterloo, ON N2J 3H8
Tel: 226-240-7736; *Fax:* 519-886-5674
Toll-Free: 800-617-5864
www.petkerlaw.com

Waterloo: James E. Pitcher - *1
420 Weber St. N, Waterloo, ON N2J 4E7
Tel: 519-725-9444; *Fax:* 519-725-2379

Waterloo: Richard B. Strype - *2
P.O. Box 547, 92 Erb St. East, Waterloo, ON N2J 4B8
Tel: 519-886-1590; *Fax:* 519-886-8545
rstrype@strypelaw.com

Waterloo: Verbanac Law Firm - *2
#205B, 470 Weber St. North, Waterloo, ON N2L 6J2
Tel: 519-744-5588; *Fax:* 519-744-5533
info@vlawfirm.ca
www.vlawfirm.ca

Watford: Wallace B. Lang - *1
P.O. Box 449, 5290 Nauvoo Rd., Watford, ON N0M 2S0
Tel: 519-876-2742; *Fax:* 519-876-2073
www.wallacelanglawyer.ca

Welland: Vince Bellantino - *1
8 East Main St., Welland, ON L3B 3W3
Tel: 905-788-3881; *Fax:* 905-788-3885
vincebel@iaw.on.ca

Welland: Beresh & Associates - *1
P.O. Box 127, Stn. Main, 191 Division St., Welland, ON L3B
5P2
Tel: 905-735-1770; *Fax:* 905-735-7031

Welland: Blackadder Marion Wood LLP
136 East Main St., Welland, ON L3B 5R3
Tel: 905-735-3620; *Fax:* 905-735-1577

Welland: Flett Beccario - *8
190 Division St., Welland, ON L3B 4A2
Tel: 905-732-4481; *Fax:* 905-732-2020
Toll-Free: 866-473-5388
www.flettbeccario.com

Welland: William V. Frith - *1
#301, 76 Division St., Welland, ON L3B 3Z7
Tel: 905-735-7582; *Fax:* 905-735-0093
w_firth@iaw.com

Welland: Houghton, Sloniowski & Stengel
170 Division St., Welland, ON L3B 4A2
Tel: 905-734-4577; *Fax:* 905-732-3765
Toll-Free: 888-483-9770

Welland: Rodney J. Kajan - *1
60 King St., Welland, ON L3B 5P2
Tel: 905-732-1352; *Fax:* 905-732-0531

Welland: Kormos & Evans Law Office - *1
120 Thorold Rd., Welland, ON L3C 3V3
Tel: 905-732-4424
www.markevanslaw.com

Welland: Pylypuk & Associates - *2
Former Name: Pylypuk, Anthony W.
P.O. Box 605, 80 King St., Welland, ON L3B 5R4
Tel: 905-735-2300; *Fax:* 905-735-9230
www.pylypuk.com

Welland: Talmage & DiFiore
P.O. Box 97, 221 Division St., Welland, ON L3B 5P2
Tel: 905-732-4477; *Fax:* 905-732-4718
talstradi@iaw.on.ca

* indicates number of lawyers

Welland: Douglas R. Thomas - *1
9 East Main St., Welland, ON L3B 5R3
Tel: 905-732-5529; Fax: 905-732-2211
thomform@iaw.com

Westport: Barker Willson Professional Corporation - Westport - *5
P.O. Box 159, 25 Main St., Westport, ON K0G 1X0
Tel: 613-273-3166; Fax: 613-273-3676
www.barkerwillson.com

Wheatley: Joyce H. Eaton - *1
26 Erie St. South, Wheatley, ON N0P 2P0
Tel: 519-825-7032; Fax: 519-825-9570
joyce.eaton@3web.net

Whitby: David J. Gillespie - *1
P.O. Box 208, Stn. Main, 214 Dundas St. East, 2nd Fl., Whitby, ON L1N 5S1
Tel: 905-666-2221; Fax: 905-666-2344
Toll-Free: 888-880-6786
info@davidgillespie.ca
www.davidgillespie.ca/en/

Whitby: Howard Schneider - *1
107 Kent St., Whitby, ON L1N 4Y1
Tel: 905-668-1677; Fax: 905-668-2023

Whitby: Stacy Howell
916 Brock St. South, Whitby, ON L1N 8R1
Tel: 905-668-7747; Fax: 905-668-7787
showell@bellnet.ca

Whitby: Jenkins, Newman & Shipley
Former Name: Jenkins & Newman
106 Colborne St. East, Whitby, ON L1N 1V8
Tel: 905-666-8588
www.jnslaw.ca

Whitby: Johnston Montgomery - Whitby - *3
201 Byron St. South, Whitby, ON L1N 4P7
Tel: 905-666-2252; Fax: 905-430-0878
www.lawhitby.com

Whitby: Michaels & Michaels - *1
#201, 1450 Hopkins St., Whitby, ON L1N 2C3
Tel: 905-665-7711; Fax: 905-430-9100
info@michaelslaw.ca

Whitby: Rosenberg, Pringle - *2
#214, 185 Brock St. North, Whitby, ON L1N 4H3
Tel: 905-665-9594; Fax: 905-665-7124

Whitby: Edward P. Schein - *1
107 Kent St., Whitby, ON L1N 4Y1
Tel: 905-666-1266; Fax: 905-668-2023

Whitby: Sims Thomson & Babbs - *3
P.O. Box 358, Stn. Main, 117 King St., Whitby, ON L1N 5S4
Tel: 905-668-7704; Fax: 905-668-1268

Whitby: B.P. Stelmach - *1
#201, 1614 Dundas St. East, Whitby, ON L1N 8Y8
Tel: 905-430-6611; Fax: 905-430-6828
stelmach@bellnet.ca

Whitby: Debra J. Sweetman - *1
340 Byron St. South, Whitby, ON L1N 4P8
Tel: 905-666-8166; Fax: 905-666-8163

Winchester: David J. Barnhart - *1
P.O. Box 730, 489 Main St., Winchester, ON K0C 2K0
Tel: 613-774-2808; Fax: 613-774-5731

Windsor: Ballance & Melville - *2
#100, 251 Goyeau St., Windsor, ON N9A 6V2
Tel: 519-255-1414; Fax: 519-255-7404

Windsor: Barat, Farlam, Millson
#510, Westcourt Place, 251 Goyeau St., Windsor, ON N9A 6V2
Tel: 519-258-2424; Fax: 519-258-2451

Windsor: Bartlet & Richardes LLP - *17
#1000, 374 Ouellette Ave., Windsor, ON N9A 1A9
Tel: 519-253-7461; Fax: 519-253-2321
mail@bartlet.com
www.bartlet.com

Windsor: Belowus Easton English - *3
100 Ouellette Ave., 7th Fl., Windsor, ON N9A 6T3
Tel: 519-973-1900; Fax: 519-973-0225

Windsor: Bondy, Riley, Koski LLP
#310, 176 University Ave. West, Windsor, ON N9A 5P1
Tel: 519-258-1641; Fax: 519-258-1725

Windsor: A.J. Bradie - *2
691 Ouellette Ave., Windsor, ON N9A 4J4
Tel: 519-255-1542; Fax: 519-255-9888
abradie@mnsi.net

Windsor: Mario Carnevale Law Office - *2
2488 McDougall Ave., Windsor, ON N8X 3N7
Tel: 519-969-8855; Fax: 519-969-0085
carnevalelaw@cogeco.net
www.clolawoffice.com

Windsor: Maria Carroccia - *1
#602, Canada Bldg., 374 Ouellette Ave., Windsor, ON N9A 1A8
Tel: 519-258-0905; Fax: 519-258-8755
Toll-Free: 888-959-9917

Windsor: F. Michael Cervi - *1
#400, 1500 Ouellette Ave., Windsor, ON N8X 1K7
Tel: 519-258-9494; Fax: 519-258-9985
michaelcervi@on.aibn.com

Windsor: Chodola Reynolds Binder - *5
720 Walker Rd., Windsor, ON N8Y 2N3
Tel: 519-254-6433; Fax: 519-254-7990
www.facebook.com/windsorinjurylawyers,
www.linkedin.com/company/chodola-reynolds-binder

Windsor: Clarks LLP - *7
Former Name: Clarks, Barristers & Solicitors
#1200, Canada Bldg., 374 Ouellette Ave., Windsor, ON N9A 1A8
Tel: 519-254-4990; Fax: 519-254-2294
www.clarkslaw.com

Windsor: Robert J. Comartin - *1
350 Devonshire Rd., Windsor, ON N8Y 2L4
Tel: 519-253-7050; Fax: 519-253-7049

Windsor: Crown Attorney's Office - *1
200 Chatham St. E, 5th Fl., Windsor, ON N9A 2W3
Tel: 519-253-1104; Fax: 519-253-1813
russ.cornett@ontario.ca

Windsor: John Paul Corrent - *5
Former Name: Corrent & Macri
#201, 2485 Ouellette Ave., Windsor, ON N8X 1L5
Tel: 519-255-7332; Fax: 519-255-9123
jcorrent@correntmacri.com
www.jpcorrent.com

Windsor: Culmone Law - *1
410 Giles Blvd. East, Windsor, ON N9A 4C6
Tel: 519-258-3632; Fax: 519-977-1199
floro@culmonelaw.com
www.culmonelaw.com

Windsor: D'hondt & Connor - *3
#260, 2109 Ottawa St., Windsor, ON N8Y 1R8
Tel: 519-258-8220; Fax: 519-258-7788

Windsor: David Deluzio Law Firm - *1
#200, 52 Chatham St. West, Windsor, ON N9A 5M6
Tel: 519-256-1994; Fax: 519-256-7233

Windsor: Robert M. DiPietro - *1
#302, 380 Ouellette Ave., Windsor, ON N9A 6X5
Tel: 519-258-8248; Fax: 519-255-7685
robertdipietro@bellnet.ca

Windsor: Jon Dobrowolski - *1
#309, Westcourt Place, 251 Goyeau St., Windsor, ON N9A 6V2
Tel: 519-258-0034; Fax: 519-258-9133

Windsor: Donaldson, Donaldson, Greenaway - *5
547 Devonshire Rd., Windsor, ON N8Y 2L6
Tel: 519-255-7333; Fax: 519-255-7173
ddglaw@on.aibn.com

Windsor: Ducharme Fox LLP - *6
800 University Ave. West, Windsor, ON N9A 5R9
Tel: 519-259-1800; Fax: 519-259-1830
info@ducharmefox.com
www.ducharmefox.com

Windsor: Fazio Giorgi LLP - *4
333 Wyandotte St. East, Windsor, ON N9A 3H7
Tel: 519-258-5030; Fax: 519-971-9051
accounting@faziogiorgi.com
www.faziogiorgi.com

Windsor: Julie Fodor - *1
3085 Longfellow Ave., Windsor, ON N9E 2L4
Tel: 519-256-8238; Fax: 519-258-5780
jfoder.law@bellnet.com

Windsor: Gatti Law Professional Corporation - *2
Also Known As: Lisa Carnelos
#400, 267 Pelissier St., Windsor, ON N9A 4K4
Tel: 519-258-1010; Fax: 519-258-0163
arg@argatti.com

Windsor: Goldstein DeBiase Serious Injury Lawyers - *4
Former Name: Goldstein DeBiase Manzocco, The Personal Injury Law Firm
#200, 475 Devonshire Rd., Windsor, ON N8Y 2L5
Tel: 226-773-1790; Fax: 519-253-0218
Toll-Free: 866-622-4825
www.gdmlawyers.com

Windsor: Goulin & Patrick - *1
500 Windsor Ave., Windsor, ON N9A 6Y5
Tel: 519-258-8073; Fax: 519-977-0694
www.goulinpatricklawyer.com

Windsor: Greg Monforton and Partners - *8
Former Name: Monforton, Robitaille, & Skipper
#801, 1 Riverside Dr. West, Windsor, ON N9A 5K3
Tel: 519-258-6490; Fax: 519-258-4104
Toll-Free: 800-663-1145
www.gregmonforton.com
www.facebook.com/gregmonfortonpartners,
twitter.com/gregmonforton,
www.linkedin.com/pub/greg-monforton/6b/954/b73

Windsor: Jason P. Howie - *1
350 Devonshire Rd., Windsor, ON N8Y 2L4
Tel: 519-800-1039; Fax: 519-973-9905
Toll-Free: 800-335-7511
www.jasonpaulhowie.com
www.facebook.com/hjbarristerssolicitors,
www.linkedin.com/company/1605795

Windsor: Hulka Porter LLP - *3
#200, 110 Tecumseh Rd. East, Windsor, ON N8X 2P8
Tel: 519-254-5952; Fax: 519-254-3957
Toll-Free: 800-263-8723
enquire@hulkaporter.com
www.hulkaporter.com

Windsor: Jutras Legal & Mediation Inc. - Windsor - *1
#510, Westcourt Place, 251 Goyeau St., Windsor, ON N9A 1J2
Toll-Free: 866-682-3100
www.progressivemediation.ca

Windsor: Kamin, Fisher, Burnett, Ziriada & Robertson - *5
#200, 176 University Ave. West, Windsor, ON N9A 5P1
Tel: 519-252-1123; Fax: 519-977-6503
info@kaminlaw.ca

Windsor: Katzman, Wylupek LLP - *5
1427 Ouellette Ave., Windsor, ON N8X 1K1
Tel: 519-254-4878; Fax: 519-254-6774
www.katzman-wylupek.com

Windsor: Kirwin Partners LLP - *10
423 Pelissier St., Windsor, ON N9A 4L2
Tel: 519-255-9840; Fax: 519-255-1413
www.kirwinpartners.com

Windsor: Kyrtsakas Law Office - *1
5655 Tecumseh Rd. East, Windsor, ON N8T 1C8
Tel: 519-974-6303; Fax: 519-974-8644
www.kyrtsakaslaw.com

Windsor: Lisa S. Labute - *1
#444, 251 Goyeau St., Windsor, ON N9A 6V2
Tel: 519-252-6822; Fax: 519-252-2638
lslabute@mnsi.net

Windsor: Legal Assistance of Windsor - *4
Former Name: Brian Rodenhurst
#200, 443 Ouellette Ave., Windsor, ON N9A 4J2
Tel: 519-256-7831; Fax: 519-256-1387
www.legalassistanceofwindsor.com

Windsor: Anthony R. Mariotti - *1
#202, 176 University Ave. West, Windsor, ON N9A 5P1
Tel: 519-258-1931; Fax: 519-973-7575
arm.law@sympatico.ca

Windsor: Brenda A. McGinty - *1
518 Victoria Ave., Windsor, ON N9A 4M8
Tel: 519-255-1535; Fax: 519-255-1719

Windsor: McTague Law Firm LLP - *23
455 Pelissier St., Windsor, ON N9A 6Z9
Tel: 519-255-4300
info@mctaguelaw.com
www.mctaguelaw.com
www.facebook.com/mctaguelaw

Windsor: Melanie J. McWilliams - *1
#710, 100 Ouellette Ave., Windsor, ON N9A 6T3
Tel: 519-258-1100; Fax: 519-258-7384
mjmcwilliams@winlaw.ca

Windsor: Tullio Meconi - *1
349 Wyandotte St. East, Windsor, ON N9A 3H7
Tel: 519-252-7274

Windsor: Donald D. Merritt - *1
#103, 525 Windsor Ave., Windsor, ON N9A 1J4
Tel: 519-258-8060; Fax: 519-258-9877
merritt2@mnsi.net

Windsor: Miller Canfield LLP (Ontario) - *21
Former Name: Miller Canfield Paddock & Stone LLP;
Miller Canfield Paddock & Stone - Wilson Walker
#1300, 100 Ouellette Ave., Windsor, ON N9A 6T3
Tel: 519-946-2123; Fax: 519-946-2133
www.millercanfield.com
www.facebook.com/MillerCanfield, twitter.com/millercanfield,
www.linkedin.com/company/miller-canfield

Windsor: S. Frank Miller - *1
560 Chatham St. West, Windsor, ON N9A 5N2
Tel: 519-258-3044; Fax: 519-258-2350
frankmilleratlaw@earthlink.net

Windsor: Joana G. Miskinis - *1
518 Victoria Ave., Windsor, ON N9A 4M8
Tel: 519-254-3757; Fax: 519-255-1719
joanamiskinis@hotmail.com

Windsor: Mousseau DeLuca McPherson Prince LLP
- Windsor - *9
#500, Westcourt Place, 251 Goyeau, Windsor, ON N9A 6V2
Tel: 519-258-0615; Fax: 519-258-6833
lawyers@mousseaulaw.com
www.mousseaulaw.com

Windsor: Michael P. O'Hearn - *1
#A-1, P.O. Box 1212, Stn. A, 75 Riverside Dr. East, Windsor,
ON N9A 6P8
Tel: 519-255-1250; Fax: 519-971-9607
mike.ohearn@sympatico.ca

Windsor: John G. Ohler - *2
101 Tecumseh Rd. West, Windsor, ON N8X 1E8
Tel: 519-256-5496; Fax: 519-256-1492
ohlerlawfirm@bellnet.ca

Windsor: James W. Oxley
1854 Kildare Rd., Windsor, ON N8W 2W7
Tel: 519-258-7211

Windsor: Paroian Skipper Lawyers - *3
2510 Ouellette Ave., Windsor, ON N8X 1L4
Tel: 519-250-0894; Fax: 519-966-1869
skipper@therightcall.ca
therightcall.ca

Windsor: Peter Hrastovec Professional Corporation
- *1
2510 Ouellette Ave., Windsor, ON N8X 1L4
Tel: 519-966-1300; Fax: 519-966-1079
www.peterlaw.ca

Windsor: Derek R. Revait - *1
#209, Royal Windsor Terrace, 380 Pelissier, Windsor, ON
N9A 6W8
Tel: 519-258-7030; Fax: 519-258-2629
derek.revait@bellnet.ca

Windsor: Salem, McCullough & Gibson Professional
Corp. - *2
2828 Howard Ave., Windsor, ON N8X 3Y3
Tel: 519-966-3633; Fax: 519-972-7788
www.salemmcculloughgibson.com

Windsor: Daniel W. Scott - *1
#302, 380 Ouellette Ave., Windsor, ON N9A 6X5
Tel: 519-258-8248; Fax: 519-255-7685
donscott@bellnet.ca

Windsor: Stephen L. Shanfield - *1
#333, 880 Ouellette Ave., Windsor, ON N9A 1C7
Tel: 519-258-3338; Fax: 519-258-3335

Windsor: Brian Sherwell - *1
827 Pillette Rd., Windsor, ON N8Y 3B4
Tel: 519-945-1109; Fax: 519-948-0003

Windsor: Sorensen Baker Professional Corporation
- *2
1600 Wyandotte St. East, Windsor, ON N8Y 1C7
Tel: 519-256-3111; Fax: 519-256-5468
baker@cogeco.net
www.facebook.com/Sorensen.Baker

Windsor: R. Craig Stevenson - *1
#18A, 25 Amy Croft Dr., Windsor, ON N9K 1C7
Tel: 519-735-0777; Fax: 519-735-2999
rcslaw@mnsi.net
www.rcraigstevensonlawoffice.com

Windsor: Stipic, Arpino, Weisman LLP - *14
1574 Ouellette Ave., Windsor, ON N8X 1K7
Tel: 519-258-3201; Fax: 519-258-2665
sawlawyers.com

Windsor: Tamara Stomp & Associate - *2
721 Walker Rd., Windsor, ON N8Y 2N2
Tel: 519-948-9778; Fax: 519-948-9773
stomp@mnsi.net

Windsor: Strosberg Sasso Sutts LLP - Windsor - *16
Former Name: Sutts, Strosberg LLP
1561 Ouellette Ave., Windsor, ON N8X 1K5
Tel: 519-258-9333; Fax: 519-258-9527
info@strosbergco.com
www.strosbergco.com

Windsor: Gary V. Wortley - *1
2490 Talbot Rd., Windsor, ON N9H 1A6
Tel: 519-967-9410; Fax: 519-967-9431
wortley@jet2.net

Windsor: Martin Wunder, Q.C. - *1
#908, 100 Ouellette Ave., Windsor, ON N9A 6T3
Tel: 519-252-1121

Woodbridge: Gary A. Beaulne - *2
#401, 3700 Steeles Ave. West, Woodbridge, ON L4L 8K8
Tel: 905-850-5060; Fax: 905-850-5066
Toll-Free: 866-850-5006
gary@garyabeaulne.com
www.garyabeaulne.com

Woodbridge: Frank Borgatti - *1
7135 Islington Ave., 2nd Fl., Woodbridge, ON L4L 1V9
Tel: 905-851-2883; Fax: 905-851-2887

Woodbridge: Roger Bourque - *1
#300, 3800 Steeles Ave. West, Woodbridge, ON L4L 4G9
Tel: 905-856-7101; Fax: 905-856-1524
rogerbourque@bellnet.ca

Woodbridge: Capo Sgro LLP - *12
#400, 7050 Weston Rd., Woodbridge, ON L4L 8G7
Tel: 905-850-7000; Fax: 905-850-7050
www.csllp.ca

Woodbridge: Ralph Ciccia - *1
#400, 7050 Weston Rd., Woodbridge, ON L4L 8G7
Tel: 905-850-6408; Fax: 905-850-7050
rciccia@ciccia.ca

Woodbridge: Cosman & Associates - *2
Former Name: Cosman, Gray LLP
#37, 111 Zenway, Woodbridge, ON L4H 3H9
Tel: 905-850-3110; Fax: 905-850-3123
cosmanlaw.com
www.facebook.com/CosmanAssociates, twitter.com/infocosman

Woodbridge: D'Alimonte Law - *1
#27, 4300 Steeles Ave. W, Woodbridge, ON L4L 4C2
Tel: 905-264-1553; Fax: 905-264-5450
jdalimonte@bellnet.ca

Woodbridge: M. DiPaolo - *1
#400, 7050 Weston Rd., Woodbridge, ON L4L 8G7
Tel: 905-850-7575; Fax: 905-850-7050
mdipaolo@di-paolo.ca

Woodbridge: Michael A. Handler - *1
#101, 10 Director Crt., Woodbridge, ON L4L 7E8
Tel: 905-265-2242; Fax: 905-265-2235
mhandler@mhandlerlaw.com

Woodbridge: Hans Law Firm - *1
#305, 216 Chrislea Rd., Woodbridge, ON L4L 8S5
Tel: 905-790-0092; Fax: 905-605-1079
hanslaw.com

Woodbridge: Thomas F. Kowal - *1
#906, 3700 Steeles Ave. West, Woodbridge, ON L4L 8K8
Tel: 905-856-5855

Woodbridge: Mancini Associates LLP - *3
#505, 7050 Weston Rd., Woodbridge, ON L4L 8G7
Tel: 905-851-7717; Fax: 905-851-7718

Woodbridge: Massimo Panicali - *1
#4, 253 Jevlan Dr., Woodbridge, ON L4L 7Z6
Tel: 905-850-2642; Fax: 905-850-8544
mass.pan-demonium@on.aibn.com

Woodbridge: Piccin Bottos - *5
#201, 4370 Steeles Ave. West, Woodbridge, ON L4L 4Y4
Tel: 905-850-0155; Fax: 905-850-0498
www.piccinbottos.com

Woodbridge: Felix Rocca - *1
#302, 7050 Weston Rd., Woodbridge, ON L4L 8G7
Tel: 905-851-7747; Fax: 905-851-7834
felixrocca@rogers.com

Woodbridge: Rovazzi, Pallotta - *3
#901, 3700 Steeles Ave. West, Woodbridge, ON L4L 8K8
Tel: 905-850-2468; Fax: 905-850-4066

Woodbridge: Devi D. Sharma - *1
#625, 7050 Weston Rd., Woodbridge, ON L4L 8G7
Tel: 905-856-6404; Fax: 905-856-6264

Woodbridge: Stabile Professional Corporation - *2
Former Name: Stabile Partners
#905, 3700 Steeles Ave. West, Woodbridge, ON L4L 8K8
Tel: 905-851-6711; Fax: 905-851-5773
vista@stablaw.com

Woodbridge: Tanzola & Sorbara - *4
#101, 10 Director Ct., Woodbridge, ON L4L 7E8
Tel: 905-265-2252; Fax: 905-265-0667
www.tanzola-sorbara.net

Woodbridge: Turner, Brooks - *1
Former Name: Turner, Brooks Associates
#15, 4220 Steeles Ave. West, Woodbridge, ON L4L 3S8
Tel: 416-213-0524
stumer.barrister@bellnet.ca

Woodbridge: Weston Law Chambers - *9
Also Known As: Weston Law
#600, 3700 Steeles Ave. West, Woodbridge, ON L4L 8K8
Tel: 905-856-3700; Fax: 905-856-1213
info@westonlaw.ca
www.westonlaw.ca

Woodstock: George H. Bishop - *1
557 Adelaide St., Woodstock, ON N4S 4B7
Tel: 519-539-8559; Fax: 519-539-2401
angie-bishoplaw@rogers.com

Woodstock: Gregory W. Boddy - *1
Former Name: Beatty Stock & Lemon
P.O. Box 336, 487 Princess St., Woodstock, ON N4S 7X6
Tel: 519-537-6629; Fax: 519-539-2459

Woodstock: Debra A. Brown - *1
94 Graham St., Woodstock, ON N4S 6J7
Tel: 519-539-9870; Fax: 519-539-9248
debra@dabrownlaw.com

Woodstock: Peter H. Kratzmann - *1
372 Hunter St., Woodstock, ON N4S 6E2
Tel: 519-537-2221; Fax: 519-537-5150
phklaw@primus.ca

Woodstock: Gordon Lemon - *1
530 Adelaide St., Woodstock, ON N4S 8X8
Tel: 519-537-5555; Fax: 519-537-8609
glemon@beattylaw.on.ca

Woodstock: Gary D. McQuaid - *1
380 Hunter St., Woodstock, ON N4S 4G2
Tel: 519-539-1310

Woodstock: White Coad LLP - Woodstock - *4
5 Wellington St. North, Woodstock, ON N4S 6P1
Tel: 519-421-1500; Fax: 519-539-6926
main@whitecoad.com
www.whitecoad.com

indicates number of lawyers

Woodstock: R.B. Wolyniuk - *3
19 Riddell St., Woodstock, ON N4S 6L9
Tel: 519-539-7431; *Fax:* 519-539-4975

Prince Edward Island

Charlottetown: Campbell Lea Barristers & Solicitors
- *7
#400, P.O. Box 429, 65 Water St., Charlottetown, PE C1A 1A3
Tel: 902-566-3400; *Fax:* 902-367-3713
www.campbelllea.com

Charlottetown: Carr, Stevenson & MacKay - *11
P.O. Box 522, 65 Queen St., Charlottetown, PE C1A 7L1
Tel: 902-892-4156; *Fax:* 902-566-1377
www.csmlaw.com

Charlottetown: Kenneth A. Clark Law Office - *1
P.O. Box 2831, Stn. Central, 155 Queen St., 2nd Fl.,
Charlottetown, PE C1A 4B4
Tel: 902-566-9996; *Fax:* 902-566-9997

Charlottetown: Peter C. Ghiz - *1
240 Pownal St., Charlottetown, PE C1A 3X1
Tel: 902-628-6300; *Fax:* 902-628-6399
Toll-Free: 800-399-3221
peterghiz@peterghizlawyer.com
www.petercghizlawcorporation.com

Charlottetown: Key Murray Law - Charlottetown - *14
Former Name: Matheson & Murray
#202, P.O. Box 875, 119 Queen St., Charlottetown, PE C1A
7I9
Tel: 902-894-7051; *Fax:* 902-368-3762
charlottetown@keymurraylaw.com
keymurraylaw.com

Charlottetown: Macnutt & Dumont - *3
P.O. Box 965, 57 Water St., Charlottetown, PE C1A 7M4
Tel: 902-894-5003; *Fax:* 902-368-3782
info@macnuttdumont.ca
www.macnuttdumont.ca

Charlottetown: Philip Mullally, Q.C. - *1
P.O. Box 2560, Stn. Central, 51 University Ave.,
Charlottetown, PE C1A 8C2
Tel: 902-892-5452; *Fax:* 902-892-7013

Charlottetown: Paul J.D. Mullin Q.C. - *1
P.O. Box 604, Stn. Central, 14 Great George St.,
Charlottetown, PE C1A 7L3
Tel: 902-368-3221; *Fax:* 902-894-7491
mullinlaw@pei.aibn.com

Charlottetown: Brenda J. Picard - *1
P.O. Box 2000, Stn. Central, 40 Great George St.,
Charlottetown, PE C1A 7N8
Tel: 902-368-6043; *Fax:* 902-368-6122
bjpicard@gov.pe.ca

Charlottetown: Elizabeth S. Reagh Q.C. - *1
17 West St., Charlottetown, PE C1A 3S3
Tel: 902-892-7667; *Fax:* 902-368-8629

Mount Stewart: Marlene R. Clarke Q.C. - *1
P.O. Box 63, Mount Stewart, PE C0A 1T0
Tel: 902-676-2954

Summerside: Kathleen Loo Craig - *1
P.O. Box 11, Stn. Main, Summerside, PE C1N 4P6
Tel: 902-887-2900; *Fax:* 902-887-2100

Summerside: Robert McNeill - *1
251 Water St., Summerside, PE C1N 1B5
Tel: 902-436-4847; *Fax:* 902-436-8183

Québec

Alma: Sandra Bouchard, Avocate - *1
Palais de Justice, 725 Harvey ouest, Alma, QC G8B 1P5
Tél: 418-668-3334; *Téléc:* 418-662-3697

Alma: Larouche Lalancette Pilote, Avocats
s.e.n.r.c.l. - *7
Former Name: Larouche, Lalancette, Pilote & Bouchard
660, boul de Quen nord, Alma, QC G8B 6H5
Tél: 418-662-6475; *Téléc:* 418-662-9239
www.llpavocats.com

Amos: Bigué avocats - *6
Former Name: Bigué & Bigué
91, av 1re ouest, Amos, QC J9T 1T7
Tél: 819-732-8911; *Téléc:* 819-732-1470
www.bigueavocats.com

Amos: McGuire Dussault et Associés - *1
39A, av 1re ouest, Amos, QC J9T 1T7
Tél: 819-732-5258; *Téléc:* 819-732-0394

Asbestos: Denis Beaubien Avocat - *1
601, rue Simoneau, Asbestos, QC J1T 4G7
Tél: 819-879-7177
info@beaubienavocat.com
www.beaubienavocat.com

Beauport: Blouin & Associés - *3
1217, av Royal, Beauport, QC G1E 2B2
Tél: 418-663-2931; *Téléc:* 418-663-3792

Beloeil: Doré, Tourigny, Mallette & Associés - *5
#201, 347 rue Duvernay, Beloeil, QC J3G 5S8
Tél: 450-446-8474; *Téléc:* 450-467-7134

Beloeil: Morand Duval Avocats inc. - *5
Former Name: Bastien, Morand & Associés
201, boul Sir-Wilfrid-Laurier, Beloeil, QC J3G 4G8
Tél: 450-467-5849
info@morandduvalavocats.ca
www.morandduvalavocats.ca
www.facebook.com/avocatsbm

Boucherville: Lecompte Deguire Avocats - *2
1019, rue de la Ventrouze, Boucherville, QC J4B 5V3
Tél: 450-641-0065; *Téléc:* 450-641-3721
lecomptedeguire@videotron.ca

Brossard: Lord & Associes - *6
#204, 5855 boul Taschereau, Brossard, QC J4Z 1A5
Tél: 514-990-2803; *Téléc:* 450-672-5320

Châteauguay: Marie-Andrée Mallette - *1
272, boul St-Jean-Baptiste, Châteauguay, QC J6K 3C2
Tél: 450-699-9499; *Téléc:* 450-699-9710
marieandreemallette@videotron.ca

Coaticook: Gérin Custeau Francoeur - *3
#110, 38, rue Child, Coaticook, QC J1A 2B1
Tél: 819-849-4855

Cowansville: Claude Boulet - *1
#330, 104, rue du Sud, Cowansville, QC J2K 2X2
Tél: 450-263-0061; *Téléc:* 450-263-9468
c.boulet@endirect.qc.ca

Dolbeau-Mistassini: Bouchard Voyer Boily - *3
1273, boul Wallberg, Dolbeau-Mistassini, QC G8L 1H3
Tél: 418-276-2234; *Téléc:* 418-276-3582
www.facebook.com/466405646899980

Dolbeau-Mistassini: Simard Boivin Lemieux Avocats
- Dolbeau-Mistassini - *27
Former Name: Boivin, Lussier, Hébert
112, av de l'Église, Dolbeau-Mistassini, QC G8L 4W4
Tél: 418-276-2570; *Téléc:* 418-276-8797
Ligne sans frais: 877-276-2570
dolmis@sblavocats.com
www.sblavocats.com
www.facebook.com/sblavocats,
www.linkedin.com/company/sbl-avocats

Donnacona: Bernatchez Associés - Avocats - *1
Former Name: Yves Bernatchez
#120, 100, rte 138, Donnacona, QC G3M 1B5
Tél: 418-462-1010; *Téléc:* 418-462-1011
avocats@avoc.ca
www.avoc.ca
www.facebook.com/BernatchezAssociesAvocats,
twitter.com/BernatchezAvoc,
www.linkedin.com/company/2655304

Donnacona: Claude Dussault - *1
220, av Ste-Marie, Donnacona, QC G3M 2M2
Tél: 418-284-4841

Dorval: Amaron, Viberg & Pecho - *1
#200, 280, av Dorval, Dorval, QC H9S 3H4
Tél: 514-636-4992; *Téléc:* 514-636-8122

Drummondville: Biron & Associé Avocats - *1
#195, 350, rue St-Jean, Drummondville, QC J2B 5L4
Tél: 819-477-8741; *Téléc:* 819-477-7166
bironavocats@cgocable.ca
www.bironetassocieavocats.ca

Drummondville: Boudreau, Méthot, Tourigny - *2
Former Name: Boudreau, Méthot
83, rue St-Damase, Drummondville, QC J2B 6E5
Tél: 819-477-3517; *Téléc:* 819-477-0700

Drummondville: Hinse Tousignant et Associés - *3
360, rue Marchand, Drummondville, QC J2C 4N9
Tél: 819-477-3424; *Téléc:* 819-477-7728
Ligne sans frais: 888-488-3424
hinsetousignant@bellnet.ca
www.hinsetousignantavocats.com

Drummondville: Jutras et Associés - *4
449, rue Hériot, Drummondville, QC J2B 1B4
Tél: 819-477-6321; *Téléc:* 819-474-5691
info@jutras.ca
www.jutras.ca

Gatineau: Jean-Paul Aubry - *1
175, rue Champlain, Gatineau, QC J8X 3R3
Tél: 819-771-8645; *Téléc:* 819-771-9338

Gatineau: Christine M. Auger - *1
#200, 525 boul Maloney est, Gatineau, QC J8P 1E8
Tél: 819-770-4022; *Téléc:* 819-669-9627

Gatineau: Beaudry, Bertrand, s.e.n.c.r.l. - *11
#107, 160, boul de l'Hôpital, Gatineau, QC J8T 8J1
Tél: 819-770-4880; *Fax:* 819-595-4979
www.beaudry-bertrand.com

Gatineau: Robert Bélanger, Avocat - *1
307, boul Saint-Joseph, Gatineau, QC J8Y 3Y6
Tél: 819-771-6679; *Téléc:* 819-771-9675
robert.belanger.avocat@sympatico.ca

Gatineau: Pierre Fontaine - *1
25, rue Bernier, Gatineau, QC J8Z 1E7
Tél: 819-771-6578
pierre14f@yahoo.com

Gatineau: Gaudreau - *2
167, rue Notre-Dame-de-l'Ile, Gatineau, QC J8X 3T3
Tél: 819-770-7928; *Téléc:* 819-770-1424
bergeron.gaudreau@qc.aira.com

Gatineau: André Gingras - *1
30, rue Maricourt, Gatineau, QC J29 1R9
Tél: 819-595-4748; *Téléc:* 819-772-4193
mariannamerica@videotron.ca

Gatineau: Leduc, Bouthillette - *9
#301, 200, rue Montcalm, Gatineau, QC J8Y 3B5
Tél: 819-778-1870; *Téléc:* 819-778-8860
LB@auocats.ca

Gatineau: Letellier Gosselin - *7
#127, 139, boul de l'Hôpital, Gatineau, QC J8T 8A3
Tél: 819-243-1336; *Téléc:* 819-243-9425
mgosselin@letellier.com
www.letellier.com

Gatineau: Lora, Houle, Jacques - *3
Former Name: Lora, E. Wayne
175, rue Champlain, Gatineau, QC J8X 3R3
Tél: 819-778-6511; *Téléc:* 819-770-5703
wlora@mac.com

Gatineau: Pharand Joyal - *5
166, rue Wellington, Gatineau, QC J8X 2J4
Tél: 819-771-7781; *Téléc:* 819-771-0608
pharand.joyal@qc.aira.com

Gatineau: Ste-Marie & Lacombe - *2
175, rue Champlain, Gatineau, QC J8X 3R3
Tél: 819-770-7800; *Téléc:* 819-770-5703

Gatineau: Sarrazin & Charlebois - *2
162, rue Wellington, Gatineau, QC J8X 2J4
Tél: 819-770-4888; *Téléc:* 819-770-0712
sarrazin-charlebois@videotron.ca

Gracefield: Louise Major - *1
40, rue Principale, Gracefield, QC J0X 1W0
Tél: 819-463-3477; *Téléc:* 819-463-4603

Granby: Gaudet Cabanac - *3
Former Name: Gaudet Galipeau Parcel - Avocats;
Gaudet & Associés
18, rue Court, Granby, QC J2G 4Y5
Tél: 450-777-1070; *Téléc:* 450-777-5960
www.gaudetavocats.com

indicates number of lawyers

Granby: Gilles Viens - *1
#204, 160 rue Principale, Granby, QC J2G 2V6
Tél: 450-770-2121; Téléc: 450-770-0088
gilles@fournierleclerc.ca

Hampstead: Judith Lifshitz - *1
30, ch Belsize, Hampstead, QC H3X 3J8
Tél: 514-488-8561; Téléc: 514-488-0121

Joliette: Asselin Avocats - *5
Former Name: Asselin, Asselin & Germain
569, rue Archambault, Joliette, QC J6E 2W7
Tél: 450-755-5050; Téléc: 450-755-5111
info@asselinavocats.ca
asselinavocats.ca

Joliette: Boulard & Richer - Avocates - *2
198, rue St-Joseph, Joliette, QC J6E 5C6
Tél: 450-753-8360; Téléc: 450-753-8359
boulard_richer_sb@videotron.ca
www.boulardetricheravocates.com

Joliette: Claudette Vincelette - *1
Former Name: Vincelette, Marois
125, rue Beaudry nord, Joliette, QC J6E 6A4
Tél: 450-759-3958; Téléc: 450-756-2933

Kahnawake: Mohawk Council of Kahnawake Legal Services
CP 720, Kahnawake, QC J0L 1B0
Tél: 450-632-7500; Téléc: 450-638-3663
communications@mck.ca
www.kahnawake.com/org/lsu
twitter.com/mckahnawake

L'Ile Perrot: Aumais Chartrand - Avocats - *6
#12, 100, boul Don Quichotte, L'Ile Perrot, QC J7V 6L7
Tél: 514-425-2233; Téléc: 514-453-0977

La Malbaie: Marie-Claude Dallaire - *1
#220, CP 237, 251, rue John-Nairne, La Malbaie, QC G5A 1M4
Tél: 418-665-6417; Téléc: 418-665-6174
marieclaude.dallaire@ccjg.qc.ca

Lac-Beauport: Alain Baccigalupo - *1
27, ch le Tour du Lac, Lac-Beauport, QC G0A 2C0
Tél: 418-849-0396; Téléc: 418-656-7861

Lac-Mégantic: Daniel Drouin - *1
4927, rue Laval, Lac-Mégantic, QC G6B 1E2
Tél: 819-583-0787; Téléc: 819-583-4631
ddrouin@notarius.net

Lac-Simon: Sylvie Savoie - *1
1428, ch Du Tour-Du-Lac, Lac-Simon, QC J5A 2G9
Tél: 819-428-9366

Lachine: Louise Saint-Amour - *1
#3, 1375, rue Notre-Dame, Lachine, QC H8S 2C9
Tél: 514-634-8243; Téléc: 514-634-3044
saintamourlouise@yahoo.ca

Lachute: William M.C. Steeves - *1
18, boul de la Providence, Lachute, QC J8H 3K9
Tél: 450-562-2465; Téléc: 450-562-2467

Laval: Alepin Gauthier Avocats Inc - *26
#400, 3080, boul Le Carrefour, Laval, QC H7T 2R5
Tél: 450-231-1277; Téléc: 450-681-1476
www.alepin.com
www.facebook.com/AlepinGauthierAvocats
twitter.com/AlepinGauthier,
www.linkedin.com/company/alepin-gauthier-avocats

Laval: Bélanger, Garceau - *2
#309, 400, boul St-Martin ouest, Laval, QC H7M 3Y8
Tél: 450-669-1313; Téléc: 450-669-1122
belangergarceau@videotron.ca

Laval: François Bordeleau - *1
60, rue Alexandre, Laval, QC H7G 3K9
Ligne sans frais: 877-975-2060

Laval: Cholette Robidoux avocats s.e.n.c. - *6
Former Name: Cholette Côté & associés Avocats
#650, 1, Place Laval, Laval, QC H7N 1A1
Tél: 450-668-0888; Téléc: 450-668-0048
info@choletterobidoux.com
www.choletterobidoux.com

Laval: France Cormier - *1
3682, rue Isabelle, Laval, QC H7P 4Z6
Tél: 450-622-7616; Téléc: 450-622-5254
francecormier@videotron.ca

Laval: Dagenais, Poupart - *3
#650, 2550, boul Daniel-Johnson, Laval, QC H7T 2L1
Tél: 450-978-2442; Téléc: 450-973-4010

Laval: Fournier, Diamond - *2
#1102, 2500, boul Daniel-Johnson, Laval, QC H7T 2P6
Tél: 450-682-7011; Téléc: 450-686-8566

Laval: Michel B. Fournier - *1
#204, 4150, boul St-Martin ouest, Laval, QC H7T 1C1
Tél: 450-686-2600; Téléc: 450-681-3642
mb.fournier@sympatico.ca

Laval: Massicott & Guérard - *3
134, boul des Laurentides, Laval, QC H7G 2T3
Tél: 450-663-0851

Laval: Jean Mignault - *1
#2020, 400, boul Armand Frappier, Laval, QC H7V 4B4
Tél: 514-332-4110; Téléc: 514-334-6043

Laval: Pierre Lamarche - *1
237A, boul des Prairies, Laval, QC H7N 2T8
Tél: 450-667-9802; Téléc: 450-667-5740
plamarche@g1bonavocat.com
www.g1bonavocat.com

Laval: Turcotte, Nolet - *5
#470, 500, boul St. Martin ouest, Laval, QC H7M 3Y2
Tél: 450-901-0151; Téléc: 450-901-0152
turcotte.nolet@qc.aira.com

Longueuil: Bernard & Brassard S.E.N.C.R.L. - *17
#400, 555, boul Roland-Therrien, Longueuil, QC J4H 4E7
Tél: 450-670-7900; Téléc: 450-670-0673
Ligne sans frais: 888-670-7900
info@bernard-brassard.com
www.bernard-brassard.com
www.linkedin.com/company/2067921

Longueuil: Jacques Boissonnault - *1
630, ch de Chambly, Longueuil, QC J4H 3L8
Tél: 514-831-3052; Téléc: 866-462-3192
avocat.jb@videotron.ca

Longueuil: Dubois et Associés - *3
#97, 45, Place Charles-Lemoyne, Longueuil, QC J4K 5G5
Tél: 450-646-2613; Téléc: 450-646-4225

Longueuil: Monique Fortier - *2
#95, 45, Place Charles Lemoyne, Longueuil, QC J4K 5G5
Tél: 450-651-4418; Téléc: 450-442-1125
me.mfortier@bellnet.ca

Lorraine: André J. Courtemanche - *1
107, boul Val D'Ajol, Lorraine, QC J6Z 4G4
Tél: 514-758-6884; Téléc: 450-965-6958
andre.courtemanche@videotron.ca

Lévis: Gosselin, Lagueux, Roy, notaires s.e.n.c.r.l. - Lévis - *4
CP 1247, 67, côte du Passage, Lévis, QC G6V 6R8
Tél: 418-833-0311; Téléc: 418-833-1749
info@glrnotaires.com
www.glrnotaires.com

Lévis: Pelletier D'Amours - *8
Former Name: Pelletier, Kronstro@#m, Giguère
CP 3500, 6300, boul de la Rive sud, Lévis, QC G6V 6P9
Tél: 418-835-4944; Téléc: 418-835-8847
Ligne sans frais: 800-314-4944

Matane: Deschenes & Doiron, Avocats, s.e.n.c. - *2
352, av St-Jérôme, Matane, QC G4W 3B1
Tél: 418-562-2097; Téléc: 418-562-2926
desdoiron@cgocable.ca

Mont-Laurier: Maitre Marc-André Simard - *4
Former Name: Simard, Deschênes et Barrette
445, rue du Pont, Mont-Laurier, QC J9L 2R8
Tél: 819-623-1715

Mont-Laurier: Roger Rancourt, Avocat - *1
673, Carré Laurier, Mont-Laurier, QC J9L 2W4
Tél: 819-623-4485

Montmagny: Robert Daveluy, Q.C. - *1
#22, 46, rue St-Jean-Baptiste est, Montmagny, QC G5V 1J8
Tél: 418-248-1072

Montmagny: Marcel Guimont - *2
134, rue St-Jean Baptiste est, Montmagny, QC G5V 1K6
Tél: 418-248-1530; Téléc: 418-248-4157

Montréal: Adessky Lesage - *2
#525, 4150, rue Ste-Catherine ouest, Montréal, QC H3Z 2Y5
Tél: 514-288-8070; Téléc: 514-288-8655
general@adesskylesage.com

Montréal: L'Agence Goodwin - *3
#2, 839, rue Sherbrooke est, Montréal, QC H2L 1K6
Tél: 514-598-5252; Téléc: 514-598-1878
artistes@goodwin.agent.ca
www.agencegoodwin.com

Montréal: Joseph W. Allen - *1
#203, 6855, av de l'Epée, Montréal, QC H3N 2C7
Tél: 514-274-9393; Téléc: 514-274-5614
jwallenimmlaw@bellnet.ca

Montréal: Amar & Associés - *3
625, boul René Lévesque ouest, Montréal, QC H3B 1R2
Tél: 514-878-1532; Téléc: 514-878-4761
michael@amar.ca

Montréal: Arsenault, Lemieux - *2
2328, rue Ontario est, Montréal, QC H2K 1W1
Tél: 514-527-8903; Téléc: 514-527-1410
arsenault.lemieux@qc.aira.com

Montréal: Baron Abrams - *9
#200, 4141, rue Sherbrooke ouest, Montréal, QC H3Z 1B8
Tél: 514-935-7783; Téléc: 514-989-1811

Montréal: Barsalou Lawson - *13
#1500, 2000, av McGill College, Montréal, QC H3A 3H3
Tel: 514-982-3355; Fax: 514-982-2550
www.barsalou.ca

Montréal: Howard A. Barza - *2
#450, 2015, rue Peel, Montréal, QC H3A 1T8
Tél: 514-288-9322; Téléc: 514-288-2562

Montréal: Bastien & Champagne - *2
#100, 6621, rue Sherbrooke est, Montréal, QC H1N 1C7
Tél: 514-253-0876; Téléc: 514-253-2578

Montréal: Jacques Bazinet - *1
4276, rue Fabre, Montréal, QC H2J 3T6
Tél: 514-527-1702; Téléc: 514-597-1352

Montréal: Beaudry Dessurealt - *3
#304, 480, boul St-Laurent, Montréal, QC H2Y 3Y7
Tél: 514-282-0727; Téléc: 514-282-9363

Montréal: Bélanger Sauvé - Montréal - *57
#900, 5, Place Ville Marie, Montréal, QC H3B 2G2
Tel: 514-878-3081; Fax: 514-878-3053
info@belangersauve.com
www.belangersauve.com

Montréal: Belanger, Fiore - *2
#300, 685, boul Décarie, Montréal, QC H4L 5G4
Tél: 514-744-0825; Téléc: 514-744-9861

Montréal: Peter J. Bellan - *1
#1A, 5130, rue Charleroi, Montréal, QC H1G 2Z8
Tél: 514-955-0691; Téléc: 514-955-6921

Montréal: Nicole Benchimol - *1
#1200, 2015, rue Peel, Montréal, QC H3A 1T8
Tél: 514-844-1515; Téléc: 514-845-4472

Montréal: Bérard Avocats - *2
417, rue des Seigneurs, 2e étage, Montréal, QC H3J 1X7
Tél: 514-934-1760; Téléc: 514-934-1212

Montréal: Berger & Winston - *2
#1150, 615, boul René-Lévesque ouest, Montréal, QC H3B 1P5
Tél: 514-288-4177; Téléc: 514-876-1090

Montréal: Jean Bernier - *1
425, rue Saint-Sulpice, Montréal, QC H2Y 2V7
Tél: 514-395-2290

Montréal: Elaine Bissonnette - *1
3892, rue Monselet, Montréal, QC H1H 2C1
Tél: 514-323-8770; Téléc: 514-323-8700
avocatebissonnette@qc.aira.com
www.avocatebissonnette.com

Montréal: Marc Bissonnette - *1
4, rue Notre-Dame est, Montréal, QC H2Y 1B8
Tél: 514-871-8250
marc.bissonnette@sympatico.ca
www.marcbissonnette.com

* indicates number of lawyers

Montréal: Harry Blank, Q.C. - *1
#1416, 1255, rue University, Montréal, QC H3B 3X1
Tél: 514-866-1125; Téléc: 514-866-6898
hablank@videotron.ca

Montréal: Blitt Héroux - *2
4770, av de Kent, Montréal, QC H3W 1H2
Tél: 514-483-2444; Téléc: 514-483-2477

Montréal: Bloomfield & Avocats - *2
Former Name: Harry J.F. Bloomfield
#1310, 1155, rue University, Montréal, QC H3B 3A7
Tél: 514-871-9571; Téléc: 514-397-0816
hbloomfield@fieldbloom.com
www.bloomfieldandassociates.ca

Montréal: Sonia, Bogdaniec - *1
#400, 460, rue St-Gabriel, Montréal, QC H2Y 2Z9
Tél: 514-393-3326; Téléc: 514-392-7766

Montréal: Rika Bohbot - *1
555, rue Chabanel ouest, Montréal, QC H2N 2L1
Tél: 514-385-3000; Téléc: 514-385-6625

Montréal: Gaston E. Bouchard - *1
1015, rue Champigny, Montréal, QC H4L 4P3
Tél: 514-744-0918; Téléc: 514-345-4718

Montréal: Boucher Harper - *6
#610, 630, rue Sherbrooke ouest, Montréal, QC H3A 1E4
Tél: 514-878-1900; Téléc: 514-878-3679

Montréal: Pierre-Paul Boucher - *1
7568, rue St-Denis, Montréal, QC H2R 2E6
Tél: 514-495-8900; Téléc: 514-495-8367

Montréal: François Bourdon - *1
2308, rue Sherbrooke est, Montréal, QC H2K 1E5
Tél: 514-526-0821; Téléc: 514-521-5397

Montréal: Jacques Bourgault - *1
7575, rue des Ecores, Montréal, QC H2E 2W5
Tél: 438-490-3903
jacques.bourgault@videotron.ca
www.jacquesbourgaultavocatlawyer.com

Montréal: Boyer Gariépy - *4
#200, 417, rue St-Nicolas, Montréal, QC H2Y 2P4
Tél: 514-287-9585; Téléc: 514-844-5243
boga@bellnet.ca

Montréal: Diane Brais - *1
Former Name: Brais, Shindler
282 rue Notre-Dame ouest, Montréal, QC H2Y 1T7
Tél: 514-985-5454; Téléc: 514-985-5433
info@braislaw.ca
www.braislaw.ca

Montréal: Sarto Brisebois - *2
#301, 60, rue St-Jacques, Montréal, QC H2Y 1L5
Tél: 514-849-9444; Téléc: 514-849-0119

Montréal: Brisset Bishop - *5
#2020, 2020, boul Robert Bourassa, Montréal, QC H3A 2A5
Tel: 514-393-3700; Fax: 514-393-1211
general@brissetbishop.com
www.brissetbishop.com

Montréal: Jacques Brunet - *1
#103, 3714, rue Ontario est, Montréal, QC H1W 1R9
Tél: 514-524-6638

Montréal: Rebecca Butovsky - *1
3562, av de Vendome, Montréal, QC H4A 3M7
Tél: 514-484-2942

Montréal: Diane G. Cameron - *1
#206, 4700, av Bonavista, Montréal, QC H3W 2C5
Tél: 514-483-2619; Téléc: 514-483-3616

Montréal: Campbell Cohen Law Firm Inc. - *4
#800, 1980, rue Sherbrooke ouest, Montréal, QC H3H 1E8
Tél: 514-937-9445; Téléc: 514-937-2618

Montréal: Andre Carbonneau - *1
2567, rue Ontario est, Montréal, QC H2K 1W6
Tél: 514-528-2600

Montréal: Carette Desjardins - *7
Former Name: Lepage Carette; Hébert, Downs, Lepage,
Soulière & Carette
#2830, 500, place d'Armes, Montréal, QC H2Y 2W2
Tél: 514-284-2351; Téléc: 514-284-2354
www.carettedesjardins.com

Montréal: Pauline Cazelais, Q.C. - *1
2339, Terrasse Guindon, Montréal, QC H1H 1L7
Tél: 514-522-5427

Montréal: Cerundolo & Maiorino - *2
1807, rue Jean-Talon est, Montréal, QC H1E 1T4
Tél: 514-376-0335; Téléc: 514-376-6334
avocatscema.com

Montréal: Chalifoux Montpetit Vaillancourt Paradis &
Ass SENCRL - *12
Former Name: Chalifoux, Carette & Montpetit
#200, 28, rue Notre-Dame est, Montréal, QC H2Y 1B9
Tél: 514-842-1006; Téléc: 514-842-1811

Montréal: Chapados Avocats - *1
#2350, 1010, rue Sherbrooke ouest, Montréal, QC H3A 2R7
Tél: 514-849-2350; Téléc: 514-549-3589

Montréal: Charbonneau SA Avocats - *2
#345, 32, rue Saint-Charles ouest, Montréal, QC J4H 1C6
Tél: 514-527-4561
nathalie@charbonneau-sa.com
www.facebook.com/charbonneau.sa

Montréal: Charness, Charness & Charness - *5
#500, 614, rue St-Jacques, Montréal, QC H3C 1E2
Tél: 514-878-1808; Téléc: 514-871-1149
info@charnesslaw.com
charnesslaw.com

Montréal: Maurice Chevalier - *1
#1407, 3555, rue Berri, Montréal, QC H2L 4G4
Tél: 514-845-5551

Montréal: Choquette Beaupré Rheaume - *3
#200, 5316, av du Parc, Montréal, QC H2V 4G7
Tél: 514-270-3192; Téléc: 514-270-8876

Montréal: Clyde & Cie Canada, S.E.N.C.R.L / LLP -
Montréal - *65
#1700, 630, boul René-Lévesque ouest, Montréal, QC H3B
1S6
Tél: 514-843-3777; Téléc: 514-843-6110
info@clydeco.ca
www.clydeco.ca

Montréal: Colby, Monet, Demers, Delage & Crevier -
*15
Also Known As: Colby Monet
#2900, Tour McGill College, 1501, av McGill College,
Montréal, QC H3A 3M8
Tel: 514-284-3663; Fax: 514-284-1961
cmddc@colby-monet.com
www.colby-monet.com

Montréal: Commission des services juridiques
CP 123, Stn. Desjardins, Montréal, QC H5B 1B3
Tél: 514-873-3562
info@csj.qc.ca
www.csj.qc.ca

Montréal: Lulu Cornellier - *1
#2821, 1, Place Ville Marie, Montréal, QC H3B 4R4
Tél: 514-842-1822; Téléc: 514-842-0052
lulucor@videotron.ca

Montréal: Côté Benoit - *1
1252, rue Beaubien est, Montréal, QC H2S 1T9
Tél: 514-272-5755
benoit.cote@bellnet.ca

Montréal: Daigneault, avocats inc. - *5
Also Known As: Daigneault, Lawyers Inc.
Former Name: Robert Daigneault, Cabinet D'Avocats
#400, Place D'Youville, 353, rue Saint-Nicolas, Montréal, QC
H2Y 2P1
Tél: 514-985-2929; Téléc: 514-985-0595
Ligne sans frais: 888-228-5834
enviro@daigneaultinc.com
www.daigneaultinc.com

Montréal: Jean-Louis Daunais - *1
#100, 10550, rue Iberville, Montréal, QC H2B 2V1
Tél: 514-385-1601

Montréal: David & Touchette - *2
#1500, 1255, boul Robert-Bourassa, Montréal, QC H3B 3X2
Tél: 514-871-8174; Téléc: 514-683-9669
www.davidtouchette.com

Montréal: De Grandpré Chait SENCRL-LLP - *68
Former Name: De Grandpré Godin
#2900, 1000, rue de la Gauchetière ouest, Montréal, QC H3B
4W5
Tel: 514-878-4311; Fax: 514-878-4333
info@degrandpre.com
www.degrandpre.com

Montréal: Claude de la Madeleine - *1
3600, boul Henri-Bourassa est, Montréal, QC H1H 1J4
Tél: 514-323-2112

Montréal: Charles Derome - *1
5064, av du Parc, Montréal, QC H2V 4G1
Tél: 514-271-4700; Téléc: 514-271-4708
charles.derome@videotron.ca
www.facebook.com/252601218177492

Montréal: Claude Des Marais - *1
1206, boul St. Joseph est, Montréal, QC H2J 1L6
Tél: 514-521-0047; Téléc: 514-521-0047

Montréal: Desjardins, Lapointe, Mousseau, Bélanger
- *6
#2185, 600, rue de la Gauchetière ouest, Montréal, QC H3B
4L8
Tél: 514-875-5404; Téléc: 514-875-5647

Montréal: Desrosiers, Joncas, Massicotte, Avocats -
*6
Former Name: Desrosiers, Turcotte, Marachand,
Massicotte
#503, 480, boul St. Laurent, Montréal, QC H2Y 3Y7
Tél: 514-387-9284; Téléc: 514-397-9922

Montréal: Donato Di Tullio - *1
7647, boul Gouin est, Montréal, QC H1E 1A7
Tél: 514-648-1048; Téléc: 514-648-1048
donatoditullio@gmail.com

Montréal: Doyon Izzi Nivoix - *5
#501, 6455, rue Jean-Talon est, Montréal, QC H1S 3E8
Tél: 514-253-3338; Téléc: 514-251-0560
info@dinlex.com
www.dinlex.com

Montréal: Mario Du Mesnil - *1
1595, rue St-Hubert, 4e étage, Montréal, QC H2L 3Z2
Tél: 514-526-6625; Téléc: 514-524-4341

Montréal: Duceppe, Théoret & Associés - *3
1595, rue St-Hubert, 4e étage, Montréal, QC H2L 3Z2
Tél: 514-526-6621; Téléc: 514-524-4341

Montréal: Emile J. Fattal - *1
#705, 1134, rue Ste-Catherine ouest, Montréal, QC H3B 1H4
Tél: 514-861-4545; Téléc: 514-874-1639
occidental@europe.com

Montréal: Jon M. Feldman - *1
#1500, 1 Westmount Sq., Montréal, QC H3Z 2P9
Tél: 514-935-6222; Téléc: 514-935-2314
jfeldman@jilaw.ca

Montréal: Ferland Marois Lanctot Avocats - *17
Montréal, QC
Tél: 514-861-1110
dsucces@fml.ca
www.fml.ca

Montréal: Filteau & Belleau - *2
Former Name: Filteau, Belleau, Normandeau &
Daudelin
#301, 28, rue Notre-Dame est, Montréal, QC H2Y 1B9
Tél: 514-843-7877; Téléc: 514-499-1889

Montréal: Finkelberg, Light - *2
#1200, 1, Westmount Sq., Montréal, QC H3Z 2P9
Tél: 514-932-7392; Téléc: 514-932-0990
plight@sympatico.ca

Montréal: Fishman Flanz Meland Paquin LLP - *14
Former Name: Goldstein, Flanz & Fishman
SENCRL/LLP
#4100, 1250, boul René-Lévesque ouest, Montréal, QC H3B
4W8
Tel: 514-932-4100; Fax: 514-932-4170
info@ffmp.ca
www.ffmp.ca

Montréal: Frankel & Spina - *2
#401, 60, rue St-Jacques, Montréal, QC H2Y 1L5
Tél: 514-849-3544; Téléc: 514-849-4457
plvspina@frankelspina.ca

Montréal: Franklin & Franklin - *4
#545, 4141, rue Sherbrooke ouest, Montréal, QC H3Z 1B8
Tél: 514-935-3576; *Téléc:* 514-935-6862
Ligne sans frais: 800-935-3576
info@franklinlegal.com
franklinlegal.com

Montréal: Frumkin, Feldman & Glazman - *3
#2270, Place du Canada, 1010, rue de la Gauchetière ouest, Montréal, QC H3Z 1T3
Tél: 514-861-2812; *Téléc:* 514-861-6062
ffg@bellnet.ca

Montréal: Gasco Goodhue St-Germain - *19
Former Name: Gasco Goodhue Provost
#800, 1000, rue Sherbrooke ouest, Montréal, QC H3A 3G4
Tél: 514-397-0066; *Téléc:* 514-397-0393
info@gasco.qc.ca
www.gasco.qc.ca

Montréal: Ulrich Gautier - *1
#2350, 500, place D'Armes, Montréal, QC H2Y 2W2
Tél: 514-288-3344; *Téléc:* 514-288-7772
ugautier@videotron.ca

Montréal: Gendron, Carpentier, S.E.N.C - *2
#300, 615, boul René-Lévesque ouest, Montréal, QC H3B 1P5
Tél: 514-395-4527; *Téléc:* 514-395-6031

Montréal: Gervais & Gervais - *1
#2100, 500, place d'Armes, Montréal, QC H2Y 2W2
Tél: 514-288-4241; *Téléc:* 514-849-9984

Montréal: Gingras Ouellet - *2
4141, av Pierre-de-Coubertin, Montréal, QC H1V 3N7
Tél: 514-252-4638; *Téléc:* 514-252-6906

Montréal: Goldwater, Dubé - *12
#2310, 3500, de Maisonneuve ouest, Montréal, QC H3Z 3C1
Tél: 514-600-6621; *Téléc:* 514-861-7601
www.goldwaterdube.com

Montréal: Gottlieb & Associés
#1920, 2020, rue University, Montréal, QC H3A 2A5
gottliebtradeandcustoms.com

Montréal: Gouveia, Gouveia - *3
#1704, 507, Place d'Armes, Montréal, QC H2Y 2W8
Tél: 514-844-0116; *Téléc:* 514-844-9053

Montréal: Elizabeth Greene - *1
#650, 4141, rue Sherbrooke ouest, Montréal, QC H3Z 1B8
Tél: 514-934-4852; *Téléc:* 514-935-3559

Montréal: Grenier, Gagnon - *4
#1410, 625, boul René-Lévesque ouest, Montréal, QC H3B 1R2
Tél: 514-875-4949; *Téléc:* 514-875-0313
info@greniergagnon.com
www.greniergagnon.com

Montréal: Gurman, Crevier Inc. - *2
#200, 5000 Jean-Talon St. ouest, Montréal, QC H4P 1W9
Tél: 514-858-1118; *Téléc:* 514-858-1121
agurman@gurman-crevier.com

Montréal: Calliope Hadjis - *1
Former Name: Hadjis & Hadjis
#707, 1117, rue Ste-Catherine ouest, Montréal, QC H3B 1H9
Tél: 514-849-3526; *Téléc:* 514-849-1595
info@hadjislaw.ca
www.hadjislaw.ca

Montréal: Martine Hamel - *1
#300, 13301, rue Sherbrooke est, Montréal, QC H1A 1C2
Tél: 514-642-4473; *Téléc:* 514-642-1663
martinehamel@vocate.com

Montréal: Hamilton, Cooper, Ashkenazy - *3
#401, 4226, boul St-Jean, Montréal, QC H9G 1X5
Tél: 514-626-0266; *Téléc:* 514-626-0011
info@hcalaw.ca

Montréal: Handelman, Handelman & Schiller
#630, 5160, boul Decarie, Montréal, QC H3X 2H9
Tél: 514-866-5071; *Téléc:* 514-866-4210
rs@hhslaw.ca
www.hhslaw.ca

Montréal: Hanna Glasz & Sher - *5
#2260, 1010, rue de la Gauchetière ouest, Montréal, QC H3B 2N2
Tél: 514-284-9551; *Téléc:* 514-284-3419

Montréal: Linda Hoddes - *3
1070, rue Mathieu, Montréal, QC H3H 2S8
Tél: 514-842-1714; *Téléc:* 514-842-1718

Montréal: Hutchins Legal Inc. - *11
Former Name: Hutchins Caron & Associés; Hutchins Grant & Associates; Hutchins, Soroka & Grant
424, rue Saint-François-Xavier, Montréal, QC H2Y 2S9
Tel: 514-849-2403; *Fax:* 514-849-4907
admin@hutchinslegal.ca
www.hutchinslegal.ca

Montréal: Michel A. Iacono - *1
#2001, 1 place Ville Marie, Montréal, QC H3B 2C4
Tél: 514-288-1414; *Téléc:* 514-288-0328
mmc.iacono@sympatico.ca

Montréal: Irving Mitchell Kalichman, SENCRL/LLP - *19
#1400, Place Alexis Nihon, Tower 2, 3500, boul de Maisonneuve ouest, Montréal, QC H3Z 3C1
Tél: 514-935-4460; *Téléc:* 514-935-2999
info@imk.ca
www.imk.ca

Montréal: Jeansonne Avocats inc. - *7
1401, av McGill College, Montréal, QC H3A 1Z4
Tél: 514-907-6175; *Téléc:* 514-840-9040
www.jeansonnelaw.ca

Montréal: Kierans & Guay - *2
#440, 606, rue Cathcart, Montréal, QC H3B 1K9
Tél: 514-866-3394; *Téléc:* 514-866-3398

Montréal: Leonard Kliger - *3
#808, 1255, carré Phillips, Montréal, QC H3B 3G1
Tél: 514-281-1720; *Téléc:* 514-281-0678
info@leonardkliger.com
leonardkliger.com

Montréal: Kounadis Perreault - *5
#740, 1010, rue Ste-Catherine ouest, Montréal, QC H3B 0C8
Tél: 514-844-8631
info@kpa-law.com
www.kpa-law.com

Montréal: Kravitz & Kravitz - *2
#350, 750, boul Marcel-Laurin, Montréal, QC H4M 2M4
Tél: 514-748-2889; *Téléc:* 514-748-5191
kravitz@centra.ca

Montréal: Kugler Kandestin - *14
#1170, 1, Place Ville-Marie, Montréal, QC H3B 2A7
Tél: 514-878-2861; *Téléc:* 514-875-8424
info@kklex.com
kklex.com

Montréal: Lucien Lachapelle - *1
5971, rue St-Hubert, Montréal, QC H2S 2L8
Tél: 514-277-2164; *Téléc:* 514-227-1120

Montréal: Gaetan Lagarde - *2
#201, 1554, boul Mont-Royal est, Montréal, QC H2J 1Z2
Tél: 514-521-2442; *Téléc:* 514-525-5561
gaela@videotron.ca

Montréal: Lamarre Perron Lambert Vincent - *6
Also Known As: LPLV
#200, 480, boul St-Laurent, Montréal, QC H2Y 3Y7
Tél: 514-798-1515; *Téléc:* 514-798-5599
www.lplv.com
www.facebook.com/LPLVavocats

Montréal: Raymond Landry - *1
74, ch de la Côte Sainte-Catherine, Montréal, QC H2V 2A3
Tel: 514-908-2171; *Fax:* 514-940-7044
info@raymondlandry-avocat.com
www.raymondlandry-avocat.com

Montréal: Lapointe Rosenstein Marchand Melançon - *64
Former Name: Lapointe Rosenstein; Marchand Melançon Forget
#1300, 1 Place Ville Marie, Montréal, QC H3B 5E9
Tel: 514-925-6300; *Fax:* 514-925-9001
Toll-Free: 800-728-6228
www.lrmm.com

Montréal: LaSalle Sokol - *2
Former Name: Moisan Lasalle Perreault
#280, 450, rue Sherbrooke est, Montréal, QC H2L 1J8
Tél: 514-844-3077; *Téléc:* 514-844-1018

Montréal: LaTraverse Avocat Indépendant - *2
Former Name: LaTraverse Avocats
#1510, 1010, rue Sherbrooke ouest, Montréal, QC H3A 2R7
Tél: 514-938-1313; *Téléc:* 514-938-3691
latraverse@latraverse.ca
www.latraverse.ca

Montréal: Laurier, Côté & Couturier - *3
356, 90e av, Montréal, QC H8R 2Z7
Tél: 514-363-0220; *Téléc:* 514-363-9495

Montréal: Lauzon Bélanger Lespérance inc. - *4
#100, 286, Saint-Paul ouestWest, Montréal, QC H2Y 2A3
Tel: 514-844-4646; *Fax:* 514-844-7009
info@lblavocats.ca
lblavocats.ca

Montréal: Lazare & Altschuler - *2
#2210, 1010, rue Sherbrooke ouest, Montréal, QC H3A 2R7
Tél: 514-878-3341; *Téléc:* 514-878-3314
lazare@lazalt.com

Montréal: John E. Lechter - *1
2015, rue Drummond, Montréal, QC H3G 1W7
Tél: 514-845-4287; *Téléc:* 514-845-1803

Montréal: Legros, St-Gelais, Charbonneau, avocats - *7
Former Name: Dugas & Legros
CP 1000, Stn. M, 4545, av Pierre-de-Coubertin, Montréal, QC H1V 3R2
Tél: 514-252-3000; *Téléc:* 514-252-0242
juridique@loisirquebec.qc.ca

Montréal: Liebman Légal Inc. - *1
#1500, 1, carré Westmount, Montréal, QC H3Z 2P9
Tél: 514-846-0666; *Téléc:* 514-935-2314
info@liebmanlegal.com
www.liebmanlegal.com

Montréal: Robert Loulou - *1
#1, 7924, rue St-Denis, Montréal, QC H2R 2G1
Tél: 514-388-3511; *Téléc:* 514-388-3211

Montréal: Lozeau Gonthier Masse Richard - *9
#1900, 1010, rue de la Gauchetière ouest, Montréal, QC H3B 2N2
Tél: 514-981-5600; *Téléc:* 514-981-5601

Montréal: Mannella & Associés - *3
3055, boul de l'Assomption, Montréal, QC H1N 2H1
Tél: 514-899-5375; *Téléc:* 514-899-0476
mannella@qc.aira.com

Montréal: Marchi Bellemare - *2
#200, 400, av McGill, Montréal, QC H2Y 2G1
Tél: 514-288-5753; *Téléc:* 514-284-6606
www.marchibellemare.com

Montréal: Martin Camirand Pelletier Lawyers - *7
#600, 460, rue St-Gabriel, Montréal, QC H2Y 2Z9
Tél: 514-847-8989; *Téléc:* 514-847-8990
mcp@mcp-avocats.com
www.mcp-avocats.com

Montréal: Melançon, Marceau, Grenier & Sciortino - Montréal - *17
#300, 1717, boul René-Lévesque est, Montréal, QC H2L 4T3
Tél: 514-525-3414; *Téléc:* 514-525-2803
www.mmgs.qc.ca

Montréal: Jean Mercier - *1
#202, 4059, rue Hochelaga, Montréal, QC H1W 1K4
Tél: 514-252-0888; *Téléc:* 514-252-5010

Montréal: Miller & Khazzam - *2
#525, 4150, Ste-Catherine ouest, Montréal, QC H3Z 2Y5
Tél: 514-875-8040; *Téléc:* 514-875-8044

Montréal: Monette Barakett, Avocats S.E.N.C. - *22
Former Name: Monette, Barakett, Lévesque, Bourque, Pedneault
#600, 4, Place Ville Marie, Montréal, QC H3B 2E7
Tél: 514-878-9381; *Téléc:* 514-878-3957
info@mbavocats.ca
www.monette-barakett.com
www.linkedin.com/company/monette-barakett-senc

Montréal: Myszka & Tepner - *2
#204, 4781, av Van Horne, Montréal, QC H3W 1J1
Tél: 514-737-4069

* indicates number of lawyers

Montréal: **Irving Narvey**
Also Known As: Druker, Narvey, Green, Schwartz
#605, 1255, carré Phillips, Montréal, QC H3B 3G5
Tél: 514-871-1300; Téléc: 514-871-1304
inarvey@dngslaw.com
irvingnarvey.com
www.facebook.com/IrvingNarveylaw

Montréal: **Nudleman Lamontagne - *2**
Former Name: Nudleman, Lamontagne & Grenier
#716, 1010, rue Sherbrooke ouest, Montréal, QC H3A 2R7
Tél: 514-866-6674; Téléc: 514-866-9822
info@nlglegal.ca
www.nlglegal.ca

Montréal: **O'Reilly & Associés - *4**
#1007, 1155, rue University, Montréal, QC H3B 3A7
Tél: 514-871-8117; Téléc: 514-871-9177

Montréal: **Pasquin Viens - *7**
204, Place d'Youville, Montréal, QC H2Y 2B4
Tél: 514-845-5171; Téléc: 514-845-5578
info@pasquinviens.com
www.pasquinviens.com

Montréal: **Pateras & Iezzoni - *5**
#2314, B.C. nord Bldg., 500, place d'Armes, Montréal, QC H2Y 2W2
Tél: 514-284-0860; Téléc: 514-843-7990

Montréal: **Yvan Pelletier - *1**
#600, CP 1390, Stn. Succ., 1801, ave. McGill Collège, Montréal, QC H3B 3L2
Tél: 514-879-2901; Téléc: 514-879-1923

Montréal: **John J. Pepper, Q.C & Associates - *1**
CP 2500, 1155, boul René-Lévesque ouest, Montréal, QC H3B 2K4
Tél: 514-875-5454; Téléc: 514-282-0053

Montréal: **Phillips, Friedman, Kotler - *16**
#900, Place du Canada, 1010, rue de la Gauchetière ouest, Montréal, QC H3B 2P8
Tél: 514-878-3371; Téléc: 514-878-4676
info@pfklaw.com
www.pfklaw.com

Montréal: **Marcel Plante - *1**
6915, rue Saint-Denis, Montréal, QC H2S 2S3
Tél: 514-272-8217

Montréal: **Polisuk, Lord - *2**
#2650, 1155, boul René-Lévesque ouest, Montréal, QC H3B 4S5
Tél: 514-861-8546; Téléc: 514-861-1298
info@polisuklord.com
www.polisuklord.com

Montréal: **Jacques Ranger - *1**
5694, av Laurendeau, Montréal, QC H4E 3W4
Tél: 514-766-0756

Montréal: **Renaud Dupuis Rioux - *6**
Former Name: Dupuis Brodeur S.E.N.C.
#3000, 315, rue du Saint-Sacrement, Montréal, QC H2Y 1Y1
Tél: 514-849-5140; Téléc: 514-849-3633
www.renaudbrodeur.com

Montréal: **Robic LLP - *40**
Centre CDP Capital, Bloc E, 8e étage, 1001, Square-Victoria, Montréal, QC H2Z 2B7
Tél: 514-987-6242; Téléc: 514-845-7874
info@robic.com
www.robic.ca
www.facebook.com/ROBICCanada, twitter.com/robiccanada, www.linkedin.com/company/robic

Montréal: **Robinson Sheppard Shapiro LLP - Montréal - *87**
#4600, 800, du Square Victoria, Montréal, QC H4Z 1H6
Tel: 514-878-2631; Fax: 514-878-1865
info@rsslex.com
www.rsslex.com

Montréal: **Rougeau Lambert Leborgne Avocats - *6**
#200, 402, rue Notre-Dame est, Montréal, QC H2Y 1C8
Tél: 514-840-9119; Téléc: 514-840-0177

Montréal: **Johanne St. Pierre - *1**
#101, 1395, rue Fleury est, Montréal, QC H2C 1R7
Tél: 514-388-8922; Téléc: 514-388-3672
johannestpierre47@gmail.com

Montréal: **Jean Saulnier - *1**
7190, rue St-Denis, Montréal, QC H2R 2E2
Tél: 514-273-1525; Téléc: 514-273-1673

Montréal: **Seidman Avocats inc. - *3**
Former Name: Seal Seidman G.P.
#300, 4060, rue Sainte-Catherine ouest, Montréal, QC H3Z 2Z3
Tél: 514-842-8861; Téléc: 514-288-1708
seidlaw.ca

Montréal: **Ian M. Solloway - *1**
#1700, 700, rue Sherbrooke ouest, Montréal, QC H3A 1G1
Tél: 514-906-1701; Téléc: 514-844-7290
info@sollaw.ca
www.sollaw.ca
twitter.com/sollowaylaw

Montréal: **Spiegel Sohmer - *49**
#1000, 1255, rue Peel, Montréal, QC H3B 2T9
Tél: 514-875-2100; Téléc: 514-875-8237
www.spiegelsohmer.com
www.facebook.com/Spiegel-Sohmer-Inc-128016573934088/,
twitter.com/SpiegelSohmerI, www.linkedin.com/company/108294

Montréal: **Stern & Blumer - *2**
#1825, 300, av Leo-Pariseau, Montréal, QC H3L 1R9
Tél: 514-842-1133; Téléc: 514-842-3105

Montréal: **Sternthal Katznelson Montigny s.e.n.c.r.l. - *13**
#1020, Place du Canada, 1010, rue de la Gauchetière ouest, Montréal, QC H3B 2N2
Tél: 514-878-1011; Téléc: 514-878-9195
litige@skm.ca
www.skm.ca

Montréal: **Mark Sumbulian - *1**
Former Name: Sumbulian & Sumbulian; Sumbulian, Hayk
#1610, 1350, rue Sherbrooke ouest, Montréal, QC H3G 1J1
Tél: 514-281-1955; Téléc: 514-281-1956

Montréal: **Tassé & Vescio - *2**
Former Name: Tassé & Themens
2421, rue Allard, Montréal, QC H4E 2L3
Tél: 514-769-9654; Téléc: 514-769-7363

Montréal: **Tiger Banon Inc. - *2**
Former Name: Tiger Goldman
#716, 1010, rue Sherbrooke ouest, Montréal, QC H3A 2R7
Tél: 514-284-8401
www.tigerbanon.com

Montréal: **Harvey Touch - *1**
Former Name: Toulch & Associates
#406, 1117, rue Ste-Catherine ouest, Montréal, QC H3B 1H9
Tél: 514-849-1289; Téléc: 514-849-3101
harvey.toulch@videotron.ca

Montréal: **Trudel Avocats S.E.N.C.R.L. - *6**
Former Name: Trudel Nadeau Avocats S.E.N.C.R.L.
#2500, Place du Parc, 300, rue Léo-Pariseau, Montréal, QC H2X 4B7
Tél: 514-849-5754; Téléc: 514-499-0312
info@trudelavocats.com
www.trudelavocats.com

Montréal: **Tucci & Associés - *3**
Former Name: Sergio Tucci & Associates
201, rue St-Zotique est, Montréal, QC H2S 1L2
Tél: 514-271-0650
info@tucci.ca
www.tucci.ca

Montréal: **Peter H. Turner - *1**
256, rue Devon, Montréal, QC H3R 1B9
Tél: 514-731-3544; Téléc: 514-737-3770

Montréal: **Unterberg, Carisse, Labelle, Dessureault, Lebeau & Petit**
Former Name: Unterberg, Labelle, Lebeau
#700, 1980, rue Sherbrooke ouest, Montréal, QC H3H 1E8
Tél: 514-934-0841; Téléc: 514-937-6547

Montréal: **Woods LLP - *24**
#1700, 2000, av McGill College, Montréal, QC H3A 3H3
Tél: 514-982-4545; Téléc: 514-284-2046
general@woods.qc.ca
www.litigationboutique.com

Paspébiac: **Gilles Moulin - *1**
CP 880, Paspébiac, QC G0C 2K0
Tél: 418-752-2244

Pointe-Claire: **Stanley Gelfand - *1**
#306, 189, boul Hymus, Pointe-Claire, QC H9R 1E9
Tél: 514-695-4542; Téléc: 514-695-7975

Québec: **Beauvais Truchon - *31**
#200, CP 1000, 79, boul René-Lévesque est, Québec, QC G1R 4T4
Tél: 418-692-4180; Téléc: 418-692-5321
www.beauvaistruchon.com
www.linkedin.com/company/beauvais-truchon-s-e-n-c-r-l-

Québec: **Herman Bedard - *1**
#206, 51, rue des Jardins, Québec, QC G1R 4L6
Tél: 418-692-2425; Téléc: 418-692-2528
hermanbedard@qc.aira.com
www.hermanbedard.com

Québec: **André Bernatchez - *1**
#220, 157, rue des Chênes ouest, Québec, QC G1L 1K6
Tél: 418-628-4575

Québec: **Maurice Bernatchez - *1**
#2, 1460, av de la Verendrye, Québec, QC G1J 4V8
Tél: 418-667-7830

Québec: **Yvan Bilodeau - *1**
#180, 801, ch St-Louis, Québec, QC G1S 1C1
Tél: 418-686-4875; Téléc: 418-686-6160

Québec: **Bouchard Pagé Tremblay, S.E.N.C. - Avocats - *10**
#510, 825, boul Lebourgneuf, Québec, QC G2J 0B9
Tél: 418-622-6699; Téléc: 418-628-1912
bouchardpagetremblay@bptavocats.com
www.bouchardpagetremblay.com
www.facebook.com/BouchardAvocats

Québec: **J. Michel Bouchard - *1**
1753 ave. Industrielle, Québec, QC G3K 1L8
Tél: 418-842-0996

Québec: **Roland Cote - *1**
1445, rue Maine, Québec, QC G1G 2J6
Tél: 418-628-2321

Québec: **Norman Dumais - *1**
#7, CP 18500, Stn. Terminus, 400 boul Jean-Lesage, Québec, QC G1K 7Z5
Tél: 418-643-4933; Téléc: 418-646-3678
norman.dumais@cnt.gouv.qc.ca

Québec: **Dussault Gervais Thivierge - *11**
Former Name: Brochet Dussault Lemieux Larochelle
#450, 2795, boul Laurier, Québec, QC G1V 4M7
Tél: 418-657-2424; Téléc: 418-657-1793
avocats@dlgt.ca
www.lesavocats.ca

Québec: **Gagné Letarte S.E.N.C.R.L. - Québec - *8**
#400, 79, boul René-Lévesque est, Québec, QC G1R 5N5
Tél: 418-522-7900; Téléc: 418-523-7900
www.gagneletarte.qc.ca

Québec: **Gagnon Girard Julien & Matte Avocats Avocates - *7**
#301, 1535, ch Ste-Foy, Québec, QC G1S 2P1
Tél: 418-681-0037; Téléc: 418-681-0539
www.ggjmavocats.ca

Québec: **La Société d'Avocats Garneau, Verdon, Michaud, Samson - *10**
67, rue Ste-Ursule, Québec, QC G1R 4E7
Tél: 418-692-3010; Téléc: 418-692-1742
gvm@qc.aira.com

Québec: **Giasson et Associés - *24**
#551, 2, rue des Jardins, Québec, QC G1R 4S9
Tél: 418-641-6156; Téléc: 418-641-6353

Québec: **Gosselin, Bussières, Bedard, Ouellet - *4**
#315, 400, boul Jean-Lesage, Québec, QC G1K 8W1
Tél: 418-529-9968; Téléc: 418-524-5243

Québec: **Hickson, Martin, Blanchard - *6**
Former Name: Hickson Noonan
1170 Grande Allée ouest, Québec, QC G1S 1E5
Tél: 418-681-9671; Téléc: 418-527-6938
wnoonan@oricom.ca
hickson-noonan.com

* indicates number of lawyers

Québec: Joli-Coeur Lacasse Avocats - Québec - *59
#600, 1134, Grande-Allée ouest, Québec, QC G1S 1E5
Tél: 418-681-7007; *Téléc:* 418-681-7100
infos@jolicoeurlacasse.com
www.jolicoeurlacasse.com
www.facebook.com/jolicoeurlacasse
www.linkedin.com/company/joli-coeur-lacasse-avocats

Québec: Micheline Anne Montreuil - *1
1050, rue François-Blondeau, Québec, QC G1H 2H2
Tél: 418-621-5032; *Téléc:* 418-621-5092
helene@maitremontreuil.ca
www.maitremontreuil.ca

Québec: Morency Société d'Avocats - Québec - *58
Former Name: Pothier Delisle Société D'Avocats
#400, 3075, ch des Quatre-Bourgeois, Québec, QC G1W 4X5
Tél: 418-651-9900; *Téléc:* 418-651-5184
avocats@morencyavocats.com
www.morencyavocats.com
www.facebook.com/MorencySocieteAvocats,
twitter.com/morencyavocats

Québec: O'Brien avocats, S.E.N.C.R.L. - *11
#600, 140, Grande Allée est, Québec, QC G1R 5M8
Tél: 418-648-1511; *Téléc:* 418-648-9335
dobrien@obrienavocats.qc.ca
obrienavocats.qc.ca

Québec: Gregoire Perron & Associes - *1
Former Name: Perron & Associés
2300, de l'Église, Québec, QC J0T 2N0
Tel: 819-322-5409; *Fax:* 514-285-6441
info@gregoireperron.com
www.gregoireperron.com

Québec: Poudrier Bradet - Québec - *25
#100, 70, rue Dalhousie, Québec, QC G1K 4B2
Tél: 418-780-3333; *Téléc:* 418-780-3334
www.poudrierbradet.com

Québec: Provencal Breton Murray - *5
#204, 2500, rue Jean-Perrin, Québec, QC G2C 1X1
Tél: 418-871-2955; *Téléc:* 418-871-7352

**Québec: Tremblay Bois Mignault Lemay
S.E.N.C.R.L. - *36**
#200, Iberville Un, 1195, av Lavigerie, Québec, QC G1V 4N3
Tél: 418-658-9966; *Téléc:* 418-658-6100
avocats@tremblaybois.qc.ca
www.tremblaybois.qc.ca

Repentigny: Robert Toupin - *1
#307, 579A, rue Notre-Dame, Repentigny, QC J6A 7L4
Tél: 450-654-9661; *Téléc:* 450-654-9657

Rimouski: Jean Blouin - *1
216, av de la Cathedrale, Rimouski, QC G5L 5J2
Tél: 418-724-2031; *Téléc:* 418-723-4621

Rivière-du-Loup: Belzile & Associés - *3
110, rue Lafontaine, Rivière-du-Loup, QC G5R 3A1
Tél: 418-862-9460; *Téléc:* 418-862-9939

Rivière-du-Loup: Moreau Avocats inc. - *6
CP 487, 12, rue de la Cour, Rivière-du-Loup, QC G5R 3Z1
Tél: 418-862-3565; *Téléc:* 418-862-4408
www.moreauavocats.com

Rouyn-Noranda: Daoust Parayre Avocats - *3
Former Name: Daoust, Boulianne, Parayre avocats
201, av Murdoch, Rouyn-Noranda, QC J9X 1E5
Tél: 819-762-8294; *Téléc:* 819-762-8296
info@mdbpavocats.com
www.avocatsrn.com

Saint-Hyacinthe: Claude L. Bédard Avocat - *1
1782, rue Girouard ouest, Saint-Hyacinthe, QC J2S 3A1
Tél: 450-774-2749; *Téléc:* 450-774-9533
claudebedardavocat@cgocable.ca

**Saint-Hyacinthe: Sylvestre & Associés Avocats
S.E.N.C. - Saint-Hyacinthe - *16**
#236, 1600, rue Girouard ouest, Saint-Hyacinthe, QC J2S
2Z8
Tél: 450-773-8445; *Téléc:* 450-773-2112
etude@jurisylvestre.ca
www.jurisylvestre.com

**Saint-Jean-Port-Joli: Les Avocats Blanchet
Gaudreault - *2**
512, route de l'Eglise, Saint-Jean-Port-Joli, QC G0R 3G0
Tél: 418-598-7004; *Téléc:* 418-598-7390
blanchet.gaudreault@globetrotter.net

Saint-Jean-sur-Richelieu: Paul Claude Bérubé
#225, 145, boul St-Joseph, Saint-Jean-sur-Richelieu, QC
J3B 1W5
Tél: 450-359-7171; *Téléc:* 450-359-9957

Saint-Jean-sur-Richelieu: Lachance & Morin - *2
108, rue St-Charles, Saint-Jean-sur-Richelieu, QC J3B 2C1
Tél: 450-346-4464; *Téléc:* 450-346-5824

Saint-Jean-sur-Richelieu: Claude Lauzon - *1
160, rue Longueuil, Saint-Jean-sur-Richelieu, QC J3B 6P1
Tél: 450-347-2344; *Téléc:* 450-347-4132

**Saint-Joseph-de-Beauce: Bureau d' Aide juridique -
Saint-Joseph-de-Beauce - *3**
#100, 700, av Robert-Cliche, Saint-Joseph-de-Beauce, QC
G0S 2V0
Tél: 418-397-7288; *Téléc:* 418-397-7283
bajstjoseph@ccjq.qc.ca

**Saint-Joseph-de-Beauce: Cliche, Laflamme &
Loubier - *8**
CP 160, 109, rue Verreault, Saint-Joseph-de-Beauce, QC
G0S 2V0
Tél: 418-397-5264; *Téléc:* 418-397-5269
info@clichelaflamme.com
clichelaflamme.com

**Saint-Jérôme: Lalonde Geraghty Riendeau Avocats -
*8**
Former Name: Lalonde Geraghty Riendeau Lapierre
Avocats
44, rue de Martigny ouest, Saint-Jérôme, QC J7Z 2E9
Tél: 450-436-8022; *Téléc:* 450-436-5185
info@lgra.ca
www.lgra.ca

Saint-Jérôme: Prévost Fortin D'Aoust - *41
Former Name: Prévost Auclair Fortin D'Aoust
#400, 55, rue Castonguay, Saint-Jérôme, QC J7Y 2H9
Tel: 450-436-8244; *Fax:* 450-436-9735
info@pfdlex.com
www.pfdlex.com

Saint-Lambert: André Demers - *1
439, av Notre-Dame, Saint-Lambert, QC J4P 2K5
Tél: 514-875-2007; *Téléc:* 450-466-7315

Saint-Lambert: Paul Joffe - *1
360, av Putney, Saint-Lambert, QC J4P 3B6
Tél: 450-465-3654; *Téléc:* 450-465-5730
pjoffe@joffelaw.ca

Sainte-Foy: Claude Berlinguette - *1
1429, rue du Nordet, Sainte-Foy, QC G2G 2C2
Tél: 418-871-1478

Sainte-Julie: Roland Boyer - *1
69, av Mont Bruno, RR#3, Sainte-Julie, QC J3E 3A1
Tél: 450-649-3772; *Téléc:* 450-649-0101
rolandboyer@yahoo.com

**Sainte-Marie: Sylvain Parent Gobeil Simard
S.E.N.C.R.L.**
225, av du College, Sainte-Marie, QC G6E 3X9
Tél: 418-387-2727; *Téléc:* 418-387-7070
www.spgs.ca

**Salaberry-de-Valleyfield: Rancourt Legault Joncas -
*6**
Former Name: Les Avocats Rancourt, Legault &
St-Onge; Rancourt, Legault, Boucher & St-Onge
303, rue Victoria, Salaberry-de-Valleyfield, QC J6T 1B2
Tél: 450-371-2221; *Téléc:* 450-371-2094
info@rancourtlegault.com
www.rancourtlegault.com

**Salaberry-de-Valleyfield: Vachon, Martin & Besner
Avocats - *4**
57, rue St-Jean-Baptiste, Salaberry-de-Valleyfield, QC J6T
1Z6
Tél: 514-371-7771; *Téléc:* 514-371-2438
info@vmbavocats.com
www.vmbavocats.com

Sept-Iles: Besnier, Dion, Rondeau - *5
865, boul Laure, Sept-Iles, QC G4R 1Y6
Tél: 418-962-9775; *Téléc:* 418-968-6806

Sept-Iles: Desrosiers & Associés - *3
#201, 440, av Brochu, Sept-Iles, QC G4R 2W8
Tél: 418-962-7392; *Téléc:* 418-962-6100
desricar@globetrotter.qc.ca

Sherbrooke: Claude R. Beauchamp - *1
#101, 380, rue King ouest, Sherbrooke, QC J1H 1R4
Tél: 819-563-7733; *Téléc:* 819-563-7734

Sherbrooke: Pierre Belhumeur - *1
53 rue Peel, Sherbrooke, QC J1H 4J9
Tél: 819-566-1676; *Téléc:* 819-575-0610
pbelhumeuravocat@videotron.ca

Sherbrooke: Gerard G. Boudreau - *1
2571, boul Portland, Sherbrooke, QC J1J 1V6
Tél: 819-562-0848; *Téléc:* 819-569-3580

Sherbrooke: Delorme, LeBel, Bureau, Savoie - *9
#100, 2355, rue King ouest, Sherbrooke, QC J1J 2G6
Tél: 819-566-6222; *Téléc:* 819-566-4221
dlb@dlbavocats.com
www.dlbavocats.com

Sherbrooke: Fontaine, Panneton & Associes - *8
#220, 2050, rue King ouest, Sherbrooke, QC J1J 2E8
Tél: 819-564-1222; *Téléc:* 819-822-2180

Sherbrooke: Gallant Morin Avocats
731, rue Galt ouest, Sherbrooke, QC J1H 1Z1
Tél: 819-565-1808; *Téléc:* 819-565-2729
gcgm@globetrotter.net

Sherbrooke: Hackett, Campbell & Bouchard - *5
80, rue Peel, Sherbrooke, QC J1H 4K1
Tél: 819-565-7885; *Téléc:* 819-566-0888
info@hcblegal.com

Sherbrooke: Frédéric-Antoine Lemieux - *2
18, rue Wellington nord, Sherbrooke, QC J1H 5B7
Tél: 819-566-3939
m.mefrederic-antoinelemieux.ca

Sherbrooke: Linda Boulanger - *1
#3, 30, rue Vaudry, Sherbrooke, QC J1M 1B2
Tél: 819-820-2661; *Téléc:* 819-820-8330
lindaboulangeravocate@yahoo.ca

**Sherbrooke: Monty Sylvestre, conseillers juridiques
- Sherbrooke - *30**
Former Name: Monty Coulombe s.e.n.c.
#200, 455, rue King ouest, Sherbrooke, QC J1H 6E9
Tél: 819-566-4466; *Téléc:* 819-565-2891
sherbrooke@montysylvestre.com
www.montysylvestre.com
www.facebook.com/montysylvestre,
www.linkedin.com/company/5347097

Sorel-Tracy: Carole Lepage - *1
96, rue George, Sorel-Tracy, QC J3P 1C3
Tél: 450-742-3766; *Téléc:* 450-742-1133

St-Georges-de-Beauce: Jêrôme Poirier - *1
Former Name: Lebel, Poirier
11720, 1re av, St-Georges-de-Beauce, QC G5Y 2C8
Tél: 418-228-3123; *Téléc:* 418-228-0494
jerome.poirier@globetrotter.net

St-Léonard: DiPace, Mercadente - *6
#202, 5450, rue Jarry est, St-Léonard, QC H1P 1T9
Tél: 514-326-3300; *Téléc:* 514-326-4706

St-Léonard: Carmelo Morabito - *1
#3001, 5095, rue Jean-Talon est, St-Léonard, QC H1S 3G4
Tél: 514-727-0332; *Téléc:* 514-727-9315
carmorab@total.net

Terrebonne: Talbot Kingsbury Avocats - *2
#101, 227, boul des Braves, Terrebonne, QC J6W 3H6
Tél: 450-964-0414; *Téléc:* 450-964-5739
etude@tkavocats.com
www.tkavocats.com

Trois-Rivières: Biron Spain - *5
Former Name: Biron, Spain & Associés
154, rue Radisson, Trois-Rivières, QC G9A 5G4
Tél: 819-375-4187; *Téléc:* 819-375-7395
www.bironspainavocats.com

Trois-Rivières: Braun & Bélisle - *2
#4, 1185, rue Hart, Trois-Rivières, QC G9A 4S4
Tél: 819-691-1390; *Téléc:* 819-378-7344

Trois-Rivières: Godin, Brunet - *2
190, rue Bonaventure, Trois-Rivières, QC G9A 2B1
Tél: 819-379-5225; *Téléc:* 819-379-4545
dgodin@godinbrunet.comm

* indicates number of lawyers

Trois-Rivières: Louis Hénaire - *1
Also Known As: Hénaire, Avocats
983, rue Hart, Trois-Rivières, QC G9A 4S3
Tél: 819-379-3355; *Téléc:* 819-379-1227

Val-d'Or: Cliche Lortie Ladouceur inc. - *11
1121, 6e rue, Val-d'Or, QC J9P 3W8
Tél: 819-825-3010; *Téléc:* 819-825-7375
Ligne sans frais: 800-692-3010
info@cll-avocats.ca
www.clicheavocats.com

Val-d'Or: Cossette, Claude - *1
795, 3e av, Val-d'Or, QC J9P 1S8
Tél: 819-825-2787; *Téléc:* 819-874-4160

Verdun: Robert Beaudet - *2
5331, rue Bannantyne, Verdun, QC H4H 1E8
Tél: 514-769-8527; *Téléc:* 514-769-7466

Westmount: Robert Berger - *1
#220, 4823 rue Sherbrooke ouest, Westmount, QC H3Z 1G7
Tél: 514-931-5660; *Téléc:* 514-932-6570
rberger@segberg.com

Westmount: Luisa Biasutti - *1
#410, 4115, rue Sherbrooke ouest, Westmount, QC H3Z 1K9
Tél: 514-933-3838; *Téléc:* 514-933-2668
biasutti@groupeteq.com

Westmount: Morris Chaikelson - *1
#400, 4120, rue Sainte-Catherine ouest, Westmount, QC H3Z 1P4
Tél: 514-288-3838; *Téléc:* 415-288-3433
chaimor@videotron.ca

Westmount: Paul B. Cohen - *1
#809, 4000, boul de Maisonneuve ouest, Westmount, QC H3Z 1J9
Tél: 514-931-3691; *Téléc:* 514-931-3637
paulcohen@bellnet.ca

Westmount: A. Barry Coleman - *1
#660, 4141, rue Sherbrooke ouest, Westmount, QC H3Z 1B8
Tél: 514-620-6002; *Téléc:* 514-935-3559

Westmount: André R. Dorais Avocats - *3
#2000, 1, carré Westmount, Westmount, QC H3Z 2P9
Tél: 514-938-0808; *Téléc:* 514-938-8888
adorais@ardavocats.ca

Westmount: Linda Hammerschmid - *4
#1290, 1 Westmount Sq., Westmount, QC H3Z 2P9
Tél: 514-846-1013; *Téléc:* 514-846-1803

Westmount: Orna Hilberger - *1
#939, 1, carré Westmount, Westmount, QC H3Z 2P9
Tél: 514-932-7392
hilbergerlaw@gmail.com
www.montrealdivorcelaw.ca

Westmount: Stein & Stein Inc. - *3
4101, rue Sherbrooke ouest, Westmount, QC H3Z 1A7
Tél: 514-866-9806; *Téléc:* 514-875-8218
www.steinandstein.com

Westmount: Rosalie Szewczuk - *1
4420, rue Ste-Catherine ouest, Westmount, QC H3Z 1R2
Tél: 514-933-4453; *Téléc:* 514-934-3134
rosiesz@videotron.ca

Saskatchewan

Assiniboia: Lewans & Ford - *2
P.O. Box 759, 228 Centre St., Assiniboia, SK S0H 0B0
Tel: 306-642-3543; *Fax:* 306-642-5777

Assiniboia: Marlin Law Office - *1
P.O. Box 1088, 200 Centre St., Assiniboia, SK S0H 0B0
Tel: 306-642-3933; *Fax:* 306-642-5399

Assiniboia: Mountain & Mountain - *2
P.O. Box 459, 101 - 4 Ave. West, Assiniboia, SK S0H 0B0
Tel: 306-642-3866; *Fax:* 306-642-5848
mountainlawoffice@sasktel.net

Biggar: Busse Law Professional Corporation - *2
P.O. Box 669, 302 Main St., Biggar, SK S0K 0M0
Tel: 306-948-3346; *Fax:* 306-948-3366
reception@busselaw.net
busselaw.net

Broadview: Gary G. Moore - *1
P.O. Box 610, 616 Main St., Broadview, SK S0G 0K0
Tel: 306-696-2454; *Fax:* 306-696-3105

Davidson: Dellene S. Church - *1
P.O. Box 724, 200 Garfield St., Davidson, SK S0G 1A0
Tel: 306-567-5554; *Fax:* 306-567-2831
dsc-law@sasktel.net

Estevan: Kohaly, Elash & Ludwig Law Firm LLP - Estevan - *2
1312 - 4th St., Estevan, SK S4A 0X2
Tel: 306-634-3631; *Fax:* 306-634-6901
www.kohalyelash.com

Estevan: Orlowski Law Office - *2
1215 - 5th St., Estevan, SK S4A 0Z5
Tel: 306-634-3353; *Fax:* 306-634-7714
orlowski.law@sasktel.net

Eston: Hughes Law Office - *1
Also Known As: Hughes Agencies Ltd.
P.O. Box 729, 305 Main St. South, Eston, SK S0L 1A0
Tel: 306-962-4111; *Fax:* 306-962-3302
hugheslaw@sasktel.net
www.hughesagencies.saskbrokers.com

Fort Qu'appelle: Halford Law Office - *1
P.O. Box 617, Fort Qu'appelle, SK S0G 1S0
Tel: 306-332-5661; *Fax:* 306-332-4293

Humboldt: Behiel, Will & Biemans - Humboldt - *4
Former Name: Behiel, Munkler & Will
P.O. Box 878, 602 - 9th St., Humboldt, SK S0K 2A0
Tel: 306-682-2642; *Fax:* 306-682-5165
office_bmwlaw@sasktel.net
www.behielwill.com

Kamsack: Rosowsky, Campbell & Seidle - *3
P.O. Box 399, 445 2nd St., Kamsack, SK S0A 1S0
Tel: 306-542-2646; *Fax:* 306-542-2510

Kindersley: Ard Law Office - *1
P.O. Box 1898, Kindersley, SK S0L 1S0
Tel: 306-463-2626; *Fax:* 306-463-4917
ard.law@sasktel.net

Kindersley: Sheppard & Millar - *2
P.O. Box 1510, 113 - 1 Ave. East., Kindersley, SK S0L 1S0
Tel: 306-463-4647; *Fax:* 306-463-6133
kindersley.law@sasktel.net

La Ronge: Buckle Law Office - *1
P.O. Box 960, La Ronge, SK S0J 1L0
Tel: 306-425-5959; *Fax:* 306-425-2840

Langenburg: Layh & Associates - *3
Former Name: Layh Law Office
Welke House, P.O. Box 250, 216 Road Ave. East, Langenburg, SK S0A 2A0
Tel: 306-743-5520; *Fax:* 306-743-5589
info@layhlaw.com
www.layhlaw.com

Lloydminster: Fox Wakefield - *2
Former Name: Bennett Fox Wakefield
P.O. Box 500, Stn. Main, 5105 - 49 St., Lloydminster, SK S9V 0Y6
Tel: 780-875-9105; *Fax:* 780-875-6748

Meadow Lake: Francis & Company - *2
Former Name: Francis
P.O. Box 310, Stn. Main, 822 - 9th Ave. West, Meadow Lake, SK S9X 1Y3
Tel: 306-236-5540; *Fax:* 306-236-5571
info@franciscolaw.ca

Meadow Lake: Gerald R. Perkins - *1
#2, 132 Centre St., Meadow Lake, SK S9X 1Z7
Tel: 306-236-4040; *Fax:* 306-236-4878
perkinslawoffice@sasktel.net

Melfort: Annand Law Office - *4
P.O. Box 69, 208 Main St., Melfort, SK S0E 1A0
Tel: 306-752-2707; *Fax:* 306-752-4484
info@annandlawoffice.com
www.annandlawoffice.com

Melfort: Carson Law Office - *1
803 Main St., Melfort, SK S0E 1A0
Tel: 306-752-5781

Melfort: Kapoor Selnes Klimm - *4
Former Name: Kapoor Selnes Klimm
417 Main St., Melfort, SK S0E 1A0
Tel: 306-752-5777; *Fax:* 306-752-2712

Melfort: Ronald Price-Jones - *1
P.O. Box 129, #3 Hwy. East, Melfort, SK S0E 1A0
Tel: 306-752-5701; *Fax:* 306-752-2444
ronp-j@sasktel.net

Melville: Bell, Kreklewich & Chambers - *3
Former Name: Bell, Kreklewich & Company
147 - 3 Ave. East, Melville, SK S0A 2P0
Tel: 306-728-5468; *Fax:* 306-728-4444
bell.kreklewich_bkc@sasktel.net
www.bellkreklewichandchambers.ca

Melville: Schmidt Law Office - *1
P.O. Box 160, 101C 3rd Ave. West, Melville, SK S0A 2P0
Tel: 306-728-5481
schmidtlaw.ca

Moose Jaw: Curran & Fielding - *2
#108, 54 Ominica St. West, Moose Jaw, SK S6H 1W9
Tel: 306-693-7181; *Fax:* 306-691-0187

Moose Jaw: Grayson & Company - *5
Former Name: Grayson, Rushford, Cooper, Arendt, Cornea & Patterson
350 Langdon Cres., Moose Jaw, SK S6H 0X4
Tel: 306-693-6176; *Fax:* 306-693-1515
www.graysonandcompany.com

Moose Jaw: Terrance Ocrane Law Office - *1
#414, 310 Main St. North, Moose Jaw, SK S6H 3K1
Tel: 306-694-4922; *Fax:* 306-692-6386
ocranelawoffice@sasktel.net

Moose Jaw: Walper-Bossence Law Office Prof. Corp. - *1
84 Athabasca St. West, Moose Jaw, SK S6H 2B5
Tel: 306-693-7288
www.walperlaw.ca

Moose Jaw: Wheatley Law Firm - *1
P.O. Box 1648, Stn. Main, Moose Jaw, SK S6H 7K7
Tel: 306-692-0113; *Fax:* 306-692-0113

Moose Jaw: Whittaker, Craik, MacLowich & Hughes - *3
P.O. Box 1178, 109 Ominica St. West, Moose Jaw, SK S6H 4P9
Tel: 306-694-4677; *Fax:* 306-694-5747

Moosomin: Osman & Co.
Former Name: Osman, Gordon & Co.
1103 Broadway Ave., Moosomin, SK S0G 3N0
Tel: 306-435-3851; *Fax:* 306-435-3962

Nipawin: Eremko & Eremko - *1
P.O. Box 250, Nipawin, SK S0E 1E0
Tel: 306-862-4422; *Fax:* 306-862-4477

North Battleford: Cawood Demmans Baldwin Friedman - *5
#201, P.O. Box 905, 1291 - 102 St., North Battleford, SK S9A 2Z3
Tel: 306-445-6177; *Fax:* 306-445-7076
cawood.et.al@sasktel.net
cdbf.ca

North Battleford: Holm Meiklejohn Law Office - *1
Former Name: Jones & Hudec
#103, 1501 - 100th St., North Battleford, SK S9A 0W3
Tel: 306-445-7300; *Fax:* 306-445-7302
holmlaw@sasktel.net

North Battleford: Hudec Law Office - *2
#10211, 12th Ave., 2nd Fl., North Battleford, SK S9A 3X5
Tel: 306-446-2555; *Fax:* 306-446-2556
hudeclaw@sasktel.net

North Battleford: Matrix Law Group - *5
Former Name: Clifford Holm Law Office; Lindgren, Blais, Frank & Illingworth
1421 - 101 St., North Battleford, SK S9A 1A1
Tel: 306-445-7300; *Fax:* 306-445-7302
reception@matrixlawgroup.ca
matrixlawgroup.ca

North Battleford: Migneault Law Office
Former Name: Migneault Greenwood
1391 - 101st St., North Battleford, SK S9A 0Z9
Tel: 306-445-4436
www.migneaultlawoffice.ca

Preeceville: Peet Law Firm - *1
P.O. Box 1210, 17 First Ave. NW, Preeceville, SK S0A 3B0
Tel: 306-547-3322

* indicates number of lawyers

Prince Albert: **Cherkewich, Ronald, Legal Services - *1**
#202, 1000 - 1st Ave. East, Prince Albert, SK S6V 2A7
Tel: 306-764-1537; Fax: 306-763-0505

Prince Albert: **Novus Law Group - Central Ave. - *14**
Also Known As: Wilcox Holash Chovin McCullagh
Former Name: Holash Logue McCullagh Law Office;
Wilcox & Chovin Law Office; Harradence Logue Holash;
Holash Logue
1200 Central Ave., Prince Albert, SK S6V 4V8
Tel: 306-922-4700
princealbert@novuslaw.ca
www.novuslaw.ca

Prince Albert: **Parchomchuk Sherdahl Hunter - Prince Albert - *7**
Former Name: Sanderson Balicki Parchomchuk
110 - 11 St. East, Prince Albert, SK S6V 1A1
Tel: 306-764-2222; Fax: 306-764-2221
psh.psh@sasktel.net
www.pshlaw.ca

Prince Albert: **Stephens Law Office - *1**
Former Name: Stephens Arnot Heffernan
#3, 27 - 11th St. West, Prince Albert, SK S6V 3A8
Tel: 306-764-3456; Fax: 306-922-3772

Prince Albert: **West, Siwak - *2**
1109 Central Ave., Prince Albert, SK S6V 4V7
Tel: 306-763-7467; Fax: 306-763-7469

Prince Albert: **Zatlyn Law Office - *4**
#231, 1061 Central Ave., Prince Albert, SK S6V 4V4
Tel: 306-922-1444; Fax: 306-922-5848
zatlyn@sasktel.net

Regina: **Beke Law Firm - *1**
#700, 2103 - 11th Ave., Regina, SK S4P 4G1
Tel: 306-347-8325
bekelaw@sasktel.net

Regina: **Dahlem Findlay - *1**
2100 Smith St., Regina, SK S4P 2P2
Tel: 306-522-3631; Fax: 306-565-2616
don.findlay@sasktel.net
www.donfindlay.ca

Regina: **Duchin, Bayda & Kroczynski - *4**
Also Known As: DBK Law
2515 Victoria Ave., Regina, SK S4P 0T2
Tel: 306-359-3131; Fax: 306-359-3372
www.dbklaw.com

Regina: **Duncan Bonneau Law - *2**
#1580, 2002 Victoria Ave., Regina, SK S4P 0R7
Tel: 306-525-8500; Fax: 306-525-8585
www.duncanbonneaulaw.com

Regina: **Duncan Reimber Canham - *3**
116 Albert St., Regina, SK S4R 2N2
Tel: 306-791-2503; Fax: 306-543-9655

Regina: **Gates & Company - *4**
Avonhurst Plaza, 3132 Avonhurst Dr., Regina, SK S4R 3J7
Tel: 306-949-5544; Fax: 306-775-2995
office@gateslaw.ca

Regina: **Gerrand Rath Johnson LLP - *20**
Former Name: Gerrand Mulatz
#400, 1900 Albert St., Regina, SK S4P 4K8
Tel: 306-522-3030; Fax: 306-522-3555
www.grj.ca

Regina: **Griffin Toews Maddigan Brabant - *6**
Former Name: Griffin Toews Maddigan
1530 Angus St., Regina, SK S4T 1Z1
Tel: 306-525-6125; Fax: 306-525-5226
griffin.toews@sasktel.net

Regina: **Cindy M. Haynes Law Office - *1**
320 Gardiner Park Crt., Regina, SK S4V 1R9
Tel: 306-789-2242; Fax: 306-789-4950
cindym.haynes@sasktel.net

Regina: **Jaques Law Office - *2**
2912 Rae St., Regina, SK S4S 1R5
Tel: 306-359-3041; Fax: 306-525-4173
jaques@hierlaw.com
www.hierlaw.com

Regina: **Kanuka Thuringer LLP, Barristers & Solicitors - *26**
#1400, 2500 Victoria Ave., Regina, SK S4P 3X2
Tel: 306-525-7200; Fax: 306-359-0590
firm@ktllp.ca
www.kanukathuringer.com

Regina: **kmpLaw - *9**
2600 Victoria Ave., Regina, SK S4T 1K2
Tel: 306-761-6200; Fax: 306-761-6222
reception@kmplaw.com
kmplaw.com

Regina: **Kowalishen Law Firm**
1954 Angus St., Regina, SK S4T 1Z6
Tel: 306-525-2385; Fax: 306-525-2386

Regina: **MacKay & McLean Barristers & Solicitors - *4**
2042 Cornwall St., Regina, SK S4P 2K5
Tel: 306-569-1301; Fax: 306-569-8560
www.mackaymclean.com

Regina: **MacLean Keith - *6**
2398 Scarth St., Regina, SK S4P 2J7
Tel: 306-757-1611; Fax: 306-757-0712
www.macleankeith.com

Regina: **McDougall Gauley - Regina - *80**
#1500, 1881 Scarth St., Regina, SK S4P 4K9
Tel: 306-757-1641; Fax: 306-359-0785
www.mcdougallgauley.com

Regina: **Mellor Law Firm - *1**
The Anson House, 1547 Anson Rd., Regina, SK S4P 0E1
Tel: 306-569-5299; Fax: 306-546-4411
k.mellor@mellorlaw.net
www.mellorlaw.net

Regina: **Merchant Law Group LLP - Regina - *35**
#100, Saskatchewan Drive Plaza, 2401 Saskatchewan Dr.,
Regina, SK S4P 4H8
Tel: 306-359-7777; Fax: 306-522-3299
Toll-Free: 888-567-7777
info@merchantlaw.com
www.merchantlaw.com

Regina: **Mercier Law Office - *1**
#1, 2080 Rae St., Regina, SK S4T 2E5
Tel: 306-551-8001; Fax: 877-408-9431
louis@mercierlaw.ca
www.mercierlaw.ca

Regina: **Donald R. Morgan - *1**
#361, Legislative Bldg., Minister's Office, 2405 Legislative
Dr., Regina, SK S4S 0B3
Tel: 306-787-0613; Fax: 306-787-6946
minister.ae@gov.sk.ca

Regina: **Morgan, Khaladkar & Skinner - *2**
2510 - 13 Ave., Regina, SK S4P 0W2
Tel: 306-525-9191; Fax: 306-525-0006

Regina: **Noble, Johnston & Associates - *5**
1143 Lakewood Ct. North, Regina, SK S4X 3S3
Tel: 306-949-5616; Fax: 306-775-2234
info@noblejohnston.com
www.noblejohnston.com

Regina: **Olive Waller Zinkhan & Waller LLP - *18**
#1000, 2002 Victoria Ave., Regina, SK S4P 0R7
Tel: 306-359-1888; Fax: 306-352-0771
owzw@owzw.com
www.owzw.com

Regina: **Phillips & Co. - *2**
Haldane House, 2100 Scarth St., Regina, SK S4P 2H6
Tel: 306-569-0811; Fax: 306-565-3434
phillipsco@phillipsco.ca

Regina: **Ann Phillips - *1**
#205, 2022 Cornwall St., Regina, SK S4P 2K5
Tel: 306-791-2626; Fax: 306-352-2020
annphillips@attglobal.net

Regina: **Richmond Nychuk - *8**
#100, 2255 Albert St., Regina, SK S4P 2V5
Tel: 306-359-0202; Fax: 306-359-0330
lawoffice@richmondnychuk.com
www.richmondnychuk.com

Regina: **Sheppard, Braun, Muma - *2**
#204, 3988 Albert St., Regina, SK S4S 3R1
Tel: 306-586-6020; Fax: 306-586-8525
sbmlaw@sasktel.net

Regina: **Silversides & Cox - *2**
Former Name: Woloshyn & Company
#280, Saskatchewan Pl., 1870 Albert St., Regina, SK S4P
4B7
Tel: 306-337-4560; Fax: 306-337-4568

Regina: **Tulloch, Tulloch & Horvath Law Firm - *4**
Also Known As: TTH Law
Former Name: Willows Tulloch & Howe
2012 McIntyre St., Regina, SK S4P 2R6
Tel: 306-924-8600; Fax: 306-924-8601
info@tthlaw.ca
tthlaw.ca

Regina: **Walker, Singer & McCannell - *3**
1872 Angus St., Regina, SK S4T 1Z4
Tel: 306-352-8109; Fax: 306-352-7339

Regina: **Willows Wellsch Orr & Brundige LLP - *14**
Former Name: Rendek McCrank; Stewart Johnson
Brundige
#401, 1916 Dewdney Ave., Regina, SK S4R 1G9
Tel: 306-525-2191; Fax: 306-757-8138
www.willowswellsch.com

Rosetown: **Skelton Turner Mescall - *2**
P.O. Box 1120, 314 Main St., Rosetown, SK S0L 2V0
Tel: 306-882-4244; Fax: 306-882-3969

Saskatoon: **A.S.K. Law - *2**
#210, 75 - 24th St. East, Saskatoon, SK S7K 0K3
Tel: 306-933-3933; Fax: 306-933-9505
www.asklaw.ca

Saskatoon: **Murray D. Acton - *1**
Also Known As: Acton Law Office
520 Spadina Cres. East, Saskatoon, SK S7K 3G7
Tel: 306-933-5155; Fax: 306-933-5725

Saskatoon: **Bodnar & Campbell - *2**
Former Name: Bodnar, Wanhella & Cutforth
#400, 245 - 3 Ave. South, Saskatoon, SK S7K 1M4
Tel: 306-664-3314; Fax: 306-664-3354
mbodnarlaw@sasktel.net

Saskatoon: **Bodnar & Campbell - *1**
#400, 235 - 3 Ave. South, Saskatoon, SK S7K 1M4
Tel: 306-664-3314; Fax: 306-664-3354
wjcampbell@sasktel.net

Saskatoon: **Brayford Shapiro - *2**
311 - 21 St. East., Saskatoon, SK S7K 0C1
Tel: 306-244-5656; Fax: 306-244-5644
www.brayfordshapiro.ca

Saskatoon: **Burlingham Cuelenaere - *2**
1043 - 8 St. East, Saskatoon, SK S7H 0S2
Tel: 306-343-9581; Fax: 306-343-1947
office@bclawsk.com
www.bclawsk.com

Saskatoon: **Cuelenaere LLP - *24**
Former Name: Cuelenaere, Kendall, Katzman & Watson
#200, Nexus Bldg., 450 - 2nd Ave. North, Saskatoon, SK S7K
2C3
Tel: 306-653-5000; Fax: 306-652-4171
www.cuelenaere.com

Saskatoon: **Halyk Kennedy Knox - *3**
321 - 6 Ave. North, Saskatoon, SK S7K 2S3
Tel: 306-665-3434; Fax: 306-652-1915
halyk@sasktel.net

Saskatoon: **Hnatyshyn Gough - *8**
#601, 402 - 21st St. East, Saskatoon, SK S7K 0C3
Tel: 306-653-5150; Fax: 306-652-5859
hglaw@hglaw.ca
www.hglaw.ca

Saskatoon: **Kloppenburg & Kloppenburg - *2**
#2, 527 Main St., Saskatoon, SK S7N 0C2
Tel: 306-665-7600; Fax: 306-665-7800
juristen@kloppenburg.ca
www.kloppenburg.ca

Saskatoon: **Knott den Hollander - *3**
215 Wall St., Saskatoon, SK S7K 1N5
Tel: 306-664-6900; Fax: 306-653-4599
kddlaw@sasktel.net
www.kdqsaskatoonlaw.com

* indicates number of lawyers

Saskatoon: Koskie Helms - *2
Former Name: Koskie & Company
#3, 501 Gray Ave., Saskatoon, SK S7N 2H8
Tel: 306-242-8478; Fax: 306-653-2120
firm@koskie.com
www.koskie.com

Saskatoon: Leland Kimpinski LLP - *9
336 - 6th Ave. North, Saskatoon, SK S7K 2S5
Tel: 306-244-6686; Fax: 306-653-7008
info@lelandlaw.ca
www.lelandlaw.ca

Saskatoon: MacDermid Lamarsh - *6
301 - 3rd Ave. South, Saskatoon, SK S7K 1M6
Tel: 306-652-9422; Fax: 306-242-1554
macmarsh@macmarsh.com
www.macdermidlamarsh.com

Saskatoon: Mathiason, Valkenburg & Polishchuk - *1
Former Name: Mathiason, Valkenburg & McLeod
#705, 230 - 22nd St. East, Saskatoon, SK S7K 0E9
Tel: 306-242-1202; Fax: 306-244-4423
mvplaw@sasktel.net

Saskatoon: McKercher LLP - Saskatoon - *59
374 Third Ave. South, Saskatoon, SK S7K 1M5
Tel: 306-653-2000; Fax: 306-653-2669
info@mckercher.ca
www.mckercher.ca
www.linkedin.com/company/mckercher-llp

Saskatoon: Nussbaum & Company - *2
#204, 2102 - 8 St. East, Saskatoon, SK S7H 0V1
Tel: 306-955-8890; Fax: 306-955-1293
nussbaum@sasktel.net

Saskatoon: Piche & Company - *1
#204, 611 University Dr., Saskatoon, SK S7N 3Z1
Tel: 306-955-7667; Fax: 306-955-7727
Toll-Free: 866-234-3444
pichelaw@sasktel.net

Saskatoon: Plaxton Jensen - *2
Former Name: Plaxton & Company Lawyers
#500, 402 - 21 St. East, Saskatoon, SK S7K 0C3
Tel: 306-653-1500; Fax: 306-664-6659
contactus@plaxtonlaw.com
www.plaxtonlaw.com

Saskatoon: Quon Ferguson - *2
Former Name: Quon Ferguson Owens
#704, 224 - 4th Ave. South, Saskatoon, SK S7K 5M5
Tel: 306-665-8828; Fax: 306-665-8835

Saskatoon: Robertson Stromberg LLP - *28
#600, Canada Building, 105 - 21st St. East, Saskatoon, SK S7K 0B3
Tel: 306-652-7575; Fax: 306-652-2445
Toll-Free: 800-667-0070
www.rslaw.com
www.facebook.com/Robertsonstromberg, twitter.com/RSLLP, www.linkedin.com/company/robertson-stromberg-llp

Saskatoon: Rozdilsky, Baniak - *2
#301, 220 - 3rd Ave. South, Saskatoon, SK S7K 1M1
Tel: 306-664-9900

Saskatoon: Scharfstein Gibbings Walen Fisher LLP - *19
#200, 123 - 2 Ave. South, Saskatoon, SK S7K 7E6
Tel: 306-653-2838; Fax: 306-652-4747
lawyers@scharfsteinlaw.com
www.scharfsteinlaw.com

Saskatoon: Scott & Beaven Law Office - *3
Former Name: Scott, Ludlow, Fehr
211A - 33 St. West, Saskatoon, SK S7L 0V2
Tel: 306-955-6822; Fax: 306-955-6823
www.sblo.ca

Saskatoon: Scott Phelps & Mason Barristers & Solicitors - *6
306 Ontario Ave., Main Fl., Saskatoon, SK S7K 2H5
Tel: 306-244-2201; Fax: 306-244-2420
barristers@spmlaw.ca
www.spmlaw.ca

Saskatoon: Sonnenschein Law Office - *1
Lincoln's Inn, 313 - 20th St. East, Saskatoon, SK S7K 0A9
Tel: 306-652-4730; Fax: 306-653-5760

Saskatoon: Stevenson Hood Thornton Beaubier LLP - *21
#500, 123 - 2nd Ave. South, Saskatoon, SK S7K 7E6
Tel: 306-244-0132; Fax: 306-653-1118
info@shtb-law.com
www.shtb-law.com

Saskatoon: Stooshinoff Law Office - *2
#300, 416 - 21st St. East, Saskatoon, SK S7K 0C2
Tel: 306-653-9000; Fax: 306-653-5284

Saskatoon: The W Law Group - *15
Former Name: Woloshyn & Company
#300, 110 - 21st St. East, Saskatoon, SK S7K 0B6
Tel: 306-244-2242; Fax: 306-652-0332
Toll-Free: 888-244-2242
info@wlawgroup.com
wlawgroup.com

Saskatoon: Wallace Meschishnick Clackson Zawada - *19
#410, 475 - 2nd Ave. South, Saskatoon, SK S7K 1P4
Tel: 306-933-0004; Fax: 306-933-2006
info@wmcz.com
www.wmcz.com
twitter.com/wmcz, www.linkedin.com/company/1772083

Saskatoon: Steven J. Wilson - *1
2120 York Ave., Saskatoon, SK S7J 1H8
Tel: 306-956-3345; Fax: 306-955-1699

Shaunavon: Coralie O. Geving - *1
Also Known As: Geving Law Office
23 - 3 Ave. East, Shaunavon, SK S0N 2M0
Tel: 306-297-2205; Fax: 306-297-2411

Swift Current: Anderson & Company - Swift Current - *6
51 - 1st Ave. NW, Swift Current, SK S9H 0M5
Tel: 306-773-2891; Fax: 306-778-3364
anderson.company@andlaw.ca
www.andersonandcompany.ca

Swift Current: Holland Law Office - *1
#15, 600 Chaplin St. East, Swift Current, SK S9H 1J3
Tel: 306-773-0661; Fax: 306-773-9630

Swift Current: MacBean Tessem - Swift Current - *6
P.O. Box 550, 151 First Ave. NE, Swift Current, SK S9H 2B1
Tel: 306-773-9343; Fax: 306-778-3828
www.macbeantessem.com

Unity: Neil Law Office - *1
Former Name: Hepting Neil & Jeanson
P.O. Box 600, 206 - 2nd Ave. West, Unity, SK S0K 4L0
Tel: 306-228-2631; Fax: 306-228-4449
neillawoffice@saktel.net

Weyburn: Nimegeers Schuck Wormsbecker Bobbitt - *3
Also Known As: NSWB Law Firm
Former Name: Nimegeers & Schuck; Nimegeers & Grant
P.O. Box 8, 319 Souris Ave., Weyburn, SK S4H 2J8
Tel: 306-842-4654; Fax: 306-842-0522
law@nswb.com
www.nswb.com
www.facebook.com/NSWBlawfirm

Wynyard: Klebeck Law Office - *1
P.O. Box 1120, 115 Ave. B East, Wynyard, SK S0A 4T0
Tel: 306-554-2523; Fax: 306-554-2099
klebeck.law.office@sasktel.net

Wynyard: Paulson & Ferraton - *1
P.O. Box 460, 106 Main St., Wynyard, SK S0A 4T0
Tel: 306-554-2134; Fax: 306-554-2342
paulson.ferraton@sasktel.net

Yorkton: Leland Campbell Kondratoff Persick LLP - Yorkton - *7
Former Name: Leland Campbell LLP
P.O. Box 188, 36 - 4th Ave. North, Yorkton, SK S3N 2V7
Tel: 306-783-8541; Fax: 306-786-7484
reception@lelandcampbell.com
www.lelandcampbell.com

Yorkton: Tourney, Dellow - *2
#2, 16 - 3rd Ave. North, Yorkton, SK S3N 0A1
Tel: 306-782-2211; Fax: 306-782-2213
tourneydellow@sasktel.net

Yukon Territory

Whitehorse: Austring, Fendrick & Fairman - *7
3081 - 3 Ave., Whitehorse, YT Y1A 4Z7
Tel: 867-668-4405; Fax: 867-668-3710
info@lawyukon.com
www.lawyukon.com

Whitehorse: Cabott & Cabott - *5
#101, 2131 - 2nd Ave., Whitehorse, YT Y1A 1C3
Tel: 867-456-3100; Fax: 867-456-7093
Toll-Free: 877-456-3105
tina.escareal@northwestel.net
www.cabottandcabott.com

Whitehorse: Lackowicz & Hoffman
Former Name: Preston Lackowicz & Shier
#300, 204 Black St., Whitehorse, YT Y1A 2M9
Tel: 867-668-5252; Fax: 867-668-5251

Whitehorse: Lamarche Pearson
505 Lambert St., Whitehorse, YT Y1A 1Z8
Tel: 867-456-3300
slamarche@lamarchepearson.com

Whitehorse: Macdonald & Company
#200, 204 Lambert St., Whitehorse, YT Y1A 3T2
Tel: 867-667-7885; Fax: 867-667-7600

Whitehorse: Roothman & Company - *2
#203, 4133 - 4th Ave, Whitehorse, YT Y1A 1H8
Tel: 867-667-4664
info@roothmanlaw.ca
www.roothmanlaw.ca/en/

Whitehorse: Tucker & Company - *5
#102, 205 Hawkins St., Whitehorse, YT Y1A 1X3
Tel: 867-667-2099; Fax: 867-667-2109
info@tuckerandcompany.ca
tuckerandcompany.ca
www.facebook.com/tuckerandcompany,
www.linkedin.com/company/tucker-&-company

Whitehorse: Whittle & Company
#203, 107 Main St., Whitehorse, YT Y1A 2A7
Tel: 867-633-4199

SECTION 12
LIBRARIES

Library & Archives Canada: 1657

Government Departments in Charge of Libraries: 1657

Library listings are arranged by province. Each province includes the following categories

Regional Systems

Public Libraries

Archives

Library & Archives Canada/Bibliothèque et Archives Canada
395 Wellington St., Ottawa ON K1A 0N4
613-996-5115; Fax: 613-995-6274
Toll-Free 866-578-7777; TTY 613-992-6969
www.bac-lac.gc.ca
Librarian & Archivist of Canada, Leslie Weir
www.facebook.com/LibraryArchives
twitter.com/@LibraryArchives;
www.youtube.com/user/LibraryArchiveCanada

Aurora: 613-996-5115; Fax: 613-995-6274;
bac-lac.on.worldcat.org/discovery

Canadian Cataloguing in Publications Program (CIP):
819-994-6881; BAC.CIP.LAC@canada.ca;
www.bac-lac.gc.ca/eng/services/cip; Symbol: OONL

Canadiana: The National Bibliography of Canada: Fax:
819-934-4388;
BAC.Descriptiondesressources-Resourcedescription.LAC@c
anada.ca; www.bac-lac.gc.ca/eng/services/canadiana;
Symbol: OONL; Manager, Published Canadiana, Karin
MacLeod, karin.macleod@canada.ca

Cataloguing & Metadata: Fax: 819-934-4388;
BAC.Normesdecatalogage-Cataloguingstandards.LAC@cana
da.ca; www.bac-lac.gc.ca/eng/services/cataloguing-metadata;
Symbol: OONL

Gifts: 819-934-5793; BAC.Dons-Gifts.LAC@canada.ca;
www.bac-lac.gc.ca/eng/about-us/about-collection/make_a_do
nation; Symbol: OONL

Government Information Management & Disposition:
819-934-7519; Fax: 819-934-7535;
BAC.Centredeliaison-Liaisoncentre.LAC@canada.ca;
www.bac-lac.gc.ca/eng/services/government-information-reso
urces; Symbol: OONL

Interlibrary Loan (ILL): 613-996-5115; Fax: 613-996-4424;
www.bac-lac.gc.ca/eng/services/loans-other-institutions/Page
s/loans-other-institutions.aspx; Symbol: OONL

International Standard Book Number (ISBN): 819-994-6872;
Fax: 819-934-7535; BAC.ISBN.LAC@canada.ca;
www.bac-lac.gc.ca/eng/services/isbn-canada; Symbol:
OONL; ISBN Technician, Heidi Poapst,
heidi.poapst@canada.ca

International Standard Music Number (ISMN): 819-994-6872;
Fax: 819-997-7019; BAC.ISMN.LAC@canada.ca;
www.bac-lac.gc.ca/eng/services/ismn-canada; Symbol:
OONL

International Standard Serial Number (ISSN): 819-994-6895;
Fax: 819-997-6209; BAC.ISSN.LAC@canada.ca;
www.bac-lac.gc.ca/eng/services/issn-canada; Symbol: OONL

Jacob M. Lowy Collection: 613-995-7960; Fax: 613-943-1112;
BAC.Lowy.LAC@canada.ca;
www.bac-lac.gc.ca/eng/lowy-collection; Symbol: OONL;
Curator, Michael Kent, michael.kent2@canada.ca

Legal Deposit: 819-997-9565; Fax: 819-997-7019;
BAC.Depotlegal-LegalDeposit.LAC@canada.ca;
www.bac-lac.gc.ca/eng/services/legal-deposit; Symbol: OONL

Literary Archives: bac.reference.lac@canada.ca;
www.bac-lac.gc.ca/eng/discover/archives-literary; Symbol:
OONL

MARC 21 Standards: 819-994-6936; Fax: 819-934-4388;
marc@bac-lac.gc.ca; www.marc21.ca/index-e.html; Symbol:
OONL

Multi-Institution Disposition Authorities: 819-934-7519; Fax:
819-934-7535;
BAC.Centredeliaison-Liaisoncentre.LAC@canada.ca;
www.bac-lac.gc.ca/eng/services/government-information-reso
urces/disposition/Pages/mida.aspx; Symbol: OONL

The Rare Book Collection: 613-996-5115; Fax: 613-995-6274;
bac.reference.lac@canada.ca;
www.bac-lac.gc.ca/eng/discover/rare-book; Symbol: OONL

Reference Services: 613-996-5115; Fax: 613-995-6274;
bac.reference.lac@canada.ca;
www.bac-lac.gc.ca/eng/services/reference-public; Symbol: OONL;
Alison Pier, Reference Librarian, alison.pier@canada.ca

Theses Canada: 819-994-6882; Fax: 819-997-2395;
BAC.ThesesCanada-ThesesCanada.LAC@canada.ca;
www.bac-lac.gc.ca/eng/services/theses; Symbol: OONL

Voilà - The National Union Catalogue: 819-934-5851; Fax:
819-934-4388;
BAC.Cataloguecollectif-UnionCatalogue.LAC@canada.ca;

www.bac-lac.gc.ca/eng/services/national-union-catalogue;
Symbol: OONL

Government Departments in Charge of Libraries

ALBERTA: Alberta Public Library Services, #803, Standard Life
Centre, 10405 Jasper Ave., Edmonton, AB T5J 4R7,
780-427-4871; Fax: 780-415-8594, libraries@gov.ab.ca,
www.alberta.ca/public-library-services-branch.aspx; Director,
Diana Davidson

BRITISH COLUMBIA: Ministry of Education, Libraries Branch,
PO Box 9831, Stn. Provincial Government, Victoria, BC V8W
9T1, 250-356-1791; Fax: 250-953-4985; Toll Free:
800-663-7051, llb@gov.bc.ca, www2.gov.bc.ca;
twitter.com/MyBCLibrary; Director, Library Services, Mari
Martin

MANITOBA: Manitoba Public Library Services, 340 - 9th St.,
#B10, Brandon, MB R7A 0L5, 204-726-6590, Fax:
204-726-6868, pls@gov.mb.ca, www.gov.mb.ca/chc/pls;
Director, Trevor Surgenor

NEW BRUNSWICK: New Brunswick Public Library Service,
Provincial Office, #2, 570 Two Nations Crossing, Fredericton,
NB E3A 0X9, 506-453-2354, Fax: 506-444-4064,
NBPLS-SBPNB@gnb.ca,
www2.gnb.ca/content/gnb/en/departments/nbpl.html; Acting
Executive Director, Ella Nason

NEWFOUNDLAND & LABRADOR: Newfoundland & Labrador
Public Libraries, 48 St. George's Ave., Stephenville NL A2N
1K9, 709-643-0900, Fax: 709-643-0925, www.nlpl.ca;
Executive Director, Andrew Hunt, ahunt@nlpl.ca

NORTHWEST TERRITORIES: Northwest Territories Public
Library Services, 75 Woodland Dr., Hay River NT X0E 1G1,
867-874-6531, Fax: 867-874-3321, Toll Free: 866-297-0232,
www.ece.gov.nt.ca/en/services/nwt-public-libraries; Territorial
Librarian, Brian Dawson, Brian_Dawson@gov.nt.ca

NOVA SCOTIA: Nova Scotia Provincial Library, 6016 University
Ave., 5th Fl., Halifax NS B3H 1W4, 902-424-2457, Fax:
902-424-0633, nspl@novascotia.ca, library.novascotia.ca

NUNAVUT: Nunavut Public Library Services, PO Box 270, Baker
Lake NU X0C 0A0, 867-793-3353, Fax: 867-793-3360,
www.publiclibraries.nu.ca; Manager, Library Services, Ron
Knowling, rknowling@gov.nu.ca

ONTARIO: Ontario Public Libraries, #1700, 401 Bay St.,
Toronto, ON M7A 0A7, 416-314-7620, Fax: 416-212-1802,
www.mtc.gov.on.ca/en/libraries/libraries.shtml; Manager,
Libraries, Arts & Heritage Services Unit, Sarah Cossette,
sarah.cossette@ontario.ca

PRINCE EDWARD ISLAND: Public Library Service, PO Box
7500, Morell PE C0A 1S0, 902-961-7320, Fax: 902-961-7322,
plshq@gov.pe.ca,
www.princeedwardisland.ca/en/topic/libraries-and-archives;
twitter.com/PEILibrary; www.facebook.com/PEILibrary

QUÉBEC: Ministère de la culture et communications,
Bibliothèque ministérielle, Direction de la coordination et du
soutien à la gestion des programmes, Édifice Guy-Frégault,
225, Grande Allée est, Bloc C, sous-sol, Québec QC G1R
5G5, 418-380-2325, Téle: 418-380-2326,
biblio@mcc.gouv.qc.ca; www.mcc.gouv.qc.ca; Directrice,
Technologies de l'information et gestion documentaire,
Carolyne Gignac

SASKATCHEWAN: Provincial Library & Literacy Office, 409A
Park St., Regina, SK S4N 5B2, 306-787-2976, Fax:
306-787-2029,
www.saskatchewan.ca/residents/education-and-learning;
Provincial Librarian & Executive Director, Alison Hopkins,
alison.hopkins@gov.sk.ca

YUKON: Yukon Public Libraries, PO Box 2703, Whitehorse YT
Y1A 2C6, 867-667-5239, Fax: 867-393-6333, Toll Free (in
Yukon): 800-661-0408, whitehorselibrary@yukon.ca,
yukon.ca/en/yukon-public-libraries

Alberta

Regional Systems

Chinook Arch Regional Library System
2902 - 7th Ave. North, Lethbridge, AB T1H 5C6
Tel: 403-380-1500; *Fax:* 403-380-3550
Toll-Free: 888-458-1500
arch@chinookarch.ca
chinookarch.ca
twitter.com/chinooklibs; www.facebook.com/chinook.arch.7

Robin Hepher, Chief Executive Officer
rhepher@chinookarch.ca
403-380-1505
Lisa Weekes, Manager, Partnerships & Community
Development
lweekes@chinookarch.ca
403-380-1506
Pat Wauters, Manager, Bibliographic Services
pwauters@chinookarch.ca
403-380-1515

Marigold Library System
710 - 2nd St., Strathmore, AB T1P 1K4
Tel: 403-934-5334; *Toll-Free:* 855-934-5334
admin@marigold.ab.ca
marigold.ab.ca
www.instagram.com/marigoldlibrarysystem;
twitter.com/MarigoldLibSys;
www.facebook.com/MarigoldLibrarySystem;
www.linkedin.com/company/marigoldlibrarysystem
Michelle Toombs, Chief Executive Officer
michelle@marigold.ab.ca
403-934-5334 ext. 224
Laura Taylor, Deputy Chief Executive Officer
laura@marigold.ab.ca
403-934-5334 ext. 242
Lynne Price, Director, Delivery Service
lynne@marigold.ab.ca
403-934-5334 ext. 248

Northern Lights Library System (NLLS)
5615 - 48th St., Elk Point, AB T0A 1A0
Tel: 780-724-2596; *Fax:* 780-724-2597
Toll-Free: 800-561-0387
www.nlls.ab.ca
www.instagram.com/nlls_alberta; twitter.com/nlls_alberta;
www.facebook.com/NLLS.47;
www.linkedin.com/company/northern-lights-library-system
James MacDonald, Executive Director
780-724-2596 ext. 2112

Parkland Regional Library System
4565 - 46th St., Lacombe, AB T4L 0K2
Tel: 403-782-3850; *Toll-Free:* 800-567-9024
www.prl.ab.ca
www.youtube.com/user/PRLLibrary; twitter.com/PrlLibrary;
www.facebook.com/prl.library
Ronald Sheppard, Director
rsheppard@prl.ab.ca

Peace Library System
8301 - 110th St., Grande Prairie, AB T8W 6T2
Tel: 780-538-4656; *Fax:* 780-539-5285
Toll-Free: 800-422-6875
peacelib@peacelibrarysystem.ab.ca
www.peacelibrarysystem.ab.ca
www.pinterest.ca/peacelibrarysys; twitter.com/PeaceLibrarySys;
www.facebook.com/peacelibrarysystem
Louisa Robinson, Chief Executive Officer
lrobison@peacelibrarysystem.ab.ca
780-538-4656 ext. 102
Samantha Mercer, Librarian, Digital Learning & Outreach
smercer@peacelibrarysystem.ab.ca
780-538-4656 ext. 107
Janet Ayles, Manager, Technical Services
jayles@peacelibrarysystem.ab.ca
780-538-4656 ext. 106

Shortgrass Library System
2375 - 10th Ave. SW, Medicine Hat, AB T1A 8G2
Tel: 403-529-0550; *Fax:* 403-528-2473
Toll-Free: 866-529-0550
shortgrass.ca
www.youtube.com/user/ShortgrassLibrary;
twitter.com/shortgrassnews;
www.facebook.com/shortgrasslibsystem
Petra Mauerhoff, Chief Executive Officer
petra@shortgrass.ca
403-529-0550 ext. 101
Chris Field, Manager, Systems & Technical Services
chris@shortgrass.ca
403-529-0550 ext. 102
Kait McClary, Librarian, Client Services
kaitm@shortgrass.ca
403-529-0550 ext. 104

Wood Buffalo Regional Library
1 C.A. Knight Way, Fort McMurray, AB T9H 5C5
Tel: 780-743-7800
customer.service@wbrl.ca
www.wbrl.ca
www.instagram.com/wbrl_ab; twitter.com/wbrl_ab;
www.facebook.com/wbrlab

Melissa Flett, Director
melissa.flett@wbrl.ca

Yellowhead Regional Library
433 King St., Spruce Grove, AB T7X 2Y1
Tel: 780-962-2003; Fax: 780-962-2770
Toll-Free: 877-962-2003
askyrl@yrl.ab.ca
yrl.ab.ca
twitter.com/YRLnow

Karla Palichuk, Director
kpalichuk@yrl.ab.ca
780-982-2003 ext. 226
Wendy Sears Ilnicki, Deputy Director & Manager, Administrative
Services
wsears@yrl.ab.ca
780-962-2003 ext. 225

Public Libraries

Acadia Valley: Acadia Municipal Library
Warren Peers School, 103 - 1st Ave. North, Acadia Valley,
AB T0J 0A0
Tel: 403-972-3744
aavalibrary@marigold.ab.ca
www.acadialibrary.ca

Acme: Acme Municipal Library
610 Walsh Ave., Acme, AB T0M 0A0
Tel: 403-546-3879
aamlibrary@marigold.ab.ca
www.acmelibrary.ca
www.facebook.com/acmelibrary

Airdrie: Airdrie Public Library
#111, 304 Main St. SE, Airdrie, AB T4B 3C3
Tel: 403-948-0600
info@airdriepubliclibrary.ca
airdriepubliclibrary.ca
twitter.com/AirdrieLibrary;
www.facebook.com/AirdriePublicLibrary
Pam Medland, Director
pamela.medland@airdriepubliclibrary.ca

Alberta Beach: Alberta Beach Municipal Library
4815 - 50th Ave., Alberta Beach, AB T0E 0A0
Tel: 780-924-3491
ablibrary@yrl.ab.ca
albertabeachlibrary.ca
www.facebook.com/alberta.beach.58;

Alder Flats: Alder Flats Public Library
PO Box 148, Alder Flats, AB T0C 0A0
Tel: 780-388-3881
alderflatslibrary@yrl.ab.ca
alderflatslibrary.ab.ca
www.facebook.com/alderflatslibrary
Jean Sargeant, Chair

Alix: Alix Public Library
4928 - 50th St., Alix, AB T0C 0B0
Tel: 403-747-3233
alixpublic@prl.ab.ca
alixpublic.prl.ab.ca
www.facebook.com/alixpubliclibrary
Sue Duncan, Library Manager

Alliance: Alliance Public Library
101 - 1st Ave. East, Alliance, AB T0B 0A0
Tel: 403-747-3233
alliancelibrary@prl.ab.ca
alliance.prl.ab.ca
www.facebook.com/107890867635075
Libby Whittall, Library Manager

Amisk: Amisk Public Library
5005 - 50th St., Amisk, AB T0B 0B0
Tel: 780-628-5457
amiskpubliclibrary@prl.ab.ca
amisklibrary.prl.ab.ca
www.facebook.com/196095401013105
Jacquie Chastellaine, Library Manager

Andrew: Andrew Municipal Public Library
5021 - 50th Ave., Andrew, AB T0B 0C0
Tel: 780-365-3501; Fax: 780-365-3734
info@andrewpubliclibrary.ca
www.andrewpubliclibrary.ca
C. Forst, Library Manager

Arrowwood: Arrowwood Municipal Library
22 Centre St., Arrowwood, AB T0L 0B0
Tel: 403-534-3932
help@arrowwoodlibrary.ca
arrowwoodlibrary.ca

Ashmont: Ashmont Community Library
Main St., Ashmont, AB T0A 0C0
Tel: 780-726-3877; Fax: 780-726-3818
info@ashmontlibrary.ab.ca
www.ashmontlibrary.ab.ca
www.facebook.com/2225686817644131

Athabasca: Alice B. Donahue Library & Archives
4716 - 48th St., Athabasca, AB T9S 1R2
Tel: 780-675-2735
librarian@athabascalibrary.ab.ca
www.athabascalibrary.ab.ca
twitter.com/alice_archives;
www.facebook.com/AliceB.DonahueLibrary

Banff: Banff Public Library
101 Bear St., Banff, AB T1L 1H3
Tel: 403-762-2661
info@bannflibrary.ab.ca
www.bannflibrary.ab.ca
twitter.com/BanffLibrary; www.facebook.com/bannflibrary
Sarah McCormack, Library Director
Carey Anne Lees, Assistant Library Director

Barnwell: Barnwell Municipal Library
320 Heritage Rd., Barnwell, AB T0K 0B0
Tel: 403-223-2902
help@barnwelllibrary.ca
barnwelllibrary.ca
www.facebook.com/barnwellpubliclibrary
Kim Shimbashi, Library Manager

Barrhead: Barrhead Public Library
5103 - 53rd Ave., Barrhead, AB T7N 1N9
Tel: 780-674-8519; Fax: 780-674-8520
library@barrheadpubliclibrary.ca
barrheadpubliclibrary.ca
www.facebook.com/BarrheadPublicLibrary
Elaine Dickie, Library Director

Bashaw: Bashaw Municipal Library
5112 - 52nd St., Bashaw, AB T0B 0H0
Tel: 780-372-4055
bashawlibrary.prl.ab.ca
www.facebook.com/Bashawmunicipallibrary
Cindy Hunter, Library Manager

Bassano: Bassano Memorial Library
522 - 2nd Ave., Bassano, AB T0J 0B0
Tel: 403-641-4065; Fax: 403-641-4065
bassano.shortgrass.ca
www.facebook.com/BassanoMemorialLibrary
Mandy Galarneau, Chief Librarian
bassano.manager@shortgrass.ca

Bawlf: Bawlf Public Library
203 Hanson St., Bawlf, AB T0B 0J0
Tel: 780-373-3882
bawlflibrary@prl.ab.ca
bawlflibrary.prl.ab.ca
www.facebook.com/108324264375518
Kait Davies, Library Manager

Bear Canyon: Bear Point Community Library
833075 Range Rd. 123, Bear Canyon, AB T0H 0B0
Tel: 780-595-3771
librarian@bearpointlibrary.ab.ca
www.bearpointlibrary.ab.ca

Beaumont: Bibliothèque de Beaumont Library
5700 - 49th St., Beaumont, AB T4X 1S7
Tel: 780-929-2665; Fax: 780-929-1291
library@beaumontlibrary.com
beaumontlibrary.com
www.facebook.com/BeaumontLibrary
Aruna Brennan, Chair
Laura Winton, Library Manager
laura@beaumontlibrary.com
Andrea Ciochetti, Program Coordinator
andrea@beaumontlibrary.com
Jo-Anne Knieper, Contact, Interlibrary Loans
jo-anne@beaumontlibrary.com

Beaverlodge: Beaverlodge Public Library
406 - 10th St., Beaverlodge, AB T0H 0C0
Tel: 780-354-2569; Fax: 780-354-3078
librarian@beaverlodgelibrary.ab.ca
www.beaverlodgelibrary.ab.ca
www.facebook.com/BeaverlodgeLibrary
Tracy Deets, Library Manager

Beiseker: Beiseker Municipal Library
401 - 5th St., Beiseker, AB T0M 0G0
Tel: 403-947-3230
abemlibrary@marigold.ab.ca
www.beisekerlibrary.ca
www.facebook.com/beisekermunicipallibrary

Bentley: Bentley Municipal Library
5014 - 49th Ave., Bentley, AB T0C 0J0
Tel: 403-748-4626
bentleylibrary.prl.ab.ca
www.facebook.com/BentleyMunicipalLibrary

Berwyn: Berwyn W.I. Municipal Library
5105 - 51st St., Berwyn, AB T0H 0E0
Tel: 780-338-3616
librarian@berwynlibrary.ab.ca
www.berwynlibrary.ab.ca
www.facebook.com/Berwyn.I
Laurie Crowder, Library Manager

Big Valley: Big Valley Municipal Library
29 - 1st Ave. South, Big Valley, AB T0J 0G0
Tel: 403-876-2642
bigvalleylibrary@prl.ab.ca
bvlibrary.prl.ab.ca
Cordelle Rotvik, Library Manager

Blackfalds: Blackfalds Public Library
5018 Waghorn St., Blackfalds, AB T0M 0J0
Tel: 403-885-2343
library@blackfaldslibrary.ca
www.blackfaldslibrary.ca
twitter.com/blkfaldslibrary;
www.facebook.com/blackfaldspubliclibrary
Carley Binder, Library Manager

Blairmore: Crowsnest Community Library
2114 - 127th St., Blairmore, AB T0K 0E0
Tel: 403-562-8393; Fax: 403-562-8397
help@crowsnestpasslibrary.ca
crowsnestpasslibrary.ca
twitter.com/LibraryCNP; www.facebook.com/CNPLibrary
Diane DeLauw, Library Manager

Blue Ridge: Blue Ridge Community Library
117 - 2nd Ave., Blue Ridge, AB T0E 0B0
Tel: 780-648-3991
blueridgelibrary@yrl.ab.ca
blueridgelibrary.ab.ca
www.facebook.com/blueridgelibrary
Jenna Wilson, Acting Library Manager

Bon Accord: Bon Accord Public Library
5025 - 50th Ave., Bon Accord, AB T0A 0K0
Tel: 780-921-2540; Fax: 780-921-2580
librarian@bonaccordlibrary.ab.ca
www.bonaccordlibrary.ab.ca
www.facebook.com/116653245031620
Brenda Gosbjorn, Chair
Joyce Curtis-Bonardi, Library Manager

Bonanza: Bonanza Municipal Library
PO Box 53, Bonanza, AB T0H 0K0
Tel: 780-353-3067
librarian@bonanzalibrary.ca
www.bonanzalibrary.ca

Bonnyville: Bonnyville Municipal Library
4804 - 49th Ave., Bonnyville, AB T9N 2J3
Tel: 780-826-3071; Fax: 780-826-2058
www.bonnyvillelibrary.ab.ca
www.facebook.com/bonnyvillelibrary
Leah Woodford, Library Manager

Bow Island: Bow Island Municipal Library
510 Centre St., Bow Island, AB T0K 0G0
Tel: 403-545-2828; Fax: 403-545-6642
bowlib@shortgrass.ca
bowisland.shortgrass.ca
www.facebook.com/BowIslandLibrary
Kathryn Van Dorp, Library Manager
bowisland.manager@shortgrass.ca

Bowden: **Bowden Public Library**
Bay #2, 2101 20th Ave., Bowden, AB T0M 0K0
Tel: 403-224-3688
bowdenlibrary.prl.ab.ca
www.facebook.com/BowdenLibrary
Julie Hamblin, Library Manager

Boyle: **Boyle Public Library**
4800 - 3rd St., Boyle, AB T0A 0M0
Tel: 780-689-4161; *Fax:* 780-689-5660
librarian@boylepublib.ca
www.boylelibrary.ca
www.facebook.com/Boylepubliclibrary

Breton: **Breton Municipal Library**
4916 - 50th Ave., Breton, AB T0C 0P0
Tel: 780-696-3740; *Fax:* 780-696-3590
bretonlibrary@yrl.ab.ca
bretonlibrary.ab.ca
www.facebook.com/BretonLibrary
Katelynn Watts, Library Director

Brooks: **Brooks Public Library**
323 First St. East, Brooks, AB T1R 1C5
Tel: 403-362-2947; *Fax:* 403-362-8111
brolib@shortgrass.ca
brooks.shortgrass.ca
www.facebook.com/BrooksPublicLibrary
Lisa Patton, Library Manager
brooks.manager@shortgrass.ca

Brownfield: **Brownfield Community Library**
5001 Main St., Brownfield, AB T0C 0R0
Tel: 403-578-2247
brownfieldlibrary.prl.ab.ca
www.facebook.com/BrownfieldPublicLibrary
Darvy Gilbertson, Library Manager

Brownvale: **Brownvale Community Library**
300 - 4th Ave., Brownvale, AB T0H 0L0
Tel: 780-618-6216
brownvalelibrary@wispernet.ca
www.brownvalelibrary.ab.ca

Bruderheim: **Metro Kalyn Community Library**
5017 - 49th St., Bruderheim, AB T0B 0S0
Tel: 780-796-3032; *Fax:* 780-796-3032
info@bruderheimpl.ab.ca
www.bruderheimpl.ab.ca

Cadogan: **Cadogan Public Library**
112 - 2nd St., Cadogan, AB T0B 0T0
Tel: 780-753-6933
cadoganlibrary.prl.ab.ca
www.facebook.com/cadoganlibrary15
Rochelle Scammell, Library Manager

Calgary: **Calgary Public Library**
800 - 3rd St. SE, Calgary, AB T2G 2E7
Tel: 403-260-2600
calgarylibrary.ca
www.instagram.com/calgarylibrary; twitter.com/calgarylibrary;
www.facebook.com/calgarylibrary;
www.linkedin.com/company/calgary-public-library
Sarah Meilleur, Interim Chief Executive Officer
Mary Kapusta, Director, Communications
Paul Lane, Director, Corporate Services
Heather Robertson, Director, Service Design

Calling Lake: **Calling Lake Public Library**
2824 Central Dr., Calling Lake, AB T0G 0K0
Tel: 780-331-3027; *Fax:* 780-331-3029
librarian@callinglakelibrary.ab.ca
www.callinglakelibrary.ab.ca
www.instagram.com/cllibrary;
www.facebook.com/callinglakelibrary.ab.ca

Calmar: **Calmar Public Library**
4705 - 50th Ave., Calmar, AB T0C 0V0
Tel: 780-985-3472; *Fax:* 780-985-2859
circulation@calmarpubliclibrary.ca
calmarpubliclibrary.ca
www.facebook.com/calmarlibrary
Susan Parkinson, Manager
sparkinson@calmarpubliclibrary.ca

Camrose: **Camrose Public Library**
4710 - 50th Ave., Camrose, AB T4V 0R8
Tel: 780-672-4214; *Fax:* 780-672-9165
cpl.prl.ab.ca
www.facebook.com/CamroseLibrary
Robyn Gray, Library Director
Cheryl Hamel, Manager

Canmore: **Canmore Public Library**
#101, 700 Railway Ave., Canmore, AB T1W 1P4
Tel: 403-678-2468
info@canmorelibrary.ab.ca
www.canmorelibrary.ab.ca
www.pinterest.com/canmorelibrary; twitter.com/CanmoreLibrary;
www.facebook.com/canmorelibrary
Anne Baker, Chair
Michelle Preston, Library Director
mpreston@canmorelibrary.ab.ca

Carbon: **Village of Carbon Library**
Carbon Community Centre, 718 Glengarry St., Carbon, AB
T0M 0L0
Tel: 403-572-3440
acarmlibrary@marigold.ab.ca
www.carbonlibrary.ca
www.facebook.com/carbonmunicipallibrary
Julie Wiebe, Chair

Cardston: **Jim & Mary Kearl Library of Cardston**
25 - 3rd Ave. West, Cardston, AB T0K 0K0
Tel: 403-653-4775; *Fax:* 403-653-4716
help@cardstonlibrary.ca
cardstonlibrary.ca
www.facebook.com/CardstonJimandMaryKearlLibrary
Donna Beazer, Library Manager
Elizabeth Bectell, Children's Programming Advisor

Carmangay: **Carmangay & District Municipal Library**
416 Grand Ave., Carmangay, AB T0L 0N0
Tel: 403-643-3777
help@carmangaylibrary.ca
carmangaylibrary.ca
Kelsey Chic, Library Manager

Caroline: **Caroline Municipal Library**
5023 - 50th Ave., Caroline, AB T0M 0M0
Tel: 403-722-4060
carolinelibrary@prl.ab.ca
carolinelibrary.prl.ab.ca
www.facebook.com/carolinemunicipallibrary
Amanda Archibald, Manager
Allison Farr, Manager

Carseland: **Carseland Community Library**
Carseland Community Hall, 330 Railway Ave. West,
Carseland, AB T0J 0M0
Tel: 403-934-6007
acarselibrary@marigold.ca
www.carselandlibrary.ca
www.facebook.com/104146987676126

Carstairs: **Carstairs Public Library**
1402 Scarlett Ranch Blvd., Carstairs, AB T0M 0N0
Tel: 403-337-3943
carstairs@prl.ab.ca
carstairspublic.prl.ab.ca
www.facebook.com/CarstairsLibrary
Megan Ginther, Library Manager

Castor: **Castor Public Library**
4905 - 50th Ave., Castor, AB T0C 0X0
Tel: 403-882-3999
castorlibrary@prl.ab.ca
castorlibrary.prl.ab.ca
www.facebook.com/castorlibrary
Tess Griebel, Library Manager

Cessford: **Berry Creek Community School Library**
Berry Creek Community School, 116 - 1st Ave., Cessford,
AB T1R 1E2
Toll-Free: 844-566-3743
bccslibrary@plrd.ab.ca
www.berrycreeklibrary.ca
www.facebook.com/berrycreekcommunitylibrary

Champion: **Champion Municipal Library**
132A - 2nd St. South, Champion, AB T0L 0R0
Tel: 403-897-3099
help@championlibrary.ca
championlibrary.ca
Patty Abel, Library Manager

Chauvin: **Chauvin Municipal Library**
Dr. Folkins Community School, 5200 - 4th Ave. North,
Chauvin, AB T0B 0V0
Tel: 780-858-3746; *Fax:* 780-858-2392
librarian@chauvinmunicipallibrary.ab.ca
www.chauvinmunicipallibrary.ab.ca
www.facebook.com/chauvinmunicipallibrary
Heather Winacott, Chair
Jennifer Waters, Library Manager

Chestermere: **Chestermere Public Library**
105B Marina Rd., Chestermere, AB T1X 1V7
Tel: 403-272-9025
info@chestermerepubliclibrary.com
chestermerepubliclibrary.com
twitter.com/ChestermereLib;
www.facebook.com/ChestermerePublicLibrary

Claresholm: **Claresholm Public Library**
211 - 49th Ave. West, Claresholm, AB T0L 0T0
Tel: 403-625-4168; *Fax:* 403-625-2939
help@claresholmlibrary.ca
claresholmlibrary.ca
twitter.com/clarlibrary; www.facebook.com/clarlibrary
Jay Sawatzky, Library Manager
Barb Kemery, Program Coordinator

Cleardale: **Menno-Simons Public Library**
521 Cleardale Dr., Cleardale, AB T0H 3Y0
Tel: 780-685-2340; *Fax:* 780-685-3665
librarian@mennosimonslibrary.ca
www.mennosimonslibrary.ca
www.facebook.com/2038360089786696

Clive: **Clive Public Library**
5107 - 50th St., Clive, AB T0C 0Y0
Tel: 780-784-3131
clivepublib.prl.ab.ca
www.facebook.com/clivelibrarybuilding
Melanie Ash, Manager

Coaldale: **Coaldale Public Library**
2014 - 18th St., Coaldale, AB T1M 1N1
Tel: 403-345-1340; *Fax:* 403-345-1342
help@coaldalelibrary.ca
coaldalelibrary.ca
twitter.com/CoaldaleLibrary;
www.facebook.com/CoaldalePublicLibrary
Dothlyn McFarlane, Head Librarian

Cochrane: **Cochrane Public Library**
405 Railway St. West, Cochrane, AB T4C 2E2
Tel: 403-932-4353
info@cochranepubliclibrary.ca
www.cochranepubliclibrary.ca
twitter.com/LibraryCochrane;
www.facebook.com/CochranePublicLibrary
Jeri Maitland, Executive Director
jeri.maitland@cochranepubliclibrary.ca

Cold Lake: **Cold Lake Public Library**
5513B - 48th Ave., Cold Lake, AB T9M 1X9
Tel: 780-594-5101; *Fax:* 780-594-7787
www.coldlakelibrary.ca
twitter.com/CLPublicLibrary
Leslie Price, Director
director@library.coldlake.ab.ca

Consort: **Consort Municipal Library**
Consort School, 5215 - 50th St., Consort, AB T0C 1B0
Tel: 403-577-2501
aconmlibrary@marigold.ab.ca
www.consortlibrary.ca
www.facebook.com/consortlibrary

Coronation: **Coronation Memorial Library**
5001 Royal St., Coronation, AB T0C 1C0
Tel: 403-578-3445
coronationlibrary@prl.ab.ca
coronationlib.prl.ab.ca
www.facebook.com/CoronationLibrary
Jordan Stonehouse, Library Manager

Coutts: **Coutts Municipal Library**
218 - 1st Ave. South, Coutts, AB T0K 0N0
Tel: 403-344-3804
help@couttslibrary.ca
couttslibrary.ca
www.facebook.com/couttslibrary
Sharon Wollersheim, Library Manager

Cremona: **Cremona Municipal Library**
Municipal Bldg., 205 - 1st St. East, Cremona, AB T0M 0R0
Tel: 403-637-3100
cremonalibrary@prl.ab.ca
cremonalibrary.prl.ab.ca
Tracy Westerson, Library Manager

Crossfield: **Crossfield Municipal Library**
1210 Railway St., Crossfield, AB T0M 0S0
Tel: 403-946-4232; *Fax:* 403-946-4212
admin@crossfieldlibrary.ca
www.crossfieldlibrary.ca
www.facebook.com/156681641025114;

Czar: Czar Public Library
5005 - 49th Ave., Czar, AB T0B 0Z0
Tel: 780-857-2895
czarlibrary@prl.ab.ca
czarlibrary.prl.ab.ca
www.facebook.com/385344075341282
Jackie Almberg, Library Manager

Darwell: Darwell Public Library
Darwell Community Hall, #54, 225B Hwy. 765, Darwell, AB T0E 0L0
Tel: 780-892-3746; *Fax:* 780-892-3743
adarlibrary@yrl.ab.ca
www.darwellpubliclibrary.ab.ca
www.facebook.com/DarwellPublicLibrary
Sandra Stepaniuk, Library Manager

Daysland: Daysland Public Library
5130 - 50th St., Daysland, AB T0B 1A0
Tel: 780-781-0005
dayslandlibrary@prl.ab.ca
dayslandlibrary.prl.ab.ca
www.facebook.com/DayslandPublicLibrary
Christi Elley, Library Manager

Debolt: DeBolt Public Library
65 Alberta Ave., Debolt, AB T0H 1B0
Tel: 780-957-3770; *Fax:* 780-957-3770
librarian@deboltlibrary.ab.ca
deboltlibrary.ab.ca
www.facebook.com/1446320978995505

Delburne: Delburne Municipal Library
2210 - 20th St., Delburne, AB T0M 0V0
Tel: 403-749-3848
delburnelibrary@prl.ab.ca
delburnelibrary.prl.ab.ca
Judy Nicklom, Library Manager

Delia: Delia Municipal Library
Delia School, 205 - 3rd Ave. North, Delia, AB T0J 0W0
Tel: 403-364-3777
adm.library@plrd.ab.ca
www.delialibrary.ca
www.pinterest.com/delialibrary; twitter.com/DeliaLibrary;
www.facebook.com/admlibrary
Janice Hoover, Chair
Leah Hunter, Library Manager

Devon: Devon Public Library
#101, 17 Athabasca Ave., Devon, AB T9G 1G5
Tel: 780-987-3720
devon@devonpubliclibrary.ca
devonpubliclibrary.ca
twitter.com/dp_library; www.facebook.com/DevonLibrary
Barbara London, Chair
Stephanie Johnson, Director
stephanie@devonpubliclibrary.ca
Holly Gilmour, Coordinator, Early Childhood & Seniors Program
Kammi Rosentreter, Coordinator, Adult & Young Adult Program

Didsbury: Didsbury Municipal Library
2033 - 19th Ave., Didsbury, AB T0M 0W0
Tel: 403-335-3142
didsburylibrary@prl.ab.ca
dml.prl.ab.ca
www.pinterest.ca/didsburylibrary; twitter.com/DidsburyLibrary;
www.facebook.com/DidsburyLibrary
Monique Fiedler, Library Manager

Dixonville: Dixonville Community Library
PO Box 206, Dixonville, AB T0H 1E0
Tel: 780-971-2593; *Fax:* 780-971-2048
librarian@dixonvillelibrary.ab.ca
www.dixonvillelibrary.ab.ca
www.facebook.com/DixonvilleCommunityLibrary
Cayley Russell, Library Manager

Donalda: Donalda Public Library
5001 Main St., Donalda, AB T0B 1H0
Tel: 403-883-2665
donaldalibrary@prl.ab.ca
donaldalibrary.prl.ab.ca
www.facebook.com/DonaldaLibrary
Naomi LaBelle, Library Manager

Drayton Valley: Drayton Valley Municipal Library
5120 - 52nd St., Drayton Valley, AB T7A 1R7
Tel: 780-514-2722; *Fax:* 780-514-2790
dvml@draytonvalleylibrary.ca
draytonvalleylibrary.ca
twitter.com/dvlibrary; www.facebook.com/dvlibrary
Doug Whistance-Smith, Library Director

Drumheller: Drumheller Public Library
80 Veterans Way, Drumheller, AB T0J 0Y2
Tel: 403-823-1371; *Fax:* 403-823-1374
librarystaff@drumhellerlibrary.ca
www.drumhellerlibrary.ca
twitter.com/DrumPubLibrary;
www.facebook.com/110077339080350
Samantha Haddon, Chair
Emily Hollingshead, Director, Library Services
director@drumhellerlibrary.ca

Duchess: Duchess & District Public Library
256 Louise Ave., Duchess, AB T0J 0Z0
Tel: 403-378-4369; *Fax:* 403-378-4369
duclib@shortgrass.ca
duchess.shortgrass.ca
www.facebook.com/www.shortgrass.ca
Lorraine Samis, Chair
Daryl Kimura, Library Manager

Duffield: Parkland County Libraries
1 Main St., Duffield, AB T0E 0N0
Tel: 780-892-2644
duffieldlibrary@pclibraries.ca
pclibraries.ca
Sarah Leteta, Chair
sleteta@gmail.com
Kathy Gardiner, Library Director
kgardiner@pclibraries.ca
Brenda Baron, Library Manager

Eaglesham: Eaglesham Public Library
4902 - 53rd Ave., Eaglesham, AB T0H 1H0
Tel: 780-359-3792; *Fax:* 780-359-3745
librarian@eagleshamlibrary.ab.ca
www.eagleshamlibrary.ab.ca
www.facebook.com/EagleshamPublicLibrary

Eckville: Eckville Public Library
4855 - 51st Ave., Eckville, AB T0M 0X0
Tel: 403-746-3240
eckvillelibrary@prl.ab.ca
eckvillelibrary.prl.ab.ca
www.facebook.com/eckvillelibrary
Patti Skocdopole, Library Manager

Edberg: Edberg Public Library
48 - 1st Ave. West, Edberg, AB T0B 1J0
Tel: 780-678-5606
edberglibrary.prl.ab.ca
Pam Fankhanel, Library Manager

Edgerton: Edgerton Public Library
5037 - 50th Ave., Edgerton, AB T0B 1K0
Tel: 780-755-3933; *Fax:* 780-755-3750
librarian@edgertonlibrary.ab.ca
www.edgertonlibrary.ab.ca
www.facebook.com/edgertonpubliclibrary

Edmonton: Alberta Public Library Services
#803, 10405 Jasper Ave., Edmonton, AB T5J 4R7
Tel: 780-427-4871; *Fax:* 780-415-8594
libraries@gov.ab.ca
www.alberta.ca/public-library-services.aspx
Diana Davidson, Director
diana.davidson@gov.ab.ca
Kerry Anderson, Assistant Director
kerry.anderson@gov.ab.ca
Jen Anderson, Manager, Public Library Grants Program
jen.anderson@gov.ab.ca
Colette Poitras, Manager, Indigenous Public Library Outreach
colette.poitras@gov.ab.ca

Edmonton: Edmonton Public Library
7 Sir Winston Churchill Sq., Edmonton, AB T5J 2V4
Tel: 780-496-7000
Other Numbers: Text: 780-800-4929
www.epl.ca
www.youtube.com/user/edmontonpl; twitter.com/EPLdotCA;
www.facebook.com/EPLdotCA;
www.linkedin.com/company/edmonton-public-library
Pilar Martinez, Chief Executive Officer
780-496-7050
Deborah Rhodes, Chief Financial Officer & Executive Director, Shared Services
780-496-7097
Tina Thomas, Executive Director, Customer Experience
780-496-7046
Anna Alfonso, Director, Marketing & Communications
780-508-9166
Sharon Day, Director, Branch Services & Collections
780-496-5522

Chrissy Hodgins, Director, Branch Services & Community Engagement
780-442-6850
Mike Lewis, Director, Human Resource Services
780-496-7066
Roman Szczepanik, Director, Facilities & Operations
780-496-1846
Steve Till-Rogers, Director, Technology Services
780-442-6280

Edson: Edson & District Public Library
4726 - 8th Ave., Edson, AB T7E 1E3
Tel: 780-723-6691
mgagne@edsonlibrary.ca
edsonlibrary.ca
www.facebook.com/EdsonPublicLibrary
Robin Corser, Chair
Michael Baird, Library Manager
mbaird@edsonlibrary.ca

Elk Point: Elk Point Municipal Library
5123 - 50th Ave., Elk Point, AB T0A 1A0
Tel: 780-724-3737; *Fax:* 780-724-3739
info@elkpointlibrary.ab.ca
www.elkpointlibrary.ab.ca
www.facebook.com/elkpointlibrary

Elmworth: Elmworth Community Library
113036 Hwy. 722, Elmworth, AB T0H 1J0
Tel: 780-354-2930; *Fax:* 780-354-3639
librarian@elmworthlibrary.ab.ca
www.elmworthlibrary.ab.ca
www.facebook.com/ElmworthCommunityLibrary

Elnora: Elnora Public Library
210 Main St., Elnora, AB T0M 0Y0
Tel: 403-773-3966
elnoralibrary@prl.ab.ca
elnoralibrary.prl.ab.ca
www.facebook.com/ElnoraLibrary
Wanda Strandquist, Library Manager

Empress: Empress Municipal Library
6 - 3rd Ave., Empress, AB T0J 1E0
Tel: 403-565-3936
aemlibrary@marigold.ab.ca
www.empresslibrary.ca

Enchant: Enchant Community Library
134 Centre St., Enchant, AB T0K 0V0
Tel: 403-739-3835; *Fax:* 403-739-2585
help@enchantlibrary.ca
enchantlibrary.ca
www.facebook.com/Enchantcommunitylibrary
Sharon Hagen, Library Manager

Evansburg: Evansburg Public Library
4707 - 46th Ave., Evansburg, AB T0E 0T0
Tel: 780-727-2030; *Fax:* 780-727-2060
melirona@gypsd.ca
evansburglibrary.ca
twitter.com/evansburglib; www.facebook.com/EvansburgLibrary
Melissa Ronayne, Library Manager
melirona@gypsd.ca

Exshaw: Bighorn Library
2 Heart Mountain Dr., Exshaw, AB T0L 2C0
Tel: 403-673-3571
aexclibrary@marigold.ab.ca
www.bighornlibrary.ca
www.facebook.com/BighornLibrary;

Fairview: Fairview Public Library
10209 - 109th St., Fairview, AB T0H 1L0
Tel: 780-835-2613; *Fax:* 780-835-2613
librarian@fairviewlibrary.ab.ca
www.fairviewlibrary.ab.ca
www.facebook.com/368794109881543
Chris Burkholder, Library Manager

Falher: Bibliothèque Dentinger/Falher Library
27 Central Ave. SE, Falher, AB T0H 1M0
Tel: 780-837-2776; *Fax:* 780-837-8755
librarian@falherlibrary.ab.ca
falherlibrary.ab.ca
www.facebook.com/FalherBibliotheque
Doreen Horvath, Library Manager & Coordinator, CRC
crc@falherlibrary.ab.ca

Flatbush: Flatbush Community Library
661001 Hwy. 44, Flatbush, AB T0G 0Z0
Tel: 780-681-3756; *Fax:* 780-681-3756
librarian@flatbushlibrary.ab.ca
www.flatbushlibrary.ab.ca
www.facebook.com/FlatbushCommunityLibrary

Foremost: Foremost Municipal Library
103 - 1st Ave., Foremost, AB T0K 0X0
Tel: 403-867-3855
forlib@shortgrass.ca
foremost.shortgrass.ca
www.facebook.com/foremostlibrary
Joan Beutler, Library Manager
foremost.manager@shortgrass

Forestburg: Forestburg Public Library
Farvolden Centre, 4901 - 50th St., Forestburg, AB T0B 1N0
Tel: 780-582-4110
forestburglibrary@prl.ab.ca
forestburglibrary.prl.ab.ca
www.facebook.com/ForestburgLibrary
Sarah Tonowski, Library Manager

Fort Assiniboine: Fort Assiniboine Public Library
20 - 1st St., Fort Assiniboine, AB T0G 1A0
Tel: 780-584-2227; *Fax:* 780-674-8575
fortassiniboinelibrary@yrl.ab.ca
fortassiniboinelibrary.ab.ca
Megan Petryshen, Library Manager

Fort MacLeod: Fort MacLeod Public Library
264 - 24th St., Fort MacLeod, AB T0L 0Z0
Tel: 403-553-3880
help@fortmacleodlibrary.ca
fortmacleodlibrary.ca
www.facebook.com/FortMacleodLibrary
Darlene Hofer, Library Manager

Fort Saskatchewan: Fort Saskatchewan Public Library
10011 - 102nd St., Fort Saskatchewan, AB T8L 2C5
Tel: 780-998-4275
fsasklib@fspl.ca
fspl.ca
twitter.com/FSaskLib; www.facebook.com/FortSaskLibrary
Michele Fedyk, Library Director
mfedyk@fspl.ca

Fort Vermilion: Fort Vermilion Community Library
5103 River Rd., Fort Vermilion, AB T0H 1N0
Tel: 780-927-4279; *Fax:* 780-927-4746
afvclibrary@incentre.net
www.fvclibrary.com
www.facebook.com/FortVermilionCommunityLibrary

Fox Creek: Fox Creek Municipal Library
Fox Creek Greenview Multiplex, 103 - 2A Ave., 2nd Fl., Fox Creek, AB T0H 1P0
Tel: 780-622-2343; *Fax:* 780-622-4160
foxcreeklibrary@yahoo.com
www.foxcreeklibrary.ca
www.facebook.com/383125811771324
Mandy Miskelly, Library Manager

Gem: Gem Jubilee Library
125 Center St., Gem, AB T0J 1M0
Tel: 403-641-3245
gem.manager@shortgrass.ca
gem.shortgrass.ca
Kim Biette, Library Manager
403-641-2053

Gibbons: Gibbons Municipal Library
5115 - 51st St., Gibbons, AB T0A 1N0
Tel: 780-923-2004
info@gibbonslibrary.ab.ca
www.gibbonslibrary.ab.ca
Ryan Edmonds, Library Manager

Gleichen: Gleichen & District Library
404 Main St., Gleichen, AB T0J 1N0
Tel: 403-734-2390
agmlibrary@marigold.ab.ca
www.gleichenlibrary.ca
www.facebook.com/111462155589014

Glenwood: Glenwood Municipal Library
59 Main Ave., Glenwood, AB T0K 2R0
Tel: 403-942-8033
help@glenwoodlibrary.ca
www.glenwoodlibrary.ca
www.facebook.com/GlenwoodMunicipalLibrary
Nikki Francis, Library Manager

Grande Cache: Grande Cache Municipal Library
10601 Shand Ave., Grande Cache, AB T0E 0Y0
Tel: 780-827-2081; *Fax:* 780-827-3112
grandecachelibrary@gmail.com
www.grandecachelibrary.ab.ca
twitter.com/GCMuniLibrary;
www.facebook.com/gcmunicipallibrary
Laurel Kelsch, Library Manager
laurkels@gypsd.ca

Grande Prairie: Grande Prairie Public Library
#101, 9839 - 103rd Ave., Grande Prairie, AB T8V 6M7
Tel: 780-532-3580
info@gppl.ca
www.gppl.ca
www.youtube.com/user/GPPublicLibrary;
twitter.com/GPPublicLibrary; www.facebook.com/GPPL.ca
Deb Cryderman, Library Director
dcryderman@gppl.ca
780-357-7463
Jacob Fehr, Head, Children's & Teen Services
jfehr@gppl.ca
780-357-7477
Hailey McCullough, Head, Adult Services
hmccullough@gppl.ca
780-357-7474
Tara Wiebe, Head, Customer Services
twiebe@gppl.ca
780-357-7462
Belinda Blackbourn, Coordinator, Technical Services
bblackbourn@gppl.ca
780-357-7460

Granum: Granum Public Library
310 Railway Ave., Granum, AB T0L 1A0
Tel: 403-687-3912; *Fax:* 403-687-3914
help@granumlibrary.ca
granumlibrary.ca
www.facebook.com/granumpubliclibrary
Donna Pavey, Library Manager

Grassland: Grassland Public Library
Hwy. 63, Grassland, AB T0A 1V0
Tel: 780-525-3733; *Fax:* 780-525-3750
www.grasslandlibrary.ab.ca

Grassy Lake: Grassy Lake Public Library
512 - 3rd St. South, Grassy Lake, AB T0K 0Z0
Tel: 403-655-2232; *Fax:* 403-655-2259
help@grassylakelibrary.ca
grassylakelibrary.ca
Nancy Nelson, Library Manager

Grimshaw: Grimshaw Municipal Library
4412A - 50th St., Grimshaw, AB T0H 1W0
Tel: 780-332-4553; *Fax:* 780-332-1687
read@grimshawlibrary.ab.ca
www.grimshawlibrary.ab.ca
www.facebook.com/GrimshawLibrary
Linda Chmilar, Library Manager
Vivianne Gayton, Assistant Manager & Program Coordinator
connect@grimshawlibrary.ab.ca

Gunn: Rich Valley Public Library
Rich Valley Community Hall, RR#1, Gunn, AB T0E 1A0
Tel: 780-967-3525
rvpublib@yrl.ab.ca
richvalleylibrary.ab.ca
www.instagram.com/richvalleylibrary;
www.facebook.com/rvpublib

Hanna: Hanna Municipal Library
202 - 1st St. West, Hanna, AB T0J 1P0
Tel: 403-854-3865
library@hanna.ca
www.hannalibrary.ca
www.facebook.com/HannaLibrary
Melanie Jensen, Chair
Carley Angelstad, Director
Jenn Steinbrecker, Contact, Interlibrary Loans

Hardisty: Hardisty Public Library
5027 - 50th St., Hardisty, AB T0B 1V0
Tel: 780-888-3947
hardistylibrary@prl.ab.ca
hardistylib.prl.ab.ca
www.facebook.com/HardistyLibrary
Kelly McDowell, Library Manager

Hay Lakes: Hay Lakes Municipal Library
110 Main St., Hay Lakes, AB T0B 1W0
Tel: 780-878-2665
haylakeslibrary@prl.ab.ca
haylakeslibrary.prl.ab.ca
www.facebook.com/Haylakeslibrary
Beth Schultz, Library Manager

Hays: Hays Public Library
210 - 2nd Ave., Hays, AB T0K 1B0
Tel: 403-725-3744
help@hayslibrary.ca
hayslibrary.ca
Diane Wickenheiser, Library Manager

Heinsburg: Heinsburg Community Library
General Delivery, Heinsburg, AB T0A 1X0
Tel: 780-943-3913; *Fax:* 780-943-3773
www.heinsburgschool.ca/library-learning-commons

Heisler: Heisler Municipal Library
100 Haultain Ave., Heisler, AB T0B 2A0
Tel: 780-889-3925
heislerlibrary.prl.ab.ca
www.facebook.com/HeislerLibrary
Dixie Wolbeck, Library Manager

High Level: High Level Municipal Library
10601 - 103rd St., High Level, AB T0H 1Z0
Tel: 780-926-2097
librarian@highlevellibrary.ab.ca
www.highlevellibrary.ab.ca
twitter.com/HLLibraryAB; www.facebook.com/373315752685440
ShawnaLee Jessiman, Chair
Amanda Ebert, Library Manager

High Prairie: High Prairie Municipal Library
4723 - 53rd Ave., High Prairie, AB T0G 1E0
Tel: 780-523-3838; *Fax:* 780-523-2537
librarian@highprairielibrary.ab.ca
www.highprairielibrary.ab.ca
www.facebook.com/194353513915591
Tracy Ireland, Library Manager
Diana Palisoc, Contact, Interlibrary Loans
ill@highprairielibrary.ab.ca

High River: High River Library
909 - 1st St. SW, High River, AB T1V 1A5
Tel: 403-652-2917
library@highriverlibrary.ca
www.highriverlibrary.ca
twitter.com/HighRiverLib; www.facebook.com/highriverlibrary
Mary Zazelenchuk, Director
maryz@highriverlibrary.ca

Hines Creek: Hines Creek Municipal Library
212 - 10th St., Hines Creek, AB T0H 2A0
Tel: 780-494-3879
librarian@hinescreeklibrary.ab.ca
www.hinescreeklibrary.ab.ca
Denise Wiseman, Library Manager

Hinton: Hinton Municipal Library
803 Switzer Dr., Hinton, AB T7V 1V1
Tel: 780-865-2363; *Fax:* 780-865-4292
info@hintonlibrary.org
www.hintonlibrary.org
twitter.com/hintonlibrary; www.facebook.com/HintonLibrary
Hank Smit, Chair
Anayo Ugboma, Manager, Library Services
augboma@hintonlibrary.org
780-865-6051
Lindsey Bennett, Librarian
lbennett@hintonlibrary.org
780-865-6954
Corina Bowman, Librarian
coribowm@hintonlibrary.org
780-865-6050

Holden: Holden Municipal Library
4912 - 50th St., Holden, AB T0B 2C0
Tel: 780-688-3838; *Fax:* 780-688-3838
info@holdenlibrary.ab.ca
www.holdenlibrary.ab.ca
www.facebook.com/HoldenMunicipalLibrary

Hughenden: Hughenden Public Library
7 Mackenzie Ave., Hughenden, AB T0B 2E0
Tel: 780-856-2435
hughendenlibrary.prl.ab.ca
hughendenlibrary.prl.ab.ca
www.facebook.com/HughendenLibrary
Naomi Degenhardt, Library Manager
Marina Jones, Library Assistant

Hussar: Hussar Municipal Library
111 Centre St., Hussar, AB T0J 1S0
Toll-Free: 855-934-5334
librarylendinglockers@marigold.ab.ca
hussarlibrary.ca
Tim Frank, Chair

Hythe: Hythe Public Library
10013 - 100th St., Hythe, AB T0H 2C0
Tel: 780-356-3014; *Fax:* 780-356-3014
manager@hythelibrary.ca
www.hythelibrary.ab.ca
www.facebook.com/hythepubliclibrary

Innisfail: Innisfail Public Library
5300A - 55th St. Close, Innisfail, AB T4G 1R6
Tel: 403-227-4407
innisfail@prl.ab.ca
ipl.prl.ab.ca
www.facebook.com/innisfailpubliclibrary
Tara Downs, Library Manager

Innisfree: Innisfree Public Library
Millennium Bldg., 5317 - 48th Ave., Innisfree, AB T0B 2G0
Tel: 780-592-2122
librarian@innisfreelibrary.ca
www.innisfreelibrary.ca
www.facebook.com/VillageofInnisfreeLibrary
Marilyn Newton, Library Manager

Irma: Irma Municipal Library (Phyllis Craig Legacy Library)
5011 - 53rd Ave., Irma, AB T0B 2H0
Tel: 780-754-3746
librarian@irmalibrary.ca
www.irmalibrary.ca
www.facebook.com/irmalibrary

Irricana: Irricana Municipal Library
226 - 2nd St., Irricana, AB T0M 1B0
Tel: 403-935-4818; *Fax:* 403-935-4818
aimanager@marigold.ab.ca
www.irricanalibrary.ca
www.pinterest.com/IrricanaLibrary; twitter.com/IrricanaLibrary;
www.facebook.com/irricanalibrary
Papari Borthakur, Library Manager

Jasper: Jasper Municipal Library
500 Robson St., Jasper, AB T0E 1E0
Tel: 780-852-3652; *Fax:* 780-852-5841
jasperlibrary@town.jasper.ab.ca
www.jasperlibrary.ab.ca
twitter.com/jasperlib; www.facebook.com/jaspermunicipallibrary
Angie Thom, Director, Library Services

Keg River: Keg River Community Library
PO Box 68, Keg River, AB T0H 2G0
Tel: 780-981-2128
Susan MacDougall, Manager

Killam: Killam Municipal Library
5017 - 49th Ave., Killam, AB T0B 2L0
Tel: 780-385-3032
killamlibrary@prl.ab.ca
killamlibrary.prl.ab.ca
www.facebook.com/KillamPublicLibrary
Barb Cox, Library Manager

Kinuso: Kinuso Municipal Library
15 Kinuso Ave., Kinuso, AB T0G 1K0
Tel: 780-775-3694; *Fax:* 780-775-3650
librarian@kinusolibrary.ab.ca
www.kinusolibrary.ab.ca
www.facebook.com/307363213020733

Kitscoty: Kitscoty Public Library
4910 - 51st St., Kitscoty, AB T0B 2P0
Tel: 780-846-2822; *Fax:* 780-846-2215
librarian@kitscotypubliclibrary.ab.ca
www.kitscotypubliclibrary.ab.ca
www.facebook.com/1010819015770982

La Crete: La Crete Community Library
10102 - 100th Ave., La Crete, AB T0H 2H0
Tel: 780-928-3166
info@lacretelibrary.com
www.lacretelibrary.com
www.facebook.com/321429834622466

La Glace: La Glace Community Library
9924 - 97th Ave., La Glace, AB T0H 2J0
Tel: 780-568-4696; *Fax:* 780-568-4707
librarian@laglacelibrary.ca
www.laglacelibrary.ab.ca
www.facebook.com/LaGlaceCommunityLibrary;

Lac La Biche: Lac La Biche County Libraries
8702 - 91st Ave., Lac La Biche, AB T0A 2C0
Tel: 780-623-7467; *Fax:* 780-623-7497
www.llbcl.ca
twitter.com/LLBC_Libraries;
www.facebook.com/LacLaBicheCountyLibraries
Maureen Penn, Library Director

Lacombe: Mary C. Moore Public Library
#101, 5214 - 50th Ave., Lacombe, AB T4L 0B6
Tel: 403-782-3433; *Fax:* 403-782-3329
mcmpl@prl.ab.ca
www.lacombelibrary.com
twitter.com/MCM_PubLibrary; www.facebook.com/MCMPL

Lamont: Lamont Public Library
4801 - 50th Ave., Lamont, AB T0B 2R0
Tel: 780-895-2299; *Fax:* 780-895-2600
info@lamontpubliclibrary.ca
www.lamontpubliclibrary.ca
www.facebook.com/lamontpubliclibrary

Lancaster Park: Edmonton Garrison Community Library
#32, Bldg. 161, Lancaster Park, AB T0A 2H0
Tel: 780-973-4011
librarian@garrisonlibrary.ab.ca
www.garrisonlibrary.ab.ca
www.facebook.com/121932424548779

Leduc: Leduc Public Library
2 Alexandra Park, Leduc, AB T9E 4C4
Tel: 780-986-2637; *Fax:* 780-986-3462
infodesk@leduclibrary.ca
leduclibrary.ca
www.pinterest.com/leduclibrary; twitter.com/LeducLibrary;
www.facebook.com/LeducLibrary
Carla Frybort, Library Director
cfrybort@leduclibrary.ca

Lethbridge: Lethbridge Public Library
810 - 5th Ave. South, Lethbridge, AB T1J 4C4
Tel: 403-380-7310; *Fax:* 403-329-1478
questions@lethlib.ca
www.lethlib.ca
www.youtube.com/user/lethlib; twitter.com/lethlib;
www.facebook.com/lethlib
Terra Plato, Chief Executive Officer

Lethbridge: Médiathèque Françophone de Lethbridge
2104, 6e av sud, Lethbridge, AB T1J 1C3
Tél: 403-388-2921
mediatheque@scfl.ca
citedesprairies.info
www.facebook.com/mediathequelethbridge

Linden: Linden Municipal Library
Dr. Elliot School, 215 - 1st St. SE, Linden, AB T0M 1J0
Tel: 403-546-3757
almlibrary@marigold.ab.ca
lindenlibrary.ca
Wanda Malsbury, Chair

Lomond: Lomond Community Library
2 Railway Ave. North, Lomond, AB T0L 1G0
Tel: 403-792-3934
help@lomondlibrary.ca
lomondlibrary.ca
www.facebook.com/lomond.community.library
Kate Koch, Library Manager

Longview: Longview Municipal Library
128 Morrison Pl., Longview, AB T0L 1H0
Tel: 403-558-3927; *Fax:* 403-558-3927
alomlibrary@marigold.ab.ca
www.longviewlibrary.ca
www.facebook.com/LongviewMunicipalLibrary
Erika Smith, Chair

Lougheed: Lougheed Public Library
5004 - 50th St., Lougheed, AB T0B 2V0
Tel: 780-386-2498
lougheedlibrary@prl.ab.ca
lougheedlibrary.prl.ab.ca
www.facebook.com/LougheedLibrary
Barb McConnell, Library Manager

Ma-Me-O Beach: Pigeon Lake Public Library
603 - 2nd Ave., Ma-Me-O Beach, AB T0C 1X0
Tel: 780-586-3778; *Fax:* 888-452-0989
pigeonlakelibrary@yrl.ab.ca
pigeonlakepubliclibrary.ab.ca
www.facebook.com/pigeonlakelibrary
Cheryl McKerrall, Library Manager

Magrath: Magrath Public Library
27 South Centre St., Magrath, AB T0K 1J0
Tel: 403-758-6498
help@magrathlibrary.ca
magrathlibrary.ca
www.facebook.com/magrathlibrary.ca
Stephanie Humphreys, Library Manager

Mallaig: Mallaig Public Library
3110 - 1st St. East, Mallaig, AB T0A 2K0
Tel: 780-635-3858; *Fax:* 780-635-3938
www.mallaiglibrary.ab.ca

Manning: Manning Municipal Library
407 Main St., Manning, AB T0H 2M0
Tel: 780-836-3054; *Fax:* 780-836-0071
librarian@manninglibrary.ab.ca
manninglibrary.ab.ca
www.facebook.com/ManningMunicipalLibrary
Julie Gummesen, Chair
jgummesen@me.com
Crystal Jacobson, Library Manager

Mannville: Mannville Centennial Public Library
5029 - 50th St., Mannville, AB T0B 2W0
Tel: 780-763-3611; *Fax:* 780-763-3688
info@mannvillelibrary.ab.cab.ca
www.mannvillelibrary.ab.ca
www.facebook.com/MannvilleCentennialPublicLibrary

Marwayne: Marwayne Public Library
105 - 2nd St. South, Marwayne, AB T0B 2X0
Tel: 780-847-3930; *Fax:* 780-847-3796
www.marwaynelibrary.ab.ca
www.facebook.com/351184388234712;

Mayerthorpe: Mayerthorpe Public Library
4601 - 52nd St., Mayerthorpe, AB T0E 1N0
Tel: 780-786-2404
mayerthorpepl@yrl.ab.ca
mayerthorpelibrary.ab.ca
www.facebook.com/Mayerthorpe.Public.Library

McLennan: McLennan Municipal Library
19 - 1st Ave. NW, McLennan, AB T0H 2L0
Tel: 780-324-3767; *Fax:* 780-324-2288
librarian@mclennanlibrary.ab.ca
www.mclennanlibrary.ab.ca

Medicine Hat: Medicine Hat Public Library
414 - 1st St. SE, Medicine Hat, AB T1A 0A8
Tel: 403-502-8525
mhpl.shortgrass.ca
www.youtube.com/user/MHPublicLibrary;
twitter.com/mhpubliclibrary; www.facebook.com/MHPublicLibrary
Ken Feser, Chief Librarian
kenf@shortgrass.ca
403-502-8528
Carol Ann Cross-Roen, Head, Youth Services
carolannc@shortgrass.ca
403-502-8532
Keith McLean, Head, Fiction Services
keithm@shortgrass.ca
403-502-8531
Annette Ziegler, Manager, Circulation Services
annettez@shortgrass.ca
403-502-8539

Milk River: Milk River Municipal Library
321 - 3rd Ave. NE, Milk River, AB T0K 1M0
Tel: 403-647-3793
help@milkriverlibrary.ca
milkriverlibrary.ca
Peter Denmark, Library Manager

Millarville: Millarville Community Library
Millarville Community School, 130 Millarville Rd., Millarville, AB T0L 1K0
Tel: 403-931-3919
amclibrary@marigold.ab.ca
www.millarvillelibrary.ca
www.facebook.com/millarvillecommunitylibrary

Millet: Millet Public Library
4528 - 51st St., Millet, AB T0C 1Z0
Tel: 780-387-5222
millet@yrl.ab.ca
milletlibrary.ca
www.facebook.com/milletlibrary
Margaret Blackstock, Assistant Manager

Milo: Milo Library
116 Centre St., Milo, AB T0L 1L0
Tel: 403-599-3850; *Fax:* 403-599-3924
help@milolibrary.ca
milolibrary.ca
Joanne Monner, Library Manager

Mirror: Mirror Public Library
5003 - 50th Ave., Mirror, AB T0B 3C0
Tel: 403-788-3044

Morinville: Morinville Public Library
10125 - 100th Ave., Morinville, AB T8R 1P8
Tel: 780-939-3292; *Fax:* 780-939-2757
info@morinvillelibrary.ca
www.morinvillelibrary.ca
www.facebook.com/MoriLibrary

Morrin: Morrin Municipal Library
113 Main St., Morrin, AB T0J 2B0
Tel: 403-772-3922
amomlibrary@marigold.ab.ca
www.morrinlibrary.ca
www.pinterest.com/amomlibrary;
www.facebook.com/152196974828164

Mundare: Mundare Municipal Public Library
5128 - 50th St., Mundare, AB T0B 3H0
Tel: 780-764-3929; *Fax:* 780-764-2003
www.mundarelibrary.ab.ca

Myrnam: Myrnam Community Library
New Myrnam School, 5105 - 50th St., Myrnam, AB T0B 3K0
Tel: 780-366-3801; *Fax:* 780-366-2332
www.myrnamlibrary.ab.ca

Nampa: Nampa Municipal Library
10203 - 99th Ave., Nampa, AB T0H 2R0
Tel: 780-322-3805; *Fax:* 780-322-3955
nlibrary@nampalibrary.ca
www.nampalibrary.ab.ca
Cathy Armstrong, Library Manager

Nanton: Nanton Thelma Fanning Memorial Library
1907 - 21st Ave., Nanton, AB T0L 1R0
Tel: 403-646-5535; *Fax:* 403-646-2653
help@nantonlibrary.ca
nantonlibrary.ca
Gloria McGowan, Library Manager

Neerlandia: Neerlandia Public Library
4918 - 50th St., Neerlandia, AB T0G 1R0
Tel: 780-674-5384
neerlandialibrary1@gmail.com
neerlandialibrary.ab.ca
www.facebook.com/Neerlandiapublic

New Sarepta: New Sarepta Community Library
c/o New Sarepta Community High School, 5150 Centre St.,
New Sarepta, AB T0B 3M0
Tel: 780-975-7513; *Fax:* 780-941-2224
newsareptalibrary@yrl.ab.ca
newsareptalibrary.ca
www.facebook.com/newsareptalibrary
Angie Guderjan, Library Director

Newbrook: Newbrook Public Library
4805 - 50th St., Newbrook, AB T0A 2P0
Tel: 780-576-3772
librarian@newbrooklibrary.ab.ca
www.newbrooklibrary.ab.ca
twitter.com/newbrooklibrary;
www.facebook.com/541816375897592;

Niton Junction: Green Grove Public Library
5307 - 50th St., Niton Junction, AB T0E 1S0
Tel: 780-795-2474; *Fax:* 780-795-3933
nitonlibrary.ca
Toni Smigelski, Library Manager
toniice@gypsd.ca

Nordegg: Nordegg Public Library
#101, 5214 - 50th Ave., Nordegg, AB T4L 0B6
Tel: 403-800-3667
nordegglibrary.prl.ab.ca
Heather Clement, Library Manager

Okotoks: Okotoks Public Library
7 Riverside Dr. West, Okotoks, AB T1S 1A6
Tel: 403-938-2220
librarian@okotokslibrary.ca
www.okotokslibrary.ca
twitter.com/OkotoksLibrary;
www.facebook.com/OkotoksPublicLibrary
Lara Grunow, Director

Olds: Olds Municipal Library
5217 - 52nd St., Olds, AB T4H 1H7
Tel: 403-556-6460
oml@prl.ab.ca
oml.prl.ab.ca
twitter.com/oldslibrary; www.facebook.com/OldsMunicipalLibrary
Lesley Winfield, Library Manager
lwinfield@prl.ab.ca

Onoway: Onoway Public Library
4708 Lac Ste. Anne Trail North, Onoway, AB T0E 1V0
Tel: 780-967-2445; *Fax:* 888-467-1389
onowaylibrary@yrl.ab.ca
onowaylibrary.ab.ca
www.facebook.com/onowaypubliclibrary
Kelly Huxley, Library Manager

Paddle Prairie: Paddle Prairie Public Library
PO Box 58, Paddle Prairie, AB T0H 2W0
Tel: 780-981-3100; *Fax:* 780-981-3737
librarian@paddleprairielibrary.ab.ca
www.paddleprairielibrary.ab.ca

Paradise Valley: Three Cities Public Library
PO Box 89, Paradise Valley, AB T0B 3R0
Tel: 780-745-2277; *Fax:* 780-745-2641
threecitiespubliclibrary@gmail.com
www.paradisevalleylibrary.ab.ca
www.facebook.com/3citiespubliclibrary

Peace River: Peace River Municipal Library
9807 - 97th Ave., Peace River, AB T8S 1H6
Tel: 780-624-4076; *Fax:* 780-624-4086
info@prmlibrary.ab.ca
www.prmlibrary.ab.ca
www.instagram.com/peacerivermunicipallibrary;
www.facebook.com/peacerivermunicipallibrary
Johanna Downing, Chair
Channing Stenhouse, Library Director
director@prmlibrary.ab.ca

Penhold: Penhold & District Public Library
1 Waskasoo Ave., Penhold, AB T0M 1R0
Tel: 403-886-2636; *Fax:* 403-886-2638
penholdlibrary@prl.ab.ca
penholdlibrary.ca
www.facebook.com/penholdlibrary

Picture Butte: Picture Butte Municipal Library
120 - 4th St. South, Picture Butte, AB T0K 1V0
Tel: 403-732-4141
help@picturebuttelibrary.ca
picturebuttelibrary.ca
www.facebook.com/picturebuttelibrary
Cheryl Garratt, Library Manager

Pincher Creek: Pincher Creek Municipal Library
899 Main St., Pincher Creek, AB T0K 1W0
Tel: 403-627-3813
help@pinchercreeklibrary.ca
www.pinchercreeklibrary.ca
www.facebook.com/pinchercreeklibrary
Janice Day, Library Manager

Ponoka: Ponoka Jubilee Library
5604 - 50th St., Ponoka, AB T4J 1G5
Tel: 403-783-3843
ponokalibrary@prl.ab.ca
www.ponokalibrary.com
twitter.com/PonokaJubilee;
www.facebook.com/ponokajubileelibrary

Provost: Provost Municipal Library
5035 - 49th St., Provost, AB T0B 3S0
Tel: 780-753-2801
provostlibrary@prl.ab.ca
provostlibrary.prl.ab.ca
www.facebook.com/ProvostLibrary
Donna Engel, Library Manager

Radway: Radway Public Library
4915 - 50th St., Radway, AB T0A 2V0
Tel: 780-736-3548; *Fax:* 780-736-3858
librarian@radwaylibrary.ab.ca
www.radwaylibrary.ab.ca
www.facebook.com/radwaylibrary

Rainbow Lake: Rainbow Lake Municipal Library
1 Atco Rd., Rainbow Lake, AB T0H 2Y0
Tel: 780-956-3656
librarian@rainbowlakelibrary.ab.ca
www.rainbowlakelibrary.ab.ca
www.facebook.com/332382394231661
Michelle Farris, Chair
Kelly Drynan, Library Manager

Rainier: Alcoma Community Library
Alcoma School, Rainier, AB T0J 2M0
Tel: 403-362-3741
alcoma.shortgrass.ca
Janet Wagner, Library Manager
alcoma.manager@shortgrass.ca

Ralston: Graham Community Library
Ralston Community Centre, 35R Dugway Dr., Ralston, AB
T0J 2N0
Tel: 403-544-3670; *Fax:* 403-544-3814
graham.shortgrass.ca
www.facebook.com/GrahamCommunityLibrary
Stefanie Schranz, Library Manager
stefanie@shortgrass.ca

Raymond: Raymond Public Library
15 Broadway South, Raymond, AB T0K 2S0
Tel: 403-752-4785; *Fax:* 587-271-4710
help@raymondlibrary.ca
raymondlibrary.ca
www.facebook.com/RaymondPublicLibraryandArchives
Faye Geddes, Library Manager

Red Deer: Red Deer Public Library
4818 - 49th St., Red Deer, AB T4N 1T9
Tel: 403-346-4576; *Fax:* 403-341-3110
inquiries@rdpl.org
www.rdpl.org
twitter.com/rdpl; www.facebook.com/reddeerpubliclibrary
Shelley Ross, CEO

Red Earth Creek: Red Earth Public Library
115 Sandy Lane, Red Earth Creek, AB T0G 1X0
Tel: 780-694-3898; *Fax:* 780-694-3860
librarian@redearthlibrary.ab.ca
www.redearthlibrary.ab.ca

Redcliff: Redcliff Public Library
131 Main St. South, Redcliff, AB T0J 2P0
Tel: 403-548-3335; *Fax:* 403-548-6295
redcliff.manager@shortgrass.ca
redcliff.shortgrass.ca
www.instagram.com/redcliffablibrary; twitter.com/redcliflibrary;
www.facebook.com/RedcliffPublicLibrary
Tracy Laturnus, Library Manager

Redwater: Redwater Public Library
4915 - 48th St., Redwater, AB T0A 2W0
Tel: 780-942-3464; *Fax:* 888-759-5593
director@redwaterlibrary.ab.ca
www.redwaterlibrary.ab.ca
twitter.com/redwaterlibrary; www.facebook.com/RedwaterLibrary
Alicea Paszek, Director, Library Services

Rimbey: Rimbey Municipal Library
4938 - 50 Ave., Rimbey, AB T0C 2J0
Tel: 403-843-2841
rimbeylibrary.prl.ab.ca
www.pinterest.ca/rimbeylibrary; twitter.com/RimbeyLibrary;
www.facebook.com/rimbeylibrary
Jean Keetch, Library Manager

Rochester: Rochester Municipal Library
Rochester School, Hwy. 661, Rochester, AB T0G 1Z0
Tel: 780-698-3970; *Fax:* 780-698-2290
librarian@rochesterlibrary.ab.ca
www.rochesterlibrary.ab.ca

**Rocky Mountain House: Rocky Mountain House
Public Library**
4922 - 52nd St., Rocky Mountain House, AB T4T 1B1
Tel: 403-845-2042; *Fax:* 403-845-5633
armh@prl.ab.ca
rmhlibrary.prl.ab.ca
twitter.com/RockyLibrary; www.facebook.com/rockypubliclibrary
Ben Worth, Library Manager

Rockyford: Rockyford Municipal Library
Rockyford Community Centre, 412 Serviceberry Trail,
Rockyford, AB T0J 2R0
Tel: 403-533-3964
rockyford.library@marigold.ab.ca
www.rockyfordlibrary.ca
www.pinterest.com/rockyfordlib; twitter.com/Rockyford_AB;
www.facebook.com/RockyfordLibrary

Rolling Hills: Rolling Hills Public Library
322 - 4th St., Rolling Hills, AB T0J 2S0
Tel: 403-964-2186
rolcirc@shortgrass.ca
rollinghills.shortgrass.ca
Johnene Amulung, Library Manager
rollinghills.manager@shortgrass.ca

Rosemary: Rosemary Community Library
Rosemary Academic School, Block 6, Dahlia St., Rosemary,
AB T0J 2W0
Tel: 403-378-4493
rosemary.manager@shortgrass.ca
rosemary.shortgrass.ca
www.facebook.com/RosemaryLibrary
Vanessa Plett, Library Manager

Rumsey: Rumsey Community Library
229 Main St., Rumsey, AB T0J 2Y0
Tel: 403-368-3939
arumlibrary@marigold.ab.ca
www.rumseylibrary.ca
www.facebook.com/113046358725666

Rycroft: Rycroft Municipal Library
PO Box 248, Rycroft, AB T0H 3A0
Tel: 780-765-3973
librarian@rycroftlibrary.ab.ca
www.rycroftlibrary.ab.ca
www.facebook.com/RycroftMunicipalLibrary

Ryley: McPherson Municipal Library
5113 - 50th St., Ryley, AB T0B 4A0
Tel: 780-663-3999; *Fax:* 780-663-3909
www.mcphersonlibrary.ab.ca
Kimberly Murphy, Contact
librarian@mcphersonlibrary.ab.ca

Sangudo: Sangudo Public Library
5028 - 50th Ave., Sangudo, AB T0E 2A0
Tel: 780-785-2955
sangudolibrary@yrl.ab.ca
sangudolibrary.ca
www.facebook.com/SangudoPublicLibrary
Sandra Stepaniuk, Library Manager

Seba Beach: Seba Beach Public Library
140 - 3rd St. South, Seba Beach, AB T0E 2B0
Tel: 780-797-3940; *Fax:* 780-797-3800
sebabeachlibrary@yrl.ab.ca
sebabeachlibrary.ca
www.facebook.com/summervillageofsebabeachpubliclibrary
Lana Bouma, Library Manager

Sedgewick: Sedgewick & District Municipal Library
5301 - 51st Ave., Sedgewick, AB T0B 4C0
Tel: 780-384-3003
sedgewicklibrary@prl.ab.ca
sedgpublib.prl.ab.ca
www.facebook.com/SedgewickLibrary
Carol Williams, Chair
Barb McConnell, Library Manager

Sexsmith: Shannon Municipal Library
Sexsmith Civic Centre, 9917 - 99th Ave., Sexsmith, AB T0H
3C0
Tel: 780-568-4333; *Fax:* 780-568-7249
librarian@shannonlibrary.ab.ca
www.shannonlibrary.ab.ca
www.pinterest.ca/shannonlibrary;
www.facebook.com/shannonlibrary
Sheryl Pelletier, Library Director

Sherwood Park: Strathcona County Library (SCL)
Community Centre, 401 Festival Lane, Sherwood Park, AB
T8A 5P7
Tel: 780-410-8600; *Fax:* 780-467-6861
info@sclibrary.ca
www.sclibrary.ca
www.youtube.com/user/strathcolibrary; twitter.com/sc_library;
www.facebook.com/StrathconaCountyLibrary
Meagan Olive, Chair

Silver Valley: Savanna Municipal Library
PO Box 49, Silver Valley, AB T0H 3E0
Tel: 780-351-3771
librarian@savannalibrary.ca
www.savannalibrary.ca

Slave Lake: Rotary Club of Slave Lake Public Library
Government Centre, 50 Main St. SW, Slave Lake, AB T0G
2A0
Tel: 780-849-5250; *Fax:* 780-849-3275
librarian@slavelakelibrary.ab.ca
www.slavelakelibrary.ab.ca
www.facebook.com/RotaryClubOfSlaveLakePublicLibrary
Kendra McRee, Manager

Smith: Smith Community Library
1005 - 9th St., Smith, AB T0G 2B0
Tel: 780-829-2389; *Fax:* 780-829-2389
librarian@smithlibrary.ab.ca
www.facebook.com/SmithCommunityLibrary
Kendra McRee, Library Manager

Smoky Lake: Smoky Lake Municipal Library
5010 - 50th St., Smoky Lake, AB T0A 3C0
Tel: 780-656-4212; *Fax:* 780-656-4212
librarian@smokylakelibrary.ab.ca
www.smokylakelibrary.ab.ca
www.facebook.com/smokylakepubliclibrary
Lise van der Vaart, Library Manager

Spirit River: Spirit River Municipal Library
4816 - 44th Ave., Spirit River, AB T0H 3G0
Tel: 780-864-4038; *Fax:* 780-864-3006
librarian@spiritriverlibrary.ab.ca
www.spiritriverlibrary.ab.ca
www.facebook.com/1500693876884728

Spruce Grove: Spruce Grove Public Library
Melcor Cultural Centre, 35 - 5th Ave., Spruce Grove, AB T7X
2C5
Tel: 780-962-4423
library@sgpl.ca
sgpl.ca
www.youtube.com/user/SpruceGroveLibrary61;
twitter.com/SG_Library; www.facebook.com/SpruceGroveLibrary
Leanne Myggland-Carter, Director, Library Services
leanne@sgpl.ca
780-962-4423 ext. 202

Spruce View: Spruce View Community Library
Hwy. 54, Spruce View, AB T0M 1V0
Tel: 403-728-0012
svlibrary@prl.ab.ca
svlibrary.prl.ab.ca
www.facebook.com/spruceviewcommunitylibrary
Paddy Birkeland, Library Manager

St Albert: St Albert Public Library
5 St Anne St., St Albert, AB T8N 3Z9
Tel: 780-459-1530; *Fax:* 780-458-5772
sapl@sapl.ca
www.sapl.ca
twitter.com/stalbertlibrary;
www.facebook.com/stalbertpubliclibrary
Janice Marschner, Chair
Peter Bailey, Chief Executive Officer
pbailey@sapl.ca
780-459-1681
Stephanie Foremsky, Manager, Public Services
780-459-1686
Kathleen Troppmann, Manager, Customer Services
ktroppmann@sapl.ca
780-459-1537

St Isidore: St Isidore Community Library/Bibliothèque de St Isidore
4, rue Bouchard, St Isidore, AB T0H 3B0
Tel: 780-624-8182; *Fax:* 780-624-8192
librarian@bibliothequestisidore.ab.ca
www.bibliothequestisidore.ab.ca

St Paul: St Paul Municipal Library
4802 - 53rd St., St Paul, AB T0A 3A0
Tel: 780-645-4904; *Fax:* 780-645-5198
librarian@stpaullibrary.ab.ca
www.stpaullibrary.ab.ca
www.instagram.com/stpaulablibrary;
www.facebook.com/Stpaulablibrary
Madeleine Bombay, Chair

Standard: Standard Municipal Library
822 The Broadway, Standard, AB T0J 3G0
Tel: 403-644-3995
astmlibrary@marigold.ab.ca
www.standardlibrary.ca
www.facebook.com/1010036936653357
Lori Bach, Chair

Standoff: Kainai Public Library
Shot Both Sides Bldg., #1, Hwy. 2, Standoff, AB T0L 1Y0
Tel: 403-737-8351
help@kainailibrary.ca
kainailibrary.ca
www.facebook.com/KainaiPublicLibrary
Kathy Goodstriker, Library Manager
Linda Weaselhead, Learning Commons Manager
Candice Shouting, Library Technician

Stavely: Stavely Municipal Library
4823 - 49th St., Stavely, AB T0L 1Z0
Tel: 403-549-2190
help@stavelylibrary.ca
stavelylibrary.ca
Bev Olsen, Library Manager

Stettler: Stettler Public Library
6202 - 44th Ave., Stettler, AB T0C 2L1
Tel: 403-742-2292
spl@prl.ab.ca
spl.prl.ab.ca
www.pinterest.ca/stettlerlibrary; twitter.com/stettlerlibrary;
www.facebook.com/StettlerPublicLibrary
Rhonda O'Neill, Library Manager

Stirling: Stirling Theodore Brandley Municipal Library
409 - 2nd St., Stirling, AB T0K 2E0
Tel: 403-756-3665
help@stirlinglibrary.ca
stirlinglibrary.ca
Laura Quinton, Library Manager

Stony Plain: Stony Plain Public Library
5216 - 50th St., Stony Plain, AB T7Z 0N5
Tel: 780-963-5440; *Fax:* 780-963-1746
info@mysppl.ca
mysppl.ca
www.instagram.com/stonyplainlibrary; twitter.com/stonyplainlib;
www.facebook.com/StonyPlainLibrary
Shauna Johnstone, Chair
Mark McHale, Director
markm@mysppl.ca
780-963-5440 ext. 101

Strathmore: Strathmore Municipal Library
85 Lakeside Blvd., Strathmore, AB T1P 1A1
Tel: 403-934-5440; *Fax:* 403-934-1908
info@strathmorelibrary.ca
www.strathmorelibrary.ca
www.instagram.com/strathmorelib;
www.facebook.com/strathmorelibrary
Rachel Dick Hughes, Director, Library Services
director@strathmorelibrary.ca

Sundre: Sundre Municipal Library
#2, 96 - 2nd Ave. NW, Sundre, AB T0M 1X0
Tel: 403-638-4000; *Fax:* 403-638-5755
sundrelibrary@prl.ab.ca
sundre.prl.ab.ca
twitter.com/SundreLibrary; www.facebook.com/sundrelibrary
Karen Tubb, Library Manager

Swan Hills: Swan Hills Public Library
5536 Main St., Swan Hills, AB T0G 2C0
Tel: 780-333-4505; *Fax:* 780-333-4551
swanhillslibrary.ab.ca
www.facebook.com/swanhillslibrary
April Wharton, Library Director
awharton.swanhillslibrary@yrl.ab.ca

Sylvan Lake: Sylvan Lake Municipal Library
4715 - 50th Ave., Sylvan Lake, AB T4S 1A2
Tel: 403-887-2130; *Fax:* 403-887-0537
sylvan.library@prl.ab.ca
www.sylvanlibrary.ca
twitter.com/SylvanLib
www.facebook.com/SylvanLakeMunicipalLibrary
Andrea Newland, Director

Taber: Taber Public Library
5415 - 50th Ave., Taber, AB T1G 1V2
Tel: 403-223-4343; *Fax:* 403-223-4314
help@taberlibrary.ca
taberlibrary.ca
twitter.com/TaberLibrary; www.facebook.com/TaberPublicLibrary
Dawn Kondas, Program Coordinator
dkondas@taberlibrary.ca

Tangent: Tangent Community Library
1009 Railway Ave., Tangent, AB T0H 3J0
Tel: 780-359-2666
librarian@tangentlibrary.ab.ca
www.tangentlibrary.ab.ca
www.facebook.com/546255662397397

Thorhild: Thorhild Library
210 - 7th Ave., Thorhild, AB T0A 3J0
Tel: 780-398-3502
librarian@thorhildlibrary.ab.ca
www.thorhildlibrary.ab.ca
www.facebook.com/515491841853129

Thorsby: Thorsby Municipal Library
4901 - 48th Ave., Thorsby, AB T0C 2P0
Tel: 780-789-3808
thorsbypublib@yrl.ab.ca
thorsbymunicipallibrary.ab.ca
www.facebook.com/ThorsbyLibrary
Gayle Sacuta, Interim Library Manager

Three Hills: Three Hills Municipal Library
135 - 2nd Ave. South, Three Hills, AB T0M 2A0
Tel: 403-443-2360
athmlibrary@marigold.ab.ca
www.3hillslibrary.com
www.pinterest.com/3HillsLibrary; twitter.com/3hillslibrary;
www.facebook.com/ThreeHillsLibrary
Karen Nickel, Library Manager

Tilley: Tilley Public Library
148 - 1st Ave. East, Tilley, AB T0J 3K0
Tel: 403-377-2233
tilleypubliclibrary@shortgrass.ca
tilley.shortgrass.ca
www.facebook.com/TilleyandDistrictPublicLibrary
Anita Chappell, Library Manager
tilley.manager@shortgrass.ca

Tofield: Tofield Municipal Library
5407 - 50th St., Tofield, AB T0B 4J0
Tel: 780-662-3838; *Fax:* 780-662-3929
www.tofieldlibrary.ca
www.facebook.com/tofieldlibrary

Trochu: Trochu Municipal Library
317 Main St., Trochu, AB T0M 2C0
Tel: 403-442-2458
atrmlibrary@marigold.ab.ca
www.trochulibrary.ca

Turner Valley: Sheep River Community Library
129 Main St. NE, Turner Valley, AB T0L 2A0
Tel: 403-933-3278; *Fax:* 403-933-3298
abdsrclibrary@marigold.ab.ca
www.sheepriverlibrary.ca
www.facebook.com/SheepRiverLibrary

Two Hills: Alice Melnyk Public Library
5009 Diefenbaker (50th) Ave., Two Hills, AB T0B 4K0
Tel: 780-657-3553; *Fax:* 780-657-3553
librarian@twohillslibrary.ab.ca
www.twohillslibrary.ab.ca

Valhalla Centre: Valhalla Community Library
9702 - 100th Ave., Valhalla Centre, AB T0H 3M0
Tel: 780-356-3834; *Fax:* 780-356-3834
librarian@valhallalibrary.ab.ca
www.valhallalibrary.ab.ca
www.facebook.com/ValhallaCommunityLibrary

Valleyview: Valleyview Municipal Library
4804 - 50th Ave., Valleyview, AB T0H 3N0
Tel: 780-524-3033; *Fax:* 780-524-4563
librarian@valleyviewlibrary.ab.ca
www.valleyviewlibrary.ab.ca
www.facebook.com/ValleyviewMunicipalLibrary
Kerri Danner, Library Manager

Vauxhall: Vauxhall Public Library
504 - 2nd Ave. North, Vauxhall, AB T0K 2K0
Tel: 403-654-2370; *Fax:* 403-654-2192
help@vauxhalllibrary.ca
vauxhalllibrary.ca

Gen Durupt, Acting Library Manager

Vegreville: Vegreville Centennial Library
4709 - 50th St., Vegreville, AB T9C 1R1
Tel: 780-632-3491
www.vegrevillelibrary.ab.ca
twitter.com/VegLibrary
Mike Cooper, Chair

Vermilion: Vermilion Public Library
5001 - 49th Ave., Vermilion, AB T9X 1B8
Tel: 780-853-4288; *Fax:* 833-792-7170
info@vermilionpubliclibrary.ca
www.vplibrary.ca
www.facebook.com/vermilionpl
Stuart Pauls, Library Manager
librarian@vplibrary.ca

Veteran: Veteran Municipal Library
201 Luckow St., Veteran, AB T0C 2S0
Tel: 403-575-3915

Viking: Viking Municipal Library
Viking Carena Complex, 5120 - 45th St., Viking, AB T0B 4N0
Tel: 780-336-4992; *Fax:* 780-336-4992
www.vikinglibrary.ab.ca
www.facebook.com/180715135371094
Jeanne Congdon, Chair
Barb Chrystian, Library Manager

Vilna: Vilna Municipal Library
Cultural Center, 5431 - 50th St., Vilna, AB T0A 3L0
Tel: 780-636-2077; *Fax:* 780-636-3243
librarian@vilnapubliclibrary.ab.ca
www.vilnapubliclibrary.ab.ca
www.facebook.com/vilnapubliclibrary
Marion Vinette, Chair

Vulcan: Vulcan Municipal Library
303 Centre St., Vulcan, AB T0L 2B0
Tel: 403-485-2571; *Fax:* 403-485-5013
help@vulcanlibrary.ca
vulcanlibrary.ca
www.facebook.com/VulcanMunicipalLibrary
Connie Clement, Library Manager
Dorothy Way, Assistant Librarian

Wabasca: Wabasca Public Library
2853 Alook Dr., Wabasca, AB T0G 2K0
Tel: 780-891-2203; *Fax:* 780-891-2402
librarian@wabascalibrary.ab.ca
www.wabascalibrary.ab.ca
www.instagram.com/wabascalibrary;
www.facebook.com/225869701414525
Brenda Bladon, Chair
brendabladon@gmail.com

Wainwright: Wainwright Public Library
921 - 3rd Ave., Wainwright, AB T9W 1C5
Tel: 780-842-2673; *Fax:* 780-842-2340
librarian@wainwrightlibrary.ab.ca
www.wainwrightlibrary.ab.ca
www.facebook.com/WainwrightPublicLibrary
Linda White, Chair
Jodi Dahlgren, Library Manager

Wandering River: Wandering River Women's Institute Community Library
Wandering River School, Wandering River, AB T0A 3M0
Tel: 780-771-3939
librarian@wanderingriverlibrary.ab.ca
www.wanderingriverlibrary.ab.ca
www.facebook.com/WanderingRiverLibrary
Cheryl Ballard, Library Manager

Warburg: Warburg Public Library
5212 - 50th Ave., Warburg, AB T0C 2T0
Tel: 780-848-2391
warburglibrary@yrl.ab.ca
warburglibrary.ab.ca
www.facebook.com/WarburgPublicLibrary

Warner: Warner Memorial Library
206 - 3rd Ave., Warner, AB T0K 2L0
Tel: 403-642-3988
help@warnerlibrary.ca
www.warnerlibrary.ca
www.facebook.com/a.tapp968
Andrea Tapp, Library Manager

Waskatenau: Anne Chorney Public Library
PO Box 130, Waskatenau, AB T0A 3P0
Tel: 780-358-2777; *Fax:* 780-358-2777
librarian@waskatenaulibrary.ab.ca
www.waskatenaulibrary.ab.ca
www.facebook.com/annechorneypubliclibrary
Tracy Wilhelm, Library Manager

Water Valley: Water Valley Public Library
PO Box 250, Water Valley, AB T0M 2E0
Tel: 403-637-3899
watervalleylibrary@prl.ab.ca
watervalleylibrary.prl.ab.ca
www.facebook.com/WaterValleyLibrary
Lisette Neva McCracken, Library Manager

Wembley: Wembley Public Library
9719 - 99th Ave., Wembley, AB T0H 3S0
Tel: 780-766-3553; *Fax:* 780-776-3543
librarian@wembleypubliclibrary.ab.ca
www.wembleypubliclibrary.ab.ca

Westlock: Westlock Libraries
#1, 10007 - 100th Ave., Westlock, AB T7P 2H5
Tel: 780-349-3060; *Fax:* 780-349-5291
info@westlocklibrary.ca
westlocklibrary.ca
www.pinterest.com/westlocklibrary; twitter.com/westlocklibrary;
www.facebook.com/westlocklibraries
Tanya Pollard, Chair
Lisa Old, Library Director
lold@westlocklibrary.ca

Wetaskiwin: Wetaskiwin Public Library
5002 - 51st Ave., Wetaskiwin, AB T9A 0V1
Tel: 780-361-4446; *Fax:* 780-352-3266
library@wetaskiwin.ca
wetaskiwinpubliclibrary.ab.ca
twitter.com/awpubliclibrary;
www.facebook.com/wetaskiwinpubliclibrary
Svea Beson, Manager, Administrative Services
Christine Hutchinson, Librarian, Public Services
christine.hutchinson@wetaskiwin.ca
Kat MacCallum, Coordinator, Children's Services
kat.maccallum@wetaskiwin.ca

Whitecourt: Whitecourt & District Public Library
5201 - 49th St., Whitecourt, AB T7S 1N3
Tel: 780-778-2900
info@whitecourtlibrary.ab.ca
whitecourtlibrary.ab.ca
www.facebook.com/whitecourtlibrary
Serena Lapointe, Chair
Joseph Kubelka, Library Director
jkubelka@whitecourtlibrary.ab.ca

Wildwood: Wildwood Public Library
5215 - 50th St., Wildwood, AB T0E 2M0
Tel: 780-325-3882; *Fax:* 780-325-3880
wildwoodlibrary.ab.ca
www.facebook.com/WildwoodPublicLibrary
Susannah Kotyk, Library Manager
skotyk.wildwoodlibrary@yrl.ab.ca

Winfield: Winfield Community Library
401 - 4th Ave. East, Winfield, AB T0C 2X0
Tel: 780-682-2498
winfieldlibrary@yrl.ab.ca
winfieldlibrary.ab.ca
www.facebook.com/WinfieldCommunityLibrary
Joyce Brown, Library Manager

Woking: Woking Municipal Library
#10, 5245 - 51st St., Woking, AB T0H 3V0
Tel: 780-774-3932
librarian@wokinglibrary.ca
www.wokinglibrary.ca
www.facebook.com/913173865445908

Worsley: Worsley & District Library
216 Alberta Ave., Worsley, AB T0H 3W0
Tel: 780-685-3842
awdlib@hotmail.com
www.worsleylibrary.ab.ca
www.facebook.com/WorsleyLibrary

Wrentham: Wrentham Public Library
101 Caragan Ave., Wrentham, AB T0K 2P0
Tel: 403-222-2485; *Fax:* 403-222-2101
help@wrenthamlibrary.ca
wrenthamlibrary.ca
Marsha Edwards, Library Manager

Youngstown: **Youngstown Municipal Library**
218 Main St., Youngstown, AB T0J 3R0
Tel: 403-779-3864; *Fax:* 403-779-3864
aymlibrary@marigold.ab.ca
www.youngstownlibrary.ca

Zama City: **Zama Community Library**
1025 Aspen Dr., Zama City, AB T0H 4E0
Tel: 780-683-2888
mclboard.com/municipal-libraries/zama-library
www.facebook.com/ZamaCityLibrary

Archives

Banff: **The Banff Centre (Paul D. Fleck Library & Archives)**
107 Tunnel Mountain Dr., Banff, AB T1L 1H5
Tel: 403-762-6265; *Fax:* 403-762-6266
Other Numbers: Archives: 403-762-6440
library@banffcentre.ca
www.banffcentre.ca/library-and-archives

Banff: **Whyte Museum of the Canadian Rockies**
111 Bear St., Banff, AB T1L 1A3
Tel: 403-762-2291; *Fax:* 403-762-2339
archives@whyte.org
www.whyte.org/research-collections
www.youtube.com/user/WhyteMuseum;
twitter.com/whytemuseum; www.facebook.com/WhyteMuseum
Jennifer Rutkair, Head Archivist
jrutkair@whyte.org

Brooks: **Eastern Irrigation District Archives & Library**
550 Industrial Rd. West, Brooks, AB T1R 1B2
Tel: 403-362-1400; *Fax:* 403-362-6206
www.eid.ca

Calgary: **Calgary Highlanders Regimental Museum & Archives**
4520 Crowchild Trail SW, Calgary, AB T3E 1T8
Tel: 403-410-2340
museum@calgaryhighlanders.com
calgaryhighlanders.com/regimental-organizations/museum
Kent Griffiths, Curator

Calgary: **The City of Calgary**
Administration Bldg., 313 - 7th Ave. SE, Main Fl., Calgary, AB T2G 0J1
Tel: 403-268-8180; *Fax:* 403-268-6731
archives@calgary.ca
www.calgary.ca

Lynn Bullock, Archivist
lynn.bullock@calgary.ca
403-268-8185

Calgary: **Glenbow Museum**
130 - 9th Ave. SE, Calgary, AB T2G 0P3
Tel: 403-268-4204; *Fax:* 403-232-6569
archives@glenbow.org
www.glenbow.org/collections/archives
Daryl Betenia, Manager, Collections
dbetenia@glenbow.org

Calgary: **Heritage Park Society**
1900 Heritage Dr. SW, Calgary, AB T2V 2X3
Tel: 403-268-8500; *Fax:* 403-268-8501
info@heritagepark.ab.ca
www.heritagepark.ca
twitter.com/HeritageParkYYC;
www.facebook.com/HeritageParkYYC

Calgary: **Jewish Historical Society of Southern Alberta**
1607 - 90th Ave. SW, Calgary, AB T2V 4V7
Tel: 403-444-3171; *Fax:* 403-253-7915
jhssa@shaw.ca
jhssa.org
Roberta Kerr, Librarian & Archivist
Katie Baker, Office Administrator

Calgary: **Legal Archives Society of Alberta**
#400, 1015 - 4th St. SW, Calgary, AB T2R 1J4
Tel: 403-244-5510; *Fax:* 403-454-4419
lasa@legalarchives.ca
www.legalarchives.ca
Stacy Kaufeld, Executive Director
stacy.kaufeld@legalarchives.ca
403-244-5510
Brenda McCafferty, Archivist
brenda.mccafferty@legalarchives.ca
403-244-5510

Calgary: **Lord Strathcona's Horse Regimental Museum**
4520 Crowchild Trail SW, Calgary, AB T2T 5J4
Tel: 403-410-2340; *Fax:* 403-410-2359
archives@strathconas.ca
www.strathconas.ca/strathcona-museum
P.J. (Phil) Webster, Curator
Todd Giberson, Manager, Collections

Calgary: **The Military Museums**
4520 Crowchild Trail SW, Calgary, AB T2T 5J4
Tel: 403-410-2340
themilitarymuseums.ca/visit/library
Jason Nisenson, Head Librarian & Senior Archivist
jason.nisenson@ucalgary.ca

Calgary: **Naval Museum of Alberta**
4520 Crowchild Trail SW, Calgary, AB T2T 5J4
Tel: 403-410-2340
nma@themilitarymuseums.ca
www.themilitarymuseums.ca/visit/tmm-galleries/navy
Brad Froggatt, Curator
nma@themilitarymuseums.ca

Calgary: **YouthLink Calgary**
5151 - 47th St. NE, Calgary, AB T3J 3R2
Tel: 403-428-4530; *Fax:* 403-974-0508
youthlink@calgarypolice.ca
www.youthlinkcalgary.com
www.instagram.com/YouthLinkYYC; twitter.com/YouthLinkYYC;
www.facebook.com/YouthLinkYYC
Tara Robinson, Executive Director

Edmonton: **Canadian Moravian Historical Society Archives**
2304 - 38th St., Edmonton, AB T6L 4K9
Tel: 780-440-3050; *Fax:* 780-463-2143
historical@moravian.ca
www.moravian.org/canada

Edmonton: **City of Edmonton Archives/Archives de la ville d'Edmonton**
#200, 10440 - 108th Ave., Edmonton, AB T5H 3Z9
Tel: 780-496-8711
cms.archives@edmonton.ca
www.edmonton.ca/archives
Kathryn Ivany, City Archivist
kathryn.ivany@edmonton.ca
780-496-8718

Edmonton: **Edmonton Public Schools**
McKay Ave. School, 10425 - 99th Ave. NW, Edmonton, AB T5K 0E5
Tel: 780-422-1970
archivesmuseum@epsb.ca
archivesmuseum.epsb.ca
twitter.com/EPSB_McKay

Edmonton: **The Edmonton Sun**
10006 - 101st St., Edmonton, AB T5J 0S1
Tel: 780-468-0100
licensing@postmedia.com
www.edmontonsun.com

Edmonton: **Provincial Archives of Alberta**
8555 Roper Rd., Edmonton, AB T6E 5W1
Tel: 780-427-1750
paa@gov.ab.ca
provincialarchives.alberta.ca
twitter.com/ProvArchivesAB;
www.facebook.com/www.provincialarchivesofalberta
Tom Anderson, Manager, Private Records
tom.anderson@gov.ab.ca
Glynys Hohmann, Manager, Government Records
glynys.hohmann@gov.ab.ca
Angie Friesen, Access Archivist

Jasper: **Jasper-Yellowhead Museum & Archives**
400 Bonhomme St., Jasper, AB T0E 1E0
Tel: 780-852-3013
archives@jaspermuseum.org
www.jaspermuseum.org/archives.html
www.facebook.com/123561747657136

Lethbridge: **Galt Museum & Archives**
502 - 1st St. South, Lethbridge, AB T1J 1Y4
Tel: 403-320-3954; *Fax:* 403-329-4958
Toll-Free: 866-320-3898
archives@galtmuseum.com
www.galtmuseum.com/research
www.flickr.com/photos/galtmuseum; twitter.com/GaltMuseum;
www.facebook.com/GaltMuseum
Andrew Chernevych, Archivist
403-329-7302

Medicine Hat: **Esplanade Arts & Heritage Centre**
401 - 1st St. SE, Medicine Hat, AB T1A 8W2
Tel: 403-502-8582; *Fax:* 403-502-8589
archives@medicinehat.ca
www.esplanade.ca/archives
twitter.com/MedHatEsplanade;
www.facebook.com/MedHatEsplanade

Millet: **Millet & District Museum & Archives**
5120 - 50th St., Millet, AB T0C 1Z0
Tel: 780-387-5558; *Fax:* 780-387-5548
info@milletmuseum.ca
www.milletmuseum.ca/archives
twitter.com/milletmuseum;
www.facebook.com/221092931274232
Tracey Leavitt, Executive Director & Curator

Olds: **Mountain View Museum & Archives**
5038 - 50th St., Olds, AB T4H 1P6
Tel: 403-556-8464
archives@oldsmuseum.ca
www.oldsmuseum.ca
www.facebook.com/353511488101429

Red Deer: **Red Deer & District Archives**
4725 - 49th St., Red Deer, AB T4N 1T6
Tel: 403-309-8403; *Fax:* 403-340-8728
archives@reddeer.ca
www.reddeer.ca/about-red-deer/history/archives

St Albert: **Musée Héritage Museum**
5 St Anne St., St Albert, AB T8N 3Z9
Tel: 780-459-1528; *Fax:* 780-459-1232
archives@artsandheritage.ca
museeheritage.ca/archives-collections
twitter.com/artsandheritage;
www.facebook.com/ArtsAndHeritageStAlbert

Stony Plain: **The Multicultural Heritage Centre**
5411 - 51st St., Stony Plain, AB T7Z 1X7
Tel: 780-963-2777; *Fax:* 780-963-0233
info@multicentre.org
multicentre.org/museum/library-and-archives
twitter.com/MultiCentre; www.facebook.com/MultiCentre1974
Joel Wynngarden, Contact, Archives, Historical Research
joel@multicentre.org

Taber: **Taber & District Museum Society**
4702 - 50th St., Taber, AB T1G 2B6
Tel: 403-223-5708; *Fax:* 403-223-0529
tiimchin@telusplanet.net
www.facebook.com/569300306428531

Wetaskiwin: **City of Wetaskiwin Archives**
4904 - 51 St., Wetaskiwin, AB T9A 1L2
Tel: 780-361-4423
archives@wetaskiwin.ca
www.wetaskiwin.ca/107/Wetaskiwin-Archives
www.facebook.com/WetaskiwinArchives

British Columbia

Regional Systems

Cariboo Regional District Library
180 - 3rd Ave. North, #A, Williams Lake, BC V2G 2A4
Tel: 250-392-3351; *Fax:* 250-392-7399
www.cln.bc.ca
Wanda Davis, Manager, Library Services
wdavis@cariboord.bc.ca

Fraser Valley Regional Library
34589 DeLair Rd., Abbotsford, BC V2S 5Y1
Tel: 604-859-7141; *Fax:* 604-852-5701
Toll-Free: 888-668-4141
www.fvrl.bc.ca
www.youtube.com/user/FraserValleyLibrary
twitter.com/readlearnplay; www.facebook.com/ReadLearnPlay
Scott Hargrove, Chief Executive Officer
scott.hargrove@fvrl.bc.ca
Jeff Narver, Director, Infrastructure & Resources
jeff.narver@fvrl.bc.ca
Cathy Renshaw, Director, Organizational Development
cathy.renshaw@fvrl.bc.ca
Heather Scoular, Director, Customer Experience
heather.scoular@fvrl.bc.ca
Brad Fenrick, Manager, Information Technology
brad.fenrick@fvrl.bc.ca
Dean Kelly, Manager, Collections, Access & Digital Services
dean.kelly@fvrl.bc.ca

IslandLink Library Federation
3185 West Rd., Nanaimo, BC V9R 6X1
Toll-Free: 855-927-2005
islandlink.bc.libraries.coop
Laura Beswick, Manager
lbeswick@islandlink.ca
855-927-2005

Kootenay Library Federation (KLF)
PO Box 3125, Castlegar, BC V1N 3H4
Tel: 250-443-1428
klf.bc.libraries.coop
Melanie Reaveley, Executive Director
director@klf.bclibrary.ca
250-608-4490

North East Library Federation
106 Wade St., Prince George, BC V2M 6C7
Tel: 250-383-9409; *Toll-Free:* 888-387-8772
nelf.ca
Edel Toner-Rogala, Manager
etoner-rogala@nelf.ca

Northwest Library Federation
12495 Budds Rd., Prince George, BC V2N 6K7
Tel: 250-988-1860
director@nwlf.ca
nwlf.ca
Anna Babluck, Director

Okanagan Regional Library
1430 KLO Rd., Kelowna, BC V1W 3P6
Tel: 250-860-4033; *Fax:* 250-861-8696
info@orl.bc.ca
orl.bc.ca
twitter.com/ORLreads; www.facebook.com/OKRegLib
Don Nettleton, Chief Executive Officer
dnettleton@orl.bc.ca
250-860-4033 ext. 2491
James Laitinen, Head, Collection Department
jlaitinen@orl.bc.ca

Public Library InterLINK
#158, 5489 Byrne Rd., Burnaby, BC V5J 3J1
Tel: 604-437-8441; *Fax:* 604-437-8410
info@interlinklibraries.ca
www.interlinklibraries.ca
Michael Burris, Executive Director
michael.burris@interlinklibraries.ca
Allie Douglas, Office Manager
allie.douglas@interlinklibraries.ca
Candice Stenstrom, Program Coordinator
candice.stenstrom@interlinklibraries.ca

Southern Gulf Islands Community Libraries
4407 Bedwell Harbour Rd., Pender Island, BC V0N 2M1
Tel: 250-629-3722
penderislandlibrary@crd.bc.ca
sgicl.bc.libraries.coop
Carmen Oleskevich, Library Director
coleskevich@crd.bc.ca
Colette Clarke, Library Technician
cclarke@crd.bc.ca

Thompson-Nicola Regional District Library System
#100, 465 Victoria St., Kamloops, BC V2C 2A9
Tel: 250-372-5145
questions@tnrd.ca
www.tnrl.ca
www.instagram.com/tnrlibrary; twitter.com/TNRD;
www.facebook.com/tnrl.ca
Judy Moore, Chief Librarian
jmoore@tnrd.ca
250-377-7070

Vancouver Island Regional Library
6250 Hammond Bay Rd., Nanaimo, BC V9T 6M9
Tel: 250-758-4697; *Toll-Free:* 877-415-8475
info@virl.bc.ca
virl.bc.ca
www.instagram.com/vilibrary; twitter.com/VI_Library;
www.facebook.com/MyVIRL;
www.linkedin.com/company/vancouver-island-regional-library
Rosemary Bonanno, Executive Director
executivedirector@virl.bc.ca
Joel Adams, Director, Finance
jadams@virl.bc.ca
David Carson, Director, Corporate Communications & Strategic Initiatives
dcarson@virl.bc.ca
Melissa Legacy, Director, Library Services & Planning
mjlegacy@virl.bc.ca

Public Libraries

Alert Bay: **Alert Bay Public Library & Museum**
116 Fir St., Alert Bay, BC V0N 1A0
Tel: 250-974-5721
abplb@island.net
alertbay.bc.libraries.coop
www.facebook.com/alertbaypubliclibrary
Joyce Wilby, Library Director & Community Librarian

Atlin: **Atlin Library**
Courthouse Bldg., Atlin, BC V0W 1A0

Bowen Island: **Bowen Island Public Library**
430 Bowen Trunk Rd., Bowen Island, BC V0N 1G0
Tel: 604-947-9788
info@bowenlibrary.ca
bowenlibrary.ca
www.facebook.com/bowenislandpubliclibrary
Tina Nielsen, Chief Librarian

Burnaby: **Burnaby Public Library**
6100 Willingdon Ave., Burnaby, BC V5H 4N5
Tel: 604-436-5427; *Fax:* 604-436-2961
Other Numbers: Telcirc: 604-293-0034
bpl@bpl.bc.ca
www.bpl.bc.ca
twitter.com/burnabypl; www.facebook.com/burnabypubliclibrary
Beth Davies, Chief Librarian
beth.davies@bpl.bc.ca
604-436-5431
Trish Mau, Assistant Director, Collections & Technology
trish.mau@bpl.bc.ca
Heidi Schiller, Assistant Director, Public Service
heidi.schiller@bpl.bc.ca
604-436-5432

Burns Lake: **Burns Lake Public Library**
585 Government St., Burns Lake, BC V0J 1E0
Tel: 250-692-3192; *Fax:* 250-692-7488
libraryn@burnslakelibrary.com
burnslake.bc.libraries.coop
www.facebook.com/outofthelibrary
Monika Willner, Library Director
monika@burnslakelibray.com
Robert McKenzie, Acting Assistant Director
roberta@burnslakelibrary.com
Bonny Remple, Children's Librarian
bonny@burnslakelibrary.com

Castlegar: **Castlegar & District Public Library**
1005 - 3rd St., Castlegar, BC V1N 2A2
Tel: 250-365-6611; *Fax:* 250-365-7765
info@castlegarlibrary.com
castlegar.bc.libraries.coop
www.facebook.com/castlegarlibrary
Kimberly Partanen, Library Director
director@castlegarlibrary.com
Julie Kalesnikoff, Librarian
Vera Terpin, Librarian

Chetwynd: **Chetwynd Public Library**
5012 - 46th St., Chetwynd, BC V0C 1J0
Tel: 250-788-2559; *Fax:* 250-788-2186
cpl@chetwynd.bclibrary.ca
chetwynd.bc.libraries.coop
www.pinterest.com/chetwyndlibrary;
twitter.com/ChetwyndLibrary;
www.facebook.com/chetwyndpubliclibrary
Dana Bergen, Chair
Melissa Millsap, Director
librarydirector@chetwynd.bclibrary.ca

Coquitlam: **Coquitlam Public Library**
575 Poirier St., Coquitlam, BC V3J 6A9
Tel: 604-937-4141
askalibrarian@coqlibrary.ca
www.coqlibrary.ca
www.instagram.com/coqlibrary; twitter.com/CoqLibrary;
www.facebook.com/CoqLibrary
Todd Gnissios, Executive Director
tgnissios@coqlibrary.ca
604-937-4130
Silvana Harwood, Deputy Director
sharwood@coqlibrary.ca
604-937-4130
Anthea Goffe, Director, Community Engagement
agoffe@coqlibrary.ca
604-554-7347

Cranbrook: **Cranbrook Public Library**
1212 - 2nd St. North, Cranbrook, BC V1C 4T6
Tel: 250-426-4063; *Fax:* 250-426-2098
staff@cranbrookpubliclibrary.ca
cranbrookpubliclibrary.ca
www.facebook.com/CranbrookPublicLibrary

Crawford Bay: **East Shore Community Library (Reading Centre)**
16234 King Rd., Crawford Bay, BC V0B 1E0
Tel: 250-777-7741
escomlib@gmail.com
www.facebook.com/escomlib

Creston: **Creston Public Library**
531 - 16th Ave. South, Creston, BC V0B 1G5
Tel: 250-428-4141; *Fax:* 250-428-4703
info@crestonlibrary.com
www.crestonlibrary.com
www.facebook.com/crestonlibrary
Saara Itkonen, Library Director
saara@crestonlibrary.com

Dawson Creek: **Dawson Creek Municipal Public Library**
1001 McKellar Ave., Dawson Creek, BC V1G 4W7
Tel: 250-782-4661; *Fax:* 250-782-4667
dclib@pris.ca
dawsoncreek.bc.libraries.coop
www.facebook.com/183700895048680
Pamela Morris, Head Librarian
Laurie Youb, Assistant Librarian

Edgewood: **Inonoaklin Valley Reading Centre**
409 Monashee Ave., Edgewood, BC V0G 1J0
Tel: 250-269-7212; *Fax:* 250-269-7633

Elkford: **Elkford Public Library**
816 Michel Rd., Elkford, BC V0B 1H0
Tel: 250-865-2912; *Fax:* 250-865-2460
info@elkfordlibrary.org
elkford.bc.libraries.coop
www.facebook.com/elkfordlibrary
Alexandra Faucher, Director
Jeanette Fairbairn, Library Clerk
Paula Nyuli, Library Clerk

Fernie: **Fernie Heritage Library**
492 - 3rd Ave., Fernie, BC V0B 1M0
Tel: 250-423-4458; *Fax:* 250-423-7906
information@fernieheritagelibrary.com
fernie.bc.libraries.coop
www.facebook.com/FernieHeritageLibrary
Emma Dressler, Director

Fort Nelson: **Fort Nelson Public Library**
Municipal Square, 5315 - 50th Ave. South, #A2, Fort Nelson, BC V0C 1R0
Tel: 250-774-6777; *Fax:* 250-774-6777
fnpl@fortnelson.bclibrary.ca
fortnelson.bc.libraries.coop
www.facebook.com/FNPLibrary
Shirley Kenney, Chair
Danika Andrews, Library Director
librarian@fortnelson.bclibrary.ca
Everly Radford, Librarian, Adult Services & Local History
eradford@fortnelson.bclibrary.ca
Shannon Chabot, Librarian, Children & Youth Services
schabot@fortnelson.bclibrary.ca
Hannah Waughtal, Contact, Interlibrary Loans
bfn.ill@fortnelson.bclibrary.ca

Fort St James: **Fort St James Public Library**
425 Manson St., Fort St James, BC V0J 1P0
Tel: 250-996-7431; *Fax:* 250-996-7484
librarian@fortstjames.bclibrary.ca
fortstjames.bc.libraries.coop
www.facebook.com/FortStJamesLibrary
Louise Evans-Salt, Chair
Karli Fisher, Library Director

Fort St John: **Fort St John Public Library**
10015 - 100th Ave., Fort St John, BC V1J 1Y7
Tel: 250-785-3731; *Fax:* 250-785-7982
www.fsjpl.ca
www.facebook.com/fsjlibrary
Matthew Rankin, Director

Fraser Lake: **Fraser Lake Public Library**
228 Endako Ave., Fraser Lake, BC V0J 1S0
Tel: 250-699-8888; *Fax:* 250-699-8899
fllibrarian@bcgroup.net
fraserlake.bc.libraries.coop
www.facebook.com/fraserlake.ca

Anne Marie Pond, Chair
Audrey Fennema, Chief Librarian
Jesii Gammie, Library Assistant
Irene Greenlees, Library Assistant
Teri Poncia, Library Assistant

Fruitvale: Beaver Valley Public Library
1847 - 1st St., Fruitvale, BC V0G 1L0
Tel: 250-367-7114; *Fax:* 250-367-7130
bvpublic@telus.net
beavervalley.bc.libraries.coop
www.facebook.com/527274463973725
Darrel Ganzert, Chair
Marie Onyett, Head Librarian

Galiano Island: Galiano Island Community Library
#2, 1290 Sturdies Bay Rd., Galiano Island, BC V0N 1P0
Tel: 250-539-2141
galianolibrary@gmail.com
sgicl.bc.libraries.coop
www.facebook.com/galianolibrary

Gibsons: Gibsons & District Public Library
470 South Fletcher Rd., Gibsons, BC V0N 1V0
Tel: 604-886-2130; *Fax:* 604-886-2689
gdplinfo@gibsons.bclibrary.ca
gibsons.bc.libraries.coop
www.facebook.com/gibsonslibrary
Heather Evans-Cullen, Library Director
Susanne Larose-Cloherty, Coordinator, Circulation Services

Grand Forks: Grand Forks & District Public Library
7342 - 5th St., Grand Forks, BC V0H 1H0
Tel: 250-442-3944
library@gfpl.ca
grandforks.bc.libraries.coop
www.facebook.com/grandforkslibrary
Mary Kierans, Chair
Cari Lynn Gawletz, Library Director
director@gfpl.ca

Granisle: Granisle Public Library
#2 Village Sq., McDonald Ave., Granisle, BC V0J 1W0
Tel: 250-697-2713
library@granisle.net
granisle.bc.libraries.coop
www.facebook.com/granislepublib
Lora Hunsakerl, Chair
Lisa Rees, Chief Librarian

Grasmere: Grasmere Reading Centre
PO Box 75, Grasmere, BC V0B 1R0
Tel: 250-887-3487

Greenwood: Greenwood Public Library
346 South Copper Ave., Greenwood, BC V0H 1J0
Tel: 250-445-6111; *Fax:* 250-445-6111
greenlib@shaw.ca
greenwood.bc.libraries.coop
www.facebook.com/1002320859873941
Judy Foucher, Library Director

Hazelton: Hazelton & District Public Library
4255 Government St., Hazelton, BC V0J 1Y0
Tel: 250-842-5961; *Fax:* 250-842-2176
hazlib@citywest.ca
hazelton.bc.libraries.coop
www.facebook.com/hazeltonpubliclibrary
Braunwyn Henwood, Chair
Brian Butler, Head Librarian

Houston: Houston Public Library
3150 - 14th St., Houston, BC V0J 1Z0
Tel: 250-845-2256; *Fax:* 250-845-2088
admin@houstonlibrary.ca
houston.bc.libraries.coop
www.facebook.com/Gr8reads
Allen Elliott, Chair
Sara Lewis, Library Director

Hudson's Hope: Hudson's Hope Public Library
9905 Dudley Dr., Hudson's Hope, BC V0C 1V0
Tel: 250-783-9414; *Fax:* 250-783-5272
director.hhpl@pris.ca
hudsonshope.bc.libraries.coop
www.facebook.com/hudsonshopepubliclibrary
Amber Norton, Library Director

Invermere: Invermere Public Library
646 - 4th St., Invermere, BC V0A 1K0
Tel: 250-342-6416; *Fax:* 250-342-6461
publiclibrary@invermere.net
invermere.bc.libraries.coop
www.pinterest.com/InvLibrary; twitter.com/invermerelib;
www.facebook.com/invermerelibrary
Anne Rogers, Library Director
Virginia Walker, Librarian

Kaslo: Kaslo & District Public Library
Kaslo Village Hall, 413 - 4th St., Kaslo, BC V0G 1M0
Tel: 250-353-2942; *Fax:* 250-353-2943
info@kaslo.bclibrary.ca
kaslo.bc.libraries.coop
www.facebook.com/209955515837450
Eva Kelemen, Library Director
Angela Bennett, Program Coordinator

Kimberley: Kimberley Public Library
115 Spokane St., Kimberley, BC V1A 2E5
Tel: 250-427-3112; *Fax:* 250-427-7157
staff@kimberleylibrary.net
kimberley.bc.libraries.coop
twitter.com/Library_KPL;
www.facebook.com/kimberleylibrary.net
Karin von Wittgenstein, Chief Librarian & Library Director

Kitimat: Kitimat Public Library
940 Wakashan Ave., Kitimat, BC V8C 2G3
Tel: 250-632-8985; *Fax:* 250-632-2630
ask@kitimatlibrary.ca
kitimatlibrary.ca
www.facebook.com/kitimatlibrary
Virginia Charron, Director
vcharron@kitimatlibrary.ca

Kitwanga: Gitanyow Independent School Reading Centre
PO Box 369, Kitwanga, BC V0J 3A0
Tel: 250-849-5528; *Fax:* 250-849-5870
Other Numbers: Administration: 250-849-5384
www.gitanyow.ca
Jacqueline Smith, Administrator
jsmith@gitanyow.ca

Lillooet: Lillooet & Area Public Library Association
930 Main St., Lillooet, BC V0K 1V0
Tel: 250-256-7944; *Fax:* 866-704-3340
lala@lillooet.bclibrary.ca
lillooet.bc.libraries.coop
www.facebook.com/LillooetPublicLibrary
Toby Mueller, Library Director
Stephanie Witt, Branch & Community Librarian
Cindy MacDonald, Community Librarian
Michelle Smith, Community Librarian
Christina Timms, Librarian, Children & Outreach

Mackenzie: MacKenzie Public Library
Recreation Centre, 400 Skeena Dr., Mackenzie, BC V0J 2C0
Tel: 250-997-6343; *Fax:* 250-997-5792
mackenziepubliclibrary@gmail.com
mackenzie.bc.libraries.coop
www.facebook.com/MackenziePublicLibrary
Alice Pek, Acting Library Director
alice.pek@mackenzie.bc.libraries.coop

Madeira Park: Pender Harbour Reading Centre
12952 Madeira Park Rd., Madeira Park, BC V0N 2H1
Tel: 604-883-2983
phrclibrary@gmail.com
penderharbourlibrary.ca
Karen Dyck, Chair

Mayne Island: Mayne Island Community Library
411 Naylor Rd., Mayne Island, BC V0N 2J0
Tel: 250-539-2597
mipl@shaw.ca
sgicl.bc.libraries.coop
www.facebook.com/1583884845158917

McBride: McBride & District Public Library
521 Main St., McBride, BC V0J 2E0
Tel: 250-569-2411; *Fax:* 250-569-0000
library@mcbridebc.org
mcbride.bc.libraries.coop
Abi Ward, Library Director
Doreen Beck, Assistant Librarian, Acquisitions & Collections Management

Midway: Midway Public Library
612 - 6th Ave., Midway, BC V0H 1M0
Tel: 250-449-2620; *Fax:* 250-449-2389
midwaypubliclibrary@gmail.com
midway.bc.libraries.coop
Sasha Tauzer, Director

Nakusp: Nakusp Public Library Association
92 - 6th Ave. NW, Nakusp, BC V0G 1R0
Tel: 250-265-3363
contact@nakusplibrary.ca
nakusplibrary.ca
www.facebook.com/NakuspPublicLibrary
Claire Paradis, Library Director
Susan Rogers, Librarian

Nelson: Nelson Public Library
602 Stanley St., Nelson, BC V1L 1N4
Tel: 250-352-6333
info@nelson.ca
nelson.bc.libraries.coop
twitter.com/NelsonPLibrary;
www.facebook.com/nelsonpubliclibrary
Tracey Therrien, Chief Librarian

New Denver: New Denver Reading Centre
521 - 6th Ave., New Denver, BC V0G 1S0
Tel: 250-358-2221
newdenver.ca/amenities/the-reading-centre

New Westminster: New Westminster Public Library
716 - 6th Ave., New Westminster, BC V3M 2B3
Tel: 604-527-4660
askus@nwpl.ca
www.nwpl.ca
twitter.com/nwplibrary; www.facebook.com/NWPLibrary
Julie Spurrell, Chief Librarian
jspurrell@nwpl.ca
604-527-4675
Susan Buss, Deputy Chief Librarian
sbuss@nwpl.ca
604-527-4669
Adam Farrell, Manager, Technology & Technical Services
afarrell@nwpl.ca
604-527-4671
Christopher Koth, Manager, Programs & Community Development
ckoth@nwpl.ca
604-527-4678
Shelley Wilson-Roberts, Manager, Public Services
swilson-roberts@nwpl.ca
604-527-4661

North Vancouver: North Vancouver City Library
120 - 14th St. West, North Vancouver, BC V7M 1N9
Tel: 604-998-3450; *Fax:* 604-983-3624
info@nvcl.ca
www.nvcl.ca
www.pinterest.com/nvcitylibrary; twitter.com/NorthVanCityLib;
www.facebook.com/NorthVanCityLibrary
Deb Hutchison Koep, Chief Librarian
dkoep@cnv.org
604-990-4226

North Vancouver: North Vancouver District Public Library
#300, 1277 Lynn Valley Rd., North Vancouver, BC V7J 0A2
Tel: 604-990-5800; *Fax:* 604-984-7600
info@nvdpl.ca
nvdpl.ca
twitter.com/nvdpl; www.facebook.com/nvdpl
Jacqueline van Dyk, Director, Library Services
jvandyk@nvdpl.ca
604-990-3740
Alison Campbell, Manager, Community Connections
alicam@nvdpl.ca
604-990-5800 ext. 8118

Pemberton: Pemberton & District Public Library
7390A Cottonwood St., Pemberton, BC V0N 2L0
Tel: 604-894-6916
library@pemberton.bclibrary.ca
pemberton.bc.libraries.coop
www.instagram.com/pembylibrary; twitter.com/pembylibrary;
www.facebook.com/pembertonlibrary
Emma Gillis, Library Director
egillis@pemberton.bclibrary.ca
Gen Zichy, Senior Library Assistant
gzichy@pemberton.bclibrary.ca

Pender Island: Pender Island Public Library
4407 Bedwell Harbour Rd., Pender Island, BC V0N 2M1
Tel: 250-629-3722
penderislandlibrary@crd.bc.ca
sgicl.bc.libraries.coop
www.facebook.com/946941972027284

Penticton: Penticton Public Library
785 Main St., Penticton, BC V2A 5E3
Tel: 250-770-7781
info@pentictonlibrary.ca
pentictonlibrary.ca
www.facebook.com/PentictonPublicLibrary
Heather Buzzell, Chief Librarian

Port Moody: Port Moody Public Library
100 Newport Dr., Port Moody, BC V3H 5C3
Tel: 604-469-4577; *Fax:* 604-469-4576
Other Numbers: Admin: 604-469-4686
askthelibrary@portmoody.ca
library.portmoody.ca
twitter.com/PoMoLibrary; www.facebook.com/pomolibrary;
www.linkedin.com/company/port-moody-public-library
Marc Saunders, Director, Library Services
604-469-4580

Pouce Coupe: Pouce Coupe Public Library
5010 - 52nd Ave., Pouce Coupe, BC V0C 2C0
Tel: 250-786-5765; *Fax:* 250-786-5761
bpoc.ill@pris.bc.ca
poucecoupe.bc.libraries.coop
www.facebook.com/PouceCoupePublicLibrary
Cindy Blayney, Chair
Courtenay Johnston, Library Director

Powell River: Powell River Public Library
#100, 6975 Alberni St., Powell River, BC V8A 2B8
Tel: 604-485-4796
info@prpl.ca
prpl.ca
twitter.com/PRPublicLibrary;
www.facebook.com/PowellRiverPublicLibrary
Rebecca Burbank, Chief Librarian
604-485-4796 ext. 202

Prince George: Prince George Public Library
888 Canada Games Way, Prince George, BC V2L 5T6
Tel: 250-563-9251
ask@pgpl.ca
www.pgpl.ca
www.youtube.com/user/pglibrary; twitter.com/pg_library;
www.facebook.com/pglibrary
Paul Burry, Library Director
pburry@pgpl.ca
250-563-9251 ext. 130
Ignacio Albarracin, Manager, Collections & Technology
ialbarracin@pgpl.ca
250-563-9251 ext. 158
Amy Dhanjal, Manager, Communications & Engagement
adhanjal@pgpl.ca
250-563-9251 ext. 128
Sheila Littler, Manager, Customer Experience & Service Delivery
slittler@pgpl.ca
250-563-9251 ext. 143
Jody Tindill, Manager, Finance & Facilities
jtindill@pgpl.ca
250-563-9251 ext. 122

Prince Rupert: Prince Rupert Public Library
101 - 6th Ave. West, Prince Rupert, BC V8J 1Y9
Tel: 250-627-1345; *Fax:* 250-627-7851
info@princerupertlibrary.ca
www.princerupertlibrary.ca
www.instagram.com/princerupertlibrary;
www.facebook.com/PrinceRupertLibrary
Joe Zelwietro, Chief Librarian
Kathleen Larkin, Deputy Librarian

Radium Hot Springs: Radium Public Library
4863 Stanley St., Radium Hot Springs, BC V0A 1M0
Tel: 250-347-2434
info@radium.bclibrary.ca
radium.bc.libraries.coop
www.facebook.com/RadiumPublicLibrary
Jacqueline Wagner, Director

Richmond: Richmond Public Library
#100, 7700 Minoru Gate, Richmond, BC V6Y 1R8
Tel: 604-231-6422
Other Numbers: Adult Ask Me Desk: 604-231-6413
rpl.yourlibrary.ca
www.instagram.com/rplbc; twitter.com/RPLBC;
www.facebook.com/yourlibraryRichmond

Susan Walters, Chief Librarian & Secretary to the Board
Mark Ellis, Manager, Information Technology
Shaneena Rahman, Manager, Customer Experience

Riondel: Riondel Community Library
PO Box 29, Riondel, BC V0B 2B0
Tel: 250-225-3242
the_librarian@bluebell.ca
library.riondel.ca

Roberts Creek: Roberts Creek Community Library
1044 Roberts Creek Rd., Roberts Creek, BC V0N 2W0
Tel: 604-885-9401
www.robertscreekcommunity.com/the-library
www.facebook.com/RobertsCreekCommunityLibrary

Rossland: Rossland Public Library
2180 Columbia Ave., Rossland, BC V0G 1Y0
Tel: 250-362-7611
info@rossland.bclibrary.ca
rossland.bc.libraries.coop
www.instagram.com/rosslandpubliclibrary;
twitter.com/RosslandLibrary;
www.facebook.com/RosslandPublicLibrary
Stacey Boden, Library Director
director@rossland.bclibrary.ca
Lynn Amann, Children's Librarian
children@rossland.bclibrary.ca

Salmo: Salmo Valley Public Library
104 - 4th St., Salmo, BC V0G 1Z0
Tel: 250-357-2312; *Fax:* 250-357-2312
salmolibrary@salmo.bc.libraries.coop
salmo.bc.libraries.coop
www.facebook.com/salmolibrary
Taylor Caron, Library Director
tcaron@salmo.bc.libraries.coop

Salt Spring Island: Salt Spring Island Public Library
129 McPhillips Ave., Salt Spring Island, BC V8K 2T6
Tel: 250-537-4666
info@saltspringlibrary.com
saltspring.bc.libraries.coop
twitter.com/ssilibrary;
www.facebook.com/SaltSpringIslandPublicLibrary
Karen Hudson, Chief Librarian
khudson@saltspringlibrary.com
Nikky McCarvill, Librarian
nmccarvill@saltspringlibrary.com

Saturna Island: Saturna Island Community Library
140 East Point Rd., Saturna Island, BC V0N 2Y0
Tel: 250-539-5312
saturnaislandlibrary@gmail.com
sgicl.bc.libraries.coop
www.facebook.com/103170521250035

Sechelt: Sechelt Public Library
5797 Cowrie St., Sechelt, BC V0N 3A0
Tel: 604-885-3260; *Fax:* 604-885-5183
info@sechelt.bclibrary.ca
sechelt.bc.libraries.coop
twitter.com/SecheltLibrary; www.facebook.com/secheltlibrary
Leianne Emery, Library Director
leianne.emery@secheltlibrary.ca

Sidney: Piers Island Community Library
PO Box 2223, Sidney, BC V8L 3S8
libraryonpiers@gmail.com
sgicl.bc.libraries.coop
www.facebook.com/104362414768957

Smithers: Smithers Public Library
3817 Alfred Ave., Smithers, BC V0J 2N0
Tel: 250-847-3043; *Fax:* 250-847-1533
contact@smitherslibrary.ca
smithers.bc.libraries.coop
twitter.com/smitherslibrary; www.facebook.com/smitherslibrary
Wendy Wright, Library Director
director@smitherslibrary.ca

Sparwood: Sparwood Public Library
110 Pine Ave., Sparwood, BC V0B 2G0
Tel: 250-425-2299; *Fax:* 250-425-0229
sparwood.bc.libraries.coop
www.facebook.com/groups/sparwoodlibrary
James Bertoia, Head Librarian
jb@sparwoodlibrary.ca

Squamish: Squamish Public Library
37907 - 2nd Ave., Squamish, BC V8B 0A7
Tel: 604-892-3110; *Fax:* 604-892-9376
library@squamish.ca
squamishlibrary.ca
twitter.com/squamishlibrary;
www.facebook.com/SquamishLibrary
Hilary Bloom, Director, Library Services
librarydirector@squamish.ca
604-892-3110 ext. 5303

Stewart: Stewart Public Library
322 - 5th Ave., Stewart, BC V0T 1W0
Tel: 236-636-2380
stewartpubliclibrary@gmail.com
stewart.bc.libraries.coop
Rebecca Mitchell, Director

Surrey: Surrey Libraries
City Centre Library, 10350 University Dr., 3rd Fl., Surrey, BC V3T 4B8
Tel: 604-598-7901
www.surreylibraries.ca
www.instagram.com/surreylibraries; twitter.com/surreylibrary;
www.facebook.com/surreylibraries
Surinder Bhogal, Chief Librarian
sbhogal@surrey.ca

Taylor: Taylor Public Library
10008 - 104th Ave., Taylor, BC V0C 2K0
Tel: 250-789-9878
library@districtoftaylor.com
taylor.bc.libraries.coop
twitter.com/TaylorBCLibrary;
www.facebook.com/325257110840343
Sherry Murphy, Library Director

Terrace: Terrace Public Library Association
4610 Park Ave., Terrace, BC V8G 1V6
Tel: 250-638-8177; *Fax:* 250-635-6207
library@terracelibrary.ca
www.terracelibrary.ca
www.facebook.com/TerracePublicLibrary

Trail: Trail & District Public Library
1505 Bay Ave., Trail, BC V1R 4B2
Tel: 250-364-1731
www.traillibrary.com
twitter.com/TrailPublic; www.facebook.com/TrailLibrary

Tumbler Ridge: Tumbler Ridge Public Library
340 Front St., Tumbler Ridge, BC V0C 2W0
Tel: 250-242-4778; *Fax:* 250-242-4707
info@trlibrary.org
tumblerridgelibrary.org
www.facebook.com/TumblerRidgePublicLibrary
Paula Coutts, Head Librarian
Chris Norbury, Children's Librarian

Valemount: Valemount Public Library
1090A Main St., Valemount, BC V0E 2Z0
Tel: 250-566-4367; *Fax:* 250-566-4278
library@valemount.ca
valemount.bc.libraries.coop
www.facebook.com/218260084896402
Wendy Cinnamon, Chief Librarian

Vancouver: Isaac Waldman Jewish Public Library
Jewish Community Centre of Greater Vancouver, 950 West 41st Ave., 2nd Fl., Vancouver, BC V5Z 2N7
Tel: 604-257-5181
library@jccgv.bc.ca
www.jccgv.com/art-and-culture/library
www.facebook.com/IWJPL;

Vancouver: Vancouver Public Library
350 West Georgia St., Vancouver, BC V6B 6B1
Tel: 604-331-3603
info@vpl.ca
www.vpl.ca
www.youtube.com/user/vancouverlibrary; twitter.com/VPL;
www.facebook.com/vancouverpubliclibrary
Christina de Castell, Chief Librarian & CEO
christina.decastell@vpl.ca
604-331-4003
Kay Cahill, Director, Collections & Technology
kay.cahill@vpl.ca
604-331-4070
Julie Iannacone, Director, Neighbourhood & Youth Services
julie.iannacone@vpl.ca
604-331-4005
Dawn Ibey, Director, Library Experience
dawn.ibey@vpl.ca
604-331-4004

Julia Morrison, Director, Corporate Services & Facilities
julia.morrison@vpl.ca
604-331-3761
Carol Nelson, Director, Planning & Communications
carol.nelson@vpl.ca
604-331-4006
Balwinder Rai, Director, Human Resources
balwinder.rai@vpl.ca
604-331-4051

Vanderhoof: Vanderhoof Public Library
230 Stewart St. East, Vanderhoof, BC V0J 3A0
Tel: 250-567-4060
info@vanderhooflibrary.com
www.vanderhooflibrary.com
www.facebook.com/109105738170
Donna Klingspohn, Chair
Jennifer Barg, Chief Librarian
jennifer@vanderhooflibrary.com
Sara Hara, Librarian
sara@vanderhooflibrary.com

Victoria: British Columbia Ministry of Education
PO Box 9831, Stn Provincial Government, Victoria, BC V8W 9T1
Tel: 250-356-1791; *Fax:* 250-953-4985
Toll-Free: 800-663-7051
llb@gov.bc.ca
www2.gov.bc.ca/gov/content/sports-culture
twitter.com/MyBCLibrary
Mari Martin, Director
mari.martin@gov.bc.ca

Victoria: Greater Victoria Public Library
735 Broughton St., Victoria, BC V8W 3H2
Tel: 250-940-4875
www.gvpl.ca
twitter.com/gvpl; www.facebook.com/greatervictoriapubliclibrary
Maureen Sawa, Chief Executive Officer
msawa@gvpl.ca
250-940-1193
Debbie Main, Director, People & Culture
dmain@gvpl.ca
250-413-0359
Paul McKinnon, Director, Finance & Facilities
pmckinnon@gvpl.ca
250-413-0355
Jennifer Windecker, Director, Innovation & Delivery
jwindecker@gvpl.ca
250-413-0382
Daphne Wood, Director, Information Technology
dwood@gvpl.ca
250-413-0370

Victoria: View Royal Reading Centre
266 Island Hwy., Victoria, BC V9B 1G5
Tel: 250-479-2723
vivr.ill@shaw.ca
www.viewroyal.ca/EN/main/discover/public-facilities/libraries.html
www.facebook.com/libraryviewroyal

West Vancouver: West Vancouver Memorial Library
1950 Marine Dr., West Vancouver, BC V7V 1J8
Tel: 604-925-7400; *Fax:* 604-925-5933
info@westvanlibrary.ca
westvanlibrary.ca
www.instagram.com/westvanlibrary; twitter.com/westvanlibrary;
www.facebook.com/WestVancouverMemorialLibrary
Stephanie Hall, Director
shall@westvanlibrary.ca
604-925-7424
Sukh Gill, Head, Finance & Facilities
sgill@westvanlibrary.ca
604-925-7431
Tara Matsuzaki, Head, Customer & Community Experience
tmatsuzaki@westvanlibrary.ca
604-921-2143
Michelle Yule, Head, Collections
myule@westvanlibrary.ca
604-925-7420

Whistler: Whistler Public Library
4329 Main St., Whistler, BC V0N 1B4
Tel: 604-935-8435
publicservices@whistlerlibrary.ca
www.whistlerlibrary.ca
www.facebook.com/whistlerpubliclibrary
Elizabeth Tracy, Library Director
etracy@whistlerlibrary.ca
604-935-8438

Timothy Kuelker, Librarian, Technology & Support Services
tkuelker@whistlerlibrary.ca
604-935-8433 ext. 8729
Kaley O'Brien, Librarian, Youth Services
kobrien@whistlerlibrary.ca
604-935-8433 ext. 8726
Nadine White, Librarian, Public Services
nwhite@whistlerlibrary.ca
604-935-8433 ext. 8725

Archives

Abbotsford: Heritage Abbostsford Society - Trethewey House Heritage Site
2313 Ware St., Abbotsford, BC V2S 3C6
Tel: 604-853-0313; *Fax:* 866-373-2771
communications@heritageabbotsford.ca
www.tretheweyhouse.ca
twitter.com/TretheweyHouse;
www.facebook.com/TretheweyHeritageSite
Christina Reid, Executive Director
creid@tretheweyhouse.ca
Lorisa Williams, Manager, Collections
admin@tretheweyhouse.ca

Alert Bay: U'mista Cultural Centre
1 Front St., Alert Bay, BC V0N 1A0
Tel: 250-974-5403; *Fax:* 250-974-5499
Toll-Free: 800-690-8222
info@umista.ca
www.umista.ca
www.facebook.com/Umista.Cultural.Society
Juanita Johnston, Director, Collections & Tourism
juanita@umista.ca

Ashcroft: Ashcroft Museum
402 Brink St., Ashcroft, BC V0K 1A0
Tel: 250-453-9232
museum@ashcroftbc.ca
ashcroftbc.ca/museum
Kathy Paulos, Curator

Barkerville: Barkerville Historic Town
14301 Hwy. 26 East, Barkerville, BC V0K 1B0
Tel: 604-994-3332; *Fax:* 250-994-3435
Toll-Free: 888-994-3332
barkerville@barkerville.ca
www.barkerville.ca/archives
twitter.com/BarkervilleBC
Mandy Kilsby, Curator
mandy.kilsby@barkerville.ca
888-994-3332 ext. 35

Bella Bella: Heiltsuk Cultural Education Centre
PO Box 880, Bella Bella, BC V0T 1Z0
Tel: 250-957-2626; *Fax:* 250-957-2780
hcec.bellabella@gmail.com
hcec.ca
Jennifer Carpenter, Director
jennifer.carpenter@heiltsuk.ca

Burnaby: Nikkei National Museum & Cultural Centre
6688 Southoaks Cres., Burnaby, BC V5E 4M7
Tel: 604-777-7000; *Fax:* 604-777-7001
info@nikkeiplace.org
centre.nikkeiplace.org
www.youtube.com/user/nikkeimuse; twitter.com/nikkeimuse;
www.facebook.com/NNMCC
Karah Goshinmon Foster, Executive Director
kgoshinmon@nikkeiplace.org
604-777-7000 ext. 110
Sherri Kajiwara, Director & Curator
skajiwara@nikkeiplace.org
604-777-7000 ext. 112
Linda Kawamoto Reid, Research Archivist
lreid@nikkeiplace.org
604-777-7000 ext. 111

Campbell River: Museum at Campbell River
470 Island Hwy., Campbell River, BC V9W 2B7
Tel: 250-287-3103; *Fax:* 250-286-0109
general.inquiries@crmuseum.ca
crmuseum.ca/learn/archives-research-centre
www.instagram.com/museumatcampbellriver;
twitter.com/crmuseum1;
www.facebook.com/museumatcampbellriver
Megan Purcell, Collections Manager
megan.purcell@crmuseum.ca
Beth Boyce, Curator & Education Manager
beth.boyce@crmuseum.ca

Chilliwack: Chilliwack Archives
Evergreen Hall, 9291 Corbould St., Chilliwack, BC V2P 4A6
Tel: 604-795-5210
www.chilliwackmuseum.ca/research/archives
Tristan Evans, Archivist
tristan@chilliwackmuseum.ca
604-795-5210 ext. 104

Cranbrook: Canadian Museum of Rail Travel
57 Van Horne St. South, Cranbrook, BC V1C 4H9
Tel: 250-489-3918; *Fax:* 250-489-5744
www.cranbrookhistorycentre.com
www.cranbrookhistorycentre.com/learn/archives-collections
Honor Neve, Chief Curator

Cumberland: Cumberland Museum & Archives
2680 Dunsmuir Ave., Cumberland, BC V0R 1S0
Tel: 250-336-2445
info@cumberlandmuseum.ca
www.cumberlandmuseum.ca
www.facebook.com/cumberlandbc.museum
Rosslyn Shipp, Executive Director
director@cumberlandmuseum.ca
Lia Tarle, Curator
curator@cumberlandmuseum.ca

Delta: City of Delta
4450 Clarence Taylor Cres., Delta, BC V4K 3W3
Tel: 604-952-3836
deltaarchives@delta.ca
www.delta.ca/discover-delta/archives
Robert Sullivan, Manager, Cultural Services
rsullivan@delta.ca
604-952-3540
Michelle Taylor, Curator
rsullivan@delta.ca
604-952-3837
Kevin Hicks, Assistant, Collections
khicks@delta.ca
604-952-3829

Duncan: Cowichan Valley Museum & Archives
Duncan City Hall, 3rd Fl., Duncan, BC V9L 3Y2
Tel: 250-746-6612; *Fax:* 250-746-6612
www.cowichanvalleymuseum.bc.ca/archives

Esquimalt: Township of Esquimalt
1149A Esquimalt Rd., Esquimalt, BC V9A 3N6
Tel: 250-412-8540; *Fax:* 250-414-7111
archives@esquimalt.ca
www.esquimalt.ca/culture-heritage/archives
Jessica Nichol, Archivist & Records Coordinator

Fort Langley: Langley Centennial Museum & National Exhibition Centre
9135 King St., Fort Langley, BC V1M 2S2
Tel: 604-532-3536
museum@tol.ca
museum.tol.ca

Fort St John: Fort St John - North Peace Museum
9323 - 100th St., Fort St John, BC V1J 4N4
Tel: 250-787-0430
fsjnpmuseum@fsjmail.com
fsjmuseum.com
www.facebook.com/FSJMuseum
Heather Sjoblom, Manager & Curator

Fort Steele: Fort Steele Heritage Town
9851 Hwy. 93/95, Fort Steele, BC V0B 1N0
Tel: 250-417-6000
info@fortsteele.bc.ca
fortsteele.ca
www.facebook.com/fortsteeleheritagetown
Jessica Marusyk, Manager
jessica.johnson@fortsteele.bc.ca
Jessica VanOostwaard, Curator
jessica.vanoostwaard@fortsteele.bc.ca

Golden: Golden Museum & Archives
PO Box 992, Golden, BC V0A 1H0
Tel: 250-344-5169
museum.golden@gmail.com
goldenbcmuseums.com
www.facebook.com/museum.golden

Harrison Mills: Kilby Historic Site Museum
215 Kilby Rd., Harrison Mills, BC V0M 1L0
Tel: 604-796-9576; *Fax:* 604-796-9592
info@kilby.ca
www.kilby.ca
www.instagram.com/kilbyhistoricsite; twitter.com/kilbyhistoricsi;
www.facebook.com/kilbyhistoricsite
Jo-Anne Leon, Curator

Hazelton: 'Ksan Historical Village & Museum
PO Box 440, Hazelton, BC V0J 1Y0
Tel: 250-842-5544; *Toll-Free:* 877-842-5518
ksan@gitanmaax.com

Kamloops: Kamloops Museum & Archives
207 Seymour St., Kamloops, BC V2C 2E7
Tel: 250-828-3576; *Fax:* 250-828-3760
museum@kamloops.ca
www.kamloops.ca/museum
twitter.com/kamloopsmuseum;
www.facebook.com/kamloopsmuseum
Jaimie Fedorak, Archivist

Kaslo: Kootenay Lake Archives
312 - 4th St., Kaslo, BC V0G 1M0
Tel: 250-353-3204
archives@klhs.bc.ca
www.klhs.bc.ca/archives
Elizabeth Scarlett, Archivist
250-353-2563

Kelowna: Kelowna Public Archives
470 Queensway Ave., Kelowna, BC V1Y 6S7
Tel: 250-763-2417
info@kelownamuseums.ca
www.kelownamuseums.ca/archives/kelowna-public-archives-2
twitter.com/kelownamuseums
Tara Hurley, Archivist
thurley@kelownamuseums.ca
250-763-2417 ext. 25

Kelowna: Roman Catholic Diocese of Nelson
3665 Benvoulin Rd., Kelowna, BC V1L 4M7
Tel: 250-448-2725
archives@nelsondiocese.org
www.nelsondiocese.org
Marcel Cote, Archivist

Kitimat: Kitimat Museum & Archives
293 City Centre, Kitimat, BC V8C 1T6
Tel: 250-632-8950
info@kitimatmuseum.ca
www.kitimatmuseum.ca
www.instagram.com/kitimatmuseum;
www.facebook.com/kitimatmuseum
Louise Avery, Executive Director
lavery@kitimatmuseum.ca
Angela Eastman, Contact, Collections & Programming
aeastman@kitimatmuseum.ca

Lake Cowichan: Kaatza Historical Society
125 South Shore Rd., Lake Cowichan, BC V0R 2G0
Tel: 250-749-6142
kaatzamuseum@shaw.ca
www.kaatzastationmuseum.ca
www.facebook.com/kaatzastation

Maple Ridge: Maple Ridge Museum & Community Archives
22520 - 116th Ave., Maple Ridge, BC V2X 0S4
Tel: 604-463-5311
mrmuseum@gmail.com
mapleridgemuseum.org
www.instagram.com/mapleridgemuseum;
twitter.com/MRMArchives;
www.facebook.com/mapleridgemuseum
Melissa Rollit, Curator
mrmcurator@gmail.com

Merritt: Nicola Valley Museum & Archives
1675 Tutill Ct., Merritt, BC V1K 1B8
Tel: 250-378-4145
www.nicolavalleymuseum.org
www.facebook.com/NVMuseum
Barb Watson, Office Administrator
Jo Atkinson, Assistant Administrator

Merritt: Scw'exmx Tribal Council
2090 Coutlee Ave., Merritt, BC V1K 1B8
Tel: 250-378-4235; *Fax:* 250-378-9119
www.scwexmxtribal.com
Arlene Johnston, Executive Director
250-378-4235 ext. 107

Mission: Mission Community Archives
33215 - 2nd Ave., Mission, BC V2V 4L1
Tel: 604-820-2621
mca@missionarchives.com
www.missionarchives.com

Nakusp: Arrow Lakes Historical Society
92 - 6th Ave. NW, Nakusp, BC V0G 1R0
Tel: 250-265-0110; *Fax:* 250-265-0110
Other Numbers: Off-Hours: 250-265-3323
alhs1234@telus.net
alhs-archives.com
www.facebook.com/arrowlakeshistoricalsociety
Marilyn Taylor, President
Kathleen Bone, Secretary

Nelson: Touchstones Nelson Museum of Art & History
502 Vernon St., Nelson, BC V1L 4E7
Tel: 250-352-9813
info@touchstonesnelson.ca
touchstonesnelson.ca/archives/shawn-lamb-archives
www.flickr.com/photos/touchstonesnelson;
www.facebook.com/touchstonesnelson
Jean-Philippe Stienne, Archivist & Collections Manager
collections@touchstonesnelson.ca
Arin Fay, Curator
curator@touchstonesnelson.ca

New Westminster: New Westminster Museum & Archives
777 Columbia St., New Westminster, BC V3M 1B6
Tel: 604-527-4640
museum@newwestcity.ca
www.newwestcity.ca/services/arts-and-heritage/museums-and-archives
www.instagram.com/newwestmuseum;
www.facebook.com/NWMuseumandArchives
Barry Dykes, Archivist
bdykes@newwestcity.ca
604-527-4642

North Vancouver: North Vancouver Museum & Archives
Community History Centre, 3203 Institute Rd., North Vancouver, BC V7K 3E5
Tel: 604-990-3700; *Fax:* 604-987-5688
nvma.ca
twitter.com/NorthVanMuseum;
www.facebook.com/NorthVancouverMuseumArchives
Jessica Bushey, Archivist
busheyj@dnv.org
Daien Ide, Reference Historian
ided@dnv.org

Penticton: Penticton Museum & Archives
785 Main St., Penticton, BC V2A 5E3
Tel: 250-490-2451; *Fax:* 250-490-2442
www.pentictonmuseum.com
www.facebook.com/108559494129
Dennis Oomen, Manager & Curator
Chandra Wong, Museum Assistant

Port Alberni: Alberni District Historical Society
4255 Wallace St., Port Alberni, BC V9Y 3Y6
Tel: 250-723-2181
aadhs1@gmail.com
www.memorybc.ca/alberni-district-historical-society-archives

Port Clements: Port Clements Historical Society
45 Bayview Dr., Port Clements, BC V0T 1R0
Tel: 250-557-4576
portclementshistoricalsociety@gmail.com
www.portclementsmuseum.com
www.facebook.com/175359227203

Powell River: Powell River Historical Museum & Archives
4798 Marine Ave., Powell River, BC V8A 4Z5
Tel: 604-485-2222; *Fax:* 604-485-2327
info@powellrivermuseum.ca
www.powellrivermuseum.ca
Nikita Johnston, Collections Manager

Prince George: Exploration Place
333 Becott Pl., Prince George, BC V2L 4V7
Tel: 250-562-1612; *Fax:* 250-562-6395
Toll-Free: 866-562-1612
curatorial@theexplorationplace.com
www.theexplorationplace.com/collections/archives-collection
twitter.com/ExplorationPG;
www.facebook.com/TheExplorationPlace
Alyssa Tobin-Leier, Curator
alyssa.tobin@theexplorationplace.com

Prince Rupert: Prince Rupert City & Regional Archives
424 - 3rd Ave. West, Prince Rupert, BC V8J 1L7
Tel: 250-624-3326; *Fax:* 250-624-3706
info@princerupertarchives.ca
www.princerupertarchives.ca
Jean Eiers-Page, Archivist
archives@citywest.ca
250-624-3326

Quesnel: Quesnel & District Museum & Archives
705 Carson Ave., Quesnel, BC V2J 2B6
Tel: 250-992-9580
www.quesnelmuseum.ca
www.facebook.com/350659608390264
Elizabeth Hunter, Museum & Heritage Manager
ehunter@quesnel.ca
250-992-9580
Brandee Shutz, Museum Assistant
bshutz@quesnel.ca
250-992-9580

Revelstoke: Revelstoke Museum & Archives
315 - 1st St. West, Revelstoke, BC V0E 2S0
Tel: 250-837-3067; *Fax:* 250-837-3094
info@revelstokemuseum.ca
www.revelstokemuseum.ca
twitter.com/revmuseum; www.facebook.com/144528853796

Richmond: City of Richmond Archives
7700 Minoru Gate, Richmond, BC V6Y 1R9
Tel: 604-247-8305
archives@richmond.ca
www.richmond.ca/cityhall/archives/about/about.htm
www.youtube.com/user/richmondarchives;
www.facebook.com/FriendsofTheRichmondArchives

Rossland: Rossland Historical Museum & Archives Association
1100 Hwy. 3B, Rossland, BC V0G 1Y0
Tel: 250-362-7722; *Toll-Free:* 888-448-7444
archives@rosslandmuseum.ca
www.rosslandmuseum.ca
twitter.com/rosslandmuseum;
www.facebook.com/rosslandmuseum
Joelle Hodgins, Museum Director
museumdirector@rosslandmuseum.ca
Sarah Taekema, Manager, Research
Sara Wright, Manager, Collections

Sooke: Sooke Region Museum & Visitor Centre
2070 Phillips Rd., Sooke, BC V9Z 0Y3
Tel: 250-642-6351; *Fax:* 250-642-7089
Toll-Free: 866-888-4748
info@sookeregionmuseum.ca
www.sookeregionmuseum.ca
twitter.com/SookeRegionMuse;
www.facebook.com/118482471530145
Lee Boyko, Executive Director

Summerland: Summerland Museum & Archives
9521 Wharton St., Summerland, BC V0H 1Z0
Tel: 250-494-9395; *Fax:* 250-494-9326
archives@summerlandmuseum.org
www.summerlandmuseum.org
www.instagram.com/summerlandmuseum;
www.facebook.com/summerlandmuseumandarchives
Stephanie Normandeau, Archives Registrar
archives@summerlandmuseum.org

Surrey: City of Surrey Archives
17671 - 56th Ave., Surrey, BC V3S 1C9
Tel: 604-502-6459
archives@surrey.ca
www.surrey.ca/culture-recreation/2394.aspx
www.youtube.com/surreyarchives

Trail: Trail Historical Society
Riverfront Centre, 1505 Bay Ave., Trail, BC V1R 4B2
Tel: 250-364-0821
collections@trail.ca
www.trailhistory.com/archives
www.facebook.com/1677965719131625

Vancouver: British Columbia Sports Hall of Fame & Museum
777 Pacific Blvd. South, Vancouver, BC V6B 4Y8
Tel: 604-687-5520; *Fax:* 604-687-5510
guestservices@bcsportshall.com
bcsportshall.com
www.instagram.com/bcsportshall; twitter.com/BCSportsHall;
www.facebook.com/bcsportshall
Jason Beck, Curator

Vancouver: City of Vancouver Archives
1150 Chestnut St., Vancouver, BC V6J 3J9
Tel: 604-736-8561
archives@vancouver.ca
vancouver.ca/your-government/city-of-vancouver-archives.aspx
www.youtube.com/user/VancouverArchives;
twitter.com/VanArchives; www.facebook.com/VanArchives;

Vancouver: Jewish Historical Society of BC
6184 Ash St., Vancouver, BC V5Z 3G9
Tel: 604-257-5199
archives@jewishmuseum.ca
jewishmuseum.ca/archives
www.instagram.com/jewishmuseumbc; twitter.com/JMA_BC;
www.facebook.com/JewishBC
Alysa Routtenberg, Archivist

Vancouver: Roman Catholic Archdiocese of Vancouver
4885 Saint John Paul II Way, Vancouver, BC V5Z 0G3
Tel: 604-683-0281; *Fax:* 604-683-4288
rcav.org/archives-office

Vancouver: Satellite Video Exchange Society
2625 Kaslo St., Vancouver, BC V5M 3G9
Tel: 604-872-8337; *Fax:* 604-876-1185
library@vivomediaarts.com
www.vivomediaarts.com
Kendra Place, General Manager
admin@vivomediaarts.com
Syr Reifsteck, Archivist

Vancouver: Union of British Columbia Indian Chiefs
#401, 312 Main St., Vancouver, BC V6A 2T2
Tel: 604-684-0231
library@ubcic.bc.ca
www.ubcic.bc.ca/library

Vancouver: Unitarian Church of Vancouver
#949, West 49th Ave., Vancouver, BC V5Z 2T1
Tel: 604-261-7204
info@vancouverunitarians.ca
vancouverunitarians.ca/community/engaging/library-archives
David Buchanan, Library Committee Chair
davidfbuchanan@gmail.com

Vancouver: Vancouver Ballet Society
677 Davie St., 6th Fl., Vancouver, BC V6B 2G6
Tel: 604-681-1525; *Fax:* 604-681-7732
vbs@telus.net
www.vancouverballetsociety.ca/about-vbs
Maureen Allen, Contact
604-681-1581

Vernon: Greater Vernon Museum & Archives
3009 - 32nd Ave., Vernon, BC V1T 2L8
Tel: 250-542-3142
mail@vernonmuseum.ca
www.vernonmuseum.ca
www.facebook.com/vernonmuseum
Barbara Bell, Senior Archivist
barbara.bell@vernonmuseum.ca

Victoria: City of Victoria Archives
8 Centennial Sq., Victoria, BC V8W 1P6
Tel: 250-361-0375; *Fax:* 250-361-0367
archives@victoria.ca
www.victoria.ca/EN/main/residents/archives.html

Victoria: Roman Catholic Diocese of Victoria
#1, 4044 Nelthorpe St., Victoria, BC V8X 2A1
Tel: 250-479-1331; *Fax:* 250-479-5423
www.rcdvictoria.org/archives
Theresa Vogel, Manager, Archives
250-479-1331 ext. 229

Victoria: Saanich Municipal Archives
3100 Tillicum Rd., Victoria, BC V9A 6T2
Tel: 250-475-5494
archives@saanich.ca
www.saanich.ca/archives

Victoria: Sisters of St. Ann Archives/Archives des Soeurs de Sainte-Anne à Victoria
675 Belleville St., Victoria, BC V8R 9W2
Tel: 250-592-0685
archives@ssabc.ca
www.royalbcmuseum.bc.ca/bc-archives/info/sisters-st-ann-archives
Beverly Paty, Manager, Archives Collections
bpaty@royalbcmuseum.bc.ca
Lauren Buttle, Archival Conservator
lbuttle@royalbcmuseum.bc.ca

West Vancouver: West Vancouver Archives
680 - 17th St., West Vancouver, BC V7V 3T2
Tel: 604-925-7298
archives@westvancouver.ca
westvancouver.ca/arts-culture/heritage/archives

White Rock: White Rock Museum & Archives Society
14970 Marine Dr., White Rock, BC V4B 1C4
Tel: 604-541-2221; *Fax:* 604-541-2223
archives@whiterockmuseum.ca
www.whiterockmuseum.ca
www.instagram.com/whiterockmuseum;
www.facebook.com/whiterockmuseumandarchives
Hugh Ellenwood, Archives Manager
archives@whiterockmuseum.ca
604-541-2225
Charlene Garvey, Curator
curator@whiterockmuseum.ca
604-541-2230

Manitoba

Regional Systems

Border Regional Library
312 - 7th Ave., Virden, MB R0M 2C0
Tel: 204-748-3862
brlcoord@rfnow.com
www.borderregionallibrary.ca
www.instagram.com/borderregionallibrary;
www.facebook.com/558622490862434

Evergreen Regional Library
55 - 1st Ave., Gimli, MB R0C 1B0
Tel: 204-642-7912; *Fax:* 204-642-8319
gimli.library@mts.net
erlibrary.ca
Becky Barrett, Chair
Sandra Reykdal, Head Librarian
Lindsay Struhan, Library Clerk

Lac du Bonnet Regional Library
84 - 3rd St., Lac du Bonnet, MB R0E 1A0
Tel: 204-345-2653; *Fax:* 204-345-6827
mldb@mymts.net
www.lacdubonnetlibrary.ca
www.facebook.com/lacdubonnetlibrary
Vickie Short, Head Librarian

Lakeland Regional Library
318 Williams Ave., Killarney, MB R0K 1G0
Tel: 204-523-4949; *Fax:* 204-523-7460
info@lakelandregionallibrary.ca
www.lakelandregionallibrary.ca
www.instagram.com/lakelandregionallibrary;
www.facebook.com/LakelandRegionalLibrary
Krista Law, Library Administrator

Parkland Regional Library
504 Main St. North, Dauphin, MB R7N 1C9
Tel: 204-638-6410; *Toll-Free:* 866-638-6410
prlhq@parklandlib.mb.ca
parklandlib.mb.ca
Alison Moss, Director

South Central Regional Library
160 Main St., Winkler, MB R6W 0M3
Tel: 204-325-7174
winklerlib@gmail.com
scrl.mb.libraries.coop
twitter.com/SCRL_Library; www.facebook.com/scrllibrary
Cathy Ching, Director, Library Services
scrldirector@gmail.com

Southwestern Manitoba Regional Library
149 Main St., Melita, MB R0M 1L0
Tel: 204-522-3923; *Fax:* 204-522-3923
swmblib@wcgwave.ca
southwestern.mb.libraries.coop
www.facebook.com/MelitaLibrary
Sandra Sterling, Head Librarian

Western Manitoba Regional Library
#1, 710 Rosser Ave., Brandon, MB R7A 0K9
Tel: 204-727-6648
info@wmrl.ca
www.wmrl.ca
twitter.com/wmrlibrary; www.facebook.com/wmrlibrary
Danielle Hubbard, Director, Library Services
danielle@wmrl.ca

Public Libraries

Baldur: Regional Municipality of Argyle Public Library
627 Elizabeth Ave. East, Baldur, MB R0K 0B0
Tel: 204-535-2314; *Fax:* 204-535-2242
rmargyle@gmail.com
rmargyle.wix.com/rmargyle

Beausejour: Brokenhead River Regional Library
427 Park Ave., Beausejour, MB R0E 0C0
Tel: 204-268-7570
brrlibr2@mymts.net
www.brrlibrary.ca
www.facebook.com/1024119984324151
Kristy Mazur, Head Librarian
kmazurbrrl@mymts.net

Boissevain: Boissevain & Morton Regional Library
409 South Railway St., Boissevain, MB R0K 0E0
Tel: 204-534-6478
mail@bmlibrary.ca
bmlibrary.ca
www.facebook.com/bmlibrary

Brandon: Manitoba Public Library Services
340 - 9th St., #B10, Brandon, MB R7A 6C2
Tel: 204-726-6590; *Fax:* 204-726-6868
Toll-Free: 800-252-9998
pls@gov.mb.ca
www.gov.mb.ca/chc/pls
Trevor Surgenor, Director
204-573-2814

Carman: Boyne Regional Library
15 - 1st Ave. SW, Carman, MB R0G 0J0
Tel: 204-745-3504
boyneregionallibrary@outlook.com
sites.google.com/site/boyneregionallibrary
www.facebook.com/boynelibrarycarman

Cartwright: Cartwright Branch Library
483 Veteran Dr., Cartwright, MB R0K 0L0
Tel: 204-529-2261
cartlib@mymts.net
www.lakelandregionallibrary.ca
Gloria Kinley, Branch Librarian

Churchill: Churchill Public Library
180 Laverendry Ave., Churchill, MB R0B 0E0
Tel: 204-675-2731
mchlibrary@yahoo.com
www.churchill.ca/p/public-library
www.facebook.com/churchillpubliclibrary

Deloraine: Bren Del Win Centennial Library
211 North Railway West, Deloraine, MB R0M 0M0
Tel: 204-747-2415
bdwlib@gmail.com
delorainelibrary.com
www.facebook.com/BrenDelWinLibrary

Easterville: Chemawawin Public Library
1A Cree Cres., Easterville, MB R0C 0V0
Tel: 204-329-2995
www.ucn.ca
Anthony Zong, Librarian
azong@ucn.ca

Eriksdale: Eriksdale Public Library
9 Main St., Eriksdale, MB R0C 0W0
Tel: 204-739-2668
epl1@mymts.net
www.facebook.com/523666644387159

Flin Flon: Flin Flon Public Library
58 Main St., Flin Flon, MB R8A 1J8
Fax: 888-293-4070
Toll-Free: 833-960-3519
ffpl@shaw.ca
www.flinflonpubliclibrary.ca
www.facebook.com/FlinFlonPublicLibrary
Elizabeth Andres, Library Administrator
ffpl-admin@shaw.ca
833-960-3519 ext. 333

Gillam: Bette Winner Public Library
206 Button Ave., Gillam, MB R0B 0L0
Tel: 204-652-2617
library@townofgillam.com
www.townofgillam.com/p/bette-winner-public-library-
Dawna Gray McDonald, Head Librarian
Lisa Wiwchar, Assistant Librarian

Headingley: Headingley Municipal Library
49 Alboro St., Headingley, MB R4J 1A3
Tel: 204-888-5410
hml@headingleylibrary.ca
headingleylibrary.ca

Alison Au, Head Librarian

Holland: Victoria Municipal Library
102 Stewart Ave., Holland, MB R0G 0X0
Tel: 204-526-2011
victorialibrary@rmofvictoria.com
www.rmofvictoria.com/p/library-services
www.facebook.com/victoriamunicipallibrary

Ile-des-Chênes: Bibliothèque Ritchot Library
École Gabrielle-Roy, 310 Lamoureux Rd., Ile-des-Chênes, MB R0A 0T0
Tél: 204-878-2147
ritchotlib@hotmail.com
www.ritchot.com/p/libraries
www.facebook.com/529151163863745

La Broquerie: Bibliothèque Saint-Joachim Library
29, baie Normandeau, La Broquerie, MB R0A 0W0
Tel: 204-424-9533; *Fax:* 204-424-5610
bsjl@bsjl.ca
www.bsjl.ca
www.instagram.com/bsjl.ca; twitter.com/mybsjl;
www.facebook.com/363462824450180

Yolande Tétrault, Présidente

Leaf Rapids: Leaf Rapids Public Library
20 Town Centre, Leaf Rapids, MB R0B 1W0
Tel: 204-473-2742
lrlib@mts.net

Lorette: Bibliothèque Taché Library
1082, ch Dawson, Lorette, MB R0A 0Y0
Tel: 204-878-9488
btl@srsd.ca
www.bibliotachelibrary.ca

Jo-Dee Huberdeau, Chair
Shaunda Brommell, Librarian

Lundar: Pauline Johnson Library
23 Main St., Lundar, MB R0C 1Y0
Tel: 204-762-5367
mlpj@mymts.net
www.facebook.com/paulinejohnsonlibrary

Lynn Lake: Lynn Lake Centennial Library
PO Box 1127, Lynn Lake, MB R0B 0W0
Tel: 204-356-8222

MacGregor: North Norfolk MacGregor Regional Library
35 Hampton St. East, MacGregor, MB R0H 0R0
Tel: 204-685-2796; *Fax:* 204-685-2478
maclib@mts.net
nnmrl.net
twitter.com/nn_mac

Minnedosa: Minnedosa Regional Library
45 - 1st Ave. SE, Minnedosa, MB R0J 1E0
Tel: 204-867-2585; *Fax:* 204-867-6140
mmr@mts.net
www.minnedosaregionallibrary.com
www.facebook.com/103641533063836

Morris: Valley Regional Library
141 Main St. South, Morris, MB R0G 1K0
Tel: 204-746-2136
valleyregionallibrary@gmail.com
valley.mb.libraries.coop

Diane Ali, Head Librarian

Norway House: Norway House Public Library
University College of the North (UCN), Norway House, MB R0B 1B0
Tel: 204-359-6296; *Fax:* 204-359-6262
library@ucn.ca
www.ucn.ca/sites/library
www.facebook.com/nhpubliclibrary

Fiona Godwin, Librarian
fgodwin@ucn.ca

Notre-Dame-de-Lourdes: Bibliothèque Père Champagne/Père Champagne Library
44 Rogers St., Notre-Dame-de-Lourdes, MB R0G 1M0
Tel: 204-248-2386
bpcndlib@gmail.com
bpcl.fbmb.ca
www.facebook.com/194725747351803

Diane Bazin, Chair

Pilot Mound: Louise Public Library
148 Moffat Ave., Pilot Mound, MB R0G 1P0
Tel: 204-825-2035
louiselibrary@gmail.com
louiselibrary.ca
www.facebook.com/louisepubliclibrary

Karen Potter, Chair
Susanne Fortin, Chief Librarian

Pinawa: Pinawa Public Library
Community Centre, Vanier Ave., Pinawa, MB R0E 1L0
Tel: 204-753-2496
email@pinawapubliclibrary.com
pinawapubliclibrary.com
www.facebook.com/166929396717731

Lois Bernardin, Head Librarian

Portage la Prairie: Portage la Prairie Regional Library
40B Royal Rd. North, Portage la Prairie, MB R1N 1V1
Tel: 204-857-4271
portlib@portagelibrary.com
www.portagelibrary.com
www.facebook.com/plaplibrary

Rapid City: Rapid City Regional Library
425 - 3rd Ave., Rapid City, MB R0K 1W0
Tel: 404-826-2732
rclib@wcgwave.ca
www.rclibrary.ca
www.facebook.com/rclib

Donna Anderson, Chair
Shirley Martin, Librarian

Reston: Reston & District Library
220 - 4th St., Reston, MB R0M 1X0
Tel: 204-877-3673
restonlb@yahoo.ca
restondistrictlibrary.ca
www.facebook.com/1716067108435799

Laura Jean Campbell, Chair

Rivers: Prairie Crocus Regional Library
137 Main St., Rivers, MB R0K 1X0
Tel: 204-328-7613
pclibrary@wcgwave.ca
riverslibrary.ca
www.facebook.com/PCRLRivers

Sherri Dzier, Librarian
Michelle Willows, Assistant Librarian

Saint Jean Baptiste: Bibliothèque Montcalm Library
113, 2e av, Saint Jean Baptiste, MB R0G 2B0
Tél: 204-758-3137; *Téléc:* 204-758-3574
bibliomontcalm@hotmail.ca
bml.fbmb.ca

Saint-Claude: Bibliothèque Saint-Claude/St. Claude Library
50 - 1st St., Saint-Claude, MB R0G 1Z0
Tel: 204-379-2524; *Fax:* 204-379-2524
stclib@mymts.net
stclaude.mb.libraries.coop

Roger Bazin, Chair
Lynn Gobin, Librarian

Selkirk: Gaynor Family Regional Library
806 Manitoba Ave., Selkirk, MB R1A 2H4
Tel: 204-482-3522
library@gfrl.org
gfrl.org
twitter.com/GaynorLibraryMB;
www.facebook.com/GaynorLibraryMB

Ken Kuryliw, Director, Library Services

Shilo: Shilo Community Library
Community Centre Bldg., 114 Notre Dame Ave., #T, Shilo, MB R0K 2A0
Tel: 204-765-3000
shilolibrary@gmail.com

Snow Lake: Snow Lake Community Library
Joseph H. Kerr School, 201 Cherry Ave., Snow Lake, MB R0B 1M0
Tel: 204-358-2322; *Fax:* 204-358-2116
www.facebook.com/SnowLakeCommunityLibrary

Souris: Glenwood & Souris Regional Library
#18, 114 - 2nd St. South, Souris, MB R0K 2C0
Tel: 204-483-2757; *Fax:* 204-709-0120
frontdesk@sourislibrary.mb.ca
www.sourislibrary.mb.ca
www.facebook.com/LibrarySouris

Robert Enns, Chair

Connie Bradshaw, Head Librarian
Debra Wright, Assistant Librarian

St Georges: Bibliothèque Allard Regional Library
104086 PTH 11, St Georges, MB R0E 1V0
Tel: 204-367-8443; *Fax:* 204-367-1780
info@allardlibrary.com
www.allardlibrary.com
www.facebook.com/144949018850811

Kelly Murray, Head Librarian

St Pierre Jolys: Jolys Regional Library/Bibliothèque régionale Jolys
505 Hébert Ave. North, St Pierre Jolys, MB R0A 1V0
Tel: 204-433-7729; *Fax:* 204-433-7412
stplibrary@jrlibrary.mb.ca
www.jrlibrary.mb.ca
www.facebook.com/BibliothequeRegionaleJolys

Paule Peloquin, Head Librarian
204-433-3089

Ste Rose du Lac: Ste. Rose Regional Library
580 Central Ave., Ste Rose du Lac, MB R0L 1S0
Tel: 204-447-2527; *Fax:* 450-447-2527
steroselibrary@hotmail.com
www.sterose.ca/p/ste-rose-regional-library

Michelle Bonin-LeGall, Librarian

Ste-Anne-des-Chênes: Bibliothèque Ste-Anne Library
16 de l'Eglise St., Ste-Anne-des-Chênes, MB R5H 1H8
Tel: 204-422-9958
library@steanne.ca
bibliothequesteannelibrary.ca
www.facebook.com/342314585816253

Steinbach: Jake Epp Library
255 Elmdale St., Steinbach, MB R5G 0C9
Tel: 204-326-6841; *Fax:* 204-326-6859
librarian@jakeepplibrary.com
www.jakeepplibrary.com
www.instagram.com/jakeepplibrary;
www.facebook.com/jakeepplibrary

Cindy Blatz, Chair
Chrystie Kroeker Boggs, Library Director

Stonewall: South Interlake Regional Library
419 Main St., Stonewall, MB R0C 2Z0
Tel: 204-467-8415; *Fax:* 204-467-9809
circ@sirlibrary.com
www.sirlibrary.com
www.facebook.com/sirlstonewall

Raquel Dumas, Library Director
rdumas@sirlibrary.com
Joan Ransom, Branch Librarian
Pam Palcat, Bookmobile Librarian
bookmobile@sirlibrary.com

Swan River: North-West Regional Library
610 - 1st St. North, Swan River, MB R0L 1Z0
Tel: 204-734-3880; *Fax:* 204-734-3880
email@swanriverlibrary.ca
swanriverlibrary.ca
www.facebook.com/SwanRiverLibrary

Kathy Sterma, Head Librarian

The Pas: The Pas Regional Library
53 Edwards Ave., The Pas, MB R9A 1R2
Tel: 204-623-2023; *Fax:* 204-623-4594
library@mymts.net
www.thepasregionallibrary.com
www.instagram.com/thepasregionallibrary;
www.facebook.com/ThePasRegionalLibrary

Thompson: Thompson Public Library
81 Thompson Dr. North, Thompson, MB R8N 0C3
Tel: 204-677-3717
info@thompsonlibrary.com
www.thompsonlibrary.com
www.instagram.com/thompsonlibrary;
twitter.com/LibraryThompson;
www.facebook.com/Library.Thompson

Cheryl Davies, Administrator

Winnipeg: Winnipeg Public Library
251 Donald St., Winnipeg, MB R3C 3P5
Tel: 204-986-6462; *Fax:* 204-942-5671
wpl.winnipeg.ca/library
www.instagram.com/winnipegpubliclibrary;
twitter.com/wpglibrary; www.facebook.com/winnipegpubliclibrary
Ed Cuddy, Manager, Library Services
ecuddy@winnipeg.ca
Karin Borland, Coordinator, Youth Services
kborland@winnipeg.ca

Sophie Firby, Coordinator, Information & Virtual Services
sophiefirby@winnipeg.ca
Irmy Nikkel, Coordinator, Support Services
inikkel@winnipeg.ca
Betty Parry, Coordinator, Public Services & Collection
Development
bparry@winnipeg.ca
Kathleen Williams, Coordinator, Adult Programming & Outreach
kathleenwilliams@winnipeg.ca

Archives

Boissevain: **Boissevain Community Archives**
409 South Railway St., Boissevain, MB R0K 0E0
Tel: 204-534-6478
mail@bmlibrary.ca
bmlibrary.ca/resources/community-archives
www.facebook.com/bmlibrary

Brandon: **Brandon General Museum & Archives Inc.**
#101, 19 - 9th St., Brandon, MB R7A 4A3
Tel: 204-717-1514
bgmainfo@wcgwave.ca
brandongeneralmuseum.ca
twitter.com/TheBGMA;
www.facebook.com/brandongeneralmuseum

Brandon: **Magnacca Research Centre**
122 - 18th St., Brandon, MB R7A 5A4
Tel: 204-727-1722; *Fax:* 204-727-1722
archives@wcgwave.ca
www.dalyhousemuseum.ca/wordpress/archives
twitter.com/DalyHouseMuseum; www.facebook.com/dalyhouse
Eileen Trott, Curator

Brandon: **X11 Manitoba Dragoons & 26 Field
Regiment Museum**
**Brandon Armoury, 1116 Victoria Ave., 1st Fl., Brandon, MB
R7A 1B2**
26fdlibrary@wcgwave.ca
www.12mbdragoons.com
www.facebook.com/369782049790739
Edd McArthur, Curator
26fdregCurator@wcgwave.ca
204-717-4579
Ted Krasicki, Contact, Research
krasicki@mymts.net

Carberry: **Carberry Plains Archives**
122 Main St., Carberry, MB R0K 0H0
Tel: 204-834-6614
cparchives@mymts.net
www.townofcarberry.ca/archives
www.facebook.com/240790079590929
Valerie Andrey, Archivist

Churchill: **Diocese of Churchill - Hudson Bay**
242 La Verendrye Ave., Churchill, MB R0B 0E0
Tel: 204-675-2030; *Fax:* 204-675-2140
chhbay@mts.net
dioceseofchurchillhudsonbay.wordpress.com/museum

Killarney: **J.A.V. David Museum**
414 William St., Killarney, MB R0K 1G0
Tel: 204-523-7325
javdavidmuseum@outlook.com
www.facebook.com/javdavidmuseumatkillarneymb

Selkirk: **Selkirk Mental Health Centre Archives
Collection Inc.**
825 Manitoba Ave., Selkirk, MB R1A 0Z3
Tel: 204-482-3810
smhc-archives.com

Shilo: **Royal Canadian Artillery Museum/Le Musée
de l'artillerie du Canada**
**Bldg. N, Canadian Forces Base Shilo, 118 Patricia Rd.,
Shilo, MB R0K 2A0**
Tel: 204-765-3000
rcamuseum@forces.gc.ca
www.rcamuseum.com

Steinbach: **Mennonite Heritage Village**
231 PTH 12 North, Steinbach, MB R5G 1T8
Tel: 204-326-9661; *Fax:* 204-326-5046
info@mhv.ca
mennoniteheritagevillage.com
twitter.com/MHVSteinbach; www.facebook.com/MHVSteinbach
Andrea Klassen, Senior Curator
andreak@mhv.ca
204-326-9661 ext. 226

Thompson: **Heritage North Museum**
162 Princeton Dr., Thompson, MB R8N 2A4
Tel: 204-677-2216
hnmuseum@mts.net
heritagenorthmuseum.ca
Tanna Teneycke, Executive Director

Winnipeg: **Archevêché de St-Boniface**
151, av de la Cathédrale, Winnipeg, MB R2H 0H6
Tél: 204-237-9851; *Téléc:* 204-231-8550
pastorale@archsaintboniface.ca
www.archsaintboniface.ca/resources/fr
Katelyn Sutton, Adjoint administratif
ajohns@archsaintboniface.ca

Winnipeg: **Archives of Manitoba/Archives du
Manitoba**
#130, 200 Vaughan St., Winnipeg, MB R3C 1T5
Tel: 204-945-3971; *Fax:* 204-948-2672
Toll-Free: 800-617-3588
archives@gov.mb.ca
www.gov.mb.ca/chc/archives
twitter.com/MBGovArchives

Winnipeg: **Centre for Mennonite Brethren Studies**
1310 Taylor Ave., Winnipeg, MB R3M 3Z6
Tel: 204-669-6575; *Fax:* 204-654-1865
Toll-Free: 888-669-6575
cmbs@mbchurches.ca
cmbs.mennonitebrethren.ca
Jon Isaak, Director
jon.isaak@mbchurches.ca

Winnipeg: **City of Winnipeg**
50 Myrtle St., Winnipeg, MB R3E 2R2
Tel: 204-986-5325; *Fax:* 204-986-7133
www.winnipeg.ca/clerks/toc/archives.stm

Winnipeg: **Fire Fighters Historical Society of
Winnipeg**
56 Maple St., Winnipeg, MB R3B 0Y8
Tel: 204-942-4817
firemuseum@gatewest.net
wpgfiremuseum.ca/archives

Winnipeg: **Fort Garry Horse Museum & Archives**
551 Machray Ave., Winnipeg, MB R2W 1A8
Tel: 204-586-6298
fortgarryhorse.ca/wp/museum-and-archives
www.facebook.com/fghmuseum
Gordon Crossley, Museum Director
museum.director@fortgarryhorse.ca

Winnipeg: **Grand Lodge of Manitoba**
420 Corydon Ave., Winnipeg, MB R3L 0N8
Tel: 204-832-0134; *Fax:* 204-284-3527
archivistgrandlodgemb@outlook.com
www.glmb.ca/archives.html
John Drew, Archivist

Winnipeg: **Jewish Heritage Centre of Western
Canada**
123 Doncaster St., #C140, Winnipeg, MB R3N 2B2
Tel: 204-477-7461
jewishheritage@jhcwc.org
www.jhcwc.org/research/collections-library
Andrew Morrison, Archivist
amorrison@jhcwc.org

Winnipeg: **Manitoba Museum**
190 Rupert Ave., Winnipeg, MB R3B 0N2
Tel: 204-988-0692; *Fax:* 204-942-3679
info@manitobamuseum.ca
www.manitobamuseum.ca
Nancy Anderson, Manager, Information Services
nanderson@manitobamuseum.ca

Winnipeg: **Mennonite Heritage Centre**
600 Shaftesbury Blvd., Winnipeg, MB R3P 0M4
Tel: 204-560-1998; *Fax:* 204-831-5675
Toll-Free: 866-888-6785
archives.mennonitechurch.ca
Conrad Stoesz, Archivist
cstoesz@cmu.ca
Selenna Wolfe, Administrative Assistant
swolfe@mharchives.ca

Winnipeg: **Rainbow Resource Centre**
170 Scott St., Winnipeg, MB R3L 0L3
Tel: 204-474-0212; *Fax:* 204-478-1160
Toll-Free: 855-437-8523
info@rainbowresourcecentre.org
rainbowresourcecentre.org/programs/library
www.instagram.com/rainbowresourcecentre;
twitter.com/RainbowResCtr; www.facebook.com/rrclibrary
Noreen Mian, Executive Director
noreenm@rainbowresourcecentre.org
204-474-0212 ext. 208
Alberto Forzan, Information & Intake Assessment Coordinator

Winnipeg: **Royal Aviation Museum of Western
Canada**
Hangar T-2, 958 Ferry Rd., Winnipeg, MB R3H 0Y8
Tel: 204-786-5503; *Fax:* 204-775-4761
info@royalaviationmuseum.com
www.royalaviationmuseum.com

Winnipeg: **Sisters of Our Lady of the
Missions/Religieuses de Notre Dame des Missions**
393 Gaboury Pl., Winnipeg, MB R2H 0L5
Tel: 204-786-6051; *Fax:* 204-691-0640
canrndm@shaw.ca
www.rndmcanada.org

Winnipeg: **Soeurs Missionnaires Oblates du
Sacré-Coeur et de Marie Immaculée/Missionary
Oblate Sisters of the Sacred Heart & of Mary
Immaculate**
**Les Missionnaires Oblates Saint Boniface, #3, 601 Aulneau
St., Winnipeg, MB R2H 2V5**
Tél: 204-233-7287
www.missionaryoblatesisters.ca
Léa Archambault, Contact
llarchambault@hotmail.com

Winnipeg: **Transcona Historical Museum Inc.**
141 Regent Ave. West, Winnipeg, MB R2C 1R1
Tel: 204-222-0423; *Fax:* 204-222-0208
info@transconamuseum.mb.ca
www.transconamuseum.mb.ca
www.youtube.com/user/TransconaMuseum;
www.facebook.com/transconamuseum
Alanna Horejda, Curator
Jennifer Maxwell, Assistant Curator

Winnipeg: **Ukrainian Catholic Church Archeparchy
of Winnipeg**
233 Scotia St., Winnipeg, MB R2V 1V7
Tel: 204-338-7801; *Fax:* 204-339-4006
uccarchives@gmail.com
www.archeparchy.ca/page.php?id=30
Gloria Romaniuk, Archivist

Winnipeg: **Ukrainian Cultural & Educational Centre**
184 Alexander Ave. East, Winnipeg, MB R3B 0L6
Tel: 204-942-0218
info@oseredok.ca
www.oseredok.ca
www.facebook.com/oseredok

New Brunswick

Regional Systems

**Albert-Westmorland-Kent Library Regional
Office/Région de bibliothèques AWK**
#201, 644 Main St., Moncton, NB E1C 1E2
Tel: 506-869-6032; *Fax:* 506-869-6022
nbplsawkadministrativestaff@gnb.ca
Nadine Goguen, Regional Director
Robin Illsley, Librarian, Public Services

**Chaleur Library Regional Office/Région de
bibliothèques Chaleur**
113A Roseberry St., Campbellton, NB E3N 2G6
Tel: 506-789-6599; *Fax:* 506-789-7318
nbplschaleuradministrativestaff@gnb.ca
Georgette Lavail, Regional Director
Simon Marsolais, Librarian, Collections Management

**Fundy Library Region/Région de bibliothèques de
Fundy**
1 Market Sq., Saint John, NB E2L 4Z6
Tel: 506-643-7222; *Fax:* 506-643-7225
nbplsfundyadministrativestaff@gnb.ca
Brian Steeves, Regional Director
Amy Heans, Acting Assistant Regional Director
Nora Kennedy, Librarian, Public Services
Robin Sexton-Mayes, Acting Librarian, Collections Management

Haut-Saint-Jean Library Region/Région de bibliothèques Haut-Saint-Jean
#102, 15 de l'Église St., Edmundston, NB E3V 1J3
Tel: 506-735-2074; *Fax:* 506-735-2193
nbplshsjadministrativestaff@gnb.ca
Patrick Provencher, Regional Director
Sarah Dereumetz, Acting Assistant Regional Director
Alexandra Ferguson, Librarian, Collections Management

York Library Region/Région de bibliothèques York
#1, 570 Two Nations Crossing, Fredericton, NB E3A 0X9
Tel: 506-453-5380; *Fax:* 506-457-4878
nbplsyorkadministrativestaff@gnb.ca
Sarah Kilfoil, Regional Director
Tyler Griffin, Assistant Regional Director
Mikey Colborne, Librarian, Public Services
Annette McAllister, Coordinator, Interlibrary Loan Service

Public Libraries

Atholville: Bibliothèque publique de Raymond Lagacé/Raymond Lagacé Public Library
275, rue Notre-Dame, Atholville, NB E3N 4T1
Tél: 506-789-2914; *Téléc:* 506-789-2056
biblioda@gnb.ca
www.facebook.com/bibliothequeatholville
Kevin Soussana, Gestionnaire de bibliothèque

Bas-Caraquet: Bibliothèque publique Claude-LeBouthillier/Claude LeBouthillier Public Library
#8185, 2, rue St-Paul, Bas-Caraquet, NB E1W 6C4
Tél: 506-726-2775; *Téléc:* 506-726-2770
bibliobc@gnb.ca
www.facebook.com/BibliothequeBasCaraquet
Mylène May Gionet, Gestionnaire de bibliothèque

Bathurst: Bibliothèque publique de Bathurst/Bathurst Public Library
#1, 150, rue St-George, Bathurst, NB E2A 1B5
Tél: 506-548-0706; *Téléc:* 506-548-0708
bibliocn@gnb.ca
www.facebook.com/BiblioBathurst
Laura Little, Directrice par interim

Beresford: Bibliothèque publique Mgr-Robichaud/Mgr. Robichaud Public Library
#3, 855, rue Principale, Beresford, NB E8K 1T3
Tél: 506-542-2704; *Téléc:* 506-542-2714
bibliomr@gnb.ca
www.facebook.com/bibliomr
Julia Maury, Directrice

Bouctouche: Gérald Leblanc Public Library/Bibliothèque publique Gérald-Leblanc
#100, 84 Irving Blvd., Bouctouche, NB E4S 3L4
Tél: 506-743-7263; *Fax:* 506-743-7263
bibliopb@gnb.ca
www.facebook.com/bibliothequepubliquegeraldleblanc
Monique Langis, Manager

Campbellton: Bibliothèque du Centenaire de Campbellton/Campbellton Centennial Library
#100, 19, rue Aberdeen, Campbellton, NB E3N 2J6
Tél: 506-753-5253; *Téléc:* 506-753-3803
bibliocc@gnb.ca
bibliothequecentenairecampbellton.wordpress.com
www.facebook.com/bibliocampbellton
Stéphane Dupuy, Directeur
François Forest, Chef, Services pour enfants par intérim
Karine Lelièvre, Chef, Services pour jeunes adultes et adultes

Campobello: Campobello Public Library
3 Welshpool St., Campobello, NB E5E 1G3
Tel: 506-752-7082; *Fax:* 506-752-7083
campbopl@gnb.ca
www.facebook.com/CampobelloLibrary
Stephanie Gough, Acting Manager

Cap-Pelé: Cap-Pelé Public Library
2638 Acadie Rd., Cap-Pelé, NB E4N 1E3
Tel: 506-577-2090; *Fax:* 506-577-2094
bibliocp@gnb.ca
www.facebook.com/cappelepubliclibrary
Michele-Ann Goguen, Library Manager

Caraquet: Bibliothèque publique Mgr-Paquet/Mgr. Paquet Public Library
10A, rue du Colisée, Caraquet, NB E1W 1A5
Tél: 506-726-2681; *Téléc:* 506-726-2685
bibliock@gnb.ca
www.facebook.com/166611596794336
Irène Guraliuc, Directrice

Chipman: Chipman Public Library
8 King St., Chipman, NB E4A 2H3
Tel: 506-339-5852; *Fax:* 506-339-9804
chipman.publiclibrary@gnb.ca
www.facebook.com/336393173148889
Krista Blyth, Manager

Dalhousie: Bibliothèque du centenaire de Dalhousie/Dalhousie Centennial Library
403, rue Adelaide, Dalhousie, NB E8C 1B6
Tel: 506-684-7370; *Fax:* 506-684-7374
bibliocd@gnb.ca
www.facebook.com/bibliodalhousie
Joanie Tanguay, Gestionnaire de bibliothèque

Dieppe: Dieppe Public Library/Bibliothèque publique de Dieppe
333 Acadie Ave., Dieppe, NB E1A 1G9
Tel: 506-877-7945; *Fax:* 506-877-7897
bibliopd@gnb.ca
twitter.com/DieppeLibrary;
www.facebook.com/dieppepubliclibrary
Nathalie Brun, Director

Doaktown: Doaktown Community - School Library
430 Main St., Doaktown, NB E9C 1E8
Tel: 506-365-2018; *Fax:* 506-365-2054
dtcslib@gnb.ca
www.facebook.com/DoaktownCommunitySchoolLibrary
Angela Nodwell-Beek, Library Manager

Dorchester: Dorchester Public Library
3516 Cape Rd., Dorchester, NB E4K 2X7
Tel: 506-379-3032; *Fax:* 506-379-3033
dorchpl@gnb.ca
www.facebook.com/BiblioLibraryDorchester
Krista Johansen, Manager

Edmundston: Mgr. W.J. Conway Public Library/Bibliothèque publique Mgr-W.-J. Conway
33 Irène St., Edmundston, NB E3V 1B7
Tel: 506-735-4713; *Fax:* 506-737-6848
biblioed@gnb.ca
www.bibliotheque-edmundston.ca
www.facebook.com/biblioed
Marc Cool, Library Director & Acting Head, Children's Services
Tanya Eindiguer, Head, Young Adult & Adult Services
Véronique Thibault, Head, Children's Services
Louis Roy, Supervisor, Circulation

Florenceville: Andrew & Laura McCain Public Library/Bibliothèque publique Andrew-et-Laura-McCain
8 McCain St., Florenceville, NB E7L 3H6
Tel: 506-392-5294; *Fax:* 506-392-8108
florenpl@gnb.ca
www.facebook.com/ALMcCainPublicLibrary
Julie Craig, Manager

Fredericton: Dre Marguerite Michaud Library/Bibliothèque Dr Marguerite Michaud
Centre communautaire Sainte-Anne, 715 Priestman St., Fredericton, NB E3B 5W7
Tél: 506-453-7100; *Téléc:* 506-453-3958
bibliodmm@gnb.ca
Olena Bedoieva, Director

Fredericton: Fredericton Public Library
12 Carleton St., Fredericton, NB E3B 5P4
Tel: 506-460-2800; *Fax:* 506-460-2801
ftonpub@gnb.ca
twitter.com/FredLibrary; www.facebook.com/FredLibrary
Julia Stewart, Library Director
Stephanie Furrow, Head, Reference Services
Erin Smith, Head, Young Adult & Adult Services
Sheila Grondin-Lyons, Supervisor, Circulation

Fredericton: Fredericton Public Library - Nashwaaksis
324 Fulton Ave., Fredericton, NB E3A 5J4
Tel: 506-453-3241; *Fax:* 506-444-4129
nashwaaksis.library@gnb.ca
www.facebook.com/NasisLibrary
Candace Hare, Director

Fredericton: New Brunswick Public Library Service (NBPLS)/Service des bibliothèques publiques du Nouveau-Brunswick
#2, 570 Two Nations Crossing, Fredericton, NB E3A 0X9
Tel: 506-453-2354; *Fax:* 506-444-4064
nbpls-sbpnb@gnb.ca
www2.gnb.ca/content/gnb/en/departments/nbpl.html

Ella Nason, Acting Executive Director
ella.nason@gnb.ca
Emanuel Actarian, Head, Collections Management
emanuel.actarian@gnb.ca
Lorraine Morehouse, Head, Circulation & Access Services
lorraine.morehouse@gnb.ca
Kate Thompson, Head, Public Services Development
kate.thompson@gnb.ca
Teresa Johnson, Director, Research & Planning
teresa.johnson@gnb.ca

Grand Falls: Grand Falls Public Library/Bibliothèque publique de Grand-Sault
#201, 131 Pleasant St., Grand Falls, NB E3Z 1G6
Tel: 506-475-7781; *Fax:* 506-475-7783
gfplib@gnb.ca
www.facebook.com/bibliograndsault.grandfallslib
Audrée-Ann Ramacieri-Tremblay, Library Director

Grand Manan: Grand Manan Library
1144 Rte. 776, Grand Manan, NB E5G 4E8
Tel: 506-662-7099; *Fax:* 506-662-7094
grandmananlibrary@gnb.ca
www.facebook.com/GrandMananFreePublicLibrary
Kendra Neves, Manager

Hartland: Dr. Walter Chestnut Public Library/Bibliothèque publique Dr-Walter-Chestnut
#1, 395 Main St., Hartland, NB E7P 2N3
Tel: 506-375-4876; *Fax:* 506-375-6816
hartlandl@gnb.ca
www.facebook.com/165459630180967
Marsha MacDonald-Nason, Manager

Harvey: Harvey Community Library
Harvey High School, 2055 Rte. 3, Harvey, NB E6K 1L1
Tel: 506-366-2206; *Fax:* 506-366-2210
harvey.library@gnb.ca
www.facebook.com/433288416758301
Jennifer Hunter, Acting Manager

Hillsborough: Hillsborough Public Library
#2, 2849 Main St., Hillsborough, NB E4H 2X7
Tel: 506-734-3722; *Fax:* 506-734-3711
hillsborough.publiclibrary@gnb.ca
www.facebook.com/hillsboroughpubliclibrary
Rebekah Wheaton, Acting Manager

Kedgwick: Kedgwick Public Library/Bibliothèque publique de Kedgwick
116 Notre-Dame St., #P, Kedgwick, NB E8B 1H8
Tel: 506-284-2757; *Fax:* 506-284-4557
bibliopk@gnb.ca
Diane Thompson, Manager

Lamèque: Bibliothèque publique de Lamèque/Lamèque Public Library
46, rue du Pêcheur nord, Lamèque, NB E8T 1J3
Tél: 506-344-3262; *Téléc:* 506-344-3263
bibliopl@gnb.ca
www.facebook.com/bibliolameque
Lison Gaudet, Gestionnaire de bibliothèque

McAdam: McAdam Public Library
Municipal Bldg., 146 Saunders Rd., McAdam, NB E6J 1L2
Tel: 506-784-1403; *Fax:* 506-784-1402
mcadam.library@gnb.ca
www.facebook.com/McAdamPublicLibrary
Julian Christie, Manager

Memramcook: Memramcook Public Library/Bibliothèque publique de Memramcook
#1, 540 Centrale St., Memramcook, NB E4K 3S6
Tel: 506-758-4029; *Fax:* 506-758-4030
bibliopm@gnb.ca
www.facebook.com/BiblioMemramcook

Minto: Minto Public Library
Municipal Bldg., #2, 420 Pleasant Dr., Minto, NB E4B 2T3
Tel: 506-327-3220; *Fax:* 506-327-3041
minto.publiclibrary@gnb.ca
www.facebook.com/MintoPublicLibrary
Mary Lambropoulos, Manager

Miramichi: Chatham Public Library
24 King St., Miramichi, NB E1N 2N1
Tel: 506-773-6274; *Fax:* 506-773-6963
chathmpl@gnb.ca
www.facebook.com/chathampubliclibrary
Jennifer Wilcox, Director

Miramichi: Médiathèque Père-Louis-Lamontagne
Centre communautaire Carrefour Beausoleil, 300
Beaverbrook Rd., Miramichi, NB E1V 1A1
Tel: 506-627-4084; *Fax:* 506-627-4592
mediathequep@gnb.ca
www.facebook.com/602676229862235
Geneviève Thériault-McGraw, Director

Miramichi: Newcastle Public Library
100 Fountain Head Lane, Miramichi, NB E1V 4A1
Tel: 506-623-2450; *Fax:* 506-623-2335
npublib@gnb.ca
www.facebook.com/NewcastlePublicLibrary
Maureen Wallace, Director

Moncton: Moncton Public Library/Bibliothèque
publique de Moncton
#101, 644 Main St., Moncton, NB E1C 1E2
Tel: 506-869-6000; *Fax:* 506-869-6040
mplib@gnb.ca
monctonpubliclibrary.ca
www.instagram.com/bibliomonctonlibrary;
twitter.com/MonctonLibrary;
www.facebook.com/monctonpubliclibrary
Chantale Bellemare, Director
Katelynn Siddall, Head, Young Adult & Adult Services
Lindsay Warner, Head, Children's Services

Nackawic: Nackawic Public - School
Library/Bibliothèque publique-scolaire de Nackawic
30 Landegger Dr., Nackawic, NB E6G 1E9
Tel: 506-575-2136; *Fax:* 506-575-2336
nackawic.library@gnb.ca
www.facebook.com/173718052683180
Paulette Tonner, Manager

New Bandon: Upper Miramichi Community Library
#1, 7263 Rte. 8, New Bandon, NB E9C 2A7
Tel: 506-365-2096; *Fax:* 506-365-2052
uppermiramichi.communitylibrary@gnb.ca
www.facebook.com/UpperMiramichiCommunityLibrary
Tabatha Sheffroth, Manager

Oromocto: Fay Tidd Public Library
54 Miramichi Rd., Oromocto, NB E2V 1S2
Tel: 506-357-3329; *Fax:* 506-357-5161
oromocto.publiclibrary@gnb.ca
www.facebook.com/OromoctoPublicLibraryBibliotequePubliqueO
romocto
Christin Sheridan, Library Director

Perth-Andover: Perth-Andover Public
Library/Bibliothèque publique de Perth-Andover
642 East Riverside Dr., Perth-Andover, NB E7H 1Z6
Tel: 506-273-2843; *Fax:* 506-273-1913
paplib@gnb.ca
www.facebook.com/173921195993003
Tammie Wright, Manager

Petit-Rocher: Bibliothèque publique de
Petit-Rocher/Petit-Rocher Public Library
57, rue Rochette, Petit-Rocher, NB E8J 1J5
Tél: 506-542-2744; *Téléc:* 506-542-2745
bibliopr@gnb.ca
www.facebook.com/bibliopr
Sonia Godin, Gestionnaire de bibliothèque

Petitcodiac: Petitcodiac Public Library
#101, 6 Kay St., Petitcodiac, NB E4Z 4K6
Tel: 506-756-3144; *Fax:* 506-756-3142
petitcodiac.publiclibrary@gnb.ca
twitter.com/PetitcodiacLib;
www.facebook.com/PetitcodiacPublicLibrary
Danny Jacobs, Manager

Plaster Rock: Plaster Rock Public - School
Library/Bibliothèque publique-scolaire de Plaster
Rock
290A Main St., Plaster Rock, NB E7G 2C6
Tel: 506-356-6018; *Fax:* 506-356-6019
prplib@gnb.ca
www.facebook.com/221659757862270
Patricia Corey, Manager

Port Elgin: Port Elgin Public Library
33 Moore Rd., Port Elgin, NB E4M 2E6
Tel: 506-538-9001
portepl@gnb.ca
www.facebook.com/portelginlibrary
Kathleen Grigg, Manager

Quispamsis: Kennebecasis Public Library
1 Landing Ct., Quispamsis, NB E2E 4R2
Tel: 506-849-5314
kennebpl@gnb.ca
twitter.com/kvlibrary; www.facebook.com/kennebpl
Laura Corscadden, Director

Richibucto: Richibucto Public Library/Bibliothèque
publique de Richibucto
9376 Main St., Richibucto, NB E4W 4C9
Tel: 506-523-7851; *Fax:* 506-523-2019
bibliori@gnb.ca
www.facebook.com/richibuctopubliclibrary
Sylvie Bourque, Manager

Riverview: Riverview Public Library
34 Honour House Ct., Riverview, NB E1B 3Y9
Tel: 506-387-2108; *Fax:* 506-387-7120
rplib@gnb.ca
www.facebook.com/riverviewpubliclibrary
Elizabeth Boutilier, Director

Rogersville: Rogersville Public Library
#1, 28 Boucher St., Rogersville, NB E4Y 1X5
Tel: 506-775-2102; *Fax:* 506-775-2087
bibliorog@gnb.ca
www.facebook.com/bibliothequepubliquederogersvillepubliclibrar
y
Maribeth Maillet, Manager

Sackville: Sackville Public Library
66 Main St., Sackville, NB E4L 4A7
Tel: 506-364-4915
spublib@gnb.ca
www.facebook.com/sackvillepubliclibrary
Allan Alward, Manager

Saint John: Le Cormoran Library
67 Ragged Point Rd., Saint John, NB E2K 5C3
Tel: 506-658-4610; *Fax:* 506-658-3984
bibliolc@gnb.ca
Mireille Mercure, Director

Saint John: Saint John Free Public Library
1 Market Sq., Saint John, NB E2L 4Z6
Tel: 506-643-7236; *Fax:* 506-643-7225
sjfpl@gnb.ca
twitter.com/saintjohnfpl; www.facebook.com/sjfpl
Laura Corscadden, Library Director
Keith MacKinnon, Head, Reference Services
Heather McKend, Head, Children's Services
Daniel Teed, Head, Young Adult & Adult Services
Mark Goodfellow, Supervisor, Circulation
Tina Kieffer, Supervisor, Circulation

Saint John: Saint John Free Public Library
55 McDonald St., Saint John, NB E2J 0C7
Tel: 506-643-7250; *Fax:* 506-643-7225
eastbranch.publiclibrary@gnb.ca
twitter.com/EastSJLibrary;
www.facebook.com/290748454326495
Emily King, Manager

Saint John: Saint John Free Public Library
Lancaster Mall, 621 Fairville Blvd., Saint John, NB E2M 4X5
Tel: 506-643-7260; *Fax:* 506-643-7225
westbranch.publiclibrary@gnb.ca
www.facebook.com/westbranchlibrarysj
Robin Sexton-Mayes, Director

Saint-Antoine: Omer-Léger Public
Library/Bibliothèque publique de Omer-Léger
#100, 4556 Principale St., Saint-Antoine, NB E4V 1R3
Tel: 506-525-4028; *Fax:* 506-525-4199
bibliosa@gnb.ca
www.facebook.com/BibliothequePubliqueOmerLegerPublicLibrar
y
Sylvie Hébert, Manager

Saint-François: Mgr. Plourde Public
Library/Bibliothèque publique Mgr-Plourde
15 Bellevue St., Saint-François, NB E7A 1A4
Tel: 506-992-6052; *Fax:* 506-992-6047
stfplib@gnb.ca
Tania St-Onge, Manager

Saint-Léonard: Dr. Lorne J. Violette Public
Library/Bibliothèque publique Dr.-Lorne-J.-Violette
180 St-Jean St., Saint-Léonard, NB E7E 2B9
Tel: 506-423-3025; *Fax:* 506-423-3026
stlplib@gnb.ca
Sophie-Michele Cyr, Manager

Saint-Quentin: La Moisson Public
Library/Bibliothèque publique La Moisson de
Saint-Quentin
206 Canada St., Saint-Quentin, NB E8A 1H1
Tel: 506-235-1955; *Fax:* 506-235-1957
bibliolm@gnb.ca
Hélène DuRepos Thériault, Manager

Salisbury: Salisbury Public Library
3215 Main St., Salisbury, NB E4J 2K7
Tel: 506-372-3240; *Fax:* 506-372-3261
salisbury.publiclibrary@gnb.ca
www.salisburylibrary.org
www.instagram.com/salisburypubliclibrary;
www.facebook.com/SalisburyPublicLibrary
Cathy MacDonald, Manager

Shediac: Shediac Public Library/Bibliothèque
publique de Shediac
#100, 290 Main St., Shediac, NB E4P 2E3
Tel: 506-532-7014; *Fax:* 506-532-8400
Other Numbers: 506-532-7000
bibliosh@gnb.ca
biblioshediaclibrary.ca
twitter.com/shediaclibrary; www.facebook.com/ShediacLibrary
Gabrielle LeBlanc, Manager

Shippagan: Bibliothèque publique Laval
Goupil/Laval Goupil Public Library
128, rue Mgr-Chiasson, Shippagan, NB E8S 1X7
Tél: 506-336-3920; *Téléc:* 506-336-3921
bibliops@gnb.ca
www.facebook.com/BibliothequepubliqueLavalGoupil
Nadine Robichaud, Gestionnaire

St Andrews: Ross Memorial Library
110 King St., St Andrews, NB E5B 1Y6
Tel: 506-529-5125; *Fax:* 506-529-5129
standrpl@gnb.ca
www.facebook.com/rossmemlibrary
Lesley Wells, Manager

St Stephen: St Croix Public Library
11 King St., St Stephen, NB E3L 2C1
Tel: 506-466-7529; *Fax:* 506-466-7574
ststeppl@gnb.ca
www.facebook.com/ststephenlibrary
Rebekah Wheaton, Director

Stanley: Stanley Community Library
#2, 28 Bridge St., Stanley, NB E6B 1B2
Tel: 506-367-2492; *Fax:* 506-367-2764
stanley.library@gnb.ca
www.facebook.com/StanleyCommunityLibrary
Tim Sarty, Manager

Sussex: Sussex Regional Library
46 Magnolia Ave., Sussex, NB E4E 2H2
Tel: 506-432-4585; *Fax:* 506-432-4583
sussexpl@gnb.ca
www.facebook.com/BibSussexPl
Vanessa Black, Director

Tracadie: Bibliothèque publique de
Tracadie/Tracadie Public Library
3620, rue Principale, Tracadie, NB E1X 1G5
Tél: 506-394-4005; *Téléc:* 506-394-4009
bibliots@gnb.ca
www.facebook.com/bibliotracadie
Marie-Claude Gagnon, Directrice

Woodstock: L.P. Fisher Public Library/Bibliothèque
publique L.-P.-Fisher
679 Main St., Woodstock, NB E7M 2E1
Tel: 506-325-4777; *Fax:* 506-325-4811
lpfisher.library@gnb.ca
www.facebook.com/L.P.Fisher.Library
Jennifer Carson, Director

Archives

Bathurst: Herman J. Good, VC, Royal Canadian
Legion
575 St Peters Ave., Bathurst, NB E2A 2Y5
Tel: 506-546-3135; *Fax:* 506-546-1011
hermanjgoodvc.tripod.com/museum.html

Bouctouche: Musée de Kent
150, ch du Couvent, Bouctouche, NB E4S 3C1
Tél: 506-743-5005
museedekent@gmail.com
museedekent.wixsite.com
www.facebook.com/museedekent

Dalhousie: **Restigouche Regional Museum**
115 George St., Dalhousie, NB E8C 1R6
Tel: 506-684-7490
info.rrm.mrr@gmail.com
www.facebook.com/restigoucheregionalmuseum

Edmundston: **Centre de documentation et d'études Madawaskayennes**
Bibliothèque Rhéa-Larose, 165, boul Hébert, Edmundston, NB E3V 2S8
Tél: 506-737-5058; *Téléc:* 506-737-5373
brl-ce@umoncton.ca
www.umoncton.ca/umce-bibliotheque/cdem
Émilie Lefrançois, Responsable
emilie.lefrancois@umoncton.ca
506-737-5266 ext. 5266
Claire Charest, Assistance aux chercheures
claire.d.charest@umoncton.ca
506-737-5050 ext. 5247

Fredericton: **Provincial Archives of New Brunswick/Archives provinciales du Nouveau-Brunswick**
University of New Brunswick, Bonar Law-Bennett Bldg., 23 Dineen Dr., Fredericton, NB E3B 5H1
Tel: 506-453-2122
provincial.archives@gnb.ca
archives.gnb.ca
Joanna Aiton Kerr, Manager
joanna.aitonkerr@gnb.ca
506-453-8431

Grand Falls: **Grand Falls Museum/Musée de Grand-Sault**
68 Madawaska Rd., Grand Falls, NB E3Y 1C6
Tel: 506-473-5265
www.facebook.com/103286554538362

Grand Manan: **Grand Manan Museum**
1141 Rte. 776, Grand Manan, NB E5G 4E9
Tel: 506-662-5277
gmadmin@grandmananmuseum.ca
www.grandmananmuseum.ca/museum—archives-collection
twitter.com/GMMuseum;
www.facebook.com/GrandMananMuseum
M.J. Edwards, Director & Curator
Ava Sturgeon, Archivist

Miramichi: **St Michael's Museum, Genealogical Centre & Catholic Bookstore**
10 Howard St., Miramichi, NB E1N 3A7
Tel: 506-778-5152
mmuseum@nbnet.nb.ca

Saint John: **New Brunswick Museum/Musée du Nouveau-Brunswick**
277 Douglas Ave., Saint John, NB E2K 1E5
Tel: 506-643-2322; *Fax:* 506-643-2360
Toll-Free: 888-268-9595
archives@nbm-mnb.ca
www.nbm-mnb.ca
twitter.com/nbmmnb; www.facebook.com/nbmmnb
Felicity Osepchook, Curator, Archives & Manager, Research Library
felicity.osepchook@nbm-mnb.ca
506-643-2324
Mary Kuna, Library & Archival Assistant
mary.kuna@nbm-mnb.ca
506-643-2324
Jennifer Longon, Library & Archival Assistant
jennifer.longon@nbm-mnb.ca
506-643-2397

Saint John: **Roman Catholic Diocese of Saint John**
1 Bayard Dr., Saint John, NB E2L 3L5
Tel: 506-653-6807; *Fax:* 506-653-6812
archives@dioceseofsaintjohn.org
www.dioceseofsaintjohn.org
Mary Kilfoil McDevitt, Archivist

Saint John: **Saint John Jewish Historical Society Inc.**
91 Leinster St., Saint John, NB E2L 1J2
Tel: 506-633-1833; *Fax:* 506-642-9926
sjjhm@nbnet.nb.ca
jewishmuseumsj.com
Katherine Biggs-Craft, Curator

Shippagan: **Société historique Nicolas-Denys**
218, boul J.-D.-Gauthier, #PIL061, Shippagan, NB E8S 1P6
Tél: 506-336-3461; *Téléc:* 506-336-3603
shnd@umoncton.ca
www.shnd.ca

Raymond Léger, Président par interim
Nathalie Lanteigne, Secrétaire administrative

St Andrews: **Charlotte County Historical Society, Inc.**
123 Frederick St., St Andrews, NB E5B 1Z1
Tel: 506-529-4248
contact@ccarchives.ca
www.ccarchives.ca

Woodstock: **Carleton County Historical Society**
128 Connell St., Woodstock, NB E7M 1L5
Tel: 506-328-9706; *Fax:* 506-328-2942
cchs@nb.aibn.com
www.cchsnb.ca

Newfoundland & Labrador

Regional Systems

Provincial Information & Library Resources Board
48 St Georges Ave., Stephenville, NL A2N 1K9
Tel: 709-643-0900; *Fax:* 709-643-0925
nlpl.ca
Andrew Hunt, Executive Director
ahunt@nlpl.ca
Keith Sweetland, Director, Information Technology
ksweetland@nlpl.ca

Public Libraries

Arnold's Cove: **Arnold's Cove Public Library**
5 Highliner Dr., Arnold's Cove, NL A0B 1A0
Tel: 709-463-8707
arnoldscove@nlpl.ca
nlpl.ca
www.facebook.com/202329123122799
Beverly Best, Librarian

Baie Verte: **Baie Verte Public Library**
Hwy. 410, Baie Verte, NL A0K 1B0
Tel: 709-532-8361
baieverte@nlpl.ca
nlpl.ca
www.facebook.com/294244900591746
Terri-Lynn Pinksen, Librarian

Bay Roberts: **Bay Roberts Public Library**
76 Cross Rd., Bay Roberts, NL A0A 1G0
Tel: 709-786-9629
bayroberts@nlpl.ca
nlpl.ca
www.facebook.com/bayrobertspubliclibrary
Marilyn Clarke, Librarian

Bell Island: **Bell Island Public Library**
Provincial Bldg., 20 Bennett St., Bell Island, NL A0A 4H0
Tel: 709-488-2413
bellisland@nlpl.ca
nlpl.ca
www.facebook.com/121841385143273
Melanie Butler, Librarian

Bishop's Falls: **Bishop's Falls Public Library**
Town Hall, 445 Main St., Bishop's Falls, NL A0H 1C0
Tel: 709-258-6244
bishopsfalls@nlpl.ca
nlpl.ca
www.facebook.com/196092067069090
Elizabeth John, Librarian

Bonavista: **Bonavista Memorial Public Library**
PO Box 400, Bonavista, NL A0C 1B0
Tel: 709-468-2185
bonavista@nlpl.ca
nlpl.ca
www.facebook.com/BonavistaPublicLibrary
Brenda Wilton, Librarian

Botwood: **Botwood Kinsmen Public Library**
240 Water St., Botwood, NL A0H 1E0
Tel: 709-257-2091
botwood@nlpl.ca
nlpl.ca
www.facebook.com/277034772326408
Patricia Lanning, Librarian

Brigus: **Brigus Public Library**
7 South St., Brigus, NL A0A 1K0
Tel: 709-528-3156
brigus@nlpl.ca
nlpl.ca
www.facebook.com/293485244001700

Raelene Wall, Librarian

Buchans: **Buchans Public Library**
Lakeside Academy, Buchans, NL A0H 1G0
Tel: 709-672-3859
nlpl.ca
www.facebook.com/166209073464618
Dawn Pennell, Librarian

Burgeo: **Burgeo Public Library**
1 School Rd., Burgeo, NL A0N 2H0
Tel: 709-886-2730
nlpl.ca
www.facebook.com/burgeopubliclibrary
Freda MacDonald, Librarian

Burin: **Burin Public Library**
Pearce Junior High School, 48B Main St., Burin, NL A0E 1G0
Tel: 709-891-1924
burin@nlpl.ca
nlpl.ca/component/jumi/library.html?site_id=bbn
www.facebook.com/164399110273548
Patricia Peddle, Librarian

Cape St George: **Cape St George Public Library**
879 Oceanview Dr., Cape St George, NL A0N 1T1
Tel: 709-644-2852
capestgeorge@nlpl.ca
nlpl.ca
www.facebook.com/capestgeorgepubliclibrary
Elizabeth Cornect, Librarian

Carbonear: **Carbonear Public Library**
256 Water St., Carbonear, NL A1Y 1C4
Tel: 709-596-3382
carbonear@nlpl.ca
nlpl.ca
www.facebook.com/180339618708886
Tracey Vaughan-Evans, Librarian

Carmanville: **Carmanville Public Library**
Phoenix Academy, 95-97 Main St., Carmanville, NL A0G 1N0
Tel: 709-534-2370
carmanville@nlpl.ca
nlpl.ca
www.facebook.com/nlpl
Daphne Brown, Librarian

Cartwright: **Cartwright Public Library**
Henry Gordon Academy, Cartwright, NL A0K 1V0
Tel: 709-938-7219
cartwright@nlpl.ca
nlpl.ca
www.facebook.com/CartwrightPublicLibrary
Hazel Dyson, Librarian

Centreville: **Centreville Public Library**
Centreville Academy, 2 Memory Lane, Centreville, NL A0G 4P0
Tel: 709-678-2700
centreville@nlpl.ca
nlpl.ca
www.facebook.com/162023927217777
Veronica Rogers, Librarian

Change Islands: **Change Islands Public Library**
A.R. Scammell Academy, Main St., Change Islands, NL A0G 1R0
Tel: 709-621-5566
nlpl.ca
www.facebook.com/201802779889508
Amanda Hurley, Librarian

Churchill Falls: **Churchill Falls Library**
Town Centre, Churchill Falls, NL A0R 1A0
Tel: 709-925-3281; *Fax:* 709-925-3487
churchillfallslibrary@gmail.com
www.facebook.com/cflibrary
Katie Noel, Head Librarian
Danni Ricketts, Assistant Librarian

Clarenville: **Clarenville Public Library**
98 Manitoba Dr., Clarenville, NL A5A 1K7
Tel: 709-466-7634
clarenville@nlpl.ca
nlpl.ca
www.facebook.com/ClarenvillePublicLibrary
Kaitlyn Penney, Librarian

Conception Bay South: Conception Bay South Public Library
110 Conception Bay Hwy., Conception Bay South, NL A1W 3A5
Tel: 709-834-4241
conceptionbaysouth@nlpl.ca
nlpl.ca
www.facebook.com/CBSPublicLibrary
Rebecca Stone, Librarian

Cormack: Cormack Public Library
280A Veterans Dr., Cormack, NL A8A 2R4
Tel: 709-635-7022
cormack@nlpl.ca
nlpl.ca
www.facebook.com/cormackpubliclibrary
Amanda Wellon, Librarian

Corner Brook: Corner Brook Public Library
4 West St., Corner Brook, NL A2H 0C1
Tel: 709-634-0013
cornerbrook@nlpl.ca
nlpl.ca
www.facebook.com/CornerBrookPublicLibrary
Cathy Regular, Librarian

Cow Head: Cow Head Public Library
119 Main St., Cow Head, NL A0K 2A0
Tel: 709-243-2467
cowhead@nlpl.ca
nlpl.ca
www.facebook.com/cowheadpubliclibrary
Nora Shears, Librarian

Daniels Harbour: Daniels Harbour Public Library
15 Church Lane, Daniels Harbour, NL A0K 2C0
Tel: 709-898-2283
danielsharbour@nlpl.ca
nlpl.ca
www.facebook.com/DanielsHarbourPublicLibrary
Sharon Humber, Librarian

Deer Lake: Deer Lake Public Library
4 Poplar Rd., Deer Lake, NL A8A 1Z4
Tel: 709-635-3671
deerlake@nlpl.ca
nlpl.ca
www.facebook.com/DeerLakePublicLibrary
Worneta Cramm, Librarian

Doyles: Codroy Valley Public Library
Belanger Memorial School, Doyles, NL A0N 1J0
Tel: 709-955-3158
codroyvalley@nlpl.ca
nlpl.ca
www.facebook.com/CodroyValleyPublicLibrary
Danielle Peddle, Librarian

Fogo Island: Fogo Island Public Library
Fogo Island Central Academy, 1 Iceberg Arena Rd., Fogo Island, NL A0G 2B0
Tel: 709-266-2210
fogoisland@nlpl.ca
nlpl.ca
www.facebook.com/293454134002404
Melissa Collins, Librarian

Fortune: Fortune Public Library
1 Temple St., Fortune, NL A0E 1P0
Tel: 709-832-0232
fortune@nlpl.ca
nlpl.ca
www.facebook.com/1638258466449638
Candace Bennett Weed, Librarian

Fox Harbour: Fox Harbour Public Library
2 Southside Rd., Fox Harbour, NL A0B 1V0
Tel: 709-227-2135
foxharbour@nlpl.ca
nlpl.ca
www.facebook.com/2051537098404597
Catherine Murray, Librarian

Gambo: Gambo Public Library
6 Centennial Rd., Gambo, NL A0G 1T0
Tel: 709-674-5052
gambo@nlpl.ca
nlpl.ca
www.facebook.com/Gambolibrary
April Hunt, Librarian

Gander: Gander Public Library
6 Bell Pl., Gander, NL A1V 1X2
Tel: 709-651-5354
gander@nlpl.ca
nlpl.ca
www.facebook.com/Ganderlibrary
Michelle Stuckless, Librarian

Garnish: Garnish (Greta Hollett) Memorial Library
PO Box 40, Garnish, NL A0E 1T0
Tel: 709-826-2371
garnish@nlpl.ca
nlpl.ca
www.facebook.com/GarnishPublicLibrary
Linda Nolan, Librarian

Gaultois: Gaultois Public Library
Gaultlois Town Council Bldg., 10 Valley Rd., Gaultois, NL A0H 1N0
Tel: 709-841-3311
gaultois@nlpl.ca
nlpl.ca
www.facebook.com/120849931351864

Glenwood: Glenwood Public Library
26 Main St., Glenwood, NL A0G 2K0
Tel: 709-679-5700
glenwood@nlpl.ca
nlpl.ca
www.facebook.com/918371634916094
Kelly Gillingham, Librarian

Glovertown: Glovertown Public Library
Glovertown Academy, 10 Penney's Brook Rd., Glovertown, NL A0G 2L0
Tel: 709-533-6688
nlpl.ca
Kim Pollard, Librarian

Grand Bank: Grand Bank Public Library
19 Church St., Grand Bank, NL A0E 1W0
Tel: 709-832-0310
grandbank@nlpl.ca
nlpl.ca
www.facebook.com/GrandBankPublicLibrary
Karen Anderson, Librarian

Grand Falls-Windsor: Grand Falls-Windsor Public Library
Gordon Pinsent Centre for the Arts, 1 Cromer Ave., 2nd Fl., Grand Falls-Windsor, NL A2A 1W9
Tel: 709-489-2303
nlpl.ca
Nancy Barker, Librarian

Greenspond: Greenspond Memorial Library
32 Main St., Greenspond, NL A0G 2N0
Tel: 709-269-3434
greenspond@nlpl.ca
nlpl.ca
www.facebook.com/112046647267341
Roxane Hounsell, Librarian

Happy Valley-Goose Bay: Happy Valley-Goose Bay Public Library
Elizabeth Goudie Bldg., 141 Hamilton River Rd., Happy Valley-Goose Bay, NL A0P 1E0
Tel: 709-896-8045
nlpl.ca
Hyra Skoglund, Librarian

Harbour Breton: Harbour Breton Public Library
King Academy High School, 43 Main Rd. North, 2nd Fl., Harbour Breton, NL A0H 1P0
Tel: 709-885-2165
harbourbreton@nlpl.ca
nlpl.ca
www.facebook.com/106888722722378
Kerri Hunt, Librarian

Harbour Grace: Harbour Grace Public Library
106 Harvey St., Harbour Grace, NL A0A 2M0
Tel: 709-596-3894
harbourgrace@nlpl.ca
nlpl.ca
www.facebook.com/561859537294615
Doreen Quinn, Librarian

Hare Bay: Hare Bay / Dover Public Library
Jane Collins Academy, 22 Anstey's Rd., Hare Bay, NL A0G 2P0
Tel: 709-537-2391
harebay@nlpl.ca
nlpl.ca
www.facebook.com/1510720842579078
Jane Rogers-Willis, Librarian

Harry's Harbour: Harry's Harbour Public Library
17 Harry's Harbour Rd., Harry's Harbour, NL A0J 1E0
Tel: 709-624-5464
harrysharbour@nlpl.ca
nlpl.ca
www.facebook.com/1198264615394430
Janice Sharpe, Librarian

Hermitage: Hermitage Public Library
John Watkins Academy, 10 Boys Rd., Hermitage, NL A0H 1S0
Tel: 709-883-2421
hermitage@nlpl.ca
nlpl.ca
www.facebook.com/544831812340427
Bernice Willmott, Librarian

Holyrood: Holyrood Public Library
5 Liam Hickey Dr., TCH Access Rd., Holyrood, NL A0A 2R0
Tel: 709-229-7852
holyrood@nlpl.ca
nlpl.ca
www.facebook.com/HolyroodPublicLibrary
Michelle Potter, Librarian

King's Point: King's Point Public Library
108 Main St., King's Point, NL A0J 1H0
Tel: 709-268-2282
nlpl.ca
Patsy Bowers, Librarian

L'Anse au Loup: L'Anse Au Loup Public Library
Lawrence D. O'Brien Town Center, 11 Branch Rd., L'Anse au Loup, NL A0K 3L0
Tel: 709-927-5542
lanseauloup@nlpl.ca
nlpl.ca
www.facebook.com/LabradorSouthPublicLibrary
Lauralee Wellman, Librarian

La Scie: La Scie Public Library
Town Hall, 7 Church Rd., La Scie, NL A0K 3M0
Tel: 709-675-2004
lascie@nlpl.ca
nlpl.ca
www.facebook.com/241047925952012
Krista-Lee Haas, Librarian

Labrador City: Labrador City Public Library
306 Hudson Dr., Labrador City, NL A2V 1L5
Tel: 709-944-2190
labradorcity@nlpl.ca
nlpl.ca
www.facebook.com/labradorcitylibrary
Trudy Andrews, Librarian

Lark Harbour: Lark Harbour Public Library
St. James All Grade School, Main St., Lark Harbour, NL A0L 1H0
Tel: 709-681-2147
larkharbour@nlpl.ca
nlpl.ca
www.facebook.com/LarkHarbourPublicLibrary
Roxanne Sheppard, Librarian

Lewisporte: Lewisporte Public Library
Town Hall, 152 Main St., Lewisporte, NL A0G 3A0
Tel: 709-535-2519
nlpl.ca
www.facebook.com/149315705125296
Bobbi Benson, Librarian

Lourdes: Lourdes Public Library
Lourdes Elementary School, 82 Main St., Lourdes, NL A0N 1R0
Tel: 709-642-5388
lourdes@nlpl.ca
nlpl.ca
www.facebook.com/LourdesPublicLibrary
Sabrina Rowsell, Librarian

Lumsden: Lumsden Public Library
Lumsden Academy, Forest Rd., Lumsden, NL A0G 3E0
Tel: 709-530-2617
lumsden@nlpl.ca
nlpl.ca
www.facebook.com/780839978704898
Kay Stagg, Librarian

Marystown: Marystown Public Library
Sacred Heart Elementary School, Columbia Dr., Marystown, NL A0E 2M0
Tel: 709-279-1507
marystown@nlpl.ca
nlpl.ca
www.facebook.com/1484545131855743
Patsy Mayo, Librarian

McKays: Bay St. George South Public Library
E. A. Butler School, 615 Main Rd., McKays, NL A0N 1G0
Tel: 709-645-2186
baystgeorgesouth@nlpl.ca
nlpl.ca
www.facebook.com/BayStGeorgeSouthPublicLibrary
Leanda Shears, Librarian

Mount Pearl: Mount Pearl (Ross King) Memorial Public Library
65 Olympic Dr., Mount Pearl, NL A1N 5H6
Tel: 709-368-3603
mountpearl@nlpl.ca
nlpl.ca
www.facebook.com/MountPearlPublicLibrary
Gwen Mitchell, Librarian

Musgrave Harbour: John B. Wheeler Public Library
17 Lady Peace Ave., Musgrave Harbour, NL A0G 3J0
Tel: 709-655-2730
nlpl.ca
Eunice Abbott, Librarian

Norris Arm: Norris Arm Public Library
65 Norris Ave., Norris Arm, NL A0G 3M0
Tel: 709-653-2531
nlpl.ca
Joanne Barrett, Librarian

Norris Point: Norris Point Public Library
Julia Ann Walsh Centre, #2, 6 Hospital Rd., Norris Point, NL A0K 3V0
Tel: 709-458-3368
norrispoint@nlpl.ca
nlpl.ca
www.facebook.com/norrispointpubliclibrary
Judy Samms, Librarian

North West River: North West River Library & CAP Site
PO Box 410, North West River, NL A0P 1M0
Tel: 709-497-8705; Fax: 709-497-8705
nwrvollibrary@hotmail.com
northwestriverlibrary.weebly.com
Wendy Mitchell, Librarian

Old Perlican: Old Perlican Public Library
Town Hall, 299 Blow Me Down Dr., Old Perlican, NL A0A 3G0
Tel: 709-587-2028
oldperlican@nlpl.ca
nlpl.ca
www.facebook.com/148308438552459
Cathy Hatch, Librarian

Pasadena: Pasadena Public Library
Town Council Bldg., 16 - 10th Ave., Pasadena, NL A0L 1K0
Tel: 709-686-2792
pasadena@nlpl.ca
nlpl.ca
www.facebook.com/pasadenanllibrary
Angela Menchion, Librarian

Placentia: Placentia Public Library
14 Atlantic Ave., Placentia, NL A0B 2Y0
Tel: 709-227-3621
placentia@nlpl.ca
nlpl.ca
www.facebook.com/1714616768597520
Melinda Goodland, Librarian

Point Leamington: Point Leamington Public Library
Point Leamington Academy, 1 Rices Lane, Point Leamington, NL A0H 1Z0
Tel: 709-484-3541
pointleamington@nlpl.ca
nlpl.ca
www.facebook.com/1158482777502327

Karen Smith, Librarian

Port au Port: Port au Port Public Library
St. Thomas Aquinas School, 290 Main St., Port au Port, NL A0N 1T0
Tel: 709-648-2472
portauport@nlpl.ca
nlpl.ca
www.facebook.com/portauportpubliclibrary
Janice Clarke, Librarian

Port Saunders: Port Saunders (Ingornachoix) Public Library
Main St., Port Saunders, NL A0K 4H0
Tel: 709-861-3690
portsaunders@nlpl.ca
nlpl.ca
www.facebook.com/PortSaundersPublicLibrary
Evelyn Biggin, Librarian

Port-aux-Basques: Port aux Basques Public Library
8 Grand Bay Rd., Port-aux-Basques, NL A0M 1C0
Tel: 709-695-3471
portauxbasques@nlpl.ca
nlpl.ca
www.facebook.com/PortauxBasquesPublicLibrary
Jodi McNeil, Librarian

Pouch Cove: Pouch Cove Public Library
PO Box 40, Pouch Cove, NL A0A 3L0
Tel: 709-335-2652
pouchcove@nlpl.ca
nlpl.ca
www.facebook.com/125102087554464
Laura Bragg, Librarian

Ramea: Ramea Public Library
St. Boniface All Grade School, 10 School Rd., Ramea, NL A0N 2J0
Tel: 709-625-2344
ramea@nlpl.ca
nlpl.ca
www.facebook.com/RameaPublicLibrary
Ann Margaret Cutler, Librarian

Robert's Arm: Robert's Arm Public Library
14 School Rd., Robert's Arm, NL A0J 1R0
Tel: 709-652-3100
robertsarm@nlpl.ca
nlpl.ca
www.facebook.com/106575097795003
Helen Suley, Librarian

Rocky Harbour: Rocky Harbour Public Library
Gros Morne Academy, 5 Parson's Lane, Rocky Harbour, NL A0K 4N0
Tel: 709-458-2900
rockyharbour@nlpl.ca
nlpl.ca
www.facebook.com/rockyharbourpubliclibrary
Judy Samms, Librarian

Seal Cove: Seal Cove Public Library
Seal Cove Town Council Bldg., 2 Council Rd., Seal Cove, NL A0K 5E0
Tel: 709-531-2505
sealcove@nlpl.ca
nlpl.ca
www.facebook.com/157431877976249
Karen Pinksen, Librarian

Sop's Arm: Sop's Arm Public Library
Main River Academy, 33 Academy Dr., Sop's Arm, NL A0K 5K0
Tel: 709-482-2225
sopsarm@nlpl.ca
nlpl.ca
www.facebook.com/SopsArmPublicLibrary
Diane White, Librarian

Southern Harbour: Southern Harbour Public Library
Community Centre, 1 Municipal Dr., Southern Harbour, NL A0B 3H0
Tel: 709-463-8814
nlpl.ca
www.facebook.com/187626111269277

Springdale: Springdale Public Library
Indian River High School, 10 Grant Ave., Springdale, NL A0J 1T0
Tel: 709-673-4169
springdale@nlpl.ca
nlpl.ca
www.facebook.com/183383428341681

Jennifer Brett, Librarian

St Alban's: St Alban's Public Library
Town Hall Bldg., 14 Church Rd., St Alban's, NL A0H 2E0
Tel: 709-538-3034
stalbans@nlpl.ca
nlpl.ca
www.facebook.com/164395240275009
Kerri-Ann King, Librarian
kking@nlpl.ca

St Anthony: St Anthony Public Library
St Anthony Town Council Bldg., 95 West St., St Anthony, NL A0K 4S0
Tel: 709-454-3025
stanthony@nlpl.ca
nlpl.ca
www.facebook.com/StAnthonyPublicLibrary
Jocelyn Elliott, Librarian

St Bride's: St Brides Public Library
Council Bldg., Main Rd., St Bride's, NL A0B 1E0
Tel: 709-337-2360
nlpl.ca
www.facebook.com/1058030284216285
Jacqueline Nash, Librarian

St George's: St George's Public Library
Town Office, 93 Main St., St George's, NL A0N 1Z0
Tel: 709-647-3808
stgeorges@nlpl.ca
nlpl.ca
www.facebook.com/StGeorgesPublicLibrary
Heather Parsons, Librarian

St Lawrence: St Lawrence Public Library
St Lawrence Academy, St Lawrence, NL A0E 2V0
Tel: 709-873-2650
nlpl.ca
www.facebook.com/149095271806633
Vicki Lockyer, Librarian
vlockyer@nlpl.ca

St. John's: St John's Public Libraries
Arts & Culture Centre, 125 Allandale Rd., St. John's, NL A1B 3A3
Tel: 709-737-2133
achunter@nlpl.ca
nlpl.ca
www.facebook.com/ACHunterPublicLibrary

Stephenville: Newfoundland & Labrador Public Libraries
48 St Georges Ave., Stephenville, NL A2N 1K9
Tel: 709-643-0900; Fax: 709-643-0925
nlpl.ca
twitter.com/NLPubLibraries
Andrew Hunt, Executive Director
ahunt@nlpl.ca
Keith Sweetland, Director, Information Technology
ksweetland@nlpl.ca

Stephenville: Stephenville Public Library
45 Carolina Ave., Stephenville, NL A2N 3P8
Tel: 709-643-4262
stephenville@nlpl.ca
nlpl.ca
www.facebook.com/kindalepubliclibrary
Jaime Bourgeois, Librarian

Stephenville Crossing: Stephenville Crossing Public Library
Town Council Office, 73 West St., Stephenville Crossing, NL A0N 2C0
Tel: 709-646-2173
stephenvillecrossing@nlpl.ca
nlpl.ca
www.facebook.com/stephenvillecrossinglibrary
James Dennison, Librarian

Summerford: Summerford Public Library
Summerford Community Bldg., Main St., Summerford, NL A0G 4E0
Tel: 709-629-3244
summerford@nlpl.ca
nlpl.ca
www.facebook.com/SummerfordPublicLibrary
Mavis Boyd, Librarian
mboyd@nlpl.ca

Torbay: Torbay Public Library
1339C Torbay Rd., Torbay, NL A1K 1B2
Tel: 709-437-6571
torbay@nlpl.ca
nlpl.ca
www.facebook.com/Torbaypubliclibrary
M. Harris, Librarian

Trepassey: Trepassey Public Library
PO Box 183, Trepassey, NL A0A 4B0
Tel: 709-438-2224
trepassey@nlpl.ca
nlpl.ca
www.facebook.com/1594645407286531
Patricia McCormack, Librarian

Trinity Bay North: Trinity Bay North Public Library
PO Box 69, Trinity Bay North, NL A0C 1J0
Tel: 709-469-3045
trinitybaynorth@nlpl.ca
nlpl.ca
www.facebook.com/153591621401962
Kimberley Johnson, Librarian

Twillingate: Twillingate Public Library
J.M. Olds Collegiate, 97 Main St., Twillingate, NL A0G 4M0
Tel: 709-884-2353
twillingate@nlpl.ca
nlpl.ca
www.facebook.com/TwillingatePublicLibrary
Ashley Whitt, Librarian

Victoria: Victoria Public Library
PO Box 190, Victoria, NL A0A 4G0
Tel: 709-596-3682
nlpl.ca
www.facebook.com/1718393198381120
Shona Colbourne, Librarian

Wabush: Wabush Public Library
15 Whiteway Dr., Wabush, NL A0R 1B0
Tel: 709-282-3479
wabush@nlpl.ca
nlpl.ca
www.facebook.com/WabushPublicLibrary
Kelly Roberts, Librarian

Wesleyville: New-Wes-Valley Public Library
Pearson Academy, 139-143 Main St., Wesleyville, NL A0G 4R0
Tel: 709-536-5777
nlpl.ca
Austin King, Librarian

Whitbourne: Whitbourne Public Library
494 Main St., Whitbourne, NL A0B 3K0
Tel: 709-759-2461
whitbourne@nlpl.ca
nlpl.ca
www.facebook.com/144844512243474
Gloria Somerton, Librarian

Winterton: Winterton Public Library
Perlwin Elementary School, 102 Main Rd., Winterton, NL A0B 3M0
Tel: 709-583-2119
nlpl.ca
www.facebook.com/170470796905112
Glennys Coates, Librarian

Woody Point: Woody Point Public Library (E.L. Roberts Memorial Library)
Water St., Woody Point, NL A0K 1P0
Tel: 709-453-2556
woodypoint@nlpl.ca
nlpl.ca
www.facebook.com/WoodyPointLibrary
Michelle Harris, Librarian

Archives

Bonavista: Bonavista Historical Society
PO Box 2957, Bonavista, NL A0C 1B0
Tel: 709-468-7747; *Fax:* 709-468-2495
bonavistaarchives@outlook.com
townofbonavista.com/bonavista-archives
Crystal Fudge, Contact

Botwood: Botwood Heritage Society Archive
12 Airbase Pl., Botwood, NL A0H 1E0
Tel: 709-257-4612
Other Numbers: Off Season: 709-257-2839, ext. 224
botwoodheritage@hotmail.com
www.botwoodnl.ca/botwood-heritage-society.html
www.facebook.com/217449774933206

Happy Valley-Goose Bay: Them Days Incorporated
3 Courte Manche St., Happy Valley-Goose Bay, NL A0P 1E0
Tel: 709-896-8531; *Fax:* 709-896-4970
www.themdays.com
Tabbea Aggek, Archive Technician-Administrator

Harbour Grace: Conception Bay Museum
PO Box 298, Harbour Grace, NL A0A 2M0
Tel: 709-596-5465; *Fax:* 709-596-5465
Other Numbers: Off season: 709-595-2261
conceptionbaymuseum@outlook.com
conceptionbaymuseum.com/archive
www.instagram.com/conceptionbaymuseum;
twitter.com/cbmuseum1870;
www.facebook.com/conceptionbaymuseum
Patrick J. Collins, Chair
pjcollins@eastlink.ca

Musgrave Harbour: Fisherman's Museum
239 Main Rd., Musgrave Harbour, NL A0G 3J0
Tel: 709-655-2589; *Fax:* 709-655-2064
bantinghti@nf.aibn.com
www.musgraveharbour.com/museum.html
Mitzi Abbott, Contact

St. John's: City of St John's Archives
15 Terra Nova Rd., St. John's, NL A1B 1E7
Tel: 709-576-8167; *Fax:* 709-576-8254
archives@stjohns.ca
www.stjohns.ca/living-st-johns/city-services/archives

St. John's: Congregation of Sisters of Mercy of Newfoundland
Littledale Complex, Waterford Bridge Rd., St. John's, NL A1C 5P5
Tel: 709-726-7320; *Fax:* 709-726-4414
mercygeneralate@sistersofmercynf.org
www.sistersofmercynf.org
Elizabeth Davis, Congregational Leader

St. John's: Newfoundland Historical Society
PO Box 23154, Churchill Square, St. John's, NL A1B 4J9
Tel: 709-722-3191; *Fax:* 709-722-9035
nlhistsociety@gmail.com
www.nlhistory.ca
twitter.com/nlhistsoc; www.facebook.com/nfhistsoc
Uli Brown, Office Manager

St. John's: Presentation Congregation Archives
Cathedral Sq., Presentation Convent, 170 Military Rd., St. John's, NL A1C 5L4
Tel: 709-753-7291
presentationarchivesnl@gmail.com
www.presentationsisters.ca
Marilyn Doyle, Assistant Archivist

St. John's: Provincial Archives of Newfoundland & Labrador
9 Bonaventure Ave., St. John's, NL A1C 5P9
Tel: 709-757-8030; *Fax:* 709-757-8017
archives@therooms.ca
www.therooms.ca

St. John's: Queen's College
Archives & Special Collections, Queen Elizabeth II Library, Memorial University of Newfoundland, St. John's, NL A1B 3Y1
Tel: 709-864-4349; *Fax:* 709-864-2153
archives@mun.ca
queenscollegenl.ca
twitter.com/MUN_asc;
www.facebook.com/MUNarchivesandspecialcollections
Colleen Quigley, Division Head, Archives & Special Collections
csquigley@mun.ca
709-864-3238

St. John's: Roman Catholic Archdiocese of St John's
200 Military Rd., St. John's, NL A1C 5H5
Tel: 709-726-3660; *Fax:* 709-729-8021
rcsj.org/archives-research
Emily Gushue, Archivist
egushue@rcsj.org
709-726-3660 ext. 225

St. John's: Sport Archives of Newfoundland & Labrador
The Rooms Provincial Archives Division, 9 Bonaventure Ave., St. John's, NL A1C 5P9
Tel: 709-757-8030; *Fax:* 709-757-8017
Other Numbers: Archives Reference Desk: 709-757-8088
archives@therooms.ca
www.therooms.ca/collections-research

Trinity: Trinity Historical Society Archives
Lester-Garland House, 3rd Fl., Trinity, NL A0C 2S0
Tel: 709-464-3599; *Fax:* 709-464-3599
info@trinityhistoricalsociety.com
www.trinityhistoricalsociety.com

Northwest Territories

Regional Systems

Northwest Territories Public Library Services
75 Woodland Dr., Hay River, NT X0E 1G1
Tel: 867-874-6531; *Fax:* 867-874-3321
Toll-Free: 866-297-0232
www.ece.gov.nt.ca/en/services/nwt-public-libraries
Brian Dawson, Territorial Librarian
brian_dawson@gov.nt.ca
Louis Dolbec, Head, Technical Services
ouis-nicolas_dolbec@gov.nt.ca
Heather Hirst, Clerk, Acquisitions
heather_hirst@gov.nt.ca
Kevin Lafferty, Clerk, Interlibrary Loans
kevin_lafferty@gov.nt.ca
Janine Hoff, Coordinator, Community Library Literacy
janine_hoff@gov.nt.ca

Public Libraries

Aklavik: Aklavik Community Library
Moose Kerr School, Aklavik, NT X0E 0A0
Tel: 867-978-2536; *Fax:* 867-978-2829

Behchoko: Behchoko Community Library
c/o Chief Jimmy Bruneau School, Behchoko, NT X0E 0Y0
Tel: 867-371-4511

Deline: Deline Community Library
Ehtseo Ayha School, Deline, NT X0E 0G0
Tel: 867-589-3391; *Fax:* 867-589-4867

Fort Good Hope: Fort Good Hope Community Library
Chief T'Selehye School, Fort Good Hope, NT X0E 0H0
Tel: 867-598-2288

Fort Liard: Fort Liard Community Library
327 Valley Main St., Fort Liard, NT X0G 0A0
Tel: 867-770-4104

Fort McPherson: Fort McPherson Community Library
c/o Chief Julius School, Fort McPherson, NT X0E 0J0
Tel: 867-952-2131

Fort Providence: Zhahti Koe Community Library
Deh Gáh Elementary & Secondary School, Fort Providence, NT X0E 0L0
Tel: 867-699-3131; *Fax:* 867-699-3525
www.facebook.com/groups/312982702992631

Fort Resolution: Fort Resolution Community Library
c/o Deninu School, Fort Resolution, NT X0E 0M0
Tel: 867-394-4501
fortresolutionlibrary@gmail.com
www.facebook.com/504121656438059

Fort Simpson: John Tsetso Memorial Library
#96 - 100th St., Fort Simpson, NT X0E 0N0
Tel: 867-695-3276

Fort Smith: Mary Kaeser Library
170 McDougal Rd., Fort Smith, NT X0E 0P0
Tel: 867-872-2296; *Fax:* 867-872-5303
www.fortsmith.ca/attraction/mary-kaeser-library

Gameti: Gameti Community Library
c/o Jean Wetrade Gameti School, Gameti, NT X0E 1R0
Tel: 867-997-3600

Hay River: **Hay River Centennial Library**
75 Woodland Dr., Hay River, NT X0E 1G1
Tel: 867-874-6486
programs@hrlibrary.org
hayriver.com/library
www.facebook.com/117573528267995

Hay River: **Hay River Dene Reserve Community Library**
Chief Sunrise Education Centre, Hay River, NT X0E 1G4
Tel: 867-874-6444

Inuvik: **Inuvik Centennial Library**
100 MacKenzie Rd., Inuvik, NT X0E 0T0
Tel: 867-777-8620; *Fax:* 867-777-8621
lfrontdesk@inuvik.ca
www.inuvik.ca/en/getting-active/Library.asp

Norman Wells: **Norman Wells Community Library**
Mackenzie Mountain School, Norman Wells, NT X0E 0V0
Tel: 867-587-3714

Tuktoyaktuk: **Tuktoyaktuk Community Library**
c/o Mangilaluk School, Tuktoyaktuk, NT X0E 1C0
Tel: 867-977-2255
tuklibrary@outlook.com
www.facebook.com/TuktoyaktukCommunityLibrary

Tulita: **Tulita Community Library**
Chief Albert Wright School, Tulita, NT X0E 0K0
Tel: 867-588-4361

Ulukhaktok: **Ulukhaktok Community Library**
Helen Kalvak Elihakvik School, Ulukhaktok, NT X0E 0S0
Tel: 867-396-3804
ulukhaktoklibrary@gmail.com
www.facebook.com/ULU.HKE.Library

Wha Ti: **Wha Ti Community Library**
c/o Mezi Community School, Wha Ti, NT X0E 1P0
Tel: 867-573-3131

Yellowknife: **Yellowknife Public Library**
Centre Square Mall, 5022 - 49th St., 2nd Fl., Yellowknife, NT X1A 3R8
Tel: 867-920-5642
library@yellowknife.ca
www.yellowknife.ca/en/living-here/public-library.asp

Archives

Fort Smith: **Northern Life Museum & Cultural Centre**
110 King St., Fort Smith, NT X0E 0P0
Tel: 867-872-2859
info@nlmcc.ca
nlmcc.ca
twitter.com/NorthernLifeMus; www.facebook.com/NLMCC
Jeri Miltenberger, Manager

Yellowknife: **Prince of Wales Northern Heritage Centre**
4750 - 48th St., Yellowknife, NT X1A 2L9
Tel: 867-767-9347; *Fax:* 867-873-0660
nwtarchives@gov.nt.ca
www.nwtarchives.ca
www.facebook.com/nwtarchives
Erin Suliak, Territorial Archivist
erin_suliak@gov.nt.ca
867-767-9347 ext. 71210
Robin Weber, Archival & Library Technician
robin_weber@gov.nt.ca
867-767-9347 ext. 71211
Elizabeth Ferch, Senior Archivist
elizabeth_ferch@gov.nt.ca
867-767-9347 ext. 71215
Leslie Gordon, Senior Archivist
leslie_gordon@gov.nt.ca
867-767-9347 ext. 71213
Tiffany Champagne, Digital Records Archivist
tiffany_champagne@gov.nt.ca
867-767-9347 ext. 71212

Nova Scotia

Regional Systems

Annapolis Valley Regional Library
236 Commercial St., Berwick, NS B0P 1E0
Tel: 902-538-2665; *Fax:* 902-665-4899
Toll-Free: 866-922-0229
administration@valleylibrary.ca
www.valleylibrary.ca
www.instagram.com/avrlibrary; twitter.com/valleylibs;
www.facebook.com/AVRLibrary
Ann-Marie Mathieu, Chief Executive Officer
amathieu@valleylibrary.ca
902-538-2665 ext. 1101
Charlotte Janes, Coordinator, Systems & Collections Access
cjanes@valleylibrary.ca
902-538-2665 ext. 104
Angela Reynolds, Coordinator, Community Engagement
areynolds@valleylibrary.ca
902-538-2665 ext. 1102

Cape Breton Regional Library
50 Falmouth St., Sydney, NS B1P 6X9
Tel: 902-562-3279; *Fax:* 902-564-0765
info@cbrl.ca
cbrl.ca
www.instagram.com/cbrlibrary; twitter.com/CBRLibrary;
www.facebook.com/cbrlibrary
Eldon MacDonald, Chair

Colchester-East Hants Public Library
754 Prince St., Truro, NS B2N 1G9
Tel: 902-895-0235; *Fax:* 902-895-7149
Toll-Free: 888-632-9088
info@cehpubliclibrary.ca
lovemylibrary.ca
www.youtube.com/user/CEHPL; www.facebook.com/cehpl
Tiffany Bartlett, Chief Executive Officer
tbartlett@cehpubliclibrary.ca

Cumberland Public Libraries
PO Box 220, Amherst, NS B4H 3Z2
Tel: 902-667-2135; *Fax:* 902-667-1360
information@cumberlandpubliclibraries.ca
www.cumberlandpubliclibraries.ca
twitter.com/CumberlandPL;
www.facebook.com/CumberlandPublicLibraries

Eastern Counties Regional Library
390 Murray St., Mulgrave, NS B0E 2G0
Tel: 902-747-2597; *Toll-Free:* 855-787-7323
www.ecrl.library.ns.ca
www.facebook.com/ECRLibrary
Shirley McNamara, Chair

Halifax Public Libraries
60 Alderney Dr., Dartmouth, NS B2Y 4P8
Tel: 902-490-5744
asklib@halifax.ca
www.halifaxpubliclibraries.ca
www.youtube.com/user/hfxpublib; twitter.com/hfxpublib;
www.facebook.com/hfxpublib
Åsa Kachan, Chief Librarian & CEO
libraryceo@halifax.ca
902-490-5868
Mairead Barry, Senior Manager, Strategy
barryma@halifax.ca
902-490-5898
Karen Dahl, Senior Manager, Programming & Community Engagement
dahlk@halifax.ca
902-490-5864
Terry Gallagher, Senior Manager, Finance & Facilities
gallagt@halifax.ca
902-476-4067
Sara Gillis, Senior Manager, People & Culture
gillissar@halifax.ca
902-490-6339
Debbie LeBel, Senior Manager, Access
lebeld@halifax.ca
902-490-2946

Nova Scotia Provincial Library
6016 University Ave., 5th Fl., Halifax, NS B3H 1W4
Tel: 902-424-2457; *Fax:* 902-424-0633
nspl@novascotia.ca
library.novascotia.ca

Pictou-Antigonish Regional Library
PO Box 276, 182 Dalhousie St., New Glasgow, NS B2H 5E3
Tel: 902-755-6031; *Toll-Free:* 866-779-7761
info@parl.ns.ca
www.parl.ns.ca
twitter.com/parlevents; www.facebook.com/PARLevents
Eric Stackhouse, Chief Librarian
estackhouse@parl.ns.ca
Kristel Fleuren-Hunter, Librarian, Children's Services
Trecia Schell, Librarian, Community Services
Jess Davey, Manager, Web Services
Melanie Pauls, Manager, Community Technology

South Shore Public Libraries
135 North Park St., Bridgewater, NS B4V 9B3
Tel: 902-543-2548; *Toll-Free:* 877-455-2548
info@ssplibraries.ca
www.southshorepubliclibraries.ca
www.instagram.com/south.shore; twitter.com/ssplibraries;
www.facebook.com/southshorepubliclibraries
Troy Myers, CEO & Chief Librarian
troy.myers@southshorepubliclibraries.ca
Jeff Mercer, Deputy Chief Librarian
jeff.mercer@southshorepubliclibraries.ca
902-240-5774

Western Counties Regional Library
405 Main St., Yarmouth, NS B5A 1G3
Tel: 902-742-2486; *Fax:* 902-742-6920
officemanager@westerncounties.ca
westerncounties.ca
www.youtube.com/irwhite62; twitter.com/wcrlibrary;
www.facebook.com/62520112493
Erin Comeau, Regional Library Director
director@westerncounties.ca
Yvonne LeBlanc, Manager, Office
officemanager@westerncounties.ca
Ian White, Manager, Public Relations
publicrelations@westerncounties.ca
Carol Surette, Bookkeeper
bookkeeper@westerncounties.ca

Archives

Amherst: **Cumberland County Museum & Archives**
150 Church St., Amherst, NS B4H 3C4
Tel: 902-667-2561
cumberlandmuseumsociety.ca
www.facebook.com/CumberlandMuseumSociety
Rebecca Taylor, Manager
manager@cumberlandmuseumsociety.ca

Annapolis Royal: **Annapolis Heritage Society**
O'Dell House Museum, 136 St. George St., Annapolis Royal, NS B0S 1A0
Tel: 902-532-7754
annapolisheritage@gmail.com
annapolisheritagesociety.com/collections/archives
www.facebook.com/AnnapolisHeritage

Antigonish: **Antigonish Heritage Museum**
20 East Main St., Antigonish, NS B2G 2E9
Tel: 902-863-6160
antheritage@parl.ns.ca
www.antigonishheritage.org/antigonish-heritage-museum
www.youtube.com/user/AntigonishHeriMuseum;
www.facebook.com/AntigonishHeritageMuseum

Baddeck: **Alexander Graham Bell National Historic Site/Lieu Historique National Alexander Graham Bell**
559 Chebucto St., Baddeck, NS B0E 1B0
Tel: 902-295-2069; *Fax:* 902-295-3496
pc.information.pc@canada.ca
www.pc.gc.ca/eng/lhn-nhs/ns/grahambell
www.facebook.com/AGBNHS

Barrington: **Cape Sable Historical Society Centre**
2401 Hwy. 3, Barrington, NS B0W 1E0
Tel: 902-637-2185
barmuseumcomplex@eastlink.ca
capesablehistoricalsociety.com
www.facebook.com/barringtonmuseumcomplex

Bridgetown: **Bridgetown & Area Historical Society**
12 Queen St., Bridgetown, NS B0S 1C0
Tel: 902-665-4530
info@jameshousemuseum.com
www.jameshousemuseum.com
www.facebook.com/jameshousemuseum1835

Bridgewater: DesBrisay Museum
130 Jubilee Rd., Bridgewater, NS B4V 3X9
Tel: 902-543-4619; Fax: 902-543-4713
Other Numbers: Archives: 902-543-4033
museum@bridgewater.ca
www.desbrisaymuseum.ca/contact-us/archives-research
twitter.com/DesBrisayMuseum;
www.facebook.com/DesBrisayMuseumNS

Canso: Canso Historical Society
90 Union St., Canso, NS B0H 1H0
Tel: 902-366-2170
www.facebook.com/cansohistoricalsociety

Centreville: Archelaus Smith Museum
915 Hwy. 330, Centreville, NS B0W 1P0
Tel: 902-745-3361
archsmithmuseum@gmail.com
www.facebook.com/ArchelausSmithMuseum

Cherry Brook: Black Cultural Centre for Nova Scotia
10 Cherry Brook Rd., Cherry Brook, NS B2Z 1A8
Tel: 902-434-6223; Fax: 902-434-2306
Toll-Free: 800-465-0767
contact@bccns.com
www.bccns.com
twitter.com/BCC_NS; www.facebook.com/bccnsmuseum
Russell Grosse, Executive Director

Church Point: St Mary's Museum/Le Musée Sainte Marie
1713 Hwy. 1, Church Point, NS B0W 1M0
Tel: 902-769-2378; Fax: 902-769-0048
www.museeeglisesaintemariemuseum.ca

Dartmouth: Cole Harbour Rural Heritage Society
471 Poplar Dr., Dartmouth, NS B2W 4L2
Tel: 905-434-0222
hello@coleharbourfarmmuseum.ca
coleharbourfarmmuseum.ca
twitter.com/coleharbourfarm;
www.facebook.com/TheFarmMuseum

Dartmouth: Dartmouth Heritage Museum
26 Newcastle St., Dartmouth, NS B2Y 3M5
Tel: 902-464-2300; Fax: 902-464-8210
info@dartmouthmuseum.ca
www.dartmouthheritagemuseum.ns.ca
www.facebook.com/dartmouthheritagemuseum
Terry Eyland, Manager & Curator
manager@dartmouthmuseum.ca
902-464-2916

Dartmouth: Genealogical Association of Nova Scotia
#100, 33 Ochterloney St., Dartmouth, NS B2Y 4P5
Tel: 902-454-0322
info@novascotiaancestors.ca
novascotiaancestors.ca
Joseph Ballard, President
admin@novascotiaancestors.ca

Halifax: Canadian Museum of Immigration at Pier 21
1055 Marginal Rd., Halifax, NS B3H 4P7
Tel: 902-425-7770; Fax: 902-423-4045
Toll-Free: 855-526-4721
sfhc@pier21.ca
www.pier21.ca
Cara MacDonald, Manager, Reference Services
caramacdonald@pier21.ca
902-425-7770 ext. 224

Halifax: Halifax Regional Municipality
Burnside Industrial Park, #11, 81 Isley Ave., Halifax, NS B3B 1L5
Tel: 902-490-4643
archives@halifax.ca
www.halifax.ca/about-halifax/municipal-archives
Susan McClure, Municipal Archivist

Halifax: Nova Scotia Archives & Records Management
6016 University Ave., Halifax, NS B3H 1W4
Tel: 902-424-6060; Fax: 902-424-0628
archives@novascotia.ca
archives.novascotia.ca
www.youtube.com/c/nsarchives; twitter.com/NS_Archives;
www.facebook.com/novascotiaarchives

Halifax: Nova Scotia Sport Hall of Fame
#446, 1800 Argyle St., Halifax, NS B3J 3N8
Tel: 902-421-1266; Fax: 902-425-1148
info@nsshf.com
nsshf.com
www.youtube.com/user/NSSportHallofFame;
twitter.com/NSSHF; www.facebook.com/nsshf;
www.linkedin.com/company/nova-scotia-sport-hall-of-fame
Katie Tanner, Museum & Communications Coordinator
katie@nsshf.com

Halifax: Shambhala Archives
1084 Tower Rd., Halifax, NS B3H 2Y5
Tel: 902-420-1118
archives@shambhala.org
shambhalaarchives.org
www.facebook.com/ShambhalaArchives
Jeanne Riord, Archival Specialist

Halifax: Sisters of Charity - Halifax
Sisters of Charity Centre, 215 Seton Rd., Halifax, NS B3M 0C9
Tel: 902-406-8136
communications@schalifax.ca
schalifax.ca/archives
Mary Flynn, Congregational Archivist
mflynn@schalifax.ca

Kentville: Kings County Historical Society
The Kings County Museum, 37 Cornwallis St., Kentville, NS B4N 2E2
Tel: 902-678-6237; Fax: 902-678-2764
info@kingscountymuseum.ca
www.kingscountymuseum.ca
www.facebook.com/kingscountymuseum

Liverpool: Thomas H. Raddall Research Centre
109 Main St., Liverpool, NS B0T 1K0
Tel: 902-354-4058; Fax: 902-354-2050
www.raddallresearchcentre.com
www.facebook.com/223194214399105
Linda Rafuse, Director
linda.a.rafuse@novascotia.ca
902-354-4058

Maplewood: Parkdale-Maplewood Community Museum
3005 Barss Corner Rd., RR#1, Maplewood, NS B0R 1A0
Tel: 902-644-2893; Fax: 902-644-3422
Other Numbers: Off-season: 902-644-3421
p-mcm@hotmail.com
parkdale.ednet.ns.ca
www.facebook.com/94020106181
Donna Arenburg, Curator
Suzanne Isaacs, Museum Assistant

Middleton: Annapolis Valley Macdonald Museum
21 School St., Middleton, NS B0S 1P0
Tel: 902-825-6116; Fax: 902-825-0531
contact@macdonaldmuseum.ca
macdonaldmuseum.ca/geneology-research-library
www.facebook.com/AnnapolisValleyMacdonaldMuseum

Parrsboro: Parrsborough Shore Historical Society
1155 Whitehall Rd., Parrsboro, NS B0M 1S0
Tel: 902-254-2376
ottawa.house@ns.sympatico.ca
www.ottawahousemuseum.ca/archival-holdings
www.facebook.com/518524778304980

Pictou: McCulloch House Museum & Genealogy Centre
86 Haliburton Rd., Pictou, NS B0K 1H0
Tel: 902-485-4563
pcghs@gov.ns.ca
www.mccullochcentre.ca
twitter.com/McCullochCentre;
www.facebook.com/mccullochcentre
Michelle Davey, Curator & Site Manager
michelle.davey@novascotia.ca

Port Hastings: Strait Area Museum
24 Hwy. 19, Port Hastings, NS B9A 1M1
Tel: 902-625-1295
straitareamuseum@gmail.com
sites.google.com/view/strait-area-museum
www.facebook.com/PortHastingsMuseum
Karen Mudge, President

Shearwater: Shearwater Aviation Museum
34 Bonaventure St., Shearwater, NS B0J 3A0
Tel: 902-720-2165; Fax: 902-720-2037
library@shearwateraviationmuseum.ns.ca
www.shearwateraviationmuseum.ns.ca
twitter.com/YAWmuseum;
www.facebook.com/shearwateraviationmuseum

Truro: Colchester Historical Society Museum & Archives
29 Young St., 2nd Fl., Truro, NS B2N 3W3
Tel: 902-895-6284
colchesterhistoreum.ca/archives
twitter.com/Col_Historeum
Margaret Mulrooney, Curator
curator@colchesterhistoreum.ca
Ashley Sutherland, Archivist
archivist@colchesterhistoreum.ca
902-895-9530

Tusket: Argyle Township Court House Archives
8162 Hwy. 3, Tusket, NS B0W 3M0
Tel: 902-648-2493
www.argylecourthouse.com/content/argyle-archives-information
www.facebook.com/argylecourthouse
Judy Frotten, Heritage Development Officer
jfrotten@argylecourthouse.com

Windsor: West Hants Historical Society
281 King St., Windsor, NS B0N 2T0
Tel: 902-798-4706
info@westhantshistoricalsociety.ca
westhantshistoricalsociety.ca/genealogy-services
www.youtube.com/user/westhantshistorical;
www.facebook.com/westhantshistoricalsociety;

Yarmouth: Yarmouth County Museum & Archives
22 Collins St., Yarmouth, NS B5A 3C8
Tel: 902-742-5539; Fax: 902-749-1120
ycarchives@eastlink.ca
yarmouthcountymuseum.ca
www.facebook.com/92402018979
Nadine Gates, Director & Curator
ycmuseum@eastlink.ca
Lisette Gaudet, Archivist
ycarchives@eastlink.ca

Ontario

Public Libraries

Ajax: Ajax Public Library
55 Harwood Ave. South, Ajax, ON L1S 2H8
Tel: 905-683-4000; Fax: 905-683-6944
TTY: 866-460-4489
www.ajaxlibrary.ca
twitter.com/ajax_library; www.facebook.com/ajaxpubliclibrary
Noel Green, Chair
Sarah Vaisler, Chief Librarian & CEO
sarah.vaisler@ajaxlibrary.ca
905-683-4000 ext. 8825
Jason Tooral, Manager, Corporate Services
jason.tooral@ajaxlibrary.ca
905-683-4000 ext. 8822
Cindy Poon, Manager, Public Services
cindy.poon@ajaxlibrary.ca
905-683-4000 ext. 8801

Alban: French River Public Library/Bibliothèque publique de la Rivière-des-français
796 Hwy. 64, #A, Alban, ON P0M 1A0
Tel: 705-857-1771; Fax: 705-857-1771
library@frenchriverlibrary.ca
www.frenchriver.ca/p/french-river-public-library
www.facebook.com/286132221488267
Linda Keenan, Chief Executive Officer

Alfred: Bibliothèque publique du Canton d'Alfred et Plantagenet/Alfred & Plantagenet Public Library
330, rue St-Phillipe, Alfred, ON K0B 1A0
Tél: 613-679-2663; Téléc: 613-679-2663
www.alfred-plantagenet.ca
www.facebook.com/302328049891593
Dominique Lacelle, Directrice générale
Ginette Péladeau, Responsable
peladeaug@yahoo.ca

Alliston: New Tecumseth Public Library
17 Victoria St. East, Alliston, ON L9R 1T3
Tel: 705-435-5651; *Fax:* 705-435-0750
Other Numbers: Administration: 705-435-5650
info@ntpl.ca
ntpl.ca
www.facebook.com/newteclibrary
Graeme Peters, Chief Executive Officer & Branch Manager
gpeters@ntpl.ca

Almonte: Mississippi Mills Public Library
155 High St., Almonte, ON K0A 1A0
Tel: 613-256-1037
almontelib@missmillslibrary.com
www.missmillslibrary.com
twitter.com/mmpublib;
www.facebook.com/mississippimillspubliclibrary
Christine Row, Chief Executive Officer
crow@mississippimills.ca
Monica Blackburn, Deputy Chief Executive Officer
mblackburn@mississippimills.ca

Angus: Essa Public Library
#1, 8505 County Rd. 10, Angus, ON L0M 1B1
Tel: 705-424-6531; *Fax:* 705-424-5512
essalib@essa.library.on.ca
www.essa.library.on.ca
twitter.com/essalibrary; www.facebook.com/essapubliclibrary
Laura Wark, Chief Executive Officer
ceo@essa.library.on.ca
Glenda Newbatt, Manager, Library Services
gnewbatt@essa.library.on.ca
Angie Wishart, Coordinator, Facility & Support Services
awishart@essa.library.on.ca

Apsley: North Kawartha Public Library
175 Burleigh St., Apsley, ON K0L 1A0
Tel: 705-656-4333; *Fax:* 705-656-2538
www.northkawarthalibrary.com
twitter.com/NorthKawartha; www.facebook.com/NorthKawartha
Catherine Leard, Chair
Debbie Hall, Librarian & CEO

Arnprior: Arnprior Public Library
21 Madawaska St., Arnprior, ON K7S 1R6
Tel: 613-623-2279; *Fax:* 613-623-0281
library@arnpriorlibrary.ca
www.arnpriorlibrary.ca
twitter.com/arnpriorlibrary; www.facebook.com/arnpriorlibrary
Karen DeLuca, Librarian & CEO
Carolyn Swayze, Librarian, Youth Services
Tracey Telgen, Librarian, Interlibrary Loans

Astorville: East Ferris Public Library/Bibliothèque
publique d'East Ferris
1257 Village Rd., Astorville, ON P0H 1B0
Tel: 705-752-2042
library@eastferris.ca
www.efpl.ca
www.facebook.com/EastFerrisPublicLibrary
Jennifer Laporte, CEO

Athens: Athens Public Library
5 Central St., Athens, ON K0E 1B0
Tel: 613-924-2048
athenspl@bellnet.ca
www.athenslibrary.ca
Julianna McAleese, Chair
Diane Benschop, Head Librarian
Karen DeJong, Children's Librarian

Atikokan: Atikokan Public Library
Civic Centre, Atikokan, ON P0T 1C0
Tel: 807-597-4406; *Fax:* 807-597-1415
aplibrary.org
www.facebook.com/139703726078003
Tracey Sinclair, Acting CEO/Librarian
Shelly Palmai, Head of Youth Services

Aundeck OmniKaning First Na: Aundeck Omni
Kaning First Nation Library
1300 Hwy. 540, Aundeck OmniKaning First Na, ON P0P 1K0
Tel: 705-368-3696; *Fax:* 705-368-3563

Aurora: Aurora Public Library
15145 Yonge St., Aurora, ON L4G 1M1
Tel: 905-727-9494
info@aurorapl.ca
www.library.aurora.on.ca
www.youtube.com/user/AuroraPubLib; twitter.com/APLtweets;
www.facebook.com/aurorapubliclibrary
Bruce Gorman, Chief Executive Officer
bgorman@aurorapl.ca

Baden: Region of Waterloo Library
2017 Nafziger Rd., Baden, ON N3A 3H4
Tel: 519-575-4590; *Fax:* 519-634-5371
TTY: 519-575-4608
libhq@regionofwaterloo.ca
www.rwlibrary.ca
twitter.com/rwlibrary; www.facebook.com/RWLibrary.ca
Sheryl Tilley, Manager, Library Services
Jennifer Cyr, Coordinator, Library Collections
jcyr@regionofwaterloo.ca

Bala: Wahta Mohawks Public Library
2664 Muskoka Rd. 38, Bala, ON P0C 1A0
Tel: 705-762-2354; *Fax:* 705-762-2376
Carol Holmes, Education Coordinator
carol.holmes@wahtamohawks.ca

Bancroft: North Hastings Public Library
14 Flint St., Bancroft, ON K0L 1C0
Tel: 613-332-3380; *Fax:* 613-332-5473
info@northhastingslibrary.ca
www.northhastingslibrary.ca
www.facebook.com/OfficialBancroftPublicLibrary
Kimberly McMunn, Head Librarian & CEO
nhpl.ceo@gmail.com
Beverly Creighton, Librarian & InterLibrary Loan Officer
Shirley McRandall, Assistant Librarian
Louise Villeneuve, Coordinator, Events

Barrie: Barrie Public Library
60 Worsley St., Barrie, ON L4M 1L6
Tel: 705-728-1010
askus@barrielibrary.ca
www.barrielibrary.ca
www.instagram.com/barriepubliclibrary;
twitter.com/BPL_inthecity; www.facebook.com/barriepubliclibrary
Lauren Jessop, Chief Executive Officer
705-728-1010 ext. 2100
Karen Barratt, Director, Innovation & Technology
collections@barrielibrary.ca
705-728-1010 ext. 2400
Alison Schroeder, Director, Customer Experience
705-728-1010 ext. 2300
Chris Vanderkruys, Director, Business & Development
705-728-1010 ext. 2200

Barry's Bay: Barry's Bay - Madawaska Valley Public
Library
19474 Opeongo Line, Barry's Bay, ON K0J 1B0
Tel: 613-756-2000; *Fax:* 613-756-2000
admin@madawaskavalleylibrary.ca
www.madawaskavalleylibrary.ca
www.facebook.com/441487465920394
Karen Filipkowski, Head Librarian & CEO

Baysville: Lake of Bays Public Library
Community Centre, 10 University St., Baysville, ON P0B 1A0
Tel: 705-767-2361; *Fax:* 705-767-2361
baysville@lakeofbayslibrary.ca
www.lakeofbayslibrary.ca
twitter.com/baysvillepl;
www.facebook.com/BaysvilleBranchLakeofBaysLibrary
Linda Lacroix, Chief Executive Officer
linla@vianet.ca

Beachburg: Township of Whitewater Region Public
Libraries
20 Cameron St., Beachburg, ON K0J 1C0
Tel: 613-582-7090
bblib@nrtco.net
whitewaterregion.ca/library
www.facebook.com/565700196806968
Debbi McLaughlin, Chief Executive Officer
whitewaterpl@nrtco.net

Beamsville: Lincoln Public Library
5020 Serena Dr., Beamsville, ON L0R 1B0
Tel: 905-563-7014; *Fax:* 905-563-1810
info@lincoln.library.on.ca
lincoln.library.on.ca
twitter.com/lincolnlibrary1; www.facebook.com/LincolnLibraryON
Donna Burton, Chair
Julie Andrews, Chief Executive Officer
andrews@lincoln.library.on.ca

Beaverton: Brock Township Public Libraries
401 Simcoe St., Beaverton, ON L0K 1A0
Tel: 705-426-9283; *Fax:* 705-426-9353
info@brocklibraries.ca
www.brocklibraries.ca
www.facebook.com/BrockTownshipPublicLibraries
Karen Enss, Chair

Brian Harding, Chief Executive Officer
brianharding@brocklibraries.ca
705-426-9283

Belleville: Belleville Public Library (BPL)
254 Pinnacle St., Belleville, ON K8N 3B1
Tel: 613-968-6731; *Fax:* 613-968-6841
Toll-Free: 866-979-5877
infoserv@bellevillelibrary.ca
bellevillelibrary.ca
twitter.com/BellevillePL; www.facebook.com/219197338115817
Trevor Pross, Chief Executive Officer
tpross@bellevillelibrary.ca
613-968-6731 ext. 2022
Holly Dewar, Manager, Public Services
hdewar@bellevillelibrary.ca
613-968-6731 ext. 2041
Shannon Bryan, Coordinator, Information & Web Services
sbryan@bellevillelibrary.ca
613-968-6731 ext. 2049
Jonathan Powell, Acting Coordinator, Children's, Youth &
Readers' Services
jpowell@bellevillelibrary.ca
613-968-6731 ext. 2046
Wendy Rayson-Kerr, Acting Curator, John M. Parrot Art Gallery
gallery@bellevillelibrary.ca
613-968-6731 ext. 2039

Birch Island: Whitefish River First Nation Public
Library
212 Rainbow Ridge Rd., Birch Island, ON P0P 1A0
Tel: 705-285-0028; *Fax:* 705-285-4532
whitefishriverfirstnationlibrary@hotmail.com
www.whitefishriver.ca
Evelyn Jacko, Librarian
evelynj@whitefishriver.ca

Blenheim: Caldwell First Nation Public Library
1029 Talbot Rd., RR#2, Blenheim, ON N0P 1A0
Tel: 519-676-5499

Blind River: Blind River Public Library/Bibliothèque
de Blind River
8 Woodward Ave., Blind River, ON P0R 1B0
Tel: 705-356-7616
brplcirc@ontera.net
blindriver.olsn.ca
www.facebook.com/blindriverpl

Blind River: Mississauga First Nation Public Library
152 Village Rd., Blind River, ON P0R 1B0
Tel: 705-356-1621; *Fax:* 705-356-1742
mfnlibrary@mississaugi.com
www.mississaugi.com/library.html

Bolton: Caledon Public Library
150 Queen St. South, Bolton, ON L7E 1E3
Tel: 905-857-1400
bolton@caledon.library.on.ca
www.caledon.library.on.ca
www.youtube.com/user/caledonpubliclibrary;
twitter.com/caledonlibrary;
www.facebook.com/CaledonPublicLibrary
Colleen Lipp, Chief Librarian & CEO
clipp@caledon.library.on.ca
905-857-1400 ext. 215
Laurie Groe, Contact, Youth Services
lgroe@caledon.library.on.ca
905-857-1400 ext. 231
Mary Maw, Contact, Communications & Community
Development
mmaw@caledon.library.on.ca
905-857-1400 ext. 228
Kelley Potter, Contact, Public Service
kpotter@caledon.library.on.ca
905-857-1400 ext. 238
Megan Renkema, Contact, Information Services
mrenkema@caledon.library.on.ca
905-857-1400 ext. 232
Mojgan Schmalenberg, Contact, Information Technology
mschmale@caledon.library.on.ca
905-857-1400 ext. 237

Bonfield: Bonfield Public Library
365 Hwy. 531, Bonfield, ON P0H 1E0
Tel: 705-776-2396; *Fax:* 705-776-1154
bonfieldlibrary@gmail.com
bonfield.olsn.ca
www.facebook.com/bonfieldpubliclibrary
Leslie Larocque, Chair
Jeannette Shields, Librarian & CEO

Borden: Borden Public & Military
Library/Bibliothèque publique et militaire de Borden
41 Kapyong Rd., Borden, ON L0M 1C0
Tel: 705-424-1200; *Fax:* 705-423-3432
www.cafconnection.ca/Borden/Facilities/Library.aspx
Donald Allen, Chief Librarian
don.allen@forces.gc.ca

Bowmanville: Clarington Public Library
163 Church St., Bowmanville, ON L1C 1T7
Tel: 905-623-7322; *Fax:* 905-623-8608
info@clarington-library.on.ca
www.clarington-library.on.ca
www.youtube.com/c/ClaringtonLib; twitter.com/ClaringtonLib;
www.facebook.com/ClaringtonPublicLibrary
Linda Kent, Chief Executive Officer
905-623-7322 ext. 2702
Melissa Redden, Deputy Director
905-623-7322 ext. 2714
Megan Elliott, Manager, Business Administration
905-623-7322 ext. 2701
Nancy Sandercock, Manager, Human Resources
905-623-7322 ext. 2704
Samantha Aitken, Coordinator, Community Engagement
905-623-7322 ext. 2708
Alison Dee, Coordinator, Collections
905-987-4844 ext. 223

Bracebridge: Bracebridge Public Library
94 Manitoba St., Bracebridge, ON P1L 2B5
Tel: 705-645-4171; *Fax:* 705-645-6551
info@bracebridgelibrary.ca
bracebridgelibrary.ca
twitter.com/bracebridgepl;
www.facebook.com/BracebridgePublicLibrary
Cathryn Rodney, Chief Librarian & CEO
cathryn.rodney@bracebridgelibrary.ca
Cindy Buhne, Librarian, Information & Digital Services
Ashleigh Whipp, Librarian, Children & Youth Services
ashleigh.whipp@bracebridgelibrary.ca
Carolyn Dawkins, Office Manager
carolyn.dawkins@bracebridgelibrary.ca

Bradford: Bradford-West Gwillimbury Public Library
425 Holland St. West, Bradford, ON L3Z 0J2
Tel: 905-775-3328
bwgmailbox@bradford.library.on.ca
www.bradford.library.on.ca
www.facebook.com/bwglibrary
Jennifer Harrison, Chair
Matthew Corbett, Chief Executive Officer
mcorbett@bradford.library.on.ca
905-775-3328 ext. 6101
Nina Cunniff, Deputy CEO
ncunniff@bradford.library.on.ca
905-775-3328 ext. 6105
Andrea Ciurria, Manager, Borrower & Technical Services
aciurria@bradford.library.on.ca
905-775-3328 ext. 6106
Elizabeth Campbell, Librarian, Information Services
ecampbell@bradford.library.on.ca
905-775-3328 ext. 6122
Sarah Petryshyn, Librarian, Emerging Technologies
spetryshyn@bradford.library.on.ca
905-775-3328 ext. 6113
Bailey Shaw, Librarian, Children's Services
bshaw@bradford.library.on.ca
905-775-3328 ext. 6114
Wendy Zwaal, Librarian, Adult Services
wzwaal@bradford.library.on.ca
905-775-3328 ext. 6108

Brampton: Brampton Library
65 Queen St. East, Brampton, ON L6W 3L6
Tel: 905-793-4636
TTY: 866-959-9994
info@bramlib.on.ca
www.bramptonlibrary.ca
www.instagram.com/bramptonlibrary;
twitter.com/BramptonLibrary;
www.facebook.com/bramptonlibrary
Todd Kyle, Chief Executive Officer
chieflib@bramlib.on.ca
Susan Bartoletta, Director, Branch & Neighbourhood Services
sbartoletta@bramlib.on.ca
905-793-4636 ext. 74406
Jason Baty, Director, Innovation & Technology
jbaty@bramlib.on.ca
905-793-4636 ext. 74107
John Simone, Director, Business Management & Operations
jsimone@bramlib.on.ca
905-793-4636 ext. 74716

Sarala Uttangi, Director, Community Engagement & Partnerships
suttangi@bramlib.on.ca
905-793-4636 ext. 74256

Brantford: Brantford Public Library
173 Colborne St., Brantford, ON N3T 2G8
Tel: 519-756-2220; *Fax:* 519-756-4979
info@brantford.library.on.ca
www.brantfordlibrary.ca
twitter.com/BtfdLibrary;
www.facebook.com/BrantfordPublicLibrary
Rae-Lynne Aramburo, Chief Libarian & CEO
raramburo@brantford.library.on.ca
519-756-2220 ext. 3319
James Clark, Manager, Communications & Community Engagement
jclark@brantfordlibrary.ca
519-756-2220 ext. 3343
Kelly Nielsen, Manager, Public Services
519-756-2220 ext. 3309
Zile Ozols, Manager, Programming & Outreach
519-756-2220 ext. 3314

Bridgenorth: Selwyn Public Library
836 Charles St., Bridgenorth, ON K0L 1H0
Tel: 705-292-5065; *Fax:* 705-292-6695
librarian@mypubliclibrary.ca
www.selwyntownship.ca/en/library/library.aspx
www.pinterest.com/mypubliclibrary; twitter.com/selwynlibrary;
www.facebook.com/SelwynPublicLibrary
Sarah Hennessey, Chief Librarian & CEO
Heather Jamieson, Branch Librarian

Brighton: Brighton Public Library
35 Alice St., Brighton, ON K0K 1H0
Tel: 613-475-2511
www.brighton.library.on.ca
www.facebook.com/BrightonPublicLibrary
Heather Ratz, Chief Executive Officer
brightonceo@brighton.library.on.ca

Britt: Britt Public Library
841 Riverside Dr., Britt, ON P0G 1A0
Tel: 705-383-2432; *Fax:* 705-383-0077

Brockville: Augusta Township Public Library
4500 County Rd. 15, RR#2, Brockville, ON K6V 5T2
Tel: 613-926-2449; *Fax:* 613-702-0441
staff@augustalibrary.com
augustalibrary.com
www.facebook.com/AugustaTownshipPublicLibrary
Kimberley Craig, Librarian
Corwin Gonneau, Librarian
Angie Knights, Librarian

Brockville: Brockville Public Library
23 Buell St., Brockville, ON K6V 5T7
Tel: 613-342-3936; *Fax:* 613-342-6096
info@brockvillelibrary.ca
brockvillelibrary.ca
twitter.com/BrockvillePL;
www.facebook.com/BrockvillePublicLibrary;
www.linkedin.com/company/brockville-public-library
Andreas von Cramon, Acting Chair
Emily Farrell, Chief Executive Officer
emily@brockvillelibrary.ca
Laura Julien, Manager, Customer Experience
laura@brockvillelibrary.ca
613-342-3936 ext. 6431
Lisa Cirka, Coordinator, Youth Engagement
lisa@brockvillelibrary.ca
613-342-3936 ext. 6424

Brockville: Elizabethtown-Kitley Township Public Library
4103 Country Rd. 29, Brockville, ON K6V 5T4
Tel: 613-498-3338
elizndub@ektwp.ca
ektwp.ca/living/public-library
www.facebook.com/453942774763236
Ruth Blanchard, Librarian

Bruce Mines: Bruce Mines & Plummer Additional Union Public Library
33 Desbarats St., Bruce Mines, ON P0R 1C0
Tel: 705-785-3370; *Fax:* 705-785-3370
info@bmpaupl.ca
brucemines.olsn.ca
www.facebook.com/BMPAUPL

Buckhorn: Trent Lakes Public Libraries
5 George St., Buckhorn, ON K0L 1J0
Tel: 705-657-3695; *Fax:* 705-657-3695
library@trentlakes.ca
www.trentlakeslibrary.ca
twitter.com/TrentLakesLib;
www.facebook.com/TrentLakesLibrary
Stephanie McPherson, Head Librarian & CEO
smcpherson@trentlakes.ca

Burks Falls: Burks Falls, Armour & Ryerson Union Public Library
39 Copeland St., Burks Falls, ON P0A 1C0
Tel: 705-382-3327; *Fax:* 705-382-3327
burksfallslibrary@gmail.com
www.burksfallslibrary.com
twitter.com/BurksFallsLibra; www.facebook.com/burksfallslibrary
Nieves Guijarro, Chief Executive Officer

Burlington: Burlington Public Library
2331 New St., Burlington, ON L7R 1J4
Tel: 905-639-3611; *Fax:* 905-681-7277
www.bpl.on.ca
www.instagram.com/burlonlibrary; twitter.com/BurlingtonPL;
www.facebook.com/BurlOnLibrary
Catharine Benzie, Chair
board@bpl.on.ca
Lita Barrie, Chief Executive Officer
barriel@bpl.on.ca
905-639-3611 ext. 1100
Heather Martyn, Manager, Central Branch

Calabogie: Greater Madawaska Public Library
12629 Lanark Rd., Calabogie, ON K0J 1H0
Tel: 613-752-2317
gmpl@bellnet.ca
www.greatermadawaska.com/library
www.facebook.com/GreaterMadawaskaPublicLibrary
Sharon Shalla, Chief Librarian & CEO

Callander: Callander Public Library
30 Catherine St. West, Callander, ON P0H 1H0
Tel: 705-752-2544
callanderlibrary@gmail.com
www.mycallander.ca/library/home
twitter.com/ourcplibrary;
www.facebook.com/callanderpubliclibrary
Melissa Sones, Chief Librarian & CEO

Cambridge: Idea Exchange
1 North Sq., Cambridge, ON N1S 2K6
Tel: 519-621-0460; *Fax:* 519-621-2080
askalibrarian@ideaexchange.org
ideaexchange.org
twitter.com/IdeaXchng; www.facebook.com/IdeaXchng
Gary Price, Chair
board@ideaexchange.org
Helen Kelly, Chief Executive Officer
hkelly@ideaexchange.org
519-621-0460 ext. 120
Marcie Bronson, Director, Cambridge Art Galleries
mbronson@ideaexchange.org
519-621-0460 ext. 129
Jamie Kamula, Director, Public Services
jkamula@ideaexchange.org
226-533-2767 ext. 139
Ellen Lehman, Director, Finance & Facilities
elehman@ideaexchange.org
519-621-0460 ext. 131
Jaime Griffis, Director, Programming & Promotion
jgriffis@ideaexchange.org
519-621-0460 ext. 145
Caitlyn Hicks, Branch Manager, Queen's Square
cehicks@ideaexchange.org
519-621-0460 ext. 118

Campbellford: Trent Hills Public Library
98 Bridge St. East, Campbellford, ON K0L 1L0
Tel: 705-653-3611; *Fax:* 705-653-4611
trenthillslibrary@trenthills.ca
trenthillslibrary.ca
www.facebook.com/1300817283346199
Brianne Parr, Acting Chief Executive Officer

Cardinal: Edwardsburgh Cardinal Public Library
618 County Rd. 2, Cardinal, ON K0E 1E0
Tel: 613-657-3822
cardinal@edcarlibrary.ca
www.edcarlibrary.ca
www.facebook.com/edcarlibrary
Donna Gladstone, Chief Executive Officer
donna.gladstone@edcarlibrary.ca
Margaret Ann Gaylord, Supervisor

Carleton Place: Carleton Place Public Library
101 Beckwith St., Carleton Place, ON K7C 2T3
Tel: 613-257-2702
library@carletonplace.ca
www.carletonplacelibrary.ca
www.facebook.com/CarletonPlacePublicLibrary
Meriah Caswell, Chief Executive Officer
mcaswell@carletonplace.ca

Casselman: Bibliothèque publique de Casselman/Casselman Public Library
764, rue Brébeuf, Casselman, ON K0A 1M0
Tél: 613-764-5505; *Téléc:* 613-764-5507
infobiblio@casselman.ca
bibliocasselman.ca
www.facebook.com/bibliocasselman
Linda Desjardins-Bergero, Directrice

Castleton: Cramahe Township Public Library
Castleton Town Hall, 1780 Percy St., Castleton, ON K0K 1M0
Tel: 905-344-7320
info@cramahelibrary.ca
www.cramahelibrary.ca
www.facebook.com/cramahelibrary

Chapleau: Chapleau Public Library
20 Pine St. East, Chapleau, ON P0M 1K0
Tel: 705-864-0852; *Fax:* 705-864-0295
library@chapleau.ca
www.chapleau.ca/en/townshipservices/library-new.asp
www.facebook.com/138198009599471
Kimberly Jean, Librarian

Chatham: Chatham-Kent Public Library
120 Queen St., Chatham, ON N7M 2G6
Tel: 519-354-2940; *Fax:* 519-354-2602
cklibrary@chatham-kent.ca
www.chatham-kent.ca/library
twitter.com/cklibrary; www.facebook.com/CKPLibrary
Tania Sharpe, Chief Librarian & CEO
tanias@chatham-kent.ca
Cassey Beauvais, Manager, Public Services
casseyb@chatham-kent.ca
Sarah Hart Coatsworth, Manager, Marketing, Outreach & Programs
Heidi Wyma, Manager, Support Services
heidiw@chatham-kent.ca

Christian Island: Beausoleil First Nation Library
150 Mkade Kegwin Miikaan, Christian Island, ON L9M 0A9
Tel: 705-247-2255; *Fax:* 705-247-2772
librarysupport@chimnissing.ca
beausoleil.olsn.ca
www.facebook.com/111588630296087
Kathleen Peters, Librarian & CEO
librarian@chimnissing.ca

Clinton: Huron County Library
77722B London Rd., RR#5, Clinton, ON N0M 1L0
Tel: 519-482-5457
libraryadmin@huroncounty.ca
www.huroncounty.ca/library
twitter.com/huroncountylib;
www.facebook.com/HuronCountyLibrary

Cobalt: Cobalt Public Library/Bibliothèque publique du Cobalt
30 Lang St., Cobalt, ON P0J 1C0
Tel: 705-679-8120; *Fax:* 705-679-8120
cobaltpubliclibrary@gmail.com
cobalt.olsn.ca
www.facebook.com/cobaltlibrary
Kendra Lacarte, Librarian & CEO

Cobourg: Cobourg Public Library
200 Ontario St., Cobourg, ON K9A 5P4
Tel: 905-372-9271; *Fax:* 905-372-4538
ref@cobourg.library.on.ca
www.cobourg.ca/en/Library.aspx
twitter.com/cobourgPL; www.facebook.com/CobourgPubliclibrary
Tammy Robinson, Chief Executive Officer
trobinson@cobourg.library.on.ca
905-372-9271 ext. 6200
Kate Davis, Manager, Public Services
kdavis@cobourg.library.on.ca
905-372-9271 ext. 6260
Heather Viscount, Manager, Support Services
hviscount@cobourg.library.on.ca
905-372-9271 ext. 6230

Cochrane: Cochrane Public Library/Bibliothèque publique de Cochrane
178 - 4th Ave., Cochrane, ON P0L 1C0
Tel: 705-272-4178; *Fax:* 705-272-4165
library@cochraneontario.com
cochrane.olsn.ca
www.youtube.com/user/CochraneLibraryCAP;
www.facebook.com/TheCochranePublicLibrary
Christina Blazecka, Chief Executive Officer
christina.blazecka@cochraneontario.com
705-272-4178 ext. 28

Coe Hill: Wollaston Public Library
5629-A Hwy. 620, Coe Hill, ON K0L 1P0
Tel: 613-337-5183; *Fax:* 613-337-5183
wollastonpubliclibrary@gmail.com
www.wollastonpubliclibrary.ca
twitter.com/publicwollaston;
www.facebook.com/WollastonPublicLibrary
Temple Cameron, Librarian & CEO

Coldwater: Township of Severn
31 Coldwater Rd., Coldwater, ON L0K 1E0
Tel: 705-686-3601; *Fax:* 705-686-3741
library@severn.ca
www.coldwater.library.on.ca
www.facebook.com/SevernTownshipPublicLibrary
Adah Silk, Chair

Collingwood: Collingwood Public Library
55 Ste Marie St., Collingwood, ON L9Y 0W6
Tel: 705-445-1571; *Fax:* 705-445-3704
info@collingwoodpubliclibrary.ca
www.collingwoodpubliclibrary.ca
twitter.com/collingwoodpl;
www.facebook.com/collingwoodpubliclibrary
Nina Robitaille, Chair
Ashley Kulchycki, Acting Chief Executive Officer
khaigh@collingwood.ca
705-445-1571 ext. 6234
Lynda Reid, Manager, Collection & Facility Services
lreid@collingwood.ca
705-445-1571 ext. 6223

Constance Lake: Constance Lake First Nation Public Library
2 Musko St., Constance Lake, ON P0L 1B0
Tel: 705-463-1199; *Fax:* 705-463-2077
Lizzie Sutherland, Librarian
lizzie.sutherland@clfn.on.ca

Cornwall: Cornwall Public Library (Ontario)/Bibliothèque publique de Cornwall
45 - 2nd St. East, Cornwall, ON K6H 5V1
Tel: 613-932-4796; *Fax:* 613-932-2715
generalmail@library.cornwall.on.ca
www.library.cornwall.on.ca
twitter.com/CornwallPubLibr;
www.facebook.com/librarycornwallontario
Jennifer Jarvis, Chair
board@library.cornwall.on.ca

Cornwall: Stormont, Dundas & Glengarry County Library/Bibliothèque des comtés unis Stormont, Dundas et Glengarry
#106, 26 Pitt St., Cornwall, ON K6J 3P2
Tel: 613-936-8777; *Fax:* 613-936-2532
generalinfo@sdglibrary.ca
sdglibrary.ca
www.youtube.com/user/sdgcountylibrary; twitter.com/sdglibrary;
www.facebook.com/sdglibrary
Karen Franklin, Director, Library Services
kfranklin@sdglibrary.ca
613-936-8777 ext. 211
Margaret Piper, Librarian, Systems
mpiper@sdglibrary.ca
613-936-8777 ext. 239
Susan Wallwork, Librarian, Community
swallwork@sdglibrary.ca
613-936-8777 ext. 226

Curve Lake: Curve Lake First Nation Public Library
65 Chemong St. South, Curve Lake, ON K0L 1R0
Tel: 705-657-3217; *Fax:* 705-657-8708
library@curvelake.ca
curvelakefirstnation.ca
www.facebook.com/clfnpubliclibrary
Krista Commanda, Librarian

Cutler: Serpent River First Nation Public Library
49 Village Rd., Cutler, ON P0P 1B0
Tel: 705-844-2009
library@serpentriverfn.com
serpentriverfn.com/meetup/education-library
Karel Grant, Librarian

Deep River: Deep River Public Library (W.B. Lewis Public Library)
55 Ridge Rd., Deep River, ON K0J 1P0
Tel: 613-584-4244
info@deepriverlibrary.ca
www.deepriverlibrary.ca
www.facebook.com/DeepRiverLibrary
Naomi Balla-Boudreau, Chief Executive Officer
nballa-boudreau@deepriverlibrary.ca

Deep River: Laurentian Hills Public Library
34465 Hwy. 17, RR#1, Deep River, ON K0J 1P0
Tel: 613-584-2714; *Fax:* 613-584-9145
library@laurentianhills.ca
library.laurentianhills.ca
www.facebook.com/laurentianhillslibrary

Deseronto: Deseronto Public Library
358 Main St., Deseronto, ON K0K 1X0
Tel: 613-396-2744
info@deserontopubliclibrary.ca
www.deserontopubliclibrary.ca
www.facebook.com/DeserontoPublicLibrary
Steven Everhardus, Chair
Amy McDonald, Chief Executive Officer
amcdonald@deserontopubliclibrary.ca

Dobie: Dobie Public Library
92 McPherson St., Dobie, ON P0K 1B0
Tel: 705-568-8951; *Fax:* 705-568-8951

Dokis: Dokis First Nation Public Library
930 Main St., Dokis, ON P0M 2N1
Tel: 705-763-2511
dokislibrary@netspectrum.ca
www.dokis.ca
www.facebook.com/dokislib
Jason Restoule, Librarian

Dorion: Dorion Public Library
170 Dorion Loop Rd., Dorion, ON P0T 1K0
Tel: 807-857-2289; *Fax:* 807-857-2203
dorlib@tbaytel.net
doriontownship.ca/living/library
www.facebook.com/dorionpubliclibrary

Douglas: Admaston-Bromley Public Library
5346 Queen St., Douglas, ON K0J 1S0
Tel: 613-649-2576
info@admastonbromleylibrary.com
admastonbromleylibrary.com
Jane Wouda, Chief Executive Officer

Douro: Douro-Dummer Public Library
435 Fourth Line, Douro, ON K0L 2H0
Tel: 705-652-8599
library@dourodummer.on.ca
www.dourodummer.on.ca/services-departments/library
twitter.com/DouroDummerLib;
www.facebook.com/DouroDummerLibrary
Anne Landry, Chief Executive Officer
alandry@dourodummer.on.ca

Dryden: Dryden Public Library
36 Van Horne Ave., Dryden, ON P8N 2A7
Tel: 807-223-1475; *Fax:* 807-223-4312
library@dryden.ca
www.dryden.ca/en/explore/library.aspx
twitter.com/dpl1966; www.facebook.com/drydenlibrary
Matthew Benson, Chair

Dubreuilville: Bibliothèque publique de Dubreuilville/Dubreuilville Public Library
120, rue Magpie, Dubreuilville, ON P0S 1B0
Tél: 705-884-1435; *Téléc:* 705-884-1437
Ligne sans frais: 877-637-8010
dpl@dubreuilville.ca

Dunchurch: Whitestone Hagerman Memorial Public Library
2206 Hwy. 124, Dunchurch, ON P0A 1G0
Tel: 705-389-3311; *Fax:* 705-389-3311
whitestonelibrary@vianet.ca
whitestone.olsn.ca
twitter.com/whitestonelib; www.facebook.com/whitestonelib
Lori Guillemette, CEO

Dundalk: Southgate Public Library
80 Proton St. North, Dundalk, ON N0C 1B0
Tel: 519-923-3248
library@southgate.ca
southgate.ca/en/municipal-services/southgate-public-library.aspx
www.pinterest.com/southgatepl; twitter.com/southgatepl;
www.facebook.com/113603805368473
Charles Fernandes, Chair

Dunnville: Haldimand County Public Library
317 Chestnut St., Dunnville, ON N1A 2H4
Tel: 289-674-0400
library@haldimandcounty.on.ca
www.haldimandcounty.ca/haldimand-county-public-library
www.facebook.com/HaldimandLibrary
Linda Van Ede, Chair
Paul Diette, Chief Executive Officer
pdiette@haldimandcounty.on.ca
905-318-5932 ext. 6111

Durham: West Grey Public Library
453 Garafraxa St. North, Durham, ON N0G 1R0
Tel: 519-369-2107; *Fax:* 519-369-9966
info@westgreylibrary.com
www.westgreylibrary.com
www.facebook.com/west.greylibrary
Kim Storz, Chief Librarian & CEO
kim@westgreylibrary.com

Eabamet Lake: Fort Hope First Nation Public Library
John C. Yesno Education Centre, Eabamet Lake, ON P0T 1L0
Tel: 807-242-8421; *Fax:* 807-242-1592
jcy.efnea64@gmail.com
efnea64.com/index.php/jcy
www.facebook.com/jcyschool

Ear Falls: Ear Falls Public Library
2 Willow Cres., Ear Falls, ON P0V 1T0
Tel: 807-222-3209; *Fax:* 807-222-3432
efpl@hotmail.ca
ear-falls.com/residents/community-services/library-services
www.facebook.com/earfallspubliclibrary
Susan Carey, Library Director & CEO

Earlton: Earlton Public Library/La bibliothèque publique du canton d'Armstrong
35 - 10th St., Earlton, ON P0J 1E0
Tel: 705-563-2717
library@armstrong.ca
armstrongtownship.com/index.php/2-uncategorised/13-library
www.facebook.com/1383337388662703
Bernice Lockhart, Assistant Librarian

Eganville: Bonnechere Union Public Library
74A Maple St., Eganville, ON K0J 1T0
Tel: 613-628-2400
info@bonnechereupl.com
www.bonnechereupl.com
twitter.com/bonnechereupl; www.facebook.com/BonnechereUPL
Nikolina Likarezic, Chief Executive Officer
ceo@bonnechereupl.com

Elgin: Rideau Lakes Public Library
26 Halladay St., Elgin, ON K0G 1E0
Tel: 613-359-5315; *Fax:* 613-359-5418
info@rlpl.ca
rideaulakeslibrary.ca
twitter.com/rideaulibrary1;
www.facebook.com/rideaulakespubliclibrary
Maxine Weber, Chair
maxineweber4@gmail.com
Vicki Stevenson, Chief Executive Officer
vicki@rlpl.ca
Joan Cochrane, Manager, Circulation
joan@rlpl.ca
Laura Lee Davies, Manager, Programs & Community Outreach
lauralee@rlpl.ca

Elk Lake: James Township Public Library
19 - 1st St., Elk Lake, ON P0J 1G0
Tel: 705-678-2340
jamestwppl@gmail.com
www.elklake.ca/library.html
www.facebook.com/24First
Cyndi Stockman, Chief Executive Officer
Dana Levesque, Library Assistant

Elliot Lake: Elliot Lake Public Library
Pearson Plaza, 40 Hillside Dr., Elliot Lake, ON P5A 1M7
Tel: 705-848-2287
www.elliotlake.ca/en/library
Pat McGurk, Chief Librarian
705-848-2287 ext. 2801

Emo: Emo Public Library
36 Front St., Emo, ON P0W 1E0
Tel: 807-482-2575; *Fax:* 807-482-2575
emolib@bellnet.ca
emo.ca/emo-public-library
Kathy Leek, Librarian

Emsdale: Perry Township (Emsdale) Public Library
25 Joseph St., Emsdale, ON P0A 1J0
Tel: 705-636-5454
library@townshipofperry.ca
www.perrylibrary.ca
www.facebook.com/perrytwplibrary
Annette Gilpin, Chief Executive Officer

Englehart: Englehart Public Library/Bibliothèque publique d'Englehart
71 - 4th Ave., Englehart, ON P0J 1H0
Tel: 705-544-2100; *Fax:* 705-544-2238
www.englehartpubliclibrary.ca
Sharon Williams, Chief Executive Officer
swilliams@englehartpubliclibrary.ca
Karen Watchorn, Clerk
Kassandra Young, Clerk

Espanola: Espanola Public Library
245 Avery Dr., Espanola, ON P5E 1S4
Tel: 705-869-2940; *Fax:* 705-869-6463
library@espanola.ca
www.espanola.ca/services/library
www.facebook.com/EspanolaPublicLibrary
Rosemary Rae, Chief Executive Officer

Essex: Essex County Public Library
#101, 360 Fairview Ave. West, Essex, ON N8M 1Y3
Tel: 519-776-5241; *Fax:* 519-776-6851
www.essexcountylibrary.ca
twitter.com/EssexCountyLib;
www.facebook.com/EssexCountyLibrary
Robin Greenall, Chief Librarian & CEO
rgreenall@essexcountylibrary.ca

Fauquier: Bibliothèque publique de Fauquier-Strickland/Fauquier-Strickland Public Library
25, rue Grzela, Fauquier, ON P0L 1G0
Tél: 705-339-2522; *Téléc:* 705-339-2421
bibliothequefauquier@gmail.com
bibliofauquier.weebly.com
Nicole Lamontagne, Directrice des services
Lise B. Gagnon, Aide-bibliothécaire

Fergus: Wellington County Library
190 St Andrew St. West, Fergus, ON N1M 1N5
Tel: 519-787-7805; *Fax:* 519-787-4608
www.wellington.ca/en/library.aspx
Rebecca Hine, Chief Librarian
rebeccah@wellington.ca
519-787-7805 ext. 6224
Chanda Gilpin, Assistant Chief Librarian
chandag@wellington.ca
519-787-7805 ext. 6229
Janice Ellison, Library Technician
janicee@wellington.ca
519-787-7805 ext. 6227

Flesherton: Grey Highlands Public Library
101 Highland Dr., Flesherton, ON N0C 1E0
Tel: 519-924-2241; *Fax:* 519-924-2562
contact@greyhighlandspubliclibrary.com
www.greyhighlandspubliclibrary.com
twitter.com/GreyHighlandsPL;
www.facebook.com/GreyHighlandsPL
Kevin Land, Chair
Wilda Allen, Chief Librarian & CEO

Flinton: Addington Highlands Public Library
3641 Flinton Rd., Flinton, ON K0H 1P0
Tel: 613-336-1091
flintonl@hotmail.com
www.addingtonhighlandspubliclibrary.ca
www.facebook.com/445455308804599
Carol Lessard, Chair

Fonthill: Pelham Public Library
43 Pelham Town Sq., Fonthill, ON L0S 1E0
Tel: 905-892-6443; *Fax:* 905-892-3392
admin@pelhamlibrary.on.ca
pelhamlibrary.on.ca
www.instagram.com/pelhamlibrary; twitter.com/Pelham_Library;
www.facebook.com/pelhampubliclibrary
Amy Guilmette, Acting Chief Executive Officer
aguilmette@pelhamlibrary.on.ca

Jo-Anne Teeuwsen, Acting Deputy CEO & Manager, Technical Services
jteeuwsen@pelhamlibrary.on.ca
Jennifer Bennett, Coordinator, Children & Youth
jbennett@pelhamlibrary.on.ca
Melanie Taylor-Ridgway, Coordinator, Volunteer & Development
mtaylorridgway@pelhamlibrary.on.ca

Fort Erie: Fort Erie Public Library
136 Gilmore Rd., Fort Erie, ON L2A 2M1
Tel: 905-871-2546
info@fepl.ca
www.fepl.ca
twitter.com/fepl; www.facebook.com/forteriepubliclibrary
Craig Shufelt, Chief Executive Officer
cshufelt@fepl.ca
905-871-2546 ext. 303
Maria Brigantino, Business Administrator
mbrigantino@fepl.ca
905-871-2546 ext. 307
Michael Schell, Systems Administrator
mschell@fepl.ca
905-871-2546 ext. 301
Dawn Gangarossa, Coordinator, Branch Services
dgangarossa@fepl.ca
905-871-2546 ext. 310
Ashley Dunk, Librarian, Children's & Teen
adunk@fepl.ca
905-871-2546 ext. 306
Sean Fleming, Librarian, Adult Services
sfleming@fepl.ca
905-871-2546 ext. 304
Laura Trabucco, Librarian, Community Engagement
ltrabucco@fepl.ca
905-871-2546 ext. 309
Amy Baker, Library Technician
abaker@fepl.ca
905-871-2546 ext. 314

Fort Frances: Fort Frances Library Technology Centre
601 Reid Ave., Fort Frances, ON P9A 0A2
Tel: 807-274-9879; *Fax:* 807-274-4496
ffpltc@gmail.com
www.ffpltc.ca
twitter.com/ffpltc; www.facebook.com/ffpltc
Jean MacLean, Chief Executive Officer
jmaclean@ffpltc.ca
807-274-9879 ext. 1610

Gananoque: Gananoque Public Library
100 Park St., Gananoque, ON K7G 2Y5
Tel: 613-382-2436
gplbl@bellnet.ca
www.gananoquelibrary.ca
twitter.com/GPLlibrary; www.facebook.com/439276356177743

Garden River: Garden River First Nation Public Library
48 Syrette Lake Rd., Garden River, ON P6A 7A1
Tel: 705-946-3933; *Fax:* 705-946-0413
Irene Gray, Coordinator, Resource Centre

Garden Village: Nipissing First Nation Public Library
24 Semo Rd., Garden Village, ON P2B 3K2
Tel: 705-753-6997; *Fax:* 705-753-3755
www.kendaaswin.ca
Randy Penasse, Librarian
705-753-2050 ext. 1231

Georgetown: Halton Hills Public Library
9 Church St., Georgetown, ON L7G 2A3
Tel: 905-873-2681; *Fax:* 905-873-6118
www.hhpl.on.ca
twitter.com/HaltonHillsPL;
www.facebook.com/HaltonHillsPublicLibrary
Melanie Southern, Chief Librarian
905-873-2681 ext. 2513
Clare Hanman, Manager, Content & Technologies
clare.hanman@haltonhills.ca
905-873-2681 ext. 2512
Beverley King, Manager, Community Engagement
beverley.king@haltonhills.ca
905-873-2681 ext. 2522
Mary Querques, Manager, Business Services
905-873-2681 ext. 2510
Dani Austin, Librarian, Children's Services
905-873-2681 ext. 2552
Jen Corrin, Librarian, Systems
jen.corrin@haltonhills.ca
905-873-2681 ext. 2968

Danielle Dawe, Librarian, Adult Services
danielle.dawe@haltonhills.ca
905-873-2681 ext. 2531
Brandi Gillett, Librarian, Community
905-873-2681 ext. 2544
Jodie Mandarino, Librarian, Youth Services
905-873-2681 ext. 2501
Sherry Farago, Branch Supervisor
905-873-2681 ext. 2514

Georgina Island: Chippewas of Georgina Island First Nation Public Library
830 Joseph Snake Rd., Georgina Island, ON L0E 1N0
Tel: 705-437-4327
www.georginaisland.com/community-services/library
Karen Foster, Librarian
Lynn Mooney, Literacy Coordinator

Geraldton: Greenstone Public Library
405 - 2nd St. West, Geraldton, ON P0T 1M0
Tel: 807-854-1490; *Fax:* 807-854-2351
greenstonepl@hotmail.com
www.greenstone.ca/content/greenstone-public-library
www.facebook.com/1540237069589541
Mari Mannisto, Chief Executive Officer
Maria Smith, Branch Librarian

Gilmour: Tudor & Cashel Public Library
371 Weslemkoon Lake Rd., Gilmour, ON K0L 1W0
Tel: 613-474-1096
library@tudorandcashel.com
tudorandcashel.com/services/library
www.facebook.com/101544304768398
Leanne Golan, Librarian

Gogama: Gogama Public Library/Bibliothèque publique de Gogama
15 Low Ave., Gogama, ON P0M 1W0
Tel: 705-894-2448; *Fax:* 705-894-2448
glibrary@ontera.net

Gore Bay: Gore Bay Union Public Library
15 Water St., Gore Bay, ON P0P 1H0
Tel: 705-282-2221
gorebaylibrary@gorebaycable.com
gorebayunionpubliclibrary.ca
www.facebook.com/528005707735659
Johanna Allison, Chief Librarian

Grafton: Alnwick-Haldimand Public Libraries
Centreton Community Hall, 2363 County Rd. #23, Grafton, ON K0K 2G0
Tel: 905-349-2976
publiclibraryoffice@ahtwp.ca
www.ahtwp.ca/en/explore-and-play/library.aspx
www.facebook.com/190046424350622
Elaine Skinner, Chief Executive Officer

Grand Valley: Grand Valley Public Library
4 Amaranth St. East, Grand Valley, ON L9W 5L2
Tel: 519-928-5622; *Fax:* 519-928-2586
info@grandvalley.org
www.townofgrandvalley.ca/en/library-landing.aspx
www.facebook.com/GrandValleyPublicLibrary
Joanne Stevenson, Chief Executive Officer

Gravenhurst: Gravenhurst Public Library
180 Sharpe St. West, Gravenhurst, ON P1P 1J1
Tel: 705-687-3382
library@gravenhurst.ca
www.gravenhurst.ca/en/explore-and-play/library.aspx
twitter.com/gravenhurstlib
www.facebook.com/gravenhurstpubliclibrary
David Hammill, Chair

Grimsby: Grimsby Public Library
18 Carnegie Lane, Grimsby, ON L3M 1Y1
Tel: 905-945-5142
gen-library@grimsby.ca
www.grimsby.ca/en/parks-recreation-culture/library.aspx
twitter.com/GrimsbyLibrary; www.facebook.com/GrimsbyLibrary
Gordana Mosher, Board Chair
Kathryn Drury, CEO & Chief Librarian
905-309-2065

Guelph: Guelph Public Library
100 Norfolk St., Guelph, ON N1H 4J6
Tel: 519-824-6220
Other Numbers: Text: 613-519-0059
askus@guelphpl.ca
www.guelphpl.ca
www.youtube.com/user/GuelphPublicLibrary;
twitter.com/GuelphLibrary; www.facebook.com/GuelphLibrary

Steven Kraft, Chief Executive Officer
519-824-6220 ext. 224
Dan Atkins, Deputy CEO
519-824-6220 ext. 313
Darcy Hiltz, Archivist
519-824-6220 ext. 245
Deb Quaile, Contact, Interlibrary Loans
519-824-6220 ext. 261

Hagersville: Mississaugas of the New Credit First Nation Public Library
2789 Mississauga Rd., RR#6, Hagersville, ON N0A 1H0
Tel: 905-768-5686
newcreditpl@gmail.com
mncfn.ca
Darin P. Wybenga, Coordinator, Traditional Knowledge & Land Use
darin.wybenga@mncfn.ca

Haileybury: Temiskaming Shores Public Library/Bibliothèque publique de Temiskaming Shores
285 Whitewood Ave West., Haileybury, ON P0J 1K0
Tel: 705-647-4215
info@temisklibrary.com
www.temiskamingshores.ca
www.facebook.com/TemiskamingShoresLibrary
Brigid Wilkinson, Chair
chair@temisklibrary.com
Rebecca Hunt, Chief Executive Officer
rhunt@temiskamingshores.ca

Haliburton: Haliburton County Public Library
78 Maple Ave., Haliburton, ON K0M 1S0
Tel: 705-457-2241
info@haliburtonlibrary.ca
www.haliburtonlibrary.ca
haliburtonlibrary.wordpress.com; twitter.com/HaliburtonCPL;
www.facebook.com/haliburtonlibrary
Sally Howson, Chair
Bessie Sullivan, County Librarian & CEO
bsullivan@haliburtonlibrary.ca
Erin Kernohan-Berning, Branch Services Librarian & Deputy CEO
ekernohan@haliburtonlibrary.ca

Hamilton: Hamilton Public Library
55 York Blvd., Hamilton, ON L8N 4E4
Tel: 905-546-3200; *Fax:* 905-546-3202
TTY: 905-546-3474
askhpl@hpl.ca
www.hpl.ca
www.youtube.com/c/HamiltonLibraryVideo;
twitter.com/HamiltonLibrary;
www.facebook.com/hamiltonpubliclibrary
Paul Takala, Chief Librarian & CEO
ptakala@hpl.ca
905-546-3200 ext. 3215
Tony Del Monaco, Director, Finance & Facilities
tdelmona@hpl.ca
905-546-3200 ext. 3226
Lisa DuPelle, Director, Human Resources & Information Services
ldupelle@hpl.ca
905-546-3200 ext. 3290
Sherry Fahim, Director, Digital Technology & Creation
sfahim@hpl.ca
905-546-3200 ext. 3557
Dawna Wark, Director, Public Services
dwark@hpl.ca
905-546-3200 ext. 3285
Lisa Weaver, Director, Collections & Program Development
lweaver@hpl.ca
905-546-3200 ext. 3442

Hanover: Hanover Public Library
Civic Centre, 451 - 10th Ave., Hanover, ON N4N 2P1
Tel: 519-364-1420; *Fax:* 519-364-1747
hanpub@hanover.ca
hanoverlibrary.ca
twitter.com/HanoverLibrary;
www.facebook.com/HanoverPublicLibrary
Kathi Maskell, Chair
Agnes Rivers-Moore, Chief Librarian & CEO
arm@hanover.ca

Havelock: Havelock-Belmont-Methuen Township Public Library
13 Quebec St., Havelock, ON K0L 1Z0
Tel: 705-778-2621; *Fax:* 705-778-2621
habellib@nexicom.net
www.hbmlibrary.on.ca
Sandra Harris, Chief Librarian & CEO

Hawkesbury: Bibliothèque publique de Hawkesbury/Hawkesbury Public Library
550 Higginson St., Hawkesbury, ON K6A 1H1
Tél: 613-632-0106; *Téléc:* 613-636-2097
info@bibliotheque.hawkesbury.on.ca
www.bibliotheque.hawkesbury.on.ca
www.facebook.com/BibHawkesbury
Yvon Léonard, Président
Lynn Belle-Isle, Directrice générale
Madeline Laflèche, Bibliotechnicienne
Nathalie St-Jacques, Bibliotechnicienne

Hearst: Bibliothèque publique de Hearst/Hearst Public Library
801 George St., Hearst, ON P0L 1N0
Tel: 705-372-2843; *Fax:* 705-372-2833
bibliohearst.on.ca
www.facebook.com/bibliohearst
Julie Portelance, Director, Library Services
director@bibliohearst.on.ca
Chloé Vachon, Library Services Technician
tech@bibliohearst.on.ca

Hermon: Carlow-Mayo Public Library
124 Fort Stewart Rd., Hermon, ON K0L 1C0
Tel: 613-332-2544
carlowmayopl@gmail.com
carlowmayo.ca/services/library
Carrie McKenzie, Head Librarian

Heron Bay: Ojibways of the Pic River First Nation Public Library
Pic River Elementary School, 21 Rabbit Dr., Heron Bay, ON P0T 1R0
Tel: 807-229-0630; *Fax:* 807-229-1944
Glenda Michano-Nabigon, Chief Executive Officer

Hilton Beach: Hilton Union Public Library
3085 Marks St., Hilton Beach, ON P0R 1G0
Tel: 705-255-3520
hiltonlibrary@hotmail.ca
hiltonunion.library.on.ca
www.facebook.com/1629569227328783
Kim McHale, Chief Executive Officer

Holland Landing: East Gwillimbury Public Library
19513 Yonge St., Holland Landing, ON L9N 1P2
Tel: 905-836-6492
info@egpl.ca
www.egpl.ca
twitter.com/EGPublicLibrary;
www.facebook.com/eastgwillimburylibrary
Monika Machacek, CEO
mmachacek@egpl.ca
905-836-6492 ext. 110
Angela Ramsey, Deputy CEO
aramsey@egpl.ca
905-836-6492 ext. 105
Heather Alblas, Manager, Collections & Resources
halblas@egpl.ca
905-836-6492 ext. 112
Stephanie Clare, Manager, Programs & Community Engagement
sclare@egpl.ca
905-836-6492 ext. 115
Lyndsay Irvine, Manager, Customer Experience
lirvine@egpl.ca
905-836-6492 ext. 117
Ben Van Gorp, Librarian
bvangorp@egpl.ca
905-836-6492 ext. 109

Hornepayne: Hornepayne Township Public Library
68 Front St., Hornepayne, ON P0M 1Z0
Tel: 807-868-2332
hornepaynepl@gmail.com
hornepayne.olsn.ca
www.facebook.com/HornepaynePublicLibrary
David Turgeon, Chair
Darnelle Hill, Chief Executive Officer

Huntsville: Huntsville Public Library
7 Minerva St. East, Huntsville, ON P1H 1W1
Tel: 705-789-5232
comments@huntsvillelibrary.ca
www.huntsvillelibrary.ca
twitter.com/HuntsvillePL; www.facebook.com/huntsvillelibrary
David Purchase, Chair
David Tremblay, Chief Librarian & CEO
705-789-5232 ext. 3407
Cortney LeGros, Coordinator, Community Engagement
705-789-5232 ext. 3408

Julie Manczak, eLibrarian
705-789-5232 ext. 3404
Amber McNair, Librarian, Youth Services
705-789-5232 ext. 3406

Ignace: Ignace Public Library
36 Main St., Ignace, ON P0T 1T0
Tel: 807-934-2280
ignace.olsn.ca

Cindy Stark, Chair
Tina Richards, Chief Executive Officer
ceoignacelibrary@gmail.com

Innisfil: Innisfil ideaLAB & Library
967 Innisfil Beach Rd., Innisfil, ON L9S 1V3
Tel: 705-431-7410
info@innisfilidealab.ca
www.innisfilidealab.ca
www.youtube.com/c/InnisfilideaLABLibrary;
twitter.com/Innisfildealab;
www.facebook.com/InnisfilideaLABLibrary
Erin Scuccimarri, Chief Librarian & CEO
escuccimarri@innisfilidealab.ca
Susan Baues, Deputy Chief Librarian
sbaues@innisfilidealab.ca
Megan Legg, Manager, Programming & Outreach
mlegg@innisfilidealab.ca
Mandy Pethick, Manager, Collections & Customer Experience
mpethick@innisfilidealab.ca
Kathryn Schousten, Manager, Engagement & Community
Development
kshousten@innisfilidealab.ca
John van Rassel, Manager, Information Technology
jvanrassel@innisfil.library.on.ca

**Iroquois Falls: Bibliothèque publique d'Iroquois
Falls Public Library**
725 Synagogue Ave., Iroquois Falls, ON P0K 1G0
Tel: 705-232-5722; *Fax:* 705-232-7166
ifplibrary1@gmail.com
www.iroquoisfalls.com/iroquois-falls-public-library
www.facebook.com/IFPLibrary
Diane Gagnon, Chief Executive Officer
Haley Irvine-Montreuil, Assistant Librarian

Kagawong: Billings Township Public Library
18 Upper St., Kagawong, ON P0P 1J0
Tel: 705-282-2944
billingslibrary@vianet.ca
billingstwp.ca/services/billings-public-library
www.facebook.com/kagawonglibrary

**Kapuskasing: Kapuskasing Public
Library/Bibliothèque publique de Kapuskasing**
24 Mundy Ave., Kapuskasing, ON P5N 1P9
Tel: 705-335-3363; *Fax:* 705-335-2464
library@kapuskasing.ca
www.kapuskasing.olsn.ca
www.facebook.com/bibliothequepubliquekapuskasingpubliclibrar
y

Kearney: Kearney & Area Public Library
Kearney Community Centre, 8 Main St., Kearney, ON P0A
1M0
Tel: 705-636-5849
kearneylibrary@hotmail.ca
kearney.olsn.ca
Brandi Nolan, Librarian & CEO

Keene: Otonabee-South Monaghan Public Library
3252 County Rd. 2, Keene, ON K0L 2G0
Tel: 705-295-6814
keene_library@nexicom.net
www.otosoumon.library.on.ca
twitter.com/LibraryOtonSMon;
www.facebook.com/osmpubliclibrary
Val Crowley, Chair
brianval@sympatico.ca
Carolanne Nadeau, Chief Executive Officer

Kemptville: North Grenville Public Library
1 Water St., Kemptville, ON K0G 1J0
Tel: 613-258-4711; *Fax:* 613-258-4134
info@ngpl.ca
ngpl.ca
twitter.com/NGPLStaff; www.facebook.com/NorthGrenvillePL
Rachel Brown, Chief Executive Officer
rbrown@ngpl.ca
Patricia Evans, Manager, Information Services
pevans@ngpl.ca
Sierra Jones, Manager, Service Delivery
sjones@ngpl.ca

Kenora: City of Kenora Public Library
24 Main St. South, Kenora, ON P9N 1S7
Tel: 807-467-2081; *Fax:* 807-467-2085
kpl@kenora.ca
kenorapubliclibrary.org

Keswick: Georgina Public Library
90 Wexford Dr., Keswick, ON L4P 3P7
Tel: 905-476-7233; *Fax:* 905-476-8724
eservicesupport@georgina.ca
www.georginalibrary.ca
twitter.com/georginalibrary; www.facebook.com/GeorginaPL
Val Stevens, CEO & Director, Library Services
905-476-7233 ext. 4521

**Kettle & Stony Point: Chippewas of Kettle & Stony
Point Library**
#6, 9111 West Ipperwash Rd., Kettle & Stony Point, ON N0N
1J0
Tel: 519-786-2955; *Fax:* 519-786-6904
Other Numbers: 519-786-6903
kettlepoint.org/kettle-stony-point-education-services

Killaloe: Killaloe & District Public Library
1 John St., Killaloe, ON K0J 2A0
Tel: 613-757-2211
info@killaloelibrary.ca
killaloelibrary.ca
www.facebook.com/166579606709402
Glenn Allen, Chair
Nicole Zummach, Librarian & CEO
librarian@killaloelibrary.ca
Cheryl Keetch, Assistant Librarian
cheryl@killaloelibrary.ca

King City: King Township Public Library
1970 King Rd., King City, ON L7B 1K9
Tel: 905-833-5101; *Fax:* 905-833-0824
info@kinglibrary.ca
www.kinglibrary.ca
twitter.com/KingLibraries; www.facebook.com/KTPLibrary
Adele Reid, Manager, Administrative & Branch Services
a.reid@kinglibrary.ca
905-833-5101 ext. 2103

Kingston: Kingston Frontenac Public Library
130 Johnson St., Kingston, ON K7L 1X8
Tel: 613-549-8888
contact@kfpl.ca
www.kfpl.ca
www.youtube.com/c/KingstonFrontenacPublicLibrary;
twitter.com/KFPL; www.facebook.com/KingstonFrontenacPL
Laura Carter, Chief Librarian & CEO
lcarter@kfpl.ca
Nicole Charles, Director, Branch Experience
ncharles@kfpl.ca
Shelagh Quigley, Director, Human Resources
squigley@kfpl.ca
Lester Webb, Director, Outreach & Technology
lwebb@kfpl.ca
Elizabeth Coates, Manager, Branch Operations
lcoates@kfpl.ca
Andrew Morton, Manager, Facilities
amorton@kfpl.ca
Kimberly Sutherland Mills, Manager, Programming & Outreach
kmills@kfpl.ca

Kirkland Lake: Teck Centennial Library
10 Kirkland St. East, Kirkland Lake, ON P2N 1P1
Tel: 705-567-7966; *Fax:* 705-568-6303
library@tkl.ca
teckcentennialpl.ca
twitter.com/lake_kirkland;
www.facebook.com/TeckCentennialLibrary
Cheryl Lafreniere, Chief Executive Officer

Kitchener: Kitchener Public Library
85 Queen St. North, Kitchener, ON N2H 2H1
Tel: 519-743-0271; *Fax:* 519-743-1261
TTY: 877-614-4832
askkpl@kpl.org
www.kpl.org
www.youtube.com/user/kitchenerlibrary; twitter.com/KitchLibrary;
www.facebook.com/kitchenerlibrary
Mary Chevreau, Chief Executive Officer
libraryceo@kpl.org
519-743-0271 ext. 244
Penny-Lynn Fielding, Deputy CEO
penny-lynn.fielding@kpl.org
519-743-0271 ext. 274
Lesa Balch, Director, Innovation & Integration
lesa.balch@kpl.org
519-743-0271 ext. 231

Angela Riddell, Director, Business Services & Infrastructure
angela.riddell@kpl.org
519-743-0271 ext. 240
Lisa Wallace, Manager, Information Technology
lisa.wallace@kpl.org
519-743-0271 ext. 242

**Lake Temagami: Temagami First Nation Public
Library/Bibliothèque publique de Tribu Temagami**
General Delivery, Bear Island, Lake Temagami, ON P0H 1C0
Tel: 705-237-8943
librarian@temagamifirstnation.ca
www.temagamifirstnation.ca/library

Lanark Village: Lanark Highlands Public Library
75 George St., 2nd Fl., Lanark Village, ON K0G 1K0
Tel: 613-259-3068
general@lanarklibrary.ca
lanarklibrary.ca
www.facebook.com/LanarkHighlandsPublicLibrary
Bob Mezzatesta, Chair
Amanda Robinson, Chief Executive Officer
ceo@lanarklibrary.ca

**Lansdowne: Leeds & the Thousand Islands Public
Library**
1B Jessie St., Lansdowne, ON K0E 1L0
Tel: 613-659-3885; *Fax:* 613-659-4192
staff@ltipl.net
www.ltipl.net
www.facebook.com/leeds1000islandspubliclibrary
Linda Chadwick, Interim Chief Executive Officer
linda@ltipl.net

Larder Lake: Larder Lake Public Library
Larder Lake Municipal Complex, 69 - 4th Ave., Larder Lake,
ON P0K 1L0
Tel: 705-643-2222; *Fax:* 705-643-2311
www.larderlakepubliclibrary.ca
www.facebook.com/LarderLakePublicLibrary
Tracey Reid, Chair

Lindsay: City of Kawartha Lakes Public Library
190 Kent St. West, Lindsay, ON K9V 2Y6
Tel: 705-324-9411; *Fax:* 705-878-1859
Toll-Free: 888-822-2225
libraryadministration@kawarthalakes.ca
www.kawarthalakeslibrary.ca
twitter.com/kawarthalibrary; www.facebook.com/kawarthalibrary
Susan Ferguson, Chair
Jamie Anderson, Library Director & CEO
705-324-9411 ext. 1260

Listowel: North Perth Public Library
260 Main St. West, Listowel, ON N4W 1A1
Tel: 519-291-4621; *Fax:* 519-291-2235
Toll-Free: 888-714-1993
www.northperth.ca
twitter.com/NorthPerthLib
Terrance Ritchie, Chair
Ellen Whelan, Interim Chief Executive Officer

**Little Current: Northeastern Manitoulin & the Islands
(NEMI) Public Library**
50 Meredith St. West, Little Current, ON P0P 1K0
Tel: 705-368-2444; *Fax:* 705-368-0708
nemilib@vianet.on.ca
www.townofnemi.on.ca/p/library
www.facebook.com/NEMILibrary
Kathy Berry, Chief Executive Officer

London: London Public Library
251 Dundas St., London, ON N6A 6H9
Tel: 519-661-4600; *Fax:* 519-663-9013
TTY: 519-432-8835
info@lpl.ca
www.londonpubliclibrary.ca
www.youtube.com/user/LondonPublicLibrary;
twitter.com/londonlibrary; www.facebook.com/londonlibrary
Michael Ciccone, CEO & Chief Librarian
michael.ciccone@lpl.ca
519-661-5143
Nancy Collister, Director, Customer Services & Branch
Operations
nancy.collister@lpl.ca
519-661-5100 ext. 5136
Tom Travers, Acting Director, Information Technology Services
jon.macdonald@lpl.ca
519-661-5100 ext. 6475
Emily Schinbein, Director, Financial Services
emily.schinbein@lpl.ca
519-661-5100 ext. 5144

M'Chigeeng: M'Chigeeng First Nation Public Library
18 Lakeview Dr., M'Chigeeng, ON P0P 1G0
Tel: 705-377-5540; *Fax:* 705-377-5080
mchigeeng.ca

MacTier: Township of Georgian Bay Public Library
12 Muskoka Rd., MacTier, ON P0C 1H0
Tel: 705-375-5430; *Fax:* 705-375-5430
georgianbaypl@gmail.com
www.gbpl.ca
www.facebook.com/200394210063297
Sarah Papple, Chief Executive Officer
Carol McCron, Librarian
Mandy Near, Librarian
Nadine Triemstra, Librarian

Madoc: Madoc Public Library
20 Davidson St., Madoc, ON K0K 2K0
Tel: 613-473-4456
info@madocpubliclibrary.ca
madocpubliclibrary.ca
www.facebook.com/madoclibrary
Gayle Ketcheson, Chair
Tammie Adams-Wagner, Librarian & CEO
ceo@madocpubliclibrary.ca
Leigh Anne Lavender, Assistant Librarian

Magnetawan: Magnetawan Public Library
4304 Sparks St. North, Magnetawan, ON P0A 1P0
Tel: 705-387-4411; *Fax:* 705-387-0636
magcap@ontera.net
magnetawanlibrary.ca
twitter.com/MagnetawanPL; www.facebook.com/41591429313
Julie Ferris, Board Chair
Lorinda Makoviczki, Head Librarian & CEO
Karen Hoffman, Library Assistant

Mallorytown: Front of Yonge Public Library
76 County Rd. 5 South, Mallorytown, ON K0E 1R0
Tel: 613-923-1790; *Fax:* 613-923-2691
library@frontofyonge.com
www.library.frontofyonge.com
www.facebook.com/FOYLibrary
Lisa Marston, Chief Executive Officer

Manitouwadge: Manitouwadge Public Library
Community Centre, 2 Manitou Rd., Manitouwadge, ON P0T 2C0
Tel: 807-826-3913; *Fax:* 807-826-4640
library@manitouwadge.ca
manitouwadge.olsn.ca
www.facebook.com/ManitouwadgePublicLibrary
Elizabeth Bierworth, Librarian & CEO
libadmin@manitouwadge.ca

Manitowaning: Assiginack Public Library
25 Spragge St., Manitowaning, ON P0P 1N0
Tel: 705-859-2110
aplgoodtomes@email.com
www.assiginack.ca/services/public-library
Debbie Robinson, Head Librarian & CEO

Marathon: Marathon Public Library
22 Peninsula Rd., Marathon, ON P0T 2E0
Tel: 807-229-0740; *Fax:* 807-229-3336
marpublib@shaw.ca
marathon.olsn.ca
twitter.com/Marathon_PL0740; www.facebook.com/marpublib
Amy Mackie, Chair
Tamara Needham, Head Librarian & CEO
marpublib.ceo@outlook.com
807-229-1340 ext. 2266

Markham: Markham Public Library
6031 Hwy. 7, Markham, ON L3P 3A7
Tel: 905-513-7977; *Fax:* 905-471-9015
comments@markham.library.on.ca
www.markhampubliclibrary.ca
twitter.com/markhamlibrary; www.facebook.com/markhamlibrary
Catherine Biss, Chief Executive Officer
cbiss@markham.library.on.ca
905-513-7977 ext. 5999
Andrea Cecchetto, Director, Service Excellence
acecch@markham.library.on.ca
905-513-7977 ext. 4997
Diane Macklin, Director, Community Engagement
dmacklin@markham.library.on.ca
905-513-7977 ext. 3912
Michelle Sawh, Director, Administration
msawh@markham.library.on.ca
905-513-7977 ext. 4233

Deborah Walker, Director, Strategy & Planning
dwalker@markham.library.on.ca
905-513-7977 ext. 4414

Markstay: Markstay Public Library
7 Pioneer St. East, Markstay, ON P0M 2G0
Tel: 705-599-3009
library@markstay-warren.ca
markstaywarren.olsn.ca
www.facebook.com/MarkstayWarrenLibrary

Marmora: Marmora & Lake Public Library
37 Forsyth St., Marmora, ON K0K 2M0
Tel: 613-472-3122
info@marmoralibrary.ca
marmoralibrary.ca
www.facebook.com/marmoralibrary
Rene Young, Chair
Kathy Farrell, Librarian & CEO
ceo@marmoralibrary.ca
Megan Haines, Assistant Librarian
assistlib@marmoralibrary.ca

Massey: Massey & Township Public Library
185 Grove St., Massey, ON P0P 1P0
Tel: 705-865-2641; *Fax:* 705-865-1781
infomasseylibrary@gmail.com
masseylibrary.com
www.facebook.com/masseyandtownshippubliclibrary
Kevin Burke, Chair
Serena Mariage, Chief Librarian & CEO

Massey: Sagamok Anishnawbek First Nation Public Library
4008 Espaniel Rd., Massey, ON P0P 1P0
Tel: 705-865-2970; *Fax:* 705-865-3307
sagamokeducation.ca/programs-services/library
Colleen Eshkakogan, Chief Executive Officer
eshkakogan_colleen@sagamok.ca

Matheson: Black River-Matheson Public Library
352 - 2nd St., Matheson, ON P0K 1N0
Tel: 705-273-2760; *Fax:* 705-273-2760
brmlibrary@gmail.com
www.blackriver-matheson.com/library.php
www.facebook.com/brmlibrary
Margaret-Anne Friese, Librarian & CEO

Mattagami: Mattagami First Nation Public Library
PO Box 250, Mattagami, ON P0M 1W0
Tel: 705-894-2003; *Fax:* 705-894-2386

Mattawa: Mattawa Public Library
370 Pine St., Mattawa, ON P0H 1V0
Tel: 705-744-5550; *Fax:* 705-744-1714
mplibrary@efni.com
www.facebook.com/JohnDixonPublicLibrary

Mattice: Mattice - Val Côté Public Library/Bibliothèque publique de Mattice - Val Côté
189 Balmoral Ave., Mattice, ON P0L 1T0
Tel: 705-364-5301; *Fax:* 705-364-6431
biblimat@matticevalcote.ca
matticevalcote.ca/mattice/?page_id=1540
Michelle Salonen, Librarian

Maynooth: Hastings Highlands Public Library
33011 Hwy. 62 North, Maynooth, ON K0L 2S0
Tel: 613-338-2262; *Fax:* 613-338-5534
info@hastingshighlandslibrary.ca
www.hastingshighlandslibrary.ca
www.facebook.com/HastingsHighlandsPublicLibrary
Rod Moffitt, Chief Executive Officer
ceo@hastingshighlandslibrary.ca
Kristin Seaborn, Assistant Librarian
librarian@hastingshighlandslibrary.ca

McKellar: McKellar Township Public Library
701 Hwy. 124, McKellar, ON P0G 1C0
Tel: 705-389-2611; *Fax:* 705-389-2611
mckellarlib@vianet.ca
mckellarpubliclibrary.ca
www.facebook.com/434102280347130
Terri Short, Librarian & CEO
Lynne Campbell, Assistant Librarian

Meaford: Meaford Public Library
11 Sykes St. North, Meaford, ON N4L 1V6
Tel: 519-538-3500
libraryinfo@meaford.ca
www.meaford.ca/en/explore-play/library.aspx
www.pinterest.com/meafordlibrary; twitter.com/meafordlibrary;
www.facebook.com/meafordpubliclibrary
Mike Poetker, Chair

Cathie Lee, Chief Executive Officer

Merrickville: Merrickville Public Library
446 Main St. West, Merrickville, ON K0G 1N0
Tel: 613-269-3326
merrickville_library@bellnet.ca
merrickvillelibrary.ca
www.facebook.com/Merrickville.Library
Mary Kate Laphen, Chief Executive Officer

Midhurst: Springwater Township Public Library
12 Finlay Mill Rd., Midhurst, ON L9X 0N7
Tel: 705-737-5650; *Fax:* 705-737-3594
info-library@springwater.ca
www.springwater.library.on.ca
www.pinterest.com/springwaterpl; twitter.com/SpringwaterLib;
www.facebook.com/257744667668662
Jodie Player Delgado, Chief Executive Officer

Midland: Midland Public Library
320 King St., Midland, ON L4R 3M6
Tel: 705-526-4216; *Fax:* 705-526-1474
www.midlandlibrary.com
twitter.com/midland_library; www.facebook.com/midlandlibrary
Crystal Bergstrome, Chief Librarian & CEO

Millbrook: Cavan Monaghan Libraries
Old Millbrook School, 1 Dufferin St., Millbrook, ON L0A 1G0
Tel: 705-932-2919
questions@cavanmonaghanlibraries.ca
www.cavanmonaghanlibraries.ca
www.facebook.com/CavanMonaghanLibraries
Karla Buckborough, Librarian & CEO
Erin Stewart, Branch Librarian

Milton: Milton Public Library
1010 Main St. East, Milton, ON L9T 6H7
Tel: 905-875-2665; *Fax:* 905-875-4324
TTY: 905-875-1550
information@beinspired.ca
www.mpl.on.ca
www.instagram.com/miltonpubliclibrary;
twitter.com/Milton_Library;
www.facebook.com/MiltonPublicLibrary
Mark Williams, Chief Librarian & CEO
mark.williams@mpl.on.ca
905-875-2665 ext. 3265
Dave Hook, Deputy Chief Librarian
dave.hook@mpl.on.ca
905-875-2665 ext. 3233
Vito Montesano, Senior Manager, Human Resources
vito.montesano@mpl.on.ca
905-875-2665 ext. 3232
Maria Petricko, Manager, Branches
maria.petricko@mpl.on.ca
905-875-2665 ext. 3290
Lee Puddephatt, Manager, Public Service
lee.puddephatt@mpl.on.ca
905-875-2665 ext. 3260

Milverton: Perth East Public Library
19 Mill St. East, Milverton, ON N0K 1M0
Tel: 519-595-8395; *Fax:* 519-595-2943
pel@pcin.on.ca
pertheastpl.ca
www.instagram.com/pepllibrary; twitter.com/pepllibrary;
www.facebook.com/PerthEastPublicLibrary
Hugh McDermid, Chair
Allie Fallis, Chief Executive Officer

Mindemoya: Central Manitoulin Public Libraries
6020 Hwy. 542, Mindemoya, ON P0P 1S0
Tel: 705-377-5334; *Fax:* 705-377-5334
bookworm@amtelecom.net
www.centralmanitoulin.ca/central-manitoulin/library
www.facebook.com/CentralManitoulinLibraries
Claire Cline, Chief Librarian & CEO
Christine Taylor, Assistant Librarian

Mine Centre: Seine River First Nation Public Library
25 Learning Centre Rd., Mine Centre, ON P0W 1H0
Tel: 807-599-2224; *Fax:* 807-599-2871
Toll-Free: 800-465-3349
srlibrary@bellnet.ca
seineriverfirstnation.ca

Mississauga: Mississauga Library System
301 Burnhamthorpe Rd. West, Mississauga, ON L5B 3Y3
Tel: 905-615-3500; *Fax:* 905-615-3625
support.library@mississauga.ca
web.mississauga.ca/library
www.instagram.com/mississaugalib; twitter.com/mississaugalib;
www.facebook.com/mississaugalibrary

Jennifer Stirling, Director, Library Services
jennifer.stirling@mississauga.ca
905-615-3200 ext. 3605
Sue Coles, Manager, Library Facilities & Operations
sue.coles@mississauga.ca
905-615-3200 ext. 2082
James Cooper, Manager, Digital Library Services & Collections
james.cooper@mississauga.ca
647-969-9531
Michael Menary, Manager, Library Planning, Development &
Analysis
michael.menary@mississauga.ca
905-615-3200 ext. 4822
Laura Reed, Manager, Central Library & Community
Development
laura.reed@mississauga.ca
905-615-3200 ext. 4520

Mitchell: West Perth Public Library
105 St Andrew St., Mitchell, ON N0K 1N0
Tel: 519-348-9234; *Fax:* 519-348-4540
askwppl@pcin.on.ca
westperthpl.ca
Jesse Britton, Chair
Rosemary Minnella, Chief Executive Officer
rminnella@pcin.on.ca

Mobert: Pic Mobert First Nation Public Library
PO Box 615, Mobert, ON P0M 2J0
Tel: 807-822-2011; *Fax:* 807-822-2710
principal@picmobert.ca

Moonbeam: Bibliothèque de Moonbeam/Moonbeam Public Library
53, av St-Aubin, Moonbeam, ON P0L 1V0
Tél: 705-367-2462; *Téléc:* 705-367-2120
biblio@moonbeam.ca
biblio.moonbeam.ca
Gisèle Belisle, Directrice-Responsable
Angèle Albert, Directrice adjointe

Morson: Big Grassy First Nation Public Library
Pegamigaabo School, 513 Beach Rd., Morson, ON P0W 1J0
Tel: 807-488-5916; *Fax:* 807-488-5345
biggrassy.ca/library
Angeline Andy, Chief Executive Officer
angandy76@hotmail.com

Muncey: Chippewas of the Thames
328 Chippewa Rd., Muncey, ON N0L 1Y0
Tel: 519-289-2929
info@cottfn.com
www.cottfn.com

Murillo: Oliver Paipoonge Public Library
4569 Oliver Rd., Murillo, ON P0T 2G0
Tel: 807-935-2729
oliverpaipoongelibrary@gmail.com
oliverpaipoonge.olsn.ca
www.facebook.com/317003395098369

Napanee: Lennox & Addington County Library
97 Thomas St. East, Napanee, ON K7R 4B9
Tel: 613-354-4883; *Fax:* 613-354-3112
lennox-addington.on.ca/library-services
www.instagram.com/LandALibrary; twitter.com/LandALibrary;
www.facebook.com/LandALibrary
Catherine Coles, Manager, Library Services
ccoles@lennox-addington.on.ca
613-354-4883 ext. 3237

Naughton: Atikameksheng Anishnawbek First Nation Public Library
212 Maani St., RR#1, Naughton, ON P0M 2M0
Tel: 705-692-9901; *Fax:* 705-692-5010
library@wlfn.com
atikamekshenganishnawbek.ca/service/library
Mary Fraser, Librarian
mfraser@wlfn.com

Nestor Falls: Ojibways of Onigaming First Nation Public Library
Mikinaak Onigaming School, 212 Mikinaak Rd., Nestor Falls, ON P0X 1K0
Tel: 807-484-2612; *Fax:* 807-484-2737
onigamingfn@yahoo.com
www.onigaming.ca

Newmarket: Newmarket Public Library
438 Park Ave., Newmarket, ON L3Y 1W1
Tel: 905-953-5110; *Fax:* 905-953-5104
npl@newmarketpl.ca
www.instagram.com/newmarketlibrary;
twitter.com/NewmarketPL; www.facebook.com/247080242075
Linda Peppiatt, Chief Executive Officer
905-953-5110 ext. 4670

Neyaashiinigmiing: Ninda Kikaendjigae Wigammik Library
25 Maadookii Subdivision, RR#5, Neyaashiinigmiing, ON N0H 2T0
Tel: 519-534-1508; *Fax:* 519-534-2130
library@nawashfn.ca
www.nawash.ca/library
Priscilla Ashkewe, Librarian

Niagara Falls: Niagara Falls Public Library
4848 Victoria Ave., Niagara Falls, ON L2E 4C5
Tel: 905-356-8080; *Fax:* 905-356-9498
my.nflibrary.ca
www.youtube.com/user/NFPublicLibraryCA;
twitter.com/NFLibrary; www.facebook.com/NFPublicLibrary
Alicia Kilgour, CEO & Chief Librarian
Susan DiBattista, Manager, Customer Service
Ashleigh Dronyk, Manager, Information Resources &
Connections
Laura Martin, Manager, Community Development &
Programming

Niagara on the Lake: Niagara on the Lake Public Library
10 Anderson Lane, Niagara on the Lake, ON L0S 1J0
Tel: 905-468-2023; *Fax:* 905-468-3334
notllibrary@gmail.com
notlpubliclibrary.org
www.pinterest.com/notlpl; twitter.com/notl_library;
www.facebook.com/notlpubliclibrary
Cathy Simpson, Chief Librarian
csimpson@notlpl.org
905-468-2023 ext. 203
Laura Tait, Library Manager
ltait@notlpl.org
905-468-2023 ext. 206

Nipigon: Nipigon Public Library
52 Front St., Nipigon, ON P0T 2J0
Tel: 807-887-3142
nipigonpl@gmail.com
www.nipigon.net/residents/nipigon-public-library
Sumiye Sugawara, Librarian & CEO

Nobel: Shawanaga First Nation Public Library
2 Church St., Nobel, ON P0G 1G0
Tel: 705-366-2029

North Bay: North Bay Public Library
271 Worthington St. East, North Bay, ON P1B 1H1
Tel: 705-474-4830; *Fax:* 705-495-4010
library@northbay.ca
library.cityofnorthbay.ca
twitter.com/North_BayPL
www.facebook.com/NorthBayPublicLibrary
Ravil Veli, Chief Executive Officer
ravil.veli@northbay.ca
Judith Bouman, Manager, Adult & Technical Services
judith.bouman@northbay.ca
Nora Elliott-Coutts, Manager, Children's Services
nora.elliott-coutts@northbay.ca
Carrie James, Manager, Administrative Services
carrie.james@northbay.ca
Rebecca Larocque, Manager, Digital Services & Facilities
rebecca.larocque@northbay.ca

Norwood: Asphodel-Norwood Public Library
2363 County Rd. #45, Norwood, ON K0L 2V0
Tel: 705-639-2228
info@anpl.org
anpl.org
twitter.com/AsphodelLibrary;
www.facebook.com/AsphodelNorwoodPublicLibrary
Mary Hay, Chair
Kris Van Luven, Head Librarian & CEO

Oakville: Oakville Public Library
120 Navy St., Oakville, ON L6J 2Z4
Tel: 905-815-2042; *Fax:* 905-815-2024
oplreference@oakville.ca
www.opl.on.ca
www.instagram.com/oakvillelibrary; twitter.com/OakvilleLibrary;
www.facebook.com/oakville.library

Tara Wong, Chief Executive Officer
tara.wong@oakville.ca
905-815-2042 ext. 2027
Simona Dinu, Director, Customer Experience
simona.dinu@oakville.ca
905-815-2042 ext. 2035
Joseph Moncada, Director, Innovation & Integration
joseph.moncada@oakville.ca
905-815-2042 ext. 2014

Ohsweken: Six Nations Public Library
1679 Chiefswood Rd., Ohsweken, ON N0A 1M0
Tel: 519-445-2954; *Fax:* 519-445-2872
info@snpl.ca
snpl.ca
twitter.com/6NationsLibrary; www.facebook.com/6NationsPL
Donald D. Lynch, Chair
chair@snpl.ca
Feather Maracle, Chief Executive Officer
director@snpl.ca

Opasatika: Opasatika Public Library/La Bibliothèque d'Opasatika
6 St Antoine St., Opasatika, ON P0L 1Z0
Fax: 705-369-3098
opasatikabiblio@hotmail.ca
www.opasatika.net/library

Orangeville: Orangeville Public Library
1 Mill St., Orangeville, ON L9W 2M2
Tel: 519-941-0610
infolibrary@orangeville.ca
www.orangevillelibrary.ca
www.facebook.com/ovillelibrary
Darla Fraser, Chief Librarian & CEO
dfraser@orangeville.ca
519-941-0610 ext. 5222
Kim Carson, Librarian, Collection & Systems
519-941-0610 ext. 5226
Kathryn Creelman, Librarian, Public Services
kcreelman@orangeville.ca
519-941-0610 ext. 5232
Lauren Tilly, Librarian, Program & Research
519-941-0610 ext. 5230

Orillia: Orillia Public Library
36 Mississaga St. West, Orillia, ON L3V 3A6
Tel: 705-325-2338; *Fax:* 705-327-1744
info@orilliapubliclibrary.ca
www.orilliapubliclibrary.ca
twitter.com/orillialibrary; www.facebook.com/OrilliaPublicLibrary
Suzanne Campbell, Chief Executive Officer

Oshawa: Oshawa Public Libraries
65 Bagot St., Oshawa, ON L1H 1N2
Tel: 905-579-6111; *Fax:* 905-433-8107
ask@oshawalibrary.on.ca
oshlib.ca
www.youtube.com/user/OshawaLibraryTV;
twitter.com/OshawaLibraries;
www.facebook.com/oshawapubliclibrary
Frances Newman, Chief Executive Officer
Ellen Stroud, Director, Service Design & Delivery
Jennifer Green, Manager, Collections & Access
Tracy Munusami, Manager, Service Excellence

Ottawa: Ottawa Public Library/Bibliothèque publique d'Ottawa
120 Metcalfe St., Ottawa, ON K1P 5M2
Tel: 613-580-2940
infoservice@bibliottawalibrary.ca
bibliottawalibrary.ca
www.youtube.com/user/BiblioOttawaLibrary;
twitter.com/opl_bpo; www.facebook.com/BiblioOttawaLibrary
Danielle McDonald, Chief Executive Officer
danielle.mcdonald@bibliottawalibrary.ca
Anna Basile, Division Manager, Corporate Services
anna.basile@bibliottawalibrary.ca
Donna Clark, Division Manager, Branch Operations
Craig Ginther, Division Manager, Central Library Project
craig.ginther@bibliottawalibrary.ca
Catherine Seaman, Division Manager, Customer Experience
Karen Beiles, Branch Manager, South West
Sharon Campbell, Acting Branch Manager, South East
Catherine Flegg, Branch Manager, West
Sarah Macintyre, Branch Manager, East
Philip Robert, Branch Manager, Urban East
Yvonne van Lith, Branch Manager, Urban West
Tony Westenbroek, Branch Manager, Central

Owen Sound: Owen Sound & North Grey Union Public Library
824 - 1st Ave. West, Owen Sound, ON N4K 4K4
Tel: 519-376-6623; *Fax:* 519-376-7170
info@owensound.library.on.ca
www.owensound.library.on.ca
www.facebook.com/OSNGUPL
Tim Nicholls Harrison, Chief Librarian & CEO

Paris: County of Brant Public Library
12 William St., Paris, ON N3L 1K7
Tel: 519-442-2433; *Fax:* 519-442-7582
brantlibrary@brant.ca
www.brantlibrary.ca
www.youtube.com/user/BrantLibrary; twitter.com/brantlibrary;
www.facebook.com/brantlibrary
Fred Gladding, Chair
Kelly Bernstein, Chief Executive Officer
kelly.bernstein@brant.ca
Karen Scott, Director, Public Services

Parry Sound: Parry Sound Public Library
29 Mary St., Parry Sound, ON P2A 1E3
Tel: 705-746-9601; *Fax:* 705-746-9601
pspl@vianet.ca
www.parrysoundlibrary.com
www.facebook.com/parrysoundpubliclibrary
Tom Lundy, Chair
tomlundy@sympatico.ca
Rita Orr, Chief Executive Officer
pslibrary@vianet.ca

Parry Sound: Wasauksing First Nation Public Library
1508 Geewadin Rd., Lane G, Parry Sound, ON P2A 2X4
Tel: 705-746-2531
librarian@wasauksing.ca
wasauksing.ca
Francine King, Library Technician

Pawitik: Naotkamegwanning First Nation Public Library
1004 Baibombeh Rd., Pawitik, ON P0X 1L0
Tel: 807-226-5710; *Fax:* 807-226-1066
naotkam@bellnet.ca
www.naotkameg.wanning.ca

Pembroke: Pembroke Public Library
237 Victoria St., Pembroke, ON K8A 4K5
Tel: 613-732-8844; *Fax:* 613-732-1116
fineprint@pembrokelibrary.ca
pembrokelibrary.ca
www.facebook.com/PembrokePublicLibrary
Karthi Rajamani, Chief Executive Officer
krajamani@pembrokelibrary.ca
613-732-8844 ext. 3
Sara Hosseini, Contact, Interlibrary Loans
shosseini@pembrokelibrary.ca
613-732-8844 ext. 1

Penetanguishene: Penetanguishene Public Library
24 Simcoe St., Penetanguishene, ON L9M 1R6
Tel: 705-549-7164; *Fax:* 705-549-3932
penlibbk@gmail.com
www.penetanguishene.library.on.ca
twitter.com/PPLlibrarystaff
www.facebook.com/penetanguishene.librarystaff
Linda Keenan, Chief Executive Officer
lkeenan@penetanguishene.library.on.ca

Perth: Perth & District Union Public Library
30 Herriott St., Perth, ON K7H 1T2
Tel: 613-267-1224
info@perthunionlibrary.ca
www.perthunionlibrary.ca
www.facebook.com/perthlibrary
Erika Heesen, Chief Librarian & CEO
eheesen@perthunionlibrary.ca

Petawawa: Petawawa Public Library
16 Civic Centre Rd., Petawawa, ON K8H 3H5
Tel: 613-687-2227; *Fax:* 613-687-2527
info@petawawapubliclibrary.ca
petawawapubliclibrary.ca
www.facebook.com/petawawapubliclibrary
Lisa Worobec, Chief Executive Officer
ceo@petawawapubliclibrary.ca
613-687-227 ext. 2202

Peterborough: Peterborough Public Library
345 Aylmer St. North, Peterborough, ON K9H 3V7
Tel: 705-745-5382; *Fax:* 705-745-8958
libraryinfo@peterborough.ca
www.ptbolibrary.ca
twitter.com/ptbolibrary; www.facebook.com/PtboLibrary
Jennifer Jones, Chief Executive Officer
705-745-5382 ext. 2370
Mark Stewart, Manager, Library Services
705-745-5382 ext. 2380
Becky Waldman, Coordinator, Marketing & Communications
705-745-5382 ext. 2324

Pickerel: Henvey Inlet First Nation Public Library
295 Pickerel River Rd., Pickerel, ON P0G 1J0
Tel: 705-857-2222
www.hifn.ca/departments-2/library.html
Debbie Fox, Librarian
maheengun12@hotmail.com

Pickering: Pickering Public Library
1 The Esplanade, Pickering, ON L1V 6K7
Tel: 905-831-6265; *Fax:* 905-831-6927
Toll-Free: 888-831-6266
TTY: 905-831-2789
Other Numbers: Renewals: 905-831-8209
help@pickeringlibrary.ca
pickeringlibrary.ca
www.youtube.com/user/PickeringLibrary;
twitter.com/pickeringlibs; www.facebook.com/pickeringlibs
Jackie Flowers, Chief Executive Officer
jackieflowers@pickeringlibrary.ca
905-831-6265 ext. 6222
Elaine Bird, Director, Support Services
elainebird@pickeringlibrary.ca
905-831-6265 ext. 6231
Kathy Williams, Director, Public Services
kathywilliams@pickeringlibrary.ca
905-831-6265 ext. 6251

Picton: Prince Edward County Public Library
208 Main St., Picton, ON K0K 2T0
Tel: 613-476-5962; *Fax:* 613-476-3325
www.peclibrary.org
www.facebook.com/peclibrary

Pikwàkanagàn: Algonquins of Pikwakanagan Library
1657A Mishomis Inamo, Pikwàkanagàn, ON K0J 1X0
Tel: 613-625-2402
library@pikwakanagan.ca
www.algonquinsofpikwakanagan.com
Estelle Amikons, Librarian
613-625-2800 ext. 244

Port Carling: Township of Muskoka Lakes Libraries
69 Joseph St., Port Carling, ON P0B 1J0
Tel: 705-765-5650
muskokalakes@pclib.ca
www.muskokalakes.ca/en/recreation/library.aspx
www.facebook.com/155634271143907
Valerie Duke, Chair
Cathy Duck, Chief Librarian & CEO
cduck@pclib.ca

Port Colborne: Port Colborne Public Library
310 King St., Port Colborne, ON L3K 4H1
Tel: 905-834-6512; *Fax:* 905-835-5775
library@portcolborne.ca
www.portcolborne.ca/en/recreation-and-leisure/library.aspx
twitter.com/PortColborneLib;
www.facebook.com/PortColbornePublicLibrary
Michael Cooper, Chair
Scott Luey, Chief Executive Officer
cao@portcolborne.ca
Susan Therrien, Director, Library Services
susantherrien@portcolborne.ca

Port Elgin: Bruce County Public Library
1243 Mackenzie Rd., Port Elgin, ON N0H 2C6
Tel: 519-832-6935
libraryinfo@brucecounty.on.ca
library.brucecounty.on.ca
www.instagram.com/brucecountypubliclibrary;
twitter.com/BruceCountyLib
www.facebook.com/BruceCountyPublicLibrary
Brooke McLean, Director, Library Services
bmclean@brucecounty.on.ca

Port Hope: Port Hope Public Library
31 Queen St., Port Hope, ON L1A 2Y8
Tel: 905-885-4712
library@porthope.ca
porthopepubliclibrary.ca
twitter.com/porthopelibrary; www.facebook.com/PortHopeLibrary
Margaret Scott, Chief Librarian & CEO
mscott@porthope.ca

Port Loring: Port Loring & District (Argyle) Public Library
11767 Hwy. 522, Port Loring, ON P0H 1Y0
Tel: 705-472-8170
argylecommunitylibrary@hotmail.com
www.argylecommunitylibrary.ca
www.facebook.com/139348189451348
Jennifer Fry, Librarian

Port McNicoll: Tay Township Public Libraries
715 - 4th Ave., Port McNicoll, ON L0K 1R0
Tel: 705-534-3511; *Fax:* 705-534-3511
library@tay.ca
www.tay.library.on.ca
www.facebook.com/TayTownshipPL
Jody Bressette, Acting Chief Executive Officer
705-534-7248 ext. 401
Heather Delong, Branch Librarian

Port Perry: Mississaugas of Scugog Island First Nation Library
Health & Resource Centre, 22600 Island Rd., Port Perry, ON L9L 1B6
Tel: 905-985-1826; *Fax:* 905-985-7958
www.scugogfirstnation.com/Public/LibraryComputer
Monica McLean, Contact
mmclean@scugogfirstnation.com

Port Perry: Scugog Memorial Public Library
231 Water St., Port Perry, ON L9L 1A8
Tel: 905-985-7686
info@scugoglibrary.ca
www.scugoglibrary.ca
twitter.com/ScugogLibrary; www.facebook.com/scugoglibrary
Deborah Anne Watson, Chair
Amy Caughlin, Chief Executive Officer
acaughlin@scugoglibrary.ca
905-985-7686 ext. 102
Sarah White, Manager, Public Services
swhite@scugoglibrary.ca
905-985-7686 ext. 103

Powassan: Powassan & District Union Public Library
324 Clark St., Powassan, ON P0H 1Z0
Tel: 705-724-3618; *Fax:* 705-724-5525
powlib@gmail.com
www.powassanlibrary.com
www.instagram.com/powassanlibrary;
twitter.com/powassanlibrary;
www.facebook.com/powassanlibrary
Tina Martin, Chair

Prescott: Prescott Public Library
360 Dibble St. West, Prescott, ON K0E 1T0
Tel: 613-925-4340; *Fax:* 613-925-0100
library@prescott.ca
www.prescott.ca/en/play-here/Library.asp
www.facebook.com/TownofPrescottPublicLibrary
Jane McGuire, Chief Librarian & CEO

Rainy River: Rainy River Public Library
334 - 4th St., Rainy River, ON P0W 1L0
Tel: 807-852-3375; *Fax:* 807-852-3375
libraryrr@gmail.com
www.rainyriverlibrary.com
www.facebook.com/164559081453

Rama: Chippewas of Rama First Nation Public Library
6147 Rama Rd., Rama, ON L3V 6H6
Tel: 705-325-3611; *Fax:* 705-325-2801
library@ramafirstnation.ca
www.ramafirstnation.ca/rama-public-library

Ramara: Ramara Township Public Library
5482 Hwy. 12 South, Ramara, ON L3V 0S2
Tel: 705-325-5776; *Fax:* 705-325-8176
info@ramarapubliclibrary.org
www.ramarapubliclibrary.org
www.instagram.com/ramaralibrarys; twitter.com/RamaraPL;
www.facebook.com/ramarapubliclibrary
Anne Belanger, Chair

Janet Banfield, Chief Executive Officer
banfieldj@ramarapubliclibrary.org

Red Lake: Red Lake Public Library
117 Howey St., Red Lake, ON P0V 2M0
Tel: 807-727-2230; Fax: 807-727-2230
rllib212@yahoo.com
www.redlake.ca/web/libraries.php
www.facebook.com/323418081416112

Red Rock: Red Rock Public Library
42 Salls St., Red Rock, ON P0T 2P0
Tel: 807-886-2558
rrocklib@gmail.com
redrock.olsn.ca
www.pinterest.com/redrocklib; twitter.com/RedRockLibrary;
www.facebook.com/142529769158602
Nancy Carrier, Head Librarian & CEO

Redbridge: Phelps Public Library
9315 Hwy. 63, Redbridge, ON P0H 2A0
Tel: 705-663-2220
phelpspubliclibrary@intera.net
phelpstownship.ca
Beverly Reynolds, Chief Executive Officer

Renfrew: Renfrew Public Library
13 Railway Ave. East, Renfrew, ON K7V 3A9
Tel: 613-432-8151
info@renfrewlibrary.ca
www.renfrew.ca/library.cfm
www.instagram.com/renfrewpubliclibrary;
twitter.com/renfrewreads;
www.facebook.com/renfrewpubliclibrary
Kelly Thompson, Chief Librarian & CEO
kthompson@renfrewlibrary.ca
Susan Klinck, Head, Children's Department
sklinck@renfrewlibrary.ca

Richard's Landing: St Joseph Township Public Library
1240 Richard St., Richard's Landing, ON P0R 1J0
Tel: 705-246-2353
sjtlibrary@gmail.com
stjosephtownship.com/community/libraries
www.facebook.com/SJTPublicLibrary
Pam Heart, Chair

Richmond Hill: Richmond Hill Public Library
1 Atkinson St., Richmond Hill, ON L4C 0H5
Tel: 905-884-9288; Fax: 905-884-6544
uasked@rhpl.ca
www.rhpl.ca
twitter.com/rhpltweets; www.facebook.com/rhpl.news
Mary Jane Celsie, Director, Content
mjcelsie@rhpl.ca
905-884-9288 ext. 4980
Catherine Charles, Director, Community Connections
ccharles@rhpl.ca
905-884-9288 ext. 4996
Yunmi Hwang, Director, Branch Services
yhwang@rhpl.ca
905-884-9288 ext. 5047
Barbara Ransom, Director, Customer Experiences
bransom@rhpl.ca
905-884-9288 ext. 5046
Greg Patterson, Manager, Central Library
gpatterson@rhpl.ca
905-884-9288 ext. 5071

Rockland: Clarence-Rockland Public Library/Bibliothèque publique de Clarence-Rockland
#2, 1525 du Parc Ave., Rockland, ON K4K 1C3
Tel: 613-446-5680
biblioinfo@bpcrpl.ca
bpcrpl.ca
twitter.com/BPCRPL; www.facebook.com/bpcrpl.ca
Sylvie Archambault, Chair
Catherina Rouse, Chief Executive Officer
ceo@bpcrpl.ca

Roseneath: Alderville First Nation Library
11696 - 2nd Line Rd., Roseneath, ON K0K 2X0
Tel: 905-352-2488; Fax: 905-352-1080
alderville.ca/our-offices-services/library

Russell: Russell Township Public Library/Bibliothèque publique du Canton de Russell
1053 Concession St., Russell, ON K4R 1E1
Tel: 613-445-5331; Fax: 613-445-8014
mylibrary@russellbiblio.com
russellbiblio.com
www.pinterest.ca/russellbiblio; www.facebook.com/russellbiblio

---

France Séguin, Chief Executive Officer
france.seguin@russellbiblio.com
Hélène Quesnel, Branch Head
helene.quesnel@russellbiblio.com

Sachigo Lake: Sachigo Lake First Nation Public Library
c/o Martin McKay Memorial School, Sachigo Lake, ON P0V 2P0
Tel: 807-595-2526; Fax: 807-595-1305
olsn.ent.sirsidynix.net/client/en_US/sachigo
Annie Tait, Librarian
taitannie@gmail.com

Saint-Isidore: Bibliothèque publique de la municipalité de La Nation/Nation Municipality Public Library
4531, rue Ste-Catherine, Saint-Isidore, ON K0C 2B0
Tel: 613-524-2252; Fax: 613-524-2545
biblioinfo@nationmun.ca
www.nationmunbiblio.ca
France Lamoureux, Présidente
flamoureux@nationmun.ca
Jeanne Leroux, Directrice général
jeanneleroux@nationmun.ca
613-254-2252

Saugeen: Saugeen First Nation Library
812 French Bay Rd., Saugeen, ON N0H 2L0
Tel: 519-797-5986
saugeenfirstnation.ca/departments/library

Sault Ste Marie: Batchewana First Nation
15 Jean St., Sault Ste Marie, ON P6B 4B1
Tel: 705-759-7285; Fax: 705-759-9982
batchewana.ca/departments/education/learning

Sault Ste Marie: Prince Township Library/Bibliothèque publique du Canton Prince
3042 - 2nd Line West, Sault Ste Marie, ON P6A 6K4
Tel: 705-779-3653
ptpl@twp.prince.on.ca
www.ptpl.ca
Rita Wagner, Chief Executive Officer

Sault Ste Marie: Sault Ste Marie Public Library
50 East St., Sault Ste Marie, ON P6A 3C3
Tel: 705-759-5230; Fax: 705-759-8752
admin.library@cityssm.on.ca
www.ssmpl.ca
www.facebook.com/SSMPL
Matthew MacDonald, Chief Executive Office
m.macdonald@cityssm.on.ca
705-759-5246
Chris Rumas, Manager, Digital Literacy
c.rumas@cityssm.on.ca
705-759-5245
Julie Ringrose, Librarian, Collections
j.ringrose@cityssm.on.ca
705-759-5234

Savant Lake: Savant Lake Community Library
General Delivery, Savant Lake, ON P0V 2S0
Tel: 807-584-2242

Schreiber: Schreiber Public Library
314 Scotia St., Schreiber, ON P0T 2S0
Tel: 807-824-2477; Fax: 807-824-2996
libinfo@schreiber.ca
www.schreiberlibrary.ca
www.youtube.com/user/schreiberlibrary;
www.facebook.com/schreiberontario
Donna Mikeluk, Head Librarian & CEO

Seguin: Seguin Township Public Library
15 Humphrey Dr., Seguin, ON P2A 2W8
Tel: 705-732-4526
seguinplstaff@gmail.com
seguinpubliclibraries.ca
twitter.com/SeguinPL; www.facebook.com/SeguinPublicLibraries
Stefanie Veneranda, Chief Executive Officer
ceo@seguinpubliclibraries.ca

Shannonville: Tyendinaga Township Public Library
852 Melrose Rd., Shannonville, ON K0K 3A0
Tel: 613-967-0606
tyendinagatwplibrary@xplornet.ca
www.ttpl.ca
www.facebook.com/tyendinagatownshippubliclibrary
Jessica Walsh, Chief Executive Officer

Shelburne: Shelburne Public Library
201 Owen Sound St., Shelburne, ON L9V 3L2
Tel: 519-925-2168; Fax: 519-925-6555
info@shelburnelibrary.ca
www.shelburnelibrary.ca
twitter.com/ShelburnePL; www.facebook.com/shelburnelibrary
Rose Dotten, Head Librarian & CEO
rdotten@shelburnelibrary.ca

Sheshegwaning: Sheshegwaning Public Library
PO Box 1, Sheshegwaning, ON P0P 1X0
Tel: 705-283-3014; Fax: 705-283-4038
www.sheshegwaning.org

Shoal Lake: Iskatewizaagegan #39 First Nation Community Public Library
Kejick Post Office, Shoal Lake, ON P0X 1E0
Tel: 807-733-3621; Fax: 807-733-3106
Irene Ross, Librarian
i_ross38@hotmail.com

Simcoe: Norfolk County Public Library
46 Colborne St. South, Simcoe, ON N3Y 4H3
Tel: 519-426-3506; Fax: 519-582-8376
norfolk.library@norfolkcounty.ca
olc.ncpl.ca
www.youtube.com/user/norfolkcpl; twitter.com/norfoldlibrary;
www.facebook.com/NorfolkLibrary
Heather King, Chief Executive Officer
heather.king@norfolkcounty.ca
519-426-3506 ext. 1253
Janet Cowan, Manager, Facilities & Operations
janet.cowan@norfolkcounty.ca
519-426-3506 ext. 1251
Heidi Goodale, Manager, Collection Development & Technology
heidi.goodale@norfolkcounty.ca
519-426-3506 ext. 1250
Kasey Whitwell, Coordinator, Administration
kasey.whitwell@norfolkcounty.ca
519-426-3506 ext. 1258

Sioux Lookout: Sioux Lookout Public Library
21 - 5th Ave., Sioux Lookout, ON P8T 1B3
Tel: 807-737-3660; Fax: 807-737-4046
info@slpl.on.ca
www.slpl.on.ca
www.youtube.com/user/SLPublicLibrary;
www.facebook.com/SiouxLookoutPublicLibrary
Mike Laverty, Chief Librarian & CEO
ceo@siouxlibrary.com
807-737-3660 ext. 4401

Sioux Narrows: Sioux Narrows Public Library
Sioux Narrows Public School, 5689 Hwy. 71, Sioux Narrows, ON P0X 1N0
Tel: 807-484-2777
library@kmts.ca
www.snnf.ca/art-and-culture/library

Smiths Falls: Smiths Falls Public Library
81 Beckwith St. North, Smiths Falls, ON K7A 2B9
Tel: 613-283-2911; Fax: 613-283-9834
info@smithsfallslibrary.ca
www.smithsfallslibrary.ca
www.facebook.com/SmithsFallsLibrary
Amanda Guerin, Chair
Amanda Foster, Head Librarian & CEO

Smithville: West Lincoln Public Library
177 West St., Smithville, ON L0R 2A0
Tel: 905-957-3756
smithville@westlincolnlibrary.ca
www.westlincolnlibrary.ca
www.instagram.com/westlincolnpubliclibrary;
twitter.com/WLPLibrary; www.facebook.com/WLPLibrary
Vanessa Holm, Chief Executive Officer

Smooth Rock Falls: Smooth Rock Falls Public Library/Bibliothèque publique de Smooth Rock Falls
120 Ross Rd., Smooth Rock Falls, ON P0L 2B0
Tel: 705-338-2318; Fax: 705-338-2330
www.smoothrockfalls.ca/living-here/recreation-activities/library
Lise Gagnon, Librarian & CEO
lgagnon@townsrf.ca

South River: South River-Machar Union Public Library
63 Marie St., South River, ON P0A 1X0
Tel: 705-386-0222; Fax: 705-386-0222
osrmlibrary@hotmail.com
southriver.olsn.ca
www.facebook.com/288691530122

Southwold: Onyota'a:ka Community Library
Onyota'a:ka Language & Cultural Centre, Southwold, ON
N0L 2G0

www.oneida.on.ca

Spanish: Spanish Public Library/Bibliothèque
publique du Spanish
8 Trunk Rd., Spanish, ON P0P 2A0
Tel: 705-844-2555; *Fax:* 705-844-2550
library@townofspanish.com
www.townofspanish.com/residents/public-library
www.facebook.com/SpanishLibraryHistory

St Catharines: St. Catharines Public Library
54 Church St., St Catharines, ON L2R 7K2
Tel: 905-688-6103; *Fax:* 905-688-6292
info@myscpl.ca
www.myscpl.ca
www.youtube.com/c/StCatharinesPublicLibrary;
twitter.com/stcathlibrary; www.facebook.com/stcathlibrary
Qingyi (Ken) Su, Chief Executive Officer

St Charles: St Charles Public Library
22 Ste Anne St., St Charles, ON P0M 2W0
Tel: 705-867-5332; *Fax:* 705-867-2511
stcharles_library@yahoo.ca
stcharlesontario.ca/resident-services/public-library
Nicole Lafontaine, Chief Librarian

St Marys: St Marys Public Library
15 Church St. North, St Marys, ON N4X 1B4
Tel: 519-284-3346; *Fax:* 519-284-2630
libraryinfo@stmaryspubliclibrary.ca
www.townofstmarys.com/en/recreation-and-culture/Library.aspx
twitter.com/stmaryspl; www.facebook.com/StMarysPublicLibrary
Cole Atlin, Chair
Matthew Corbett, Chief Executive Officer
Rebecca Webb, Coordinator, Library Services

St Thomas: Elgin County Library
450 Sunset Dr., St Thomas, ON N5R 5V1
Tel: 519-631-1460
www.elgincounty.ca/library
www.youtube.com/user/ElginLibrary;
twitter.com/LibrElginCounty;
www.facebook.com/ElginCountyLibrary
Brian Masschaele, Director, Community & Cultural Events
bmasschaele@elgin-county.on.ca
Natalie Marlowe, Library Coordinator
Sandra Poczobut, Manager, Library Programming & Community
Development

St Thomas: St Thomas Public Library
153 Curtis St., St Thomas, ON N5P 3Z7
Tel: 519-631-6050
info@stthomaspubliclibrary.ca
stthomaspubliclibrary.ca
www.facebook.com/stthomaspubliclibrary
Heather Robinson, Chief Executive Officer
hrobinson@stthomaspubliclibrary.ca
519-631-6050 ext. 8027
Aaron DeVries, Manager, Digital & Support Services
adevries@stthomaspubliclibrary.ca
519-631-6050 ext. 8016
Nadine Poulos, Manager, Customer Engagement & Collections
npoulos@stthomaspubliclibrary.ca
519-631-6050 ext. 8022
Dana Vanzanten, Manager, Programming & Community
Development
dvanzanten@stthomaspubliclibrary.ca
519-631-6050 ext. 8012

Stayner: Clearview Public Library
269 Regina St., Stayner, ON L0M 1S0
Tel: 705-428-3595
interlibraryloans@clearview.ca
www.clearview.library.on.ca
www.instagram.com/clearviewpubliclibrary;
twitter.com/Clearview_Lib;
www.facebook.com/clearviewpubliclibrary
Diane Kelly, Chair
Jennifer LaChapelle, Chief Executive Officer
jlachapelle@clearview.ca

Stirling: Stirling-Rawdon Public Library
43 West Front St., Stirling, ON K0K 3E0
Tel: 613-395-2837
info@stirlinglibrary.com
stirlinglibrary.com
www.instagram.com/stirling_library;
www.facebook.com/StirlingRawdonPublicLibrary
Andrew Marre, Chair

Jaye Bannon, Chief Executive Officer
jaye@stirlinglibrary.com

Stonecliffe: Head, Clara & Maria Public Library
15 Township Hall Rd., Stonecliffe, ON K0J 2K0
Tel: 613-586-1950
hcmlibra13@gmail.com
hcmpubliclibrary.ca
www.facebook.com/hcmpubliclibrary
Melanie Theil, Chief Librarian & CEO

Stouffville: Whitchurch-Stouffville Public Library
2 Park Dr., Stouffville, ON L4A 4K1
Tel: 905-642-7323; *Fax:* 905-640-1384
Toll-Free: 888-603-4292
wsplinfo@wsplibrary.ca
www.wsplibrary.ca
twitter.com/WhitStoufLibrar; www.facebook.com/WSPLibrary
Sandra Liaros, Chair
Margaret Wallace, Chief Executive Officer

Stratford: Stratford Public Library
19 St Andrew St., Stratford, ON N5A 1A2
Tel: 519-271-0220; *Fax:* 519-271-3843
askspl@pcin.on.ca
spplibrary.ca
www.youtube.com/user/StratfordPubLib; twitter.com/SPLibrary;
www.facebook.com/stratfordpubliclibrary;
www.linkedin.com/company/splibrary
Zac Gribble, Chair
Julia Merritt, Library Director & CEO
jmerritt@stratfordcanada.ca
519-271-0220 ext. 110

Strathroy: Middlesex County Public Library
Headquarters
34 Frank St., Strathroy, ON N7G 2R4
Tel: 519-245-1290
librarian@middlesex.ca
library.middlesex.ca
twitter.com/mxcountylibrary;
www.facebook.com/MiddlesexCountyLibrary
Lindsay Brock, Director, Library Services
lbrock@middlesex.ca
519-245-8237 ext. 4022
Liz Adema, Coordinator, Public Services
eadema@middlesex.ca
519-245-8237 ext. 4021
Liz Adema, Branch Supervisor
jmoir@middlesex.ca

Sturgeon Falls: West Nipissing Public
Library/Bibliothèque publique de Nipissing Ouest
#107, 225 Holditch St., Sturgeon Falls, ON P2B 1T1
Tel: 705-753-2620; *Fax:* 705-753-2131
mail@wnpl.ca
www.wnpl.ca
www.facebook.com/205021066285255
Émélie Keenan, Chief Executive Officer
ekeenan@wnpl.ca

Sudbury: Greater Sudbury Public
Library/Bibliothèque publique du grand Sudbury
74 Mackenzie St., Sudbury, ON P3C 4X8
Tel: 705-673-1155; *Fax:* 705-673-0554
mackenzie.infodesk1@greatersudbury.ca
www.sudburylibraries.ca
www.youtube.com/gsplibrary; twitter.com/GSPLibrary;
www.facebook.com/GSPLibrary
Mette Krüger, Manager, Libraries & Heritage Resources
705-673-1155 ext. 4769
Rick Clouthier, Manager, Citizen Service Centres
705-673-1155 ext. 4720
Mary Searle, Coordinator, Library Collections
705-673-1155 ext. 4782

Sundridge: Sundridge-Strong Union Public Library
110 Main St., Sundridge, ON P0A 1Z0
Tel: 705-384-7311; *Fax:* 705-384-7311
sundridgelibrary@gmail.com
sundridge.olsn.ca
www.facebook.com/332738433516395
Fraser Williamson, Chair
Melinda Kent, Librarian & CEO

Tehkummah: Tehkummah Township Public Library
Municipal Offices Bldg., RR#1, Tehkummah, ON P0P 2C0
Tel: 705-859-3301; *Fax:* 705-859-2605
tehklib@yahoo.ca
www.facebook.com/273818416372891

Temagami: Temagami Public Library
Welcome Centre, 7 Lakeshore Dr., Temagami, ON P0H 2H0
Tel: 705-569-2945
library@temagami.ca
temagami.library.on.ca
www.facebook.com/740642365976429

Terrace Bay: Terrace Bay Public Library
13 Selkirk Ave., Terrace Bay, ON P0T 2W0
Tel: 807-825-3315; *Fax:* 807-825-1249
library@terracebay.ca
terracebay.library.on.ca
www.facebook.com/TerraceBayPL
Mary Deschatelets, Chief Executive Officer
m.deschatelets@terracebay.ca
807-825-3315 ext. 234

Thamesville: Delaware First Nation Public Library
RR#3, Thamesville, ON N0P 2K0
Tel: 519-692-3411
library@delawarenation.on.ca
delawarenation.on.ca
www.facebook.com/96103201022911

Thessalon: Thessalon First Nation Public Library
35 Sugarbush Rd., Thessalon, ON P0R 1L0
Tel: 705-842-1258; *Fax:* 705-842-0178
thessalonfirstnationlibrary@hotmail.com
www.thessalonfirstnation.ca/library2.html
Michelle Bouillon, Librarian
m.bouillon.tfn@vianet.ca

Thessalon: Thessalon Public Library
187 Main St., Thessalon, ON P0R 1L0
Tel: 705-842-2306; *Fax:* 705-842-5690
thessalonlib@thessalonlibrary.ca
thessalonlibrary.ca
www.facebook.com/104998919541074

Thornbury: The Blue Mountains Public Library
173 Bruce St. South, Thornbury, ON N0H 2P0
Tel: 519-599-3681; *Fax:* 519-599-7951
libraryinfo@thebluemountains.ca
www.thebluemountainslibrary.ca
twitter.com/le_shore;
www.facebook.com/thebluemountainslibrary
Maurice Pepper, Chair
Sabrina Saunders, Chief Executive Officer
libraryceo@thebluemountains.ca
519-599-3681 ext. 148
Mary Dodge, Acting Manager, Public Services & Community
Outreach
libraryprograms@thebluemountains.ca
519-599-3681 ext. 145
Elisa Chandler, Manager, Technical & Virtual Services
librarytech@thebluemountains.ca
519-599-3681 ext. 143

Thorold: Thorold Public Library
14 Ormond St. North, Thorold, ON L2V 1Y8
Tel: 905-227-2581; *Fax:* 905-227-2311
info@thoroldpubliclibrary.ca
www.thoroldpubliclibrary.ca
www.instagram.com/thoroldpubliclibrary;
twitter.com/ThoroldLibrary;
www.facebook.com/thoroldpubliclibrary
Joanne DeQuadros, Chief Librarian
jdequadros@thoroldpubliclibrary.ca
Rebecca Lazarenko, Librarian, Public Services

Thunder Bay: Thunder Bay Public Library
285 Red River Rd., Thunder Bay, ON P7B 1A9
Tel: 807-345-8275
comments@tbpl.ca
www.tbpl.ca
www.facebook.com/TBayPL
John Pateman, Chief Librarian & CEO
jpateman@tbpl.ca
807-630-4619
Cherri Braye, Director, Resources
cbraye@tbpl.ca
807-684-6804
Stephen Hurrell, Director, Systems
shurrell@tbpl.ca
807-684-6807
Angela Meady, Director, Collections
ameady@tbpl.ca
807-684-6810
Tina Maronese, Director, Communities
tmaronese@tbpl.ca
807-684-6813

Tyler Fallen, Community Hub Manager, Facilities
tfallen@tbpl.ca
807-624-4202
Amy Ongaro, Community Hub Librarian, Relationships
aongaro@tbpl.ca
807-684-6811
Sylvia Renaud, Community Hub Librarian, Collections
srenaud@tbpl.ca
807-684-6808

Timmins: Timmins Public Library/Bibliothèque municipale de Timmins
320 - 2nd Ave., Timmins, ON P4N 8A4
Tel: 705-360-2623; *Fax:* 705-360-2688
refdesk@timmins.ca
tpl.timmins.ca

Carole-Ann Churcher, Chief Executive Officer
caroleann.churcher@timmins.ca
Chantal Benson, Head, Technical Support & Services
chantal.benson@timmins.ca

Toronto: Holocaust Education Centre
Sarah & Chaim Neuberger Holocaust Education Centre, UJA Federation, 4600 Bathurst St., 4th Fl., Toronto, ON M2R 3V2
Tel: 416-635-2996
www.holocaustcentre.com/library

Toronto: Ontario Public Libraries
#1700, 401 Bay St., Toronto, ON M7A 0A7
Tel: 416-314-7620; *Fax:* 416-212-1802
www.mtc.gov.on.ca/en/libraries/libraries.shtml

Toronto: Toronto Public Library/Bibliothèque publique de Toronto
789 Yonge St., Toronto, ON M4W 2G8
Tel: 416-393-7131; *Fax:* 416-393-7083
TTY: 416-393-7030
answerline@tpl.ca
www.torontopubliclibrary.ca
www.instagram.com/torontolibrary; twitter.com/torontolibrary;
www.facebook.com/torontopubliclibrary;
www.linkedin.com/company/toronto-public-library
Vickery Bowles, City Librarian
citylibrarian@tpl.ca
416-393-7032
Brian Daly, Director, Human Resources
bdaly@tpl.ca
416-395-5850
Elizabeth Glass, Director, Policy, Planning & Performance Management
eglass@tpl.ca
416-395-5602
Linda Hazzan, Director, Communications, Programming & Customer Engagement
lhazzan@tpl.ca
416-393-7214
Moe Hosseini-Ara, Director, Branch Operations & Customer Experience
branchoperations@tpl.ca
416-397-5944
Larry Hughsam, Director, Finance & Treasurer
lhughsam@tpl.ca
416-397-5946
Shawn Mitchell, Director, Collections & Membership Services
smitchell@tpl.ca
416-395-5506
Pam Ryan, Director, Service Development & Innovation
pryan@tpl.ca
416-393-7133
Jennifer Jones, President, Toronto Public Library Foundation
jjones@tpl.ca
416-393-7134

Trenton: Quinte West Public Library
7 Creswell Dr., Trenton, ON K8V 6X5
Tel: 613-394-3381; *Fax:* 613-394-2079
illo@quintewest.ca
www.library.quintewest.ca
www.facebook.com/QuesteWestPublicLibrary
Doug Couture, Chair
Suzanne Humphreys, Chief Executive Officer
suzanneh@quintewest.ca

Tweed: Tweed Public Library
230 Metcalf St., Tweed, ON K0K 3J0
Tel: 613-478-1066
tweedlibrary@vianet.ca
www.tweedlibrary.ca
www.facebook.com/TweedPublicLibrary
Al McNeil, Chair
Shannon Ruttle, Chief Executive Officer

Tyendinaga: Kanhiote / Tyendinaga Territory Public Library
1658 York Rd., RR#1, Tyendinaga, ON K0K 1X0
Tel: 613-967-6264; *Fax:* 613-396-3627
kanhiotelibrary@gmail.com
kanhiote.ca
www.facebook.com/kanhiote
Kelly-Anne Whalen, Chief Executive Officer

Uxbridge: Uxbridge Township Public Library
9 Toronto St. South, Uxbridge, ON L9P 1P7
Tel: 905-852-9747
uxbridgelibrary@uxlib.com
uxlib.com
www.instagram.com/theuxbridgelibrary;
twitter.com/uxbridgelibrary;
www.facebook.com/181717581870540
Amanda Ferraro, Interim Chief Executive Officer
aferraro@uxbridge.ca
905-852-9747 ext. 204
Corrinne Morrison, Acting Library Manager
corrinne.morrison@uxlib.com
905-852-9747 ext. 203
Leslie Nagle, Contact, Interlibrary Loans
leslie@uxlib.com
905-852-9747 ext. 205

Val Rita: Val Rita-Harty Public Library/Bibliothèque municipale de Val Rita-Harty
106 Government Rd., Val Rita, ON P0L 2G0
Tel: 705-335-8700
bibliovalrita@gmail.com
valharty.ca/municipality/library
Cécile Lamontagne, Chief Executive Officer

Vankleek Hill: Champlain Township Public Library/Bibliothèque Champlain
94 Main St. East, Vankleek Hill, ON K0B 1R0
Tel: 613-678-2216; *Fax:* 613-678-2216
library@bc-cl.ca
bc-cl.ca
www.instagram.com/champlain_library;
www.facebook.com/159615927424618/
Michelle Landriault, Chair
Cynthia Martin, Head Librarian & CEO
cmartin@bc-cl.ca
Alicia Heinzle, Librarian, Children's Services
aheinzle@bc-cl.ca
Anne Smith, Librarian, Adult Services
asmith@bc-cl.ca

Vaughan: Vaughan Public Libraries
2191 Major Mackenzie Dr., Vaughan, ON L6A 4W2
Tel: 905-653-7323
www.vaughanpl.info
www.instagram.com/vaughanpubliclibraries;
twitter.com/vaughanpl; www.facebook.com/vaughanpl
Margie Singleton, Chief Executive Officer
margie.singleton@vaughan.ca
905-653-7323 ext. 4601
Aleksandra Dowiat Vine, Director, Growth & Communications
aleksandra.dowiat-vine@vaughan.ca
905-653-7323 ext. 4620
Marilyn Guy, Director, Innovative Technologies & Collections
marilyn.guy@vaughan.ca
905-653-7323 ext. 4114
Lisa McDonough, Director, Customer Experience
lisa.mcdonough@vaughan.ca
905-653-7323 ext. 4624

Wainfleet: Wainfleet Township Public Library
31909 Park St., Wainfleet, ON L0S 1V0
Tel: 905-899-1277; *Fax:* 905-899-2495
wainfleetlibrary.ca
www.facebook.com/WainfleetTownshipPublicLibrary
Lorrie Atkinson, Chief Librarian & CEO
latkinson@wainfleetlibrary.ca
905-899-1277 ext. 280
Carrie Mayr, Library Programmer
cmayr@wainfleetlibrary.ca
905-899-1277 ext. 281
Cheryl Davis-Catchpaw, Secretary & Library Clerk
cdavis-catchpaw@wainfleetlibrary.ca
905-899-1277 ext. 282
Dariusz Zelichowski, IT Specialist
darius@wainfleet.ca
905-899-1277 ext. 220

Walker's Point: Walker's Point Community Library
Walker's Point Community Centre, 1074 Walker's Point Rd., Walker's Point, ON P1P 1P5
Tel: 705-687-9965
walkerspointlibrary@gmail.com
walkerspointlibrary.com
Pat Young, Chair

Wallaceburg: Bkejwanong First Nation Public Library
Walpole Island First Nation, 136 Tecumseh Rd., RR#3, Wallaceburg, ON N8A 4K9
Tel: 519-627-7034; *Fax:* 519-627-7035
library@wifn.org
bkejwanonglibrary.ca

Wasaga Beach: Wasaga Beach Public Library
120 Glenwood Dr., Wasaga Beach, ON L9Z 2K5
Tel: 705-429-5481; *Fax:* 705-429-5481
info.wbpl@wasagabeach.com
www.wasagabeach.library.on.ca
twitter.com/BeyondBooksWBPL;
www.facebook.com/wasagabeachpubliclibrary
Pamela Pal, Chief Librarian & CEO
ceo.wbpl@wasagabeach.com
705-429-5481 ext. 2404

Waterloo: Waterloo Public Library
35 Albert St., Waterloo, ON N2L 5E2
Tel: 519-886-1310; *Fax:* 519-886-7936
TTY: 866-786-3941
askus@wpl.ca
www.wpl.ca
www.instagram.com/waterloolibrary; twitter.com/waterloolibrary;
www.facebook.com/WaterlooLibraryON
Laurie Clarke, Chief Executive Officer
lclarke@wpl.ca
519-886-1310 ext. 123
Gloria Van Eek-Meijers, Deputy CEO
gvaneek@wpl.ca
Alannah d'Ailly, Manager, Collections
adailly@wpl.ca
Laura Dick, Manager, Branches
ldick@wpl.ca
Anjana Kipfer, Manager, Marketing & Communications
akipfer@wpl.ca
Janet Seally, Manager, Information Services
jseally@wpl.ca

Wawa: Michipicoten First Nation Public Library
107 Hiawatha Dr., RR#1, Wawa, ON P0S 1K0
Tel: 705-856-1993; *Fax:* 705-856-1642
library@michipicoten.com
michipicoten.com
Deanna Buonomo, Librarian
d.buonomo@michipicoten.com

Wawa: Wawa Public Library
40 Broadway Ave., Wawa, ON P0S 1K0
Tel: 705-856-2244
wawa.olsn.ca
Colleen Abbott, Head Librarian
cabbott@wawa.cc
905-856-2244 ext. 291

Weagamow Lake: North Caribou First Nation Public Library
PO Box 158, Weagamow Lake, ON P0V 2Y0
Tel: 807-469-1288; *Fax:* 807-469-1132
northcariboulakefirstnation@knet.ca
weagamow.firstnation.ca/publiclibrary
Beatrice Kanate, Librarian

Welland: Welland Public Library
50 The Boardwalk, Welland, ON L3B 6J1
Tel: 905-734-6210; *Fax:* 905-734-8955
info@wellandlibrary.ca
wellandlibrary.ca
www.youtube.com/user/wellandpubliclibrary;
twitter.com/wellandlibrary;
www.facebook.com/wellandpubliclibrary
Julianne Brunet, Chief Executive Officer
jbrunet@wellandlibrary.ca
905-734-6210 ext. 2500
David Beaudoin, Manager, Information Technology & Systems
dbeaudoin@wellandlibrary.ca
905-734-6210 ext. 2510
Conor Echlin, Manager, Customer Experience
cechlin@wellandlibrary.ca
905-734-6210 ext. 2509
Daniella Liebregts-Hamilton, Manager, Programming & Outreach
dliebregts@wellandlibrary.ca
905-734-6210 ext. 2508

Westport: **Westport Public Library**
3 Spring St., Westport, ON K0G 1X0
Tel: 613-273-3223
library@rideau.net
westportontariolibrary.wordpress.com
www.facebook.com/155845464448129
Pamela Stuffles, Chief Executive Officer

Whitby: **Whitby Public Library**
405 Dundas St. West, Whitby, ON L1N 6A1
Tel: 905-668-6531; *Fax:* 905-668-7445
admin@whitbylibrary.ca
www.whitbylibrary.ca
www.instagram.com/whitbylibrary; twitter.com/whitbylibrary;
www.facebook.com/whitbylibrary
Rhonda Jessup, CEO & Chief Librarian
Donna Bolton-Steele, Manager, Community & Service
Development
Michelle Frenette, Manager, Corporate Services
Elaine Yatulis Dobbin, Manager, Technical Services & Systems
Support

White River: **White River Public Library**
123 Superior St., White River, ON P0M 3G0
Tel: 807-822-1113; *Fax:* 807-822-1113
whiteriverlibrary@bellnet.ca
www.whiteriverlibrary.ca
www.facebook.com/whiteriverlibrary
Jan Ramage, Chief Executive Officer

Whitney: **South Algonquin Public Library**
33 Medical Centre Rd., Whitney, ON K0J 2M0
Tel: 613-637-5471; *Fax:* 613-637-5471
whitneylibrary@southalgonquin.ca
www.southalgonquin.ca/library
www.facebook.com/TownshipofSouthAlgonquinPublicLibrary
Charlene Alexander, Head Librarian & CEO

Wikwemikong: **Wikwemikong First Nation Public
Library**
34 Henry St., Wikwemikong, ON P0P 2J0
Tel: 705-859-2692; *Fax:* 705-859-3851
publiclibrary@wiikwemkoong.ca
wikwemikong.olsn.ca
www.facebook.com/wikylibrary
Danielle Mhiingan, Librarian

Windsor: **Windsor Public Library**
850 Ouellette Ave., Windsor, ON N9A 4M9
Tel: 519-255-6770
TTY: 800-855-0511
customerservice@windsorpubliclibrary.com
www.windsorpubliclibrary.com
www.youtube.com/user/wplwindsor; twitter.com/windsorpublib;
www.facebook.com/windsorpl
Kitty Pope, Chief Executive Officer
kpope@windsorpubliclibrary.com
Chris Woodrow, Director, Corporate Services
cwoodrow@windsorpubliclibrary.com
Kimberley Brydon, Manager, Financial Accounting
kbrydon@windsorpubliclibrary.com
Adam Craig, Manager, Public Services, Central Branch
acraig@windsorpubliclibrary.com
Andrea O'Brien, Manager, Operations
aobrien@windsorpubliclibrary.com
Leisa Pieczonka, Manager, Public Services, Branches
lpieczonka@windsorpubliclibrary.com
Christine Rideout-Arkell, Manager, Public Services
carkell@windsorpubliclibrary.com

Woodstock: **Oxford County Library**
Oxford County Administration Bldg., 21 Reeve St.,
Woodstock, ON N4S 3G1
Tel: 519-539-9800; *Fax:* 519-421-4712
www.ocl.net
www.instagram.com/oxfordcountylibrary; twitter.com/_OCL;
www.facebook.com/OxfordCountyLibrary
Marcus Ryan, Chair
mryan@zorra.on.ca
Lisa Miettinen, Chief Librarian & CEO
lmiettinen@ocl.net
519-539-9800 ext. 3260
Cristina McLaren, Branch Services Librarian
cmclaren@ocl.net
519-539-9800 ext. 3266

Woodstock: **Woodstock Public Library**
445 Hunter St., Woodstock, ON N4S 4G7
Tel: 519-539-4801; *Fax:* 519-539-5246
info@mywpl.ca
www.mywpl.ca
www.pinterest.com/mywpl; twitter.com/WoodstockLib;
www.facebook.com/myWPL

David Harvie, Chief Librarian & CEO
dharvie@mywpl.ca
519-539-4801 ext. 3000
Noelle Carr-Rivard, Head, Circulation
ncarr-rivard@mywpl.ca
519-539-4801 ext. 3011
Lindsay Harris, Manager, Operations
lharris@mywpl.ca
519-539-4801 ext. 3012
Darlene Pretty, Manager, Public Services
dpretty@mywpl.ca
519-539-4801 ext. 3009

Wyoming: **Lambton County Library**
787 Broadway St., Wyoming, ON N0N 1T0
Tel: 519-845-3324; *Fax:* 519-845-0700
Toll-Free: 866-324-6912
www.lclibrary.ca
twitter.com/LCLibraryca; www.facebook.com/LCLibraryca
Darlene Coke, Manager, Libraries
darlene.coke@county-lambton.on.ca
519-845-3324 ext. 5238

Archives

Alexandria: **Glengarry County Archives**
28 Kenyon St. East, Alexandria, ON K0C 1A0
Tel: 613-209-0202
glengarrycountyarchives@gmail.com
www.glengarrycountyarchives.ca
www.facebook.com/684597058380319
Allan MacDonald, County Archivist

Ameliasburgh: **Quinte Educational Museum &
Archives**
13 Coleman St. Group Box 14, Ameliasburgh, ON K0K 1A0
Tel: 613-966-5501
info@qema1978.com
www.qema1978.org/the-museum-and-archives
twitter.com/QEMA1978; www.facebook.com/qema1978

Amherstburg: **Amherstburg Freedom Museum**
277 King St., Amherstburg, ON N9V 2C7
Tel: 519-736-5433; *Toll-Free:* 800-713-6336
amherstburgfreedom.org
twitter.com/Aburgfreedom;
www.facebook.com/AmherstburgFreedom

Amherstburg: **Marsh Collection Society**
80 Richmond St., Amherstburg, ON N9V 1E9
Tel: 519-736-9191
research@marshcollection.org
www.marshcollection.org
www.facebook.com/968976766461303

Aylmer: **Aylmer-Malahide Museum & Archives**
14 East St., Aylmer, ON N5H 1W2
Tel: 519-773-9723
aylmermuseum@amtelecom.net
aylmermuseum.ca
twitter.com/AylmerMuseum;
www.facebook.com/AylmerMalahideMuseumArchives
Amanda VandenWyngaert, Curator
Sarah Bentley, Digital Archivist & Collections Manager

Bayfield: **Bayfield Historical Society & Archives**
20 Main St. North, Bayfield, ON N0M 1G0
Tel: 519-441-3224
bayarchives@tcc.on.ca
www.bayfieldhistorical.ca
www.facebook.com/bayfieldarchives
Julia Armstrong, Archivist
Claudia Barrett, Assistant Archivist

Bowmanville: **Clarington Museums & Archives**
Sarah Jane Williams Heritage Centre, 62 Temperance St.,
Bowmanville, ON L1C 3A8
Tel: 905-623-2734
info@claringtonmuseums.com
www.claringtonmuseums.com
twitter.com/ClarMuseum; www.facebook.com/clarmus
Heather Ridge, Executive Director

Brampton: **Region of Peel Art Gallery, Museum &
Archives**
The Peel Heritage Complex, 9 Wellington St. East,
Brampton, ON L6W 1Y1
Tel: 905-791-4055; *Fax:* 905-451-4931
infopama@peelregion.ca
pama.peelregion.ca
twitter.com/visitpama; www.facebook.com/visitPAMA

Jim Leonard, Supervisor, Archives Services
james.leonard@peelregion.ca
905-791-4055 ext. 3629
Kyle Neill, Senior Archivist
kyle.neill@peelregion.ca
905-791-4055 ext. 4677
Samantha Thompson, Archivist
samantha.thompson@peelregion.ca
905-791-4055 ext. 3780

Brantford: **Brant Historical Society**
57 Charlotte St., Brantford, ON N3T 2W6
Tel: 519-752-2483
information@brantmuseums.ca
www.brantmuseum.ca
twitter.com/branthistorical;
www.facebook.com/BrantHistoricalSociety
Nathan Etherington, Programming & Community Coordinator
nathan.etherington@brantmuseums.ca

Bridgenorth: **Smith Ennismore Historical Society**
826 Ward St., Bridgenorth, ON K0L 1H0
Tel: 705-292-9430
feedback@sehs.on.ca
www.sehs.on.ca/heritage-learning-centre

Brockville: **Brockville Museum**
5 Henry St., Brockville, ON K6V 6M4
Tel: 613-342-4397
museum@brockville.com
www.brockvillemuseum.com
Natalie Wood, Curator & Director
Peggy Hause, Coordinator, Interpretation & Public Program

Burlington: **Joseph Brant Museum**
1240 North Shore Blvd. East, Burlington, ON L7S 1C5
Tel: 905-634-3556
museuminfo@burlington.ca
museumsofburlington.ca/visitor-information/joseph-brant-museu
m
Kimberly Watson, Director
kimberly.watson@burlington.ca
Chris Selman, Curator
chris.selman@burlington.ca

Cambridge: **Cambridge Archives**
46 Dickson St., 2nd Fl., Cambridge, ON N1R 1T7
Tel: 519-740-4680
archives@cambridge.ca
www.cambridge.ca/en/learn-about/cambridge-archives.aspx

Cannington: **Cannington & Area Historical Society**
21 Laidlaw St. South, Cannington, ON L0E 1E0
Tel: 705-432-3136
canningtonhistoricalsociety@hotmail.com
www.canningtonhistoricalsociety.ca

Chatham: **Chatham-Kent Museum**
75 William St. North, Chatham, ON N7M 4L4
Tel: 519-360-1998; *Fax:* 519-354-4170
Toll-Free: 800-714-7497
ckcccmuseum@chatham-kent.ca
www.chatham-kent.ca/explore/museums
twitter.com/culturalcentre1;
www.facebook.com/ChathamCulturalCentre

Combermere: **Madonna House**
2888 Dafoe Rd. RR#2, Combermere, ON K0J 1L0
Tel: 613-756-3713; *Fax:* 613-756-0211
archives@madonnahouse.org
www.madonnahouse.org
www.youtube.com/MadonnaHouseCanada;
twitter.com/madonnahouse; www.facebook.com/MadonnaHouse

Delhi: **Delhi Tobacco Museum & Heritage Centre**
200 Talbot Rd., Delhi, ON N4B 2A2
Tel: 519-582-0278; *Fax:* 519-582-0122
delhi.museum@norfolkcounty.ca
delhimuseum.ca
www.facebook.com/delhimuseum

Fergus: **Wellington County Museum & Archives**
0536 County Rd. 18, RR#1, Fergus, ON N1M 2W3
Tel: 519-846-0916; *Fax:* 519-846-9630
Toll-Free: 800-663-0750
www.wellington.ca/en/museum-and-archives.aspx

Fort Frances: **Fort Frances Museum & Cultural
Centre**
259 Scott St., Fort Frances, ON P9A 1G8
Tel: 807-274-7891
ffmuseum@fort-frances.com
fortfrances.ca/experience/activities-amenities/museum
www.facebook.com/FortFrancesMuseum

Beverley Cochrane, Contact

Gatineau: Canadian Museum of Nature/Musée canadien de la nature
1740, rue Pink, Gatineau, ON J9J 3N7
Tel: 613-364-4734; Fax: 613-364-4026
Other Numbers: Archives: 613-364-4047
cmnlib@nature.ca
nature.ca/en/research-collections/collections/library-archives

Georgetown: Esquesing Historical Society
9 Church St., Georgetown, ON L7G 2A3
Tel: 905-877-9510
esquesinghs@gmail.com
esquesinghistoricalsociety.com/about-us
Stephen Blake, President, Esquesing Historical Society
905-877-8251
J. Mark Rowe, Archivist
mrowe6@sympatico.ca

Goderich: Huron County Museum Archives
110 North St., Goderich, ON N7A 2T8
Tel: 519-524-2686
museum@huroncounty.ca
www.huroncountymuseum.ca/huron-county-archives
www.instagram.com/huroncountymuseum;
twitter.com/hcmuseum;
www.facebook.com/huroncountymuseum
Michael Molnar, Archivist
mmolnar@huroncounty.ca

Gravenhurst: Gravenhurst Archives
Gravenhurst Public Library, 180 Sharpe St. West,
Gravenhurst, ON P1P 1J1
Tel: 705-687-6289
gravenhurstarchives@gmail.com
www.gravenhurst.ca/en/explore-and-play/archives.aspx
Judy Humphries, Chair, Archives

Guelph: Guelph Civic Museum
52 Norfolk St., Guelph, ON N1H 4H8
Tel: 519-836-1221; Fax: 519-836-5280
museum@guelph.ca
guelphmuseums.ca
twitter.com/guelphmuseums;
www.facebook.com/guelphmuseums
Tammy Adkin, Manager
tammy.adkin@guelph.ca
519-836-1221 ext. 2775
Dawn Owen, Curator
dawn.owen@guelph.ca
519-836-1221 ext. 2774
Luke Stempien, Coordinator, Collections & Research
luke.stempien@guelph.ca
519-836-1221 ext. 2776
Val Harrison, Supervisor, Visitor Experiences
val.harrison@guelph.ca
519-836-1221 ext. 2773

Haliburton: Haliburton Highlands Museum
66 Museum Rd., Haliburton, ON K0M 1S0
Tel: 705-457-2760
info@haliburtonhighlandsmuseum.com
www.haliburtonhighlandsmuseum.com
twitter.com/HH_Museum;
www.facebook.com/HaliburtonMuseum
Kate Butler, Director
Stephen Hill, Curator

Hamilton: Canadian Baptist Archives/Archives baptistes canadiennes
c/o McMaster Divinity College, 1280 Main St. West,
Hamilton, ON L8S 4K1
Tel: 905-525-9140
cbarch@mcmaster.ca
www.mcmasterdivinity.ca/welcome/canadian-baptist-archives
Adam McCulloch, Archivist
amcull@mcmaster.ca
905-525-9140 ext. 23511

Kenora: Lake of the Woods Museum
300 Main St. South, Kenora, ON P9N 3X5
Tel: 807-467-2105; Fax: 807-467-2109
info@themusekenora.ca
themusekenora.ca
Lori Nelson, Director
Braden Murray, Museum Educator

Kingston: Marine Museum of the Great Lakes at Kingston
53 Yonge St., Kingston, ON K7M 6G4
Tel: 613-542-2261
marmus@marmuseum.ca
marmuseum.ca

Doug Cowie, Manager
manager@marmuseum.ca

Kingston: The Original Hockey Hall of Fame & Museum
1350 Gardiners Rd., 2nd Fl., Kingston, ON K7P 0E5
Tel: 613-507-1943
info@originalhockeyhalloffame.com
www.originalhockeyhalloffame.com
www.facebook.com/207141552735961
Mike Postovit, Curator
J.W. (Bill) Fitsell, Historian

Kingston: Sisters of Providence of St. Vincent de Paul
1200 Princess St., Kingston, ON K7M 3C9
Tel: 613-544-4525; Fax: 613-531-9805
archives@providence.ca
www.providence.ca/our-story/archives
Veronica Stienburg, Archivist

Kitchener: Ken Seiling Waterloo Region Museum
10 Huron Rd., Kitchener, ON N2P 2R7
Tel: 519-748-1914; Fax: 519-748-0009
TTY: 519-575-4608
waterlooregionmuseum@regionofwaterloo.ca
www.waterlooregionmuseum.ca
www.youtube.com/user/WaterlooRegionMuseum
twitter.com/WRegionMuseum;
www.facebook.com/WaterlooRegionMuseum
Keri Solomon, Manager
519-748-1914 ext. 3878
Stacy McLennan, Collections Curator & Registrar
smclennan@regionofwaterloo.ca
519-748-1914 ext. 3268
James Jensen, Supervisor, Historic Sites
519-748-1914 ext. 3271

Kleinburg: McMichael Canadian Art Collection/Collection McMichael d'Art Canadien
10365 Islington Ave., Kleinburg, ON L0J 1C0
Tel: 905-893-1121; Fax: 905-893-0692
library@mcmichael.com
www.mcmichael.com
www.youtube.com/mcmichaelgallery; twitter.com/mcacgallery;
www.facebook.com/mcmichaelgallery
Linda Morita, Librarian & Archivist

London: Museum London
421 Ridout St. North, London, ON N6A 5H4
Tel: 519-661-0333
museumlondon.ca
www.instagram.com/museumlondon;
twitter.com/MuseumLondon;
www.facebook.com/MuseumLondon
Janette Cousins Ewan, Art Registrar
jcewans@museumlondon.ca
519-661-0333 ext. 4269

London: The Royal Canadian Regiment Museum/Musée du Royal Canadian Regiment
Wolseley Barracks, 701 Oxford St. East, London, ON N5Y 4T7
Tel: 519-660-5275; Fax: 519-660-5344
info@thercrmuseum.ca
www.thercrmuseum.ca
twitter.com/RCRMuseum; www.facebook.com/RCRMuseum
Georgiana Stanciu, Executive Director
director@thercrmuseum.ca
519-660-5275 ext. 5015

Midland: Huronia Museum
549 Little Lake Park, Midland, ON L4R 4P4
Tel: 705-526-2844; Fax: 705-527-6622
huroniamuseum@gmail.com
huroniamuseum.com/about-2/huronia-museum-library-and-archives
www.flickr.com/photos/huroniamuseum;
twitter.com/HuroniaMuseum;
www.facebook.com/huroniamuseum

Milton: Halton Region Heritage Services
5181 Kelso Rd., RR#3, Milton, ON L9T 2X7
Tel: 905-825-6000; Toll-Free: 866-442-5866
museum@halton.ca
www.halton.ca/The-Region/Heritage-Services

Milton: Ontario Electric Railway Historical Association
13629 Guelph Line, Milton, ON L0P 1B0
Tel: 519-856-9802; Fax: 519-856-1399
archives@hcry.org
hcry.org

Minesing: County of Simcoe
1149 Hwy. 26, Minesing, ON L9X 0Z7
Tel: 705-726-9331; Fax: 705-725-5341
Toll-Free: 866-893-9300
archives@simcoe.ca
www.simcoe.ca/dpt/arc
Matthew Fells, County Archivist
matthew.fells@simcoe.ca
705-726-9300 ext. 1285

Mississauga: Pentecostal Assemblies of Canada
2450 Milltower Ct., Mississauga, ON L5N 5Z6
Tel: 905-542-7400; Fax: 905-542-7313
archives@paoc.org
paoc.org/family/archives/about
James Craig, Archivist

Napanee: Lennox & Addington County Museum & Archives
97 Thomas St. East, Napanee, ON K7R 4B9
Tel: 613-354-3027; Fax: 613-354-3112
archives@lennox-addington.on.ca
www.lennox-addington.on.ca/museum-archives
www.facebook.com/CountyMuseum
Amber Meyer, Manager
JoAnne Himmelman, Curator
jhimmelman@lennox-addington.on.ca
Lisa Lawlis, Archivist

Niagara on the Lake: Shaw Festival Theatre Foundation Library
10 Queen's Parade, Niagara on the Lake, ON L0S 1J0
Tel: 905-468-2153; Fax: 905-468-5438
Toll-Free: 800-657-1106
www.shawfest.com
Nancy Butler, Librarian

North Bay: Discovery North Bay Museum
100 Ferguson St., North Bay, ON P1B 1W8
Tel: 705-476-2323
discover@northbaymuseum.com
www.discoverynorthbay.com
www.facebook.com/discovery.n.bay
Naomi Hehn, Director & Curator
naomi@northbaymuseum.com

Norwich: Norwich & District Historical Society
91 Stover St. North, RR#3, Norwich, ON N0J 1P0
Tel: 519-863-3638; Fax: 519-863-2343
archives@norwichdhs.ca
www.norwichdhs.ca/archives.html
twitter.com/norwichdhs; www.facebook.com/NorwichDHS

Orillia: Mariposa Folk Foundation
10 Peter St. South, Orillia, ON L3V 5A9
Tel: 705-326-3655; Fax: 705-326-5963
mff@mariposafolk.com
mariposafolk.com

Orillia: Stephen Leacock Museum
50 Museum Dr., Orillia, ON L3V 7T9
Tel: 705-329-1908
www.orillia.ca/en/visiting/leacock-museum.aspx
www.facebook.com/LeacockMuseum
Jenny Martynyshyn, Coordinator
jmartynyshyn@orillia.ca
Tom Rose, Collections & Program Supervisor
trose@orillia.ca

Oshawa: Oshawa Community Museum & Archives
1450 Simcoe St. South, Oshawa, ON L1H 8S8
Tel: 905-436-7624; Fax: 905-436-7625
programming@oshawamuseum.org
oshawamuseum.org
twitter.com/oshawamuseum;
www.facebook.com/OshawaMuseum
Melissa Cole, Curator
curator@oshawamuseum.org
905-436-7624 ext. 103
Jennifer Weymark, Archivist
archivist@oshawamuseum.org
905-436-7624 ext. 100

Oshawa: Robert McLaughlin Gallery
Civic Centre, 72 Queen St., Oshawa, ON L1H 3Z3
Tel: 905-576-3000; Fax: 905-576-9774
communications@rmg.on.ca
rmg.on.ca
www.youtube.com/c/RMGOshawa; twitter.com/theRMG;
www.facebook.com/TheRMG
www.linkedin.com/company/the-rmg-robert-mclaughlin-gallery-

Leila Timmins, Senior Curator
ltimmins@rmg.on.ca
905-576-3000 ext. 111
Sonya Jones, Curator, Collections
sjones@rmg.on.ca
905-576-3000 ext. 110

Ottawa: Bytown Railway Society
PO Box 47076, Ottawa, ON K1B 5P9
Tel: 613-745-1201; Fax: 613-745-1201
info@bytownrailwaysociety.ca
www.bytownrailwaysociety.ca
www.youtube.com/user/bytownrailwaysociety;
twitter.com/BytownRSociety;
www.facebook.com/bytownrailwaysociety

Ottawa: C. Robert Craig Memorial Library
Ottawa City Archives, 100 Tallwood Dr., Ottawa, ON K2G
4R7

librarian@crcml.org
www.crcml.org

Ottawa: Canadian Institute of Geomatics/Association canadienne des sciences géomatiques
#100D, 900 Dynes Rd., Ottawa, ON K2C 3L6
Tel: 613-224-9851; Fax: 613-224-9577
admin@cig-acsg.ca
www.cig-acsg.ca

Ottawa: Canadian Intergovernmental Conference Secretariat/Secrétariat des conférences intergouvernementales Canadiennes
222 Queen St., 10th Fl., Ottawa, ON K1P 5V9
Tel: 613-995-2341; Fax: 613-996-6091
info@scics.ca
www.scics.ca

Mario Giasson, Director, Information Services

Ottawa: Canadian Women's Movement Archives/Archives canadiennes du mouvement des femmes
Archives Special Collections, Morisset Hall, University of
Ottawa, #039, 65 University Pvt, Ottawa, ON K1N 6N5
Tel: 613-562-5910
arcs@uottawa.ca
biblio.uottawa.ca/en/archives-and-special-collections
Lucie Desjardins, Interim Chief Archivist
lucie.desjardins@uottawa.ca
613-562-5800 ext. 6465

Ottawa: Chaise de recherche en histoire religieuse du Canada/Research Chair in Religious History of Canada
Université St-Paul, 223, rue Main, Ottawa, ON K1S 1C4
Tél: 613-236-1393; Téléc: 613-782-3005
Ligne sans frais: 800-637-6859
crh-rc-rhc@ustpaul.ca
www.ustpaul.ca

Pierre Hurtubise, Directeur
Denis Castonguay, Secrétaire

Ottawa: City of Ottawa Archives/Archives municipales d'Ottawa
100 Tallwood Dr., Ottawa, ON K2G 4R7
Tel: 613-580-2857; Fax: 613-580-2614
archives@ottawa.ca
ottawa.ca/en/arts-heritage-and-events/city-ottawa-archives
www.facebook.com/OttawaArchives
Paul Henry, City Archivist
paul.henry@ottawa.ca

Ottawa: Grey Sisters of the Immaculate Conception
#503, 440 Gloucester St., Ottawa, ON K1R 7T8
Tel: 613-231-3347

Mary Ruddy, Manager, Archives

Ottawa: National Archival Appraisal Board/Conseil national d'évaluation des archives
c/o CCA, #1912, 130 Albert St., Ottawa, ON K1P 5G4
Tel: 613-565-1222; Fax: 613-565-5445
Toll-Free: 866-254-1403
naab@archivescanada.ca
naab.ca

Ottawa: Ottawa Jewish Archives
21 Nadolny Sachs Private, Ottawa, ON K2A 1R9
Tel: 613-798-4696; Fax: 613-798-4695
archives@jewishottawa.com
jewishottawa.com/ottawa-jewish-archives
www.facebook.com/ottawajewisharchives

Teigan Goldsmith, Archivist
archives@jewishottawa.com
613-798-4696 ext. 260

Ottawa: Parent Finders Ottawa
PO Box 21025, Ottawa South Postal Outlet, Ottawa, ON K1S
5N1
Tel: 613-730-8305
pfncr@yahoo.com
www.parentfindersottawa.ca
www.facebook.com/120530528033309

Ottawa: Roman Catholic Archdiocese of Ottawa/Corporation Episcopale Catholique Romaine d'Ottawa
1244 Kilborn Pl., Ottawa, ON K1H 6K9
Tel: 613-738-5025; Fax: 613-738-0130
archiviste@archottawa.ca
archoc.ca

Ottawa: The Royal College of Physicians & Surgeons of Canada
774 Echo Dr., Ottawa, ON K1S 5N8
Tel: 613-730-8177; Fax: 613-730-8830
Toll-Free: 800-668-3740
researchunit@royalcollege.ca
www.royalcollege.ca

Ottawa: Scouts Canada
1345 Baseline Rd., Ottawa, ON K2C 0A7
Tel: 613-224-5134
www.scouts.ca

Owen Sound: Grey Roots Museum & Archives
102599 Grey Rd. 18, RR#4, Owen Sound, ON N4K 5N6
Tel: 519-376-3690; Fax: 519-376-4654
Toll-Free: 877-473-9766
archives@greyroots.com
greyroots.com
www.instagram.com/greyroots; twitter.com/greyrootsmuseum;
www.facebook.com/grey.roots
Karin Noble, Archivist
karin.noble@greyroots.com
519-376-3690 ext. 6113
Kate Jackson, Assistant Archivist
kate.jackson@greyroots.com
519-376-3690 ext. 6111
Sarina King, Assistant Archivist
sarina.king@greyroots.com
519-376-3690 ext. 6111

Perth: Perth Museum & Archives
11 Gore St. East, Perth, ON K7H 1H4
Tel: 613-267-1947; Toll-Free: 855-326-1947
www.perth.ca/en/explore-perth/Museum.aspx
twitter.com/perthmuseum; www.facebook.com/ThePerthMuseum

Peterborough: Peterborough Museum & Archives
Ashburnham Memorial Park, 300 Hunter St. East,
Peterborough, ON K9H 6Y5
Tel: 705-743-5180; Fax: 705-743-2614
Toll-Free: 855-738-3755
www.peterborough.ca/en/explore-and-play/museum-and-archive
s.aspx
twitter.com/PtboMuseum;
www.facebook.com/PTBOMuseumArchives

Picton: Burgee Data Archives
Naval Marine Archive, 205 Main St., Picton, ON K0K 2T0

info@navalmarinearchive.com
opac.navalmarinearchive.com

Prescott: Grenville County Historical Society
500 Railway Ave., Prescott, ON K0E 1T0
Tel: 613-925-0489
gchs@truespeed.ca
www.grenvillecountyarchives.ca
Bonnie Gaylord, Research Chair

Sault Ste Marie: Sault Ste Marie & 49th Field Regiment R.C.A. Historical Society, Sault Ste Marie Museum
690 Queen St. East, Sault Ste Marie, ON P6A 2A4
Tel: 705-759-7278; Fax: 705-759-3058
info@saultmuseum.ca
www.saultmuseum.com
www.youtube.com/user/saultmuseum; twitter.com/SaultMuseum;
www.facebook.com/saultmuseum
William Hollingshead, Executive Director & Chief Curator
william@saultmuseum.ca

Simcoe: Norfolk County Archives
109 Norfolk St. South, Simcoe, ON N3Y 2W3
Tel: 519-426-1583
archives@norfolkcounty.ca
www.nca-ebdm.ca
Joshua Klar, Archivist

Southampton: Bruce County Museum & Cultural Centre
33 Victoria St. North, Southampton, ON N0H 2L0
Tel: 519-797-2080; Fax: 519-797-2191
Toll-Free: 866-318-8889
museum@brucecounty.on.ca
www.brucemuseum.ca
twitter.com/brucemuseum;
www.facebook.com/BruceCountyMuseum
Deb Sturdevant, Archivist
dsturdevant@brucecounty.on.ca

St Catharines: St Catharines Museum & Welland Canals Centre
1932 Welland Canals Pkwy., St Catharines, ON L2R 7K6
Tel: 905-984-8880; Fax: 905-984-6910
Toll-Free: 800-305-5134
TTY: 905-688-4889
museum@stcatharines.ca
www.stcatharines.ca/en/experiencein/MuseumCollections.asp
twitter.com/stcmuseum;
www.facebook.com/stcatharinesmuseum
Kathleen Powell, Supervisor & Curator
kpowell@stcatharines.ca

Stratford: Stratford Shakespeare Festival
350 Douro St., Stratford, ON N5A 3S7
Tel: 519-271-4040
www.stratfordfestival.ca
www.instagram.com/stratfest; twitter.com/stratfest;
www.facebook.com/StratfordFestival
Liza Giffen, Archives Director
lgiffen@stratfordfestival.ca
Christine Schindler, Archives Coordinator
cschindler@stratfordfestival.ca
Nora Polley, Archives Assistant
npolley@stratfordfestival.ca

Stratford: Stratford-Perth Archives
4273 Line 34, RR#5, Stratford, ON N5A 6S6
Tel: 519-271-0531; Fax: 519-273-5746
archives@perthcounty.ca
www.stratfordpertharchives.on.ca
Betty Jo Belton, Archivist
519-271-0531 ext. 250

Teeterville: Teeterville Pioneer Museum
194 Teeter St., Teeterville, ON N0E 1S0
Tel: 519-426-5870; Fax: 519-428-3069
Other Numbers: Summer Hours: 519-443-4400
teeterville.museum@norfolkcounty.ca
www.teetervillemuseum.ca
www.facebook.com/teetervillemuseum

Thunder Bay: City of Thunder Bay
235 Vickers St. North, Thunder Bay, ON P7C 4B1
Tel: 807-625-2270
archives@thunderbay.ca
www.thunderbay.ca/en/city-hall/city-archives.aspx
www.flickr.com/photos/thunderbayarchives
Matt Szybalski, Manager, Corporate Records & City Archivist
807-625-3390

Thunder Bay: Northwestern Ontario Sports Hall of Fame
219 May St. South, Thunder Bay, ON P7E 1B5
Tel: 807-622-2852; Fax: 807-622-2736
nwosport@tbaytel.net
www.nwosportshalloffame.com/museum-and-archives
www.youtube.com/user/nwosport; twitter.com/nwosports;
www.facebook.com/nwosport
Diane Imrie, Executive Director
Kathryn Dwyer, Curator

Thunder Bay: Thunder Bay Historical Museum
425 Donald St. East, Thunder Bay, ON P7E 5V1
Tel: 807-623-0801; Fax: 807-622-6880
info@thunderbaymuseum.com
www.thunderbaymuseum.com/artifacts-archives
www.instagram.com/thunderbaymuseum;
twitter.com/TBayMuseum;
www.facebook.com/Thunderbaymuseum
Scott Bradley, Executive Director
director@thunderbaymuseum.com
807-623-0801 ext. 13

Michael deJong, Archivist & Curator
curatorial@thunderbaymuseum.com
807-623-0801 ext. 11

Toronto: Anglican General Synod Archives
80 Hayden St., Toronto, ON M4Y 3G2
Tel: 416-924-9199; *Fax:* 416-968-7983
archives@national.anglican.ca
www.anglican.ca/archives

Laurel Parson, Archivist
lparson@national.anglican.ca
416-924-9199 ext. 278

Toronto: Archives of Ontario
134 Ian Macdonald Blvd., Toronto, ON M7A 2C5
Tel: 416-327-1600; *Fax:* 416-327-1999
Toll-Free: 800-668-9933
reference@ontario.ca
www.archives.gov.on.ca
www.youtube.com/ArchivesOfOntario;
twitter.com/ArchivesOntario;
www.facebook.com/ArchivesOntario

John Roberts, Archivist
john.roberts@ontario.ca
647-983-6694

Toronto: The ArQuives
34 Isabella St., Toronto, ON M4Y 1N1
Tel: 416-777-2755
queeries@clga.ca
arquives.ca
www.instagram.com/thearquives; twitter.com/TheArQuives;
www.facebook.com/TheArQuives
Raegan Swanson, Executive Director
executivedirector@clga.ca
Lucie Handley-Girard, Archivist
archivist@arquives.ca

Toronto: Art Gallery of Ontario/Musée des beaux-arts de l'Ontario
317 Dundas St. West, Toronto, ON M5T 1G4
Tel: 416-979-6642; *Fax:* 416-979-6602
library.archives@ago.ca
ago.ca/research/library-and-archives
twitter.com/agotoronto; www.facebook.com/AGOToronto

Toronto: Arts & Letters Club
14 Elm St., Toronto, ON M5G 1G7
Tel: 416-597-0223; *Fax:* 416-597-9544
info@artsandlettersclub.ca
artsandlettersclub.ca

Scott James, Archivist

Toronto: Beth Tzedec Congregation
1700 Bathurst St., Toronto, ON M5P 3K3
Tel: 416-781-3514; *Fax:* 416-781-0150
www.beth-tzedec.org/page/museum
Dorion Liebgott, Curator
dliebgott@beth-tzedec.org

Toronto: Canadian Children's Book Centre
#217, 40 Orchard View Blvd., Toronto, ON M4R 1B9
Tel: 416-975-0010; *Fax:* 416-975-8970
info@bookcentre.ca
www.bookcentre.ca

Rose Vespa, Executive Director
rose@bookcentre.ca
Meghan Howe, Library Coordinator
meghan@bookcentre.ca

Toronto: Canadian Opera Company/La compagnie d'opéra canadienne
227 Front St. East, Toronto, ON M5A 1E8
Tel: 416-363-6671; *Fax:* 416-363-5584
www.coc.ca
twitter.com/canadianopera;
www.facebook.com/canadianoperacompany
Birthe Joergensen, Archivist
birthej@coc.ca

Toronto: City of Toronto Archives
255 Spadina Rd., Toronto, ON M5R 2V3
Tel: 416-397-0778; *Fax:* 416-392-9685
archives@toronto.ca
www.toronto.ca/archives
flickr.com/photos/torontohistory; twitter.com/TorontoArchives
Carol Radford-Grant, Archivist
416-397-7393

Toronto: College of Physicians & Surgeons of Ontario
80 College St., Toronto, ON M5G 2E2
Tel: 416-967-2600; *Fax:* 416-961-3330
Toll-Free: 800-268-7096
www.cpso.on.ca

Toronto: Etobicoke Historical Society
c/o Montgomery's Inn, 4709 Dundas St. West, Toronto, ON M9A 1A8

www.etobicokehistorical.com
twitter.com/EtobHistory; www.facebook.com/etobicokehistory
Denise Harris, Chief Historian
Philip Enros, Archivist

Toronto: Exhibition Place
#1, 100 Princes' Blvd., Toronto, ON M6K 3C3
Tel: 416-263-3676
www.explace.on.ca/about/history/records-and-archives
twitter.com/explaceTO; www.facebook.com/ExPlaceTO

Toronto: The Film Reference Library
TIFF Bell Lightbox, 350 King St. West, 4th Fl., Toronto, ON M5V 3X5
Tel: 416-599-8433
libraryservices@tiff.net
tiff.net/library

Toronto: General Archives of the Basilian Fathers
95 St Joseph St., Toronto, ON M5S 3C2
Tel: 416-925-4368
archives@basilian.org
www.basilian.org
Michelle Sawyers, Archivist

Toronto: Hockey Hall of Fame
400 Kipling Ave., Toronto, ON M8V 3L1
Tel: 416-360-7735; *Fax:* 416-251-5770
acquisitions@hhof.com
www.hhof.com/htmlrescentre/rc00.shtml
Samantha Chianta, Archivist & Collections Registrar
schianta@hhof.com
Craig Campbell, Manager, Resource Centre & Archives
campbellc@hhof.com
Steve Poirier, Coordinator, HHOF Images & Archival Services
spoirier@hhof.com
Izak Westgate, Manager, Outreach Exhibits & Assistant Curator
iwestgate@hhof.com

Toronto: Holy Blossom Temple
1950 Bathurst St., Toronto, ON M5P 3K9
Tel: 416-789-3291
templemail@holyblossom.org
www.holyblossom.org
www.youtube.com/user/holyblossomtemple;
twitter.com/holyblossom;
www.facebook.com/holyblossomtemple
Ron Polster, Executive Director
rpolster@holyblossom.org
416-789-3291 ext. 226
Neomi Offman, Education Department Administrator
noffman@holyblossom.org
416-789-3291 ext. 237

Toronto: Institute of the Blessed Virgin Mary in North America (Loretto Sisters)
101 Mason Blvd., Toronto, ON M5M 3E2
Tel: 416-483-2238; *Fax:* 416-485-9884
ibvmadm@rogers.com
www.ibvm.ca/institute-archives

Toronto: Montgomery's Inn Museum
4709 Dundas St. West, Toronto, ON M9A 1A8
Tel: 416-394-8113; *Fax:* 416-394-6027
montinn@toronto.ca
montgomerysinn.com/library
twitter.com/MontINNTO; www.facebook.com/montgomerysinn

Toronto: The Multicultural History Society of Ontario (MHSO)
901 Lawrence Ave. West, Toronto, ON M6A 1C3
Tel: 416-979-2973; *Fax:* 416-979-7947
info@mhso.ca
www.mhso.ca
www.facebook.com/multiculturalhistorysociety
Dennis Moore, Archivist
dennis.moore@mhso.ca
Elizabeth Price, Manager, Development
elizabeth.price@mhso.ca

Toronto: National Ballet of Canada/Ballet national du Canada
470 Queens Quay West, Toronto, ON M5V 3K4
Tel: 416-345-9686
archives@national.ballet.ca
national.ballet.ca/archives
Katherine Wilson, Archivist

Toronto: Ontario Genealogical Society
Humanities & Social Sciences Dept., Toronto Reference Library, 789 Yonge St., Toronto, ON M4W 2G8
Tel: 416-489-0734; *Toll-Free:* 855-697-6687
trlhss@torontopubliclibrary.ca
ogs.on.ca/resources/ogs-libraries

Toronto: Ontario Jewish Archives
Sherman Campus, UJA Federation of Greater Toronto, 4600 Bathurst St., Toronto, ON M2R 3V2
Tel: 416-635-5391; *Fax:* 416-849-1006
ojainquiries@ujafed.org
ontariojewisharchives.org
www.facebook.com/OntarioJewishArchives
Dara Solomon, Executive Director
Faye Blum, Archivist
Michael Friesen, Archivist

Toronto: Ports Toronto
60 Harbour St., Toronto, ON M5J 1B7
Tel: 416-863-2011; *Fax:* 416-863-0391
www.portstoronto.com

Toronto: The Presbyterian Church in Canada
50 Wynford Dr., Toronto, ON M3C 1J7
Tel: 416-441-1111; *Toll-Free:* 800-619-7301
www.presbyterianarchives.ca
Kim Arnold, Archivist & Records Administrator
karnold@presbyterian.ca
416-441-1111 ext. 310
Bob Anger, Assistant Archivist
banger@presbyterian.ca
416-441-1111 ext. 266

Toronto: Queen's Own Rifles of Canada Regimental Museum
1 Austin Terrace, Toronto, ON M5R 1X8

museum@qormuseum.org
qormuseum.org/research/archives
www.flickr.com/photos/qormuseum; twitter.com/qormuseum;
www.facebook.com/qormuseum
John Stephens, Curator

Toronto: Queen's York Rangers (1st American Regiment) Museum
CFA Fort York, 660 Fleet St. West, Toronto, ON M5V 1A9
Tel: 416-203-4629
info@qyrang.ca
qyrangmuseum.com
Phil Halton, Curator

Toronto: Roman Catholic Archdiocese of Toronto
Catholic Pastoral Centre, #505, 1155 Yonge St., Toronto, ON M4T 1W2
Tel: 416-934-3400; *Fax:* 416-934-3434
archives@archtoronto.org
www.archtoronto.org/archives
Gillian Hearns, Director

Toronto: The Royal Canadian Yacht Club
141 St. George St., Toronto, ON M5R 2L8
Tel: 416-967-7245
heritage@rcyc.ca
www.rcyc.ca
Beverley Darville, Archivist
beverley.darville@rcyc.ca
416-967-7245 ext. 351

Toronto: Royal Ontario Museum/Musée royal de l'Ontario
100 Queen's Park Cres., Toronto, ON M5S 2C6
Tel: 416-586-5595; *Fax:* 416-586-5519
library@rom.on.ca
www.rom.on.ca/en/collections-research/library-archives
twitter.com/ROMLibrary; www.facebook.com/ROMLibrary
Max Dionisio, Acting Head, Library & Archives
416-586-7931
Charlotte Chaffey, Archivist
416-586-5596

Toronto: The Salvation Army
26 Howden Rd., Toronto, ON M1R 3E4
Tel: 416-285-4344
heritage.centre@salvationarmy.ca
salvationist.ca/archives-and-museum
twitter.com/ArchivesCab; www.facebook.com/ArchivesCAB
Ron Millar, Director

Toronto: Scarboro Mission Society
2685 Kingston Rd., Toronto, ON M1M 1M4
Tel: 416-261-7135; *Fax:* 416-261-0820
Toll-Free: 800-260-4815
www.scarboromissions.ca/archives
Mike Traher, Secretary General
mtraher@scarboromissions.ca

Toronto: Scarborough Historical Society
6282 Kingston Rd., Toronto, ON M1C 1K9
Tel: 416-995-6930
archives@scarboroughhistorical.ca
scarboroughhistorical.ca/archives-2
www.facebook.com/scarborough.lookingback
Rick Schofield, Archivist
rickschofield@rogers.com

Toronto: Sculptors Society of Canada/La Société des sculpteurs du Canada
19 Mill St., Toronto, ON M5A 3R3
Tel: 647-435-5858
cansculpt@gmail.com
www.sculptorssocietyofcanada.org
Judi Michelle Young, President
Bastien Martel, Vice-President

Toronto: The Sisterhood of St. John the Divine Convent
233 Cummer Ave., Toronto, ON M2M 2E8
Tel: 416-226-2201; *Fax:* 416-226-2131
convent@ssjd.ca
ssjd.ca/about-us/the-convent

Toronto: Sisters of St. Joseph of Toronto
101 Thorncliffe Park Dr., Toronto, ON M4H 1M2
Tel: 416-467-2643; *Fax:* 416-429-7921
info@csj-to.ca
www.csj-to.ca/archives
www.youtube.com/user/CSJTO; twitter.com/csjto;
www.facebook.com/csjto
Linda Wicks, Archivist
lwicks@csj-to.ca

Toronto: Sisters Servants of Mary Immaculate
5 Austin Terrace, Toronto, ON M5R 1Y1
Tel: 416-924-7422; *Fax:* 416-928-9261
ssmican@pathcom.com
www.ssmi.org

Toronto: Tartu Institute
310 Bloor St. West, Toronto, ON M5S 1W4
Tel: 416-925-9405; *Fax:* 416-925-2295
vemu@tartucollege.ca
www.tartuinstitute.ca
Piret Noorhani, Head Archivist
piret@tartucollege.ca
Roland Weiler, Archivist
905-627-3856

Toronto: Todmorden Mills Heritage Site
67 Pottery Rd., Toronto, ON M4K 2B9
Tel: 416-396-2819
todmorden@toronto.ca
www.toronto.ca/explore-enjoy/history-art-culture/museums

Toronto: The Toronto Sun
365 Bloor St. East, Toronto, ON M4W 3L4
Tel: 416-947-2258
licensing@postmedia.com
www.torontosun.com

Toronto: Toronto Symphony Orchestra
212 King St. West, 6th Fl., Toronto, ON M5H 1K5
Tel: 416-593-7769; *Fax:* 416-977-2912
www.tso.ca
John Sharpe, Archivist
jsharpe@tso.ca

Toronto: United Church of Canada Archives
40 Oak St., Toronto, ON M5A 2C6
Tel: 416-231-7680; *Fax:* 416-231-3103
Toll-Free: 800-268-3781
archives@united-church.ca
www.unitedchurcharchives.ca
Erin Greeno, Archivist
egreeno@united-church.ca

Robin Brunelle, Assistant Archivist
rbrunelle@united-church.ca
Elizabeth Mathew, Reference Assistant
emathew@united-church.ca

Toronto: Upper Canada College Archives
200 Lonsdale Rd., Toronto, ON M4V 1W6
Tel: 416-488-1125
www.ucc.on.ca
Jill Spellman, Archivist
jspellman@ucc.on.ca

Toronto: Weston Historical Society
1901 Weston Rd., Toronto, ON M9N 3P1
Tel: 416-241-7618
info@heritageweston.com
heritageweston.com/WHS_Aboutus.aspx
www.facebook.com/113972951953777
Cherri Hurst, President

Toronto: York Pioneer & Historical Society
2482 Yonge St., Toronto, ON M4P 3E3
Tel: 416-656-2954
yorkpioneers@gmail.com
www.yorkpioneers.org
twitter.com/YorkPioneers; www.facebook.com/yorkpioneers

Tweed: Tweed & Area Heritage Centre
40 Victoria St. North, Tweed, ON K0K 3J0
Tel: 613-478-3989
tweedheritageinfo@on.aibn.com
www.facebook.com/1665668286912152
Evan Morton, Curator

Uxbridge: Uxbridge Historical Centre
7239 Concession 6, Uxbridge, ON L9P 1N5
Tel: 905-852-5854
museum@uxbridge.on.ca
uxbridgehistoricalcentre.com
twitter.com/UxbridgeMuseum;
www.facebook.com/uxbridgehistoricalcentre
Pat Neal, Manager & Curator
pneal@uxbridge.ca

Vaughan: City of Vaughan Archives
City Hall, Level 000, 2141 Major Mackenzie Dr., Vaughan, ON L6A 1T1
Tel: 905-832-2281
archives@vaughan.ca
www.vaughan.ca/services/vaughan_archives

Vernon: Osgoode Township Historical Society & Museum
7814 Lawrence St., Vernon, ON K0A 3J0
Tel: 613-821-4062
osgoodemuseum.ca
twitter.com/osgoodemuseum;
www.facebook.com/osgoodemuseum
Jillian Metcalfe, Executive Director
manager@osgoodemuseum.ca
Ann Robinson, Administrator
administration@osgoodemuseum.ca

Waterford: Waterford Heritage & Agricultural Museum
159 Nichol St., Waterford, ON N0E 1Y0
Tel: 519-443-4211
waterford.museum@norfolkcounty.ca
waterfordmuseum.ca
www.facebook.com/WHAMuseum

Waterloo: Evangelical Lutheran Church in Canada
Wilfred Laurier University, 75 University Ave. West, Waterloo, ON N2L 3C5
Tel: 519-884-0710
easternsynod.org
Karen Kuhnert, Archivist

Waterloo: Mennonite Archives of Ontario
Conrad Grebel University College, 140 Westmount Rd. North, Waterloo, ON N2L 3G6
Tel: 519-885-0220
marchive@uwaterloo.ca
uwaterloo.ca/mennonite-archives-ontario
Laureen Harder-Gissing, Librarian & Archivist
lharderg@uwaterloo.ca

Wellington: Prince Edward County Archives
28 East St., Wellington, ON
Tel: 613-399-2023
pecarchives.org
Molly McGowan, Archivist
mmcgowan@peclibrary.org

Whitby: Town of Whitby Archives
Whitby Public Library, 405 Dundas St. West, Whitby, ON L1N 6A1
Tel: 905-668-6531; *Fax:* 905-668-7445
archives@whitbylibrary.ca
www.whitbylibrary.ca/archives-and-local-history
Sarah Ferencz, Archivist

Windsor: Assumption University Archives
400 Huron Church Rd., Windsor, ON N9C 2J9
Tel: 519-973-7033; *Fax:* 519-973-7089
info@assumptionu.ca
www.assumptionu.ca
Dinh G. Votran, University Archivist
vtgdinh@assumption.edu

Windsor: Serbian Heritage Museum
6770 Tecumseh Rd. East, Windsor, ON N8T 1E6
Tel: 519-944-4884
info@serbianheritagemuseum.com
www.serbianheritagemuseum.com
www.youtube.com/user/shmuseum;
www.facebook.com/shmuseum
Anne Dube, President
519-819-5819

Windsor: Windsor's Community Museum/Le Musée communautaire de Windsor
François Baby House, 254 Pitt St. West, Windsor, ON N9A 5L5
Tel: 519-253-1812
wmuseum@city.windsor.on.ca
www.citywindsor.ca
Madelyn Della Valle, Museum Curator
mdellavalle@citywindsor.ca

Woodstock: County of Oxford
82 Light St., 2nd Fl., Woodstock, ON N4S 6H1
Tel: 519-539-9800
archives@oxfordcounty.ca
oxfordcounty.ca/archives
www.instagram.com/oxfordcountyarchives
Liz Dommasch, Archivist
Megan Lockhart, Archives Technician
519-539-9800 ext. 3070

Wyoming: Lambton County Museums
787 Broadway St., Wyoming, ON N0N 1T0
Tel: 519-845-5426; *Fax:* 519-845-0700
Toll-Free: 866-324-6912
archives@county-lambton.on.ca
www.lambtonmuseums.ca/lambton-county-archives
www.youtube.com/user/lambtonroom;
twitter.com/HeritageLambton;
www.facebook.com/LambtonCountyArchives

Prince Edward Island

Regional Systems

Prince Edward Island Public Library Service
89 Red Head Rd., Morell, PE C0A 1S0
Tel: 902-961-7320; *Fax:* 902-961-7322
plshq@gov.pe.ca
www.princeedwardisland.ca/en/topic/libraries-and-archives
www.pinterest.com/peilibrary; twitter.com/PEILibrary;
www.facebook.com/PEILibrary

Public Libraries

Alberton: Alberton Public Library
11 Railway St., Alberton, PE C0B 1B0
Tel: 902-231-2090
alberton@gov.pe.ca

Borden: Borden-Carleton Public Library
244 Borden Ave., Borden, PE C0B 1X0
Tel: 902-437-6492
borden-carleton@gov.pe.ca

Breadalbane: Breadalbane Public Library
4023 Dixon Rd., Breadalbane, PE C0A 1E0
Tel: 902-964-2520
breadalbane@gov.pe.ca

Charlottetown: Bibliothèque publique Dr. J. Edmond Arsenault
5 Acadian Dr., Charlottetown, PE C1C 1M2
Tél: 902-368-6092
carrefour@gov.pe.ca

Charlottetown: Confederation Centre Public Library
145A Richmond St., Charlottetown, PE C1A 8G8
Tel: 902-368-4642
ccpl@gov.pe.ca

Cornwall: Cornwall Public Library (PEI)
15 Mercedes Dr., Cornwall, PE C0A 1H0
Tel: 902-629-8415
cornwall@gov.pe.ca

Crapaud: Crapaud Public Library
20424 Trans Canada Hwy., Crapaud, PE C0A 1J0
Tel: 902-658-2297
crapaud@gov.pe.ca

Georgetown: Georgetown Genevieve Soloman Memorial Library
36 Kent St., Georgetown, PE C0A 1L0
Tel: 902-652-2832
georgetown@gov.pe.ca

Hunter River: Hunter River Memorial Library
19816 Rte. 2, Hunter River, PE C0A 1N0
Tel: 902-964-2800
hunter_river@gov.pe.ca

Kensington: Kensington Public Library
6 Commercial St., Kensington, PE C0B 1M0
Tel: 902-836-3721
kensington@gov.pe.ca

Kinkora: Kinkora Public Library
45 Anderson Rd., Kinkora, PE C0B 1N0
Tel: 902-887-2172
kinkora@gov.pe.ca

Montague: Montague Rotary Library
21 Sullivan Lane, Montague, PE C0A 1R0
Tel: 902-838-2928
montague@gov.pe.ca

Morell: Morell Public Library
89 Red Head Rd., Morell, PE C0A 1S0
Tel: 902-961-3389
morell@gov.pe.ca

Mount Stewart: Mount Stewart Public Library
104 Main St., Mount Stewart, PE C0A 1T0
Tel: 902-676-2050
mtstewart@gov.pe.ca

Murray Harbour: Murray Harbour Public Library
27 Faye Fraser Dr., Murray Harbour, PE C0A 1V0
Tel: 902-962-3875
murray_harbour@gov.pe.ca

Murray River: Murray River Leona Giddings Memorial Library
1066 McInnis Rd., Murray River, PE C0A 1W0
Tel: 902-962-2667
murray_river@gov.pe.ca

O'Leary: O'Leary Public Library
18 Community St., O'Leary, PE C0B 1V0
Tel: 902-859-8788
o'leary@gov.pe.ca

Souris: Souris Public Library
75 Main St., Souris, PE C0A 2B0
Tel: 902-687-2157
souris@gov.pe.ca

St. Peters Bay: St. Peters Public Library
1968 Cardigan Rd., St. Peters Bay, PE C0A 2A0
Tel: 902-961-3415
st_peter's@gov.pe.ca

Stratford: Stratford Public Library (PEI)
25 Hopeton Rd., Stratford, PE C1B 1T6
Tel: 902-569-7441
stratford@gov.pe.ca

Summerside: Bibliothèque J.-Henri-Blanchard
5 Maris Stella Ave., Summerside, PE C1N 6M9
Tel: 902-432-2748
blanchard@gov.pe.ca

Summerside: Summerside Rotary Library
57 Central St., Summerside, PE C1N 1B1
Tel: 902-436-7323
summerside@gov.pe.ca

Tignish: Tignish Public Library
103 School St., Tignish, PE C0B 2B0
Tel: 902-882-7363
tignish@gov.pe.ca

Tyne Valley: Tyne Valley Public Library
19 Allen Rd., Tyne Valley, PE C0B 2C0
Tel: 902-831-3338
tyne_valley@gov.pe.ca

Wellington: Bibliothèque publique d'Abram-Village
a/s École Évangéline, 1596 Rte. 124, Wellington, PE C0B 2E0
Tél: 902-854-2491
abram@gov.pe.ca

Archives

Charlottetown: Prince Edward Island Public Archives & Records Office
175 Richmond St., Charlottetown, PE C1A 1J1
Tel: 902-368-4290; Fax: 902-368-6327
archives@gov.pe.ca
www.princeedwardisland.ca/en/topic/libraries-and-archives
Jill MacMicken-Wilson, Provincial Archivist
jswilson@gov.pe.ca
902-368-4351

Québec

Regional Systems

Réseau BIBLIO de l'Abitibi-Témiscamingue-Nord-du-Québec
20, av Québec, Rouyn-Noranda, QC J9X 2E6
Tél: 819-762-4305; Télec: 819-762-5309
info@reseaubiblioatnq.qc.ca
mabiblio.quebec
www.youtube.com/user/Mouvi1;
www.facebook.com/reseaubiblioatnq
Cloé Gingras, Directrice générale
cloe.gingras@reseaubiblioatnq.qc.ca
819-762-4305 ext. 23

Réseau BIBLIO de l'Estrie
4155, rue Brodeur, Sherbrooke, QC J1L 1K4
Tél: 819-565-9744; Télec: 819-565-9157
crsbpe@reseaubiblioestrie.qc.ca
www.reseaubiblioestrie.qc.ca
Joelle Thivierge, Directrice générale
jthivierge@reseaubiblioestrie.qc.ca
819-565-9744 ext. 102
Alla Kadouchkina, Service à la clientele et support Symphony
alla@reseaubiblioestrie.qc.ca
819-565-9744 ext. 101
France Lachance, Service à la clientèle et prêt entre bibliothèques
flachance@reseaubiblioestrie.qc.ca
819-565-9744 ext. 103

Réseau BIBLIO de l'Outaouais
2295, rue Saint-Louis, Gatineau, QC J8T 5L8
Tél: 819-561-6008; Télec: 819-561-6767
biblio@crsbpo.qc.ca
www.reseaubibliooutaouais.qc.ca
www.facebook.com/ReseauBiblioOutaouais
Sylvie Thibault, Directrice générale
sylvie.thibault@crsbpo.qc.ca
819-561-6008 ext. 222
Stéphanie Bellemare, Responsable, services au réseau
reception@crsbpo.qc.ca
819-561-6008 ext. 233
Pascal Demers, Technicien, soutien technique des bibliothèques
pascal.demers@crsbpo.qc.ca
819-561-6008 ext. 227

Réseau BIBLIO de la Capitale-Nationale et de la Chaudière-Appalaches
3189, rue Albert-Demers, Lévis, QC G6X 3A1
Tél: 418-832-6166; Télec: 418-832-6168
Ligne sans frais: 866-446-6166
info@reseaubibliocnca.qc.ca
www.reseaubibliocnca.qc.ca
www.facebook.com/reseaubibliocnca
Isabelle Poirier, Directrice générale
ipoirier@reseaubibliocnca.qc.ca
Marc Hébert, Agent culturel et de développement
mhebert@reseaubibliocnca.qc.ca

Réseau BIBLIO de la Côte-Nord
59, rue Napoléon, Sept-Iles, QC G4R 5C5
Tél: 418-962-1020
biblio@reseaubibliocn.qc.ca
www.reseaubibliocn.qc.ca
Marie-Soleil Vigneault, Directeur général
msvigneault@reseaubibliocn.qc.ca

Chantal Hould, Technicienne en documentation
chantalh@reseaubibliocn.qc.ca

Réseau BIBLIO de la Gaspésie-Iles-de-la-Madeleine
31, rue des Écoliers, Cap-Chat, QC G0J 1E0
Tél: 418-786-5597; Ligne sans frais: 855-737-3281
info@reseaubibliogim.qc.ca
www.reseaubibliogim.qc.ca
www.facebook.com/ReseauBIBLIOGIM
Julie Blais, Directrice générale
julie.blais@reseaubibliogim.qc.ca
Monique Demers, Responsable, soutien aux bibliothèques
monique.demers@reseaubibliogim.qc.ca
Sabrina Mallette, Responsable, service de prêt entre bibliothèques
sabrina.mallette@reseaubibliogim.qc.ca

Réseau BIBLIO de la Montérégie
275, rue Conrad-Pelletier, La Prairie, QC J5R 4V1
Tél: 450-444-5433; Télec: 450-659-3364
crsaide@reseaubibliomonteregie.qc.ca
www.reseaubibliomonteregie.qc.ca
www.youtube.com/user/RBMonteregie;
twitter.com/RBMonteregie;
www.facebook.com/ReseauBiblioMonteregie;
www.linkedin.com/company/réseau-biblio-de-la-montérégie
Sylvain Meunier, Directrice générale
sylvain.meunier@reseaubibliomonteregie.qc.ca
Mohamed Meziani, Directeur, Service des technologies de l'information
mohamed.meziani@reseaubibliomonteregie.qc.ca

Réseau BIBLIO des Laurentides
29, rue Brissette, Sainte-Agathe-des-Monts, QC J8C 3L1
Tél: 819-326-6440; Télec: 819-326-0885
info@crsbpl.qc.ca
www.mabiblioamoi.ca
JoAnne Turnbull, Directrice générale
jturnbull@crsbpl.qc.ca

Réseau BIBLIO du Bas-Saint-Laurent
465, rue St-Pierre, Rivière-du-Loup, QC G5R 4T6
Tél: 418-867-1682; Télec: 418-867-3434
crsbp@crsbp.net
www.reseaubibliobsl.qc.ca
www.facebook.com/reseaubibliobsl
Jacques Côté, Directeur général
jacques.cote@crsbp.net
418-867-1682 ext. 112

Réseau BIBLIO du Centre-du-Québec, de Lanaudière et de la Mauricie
3125, rue Girard, Trois-Rivières, QC G8Z 2M4
Tél: 819-375-9623; Télec: 819-375-0132
Ligne sans frais: 877-324-2546
crsbp@reseaubibliocqlm.qc.ca
reseaubibliocqlm.qc.ca
www.facebook.com/reseaubibliocqlm
France René, Directrice générale
france.rene@reseaubibliocqlm.qc.ca

Réseau BIBLIO du Saguenay-Lac-Saint-Jean
100, rue Price ouest, Alma, QC G8B 4S1
Tél: 418-662-6425; Ligne sans frais: 800-563-6425
info@reseaubiblioslsj.qc.ca
www.reseaubiblioslsj.qc.ca
www.facebook.com/reseaubiblioSLSJ
Sophie Bolduc, Directrice générale
sbolduc@reseaubiblioslsj.qc.ca
418-662-6425 ext. 227
Julie Macquart, Responsable, services administratifs et Adjointe à la direction
jmacquart@reseaubiblioslsj.qc.ca
418-662-6425 ext. 223
Lily Lachance, Conseillère aux bibliothèques
llachance@reseaubiblioslsj.qc.ca
418-662-6425 ext. 234
Karine Labonté, Technicienne en documentation
klabonte@reseaubiblioslsj.qc.ca
418-662-6425 ext. 225

Public Libraries

Acton Vale: Bibliothèque d'Acton Vale
1093A, rue Saint-André, Acton Vale, QC J0H 1A0
Tél: 450-546-2703; Télec: 450-642-1165
biblio@ville.actonvale.qc.ca
ville.actonvale.qc.ca/categories/bibliotheque
www.facebook.com/biblioActonVale
Sophia Bédard, Coordonnatrice
sophia.bedard@ville.actonvale.qc.ca
450-546-2703 ext. 251

Aguanish: Bibliothèque d'Aguanish (Victor Lachance)
106, rue Jacques-Cartier, Aguanish, QC G0G 1A0
Tél: 418-533-2323
info@mun.aguanish.org
www.aguanish.org/bibliothèque-victor-lachance
Delvie Blais, Responsable

Albanel: Bibliothèque Denis-Lebrun
153A, rue Principale, Albanel, QC G8M 3J3
Tél: 613-279-5250; Téléc: 418-279-3147
albanel@reseaubiblioslsj.qc.ca
albanel.ca/bibliotheque-denis-lebrun
www.facebook.com/236993253109274
Rachel Lavoie, Responsable

Albertville: Bibliothèque d'Albertville
1058, rue Principale, Albertville, QC G0J 1A0
Tél: 418-756-6015
biblio.albert@crsbp.net
www.facebook.com/BiblioAlbertville
Valérie Delisle-Gagnon, Responsable

Alma: Bibliothèque municipale d'Alma
500, rue Collard ouest, Alma, QC G8B 1N2
Tél: 418-669-5140; Téléc: 418-669-5089
bibliotheque@ville.alma.qc.ca
www.ville.alma.qc.ca/biblio
www.facebook.com/biblio.alma
Emilie Guertin, Coordonnatrice des bibliothèques
emilie.guertin@ville.alma.qc.ca
418-669-5140 ext. 5139

Alma: Bibliothèque publique de Delisle
221, rue des Bruyères, Alma, QC G8E 1J9
Tél: 418-668-2697
delisle@reseaubiblioslsj.qc.ca

Alma: Bibliothèque publique de Saint-Coeur-de-Marie
#105, 5791, av du Pont nord, Alma, QC G8E 1X1
Tél: 418-347-3729
stcoeur@reseaubiblioslsj.qc.ca

Amherst: Bibliothèque de Saint-Rémi
259, rue Amherst, Amherst, QC J0T 2L0
Tél: 819-681-3372
bibliostremi@municipalite.amherst.qc.ca

Amqui: Bibliothèque Madeleine-Gagnon
24, promenade Marcel-Rioux, Amqui, QC G5J 3E1
Tél: 418-629-4242; Téléc: 418-629-4090
bibliotheque@ville.amqui.qc.ca
www.ville.amqui.qc.ca
Roy Mike, Responsable

Angliers: Bibliothèque d'Angliers
14, rue Baie Miller, Angliers, QC J0Y 1A0
angliers@reseaubiblioatnq.qc.ca
www.angliers.fr/bibliotheque

Armagh: Bibliothèque Armagimo
9, rue de la Salle, Armagh, QC G0R 1A0
Tél: 418-466-3004; Téléc: 418-466-2409
armagimobibliotheque@gmail.com
www.mabibliotheque.ca/armagh
www.facebook.com/bibliothequearmagimo

Arundel: Bibliothèque d'Arundel/Arundel Library
2, rue du Village, Arundel, QC J0T 1A0
Tél: 819-681-3390; Téléc: 819-687-8760
biblio@arundel.ca
arundel.ca/services-municipaux/bibliotheque
France Jones, Responsable

Ascot Corner: Bibliothèque municipale d'Ascot Corner
5699, rue Principale, Ascot Corner, QC J0B 1A0
Tél: 819-560-8562; Téléc: 819-560-8563
biblio008@reseaubiblioestrie.qc.ca
ascot-corner.com/sport-loisir-et-culture/bibliotheque-municipale

Aston-Jonction: Bibliothèque d'Aston-Jonction
210, rue Lemire, Aston-Jonction, QC G0Z 1A0
Tél: 819-489-1103
biblio070@reseaubibliocqlm.qc.ca
www.aston-jonction.ca/bibliotheque-daston-jonction
www.facebook.com/biblio.astonjonction

Auclair: Bibliothèque d'Auclair
777, rue du Clocher, Auclair, QC G0L 1A0
Tél: 418-899-0847
biblio.auclair@crsbp.net

Aumond: Bibliothèque d'Aumond
664, rte Principale, Aumond, QC J0W 1W0
Tél: 819-441-2300; Téléc: 819-449-7448
admaumond@crsbpo.qc.ca
aumond.ca/services_municipaux/bibliotheque_d_aumond.php
Linda Lemieux, Responsable

Baie-Comeau: Bibliothèque municipale Alice-Lane
6, av Radisson, Baie-Comeau, QC G4Z 1W4
Tél: 418-296-8304
biblio@ville.baie-comeau.qc.ca
biblio.ville.baie-comeau.qc.ca
www.facebook.com/bibliothequealicelane

Baie-des-Sables: Bibliothèque de Baie-des-Sables
20, rue de Couvent, Baie-des-Sables, QC G0J 1C0
Tél: 418-772-6218
biblio.sables@crsbp.net
www.facebook.com/998819040264946

Baie-du-Febvre: Bibliothèque de Baie-du-Febvre
23, rue de l'Église, Baie-du-Febvre, QC J0G 1A0
Tél: 819-519-6422
biblio032@reseaubibliocqlm.qc.ca
bibletcie.ca/biblio/bibliotheque-de-baie-du-febvre
Lyne Bergeron, Responsable

Baie-Johan-Beetz: Bibliothèque Baie-Johan-Beetz
12, rue Tanguay, Baie-Johan-Beetz, QC G0G 1B0
Tél: 418-539-0125; Téléc: 418-539-0205
bibliotheque@baiejohanbeetz.qc.ca
Sylvain Roy, Responsable

Baie-Saint-Paul: Bibliothèque René-Richard
9, rue Forget, Baie-Saint-Paul, QC G3Z 1T4
Tél: 418-435-5858; Téléc: 418-435-0010
www.baiesaintpaul.com/loisirs-et-culture/bibliotheque-rene-richard
www.facebook.com/Bibliothequerenerichard
Denise Ouellet, Responsable
deniseouellet@baiesaintpaul.com

Baie-Sainte-Catherine: Bibliothèque municipale Bernadette-Dallaire
304, rue Leclerc, Baie-Sainte-Catherine, QC G0T 1A0
Tél: 418-237-4241; Téléc: 418-237-4223
biblio15762@outlook.fr

Baie-Trinité: Bibliothèque de Baie-Trinité
28, rte 138, Baie-Trinité, QC G0H 1A0
Tél: 418-939-2231; Téléc: 418-939-2616
bibliobtrinite@gmail.com
www.facebook.com/bibliotheque.baietrinite
Pierrette Bureau, Responsable

Barraute: Bibliothèque Barraute
600, 1e rue ouest, Barraute, QC J0Y 1A0
Tél: 819-734-6762; Téléc: 819-734-6762
barraute@reseaubiblioatnq.qc.ca
Lilaine Cayouette, Responsable

Batiscan: Bibliothèque municipale de Batiscan
791, place de la Solidarité, Batiscan, QC G0X 1A0
Tél: 819-840-0600
biblio025@reseaubibliocqlm.qc.ca
www.batiscan.ca/fr/loisirs/organismes/bibliotheque
www.facebook.com/bibliothequedebatiscan

Beaconsfield: Beaconsfield Library/Bibliothèque de Beaconsfield
303, boul Beaconsfield, Beaconsfield, QC H9W 4A7
Tél: 514-428-4460
bibliotheque@beaconsfield.ca
www.beaconsfield.ca/en/305-culture-and-leisure-fields/library

Beaucanton: Bibliothèque Beaucanton
2709, boul McDuff, #C, Beaucanton, QC J0Z 1H0
Tél: 819-941-2101; Téléc: 819-941-2485
beaucanton@reseaubiblioatnq.qc.ca
Annie Lavoie, Coordonnatrice

Beauceville: Bibliothèque Madeleine-Doyon
100, place de l'Église, Beauceville, QC G5X 1X3
Tél: 418-774-9137; Téléc: 418-774-2499
biblio@ville.beauceville.qc.ca
ville.beauceville.qc.ca/bibliotheque-madeleine-doyon

Beauharnois: Bibliothèque de Beauharnois
39, rue Richardson, Beauharnois, QC J6N 2T3
Tél: 450-429-3546
biblio@ville.beauharnois.qc.ca
ville.beauharnois.qc.ca/bibliotheque-beauharnois
Caroline Ménard, Bibliotechnicienne
450-429-3546 ext. 259

Beaumont: Bibliothèque Luc-Lacourcière
64, ch du Domaine, Beaumont, QC G0R 1C0
Tél: 418-837-2658
biblio@beaumont-qc.com
www.mabibliotheque.ca/beaumont
www.facebook.com/bibliobeaumont

Beaupré: Bibliothèque La Plume d'Oie (Bibliothèque de Beaupré et Saint-Joachim)
11298, rue de La Salle, Beaupré, QC G0A 1E0
Tél: 418-827-8483; Téléc: 418-827-3818
bibliotheque@villedebeaupre.com
www.villedebeaupre.com/pages/bibliotheque

Bedford: Bibliothèque Léon-Maurice-Côté
52, rue Du Pont, Bedford, QC J0J 1A0
Tél: 450-248-4625
bibliotheque@ville.bedford.qc.ca
ville.bedford.qc.ca/loisirs/bibliotheque-leon-maurice-cote

Belcourt: Bibliothèque de Belcourt
219A, rue Communautaire, Belcourt, QC J0Y 2M0
Tél: 819-737-8894; Téléc: 819-737-4084
belcourt@reseaubiblioatnq.qc.ca
mabiblio.quebec/client/fr_CA/belcourt
Guylaine Labbée, Responsable

Belleterre: Bibliothèque de Belleterre
265, 1e av, Belleterre, QC J0Z 1L0
Tél: 819-722-2052; Téléc: 819-722-2527
belleterre@reseaubiblioatnq.qc.ca
mabiblio.quebec/client/fr_CA/belleterre
Josée Rivard, Responsable

Beloeil: Bibliothèque municipale de Beloeil
620, rue Richelieu, Beloeil, QC J3G 5E8
Tél: 450-467-7872
biblio@beloeil.ca
beloeil.ca/divertir/bibliotheque
www.facebook.com/bibliobeloeil

Berthier-sur-Mer: Bibliothèque Camille-Roy
24, boul Blais est, Berthier-sur-Mer, QC G0R 1E0
Tél: 418-259-2353; Téléc: 418-259-2038
berthiersurmer.ca/bibliotheque-camille-roy-et-reseau-biblio

Biencourt: Bibliothèque de Biencourt
#1, 2, rue Saint-Marc, Biencourt, QC G0K 1T0
Tél: 418-499-1041
biblio.biencourt@crsbp.net
www.reseaubibliobsl.qc.ca/bibliotheque/bibliotheque-de-biencourt

Blainville: Bibliothèque publique de Blainville
1003, rue de la Mairie, Blainville, QC J7C 3C7
Tél: 450-434-5275
bibliotheque@blainville.ca
biblio.ville.blainville.qc.ca

Blue Sea: Bibliothèque Blue Sea
2, ch Blue Sea Nord, Blue Sea, QC J0X 1C0
Tél: 819-463-3919; Téléc: 819-463-4345
admbluesea@crsbpo.qc.ca
www.bluesea.ca/index.php/services/bibliotheque-municipale
Nadine Martin, Responsable

Bois-Franc: Bibliothèque de Bois-Franc
466, rte 105, Bois-Franc, QC J9E 3A9
Tél: 819-441-0645; Téléc: 819-449-4407
admboisfranc@crsbpo.qc.ca
www.bois-franc.ca/services/bibliotheque
Angèle Lacaille, Responsable

Boisbriand: Bibliothèque municipale de Boisbriand
901, boul de la Grande-Allée, Boisbriand, QC J7G 1W6
Tél: 450-435-7466; Téléc: 450-435-0627
www.ville.boisbriand.qc.ca/bibliotheque

Bonaventure: Bibliothèque Françoise-Bujold
95A, av Port-Royal, Bonaventure, QC G0C 1E0
Tél: 418-534-4238
biblio@villebonaventure.ca
www.facebook.com/BibliothequeFrancoiseBujold

Bonsecours: Bibliothèque de Bonsecours
535, rte 220, Bonsecours, QC J0E 1H0
Tél: 450-532-3139; Téléc: 450-532-3139
mbonsecours@cooptel.qc.ca
municipalites-du-quebec.ca/bonsecours/bibliotheque.php

Boucherville: Bibliothèque Montarville-Boucher-De la Bruère
501, ch du Lac, Boucherville, QC J4B 6V6
Tél: 450-449-8650; *Téléc:* 450-449-6865
bibliotheque@boucherville.ca
bibliotheque.ville.boucherville.qc.ca

Bouchette: Bibliothèque de Bouchette
47, rue Principale, Bouchette, QC J0X 1E0
Tél: 819-465-5782; *Téléc:* 819-465-2318
admbouchette@crsbpo.qc.ca
www.bouchette.ca/index.php/fr/services/bibliotheque
Chantal Leblanc, Responsable

Brigham: Bibliothèque municipale de Brigham
118, av des Cèdres, Brigham, QC J2K 4K4
Tél: 450-266-0500
info@biblio.brigham.ca
brigham.ca/bibliotheque
Céline Vaillancourt, Coordonnatrice

Bristol: Bibliothèque de Bristol/Bristol Library
32, rue d'Aylmer, Bristol, QC J0X 1G0
Tél: 819-647-5555; *Téléc:* 819-647-2424
admbristol@crsbpo.qc.ca
bristolmunicipality.qc.ca
Shiela Watt, Bibliothécaire en chef
Alina Seguin-Holmes, Bibliothécaire
Diane Wilson, Bibliothécaire

Brossard: Bibliothèque de Brossard (Georgette-Lepage)
7855, av San-Francisco, Brossard, QC J4X 2A4
Tél: 450-923-6350; *Téléc:* 450-923-7042
bibliotheque@brossard.ca
biblio.brossard.ca
www.youtube.com/user/bibliobrossard;
twitter.com/Bibliobrossard; www.facebook.com/bibliobrossard

Brownsburg-Chatham: Bibliothèque de Brownsburg-Chatham
200, rue MacVicar, Brownsburg-Chatham, QC J8G 2Z6
Tél: 450-533-5355
biblio@brownsburgchatham.ca
www.facebook.com/BiblioBrownsburgChatham

Brébeuf: Bibliothèque M.-A. Grégoire-Coupal
217, rte 323, Brébeuf, QC J0T 1B0
Tél: 819-425-9833; *Téléc:* 819-425-6611
biblio@brebeuf.ca
brebeuf.ca/bibliotheque

Buckland: Bibliothèque Biblio Buck
4340, rue Principale, Buckland, QC G0R 1G0
Tél: 418-789-3119
www.buckland.qc.ca/pages/bibliotheque-municipale
Diane Laflamme, Préposée

Bury: Bibliothèque de Bury
569, rue Main, Bury, QC J0B 1J0
Tél: 819-560-8416
biblio088@reseaubiblioestrie.qc.ca

Béarn: Bibliothèque de Béarn
38, rue Principale nord, Béarn, QC J0Z 1G0
Tél: 819-726-2251; *Téléc:* 819-726-2121
bearn@reseaubiblioatnq.qc.ca
mabiblio.quebec/client/fr_CA/bearn
Josée Gaudet, Responsable

Bécancour: Bibliothèque municipale de Bécancour
1295, av Nicolas-Perrot, Bécancour, QC G9H 1A1
Tél: 819-294-4455
www.becancour.net/citoyens/bibliotheques

Bégin: Bibliothèque publique de Bégin
120B, rue Tremblay, Bégin, QC G0V 1B0
Tél: 418-672-4503
begin@reseaubiblioslsj.qc.ca
www.begin.ca/index.php/culture-et-loisir/bibliotheque

Calixa-Lavallée: Bibliothèque municipale de Calixa-Lavallée
771, ch de la Beauce, Calixa-Lavallée, QC J0L 1A0
Tél: 450-583-6470
biblio@calixa-lavallee.ca
www.calixa-lavallee.ca/bibliotheque
Nicole Jacques, Responsable

Candiac: Bibliothèque municipale de Candiac
Centre Claude-Hébert, 59, ch Haendel, Candiac, QC J5R 1R7
Tél: 450-635-6032; *Téléc:* 450-635-0900
biblio@ville.candiac.qc.ca
www.biblio.ville.candiac.qc.ca

Cantley: Bibliothèque municipale de Cantley
6, impasse des Étoiles, Cantley, QC J8V 0C6
Tél: 819-827-3434
cantley.ca/culture-et-loisirs/espaceculturel

Cap-Chat: Bibliothèque La ruche littéraire
27, rue des Écoliers, Cap-Chat, QC G0J 1E0
Tél: 418-786-2068

Cap-d'Espoir: Bibliothèque de Cap-d'Espoir
52, rue du Curé-Poirier, Cap-d'Espoir, QC G0C 1G0
Tél: 581-353-2019
bbocesp@ville.perce.qc.ca
www.facebook.com/384621774979266

Cap-Saint-Ignace: Bibliothèque Léo-Pol-Morin
100, place de l'Église, Cap-Saint-Ignace, QC G0R 1H0
Tél: 418-246-3037; *Téléc:* 418-246-5663
biblicap@capsaintignace.ca
www.facebook.com/bibliothequecapsaintignace

Cap-Santé: Bibliothèque municipale de Cap-Santé
15, rue Marie-Fitzbach, Cap-Santé, QC G0A 1L0
Tél: 418-285-6891; *Téléc:* 418-285-0009
bibliocapsante@hotmail.com
www.mabibliothque.ca/cap-sante
www.facebook.com/bibliocapsante

Caplan: Bibliothèque Jeanne-Ferlatte
17-B, boul Perron est, Caplan, QC G0C 1H0
Tél: 418-388-2545
bibliocaplan@hotmail.com

Capucins: Bibliothèque de Capucins
294, rue du Village, Capucins, QC G0J 1H0
Tél: 418-786-2013

Carleton-sur-Mer: Bibliothèque Gabrielle-Bernard-Dubé
774, boul Perron, Carleton-sur-Mer, QC G0C 1J0
Tél: 418-364-7103
bibliotheque@carletonsurmer.com
www.facebook.com/283352675052837

Causapscal: Bibliothèque de Causapscal
3, Place de l'Église, Causapscal, QC G0J 1J0
Tél: 418-756-3444
biblio.causap@crsbp.net
www.causapscal.net
www.facebook.com/Bibliocausap

Chambly: Bibliothèque municipale de Chambly
1625, boul De Périgny, Chambly, QC J3L 1X1
Tél: 450-658-2711; *Téléc:* 450-447-4525
bibliotheque@ville.chambly.qc.ca
www.ville.chambly.qc.ca/bibliotheque
Paméla Deslauriers, Responsable

Chambord: Bibliothèque publique de Chambord
#72, 1, boul de la Montagne, Chambord, QC G0W 1G0
Tél: 418-342-6274
chambord@reseaubiblioslsj.qc.ca
www.facebook.com/bilbiothequechambord

Champlain: Bibliothèque de Champlain
963, rue Notre-Dame, Champlain, QC G0X 1C0
Tél: 819-840-0407
biblio005@reseaubibliocqim.qc.ca
www.municipalite.champlain.qc.ca/fr/bibliotheque-municipale_44
Isabelle Vézina, Coordonnatrice

Chandler: Bibliothèque municipale-scolaire de Chandler
183, rue Commerciale ouest, Chandler, QC G0C 1K0
Tél: 418-689-3808
chandbbo@villechandler.com
www.villedechandler.com/sports-loisirs/arts-culture
www.facebook.com/bibliodechandler

Chapais: Bibliothèque publique de Chapais
45, 5e av, Chapais, QC G0W 1H0
Tél: 418-745-2531
chapais@reseaubiblioslsj.qc.ca
villedechapais.com
Doris Dubé, Responsable

Charette: Bibliothèque de Charette (Armance-Samson)
390, rue Saint-Édouard, Charette, QC G0X 1E0
Tél: 819-221-2095
biblio023@reseaubibliocqlm.qc.ca
www.municipalite-charette.ca/bibliotheque
Marie Fitzgerald, Coordonnatrice

Charlemagne: Bibliothèque Camille-Laurin
84, rue du Sacré-Coeur, Charlemagne, QC J5Z 1W8
Tél: 450-581-7243; *Téléc:* 450-581-0597
biblio@ville.charlemagne.qc.ca
www.ville.charlemagne.qc.ca/fr/bibliotheque

Chartierville: Bibliothèque de Chartierville
27, Saint-Jean Baptiste, Chartierville, QC J0B 1K0
Tél: 819-560-8522; *Téléc:* 819-560-8523
biblio067@reseaubiblioestrie.qc.ca
chartierville.ca/zone-citoyen/loisirs/bibliotheque

Chelsea: Bibliothèque de Chelsea/Chelsea Library
100, ch Old Chelsea, Chelsea, QC J9B 1C1
Tél: 819-827-4019
bibliotheque@chelsea.ca
www.chelsea.ca/en/residents/service-municipaux/library
www.facebook.com/LibraryChelsea

Chertsey: Bibliothèque de Chertsey
333, av de l'Amitié, Chertsey, QC J0K 3K0
Tél: 450-882-4738
chertsey.ca/loisirs-et-culture/pret-et-location-de-salles/biblio

Chesterville: Bibliothèque de Chesterville
474, rue de l'Acceuil, Chesterville, QC G0P 1J0
Tél: 819-382-2059
biblio146@reseaubibliocqlm.qc.ca
bibletcie.ca/bibliotheque-de-chesterville
www.facebook.com/bibliothequechesterville

Chevery: Bibliothèque de Chevery
Municipalité de la Côte-Nord-du-Golfe-du-Saint-Laurent, Chevery, QC G0G 1G0
Tél: 418-787-2244; *Téléc:* 418-787-2241
Sylvie Perron, Responsable

Chibougamau: Bibliothèque municipale de Chibougamau
601, 3e rue, Chibougamau, QC G8P 0A8
Tél: 418-748-2688
bibliotheque@ville.chibougamau.qc.ca
www.ville.chibougamau.qc.ca

Chicoutimi: Bibliothèques de Saguenay
155, rue Racine est, Chicoutimi, QC G7H 1R5
Tél: 418-698-5350; *Téléc:* 418-698-5359
webbiblio@ville.saguenay.qc.ca
ville.saguenay/activites-et-loisirs/bibliotheque
Luc-Michel Belley, Chef de division, Arts, culture et bibliothèques

Chute-aux-Outardes: Bibliothèque de Chute-aux-Outardes
2, rue de l'École, Chute-aux-Outardes, QC G0H 1C0
Tél: 418-567-2525; *Téléc:* 418-567-4478
loisirs@municipalitecao.ca
Manon Finn, Responsable

Chute-Saint-Philippe: Bibliothèque de Chute-Saint-Philippe
592, ch du Progrès, Chute-Saint-Philippe, QC J0W 1A0
Tél: 819-585-3397; *Téléc:* 819-585-2209
bibliotheque@chute-saint-philippe.ca

Chénéville: Bibliothèque de Chénéville / Lac-Simon
77, rue Hôtel-de-Ville, Chénéville, QC J0V 1E0
Tél: 819-428-3583; *Téléc:* 819-428-4838
biblio@ville-cheneville.com
www.ville.cheneville.qc.ca/bibliotheque
Madeleine Tremblay, Responsable

Château-Richer: Espace culturel Richard-Verreau
177, rue de l'Église, Château-Richer, QC G0A 1N0
Tél: 418-824-4292
bibliotheque@chateauricher.qc.ca
www.chateauricher.qc.ca/pages/espace-culturel-richard-verreau
www.facebook.com/espaceculturelrichardverreau

Châteauguay: Bibliothèque municipale de Châteauguay/Châteauguay Municipal Library
25, boul Maple, Châteauguay, QC J6J 3P7
Tél: 450-698-3080
biblio@ville.chateauguay.qc.ca
ville.chateauguay.qc.ca/bibliotheque
www.facebook.com/BibliothequeRaymondLaberge

Clarenceville: Bibliothèque municipale de Saint-Georges-de-Clarenceville
1340, ch Middle, Clarenceville, QC J0J 1B0
Tél: 450-294-3200
biblio@clarenceville.qc.ca
www.facebook.com/BibliothequeClarenceville

Clermont: Bibliothèque La Chute de Mots
11, rue Jean Talon, Clermont, QC G4A 1A4
Tél: 418-439-2903
lachutedemots63@hotmail.com
www.mabibliotheque.ca/clermont
www.facebook.com/lachutedemots63

Clerval: Bibliothèque de Clerval
579-B, rang 2-3, Clerval, QC J0Z 1R0
Tél: 819-783-2069; *Téléc:* 819-783-4001
clerval@reseaubiblioatnq.qc.ca
mabiblio.quebec/client/fr_CA/clerval
Luc Barriault, Responsable

Cloridorme: Bibliothèque de Cloridorme
472, rte 132, Cloridorme, QC G0E 1G0
Tél: 418-395-2609
maire2013@hotmail.ca

Coaticook: Bibliothèque Françoise-Maurice de Coaticook
34, rue Main est, Coaticook, QC J1A 1N2
Tél: 819-849-4013; *Téléc:* 819-849-0479
biblcoat@bibliotheque.coaticook.qc.ca
bibliotheque.coaticook.qc.ca
www.facebook.com/bibliothequedecoaticook;

Colombier: Bibliothèque de Colombier
570, rue Principale, Colombier, QC G0H 1P0
Tél: 418-565-3013; *Téléc:* 418-565-3289
biblio.colombier@hotmail.com
Gina Boulianne, Responsable

Compton: Bibliothèque de Compton
#202, 29 ch de Hatley, Compton, QC J0B 1L0
Tél: 819-835-0404; *Téléc:* 819-835-0404
biblio003@reseaubiblioestrie.qc.ca
www.compton.ca/fr/citoyen/bibliotheque.php
www.facebook.com/BibliothequeEstelleBureau

Cookshire-Eaton: Bibliothèque de Cookshire-Eaton
210, rue Principale est, Cookshire-Eaton, QC J0B 1M0
Tél: 819-560-8589; *Téléc:* 819-875-5311
biblio010@reseaubiblioestrie.qc.ca
www.cookshire-eaton.qc.ca/sports-et-loisirs

Coteau-du-Lac: Bibliothèque Jules-Fournier
3, rue du Parc, Coteau-du-Lac, QC J0P 1B0
Tél: 450-763-2763; *Téléc:* 450-763-2495
bibliotheque@coteau-du-lac.com
bibliotheque.coteau-du-lac.com
www.facebook.com/bibliothequejulesfournier
Christine Gauthier, Responsable

Cowansville: Bibliothèque Gabrielle-Giroux-Bertrand
608, rue du Sud, Cowansville, QC J2K 2Y1
Tél: 450-263-4071; *Téléc:* 450-263-7477
bibliothequeggb@ville.cowansville.qc.ca
www.ville.cowansville.qc.ca

Crabtree: Bibliothèque de Crabtree
59, 16e rue, Crabtree, QC J0K 1B0
Tél: 450-754-4332
biblio114@reseaubibliocqlm.qc.ca
crabtree.quebec/loisirs-et-culture/bibliotheque

Côte Saint-Luc: Bibliothèque publique Eleanor London Côte-Saint-Luc
5851, boul Cavendish, Côte Saint-Luc, QC H4W 2X8
Tél: 514-485-6900; *Téléc:* 514-485-6966
reference@cotesaintluc.org
csllibrary.org
www.facebook.com/csllibrary
Janine West, Directrice de la bibliothèque
jwest@cotesaintluc.org
514-485-6900 ext. 4202

Danford Lake: Bibliothèque de Alleyn-et-Cawood
10, ch Jondee, Danford Lake, QC J0X 1P0
Tél: 819-467-2941; *Téléc:* 819-467-3133
admalleyncawood@crsbpo.qc.ca
www.alleyn-cawood.ca/fr/services-citoyens/bibliotheque
Jessica Vahiy, Responsable

Danville: Bibliothèque municipale de Danville
51, rue Cleveland, Danville, QC J0A 1A0
Tél: 819-839-3236; *Téléc:* 819-839-2918
biblio053@reseaubiblioestrie.qc.ca
danville.ca/bottin/services/bibliotheque

Daveluyville: Bibliothèque de Daveluyville
111, 7e av, Daveluyville, QC G0Z 1C0
Tél: 819-367-3645
biblio057@reseaubibliocqlm.qc.ca
biblietcie.ca/biblio/bibliotheque-de-daveluyville
www.facebook.com/BibliothequeDaveluyville

Delson: Bibliothèque municipale de Delson
1, 1e av, Delson, QC J5B 1M9
Tél: 450-632-1050
biblio@ville.delson.qc.ca
www.ville.delson.qc.ca

Desbiens: Bibliothèque publique de Desbiens
1058, rue Marcellin, Desbiens, QC G0W 1N0
Tél: 418-346-5739
desbiens@reseaubiblioslsj.qc.ca

Deschaillons: Bibliothèque de Deschaillons-sur-Saint-Laurent
1042A, rte Marie-Victorin, Deschaillons, QC G0S 1G0
Tél: 819-292-2483
biblio101@reseaubibliocqlm.qc.ca
biblietcie.ca/bibliotheque-de-deschaillons-sur-saint-laurent
www.facebook.com/bibliodeschaillonsS
Hélène Quesnel, Responsable par intérim

Deschambault-Grondines: Bibliothèque Du Bord de l'Eau
#1, 115, rue de l'Église, Deschambault-Grondines, QC G0A 1S0
Tél: 418-286-6938; *Téléc:* 418-286-6511
bibliodesc@hotmail.com
www.mabibliotheque.ca/deschambault
www.facebook.com/1147109648735626

Deux-Montagnes: Bibliothèque de Deux-Montagnes/Deux-Montagnes Library
200, rue Henri-Dunant, Deux-Montagnes, QC J7R 4W6
Tél: 450-473-2702; *Téléc:* 450-473-2816
biblio@ville.deux-montagnes.qc.ca
bibliotheque.ville.deux-montagnes.qc.ca
Pascale Dupuis, Directrice, culture et bibliothèque
pdupuis@ville.deux-montagnes.qc.ca
450-473-2796 ext. 5222
Valérie Schiltz, Bibliothécaire
vschiltz@ville.deux-montagnes.qc.ca
450-473-2796 ext. 5225
Guylaine Lemire, Technicienne en documentation
glemire@ville.deux-montagnes.qc.ca
450-473-2796 ext. 5226

Dolbeau-Mistassini: Bibliothèque de Dolbeau-Mistassini
175, 4e av, Dolbeau-Mistassini, QC G8L 1W6
Tél: 418-276-0160; *Téléc:* 418-276-8265
www.dolbeau.biblio.qc.ca

Dollard-des-Ormeaux: Bibliothèque publique de Dollard-des-Ormeaux/Dollard-des-Ormeaux Public Library
12001, boul De Salaberry, Dollard-des-Ormeaux, QC H9B 2A7
Tél: 514-684-1496
bibliotheque@ddo.qc.ca
webopac.ddo.qc.ca/iguana/www.main.cls?surl=Accueil
www.facebook.com/biblioddo;

Dorval: Bibliothèque de Dorval
1401, ch du Bord-du-Lac, Dorval, QC H9S 2E5
Tél: 514-633-4170
biblio@ville.dorval.qc.ca
biblioweb.ville.dorval.qc.ca
www.facebook.com/bibliodorval

Dosquet: Bibliothèque La Bouquinerie (Dosquet)
154A, rte St-Joseph, Dosquet, QC G0S 1H0
Tél: 418-415-1015
bibliothequedosquet@videotron.ca
www.facebook.com/labouquineriededosquet

Drummondville: Bibliothèque publique de Drummondville
425, rue des Forges, Drummondville, QC J2B 0G4
Tél: 819-478-6573; *Téléc:* 819-478-0399
bibliotheque@drummondville.ca
www.drummondville.ca/culture-loisirs-et-sports/bibliotheque

Drummondville: Centre de lecture Réal-Rochefort
Pavillon Jean Coutu, 565, rue Victorin, Drummondville, QC J2C 1C1
Tél: 819-477-2326
ccscharles.ca

Dudswell: Bibliothèque Claire D. Manseau
185, rue Principale est, Dudswell, QC J0B 2L0
Tél: 819-560-8484; *Téléc:* 819-560-8485
biblio093@reseaubiblioestrie.qc.ca
municipalitededudswell.ca/culture/bibliotheque-claire-d-manseau
www.facebook.com/BibliothequedeDudswell
Jasmine Marcotte, Responsable

Duhamel: Bibliothèque Duhamel
1899, rue Principale, Duhamel, QC J0V 1G0
Tél: 819-428-7100; *Téléc:* 819-428-1941
admduhamel@crsbpo.qc.ca
www.municipalite.duhamel.qc.ca/bibliotheque
Roselyne Bernard, Responsable

Dunham: Bibliothèque municipale de Dunham/Dunham Municipal Library
3638, rue Principale, Dunham, QC J0E 1M0
Tél: 450-295-2621
biblio@ville.dunham.qc.ca
www.ville.dunham.qc.ca/fr/services-2/library
www.facebook.com/centredartdedunham

Duparquet: Bibliothèque Duparquet
54, rue Principale, Duparquet, QC J0Z 1W0
Tél: 819-948-2266; *Téléc:* 819-948-2266
duparquet@reseaubiblioatnq.qc.ca
www.facebook.com/biblio56
Carmen Lacroix, Responsable

Dupuy: Bibliothèque de Dupuy
63, rue Principale, Dupuy, QC J0Z 1X0
Tél: 819-783-2595; *Téléc:* 819-783-2147
dupuy@reseaubiblioatnq.qc.ca
mabiblio.quebec/client/fr_CA/dupuy
Diane Ayotte, Responsable

Durham-Sud: Bibliothèque de Durham-Sud
77, rue de l'Église, Durham-Sud, QC J0H 2C0
Tél: 819-858-1156
biblio153@reseaubibliocqlm.qc.ca
biblietcie.ca/biblio/bibliotheque-de-durham-sud
www.facebook.com/101779388408538

Dégelis: Bibliothèque municipale de Dégelis
384, av Principale, Dégelis, QC G5T 1L3
Tél: 418-853-2380
biblio.degelis@crsbp.net
degelis.ca/culture/bibliotheque-municipale
www.facebook.com/biblio.degelis

East Broughton: Bibliothèque La Bouquinerie (East Broughton et Sacré-Coeur-de-Jésus)
372A, av du Collège, East Broughton, QC G0N 1G0
Tél: 418-427-4900
bouquinerieeb@hotmail.com
www.facebook.com/1491549084236372

East Hereford: Bibliothèque d'East Hereford
15, rue de l'Église, East Hereford, QC J0B 1S0
Tél: 819-844-2463; *Téléc:* 819-844-2463
biblio060@reseaubiblioestrie.qc.ca
easthereford.ca/fr/citoyens/bibliotheque-et-acces-internet.php

Eastman: Bibliothèque Danielle-Simard
395, rue Principale, Eastman, QC J0E 1P0
Tél: 450-297-2120; *Téléc:* 450-297-3448
biblio076@reseaubiblioestrie.qc.ca
eastman.quebec/loisirs-arts-et-culture/bibliotheque
www.facebook.com/bibliothequedeastman

Entrelacs: Bibliothèque d'Entrelacs
2351, ch Entrelacs, Entrelacs, QC J0T 2E0
Tél: 450-228-2529
biblient@entrelacs.com
www.entrelacs.com/loisirs-culture/bibliotheque

Esprit-Saint: Bibliothèque d'Esprit-Saint
1, rue des Érables, Esprit-Saint, QC G0K 1A0
Tél: 418-779-2016
biblio.esprit@crsbp.net
www.municipalite.esprit-saint.qc.ca
Tania Lord, Responsable

Fabre: Bibliothèque Le Coquelicot de Fabre
1301, rue Laurendeau, Fabre, QC J0Z 1Z0
Tél: 819-634-2745; *Téléc:* 819-634-2022
fabre@reseaubiblioatnq.qc.ca
mabiblio.quebec/client/fr_CA/fabre
Jacinthe Breton Desrochers, Responsable

Farnham: Bibliothèque municipale Louise-Hall
479, rue de l'Hôtel de Ville, Farnham, QC J2N 2H3
Tél: 450-293-3326
bibliotheque@ville.farnham.qc.ca
www.ville.farnham.qc.ca/bibliotheque-municipale-louise-hall

Fassett: Bibliothèque Fassett /
Notre-Dame-de-Bonsecours
19, rue Gendron, Fassett, QC J0V 1H0
Tél: 819-423-6943; *Téléc:* 819-423-5388
biblio@village-fassett.com
www.village-fassett.com/loisirs-et-culture/bibliotheque
Johanne Cadotte, Responsable

Ferme-Neuve: Bibliothèque de Ferme-Neuve
144, 12e rue, Ferme-Neuve, QC J0W 1C0
Tél: 819-587-3400
bibliotheque@munfn.ca
municipalite.ferme-neuve.qc.ca/bibliotheque
Renée Meilleur, Responsable

Fermont: Bibliothèque publique de Fermont
100, place Daviault, Fermont, QC G0G 1J0
Tél: 418-287-3227; *Téléc:* 418-287-3274
biblio@villedefermont.qc.ca

Forestville: Bibliothèque de Forestville
(Bibliothèque Camille-Bouchard)
#10, 10e rue, Forestville, QC G0T 1E0
Tél: 418-587-4482; *Téléc:* 418-587-2458
bibliotheque@forestville.ca
Sophie Gagnon, Responsable

Fort-Coulonge: Bibliothèque de Fort-Coulonge
134, rue Principale, Fort-Coulonge, QC J0X 1V0
Tél: 819-683-3421; *Téléc:* 819-683-3627
biblio.fc@fortcoulonge.qc.ca
www.fortcoulonge.qc.ca/-Bibliotheque-
www.facebook.com/537134273127335
Sandra Gendron, Responsable

Fortierville: Bibliothèque de Fortierville
198A, rue de la Fabrique, Fortierville, QC G0S 1J0
Tél: 819-287-4309
biblio015@reseaubibliocqlm.qc.ca
biblietcie.ca/biblio/bibliotheque-de-fortierville
www.facebook.com/721860724590057
Denise Lemay, Responsable

Fossambault-sur-le-Lac: Bibliothèque municipale de
Fossambault-sur-le-Lac ("La Source")
145, rue Gingras, Fossambault-sur-le-Lac, QC G3N 0K2
Tél: 418-875-3133
fossambault-sur-le-lac.com/bibliotheque
Monique Blouin, Responsable

Franquelin: Bibliothèque municipale de Franquelin
5, rue des Cèdres, Franquelin, QC G0H 1E0
Tél: 418-296-1421; *Téléc:* 418-296-6946
biblio.munic.franquelin@globetrotter.net
www.municipalitefranquelin.ca/loisirs-culture/bibliotheque
Diane Jourdain, Responsable

Frontenac: Bibliothèque de Frontenac
2430, rue St-Jean, Frontenac, QC G6B 2S1
Tél: 819-554-8040; *Téléc:* 819-583-0855
biblio085@reseaubiblioestrie.qc.ca
municipalitefrontenac.qc.ca/bibliotheque

Fugèreville: Bibliothèque de Fugèreville
33A, rue Principale, Fugèreville, QC J0Z 2A0
Tél: 819-748-2276; *Téléc:* 819-748-2422
fugereville@reseaubiblioatnq.qc.ca
mabiblio.quebec/client/fr_CA/fugereville
Gaétane Cloutier, Responsable

Gaspé: Bibliothèque Alma-Bourget-Costisella
10, Côte Carter, Gaspé, QC G4X 1V2
Tél: 418-368-2104
biblio.gaspe@ville.gaspe.qc.ca
ville.gaspe.qc.ca
www.facebook.com/1553422671653593

Gaspé: Bibliothèque de Cap-aux-Os
1826, boul Forillon, Gaspé, QC G4X 6L4
Tél: 418-368-2104
biblio.cao@ville.gaspe.qc.ca
ville.gaspe.qc.ca

Gaspé: Bibliothèque de L'Anse-à-Valleau
6, rue Mathurin, Gaspé, QC G4X 4A8
Tél: 418-368-2104

Gaspé: Bibliothèque de Petit-Cap
439, boul Petit-Cap, Gaspé, QC G4X 4L1
Tél: 418-368-2104
biblio.pc@ville.gaspe.qc.ca

Gaspé: Bibliothèque de Saint-Majorique
1-3, montée de Corte-Réal, Gaspé, QC G4X 6R7
Tél: 418-368-2104
biblio.stm@ville.gaspe.qc.ca
ville.gaspe.qc.ca

Gatineau: Bibliothèque municipale de Gatineau
25, rue Laurier, Gatineau, QC J8X 4A6
Tél: 819-595-7460
bibliotheque.gatineau.ca

Girardville: Bibliothèque publique de Girardville
180, rue Principale, Girardville, QC G0W 1R0
Tél: 418-258-3222
girardv@reseaubiblioslsj.qc.ca
ville.girardville.qc.ca/entreprises/bibliotheque
www.facebook.com/BibliothequeMunicipaleDeGirardville;

Godbout: Bibliothèque de Godbout
101, rue Levack, Godbout, QC G0H 1G0
Tél: 418-568-7670
biblio.godbout@hotmail.com
Marie-Anne Morin, Responsable

Gracefield: Bibliothèque de Gracefield
3, rue de la Polyvalente, Gracefield, QC J0X 1W0
Tél: 819-463-1180; *Téléc:* 819-463-4236
admgracefield@crsbpo.qc.ca
www.gracefield.ca/index.php/citoyens/loisir-et-culture
www.facebook.com/villegracefield
Stéphanie Pétrin, Responsable

Granby: Bibliothèque Paul-O.-Trépanier
11, rue Dufferin, Granby, QC J2G 4W5
Tél: 450-776-8320
bibliotheque@ville.granby.qc.ca
biblio.granby.ca
www.facebook.com/bibliogranby

Grand-Remous: Bibliothèque de Grand-Remous
1508, rte Transcanadienne, Grand-Remous, QC J0W 1E0
Tél: 819-438-2168; *Téléc:* 418-438-2364
admgrandremous@crsbpo.qc.ca
www.grandremous.ca/index.php/citoyens/la-bibliotheque
www.facebook.com/361352314969717
Cassey O'Brien, Responsable

Grande-Rivière: Bibliothèque municipale de
Grande-Rivière
210B, rue du Carrefour, Grande-Rivière, QC G0C 1V0
Tél: 418-385-3833
biblio.grande.riviere@gmail.com
www.facebook.com/bibliogr

Grande-Vallée: Bibliothèque Esdras-Minville
18A, rue St-François-Xavier est, Grande-Vallée, QC G0E 1K0
Tél: 418-393-2161
biblio@grande-vallee.ca

Grandes-Piles: Bibliothèque de Grandes-Piles
650, 4e av, Grandes-Piles, QC G0X 1H0
Tél: 819-533-3697; *Téléc:* 819-538-6947
biblio030@reseaubiblio.qc.ca
biblietcie.ca/biblio/bibliotheque-de-grandes-piles
Claudette Côté, Responsable

Grenville: Bibliothèque de Grenville
18, rue Tri-Jean, Grenville, QC J0V 1J0
Tél: 819-242-2146
biblio@grenville.ca

Grenville-sur-la-Rouge: Bibliothèque de Calumet
435, rue Principale, Grenville-sur-la-Rouge, QC J0V 1B0
Tél: 819-242-8088; *Téléc:* 819-242-1232
bibliocalumet@gslr.ca

Grenville-sur-la-Rouge: Bibliothèque de
Pointe-au-Chêne
2710A, rte 148, Grenville-sur-la-Rouge, QC J0V 1B0
Tél: 819-242-3232
bibliopointeauchêne@gslr.ca

Grondines: Bibliothèque L'Ardoise
490, ch du Roy, Grondines, QC G0A 1W0
Tél: 418-268-4375
bibligron@outlook.com
deschambault-grondines.com/citoyens/bibliotheques
www.facebook.com/1176003469110027

Gros-Morne: Bibliothèque de Gros-Morne
5, rue de l'Église, Gros-Morne, QC G0E 1L0
Tél: 418-967-0232
maisonlessentielle@gmail.com

Guyenne: Bibliothèque de Guyenne
1255-F, rang 5, Guyenne, QC J0Y 1L0
Tél: 819-732-9128; *Téléc:* 819-732-0904
guyenne@reseaubiblioatnq.qc.ca
mabiblio.quebec/client/fr_CA/guyenne
Francine Simard, Responsable

Ham-Nord: Bibliothèque de Ham-Nord
474, rue Principale, Ham-Nord, QC G0P 1A0
Tél: 819-344-2424; *Téléc:* 819-344-2806
biblio150@reseaubibliocqlm.qc.ca
biblietcie.ca/biblio/bibliotheque-de-ham-nord
www.facebook.com/bibliohamnord
Francis Montpetit, Coordonnateur

Havre-aux-Maisons: Bibliothèques de la Municipalité
des Îles-de-la-Madeleine
37, ch Central, Havre-aux-Maisons, QC G4T 5H1
Tél: 418-986-3100
bibliodesiles@muniles.ca
www.muniles.ca/loisirs-et-culture/bibliotheques-et-vie-culturelle

Havre-Saint-Pierre: Bibliothèque municipale de
Havre-St-Pierre
1045, rue Dulcinée, Havre-Saint-Pierre, QC G0G 1P0
Tél: 418-538-3301
biblio.havrest-pierre@globetrotter.net
www.facebook.com/bibliohsp
Liliane Drolet, Responsable

Hemmingford: Bibliothèque municipale
d'Hemmingford/Hemmingford Community Library
552, av Goyette, Hemmingford, QC J0L 1H0
Tél: 450-247-0010
bibliotheque@hemmingford.ca
www.hemmingford.ca/canton/services-municipaux/bibliotheque
www.facebook.com/bibliohemmingford

Henryville: Bibliothèque municipale d'Henryville
#104, 854, rue St-Jean-Baptiste, Henryville, QC J0J 1E0
Tél: 450-346-4116
biblio@henryville.ca
www.facebook.com/bibliotheque.henryville;

Honfleur: Bibliothèque La Livrothèque
320, rue Saint-Jean, Honfleur, QC G0R 1N0
Tél: 418-885-8212; *Téléc:* 418-885-9195
livro@globetrotter.net

Huberdeau: Bibliothèque d'Huberdeau
101, rue Du Pont, Huberdeau, QC J0T 1G0
Tél: 819-681-3377
biblio@municipalite.huberdeau.qc.ca

Huntingdon: Little Green Library/La Petite
Bibliothèque Verte
#103, 4, rue Lorne, Huntingdon, QC J0S 1H0
Tél: 450-264-4872
pbv.lgl@gmail.com
www.pbv-lgl.org
www.facebook.com/PetiteBibliothequeVerteLittleGreenLibrary
Catherine Turgeon, President

Hérouxville: Bibliothèque de Hérouxville
1060, rue Saint-Pierre, Hérouxville, QC G0X 1J0
Tél: 418-365-7337
biblio090@reseaubibliocqlm.qc.ca
biblietcie.ca/biblio/bibliotheque-de-herouxville-la-source
www.facebook.com/451340661652376
Julie L'Heureux, Responsable

Inverness: Bibliothèque de Inverness
(L'Inverthèque)
1801, rue Dublin, Inverness, QC G0S 1K0
Tél: 418-453-2512
biblio145@reseaubibliocqlm.qc.ca
biblietcie.ca/biblio/bibliotheque-de-inverness-linvertheque
www.facebook.com/BibliothequeInverness

Issoudun: Bibliothèque La Rêverie
(Notre-Dame-de-Sacré-Coeur-d'Issoudun)
268, rue Principale, Issoudun, QC G0S 1L0
Tél: 418-728-9061; *Téléc:* 418-728-2303
biblisso@globetrotter.net
www.facebook.com/Bibliotheque.la.reverie.issoudun

Johnville: Bibliothèque de Johnville
62B, ch Jordan Hill, Johnville, QC J0B 2A0
Tél: 873-623-8555
biblio086@reseaubiblioestrie.qc.ca

Joliette: Bibliothèque Rina-Lasnier
57, rue Saint-Pierre sud, Joliette, QC J6E 5Y5
Tél: 450-755-6400
biblio@biblio.rinalasnier.qc.ca
catalogue.biblio.rinalasnier.qc.ca
www.facebook.com/bibliorinalasnier
Suzie Charbonneau, Directrice générale

Kazabazua: Bibliothèque de Kazabazua
373, rte 105, Kazabazua, QC J0X 1X0
Tél: 819-467-2852; *Téléc:* 819-467-5746
admkaz@crsbpo.qc.ca
www.kazabazua.ca/fr/bibliotheque.shtml
Guylaine Crites, Responsable

Kiamika: Bibliothèque de Kiamika
3, ch Valiquette, Kiamika, QC J0W 1G0
Tél: 819-585-3225
biblio@kiamika.ca
www.kiamika.ca/services-municipaux/bibliotheque.html

Kingsey Falls: Bibliothèque de Kingsey Falls
13, rue Caron, Kingsey Falls, QC J0A 1B0
Tél: 819-363-3818
biblio040@reseaubibliocqlm.qc.ca
biblietcie.ca/biblio/bibliotheque-de-kingsey-falls
www.facebook.com/1551868258471183

Kirkland: Bibliothèque de Kirkland
17100, boul Hymus, Kirkland, QC H9J 2W2
Tél: 514-630-2726; *Téléc:* 514-630-2716
biblioweb.ville.kirkland.qc.ca
Julie Filion, Chef de division
jfilion@ville.kirkland.qc.ca
514-694-4100 ext. 3200

L'Anse-au-Griffon: Bibliothèque de
L'Anse-au-Griffon
615, boul du Griffon, L'Anse-au-Griffon, QC G4X 6A5
Tél: 418-368-2104
biblio.aag@ville.gaspe.qc.ca
www.facebook.com/BibliothequeMunicipaleDeLAnseAuGriffon

L'Anse-Saint-Jean: Bibliothèque publique de
L'Anse-St-Jean
3, rue du Couvent, L'Anse-Saint-Jean, QC G0V 1J0
Tél: 418-272-2633
anse@reseaubiblioslsj.qc.ca

L'Ascension: Bibliothèque de l'Ascension
58, rue de l'Hôtel-de-Ville, L'Ascension, QC J0T 1W0
Tél: 819-275-3027; *Téléc:* 819-275-3489
bibliotheque@municipalite-lascension.qc.ca
www.municipalite-lascension.qc.ca/bibliotheque
Lyne Beaulieu, Responsable

L'Ascension: Bibliothèque publique de L'Ascension
900, 4e av est, L'Ascension, QC G0W 1Y0
Tél: 418-347-3482; *Téléc:* 418-347-4253
ascens@reseaubiblioslsj.qc.ca

L'Assomption: Bibliothèque Christian-Roy
375, rue St-Pierre, L'Assomption, QC J5W 1V1
Tél: 450-589-5671; *Téléc:* 450-589-4512
bibliotheque@ville.lassomption.qc.ca
www.ville.lassomption.qc.ca/bibliotheque

L'Isle-aux-Allumettes: Bibliothèque de
L'Isle-aux-Allumettes / Sheenboro
104, Notre-Dame, L'Isle-aux-Allumettes, QC J0X 1M0
Tél: 819-689-2488; *Téléc:* 819-689-5102
municipalschoollibrary@mrcpontiac.qc.ca
www.isle-aux-allumettes.com/bibliotheque
Lorie Keon-Leahey, Responsable

L'Isle-aux-Coudres: Bibliothèque 'Pour la suite du
monde'
1026, ch des Coudriers, L'Isle-aux-Coudres, QC G0A 3J0
Tél: 418-760-1062; *Téléc:* 418-760-1061
psdm@municipaliteiac.ca
www.facebook.com/1080107452108968

L'Islet: Bibliothèque Jean-Paul-Bourque
(L'Islet-sur-Mer)
16, ch des Pionniers est, L'Islet, QC G0R 2B0
Tél: 418-247-7576; *Téléc:* 418-247-5009
www.facebook.com/jeanpaulbourquedelisletsurmer

L'Islet: Bibliothèque Léon-Laberge
#1, 284, boul Nilus-Leclerc, L'Islet, QC G0R 2C0
Tél: 418-247-5345; *Téléc:* 418-247-5085

L'Épiphanie: Bibliothèque de L'Épiphanie
83, rue Amireault, L'Épiphanie, QC J5X 1A1
Tél: 450-588-4470
biblio@lepiphanie.ca
ville-de-lepiphanie.c4di.qc.ca:8213

La Conception: Bibliothèque de La Conception
1373, boul du Centenaire, La Conception, QC J0T 1M0
Tél: 819-681-3016
biblio@municipalite.laconception.qc.ca
www.facebook.com/116504845226551

La Corne: Bibliothèque municipale de la Corne
324, rte 111, La Corne, QC J0Y 1R0
Tél: 819-799-3571
lacorne@reseaubiblioatnq.qc.ca
lacorne.ca/les-comites/bibliotheque
www.facebook.com/bibliolacorne
Chantal Lessard, Responsable

La Doré: Bibliothèque publique de la Doré
4450, rue des Peupliers, La Doré, QC G8J 1E5
Tél: 418-256-3545; *Téléc:* 418-307-8003
ladore@reseaubiblioslsj.qc.ca

La Macaza: Bibliothèque de La Macaza
53, rue des Pionniers, La Macaza, QC J0T 1R0
Tél: 819-275-2077; *Téléc:* 819-275-3429
biblio@munilamacaza.ca
www.munilamacaza.ca/bibliotheque
www.facebook.com/545160822205187
Isabelle Robert, Responsable

La Malbaie: Bibliothèque Laure-Conan
395, rue St-Etienne, La Malbaie, QC G5A 1S8
Tél: 418-665-3747; *Téléc:* 418-665-6481
www.ville.lamalbaie.qc.ca/loisirs-culture/bibliotheques
www.facebook.com/BibliothequeLaMalbaie

La Minerve: Bibliothèque de La Minerve
100, ch des Fondateurs, La Minerve, QC J0T 1S0
Tél: 819-681-3380; *Téléc:* 819-274-2031
biblio@municipalite.laminerve.qc.ca
www.municipalite.laminerve.qc.ca/bibliotheque-de-la-minerve
www.facebook.com/1423606051235164

La Motte: Bibliothèque de La Motte
349, ch St-Luc, La Motte, QC J0Y 1T0
Tél: 819-732-0505; *Téléc:* 819-727-4248
lamotte@reseaubiblioatnq.qc.ca
mabiblio.quebec/client/fr_CA/lamotte
Nicole Richard, Responsable

La Patrie: Bibliothèque de La Patrie
44-2, rue Garneau, La Patrie, QC J0B 1Y0
Tél: 819-560-8520; *Téléc:* 819-888-2697
biblio041@reseaubiblioestrie.qc.ca
www.lapatrie.ca/fr/bibliotheque.htm
Paméla Blais, Responsable
Lisette Blouin, Responsable

La Pocatière: Bibliothèque municipale de La
Pocatière
#4, 900, 6e av, La Pocatière, QC G0R 1Z0
Tél: 418-856-3394
biblio@lapocatiere.ca
www.lapocatiere.ca/loisirs-et-culture/bibliotheque-municipale
www.facebook.com/BiblioLaPoc
Julie Garon, Responsable

La Prairie: Bibliothèque Léo-Lecavalier
Centre multifonctionnel Guy-Dupré, 500, rue Saint-Laurent,
La Prairie, QC J5R 5X2
Tél: 450-444-6710; *Téléc:* 450-444-6708
biblio@ville.laprairie.qc.ca
catalogue.ville.laprairie.qc.ca/in/fr

La Pêche: Bibliothèque de Sainte-Cécile-de-Masham
(La Pêche)
5, rte Principale ouest, La Pêche, QC J0X 2W0
Tél: 819-456-2627; *Téléc:* 819-456-4228
admmasham@crsbpo.qc.ca
www.villelapeche.qc.ca/fr/vie-municipale/bibliotheques
Gisèle Duguay, Responsable

La Pêche: Bibliothèque Lac-des-Loups (La Pêche)
275, rue Pontbriand, La Pêche, QC J0X 3K0
Tél: 819-456-3222
admlac-des-loups@crsbpo.qc.ca
www.villelapeche.qc.ca/fr/vie-municipale/bibliotheques

Carole Renaud, Responsable

La Reine: Bibliothèque La Reine
1, 3e av ouest, La Reine, QC J0Z 2L0
Tél: 819-947-5271; *Téléc:* 819-947-5271
lareine@reseaubiblioatnq.qc.ca
Solange Perreault, Responsable

La Sarre: Bibliothèque municipale Richelieu de La
Sarre
195, rue Principale, La Sarre, QC J9Z 1Y3
Tél: 819-333-2282
biblio@ville.lasarre.qc.ca
www.ville.lasarre.qc.ca

La Trinité-des-Monts: Bibliothèque de La
Trinité-des-Monts
12, rue Principale ouest, La Trinité-des-Monts, QC G0K 1B0
Tél: 418-779-2421
biblio.trinite@crsbp.net
www.la-trinite-des-monts.ca/Citoyens.php
Johanne Frappier, Responsable

La Tuque: Bibliothèque municipale de La Tuque
(Annie-St-Arneault)
575, rue St-Eugène, La Tuque, QC G9X 1L5
Tél: 819-523-3100; *Téléc:* 819-523-4487
bibliotheque@ville.latuque.qc.ca
www.ville.latuque.qc.ca
www.facebook.com/bibliotheque.latuque

Labelle: Bibliothèque de Labelle
7393, boul du Curé-Labelle, Labelle, QC J0T 1H0
Tél: 819-681-3371; *Téléc:* 819-686-3820
biblio@municipalite.labelle.qc.ca
www.municipalite.labelle.qc.ca/services-municipaux/bibliotheque
Nathalie Robson, Directrice

Labrecque: Bibliothèque publique de Labrecque
3425, rue Ambroise, Labrecque, QC G0W 2S0
Tél: 418-481-1618
labrecque@reseaubiblioslsj.qc.ca
www.ville.labrecque.qc.ca/bibliotheque-municipale
www.facebook.com/113461298682613

Lac-au-Saumon: Bibliothèque Bertrand-Leblanc
20, Place de la Municipalité, Lac-au-Saumon, QC G0J 1M0
Tél: 418-778-3378
biblio.saumon@crsbp.net
municipalites-du-quebec.ca/lac-au-saumon

Lac-aux-Sables: Bibliothèque de Lac-aux-Sables
820, rue Saint-Alphonse, Lac-aux-Sables, QC G0X 1M0
Tél: 418-336-3299
biblio045@reseaubibliocqlm.qc.ca
biblietcie.ca/bibliotheque-de-lac-aux-sables-rita-brouillette
www.facebook.com/BiblioRitaBrouillette

Lac-Beauport: Bibliothèque municipale L'Écrin
50, ch du Village, Lac-Beauport, QC G3B 1R2
Tél: 418-849-7141
bibliothequeecrin@lacbeauport.net
lac-beauport.quebec

Lac-Bouchette: Bibliothèque publique de
Lac-Bouchette
#110, 258, rue Principale, Lac-Bouchette, QC G0W 1V0
Tél: 418-348-6306
lac.bouchett@reseaubiblioslsj.qc.ca

Lac-Brome: Bibliothèque Commémorative
Pettes/Pettes Memorial Library
276, ch Knowlton, Lac-Brome, QC J0E 1V0
Tél: 450-243-6128
pettes.bpl@gmail.com
www.pettes.ca
www.facebook.com/petteslibrary
Jana Valasek, Directrice générale
jana@pettes.ca

Lac-des-Aigles: Bibliothèque Lac-des-Aigles
75A, rue Principale, Lac-des-Aigles, QC G0K 1V0
Tél: 418-779-2300
biblio.aigles@crsbp.net
www.lacdesaigles.ca/sports-culture-et-loisirs/bibliotheque
www.facebook.com/bibliothequelacdesaigles

Lac-des-Plages: Bibliothèque Lac-des-Plages
2053, ch Tour-du-Lac, Lac-des-Plages, QC J0T 1K0
Tél: 819-426-2391; *Téléc:* 819-426-2085
bibliodesplages@crsbpo.qc.ca
lacdesplages.com/ressources-et-communaute/bibliotheque
Nicole Bourgeois, Responsable

Lac-des-Seize-Iles: Bibliothèque de
Lac-des-Seize-Iles
47, rue de l'Église, Lac-des-Seize-Iles, QC J0T 2M0
Tél: 450-226-6848
bibliotheque@lac-des-seize-iles.com
www.lac-des-seize-iles.com/loisirs-et-culture/bibliotheque

Lac-des-Écorces: Bibliothèque de Lac-des-Écorces
570, boul St-François, Lac-des-Écorces, QC J0W 1H0
Tél: 819-585-2555
bibliolde@lacdesecorces.ca
www.lacdesecorces.ca/bibliotheques

Lac-des-Écorces: Bibliothèque de Val-Barrette
135, rue St-Joseph, Lac-des-Écorces, QC J0W 1H0
Tél: 819-585-3131
bibliovb@lacdesecorces.ca
www.lacdesecorces.ca/bibliotheque
www.facebook.com/biblio.valbarrette

Lac-Drolet: Bibliothèque de Lac-Drolet
685A, rue Principale, Lac-Drolet, QC G0Y 1C0
Tél: 819-549-2332; *Téléc:* 819-549-1012
biblio013@reseaubiblioestrie.qc.ca
lacdrolet.ca/loisirs-et-culture
Josée Bégin, Responsable

Lac-du-Cerf: Bibliothèque de Lac-du-Cerf
15, rue Émard, Lac-du-Cerf, QC J0W 1S1
Tél: 819-597-4163; *Téléc:* 819-597-4163
biblio@lac-du-cerf.ca
www.lacducerf.ca/bibliotheque
Rolande Huberdeau, Responsable

Lac-Etchemin: Bibliothèque L'Élan
208A, 2e av, Lac-Etchemin, QC G0R 1S0
Tél: 418-625-5325; *Téléc:* 418-625-3175
biblio@sogetel.net

Lac-Mégantic: Médiathèque municipale Nelly-Arcan
3700, rue Lemieux, Lac-Mégantic, QC G6B 1S7
Tél: 819-583-0876
info@mediathequenellyarcan.ca
www.mediathequenellyarcan.ca
www.facebook.com/mediathequenellyarcan
Daniel Lavoie, Directeur et Bibliothécaire
directeur@mediathequenellyarcan.ca
819-583-0876 ext. 24
Christyne Lafond, Technicienne en documentation
christyne.lafond@mediathequenellyarcan.ca
819-583-0876 ext. 23
Annie Trudel, Technicienne en documentation
annie.trudel@mediathequenellyarcan.ca
819-583-0876 ext. 25

Lac-Saguay: Bibliothèque de Lac-Saguay
257A, rte 117, Lac-Saguay, QC J0W 1L0
Tél: 819-278-3972
biblio@lacsaguay.qc.ca
www.lacsaguay.qc.ca/bibliotheque.html

Lac-Sainte-Marie: Bibliothèque municipale de
Lac-Sainte-Marie
121, ch Lac-Sainte-Marie, Lac-Sainte-Marie, QC J0X 1Z0
Tél: 819-467-5437; *Téléc:* 819-467-4826
admstemarie@crsbpo.qc.ca
www.lac-sainte-marie.com/fr/bibliotheque_de_lac-sainte-marie.php
Marie-Pold Lacaille, Responsable

Lac-Supérieur: Bibliothèque de Lac-Supérieur
1277, ch du Lac-Supérieur, Lac-Supérieur, QC J0T 1J0
Tél: 819-681-3370; *Téléc:* 819-688-3010
biblio@muni.lacsuperieur.qc.ca
www.muni.lacsuperieur.qc.ca/bibliotheque
www.facebook.com/biblioLacSuperieur
Johanne Nolet, Responsable

Lac-à-la-Croix: Bibliothèque publique de
Lac-à-la-Croix
#002, 335, rue de Rouillac, Lac-à-la-Croix, QC G8G 2B5
Tél: 418-349-8495
lac.croix@reseaubiblioslsj.qc.ca

Lac-Édouard: Bibliothèque de Lac-Édouard
195, rue Principale, Lac-Édouard, QC G0X 3N0
Tél: 819-653-2238
biblio024@reseaubibliocqlm.qc.ca
biblietcie.ca/biblio/bibliotheque-de-lac-edouard-marie-desbiens
www.facebook.com/320047861504727

Lachute: Bibliothèque Jean-Marc-Belzile
378, rue Principale, Lachute, QC J8H 1Y2
Tél: 450-562-4578; 450-562-1431
biblio@ville.lachute.qc.ca
www.ville.lachute.qc.ca/biblio/votre-bibliotheque
www.facebook.com/BiblioLachute
Claudia Tremblay, Chef de service de la bibliothèque et des
activités culturelles
450-562-3781 ext. 255
Chantal Bélisle, Technicienne en documentation
cbelisle@ville.lachute.qc.ca
450-562-3781 ext. 214

Lacolle: Bibliothèque municipale de Lacolle
3, rue du Collège, Lacolle, QC J0J 1J0
Tél: 450-515-8050
biblio@lacolle.com
www.lacolle.com/services/?id=45

Laforce: Bibliothèque Laforce
703, rue Principale, Laforce, QC J0Z 2J0
Tél: 819-722-2461; *Téléc:* 819-722-2462
laforce@reseaubiblioatnq.qc.ca
Ginette Morin, Responsable

Lamarche: Bibliothèque publique de Lamarche
102, rue Principale, Lamarche, QC G0W 1X0
Tél: 418-481-2861
lamarche@reseaubiblioslsj.qc.ca

Lambton: Bibliothèque de Lambton
215, rue de l'Aréna, Lambton, QC G0M 1H0
Tél: 418-486-2750; *Téléc:* 418-486-7440
biblio005@reseaubiblioestrie.qc.ca
www.lambton.ca/le-citoyen/arts-et-culture/bibliotheque
Claire Boulanger, Responsable

Landrienne: Bibliothèque Landrienne
158, rue Principale est, Landrienne, QC J0Y 1V0
Tél: 819-732-4357; *Téléc:* 819-732-3866
landrienne@reseaubiblioatnq.qc.ca
www.landrienne.com/cultures-et-loisirs/bibliotheque
Linda Perron, Responsable

Lanoraie: Bibliothèque de Lanoraie
(Ginette-Rivard-Tremblay)
#100, 12, rue Louis-Joseph-Doucet, Lanoraie, QC J0K 1E0
Tél: 450-887-1100; *Téléc:* 450-836-5229
biblio060@reseaubibliocqlm.qc.ca
www.lanoraie.ca/fr/bibliotheque-ginette-rivard-tremblay
Marie-France Letreiz, Responsable
mfletreiz@lanoraie.ca
450-887-1100 ext. 3017

Larouche: Bibliothèque publique de Larouche
#214, 610, rue Lévesque, Larouche, QC G0W 1Z0
Tél: 418-695-2201
larouche@reseaubiblioslsj.qc.ca
www.facebook.com/547293838619940
Sylvie Voisine, Responsable

Latulipe: Bibliothèque Latulipe-et-Gaboury
5, rue du Carrefour nord, Latulipe, QC J0Z 2N0
Tél: 819-629-2472
latulipe@reseaubiblioatnq.qc.ca
Daniel Gauthier, Responsable

Laurier-Station: Bibliothèque Wilfrid Laurier
147, rue Saint-Denis, Laurier-Station, QC G0S 1N0
Tél: 418-728-5939; *Téléc:* 418-728-4801
bwlaurier@globetrotter.net
www.ville.laurier-station.qc.ca/bibliotheque
www.facebook.com/bibliothequelaurier;

Laurierville: Bibliothèque de Laurierville
148A, rue Grenier, Laurierville, QC G0S 1P0
Tél: 819-365-4646
biblio122@reseaubibliocqlm.qc.ca
biblietcie.ca/biblio/bibliotheque-de-laurierville
Dominique Martel, Coordonnatrice

Laval: Bibliothèques Ville de Laval
1535, boul Chomedey, 1e étage, Laval, QC H7V 3Z4
Tél: 450-978-6088; *Téléc:* 450-978-5835
www.biblio.ville.laval.qc.ca
www.facebook.com/bibliothequeslaval

Lavaltrie: Bibliothèque de Lavaltrie
241, rue Saint-Antoine nord, Lavaltrie, QC J5T 2G7
Tél: 450-586-2921; *Téléc:* 450-586-4060
bibliotheque@ville.lavaltrie.qc.ca
www.ville.lavaltrie.qc.ca/services-citoyens/bibliotheque

Laverlochère: Bibliothèque de Laverlochère
3, rue Principale sud, Laverlochère, QC J0Z 2P0
Tél: 819-765-2549; *Téléc:* 819-765-2089
laverlochere@reseaubiblioatnq.qc.ca
mabiblio.quebec/client/fr_CA/laverlochere
Lauriane Rivest, Responsable

Lebel-sur-Quévillon: Bibliothèque
Lebel-sur-Quévillon
500, Place Quévillon, Lebel-sur-Quévillon, QC J0Y 1X0
Tél: 819-755-4826; *Téléc:* 819-755-8124
biblio@lsq.quebec
Ghislaine Blouin, Responsable

Lefebvre: Bibliothèque de Lefebvre
200, 10e rang, Lefebvre, QC J0H 2C0
Tél: 819-394-3354; *Téléc:* 819-394-2782
municipalites-du-quebec.ca/lefebvre/bibliotheque.php

Lejeune: Bibliothèque de Lejeune
69, rue de la Grande-Coulée, Lejeune, QC G0L 1S0
Tél: 418-855-2428
biblio.lejeune@crsbp.net
www.municipalitelejeune.com

Lemieux: Bibliothèque de Lemieux
526, rue de l'Eglise, Lemieux, QC G0X 1S0
Tél: 819-283-2506; *Téléc:* 819-283-2029
biblio138@reseaubibliocqlm.qc.ca
www.municipalitelemieux.ca/?page=bibliotheque-de-lemieux

Les Bergeronnes: Bibliothèque Les Bergeronnes
514, rue du Boisé, Les Bergeronnes, QC G0T 1G0
Tél: 418-232-1165
bergeronnes.net/bibliothèque-1
www.facebook.com/2011242039203282
Sara Brisson, Responsable

Les Coteaux: Bibliothèque municipale Des Coteaux
65, rte 338, Les Coteaux, QC J7X 1A2
Tél: 450-267-1414; *Téléc:* 450-267-3532
bibliodescoteaux@videotron.ca
www.facebook.com/409988992541789

Les Cèdres: Bibliothèque des Cèdres (Bibliothèque
Gaby-Farmer-Denis)
141, rue Valade, Les Cèdres, QC J7T 1S9
Tél: 450-452-4250
bibliogabyfarmerdenis@ville.lescedres.qc.ca
www.facebook.com/bibliolescedres
Odette Marois, Responsable
omarois@ville.lescedres.qc.ca
450-452-4250 ext. 222

Les Escoumins: Bibliothèque municipale des
Escoumins
2, rue de la Rivère, Les Escoumins, QC G0T 1K0
Tél: 581-322-1080; *Téléc:* 418-233-3273
www.escoumins.ca/citoyens/loisirs-et-cultures/bibliotheque
Odile Boisvert, Responsable
odilepoirier01@hotmail.com

Les Méchins: Bibliothèque municipale de Les
Méchins
164, rue Principale, Les Méchins, QC G0J 1T0
Tél: 418-729-1346

Les Éboulements: Bibliothèque
Félix-Antoine-Savard
#210, 2335, rte du Fleuve, Les Éboulements, QC G0A 2M0
Tél: 418-489-2990; *Téléc:* 418-489-2989
bibliotheque@leseboulements.com
www.mabibliotheque.ca/leseboulements
www.facebook.com/273864379927414

Lingwick: Bibliothèque de Lingwick Canton
72, rte 108, Lingwick, QC J0B 2Z0
Tél: 819-560-8422; *Téléc:* 819-877-3315
biblio050@reseaubiblioestrie.qc.ca
www.cantondelingwick.com

Longue-Pointe-de-Mingan: Bibliothèque de
Longue-Pointe-de-Mingan
878, ch du Roi, Longue-Pointe-de-Mingan, QC G0G 1V0
Tél: 418-949-2437; *Téléc:* 418-949-2166
biblipte@hotmail.com
www.facebook.com/114682923245575
Pauline Vachon, Responsable

Longueuil: Réseau des bibliothèques publiques de Longueuil
1100, rue Beauregard, Longueuil, QC J4K 2L1
Tél: 450-463-7180
www.longueuil.quebec/bibliotheques
www.facebook.com/BibliothequesLongueuil

Lorraine: Bibliothèque municipale de Lorraine
31, boul de Gaulle, Lorraine, QC J6Z 3W9
Tél: 450-621-1071
bibliotheque@ville.lorraine.qc.ca
www.ville.lorraine.qc.ca/loisirs-et-culture/bibliotheque
Véronique Bergeron, Chef de service

Lorrainville: Bibliothèque Lorrainville
8, rue de l'Église sud, Lorrainville, QC J0Z 2R0
Tél: 819-625-2401; *Téléc:* 819-625-2380
lorrainville@reseaubiblioatnq.qc.ca
www.facebook.com/BiblioLorrainville
Josée Beauregard, Responsable

Lotbinière: Bibliothèque 'Au fil des pages'
#100, 30, rue Joly, Lotbinière, QC G0S 1S0
Tél: 418-796-2912; *Téléc:* 418-796-2198
bibliotheque.lotbiniere@gmail.com
www.mabibliotheque.ca/lotbiniere
www.facebook.com/1039885672716432

Lourdes-de-Blanc-Sablon: Bibliothèque de Blanc-Sablon
20, rue Mgr Scheffer, Lourdes-de-Blanc-Sablon, QC G0G 1W0
Tél: 418-461-2030; *Téléc:* 418-461-2529
scheffer@globetrotter.net
Vincent Joncas, Responsable

Low: Bibliothèque municipale de Low
4A, ch D'Amour, Low, QC J0X 2C0
Tél: 819-422-3218; *Téléc:* 819-422-3796
admlow@crsbpo.qc.ca
www.lowquebec.ca/pages_fr/loisirs_et_culture.php
Lise Legros, Responsable

Lyster: Bibliothèque de Lyster (Graziella-Ouellet)
2375, rue Bécancour, Lyster, QC G0S 1V0
Tél: 819-389-5787; *Téléc:* 819-389-5981
biblio144@reseaubibliocqlm.qc.ca
lyster.ca/loisir-sport-et-culture/bibliotheque-graziella-ouellet
Pierrette Fradette, Coordonnatrice

Lévis: Bibliothèques Lévis
7, rue Monseigneur-Gosselin, Lévis, QC G6V 5J9
Tél: 418-835-8570
bibliolevis@ville.levis.qc.ca
www.ville.levis.qc.ca/culture/bibliotheques

Macamic: Bibliothèque de Colombourg
705, Rang 2-3 ouest, Macamic, QC J0Z 2S0
Tél: 819-333-5783; *Téléc:* 819-333-1075
colombourg@reseaubiblioatnq.qc.ca
mabiblio.quebec/client/fr_CA/colombourg
Noëlla Royer, Responsable

Macamic: Bibliothèque municipale Desjardins
6, 7e av est, Macamic, QC J0Z 2S0
Tél: 819-782-4604; *Téléc:* 819-782-4464
macamic@reseaubiblioatnq.qc.ca
mabiblio.quebec/client/fr_CA/macamic
www.facebook.com/340634119469188
Sylvie Paquin, Responsable

Madeleine-Centre: Bibliothèque Jacques-Ferron
104, rte Principale, Madeleine-Centre, QC G0E 1P0
Tél: 418-393-3269

Magog: Bibliothèque municipale Memphrémagog
90, rue Saint-David, Magog, QC J1X 0H9
Tél: 819-843-1330
biblio@ville.magog.qc.ca
www.ville.magog.qc.ca/bibliotheque
Françoise Ménard, Chef de section, bibliothèque Memphrémagog
f.menard@ville.magog.qc.ca
819-843-3333 ext. 897

Malartic: Bibliothèque Malartic
640, rue de la Paix, Malartic, QC J0Y 1Z0
Tél: 819-757-3611; *Téléc:* 819-757-3084
malartic@reseaubiblioatnq.qc.ca
mabiblio.quebec/client/fr_CA/malartic
Cindy-Kim Turpin, Responsable

Mandeville: Bibliothèque municipale de Mandeville
162, rue Desjardins, Mandeville, QC J0K 1L0
Tél: 450-835-2055
bibliotheque@mandeville.ca
www.mandeville.ca/Bibliotheque-municipale-de-mandeville.php
Monique Bessette, Coordonnatrice

Maniwaki: Bibliothèque de Maniwaki / Déléage / Egan-Sud
14, rue Comeau, Maniwaki, QC J9E 2R8
Tél: 819-449-2738; *Téléc:* 819-449-7626
admmaniwaki@crsbpo.qc.ca
Colette Archambault, Responsable

Manseau: Bibliothèque de Manseau
200A, rue Roux, Manseau, QC G0X 1V0
Tél: 819-356-2450
biblio084@reseaubibliocqlm.qc.ca
municipalites-du-quebec.org/manseau/loisirs-culture.php
Denise Bernier, Responsable

Mansfield: Bibliothèque Mansfield-et-Pontefract
314, rue Principale, Mansfield, QC J0X 1R0
Tél: 819-683-3491; *Téléc:* 819-683-3590
admmansfield@crsbpo.qc.ca
www.facebook.com/BiblioMansfield
Martine Laroche, Responsable

Maria: Bibliothèque Noël-Audet
#475, 1, rue des Chardonnerets, Maria, QC G0C 1Y0
Tél: 418-759-3282
biblio@mariaquebec.com
www.mariaquebec.com/bibliotheque-noel-audet
Sylvie Boudreau, Responsable

Marieville: Bibliothèque Commémorative Desautels
603, rue Claude-De Ramezay, Marieville, QC J3M 1J7
Tél: 450-460-4444; *Téléc:* 450-460-3526
biblio-marieville@ville.marieville.qc.ca
www.ville.marieville.qc.ca/fr/loisirs-et-culture/bibliotheque

Marsoui: Bibliothèque Mariette-Lever
8, rte Principale est, Marsoui, QC G0E 1S0
Tél: 418-288-5508
Anne Sohier, Responsable
annesohier@hotmail.com

Marston: Bibliothèque de Marston
156, rte 263 sud, Marston, QC G0Y 1G0
Tél: 819-583-0425; *Téléc:* 819-583-6604
biblio107@reseaubiblioestrie.qc.ca
www.munmarston.qc.ca/pages/bibliotheque

Martinville: Bibliothèque de Martinville
223, rue Principale est, Martinville, QC J0B 2A0
Tél: 819-501-8585
biblio066@reseaubiblioestrie.qc.ca
municipalites-du-quebec.ca/martinville/bibliotheque.php

Mascouche: Bibliothèque Bernard-Patenaude
3015, av des Ancêtres, Mascouche, QC J7K 1X6
Tél: 450-474-4159
biblio@ville.mascouche.qc.ca
ville.mascouche.qc.ca/culture-vie-communautaire/bibliotheque

Mashteuiatsh: Bibliothèque publique de Mashteuiatsh
507, rue Uapileu, Mashteuiatsh, QC G0W 2H0
Tél: 418-275-5386; *Téléc:* 418-275-0097
masht@reseaubiblioslsj.qc.ca

Maskinongé: Bibliothèque de Maskinongé
11, rue Marcel, Maskinongé, QC J0K 1N0
Tél: 819-227-4656
biblio059@reseaubibliocqlm.qc.ca
biblietcie.ca/biblio/bibliotheque-de-maskinonge
www.facebook.com/1464514637112759
Nicole Dessailliers, Responsable

Massueville: Bibliothèque municipale de Massueville et St-Aimé
846A, rue de l'Église, Massueville, QC J0G 1K0
Tél: 450-788-3120
bibliosam@massueville.net
www.facebook.com/bibliodeSAM

Matane: Bibliothèque municipale de Matane (Fonds de Solidarité FTQ)
Complexe culturel Joseph-Rouleau, 520, av Saint-Jérôme, Matane, QC G4W 3B5
Tél: 418-562-9233; *Téléc:* 418-566-2064
www.ville.matane.qc.ca
www.facebook.com/BiblioFTQMatane

Christiane Melançon, Responsable
c.melancon@ville.matane.qc.ca

Matapédia: Bibliothèque de Matapédia
5, rue de l'Hôtel-de-Ville, Matapédia, QC G0J 1V0
Tél: 418-865-2717
bbomatap@globetrotter.net

Mercier: Bibliothèque municipale de Mercier
16, rue du Parc, Mercier, QC J6R 1E5
Tél: 450-691-6090; *Téléc:* 450-691-6529
bibliotheque@ville.mercier.qc.ca
www.ville.mercier.qc.ca/loisirs-et-culture/bibliotheque

Messines: Bibliothèque de Messines
3, ch de la Ferme, Messines, QC J0X 2J0
Tél: 819-465-2637; *Téléc:* 819-465-2943
admmessines@crsbpo.qc.ca
www.messines.ca/fr/services/bibliotheque-municipale
www.facebook.com/311882156290750
Claire Lacroix, Responsable

Milan: Bibliothèque municipale de Milan
405, rang Sainte-Marie, Milan, QC G0Y 1E0
Tél: 819-657-4527; *Téléc:* 819-657-2987
biblio023@reseaubiblioestrie.qc.ca
www.munmilan.qc.ca/indexFr.asp?numero=31
Louise Denis, Responsable

Mirabel: Bibliothèque municipale de Mirabel
17710, rue du Val-d'Espoir, Mirabel, QC J7J 1V7
Tél: 450-475-2011
biblio@ville.mirabel.qc.ca
mirabel.ca/bibliotheque

Mont-Carmel: Bibliothèque Odile-Boucher
22, rue de la Fabrique, Mont-Carmel, QC G0L 1W0
Tél: 418-498-2050
mont-carmel.ca/services-aux-citoyens/bibliotheque-odile-boucher
Huguette Massé, Responsable

Mont-Joli: Bibliothèque Jean-Louis-Desrosiers de Mont-Joli
1477, boul Jacques-Cartier, Mont-Joli, QC G5H 3L3
Tél: 418-775-7285
bibliomj@ville.mont-joli.qc.ca
ville.mont-joli.qc.ca

Mont-Laurier: Bibliothèque municipale de Mont-Laurier
385, rue Du Pont, Mont-Laurier, QC J9L 2R5
Tél: 819-623-1221
bibliotheque@villemontlaurier.qc.ca
biblio.villemontlaurier.qc.ca
www.facebook.com/bibliothequesMontLaurier

Mont-Saint-Hilaire: Bibliothèque Armand-Cardinal
150, rue du Centre Civique, Mont-Saint-Hilaire, QC J3H 5Z5
Tél: 450-467-2854
bibliotheque@villemsh.ca
www.villemsh.ca
www.facebook.com/BibliothequeArmandCardinal;

Mont-Saint-Michel: Bibliothèque de Mont-Saint-Michel
73, rue Principale, Mont-Saint-Michel, QC J0W 1P0
Tél: 819-587-3093; *Téléc:* 819-587-3781
biblio@montsaintmichel.ca
www.montsaintmichel.ca/bibliotheque
www.facebook.com/bibliomontsaintmichel
Marlène Paquin, Responsable

Mont-Saint-Pierre: Bibliothèque Kevin Pouliot-Bernatchez
102, rue Prudent Cloutier, Mont-Saint-Pierre, QC G0E 1V0
Tél: 418-797-2898
www.facebook.com/bibliothequemsp

Mont-Tremblant: Bibliothèque du Couvent
1875, ch du Village, Mont-Tremblant, QC J8E 1K4
Tél: 819-425-8614
cultureetloisirs@villedemont-tremblant.qc.ca

Mont-Tremblant: Bibliothèque Samuel-Ouimet
1145, rue de Saint-Jovite, Mont-Tremblant, QC J8E 1V1
Tél: 819-425-8614; *Téléc:* 819-425-1391
cultureetloisirs@villedemont-tremblant.qc.ca
www.villedemont-tremblant.qc.ca

Montcalm: Bibliothèque de Montcalm
30, rte du Lac-Rond nord, Montcalm, QC J0T 2V0
Tél: 819-681-3383; *Téléc:* 819-687-2374
biblio@municipalite.montcalm.qc.ca

Montcerf-Lytton: **Bibliothèque Montcerf-Lytton**
16, rue Principale nord, 2e étage, Montcerf-Lytton, QC J0W
1N0
Tél: 819-449-2065; *Télec:* 819-449-7310
admmontcerf@crsbpo.qc.ca
www.montcerf-lytton.com/index.php/services/bibliotheque
Angèle Lacaille, Responsable

Montebello: **Bibliothèque de Montebello**
220, rue Bonsecours, Montebello, QC J0V 1L0
Tél: 819-423-5123
biblio@montebello.ca
www.montebello.ca/bibliotheque.php
Diane Thivierge, Responsable

Montpellier: **Bibliothèque de Montpellier**
4B, rue du Bosquet, Montpellier, QC J0V 1M0
Tél: 819-428-3663; *Télec:* 819-428-1221
biblio@montpellier.ca
montpellier.ca/bibliotheque
Nicole Touchette, Responsable

Montréal: **Atwater Library & Computer
Centre/Bibliothèque et centre d'informatique
Atwater**
1200, av Atwater, Montréal, QC H3Z 1X4
Tel: 514-935-7344; *Fax:* 514-935-1960
info@atwaterlibrary.ca
www.atwaterlibrary.ca
www.facebook.com/197740473587129
Kimberley Ryan, Head Librarian
kryan@atwaterlibrary.ca
514-935-7344 ext. 205

Montréal: **Bibliothèque de Baie-D'Urfé**
20551, ch Lakeshore, Montréal, QC H9X 1R3
Tél: 514-457-3274
biblio@baie-durfe.qc.ca
www.bibliobaiedurfe.com
twitter.com/bibliobaiedurfe; www.facebook.com/bibliobaiedurfe

Montréal: **Bibliothèque et Archives nationales du
Québec**
2275, rue Holt, Montréal, QC H2G 3H1
Tél: 514-873-1100; *Ligne sans frais:* 800-363-9028
collectionspeciale@banq.qc.ca
www.banq.qc.ca
www.youtube.com/user/BAnQweb20; twitter.com/_BAnQ;
www.facebook.com/banqweb20
Jean-Louis Roy, Président-directeur général
pdg@banq.qc.ca

Montréal: **Bibliothèque publique de Pointe-Claire**
100, av Douglas-Shand, Montréal, QC H9R 4V1
Tél: 514-630-1218; *Télec:* 514-630-1261
bibliotheque@pointe-claire.ca
www.pointe-claire.ca/fr/culture-loisirs/bibliotheque
Katya Borrás, Coordonnatrice
katya.borras@pointe-claire.ca
514-630-1218 ext. 1217
Mary Pupil, Bibliotechnicienne principale, Comptoir du prêt
mary.pupil@pointe-claire.ca
514-630-1218 ext. 1626
Susan Hunter, Bibliotechnicienne, Prêt entre bibliothèques
ill@pointe-claire.ca
514-630-1218 ext. 1879

Montréal: **Bibliothèque Reginald J.P. Dawson**
1967, boul Graham, Montréal, QC H3R 1G9
Tél: 514-734-2967; *Télec:* 514-734-3089
bibliotheque@ville.mont-royal.qc.ca
www.ville.mont-royal.qc.ca/fr/services-residents/bibliotheque
www.facebook.com/VMR.biblio
Denis Chouinard, Chef de division
denis.chouinard@ville.mont-royal.qc.ca

Montréal: **Bibliothèques de Montréal/Montreal Public
Libraries Network**
Pavillon Prince, 801, rue Brennan, 5e étage, Montréal, QC
H3C 0G4
bibliomontreal.com
www.instagram.com/bibliomontreal; twitter.com/bibliomontreal;
www.facebook.com/bibliomontreal

Montréal: **The Fraser-Hickson Institute/Institut
Fraser-Hickson**
#102, 3755 Botrel St., Montréal, QC H4A 3G8
Tél: 514-872-0517
biblio@minibiblioplus.org
minibiblioplus.org
www.linkedin.com/company/minibiblioplus
Marco De Petrillo, Librarian

Montréal: **Jewish Public Library (Montréal)/La
Bibliothèque publique juive (Montréal)**
5151, ch de la Côte Ste-Catherine, Montréal, QC H3W 1M6
Tel: 514-345-2627
info@jplmontreal.org
jewishpubliclibrary.org
twitter.com/jpl_montreal; www.facebook.com/jpl.montreal
Michael Crelinsten, Executive Director

Montréal-Est: **Bibliothèque Micheline-Gagnon**
11370, rue Notre-Dame est, 3e étage, Montréal-Est, QC H1B
2W6
Tél: 514-905-2145
bibliotheque.montreal-est@montreal-est.ca

Morin-Heights: **Bibliothèque de Morin-Heights**
823, ch du Village, Morin-Heights, QC J0R 1H0
Tél: 450-226-3232; *Télec:* 450-226-8786
bibliotheque@morinheights.com
www.morinheights.com/bibliotheque-municipale
Lois Russell, Responsable

Murdochville: **Bibliothèque de Murdochville**
635, 5e rue, Murdochville, QC G0E 1W0
Tél: 418-784-2866
bibliotheque@murdochville.com

Métabetchouan-Lac-à-la-Croi: **Bibliothèque publique
de Métabetchouan**
87, rue Saint-André, Métabetchouan-Lac-à-la-Croi, QC G8G
1A1
Tél: 418-349-8495
metabet@reseaubiblioslsj.qc.ca

Métis-sur-Mer: **Bibliothèque Métis-sur-Mer**
130, rue Principale, Métis-sur-Mer, QC G0J 1S0
Tél: 418-936-3239
biblio.metis@crsbp.net

Namur: **Bibliothèque Namur/Namur Library**
331, rue Hôtel-de-Ville, Namur, QC J0V 1N0
Tél: 819-426-2996; *Télec:* 819-426-3074
biblio@namur.ca
namur.ca/bibliotheque
Tammie Leggett, Responsable

Nantes: **Bibliothèque de Nantes - Centre des loisirs**
2371, rue Laval, Nantes, QC G6B 2V4
Tél: 819-554-8897
biblio115@reseaubiblioestrie.qc.ca
municipalites-du-quebec.org/nantes/bibliotheque.php
Nicole Nolet, Responsable

Nantes: **Bibliothèque de Nantes - Municipale village**
1242, rue Principale, Nantes, QC G0Y 1G0
Tél: 819-547-3855
biblio109@reseaubiblioestrie.qc.ca
municipalites-du-quebec.org/nantes/bibliotheque.php
Céline Gendron, Responsable

Napierville: **Bibliothèque municipale de Napierville**
290, rue St-Alexandre, Napierville, QC J0J 1L0
Tél: 450-245-0030; *Télec:* 450-245-3777
bibliotheque@napierville.ca
www.facebook.com/biblionapierville

Natashquan: **Bibliothèque de Natashquan**
29, ch d'en Haut, Natashquan, QC G0G 2E0
Tél: 418-726-3362; *Télec:* 418-726-3698
biblionatashquan@gmail.com
www.natashquan.ca/bibliotheque
www.facebook.com/500030133831933
Louise Gagnon, Responsable

Neuville: **Bibliothèque Félicité-Angers**
704, rue des Érables, Neuville, QC G0A 2R0
Tél: 418-876-4750
biblio@ville.neuville.qc.ca
www.ville.neuville.qc.ca/loisirs-et-activites/bibliotheque
www.facebook.com/1793606744186115

New Richmond: **Bibliothèque du Vieux-Couvent**
99, place Suzanne-Guité, New Richmond, QC G0C 2B0
Tél: 581-355-0051
biblio@villenewrichmond.com
villenewrichmond.com/activities/bibliotheque-municipale

Newport: **Bibliothèque municipale-scolaire de
Newport**
École primaire Sacré-Coeur, 317, rte 132, Newport, QC G0C
2A0
Tél: 418-777-2280; *Télec:* 418-689-3639
bbonewpt@globetrotter.net
www.villedechandler.ca/sports-loisirs/arts-culture

Nicolet: **Bibliothèque de Nicolet**
180, rue de Monseigneur-Panet, Nicolet, QC J3T 1S6
Tél: 819-293-6901
biblio072@reseaubibliocqlm.qc.ca
nicolet.ca/fr/services-a-la-communaute/bibliotheque-municipale
www.facebook.com/1033759243405808

Nominingue: **Bibliothèque de Nominingue**
2112, ch du Tour du Lac, Nominingue, QC J0W 1R0
Tél: 819-278-3384
biblio@municipalitenominingue.qc.ca

Normandin: **Bibliothèque municipale de Normandin**
1156, av Valois, Normandin, QC G8M 3Z8
Tél: 418-274-2004
bibliotheque@ville.normandin.qc.ca
ville.normandin.qc.ca/bibliotheque

Normétal: **Bibliothèque Normétal**
36A, rue Principale, Normétal, QC J0Z 3A0
Tél: 819-788-2505; *Télec:* 819-788-2730
normetal@reseaubiblioatnq.qc.ca
Louise Nolet, Responsable

North Hatley: **Bibliothèque de North Hatley/North
Hatley Library**
165, rue Main, North Hatley, QC J0B 2C0
Tél: 819-842-2110
biblio@nhlibrary.qc.ca
www.nhlibrary.qc.ca
www.facebook.com/north.hatley.bibliotheque.library;

Notre-Dame-de-Ham: **Bibliothèque de
Notre-Dame-de-Ham**
25, rue de l'Église, Notre-Dame-de-Ham, QC G0P 1C0
Tél: 819-344-5010
biblio149@reseaubibliocqlm.qc.ca
biblietcie/biblio/bibliotheque-de-notre-dame-de-ham

Notre-Dame-de-la-Merci: **Bibliothèque de
Notre-Dame-de-la-Merci**
1900, Montée de la Réserve, Notre-Dame-de-la-Merci, QC
J0T 2A0
Tél: 819-424-2113
biblio@mun-ndm.ca
www.mun-ndm.ca/services/bibliotheque-culture

Notre-Dame-de-la-Paix: **Bibliothèque
Notre-Dame-de-la-Paix**
10, rue Saint-Jean-Baptiste, Notre-Dame-de-la-Paix, QC J0V
1P0
Tél: 819-522-6610; *Télec:* 819-522-6710
biblio@ndlapaix.ca
www.notredamedelapaix.qc.ca/bibliotheque
France Legault, Responsable

Notre-Dame-de-la-Salette: **Bibliothèque de
Notre-Dame-de-la-Salette**
68, rue des Saules, Notre-Dame-de-la-Salette, QC J0X 2L0
Tél: 819-766-2872; *Télec:* 819-766-2983
admsalette@crsbpo.qc.ca
www.muni-ndsalette.qc.ca/communautaire/loisirs-et-culture
www.facebook.com/biblioN.D.delaSalette
France Desormeaux, Responsable

Notre-Dame-de-Lorette: **Bibliothèque publique de
Notre-Dame-de-Lorette**
Couvent Maria-Goretti, 22, rue Principale,
Notre-Dame-de-Lorette, QC G0W 1B0
Tél: 418-276-1934
ndlorette@reseaubiblioslsj.qc.ca

Notre-Dame-de-Lourdes: **Bibliothèque
Notre-Dame-de-Lourdes**
3971, rue Principale, Notre-Dame-de-Lourdes, QC J0K 1K0
Tél: 450-759-7864
www.notredamedelourdes.ca/services-biblio.asp
www.facebook.com/622069297872428
Marlène Anglehart, Responsable

Notre-Dame-de-Montauban: **Bibliothèque de
Notre-Dame-de-Montauban**
550, av des Loisirs, Notre-Dame-de-Montauban, QC G0X
1W0
Tél: 418-336-1211
biblio058@reseaubibliocqlm.qc.ca
biblietcie/biblio/bibliotheque-de-notre-dame-de-montauban
Denise Villemure, Coordonnatrice

Notre-Dame-de-Pontmain: **Bibliothèque de Notre-Dame-de-Pontmain**
1027, rue Principale, Notre-Dame-de-Pontmain, QC J0W 1S0
Tél: 819-597-2382
bibliotheque@munpontmain.qc.ca
www.munpontmain.qc.ca/en/directory/bibliotheque-municipale

Notre-Dame-des-Bois: **Bibliothèque de Notre-Dame-des-Bois**
27, rte de l'Église, Notre-Dame-des-Bois, QC J0B 2E0
Tél: 819-875-3033
biblio009@reseaubiblioestrie.qc.ca
www.notredamedesbois.qc.ca/fr/loisirs-et-culture/bibliotheque
www.facebook.com/231847027296348

Notre-Dame-des-Monts: **Bibliothèque La Girouette**
87, rue Notre-Dame, Notre-Dame-des-Monts, QC G0T 1L0
Tél: 418-489-2011; *Télec:* 418-439-0883

Notre-Dame-des-Pins: **Bibliothèque Le Signet (Notre-Dame-des-Pins & Saint-Simon-les-Mines)**
3015, 1e av, Notre-Dame-des-Pins, QC G0M 1K0
Tél: 418-774-9454
biblnddp@sogetel.net
www.facebook.com/1204668799563086

Notre-Dame-des-Sept-Douleur: **Bibliothèque de Notre-Dame-des-Sept-Douleurs**
6203, ch de L'Ile, Notre-Dame-des-Sept-Douleur, QC G0L 1K0
Tél: 418-898-3451
biblio.douleurs@crsbp.net
www.ileverte-municipalite.com
Louise Alain, Coordonnatrice

Notre-Dame-du-Bon-Conseil: **Bibliothèque de Notre-Dame-du-Bon-Conseil**
541, rue Notre-Dame, Notre-Dame-du-Bon-Conseil, QC J0C 1A0
Tél: 819-336-2967
bibliobonconseil@hotmail.com
www.notre-dame-du-bon-conseil-village.qc.ca/services/?id=17
www.facebook.com/bibliothequebonconseil
Jacinthe Dufort, Coordinatrice

Notre-Dame-du-Laus: **Bibliothèque de Notre-Dame-du-Laus**
11, ch Ruisseau Serpent, Notre-Dame-du-Laus, QC J0X 2M0
Tél: 819-767-2772
biblio@mun-ndl.ca
www.notre-dame-du-laus.ca/bibliotheque
www.facebook.com/bibliondl
France Drouin, Responsable

Notre-Dame-du-Nord: **Bibliothèque Notre-Dame-du-Nord**
15A, rue Desjardins, Notre-Dame-du-Nord, QC J0Z 3B0
Tél: 819-723-2408; *Télec:* 819-723-2483
nord@reseaubiblioatnq.qc.ca
Carmen Laliberté, Responsable

Notre-Dame-du-Portage: **Bibliothèque de Notre-Dame-du-Portage**
560, rte de la Montagne, Notre-Dame-du-Portage, QC G0L 1Y0
Tél: 418-862-9163
biblio.portage@crsbp.net
www.municipalite.notre-dame-du-portage.qc.ca
Madeline Lepage, Responsable
418-862-4670

Nouvelle: **Bibliothèque municipale-scolaire de Nouvelle**
14, rue de l'Église, Nouvelle, QC G0C 2E0
Tél: 418-794-2244
bbonouv@globetrotter.net
nouvellegaspesie.com/horaires/bibliotheque

Noyan: **Bibliothèque municipale de Noyan/Noyan Public Library**
1312, ch de la Petite-France, Noyan, QC J0J 1B0
Tél: 450-291-4504; *Télec:* 450-291-4505
bibio14@ville.noyan.qc.ca
www.ville.noyan.qc.ca/bibliotheque
www.facebook.com/128784550520545

Nédélec: **Bibliothèque de Nédélec**
68, rue Principale, Nédélec, QC J0Z 2Z0
Tél: 819-784-3351; *Télec:* 819-784-2126
nedelec@reseaubiblioatnq.qc.ca
mabiblio.quebec/client/fr_CA/nedelec
Gaétane Marcoux, Responsable

Odanak: **Bibliothèque de Odanak**
102B, rue Sibosis, Odanak, QC J0G 1H0
Tél: 450-568-0107
biblio139@reseaubibliocqlm.qc.ca
caodanak.com/salle-familiale-3
www.facebook.com/biblioodanak
Marcelle O'Bomsawin, Responsable

Old Fort: **Bibliothèque de Old Fort**
Livraison Generale, Old Fort, QC G0G 2G0
Tél: 418-379-2911; *Télec:* 418-379-2959
René Fequet, Responsable

Opitciwan: **Bibliothèque de Opitciwan**
22, rue Tcikatnaw, Opitciwan, QC G0W 3B0
Tél: 819-974-1221
biblio065@reseaubibliocqlm.qc.ca
biblietcie.ca/biblio/bibliotheque-de-opitciwan

Ormstown: **Bibliothèque municipale d'Ormstown**
85, rue Roy, Ormstown, QC J0S 1K0
Tél: 450-829-3249
biblio@ormstown.ca
www.facebook.com/1448920602061184

Otter Lake: **Bibliothèque Otter Lake**
340, av Martineau, Otter Lake, QC J0X 2P0
Tél: 819-453-7344; *Télec:* 819-453-7311
admotterlake@crsbpo.qc.ca
www.otterlakequebec.ca/library
www.facebook.com/OtterLakeLibrary
Esther Dubeau, Responsable

Ouje-Bougoumou: **Bibliothèque Oujé-Bougoumou**
205, Opemiska Meskino, Ouje-Bougoumou, QC G0W 3C0
Tél: 418-745-2444
mabiblio.quebec/client/fr_CA/ouje-bougoumou
Annie Bosum, Responsable
annie.bosum@creeculture.ca

Packington: **Bibliothèque Packington**
115, rue Soucy, Packington, QC G0L 1Z0
Tél: 418-854-8456
biblio.packing@crsbp.net

Padoue: **Bibliothèque de Padoue**
215, rue Beaulieu, Padoue, QC G0J 1X0
Tél: 418-775-8188
padoue@mitis.qc.ca

Palmarolle: **Bibliothèque Palmarolle**
115, rue Principale, Palmarolle, QC J0Z 3C0
Tél: 819-787-3459; *Télec:* 819-787-2412
palmarolle@reseaubiblioatnq.qc.ca
Ghislaine Bégin, Responsable

Papineauville: **Bibliothèque de Papineauville / Lochaber**
294, rue Papineau, Papineauville, QC J0V 1R0
Tél: 819-427-5511
bibliotheque@papineauville.ca
www.papineauville.ca/loisirs-culture/bibliotheque.php
www.facebook.com/284798808312015
Francine Denis, Responsable

Parisville: **Bibliothèque de Parisville**
1260, rue Saint-Jacques, Parisville, QC G0S 1X0
Tél: 819-292-2644
biblio103@reseaubibliocqlm.qc.ca
www.municipalite.parisville.qc.ca/bibliotheque
Diane Auger, Responsable

Paspébiac: **Bibliothèque de Paspébiac**
95, boul Gérard-D.-Lévesque ouest, Paspébiac, QC G0C 2K0
Tél: 418-752-6747
bibliotheque@villepasbepiac.ca
villepaspebiac.ca/vie-culturelle/bibliotheque-municipale

Percé: **Bibliothèque de Percé**
137, rte 132 Ouest, Percé, QC G0C 2L0
Tél: 418-782-2933
bboperce@ville.perce.qc.ca
www.facebook.com/1401154396824528

Petit-Saguenay: **Bibliothèque publique de Petit-Saguenay**
50, rue Tremblay, Petit-Saguenay, QC G0V 1N0
Tél: 418-272-2323
petitsag@reseaubiblioslsj.qc.ca

Petite-Rivière-St-François: **Bibliothèque Gabrielle-Roy (Petite-Rivière-Saint-François)**
1069, rue Principale, Petite-Rivière-Saint-François, QC G0A 2L0
Tél: 418-760-1050; *Télec:* 418-760-1051
biblioprsf@hotmail.com
www.facebook.com/1519741135013966;

Petite-Vallée: **Bibliothèque de Petite-Vallée**
45, rue Principale, Petite-Vallée, QC G0E 1Y0
Tél: 418-393-2949
bibliopv@globetrotter.net

Pierreville: **Bibliothèque de Pierreville**
26, rue Ally, Pierreville, QC J0G 1J0
Tél: 450-568-3500
biblio051@reseaubibliocqlm.qc.ca
biblietcie.ca/bibliotheque-de-pierreville-jean-luc-precourt
www.facebook.com/biblietcie.ca
Chantale Bellamy, Responsable

Pincourt: **Bibliothèque de Pincourt/Pincourt Library**
225, boul Pincourt, Pincourt, QC J7W 9T2
Tél: 514-425-1104
bibliotheque@villepincourt.qc.ca
www.villepincourt.qc.ca/fr/loisirs-et-culture/bibliotheque

Piopolis: **Bibliothèque de Piopolis**
403, rue Principale, Piopolis, QC G0Y 1H0
Tél: 819-583-3953; *Télec:* 819-583-1467
biblio019@reseaubiblioestrie.qc.ca
piopolis.quebec/content/bibliothèque

Plaisance: **Bibliothèque de Plaisance**
281, rue Desjardins, Plaisance, QC J0V 1S0
Tél: 819-427-5363; *Télec:* 819-427-5015
biblio@villeplaisance.com
ville.plaisance.qc.ca/loisirs-et-cultures/bibliotheque
Pierrette Charlebois, Responsable

Plessisville: **Bibliothèque Linette-Jutras-Laperle**
1800, rue Saint-Calixte, Plessisville, QC G6L 1R6
Tél: 819-362-6628
bibliotheque@plessisville.quebec
plessisville.quebec/loisirs-culture/bibliotheque
www.facebook.com/bibliothequelinettejutraslaperle
Suzanne Bédard, Coordonnatrice culturelle
sbedard@plessisville.quebec

Pointe-aux-Outardes: **Bibliothèque de Pointe-aux-Outardes**
481, ch Principal, 2e étage, Pointe-aux-Outardes, QC G0H 1H0
Tél: 418-567-2281; *Télec:* 418-567-4409
loisirs@pointe-aux-outardes.ca
www.pointe-aux-outardes.ca/bibliotheque
Lisette Bouchard, Responsable

Pointe-Calumet: **Bibliothèque La Sablière**
190, 41e av, Pointe-Calumet, QC J0N 1G2
Tél: 450-473-5918; *Télec:* 450-473-6571
bibliotheque@pointe-calumet.ca
www.pointe-calumet.ca
Brigitte Lessard, Directrice
450-473-5918 ext. 261

Pointe-des-Cascades: **Bibliothèque Adrienne Demontigny-Clément**
52, ch du Fleuve, Pointe-des-Cascades, QC J0P 1M0
Tél: 450-455-5310
biblio@pointe-des-cascades.com
www.facebook.com/bibliothequepointedescascades

Pointe-Lebel: **Bibliothèque de Pointe-Lebel**
380, rue Granier, Pointe-Lebel, QC G0H 1N0
Tél: 418-589-2325; *Télec:* 418-589-6154
www.facebook.com/747657062029045
Lise Therrien, Responsable
lise.therrien@pointelebel.com

Pointe-à-la-Croix: **Bibliothèque de La Petite-Rochelle**
44A, rue Lasalle, Pointe-à-la-Croix, QC G0C 1L0
Tél: 418-788-2931
biblio.41@hotmail.com
www.facebook.com/673458772794175

Pont-Rouge: **Bibliothèque Auguste-Honoré-Gosselin**
189, rue Dupont, Pont-Rouge, QC G3H 1N4
Tél: 418-873-4067
bibliotheque@ville.pontrouge.qc.ca
www.ville.pontrouge.qc.ca/loisirs/culture/bibliotheque
www.facebook.com/bibliopontrouge
Sylvain Brousseau, Responsable
sylvain.brousseau@ville.pontrouge.qc.ca

Pontiac: Bibliothèque de Luskville
2024, rte 148, Pontiac, QC J0X 2G0
Tél: 819-455-2370; *Téléc:* 819-455-9756
admluskville@crsbpo.qc.ca
municipalitepontiac.com/bibliotheques
Louise Ramsay, Responsable

Pontiac: Bibliothèque municipale de Quyon
12, rue Saint-John, Pontiac, QC J0X 2V0
Tél: 819-458-1227; *Téléc:* 819-458-9756
biblioquyon@gmail.com
municipalitepontiac.com/bibliotheques
www.facebook.com/biblioquyon
Glenda Nitschke, Responsable

Port-Cartier: Bibliothèque municipale de Port-Cartier (Le Manuscrit)
21, rue des Cèdres, Port-Cartier, QC G5B 2W5
Tél: 418-766-3366; *Téléc:* 418-766-3561
loisirsculture@villeport-cartier.com
www.villeport-cartier.com
Chantal Maltais, Bibliothecnicienne
chantalmaltais@villeport-cartier.com

Port-Menier: Bibliothèque municipale de l'Ile d'Anticosti
4B, rue Savoy, Port-Menier, QC G0G 2Y0
Tél: 418-535-0048; *Téléc:* 418-535-0381
maisondelacommunaute@hotmail.ca
municipalite-anticosti.org/citoyens/bibliotheque
Isabelle Plante, Responsable

Portneuf: Bibliothèque La Découverte
297, 1e av, Portneuf, QC G0A 2Y0
Tél: 418-286-4452
bibliodecouv@globetrotter.net

Portneuf-sur-Mer: Bibliothèque de Portneuf-sur-Mer
170, rue Principale, Portneuf-sur-Mer, QC G0T 1P0
Tél: 418-238-5303; *Téléc:* 418-238-5319
bibliopsmer@hotmail.com
Christine Olivier, Responsable

Poularies: Bibliothèque Poularies
990, rue Principale, Poularies, QC J0Z 3E0
Tél: 819-782-5159; *Téléc:* 819-782-5063
poularies@reseaubiblioatnq.qc.ca
Kate Morin, Responsable

Price: Bibliothèque de Price
1, rue du Centre, Price, QC G0J 1Z0
Tél: 418-775-2144
biblio.price@crsbp.net
www.municipaliteprice.com/fr/activites-et-culture/bibliotheque

Princeville: Bibliothèque de Princeville (Madeleine-Bélanger)
140, rue Saint-Jean-Baptiste Sud, Princeville, QC G6L 5A5
Tél: 819-364-3333
biblio079@reseaubiblioclm.qc.ca
villedeprinceville.qc.ca/bibliotheque

Préissac Sud: Bibliothèque de Preissac Sud
186, av du Lac, Préissac Sud, QC J0Y 2E0
Tél: 819-759-4138; *Téléc:* 819-759-4138
preissacs@reseaubiblioatnq.qc.ca
preissac.com/sports-loisirs-et-plein-air/bibliothque-municipale
Nicole Marcil, Responsable

Prévost: Bibliothèque Jean-Charles-Des Roches
2945, boul du Curé-Labelle, Prévost, QC J0R 1T0
Tél: 450-224-8888
biblio@ville.prevost.qc.ca
www.ville.prevost.qc.ca

Péribonka: Bibliothèque publique de Péribonka
296A, Édouard-Niquet, Péribonka, QC G0W 2G0
Tél: 418-374-2967
peribonk@reseaubibliolsj.qc.ca
www.facebook.com/BiblioPeribonka
Cynthia Gauthier, Responsable

Québec: Bibliothèque de Québec
350, rue Saint-Joseph est, Québec, QC G1K 3B2
Tél: 418-641-6789
courrier@bibliothequedequebec.qc.ca
www.bibliothequedequebec.qc.ca
www.facebook.com/bibliothequedequebec
Éric Therrien, Directeur

Ragueneau: Bibliothèque de Ragueneau
13, rue des Loisirs, Ragueneau, QC G0H 1S0
Tél: 418-567-2291; *Téléc:* 418-567-2344
biblio@municipalite.ragueneau.qc.ca
municipalite.ragueneau.qc.ca/culture-et-loisirs/bibliotheque
www.facebook.com/biblioragueneau
Édith Martel, Responsable

Ravignan: Bibliothèque Liratu
108A, rue de l'Église, Ravignan, QC G0R 2L0
Tél: 418-267-5931; *Téléc:* 418-267-5930
biblioliratu@reseaubiblioatnq.qc.ca

Rawdon: Bibliothèque de Rawdon (Alice-Quintal)
3643, rue Queen, Rawdon, QC J0X 1S0
Tél: 450-834-2596
bibliotheque@rawdon.ca
rawdon.ca/citoyen/bibliotheque-alice-quintal

Repentigny: Bibliothèque municipale de Repentigny
1, place d'Evry, Repentigny, QC J6A 8H7
Tél: 450-470-3420
bibliotheque@ville.repentigny.qc.ca
repentigny.ca/culture-loisirs/culture/bibliotheques

Richelieu: Bibliothèque municipale Simonne-Monet-Chartrand
200, boul Richelieu, Richelieu, QC J3L 3R4
Tél: 450-658-1157
biblio@ville.richelieu.qc.ca
ville.richelieu.qc.ca/bibliotheque

Richmond: Bibliothèque RCM
820, rue Gouin, Richmond, QC J0B 2H0
Tél: 819-826-5814
bibliorcm@ville.richmond.qc.ca
www.ville.richmond.qc.ca/bibliotheque

Rigaud: Bibliothèque municipale de Rigaud
102, rue Saint-Pierre, Rigaud, QC J0P 1P0
Tél: 450-451-0869
biblio@ville.rigaud.qc.ca
www.ville.rigaud.qc.ca
www.facebook.com/BiblioRigaud

Rimouski: Bibliothèque de Pointe-au-Père
315, av Thomas-Dionne, Rimouski, QC G5M 1M8
Tél: 418-724-3164
bibliotheque.pointe-au-pere@ville.rimouski.qc.ca
biblio.rimouski.ca

Rimouski: Bibliothèque du Bic
130, rue du Mont Saint Louis, Rimouski, QC G0L 1B0
Tél: 418-724-3164
bibliotheque.bic@ville.rimouski.qc.ca
biblio.rimouski.ca

Rimouski: Bibliothèque Lisette-Morin
110, rue de l'Évêché est, Rimouski, QC G5L 7C7
Tél: 418-724-3164
bibliotheque.lisette-morin@ville.rimouski.qc.ca
biblio.rimouski.ca

Rimouski: Bibliothèque Pascal-Parent (Sainte-Blandine)
22, rue Lévesque, Rimouski, QC G5N 5S6
Tél: 418-724-3164
bibliotheque.pascal-parent@ville.rimouski.qc.ca
biblio.rimouski.ca

Ripon: Bibliothèque de Ripon
31, rue Coursol, Ripon, QC J0V 1V0
Tél: 819-983-2000; *Téléc:* 819-983-1327
admripon@crsbpo.qc.ca
ripon.ca/bibliotheque
Céline Derouin, Coordonnatrice

Rivière-au-Tonnerre: Bibliothèque de Rivière-au-Tonnerre
472, rue Jacques-Cartier, Rivière-au-Tonnerre, QC G0G 2L0
Tél: 418-465-2055; *Téléc:* 418-465-2956
bibliotheque@riviere-au-tonnerre.ca
riviere-au-tonnerre.ca/loisirs-et-vie-communautaire
Anne Desmeules, Responsable
desmeulesanne@gmail.com

Rivière-du-Loup: Bibliothèque municipale Françoise-Bédard
75, rue de l'Hôtel-de-Ville, Rivière-du-Loup, QC G5R 1L7
Tél: 418-862-4252
bibliotheque@villerdl.ca
villerdl.ca/fr/loisirs/bibliotheque/votre-bibliotheque
www.facebook.com/bibliothequefrancoisebedard

Sylvie Michaud, Bibliothécaire responsable
sylvie.michaud@villerdl.ca
418-867-6669
Marie-France April, Technicienne en documentation
marie-france.april@villerdl.ca
418-867-6670
Maxime Bélisle, Technicienne en documentation (aide à la recherche)
maxime.belisle@villerdl.ca
418-862-6529
Isabelle Moffet, Coordonnatrice à l'animation
isabelle.moffet@villerdl.ca
418-867-6668

Rivière-Héva: Bibliothèque Rivière-Héva
15A, rue du Parc, Rivière-Héva, QC J0Y 2H0
Tél: 819-735-2306; *Téléc:* 819-735-4251
heva@reseaubiblioatnq.qc.ca
www.facebook.com/106026390837457
Mélissa Vallée, Responsable

Rivière-Rouge: Bibliothèque Sainte-Véronique
2167, boul Fernand-Lafontaine, Rivière-Rouge, QC J0T 1T0
Tél: 819-275-3759
bibliolannon@riviere-rouge.ca
www.riviere-rouge.ca/bibliotheques
www.facebook.com/291730280841664
Ginette Terreault, Responsable

Rivière-St-Paul: Bibliothèque de Rivière-St-Paul
Livraison Generale, Rivière-St-Paul, QC G0G 2P0
Tél: 418-379-2911; *Téléc:* 418-379-2959
stpaulps@globetrotter.net
Gail MacDonald, Responsable

Rivière-à-Claude: Bibliothèque de Rivière-à-Claude
520, rue Principale est, Rivière-à-Claude, QC G0E 1Z0

Rivière-Éternite: Bibliothèque publique de Rivière Eternité
404, rue Principale, Rivière-Éternite, QC G0V 1P0
Tél: 418-272-1052
eternite@reseaubibliolsj.qc.ca

Roberval: Bibliothèque Georges-Henri-Lévesque
829, boul St-Joseph, Roberval, QC G8H 2L6
Tél: 418-275-0202
www.roberval.biblio.qc.ca

Rosemère: Bibliothèque municipale H J Hemens de Rosemère
339, ch de la Grande-Côte, Rosemère, QC J7A 1K2
Tél: 450-621-3500; *Téléc:* 450-621-6131
biblio@ville.rosemere.qc.ca
www.ville.rosemere.qc.ca/services-bibliotheque

Rougemont: Bibliothèque municipale de Rougemont
839, rue Principale, Rougemont, QC J0L 1M0
Tél: 450-469-3213
biblio@rougemont.ca
www.rougemont.ca/bibliotheque
www.facebook.com/bibliothequederougemont
Marie-Eve Dubuc, Responsable

Rouyn-Noranda: Biblio Rollet
12570, boul Rideau, Rouyn-Noranda, QC J0Z 3J0
Tél: 819-797-7110; *Téléc:* 819-493-1210
rollet@reseaubiblioatnq.qc.ca
mabiblio.quebec/client/fr_CA/rollet
Chantal Mongrain, Responsable

Rouyn-Noranda: Bibliothèque Cadillac
106, rue de Cadillac, Rouyn-Noranda, QC J0Y 1C0
Tél: 819-797-7110; *Téléc:* 819-759-3607
cadillac@reseaubiblioatnq.qc.ca
Josianne Rodriguez, Responsable

Rouyn-Noranda: Bibliothèque de Arntfield
15, av Fugère, Rouyn-Noranda, QC J0Y 1B0
Tél: 819-797-7110; *Téléc:* 819-279-2481
arntfield@reseaubiblioatnq.qc.ca

Rouyn-Noranda: Bibliothèque de Beaudry
6884, boul Témiscamingue, Rouyn-Noranda, QC J9Y 1N1
Tél: 819-797-7110; *Téléc:* 819-797-2108
beaudry@reseaubiblioatnq.qc.ca
www.facebook.com/310258552681179
Marguerite Petit, Responsable

Rouyn-Noranda: Bibliothèque de Bellecombe
2471, rte des Pionniers, Rouyn-Noranda, QC J0Z 1K0
Tél: 819-797-7110; *Téléc:* 819-797-6585
bellecombe@reseaubiblioatnq.qc.ca
mabiblio.quebec/client/fr_CA/bellecombe

Rouyn-Noranda: **Bibliothèque de Cléricy**
8002-B, rue du Souvenir, Rouyn-Noranda, QC J0Z 1P0
Tél: 819-797-7110; *Téléc:* 819-637-2133
clericy@reseaubiblioatnq.qc.ca
mabiblio.quebec/client/fr_CA/clericy
Lise Robin Boucher, Responsable

Rouyn-Noranda: **Bibliothèque de Cloutier**
10232-B, boul Témiscamingue, Rouyn-Noranda, QC J0Z 1S0
Tél: 819-797-8613; *Téléc:* 819-797-1299
cloutier@reseaubiblioatnq.qc.ca
Jacqueline Gaudreau, Responsable

Rouyn-Noranda: **Bibliothèque Destor**
7292, rang du Parc, Rouyn-Noranda, QC J9Y 0C8
Tél: 819-637-2279; *Téléc:* 819-637-2095
destor@reseaubiblioatnq.qc.ca
mabiblio.quebec/client/fr_CA/destor
www.facebook.com/bibliotheque.dedestor
Rita Tremblay, Responsable

Rouyn-Noranda: **Bibliothèque Montbeillard**
9632C, boul Rideau, Rouyn-Noranda, QC J0Z 2X0
Tél: 819-797-7110; *Téléc:* 819-797-2390
montbeillard@reseaubiblioatnq.qc.ca
www.facebook.com/100389824144083
Monique Trudel, Responsable

Rouyn-Noranda: **Bibliothèque Mont-Brun**
9985, rang du Berger, Rouyn-Noranda, QC J0Z 2Y0
Tél: 819-797-7110
montbrun@reseaubiblioatnq.qc.ca
Noëlla Thibault, Responsable

Rouyn-Noranda: **Bibliothèque municipale de Rouyn-Noranda**
201, av Dallaire, Rouyn-Noranda, QC J9X 4T5
Tél: 819-762-0944; *Téléc:* 819-797-7564
info@biblrn.qc.ca
www.biblrn.qc.ca
www.facebook.com/BibliRN
Esther Labrie, Directrice générale
esther.labrie@biblrn.qc.ca
819-762-0944 ext. 3333
Ginette Montigny, Responsable, Services techniques
ginette.montigny@biblrn.qc.ca
819-762-0944 ext. 3225
Diane Brazeau, Secrétaire de direction
diane.brazeau@biblrn.qc.ca
819-762-0944 ext. 3221

Roxton Pond: **Bibliothèque municipale de Roxton Pond**
905, rue Saint-Jean, Roxton Pond, QC J0E 1Z0
Tél: 450-372-6875
bibliotheque@roxtonpond.ca
www.roxtonpond.ca/bibliotheque
www.facebook.com/biblioroxtonpond
Pierre Dalpé, Responsable

Rémigny: **Bibliothèque de Rémigny**
1304, ch de l'Église, Rémigny, QC J0Z 3H0
Tél: 819-761-2331; *Téléc:* 819-761-2421
remigny@reseaubiblioatnq.qc.ca
mabiblio.quebec/client/fr_CA/remigny
Jocelyne Savignac, Responsable

Sabrevois: **Bibliothèque municipale de Sainte-Anne-de-Sabrevois**
1218, rte 133, Sabrevois, QC J0J 2G0
Tél: 450-346-0899
biblio@sabrevois.info
sainte-anne-de-sabrevois.com/bibliotheque-municipale
www.facebook.com/bibliosabrevois
Guylaine Marchand, Responsable

Sacré-Coeur: **Bibliothèque de Sacré-Coeur**
#119, 80, rue de l'Église, Sacré-Coeur, QC G0T 1Y0
Tél: 418-236-4460; *Téléc:* 418-236-9144
pier69villeneuve@hotmail.com
www.sacre-coeur.ca/bibliotheque
Émilie Gravel, Responsable

Saint-Adelphe: **Bibliothèque de Saint-Adelphe**
601, rue Principale, Saint-Adelphe, QC G0X 2G0
Tél: 418-322-5736
biblio004@reseaubibliocqlm.qc.ca
biblietcie.ca/bibliotheque-de-saint-adelphe-roger-fontaine
Suzanne Tessier, Coordonnatrice

Saint-Adolphe-d'Howard: **Bibliothèque de Saint-Adolphe-d'Howard**
1881, ch du Village, Saint-Adolphe-d'Howard, QC J0T 2B0
Tél: 819-327-2117; *Téléc:* 819-327-2282
biblio@stadolphedhoward.qc.ca
stadolphedhoward.qc.ca/26/bibliotheque
Lucie Charette, Responsable

Saint-Adrien: **Bibliothèque de Saint-Adrien**
1598, rue Principale, Saint-Adrien, QC J0A 1C0
Tél: 819-828-2872
biblio037@reseaubiblioestrie.qc.ca
st-adrien.com/notre-milieu-de-vie/bottin/bibliotheque-municipale

Saint-Aimé-des-Lacs: **Bibliothèque La Plume d'Or**
123B, rue Principale, Saint-Aimé-des-Lacs, QC G0T 1S0
Tél: 418-439-2006; *Téléc:* 418-439-1475

Saint-Aimé-du-Lac-des-Iles: **Bibliothèque de Saint-Aimé-du-Lac-des-Iles**
871, ch Diotte, Saint-Aimé-du-Lac-des-Iles, QC J0W 1J0
Tél: 819-597-4174
biblio@saint-aime-du-lac-des-iles.ca
www.saint-aime-du-lac-des-iles.ca/bibliotheque
Johanne Coté, Responsable

Saint-Alban: **Bibliothèque Biblio-Chut! (Saint-Alban)**
179, rue Principale, Saint-Alban, QC G0A 3B0
Tél: 418-268-3557; *Téléc:* 418-268-5073
www.facebook.com/195321754418153

Saint-Alexis-de-Montcalm: **Bibliothèque de Saint-Alexis**
#102, 258, rue Principale, Saint-Alexis-de-Montcalm, QC J0K 1T0
Tél: 450-839-7277
biblio@st-alexis.com
biblietcie.ca/biblio/bibliotheque-de-saint-alexis-diane-lavallee
www.facebook.com/bibliostalexis

Saint-Alexis-des-Monts: **Bibliothèque de Saint-Alexis-des-Monts (Léopold-Bellemare)**
105, rue Hôtel-de-Ville, Saint-Alexis-des-Monts, QC J0K 1V0
Tél: 819-265-2046
biblio028@reseaubibliocqlm.qc.ca
www.facebook.com/bibliotheque.stalexisdesmonts

Saint-Alphonse: **Bibliothèque de ABC du savoir**
134A, rue Principale Ouest, Saint-Alphonse, QC G0C 2V0
Tél: 418-388-5577
bbostal@globetrotter.net
www.st-alphonsegaspesie.com/loisirs-et-culture/bibliothèque.htm
www.facebook.com/204499129733271

Saint-Alphonse-de-Granby: **Bibliothèque municipale de Saint-Alphonse-de-Granby**
360, rue Principale, Saint-Alphonse-de-Granby, QC J0E 2A0
Tél: 450-375-7229; *Téléc:* 450-375-4570
biblio@st-alphonse.qc.ca
Daniel Delorme, Responsable

Saint-Alphonse-Rodriguez: **Bibliothèque de Saint-Alphonse-Rodriguez (Docteur-Jacques-Olivier)**
99, rue de la Plage, Saint-Alphonse-Rodriguez, QC J0K 1W0
Tél: 450-883-2264
biblio@munsar.ca

Saint-Amable: **Bibliothèque de Saint-Amable**
575, rue Principale, Saint-Amable, QC J0L 1N0
Tél: 450-649-3555; *Téléc:* 450-649-0203
bibliotheque@st-amable.qc.ca
www.st-amable.qc.ca/bibliotheque

Saint-Ambroise: **Bibliothèque publique de Saint-Ambroise**
156, rue Gaudreault, Saint-Ambroise, QC G7P 2J9
Tél: 418-672-2253
stambr@reseaubiblioslsj.qc.ca
st-ambroise.qc.ca

Saint-André: **Bibliothèque publique de Saint-André**
11, rue du Collège, Saint-André, QC G0W 2K0
Tél: 418-349-1019
standre@reseaubiblioslsj.qc.ca

Saint-André-Avellin: **Bibliothèque de Saint-André-Avellin**
532, rue Charles-Auguste Montreuil, Saint-André-Avellin, QC J0V 1W0
Tél: 819-983-2840; *Téléc:* 819-983-2344
biblio@st-andre-avellin.com
www.ville.st-andre-avellin.qc.ca/residents/bibliotheque-et-culture
www.facebook.com/BiblioSTAA
Adéodat Bernard, Responsable

Saint-André-de-Restigouche: **Bibliothèque de Saint-André-de-Restigouche**
163, rue Principale, Saint-André-de-Restigouche, QC G0J 2G0
Tél: 418-865-2234
m.st.and.restigouche@globetrotter.net

Saint-Anicet: **Bibliothèque municipale de Saint-Anicet**
1547, rte 132, Saint-Anicet, QC J0S 1M0
Tél: 450-264-9431; *Téléc:* 450-264-3544
biblio@stanicet.com
stanicet.com/bibliotheque

Saint-Antoine-sur-Richelieu: **Bibliothèque Hélène-Dupuis-Marion**
#2, 1060, rue du Moulin Payet, Saint-Antoine-sur-Richelieu, QC J0L 1R0
Tél: 450-787-3497; *Téléc:* 450-787-2852
bibliotheque@sasr.ca
www.facebook.com/bibliostantoinesurrichelieu

Saint-Antonin: **Bibliothèque Saint-Antonin**
261, rue Principale, Saint-Antonin, QC G0L 2J0
Tél: 418-862-1056
biblio.antonin@crsbp.net
Sylvie Ratté, Responsable

Saint-Apollinaire: **Bibliothèque Au Jardin des livres (Saint-Apollinaire)**
#102, 94, rue Principale, Saint-Apollinaire, QC G0S 2E0
Tél: 418-881-3996
bibliotheque@st-apollinaire.com
www.mabibliotheque.ca/saint-apollinaire
www.facebook.com/Aujardindeslivres

Saint-Arsène: **Bibliothèque Saint-Arsène**
49, rue de l'Église, Saint-Arsène, QC G0L 2K0
Tél: 418-867-2205
biblio.arsene@crsbp.net
Estelle Dubé, Responsable

Saint-Athanase: **Bibliothèque Saint-Athanase**
6081, ch de l'Église, Saint-Athanase, QC G0L 2L0
Tél: 418-863-7706
biblio.athanase@crsbp.net

Saint-Aubert: **Bibliothèque Charles-E.-Harpe**
14, rue des Loisirs, Saint-Aubert, QC G0R 2R0
Tél: 418-598-3623; *Téléc:* 418-598-3369
bibliotheque@saint-aubert.net
www.facebook.com/bibliothequesaintaubert

Saint-Augustin: **Bibliothèque de Saint-Augustin**
Livraison Generale, Saint-Augustin, QC G0G 2R0
Tél: 418-947-2404; *Téléc:* 418-947-2533
Julie Beaurivage, Responsable
jbeaurivage@csdulittoral.qc.ca

Saint-Augustin: **Bibliothèque publique de St-Augustin**
710, rue Principale, Saint-Augustin, QC G0W 1K0
Tél: 418-374-2147
augustin@reseaubiblioslsj.qc.ca

Saint-Augustin-de-Desmaures: **Bibliothèque Alain-Grandbois**
160, rue Jean-Juneau, Saint-Augustin-de-Desmaures, QC G3A 2P1
Tél: 418-878-5473
bibliotheque.alain-grandbois@vsad.ca
catalogue.vsad.ca
Kim Timmons-Bélair, Responsable
418-878-4662 ext. 6612

Saint-Augustin-de-Woburn: **Bibliothèque municipale de Saint-Augustin-de-Woburn**
515, rue OTJ, Saint-Augustin-de-Woburn, QC G0Y 1R0
Tél: 819-544-4741
biblio016@reseaubiblioestrie.qc.ca
www.saintaugustindewoburn.ca/pages/bibliotheque-municipale
Micheline Fortier, Responsable

Saint-Barthélemy: Bibliothèque de Saint-Barthélemy
1980, rue Bonin, Saint-Barthélemy, QC J0K 1X0
Tél: 450-885-3511
biblio.st-barthelemy@outlook.com
www.saint-barthelemy.ca
www.facebook.com/104244999653520

Saint-Basile: Bibliothèque Au fil des mots
(Saint-Basile)
41, rue Caron, Saint-Basile, QC G0A 3G0
Tél: 418-329-2858; *Téléc:* 418-329-3743
www.facebook.com/781479911983264

Saint-Basile-le-Grand: Bibliothèque Roland Leblanc
40, rue Savaria, Saint-Basile-le-Grand, QC J3N 1L8
Tél: 450-461-8000
bibliotheque@villesblg.ca
www.ville.saint-basile-le-grand.qc.ca

Saint-Benjamin: Bibliothèque La Détente
(Saint-Benjamin)
440B, rue du Collège, Saint-Benjamin, QC G0M 1N0
Tél: 418-594-6068; *Téléc:* 418-594-6068

Saint-Benoît-Labre: Bibliothèque L'Envolume
216, rte 271, Saint-Benoît-Labre, QC G0M 1P0
Tél: 418-228-9250; *Téléc:* 418-228-0518
biblistben@outlook.com
saintbenoitlabre.com/bibliotheque
Nadia Lebel, Responsable

Saint-Bernard: Bibliothèque Liratout (Saint-Bernard)
540, rue Vaillancourt, Saint-Bernard, QC G0S 2G0
Tél: 418-475-4669; *Téléc:* 418-475-5136
biblio@saint-bernard.quebec
saint-bernard.quebec/loisirs-et-activites/bibliotheque-liraout
www.facebook.com/bibliothequeliratout
Denise Dallaire, Responsable
418-475-4233

Saint-Bernard-de-Michaudvil: Bibliothèque
municipale de Saint-Bernard-de-Michaudville
390, rue Principale, Saint-Bernard-de-Michaudvil, QC J0H
1C0
Tél: 450-792-3190; *Téléc:* 450-792-3591
bibliostbernard@mrcmaskoutains.qc.ca
saintbernarddemichaudville.qc.ca/pages/o_bibliotheque.htm
www.facebook.com/bibliostbernarddemichaudville

Saint-Blaise-sur-Richelieu: Bibliothèque municipale
de Saint-Blaise-sur-Richelieu
#6, 795, rue des Loisirs, Saint-Blaise-sur-Richelieu, QC J0J
1W0
Tél: 450-291-5944; *Téléc:* 450-291-5095
bibliotheque@st-blaise.ca
www.st-blaise.ca/bibliotheque
www.facebook.com/2143585175883562

Saint-Bonaventure: Bibliothèque de
Saint-Bonaventure
110, rue Cyr, Saint-Bonaventure, QC J0C 1C0
Tél: 819-396-1676
biblio120@reseaubibliocqlm.qc.ca
www.saint-bonaventure.ca/bibliotheque
www.facebook.com/bibliostbon
Gisèle Corbin, Responsable

Saint-Boniface: Bibliothèque de Saint-Boniface
155, rue Langevin, Saint-Boniface, QC G0X 2L0
Tél: 819-535-3330
biblio021@reseaubibliocqlm.qc.ca
municipalitesaint-boniface.ca/index.php/bibliotheque-municipale
www.facebook.com/BiblioSaintBoniface

Saint-Bruno: Bibliothèque publique de Saint-Bruno
550, rue des 4H, Saint-Bruno, QC G0W 2L0
Tél: 418-212-8007
stbruno@reseaubibliolsj.qc.ca

Saint-Bruno-de-Guigues: Bibliothèque de
Saint-Bruno-de-Guigues
23B, rue Principale nord, Saint-Bruno-de-Guigues, QC J0Z
2G0
Tél: 819-728-2910; *Téléc:* 819-728-2404
guigues@reseaubiblioatnq.qc.ca
mabiblio.quebec/client/fr_CA/st-bruno-de-guigues
Lucie Loubert, Responsable

Saint-Bruno-de-Kamouraska: Bibliothèque de
Saint-Bruno-de-Kamouraska
4, rue Du Couvent, Saint-Bruno-de-Kamouraska, QC G0L
2M0
Tél: 418-492-2612
biblio.bruno@crsbp.net
www.stbrunokam.qc.ca/fr/loisirs-et-culture/bibliotheque
Diane Cardin, Responsable

Saint-Bruno-de-Montarville: Bibliothèque municipale
de Saint-Bruno-de-Montarville
82, boul Seigneurial ouest, Saint-Bruno-de-Montarville, QC
J3V 5N7
Tél: 450-645-2950; *Téléc:* 450-441-8485
bibliotheque@stbruno.ca
stbruno.ca/loisirs-et-culture/bibliotheque-municipale

Saint-Calixte: Bibliothèque de Saint-Calixte
6250, rue Hôtel-de-Ville, Saint-Calixte, QC J0K 1Z0
Tél: 450-222-2782
biblio@mscalixte.qc.ca
saint-calixte.ca/loisirs-et-culture/culture/bibliotheque

Saint-Camille: Bibliothèque municipale de
Saint-Camille
93, rue Desrivières, Saint-Camille, QC J0A 1G0
Tél: 819-286-8282
biblio043@reseaubiblioestrie.qc.ca
saint-camille.ca
www.facebook.com/bibliothequestcamille

Saint-Casimir: Bibliothèque Jean-Charles-Magnan
510, boul de la Montagne, Saint-Casimir, QC G0A 3L0
Tél: 418-339-2909; *Téléc:* 418-339-3105
jcmagnan@csportneuf.qc.ca
www.facebook.com/796365837113827
Ange-Aimée Asselin, Responsable

Saint-Charles: Bibliothèque Jacques-Labrie
2829A, av Royale, Saint-Charles, QC G0R 2T0
Tél: 418-887-6561; *Téléc:* 418-887-6779
biblstch@globetrotter.qc.ca
www.facebook.com/833311100063498

Saint-Charles-de-Bourget: Bibliothèque publique de
Saint-Charles-de-Bourget
357, rang 2, Saint-Charles-de-Bourget, QC G0V 1G0
Tél: 418-672-2624
stcharle@reseaubiblioslsj.qc.ca
www.stcharlesdebourget.ca/index/bibliotheque
Louise Breton, Responsable

Saint-Charles-Garnier: Bibliothèque de
Saint-Charles-Garnier
38, rte de Saint-Charles-Garnier, Saint-Charles-Garnier, QC
G0K 1K0
Tél: 418-798-4820
biblio.garnier@crsbp.net
www.municipalite.saint-charles-garnier.qc.ca

Saint-Claude: Bibliothèque municipale Irène Duclos
565, rang 7, Saint-Claude, QC J0B 2N0
Tél: 819-845-3259
biblio017@reseaubiblioestrie.qc.ca
www.municipalite.st-claude.ca/services-communautaires

Saint-Clet: Bibliothèque municipale de Saint-Clet
25, rue Piché, Saint-Clet, QC J0P 1S0
Tél: 450-456-3175
biblio@st-clet.com
www.st-clet.com/fr/bibliotheque
www.facebook.com/BiblioClet
Catherine Duquette, Responsable

Saint-Clément: Bibliothèque de Saint-Clément
25A, rue Saint-Pierre, Saint-Clément, QC G0L 2N0
Tél: 418-963-2258
biblio.clement@crsbp.net
Thérèse St-Pierre, Responsable

Saint-Cléophas: Bibliothèque de Saint-Cléophas
356, rue Principale, Saint-Cléophas, QC G0J 3N0
Tél: 418-536-3915
biblio.cleophas@crsbp.net
www.stcleophas.com

Saint-Cléophas-de-Brandon: Bibliothèque de
Saint-Cléophas-de-Brandon
750, rue Principale, Saint-Cléophas-de-Brandon, QC J0K
2A0
Tél: 450-889-5683
biblio107@reseaubibliocqlm.qc.ca
biblietcie.ca/biblio/bibliotheque-de-saint-cleophas-de-brandon

Saint-Colomban: Bibliothèque de Saint-Colomban
347, montée de l'Église, Saint-Colomban, QC J5K 1B1
Tél: 450-436-1453; *Téléc:* 450-432-1863
biblio@st-colomban.qc.ca
st-colomban.qc.ca/activites-loisirs-et-culture/bibliotheque
www.facebook.com/bibliothequesaintcolomban

Saint-Constant: Bibliothèque municipale de
Saint-Constant
#200, 121, rue Saint-Pierre, Saint-Constant, QC J5A 0M3
Tél: 450-638-2010
bibliotheque@saint-constant.ca
saint-constant.ca/fr/bibliotheque-municipale

Saint-Cuthbert: Bibliothèque de Saint-Cuthbert
1891, rue Principale, Saint-Cuthbert, QC J0K 2C0
Tél: 450-836-4852
biblio126@reseaubibliocqlm.qc.ca
www.st-cuthbert.qc.ca/loisirs-et-culture/bibliotheque.html

Saint-Cyprien: Bibliothèque de Saint-Cyprien
(Alphonse-Desjardins)
187, rue Principale, Saint-Cyprien, QC G0L 2P0
Tél: 418-963-2226
biblio.cyprien@crsbp.net
saintcyprien.ca/services_aux_citoyens/?id=stcyprien-bibliothequ
e
Ginette Gagné, Responsable

Saint-Cyprien: Bibliothèque municipale de
Saint-Cyprien
187, rue Principale, Saint-Cyprien, QC G0L 2P0
Tél: 418-963-2730
biblio.cyprien@crsbp.net
www.saintcyprien.ca

Saint-Célestin: Bibliothèque de Saint-Célestin
(Claude-Bouchard)
450B, rue Marquis, Saint-Célestin, QC J0C 1G0
Tél: 819-229-3403
biblio130@reseaubibliocqlm.qc.ca
www.facebook.com/928764117191372

Saint-Côme: Bibliothèque de Saint-Côme
1675, 55e rue, Saint-Côme, QC J0K 2B0
Tél: 450-883-2726
biblio054@reseaubibliocqlm.qc.ca
biblietcie.ca/biblio/bibliotheque-de-saint-come
Josianne D. Mainguy, Coordonnatrice aux loisirs
loisirs@stcomelanaudiere.ca

Saint-Côme-Linière: Bibliothèque municipale de
Saint-Côme-Linière
1375, 18e rue, Saint-Côme-Linière, QC G0M 1J0
Tél: 418-685-3825; *Téléc:* 418-685-2566
bibliostcome@hotmail.com
www.stcomeliniere.com/loisirs-et-culture/bibliotheque

Saint-Damase: Bibliothèque de Saint-Damase
377, rue de l'Église, Saint-Damase, QC G0J 2J0
Tél: 418-776-2103
biblio.damase@crsbp.net

Saint-Damase: Bibliothèque municipale de
Saint-Damase
113, rue St-Étienne, Saint-Damase, QC J0H 1J0
Tél: 418-797-3341
biblio@st-damase.qc.ca
www.facebook.com/BiblioSaintDamase
Chantal Reichel, Responsable

Saint-Damien: Bibliothèque de Saint-Damien
2045, rue Taschereau, Saint-Damien, QC J0K 2E0
Tél: 450-835-3419
bibliotheque@st-damien.com
biblietcie.ca/biblio/bibliotheque-de-saint-damien

Saint-Damien-de-Buckland: Bibliothèque Le
Bouquin d'Or (Saint-Damien-de-Buckland)
75, rue Saint-Gérard, Saint-Damien-de-Buckland, QC G0R
2Y0
Tél: 418-789-2526; *Téléc:* 418-789-2125
biblio@saint-damien.com
saint-damien.com/biblio
www.facebook.com/BouquindOr

Saint-Denis: Bibliothèque de Saint-Denis
5, rte 287, Saint-Denis, QC G0L 2R0
Tél: 418-498-2968
biblio.denis@crsbp.net
munstdenis.com/communauté/bibliothèque
Doris Rivard, Responsable

Saint-Denis-de-Brompton: Bibliothèque de
Saint-Denis de Brompton
1485, rte 222, Saint-Denis-de-Brompton, QC J0B 2P0
Tél: 819-846-3627
biblio035@reseaubiblioestrie.qc.ca
www.sddb.ca/fr/culture-loisir-et-vie-communautaire/bibliotheque

Saint-Didace: Bibliothèque de Saint-Didace
(Louis-Edmon Hamelin)
530A, rue Principale, Saint-Didace, QC J0K 2G0
Tél: 450-835-4184
biblio@saint-didace.com
biblietcie.ca/bibliotheque-de-saint-didace-louis-edmond-hamelin
Robert Roy, Coordonnateur

Saint-Dominique: Bibliothèque municipale de
Saint-Dominique
488, Saint-Dominique, Saint-Dominique, QC J0H 1L0
Tél: 450-771-0256
biblio@st-dominique.ca
www.facebook.com/bibliodominique

Saint-Donat: Bibliothèque de Saint-Donat
510, rue Desrochers, Saint-Donat, QC J0T 2C0
Tél: 819-424-3044; Téléc: 819-424-5020
biblio@saint-donat.ca
www.facebook.com/loisirsaintdonat

Saint-Donat: Bibliothèque de Saint-Donat
108, rue Bérubé, Saint-Donat, QC G0K 1L0
Tél: 418-739-3948
biblio.donat@crsbp.net
www.saintdonat.ca/recreo-communautaire/bibliotheques
Madeleine Leclerc, Responsable

Saint-Edmond-les-Plaines: Bibliothèque publique de
Saint-Edmond-les-Plaines
561, rue Principale, Saint-Edmond-les-Plaines, QC G0W 2M0
Tél: 418-274-3069
stedmond@reseaubiblioslsj.qc.ca
www.facebook.com/122060524625353

Saint-Edouard-de-Lotbinière: Bibliothèque
A.-Lachance
**105, rue de L'École, Saint-Edouard-de-Lotbinière, QC G0S
1Y0**
Tél: 418-796-2433; Téléc: 418-796-2228
loisirs@st-edouard.com
www.mabibliotheque.ca/saint-edouard
www.facebook.com/loisirs.stedouardlotbiniere

Saint-Elzéar: Bibliothèque de Saint-Elzéar
668, av Principale, Saint-Elzéar, QC G0S 2J0
Tél: 418-387-2534
st-elzear.ca/citoyens/bibliotheque

Saint-Elzéar: Bibliothèque de Saint-Elzéar
(Saint-Elzéar-de-Témiscouata)
209, rue de l'Église, Saint-Elzéar, QC G0L 2W0
Tél: 418-867-3225
biblio.elzear@crsbp.net
saintelzear.ca/bibliotheque

Saint-Esprit: Bibliothèque de Saint-Esprit
(Alice-Parizeau)
45, rue des Écoles, Saint-Esprit, QC J0K 2L0
Tél: 450-831-2274
biblio125@reseaubibliocqlm.qc.ca
biblietcie.ca/biblio/bibliotheque-de-saint-esprit-alice-parizeau
www.facebook.com/343413225730969

Saint-Eugène: Bibliothèque publique de
Saint-Eugène
#2, 469, du Pont, Saint-Eugène, QC G0W 1B0
Tél: 418-276-7790
steugene@reseaubiblioslsj.qc.ca

Saint-Eugène-de-Guigues: Bibliothèque de
Saint-Eugène-de-Guigues
4, 1e av ouest, Saint-Eugène-de-Guigues, QC J0Z 3L0
Tél: 819-785-4441; Téléc: 819-785-2301
eugene@reseaubiblioatnq.qc.ca
mabiblio.quebec/client/fr_CA/st-eugene-de-guigues
Lorraine Falardeau, Responsable

Saint-Eustache: Bibliothèque municipale
Guy-Bélisle
12, ch de la Grande-Côte, Saint-Eustache, QC J7P 1A2
Tél: 450-974-5035
infobiblio@saint-eustache.ca
www.saint-eustache.ca/citoyens/bibliotheque
www.facebook.com/bibliothequeguybelisle

Saint-Eusèbe: Bibliothèque de Saint-Eusèbe
222B, rue Principale, Saint-Eusèbe, QC G0L 2Y0
Tél: 418-899-0194
biblio.eusebe@crsbp.net

Saint-Fabien: Bibliothèque de Saint-Fabien
30, 7e av, Saint-Fabien, QC G0L 2Z0
Tél: 418-869-2602
biblio.fabien@crsbp.net
www.saint-fabien.ca/bibliotheque-municipale

Saint-Fabien-de-Panet: Bibliothèque Fabiothèque
(Saint-Fabien-de-Panet)
199, rue Bilodeau, Saint-Fabien-de-Panet, QC G0R 2J0
Tél: 418-249-4417; Téléc: 418-249-2507
www.facebook.com/bibliostfabiendepanet

Saint-Faustin-Lac-Carré: Bibliothèque du Lac
64, rue de la Culture, Saint-Faustin-Lac-Carré, QC J0T 1J1
Tél: 819-688-5434
bibliodulac@sflc.ca

Saint-Ferdinand: Bibliothèque de Saint-Ferdinand
(Onil-Garneau)
#1, 620, rue Notre-Dame, Saint-Ferdinand, QC G0N 1N0
Tél: 418-428-9607
biblio049@reseaubibliocqlm.qc.ca
biblietcie.ca/biblio/bibliotheque-de-saint-ferdinand-onil-garneau
www.facebook.com/amisdelabibliothequeonilgarneau
Lily-Ann Lambert-Boudreault, Responsable

Saint-Ferréol-les-Neiges: Bibliothèque Aux Sources
(Saint-Ferréol-les-Neiges)
33, rue de l'Église, Saint-Ferréol-les-Neiges, QC G0A 3R0
Tél: 418-826-3540; Téléc: 418-826-0489
www.facebook.com/BibliothequeAuxSources

Saint-Flavien: Bibliothèque La Flaviethèque
(Saint-Flavien)
12A, rue Roberge, Saint-Flavien, QC G0S 2M0
Tél: 418-728-4190; Téléc: 418-728-4190
laflavietheque@st-flavien.com

Saint-Fortunat: Bibliothèque municipale de
Saint-Fortunat
173, rue Principale, Saint-Fortunat, QC G0P 1G0
Tél: 819-344-5399; Téléc: 819-344-5399

Saint-François-d'Assise: Bibliothèque de
Saint-François-d'Assise
399, ch Central, Saint-François-d'Assise, QC G0J 2N0
Tél: 418-299-2066
munstfrs@globetrotter.net

Saint-François-de-Sales: Bibliothèque publique de
Saint-François-de-Sales
**255-B, rue de l'Église, Saint-François-de-Sales, QC G0W
1M0**
Tél: 418-348-6736
franco@reseaubiblioslsj.qc.ca

Saint-François-du-Lac: Bibliothèque de
Saint-François-du-Lac
480, rue Notre-Dame, Saint-François-du-Lac, QC J0G 1M0
Tél: 450-568-1130
bibliotheque@saintfrancoisdulac.ca
www.saintfrancoisdulac.ca/fr/loisirs-culture-vie-communautaire
www.facebook.com/411163719675802

Saint-Fulgence: Bibliothèque publique de
Saint-Fulgence
12, rue Saint-Basile, Saint-Fulgence, QC G0V 1S0
Tél: 418-615-0059
stfulgence@reseaubiblioslsj.qc.ca
www.facebook.com/582016365144192

Saint-Félicien: Bibliothèque municipale de
Saint-Félicien
**1209, boul Sacré Coeur, 2e étage, Saint-Félicien, QC G8K
2R5**
Tél: 418-679-2100; Téléc: 418-679-1449
biblio@ville.stfelicien.qc.ca
www.ville.stfelicien.qc.ca
Forget Bruno, Technicien en documentation
bruno.forget@ville.stfelicien.qc.ca
418-679-2100 ext. 2247

Saint-Félix-d'Otis: Bibliothèque publique de
Saint-Félix-d'Otis
455, rue Principale, Saint-Félix-d'Otis, QC G0V 1M0
Tél: 418-544-5543
stfelix@reseaubiblioslsj.qc.ca

Saint-Félix-de-Kingsey: Bibliothèque de
Saint-Félix-de-Kingsey
6115B, rue Principale, Saint-Félix-de-Kingsey, QC J0B 2T0
Tél: 819-848-1400
biblio152@reseaubibliocqlm.qc.ca
biblietcie.ca/bibliotheque-de-saint-felix-de-kingsey
www.facebook.com/827357157378068
Émilie Choquette, Coordonnatrice

Saint-Félix-de-Valois: Bibliothèque de
Saint-Félix-de-Valois
4863, rue Principale, Saint-Félix-de-Valois, QC J0K 2M0
Tél: 450-889-5589
bibliotheque@st-felix-de-valois.com
st-felix-de-valois.com/loisirs-culture-et-vie-communautaire

Saint-Gabriel: Bibliothèque de Saint-Gabriel (Au fil
des pages)
53, rue Beausoleil, Saint-Gabriel, QC J0K 2N0
Tél: 450-835-2212; Téléc: 450-835-1493
biblio013@reseaubibliocqlm.qc.ca
www.facebook.com/1481895835404193
Noëlla Ganley, Coordonnatrice

Saint-Gabriel-de-Rimouski: Bibliothèque Le
Bouquinier
103, rue Leblanc, Saint-Gabriel-de-Rimouski, QC G0K 1M0
Tél: 418-775-0148; Téléc: 418-798-4108
biblio.gabriel@crsbp.net
www.facebook.com/leBouquinier
Nycole Bouchard Meyer, Responsable

Saint-Georges: Bibliothèque municipale de
Saint-Georges
**Centre culturel Marie-Fitzbach, 250, 18e rue, Saint-Georges,
QC G5Y 4S9**
Tél: 418-226-2271
ccmf@saint-georges.ca
ccmf.saint-georges.ca/bibliotheque

Saint-Georges-de-Windsor: Bibliothèque municipale
de Saint-Georges-de-Windsor
527, rue Principale, Saint-Georges-de-Windsor, QC J0A 1J0
Tél: 819-828-2716; Téléc: 819-828-0213
biblio051@reseaubiblioestrie.qc.ca
www.st-georges-de-windsor.org/citoyens-bibliotheque.php
Lise Turcott, Responsable

Saint-Germain: Bibliothèque de Saint-Germain
506, rue Jean-Baptiste-Moreau, Saint-Germain, QC G0L 3G0
Tél: 418-952-5767
biblio.germain@crsbp.net

Saint-Germain-de-Grantham: Bibliothèque de
Saint-Germain-de-Grantham (Le Signet)
**299, rue Notre-Dame, Saint-Germain-de-Grantham, QC J0C
1K0**
Tél: 819-395-2644
biblio100@reseaubibliocqlm.qc.ca
biblietcie.ca/bibliotheque-de-saint-germain-de-grantham-le-signet
www.facebook.com/biblio.lesignet.9
Louise Gaillard-Simoneau, Responsable

Saint-Gervais: Bibliothèque Faubourg de la Cadie
36A, rue de la Fabrique est, Saint-Gervais, QC G0R 3C0
Tél: 418-887-3628; Téléc: 418-887-3628
www.facebook.com/faubourgdelacadie

Saint-Gilles: Bibliothèque Le Signet
1540, rue du Couvent, Saint-Gilles, QC G0S 2P0
Tél: 418-888-4210
www.facebook.com/272598250099555

Saint-Guillaume: Bibliothèque de Saint-Guillaume
106, rue Saint-Jean-Baptiste, Saint-Guillaume, QC J0C 1L0
Tél: 819-396-3754
biblio087@reseaubibliocqlm.qc.ca
biblietcie.ca/biblio/bibliotheque-de-saint-guillaume
www.facebook.com/393757304113420
Johanne Forcier, Responsable

Saint-Guy: Bibliothèque de Saint-Guy
54, ch Principal, Saint-Guy, QC G0K 1W0
Tél: 418-963-1490
biblio.guy@crsbp.net

Saint-Gédéon: Bibliothèque publique de
Saint-Gédéon
208, rue De Quen, Saint-Gédéon, QC G0W 2P0
Tél: 418-345-8001
stgedeon@reseaubiblioslsj.qc.ca
www.facebook.com/188664541169728

Saint-Gédéon-de-Beauce: Biblio GEDE-Livres
127A, 1e av sud, Saint-Gédéon-de-Beauce, QC G0M 1T0
Tél: 418-582-3035
biblio-st-gedeon@hotmail.com
www.facebook.com/bibliostgedeondebeauce

Saint-Henri: Bibliothèque La Reliure (Saint-Henri)
217, rue Commerciale, Saint-Henri, QC G0R 3E0
Tél: 418-882-2401; *Téléc:* 418-882-0302
bibliotheque@saint-henri.ca
www.facebook.com/maisondelaculuresthenri

Saint-Henri-de-Taillon: Bibliothèque publique de
Saint-Henri-de-Taillon
430, rue Hôtel-de-Ville, Saint-Henri-de-Taillon, QC G0W 2X0
Tél: 418-347-3243; *Téléc:* 418-347-1138
sthenri@reseaubiblioslsj.qc.ca
www.facebook.com/110712302428625

Saint-Hilarion: Bibliothèque aux Quatre Vents de
Saint-Hilarion
#1, 247, ch Principal, Saint-Hilarion, QC G0A 3V0
Tél: 418-489-2999
biblioquatrevents@gmail.com
www.facebook.com/biblioauquatrevents

Saint-Hippolyte: Bibliothèque de Saint-Hippolyte
2258, ch des Hauteurs, Saint-Hippolyte, QC J8A 2R5
Tél: 450-224-4137
biblio@saint-hippolyte.ca
saint-hippolyte.ca/services-aux-citoyens/bibliotheque-et-culture
www.facebook.com/bibliosainthippolyte

Saint-Honoré-de-Chicoutimi: Bibliothèque publique
de Saint-Honoré
100, rue Paul-Aimé Hudon, Saint-Honoré-de-Chicoutimi, QC
G0V 1L0
Tél: 418-673-3790; *Téléc:* 418-673-3871
bibliothequesthonore@hotmail.com
www.facebook.com/BibliothequeDeStHonore

Saint-Hugues: Bibliothèque municipale de
Saint-Hugues
207, rue Saint-Germain, Saint-Hugues, QC J0H 1N0
Tél: 450-794-2030
biblio@st-hugues.com
www.facebook.com/BiblioStHugues

Saint-Hyacinthe: Médiathèque maskoutaine
2720, rue Dessaulles, Saint-Hyacinthe, QC J2S 2V7
Tél: 450-773-1830; *Téléc:* 450-773-3398
info@mediatheque.qc.ca
www.mediatheque.qc.ca
www.facebook.com/mediathequemaskoutaine
Louise Struthers, Directrice générale
struthersl@mediatheque.qc.ca
450-773-1830 ext. 23
Nathalie Lespérance, Responsable, Services publics,
Bibliothèque T.-A.-St-Germain
lesperancen@mediatheque.qc.ca
450-773-1830 ext. 25

Saint-Ignace-de-Loyola: Bibliothèque de
Saint-Ignace-de-Loyola
621, rue de l'Église, Saint-Ignace-de-Loyola, QC J0K 2P0
Tél: 450-836-3376
biblio156@reseaubibliocqlm.qc.ca
bibliotcie.ca/bibliotheque-de-saint-ignace-de-loyola
www.facebook.com/1192805264069467

Saint-Irénée: Bibliothèque Adolphe-Basile-Routhier
400, rue Principale, Saint-Irénée, QC G0T 1V0
Tél: 418-620-5015; *Téléc:* 418-452-8221
bibliotheque@saintirenee.ca
saintirenee.ca/liens-rapides/bibliotheque/bibliotheque.aspx
www.facebook.com/bibliothequesaintirenee

Saint-Isidore: Bibliothèque Laurette-Nadeau-Parent
101, rue des Aigles, Saint-Isidore, QC G0S 2S0
Tél: 418-700-1018; *Téléc:* 418-882-6470
www.saint-isidore.net/la-bibliotheque-laurette-nadeau-parent
www.facebook.com/521370084539684

Saint-Isidore: Bibliothèque municipale de
Saint-Isidore
693, rang St-Régis, Saint-Isidore, QC J0L 2A0
Tél: 450-992-1323
biblio@st-isidore.ca
www.facebook.com/biblioisidore;

Saint-Isidore-de-Clifton: Bibliothèque municipale de
Saint-Isidore-de-Clifton
25, rue de l'Église, Saint-Isidore-de-Clifton, QC J0B 2X0
Tél: 819-875-5643; *Téléc:* 819-560-8559
biblio032@reseaubiblioestrie.qc.ca
www.st-isidore-clifton.qc.ca/fr/bibliotheque-municipale.htm
Hélène Dumais, Responsable

Saint-Jacques: Bibliothèque municipale
Marcel-Dugas
16, rue Maréchal, Saint-Jacques, QC J0K 2R0
Tél: 450-839-3671; *Téléc:* 450-839-2387
Other Numbers: 450-831-2296
biblio@st-jacques.org
www.st-jacques.org/bibliotheque-et-culture/general

Saint-Jacques-de-Leeds: Bibliothèque La Ressource
425, rue Principale, Saint-Jacques-de-Leeds, QC G0N 1J0
Tél: 418-424-3181; *Téléc:* 418-424-0126

Saint-Jacques-le-Mineur: Bibliothèque municipale
de Saint-Jacques-le-Mineur
89, rue Principale, Saint-Jacques-le-Mineur, QC J0J 1Z0
Tél: 450-347-5446; *Téléc:* 450-347-5754
biblio@sjlm.ca
www.facebook.com/bibliosjlm

Saint-Janvier-de-Joly: Bibliothèque Adrien-Lambert
(Saint-Janvier-de-Joly)
729, rue des Loisirs, Saint-Janvier-de-Joly, QC G0S 1M0
Tél: 418-728-2984; *Téléc:* 418-728-2984
joly@reseaubibliocnca.qc.ca
www.mabibliotheque.ca/joly
www.facebook.com/bibliothequeadrienlambert

Saint-Jean-Baptiste: Bibliothèque municipale de
Saint-Jean-Baptiste
3090, rue Principale, Saint-Jean-Baptiste, QC J0L 2B0
Tél: 450-467-1786
biblio69@msjb.qc.ca
www.msjb.qc.ca/mes-services-municipaux/bibliotheque
www.facebook.com/bibliothequesaintjeanbaptiste
Sylvie Sweeney, Responsable

Saint-Jean-de-Brébeuf: Bibliothèque
Saint-Jean-de-Brébeuf (Bibliothèque Bibliomagie)
844, rue de l'Église, Saint-Jean-de-Brébeuf, QC G6G 0A1
Tél: 418-453-2571; *Téléc:* 418-453-2339
breb@reseaubibliocnca.qc.ca
www.facebook.com/Bibliomagie

Saint-Jean-de-Dieu: Bibliothèque de
Saint-Jean-de-Dieu
75, rue Principale nord, Saint-Jean-de-Dieu, QC G0L 3M0
Tél: 418-963-3529
biblio.jeandieu@crsbp.net
Francine Rioux, Responsable

Saint-Jean-de-Matha: Bibliothèque de
Saint-Jean-de-Matha
81, rue Sainte-Louise, Saint-Jean-de-Matha, QC J0K 2S0
Tél: 450-886-5855
biblio047@reseaubibliocqlm.qc.ca
biblietcie.ca/bibliotheque-de-saint-jean-de-matha-louis-landry
www.facebook.com/bibliosaintjeandematha

Saint-Jean-Port-Joli: Bibliothèque Marie-Bonenfant
(Saint-Jean-Port-Joli)
7B, place de l'Église, Saint-Jean-Port-Joli, QC G0R 3G0
Tél: 418-598-3187; *Téléc:* 418-598-3085
biblio.stjean@globetrotter.net
www.facebook.com/bibliothequemariebonenfant

Saint-Jean-sur-Richelieu: Bibliothèques municipales
de Saint-Jean-sur-Richelieu
180, rue Laurier, Saint-Jean-sur-Richelieu, QC J3B 7B2
Tél: 450-357-2111
biblio@sjsr.ca
sjsr.ca/bibliotheques
Johanne Jacob, Chef, Division bibliothèques
j.jacob@sjsr.ca

Saint-Joseph-de-Beauce: Bibliothèque de
Saint-Joseph-de-Beauce
139, rue Sainte-Christine, Saint-Joseph-de-Beauce, QC G0S
2V0
Tél: 418-397-6160; *Téléc:* 418-397-5715
biblio@vsjb.ca
www.vsjb.ca/bibliotheque

Saint-Joseph-de-Ham-Sud: Bibliothèque municipale
de Ham-Sud
9, ch Gosford sud, Saint-Joseph-de-Ham-Sud, QC J0B 3J0
Tél: 819-877-3220; *Téléc:* 819-877-5121
biblio042@reseaubiblioestrie.qc.ca
ham-sud.ca/loisirs-et-tourisme/loisirs-et-activites/bibliotheque
Lucille Blais, Responsable

Saint-Joseph-de-Kamouraska: Bibliothèque de
Saint-Joseph-de-Kamouraska
300, rue Principale, Saint-Joseph-de-Kamouraska, QC G0L
3P0
Tél: 418-493-2214
biblio.joseph@crsbp.net
www.stjosephkam.ca
Nancy Boudreault, Responsable

Saint-Joseph-de-Lepage: Bibliothèque de
Saint-Joseph-de-Lepage
70, rue de la Rivière, Saint-Joseph-de-Lepage, QC G5H 3N8
Tél: 418-775-4171; *Téléc:* 418-775-3004
biblio.lepage@crsbp.net

Saint-Joseph-du-Lac: Bibliothèque de
Saint-Joseph-du-Lac
70, Montée du Village, Saint-Joseph-du-Lac, QC J0N 1M0
Tél: 450-623-1072
biblio@sjdl.qc.ca
sjdl.qc.ca/loisirs-et-culture/bibliotheque
Katerine Douville, Technicienne en documentation

Saint-Jude: Bibliothèque St-Jude
940, rue de Centre, Saint-Jude, QC J0H 1P0
Tél: 450-792-3855
biblio-st-jude@hotmail.com
www.saint-jude.ca/bibliotheque.html
www.facebook.com/bibliothequeeliseecourville

Saint-Julien: Bibliothèque des Z'hauteurs
794, ch Saint-Julien, Saint-Julien, QC G0N 1B0
Tél: 418-423-7474; *Téléc:* 418-423-3410
bibliotheque.des.zhauteurs@gmail.com
www.st-julien.ca/pages/bibliotheque
Michel Tremblay, Responsable

Saint-Juste-du-Lac: Bibliothèque de
Saint-Juste-du-Lac
37, ch Principal, Saint-Juste-du-Lac, QC G0L 3R0
Tél: 418-899-0375
biblio.juste@crsbp.net
Jeanne Benoist, Responsable

Saint-Juste-du-Lac: Bibliothèque Lots-Renversés
84, rte 295, Saint-Juste-du-Lac, QC G0L 1V0
Tél: 418-899-2356
biblio.lotsren@crsbp.net

Saint-Justin: Bibliothèque de Saint-Justin
590, rue Lafrenière, Saint-Justin, QC J0K 2V0
Tél: 819-227-2775
biblio056@reseaubibliocqlm.qc.ca
biblietcie.ca/biblio/bibliotheque-de-saint-justin

Saint-Jérôme: Bibliothèque publique de
Saint-Jérôme
101, place du Curé-Labelle, Saint-Jérôme, QC J7Z 1X6
Tél: 450-432-0569; *Téléc:* 450-436-1211
www.vsj.ca/fr/bibliotheques.aspx

Saint-Lambert: Bibliothèque municipale de
Saint-Lambert
490, av Mercille, Saint-Lambert, QC J4P 2L5
Tél: 450-466-3910
bibliotheque@saint-lambert.ca
www.saint-lambert.ca/fr/services-recreatifs/bibliotheque

Saint-Lazare-de-Bellechasse: Bibliothèque
Biblio-Culture
116B, rue de la Fabrique, Saint-Lazare-de-Bellechasse, QC
G0R 3J0
Tél: 418-883-2551; *Téléc:* 418-883-2551
biblio-st-lazare@globetrotter.net

Saint-Liboire: Bibliothèque municipale de
Saint-Liboire
21, place Mauriac, Saint-Liboire, QC J0H 1R0
Tél: 450-793-4751
biblio@st-liboire.ca
www.facebook.com/102653274644224

Saint-Liguori: Bibliothèque de Saint-Liguori
741, rue Principale, Saint-Liguori, QC J0K 2X0
Tél: 450-753-4446
biblio006@reseaubibliocqlm.qc.ca
www.saint-liguori.com/index.php/loisirs-et-cultures
Annie Lemarbre, Responsable

Saint-Lin-Laurentides: Bibliothèque de
Saint-Lin-Laurentides
252, rue J.H.-Corbeil, Saint-Lin-Laurentides, QC J5M 3B2
Tél: 450-439-3130
biblio@saint-lin-laurentides.com
www.saint-lin-laurentides.com/culture-et-communaute/biblio

Saint-Louis-de-Blandford: Bibliothèque de
Saint-Louis-de-Blandford
80, rue Principale, Saint-Louis-de-Blandford, QC G0Z 1B0
Tél: 819-364-7007
biblio116@reseaubibliocqlm.qc.ca
biblietcie.ca/biblio/bibliotheque-de-saint-louis-de-blandford

Saint-Louis-de-Gonzague: Bibliothèque municipale
de Saint-Louis-de-Gonzague
140, rue Principale, Saint-Louis-de-Gonzague, QC J0S 1T0
Tél: 450-371-0523
bibliotheque@saint-louis-de-gonzague.com
Marc-André Dumouchel, Responsable

Saint-Louis-du-Ha!Ha!: Bibliothèque de
Saint-Louis-du-Ha!Ha!
234, rue Commerciale, Saint-Louis-du-Ha!Ha!, QC G0L 3S0
Tél: 418-854-4031
biblio.louis@crsbp.net
saintlouisduhaha.com/bibliotheque-caci
Diane Bossé, Responsable

Saint-Luc-de-Bellechasse: Bibliothèque L'Éveil
(Saint-Luc-de-Bellechasse)
115, rue de la Fabrique, Saint-Luc-de-Bellechasse, QC G0R
1L0
Tél: 418-636-2776; *Téléc:* 418-636-2776
bibliotheque@sogetel.net

Saint-Luc-de-Vincennes: Bibliothèque de
Saint-Luc-de-Vincennes
660, rue Principale, Saint-Luc-de-Vincennes, QC G0X 3K0
Tél: 819-295-3608; *Téléc:* 819-295-3608
biblio097@reseaubibliocqlm.qc.ca
biblietcie.ca/biblio/bibliotheque-de-saint-luc-de-vincennes
www.facebook.com/1415295512024049
Colette Normandin, Coordonnatrice

Saint-Ludger: Bibliothèque municipale de
Saint-Ludger
212B, rue La Salle, 2e étage, Saint-Ludger, QC G0M 1W0
Tél: 819-548-5826; *Téléc:* 819-548-5743
biblio091@reseaubiblioestrie.qc.ca
st-ludger.qc.ca/bibliotheque-municipale
www.facebook.com/bibliothequedestludger
Jacinthe Rocheleau, Responsable

Saint-Ludger-de-Milot: Bibliothèque publique de
Saint-Ludger-de-Milot
739, rue Gaudreault, Saint-Ludger-de-Milot, QC G0W 2B0
Tél: 418-373-2266; *Téléc:* 418-373-2554
stludger@reseaubibliosIsj.qc.ca
www.facebook.com/301721619937159

Saint-Léon-de-Standon: Bibliothèque l'Étincelle
514B, rue Principale, Saint-Léon-de-Standon, QC G0R 4L0
Tél: 418-642-2708; *Téléc:* 418-642-2570
etincel@globetrotter.qc.ca
www.mabibliotheque.ca/saint-leon
www.facebook.com/bibliothequeletincelle

Saint-Léon-le-Grand: Bibliothèque de
Saint-Léon-le-Grand (Bas-Saint-Laurent)
241, rue Gendron, Saint-Léon-le-Grand, QC G0J 2W0
Tél: 418-743-2914
biblio.granleon@crsbp.net
Lise Fournier, Responsable

Saint-Léon-le-Grand: Bibliothèque de
Saint-Léon-le-Grand (Mauricie)
49, rue de la Fabrique, Saint-Léon-le-Grand, QC J0K 2W0
Tél: 819-228-3236
biblio029@reseaubibliocqlm.qc.ca
biblietcie.ca/biblio/bibliotheque-de-saint-leon-le-grand

Saint-Léonard-d'Aston: Bibliothèque de
Saint-Léonard-d'Aston (Lucille-M.-Desmarais)
440, rue de l'Exposition, Saint-Léonard-d'Aston, QC J0C
1M0
Tél: 819-399-3368
biblio089@reseaubibliocqlm.qc.ca
saint-leonard-daston.net/bibliotheque
www.facebook.com/564046327004218
Yolande Morissette, Coordonnatrice

Saint-Léonard-de-Portneuf: Bibliothèque 'Fleur de
lin'
260, rue Pettigrew, Saint-Léonard-de-Portneuf, QC G0A 4A0
Tél: 418-337-3961
bibliofleurdelin@hotmail.com

Saint-Malachie: Bibliothèque J.-A.-Kirouac
1184, rue Principale, Saint-Malachie, QC G0R 3N0
Tél: 418-642-5127; *Téléc:* 418-642-2231
bibliojakirouac@gmail.com
www.st-malachie.qc.ca/pages/bibliotheque-j-a-kirouac
www.facebook.com/BiblioJAKirouac

Saint-Malo: Bibliothèque de Saint-Malo
127, rue Principale, Saint-Malo, QC J0B 2Y0
Tél: 819-849-7280; *Téléc:* 819-658-1169
biblio070@reseaubiblioestrie.qc.ca
www.saint-malo.ca/fr/citoyen/bibliotheque-acces-internet.php

Saint-Marc-du-Lac-Long: Bibliothèque
Saint-Marc-du-Lac-Long
14A, rue de l'Église, Saint-Marc-du-Lac-Long, QC G0L 1T0
Tél: 418-893-2643
biblio.laclong@crsbp.net
Jeanne-D'Arc Poliquin, Responsable

Saint-Marc-sur-Richelieu: Bibliothèque municipale
Archambault-Trépanier (Saint-Marc-sur-Richelieu)
110, rue de la Fabrique, Saint-Marc-sur-Richelieu, QC J0L
2E0
Tél: 450-584-2258
biblio@smsr.quebec

Saint-Marcel: Bibliothèque municipale
l'Entre-Temps
46, ch Taché est, Saint-Marcel, QC G0R 3R0

www.saintmarcel.qc.ca/pages/bibliotheque-lentre-temps
Mélanie Bourgault, Responsable
418-356-5622
Solange Pelletier, Responsable
418-356-2635

Saint-Marcel-de-Richelieu: Bibliothèque
Saint-Marcel-de-Richelieu
488, rue de l'École, Saint-Marcel-de-Richelieu, QC J0G 1T0
Tél: 450-794-2832
munst-marcel@mrcmaskoutains.qc.ca
saintmarcelderichelieu.ca/bibliotheque.wfs
Nicole Beauchamp, Responsable

Saint-Marcellin: Bibliothèque de St-Marcellin
336, rte 234, Saint-Marcellin, QC G0K 1R0
Tél: 418-798-4382
biblio.marcellin@crsbp.net
www.facebook.com/1488652531248898

Saint-Martin: Bibliothèque municipale de
Saint-Martin et Saint-René
131, 1e av est, Saint-Martin, QC G0M 1B0
Tél: 418-382-5034; *Téléc:* 418-382-5561
www.st-rene.ca/pages/bibliotheque-municipale

Saint-Mathias-sur-Richelieu: Bibliothèque
Thimothée-Franchère
99, rue Lussier, Saint-Mathias-sur-Richelieu, QC J3L 6A4
Tél: 450-658-2841
bibliotheque@st-mathias.org
www.facebook.com/bibliosaintmathias

Saint-Mathieu: Bibliothèque municipale de
Saint-Mathieu
299, ch Saint-Édouard, Saint-Mathieu, QC J0L 2H0
Tél: 450-632-9528
biblio@municipalite.saint-mathieu.qc.ca
municipalite.saint-mathieu.qc.ca/bibliotheque
www.facebook.com/bibliosmathieu

Saint-Mathieu-de-Beloeil: Bibliothèque municipale
Ryane-Provost
5000, rue des Loisirs, Saint-Mathieu-de-Beloeil, QC J3G 2C9
Tél: 450-467-7490
bibliotheque@stmathieudebeloeil.ca
stmathieudebeloeil.ca/loisirs-et-communaute/bibliotheque
www.facebook.com/biblioRyaneProvost
Kathie Ferland, Responsable

Saint-Mathieu-de-Rioux: Bibliothèque de
Saint-Mathieu-de-Rioux
41, rue de l'Église, Saint-Mathieu-de-Rioux, QC G0L 3T0
Tél: 418-738-3057
biblio.mathieu@crsbp.net
www.facebook.com/BiblioSaintMathieuDeRioux

Saint-Mathieu-du-Parc: Bibliothèque de
Saint-Mathieu-du-Parc (Micheline H.-Gélinas)
600, ch de l'Esker, Saint-Mathieu-du-Parc, QC G0X 1N0
Tél: 819-299-3830
biblio093@reseaubibliocqlm.qc.ca

Saint-Maurice: Bibliothèque de Saint-Maurice
1544, rue Notre-Dame, Saint-Maurice, QC G0X 2X0
Tél: 819-378-7315
biblio026@reseaubibliocqlm.qc.ca
biblietcie.ca/biblio/bibliotheque-de-saint-maurice

Saint-Maxime-du-Mont-Louis: Bibliothèque Liratou
4, av B, Saint-Maxime-du-Mont-Louis, QC G0E 1T0
Tél: 418-797-2032
liratou.montlouis@gmail.com
www.facebook.com/bibliothequeliratou;

Saint-Michel: Bibliothèque municipale Claire-Lazure
440, place Saint-Michel, Saint-Michel, QC J0L 2J0
Tél: 450-454-7995
bibliotheque@mst-michel.ca
www.facebook.com/bibliothequeclairelazure

Saint-Michel-de-Bellechasse: Bibliothèque
Benoît-Lacroix
8, av Saint-Charles, Saint-Michel-de-Bellechasse, QC G0R
3S0
Tél: 418-884-2766; *Téléc:* 418-884-2866
biblistmic@globetrotter.net
www.facebook.com/102352034556863

Saint-Michel-des-Saints: Bibliothèque de
Saint-Michel-des-Saints (Antonio-Saint-Georges)
390B, rue Matawin, Saint-Michel-des-Saints, QC J0K 3B0
Tél: 450-833-5471
biblio044@reseaubibliocqlm.qc.ca
smds.quebec/citoyens/bibliotheque
www.facebook.com/327213797353672

Saint-Michel-du-Squatec: Bibliothèque Alma-Durand
149C, rue Saint-Joseph, Saint-Michel-du-Squatec, QC G0L
4H0
Tél: 418-855-5228
biblio.squatec@crsbp.net
Céline Morin, Responsable

Saint-Modeste: Bibliothèque municipale de
Saint-Modeste
340, rue Principale, Saint-Modeste, QC G0L 3W0
Tél: 418-867-2352
biblio.modeste@crsbp.net
www.facebook.com/100721831785241
Solange Chouinard, Responsable

Saint-Médard: Bibliothèque de Saint-Médard
1, rue Principale est, Saint-Médard, QC G0L 3V0
Tél: 418-963-1588
biblio.medard@crsbp.net
Kathy Bélisle, Responsable

Saint-Narcisse: Bibliothèque de Saint-Narcisse
(Gérard-Desrosiers)
511, rue Massicotte, #B, Saint-Narcisse, QC G0X 2Y0
Tél: 418-328-4430
biblio001@reseaubibliocqlm.qc.ca
www.saint-narcisse.com/loisirs-et-culture/bibliotheque-municipal
e

Saint-Narcisse-de-Beaurivag: Bibliothèque
municipale de Saint-Narcisse-de-Beaurivag
101, rue Curé-Beaumont, Saint-Narcisse-de-Beaurivag, QC
G0S 1W0
Tél: 418-475-6464; *Téléc:* 418-475-6880
biblio.st-narcisse@globetrotter.net
www.mabibliotheque.ca/st-narcisse
www.facebook.com/bibliosn

Saint-Nazaire: Bibliothèque publique de St-Nazaire
220, rue Principale, Saint-Nazaire, QC G0W 2V0
Tél: 418-662-1422; *Téléc:* 418-662-5467
nazaire@reseaubiblioslsj.qc.ca
mediatheque.mairie-saintnazaire.fr

Saint-Nazaire-d'Acton: Bibliothèque municipale de
Saint-Nazaire-d'Acton
715, rue des Loisirs, Saint-Nazaire-d'Acton, QC J0H 1V0
Tél: 819-392-2090
biblio92@mun-nazaire.qc.ca
www.facebook.com/saintnazairedacton

Saint-Norbert-d'Arthabaska: Bibliothèque de
Saint-Norbert-d'Arthabaska
42, rue Landry, Saint-Norbert-d'Arthabaska, QC G0P 1B0
Tél: 819-261-0560
biblio147@reseaubibliocqlm.qc.ca
biblietcie.ca/biblio/bibliotheque-de-saint-norbert-darthabaska

Saint-Noël: Bibliothèque de Saint-Noël
25, rue de l'Église, Saint-Noël, QC G0J 3A0
Tél: 418-776-2549
biblio.noel@crsbp.net
Jennifer Bérubé, Responsable

Saint-Nérée-de-Bellechasse: Bibliothèque Biblio Du
Centenaire
2139, rte Principale, Saint-Nérée-de-Bellechasse, QC G0R
3V0
Tél: 418-243-3649; *Téléc:* 418-243-2136
Julie Drapeau, Adjointe

Saint-Odilon: Bibliothèque L'Intello
(Saint-Odilon-de-Cranbourne)
111, rue de l'Hôtel-de-Ville, Saint-Odilon, QC G0S 3A0
Tél: 418-464-4803; *Téléc:* 418-464-4800
bibliolintello@hotmail.com
www.facebook.com/105225754194438

Saint-Omer: Bibliothèque de Saint-Omer
106B, rte 132 Est, Saint-Omer, QC G0C 2Z0
Tél: 418-364-6485
bibliostomer@globetrotter.net

Saint-Ours: Bibliothèque municipale de Saint-Ours
2540, rue de l'Immaculée-Conception, Saint-Ours, QC J0G
1P0
Tél: 450-785-2779
biblio@saintours.qc.ca
ville.saintours.qc.ca/bibliotheque
www.facebook.com/bibliothequedesaintours

Saint-Pacôme: Bibliothèque de Saint-Pacôme
201, boul Bégin, Saint-Pacôme, QC G0L 3X0
Tél: 418-315-0579
biblio.pacome@crsbp.net
www.st-pacome.ca/bibliotheque-mathilde-masse

Saint-Pamphile: Bibliothèque Marie-Louise-Gagnon /
Saint-Pamphile
3, rte Elgin sud, Saint-Pamphile, QC G0R 3X0
Tél: 418-356-5403
saintpamphile.ca/citoyens/bibliotheque-marie-louise-gagnon
Marthe Dupont, Responsable
Marie-Lise Pelletier, Responsable

Saint-Pascal: Bibliothèque de Saint-Pascal
470, rue Notre-Dame, Saint-Pascal, QC G0L 3Y0
Tél: 418-492-2312
biblio.pascal@crsbp.net

Saint-Patrice-de-Beaurivage: Bibliothèque
Florence-Guay (Saint-Patrice-de-Beaurivage)
470, du Manoir, Saint-Patrice-de-Beaurivage, QC G0S 1B0
Tél: 418-596-2439; *Téléc:* 418-596-2430
borivage@globetrotter.qc.ca

Saint-Paul: Bibliothèque de Saint-Paul
790, boul de l'Industrie, Saint-Paul, QC J0K 3E0
Tél: 450-759-3333
biblio071@reseaubibliocqlm.qc.ca
saintpaul.quebec/loisirs-et-culture/bibliotheque
Sylvie Labelle, Coordonnatrice
450-759-4040 ext. 331

Saint-Paul de l'île-aux-Noi: Bibliothèque
Lucile-Langlois-Éthier
959C, rue Principale, Saint-Paul de l'île-aux-Noi, QC J0J 1G0
Tél: 450-291-5585
biblio@ileauxnoix.qc.ca
www.facebook.com/bibliolle

Saint-Paul-de-la-Croix: Bibliothèque de
Saint-Paul-de-la-Croix
1, rue du Parc, Saint-Paul-de-la-Croix, QC G0L 3Z0
Tél: 418-898-3095
biblio.croix@crsbp.net
Johanne Lagacé, Responsable

Saint-Paulin: Bibliothèque de Saint-Paulin
(Jeannine-Julien)
3051, rue Bergeron, Saint-Paulin, QC J0K 3G0
Tél: 819-268-2425
biblio118@reseaubibliocqlm.qc.ca
biblietcie.ca/biblio/bibliotheque-de-saint-paulin-jeannine-julien
www.facebook.com/bibliothequesaintpaulin
Franziska Dellinger, Coordonnatrice

Saint-Philippe: Bibliothèque Saint-Philippe / Le
Vaisseau d'Or
2223, rte Édouard VII, Saint-Philippe, QC J0L 2K0
Tél: 450-659-7701
bibliotheque@ville.saintphilippe.quebec
ville.saintphilippe.quebec/bibliotheque

Saint-Philippe-de-Néri: Bibliothèque
Claude-Béchard
11, Côte de l'Église, Saint-Philippe-de-Néri, QC G0L 4A0
Tél: 418-498-2744
biblio.philip@crsbp.net
Mariette Dumais, Responsable

Saint-Philippe-de-Néri: Bibliothèque de
St-Philippe-de-Néri
11, Côte de l'Église, Saint-Philippe-de-Néri, QC G0L 4A0
Tél: 418-498-2744
biblio.philip@crsbp.net
www.reseaubiblioduquebec.qc.ca
Mariette Dumais, Présidente

Saint-Philémon: Bibliothèque des Sous-Bois
1460, rue St-Louis, Saint-Philémon, QC G0R 4A0
Tél: 418-469-2443

Saint-Pie: Bibliothèque municipale de Saint-Pie
309, rue Notre-Dame, Saint-Pie, QC J0H 1W0
Tél: 450-772-2332
biblio@villest-pie.ca

Saint-Pierre-de-Broughton: Bibliothèque
Maurice-Couture (Saint-Pierre-de-Broughton)
6, du Couvent, Saint-Pierre-de-Broughton, QC G0N 1T0
Tél: 418-424-3450; *Téléc:* 418-424-0389
biblio.m.couture@cgocable.ca
www.facebook.com/BibliothequeMauriceCoutureStPierreDeBrou
ghton

Saint-Pierre-de-l'Ile-d'Orl: Bibliothèque
Oscar-Ferland
515, rte des Prêtres, Saint-Pierre-de-l'Ile-d'Orl, QC G0A 4E0
Tél: 418-828-2855; *Téléc:* 418-828-0724

Saint-Pierre-les-Becquets: Bibliothèque de
Saint-Pierre-les-Becquets
108, rue des Loisirs, Saint-Pierre-les-Becquets, QC G0X 2Z0
Tél: 819-263-0797
biblio086@reseaubibliocqlm.qc.ca
st-pierre-les-becquets.qc.ca/services-aux-citoyens/bibliotheque
www.facebook.com/bibliolesbecquets
Francine Bergeron, Responsable

Saint-Placide: Bibliothèque de Saint-Placide
73, rue de l'Église, Saint-Placide, QC J0V 2B0
Tél: 450-258-1780; *Téléc:* 450-258-0364
biblio@saintplacide.ca
saintplacide.ca/liens-rapides/bibliotheque
Chantal Breault, Responsable

Saint-Polycarpe: Bibliothèque municipale de
Saint-Polycarpe
7, rue Ste-Catherine, Saint-Polycarpe, QC J0P 1X0
Tél: 450-265-3444
biblio@stpolycarpe.ca

Saint-Prime: Bibliothèque publique de Saint-Prime
616, rue Principale, Saint-Prime, QC G8J 1T4
Tél: 418-251-2116
stprime@reseaubiblioslsj.qc.ca

Saint-Prosper-de-Champlain: Bibliothèque de
Saint-Prosper-de-Champlain (Livresque)
#100, 371, rue de l'Église, Saint-Prosper-de-Champlain, QC
G0X 3A0
Tél: 819-840-0408; *Téléc:* 418-328-4219
biblio012@reseaubibliocqlm.qc.ca
www.st-prosper.ca/fr/la-bibliotheque-livresque_12.html
www.facebook.com/272728089429330;

Saint-Raphaël: Bibliothèque
Jeannine-Marquis-Garant
88, rue du Foyer, Saint-Raphaël, QC G0R 4C0
Tél: 418-243-3437; *Téléc:* 418-243-2605
bibliotheque.straphael@outlook.com
www.saint-raphael.ca/pages/bibliotheque-jeannine-marquis-gara
nt

Saint-René-de-Matane: Bibliothèque de
Saint-René-de-Matane
178, av Saint-René, Saint-René-de-Matane, QC G0J 3E0
Tél: 418-224-1339
www.saintrene.ca

Saint-Robert: Bibliothèque municipale de
Saint-Robert
1, rue Aggée-Pelletier, Saint-Robert, QC J0G 1S0
Tél: 450-782-2562
www.saintrobert.qc.ca
Nathalie Cheyney, Responsable

Saint-Robert-Bellarmin: Bibliothèque municipale de
Saint-Robert-Bellarmin
10, rue Nadeau, Saint-Robert-Bellarmin, QC G0M 2E0
Tél: 418-582-6685; *Téléc:* 418-582-0052
biblio106@reseaubiblioestrie.qc.ca
www.st-robertbellarmin.qc.ca/pages/bibliotheque-municipale

Saint-Roch-de-l'Achigan: Bibliothèque de
Saint-Roch-de-l'Achigan
31, rue Gariepy, Saint-Roch-de-l'Achigan, QC J0K 3H0
Tél: 450-588-5838
biblio109@reseaubibliocqlm.qc.ca
biblietcie.ca/biblio/bibliotheque-de-saint-roch-de-lachigan

Saint-Roch-de-Mékinac: Bibliothèque de
Saint-Roch-de-Mékinac
1216, rue Principale, Saint-Roch-de-Mékinac, QC G0X 2E0
Tél: 418-507-9868
biblio033@reseaubibliocqlm.qc.ca
biblietcie.ca/biblio/bibliotheque-de-saint-roch-de-mekinac

Saint-Roch-de-Richelieu: Bibliothèque municipale
de Saint-Roch-de-Richelieu
890B, rue Saint-Pierre, Saint-Roch-de-Richelieu, QC J0L
2M0
Tél: 450-785-2755
biblio@saintrochderichelieu.com
www.facebook.com/bibliostrochderichelieu

Saint-Roch-des-Aulnaies: Bibliothèque
Bibli-Aulnaies (Saint-Roch-des-Aulnaies)
379, rte de l'Église, Saint-Roch-des-Aulnaies, QC G0R 4E0
Tél: 418-354-1831; *Téléc:* 418-354-2059
bibliosrda@gmail.com
www.facebook.com/264662480655565

Saint-Romain: Bibliothèque municipale de
Saint-Romain
325, rue Principale, Saint-Romain, QC G0Y 1L0
Tél: 418-486-7300; *Téléc:* 418-486-2718
biblio082@reseaubiblioestrie.qc.ca
www.st-romain.ca/pages/bibliotheque
www.facebook.com/bmsaintromaingal
Danielle Nault, Responsable

Saint-Rosaire: Bibliothèque municipale de
Saint-Rosaire
214, 6e rang, Saint-Rosaire, QC G0Z 1K0
Tél: 819-752-6178
www.strosaire.ca/bibliotheque-municipale
Jean-Philippe Bouffard, Responsable

Saint-Rémi: Bibliothèque municipale de Saint-Rémi
25, rue Saint-Sauveur, Saint-Rémi, QC J0L 2L0
Tél: 450-454-3993
bibliotheque@ville.saint-remi.qc.ca
www.ville.saint-remi.qc.ca/services-municipaux/bibliotheque

Saint-Samuel: Bibliothèque de Saint-Samuel
141, rue de l'Église, Saint-Samuel, QC G0Z 1G0
Tél: 819-353-2642
biblio137@reseaubibliocqlm.qc.ca
www.saint-samuel.ca/bibliotheque-municipale
Pierrette Doucet, Responsable

Saint-Sauveur: Bibliothèque de Saint-Sauveur
Chalet Pauline-Vanier, 33, av de l'Église, Saint-Sauveur, QC
J0R 1R0
Tél: 450-227-4633; Téléc: 866-313-6267
bibliotheque@ville.saint-sauveur.qc.ca
www.ville.saint-sauveur.qc.ca

Saint-Simon: Bibliothèque de Saint-Simon
19, rue de l'Église, Saint-Simon, QC G0L 4C0
Tél: 418-738-2249
biblio.simon@crsbp.net
www.st-simon.qc.ca/services/?id=stsimon-bibliotheque
France Beauchesne, Responsable

Saint-Simon: Bibliothèque municipale
Lise-Bourque-St-Pierre
47, rue du Couvent, 2e étage, Saint-Simon, QC J0H 1Y0
Tél: 450-798-2276
www.saint-simon.ca/loisirs-culture.html

Saint-Siméon: Bibliothèque Henri-Brassard
505A, rue Saint-Laurent, Saint-Siméon, QC G0T 1X0
Tél: 418-471-0550
bibliotheque@saintsimeon.ca
www.facebook.com/biblioSaintSimeon

Saint-Siméon-de-Bonaventure: Bibliothèque de
Saint-Siméon
116, rue Bélanger, Saint-Siméon-de-Bonaventure, QC G0C
3A0
Tél: 418-534-2606
bbostsim@globetrotter.net
www.stsimeon.ca/bibliotheque
www.facebook.com/1736478126669395

Saint-Stanislas: Bibliothèque publique de
Saint-Stanislas
170, ch Rousseau, Saint-Stanislas, QC G8L 7C2
Tél: 418-276-1530; Téléc: 418-276-4476
stanisla@reseaubiblioslsj.qc.ca

Saint-Stanislas: Bibliothèque Saint-Stanislas
(Émile-Bordeleau)
8, rue Saint-Gabriel, Saint-Stanislas, QC G0X 3E0
Tél: 418-328-0008
biblio002@reseaubibliocqlm.qc.ca
www.facebook.com/1481825412125119;

Saint-Stanislas-de-Kostka: Bibliothèque
Maxime-Raymond
117, rue Centrale, Saint-Stanislas-de-Kostka, QC J0S 1W0
Tél: 450-370-4650
bibliotheque@st-stanislas-de-kostka.ca
st-stanislas-de-kostka.ca/vie-communautaire/bibliotheque
www.facebook.com/bibliomaximeraymond

Saint-Sulpice: Bibliothèque de Saint-Sulpice
215, rue des Loisirs, Saint-Sulpice, QC J5W 6C9
Tél: 450-589-7816
biblio133@reseaubibliocqlm.qc.ca
biblietcie.ca/biblio/bibliotheque-de-saint-sulpice
www.facebook.com/2375998725990337
Nathalie Robidoux, Directrice

Saint-Sylvère: Bibliothèque de Saint-Sylvère
756, rue Principale, Saint-Sylvère, QC G0Z 1H0
Tél: 819-285-2075
biblio037@reseaubibliocqlm.qc.ca
biblietcie.ca/biblio/bibliotheque-de-saint-sylvere
www.facebook.com/bibliothequesaintsylvere
Maryse Désilets, Responsable

Saint-Sébastien: Bibliothèque municipale de
Saint-Sébastien
595, rue de La Fabrique, Saint-Sébastien, QC G0Y 1M0
biblio092@reseaubiblioestrie.qc.ca

Saint-Séverin: Bibliothèque de Saint-Séverin
40, rue Saint-François, Saint-Séverin, QC G0X 2B0
Tél: 418-365-6417
biblio008@reseaubibliocqlm.qc.ca
biblietcie.ca/biblio/bibliotheque-de-saint-severin
www.facebook.com/531155126942784

Saint-Séverin: Bibliothèque La Voluthèque
(Saint-Séverin)
900, rue des Lacs, Saint-Séverin, QC G0N 1V0
Tél: 418-426-2423; Téléc: 418-426-1274
biblio-st-severin.qc.ca
www.mabibliotheque.ca/st-severin
www.facebook.com/2218835225071768
Cécile Couture, Responsable

Saint-Sévère: Bibliothèque de Saint-Sévère
59, rue Principale, Saint-Sévère, QC G0X 3B0
Tél: 819-264-5656
biblio119@reseaubibliocqlm.qc.ca
biblietcie.ca/bibliotheque-de-saint-severe-denise-l-noel
Jocelyne Lavigne, Coordonnatrice

Saint-Thomas-de-Joliette: Bibliothèque de
Saint-Thomas (Jacqueline-Plante)
#941, 10, rue Principale, Saint-Thomas-de-Joliette, QC J0K
3L0
Tél: 450-759-8173
biblio117@reseaubibliocqlm.qc.ca
www.facebook.com/263931613689729

Saint-Thomas-Didyme: Bibliothèque publique de
Saint-Thomas-de-Didyme
#1, 31, av du Moulin, Saint-Thomas-Didyme, QC G0W 1P0
Tél: 418-274-3638
thomas@reseaubiblioslsj.qc.ca
stthomasdidyme.qc.ca/vie-communautaire/bibliotheque
Denise Bergeron, Responsable
418-274-3113

Saint-Théodore-d-Acton: Bibliothèque autonome de
Saint-Théodore-d'Acton
1803, rue Principale, Saint-Théodore-d-Acton, QC J0H 1Z0
Tél: 450-546-5643
biblio.st-theodore@mrcacton.qc.ca
st-theodore.com/services-municipaux/bibliotheque
www.facebook.com/bibliosttheo

Saint-Tite: Bibliothèque de Saint-Tite
(Marielle-Brouillette)
330, rue du Moulin, Saint-Tite, QC G0X 3H0
Tél: 418-365-6203
biblio017@reseaubibliocqlm.qc.ca
www.facebook.com/1701905803433562
Denise Groleau, Responsable

Saint-Ubalde: Bibliothèque Guy-Laviolette
425, rue St-Paul, Saint-Ubalde, QC G0A 4L0
Tél: 418-277-2124; Téléc: 418-277-2055
www.facebook.com/314729798896658

Saint-Valentin: Bibliothèque municipale de
Saint-Valentin
790, 4e Ligne, Saint-Valentin, QC J0J 2E0
Tél: 450-291-3948
biblio@municipalite.saint-valentin.qc.ca

Saint-Vallier: Bibliothèque
Marie-Josephte-Corrivaux
365, av de l'Église, Saint-Vallier, QC G0R 4J0
Tél: 418-884-3190; Téléc: 418-884-2454
biblstva@globetrotter.qc.ca
www.facebook.com/bibliostvallier

Saint-Valérien: Bibliothèque de Saint-Valérien
122, rue Principale, Saint-Valérien, QC G0L 4E0
Tél: 418-736-5047
biblio.valerien@crsbp.net
www.reseaubibliobsl.qc.ca/bibliotheque/bibliotheque-de-st-valerien
Sylvie Ledru, Responsable
418-736-8170

Saint-Valère: Bibliothèque de Saint-Valère
2A, rue du Parc, Saint-Valère, QC G0P 1M0
Tél: 819-353-3464; Téléc: 819-353-3465
biblio127@reseaubibliocqlm.qc.ca
www.msvalere.qc.ca/lieux/bibliotheque-municipale-de-saint-valere
www.facebook.com/2229607127305967
Marlène Chouinard, Coordonnatrice

Saint-Venant-de-Paquette: Bibliothèque de
Saint-Venant-de-Paquette
5, ch du Village, Saint-Venant-de-Paquette, QC J0B 1S0
Tél: 819-658-3660; Téléc: 819-658-0985
biblio064@reseaubiblioestrie.qc.ca
municipalites-du-quebec.org/st-venant-de-paquette/bibliotheque.php

Saint-Vianney: Bibliothèque de Saint-Vianney
170-B, av Centrale, Saint-Vianney, QC G0J 3J0
Tél: 418-629-4082
biblio.vianney@crsbp.net
Estelle Allaire, Responsable

Saint-Victor: Bibliothèque Biblio Luc-Lacourcière
(Saint-Victor)
287, rue Marchand, Saint-Victor, QC G0M 2B0
Tél: 418-588-6854; Téléc: 418-588-6855
sports@st-victor.qc.ca
www.facebook.com/521954474652416

Saint-Wenceslas: Bibliothèque de Saint-Wenceslas
1035, rue Hébert, Saint-Wenceslas, QC G0Z 1J0
Tél: 819-224-4169
biblio073@reseaubibliocqlm.qc.ca
biblietcie.ca/biblio/bibliotheque-de-saint-wenceslas-jeanne-hebert
www.facebook.com/102714257875321
Diane Renaud, Coordonnatrice

Saint-Zotique: Bibliothèque municipale de
Saint-Zotique
30, av des Maîtres, Saint-Zotique, QC J0P 1Z0
Tél: 450-267-9335
biblio@st-zotique.com
st-zotique.com/bibliotheque-renseignements-generaux
www.facebook.com/biblio.stzo
Lyne Cadieux, Directrice
450-267-9335 ext. 262

Saint-Zénon: Bibliothèque de Saint-Zénon
(Danièle-Bruneau)
6191, rue Principale, Saint-Zénon, QC J0K 3N0
Tél: 450-884-0328; Téléc: 450-884-5285
biblio048@reseaubibliocqlm.qc.ca
biblietcie.ca/biblio/bibliotheque-de-saint-zenon-daniele-bruneau
www.facebook.com/494363934079856

Saint-Zéphirin-de-Courval: Bibliothèque de
Saint-Zéphirin-de-Courval
950B, rue des Loisirs, Saint-Zéphirin-de-Courval, QC J0G
1V0
Tél: 450-564-2401
biblio092@reseaubibliocqlm.qc.ca
biblietcie.ca/biblio/bibliotheque-de-saint-zephirin-de-courval
www.facebook.com/953134041391906
Angèle Lefebvre, Responsable

Saint-Édouard: Bibliothèque municipale de
Saint-Édouard
405B, Montée Lussier, Saint-Édouard, QC J0L 1Y0
Tél: 450-454-6333
biblio@saintedouard.ca
www.saintedouard.ca/bibliotheque
www.facebook.com/320047861504727
Mylène Lavallée, Responsable

Saint-Édouard-de-Maskinongé: Bibliothèque de
Saint-Édouard-de-Maskinongé
3851, rue Notre-Dame, Saint-Édouard-de-Maskinongé, QC
J0K 2H0
Tél: 819-268-2833
biblio123@reseaubibliocqlm.qc.ca
biblietcie.ca/biblio/bibliotheque-de-saint-edouard-de-maskinonge
www.facebook.com/bibliostedouardmaskinonge

Saint-Élie-de-Caxton: Bibliothèque de
Saint-Élie-de-Caxton
2240, av Principale, Saint-Élie-de-Caxton, QC G0X 2N0
Tél: 819-221-2701
biblio115@reseaubibliocqlm.qc.ca
biblietcie.ca/bibliotheque-de-saint-elie-de-caxton
Suzanne Arel, Coordonnatrice

Saint-Éloi: Bibliothèque de Saint-Éloi
456, rue Principale, Saint-Éloi, QC G0L 2V0
Tél: 418-898-2734
biblio.eloi@crsbp.net
www.municipalite-st-eloi.com/salle-municipale
Josée Parent, Responsable

Saint-Émile-de-Suffolk: Bibliothèque de
Saint-Émile-de-Suffolk
299, rte des Cantons, Saint-Émile-de-Suffolk, QC J0V 1Y0
Tél: 819-426-2947; Téléc: 819-426-3447
admstemile@crsbpo.qc.ca
www.st-emile-de-suffolk.com/bibliotheque
France Legault, Responsable

Saint-Éphrem-de-Beauce: Bibliothèque La Voûte de
l'Imaginaire
#14, 34, rte 271 sud, Saint-Éphrem-de-Beauce, QC G0M 1R0
Tél: 418-484-5716
www.saint-ephrem.com/pages/bibliotheque
www.facebook.com/1668475243216356

Saint-Épiphane: **Bibliothèque de Saint-Épiphane**
216, rue du Couvent, Saint-Épiphane, QC G0L 2X0
Tél: 418-862-0052
biblio.epiphane@crsbp.net

Saint-Étienne-de-Beauharnois: **Bibliothèque municipale de Saint-Étienne-de-Beauharnois**
489, ch de l'Église, Saint-Étienne-de-Beauharnoi, QC J0S 1S0
Tél: 450-429-6384; *Téléc:* 450-429-6384
biblio.stetienne@videotron.ca
www.st-etiennedebeauharnois.qc.ca/bibliotheque
www.facebook.com/bibliostetienne
Martine Lalande, Responsable

Saint-Étienne-des-Grès: **Bibliothèque de Saint-Étienne-des-Grès**
#300, 190, rue Saint-Honoré, Saint-Étienne-des-Grès, QC G0X 2P0
Tél: 819-299-3854
biblio019@reseaubibliocqlm.qc.ca
biblietcie.ca/biblio/bibliotheque-de-saint-etienne-des-gres

Sainte-Adèle: **Bibliothèque Claude-Henri-Grignon**
#118, 555 boul de Sainte-Adèle, Sainte-Adèle, QC J8B 1A7
Tél: 450-229-2921; *Téléc:* 450-229-2283
responsablebiblio@ville.sainte-adele.qc.ca
ville.sainte-adele.qc.ca/bibliotheque.php
Sylvie Caron, Responsable
450-229-2921 ext. 7248
Justin Trottier, Technicien en documentation
catalogage@ville.sainte-adele.qc.ca
450-229-2921 ext. 7242

Sainte-Agathe-de-Lotbinière: **Bibliothèque municipale Rayons d'Art**
402A, rue Gosford ouest, Sainte-Agathe-de-Lotbinière, QC G0S 2A0
Tél: 418-599-2830; *Téléc:* 418-599-2905
www.mabibliotheque.ca/sainte-agathe

Sainte-Agathe-des-Monts: **Bibliothèque municipale Gaston-Miron/Gaston-Miron Public Library**
10, rue St-Donat, Sainte-Agathe-des-Monts, QC J8C 1P5
Tél: 819-326-4595; *Téléc:* 819-326-1379
bibliotheque@vsadm.ca
ville.sainte-agathe-des-monts.qc.ca

Sainte-Angèle-de-Monnoir: **Bibliothèque Sainte-Angèle-de-Monnoir**
7, ch du Vide, Sainte-Angèle-de-Monnoir, QC J0L 1P0
Tél: 450-460-3644; *Téléc:* 450-460-3853
biblio@sainte-angele-de-monnoir.ca
www.sainte-angele-de-monnoir.ca/bibliotheque
François Lachance, Responsable

Sainte-Angèle-de-Prémont: **Bibliothèque de Sainte-Angèle-de-Prémont**
2451, rue Camirand, Sainte-Angèle-de-Prémont, QC J0K 1R0
Tél: 819-268-5526
biblio124@reseaubibliocqlm.qc.ca
biblietcie.ca/biblio/bibliotheque-de-sainte-angele-de-premont
www.facebook.com/biblioSteAngeledePremont
Julie Pigeon, Responsable
819-268-5526 ext. 2607

Sainte-Anne-de-Bellevue: **Bibliothèque de Sainte-Anne-de-Bellevue**
40, rue Saint-Pierre, Sainte-Anne-de-Bellevue, QC H9X 1Y6
Tél: 514-457-1940; *Téléc:* 514-457-7146
biblio@sadb.ca
www.ville.sainte-anne-de-bellevue.qc.ca

Sainte-Anne-de-la-Pérade: **Bibliothèque de Sainte-Anne-de-la-Pérade (Armand-Goulet)**
100, rue de la Fabrique, Sainte-Anne-de-la-Pérade, QC G0X 2J0
Tél: 418-325-6666
biblio014@reseaubibliocqlm.qc.ca
sadlp.ca/fr/repertoire/2860/bibliotheque-armand-goulet

Sainte-Anne-des-Lacs: **Bibliothèque de Sainte-Anne-des-Lacs**
723, ch Ste-Anne-des-Lacs, Sainte-Anne-des-Lacs, QC J0R 1B0
Tél: 450-224-2675
biblio@sadl.qc.ca
www.sadl.qc.ca/vie-citoyenne/bibliotheque

Sainte-Anne-des-Monts: **Bibliothèque municipale Blanche-Lamontagne**
120, 7e rue ouest, Sainte-Anne-des-Monts, QC G4V 2L2
Tél: 418-763-3810
bibliotheque@villesadm.net
www.maisondelaculture.net/bibliotheque
www.facebook.com/BIBLIOSADMONTS

Sainte-Anne-des-Plaines: **Bibliothèque publique de Sainte-Anne-des-Plaines**
155, rue des Cèdres, Sainte-Anne-des-Plaines, QC J0N 1H0
Tél: 450-478-4337
bibliotheque@villesadp.ca
www.villesadp.ca/services-citoyens/bibliotheque

Sainte-Anne-du-Lac: **Bibliothèque de Sainte-Anne-du-Lac**
1B, rue St-François-Xavier, Sainte-Anne-du-Lac, QC J0W 1V0
Tél: 819-586-2110
biblio@steannedulac.ca
www.steannedulac.ca/bibliotheque-lida-touchette
www.facebook.com/bibsadl.steannedulac
Karine Quevillon, Responsable

Sainte-Aurélie: **Bibliothèque Le Maillon**
151B, ch des Bois-Francs, Sainte-Aurélie, QC G0M 1M0
Tél: 418-593-3021; *Téléc:* 418-593-3961
maillon@sogetel.net
www.facebook.com/109123257106642
JoAnne Leclerc, Responsable
Pierrette Morin, Adjointe

Sainte-Barbe: **Bibliothèque municipale Lucie Benoît**
468, ch de l'Église, Sainte-Barbe, QC J0S 1P0
Tél: 450-371-2324
biblio@ste-barbe.com
www.ste-barbe.com/bibliotheque-municipale-lucie-benoit

Sainte-Brigide-d'Iberville: **Bibliothèque de Sainte-Brigide-d'Iberville**
509, 9e rang, Sainte-Brigide-d'Iberville, QC J0J 1X0
Tél: 450-293-4604
reception@sainte-brigide.qc.ca
www.sainte-brigide.qc.ca/services

Sainte-Brigitte-de-Laval: **Bibliothèque Le Trivent**
3, rue du Couvent, Sainte-Brigitte-de-Laval, QC G0A 3K0
Tél: 418-666-4666; *Téléc:* 418-825-3114
trivent.bibliotheque@csdps.qc.ca
sbdl.net/bibliotheque-municipale
www.facebook.com/BiblioTrivent

Sainte-Brigitte-des-Saults: **Bibliothèque de Sainte-Brigitte-des-Saults (Michel-David)**
400, rue Principale, Sainte-Brigitte-des-Saults, QC J0C 1E0
Tél: 819-336-7145
biblio043@reseaubibliocqlm.qc.ca
www.saintebrigittedessaults.ca/lieux/biblioheque
www.facebook.com/466708776680988

Sainte-Béatrix: **Bibliothèque de Sainte-Béatrix**
861, rue de l'Église, Sainte-Béatrix, QC J0K 1Y0
Tél: 450-883-2245
biblio069@reseaubibliocqlm.qc.ca
biblietcie.ca/biblio/bibliotheque-de-sainte-beatrix
www.facebook.com/BiblioSteBeatrix

Sainte-Catherine: **Bibliothèque de Ville de Sainte-Catherine**
5365, boul St-Laurent, Sainte-Catherine, QC J5C 1A6
Tél: 450-632-0590; *Téléc:* 450-632-9908
bibliotheque@ville.sainte-catherine.qc.ca
www.ville.sainte-catherine.qc.ca

Sainte-Christine: **Bibliothèque municipale de Sainte-Christine**
629, rue des Loisirs, Sainte-Christine, QC J0H 1H0
Tél: 819-248-1008
bibliostechristine2020@gmail.com
ste-christine.com/bibliotheque
www.facebook.com/BibliothequeSteChristine
Rosalie Proulx, Responsable

Sainte-Claire: **Bibliothèque municipale de Sainte-Claire**
55, rue de la Fabrique, Sainte-Claire, QC G0R 2V0
Tél: 418-883-2275; *Téléc:* 418-883-3845
ste-claire.ca/culture-et-patrimoine-2/bibliotheque
www.facebook.com/1634974400095092

Sainte-Clotilde-de-Beauce: **Bibliothèque Jeanne-Édith-Audet**
307C, rue du Couvent, Sainte-Clotilde-de-Beauce, QC G0N 1C0
Tél: 418-427-2181; *Téléc:* 418-427-2495

Sainte-Clotilde-de-Horton: **Bibliothèque de Sainte-Clotilde-de-Horton**
27A, rue Saint-Denis, Sainte-Clotilde-de-Horton, QC J0A 1H0
Tél: 819-336-5363
biblio161@reseaubibliocqlm.qc.ca
biblietcie.ca/biblio/bibliotheque-de-sainte-clotilde-de-horton
www.facebook.com/BibliothequeMunicipaleDeSainteClotildeDeHorton
Marthe Désilets, Coordonnatrice

Sainte-Cécile-de-Lévrard: **Bibliothèque de Sainte-Cécile-de-Lévrard**
234, rue Principale, Sainte-Cécile-de-Lévrard, QC G0X 2M0
Tél: 819-263-0368
biblio113@reseaubibliocqlm.qc.ca
biblietcie.ca/biblio/bibliotheque-de-sainte-cecile-de-levrard
www.facebook.com/SteCecileDeLevrard

Sainte-Cécile-de-Whitton: **Bibliothèque de Sainte-Cécile-de-Whitton**
4559, rue Principale, Sainte-Cécile-de-Whitton, QC G0Y 1J0
Tél: 819-583-4149
biblio089@reseaubiblioestrie.qc.ca
www.stececiledewhitton.qc.ca/pages/bibliotheque-municipale
www.facebook.com/Bibliostececile

Sainte-Elisabeth-de-Proulx: **Bibliothèque publique de Sainte-Elisabeth-de-Proulx**
1254, rue Principale, Sainte-Elisabeth-de-Proulx, QC G8L 8A5
Tél: 418-276-9494
elisabeth@reseaubiblioslsj.qc.ca

Sainte-Eulalie: **Bibliothèque de Sainte-Eulalie**
757A, rue des Bouleaux, Sainte-Eulalie, QC G0Z 1E0
Tél: 819-225-4345
biblio074@reseaubibliocqlm.qc.ca
biblietcie.ca/biblio/bibliotheque-de-sainte-eulalie

Sainte-Famille: **Bibliothèque Marie-Barbier**
#2482, 1, ch Royal, Sainte-Famille, QC G0A 3P0
Tél: 418-666-4666; *Téléc:* 418-829-2513
www.mabibliotheque.ca/sainte-famille

Sainte-Flavie: **Bibliothèque Olivar-Asselin**
505, rte de la Mer, Sainte-Flavie, QC G0J 2L0
Tél: 418-775-7050; *Téléc:* 418-775-5672
biblio.flavie@crsbp.net
www.sainte-flavie.net/vie/115-comite-de-la-bibliotheque
Liz Fortin, Responsable

Sainte-Florence: **Bibliothèque de Sainte-Florence**
29, rue des Loisirs, Sainte-Florence, QC G0J 2M0
Tél: 418-756-5079
biblio.florence@crsbp.net
Réjeanne Doiron, Responsable

Sainte-Françoise: **Bibliothèque de Sainte-Françoise (Bas-Saint-Laurent)**
31, rue Principale, Sainte-Françoise, QC G0L 3B0
Tél: 418-851-3878
biblio.francoise@crsbp.net

Sainte-Françoise: **Bibliothèque de Sainte-Françoise (Centre-du-Québec)**
563, rue Principale, Sainte-Françoise, QC G0S 2N0
Tél: 819-287-0126
biblio104@reseaubibliocqlm.qc.ca
biblietcie.ca/biblio/bibliotheque-de-sainte-francoise

Sainte-Geneviève-de-Batiscan: **Bibliothèque de Sainte-Geneviève-de-Batiscan (Clément-Marchand)**
91, rue de l'Église, Sainte-Geneviève-de-Batisca, QC G0X 2R0
Tél: 819-840-0476
biblio036@reseaubibliocqlm.qc.ca
www.facebook.com/1794169287467408

Sainte-Geneviève-de-Berthie: **Bibliothèque de Sainte-Geneviève-de-Berthier (Léo-Paul-Desrosiers)**
391, rang de la Rivière-Bayonne sud, Sainte-Geneviève-de-Berthie, QC J0K 1A0
Tél: 450-836-4333
biblio066@reseaubibliocqlm.qc.ca
www.facebook.com/biblioleopauldesrosiers

Sainte-Germaine-Boulé: Bibliothèque de
Sainte-Germaine-Boulé
240B, rue Roy, Sainte-Germaine-Boulé, QC J0Z 1M0
Tél: 819-787-6477; *Téléc:* 819-787-6477
boule@reseaubiblioatnq.qc.ca
mabiblio.quebec/client/fr_CA/ste-germaine-boule
Odette Rancourt, Responsable

Sainte-Hedwidge: Bibliothèque publique de
Sainte-Hedwidge
#205, 1090, rue Principale, Sainte-Hedwidge, QC G0W 2R0
Tél: 418-275-3020
hedwidge@reseaubablioslsj.qc.ca
www.facebook.com/bibliothequeSainteHedwidge

Sainte-Hélène: Bibliothèque de Sainte-Hélène
707, rue du Couvent, Sainte-Hélène, QC G0L 3J0
Tél: 418-856-7057
biblio.helene@crsbp.net
sainte-helene.net/loisirs-et-vie-communautaire/bibliotheque
www.facebook.com/314089539198676

Sainte-Hélène-de-Bagot: Bibliothèque municipale de
Sainte-Hélène-de-Bagot
384, 6e av, Sainte-Hélène-de-Bagot, QC J0H 1M0
Tél: 450-791-2455
saintehelenedebagot.com/services-municipaux/bibliotheque

Sainte-Hénédine: Bibliothèque La Détente
(Sainte-Hénédine)
111D, rue Principale, Sainte-Hénédine, QC G0S 2R0
Tél: 418-935-3993; *Téléc:* 418-935-3113
bibliohenedine@hotmail.com
www.ste-henedine.com/fr/bibliotheque-la-detente
www.facebook.com/438394393030205
Doris Drouin-Dubreuil, Responsable

Sainte-Jeanne-D'Arc: Bibliothèque publique de
Sainte-Jeanne-D'Arc
#13, 400, rue Verreault, Sainte-Jeanne-D'Arc, QC G0W 1E0
Tél: 418-276-3166
jeanne@reseaubablioslsj.qc.ca
stejeannedarc.qc.ca/bibliotheque

Sainte-Julie: Bibliothèque municipale de
Sainte-Julie
1600, ch du Fer-à-Cheval, Sainte-Julie, QC J3E 0A3
Tél: 450-922-7070; *Téléc:* 450-922-7077
biblio@ville.sainte-julie.qc.ca
www.ville.sainte-julie.qc.ca/bibliotheque
www.facebook.com/bibliosaintejulie
Marie-Hélène Parent, Bibliothécaire en chef

Sainte-Julienne: Bibliothèque Gisèle-Paré
2550, rue Eugène-Marsan, Sainte-Julienne, QC J0K 2T0
Tél: 450-831-3811; *Téléc:* 450-831-4433
bibliotheque@sainte-julienne.com
www.sainte-julienne.com/loisirs-et-culture/bibliotheque
Jean-François Caron, Responsable
jean-françois.caron@sainte-julienne.com
450-831-2688 ext. 7181

Sainte-Justine: Bibliothèque Roch-Carrier
250, rue Principale, Sainte-Justine, QC G0R 1Y0
Tél: 418-383-5399
bibliorochcarrier@sogetel.net
www.stejustine.net/bibliotheque
www.facebook.com/109791477115264

Sainte-Louise: Bibliothèque Idée-Lire
506, rue Principale, Sainte-Louise, QC G0R 3K0
Tél: 418-856-7048; *Téléc:* 418-354-7730

Sainte-Luce: Bibliothèque de Luceville
67, rue Saint-Pierre est, Sainte-Luce, QC G0K 1P0
Tél: 418-739-4420
biblio.luceville@crsbp.net
sainteluce.ca/loisir/bibliotheque.php

Sainte-Luce: Bibliothèque de Sainte-Luce
#200, 1, rue Langlois, Sainte-Luce, QC G0K 1P0
Tél: 418-739-4420
biblio.luce@crsbp.net
sainteluce.ca/loisir/bibliotheque.php

Sainte-Lucie-de-Beauregard: Bibliothèque A la
Bouquinerie (Sainte-Lucie-de-Beauregard)
21, rte des Chutes, Sainte-Lucie-de-Beauregard, QC G0R
3L0
Tél: 418-223-3122; *Téléc:* 418-223-3121
alabouquinerie@hotmail.com
Nicole Gaudreau, Responsable

Sainte-Madeleine: Bibliothèque municipale de
Sainte-Madeleine
1040A, rue Saint-Simon, Sainte-Madeleine, QC J0H 1S0
Tél: 450-795-3959
biblio@stemadeleine.quebec

Sainte-Marcelline-de-Kildar: Bibliothèque de
Sainte-Marcelline-de-Kildar (Bibliothèque Gisèle
Labine)
435, 1e av Pied-de-la-Montagne, Sainte-Marcelline-de-Kildar,
QC J0K 2Y0
Tél: 450-883-0247
biblio135@reseaubibliocqlm.qc.ca
biblietcie.ca/biblio/bibliotheque-de-sainte-marcelline-de-kildare
Vanessa Arbour, Responsable
varbour@ste-marcelline.com
450-883-2241 ext. 7562

Sainte-Marguerite: Biblio La Bouquine
(Sainte-Marguerite)
268, rue Saint-Jacques, Sainte-Marguerite, QC G0S 2X0
Tél: 418-935-7089; *Téléc:* 418-935-3709
www.mabibliotheque.ca/sainte-marguerite
www.facebook.com/BibliothequeLaBouquineSteMarguerite
Michelle Lavoie, Responsable
418-935-7005

Sainte-Marguerite: Bibliothèque de
Sainte-Marguerite
15, rue de la Vérendrye, Sainte-Marguerite, QC G0J 2Y0
Tél: 418-756-3364
biblio.margot@crsbp.net

Sainte-Marie: Bibliothèque Honorius-Provost
80, rue St-Antoine, Sainte-Marie, QC G6E 4B8
Tél: 418-387-2240
info-biblio@sante-marie.ca
www.sainte-marie.ca/bibliotheque-honorius-provost
Johanne Labbé, Responsable

Sainte-Marie-de-Blandford: Bibliothèque de
Sainte-Marie-de-Blandford
492, rue des Bosquets, Sainte-Marie-de-Blandford, QC G0X
2W0
Tél: 819-519-2127
biblio108@reseaubibliocqlm.qc.ca
biblietcie.ca/biblio/bibliotheque-de-sainte-marie-de-blandford

Sainte-Marie-Salomé: Bibliothèque de
Sainte-Marie-Salomé
652, ch Saint-Jean, Sainte-Marie-Salomé, QC J0K 2Z0
Tél: 450-839-6212
biblio050@reseaubibliocqlm.qc.ca
biblietcie.ca/biblio/bibliotheque-de-sainte-marie-salome
www.facebook.com/BibliothequeSTE.MARIE.SALOME
Diane Éthier, Responsable

Sainte-Marthe-sur-le-Lac: Bibliothèque municipale
de Sainte-Marthe-sur-le-Lac
#103, 3003, ch d'Oka, Sainte-Marthe-sur-le-Lac, QC J0N 1P0
Tél: 450-472-7310
bibliotheque@vsmsll.ca
www.ville.sainte-marthe-sur-le-lac.qc.ca/bibliotheque

Sainte-Monique: Bibliothèque de Sainte-Monique
247, rue Principale, Sainte-Monique, QC J0G 1N0
Tél: 819-289-2051
biblio052@reseaubibliocqlm.qc.ca
biblietcie.ca/biblio/bibliotheque-de-sainte-monique

Sainte-Monique: Bibliothèque publique de
Sainte-Monique
138, rue Honfleur, Sainte-Monique, QC G0W 2T0
Tél: 418-347-4391
monique@reseaubablioslsj.qc.ca

Sainte-Mélanie: Bibliothèque de Sainte-Mélanie
(Louise-Amélie-Panet)
940, rue Principale, Sainte-Mélanie, QC J0K 3A0
Tél: 450-889-5871
biblio111@reseaubibliocqlm.qc.ca
www.sainte-melanie.ca/bibliotheque-louise-amelie-panet
Ghislaine Beaufort, Responsable
450-889-5871 ext. 239

Sainte-Paule: Bibliothèque de Sainte-Paule
102, rue Banville, Sainte-Paule, QC G0J 3C0
Tél: 418-737-1378
biblio.paule@crsbp.net

Carmen Côté-D'Amours, Responsable

Sainte-Perpétue: Bibliothèque de Sainte-Perpétue
2504, rang St-Joseph, Sainte-Perpétue, QC J0C 1R0
Tél: 819-336-6275
biblio094@reseaubibliocqlm.qc.ca
biblietcie.ca/biblio/bibliotheque-de-sainte-perpetue
www.facebook.com/cqlmbiblio094
Louiselle Robichaud, Responsable

Sainte-Pétronille: Bibliothèque municipale de
Sainte-Pétronille
8436, ch Royal, Sainte-Pétronille, QC G0A 4C0
Tél: 418-828-8888; *Téléc:* 418-828-1364
bibliopetronille@gmail.com

Sainte-Rita: Bibliothèque Sainte-Rita
5, rue de L'Église ouest, Sainte-Rita, QC G0L 4G0
Tél: 418-963-2967
biblio.rita@crsbp.net

Lucille Turcotte, Responsable

Sainte-Rose-de-Watford: Bibliothèque municipale de
Sainte-Rose-de-Watford
693, rue Carrier, Sainte-Rose-de-Watford, QC G0R 4G0
Tél: 418-267-5264; *Téléc:* 418-267-5812
www.mabibliotheque.ca/sainte-rose

Sainte-Rose-du-Nord: Bibliothèque publique de
Ste-Rose-du-Nord
126, rue Descente-des-Femmes, Sainte-Rose-du-Nord, QC
G0V 1T0
Tél: 418-675-2250
ste-rose@reseaubablioslsj.qc.ca

Sainte-Sabine: Bibliothèque Sabithèque
#203, 4, rue St-Charles, Sainte-Sabine, QC G0R 4H0
Tél: 418-383-5788; *Téléc:* 418-383-5488
sabitheque@hotmail.com

Sainte-Sophie-de-Lévrard: Bibliothèque de
Sainte-Sophie-de-Lévrard
184A, rue Saint-Antoine, Sainte-Sophie-de-Lévrard, QC G0X
3C0
Tél: 819-288-0334
biblio102@reseaubibliocqlm.qc.ca
biblietcie.ca/biblio/bibliotheque-de-sainte-sophie-de-levrard
www.facebook.com/271989235141 6648

Sainte-Séraphine: Bibliothèque de Sainte-Séraphine
2660, rue Centre communautaire, Sainte-Séraphine, QC J0A
1E0
Tél: 819-336-3222
biblio085@reseaubibliocqlm.qc.ca
biblietcie.ca/biblio/bibliotheque-de-sainte-seraphine

Sainte-Thérèse: Bibliothèque municipale de
Sainte-Thérèse/Sainte-Thérèse Public Library
150, boul du Séminaire, Sainte-Thérèse, QC J7E 1Z2
Tél: 450-434-1440
biblio@sainte-therese.ca
biblio.sainte-therese.ca

Sainte-Thècle: Bibliothèque de Sainte-Thècle
301, rue Saint-Jacques, Sainte-Thècle, QC G0X 3G0
Tél: 418-289-3717
biblio016@reseaubibliocqlm.qc.ca
biblietcie.ca/biblio/bibliotheque-de-sainte-thecle
www.facebook.com/bibliothequemunicipalesaintethecle

Sainte-Ursule: Bibliothèque de Sainte-Ursule (C.-J.
Magnan)
#1, 215, rue Lessard, Sainte-Ursule, QC J0K 3M0
Tél: 819-228-4345
biblio031@reseaubibliocqlm.qc.ca
biblietcie.ca/biblio/bibliotheque-de-sainte-ursule-c-j-magnan

Sainte-Victoire-de-Sorel: Bibliothèque municipale de
Sainte-Victoire-de-Sorel
519, rang Sud, Sainte-Victoire-de-Sorel, QC J0G 1T0
Tél: 450-782-3111
victoire@reseaubibliomonteregie.qc.ca
www.saintevictoiredesorel.qc.ca
www.facebook.com/350828121784779

Sainte-Élisabeth: Bibliothèque municipale de
Sainte-Elisabeth
2195, rue Principale, Sainte-Élisabeth, QC J0K 2J0
Tél: 450-759-2875
ste-elisabeth.qc.ca
www.facebook.com/biblio.steelisabeth

Josée Pagé, Responsable

Sainte-Élizabeth-de-Warwick: Bibliothèque de Sainte-Élizabeth-de-Warwick
228, rue Principale, Sainte-Élizabeth-de-Warwick, QC J0A 1M0
Tél: 819-358-2429
biblio141@reseaubibliocqlm.qc.ca
biblietcie.ca/biblio/bibliotheque-de-sainte-elizabeth-de-warwick

Sainte-Émélie-de-l'Énergie: Bibliothèque de Sainte-Émélie-de-l'Énergie
241, rue Coutu, Sainte-Émélie-de-l'Énergie, QC J0K 2K0
Tél: 450-886-3823
biblio053@reseaubibliocqlm.qc.ca
biblietcie.ca/biblio/bibliotheque-de-sainte-emelie-de-lenergie
www.facebook.com/bibliotheque.steemeliedelenergie
France Conochie, Responsable

Saints-Martyrs-Canadiens: Bibliothèque de Saints-Martyrs-Canadiens
13, ch du Village, Saints-Martyrs-Canadiens, QC G0P 1A1
Tél: 819-344-5171
biblio157@reseaubibliocqlm.qc.ca
biblietcie.ca/biblio/bibliotheque-de-saints-martyrs-canadiens

Sawyerville: Bibliothèque de Sawyerville
11, ch Clifton, Sawyerville, QC J0B 3A0
Tél: 819-560-8593
biblio022@reseaubiblioestrie.qc.ca

Sayabec: Bibliothèque Quilit
8, rue Keable, Sayabec, QC G0J 3K0
Tél: 418-536-5431
biblio.sayabec@crsbp.net
www.facebook.com/397015774009373
Charline Metcalfe, Responsable

Scotstown: Bibliothèque de Scotstown / Hampden
103, ch Victoria ouest, 2e étage, Scotstown, QC J0B 3B0
Tél: 819-560-8435; *Téléc:* 819-560-8434
biblio034@reseaubiblioestrie.qc.ca
scotstown.net/bibliotheque
www.facebook.com/100344318166339
Lynne Provençale, Responsable

Scott: Bibliothèque municipale de Scott
1, 8e rue, Scott, QC G0S 3G0
Tél: 418-386-2736; *Téléc:* 418-387-1837
scot@reseaubibliocnca.qc.ca
www.municipalitescott.com/municipal/bibliotheque

Senneterre: Bibliothèque de Senneterre
121, 1e rue est, Senneterre, QC J0Y 2M0
Tél: 819-737-2296; *Téléc:* 819-737-4215
senneterre@reseaubiblioatnq.qc.ca
www.ville.senneterre.qc.ca/loisirs_sports/bibliotheque
Denise Dufour, Responsable

Sept-Îles: Bibliothèque Louis-Ange-Santerre
500, av Jolliet, Sept-Îles, QC G4R 2B4
Tél: 418-964-3355
bibliotheque@septiles.ca
www.ville.sept-iles.qc.ca/fr/horaire-et-coordonnees_216
www.facebook.com/bibliothequelouisangesanterre

Shannon: Bibliothèque municipale de Shannon
40, rue St-Patrick, Shannon, QC G0A 4N0
Tél: 418-844-3778; *Téléc:* 418-844-2111
bibliotheque@shannon.ca
shannon.ca/services-aux-citoyens/bibliotheque-municipale

Shawinigan: Bibliothèques de Shawinigan
205, 6e rue de la Pointe, Shawinigan, QC G9N 6V3
Tél: 819-536-7218
biblio.shawinigan.ca

Shawville: Bibliothèque Shawville / Clarendon / Thorne
356, rue Main, Shawville, QC J0X 2Y0
Tél: 819-647-3732; *Téléc:* 819-647-3732
admshawville@crsbpo.qc.ca
town.shawville.qc.ca/fr/vivre-a-shawville/bibliotheque-archives
www.facebook.com/sclibrary

Sherbrooke: Bibliothèque de Brompton
81, rue du Curé LaRocque, Sherbrooke, QC J1C 0T2
Tél: 819-846-6645
biblio028@reseaubiblioestrie.qc.ca
bibliotheques.sherbrooke.ca/bibliotheque-gisele-bergeron
www.facebook.com/bibliothequegiselebergeron

Sherbrooke: Bibliothèques de la Ville de Sherbrooke
450, rue Marquette, Sherbrooke, QC J1H 5H9
Tél: 819-821-5596; *Téléc:* 819-822-6110
bibliotheque@ville.sherbrooke.qc.ca
bibliotheques.sherbrooke.ca
twitter.com/VilleSherbrooke;
www.facebook.com/BiblioSherbrooke

Sorel-Tracy: Bibliothèque municipale de Sorel-Tracy
145, rue George, Sorel-Tracy, QC J3P 7K1
Tél: 450-780-5600
bibliotheque@ville.sorel-tracy.qc.ca
bibliotheque.ville.sorel-tracy.qc.ca
www.facebook.com/biblio.sorel.tracy

St-Alexandre-de-Kamouraska: Bibliothèque de Saint-Alexandre-de-Kamouraska (Bertrand-Deschênes)
480, av de l'École, St-Alexandre-de-Kamouraska, QC G0L 2G0
Tél: 418-495-3123
biblio.alexi@crsbp.net
www.stalexkamouraska.com/pages/bibliotheque-municipale
www.facebook.com/828096890622772
Lisette Côté, Responsable

St-Antoine-de-l'Isle-aux-Gr: Bibliothèque La Rose des Vents (Saint-Antoine-de-L'Isle-aux-Grues)
#08, 107, ch de la Volière, St-Antoine-de-l'Isle-aux-Gr, QC G0R 1P0
Tél: 418-248-4680
isle-aux-grues.com/?s=bibliotheque

St-Barnabé-Nord: Bibliothèque de Saint-Barnabé
70, rue Duguay, St-Barnabé-Nord, QC G0X 2K0
Tél: 819-264-2085
biblio027@reseaubibliocqlm.qc.ca
www.saint-barnabe.ca/Bibliotheque.html

St-David-de-Falardeau: Bibliothèque publique Saint-David-de-Falardeau
124, boul St-David, St-David-de-Falardeau, QC G0V 1C0
Tél: 418-673-6395
stdavid@reseaubibliosisj.qc.ca
www.villefalardeau.ca/bibliotheque
www.facebook.com/325088357599921

St-Dominique-du-Rosaire: Bibliothèque de St-Dominique-du-Rosaire
235, rue Principale, St-Dominique-du-Rosaire, QC J0Y 2K0
Tél: 819-727-4144; *Téléc:* 819-727-4344
dominique@reseaubiblioatnq.qc.ca
mabiblio.quebec/client/fr_CA/st-dominique-du-rosaire
Marcelle Gravel, Responsable

St-François-Xavier-de-Viger: Bibliothèque de Saint-François-Xavier-de-Viger
125A, rue Principale, St-François-Xavier-de-Viger, QC G0L 3C0
Tél: 418-868-6855
biblio.xavier@crsbp.net
Suzie Lemelin, Responsable

St-Jean-de-l'Île-d'Orléans: Bibliothèque Vents et Marées
10, ch des Côtes, St-Jean-de-l'Île-d'Orléans, QC G0A 3W0
Tél: 418-829-3336
bibliotheque.saintjeaniledorleans.ca/opac_css
Patrick Plante, Responsable

St-Laurent-de-l'Île-d'Orléa: Bibliothèque David-Gosselin (Saint-Laurent-de-l'Île-d'Orléans)
#1, 6822, ch Royal, St-Laurent-de-l'Île-d'Orléa, QC G0A 3Z0
Tél: 418-828-2529; *Téléc:* 418-828-2170
biblio@saintlaurentio.com
saintlaurentio.com/bibliotheque

St-Pierre-de-la-Rivière-du-: Bibliothèque La Volumineuse (Saint-Pierre-de-la-Rivière-du-Sud)
620, rue Principale, St-Pierre-de-la-Rivière-du-, QC G0R 4B0
Tél: 418-241-5396; *Téléc:* 418-241-1477

Stanbridge East: Bibliothèque Denise-Larocque-Duhamel/Denise Larocque Duhamel Library
12A, rue Maple, Stanbridge East, QC J0J 2H0
Tél: 450-248-4662
bibliothequestanbridge@axion.ca
www.facebook.com/BiblioStanbridgeEast

Stanstead: Haskell Free Library Inc./Bibliotheque Haskell
1, rue Church, Stanstead, QC J0B 3E2
Tel: 888-626-2060; *Fax:* 802-873-3022
library@haskellopera.com
haskellopera.com/fr/bibliotheque
twitter.com/HaskellLibrary; www.facebook.com/Haskellopera

Ste-Catherine-de-la-J-Carti: Bibliothèque Anne-Hébert
215, rue Désiré-Juneau, Ste-Catherine-de-la-J-Carti, QC G3N 3E1
Tél: 418-875-2758
bibliotheque@villescjc.com
www.villescjc.com/culture/bibliotheque-anne-hebert

Ste-Gertrude-Manneville: Bibliothèque de Sainte-Gertrude
391, rte 395, Ste-Gertrude-Manneville, QC J0Y 2L0
Tél: 819-727-2248; *Téléc:* 819-727-2244
gertrude@reseaubiblioatnq.qc.ca
Alice Chagnon, Responsable

Ste-Hélène-de-Mancebourg: Bibliothèque de Sainte-Hélène-de-Mancebourg
459, ch des Rangs 2 et 3, Ste-Hélène-de-Mancebourg, QC J0Z 2T0
Tél: 819-333-4609; *Téléc:* 819-333-9591
mancebourg@reseaubiblioatnq.qc.ca
Ginette Fortin, Responsable

Ste-Jeanne-d'Arc: Bibliothèque de Sainte-Jeanne-d'Arc
321, rue Principale, Ste-Jeanne-d'Arc, QC G0J 2T0
Tél: 418-775-5660
biblio.jeanne@crsbp.net
Chantal Giroux, Responsable

Ste-Lucie-des-Laurentides: Bibliothèque de Sainte-Lucie-des-Laurentides
2057, ch des Hauteurs, Ste-Lucie-des-Laurentides, QC J0T 2J0
Tél: 819-326-3228; *Téléc:* 819-326-0592
biblio@msldl.ca
msldl.ca
Lorraine Beauchamp, Responsable

Ste-Marguerite-du-Lac-Masso: Bibliothèque de Sainte-Marguerite-Estérel
4, rue des Lilas, Ste-Marguerite-du-Lac-Masso, QC J0T 1L0
Tél: 450-228-4442
biblio@lacmasson.com
lacmasson.com/culture-et-loisirs/bibliotheque

Ste-Thérèse-de-la-Gatineau: Bibliothèque municipale de Sainte-Thérèse-de-la-Gatineau
#3, 29, rue Principale, Ste-Thérèse-de-la-Gatineau, QC J0X 2X0
Tél: 819-449-7964; *Téléc:* 819-449-2194
admtherese@crsbp.qc.ca
www.sainte-therese-de-la-gatineau.ca
Julie Richard, Bibliothécaire

Stoke: Bibliothèque municipale de Stoke
403, rue Principale, Stoke, QC J0B 3G0
Tél: 819-878-3390; *Téléc:* 819-878-3804
biblio002@reseaubiblioestrie.qc.ca
www.stoke.ca/Municipalite_de_Stoke/Services_aux_citoyens.html
Réjeanne Venner, Responsable

Stoneham-et-Tewkesbury: Bibliothèque Jean-Luc-Grondin
325, ch du Hibou, Stoneham-et-Tewkesbury, QC G3C 1R8
Tél: 418-848-2381; *Téléc:* 418-848-1748
ebouchard@villestoneham.com

Stornoway: Bibliothèque municipale de Stornoway
507, rte 108 ouest, Stornoway, QC G0Y 1N0
Tél: 819-652-2659; *Téléc:* 819-652-2105
biblio046@reseaubiblioestrie.qc.ca
www.munstornoway.qc.ca/pages/bibliotheque-municipale
Gilbert Sills, Responsable

Stratford: Bibliothèque de Stratford
165B, av Centrale nord, Stratford, QC G0Y 1P0
Tél: 418-443-2538; *Téléc:* 418-443-2603
biblio075@reseaubiblioestrie.qc.ca
stratford.quebec/citoyens/bibliotheque

Stukely-Sud: Bibliothèque municipale de
Stukely-Sud
101, place de la Mairie, Stukely-Sud, QC J0E 2J0
Tél: 450-297-1075; *Téléc:* 450-297-3759
biblio084@reseaubiblioestrie.qc.ca
stukely-sud.com/bibliotheque

Sutton: Bibliothèque municipale et scolaire de
Sutton
19, rue Highland, Sutton, QC J0E 2K0
Tél: 450-538-5843
bibliotheque@sutton.ca
www.facebook.com/928921117174406
Lisa Charbonneau, Responsable

Tadoussac: Bibliothèque municipale de Tadoussac
162, rue des Jésuites, Tadoussac, QC G0T 2A0
Tél: 418-235-4446; *Téléc:* 418-235-4433
biblio@tadoussac.com
municipalite.tadoussac.com
Johanne Hovington, Responsable

Taschereau: Bibliothèque de Taschereau
50B, rue Morin, Taschereau, QC J0Z 3N0
Tél: 819-796-2219; *Téléc:* 819-796-3226
taschereau@reseaubiblioatnq.qc.ca
mabiblio.quebec/client/fr_CA/taschereau
Ghislaine Tardif, Responsable

Terrasse-Vaudreuil: Bibliothèque
Terrasse-Vaudreuil
74, 7e av, Terrasse-Vaudreuil, QC J7V 3M9
Tél: 514-453-8120
terrasse-vaudreuil.ca/culture-et-loisirs/bibliotheque-municipale

Terrebonne: Bibliothèque publique de Terrebonne
3425, place Camus, Terrebonne, QC J6Y 0C8
Tél: 450-961-2001
biblio.ville.terrebonne.qc.ca

Thetford Mines: Bibliothèque de Black Lake
499, rue St-Désiré, Thetford Mines, QC G6H 1L7
Tél: 418-423-4291
villethetford.ca/vie-culturelle-sportive/bibliotheque-publiques

Thetford Mines: Bibliothèque de l'Amitié
#3, 5785, boul Frontenac est, Thetford Mines, QC G6H 4H9
Tél: 418-332-4548
biblio@villethetford.ca
www.villethetford.ca/vie-culturelle-sportive/bibliotheque-publique

Thetford Mines: Bibliothèque L'HIBOUCOU
5, rue de la Fabrique, Thetford Mines, QC G6G 2N4
Tél: 418-335-6111
biblio@villethetford.ca
www.villethetford.ca/vie-culturelle-sportive/bibliotheque-publique

Thurso: Bibliothèque de Thurso et
Lochaber-Partie-Ouest
341A, rue Victoria, Thurso, QC J0X 3B0
Tél: 819-985-2000; *Téléc:* 819-386-0134
biblio.thurso@mrcpapineau.com
www.ville.thurso.qc.ca/loisirs-et-culture/bibliotheque

Tingwick: Bibliothèque de Tingwick
1266, rue Saint-Joseph, Tingwick, QC J0A 1L0
Tél: 819-359-3225; *Téléc:* 819-359-2233
biblio083@reseaubiblioclm.qc.ca
bibletcie.ca/biblio/bibliotheque-de-tingwick
Maureen Martineau, Responsable

Tring-Jonction: Bibliothèque Livres-en-train
208, rue Principale, Tring-Jonction, QC G0N 1X0
Tél: 418-426-1500
www.facebook.com/BibliothequeLivresentrain

Trois-Pistoles: Bibliothèque Anne-Marie-D'Amours
145, rue de l'Aréna, Trois-Pistoles, QC G0L 4K0
Tél: 418-851-2374; *Téléc:* 418-851-3567
biblio.troispistoles@crsbp.net
ville-trois-pistoles.ca
Karen Dionne, Responsable
k.dionne@ville-trois-pistoles.ca
418-851-2374

Trois-Rives: Bibliothèque de
Saint-Joseph-de-Mékinac
258, rue St-Joseph, Trois-Rives, QC G0X 2C0
Tél: 819-646-5686
biblio034@reseaubibliocqlm.qc.ca
biblietcie.ca/biblio/bibliotheque-de-saint-joseph-de-mekinac
Johanne Doucet, Responsable

Trois-Rivières: Bibliothèques de Trois-Rivières
1425, Place de l'Hôtel-de-Ville, Trois-Rivières, QC G9A 5L9
Tél: 819-372-4615
bglreference@v3r.net
www.v3r.net/activites-et-loisirs/bibliotheques
www.facebook.com/bibliothequesdetroisrivieres

Très-Saint-Rédempteur: Bibliothèque municipale de
Très-Saint-Rédempteur
769, rte Principale, Très-Saint-Rédempteur, QC J0P 1P1
Tél: 450-451-5203
biblio@tressaintredempteur.ca
www.tressaintredempteur.ca/loisirs-et-culture/bibliotheque
www.facebook.com/biblio068
Gaston Soucy, Responsable

Témiscaming: Bibliothèque de Témiscaming
40, rue Boucher, Témiscaming, QC J0Z 3R0
Tél: 819-627-6623
biblio@temiscaming.net
temiscaming.net
www.facebook.com/490041997850202

Témiscouata-sur-le-Lac: Bibliothèque Cabano
34A, rue Vieux-Chemin, Témiscouata-sur-le-Lac, QC G0L 1E0
Tél: 418-854-5568
biblio.cabano@crsbp.net

Témiscouata-sur-le-Lac: Bibliothèque
Notre-Dame-du-Lac
2448, rue Commerciale sud, Témiscouata-sur-le-Lac, QC G0L 1X0
Tél: 418-899-6004
biblio.ndlac@crsbp.net

Tête-à-la-Baleine: Bibliothèque municipale de
Tête-à-la-Baleine
Centre Communautaire, Tête-à-la-Baleine, QC G0G 2W0
Tél: 418-242-2050; *Téléc:* 418-242-2020
Laurie Monger, Responsable
monlory@hotmail.com

Upton: Bibliothèque municipale d'Upton
784, rue Saint-Éphrem, Upton, QC J0H 2E0
Tél: 450-549-4537
www.upton.ca/bibliotheque
Francine Savoie, Responsable

Val-Alain: Bibliothèque L'Hiboucou
1298, rue de l'Église, Val-Alain, QC G0S 3H0
Tél: 418-744-3313; *Téléc:* 418-744-1330
bibliolhiboucou@val-alain.com
www.val-alain.com/bibliotheque
www.facebook.com/108377837213968

Val-Brillant: Bibliothèque Val-Brillant
2, rue Champagnat, Val-Brillant, QC G0J 3L0
Tél: 418-742-3279; *Téléc:* 418-742-3624
valbrillant.adm@mrcmatapedia.qc.ca
www.facebook.com/100229828073292
Nancy Pâquet, Responsable

Val-d'Espoir: Bibliothèque de Val-d'Espoir
1240-A, ch de Val d'Espoir, Val-d'Espoir, QC G0C 3G0
Tél: 418-782-2933
bibliothequevaldespoir@hotmail.com

Val-d'Or: Bibliothèque municipale de Val-d'Or
600, 7e rue, Val-d'Or, QC J9P 3P3
Tél: 819-824-2666
infobibliotheques@ville.valdor.qc.ca
www.ville.valdor.qc.ca
Maude Fiset, Bibliotechnicienne
maude.fiset@ville.valdor.qc.ca
819-824-2666 ext. 4221
Annie Labelle, Bibliotechnicienne
annie.labelle@ville.valdor.qc.ca
819-824-2666 ext. 4224

Val-David: Bibliothèque de Val-David
1355, rue de l'Académie, Val-David, QC J0T 2N0
Tél: 819-324-5678
comptoir@valdavid.com
www.valdavid.com/culture/bibliotheque

Val-des-Bois: Bibliothèque de Val-des-Bois et
Bowman
593, rte 309, Val-des-Bois, QC J0X 3C0
Tél: 819-454-2280; *Téléc:* 819-454-2211
biblio@val-des-bois.ca
www.val-des-bois.ca/services/?c=9#contn
www.facebook.com/BiblioVdB.Bowman
Josée Prévost, Responsable

Val-des-Lacs: Bibliothèque Val-des-Lacs
349, ch Val-des-Lacs, Val-des-Lacs, QC J0T 2P0
Tél: 819-326-5624
bibliotheque@municipalite.val-des-lacs.qc.ca

Val-des-Monts: Bibliothèque de Perkins
(Val-des-Monts)
17, ch du Manoir, Val-des-Monts, QC J8N 7E8
Tél: 819-671-1476; *Téléc:* 819-457-4141
biblioperkins@val-des-monts.net
www.val-des-monts.net/29-bibliothques
Marie-Claude Lachaine, Responsable

Val-des-Monts: Bibliothèque de Poltimore / Denholm
(Val-des-Monts)
2720, rte Principale, Val-des-Monts, QC J8N 3B6
Tél: 819-457-4467; *Téléc:* 819-457-4141
bibliopoltimore@val-des-monts.net
www.val-des-monts.net/29-bibliothque
Alexandra Éthier Deragon, Responsable

Val-des-Monts: Bibliothèque de
Saint-Pierre-de-Wakefield (Val-des-Monts)
24, ch du Parc, Val-des-Monts, QC J8N 4H8
Tél: 819-457-1911; *Téléc:* 819-457-9113
bibliost-pierre@val-des-monts.net
www.val-des-monts.net/29-bibliothque
Alexandra Éthier Deragon, Responsable

Val-des-Sources: Bibliothèque municipale de
Val-des-Sources
351, boul Saint-Luc, Val-des-Sources, QC J1T 2W4
Tél: 819-879-7171; *Téléc:* 819-879-2343
infobiblio@valdessources.ca
valdessources.ca/culture-et-loisirs/bibliotheque

Val-Morin: Bibliothèque Francine Paquette
6160, rue Morin, Val-Morin, QC J0T 2R0
Tél: 819-324-5672
biblio@val-morin.ca

Val-Saint-Gilles: Bibliothèque de Val-Saint-Gilles
801, rue Principale, Val-Saint-Gilles, QC J0Z 3T0
Tél: 819-333-5676; *Téléc:* 819-333-3116
gilles@reseaubiblioatnq.qc.ca
Nicole Richer, Responsable

Valcourt: Bibliothèque publique Yvonne L.
Bombardier
1002, av J.A. Bombardier, Valcourt, QC J0E 2L0
Tél: 450-532-2250
bylb@fjab.qc.ca
centreculturelbombardier.com/bibliotheque-accueil

Varennes: Bibliothèque de Varennes
2221, boul René-Gaultier, Varennes, QC J3X 1E3
Tél: 450-652-3949
biblio@ville.varennes.qc.ca
www.ville.varennes.qc.ca/activites/bibliotheque
Chantal Pelletier, Bibliothécaire, chef de division
chantal.pelletier@ville.varennes.qc.ca
450-652-3949 ext. 5166

Vaudreuil-Dorion: Bibliothèque municipale de
Vaudreuil-Dorion
51, rue Jeannotte, Vaudreuil-Dorion, QC J7V 6E6
Tél: 450-455-3371
biblio@ville.vaudreuil-dorion.qc.ca
ville.vaudreuil-dorion.qc.ca/fr/loisirs-et-culture/bibliotheque
www.facebook.com/bibliothequevaudreuildorion;

Vendée: Bibliothèque de Vendée
1800, ch du Village, Vendée, QC J0T 2T0
Tél: 819-681-3372
bibliovendee@municipalite.amherst.qc.ca

Venise-en-Québec: Bibliothèque de
Venise-en-Québec
237, 16e av, Venise-en-Québec, QC J0J 2K0
Tél: 450-346-4260
bibliotheque@venise-en-quebec.ca
veniseenquebec.ca/directory/bibliotheque-municipale
www.facebook.com/biblioveniseenquebec

Verchères: Bibliothèque municipale-scolaire
Dansereau-Larose
36, rue Dalpé, Verchères, QC J0L 2R0
Tél: 450-583-3309; *Téléc:* 450-583-3637
biblio@ville.vercheres.qc.ca
mabibliotheque.ca/vercheres
Sylvie Bissonnette, Directrice

Victoriaville: **Bibliothèque publique de Victoriaville**
2, rue de l'Ermitage, Victoriaville, QC G6P 6T2
Tél: 819-758-8441; *Téléc:* 819-758-9432
bibliotheque@victoriaville.ca
www.victoriaville.ca/page/865/bibliotheques.aspx
www.facebook.com/bibliothequesvicto

Ville-Marie: **Bibliothèque Ville-Marie 'La Bouquine'**
50, rue Notre-Dame de Lourdes, Ville-Marie, QC J9V 1X9
Tél: 819-629-2881
villemarie@reseaubiblioatnq.qc.ca
villevillemarie.org/loisirs-et-culture/bibliotheque-la-bouquine
www.facebook.com/634330910037379
Josianne Bergeron, Responsable

Villebois: **Bibliothèque de Villebois**
3897, rte de l'Église, Villebois, QC J0Z 3V0
Tél: 819-941-2040; *Téléc:* 819-941-2685
villebois@reseaubiblioatnq.qc.ca
mabiblio.quebec/client/fr_CA/villebois
Sylvie Mailhot, Responsable

Wakefield: **Wakefield Library/Bibliothèque de Wakefield (La Pêche)**
#1, 38 ch de la Vallée, Wakefield, QC J0X 3G0
Tel: 819-459-3266; *Fax:* 819-459-8832
contact@wakefieldlibrary.ca
bibliowakefieldlibrary.ca
www.facebook.com/bibliowakefield
Amy Carver, Responsable
Claus Jobes, Responsable

Warwick: **Bibliothèque de Warwick (P.-Rodolphe-Baril)**
181, rue Saint-Louis, Warwick, QC J0A 1M0
Tél: 819-358-4325
bibliotheque@ville.warwick.qc.ca
villedewarwick.quebec/bibliotheque-p-rodolphe-baril
www.facebook.com/bibliwarwick

Waterloo: **Bibliothèque publique de Waterloo**
650, rue de la Cour, Waterloo, QC J0E 2N0
Tél: 450-539-2268
biblio@cacwaterloo.qc.ca

Waterville: **Bibliothèque municipale de Waterville**
150, rue Compton est, Waterville, QC J0B 3H0
Tél: 819-837-0557
biblio004@reseaubiblioestrie.qc.ca
www.waterville.ca/fr/millieu-de-vie/bibliotheque.php
www.facebook.com/bibliothequeWaterville

Weedon: **Bibliothèque de Weedon**
#208, 209, des Erables, Weedon, QC J0B 3J0
Tél: 819-560-8552
biblio015@reseaubiblioestrie.qc.ca
weedon.ca/loisirs-et-culturel/bibliotheque
www.facebook.com/BiblioWeedon

Weedon: **Bibliothèque Saint-Gérard**
249A, rue Principale, Weedon, QC J0B 3J0
Tél: 819-877-5704
biblio024@reseaubiblioestrie.qc.ca
www.facebook.com/BiblioStGerard

Wemotaci: **Bibliothèque de Wemotaci**
CP 222, Wemotaci, QC G0X 3R0
Tél: 819-666-2232
biblio064@reseaubibliocqlm.qc.ca
bibliotcie.ca/biblio/bibliotheque-de-wemotaci

Wentworth-Nord: **Bibliothèque de Wentworth-Nord**
3486, rte Principale, Wentworth-Nord, QC J0T 1Y0
Tél: 450-226-2416

Westmount: **Bibliothèque publique de Westmount/Westmount Public Library**
4574, rue Sherbrooke ouest, Westmount, QC H3Z 1G1
Tél: 514-989-5300
wpl@westmount.org
www.westlib.org
www.youtube.com/user/bibliowestmount;
www.facebook.com/bibliowestmount
Julie-Anne Cardella, Directrice
jacardella@westmount.org
514-989-5429
Mai Jay, Bibliothécaire de référence
mjay@westmount.org
514-989-5296

Wickham: **Bibliothèque de Wickham**
893, rue Moreau, Wickham, QC J0C 1S0
Tél: 819-741-0202
bibliothequewickham@gmail.com
www.wickham.ca/loisirs-culture-vie-communautaire/mediatheque
www.facebook.com/BiblioWickham
Martine Lamy, Coordonnatrice

Windsor: **Bibliothèque municipale Patrick-Dignan de Windsor**
52, rue St-Georges, Windsor, QC J1S 1J5
Tél: 819-845-7888; *Téléc:* 819-845-5516
info@bibliotheque.windsor.qc.ca
bibliotheque.windsor.qc.ca
Jacynthe Dubois, Technicienne en documentation
jacynthe@bibliotheque.windsor.qc.ca

Wotton: **Bibliothèque Wotton**
398, Mgr. l'Heureux, Wotton, QC J0A 1N0
Tél: 819-828-0693; *Téléc:* 819-828-3594
biblio055@reseaubiblioestrie.qc.ca
www.facebook.com/biblio055Wotton

Yamachiche: **Bibliothèque de Yamachiche (J.-Alide-Pellerin)**
440, rue Sainte-Anne, Yamachiche, QC G0X 3L0
Tél: 819-296-3580
biblio020@reseaubibliocqlm.qc.ca
bibliotcie.ca/biblio/bibliotheque-de-yamachiche-j-alide-pellerin
www.facebook.com/loisirs.yamachiche

Ile-du-Grand-Calumet: **Bibliothèque Ile-du-Grand-Calumet**
2, rue Brizard, Ile-du-Grand-Calumet, QC J0X 1J0
Tél: 819-648-5966; *Téléc:* 819-648-2659
admcalumet@crsbpo.qc.ca
île-du-grand-calumet.ca/community/bibliotheque
Cécile La Salle, Responsable

Archives

Alma: **Société d'histoire du Lac-Saint-Jean**
1671, av du Pont nord, Alma, QC G8B 5G2
Tél: 418-668-2606; *Téléc:* 418-668-5851
Ligne sans frais: 866-668-2606
info.archives@shlsj.org
www.shlsj.org
www.facebook.com/shlsj.org
Allyson D'Amours, Directrice, Service d'archives et de généalogie et Archiviste
adamours@shlsj.org
418-668-2606 ext. 231
Olivier Dallaire-Lavoie, Archiviste-historien
418-668-2606 ext. 229
Nancy Darveau, Archiviste du service de consultant
ndarveau@shlsj.org
418-668-2606 ext. 230

Amos: **Société d'histoire d'Amos**
Édifice de la Maison de la culture, 222, 1e av est, Amos, QC J9T 1H3
Tél: 819-732-6070
societe.histoire@cableamos.com
societehistoireamos.com/documentation/archives
www.youtube.com/c/societehistoireamos1980;
www.facebook.com/societehistoireamos
Geneviève Dubé, Archiviste responsable

Baie-Comeau: **Société historique de la Côte-Nord**
2, place La Salle, Baie-Comeau, QC G4Z 1K3
Tél: 418-296-8228; *Téléc:* 418-294-4187
shcn@globetrotter.net
www.shcote-nord.org
www.facebook.com/shcotenord
Catherine Pellerin, Archiviste
catherine.pellerin@shcote-nord.org

Baie-Comeau: **Ville de Baie-Comeau**
2, place La Salle, Baie-Comeau, QC G4Z 1K3
Tél: 418-296-8298; *Téléc:* 418-296-8120
www.ville.baie-comeau.qc.ca
Annick Tremblay, Greffière
antremblay@ville.baie-comeau.qc.ca

Chambly: **Société d'histoire de la Seigneurie de Chambly**
2445, rue Bourgogne, Chambly, QC J3L 2A5
Tél: 450-658-2666
shsc@histoireseigneuriechambly.org
www.histoireseigneuriechambly.org
www.facebook.com/societehistoirechambly
René Fournier, Président

Chicoutimi: **Diocèse de Chicoutimi**
602, rue Racine est, Chicoutimi, QC G7H 1V1
Tél: 418-543-0783; *Téléc:* 418-543-2141
diocese.chicoutimi@evechedechicoutimi.qc.ca
www.evechedechicoutimi.qc.ca/page/service-des-archives
Nathalie Lévesque, Responsable
nathalie.levesque@evechedechicoutimi.qc.ca

Chicoutimi: **Séminaire de Chicoutimi**
679, rue Chabanel, Chicoutimi, QC G7H 1Z7
Tél: 418-549-0190; *Téléc:* 418-549-1524
info@sdec.education
seminairedechicoutimi.ca

Chicoutimi: **Société historique du Saguenay**
930, rue Jacques Cartier est, Chicoutimi, QC G7H 7K9
Tél: 418-549-2805; *Téléc:* 418-698-3758
shs@shistoriquesaguenay.com
shistoriquesaguenay.com/recherche
Sara-Jeanne Lemieux, Archiviste

Gaspé: **Centre d'archives du Musée de la Gaspésie**
80, boul de Gaspé, Gaspé, QC G4X 1A9
Tel: 418-368-1534
archives@museedelagaspesie.ca
museedelagaspesie.ca/pages/archives
www.youtube.com/user/musee1534; twitter.com/MG1534;
www.facebook.com/museegaspesie
Marie-Pierre Huard, Archiviste

Gatineau: **Archives municipales de la Ville de Gatineau**
855, boul de la Gappe, Gatineau, QC J8T 8H9
Tél: 819-243-2329; *Téléc:* 819-243-2341
archives@gatineau.ca
www.gatineau.ca/portail/default.aspx?p=guichet_municipal/archives

Gatineau: **Western Québec School Board**
15, rue Katimavik, Gatineau, QC J9J 0E9
Tél: 819-864-2336; *Fax:* 819-684-1328
Toll-Free: 800-363-9111
westernquebec.ca
Pascal Proulx, Director, Buildings, Technology & Archives
pproulx@wqsb.qc.ca

Granby: **Société d'histoire de la Haute-Yamaska**
135, rue Principale, Granby, QC J2G 2V1
Tél: 450-372-4500
info@shhy.org
www.shhy.info/fonds-et-collections-d-archives
Cecilia Capocchi, Directrice générale
cecilia.capocchi@shhy.info
Mario Gendron, Historien
mario.gendron@shhy.info

Jonquière: **La Commission scolaire de la Jonquière**
1955, rue Bourassa, Jonquière, QC G7X 4E1
Tél: 418-695-1801; *Téléc:* 418-695-2549
gdocuments@csjonquiere.qc.ca
www.csjonquiere.qc.ca
Jonathan Nault, Directeur
sgeneral@csjonquiere.qc.ca
418-542-7551 ext. 4302

Knowlton: **Brome County Historical Society**
130, ch Lakeside, Knowlton, QC J0E 1V0
Tél: 450-243-6782
info@shcb.com
www.bromemuseum.com/archives
Arlene Royea, Managing Director & Archivist
Anne-Marie Charuest, Archivist

La Pocatière: **Evêché de Sainte-Anne-de-la-Pocatière**
#1200, 4e av Painchaud, La Pocatière, QC G0R 1Z0
Tél: 418-856-1811; *Téléc:* 418-856-5863
diocese@diocese-ste-anne.net
www.diocese-ste-anne.net

La Pocatière: **Société historique de la Côte-du-Sud**
100, 4e av Painchaud, La Pocatière, QC G0R 1Z0
Tél: 418-856-2104; *Téléc:* 418-856-2104
archsud@bellnet.ca
www.shcds.org
www.facebook.com/shcds
François Taillon, Directeur, Centre des archives

La Prairie: **Archives des Frères de l'Instruction chrétienne**
870, ch de Saint-Jean, La Prairie, QC J5R 2L5
Tél: 450-659-1922
www.provincejdlm.com/Archives.htm

Janine Mazenc, Branch Librarian

Redvers: Redvers Library
23B Railway Ave., Redvers, SK S0C 2H0
Tel: 306-452-3255
redvers@southeastlibrary.ca
southeastlibrary.ca/spm/branch/355
www.facebook.com/205826132823308
Michelle Jensen, Librarian

Regina: Regina Public Library
2311 - 12th Ave., Regina, SK S4P 0N3
Tel: 306-777-6000; *Fax:* 306-949-7260
askalibrarian@reginalibrary.ca
www.reginalibrary.ca
twitter.com/OfficialRPL; www.facebook.com/ReginaPublicLibrary
Jeff Barber, CEO & Library Director
jbarber@reginalibrary.ca
306-777-6099
Julie McKenna, Deputy Library Director
jmckenna@reginalibrary.ca
306-777-6074
Kevin Saunderson, Senior Manager, Corporate Services
ksaunderson@reginalibrary.ca
306-777-6222
Robert Borges, Manager, Information Technology
rborges@reginalibrary.ca
306-777-6056
Jeff Demitor, Manager, E-Services
jdemitor@reginalibrary.ca
306-777-6073
Nancy MacKenzie, Manager, Community Engagement &
Programming
nmackenzie@reginalibrary.ca
306-777-6071

Regina: Saskatchewan Provincial Library & Literacy Office
409A Park St., Regina, SK S4N 5B2
Tel: 306-787-2976; *Fax:* 306-787-2029
saskliteracy@gov.sk.ca
www.saskatchewan.ca/residents/education-and-learning
Alison Hopkins, Provincial Librarian & Executive Director
alison.hopkins@gov.sk.ca
Julie Arie, Director, Public Library Planning
julie.arie@gov.sk.ca
306-787-3005
Flo Woods, Director, Library Accountability & Administration
flo.woods@gov.sk.ca
306-787-2029
Merla Parker, Program Manager, Literacy Office
merla.parker@gov.sk.ca
306-787-2513
Debbie Kraus, Executive Coordinator
debbie.kraus@gov.sk.ca
306-787-2514

Regina Beach: Regina Beach Branch Library
133 Donovel Cres., Regina Beach, SK S0C 4C0
Tel: 306-729-2062
reginabeach@southeastlibrary.ca
southeastlibrary.ca/branch/354
www.facebook.com/264884513548181
Laura Davies, Librarian

Riverhurst: Riverhurst Branch Library
The Village Square, 324 Teck St., Riverhurst, SK S0H 3P0
Tel: 306-353-2130
riverhurst@palliserlibrary.ca
palliserlibrary.ca/branch/232
www.facebook.com/riverhurst.library
Valerie Bennett, Librarian

Rocanville: Rocanville Branch Library
218 Ellice St., Rocanville, SK S0A 3L0
Tel: 306-645-2088
rocanville@southeastlibrary.ca
southeastlibrary.ca/branch/356
www.facebook.com/274115229287229
Jeri Waldo, Librarian

Rockglen: Rockglen Branch Library
1018 Centre St., Rockglen, SK S0H 3R0
Tel: 306-476-2350
rockglen@palliserlibrary.ca
palliserlibrary.ca/branch/231
www.facebook.com/RockglenLibrary
Angela Stewart, Librarian

Rouleau: Rouleau Branch Library
204 Main St., Rouleau, SK S0G 4H0
Tel: 306-776-2322; *Fax:* 306-776-0003
rouleau@palliserlibrary.ca
palliserlibrary.ca/branch/233
www.facebook.com/RouleauLibrary
Marla Gellvear, Librarian

Sandy Bay: Ayamicikiwikamik Public Library
PO Box 240, Sandy Bay, SK S0P 0G0
Tel: 306-754-2139; *Fax:* 306-754-2130
ssbp@pnls.lib.sk.ca
pahkisimon.ca/branch/199

Saskatoon: Saskatoon Public Library
311 - 23rd St. East, Saskatoon, SK S7K 0J6
Tel: 306-975-7558
askus@saskatoonlibrary.ca
saskatoonlibrary.ca
www.instagram.com/stoonlibrary; twitter.com/stoonlibrary;
www.facebook.com/stoonlibrary
Carol Cooley, CEO & Director of Libraries

Sedley: Sedley Branch Library
224 Broadway St., Sedley, SK S0G 4K0
Tel: 306-885-4505
sedley@southeastlibrary.ca
southeastlibrary.ca/branch/359
www.facebook.com/281851975179696
Stephanie Makellky, Librarian

Stanley Mission: Keethanow Public Library
PO Box 70, Stanley Mission, SK S0M 1G0
Tel: 306-635-2104; *Fax:* 306-635-2050
ssk@pnls.lib.sk.ca
pahkisimon.ca/branch/205
Lucy Ratt, Branch Librarian

Stoughton: Stoughton Branch Library
232 Main St., Stoughton, SK S0G 4T0
Tel: 306-457-2484
stoughton@southeastlibrary.ca
southeastlibrary.ca/branch/358
www.facebook.com/292105920817879
Rheanelle Callfas, Librarian

Tugaske: Tugaske Branch Library
106 Ogema St., Tugaske, SK S0H 4B0
Tel: 306-759-2215
tugaske@palliserlibrary.ca
palliserlibrary.ca/branch/234
Violet Beaudry, Branch Librarian
vi7@sasktel.net
Nola Rudd, Librarian

Vibank: Vibank Branch Library
101 - 2nd Ave., Vibank, SK S0G 4Y0
Tel: 306-762-2270
vibank@southeastlibrary.ca
southeastlibrary.ca/branch/361
www.facebook.com/299516580073965
Betty Kuntz, Librarian

Wapella: Wapella Branch Library
519 Railway St. South, Wapella, SK S0G 4Z0
Tel: 306-532-4419
wapella@southeastlibrary.ca
southeastlibrary.ca/branch/362
twitter.com/WapellaLibrary;
www.facebook.com/252057424840055
Sharon Matheson, Librarian

Wawota: Wawota Branch Library
308 Railway Ave., Wawota, SK S0G 5A0
Tel: 306-739-2375
wawota@southeastlibrary.ca
southeastlibrary.ca/branch/367
www.facebook.com/286787141339067
Shirley Palendat, Chair
Kayla Porter, Librarian

Weyburn: Weyburn Public Library
45 Bison Ave., Weyburn, SK S4H 0H9
Tel: 306-842-4352; *Fax:* 306-842-1255
weyburn@southeastlibrary.ca
weyburnpubliclibrary.weebly.com
www.facebook.com/189593097722161
Katherine Wagner, Librarian
wplmanager@southeastlibrary.ca

White City: White City Branch Library
White City Community Centre, 12 Ramm Ave., White City,
SK S4L 5B1
Tel: 306-781-2118
whitecity@southeastlibrary.ca
southeastlibrary.ca/branch/363
www.facebook.com/269027146468715
Lori-Lee Harris, Branch Librarian

Whitewood: Whitewood Library
731 Lalonde St., Whitewood, SK S0G 5C0
Tel: 306-735-4233
whitewood@southeastlibrary.ca
southeastlibrary.ca/branch/364
www.facebook.com/WhitewoodPublicLibrary
Erica Duncan, Branch Librarian

Willow Bunch: Willow Bunch Branch Library
2 Ave. F South, Willow Bunch, SK S0H 4K0
Tel: 306-473-2393
willowbunch@palliserlibrary.ca
palliserlibrary.ca/branch/235
www.facebook.com/WillowBunchlibrary
Barb Gibbons, Branch Librarian

Windthorst: Windthorst Branch Library
202 Angus St., Windthorst, SK S0G 5G0
Tel: 306-224-2159
windthorst@southeastlibrary.ca
southeastlibrary.ca/branch/365
www.facebook.com/165951236831916
Joanne Smith, Interim Branch Librarian

Wolseley: Wolseley Branch Library
500 Front St., Wolseley, SK S0G 5H0
Tel: 306-698-2221
wolseley@southeastlibrary.ca
southeastlibrary.ca/branch/366
www.facebook.com/236619326394875
Cambie Lam, Interim Librarian

Wood Mountain: Wood Mountain Branch Library
2 - 2nd Ave., Wood Mountain, SK S0H 4L0
Tel: 306-266-2110
woodmountain@palliserlibrary.ca
palliserlibrary.ca/branch/236
www.facebook.com/139580349558483
Jocelyn Todd, Librarian

Yellow Grass: Yellow Grass Branch Library
213 Souris St., Yellow Grass, SK S0G 5J0
Tel: 306-465-2574
yellow.grass@southeastlibrary.ca
southeastlibrary.ca/branch/369
twitter.com/YellowGrassLib;
www.facebook.com/278686295488027
Betty Guest, Librarian

Archives

Duck Lake: Duck Lake Historical Society
PO Box 328, Duck Lake, SK S0K 1J0
Toll-Free: 866-467-2057
info@ducklakemuseum.com
www.ducklakemuseum.ca
www.facebook.com/DuckLakeRIC

Prince Albert: Prince Albert Historical Society
10 River St. East, Prince Albert, SK S6V 8A9
Tel: 306-764-2992
historypa@citypa.com
www.historypa.com
twitter.com/historypa;
www.facebook.com/PrinceAlbertHistoricalSociety
Michelle Taylor, Manager/Curator

Regina: Provincial Archives of Saskatchewan
2440 Broad St., Regina, SK S4P 0A5
Tel: 306-787-4068; *Fax:* 306-787-1975
www.saskarchives.com
Linda McIntyre, Provincial Archivist
lmcintyre@archives.gov.sk.ca

Regina: RCMP Heritage Centre/Centre du Patrimoine de la GRC
5600 - 11th Ave., Regina, SK S4P 3J7
Tel: 306-522-7333; *Fax:* 306-585-3052
Toll-Free: 866-567-7267
rcmphc.com/about/historical-collections-unit
Jodi Anne Eskritt, Curator

Regina: Saskatchewan Genealogical Society
#110, 1514 - 11th Ave., Regina, SK S4P 0H2
Tel: 306-780-9207
saskgenealogy@sasktel.net
www.saskgenealogy.com/index.php/library-catalogues
www.facebook.com/216892188363312

Saskatoon: City of Saskatoon Archives
224 Cardinal Cr., Saskatoon, SK S7L 6H8
Tel: 306-975-7811; *Fax:* 306-975-2612
city.archives@saskatoon.ca
saskatoon.ca/community-culture-heritage/saskatoon-history-arch
ives
twitter.com/cityofsaskatoon

Saskatoon: Diefenbaker Canada Centre
University of Saskatchewan, 101 Diefenbaker Pl.,
Saskatoon, SK S7N 5B8
Tel: 306-966-8384
dief.centre@usask.ca
diefenbaker.usask.ca
www.instagram.com/diefcentre; twitter.com/DiefCentre;
www.facebook.com/diefenbakercentre
Helanna Gessner, Curator & Manager, Exhibits & Collections
helanna.gessner@usask.ca

Saskatoon: Mohyla Institute
1240 Temperance St., Saskatoon, SK S7N 0P1
Tel: 306-653-1944; *Fax:* 306-653-1902
info@mohylainstitute.ca
www.mohylainstitute.ca

Verigin: National Doukhobour Heritage Village Inc.
PO Box 99, Verigin, SK S0A 4H0
Tel: 306-542-4441
ndhv@yourlink.ca
www.ndhv.ca

Weyburn: Soo Line Historical Museum
411 Riverfront Rd., Weyburn, SK S4H 2L2
Tel: 306-842-2922; *Fax:* 306-842-2001
slhm@sasktel.net
weyburn.ca/soo-line-historical-museum

Yukon Territory

Public Libraries

Whitehorse: Yukon Public Libraries
1171 Front St., Whitehorse, YT Y1A 2C6
Tel: 867-667-5239; *Fax:* 867-393-6333
Toll-Free: 800-661-0408
whitehorse.library@gov.yk.ca
www.pac.gov.yk.ca
twitter.com/YukonLibraries;
www.facebook.com/yukonpubliclibraries

Archives

Dawson City: Dawson City Museum
595 - 5th Ave., Dawson City, YT Y0B 1G0
Tel: 867-993-5291; *Fax:* 867-993-5839
info@dawsonmuseum.ca
www.dawsonmuseum.ca
twitter.com/dcmuseum; www.facebook.com/DawsonCityMuseum
Alex Somerville, Executive Director
asomerville@dawsonmuseum.ca
867-993-5291 ext. 21

Whitehorse: Yukon Tourism & Culture
400 University Dr., Whitehorse, YT Y1A 3K5
Tel: 867-667-5321; *Fax:* 867-393-6253
Toll-Free: 800-661-0408
yukon.archives@gov.yk.ca
yukon.ca/archives
David Schlosser, Territorial Archivist
david.schlosser@gov.yk.ca
867-667-5275
Lesley Buchan, Archivist, Private Records
lesley.buchan@gov.yk.ca
867-667-5641
Susan Gordon, Archivist, Private Records
susan.gordon@gov.yk.ca
867-456-6740
Nadine Helm, Archivist, Reference
nadine.helm@gov.yk.ca
867-667-5839
Heather LeDuc, Archivist, Government Records
heather.leduc@yukon.ca
867-667-8959
Kaitlin Normandin, Archivist, Government Records
kaitlin.normandin@yukon.ca
867-667-8063
Elizabeth Walker, Archivist, Digital
elizabeth.walker@yukon.ca
867-667-8958
Anne Barkworth, Archives Librarian
anne.barkworth@gov.yk.ca
867-667-5625

SECTION PUBLISHING 13

Publishers

Book Publishers

AB collector publishing
5835 Grant St., Halifax, NS B3H 1C9
Tel: 902-429-5768; *Fax:* 506-385-1981
Toll-Free: 888-748-5514
darklady@nbnet.nb.ca
www.abcollectorpublishing.ca
Publisher of poetry, short stories, biography, drama, works relating to photography, ceramics, art & history, in English, French, German
Astrid Brunner, Publisher

ABC Publishing (Anglican Book Centre)
Owned By: Augsburg Fortress Canada
80 Hayden St., Toronto, ON M4Y 3G2
Tel: 416-924-9199; *Fax:* 416-968-7983
www.abcpublishing.com
ISBNs: 0-919030, 0-919891, 0-921846
ABC Publishing (Anglican Book Centre) produces liturgical resources (prayer books, hymn books, lectionary aids), institutional materials & parish leadership resources (congregational development, biblical reflection, church school materials).

Able Sense Publishing
#300, 1559 Brunswick St., Halifax, NS B3J 2G1
Tel: 902-442-9356
info@ablesensepublishing.com
www.ablesensepublishing.com
www.pinterest.ca/AbleSensePub
twitter.com/AbleSensePub
www.facebook.co m/ablesensepublishing
Publishes specialized how-to books.

Acadiensis Press
Campus House, University of New Brunswick, PO Box 4400, 11 Garland Ct., Fredericton, NB E3B 5A3
Tel: 506-453-4978
acadnsis@unb.ca
www.lib.unb.ca/Texts/Acadiensis
twitter.com/acadiensis
www.facebook.com/Acadiensis
ISSN: 0044-5871
Publisher of ACADIENSIS: The Journal of the History of the Atlantic Region & books on the culture & history of Atlantic Canada.
Stephen Dutcher, Managing Editor, 506-458-7199

Acorn Press
PO Box 22024, Charlottetown, PE C1A 9J2
Tel: 902-221-1061
info@acompresscanada.com
acornpresscanada.com
twitter.com/AcornPress
www.facebook.com/146624385354176
ISBNs: 1-894838014-9; 1-894838-16-5-64
Publishing books about Prince Edward Island, with emphasis on Prince Edward Island authors, Acorn Press lists works of fiction, poetry, folklore, history & literature for children. Canadian and US distribution by Nimbus Publishing
Terrilee Bulger, Publisher

Actualisation
Édifice Steel, #300, 4080 rue Wellington, Montréal, QC H4G 1V4
Ligne sans frais: 877-688-0101
www.actualisation.com
www.linkedin.com/company/actualisation-idh
twitter.com/ActualisationRH
www.facebook.com/ActualisationIDH
Matériel pour animer des formations, destiné aux formateurs, éducateurs et conseillers en ressources humaines: guides, manuels, questionnaires.
Louis Fortin, Président

Alpine Book Peddlers
#140, 105 Bow Meadows Cres., Canmore, AB T1W 2W8
Tel: 403-678-2280; *Fax:* 403-678-2840
Toll-Free: 866-478-2280
info@alpinebookpeddlers.ca
www.alpinebookpeddlers.ca
Other information: Toll-Free Fax: 866-978-2840
ISBNs: 0-9699368, 0-9692631, 0-919934, 0-9692457; SAN: 1187546
Distributor of books, journals, maps, posters, & cards
Heather Lohnes, Operator
Tobias Toleman, Operator

Annick Press Ltd.
15 Patricia Ave., Toronto, ON M2M 1H9
Tel: 416-221-4802; *Fax:* 416-221-8400
annickpress@annickpress.com
www.annickpress.com
www.instagram.com/annick_press
twitter.com/AnnickPress
www.facebook.com/AnnickPress
ISBNs: 0-920236, 920303, 1-55037; SAN: 115-0065
Publishers of fiction & nonfiction for children & young adults. Editorial offices in Toronto & Vancouver.
David Wichman, Editor

Anvil Press
278 East First Ave., Vancouver, BC V5T 1A6
Tel: 604-876-8710; *Fax:* 604-879-2667
info@anvilpress.com
www.anvilpress.com
twitter.com/anvilpress
ISBNs: 1-895636
Brian Kaufman, Publisher

Apple Press Publishing
810 Landresse Ct., Newmarket, ON L3X 1M6
Tel: 905-853-7979; *Fax:* 905-853-1175
Toll-Free: 866-222-8883
ISBNs: 0-919972
George Quinn, President, 905-853-7979

Aquila Communications Ltd.
176 Beacon Hill, Beaconsfield, QC H9W 1T6
Toll-Free: 800-667-7071
mike@aquilacommunications.com
www.fsldigitalbooks.com
www.facebook.com/aquilafsl
ISBNs: 0-88510, 2-89054; SAN: 115-2483, 115-8295
Publishes French as a Second Language reading materials, for grades 4 through college.
Sami Kelada, President & CEO
Mike Kelada, Vice-President & General Manager

Arbeiter Ring Publishing
#201E, 121 Osborne St., Winnipeg, MB R3L 1Y4
Tel: 204-942-7058; *Fax:* 204-944-9198
info@arpbooks.org
arpbooks.org
twitter.com/arpbooks
www.facebook.com/arpbooks
ISBNs: 1-894037
Publishers of books on contemporary politics, culture, and social issues.

Arsenal Pulp Press Ltd.
#202, 211 East Georgia St., Vancouver, BC V6A 1Z6
Tel: 604-687-4233; *Fax:* 604-687-4283
info@arsenalpulp.com
www.arsenalpulp.com
twitter.com/arsenalpulp
www.facebook.com/arsenalpulp
ISBNs: 0-88978, 1-55152; SAN: 115-0847
Publisher with over 200 titles in print, including literary fiction & non-fiction; cultural & gender studies; gay, lesbian & multicultural literature; cookbooks & guidebooks.
Brian Lam, Publisher

Art Metropole
#135, 163 Sterling Rd., Toronto, ON M6R 2B2
Tel: 416-703-4400; *Fax:* 416-703-4404
info@artmetropole.com
www.artmetropole.com
Publisher of art books & publications
Danielle St-Amour, Executive Director,
danielle@artmetropole.com

Artexte / Centre d'information Artexte
#301, 2 Sainte-Catherine est, Montréal, QC H2X 1K4
Tél: 514-874-0049
info@artexte.ca
www.artexte.ca
www.instagram.com/artexte
www.facebook.com/artextemtl
Artexte est attachée à la compréhension et à la promotion des arts visuels grâce à des sources d'information fiables.
Sarah Watson, Directrice, swatson@artexte.ca

Artistic Warrior
#207, 2475 Dobbin Rd., West Kelowna, BC V4T 2E9
Tel: 778-587-5911
publisher@artisticwarrior.com
www.artisticwarrior.com
www.facebook.com/ArtisticWarriorPublishing
Publisher of new & emerging Canadian authors with a focus on BC authors.

Darcy Nybo, Publisher

Asteroid Publishing Inc.
PO Box 3, Richmond Hill, ON L4C 4X9
Tel: 416-319-5911; *Fax:* 416-352-1561
editor@asteroidpublishing.ca
asteroidpublishing.ca
twitter.com/asteroidpublish
Publisher of literary fiction & non-fiction books.

Athabasca University Press
Edmonton Learning Centre, Peace Hills Trust Tower, #1200, 10011 - 109th St., Edmonton, AB T5J 3S8
Tel: 780-497-3412; *Fax:* 780-421-3298
aupress@athabascau.ca
www.aupress.ca
www.instagram.com/au_press
twitter.com/au_press
www.facebook.com/aupre ss1
ISBNs: 0-919737
Megan Hall, Acting Director, director.aupress@athabascau.ca
Pamela Holway, Senior Acquisitions Editor, editor.aupress@athabascau.ca

Augsburg Fortress Publishers
Canadian Office
55 Woodslee Ave., Paris, ON N3L 35E
Tel: 519-748-2200; *Fax:* 519-748-9835
Toll-Free: 800-265-6397
custserv@davidccook.ca
www.afcanada.com
Other information: kitchenerstore@augsburgfortress.org
www.youtube.com/user/AugsburgFortress
twitter.com/augsburgfortres
www.facebook.com/augsburgfortress
The publishing wing of the Evangelical Lutheran Church in America, Augsburg Fortress also services the Evangelical Lutheran Church in Canada & publishes Bibles, Bible study resources, multicultural materials, music & seasonal & special occasion books.

Augustine Hand Press
62 Walter Copp Cres., Winnipeg, MB R2K 4H6
ISBNs: 0973151900, 0973151919

Aviation Publishers Co. Ltd.
PO Box 1361 B, Ottawa, ON K1P 5R4
Tel: 613-244-8280; *Fax:* 613-244-8281
info@aviationpublishers.com
www.aviationpublishers.com
www.linkedin.com/company/aviation-publishers-co.-ltd.
twitter.com/aviation_pub
ISBNs: 0-9690054
Publisher of the ground school flight training manual "From the Ground Up" as well as other books on flight training & aeronautical theory.
Graeme Peppler, Owner & General Manager

Backroad Mapbooks
Owned By: Mussio Ventures Ltd.
#106, 1500 Hartley Ave., Coquitlam, BC V3K 7A1
Tel: 604-521-6277; *Fax:* 604-521-6260
Toll-Free: 877-520-5670
info@backroadmapbooks.com
www.backroadmapbooks.com
www.linkedin.com/company/backroad-mapbooks
twitter.com/backroadmapbook
www.facebook.com/backroadmapbooks
Backroad Mapbooks produces outdoor recreation Canadian maps & guidebooks.
Russell Mussio, President, rmussio@backroadmapbooks.com
Chris Taylor, Vice-President, ctaylor@backroadmapbooks.com

Bacon & Hughes Limited
13 Deerlane Ave., Ottawa, ON K2E 6W7
Tel: 613-226-8136; *Fax:* 613-226-8121
Toll-Free: 800-563-2468
sales@baconandhughes.ca
www.baconandhughes.ca
Bacon & Hughes Limited provides learning resources from early childhood to the secondary level. Teacher resources & French literature are also available.
Jos Bacon, President, jos.bacon@baconandhughes.ca

Bahá'í Distribution Service (BDS) / Service de distribution bahá'í
Previous Name: Unity Arts Inc.
7200 Leslie St., Thornhill, ON L3T 6L8
Tel: 905-889-8168; *Toll-Free:* 800-465-3287
bds-admin@cdnbnc.org
bookstore.bahai.ca
Publishes books about the Bahá'í faith

Banff Centre Press
The Banff Centre, PO Box 1020 21, 107 Tunnel Mountain Dr., Banff, AB T1L 1H5
Tel: 403-762-6408
press@banffcentre.ca
www.banffcentre.ca/press
www.instagram.com/banffcentre
twitter.com/banffcentre
www.facebook.com /banffcentre
The Banff Centre Press publishes books of contemporary art, culture, & literature.
Janice Price, President/CEO, Banff Centre

Baraka Books
6977, rue Lacroix, Montréal, QC H4E 2V4
Tel: 514-808-8504
info@barakabooks.com
www.barakabooks.com
twitter.com/barakabooks
www.facebook.com/728056780560267
Specializes in creative & political non-fiction, history & historical fiction, & fiction.
Robin Philpot, President & Publisher

The Battered Silicon Dispatch Box
159 Blue Mountain Maples Rd., Flesherton, ON N0C 1E0
www.batteredbox.com
www.facebook.com/289010754883
ISBNs: 1-55246
Publisher of Sherlock Holmes & other out-of-print works by Canadian & international authors
George A. Vanderburgh, Publisher,
george.vanderburgh@gmail.com

Bayeux Arts Inc.
2403, 510-6th Ave. SE, Calgary, AB T2G 1L7
mail@bayeux.com
www.bayeux.com
Eclectic & avant-garde books.
Ashis Gupta, Publisher, agupta@bayeux.com
Swapna Gupta, Co-Publisher & Director

Be That Books Publishing
#91033, 125 - 8888 Country Hills Blvd. NW, Calgary, AB T3G 5T0
Tel: 403-699-8845
admin@bethatbooks.com
bethatbooks.com
www.pinterest.com/bethatbooks
twitter.com/BeThatBooks
www.facebook. com/BeThatBooks
Publisher of self-help books
Tina O'Conner, President & CEO

Béliveau Éditeur
Anciennement: Éditions Sciences et Culture inc.; Iris Diffusion
567, rue de Bienville, Boucherville, QC J4B 2Z5
Tél: 450-679-1933
admin@beliveauediteur.com
www.beliveauediteur.com
ISBNs: 2-89092
Spécialités: Affaires, finances, biographies, psychologie et sciences humaines, religion, mathématiques, physique, chimie
Mathieu Béliveau, Président-directeur général,
mbeliveau@beliveauediteur.com

The Best of Bridge Publishing Ltd.
Owned By: Robert Rose Inc.
#800, 120 Eglinton Ave. East, Toronto, ON M4P 1E2
Tel: 416-322-6552; *Fax:* 416-322-6936
www.bestofbridge.com
www.instagram.com/bestofbridge
twitter.com/thebestofbridge
www.facebook.com/102901496565355
ISBNs: 0-9690425
Publisher of cookbooks

Between the Lines (BTL)
#281, 401 Richmond St. West, Toronto, ON M5V 3A8
Tel: 416-535-9914; *Toll-Free:* 800-718-7201
info@btlbooks.com
www.btlbooks.com
www.youtube.com/BTLbooks
twitter.com/readBTLbooks
www.facebook.com/BTL books
Between the Lines provides books with critical perspectives on culture, economics & society.
Amanda Crocker, Managing Editor

Biblioasis
#100, 1686 Ottawa St., Windsor, ON N8Y 1R1
Tel: 519-915-3930
info@biblioasis.com
www.biblioasis.com
twitter.com/biblioasis
www.facebook.com/groups/2409174840
Publisher of poetry, fiction & non-fiction.
Daniel Wells, Publisher

Bibliothèque et Archives nationales du Québec
2275, rue Holt, Montréal, QC H2G 3H1
Tel: 514-873-1100; *Fax:* 514-873-9312
Toll-Free: 800-363-9028
www.banq.qc.ca
www.youtube.com/user/BAnQweb20
twitter.com/_BAnQ
www.facebook.com/banq web20
ISBNs: 2-550, 2-551
Jean-Louis Roy, Président-directeur général

Black Moss Press
2450 Byng Rd., Windsor, ON N8W 3E8
Tel: 519-252-2551
salfini@blackmosspress.com
www.blackmosspress.com
www.youtube.com/blackmosswindsor
twitter.com/readblackmoss
The literary press publishes Canadian literature, including poetry & short story anthologies.
Marty Gervais, Publisher

Black Rose Books
PO Box 35788 Léo Pariseau, Montréal, QC H2X 0A4
www.blackrosebooks.net
twitter.com/blackrosebooks
www.facebook.com/blackrosebookspublishing
Black Rose Books publishes critical writing on topics such as philosophy, politics, history, sociology & the environment.

Blue Heron Press
Toronto, ON
lorne.blueheron@gmail.com
www.blueheronpress.ca
The literary press specializes in Canadian literature.
Lorne Shirinian, Owner & Publisher, lorne.blueheron@gmail.com

Blue Moon Publishers
Stratford, ON
info@barakabooks.com
www.bluemoonpublishers.com
twitter.com/bluemoonpbh
www.facebook.com/17422795939274
Literary fiction & non-fiction; women's fiction, Young Adult, New Adult, Middle Grade fiction

Bodhi Publishing
PO Box 144, 124 Reid St., Kinmount, ON K0M 2A0
kcw@bodhipublishing.org
www.bodhipublishing.org
The charitable organization publishes books by Venerable Namgyal Rinpoche.

BookLand Press
#600, 15 Allstate Pkwy., Markham, ON L3R 5B4
Tel: 905-943-0950; *Fax:* 905-248-1215
Toll-Free: 800-535-1774
books@booklandpress.com
www.booklandpress.com
twitter.com/booklandpress
Publishes Canadian works that range from poetry to translations.

BookThug
260 Ryding Ave., Toronto, ON M6N 1H5
www.bookthug.ca
Other information: Submissions, Email:
submissions@bookthug.ca
www.instagram.com/bookthug_press
twitter.com/bookthug
www.facebook.com /bookthug
Independent literary press specializing in poetry, prose, creative critism, experimental literature
Jay Millar, Publisher

Boomerang Éditeur Jeunesse inc.
QC
Tél: 450-640-1234; *Ligne sans frais:* 800-771-3022
info@boomerangjeunesse.com
www.boomerangjeunesse.com
www.instagram.com/boomerang_editeur_jeunesse
www.facebook.com/boomera ngediteurjeunesse
Publie des livres pour la jeunesse
Manon Bergeron, Édition et production,
mbergeron@boomerangjeunesse.com

Danielle Lalande, Gestion et administration,
dlalande@boomerangjeunesse.com
Caroline Lafrance, Promotion et marketing,
clafrance@boomerangjeunesse.com

Borealis Book Publishers
8 Mohawk Cres., Nepean, ON K2H 7G6
Tel: 613-829-0150; *Fax:* 613-829-7783
Toll-Free: 877-696-2585
drt@borealispress.com
www.borealispress.com
Borealis Book Publishers consists of Borealis Books, Tecumseh Books, Publishing Advisors Inc., Journal of Canadian Poetry, Canadian Critical Editions & the Parliamentary Handbook / Répertoire Parlementaire Canadien.

Boston Mills Press
Firefly Books Ltd., #1, 50 Staples Ave., Richmond Hill, ON L4B 0A7
Tel: 416-499-8412; *Fax:* 416-499-8313
Toll-Free: 800-387-6192
service@fireflybooks.com
www.fireflybooks.com
twitter.com/FireflyBooks
www.facebook.com/FireflyBooksLtd
ISBNs: 0-919783; 0-919822
Boston Mills Press publishes nonfiction books for adults, including nature, history, travel, & transportation titles. It is a client publisher of Firefly Books.
Michael J Bazinet, Senior Operations Manager

Boulder Publications Ltd.
198 Neary's Pond Rd., Portugal Cove-St. Philip's, NL A1M 2Y5
Tel: 709-895-6483; *Fax:* 709-895-8047
info@boulderpublications.ca
boulderbooks.ca/ons.ca
twitter.com/Boulder_Books
www.facebook.com/BoulderBooks.ca
Boulder Publications specializes in publishing fiction, field guides & historical works.
Gavin Will, President

Breakwater Books Ltd.
Previous Name: Summerhill Books
PO Box 2188, St. John's, NL A1C 6E6
Tel: 709-722-6680; *Fax:* 709-753-0708
Toll-Free: 800-563-3333
info@breakwaterbooks.com
www.breakwaterbooks.com
twitter.com/breakwaterbooks
www.facebook.com/29596022506
ISBNs: 0-919519, 0-920911, 1-55081; SAN 115-0154
Newfoundland's first publishing house; specializing in educational & curriculum materials, and resources with an emphasis on the history & unique culture of Newfoundland & Labrador
Rebecca Rose, President

Brick Books
PO Box 20081, 431 Boler Rd., London, ON N6K 4G6
Tel: 519-657-8579
brick.books@sympatico.ca
www.brickbooks.ca
www.youtube.com/brickbooks
twitter.com/brickbooks
www.facebook.com/brickbooks
ISBNs: 0-919626, 1-894078; SAN: 115-0162
Small literary press devoted to the work of Canadian poets
Kitty Lewis, General Manager

Brindle & Glass Publishing Ltd.
Owned By: TouchWood Editions Ltd.
#103, 1075 Pendergast St., Victoria, BC V8V 0A1
Tel: 250-360-0829; *Fax:* 250-386-0829
info@brindleandglass.com
www.brindleandglass.com
www.facebook.com/brindleandglass
An imprint of TouchWood Editions; publishes fiction & literary non-fiction
Taryn Boyd, Publisher, TouchWood Editions Ltd.

Broadview Press
PO Box 1243, #5, 280 Perry St., Peterborough, ON K9J 7H5
Tel: 705-743-8990; *Fax:* 705-743-8353
customerservice@broadviewpress.com
www.broadviewpress.com
twitter.com/broadviewpress
www.facebook.com/316561361724692
ISBNs: 0-921149, 1-55111; SAN: 115-6772
With additional offices in Guelph, Nanaimo, Wolfville & Calgary; specializing in English Studies & Philosophy
Don LePan, President

Broken Jaw Press Inc. (BJP)
Previous Name: Maritimes Arts Projects Productions
PO Box 596 A, Fredericton, NB E3B 5A6
Tel: 506-454-5127; *Fax:* 506-454-5134
editors@brokenjaw.com
www.brokenjaw.com
www.facebook.com/190837609905
ISBNs: 0-921411, 1-896647, 1-55391; SAN: 117-1437
Joe Blades, Publisher

Broquet inc. / Broquet Publishing Company Inc.
97-B, Montée des Bouleaux, Saint-Constant, QC J5A 1A9
Tél: 450-638-3338; *Téléc:* 450-638-4338
Ligne sans frais: 800-363-2864
info@broquet.qc.ca
www.broquet.qc.ca
www.instagram.com/editions_broquet
www.facebook.com/EditionsBroquet
ISBNs: 2-89000
Ouvrages qui traitent des sciences de la nature, d'horticulture, d'hornithologie, de cuisine, de santé, de bricolage, de sport, de techniques artistiques, de livres jeunesse et de tout autres sujets pratiques.
Antoine Broquet, Éditeur, 450 638 3338, info@broquet.qc.ca
Caroline Broquet, Adjointe à l'édition, 450 638 3338, caroline@broquet.qc.ca

The Brucedale Press
Owned By: Broad Horizons Books
PO Box 2259, Port Elgin, ON N0H 2C0
Tel: 519-832-6025; *Toll-Free:* 866-832-6025
info@brucedalepress.ca
www.brucedalepress.ca
ISBNs: 0-9698716, 1-896922
Specializes in works from Bruce Peninsula & Queen's Bush writers, artists & photographers

Brush Education Inc.
Previous Name: Detselig Enterprises Ltd.
6531 - 111th St., Edmonton, AB T6H 4R5
Tel: 780-989-0910; *Fax:* 780-989-0930
Toll-Free: 855-283-0900
contact@brusheducation.ca
www.brusheducation.ca
ISBNs: 0-920490, 1-55059; SAN: 115-0324
Specializes in general trade & academic books written by authors from Canada, the U.S., & Europe.
Glenn Rollans, Partner
Lauri Seidlitz, Managing Editor, lauri.seidlitz@brusheducation.ca

Bungalo Books
RR#1, Hartington, ON K0H 1W0
publisher@bungalobooks.com
www.bungalobooks.com
twitter.com/FrankBEdwards
www.facebook.com/BungaloBooks
Books for children
Frank Edwards, Publisher

Burnstown Publishing House
Previous Name: General Store Publishing House
5 Leckie Lane, Burnstown, ON K0J 1G0
Tel: 613-509-1090
info@burnstownpublishing.com
www.burnstownpublishing.com
ISBNs: 1-896182, 1-897113, 1-894263
Tim Gordon, President, timgordon@burnstownpublishing.com

BuschekBooks
PO Box 74053, 5 Beechwood Ave., Ottawa, ON K1M 2H9
Tel: 613-744-2589; *Fax:* 613-744-2967
contact@buschekbooks.com
www.buschekbooks.com
ISBNs: 0-9699904, 1-894543
Publishers of poetry, fiction & translations by first time authors & translators.

Caitlin Press Inc.
8100 Alderwood Rd., Halfmoon Bay, BC V0N 1Y1
Tel: 604-885-9194; *Toll-Free:* 877-964-4953
www.caitlin-press.com
twitter.com/caitlinpress
www.facebook.com/caitlinbooks
ISBNs: 1-894759, 0-920576; SAN: 115-2793
Specializing in BC women's literature, Caitlin Press publishes fiction, non-fiction, & poetry, as well as children's & young adult titles.
Vici Johnstone, Publisher, vici@caitlin-press.com
Sarah Corsie, Editorial/Production Manager, sarah@caitlin-press.com
Monica Miller, marketer/publicist, monica@caitlin-press.com

Callawind Publications Inc. / Publications Callawind inc.
#179, 3551, boul St. Charles, Kirkland, QC H9H 3C4
Tel: 844-833-9109
info@callawind.com
www.callawind.com
www.linkedin.com/company/callawind-publications-inc.
www.facebook.com/ca llawindbookpublishing
ISBNs: 1-896511
Specializes in cookbooks. Also publishes children's books, coffee table books, textbooks, business books & how-to books.
Marcy Claman, Owner

Canadian Bible Society (CBS)
10 Carnforth Rd., Toronto, ON M4A 2S4
Tel: 416-757-4171; *Fax:* 416-757-3376
Toll-Free: 800-465-2425
info@biblesociety.ca
www.biblesociety.ca
twitter.com/canadianbible
www.facebook.com/CanadianBibleSociety
ISBNs: 0-88834; SAN: 112-5559
The Society translates, publishes, & distributes the Bible throughout Canada.
Dr. Rupen Das., Executive Director
Nelly Safari, Senior Publishing Manager
Myles Leitch, Director of Scriptural Translation

Canadian Institute of Ukrainian Studies Press (CIUS Press)
Editorial Office, University of Toronto, #308, 256 McCaul St., Toronto, ON M5T 1W5
Tel: 780-492-2973; *Fax:* 780-492-4967
ciuspress.com
ISBNs: 0-920862, 1-895571, 1-894301, 1-894865; SAN: 115-2920
CIUS Press is the Canadian Institute of Ukrainian Studies' publishing arm. It publishes scholarly books about Ukrainian history, language, literature, contemporary Ukraine & Ukrainians in Canada. It also publishes English translations of Ukrainian monographs & memoirs.

Canadian Museum of History
Previous Name: Canadian Museum of Civilization
100, rue Laurier, Gatineau, QC K1A 0M8
Tel: 819-776-7000; *Toll-Free:* 800-555-5621
www.historymuseum.ca
Other information: TTY: 819-776-7003
www.instagram.com/canmushistory
twitter.com/CanMusHistory
www.facebook.com/CanMusHistory
ISBNs: 0-660; SAN: 115-4532
The Canadian Museum of History publishes a range of books, papers, essays, journals & reports with a focus on Canadian history, prehistory & civilization for both adults & children.
Mark O'Neill, President & CEO

Canadian Scholars' Press Inc. (CSPI)
#200, 425 Adelaide St. West, Toronto, ON M5V 3C1
Tel: 416-929-2774; *Fax:* 416-929-1926
www.canadianscholars.ca
twitter.com/canadianscholar
www.facebook.com/canadianscholar
ISBNs: 1-55130, 0-921627, 1-894184
Canadian Scholars is an independent publisher of texts, scholarly works, and titles that present themes and issues of interest to the general Canadian market. It also imprints Women's Pressm which focuses on feminist Canadian writing and scholarship, and Scholars Coursepack, which allows college/university instructors to choose readings from multiple sources and combine them into coursepacks, optimizing course material.
Andrew Wayne, President, awayne@canadianscholars.ca
Lily Bergh, Vice-President & Publisher, lily.bergh@canadianscholars.ca

Canadian University Press
3570 Skelding Rd., Orono, ON L0B 1M0
Tel: 416-962-2287; *Fax:* 416-966-3699
Toll-Free: 866-250-5595
president@cup.ca
www.cup.ca
twitter.com/canunipress
www.facebook.com/canadianuniversitypress
Canadian University Press is a national, non-profit co-operative, owned & operated by more than 80 student newspapers from coast to coast.
Emma McPhee, Vice-President, emma.mcphee@cup.ca
Erik Preston, President & Chair, erik.preston@cup.ca

Canadian Urban Institute / Institut urbain du Canada
#500, 30 St Patrick St., Toronto, ON M5T 3A3
Tel: 416-365-0816; *Fax:* 416-365-0650
cui@canurb.org
canurb.org
www.linkedin.com/company/canadian-urban-institute
twitter.com/canurb
www.facebook.com/canurb
ISBNs: 1-895446
Non-profit organization with annual publications to improve urban regions.
Mary Rowe, President & CEO
Lisa Cavicchia, Program Director, lcavicchia@canurb.org

CANAV Books (CANAV)
51 Balsam Ave., Toronto, ON M4E 3B6
Tel: 416-698-7559
larry@canavbooks.com
www.canavbooks.com
canavbooks.wordpress.com
ISBNs: 0-9690703, 0-921022; SAN: 115-3021
Publishers of books on aviation history
Larry Milberry, Publisher, larry@canavbooks.com

Cape Breton Books
Previous Name: Breton Books & Music
Wreck Cove, NS B0C 1H0
Fax: 902-562-3969
Toll-Free: 800-565-5140
bretonbooks@gmail.com
www.capebretonbooks.com
ISBNs: 1-895415
Showcases Cape Breton authors
Ronald Caplan, Publisher

Captus Press
#14-15, 1600 Steeles Ave. West, Concord, ON L4K 4M2
Tel: 416-736-5537; *Fax:* 416-736-5793
info@captus.com
www.captus.com
ISBNs: 0-921801, 1-895712, 1-896691, 1-55322
Captus is a publisher of textbooks which provide a Canadian context for university & college courses in various subjects, including business, law, disability studies, & Aboriginal economic development.

Centre for Addiction & Mental Health (CAMH)
Previous Name: Addiction Research Foundation
33 Russell St., Toronto, ON M5S 2S1
Tel: 416-535-8501; *Toll-Free:* 800-463-2338
info@camh.ca
www.camh.ca
www.linkedin.com/company/camh
twitter.com/CAMHnews
www.facebook.com/Ce ntreforAddictionandMentalHealth
ISBNs: 978-1-77052-003-5
CAMH publishes resources for therapists, doctors, nurses, front-line workers, & other professionals in the fields of addictions & mental health. Materials include research papers, pamphlets, newsletters, & journals.
Dr. Deborah Gillis, President & CEO
Dr. Sanjeev Sockalingam, Vice-President, Education

Centre for Reformation & Renaissance Studies (CRRS)
Previous Name: Dovehouse Editions Inc.
Victoria University in the University of Toronto, #301, 71 Queen's Park Cres. East, Toronto, ON M5S 1K7
Tel: 416-585-4465; *Fax:* 416-585-4430
crrs.info@vicu.utoronto.ca
www.crrs.ca
twitter.com/CRRS_Toronto
ISBNs: 0-919473, 1-895537
Researches, teaches, & publishes series about the time period between 1350-1700
Ethan Matt Kavaler, Director

Centre FORA
#4, 800, rue Notre Dame, Hammer, ON P3P 1X5
Tél: 705-524-3672; *Téléc:* 705-524-8535
Ligne sans frais: 888-814-4422
info@centrefora.on.ca
www.centrefora.on.ca
ISBNs: 2-921706
Centre francophone d'édition en éducation de base des adultes, et de diffusion de matériel éducatif pour tout âge. Service d'édition: coordination de projects, production, impression, rédaction, etc. Service de diffusion. Bureaux: Sudbury, North Bay.
Jacqueline Gauthier, Directrice générale, jgauthier@centrefora.on.ca

Centre franco-ontarien de ressources pédagogiques
435, rue Donald, Ottawa, ON K1K 4X5
Tél: 613-747-8000; *Téléc:* 613-747-2808
Ligne sans frais: 877-742-3677
www.instagram.com/cforp
twitter.com/cforp
www.facebook.com/cforp
Centre multiservices en éducation; développement, édition;
production multimedia; programmation; formation
professionnelle; imprimerie
Claude Deschamps, Directeur général et secrétaire-trésorier
Hubert Lalande, Directeur, Édition

CGS Communications, Inc.
Previous Name: Canadian Guidance Services
2521 Nicklaus Ct., Burlington, ON L7M 4V1
Tel: 905-332-0083; *Fax:* 905-319-1641
info@cgscommunications.com
www.cgscommunications.com
ISBNs: 0-929079
Publishes books on career / educational planning & scholarship
information.
Brian Harris, President, 905-483-7331,
brian@cgscommunications.com

The Charlton Press
991 Victoria St. North, Kitchener, ON N2B 3C7
Tel: 416-962-2665; *Fax:* 519-579-0532
Toll-Free: 866-663-8827
chpress@charltonpress.com
www.charltonpress.com
Publishers of catalogues on 20th century collectables including
coins, bank notes & others
Mark Drake, Publisher

Chaudiere Books
2423 Alta Vista Dr., Ottawa, ON K1H 7M9
info@chaudierebooks.com
www.chaudierebooks.com
www.myspace.com/chaudierebooks
twitter.com/ChaudiereBooks
Literary publisher.
Rob McLennan, Publisher Editor, rob@chaudierebooks.com
Christine McNair, Publisher, christine@chaudierebooks.com

Chenelière Éducation
Anciennement: Éditions de la Chenelière inc.
#900, 5800, rue Saint-Denis, Montréal, QC H2S 3L5
Tél: 514-273-1066; *Téléc:* 514-276-0324
Ligne sans frais: 800-565-5531
info@cheneliere.ca
www.cheneliere.ca
Autre information: Toll-Free Fax: 800-814-0324
www.linkedin.com/company/cheneli-re-ducation
twitter.com/cheneliere
ww w.facebook.com/CheneliereEducationPrimaire
ISBNs: 2-89310, 2-89461
Y compris Groupe Beauchemin, Gaëtan Morin Éditeur, et les
Publications Graficor
Michel Carl Perron, Vice-président, Production,
mcperron@cheneliere.ca

Chestnut Publishing Group Inc.
#297, 44 Stubbs Dr., Toronto, ON M2L 2R3
Tel: 416-224-5824
www.facebook.com/chestnutpublishing
ISBNs: 1-894601, 0-9731237, 0-9689552, 0-9688946
CPG publishes educational material for both adult & children,
ESL materials, as well as novels & teacher's guides targeted at
reluctant readers. It has 4 imprints: Chestnut Publishing, High
Interest Publishing (HIP), Lynx Publishing and Patnor Books with
its New Start Suspense Series.
Stanley Starkman, President & CEO, sharkstark@sympatico.ca

ChiZine Publications
Peterborough, ON
www.chizinepub.com
www.youtube.com/user/chizinepub
twitter.com/chizinepub
www.facebook.co m/pg/chizinepub/about
CZP publishes weird, subtle, surreal & disturbing dark fiction and
fantasy.
Sandra Kasturi, Co-Owner & Publisher
Brett Savory, Co-Owner & Editor

Clifford Ford Publications
#2004, 530 Laurier Ave. West, Ottawa, ON K1R 7T1
www.cliffordfordpublications.ca
ISBNs: 0-919883
Publisher of a wide range of sheet music, including Canadian
historical anthologies, choral collections & pedagogical music, as
well as works composed by Clifford Ford.

Clifford Ford, Publisher, crford@cliffordfordpublications.ca

CMP Publications
PO Box 34097, Halifax, NS B3J 3S1
Tel: 902-425-1320; *Fax:* 902-425-1325
info@cmppublications.com
www.cmppublications.com
ISBNs: 0-9693595, 0-9739494
The company focuses on the research, publishing, &/or
distribution of information related to the natural & social
sciences. Titles include themes on fisheries, agriculture,
construction, environment, recycling, & more.

Coach House Books
80 bpNichol Lane, Toronto, ON M5S 3J4
Tel: 416-979-2217; *Fax:* 416-977-1158
Toll-Free: 800-367-6360
mail@chbooks.com
www.chbooks.com
www.goodreads.com/chbooks
twitter.com/coachhousebooks
www.facebook.com/coachhousebooks
ISBNs: 1-55245, 1-897439, 1-77056
Coach House Books publishes Canadian content across a
variety of fields: fiction, poetry, art & architecture, drama &
performing arts, children's, social science & travel, including a
series of books about Toronto.
Stan Bevington, Publisher, stan@chbooks.com
Alana Wilcox, Editorial Director, alana@chbooks.com

Colombo & Company
42 Dell Park Ave., Toronto, ON M6B 2T6
Tel: 416-782-6853; *Fax:* 416-782-0285
www.colombo.ca
ISBNs: 1-894540, 0-9695092, 1-896308
Publishing imprint for books by John Robert Colombo &
colleagues, including poetry & poetry anthologies, Canadiana,
reference works & quotation collections, mysteries, humour &
translations.
John Robert Colombo, Publisher, jrc@colombo.ca

Commodore Books
English
Simon Fraser University, 8888 University Dr., Burnaby, BC
V5A 1S6
Tel: 778-782-4988; *Fax:* 604-291-5737
info@commodorebooks.com
www.commodorebooks.com
Literary Press that celebrates and champions black writers in
BC.
David Chariandy, Owner
Wayde Compton, Owner
Karina Vernon, Owner

Commoners' Publishing Society Inc.
631 Tubman Cres., Ottawa, ON K1V 8L5
Tel: 613-523-2444; *Fax:* 888-613-0329
sales@commonerspublishing.com
www.commonerspublishing.com
ISBNs: 0-88970; SAN: 115-0243
Commoners Publishing is a book publisher, distributor, designer,
& editor of books across a variety of topics, including parenting,
marriage, divorce, public policy, history, immigration, business,
language, & urban planning.
Glenn Cheriton, President/Editor

Company's Coming Publishing Limited
C/O BookLogic, 1141 - 119th St., Edmonton, AB V6A 1S9
Tel: 800-875-7108; *Fax:* 780-450-1857
accounts@companyscoming.com
www.companyscoming.com
www.facebook.com/companyscomingcookbooks
ISBNs: 1-896891, 1-897069, 1-895455, 0-9690695, 0-9693322,
1-897477
Publishes an extensive array of cookbooks, including a selection
of series, with Healthy Cooking, Wild Canada, & Focus as
examples. In addition, Company's Coming publishes a series of
craft books.

Conundrum Press
10224 Highway #1, Wolfville, NS B4P 2R2
Toll-Free: 800-591-6250
andy@conundrumpress.com
www.conundrumpress.com
twitter.com/ConundrumCanada
www.facebook.com/ConundrumPressCanada
Publishes a wide range of books which include graphic novels,
artist projects, fiction, books about cultural history & the spoken
word.
Andy Brown, Founder & Publisher, andy@conundrumpress.com

Copp Clark Limited
Owned By: Pearson Canada Inc.
#1, 1675 Sismet Rd., Mississauga, ON L4W 4K8
Tel: 905-238-2882
www.coppclark.com
ISBNs: 0-7730, 0-273
Copp Clark publishes resources for the financial trading
community & information on holiday observances.

Cormorant Books Inc.
#615, 10 St Mary St., Toronto, ON M4Y 1P9
Tel: 416-925-8887
www.cormorantbooks.com
twitter.com/cormorantbooks
www.facebook.com/cormorantbooks
ISBNs: 0-920953, 1-896951, 1-897151; SAN: 115-4176
Cormorant Books specializes in fiction emerging Canadian
writers, reissues of Canadian literary classics, and English
translations of works by Quebec writers. There is a selection of
gay & lesbian literature, as well as non-fiction titles, including
historical biographies and memoirs.
Marc Coté, President & Publisher

Coteau Books
Owned By: Thunder Creek Publishing Cooperative
2517 Victoria Ave., Regina, SK S4P 0T2
Tel: 306-777-0170; *Fax:* 306-522-5152
coteau@coteaubooks.com
www.coteaubooks.com
www.instagram.com/coteaubooks
twitter.com/coteaubooks
www.facebook.com /coteaubookspub
ISBNs: 0-919926, 1-55050
Coteau Books is a not-for-profit, cooperatively run press
specializing in fiction, poetry, drama & fiction for young readers,
with some emphasis on Saskatchewan writers.
John Agnew, Publisher, publisher@coteaubooks.com
MacKenzie Hamon, Marketing Manager,
publicist@coteaubooks.com

Crabtree Publishing
616 Welland Ave., St Catharines, ON L2M 5V6
Tel: 905-682-5221; *Fax:* 800-355-7166
Toll-Free: 800-387-7650
custserv@crabtreebooks.com
www.crabtreebooks.com
twitter.com/CrabtreePub
www.facebook.com/CrabtreePublishing
ISBNs: 0-7787, 0-86505, 1-4271; SAN: 115-1436
With offices in the U.S., Canada, the U.K. and Australia,
Crabtreespecializes in children's non-fiction work & educational
products on many curriculum subjects. Material is published in
an audio format and in several languages, including Spanish and
French. Imprints include: A Bobbie Kalman Book; Leaps and
Bounds Books; and Look, Listen, & Learn.

Cranberry Tree Press
#173, 5060 Tecumseh Rd. East, Windsor, ON N8T 1C1
Fax: 519-945-6207
mail@cranberrytreepress.com
www.cranberrytreepress.com
ISBNs: 0-9681325, 0-9684218, 1-894668
Cranberry Tree Press is a contract, co-operative publishing
service with editors & designers on staff.
Lenore Langs, Publisher & Editor
Laurie Smith, Publisher & Editor

Crown Publications Inc.
PO Box 9452 Prov Govt, Victoria, BC V8W 9V7
Tel: 250-387-6409; *Fax:* 250-387-1120
Toll-Free: 800-663-6105
crownpub@gov.bc.ca
www.crownpub.bc.ca
ISBNs: 0-9696417
Crown Publications is the authorized distributor of British
Columbia acts, regulations & related legislative publications, &
an authorized agent for Canadian Federal Government
publications.

Curio.ca
PO Box 500 A, Toronto, ON M5W 1E6
curio.ca
twitter.com/CurioCBC
www.facebook.com/CurioCBC
Publishes resources related to CBC programs & programming

Dalhousie Architectural Press
Previous Name: Tuns Press
Faculty of Architecture & Planning, Dalhousie University,
PO Box 15000, 5410 Spring Garden Rd., Halifax, NS B3J 4R2
Tel: 902-494-3925; *Fax:* 902-423-6672
archpress@dal.ca
www.dal.ca/faculty/architecture-planning/dalhousie-arch
itectural-press.html
ISBNs: 0-929112
Publishing arm of the Faculty of Architecture & Planning at
Dalhousie University

Dance Collection Danse Publishing
#301, 149 Church St., Toronto, ON M5B 1Y4
Tel: 416-365-3233; *Toll-Free:* 800-665-5320
talk@dcd.ca
www.dcd.ca
www.instagram.com/dancecollectiondanse
twitter.com/dancecollection
www .facebook.com/dancecollectiondanse1
ISBNs: 0-929003
Publisher of "Dance Collection Danse Magazine," & books on
dance.
Miriam Adams, Co-Founder/Director C.M.
Amy Bowring, Director, Collections & Research

Database Directories
588 Dufferin Ave., London, ON N6B 2A4
Tel: 519-433-1666; *Fax:* 519-430-1131
mail@databasedirectory.com
www.databasedirectory.com
ISBNs: 1-896537
Publisher of current contact information on Canadian schools,
libraries, book retailers & municipalities.
Lesley Classic, Chief Executive Officer,
lclassic@databasedirectory.com

Davus Publishing
150 Norfolk St. South, Simcoe, ON N3Y 2W2
Tel: 519-426-2077; *Fax:* 519-426-0105
davuspub@sympatico.ca
www.davuspublishing.com
ISBNs: 0-915317
Featuring the works of David Beasley, and Major John
Richardson, Canada's first novelist.
David R. Beasley, President & Publisher,
davuspub@sympatico.ca

DC Books
5, av Fenwick, Montréal, QC H4X 1P3
Tel: 514-939-3990
dcbookscanada@gmail.com
www.dcbooks.ca
www.facebook.com/dcbookscanada
ISBNs: 0-919688, 1-897190; SAN: 115-8988
DC Books publishes poetry & prose with innovative Canadian
emphasis, histories, memoirs, & drama. Also offered are Railfare
DC Books about railways & Moosehead Anthology. The house is
a Member of the Association of English Editors of Quebec, & the
Literary Press Group. Books are distributed by Fitzhenry &
Whiteside.
Keith Henderson, Managing Editor

Decker Intellectual Properties Inc.
372 Richmond St. West, Toronto, ON M5V 2L7
Tel: 905-522-8526; *Toll-Free:* 855-647-6511
customercare@deckermed.com
www.deckerip.com
Offers the ACP Medicine & ACS Surgery book products in both
print & digital editions, as well as specialty medical journals &
databases, to serve the informational needs of health care
professionals & students.
Ryan T. Decker, Chief Content Officer
Jeffrey B. Decker, Chief Technology Officer

Demeter Press
PO Box 13022, 2546 - 10th Line, Bradford, ON L3Z 3L3
Tel: 289-383-0134
info@demeterpress.org
www.demeterpress.org
twitter.com/DemeterPress
www.facebook.com/MIRCIDemeterPress
Demeter Press is an independent feminist press focused
specifically on mothering, reproduction, sexuality, family &
motherhood.
Andrea O'Reilly, Founder & Editor-in-Chief

Deux Voiliers Publishing (DVP)
Gatineau, QC
Tel: 819-684-7688
deuxvoiliers@gmail.com
www.deuxvoilierspublishing.com
www.linkedin.com/pub/deux-voiliers/41/76b/134
www.facebook.com/DeuxVoili ersPublishing
A small print press specializing in first-time Canadian novelists.
Ian Thomas Shaw, Founder

Diffusion Dimedia inc.
539, boul Lebeau, Montréal, QC H4N 1S2
Tel: 514-336-3941; *Fax:* 514-331-3916
general@dimedia.qc.ca
www.dimedia.qc.ca
Diffuse & distribue des livres de langue française au Canada

Diffusion Inter-Livres
1701, rue Belleville, Lemoyne, QC J4P 3M2
Tél: 450-465-0037; *Téléc:* 450-923-8966
Ligne sans frais: 866-465-5579
interlivres@llbquebec.com
www.inter-livres.ca
www.instagram.com/interlivres
www.facebook.com/diffusioninterlivres
Ministère de la Ligue pour la lecture de la Bible et du Canada
français dans le but principal d'aider les librairies chrétiennes qui
étaient de fournir des livres en langue française directement à
partir de l'Europe.

Doubleday Canada Ltd.
c/o Penguin Random House of Canada, #1400, 320 Front St.
West, Toronto, ON M5V 3B6
Tel: 416-364-4449; *Fax:* 416-598-7764
www.penguinrandomhouse.ca
www.youtube.com/user/BookLounge
twitter.com/RandomHouseCA
www.facebook .com/RandomHouseOfCanada
Publishes Canadian literary & commercial fiction from new &
established writers, as well as memoirs, history, business, &
social & political journalism
Martha Kanya-Forstner, Editor-in-Chief

Douglas & McIntyre (2013) Ltd.
PO Box 219, 4437 Rondeview Rd., Madeira Park, BC V0N
2H0
Toll-Free: 800-667-2988
info@douglas-mcintyre.com
www.douglas-mcintyre.com
twitter.com/DMPublishers
www.facebook.com/DMPublishers
ISBNs: 0-88894, 1-55054, 1-55365; SAN: 115-1886, 115-026X
Specializing in Canadian fiction & non-fiction. Harbour Publishing
acquired Douglas & McIntyre in 2013 from D&M Publishers Inc.
Howard White, Publisher

Dragon Hill Publishing Ltd.
9827 - 74th Ave. NW, Edmonton, AB T6E 1G1
Toll-Free: 800-661-9017
www.dragonhillpublishing.com
www.facebook.com/1426517867598172
ISBNs: 1-896124
Publishing for the popular adult & youth markets, in the subject
areas of self-help, biography, success guides & traditional
cultures.
Marina Michaelides, President,
marinam@dragonhillpublishing.com

Drawn & Quarterly
PO Box 48056, #201, 6750 Esplanade, Montréal, QC H2V
4M1
Tel: 514-279-2221
info@drawnandquarterly.com
www.drawnandquarterly.com
www.instagram.com/drawnandquarterly
twitter.com/dandq
www.facebook.com /drawnandquarterly
ISBNs: 1-896597
Publisher of comic books & graphic novels.
Peggy Burns, Publisher

Dundurn Group
#500, 3 Church St., Toronto, ON M5E 1M2
Tel: 416-214-5544; *Fax:* 416-214-5556
info@dundurn.com
www.dundurn.com
twitter.com/dundurnpress
www.facebook.com/dundurnpress
Dundurn Press, a small Canadian publisher,specializes in
publishing YA fiction, adult fiction, history and mysteries.
Kirk Howard, President & Publisher
C. Dick Yu, Director of Finance
Margaret Bryant, Director of Sales & Marketing

eastendbooks
45 Fernwood Park Ave., Toronto, ON M4E 3E9
www.eastendbooks.com
ISBNs: 1-896973
A small-press with an Ontario focus, publishing material in a
range of subjects, including fiction, travel, current events &
modern jazz
Jeanne MacDonald, Managing Partner,
jmacdonald@eastendbooks.com

Écrits des Forges
992-A, rue Royale, Trois-Rivières, QC G9A 4H9
Tél: 819-840-8492
ecritsdesforges@gmail.com
www.ecritsdesforges.com
www.instagram.com/ecritsdesforges
twitter.com/EcritsdesForges
www.face book.com/editions.ecritsdesforges
ISBNs: 2-89046
Poésie, et essais en poésie
Etienne Poirier, Directeur exécutif chez Ecrits Des Forges (Les)

ECW Press (ECW)
665 Gerrard St. East, Toronto, ON M4M 1Y2
Tel: 416-694-3348; *Fax:* 416-698-9906
info@ecwpress.com
www.ecwpress.com
www.instagram.com/ecwpress
twitter.com/ecwpress
www.facebook.com/ecwpr ess
Publishing House that focuses on poetry, fiction, biography,
travel guides & sports.
David Caron, Co-Publisher & President, david@ecwpress.com
Jack David, Co-Publisher, jack@ecwpress.com
Michael Holmes, Executive Editor, michael@ecwpress.com

Éditions Anne Sigier inc.
Détenteur: Éditions Médiaspaul
a/s Éditions Médiaspaul, 3965, boul Henri-Bourassa est,
Montréal, QC H1H 1L1
Tél: 514-322-7341; *Téléc:* 514-322-4281
editeur@mediaspaul.qc.ca
www.mediaspaul.ca
ISBNs: 2-89129
Bibles, livres de spiritualité chrétienne, beaux-livres
Gilles Collicelli, Éditeur

Les Éditions Ariane / Ariane Editions Inc.
#101, 1217 av Bernard ouest, Outremont, QC H2V 1V7
Tél: 514-276-2949; *Téléc:* 514-276-4121
www.editions-ariane.com
twitter.com/ArianeEditions
www.facebook.com/EditionsAriane
ISBNs: 2-920987
Offre une variété de cours liés à la spiritualité, le développement
personnel, la santé mondiale et l'émergence d'un nouveau
monde et un monde plus juste, durable et société plus verte
Marc Vallée, Président

Les Éditions Cap-aux-Diamants Inc.
CP 26 Haute-Ville, #212, 3, rue de la Vieille-Université,
Québec, QC G1R 5K1
Tél: 418-656-5040
revue.cap-aux-diamants@hst.ulaval.ca
www.capauxdiamants.org
www.facebook.com/460428417363862
ISBNs: 2-920069
Yves Beauregard, Contact,
revue.cap-aux-diamants@hst.ulaval.ca

Les Éditions CEC inc.
Une compagnie de Quebecor Media
Owned By: Quebecor Media
9001, boul Louis-H.-La Fontaine, Anjou, QC H1J 2C5
Tel: 514-351-6010; *Fax:* 514-351-3534
Toll-Free: 800-363-0494
sac@editionscec.com
www.editionscec.com
Other information: Toll-Free Fax: 877-913-5920
ISBNs: 0-7751, 2-7617
Ouvrages pour tous les ordres d'enseignement - manuels
scolaires, ouvrages de référence, grammaires, anthologies
littéraires

Les Éditions Chouette
1001, rue Lenoir, #B-238, Montréal, QC H4C 2Z6
Tel: 514-925-3325; *Fax:* 514-925-3323
info@editions-chouette.com
www.editions-chouette.com
Livres Caillou

Exile Editions Ltd.
134 Eastbourne Ave., Toronto, ON M5P 2G6
info@exileeditions.com
www.exileeditions.com
www.youtube.com/user/exilewritersseries
www.facebook.com/exile.writers
Specializing in fiction, poetry, drama, non-fiction & translations, from established & new writers
Michael Callaghan, Publisher

Fernwood Publishing Company Limited
748 Broadway Ave., Winnipeg, MB R3G 0X3
Tel: 204-474-2958; Fax: 204-475-2813
info@fernpub.ca
www.fernwoodpublishing.ca
www.instagram.com/fernpub
twitter.com/fernpub
www.facebook.com/fernwoo d.publishing
ISBNs: 0-9694180, 1-896496
Small publishing house; Publishes plays & fiction & non-fiction books of local interest
Errol Sharpe, Co-Publisher
Wayne Antony, Co-Publisher

Fifth House Publishers
Owned By: Fitzhenry & Whiteside Limited
195 Allstate Pkwy., Markham, ON L3R 4T8
Fax: 800-260-9777
Toll-Free: 800-387-9776
bookinfo@fitzhenry.ca
www.fifthhousepublishers.ca
twitter.com/fifthhousebooks
www.facebook.com/fifthhousepublishers
ISBNs: 0-920079, 1-894004, 1-894856, 1-895618; SAN: 115-1134
Specializing in non-fiction with a Western Canadian emphasis
Sharon Fitzhenry, Publisher, sfitz@fifthhousepublishers.ca
Katherine Cole, Publisher

Firefly Books Ltd.
#1, 50 Staples Ave., Richmond Hill, ON L4B 0A7
Tel: 416-499-8412; Fax: 416-499-8313
Toll-Free: 800-387-6192
service@fireflybooks.com
www.fireflybooks.com
ISBNs: 0-920668; 1-895565; 1-55209; 1-55297; 1-55407
Firefly Books publishes non-fiction books & distributes non-fiction & children's books.

Fitzhenry & Whiteside Limited
195 Allstate Pkwy., Markham, ON L3R 4T8
Tel: 905-477-9700; Fax: 905-477-2834
Toll-Free: 800-387-9776
bookinfo@fitzhenry.ca
www.fitzhenry.ca
www.instagram.com/fitzwhits
twitter.com/fitzwhits
www.facebook.com/fitzwhits
ISBNs: 0-55041, 0-88902, 1-55005, 1-894004, 1-895618, 0-7737
Specializing in history, biography, poety, sports, photography, reference resources, and children's and young adult material.
Publisher of books from: Red Deer Press, Fifth House Publishers and Whitecap Books.
Sharon Fitzhenry, CEO, sfitz@fitzhenry.ca

Flanker Press Ltd.
#1, 1243 Kenmount Rd., Paradise, NL A1L 0V8
Tel: 709-739-4477; Fax: 709-739-4420
Toll-Free: 866-739-4420
info@flankerpress.com
www.flankerpress.com
twitter.com/flankerpress
www.facebook.com/flankerpress
ISBNs: 0-9698767, 1-894463
Specializing in regional Newfoundland & Labrador historical fiction & non-fiction titles; imprints include Pennywell Books, & Brazen Books
Garry Cranford, President

Folklore Publishing
11717 - 90 Ave. NW, Edmonton, AB T6J 7B7
Tel: 780-435-2376; Fax: 780-435-0674
fboer@folklorepublishing.com
www.folklorepublishing.com
Publishes books about North American history.
Faye Boer, Publisher

Formac Publishing Company Limited
5502 Atlantic St., Halifax, NS B3H 1G4
Tel: 902-421-7022; Fax: 902-425-0166
Toll-Free: 800-565-1975
orderdesk@formac.ca
www.formac.ca

ISBNs: 0-8878, 0-921921; SAN: 115-1371
Publishers & distributors of cooking, travel, regional interest, biographical, fiction, historical, nature, Maritime politics, natural history, children, & teen books
James Lorimer, Publisher, 902-421-7022 ext. 29, jlorimer@formac.ca
Dan Campbell, Sales Coordinator, 902-421-7022 ext. 21, customerservice@formac.ca
Robin Spitall, Publicist, 902-421-7022, promo@formac.ca

The Fraser Institute
1770 Burrard St., 4th Fl., Vancouver, BC V6J 3G7
Tel: 604-688-0221; Fax: 604-688-8539
Toll-Free: 800-665-3558
info@fraserinstitute.org
www.fraserinstitute.org
www.youtube.com/user/FraserInstitute
twitter.com/fraserinstitute
www.facebook.com/FraserInstitute
ISBNs: 0-88975; SAN: 115-3498
Offices in Vancouver, Calgary, Toronto, Montreal; engaged in research & publication with emphasis on economics, public policy & other issues that affect Canadians
Niels Veldhuis, President, niels.veldhuis@fraserinstitute.org

The Frederick Harris Music Co. Limited
273 Bloor St. West, Toronto, ON M5S 1W2
Toll-Free: 800-387-4013
publishing@rcmusic.ca
www.rcmusic.com/about-us/rcm-publishing
Catalogues of music repertoire for ear training, sight reading, technique, theory, harmony & music history

Free World Publishing Inc.
World Exchange Plaza, PO Box 81101, Ottawa, ON K1P 1B1
fwp@freeworldpublishing.com
www.freeworldpublishing.com
Free World Publishing is a Canadian publishing house with Academic& Fiction divisions.

Freehand Books
#515, 815 1st St. SW, Calgary, AB T2P 1N3
Tel: 403-452-5662
kelsey@freehand-books.com
www.freehand-books.com
twitter.com/fhbooks
www.facebook.com/freehandbooks
Publishes Canadian fiction, poetry & creative nonfiction by new & seasoned writers.
Kelsey Attard, Managing Editor, kelsey@freehand-books.com

Frontenac House
1648 Bowness Rd. NW, Calgary, AB T2N 3J9
Tel: 403-263-7025
connect@frontenachouse.com
www.frontenachouse.com
twitter.com/frontenachouse
www.facebook.com/frontenac.house
Publishes a variety of books including those about art, photography, fiction, aviation, political satire & poetry.
Neil Petrunia, Publisher
Terry Davies, Managing Editor

Fundy Guild Inc.
Fundy National Park, #2, 8642 Rte. 114, Alma, NB E4H 4V2
Tel: 506-887-6094; Fax: 506-887-6008
www.fundyguild.ca
www.instagram.com/friendsoffundy
www.facebook.com/FundyFriends
ISBNs: 0-920383
Publishes books related to the Bay of Fundy & Fundy National Park

Gaspereau Press Ltd.
47 Church Ave., Kentville, NS B4N 2M7
Tel: 902-678-6002; Fax: 902-678-7845
Toll-Free: 877-230-8232
info@gaspereau.com
www.gaspereau.com
www.facebook.com/gaspereaupress
ISBNs: 1-894031
Specializing in contemporary literature by emerging & established Canadian authors, with publishing & printing under one roof
Gary Dunfield, Co-Publisher
Andrew Steeves, Co-Publisher

Georgetown Publications Inc.
Owned By: The Georgetown Group Limited
34 Armstrong Ave., Georgetown, ON L7G 4R9
Tel: 905-873-8498; Fax: 888-595-3009
Toll-Free: 888-595-3008
info@georgetownpublications.com
www.georgetownpublications.com
twitter.com/georgetownpubl
www.facebook.com/202057239829417
ISBNs: 0-9731994, 0-9733149
Distributor for Allison & Busby, American Girl Pubishing, Hampton Roads Publishing, & Large Print Press, among others
Larry Sisnett, President

The Ginger Press
848 - 2 Ave. East, Owen Sound, ON N4K 2H3
Tel: 519-376-4233; Fax: 519-376-9871
Toll-Free: 800-463-9937
www.gingerpress.com
www.facebook.com/190286531057443
ISBNs: 0-921773
A bookshop, café, & publishing house, specializing in Owen Sound & area writers & subjects
Maryann Thomas, Publisher, maryann@gingerpress.com

Godwin Books
PO Box 50021, #15, 1594 Fairfield Mall, Victoria, BC V8S 5L8
Tel: 250-370-7753
www.godwinbooks.com
ISBNs: 0-9696774
Featuring books by Robert Thomson & George Godwin
Robert Stuart Thomson, Publisher & Editor Ph.D., 250-370-7753, rthomson@islandnet.com

Goose Lane Editions
Previous Name: Fiddlehead Poetry Books
#330, 500 Beaverbrook Ct., Fredericton, NB E3B 5X4
Tel: 506-450-4251; Fax: 506-459-4991
Toll-Free: 888-926-8377
info@gooselane.com
www.gooselane.com
www.instagram.com/goose_lane
twitter.com/goose_lane
www.facebook.co m/gooselaneditions
ISBNs: 0-919197, 0-86492, 0-920110; SAN: 115-3420
Small independent publisher of high-quality, award-winning books.
Susanne Alexander, Publisher, s.alexander@gooselane.com

Government of Canada Publications
Publishing and Depository Services Directorate, Ottawa, ON K1A 0S5
Tel: 613-941-5995; Fax: 613-998-1450
Toll-Free: 800-635-7943
publications.gc.ca
ISBNs: 0-660, 0-662; SAN: 115-2882
The official publisher for the Government of Canada. As of March 7, 2014, Publishing and Depository Services is no longer selling or distributing Government of Canada publications in tangible formats. The publisher directory has over 430,000 publications, including 310,000 digital publications.

Grand Duc en ligne
Anciennement: Éditions Agence d'Arc
#350, 1699, boul Le Corbusier, Laval, QC H7S 1Z3
Tél: 514-334-8466; Téléc: 514-334-8387
www.grandducenligne.com
twitter.com/grandducligne
www.facebook.com/GrandDucenligne
ISBNs: 2-7607, 0-88586, 0-289022, 0-0392

Granville Island Publishing
#212, 1656 Duranleau St., Vancouver, BC V6H 3S4
Tel: 604-688-0320; Fax: 604-668-0132
Toll-Free: 877-688-0320
www.granvilleislandpublishing.com
twitter.com/GIPLbooks
Granville Island Publishing manages book projects for clients such as individuals, corporations, & other orgnaizations.
Jo Blackmore, Publisher

Grass Roots Press
Owned By: Literacy Services of Canada Ltd.
6520 - 82 Ave., Main Fl., Edmonton, AB T6B 0E7
Tel: 780-413-6491; Fax: 780-413-6582
Toll-Free: 888-303-3213
info@grassrootsbooks.net
www.grassrootsbooks.net
www.facebook.com/187241824635013
Specializing in adult literacy & ESL resources
Pat Campbell, President

Great Plains Publications Ltd.
1173 Wolseley Ave., Winnipeg, MB R3G 1H1
Tel: 204-475-6799
info@greatplains.mb.ca
www.greatplains.mb.ca
twitter.com/greatplainspub
www.facebook.com/greatplainspublications
ISBNs: 0-9697804, 1-894283
Specializing in the best books from the Prairies & authors from across Canada
Catharina de Bakker, Editorial Director

Grey House Publishing Canada
411 Queen St. West, Toronto, ON M5V 2A5
Tel: 416-644-6479; *Fax:* 416-644-1904
Toll-Free: 866-433-4739
info@greyhouse.ca
Other information: circ.greyhouse.ca
www.linkedin.com/company/grey-house-publishing-canada
twitter.com/greyhousecanada
www.facebook.com/GreyHouseCanada
ISBNs: 978-1-61925, 978-1-68217, 978-1-64265
Publisher of a number of comprehensive Canadian directories including the Canadian Almanac & Directory, Canadian Who's Who, Associations Canada, Libraries Canada, Cannabis Canada & the Canadian Parliamentary Guide. Also the publisher of a range of Financial Post titles, including the Directory of Directors & the FPbonds & FPsurvey series.
Bryon Moore, General Manager
Stuart Paterson, Managing Editor

Greystone Books Ltd.
#201, 343 Railway St., Vancouver, BC V6A 1A4
Tel: 604-875-1550
info@greystonebooks.com
www.greystonebooks.com
twitter.com/greystonebooks
www.facebook.com/GreystoneBooks
Books about nature, the environment, travel, sports, popular culture & current issues. Greystone Books was acquired by Heritage House Publishing in 2013.
Rob Sanders, Publisher
Jennifer Croll, Editorial Director
Paula Ayer, Editor
Nancy Flight, Editor Emerita

Groupe d'édition la courte échelle
#315, 4388, rue Saint-Denis, Montréal, QC H2J 2L1
Tél: 514-312-6950
info@courteechelle.com
www.courteechelle.com
twitter.com/Courte_echelle
www.facebook.com/courteechelle
ISBNs: 2-89021; SAN: 116-0249
Un leader de la littérature jeunesse francophone - livres pour les trois à six ans; collection adulte
Mariève Talbot, Directrice générale
Caroline Tremblay, Éditrice jeunesse et directrice littéraire

Groupe Éducalivres inc.
Anciennement: Éditions Agence d'Arc
#350, 1699, boul Le Corbusier, Laval, QC H7S 1Z3
Tél: 514-334-8466; *Téléc:* 514-334-8387
infoservice@grandduc.com
www.educalivres.com
ISBNs: 2-7607, 0-88586, 0-289022, 0-0392
Conçoivent, publient et distribuent du matériel pédagogique destiné aux élèves du primaire, du secondaire et de l'éducation aux adultes.

Groupe Fides Inc.
#100, 7333, place des Roseraies, Anjou, QC H1M 2X6
Tél: 514-745-4290; *Téléc:* 514-745-4299
editions@groupefides.com
www.groupefides.com
twitter.com/editionsFides
www.facebook.com/344202282311782
ISBNs: 2-89137, 2-89035, 2-7621, 2-923694, 2-923989
Maison d'édition dont les spécialités sont : ouvrages de fiction, de référence, de spiritualité, essais, beaux livres, manuels d'enseignement collégial et universitaire.
Claude Rhéaume, Directeur général

Groupe Modus
Previous Name: Les Éditions Modus Vivendi inc
55, rue Jean-Talon ouest, Montréal, QC H2R 2W8
Tel: 514-272-0433
info@groupemodus.com
www.groupemodus.com
www.linkedin.com/company/groupe-modus
twitter.com/groupemodus
www.face book.com/GroupeModus

ISBNs: 2-921556, 2-89523, 2-922148 (Presses Aventure)
Publisher of books covering topics such as arts & crafts, cooking, food & wine, diet & health, games & activities, home renovations & others.
Marc Alain, President & CEO

GTK Press
#109, 18 Wynford Dr., Toronto, ON M3C 3S2
Tel: 416-385-1313; *Fax:* 416-385-1319
Toll-Free: 866-485-7737
info@gtkpress.com
www.gtkpress.com
ISBNs: 1-894318, 1-55137
Publisher of curriculum resources, notably science, technology, mathematics
K.L. Kwong, President

Guérin éditeur ltée
#200, 800, boul Industriel, Saint-Jean-sur-Richelieu, QC J3B 8G4
Tél: 514-842-3481; *Téléc:* 514-842-4923
Ligne sans frais: 800-398-8337
www.guerin-editeur.qc.ca
ISBNs: 2-7601
L'éditeur des écoles. Groupe Guérin: Guérin, éditeur limitée, Les Éditions La Pensée Inc., et LIDEC Inc.

Guernica Editions Inc.
1569 Heritage Way, Oakville, ON L6M 2Z7
Tel: 416-658-9888; *Fax:* 416-657-8885
Toll-Free: 800-565-9523
www.guernicaeditions.com
www.youtube.com/user/guernicaed
twitter.com/guernica_ed
www.facebook.c om/guernicaed
ISBNs: 0-919349, 2-89135, 0-920717, 1-55071; SAN: 115-0421
Michael Mirolla, Editor-in-Chief/Publisher,
michaelmirolla@guernicaeditions.com
Connie McParland, Publisher/Editor-in-Chief,
conniemcparland@guernicaeditions.com

Guides de voyage Ulysse inc.
4176, rue Saint-Denis, Montréal, QC H2W 2M5
Tel: 514-843-9447
st-denis@ulysse.ca
www.guidesulysse.com
www.youtube.com/user/guidesulysse
twitter.com/guidesulysse
www.facebook.com/GuidesUlysse
ISBNs: 2-921444, 2-89464; SAN: 115-7167
Publishers of Canadian travel guides covering all areas of the country with a focus on Québec

Guy Saint-Jean Éditeur
4490, rue Garand, Laval, QC H7L 5Z6
Tél: 450-663-1777
info@saint-jeanediteur.com
www.saint-jeanediteur.com
twitter.com/guysaintjean
www.facebook.com/saintjeanediteur
ISBNs: 2-920340, 2-89455
Guides pratiques sur la santé, la psychologie populaire, le sport, le jardinage; beaux-livres; littérature; Green Frog Publishing (www.greenfrogpublishing.com) et MarieGray (www.mariegray.com)
Nicole Saint-Jean, Présidente, nicole@saint-jeanediteur.com
Jean Paré, Directeur général, jean.pare@saint-jeanediteur.com

Hades Publications, Inc.
PO Box 1414 M, Calgary, AB T2P 2L6
Tel: 403-254-0160; *Fax:* 403-254-0456
admin@hadespublications.com
www.trickster.com
ISBNs: 0-919230, 0-921298
Publishes books & other materials on Magic, Illusion, Conjuring & Variety Arts. It has four imprints: Edge Science Fiction & Fantasy, Dragon Moon Press, Absolute Xpress & Trickster.
Brian Hades, Publisher

Hagios Press
PO Box 33024, Regina, SK S4T 7X2
Tel: 306-522-5055
hagiospress@myaccess.ca
www.lpg.ca/house-hagios-press
twitter.com/hagiospress
Publisher of poetry, art books, short-fiction & literary non-fiction, with a particular focus on books that advance a spiritual connection with the world.
Paul Wilson, Managing Editor

Hancock House Publishers Ltd.
19313 Zero Ave., Surrey, BC V3S 9R9
Tel: 604-538-1114; *Fax:* 604-538-2262
Toll-Free: 800-938-1114
info@hancockhouse.com
www.hancockhouse.com
Publishers of nonfiction regional titles, focusing on western & northern hisory, biography, wildlife & nature
David Hancock, President

Hans Schafler & Co. Ltd.
248 Overton Place, Oakville, ON L6L 1E9
Tel: 905-844-4682
info@schafler.com
www.schafler.com
Publishes curriculum books for schools
Lisbeth Schafler, President

Harbour Publishing Co. Ltd.
PO Box 219, Madeira Park, BC V0N 2H0
Tel: 604-883-2730; *Fax:* 604-883-9451
Toll-Free: 800-667-2988
info@harbourpublishing.com
www.harbourpublishing.com
twitter.com/harbour_publish
ISBNs: 0-920080, 1-55017
Specializing in BC authors & books of the Pacific Northwest
Howard White, President

Harlequin Enterprises Limited
Owned By: News Corp.
PO Box 603, Fort Erie, ON L2A 5X3
Toll-Free: 888-432-4879
customerservice@Harlequin.com
www.harlequin.com
www.linkedin.com/company/harlequin
twitter.com/harlequinbooks
www.facebook.com/HarlequinBooks
ISBNs: 978-0-778
Specializing in fiction for women, in 29 languages & 107 international markets.
Craig Swinwood, Publisher & Chief Executive Officer

HarperCollins Publishers Ltd.
Owned By: News Corp.
22 Adelaide St. West, 41st Fl., Toronto, ON M5H 4E3
Tel: 416-975-9334; *Fax:* 855-822-0957
Toll-Free: 844-327-5757
hcorder@harpercollins.com
www.harpercollins.ca
www.youtube.com/harpercollinscanada
twitter.com/harpercollinsca
www .facebook.com/HarperCollinsCanada
ISBNs: 978-1-44341; 1-44341
Canadian imprints include Avon, Greenwillow Books, HarperAudio, HarperBusiness, HarperLargePrint, William Morrow, among many others; specializing in Canadian fiction & non-fiction, for adults & children
Brian Murray, President & CEO

Hartley & Marks Group
#400, 948 Homer St., Vancouver, BC V6B 2W7
Toll-Free: 800-277-5887
pbdesk@hartleyandmarks.com
www.hartleyandmarksgroup.com
Publisher of The Elements of Typographic Style & The Complete Japanese Joinery. Hartley & Marks no longer publishes new book titles.

HealthCareCAN
Previous Name: Canadian Healthcare Association
#100, 17 York St., 3rd Fl., Ottawa, ON K1N 5S7
Tel: 613-241-8005; *Fax:* 613-241-5055
Toll-Free: 855-236-0213
info@healthcarecan.ca
www.healthcarecan.ca
twitter.com/HealthCareCAN
www.facebook.com/healthcarecan.soinssantecan
ISBNs: 1-896151
HealthCareCAN was created from the 2014 merger of the Canadian Healthcare Association & the Association of Canadian Academic Healthcare Organizations. The organization publishes books on healthcare issues & health management, as well as other resources, including reports, fact sheets, policy documents & an online healthcare facilities guide.
Paul-Émile Cloutier, President & CEO,
pecloutier@healthcarecan.ca
Dale Schierbeck, Vice-President, Learning & Development,
dschierbeck@healthcarecan.ca

Hedgerow Press
PO Box 2471, 10876 Madrona Dr., North Saanich, BC V8L 5N9
Tel: 250-656-9320
hedgep@telus.net
www.hedgerowpress.com
Celebrates & publishes books by BC writers & artists.
Joan Coldwell, Publisher

Herald Press
Owned By: MennoMedia
1251 Virginia Ave., Harrisonburg, VA
Fax: 877-271-0760
Toll-Free: 800-245-7894
info@MennoMedia.org
www.mennomedia.org
www.youtube.com/user/mennomedia
twitter.com/MennoMedia
www.facebook.co m/MennoMedia
ISBNs: 978-8-08361
Specializing in resources with emphasis on the Anabaptist perspective, biblical studies, mission, family & church life
Amys Gingerich, Executive Director & Publisher

Heritage House Publishing Co. Ltd.
#103, 1075 Pendergast St., Victoria, BC V8V 0A1
Tel: 250-360-0829; Fax: 250-386-0829
Toll-Free: 800-665-3302
heritage@heritagehouse.ca
www.heritagehouse.ca
www.facebook.com/heritagehousebooks
ISBNs: 0-919214, 1-895811, 1-894384; SAN: 115-8287
Specializing in Western Canadian non-fiction subjects & authors
Rodger Touchie, President/Publisher

HikingCamping.com
PO Box 8563, Canmore, AB T1W 2V3
Fax: 866-431-3894
nomads@hikingcamping.com
www.hikingcamping.com
www.instagram.com/nomadhikers
twitter.com/nomadhikers
www.facebook.com /utahslickrockguides
Specializing in guidebooks for hikers & campers, works of inspiration, insight & philosophy, & photography

Hogrefe Publishing
Previous Name: Hogrefe & Huber Publishers
82 Laird Dr., Toronto, ON M4G 3V2
customerservice@hogrefe-publishing.com
www.hogrefe.com
www.linkedin.com/company/hogrefe-publishing
twitter.com/hogrefe_publ
Publishes books & journals on psychology, mental health & tests
Dr. G.Jürgen Hogrefe, Publisher & CEO,
juergen.hogrefe@hogrefe.com

House of Anansi Press & Groundwood Books
Owned By: Stoddart Publishing
128 Sterling Rd., Toronto, ON M5V 2K4
Tel: 416-363-4343; Fax: 416-363-1017
Toll-Free: 800-663-5714
customerservice@houseofanansi.com
www.houseofanansi.com
www.youtube.com/HouseOfAnansi
twitter.com/houseofanansi
www.facebook.com/houseofanansi
ISBNs: 0-88784; SAN: 115-0391
Specializing in new & established Canadian writers of fiction, non-fiction & poetry, & French-Canadian works in translation
Sarah MacLachlan, President & Publisher

Human Kinetics Canada
#100, 475 Devonshire Rd., Windsor, ON N8Y 2L5
Tel: 519-971-9500; Fax: 519-971-9797
Toll-Free: 800-465-7301
info@khcanada.com
www.humankinetics.com
Publishes information about psychology & phisiology of physical activity
Skip Maier, CEO

Hungry I Books
#215, 1590 Dr. Penfield Ave., Montréal, QC H3G 1C5
Tel: 514-848-2424
hungryibooks@hotmail.com
cjs.concordia.ca/publications/hungry-i-books
Hungry I Books is a publishing arm of the Institute for Canadian Jewish Studies.

Iguana Books
CSI Annex, 720 Bathurst St., 3rd Fl., Toronto, ON M5S 2R4
Tel: 416-214-0760
info@iguanabooks.com
www.iguanabooks.ca
www.linkedin.com/company/iguana-books
twitter.com/Iguana_Books
www.fac ebook.com/iguanaslikebooks
Iguana Books is a publishing services house. It published its 100th book in 2017.
Greg Ioannou, President
Lee Parpart, Editor
Paula Chiarcos, Editor

Inanna Publications
York University, 4700 Keele St., Toronto, ON M3J 1P3
Tel: 416-736-5356; Fax: 416-736-5765
inanna.publications@inanna.ca
www.inanna.ca
www.pinterest.com/readinannabooks
twitter.com/InannaPub
Independent feminist press.
Luciana Ricciutelli, Editor-in-Chief, luciana@inanna.ca

Inclusion Press International
47 Indian Trail, Toronto, ON M6R 1Z8
Tel: 416-658-5363; Fax: 416-658-5067
inclusionpress@inclusion.com
www.inclusion.com
twitter.com/inclusionpress
www.facebook.com/InclusionPress
ISBNs: 1-895418, 1-927771
Resource materials with emphasis on diversity, inclusion & community, for educational institutions, government agencies, human service agencies, First Nations organizations
Jack Pearpoint, Co-Publisher, jack@inclusion.com
Lynda Kahn, Director, Marketing, lynda@inclusion.com
Cathy Hollands, Managing Director, cathy@inclusion.com

Indigenous Law Centre (ILC)
Previous Name: Native Law Centre
Law Bldg., University of Saskatchewan, #160, 15 Campus Dr., Saskatoon, SK S7N 5A6
Tel: 306-966-6189; Fax: 306-966-6207
indigenouslawcentre@usask.ca
indigenouslaw.usask.ca
www.linkedin.com/in/nativelawcentre
twitter.com/NativeLawCentre
www .facebook.com/nativelawcentre
ISBNs: 0-88880; SAN: 115-4540
Publisher of materials relating to First Nations & Aboriginal Law in Canada.
Marilyn Poitras, Director, 306-966-5806,
marilyn.poitras@usask.ca

Inhabit Education
PO Box 11125, 2475 Kalla Lane, Iqaluit, NU X0A 1H0
Tel: 647-352-0600
info@inhabitmedia.com
www.inhabiteducation.com
www.instagram.com/inhabit_ed
twitter.com/inhabit_ed
www.facebook.com/I nhabitEducation
Educational arm of Inuit-owned publishing company Inhabit Media.
Neil Christopher, Publisher/Managing Partner

Inhabit Media
PO Box 11125, 2475 Kalla Lane, Iqaluit, NU X0A 1H0
Tel: 647-352-0600
info@inhabitmedia.com
www.inhabitmedia.com
www.instagram.com/inhabit_media
twitter.com/Inhabit_Media
www.facebook .com/inhabitmedia
This is an Inuit-owned publishing company. It's aim is to preserve & promote the stories, knowledge & talent of Inuit & northern Canada.
Neil Christopher, Publisher/Managing Partner

Inner City Books
53 Alvin Ave., Toronto, ON M4T 2A8
Tel: 416-927-0355; Fax: 416-924-1814
info@innercitybooks.net
www.innercitybooks.net
twitter.com/innercitybooks
www.facebook.com/587527457924185
ISBNs: 0-919123, 1-894574; SAN: 115-3870
Publishers of studies in Jungian Psychology by Jungian Analysts.
Daryl Sharp, President

Insomniac Press
520 Princess Ave., London, ON N6B 2B8
www.insomniacpress.com
ISBNs: 1-895837, 1-894663
Independent press that publishes non-fiction, poetry & fiction
Mike O'Connor, Founder/Publisher, mike@insomniacpress.com

Institut de recherches psychologiques, inc. / Institute of Psychological Research Inc.
PO Box 68 St-Dominique, Montréal, QC H2S 3K6
Tel: 514-382-3000
info@irpcanada.com
www.irpcanada.com
www.facebook.com/1382041728710539
ISBNs: 0-88509, 2-89109
Un institut de recherche axée sur le développement d'outils d'évaluation psychométrique
Patricia Bergeron, Présidente et directrice,
patricia@irpcanada.com
Paul Goldman, Éditeur

The Institute for Research on Public Policy / L'Institut de recherche en politiques publiques
#200, 1470, rue Peel, Montréal, QC H3A 1T1
Tel: 514-985-2461
irpp@irpp.org
irpp.org
twitter.com/irpp
www.facebook.com/IRPP.org
ISBNs: 0-920380, 0-88645; SAN: 115-3889, 115-0537
Specializing in research & publications with emphasis on Canadian public policy, Canadian federalism, economic policy, international relations; publisher of Policy Options journal
Graham Fox, President & CEO, 514-787-0741, gfox@irpp.org
Suzanne Ostiguy-McIntyre, Vice-President, Operations,
smcintyre@irpp.org

International Development Research Centre (IDRC) / Le Centre de recherches pour le développement international
150 Kent St., Ottawa, ON K1P 0B2
Tel: 613-236-6163; Fax: 613-238-7230
info@idrc.ca
www.idrc.ca
www.linkedin.com/company/idrc
twitter.com/idrc_crdi
www.facebook.com/I DRC.CRDI
ISBNs: 0-88936, 1-55250
Publisher of IDRC Bulletin, & resources with emphasis on international development, sustainable development, food, health & social issues.
Jean Lebel, President

Invisible Publishing
#1, 289 Main St., Picton, PE K0K 2T0
info@invisiblepublishing.com
invisiblepublishing.com
www.instagram.com/invisibooks
twitter.com/invisibooks
www.facebook.com/invisibooks
This is a non-profit publisher that focuses on cool & contemporaryCanadian fiction as well as poetry & non-fiction.
Nic Boshart, Founder
Leigh Nash, Publisher
Robbie MacGregor, Director
Bryan Ibeas, Editor

Irwin Law Inc.
#206, 14 Duncan St., Toronto, ON M5H 3G8
Tel: 416-862-7690; Fax: 416-862-9236
Toll-Free: 888-314-9014
contact@irwinlaw.com
irwinlaw.com
www.linkedin.com/company/irwinlawinc
twitter.com/irwinlaw
www.facebook .com/IrwinLawInc
ISBNs: 1-55221
Publishes books on law for students & legal practitioners.
Jeffrey Miller, Publisher

Is Five Communications
Owned By: Is Five Foundation
1170 Birchmount Rd., Toronto, ON M1P 5E3
Tel: 416-480-2408; Fax: 416-480-2546
www.isfive.com
ISBNs: 0-920934; SAN: 115-3943
Writes, designs & produces educational materials, brochures, annual reports, posters & other materials needed for businesses
Shelly Medeiros, Managing Director, shelly@isfive.com

ISER Books
Memorial University of Newfoundland
Faculty of Arts Arts Publications, 297 Mount Scio Rd., St. John's, NL A1C 5S7
Tel: 709-864-3453; *Fax:* 709-864-4342
iser-books@mun.ca
www.arts.mun.ca/iserbooks
ISBNs: 1-894725, 0-919666; *SAN:* 115-3897
Research on social economic questions regarding cultural, geographic & economic circumstances in the North Atlantic region
Alison Carr, Managing Editor, acarr@mun.ca

Island Studies Press (ISP)
University of Prince Edward Island, #204, 550 University Ave., Charlottetown, PE C1A 4P3
Tel: 902-566-0386; *Fax:* 902-566-0756
ispstaff@upei.ca
projects.upei.ca/isp
ISBNs: 0-919013
Publisher of books on the history, literature, culture & environment of Prince Edward Island.

ITMB Publishing Ltd.
12300 Bridgeport Rd., Richmond, BC V6V 1J5
Tel: 604-273-1400; *Fax:* 604-273-1488
itmb@itmb.com
www.itmb.ca
www.linkedin.com/company/itmb-canada
twitter.com/ITMBCanada
www.facebook.com/ITMBPublishingLtd
ISBNs: 978-1-55341
Publisher of travel maps
Jack Joyce, President

J. Gordon Shillingford Publishing Inc.
Previous Name: The Muses' Company
PO Box 86, RPO Corydon Avenue, Winnipeg, MB R3M 3S3
Tel: 204-779-6967
jgshill2@mymts.net
jgshillingford.com
ISBNs: 1-896239, 0-919754, 0-969761, 0-920486, 0-968942
Primarily a literary publisher; publishes on average 14 titles/year.
J. Gordon Shillingford, President

Jack The Bookman Ltd.
c/o Jack the Bookman, Route E, #4, 1150 Kerrisdale Blvd., Newmarket, ON L3Y 8Z9
Tel: 905-836-5999; *Fax:* 905-836-1152
Toll-Free: 800-563-5168
info@jackthebookman.com
www.jackthebookman.com
Library wholesalers
Mark Davey, President, markd@jackthebookman.com
Scott Davey, Vice-President, scottd@jackthebookman.com

James Lorimer & Co. Ltd., Publishers
#304, 117 Peter St., Toronto, ON M5V 0M3
Tel: 416-362-4762; *Fax:* 416-362-3939
Toll-Free: 800-565-1975
info@lorimer.ca
www.lorimer.ca
twitter.com/lorimerbooks
www.facebook.com/lorimerbooks
ISBNs: 0-88862, 1-55028; *SAN:* 115-1134
Literature for children and adults.
James Lorimer, Publisher, jlorimer@lorimer.ca

John Wiley & Sons Inc.
#300, 90 Eglinton Ave. East, Toronto, ON M4P 2Y3
Tel: 416-236-4433; *Fax:* 416-236-4446
Toll-Free: 800-567-4797
www.wiley.com/en-ca
Other information: Toll-Free Fax: 800-565-6802
ISBNs: 0-471; *SAN:* 115-1185
Scientific, mechanical, technical & scholarly content in articles, journals, books & databases
Brian Napack, President & CEO
John Kritzmacher, Chief Financial Officer & Executive Vice-President, Operations
Danielle McMahan, Executive Vice-President & Chief People Officer
Deirdre Silver, Executive Vice-President & General Counsel
Christopher Caridi, Senior Vice-President & Corporate Controller
Vincent Marzano, Senior Vice-President & Treasurer
Joanna Jia, Corporate Secretary

Kegedonce Press
Neyaashiinigmiing, Chippewas of Nawash First Nation, 11 Park Rd., Neyaashiinigmiing, ON NOH 2TO
info@kegedonce.com
www.kegedonce.com
twitter.com/KegedoncePress
www.facebook.com/Kegedonce
Publishes the work of Indigenous writers nationally & internationally.
Kateri Akiwenzie-Damm, Owner

Keng Seng Enterprises Inc.
#103, 4000, rue St-Ambroise, Montréal, QC H4C 2C7
Tel: 514-939-3971
canada@kengseng.com
www.kengseng.com
ISBNs: 1-895494

The Key Publishing House Inc. (KPH)
161 Bay St., Toronto, ON M5J 2S1
Tel: 416-935-1790; *Fax:* 416-935-1790
info@thekeypublish.com
www.thekeypublish.com
The Key publishes a wide variety of academic, non-fiction & literary fiction as well as young adult & children's books.

Kids Can Press Ltd.
Owned By: Corus Entertainment Inc.
25 Dockside Dr., Toronto, ON M5A 0B5
Tel: 416-479-7000; *Fax:* 416-960-5437
customerservice@kidscan.com
www.kidscanpress.com
www.youtube.com/KidsCanPressMovies
twitter.com/KidsCanPress
www.fac ebook.com/KidsCanBooks
ISBNs: 0-919964, 0-55337, 1-55074; *SAN:* 115-4001
Specializes in children's literature & children's books

Kindred Productions
1310 Taylor Ave., Winnipeg, MB R3M 3Z6
Tel: 204-669-6575; *Fax:* 204-654-1865
Toll-Free: 800-545-7322
kindred@mbchurches.ca
www.kindredproductions.com
ISBNs: 0-919797, 0-921788, 1-894791
Publishing & distribution arm of the Mennonite Brethren Churches in North America.

Kinésis Éducation Inc. / Brault & Bouthillier Publishing
Previous Name: Les Éditions Brault & Bouthillier
#275, 4823, rue Sherbrooke ouest, Montréal, QC H3Z 1G7
Tel: 514-932-9466; *Fax:* 514-932-5929
Toll-Free: 866-750-9466
editions@ebbp.ca
www.ebbp.ca
ISBNs: 0-88537, 2-7615
Manuels scolaires, ouvrages pédagogiques / parascolaires; français et anglais

KO Éditions
Owned By: KO Média Inc.
#100, 651, rue Notre-Dame ouest, Montréal, QC H3C 1H9
Tel: 514-933-2462
info@ko-editions.ca
www.ko-media.ca/livres
Louis Morissette, Président
Sophie Banford, Directrice générale et éditrice

Lachesis Publishing
Ottawa, ON
www.lachesispublishing.com
twitter.com/lachesispub
www.facebook.com/lachesispublishing
Mystery, thriller, suspence & romance fiction.

Lancaster House
#200, 1881 Yonge St., Toronto, ON M4S 3C4
Tel: 416-977-6618; *Fax:* 416-977-5873
Toll-Free: 888-298-8841
customerservice@lancasterhouse.com
www.linkedin.com/company/lancaster-house-publishing
www.lancasterhouse.com
twitter.com/LancasterCanada
ISBNs: 0-920450
Publishes information & hosts conferences in the areas of labour & employment law.
Jeffrey Sack, President
Boris Bohuslawsky, Senior Editor
Rachel Cardozo, Senior Editorial Administrator
Paula Chapman, Editorial Director & Corporate Counsel

LandOwner Resource Centre (LRC)
PO Box 599, 3889 Rideau Valley Dr., Manotick, ON K4M 1A5
Tel: 613-692-3571; *Fax:* 613-692-0831
Toll-Free: 800-267-3504
info@lrconline.com
www.lrconline.com
ISBNs: 0-9680992
Publishes information on forestry, agriculture, wildlife, water, soil & other land management issues.

Latitude 46 Publishing
#205, 109 Elm St., Sudbury, ON P3C 1T4
Tel: 705-885-5658
www.latitude46publishing.com
twitter.com/Lat46Publishing
www.facebook.com/latitude46publishing
Heather Campbell, Publisher & Manager, Production, heather@latitude46publishing.com
Mitchell Gauvin, Consulting Editorer, Editorial, mitchell@latitude46publishing.com

Lazara Press
PO Box 2269, Vancouver, BC V6B 3W2
Tel: 416-817-1151
publisher@lazarapress.ca
www.lazarapress.ca
ISBNs: 0-920999
Small, progressive publishing house located in Vancouver. Publisher of poetry, literature, broadsides & chapbooks. Aims to publish & distribute works that might not otherwise be available.
Penny Goldsmith, Owner

Leaf Press
PO Box 416, 7727 Lantzville Rd., Lantzville, BC V0R 2H0
Tel: 250-390-3028
poems@leafpress.ca
www.leafpress.ca
www.facebook.com/Leaf.Press
Poetry chapbook publisher.
Ursula Vaira, Founder

Legacy Project
The Cedars, 20200 Marsh Hill Rd., Uxbridge, ON L9P 1R3
Tel: 905-852-3777; *Fax:* 866-590-2922
Toll-Free: 800-772-7765
admin@legacyproject.org
www.legacyproject.org
www.instagram.com/legacycubed
twitter.com/legacycubed
www.facebook.com/legacycubed
ISBNs: 1-896232
A research & education group, with an independent press, dedicated to quality books for children & adults in the areas of literacy, science education, life course & intergenerational relationships
Brian Puppa, Executive Director

Leméac Éditeur
4609, rue d'Iberville, 1er étage, Montréal, QC H2H 2L9
Tél: 514-524-5558; *Téléc:* 514-524-3145
lemeac@lemeac.com
www.lemeac.com
ISBNs: 2-7609, 0-7761
Éditeur de langue française spécialisé dans la littérature
Pierre Filion, Directions générale et éditoriale

LexisNexis Canada Inc.
Previous Name: Lexis Nexis Butterworths; Butterworths Canada Ltd
#900, 111 Gordon Baker Rd., Toronto, ON M2H 3R1
Tel: 905-479-2665; *Toll-Free:* 800-668-6481
www.lexisnexis.ca
www.linkedin.com/company/lexisnexis-canada-inc-
twitter.com/lexisnexisca n
www.facebook.com/lexisnexiscanada
Provider of information & services to law professionals, corporations, government, & academic institutions through books & online products.
Eric Wright, CEO, Risk Solutions
Mike Walsh, CEO, Legal & Professional

Librairie Gallimard de Montréal
3700, boul Saint-Laurent, Montréal, QC H2X 2V4
Tél: 514-499-2012; *Téléc:* 514-499-1535
librairie@gallimardmontreal.com
www.gallimardmontreal.com
www.facebook.com/LibrairieGallimardMontreal
La librairie Gallimard de Montréal est un lieu pour poésie, théâtre, philosophie, histoire, littérature, sciences humaines sont de véritables niches qui révèlent un fonds accumulé par une longue expérience.

Oolichan Books
PO Box 2278, Fernie, BC V0B 1M0

Tel: 250-423-6113
info@oolichan.com
www.oolichan.com
twitter.com/oolichanbooks
www.facebook.com/181252759556
ISBNs: 0-88982; *SAN:* 115-4680
Publishes poetry, fiction & non-fiction titles including literary criticism, memoirs & books on regional history
Randal Macnair, Publisher
Ron Smith, Editor
Pat Smith, Consulting Editor

Orca Book Publishers Canada
1601 Balmoral Rd., Victoria, BC V8T 1A8

Fax: 877-408-1551
Toll-Free: 800-210-5277
orca@orcabook.com
www.orcabook.com
www.instagram.com/orcabookpublishers
twitter.com/orcabook
www.facebook.com/orcabook
ISBNs: 0-920501, 1-55143; *SAN:* 115-7485
Publishers of children's books; with over 350 titles in print & 60 new titles per year. Picturebooks, Early chapter books, teen novels
Bob Tyrrell, President
Andrew Wooldridge, Publisher

Organisation for Economic Cooperation & Development (OECD)
OECD Washington Center, #450, 1776 Eye St. NW, Washington, DC

Tel: 202-785-6323
washington.contact@oecd.org
www.oecd.org/washington
ISBNs: 92-64
Serving as the OECD liaison to the US & Canada, the Washington Center publishes books in the fields of economics & public affairs, as well as statistical tables & databases.
Will Davis, Head, will.davis@oecd.org
Miguel Gorman, Senior Manager, Public Affairs & Media, miguel.gorman@oecd.org
Jean-Marie Le Grand, Office Manager, jean-marie.legrand@oecd.org
Iain Williamson, Manager, Sales & Marketing, iain.williamson@oecd.org

Owlkids Books
Previous Name: Maple Tree Press Inc.
#400, 10 Lower Spadina Ave., Toronto, ON M5V 2Z2

Tel: 416-340-2700; *Fax:* 416-340-9769
owlkids@owlkids.com
owlkidsbooks.com
www.instagram.com/owlkidspublishing
www.facebook.com/owlkids
ISBNs: 0-919872, 0-920775, 1-895688, 1-897066, 1-894379; *SAN:* 1
Publishers of non-fiction books for children covering a wide variety of topics including Sports, Humor, Science, Crafts, Canada, History & Culture.
Angela Keenlyside, Group Publisher, Owlkids
Karen Boersma, Publisher, Owlkids Books

Oxford University Press - Canada
#204, 8 Sampson Mews, Toronto, ON M3C 0H5

Tel: 416-441-2941; *Fax:* 416-444-0427
Toll-Free: 800-387-8020
customer.service@oup.com
www.oupcanada.com
ISBNs: 0-19; *SAN:* 115-731
One of the oldest publishing companies in the world; Publishers of non-fiction & educational material
Geoff Forguson, General Manager

Pacific Edge Publishing Ltd.
1773 El Verano Dr., Gabriola, BC V0R 1X6

Toll-Free: 800-668-8806
pacificedgepublishing.com
ISBNs: 1-895110
Publisher & distributor of educational resources for K-12 teachers
Ron Mumford, Publisher

Pacific Educational Press
University of British Columbia, 2029 West Mall, Vancouver, BC V6T 1Z2

Tel: 604-822-5959
pep.admin@ubc.ca
pacificedpress.ca
twitter.com/PacificEdPress

ISBNs: 0-88865, 1-895766; *SAN:* 115-1266
Publishing house of the Faculty of Education at the University of British Columbia and an imprint of UBC Press; Publishes educational resources
Catherine Edwards, Director

Pajama Press
#251, 181 Carlaw Ave., Toronto, ON M4M 2S1

Tel: 416-466-2222
info@pajamapress.ca
pajamapress.ca
www.youtube.com/user/PajamaPress
twitter.com/PajamaPress1
www.faceb ook.com/PajamaPress
Publisher of all formats of children's books including the following genres: picture books, board books, middle grade novels, young adult novels, non-fiction for all juvenile categories.
Gail Winskill, Publisher, gailwinskill@pajamapress.ca
Richard Jones, President
Ann Featherstone, Editor, annfeatherstone@pajamapress.ca
Pat Thornton Jones, Administration

Palimpsest Press
1171 Eastlawn Ave., Windsor, ON N8S 3J1

publicity@palimpsestpress.ca
www.palimpsestpress.ca
twitter.com/palimpsestpress
www.facebook.com/palimpsestpress
Poetry, fiction & select non-fiction titles, including essays/memoirs from poets. Focus on books that examine Canadian poetry & the Canadian cultural landscape
Aimée Parent Dunn, Publisher
Shaun Dunn, Manager

Pandora Press
47 Water St. North, Kitchener, ON N2H 5A6

Tel: 519-745-1560; *Fax:* 519-578-1826
Toll-Free: 866-696-1678
christian@pandorapress.com
www.pandorapress.com
ISBNs: 0-9698762, 0-9685543, 1-894710

Paperplates Books
Toronto, ON

info@paperplates-books.com
www.paperplates-books.com
Publisher of contemporary literary fiction (short story collections or short- to medium-length novels).

Parkland Publishing
501 Mount Allison Pl., Saskatoon, SK S7H 4A9

Tel: 306-242-7731
info@parklandpublishing.com
www.parklandpublishing.com
www.instagram.com/karpanphotojourneys
twitter.com/karpanparkland
www.f acebook.com/karpanphotojourneys
Publishes non-fiction books about Saskatchewan, hiking in Saskatchewan & trivia about Saskatchewan
Robin Kaplan, Co-Founder
Arlene Kaplan, Co-Founder

Pearson Canada Inc.
Previous Name: Prentice-Hall Canada;
Addison-Wesley Publishers
Owned By: Pearson Canada
26 Prince Andrew Pl., Don Mills, ON M3C 2T8

Tel: 416-447-5101; *Fax:* 416-443-0948
Toll-Free: 800-263-9965
www.pearsoncanada.ca
www.linkedin.com/company/pearson
twitter.com/pearson
www.facebook.com/ pearsonplc
ISBNs: 9780131113497; 9780131228436; 9780131280397
A Pearson Canada imprint, Pearson Education Canada Inc. is the largest publisher of print & electronic curriculum materials in Canada
Dan Lee, President & CEO, Pearson Canada

Pearson Éditions du Renouveau Pédagogique inc. (ERPI)
Anciennement: Editions Pierre Tisseyre
1611, boul Crémazie est, 10e étage, Montréal, QC H2M 2P2

Tél: 514-334-2690; *Téléc:* 514-334-4720
Ligne sans frais: 800-263-3678
bienvenue@pearsonerpi.com
www.pearsonerpi.com
Autre information: Télécopieur: 800-643-4720
www.linkedin.com/company/pearson-erpi
ISBNs: 2-7613
Maison d'édition scolaire; matériel didactique pour tous les niveaux d'enseignement

Pearson Education Canada
Owned By: Pearson Canada
26 Prince Andrew Pl., Toronto, ON M3C 2H4

Tel: 416-447-5101; *Fax:* 416-443-0948
Toll-Free: 800-263-9965
www.pearson.com/ca/en.html
twitter.com/pearsoncanada
www.facebook.com/pearsonplc
Pearson is a provider of educational products, including textbooks, digital services, teaching & training materials, & resources for professionals. Academic titles include astronomy, mathematics & statistics, economics, & finance.
James Reeve, Managing Director

Pedlar Press
113 Bond St., St. John's, NL A1C 1T6

www.pedlarpress.com
ISBNs: 0-9681884, 0-9686522, 0-9732140
Publishes contemporary Canadian fiction & poetry
Beth Follett, Contact, feralgrl@interlog.com

Pembroke Publishers Limited
538 Hood Rd., Markham, ON L3R 3K9

Tel: 905-477-0650; *Fax:* 905-477-3691
Toll-Free: 800-997-9807
www.pembrokepublishers.com
twitter.com/pembrokepublish
www.facebook.com/pembrokepublishers
ISBNs: 0-921217, 1-55138
Publisher of educational resources for parents & teachers covering: Reading & Writing; Grammar & Speaking; Thinking & drama; Classroom management & major issues in education
Claudia Connolly, General Manager
Mary Macchiusi, President

Pemmican Publications Inc.
150 Henry Ave., Winnipeg, MB R3B 0J7

Tel: 204-589-6346; *Fax:* 204-589-2063
pemmican@pemmican.mb.ca
www.pemmicanpublications.ca
ISBNs: 0-91943, 0-921827; *SAN:* 115-1657
Published more than 150 titles, including history, biography, Canadian cultural and linguistic studies, adult fiction, poetry and illustrated stories for young and early readers. Pemmican is the only dedicated Metis publishing house in Canada.
Randal McIlroy, Managing Editor

Penguin Random House
Previous Name: Random House Canada Ltd. & Penguin Canada
Owned By: Bertelsmann & Pearson PLC
Penguin Random House Canada, #1400, 320 Front St. West, Toronto, ON M5V 3B6

Tel: 416-364-4449; *Fax:* 416-364-6863
customerservicescanada@penguinrandomhouse.com
www.penguinrandomhouse.com
twitter.com/PenguinRandomCA
www.facebook.com/PenguinRandomCA
ISBNs: 0-394, 0-679; *SAN:* 115-088X
After merging with Penguin in July 2013, Random House has become Penguin Random House & still publishes numerous titles each month
Kristin Cochrane, CEO, Penguin Random House Canada

Penumbra Press
PO Box 20011, 1 King Ave. East, Newcastle, ON L1B 1M3

Tel: 613-692-5590; *Fax:* 613-692-5589
www.penumbrapress.com
twitter.com/penumbra_press
ISBNs: 0-921254, 0-929806, 1-894131; *SAN:* 115-0774
Small fine-art & literary publishing house; Publishes Northern and Native literatures; children's literature; poetry; translations of Scandinavian literature; history; mythology; art books
John Flood, President, john@penumbrapress.ca

Playfort Publishing
PO Box 576, 362 Alexander St. NE, Salmon Arm, BC V1E 4N7

Tel: 250-833-5554; *Fax:* 250-833-4915
playfortpublishing.ca
www.pinterest.com/playfort
twitter.com/FriendlyFiction
www.facebook.com/PlayfortPublishing
Children's publisher.

Playwrights Canada Press
Previous Name: Playwrights Union of Canada
#202, 269 Richmond St. West, Toronto, ON M5V 1X1
Tel: 416-703-0013; *Fax:* 416-408-3402
info@playwrightscanada.com
www.playwrightscanada.com
www.instagram.com/playcanpress
twitter.com/playcanpress
www.facebook.com/plcnp
ISBNs: 0-88754, 0-919834
Publishes roughly 32 books of plays, theatre history & criticism annually
Annie Gibson, Publisher, annie@playwrightscanada.com
Blake Sproule, Managing Editor, blake@playwrightscanada.com

Pontifical Institute of Mediaeval Studies Publications
59 Queen's Park Cres. East, Toronto, ON M5S 2C4
Tel: 416-926-7142; *Fax:* 416-926-7292
pontifex@chass.utoronto.ca
pims.ca
twitter.com/PIMS_Mediaeval
ISBNs: 0-88844; SAN: 115-0804
Small university press that publishes research, texts, translations, reference works & articles about the Middle Ages
Richard M.H. Alway, President, 416-926-7147,
richard.alway@utoronto.ca
Bill Harnum, Director, Publications, 416-926-7126,
bill.harnum@gmail.com

Porcupine's Quill Inc.
PO Box 160, 68 Main St., Erin, ON N0B 1T0
Tel: 519-833-9158; *Fax:* 519-833-9845
pql@sentex.net
porcupinesquill.ca
twitter.com/porcupinesquill
www.facebook.com/theporcupinesquill
ISBNs: 0-88984; SAN: 115-0820
Small publishing house; Publishers of Canadian poetry & literature
Tim Inkster, Publisher
Elke Inkster, Publisher

Portage & Main Press
Previous Name: Peguis Publishers Limited
#100, 318 McDermot Ave., Winnipeg, MB R3A 0A2
Tel: 204-987-3500; *Fax:* 866-734-8477
Toll-Free: 800-667-9673
customerservice@portageandmainpress.com
www.portageandmainpress.com
www.instagram.com/highwaterpress
twitter.com/PortageMainPres
www.facebook.com/PortageandMainPress
ISBNs: 0-919566, 1-89110, 1-895411, 1-55379
Publishers of educational books & resources for teachers
Annalee Greenberg, Editorial Director

Potlatch Publications Limited
2 Campview Rd., Stoney Creek, ON L8E 5E2
Tel: 905-643-5425
www.potlatchpublications.wordpress.com
ISBNs: 0-919676; SAN: 115-1355
Robert Nielsen, President, robtnielsen@aol.com

Pottersfield Press
83 Leslie Rd., East Lawrencetown, NS B2Z 1P8
Tel: 902-827-4517; *Fax:* 902-455-3652
Toll-Free: 800-646-2879
www.pottersfieldpress.com
twitter.com/potterspress
www.facebook.com/pottersfieldpress
ISBNs: 0-919001, 1-895900; SAN: 115-0790
Publishers of fiction, non-fiction, poetry and Maritime interest books, with a focus on African Nova Scotian and Mi'kmaq tradition
Lesley Choyce

Pow Pow Press
Montréal, QC
info@editionspowpow.com
www.powpowpress.com
French-language graphic novels
Luc Bossé, Publisher

Power Engineering Books Ltd.
7 Perron St., St Albert, AB T8N 1E3
Tel: 780-458-3155; *Fax:* 780-460-2530
Toll-Free: 800-667-3155
power@nucleus.com
www.powerengbooks.com
ISBNs: SAN: 115-4850
Publisher of technical books & supplier of codes & standards to private, trade & public businesses across Canada

The Press of the Nova Scotia College of Art & Design (NSCAD)
5163 Duke St., Halifax, NS B3J 3J6
Tel: 902-444-9600; *Fax:* 902-425-2420
thepress@nscad.ca
nscad.ca
ISBNs: 0-919616
Publisher of scholarly works in the fields of contemporary art, craft & design.

Les Presses de l'Université de Montréal
#100, 5450, ch de la Côte-des-Neiges, Montréal, QC H3T 1Y6
Tél: 514-343-6933; *Téléc:* 514-343-2232
pum@umontreal.ca
www.pum.umontreal.ca
twitter.com/PressesUdeM
www.facebook.com/1485468251667307
ISBNs: 0-7770, 2-7605, 2-920073
A pour mandat le diffusion des résultats de la recherche universitaire (livres, revues, édition électronique); la transférence des connaissances scientifiques à un large public; participation à la vie de la Cité; et contribution au rayonnement national et international de l'Université de Montréal
Patrick Poirier, Directeur général, poirierp@editionspum.ca

Les Presses de l'Université Laval
Pavillon de l'Est, 2180, ch Sainte-Foy, 1é étage, Québec, QC G1V 0A6
Tél: 418-656-2803; *Téléc:* 418-656-3305
presses@pul.ulaval.ca
www.pulaval.com
twitter.com/pulaval
www.facebook.com/pulaval
ISBNs: 2-7637, 2-89224
Ouvrages didactiques, manuels, travaux savants; diffuseur et distributeur
Denis Dion, Directeur général, denis.dion@pul.ulaval.ca
Dominique Gingras, Directrice administrative,
dominique.gingras@pul.ulaval.ca

Prise de Parole
#205, 109, rue Elm, Sudbury, ON P3C 1T4
Tél: 705-675-6491; *Téléc:* 705-673-1817
info@prisedeparole.ca
www.prisedeparole.ca
twitter.com/prisedeparole
www.facebook.com/editionsPrisedeparole
ISBNs: 0-920814, 0-921573, 2-89423
Bandes dessinées, beaux livres, contes traditionnels, enfants, ados, études littéraires, poésie, revues, romans
Denise Truax, Codirectrice générale, dtruax@prisedeparole.ca
Stéphane Cormier, Codirecteur général,
scormier@prisedeparole.ca
Alain Mayotte, Contrôleur-comptable,
amayotte@prisedeparole.ca

Probe International
225 Brunswick Ave., Toronto, ON M5S 2M6
www.probeinternational.org
twitter.com/ProbeIntl
www.facebook.com/ProbeInternational
ISBNs: 0-919849, 1-85383, 0-7656
Publishes books & articles promoting social, economic & environmental well-being in Canada & around the world.
Patricia Adams, Executive Director,
patriciaadams@probeinternational.org

Productive Publications
380 Brooke Ave., Toronto, ON M5M 2L6
Tel: 416-483-0634; *Fax:* 416-322-7434
productivepubs@rogers.com
www.productivepublications.ca
ISBNs: 0-920847, 1-896210, 1-55270; SAN: 117-1712
Iain Williamson, Publisher

Promontory Press Inc.
Victoria, BC
www.promontorypress.com
www.linkedin.com/company/promontory-press
witter.com/promontorypress
www.facebook.com/promontorypress
Fiction, non-fiction, poetry; focuses on publishing first-time authors
Bennett R. Coles, Founder

Publications Ontario
222 Jarvis St., 8th Fl., Toronto, ON M7A 0B6
Tel: 416-326-5300; *Toll-Free:* 800-668-9938
webpubont@ontario.ca
www.publications.gov.on.ca
Other information: TTY: 800-268-7095
ISBNs: 0-7743, 0-7729, 0-7778
Publisher of government publications, including driver's

handbook, fire codes, building codes, agricultural publications, employment standards & occupational health & safety regulations

Publishers Group Canada
Previous Name: Publishers Group West
#300, 76 Stratford St., Toronto, ON M6J 2S1
Tel: 416-934-9900; *Fax:* 416-934-1410
Toll-Free: 800-747-8147
info@pgcbooks.ca
www.pgcbooks.ca
www.instagram.com/pgcbooks
twitter.com/pgcbooks
www.facebook.com/162713432414
ISBNs: SAN: 117-0171
Distributors of a large number of non-fiction, fiction & children's books for a large number of publishers.
Graham Fidler, Executive Vice-President, graham@pgcbooks.ca

QC Fiction
Owned By: Baraka Books
6977, rue Lacroix, Montréal, QC H4E 2V4
www.qcfiction.com
twitter.com/qcfiction
www.facebook.com/qcfictionimprint
An imprint of Baraka Books, QC Fiction publishes contemporary Québec fiction in English translations.
Peter McCambridge, Editor, peter@petermccambridge.com

Qualitas Publishing
195 Cardiff Dr. NW, Calgary, AB T2K 1S1
Tel: 403-618-3830
info@qualitaspublishing.com
www.qualitaspublishing.com
Publishes classics.

Quattro Books
12 Concord Ave., 2nd Fl., Toronto, ON M6H 2P1
Tel: 647-748-7484
info@quattrobooks.ca
www.quattrobooks.ca
www.youtube.com/quattrobooks
twitter.com/quattrobooks
awww.facebook .com/quattrobooks
Allan Briesmaster, Vice-President/Publisher,
allan@quattrobooks.ca
Luciano Iacobellli, Publisher/Executive Director,
allan@quattrobooks.ca

Québec dans le Monde
#200, 511, rue Saint-Joseph est, Québec, QC G1K 3B7
info@quebecmonde.com
www.quebecmonde.com
ISBNs: 2-921309, 2-89525, 2-9801130; SAN: 116-8657
Une organisation à but non lucratif livres de l'édition de référence sur le Québec, la promotion des entreprises locales du Québec et a récemment ouvert une école internationale d'immersion en français à Québec
Robert Laliberté, Président
Lise Gravel, Vice-Présidente

Québec Science
1251, rue Rachel est, Montréal, QC H2L 2J9
Tél: 514-521-8356; *Ligne sans frais:* 800-567-8356
courrier@quebecscience.qc.ca
www.quebecscience.qc.ca
twitter.com/quebecscience
www.facebook.com/QuebecScience
ISBNs: 2-920073
Québec Science aborde toutes les questions liées à la science et à la technologie et est un regard scientifique sur les grandes questions
Marie Lambert-Chan, Rédactrice en chef,
mlchan@quebecscience.qc.ca

Rattling Books
Owned By: Alca Productions Inc.
NL
www.rattlingbooks.com
soundcloud.com/rattlingbooks
www.facebook.com/pg/RattlingBooks
Audio Book publisher.

Red Deer Press
195 Allstate Pkwy., Markham, ON L3R 4T8
Toll-Free: 800-387-9776
rdp@reddeerpress.com
www.reddeerpress.com
ISBNs: 0-88995; SAN: 115-0871
Publishes picture books, junior, juvenile, Young Adult fiction and non-fiction and adult non-fiction titles. Was purchased by Fitzhenry & Whiteside in 2005.
Richard Dionne, Publisher, dionne@reddeerpress.com

Peter Carver, Children's Editor

Reference Press
PO Box 70, Teeswater, ON N0G 2S0
Tel: 519-392-6634
www.libris.ca/refpress
ISBNs: 0-919981; SAN: 115-687X
Publisher of Canadian reference materials & software for use in
school & public libraries
Gordon Ripley, Contact

Renouf Publishing Co. Ltd. / Éditions Renouf limitées
#22, 1010 Polytek St., Ottawa, ON K1J 9J3
Tel: 613-745-2665; *Fax:* 613-745-7660
Toll-Free: 866-767-6766
orders@renoufbooks.com
www.renoufbooks.com
twitter.com/renoufbooks
ISBNs: 0-88852; SAN: 170-8066
Publisher of over 35 international organizations' publications &
documents

The Resource Centre
PO Box 190, Waterloo, ON N2J 3Z9
Tel: 519-885-0826; *Fax:* 519-747-5629
Toll-Free: 800-923-0330
sales@theresourcecentre.com
www.theresourcecentre.com
ISBNs: 0-920701; SAN: 115-5032
Publisher of educational resources, including the Canadian
Handwriting series

Retromedia Inc.
PO Box 471, 111 Richmond, Charlottetown, PE C1A 7L1
Tel: 902-394-3855
www.retromedia.ca
Publishes a variety of books, from provincial politics to sports.
Larry Resnitzky, Owner & Publisher

Riverwood Publishers Ltd.
471 Eagle St., Newmarket, ON L3Y 1K7
Toll-Free: 800-561-2674
consultantsupport@usbornebooksathome.ca
usbornebooksathome.ca
ISBNs: 1-895121; SAN: 116-1288
Publisher of children's books & Canadian distributor of Usborne
Books, a children's book publisher.
Ron Charlesworth, President

RK Publishing Inc.
#308, 3089 Bathurst St., Toronto, ON M6A 2A4
Tel: 416-785-0312; *Fax:* 416-785-0317
Toll-Free: 866-696-9549
frenchtextbooks@rkpublishing.com
www.rkpublishing.com
twitter.com/rkpublishing
www.facebook.com/RKPublishingInc
Publishing company that specializes in Canadian French books.

Robert Rose, Inc.
#800, 120 Eglinton Ave. East, Toronto, ON M4P 1E2
Tel: 416-322-6552; *Fax:* 416-322-6936
www.robertrose.ca
www.instagram.com/robertrose
twitter.com/robert_rose
www.facebook.c om/robert.roseinc
Publisher of cookbooks & health books.
Meredith Dees, Senior Editor

Robin Brass Studio Inc.
56, rue Faillon, Montréal, QC H2R 1K6
Tel: 514-272-7463
rbrass@sympatico.ca
www.robinbrassstudio.com
ISBNs: 1-896941; SAN: 115-5040
Small publishing house producing primarily non-fiction,
especially within the area of military history & other Canadian
history; also designs & produces books under contract for other
publishers & organizations.

Rocky Mountain Books
414 - 13th Ave. NE, Calgary, AB T2E 1C2
Tel: 250-360-0829; *Fax:* 250-386-0829
Toll-Free: 800-665-3302
distribution@heritagehouse.ca
www.rmbooks.com
www.instagram.com/rm_books
twitter.com/rmbooks
www.facebook.com/rmb ooks
ISBNs: 0-921102; SAN: 115-5040
Publisher of outdoor activity guidebooks, historical accounts of
Canadian mountaineering and other adventures, biographies &
related non-fiction

Don Gorman, Publisher, don@rmbooks.com
Joe Wilderson, Senior Editor, joe@rmbooks.com

Ronsdale Press
Previous Name: Cacanadadada Press
3350 West 21st Ave., Vancouver, BC V6S 1G7
Tel: 604-738-4688; *Fax:* 604-731-4548
ronsdale@shaw.ca
www.ronsdalepress.com
twitter.com/ronsdalepress
www.facebook.com/ronsdalepress
ISBNs: 0-921870, 1-55380; SAN: 116-2454
Publisher of books about & from across Canada, including
fiction, poetry, regional history, biography & autobiography, &
children's books.
Ronald B. Hatch, Publisher

Roseway Publishing
Fernwood Publishing
32 Oceanvista Lane, Black Point, NS B0J 1B0
Tel: 902-857-1388; *Fax:* 902-857-1328
roseway@fernpub.ca
www.fernwoodpublishing.ca/roseway
www.instagram.com/fernpub
twitter.com/fernpub
www.facebook.com/roseway.publishing
ISBNs: 1-895686, 1-55266
Fiction imprint of Fernwood

The Royal Astronomical Society of Canada (RASC)
#203, 4920 Dundas St. West, Toronto, ON M9A 1B7
Tel: 416-924-7973; *Toll-Free:* 888-924-7272
www.rasc.ca
www.youtube.com/user/RASCANADA
twitter.com/rasc
www.facebook.com/theRoyalAstronomicalSocietyofCanada
Publishes journals & guides relating to astronomy
Phil Groff, Executive Director

Rubicon Publishing Inc.
2040 Speers Rd., Oakville, ON L6L 2X8
Tel: 905-849-8777; *Fax:* 800-336-0980
Toll-Free: 800-336-0980
contact@rubiconpublishing.com
www.rubiconpublishing.com
ISBNs: 0-921156; SAN: 115-432X
Publisher of educational resources for students & educators for
grades K-12.

Running the Goat Books & Broadsides
General Delivery, Tors Cove, NL A0A 4A0
Tel: 709-334-3239
www.runningthegoat.com
Micro press publishing children's literature, letterpress-printed
books & broadsides; specializes in celebrating the life & culture
of Newfoundland & Atlantic Canada
Marnie Parsons, Contact, marnie.parsons@mac.com

Sandhill Book Marketing Ltd.
Millcreek Industrial Park, #4, 3308 Appaloosa Rd., Kelowna,
BC V1V 2W5
Tel: 250-491-1446; *Fax:* 250-491-4066
Toll-Free: 800-667-3848
info@sandhillbooks.com
www.sandhillbooks.com
ISBNs: 0-920923; SAN: 115-2181
Distributor for small press & independent publishers
Nancy Wise, Owner, nwise@sandhillbooks.com

Sara Jordan Publishing
Owned By: Jordan Music Productions Inc.
PO Box 28105 RPO Lakeport, 600 Ontario St., St Catharines,
ON L2N 7P8
Tel: 905-938-9555; *Fax:* 905-938-9970
Toll-Free: 800-567-7733
info@songsthatteach.com
www.songsthatteach.com
www.facebook.com/songsthatteach
ISBNs: 1-895523, 1-894262, 1-533860; SAN: 118-959X
Publisher & producer of educational songs & music
Sara Jordan, Publisher

Saunders Book Company
PO Box 9, 29 Stewart Rd., Collingwood, ON L9Y 3Z7
Tel: 705-445-4777; *Fax:* 705-445-9569
Toll-Free: 800-461-9120
info@saundersbook.ca
www.saundersbook.ca
twitter.com/saundersbookco
www.facebook.com/saundersbook
ISBNs: SAN: 169-9768
Publishers of books for educational books & fiction for K-12
schools & libraries

John Saunders, President

Scholar's Choice
2323 Trafalgar St., London, ON N5Y 5S7
Tel: 519-453-7470; *Fax:* 800-363-3398
Toll-Free: 800-265-1095
customerservice@scholarschoice.ca
www.scholarschoice.ca
www.pinterest.com/scholarschoice
twitter.com/scholarschoice
www.facebook.com/scholarschoice.ca
ISBNs: 0-88809; SAN: 170-0014
Publisher & retailer of educational materials
Scott Webster, President
Cindy Webster, Chief Financial Officer

Scholastic Canada Ltd. / Éditions Scholastic
175 Hillmount Rd., Markham, ON L6C 1Z7
Tel: 905-887-7323; *Fax:* 800-387-4944
Toll-Free: 800-268-3660
custserve@scholastic.ca
www.scholastic.ca
twitter.com/scholasticCDA
www.facebook.com/ScholasticCanada
ISBNs: 0-590; SAN: 115-5164
Leading publishers & distributors of children's books &
educational materials in French & English
Richard Robinson, Chairman of the Board, President, & CEO
Kenneth J. Cleary, Chief Financial Officer
Iole Lucchese, Chief Strategy Officer
Satbir Bedi, Executive Vice President & Chief Technology
Officer
Ellie Berger, Executive Vice-President and President, Trade
Publishin
Alan Boyko, President, Scholastic Book Fairs

Second Story Press
#401, 20 Maud St., Toronto, ON M5V 2M5
Tel: 416-537-7850; *Fax:* 416-537-0588
info@secondstorypress.ca
secondstorypress.ca
www.linkedin.com/company/second-story-feminist-press
twitter.com/_second story
www.facebook.com/SecondStoryPress
ISBNs: 0-929005, 1-896764
Publisher of feminist-inspired adult fiction & non-fiction;
children's fiction, non-fiction, & picture books; & young adult
fiction & non-fiction. Special interest areas include social justice,
human rights, equality & ability issues.
Margie Wolfe, Publisher
Phuong Truong, General Manager
Melissa Kaita, Manager, Production
Gillian Rodgerson, Managing Editor
Emma Rodgers, Manager, Marketing & Promotions
Yasmine Lee, Coordinator, Marketing & Promotions

The Secret Mountain
3816 Royal Ave., Montréal, QC H4A 2M2
Tel: 514-483-9281
info@thesecretmountain.com
www.thesecretmountain.com
www.youtube.com/user/TheSecretMountain
twitter.com/secretmountain
www. facebook.com/TheSecretMountain
The Secret Mountain publishes children's books, videos & audio
recordings.

Self-Counsel Press Ltd.
1481 Charlotte Rd., North Vancouver, BC V7J 1H1
Tel: 604-986-3366; *Fax:* 604-986-3947
Toll-Free: 800-663-3007
orders@self-counsel.com
www.self-counsel.com
www.linkedin.com/company/self-counsel-press
twitter.com/selfcounsel
www.facebook.com/selfcounselpress
ISBNs: 0-88908, 1-55180; SAN: 115-0545
Publisher of self-help law books & books for small business
Diana R. Douglas, President

Selkirk Stories
678 PE-19, Meadow Bank, PE C0A 1H1
Tel: 902-368-2490
info@selkirkstories.com
www.selkirkstories.com
twitter.com/SelkirkStories
www.facebook.com/selkirkstories
Publishes stories of Prince Edward Island, both in fiction and
new editions of obscure works of genealogy and Island history.
John Westlie, Publisher

Septembre éditeur inc.
#901, 305, boul Charest est, Québec, QC G1N 2C9
Tél: 418-658-7272; *Téléc:* 418-652-0986
Ligne sans frais: 800-361-7755
editions@septembre.com
www.septembre.com
ISBNs: 2-930433, 2-89471
Matériel didactique; éducation; emplois; formation; littérature jeunesse; management; ressources humaines; métiers; orientation; outils pédagogiques
Annik De Celles, Directrice générale, annik@septembre.com

Seraphim Editions
4456 Park St., Niagara Falls, ON L2E 2P6
Tel: 519-290-5509; *Fax:* 519-290-5509
info@seraphimeditions.com
www.seraphimeditions.com
www.instagram.com/seraphimeditions
Celebrates & publishes the works of Canadian authors & artists.
Maureen Whyte, Founder

Services documentaires multimédias inc. (SDM)
#620, 5650, rue d'Iberville, Montréal, QC H2G 2B3
Tel: 514-382-0895; *Fax:* 514-384-9139
informations@sdm.qc.ca
www.sdm.qc.ca
ISBNs: 2-89059, 0-88523
SDM a des bases de données et d'autres produits de pointe pour aider à gérer les documents publiés dans le monde de langue française
Philippe Sauvageau, Chef de Direction,
philippe.sauvageau@sdm.qc.ca

Shoreline Press
23, rue Sainte-Anne, Sainte-Anne-de-Bellevue, QC H9X 1L1
Tel: 514-457-5733
info@shorelinepress.ca
www.shorelinepress.ca
ISBNs: 0-9695180, 0-9698752, 1-896754; SAN 116-9564
Independent press specializing in memoirs & titles of local interest
Judith Isherwood, Owner & Senior Editor

Signature Editions
Previous Name: Nuage Éditions
PO Box 206, Winnipeg, MB R3M 3S7
Tel: 204-779-7803; *Fax:* 204-779-6970
signature@allstream.net
www.signature-editions.com
twitter.com/sigeditions
www.facebook.com/154009474633646
ISBNs: 0-921833, 1-897109; SAN: 115-0723
Signature Editions is a literary press with an eclectic list of fiction, non-fiction, poetry and drama.
Karen Haughian, Publisher

Simon & Schuster Canada
Owned By: Simon & Schuster
#300, 166 King St. East, Toronto, ON M5A 1J3
Tel: 647-427-8882; *Fax:* 647-430-9446
Toll-Free: 800-387-0446
www.simonschustercanada.ca
www.instagram.com/simonschusterca
twitter.com/SimonSchusterCA
www.face book.com/simonandschustercanada
Publishers of a large catalog of books covering all aspects of fiction & non-fiction; as of May 2013, they can now publish Canadian content domestically.
Kevin Hanson, President & Publisher
Nita Pronovost, Editorial Director
Patricia Ocampo, Managing Editor

Socadis Inc.
420, rue Stinson, Montréal, QC H4N 3L7
Tel: 514-331-3300; *Fax:* 514-745-3282
Toll-Free: 800-361-2847
socinfo@socadis.com
www.socadis.com
Other information: Toll-Free Fax: 866-803-5422
www.facebook.com/socadis
Distributes French-language books to Canadian retailers

Sono Nis Press
PO Box 160, Winlaw, BC V0G 2J0
Tel: 250-226-0077; *Fax:* 250-226-0074
Toll-Free: 800-370-5228
books@sononis.com
www.sononis.com
twitter.com/sononispress
A literary house specializing in poetry, fiction & regional non-fiction.
Diane Morriss, Owner & Publisher

Spotted Cow Press
4216 - 121 St., Edmonton, AB T6J 1Y8
Tel: 780-434-3858
jmartin@spottedcowpress.ca
www.spottedcowpress.ca
Publishes books about the Great Plains of North America.
Jerome Martin, Publisher, jmartin@spottedcowpress.ca

Stanton Atkins & Dosil Publishers (SA&D)
2632 Bronte Dr., North Vancouver, BC V7H 1M4
Tel: 604-881-7067; *Fax:* 604-881-7068
Toll-Free: 800-665-3302
info@s-a-d-publishers.ca
www.s-a-d-publishers.ca
Specializes in written & illustrated books about Canada.
Mark Stanton, Owner
Don Atkins, Owner

Statistics Canada
150 Tunney's Pasture Driveway, Ottawa, ON K1A 0T6
Tel: 514-283-8300; *Fax:* 514-283-9350
Toll-Free: 800-263-1136
statcan.infostats-infostats.statcan@canada.ca
www.statcan.gc.ca
Other information: TTY: 800-363-7629
www.linkedin.com/company/statcan
twitter.com/statcan_eng
www.facebook. com/StatisticsCanada
ISBNs: 0-660, 0-662
Publishes information & research conducted by Statistics Canada

Stonehouse Publishing
Bonnie Doon Shopping Centre, PO Box 68092, Edmonton, AB T6C 4N6
Tel: 780-628-7024
info@stonehousepublishing.ca
www.stonehousepublishing.ca
Literary & trade fiction, with a focus on historical fiction; publishes 5-8 titles annually
Bruce Valpy, Publisher
Mike Bryant, Editor

Strategic Studies Working Group
Previous Name: Canadian Institute of Strategic Studies
Canadian Global Affairs Institute, #1800, 421 - 7th Ave. SW, Calgary, AB T2P 4K9
Tel: 613-288-2529
www.cgai.ca/sswg
Publishes research on security, defence & other international issues
Kelly J. Ogle, President, kogle@cgai.ca
David Perry, Vice-President & Senior Analyst, dperry@cgai.ca
Colin Robertson, Vice-President, crobertson@cgai.ca
Adam Frost, Managing Editor & Program Coordinator, afrost@cgai.ca

Sumach Press
Owned By: Three O'Clock Press
#20, 425 Adelaide St. West, Toronto, ON M5V 3C1
Tel: 416-929-2964; *Fax:* 416-929-1926
www.threeoclockpress.com
twitter.com/3oclockpress
www.facebook.com/threeoclockbooks
ISBNs: 1-894549, 1-896764, 0-929005; SAN: 115-1134
Publishers of feminist writing

Summerthought Publishing
PO Box 2309, Banff, AB T1L 1C1
Tel: 403-762-0535; *Fax:* 403-762-3095
info@summerthought.com
www.summerthought.com
www.facebook.com/thecanadianrockies
ISBNs: 0-919934; SAN: 115-2149
Specializing in the publication of Canadian Rockies non-fiction books.
Andrew Hempstead, Publisher

Sybertooth Inc.
59 Salem St., Sackville, NB E4L 4J6
www.sybertooth.ca
twitter.com/sybertoothbooks
A publisher of fiction, non-fiction, poetry & plays.

Talon Books Ltd.
PO Box 2076, 278 East 1st Ave., Vancouver, BC V6B 3S3
Tel: 604-444-4889; *Fax:* 604-444-4119
Toll-Free: 888-445-4176
info@talonbooks.com
www.talonbooks.com
twitter.com/talonbooks
www.facebook.com/talonbooks

ISBNs: 0-88922; SAN: 115-5334; Telebook: S1150391
Publishers specializing in poetry, drama & literary criticism. Also publishes fiction & non-fiction
Kevin Williams, President/Publisher, kevin@talonbooks.com

TechnoKids Inc.
2097 Bates Common, Burlington, ON L7R 0A5
Tel: 905-631-9112; *Fax:* 905-631-9113
Toll-Free: 800-221-7921
information@technokids.com
www.technokids.com
www.linkedin.com/company/technokids-inc-
twitter.com/technokidsinc
www.facebook.com/technokidscomputercurriculum
ISBNs: 1-894995
Publisher of technology cirriculum for schools. Publish K-12 Microsoft Office technology projects. Over 60 titles available.
Scott Gerard, President

Ten Speed Press
1745 Broadway, New York, NY 10019
Tel: 212-782-9000
crownpublishing.com/archives/imprint/ten-speed-press
twitter.com/TenSpeedPress
ISBNs: 0-89815, 1-58008, 0-89087, 1-883672, 1-58246, 1-58761
Division of Penguin Random House & part of The Crown Publishing Group, Ten Speed Press publishes cookbooks, guides & manuals. Books available in Canada through Penguin Random House, #1400, 320 Front St. West, Toronto, ON M5V 3B6, 416-364-4449.

Theytus Books
Green Mountain Rd., Lot 45, RR#2, Comp. 8, Site 50, Penticton, BC V2A 6J7
Tel: 250-493-7181; *Fax:* 250-493-5302
info@theytus.com
www.theytus.com
twitter.com/theytusbooks
www.facebook.com/theytusboks
ISBNs: 0-919441, 1-894778; SAN: 115-1517
Aboriginal-owned & operated publishing house; Focus is on publishing books of Aboriginal literature, children's books, history, culture, politics & educational materials

Third Sector Publishing
c/o Communitech Data Hub, 14 Erb St. West, Waterloo, ON N2L 1S7
Tel: 705-325-5552
info@thirdsectorpublishing.ca
www.thirdsectorpublishing.ca
www.linkedin.com/company/third-sector-publishing
twitter.com/thirdsector_
www.facebook.com/thirdsectorpublishing
Publisher of information regarding Canada's registered charities & those who donate to them.
Anderson Charters, Owner & Publisher
Susan Charters, Owner

Thistledown Press Ltd.
410 - 2nd Ave. North, Saskatoon, SK S7K 2C3
Tel: 306-244-1722; *Fax:* 306-244-1762
www.thistledownpress.com
twitter.com/readthistledown
www.facebook.com/thistledown.press
ISBNs: 0-920066, 1-894345, 0-920633, 1-895449
Publishes poetry & fiction for adults & young adults by Canadian writers; Also publishes resources for teachers
Allan Forrie, Publisher, editorial@thistledownpress.com
Jackie Forrie, Publishing & Production Manager, tdpress@thistledownpress.com

Thomas Allen & Son Ltd.
195 Allstate Pkwy., Markham, ON L3R 4T8
Tel: 905-475-9126; *Toll-Free:* 800-387-4333
info@t-allen.com
www.thomasallen.ca
ISBNs: 0-919028, 088762; SAN: 115-1762
Distributor of self-help books, fiction & non-fiction books, calendars & stationery

Thompson Educational Publishing, Inc.
20 Ripley Ave., Toronto, ON M6S 3N9
Tel: 416-766-2763; *Fax:* 416-766-0398
Toll-Free: 877-366-2763
info@thompsonbooks.com
thompsonbooks.com
ISBNs: 1-55077; SAN: 115-0391
Publishes educational texts in the social sciences & humanities
Keith Thompson, President
Ted Temertzoglou, Vice-President

Three O'Clock Press
#200, 425 Adelaide St. West, Toronto, ON M5V 3C1
Tel: 416-929-2964
info@threeoclockpress.com
www.threeoclockpress.com
twitter.com/3oclockpress
www.facebook.com/threeoclockpress
Feminist writing.

Tikka Books
3866 Claude, Verdun, QC H4G 1H1
Tel: 514-767-2125
www.tikkabooks.com

ISBNs: 1-896106; 0-921993
Independent publishing house specializing in how-to books for crafts, sewing, cooking & Halloween
Leila Peltosaari, Publisher, leila@tikkabooks.com

Timeless Books
PO Box 9, Walker's Landing Rd., Kootenay, BC V0B 1X0
Tel: 250-227-9224; *Fax:* 250-227-9494
Toll-Free: 800-661-8711
bookstore@timeless.org
www.timeless.org

ISBNs: 0-931454
Publisher of teachings on yoga, including poetry & spiritual biography; also publishes classic books & audio

TouchWood Editions Ltd.
Previous Name: Horsdal & Schubart Publishers Ltd.
#103, 1075 Pendergast St., Victoria, BC V8V 0A1
Tel: 250-360-0829; *Fax:* 250-386-0829
info@touchwoodeditions.com
www.touchwoodeditions.com
twitter.com/touchwooded
www.facebook.com/touchwoodeditions

ISBNs: 0-920663, 1-894898
Publishes books with a focus on history, historical fiction, biography, food, nautical subjects, mysteries & art/architecture
Taryn Boyd, Publisher

Tradewind Books
#202, 1807 Maritime Mews, Vancouver, BC V6H 3W7
Tel: 604-662-4405
www.tradewindbooks.com
twitter.com/tradewindbooks
www.facebook.com/164946283181

ISBNs: 1-896580
Publishers of children's literature recognized internationally
Michael Katz, Publisher

Tree House Press Inc.
195 Allstate Pkwy., Markham, ON L3R 4T8
Fax: 905-574-0228
Toll-Free: 800-776-8733
contact@treehousepress.com
www.treehousepress.com
www.youtube.com/mytreehousepress
www.facebook.com/treehousepress

ISBNs: 1-895165
Publisher of educational resources
Patrick Lashmar, President & Chief Executive Officer

Tundra Books
Owned By: McClelland & Stewart Ltd.
#1400, 320 Front St. West, Toronto, ON M5V 3B6
Tel: 416-364-4449; *Toll-Free:* 888-523-9292
tundra@mcclelland.com
www.tundrabooks.com
www.instagram.com/tundrabooks
twitter.com/TundraBooks
www.facebook.com /TundraBooks
Publishes children's books.
Kathryn Cole, Publisher

Turnstone Press
#206, 100 Arthur St., Winnipeg, MB R3B 1H3
Tel: 204-947-1555; *Fax:* 204-942-1555
www.turnstonepress.com
www.instagram.com/turnstone_press
twitter.com/turnstonepress
www.faceb ook.com/turnstone.press.3
ISBNs: 0-88801; SAN: 115-1096
Publishers of fiction, literary criticism, poetry & non-fiction; Imprints include Turnstone Press which publishes mysteries, thrillers & noir fiction

Ulverscroft Large Print Books Ltd.
Canada
PO Box 1230, West Seneca, NY
Tel: 905-637-8734; *Fax:* 905-333-6788
Toll-Free: 888-860-3365
sales@ulverscroftcanada.com
www.ulverscroft.com
twitter.com/UlverscroftCA
www.facebook.com/Ulverscroft

ISBNs: 0-7089
Publisher of large print & audio books

United Church Publishing House
#300, 3250 Bloor St. West, Toronto, ON M8X 2Y4
Tel: 416-253-5456; *Fax:* 416-231-3103
Toll-Free: 800-288-7365
info@ucrdstore.ca
www.ucrdstore.ca
Other information: Toll-Free Fax: 888-858-8358
www.youtube.com/unitedchurchofcanada
twitter.com/UnitedChurchCda
www.f acebook.com/UnitedChurchCda
ISBNs: 0-919000, 1-55134; SAN: 111-6002

University of Alberta Press
University of Alberta, Ring House 2, Edmonton, AB T6G 2E1
Tel: 780-492-3662; *Fax:* 780-492-0719
www.uap.ualberta.ca
twitter.com/ualbertapress
www.facebook.com/18764314500

ISBNs: 0-88864; SAN: 118-9794
Academic unit of Learning Services at the University of Alberta; contemporary university press with publications that have scholarly impact & achieve creative distinction
Douglas Hildebrand, Director & Publisher, 780-492-0717, dhildebr@ualberta.ca

University of British Columbia Press
2029 West Mall, Vancouver, BC V6T 1Z2
Tel: 604-822-5959; *Fax:* 604-822-6083
Toll-Free: 877-377-9378
frontdesk@ubcpress.ca
www.ubcpress.ca
Other information: Toll-Free Fax: 800-668-0821
www.instagram.com/ubcpress
twitter.com/ubcpress
www.facebook.com/UBCPr ess

ISBNs: 0-7748; SAN: 115-1118
Publishing branch of the University of British Columbia. Specialties include political science, Native studies, forestry, Asian studies, Canadian history, environmental studies, planning & urban studies.
Melissa Pitts, Director, 604-822-6376, pitts@ubcpress.ca

University of Calgary Press
2500 University Dr. NW, Calgary, AB T2N 1N4
Tel: 403-220-7578; *Fax:* 403-282-0085
ucpbooks@ucalgary.ca
press.ucalgary.ca

Publishing arm of the University of Calgary
Brian Scrivener, Director, 403-220-3511,
brian.scrivener@ucalgary.ca
Helen Hajnoczky, Coordinator, Editorial, 403-220-4208,
helen.hajnoczky@ucalgary.ca

University of Manitoba Press
University of Manitoba, 92 Dysart Rd., Winnipeg, MB R3T 2M5
Fax: 204-474-7566
uofmpress@umanitoba.ca
www.uofmpress.ca
twitter.com/umanitobapress

ISBNs: 0-88755; SAN: 115-5474
Publishing arm of the University of Manitoba. Focuses on publishing books on Indigenous & Canadian history, as well as ethnic & immigration studies, Canadian literary studies, Indigenous languages, environment, land use & food studies.
David Carr, Director, 204-474-9242, david.carr@umanitoba.ca
Glenn Bergen, Managing Editor, 204-474-7338,
glenn_bergen@umanitoba.ca
Jill McConkey, Acquisitions Editor, 204-474-8804,
jill.mcconkey@umanitoba.ca

University of Ottawa Press (UOP/PUO) / Presses de l'Université d'Ottawa
542 King Edward Ave., Ottawa, ON K1N 6N5
Tel: 613-562-5246; *Fax:* 613-562-5247
Toll-Free: 800-565-9523
puo-uop@uottawa.ca
www.press.uottawa.ca
twitter.com/uottawapress
www.facebook.com/uottawapress

ISBNs: 0-7766, 2-7603
Canada's oldest French Language university press & the only Bilingual University press in North America.
Lara Mainville, Director, 613-562-5663,
lara.mainville@uottawa.ca

University of Regina Press
Previous Name: Canadian Plains Research Center Press
University of Regina, 3737 Wascana Pkwy., Regina, SK S4S 0A2
Tel: 306-585-4758; *Fax:* 306-585-4699
Toll-Free: 866-874-2257
uofrpress@uregina.ca
www.uofrpress.ca
twitter.com/UofRPress
www.facebook.com/UofRPress

ISBNs: 0-88977
The University of Regina Press is the publishing arm of the University of Regina. It publishes regional non-fiction trade titles concerning Aboriginal issues, the environment & other topics.
Kristine Luecker, Director, 306-585-4795,
kristine.luecker@uregina.ca
Kelly Laycock, Managing Editor, 306-585-4787,
kelly.laycock@uregina.ca

University of Toronto Press (UTP)
#700, 10 St Mary St., Toronto, ON M4Y 2W8
Tel: 416-978-2239; *Fax:* 416-978-4738
utorontopress.com
twitter.com/utpress
www.facebook.com/utpress

ISBNs: ISBN: 0-8020; SAN: 115-1134, 115-3234
UTP publishes scholarly, reference and general interest books in Canadian history and literature, medieval studies, social sciences, etc., as well as scholarly journals.
John Yates, President; Publisher & Chief Executive Officer, 416-978-2239 ext.222, jyates@utpress.utoronto.ca
Lynn Fisher, Vice President, Book Publishing Division, 416-978-2239 ex.2234, lfisher@utorontopress.com
Alexandra Grieve, Editorial Assistant, Book Publishing Division, 416-978-2239 ex.4235

Véhicule Press
CP 42094 Roy, Montréal, QC H2W 2T3
Tél: 514-844-6073; *Téléc:* 514-844-7543
admin@vehiculepress.com
www.vehiculepress.com
twitter.com/vehiculepress
www.facebook.com/vehiculepress

ISBNs: 0-919890, 1-55065; SAN: 115-1150
Simon Dardick, Publisher, sd@vehiculepress.com

VLB Éditeur
Une compagnie de Quebecor Media
Anciennement: Editions Quinze
Détenteur: Quebecor Media
#300, 1055 boul René-Lévesque est, Montréal, QC H2L 4S5
Tél: 514-849-5259
adpcommandes@messageries-adp.com
www.edvlb.com
www.facebook.com/vlbediteur

ISBNs: 2-89005
Publie des romans, des essais et des nouvelles.
Martin Balthazar, Vice-président, Édition

Voyageur Publishing
1474 Clayton Rd., RR#1, Almonte, ON K0A 1A0
Tel: 613-256-9435
www.voyageurpublishing.weebly.com

ISBNs: 0-921842
Publisher of Canadian history books with a Christian perspective
Vincent Marquis, Contact, 613-297-2138,
vmarquismin@gmail.com

Whitecap Books Ltd.
Owned By: Fitzhenry & Whiteside Limited
#209, 314 West Cordova St., Vancouver, BC V6B 1E8
Toll-Free: 800-387-9776
bookinfo@whitecap.ca
www.whitecap.ca
twitter.com/whitecapbooks
www.facebook.com/whitecapbooks
ISBNs: 1-895099, 1-55110, 1-55285; SAN: 115-1290
Currently publishes more than 300 Canadian & foreign titles; Primary emphasis is in the areas of food & wine, but also publish children's fiction & non-fiction; travel sports & transportation.
Nick Rundall, Publisher, nickr@whitecap.ca

Wilfrid Laurier University Press
75 University Ave. West, Waterloo, ON N2L 3C5
Tel: 519-884-0710; *Fax:* 519-725-1399
press@wlu.ca
www.wlupress.wlu.ca
twitter.com/wlupress
www.facebook.com/wlupress

ISBNs: 0-88920; SAN: 115-1525
Publishing arm of Wilfrid Laurier University; Publishes 28-30 titles annually in the fields of history, literature, sociology, social work, life writing, film and media studies, aboriginal studies, women's studies, philosophy, & religious studies
Lisa Quinn, Director, Rights & Permissions, lquinn@wlu.ca
Rob Kohlmeier, Managing Editor, rkohlmeier@wlu.ca
Siobhan McMenemy, Senior Editor, smcmenemy@wlu.ca
Clare Hitchens, Sales & Marketing Coordinator,
chitchens@wlu.ca

Winding Trail Press
1304 St-Jacques Rd., Embrun, ON K0A 1W0
Tel: 613-443-4484; *Fax:* 800-565-9523
Toll-Free: 800-221-9985
contact@windingtrailpress.com
www.windingtrailpress.geliefan.net
Publishes Canadian literature & non-fiction.
Ruth Bradley-St. Cyr, Publisher

Wolsak & Wynn Publishers Ltd.
280 James St. North, Hamilton, ON L8R 2L3
Tel: 905-972-9885; *Fax:* 905-972-8589
info@wolsakandwynn.ca
www.wolsakandwynn.ca
www.instagram.com/wolsakandwynn
twitter.com/wolsakandwynn
www.facebook.com/24466746964

ISBNs: 0-919897
Publishes mostly poetry and non-fiction.
Noelle Allen, Publisher

Wolters Kluwer
Previous Name: CCH Canadian Limited
#300, 90 Sheppard Ave. East, Toronto, ON M2N 6X1
Tel: 800-461-4131; *Fax:* 416-224-2243
Toll-Free: 800-268-4522
cservice@wolterskluwer.com
wolterskluwer.ca
Other information: Toll-Free Fax: 800-461-4131
ISBNs: 1-55367, 1-55141, 0-88796, 1-55496; SAN: 115-2785
Publishers of professional information products involving tax, accounting, law, financial planning & human resources
Nancy Mckinstry, CEO & Chairman of the Executive Board
Kevin Entricken, CFO & Chairman of the Executive Board

Women's Press
Owned By: Canadian Scholars' Press Inc.
#200, 245 Adelaide St. West, Toronto, ON M5V 3C1
Tel: 416-929-2774
info@canadianscholars.ca
www.womenspress.canadianscholars.ca
twitter.com/canadianscholar
www.facebook.com/canadianscholar
ISBNs: 0-88961, 0-921881, 0-7737, 0-921556; SAN: 115-5628
Publishes high-quality feminist writing
Andrew Wayne, President, Canadian Scholars' Press Inc.

Wood Lake Publishing Inc.
485 Beaver Lake Rd., Kelowna, BC V4V 1S5
Fax: 888-841-9991
Toll-Free: 800-663-2775
customerservice@woodlake.com
www.woodlakebooks.com
twitter.com/woodlakebooks
www.facebook.com/woodlakepublishinginc
ISBNs: 1-55145, 1-896836; SAN: 117-7436
Publishers of religious books and religious education tools.
Imprints: WoodLake | Northstone | CopperHouse | Seasons of the Spirit | The Best of Whole People of God Online.

YYZBOOKS
#140, 401 Richmond St. West, Toronto, ON M5V 3A8
Tel: 416-598-4546; *Fax:* 416-598-2282
publish@yyzartistsoutlet.org
www.yyzbooks.com
www.facebook.com/yyzartistsoutlet
ISBNs: 0-920397
Publishes a variety of current writing focusing on art & culture
Ana Barajas, Director

Zygote Publishing
PO Box 4049, 10101 Saskatchewan Dr. NW, Edmonton, AB T6E 4R6
Tel: 780-439-7580; *Fax:* 780-439-7529
publish@zygotepublishing.com
www.zygotepublishing.com
Publishes unique Canadian books.

Magazine & Newspaper Publishers

Aberdeen Publishing Inc.
6379 Main St., Oliver, BC V0H 1T0
Tel: 778-439-2129
info@aberdeenpublishing.com
www.aberdeenpublishing.com
Robert W. Doull, President, rdoull@aberdeenpublishing.com

Acadie Média
860 Main St., Moncton, NB E1C 1G2
Tél: 506-383-1955; *Téléc:* 506-383-7440

Advocate Media Inc.
Owned By: Advocate Printing & Publishing Co.
PO Box 1000, 181 Brown's Point Rd., Pictou, NS B0K 1H0
Tel: 902-485-1990; *Fax:* 902-485-6353
Toll-Free: 800-236-9526
advocatemediainc.com
twitter.com/advocate1891
www.facebook.com/advocatecompanies
Publishes 11 newspapers & over 20 magazines.
Sean Murray, President & CEO, Advocate Printing & Publishing Co., seanmurray@advocateprinting.com

Advocate Printing & Publishing Co.
PO Box 1000, 181 Brown's Point Rd., Pictou, NS B0K 1H0
Tel: 902-485-1990; *Fax:* 902-485-6353
Toll-Free: 800-236-9526
advocateprinting.com
twitter.com/advocate1891
www.facebook.com/advocatecompanies
Divisions include Advocate Media Inc. & Metro Guide Publishing.
Sean Murray, President & CEO,
seanmurray@advocateprinting.com

AgMedia Inc.
Previous Name: AgMedia Co-operative Inc.
Owned By: Farms.com
ON
Toll-Free: 888-248-4893
www.betterfarming.com
Focus on the Ontario agricultural community, with industry magazines, trade show guides, custom publishing & database services. Magazines include "Better Farming" & "Better Pork".
Paul Nolan, Publisher & Editorial Director,
paul.nolan@betterfarming.com

Alta Newspaper Group LP
Owned By: Glacier Media Inc.
#920, 1200 - 73rd Ave. West, Vancouver, BC V6P 6G5
Tel: 604-732-4443;

Andrew John Publishing Inc.
40 Bloomsbury Way, London, UK WC1A 2SE
info@andrewjohnpublishing.com
www.andrewjohnpublishing.com
www.linkedin.com/company/andrew-john-publishing
twitter.com/andrewjohnpub
Andrew John Publishing Inc. is a trade oriented publishing house with a focus on health sciences & specializing in association & society publishing. Publications include "Canadian Hearing Report", "Allied Hearing Health", "Vibes" & "Listen/Écoute"

Annex Business Media
Previous Name: Annex Media & Printing Inc.
PO Box 530, 105 Donly Dr. South, Simcoe, ON N3Y 4N5
Tel: 519-429-3966; *Fax:* 519-429-3094
Toll-Free: 800-265-2827
www.annexbusinessmedia.com
Mike Fredericks, President & CEO
Paul Grossinger, Editorial Director & Group Publisher

Bale Communications Inc.
#1463, 1011 Upper Middle Rd. East, Oakville, ON L6H 5Z9
info@adnews.com
www.adnews.com
Publishes Adnews, a daily advertising & marketing news publication.
Robert Bale, Publisher
Derek Winkler, Editor

Baum Publications Ltd.
#124, 2323 Boundary Rd., Vancouver, BC V5M 4V8
Tel: 604-291-9900; *Fax:* 604-291-1906
Toll-Free: 888-286-3630
www.baumpub.com
Baum Publications Ltd. publishes specialty trade publications for manufacturers in the construction, oil & gas, recycling & solid waste & underground infrastructure sectors.
Ken Singer, Publisher & President, ksinger@baumpub.com
Melvin Date Chong, Controller & Vice-President,
mdatechong@baumpub.com
Lawrence Buser, Editorial Director, Heavy Equipment Guide,
lbuser@baumpub.com

Baxter Publications Inc.
310 Dupont St., Toronto, ON M5R 1V9
Tel: 416-968-7252; *Fax:* 416-968-2377
info@baxter.net
baxter.net
www.linkedin.com/company/baxtermediaca
twitter.cdn/CdnTravelPress
Baxter Publications is the publisher of education products & travel industry products. Services include web design & development, web hosting & digital publishing.

Bayard Presse Canada Inc.
4475, rue Frontenac, Montréal, QC H2H 2S2
Tel: 514-278-3025; *Fax:* 514-522-1761
www.bayardcanada.ca
www.linkedin.com/company/bayard-canada
twitter.com/bayardjca
www.faceb ook.com/bayard.jeunesse.canada
Hugues de Foucauld, Chief Executive Officer

Becker Associates
Previous Name: Publishing & Printing Services
#202, 10 Morrow Ave., Toronto, ON M6R 2J1
Tel: 416-538-1650; *Fax:* 416-489-1713
Toll-Free: 844-538-1650
info@beckerassociates.ca
beckerassociates.ca
www.linkedin.com/company/becker-associates
twitter.com/beckerassoc
www.facebook.com/beckerassociates
Becker Associates offers services such as editorial management, production management & web-based publishing for publications & scholarly journals.
Adam Becker, President & CTO

Black Press Group Ltd.
#210, 15288 - 54A Ave., Surrey, BC V3S 6T4
Tel: 604-575-2744
www.blackpress.ca
Publishes over 170 newspapers throughout British Columbia, Alberta, Yukon & Washington state.
Rick O'Connor, President & CEO, coconnor@blackpress.ca

Breton Communications Inc.
4660, Montée St-Hubert, St-Hubert, QC J3Y 1V1
Tel: 450-629-6005; *Fax:* 514-360-6523
Toll-Free: 888-462-2112
editorial@bretoncom.com
bretoncommunications.com
www.linkedin.com/company/803726
twitter.com/BretonCom
www.facebook.com/BretonCom
Media & publishing company specializing in optometry
Martine Breton, President, martine@bretoncom.com

Brunico Communications Ltd.
#100, 366 Adelaide St. West, Toronto, ON M5V 1R9
Tel: 416-408-2300; *Fax:* 416-408-0870
www.brunico.com
www.linkedin.com/company/brunico-communications
Brunico Communications Ltd. produces print & electronic publications on the entertainment & marketing industries. Its subsidiary, Brunico Marketing Inc., organizes entertainment & marketing conferences in cities across the U.S.
Russell Goldstein, President & CEO, rgoldstein@brunico.com
Mary Maddever, Senior Vice-President, Editorial Director & Publisher, Strategy, mmaddever@brunico.com
Jocelyn Christie, Vice-President & Publisher, Kidscreen, jchristie@brunico.com
Linda Lovegrove, Vice-President, Finance & Administration, llovegrove@brunico.com
Claire Macdonald, Vice-President & Publisher, Realscreen, cmacdonald@brunico.com

Brunswick News Inc. (BNI)
PO Box 1001, 939 Main St., Moncton, NB E1C 8P3
Tel: 506-859-4900; *Fax:* 506-859-4899
Toll-Free: 888-923-4900
www.linkedin.com/company/brunswick-news-inc-

Mike Powers, Publisher & Editor-in-Chief
Jamie Irving, Vice-President

Business Link Media Group
#101, 4056 Dorchester Rd., Niagara Falls, ON L2E 6M9
Tel: 905-646-9366; *Fax:* 905-646-5486
info@businesslinkmedia.com
businesslinkmedia.com
www.linkedin.com/company/businesslinkmediagroup
twitter.com/TheBusine ssLink
www.facebook.com/BusinessLinkMedia
Publishes digital & print media, including Business Link
Magazine.

Byrne Publishing Group Inc.
814 Lawrence Ave., Kelowna, BC V1Y 6L9
Tel: 250-861-5399; *Fax:* 250-868-3040
info@okanaganlife.com
okanaganlife.com
Publishes Okanagan Life Magazine.
Paul Byrne, Publisher & Editor, paul@okanaganlife.com

Canada Wide Media Limited
Previous Name: Canada Wide Magazines &
Communications Ltd.
#230, 4321 Still Creek Dr., Burnaby, BC V5C 6S7
Tel: 604-299-7311; *Fax:* 604-299-9188
cwm@canadawide.com
www.canadawide.com
Canada Wide Media provides a range of media services &
products, in printed publications & digital media.
Peter Legge, Chair & CEO LL.D, plegge@canadawide.com

Canadian Committee on Labour History
**Peace Hills Trust Tower, Athabasca University, 1200, 10011 -
109th St., Edmonton, AB T5J 3S8**
cclh@athabascau.ca
www.cclh.ca
twitter.com/cclhtweets
ISBNs: 0-9692060, 0-9695835, 1-894000; SAN: 115-4168
Publisher of "Labour/Le Travail: Journal of Canadian Labour
Studies", as well as books & bulletins around the subject of
labour history.

Canadian Energy Research Institute (CERI)
#150, 3512 - 33rd St. NW, Calgary, AB T2L 2A6
Tel: 403-282-1231; *Fax:* 403-284-4181
info@ceri.ca
ceri.ca
www.linkedin.com/company/1945878
twitter.com/ceri_canada
ISBNs: 0-920522, 1-896091; SAN: 115-2866
CERI is an independent, not-for-profit research organization
formed through a partnership of industry, academia &
government. It aims to conduct economic research on energy &
related environmental issues for the benefit of academia,
business, government & the public.
Allan Fogwill, President & CEO
Dinara Millington, Vice-President, Research
Lisa Rollins, Vice-President, External Relations

Canadian Institute of Resources Law
**Murray Fraser Hall, University of Calgary, #3353, 2500
University Dr. NW, Calgary, AB T2N 1N4**
Tel: 403-220-3200; *Fax:* 403-282-6182
cirl@ucalgary.ca
cirl.ca
ISBNs: 0-919269; SAN: 115-2904
Publishes research & proceedings of sponsored conferences on
the topic of Natural Resources Law. Titles include "Canada
Energy Law Service" & "Resources".
Allan Ingelson, Executive Director

Canadian Science Publishing (CSP)
Previous Name: NRC Research Press
#1, 1840 Woodward Dr., Ottawa, ON K2C 0P7
Tel: 613-656-9846; *Fax:* 613-656-9838
contact@cdnsciencepub.com
cdnsciencepub.com
www.linkedin.com/company/canadian-science-publishing
twitter.com/cdnscie ncepub
www.facebook.com/cdnsciencepub
The publisher is a not-for-profit organization that publishes 24
journals in a wide range of discipliines. It was the publishing
division of the National Research Council until it was spun off in
2010. It is affiliated with over 25 other Canadian & international
societies & associations.
Suzanne Kettley, Executive Director
James J. Germida, Executive Editor-in-Chief

Canstar Community News Ltd.
Owned By: FP Canadian Newspapers
1355 Mountain Ave., Winnipeg, MB R2X 3B6
Tel: 204-697-7000; *Fax:* 204-953-4300
www.winnipegfreepress.com
Published titles include such community newspapers as The
Herald, The Lance, The Sou'wester, The Headliner, The Metro &
The Times.

Capamara Communications Inc.
4623 William Head Rd., Victoria, BC V9C 3Y7
Tel: 250-478-3973
info@capamara.com
capamara.com
This publisher offers specialty magazines & trade newspapers
for various industries in Canada & around the world. Titles
include: Service Truck Magazine, Tree Service Canada & Small
Farm Canada.

CCMC Sports
#101, 5397 Eglinton Ave. West, Toronto, ON M9C 5K6
Tel: 416-928-2909; *Fax:* 416-966-1118
Toll-Free: 800-320-6420
info@ccmcsports.com
ccmcsports.ca
A sports & entertainment marketing company working in
publishing, radio & television, internet, event production & media
creation. Published products include SCOREGolf & CFL
Illustrated.
Kim Locke, President
Cliff Kivell, Vice-President & General Manager

Centre for Criminology & Sociolegal Studies
**University of Toronto, 14 Queen's Park Cres. West, 2nd Fl.,
Toronto, ON M5S 3K9**
Fax: 416-978-4195
crim@utoronto.ca
www.criminology.utoronto.ca
In-house publishing facility to showcase research of Centre
faculty & graduate students.
Audrey Macklin, Director, audrey.macklin@utoronto.ca

Chronicle Information Resources Ltd.
#306, 555 Burnhamthorpe Rd., Toronto, ON M9C 2Y3
Fax: 416-352-6199
Toll-Free: 866-632-4766
health@chronicle.org
www.chronicle.ca
ISBNs: 0-9685848
An independent producer of periodicals, newsletters, websites &
information for medical practitioners as well as the
pharmaceutical & biotech industries. Publications include: "The
Chronicle of Skin & Allergy," "Chronicle of Cosmetic Medicine +
Surgery" & "Pediatric Chronicle".

CNIB
1929 Bayview Ave., Toronto, ON M4G 3E8
Toll-Free: 800-563-2642
info@cnib.ca
cnib.ca
www.linkedin.com/company/cnib
twitter.com/cnib
www.facebook.com/mycnib
ISBNs: 0-616, 0-921122
Produces accessible & alternative publishing for people with
print disabilities, including in formats like Braille, DAISY,
audiobooks & e-books.
John M. Rafferty, President & CEO

Continental Newspapers Canada Ltd.
550 Doyle Ave., Kelowna, BC V1Y 7V1
David Radler, Founder

Coopérative nationale de l'information indépendante (CN2i)
QC

Cottage Life Media
Owned By: Blue Ant Media
#200, 130 Merton St., Toronto, ON M4S 1A4
Tel: 416-599-2000; *Toll-Free:* 800-267-0393
service@cottagelife.com
cottagelife.com
www.instagram.com/cottagelife
twitter.com/cottagelife
www.facebook.com /cottagelife
ISBNs: 0-9696922
Publishes "Cottage Life" magazine & website as well as
distributing a selection of cottage-related books & television
shows.
Al Zikovitz, President & Chief Executive Officer

Coyle Media Group (CMG)
67 Neil Ave., Stittsville, ON K2S 1B9
Tel: 613-271-8903; *Fax:* 613-271-8905
info@coylemediagroup.com
www.coylemediagroup.com
twitter.com/coylemediagroup
www.facebook.com/CoyleMediaGroup
CMG is a publisher of print & digital media. It also produces the
Fifty-Five Plus Lifestyle Show twice each year.
George Coyle, President, george@coylemediagroup.com
Bryan Wiltsie, Director, Operations, Digital Media & Publishing,
bwiltsie@coylemediagroup.com
Pam Dillon, Editor, pam@coylemediagroup.com

Craig Kelman & Associates Ltd.
2020 Portage Ave., 3rd Fl., Winnipeg, MB R3J 0K4
Tel: 866-985-9780; *Fax:* 866-985-9799
info@kelman.ca
www.kelman.ca
www.linkedin.com/company/craig-kelman-&-associates
Craig Kelman & Associates is a contract publisher of magazines,
directories & newsletters.
Chris Kelman, Contact, 866-985-9781, chris@kelman.ca

CTC Communications Corporation
#200, 2110 Matheson Blvd. East, Mississauga, ON L4W 5E1
Tel: 905-712-3636; *Fax:* 905-712-1679
Toll-Free: 800-561-7516
info@ctccomm.com
ctccomm.com
www.linkedin.com/company/ctc-communications-corporation
Medical communications company with a focus on branding
through education
Joseph Duz, President

DBC Communications Inc.
655, av Sainte-Anne, Saint-Hyacinthe, QC J2S 5G4
Tél: 450-773-6028; *Téléc:* 450-773-3115
admin@dbccomm.qc.ca
www.dbc.ca
Benoit Chartier, Président et directeur général

DEL Communications Inc.
6 Roslyn Rd., Winnipeg, MB R3L 0G5
Tel: 204-254-7170; *Toll-Free:* 866-424-6398
delcommunications.com
www.linkedin.com/company/del-communications-inc-
twitter.com/delcomminc
www.facebook.com/DELCommunications
Publishes magazines & offers sales & editorial services.

Department of National Defence (DND)
**National Defence Headquarters, 101 Colonel By Dr., Ottawa,
ON K1A 0K2**
information@forces.gc.ca
www.canada.ca/en/department-national-defence.html

DvL Publishing Inc.
PO Box 1509, Liverpool, NS B0T 1K0
Tel: 902-354-5411
dvlpublishing.office@gmail.com
www.rurallife.ca
Publisher of farm & country magazines: "Rural Delivery", "Horse
& Pony", "Atlantic Beef" & "Atlantic Forestry"

E.J. Lewchuck & Associates Ltd.
PO Box 3595, #6, 40 South Ave., Spruce Grove, AB T7X 3A8
Tel: 780-962-9228; *Fax:* 780-962-1021
www.com-voice.com

Les Éditions Apex inc. / Apex Publications Inc.
#102, 171, rue Saint-Paul, Québec, QC G1K 3W2
Fax: 800-664-2739
Toll-Free: 800-905-7468
info@photolife.com
www.photolife.com
www.facebook.com/photolifemag
Éditeur de périodiques: "Photo Life", et "Photo Solution"
Valérie Racine, Publisher & Director, Marketing,
vracine@photolife.com
Guy Langevin, Editor-in-Chief & Director, Art,
glangevin@photolife.com

Les Éditions du Journal de l'assurance
#100, 321, rue de la Commune ouest, Montréal, QC H2Y 2E1
Tél: 514-289-9595
service@portail-assurance.ca
portail-assurance.ca
twitter.com/journ_assurance
www.facebook.com/journalassurance
Publications: "FlashFinance.ca", "Le Journal de l'assurance",
"Répertoire des services en assurance des dommages" & "The
Insurance & Investment Journal". Conventions: "Le Congrès de

l'assurance et de l'investissement", "Canada Sales Conference" et "Journée de l'assurance de dommages".

Les Éditions forestières
#203, 1175, rue Lavigerie, Québec, QC G1V 4P1
Tél: 418-877-4583; *Téléc:* 418-877-6449
www.lemondeforestier.ca
www.facebook.com/LeMondeForestier
Le Monde Forestier est le journal mensuel québécois dédié à la foresterie
Roger Robitaille, Directeur des ventes,
roger@lemondeforestier.ca

EGS Press
#118, 283 Danforth Ave., Toronto, ON M4K 1N2
Tel: 416-829-8014
info@egspress.com
egspress.com

ISBNs: 0-9685330
Publisher of research material in the fields of media, the arts & therapy from the European Graduate School, Switzerland & the annual journal "Poiesis: A Journal of the Arts & Communication".
Steve Levine, Editor-in-Chief

EMC Publications
19073 - 63rd Ave., Surrey, BC V3S 8G7
Tel: 604-574-4577; *Fax:* 604-574-2196
Toll-Free: 800-667-0955
www.emcmarketing.com
Trade publisher serving the hospitality industry. Publications include The Publican, Liquor Retailer, InnFocus, Cannabis Retailer, ABLE BC Buyer's Guide & BCHA Buyers' Guide, as well as LiquorRetailer.com.
Joyce Hayne, Publisher, joyce@emcmarketing.com

EnsembleIQ
Previous Name: Stagnito Business Information & Edgell Communications
#1800, 20 Eglinton Ave. West, Toronto, ON M4R 1K8
Fax: 888-889-9522
Toll-Free: 877-687-7321
ensembleiq.com
www.linkedin.com/company/stagnito-media
Provides business resources for retailers, retail suppliers, & technology vendors, including a variety of trade publications.
Jennifer Litterick, Chief Executive Officer

FMA Communications Canada, Inc.
#416, 1154 Warden Ave., Toronto, ON M1R 0A1
Tel: 815-399-8700; *Toll-Free:* 888-394-4362
info@canadianmetalworking.com
www.canadianmetalworking.com

FMG Publishing Inc.
#300, 7071 Bayers Rd., Halifax, NS B3L 2C2
Tel: 647-479-2163
www.fmgpublishing.com
Other information: Advertising: accounts@fmgpublishing.com
www.linkedin.com/company/focus-media-group-pty-ltd

FP Newspapers Inc. (FPI)
PO Box 11583, #2900, 650 West Georgia St., Vancouver, BC V6B 4N8
www.fpnewspapers.com
Daniel Koshowski, Chief Financial Officer, 204-771-1897

Fulcrum Media Inc.
Previous Name: Fulcrum Publishing Inc.
#201, 508 Lawrence Ave. West, Toronto, ON M6A 1A1
Tel: 416-504-0504; *Fax:* 416-256-3002
Toll-Free: 866-688-0504
info@fulcrum.ca
fulcrum.ca
Other information: Vancouver, Email: info@eat-vancouver.com
New media company targeting the food & beverage industries, with print & digital publications, social media & live events.
Alan Fogel, Group Publisher, afogel@fulcrum.ca
Russell Hoffman, Genreal Manager, rhoffman@fulcrum.ca

Glacier FarmMedia LP
Previous Name: Farm Business Communications
Owned By: Glacier Media Inc.
PO Box 9800, 1666 Dublin Ave., Winnipeg, MB R3H 0H1
Tel: 204-954-1400; *Fax:* 204-945-4142
farmmedia.com
www.linkedin.com/company/farm-business-communications
twitter.com/glacie rfarmedia
Agriculture & livestock publications, digital media & consumer shows
Bob Willcox, President, 204-944-5751,
bwillcox@farmmedia.com

Glacier Media Inc.
2188 Yukon St., Vancouver, BC V5Y 3P1
Tel: 604-872-8565
info@glaciermedia.ca
www.glaciermedia.ca

Jonathon Kennedy, President & CEO

The Globe & Mail Inc.
Owned By: Woodbridge Company Limited
#1600, 351 King St. East, Toronto, ON M5A 0N1
Tel: 416-585-5000
newsroom@globeandmail.com
www.theglobeandmail.com
Phillip Crawley, Publisher & CEO
David Walmsley, Editor-in-Chief, dwalmsley@globeandmail.com

Globe Media Group
Owned By: The Globe & Mail Inc.
#1600, 351 King St. East, Toronto, ON M5A 0N1
Tel: 416-585-5600; *Fax:* 888-391-0122
Toll-Free: 866-999-9237
advertising@globeandmail.com
globelink.ca
www.linkedin.com/company/globemediagroup
twitter.com/globemediagroup
www.facebook.com/globemediagroup
Globe Media Group is the advertising arm of the Globe & Mail. It advertises through original magazines, newspapers, digital & mobile platforms.

Gravité Média
#215, 215, boul Jean-Leman, Candiac, QC J5R 6Z8
Ligne sans frais: 855-472-8483
info@gravitemedia.com
gravitemarketing.com
www.linkedin.com/company/gravitemarketing
www.facebook.com/gravitemedia
Julie Voyer, Fondatrice et Présidente-directrice générale

Great West Newspapers LP
Owned By: Glacier Media Inc. / Jamison Newspapers Inc.
340 Carleton Dr., St Albert, AB T8N 7L3
Tel: 780-460-5500; *Fax:* 780-460-8220
www.greatwest.ca
Great West Newspapers Limited Partnership is a Canadian community newspaper publishing company. Its three subsidiaries are Rocky View Publishing Ltd., Mountain View Publishing Inc. & Alberta Business Research Ltd.
Duff Jamison, Chief Executive Officer, 780-460-5519

Groupe Constructo
Détenteur: TC Media
#900, rue Saint-Denis, Montréal, QC H2S 3L5
Tél: 514-856-6600; *Téléc:* 514-257-8544
Ligne sans frais: 800-669-7326
www.constructo.ca
Directory for the construction industry

Groupe Contex Inc. / Contex Group Inc.
1000, boul René-Lévesque ouest, Montréal, QC H3B 4X9
Tél: 514-392-2009
www.linkedin.com/company/groupe-contex
Pierre Marcoux, Président, pierre.marcoux@tc.tc

Groupe Lexis Média Inc. / Lexis Media Group Inc.
#103, 7750, boul Cousineau, Saint-Hubert, QC J3Z 0C8
Tél: 514-394-7156; *Téléc:* 514-394-7157
Ligne sans frais: 888-767-7156
contact@lexismedia.ca
lexismedia.ca
www.linkedin.com/company/lexismedia
www.facebook.com/groupelexismedia

HAB Press Limited
Owned By: Key Media Canada
www.habpress.ca
Publishes information for HR, business & law industries.

HOMES Publishing Group (HPG)
#401, 610 Applewood Cres., Concord, ON L4K 0E3
Tel: 905-479-4663; *Toll-Free:* 800-363-4663
myhomepage.ca
www.linkedin.com/company/homes-publishing-group
twitter.com/homespublish ing
www.facebook.com/homespublishing
Homes Publishing Group publishes titles such as "Reno & Decor", "Renovation Contractor", Ontario Design", "Condo Life" & "HOMES Magazine".
Michael Rosset, President & Publisher,
mrosset@homesmag.com

Horse Publications Group
Previous Name: Corinthian Publishing Co. Ltd.
PO Box 670, Aurora, ON L4G 4J9
Tel: 905-727-0107; *Toll-Free:* 800-505-7428
www.horse-canada.com
www.instagram.com/horsecanadamagazine
twitter.com/HorseCanada
www.face book.com/HorseCanada
Publications include Horse Sport, Horse Canada, & Canadian Thoroughbred.

House & Home Media
354 Davenport Rd., #G1, Toronto, ON M5R 1K6
Tel: 416-593-0204; *Fax:* 416-591-1630
Toll-Free: 800-559-8868
letters@hhmedia.com
houseandhome.com
www.instagram.com/houseandhomemag
twitter.com/HouseandHome
www.facebook.com/houseandhomemagazine
Design & lifestyle brand; publisher of House & Home magazine
Lynda Reeves, President & Publisher

In Médias
QC
ev.inmedias.ca
Corrado Paina, Editorial Director, paina@italchambers.ca

Infopresse
4316, boul St-Laurent, Montréal, QC H2W 1Z3
Tél: 514-842-5873
redaction@infopresse.com
www.infopresse.com
www.linkedin.com/company/infopresse
twitter.com/Infopresse
www.facebook.com/Infopresse
Le mensuell du marketing, de la publicité et des communications
Arnaud Granata, Président

Institute of Intergovernmental Relations
Robert Sutherland Hall, School of Policy Studies, Queen's University, #412, 138 Union St., Kingston, ON K7L 3N6
Tel: 613-533-2080
iigr@queensu.ca
www.queensu.ca/iigr
twitter.com/iigr_queensu
www.facebook.com/IIGR.QU

ISBNs: 0-88911, 1-55339
Specializing in research & publication, with emphasis on Canadian federalism, intergovernmental relations, constitutional reform & social union
Christian Leuprecht, Director, leuprech@queensu.ca

Investment Executive
Owned By: Newcom Media Inc.
#400, 5353 Dundas St. West, Toronto, ON M9B 6H8
Tel: 416-847-8038
editorial_investmentexecutive@newcom.ca
www.investmentexecutive.com
www.linkedin.com/company/investment-executive
twitter.com/IE_Canada

Issues Ink
#403, 313 Pacific Ave., Winnipeg, MB R3A 0M2
Tel: 204-453-1965; *Fax:* 204-475-5247
Toll-Free: 877-710-3222
issues@issuesink.com
www.issuesink.com
www.linkedin.com/company/issues-ink
twitter.com/issuesink
www.facebook .com/issuesink
Publishing & consulting company. Magazines include "Seed World", "Germination", "Spud Smart", "European Seed" & "Alberta Seed Guide".
Shawn Brook, President, sbrook@issuesink.com
Michelle Clark, Managing Editor, sbrook@issuesink.com

Jamison Newspapers Inc.
340 Carleton Dr., St Albert, AB T8N 7L3
Duff Jamison, President

Journal l'Édition des gens d'affaires
Anciennement: Journal la Nouvelle Édition
Montréal, QC
Tél: 514-257-1000; *Téléc:* 514-257-7505
www.journaledition.com
Actualités économiques
Alain Dulong, Président/Éditeur, a.dulong@journaledition.com

Kenilworth Media Inc.
#710, 15 Wertheim Ct., Richmond Hill, ON L4B 3H7
Tel: 905-771-7333; Fax: 905-771-7336
Toll-Free: 800-409-8688
kenilworth.com
www.linkedin.com/company/kenilworth-media-inc
Magazines include "Sign Media" & "Construction Canada".
Ellen Kral, Chief Executive Officer

Kerrwil Publications Ltd.
538 Elizabeth St., Midland, ON L4R 2A3
Tel: 705-527-7666
www.kerrwil.com
www.linkedin.com/company/kerrwil-publications-limited
Publisher of Canadian Yachting; Boating Industry Canada;
Electrical Industry Canada; Canadian Electrical Wholesaler;
Lighting Design & Specification
John W. Kerr, President, 705-527-7677, johnkerr@kerrwil.com

Key Media Canada
Owned By: Key Media Pty Ltd.
20 Duncan St., 3rd Fl., Toronto, ON M5H 3G8
Tel: 416-644-8740
www.keymedia.com
www.linkedin.com/company/key-media
www.facebook.com/keymediainternational
Specializes in business-to-business & consumer publications.
Mike Shipley, Chief Executive Officer

KO Média Inc.
#100, 651, rue Notre-Dame ouest, Montréal, QC H3C 1H9
Tel: 514-933-2462
info@ko-media.ca
www.ko-media.ca
Louis Morissette, Président
Sophie Banford, Directrice générale et éditrice

Kostuch Media Ltd. (KML)
Previous Name: Kostuch Publications Ltd.
#404, 23 Lesmill Rd., Toronto, ON M3B 3P6
Tel: 416-447-0888
www.kostuchmedia.com
www.linkedin.com/company/kostuch-media-ltd-
Publisher serving the foodservice & hospitality markets in
Canada such as "Foodservice & Hospitality" & "Hotelier".
Rosanna Caira, Editor & Publisher, rcaira@foodservice.ca

Kylix Media Inc
#500, 5165, rue Sherbrooke ouest, Montréal, QC H4A 1T6
Tél: 514-481-5892; Téléc: 514-481-9699

LexisNexis Canada Ltd.
#900, 111 Gordon Baker Rd., Toronto, ON M2H 3R1
Tel: 905-479-2665; Toll-Free: 800-668-6481
customerservice@lexisnexis.ca
www.lexisnexis.ca
www.linkedin.com/company/lexisnexis-canada-inc-
twitter.com/lexisnexi scan
www.facebook.com/lexisnexiscanada
Eric Wright, Chief Executive Officer
Paula Sloss, Account Executive, paula.sloss@lexisnexis.ca

Lighthouse Publishing Limited
Owned By: Advocate Media Inc.
353 York St., Bridgewater, NS B4V 3K2
Tel: 902-543-2457; Fax: 902-543-2228
hello@lighthousenow.ca
lighthousenow.ca
www.linkedin.com/company/lighthousenow
twitter.com/lhnownews
www.faceb ook.com/lighthousenow
Charles Mandel, Editor, charles.mandel@lighthousenow.ca

Lloydmedia, Inc.
137 Main St. North, 3rd Fl., Markham, ON L3P 1Y2
Tel: 905-201-6600; Fax: 905-201-6601
Toll-Free: 800-668-1838
dmn.ca
Media company with an audience of more than 100,000 readers;
publishes four magazines & three industry directories.
Steve Lloyd, President, 905-201-6600 x225, steve@dmn.ca

Mackenzie Report Inc.
10006 - 97th St., High Level, AB T0H 1Z0
Tel: 780-926-2000; Fax: 780-926-2001
publisher@mrnews.ca
www.mrnews.ca

Martin Charlton Communications
Previous Name: Charlton Communications
#300, 1914 Hamilton St., Regina, SK S4N 3N6
Tel: 306-584-1000; Fax: 306-352-4110
hello@martincharlton.ca
www.martincharlton.ca
www.linkedin.com/company/martin-charlton-communications
twitter.com/m artincharlton_
www.facebook.com/martincharltonca
Public relations consultant with services including writing,
graphic design, media training & communications planning,
among others.
Mary-Lynn Charlton, President & CEO,
marylynn@martincharlton.ca

Media Classified Corporation
#401, 610 Applewood Cres., Toronto, ON L4K 0E3
Tel: 905-761-3313; Fax: 905-761-5038
Toll-Free: 888-761-3313
mediaclassified.ca
twitter.com/mediaclassified
www.facebook.com/MediaClassified
Offers 11 website & 80 publications nationwide.
Leo Racioppo, Publisher & CEO

MediaEdge Communications Inc.
#500, 2001 Sheppard Ave. East, Toronto, ON M2J 4Z8
Tel: 416-512-8186; Fax: 416-512-8344
info@mediaedge.ca
www.mediaedge.ca
www.linkedin.com/company/mediaedge-communications
twitter.com/MediaEdgeT OR
www.facebook.com/mediaedginc
Publications including Services Magazine, Canadian Apartment
Magazine, CondoBusiness, Construction Business & Design
Quarterly.
Kevin Brown, President

Mercury Publications Ltd.
#16, 1313 Border St., Winnipeg, MB R3H 0X4
Tel: 204-954-2085; Fax: 204-954-2057
Toll-Free: 800-337-6372
mp@mercury.mb.ca
www.mercury.mb.ca
Specializes in business-to-business communications.
Frank Yeo, President & CEO, fyeo@mercury.mb.ca

Metro Guide Publishing
Owned By: Advocate Media Inc.
2882 Gottingen St., Halifax, NS B3K 3E2
Tel: 902-420-9943
publishers@metroguide.ca
metroguide.ca
Magazines include "East Coast Living", "Halifax Magazine", "Our
Children", "Positive Aging", "Alumni Anchor".
Crystal Murray, President, crystalmurray@advocateprinting.com
Fred Fiander, Publisher & Director, Media Operations,
fredfiander@advocateprinting.com

Métro Média
#320, 101, boul Marcel-Laurin, Montréal, QC H4N 2M3
Tél: 514-286-1066
ventes_montreal@metromedia.ca
metromedia.ca
Autre information: Bureau de Québec, courriel:
ventes_quebec@metromedia.ca
www.linkedin.com/company/metro-media-canada
Nachmi Artzy, Publisher

Metroland Media Group Ltd.
Owned By: Torstar Corporation
#6, 3715 Laird Rd., Mississauga, ON L5L 0A3
Toll-Free: 866-838-8960
customerservice@metroland.com
metroland.com
www.linkedin.com/company/metroland
Metroland Media Group is a media, publishing & distribution
company that publishes daily & weekly local newspapers across
Ontario, as well as prints commercial flyers & magazines.
Ian Oliver, Executive Vice-President & President, Torstar,
Community Brands

Moorshead Magazines Ltd.
33 Angus Dr., Ajax, ON L1S 5C4
Toll-Free: 888-326-2476
www.moorshead.com
Publications include "Your Genealogy", "Internet Genealogy",
"History Magazine".
Edward Zapletal, Publisher & Editor, edward@moorshead.com

MPM Group of Brands Inc.
PO Box 57096, Vancouver, BC V5K 5G6
Toll-Free: 888-924-7524
contact@mypassionmedia.com
www.mypassionmedia.com

The Neepawa Press
423 Mountain Ave., Neepawa, MB R0J 1H0
Tel: 204-476-3401; Fax: 204-476-5073
www.mywestman.ca
Publications such as the mywestman.ca, Neepawa Banner &
Press & Rivers Banner
Ken Waddell, Publisher & Owner
Christine Waddell, Publisher & Owner

Néomédia
9085, boul Lacroix, Saint-Georges, QC G5Y 2B4
Tél: 418-222-5515; Téléc: 418-222-5699
Ligne sans frais: 866-327-0660
www.neomedia.com
Néomédia publishes 17 100% Web-based daily newspapers in
Québec.

Nesbitt Publishing Ltd.
PO Box 160, Shoal Lake, MB R0J 1Z0
Tel: 204-759-2644; Fax: 204-759-2521
www.crossroadsthisweek.com
Greg Nesbitt, Manager, gnesbitt@mb.sympatico.ca

Newcom Media Inc.
#400, 5353 Dundas St. West, Toronto, ON M9B 6H8
Tel: 416-614-2200; Fax: 416-614-8861
www.newcom.ca
www.linkedin.com/company/newcom-media
Specializes in business magazines, directories & databases. In
2019, Newcom acquired a number of TC Transcontinental
publications.
Mike Fredericks, CEO

News Canada Inc.
Head Office
#509, 920 Yonge St., Toronto, ON M4W 3C7
Tel: 416-599-9900; Toll-Free: 888-855-6397
content@newscanada.com
www.newscanada.com
Provides copyright-free Canadian lifestyle content for people or
organizations in search of print & digital content.

Norris-Whitney Communications Inc. (NWC)
#202, 4056 Dorchester Rd., Niagara Falls, ON L2E 6M9
Tel: 905-374-8878; Fax: 888-665-1307
info@nwcworld.com
nwcworld.com
www.linkedin.com/company/nwcworld
www.facebook.com/NWCWorld
Publishes "Canadian Musician", "Professional Sound",
"Professional Lighting & Production" & "Canadian Music Trade"
magazines
Andrew King, Editor-in-Chief, aking@nwcworld.com

North Huron Publishing Inc.
404 Queen St., Blyth, ON N0M 1H0
Tel: 519-523-4792
info@northhuron.on.ca
www.huroncitizen.ca
Publications include The Citizen, The Rural Voice & Stops Along
the Way.
Deb Sholdice, Publisher, deb@northhuron.on.ca

North Island Publishing Ltd.
Previous Name: North Island Sound Ltd.
#8, 1606 Sedlescomb Dr., Mississauga, ON L4X 1M6
Tel: 905-625-7070; Fax: 905-625-4856
Toll-Free: 800-331-7408
www.northisland.ca
Serves commercial printing & magazine publishing industries;
has staff in editorial, design, online publishing, production,
circulation, sales & administration
Sandy Donald, President & Owner

North Superior Publishing Inc.
#2506, 2260 Sleeping Giant Pkwy., Thunder Bay, ON P7A
0E7
Tel: 807-623-2348; Fax: 807-623-7515
nspinc@tbaytel.net
www.northsuperiorpublishing.com
www.facebook.com/NorthSuperiorPublishing
Publishes "Golfing News" & "Snowmobile News".
Scott A. Sumner, Publisher & Editor

The Northern Miner Group
Owned By: Glacier Media Inc.
#320, 225 Duncan Mill Rd., Toronto, ON M3B 3K9
Tel: 416-510-6789; Fax: 416-510-5138
Toll-Free: 888-502-3456
northernminer2@northernminer.com
www.northernminer.com
Anthony Vaccaro, Group Publisher, 416-442-2098, avaccaro@northernminer.com
Trish Saywell, Editor-in-Chief, 416-510-6741, tsaywell@northernminer.com

Northern Star Publications Ltd.
Previous Name: Northern Star Communications Ltd.
900 - 6th Ave. SW, 5th Fl., Calgary, AB T2P 3K2
Tel: 403-263-6881; Fax: 403-263-6886
Toll-Free: 800-526-4177
reception@northernstar.ab.ca
www.northernstar.ab.ca
Three oilpatch magazines: "The Roughneck", "Energy Processing Canada" & "Propane Canada"
Scott Jeffrey, Publisher & Owner, scott@northernstar.ab.ca

Ontario Historical Society (OHS)
34 Parkview Ave., Toronto, ON M2N 3Y2
Tel: 416-226-9011; Fax: 416-226-2740
Toll-Free: 866-955-2755
ohs@historicalsociety.ca
ontariohistoricalsociety.ca
twitter.com/ontariohistory
www.facebook.com/ontariohistoricalsociety
Rob Leverty, Executive Director

OP Media Group Ltd.
#802, 1166 Alberni St., Vancouver, BC V6E 3Z3
Tel: 604-428-0259; Fax: 604-620-0425
www.opmediagroup.ca
Publishes magazines such as "Pacific Yachting" & "British Columbia Magazine".
Mark Yelic, Publisher & President, myelic@opmediagroup.ca

Orinha Média
36, ch de Salzbourg est, Wentworth, QC J8H 0G7
www.orinhamedia.com
Pierre Hamel, Éditeur, phamel@orinhamedia.com

OT Communications
101 - 6th Ave. SW, Calgary, AB T2P 3P4
Tel: 403-264-3270; Fax: 403-264-3276
Toll-Free: 800-465-0322
info@otcommunications.com
www.otcommunications.com
Publications include: "Canadian Funeral News", Network", "Frontline", "Courage", "The Communicator", "Business in Calgary", "Business in Edmonton", "Farming for Tomorrow"
Pat Ottman, Co-Publisher, pat@businessincalgary.com
Tim Ottman, Co-Publisher, tim@businessincalgary.com

Our Kids Media
Previous Name: Our Kids Publications Ltd.
4242 Rockwood Rd., Mississauga, ON L4W 1L8
info@ourkidsmedia.com
www.ourkidsmedia.com
www.linkedin.com/company/our-kids-media
twitter.com/ourkidsnet
www.facebook.com/ourkidsnet
Publisher of consumer magazines, online portals, social channels, videos & school directories.

Outdoor Group Media Ltd.
#802, 1166 Alberni St., Vancouver, BC V6E 3Z3
Tel: 604-428-0259
www.outdoorgroupmedia.com

Parkhurst Publishing
Previous Name: C.M.E. Publishing
400 rue McGill, Montréal, QC H2Y 2G1
Tel: 514-397-8833
www.doctorsreview.com
ISBNs: 0-9688648, 0-9698972, 0-9732870
Parkhurst is a medical publishing house providing a range of medical media journals & educational communications to physicians & patients

Pink Triangle Press
#1600, 2 Carlton St., Toronto, ON M5B 1J3
Fax: 416-925-6674
Toll-Free: 800-268-9872
pinktrianglepress@dailyxtra.com
pinktrianglepress.com
www.linkedin.com/company/pink-triangle-press
David Walberg, Executive Director

Playhouse Publications
Owned By: Suggitt Publishing Ltd.
10177 - 105th St. NW, Edmonton, AB T5J 1E2
Tel: 780-423-5834; Fax: 780-413-6185
info@playhousepublications.ca
playhousepublications.ca
Specializes in playbills for theatre & opera companies.

Post City Magazines Inc.
30 Lesmill Rd., Toronto, ON M3B 2T6
Tel: 416-250-7979
postcitymagazines.com
www.linkedin.com/company/post-city-magazines
twitter.com/postcity
Publishes 8 magazines for the Greater Toronto Area as well as operating trnto.com.
Lorne London, Publisher

Postmedia Network Canada Corp.
365 Bloor St. East, Toronto, ON M4W 3L4
Tel: 416-383-2300
www.postmedia.com
www.linkedin.com/company/postmedia-network-inc.
twitter.com/postmedianet
www.facebook.com/Postmedia

Postmedia Network Inc.
Owned By: Postmedia Network Canada Corp.
365 Bloor St. East, Toronto, ON M4W 3L4
Tel: 416-383-2300
www.postmedia.com
www.linkedin.com/company/postmedia-network-inc.
twitter.com/postmedianet
www.facebook.com/postmedia
Publishes English-language daily newspapers across Canada with over 150 brands in print, digital & mobile platforms.
Andrew MacLeod, Executive Chair & CEO
Mary Anne Lavallee, Executive Vice-President & COO

Power Corporation of Canada
#5000, 161 Bay St., Toronto, ON M5J 2S1
Tel: 416-607-2250
www.powercorporation.com
www.linkedin.com/company/power-corporation-of-canada
R. Jeffrey Orr, President & CEO

Powershift Communications Inc.
245 Fairview Mall Dr., 5th Fl., Toronto, ON M2J 4T1
Tel: 416-494-1066; Fax: 416-494-2536
www.powershift.ca
Publications that serve the group employee benefits plan management & group pension fund investment sectors.
Publications include "Benefits & Pensions Monitor".
D. Brian McKerchar, President & CEO, dbm@powershift.ca

Québecor Media Inc.
612, rue Saint-Jacques, Montréal, QC H3C 4M8
Tel: 514-380-1999
www.quebecor.com
www.linkedin.com/company/quebecor-media-inc
twitter.com/Quebecor
Pierre Karl Péladeau, President & CEO

Rogers Media Inc.
1 Mount Pleasant Rd., Toronto, ON M4Y 2Y5
Tel: 416-764-2000
www.rogerssportsandmedia.com
www.linkedin.com/company/rogers-media
Publications include "Canadian Business", "Chatelaine", "HELLO! Canada", "Today's Parent", "Macleans", "Walmart Live Better/Vivre mieux", "Véro", "L'actualité".
Jordan Banks, President

Roustan Media Ltd.
contact@roustan.media
roustan.media
W. Graeme Roustan, Chair, Owner & Publisher

St. Joseph Media
Owned By: St. Joseph Communications
15 Benton Rd., Toronto, ON M6M 3G2
Toll-Free: 833-632-0833
www.stjoseph.com/divisions/media
Ken Hunt, President & Publisher

Salon Communications Inc.
#202, 183 Bathurst St., Toronto, ON M5T 2R7
Tel: 416-869-3131
info@salonmagazine.ca
www.salonmagazine.ca
www.linkedin.com/company/salon-communications-inc-
Salon Communications Inc. publishes "Salon Magazine", salonmagazine.ca, beautynet.com, Elevate Magazine & elevatemagazine.com.

Laura Dunphy, Group Publisher, 416-869-3131 x110, laura@salonmagazine.ca

SaltWire Network
PO Box 610, 2717 Joseph Howe Dr., Halifax, NS B3L 4T9
Tel: 902-426-2811
hello@saltwire.com
www.saltwire.com
www.linkedin.com/company/saltwire-network
twitter.com/saltwirenetwork
www.facebook.com/saltwirenetwork
SaltWire network owns & publishes 32 daily & weekly newspapers in Atlantic Canada.
Mark Lever, President & CEO

Shoetrades Publications
Montréal, QC
Tel: 514-754-6401; Fax: 705-417-1997
books@shoetrades.com
www.shoetrades.com
Books & magazine for the leather / footwear industries

Sing Tao Media Group Canada
221 Whitehall Dr., Markham, ON L3R 9T1
Tel: 416-861-8168; Fax: 905-752-3888
info@singtao.ca
eng.singtao.ca
www.linkedin.com/company/sing-tao-canada
Publishes Sing Tao Daily, Singtao.ca & Sing Tao A1 Chinese Radio.

snapd Inc.
505 Queen St., Newmarket, ON L3Y 2H3
Tel: 905-953-7977; Toll-Free: 866-953-8509
info@snapd.com
snapd.com
www.linkedin.com/company/snap-newspaper-group-inc-
twitter.com/getsnapd
www.facebook.com/getsnapd
J. Paul Dutton, President & CEO

STA HealthCare Communications
#310, 6500 Trans-Canada Hwy., Pointe-Claire, QC H9R 0A5
Tel: 514-695-7623; Fax: 514-695-8554
www.stacommunications.com
Journals include "Diagnosis", "CME", "Canadian Pharmaceutical Marketing".
Paul Brand, Contact, paulb@sta.ca

Suggitt Publishing Ltd.
10177 - 105th St. NW, Edmonton, AB T5J 1E2
Tel: 780-413-6163; Fax: 780-413-6185
Toll-Free: 877-784-4488
reception@suggitt.com
www.suggitt.com
Consumer magazines on the arts, sports, & community services.
Tom Suggitt, President & CEO, tom@suggitt.com
Rob Suggitt, President & CFO, rob@suggitt.com

Sunrise Publishing
Previous Name: Saskatchewan Business Magazine
255 Robin Cres., Saskatoon, SK S7L 6M8
Tel: 306-244-5668; Fax: 306-244-5679
Toll-Free: 800-247-5743
sunrisepublish.com
Publishes information on Saskatchewan's businesses
Twila Reddekopp, Publisher

Taylor Publishing Group (TPG)
#44, 268 Crawford Cres., Campbellville, ON L0P 1B0
Tel: 905-844-8218
www.taylorpublishinggroup.com
William Taylor, Owner & Publisher

Torstar Corporation
1 Yonge St., Toronto, ON M5E 1E6
Tel: 416-869-4010; Fax: 416-869-4183
www.torstar.com
Torstar Corporation is a media & publishing company that publishes the Toronto Star, as well as community newspapers & daily newspapers
John Boynton, President, CEO & Publisher, Toronto Star
Lorenzo DeMarchi, Executive Vice-President & CFO

Trajan Publishing Corp.
#2, 459 Prince Charles Dr. South, Welland, ON L3B 5X1
Tel: 905-646-7744; Fax: 905-646-0995
Toll-Free: 800-408-0352
info@trajan.ca
trajan.com
Produces "Antique & Collectibles Showcase" & "Canadian Coin News & Canadian Stamp News".
Bret Evans, Managing Editor, bret@trajan.ca

Transcontinental Inc.
#3240, 1, Place Ville Marie, Montréal, QC H3B 0G1
Tel: 514-954-4000; *Fax:* 514-954-4016
communications@tc.tc
tctranscontinental.com
www.linkedin.com/company/tc-transcontinental
twitter.com/tctranscontinen
www.facebook.com/tc.transcontinental
François Olivier, President & CEO

Trium Médias
100, rue Saint-Joseph, Alma, QC G8B 7A6
Tel: 416-668-4545
ventes@trium.media
www.trium.media
www.facebook.com/TriumMedias

Turnkey Media Solutions Inc.
48 Lumsden Cres., Whitby, ON L1R 1G5
www.autoserviceworld.com
www.linkedin.com/company/turnkey-media-ca
Publisher of automotive magazines "CARS", "Jobber News" &
"L'automobile".
Allan Janssen, Editorial Director, Automotive Group,
416-614-5814, allan@carsmagazine.ca

TVA Publications inc.
Anciennement: Trustar Ltd
Détenteur: Québecor Média
QC
www.groupetva.ca/legroupe/publications
France Lauzière, Présidente et chef de la direction, Groupe TVA
Inc.

2M.Media
2700, av Francis-Hughes, Laval, QC H7L 3S8
Tél: 450-667-4360
2m.media
Martin Olivier, Président, molivier@2m.media

University of Calgary Press
2500 University Dr. NW, Calgary, AB T2N 1N4
Tel: 403-220-7578; *Fax:* 403-282-0085
ucpbooks@ucalgary.ca
www.press.ucalgary.ca
Brian Scrivener, Director

Up Here Publishing Ltd.
Previous Name: Outcrop, The Northern Publishers
#102, 4510 - 50th Ave., Yellowknife, NT X1A 1B9
Tel: 867-766-6710; *Fax:* 867-669-0626
editor@uphere.ca
www.uphere.ca
www.instagram.com/upheremag
twitter.com/upheremag
www.facebook.com/uph ere
Publisher of "Up Here" magazine, which features articles on
Canada's North.
Herb Mathisen, Editor, herb@uphere.ca

Vélo Québec Éditions
Maison des Cyclistes, 1251, rue Rachel est, Montréal, QC
H2J 2J9
Tél: 514-521-8356; *Téléc:* 514-521-5711
www.velo.qc.ca/fr/publication.php
twitter.com/VeloQuebec
www.facebook.com/VeloQuebec

York Region Media Group
Owned By: Metroland Media Group Ltd.
580B Steven Ct., Newmarket, ON L3Y 4X1
Tel: 905-773-7627
www.yorkregion.com
twitter.com/yorkregion
www.facebook.com/YorkRegionNews
Information provider in York Region's nine municipalities;
publications include community newspapers, mass flyers,
printing & specialty publications like directories & guides.
Dana Robbins, Vice-President & Regional Publisher,
dana.robbins@metroland.com
Joanne Burghardt, Regional Editor-in-Chief,
jburghardt@metroland.com

Newspapers

Alberta

Daily Newspapers in Alberta

Calgary: Calgary Herald
Owned By: Postmedia Network Inc.
215 - 16th St. SE, Calgary, AB T2E 7P5
Tel: 403-235-7323 *Toll-Free:* 800-372-9219
submit@calgaryherald.com
calgaryherald.com
twitter.com/calgaryherald
www.facebook.com/yycherald
Frequency: Monday-Saturday
Lorne Motley, Editor
403-235-7546

Calgary: Calgary Sun
Owned By: Postmedia Network Inc.
215 - 16th St. SE, Calgary, AB T2E 7P5
Tel: 403-235-7100 *Toll-Free:* 800-590-4419
calgaryadvertising@postmedia.com
calgarysun.com
twitter.com/calgarysun
www.facebook.com/thecalgarysun
Frequency: Daily
Calgary's daily newspaper
Lorne Motley, Editor-in-chief
lmotley@postmedia.com
Martin Hudson, Managing Editor
mhudson@postmedia.com

Calgary: Sing Tao Daily Calgary
Owned By: Sing Tao Media Group Canada
#954 - 55th Ave. NE, Calgary, AB T2E 6Y4
Tel: 403-263-1668; *Fax:* 403-233-8603
calprod@singtao.ca
www.singtao.ca/calgary
Frequency: Daily
Chinese daily newspaper.

Edmonton: The Edmonton Journal
Owned By: Postmedia Network Inc.
10006 - 101st St., Edmonton, AB T5J 0S1
Tel: 780-498-5500 *Toll-Free:* 800-249-4695
edmontonjournal.com
www.youtube.com/user/EdJournal
twitter.com/edmontonjournal
www.facebook.com/edmontonjournal
Frequency: Monday-Saturday
Mark Iype, Editor-in-Chief
Dave Breakenridge, Managing Editor

Edmonton: Edmonton Sun
Owned By: Postmedia Network Inc.
10006 - 101st St., Edmonton, AB T5J 0S1
Tel: 780-468-0100
edmontonsun.com
twitter.com/edmontonsun
www.facebook.com/edmontonsun
Frequency: Daily
Lorne Motley, Editor-in-Chief
Dave Breakenridge, Managing Editor
780-468-0107
dave.breakenridge@sunmedia.ca

Fort McMurray: Fort McMurray Today
Owned By: Postmedia Network Inc.
Fort McMurray, AB
today@fortmcmurraytoday.com
www.fortmcmurraytoday.com
twitter.com/Fortmactoday
www.facebook.com/FortMacToday
Frequency: Monday-Friday

Lethbridge: Lethbridge Herald
Owned By: Alta Newspaper Group LP
504 - 7th St. South, Lethbridge, AB T1J 2H1
Tel: 403-328-4411
editor@lethbridgeherald.com
lethbridgeherald.com
twitter.com/Leth_Herald
www.facebook.com/LethbridgeHerald
Frequency: Daily

Medicine Hat: The Medicine Hat News
Owned By: Alta Newspaper Group LP
3257 Dunmore Rd. SE, Medicine Hat, AB T1B 3R2
Tel: 403-527-1101; *Fax:* 403-528-5696
medicinehatnews.com
twitter.com/medicinehatnews
www.facebook.com/MedicineHatNews
Frequency: Monday-Saturday

Red Deer: Red Deer Advocate
Owned By: Black Press Group Ltd.
2950 Bremner Ave., Red Deer, AB T4R 1M9
Tel: 403-343-2400
editorial@reddeeradvocate.com
www.reddeeradvocate.com
twitter.com/RedDeerAdvocate
www.facebook.com/RDAdvocate
Frequency: Monday-Saturday
Central Alberta's news
Mary Kemmis, Publisher
403-314-4311
mary.kemmis@blackpress.ca
Mamta Lulla, Managing Editor
403-314-4332
mamta.lulla@reddeeradvocate.com

Other Newspapers in Alberta

Airdrie: Airdrie City View
Owned By: Great West Newspapers LP
#403, 2903 Kingview Blvd., Airdrie, AB T4A 0C4
Tel: 403-948-1885; *Fax:* 403-948-2554
sales@airdrie.greatwest.ca
www.airdriecityview.com
www.facebook.com/airdriecityviewnewspaper
Circulation: 17,000 *Frequency:* Thurs.
Cameron Christianson, Publisher
cchristianson@airdrie.greatwest.ca
Stacie Snow, Editor
ssnow@airdrie.greatwest.ca

Airdrie: Airdrie Echo
Owned By: Postmedia Network Inc.
112 - 1st Ave. NE, Airdrie, AB T4B 0R6
Tel: 403-948-7280; *Fax:* 403-912-2341
www.airdrieecho.com
twitter.com/Airdrie_Echo
www.facebook.com/AirdrieEcho
Circulation: 17,035 *Frequency:* Wednesday
Airdrie's weekly newspaper
Ed Huculak, Publisher
403-250-4240
ed.huculak@sunmedia.ca

Airdrie: Rocky View Weekly
Owned By: Great West Newspapers LP
#403, 2903 Kingsview Blvd., Airdrie, AB T4A 0C4
Tel: 403-948-1885; *Fax:* 403-948-2554
www.rockyviewweekly.com
twitter.com/RV_Publishing
www.facebook.com/rockyviewweekly
Circulation: 18,079 *Frequency:* Weekly; Tuesday
Shows local news around Airdrie & Rocky View, AB.

Athabasca: Athabasca Advocate
Owned By: Great West Newspapers LP
4917B - 49th St., Athabasca, AB T9S 1C5
Tel: 780-675-9222; *Fax:* 780-675-3143
advocate@athabasca.greatwest.ca
www.athabascaadvocate.com
twitter.com/athaadvocate
www.facebook.com/122608544476186
Circulation: 2,800 *Frequency:* Tues.
The newspaper serves the Alberta communities of Athabasca &
Boyle, & the surrounding area.
Ross Hunter, Publisher
rhunter@athabasca.greatwest.ca
Meghan McIvor, Manager, Production
production@athabasca.greatwest.ca

Barrhead: The Barrhead Leader
Previous Name: Barrhead News
Owned By: Great West Newspapers LP
PO Box 4520, 5015 - 51 St., Barrhead, AB T7N 1A4
Tel: 780-674-3823; *Fax:* 780-674-6337
www.barrheadleader.com
www.youtube.com/barrheadleader
twitter.com/barrheadleader
www.facebook .com/BarrheadLeader
Circulation: 3,737 *Frequency:* Weekly
Barrhead's weekly newspaper
Carol Farnalls, Publisher
farnalls@barrhead.greatwest.ca

Marcus Day, Editor
mday@barrhead.greatwest.ca
Amy Newton, Manager, Sales
sales@barrhead.greatwest.ca

Beaumont: La Nouvelle Beaumont News
Owned By: Postmedia Network Inc.
4908 - 50th Ave., Beaumont, AB T4X 1J9
Tel: 780-929-6632; *Fax:* 780-929-6634
www.thebeaumontnews.ca
twitter.com/BeaumontNews
www.facebook.com/LaNouvelleBeaumontNews
Circulation: 6,305 *Frequency:* Friday
Beaumont's weekly news
Bobby Roy, Regional Managing Editor
leducrep.editor@sunmedia.ca

Blairmore: Crowsnest Pass Herald
Owned By: The Pass Herald Ltd.
PO Box 960, 12925 - 20th Ave., Blairmore, AB T0K 0E0
Tel: 403-562-2248; *Fax:* 403-562-8379
news@passherald.ca
www.passherald.ca
www.facebook.com/398857086794980
Circulation: 1,966 *Frequency:* Tuesday
Blairmore's weekly newspaper
Lisa Sygutek, Publisher
Trevor Slapak, Editor

Bonnyville: Bonnyville Nouvelle
Owned By: Great West Newspapers LP
5304 - 50th Ave., Bonnyville, AB T9N 1Y4
Tel: 780-826-3876; *Fax:* 780-826-7062
nouvelle@bonnyville.greatwest.ca
www.bonnyvillenouvelle.ca
Other information: Advertising, Email:
advertising@bonnyville.greatwest.ca
twitter.com/BvilleNouvelle
www.facebook.com/294955134326
Circulation: 2,808 *Frequency:* Tuesday
The Bonnyville Nouvelle serves communities in northeastern Alberta, including Bonnyville, Cold Lake, Ardmore, La Corey, Fort Kent, Glendon, & Iron River.
Clare Gauvreau, Publisher
Melissa Barr, Editor & Reporter
Nora Chachula, Manager, Production
Brandon MacLeod, Sports Reporter
Amber Cook, Sales Associate
Breanna Ernst, Sales Associate

Bow Island: The 40-Mile County Commentator
Previous Name: County Commentator & Cypress Courier
Owned By: Alta Newspaper Group
PO Box 580, 147 - 5th Ave., Bow Island, AB T0K 0G0
Tel: 403-545-2258; *Fax:* 403-545-6886
www.bowislandcommentator.com
Circulation: 5,700 *Frequency:* Tues.
Coleen Campbell, Publisher
403-545-2258
ccampbell@tabertimes.com
Jamie Rieger, Editor
editor@bowislandcommentator.com

Brooks: Brooks & County Chronicle
PO Box 1568 Main, 619 - 1st St. West, Brooks, AB T1R 1C4
Tel: 403-793-2252; *Fax:* 403-793-2288
thechronicle@telusplanet.net
www.brooksinthenews.com
Circulation: 11,300 *Frequency:* Sun.
The newspaper serves Brooks, Alberta & the surrounding communities.
M. Joan Brees, Publisher & Editor

Brooks: The Brooks Bulletin
Owned By: Nesbitt Publishing Ltd.
PO Box 1450, Brooks, AB T1R 1C3
Tel: 403-362-5571; *Fax:* 403-362-5080
editor@brooksbulletin.com
www.brooksbulletin.com
Frequency: Weekly
Part of the Alberta Weekly Newspaper's Association

Camrose: The Camrose Booster
4925 - 48 St., Camrose, AB T4V 1L7
Tel: 780-672-3142; *Fax:* 780-672-2518
ads@camrosebooster.com
www.camrosebooster.com
Circulation: 12,729 *Frequency:* Weekly; Tuesday
Daily newspaper in Camrose, Alberta
Blain Fowler, Publisher
Ron Pilger, Sales Manager

Canmore: Rocky Mountain Outlook
Owned By: Great West Newspapers LP
PO Box 8610, #201, 1001 - 6th Ave., Canmore, AB T1W 2V3
Tel: 403-609-0220
www.rmoutlook.com
twitter.com/rmoutlook
www.facebook.com/113146002044547
Circulation: 9,400 *Frequency:* Thurs.
The newspaper serves the communities of Banff, Lake Louise, Canmore, & Kananaskis.
Jason Lyon, Publisher
jlyon@outlook.greatwest.ca
Dave Whitfield, Editor
dwhitfield@outlook.greatwest.ca
Craig Douce, Photojournalist
cdouce@outlook.greatwest.ca
Erin Buehler, Contact, Sales
swhite@outlook.greatwest.ca

Cardston: Temple City Star
PO Box 2060, 311 Main St., Cardston, AB T0K 0K0
Tel: 403-653-4664; *Fax:* 403-653-3162
info@templecitystar.net
www.templecitystar.net
Circulation: 803 *Frequency:* Weekly; Thursday
Cardston & Area newspaper
Robert T. Smith, Owner & Publisher

Carstairs: Carstairs Courier
Owned By: Great West Newspapers LP
PO Box 114, 320 - 10th St. South, Carstairs, AB T0M 0N0
Tel: 403-337-2806; *Fax:* 403-337-3160
www.carstairscourier.ca
Circulation: 3,257 *Frequency:* Weekly; Tuesday

Claresholm: Claresholm Local Press
PO Box 520, Claresholm, AB T0L 0T0
Tel: 403-625-4474; *Fax:* 403-625-2828
info@claresholmlocalpress.ca
www.claresholmlocalpress.ca
www.facebook.com/ClaresholmLocalPress
Circulation: 1,610 *Frequency:* Weekly; Wednesday
The newspaper serves the Alberta communities of Claresholm, Stavely, & Granum.
Roxanne Thompson, Owner & Publisher

Coaldale: Sunny South News
Owned By: Alta Newspaper Group LP
1802 - 20th Ave., Coaldale, AB T1M 1M2
Tel: 403-732-4045
office@sunnysouthnews.com
www.sunnysouthnews.com
twitter.com/SunnySouthNews
Circulation: 3,713 *Frequency:* Weekly; Tuesday
Serves the towns of Coaldale and Picture Butte as well as the villages and hamlets within the County of Lethbridge.
Coleen Campbell, Publisher
403-223-9659
ccampbell@abnewsgroup.com

Cochrane: Cochrane Eagle
Owned By: Great West Newspapers LP
126A River Ave., Cochrane, AB T4C 2C2
Tel: 403-932-6588; *Fax:* 403-851-6520
letters@cochrane.greatwest.ca
www.cochraneeagle.com
Other information: Advertising, Email:
advertising@cochrane.greatwest.ca
twitter.com/CochraneEagle
www.facebook.com/175941871603
Circulation: 10,600 *Frequency:* Thurs.
Brenda Tennant, Publisher
btennant@cochrane.greatwest.ca
Derek Clouthier, Editor
dclouthier@cochrane.greatwest.ca
Lindsay Seewalt, Reporter
lseewalt@cochrane.greatwest.ca
Brendan Nagle, Reporter, Sports
sports@cochrane.greatwest.ca
Carrie Anderson, Contact, Administration & Circulation
classifieds@cochrane.greatwest.ca
Jodi Collins, Contact, Accounting
accounting@cochrane.greatwest.ca

Cochrane: The Cochrane Times
Bay 8, 206 - 5th Ave. West, Cochrane, AB T4C 1X3
Tel: 403-932-3500; *Fax:* 403-932-3935
www.cochranetimes.com
twitter.com/CochraneTimes
Frequency: Wednesday
The Cochrane Times is a member of Canoe Sun Media Community Newspapers.

Shawn Cornell, Publisher
403-932-3500 ext.245
shawn.cornell@sunmedia.ca
Noel Edey, City Editor
403-932-3500 ext.227
noel.edey@sunmedia.ca

Cold Lake: Cold Lake Sun
Owned By: Postmedia Network Inc.
PO Box 268, Cold Lake, AB T9M 1P1
Tel: 780-594-5881; *Fax:* 780-594-2120
www.coldlakesun.com
twitter.com/ColdLakeSun
www.facebook.com/ColdLakeSun
Circulation: 6,458 *Frequency:* Weekly; Tuesday
The Cold Lake Sun is a member of Canoe Sun Media Community Newspapers. A PDF version of the newspaper is produced each week.
Peter Lozinski, Editor
peter.lozinski@sunmedia.ca

Cold Lake: The Courier
Owned By: Department of National Defence
Centennial Bldg. #67, PO Box 6190 Forces, Cold Lake, AB T9M 2C5
Tel: 780-594-5206; *Fax:* 780-594-2139
thecourier@telus.net
www.thecouriernewspaper.ca
Circulation: 2,126 *Frequency:* Weekly; Tuesday
The Courier serves the military community of Cold Lake, Alberta.
Connie Lavigne, Manager
780-840-8000; Fax: 780-594-2139
Connie.Lavigne@forces.gc.ca
Jeff Gaye, Editor & Reporter
780-594-5206; Fax: 780-594-2139
thecourier@telus.net

Consort: Consort Enterprise
PO Box 129, Consort, AB T0C 1B0
Tel: 403-577-3337; *Fax:* 403-577-3611
www.consortenterprise.com
Circulation: 1,080 *Frequency:* Weekly; Wednesday
The Consort Enterprise serves the Alberta communities of Consort, Monitor, Altario, Veteran, Kirriemuir, & Compeer.
Carol Bruha, Co-publisher
Dave Bruha, Co-publisher

Coronation: East Central Alberta Review
Owned By: Coronation Review Limited
PO Box 70, 4923 Victoria Ave., Coronation, AB T0C 1C0
Tel: 403-578-4111; *Fax:* 403-578-2088
www.ecareview.com
twitter.com/ECA_review
www.facebook.com/EcaReview
Circulation: 26,826 *Frequency:* Weekly; Thursday
ECA Review provides a source of for news and entertainment in Central Alberta.
Joyce Webster, Publisher & Editor
publisher@ecareview.com

Didsbury: Didsbury Review
Owned By: Great West Newspapers LP
PO Box 760, 2017 - 19th Ave., Didsbury, AB T0M 0W0
Tel: 403-335-3301; *Fax:* 403-335-8143
www.didsburyreview.ca
twitter.com/didsburyreview
Circulation: 3,101 *Frequency:* Weekly; Tuesday
Part of Mountain View Publishing Inc.

Drayton Valley: Drayton Valley Western Review
Owned By: Postmedia Network Inc.
PO Box 6960, 4905 - 52nd Ave., Drayton Valley, AB T7A 1S3
Tel: 780-542-5380; *Fax:* 780-542-9200
www.draytonvalleywesternreview.com
twitter.com/Western_Review
The Drayton Valley Western Review is a member of Canoe Sun Media Community Newspapers. A digital edition of the newspaper is also produced each week.
Courtney Whalen, City Editor
courtney.whalen@sunmedia.ca

Drumheller: Drumheller Mail
Previous Name: The Munson Mail
PO Box 1629, 515 Hwy. 10 East, Drumheller, AB T0J 0Y0
Tel: 403-823-2580; *Fax:* 403-823-3864
www.drumhellermail.com
twitter.com/DrumhellerMail
www.facebook.com/drumhellermail
Circulation: 4,104 *Frequency:* Weekly; Wednesday
Online & print editions of weekly news in Drumheller
Ossie Sheddy, Publisher
Bob Sheddy, Managing Editor

Edmonton: The Edmonton Examiner
Previous Name: West Edmonton Examiner
Owned By: Postmedia Network Inc.
#350, 4990 - 92nd Ave., Edmonton, AB T6B 3A1
Tel: 780-468-0100; Fax: 780-451-4574
www.edmontonexaminer.com
twitter.com/edm_examiner
www.facebook.com/edmontonexaminer
Circulation: 125,824 *Frequency:* Weekly; Monday
The Edmonton Examiner is a member of Canoe Sun Media
Community Newspapers. Each week, seven versions of the
newspaper are published for seven city zones. The newspaper
employs over 90 people.
Dave Breakenridge, Editor-in-Chief
dave.breakenridge@sunmedia.ca

Edmonton: Le Franco
#312, 8627 - rue 91, Edmonton, AB T6C 3N1
Tél: 780-465-6581; Téléc: 780-469-1129
journal@lefranco.ab.ca
twitter.com/JournalLeFranco
www.facebook.com/225495297491230
Tirage: 3 508 *Fréquence:* Weekly; Thursday
Le Franco est un journal indépendant sur les plans administratif
et rédactionnel.
Étienne Alary, Director
direction@lefranco.ab.ca
Lysane Sénécal Mastropaolo, Journaliste
redaction@lefranco.ab.ca

Edson: The Edson Leader
Owned By: Postmedia Network Inc.
4820 - 3rd Ave., Edson, AB T7E 1T8
Tel: 780-723-3301; Fax: 780-723-5171
leadernews@telusplanet.net
www.edsonleader.com
twitter.com/Edson_Leader
www.facebook.com/edsonleader
Circulation: 5,831 *Frequency:* Weekly; Wednesday
The Edson Leader is a member of Canoe Sun Media
Community Newspapers. A PDF version of the newspaper is
produced each week.
Ian Mcinnes, Editor
ian.mcinnes@sunmedia.ca

Edson: The Weekly Anchor
PO Box 6870, 5040 - 3rd Ave., Edson, AB T7E 1V2
Tel: 780-723-5787; Fax: 780-723-5725
anchorwk@telusplanet.net
www.weeklyanchor.com
www.facebook.com/weeklyanchor
Circulation: 5,796 *Frequency:* Weekly; Monday
The independent newspaper serves the Alberta communities of
Edson, Robb, Evansburg, Marlboro, Entwistle, Nojack,
Wildwood, Carrot Creek, Peers, & Niton Junction.

Fairview: Fairview Post
Owned By: Postmedia Network Inc.
PO Box 1900, 10915 - 102 Ave., Fairview, AB T0H 1L0
Tel: 780-835-4925; Fax: 780-835-4227
www.fairviewpost.com
twitter.com/fairviewpost
www.facebook.com/fairviewpost
Circulation: 1,672 *Frequency:* Weekly; Wednesday
The Fairview Post is a member of Canoe Sun Media Community
Newspapers. A digital edition of the newspaper is available each
week.
Chris Eakin, Editor
chris.eakin@sunmedia.ca

Falher: Smoky River Express
Owned By: South Peace News Ltd.
PO Box 644, Falher, AB T0H 1M0
Tel: 780-837-2585; Fax: 780-837-2102
www.smokyriverexpress.com
www.facebook.com/SmokyRiverExpress
Circulation: 2,063 *Frequency:* Weekly; Wednesday
The newspaper serves the Municipal District of Smoky River.
Mary Burgar, Publisher
spn@cablecomet.com

Fort Macleod: The Macleod Gazette
PO Box 720, 310 Col. Macleod Blvd., Fort Macleod, AB T0L
0Z0
Tel: 403-553-3391; Fax: 403-553-2961
ftmgazet@telusplanet.net
www.fortmacleodgazette.com
Circulation: 1,192 *Frequency:* Weekly; Wednesday
Independent newspaper published weekly
Frank McTighe, Publisher & Editor
Emily McTighe, Manager

Fort Saskatchewan: Fort Saskatchewan Record
Owned By: Postmedia Network Inc.
#168A, 10404 - 99th Ave., Fort Saskatchewan, AB T8L 3W2
Tel: 780-998-7070; Fax: 780-998-5515
www.fortsaskatchewanrecord.com
twitter.com/Fort_Record
www.facebook.com/FortSaskatchewanRecord
Circulation: 8,750 *Frequency:* Weekly; Thursday
Fort Saskatchewan's weekly newspaper
Ben Proulx, Editor
ben.proulx@sunmedia.ca

Grande Prairie: Peace Country Sun
Owned By: Postmedia Network Inc.
PO Box 3000, 10604 - 100th St., Grande Prairie, AB T8V 6V4
Tel: 780-532-1110; Fax: 780-532-2120
www.peacecountrysun.com
twitter.com/peacecountrysun
www.facebook.com/PeaceCountrySun
Circulation: 18,668 *Frequency:* Weekly; Friday
The Peace Country Sun is a member of Canoe Sun Media
Community Newspapers.
Fred Rinne, Regional Managing Editor
fred.rinne@sunmedia.ca

Grimshaw: The Mile Zero News
Owned By: Mackenzie Report Inc.
4921 - 54th Ave., Grimshaw, AB T0H 1W0
Tel: 780-332-2215
www.mrnews.ca/mile-zero-news
Circulation: 1,672 *Frequency:* Weekly; Wednesday
Tom Mihaly, Publisher

Hanna: Hanna Herald
Owned By: Postmedia Network Inc.
PO Box 790, 113 - 1st Ave., Hanna, AB T0J 1P0
Tel: 403-854-3366; Fax: 403-854-3256
www.hannaherald.com
twitter.com/HannaHerald
www.facebook.com/134487243289016
Circulation: 900 *Frequency:* Weekly; Wednesday
The Hanna Herald is a member of Canoe Sun Media Community
Newspapers. A PDF version of the newspaper is produced each
week.

High Level: The Echo-Pioneer
Owned By: Mackenzie Report Inc.
10006 - 97th St., High Level, AB T0H 1Z0
Tel: 780-926-2000
www.mrnews.ca/the-echo-mrnews-pioneer
Circulation: 2,000 *Frequency:* Weekly; Wednesday

High Prairie: South Peace News
Owned By: South Peace News Ltd.
PO Box 1000, High Prairie, AB T0G 1E0
Tel: 780-523-4484; Fax: 780-523-3039
www.southpeacenews.com
twitter.com/SouthPeaceNews
Circulation: 1,358 *Frequency:* Weekly; Wednesday
Mary Burgar, Publisher
spn@cablecomet.com

High River: High River Times
Owned By: Postmedia Network Inc.
618 Centre St. South, High River, AB T1V 1E9
Tel: 403-652-2034; Fax: 403-652-3962
www.highrivertimes.com
twitter.com/highrivertimes
www.facebook.com/highrivertimes
Circulation: 13,231 *Frequency:* Weekly
The High River Times is a member of Canoe Sun Media
Community Newspapers, which is part of Postmedia Network.
The newspaper serves the Alberta communities of High River,
Cayley, Blackie, & Longview.

Hinton: The Hinton Parklander
Owned By: Postmedia Network Inc.
387 Drinnan Way, Hinton, AB T7V 2A3
Tel: 780-865-3115; Fax: 780-865-1252
news@hintonparklander.com
www.hintonparklander.com
twitter.com/H_Parklander
Circulation: 4,078 *Frequency:* Weekly; Monday
The Hinton Parklander is a member of Canoe Sun Media
Community Newspapers. The newspaper serves the town of
Hinton in Alberta & its surrounding area.
Gord Fortin, Editor
780-723-3301
gord.fortin@sunmedia.ca

Innisfail: Innisfail Province
Owned By: Great West Newspapers LP
5036 - 48th St., Innisfail, AB T4G 1M8
Tel: 403-227-3477; Fax: 403-227-3330
www.innisfailprovince.ca
twitter.com/innisfailprovin
www.facebook.com/621035251342433
Circulation: 8,306 *Frequency:* Tuesday
Ray Brinson, Publisher
Lea Smaldon, Managing Editor
Johnnie Bachusky, Editor

La Crete: The Northern Pioneer
Owned By: Mackenzie Report Inc.
PO Box 571, 10303 - 100 St., La Crete, AB T0H 2H0
Tel: 780-928-4000; Fax: 780-928-4001
pioneer@mackreport.ab.ca
mrnews.ca/the-northern-pioneer-mrnews
Circulation: 900 *Frequency:* Wed.
The Northern Pioneer serves the Alberta communities of La
Crete & Fort Vermilion.
Tom Mihaly, Publisher & Editor
publisher@mrnews.ca
Lisa Neufeld, Contact, Office, Advertising
northernpioneer@mrnews.ca

Lac La Biche: The Lac La Biche Post
Owned By: Great West Newspapers LP
PO Box 508, 10211 - 101st St., Lac La Biche, AB T0A 2C0
Tel: 780-623-4221; Fax: 780-623-4230
production@llb.greatwest.ca
www.laclabichepost.com
www.youtube.com/user/LLBPostNews
twitter.com/LLBPOSTnews
Circulation: 2,218 *Frequency:* Weekly; Tuesday
Covering events & businesses in Lac La Biche, Plamondon, Owl
River, Wandering River, Kikino, Beaver Lake, Buffalo Lake, Hylo,
Casian, Atmore, Rich Lake & Heart Lake
Rob McKinley, Publisher

Lacombe: Lacombe Globe
Owned By: Postmedia Network Inc.
5019 - 50th St., Lacombe, AB T4L 1W9
Tel: 403-782-3498; Fax: 403-782-5850
www.lacombeglobe.com
twitter.com/LacombeGlobe
www.facebook.com/lacombe.globe
Circulation: 7,100 *Frequency:* Thurs.
Nick Goetz, Publisher
nick.goetz@sunmedia.ca
Vince Burke, Editor
vince.burke@sunmedia.ca

Lamont: Lamont Farm 'n' Friends
Owned By: W & E Cowley Publishing Ltd.
PO Box 800, Lamont, AB T0B 2R0
Tel: 780-943-2032; Fax: 780-942-2515
redwater@shaw.ca
www.cowleynewspapers.com/farm-n-friends
Circulation: 19,200 *Frequency:* Fri.
Serves the counties of Sturgeon, Thorhild, Smoky Lake, Lamont
& Beaver.
Ed Cowley, Publisher & Editor

Leduc: The Leduc Rep
Previous Name: Leduc Representative
Owned By: Postmedia Network Inc.
4504 - 61st Ave., Leduc, AB T9E 3Z1
Tel: 780-986-2271; Fax: 780-986-6397
www.leducrep.com
twitter.com/LeducRep
www.facebook.com/LeducRep
Circulation: 16,795 *Frequency:* Weekly; Friday
The Leduc Representative is a member of Canoe Sun Media
Community Newspapers. The newspaper serves Leduc & Leduc
County in Alberta.
Bobby Roy, Editor
leducrep.editor@sunmedia.ca

Lethbridge: The Lethbridge Shopper
234A - 12B St. North, Lethbridge, AB T1H 2K7
Tel: 403-329-8225; Fax: 403-329-8211
www.shoppergroup.com
Frequency: Weekly
The Lethbridge Shopper publishes classifieds for Lethbridge and
surrounding area

Lloydminster: Lloydminster Meridian Booster
Owned By: Postmedia Network Inc.
5714 - 44th St., Lloydminster, AB T9V 0B6
Tel: 780-875-3362; *Fax:* 780-875-3423
www.meridianbooster.com
twitter.com/meridianbooster
www.facebook.com/170487056316788
Circulation: 39,800 *Frequency:* Mon., Wed., Fri.
Mary-Ann Kostiuk, Publisher
mary-ann.kostiuk@sunmedia.ca
Dana Smith, Managing Editor
dana.smith@sunmedia.ca

Manning: The Banner Post
Owned By: Mackenzie Report Inc.
413 Main St., Manning, AB T0H 2M0
Tel: 780-836-3588
www.mrnews.ca/the-banner-post
Circulation: 1,125 *Frequency:* Weekly; Wednesday

Medicine Hat: Holmes Publishing Co. Ltd.
1577 Dunmore Rd. SE, Medicine Hat, AB T1A 1Z8
Tel: 403-526-5937

Medicine Hat: Medicine Hat Shopper
922 Allowance Ave. SE, Medicine Hat, AB T1A 3G7
Tel: 403-527-5777; *Fax:* 403-526-7352
www.shoppergroup.com
Frequency: Weekly
Classified advertisements also appear on the web site.

Morinville: The Free Press Newspaper
Owned By: W & E Cowley Publishing Ltd.
PO Box 3005, 10126 - 100th Ave., Morinville, AB T8R 1R9
Tel: 780-939-3309; *Fax:* 780-939-3093
morinville@shaw.ca
www.cowleynewspapers.com
Circulation: 11,987 *Frequency:* Weekly; Tuesday
The newspaper serves residents of Alberta's Sturgeon County.

Morinville: The Morinville News
PO Box 3135, Morinville, AB T8R 1S1
Tel: 780-800-3619
editor@morinvillenews.com
morinvillenews.com
www.youtube.com/user/MorinvilleNews
twitter.com/MorinvilleNews
www.fac ebook.com/MorinvilleNews
Stephen A. Dafoe, Owner & Publisher

Nanton: Nanton News
Owned By: Postmedia Network Inc.
1902 - 21st Ave., Nanton, AB T0L 1R0
Tel: 403-646-2023; *Fax:* 403-646-2848
www.nantonnews.com
twitter.com/NantonNews
www.facebook.com/224526534248789
Circulation: 560 *Frequency:* Weekly; Wednesday
Nanton community news
Sheena Read, City Editor
sheena.read@sunmedia.ca

Okotoks: Okotoks Western Wheel
Owned By: Great West Newspapers LP
PO Box 150, Okotoks, AB T1S 2A2
Tel: 403-938-6397; *Fax:* 403-938-2518
www.westernwheel.com
Circulation: 16,284 *Frequency:* Weekly; Wednesday
Okotoks' weekly newspaper
Matt Rockley, Publisher
mrockley@okotoks.greatwest.ca

Olds: Mountain View Gazette
Owned By: Great West Newspapers LP
5013 - 51st St., Olds, AB T4H 1P6
Tel: 403-556-7510; *Fax:* 403-556-7515
www.mountainviewgazette.ca
twitter.com/mtnviewgazette
Circulation: 23,000 *Frequency:* Weekly; Tuesday
Alberta's Mountain View & Red Deer Counties are served by the
Mountain View Gazette.
Dan Singleton, Editor
dsingleton@olds.greatwest.ca

Olds: Olds Albertan
Owned By: Great West Newspapers LP
5013 - 51st St., Olds, AB T4H 1P6
Tel: 403-556-7510; *Fax:* 403-556-7515
www.oldsalbertan.ca
twitter.com/oldsalbertan
www.facebook.com/OldsAlbertan

Circulation: 6,611 *Frequency:* Weekly; Tuesday
The free newspaper serves the Alberta communities of Olds,
Wimborne, Torrington, & Bowden & the surrounding region.
Doug Collie, Editor
dcollie@olds.greatwest.ca

Oyen: Oyen Echo
Owned By: Holmes Publishing Co. Ltd.
PO Box 420, Oyen, AB T0J 2J0
Tel: 403-664-3622
oyenecho@telusplanet.net
www.oyenecho.ca
Circulation: 1,306 *Frequency:* Weekly; Tuesday
Oyen Echo's classifieds

Peace River: Peace River Record-Gazette
Owned By: Postmedia Network Inc.
PO Box 6870, 10002 - 100th St., Peace River, AB T8S 1S6
Tel: 780-624-2591; *Fax:* 780-624-8600
www.prrecordgazette.com
twitter.com/PRRecordGazette
www.facebook.com/peaceriverrecordgazette
Circulation: 1,500 *Frequency:* Wed.
Peter Meyerhoffer, Publisher
peter.meyerhoffer@sunmedia.ca
Fred Rinne, Editor, City
fred.rinne@sunmedia.ca

Pincher Creek: Pincher Creek Echo
Owned By: Postmedia Network Inc.
PO Box 1000, Pincher Creek, AB T0K 1W0
Tel: 403-627-3252; *Fax:* 403-627-3949
www.pinchercreekecho.com
twitter.com/PCEcho
www.facebook.com/pinchercreekecho1
Circulation: 1,091 *Frequency:* Weekly; Friday
Pincher Creek's weekly newspaper
Greg Cowan, Managing Editor
greg.cowan@sunmedia.ca

Ponoka: Ponoka News
Owned By: Black Press Group Ltd.
PO Box 4217, Ponoka, AB T4J 1R6
Tel: 403-783-3311; *Fax:* 403-783-6300
www.ponokanews.com
twitter.com/PonokaNews
www.facebook.com/476641985724647
Circulation: 5,885 *Frequency:* Weekly; Wednesday
Free weekly publication
Mustafa Eric, Editor
403-783-3311
editorial@ponokanews.com

Provost: The Provost News
Owned By: Holmes Publishing Co. Ltd.
PO Box 180, 5111 - 50th St., Provost, AB T0B 3S0
Tel: 780-753-2564; *Fax:* 780-753-6117
advertising@provostnews.ca
www.provostnews.ca
Circulation: 1,746 *Frequency:* Weekly; Wednesday
Richard Holmes, Managing Editor
rcholmes@agt.net

Red Deer: Red Deer Express
Owned By: Black Press Group Ltd.
#121, 5301 - 43rd St., Red Deer, AB T4N 1C8
Tel: 403-346-3356
advertising@reddeerexpress.com
www.reddeerexpress.com
twitter.com/reddeerexpress
www.facebook.com/12133222553
Circulation: 25,000 *Frequency:* Wednesday
The Red Deer Express is a community newspaper & online
news source that serves Red Deer & central Alberta.
Tracy Scheveers, Publisher
tscheveers@reddeerexpress.com
Erin Fawcett, Co-Editor
1-403-309-5457
efawcett@reddeerexpress.com
Mark Weber, Co-Editor
1-403-309-5455
editor@reddeerexpress.com

Red Deer: Red Deer Life
2950 Bremner Ave., Red Deer, AB T4R 1M9
Tel: 403-343-2400
editorial@reddeeradvocate.com
www.reddeeradvocate.com
twitter.com/RedDeerAdvocate
www.facebook.com/RDAdvocate
Circulation: 26,000+ *Frequency:* Sun.
The community newspaper is delivered to homes in Red Deer &
rural regions.

Fred Gorman, Publisher
fgorman@reddeeradvocate.com
John Stewart, Managing Editor
jstewart@reddeeradvocate.com

Redwater: The Review
Owned By: W & E Cowley Publishing Ltd.
PO Box 850, 4720 - 50th Ave., Redwater, AB T0A 2W0
Tel: 780-942-2023; *Fax:* 780-942-2515
redwater@shaw.ca
www.cowleynewspapers.com
Circulation: 4,437 *Frequency:* Weekly; Tuesday
Redwater's The Review serves residents in the Counties of
Smoky Lake & Thorhild.

Rimbey: Rimbey Review
Owned By: Black Press Group Ltd.
PO Box 244, 5001 - 50th Ave., Rimbey, AB T0C 2J0
Tel: 403-843-4909
twitter.com/RedDeerAdvocate
www.facebook.com/397611640365446
Circulation: 5,500 *Frequency:* Tues.
The free community newspaper provides news & information to
readers in Rimbey & west central Alberta.
Michele Rosenthal, Publisher
publisher@sylvanlakenews.com
Treena Mielke, Editor
reporter@rimbeyreview.com
Treena Mielke, Reporter
reporter@rimbeyreview.com
Susan Whitecotton, Contact, Classifieds
sales@rimbeyreview.com

Rocky Mountain House: The Mountaineer
Owned By: The Mountaineer Publishing Company
4814 - 49th St., Rocky Mountain House, AB T4T 1S8
Tel: 403-845-3334; *Fax:* 403-845-5570
advertising@mountaineer.bz
www.rock-e.ca
twitter.com/RMH_Mountaineer
www.facebook.com/RMHMountaineer
Circulation: 3,353 *Frequency:* Weekly; Tuesday
The newspapers covers news from Clearwater County, the Town
of Rocky Mountain House, & the Village of Caroline.
Glen Mazza, Publisher
publish@mountaineer.bz

Rycroft: The Central Peace Signal
PO Box 250, Rycroft, AB T0H 3A0
Tel: 780-765-3604
signalnews@abnorth.com
Circulation: 2,650 *Frequency:* Tues.
Danny Zahara, Publisher

Sedgewick: The Community Press
Previous Name: The Sedgewick Sentinel
Owned By: Caribou Publishing
PO Box 99, Sedgewick, AB T0B 4C0
Tel: 780-385-6693; *Fax:* 780-385-3107
news@thecommunitypress.com
www.thecommunitypress.com
Other information: Phone: 780-384-3641; Fax: 780-384-2244
twitter.com/CPresstweet
www.facebook.com/TheCommPress
Circulation: 2,468 *Frequency:* Weekly; Tuesday
The newspaper serves Alberta's Flagstaff County & the
surrounding region. The Community Press is part of a
multi-newspaper collective known as Caribou Publishing.
Eric Anderson, Publisher
Leslie Cholowsky, Editor

**Sherwood Park: The Sherwood Park/Strathcona
County News**
Owned By: Postmedia Network Inc.
168 Kaska Rd., Sherwood Park, AB T8A 4G7
Tel: 780-464-0033; *Fax:* 780-464-8512
www.sherwoodparknews.com
twitter.com/SHPk_News
www.facebook.com/SherwoodParkNews
Circulation: Tues. 25,869; Fri. 27,981 *Frequency:* Tuesday,
Friday
The two newspapers, Sherwood Park News & Strathcona
County News This Week, merged in 2007 to become Sherwood Park -
Strathcona County News. The newspaper is a member of Canoe
Sun Media Community Newspapers.
Michael Di Massa, Regional Managing Editor
michael.dimassa@sunmedia.ca

Slave Lake: Lakeside Leader
Owned By: South Peace News Ltd.
PO Box 849, 103 - 3rd St. NE, Slave Lake, AB T0G 2A0
Tel: 780-849-4380; *Fax:* 780-849-3903
lsleader@telusplanet.net
www.lakesideleader.com
Circulation: 2,775 *Frequency:* Weekly; Wednesday
Slave Lake's weekly newspaper
Mary Burgar, Publisher
spn@cablecomet.com

Smoky Lake: Smoky Lake Signal
PO Box 328, Smoky Lake, AB T0A 3C0
Tel: 780-656-4114; *Fax:* 780-656-4361
signal@mcsnet.ca
www.smokylake.com
Circulation: 1,347 *Frequency:* Weekly; Wednesday
Smoky Lake's local news
Lorne Taylor, Publisher

Spruce Grove: Calmar Community Voice
Owned By: E.J. Lewchuck & Associates Ltd.
c/o E.J. Lewchuck & Associates Ltd., PO Box 3595, 45
South Ave., Bay C, Spruce Grove, AB T7X 3A3
Tel: 780-962-9228; *Fax:* 780-962-1021
news@com-voice.com
www.com-voice.com
Other information: Classifieds Phone: 780-962-9229
Circulation: 4,000 *Frequency:* Biweekly
Bi-weekly newspaper

Spruce Grove: Onoway Community Voice
Owned By: E.J. Lewchuck & Associates Ltd.
c/o E.J. Lewchuck & Associates Ltd., PO Box 3595, 45
South Ave., Bay C, Spruce Grove, AB T7X 3A3
Tel: 780-962-9228; *Fax:* 780-962-1021
news@com-voice.com
www.com-voice.com
Other information: Classifieds Phone: 780-962-9229
Circulation: 6,000 *Frequency:* Biweekly
Bi-weekly newspaper

Spruce Grove: The Spruce Grove Examiner
Owned By: Postmedia Network Inc.
PO Box 4206, #1, 420 King St., Spruce Grove, AB T7X 3B4
Tel: 780-962-4257; *Fax:* 780-962-0658
www.sprucegroveexaminer.com
twitter.com/RepEx1
www.facebook.com/153508004671004
Circulation: 10,970 *Frequency:* Weekly; Friday
The Grove Examiner is Spruce Grove's weekly newspaper
Thomas Miller, Publisher
thomas.miller@sunmedia.ca

Spruce Grove: The Stony Plain Reporter
Owned By: Postmedia Network Inc.
PO Box 4206, #1, 420 King St., Spruce Grove, AB T7X 3B4
Tel: 780-962-4257; *Fax:* 780-962-0658
www.stonyplainreporter.com
twitter.com/StonyPlain
www.facebook.com/153508004671004
Circulation: 10,195 *Frequency:* Weekly; Friday
Spruce Grove's weekly newspaper
Thomas Miller, Publisher
thomas.miller@sunmedia.ca

Spruce Grove: Wabamun Community Voice
Owned By: E.J. Lewchuck & Associates Ltd.
c/o E.J. Lewchuck & Associates Ltd., PO Box 3595, 45
South Ave., Bay C, Spruce Grove, AB T7X 3A3
Tel: 780-962-9228; *Fax:* 780-962-1021
news@com-voice.com
www.com-voice.com
Other information: Classifieds Phone: 780-962-9229
Circulation: 6,000 *Frequency:* Biweekly
Bi-weekly newspaper

St Paul: St. Paul Journal
Owned By: Great West Newspapers LP
PO Box 159, 4813 - 50th Ave., St Paul, AB T0A 3A0
Tel: 780-645-3342; *Fax:* 780-645-2346
www.spjournal.com
twitter.com/StPaulJournal
www.facebook.com/312421611441
Circulation: 3,599 *Frequency:* Weekly; Tuesday
The community newspaper provides news & information about
the County & Town of St. Paul.
Janani Whitfield, Publisher
jwhitfield@stpaul.greatwest.ca

St. Albert: St. Albert Gazette
Owned By: Great West Newspapers LP
340 Carleton Dr., St. Albert, AB T8N 7L3
Tel: 780-460-5500; *Fax:* 780-460-8220
www.stalbertgazette.com
twitter.com/StAlbertGazette
www.facebook.com/stalbertgazettenews
Circulation: 28,314 *Frequency:* Weekly; Wednesday
St. Albert's weekly newspaper
Brian Bachynski, Publisher
bbachynski@greatwest.ca

Stettler: Stettler Independent
Owned By: Black Press Group Ltd.
PO Box 310, 4810 - 50th St., Stettler, AB T0C 2L0
Tel: 403-742-2395
editorial@reddeeradvocate.com
www.stettlerindependent.com
twitter.com/RedDeerAdvocate
www.facebook.com/RDAdvocate
Circulation: 2,163 *Frequency:* Weekly; Wednesday
Settler's weekly newspaper
Randy Holt, Publisher
Mustafa Eric, Editor

Sundre: Sundre Round Up
Owned By: Great West Newspapers LP
PO Box 599, 103 - 2nd St. NW, Sundre, AB T0M 1X0
Tel: 403-638-3577; *Fax:* 403-638-3077
www.sundreroundup.ca
twitter.com/sundreroundup
www.facebook.com/1469549416644673
Circulation: 1,487 *Frequency:* Weekly; Tuesday
Sundre Round Up is one of six newspapers published by
Mountain View Publishing, which is a subsidiary of Great West
Newspapers LP. The newspaper features information from the
town of Sundre & the surrounding region in west central Alberta.
Simon Ducatel, Editor
sducatel@sundre.greatwest.ca

Swan Hills: Swan Hills Grizzly Gazette
Owned By: Grizzly Gazette (1990) Inc.
PO Box 1000, 5435 Plaza Ave., Swan Hills, AB T0G 2C0
Tel: 780-333-2100; *Fax:* 780-333-2111
sgazette@telusplanet.net
Circulation: 526 *Frequency:* Weekly; Tuesday
Carol Webster, Publisher

Sylvan Lake: Eckville Echo
Owned By: Sylvan Lake News Ltd.
#103, 5020 - 50A St., Sylvan Lake, AB T4S 1R2
Tel: 403-887-2331; *Fax:* 403-887-2081
Toll-Free: 888-882-2331
Other information: Toll-Free Fax: 888-999-2081
Circulation: 2,500 *Frequency:* Thurs.
Sylvan Lake News Ltd. publishes the Eckville Echo.
Michele Rosenthal, Publisher
publisher@sylvanlakenews.com

Sylvan Lake: Sylvan Lake News
Owned By: Black Press Group Ltd.
#103, 5020 - 50A St., Sylvan Lake, AB T4S 1R2
Tel: 403-887-2331
www.sylvanlakenews.com
twitter.com/RedDeerAdvocate
www.facebook.com/SylvanLakeNews
Circulation: 7,778 *Frequency:* Weekly; Friday
News is presented from the town of Sylvan Lake & the
surrounding region, from Red Deer to Benalto.
Randy Holt, Publisher
Stuart Fullarton, Editor

Taber: The Taber Times
Owned By: Alta Newspaper Group LP
4822 - 53rd St., Taber, AB T1G 1W4
Tel: 403-223-2266; *Fax:* 403-223-1408
www.tabertimes.com
Other information: Alternate Phone: 403-223-9659
www.youtube.com/user/TheTaberTimes
twitter.com/tabertimes
www.faceb ook.com/TheTaberTimes
Circulation: 2,104 *Frequency:* Weekly; Wednesday
Coleen Campbell, Publisher
ccampbell@abnewsgroup.com
Greg Price, Editor
gprice@tabertimes.com

Three Hills: The Capital
Owned By: Capital Printers Ltd.
411 Main St., Three Hills, AB T0M 2A0
Tel: 403-443-5133; *Fax:* 403-443-7331
info@threehillscapital.com
www.threehillscapital.com

Circulation: 3,744 *Frequency:* Weekly; Wednesday
The Capital is also available through electronic subscription.
Timothy J. Shearlaw, Publisher & Editor

Tofield: The Tofield Mercury
Owned By: Caribou Publishing
PO Box 150, 5312 - 50th St., Tofield, AB T0B 4J0
Tel: 780-662-4046; *Fax:* 780-662-3735
adsmercury@gmail.com
www.tofieldmerc.com
twitter.com/tofieldmercury
www.facebook.com/TofieldMercury
Circulation: 1,106 *Frequency:* Weekly; Tuesday
The newspaper is part of Caribou Publishing. It serves the
Alberta communities of Tofield, Ryley, & Holden & the
surrounding region.
Kerry Anderson, Publisher
Patricia Harcourt, Editor

Two Hills: Two Hills & County Chronicle
PO Box 668, 4708 - 50 St., Two Hills, AB T0B 4K0
Tel: 780-657-2524; *Fax:* 780-657-2534
Circulation: 1,300 *Frequency:* Tuesday
Ruven Rajoo, Publisher
Sonny Rajoo, Editor

Vauxhall: The Vauxhall Advance
Owned By: Alta Newspaper Group LP
516 - 2nd Ave. North, Vauxhall, AB T0K 2K0
Tel: 403-654-2122
office@vauxhalladvance.com
www.vauxhalladvance.com
Circulation: 496 *Frequency:* Weekly; Thursday
Weekly paper published by the Alta Newspaper Group Ltd.
Partnership
Coleen Campbell, Publisher
ccampbell@abnewsgroup.com
Greg Price, Editor
gprice@tabertimes.com

Vegreville: Vegreville News Advertiser Ltd.
PO Box 810, 5110 - 50th St., Vegreville, AB T9C 1R9
Tel: 780-632-2861; *Fax:* 780-632-7981
Toll-Free: 800-522-4127
editor@newsadvertiser.com
www.newsadvertiser.com
Other information: Alt. Email: news@newsadvertiser.com
Circulation: 7,433 *Frequency:* Weekly; Wednesday
Weekly newspaper for Vegreville
Dan Beaudette, Publisher & Editor
dan@newsadvertiser.com
Michael Simpson, Editorial Manager
michael@newsadvertiser.com

Vermilion: Vermilion Standard
Owned By: Postmedia Network Inc.
4917 - 50th Ave., Vermilion, AB T9X 1A6
Tel: 780-853-5344; *Fax:* 780-853-5203
www.vermilionstandard.com
twitter.com/Vermstand
www.facebook.com/VermilionStandard
Circulation: 4,098 *Frequency:* Weekly; Tuesday
Vermillion weekly newspaper
Chris Roberts, Regional Managing Editor
chris.roberts@sunmedia.ca

Veteran: The Veteran Eagle
PO Box 322, Veteran, AB T0C 2S0
Tel: 403-575-5632
veteraneagle@gmail.com
www.facebook.com/theveteraneagle
Circulation: 525 *Frequency:* Weekly; Thursday
Veteran weekly newspaper

Viking: The Weekly Review
Owned By: Caribou Publishing
PO Box 240, 5311 - 50th St., Viking, AB T0B 4N0
Tel: 780-336-3422; *Fax:* 780-336-3223
vikingreview@gmail.com
www.weeklyreview.ca
twitter.com/vikingweekly
www.facebook.com/VikingWeeklyReview
Circulation: 1,097 *Frequency:* Weekly; Tuesday
The newspaper reports on the Alberta communities of Viking,
Ryley, Kinsella, Irma, Holden, & Bruce. Both regular & online
subscriptions are available. The Weekly Review is part of
Caribou Publishing.
Kerry Anderson, Owner & Publisher
Lorraine Poulsen, Managing Editor

Vulcan: **Vulcan Advocate**
Owned By: Postmedia Network Inc.
112 - 3rd Ave. North, Vulcan, AB T0L 2B0
Tel: 403-485-2036; *Fax:* 403-485-6938
www.vulcanadvocate.com
twitter.com/Vulcanadvocate
www.facebook.com/177296522292461
Circulation: 1,043 *Frequency:* Weekly; Wednesday
Vulcan Alberta's daily newspaper for citizens and Star Trek fans
alike
Josh Chalmers, Assistant Manager
josh.chalmers@sunmedia.ca

Wainwright: **Star News Inc.**
1027 - 3rd Ave., Wainwright, AB T9W 1T6
Tel: 780-842-4465; *Fax:* 780-842-2760
info@starnews.ca
www.starnews.ca
Rogers Holmes, Publisher
roger@starpress.ca
Kelly Clemmer, Editor-in-Chief
kelly@starnews.ca

Wainwright: **Wainwright StarEDGE**
Owned By: Star News Inc.
1027 - 3rd Ave., Wainwright, AB T9W 1T6
Tel: 780-842-4465; *Fax:* 780-842-2760
classifieds@starnews.ca
www.starnews.ca
www.facebook.com/WainwrightStarNews
Circulation: 6,650 *Frequency:* Fri.
Roger Holmes, Publisher
roger@starpress.ca
Patrick Moroz, Associate Publisher & Manager, Sales
patrick@starnews.ca
Kelly Clemmer, Editor-in-Chief
kelly@starnews.ca
Terry Hunka, Manager, Composition
terry@starnews.ca
Sandy Olejnik, Manager, Finance
sandy@starnews.ca
Carrie Baumgartner, Graphic Designer
carrie@starnews.ca
Sherry Schatz, Contact, Sales & Promotions
sherry@starnews.ca

Westlock: **The Westlock News**
Owned By: Great West Newspapers LP
9871 - 107th St., Westlock, AB T7P 1R9
Tel: 780-349-3033; *Fax:* 780-349-3677
www.westlocknews.com
www.youtube.com/user/WestlockNews
twitter.com/westlocknews
www.facebook.com/130628693670762
Circulation: 3,085 *Frequency:* Weekly; Tuesday
The town & county of Westlock & the village of Clyde are served
by the newspaper.
George Blais, Publisher
gblais@westlock.greatwest.ca
Doug Neuman, Editor
dneuman@westlock.greatwest.ca

Wetaskiwin: **Wetaskiwin Times**
Owned By: Postmedia Network Inc.
5013 - 51st St., Wetaskiwin, AB T9A 1L4
Tel: 780-352-2231; *Fax:* 780-352-4333
www.wetaskiwintimes.com
twitter.com/WetaskiwinTimes
Circulation: 10,689 *Frequency:* Weekly; Wednesday
Wetaskiwin's weekly newspaper
Jerold Leblanc, City Editor
wtimes.editor@sunmedia.ca

Whitecourt: **Mayerthorpe Freelancer**
Owned By: Postmedia Network Inc.
PO Box 630, 4732 - 50th Ave., Whitecourt, AB T7S 1N7
Tel: 780-778-3977; *Fax:* 780-778-6459
www.mayerthorpefreelancer.com
twitter.com/M_Freelancer
www.facebook.com/145871818816228
Circulation: 671 *Frequency:* Weekly; Wednesday
Mayerthore's weekly newspaper
Ann Harvey, Editor
ann.harvey@sunmedia.ca

Whitecourt: **The Whitecourt Star**
Owned By: Postmedia Network Inc.
PO Box 630, 4732 - 50th Ave., Whitecourt, AB T7S 1N7
Tel: 780-778-3977; *Fax:* 780-778-6459
www.whitecourtstar.com
twitter.com/Whitecourtstar
www.facebook.com/244728762259644

Circulation: 1,643 *Frequency:* Weekly; Wednesday
Weekly newspaper for Whitecourt
Pam Allain, Regional Director of Advertising
pamela.allain@sunmedia.ca
Christopher King, Editor
christopher.king@sunmedia.ca

British Columbia

Daily Newspapers in British Columbia

Fort St. John: **Alaska Highway News**
Previous Name: Dawson Creek Daily News; Peace
River Block News
Owned By: Glacier Media Inc.
9916 - 98th St., Fort St. John, BC V1J 3T8
Tel: 250-782-5631; *Fax:* 250-782-3522
www.alaskahighwaynews.ca
twitter.com/AHNnewspaper
www.facebook.com/AlaskaHighwayNews
Circulation: 12,000 total *Frequency:* Monday-Friday
Serving Dawson Creek, Fort St. John & surrounding
communities
William Julian, Regional Manager
wj@ahnfsj.ca
Matt Preprost, Managing Editor
250-785-5631
editor@ahnfsj.ca

Kelowna: **The Daily Courier**
Owned By: Continental Newspapers Canada Ltd.
2253 Leckie Rd., Kelowna, BC V1X 6Y5
Tel: 250-762-4445; *Fax:* 250-762-3866
www.kelownadailycourier.ca
twitter.com/KelownaCourier
www.facebook.com/KelownaDailyCourier
Frequency: Tuesday-Saturday
The Daily Courier is distributed Monday to Friday, & the
Okanagan Saturday & the Okanagan Sunday are distributed on
weekends.
Stephanie Goodban, General Manager
stephanie.goodban@ok.bc.ca
Pat Bulmer, City Editor
city.desk@ok.bc.ca

Kimberley: **Kimberley Daily Bulletin**
Owned By: Black Press Group Ltd.
335 Spokane St., Kimberley, BC V1A 1Y9
Tel: 250-427-5333
www.kimberleybulletin.com
www.instagram.com/thekimberleybulletin
twitter.com/kbulletin
Frequency: Monday-Friday
Zena Williams, Publisher
zena.williams@blackpress.ca
Carolyn Grant, Editor
carolyn.grant@kimberleybulletin.com

Penticton: **Penticton Herald**
Previous Name: Penticton Press
Owned By: Continental Newspapers Canada Ltd.
#101, 186 Nanaimo Ave. West, Penticton, BC V2A 1N4
Tel: 250-492-4002; *Fax:* 250-492-2403
csr@ok.bc.ca
www.pentictonherald.ca
Other information: Classified, Phone: 250-493-4332; Circulation:
250-493-6737
twitter.com/pentictonherald
www.facebook.com/pentictonherald
Frequency: Tuesday-Saturday
James Miller, Managing Editor
james.miller@ok.bc.ca

Trail: **Trail Daily Times**
Owned By: Black Press Group Ltd.
1163 Cedar Ave., Trail, BC V1R 4B8
Tel: 250-368-8551
www.traildailytimes.ca
twitter.com/traildailytimes
www.facebook.com/trailtimes
Frequency: Tuesday-Friday
The British Columbia communities of Trail, Rossland, Montrose,
Warfiels & Fruitvale are served by the newspaper.
Barb Blatchford, Publisher
publisher@trailtimes.ca
Guy Bertrand, Editor
editor@trailtimes.ca
Michelle Bedford, Manager, Circulation
circulation@trailtimes.ca

Vancouver: **The Province**
Owned By: Postmedia Network Inc.
#400, 2985 Virtual Way, Vancouver, BC V5M 4X7
Tel: 604-605-7381 *Toll-Free:* 800-663-2662
contactus@sunprovince.com
theprovince.com
www.youtube.com/user/TheProvinceOnline
twitter.com/theprovince
www.fac ebook.com/TheProvince
Frequency: Monday-Friday, Sunday
Harold Munro, Editor-in-Chief
hmunro@postmedia.com

Vancouver: **Sing Tao Daily Vancouver**
Owned By: Sing Tao Media Group Canada
8508 Ash St., Vancouver, BC V6P 3M2
Tel: 604-321-1111; *Fax:* 604-321-1178
vanadmin@singtao.ca
www.singtao.ca/vancouver
Frequency: Daily
Chinese daily newspaper.

Vancouver: **The Vancouver Sun**
Owned By: Postmedia Network Inc.
#400, 2985 Virtual Way, Vancouver, BC V5M 4X7
Tel: 604-605-7381 *Toll-Free:* 800-663-2662
contactus@sunprovince.com
vancouversun.com
twitter.com/VancouverSun
www.facebook.com/VancouverSun
Frequency: Monday-Saturday
Gordon Fisher, President
604-605-2480; Fax: 604-605-2633
gfisher@postmedia.com
Harold Munro, Editor-in-Chief
604-605-2185; Fax: 604-605-2323
hmunro@vancouversun.com

Victoria: **Times Colonist**
Previous Name: Victoria Daily Times; British Colonist
Owned By: Glacier Media Inc.
#201, 655 Tyee Rd., Victoria, BC V9A 6X5
Tel: 250-380-5211 *Toll-Free:* 800-663-6384
customerservice@timescolonist.com
www.timescolonist.com
www.linkedin.com/company/times-colonist-victoria
twitter.com/timescolonist
www.facebook.com/timescolonist
Circulation: 60,790 *Frequency:* Tuesday-Sunday
The oldest daily newspaper in Western Canada.
Dave Obee, Editor & Publisher
dobee@timescolonist.com

Other Newspapers in British Columbia

100 Mile House: **100 Mile House Free Press**
Owned By: Black Press Group Ltd.
PO Box 459, 100 Mile House, BC V0K 2E3
Tel: 250-395-2219; *Fax:* 250-395-3939
circulation@100milefreepress.net
www.100milefreepress.net
twitter.com/100mile
www.facebook.com/100MileFreePress
Frequency: Wednesday
The 100 Mile House Free Press covers the South Cariboo
region, from Lac la Hache to Clinton.
Chris Nickless, Publisher & Manager, Sales
publisher@100milefreepress.net
Ken Alexander, Editor
newsroom@100milefreepress.net
Heather Nelson, Contact, Advertising Sales
heather@100milefreepress.net

Abbotsford: **Abbotsford News**
Owned By: Black Press Group Ltd.
34375 Gladys Ave., Abbotsford, BC V2S 2H5
Tel: 604-853-1144
www.abbynews.com
twitter.com/abbynews
www.facebook.com/myabbynews
Circulation: Wed. 44,800; Fri. 46,000 *Frequency:* Biweekly
Full printed editions of the newspaper are also available online.
Andrew Franklin, Publisher
publisher@abbynews.com
Andrew Holota, Editor
604-851-4522
newsroom@abbynews.com

Houston: Houston Today Newspaper
Owned By: Black Press Group Ltd.
PO Box 899, 3232 Hwy. 16, Houston, BC V0J 1Z1
Tel: 250-845-2890
newsroom@houston-today.com
www.houston-today.com
twitter.com/houstonnews1
www.facebook.com/HoustonToday
Circulation: 1020 *Frequency:* Wednesday, Weekly
Andrew Hudson, Reporter

Invermere: The Valley Echo
Owned By: Black Press Group Ltd.
PO Box 70, #8, 1008 - 8th Ave., Invermere, BC V0A 1K0
Tel: 250-341-6299
nicole@invermerevalleyecho.com
www.invermerevalleyecho.com
twitter.com/TheValleyEcho
www.facebook.com/InvermereValleyEcho
Circulation: 1397 *Frequency:* Wednesday, Weekly
The Valley Echo serves the British Columbia communities of
Invermere, Fairmont Hot Springs, Windermere, Radium Hot
Springs, & Wilmer.
Rose-Marie Regitnig, Publisher
publisher@invermerevalleyecho.com
Nicole Trigg, Editor
nicole@invermerevalleyecho.com

Kamloops: Kamloops This Week
Owned By: Aberdeen Publishing Inc.
1365B Dalhousie Dr., Kamloops, BC V2C 5P6
Tel: 250-374-7467
www.kamloopsthisweek.com
www.youtube.com/user/KamloopsThisWeek
twitter.com/kamthisweek
www.facebook.com/kamloopsthisweek
Circulation: 58,650 *Frequency:* Biweekly
Kelly Hall, Publisher
publisher@kamloopsthisweek.com
Christopher Foulds, Editor
editor@kamloopsthisweek.com

Kelowna: Capital News
Owned By: Black Press Group Ltd.
2495 Enterprise Way, Kelowna, BC V1X 7K2
Tel: 250-763-3212
nlark@kelownacapnews.com
www.kelownacapnews.com
twitter.com/kelownacapnews
www.facebook.com/newskelowna
Circulation: 144,660 *Frequency:* Tuesday, Thursday, & Friday
Kelowna & its surrounding communities of Peachland, the
Westside, & Lake Country are served by the newspaper.
Karen Hill, Publisher
250-763-3212
khill@kelownacapnews.com
Barry Gerding, Managing Editor & Columnist
205-763-3212
bgerding@kelownacapnews.com
Alistair Waters, Assistant Editor
awaters@kelownacapnews.com
Glenn Beaudry, Manager, Circulation
250-763-3212
gbeaudry@kelownacapnews.com
Sean Connor, Photographer
photodesk@kelownacapnews.com

Kelowna: Lake Country Calendar
Owned By: Black Press Group Ltd.
2495 Enterprise Way, Kelowna, BC V1X 7K2
Tel: 250-766-4688; *Fax:* 250-766-4645
production@lakecountrynews.com
www.lakecountrycalendar.com
Other information: Classifieds & Community Events, Email:
classified@lakecountrynews.net
www.facebook.com/LakeCountryCalendar
Circulation: 3,600 *Frequency:* Wednesday
The area covered by the Lake Country Calendar includes the
communities of Winfield, Oyama, Okanagan Centre, & Carr's
Landing.
Barry Gerding, Editor
250-979-7302
newsroom@lakecountrynews.net

Kelowna: Westside Weekly
Owned By: Continental Newspapers Canada Inc.
550 Doyle Ave., Kelowna, BC V1Y 7V1
Tel: 250-762-4445; *Fax:* 250-762-3866
westside@ok.bc.ca
www.kelownadailycourier.ca
twitter.com/Westside_Weekly
www.facebook.com/westsideweekly

Circulation: 13,600 *Frequency:* Thurs., Sun.
The Westside Weekly serves West Kelowna, Peachland, & the
Westbank First Nation.
Terry Armstrong, Group Publisher
terry.armstrong@ok.bc.ca
Dave Trifunov, Editor

Keremeos: The Review
Owned By: Black Press Group Ltd.
PO Box 130, 605 - 7th Ave., Keremeos, BC V0X 1N0
Tel: 250-499-2653; *Fax:* 250-499-2645
www.keremeosreview.com
twitter.com/keremeosnews
www.facebook.com/144834348947774
Circulation: 850 *Frequency:* Thurs.
Don Kendall, Publisher
1-250-492-0444
dkendall@blackpress.ca
Tammy Sparkes, Associate Publisher
publisher@keremeosreview.com
Steve Arstad, Editor
news@keremeosreview.com
Tammy Hartfield, Manager, Composing
ads@keremeosreview.com
Sandi Nolen, Representative, Advertising Sales
sales@keremeosreview.com

Kitimat: Northern Sentinel
Owned By: Black Press Group Ltd.
626 Enterprise Ave., Kitimat, BC V8C 2E4
Tel: 250-632-6144
newsroom@northernsentinel.com
www.northernsentinel.com
twitter.com/kitimatnews
www.facebook.com/KitimatNews
Circulation: 805 *Frequency:* Wednesday
Louisa Genzale, Publisher & Contact, Ad Management
250-632-6144
publisher@northernsentinel.com
Cameron Orr, Editor
250-632-6144
newsroom@northernsentinel.com

Ladner: The Delta Optimist
Owned By: Glacier Media Inc.
5008 - 47A Ave., Ladner, BC V4K 1T8
Tel: 604-946-4451; *Fax:* 604-946-5680
production@delta-optimist.com
www.delta-optimist.com
Other information: Classifieds, Phone: 604-630-3300;
Distribution: 604-249-3332
twitter.com/DeltaOptimist
www.facebook.com/TheDeltaOptimist
Circulation: Wed. 17,140; Fri. 17,050 *Frequency:* Wednesday,
Friday
The newspaper covers community news & events in Ladner &
Tsawwassen.
Alvin Brouwer, Publisher
abrouwer@delta-optimist.com
Ted Murphy, Editor
tmurphy@delta-optimist.com

Ladysmith: Ladysmith-Chemainus Chronicle
Owned By: Black Press Group Ltd.
PO Box 400, 940 Oyster Bay Dr., Ladysmith, BC V9G 1A3
Tel: 250-245-2277
www.ladysmithchronicle.com
twitter.com/LC_Chronicle
Circulation: 1431 *Frequency:* Tuesday, Weekly
A print edition & an e-edition of the newspaper are available.
Teresa McKinley, Publisher
250-245-2277
publisher@ladysmithchronicle.com
Lindsay Chung, Editor
250-245-2277
editor@ladysmithchronicle.com
Doug Kent, Manager, Production
250-245-2277
Colleen Wheeler, Manager, Circulation & Office
250-245-2277
circulation@ladysmithchronicle.com
Niomi Pearson, Reporter
news@ladysmithchronicle.com

Lake Cowichan: Lake Cowichan Gazette
Owned By: Black Press Group Ltd.
PO Box 10, 170 Cowichan Lake Rd., Lake Cowichan, BC
V0R 2G0
Tel: 250-749-4383
office@lakecowichangazette.com
www.lakecowichangazette.com
twitter.com/lakecowichannew
www.facebook.com/117628711667898

Circulation: 730 *Frequency:* Wed.
Local news is provided for the British Columbia communities of
Lake Cowichan, Honeymoon Bay, Caycuse, Skutz Falls,
Youbou, & Mesachie Lake. A print edition & an e-dition of the
newspaper are available.
Dennis Skalicky, Publisher & Editor
publisher@lakecowichangazette.com
Karen Brouwer, Office Manager

Langley: Langley Advance
Owned By: Glacier Media Inc.
#112, 6375 - 202nd St., Langley, BC V2Y 1N1
Tel: 604-534-8641; *Fax:* 604-534-0824
editorial@langleyadvance.com
www.langleyadvance.com
twitter.com/LangleyAdvance
www.facebook.com/LangleyAdvance
Circulation: 80125 *Frequency:* Tuesday, Thursday
The City of Langley, Langley Township, & Cloverdale are served
by the newspaper.
Ryan McAdams, General Manager
rmcadams@langleyadvance.com
Bob Groeneveld, Editor
604-994-1050
editorial@langleyadvance.com
Jackie McKinley, Contact, Delivery
604-994-1045
jmckinley@langleyadvance.com

Langley: Langley Times
Owned By: Black Press Group Ltd.
PO Box 3097, 20258 Fraser Hwy., Langley, BC V3A 4E6
Tel: 604-533-4157
newsroom@langleytimes.com
www.langleytimes.com
twitter.com/langleytimes
www.facebook.com/LangleyAdvanceTimes
Circulation: 35,823 *Frequency:* Tuesday, Thursday
Dwane Weidendorf, Publisher
604-514-6750
publisher@langleytimes.com
Frank Bucholtz, Editor
604-514-6751
newsroom@langleytimes.com

Lantzville: The Lantzville Log
PO Box 214, Lantzville, BC V0R 2H0
Tel: 250-390-5336; *Fax:* 250-390-2847
editor@thelog.ca
www.thelog.ca
www.facebook.com/LantzvilleLoggers
Circulation: 2,000 *Frequency:* 11 times a year
Julie Winkel, Owner & Publisher

Lazo: Totem Times
Owned By: Department of National Defence
PO Box 1000 Main, 19 Wing Comox, Lazo, BC V0R 2K0
Tel: 250-339-2541
totemtimes@gmail.com
www.cg.cfpsa.ca
Circulation: 1,800 *Frequency:* Semimonthly; Tuesday
The newspaper is distributed at 19 Wing in the Comox Valley,
Canadian Forces bases throughout Canada, & Canadian Forces
deployments around the world.
Camille Douglas, Managing Editor
camille.douglas@forces.gc.ca

Lillooet: Bridge River-Lillooet News
Owned By: Glacier Newspaper Group
PO Box 709, 979 Main St., Lillooet, BC V0K 1V0
Tel: 250-256-4219; *Fax:* 250-256-4210
Toll-Free: 877-300-8569
lillooetnews@cablelan.net
www.lillooetnews.net
twitter.com/lillooetnews
www.facebook.com/BridgeRiverLIllooetNews
Circulation: 1,058 *Frequency:* Wednesday
Bruce MacLennan, Publisher
pub@lillooetnews.net
Wendy Fraser, Editor
editor@lillooetnews.net

Lumby: Lumby Valley Times
PO Box 408, 2062 Park Ave., Lumby, BC V0E 2G0
Tel: 250-307-0163
lvt@telus.net
www.lumbyvalleytimes.ca
Circulation: 2,700 *Frequency:* Fri.
Rod Neufeld, Publisher

Mackenzie: Mackenzie Times
PO Box 609, #125, 403 Mackenzie Blvd., Mackenzie, BC V0J 2C0
Tel: 250-997-6675; Fax: 250-997-4747
ads@mackenzietimes.com
Circulation: 1,000 *Frequency:* Wednesday
Jackie Benton, Editor
Kathy Dugan, Contact, Advertising

Maple Ridge: Maple Ridge - Pitt Meadows Times
Owned By: Glacier Media Inc.
#2, 22345 North Ave., Maple Ridge, BC V2X 8T2
Tel: 604-463-2281; Fax: 604-463-9943
www.mrtimes.com
Other information: Classified Advertising, Phone: 604-998-0218
twitter.com/mapleridgetimes
Circulation: 30,089 *Frequency:* Tuesday, Thursday
The newspaper is a division of Postmedia Nework Inc.
Shannon Balla, Publisher
sballa@mrtimes.com
Bob Groeneveld, Editor
bgroeneveld@mrtimes.com
Roxanne Hooper, Assistant Editor
rhooper@mrtimes.com
Ralph DeAdder, Advertising Representative
rdeadder@mrtimes.com
Wendy Bradley, Contact, Delivery
wbradley@van.net

Maple Ridge: The News
Owned By: Black Press Group Ltd.
22611, Dewdney Trunk Rd., Maple Ridge, BC V2X 3K1
Tel: 604-467-1122
newsroom@mapleridgenews.com
www.mapleridgenews.com
twitter.com/mapleridgenews
www.facebook.com/MapleRidgeNews
Circulation: 30,500 *Frequency:* Wed., Fri.
The News is distributed in the communities of Maple Ridge & Pitt Meadows, British Columbia. An e-edition is also available.
Jim Coulter, Publisher
1-604-476-2720
publisher@mapleridgenews.com
Michael Hall, Editor
1-604-476-2733
editor@mapleridgenews.com
Lisa Prophet, Manager, Advertising & Creative Services
admanager@mapleridgenews.com
Brian Yip, Manager, Circulation
circulation@mapleridgenews.com

Merritt: Merritt Herald
Owned By: Black Press Group Ltd.
PO Box 9, 2090 Granite Ave., Merritt, BC V1K 1B8
Tel: 250-378-4241; Fax: 250-378-6818
www.merrittherald.com
twitter.com/merrittherald
www.facebook.com/themerrittherald
Circulation: 6054 *Frequency:* Thursday, Weekly
News, community events, & sports are presented from Merritt & the Nicola Valley.
Theresa Arnold, Publisher
publisher@merrittherald.com
Emily Wessel, Editor
newsroom@merrittherald.com
Carol Soames, Manager, Office & Classifieds
classifieds@merrittherald.com

Mission: Mission City Record
Owned By: Black Press Group Ltd.
33047 - 1st Ave., Mission, BC V2V 1G2
Tel: 604-826-6221
adcontrol@missioncityrecord.com
www.missioncityrecord.com
twitter.com/missionrecord
www.facebook.com/123079451105629
Circulation: 10,000+ *Frequency:* Thursday
A print edition & an e-edition are available.
Andrew Franklin, Publisher
1-604-851-4538
publisher@missioncityrecord.com
Andrew Holota, Editor
editor@abbynews.com
Carol Aun, Editor, Arts
arts@missioncityrecord.com
Crystal Orchison, Contact, Advertising
crystal@missioncityrecord.com

Nakusp: Arrow Lakes News
Owned By: Black Press Group Ltd.
PO Box 189, 203 Broadway, Nakusp, BC V0G 1R0
Tel: 250-265-3823
www.arrowlakesnews.com
www.facebook.com/ArrowLakesNews
Circulation: 605 *Frequency:* Wednesday, Weekly
The British Columbia communities of Naskusp, New Denver, Trout Lake, Silverton, Burton, Fauquier, Arrow Park, & Edgewood are served by the newspaper.
Mavis Cann, Publisher & Manager, Ads
publisher@arrowlakesnews.com
Aaron Orlando, Editor
newsroom@arrowlakesnews.com

Nanaimo: Harbour City Star
Owned By: Glacier Newspaper Group
c/o Nanaimo Daily News, 2575 McCullough Rd., #B1, Nanaimo, BC V9S 5W5
Tel: 250-729-4200; Fax: 250-729-4256
www.nanaimodailynews.com
Other information: Classifieds, Phone: 250-729-4222;
Circulation: 250-729-4266
twitter.com/NanaimoDaily
www.facebook.com/150301821648264
Circulation: 27,800 *Frequency:* Fri.
Hugh Nicholson, Publisher
250-729-4257
hnicholson@glaciermedia.ca
Mark MacDonald, Managing Editor
mamacdonald@nanaimodailynews.com
Wendy King, Manager, Production
wking@nanaimodailynews.com
Rachel Mason, Manager, Business
rmason@nanaimodailynews.com
Andrea Rosato-Taylor, Manager, Advertising
arosato-taylor@nanaimodailynews.com

Nanaimo: Nanaimo News Bulletin
Owned By: Black Press Group Ltd.
777 Poplar St., Nanaimo, BC V9S 2H7
Tel: 250-753-3707
editor@nanaimobulletin.com
www.nanaimobulletin.com
twitter.com/nanaimobulletin
www.facebook.com/nanaimobulletin
Circulation: 30,000 *Frequency:* Tuesday, Thursday, Saturday
The Nanaimo New Bulletin is available in print & online.
Maurice Donn, Publisher
250-734-4600
publisher@nanaimobulletin.com
Melissa Fryer, Editor
250-734-4621
editor@nanaimobulletin.com
Michael Kelly, Manager, Circulation
250-734-4620
circulation@nanaimobulletin.com
Sean McCue, Manager, Sales
salesmgr@nanaimobulletin.com
Chris Bush, Photographer
250-734-4625
photos@nanaimobulletin.com

Nelson: Express
554 Ward St., Nelson, BC V1L 1S9
Tel: 250-354-3910; Fax: 250-352-5075
Toll-Free: 800-665-3288
express@expressnews.bc.ca
www.expressnews.ca
Other information: Editorial, Phone: 250-354-1118
www.youtube.com/user/expressnewsupdate
Frequency: Weekly
Nelson Becker, Publisher

Nelson: Nelson Star
Owned By: Black Press Group Ltd.
514 Hall St., Nelson, BC V1L 1Z2
Tel: 250-352-1890
www.nelsonstar.com
twitter.com/nelsonstarnews
www.facebook.com/nelsonstarnews
Circulation: 9,000 *Frequency:* Wednesday, Friday
Twice weekly newspaper for Nelson, BC
Karen Bennett, Publisher
250-352-1890
advertising@nelsonstar.com
Greg Nesteroff, Editor
250-551-4137
editor@nelsonstar.com

North Vancouver: North Shore News
Owned By: Glacier Newspaper Group
#100, 126 East 15th St., North Vancouver, BC V7L 2P9
Tel: 604-985-2131; Fax: 604-985-3227
distribution@nsnews.com
Other information: Classified, Phone: 604-630-3300; Real Estates Ads: 604-985-6982
twitter.com/NorthShoreNews
www.facebook.com/northshorenews
Circulation: 62,725 *Frequency:* Wednesday, Friday, Sunday
Doug Foot, Publisher
604-998-3550
dfoot@nsnews.com
Terry Peters, Managing Editor
604-998-3530
tpeters@nsnews.com
Vicki Magnison, Director, Sales & Marketing
604-998-3520
vmagnison@nsnews.com
Rick Anderson, Manager, Real Estate
604-998-3580
randerson@nsnews.com

Oliver: Oliver Chronicle
Owned By: Aberdeen Publishing Inc.
6379 Main St., Oliver, BC V0H 1T0
Tel: 250-498-3711; Fax: 250-498-3966
www.timeschronicle.ca
twitter.com/OliverChronicle
www.facebook.com/OliverChronicle
Circulation: 1722 *Frequency:* Wednesday
Both paper & online editions are available.
Steve Ceron, Publisher
publisher@oliverchronicle.com
Lyonel Doherty, Editor
editor@oliverchronicle.com
Derrick Robson, Contact, Production
production@oliverchronicle.com
Marilyn Swartz, Contact, Sales
sales@oliverchronicle.com

Osoyoos: Osoyoos Times
Owned By: Aberdeen Publishing Group
PO Box 359, 8712 Main St., Osoyoos, BC V0H 1V0
Tel: 250-495-7225; Fax: 250-495-6616
ads@osoyoostimes.com
www.osoyoostimes.com
Circulation: 1911 *Frequency:* Wednesday
Steve Ceron, Publisher
sceron@osoyoostimes.com
Keith Lacey, Editor
news@osoyoostimes.com
Richard McGuire, Reporter & Photographer
reporter@osoyoostimes.com
Jocelyn Merit, Office Administrator
admin@osoyoostimes.com
Sherry Anderson, Contact, Newspaper Circulation & Delivery
Ken Baker, Contact, Advertising Sales & Layout
sales@osoyoostimes.com

Parksville: The Parksville Qualicum Beach News
Previous Name: Oceanside Star
Owned By: Black Press Group Ltd.
PO Box 1180, #4, 154 Middleton, Parksville, BC V9P 2H2
Tel: 250-248-4341
www.pqbnews.com
Circulation: 16,243 *Frequency:* Weekly; Thursday
Peter McCully, Publisher
250-905-0018
publisher@pqbnews.com
John Harding, Editor
editor@pqbnews.com

Parksville: Parksville Qualicum News
Owned By: Black Press Group Ltd.
PO Box 1180, #4, 154 Middleton Ave., Parksville, BC V9P 2H2
Tel: 250-248-4341
www.pqbnews.com
twitter.com/parksvillenews
www.facebook.com/PQBNews
Circulation: 15800+ *Frequency:* Tuesday, Friday, Thursday
The Parksville Qualicum News is available inprint & online. The newspaper serves the City of Parksville, the Town of Qualicum Beach, & the Vancouver Island communities of Deep Bay, Qualicum Bay, Errington, Hilliers, Coombs, & Whiskey Creek.
Peter McCully, Publisher
250-905-0018
publisher@pqbnews.com

John Harding, Editor
250-905-0019
editor@pqbnews.com
Lissa Alexander, Reporter
250-905-0028
reporter@pqbnews.com
Auren Ruvinsky, Reporter
250-905-0026
writer@pqbnews.com
Peggy Sidbeck, Manager, Production
250-905-0016
production@pqbnews.com
Grant DeGagne, Representative, Advertising
250-905-0015
gdegagne@pqbnews.com

Peachland: The Peachland Signal
PO Box 800, #3, 4478 Third St., Peachland, BC V0H 1X0
Tel: 250-767-2004; *Fax:* 250-767-3306
signal@cablelan.net
Circulation: 1,308 *Frequency:* Weekly
Darren Bayrack, Publisher

Peachland: Peachland View
Owned By: Aberdeen Publishing Group
PO Box 1150, 4437 - 3rd St., Peachland, BC V0H 1X7
Tel: 250-767-7771
publisher.peachlandview@shaw.ca
www.peachlandview.com
twitter.com/peachlandview
www.facebook.com/ThePeachlandView
Circulation: 3,100 *Frequency:* Fri.
The independently owned, free community newspaper is
distributed to Peachland's residences & businesses, as well as
businesses in Westbank.
Steve Ceron, Group Publisher
sceron@aberdeenpublishing.com
Erin Christie, Editor
editor@peachlandview.ca
Joanne Layh, Manager, Sales
sales@peachlandview.ca

Pender Island: Island Tides
PO Box 55, Pender Island, BC V0N 2M1
Tel: 250-216-2267; *Fax:* 250-629-3838
islandtides@islandtides.com
www.islandtides.com
Circulation: 14,600 *Frequency:* Thurs., bi-weekly
Island Tides presents news & views from British Columbia's west
coast. The newspaper is available around the Strait of Georgia.
Christa Grace-Warrick, Publisher

Penticton: Penticton Western News
Owned By: Black Press Group Ltd.
2250 Camrose St., Penticton, BC V2A 8R1
Tel: 250-492-3636
region@pentictonwesternnews.com
www.pentictonwesternnews.com
Other information: Classifieds, Email:
classifieds@pentictonwesternnews.com
twitter.com/pentictonnews
www.facebook.com/pentictonnews
Circulation: 20,000+ *Frequency:* Wednesday, Friday
News, sports, & entertainment in Penticton & the South
Okanagan are covered by the newspaper.
Don Kendall, Publisher
250-492-0444
dkendall@blackpress.ca
Percy Hébert, Editor & Columnist
editor@pentictonwesternnews.com
Emanuel Sequeira, Sports Editor & Columnist
250-492-3636
sports@pentictonwesternnews.com
Larry Mercier, Manager, Sales
250-492-0444
larry@pentictonwesternnews.com
Kirk Myltoft, Composing Manager, Creative Services
kirk@pentictonwesternnews.com
Sue Kovacs, Manager, Circulation
circulation@pentictonwesternnews.com
Mark Brett, Photographer
photos@pentictonwesternnews.com

Port Coquitlam: The Tri-City News
Owned By: Glacier Media Inc.
#115, 1525 Broadway St., Port Coquitlam, BC V3C 6L6
Tel: 604-525-6397
www.tricitynews.com
twitter.com/tricitynews
www.facebook.com/tricitynewsBC
Circulation: Wed. 52,310; Fri. 52,297 *Frequency:* Wednesday,
Friday
The newpaper covers happenings in the British Columbia

communities of Port Coquitlam, Coquitlam, Anmore, Port Moody,
& Belcarra.
Nigel Lark, Publisher
publisher@tricitynews.com
Richard Dal Monte, Editor
newsroom@tricitynews.com

Port Hardy: North Island Gazette
Owned By: Black Press Group Ltd.
PO Box 458, 7305 Market St., Port Hardy, BC V0N 2P0
Tel: 250-949-6225
www.northislandgazette.com
twitter.com/nigazette
www.facebook.com/NorthIslandGazette
Circulation: 1,500 *Frequency:* Thursday
The newspaper serves the northern part of Vancouver Island,
including the communities of Port McNeill, Port Hardy, Port Alice,
Sointula, & Alert Bay.
Sandy Grenier, Publisher
publisher@northislandgazette.com
J.R. Rardon, Editor
editor@northislandgazette.com
Annae Marchand, Manager, Production
production@northislandgazette.com
Aidan O'Toole, Reporter
reporter@northislandgazette.com
Lisa Harrison, Representative, Sales
sales@northislandgazette.com

Port Moody: The Tri-Cities Now
Owned By: Glacier Media Inc.
#216, 3190 St. Johns St., Port Moody, BC V3H 2C7
Tel: 604-492-4492
www.thenownews.com
Other information: Classified Advertising, Email:
classified@van.net
twitter.com/TheTriCitiesNow
www.facebook.com/TheTriCitiesNOW
Circulation: 54,989 *Frequency:* Wednesday, Friday
News is provided for the British Columbia communities of
Coquitlam, Port Moody & Port Coquitlam.
Shannon Balla, Publisher
604-492-4229
publisher@thenownews.com
Leneen Robb, Editor
604-492-4967
editorial@thenownews.com

Powell River: Powell River Peak
Owned By: Glacier Media Inc.
4400 Marine Ave., Powell River, BC V8A 2K1
Tel: 604-485-5313; *Fax:* 604-485-5007
editor@prpeak.com
www.prpeak.com
Other information: Administration, Email: admin@prpeak.com
twitter.com/Peak_Aboo
www.facebook.com/168767440173
Circulation: 2,850 *Frequency:* Wed.
Joyce Carlson, Publisher

Prince George: Pipeline News North
Owned By: Glacier Media Inc.
PO Box 5700, Prince George, BC V2L 5K9
Tel: 250-785-5631
editor@pipelinenewsnorth.ca
www.pipelinenewsnorth.ca
twitter.com/PipelineNN
www.facebook.com/PipelineNewsNorth
Circulation: 14,000 *Frequency:* Monthly
Discusses petroleum news in northern British Columbia &
Alberta.
Matt Prepost, Managing Editor
editor@ahnfsj.ca

Prince George: The Prince George Citizen
Owned By: Glacier Media Inc.
505 - 4th Ave., Prince George, BC V2L 3H2
Tel: 250-562-2441
info@pgcitizen.ca
www.princegeorgecitizen.com
twitter.com/pgcitizen
www.facebook.com/pgcitizen
Frequency: Thursday
Colleen Sparrow, Publisher
csparrow@pgcitizen.ca

Prince George: Prince George Free Press
Owned By: Black Press Group Ltd.
1773 South Lyon St., Prince George, BC V2N 1T3
Tel: 250-564-0005; *Fax:* 250-562-0025
editor@pgfreepress.com
pgfreepress.com
twitter.com/pgfreepress
www.facebook.com/140123662713095
Circulation: 56,000 *Frequency:* Wed., Fri.
Ron Drillen, General Manager
publisher@pgfreepress.com
Bill Phillips, Editor

Princeton: Similkameen News Leader
Owned By: Black Press Ltd.
PO Box 956, 226A Bridge St., Princeton, BC V0X 1W0
Tel: 250-295-4149; *Fax:* 250-295-4103
Toll-Free: 888-350-9969
editor@thenewsleader.ca
www.thenewsleader.ca
Other information: Advertising Department, Email:
ads@thenewsleader.ca
twitter.com/PrincetonBCNews
www.facebook.com/thenewsleader1
Circulation: 1,000 *Frequency:* Wed.
The tabloid newspaper is distributed in the Similkameen Valley,
including Princeton, Cawston, Coalmont, Keremeos, Hedley, &
Tulameen.
W. George Elliott, Publisher
george@thenewsleader.ca
Brenda Engel, Office Administrator
brenda@thenewsleader.ca

Princeton: Similkameen Spotlight
Owned By: Black Press Group Ltd.
PO Box 340, 282 Bridge St., Princeton, BC V0X 1W0
Tel: 250-295-3535
classifieds@similkameenspotlight.com
www.similkameenspotlight.com
twitter.com/similkameennews
www.facebook.com/SimilkameenSpotlight
Circulation: 1000+ *Frequency:* Wednesday, Weekly
The Similkameen Spotlight serves the Similkameen Valley,
including Coalmont, Princeton, Tulameen, Keremeos, & Hedley.
Lisa Carleton, Editor & Associate Publisher
lisa@similkameenspotlight.com
Sandi Nolan, Consultant, Advertising
advertising@similkameenspotlight.com

Queen Charlotte: Haida Gwaii Observer
Owned By: Observer Publishing Co. Ltd.
PO Box 205, 623 - 7th St., Queen Charlotte, BC V0T 1S0
Tel: 250-559-4680; *Fax:* 250-559-8433
Toll-Free: 888-529-4747
observer@haidagwaii.ca
www.qciobserver.com
www.facebook.com/haidagwaiiobserver
Circulation: 900 *Frequency:* Thursday, Weekly
Formerly the Queen Charlotte Islands Observer
Jeff King, Manager, Advertising

Quesnel: Cariboo Observer
Owned By: Black Press Group Ltd.
188 Carson Ave., Quesnel, BC V2J 2A8
Tel: 250-992-2121
editor@quesnelobserver.com
www.quesnelobserver.com
twitter.com/quesnelnews
www.facebook.com/QuesnelCaribooObserver
Circulation: 9000+ *Frequency:* Wednesday, Friday
News is provided about Quesnel & area, British Columbia.
Tracey Roberts, Publisher & Manager, Sales
publisher@quesnelobserver.com
Autumn MacDonald, Editor
editor@quesnelobserver.com
Whitney Griffiths, Reporter, Sports
sports@quesnelobserver.com

Revelstoke: Revelstoke Times Review
Owned By: Black Press Group Ltd.
PO Box 20, 518 - 2nd St. West, Revelstoke, BC V0E 2S0
Tel: 250-837-4667
www.revelstoketimesreview.com
twitter.com/revelstoketimes
www.facebook.com/RevelstokeTimesReview
Circulation: 1,200+ *Frequency:* Wednesday
The Revelstoke Review, which was founded in 1914, merged
with the Revelstoke Times in 2003 to create the Revelstoke
Times Review.
Mavis Cann, Publisher
mavis@revelstoketimesreview.com

Alex Cooper, Editor
editor@revelstoketimesreview.com
Fran Carlson, Manager, Office
circulation@revelstoketimesreview.com
Rob Stokes, Contact, Production
production@revelstoketimesreview.com

Richmond: Richmond News
Owned By: Glacier Media Inc.
5731, No. 3 Road, Richmond, BC V6X 2C9
Tel: 604-270-8031; *Fax:* 604-270-2248
editor@richmond-news.com
www.richmond-news.com
Frequency: Biweekly; Wednesday, Friday
Discusses local news in & around Richmond.
Pierre Pelletier, Publisher
604-249-3336
ppelletier@richmond-news.com

Richmond: Richmond Review
Owned By: Black Press Group Ltd.
#1, 3671 Viking Way, Richmond, BC V6V 2J5
Tel: 604-247-3700
news@richmondreview.com
www.richmondreview.com
Other information: Newsroom, Phone: 604-247-3730; Classified
Advertising: 604-575-5555
twitter.com/richmondreview
www.facebook.com/richmondreview
Circulation: 93,500 *Frequency:* Wed., Fri.
Mary Kemmis, Publisher
publisher@richmondreview.com
Bhreandain Clugston, Editor
Jaana Bjork, Manager, Creative Services
jaana@richmondreview.com
Kristene Murray, Manager, Circulation
circulation@richmondreview.com
Elana Gold, Assistant Manager, Advertising
admanager@richmondreview.com

Salmon Arm: Salmon Arm Observer
Owned By: Black Press Group Ltd.
PO Box 550, 171 Shuswap St., Salmon Arm, BC V1E 4H7
Tel: 250-832-2131
circulation@saobserver.net
www.saobserver.net
twitter.com/salmonarm
www.facebook.com/SalmonArmObserver
Circulation: 2400+ *Frequency:* Wednesday
Tracy Hughes, Editor & Columnist
newsroom@saobserver.net
Penny Brown, Contact, Advertising Sales
pennyjb@saobserver.net

Salmon Arm: The Shuswap Market News
Owned By: Black Press Group Ltd.
171 Shuswap St., Salmon Arm, BC V1E 4H7
Tel: 250-832-2131
www.saobserver.net
Circulation: 14,000 *Frequency:* Friday
The Shuswap Market News is a free paper.
Tracy Hughes, Editor & Columnist
newsroom@saobserver.net
Sherry Kaufmam, Contact, Advertising Sales
sherry@saobserver.net

Salt Spring Island: Gulf Islands Driftwood
Owned By: Black Press Group Ltd.
328 Lower Ganges Rd., Salt Spring Island, BC V8K 2V3
Tel: 250-537-9933
info@driftwoodgimedia.com
www.gulfislandsdriftwood.com
twitter.com/gidriftwood
www.facebook.com/gulfislandsdriftwood
Circulation: 2996 *Frequency:* Wednesday
The community newspaper is available in print & online. The
Gulf Island Driftwood serves the British Columbia islands of
Mayne, Salt Spring, Pender, Saturna, & Galiano.
Amber Ogilvie, Publisher
aogilvie@gulfislandsdriftwood.com
Gail Sjuberg, Managing Editor
gsjuberg@gulfislands.net
Lorraine Sullivan, Manager, Production
production@gulfislands.net

Sechelt: Coast Reporter
Previous Name: Coast Independent
Owned By: Glacier Media Inc.
PO Box 1388, 5485 Wharf Rd., Sechelt, BC V0N 3A0
Tel: 604-885-4811; *Fax:* 604-885-4818
www.coastreporter.net
twitter.com/coast_reporter
www.facebook.com/coastreporter

Circulation: 11,900 *Frequency:* Fri.
Peter Kvarnstrom, Publisher
pkvarnstrom@coastreporter.net
Ian Jacques, Editor
editor@coastreporter.net

Sicamous: Eagle Valley News
Owned By: Black Press Group Ltd.
PO Box 113, 1133 Parksville St., Sicamous, BC V0E 2V0
Tel: 250-836-2570; *Fax:* 250-836-2661
classifieds@eaglevalleynews.com
www.eaglevalleynews.com
Circulation: 500 *Frequency:* Wednesday
Lavigne Laura, Contact, Sales
laura@saobserver.net
Lachlan Labere, Reporter
circulation@saobserver.net

Sidney: Peninsula News Review
Previous Name: Sidney Review
Owned By: Black Press Group Ltd.
#6, 9843 - 2nd St., Sidney, BC V8L 3C7
Tel: 250-656-1151
victorianews.com
twitter.com/peninsulanews
www.facebook.com/PeninsulaNewsReview
The newspaper serves the British Columbia communities of
Sidney, North Saanich, & Central Saanich.
Jim Parker, Publisher
publisher@peninsulanewsreview.com
Steven Heywood, Editor
editor@peninsulanewsreview.com
Arlene Smith, Manager, Circulation
circulation@peninsulanewsreview.com
Devon MacKenzie, Reporter
reporter@peninsulanewsreview.com

Smithers: Interior News
Owned By: Black Press Group Ltd.
PO Box 2560, 3764 Broadway, Smithers, BC V0J 2N0
Tel: 250-847-3266; *Fax:* 250-847-2995
advertising@interior-news.com
www.interior-news.com
twitter.com/smithersnews
www.facebook.com/SmithersInteriorNews
Circulation: 2,700 *Frequency:* Wednesday
Grant Harris, Publisher
publisher@interior-news.com
Ryan Jensen, Editor
editor@interior-news.com

Sooke: Sooke News Mirror
Owned By: Black Press Group Ltd.
#4, 6631 Sooke Rd., Sooke, BC V9Z 0A3
Tel: 250-642-5752; *Fax:* 250-642-4767
www.sookenewsmirror.com
twitter.com/sookenews
www.facebook.com/SookeNewsMirror
Circulation: 5700+ *Frequency:* Wednesday
The Sooke News Mirror serves the District of Sooke & its
surrounding area.
Rod Sluggett, Publisher
publisher@sookenewsmirror.com
Pirjo Raits, Editor
editor@sookenewsmirror.com
Britt Santowski, Reporter
news@sookenewsmirror.com
Harla Eve, Contact, Office Administration
office@sookenewsmirror.com
Joan Gamache, Advertising Representative & Contact,
Circulation
sales@sookenewsmirror.comm

Squamish: Squamish Chief
Owned By: Glacier Newspapers Group
PO Box 3500, 38117 - 2nd Ave., Squamish, BC V8B 0B9
Tel: 604-892-9161; *Fax:* 604-892-8483
lpasko@squamishchief.com
www.squamishchief.com
twitter.com/squamishchief
www.facebook.com/squamishchief
Circulation: 2,846 *Frequency:* Friday
Darren Roberts, Publisher
publisher@squamishchief.com
David Burke, Editor
dburke@squamishchief.com

Summerland: Summerland Review
Owned By: Black Press Group Ltd.
PO Box 309, Summerland, BC V0H 1Z0
Tel: 250-494-5406
www.summerlandreview.com
twitter.com/summerlandnews
www.facebook.com/SummerlandReview
Circulation: 1,700 *Frequency:* Thursday
A print edition & an e-edition are available.
Don Kendall, Publisher
dkendall1@hotmail.com
John Arendt, Editor
news@summerlandreview.com
Nan Cogbill, Manager, Circulation & Classified
class@summerlandreview.com
Jo Freed, Manager, Sales
ads@summerlandreview.com

Surrey: Cloverdale Reporter
Owned By: Black Press Group Ltd.
17586 - 56A Ave., Surrey, BC V3S 1G3
Tel: 604-575-2405
editor@cloverdalereporter.com
www.cloverdalereporter.com
twitter.com/cloverdalenews
www.facebook.com/CloverdaleReporter
Circulation: 20,000 *Frequency:* Thurs.
News is reported from the Cloverdale area of Surrey, British
Columbia in both print & e-editions.
Jennifer Lang, Editor
editor@cloverdalereporter.com
Ursula Maxwell-Lewis, Founding Editor
604-575-2405
Lyliane Ward, Consultant, Advertising
604-575-2423
sales@cloverdalereporter.com

Surrey: The Indo-Canadian Voice
#102, 9360 - 120th St., Surrey, BC V3V 4B9
Tel: 604-502-6100; *Fax:* 604-501-6111
editor@voiceonline.com
www.voiceonline.com
twitter.com/indocanvoice
www.facebook.com/indocanadianvoice
Circulation: 18,500 *Frequency:* Weekly
The VOICE caters to the South Asian population of Vancouver
and British Columbia
Rattan Mall, Editor
newsdesk@voiceonline.com
Vinnie Combow, General Manager
rcombow@gmail.com

Surrey: The Leader
Owned By: Black Press Group Ltd.
#200, 5450 - 152nd St., Surrey, BC V3S 5J9
Tel: 604-575-2744
newsroom@surreyleader.com
www.surreyleader.com
twitter.com/surreyleader
www.facebook.com/surreyleader
Circulation: 80,000+ *Frequency:* Tuesday, Thursday
The Leader covers news for Surrey & North Delta, British
Columbia. Editions are available in print & online.
Jim Mihaly, Publisher
publisher@surreyleader.com
Paula Carlson, Editor
604-575-5337
pcarlson@surreyleader.com
Sheila Reynolds, Assistant Editor
604-575-5332
sreynolds@surreyleader.com
Jeff Nagel, Regional Reporter
604-575-5334
jnagel@surreyleader.com
Boaz Joseph, Multimedia Journalist
604-575-5340
bjoseph@surreyleader.com

Surrey: The Link
#203, 12725 - 80th Ave., Surrey, BC V3W 3A6
Tel: 604-591-5160; *Fax:* 604-591-2113
ads@thelinkpaper.ca
www.thelinkpaper.ca
Focus on both British Columbia & international South Asian
news & issues
Paul R. Dhillon, Editor-in-chief
editor@thelinkpaper.ca

Surrey: The Now
Owned By: Glacier Newspapers Group
#201, 7889 - 132nd St., Surrey, BC V3W 4N2
Tel: 604-572-0064
delivery@thenownewspaper.com
www.thenownewspaper.com
Other information: Distribution, Phone: 604-534-6493;
Classifieds: 604-444-3000
twitter.com/TheNowNewspaper
www.facebook.com/thesurreynow
Circulation: 116,000+ *Frequency:* Tuesday, Friday
The area covered by the newspaper includes Surrey, Whiterock,
& Noth Delta, British Columbia.
Gary Hollick, Publisher
ghollick@thenownewspaper.com
Beau Simpson, Editor
bsimpson@thenownewspaper.com

Surrey: The Peace Arch News
Owned By: Black Press Group Ltd.
#200, 2411 - 160th St., Surrey, BC V3S 0C8
Tel: 604-531-1711
www.peacearchnews.com
twitter.com/whiterocknews
www.facebook.com/peacearchnews
Circulation: 37,000+ *Frequency:* Tuesday, Thursday
The Peace Arch News serves communities on the Semiahmoo
Peninsula, including South Surrey & White Rock.
Rita Walters, Publisher
publisher@peacearchnews.com
Lance Peverley, Editor & Columnist
604-542-7402
lpeverley@peacearchnews.com
Jim Chmelyk, Manager, Creative Services
604-542-7420
jim@peacearchnews.com
Marilou Pasion, Manager, Circulation
604-542-7430
marilou@peacearchnews.com

Terrace: Terrace Standard
Owned By: Black Press Group Ltd.
3210 Clinton Ave., Terrace, BC V8G 5R2
Tel: 250-638-7283; *Fax:* 250-638-8432
www.terracestandard.com
twitter.com/terracestandard
www.facebook.com/TerraceStandard
Circulation: 8,000 *Frequency:* Wednesday
The newspaper employs fifteen staff members in its Terrace
office.
Rod Link, Publisher & Editor
rodlink@terracestandard.com
Brian Lindenbach, Manager, Sales
brianl@terracestandard.com
Margaret Speirs, Community Reporter
newsroom@terracestandard.com

Tumbler Ridge: Tumbler Ridge News
#120, 230 Main St., Tumbler Ridge, BC V0C 2W0
Tel: 250-242-5343; *Fax:* 250-242-5340
mail@tumblerridgenews.com
www.tumblerridgenews.com
www.facebook.com/TumblerRidgeNews
Circulation: 1,500 *Frequency:* Wednesday
Loraine Funk, Publisher
Trent Ernst, Editor
250-242-5597
editor@tumblerridgenews.com
Colette Ernst, Manager
250-242-5300
sales@tumblerridgenews.com
Roxanne Braam, Contact, Classifieds
250-242-5343
frontdesk@tumblerridgenews.com

Ucluelet: Tofino-Ucluelet Westerly News
Owned By: Glacier Newspapers Group
PO Box 317, #1, 1920 Lyche Rd., Ucluelet, BC V0R 3A0
Tel: 250-726-7029; *Fax:* 250-726-4282
office@westerlynews.ca
www.westerlynews.ca
Other information: Classifieds, Email: classifieds@van.net
twitter.com/WesterlyNews
Circulation: 987 *Frequency:* Thursday
Hugh Nicholson, Publisher
250-729-4257
hnicholson@glaciermedia.ca
Jacqueline Carmichael, Editor

Valemount: The Valley Sentinel
Owned By: Aberdeen Publishig Group
PO Box 688, 1012 Commercial Dr., Valemount, BC V0E 2Z0
Tel: 250-566-4425; *Fax:* 250-566-4528
Toll-Free: 800-226-2129
ads@thevalleysentinel.com
www.thevalleysentinel.com
www.linkedin.com/company/the-valley-sentinel
twitter.com/ValleySentinel
www.facebook.com/valleysentinelnewspaper
Circulation: 690 *Frequency:* Wednesday
The Valley Sentinel Robson Valley communities, including
Valemount & McBride.
Kelly Hall, Publisher
publisher@thevalleysentinel.com
Daniel Betts, Editor
editor@thevalleysentinel.com

Vancouver: Apna Roots
PO Box 2296, Vancouver, BC V6B 3W5
Tel: 604-599-5408; *Fax:* 604-599-5415
indo@telus.net
www.apnaroots.com
Circulation: 15,000 *Frequency:* Fri., bi-weekly
Published for an Indo-Canadian/South Asian audience; covers
developments in Science & Technology, Education & Careers,
Health & Fitness, Parenting, & Beauty & Lifestyle. Also features
editorials that discuss serious issues confronting ethnic
communities, e.g. terrorism, the role of women, gangs, drug
problems, etc.
Rue Hayer Bains, Publisher

Vancouver: Country Life in BC
1120 East 13th Ave., Vancouver, BC V5T 2M1
Tel: 250-871-0001; *Fax:* 250-871-0003
countrylifeinbc@shaw.ca
www.countrylifeinbc.com
Frequency: Monthly
Country Life in BC provides agricultural news for farmers in
British Columbia.
Peter Wilding, Publisher & Editor
604-871-0001; Fax: 604-871-0003
David Schmidt, Associate Editor
604-793-9193
davidschmidt@shaw.ca
Cathy Glover, Contact
604-328-3814; Fax: 604-946-5919
cathyglover@telus.net

Vancouver: L'Express du Pacifique
#227A, 1555, 7e av ouest, Vancouver, BC V6J 1S1
Tél: 604-736-3734; *Téléc:* 604-736-3740
administration@lexpress.org
www.lexpress.org
Tirage: 1 800 *Fréquence:* Lundi; aux deux semaines
Stéphanie Descôteaux
Raphael Perdrau, directeur de la publication
Cécil Lepage, journaliste

Vancouver: Indo-Canadian Times
PO Box 2296, Vancouver, BC V6B 3W5
Tel: 604-599-5408; *Fax:* 604-599-5415
indo@telus.net
blogs.vancouversun.com/tag/indo-canadian-times
Circulation: 32,000 *Frequency:* Wed.
Oldest and largest circulating Punjabi newspaper in Canada
Rupinder Hayer, Publisher

Vancouver: Jewish Independent
Previous Name: Jewish Western Bulletin
#99, 291 East 2nd Ave., Vancouver, BC V5T 1B8
Tel: 604-689-1520
editor@jewishindependent.ca
jewishindependent.ca
twitter.com/jiviews
www.facebook.com/JewishIndie
Circulation: 5,000 *Frequency:* Weekly
Cynthia Ramsay, Publisher
cramsay@jewishindependent.ca
Basya Laye, Editor
editor@jewishindependent.ca
Leanne Jacobsen, Contact, Advertising
sales@jewishindependent.ca
Steve Freedman, Contact, Classified Advertising
sfreedman@jewishindependent.ca

Vancouver: The Vancouver Courier
Owned By: Glacier Newspapers Group
1574 West 6th Ave., Vancouver, BC V6J 1R2
Tel: 604-738-1411
delivery@vancourier.com
www.vancourier.com
twitter.com/VanCourierNews
www.facebook.com/TheVancouverCourierNew spaper
Circulation: 123,092 *Frequency:* Wednesday, Friday
Dee Dhaliwal, Publisher
604-630-3521
ddhaliwal@vancourier.com
Barry Link, Editor
blink@vancourier.com
Tara Lalanne, Director
tlalanne@vancourier.com

Vancouver: Westside Revue
1736A East 33rd Ave., Vancouver, BC V5N 3E2
Tel: 604-327-1665
Circulation: 7,600 *Frequency:* Bi-weekly
Rod Raglin, Publisher & Editor

Vanderhoof: Omineca Express
Owned By: Black Press Group Ltd.
PO Box 1007, 150 Columbia St. West, Vanderhoof, BC V0J 3A0
Tel: 250-567-9258; *Fax:* 250-567-2070
newsroom@ominecaexpress.com
www.ominecaexpress.com
twitter.com/vanderhoofnews
www.facebook.com/VanderhoofOminecaExpress
Circulation: 890 *Frequency:* Wednesday
The newspaper serves the British Columbia communities of
Vanderhoof, Fraser Lake, & Fort Fraser.
Pam Berger, Publisher & Manager, Sales
publisher@ominecaexpress.com
Sam Redding, Editor
newsroom@ominecaexpress.com
Wendy Haslam, Contact, Production Department
wendy@ominecaexpress.com
Anne Stevens, Contact, Front Office, Circulation Sales &
Classified Sales
office@ominecaexpress.com

Vernon: The Morning Star
Owned By: Black Press Group Ltd.
4407 - 25th Ave., Vernon, BC V1T 1P5
Tel: 250-545-3322
newsroom@vernonmorningstar.com
www.vernonmorningstar.com
twitter.com/vernonnews
www.facebook.com/vernonmorningstar
Circulation: 30,000+ *Frequency:* Sunday, Wednesday, Friday
News is covered in the North Okanagan communities of Vernon,
Oyama, Cherryville, Lavington, Coldstream, Silver Star,
Armstrong, Falkland Lumby, Enderby, North Westside, Grindrod,
Kingfisher, Ashton Creek, Mabel Lake, the Okanagan Indian
Band, Spallumcheen, & the Splatsin First Nation.
Ian Jensen, Publisher
250-550-7906
publisher@vernonmorningstar.com
Glenn Mitchell, Managing Editor & Columnist
250-550-7920
glenn@vernonmorningstar.com
Kristin Froneman, Entertainment Editor & Columnist
250-550-7923
entertainment@vernonmorningstar.com
Roger Knox, Web Editor & Columnist
250-550-7922
roger@vernonmorningstar.com
Kevin Mitchell, Sports Editor
250-550-7902
sports@vernonmorningstar.com
Tammy Stelmachowich, Circulation Manager
250-550-7901
circulation@vernonmorningstar.com
Carol Williment, Classified Manager
250-550-7900
classifieds@vernonmorningstar.com
Lisa VanderVelde, Reporter & Photographer
250-550-7909
lisa@vernonmorningstar.comtar.com

Victoria: Lookout
c/o CFB Esquimalt, PO Box 17000 Forces, 1522 Esquimalt Rd., Victoria, BC V9A 7N2
Tel: 250-363-3127; *Fax:* 250-363-3015
frontoffice@lookoutnewspaper.com
www.lookoutnewspaper.com
twitter.com/Lookout_news
www.facebook.com/lookout.newspaper

Frequency: Monday
The newspaper contains news & information about the Canadian Navy.
Melissa Atkinson, Publisher
melissa.atkinson@forces.gc.ca
Shawn O'Hara, Writer
250-363-3672
shawn.ohara3@forces.gc.ca
Raquel Tirado, Supervisor, Office Accounts
raquel.tirado@forces.gc.ca
Ivan Groth, Sales Representative
sales@lookoutnewspaper.com

Victoria: **Oak Bay News**
Previous Name: Oak Bay Star
Owned By: Black Press Group Ltd.
818 Broughton St., Victoria, BC V8W 1E4
Tel: 250-381-3484
www.oakbaynews.com
twitter.com/oakbaynews
www.facebook.com/OakBayNews
Circulation: 6304 *Frequency:* Wednesday, Friday
Laura Lavin, Editor
editor@oakbaynews.com

Victoria: **Saanich News**
Owned By: Black Press News Group Ltd.
818 Broughton St., Victoria, BC V8W 1E4
Tel: 250-381-3484
www.vicnews.com
twitter.com/saanichnews
www.facebook.com/saanichnews
Circulation: 30,000+ *Frequency:* Wednesday & Friday, Weekly
News is featured from the Vancouver Island municipality of Saanich. A print & an e-edition are available. Formerly Saanich News.
Penny Sakamoto, Publisher
250-480-3204
publisher@saanichnews.com
Edward Hill, Editor
250-480-3238
editor@saanichnews.com
Oliver Sommer, Contact, Advertising
250-480-3274
osommer@saanichnews.com

Victoria: **Victoria News**
Owned By: Black Press Group Ltd.
818 Broughton St., Victoria, BC V8W 1E4
Tel: 250-386-3484
editor@vicnews.com
www.vicnews.com
twitter.com/victorianews
www.facebook.com/victorianews
News is provided about Victoria & Equimalt, British Columbia. An e-edition is available.
Penny Sakamoto, Publisher
psakamoto@blackpress.ca
Don Descoteau, Editor
editor@vicnews.com
Bruce Hogarth, Director, Circulation
distribution@vicnews.com
Oliver Sommer, Director, Sales
osommer@blackpress.ca

Williams Lake: **The Cariboo Advisor**
Owned By: Black Press Group Ltd.
68 North Broadway Ave., Williams Lake, BC V2G 1C1
Tel: 250-398-5516
wltribune.com
www.facebook.com/284148154946870
Circulation: 10,200 *Frequency:* Fri.
Amalgamated with the Williams Lake Tribune (Wed., weekly) in 2013
Kathy McLean, Publisher
Rob DeMone, Editor

Williams Lake: **Williams Lake Tribune**
Owned By: Black Press Group Ltd.
188 North 1st Ave., Williams Lake, BC V2G 1Y8
Tel: 250-392-2331
editor@wltribune.com
www.wltribune.com
twitter.com/williamslnews
www.facebook.com/WLTribune
Circulation: 7,200 *Frequency:* Wednesday
The Williams Lake Tribune employs 45 full & part-time people.
Lisa Bowering, Publisher & Manager, Advertising
publisher@wltribune.com
Angie Mindus, Acting Editor
editor@wltribune.com

Gaeil Farrar, Community Editor
community@wltribune.com
Lynn Bolt, Contact, Classifieds
classifieds@wltribune.com

Manitoba

Daily Newspapers in Manitoba

Brandon: **Brandon Sun**
Owned By: FP Newspapers Inc.
501 Rosser Ave., Brandon, MB R7A 0K4
Tel: 204-727-2451
circ@brandonsun.com
www.brandonsun.com
Other information: Classified Advertising, Phone: 204-571-7400
www.linkedin.com/company/brandon-sun
twitter.com/thebrandonsun
www.fac ebook.com/thebrandonsun
Frequency: Monday-Saturday
Jim Mihaly, Publisher
jmihaly@brandonsun.com

Flin Flon: **The Reminder**
Owned By: Glacier Media Inc.
14 North Ave., Flin Flon, MB R8A 0T2
Tel: 204-687-3454; *Fax:* 204-687-4473
ads@thereminder.ca
www.thereminder.ca
www.facebook.com/FlinFlonReminder
Circulation: 1,450 *Frequency:* Wednesday
Communities served by The Reminder include Flin Flon, Denare Beach, Snow Lake, Creighton & Cranberry Portage, Manitoba.
Nancy Johnson, Publisher
publisher@thereminder.ca

Winnipeg: **Winnipeg Free Press**
Owned By: FP Newspapers Inc.
1355 Mountain Ave., Winnipeg, MB R2X 3B6
Tel: 204-697-7000 *Toll-Free:* 800-542-8900
city.desk@freepress.mb.ca
www.winnipegfreepress.com
www.youtube.com/user/WinnipegFreePress
twitter.com/WinnipegNews
www .facebook.com/winnipegfreepress
Circulation: 141,000 M-F; 225,000 Sa *Frequency:*
Monday-Saturday
Bob Cox, Publisher
204-697-7547
bob.cox@freepress.mb.ca
Paul Samyn, Editor
204-697-7295
paul.samyn@freepress.mb.ca

Winnipeg: **The Winnipeg Sun**
Owned By: Postmedia Network Inc.
1700 Church Ave., Winnipeg, MB R2X 3A2
Tel: 204-632-2780 *Toll-Free:* 800-921-9294
winnipegsun.com
twitter.com/WinnipegSun
www.facebook.com/wpgsun
Frequency: Daily
Mark Hamm, Editor
mark.hamm@sunmedia.ca

Other Newspapers in Manitoba

Altona: **The Red River Valley Echo**
Owned By: Postmedia Network Inc.
PO Box 700, Altona, MB R0G 0B0
Tel: 204-324-5001; *Fax:* 204-324-1402
www.altonaecho.com
twitter.com/AltonaEcho
www.facebook.com/RedRiverValleyEcho
Circulation: 4,500 *Frequency:* Thursday
Darcie Morris, Publisher
darcie.morris@sunmedia.ca
Don Radford, Regional Managing Editor
winkler.news@sunmedia.ca
Greg Vandermeulen, City Editor
altona.news@sunmedia.ca

Baldur: **Baldur-Glenboro Gazette**
Previous Name: Baldur Gazette; Baldur Gazette News
PO Box 280, 223 Elizabeth Ave., Baldur, MB R0K 0B0
Tel: 204-535-2127; *Fax:* 204-535-2350
gazette@mts.net
www.baldur-glenborogazette.ca
Other information: Glenboro Office, Phone: 204-827-2343, Email: gazette2@mts.net
Circulation: 1,500 *Frequency:* Tuesday
The Baldur Gazette News amalgamated with the Glenboro Gazette in 2003 to create the Baldur-Glenboro Gazette. The

newspaper serves the southwestern Manitoba communities of Baldur, Glenboro, Belmont, Glenora, Cypress River, Stockton, Ninette, Wawanesa, & Treesbank.
Mike Johnson, Co-Publisher & Editor
Travis Johnson, Co-Publisher & Assistant Editor

Beausejour: **The Clipper Weekly**
Owned By: Clipper Publishing Corp.
PO Box 2033, 27A - 3rd St. South, Beausejour, MB R0E 0C0
Tel: 204-268-4700; *Fax:* 204-268-3858
mail@clipper.mb.ca
www.clipper.mb.ca
www.facebook.com/clipperweekly
Circulation: 12,000+ *Frequency:* Thurs.
Community news is provided to the North Eastman Region of Manitoba, including the communities of Beausejour, Dugald, Tyndall, Whitemouth, Oakbank, Anola, Garson, & Lac du Bonnet. Readership stands at 83%.
Kim MacAulay, Publisher
macaulay@clipper.mb.ca
Mark T. Buss, Editor
news@clipper.mb.ca
Jennifer Kuhn, Manager, Office
Traci Klimchuk, Contact, Display Advertising
traci@clipper.mb.ca

Boissevain: **Boissevain Recorder**
Boissevain Recorder Inc., PO Box 220, 425 South Railway St., Boissevain, MB R0K 0E0
Tel: 204-534-6479; *Fax:* 204-534-2977
news@therecorder.ca
www.therecorder.ca
Other information: Classifieds, Email: classifieds@therecorder.ca
Circulation: 1,200 *Frequency:* Friday
Lorraine Houston, Editor
editor@therecorder.ca
Paul Rayner, Reporter
prayner@therecorder.ca
Julie Watt, Contact, Circulation & Accounts
mail@therecorder.ca
Christie Paskewitz-Smith, Contact, Advertising & Printing
ads@therecorder.ca

Brandon: **Westman Journal**
Previous Name: Wheat City Journal
Owned By: Glacier Newspapers Group
315 College Ave., #D, Brandon, MB R7A 1E7
Tel: 204-725-0209; *Fax:* 204-725-3021
info@wheatcityjournal.ca
www.westmanjournal.com
twitter.com/ChrisTataryn
www.facebook.com/222064044474022
Circulation: 15,000 *Frequency:* Wed.
Todd Hamilton, Editor
newsroom@wheatcityjournal.ca
Lorraine Dillabough, Manager, Production
ldillabough@wheatcityjournal.ca

Carberry: **The Carberry News-Express**
Owned By: FP Newspapers Inc.
Carberry News-Express Ltd., 34 Main St., Carberry, MB R0K 0H0
Tel: 204-834-2153; *Fax:* 204-834-2714
info@carberrynews.ca
www.carberrynews.ca
Circulation: 930 *Frequency:* Weekly; Monday
Kathy Carr, General Manager
kathy@carberrynews.ca

Carman: **The Valley Leader**
Owned By: Postmedia Network Inc.
70 Main St., Carman, MB R0G 0J0
Tel: 204-745-2051; *Fax:* 204-745-3976
www.carmanvalleyleader.com
Circulation: 5,852 *Frequency:* Friday
Darcie Morris, Publisher
darcie.morris@suntimes.ca
Don Radford, Regional Managing Editor
winkler.news@suntimes.ca
Gene Still, City Editor
carmanvl.news@suntimes.ca

Cartwright: **Southern Manitoba Review**
PO Box 249, Cartwright, MB R0K 0L0
Tel: 204-529-2342; *Fax:* 204-529-2029
cartnews@mts.net
www.southernmanitobareview.com
Circulation: 785 *Frequency:* Thursday
Vicky M. Wallace, Publisher

Darlingford: The Southern Shopper & Review
RR#2, Darlingford, MB R0G 0L0
Tel: 204-362-2666; *Fax:* 204-246-2018
southernshopper@mts.net
www.southernshopperonline.ca

Frequency: Bi-weekly
The Southern Shopper & Review serves communities in southern Manitoba.

Dauphin: The Dauphin Herald
Previous Name: The Weekly News; The Spectator; Dauphin Herald & Press
Owned By: Gilroy Publishing
PO Box 548, 120 - 1st Ave. NE, Dauphin, MB R7N 1A5
Tel: 204-638-4420; *Fax:* 204-638-8760
dherald@mts.net
www.dauphinherald.com

Circulation: 4,143 *Frequency:* Tuesday
Shawn Bailey, Editor
shawn@dauphinherald.com
Mandy Carberry, Manager, Circulation & Distribution
circ@dauphinherald.com
Bob Gilroy, Manager, Print Shop
bob@dauphinherald.com
Brent Wright, Manager, Advertising
displayads@dauphinherald.com
Samantha Gallaway-Boulbria, Contact, Classified Advertising
classifieds@dauphinherald.com

Deloraine: Deloraine Times & Star
Owned By: Glacier Newspaper Group
PO Box 407, 122 Broadway St. North, Deloraine, MB R0M 0M0
Tel: 204-747-2249; *Fax:* 204-747-3999
Circulation: 746 *Frequency:* Friday
Judy Wells, Publisher
cpocket@mts.net
Marlene Tibury, Contact, Sales
204-522-3491
ads.cpocket@mts.net

Emerson: The Southeast Journal
PO Box 68, 104 1/2 Dominion St., Emerson, MB R0A 0L0
Tel: 204-373-2493; *Fax:* 204-373-2084
sej@mts.net
www.southeastjournal.ca

Circulation: 3,390 *Frequency:* Sat.
News is covered in the Manitoba communities of Emerson, Morris, Dominion City, Tolstoi, Woodmore, Riverside/Rosenort, & Ridgeville.
Brenda Piett, Co-Publisher & Contact, Sales & Circulation
Don Piett, Co-Publisher & Editor

Grandview: Grandview Exponent
Owned By: Chaloner Publishers
PO Box 39, Grandview, MB R0L 0Y0
Tel: 204-546-2555; *Fax:* 204-546-3081
expos@mts.net
www.grandviewexponent.com

Circulation: 1,000 *Frequency:* Tuesday
Clayton Chaloner, Publisher & Editor

Killarney: The Guide
Struth Publishing Ltd., PO Box 670, 336 Park St. East, Killarney, MB R0K 1G0
Tel: 204-523-4611; *Fax:* 204-523-4445
info@killarneyguide.ca
www.killarneyguide.ca

Circulation: 1,655 *Frequency:* Friday
The newspaper is available in print & online.
Jay Struth, Editor
news@killarneyguide.ca
Curt Struth, Manager, Printing & Advertising
printing@killarneyguide.ca

Manitou: Manitou Western Canadian
Owned By: BKS Publishing Ltd.
PO Box 190, 424 Ellis Ave. East, Manitou, MB R0G 1G0
Tel: 204-242-2555; *Fax:* 204-242-3137
westerncanadian@goinet.ca

Circulation: 1,245 *Frequency:* Tuesday
Grant Howatt, Publisher

Melita: Corner Pocket
Owned By: Glacier Media Inc.
PO Box 820, 128 Main St., Melita, MB R0M 1L0
Tel: 204-522-3491; *Fax:* 204-522-3648
cpocket@mts.net
www.glaciermedia.ca/advertisers/local-newspapers/corner-pocket

Circulation: 20,000 *Frequency:* Monthly
Sent to households in Southwestern Manitoba & Southeastern Saskatchewan.

Melita: Melita New Era
Owned By: Glacier Newspaper Group
PO Box 820, 128 Main St. South, Melita, MB R0M 1L0
Tel: 204-522-3491; *Fax:* 204-522-3648
Circulation: 1,104 *Frequency:* Friday
The newspaper serves southwestern Manitoba & southeastern Saskatchewan.
G. Longmuir, Manager
cpocket@mts.net
Marlene Tilbury, Contact, Sales
ads.cpocket@mts.net

Minnedosa: Minnedosa Tribune
PO Box 930, 14 - 3rd Ave. SW, Minnedosa, MB R0J 1E0
Tel: 204-867-3816; *Fax:* 204-867-5171
www.minnedosatribune.com

Circulation: 2,480 *Frequency:* Friday
Darryl Holyk, Publisher & Editor
editor@minnedosatribune.com
Gloria Kerluke, Office Manager & Contact, Classifieds
class@minnedosatribune.com
Jennifer Page, Reporter & Photographer
reporter@minnedosatribune.com
Nathalie Loughlin, Contact, Graphic Design & Ad Sales
adsales@minnedosatribune.com

Morden: The Morden Times
Owned By: Postmedia Network Inc.
104 - 8th St., Morden, MB R6M 1Y7
Tel: 204-822-4421; *Fax:* 204-822-4079
www.mordentimes.com
twitter.com/MordenTimes
www.facebook.com/mordentimes

Circulation: 5,600 *Frequency:* Thursday
Jack Neufeld, Publisher & Advertising Director
jack.neufeld@sunmedia.ca
Lorne Stelmach, City Editor
mordentimes.new@sunmedia.ca

Neepawa: Neepawa Banner
Owned By: 3259545 (Manitoba) Ltd.
PO Box 699, 243 Hamilton St., Neepawa, MB R0J 1H0
Tel: 204-476-3401; *Fax:* 204-476-5073
Toll-Free: 888-436-4242
www.neepawabanner.com
www.youtube.com/TheNeepawaBanner
twitter.com/NeepawaBanner
www.facebook.com/neepawabanner

Circulation: 8,228 *Frequency:* Friday
Ken Waddell, Owner, Publisher, & Contact, Sales
kwaddell@neepawabanner.com
Kate Jackman-Atkinson, Reporter & Photographer
news@neepawabanner.com
Kay De'Ath, Contact, Accounts & Circulation
accounts@neepawabanner.com
Lanny Stewart, Contact, Sports
sports@neepawabanner.com
Sandra Unger, Contact, Front Desk
print@neepawabanner.com

Neepawa: Neepawa Press
Owned By: Glacier Newspaper Group
PO Box 939, 423 Mountain Ave., Neepawa, MB R0J 1H0
Tel: 204-476-2309; *Fax:* 204-476-5802
office@neepawapress.com
www.neepawapress.com
Other information: Classified Advertising, Email: classified@neepawapress.com

Circulation: 7,200 *Frequency:* Wednesday
Brent Fitzpatrick, Regional Publisher
pub@sasktel.net
Darren Graham, General Manager
advertising@neepawapress.com
Jean Seaborn, Manager, Office
office@neepawapress.com

Pilot Mound: The Sentinel Courier
PO Box 179, 13 Railway St. South, Pilot Mound, MB R0G 1P0
Tel: 204-825-2772; *Fax:* 204-825-2439
sentinel@sentinelcourier.com
www.sentinelcourier.com

Circulation: 1,100 *Frequency:* Tuesday
The Sentinel Courier serves the Manitoba communities of Pilot Mound, Clearwater, Mariapolis, La Riviere, & Crystal City.
Susan Peterson, Publisher

Portage la Prairie: Central Manitoba Shopper & News
1943 Saskatchewan Ave. West, Portage la Prairie, MB R1N 0R7
Tel: 204-857-7582; *Fax:* 204-239-5437
cmshopper@shawcable.com

Frequency: Weekly

Reston: Reston Recorder
Owned By: Glacier Newspaper Group
PO Box 10, 330 - 4th St., Reston, MB R0M 1X0
Tel: 204-877-3321; *Fax:* 204-522-3648
Circulation: 570 *Frequency:* Friday
Dolores Caldwell, Manager
cpocket@mts.net
Donna Anderson, Contact, Sales
ads.cpocket@mts.net

Rivers: Gilroy Publishing
526 - 2nd Ave., Rivers, MB R0K 1X0
Tel: 204-328-7494

Rivers: Rivers Banner
Owned By: 3259545 (Manitoba) Ltd.
PO Box 70, Rivers, MB R0K 1X0
Tel: 204-328-7494; *Fax:* 204-328-5212
info@riversbanner.com
www.riversbanner.com
www.youtube.com/TheNeepawaBanner

Circulation: 1,683 *Frequency:* Weekly; Friday
Ken Waddell, Owner & Publisher

Rivers: 3259545 (Manitoba) Ltd.
526 - 2nd Ave., Rivers, MB R0K 1X0
Tel: 204-328-7494

Roblin: The Roblin Review
Owned By: Gilroy Publishing
PO Box 938, 119 - 1st Ave., Roblin, MB R0L 1P0
Tel: 204-937-8377; *Fax:* 204-937-8212
www.theroblinreview.com

Circulation: 1,635 *Frequency:* Tuesday
Robert Gilroy, Publisher
Brent Wright, General Manager
Ed Doering, Editor

Russell: Russell Banner
Owned By: Gilroy Publishing
PO Box 100, 455 Main St. North, Russell, MB R0J 1W0
Tel: 204-773-2069; *Fax:* 204-773-2645
www.russellbanner.com

Circulation: 1,411 *Frequency:* Tuesday
Terrie Welwood, Editor & Reporter
rbeditor@mts.net
Jessica Shaw, Contact, Advertising
rbanner@mts.net
Jenna Simard, Contact, Subscriptions & Accounts
russellbanner@mts.net

Selkirk: The Selkirk Journal
Owned By: Postmedia Network Inc.
PO Box 352, 510 Greenwood Ave., Selkirk, MB R1A 2B3
Tel: 204-467-2421; *Fax:* 204-482-3336
www.selkirkjournal.com
twitter.com/SelkirkJournal

Circulation: 15,700 *Frequency:* Thursday
Jenifer Bilsky, Publisher
jenifer.bilsky@sunmedia.ca
Glen Hallick, Group Editor
glen.hallick@sunmedia.ca
Amanda Lefley, City Editor
amanda.lefley@sunmedia.ca

Shilo: Shilo Stag
PO Box 5000 Main, CFB Shilo, Shilo, MB R0K 2A0
Tel: 204-765-3000; *Fax:* 204-765-3814
stag@mymts.net
www.cfcommunitygeteway.ca
Other information: Phone Ext.3093
www.facebook.com/ShiloSTAG

Circulation: 3,000 *Frequency:* Bi-weekly; Thursday
The Canadian Forces newspaper serves the military & civilian communities of CFB Shilo, Wawanesa, Sprucewoods, Cottonwoods, & Douglas.
Jules Xavier, Managing Editor
204-765-3000; Fax: 204-765-3814
jules.xavier@forces.gc.ca
Jillian Driessen, Reporter & Photographer, Editorial
204-365-3000; Fax: 204-765-3814
jillian.driessen@forces.gc.ca

Shoal Lake: Crossroads This Week
Previous Name: Birtle Eye-Witness
Owned By: Nesbitt Publishing Ltd.
PO Box 160, 353 Station Rd., Shoal Lake, MB R0J 1Z0
Tel: 204-759-2644; *Fax:* 204-759-2521
ctwnews@mts.net
www.crossroadsthisweek.com

Circulation: 2,525 *Frequency:* Weekly; Friday

Greg Nesbitt, Publisher
ctwnews@mts.net

Souris: Souris Plaindealer
Owned By: Glacier Media Inc.
PO Box 488, 35 Crescent Ave. West, Souris, MB R0K 2C0
Tel: 204-483-2070; Fax: 204-483-3866
Circulation: 789 Frequency: Friday
Darci Semeschuk, Manager
204-483-2070
cpocket@mts.net
Marlene Tilbury, Contact, Sales
204-522-3491
ads.cpocket@mts.net

St-Boniface: La Liberté
Owned By: Presse Ouest Ltée.
PO Box 190, #105, 420, rue des Meurons, St-Boniface, MB R2H 3B4
Tel: 204-237-4823; Fax: 204-231-1998
Toll-Free: 800-523-3355
la-liberte@la-liberte.mb.ca
www.la-liberte.mb.ca/le-journal
www.youtube.com/user/LaLiberteMB
twitter.com/LaLiberteMB
www.facebook.com/LaLiberteManitoba
Circulation: 5000 Frequency: Weekly
La Liberté is a French language newspaper.
Sophie Gaulin, Editor
la-liberte@la-liberte.mb.ca
Lysiane Romain, Assistant Editor & Coordinator, Special Projects
promotions@la-liberte.mb.ca
Véronique Togneri, Production Manager & Graphics Specialist

Steinbach: The Carillon
377 Main St., Steinbach, MB R5G 1A5
Tel: 204-326-3421; Fax: 204-326-4860
info@thecarillon.com
www.thecarillon.com
Other information: Advertising, Email: ads@thecarillon.com
www.facebook.com/thecarillon
Circulation: 6,000 Frequency: Thursday
The Carillon serves Steinbach southeastern Manitoba. Derksen Printers & Publishers publishes the newspaper.
Glenn Buffie, Publisher & General Manager
gbuffie@thecarillon.com
Grant Burr, Editor
gburr@thecarillon.com
Terry Frey, Editor, Sports
tfrey@thecarillon.com
Carol Martens, Editor, Community News
cmartens@thecarillon.com
Kelsey Wynn, Manager, Circulation
kwynn@thecarillon.com

Stonewall: The Interlake Spectator
Owned By: Postmedia Network Inc.
PO Box 190, #3, 411 - 3rd Ave., Stonewall, MB R0C 2Z0
Tel: 204-642-2421
www.interlakespectator.com
Circulation: 14,341 Frequency: Friday
Jenifer Bilsky, Publisher
jenifer.bilsky@sunmedia.ca
Glen Hallick, Group Editor
glen.halick@sunmedia.ca

Swan River: The Swan Valley Star & Times
Owned By: Gilroy Publishing
PO Box 670, 704 Main St., Swan River, MB R0L 1Z0
Tel: 204-734-3858; Fax: 204-734-4935
info@starandtimes.ca
www.starandtimes.ca
Circulation: 2,985 Frequency: Tuesday
Brian Gilroy, Publisher & General Manager
brian@starandtimes.ca
Danielle Gordon-Broome, Editor
editor@starandtimes.ca
Tara Grey, Reporter & Photographer
reporter@starandtimes.ca
Kelley Hagglund, Contact, Classified Advertising
classifieds@starandtimes.ca

The Pas: Opasquia Times
Owned By: Gilroy Publishing
PO Box 750, 148 Fischer Ave., The Pas, MB R9A 1K8
Tel: 204-623-3435; Fax: 204-623-5601
opads@mts.net
www.opasquiatimes.com
Circulation: 2,609 Frequency: Biweekly; Wednesday, Friday
Opasquia Times presents news & information from the Opaskwayak Cree Nation, The Pas, the Rural Municipality of Kelsey, & the surrounding region.

Jennifer Cook, General Manager
optimes@mts.net
Trent Allen, Editor
opeditor@mts.net

Thompson: Nickel Belt News
Owned By: Glacier Media Inc.
PO Box 887, 141 Commercial Pl., Thompson, MB R8N 1N8
Tel: 204-677-4534
Circulation: 7,000 Frequency: Friday
The Nickel Belt News is a free publication that circulates in Thompson & throughout northern Manitoba.
Brent Fitzpatrick, Publisher
Lynn Taylor, General Manager
generalmanager@thompsoncitizen.net
John Barker, Editor
editor@thompsoncitizen.net

Thompson: Thompson Citizen
Owned By: Glacier Media Inc.
PO Box 887, 141 Commercial Pl., Thompson, MB R8N 1N8
Tel: 204-677-4534; Fax: 204-677-3681
ads@thompsoncitizen.net
www.thompsoncitizen.net
twitter.com/ThompsonCitizen
Circulation: 4,500 Frequency: Wednesday
Brent Fitzpatrick, Regional Publisher
pub@sasktel.net
Lynn Taylor, General Manager
generalmanager@thompsoncitizen.net
John Barker, Editor
editor@thompsoncitizen.net
Ryan Lynds, Manager, Production
production@thompsoncitizen.net
Ian Graham, Contact, Sports
sports@thompsoncitizen.net
Ashley Rust-McIvor, Contact, Classified Advertising
classified@thompsoncitizen.net

Treherne: The Times
PO Box 50, 194 Broadway St., Treherne, MB R0G 2V0
Tel: 204-723-2542; Fax: 204-723-2754
trehernetimes@mts.net
www.trehernetimes.ca
Circulation: 2500 Frequency: Monday
The Times circulates in the Manitoba rural municipalities of South Norfolk, Victoria, Lorne, & Grey. The newspaper is available in print & online.
Daxley Lodwick, Editor

Virden: Virden Empire-Advance
Owned By: Glacier Media Inc.
PO Box 250, #4, 585 Seventh Ave. South, Virden, MB R0M 2C0
Tel: 204-748-3931; Fax: 204-748-1816
www.empireadvance.ca
Circulation: 2,158 Frequency: Weekly; Friday
The newspaper serves the southwestern Manitoba communities of Virden, Elkhorn, Oak Lake, Reston, Pipestone, Miniota, Kenton, & Lenore.
Cheryl Rushing, General Manager
manager@empireadvance.ca

Winnipeg: Headingley Headliner
1355 Mountain Ave., Winnipeg, MB R2X 3B6
Tel: 204-697-7009; Fax: 204-953-4300
www.winnipegfreepress.com/our-communities/headliner
Circulation: 5,500 Frequency: Friday
Michelle Pereira, Publisher
John Kendle, Editor

Winnipeg: The Herald
Owned By: FP Newspapers Inc.
1355 Mountain Ave., Winnipeg, MB R2X 3B6
Tel: 204-697-7009; Fax: 204-953-4300
classifieds@canstarnews.com
www.winnipegfreepress.com/our-communities/he rald
twitter.com/HeraldWPG
www.facebook.com/TheHeraldWpg
Circulation: 44,300 Frequency: Wednesday
Laurie Finley, Vice President, Sales & Marketing
204-697-7044
John Kendle, Managing Editor
204-697-7093

Winnipeg: The Jewish Post & News
#11, 395 Berry St., Winnipeg, MB R3J 1N6
Tel: 204-694-3332; Fax: 204-694-3916
jewishp@mymts.net
www.jewishpostandnews.ca
www.youtube.com/user/JewishPostWpg
twitter.com/JewishPostWpg
www.faceb ook.com/TheJewishPost

Circulation: 2,779 Frequency: Weekly
The newspaper features local news & news from Israel, as well as features & opinions of interest to the Jewish community.
Bernie Bellan, Publisher
Matt Bellan, Publisher & Editor

Winnipeg: The Lance
Owned By: FP Newspapers Inc.
1355 Mountain Ave., Winnipeg, MB R2X 3B6
Tel: 204-697-7009; Fax: 204-953-4300
www.winnipegfreepress.com/our-communities/lance
twitter.com/lanceWPG
www.facebook.com/TheLanceWpg
Circulation: 38,000 Frequency: Wed.
Laura Finley, Vice President, Sales & Marketing
laurie.finley@winnipegfreepress.com
John Kendle, Editor
john.kendle@canstarnews.com

Winnipeg: The Metro
Owned By: FP Newspapers Inc.
1355 Mountain Ave., Winnipeg, MB R2X 3B6
Tel: 204-697-7009; Fax: 204-953-4300
www.winnipegfreepress.com/our-communities/metro
twitter.com/metroWPG
www.facebook.com/TheMetroWPG
Circulation: 35,500 Frequency: Wed.
Laurie Finley, Vice President, Sales & Marketing
laurie.finley@winnipegfreepress.com
John Kendle, Managing Editor
204-697-7093
john.kendle@canstarnews.com

Winnipeg: The Times
Owned By: FP Newspapers Inc.
1355 Mountain Ave., Winnipeg, MB R2X 3B6
Tel: 204-697-7009; Fax: 204-953-4300
www.winnipegfreepress.com/our-communities/times
twitter.com/timesWPG
www.facebook.com/TheTimesWpg
Circulation: 37,400 Frequency: Wednesday
Laurie Finley, Vice President, Sales & Marketing
204-697-7164
laurie.finley@winnipegfreepress.com
John Kendle, Managing Editor
204-697-7093
john.kendle@canstarnews.com

Winnipeg: The Voxair
PO Box 17000 Forces, #105, Bldg. 63, 17 Wing Winnipeg, Winnipeg, MB R3J 3Y5
Tel: 204-833-2500; Fax: 204-833-2809
voxair@mymts.net
www.thevoxair.ca
Other information: Accounting: accountsvoxair@gmail.com
www.facebook.com/thevoxair
Frequency: Bi-weekly; Wednesday
The Voxair is a community newspaper for Royal Canadian Air Force personnel at 17 Wing Winnipeg.
Michael Sherby, Voxair Manager
Michael.Sherby@forces.gc.ca

New Brunswick

Daily Newspapers in New Brunswick

Caraquet: L'Acadie Nouvelle
Détenteur: Acadie Média
CP 5536, 476, boul Saint-Pierre ouest, Caraquet, NB E1W 1A3
Tél: 506-727-4444; Téléc: 506-727-7620
Ligne sans frais: 800-561-2255
info@acadiemedia.com
www.acadienouvelle.com
Autre information: Bureau du Sud-Est, Téléphone: 800-561-2255, Télécopieur: 506-383-7440
www.linkedin.com/company/acadie-nouvelle
twitter.com/acadienouvelle
www.facebook.com/acadienouvelle
Tirage: 71 000 total Fréquence: lundi-samedi
Le journal L'Acadie Nouvelle est le seul quotidien francophone du Nouveau-Brunswick.
Francis Sonier, Éditeur-directeur général
francis.sonier@acadiemedia.com
Gaétan Chiasson, Directeur, Rédaction et des nouveaux médias
gaetan.chiasson@acadienouvelle.com

Fredericton: The Daily Gleaner
Owned By: Brunswick News Inc.
PO Box 3370, 984 Prospect St. West, Fredericton, NB E3B 2T8
Tel: 506-452-6671; *Fax:* 506-452-7405
Toll-Free: 800-565-9399
customerservice@brunswicknews.com
tj.news/daily-gleaner
twitter.com/dailygleaner
www.facebook.com/DailyGleaner
Circulation: 55,000 total *Frequency:* Monday-Saturday
The Daily Gleaner serves Fredericton & the surrounding region with local & international news.
Ted Rath, Managing Editor

Moncton: Times & Transcript
Previous Name: Moncton Weekly Times; Moncton Daily Transcript
Owned By: Brunswick News Inc.
PO Box 1001, 939 Main St., Moncton, NB E1C 8P3
Tel: 506-859-4905 *Toll-Free:* 800-322-3329
customerservice@brunswicknews.com
tj.news/timesandtranscript
twitter.com/TimesTranscript
www.facebook.com/TimesTranscript
Frequency: Monday-Saturday
Southeastern New Brunswick
Jessie Robichaud, Legislative Reporter
506-450-4132

Saint John: The Telegraph-Journal
Owned By: Brunswick News Inc.
PO Box 2350, 210 Crown St., Saint John, NB E2L 2X7
Tel: 506-632-8888; *Fax:* 506-633-5741
Toll-Free: 877-389-6397
customerservice@brunswicknews.com
tj.news
www.facebook.com/TelegraphJournal
Frequency: Monday-Saturday
New Brunswick's provincial newspaper

Other Newspapers in New Brunswick

Bathurst: The Northern Light
Owned By: Brunswick News Inc.
355 King Ave., Bathurst, NB E2A 1P4
Tel: 506-546-4491; *Fax:* 506-546-1491
www.telegraphjournal.com
Circulation: 3,358 *Frequency:* Tuesday
Maurice Aube, Publisher
Greg Mulock, Editor

Campbellton: The Tribune
Owned By: Brunswick News Inc.
PO Box 486, 6 Shannon St., Campbellton, NB E3N 2G6
Tel: 506-753-4413; *Fax:* 506-759-9595
www.telegraphjournal.com
Circulation: 2,700 *Frequency:* Friday
Subscriptions are available for both the print & online edition.
Peter MacIntosh, Publisher
Tim Jaques, Editor

Edmundston: Le Journal Madawaska
Détenteur: Brunswick News Inc.
20, rue St. François, Edmundston, NB E3V 1E3
Tél: 506-735-5575; *Téléc:* 506-735-8086
www.telegraphjournal.com
Tirage: 2700 *Fréquence:* Mercredi
Hermel Volpé, Publisher
Christine Theriault, Editor

Grand Falls: The Victoria Star
Owned By: Brunswick News Inc.
PO Box 7363, 229 Broadway Blvd., Grand Falls, NB E3Z 2K1
Tel: 506-473-3083
www.telegraphjournal.com
Circulation: 2,270 *Frequency:* Wednesday
The Victoria Star provides community news & information to the northwestern New Brunswick town of Grand Falls & Victoria County.
Matt Hemphill, Publisher
Mark Rickard, Editor

Grand Sault: La Cataracte
Détenteur: Brunswick News Inc.
CP 7363, 229, boul Broadway, Grand Sault, NB E3Z 2K1
Tél: 506-473-3083
Tirage: 6 300 *Fréquence:* Thursday
Jamie Irving, Publisher
Madeleine Leclerc, Editor

Hampton: Ossekeag Publishing Co. Ltd.
242 Main St., Hampton, NB E5N 6B8
Tel: 506-832-5613; *Fax:* 506-832-3353
info@ossekeag.ca
The newspaper is distributed in the Town of Hampton & the neighbouring communities of Hatfield Point, Titusville, Belleisle, Smithtown, Bloomfield, Norton, Nauwigewauk, & Bloomfield.
Debbie Hickey, President
506-832-5613
debbie@ossekeag.ca
Mike Hickey, Vice-president
506-832-5613
mike@ossekeag.ca

Hampton: The Sussex Herald
242 Main St., Hampton, NB E5N 6B8
Tel: 506-832-5613; *Fax:* 506-832-3353
Toll-Free: 888-289-2555
info@ossekeag.ca
www.facebook.com/Ossekeag
Circulation: 10,794 *Frequency:* Bi-weekly
The Sussex Herald serves Sussex, New Brunswick & the neighbouring communities of Petitcodiac, Havelock, Cambridge-Narrows, Apohaqui, & Salisbury.
Debbie Hickey, Co-Owner & Operator, Ossekeag Publishing
debbie@ossekeag.ca
Mike Hickey, Co-Owner & Operator, Ossekeag Publishing
mike@ossekeag.ca

Miramichi: Miramichi Leader
Owned By: Brunswick News Inc.
2428 King George Hwy., Miramichi, NB E1V 6V9
Tel: 506-622-2600 *Toll-Free:* 888-295-8665
www.telegraphjournal.com
Circulation: 3900 *Frequency:* Monday, Wednesday; Friday (Miramichi Weekend)
The Miramichi Leader & the Miramichi Weekend provide news for residents of New Brunswick's Miramichi Valley.
Bill MacIntosh, Publisher
Gail Savoy, Editor

Oromocto: The Post-Gazette
Owned By: Brunswick News Inc.
281 Restigouche Rd., Oromocto, NB E2V 2H5
Tel: 506-357-9813
Circulation: 12,844 *Frequency:* Thursday
The greater Fredericton area of New Brunswick is served by Oromocto's community newspaper.
Shelley Wood, Publisher
Heather Gratton, Editor

Richibucto: L'Étoile de Kent
#2, 9406, rue Principale, Richibucto, NB E4W 4E1
Tél: 506-523-6231; *Téléc:* 506-523-6520
redaction@journaletoile.com
Tirage: 100 000+ *Fréquence:* Weekly, Thursday
Mario Tardiff

Sackville: Sackville Tribune Post
Owned By: SaltWire Network
80 Main St., Sackville, NB E4L 4A7
Tel: 506-536-2500; *Fax:* 506-536-4024
www.sackvilletribunepost.com
www.facebook.com/sackvilletribunepost
Circulation: 2,250 *Frequency:* Wednesday
Scott Doherty, Editor
sdoherty@sackvilletribunepost.com

Shediac: Le Moniteur Acadien
Détenteur: Les Editions de Moniteur Acadien Inc.
CP 5191, 817 Boudreau Oest, Rt. 133, Shediac, NB E4P 8T9
Tél: 506-532-6680; *Téléc:* 506-532-6681
moniteur@rogers.com
www.moniteuracadien.com
Tirage: 5000 *Fréquence:* Mercredi
Gilles Hache, Éditeur

St Stephen: International Money Saver
57 King St., St Stephen, NB E3L 2L4
Tel: 506-466-5072; *Fax:* 506-466-9950
moneysav@nbnet.nb.ca
Circulation: 15,000 *Frequency:* Saturday

St Stephen: St. Croix Courier
Owned By: Advocate Media Inc.
PO Box 250, 47 Milltown Blvd., St Stephen, NB E3L 2X2
Tel: 506-466-3220
editor@stcroixcourier.ca
stcroixcourier.ca
twitter.com/stcroixcourier
www.facebook.com/stcroixcourier

Circulation: 3,324 Tu; 2,193 F *Frequency:* Tuesday; Friday (Courier Weekend)

Sussex: Kings County Record
Owned By: Brunswick News Inc.
593 Main St., Sussex, NB E4E 7H5
Tel: 506-433-1070; *Fax:* 506-432-3532
www.telegraphjournal.com
Frequency: Tuesday; Friday (Kings County Record Weekender)
David Kelly, Editor
Bill Ballard, Manager, Sales
ballard.william@brunswicknews.com

Woodstock: Bugle-Observer
Previous Name: The Bugle; The Observer
Owned By: Brunswick News Inc.
110 Carleton St., Woodstock, NB E7M 1E4
Tel: 506-328-8863
www.telegraphjournal.com
twitter.com/BugleObserver1
Circulation: 2,700 *Frequency:* Tuesday; Friday (Bugle-Observer Weekend)
The Bugle-Observer provides news to New Brunswick's Carleton County.
Peter Macintosh, Publisher
Jim Dumville, Editor

Newfoundland & Labrador

Daily Newspapers in Newfoundland & Labrador

St. John's: The Telegram
Owned By: SaltWire Network
PO Box 8660 A, 36 Austin St., St. John's, NL A1B 3T7
Tel: 709-364-6300
telegram@thetelegram.com
www.saltwire.com/newfoundland-labrador
twitter.com/stjohnstelegram
www.facebook.com/stjohnstelegram
Frequency: Monday-Saturday

Other Newspapers in Newfoundland & Labrador

Carbonear: The Compass
Owned By: SaltWire Network
PO Box 760, 176 Water St., Carbonear, NL A1Y 1C3
Tel: 709-596-6458; *Fax:* 709-596-1700
www.cbncompass.ca
twitter.com/cbncompass
Circulation: 3,200 *Frequency:* Tuesday
Terry Roberts, Editor
editor@cbncompass.ca

Channel-Port-aux-Basques: The Gulf News
Owned By: SaltWire Network
PO Box 1090, 17 Grand Bay Rd.,
Channel-Port-aux-Basques, NL A0M 1C0
Tel: 709-695-3671; *Fax:* 709-695-7901
info@gulfnews.ca
www.gulfnews.ca
twitter.com/thegulfnews
Circulation: 2,300 *Frequency:* Monday
The Gulf News provides news & information to Channel-Port-aux-Basques & communities in southwestern Newfoundland & Labrador.
Chris Noseworthy, Contact, Advertising
chris.noseworthy@thewesternstar.com

Clarenville: The Packet
Owned By: SaltWire Network
8B Thompson St., Clarenville, NL A5A 1Y9
Tel: 709-466-2243; *Fax:* 709-466-2717
editor@thepacket.ca
www.thepacket.ca
twitter.com/nlpacket
www.facebook.com/packet.newspapers
Circulation: 3,500 *Frequency:* Thursday
Newfoundland & Labrador communities on Trinity Bay, Bonavista Bay, & Placentia Bay are served by The Packet.

Happy Valley-Goose Bay: The Labradorian
Owned By: SaltWire Network
PO Box 39 B, 2 Hillcrest Rd., Happy Valley-Goose Bay, NL A0P 1E0
Tel: 709-896-3341; *Fax:* 709-896-8781
www.thelabradorian.ca
Circulation: 1,500 *Frequency:* Monday
The newspaper serves coastal & central Labrador.
Sharon Gallant, Contact
sharon.gallant@thelabradorian.ca

Labrador City: The Aurora
Owned By: SaltWire Network
PO Box 423, Labrador City, NL A2V 2K7
Tel: 709-944-2957; *Fax:* 709-944-2958
www.theaurora.ca
twitter.com/auroranl
Circulation: 1,200 *Frequency:* Monday
The Aurora serves residents of western Labrador.

Marystown: The Southern Gazette
Owned By: SaltWire Network
PO Box 1116, Ville Marie Dr., Marystown, NL A0E 2M0
Tel: 709-279-3188; *Fax:* 709-279-2628
editor@southerngazette.ca
www.southerngazette.ca
twitter.com/southerngazette
Circulation: 2,800 *Frequency:* Tues.
Lindsey Bunin, Manager, Custom & Community Publishing
lbunin@herald.ca

Paradise: The Shoreline News
PO Box 3065, Paradise, NL A1L 3W2
Tel: 709-834-2169
tsnews@nf.aibn.com
www.theshorelinenews.com
Circulation: 16,000 *Frequency:* Saturday
The Shoreline News serves the residents of Paradise, Conception Bay South, Conception Bay Centre, & St. Mary's Bay. Subscriptions are available for both the print & online editions of the newspaper.
Frank Petten, Publisher

St Anthony: The Northern Pen
Owned By: SaltWire Network
PO Box 520, 10-12 North St., St Anthony, NL A0K 4S0
Tel: 709-454-2191; *Fax:* 709-454-3718
info@northernpen.ca
www.northernpen.ca
twitter.com/northernpen
Circulation: 4,144 *Frequency:* Monday
Newfoundland & Labrador's northern peninsula & southern Labrador are served by The Northern Pen newspaper.

St-Jean: Le Gaboteur
Détenteur: Le Gaboteur Inc.
#254, 65 ch Ridge, St-Jean, NL A1B 4P5
Tél: 709-753-9585; *Téléc:* 709-753-9586
gaboteur@nf.sympatico.ca
www.gaboteur.ca
www.youtube.com/Legaboteur
www.facebook.com/gaboteur
Tirage: 731 *Fréquence:* Lundi, bi-mensuel
Jacinthe Tremblay, Codirectrice (rédaction)
jacinthe@gaboteur.ca
Steven Watt, Corecteur (administration)
steven@gaboteur.ca
Jordan Elliott, Adjoint administratif
jordan@gaboteur.ca

Northwest Territories

Other Newspapers in Northwest Territories

Fort Smith: Northern Journal
Owned By: Cascade Publishing Limited
PO Box 990, 207 McDougall Rd., Fort Smith, NT X0E 0P0
Tel: 867-872-2784
news@norj.ca
www.srji.com
twitter.com/NorthernJournal
www.facebook.com/NorthernJournal
Circulation: 4,346 *Frequency:* Tuesday
Formerly the Slave River Journal
Don Jaque, Publisher
don@norj.ca
Meagan Wohlberg, Managing Editor
news@norj.ca

Yellowknife: L'Aquilon
CP 456, Yellowknife, NT X1A 2N4
Tél: 867-873-6603; *Téléc:* 867-873-6663
ykjournaliste@northwestel.net
www.aquilon.nt.ca
Tirage: 1 000 *Fréquence:* Vendredi
Alain Bessette, Publisher
Denis Lord, Reporter
ykjournaliste@northwestel.net
Alain Bessette, Officer, Administration
direction_aquilon@northwestel.net

Yellowknife: Hay River Hub
Owned By: Northern News Services Ltd.
PO Box 2820, Yellowknife, NT X1A 2R1
Tel: 867-873-4031; *Fax:* 867-873-8507
editorial@nnsl.com
www.nnsl.com/hayriverhub
twitter.com/nnslonline
www.facebook.com/nnslonline
Bruce Valpy, Publisher
Mike Bryant, Managing Editor

Yellowknife: Inuvik Drum
Owned By: Northern News Services Ltd.
PO Box 2820, Yellowknife, NT X1A 2R1
Tel: 867-873-4031; *Fax:* 867-873-8507
editorial@nnsl.com
www.nnsl.com/inuvikdrum
Other information: Alt. Email: nnsl@nnsl.com
twitter.com/nnslonline
www.facebook.com/nnslonline
Bruce Valpy, Publisher
Mike Bryant, Managing Editor

Yellowknife: Kivalliq News
Owned By: Northern News Services Ltd.
PO Box 2820, Yellowknife, NT X1A 2R1
Tel: 867-873-4031; *Fax:* 867-873-8507
editorial@nnsl.com
www.nnsl.com/kivalliq-news
Other information: Alt. Email: nnsl@nnsl.com
twitter.com/nnslonline
www.facebook.com/nnslonline
Bruce Valpy, Publisher
Mike Bryant, Managing Editor

Yellowknife: Nunavut News
Owned By: Northern News Services Ltd.
PO Box 2820, Yellowknife, NT X1A 2R1
Tel: 867-873-4031; *Fax:* 867-873-8507
editorial@nnsl.com
www.nnsl.com/nunavut-news
Other information: Alt. Email: nnsl@nnsl.com
twitter.com/nnslonline
www.facebook.com/nnslonline
Bruce Valpy, Publisher
Mike Bryant, Managing Editor
editor@nunavutnews.com

Yellowknife: NWT News North
Owned By: Northern News Services Ltd.
PO Box 2820, Yellowknife, NT X1A 2R1
Tel: 867-873-4031; *Fax:* 867-873-8507
editorial@nnsl.com
www.nnsl.com/nwt-news
Other information: Alt. Email: nnsl@nnsl.com
twitter.com/nnslonline
www.facebook.com/nnslonline
Bruce Valpy, Publisher
Mike Bryant, Managing Editor

Yellowknife: Yellowknifer
Owned By: Northern News Services Ltd.
PO Box 2820, Yellowknife, NT X1A 2R1
Tel: 867-873-4031; *Fax:* 867-873-8507
editorial@nnsl.com
www.nnsl.com/yellowknife-news
Other information: Alt. Email: nnsl@nnsl.com
twitter.com/nnslonline
www.facebook.com/nnslonline
Brucr Valpy, Publisher
Mike Bryant, Managing Editor

Nova Scotia

Daily Newspapers in Nova Scotia

Truro News
Owned By: SaltWire Network
NS
news@trurodaily.com
www.saltwire.com/nova-scotia
twitter.com/trurodaily
The newspaper covers Truro, Tatamagouche & Colchester County.

Halifax: The Chronicle Herald
Owned By: SaltWire Network
2717 Joseph Howe Dr., Halifax, NS B3J 2T2
Tel: 902-426-2811; *Fax:* 902-426-1164
newsroom@herald.ca
www.saltwire.com/halifax
Other information: Classifieds, Email: classified@herald.ca
twitter.com/chronicleherald
www.facebook.com/thechronicleherald
Frequency: Monday-Saturday
Broadsheet newspaper serving readers in Halifax. After The Chronicle Herald acquired 27 regional newspapers from TC Media, SaltWire Network was formed as a parent company of The Chronicle & its acquisitions.
Mark Lever, President & CEO, SaltWire Network

Sydney: Cape Breton Post
Owned By: SaltWire Network
PO Box 1500, 255 George St., Sydney, NS B1P 1J7
Tel: 902-564-9670
news@cbpost.com
www.saltwire.com/cape-breton
Other information: Advertising, Phone: 902-563-3874
twitter.com/capebretonpost
www.facebook.com/thecapebretonpost
Frequency: Monday-Saturday
The Cape Breton Post is Cape Breton Island's only local daily newspaper.

Other Newspapers in Nova Scotia

The News
Previous Name: The Evening News
Owned By: SaltWire Network
NS
Tel: 902-752-3000
news@ngnews.ca
www.saltwire.com/nova-scotia
Other information: Classifieds, Email: class@ngnews.ca
twitter.com/ngnews
www.facebook.com/newglasgownews
Frequency: Thursday
Nova Scotia's Pictou County is served by the daily newspaper.

Amherst: The Citizen-Record
Owned By: SaltWire Network
147 South Albion St., Amherst, NS B4H 2X2
Tel: 902-667-5102; *Fax:* 902-667-0419
www.cumberlandnewsnow.com
twitter.com/ADNandrew
Frequency: Thursday
In 2011, The Citizen & The Record community newspapers merged to create The Citizen-Record. The newspaper covers Nova Scotia's Cumberland County. The Citizen-Record is available in print & online.
Richard Russell, Group Publisher, Transcontinental Nova Scotia Media Group Inc.
902-896-7526
rrussell@ngnews.ca
Christopher Gooding, Co-Editor
902-597-3731
Andrew Wagstaff, Co-Editor
902-661-5440
Gladys Coish, Regional Manager, Sales
gcoish@amherstdaily.com

Antigonish: The Casket
Owned By: The Chronicle Herald
88 College St., Antigonish, NS B2G 2L7
Tel: 902-863-4370; *Fax:* 902-863-1943
www.thecasket.ca
twitter.com/casketeditor
www.facebook.com/quadcocasket
Circulation: 3,427 *Frequency:* Weekly; Wednesday
The Casket serves the town & county of Antigonish in Nova Scotia.
Richard Mac, Contact
richardmac@thecasket.ca

Bass River: The Shoreline Journal
Previous Name: West Colchester Free Press
PO Box 41, RR#1, Bass River, NS B0M 1B0
Tel: 902-647-2968
www.theshorelinejournal.com
twitter.com/mauriceres
www.facebook.com/theshorelinejournal
Circulation: 1,363 *Frequency:* Monthly
The community newspaper serves Nova Scotia's Fundy Shore, including the communities of Bass River, Truro, Parrsboro, Belmont, Masstown, Debert, & Onslow.
Dorothy Rees, Co-Manager

Maurice Rees, Co-Manager
maurice@theshorelinejournal.com

Bridgetown: Monitor-Examiner
Previous Name: Bridgetown Monitor
PO Box 250, 29 Queen St., Bridgetown, NS B0S 1C0
Tel: 902-665-4441; *Fax:* 902-665-4014
Frequency: Weekly
Susanne Wagner, Publisher

Enfield: The Laker
Owned By: Advocate Media Inc.
287 Hwy. 2, Enfield, NS B2T 1C9
Tel: 902-883-3181; *Fax:* 902-883-3180
advertising@enfieldweeklypress.com
www.thelaker.ca
twitter.com/TheLakerNews
Circulation: 7,600 *Frequency:* Monthly, first Thursday
The community newspaper serves Nova Scotia's Lakes area,
including Waverley, Windsor Junction, Beaver Bank, Fall River,
& Wellington. The Laker is published the first week of each
month.
Leith Orr, Publisher
leith@advocatemediainc.com
Abby Cameron, Editor
editor@enfieldweeklypress.com
Scott MacKinnon, Manager, Advertising
scott@advocatemediainc.com om
Angela Isenor, Contact, Design & Production
design@enfieldweeklypress.com
Danielle Shreenan, Contact, Classified & Circulation
admin@enfieldweeklypress.com

Enfield: The Weekly Press
Owned By: Advocate Media Inc.
287 Hwy. 2, Enfield, NS B2T 1C9
Tel: 902-883-3181; *Fax:* 902-883-3180
editor@enfieldweeklypress.com
www.enfieldweeklypress.com
Circulation: 1,458 *Frequency:* Weekly; Wednesday
Fred Fiander, Publisher
fredfiander@advocatemediainc.com
Abby Cameron, Editor
editor@enfieldweeklypress.com

Greenwood: The Aurora
Owned By: Department of National Defence
PO Box 99, 14 Wing, Greenwood, NS B0P 1N0
Tel: 902-765-1494; *Fax:* 902-765-1717
www.auroranewspaper.com
Circulation: 5,900 *Frequency:* Monday
The Aurora is a free newspaper that serves the personnel of 14
Wing Greenwood, Nova Scotia.
Sara Keddy, Managing Editor
auroraeditor@ns.aliantzinc.ca
LT. Sylvain Rousseau, Editorial Advisor
9027651494
Brian Graves, Coordinator, Production
auroraproduction@ns.aliantzinc.ca
Anne Kempton, Contact, Business & Advertising
auroramarketing@ns.aliantzinc.ca
Candance May Timmins, Administrative Clerk
auroranews@ns.aliantzinc.ca

Guysborough: Guysborough Journal
Owned By: Addington Publications
PO Box 210, 48 Main St., Guysborough, NS B0H 1N0
Tel: 902-533-2851; *Fax:* 902-533-2750
news@guysboroughjournal.ca
www.guysboroughjournal.com
Other information: Subscriptions, Email:
subscribe@guysboroughjournal.ca
twitter.com/GysboroJournal
Circulation: 970 *Frequency:* Wed.
The community newspaper covers Nova Scotia's Guysborough
County. Print & digital editions are available.
Helen Murphy, Publisher, Manager, & Editor
Sharon Heighton, Manager, Office & Circulation
Dorothy Ostewig, Coordinator, Production
Navneet Kaur, Contact, Advertising
advertising@guysboroughjournal.ca

Halifax: Annapolis County Spectator
c/o SaltWire Network
Owned By: Valley Journal Advertiser/Annapolis Valley
Register
2717 Joseph Howe Dr., Halifax, NS B3J 2T2
Tel: 902-825-7122
www.annapoliscountyspectator.ca
Serves residents of Annapolis County
Lawrence Powell, Contact
lawrence.powell@annapolisspectator.ca

Halifax: Bedford-Sackville Observer
c/o The Chronicle Herald
Owned By: The Chronicle Herald
PO Box 610, 2717 Joseph Howe Dr., Halifax, NS B3J 2T2
Tel: 902-429-2811
communities@herald.ca
www.thechronicleherald.ca/community/bedfordsackvilleobserver
www.facebook.com/bedfordsackvilleobserver

Halifax: The Central Voice
Owned By: SaltWire Network
217 Joseph Howe Dr., Halifax, NS B3J 2T2
www.saltwire.com
The Central Voice launched in August 2018 after four
Newfoundland newspapers (The Pilot, The Advertiser, The
Nor'wester & The Beacon) closed. The Central Voice serves
residents of central Newfoundland.
Steve Bartlett, Managing Editor

Halifax: The Coast
5567 Cunard St., Halifax, NS B3K 1C5
Tel: 902-422-6278; *Fax:* 902-425-0013
frontdesk@thecoast.ca
www.thecoast.ca
twitter.com/TwitCoast
www.facebook.com/TheCoastHalifax
Circulation: 22,000 *Frequency:* Thursday
The Coast is an independent, locally owned paper that features
news, reports on the arts, & movie, theatre, music, gallery, &
museum listings for Halifax, Nova Scotia. The free newspaper is
distributed each week at over 650 locations. The Coast is a
member of the international Association of Alternative
Newsweeklies.
Catherine Salisbury, President
cathsalis@thecoast.ca
Christine Oreskovich, Publisher
christineo@thecoast.ca
Kyle Shaw, Editor
editor@thecoast.ca
Stephanie Johns, Editor, Arts
arts@thecoast.ca
Lindsay Raining Bird, Editor, Listings
listings@thecoast.ca
Jessica Tasker, Manager, Distribution
distribution@thecoast.ca
Bethany Stout, Director, Advertising
bethanys@thecoast.ca

Halifax: Dartmouth Tribune
c/o The Chronicle Herald
Owned By: The Chronicle Herald
PO Box 610, 2717 Joseph Howe Dr., Halifax, NS B3J 2T2
Tel: 902-426-2811
communities@herald.ca
www.thechronicleherald.ca/community/dartmouthtribune
www.facebook.com/dartmouthtribune

Halifax: Halifax Citizen
c/o The Chronicle Herald
Owned By: The Chronicle Herald
PO Box 610, 2717 Joseph Howe Dr., Halifax, NS B3J 2T2
Tel: 902-426-2811
communities@herald.ca
www.thechronicleherald.ca/community/halifaxcitizen
www.facebook.com/halifaxcitizen

Halifax: South Shore Breaker
c/o The Chronicle Herald
Owned By: The Chronicle Herald
PO Box 610, 2717 Joseph Howe Dr., Halifax, NS B3J 2T2
Tel: 902-426-2811
editor@southshorebreaker.ca
www.southshorebreaker.ca
www.facebook.com/valleyharvester

Halifax: Trident Newspaper
Owned By: Advocate Media Inc.
**CFB Halifax, PO Box 99000, 2740 Barrington St., Halifax, NS
B3K 5X5**
Tel: 902-427-4235
tridentnewspaper.com
twitter.com/trident_news
www.facebook.com/202801813483
The newspaper of Maritime Forces Atlantic
Virginia Beaton, Editor
virginia.beaton@forces.gc.ca

Halifax: Valley Harvester
c/o The Chronicle Herald
Owned By: The Chronicle Herald
PO Box 610, 2717 Joseph Howe Dr., Halifax, NS B3J 2T2
Tel: 902-426-2811
communities@herald.ca
www.thechronicleherald.ca/community/valleyharvester
www.facebook.com/valleyharvester

Halifax: Valley Journal Advertiser/Annapolis Valley
Register
c/o SaltWire Network
Owned By: SaltWire Network
2717 Joseph Howe Dr., Halifax, NS B3J 2T2
www.journaladvertiser.ca
Serves residents of Hants, Kings & Annapolis counties.
County-specific publications under this banner include:
Annapolis County Spectator, Hants Journal & Kings County
Advertiser/Kings County Register

Inverness: The Inverness Oran
Owned By: Inverness Communications Ltd.
PO Box 100, 15767 Central Ave., Inverness, NS B0E 1N0
Tel: 902-258-2253; *Fax:* 902-258-2632
oran@ns.aliantzinc.ca
www.oran.ca
Other information: Advertising Email:
oran-advertising@ns.aliantzinc.ca
www.facebook.com/invernessoran
Circulation: 3,500 *Frequency:* Wednesday
Rankin MacDonald, President & Editor
editor@oran.ca
Eleanor MacDonald, Publisher & Secretary
Bill Dunphy, Editor, Sports
oran-sports@ns.aliantzinc.ca
Ann Morrison, Accountant
ann@oran.ca
Kelly MacGillivray, Contact, Advertising & Circulation
Diane Mouland, Contact, Production

Kentville: Kings County Advertiser/Kings County
Register
Owned By: Valley Journal Advertiser/Annapolis Valley
Register
#6, Aberdeen St., Kentville, NS B4N 2T1
Tel: 902-681-2121; *Fax:* 902-681-0923
events@kentvilleadvertiser.ca
www.kingscountynews.ca
Serves residents of Kings County

Liverpool: South Shore Breaker
Owned By: SaltWire Network
271 Main St., Liverpool, NS B0T 1K0
Tel: 902-521-7711
editor@southshorebreaker.ca
www.southshorebreaker.ca
twitter.com/ssbreaker
Circulation: 1,560 *Frequency:* Tuesday
The Queen's County Advance merged with the South Shore
Breaker in June 2018.
Baillie Saunders, Editor
bsaunders@herald.ca

Meteghan River: Le Courrier de la Nouvelle-Écosse
9250, rte 1, Meteghan River, NS B0W 2L0
Tél: 902-769-3078; *Téléc:* 902-769-3869
adminstration@lecourrier.com
www.lecourrier.com
twitter.com/CourrierNE1937
www.facebook.com/lecourrier
Tirage: 1 325 *Fréquence:* vendredi
Denise Comeau-Desautels, Directrice générale; Rédactrice en
chef; Directrice, des ventes

Middleton: The Annapolis County Spectator
Owned By: SaltWire Network
PO Box 880, 87 Commercial St., Middleton, NS B0S 1P0
Tel: 902-825-7122
editor@annapolisspectator.ca
www.annapoliscountyspectator.ca
twitter.com/spectatorns
www.facebook.com/annapoliscountyspectator
Circulation: 1,800 *Frequency:* Thursday
Serves Annapolis County, including Middleton, Annapolis Royal,
Bridgetown, Lawrence & surrounding communities

Oxford: The Oxford Journal
Owned By: Oxford Journal Ltd.
PO Box 10, 111 Rideau St., Oxford, NS B0M 1P0
Tel: 902-447-2051; *Fax:* 902-447-2055
www.oxfordjournal.ca

Circulation: 1,750 Frequency: Wednesday
The Oxford Journal serves central & eastern Cumberland County in Nova Scotia.
Paul Marchant, Publisher
Charles Weeks, Editor

Pictou: The Advocate
Owned By: Advocate Media Inc.
PO Box 1000, 21 George St., Pictou, NS B0K 1H0
Tel: 902-485-8014; Fax: 902-752-4816
www.pictouadvocate.com
twitter.com/pictouadvocate
www.facebook.com/ThePictouAdvocate
Circulation: 2,624 Frequency: Wednesday
Leith Orr, Publisher
leith@advocatemediainc.com
Jackie Jardine, Editor
editor@pictouadvocate.com
Lorraine Van Veen, Manager, Circulation
circul@pictouadvocate.com

Pictou: The Light
Owned By: Advocate Media Inc.
PO Box 1000, 21 George St., Pictou, NS B0K 1H0
Tel: 902-956-8099; Fax: 902-257-2832
circul@advocateprinting.ns.ca
www.tatamagouchelight.com
Other information: Subscriptions, Phone: 902-485-8014;
Advertising: 902-657-2593
twitter.com/TheLightNews
Circulation: 4,412 Frequency: Monthly, first Wednesday
The Light is a free newspaper that provides news & information to the Nova Scotia communities of Tatamagouche, Pugwash, Malagash, Earltown, River John, Wentworth, & Wallace.
Leith Orr, Publisher
leith@advocatemediainc.com
Scott MacKinnon, Manager, Advertising
scott@advocatemediainc.com

Port Hawkesbury: The Reporter
Owned By: Advocate Media Inc.
2 MacLean Ct., Port Hawkesbury, NS B9A 3K2
Tel: 902-625-3300; Fax: 902-625-1701
www.porthawkesburyreporter.com
www.facebook.com/porthawkesburyreporter
Circulation: 2,100 Frequency: Wednesday
Jake Boudrot, Editor
jake@porthawkesburyreporter.com

Truro: Hub Now
Owned By: Advocate Media Inc.
Truro, NS
Tel: 902-305-6177
www.hubnow.ca
www.facebook.com/hubnownewspaper
Circulation: 5,000 Frequency: Monthly
Free local publication dedicated to matters affecting Colchester County.
Raissa Tetanish, Editor
raissatetanish@tatamagouchelight.com

Windsor: Hants Journal
Owned By: Valley Journal Advertiser/Annapolis Valley Register
PO Box 550, 86 Gerrish St., Windsor, NS B0N 2T0
Tel: 902-798-8371; Fax: 902-798-5451
info@hantsjournal.ca
www.hantsjournal.ca
Serves residents of Hants County

Yarmouth: Tri-County Vanguard
Owned By: SaltWire Network
2 Second St., Yarmouth, NS B5A 4B1
Tel: 902-742-7111; Fax: 902-742-2311
info@tricountyvanguard.ca
www.thevanguard.ca
Other information: Advertising, Fax: 902-742-6527
www.facebook.com/yarmouthvanguard
Circulation: 3,800 Frequency: Tuesday
The Yarmouth County Vanguard, the Digby County Courier & the Shelburne County Coast Guard merged to create the Tri-County Vanguard in 2016.
Tina Comeau, Editor

Nunavut

Other Newspapers in Nunavut

Iqaluit: Nunatsiaq News
Owned By: Nortext Publishing Corporation
PO Box 8, Iqaluit, NU X0A 0H0
Tel: 867-979-5357; Fax: 867-979-4763
editor@nunatsiaqonline.ca
www.nunatsiaqonline.ca
Other information: Advertising, Toll-Free: 800-263-1452, ext. 131; Fax: 800-417-2474
twitter.com/nunatsiaqnews
www.facebook.com/NunatsiaqNews
Circulation: 6,228 Frequency: Friday
The newspaper of the eastern Arctic is published weekly in English & Inuktitut. Stories are published online each day, and a virtual paper delivered by email is also available weekly.
Steven Roberts, Publisher
Jim Bell, Editor

Ontario

Daily Newspapers in Ontario

Belleville: The Belleville Intelligencer
Owned By: Postmedia Network Inc.
#118, 199 Front St., Belleville, ON K8N 5H5
Tel: 613-962-9171 Toll-Free: 866-511-1963
www.intelligencer.ca
www.facebook.com/TheBellevilleIntelligencer
Frequency: Tuesday-Saturday

Chatham: Chatham Daily News
Owned By: Postmedia Network Inc.
138 King St. West, Chatham, ON N7M 1E3
Tel: 519-354-2000 Toll-Free: 866-511-1957
www.chathamdailynews.ca
twitter.com/ChathamNews
www.facebook.com/ChathamDailyNews
Frequency: Tuesday, Thursday-Saturday

Hamilton: The Hamilton Spectator
Owned By: Metroland Media Group Ltd.
#4, 211 Pritchard Rd., Hamilton, ON L8J 0G5
Tel: 905-526-3333
circ@thespec.com
www.thespec.com
twitter.com/thespec
www.facebook.com/hamiltonspectator
Frequency: Monday-Saturday
Neil Oliver, Publisher
noliver@metroland.com
Paul Berton, Editor-in-Chief
pberton@thespec.com

Kitchener: Waterloo Region Record
Previous Name: The Record; Kitchener Daily Record
Owned By: Metroland Media Group Ltd.
PO Box 25069, Kitchener, ON N2A 4A5
Tel: 519-894-2250 Toll-Free: 800-265-8261
www.therecord.com
twitter.com/wr_record
www.facebook.com/waterlooregionrecord
Frequency: Monday-Saturday
Donna Luelo, Publisher
dluelo@therecord.com
Jim Poling, Editor-in-Chief
jpoling@therecord.com

London: The London Free Press
Owned By: Postmedia Network Inc.
#201, 210 Dundas St., London, ON N6A 5J3
Tel: 519-679-1999 Toll-Free: 877-679-1999
lfpress.com
twitter.com/lfpress
www.facebook.com/lfpress
Circulation: 362,348 total Frequency: Monday-Saturday
Joe Ruscitti, Editor-in-chief
jruscitti@postmedia.com

Markham: Sing Tao Daily Toronto
Owned By: Sing Tao Media Group Canada
221 Whitehall Dr., Markham, ON L3R 9T1
Tel: 416-596-8140; Fax: 416-599-6688
singtaoadmin@singtao.ca
www.singtao.ca/toronto
Frequency: Daily
Chinese daily newspaper.

North Bay: The North Bay Nugget
Owned By: Postmedia Network Inc.
259 Worthington St. West, North Bay, ON P1B 3B5
Tel: 705-472-3200 Toll-Free: 866-381-4024
www.nugget.ca
twitter.com/northbaynugget
www.facebook.com/NBNugget
Frequency: Tuesday-Saturday

Ottawa: Le Droit
Détenteur: Coopérative nationale de l'information indépendante
#201, 425, boul St-Joseph, Ottawa, ON K1N 3J9
Tél: 613-562-0111
nouvelles@ledroit.com
www.ledroit.com
twitter.com/LeDroitca
Fréquence: lundi-samedi
Éric Brousseau, Directeur général
ebrousseau@ledroit.com
Marie-Claude Lortie, Rédactrice en chef
mclortie@ledroit.com

Ottawa: Ottawa Citizen
Owned By: Postmedia Network Inc.
PO Box 5020, 1101 Baxter Rd., Ottawa, ON K2C 3M4
Tel: 613-829-9100 Toll-Free: 800-267-6100
ottawacitizen.com
www.youtube.com/c/ottawacitizen
twitter.com/OttawaCitizen
www.facebook .com/TheOttawaCitizen
Frequency: Monday-Saturday

Ottawa: The Ottawa Sun
Owned By: Postmedia Network Inc.
1101 Baxter Rd., Ottawa, ON K2C 3M4
Tel: 613-739-7200 Toll-Free: 800-267-4669
adinquiries@postmedia.com
ottawasun.com
twitter.com/ottawasuncom
www.facebook.com/OttawaSun
Circulation: 141,700 Frequency: Daily
Nicole MacAdam, Editor-in-Chief

Owen Sound: The Sun Times
Owned By: Postmedia Network Inc.
290 - 9th St. East, Owen Sound, ON N4K 5P2
Tel: 519-376-2250 Toll-Free: 866-381-3710
www.owensoundsuntimes.com
twitter.com/OwenSoundST
www.facebook.com/105811502783909
Frequency: Tuesday-Saturday
Doug Edgar, Managing Editor
doug.edgar@sunmedia.ca

Peterborough: The Peterborough Examiner
Owned By: Metroland Media Group Ltd.
c/o Package Plus Inc., #125, 171A Rink St., Peterborough, ON K9J 2J6
Tel: 705-745-4641
news@peterboroughdaily.com
www.thepeterboroughexaminer.com
twitter.com/ptboexaminer
www.facebook.com/peterboroughexaminer
Frequency: Monday-Saturday
Kennedy Gordon, Managing Editor
kennedy.gordon@peterboroughdaily.com

Sarnia: The Sarnia Observer
Owned By: Postmedia Network Inc.
140 South Front St., Sarnia, ON N7T 7M8
Tel: 519-344-3641 Toll-Free: 866-511-1960
www.theobserver.ca
twitter.com/sarniaObserver
www.facebook.com/sarniaobserver
Frequency: Tuesday-Saturday

Sault Ste. Marie: The Sault Star
Owned By: Postmedia Network Inc.
145 Old Garden River Rd., Sault Ste. Marie, ON P6A 5M5
Tel: 705-759-3030 Toll-Free: 866-381-4090
www.saultstar.com
twitter.com/SaultStar
www.facebook.com/SaultStar
Frequency: Tuesday-Saturday

St Catharaines: Niagara Falls Review
Owned By: Metroland Media Group Ltd.
PO Box 5031 Main, St Catharaines, ON L2R 7T4
Tel: 905-358-5711
www.niagarafallsreview.ca
twitter.com/niafallsreview
www.facebook.com/niagarafallsreview

Frequency: Monday-Saturday
Angus Scott, Editor-in-Chief
angus.scott@nigaradailies.com

St Catharines: The St. Catharines Standard
Owned By: Metroland Media Group Ltd.
PO Box 5031 Main, St Catharines, ON L2R 7T4
Tel: 905-684-7251
www.stcatharinesstandard.ca
twitter.com/stcatstandard
www.facebook.com/stcatharinesstandard
Frequency: Monday-Saturday
Angus Scott, Editor-in-Chief
angus.scott@niagaradailies.com

St Catharines: Welland Tribune
Previous Name: Welland-Port Colborne Tribune
Owned By: Metroland Media Group Ltd.
PO Box 5031 Main, St Catharines, ON L2R 7T4
Tel: 905-732-2411
www.wellandtribune.ca
twitter.com/wellandtribune
www.facebook.com/wellandtribune
Circulation: 62,762 total *Frequency:* Monday-Saturday
Angus Scott, Editor-in-Chief
angus.scott@niagaradailies.com

St Thomas: The St. Thomas Times-Journal
Owned By: Postmedia Network Inc.
28 Princess Ave., St Thomas, ON N5R 3V4
Tel: 519-631-2790
timesjournal@postmedia.com
www.stthomastimesjournal.com
twitter.com/Timesjournal
www.facebook.com/stthomastimesjournal
Frequency: Tuesday-Friday

Stratford: Stratford Beacon Herald
Owned By: Postmedia Network Inc.
59 Lorne Ave., #C, Stratford, ON N5A 6S4
Tel: 519-271-2222 *Toll-Free:* 800-265-8577
www.stratfordbeaconherald.com
twitter.com/ThebeaconHerald
www.facebook.com/stratfordbeaconherald
Frequency: Monday-Saturday

Sudbury: The Sudbury Star
Owned By: Postmedia Network Inc.
#103, 888 Regent St., Sudbury, ON P3E 6C6
Tel: 705-674-5271 *Toll-Free:* 800-461-1155
www.thesudburystar.com
twitter.com/sudburystar
www.facebook.com/thesudburystar
Frequency: Tuesday-Saturday
Don MacDonald, Managing Editor
don.macdonald@sunmedia.ca

Thunder Bay: The Chronicle-Journal
Previous Name: Times-News
Owned By: Continental Newspapers Canada Ltd.
75 South Cumberland St., Thunder Bay, ON P7B 1A3
Tel: 807-343-6200
circulation@chroniclejournal.com
www.chroniclejournal.com
twitter.com/cj_thunderbay
www.facebook.com/chroniclejournal
Frequency: Daily
Hilda Caverly, General Manager & Director, Finance &
Circulation
Greg Giddens, Managing Editor
ggiddens@chroniclejournal.com

Timmins: Timmins Daily Press
Owned By: Postmedia Network Inc.
187 Cedar St. South, Timmins, ON P4N 7G1
Tel: 705-268-5050 *Toll-Free:* 866-511-1972
www.timminspress.com
twitter.com/TimminsPress
www.facebook.com/TimminsDailyPress
Frequency: Tuesday-Saturday

Toronto: Brantford Expositor
Owned By: Postmedia Network Inc.
365 Bloor St. East, Toronto, ON M4W 3L4
Tel: 519-756-2020 *Toll-Free:* 866-381-3658
brantford.advertising@postmedia.com
www.brantfordexpositor.ca
twitter.com/theexpositor
www.facebook.com/BrantfordExpositor
Frequency: Tuesday-Saturday

Toronto: The Kingston Whig-Standard
Owned By: Postmedia Network Inc.
365 Bloor St. East, Toronto, ON M4W 3L4
Tel: 613-544-5000 *Toll-Free:* 866-511-1965
www.thewhig.com
www.facebook.com/whigstandard
www.facebook.com/KingstonWhigStandard
Frequency: Tuesday-Saturday
Steve Serviss, Managing Editor

Toronto: National Post
Owned By: Postmedia Network Inc.
365 Bloor St. East, 3rd Fl., Toronto, ON M4W 3L4
Tel: 416-383-2500 *Toll-Free:* 800-668-7678
www.nationalpost.com
www.youtube.com/user/nationalpost
twitter.com/nationalpost
www.facebook.com/NationalPost
Frequency: Tuesday-Saturday
National paper, with the Toronto edition containing local content
not published in the rest of the country.
Rob Roberts, Editor-in-Chief

Toronto: Simcoe Reformer
Owned By: Postmedia Network Inc.
365 Bloor St. East, Toronto, ON M4W 3L4
Tel: 519-426-5710
www.simcoereformer.ca
twitter.com/simcoe_reformer
www.facebook.com/simcoereformer
Frequency: Tuesday-Friday
Kim Novak, Managing Editor
knovak@postmedia.com

Toront o: Standard-Freeholder
Owned By: Postmedia Network Inc.
365 Bloor St. East, Toronto, ON M4W 3L4
Tel: 613-933-3160 *Toll-Free:* 866-381-3860
www.standard-freeholder.com
www.facebook.com/standardfreeholder
Frequency: Tuesday-Saturday
Hugo Rodrigues, Managing Editor
hugo.rodrigues@sunmedia.ca

Toronto: The Toronto Star
Owned By: Torstar Corporation
1 Yonge St., Toronto, ON M5E 1E6
Tel: 416-367-2000; *Fax:* 416-869-4328
Toll-Free: 800-268-9213
city@thestar.ca
www.thestar.com
twitter.com/torontostar
www.facebook.com/torontostar
Circulation: 847,000 M-F; 1,580,000 Sa; 1,264,000 Su
Frequency: Daily
Canada's largest daily newspaper
Jordan Bitove, Publisher
Anne Marie Owens, Editor

Toronto: The Toronto Sun
Owned By: Postmedia Network Inc.
365 Bloor St. East, 6th Fl., Toronto, ON M4W 3L4
Tel: 416-947-2111 *Toll-Free:* 800-668-0786
www.torontosun.com
twitter.com/TheTorontoSun
www.facebook.com/torontosun
Frequency: Daily
Adrienne Batra, Editor-in-Chief

Toronto: The Woodstock Sentinel Review
Previous Name: Woodstock-Ingersoll Daily Sentinel
Review
Owned By: Postmedia Network Inc.
365 Bloor St. East, Toronto, ON M4W 3L4
Tel: 519-537-2341
www.woodstocksentinelreview.com
twitter.com/woodstocksr
www.facebook.com/sentinelreview
Frequency: Tuesday-Friday
Bruce Urquhart, Managing Editor
burquhart@postmedia.com

Windsor: The Windsor Star
Owned By: Postmedia Network Inc.
300 Ouellette Ave., Windsor, ON N9A 7B4
Tel: 519-255-5774 *Toll-Free:* 800-265-5647
windsorstar.com
www.youtube.com/user/TheWindsorStar
twitter.com/TheWindsorStar
www.fac ebook.com/windsorstar
Frequency: Tuesday-Saturday

Craig Pearson, Managing Editor
519-255-5767
cpearson@postmedia.com

Other Newspapers in Ontario

Ailsa Craig: Middlesex Banner
Owned By: Banner Publications
PO Box 433, 175 Main St., Ailsa Craig, ON N0M 1A0
Tel: 519-293-1095; *Fax:* 519-293-1095
editor@banner.on.ca
www.banner.on.ca
Circulation: 1,170 *Frequency:* Wed.
Brad Harness, Publisher & Editor

Alexandria: Glengarry News
Owned By: Glengarry News Ltd.
PO Box 10, 3 Main St., Alexandria, ON K0C 1A0
Tel: 613-525-2020; *Fax:* 613-525-3824
gnews@glengarrynews.ca
www.glengarrynews.ca
www.facebook.com/glengarrynews
Circulation: 4,700 *Frequency:* Wednesday
Kevin Macdonald, President
J.T. Grossmith, Publisher
Steven Warburton, Managing Editor

Arnprior: Arnprior Chronicle-Guide
Owned By: Metroland Media Group Ltd.
8 McGonigal St. West, Arnprior, ON K7S 1L8
Tel: 613-623-6571
issuu.com/arnpriorchronicleguide
Circulation: 7,941 *Frequency:* Thursday
Cindy Manor, General Manager
cmanor@metroland.com
Ryland Coyne, Editor-in-Chief
rcoyne@metroland.com

Arnprior: West Carleton Review
Previous Name: West Carleton Review, West Carleton
8 McGonigal St., Arnprior, ON K7S 1L8
Tel: 613-623-6571
issuu.com/westcarletonreview
twitter.com/emcnews
www.facebook.com/emcnewspaper
Frequency: Weekly
Mike Tracy, General Manager
mike.tracy@metroland.com
Ryland Coyne, Editor-in-Chief
rcoyne@metroland.com

Atikokan: Atikokan Progress
Owned By: Atikokan Printing (1994) Ltd.
PO Box 220, 109 Main St. East, Atikokan, ON P0T 1C0
Tel: 807-597-2731; *Fax:* 807-597-6103
info@atikokanprogress.ca
www.atikokanprogress.ca
www.facebook.com/atikokanprogress
Circulation: 1,260 *Frequency:* Monday
Eve Shine, Publisher
Michael P. McKinnon, Editor

Aurora: Aurora Banner
Owned By: York Region Media Group
250 Industrial Pkwy. North, Aurora, ON L4G 4C3
Tel: 905-727-0819; *Fax:* 905-727-2909
yrcustomerservice@yrmg.com
www.yorkregion.com
Frequency: Twice a week, Thursday and Sunday
Tracy Kibble, Managing Editor

Aurora: The Auroran
#8, 15213 Yonge St., Aurora, ON L4G 1L8
Tel: 905-727-3300
www.auroran.com
Circulation: 19,160 *Frequency:* Wed.
The Auroran is an independent community newspaper.
Bob Ince, General Manager & Contact, Advertising
bob@auroran.com
Cynthia Proctor, Manager, Production
cynthia@auroran.com
Zach Shoub, Manager, Operations
zach@auroran.com
Brock Weir, Editor
brock@auroran.com

Aylmer: Aylmer Express
Owned By: Aylmer Express
PO Box 160, 390 Talbot St. East, Aylmer, ON N5H 2R9
Tel: 519-773-3126; *Fax:* 519-773-3147
Toll-Free: 800-465-9433
www.aylmerexpress.com
Circulation: 3,400 *Frequency:* Wednesday

John Hueston, Publisher & Editor

Ayr: The Ayr News
Owned By: Ayr News Ltd.
PO Box 1173, 40 Piper St., Ayr, ON N0B 1E0
Tel: 519-632-7432; Fax: 519-632-7743
ayrnews@golden.net
www.ayrnews.ca
Circulation: 3,100 *Frequency:* Wednesday
Heidi Schmidt, President & Editor
James W. Schmidt, Publisher
jw.schmidt@ayrnews.ca

Bancroft: Bancroft This Week
Previous Name: Bancroft Times
PO Box 1254, 254 Hastings St., Bancroft, ON K0L 1C0
Tel: 613-332-2002; Fax: 613-332-1710
bancroft-times@sympatico.ca
www.bancroftthisweek.com
twitter.com/BancroftTWeek
www.facebook.com/bancroftthisweek
Circulation: 7,870 *Frequency:* Friday
David Zilstra, Publisher
david.zilstra@gmail.com
Jenn Watt, Managing Editor
jenn@haliburtonpress.com

Barry's Bay: The Valley Gazette
Owned By: Postmedia Network Inc.
PO Box 375, 19574 Opeongo Line, Barry's Bay, ON K0J 1B0
Tel: 613-756-0256
www.thevalleygazette.ca
www.youtube.com/user/ValleyGazette
twitter.com/valleygazette1
www.facebook.com/TheValleyGazette
Circulation: 1,400 *Frequency:* Wednesday
Michel Lavigne, Publisher & Editor
michel@thevalleygazette.ca

Beamsville: Lincoln Post Express
PO Box 400, 4309 Central Ave., Beamsville, ON L0R 1B0
Tel: 905-563-5393; Fax: 905-563-7977
Circulation: 16,000 *Frequency:* Weekly
Tim Dundas, Publisher
Tom Wilkinson, Editor

Beeton: Beeton/New Tecumseth Times
Previous Name: Tottenham Times, New Tecumseth Times
Owned By: Simcoe-York Printing and Publishing Ltd.
34 Main St. West, Beeton, ON L0G 1A0
Tel: 905-729-2287; Fax: 905-729-2541
editor.syp@rogers.com
newspapers-online.com/tecumseth
twitter.com/NewTecTimes
www.facebook.com/newtectimes
Circulation: 1,400 *Frequency:* Thurs.
John Miles, General Manager
Wendy Soloduik, News Editor
wendy@simcoeyorkprinting.com
Annette Derraugh, Contact, Advertising
annette@simcoeyorkprinting.com

Beeton: Woodbridge Advertiser
PO Box 379, 2 Main St. West, Beeton, ON L0G 1A0
Tel: 905-729-4501 *Toll-Free:* 888-285-4501
wa@csolve.net
auctionsontario.ca
twitter.com/OntarioAuctions
www.facebook.com/WoodbridgeAdvertiser
Circulation: 5,500 *Frequency:* Thu.
Karl Mallette, Publisher
info@ontariosauctionpaper.com
Tina Dedels, Editor

Belle River: Lakeshore News
Previous Name: North Essex News
Owned By: Postmedia Network Inc.
473 Notre Dame, Belle River, ON N0R 1A0
Tel: 519-728-1082; Fax: 519-728-4551
lakeshore@windsoressexnews.com
lakeshore-news-belle-river.windsordirect. info
Circulation: 9,300 *Frequency:* Thursday
Bob Thwaites, Publisher
William Harris, Editor
Wendie Conliffe, Contact

Belleville: Belleville News
Owned By: Metroland Media Group Ltd.
PO Box 25009, 250 Sidney St., Belleville, ON K8P 5E0
Tel: 613-966-2034; Fax: 613-966-8747
www.emcbelleville.com
twitter.com/emcnews
www.facebook.com/emcnewspaper
Circulation: 24,100 *Frequency:* Thurs.
Mike Mount, Vice-President & Regional Publisher
John Kearns, Publisher
jkearns@theemc.ca
Terry Bush, Regional Managing Editor
tbush@theemc.ca

Belleville: Belleville Shopper's Market
PO Box 446, 365 North Front St., Belleville, ON K8N 5A5
Tel: 866-541-6757; Fax: 866-757-0227
www.shoppersmarket.on.ca
Circulation: 42,800 *Frequency:* Saturday
Charles Parker, General Manager

Belleville: The Community Press
Owned By: Postmedia Network Inc.
#33, 199 Front St., Belleville, ON K8N 5H5
Tel: 613-962-9171; Fax: 613-962-9652
www.communitypress.ca
twitter.com/community_press
www.facebook.com/TheCommunityPress
Circulation: 45,400 *Frequency:* Thurs.
THe Community Press is a member of Canoe Sun Media Community Newspapers.
Darren Murphy, Publisher
Bill Glisky, Regional Managing Editor
bill.glisky@sunmedia.ca
Janet Richards, City Editor
janet.richards@sunmedia.ca

Belleville: Trentonian
Owned By: Postmedia Network Inc.
#535, 199 Front St., Belleville, ON K8V 5H5
Tel: 613-392-6501; Fax: 613-392-0505
tren.newsroom@sunmedia.ca
www.trentonian.ca
twitter.com/TheTrentonian
www.facebook.com/164324826919177
Circulation: 14,000 *Frequency:* Thurs.
Bill Glisky, Regional Managing Editor
bill.glisky@sunmedia.ca
Tim Meeks, City Editor
tim.meeks@sunmedia.ca

Blenheim: Blenheim News-Tribune
Owned By: Blenheim Publishers
PO Box 160, 62 Talbot St. West, Blenheim, ON N0P 1A0
Tel: 519-676-3321; Fax: 519-676-3454
tribune@southkent.net
Circulation: 2,270 *Frequency:* Wednesday
Peter Laurie, Editor

Blyth: The Citizen
Owned By: North Huron Publishing Inc.
PO Box 429, Blyth, ON N0M 1H0
Tel: 519-523-4792; Fax: 519-523-9140
info@northhuron.on.ca
www.northhuron.on.ca
Circulation: 1,800 *Frequency:* Thursday
Keith Roulston, Publisher
Shawn Loughlin, Editor

Bolton: Caledon Citizen
Owned By: Caledon Publishing Ltd.
25 Queen St., Bolton, ON L7E 1C1
Tel: 905-857-6626; Fax: 905-857-6363
admin@caledoncitizen.com
www.caledoncitizen.com
Circulation: 17,000 *Frequency:* Thursday
Alan Claridge, Publisher
publisher@citizen.on.ca
Bill Rea, Editor
416-458-3944
editor@caledoncitizen.com

Bolton: Caledon Enterprise
Previous Name: Bolton Entrprise
Owned By: Metroland Media Group Ltd.
PO Box 99, #4A, 12612 Hwy. 50, Bolton, ON L7E 5T1
Tel: 905-454-4344
advertising@caledonenterprise.com
caledonenterprise.com
Other information: Classifieds, Email:
classified@caledonenterprise.com
twitter.com/CaledonNews
www.facebook.com/CaledonEnterpriseNews

Bolton: Caledon Enterprise
Owned By: Metroland Media Group Ltd.
PO Box 99, Bolton, ON L7E 5T1
Tel: 905-857-3433
www.caledonenterprise.com
twitter.com/caledonnews
www.facebook.com/caledonenterprisenews
Servces readers in Caledon
Kelly Montague, Publisher
kmontague@metroland.com

Bolton: King Weekly Sentinel
Previous Name: King Township Sentinel
Owned By: Simcoe-York Printing & Publishing Ltd.
25 Queen St. North, Bolton, ON L7E 1C1
Tel: 905-857-6626; Fax: 905-729-2541
www.kingsentinel.com
www.facebook.com/thekingsentinel
Circulation: 7,800 *Frequency:* Wed.
Mark Pavilons, Editor
editor@kingsentinel.com

Bracebridge: Bracebridge Examiner
Owned By: Metroland Media Group Ltd.
PO Box 1049, 34 E.P. Lee Dr., Bracebridge, ON P1L 1V2
Tel: 705-645-8771; Fax: 705-645-1718
examnews@muskoka.com
www.muskokaregion.com/bracebridge-on
twitter.com/BracebridgeExam
www.facebook.com/examinerbannernews
Circulation: 9,400 *Frequency:* Wednesday
Maureen Christie, Publisher
mchristie@metroland.com
Jack Tynan, Editor-in-Chief
jtynan@metrolandnorthmedia.com
Kim Good, Sub-editor
kgood@metrolandmedia.com

Bracebridge: Muskoka Sun
Previous Name: Muskoka Sun
Owned By: Metroland Media
34 E.P. Lee Dr., Bracebridge, ON P1L 1V2
Tel: 705-645-4463; Fax: 705-645-1718
sun@muskoka.com
www.cottagecountrynow.ca/topic/MuskokaSun
twitter.com/TheMuskokaSun
Circulation: 11,000 *Frequency:* Weekly
Shaun Sauve, Regional General Manager
ssauve@metroland.com
Kim Good, Sub-editor
kgood@metrolandmedia.com

Bracebridge: The Muskokan
Owned By: Metroland Media
PO Box 1049, 34 E.P. Lee Dr., Bracebridge, ON P1L 1V2
Tel: 705-645-8771; Fax: 705-645-1718
www.muskokaregion.com
Circulation: 25,000 *Frequency:* Weekly; Thursday
Maureen Christie, General Manager
mchristie@metroland.com
Jack Tynan, Editor-in-Chief
jtynan@metrolandnorthmedia.com
Kim Good, Sub-editor
kgood@metrolandnorthmedia.com

Bradford: Bradford West Gwillimbury Times
PO Box 1570, 74 John St. West, Bradford, ON L3Z 2B8
Tel: 905-775-4471; Fax: 905-775-4489
www.bradfordtimes.ca
Circulation: 11,000 *Frequency:* Saturday
Miriam King, Editor
905-775-4471 ext 223
David Zilstra, Publisher
905-775-4471 ext 263

Brantford: The Paris Star
Owned By: Postmedia Network Inc.
#1, 195 Henry St., Brantford, ON N3S 5C9
Tel: 519-442-7866; Fax: 519-442-3100
www.parisstaronline.com
twitter.com/ParisStar
www.facebook.com/114234248620217
Circulation: 775 *Frequency:* Wednesday
Ken Koyama, Publisher
ken.koyama@sunmedia.ca
Michael Peeling, Editor
michael.peeling@sunmedia.ca

Circulation: 30,000 *Frequency:* Tuesday, Thursday
Steve Foreman, General Manager
Chris Vernon, Regional Managing Editor
editorial@caledonenterprise.com

Brighton: The Independent
Owned By: Metroland Media Group Ltd.
PO Box 1030, 1 Young St., Brighton, ON K0K 1H0
Tel: 613-475-0255; Fax: 613-475-4546
www.northumberlandnews.com
Circulation: 17,000 Frequency: Thursday
Tim Whittaker, Publisher
Crystal Crimi, Editor

Brockville: The Recorder & Times
Owned By: Postmedia Network Inc.
2479 Parkedale Ave., Brockville, ON K6V 3H2
Tel: 613-342-4441; Fax: 613-342-4456
www.recorder.ca
twitter.com/recordertimes
Frequency: Daily
The Recorder & Times serves readers in Brockville.

Brockville: St. Lawrence News
Owned By: Metroland Media
7712 Kent Blvd., Brockville, ON K6V 7H6
Tel: 613-342-0305; Fax: 613-498-0307
Toll-Free: 866-242-0262
www.emcstlawrence.ca
twitter.com/emcnews
www.facebook.com/emcnewspaper
Circulation: 29,500 Frequency: Thurs.
Richard Squires, Supervisor, Distribution
richard.rquires@metroland.com
Marla Dowdall, News Editor
mdowdall@perfprint.ca

Burk's Falls: North Bay Nipissing News
Owned By: Metroland Media Group Ltd.
59 Ontario St., Burk's Falls, ON P0A 1C0
www.northbaynipissing.com
www.facebook.com/northbaynip
www.facebook.com/almaguinnipissingnews
Online community newspaper in North Bay, Almaguin &
Nipissing
Dana Robbins, Vice-President & Regional Publisher
dana.robbins@metroland.com

Burks Falls: Almaguin Highlands News
Previous Name: Burks Falls-Powasson Almaguin News
Owned By: Metroland Media Group Ltd.
59 Ontario St., Burks Falls, ON P0A 1C0
Tel: 705-382-9996; Fax: 705-382-9997
Toll-Free: 800-731-6397
www.northbaynipissing.com/almaguinhighlands-on
Circulation: 2,500 Frequency: Thursday
Scott Sauve, Regional General Manager
ssauve@metrolandmedia.com
Jack Tynan, Editor-in-Chief
jtynan@metrolandmedia.com

Burlington: Burlington Post
Owned By: Metroland Media Group Ltd.
#1, 5040 Mainway, Burlington, ON L7L 7G5
Tel: 905-632-4444; Fax: 905-632-9162
letters@burlingtonpost.com
www.insidehalton.com/burlington-on
Other information: Classifieds, Email:
classified@haltonsearch.com
twitter.com/InsideHalton
www.facebook.com/HaltonPhotog
Circulation: 60,000 Frequency: Wednesday, Thursday, Friday
Neil Oliver, Publisher
Jill Davis, Editor-in-Chief
jdavis@burlingtonpost.com
Debbi Koppejan, Director, Advertising
dkoppejan@metroland.com

Burlington: Flamborough Review
Owned By: Metroland Media Group Ltd.
#2, 5046 Mainway, Burlington, ON L7L 5Z1
www.flamboroughreview.com
twitter.com/flamreview
www.facebook.com/flamboroughreview
Serves readers in Flamborough
Catherine O'Hara, Regional Managing Editor, Halton Division
cohara@metroland.com

Burlington: Inside Halton
Owned By: Metroland Media Group Ltd.
901 Guelph Line, Burlington, ON L7R 3N8
www.insidehalton.com
twitter.com/insidehalton
www.facebook.com/insidehalton
Community newspapers published under this banner include the
Burlington Post, the Milton Canadian Champion & the Oakville
Beaver

Catherine O'Hara, Managing Editor, Halton Division
editor@miltoncanadianchampion.com

Caledonia: The Sachem
Owned By: Metroland Media Group Ltd.
3 Sutherland St. West, Caledonia, ON N3W 1C1
Tel: 905-765-4441
www.sachem.ca
twitter.com/sachemnews
www.facebook.com/thesachem
Serves readers in Haldimand County
Gordon Cameron, Group Managing Editor
gocameron@hamiltonnews.com

Cambridge: Cambridge Times
Owned By: Metroland Media Group Ltd.
475 Thompson Dr., Cambridge, ON N1T 2K7
www.cambridgetimes.ca
twitter.com/cambridgetimes
www.facebook.com/cambridgetimesont
Serves readers in Cambridge
Kelly Montague, Publisher
kmontague@metroland.com

Cannington: Brock Citizen
Owned By: Metroland Media Group Ltd.
2D Cameron St. East, Cannington, ON L0E 1E0
Tel: 705-432-8842; Fax: 705-432-2942
www.mykawartha.com
twitter.com/BrockCitizen
Circulation: 5,400 Frequency: Thursday
Mike Mount, Publisher
mike.mount@mykawartha.com
Scott Howard, Editor
showard@mykawartha.com

Chatham: Chatham Smart Shopper
Owned By: Postmedia Network Inc.
138 King St. West, 2nd Fl., Chatham, ON N7M 1E3
Tel: 519-351-4362; Fax: 519-351-7774
Toll-Free: 877-351-7331
classifieds.chathamsmartshopper.com
Dean Muharrem, Manager, Advertising
dean.muharrem@sunmedia.com

Chatham: Chatham This Week
Owned By: Postmedia Network Inc.
138 King St. West, Chatham, ON N7M 1E3
Tel: 519-351-7331; Fax: 519-351-7774
www.chathamthisweek.com
twitter.com/ctw_news
www.facebook.com/ctwnews
Circulation: 19,600 Frequency: Wednesday
Dean Muharrem, Publisher
519-598-4700
dead.muharrem@sunmedia.ca
Peter Epp, Editor
519-598-4727
peter.epp@sunmedia.ca

Chatham: Wallaceburg Courier Press
Owned By: Postmedia Network Inc.
138 King St. West, Chatham, ON N7M 1E3
Tel: 519-351-7331; Fax: 519-351-7334
www.wallaceburgcourierpress.com
twitter.com/w_courierpress
www.facebook.com/152594691460732
Circulation: 8,900 Frequency: Thurs.
Dean Muharrem, Publisher
dean.muharrem@sunmedia.ca
Peter Epp, Editor
peter.epp@sunmedia.ca

Chesterville: Chesterville Record
Owned By: Etcetera Publications
PO Box 368, 7 King St., Chesterville, ON K0C 1H0
Tel: 613-448-2322 Toll-Free: 866-307-3541
chestervillerecord.com
Circulation: 1,900 Frequency: Wednesday
Robin Morris, Publisher
record@storm.ca
Nelson Zandbergen, Editor

Chesterville: The Villager
Previous Name: Russell Villager
Owned By: County Media
PO Box 368, 7 King St. St., Chesterville, ON K0C 2K0
Tel: 613-445-3804
adsrussellvillager@gmail.com
russellvillager.com
www.facebook.com/TheRussellVillager
Circulation: 800 Frequency: Wed.
Serving Russell Village and Township and surrounding areas.

Robin Morris, Managing Publisher
record@storm.ca
Nelson Zandbergen, Editor
thevillager.editor@gmail.com

Clinton: Clinton News-Record
Owned By: Postmedia Network Inc.
53 Albert St., Clinton, ON N0M 1L0
Tel: 519-482-3443
www.clintonnewsrecord.com
twitter.com/clintonnewsreco
www.facebook.com/ClintonNewsRecord
Circulation: 1,400 Frequency: Wednesday
Neil H. Clifford, Publisher
neil.clifford@sunmedia.ca
Cheryl Heath, Editor
clinton.news@sunmedia.ca

Cobden: The Pulse
Owned By: The Cobden Sun Ltd.
PO Box 100, Crawford St., Cobden, ON K0J 1K0
Tel: 613-646-2380; Fax: 613-628-3291
Circulation: 1,374 Frequency: Wednesday
Formerly the Cobden Sun
Ron Tracey, Publisher

Cobourg: The Northumberland News
Owned By: Metroland Media Group Ltd.
#212, 884 Division St., Cobourg, ON K9A 5V6
Tel: 905-373-7355
www.northumberlandnews.com
twitter.com/north_news
www.facebook.com/northnews
Circulation: 22,800 Frequency: Thurs., Fri.
Serves readers in Cobourg, Port Hope, Cramahe, Hamilton
Township & Alnwick/Haldimand
Tim Whittaker, Publisher
twhittaker@durhamregion.com

Cochrane: Cochrane Times-Post
Previous Name: Cochrane Times
Owned By: Postmedia Network Inc.
143 - 6th Ave., Cochrane, ON P0L 1C0
Tel: 705-272-3344; Fax: 705-272-3434
www.cochranetimespost.com
twitter.com/CTimesPost
Circulation: 11,300 Frequency: Wed.
Wayne Major, Publisher
wayne.major@sunmedia.ca
Kevin Anderson, Regional Managing Editor
kevin.anderson@sunmedia.ca

Collingwood: The Enterprise-Bulletin
Owned By: Postmedia Network Inc.
PO Box 98, 77 Simcoe St., Collingwood, ON L9Y 3J9
Tel: 705-445-4611; Fax: 705-444-6477
www.theenterprisebulletin.com
twitter.com/EnterpriseBulle
www.facebook.com/theenterprisebulletin
Circulation: 18,800 Frequency: Tuesday, Friday
Sandy Davies, Publisher
Ian Adams, Managing Editor
ian.adams@sunmedia.ca

Cornwall: Le Journal de Cornwall
Détenteur: Campagnie d'Edition André Paquette
113 rue de Montréal, Cornwall, ON K6H 1B2
Tél: 613-938-1433; Téléc: 613-938-2798
jcornwall@eap.on.ca
editionap.ca/en/newspaper/35
Tirage: 23 000 Fréquence: Jeudi
Roger Duplantie, President
roger.duplantie@eap.on.ca

Cornwall: Seaway News
Owned By: J.G.F. Holdings Inc.
29 - 2nd St. East, Cornwall, ON K6H 1Y2
Tel: 613-933-0014; Fax: 613-933-0024
www.cornwallseawaynews.com
twitter.com/SeawayNews
www.facebook.com/cornwallseawaynews
Circulation: 36,500 Frequency: Thursday
Rick Shaver, Editor & General Manager
rshaver@conwallseawaynews.com
Joel Herrington, Editor

Deep River: North Renfrew Times
Owned By: Deep River Community Assn. Inc.
PO Box 310, 21 Champlain St., Deep River, ON K0J 1P0
Tel: 613-584-4161; Fax: 613-584-1062
nrt@magma.ca
www.northrenfrewtimes.com
Circulation: 1,845 Frequency: Wednesday

Terry Myers, Editor-in-Chief
Kelly Lapping, General Manager

Delhi: Delhi News-Record
Owned By: Postmedia Network Inc.
237 Main St., Delhi, ON N4B 2M4

Tel: 519-582-2510
www.delhinewsrecord.com
twitter.com/DelhiNewsRecord
www.facebook.com/DelhiNewsRecord

Circulation: 503 Frequency: Wednesday
Ken Koyama, Publisher
ken.koyama@sunmedia.ca
Kim Novak, Managing Editor
kim.novak@sunmedia.ca

Dorchester: Dorchester Signpost
Owned By: Dorchester Signpost
15 Bridge St., Dorchester, ON N0L 1G2

Tel: 519-268-7337; Fax: 519-268-3260
info@dorchestersignpost.com
www.dorchestersignpost.com

Circulation: 1,670 Frequency: Wednesday
Fred Huxley, Publisher
Wendy Spence, Editor
news@dorchestersignpost.com

Drayton: The Community News
Owned By: W.H.A. Publications Ltd.
PO Box 169, 41 Wellington St. North, Drayton, ON N0G 1P0

Tel: 519-638-3066; Fax: 519-638-3066
Toll-Free: 800-708-9555
news@wellingtonadvertiser.com
www.wellingtonadvertiser.com
Other information: Ads: advertising@wellingtonadvertiser.com

Circulation: 5,400 Frequency: Friday
William H. Adsett, Publisher
David L. Adsett, Editor & General Manager
editor@wellingtonadvertiser.com

Dryden: Dryden Observer
Owned By: Alex Wilson Coldstream Ltd.
PO Box 3009, #1, 32 Colonization Ave, Dryden, ON P8N 2Y9

Tel: 807-223-2381; Fax: 807-223-2907
Toll-Free: 800-465-7230
www.drydenobserver.ca
twitter.com/DrydenObserver

Circulation: 2,460 Frequency: Wednesday
Chris Marchand, Editor
807-221-7334
chrism@drydenobserver.ca
Graham Mackenzie, General Manager

Dundalk: Dundalk Herald
Owned By: Dundalk Herald Publishing
PO Box 280, 260 Main St. East, Dundalk, ON N0C 1B0

Tel: 519-923-2203; Fax: 519-923-2747
dundalk.heraldnews@gmail.com
dundalkherald.ca
Other information: Ads: dundaldkherald@gmail.com

Circulation: 1,700 Frequency: Wednesday
Matthew Walls, Publisher
Mary Fowler, Editor

Dundalk: The Flesherton Advance
PO Box 280, 260 Main St. East, Dundalk, ON N0C 1B0

Tel: 519-923-2203; Fax: 519-923-2747
dundalk.heraldnews@gmail.com
www.dundalkherald.ca
Other information: Ads: dundalk.herald@gmail.com

Circulation: 1,700 Frequency: Wednesday
Matt Walls, Publisher
Cathy Walls, General Manager

Eganville: Eganville Leader
Owned By: The Eganville Leader Publishing Ltd.
PO Box 310, 150 John St., Eganville, ON K0J 1T0

Tel: 613-628-2332; Fax: 613-628-3291
leader@nrtco.net
www.eganvilleleader.com

Circulation: 5,800 Frequency: Wednesday
Gerald Tracey, Editor & Co-Publisher

Elliot Lake: Elliot Lake Standard
Owned By: Postmedia Network Inc.
14 Hillside Dr. South, Elliot Lake, ON P5A 1M6

Tel: 705-848-7195; Fax: 705-848-0249
news@elliotlakestandard.ca
www.elliotlakestandard.ca
twitter.com/ELStandard

Circulation: 3,400 Frequency: Wednesday
Karsten Johansen, Publisher
karsten.johansen@sunmedia.ca

Kevin McSheffrey, Editor
kevin.mcsheffrey@sunmedia.ca

Elmira: Observer
20B Arthur St. North, Elmira, ON N3B 1Z9

Tel: 519-669-5790; Fax: 519-669-5753
Toll-Free: 888-966-5942
info@woolwichobserver.com
www.observerxtra.com
Other information: Advertising, Email:
sales@woolwichobserver.com
twitter.com/woolwichnews
www.facebook.com/ObserverXtra

Circulation: 15,200 Frequency: Sat.
The community newspaper serves Woolwich & Wellesley
Townships in Ontario.
Joe Merlihan, Publisher
jmerlihan@woolwichobserver.com
Steve Kannon, Editor
skannon@woolwichobserver.com

Erin: Erin Advocate
Owned By: Metroland Media Group Ltd.
PO Box 578, #1A, Spring St., Erin, ON N0B 1T0

Tel: 519-833-9603; Fax: 519-833-9605
www.erinadvocate.com

Circulation: 1,900 Frequency: Thursday
Dana Robbins, Vice President & Regional Publisher
Joan Murray, Managing Editor

Espanola: Mid-North Monitor
Owned By: Postmedia Network Inc.
#1, 46 Mead Blvd., Espanola, ON P5E 1E8

Tel: 705-869-0588; Fax: 705-869-0587
www.midnorthmonitor.com
twitter.com/MidNorthMonitor
www.facebook.com/MidNorthMonitor

Circulation: 1,000 Frequency: Thursday
Karsten Johansen, Publisher
karsten.johansen@sunmedia.ca
Kevin McSheffery, Editor
mnm.editor@sunmedia.ca

Essex: Essex Free Press
Owned By: The Essex Free Press Limited
PO Box 115, 16 Centre St., Essex, ON N8M 2Y1

Tel: 519-776-4268; Fax: 519-776-4014
essexfreepress@on.aibn.com
sxfreepress.com
www.youtube.com/user/essexfreepress
twitter.com/essexfreepress
www.fac ebook.com/theessexfreepress

Circulation: 9,950 Frequency: Thursday
Richard Parkinson, Editor & Co-Publisher

Fergus: The Wellington Advertiser
Owned By: W.H.A. Publications Ltd.
PO Box 252, 905 Gartshore St., Fergus, ON N1M 2W8

Tel: 519-843-5410; Fax: 519-843-7607
news@wellingtonadvertiser.com
www.wellingtonadvertiser.com
Other information: Ads, Email:
advertising@wellingtonadvertiser.com
twitter.com/WellyAdvertiser

Circulation: 40,470 Frequency: Friday
David L. Adsett, Publisher
Chris Daponte, Editor
editor@wellingtonadvertiser.com

Fonthill: The Voice
#8, 209 Hwy. 20 East, Fonthill, ON L0S 1E6

Tel: 905-892-8690; Fax: 905-892-0823
classified@thevoiceofpelham.ca
www.thevoiceofpelham.ca
www.facebook.com/voiceofpelham

Circulation: 5,500 Frequency: Wed.
Sarah Murrell, Publisher & Editor
Stephen Dyell, Reporter
editor@thevoiceofpelham.ca
Leslie Chiappetta, Manager, Office
office@thevoiceofpelham.ca
Warren Mason, Contact, Advertising Sales
advertising@thevoiceofpelham.ca

Forest: Forest Standard
Owned By: Hayter-Walden Publications Inc.
1 King St. West, Forest, ON N0N 1J0

Tel: 519-786-5242; Fax: 519-786-4884
standard@execulink.com
hayterwalden.com

Circulation: 1,900 Frequency: Thursday
Dale Hayter, Publisher
Kimberly Powell, Editor

Fort Frances: Fort Frances Times
Owned By: London Publishing
PO Box 339, 116 - 1st St. East, Fort Frances, ON P9A 1K2

Tel: 807-274-5373; Fax: 807-274-7286
Toll-Free: 800-465-8508
info@fortfrances.com
fftimes.com
twitter.com/fftimes
www.facebook.com/fortfrancestimes

Circulation: 3,000 Frequency: Weekly, Wednesday
News from Fort Frances & the Rainy River District
Lincoln Dunn, General Manager
ldunn@fortfrances.com
Megan Walchuk, Editor
mwalchuk@fortfrances.com

Fort Frances: Fort Frances Times
Owned By: Fort Frances Times Ltd.
116 - 1st St. East, Fort Frances, ON P9A 3M7

Tel: 807-274-5373; Fax: 807-274-7286
Toll-Free: 800-465-8508
fftimes.com
twitter.com/hashtag/fortfrances
www.facebook.com/fortfrancestimes

Circulation: 3,990 Frequency: Wednesday
Jim Cumming, Publisher
jcumming@fortfrances.com
Mike Behan, Editor
mbehan@fortfrances.com

Gananoque: Gananoque Reporter
Owned By: Postmedia Network Inc.
79 King St. East, Gananoque, ON K7G 1E8

Tel: 613-389-7400; Fax: 613-382-3010
editor@gananoquereporter.com
www.gananoquereporter.com
twitter.com/GanReporter

Circulation: 7,500 Frequency: Wednesday
Liza Nelson, Publisher
liza.nelson@sunmedia.ca
Mike Beaudin, Managing Editor
mike.beaudin@sunmedi.ca

Georgetown: The Independent & Free Press
Previous Name: Georgetown Independent/Acton Free
Press
Owned By: Metroland Media Group Ltd.
#77, 280 Guelph St., Georgetown, ON L7G 4B1

Tel: 905-873-0301
newsroom@theifp.ca
www.theifp.ca
twitter.com/ifp_11
www.facebook.com/IndependentAndFreePress

Circulation: 22,000 Frequency: Tuesday, Thursday
Kelly Montague, Publisher
kmontague@metroland.com

Geraldton: Times Star
Owned By: Time Star Publishing
PO Box 340, 401 Main St., Geraldton, ON P0T 1M0

Tel: 807-854-1919; Fax: 807-854-1682
web@thetimestar.ca
thetimestar.ca

Circulation: 938 Frequency: Wednesday
Eric Pietsch, Publisher & Editor
editor@thetimestar.ca

Glencoe: Transcript & Free Press
Owned By: Hayter-Walden Publications Inc.
PO Box 400, 243 Main St., Glencoe, ON N0L 1M0

Tel: 519-287-2615; Fax: 519-287-2408
tfp@execulink.com
hayterwalden.com

Circulation: 1,100 Frequency: Thursday
Dale Hayter, Publisher
Marie Williams-Gagnon, Editor

Goderich: The Goderich Signal-Star
Owned By: Postmedia Network Inc.
120 Huckins St., Goderich, ON N7A 3X8

Tel: 519-524-2614; Fax: 519-524-9175
www.goderichsignalstar.com
twitter.com/goderichsignals

Circulation: 4000 Frequency: Wed; also Focus (every other Fri.)
John Bauman, Publisher
john.bauman@sunmedia.ca
Paul Cluff, Editor

Grand Bend: **The Lakeshore Advance**
Owned By: Postmedia Network Inc.
PO Box 1195, 58 Ontario St. North, Grand Bend, ON N0M 1T0
Tel: 519-238-5383; *Fax:* 519-238-5131
lakeshore.advance@sunmedia.ca
www.lakeshoreadvance.com
twitter.com/lakeshoreadvanc
www.facebook.com/180897961958469
Circulation: 1,000 *Frequency:* Wednesday
Neil H. Clifford, Publisher
neil.clifford@sunmedia.ca
Lynda Hillman-Rapley, Editor
lakeshore.advance@sunmedia.ca

Gravenhurst: **Gravenhurst Banner**
Owned By: Metroland Media Group Ltd.
140 Muskoka Rd. South, Gravenhurst, ON P1P 1X2
Tel: 705-687-6674
www.muskokaregion.com/gravenhurst-on
Circulation: 3,043 *Frequency:* Wednesday
Joe Anderson, Publisher

Gravenhurst: **Muskoka Today**
PO Box 34, Gravenhurst, ON P1P 1H5
Tel: 705-687-5777 *Toll-Free:* 800-240-2329
news@muskokatoday.com
www.muskokatoday.com
Other information: Advertising, Email: ads@muskokatoday.com
Circulation: 10,000
Mark Clairmont, Publisher

Grimsby: **Grimsby Lincoln News**
Owned By: Metroland Media Group Ltd.
32 Main St. West, Grimsby, ON L3M 1R4
Tel: 905-945-8392; *Fax:* 905-945-3916
www.niagarathisweek.com/community/grimsby
www.facebook.com/GrimsbyLincolnNews
Circulation: 161,000 *Frequency:* Wed., Fri.
The Grimsby Lincoln News is a free tabloid newspaper delivered to every home in the region.
Neil Oliver, Publisher
David Bos, General Manager
Joel Billinghurst, Manager, Production
Melissa Duemo, Manager, Business
Tracy Travis-Scott, Manager, Circulation
Dave Hawkins, Director, Advertising

Grimsby: **newsnow**
Owned By: 16002207 Ontario Ltd.
49 Main St. West, Grimsby, ON L3M 1R3
Tel: 289-235-9500
wn3.ca
twitter.com/MikesNiagara
Circulation: 25,733 *Frequency:* Thursday
100% Niagara owned, operated & printed
Mike Williscraft, Publisher
289-442-4244

Guelph: **Guelph Mercury Tribune**
Owned By: Metroland Media Group Ltd.
#7, 367 Woodlawn Rd. West, Guelph, ON N1H 7K9
Tel: 519-763-3333; *Fax:* 519-763-4814
www.guelphmercury.com
twitter.com/guelphtribune
Circulation: 44,700 *Frequency:* Thursday
Chris Clark, Editor
519-763-3333 ext 230
cclark@guelphtribune.ca
Peter Winkler, Publisher

Guelph: **Guelph Mercury Tribune**
Owned By: Metroland Media Group Ltd.
#1, 367 Woodlawn Rd., Guelph, ON N1H 7K9
www.guelphmercury.com
twitter.com/mercurytribune
www.facebook.com/guelphmercurytribune
Serves readers in Guelph
Doug Coxson, Editor
dcoxson@guelphmercurytribune.com

Haliburton: **Haliburton Echo**
Previous Name: Haliburton County Echo
Owned By: Postmedia Network Inc.
PO Box 136, 146 Highland St., Haliburton, ON K0M 1S0
Tel: 705-457-1037; *Fax:* 705-457-3275
info@haliburtonecho.on.ca
www.haliburtonecho.on.ca
twitter.com/haliburtonecho
www.facebook.com/HaliburtonEcho
Circulation: 2,100 *Frequency:* Tuesday
David Zilstra, Publisher
david.zilstra@gmail.com

Jenn Watt, Editor
jenn@haliburtonpress.com

Hamilton: **Le Régional**
Hamilton Branch
970 rue King Est, Hamilton, ON L8M 1C4
Tél: 905-549-7002; *Téléc:* 905-790-9127
info@leregional.com
www.leregional.com
www.facebook.com/leregionalontario
Tirage: 10 000 *Fréquence:* Mercredi
Christiane Beaupré, Rédactrice en chef

Hanover: **The Post (Hanover)**
Owned By: Postmedia Network Inc.
413 - 18th Ave., Hanover, ON N4N 3S5
Tel: 519-364-2001; *Fax:* 519-364-6950
postedit@thepost.on.ca
www.thepost.on.ca
twitter.com/hanoverthepost
www.facebook.com/HanoverPost
Circulation: 15,500 *Frequency:* Thursday
Patrick Bales, Managing Editor
patrick.bales@sunmedia.ca
Marie David, Publisher
marie.david@sunmedia.ca

Harrow: **Harrow News**
Owned By: Harrownews Publishing Co. Inc.
PO Box 310, 563 Queen St., Harrow, ON N0R 1G0
Tel: 519-738-2542; *Fax:* 519-738-3874
harnews@mnsi.net
Circulation: 1,300 *Frequency:* Tuesday
Cecil MacKenzie, Publisher & Co-Editor

Hawkesbury: **Le Carillon**
Détenteur: La Comp. D'Edition Andre Paquette Inc.
CP 1000, 1100 Aberdeen, Hawkesbury, ON K6H 3H1
Tél: 613-632-4155; *Téléc:* 613-632-6122
nouvelles@eap.on.ca
www.lecarillon.ca
www.facebook.com/LeCarillonTribuneExpress
Tirage: 19 500 *Fréquence:* Mercredi
Yvan Joly, Directeur
yvan.joly@eap.on.ca

Hawkesbury: **Le/The Regional**
124, rue Principale est, Hawkesbury, ON K6A 1A3
Tel: 613-632-0112; *Fax:* 613-632-0277
Toll-Free: 888-477-3566
pub@le-regional.ca
www.le-regional.ca
www.facebook.com/266630786710813
Circulation: 27,000 *Frequency:* Fri.
André Cayer
Sylvain Roy

Hawkesbury: **Tribune-Express**
édition Ontario
Previous Name: Hawkesbury Tribune/Express
PO Box 1000, 1100 Aberdeen, Hawkesbury, ON K6H 3H1
Tel: 613-632-4155; *Fax:* 613-632-8601
nouvelles@eap.on.ca
editionap.ca/fr/newspaper/32
www.facebook.com/LeCarillonTribuneExpress
Circulation: 24,100 *Frequency:* Friday
Yvan Joly, Directeur
yvan.joly@eap.on.ca

Hearst: **Le Nord**
Détenteur: Le Nord Inc.
CP 2320, 813, rue Georges, Hearst, ON P0L 1N0
Tél: 705-372-1233; *Téléc:* 705-362-5954
lenord@lenord.on.ca
www.lenord.on.ca
www.facebook.com/lejournallenord
Tirage: 1 480 *Fréquence:* Mercredi
Omer Cantin, Éditeur
705-372-1234 ext 222
ocantin@lenord.on.ca
Marlène Bélanger, Gérante
705-372-1237 ext 229
mbelanger@lenord.on.ca

Huntsville: **Huntsville Forester**
Owned By: Metroland Media Group Ltd.
11 Main St. West, Huntsville, ON P1H 2C5
Tel: 705-789-5541; *Fax:* 705-789-9381
www.muskokaregion.com/huntsville-on
Circulation: 10,300 *Frequency:* Wednesday
Shaun Sauve, Regional General Manager
705-645-8771 ext 227
ssauve@metroland.com

Jack Tynan, Editor-in-Chief
705-645-8771 ext 247
jtynan@metrolandnorthmedia.com

Iroquois Falls: **The Enterprise**
Owned By: William C. Cavell Enterprises Ltd.
PO Box 834, 727 Synagogue St., Iroquois Falls, ON P0K 1G0
Tel: 705-232-4081
Circulation: 2,130 *Frequency:* Thursday
William C. Cavell, Publisher
Tony Delaurier, General Manager

Johnstown: **Barrhaven Independent**
Owned By: The Morris Group
3201 County Rd. 2, Johnstown, ON K0E 1T0
Tel: 613-692-6000
newsfile@bellnet.ca
www.barrhavenindependent.on.ca
www.facebook.com/142393275816516
Circulation: 17,138 *Frequency:* Semimonthly
Now available only online.
Jeffrey Morris, Publisher & Editor

Johnstown: **Prescott Journal**
Owned By: St. Lawrence Printing Co. Ltd.
PO Box 549, Johnstown, ON K0E 1T0
Tel: 613-925-4265; *Fax:* 613-925-2837
editor@prescottjournal.com
www.prescottjournal.com
Circulation: 1,400 *Frequency:* Wed.
Lisa D. Taylor, Publisher
Jeff Morris, Editor
newsfile@bellnet.ca

Kenora: **Lake of the Woods Enterprise**
Owned By: Postmedia Network Inc.
33 Main St., Kenora, ON P9N 3X7
Tel: 807-468-5555; *Fax:* 807-468-4318
info@kenoraenterprise.com
www.kenoradailyminerandnews.com
Circulation: 8,700 *Frequency:* Thurs.
Daria Zmiyiwsky, Publisher
daria.zmiyiwsky@sunmedia.ca
Lloyd Mack, Regional Managing Editor
lloyd.mack@sunmedia.ca

Keswick: **Georgina Advocate**
Owned By: York Region Media Group
184 Simcoe Ave., Keswick, ON L4P 2H7
Tel: 905-476-7753; *Fax:* 905-476-5785
www.yorkregion.com
Circulation: 28,500 *Frequency:* Thursday, Sunday
Ian Proudfoot, Publisher
Tracy Kibble, Editor
tkibble@yrmg.com
Tanya Pacheco, Director, Circulation
tpacheco@yrmg.com

Kincardine: **The Kincardine Independent**
Owned By: Kincardine Publishing Company Ltd.
PO Box 1240, 840 Queen St., Kincardine, ON N2Z 2Z4
Tel: 519-396-3111; *Fax:* 519-396-3899
indepen@bmts.com
www.independent.on.ca
Circulation: 2,368 *Frequency:* Wednesday
Eric Howald, Publisher
John Miles, Regional Manager

Kincardine: **Kincardine News**
Owned By: Postmedia Network Inc.
719 Queen St., Kincardine, ON N2Z 1Z9
Tel: 519-396-2963; *Fax:* 519-396-6865
kincardine.news@sunmedia.ca
www.kincardinenews.ca
twitter.com/Kincardinenews
www.facebook.com/kincardinenews
Circulation: 5,676 *Frequency:* Thursday
Marie David, Publisher
marie.david@sunmedia.ca
Troy Patterson, Editor
kincardine.news@sunmedia.ca

Kingston: **Kingston This Week**
Owned By: Postmedia Network Inc.
Kingston Publications, 6 Cataraqui St., Kingston, ON K7K 6C4
Tel: 613-389-7400; *Fax:* 613-389-7507
news@kingstonthisweek.com
www.kingstonthisweek.com
Circulation: 50,200 *Frequency:* Thursday
Liza Nelson, Publisher
liza.nelson@sunmedia.ca

Mike Beaudin, Managing Editor
mike.beaudin@sunmedia.ca

Kingsville: Kingsville Reporter
Owned By: Postmedia Network Inc.
17 Chestnut St., Kingsville, ON N9Y 1J9
Tel: 519-733-2211; *Fax:* 519-733-6464
kingsvillereporter@kingsvillereporter.com
kingsvillereporter.com
Other information: Ads: rsims@kingsvillereporter.com
Circulation: 1,420 *Frequency:* Tuesday
Nelson Santos, Editor
519-733-2211 ext 24
nsantos@kingsvillereporter.com

Kitchener: Kitchener Post
Owned By: Metroland Media Group Ltd.
#104, 630 Riverbend Dr., Kitchener, ON N2K 3S2
www.kitchenerpost.ca
twitter.com/kitchenerpost
www.facebook.com/thepostinkitchener
Online community newspaper in Kitchener
Bob Vrbanac, Managing Editor
bvrbanac@kitchenerpost.ca

Kitchener: Waterloo Chronicle
Owned By: Metroland Media Group Ltd.
#104, 630 Riverbend Dr., Kitchener, ON N2K 3S2
www.waterloochronicle.ca
twitter.com/wlchronicle
www.facebook.com/waterloochronicle
Online community newspaper in Waterloo
Bob Vrbanac, Editor
bvrbanac@waterloochronicle.ca

Lakefield: Lakefield Herald
Previous Name: Katchewanooka Herald
Owned By: Lakefield Herald Ltd.
PO Box 1000, 74 Bridge St., Lakefield, ON K0L 2H0
Tel: 705-652-6594; *Fax:* 705-652-6912
Toll-Free: 877-652-5114
info@lakefieldherald.com
www.lakefieldherald.com
twitter.com/LakefieldHerald
www.facebook.com/LakefieldHerald
Circulation: 940 *Frequency:* Friday
Simon Conolly, Publisher
sconolly@lakefieldherald.com

Listowel: Midwestern Newspapers Corp.
185 Wallace Ave., Listowel, ON N4W 1K8
Tel: 519-291-1660
midwesternnewspapers.com
Circulation: 420 *Frequency:* Wednesday
Bill Huether, General Manager
bhuether@mountforest.com
Dianne Hatch, Manager, Classifieds, Circulation
dhatch@mountforest.com

Little Current: The Manitoulin Expositor
Previous Name: The Manitoulin West Recorder
Owned By: Manitoulin Publishing Co. Ltd.
PO Box 369, 1 Manitowaning Rd., Little Current, ON P0P 1K0
Tel: 705-368-2744; *Fax:* 705-368-3822
expositor@manitoulin.ca
www.manitoulin.ca
twitter.com/man_expositor
www.facebook.com/ManitoulinExpositor
Circulation: 5,480 *Frequency:* Wednesday
Rick McCutcheon, Publisher
Alicia McCutcheon, Editor
editor@manitoulin.ca

London: London Pennysaver
PO Box 2280, 369 York St., London, ON N6A 4G1
Tel: 519-685-2020; *Fax:* 519-667-4573
pennyreaderads@londonpennysaver.com
www.londonpennysaver.com
Frequency: Friday
Cathy Forster, Manager, Sales
cforster@lfpress.com

London: The Londoner
Owned By: Postmedia Network Inc.
369 York St., London, ON N6A 4G1
Tel: 519-673-5005; *Fax:* 519-673-4624
www.thelondoner.ca
twitter.com/londoneronline
www.facebook.com/londoneronline
Circulation: 140,000 *Frequency:* Thurs.
Chris Montanini, Regional Managing Editor
cmontanini@sunmedia.ca

Lucknow: Lucknow Sentinel
Owned By: Postmedia Network Inc.
619 Campbell St., Lucknow, ON N0G 2H0
Tel: 519-528-2822; *Fax:* 519-528-3529
lucknow.editorial@sunmedia.ca
www.lucknowsentinel.com
twitter.com/LucknowSentine1
www.facebook.com/LucknowSentinel
Circulation: 1,160 *Frequency:* Wednesday
Marie David, Publisher
519-364-2001 ext 24
marie.david@sunmedia.ca

Manotick: Manotick Messenger
Owned By: The Morris Group
PO Box 567, 1165 Beaverwood Rd., Manotick, ON K4M 1A5
Tel: 613-692-6000; *Fax:* 613-692-3758
newsfile@bellnet.ca
www.manotickmessenger.on.ca
Other information: Classified Advertising, Phone: 613-925-4265
twitter.com/ManotickMessngr
www.facebook.com/267448403344583
Circulation: 8,000 *Frequency:* Thurs.
Beth Morris, Owner
Jeff Morris, Publisher
Bev McRae, Journalist & Photographer
Gary Coulombe, Representative, Advertising
advert@bellnet.ca

Markham: Markham Economist & Sun
Owned By: York Region Media Group
#115, 50 McIntosh Dr., Markham, ON L3R 9T3
Tel: 905-294-2200; *Fax:* 905-294-1538
www.yorkregion.com
Circulation: 135,000 *Frequency:* Thursday, Saturday
Ian Proudfoot, Publisher
Bernie O'Neill, Editor
boneill@yrmg.com

Mattawa: Mattawa Recorder
PO Box 64, 341 McConnell St., Mattawa, ON P0H 1V0
Tel: 705-744-5361; *Fax:* 705-744-5361
recorder@bellnet.ca
mattawa.ca
www.facebook.com/mattawa.recorder
Circulation: 1,050 *Frequency:* Sunday
Heather Edwards, Publisher
Tom Edwards, Publisher

Meaford: Blue Mountains Courier-Herald
Previous Name: The Courier Herald
Owned By: Metroland Media Group Ltd.
#6, 24 Trowbridge St., Meaford, ON N4L 1Y1
Tel: 519-599-3760; *Fax:* 519-538-5028
courierherald@simcoe.com
www.simcoe.com/bluemountains-on
Circulation: 480 *Frequency:* Wed.; also Meaford Express (Wed., circ. 2,521)
Carol Lamb, General Manager
clamb@simcoe.com
Scott Woodhouse, Editor
swoodhouse@simcoe.com

Meaford: Meaford Express
Owned By: Metroland Media Group Ltd.
#6, 24 Trowbridge St. West, Meaford, ON N4L 1Y1
Tel: 519-538-1421; *Fax:* 519-538-5028
www.simcoe.com/community/meaford
twitter.com/meafordexpress
www.facebook.com/TheMeafordExpress
Circulation: 1,200 *Frequency:* Wed.
Ian Proudfoot, Publisher
iproudfoot@metroland.com
Chris Fell, Editor
cfell@simcoe.com
Carol Lamb, General Manager
clamb@simcoe.com
Cheryl McMenemy, Manager, Sales
cmcmenemy@simcoe.com

Mildmay: Mildmay Town & Country Crier
Owned By: Mildmay Town and Country Crier
PO Box 190, 100 Elora St., Mildmay, ON N0G 2J0
Tel: 519-367-2681; *Fax:* 519-367-5417
thecrier@wightman.ca
Circulation: 1,350 *Frequency:* Wednesday
Susan Bross, Publisher

Millbrook: Millbrook Times
Owned By: Millbrook Times
PO Box 285, 1 King St. West, Millbrook, ON L0A 1G0
Tel: 705-932-3001; *Fax:* 705-932-8816
thetimes@nexicom.net
themillbrooktimes.ca
www.facebook.com/themillbrooktimes
Circulation: 1,816 *Frequency:* Thu.
Karen Graham, Publisher
Celia Hunter, Editor

Milton: Milton Canadian Champion
Owned By: Metroland Media Group Ltd.
555 Industrial Dr., Milton, ON L9T 5E1
Tel: 905-878-2341
www.insidehalton.com
twitter.com/Milton_Champion
Circulation: 28,600 *Frequency:* Tuesday, Thursday
Jill Davis, Editor-in-Chief
jdavis@metroland.com
David Harvey, Regional Group Manager
dharvey@metroland.com
Karen Miceli, Editor
kmiceli@metroland.com

Minden: Minden Times
Owned By: Postmedia Network Inc.
PO Box 97, 2 IGA Rd., Minden, ON K0M 2K0
Tel: 705-286-1288; *Fax:* 705-286-4768
www.mindentimes.ca
twitter.com/mindentimes
www.facebook.com/MindenTimes
Circulation: 1,500 *Frequency:* Wednesday
Jenn Watt, Editor
jenn.watt@sunmedia.ca
David Zilstra, Publisher
david.zilstra@gmail.com
Don Smith, Publisher

Mississauga: The Brampton Guardian
Owned By: Metroland Media Group Ltd.
3145 Wolfedale Rd., Mississauga, ON L5C 3A9
Tel: 905-273-8815
www.thebramptonguardian.com
twitter.com/brmptguardian
www.facebook.com/bramptonguardian
Serves readers in Brampton
Dana Robbins, Publisher
dana.robbins@metroland.com

Mississauga: Metroland North Media Group
Owned By: Metroland Media Group Ltd.
3145 Wolfedale Rd., Mississauga, ON L5C 3A9
www.muskokaregion.com
twitter.com/muskokaregion
www.facebook.com/muskokaregion
Community newspapers under the Metroland North Media Group banner include: Bracebridge Examiner, Gravenhurst Banner, Huntsville Forester and The Muskokan
Dana Robbins, Vice-President & Regional Publisher
dana.robbins@metroland.com
Jack Tynan, Publication Manager/Editor-in-Chief
jtynan@metrolandnorthmedia.com

Mississauga: The Mississauga News
Owned By: Metroland Media Group Ltd.
3145 Wolfedale Rd., Mississauga, ON L5C 3A9
Tel: 905-273-8111; *Fax:* 905-277-0146
www.mississauga.com
twitter.com/MissiNewsRoom
www.facebook.com/MissiNewsRoom
Circulation: 124,000 *Frequency:* Wed., Fri.
The News is a perennial newspaper award winner, including best newspaper in Ontario & Canada, on several occasions. The Mississauga News is delivered three times a week to houses. A separate edition called The Mississauga News This Week is delivered Thursdays to apartments.
Dana Robbins, Publisher
dana.robbins@metroland.com
Bill Anderson, General Manager
banderson@metroland.com

Mississauga: Mississauga News
Owned By: Metroland Media Group Ltd.
3145 Wolfedale Rd., Mississauga, ON L5C 3A9
www.mississauga.com
twitter.com/missinewsroom
www.facebook.com/missinewsroom
Serves readers in Mississauga
Patricia Lonergan, Editor-in-Chief
plonergan@metroland.com

Mississauga: The Weekly Voice
#16, 7015 Tranmere Dr., Mississauga, ON L5S 1T7
Tel: 905-795-8282; Fax: 905-795-9801
info@weeklyvoice.com
www.weeklyvoice.com
Circulation: 10,100 W; 29,900 Sa; 40,000 total Frequency: Wed., Sat.
The free newspaper presents information & views of intererst to the South Asian community of the Greater Toronto Area. The Weekly Voice is distributed at major South Asian grocery stores, transit stations, libraries, & community centres.
Sudhir Anand, Publisher
sudhir@weeklyvoice.com
Binoy Thomas, Editor in Chief
Dhruv Ghosh, General Manager
dhruv@weeklyvoice.com
Harsimrat Panfer, Contact, Classifieds
admin@weeklyvoice.com
Asha Singhh, Contact, Accounts
accounts@weeklyvoice.com

Mitchell: Mitchell Advocate
Owned By: Postmedia Network Inc.
PO Box 669, 42 Montreal St., Mitchell, ON N0K 1N0
Tel: 519-348-8431; Fax: 519-348-8836
www.mitchelladvocate.com
twitter.com/mitchellpaper
www.facebook.com/MitchellAdvocate
Circulation: 2,050 Frequency: Wednesday
Andy Bader, Publisher/Editor
andy.bader@sunmedia.ca

Morrisburg: Morrisburg Leader
Owned By: The Morrisburg Leader Ltd.
PO Box 891, 41 Main St., Morrisburg, ON K0C 1X0
Tel: 613-543-2987
info@morrisburgleader.ca
www.morrisburgleader.ca
twitter.com/theleader_ca
www.facebook.com/morrisburgleader
Circulation: 1,900 Frequency: Wednesday
Sam Laurin, Publisher & Editor
Bonnie McNairn, Managing Editor

Napanee: Napanee Beaver
Owned By: 543570 Ont. Inc.
72 Dundas St. East, Napanee, ON K7R 1H9
Tel: 613-354-6641; Fax: 613-354-2622
www.napaneebeaver.com
Circulation: 15,700 Frequency: Thursday
Jean Morrison, Publisher
Seth Duchene, Editor

Napanee: The Napanee Guide
Owned By: Postmedia Network Inc.
#11, 2 Dairy Ave., Napanee, ON K7R 3T1
Tel: 613-354-6648; Fax: 613-354-6708
www.napaneeguide.com
twitter.com/napaneeguide
Circulation: 14,900 Frequency: Thursday
Liza Nelson, Publisher
liza.nelson@sunmedia.ca

Nepean: Alta Vista Canterbury News
Previous Name: Alta Vista News
Owned By: Ottawa News Publishing
#3B, 15 Antares Dr., Nepean, ON K2E 7Y9
Tel: 613-723-5970; Fax: 613-723-1862
Circulation: 36,000 Frequency: Every other Thu.; also Britannia/Lincoln Heights News, Carlingwood/Baseline News, Glebe & Ottawa South News, Westboro/Hampton Park News
Michael Wollock, Publisher
Tom Collins, Editor

Nepean: Nepean/Barrhaven News
Owned By: Metroland Media Group Ltd.
#4, 80 Colonnade Rd. North, Nepean, ON K2E 7L2
Tel: 613-224-3330; Fax: 613-224-2265
www.emcbarrhaven.ca
twitter.com/emcnews
www.facebook.com/emcnewspaper
Circulation: 50,000 Frequency: Thurs.
In 2011, the Nepean / Barrhaven EMC merged with the Nepean & Barrhaven editions of Ottawa This Week.
Mike Mount, Vice-President & Regional Publisher
Theresa Fritz, Managing Editor
theresa.fritz@metroland.com
Mike Tracy, General Manager
mtracy@perfprint.ca

Nepean: Ottawa South News
Owned By: Metroland Media Group Ltd.
#4, 80 Colonnade Rd., Nepean, ON K2E 7L2
Tel: 613-224-3330; Fax: 613-723-1862
www.emcottawasouth.ca/news
twitter.com/emcnews
www.facebook.com/emcnewspaper
Circulation: 41,500 Frequency: Thurs.
Mike Tracy, Publisher & General Manager
613-283-3182 x164
dweir@perfprint.ca
Theresa Fritz, Managing Editor
theresa.fritz@metroland.com

Nepean: Stittsville News
Previous Name: Stittsville EMC
#4, 80 Colonnade Rd., Nepean, ON K2E 7L2
Tel: 613-224-3330; Fax: 613-224-2265
stittsvillecentral.ca
Circulation: 13,446 Frequency: Weekly; Thursday
Mike Tracy, General Manager
mike.tracy@metroland.com
Ryland Coyne, Editor-in-Chief
rcoyne@metroland.com

New Hamburg: The New Hamburg Independent
Owned By: Metroland Media Group Ltd.
77 Peel St., New Hamburg, ON N3A 1B7
Tel: 519-662-1240
editor@newhamburgindependent.ca
www.newhamburgindependent.ca
twitter.com/newhamburgindy
www.facebook.com/newhamburgindependent
Serves readers in Wilmot Township
Kelly Montague, Publisher
kmontague@metroland.com
Bob Vrbanac, Managing Editor
bvrbanac@kitchenerpost.ca

New Liskeard: The Temiskaming Speaker
Owned By: Temiskaming Printing Co.
PO Box 580, 18 Wellington St. South, New Liskeard, ON P0J 1P0
Tel: 705-647-6791; Fax: 705-647-9669
speaker.northernontario.ca
Circulation: 3,150 Frequency: Wednesday
Dave Armstrong, Publisher
Gordon Black, Editor
Lois Perry, General Manager

Newmarket: York Region Media Group
Owned By: Metroland Media Group Ltd.
580B Steven Ct., Newmarket, ON L3Y 4X1
www.yorkregion.com
twitter.com/yorkregion
www.facebook.com/yrmgnews
Community newspapers under the York Region Media Group banner include: Markham Economist & Sun, Newmarket Era, Aurora Banner, Stouffville Sun-Tribune, Georgina Advocate, Richmond Hill Liberal, Thornhill Liberal & Vaughan Citizen
Lee Ann Waterman, Editor-in-Chief, York Region
lwaterman@metroland.com

Niagara Falls: Niagara Shopping News
Owned By: Postmedia Network Inc.
4949 Victoria Ave., Niagara Falls, ON L2E 4C7
Tel: 905-357-2440; Fax: 905-357-1620
placeit@classifiedextra.ca
niagarashoppingnews.classifiedextra.ca
Circulation: 28,000 Frequency: Friday
Mark Munson

Nipigon: Nipigon-Red Rock Gazette
Owned By: Lakeshore Community Publishing Ltd.
PO Box 1057, 20 Riverview St., Nipigon, ON P0T 2J0
Tel: 807-887-3583; Fax: 807-887-3720
nipigongazette@shaw.ca
Circulation: 810 Frequency: Tuesday
Linda Harbison, Publisher
Paulette Forsythe, Editor

Oakville: Milton Shopping News
c/o The Shopping News, 467 Speers Rd., 2nd Fl., Oakville, ON L6K 3S4
Tel: 905-878-8855; Fax: 905-878-6727
smillen@haltonsearch.com
miltonshoppingnews.com
Circulation: 16,500 Frequency: Thursday
Lars Melander, General Manager
905-337-5555

Oakville: Oakville Beaver
Owned By: Metroland Media Group Ltd.
467 Speers Rd., 2nd Fl., Oakville, ON L6K 3S4
Tel: 905-825-2229; Fax: 905-825-8315
www.insidehalton.com/community/oakvilletoday
twitter.com/OakvilleBeaver
www.facebook.com/OakvilleBeav
Circulation: 50,000 Frequency: Wed., Thurs., Fri.
The newspaper is delivered to residences in northern Oakville.
Neil Oliver, Publisher
noliver@metroland.com
David Harvey, Regional Group Manager
dharvey@metroland.com
Jill Davis, Editor-in-Chief
jdavis@metroland.com
Charlene Hall, Manager, Distribution
charlenehall@metroland.com
Sandy Pare, Manager, Business
spare@metrolandwest.com
Manuel Garcia, Manager, Production
mgarcia@metroland.com

Oakville: Oakville Shopping News
2526 Speers Rd., Oakville, ON L6L 5M2
Tel: 905-827-6090; Fax: 905-827-7318
Bill Whitaker Sr.

Orangeville: Orangeville Banner
Owned By: Metroland Media Group Ltd.
37 Mill St., Orangeville, ON L9W 2M4
Tel: 519-941-1350
www.orangeville.com
twitter.com/ovillebanner
www.facebook.com/theorangevillebanner
Serves readers in Orangeville
Steve Foreman, General Manager
sforeman@metroland.com
Chris Vernon, Managing Editor
cvernon@metroland.com

Orangeville: Orangeville Citizen
Owned By: Claridge Community Newspaper Ltd.
10 - 1st St., Orangeville, ON L9W 2C4
Tel: 519-941-2230; Fax: 519-941-9361
www.citizen.on.ca
twitter.com/OvilleCitizen
www.facebook.com/Citizen.on.ca
Circulation: 17,300 Frequency: Thursday
Tom Claridge, Editor
editor@citizen.on.ca
Alan Claridge, Publisher
publisher@citizen.on.ca

Orono: Orono Weekly Times
Owned By: Orono Weekly Times
PO Box 209, 5310 Main St., Orono, ON L0B 1M0
Tel: 905-983-5301; Fax: 905-983-5301
oronotimes@rogers.com
www.oronoweeklytimes.com
twitter.com/oronotimes
www.facebook.com/oronotimes
Circulation: 930 Frequency: Wednesday
Margaret Zwart, Publisher

Oshawa: Clarington This Week
Owned By: Metroland Media Group Ltd.
PO Box 481, 865 Farewell Ave., Oshawa, ON L1H 7L5
Tel: 905-579-4400; Fax: 905-579-2238
www.durhamregion.com
Circulation: 24,550 Frequency: Thursday, Wednesday

Oshawa: Metroland Durham Region Media Group
Owned By: Metroland Media Group Ltd.
865 Farewell St., Oshawa, ON L1H 7L5
www.durhamregion.com
www.instagram.com/newsdurham
twitter.com/newsdurham
www.facebook.com/n ewsdurham
Online community newspaper in Durham Region, offering news to residents of Ajax, Clarington, Oshawa, Pickering, Scugog, Uxbridge & Whitby. Community newspapers published under the Metroland Durham Region Media Group include the Ajax-Pickering News Advertiser, Oshawa This Week, Whitby This Week, Clarington This Week, Uxbridge Times-Journal & the Port Perry Star
Tim Whittaker, Publisher
twhittaker@durhamregion.com

Oshawa: Oshawa Express
Owned By: Dowellman Publishing Corp.
774 Simcoe St. South, Oshawa, ON L1H 4K6
Tel: 905-571-7334; *Fax:* 905-571-0255
editor@oshawaexpress.ca
www.oshawaexpress.ca
www.facebook.com/218913348146817
Circulation: 35,000 *Frequency:* Wed.
Greg McDowell, Publisher
Lindsey Cole, Editor

Oshawa: Oshawa This Week
Owned By: Metroland Media Group Ltd.
PO Box 481, 865 Farewell Ave., Oshawa, ON L1H 7L5
Tel: 905-579-4400; *Fax:* 905-579-2238
www.durhamregion.com
Circulation: 121,000 *Frequency:* Wednesday, Thursday, Friday
Tim Whittaker, Publisher
Joanne Burghardt, Editor-in-chief

Oshawa: Whitby This Week
Owned By: Metroland Media Group Ltd.
PO Box 481, 865 Farewell Ave., Oshawa, ON L1H 7L5
Tel: 905-579-4400; *Fax:* 905-579-2238
www.durhamregion.com
Circulation: 121,000 *Frequency:* Wednesday, Thursday, Friday

Ottawa: Centretown News
St. Patrick's Bldg., #303, 1125 Colonel By Dr., Ottawa, ON K1S 5B6
Tel: 613-520-7410; *Fax:* 613-520-4068
ctown@carleton.ca
www.centretownnews.ca
twitter.com/CentretownNews
www.facebook.com/CentretownNews
Circulation: 17,000 *Frequency:* Fri., bi-weekly from Sept.-April
The content of Centretown News is produced by third & fourth year students from Carleton University's School of Journalism & Communication. The community newspaper is delivered to homes & businesses in the Ottawa-Carleton region between September & April.
Klaus Pohle, Publisher
Brian Platt, Editor
Hanna Lange-Chenier, Editor, Photos
Meagan Curran, Editor, Insight
Francesa Weigensberg, Editor, Sports
Sara Louden, Editor, Online
Mireille Sylvester, Editor, News
Julia Green, Editor, Business
Kelly Fleck, Editor, Arts
Sara Louden, Manager, Advertising

Ottawa: The Hill Times
Owned By: The Hill Times Publishing Inc.
69 Sparks St., Ottawa, ON K1P 5A5
Tel: 613-232-5952; *Fax:* 613-232-9055
news@hilltimes.com
www.thehilltimes.ca
twitter.com/thehilltimes
www.facebook.com/thehilltimes
Circulation: 8,370 *Frequency:* Monday
Independently-owned political & government newspaper.
Andrew Morrow, General Manager
613-688-8844
amorrow@hilltimes.com
Kate Malloy, Editor
613-688-8838
kmalloy@hilltimes.com

Parkhill: Parkhill Gazette
Owned By: Hayter-Walden Publications Inc.
PO Box 400, 165 Parkhill King St., Parkhill, ON N0M 2K0
Tel: 519-294-6264; *Fax:* 519-294-6391
gazette@execulink.com
hayterwalden.com
Circulation: 890 *Frequency:* Thurs.
Dale Hayter, Publisher
Terry Heffernan, Editor

Parry Sound: Parry Sound Beacon Star
Owned By: Metroland Media Group Ltd.
PO Box 370, 66A Bowes St., Parry Sound, ON P2A 2L3
Tel: 705-746-2104; *Fax:* 705-746-8369
parrysound.com
Circulation: 7,700 *Frequency:* Friday
Shaun Sauve, Regional General Manager
705-645-8771 ext 227
ssauve@metroland.com
Janice Heidman, General Manager
jheidman@metroland.com
Jack Tynan, Editor-in-Chief
jtynan@metroland.com

Parry Sound: Parry Sound North Star
Owned By: Metroland Media Group Ltd.
PO Box 370, 66A Bowes St., Parry Sound, ON P2A 2L3
Tel: 705-746-2104; *Fax:* 705-746-8369
parrysound.com
www.facebook.com/PSNorthStar
Circulation: 2,600 *Frequency:* Wednesday
Shaun Sauve, Regional General Manager
ssauve@metroland.com
Janice Heidman, General Manager
jheidman@metroland.com
Jack Tynan, Editorin-Chief
jtynan@metroland.com

Parry Sound: Parry Sound North Star
Owned By: Metroland Media Group Ltd.
66A Bowes St., Parry Sound, ON P2A 2L3
www.parrysound.com
twitter.com/parrysoundns
www.facebook.com/psnorthstar
Serves readers in Parry Sound
Dana Robbins, Vice-President & Regional Publisher
dana.robbins@metroland.com

Perth: Perth Courier
Owned By: Metroland Media Group Ltd.
PO Box 158, 65 Lorne St., Perth, ON K7A 4T1
Tel: 613-283-3182; *Fax:* 613-267-3986
www.insideottawavalley.com/perth-on
Circulation: 12,800 *Frequency:* Thursday
Duncan Weir, Group Publisher
Cindy Manor, General Manager
cmanor@metroland.com
Marla Dowdall, Managing Editor
mdowdall@perfprint.ca

Petawawa: Petawawa Post
Bldg. P-106, CFB Petawawa, Petawawa, ON K8H 2X3
Tel: 613-687-5511; *Fax:* 613-588-6966
petawawapost@bellnet.ca
cg.cfpsa.ca
Circulation: 7,700 *Frequency:* Tuesday
Bruce Peever, Manager
bruce.peever@forces.qc.ca
Lisa Brazeau, Assistant Editor

Peterborough: Metroland Kawartha Media Group
Previous Name: Kawartha Lakes This Week
Owned By: Metroland Media Group Ltd.
884 Ford St., Peterborough, ON K9V 5V3
Tel: 705-749-3383
www.mykawartha.com
twitter.com/kawarthanews
www.facebook.com/peteroroughnews
Metroland Kawartha Media Group publishes Peterborough This Week, Kawartha Lakes This Week and the Brock Citizen
Peter Bishop, Publisher
pbishop@metroland.com

Peterborough: Peterborough This Week
Owned By: Metroland Media Group Ltd.
884 Ford St., Peterborough, ON K9J 5V3
Tel: 705-749-3383; *Fax:* 705-749-0074
www.mykawartha.com
www.pinterest.com/rellman
twitter.com/kawarthanews
www.facebook.com/mykawartha.peterboroughnews
Circulation: 91,100 *Frequency:* Wed., Fri.
Mike Mount, Publisher
mike.mount@metroland.com
Mary Babcock, Regional General Manager
mbabcock@mykawartha.com
Lois Tuffin, Editor-in-Chief
ltuffin@mykawartha.com

Picton: Picton Gazette
Owned By: Picton Gazette
267 Main St., Picton, ON K0K 2T0
Tel: 613-476-3201; *Fax:* 613-476-3464
gazette@connect.reach.net
www.pictongazette.com
twitter.com/Gazettenews
www.facebook.com/PictonGazette
Circulation: 12,000 *Frequency:* Thursday; The Picton Gazette Regional (Sat., circ. 10,602)
Jean Morrison, Publisher
dmccann1@bellnet.ca
Adam Bramburger, Editor

Port Dover: Port Dover Maple Leaf
Owned By: Port Dover Maple Leaf Limited
PO Box 70, 351 Main St., Port Dover, ON N0A 1N0
Tel: 519-583-0112; *Fax:* 519-583-3200
news@portdovermapleleaf.com
www.portdovermapleleaf.com
twitter.com/PDMapleLeaf
www.facebook.com/PortDoverMapleLeaf
Circulation: 3,163 *Frequency:* Wed.
Stan Morris, Publisher

Port Elgin: Shoreline Beacon
Previous Name: Shoreline News
Owned By: Postmedia Network Inc.
694 Goderich St., Port Elgin, ON N0H 2C0
Tel: 519-832-9001; *Fax:* 519-389-4793
shorelinebeacon.news@sunmedia.ca
www.shorelinebeacon.com
twitter.com/shorelinebeacon
www.facebook.com/shorelinebeacon
Circulation: 3,250 *Frequency:* Tuesday
Kiera Merriam, Publisher
kiera.merriam@sunmedia.ca
Patrick Bales, Editor
patrick.bales@sunmedia.ca

Rainy River: Rainy River Record
Owned By: Fort Frances Times Ltd.
PO Box 280, 312 - 3rd St., Rainy River, ON P0W 1L0
Tel: 807-852-3366; *Fax:* 807-852-4434
info@rainyriverrecord.com
www.rainyriverrecord.com
Other information: Ads, Email: advertising@rainyriverrecord.com
www.facebook.com/rainyriverrecord
Circulation: 600 *Frequency:* Tuesday
J.R. Cumming, Publisher
Ken Johnston, Editor

Rainy River: The Westend Weekly
PO Box 66, Rainy River, ON P0W 1L0
Tel: 807-852-3815; *Fax:* 807-852-1863
westendweekly@tbaytel.net
www.westendweekly.ca
Circulation: 8,600 *Frequency:* Wed.
Jacquie Dufresne, Editor-in-chief

Renfrew: Metroland Eastern Ontario Media Group
Owned By: Metroland Media Group Ltd.
35 Opeongo Rd., Renfrew, ON K7Z 2T2
www.insideottawavalley.com
twitter.com/inottvalley
Community newspapers published under the Metroland Eastern Ontario Media Group include the Arnprior Chronicle-Guide, the Brighton Independent, the Carleton Place/Almonte Canadian-Gazette, the Kemptville Advance, the Perth Courier, the Renfrew Mercury & the Smiths Falls Record News
Peter Bishop, Vice-President & Regional Publisher
pbishop@metroland.com

Renfrew: Renfrew Mercury
Previous Name: Renfrew Mercury/Mercury Weekender
Owned By: Metroland Media Group Ltd.
35 Opeongo Rd., Renfrew, ON K7V 2T2
Tel: 613-432-3655; *Fax:* 613-432-6689
www.insideottawavalley.com/renfrew-on
Circulation: 15,300 *Frequency:* Tuesday
Mike Tracy, Publisher
Tom O'Malley, Regional Manager

Ridgetown: The Ridgetown Independent News
PO Box 609, 1 Main St. West, Ridgetown, ON N0P 2C0
Tel: 519-674-5205; *Fax:* 519-674-2573
Circulation: 1,850 *Frequency:* Wed.
Jim Brown, Owner & Publisher
Gord Brown, General Manager
Barb Brown, Editor

Rockland: Le Journal Vision
PO Box 897, 1315 rue Laurier, Rockland, ON K4K 1L5
Tel: 613-446-6456; *Fax:* 613-446-1381
Toll-Free: 800-365-9970
vision@eap.on.ca
editionap.ca
Circulation: 28,100 *Frequency:* Weekly
The newspaper is bilingual.
Paulo Casimiro, Director & Editor
paulo.casimiro@eap.on.ca

Sarnia: The Sarnia & Lambton County This Week
Previous Name: Sarnia This Week
Owned By: Postmedia Network Inc.
140 Front St. South, Sarnia, ON N7T 7M8
Tel: 519-336-1100; *Fax:* 519-336-1833
www.sarniathisweek.com
twitter.com/STW_Heather
www.facebook.com/SarniaThisWeek
Circulation: 40,240 *Frequency:* Wed.
Linda Leblanc, Publisher
linda.leblanc@sunmedia.ca
Peter Epp, Editor

Sault Ste Marie: Sault Ste Marie This Week
Owned By: Postmedia Network Inc.
145 Old Garden River Rd., Sault Ste Marie, ON P6A 5M5
Tel: 705-759-3030; *Fax:* 705-942-8596
www.saultthisweek.com
Circulation: 30,800 *Frequency:* Wed.
Mike Kennedy, Publisher
mike.kennedy@sunmedia.ca
Frank Rupnik, Regional Managing Editor
frank.rupnik@sunmedia.ca

Schreiber: Terrace Bay Schreiber News
Owned By: Lakeshore Community Publishing Ltd.
PO Box 930, 303 Scotia St., Schreiber, ON P0T 2S0
Tel: 807-824-2021; *Fax:* 807-824-2162
Circulation: 328 *Frequency:* Tues.
The Ontario community newspaper publishes local stories of interest to readers in Terrace Bay, Schreiber, Rossport, & the surrounding area.
Linda Harbinson, Publisher
Paulette Forsythe, Editor

Seaforth: The Huron Expositor
Owned By: Postmedia Network Inc.
8 Main St., Seaforth, ON N0K 1W0
Tel: 519-527-0240; *Fax:* 519-527-2858
www.seaforthhuronexpositor.com
twitter.com/C4thExp
www.facebook.com/TheHuronExpositor
Circulation: 1,400 *Frequency:* Wed.
Neil H. Clifford, Publisher
neil.clifford@sunmedia.ca
Susan Hundertmark, Editor
seaforth.news@sunmedia.ca

Shelburne: Shelburne Free Press & Economist
Owned By: Claridge Community Newspapers Ltd.
PO Box 100, #1, 143 Main St. West, Shelburne, ON L9V 3K3
Tel: 519-925-2832; *Fax:* 519-925-5500
email@shelburnefreepress.ca
shelburnefreepress.ca
www.facebook.com/ShelburneFreePress
Circulation: 3,400 *Frequency:* Thurs.
Karin Rossi, Publisher
Wendy Gabrek, Editor
wendy@simcoeworkprinting.com

Sioux Lookout: Sioux Lookout Bulletin
Owned By: 948892 Ontario Inc.
PO Box 1389, 40 Front St., Sioux Lookout, ON P8T 1B9
Tel: 807-737-3209; *Fax:* 807-737-3084
bulletin@siouxbulletin.com
www.siouxbulletin.com
Other information: Accounts: office@siouxbulletin.com; Ads: advertising@siouxbulletin.com
Circulation: 4,460 *Frequency:* Wed.
Dick MacKenzie, Editor
dick@siouxbulletin.com

Sioux Lookout: Wawatay News
Owned By: Wataway Native Communications Society
Wawatay Native Communications Society, PO Box 1180, 16 - 5th Ave., Sioux Lookout, ON P8T 1B7
Tel: 807-737-2951; *Fax:* 807-737-3224
editor@wawatay.on.ca
www.wawatay.on.ca
twitter.com/wawataynews
Circulation: 6,500 *Frequency:* Every other Thu.; English, Ojibwe & Cree
Distributed by the Sioux Lookout
Lenny Carpenter, Publisher/Editor
lennyc@wataway.on.ca

Smiths Falls: Carleton Place-Almonte Canadian Gazette
Owned By: Metroland Media Group Ltd.
PO Box 158, 65 Lorne St., Smiths Falls, ON K7A 4T1
Tel: 613-283-3182
ottawacommunitynews.com/ottawaregion
twitter.com/cdngazette
www.facebook.com/canadiangazette
Circulation: 12,800 *Frequency:* Thurs.
In 2011, The Carleton Place EMC & The Canadian merged to create the Carleton Place EMC & Canadian-Gazette newspaper.
Mike Mount, Publisher
Marla Dowdall, Managing Editor
mdowdall@perfprint.ca
Cindy Manor, General Manager
cmanor@metroland.com

Smiths Falls: Smiths Falls Record News
Owned By: Performance Printing Ltd.
PO Box 158, 65 Lorne St., Smiths Falls, ON K7A 4T1
Tel: 613-283-6222; *Fax:* 613-267-3986
insideottawavalley.com
twitter.com/ljweir
www.facebook.com/535833289857070
Circulation: 12,600 *Frequency:* Tuesday
Duncan Weir, Publisher
Ryland Coyne, Regional Editor
Marla Dowdall, Managing Editor
mdowdall@perfprint.ca

St Thomas: Elgin County Market
Owned By: Postmedia Network Inc.
16 Hincks St., St Thomas, ON N5R 5Z2
Tel: 519-631-3782; *Fax:* 519-631-3759
www.elgincountymarket.com
Circulation: 30,600
Linda Axelson, Publisher

Stoney Creek: Ancaster News
Owned By: Metroland Media Group Ltd.
333 Arvin Ave., Stoney Creek, ON L8E 2M6
Tel: 905-664-8800; *Fax:* 905-523-4014
www.hamiltonnews.com/community/ancaster
Circulation: 12,900 *Frequency:* Thursday
Debra Downey, Editor
ddowney@hamiltonnews.com

Stoney Creek: Dundas Star News
Owned By: Metroland Media Group Ltd.
333 Arvin Ave., Stoney Creek, ON L8E 2M6
Tel: 905-523-4014
www.hamiltonnews.com/dundas-on
Circulation: 15,700 *Frequency:* Thursday
Neil Oliver, Publisher
Debra Downey, Editor
ddowney@hamiltonnews.com

Stoney Creek: Hamilton Mountain News
Owned By: Metroland Media Group Ltd.
333 Arvin Ave., Stoney Creek, ON L8E 2M6
Tel: 905-523-5800; *Fax:* 905-523-4014
www.hamiltonnews.com/hamiltonmountain-on
Circulation: 50,500 *Frequency:* Thursday
Gord Bowes, Senior Editor
editor@hamiltonmountainnews.com
Neil Oliver, Publisher

Stoney Creek: Hamilton News
Owned By: Metroland Media Group Ltd.
33 Arvin Ave., Stoney Creek, ON L8E 2M6
www.hamiltonnews.com
twitter.com/hamontcomnews
www.facebook.com/hamiltoncommunitynewsofficial
Community newspapers published under this banner include Ancaster News, Dundas Star News, Hamilton Mountain News & Stoney Creek News.
Holly Chriss, Director, Advertising
hollyc@hamiltonnews.com

Stoney Creek: Stoney Creek News
Owned By: Metroland Media Group Ltd.
333 Arvin Ave., Stoney Creek, ON L6E 2M6
Fax: 905-523-4014
www.hamiltonnews.com/stoneycreek-on
twitter.com/StoneyCreekNews
www.facebook.com/StoneyCreekNews
Circulation: 30,500 *Frequency:* Thurs.
Neil Oliver, Publisher
Mike Pearson, News Editor
mpearson@hamiltonnews.com

Stratford: Inside Stratford / Perth
PO Box 23016, 285 Lorne Ave. East, Stratford, ON N5A 7V8
Tel: 519-272-0051; *Fax:* 519-272-0067
Circulation: 24,000+ *Frequency:* Weekly
The community newspaper serves Stratford & Perth County.
Richard Johnson, Publisher & Editor

Stratford: Stratford Gazette
Owned By: Metroland Media Group Ltd.
#106, 10 Downie St., Stratford, ON N5A 7K4
Tel: 519-271-8002; *Fax:* 519-271-5636
www.southwesternontario.ca/community/stratford-gazette
twitter.com/StratGazette
www.facebook.com/188314707972056
Circulation: 19,500 *Frequency:* Fri.
Doug Rowe, Regional Managing Editor
drowe@southwesternontario.ca
Laura Carter, Manager, Distribution

Strathroy: Strathroy Age Dispatch
Owned By: Postmedia Network Inc.
73 Front St. West, Strathroy, ON N7G 1X6
Tel: 519-245-2370; *Fax:* 519-245-1647
www.strathroyagedispatch.com
twitter.com/AgeDispatch
www.facebook.com/120981181268443
Circulation: 1,800 *Frequency:* Thurs.
Linda LeBlanc, Publisher
linda.leblanc@sunmedia.ca
Don Biggs, Editor
don.biggs@sunmedia.ca

Sturgeon Falls: West Nipissing Tribune
Previous Name: Sturgeon Falls Tribune
Owned By: 1102282 Ontario Inc.
206 King St., Sturgeon Falls, ON P2B 1R7
Tel: 705-753-2930; *Fax:* 705-753-5231
tribune@westnipissing.com
westnipissing.com
www.facebook.com/282577981766818
Circulation: 1,800 *Frequency:* Wednesday
Suzanne Gammon, Publisher & Editor

Sudbury: Journal Le Voyageur
Détenteur: Publications Voyageur Inc.
302-336, rue Pine, Sudbury, ON P3C 5L1
Tél: 705-673-3377; *Téléc:* 705-673-5854
Ligne sans frais: 866-688-7027
levoyageur@levoyageur.ca
www.levoyageur.ca
twitter.com/voyagersudbury
www.facebook.com/130564328071
Tirage: 8 400 *Fréquence:* Mercredi
Paul Lefebvre, Editor

Sudbury: Northern Life
Owned By: Laurentian Media Group
158 Elgin St., Sudbury, ON P3E 3N5
Tel: 705-673-5667; *Fax:* 705-673-4652
www.northernlife.ca
twitter.com/northern_life
www.facebook.com/northernlife.ca
Circulation: 85,900 *Frequency:* Tue., Thu.
Abbas Homayed, Publisher
Mark Gentili, Managing Editor

Tavistock: Tavistock Gazette
Owned By: Tavistock Gazette Ltd.
PO Box 70, 119 Woodstock South, Tavistock, ON N0B 2R0
Tel: 519-655-2341; *Fax:* 519-655-3070
gazette@tavistock.on.ca
www.tavistock.on.ca
Circulation: 1,250 *Frequency:* Wed.
William Gladding, Publisher

Tecumseh: LaSalle Post
Owned By: Postmedia Network Inc.
1116 Lesperance Rd., Tecumseh, ON N8N 1X2
Tel: 519-735-2080; *Fax:* 519-735-2082
lasallepost@postmedia.com
www.windsoressexnews.com/LasallePost.aspx
twitter.com/TheLaSallePost
www.facebook.com/LaSallePost
Circulation: 11,100 *Frequency:* Fri.
Bob Thwaites, Publisher
Kari Bowden, Editor

Tecumseh: Shoreline Week
Owned By: Postmedia Network Inc.
1116 Lesperance Rd., Tecumseh, ON N8N 1X2
Tel: 519-735-2080; *Fax:* 519-735-2082
mamcleod@postmedia.com
www.windsoressexnews.com

Circulation: 15,024 Frequency: Fri.
David Calibaba, Publisher
Bill England, Editor

Tecumseh: Tilbury Times
Owned By: Postmedia Network Inc.
1116 Lesperance Rd., Tecumseh, ON N8N 1X2
Tel: 519-753-2080; *Fax:* 519-682-3633
tilburytimes@postmedia.com
www.facebook.com/TilburyTimes
Circulation: 1,170 Frequency: Tue.
Garry Baxter, General Manager
Gerry Harvieux, Editor

Thamesville: Thamesville Herald
PO Box 580, 105 Elizabeth St., Thamesville, ON N0P 2K0
Tel: 519-692-3825; *Fax:* 519-692-9515
thamesvilleherald@sympatico.ca
Circulation: 670 Frequency: Wed.
Allison Humphrey, Publisher

Thessalon: The North Shore Sentinel
Owned By: Rankin Publications
359 River Rd. North, Thessalon, ON P0R 1L0
Tel: 705-842-2504; *Fax:* 705-842-2679
ns-sentinel@bellnet.ca
Circulation: 1,950 Frequency: Wed.
Randy Rankin, Publisher

Thorold: Fort Erie Post
Owned By: Metroland Media Group Ltd.
#1B, 3300 Merrittville Hwy., Thorold, ON L2V 4Y6
Tel: 905-688-2444
www.niagarathisweek.com/forterie-on/
Circulation: 161,000 Frequency: Weekly, Thurs.
David Bos, General Manager

Thorold: Niagara This Week
Owned By: Metroland Media Group Ltd.
#1B, 3300 Merrittville Hwy., Thorold, ON L2V 4Y6
Tel: 905-688-2444
www.niagarathisweek.com
twitter.com/NiagarathisWeek
www.facebook.com/163184140529
Circulation: 180,000 Frequency: Wed., Thurs.
David Bos, General Manager
dbos@niagarathisweek.com
Melissa Duemo, Manager, Office
mduemo@niagarathisweek.com
Neil Oliver, Publisher
noliver@metroland.com

Thorold: Niagara This Week
Owned By: Metroland Media Group Ltd.
#1B, 3300 Merrittville Hwy., Thorold, ON L2V 4Y6
www.niagarathisweek.com
twitter.com/niagarathisweek
www.facebook.com/niagarathisweek
Community newspapers published under the Niagara This Week
banner include Fort Erie Post, Grimsby Lincoln News, Niagara
This Week, Niagara-on-the-Lake Town Crier & the Port Colborne
Leader
Scott Rosts, Managing Editor
srosts@niagarathisweek.com

Thunder Bay: Thunder Bay Source
Owned By: Dougall Media
87 North Hill St., Thunder Bay, ON P7A 5V6
Tel: 807-346-2600; *Fax:* 807-345-9923
www.tbnewswatch.com
twitter.com/tbnewswatch
www.facebook.com/tbnewswatch
Circulation: 43,700 Frequency: Thurs.
Free weekly
Leith Dunick, Publisher
ldunick@dougallmedia.com

Tillsonburg: Tillsonburg News
Owned By: Postmedia Network Inc.
25 Townline Rd., Tillsonburg, ON N4G 4H6
Tel: 519-688-6397
www.tillsonburgnews.com
twitter.com/TillsonburgNews
www.facebook.com/TillsonburgNews
Circulation: 4,150 Frequency: Mon., Fri.
Ken Koyama, Publisher
ken.koyama@sunmedia.ca
Kim Novak, Editor
kim.novak@sunmedia.ca

Timmins: Les Nouvelles
187, rue Cedar, Timmins, ON P4N 7G1
Tél: 705-268-2955; *Téléc:* 705-268-3614
lesnouv@vianet.ca
journaux.apf.ca/lesnouvelles
Fréquence: Mercredi
Doris Bouchard, Rédactrice en chef
Bruce Cowan, Publisher

Timmins: Timmins Times
Owned By: Postmedia Network Inc.
187 Cedar St. South, Timmins, ON P4N 7G1
Tel: 705-268-6252; *Fax:* 705-268-2255
www.timminstimes.com
twitter.com/timminspress
www.facebook.com/213004885393148
Circulation: 16,300 Frequency: Thurs.
Lisa Wilson, Publisher
lisa.wilson@sunmedia.ca
Thomas Perry, Regional Managing Editor
thomas.perry@sunmedia.ca

Tiny: Le Goût de Vivre
Détenteur: Comité d'action Place Lafontaine
343 rue Lafontaine ouest, Tiny, ON L9M 0H1
Tél: 705-533-3349; *Téléc:* 705-533-3422
legoutdevivre@bellnet.ca
legoutdevivre.com
Tirage: 912 Fréquence: 1er et 3e jeudi du mois

Tobermory: The Bruce Peninsula Press
PO Box 89, 39 Legion St., Tobermory, ON N0H 2R0
Tel: 519-596-2658; *Fax:* 519-596-8030
Toll-Free: 800-794-4480
info@tobermorypress.com
brucepeninsulapress.com
Circulation: 3,000 Frequency: Tuesday (bi-monthly)
The community newspaper serves the northern Bruce
Peninsula.
John Francis, Publisher & Editor
Trudy Watson, Contact, Advertising & Sales

Toronto: Annex Gleaner
581 Bloor St. West, Toronto, ON M6G 1K3
Tel: 416-504-6987; *Fax:* 416-504-8792
gleanereditor@gmail.com
www.gleanernews.ca
Other information: Display & Classified Advertising, Email:
gleanerpub@gmail.com
twitter.com/gleanernews
Circulation: 33,500 Frequency: Monthly
Community news is provided to Toronto western downtown
neighbourhood. The Annex Gleaner is a free publication that is
delivered to residents & businesses.
Rebecca Payne, Editor-in-Chief
Justin Crann, Contributing Editor
justin.gleaner@gmail.com
Monika Warzecha, Online Editor
monika.gleaner@gmail.com

Toronto: The Bay Street Times
#514, 5334 Yonge St., Toronto, ON M2N 6V1
Tel: 416-949-6332; *Fax:* 416-997-6697
editor@baystreetimes.com
www.baystreetimes.com
Frequency: Monthly

Toronto: Beach Metro Community News
2196 Gerrard St. East, Toronto, ON M4E 2C7
Tel: 416-698-1164; *Fax:* 416-698-1253
admin@beachmetro.com
www.beachmetro.com
www.youtube.com/BeachMetroNews
twitter.com/BeachMetroNews
www.facebook .com/BeachMetroNews
Circulation: 30,000 Frequency: 23 per year
Phil Lameira, General Manager
phil@beachmetro.com
Jon Muldoon, Editor
jon@beachmetro.com

Toronto: Bloor West Villager
Owned By: Metroland Media Group Ltd.
175 Gordon Baker Rd., Toronto, ON M2H 0A2
Tel: 416-675-4390; *Fax:* 416-675-9262
www.insidetoronto.com
twitter.com/BWVillager
www.facebook.com/BloorWestVillager
Circulation: 33,100 Frequency: Thurs.
The Toronto neighbourhoods of Bloor West, Roncesvalles, &
The Juncion are served by the newspaper.
Ian Proudfoot, Publisher

Grace Peacock, Managing Editor
gpeacock@insidetoronto.com

Toronto: Downtown Bulletin
Previous Name: Toronto St. Lawrence & Downtown
Community Bulletin
Owned By: Community Bulletin Newspaper Group Inc.
#121, 260 Adelaide St. East, Toronto, ON M5A 1N1
Tel: 416-929-0011
info@communitybulletin.ca
www.thebulletin.ca
twitter.com/TheBulletinca
www.facebook.com/36287801341
Circulation: 51,300 Frequency: Monthly, Mon.
Frank Touby, Editor
Paulette Touby, Publisher

Toronto: East York Mirror
Owned By: Metroland Media Group Ltd.
175 Gordon Baker Rd., Toronto, ON M2H 0A2
Tel: 416-493-4400; *Fax:* 416-493-6190
www.insidetoronto.com
twitter.com/EastYorkMirror
www.facebook.com/EastYorkMirror
Circulation: 34,820 Frequency: Thurs.
The newspaper covers the Toronto neighbourhoods of East
York, Riverdale, & Leaside.
Ian Proudfoot, Publisher
Alan Shackleton, Managing Editor
asackleton@insidetoronto.com

Toronto: Etobicoke Guardian
Previous Name: Etobicoke Advertiser-Guardian
Owned By: Metroland Media Group Ltd.
175 Gordon Baker Rd., Toronto, ON M2H 0A2
Tel: 416-493-4400; *Fax:* 416-675-9262
etg@insidetoronto.com
www.toronto.com/etobicoke-toronto-on
twitter.com/ETGuardian
www.facebook.com/EtobicokeGuardian
Circulation: 71,000 Frequency: Thurs.
Grace Peacock, Managing Editor
gpeacock@insidetoronto.com
Ian Proudfoot, Publisher
iproudfoot@yrmg.com
Marg Middleton, General Manager

Toronto: L'Express
888 Ave. Eastern, Toronto, ON M4L 1A3
Tél: 416-465-2107; *Téléc:* 416-465-3778
info@lexpress.to
www.lexpress.to
twitter.com/LExpressToronto
www.facebook.com/LExpressDeToronto
Tirage: 22 000 Fréquence: Mardi
Jean-Pierre Mazare, Publisher
Francois Bergeron, Editor

Toronto: Hi-Rise
Owned By: Val Publications Ltd.
#121, 95 Leeward Glenway, Toronto, ON M3C 2Z6
Tel: 416-424-1393; *Fax:* 416-467-8262
sec.valdunn@vif.com
www.hi-risenews.com
Circulation: 50,000+ Frequency: Monthly
Distributed free of charge to the apartment/townhouse
community of the GTA
Valerie Dunn

Toronto: Kenora Miner & News
Previous Name: Daily Miner & News
Owned By: Postmedia Network Inc.
365 Bloor St. East, Toronto, ON M4W 3L4
Tel: 807-468-5555; *Fax:* 807-468-4318
www.kenominerandnews.com
twitter.com/Kenora_Daily
www.facebook.com/KenoraDailyMiner
Frequency: Thursday

Toronto: The Korea Times Daily
287 Bridgeland Ave., Toronto, ON M6A 1Z6
Tel: 416-787-1111; *Fax:* 416-781-8434
www.koreatimes.net
twitter.com/ktimesca
www.facebook.com/ktimesca

Toronto: Metroland Media Toronto
Owned By: Metroland Media Group Ltd.
175 Gordon Baker Rd., Toronto, ON M2H 0A2
www.toronto.com
www.instagram.com/torontodotcom
twitter.com/torontodotcom
www.facebook .com/torontodotcom

Community newspapers under the Metroland Media Toronto banner include: Beach Mirror, Bloor West Villager, City Centre Mirror, East York Mirror, Etobicoke Guardian, North York Mirror, Scarborough Mirror, Parkdale Villager & York Guardian
Joanne Burghardt, Editor-in-Chief
jburghardt@metroland.com

Toronto: North York Mirror
Owned By: Metroland Media Group Ltd.
175 Gordon Baker Rd., Toronto, ON M2H 0A2
Tel: 416-495-6526; Fax: 416-493-6190
www.insidetoronto.com/community/northyork
twitter.com/NorthYorkMirror
www.facebook.com/northyorkmirror
Circulation: 94,700 Frequency: Thurs., Fri.
The community newspaper is distributed to homes in the former city of North York, Ontario.
Ian Proudfoot, Publisher
Paul Futhey, Managing Editor
pfuthey@insidetoronto.com

Toronto: Our Toronto Free Press
#202, 49 Elm St., Toronto, ON M5G 1H1
Tel: 416-977-0183
letters@torontofreepress.com
www.torontofreepress.com
Frequency: Tues.
Judi McLeod, Editor & Owner
tfp@torontofreepress.com

Toronto: Our Windsor
Owned By: Metroland Media Group Ltd.
175 Gordon Baker Rd., Toronto, ON M2H 0A2
contactus@ourwindsor.ca
www.ourwindsor.ca
twitter.com/ourwindsoron
www.facebook.com/ourwindsor
Online community newspaper in Windsor

Toronto: Share
658 Vaughan Rd., Toronto, ON M6E 2Y5
Tel: 416-656-3400; Fax: 416-656-3711
share@interlog.com
www.sharenews.com
twitter.com/sharenews
www.facebook.com/357983747577821
Circulation: 50,000 Frequency: Weekly
Serves the Black and Caribbean community in the GTA.
Arnold A. Auguste, Publisher

Toronto: Toronto Street News
c/o LoveCry, 1024 Queen St. East, Toronto, ON M4M 1K4
Tel: 416-406-0099
info@torontostreetnews.net
www.torontostreetnews.net
Circulation: 3,000 Frequency: Weekly
Available free to homeless, handicapped, underemployed and dying so that they can sell for income.
Victor Fletcher, Publisher

Toronto: Town Crier
Owned By: Streeter Publications
c/o Streeter Publications, #204, 46 St. Clair Ave. East, Toronto, ON M4T 1M9
Tel: 416-901-8182
news@MyTownCrier.ca
www.mytowncrier.ca
twitter.com/mytowncrier
www.facebook.com/TownCriersTownSports
Circulation: 60,000 Frequency: Bimonthly
Serving the neighbourhoods of Leaside-Rosedale, North Toronto and Forest Hill.
Lori Abittan, President & Publisher
Eric McMillan, Managing Editor

Toronto: Village Living Magazines
Toronto, ON
Toll-Free: 866-933-1652
villagelivingmagazine.ca
www.pinterest.com/villagelivinmag
twitter.com/villagelivinmag
www.face book.com/VillageLivingMagazines
Frequency: Bi-Monthly
Free community newspaper serving the areas of Forest Hill, Hillcrest Village, Wychwood Heights, Regal Heights, and Upper Village.
Andrew Fishman, Publisher
1-866-933-1652 ext 2
Iris Zimmer-Fishman, Associate Publisher
1-866-933-1652 ext 3

Toronto: The Women's Post
#214, 501 Yonge St., Toronto, ON M4Y 1Y4
Tel: 416-900-1088; Fax: 416-645-7046
www.womenspost.ca
www.facebook.com/womenspost
Circulation: 71,818 Frequency: Bi-monthly
Sarah Whatmough-Thomson, Editor
editor@womenspost.ca
Greg Thomson, Chief Financial Officer
gthomson@womenspost.ca

Toronto: York Guardian
Owned By: Metroland Media Group Ltd.
175 Gordon Baker Rd., Toronto, ON M2H 0A2
Tel: 416-493-4400
wwww.insidetoronto.com
twitter.com/YorkGuardian
www.facebook.com/yorkguardian
Circulation: 28,550 Frequency: Thurs.
The newspaper is delivered to homes in Toronto.
Ian Proudfoot, Publisher
Paul Futhey, Managing Editor
pfuthey@insidetoronto.com

Tweed: Tweed News
Owned By: Tweed News Publishing Co. Ltd.
PO Box 550, 242 Victoria St. North, Tweed, ON K0K 3J0
Tel: 613-478-2017; Fax: 613-478-2749
info@thetweednews.ca
www.thetweednews.ca
twitter.com/TheTweedNews
Circulation: 900 Frequency: Wed.
Rodger Hanna, Publisher & Editor

Uxbridge: Uxbridge Times-Journal
Previous Name: Uxbridge Times-Journal
Owned By: Metroland Media Group Ltd.
PO Box 459, 16 Bascom St., Uxbridge, ON L9P 1M9
Tel: 905-852-9141; Fax: 905-852-9341
www.durhamregion.com/uxbridge-on
Circulation: 9,000 Frequency: Thurs.
Tim Whittaker, Publisher
twhittaker@durhamregion.com
Joanne Burghardt, Editor-in-Chief
jburghardt@durhamregion.com

Vankleek Hill: The Review
Previous Name: Vankleek Hill Review
Owned By: The Review (996963 Ontario Inc.)
PO Box 160, 76 Main St. East, Vankleek Hill, ON K0B 1R0
Tel: 613-678-3327; Fax: 613-937-2591
Toll-Free: 877-678-3327
review@thereview.ca
www.thereview.on.ca
www.youtube.com/user/VKHReview
twitter.com/vkhreview
www.facebook.com/ vkhreview
Circulation: 3,200 Frequency: Wed.
Louise Sproule, Publisher
lsproule@thereview.ca
Richard Mahoney, Editor
editor@thereview.ca

Vaughan: Vaughan Citizen
Owned By: York Region Media Group
#29, 8611 Weston Rd., Vaughan, ON L4L 9P1
Tel: 905-264-8703; Fax: 905-264-9453
www.yorkregion.com
twitter.com/VaughanEditor
www.facebook.com/TheVaughanCitizen
Circulation: 51,000 Frequency: Wed., Thurs.
Kim Champion, Editor
kchampion@yrmg.com
John Willems, Regional General Manager
john.willems@metroland.com
Robert Lazurko, Manager, Business

Walkerton: Walkerton Herald-Times
Owned By: Metroland Media Group Ltd.
PO Box 190, 10 Victoria St., Walkerton, ON N0G 2V0
Tel: 519-881-1600; Fax: 519-881-0276
southwesternontario.ca/community/walkerton-herald-times
www.facebook.com/WHTnews
Circulation: 1,600 Frequency: Wed.
John McPhee, General Manager
editor@walkerton.com
Doug Rowe, General Manager, Southwestern Division
drowe@southwesternontario.ca
Cathy Spitzig, Contact, Circulation
classifieds@walkerton.com

Wallaceburg: Wallaceburg News
538 James St., Wallaceburg, ON N8A 2N9
Tel: 519-627-2557; Fax: 519-627-1261
www.thewallaceburgnews.ca
Frequency: Wed.
Wayne Snider, Managing Editor
Daryl Smith, Publisher

Wasaga Beach: Stayner Sun
Previous Name: Angus-Borden Sun
Owned By: Metroland Media
#10, 1 Market Lane, Wasaga Beach, ON L9Z 0B6
Tel: 705-428-2638; Fax: 705-422-2446
www.simcoe.com/community/stayner
twitter.com/staynersun
www.facebook.com/145839558780312
Circulation: 4000 Frequency: Thurs.
Carol Lamb, General Manager
clamb@simcoe.com
Mike Gennings, Editor
mgennings@simcoe.com

Wasaga Beach: The Wasaga Sun
Owned By: Metroland Media Group Ltd.
#10, 1 Market Lane, Wasaga Beach, ON L9Z 2B9
Tel: 705-429-1688; Fax: 705-422-2446
www.simcoe.com/community/wasagabeach
twitter.com/WasagaSun
www.facebook.com/WasagaSunnews
Circulation: 8,200 Frequency: Thurs.
Carol Lamb, General Manager
clamb@simcoe.com
Mike Gennings, Editor
mgennings@simcoe.com

Waterdown: Flamborough Review
Owned By: Metroland Media Group Ltd.
PO Box 20, 30 Main St. North, Waterdown, ON L0R 2H0
Tel: 905-689-4841; Fax: 905-689-3110
www.flamboroughreview.com
twitter.com/FlamReview
www.facebook.com/FlamboroughReview
Circulation: 13,700 Frequency: Thurs.
Neil Oliver, Publisher
noliver@metroland.com
Brenda Jeffries, Editor
editor@flamboroughreview.com

Waterloo: Waterloo Chronicle
Owned By: Metroland Media Group Ltd.
#20, 279 Weber St. North, Waterloo, ON N2J 3H8
Tel: 519-886-2830; Fax: 519-886-9383
www.waterloochronicle.ca
twitter.com/wlchronicle
www.facebook.com/199981043371187
Circulation: 30,500 Frequency: Wed.
Peter Winkler, Publisher
Bob Vrbanac, Editor
bvrbanac@waterloochronicle.ca

Watford: Watford Guide-Advocate
Owned By: Hayter-Walden Publications Inc.
PO Box 99, 5292 Nauvoo Rd., Watford, ON N0M 2S0
Tel: 519-876-2809; Fax: 519-876-2322
guideadvocate@execulink.com
hayterwalden.com
Circulation: 920 Frequency: Thurs.
Dale Hayter, Publisher
Stephanie Cattrysee, Editor

West Lorne: The West Elgin Chronicle
Owned By: Postmedia Network Inc.
168 Main St., West Lorne, ON N0L 2P0
Tel: 519-768-2220; Fax: 519-768-2221
www.thechronicle-online.com
twitter.com/WE_TheChronicle
www.facebook.com/TheWestElginChronicle
Circulation: 5,500 Frequency: Thu.
Linda Leblanc, Publisher
519-474-5371 x242
linda.leblanc@sunmedia.ca
Ian McCallum, Editor
519-631-2790 x248
ian.mccallum@sunmedia.ca

Westport: The Review-Mirror
Owned By: The Mirror Group
PO Box 130, 43 Bedford St., Westport, ON K0G 1X0
Tel: 613-273-8000; Fax: 613-273-8001
Toll-Free: 800-387-0796
info@review-mirror.com
www.review-mirror.com

Circulation: 1,550 *Frequency:* Thursday
The Review Mirror serves Westport, the Rideau Valley, & the Rideau Lakes in Ontario. Print & electronic subscriptions are available.
Howard Crichton, Publisher & Managing Editor
Margaret Brand, Reporter & Photographer
mbrand@review-mirror.com
Marco Smits, Reporter & Photographer
msmits@review-mirror.com
Louise Haughton, Contact, Office
lhaughton@review-mirror.com
Bill Ritchie, Contact, Advertising Sales
advertising@review-mirror.com

Wheatley: **Wheatley Journal**
Owned By: Wheatley Journal
PO Box 10, 14 Talbot West, Wheatley, ON N0P 2P0
Tel: 519-825-4541; *Fax:* 519-825-4546
journal@mnsi.net
www.facebook.com/wheatleyjournal
Circulation: 700 *Frequency:* Wed.
Jim Heynes, Publisher
jim@southpoint.ca
Sheila McBrayne, Editor
sheila@southpointsun.ca

Wiarton: **Wiarton Echo**
Owned By: Postmedia Network Inc.
PO Box 220, 573 Berford St., Wiarton, ON N0H 2T0
Tel: 519-534-1560; *Fax:* 519-534-4616
www.wiartonecho.com
twitter.com/wiartonecho
www.facebook.com/334537066702
Circulation: 1,700 *Frequency:* Tues.
Nelson Phillips, Publisher
nelson.phillips@sunmedia.ca
Keith Gilbert, Managing Editor
keith.gilbert@sunmedia.ca

Winchester: **Winchester Press**
Owned By: Manotick Messenger Inc.
PO Box 399, 545 Lawrence St., Winchester, ON K0C 2K0
Tel: 613-774-2524; *Fax:* 613-774-3967
advert@winchesterpress.on.ca
www.winchesterpress.on.ca
www.facebook.com/WinchesterPress
Circulation: 3,200 *Frequency:* Wed.
Beth Morris, Owner & President
Matthew Uhrig, Editor
news@winchesterpress.on.co

Windsor: **Journal Le Rempart**
Anciennement: Le Rempart
7515, ch Forest Glade, Windsor, ON N8T 3P5
Tél: 519-948-4139; *Téléc:* 519-948-0628
info@lerempart.ca
www.lerempart.ca
www.facebook.com/184833808388836
Tirage: 6 500 *Fréquence:* Mercredi
Denis Poirier, Publisher

Windsor: **Windsor Pennysaver**
4525 Rhodes Dr., Windsor, ON N8W 5R8
Tel: 519-966-4500; *Fax:* 519-966-3660
classified@windsorpennysaver.com
shopinwindsor.com/Windsor-Essex-County-Pennysaver/344420.htm
Circulation: 119,000 *Frequency:* Fri.
Shannon Ricker, Publisher
Rod Hilts, Regional Managing Editor

Wingham: **Wingham Advance-Times**
Owned By: Metroland Media Group Ltd.
PO Box 390, 11 Veterans Rd., Wingham, ON N0G 2W0
Tel: 519-357-2320; *Fax:* 519-357-2900
www.southwesternontario.ca
www.facebook.com/WinghamAdvanceTimes
Circulation: 1,200 *Frequency:* Wed.
Pauline Kerr, Editor
pkerr@wingham.com
Bill Huether, General Manager
bhuether@northperth.com

Woodstock: **Oxford Shopping News**
Owned By: Postmedia Network Inc.
16 Brock St., Woodstock, ON N4S 3B4
Tel: 519-537-6657; *Fax:* 519-537-8542
www.oxfordshoppingnews.com
Circulation: 26,800 *Frequency:* Tues.
Distributed by the Woodstock Sentinel Review
Ken Koyama, Publisher
ken.koyama@sunmedia.ca

Gord McCreary, Director, Advertising
gord.mccreary@sunmedia.ca

Multicultural Newspapers in Ontario

Brampton: **Gujarat Express**
20 Eldwood Pl., Brampton, ON L6V 3N3
Tel: 647-298-9887
gujaratexp@gmail.com
gujaratexpress.ca
Frequency: Weekly
Gujarat Express serves new immigrants to Canada & the South Asian community.
Amit Bhatt, Editor-in-Chief

University & College Newspapers in Ontario

Hamilton: **Ignite**
Owned By: Mohawk College
Hamilton, ON L9N 3T2
journalism@mohawkcollege.ca
www.ignitenews.ca
www.youtube.com/user/IgniteNewsCanada
www.facebook.com/IgniteNews
Mohawk College newspaper.

London: **The Interrobang**
Owned By: Fanshawe College
PO Box 7005, 1001 Fanshawe College Blvd., London, ON N5Y 5R6
www.theinterrobang.ca
twitter.com/interrobang_fsu
www.facebook.com/fsuinterrobang
Frequency: Weekly
Fanshawe College newspaper.
Hannah Theodore, Editor
h_theodore@fanshawec.ca
John Said, Manager, Publications & Communications
jsaid@fanshawec.ca

Oshawa: **The Chronicle**
Owned By: Durham College
PO Box 385, 2000 Simcoe St. North, Oshawa, ON L1H 7K4
Tel: 905-721-3068; *Fax:* 905-721-3113
chronicle.durhamcollege.ca
twitter.com/DCUOITChronicle
Durham College newspaper.
Brian Legree, Editor-in-Chief
brian.legree@durhamcollege.ca

Ottawa: **The Charlatan**
Owned By: Carleton University
Unicentre Bldg., #531, 1125 Colonel By Dr., Ottawa, ON K1S 5B6
Tel: 613-520-6680
editor.charlatan@gmail.com
charlatan.ca
twitter.com/CharlatanLive
www.facebook.com/CharlatanLive
Carleton University newspaper.
Jillian Piper, Editor-in-Chief

St Catharines: **Brock Press**
Owned By: Brock University
St Catharines, ON
Tel: 905-688-5550; *Fax:* 905-984-4853
editor@brockpress.com
www.brockpress.com
www.instagram.com/thebrockpress
twitter.com/TheBrockPress
www.facebook.com/TheBrockPress
Brock University newspaper.
Noah Nickel, Editor-in-Chief

Thunder Bay: **The Argus**
Owned By: Lakehead University
955 Oliver Rd., #UC-2014B, Thunder Bay, ON P7B 5E1
editor@theargus.ca
www.theargus.ca
www.instagram.com/theargusnewspaper
www.facebook.com/theargus
Circulation: 3,000
Lakehead University newspaper.
Sarah McPherson, Editor-In-Chief

Toronto: **Dialog Newspaper**
Owned By: George Brown College
142 Kendal Ave., #E122, Toronto, ON M5R 1M3
Tel: 416-415-5000
dialognews.ca
twitter.com/dialoggbc
www.facebook.com/thedialogonline

Frequency: Monthly (Aug.-April)
George Brown College student newspaper.
Victoria Surla, Editor
editor@dialognews.ca

Toronto: **EtCetera**
Owned By: Humber College
Faculty of Media & Creative Arts, Humber College, 205 Humber College Blvd., Toronto, ON M9W 5L7
etc.humber@gmail.com
humberetc.ca
www.youtube.com/user/HumberNews
twitter.com/humberetc
www.facebook.com/HumberEtCetera
Frequency: 10 times per term (fall & winter)
Jared Dodds, Editor-in-Chief

Prince Edward Island

Daily Newspapers in Prince Edward Island

Charlottetown: **The Guardian**
Previous Name: The Evening Patriot
Owned By: SaltWire Network
165 Prince St., Charlottetown, PE C1A 4R7
Tel: 902-629-6000
newsroom@theguardian.pe.ca
www.theguardian.pe.ca
twitter.com/peiguardian
www.facebook.com/pei.guardian
Frequency: Monday-Saturday
Wayne Thibodeau, Managing Editor

Other Newspapers in Prince Edward Island

Alberton: **West Prince Graphic**
Owned By: Island Press Limited
PO Box 339, 491 Main St., #C, Alberton, PE C0B 1B0
Tel: 902-853-3320; *Fax:* 902-853-3071
www.peicanada.com
Circulation: 5,800 *Frequency:* Weds.
Paul MacNeill, Publisher
paul@peicanada.com
Melissa Heald, Editor
melissa@peicanada.com

Montague: **The Eastern Graphic**
Owned By: Island Press Limited
PO Box 790, 530 Main St., Montague, PE C0A 1R0
Tel: 902-838-2515; *Fax:* 902-838-4392
peicanada.com/content/eastern_graphic
twitter.com/graphicnews
www.facebook.com/peicanada
Circulation: 5,200 *Frequency:* Wed.
The publication covers news for eastern Prince Edward Island.
Paul MacNeill, Publisher
paul@peicanada.com
Heather Moore, Editor
editor@peicanada.com
Jan MacNeill, Manager, Advertising
jan@peicanada.com
Aura Lee Shepard, Coordinator, Production
auralee@peicanada.com
Sharon Riley, Account Executive
sharon@peicanada.com

Summerside: **La Voix Acadienne**
Détenteur: La Voix Acadienne
5, av Maris Stella, Summerside, PE C1N 6M9
Tél: 902-436-6005; *Téléc:* 902-888-3976
pub@lavoixacadienne.com
www.lavoixacadienne.com
twitter.com/lavoixacadienne
www.facebook.com/246332682050424
Tirage: 2 200 *Fréquence:* Mercredi
Marcia Enman, Directrice général
marcia.enman@lavoixacadienne.com

Québec

Daily Newspapers in Québec

Granby: **La Voix de L'Est**
Détenteur: Coopérative nationale de l'information indépendante
158, rue Principale, Granby, QC J2G 2V6
Tél: 450-375-4555
redaction@lavoixdelest.ca
www.lavoixdelest.ca
www.linkedin.com/company/la-voix-de-l'est
twitter.com/lavoixdelest
www .facebook.com/lavoixdelest

Fréquence: lundi-samedi
Christian Malo, Directeur général
christian.malo@lavoixdelest.ca
Isabelle Gaboriault, Rédactrice en chef
isabelle.gaboriault@lavoixdelest.ca

Montréal: Le Devoir
Détenteur: Independent
2050, de Bleury, 9e étage, Montréal, QC H3A 3M9
Tél: 514-985-3333 *Ligne sans frais:* 800-463-7559
redaction@ledevoir.com
www.ledevoir.com
twitter.com/LeDevoir
www.facebook.com/ledevoir
Tirage: 547 000 total *Fréquence:* lundi-samedi
Le Devoir est une référence en matière d'information.
André Ryan, Président
Marie-Andrée Chouinard, Rédactrice en chef

Montréal: Le Journal de Montréal
Détenteur: Québecor Media Inc.
4545, rue Frontenac, Montréal, QC H2H 2R7
Tél: 514-521-4545; *Téléc:* 514-521-4416
Ligne sans frais: 800-637-2667
www.journaldemontreal.com
twitter.com/JdeMontreal
www.facebook.com/jdemontreal
Tirage: 2 249 000 total *Fréquence:* quotidien
Lyne Robitaille, Présidente et éditrice

Montréal: Journal Métro de Montréal
Détenteur: Métro Média
#230, 101, boul Marcel-Laurin, Montréal, QC H4N 2M3
Tél: 514-286-1066
info@journalmetro.com
journalmetro.com
www.instagram.com/journalmetro
twitter.com/journalmetro
www.facebook.c om/journalmetro
Tirage: 1 144 000 total *Fréquence:* quotidien
Andrew Mulé, Président et directeur général

Montreal: Montreal Gazette
Previous Name: The Gazette
Owned By: Postmedia Network Inc.
#200, 1010, rue Ste-Catherine ouest, Montreal, QC H3B 5L1
Tel: 514-987-2400 *Toll-Free:* 800-361-8478
citynews@montrealgazette.com
montrealgazette.com
www.youtube.com/c/MontrealGazettevideos
twitter.com/mtlgazette
www.facebook.com/montrealgazette
Frequency: Monday-Saturday
Lucinda Chodan, Editor
514-987-2508
lchodan@postmedia.com
Basem Boshra, Managing Editor
514-987-2628
bboshra@postmedia.com

Québec: Le Journal de Québec
Détenteur: Québecor Media Inc.
450, rue Béchard, Québec, QC G1M 2E9
Tél: 418-683-1573
jdq-scoop@quebecormedia.com
www.journaldequebec.com
twitter.com/JdeQuebec
www.facebook.com/JdeQuebec
Tirage: 1 149 000 total *Fréquence:* quotidien

Québec: Le Soleil
Détenteur: Coopérative nationale de l'information indépendante
CP 1547 Terminus, 410, boul Charest est, Québec, QC G1K 7J6
Tél: 418-686-3233
nouvelles@lesoleil.com
www.lesoleil.com
www.linkedin.com/company/journal-le-soleil
twitter.com/cyblesoleil
www .facebook.com/lesoleildequebec
Fréquence: quotidien
Journal hebdomadaire du Québec
Gilles Carignan, Directeur général
gcarignan@lesoleil.com
Valérie Gaudreau, Rédactrice en chef
vgaudreau@lesoleil.com

Saguenay: Le Quotidien
Détenteur: Coopérative nationale de l'information indépendante
1051, boul Talbot, Saguenay, QC G7H 5C1
Tél: 418-690-8800
redaction@lequotidien.com
www.lequotidien.com
www.linkedin.com/company/le-quotidien
twitter.com/LeQuotidien_Cyb
www. facebook.com/LeQuotidienProgres
Fréquence: quotidien
Marc St-Hilaire, Directeur général et rédacteur en chef
mst-hilaire@lequotidien.com

Sainte-Marie-de-Beauce: Beauce Média
Anciennement: Journal de Beauce-Nord
Détenteur: icimédias
#707, 1078, boul Vachon nord, Sainte-Marie-de-Beauce, QC G6E 1M7
Tél: 418-387-8000; *Téléc:* 418-387-4495
info@beaucemedia.ca
www.editionbeauce.com
twitter.com/BeauceMedia
www.facebook.com/beaucemedia
Tirage: 24 000 *Fréquence:* mercredi
Caroline Gilbert, Éditrice régional
cgilbert@icimedias.ca

Sherbrooke: The Record
Owned By: Alta Newspaper Group LP
6, rue Mallory, Sherbrooke, QC J1M 2E2
Tel: 819-569-9525; *Fax:* 819-569-6345
www.sherbrookerecord.com
twitter.com/recordnewspaper
www.facebook.com/sherbrookerecord
Frequency: Monday-Friday
Sharon McCully, Publisher
outletjournal@sympatico.ca

Sherbrooke: La Tribune
Détenteur: Coopérative nationale de l'information indépendante
780, rue King ouest, Sherbrooke, QC J1H 1R7
Tél: 819-564-5450
redaction@latribune.qc.ca
www.latribune.ca
www.linkedin.com/company/la-tribune-de-sherbrooke
twitter.com/LT_LaTribu ne
Fréquence: lundi-samedi
Hugo Fontaine, Directeur général
hugo.fontaine@latribune.qc.ca
Louis-Éric Allard, Rédacteur en chef
lallard@latribune.qc.ca

Trois-Rivières: Le Nouvelliste
Détenteur: Coopérative nationale de l'information indépendante
1920, rue Bellefeuille, Trois-Rivières, QC G9A 3Y2
Tél: 819-376-2501
information@lenouvelliste.qc.ca
www.lenouvelliste.ca
twitter.com/le_nouvelliste
www.facebook.com/lenouvelliste
Fréquence: lundi-samedi
Stephan Frappier, Directeur général et Rédacteur en chef
stephan.frappier@lenouvelliste.qc.ca

Other Newspapers in Québec

Acton Vale: La Pensée de Bagot
Détenteur: DBC Communications Inc.
800, rue de Roxton, Acton Vale, QC J0H 1A0
Tél: 450-546-3271; *Téléc:* 450-546-3491
publicite@lapensee.qc.ca
www.lapensee.qc.ca
Tirage: 14 797 *Fréquence:* mercredi
Benoit Chartier, Éditeur
Michel Dorais, Directeur
mdorais@lapensee.qc.ca

Alma: Le Lac Saint-Jean
Détenteur: Trium Médias
#01, 100, rue St-Joseph sud, Alma, QC G8B 7A6
Tél: 418-668-4545; *Téléc:* 418-668-8522
lelacstjean.com
twitter.com/lelacstjean
www.facebook.com/lelacstjean
Fréquence: Samedi

Baie-Saint-Paul: L'Hebdo Charlevoisien
Détenteur: Néomedia
45, boul Raymond Mailloux, Baie-Saint-Paul, QC G3Z 1W2
Tél: 418-435-0220; *Téléc:* 418-435-3349
hebdo@charlevoix.net
www.charlevoixendirect.com
Tirage: 13 033 *Fréquence:* Saturday
Charles Warren, Directeur
418-665-1299
charles@hebdocharlevoisien.ca
Guy Charlebois, Directeur de production

Beaulac-Garthby: Journal Le Contact
9, rue de la Chapelle, Beaulac-Garthby, QC G0Y 1B0
Tél: 418-458-2737; *Téléc:* 418-458-1142
contactbg2002@yahoo.ca
www.beaulac-garthby.com
Tirage: 475 *Fréquence:* vendredi
Guy St-Onge, Rédacteur

Beaupré: Métro - Journal L'Autre Voix
Détenteur: Métro Média
#101, 10989, boul Sainte-Anne, Beaupré, QC G0A 1E0
Tél: 418-827-1511; *Téléc:* 418-827-1513
www.quebechebdo.com/local/journal-lautre-voix
Tirage: 14 390 *Fréquence:* mercredi
Michel Chalifour, Directeur général régional

Beloeil: L'Oeil Régional
Détenteur: DBC Communications Inc.
393, boul Sir-Wilfrid-Laurier, Beloeil, QC J3G 4H6
Tél: 450-467-1821; *Téléc:* 450-467-3087
www.oeilregional.com
twitter.com/oeilregional
www.facebook.com/oeilregional
Tirage: 35 000+ *Fréquence:* Samedi
Serge Landry, Éditeur; Directeur général régional, Montérégie-Est
serge.landry@tc.tc
Gilbert Desrosiers, Directeur des projets spéciaux
gilbert.desrosiers@quebecormedia.com

Boucherville: Journal La Relève Inc.
528, rue St-Charles, Boucherville, QC J4B 3M5
Tél: 450-641-4844; *Téléc:* 450-641-4849
lareleve@lareleve.qc.ca
www.lareleve.qc.ca
Tirage: 54 650 *Fréquence:* Jeudi et Vendredi
Bernard Desmarteau, Représentant
Michel Desmarteau, Représentant

Cantley: L'Écho de Cantley / The Echo of Cantley
188, montée de la Source, Boîte 1, Comp. 9, Cantley, QC J8V 3J2
Tel: 819-827-2828
info@echocantley.ca
www.echocantley.ca
Circulation: 2 400
Joël Deschênes, Rédacteur en chef
editor@echocantley.ca

Cap-aux-Meules: Le Radar
CP 8183, 110, ch Gros-Cap, Cap-aux-Meules, QC G4T 1R3
Tél: 418-986-2345; *Téléc:* 418-986-6358
Ligne sans frais: 866-986-2345
secretaire@leradar.qc.ca
www.leradar.qc.ca
www.facebook.com/radar.hebdomadaire
Tirage: 2 136 *Fréquence:* mardi
Adèle Arseneau, Rédactrice en chef
redacteur.qc.ca

Chambly: Le Journal de Chambly
Détenteur: Les Versants du Mont-Bruno Inc.
CP 175, 1685, rue Bourgogne, Chambly, QC J3L 1Y8
Tél: 450-658-6516; *Téléc:* 450-658-3785
www.journaldechambly.com
twitter.com/JournalChambly
www.facebook.com/journaldechambly
Tirage: 21 237 *Fréquence:* Mardi
Daniel Noiseux, Éditeur
daniel.noiseux@tc.tc
Serge Landry, Directeur général régional, Montérégie-Est
serge.landry@tc.tc

Châteauguay: Le Soleil de Châteauguay
Anciennement: Le Soleil du Samedi
Détenteur: Gravité Média
82, boul Salaberry sud, Châteauguay, QC J6J 4J6
Tél: 450-692-8552; *Téléc:* 450-692-3460
cybersoleil.com
twitter.com/cybersoleil
www.facebook.com/cybersoleil

Tirage: 35 000 *Fréquence:* Mercredi

Chibougamau: La Sentinelle et le Jamésien
317, 3e rue, Chibougamau, QC G8P 1N4
Tél: 418-748-6406; *Téléc:* 418-748-2421
www.lasentinelle.ca
Tirage: 1 968 *Fréquence:* mercredi
Ralph Pilote, Directeur général, Québecor Média,
Saguenay-Lac-Saint-Jean
ralph.pilote@quebecormedia.ca

Coaticook: Le Progrès de Coaticook
Détenteur: icimédias
20, rue de Manège, Coaticook, QC J1A 3B3
Tél: 819-849-9846; *Téléc:* 819-849-1041
www.leprogres.net
twitter.com/HebdoCoaticook
www.facebook.com/LeProgresDeCoaticook
Tirage: 8 600 *Fréquence:* Samedi
Monique Côté, Éditrice
monique.cote@tc.tc
Dany Jacques, Chef de pupitre
dany.jacques@transcontinental.ca

Cookshire-Eaton: Journal Le Haut-Saint-François
#101, 57, rue Craig nord, Cookshire-Eaton, QC J0B 1M0
Tél: 819-875-5501
info@journalhsf.com
journalhautsaintfrancois.com
www.facebook.com/JournalHSF
Tirage: 11 200 *Fréquence:* mercredi
Pierre Hébert, Directeur général

Courcelette: Adsum
CP 1000 Forces, #516, Garnison Valcartier, Courcelette, QC G0A 4Z0
Tél: 418-844-6934; *Téléc:* 418-844-6934
adsum@forces.gc.ca
www.journaladsum.com
www.journaladsum.com/contact.php#
Tirage: 4 200 *Fréquence:* semi-mensuelle, mercredi
Caroline Charest, Editor
caroline.charest@forces.gc.ca

Cowansville: L'Avenir et des Rivières
Détenteur: icimédias
#123, 3, rue Principale, Cowansville, QC J2K 1J3
Ligne sans frais: 800-363-4542
www.laveniretdesrivieres.com
twitter.com/HebdoFarnham
www.facebook.com/lAveniretDesRivieres
Tirage: 10 885 *Fréquence:* mercredi

Daveluyville: Le Causeur
337, rue Principale, Daveluyville, QC G0Z 1C0
Tél: 819-367-3395; *Téléc:* 819-367-3550
info@ville.daveluyville.qc.ca
www.ville.daveluyville.qc.ca/causeur_journ al_municipal.php
www.facebook.com/351233864932287
Tirage: 1 100 *Fréquence:* mensuel
Pauline Vrain, Directrice générale
dg@ville.daveluyville.qc.ca

Delson: Le Reflet
Détenteur: Gravité Média
11, rte 132, Delson, QC J5B 1G9
Tél: 450-635-9146; *Téléc:* 450-635-4619
info@lereflet.qc.ca
www.lereflet.qc.ca
twitter.com/lereflet
www.facebook.com/journallereflet
Tirage: 40 000 *Fréquence:* Mercredi

Disraéli: Le Cantonnier
888, rue St-Antoine, Disraéli, QC G0N 1E0
Tél: 418-449-1888; *Téléc:* 418-449-1889
lecantonnier@lino.com
www.lecantonnier.com
Jean-Denis Grimard, Rédacteur

Dolbeau-Mistassini: Journal Nouvelles Hebdo
Détenteur: Trium Médias
1741, rue des Pins, Dolbeau-Mistassini, QC G8L 1J7
Tél: 418-276-6211; *Téléc:* 418-276-6166
www.nouvelleshebdo.com
twitter.com/NouvellesHebdo
www.facebook.com/NouvellesHebdo
Tirage: 12 596 *Fréquence:* mercredi
Claudia Turcotte, Directrice générale
claudia.turcotte@tc.tc

Donnacona: Le Courrier de Portneuf
CP 1030, 276, rue Notre-Dame, Donnacona, QC G3M 1G7
Tél: 418-285-0211 *Ligne sans frais:* 866-577-0211
www.courrierdeportneuf.com
twitter.com/CourrierdePnf
Tirage: 27 700 *Fréquence:* Samedi
Josee-Anne Fiset, Directrice general
josee-anne.fiset@courrierdeportneuf.com

Dorval: Cités Nouvelles / City News
Owned By: Métro Média
#303, 455, boul Fénelon, Dorval, QC H9S 5T8
Tel: 514-636-7314; *Fax:* 514-636-7317
journalmetro.com/local/ouest-de-lile
twitter.com/CitesNouvelles
www.facebook.com/CitesNouvelles
Circulation: 44 400 *Frequency:* Dimanche
Sylviane Lussier, Directrice régionale
Denis Therrien, Directeur général

Dorval: Magazine Ile des Soeurs / Nuns Island Magazine
Détenteur: Métro Média
#303, 455, boul Fénelon, Dorval, QC H9S 5T8
Tél: 514-636-7314; *Téléc:* 514-636-7315
www.lemagazineiledessoeurs.com
twitter.com/LeMagazineIDS
www.facebook.com/278830125519919
Tirage: 8 148 *Fréquence:* Mercredi
Patricia-Ann Beaulieu, Éditrice
patriciaann.beaulieu@tc.tc
Normand Sauvé, Chef de pupitre
normand.sauve@tc.tc

Dorval: Le Messager de LaSalle
Détenteur: Métro Média
#303, 455, boul Fénelon, Dorval, QC H9S 5T8
Tél: 514-636-7314; *Téléc:* 514-636-7315
journalmetro.com/local/lasalle
twitter.com/MessagerLaSalle
www.facebook.com/166724190111906
Tirage: 32 200 *Fréquence:* Sunday
Patricia-Ann Beaulieu, Éditrice
patriciaann.beaulieu@tc.tc
Normand Sauvé, Chef de pupitre
normand.sauve@tc.tc

Dorval: Le Messager Lachine Dorval
Détenteur: Métro Média
#303, 455, boul Fénelon, Dorval, QC H9S 5T8
Tél: 514-636-7314; *Téléc:* 514-636-7315
journalmetro.com/local/lachine-dorval
twitter.com/MessagerLachine
www.facebook.com/166241803496061
Tirage: 23 100 *Fréquence:* Sunday
Robert Leduc, Rédacteur en chef
robert.leduc@tc.tc
Dennis Therrien, Directeur général. ouest de Montréal
denis.therrien@tc.tc

Dorval: Métro - IDS - Verdun
Détenteur: Métro Média
#303, 455, boul Fénelon, Dorval, QC H9S 5T8
Tél: 514-636-7314; *Téléc:* 514-636-7315
journalmetro.com/local/ids-verdun
twitter.com/MessagerVerdun
www.facebook.com/MessagerVerdun
Tirage: 24 443 *Fréquence:* Jeudi
Stéphane Desjardins, Directeur général
stephane.desjardins@tc.tc
Daniel Beaudin, Conseiller en solutions médias
daniel.beaudin@tc.tc

Dorval: La Voix Pop
Anciennement: La Voix Populaire
Détenteur: Métro Média
#303, 455, boul Fénelon, Dorval, QC H9S 5T8
Tél: 514-636-7314; *Téléc:* 514-636-7315
journalmetro.com/local/sud-ouest
twitter.com/VoixPop
www.facebook.com/lavoixpop
Tirage: 29 170 *Fréquence:* Dimanche
Stéphane Desjardins, Directeur général - Sud ouest de Montréal
stephane.desjardins@tc.tc
Olivier Laniel, Directeur du contenu et des relations avec la communaut
olivier.laniel@tc.tc

Drummondville: L'Express
1050, rue Cormier, Drummondville, QC J2C 2N6
Tél: 819-478-8171; *Téléc:* 819-478-4306
www.journalexpress.ca
twitter.com/JournalExpress
www.facebook.com/JournalExpressDrummond
Tirage: 48 000+ *Fréquence:* Dimanche
Jean Morisette, Directeur général
jean.morisette@tc.tc
Lise Tremblay, Chef de pupitre
lise.tremblay@tc.tc

Egan-Sud: La Gatineau
Détenteur: Les Éditions La Gatineau Ltée
135-B, rte 105, Egan-Sud, QC J9E 3A9
Tél: 819-449-1725; *Téléc:* 819-449-5108
reception@lagatineau.com
www.lagatineau.com
www.facebook.com/lagatineau
Tirage: 11 100 *Fréquence:* Vendredi
Philippe Patry, Directeur général
ppatry@lagatineau.com
Sylvie Dejouy, Rédaction
ppatry@lagatineau.com

Fermont: Journal Le Trait D'union du Nord
Détenteur: Le Trait d'union
850 Place Daviault, local 159, Fermont, QC G0G 1J0
Tél: 418-287-3655; *Téléc:* 418-287-3874
info.journaltdn@gmail.com
www.journaltdn.com
Tirage: 1 800 *Fréquence:* mercredi
Le journal des villes nordiques
Sandra Carter, Directrice générale
Véronique Dumais, Rédactrice en chef et journaliste

Forestville: Journal Haute Côte-Nord Ouest
Détenteur: Journal Haute Côte-Nord Inc.
31, rte 138, Forestville, QC G0T 1E0
Tél: 418-587-2090; *Téléc:* 418-587-6407
pub@journalhcn.com
www.journalhcnouest.com
Tirage: 5 604 *Fréquence:* mercredi
Luc Brisson, Éditeur
luc.brisson@journalhcn.com

Fort-Coulonge: Pontiac Journal du Pontiac / Le Journal de Pontiac
289, Manoir Mansfield, #RR 148, Fort-Coulonge, QC J0X 1V0
Tél: 819-683-3582; *Téléc:* 819-683-2977
editor@journalpontiac.com
journalpontiac.com
Tirage: 9 319 *Fréquence:* Bi-weekly
Journal is the only local newspaper that has both French & English editors. / C'est le seul journal local qui a des rédacteurs francophone et anglophone
Lynne Lavery, Directrice générale
info@journalpontiac.com
Fred Ryan, Éditeur
Nancy Hunt, Editor / rédactrice (English/anglais)
editor@journalpontiac.com
Andre Macron, Editor / rédacteur (French/français)
editor@journalpontiac.com

Gatineau: Bulletin d'Aylmer
#C-10, 181, rue Principale, Gatineau, QC J9H 6A6
Tel: 819-684-4755; *Fax:* 819-684-6428
Toll-Free: 800-486-7678
www.bulletinaylmer.com
Circulation: 24,700 *Frequency:* Wed.
Lynne Lavery, Office Manager
l.lavery@bulletinaylmer.com
Fred Ryan, Editor
abawqp@videotron.ca

Gatineau: Bulletin d'Aylmer
Previous Name: The West Québec Post
#C-10, 181, rue Principale, Gatineau, QC J9H 6A6
Tél: 819-684-4755; *Fax:* 819-684-6428
Toll-Free: 800-486-7678
info@bulletinaylmer.com
www.bulletinaylmer.com
Circulation: 24 543 *Frequency:* mercredi
Lily Ryan, Éditrice
info@bulletinaylmer.com

Granby: Granby Express
Anciennement: Samedi Express
Détenteur: icimédias
#127, 100, rue Robinson Sud, Granby, QC J2G 7L4
Tél: 450-777-4515
www.granbyexpress.com
www.facebook.com/GranbyExpress

Tirage: 43 245 *Fréquence:* mercredi
Cathy Bernard, Éditrice

Grande-Vallée: Journal le Phare
Anciennement: Le Phare, l'autre vision
1A, rue du Vieux Pont est, Grande-Vallée, QC G0E 1K0
Tél: 418-393-2205
redaction@journallephare.org
journallephare.org
twitter.com/journallephare
www.facebook.com/225905758286

Tirage: 1 300

Hudson: Gazette Vaudreuil-Soulanges
Previous Name: Lake of Two Mountains Gazette
Owned By: Lake of Two Mountains Gazette Ltd.
PO Box 70, 397 Main Rd., Hudson, QC J0P 1H0
Tel: 450-458-5482; *Fax:* 450-458-3337
hudsongazette@videotron.ca
gazettevaudreuilsoulanges.com
www.facebook.com/437408105332

Circulation: 16,000 *Frequency:* Wed.
First English Quebec weekly on the web.

Huntingdon: The Gleaner / Le Gleaner
Détenteur: Chateauguay Valley Community Information Services
66, rue Châteauguay, Huntingdon, QC J0S 1H0
Tél: 450-264-5364; *Téléc:* 450-264-9521
contact@the-gleaner.com
the-gleaner.com

Tirage: 4 000 *Fréquence:* Lundi
Sheri Graham, Éditrice
sheri.sheri.graham@tc.tc

Joliette: L'Action
Détenteur: Groupe Lexis Média Inc.
342, Beaudry nord, Joliette, QC J6E 6A6
Tél: 450-759-3664; *Téléc:* 450-759-3190
www.laction.com
twitter.com/journalaction
www.facebook.com/journalaction

Tirage: 46 700 *Fréquence:* Dimanche

Knowlton: Brome County News
Owned By: Sherbrooke Record
5 Victoria, Knowlton, QC J0E 1V0
Tel: 450-242-1188; *Fax:* 450-243-5155
Toll-Free: 800-463-9525
newsroom@sherbrookerecord.com
www.sherbrookerecord.com/brome
Other information: Ads, Email: classad@sherbrookerecord.com
www.facebook.com/sherbrookerecord

Circulation: 12,297 *Frequency:* Tuesday
Daniel Coulombe, Editor
dcoulombe@sherbrookerecord.com
Sharon McCully, Publisher
outletjournal@sympatico.ca

L'Islet: Journal le Hublot
Détenteur: Les Éditions des Trois Clochers
#202, 16, ch des Pionniers est, L'Islet, QC G0R 2B0
Tél: 418-247-3333; *Téléc:* 418-247-3336
clochers@globetrotter.net
www.lehublot.ca

Tirage: 1 900 *Fréquence:* mensuel
Guylaine Hudon, Directrice Générale

La Tuque: L'Écho de La Tuque
Détenteur: icimédias
324, rue St-Joseph, La Tuque, QC G9X 1L2
Tél: 819-523-6141; *Téléc:* 819-523-6143
www.lechodelatuque.com
twitter.com/lechodelatuque
www.facebook.com/246902629754

Tirage: 6 802
Michel Scarpino, Directeur du journal

Lac-Etchemin: La Voix du Sud
Détenteur: icimédias
1516A, rte 277, Lac-Etchemin, QC G0R 1S0
Tél: 418-625-7471; *Téléc:* 418-625-5200
Ligne sans frais: 866-325-8649
www.lavoixdusud.com
twitter.com/voixdusud
www.facebook.com/lavoixdusud

Tirage: 30 000+ *Fréquence:* Samedi
Caroline Gilbert, Éditeur
caroline.gilbert@tc.tc

Lac-Mégantic: L'Écho de Frontenac
5040, boul des Vétérans, Lac-Mégantic, QC G6B 2G5
Tél: 819-583-1630; *Téléc:* 819-583-1124
www.echodefrontenac.com
twitter.com/echodefrontenac
www.facebook.com/308170576707

Tirage: 9 134 *Fréquence:* Dimanche
Gaétan Poulin, Éditeur
Rémi Tremblay, Rédacteur-en-chef

Lachute: L'Argenteuil
Détenteur: La Compagnie d'édition André Paquette inc
52, rue Principale, Lachute, QC J8H 3A8
Tél: 450-562-2494; *Téléc:* 450-562-1434
argenteuil@eap.on.ca
editionap.ca

Tirage: 16 500 *Fréquence:* Mercredi
François Leblanc, Directeur
francois.leblanc@eap.on

Lachute: Tribune Express Progrès Watchman
Anciennement: The Watchman
52, rue Principale, Lachute, QC J8H 3A8
Tél: 450-562-8593; *Téléc:* 450-562-1434
Ligne sans frais: 800-561-5738

Tirage: 13 000 *Fréquence:* Samedi
Evelyne Bergeron, Editor

Laval: Courrier Laval
Détenteur: 2M.Media
#200, 2700, av Francis-Hughes, Laval, QC H7S 2B9
Tél: 450-667-4360; *Téléc:* 450-667-0845
www.courrierlaval.com
twitter.com/LeCourrierLaval
www.facebook.com/courrierlaval

Tirage: 121 172 *Fréquence:* mercredi
Benoit Caron, Directeur général régional

Laval: The Laval News
Previous Name: The Chomedey News
Owned By: Newsfirst Multimedia
3860, boul Notre-Dame, Laval, QC H7V 1S1
Tel: 450-978-9999; *Fax:* 450-687-6330
lavalnews.ca

Circulation: 33 164 *Frequency:* samedi
Laval's English newspaper since 1993
George Bakoyannis, Co-publisher
George Guzmas, Co-publisher

Laval: Nouvelles Parc-Extension News
#304, 3860, boul Notre-Dame, Laval, QC H7V 1S1
Tel: 450-978-9999; *Fax:* 450-687-6330
editor@the-news.ca
www.px-news.com

Frequency: Saturday, bi-weekly
George Bakoyannis, Co-Publisher, General Director
georgeb@the-news.ca
George S. Guzmas, Co-Publisher, Advertising Director
georgeg@the-news.ca

Laval: Vivre
828, av 79, Laval, QC H7V 3J1
Tél: 450-973-8787; *Téléc:* 450-973-8414
poste@ccvm.org
www.ccvm.org/journal-vivre
www.facebook.com/ccvm.org

Tirage: 1 000 *Fréquence:* deux fois par an
Manon Rousseau, Directrice générale

Lennoxville: The Townships Sun
PO Box 28, Lennoxville, QC J1M 1Z3
Tel: 819-566-7424
townsun@netrevolution.com
twitter.com/TownshipsSun
www.facebook.com/TheTownshipsSun

Circulation: 570 *Frequency:* Monthly
Gordon Lambie, Editor

Lévis: Le Peuple Lotbinière
Détenteur: Mélior Média Ltd.
#103B, 5790, boul Étienne-Dallaire, Lévis, QC G6V 8V6
Tél: 418-728-2131; *Téléc:* 418-728-4819
www.lepeuplelotbiniere.ca
twitter.com/Plotbiniere
www.facebook.com/plotbiniere

Tirage: 15 000 *Fréquence:* Dimanche
Paul Lessard, Éditeur
paul.lessard@tc.tc
Mathieu Galarneau, Directeur de l'information
mathieu.galarneau@tc.tc

Lingwick: Le Reflet du canton de Lingwick
72, rte 108, Lingwick, QC J0B 2Z0
Tél: 819-877-3560
info@lereflet.org
lereflet.org

Tirage: 275 *Fréquence:* neuf fois par an
Chantal Lapointe, Présidente

Longueuil: Le Courrier du Sud
Détenteur: Gravité Média
267, rue Saint-Charles ouest, Longueuil, QC J4H 1E3
Tél: 450-646-3333; *Téléc:* 450-674-0205
publicite@courrierdusud.com
www.lecourrierdusud.ca
twitter.com/LeCourrierDuSud
www.facebook.com/lecourrierdusud

Tirage: 133 000 *Fréquence:* Mercredi

Longueuil: Point Sud
#1, 674 rue Saint-Jean, Longueuil, QC J4H 2Y4
Tél: 450-677-2626; *Téléc:* 450-442-2663
info@pointsud.ca
www.pointsud.ca
twitter.com/Point_Sud
www.facebook.com/pointsud

Louiseville: L'Écho de Maskinongé
Anciennement: L'Écho D'Autray et de Maskinongé
Détenteur: icimédias
43, St-Louis, Louiseville, QC J5V 2C7
Tél: 819-228-5532; *Téléc:* 819-228-9379
www.lechodemaskinonge.com
twitter.com/EchoMaski
www.facebook.com/echomaskinonge

Tirage: 13 652 *Fréquence:* Dimanche
André Juteau, Directeur général régional
Pierre Bergeron, Directeur général
André Juteau, Directeur général régional
Marie-Ève Veillette, Chef de nouvelles

Magog: Le Reflet du Lac
Détenteur: icimédias
#104, 101, rue Du Moulin, Magog, QC J1X 4A1
Tél: 819-843-3500; *Téléc:* 819-843-3085
Ligne sans frais: 866-637-5236
www.lerefletdulac.com
twitter.com/refletdulac
www.facebook.com/LeRefletduLac

Tirage: 26 639 *Fréquence:* Samedi
Monique Côté, Éditrice
monique.cote@tc.tc
Dany Jacques, Chef de pupitre
dany.jacques@tc.tc

Malartic: Le Courrier de Malartic
CP 4020, Malartic, QC J0Y 1Z0
Tél: 819-757-4712; *Téléc:* 819-757-4712
Tirage: 1 200 *Fréquence:* Mardi
Denyse Roberge, Éditrice

Matane: L'Avantage gaspésien
Détenteur: Groupe Lexis Média Inc.
310, rue de la Gare, Matane, QC G4W 3J3
Tél: 418-562-0666
redactionmatane@lexismedia.ca
www.lavantagegaspesien.com
www.facebook.com/avantagegaspesien

Tirage: 5 013 *Fréquence:* Mercredi; aussi La Voix du dimanche

Matane: L'Avant-Poste
Détenteur: Groupe Lexis Média Inc.
305, rue de la Gare, Matane, QC G4W 3J2
Tél: 418-629-3443; *Téléc:* 418-562-4607
www.lavantposte.ca
twitter.com/LAvantPoste
www.facebook.com/lavantposte

Tirage: 8 241 *Fréquence:* mercredi

Mont-Laurier: L'Info de la Lièvre
Détenteur: In Médias
534, rue de la Madone, Mont-Laurier, QC J9L 1S5
Tél: 819-623-7374
infodelalievre.ca

Mont-Tremblant: L'Information du Nord Mont-Tremblant
Détenteur: In Médias
979, rue de Saint-Jovite, Mont-Tremblant, QC J8E 3J8
Tél: 819-425-8658
infodunordtremblant.ca
twitter.com/linfodunordmt
www.facebook.com/linfodunordmt

Tirage: 14 300 *Fréquence:* Vendredi

Johanne Régimbald, Éditrice
johanne.regimbald@tc.tc
André Guillemette, Directeur général régional, Laurentides
andre.guillemette@tc.tc

Mont-Tremblant: L'Information du Nord Valée de la Rouge
Détenteur: In Médias
979, rue de Saint-Jovite, Mont-Tremblant, QC J8E 3J8
Tél: 819-425-8658
infodunordvalleedelarouge.ca

Tirage: 8 055 *Fréquence:* Mercredi
Johanna Régimbald, Éditrice
johanne.regimbald@tc.tc
Éric Busque, Chef des nouvelles
eric.busque.a@tc.tc

Montmagny: L'Oie Blanche
70, rue de l'Anse, Montmagny, QC G5V 3S7
Tél: 418-248-8820; *Téléc:* 418-248-4033
oieblanc.sec@globetrotter.net
www.oieblanc.com
twitter.com/oieblanc
www.facebook.com/166453626708427
Tirage: 19 672 *Fréquence:* Samedi
Michel Montminy, Directeur général
mmontminy@groupermmedias.com
José Soucy, Journaliste
nouvelles@cmatv.ca

Montréal: Le Couac
6940, rue Jogues, Montréal, QC H4E 2W8
Tél: 514-596-1017
info@lecouac.org
www.lecouac.org

Montréal: Échos Montréal
387, rue Saint-Paul ouest, Montréal, QC H2Y 2A7
Tél: 514-844-2133; *Téléc:* 514-844-5858
info@echosmontreal.com
www.facebook.com/365501026942053
Denise Di Candido, Chief Editor
Vincent Di Candido, Président

Montréal: Le Flambeau Mercier-Anjou
Détenteur: Métro Média
8000, av Blaise-Pascal, Montréal, QC H1E 2S7
Tél: 514-643-0013; *Téléc:* 514-899-5001
www.flambeaudelest.com
twitter.com/Flambeaudelest
www.facebook.com/leflambeaudelest
Tirage: 56 718 *Fréquence:* mardi
Véronique Gauthier, Directrice générale

Montréal: Greek Canadian Reportage
8060, rue Birnam, Montréal, QC H3N 2T7
Tél: 514-279-7772
pages.globetrotter.net/gcradb
Circulation: 15,000 *Frequency:* Weekly
Anthony Bartzakos, Publisher & Editor

Montréal: Le Havre
#236, 410, rue Saint-Nicolas, Montréal, QC H2Y 2P5
Tél: 418-689-6686
www.journallehavre.ca
twitter.com/LeHavre
www.facebook.com/lehavre

Tirage: 8 230 *Fréquence:* Mercredi
Bernard Johnson, Éditeur
bernard.johnson@tc.tc
Alain Lavoie, Chef de nouvelles
alain.lavoie@tc.tc

Montréal: L'Informateur de Rivières-des-Prairies
Détenteur: Métro Média
8000, av Blaise-Pascal, Montréal, QC H1E 2S7
Tél: 514-643-0013; *Téléc:* 514-899-5001
www.linformateurrdp.com
twitter.com/LinformateurRDP
www.facebook.com/linformateurrdp
Tirage: 21 276 *Fréquence:* mardi
Véronique Gauthier, Directrice générale
Marie-Josée Chouinard, Directrice de l'information

Montréal: L'Itinéraire
2103, rue Ste-Catherine est, 3e étage, Montréal, QC H2K 2H9
Tél: 514-597-0238; *Téléc:* 514-597-1544
itineraire@itineraire.ca
itineraire.ca
www.youtube.com/user/itineraire1
twitter.com/LItineraire
www.facebook.com/115888658426315
Tirage: 13 000 *Fréquence:* bimensuel
Serge Lareault, Éditeur

Montréal: Le Journal de Mont-Royal
Détenteur: Proxima Publications Inc.
#206, 8180, Devonshire, Montréal, QC H4P 2K3
Tél: 514-736-1133; *Téléc:* 514-736-7855
redaction@proxima-p.qc.ca
www.proxima-p.qc.ca
www.facebook.com/113408712021778
Tristan Roy, Éditeur

Montréal: Journal de Rosemont - La Petite-Patrie
Détenteur: Métro Média
1100, boul René-Lévesque ouest, 24e étage, Montréal, QC H3B 4X9
Tél: 514-643-2300
info@journalmetro.com
journalmetro.com/local/rosemont-la-petite-patrie
twitter.com/JournalRosemont
www.facebook.com/JournaldeRosemont
Tirage: 60 041 *Fréquence:* mardi
Nicolas Faucher, Éditeur

Montréal: Métro - Ahuntsic - Cartierville
Détenteur: Métro Média
8000, av Blaise-Pascal, Montréal, QC H1E 2S7
Tél: 514-643-0013; *Téléc:* 514-899-5001
journalmetro.com/local/ahuntsic-cartierville
twitter.com/InfoAhuntsicBC
www.facebook.com/courrierahuntsicbc
Tirage: 33 552 *Fréquence:* vendredi
Denis Filion, Directeur général

Montréal: Métro - Avenir de l'Est
Détenteur: Métro Média
#210, 8770, boul Langelier, Montréal, QC H1P 3C6
Tél: 514-899-5888; *Téléc:* 514-899-5001
journalmetro.com/local/pointe-aux-trembles-montreal-est
twitter.com/avenirdelest
www.facebook.com/avenirdelest
Tirage: 28 090 *Fréquence:* Mardi
Véronique Gauthier, Éditrice

Montréal: Métro - Montréal-Nord
Anciennement: Guide de Montréal-Nord
Détenteur: Métro Média
8000, av Blaise-Pascal, Montréal, QC H1E 2S7
Tél: 514-643-0013; *Téléc:* 514-899-5001
journalmetro.com/local/montreal-nord
twitter.com/GuidemtInord
www.facebook.com/guidemtInord
Tirage: 34 730 *Fréquence:* mardi
Véronique Gauthier, Directrice générale

Montréal: Métro - Saint-Laurent
Anciennement: Les Nouvelles Saint-Laurent
Détenteur: Métro Média
#210, 8770, boul Langelier, Montréal, QC H1P 3C6
Tél: 514-855-1292; *Téléc:* 514-855-1855
journalmetro.com/local/saint-laurent
twitter.com/InfoStLaurent
www.facebook.com/NouvellesSaintLaurent
Tirage: 31 660 *Fréquence:* Jeudi
Denis Therrien, Directeur général
Serge Labrosse, Directeur de l'information

Montréal: Le Plateau Mont-Royal
Détenteur: Métro Média
1100, boul René-Lévesque ouest, 24e étage, Montréal, QC H3B 4X9
Tél: 514-643-2300
info@journalmetro.com
journalmetro.com/local/le-plateau-mont-royal
twitter.com/Journalplateau
www.facebook.com/journalduplateau
Tirage: 36 268 *Fréquence:* jeudi
Nicolas Faucher, Éditeur

Montréal: La Presse
7, rue Saint-Jacques, Montréal, QC H2X 1K9
Tél: 514-285-7000 *Ligne sans frais:* 800-361-5013
nouvelles@lapresse.ca
www.lapresse.ca
twitter.com/LP_LaPresse
www.facebook.com/LaPresseFB
Tirage: 1 734 445 total *Fréquence:* quotidien
The French-language online newspaper is a not-for-profit organization.
Guy Crevier, Président et éditeur
Éric Trottier, Vice-président et éditeur adjoint

Montréal: Progrés Villeray
Détenteur: Métro Média
#203, 1500, boul Jules-Poitras, Montréal, QC H4N 1X7
Tél: 514-855-1292; *Téléc:* 514-855-1855
www.leprogresvilleray.com
twitter.com/InfoVillerayPE
www.facebook.com/ProgresVillerayParcExtension
Tirage: 21 630 *Fréquence:* Mardi
Séverine Galus, Directrice, Contenu et des relations avec la communauté

Montréal: Reflet de Société
Anciennement: Journal de la Rue
4233, rue Ste-Catherine est, Montréal, QC H1V 1X4
Tél: 514-256-9000; *Téléc:* 514-256-9444
journal@journaldelarue.ca
www.journaldelarue.com
Raymond Viger, Éditeur et rédacteur en chef

Montréal: The Suburban
Owned By: Michael Publishing Co. Inc.
#105, 7575 Trans-Canada Hwy., Montréal, QC H4T 1V6
Tél: 514-484-1107; *Fax:* 514-484-9616
www.thesuburban.com
Circulation: East End: 26,746; West Island: 40,239; City Edition: 63,319 *Frequency:* East End: Thursday; West Island: Wednesday; City Edition: Wednesday
The largest English-language weekly in Quebec.
Sari Medicoff, Associate Publisher
sari@thesuburban.com
Beryl Wajsman, Editor-in-Chief
editor@thesuburban.com

Natashquan: Le Portageur
50, ch d'en Haut, Natashquan, QC G0G 2E0
Tél: 418-726-3736; *Téléc:* 418-726-3714
secom@globetrotter.net
leportageur.jimdo.com
Tirage: 551 *Fréquence:* mercredi

New Carlisle: The Gaspé Spec
Détenteur: Sea-Coast Publications Inc.
CP 99, 128, boul Gerard D. Levesque, New Carlisle, QC G0C 1Z0
Tél: 418-752-5400; *Téléc:* 418-752-6932
specs@globetrotter.net
www.gaspespec.com
Autre information: Alternate Phone: 418-752-5070
Tirage: 2 580 *Fréquence:* Wednesday
Sharon Renouf-Farrell, Publisher
Gilles Gagné, News Editor

Outremont: Métro - Outremont / Mont-Royal
Anciennement: L'Express d'Outremont & Mont-Royal
Détenteur: Métro Média
#203, 1500, boul Jules-Poitras, Outremont, QC H4N 1X7
Tél: 514-855-1292; *Téléc:* 514-855-1855
journalmetro.com/local/outremont-mont-royal
www.facebook.com/MetroOUTVMR
Tirage: 11 560 *Fréquence:* Jeudi, hebdo
Stéphane Desjardins, Directeur général - Sud-ouest de Montréal
stephane.desjardins@tc.tc
Marilaine Bolduc-Jacob, Rédactrice en chef
Michel-Joanny Furtin, Rédacteur-en-chef
michel.joanny-furtin@tc.tc

Preissac: Journal L'Alliance de Preissac
180, av du Lac, Preissac, QC J0Y 2E0
Tél: 819-759-4141
www.preissac.com
www.facebook.com/preissac
Fréquence: mensuel
Estelle Gelot, Président

Québec: L'Actuel
Détenteur: Métro Média
#107, 710, rue Bouvier, Québec, QC G2J 1C2
Tél: 418-628-7460
www.lactuel.com
twitter.com/l_actuel
www.facebook.com/lactuel
Tirage: 57 669 *Fréquence:* vendredi
Michel Chalifour, Directeur général régional

Québec: Beauport Express
Détenteur: Métro Média
#107, 710, rue Bouvier, Québec, QC G2J 1C2
Tél: 418-686-6400; *Téléc:* 418-686-1086
www.quebechebdo.com/local/journal-beauport-express
twitter.com/quebechebdo
www.facebook.com/quebechebdo
Tirage: 38 700 *Fréquence:* Hebdomadaire
Lilianne Laprise, Directrice des ventes

Michel Chalifour, Directeur général régional
Lynda Drouin, Directrice administrative

Québec: Le Carrefour de Québec
Détenteur: Journal Le Carrefour de Québec
799, rue 5e, Québec, QC G1J 2S9
Tél: 418-649-0775; *Téléc:* 418-649-7531
www.carrefourdequebec.com
twitter.com/LeCarrefourQc
www.facebook.com/LeCarrefourQc
Tirage: 70 000 *Fréquence:* mercredi

Québec: Charlesbourg Express
Détenteur: Métro Média
#107, 710, rue Bouvier, Québec, QC G2J 1C2
Tél: 418-686-6400; *Téléc:* 418-686-4841
www.quebechebdo.com/local/journal-charlesbourg-express
www.facebook.com/CharlesExpr
Tirage: 27 095 *Fréquence:* Mercredi
Lilianne Laprise, Éditrice

Québec: Droit de Parole
Détenteur: Communications Basse-ville
266, Saint-Vallier Ouest, Québec, QC G1K 1K2
Tél: 418-648-8043
droitdeparole.org
Tirage: 16 000 *Fréquence:* mensuel

Québec: Journal le Jacques-Cartier
Détenteur: Métro Média
#107, 710, rue Bouvier, Québec, QC G2J 1C2
Tél: 418-628-7460; *Téléc:* 418-622-1511
www.lejacquescartier.com
twitter.com/quebechebdo
www.facebook.com/LeJacquesCartier
Tirage: 9 500
Michel Chalifour, Directeur général régional

Québec: Journal Le Québec Express
Détenteur: Métro Média
#107, 710, rue Bouvier, Québec, QC G2J 1C2
Tél: 418-628-7460; *Téléc:* 418-622-1511
www.lequebecexpress.com
twitter.com/quebechebdo
www.facebook.com/lequebecexpress
Tirage: 30 259 *Fréquence:* vendredi
Michel Chalifour, Directeur général régional

Québec: Journal Québec Hebdo
Détenteur: Métro Média
5000, rue Hugues-Randin, Québec, QC G2C 2B4
Tél: 418-840-1472; *Téléc:* 418-840-1207
www.quebechebdo.com

Québec: Métro - L'Appel
Détenteur: Métro Média
#107, 710, rue Bouvier, Québec, QC G2J 1C2
Tél: 418-686-6400; *Téléc:* 418-686-1086
www.quebechebdo.com/local/journal-lappel
www.facebook.com/journallappel
Tirage: 44 360 *Fréquence:* Mercredi
Lilianne Laprise, Éditrice
Michel Chalifour, Directeur général régional

Québec: Quebec Chronicle-Telegraph
Owned By: 1764 Publications Inc.
#218, 1040 av Belvédère, Québec, QC G1S 3G3
Tel: 418-650-1764; *Fax:* 418-650-5172
info@qctonline.com
www.qctonline.com
twitter.com/QCTonline
www.facebook.com/64677421759
Circulation: 1,300 *Frequency:* Wednesday
Stacie Stanton, Editor/Publisher
editor@qctonline.com

Québec: La Quête
Détenteur: L'Archipel d'Entraide (The Archipelago of Assistance)
190, rue Saint-Joseph est, Québec, QC G1K 3A7
Tél: 418-649-9145; *Téléc:* 418-649-7770
laquetejournal@yahoo.ca
Tirage: 2 500 *Fréquence:* mensuel
Francine Chatigny, Contact

Repentigny: Hebdo Rive Nord
Anciennement: L'Artisan
Détenteur: Groupe Lexis Média Inc.
1004, rue Notre-Dame, Repentigny, QC J5Y 1S9
Tél: 450-581-5120; *Téléc:* 450-581-4515
www.hebdorivenord.com
twitter.com/hebdorivenord
www.facebook.com/hebdorn

Tirage: 56 780 *Fréquence:* Mardi
Louise Bourget, Chef de nouvelles
Olivia Nguonly, Rédactrice en chef

Richelain: Journal Servir
Détenteur: Department of National Defence
Garnison Saint-Jean, CP 100 Bureau-Chef, Richelain, QC J0J 1R0
Tél: 450-358-7099; *Téléc:* 450-358-7423
servir@forces.gc.ca
www.journalservir.com
Tirage: 3 500 *Fréquence:* mercredi
Gaëtane Dion, Rédactrice-en-chef

Rimouski: L'Avantage votre journal
Détenteur: Groupe Lexis Média Inc.
#6D, 217, av Léonidas sud, Rimouski, QC G5L 2T5
Ligne sans frais: 877-722-0205
www.lavantage.qc.ca
www.youtube.com/user/journallavantage
twitter.com/lavantageqcca
www.facebook.com/lavantageqcca
Tirage: 42 803 *Fréquence:* mercredi
Mélina de Champlain, Directrice générale
melina.dechamplain@tc.tc

Rivière-du-Loup: Info Dimanche
72, rue Fraser, Rivière-du-Loup, QC G5R 1C6
Tél: 418-862-1911; *Téléc:* 418-862-6165
journal@infodimanche.com
www.infodimanche.com
www.youtube.com/infodimanche
twitter.com/infodimanche
www.facebook.com/infodimanche
Tirage: 31 420 *Fréquence:* Mercredi
Hugo Levasseur, Éditeur
Mario Pelletier, Rédacteur-en-chef
mario@infodimanche.com

Rivière-du-Loup: Info Dimanche
Détenteur: Néomédia
72, rue Fraser, Rivière-du-Loup, QC G5R 1C6
Tél: 418-862-1911; *Téléc:* 418-862-6165
journal@infodimanche.com
www.infodimanche.com
twitter.com/infodimanche
www.facebook.com/infodimanche
Tirage: 31 860 *Fréquence:* dimanche
Hugo Levasseur, Éditeur
418-862-1911

Roberval: L'Étoile du Lac
Détenteur: Trium Médias
#101, 797, boul Saint-Joseph, Roberval, QC G8H 2L4
Tél: 418-275-2911; *Téléc:* 418-275-2834
www.letoiledulac.com
twitter.com/letoiledulac
www.facebook.com/letoiledulac
Tirage: 14 636 *Fréquence:* mercredi
Claudia Turcotte, Directrice générale
claudia.turcotte@tc.tc

Rouyn-Noranda: Le Citoyen Rouyn La Sarre
Anciennement: Le Citoyen Rouyn-Noranda; Le Citoyen
Détenteur: Groupe Lexis Média Inc.
1, rue du Terminus est, Rouyn-Noranda, QC J9X 3B5
Tél: 819-762-4361; *Téléc:* 819-797-2450
www.lecitoyenrouynlasarre.com
twitter.com/LeCitoyenRouyn
www.facebook.com/lecitoyenrouynlasarre
Tirage: 19 620 *Fréquence:* Mercredi; supplement, Journal du Nord-Ouest
Joël Caya, Éditeur
joel.caya@tc.tccormedia.com

Rouyn-Noranda: Journal Ensemble pour bâtir
CP 424, 200, rue Leblanc, Rouyn-Noranda, QC J0Z 1Y0
Tél: 819-797-7110
ensemblepb1@tlb.sympatico.ca
www.journal-ensemble.org
Tirage: 1 400
Diane Gaudet-Bergeron, Présidente

Saguenay: Le Progrès Dimanche
1051, boul Talbot, Saguenay, QC G7H 5C1
Tél: 418-545-4474
redaction@lequotidien.com
www.lapresse.ca/le-quotidien/progres-dimanche
Tirage: 44 500 *Fréquence:* Dimanche
Michel Sinard, Président et éditeur
Denis Bouchard, Rédacteur en chef

Saint-André-Avellin: L'Info Petite Nation
Anciennement: La Petite-Nation
Détenteur: In Médias
3A, rue Principale, Saint-André-Avellin, QC J0V 1W0
Tél: 819-983-2725; *Téléc:* 819-983-6844
infopetitenation.ca
twitter.com/LaPetiteNation1
www.facebook.com/infopetitenation
Tirage: 10 010 *Fréquence:* Mercredi
Eric Lacfleur, Directeur général
eric.lafleur@tc.tc
Sylvain Dupras, Directeur régional de l'information, région Ouest TC Me
sylvain.dupras@tc.tc

Saint-Bruno: Journal les Versants
Détenteur: Les Versants du Mont-Bruno Inc.
1488, rue Montarville, Saint-Bruno, QC J3V 3T5
Tél: 450-441-5300
info@versants.com
www.versants.com
twitter.com/JournalVersants
www.facebook.com/VersantsMontBruno
Tirage: 18 000
Philippe Clair, Éditeur
pclair@versants.com

Saint-Bruno-de-Kamouraska: Le Trait d'Union
Détenteur: Le Trait d'Union de Saint-Bruno inc.
CP 3, 4, rue du Couvent, Saint-Bruno-de-Kamouraska, QC G0L 2M0
Tél: 418-492-9432; *Téléc:* 418-492-9076
trdunion@globetrotter.net
www.stbrunokam.qc.ca
Diane Bossé, Présidente

Saint-Charles-de-Bellechasse: Au fil de La Boyer
8B, av Commerciale, Saint-Charles-de-Bellechasse, QC G0R 2TO
Tél: 418-948-0741
laboyer@laboyer.com
www.laboyer.com
www.facebook.com/journal.la.boyer
Tirage: 1 200 *Fréquence:* mensuel
Jean-Pierre Lamonde, Président

Saint-Denis-de-Brompton: Le Saint-Denisien
CP 244, Saint-Denis-de-Brompton, QC J0B 2P0
www.lesaintdenisien.ca
Tirage: 1 175
René Coupal, Président
819-846-3267

Saint-Donat: Journal Altitude
365, rue Principale, Saint-Donat, QC J0T 2C0
Tél: 819-424-2610; *Téléc:* 819-424-3615
journalaltitude@cgocable.ca
www.st-donat.com/journal.html
Tirage: 3 700 *Fréquence:* Vendredi
Martin Lafortune, Éditeur et chef
Nathalie Bouisson, Éditeur et chef

Saint-Eustache: La Concorde
Détenteur: Les Éditions Blainville-Deux-Montagnes Inc.
53, rue Saint-Eustache, Saint-Eustache, QC J7R 2L2
Tél: 450-472-3440; *Téléc:* 450-472-1638
infojournaux@groupejcl.com
www.leveil.com
www.facebook.com/JOURNAL.LEVEIL
Tirage: 52 470 *Fréquence:* Mercredi; aussi L'Eveil (dimanche; tirage 37 400)
Jean-Claude Langlois, Président-Éditeur
Benoît Bilodeau, Rédacteur en chef

Saint-Eustache: L'Éveil
Détenteur: Groupe JCL
53, rue St-Eustache, Saint-Eustache, QC J7R 2L2
Tél: 450-472-3440; *Téléc:* 450-472-1638
infojournaux@groupejcl.com
www.leveil.com
twitter.com/LeveilConcorde
www.facebook.com/JOURNAL.LEVEIL
Tirage: 56 735 *Fréquence:* samedi
Jean-Claude Langlois, Éditeur

Saint-Fabien-de-Panet: Journal Le Réveil
195, rue Bilodeau, Saint-Fabien-de-Panet, QC G0R 2J0
Tél: 418-249-4471; *Téléc:* 418-249-4470
saintfabiendepanet.com
Tirage: 515 *Fréquence:* mensuel

Saint-François-de-la-Rivière du Sud: L'Écho de St-François
534, ch St-François ouest, Saint-François-de-la-Rivière du Sud, QC G0R 3A0
Tél: 418-717-2659; Téléc: 418-259-2177
echosf@videotron.ca
Tirage: 725 Fréquence: mensuel
Raynald Laflamme, Directeur

Saint-Georges: L'Écho de la Rive-Nord
Détenteur: Néomédia
9085, boul Lacroix, Saint-Georges, QC G5Y 2B4
www.lechodelarivenord.ca
twitter.com/LEchoRiveNord
www.facebook.com/lechorivenord
Tirage: 64 580 Fréquence: Mercredi
Serge Cameron, Éditeur
serge.cameron@tc.tc

Saint-Georges: L'Écho de la Rive-Nord
Détenteur: Néomédia
9085, boul Lacroix, Saint-Georges, QC G5Y 2B4
Tél: 450-818-7575; Téléc: 418-222-5699
twitter.com/LEchoRiveNord
www.facebook.com/lechorivenord

Saint-Georges: L'Écho de Laval
Détenteur: Néomédia
9085, boul Lacroix, Saint-Georges, QC G5Y 2B4
www.lechodelaval.ca
twitter.com/LEchodeLaval
www.facebook.com/echolaval
Tirage: 142 135 Fréquence: Mercredi
Eric Mercier, Éditeur
eric.mercier@tc.tc
Marie-Eve Courchesne, Chef des nouvelles
marie-eve.courchesne@tc.tc

Saint-Georges: L'Écho de Trois-Rivières
Détenteur: Néomédia
9085, boul Lacroix, Saint-Georges, QC G5Y 2B4
www.lechodetroisrivieres.ca
twitter.com/lecho3rivieres
www.facebook.com/lecho3rivieres
Tirage: 68 580 Fréquence: Mercredi
Jocelyn Ouellet, Directeur de l'information
jocelyn.ouellet@tc.tc

Saint-Georges: Le Journal de Joliette
Détenteur: Néomédia
9085, boul Lacroix, Saint-Georges, QC G5Y 2B4
Téléc: 418-222-5699
Ligne sans frais: 866-327-0660
www.lejournaldejoliette.ca
twitter.com/JdeJoliette
www.facebook.com/jdejoliette
Claude Poulin, Président et directeur général
cpoulin@neomedia.com

Saint-Georges: Le Point du Lac Saint-Jean
Détenteur: Néomédia
9085, boul Lacroix, Saint-Georges, QC G5Y 2B4
Tél: 418-695-2601; Téléc: 418-222-5699
www.lepoint.ca
twitter.com/PointLacStJean
www.facebook.com/pointlacstjean
Guy Dallaire, Directeur des ventes
guy.dallaire@lepoint.ca

Saint-Georges: Le Réveil du Saguenay
Détenteur: Néomédia
9085, boul Lacroix, Saint-Georges, QC G5Y 2B4
Tél: 418-695-2601; Téléc: 418-222-5699
www.lereveil.ca
twitter.com/LeReveil
www.facebook.com/lereveil
Guy Dallaire, Directeur des ventes
guy.dallaire@lepoint.ca

Saint-Georges-de-Beauce: L'Éclaireur Progrès
Détenteur: icimédias
710, 98e rue, Saint-Georges-de-Beauce, QC G5Y 8G1
Tél: 418-228-8858; Téléc: 418-227-0268
leclaireurprogres.ca
twitter.com/EclairProgres
www.facebook.com/leclaireurprogres
Tirage: 38 147 Fréquence: Mercredi, Vendredi
Gilbert Bernier, Éditeur
gilbert.bernier@tc.tc
Simon Busque, Chef des nouvelles, Chaudière-Appalaches
simon.bisque@tc.tc

Saint-Hippolyte: Le Sentier
2264, ch des Hauteurs, Saint-Hippolyte, QC J8A 3C5
Tél: 450-563-5151; Téléc: 450-563-1059
redaction@journal-le-sentier.ca
www.journal-le-sentier.ca
Tirage: 4 000 Fréquence: mensuel
Michel Bois, Président
michel.bois@journal-le-sentier.ca

Saint-Hyacinthe: Le Clairon Regional de St-Hyacinthe
Détenteur: DBC Communications inc.
655, av Ste-Anne, Saint-Hyacinthe, QC J2S 5G4
Tél: 450-773-6028; Téléc: 450-773-3115
redaction@leclairon.qc.ca
www.leclairon.qc.ca
Tirage: 39 730 Fréquence: Mardi
Benoit Chartier, Éditeur
Guillaume Bédard, Directeur, Ventes

Saint-Hyacinthe: Le Courrier de Saint-Hyacinthe
Détenteur: DBC Communications inc.
655, rue Ste-Anne, Saint-Hyacinthe, QC J2S 5G4
Tél: 450-773-6028; Téléc: 450-773-3115
redaction@lecourrier.qc.ca
www.lecourrier.qc.ca
twitter.com/LeCourrier1853
Tirage: 13 605 Fréquence: Quotidien
Benoit Chartier, Éditeur
Martin Bourassa, Rédacteur en chef et éditorialiste
mbourassa@lecourrier.qc.ca

Saint-Jean-Port-Joli: L'Attisée
Maison Communautaire Joly, CP 954, 318, rue Verreault, Saint-Jean-Port-Joli, QC G0R 3G0
Tél: 418-598-9590; Téléc: 418-598-7588
journal.attisee@videotron.ca
www.lattisee.com
Tirage: 2 750 Fréquence: mensuel
Benedict Levesques, Président

Saint-Jean-sur-Richelieu: Le Canada Français
84, rue Richelieu, Saint-Jean-sur-Richelieu, QC J3B 6X3
Tél: 450-347-0323; Téléc: 450-347-4539
canadaf@canadafrancais.com
www.canadafrancais.com
twitter.com/Canada_Francais
www.facebook.com/lecanadafrancais
Tirage: 18 955 Fréquence: Mercredi; aussi Le Richelieu Dimanche (dimanche)
Gilles Lévesque, Rédacteur en chef
Charles Couture, Directeur général régional

Saint-Pamphile: L'Écho d'en Haut
Détenteur: Journal l'Écho d'en Haut Inc.
#209, 35, rue Principale, Saint-Pamphile, QC G0R 3X0
Tél: 418-356-5491; Téléc: 418-356-5491
echo.den.haut@globetrotter.net
www.echodenhaut.org
Tirage: 3 100 Fréquence: mensuel
Diane Bérubé, Directrice Générale

Saint-Pascal: Le Placoteux
Détenteur: Néomédia
491, av d'Anjou, Saint-Pascal, QC G0L 3Y0
Tél: 418-492-2706; Téléc: 418-492-9706
association@leplacoteux.qc.ca
www.leplacoteux.com
twitter.com/LPlacoteux
www.facebook.com/LePlacoteux
Tirage: 18 530 Fréquence: mercredi
Maurice Gagnon, Rédacteur en chef
journaliste@leplacoteux.com

Saint-Pierre-de-l'île-d'Orléans: Autour de l'île
115, 517 rte des Prêtres, Saint-Pierre-de-l'île-d'Orléans, QC G0A 4E0
Tél: 418-828-0330; Téléc: 418-828-0741
info@autourdelile.com
www.autourdelile.com
www.facebook.com/autourdelile
Tirage: 4 500 Fréquence: mensuel
Sylvain Delisle, Rédacteur en chef

Saint-Sauveur: Journal Le Nord
Anciennement: L'Annonceur
11, rue Robert, Saint-Sauveur, QC J0R 1R6
Tél: 450-438-8383; Téléc: 450-438-4174
www.journallenord.com
twitter.com/journallenord
www.facebook.com/Journallenord
Tirage: 55 388 Fréquence: mercredi

Saint-Siméon: Le Goéland
CP 250, 127-C, boul Perron ouest, Saint-Siméon, QC G0C 3A0
Tél: 418-534-2123; Téléc: 418-534-4353
journalgoeland@globetrotter.net
www.stsimeon.ca/journal-communautaire
Tirage: 650
Journal communautaire de Saint-Siméon
Antoinette Lepage, Présidente

Sainte-Anne-des-Plaines: Journal Le Point d'Impact
194B, boul Sainte-Anne, Sainte-Anne-des-Plaines, QC J0N 1H0
Tél: 450-478-3538
journallepoint@qc.aira.com
www.journallepoint.com
Tirage: 6 000 Fréquence: samedi
Serge Blondin, Éditeur

Sainte-Brigitte-de-Laval: Le Lavalois
CP 1020, Sainte-Brigitte-de-Laval, QC G0A 3K0
Tél: 418-907-7172
lelavalois@ccapcable.com
www.lelavalois.com
Tirage: 1 300 Fréquence: dix fois par an
Lucille Thomassin, Présidente
lucille@ccapcable.com

Sainte-Geneviève-de-Batiscan: Le Bulletin des Chenaux
44, ch Rivière-à-Veillet, Sainte-Geneviève-de-Batiscan, QC G0X 2R0
Tél: 819-840-3091; Téléc: 418-362-2861
info@lebulletindeschenaux.com
www.lebulletindeschenaux.com
twitter.com/BullDesChenaux
www.facebook.com/213099518727247
Tirage: 9 000
Lucien Gélinas, Directeur général

Sainte-Thérèse: Nord Info et Voix des Mille-Iles
Détenteur: Groupe JCL
50B, rue Turgeon, Sainte-Thérèse, QC J7E 3H4
Tél: 450-435-6537; Téléc: 450-435-0588
infojournaux@groupejcl.com
www.nordinfo.com
twitter.com/NordInfoVoix
www.facebook.com/NordInfoCom
Tirage: 60 033 Fréquence: Samedi
Jean-Claude Langlois, Président-Éditeur
Claude Desjardins, Rédacteur en chef

Salaberry-de-Valleyfield: Journal le Suroît
Détenteur: Les Publications du Sud-Ouest
52, rue Nicholson, Salaberry-de-Valleyfield, QC J6T 4M8
Tél: 450-371-8051; Téléc: 450-371-4237
Ligne sans frais: 877-371-8051
journal@media-sudouest.com
www.publications-sudouest.com

Salaberry-de-Valleyfield: Le Journal Saint-François
Détenteur: Gravité Média
55, rue Jacques-Cartier, Salaberry-de-Valleyfield, QC J6T 4R4
Tél: 450-371-6222; Téléc: 450-371-7254
www.journalsaint-francois.ca
www.facebook.com/journalsaintfrancois
Tirage: 34 722 Fréquence: Mercredi

Shawinigan: L'Hebdo du St-Maurice
Détenteur: icimédias
CP 10, 2102, av Champlain, Shawinigan, QC G9N 6T8
Tél: 819-537-5111; Téléc: 819-537-5471
www.lhebdodustmaurice.ca
twitter.com/HebdoStMaurice
www.facebook.com/lhebdodustmaurice
Tirage: 30 511 Fréquence: Samedi
Bernard Lepage, Éditeur
bernard-lepage@tc.tc
André Juteau, Directeur général régional
andre.juteau@tc.tc

Shawinigan: L'Hebdo Mekinac-des Chenaux
Détenteur: icimédias
1672, av St-Marc, Shawinigan, QC G9N 2H4
Tél: 819-379-1490
redaction@lhebdomekinacdeschenaux.ca
www.lhebdomekinacdeschenaux.ca
Tirage: 13 081 Fréquence: Samedi

Shawville: The Equity
Owned By: Pontiac Printshop Ltd.
133 Centre St., Shawville, QC J0X 2Y0
Tel: 819-647-2204; *Fax:* 819-647-2206
news@theequity.ca
www.theequity.ca
www.youtube.com/equitynewspaper
twitter.com/equitynewspaper
www.facebook.com/EquityNewspaper

Circulation: 3,362
Heather Dickson, Publisher
Charles Dickson, Publisher & Editor
charles.dickson@theequity.ca

Sherbrooke: Entrée Libre
#317, 187, rue Laurier, Sherbrooke, QC J1H 4Z4
Tél: 819-821-2270; *Télec:* 819-566-2664
journal@entreelibre.info
www.entreelibre.info
www.facebook.com/journalentreelibre

Tirage: 9 500 *Fréquence:* jeudi
Produit par le collectif du même nom selon une démarche
d'éducation populaire autonome, est accessible aux gens du
quartier centre-sud-ouest de Sherbrooke.
Claude Dostie, Rédacteur en chef

Sherbrooke: L'Info
CP 157, Succ. Saint-Élie d'Orford, Sherbrooke, QC J1R 1A1
Tél: 819-820-9663
journalinfo@cooptel.qc.ca
linfodesaintelie.org/Site_Journal_Linfo/Bienvenue.html
Tirage: 3 966 *Fréquence:* mensuel
Josée Dostie, Directrice générale

Sherbrooke: La Nouvelle de Sherbrooke
1950, rue Roy, Sherbrooke, QC J1K 2X8
Tél: 819-564-5450
redaction@lanouvelle.ca
www.lapresse.ca/la-tribune/la-nouvelle
twitter.com/HebdoLaNouvelle
www.facebook.com/LaPresseFB

Tirage: 52 000 *Fréquence:* Mercredi
Louise Boisvert, Présidente-éditrice
Maurice Cloutier, Rédacteur-en-chef

Shipshaw: Journal La Vie d'Ici
4681, rue Saint-Léonard, Shipshaw, QC G7P 1J4
Télec: 418-213-0701
informations@laviedici.com
www.laviedici.com

Fréquence: mensuel
Claire Duchesne, Présidente

Sorel-Tracy: Les 2 Rives
Anciennement: Les 2 Rives et la Voix
58, rue Charlotte, Sorel-Tracy, QC J3P 1G3
Tél: 450-742-9408; *Télec:* 450-742-2493
www.les2rives.com

Tirage: 30 950 *Fréquence:* Mardi
Benoit Chartier, Éditeur
Jean-Philippe Morin, Directeur de l'information

St-Léonard: Métro - Saint-Léonard
Anciennement: Progrès Saint-Léonard
Détenteur: Métro Média
#212, 8770, boul Langelier, St-Léonard, QC H1P 3C6
Tél: 514-899-5888; *Télec:* 514-899-5984
journalmetro.com/local/saint-leonard
twitter.com/progresstleo
www.facebook.com/progresstleonard

Tirage: 32 220 *Fréquence:* Mardi
Véronique Gauthier, Directrice générale
Sylviane Lussier, Directrice générale régionale pour l'île de
Montréal

St-Pierre-de-la-Rivière-du-Sud: Journal Le Pierr'Eau
645, 2e av, St-Pierre-de-la-Rivière-du-Sud, QC G0R 4B0
Tél: 418-248-8277; *Télec:* 418-248-7068
journal@stpierreriviresud.ca
www.pierreau.ca
www.facebook.com/groups/stpierreriviredusud
Christian Collin, Président

Stanstead: Stanstead Journal
269, rue Dufferin, Stanstead, QC J0B 3E2
Tél: 819-876-7514 *Ligne sans frais:* 800-567-1259
reception@stanstead-journal.com
www.stanstead-journal.com
Tirage: 2 700 *Fréquence:* Wednesday
Jean-Yves Durocher, President & Publisher
jy.durocher@stanstead-journal.com

Ste-Agathe-des-Monts: L'Information du Nord
Sainte-Agathe
Détenteur: In Médias
#72, 195, rue Brissette, Ste-Agathe-des-Monts, QC J8C 3S4
Tél: 819-425-8658
infodunordsainteagathe.ca

Tirage: 15 430 *Fréquence:* Mercredi
Johanne Régimbald, Éditrice
johanne.regimbald@tc.tc
Éric Busque, Chef des nouvelles
eric.busque.a@tc.tc

St-Étienne-des-Grès: Le Stéphanois
CP 282, St-Étienne-des-Grès, QC G0X 2P0
Tél: 819-299-3858
lestephanois@cgocable.ca
www.lestephanois.ca
Tirage: 2 000
Gérard Levesque, Président

Témiscaming: Le Contact
PO Box 566, 32, rue Simon, Témiscaming, QC J0Z 3R0
Tel: 819-627-9050; *Fax:* 819-627-1794
contact@cablevision.qc.ca
temiscamingcontact.org
Circulation: 1 000 *Frequency:* mercredi
Élaine Ouellet, Éditrice

Terrebonne: La Revue de Terrebonne
231, rue Ste-Marie, Terrebonne, QC J6W 3E4
Tél: 450-964-4444; *Télec:* 450-471-1023
www.larevue.qc.ca
Autre information: Montréal: 514-990-7314
www.linkedin.com/pub/gilles-bordonado/12/a66/556
twitter.com/revueterreb onne
www.facebook.com/revueterrebonne
Tirage: 60 000 *Fréquence:* Mercredi
Gilles Bordonado, Président-Directeur général
gbordonado@larevue.qc.ca
Daniel Soucy, Directeur développement et marketing
dsoucy@larevue.qc.ca

Thetford Mines: Le Courrier Frontenac
Détenteur: icimédias
CP 789, 541, boul Frontenac est, Thetford Mines, QC G6G
5V3
Tél: 418-338-5181; *Télec:* 418-338-5482
www.courrierfrontenac.qc.ca
twitter.com/CourFrontenac
www.facebook.com/CourrierFrontenac
Tirage: 22 950 *Fréquence:* Mercredi
Pascal Gourdeau, Rédacteur-en-chef
pascal.gourdeau@tc.tc
Laurent Raby, Directeur général
laurent.raby@tc.tc

Trois-Rivières: Le Bulletin
Détenteur: Le Tour d'y Voir
991, rue Champflour, Trois-Rivières, QC G9A 1Z8
Tél: 819-375-0484
www.tourdyvoir.ca
Tirage: 1 000

Trois-Rivières: Le Courrier-Sud
Anciennement: Nicolet Courrier-Sud
Détenteur: icimédias
#200, 6925, rue Dalpé, Trois-Rivières, QC G9A 5C9
Tél: 819-293-4551
www.lecourriersud.com
twitter.com/journalcs
www.facebook.com/LeCourrierSud
Tirage: 20 850 *Fréquence:* Mercredi
Patrick Dumais, Directeur de journal
patrick.dumas@tc.tc
Marie-Eve Veillette, Chef de nouvelles

Trois-Rivières: L'Hebdo-Journal
Détenteur: icimédias
635, rue du Père-Daniel, Trois-Rivières, QC G9A 5Z7
Tél: 819-379-1490; *Télec:* 819-379-0705
www.lhebdojournal.com
twitter.com/hebdojournal
www.facebook.com/hebdojournal
Tirage: 44 870 *Fréquence:* Samedi
Marie-Eve Veillette, Éditrice
819-379-1492 ext 242
marie-eve.veillette@tc.tc
Éric Maltais, Directeur général régional
eric.maltais@tc.tc
Carole Béliveau, Secrétaire de direction
carole.beliveau@tc.tc

Val-David: Le Journal Ski-se-Dit
#200, 2496, rue de l'Église, Val-David, QC J0R 2N0
Tél: 819-322-7969; *Télec:* 819-322-7904
ski-se-dit@cgocable.ca
www.ski-se-dit.info
www.facebook.com/skisedit
Tirage: 3 000 *Fréquence:* mensuel

Val-d'Or: Le Citoyen Val-d'Or Amos
Détenteur: Groupe Lexis Média Inc.
1723, 3e av, 2e étage, Val-d'Or, QC J9P 1W3
Tél: 819-825-3755
redactionvaldor@lexismedia.ca
www.lecitoyenvaldoramos.com
twitter.com/LeCitoyenValdOr
www.facebook.com/lecitoyenvaldoramos

Val-des-Monts: Journal l'Envol
Previous Name: L'Envol des Monts
12, Potvin, Val-des-Monts, QC J8N 7B2
Tél: 819-671-1502; *Fax:* 819-671-7463
envol.desmonts@sympatico.ca
Circulation: 11 500 *Frequency:* bimensuelle
Nicole A. Thibodeau, Éditrice

Val-des-Sources: Les Actualités
Détenteur: Néomédia
572, 1e ave, Val-des-Sources, QC J1T 4R4
Tél: 819-879-6681; *Télec:* 819-879-7235
nathalie.hurdle@quebecormedia.com
www.letincelle.qc.ca
twitter.com/LesActualites
www.facebook.com/actuasbestos
Tirage: 14 800 *Fréquence:* Samedi
Carole Pellerin, Éditrice
carole.pellerin@quebecormedia.com
Jean-Marc Bourque, Directeur régional, Québec-Est
jean-marc.bourque@tc.tc

Victoriaville: La Nouvelle Union
Anciennement: L'Union
Détenteur: icimédias
43, rue Notre-Dame est, 2e étage, Victoriaville, QC G6P 3Z4
Tél: 819-758-6211
www.lanouvelle.net
twitter.com/LaNouvelleNet
www.facebook.com/lanouvellenet
Tirage: 35 999 *Fréquence:* mercredi

Ville-Marie: Journal Le Reflet
Anciennement: Le Témiscamien
22, rue Sainte-Anne, Ville-Marie, QC J9V 2B7
Tél: 819-622-1313; *Télec:* 819-622-1333
information@journallereflet.com
www.journallereflet.com
Tirage: 8 500 *Fréquence:* Mercredi
Karen Lachapelle, Directrice générale
dg@journallereflet.com

Wakefield: The Low Down to Hull & Back News
Owned By: Performance Printing Ltd.
PO Box 99, 815 Riverside Dr., Wakefield, QC J0X 3G0
Tel: 819-459-2222; *Fax:* 819-459-3831
general@lowdownonline.com
www.lowdownonline.com
twitter.com/TrevorGreenway; twitter.com/lucyannescholey
www.facebook.com/152335818154890
Circulation: 2,990 *Frequency:* Wednesday
Nikki Mantell, Publisher
nmantell@lowdownonline.com
Liette Robert, General Manager

Windsor: L'Etincelle
193, rue St-Georges, Windsor, QC J1S 1J7
Tél: 819-845-2705; *Télec:* 819-845-5520
journal@letincelle.qc.ca
www.letincelle.qc.ca
Tirage: 10 500 *Fréquence:* Mercredi
Claude Frenette, Éditeur
cfrenette@letincelle.qc.ca
Chantal Darveau, Directrice
cdarveau@letincelle.qc.ca

Saskatchewan

Daily Newspapers in Saskatchewan

Prince Albert: The Prince Albert Daily Herald
30 - 10th St. East, Prince Albert, SK S6V 0Y5
Tel: 306-764-4276; *Fax:* 306-763-3331
editorial@paherald.sk.ca
paherald.sk.ca
twitter.com/padailyherald
www.facebook.com/PADailyHerald
Frequency: Monday-Saturday
Donna Pfeil, Publisher
donnap@paherald.sk.ca
Jason Kerr, Editor
jason.kerr@paherald.sk.ca

Regina: Regina Leader-Post
Owned By: Postmedia Network Inc.
#300, 1964 Park St., Regina, SK S4N 7M5
Tel: 306-781-5212 *Toll-Free:* 800-667-8751
www.leaderpost.com
twitter.com/leaderpost
www.facebook.com/reginaleaderpost
Frequency: Monday-Saturday
Russell Wangersky, Editor-in-Chief

Saskatoon: The StarPhoenix
Previous Name: The Saskatoon Phoenix; Saskatoon
Capital; Daily Star; Daily Phoenix
Owned By: Postmedia Network Inc.
204 - 5th Ave. North, Saskatoon, SK S7K 2P1
Tel: 306-657-6320 *Toll-Free:* 800-667-2008
citydesk@thestarphoenix.com
thestarphoenix.com
www.youtube.com/user/TheStarPhoenix
twitter.com/thestarphoenix
www. facebook.com/thestarphoenix
Frequency: Tuesday-Saturday
Heather Persson, Editor
306-657-6315
hpersson@postmedia.com

Other Newspapers in Saskatchewan

Assiniboia: Assiniboia Times
Owned By: Glacier Media Inc.
PO Box 910, 410 - 1st Ave. East, Assiniboia, SK S0H 0B0
Tel: 306-642-5901; *Fax:* 306-642-4519
Circulation: 3,400 *Frequency:* Fri.
Joyce Simard, Editor
joyce@assiniboiatimes.ca
Kevin Rasmussen, General Manager
kevin@assiniboiatimes.ca

Biggar: The Biggar Independent
Owned By: Independent Printers Ltd.
PO Box 40, 102 - 3rd Ave. West, Biggar, SK S0K 0M0
Tel: 306-948-3344; *Fax:* 306-948-2133
info@biggarindependent.ca
www.biggarindependent.ca
Circulation: 1,600 *Frequency:* Thurs.
Daryl Hasein, Co-Publisher
Margaret Hasein, Co-Publisher
Kevin Brautigam, Editor
Urla Tyler, Consultant, Advertising
tip@sasktel.net
Delta Fay Cruickshank, Contact, Production

Canora: The Canora Courier
Owned By: Glacier Media Inc.
123 First Ave. East, Canora, SK S0A 0L0
Tel: 306-563-5131; *Fax:* 306-563-5131
canoracourier@sasktel.net
Circulation: 1,200 *Frequency:* Wed.
The Saskatchewan town of Canora & the villages in its municipal
district are served by the weekly newspaper.
Ken Lewchuk, General Manager
k.lewchuk@sasktel.net
Gary Lewchuk, Editor
kamsacktimes@sasktel.net
Dan Daoust, Contact, Sales
sales.canoracourier@sasktel.net
Sonia Lewchuk, Contact, Administration
office.canoracourier@sasktel.net

Canora: Kamsack Times
Owned By: Glacier Newspaper Group
PO Box 746, 123 First Ave. East, Canora, SK S0A 0L0
Tel: 306-563-5131; *Fax:* 306-563-6144
office.canoracourier@sasktel.net

Circulation: 1,400 *Frequency:* Wed.
The Times presents community affairs for the towns of Norquay
& Kamsack, as well as nearby villages & hamlets.
Ken Lewchuk, General Manager
k.lewchuk@sasktel.net
William Koreluik, Editor
kamsacktimes@sasktel.net
Dan Daoust, Contact, Sales
sales.canoracourier@sasktel.net

Canora: Norquay North Star
PO Box 746, 18 - 1st Ave. South East, Canora, SK S0A 0L0
Tel: 306-563-5131; *Fax:* 306-563-6144
Circulation: 762 *Frequency:* Weekly
Ken Sopkow, Publisher & Editor

Canora: The Preeceville Progress
Owned By: Glacier Newspaper Group
PO Box 746, 123 - 1st Ave. East, Canora, SK S0A 0L0
Tel: 306-563-5131; *Fax:* 306-563-5131
Circulation: 1,000 *Frequency:* Thurs.
The towns of Preeceville & Sturgis, plus nearby villages &
hamlets, are served by The Preeceville Progress.
Ken Lewchuk, General Manager
k.lewchuk@sasktel.net
Gary Lewchuk, Editor
canoracourier@sasktel.net
Dan Daoust, Contact, Sales
sales@canoracourier@sasktel.net

Carlyle: Carlyle Observer
Owned By: Glacier Newspaper Group
PO Box 160, 132 Main St., Carlyle, SK S0C 0R0
Tel: 306-453-2525; *Fax:* 306-453-2938
observer@saskte.net
www.carlyleobserver.com
www.facebook.com/CarlyleObserver
Circulation: 3,200 *Frequency:* Fri.
Cindy Moffatt, Publisher
sasknew3@yahoo.com

Carnduff: Gazette Post-News
PO Box 220, 106 Broadway St., Carnduff, SK S0C 0S0
Tel: 306-482-3252; *Fax:* 306-482-3373
gazettepost.news@sasktel.net
Circulation: 1,000 *Frequency:* Fri.
Bruce Schwanke, Publisher
Bill Grass, Editor

Craik: Craik Weekly News
PO Box 360, 221 - 3rd St., Craik, SK S0G 0V0
Tel: 306-734-2313; *Fax:* 306-734-2789
craiknews@sasktel.net
Circulation: 880 *Frequency:* Monday
Harve Freidel, Publisher & Editor

Cut Knife: Highway 40 Courier
PO Box 639, 200 Steele St., Cut Knife, SK S0M 0N0
Tel: 306-398-4901; *Fax:* 306-398-4909
ckcouriernews@sasktel.net
Circulation: 490 *Frequency:* Wed.
Lorie Gibson, Publisher & Editor

Davidson: The Davidson Leader
Owned By: Davidson Publishing Ltd.
PO Box 786, 205 Washington Ave., Davidson, SK S0G 1A0
Tel: 306-567-2047; *Fax:* 306-567-2900
theleaderonline@gmail.com
www.leaderonline.ca
twitter.com/davidsonleader
www.facebook.com/DavidsonLeader
Circulation: 1,200 *Frequency:* Mon.
The Davidson Leader covers the Saskatchewan communities of
Davidson, Kenaston, Elbow, Imperial, Bladworth, Dundurn,
Craik, & Loreburn. The newspaper is available in print & as an
e-paper.
Tara de Ryk, Publisher & Editor

Esterhazy: The Miner-Journal
Owned By: Koskie Publications Ltd.
PO Box 1000, 606 Veterans Ave., Esterhazy, SK S0A 0X0
Tel: 306-745-6669; *Fax:* 306-745-2699
miner.journal@sasktel.net
www.minerjournal.com
www.facebook.com/122690607744257
Circulation: 1,530 *Frequency:* Mon.
The Miner-Journal covers news for the Saskatchewan
communities of Esterhazy, Bredenbury, Stockholm, Langenburg,
Dubuc, Churchbridge, Atwater, Rocanville, Bangor, Gerald, Spy
Hill, Yarbo, & Tantallon.
Brenda Matchett, Publisher
Christina Holmberg, General Manager
Helen Solmes, Editor

Estevan: Estevan Lifestyles
Owned By: Glacier Interactive Media
PO Box 816, 300 Kensington Ave., Estevan, SK S4A 2A7
Tel: 306-634-5112; *Fax:* 306-634-2588
lifestyles@sasktel.net
www.sasklifestyles.com
www.facebook.com/lifestyles.estevan
Circulation: 7,500 *Frequency:* Fri.
Teresa Howie, Publisher
David Willberg, Editor

Estevan: Estevan Mercury
Owned By: Glacier Interactive Media
PO Box 730, 68 Souris Ave. North, Estevan, SK S4A 2A6
Tel: 306-634-2654; *Fax:* 306-634-3934
classifieds@estevanmercury.ca
www.estevanmercury.ca
twitter.com/estevan_mercury
www.facebook.com/EstevanMercury
Circulation: 3,100 *Frequency:* Wed.
Peter Ng, Publisher
Brant Kersey, General Manager
bkersey@estevanmercury.ca
Jordan Baker, Editor
editor@estevanmercury.ca
Norm Park, Co-Editor
normpark@estevanmercury.ca

Estevan: Pipeline News
Owned By: Glacier Media Inc.
68 Souris Ave., Estevan, SK S4A 2M3
Tel: 306-634-2654; *Fax:* 306-634-3934
www.pipelinenews.ca
twitter.com/PipelineNewsSK
www.facebook.com/pipelinenews
Circulation: 28,600 *Frequency:* Monthly
Discusses petroleum news in Saskatchewan.
Brant Kersey, Publisher
bkersey@estevanmercury.ca

Estevan: The Southeast Trader Express
Owned By: Glacier Newspapers Group
PO Box 730, 68 Souris Ave. North, Estevan, SK S4A 2A6
Tel: 306-634-2654; *Fax:* 306-634-3934
mercury_merc1@sasktel.net
www.estevanmercury.ca
Circulation: 6,700 *Frequency:* Friday
Free weekly publication put out by the Estevan Mercury office.
Serves the region of Southwest Saskatchewan
Peter Ng, Publisher
Brant Kersey, General Manager
bkersey@estevanmercury.ca
Jordan Baker, Editor
editor@estevanmercury.ca

Eston: The Press Review
Owned By: Jamac Publishing Ltd.
PO Box 787, 112 Main St. West, Eston, SK S0L 1A0
Tel: 306-962-3221; *Fax:* 306-962-4445
estonpress@sasktel.net
Circulation: 840 *Frequency:* Tuesday
Stewart Crump, Publisher & General Manager
Kevin McBain, Editor

Foam Lake: Foam Lake Review
Owned By: Foam Lake Review Ltd.
PO Box 550, 325 Main St., Foam Lake, SK S0A 1A0
Tel: 306-272-3262; *Fax:* 306-272-4521
review.foamlake@sasktel.net
foamlakereview.com
Circulation: 1,370 *Frequency:* Mon.
Bob Johnson, Publisher & Editor

Fort Qu'Appelle: Fort Qu'Appelle Times
PO Box 940, 141 Broadway St. West, Fort Qu'Appelle, SK
S0G 1S0
Tel: 306-332-5526; *Fax:* 306-332-5414
forttimes@sasktel.net
bit.ly/185Iou0
Circulation: 1,100 *Frequency:* Tues.
Chris Ashfield, Publisher
George Brown, Editor

Gravelbourg: Gravelbourg Tribune
PO Box 1017, 611 Main St., Gravelbourg, SK S0H 1X0
Tel: 306-648-3479; *Fax:* 306-648-2520
gravelbourgtribune@sasktel.net
Circulation: 1,000 *Frequency:* Mon.
Paul Boisvert, Publisher & Editor
trib.editorial@sasktel.net

Gull Lake: The Gull Lake Advance
Owned By: Winquist Ventures Ltd.
PO Box 628, 1462 Conrad Ave., Gull Lake, SK S0N 1A0
Tel: 306-672-3373; Fax: 306-672-3573
glad12@sasktel.net
twitter.com/GullLakeAdvance
www.facebook.com/126675707344759
Circulation: 1,200 Frequency: Tuesday
The weekly newspaper provides news & information for Gull
Lake & southwestern Saskatchewan.
Kate Winquist, Publisher
kate.winquistventures@sasktel.net
Devin Beck, Contact, Sales & Marketing
sales.winquistventures@sasktel.net

Herbert: Herbert Herald
PO Box 399, 716 Herbert Ave., Herbert, SK S0H 2A0
Tel: 306-784-2422; Fax: 306-784-3246
herbertherald@sasktel.net
Circulation: 1,500 Frequency: Tuesday
Rhonda Ens, Owner

Hudson Bay: Hudson Bay Post Review
Owned By: Glacier Newspaper Group
20 Railway Ave., Hudson Bay, SK S0E 0Y0
Tel: 306-865-2771; Fax: 306-865-2340
Circulation: 987 Frequency: Thursday
Sherry Pilon, General Manager
postreview2@sasktel.net
Brent Fitzpatrick, Publisher
pub@sasktel.net

Humboldt: Humboldt Journal
Owned By: Glacier Newspaper Group
PO Box 970, 535 Main St., Humboldt, SK S0K 2A0
Tel: 306-682-2561; Fax: 306-682-3322
humboldt.journal@sasktel.net
www.humboldtjournal.ca
www.facebook.com/1227595078697764
Circulation: 3,000 Frequency: Friday
Al Guthro, Publisher
aguthro@humboldtjournal.ca
Kelly Friesen, Editor
kfriesen@humboldtjournal.ca

Indian Head: Indian Head - Wolseley News
PO Box 70, 508 Grand Ave., Indian Head, SK S0G 2K0
Tel: 306-695-3565; Fax: 306-695-3448
ihwnews@sasktel.net
Circulation: 1,190 Frequency: Mon.
Jodi Gendron, Publisher & Editor

Ituna: The Ituna News
Owned By: Foam Lake Review Ltd.
PO Box 413, 303 Main St. North, Ituna, SK S0A 1N0
Tel: 306-795-2412; Fax: 306-795-3621
news.ituna@sasktel.net
Circulation: 770 Frequency: Mon.
Bob Johnson, Publisher
Heidi Spilchuk, Editor

Kindersley: The Clarion
PO Box 1150, 919 Main St., Kindersley, SK S0L 1S0
Tel: 306-463-4611; Fax: 306-463-6505
ads.jamac@gmail.com
Circulation: 1,500 Frequency: Wed.
Stewart Crump, Publisher
Kevin McBain, Editor

Kindersley: Kerrobert Citizen
Owned By: Jamac Publishing
PO Box 1150, 919 Main St., Kindersley, SK S0L 1S0
Tel: 306-463-4611; Fax: 306-463-6505
ads.jamac@gmail.com
Circulation: 430 Frequency: Wed.
Stewart Crump, Publisher
Kevin McBain, Editor
publishing_jamac@sasktel.net

Kindersley: West Central Crossroads
Owned By: Jamac Publishing
PO Box 1150, 919 Main St., Kindersley, SK S0L 1S0
Tel: 306-463-4611; Fax: 306-463-6505
ads.jamac@gmail.com
Circulation: 15,300 Frequency: Fri.
Stewart Crump, Publisher
Kevin McBain, Editor
publishing_jamac@sasktel.net

Kipling: Kipling Citizen
Owned By: Glacier Newspapers Group
PO Box 329, 521 Main St., Kipling, SK S0J 2S0
Tel: 306-736-2535; Fax: 306-736-8445
thecitizen@sasktel.net
Circulation: 930 Frequency: Fri.
News & advertising from the Saskatchewan communities of
Kipling, Corning, Peebles, Kennedy, Wawota, Windthorst,
Glenavon, & Langbank are featured in the Kipling Citizen.
Laura Kish, General Manager
Terry Curzon, Representative, Advertising Sales

La Ronge: La Ronge Northerner
Owned By: Glacier Newspapers Group
PO Box 1350, 715 La Ronge Ave., La Ronge, SK S0J 1L0
Tel: 306-425-3344; Fax: 306-425-2827
northerner@sasktel.net
Other information: Sales: kdfith@sasktel.net
Circulation: 950 Frequency: Thurs.
Covers a geography of 30 communities in the northern area of
Saskatchewan
Brenda Fitch, Publisher
Debbie Parkinson, Manager, Office, Circulation
ads.northerner@sasktel.net

Langenburg: The Four-Town Journal
PO Box 68, 102 Carl Ave. West, Langenburg, SK S0A 2A0
Tel: 306-743-2617; Fax: 306-743-2299
fourtown@sasktel.net
Circulation: 1,300 Frequency: Wed.
Langenburg, Saltcoats, Bredenbury, & Churchbridge are the
communities served by The Four-Town Journal.
Bill Johnston, Publisher & Editor
Lynda Johnston, Contact, Office

Lanigan: Lanigan Advisor
PO Box 1029, 42 Main St., Lanigan, SK S0K 2M0
Tel: 306-365-2010; Fax: 306-365-3388
laniganadvisor@sasktel.net
Circulation: 880 Frequency: Mon.
Linda Mallett, Publisher & Editor

Lumsden: Lumsden Waterfront Press Regional
Newspaper
PO Box 507, 635 James St. North, Lumsden, SK S0G 3C0
Tel: 306-731-3143; Fax: 306-731-2277
watpress@sasktel.net
www.waterfrontpress.com
Circulation: 4,160 Frequency: Thurs.
Lucien Chouinard, Co-Publisher & Editor
Jacqueline Chouinard, Co-Publisher & Editor

Macklin: Macklin Mirror
Owned By: Holmes Publishing
PO Box 100, 4701 Herald St., Macklin, SK S0L 2C0
Tel: 306-753-2424; Fax: 306-753-2424
macklinmirror@sasktel.net
Circulation: 875 Frequency: Wed.
Stewart Crump, Publisher

Maple Creek: Maple Creek News
Owned By: Alta Newspaper Group Limited Partnership
PO Box 1328, 116 Harder St., Maple Creek, SK S0N 1N0
Tel: 306-662-2133; Fax: 306-662-3092
editorial@maplecreeknews.com
www.maplecreeknews.com
twitter.com/maplecreeknews
www.facebook.com/150542211683094
Other information: Ads, Email: ads@maplecreeknews.com
Circulation: 1,700 Frequency: Thurs.
Angela Litke, Manager
Della Fournier, Contact, Advertising, Sales
dfournier@maplecreeknews.com

Meadow Lake: Northern Pride
219 Centre St., Meadow Lake, SK S9X 1Z4
Tel: 306-236-5353; Fax: 306-236-5962
northern.pride@sasktel.net
www.northernprideml.com
twitter.com/NorthernPrideML
www.facebook.com/northern.pride.5
Circulation: 4,800 Frequency: Tues.
The newspaper serves Meadow Lake & northwestern
Saskatchewan.
Terry Villeneuve, Publisher
Phil Ambroziak, Editor

Melfort: The Melfort Journal
Owned By: Postmedia Network Inc.
PO Box 1300, 901 Main St., Melfort, SK S0E 1A0
Tel: 306-752-5737; Fax: 306-752-5358
www.melfortjournal.com
twitter.com/MelfortJournal
www.facebook.com/330748053648867
Circulation: 1,500 Frequency: Tues.
Ken Sorensen, Publisher, Advertising
ken.sorensen@sunmedia.ca
Greg Wiseman, Regional Managing Editor
greg.wiseman@sunmedia.ca
Greg Wiseman, Editor

Melville: Melville Advance
PO Box 1420, 218 - 3rd Ave. West, Melville, SK S0A 2P0
Tel: 306-728-5448; Fax: 306-728-4004
melvilleadvance@sasktel.net
www.melvilleadvance.com
twitter.com/MelvilleAdvance
www.facebook.com/TheMelvilleAdvance
Circulation: 2,400 Frequency: Wed.
Print & online subscriptions are available.
Chris Ashfield, Publisher & Contact, Advertising
George Brown, Managing Editor
editor.melvilleadvance@sasktel.net
Darcy Gross, Sports Reporter
sports.melvilleadvance@sasktel.net
Lloyd Schmidt, Computer Graphic Artist

Moose Jaw: The Moose Jaw Times Herald
Previous Name: Moose Jaw This Week
Owned By: Star News Publishing Inc.
44 Fairford St. West, Moose Jaw, SK S6H 1V1
Tel: 306-692-6441; Fax: 306-692-2101
www.mjtimes.sk.ca
twitter.com/MJTimesHerald
www.facebook.com/MJTHerald
Circulation: 24,000 Frequency: Wed.
Nancy Johnson, Publisher
306-691-1254; Fax: 306-692-2101
nancy.johnson@tc.tc
Lyndsay McCready, Managing Editor
editorial@mjtimes.sk.ca

Moosomin: The World-Spectator
Owned By: McKay Publications Ltd.
PO Box 250, 624 Main St., Moosomin, SK S0G 3N0
Tel: 306-435-2445; Fax: 306-435-3969
world_spectator@sasktel.net
www.world-spectator.com
Other information: Advertising, Email: ads@world-spectator.com
www.facebook.com/worldspectator
Circulation: 3,400 Frequency: Mon.
The following Saskatchewan communities are served by The
World-Spectator: Moosomin, Wawota, Maryfield, Tantallon, St.
Lazare, Elkhorn, Fleming, Manson, Kennedy, Rocanville,
Wapella, Spy Hill, Welwyn, McAuley, Kola, Kelso, Fairlight, &
Langbank.
Kevin Weedmark, Publisher & Editor
kevin@world-spectator.com

Muenster: Prairie Messenger
PO Box 190, 100 College Dr., Muenster, SK S0K 2Y0
Tel: 306-682-1772; Fax: 306-682-5285
pm@stpeterspress.ca
www.prairiemessenger.ca
Circulation: 4,800 Frequency: Wed.
Maureen Weber, Editor
pm.canadian@stpeterspress.ca
Donald Ward, Local News Editor
pm.local@stpeterspress.ca
Gail Kleefeld, Contact, Circulation
pm.circulation@stpeterspress.ca

Nipawin: The Nipawin Journal
Previous Name: Nipawin N.E. Region Community
Booster
Owned By: Postmedia Network Inc.
117 - 1st St. West, Nipawin, SK S0E 1E0
Tel: 306-862-4618; Fax: 306-862-4566
www.nipawinjournal.com
twitter.com/NipawinJournal
www.facebook.com/nipawin.journal
Circulation: 1,100 Frequency: Wed.
Ken Sorensen, Publisher
ken.sorensen@sunmedia.ca
Greg Wiseman, Regional Managing Editor
greg.wiseman@sunmedia.ca

Nokomis: **Last Mountain Times**
Owned By: Last Mountain Times Ltd.
PO Box 340, 103 - 1st Ave. West, Nokomis, SK S0G 3R0
Tel: 306-528-2020; *Fax:* 306-528-2090
lastmountaintimes.ca
www.facebook.com/lastmountaintimes
Circulation: 1,100 *Frequency:* Tues.
David Degenstien, Owner/Editor/Publisher
editor@lastmountaintimes.ca
Lynn Sonmor, Contact, Advertising
sales@lastmountaintimes.ca

Nokomis: **The Market Connection**
PO Box 340, Nokomis, SK S0G 3R0
Tel: 306-528-2020; *Fax:* 306-528-2090
editor@lastmountaintimes.ca
lastmountaintimes.ca
Other information: Classifieds email:
inbox@lastmountaintimes.ca
Circulation: 10,600 *Frequency:* 4 times a year
The Market Connection is published concurrently with an issue of Last Mountain Times.
Dave Degenstien, Publisher/Editor/Owner

North Battleford: **The Battlefords News-Optimist**
Owned By: Glacier Newspapers Group
PO Box 1029, 892 - 104 St., North Battleford, SK S9A 3E6
Tel: 306-445-7261; *Fax:* 306-445-3223
Toll-Free: 866-549-9979
battlefords.publishing@sasktel.net
www.newsoptimist.ca
Other information: Sales, Fax: 306-445-1977; Composition, Fax: 306-445-7281
twitter.com/BfordsNewsOpt
Circulation: 2,350 *Frequency:* Tues.
Alana Schweitzer, Publisher
newsoptimist.alana@sasktel.net
Becky Doig, Editor
newsoptimist.editor@sasktel.net
John Cairns, Staff Reporter
newsoptimist.john@sasktel.netet

North Battleford: **Maidstone Mirror**
Owned By: Battlefords Publishing Ltd.
PO Box 1029, 892 - 104th St., North Battleford, SK S9A 3E6
Tel: 306-445-7261; *Fax:* 306-445-3223
Toll-Free: 866-549-9979
battlefords.publishing@sasktel.net
Circulation: 777 *Frequency:* Weekly
John Webster, Publisher
Becky Doig, Editor

Outlook: **The Outlook**
Owned By: Glacier Media Inc.
PO Box 1717, Outlook, SK S0L 2N0
Tel: 306-867-8262; *Fax:* 306-867-9556
theoutlook@sasktel.net
Circulation: 1,437 *Frequency:* Thursdays
The Outlook offers news & information to west central Saskatchewan.
Delwyn Luedtke, Publisher

Pierceland: **The Beaver River Banner**
PO Box 700, 171 - 2nd St. West, Pierceland, SK S0M 2K0
Tel: 306-839-4496; *Fax:* 306-839-2306
br.banner@outlook.com
www.beaverriverbanner.com
Circulation: 2,600 *Frequency:* Tues.
Dan Birsebois, Publisher/Editor

Regina: **Journal L'eau vive**
Détenteur: La Coopérative de publ. fransaskoises
#210, 1440 - 9th Ave. North, Regina, SK S4R 8B1
Tél: 306-347-0481; *Téléc:* 306-565-3450
Ligne sans frais: 888-644-3236
www.leau-vive.ca
twitter.com/leauvive
www.facebook.com/leauvive.CPF
Tirage: 1 400 *Fréquence:* Thurs.
Jean-Pierre Picard, Directeur/Rédacteur
direction@leau-vive.ca

Regina: **Sunday Post**
Previous Name: Regina Sun
Owned By: The Leader-Post
PO Box 2020, 1964 Park St., Regina, SK S4P 3G4
Tel: 306-565-8250; *Fax:* 306-565-8350
Circulation: 78,350 *Frequency:* Sun.
A free weekly newspaper focusing on features, analysis and lengthier, weekend-style reads.
Marty Klyne, Publisher

Rosetown: **Rosetown Eagle**
Owned By: Rosetown Publishing Co. Ltd.
PO Box 130, Rosetown, SK S0L 2V0
Tel: 306-882-4202; *Fax:* 306-882-4204
editor.eagle@gmail.com
Circulation: 1,790 *Frequency:* Mon.
Stewart Crump, Publisher
Ian McKay, Editor

Rosthern: **Saskatchewan Valley News**
Previous Name: The Enterprise
PO Box 10, Rosthern, SK S0K 3R0
Tel: 306-232-4865; *Fax:* 306-232-4694
Toll-Free: 800-601-7858
info@saskvalleynews.com
www.saskvalleynews.com
Circulation: 1,750 *Frequency:* Thurs.
The Saskatchewan Valley News covers Rosthern & rural communities in the surrounding area.
Renay Kowalczyk, General Manager & Editor

Saskatoon: **The Saskatoon Express**
Previous Name: Saskatoon Neighbourhood Express
#15, 2220 Northridge Dr., Saskatoon, SK S7L 6X8
Tel: 306-244-5050; *Fax:* 306-244-5053
general@saskatoonexpress.com
www.saskatoonexpress.com
twitter.com/Sask_Express
www.facebook.com/165460726849382
Circulation: 55,000 *Frequency:* Weekly
Ryan McAdams, Publisher
Cam Hutchinson, Editor
chutchinson@saskatoonexpress.com

Shaunavon: **The Shaunavon Standard**
Owned By: Alta Newspaper Group Limited Partnership
PO Box 729, Shaunavon, SK S0N 2M0
Tel: 306-297-4144; *Fax:* 306-297-3357
www.theshaunavonstandard.com
twitter.com/The_SStandard
www.facebook.com/118598378227507
Circulation: 1,150 *Frequency:* Tues.
Paul MacNeil, Editor
standard@sasktel.net
Joanne Gregoire, Contact, Advertising & Sales
jgregoire@theshaunavonstandard.com

Shellbrook: **Shellbrook Chronicle**
Owned By: Pepperfram Limited Publications
PO Box 10, Shellbrook, SK S0J 2E0
Tel: 306-747-2442; *Fax:* 306-747-3000
chads@shellbrookchronicle.com
www.shellbrookchronicle.com
twitter.com/ShellbrookChron
www.facebook.com/SBChronicle
Circulation: 3,950 *Frequency:* Fri.
The following Saskatchewan communities are covered by the Shellbrook Chronicle: Shellbrook, Debden, Parkside, Marcelin, Holbein, Mayview, Mont Nebo, Canwook, Big River, Leask, & Blaine Lake.
C.J. Pepper, Publisher
Flavio Nienow, Editor
chnews@shellbrookchronicle.com
Madeleine Wrigley, Contact, Advertising Sales
chroniclesales@sasktel.net
Cheryl Mason, Contact, Reception & Bookkeeping

Shellbrook: **Spiritwood Herald**
Owned By: Pepperfram Limited Publications
PO Box 10, 44 Main St., Shellbrook, SK S0J 2E0
Tel: 306-747-2442; *Fax:* 306-747-3000
spiritwoodherald.com
www.facebook.com/253716234680672
Circulation: 2,570 *Frequency:* Fri.
Clark Pepper, Publisher
Tom Pierson, Editor
chnews@sbchron.com

Swift Current: **The Southwest Booster**
Owned By: Continental Newspapers Canada Ltd.
30 - 4th Ave. NW, Swift Current, SK S9H 3X4
Tel: 306-773-9321; *Fax:* 306-773-9136
www.swbooster.com
twitter.com/swbooster
www.facebook.com/163689647007012
Circulation: 18,400 *Frequency:* Thurs.
Nancy Johnson, Publisher
nancy.johnson@tc.tc
Scott Anderson, Managing Editor
sanderson@swbooster.com
Bridget Denys, Manager, Business
bdenys@swbooster.com

Mark Soper, Manager, Sales
msoper@swbooster.com
Morgan Reil, Supervisor, Commercial Print
mreil@swbooster.com
Steven Mah, Sports Reporter
smah@swbooster.com
Valerie McLearn, Coordinator, Ads
vmclearn@swbooster.com

Tisdale: **Tisdale Recorder & Parkland Review**
Owned By: Glacier Newspaper Group
PO Box 1660, 1004 - 102nd Ave., Tisdale, SK S0E 1T0
Tel: 306-873-4515; *Fax:* 306-873-4712
www.facebook.com/199458986756467
Circulation: 13,288 *Frequency:* Wed.
Brent Fitzpatrick, Publisher
pub@sasktel.net
James Tarrant, Editor
newsrecorder@sasktel.net

Unity: **The Unity-Wilkie Press Herald**
Owned By: Glacier Media Inc.
PO Box 309, 310 Main St., Unity, SK S0K 4L0
Tel: 306-228-2267; *Fax:* 306-228-2767
northwest.herald@sasktel.net
www.estevanmercury.ca/section/northwest
Circulation: 1,900 *Frequency:* Mon.
Tammi Bullerwell, General Manager
Neil Thom, Editor
editorial@website.com
Debbie Barr, Prepress Manager
prepress@website.com
Denise Allen, Accountant

Wadena: **Wadena News**
Owned By: Wadena News Ltd.
PO Box 100, 102 - 1st St. NE, Wadena, SK S0A 4J0
Tel: 306-338-2231
wadena.news@sasktel.net
www.wadenanews.ca
twitter.com/wadenanewsed
www.facebook.com/14335013609573
Circulation: 2,200 *Frequency:* Wed.
Bruce Squires, Co-Publisher
Alison Squires, Co-Publisher
Kathy Johnson, Editor

Wakaw: **Wakaw Recorder**
Owned By: Dwaymar Enterprises Ltd.
PO Box 9, 224 - 1st St. South, Wakaw, SK S0K 4P0
Tel: 306-233-4325
Circulation: 1,800 *Frequency:* Wed.
Marjorie Biccum, Publisher

Warman: **The Country Press**
PO Box 880, 520 Central St. West, Warman, SK S0K 4S0
Tel: 306-934-6191; *Fax:* 306-668-8250
countrypress@sasktel.net
Circulation: 12,300 *Frequency:* Wed.
C. Lynn Handford, Publisher & Editor

Watrous: **Watrous Manitou**
Owned By: 101026460 Saskatchewan Ltd.
PO Box 100, 309 Main St., Watrous, SK S0K 4T0
Tel: 306-946-3343; *Fax:* 306-946-2026
watrous.manitou@sasktel.net
www.twmnews.com
twitter.com/twmnews
www.facebook.com/thewatrousmanitou
Circulation: 1,400 *Frequency:* Mon.
Daniel Bushman, Publisher & Editor
Kim Bushman, Publisher & Editor
Nicole Lay, Publisher
Robin Lay, Publisher

Weyburn: **Weyburn Review**
Owned By: Glacier Interactive Media
PO Box 400, 904 East Ave., Weyburn, SK S4H 2K4
Tel: 306-842-7487; *Fax:* 306-842-0282
production@weyburnreview.com
www.weyburnreview.com
twitter.com/WeyburnReview
www.facebook.com/100299633382446
Circulation: 2,800 *Frequency:* Wed.
Darryl Ward, Publisher
Patricia Ward, Editor-in-chief

Weyburn: Weyburn This Week
115 - 2nd St. NE, Weyburn, SK S4H 0T7
Tel: 306-842-3900; *Fax:* 306-842-2515
weyburnthisweek@sasktel.net
www.weyburnthisweek.com
Other information: Advertising, Email:
advertisingthisweek@sasktel.net
Circulation: 4,600 *Frequency:* Fri.
The free publication covers local news & events in Weyburn &
surrounding communities in southeastern Saskatchewan.
Andrea Heath, Publisher & Representative, Sales
Tanya Brown, Editor & Reporter
editorialthisweek@sasktel.net
Leslie Dempsey, Contact, Graphic Design

Whitewood: Whitewood Herald
**PO Box 160, 708 South Railway St., Whitewood, SK S0G
5C0**
Tel: 306-735-2230; *Fax:* 306-735-2899
herald@whitewoodherald.com
www.whitewoodherald.com
twitter.com/WhitewoodHerald
www.facebook.com/WhitewoodHerald
Circulation: 800 *Frequency:* Mon.
Chris Ashfield, Publisher
George Brown, Editor

Wolseley: Wolseley Bulletin
PO Box 89, 219 Poplar St., Wolseley, SK S0G 5H0
Tel: 306-698-2271; *Fax:* 306-698-2808
unos@sasktel.net
www.saskfarmnews.com/id6.html
Circulation: 500 *Frequency:* Fri.
The Wolseley Bulletin is distributed in the following communities:
Wolseley, Glenavon, Indian Head, Qu'Appelle, Grenfell,
Montmartre, Sintaluta, & Regina.

Rick Dahlman, Publisher & Editor
rdahlman@sk.sympatico.ca

Wynyard: Wynyard Advance/Gazette
Owned By: Foam Lake Review Ltd.
PO Box 10, 117 Ave. B East, Wynyard, SK S0A 4T0
Tel: 306-554-2224; *Fax:* 306-554-3226
w.advance@sasktel.net
Circulation: 1,400 *Frequency:* Mon.
Bob Johnson, Publisher
Denise Mozel, Editor

Yorkton: The News Review
Owned By: Glacier Media Inc.
18 - 1st Ave. North, Yorkton, SK S3N 1J4
Tel: 306-783-7355; *Fax:* 306-783-9138
info@yorktonnews.com
www.yorktonnews.com
twitter.com/yorktonnews
www.facebook.com/yorkton.newsreview
Circulation: 6,700 *Frequency:* Thurs.
Ken Chyz, Publisher
kenchyz@yorktonnews.com
Shannon Deveau, Editor
editorial@yorktonnews.com

Yorkton: Yorkton This Week
Owned By: Glacier Newspapers Group
PO Box 1300, 20 - 3rd Ave. North, Yorkton, SK S3N 2X3
Tel: 306-782-2465; *Fax:* 306-786-1898
sales@yorktonthisweek.com
www.yorktonthisweek.com
twitter.com/yorktonthisweek
www.facebook.com/168910973121215
Circulation: 3,400 *Frequency:* Wed.
Neil Thom, Publisher & General Manager

Yukon Territory

Daily Newspapers in Yukon Territory

Whitehorse: The Whitehorse Daily Star
2149 - 2nd Ave., Whitehorse, YT Y1A 1C5
Tel: 867-668-2060; *Fax:* 867-668-7130
advertising@whitehorsestar.com
www.whitehorsestar.com
twitter.com/WhitehorseStar
www.facebook.com/WhitehorseStar
Frequency: Monday, Wednesday, Friday
Jackie Pierce, Publisher
Jim Butler, Editor
editor@whitehorsestar.com

Other Newspapers in Yukon Territory

Whitehorse: L'Aurore boréale
Détenteur: Association Franco-Yukonnaise
**Association Franco-Yukonnaise, 302, rue Strickland,
Whitehorse, YT Y1A 2K1**
Tél: 867-667-2931; *Téléc:* 867-667-2932
www.auroreboreale.ca
twitter.com/l_auroreboreale
www.facebook.com/AFY.Yukon
Tirage: 900 *Fréquence:* Bi-mensuel
Marie-Claude Nault, Coordonnatrice de la publicité
pub@auroreboreale.ca
Pierre-Luc Lafrance, Directeur
dir@auroreboreale.ca

Magazine Name Index

A

Abaka, 1833
Aberdeen Angus World, 1831
Abilities Magazine, 1823
Aboriginal Business Magazine, 1801
Above & Beyond Magazine, 1829
Acadiensis, 1836
Accès Média, 1839
Active Life, 1821
Adbusters, 1819
Adnews Online Daily, 1801
Advisor's Edge, 1803
The Advocate, 1811, 1813
Les Affaires, 1803
Affaires Plus Magazine, 1803
AGDealer Magazine, 1831
Agrobiomass, 1831
Alberta Farmer Express, 1831
Alberta Gardener, 1822
Alberta Jewish News, 1827
Alberta Native News, 1832
Alberta Oil & Gas Directory, 1812
Alberta Seed Guide, 1831
Alberta Sweetgrass, 1832
Alberta Venture, 1803
Alberta Views, 1817
Algonquin Times, 1839
Al-Mustakbal, 1833
AMA Insider, 1822
Amphora, 1816
Anglican Journal, 1827
Annals of Air & Space Law, 1836
Anthropologica, 1836
The Antigonish Review, 1825
Applied Arts, 1823
Applied Physiology, Nutrition & Metabolism, 1838
The Aquinian, 1839
Arabella, 1801
ARC Arabic Journal, 1833
Arc Poetry Magazine, 1825
Arctic Journal, 1836
The Argosy, 1839
Arthur Visual Archive, 1839
The Artichoke, 1839
The ATA Magazine, 1806
The Athenaeum, 1839
Atlantic Beef & Sheep, 1831
Atlantic Business Magazine, 1803
Atlantic Forestry Review, 1822
Atlantic Horse & Pony, 1825
Atlantic Salmon Journal, 1819
Atlantis: Critical Studies in Gender, Culture & Social Justice, 1836
Audio Ideas Guide, 1829
Avantages, 1803
Aventure chasse et pêche, 1821
Avenue, 1817
Award Magazine, 1801
AZURE, 1810

B

Backbone Magazine, 1803
Bakers Journal, 1802
Bar & Beverage Business Magazine, 1809
Bayview Post, 1817
Bazoof!, 1817
BC BookWorld, 1816
BC Christian News, 1827
BC Living, 1822
BC Outdoors, 1821
BC Parent Newsmagazine, 1820
BC Restaurant News, 1809
BC Studies: The British Columbian Quarterly, 1839

BCAA Magazine, 1829
BCBusiness, 1803
BCBusiness Magazine, 1803
Be Fabulous!, 1821
Bear Country, 1829
Benefits & Pensions Monitor, 1803
Benefits Canada, 1803
Bio Business Magazine, 1813
Biochemistry & Cell Biology, 1838
BIZ Magazine, 1804
Black Pages Directory, 1819
Blackflash, 1827
Blitz Magazine Inc, 1801
Blue Line Magazine, 1812
Boats & Places, 1816
Border Crossings, 1815
Botany, 1838
Boulevard Victoria, 1817
Bratstvo Srpsko, 1835
Briarpatch Magazine, 1827
Brick: A Literary Journal, 1825
Briefly Speaking, 1811
British Columbia Magazine, 1829
Broadcast Dialogue, 1802
Broadview, 1827
Broken Pencil, 1819
Brunswickan, 1839
BSIA News Magazine, 1802
Building Magazine, 1802
Bulgarian Horizons, 1833
Bulletin d'information du Collège Ahuntsic, 1839
Business Edge News Magazine, 1804
Business Elite Canada, 1804
Business in Calgary, 1804
Business in Edmonton, 1804
Business in Focus, 1804
Business in Vancouver, 1816
The Business Link Niagara, 1804
Business London, 1804
Business Review Canada, 1804
The Buzz, 1819

C

C Magazine, 1815
CAA Magazine, 1822
CAA Saskatchewan, 1822
CAAR Communicator, 1831
The Cadre, 1839
Calgary's Child Magazine, 1820
Camford Chemical Report, 1813
Camping Caravaning, 1816
The Campus, 1839
Canada Japan Journal, 1804
Canada Lutheran, 1827
Canada's History Magazine, 1824
The Canadian Amateur Magazine, 1824
Canadian Apartment Magazine, 1802
Canadian Architect, 1801
Canadian Art, 1815
Canadian Asian News, 1833
Canadian Auto Repair & Service Magazine, 1801
Canadian Auto World, 1801
Canadian Automotive Fleet, 1814
Canadian Aviation Historical Society Journal, 1816
Canadian Aviator Magazine, 1802
Canadian Ayrshire Review, 1831
Canadian Biker, 1815
Canadian Biomass Magazine, 1831
Canadian Business Franchise / L'entreprise, 1804
Canadian Cattlemen: The Beef Magazine, 1831
Canadian Chiropractor, 1808
Canadian Coin News, 1824

Canadian Consulting Engineer, 1807
Canadian Contractor, 1802
Canadian Cowboy Country, 1828
Canadian Cycling Magazine, 1801
Canadian Cyclist, 1828
Canadian Defence Review, 1811
Canadian Equipment Finance, 1804
Canadian Ethnic Studies, 1836
Canadian Fabricating & Welding, 1811
Canadian Family Physician, 1809
Canadian Firefighter & EMS Quarterly, 1807
Canadian Footwear Journal, 1808
Canadian Foreign Policy Journal, 1836
Canadian Forest Industries, 1808
The Canadian Funeral Director Magazine, 1808
Canadian Funeral News, 1808
Canadian Gaming Business, 1804
Canadian Geotechnical Journal, 1838
Canadian Grocer, 1808
Canadian Hairdresser Magazine, 1802
Canadian Historical Review, 1836
Canadian Horse Annual, 1825
Canadian Horse Journal - Central & Atlantic Edition, 1825
Canadian Horse Journal - Pacific & Prairie Edition, 1825
Canadian HR Reporter, 1810
Canadian Immigrant Magazine, 1822
Canadian Interiors, 1810
Canadian Journal of Chemistry, 1838
Canadian Journal of Civil Engineering, 1838
Canadian Journal of Development Studies, 1836
Canadian Journal of Earth Sciences, 1838
Canadian Journal of Economics, 1836
Canadian Journal of Fisheries & Aquatic Sciences, 1838
Canadian Journal of Higher Education, 1836
Canadian Journal of History, 1836
Canadian Journal of Information & Library Science, 1836
Canadian Journal of Law & Society, 1836
Canadian Journal of Linguistics, 1836
Canadian Journal of Mathematics, 1836
Canadian Journal of Microbiology, 1839
Canadian Journal of Neurological Sciences, 1836
The Canadian Journal of Occupational Therapy, 1809
Canadian Journal of Philosophy, 1836
Canadian Journal of Physics, 1839
Canadian Journal of Physiology & Pharmacology, 1839
Canadian Journal of Program Evaluation, 1836
Canadian Journal of Women & The Law, 1837
Canadian Journal of Zoology, 1839
Canadian Lawyer, 1811
Canadian Literature, 1837
Canadian Living, 1824
Canadian Lodging News, 1809
The Canadian Manager, 1804
Canadian Mathematical Bulletin, 1837
Canadian Meetings + Events Expo, 1806
Canadian Mennonite, 1827
Canadian Metalworking, 1811
Canadian Modern Language Review, 1837
Canadian MoneySaver, 1816

Canadian Mortgage Professional, 1813
Canadian Music Trade, 1812
Canadian Musician, 1826
Canadian Newcomer, 1822
Canadian Notes & Queries, 1825
Canadian Organic Grower, 1822
Canadian Packaging, 1812
Canadian Pizza Magazine, 1807
Canadian Plastics, 1812
Canadian Plastics Directory & Buyer's Guide, 1812
Canadian Poultry Magazine, 1831
Canadian Process Equipment & Control News, 1805
Canadian Property Management, 1802
Canadian Property Valuation, 1813
Canadian Public Policy, 1837
Canadian Real Estate Wealth, 1827
Canadian Rental Service, 1813
Canadian Review of American Studies, 1837
Canadian Running, 1814
Canadian RVing, 1816
Canadian Sailings, 1813
Canadian Security, 1813
Canadian Stamp News, 1824
Canadian Theatre Review, 1837
Canadian Trade Index, 1813
Canadian Travel Press, 1814
Canadian Traveller, 1814
Canadian Treasurer, 1804
Canadian Underwriter, 1810
Canadian Veterinary Journal, 1814
Canadian Woman Studies, 1830
Canadian Yachting, 1816
Cannabis Brightline, 1814
Cannabis Retailer, 1814
CANNAtalk, 1822
Caper Times, 1839
Capilano Courier, 1840
The Capilano Review, 1825
Caregiver Solutions, 1823
Caribbean Camera, 1833
The Carillon, 1840
Cartographica, 1837
The Cascade, 1840
The Catholic Register, 1827
Catholic Teacher Magazine, 1806
Celtic Life International, 1833
Chamber Vision, 1804
Charolais Banner, 1831
Chatelaine, 1830
Cheval Québec, 1825
chickaDEE, 1817
Chinese Canadian Times, 1833
The Chinese Journal, 1833
The Chinese Press, 1833
Chirp, 1817
Christian Courier, 1827
The Chronicle of Neurology & Psychiatry, 1809
The Chronicle of Skin & Allergy, 1809
Châtelaine, 1830
Ciel Variable, 1827
CIM Magazine, 1811
Cinema Scope, 1819
CIO Canada, 1806
City Parent, 1820
Clarion, 1827
Clin d'oeil, 1820
Collision Quarterly, 1801
Collision Repair Magazine, 1801
Columbia Journal, 1826
Comfort Life, 1821
Comics & Games Monthly, 1824
Community Digest, 1835
Computer Dealer News, 1806

Magazines

Business

Aboriginal

Aboriginal Business Magazine
Owned By: Turtle Island News Publications
c/o Turtle Island News, PO Box 329, 2208 Chiefswood Rd.,
Hagersville, ON N0A 1M0
Tel: 519-445-0868; *Fax:* 519-445-0865
aboriginalbusinessmagazine.com
www.facebook.com/AboriginalBusinessMagazine
Frequency: Quarterly
Lynda Powless, Publisher & Editor,
lynda@theturtleislandnews.com

Advertising, Marketing, Sales

Adnews Online Daily
Owned By: Bale Communications Inc.
#1463, 1011 Upper Middle Rd. E, Oakville, ON L6H 5Z9
info@adnews.com
www.adnews.com
twitter.com/Adnewscom
www.facebook.com/AdNewsAustralia
Circulation: 65,000
Frequency: Daily
Advertising, marketing, creative, research, sales, technology, PR
& media news source
Rob Bale, Publisher
Derek Winkler, Editor

Blitz Magazine Inc
1360 Bathurst St., Toronto, ON M5R 3H7
Fax: 647-435-0304
Toll-Free: 888-952-5478
editor@blitzmagazine.com
www.blitzmagazine.com
Available online only.
Troy Weston, Publisher, troy@blitzmagazine.com

Direct Marketing Magazine
Previous Name: Canadian Direct Marketing News
Owned By: Lloydmedia, Inc.
137 Main St. North, 3rd Fl., Markham, ON L3P 1Y2
Tel: 905-201-6600; *Fax:* 905-201-6601
Toll-Free: 800-688-1838
www.dmn.ca
twitter.com/directmarketmagazine
www.facebook.com/directmarketingmagazine
Circulation: 6,400
Frequency: Monthly, plus annual directory of suppliers & annual
directories The List of Lists...The DM Industry Sourcebook & the
Canadian Call Centre Industry Directory
Brendan Read, Editor, brendan@dmn.ca
Steve Lloyd, President, steve@contactmanagement.ca
Mark Henry, Contact, Ad Sales, mark@dmn.ca

Imprint Canada
Owned By: Tristan Communication Ltd.
#16, 190 Marycroft Ave., Woodbridge, ON L4L 5Y2
Tel: 905-856-2600; *Fax:* 905-856-2667
Toll-Free: 877-895-7022
feedback@imprintcanada.com
imprintcanada.com/magazine
Other information: Toll-Free Fax: 877-895-7023
twitter.com/imprint_canada
www.facebook.com/imprintcanada.shows
Tony Muccilli, Publisher

Infopresse (IP)
Détenteur: Infopresse
4310, boul Saint-Laurent, Montréal, QC H2W 1Z3
Tél: 514-842-5873; *Téléc:* 514-842-2422
www.infopresse.com
twitter.com/infopresse
www.facebook.com/Infopresse
Tirage: 7 500
Fréquence: 10 fois par an
Arnaud Granata, Président et éditeur
Melanie Rudel-Tessier, Vice-président, directeur des contenus,
melanie.rudel-tessier@infopresse.com

Kidscreen
Owned By: Brunico Communications Ltd.
#100, 366 Adelaide St. West, Toronto, ON M5V 1R9
Tel: 416-408-2300; *Fax:* 416-408-0870
Toll-Free: 800-543-4512
www.kidscreen.com
www.instagram.com/kidscreen
twitter.com/kidscreen
www.facebook.com/219 216124848853
Circulation: 12,500
Frequency: 6 times a year
Jocelyn Christie, Vice-President & Publisher,
jchristie@brunico.com
Lana Castleman, Editor, lcastleman@brunico.com

Sign Media
Also Known As: Signs Canada
Owned By: Kenilworth Media Inc.
c/o Kenilworth Media Inc., #710, 15 Wertheim Ct., Richmond
Hill, ON L4B 3H7
Tel: 905-771-7333; *Fax:* 905-771-7336
Toll-Free: 800-409-8688
editor@signmedia.ca
www.signmedia.ca
twitter.com/signmediacanada
Circulation: 11,016
Frequency: 7 times a year
Ellen Kral, Publisher
Blair Adams, Editorial Director
Erik Tolles, Sales Manager

Strategy
Owned By: Brunico Communications Ltd.
#100, 366 Adelaide St. West, Toronto, ON M5V 1R9
Tel: 416-408-2300; *Fax:* 416-408-0870
Toll-Free: 888-278-6426
strategyonline.ca
twitter.com/strategyonline
www.facebook.com/217618361606458
Circulation: 13,152
Frequency: Monthly
Russell Goldstein, President & CEO, rgoldstein@brunico.com
Mary Maddever, SVP & Editorial Director,
mmaddever@brunico.com
Jennifer Horn, Editor, jhorn@brunico.com

Architecture

Award Magazine
Owned By: Canada Wide Media Limited
#230, 4321 Still Creek Dr., Burnaby, BC V5C 6S7
Tel: 604-299-7311; *Fax:* 604-299-9188
cwm@canadawide.com
www.canadawide.com/brands/award
Circulation: 10,000
Frequency: 6 times a year
Magazine for architects, interior designers, & construction
industry professionals
Dan Chapman, Publisher, 604-473-0316,
dchapman@canadawide.com
Natalie Bruckner-Menchelli, Editor,
nbmenchelli@canadawide.com

Canadian Architect
c/o IQ Business Media, #302, 101 Duncan Mill Rd., Toronto,
ON M3B 1Z3
Tel: 416-441-2085
www.canadianarchitect.com
twitter.com/CdnArch
Frequency: Monthly
Steve Wilson, Publisher, swilson@canadianarchitect.com

Construction Canada
Owned By: Kenilworth Media Inc.
c/o Kenilworth Media Inc., #710, 15 Wertheim Ct., Richmond
Hill, ON L4B 3H7
Tel: 905-771-7333; *Fax:* 905-771-7336
Toll-Free: 800-409-8688
circulation@constructioncanada.net
www.constructioncanada.net
www.instagram.com/constructcanmag
twitter.com/constructCanMag
Frequency: Bi-monthly
Blair Adams, Editorial Director
Erik Tolles, Sales Director

Sustainable Architecture & Building Magazine
Also Known As: SAB Mag
Owned By: Janam Publications
81, rue Leduc, Gatineau, QC J8X 3A7
Tel: 819-778-5040; *Fax:* 819-595-8553
www.sabmagazine.com/magazine.html
www.youtube.com/user/SABmagazine
twitter.com/SABMagazine
www.facebook. com/sabmagcanada
Don Griffith, Publisher, 800-520-6281 ext.304,
dgriffith@sabmagazine.com
Jim Taggart, Editor, 604-874-0195, architext@telus.net

Arts, Art & Antiques

Arabella
Owned By: Arabella Publications Inc.
44 Parr St., St. Andrews, NB E5B 1L7
Tel: 506-814-0119
admin@arabelladesign.com
arabelladesign.com
www.facebook.com/107077652659400
Debra Usher, Editor-in-Chief

Automobile, Cycle, & Automotive Accessories

L'Automobile
Montréal, QC
info@lautomobile.com
www.lautomobile.ca
www.linkedin.com/company/l-automobile-magazine
www.facebook.com/magazinelautomobile
Tirage: 10 000
Fréquence: 6 fois par an
Rémy L. Rousseau, Éditeur, remyrousseau@rogers.com
Isabelle Havasy, Rédactrice en chef,
thecarfashionista@gmail.com

Canadian Auto Repair & Service Magazine
Previous Name: Canadian Technician; Service Station
& Garage Management
Owned By: Turnkey Media Solutions Inc.
451 Attwell Dr., Toronto, ON M9W 5C4
Tel: 416-614-2200; *Fax:* 416-614-8861
www.autoserviceworld.com/carsmagazine
Frequency: Monthly
Allan Janssen, Editor, allan@newcom.ca

Canadian Auto World
Owned By: Metroland Media Group Ltd.
c/o Metroland Media Group Ltd., 901 Guelph Line,
Burlington, ON L7R 3N8
Tel: 905-632-4444; *Fax:* 905-842-4432
Toll-Free: 800-693-7986
www.canadianautoworld.ca
Circulation: 4,529
Frequency: 6 times a year
Vicki Dillane, General Manager, 905-845-8536 x255,
vdillane@metroland.com

Canadian Cycling Magazine
Owned By: Gripped Publishing Inc.
75 Harbord St., Toronto, ON M5S 4G1
Tel: 416-927-0774; *Fax:* 416-927-1491
Toll-Free: 800-567-0444
info@cyclingmagazine.ca
cyclingmagazine.ca
twitter.com/CDNCyclingMag
www.facebook.com/cyclingmag
Sam Cohen, Publisher, sam@gripped.com

Collision Quarterly
Automotive Retailer Publishing Company Ltd., #1, 8980
Fraserwood Ct., Burnaby, BC V5J 5H7
Tel: 604-432-7987
publish@ara.bc.ca
www.collisionquarterly.ca
www.facebook.com/CollisionQuarterly
Circulation: 8,088
Frequency: Quarterly
Rene Young, Publisher & Editor

Collision Repair Magazine
c/o Media Matters, 455 Gilmour St., Peterborough, ON K9H
2J8
Tel: 905-370-0101
www.collisionrepairmag.com
twitter.com/CollisionMag
www.facebook.com/collisionrepairmag
Circulation: 7,400
Frequency: Bimonthly
Darryl Simmons, Publisher, publisher@collisionrepairmag.com
Mike Davey, Editor, editor@collisionrepairmag.com

dandyhorse
#813, 22 Close Ave., Toronto, ON M5K 2V4
Tel: 416-822-7910
subscribe@dandyhorsemagazine.com
dandyhorsemagazine.com
dandyhorsemagazine.com/blog
twitter.com/dandyhorse
www.facebook.com/11 6176385126268
Tammy Thorne, Editor-in-Chief,
tammy@dandyhorsemagazine.com

Jobber News
Owned By: Turnkey Media Solutions Inc.
48 Lumsden Cres., Whitby, ON L1R 1G5
www.autoserviceworld.com
twitter.com/jobbernews

Circulation: 20,000
Frequency: Monthly
Peter Bulmer, Publisher, peter@turnkey.media
Christine Hogg, Editor, christine@turnkey.media

Aviation & Aerospace

Canadian Aviator Magazine
Previous Name: Aviator Magazine
#802, 1166 Alberni St., Vancouver, BC V6E 3Z3
Tel: 604-428-0261; *Fax:* 604-620-0425
canadianaviatormagazine.com
www.facebook.com/CanadianAviatorMedia
Frequency: 6 times a year
Includes Aviators Blue Pages, a directory of aviation business,
products, services & attractions.
Steve Drinkwater, Publisher, steve@canadianaviator.com
Russ Niles, Editor, 250-546-6743, russ@canadianaviator.com

Helicopters
Owned By: Annex Business Media
PO Box 530, 105 Donly Dr. South, Simcoe, ON N3Y 4N5
Fax: 519-429-3094
Toll-Free: 888-599-2228
www.helicoptersmagazine.com
twitter.com/helicopters_mag
www.facebook.com/HelicoptersMagazine
Frequency: 5 times a year
Coverage of commercial, corporate, general & military
rotary-wing aviation in Canada & around the world.
Jon Robinson, Editor, jrobinson@annexbusinessmedia.com

Wings
Owned By: Annex Business Media
PO Box 530, 105 Donly Dr. South, Simcoe, ON N3Y 4N5
Fax: 519-429-3094
Toll-Free: 888-599-2228
www.wingsmagazine.com
www.linkedin.com/company/wings-media
twitter.com/wings_magazine
www.fa cebook.com/WingsMag
Frequency: 6 times a year
Jon Robinson, Editor, jrobinson@annexbusinessmedia.com

Baking & Bakers' Supplies

Bakers Journal
Owned By: Annex Business Media
PO Box 530, 105 Donly Dr. South, Simcoe, ON N3Y 4N5
Fax: 519-429-3094
Toll-Free: 888-599-2228
www.bakersjournal.com
www.youtube.com/user/bakersjournal
twitter.com/BakersJournal
www.faceb ook.com/BakersJournal
Frequency: 10 times a year
Martin McAnulty, Publisher,
mmcanulty@annexbusinessmedia.com
Naomi Szeben, Editor, 416-510-5244,
nszeben@annexbusinessmedia.com

Barbers & Beauticians

Canadian Hairdresser Magazine
1300 Bay St., 2nd Fl., Toronto, ON M5R 3K8
Tel: 416-923-1111
www.canhair.com
www.youtube.com/user/CanadianHairdresser
twitter.com/canhair
Circulation: 34,000
Frequency: 10 times a year
Joan Harrison, CEO & Editorial Director, joan@canhair.com

Salon Magazine
Owned By: Salon Communications Inc.
#202, 183 Bathurst St., Toronto, ON M5T 2R7
Tel: 416-869-3131; *Fax:* 416-869-3008
info@salonmagazine.ca
www.salonmagazine.ca
www.instagram.com/salonmagazine
twitter.com/Salon_Magazine
www.facebook.com/SalonMag

Frequency: 9 times a year
Laura Dunphy, Group Publisher, laura@salonmagazine.ca
Veronica Boodhan, Editor-in-Chief, veronica@salonmagazine.ca

Boating & Yachting

Poker Runs America Magazine
Owned By: Taylor Publishing Group
#2, 1121 Invicta Dr., Oakville, ON L6H 2R2
Tel: 905-844-8218; *Fax:* 905-844-8219
Toll-Free: 800-354-9145
info@pokerrunsamerica.com
www.pokerrunsamerica.com
www.youtube.com/user/steveeditor123
twitter.com/pokerrunamerica
www .facebook.com/PokerRunsAmerica

Books

Open Shelf
Previous Name: Access
Owned By: Ontario Library Association
2 Toronto St., 3rd Fl., Toronto, ON M5C 2B6
Tel: 416-363-3388; *Fax:* 416-941-9581
Toll-Free: 866-873-9867
info@accessola.com
www.accessola.org
www.youtube.com/user/ONLibraryAssoc
twitter.com/OpenShelfOLA
www.faceb ook.com/accessola
Ontario Library Association's online magazine
Martha Attridge Bufton, Editor-in-Chief

Broadcasting

Broadcast Dialogue
18 Turtle Path, Lagoon City, ON L0K 1B0
Tel: 705-484-0752
www.broadcastdialogue.com
Circulation: 7,200
Publishers for the Canadian broadcasting industry including
consultants, associations, engineers, suppliers, manufacturers &
related industry managers
Howard Christensen, Publisher,
howard@broadcastdialogue.com
Ingrid Christensen, Operations, ingrid@broadcastdialogue.com

Playback
Owned By: Brunico Communications Ltd.
#100, 366 Adelaide St. West, Toronto, ON M5V 1R9
Tel: 416-408-2300; *Fax:* 416-408-0870
Toll-Free: 888-278-6426
playbackonline.ca
www.instagram.com/playbackinstagram
twitter.com/PlaybackOnline
www.fac ebook.com/playbackonline
Jenn Kuzmyk, Publisher & Executive Director,
jkuzmyk@brunico.com
Liza Sardi, Editor-in-Chief & Director, Content,
lsardi@brunico.com

Building & Construction

BSIA News Magazine
Building Supply Industry Association of BC, #2, 19299 -
94th Ave., Surrey, BC V4N 4E6
Tel: 604-513-2205; *Fax:* 604-513-2206
Toll-Free: 888-711-5656
www.bsiabc.ca
twitter.com/BSIAofBC
www.facebook.com/BSIABC
Circulation: 1,000
Frequency: 6 times a year
Thomas Foreman, President

Building Magazine
Owned By: iQ Business Media Inc.
#302, 101 Duncan Mill Rd., Toronto, ON M3B 1Z3
Tel: 416-441-2085
circulation@building.ca
www.building.ca
twitter.com/Building_mag
www.facebook.com/buildingmagazine.canada

Circulation: 10,737
Frequency: 6 times a year
Publishes information on Canada's building products & the
companies that distribute & manufacture them
Steve Wilson, Senior Publisher, 416-441-2085 ext.105,
swilson@canadianarchitect.com
Peter Sobchak, Editor, 416-441-2085 ext.107, peter@building.ca

Canadian Apartment Magazine
Owned By: MediaEdge Communications Inc.
c/o MediaEdge Communications Inc., #500, 2001 Sheppard
Ave. East, Toronto, ON M2J 4Z8
Tel: 416-512-8186; *Fax:* 416-512-8344
Toll-Free: 866-216-0860
www.reminetwork.com/canadian-apartment-magazine
twitter.com/cdnapartmentmag
www.facebook.com/cammediaedge
Circulation: 12,000
Frequency: 6 times a year
Sean Foley, Publisher, seanf@mediaedge.ca
Erin Ruddy, Editor, erinr@mediaedge.ca

Canadian Contractor
Owned By: Annex Business Media
80 Valleybrook Dr., Toronto, ON M3B 2S9
Tel: 647-407-0754
www.canadiancontractor.ca
Circulation: 30,022
Frequency: 6 times a year
Rob Koci, Publisher, rkoci@canadiancontractor.ca
Stephen Payne, Editor, 416-442-5600 x 6784,
spayne@canadiancontractor.ca

Canadian Property Management (CPM)
Owned By: MediaEdge Communications Inc.
c/o MediaEdge Communications Inc., #500, 2001 Sheppard
Ave. East, Toronto, ON M2J 4Z8
Tel: 416-512-8186; *Fax:* 416-512-8344
Toll-Free: 866-216-0860
www.reminetwork.com/canadian-property-management
twitter.com/CDNPropMgmt
www.facebook.com/cpmmediaedge
Circulation: 12,000
Frequency: 6 times a year
Sean Foley, Publisher, seanf@mediaedge.ca
Barbara Carss, Editor-in-Chief, barbc@mediaedge.ca

CondoBusiness
Owned By: MediaEdge Communications Inc.
c/o MediaEdge Communications Inc., #500, 2001 Sheppard
Ave. East, Toronto, ON M2J 4Z8
Tel: 416-512-8186; *Fax:* 416-512-8344
Toll-Free: 866-216-0860
www.reminetwork.com/condobusiness
twitter.com/condobusiness
www.facebook.com/condomediaedge
Circulation: 6,250
Frequency: 6 times a year
Sean Foley, Publisher, seanf@mediaedge.ca
Rebecca Melnyk, Editor, rebeccam@mediaedge.ca

Construction in Focus
Owned By: FMG Publishing Inc.
7071 Bayers Rd., Halifax, NS
Tel: 647-479-2163
info@fmgpublishing.com
www.constructioninfocus.com
Other information: Advertising: accounts@fmgpublishing.com
Circulation: 112,700
Frequency: Monthly
Provides full coverage of the construction industry, including
news & events, & highlights leading construction, design, &
architectural firms
Jaime McKee, Editor

Construction411
Anciennement: Annuaire Téléphonique de la
Construction du Québec
CP 590, 22, rue St-Charles, Sainte-Thérèse, QC J7E 2A4
Tél: 450-437-1600; *Téléc:* 450-437-0723
Ligne sans frais: 800-437-0547
info@optilog.com
www.construction411.com
twitter.com/optilog
www.facebook.com/construction411
Tirage: 7 200
Fréquence: Annuellement
Directory of construction needs
Michel Vaudrin, Éditeur & Rédacteur

Construire

L'Association de la Construction du Québec, 9200, boul Métropolitain est, Montréal, QC H1K 4L2

Tél: 514-354-0609; Téléc: 514-354-8292
Ligne sans frais: 888-868-3424
info@acq.org
www.acqconstruire.com

Tirage: 25 000
Fréquence: 4 fois par an
Annie Hulmann, Rédactrice en chef

Equipment Journal

Pace Publishing Limited, #6, 5160 Explorer Dr., Mississauga, ON L4W 4T7

Tel: 905-629-7500; Fax: 800-210-5799
Toll-Free: 800-667-8541
info@equipmentjournal.com
www.equipmentjournal.com
www.linkedin.com/company/equipment-journal
twitter.com/EquipJournal
www.facebook.com/EquipmentJournal

Frequency: 17 times a year, every 3 weeks
Max Carrington, Editor, max@equipmentjournal.com

Formes

6718, rue Chambord, Montréal, QC H2G 3C3

Tél: 514-736-7637; Téléc: 514-272-3477
Ligne sans frais: 877-367-6379
www.formes.ca

Fréquence: 6 fois par an
Claude Paquin, Éditeur, cpaquin@formes.ca

Heavy Equipment Guide

Owned By: Baum Publications Ltd.
Baum Publications Ltd., 124 - 2323 Boundary Rd., Vancouver, BC V5M 4V8

Tel: 604-291-9900; Fax: 604-291-1906
Toll-Free: 888-286-3630
www.baumpub.com

Circulation: 23,000
Frequency: 9 times a year
Engelbert J. Baum, President, ebaum@baumpub.com
Ken Singer, Publisher, ksinger@baumpub.com
Lawrence Buser, Editorial Director, lbuser@baumpub.com

Journal Constructo

Tél: 514-856-6636
constructopub@tc.tc
www.groupeconstructo.com/publications/journal-constructo
Fréquence: 50 fois par an

Manufacturing in Focus

Owned By: FMG Publishing Inc.
7071 Bayers Rd., Halifax, NS

Tel: 647-479-2163
info@fmgpublishing.com
www.manufacturinginfocus.com
Other information: Advertising: accounts@fmgpublishing.com
Circulation: 128,900
Frequency: Monthly
Covers the North American manufacturing industry, including automation & distribution
Tim Hocken, Editor, tim.hocken@fmgpublishing.com

On-Site

Owned By: Annex Business Media
#400, 111 Gordon Baker Rd., Toronto, ON M2H 3R1

Tel: 416-510-6794; Fax: 416-510-5140
www.on-sitemag.com
www.linkedin.com/company/on-site-magazine
twitter.com/OnSiteMag
www.facebook.com/OnSiteMag

Circulation: 22,000
Frequency: 4 times a year
Serving the commercial construction industry.
Peter Leonard, Publisher, pleonard@on-sitemag.com
David Kennedy, Editor, dkennedy@on-sitemag.com

Ontario Home Builder

Owned By: Ontario Home Builders' Association
#101, 20 Upjohn Rd., Toronto, ON M3B 2V9

info@laureloak.ca
www.ohba.ca/magazine

Circulation: 30,000
Frequency: 6 times a year
Sheryl Humphreys, Publisher, sheryl@laureloak.ca
Ted McIntyre, Editor, ted@laureloak.ca

Ottawa Construction News

#57, 1554 Carling Ave., Ottawa, ON K1Z 7M4

Tel: 613-699-2057; Fax: 613-702-5357
Toll-Free: 888-627-8717
www.ottawaconstructionnews.com
www.linkedin.com/company/ottawa-construction-news
twitter.com/OttConNews
www.facebook.com/8494799063

Circulation: 12,000
Frequency: 12 times a year
Tim Lawlor, Contact, tlawlor@cnrgp.com
Katherine Jeffrey, Contact, kjeffrey@cnrgp.com

Business & Finance

Advisor's Edge

Owned By: Newcom Media Inc.
#400, 5353 Dundas St. West, Toronto, ON M9B 6H8

service@newcom.ca
www.advisor.ca
www.linkedin.com/company/advisor-ca
twitter.com/advisorca
www.faceb ook.com/advisorsedgemagazine

Frequency: 7 times a year
Advisor's Edge magazine is focused on the information needs of Canadian retail financial advisors (brokers, financial planners, insurance specialists, mutual fund salespeople & bank-based consultants). With an emphasis on practice management, the magazine informs on industry trends, investment insurance products & strategies, as well as marketing & client relationship best practices.
Melissa Shin, Editorial Director, mshin@newcom.ca
Mark Burgess, Managing Editor, markb@newcom.ca

Les Affaires

Détenteur: Groupe Contex Inc.
1100, boul René-Lévesque ouest, 24e étage, Montréal, QC H3B 4X9

Tél: 514-392-9000; Téléc: 514-392-1586
Ligne sans frais: 800-361-7215
lesaffaires@cdsglobal.ca
www.lesaffaires.com
www.youtube.com/user/LesAffairesTV
twitter.com/la_lesaffaires
www.face book.com/la.lesaffaires

Tirage: 77 174
Fréquence: 46 fois par an; aussi Affaires 500, PME, Affaires plus (10 fois par an, 93 288)
Il est reconnu pour sa couverture des grandes sociétés canadiennes, des petites et moyennes entreprises québécoises, de l'économie canadienne et des affaires publiques. La moitié de son contenu est consacrée aux finances personnelles et aux placements avec diverses pages spécialisées, des tableaux et des graphiques.
Sylvain Bédard, Éditeur
Géraldine Martin, Éditrice adjointe et rédactrice-en-chef

Affaires Plus Magazine

Détenteur: Groupe Contex Inc.
1100, boul René-Lévesque ouest, 24e étage, Montréal, QC H3B 4X9

Tél: 514-392-9000; Téléc: 514-392-4726
Ligne sans frais: 800-361-7215
lesaffaires@kckglobal.com
www.lesaffaires.com
www.youtube.com/user/LesAffairesTV
twitter.com/la_lesaffaires
www.face book.com/100306918236

Tirage: 77 000
Fréquence: 10 fois par an
Créé en 1978, le magazine Affaires PLUS est le magazine d'affaires au plus fort tirage et au plus fort lectorat au Québec. Le magazine est bâti autour de trois axes: mon argent, ma carrière, ma vie, qui déterminent à la fois le positionnement et le contenu d'Affaires PLUS
Sylvain Bédard, Éditeur
Géraldine Martin, Éditrice adjointe et rédactrice-en-chef

Alberta Venture

Owned By: Venture Publishing Inc.
10259 - 105 St., Edmonton, AB T5J 1E3

Tel: 780-990-0839; Fax: 780-425-4921
Toll-Free: 866-227-4276
admin@albertaventure.com
www.albertaventure.com
Other information: www.instagram.com/albertaventure
www.linkedin.com/groups/Alberta-Venture-3230251
twitter.com/AlbertaVenture
www.facebook.com/albertaventure

Circulation: 40,800
Frequency: Monthly
Alberta Venture keeps readers informed about Alberta's

business community, including trends, issues, people and events.
Ruth Kelly, President & CEO

Atlantic Business Magazine

Owned By: Communications Ten Limited
PO Box 2356 C, #302, 95 LeMarchant Rd., St. John's, NL A1C 6E7

Tel: 709-726-9300; Fax: 709-726-3013
www.atlanticbusinessmagazine.com
www.linkedin.com/company/atlantic-business-magazine
twitter.com/Atlantic Bus
www.facebook.com/atlanticbusinessmagazine

Circulation: 35,000
Frequency: Bi-monthly
An independently owned, bi-monthly glossy publication that covers all areas of business within the four Atlantic provinces.
Hubert Hutton, Publisher, 709-726-9300 ext.226, hhutton@atlanticbusinessmagazine.com
Dawn Chafe, Executive Editor, 709-726-9300 ext.224, dchafe@atlanticbusinessmagazine.com

Avantages

Détenteur: Groupe Contex Inc.
1100, boul René-Lévesque ouest, 24e étage, Montréal, QC H3B 4X9

Tél: 514-392-2009
www.avantages.ca/magazine
twitter.com/revueavantages

Fréquence: 4 fois par an
Alison Webb, Éditrice, alison.webb@groupecontex.ca
Pierre-Luc Trudel, Rédacteur en chef, pierre-luc.trudel@groupecontex.ca

Backbone Magazine

187 Rondoval Cres., North Vancouver, BC V7N 2W6

Tel: 604-986-5352; Fax: 604-986-5309
info@backbonemag.com
www.backbonemag.com
www.linkedin.com/groups/Backbone-magazine-3999379
twitter.com/BackboneMa g
www.facebook.com/backbone.canada

Circulation: 115,000
Frequency: 6 times a year
Backbone magazine's aim is to provide business people with a tangible tool to enhance the way they do business in Canada's New Economy
Steve Dietrich, Publisher & Editor in Chief, sdietrich@backbonemag.com

BCBusiness

Owned By: Canada Wide Media Limited
#230, 4321 Still Creek Dr., Burnaby, BC

Tel: 604-299-7311; Fax: 604-299-9188
www.bcbusiness.ca
twitter.com/bcbusiness
www.facebook.com/bcbusiness

Focuses on business in British Columbia. Prints annual special editions: B.C.'s Top 100 Companies, Entrepreneur of the Year, & the Best Companies to Work for in B.C.
Matt O'Grady, Editor-in-Chief, mogrady@canadawide.com

BCBusiness Magazine

Owned By: Canada Wide Media Limited
#230, 4321 Still Creek Dr., Burnaby, BC V5C 6S7

Tel: 604-299-7311; Fax: 604-299-9188
bcb@canadawide.com
www.bcbusinessonline.ca
www.youtube.com/user/BCBusinessOnline
twitter.com/bcbusiness
www.faceb ook.com/bcbusiness

Frequency: 10 times a year
Nick Rockel, Editor-in-Chief, nrockel@canadawide.com

Benefits & Pensions Monitor

Owned By: Powershift Communications Inc.
c/o Powershift Communications Inc., #501, 245 Fairview Mall Dr., Toronto, ON M2J 4T1

Tel: 416-494-1066; Fax: 416-494-2536
bpmmagazine.com

Circulation: 20,095
Frequency: 8 times a year
Brian McKerchar, President
Joe Hornyak, Associate Publisher & Executive Editor, jhornyak@powershift.ca

Benefits Canada

Owned By: Groupe Contex Inc.
1100, boul René-Lévesque ouest, Montréal, ON H3B 4X9

Tél: 514-392-2009
benefits@halldata.com
www.benefitscanada.com
twitter.com/BenCanMag

Frequency: Monthly
Provides information & analysis on pensions, benefits, healthcare & investments. The publication targets the plan sponsor community, particularly those employers with more than 500 employees.
Jennifer Paterson, Editor, jennifer.paterson@contexgroup.ca

BIZ Magazine
Previous Name: BIZ Hamilton/Halton Business Report; Hamilton Business Report
Owned By: Postmedia Network Inc.
940 Main St. West, Hamilton, ON L8S 1B1
Tel: 905-522-6117; *Fax:* 905-769-1105
www.bizmagazine.ca
twitter.com/biz_mag
Circulation: 24,000
Frequency: 4 times a year
Business publication in the Hamilton / Burlington region, with award-winning features, profiles, real-life photography & controversial opinions

Business Edge News Magazine
#201, 318 - 26th Ave. SW, Calgary, AB T2S 2T9
Tel: 403-769-9359
info@businessedge.ca
www.businessedge.ca
www.facebook.com/BusinessEdgeNewsMagazine
Circulation: 157,000
Frequency: 18 times annually
Delivered to businesses throughout Western & Central Canada.
Rob Driscoll, Publisher, Rob@BusinessEdge.ca

Business Elite Canada
4 Robert Speck Pkwy., 15th Fl., Mississauga, ON L4Z 1S1
Tel: 905-366-7301; *Fax:* 905-248-3329
info@becmag.com
www.businesselitecanada.com
twitter.com/BECMagazine
www.facebook.com/354069204610067
Circulation: 40,000
Business Elite Canada focuses on successful businesses & business leaders.
Sanjeev Amir, Publisher, samir@becmag.com
Cheryl Long, Editor, editor@becmag.com

Business in Calgary
Owned By: OT Communications
#1025, 101 - 6th Ave. SW, Calgary, AB T2P 3P4
Tel: 403-264-3270; *Fax:* 403-264-3276
info@businessincalgary.com
businessincalgary.com
www.facebook.com/BusinessinCalgary
Circulation: 28,200
Frequency: Monthly
Articles about the people, trends & events that make Calgary a prominent business centre in the west.
Pat Ottmann, Publisher, pat@businessincalgary.com
Tim Ottmann, Publisher, tim@businessincalgary.com
John Hardy, Editor, hardy@businessincalgary.com

Business in Edmonton
Owned By: OT Communications
#1780, 10020 - 101A Ave. SW, Edmonton, AB T5J 3G2
Tel: 780-638-1777; *Fax:* 587-520-5701
info@businessinedmonton.com
businessinedmonton.com
twitter.com/BusInEdmonton
www.facebook.com/businessinedmonton
Circulation: 27,000
Frequency: Monthly
Nerissa McNaughton, Editor

Business in Focus
Owned By: FMG Publishing Inc.
7071 Bayers Rd., Halifax, NS
Tel: 647-479-2163
info@fmgpublishing.com
www.businessinfocusmagazine.com
Other information: Advertising: accounts@fmgpublishing.com
Circulation: 468,200
Frequency: Monthly
Provides insight into North American business through interviews with Managers, Founders, Directors, & CEOs
Tim Hocken, Editor, tim.hocken@fmgpublishing.com

The Business Link Niagara
Owned By: Business Link Media Group
#101, 4056 Dorchester Rd., Niagara Falls, ON L2E 6M9
Tel: 905-646-9366
info@businesslinkmedia.com
businesslinkhamilton.com
Jim Shields, Publisher, jim@businesslinkmedia.com

Business London
Previous Name: London Business Magazine
Owned By: Postmedia Network Inc.
#201, 210 Dundas St., London, ON N6A 5J3
lfpress.com/category/business-london
Frequency: Monthly
Lisa Catania, Publisher, lcatania@postmedia.com
Madisyn Latham, Managing Editor, mlatham@postmedia.com

Business Review Canada (BRCA)
www.businessreviewcanada.ca
www.facebook.com/BizReviewCanada
Digital magazine aimed at business executives.
Cutter Slagle, Editor, cutter.slagle@businessreviewcanada.ca

Canada Japan Journal
Previous Name: Canada Japan Business Journal
Also Known As: Japan Advertising Ltd.
c/o Japan Advertising Ltd., #403, 602 West Hastings St., Vancouver, BC V6B 1P2
Tel: 604-688-0303; *Fax:* 604-688-1487
info@canadajournal.com
canadajournal.com
twitter.com/canadajapan
www.facebook.com/CanadaJournal
Frequency: Monthly; Japanese
Taka Aoki, Publisher

Canadian Business Franchise / L'entreprise
Owned By: Kenilworth Media Inc.
c/o Kenilworth Media Inc., #710, 15 Wertheim Ct., Richmond Hill, ON L4B 3H7
Tel: 905-771-7333; *Fax:* 905-771-3546
Toll-Free: 800-409-8688
www.franchiseinfo.ca
twitter.com/FranchiseFYI
www.facebook.com/CanadianBusinessFranchiseMagaz ine
Frequency: Bi-monthly
Features articles on franchise advice from bankers, lawyers & franchise specialists.

Canadian Equipment Finance
Owned By: Lloydmedia, Inc.
137 Main St. North, 3rd Fl., Markham, ON L3P 1Y2
Tel: 905-201-6600; *Fax:* 905-201-6601
Toll-Free: 800-668-1838
canadianequipmentfinance.com
Circulation: 6,100
Frequency: Bi-monthly
Steve Lloyd, President, steve.lloyd@lloydmedia.ca

Canadian Gaming Business
Owned By: MediaEdge Communications Inc.
c/o MediaEdge Communications Inc., #500, 2001 Sheppard Ave. East, Toronto, ON M2J 4Z8
Tel: 416-512-8186; *Fax:* 416-512-8344
Toll-Free: 866-216-0860
www.canadiangamingbusiness.com
Chuck Nervick, Publisher, chuckn@mediaedge.ca
Tom Nightingale, Managing Editor

The Canadian Manager
Canadian Institute of Management, #311, 80 Bradford St., Barrie, ON L4N 6S7
Tel: 705-725-8926; *Fax:* 705-725-8196
admin@cim.ca
www.cim.ca/resources/cim-publications/canadian-manager
Circulation: 12,000
Frequency: Quarterly

Canadian Treasurer (CT)
Owned By: Lloydmedia, Inc.
137 Main St. North, 3rd Fl., Markham, ON L3P 1Y2
Tel: 905-201-6600; *Fax:* 905-201-6601
Toll-Free: 800-668-1838
canadiantreasurer.com
Circulation: 6,000
Frequency: Quarterly
Steve Lloyd, Editor, steve@canadiantreasurer.com

Chamber Vision
Owned By: Metro Guide Publishing
Greater Moncton Chamber of Commerce, #200, 1273 Main St., Moncton, NB E1C 0P4
Tel: 506-857-2883
info@gmcc.nb.ca
gmcc.nb.ca/en-us/media/publications/chambervision.aspx
twitter.com/MonctonChamber
www.facebook.com/GreaterMonctonChamberOfCommerce
Circulation: 5000
Frequency: 6 times a year

Conseiller
Détenteur: Newcom Media Inc.
1100, boul René-Lévesque ouest, Montréal, QC H3B 4X9
Tél: 514-392-9000; *Téléc:* 514-392-4726
conseiller@newcom.ca
www.conseiller.ca
www.linkedin.com/company/conseillerca
twitter.com/Conseillerca
www.fac ebook.com/conseillerca
Fréquence: 10 fois par an

Contact Management
Owned By: Lloydmedia, Inc.
137 Main St. North, 3rd Fl., Markham, ON L3P 1Y2
Tel: 905-201-6600; *Fax:* 905-201-6601
Toll-Free: 800-668-1838
dmn.ca/contact-management
Circulation: 5,300
Frequency: Quarterly
Sarah O'Connor, Editor, sarah@contactmanagement.ca

Corporate Knights (CK)
Owned By: Corporate Knights Inc.
#207, 147 Spadina Ave., Toronto, ON M5V 2L7
Tel: 416-203-4674 *Toll-Free:* 416-946-1770
inquiries@corporateknights.com
www.corporateknights.com
www.linkedin.com/company/corporate-knights-inc
twitter.com/corporateknight
www.facebook.com/corporateknights
Circulation: 147,750
Frequency: Quarterly
The magazine's focus is corporate responsibility.
Toby Heaps, Publisher & Editor-in-Chief
Adria Vasil, Managing Editor

CPA Magazine
Previous Name: CA Magazine; CMA Management Magazine
277 Wellington St. West, Toronto, ON M5V 3H2
Tel: 416-977-3222; *Fax:* 416-977-8585
Toll-Free: 800-268-3793
www.cpacanada.ca/en/connecting-and-news/cpa-magazine
Circulation: 242,377
Frequency: 10 times a year
CPA Magazine is published by Chartered Professional Accountants Canada (CPA). Articles about careers in chartered accounting are featured while current issues are discussed & explained. The magazine also deals with a wide variety of business topics from the Chartered Accountant's perspective
Nicholas Cheung, Vice-President, Member Services, CPA Canada
Okey Chigbo, Editor

Exchange Magazine for Business
Owned By: Exchange Business Communication Inc.
c/o Exchange Business Communication Inc., PO Box 248, Waterloo, ON N2J 4A4
Tel: 519-886-0298; *Fax:* 519-886-6409
editor@exchangemagazine.com
www.exchangemagazine.com
twitter.com/ExMorningPost
Circulation: 17,500
Frequency: 9 times a year
Covers business news in the Kitchener-Waterloo area
Jon Rohr, Editor-in-chief, jon.rohr@exchangemagazine.com

Finance et Investissement
Détenteur: Newcom Media Inc.
1100, boul René-Lévesque ouest, 24e étage, Montréal, QC H3B 4X9
Tél: 514-392-9000; *Téléc:* 514-392-4726
www.finance-investissement.com
www.linkedin.com/company/finance-et-investissement
twitter.com/FI_Quebec
www.facebook.com/financeinvestissement
Tirage: 30 000
Fréquence: 16 fois par an
Le est devenu la source d'information privilégiée des représentants en épargne collective, des conseillers en valeurs mobilières, des conseillers en sécurité financière et des planificateurs financiers.
Richard Cloutier, Rédacteur en chef, richard@newcom.ca

Financial Operations
Owned By: Lloydmedia, Inc.
137 Main St. North, 3rd Fl., Markham, ON L3P 1Y2
Tel: 905-201-6600; *Fax:* 905-201-6601
Toll-Free: 800-668-1838
financialoperations.ca
Frequency: Quarterly
Karen Treml, Editorial Contact, 905-201-6600 Ext.223

Franchise Canada Directory
Canadian Franchise Association, #116, 5399 Eglinton Ave. West, Toronto, ON M9C 5K6
Tel: 416-695-2896; *Fax:* 416-695-1950
Toll-Free: 800-665-4232
info@cfa.ca
www.cfa.ca
Frequency: Annually
Lauren Huneault, Editor, editor@cfa.ca

FranchiseCanada Magazine
c/o Canadian Franchise Association, #116, 5399 Eglinton Ave. West, Toronto, ON M9C 5K6
cfa.ca/franchisecanada/franchise-canada-magazine
Frequency: Bi-monthly
The magazine is geared at entrepreneurs interested in acquiring a franchise. It contains editorial from authorities in the industry as well as tips on how to establish a successful franchise.
Joelle Kid, Editor, jkidd@cfa.ca

Investment Executive (IE)
Owned By: Newcom Media Inc.
#400, 5353 Dundas St. West, Toronto, ON M9B 6H8
Tel: 416-733-7600; *Fax:* 416-218-3624
Toll-Free: 888-366-4200
editorial_investmentexecutive@newcom.ca
www.investmentexecutive.com
www.linkedin.com/company/investment-executive
twitter.com/IE_Canada
www.facebook.com/InvestmentExecutive
Circulation: 120,000
Frequency: 16 times a year
Investment Executive is Canada's national newspaper for financial service industry professionals. Topics such as mutual funds, investment research, technology, estate planning, tax, building relationships with clients & developing products & services for the client of the future. Sister publication is Finance et Investissement.
Melissa Shin, Editorial Director, mshin@newcom.ca

Investor's Digest of Canada
Also Known As: The Digest
Owned By: MPL Communications Inc.
c/o MPL Communications Inc., #700, 133 Richmond St. West, Toronto, ON M5H 3M8
Tel: 416-869-1177 *Toll-Free:* 800-504-8846
customers@mplcomm.com
www.adviceforinvestors.com/investors-digest
Frequency: 24 times a year

Ivey Business Journal (IBJ)
Previous Name: Quarterly Review of Commerce; Business Quarterly
c/o Richard Ivey School of Business, Western University, London, ON N6A 3K7
iveybusinessjournal.com
Frequency: 6 times a year
Covers articles about e-business, managing uncertainty, knowledge management, marketing, strategy & other topics.
Thomas Watson, Editor, watson@ivey.ca

MBiz Magazine
Owned By: Manitoba Chambers of Commerce
c/o Manitoba Chambers of Commerce, 227 Portage Ave., Winnipeg, MB R3B 2A6
mbchamber.mb.ca/membership/mcc-publications
Frequency: 2 times a year
Magazine that highlights the success stories of local business & entrepreneurship. In partnership with the Winnipeg Free Press, it is distributed to all WFP subscribers, as well as the chamber of commerce members.

mbot Magazine
Previous Name: Business Bulletin
c/o Mississauga Board of Trade, #701, 77 City Centre Dr., Mississauga, ON L5B 1M5
www.mbot.com/mbot-magazine
Frequency: Quarterly
Business news & updates on MBOT activities.
Kelsey Lusk, Editor, klusk@mbot.com

MoneySense
Owned By: Rogers Media Inc.
1 Mount Pleasant Rd., 11th Fl., Toronto, ON M4Y 2Y5
Tel: 416-764-1400; *Fax:* 416-764-1376
www.moneysense.ca
www.linkedin.com/company/moneysense-magazine
twitter.com/MoneySenseMag
www.facebook.com/MoneySenseMagazine
Personal finance magazine, available online-only as of January 2017.
Ian Portsmouth, Publisher
David Thomas, Editor-in-Chief

Ottawa Business Journal (OBJ)
Owned By: Great River Media Inc.
PO Box 91585, Ottawa, ON K1W 1K0
Tel: 613-696-9494
info@obj.ca
www.obj.ca
www.linkedin.com/company/ottawa-business-journal
twitter.com/obj_news
www.facebook.com/OBJNews
Frequency: Quarterly
Ottawa Business Journal provides local business news & information for the national capital region.

Partners in Prosperity
Owned By: Manitoba Chambers of Commerce
c/o Manitoba Chambers of Commerce, 227 Portage Ave., Winnipeg, MB R3B 2A6
mbchamber.mb.ca/membership/mcc-publications
Circulation: 10,000
Frequency: Annual
The publication is a network support directory, providing information & services related to trade, tourism, education, industry, chamber affinity programs, as well as corporate member & local chamber listings.

Payments Business
Owned By: Lloydmedia, Inc.
137 Main St. North, 3rd Fl., Markham, ON L3P 1Y2
Tel: 905-201-6600; *Fax:* 905-201-6601
Toll-Free: 800-668-1838
paymentsbusiness.ca
Circulation: 9,000
Frequency: Bi-monthly
Brendan Read, Editor, brendan@dmn.ca

Port of Halifax
Owned By: Metro Guide Publishing
2882 Gottingen St., Halifax, NS B3K 3E2
Tel: 902-420-9943
publishers@metroguide.ca
metroguide.ca/port-of-halifax
Circulation: 4,000
Frequency: Quarterly
Port of Halifax Magazine features information about the Port of Halifax along with stories of interest to the international shipping community.

Québec Enterprise
269, ch de la Grande Côte, Rosemère, QC H7A 1J2
Tél: 450-420-8408; *Téléc:* 450-970-2205
magazine@quebecenterprise.com
www.quebecentreprise.ca
Tirage: 20 520
Fréquence: 5 fois par an
Magazine d'affaires couvrant les activités industrielles de toutes les régions du Québec.
Daniel Boisvert, Éditeur, 514-946-7696
François Hurtubise, Rédacteur en chef et directeur, Production

Québec Franchise
Previous Name: Québec Franchise & Microfranchise
Owned By: Top Franchise MS inc.
PO Box 72132 Atwater, Montréal, QC H3J 2Z6
Tel: 514-383-0034 *Toll-Free:* 888-575-0034
info@Quebec-Franchise.ca
www.quebec-franchise.qc.ca
twitter.com/QC_Franchise
www.facebook.com/quebecfranchise
Circulation: 7,500 copies
Frequency: 4 times a year
Spécialisé dans la franchise et les opportunités d'affaires au Québec et au Canada
Jacques Desforges, Président & Éditeur

RevolutionHer
Previous Name: MOMpreneur
#816, 420 Main St. East, Milton, ON L9T 5G3
Toll-Free: 877-247-8849
revher@revolutionher.com
revolutionher.com/magazine
www.linkedin.com/company/revolutionhertm
twitter.com/revolutionhertm
www.facebook.com/RevolutionHerTM
Frequency: Quarterly
Maria Locker, Founder & CEO

Rotman Management
Owned By: Rotman School of Management
105 St George St., Toronto, ON M5S 3E6
rotmanmag@rotman.utoronto.ca
www.rotman.utoronto.ca/connect/rotman-mag
twitter.com/RotmanMgmtMag
Frequency: 3 times a year

Karen Christensen, Editor-in-Chief, editor@rotman.utoronto.ca

Sounding Board
Owned By: Vancouver Media Group/Vancouver Board of Trade
World Trade Center, #400, 999 Canada Pl., Vancouver, BC V6C 3E1
Tel: 604-681-2111; *Fax:* 604-681-0437
contactus@boardoftrade.com
www.boardoftrade.com/publicationsresources/sounding-board.aspx
twitter.com/BoardofTrade
www.facebook.com/VancouverBoardofTrade
Circulation: 12,500
Frequency: 11 times a year
As the official monthly publication of The Vancouver Board of Trade, the Sounding Board newspaper provides analysis and discussion of regional and national issues facing the business community.
Greg Hoekstra, Manager, Communications, media@boardoftrade.com

The Taxpayer
#501, 2201 - 11th Ave., Regina, SK S4N 0N7
Tel: 306-352-7199 *Toll-Free:* 800-667-7933
admin@taxpayer.com
www.taxpayer.com/taxpayer-magazine
Frequency: 3 times a year
The Taxpayer is the flagship publication of the Canadian Taxpayers Federation (CTF). It provides updates on CTF happenings around the country as well as articles written by CTF researchers, spokespersons & guest editorials.

Thompson's World Insurance News
Owned By: First News Publishing Inc.
PO Box 1027, Waterloo, ON N2J 4S1
Tel: 519-579-2500
mpub@sympatico.ca
thompsonsnews.com
Frequency: Weekly (September-July)
An independent weekly publication for p&c insurance professionals.
Mark Publicover, Publisher & Managing Editor, mpub@rogers.com

Thunder Bay Business
Owned By: North Superior Publishing Inc.
#1402, 590 Beverly St., Thunder Bay, ON P7B 6H1
Tel: 807-623-2348; *Fax:* 807-623-7515
nspinc@tbaytel.net
www.thunderbaybusiness.ca
www.facebook.com/NorthSuperiorPublishing
Frequency: Monthly
Northwestern Ontario business publication.
Scott Sumner, President, North Superior Publishing Inc.

Up Here Business
Owned By: Up Here Publishing Ltd.
#102, 4510 - 50th Ave., Yellowknife, NT X1A 1B9
Tel: 867-766-6710; *Fax:* 867-669-0626
circ@uphere.ca
www.uphere.ca/sections/here-business

Wealth Professional
Owned By: Key Media Canada
#800, 312 Adelaide St. West, Toronto, ON M5V 1R2
Tel: 416-644-8740; *Fax:* 416-203-9083
subscriptions@kmimedia.ca
www.wealthprofessional.ca
twitter.com/wealth_proca
Frequency: Bi-Monthly
John Mackenzie, General Manager, Sales, 416-644-8740 ext.252, John.mackenzie@kmimedia.ca

Camping & Outdoor Recreation

RV Lifestyle Magazine
Owned By: Taylor Publishing Group
268.44 Crawford Cres., Milton, ON L0P 1B0
Tel: 905-844-8218; *Fax:* 905-844-5032
info@rvlifemag.com
www.rvlifemag.com
Frequency: 7 issues per year
William E. Taylor, Publisher
Norm Rosen, Editor, editor@rvlifemag.com

Chemicals & Chemical Process Industries

Canadian Process Equipment & Control News
#149, #35B, 10520 Yonge St., Richmond Hill, ON L4C 3C7
Tel: 905-770-8077; *Fax:* 905-770-8075
cpe@cpecn.com
www.cpecn.com

Circulation: 22,957
Frequency: 6 times a year
Mike Edwards, Editor, medwards@cpecn.com

Industrial Process Products & Technology
Owned By: Annex Business Media
#400, 111 Gordon Baker Rd., Toronto, ON M2H 3R1
www.ippt.ca
twitter.com/IPPTMagazine
www.facebook.com/IPPTMagazine
Frequency: 6 times a year
Don Horne, Editor, 416-510-5162, dhorne@ippt.ca

Process West
Owned By: Annex Business Media
#400, 111 Gordon Baker Rd., Toronto, ON M2H 3R1
www.processwest.ca
twitter.com/process_west
www.facebook.com/processwestmagazine
Frequency: 6 times a year
Don Horne, Editor, 416-510-5162, dhorne@ippt.ca

Clothing & Accessories

Trends Magazine
Previous Name: Canadian Apparel Magazine
Tel: 705-426-1712
www.trendsmagazine.ca
Circulation: 7,000
Business to business fashion magazine.

Computing & Technology

CIO Canada
Owned By: It World Canada Inc.
#302, 55 Town Centre Ct., Toronto, ON M1P 4X4
Tel: 416-290-0240; Fax: 416-290-0238
general@itworldcanada.com
www.itworldcanada.com/publication/cio
Circulation: 8,000
Frequency: 12 times a year
Shane Schick, Editor, sschick@itworldcanada.com

Computer Dealer News
Owned By: IT World Canada Inc.
#302, 55 Town Centre Ct., Toronto, ON M1P 4X4
Tel: 416-290-0240
www.computerdealernews.com
Paolo Del Nibletto, Editor, pdelnibletto@itwc.ca

Technologies for Worship Magazine
103 Niska Dr., Waterdown, ON L0R 2H3
Tel: 905-690-4709
www.tfwm.com
twitter.com/tfwm
www.facebook.com/TechnologiesForWorshipMagazine
Circulation: 30,000
Frequency: 10 times a year
Darryl Kirkland, Publisher
Michelle Makariak, Editor

Conventions & Meetings

Canadian Meetings + Events Expo
Previous Name: MeetingsCanada.com; M+IT
Magazine; IncentiveWorks
Owned By: Newcom Media Inc.
www.cmeexpo.ca
www.linkedin.com/company/cmeexpo
Circulation: 130,000
Sonia Audet, Editor, sonia@newcom.ca

Culture, Current Events

Eighteen Bridges
Owned By: Venture Publishing Inc.
Canadian Literature Centre, 3-5 Humanities Centre,
University of Alberta, Edmonton, AB T6G 2E5
ebmag@ualberta.ca
eighteenbridges.com
twitter.com/eighteenbridges
Curtis Gillespie, Editor & Publisher

Hush
1610 Pandora St., Vancouver, BC V5L 1L6
editor@hushmagazine.ca
www.hushmagazine.ca
www.youtube.com/user/HushMagazine
twitter.com/HUSHvancouver
www.facebook.com/HushVancouver
Barb Sligl, Editor

The Walrus
Owned By: Walrus Foundation
#B15, 411 Richmond St. E, Toronto, ON M5A 3S5
Tel: 416-971-5004 Toll-Free: 866-236-0475
info@walrusmagazine.com
walrusmagazine.com
twitter.com/walrusmagazine
www.facebook.com/thewalrusmagazine
Circulation: 60,000
Frequency: 10 times a year
Shelley Ambrose, Executive Director & Publisher, 416-971-5004
x 236, shelley.ambrose@walrusmagazine.com

Dentistry

Journal de l'Ordre des dentistes du Québec
Anciennement: Journal Dentaire du Québec
Ordre des dentistes du Québec, #1640, 800, boul
René-Lévesque ouest, Montréal, QC H3B 1X9
Tél: 514-875-8511; Téléc: 514-875-9049
journal@odq.qc.ca
www.odq.qc.ca
Tirage: 5 600
Fréquence: Quarterly
Carole Erdelyon, Rédactrice-en-chef

Oral Health Group
Owned By: Newcom Media Inc.
#400, 5353 Dundas St. West, Toronto, ON M9B 6H8
www.oralhealthgroup.com
www.linkedin.com/company/oralhealthgroup
twitter.com/Oralhealthgroup
www.facebook.com/OralHealthGroupCanada
Frequency: Monthly
Publishes Oral Health Magazine & Oral Hygiene Magazine.
Amy Bielby, Managing Editor, amy@newcom.ca

Drugs

L'Actualité pharmaceutique
Détenteur: EnsembleIQ
#800, 1200, av McGill College, Montréal, QC H3B 4G7
Ligne sans frais: 844-246-3190
www.professionsante.ca
Tirage: 8500
Fréquence: 10 fois par an
Caroline Bélisle, Directrice de marque, 514-843-2569,
cbelisle@ensembleiq.com

Pharmacy Practice + Business
Owned By: EnsembleIQ
#1510, 2300 Yonge St., Toronto, ON M4P 1E4
Tel: 416-256-9908
www.ensembleiq.com
twitter.com/PPr_Plus
www.facebook.com/PharmacyPracticePlusBusiness
Circulation: 22,375
Frequency: 6 times a year
Vicki Wood, Editor
Jackie Quemby, Publisher

Québec Pharmacie
Détenteur: EnsembleIQ
#800, 1200, av McGill College, Montréal, QC H3B 4G7
Tél: 514-843-2569
www.professionsante.ca/pharmaciens/magazines/quebec-pharm
acie
twitter.com/quebecpharmacie

Education

The ATA Magazine
The Alberta Teachers' Association, 11010 - 142nd St.,
Edmonton, AB T5N 2R1
Tel: 780-447-9400; Fax: 780-455-6481
Toll-Free: 800-232-7208
government@teachers.ab.ca
www.teachers.ab.ca
Circulation: 39,500
Frequency: 3 times a year
Joni Turville, Editor-in-Chief, joni.turville@ata.ab.ca
Cory Hare, Managing Editor, cory.hare@ata.ab.ca

Catholic Teacher Magazine
Previous Name: Agenda
c/o Ontario English Catholic Teachers' Association, #400, 65
St. Clair Ave. East, Toronto, ON M4T 2Y8
Tel: 416-925-2493; Fax: 416-925-7764
Toll-Free: 800-268-7230
contact@catholicteachers.ca
www.catholicteachers.ca
twitter.com/oecta
www.facebook.com/oecta

Circulation: 46,000
Frequency: 5 per annum
Official publication of the Ontario English Catholic Teachers'
Association; provides editorials, professional development news,
legal advice, bargaining updates, teacher profiles & feature
articles on educational, social justice & political topics
Michelle Despault, Editor

Education Forum
c/o Ontario Secondary School Teachers' Federation, 49
Mobile Dr., Toronto, ON M4A 1H5
education-forum.ca
twitter.com/EditorEdForum
www.facebook.com/EducationForum
Circulation: 60,000
Frequency: 3 times a year
Tracey Germa, Editor

ESL in Canada Directory
5750 Temperance Ave., Niagara Falls, ON L2G 4A8
Tel: 647-247-3897
www.eslincanada.com
Frequency: 2 times a year
James McBride, Coordinator

The Manitoba Teacher
c/o The Manitoba Teachers' Society, 191 Harcourt St.,
Winnipeg, MB R3J 3H2
www.mbteach.org
Circulation: 16,500
Frequency: 7 times per year (Sept.-June)
Matea Tuhtar, Contact, Advertising, advertising@mbteach.org

Professionally Speaking / Pour parler profession
c/o Ontario College of Teachers, 101 Bloor St. West,
Toronto, ON M5S 0A1
Tel: 416-961-8800; Fax: 416-961-8822
Toll-Free: 888-534-2222
info@oct.ca
professionallyspeaking.oct.ca
Frequency: Quarterly

Teach Magazine
#321, 1655 Dupont St., Toronto, ON M6P 3T1
Tel: 416-537-2103
info@teachmag.com
www.teachmag.com
Circulation: 30,000
Frequency: 6 times a year
Wili Liberman, Publisher & Editor

University Affairs / Affaires universitaires
c/o Assn. of Universities & Colleges of Canada, #1710, 350
Albert St., Ottawa, ON K1R 1B1
Tel: 613-563-1236; Fax: 613-563-9745
ua@univcan.ca
www.universityaffairs.ca
www.youtube.com/user/universityaffairsca
twitter.com/ua_magazine
www.facebook.com/universityaffairs
Frequency: 6 times a year
Philip Landon, Publisher, plandon@univcan.ca
Michel Proulx, Editor, mproulx@univcan.ca

Electrical Equipment & Electronics

Electrical Business
Owned By: Annex Business Media
#400, 111 Gordon Baker Rd., Toronto, ON M2H 3R1
Tel: 416-442-5600; Fax: 416-510-5140
www.ebmag.com
www.linkedin.com/company/electrical-business-network
twitter.com/ebmag
www.facebook.com/ElectricalBusiness
Circulation: 19,993
Frequency: 12 times a year
Anthony Capkun, Editor-Publisher, acapkun@ebmag.com

Electrical Line
Owned By: Pacific Media Publishing Inc.
Pacific Media Publishing Inc., 1785 Emerson Ct., North
Vancouver, BC V7H 2Y6
Tel: 604-924-3661; Fax: 604-924-3662
www.electricalline.com
Circulation: 20,000
Frequency: Bi-Monthly
Ken Buhr, Editor/Publisher

Electricity Today
#215, 1885 Clements Rd., Pickering, ON L1W 3V4
Tel: 905-686-1040; Fax: 905-686-1078
www.electricity-today.com
Circulation: 15,000
Frequency: 6 times a year

Randolph W. Hurst, Publisher & Executive Editor,
randy@electricityforum.com

EP&T
Also Known As: Electronic Products & Technology
Owned By: Annex Business Media
#400, 111 Gordon Baker Rd., Toronto, ON M2H 3R1
Tel: 416-442-5600; Fax: 416-510-5134
info@ept.ca
www.ept.ca
twitter.com/EPTmagazine
www.facebook.com/EPTmag
Frequency: 9 times a year
Scott Atkinson, Publisher, 416-510-5207, satkinson@ept.ca
Stephen Law, Editor, slaw@ept.ca

Engineering

Canadian Consulting Engineer
Owned By: Annex Business Media
#400, 111 Gordon Baker Rd., Toronto, ON M2H 3R1
Tel: 416-442-5600; Fax: 416-510-5140
Toll-Free: 800-268-7742
www.canadianconsultingengineer.com
twitter.com/CdnConsultEng
www.facebook.com/CanadianConsultingEngineer
Covers all engineering disiplines & all geographical areas.
Maureen Levy, Senior Publisher, 416-510-5111,
mlevy@ccemag.com
Peter Saunders, Editor, psaunders@ccemag.com

Construction Alberta News
PO Box 48109, St Albert, AB T8N 5V9
Tel: 780-460-8004; Fax: 866-860-1639
admin@conaltanews.com
www.conaltanews.com
Frequency: 2 times a year
J. Grant Bush, Publisher, grant@conaltanews.com
Beverley Williams, Editor, bev@conaltanews.com

Geomatica
Previous Name: CISM Journal
Owned By: Canadian Science Publishing
#1, 1840 Woodward Dr., Ottawa, ON K2C 0P7
Tel: 902-706-3828; Fax: 613-656-9838
geomatica@cdnsciencepub.com
cdnsciencepub.com/journal/geomat
Frequency: 4 times a year
Geomatica is dedicated to the dissemination of information on
technical advances in the geomatics sciences. It is the official
publication of the Canadian Institute of Geomatics.
Suzanne Kettley, Publisher & CEO, izaak@izaak.ca

The Ontario Technologist
#404, 10 Four Seasons Place, Toronto, ON M9B 6H7
Tel: 416-621-9621; Fax: 416-621-8694
www.oacett.org
twitter.com/OACETT
www.facebook.com/OACETT
Circulation: 24,000
Frequency: 6 times a year
Publication of the Ontario Association of Certified Engineering
Technicians & Technologists.

PLAN
Ordre des ingenieurs du Québec, Gare Windsor, #350, 1100,
av des Canadiens-de-Montréal, Montréal, QC H3B 6H7
Tél: 514-845-6141; Téléc: 514-845-1833
Ligne sans frais: 800-461-6141
www.oiq.qc.ca
Tirage: 62 000
Fréquence: 6 fois par an

Plan Canada
Canadian Institute of Planners, #1112, 141 Laurier Ave.
West, Ottawa, ON K1P 5J3
Tel: 613-237-7526; Fax: 613-237-7045
Toll-Free: 800-207-2138
general@cip-icu.ca
www.cip-icu.ca
Circulation: 4,715
Frequency: Quarterly
Beth McMahon, Executive Director, bmcmahon@cip-icu.ca
Meaghan Murphy, Coordinator, Communications,
mmurphy@cip-icu.ca

Publiquip Inc.
Anciennement: Publiquip/Roucam
490, av Gilles Villeneuve, Berthierville, QC J0C 1A0
Tél: 450-836-3666; Téléc: 450-836-7401
Ligne sans frais: 800-361-5295
production@publiquip.com
www.publiquip.com

Tirage: 51 500
Fréquence: Mensuel

Rock to Road
Owned By: Annex Business Media
PO Box 530, 105 Donly Dr. South, Simcoe, ON N3Y 4N5
Fax: 519-429-3094
Toll-Free: 888-599-2228
www.rocktoroad.com
twitter.com/RockToRoad
www.facebook.com/RockToRoadMag
Frequency: 6 times a year
Todd Humber, Group Publisher,
thumber@annexbusinessmedia.com
Andrew Snook, Editor, asnook@annexbusinessmedia.com

Supply Post
#105, 26730 - 56th Ave., Langley, BC V4W 3X5
Tel: 604-607-5577; Fax: 604-607-0533
Toll-Free: 800-663-4802
info@supplypost.com
www.supplypost.com
www.linkedin.com/company/the-supply-post-newspaper
twitter.com/supplypos t
www.facebook.com/supplypost71
Frequency: 12 times a year
The publication is provides information for the construction
equipment, trucking, forestry, mining, oil & gas, & marine
industries.
Jeff Watson, President, jeff.watson@supplypost.com

Environment & Nature

Ecoforestry
Previous Name: International Journal of Ecoforestry
Ecoforestry Institute Society, PO Box 5070 B, Victoria, BC
V8R 6N3
Tel: 250-595-0655
admin@ecoforestry.ca
www.ecoforestry.ca

EnviroLine
#369, 305 - 4625 Varsity Dr. NW, Calgary, AB T3A 0Z9
Tel: 403-263-3272; Fax: 403-263-3280
enviroline@shaw.ca
envirolinenews.ca
Circulation: 500
Frequency: 12 times a year
Provides Western Canadian resource industries with reviews of
important & up-to-date environmental issues.
Mark Lowey, Managing Editor

Vecteur Environnement
295, Place d'Youville, Montréal, QC H2Y 2B5
communications@reseau-environnement.com
www.reseau-environnement.com/publications/vecteur
Tirage: 2 000
Fréquence: 4 fois par an
Revue de l'industrie, des sciences et techniques de
l'environnement du Québec; publiée par RÉSEAU
environnement

Fashion

Zink
#2, 94, Ste-Therese, Montréal, QC H2Y 3V5
Tel: 514-759-7702
zinknews@zinkmediagroup.com
www.zinkmagazine.com
www.youtube.com/user/ZinkMag
twitter.com/ZINKMagazine
www.facebook.com /ZinkMagazine
Frequency: Monthly
Sheriff J. Ishak, Editor-in-Chief/Publisher/CEO

Fire Protection

Canadian Firefighter & EMS Quarterly
Previous Name: EMS Quarterly
Owned By: Annex Business Media
PO Box 530, 105 Donly Dr. South, Simcoe, ON N3Y 4N5
Tel: 519-428-3471; Fax: 519-429-3094
Toll-Free: 888-599-2228
www.firefightingincanada.com
twitter.com/fireincanada
www.facebook.com/firefightingincanada
Circulation: 7,500
Frequency: 4 times a year
Martin McAnulty, Publisher, mmcanulty@annexweb.com
Laura King, Editor, 289-259-8077, lking@annexweb.com

Fire Fighting in Canada
Owned By: Annex Business Media
PO Box 530, 105 Donly Dr. South, Simcoe, ON N3Y 4N5
Fax: 519-429-3094
Toll-Free: 888-599-2228
www.firefightingincanada.com
www.youtube.com/user/firefightingincanada
twitter.com/FireinCanada
www .facebook.com/firefightingincanada
Frequency: 8 times a year
The magazine provides information to educate & inform fire
chiefs, senior officers & firefighters in municipal, industrial &
military fire departments.
Laura Aiken, Editor, 416-522-1595,
laiken@annexbusinessmedia.com

Floor Coverings

Coverings
Owned By: MediaEdge Communications Inc.
c/o MediaEdge Communications Inc., #500, 2001 Sheppard
Ave. East, Toronto, ON M2J 4Z8
info@mediaedge.ca
coveringscanada.ca
Circulation: 7,926
Frequency: 6 times a year
Jason Krulicki, Publisher, jasonk@mediaedge.ca
Clare Tattersall, Editor, claret@mediaedge.ca

Food & Beverage

L'Actualité Alimentaire
Anciennement: Le Monde Alimentaire
Détenteur: Édikom inc.
615, av Notre-Dame, Saint-Lambert, QC J4P 2K8
Tél: 514-990-6967
www.actualitealimentaire.com
Tirage: 5 000
Martin Lemire, Vice-président, développement des affaires,
mlemire@edikom.ca
Sylvie Rivard, Rédactrice en chef, srivard@edikom.ca

Canadian Pizza Magazine
Owned By: Annex Business Media
PO Box 530, 105 Donly Dr. South, Simcoe, ON N3Y 4N5
Tel: 519-428-3471; Fax: 519-429-3094
Toll-Free: 888-599-2228
www.canadianpizzamag.com
twitter.com/cdnpizzamag
Circulation: 6,500
Frequency: 7 times a year
Martin McAnulty, Publisher, mmcanulty@annexweb.com
Colleen Cross, Editor, ccross@annexweb.com

Food in Canada
Owned By: Annex Business Media
#400, 111 Gordon Baker Rd., Toronto, ON M2H 3R1
Tel: 416-442-5600; Fax: 416-510-5140
www.foodincanada.com
www.linkedin.com/company/food-in-canada
twitter.com/FoodinCanada
Diane Kleer, Group Publisher, 519-403-8816,
dkleer@annexbusinessmedia.com
Nithya Caleb, Editor, 416-510-5142,
ncaleb@annexbusinessmedia.com

Grocery Business
PO Box 23103 Longworth, Bowmanville, ON L1C 0H0
Tel: 416-817-5278
www.grocerybusiness.ca
twitter.com/GroceryBusiness
Frequency: 6 times a year
Karen James, Co-Publisher & Executive Editor, 416-561-4744,
karenjames@grocerybusiness.ca
Larry Bonikowsky, Co-Publisher & Content Director,
905-697-0467, larryb@grocerybusiness.ca

Liquor Retailer
Owned By: EMC Publications
19073 - 63 Ave., Surrey, BC V3S 8G7
Tel: 604-574-4577; Fax: 604-574-2196
Toll-Free: 800-667-0955
www.emcmarketing.com/liquor-retailer
Other information: Alt. URL: liquorretailer.com
Circulation: 1,690
Frequency: Quarterly
Official magazine of the Alberta Liquor Store Association, mailed
to owners of liquor stores in Alberta.
Joyce Hayne, Publisher, joyce@emcmarketing.com

Le Must

Tél: 514-990-6967
info@lemust.ca
lemust.ca
www.instagram.com/lemustmagazine
www.facebook.com/LEmustmagazine
Fréquence: 3 fois par an

The Publican
Owned By: EMC Publications
19073 - 63 Ave., Surrey, BC V3S 8G7
Tel: 604-574-4577; *Fax:* 604-574-2196
Toll-Free: 800-667-0955
www.emcmarketing.com/publican

Circulation: 2,920
Frequency: Quarterly
Official publication of ABLE BC, distributed to liquor stores, rural agencies, pubs, bars, lounges, & nightclubs in British Columbia.
Joyce Hayne, Publisher, joyce@emcmarketing.com

Your Convenience Manager (YCM)
Owned By: Stagnito Business Information & Edgell Communications
#1510, 2300 Yonge St., Toronto, ON M4P 1E4
Tel: 416-256-9908; *Fax:* 888-889-9522
Toll-Free: 877-687-7321
ccentral.ca

Your Foodservice Manager (YFM)
Owned By: Stagnito Business Information & Edgell Communications
#1510, 2300 Yonge St., Toronto, ON M4P 1E4
Tel: 416-256-9908; *Fax:* 888-889-9522
Toll-Free: 877-687-7321
yfmonline.ca
Other information: Alt. URL: www.foodbiz.ca
twitter.com/FoodBizca
www.facebook.com/foodbizca
Circulation: 26,000
Jane Auster, Editor, jauster@stagnitomail.ca

Footwear

Canadian Footwear Journal
Previous Name: Footwear Forum
Owned By: Shoetrades Publications
241 Senneville Rd., Senneville, QC H9X 3X5
Tel: 514-457-8787
cfj@shoetrades.com
www.footwearjournal.com
Circulation: 7,000
Frequency: 15 times a year; plus Retail Buyers' Guide (annual), Shoemaking Buyers's Guide (annual)

Forest & Lumber Industries

Canadian Forest Industries (CFI)
Owned By: Annex Business Media
PO Box 530, 105 Donly Dr. South, Simcoe, ON N3Y 4N5
Fax: 519-429-3094
Toll-Free: 888-599-2228
www.woodbusiness.ca
twitter.com/CFIMag
www.facebook.com/CanadianForestIndustries
Frequency: Bi-monthly
Todd Humber, Group Publisher, 416-510-5248,
thumber@annexbusinessmedia.com
Maria Church, Editor, 226-931-1396,
mchurch@annexbusinessmedia.com

The Forestry Chronicle
c/o Canadian Institute of Forestry, PO Box 99, 6905 Hwy. 17 West, Mattawa, ON P0H 1V0
Tel: 705-744-1715; *Fax:* 705-744-1716
admin@cif-ifc.org
pubs.cif-ifc.org
Frequency: 6 times a year
A professional & scientific forestry journal.
Ron Ayling, Editor-in-Chief, forestrychronicle@cif-ifc.org

Logging & Sawmilling Journal (LSJ)
PO Box 86670, North Vancouver, BC V7L 4L2
Tel: 604-990-9970; *Fax:* 604-990-9971
forestnet.com/lsj.php
twitter.com/Forestnet2
www.facebook.com/LoggingandSawmillingJourna l
Frequency: 7 times a year
The journal is free to forestry related businesses. Information is published about forest management, logging, sawmilling, transportation, road & bridge construction, & wood manufacturing.
Anthony Anthony, Publisher & CEO, robinson@forestnet.com
Paul MacDonald, Editor, paul_macdonald@shaw.ca

Opérations forestières et de scierie
Détenteur: Annex Business Media
CP 51058, Pincourt, QC J7V 9T3
Tél: 514-425-0025; *Téléc:* 514-425-0068
www.operationsforestieres.ca
www.facebook.com/operationsforestieres
Fréquence: 4 fois par an
Guillaume Roy, Rédacteur-en-chef,
groy@annexbusinessmedia.com

Yardstick
Also Known As: WRLA YardStick
#300, 95 Cole Ave., Winnipeg, MB R2L 1J3
Tel: 204-975-0434; *Fax:* 204-949-9092
Toll-Free: 800-665-2456
wrla@wrla.org
www.wrla.org/news/yardstick-magazine
Frequency: 4 times a year
Amber McGuckin, Editor

Funeral Service

The Canadian Funeral Director Magazine
6546 Bethesda Rd., Bowmanville, ON L1C 0Y9
Tel: 905-666-8011
info@thefuneralmagazine.com
www.thefuneralmagazine.com
www.facebook.com/342543912512826
Scott Hillier, Publisher & Editor, scott@thefuneralmagazine.com

Canadian Funeral News
Owned By: OT Communications
#1025, 101 - 6th Ave. SW, Calgary, AB T2P 3P4
Tel: 403-264-3270; *Fax:* 403-264-3276
info@otcommunications.com
www.otcommunications.com/cfn
Frequency: 12 times a year
The journal provides news, articles, profiles & columns for funeral service professionals throughout Canada.
Pat Ottmann, Publisher, pat@businessincalgary.com
Tim Ottmann, Publisher, tim@businessincalgary.com

Gardening & Garden Equipment

Greenhouse Canada
Owned By: Annex Business Media
PO Box 530, 105 Donly Dr. South, Simcoe, ON N3Y 4N5
Fax: 519-429-3094
Toll-Free: 888-599-2228
greenhouse@annexweb.com
www.greenhousecanada.com
www.youtube.com/user/greenhousecanada
twitter.com/greenhousecan
www .facebook.com/GreenhouseCanada
Frequency: Monthly
Greta Chiu, Editor

Glass

Glass Canada
Owned By: Annex Business Media
PO Box 530, 105 Donly Dr. South, Simcoe, ON N3Y 4N5
Fax: 519-429-3094
Toll-Free: 888-599-2228
www.glasscanadamag.com
www.youtube.com/user/glasscanada
twitter.com/GlassCanadaMag
www.facebook.com/GlassCanada
Circulation: 4,000
Frequency: 6 times a year
Danielle Labrie, Publisher, dlabrie@annexbusinessmedia.com
Patrick Flannery, Editor, pflannery@annexbusinessmedia.com

Government

Municipal Redbook
Owned By: Reed Construction Data
c/o Reed Construction Data, #101 - 4299 Canada Way, Burnaby, ON V5G 1H3
Tel: 604-433-8164; *Fax:* 604-433-9549
Toll-Free: 888-878-2121
www.journalofcommerce.com
Circulation: 2,000
Frequency: Annually

Municipal World
42860 Sparta Line, Union, ON N0L 2L0
Tel: 519-633-0031; *Fax:* 519-633-1001
Toll-Free: 888-368-6125
www.municipalworld.com
Frequency: Monthly

Optimum Online: The Journal of Public Sector Management
The Summit Group, #100, 263 Holmwood Ave., Ottawa, ON K1S 2P8
Tel: 613-688-0763; *Fax:* 613-688-0767
www.optimumonline.ca
Circulation: 10,000
Frequency: 4 times a year
Quarterly publication on public sector management
Gilles Paquet, Editor, editor@optimumonline.ca

Parliamentary Names & Numbers
Sources, #201, 812A Bloor St. West, Toronto, ON M6G 1L9
Tel: 416-964-7799; *Fax:* 416-964-8763
sources@sources.ca
www.sources.com
Circulation: 500
Frequency: 2 times a year
Ulli Diemer, Publisher

Urba
Union des municipalitiés de Québec, #210, 2020, boul Robert-Bourassa, Montréal, QC H3A 2A5
www.umq.qc.ca/publications/magazine-urba
Tirage: 7 600
Fréquence: 4 fois par an
Ariane Duchesneau, Rédactrice, aduchesneau@umq.qc.ca

Grocery Trade

Canadian Grocer
Owned By: EnsembleIQ
#1800, 20 Eglinton Ave. West, Toronto, ON M4R 1K8
Fax: 978-671-0460
Toll-Free: 877-687-7321
canadiangrocer.com
www.linkedin.com/company/canadian-grocer-magazine
twitter.com/canadiangr ocer
Frequency: 10 times a year
Vanessa Peters, Publisher
Shellee Fitzgerald, Editor-in-Chief

Western Grocer
Owned By: Mercury Publications Ltd.
c/o Mercury Publications, #16, 1313 Border St., Winnipeg, MB R3H 0X4
Tel: 204-954-2085; *Fax:* 204-954-2057
Toll-Free: 800-337-6372
editorial@mercurypublications.ca
westerngrocer.com
Circulation: 12,657
Frequency: 6 times a year
Robin Bradley, Associate Publisher,
rbradley@mercurypublications.ca

Hardware Trade

Home Improvement Retailing
Owned By: Powershift Communications Inc.
Powershift Communications Inc., #501, 245 Fairview Mall Dr., Toronto, ON M2J 4T1
Tel: 416-494-1066; *Fax:* 416-494-2536
hir@powershift.ca
www.hirmagazine.com
Circulation: 14,127
Frequency: 6 times a year
Dante Piccinin, Publisher & Editorial Director

Quart de Rond
c/o l'AQMAT, #3, 400, rue Sainte-Hélène, Longueuil, QC J4K 3R2
Tél: 450-646-5842
information@aqmat.org
www.aqmat.org
Tirage: 2 000
Fréquence: 4 fois par an

Health & Medical

L'Actualité Médicale
Détenteur: EnsembleIQ
#800, 1200, av McGill College, Montréal, QC H3B 4G7
Ligne sans frais: 844-246-3190
www.professionsante.ca
Fréquence: 23 fois par an

Canadian Chiropractor
Owned By: Annex Business Media
PO Box 530, 105 Donly Dr. South, Simcoe, ON N3Y 4N5
Fax: 519-429-3094
Toll-Free: 888-599-2228
www.canadianchiropractor.ca
twitter.com/CanChiropractor
www.facebook.com/CanadianChiropractor

Circulation: 5,800
Frequency: 8 times a year
Jannen Belbeck, Editor, 888-599-2228 ext.211,
jbelbeck@annexbusinessmedia.com
Martin McAnulty, Publisher,
mmcanulty@annexbusinessmedia.com

Canadian Family Physician
College of Family Physicians of Canada, 2630 Skymark Ave., Mississauga, ON L4W 5A4
Tel: 905-629-0900; *Fax:* 905-629-0893
Toll-Free: 800-387-6197
CFPmedia@cfpc.ca
www.cfp.ca
twitter.com/CanFamPhysician
Frequency: Monthly
Kathryn Taylor, Managing Editor

The Canadian Journal of Occupational Therapy (CJOT) / Revue canadienne d'ergothérapie
Canadian Association of Occupational Therapists, #100, 34 Colonnade Rd., Ottawa, ON K2E 7J6
Tel: 613-523-2268; *Fax:* 613-523-2552
Toll-Free: 800-434-2268
publications@caot.ca
www.caot.ca
twitter.com/CAOT_ACE
www.facebook.com/CAOT.ca
Circulation: 7,000
Frequency: 5 times a year
Catherine Vallée, Editor-in-Chief
Helene Polatajko, Scientific Editor

The Chronicle of Neurology & Psychiatry
Owned By: Chronicle Information Resources Ltd.
#306, 555 Burnhamthorpe Rd., Toronto, ON M9C 2Y3
Tel: 416-916-2476; *Fax:* 416-352-6199
Toll-Free: 866-632-4766
health@chronicle.org
www.chronicle.org
Circulation: 6,189
Frequency: 6 times a year
Mitchell Shannon, Publisher

The Chronicle of Skin & Allergy
Owned By: Chronicle Information Resources Ltd.
#306, 555 Burnhamthorpe Rd., Toronto, ON M9C 2Y3
Tel: 416-916-2476; *Fax:* 416-352-6199
Toll-Free: 866-632-4766
health@chronicle.org
www.chronicle.org
Circulation: 6787
Frequency: 8 times a year
Mitchell Shannon, Publisher

Drugstore Canada
Owned By: Rogers Media Inc.
1 Mount Pleasant Rd., 7th Fl., Toronto, ON M4Y 2Y5
Tel: 416-764-2000; *Fax:* 416-764-3930
www.canadianhealthcarenetwork.ca
Circulation: 16,703
Frequency: 10 times a year

Fitness Business Canada
Owned By: Mill Pond Publishing Inc.
30 Mill Pond Dr., Georgetown, ON L7G 4S6
Tel: 905-873-0850; *Fax:* 905-873-8611
Toll-Free: 888-920-6537
www.fitnet.ca
Other information: www.youtube.com/user/FitnessBusinessMag
www.linkedin.com/company/fitness-business-canada
twitter.com/FBCMagazine
www.facebook.com/FitnessBusinessCanada
Circulation: 8,000+
Publication aimed at owners, directors, managers, leaders & staff of health & fitness facilities.
Graham Longwell, President & Editor
Stephen Longwell, General Manager

FMWC Newsletter
Federation of Medical Women of Canada, 1021 Thomas Spratt Pl., Ottawa, ON K1G 5L5
Tel: 613-569-5881; *Fax:* 613-249-3906
Toll-Free: 877-771-3777
fmwcmain@fmwc.ca
fmwc.ca/newsletters
Circulation: 1,000
Frequency: 3 times a year
Dr. Clover Hermans, President

Massage Therapy Canada
Owned By: Annex Business Media
PO Box 530, 105 Donly Dr. South, Simcoe, ON N3Y 4N5
Fax: 519-429-3094
Toll-Free: 888-599-2228
www.massagetherapycanada.com
www.linkedin.com/company/massage-therapy-canada
twitter.com/MTCanadaMag
www.facebook.com/MassageTherapyCanada
Circulation: 5,800
Frequency: 4 times a year
Jannen Belbeck, Editor, 888-599-2228 ext.211,
jbelbeck@annexbusinessmedia.com

The Medical Post
Owned By: EnsembleIQ
#1510, 2300 Yonge St., Toronto, ON M4P 1E4
Tel: 416-256-9908
www.ensembleiq.com
twitter.com/MedicalPost
Circulation: 47,000
Frequency: 14 times a year
Colin Leslie, Editor, cleslie@ensembleiq.com

Ontario Medical Review (OMR)
Ontario Medical Assn., #900, 150 Bloor St. West, Toronto, ON M5S 3C1
Tel: 416-599-2580; *Fax:* 416-340-2944
Toll-Free: 800-268-7215
www.oma.org
twitter.com/OntariosDoctors
www.facebook.com/Ontariosdoctors
Circulation: 33,000
Frequency: 11 times a year
Jeff Henry, Editor, jeff.henry@oma.org
Elizabeth Petruccelli, Managing Editor,
elizabeth.petruccelli@oma.org

Optical Prism
Nusand Publishing Inc., #1113, 225 the East Mall, Toronto, ON M9B 0A9
Tel: 416-233-2487; *Fax:* 416-233-1746
info@opticalprism.ca
www.opticalprism.ca
www.pinterest.com/opticalprism
twitter.com/opticalprism
www.facebook.c om/OpticalPrismMagazine
Circulation: 14,707
Frequency: 8 times a year
Robert May, Publisher, 416-432-8473, rmay@opticalprism.ca

Heating, Plumbing, Air Conditioning

Contracting Canada Magazine
114 Donjon Blvd., Port Dover, ON N0A 1N4
Tel: 905-569-2777; *Fax:* 905-569-2444
www.contractingcanada.com
Circulation: 29,000
Frequency: 4 times a year
Contracting Canada's editorial focus is on the latest industry innovations including products, service and troubleshooting techniques, system design and installation profiles, sales and marketing features. Departments include field service and installation tips, technical advice from industry experts, the latest innovations and applications of products, tools and instruments for contractors.
Don B. Beaulieu, Publisher & Editorial Director, 905-569-2777, Fax: 905-569-2444, don@contractingcanada.com

Heating Plumbing Air Conditioning
Owned By: Annex Business Media
#400, 111 Gordon Baker Rd., Toronto, ON M2H 3R1
Tel: 416-442-5600; *Fax:* 416-510-5140
www.hpacmag.com
twitter.com/hpacmag
www.facebook.com/HPACmag
Frequency: 7 times a year; also Buyers Guide (annually, Aug.)
Peter Leonard, Publisher, 416-510-6847,
pleonard@hpacmag.com
Doug Picklyk, Editor, 416-510-5218, dpicklyk@hpacmag.com

Inter-mécanique du bâtiment (CMMTQ)
8175, boul St-Laurent, Montréal, QC H2P 2M1
www.cmmtq.org
Tirage: 6 500
Fréquence: 10 fois par an

Plumbing & HVAC Product News
Previous Name: HVAC Refrigeration; Plumbing, Piping & Heating Magazine
167 Simcoe St. North, Toronto, ON L1G 4S8
Tel: 289-638-2133
plumbingandhvac.ca
www.linkedin.com/company/plumbing-and-hvac-magazine
twitter.com/Plumbing_HVAC_
www.facebook.com/PlumbingandHVAC
Frequency: 6 times a year
Mark Vreugdenhil, Publisher, mark@plumbingandhvac.ca
Simon Blake, Editor, simon@plumbingandhvac.ca

Hotels & Restaurants

Bar & Beverage Business Magazine
Owned By: Mercury Publications Ltd.
c/o Mercury Publications, #16, 1313 Border St., Winnipeg, MB R3H 0X4
Tel: 204-954-2085; *Fax:* 204-954-2057
Toll-Free: 800-337-6372
www.barandbeverage.com
Circulation: 14,500
Frequency: 6 times a year
For managers, owners & staff of nightclubs, bars, cabarets, hotels, restaurants & lounges in Canada
Elaine Dufault, Associate Publisher & National Account Manager, edufault@mercurypublications.ca

BC Restaurant News
Owned By: BC Restaurant & Food Services Association
#2, 2246 Spruce St., Vancouver, BC V6H 2P3
Tel: 604-669-2239; *Fax:* 604-669-6175
Toll-Free: 877-669-2239
info@bcrfa.com
www.bcrfa.com
www.linkedin.com/company/bc-restaurant-&-foodservices
twitter.com/BCRFA
www.facebook.com/BCRFA
Frequency: 8 times a year
Publishes information about British Columbia and its restaurants
Ian Tostenson, President & Chief Executive Officer,
itostenson@bcrfa.com

Canadian Lodging News (CLN)
info@canadianlodgingnews.com
canadianlodgingnews.com
twitter.com/Canlodgingnews
www.facebook.com/CanadianLodgingNews
Joe Baker, Editor

Foodservice & Hospitality
Previous Name: Canadian Hotel & Restaurant Product News
Owned By: Kostuch Publications Ltd.
#404, 23 Lesmill Rd., Toronto, ON M3B 3P6
Tel: 416-447-0888
info@kostuchmedia.com
www.foodserviceandhospitality.com
www.instagram.com/foodservicemag
twitter.com/foodservicemag
www.facebook.com/foodservicehospitalitymagazine
Circulation: 24,747
Frequency: 8 times a year

Hotelier
Owned By: Kostuch Publications Ltd.
#101, 23 Lesmill Rd., Toronto, ON M3B 3P6
Tel: 416-447-0888
www.hoteliermagazine.com
twitter.com/hoteliermag
www.facebook.com/HotelierMagazine
Circulation: 9,782
Frequency: 7 times a year

InnFocus
Owned By: EMC Publications
19073 - 63 Ave., Surrey, BC V3S 8G7
Tel: 604-574-4577; *Fax:* 604-574-2196
Toll-Free: 800-667-0955
www.emcmarketing.com/innfocus
Circulation: 2,050
Frequency: Quarterly
Official publication of the BC Hotel Association.
Joyce Hayne, Publisher, joyce@emcmarketing.com

Western Hotelier
Owned By: Mercury Publications Ltd.
c/o Mercury Publications, #16, 1313 Border St., Winnipeg,
MB R3H 0X4

Tel: 204-979-6071; Fax: 204-954-2057
Toll-Free: 800-337-6372
www.westernhotelier.com

Circulation: 5,200
Frequency: 5 times a year
David Bastable, Associate Publisher,
dbastable@mercurypublications.ca

Western Restaurant News
Owned By: Mercury Publications Ltd.
c/o Mercury Publications, #16, 1313 Border St., Winnipeg,
MB R3H 0X4

Tel: 204-782-2460; Fax: 204-954-2057
Toll-Free: 800-337-6372
www.westernrestaurantnews.com

Circulation: 15,000
Frequency: Quarterly
Elaine Dufault, Associate Publisher,
edufault@mercurypublications.ca

Human Resources

Canadian HR Reporter
Owned By: HAB Press Limited

Tel: 416-644-8740
www.hrreporter.com
twitter.com/hrreporter
www.facebook.com/HRReporter

Frequency: 22 times a year
Fred Crossley, Manager, fred.crossley@keymedia.com

HR Professional Magazine
Previous Name: Human Resources Professional
hrprofessionalnow.ca
Frequency: Annual (print); Monthly (digital)
MaryBeth McKenzie, Director, HRPA, Public Relations &
Communications, mmckenzie@hrpa.ca

Human Resources Magazine Canada
Also Known As: HRM Canada
Owned By: Key Media Canada
#800, 312 Adelaide St. West, Toronto, ON M5V 1R2
Tel: 416-644-8740; Fax: 416-203-9083
subscriptions@kmimedia.ca
www.hrmonline.ca
www.linkedin.com/groups/HRM-Online-Canada-8336040
twitter.com/HRMCanada
www.facebook.com/HRMOnlineCA

Circulation: 32,000
Vernon Jones, Editor, vernon.jones@kmimedia.ca

Industrial & Industrial Automation

Energy Manager
Owned By: Annex Business Media
222 Edward St., Aurora, ON LAG 1W6
Tel: 905-727-0077; Fax: 905-727-0017
Toll-Free: 800-265-2827
www.energy-manager.ca
twitter.com/manageurenergy

Circulation: 18,135
Frequency: Monthly
John MacPherson, Group Publisher, 905-713-4335,
jmacpherson@annexweb.com
Anthony Capkun, Editor, 905-713-4391,
acapkun@annexweb.com

Manufacturing Automation
Previous Name: Manufacturing & Process Automation
Owned By: Annex Business Media
#400, 111 Gordon Baker Rd., Toronto, ON M2H 3R1
Tel: 416-442-5600; Fax: 416-510-5140
www.automationmag.com
www.youtube.com/user/AutomationMagazine
twitter.com/automationmag

Circulation: 19,868
Frequency: 7 times a year
Paul Grossinger, Group Publisher,
pgrossinger@annexbusinessmedia.com
Kristina Urquhart, Editor, kurquhart@annexbusinessmedia.com

MCI
Also Known As: Magazine Circuit Industriel
Détenteur: P.A.P. Communication inc.
P.A.P. Communication Inc., 6500, boul Pierre-Bertrand,
Québec, QC G2E 1R4

Tél: 418-623-3383; Téléc: 418-623-5033
Ligne sans frais: 800-387-3383
info@magazinemci.com
www.magazinemci.com
twitter.com/MagazineMci
www.facebook.com/MagazineMCI

Tirage: 19 000
Fréquence: 6 fois par an
Éric Pageau, Président/Éditeur

Industrial Safety

OHS Canada Magazine (OH&S Canada)
Previous Name: Occupational Health & Safety Canada
Owned By: Annex Business Media
www.ohscanada.com
www.linkedin.com/in/ohscanada-media-91228b32
twitter.com/ohscanada
www .facebook.com/OHSCanadaMagazine

Frequency: 6 times a year
Paul Grossinger, Group Publisher, 416-510-5240,
pgrossinger@annexbusinessmedia.com
Marcel Vander Wier, Editor, 416-510-5115,
mvanderwier@annexbusinessmedia.com

Travail et Santé
Détenteur: Groupe de communication Sansectra inc.
3755, boul Matte, #E, Brossard, QC J4Y 2P4

Tél: 450-651-2855
info@travailetsante.net
www.travailetsante.net

Fréquence: 4 fois par an
Frédéric Lannoye, Éditeur associé,
frederic.lannoye@travailetsante.net

Workplace Safety & Prevention Services (WSPS)
5110 Creekbank Rd., Mississauga, ON L4W 0A1
Tel: 905-614-1400; Fax: 905-614-1414
Toll-Free: 877-494-9777
customercare@wsps.ca
www.wsps.ca

Frequency: Annually
Annual report of workplace safety

Insurance

Canadian Underwriter
Owned By: Newcom Media Inc.
#400, 5353 Dundas St. West, Toronto, ON M9B 6H8
www.canadianunderwriter.ca
www.linkedin.com/company/canadian-underwriter
twitter.com/CdnUnderwriter
www.facebook.com/CanadianUnderwriter

Circulation: 10,061
Frequency: Monthly; also Claims Canada, National Claims
Manual, Insurance Marketer, Annual Statistical Issue, Ontario
Insurance Directory
Canadian Underwriter is a professional Insurance & Risk
Management magazine covering all aspects of Canada's
property & casualty Insurance Market.
David Gambrill, Editor-in-Chief, 416-510-6793,
david@canadianunderwriter.ca
Adam Malik, Managing Editor, 416-510-6763,
adam@newcom.ca

Forum
Previous Name: CAIFA Forum; Office & Field
c/o Advocis, 10 Lower Spadina Ave., Toronto, ON M5V 2Z2
Tel: 416-444-5251 Toll-Free: 800-563-5822
advocisforum@gmail.com
myadvocis.ca/forum-magazine

Circulation: 21,000
Frequency: Quarterly
Peter Wilmshurst, Publisher
Deanne Gage, Editor, dgage@advocis.ca

Insurance Business Canada
Owned By: Key Media Canada
#800, 312 Adelaide St. West, Toronto, ON M5V 1R2
Tel: 416-644-8740; Fax: 416-203-9083
insurancebusiness@keymedia.com.au
www.insurancebusiness.ca
twitter.com/InsuranceBizCA
www.facebook.com/IBCanada
John Mackenzie, General Manager, Sales, 416-644-8740
Ext.252, john.mackenzie@kmimedia.ca

Le Journal de l'Assurance
Détenteur: Les Éditions du Journal de l'assurance
#100, 321, rue de la Commune ouest, Montréal, QC H2Y 2E1
Tél: 514-289-9595
reception@journal-assurance.ca
portail-assurance.ca/journal-assurance
twitter.com/journ_assurance
www.facebook.com/journalassurance

Ontario Insurance Directory
Owned By: Newcom Media Inc.
#400, 5353 Dundas St. West, Toronto, ON M9B 6H8
www.canadianunderwriter.ca

Frequency: Annually, December
Personal address & telephone book dedicated solely to the
Ontario insurance industry.

Interior Design & Decor

AZURE
#206, 213 Sterling Rd., Toronto, ON M6R 2B2
Tel: 416-203-9674
azure@azureonline.com
www.azuremagazine.com
www.linkedin.com/company/1482181
twitter.com/azuremagazine
www.facebook.com/AzureMagazine

Circulation: 18,704
Frequency: 8 times a year
Covers projects, issues, & trends relating to contemporary
architecture & design
Sergio Sgaramella, Publisher, sergio@azureonline.com

Canadian Interiors (CI)
Owned By: iQ Business Media Inc.
#302, 101 Duncan Mill Rd., Toronto, ON M3B 1Z3
Tel: 416-441-2085
circulation@canadianinteriors.com
www.canadianinteriors.com

Circulation: 13,467
Frequency: 6 times a year
Publishes information on Canada's leading interior design
professionals
Martin Spreer, Publisher, 416-441-2085 ext.108,
mspreer@canadianinteriors.com
Peter Sobchak, Editor, 416-441-2085 ext.107,
psobchak@canadianinteriors.com

Ontario Design
Owned By: Homes Publishing Group
#404, 37 Sandiford Dr., Stouffville, ON L4A 7X5
Tel: 905-479-4663; Fax: 905-591-8709
Toll-Free: 800-363-4663
info@ontariodesigntrade.com
www.ontariodesigntrade.com
www.facebook.com/OntarioDesignTradeSourcebook

Circulation: 12,000
Frequency: Annually
Michael Rosset, Publisher
Samantha Sannella, Editor

Jewellery & Giftware

Jewellery Business
Owned By: Kenilworth Media Inc.
c/o Kenilworth Media Inc., #710, 15 Wertheim Ct., Richmond
Hill, ON L4B 3H7
Tel: 905-771-7333; Fax: 905-771-7336
Toll-Free: 800-409-8688
editor@jewellerybusiness.com
www.jewellerybusiness.com
twitter.com/jewellerybizmag

Circulation: 8,079
Frequency: 6 times a year

Journalism

L'edition Nouvelles
8030, rue Marie Lefranc, Laval, QC H7Y 2C2
Tel: 450-962-7610; Fax: 450-962-7092
Toll-Free: 888-855-6397
www.newscanada.com

Circulation: 1 451
Frequency: Monthly
Ruth Douglas, President & Publisher

Media
Canadian Association of Journalists, PO Box 280,
Brantford, ON N3T 5M8
Tel: 613-526-8061; Fax: 613-521-3904
www.caj.ca

Circulation: 4,000
Frequency: Quarterly

David McKie, Editor

Landscaping

Green for Life
Owned By: Landscape Alberta Nursery Trades Association
c/o Landscape Alberta Nursery Trades Association, 18051 - 107th Ave. NW, Edmonton, AB T5S 1K3
Tel: 780-489-1991 *Toll-Free:* 800-378-3198
admin@landscape-alberta.com
www.landscape-alberta.com/membership/resourc
es/publications

Circulation: 1,500
Frequency: 6 times a year
The magazine targets persons involved in the following businesses in Manitoba, Saskatchewan & Alberta: retail & wholesale nurseries, greenhouse operators, sod farms, grounds maintenance, landscape contractors, arborists & municipal goverments.
Joel Beatson, Managing Editor

Landscape Ontario
Previous Name: Horticulture Review
Owned By: Landscape Ontario Horticultural Trades Association
7856 - 5th Line South, #RR4, Milton, ON L9T 2X8
Tel: 416-848-7575; *Fax:* 905-875-3942
Toll-Free: 800-265-5656
www.horttrades.com

Circulation: 2,300
Frequency: Monthly
Lee Ann Knudsen, Publisher
Allan Dennis, Editor, adennis@landscapeontario.com

Landscape Trades
Owned By: Landscape Ontario Horticultural Trades Association
7856 - 5th Line South, RR#4, Milton, ON L9T 2X8
comments@landscapetrades.com
landscapetrades.com

Frequency: 6 times a year
Scott Barber, Publisher, 416-848-7557,
lak@landscapeontario.com

Turf & Rec
Previous Name: Turf & Recreation
Owned By: Annex Business Media
PO Box 530, 105 Donly Dr. South, Simcoe, ON N3Y 4N5
Tel: 519-429-3094 *Toll-Free:* 888-599-2228
www.turfandrec.com
twitter.com/TurfandRec
www.facebook.com/TurfAndRec

Frequency: 7 times a year
Mike Jiggens, Editor, mjiggens@annexbusinessmedia.com

Legal

The Advocate
#1918, 1030 West Georgia St., Vancouver, BC V6E 2Y3
Tel: 604-696-6120
info@the-advocate.ca
the-advocate.ca

Circulation: 15,000
Frequency: 6 times a year
Published by the Vancouver Bar Association, The Advocate is of interest to members of the legal profession, the judiciary, courthouses & law schools in British Columbia & abroad. The Advocate features legal news & commentary.
D. Michael Bain, Editor, mbain@the-advocate.ca

Briefly Speaking
Also Known As: Just
c/o Ontario Bar Association, #300, 20 Toronto St., Toronto, ON M5C 2B8
Tel: 416-869-1047; *Fax:* 416-869-1390
Toll-Free: 800-668-8900
ccrocker@oba.org
www.oba.org/en/briefly/main/intro.aspx
Circulation: 13,000
Frequency: 3 times a year
The official, bilingual learned legal journal of the Ontario Bar Association.
Louise Harris, Editor, lharris@oba.org

Canadian Lawyer
Owned By: Key Media Canada
www.canadianlawyermag.com
www.linkedin.com/company/canadianlawyer
twitter.com/canlawmag
www.face book.com/CanLawMag
Frequency: 10 times a year
Tim Wilbur, Editor-in-chief, tim.wilbur@keymedia.com

Zena Olijnyk, Editor, zena.olijynk@keymedia.com

McGill Law Journal / Revue de droit de McGill
3644, rue Peel, Montréal, QC H3A 1W9
Tel: 514-398-7397; *Fax:* 514-398-7360
journal.law@mcgill.ca
lawjournal.mcgill.ca
www.linkedin.com/company/mlj-rdm
twitter.com/mcgill_lj
www.facebook.co m/McGillLawJournal
Frequency: 4 times a year
The McGill Law Journal is a bilingual academic legal journal run by the students of the McGill University Faculty of Law.
Nathaniel Reilly, Editor-in-chief

National
Canadian Bar Association, #1200, 66 Slater St., Ottawa, ON K1P 5H1
Tel: 613-237-2925
national@cba.org
www.nationalmagazine.ca
twitter.com/CBAnatmag
www.facebook.com/cbanatmag
Frequency: Quarterly
National is the official magazine of the Canadian Bar Association.
Yves Faguy, Editor-in-Chief, yvesf@cba.org

Ontario Legal Directory
Previous Name: Toronto Legal Directory
Also Known As: The Orange Book
University of Toronto Press, #700, 10 St Mary St., Toronto, ON M4Y 2W8
old@utpress.utoronto.ca
utpjournals.press/loi/old
Frequency: Annually, February
The directory provides over 30,000 listings of lawyers, law firms, federal & provincial courts & government offices. Entries include names, addresses, telephone & fax numbers, & email & web addresses.

The Ontario Reports
Owned By: LexisNexis Canada Ltd.
#700, 123 Commerce Valley Dr. East, Markham, ON L3T 7WB
Tel: 905-479-2665; *Fax:* 905-479-3758
Toll-Free: 800-668-6481
info@lexisnexis.ca
www.lexisnexis.ca/en-ca/products/ontario-reports.page
Frequency: Weekly
Published by the Law Society of Ontario through LexisNexis Canada, the Ontario Reports, Third Series provides information on current cases at all levels of Ontario courts. Some cases are printed in both English & French.

The Scrivener Magazine
PO Box 44, #700, 625 Howe St., Vancouver, BC V6C 2T6
Tel: 604-681-4516; *Fax:* 604-681-7258
Toll-Free: 800-663-0343
scrivener@notaries.bc.ca
www.notaries.bc.ca/scrivener
Circulation: 6,000
Frequency: 4 times a year
The Scrivener is published quarterly by The Society of Notaries Public of British Columbia. It publishes articles about points of law & the Notary profession.
Val Wilson, Editor-in-Chief

Lighting

Professional Lighting & Production
Owned By: Norris-Whitney Communications Inc.
#202, 4056 Dorchester Rd., Niagara Falls, ON L2E 6M9
Tel: 905-374-8878; *Fax:* 888-665-1307
info@nor.com
www.professional-lighting.com
twitter.com/plpmag
www.facebook.com/professionallighting
Circulation: 10,200
Frequency: 4 times a year
Jim Norris, Publisher, jnorris@nor.com

Machinery Maintenance

Machinery & Equipment MRO
Owned By: Annex Business Media
#400, 111 Gordon Baker Rd., Toronto, ON M2H 3R1
Tel: 416-510-5600; *Fax:* 416-510-5134
Toll-Free: 800-268-7742
www.mromagazine.com
www.linkedin.com/company/mro-magazine
twitter.com/MRO_Maintenance
www. facebook.com/MROMagazine

Frequency: 6 times a year
Machinery & Equipment MRO was founded to serve the industrial aftermarket (maintenance, repair and operations).
Paul Burton, Senior Publisher,
pburton@annexbusinessmedia.com
Mario Cywinski, Editor, mcywinski@annexbusinessmedia.com

Materials Handling & Distribution

Inside Logistics
Previous Name: Materials Management & Distribution
Owned By: Newcom Media Inc.
#400, 5353 Dundas St. West, Toronto, ON M9B 6H8
www.insidelogistics.ca
www.linkedin.com/company/insidelogistics-magazine
twitter.com/InsideLogi stics
Circulation: 17,271
Frequency: 6 times per year
Supply chain magazine covering information management & transportation
Emily Atkins, Editor, 416-614-5801, Emily@newcom.ca

Metalworking

Canadian Fabricating & Welding
Owned By: FMA Communications Canada, Inc.
c/o FMA Communications Canada, #416, 1154 Warden Ave., Toronto, ON M1R 0A1
Tel: 815-399-8700 *Toll-Free:* 888-394-4362
info@canadianmetalworking.com
www.canadianmetalworking.com
Circulation: 24,714
Frequency: 10 times a year
Rob Swan, Publisher, 905-315-8342,
rswan@canadianfabweld.com
Rob Colman, Editor, 905-235-0471,
rcolman@canadianfabweld.com

Canadian Metalworking
Owned By: FMA Communications Canada, Inc.
c/o FMA Communications Canada, #416, 1154 Warden Ave., Toronto, ON M1R 0A1
Tel: 815-399-8700 *Toll-Free:* 888-394-4362
info@canadianmetalworking.com
www.canadianmetalworking.com
twitter.com/CdnMetalworking
www.facebook.com/CanadianMetalworking
Circulation: 24,714
Frequency: 10 times a year
Jim Gorzek, Publisher, 815-227-8269,
jgorzek@canadianmetalworking.com
Joe Thompson, Editor, 905-315-8226,
jthompson@canadianmetalworking.com

Military

Canadian Defence Review
PO Box 305, Markham, ON L3P 3J8
Tel: 905-554-4586
info@canadiandefencereview.com
www.canadiandefencereview.com
www.linkedin.com/company/canadian-defence-review
twitter.com/CDRmagazine
www.facebook.com/CanadianDefenceReview
Frequency: 6 times a year

Mining

CIM Magazine
Previous Name: CIM Bulletin
Owned By: Canadian Institute of Mining, Metallurgy & Petroleum
#1250, 3500, boul de Maisonneuve ouest, Montréal, QC H3Z 3C1
Tel: 514-939-2710; *Fax:* 514-939-2714
cim@cim.org
magazine.cim.org
Circulation: 9,698
Frequency: 8 times a year
Ryan Bergen, Editor-in-Chief, rbergen@cim.org

The Northern Miner (TNM)
Owned By: The Northern Miner Group
#320, 225 Duncan Mill Rd., Toronto, ON M3B 3K9
Tel: 416-510-6789; *Fax:* 416-510-5138
northernminer2@northernminer.com
northernminer.com
www.linkedin.com/company/the-northern-miner
twitter.com/northernminer
www.facebook.com/NorthernMiner
Circulation: 6,000
Frequency: Bi-weekly

Anthony Vaccaro, Group Publisher, 416-442-2098, avaccaro@northernminer.com
Trish Saywell, Editor-in-Chief, 416-510-6741, tsaywell@northernminer.com

Motor Trucks & Buses

The Manitoba Trucking Guide for Shippers
Previous Name: Manitoba Ship-by-Truck Directory
Owned By: Craig Kelman & Associates Ltd.
Tel: 204-985-9791
info@trucking.mb.ca
www.trucking.mb.ca/product-truck-directory.htm
Circulation: 1,000
Frequency: Annually

Over the Road
18 Parkglen Dr., Ottawa, ON K2G 3G9
Tel: 613-224-9947; *Fax:* 613-224-8825
Toll-Free: 800-416-8712
otr@otrgroup.ca
www.overtheroad.ca
Circulation: 25,000
Frequency: 12 times a year
Peter Charboneau, Publisher, peter@otrgroup.ca
Ed Novoa, General Manager, ed@otrgroup.ca
Mary Weeks, Office Manager, mary@otrgroup.ca

Today's Trucking
Owned By: Newcom Media Inc.
#400, 5353 Dundas St. West, Toronto, ON M9B 6H8
www.trucknews.com
www.linkedin.com/company/today's-trucking
twitter.com/Todaystrucking
www.facebook.com/TodaysTrucking
Frequency: 6 times a year
Lou Smyrlis, Publisher, 416-510-6881, Fax: 416-510-5140, lou@newcom.ca
John G. Smith, Editorial Director, 416-614-5812, johng@newcom.ca

Today's Trucking
Owned By: Newcom Media Inc.
www.trucknews.com
www.youtube.com/c/TodaystruckingMagazine
twitter.com/todaystrucking
ww.facebook.com/TodaysTrucking
Frequency: 10 times a year
John G. Smith, Editorial Director, 416-614-5812, johng@newcom.ca
James Menzies, Editor, 416-510-6896, james@newcom.ca

Transport Magazine & L'Écho du Transport
Détenteur: Geyser Agence Média inc.
119, ch de la Miche, Québec, QC G3B 1J7
Tél: 418-872-6060 *Ligne sans frais:* 866-872-6060
info@transport-magazine.com
www.transport-magazine.com
www.linkedin.com/company/transport-magazine-tm
twitter.com/TransMag
www.facebook.com/transportmagazine
Fréquence: 12 fois par an

La Voix du vrac
#235, 670, rue Bouvier, Québec, QC G2J 1A7
Tél: 418-623-7923
revue@ancai.com
www.ancai.com
Tirage: 7 800
Fréquence: 6 fois par an
Gaétan Légaré, Éditeur

Western Canada Highway News
Owned By: Craig Kelman & Associates Ltd.
2020 Portage Ave., 3rd Fl., Winnipeg, MB R3J 0K4
Tel: 204-985-9715 *Toll-Free:* 866-985-9785
info@kelman.ca
www.highwaynews.ca
Circulation: 4,000
Frequency: 4 times a year
Official publication of the Alberta Motor Transport Association (AMTA), Saskatchewan Trucking Association (STA) & Manitoba Trucking Association (MTA).
Megan Funnell, Managing Editor, megan@kelman.ca

Music

Canadian Music Trade (CMT)
Owned By: Norris-Whitney Communications Inc.
#202, 4056 Dorchester Rd., Niagara Falls, ON L2E 6M9
Tel: 905-374-8878; *Fax:* 888-665-1307
mail@nwcworld.com
www.canadianmusictrade.com
twitter.com/cdnmusictrade
www.facebook.com/canadianmusictrade
Frequency: 6 times a year
Serving Canadian music dealers & suppliers.
Jim Norris, Publisher

Music Directory Canada (MDC)
Owned By: Norris-Whitney Communications Inc.
#202, 4056 Dorchester Rd., Niagara Falls, ON L2E 6M9
Tel: 905-374-8878; *Fax:* 888-665-1307
www.musicdirectorycanada.com
twitter.com/mdcanada
www.facebook.com/musicdirectorycanadaonline
Available online.
Jim Norris, Publisher, jnorris@nor.com

Professional Sound
Owned By: Norris-Whitney Communications Inc.
#202, 4056 Dorchester Rd., Niagara Falls, ON L2E 6M9
Tel: 905-374-8878; *Fax:* 888-665-1307
mail@nwcworld.com
www.professional-sound.com
www.instagram.com/profsoundmag
twitter.com/profsound
www.facebook.com/ professionalsound
Frequency: 6 times a year
Jim Norris, Publisher, jnorris@nwcworld.com
Michael Raine, Editor-in-Chief, mraine@nwcworld.com

Packaging

Canadian Packaging
Owned By: Annex Business Media
Tel: 416-510-5228
www.canadianpackaging.com
twitter.com/CdnPackaging
www.facebook.com/CanadianPackaging
Frequency: 11 times a year
Stephen Dean, Senior Publisher, 416-510-5198, Sdean@canadianpackaging.com
George Guidoni, Editor, 416-510-5227, gguidoni@canadianpackaging.com

Petroleum, Oil & Gas

Alberta Oil & Gas Directory
Owned By: DEL Communications Inc.
6 Roslyn Rd., Winnipeg, MB R3L 0G5
Circulation: 10,000
Frequency: Annually

New Technology Magazine
Owned By: JWN Energy
816 - 55th Ave. NE, 2nd Fl., Calgary, AB T2E 6Y4
Tel: 403-209-3500; *Fax:* 403-265-3706
Toll-Free: 800-387-2446
www.jwnenergy.com
Bill Whitelaw, CEO

The OGM
Previous Name: The Oil & Gas Magazine
PO Box 21178, St. John's, NL A1A 5B2
Tel: 709-770-0677
contact@theogm.com
theogm.com
www.linkedin.com/company/1801457
twitter.com/theogm
www.facebook.com/T heOGM
Frequency: 4 times a year
Tina Olivero, Publisher & Editor-in-chief, tinaolivero@theogm.com

Oil & Gas Product News
Owned By: Baum Publications Ltd.
Baum Publications Ltd., 124 - 2323 Boundary Rd., Vancouver, BC V5M 4V8
Tel: 604-291-9900; *Fax:* 604-291-1906
Toll-Free: 888-286-3630
www.oilandgasproductnews.com
Circulation: 12,000
Frequency: 6 times a year
Lee Toop, Editor, ltoop@baumpub.com

Oilweek
Owned By: JWN Energy
816 - 55th Ave. NE, 2nd Fl., Calgary, AB T2E 6Y4
Tel: 403-209-3500; *Fax:* 403-245-8666
Toll-Free: 800-387-2446
www.jwnenergy.com
Circulation: 10,000
Frequency: Monthly
Darrell Stonehouse, Editor, dstonehouse@jwnenergy.com
Bill Whitelaw, Publisher, bwhitelaw@jwnenergy.com

Propane-Canada
Owned By: Northern Star Publications Ltd.
900 - 6th Ave. SW, 4th Fl., Calgary, AB T2P 3K2
Tel: 403-263-6881; *Fax:* 403-263-6886
Toll-Free: 800-526-4177
propane@northernstar.ab.ca
www.northernstar.ab.ca/propane-canada
Circulation: 5,080
Frequency: 6 times a year
Scott Jeffrey, Publisher, scott@northernstar.ab.ca

The Roughneck
Owned By: Northern Star Publications Ltd.
900 - 6th Ave. SW, 4th Fl., Calgary, AB T2P 3K2
Tel: 780-263-6881; *Fax:* 780-423-6886
Toll-Free: 800-526-4177
roughneck@northernstar.ab.ca
www.northernstar.ab.ca/the-roughneck
Circulation: 8,460
Frequency: Monthly
Scott Jeffrey, Publisher, scott@northernstar.ab.ca

Photography

PhotoLife
Previous Name: Master Guide
#102, 171 St. Paul St., Québec, QC G1K 3W2
Tel: 418-692-2110; *Fax:* 418-692-3392
Toll-Free: 800-905-7468
www.photolife.com
twitter.com/PhotoLifeMag
www.facebook.com/photolifemag
Circulation: 6,500
Frequency: 6 times a year
Guy J. Poirier, Publisher

Plastics

Canadian Plastics
Owned By: Annex Business Media
#400, 111 Gordon Baker Rd., Toronto, ON M2H 3R1
Fax: 416-510-5134
Toll-Free: 800-268-7742
www.canplastics.com
www.linkedin.com/company/canadian-plastics
twitter.com/canplastics
www .facebook.com/CanPlastics
Frequency: 7 times a year
Diane Kleer, Group Publisher, dkleer@annexbusinessmedia.com
Mark Stephen, Editor, 416-510-5110, mstephen@canplastics.com

Canadian Plastics Directory & Buyer's Guide
Owned By: Annex Business Media
#400, 111 Gordon Baker Rd., Toronto, ON M2H 3R1
Fax: 416-510-5134
Toll-Free: 800-268-7742
www.canplastics.com
www.linkedin.com/company/canadian-plastics
twitter.com/canplastics
www .facebook.com/CanPlastics
Circulation: 10,959
Frequency: Annually
Diane Kleer, Publisher, 519-429-5177 x4177, dkleer@annexbusinessmedia.com
Mark Stephen, Editor, 416-510-5110, mstephen@canplastics.com

Police

Blue Line Magazine
80 Valleybrook Dr., Toronto, ON M3B 2S9
Tel: 416-442-5600; *Fax:* 416-442-2230
www.blueline.ca
twitter.com/Blue_LineMag
www.facebook.com/BlueLineMagazine
Circulation: 13,000
Frequency: 10 times a year
National law enforcement magazine
Paul Grossinger, Publisher, 416-510-4240, pgrossinger@annexweb.com

Renée Francoeur, Editor, 416-510-5239,
rfrancoeur@annexweb.com

Printing & Publishing

Estimators' & Buyers' Guide
Owned By: North Island Publishing Ltd.
#8, 1606 Sedlescomb Dr., Mississauga, ON L4X 1M6
Tel: 905-625-7070 *Toll-Free:* 800-331-7408
www.ebguide.ca

Frequency: Annually
Sandy Donald, Publisher, s.donald@northisland.ca

Graphic Arts Magazine
17 - 17817 Leslie St., Newmarket, ON L3Y 3E3
Fax: 905-830-9345
Toll-Free: 877-513-3999
news@graphicartsmag.com
www.graphicartsmag.com
www.linkedin.com/company/graphic-arts-magazine
twitter.com/graphicart s
www.facebook.com/graphicartsmagazine

Circulation: 10,563
Frequency: 10 times a year
Joe Mulcahy, Publisher
Tony Curcio, News Editor

Graphic Monthly
Owned By: North Island Publishing Ltd.
#8, 1606 Sedlecomb Dr., Mississauga, ON L4X 1M6
Tel: 905-625-7070 *Toll-Free:* 800-331-7408
editorgraphicmonthly.ca
www.graphicmonthly.ca

Circulation: 10,000
Frequency: 6 times a year
Sandy Donald, Publisher, s.donald@northisland.ca

Maître Imprimeur
636, rue des Vignobles, Rosemère, QC J7A 4P9
Tél: 450-818-5373; *Téléc:* 450-818-5372
info@maitreimprimeur.com
www.maitreimprimeur.com

Tirage: 5 000
Fréquence: 10 fois par an
Dédié au secteur des arts graphiques et de l'imprimerie.
Luc Saumure, Éditeur

Product Engineering & Design

Design Engineering
Owned By: Annex Business Media
www.design-engineering.com
www.linkedin.com/company/design-engineering-magazine
twitter.com/design_ eng_mag
www.facebook.com/DesignEngineering

Frequency: 6 times a year
Paul Burton, Publisher, pburton@annexbusinessmedia.com
Mike Mcleod, Editor, mmcLeod@design-engineering.com

Purchasing

Canadian Trade Index
Owned By: MacRAE'S
565 Orwell St., Unit A, Mississauga, ON L5A 2W4
Tel: 905-990-6111; *Fax:* 866-405-2203
Toll-Free: 844-990-6111
customerservice@ctidirectory.com
www.ctidirectory.com
twitter.com/CTIdirectory
www.facebook.com/240294259355914

Frequency: Annually, May

Supply Professional
Previous Name: PurchasingB2B
Owned By: iQ Business Media Inc.
#302, 101 Duncan Mill Rd., Toronto, ON M3B 1Z3
www.supplypro.ca
www.linkedin.com/company/supplyprofessional
twitter.com/supplypromag
www.facebook.com/supplyprofessional

Frequency: 10 times a year
Alex Papanou, Publisher, 416-441-2085 x101,
alex@supplypro.ca
Michael Power, Editor, 416-441-2085 x110,
michael@supplypro.ca

Real Estate

Canadian Mortgage Professional (CMP)
Owned By: Key Media Canada
#800, 312 Adelaide St. West, Toronto, ON M5V 1R2
Tel: 416-644-8740; *Fax:* 416-203-9083
www.mortgagebrokernews.ca

Circulation: 10,000
Frequency: Monthly
John Mackenzie, General Manager, Sales, 416-644-8740
ext.252, john.mackenzie@kmimedia.ca

Canadian Property Valuation
Previous Name: Canadian Appraiser
c/o Appraisal Institute of Canada, #403, 200 Catherine St.,
Ottawa, ON K2P 2K9
Tel: 613-234-6533; *Fax:* 613-234-7197
info@aicanada.ca
www.aicanada.ca/about-aic/canadian-property-valuation-m
agazine
www.linkedin.com/groups/2967439
twitter.com/AIC_Canada
www.facebook.com/AppraisalInstitute.Canada

Circulation: 5,500
Frequency: Quarterly
National magazine serving the Canadian appraisal community,
distributed to the membership of the Appraisal Institute of
Canada as well as partners, libraries & national / international
subscribers.
Craig Kelman, Managing Editor

Espace Montréal
#101, 310 av Victoria, Montréal, QC H3Z 2M9
Tél: 514-879-1559; *Téléc:* 514-879-1556
espace@espaceqc.com
www.e5pace.com

Tirage: 10 000
Fréquence: 4 fois par an
Andrew Cross, Éditeur

Espace Québec
#101, 310 av Victoria, Montréal, QC H3Z 2M9
Tél: 514-879-1559; *Téléc:* 514-879-1556
espace@espaceqc.com
www.e5pace.com

Tirage: 5 000
Fréquence: 2 fois par an
Andrew Cross, Éditeur

Real Estate Professional (REP)
Owned By: Key Media Canada
#800, 312 Adelaide St. West, Toronto, ON M5V 1R2
Tel: 416-644-8740; *Fax:* 416-203-9083
subscriptions@kmimedia.ca
www.repmag.ca
twitter.com/REPMagCA
www.facebook.com/REPmagCA

Vernon Jones, Senior Editor, 416-644-8740 ext.238,
vernon.jones@kmimedia.ca
John Mackenzie, General Manager, Sales, 416-644-8740
ext.252, john.mackenzie@kmimedia.ca

The Western Investor
Owned By: Glacier Media Inc.
303 West 5th Ave., Vancouver, BC V5Y 1J6
Tel: 604-669-8500 *Toll-Free:* 800-661-6988
info@westerninvestor.com
www.westerninvestor.com
twitter.com/westerninvestor
www.facebook.com/WesternInvestorMedia

Frequency: Monthly
Frank O'Brien, Editor, 604-669-8500

Rental & Leasing Equipment

Canadian Rental Service
Owned By: Annex Business Media
PO Box 530, 105 Donly Dr. South, Simcoe, ON N3Y 4N5
Fax: 519-429-3094
Toll-Free: 888-599-2228
www.canadianrentalservice.com
www.youtube.com/user/canadianrentalmag
twitter.com/CRSmagazine
www.fac ebook.com/CanadianRentalService

Frequency: 9 times a year
Danielle Labrie, Publisher, dlabrie@annexbusinessmedia.com
Patrick Flannery, Editor, 226-931-0545,
pflannery@annexbusinessmedia.com

Science, Research & Development

The Advocate
Previous Name: OSMT Advocate
Medical Laboratory Professionals' Association of Ontario,
PO Box 100 LCD 1, Hamilton, ON L8L 7T5
mlpao@mlpao.org
www.mlpao.org

Frequency: Annual
Blanca McArthur, Executive Director, bmcarthur@osmt.org

Bio Business Magazine
#202, 30 East Beaver Creek Rd., Richmond Hill, ON L4B 1J2
Tel: 905-886-5040; *Fax:* 905-886-6615
www.biobusinessmag.com

Circulation: 32,494
Frequency: 6 times a year
Publication serving Canada's scientific community
Christopher Forbes, Publisher, cforbes@jesmar.com

Camford Chemical Report
38 Groomsport Cres., Toronto, ON M1T 2K9
Tel: 416-291-3215; *Fax:* 416-291-3406
info@camfordinfo.com
www.camfordinformation.com

Frequency: 50 times a year
Bob Douglas, Publisher, bdouglas@camfordinfo.com
George Deligiannis, Editor, georged@camfordinfo.com

Physics in Canada (PIC) / La Physique au Canada
www.cap.ca/publications/physics-canada-pic

Circulation: 1,800
Frequency: 2 times a year
Béla JoÃ³s, Editor, bjoos@uottawa.ca

Security

Canadian Security
Owned By: Annex Business Media
#400, 111 Gordon Baker Rd., Toronto, ON M2H 3R1
Tel: 416-442-5600; *Fax:* 416-510-5140
www.canadiansecuritymag.com
www.linkedin.com/company/canadian-security-magazine
twitter.com/security ed
www.facebook.com/canadiansecmagazine

Circulation: 11,000
Frequency: 6 times a year
Paul Grossinger, Group Publisher,
pgrossinger@annexbusinessmedia.com
Neil Sutton, Editor, nsutton@annexbusinessmedia.com

FrontLine Safety & Security
Beacon Publishing Inc., 2150 Fillmore Cres., Ottawa, ON
K1J 6A4
Tel: 613-747-1138; *Fax:* 613-747-7319
info@frontline-global.com
security.frontline.online

Circulation: 16,000
Frequency: 4 times a year
FrontLine Safety & Security focuses on public safety & national
security issues. The magazine is provided to senior personnel in
the safety, security, & enforcement sectors, as well as to industry
executives that serve security agencies across Canada.
Christina MacLean, General Manager & Editor
Jonathan Calof, Executive Editor

Security Products & Technology News
Also Known As: SP&T News
Owned By: Annex Business Media
80 Valleybrook Dr., Toronto, ON M3B 2S9
Tel: 416-442-5600; *Fax:* 416-510-5140
www.sptnews.ca
twitter.com/SecurityEd

Circulation: 11,525
Frequency: 8 times a year
Source of information for dealers, installers, system integrators,
resellers, & specifiers working in the Canadian security industry.
Peter Young, Publisher, 416-510-6797, pyoung@annexweb.com
Neil Sutton, Editor, 416-510-6788, nsutton@annexweb.com

Shipping & Marine

Canadian Sailings
Also Known As: Sailings
Owned By: Great White Publications Inc.
1390, ch St-Adnre, Rivière-Beaudette, QC J0P 1R0
concentrate@sympatico.ca
canadiansailings.ca

Joyce Hammock, Publisher & Editor,
jhammock@canadiansailings.ca

Sporting Goods & Recreational Equipment

Golf Business Canada
#810, 515 Legget Dr., Ottawa, ON K2K 3G4
Tel: 613-226-3616; *Fax:* 613-226-4148
ngcoa@ngcoa.ca
www.ngcoa.ca

Circulation: 4,000
Frequency: 4 times a year
Nathalie Lavallée, Chief Operating Officer, 613-226-3616 ext 15,
nlavallee@ngcoa.ca

Piscines & Spas
Détenteur: Kenilworth Media Inc.
c/o Kenilworth Media Inc., #710, 15 Wertheim Ct., Richmond Hill, ON L4B 3H7

Tél: 905-771-7333; *Téléc:* 905-771-7336
Ligne sans frais: 800-409-8688
editor@poolspamarketing.com
www.poolspamarketing.com/piscines-spas
twitter.com/PoolSpaMktg

Fréquence: Deux fois par année
Piscines & Spas est également la publication officielle du 'Salon Splash', le salon professionnel qui se tient chaque année à l'automne au Québec.

Pool & Spa Marketing
Owned By: Kenilworth Media Inc.
c/o Kenilworth Media Inc., #710, 15 Wertheim Ct., Richmond Hill, ON L4B 3H7

Tel: 905-771-7333; *Fax:* 905-771-7336
Toll-Free: 800-409-8688
editor@poolspamarketing.com
www.poolspamarketing.com
twitter.com/PoolSpaMktg
www.facebook.com/PoolSpaMarketing

Circulation: 6,918

Pools, Spas & Patios
Owned By: Kenilworth Media Inc.
c/o Kenilworth Media Inc., #710, 15 Wertheim Ct., Richmond Hill, ON L4B 3H7

Tel: 905-771-7333; *Fax:* 905-771-7336
Toll-Free: 800-409-8688
editor@poolsspaspatios.com
www.poolsspaspatios.com
twitter.com/poolsspaspatios
www.facebook.com/PoolsSpasPatiosmagazine

Frequency: Annually

Sports & Recreation

Canadian Running
Owned By: Gripped Publishing Inc.
75 Harbord St., Toronto, ON M5S 1G4

Tel: 416-927-0774; *Fax:* 416-927-1491
Toll-Free: 800-567-0444
info@runningmagazine.ca
runningmagazine.ca
twitter.com/CanadianRunning
www.facebook.com/CanadianRunningMagazine
Michael Doyle, Editor-in-Chief, michael@runningmagazine.ca

iRun
Owned By: Sportstats Inc.
#18, 155 Colonnade Rd., Ottawa, ON K2E 7K1

Tel: 613-238-1818
ben@iRun.ca
irun.ca
www.youtube.com/user/iRunNation
twitter.com/irunnation
www.facebook.com/iRunMagazine

Circulation: 60,000
Frequency: 6 times a year
Mark Sutcliffe, Group Publisher
Ray Zahab, Editor-in-Chief

Poker Player Magazine
Owned By: HeadsUp Entertainment Inc.
#1739, 246 Stewart Green SW, Calgary, AB T3H 3C8

Tel: 403-269-9039; *Fax:* 403-269-9060
www.headsupentertainment.com
Kelly B. Kellner, President/Founder/COO

Sportsnet Magazine
Owned By: Rogers Media Inc.
1 Mount Pleasant Rd., Toronto, ON M4Y 2Y5

www.sportsnet.ca/magazine
twitter.com/Sportsnet
www.facebook.com/sportsnet
As of January 2017, Sportsnet Magazine is available online-only.

Triathlon Magazine Canada
Owned By: Gripped Publishing Inc.
PO Box 819 Main, 75 Harbord St., Markham, ON L3P 8L3

Tel: 416-927-8198; *Fax:* 416-927-1491
Toll-Free: 800-567-0444
info@triathlonmagazine.ca
triathlonmagazine.ca
twitter.com/CanadianRunning
www.facebook.com/CanadianRunningMagazi ne
Kevin Mackinnon, Editor-in-Chief, kevin@triathlonmagazine.ca

Telecommunications

Wireless Telecom
Owned By: Canadian Wireless Telecommunications Association
#1110, 130 Albert St., Ottawa, ON K1P 5G4

Tel: 613-233-4888; *Fax:* 613-233-2032
info@cwta.ca
www.cwta.ca

Circulation: 7,273
Frequency: 3 times a year

Television, Radio, Video & Home Appliances

Media Names & Numbers
#201, 812A Bloor St. West., Toronto, ON M6G 1L9

Tel: 416-964-7799; *Fax:* 416-964-8763
sources@sources.com
www.sources.com

Circulation: 500
Frequency: Annually
Ulli Diemer, Publisher

Transportation, Shipping & Distribution

Canadian Automotive Fleet
22 Marvin Dr., St Catharines, ON L2M 1Y1

Tel: 289-288-9994; *Fax:* 289-288-9996
caf@fleetbusiness.com
www.fleetbusiness.com
www.linkedin.com/company/canadian-automotive-fleet
twitter.com/CAFmagazi nes

Frequency: 7 times a year
Keith McLaughlin, Publisher, kmclaughlin@fleetbusiness.com

Maritime Magazine
#200, 4493, Sherbrooke ouest, Montréal, QC H3Z 1E7

Tel: 514-937-9009; *Fax:* 514-937-9088
info@maritimemag.com
www.maritimemag.com

Circulation: 11,000
Frequency: 4 times a year
Covers the marine transport industry in the Great Lakes/St. Lawrence region.
Leo Ryan, Rédacteur en chef, lryan@maritimemag.com

Routes et Transports
AQTR, #450, 6666, rue Saint-Urbain, Montréal, QC H2S 3H1

Tél: 514-523-6444; *Téléc:* 514-523-2666
aqtr.com/association/actualites/revue-routes-transports

Tirage: 2 500
Fréquence: 2 fois par an

Travel

Canadian Travel Press
Owned By: Baxter Publications Inc.

info@baxter.net
www.travelpress.com
Other information: Sales, Email: sales@baxter.net; Editorial: ctp@baxter.net

Frequency: Bi-weekly
Bob Mowat, Executive Editor

Canadian Traveller
Owned By: MPM Group of Brands Inc.
PO Box 57096, Vancouver, BC V5K 5G6

Toll-Free: 888-924-7524
canadiantraveller@mypassionmedia.com
www.canadiantraveller.net
twitter.com/cantravelmag

Frequency: Monthly
Jennifer Prendergast, Publisher, jenniferp@mypassionmedia.com
Terrilyn Kunopaski, Editor-in-Chief, terrilynk@mypassionmedia.com

Tourisme Plus
CP 37 Bureau-chef, La Prairie, QC J5R 3Y1

Tél: 514-881-8583; *Téléc:* 514-881-8292
info@tourismeplus.com
www.tourismeplus.com

Tirage: 9 200
Fréquence: 25 fois par an
Marie Chantal Cholette, Présidente/Éditrice, mariechantal@tourismeplus.com

University Publications

Cannabis Brightline
Owned By: FMG Publishing Inc.
#300, 7071 Bayers Rd., Halifax, NS B3L 2C2

Tel: 647-479-2163
info@fmgpublishing.com
www.cannabisbrightline.com
Other information: Advertising: accounts@fmgpublishing.com
Frequency: Monthly
Features profiles of industry leaders, businesses, new technologies, & the cannabis community as a whole

Cannabis Retailer
Owned By: EMC Publications
19073 - 63 Ave., Surrey, BC V3S 8G7

Tel: 604-574-4577; *Fax:* 604-574-2196
Toll-Free: 800-667-0055
cannabisretailer.ca
twitter.com/CannabisRetail
www.facebook.com/1992369094114147

Frequency: Quarterly
Industry publication providing advice to cannabis retail store owners
Joyce Hayne, Publisher & Editor, joyce@emcmarketing.com

Grow Opportunity
Owned By: Annex Publishing & Printing Inc.
PO Box 530, 105 Donly Dr. South, Simcoe, ON N3Y 4N5

Fax: 519-429-3094
Toll-Free: 888-599-2228
www.growopportunity.ca
twitter.com/GrowOpportunity
www.facebook.com/GrowOpportunity

Frequency: Quarterly
Magazine devoted to the legal growing of marijuana, targeting producers & their industry partners.
Mari-Len De Guzman, Editor, 289-259-1408, mdeguzman@annexbusinessmedia.com
Adam Szpakowski, National Account Manager, 289-221-6605, aszpakowski@annexbusinessmedia.com

Papers
Owned By: Business of Cannabis
#10587, 998 Bloor St. West, Toronto, ON M6H 1L0

Tel: 416-705-8382
editor@businessofcannabis.ca
www.businessofcannabis.ca/special-content/papers
Other information: Advertising: advertise@businessofcannabis.ca
www.instagram.com/businessofcannabis
twitter.com/bofc_canada
www.facebook.com/bofccanada
Print publication of the Business of Cannabis, with articles on the changing landscape of the post-prohibition cannabis industry
Blaine Pearson, Publisher
Bryan Borzykowski, Editor-at-Large

Veterinary

Canadian Veterinary Journal (CVJ) / La Revue Vétérinaire Canadienne
c/o Canadian Veterinary Medical Association, 339 Booth St., Ottawa, ON K1R 7K1

Tel: 613-236-1162; *Fax:* 613-236-9681
Toll-Free: 800-567-2862
admin@cvma-acmv.org
www.canadianveterinarians.net/cvj-cjvr-classified-ads/cvj
Circulation: 8,029
Frequency: Monthly
John Kastelic, Co-Editor-in-chief
Tim Ogilvie, Co-Editor-in-chief

Revue Le Veterinarius
#200, 800, av Ste-Anne, Saint-Hyacinthe, QC J2S 5G7

Tél: 450-774-1427; *Téléc:* 450-774-7635
Ligne sans frais: 800-267-1427
communications@omvq.qc.ca
www.omvq.qc.ca/publications/revue-le-veterinarius.html
Fréquence: 4 fois par an

Water & Wastes Treatment

Ground Water Canada
Previous Name: Canadian Water Well
Owned By: Annex Business Media
PO Box 530, 105 Donly Dr. South, Simcoe, ON N3Y 4N5

Fax: 519-429-3094
Toll-Free: 888-599-2228
www.groundwatercanada.com
twitter.com/groundwatermag
www.facebook.com/GroundWaterCanada

Frequency: 4 times a year
Serves the water well & geothermal industries.
Colleen Cross, Editor, ccross@annexbusinessmedia.com

Solid Waste & Recycling Magazine
Previous Name: Solid Waste Management
Owned By: Point One Media, Inc.
PO Box 11 A, Nanaimo, BC V9R 5K4

Toll-Free: 877-755-2762
www.solidwastemag.com
twitter.com/solidwastemag
www.facebook.com/solidwastemag

Circulation: 10,000
Frequency: 6 times a year
Solid Waste & Recycling Magazine provides environmental information to waste industry professionals. Topics include solid waste collection, hauling, processing, & disposal.
Lara Perraton, Publisher, lperraton@pointonemedia.com
Jessica Kirby, Editor, jkirby@pointonemedia.com

Woodworking

Woodworking
Owned By: Kleiser Media Inc.
62 Gray Lane, Barrie, ON L4N 7T1

Tel: 416-763-3653
info@kleisermedia.com
www.woodworkingcanada.com

Circulation: 14,108
Frequency: 6 times a year
Bert Kleiser, Publisher, 416-819-4123, bert@kleisermedia.com
Stephan Kleiser, Editor, stephan@kleisermedia.com

Consumer

Advertising, Marketing, Sales

Sparksheet
Toronto, ON

contact@sparksheet.com
sparksheet.com
www.youtube.com/user/sparksheettv
twitter.com/sparksheet
www.facebook.com/185418500634

Circulation: 120,000
Frequency: 6 times a year
For media and marketing professionals
Dan Levy, Editor

Airline Inflight

enRoute
Owned By: Spafax Canada
#707, 4200 boul. St-Laurent, Montréal, QC H2W 2R2

Tel: 514-844-2001; Fax: 514-844-6001
info@aircanadaenroute.com
enroute.aircanada.com
twitter.com/enroutemag
www.facebook.com/enroutemag

Circulation: 90,000
Frequency: Bi-Monthly
Ilana Weitzman, Editor-in-Chief

Animals

Modern Dog
#202, 343 Railway St., Vancouver, BC V6A 1A4

Tel: 604-734-3131; Fax: 604-734-3031
Toll-Free: 866-734-3131
info@moderndogmagazine.com
www.moderndogmagazine.com
twitter.com/ModernDogMag
www.facebook.com/moderndogmagazine

Frequency: 4 times a year
Connie Wilson, Editor-in-chief

Pets Magazine
Owned By: Dorman Sales & Marketing Ltd.
c/o Dorman Sales & Marketing Ltd., 100 Belliveau Beach Rd., Pointe-du-Chene, NB E4P 3W6

Tel: 506-532-6732; Fax: 506-532-4518
Toll-Free: 877-738-7624
www.petsmagazine.ca
www.instagram.com/petsmagazinecanada
www.facebook.com/petsmagazinecanada

Circulation: 36,565
Frequency: 6 times a year
Provides information for pet owners
David Dorman, Publisher, david.dorman@petsmagazine.ca
Sharron Dorman, Administrator,
sharron.dorman@petsmagazine.ca
Brad Hussey, Managing Editor, editor@petsmagazine.ca

Martin Seto, Director, Advertising,
marty.seto@reflexmediasales.com

Arts, Art & Antiques

Border Crossings
#500, 70 Arthur St., Winnipeg, MB R3B 1G7

Tel: 204-942-5778; Fax: 204-949-0793
Toll-Free: 866-825-7165
info@bordercrossingsmag.com
bordercrossingsmag.com
www.instagram.com/bordercrossingsmag
twitter.com/border_mag
www.facebook.com/BorderCrossingsmag

Circulation: 5,500
Frequency: 4 times a year
Meeka Walsh, Editor, editor@bordercrossingsmag.com
Ben Wood, Director, Operations

C Magazine
Previous Name: C international contemporary art magazine
PO Box 5 B, #444, 401 Richmond St. West, Toronto, ON M5T 2T2

Tel: 416-539-9495; Fax: 416-539-9903
Toll-Free: 800-745-6312
info@cmagazine.com
www.cmagazine.com
www.instagram.com/cmagazineart
twitter.com/cmagazineart
www.facebook.com/cmagazineart

Circulation: 2,500
Frequency: 4 times a year
Publishes criticism & writing on visual art
Kate Monro, Publisher, publisher@cmagazine.com
Kari Cwynar, Editor, editor@cmagazine.com

Canadian Art
#330, 215 Spadina Ave., Toronto, ON M5T 2C7

Tel: 416-368-8854; Fax: 416-368-6135
Toll-Free: 800-222-4762
info@canadianart.ca
www.canadianart.ca
www.instagram.com/canartca
twitter.com/canartca
www.facebook.com/canadianart

Circulation: 19,094
Frequency: 4 times a year
Publishes material that address the interests of visual artists in Ontario
Debra Rother, Publisher, debra@canadianart.ca
David Balzer, Editor-in-Chief & Publisher, david@canadianart.ca
Caoimhe Morgan-Feir, Managing Editor,
caoimhe@canadianart.ca

Dance International
Scotiabank Dance Centre, Level 6, 677 Davie St., Vancouver, BC V6B 2G6

Tel: 604-681-1525; Fax: 604-681-7732
editor@danceinternational.org
www.danceinternational.org
www.instagram.com/danceinternationalmagazine
twitter.com/DIMagazine
www.facebook.com/DanceInternationalMagazine

Circulation: 4,000
Frequency: 4 times a year
Published by the Vancouver Ballet Society
Kaija Pepper, Editor

ETC Media
CP 660, Prévost, QC J0T 1T0

Tél: 450-335-0951
etc.artactuel@videotron.ca
www.etcmedia.ca
www.facebook.com/revueetcmedia

Tirage: 3 000
Fréquence: 3 fois par an
Isabelle Lelarge, Rédacteur-en-chef, etc.lelarge@videotron.ca

Galleries West
#301, 690 Princeton Way SW, Calgary, AB T2P 5J9

Tel: 403-234-7097; Fax: 403-243-4649
Toll-Free: 866-415-3282
publisher@gallerieswest.ca
www.gallerieswest.ca

Digital magazine published every two weeks.
Portia Priegert, Editor, editor@gallerieswest.ca

Inter, art actuel
Ancienement: Intervention
Les Éditions intervention, 345, rue du Pont, Québec, QC G1K 6M4

Tél: 418-529-9680; Téléc: 418-529-6933
infos@inter-lelieu.org
www.inter-lelieu.org
www.youtube.com/user/intervention22
twitter.com/lelieuinter
www.facebook.com/inter.art.actuel

Tirage: 1 200
Fréquence: 3 fois par an
Inter, art actuel est une revue culturelle disséminant diverses formes de l'art actuel: performance, art action, installation, poésie, manouvre, multimédia, etc.
Richard Martel, Coordination artistique,
programmation@inter-lelieu.org

Muse
Canadian Museums Assn., #400, 280 Metcalfe St., Ottawa, ON K2P 1R7

Tel: 613-567-0099; Fax: 613-233-5438
Toll-Free: 888-822-2907
info@museums.ca
www.museums.ca/site/muse

Circulation: 2,500
Frequency: 6 times a year
Publication addressing the issues affecting museums, as well as industry practices & projects. Includes news, book reviews, opinion pieces, & current events coverage.

Qui Fait Quoi
CP 64002 Le Gardeur, 4841, rue Jeanne-Mance, Montréal, QC H2V 4J6

Tél: 514-842-5333; Téléc: 514-495-1069
info@qfq.com
www.qfq.com

Tirage: 8000
Fréquence: 9 fois par an
Steeve Laprise, Rédacteur en chef/éditeur, redaction@qfq.com

ROM
Previous Name: Rotunda
c/o Royal Ontario Museum, 100 Queen's Park, Toronto, ON M5S 2C6

Tel: 416-586-8000
info@rom.on.ca
www.rom.on.ca

Frequency: Quarterly

Slate
155 King St. East, Kingston, ON K7L 2Z9

Toll-Free: 800-871-8093
info@slateartguide.com
www.slateartguide.com

Frequency: 8 times a year
Allan Lochhead, Publisher, allan@slateartguide.com

Spirale
#203, 4067 boul Saint-Laurent, Montréal, QC H2W 1Y7

Tél: 438-862-4737
info@magazine-spirale.com
www.spiralemagazine.com

Tirage: 1 500
Sébastien Dulude, Directeur général

Vie des Arts
#603, 5605, av De Gaspé, Montréal, QC H2T 2A4

Tél: 514-282-0205; Téléc: 514-282-0235
redaction@viedesarts.com
viedesarts.com
www.facebook.com/viedesarts

Fréquence: 4 fois par an
Jade Boivin, Rédactrice en chef

Automobile, Cycle, & Automotive Accessories

Canadian Biker
PO Box 4122, Victoria, BC V8X 3X4

Tel: 250-384-0333
cdnbkr.ca
www.facebook.com/208957889117312

Frequency: 6 times a year

Le Monde du VTT
#260, 414 boul Sir-Wilfrid-Laurier, Mont-Saint-Hilaire, QC J3H 3N9

Tél: 450-464-1479; Téléc: 450-464-8271
Ligne sans frais: 866-522-5656
www.quadnet.ca

Tirage: 9 560
Fréquence: 6 times a year

Motocycliste
c/o Fédération Motocycliste du Québec, Lévis, QC G6K 1K5
Tél: 514-252-8121
info@fmq.ca
www.fmq.ca
Tirage: 15 500
Fréquence: 5 fois par an

Old Autos
PO Box 250, 348 Main St., Bothwell, ON N0P 1C0
info@oldautos.ca
oldautos.ca
www.facebook.com/oldautos.ca
Frequency: Bi-monthly

Pedal Magazine
#200, 260 Spadina Ave., Toronto, ON M5T 2E4
Tel: 416-977-2100; *Fax:* 416-977-9200
Toll-Free: 866-977-3325
info@pedalmag.com
www.pedalmag.com
twitter.com/pedalmagazine
www.facebook.com/101939769846530
Cycling magazine with information on races, adventure touring & recreational cycling

Pole Position
QC
Tel: 450-464-4076; *Fax:* 450-464-7742
info@poleposition.ca
www.poleposition.ca
www.instagram.com/polepositionmagazine
twitter.com/polepositionmag
www .facebook.com/polepositionmagazine
Circulation: 16,625
Frequency: 8 times a year
Philippe Brasseur, Président

Vancouver International Auto Show Guide
Owned By: Carling Media
Carling Media, 118 Dunsmuir St., Vancouver, BC V6B 1X7
Toll-Free: 877-260-1646
editorial@carlingmedia.com
www.carlingmedia.com
Circulation: 48,000
Frequency: 1 issue per year; English & Chinese
Distributed free to visitors of the Vancouver International Auto Show that runs the last week of March into early April.
Regina Chan, Editor

Vélo Mag
Détenteur: Vélo Québec Éditions
Maison des Cyclistes, 1251, rue Rachel est, Montréal, QC H2J 2J9
Tél: 514-521-8356 *Ligne sans frais:* 800-567-8356
www.velomag.com
www.facebook.com/VeloMagQc
Fréquence: 6 fois par an
Jacques Sennechael, Rédacteur-en-chef, jsennechael@velo.qc.ca

Aviation & Aerospace

Canadian Aviation Historical Society Journal
PO Box 2700 D, Ottawa, ON K1P 5W7
Tel: 519-742-6965
www.cahs.com
Frequency: Quarterly
Terry Higgins, Managing Editor & Director, Graphics

Boating & Yachting

Boats & Places
Previous Name: Today's Boating
#1, 72 Churchill Dr., Barrie, ON L4N 8Z5
Tel: 705-725-4669; *Fax:* 705-725-4996
info@lifestyleintegrated.com
www.boatsandplaces.com
twitter.com/BoatsandPlaces
www.facebook.com/BoatsandPlaces
Circulation: 24,692
Frequency: 6 times a year
Publishes information relevant to Canadian boaters
Brian Minton, President & Publisher, 705-725-4669 ext.224, brianm@lifestyleintegrated.com

Canadian Yachting
Owned By: Kerrwil Publications Limited
538 Elizabeth St., Midland, ON L4R 2A3
Tel: 705-527-7666
info@canadianyachting.ca
www.canadianyachting.ca
twitter.com/CdnYachting
Www.facebook.com/canadian.yachting

Frequency: 6 times a year
Greg Nicoll, Publisher, 877-620-9373, gnicoll@kerrwil.com
Andy Adams, Managing Editor, 416-574-7313, aadams@kerrwill.com

L'Escale Nautique
Détenteur: Les Productions Maritimes
535, route de la Montagne, Notre-Dame-du-Portage, QC G0L 1Y0
Tél: 418-863-5055; *Téléc:* 418-850-4674
redaction@escalenautique.qc.ca
www.escalenautique.qc.ca
www.facebook.com/283699044980203
Tirage: 12 000
Fréquence: 4 fois par an, plus guide nautique
Michel Sacco, Rédacteur-en-chef

Ontario Sailor Magazine
Previous Name: Lake Ontario Sailor Magazine
91 Hemmingway Dr., Courtice, ON L1E 2C2
Tel: 905-434-7409; *Fax:* 905-434-1654
sails@istar.ca
www.ontariosailormagazine.ca
Circulation: 10,000
Frequency: 7 times a year

Les Plaisanciers
Détenteur: Taylor Publishing Group
c/o Taylor Publishing Group, #268, 44 Crawford Cres., Campbellville, ON L0P 1B0
Tél: 905-844-8214
lesplaisanciers.com
Fréquence: 5 fois par an

Power Boating Canada
Owned By: Taylor Publishing Group
c/o Taylor Publishing Group, #268, 44 Crawford Cres., Campbellville, ON L0P 1B0
Toll-Free: 800-354-9145
info@powerboating.com
powerboating.com
twitter.com/PowerBoatingCan
www.facebook.com/PowerBoatingCanada
Frequency: 6 times a year
William Taylor, Publisher

Books

Amphora
c/o Alcuin Society, PO Box 3216, Vancouver, BC V6B 3X8
Tel: 604-734-1270
info@alcuinsociety.com
www.alcuinsociety.com
alcuinsociety.com/blog
twitter.com/alcuin
www.facebook.com/alcuinsociety
Circulation: 340
Frequency: 3 times a year
Amphora, the Alcuin Society's journal, presents original articles, interviews, & departments focusing on topics related to the book arts: collecting, typography, typesetting, calligraphy, papermaking, ornamentation, illustration, printing, & binding.
Peter Mitham, Editor, pmitham@telus.net

BC BookWorld
3516 West 13th Ave., Vancouver, BC V6R 2S3
Tel: 604-736-4011; *Fax:* 604-736-4011
bookworld@telus.net
www.bcbookworld.com
Circulation: 100,000
Frequency: Quarterly
Publication about books
Alan Twigg, Publisher
David Lester, Editor

Brides, Bridal

Ottawa Wedding
Owned By: Coyle Media Group
c/o Coyle Media Group, 67 Neil Ave., Stittsville, ON K2S 1B9
Tel: 613-271-8903; *Fax:* 613-271-8905
www.ottawaweddingmagazine.com
www.facebook.com/OttawaWeddingMagazine
Frequency: 2 times a year
Pam Dillon, Editor, pam@coylemediagroup.com

Today's Bride
Owned By: Newcom Media Inc.
#400, 5353 Dundas St. West, Toronto, ON M9B 6H8
Tel: 416-614-2200
info@canadianbride.com
www.todaysbride.ca
www.instagram.com/todaysbridemag
twitter.com/Todaysbridemag
www.facebook.com/todaysbridemagcanada
Frequency: 2 times a year
Amy Bielby, Editor, amy@newcom.ca

Business & Finance

Business in Vancouver (BIV)
Owned By: Glacier Media Inc.
303 West 5th Ave., Vancouver, BC V5Y 1J6
Tel: 604-688-2398
news@biv.com
www.biv.com
www.linkedin.com/company/business-in-vancouver
twitter.com/bizinvancouver
www.facebook.com/BIVMG
Frequency: Weekly, Tue.
Paul Harris, President & Publisher, 604-608-5156, pharris@biv.com
Fiona Anderson, Editor-in-Chief, 604-608-5183, fanderson@biv.com

Canadian MoneySaver
#700, 55 King St. West, Kitchener, ON N2G 4W1
Tel: 519-772-7632
moneyinfo@canadianmoneysaver.ca
www.canadianmoneysaver.ca
www.youtube.com/user/canadianmoneysaver
twitter.com/cdnmoneysaver
www.facebook.com/239193689507527
Frequency: 9 times a year
Canadian MoneySaver is an is an independent, membership-funded investment advisory magazine. Canadian MoneySaver publishes monthly with three double issues (July/August, November/December and March/April).
Peter Hodson, Editor, research@5iresearch.ca

MONEY Magazine
Money Canada Limited, #226, 7181 Woodbine Ave., Markham, ON
info@money.ca
www.money.ca
www.linkedin.com/groups/Money-Magazine-3001638
Frequency: Monthly
Finance & lifestyle magazine
James Dean, Editor-in-Chief

The Wire Report
Owned By: The Hill Times Publishing Inc.
69 Sparks St., Ottawa, ON K1P 5A5
Tel: 613-232-5952; *Fax:* 613-232-9055
roneill@hilltimes.com
www.thewirereport.ca
twitter.com/thewirereport
Circulation: 60,000
Frequency: Weekly
Anja Karadeglija, Editor, 613-688-8823, akarad@thewirereport.ca

Camping & Outdoor Recreation

Camping Caravaning
#100, 1560, rue Eiffel, Boucherville, QC J4B 5Y1
Tél: 450-650-3722; *Téléc:* 450-650-3721
Ligne sans frais: 877-650-3722
info@campingcaravaningmag.ca
www.campingcaravaningmag.ca
twitter.com/magazinecamping
www.facebook.com/Camping.Caravaning
Tirage: 46 000
Fréquence: 8 fois par an
Yvan Lafontaine, Président
André Rivest, Éditeur
Louise Gagnon, Directrice de la publication

Canadian RVing
Explorer RV Club, PO Box 800, #11, 328 Mill St., Beaverton, ON L0K 1A0
Fax: 705-426-1403
Toll-Free: 800-999-0819
info@canadianrving.com
www.canadianrving.com
Frequency: Bi-monthly
Theresa Rogers, Editor

explore
Owned By: OP Media Group Ltd.
PO Box 57096 East Hastings, Vancouver, BC V5K 5G6
Toll-Free: 888-924-7524
explore@explore-mag.com
www.explore-mag.com
www.youtube.com/user/exploremag
twitter.com/explore_mag
www.facebook.c om/exploremag
Frequency: Quarterly
Brad Liski, Publisher
David Webb, Editor

Children's

Bazoof!
Previous Name: Zamoof!
Owned By: Dream Wave Publishing Inc.
1879 West 2nd Ave., Vancouver, BC V6J 1J1
Tel: 250-762-9624; *Fax:* 905-946-1679
Toll-Free: 877-762-9624
mail@bazoof.com
www.bazoof.com
twitter.com/bazoofmag
www.facebook.com/bazoofmag
Frequency: 6 times a year

chickaDEE
Owned By: Owlkids Books
PO Box 726 Main, Markham, ON L3P 7V9
Toll-Free: 800-551-6957
owlkids@kckglobal.com
www.owlkids.com
Frequency: 10 times a year

Chirp
Owned By: Owlkids Books
#400, 10 Lower Spadina Ave., Toronto, ON M5V 2Z2
Tel: 416-340-2700; *Fax:* 416-340-9769
Toll-Free: 800-551-6957
owlkids@owlkids.com
www.owlkids.com/magazines/chirp
Circulation: 48,398
Frequency: 10 times a year
Jackie Farquhar, Editor

Les Débrouillards
Publications BLD inc., 4475, rue Frontenac, Montréal, QC H2H 2S2
Tél: 514-844-2111; *Téléc:* 514-278-3030
scientific@lesdebrouillards.com
www.lesdebrouillards.com
Tirage: 27 000
Fréquence: 11 fois par an
Magazines sur la science pour les jeunes
Félix Maltais, Éditeur, 514-844-2111 ext.263,
felix.maltais@lesdebrouillards.com
Isabelle Vaillancourt, Rédactrice en chef

Les Explorateurs
Publications BLD inc., 4475, rue Frontenac, Montréal, QC H2H 2S2
Tél: 514-844-2111; *Téléc:* 514-278-3030
lesexplorateurs@lesdebrouillards.com
www.lesexplos.com
Tirage: 24 000
Fréquence: 11 fois par an
Félix Maltais, Éditeur
Sarah Perreault, Rédactrice en chef

J'Aime Lire
Détenteur: Bayard Presse Canada Inc.
4475, rue Frontenac, Montréal, QC H2H 2S2
Ligne sans frais: 866-600-0061
redaction@bayardpresse.qc.ca
www.bayardjeunesse.ca
Tirage: 10 000
Fréquence: 10 fois par an
Hugues de Foucauld, Directeur général

Kayak: Canada's History Magazine for Kids
Bryce Hall, 515 Portage Ave., Winnipeg, MB R3B 2E9
Tel: 204-988-9300; *Fax:* 204-988-9309
Toll-Free: 866-952-3444
www.canadashistory.ca/magazines
Frequency: Quarterly

OWL Magazine
Owned By: Owlkids Books
PO Box 726 Main, Markham, ON L3P 7V9
Toll-Free: 800-551-6957
owlkids@kckglobal.com
www.owlkids.com

Frequency: 10 times a year

City Magazine

Alberta Views
#208, 320 - 23 Ave. SW, Calgary, AB T2S 0J2
Tel: 403-243-5334; *Fax:* 403-243-8599
Toll-Free: 877-212-5334
avadmin@albertaviews.ab.ca
www.albertaviews.ca
twitter.com/Alberta ViewsMag
www.facebook.com/albertaviewsmagazine
Circulation: 15,000
Frequency: 10 times a year
Magazine for the people of Alberta; discusses politics,
education, industry, public service, & the arts
Jackie Flanagan, Founding Editor
Beth Ed, Publisher

Avenue
#100, 1900 - 11th St. SE, Calgary, AB T2G 3G2
Tel: 403-240-9055; *Fax:* 403-240-9059
www.avenuemagazine.ca
twitter.com/AvenueMagazine
www.facebook.com/avenuecalgary
Frequency: Monthly
Magazine showcasing city architecture, personality, art, culture,
fashion, food, & outdoor life. Avenue Edmonton: 10221, 123 St.,
Edmonton, AB T5N 1N3, 780-451-1379, Fax: 780-482-5417,
Toll-Free: 1-866-451-1379
Joyce Byrne, Publisher, jbyrne@redpointmedia.ca
Jennifer Hamilton, Executive Editor,
jhamilton@redpointmedia.ca
Kathe Lemon, Editor, klemon@redpointmedia.ca

Bayview Post
30 Lesmill Rd., Toronto, ON M3B 2T6
Tel: 416-250-7979; *Fax:* 416-250-1737
advertising@postcity.com
www.postcity.com/Bayview-Post
Other information: Classified Advertising, Email:
classifieds@postcity.com
twitter.com/PostCity
www.facebook.com/PostCityMagazines
Circulation: 25,000
Frequency: Monthly
The magazine features news, articles, & advertising of interest to
persons of Toronto's Bayview neighbourhood.
Lorne London, Publisher, lornelondon@postcity.com
Ron Johnson, Editor, ronjohnson@postcity.com

Boulevard Victoria
Owned By: Black Press Group Ltd.
818 Broughton St., Victoria, BC V8W 1E4
Tel: 250-381-3484; *Fax:* 250-386-2624
info@blvdmag.ca
www.boulevardmagazines.com
twitter.com/boulevardmag
www.facebook.com/BoulevardMagazine
Circulation: 45,000
Frequency: Bi-monthly
Mario Gedicke, Publisher
Susan Lundy, Editor

The False Creek News
915 London St., New Westminster, BC V3M 3B5
Tel: 778-398-2000
mail@thefalsecreeknews.com
www.thefalsecreeknews.com
Other information: Advertising, Email:
adsales@thefalsecreeknews.com
Circulation: 25,000
The False Creek News features reports & information about
local issues, arts, & entertainment. The magazine is of interest to
residents of Vancouver's False Creek, Fairview Slopes, &
Granville Island neighbourhoods. Copies of the magazine are
distributed to homes, businesses, & community centres.
M. Juma, Publisher
S. Bowell, Editor
N. Ebrahim, Manager, Advertising
G. Jiwa, Manager, Administration
A. Rattanshi, Accountant
A. Thobhani, Contact, Circulation

The Georgia Straight
Owned By: Vancouver Free Press Publishing Corp.
1701 West Broadway St., Vancouver, BC V6J 1Y3
Tel: 604-730-7000; *Fax:* 604-730-7010
contact@straight.com
www.straight.com
www.linkedin.com/companies/the-georgia-straight
twitter.com/georgiastrai ght
www.facebook.com/georgiastraight

Frequency: Weekly
Dan McLeod, Publisher/Editor
Matt McLeod, General Manager

Hamilton Magazine
Previous Name: Hamilton This Month
Owned By: Postmedia Network Inc.
940 Main St. West, Hamilton, ON L8S 1B1
Tel: 905-522-6117; *Fax:* 905-769-1105
www.hamiltonmagazine.com
twitter.com/hamiltonmag
www.facebook.com/HamiltonMag
Frequency: 5 times a year

HighGrader
PO Box 20055, Timmins, ON P4N 0A5
Tel: 705-266-4950
highgrader@nt.net
www.highgradermagazine.com
Circulation: 2,500
Syl Belisle, Publisher

Island Times Magazine
PO Box 956, 1182 East Island Hwy, Parksville, BC V9P 2G9
Tel: 250-228-0995; *Fax:* 250-586-4405
publisher@islandtimesmagazine.ca
issuu.com/island-times-magazine
www.facebook.com/islandtimesmagazine.ca
Vancouver Island lifestyles magazine.
Jolene Aarbo, Publisher
Julie McManus, Editor

Kingston Life Magazine
Owned By: Postmedia Network Inc.
Kingston Publications, PO Box 2300, Kingston, ON K7L 4Z7
Tel: 613-544-5000; *Fax:* 613-530-4122
www.thewhig.com/category/magazines
twitter.com/kingston_life
www.facebook.com/KingstonLifemag
Frequency: 8 times a year
Kingston Life is delivered by controlled circulation through The
Kingston Whig-Standard, sent to subscribers & sold at selected
newsstands in Kingston, Ottawa, Toronto & Montreal.
Justine de Leyer, Editor, jdeleyer@postmedia.com

Lethbridge Living
1518 - 3rd Ave. South, Lethbridge, AB T1J 0K8
Tel: 403-381-1454; *Fax:* 403-330-3075
editor@lethbridgeliving.com
lethbridgeliving.com
twitter.com/Lethliving
www.facebook.com/lethbridge.living
Circulation: 17,000
Frequency: 6 times a year
Focus on the people and diversity of cultures in Lethbridge and
Southern Alberta.
Martin Oordt, Editor
Mary Oordt, Managing Editor

Monday Magazine
Owned By: Black Press
818 Broughton St., Victoria, BC V8W 1E4
Tel: 250-382-6188
www.mondaymag.com
twitter.com/mondaymag
www.facebook.com/MondayMagazine
Frequency: Weekly
The magazine of Victoria, British Columbia presents alternative
news & entertainment information. Print & e-editions are
available.
Penny Sakamoto, Group Publisher, publisher@mondaymag.com
Oliver Sommer, Associate Group Publisher,
osommer@blackpress.ca
Ruby Della Siega, Publisher, ruby@mondaymag.com
Sara Wilson, Editor, editor@mondaymag.com

Niagara Escarpment Views
Owned By: 1826789 Ontario Inc.
50 Ann St., Georgetown, ON L7G 2V2
Tel: 905-877-9665
www.escarpmentviews.ca
Frequency: Quarterly
The magazine is dedicated to Ontario's Niagara Escarpment
community.
Gloria Hildebrandt, Editor & Co-Publisher, 905-873-2834
Mike Davis, Co-Publisher & Accounts Manager, 905-877-9665

Niagara Life Magazine
Previous Name: The Downtowner
Owned By: Metroland West Media Group
#1B, 3300 Merrittville Hwy., Thorold, ON L2V 4Y6
Tel: 905-641-1984; *Fax:* 905-688-9272
feedback@niagaralifemag.com
www.niagarathisweek.com

Circulation: 45,000
Frequency: 8 times a year
Neil Oliver, Publisher
Melinda Cheevers, Editor-in-Chief

Northword Magazine
1412 Freeland Ave., Smithers, BC V0J 2N4
Tel: 250-847-4600
www.northword.ca

Circulation: 10,000
Frequency: 6 times a year
Serves the northern BC region.
Matt J. Simmons, Publisher & Editor-in-Chief,
matt@northword.ca

Now
Also Known As: NOW Communications Inc.
Owned By: Media Central Corp.
#503, 192 Spadina Ave., Toronto, ON M5T 2C2
Tel: 416-364-1300; *Fax:* 416-364-1166
web@nowtoronto.com
www.nowtoronto.com
www.instagram.com/nowtoronto
twitter.com/nowtoronto
www.facebook.com/n owmagazine
Frequency: Weekly; Thursday
Brian Kalish, Chief Executive Officer
Alice Klein, Owner, Editor & Publisher
Enzo Dimatteo, Editorial Director

Ottawa City Magazine
St. Joseph Media Inc., 43 Eccles St., Ottawa, ON K1R 6S3
Tel: 613-230-0333
www.ottawamagazine.com
twitter.com/ottawamag
www.facebook.com/OttawaMag
Circulation: 33,000
Frequency: 7 times a year
Dianne Wing, Publisher, dianne.wing@stjoseph.com
Dayanti Karunaratne, Editor-in-Chief,
dayanti@stjosephmedia.com

Ottawa Life Magazine
301 Metcalfe, Lower Level, Ottawa, ON K2P 1R9
Tel: 613-688-5433; *Fax:* 613-688-1994
info@ottawalife.com
www.ottawalife.com
www.instagram.com/ottawalife
twitter.com/ottawalifers
www.facebook. com/OttawaLifeMagazine
Circulation: 40,000
Frequency: 6 times a year
Dan Donovan, Publisher & Managing Editor

The Ottawa XPress
Owned By: Communications Voir Inc.
704 Somerset St. West, Ottawa, ON K1R 6P6
Tel: 613-237-8226; *Fax:* 613-237-8220
Toll-Free: 866-255-5516
info@ottawaxpress.ca
www.ottawaxpress.ca
twitter.com/ottawaxpress
www.facebook.com/ottawaxpress
Circulation: 63,500
Frequency: Weekly, Thu.
Guillaume Moffet, Managing Editor

Pique Newsmagazine
Owned By: Pique Publishing Inc.
#103, 1390 Alpha Lake Rd., Whistler, BC V0N 1B1
Tel: 604-938-0202
www.piquenewsmagazine.com
twitter.com/piquenews
www.facebook.com/PiqueNewsmagazine
Circulation: 16,500
Frequency: Weekly, Fri.
Sarah Strother, Publisher, sarah@piquenewsmagazine.com
Clare Ogilvie, Editor, edit@piquenewsmagazine.com

Planet S
Owned By: Hullabaloo Publishing Ltd.
#409, 135 - 21st St. East, Saskatoon, SK S7K 0B4
Tel: 306-651-3423; *Fax:* 306-651-3428
reception@planetsmag.com
www.planetsmag.com
twitter.com/PlanetSMagazine
www.facebook.com/40716663512
Circulation: 60,000
Stephen Whitworth, Editor, editor@planetsmag.com

the prairie dog
#201, 1836 Scarth St., Regina, SK S4P 2G3
Tel: 306-757-8522; *Fax:* 306-352-9686
reception@prairiedogmag.com
www.prairiedogmag.com
Circulation: 16,000
Frequency: Bi-weekly
Terry Morash, Publisher, tm@prairiedogmag.com
Stephen Whitworth, Editor, editor@prairiedogmag.com

Profile Kingston
Owned By: Riverview Publishing Inc.
PO Box 91, Kingston, ON K7L 4V6
Tel: 613-546-6723; *Fax:* 613-546-0707
editor@profilekingston.com
www.profilekingston.com
Circulation: 16,000
Frequency: 6 times a year
Bonnie Golomb, Publisher

Spacing
Owned By: Spacing Media
#B-02, 401 Richmond St. West, Toronto, ON M5V 3A8
Tel: 416-644-1017
info@spacing.ca
spacing.ca
www.flickr.com/groups/spacingmagpool
twitter.com/spacing
Matthew Blackett, Publisher/Creative Director, matt@spacing.ca
Todd Harrison, Managing Editor, toddharrison@spacing.ca

Thornhill Post
30 Lesmill Rd., Toronto, ON M3B 2T6
Tel: 416-250-7979; *Fax:* 416-250-1737
advertising@postcity.com
www.postcity.com/Neighbourhoods/Thornhill
Other information: Classified Advertising, Email:
classifieds@postcity.com
twitter.com/PostCity
www.facebook.com/PostCityMagazines
Circulation: 25,000
Frequency: Monthly
The magazine serves Thornhill, Ontario by featuring news &
information about local people, places, events, restaurants, &
shopping.
Lorne London, Publisher, lornelondon@postcity.com
Ron Johnson, Editor, ronjohnson@postcity.com

Thunder Bay Guest Magazine
87 North Hill St., Thunder Bay, ON P7A 5V6
Tel: 804-346-2600; *Fax:* 807-345-9923
Frequency: 9 times a year

Vancouver Magazine
Owned By: Canada Wide Media Limited
#560, 2608 Granville St., Vancouver, BC V6H 3V3
Tel: 604-877-7732; *Fax:* 604-877-4848
mail@vancouvermagazine.com
www.vanmag.co
www.instagram.com/vanmag_com
twitter.com/vanmag_com
www.facebook.com/v ancouvermagazine
Frequency: 10 times a year
Samantha Legge, Publisher
Anicka Quin, Editorial Director

Village Post
30 Lesmill Rd., Toronto, ON M3B 2T6
Tel: 416-250-7979; *Fax:* 416-250-1737
advertising@postcity.com
www.postcity.com/Neighbourhoods/Village
Other information: Classified Advertising, Email:
classifieds@postcity.com
twitter.com/PostCity
www.facebook.com/PostCityMagazines
Circulation: 25,000
Frequency: Monthly
The Forest Hill & Yorkville neighbourhoods of Toronto are served
by The Village Post, which features reports on local news,
people, & lifestyles.
Lorne London, Publisher, lornelondon@postcity.com
Ron Johnson, Editor, ronjohnson@postcity.com

Visitors' Choice
701 West George St., Vancouver, BC V7Y 1C6
Tel: 604-568-0095
info@visitorschoice.com
www.visitorschoice.com
twitter.com/VisitorsChoice
Circulation: 475,000
Frequency: 6 times a year
Publishes visitor's guides for Vancouver & BC's Lower Mainland
Randy Vannatter, Publisher
Noa Nichol, Editor

Voir Montréal
#1007, 606, rue Cathcart, Montréal, QC H3B 1K9
Tél: 514-848-1112; *Téléc:* 514-848-0533
Ligne sans frais: 877-631-8647
info@voir.ca
www.voir.ca
fr.pinterest.com/magazinevoir
twitter.com/voir
www.facebook.com/journalvoir
Tirage: 102 000
Simon Jodoin, Rédacteur-en-chef

Where Calgary
Owned By: St. Joseph Media
#206, 1201 - 5th St. SW, Calgary, AB T2R 0Y6
Tel: 403-299-1888
editor_calgary@where.ca
where.ca/alberta/calgary
twitter.com/wherecalgary
Frequency: Bi-monthly

Where Edmonton
Owned By: St. Joseph Media
#1, 9301 - 50th St., Edmonton, AB T6B 2L5
Tel: 780-465-3362
editor@whereedmonton.com
www.where.ca/promotion/edmonton
Circulation: 33,240
Frequency: 6 times a year
Rob Tanner, Publisher

Where Halifax
Owned By: St. Joseph Media
2882 Gottingen St., Halifax, NS B3K 3E2
Tel: 902-420-9943
where.ca/cover/halifax
twitter.com/Where_Halifax
Frequency: 10 times a year
Patty Baxter, Publisher

Where Ottawa
Previous Name: Where Ottawa-Hull
Owned By: St. Joseph Media
43 Eccles St., 1st Fl., Ottawa, ON K1R 6S3
Tel: 613-230-0333
where.ca/ontario/ottawa
Frequency: Bi-Monthly

Where Toronto / Muskoka / Parry Sound
Owned By: St. Joseph Media
#320, 111 Queen St. East, Toronto, ON M5C 1S2
Tel: 416-364-3333 Toll-Free: 800-387-1156
where.ca/ontario/toronto
Frequency: Monthly

Where Victoria
Previous Name: Victoria Today
Owned By: St. Joseph Media
818 Broughton St., Victoria, BC V8W 1E4
Tel: 250-383-3633
editor@wherevictoria.com
where.ca/british-columbia/victoria

Where Winnipeg
Owned By: St. Joseph Media
#400, 112 Market Ave., Winnipeg, MB R3B 0P4
Tel: 204-943-4439
where.ca/manitoba/winnipeg

Whistler, the Magazine
Owned By: Glacier Media Inc.
#103, 1390 Alpha Lake Rd., Whistler, BC V0N 1B1
Tel: 604-938-0202
www.whistlermagazine.com
twitter.com/whistlersmag
www.facebook.com/WhistlerMagazine
Circulation: 40,000
Frequency: Biannually
Leisure magazine targeted toward tourists in the Whistler resort
area.
Susan Strother, Publisher

Catherine Power-Chartrand, General Manager,
cpower@whistlerthemagazine.com
Shelley Ackerman, Managing Editor & Art Director
Cathryn Atkinson, Editor
Heidi Rode, Office Manager

Windsor Life Magazine
#318, 5060 Tecumseh Rd. East, Windsor, ON N8T 1C1
Tel: 519-979-5433; *Fax:* 519-979-9237
info@windsorlife.com
www.windsorlife.com
twitter.com/WindsorLifeMag
www.facebook.com/windsorlifemagazine

Circulation: 72,800
Frequency: 8 times a year
Robert E. Robinson, Publisher, publisher@windsorlife.com

The Yards
#1011, 10301 - 104th St. NW, Edmonton, AB T5J 1B9
info@theyardsyeg.ca
www.theyardsyeg.ca
twitter.com/theyardsyeg
www.facebook.com/theyardsyeg

Frequency: Quarterly
Collections of urban planning, development, lifestyle & cultural stories of Edmonton's transformation & growth.
Simon Yackulic, Publisher, simon@theyardsyeg.ca
Rebecca Medel, Editor, editor@theyardsyeg.ca

Computing & Technology

We Compute
1232 Kingston Rd., Toronto, ON M1N 1P3
Tel: 416-481-1955; *Fax:* 416-481-2819

Circulation: 150,000
Frequency: 12 times a year
Eric Macmillan, Editor
George Bachir, Publisher

Cosmetics

elevate magazine
Owned By: Salon Communications Inc.
#202, 183 Bathurst St., Toronto, ON M5T 2R7
Tel: 416-869-3131; *Fax:* 416-869-3008
info@elevatemagazine.com
www.elevatemagazine.com
www.instagram.com/elevatecanada
twitter.com/elevatemagazine
www.fac ebook.com/ElevateMagazine
Laura Dunphy, Publisher, laura@salonmagazine.ca
Amanpreet Dhami, Editor-in-Chief,
amanpreet@elevatemagazine.com

The Kit
Owned By: Torstar Corporation
#204, 1 Yonge St., Toronto, ON M5E 1E6
Tel: 416-945-8700
info@thekit.ca
www.thekit.ca
twitter.com/thekit
www.facebook.com/TheKITmag

Frequency: Monthly
Giorgina Bigioni, Publisher

Culture, Current Events

Adbusters
1234 West 7th Ave., Vancouver, BC V6H 1B7
Tel: 604-736-9401; *Fax:* 604-737-6021
Toll-Free: 800-663-1243
info@adbusters.org
www.adbusters.org
www.instagram.com/adbusters.magazine
twitter.com/adbusters
www.facebook.com/adbusters

Circulation: 60,000
Frequency: Bi-monthly
Non-profit & reader-supported activist magazine
Kalle Lasn, Co-Founder & Editor-in-Chief

Broken Pencil
PO Box 203 P, Toronto, ON M5S 2S7
Tel: 416-204-1700
www.brokenpencil.com

Circulation: 5,000
Frequency: 4 times a year
Devoted exclusively to underground culture & the independent arts.
Hal Niedzviecki, Publisher, hal@brokenpencil.com
Jonathan Valelly, Editor, editor@brokenpencil.com

HELLO!
Owned By: Rogers Media Inc.
1 Mount Pleasant Rd., 8th Fl., Toronto, ON M4Y 2Y5
Tel: 416-764-2863; *Fax:* 416-764-2866
contact@hellomagazine.ca
www.hellomagazine.ca
twitter.com/HELLOCanada
www.facebook.com/138543579563513

Circulation: 137,025
Frequency: 46 issues per year
Alison Eastwood, Editor-in-Chief

Maisonneuve
PO Box 53527, 1051 boul Decarie, St Laurent, QC H4L 5J9
Tel: 514-482-5089
business@maisonneuve.org
maisonneuve.org
twitter.com/maisonneuvemag
www.facebook.com/maisonneuvemagazine

Frequency: Quarterly
Jennifer Varkonyi, Publisher
Daniel Viola, Editor-in-Chief

The Newfoundland Herald
NL
Tel: 709-726-7060; *Fax:* 709-726-6971
info@nfldherald.com
nfldherald.com
twitter.com/TheNfldHerald
www.facebook.com/nfldherald

Circulation: 15,000
Frequency: Weekly
Pam Pardy-Ghent, Managing Editor, 709-570-5212,
pghent@nfldherald.com

Rural Delivery
Owned By: DvL Publishing Inc.
PO Box 1509, Liverpool, NS B0J 1K0
www.rurallife.ca/rural-delivery-tofc
www.facebook.com/287774221288330

Frequency: Monthly
Covers life in rural Atlantic Canada

Saltscapes Publishing Inc.
c/o Saltscapes, #209, 30 Damascus Rd., Bedford, NS B4A 0C1
Tel: 902-464-7258; *Fax:* 902-464-3755
www.saltscapes.com
www.instagram.com/saltscapes
twitter.com/saltscapes
www.facebook.co m/Saltscapesmagazine

Circulation: 40,000
Frequency: 6 times a year
Jim Gourlay, Publisher
Linda Gourlay, Publisher

West of the City
Owned By: Metroland Media Group Ltd.
901 Guelph Line, Burlington, ON L7R 3N8
Tel: 905-845-8536 *Toll-Free:* 800-693-7986
www.westofthecity.com
www.instagram.com/westofthecitymagazine
www.facebook.com/westofthecityma gazine
Upscale magazine targeting high-income neighbourhoods in Burlington, Oakville & Mississauga.
Cindi Campbell, Director, Media,
ccampbell@starmetrolandmedia.com
Ryan Maraj, Director, Media, rmaraj@starmetrolandmedia.com
Danielle Leonard, Editor-in-Chief, dleonard@metroland.com

Directories & Almanacs

Black Pages Directory
1390 Eglinton Ave. West, Toronto, ON M6C 2E4
Tel: 416-784-3002; *Fax:* 416-784-5719
www.blackpages.ca

Frequency: Annually
Black Pages Directory Canada is a comprehensive guide to Canada's Black & Caribbean community

Education

Life Learning Magazine
Life Media, #52, B2-125 Queensway, Toronto, ON M8Y 1H6
publisher@lifelearningmagazine.com
www.lifelearningmagazine.com
twitter.com/LifeLearningMag
www.facebook.com/LifeLearningMagazine

Circulation: 10,000
Frequency: Bi-monthly; digital
Rolf Priesnitz, Publisher
Wendy Priesnitz, Editor, editor@LifeLearningMagazine.com

Entertainment

The Buzz
160 Richmond St., Charlottetown, PE C1A 1H9
Tel: 902-628-1958
buzzon@eastlink.ca
www.buzzon.com
www.youtube.com/BUZZpei
twitter.com/buzzpei
www.facebook.com/thebuzzpe i

Circulation: Sept.-June - 15,000; July-Aug. - 26,000
Frequency: Monthly
Peter Richards, Managing Editor, 902-628-1958

Cinema Scope
465 Lytton Blvd., Toronto, ON M5N 1S5
Tel: 416-889-5430
info@cinema-scope.com
www.cinema-scope.com
twitter.com/CinemaScopeMag
www.facebook.com/205268252835971

Frequency: 4 times a year
Mark Peranson, Publisher & Editor

En Primeur
71 Barber Greene Rd., Toronto, ON M3C 2A2
Tél: 416-445-0544; *Téléc:* 416-445-2894
webmaster@enprimeur.ca
www.enprimeur.ca

Tirage: 105 000
Sandra I. Stewart, Président

Magazine Le Clap
2580, boul Laurier, Québec, QC G1V 2L1
Tél: 418-653-2470; *Téléc:* 418-653-6018
redaction@clap.ca
www.clap.qc.ca
www.youtube.com/user/LeCinemaLeClap
www.facebook.com/cinemaleclap

Fréquence: 6 fois par an

Star Cineplex
Previous Name: Cineplex Magazine
Owned By: Torstar Corporation
1 Yonge St., Toronto, ON M5E 1E6
Tel: 416-869-4010; *Fax:* 416-869-4183
www.torstar.com

Circulation: 700,000
Frequency: Monthly
Formerly known as Cineplex Magazine, Torstar bought the publication in 2021.

Star Système
Détenteur: TVA Publications inc.
1010, rue de Sérigny, 4e étage, Longueuil, QC J4K 5G7
Tél: 514-370-5823; *Téléc:* 514-270-7079
Ligne sans frais: 888-535-8634
www.tvapublications.com
www.facebook.com/StarSysteme

Fréquence: 51 fois par an

View Magazine
370 Main St. West, Hamilton, ON L8P 1K3
Tel: 905-527-3343; *Fax:* 905-527-3721
info@viewmag.com
www.viewmag.com
twitter.com/ViewHamilton
www.facebook.com/10259223335

Circulation: 30,000
Frequency: Weekly
Ron Kilpatrick, Editor, editor@viewmag.com
Sean Rosen, Publisher, seanr@viewmag.com

Vue Weekly
Owned By: Postvue Publishing Inc
#200, 11230 - 119th St. NW, Edmonton, AB T5G 2X3
Tel: 780-426-1996; *Fax:* 780-426-2889
www.vueweekly.com
www.instagram.com/vueweekly
twitter.com/vueweekly
www.facebook.com/ vueweekly

Circulation: 24,274
Frequency: Weekly
Ron Garth, Publisher & Editor, ron@vueweekly.com
Lee Butler, Interim Editor, lee@vueweekly.com

Environment & Nature

Atlantic Salmon Journal
Tel: 506-457-8737
www.asf.ca/atlantic-salmon-journal.html

Circulation: 10,500
Frequency: Quarterly

Publishes conservation-minded salmon angling & species protection articles.
Martin Silverstone, Editor, msilverstone@asf.ca

La Maison du 21e siècle
2955, rue du Domaine-du-lac-Lucerne, Sainte-Adèle, QC J8B 3K9

Tél: 514-500-4327
info@maisonsaine.ca
maisonsaine.ca
www.youtube.com/user/maison21e
twitter.com/Maison21e
www.facebook.com/ maisonsaine

Fréquence: 4 fois par an
André Fauteux, Éditeur, andre@maisonsaine.ca

Nature sauvage
Détenteur: Orinha Média
36, ch de Salzbourg est, Wentworth, QC J8H 0G7

Tél: 819-275-2177
courrier@naturesauvage.ca
www.naturesauvage.ca
www.facebook.com/1831792360476739

Fréquence: 4 fois par an
Pierre Hamel, Éditeur, phamel@orinhamedia.com

Québec Oiseaux
4545, av Pierre-De Coubertin, Montréal, QC H1V 0B2

Tél: 514-252-3190; *Téléc:* 514-251-8038
Ligne sans frais: 888-647-3289
info@quebecoiseaux.org
www.quebecoiseaux.org
www.youtube.com/user/QOiseaux
twitter.com/quebecoiseaux
www.facebook.c om/quebecoiseaux

Tirage: 30 000
Fréquence: 4 fois par an
Michel Préville, Rédacteur-en-chef

Watershed Sentinel
PO Box 1270, Comox, BC V9M 7Z8

Tel: 250-339-6117
editor@watershedsentinel.ca
watershedsentinel.ca
twitter.com/WatershSentinel
www.facebook.com/WatershedSentinelMagazine

Circulation: 5,000
Frequency: 5 times a year
This West Coast publication covers both bioregional & global perspectives on topics such as the environment, health & sustainability.
Delores Broten, Editor

Families

BC Parent Newsmagazine
PO Box 30020, Vancouver, BC V7H 2Y8

Tel: 778-855-2024
info@bcparent.ca
www.bcparent.ca
twitter.com/bcparentmag
www.facebook.com/bcparent

Circulation: 40,000
Frequency: 6 times a year
Independent parenting magazine providing information & articles on health care, education, birthing, arts, community events, & other family-related topics

Calgary's Child Magazine
#723, 710 - 20 Crowfoot Cres. NW, Calgary, AB T3G 2PG

Tel: 403-241-6066; *Fax:* 403-286-9731
calgaryschild@shaw.ca
www.calgaryschild.com
twitter.com/calgaryschild
www.facebook.com/calgaryschild

Circulation: 150,000
Frequency: 6 times a year
Ellen Percival, Publisher & Editor

City Parent
Owned By: Media Classified Corporation
#401, 610 Applewood Cres., Concord, ON L4K 0E3

Tel: 905-761-3313 *Toll-Free:* 888-761-3313
info@mediaclassified.ca
www.cityparent.com
www.instagram.com/cityparentmag
twitter.com/CityParentMag
www.facebook .com/cityparent

Circulation: 77,785
Frequency: 12 times a year

Divorce Magazine
#1179, 2255B Queen St. East, Toronto, ON M4E 1G3

Tel: 416-368-8853; *Fax:* 866-803-6667
Toll-Free: 888-803-6667
www.divorcemag.com
twitter.com/divorcemagazine
www.facebook.com/divorcemagazine

Circulation: 170,000
Frequency: 4 times a year
Dan Couvrette, CEO & Vice-President, Sales, danc@divorcemag.com
Diana Shepherd, Director, Editorial, diana@divorcemag.com

Edmonton's Child Magazine
Owned By: Gryphon Publishing
PO Box 369, 9768 - 170 St., Edmonton, AB T5T 5L4

Tel: 780-484-3360; *Fax:* 888-847-6258
info@edmontonschild.com
www.edmontonschild.com
twitter.com/edmontonschild
www.facebook.com/edmontonschild

Circulation: 33,000
Frequency: Bimonthly
Wendy Mueller, Publisher
Kerri Leland, Editor, editor@edmontonschild.com

Enfants Québec
1101, av Victoria, Saint-Lambert, QC J4R 1P8

Tél: 514-875-9612
serviceclient@enfantsquebec.com
enfantsquebec.com
www.facebook.com/enfantsquebec

Tirage: 60 506
Fréquence: 8 fois par an
Mathilde Singer, Rédactrice

Fit Parent
Toronto, ON

info@fitparentmagazine.com
www.fitparentmagazine.com

Frequency: 6 times a year
Craig Knight, Publisher, craig@fitparentmagazine.com

Our Kids: Canada's Camp & Program Guide
Owned By: Our Kids Publications Ltd.
4242 Rockwood Rd., Mississauga, ON L4W 1L8

Tel: 905-272-1843 *Toll-Free:* 877-272-1845
info@ourkidsmedia.com
www.ourkids.net
www.youtube.com/ourkidsnet
twitter.com/ourkidsnet
www.facebook.com/our kidsnet

Circulation: 200,000
Frequency: Annually
Agatha Stawicki, Publisher

Our Kids: Canada's Private School Guide
Owned By: Our Kids Publications Ltd.
4242 Rockwood Rd., Mississauga, ON L4W 1L8

Tel: 905-272-1843 *Toll-Free:* 877-272-1845
info@ourkidsmedia.com
www.ourkids.net
www.youtube.com/ourkidsnet
twitter.com/ourkidsnet
www.facebook.com/our kidsnet

Circulation: 250,000
Frequency: Annually
Agatha Stawicki, Publisher

Pomme d'Api Québec
Détenteur: Bayard Presse Canada Inc.
4475, rue Frontenac, Montréal, QC H2H 2S2

Ligne sans frais: 866-600-0061
redaction@bayardpresse.qc.ca
www.bayardjeunesse.ca

Tirage: 13 000
Fréquence: 11 par an
Hugues de Foucauld, Directeur général

7 Jours
Détenteur: TVA Publications inc.
1010, rue de Sérigny, 4e étage, Longueuil, QC J4K 5G7

Tél: 514-598-2880
7jours.ca
www.facebook.com/magazine7Jours

Fréquence: Hebdomadaire
Véronique Letter, Vice President

Today's Parent
Owned By: Rogers Media Inc.
1 Mount Pleasant Rd., 8th Fl., Toronto, ON M4Y 2Y5

Tel: 416-764-2836 *Toll-Free:* 800-567-8697
editors@todaysparent.com
www.todaysparent.com
twitter.com/Todaysparent
www.facebook.com/TodaysParent

Circulation: 160,056
Frequency: 6 times a year
Penny Hicks, Group Publisher
Sasha Emmons, Editor-in-Chief

Fashion

Clin d'oeil
Détenteur: TVA Publications inc.
1600, boul Maisonneuve est, Montréal, QC H2L 4P2

Tél: 514-596-9251
clindoeil.ca
twitter.com/Mag_clindoeil
www.facebook.com/magazineClindoeil

Fréquence: Mensuel

Dolce Magazine
Owned By: DOLCE Publishing Inc.
DOLCE Publishing Inc., #30, 111 Zenway Blvd., Vaughan, ON L4H 3H9

Tel: 905-264-6789; *Fax:* 905-264-3787
Toll-Free: 888-683-6523
www.dolcemag.com
twitter.com/dolcemag
www.facebook.com/dolceluxurymagazine

Circulation: 290,000
Frequency: Quarterly
Michelle Zerillo-Sosa, Publisher & Editor-in-Chief, michelle@dolce.ca

Fashion Magazine
Owned By: St. Joseph Media
St. Joseph Media, #320, 111 Queen St. East, Toronto, ON M5C 1S2

Tel: 416-364-3333; *Fax:* 416-594-3374
circ@fashionmagazine.com
fashionmagazine.com
www.pinterest.com/fashionmagazine
twitter.com/FashionCanada
www.facebook.com/fashioncanada

Frequency: 10 times a year
Bernadette Morra, Editor-in-Chief

Flare
Owned By: Rogers Media Inc.
One Mount Pleasant Rd., 8th Fl., Toronto, ON M4Y 2Y5

Tel: 416-764-2000; *Fax:* 416-764-2866
www.flare.com
flarefashion.tumblr.com
twitter.com/FLAREfashion
www.facebook.com/FLAREFashion

Flare is an online-only publication as of January 2017.
Melissa Ahlstrand, Group Publisher
Cameron Williamson, Editor-in-Chief

Globe Style Advisor
Owned By: Globe Media Group
444 Front St. West, Toronto, ON M5V 2S9

Tel: 416-585-5111; *Fax:* 416-585-5698
Toll-Free: 800-387-9012
advertising@globeandmail.com
www.globelink.ca/magazines/titles/styleadvi sor
twitter.com/globemediagroup
linkedin.com/company/globemediagroup

Circulation: 168,000 home subscribers
Frequency: Bi-monthly
Discusses personal style, home & design, & entertaining.

Nuvo Magazine
3055 Kingsway, Vancouver, BC V5R 5J8

Tel: 604-899-9380; *Fax:* 604-899-1450
Toll-Free: 877-205-6886
comments@nuvomagazine.com
www.nuvomagazine.com

Circulation: 50,000
Frequency: 4 times a year
Pasquale Cusano, Publisher
Claudia Cusano, Editor

Fifty-Plus Adults

Active Life
Owned By: Homes Publishing Group
#404, 37 Sandiford Dr., Stouffville, ON L4A 7X5
Tel: 905-479-4663; *Fax:* 905-591-8709
Toll-Free: 800-363-4663
info@active-life.ca
myhomepage.ca/activelife
twitter.com/ActiveLife_ON
www.facebook.com/ActiveLifeOntario

Circulation: 100,000
Frequency: 6 times a year
Michael Rosset, Publisher
Katherine Moore, Editor, katherinemoore@rogers.com

Be Fabulous!
11604 - 113 Ave., Edmonton, AB T5G 0J6
Tel: 780-470-0749; *Fax:* 780-470-0751
info@fabulousat50.com
www.fabulousat50.com/MainMenu/BeFabulousMagazine.a spx
www.youtube.com/user/Befabulousat50
twitter.com/Fabat50
www.facebook.com/86887170329
Magazine for baby boomer women over 50.
Dianna Bowes, Editor, editor@fabulousat50.com

Bel Age
Détenteur: Publications Senior Inc.
4475, rue Frontenac, Montréal, QC H2H 2S2
Tél: 514-278-9325
lebelage@kckglobal.com
www.lebelage.ca
www.youtube.com/c/LebelageCamagazine
twitter.com/BelAgeMagazine
www.fa cebook.com/belagemagazine

Fréquence: 11 fois par an
Aline Pinxteren, Rédacteur en chef,
aline.pinxteren@bayardcanada.com

Comfort Life
Owned By: Our Kids Publications Ltd.
Tel: 905-272-1843; *Fax:* 905-272-0474
Toll-Free: 877-272-1845
info@comfortlife.ca
www.comfortlife.ca
www.youtube.com/comfortlifetv
twitter.com/comfortlife
www.facebook. com/comfortlife.ca

Circulation: 30,000
Frequency: Annually

Fifty-Five Plus
Owned By: Coyle Media Group
c/o Coyle Media Group, 67 Neil Ave., Stittsville, ON K2S 1B9
Tel: 613-271-8903; *Fax:* 613-271-8905
editor@coylemediagroup.com
www.fifty-five-plus.com
twitter.com/fiftyfiveplus
www.facebook.com/fiftyfivepluslifestylemagazine
Frequency: 8 times a year
Pam Dillon, Editor, pam@coylemediagroup.com

Focus 50+
159 Marshall Rd., Midland, ON L4R 4K4
Tel: 705-322-6789
www.focus50.ca

Circulation: 14,000
Frequency: Monthly
Focus 50+ is distributed free of charge to drop-off points throughout Simcoe County.
Bonnie Stephens, Editor
Leo Stephens, Publisher

Forever Young
Owned By: Metroland Media Group Ltd.
901 Guelph Line, Burlington, ON L7R 3N8
Tel: 289-293-0634; *Fax:* 905-842-4432
www.foreveryoungnews.com
www.facebook.com/ForeverYoungNews
Circulation: 530,000
Frequency: Monthly
Jane Muller, Editor-in-chief, jmuller@metroland.com

Good Times
PO Box 11002 Anjou, Anjou, QC H1K 4H2
Toll-Free: 800-465-8443
editor@goodtimes.ca
goodtimes.ca
twitter.com/TheGoodTimesMag
www.facebook.com/thegoodtimesmagazine
Frequency: 8 times a year

Kerby News
1133 - 7th Ave. SW, Calgary, AB T2P 1B2
Tel: 403-265-0661; *Fax:* 403-705-3211
www.kerbycentre.com

Circulation: 30,000
Frequency: Monthly
Dylan Reardon, Editor, editor@kerbycentre.com

The Senior Paper
PO Box 1010 Main, Regina, SK S4P 3B2
Toll-Free: 877-908-8988
www.theseniorpaper.com
twitter.com/theseniorpaper
www.facebook.com/theseniorpaper
The publication is of interest to persons over sixty years of age. Submissions of classified advertising, special events, & milestones are welcomed. Print & electronic issues are available.

The Seniors Review
#B2, 11 Bond St., St. Catharines, ON L2R 4Z4
Tel: 905-687-9861; *Fax:* 905-687-6911
Toll-Free: 800-627-3111
www.seniorsreview.com

Circulation: 40,000
David Irwin, Publisher
Carol Anderson, Editor

Virage
4545, av Pierre-de-Coubertin, Montréal, QC H1V 3R2
Tél: 514-252-3017; *Téléc:* 514-252-3154
info@viragemagazine.com
www.viragemagazine.com

Tirage: 420 000
Fréquence: 4 fois par an
Lyne Rémillard, Rédacteur-en-chef

Zoomer Magazine
Previous Name: CARP Magazine
30 Jefferson Ave., Toronto, ON M6K 1Y4
Tel: 416-363-5562; *Fax:* 416-363-7693
comment@zoomermag.com
www.zoomermag.com
Other information: www.zoomers.ca
twitter.com/zoomermag
www.facebook.com/ZoomerMag

Circulation: 20,000
Frequency: Monthly
Susan Boyd, Editor-in-Chief

Fishing & Hunting

Aventure chasse et pêche
18660, boul Lacroix, St-Georges, QC G5Y 5B8
Tél: 418-694-5272; *Téléc:* 418-228-1003
commentaires@qacp.com
www.aventure-chasse-peche.com

Tirage: 50 600
Fréquence: Quarterly

BC Outdoors
Previous Name: BC Fishing Recreation Guide & Atlas
Owned By: Outdoor Group Media Ltd.
#201A, 7261 River Pl., Mission, BC V4S 0A2
Tel: 604-820-6453 *Toll-Free:* 800-663-7611
info@oppublishing.com
www.bcoutdoorsmagazine.com
www.facebook.com/bcoutdoorsmagazine
Frequency: 6 times a year
Mike Mitchell, Editor, 604-820-6453,
mmitchell@bcoutdoorsmagazine.com

Island Angler
30 Acacia Ave., Nanaimo, BC V9R 3L4
Tel: 250-753-2227; *Fax:* 250-753-2295
www.islandangler.net

Circulation: 15,000
Andrew Kolasinski, Publisher, kolapub@yahoo.ca

Ontario Out of Doors (OOD)
PO Box 8500, Peterborough, ON K9J 0B4
Tel: 705-748-0076; *Fax:* 705-748-9577
mail@oodmag.com
www.oodmag.com
www.youtube.com/c/Oodmagazine
twitter.com/oodmag
www.facebook.com/oodm ag

Circulation: 92,026
Frequency: 10 times a year

Outdoor Canada
Owned By: Outdoor Group Media Ltd.
#802, 1166 Alberni St., Vancouver, BC V6E 3Z3
Tel: 604-428-0259 *Toll-Free:* 800-663-7611
editorial@outdoorcanada.ca
www.outdoorcanada.ca
www.youtube.com/user/OutdoorCanadaMag
twitter.com/OutdoorCanada
www .facebook.com/outdoorcanada

Frequency: 6 times a year
National fishing & hunting magazine.
Patrick Walsh, Editor-in-Chief

Sentier Chasse-Pêche
1646, rue Michelin, Laval, QC H7L 4R3
Tél: 450-665-0271; *Téléc:* 450-665-2974
Ligne sans frais: 800-563-6738
www.sentiercp.com
www.instagram.com/sentiercp
twitter.com/sentiercp
www.facebook.com/ magazine.sentier

Tirage: 80 000
Fréquence: 11 fois par an
Louis Turbide, Rédacteur, l.turbide@sentiercp.com

Food & Beverage

Coup de Pouce
Détenteur: TVA Publications inc.
QC
www.coupdepouce.com
www.facebook.com/coupdepouce

Fréquence: 5 fois par an

Elite Wine, Food & Travel Magazine
Previous Name: Enoteca Wine & Food Magazine
88 Rosebury Ln., Vaughn, ON L4L 3Z8
Tel: 905-760-1724; *Fax:* 905-760-1718
editor@elitewinefoodtravel.com
www.elitewinefoodtravel.com

Circulation: 10,000
Frequency: 4 times a year
Anna Cavaliere, Editor

Flavours
Owned By: Fulcrum Media Inc.
#201, 508 Lawrence Ave. West, Toronto, ON M6A 1A1
Tel: 416-504-0504; *Fax:* 416-256-3002
Toll-Free: 866-688-0504
info@fulcrum.ca
fulcrum.ca
www.instagram.com/flavoursmag
twitter.com/FlavoursWorld
www.facebook.com/FlavWorld

Frequency: 4 times a year
Jane Auster, Editor, jauster@fulcrum.ca
Sheryl English Roberts, Contact, 604-728-8640,
sroberts@fulcrum.ca

Food & Drink
Liquor Control Board of Ontario, 55 Lake Shore Blvd. East, Toronto, ON M5E 1A4
Tel: 416-365-5900; *Fax:* 416-365-5935
Toll-Free: 800-668-5226
www.lcbo.com/fooddrink

Circulation: 500,000
Frequency: bi-monthly
Judy Dunn, Editor
Wayne Leek, Publisher

Food & Wine Trails
2495 Enterprise Way, Kelowna, BC V1X 7K2
Tel: 250-763-3212
www.winetrails.ca
www.facebook.com/264526741670

Circulation: 25,000
Frequency: 4 times a year
Provides information on wineries & wine tours in British Columbia
Jennifer Schell, Editor & Director, Sales,
jennifer.schell@winetrails.ca

Le Guide Cuisine (LGC)
Détenteur: Communication Duocom
Communication Duocom Inc., 72B, rue Sainte-Anne, Sainte-Anne-de-Bellevue, QC H9X 1L8
Tél: 514-457-0144; *Téléc:* 514-457-0226
Ligne sans frais: 800-558-5508
info@leguidecuisine.com
www.leguidecuisine.com
www.youtube.com/user/leguidecuisine
twitter.com/LeGuideCuisine
www.fac ebook.com/LeGuideCuisine

Tirage: 45 000
Fréquence: Cinq fois par ans
Nicolas Vallée, Rédacteur en chef

InterVin Insider
Owned By: Postmedia Network Inc.
940 Main St. West, Hamilton, ON L8S 1B1
Tel: 905-522-6117; *Fax:* 905-769-1105
www.intervin.ca
Frequency: 7 issues per year
Publication of the InterVinWine Awards.

Quench
Previous Name: Tidings
Owned By: Kylix Media Inc
#500, 5165 Sherbrooke West, Montréal, QC H4A 1T6
Tel: 514-481-5892
quench.me
www.instagram.com/quenchmagazine
twitter.com/quench_mag
www.facebook.com/quenchmag
Circulation: 35,000
Frequency: 8 times a year
Aldo Parise, Editor-in-chief

Taste
Owned By: BC Liquor Distribution Branch
2625 Rupert St., Vancouver, BC V5M 3T5
Tel: 604-252-3000
taste.magazine@bcliquorstores.com
www.bcliquorstores.com/taste/home
Magazine for BC Liquor.

Vines Magazine
Owned By: Postmedia Network Inc.
940 Main St. West, Hamilton, ON L8S 1B1
Tel: 905-522-6117; *Fax:* 905-769-1105
www.vinesmag.com
Frequency: 7 issues per year
Aimed at Canadians interested in wine.

Forest & Lumber Industries

Atlantic Forestry Review
Owned By: DvL Publishing Inc.
PO Box 1509, Liverpool, NS B0T 1K0
www.rurallife.ca/atlanticforestry
www.facebook.com/235629496526235
Frequency: Quarterly

Fraternal, Service Clubs, Associations

KIN Magazine
c/o Kin Canada, PO Box 3460, 1920 Rogers Dr., Cambridge, ON N3H 5C6
Tel: 519-653-1920; *Fax:* 519-650-1091
Toll-Free: 800-742-5546
kinhq@kincanada.ca
www.kincanada.ca
twitter.com/kincanada
www.facebook.com/kincanada
Circulation: 7,000
Frequency: 2 times a year
Jenn Martin, Editor

Gardening & Garden Equipment

Alberta Gardener
Owned By: Pegasus Publications Inc.
130A Cree Cres., Winnipeg, MB R3J 3W1
Tel: 204-940-2700; *Fax:* 204-940-2727
Toll-Free: 888-680-2008
info@pegasuspublications.net
www.albertagardener.net
www.facebook.com/AlbertaGardener
Circulation: 6,628
Frequency: 6 times a year

Canadian Organic Grower
Previous Name: Eco-Farm & Garden
#410, 100 Gloucester St., Ottawa, ON K2P 0A4
Tel: 613-216-0741; *Fax:* 613-236-0743
Toll-Free: 888-375-7383
office@cog.ca
magazine.cog.ca
twitter.com/CanadianOrganic
www.facebook.com/CanadianOrganic
Circulation: 2,500
Frequency: 3 times a year
Janet Wallace, Editor, janet@cog.ca

CANNAtalk
Owned By: CANNA Canada Corp.
#6290, 2100 Bloor St. West, Toronto, ON
www.canna.ca/cannatalk
www.facebook.com/CannaCanadaOfficial
Growing tips & general interest pieces for gardeners

Garden Making
Owned By: Inspiring Media Inc.
PO Box 808, #204, 111B Garrison Village Dr., #RR 3, Niagara on the Lake, ON L0S 1J0
Tel: 416-932-5075; *Fax:* 866-857-4262
Toll-Free: 877-832-1444
service@gardenmaking.com
www.youtube.com/gardenmaking
twitter.com/gardenmaking
www.facebook.com/gardenmaking
Circulation: 22,960
Frequency: Quarterly
Beckie Fox, Editor-in-Chief, editor@gardenmaking.com

Manitoba Gardener
Owned By: Pegasus Publications Inc.
3081 Ness Ave., Winnipeg, MB R2Y 2G3
Tel: 204-940-2700; *Fax:* 204-940-2727
Toll-Free: 888-680-2008
info@pegasuspublications.net
www.manitobagardener.net
www.facebook.com/ManitobaGardener
Circulation: 6,628
Frequency: 5 times a year
Dorothy Dobbie, Publisher
Ian Leatt, Contact

Maximum Yield
Owned By: Maximum Yield Inc.
2339 A Delinea Pl., Nanaimo, BC V9T 5L9
Tel: 250-729-2677; *Fax:* 250-729-2687
editor@maximumyield.com
www.maximumyield.com
Other information: Advertising: sales@maximumyield.com
www.instagram.com/maximumyield
twitter.com/Max_Yield
www.facebook.com/ MaximumYield
Frequency: Bi-monthly
Provides information on controlled-environment growing, including tips, instructions, & updates on current products & technologies
Toby Gorman, Editor-in-Chief

Ontario Gardener
Owned By: Pegasus Publications Inc.
3081 Ness Ave., Winnipeg, MB R2Y 2G3
Tel: 204-940-2700; *Fax:* 204-940-2727
Toll-Free: 888-680-2008
info@pegasuspublications.net
localgardener.net
www.facebook.com/OntarioGardener
Circulation: 17,700
Frequency: 5 times a year
Dorothy Dobbie, Publisher

Gay/Lesbian

être en ligne
Anciennement: R.G.
1613, rue Amherst, Montréal, QC H2L 3L4
Tél: 514-521-3873
www.etre.net
twitter.com/etremag
www.facebook.com/etremag

Fugues
1276, rue Amherst, Montréal, QC H2L 3K8
Tél: 514-848-1854; *Téléc:* 514-845-7645
Ligne sans frais: 888-848-1854
redaction@fugues.com
www.fugues.com
twitter.com/Fuguesmagazine
www.facebook.com/fugues
Tirage: 44 000
Fréquence: 12 fois par an
Maurice Nadeau, Publisher, mnadeau@fugues.com

Index: Gay & Lesbian Business Directory
Owned By: Pink Triangle Press
#1600, 2 Carlton St., Toronto, ON M5B 1J3
Tel: 416-925-5221; *Fax:* 416-925-4817
index@xtra.ca
Circulation: 34,000
Frequency: Annually
Directories for Vancouver, Toronto and Ottawa.

General Interest

AMA Insider
Previous Name: Westworld Alberta
Owned By: St. Joseph Media
St. Joseph Media, 15 Benton Rd., Toronto, ON M6M 3G2
ama.ab.ca
Circulation: 620,000
Frequency: 4 times a year
Douglas Kelly, Publisher
Kellie Davenport, Editor

BC Living
Owned By: Canada Wide Media Limited
230, 4321 Still Creek Dr., Burnaby, BC V5C 6S7
Tel: 604-299-7311
www.bcliving.ca
www.instagram.com/bcliving
twitter.com/bcliving
www.facebook.com/bcliving
The publication provides home decor & design ideas, style advice, & arts, entertainment, & restaurant recommendations for the West Coast.
Samantha Legge, Publisher, 604-473-0378, slegge@canadawide.com
Janine Verreault, Editor

CAA Magazine
Owned By: Totem Communications Group Inc.
Totem Communications Group Inc., 461 King St. West, 2nd Fl., Toronto, ON M5V 1K4
Tel: 416-360-7339; *Fax:* 416-640-6164
caamagazine@totemcontent.com
www.caasco.ca/CAA-Magazine
twitter.com/CAAMagazine
Frequency: Quarterly
Paul Ferriss, Editor, paul.ferriss@totemcontent.com

CAA Saskatchewan
Previous Name: Westworld Saskatchewan
Owned By: St. Joseph Media
200 Albert St. North, Regina, SK S4R 5E2
Tel: 306-791-4314; *Fax:* 306-949-4461
caask.ca
Circulation: 125,000
Frequency: 4 times a year
Douglas Kelly, Publisher

Canadian Immigrant Magazine
3145 Wolfedale Rd., Mississauga, ON L5C 3A9
Tel: 905-273-8111
canadianimmigrant.ca
www.youtube.com/user/cdnimmigrant
twitter.com/canimmigrant
www.face book.com/canimmigrant
Circulation: 83,000
Frequency: Monthly
Margaret Jetelina, Editor, editor@canadianimmigrant.ca

Canadian Newcomer
222 Parkview Hill Cres., Toronto, ON M4B 1R8
Tel: 416-406-4719; *Fax:* 416-757-7086
cnmag@rogers.com
www.cnmag.ca
Frequency: Quarterly
Online magazine discussing employment, housing, lifestyle, health, finance, education & media in Canada
Dale Sproule, Publisher

Continuité
82, Grande-Allée ouest, Québec, QC G1R 2G6
Tél: 418-647-4525; *Téléc:* 418-647-6483
continuite@magazinecontinuite.qc.ca
www.magazinecontinuite.com
www.linkedin.com/in/magazine-continuité-6bb15858
twitter.com/magconti nuite
www.facebook.com/magazinecontinuite
Fréquence: 4 fois par an
Josiane Ouellet, Rédactrice en chef, redaction@magazinecontinuite.qc.ca

Dernière heure
Détenteur: TVA Publications inc.
7, ch Bates, Outremont, QC H2V 4V7
Tél: 514-848-7000; *Téléc:* 514-848-9854
www.tvapublications.com
www.facebook.com/MagazineDH
Tirage: 30 000
Fréquence: Hebdomadaire

Digital Journal Magazine
PO Box 1046, Toronto, ON M5C 2K4
Tel: 416-410-9675
www.digitaljournal.com
www.facebook.com/digitaljournal
Christopher A. Hogg, Editor-in-Chief

Downhome
Previous Name: Downhomer Magazine
43 James Lane, St. John's, NL A1E 3H3
Tel: 709-726-5113; *Fax:* 709-726-2135
Toll-Free: 888-588-6353
www.downhomelife.com
twitter.com/downhomelife
www.facebook.com/downhomelife
Circulation: 225,000
Frequency: Monthly
Janice Stuckless, Editor

Going Natural/Au Naturel
PO Box 186 D, Toronto, ON M9A 4X2
Tel: 416-410-6822 *Toll-Free:* 888-512-6833
editor@fcn.ca
fcn.ca/about-the-fcn/going-natural-magazine
Circulation: 2,500
Frequency: 4 times a year

Good Life Connoisseur
#353, 15216 North Bluff Rd., White Rock, BC V4B 0A7
Toll-Free: 866-866-8755
www.goodlifeconnoisseur.com
www.linkedin.com/company/good-life-connoisseur
twitter.com/GLConnoisseur
www.facebook.com/GoodLifeConnoisseur
Circulation: 50,000
Frequency: 4 times a year
Terry Tremaine, Publisher & Editor

Humanist Perspectives
Previous Name: Humanist in Canada
Owned By: Canadian Humanist Publications
humanistperspectives.org
Frequency: 4 times a year
Madeline Weld, Editor, editor@humanistperspectives.org
Richard Young, Editor, editor@humanistperspectives.org

Legion Magazine
86 Aird Pl., Kanata, ON K2L 0A1
Tel: 613-591-0116; *Fax:* 613-591-0146
Toll-Free: 844-602-5737
info@legionmagazine.com
legionmagazine.com
www.youtube.com/user/LEGIONMAGAZINE
twitter.com/Legion_Magazine
www.facebook.com/LegionMagazine
Circulation: 177,037
Frequency: 6 times a year

Magazine Prestige
305, boul René-Lévesque ouest, Québec, QC G1S 1S1
Tél: 418-683-5333; *Téléc:* 418-683-2899
info@magazineprestige.com
www.magazineprestige.com
twitter.com/PRESTIGE_GMedia
www.facebook.com/MagazinePRESTIGE
Tirage: 45 000
Fréquence: 11 fois par an
Marie-Josée Turcotte, Rédacteur-en-chef,
redaction@magazineprestige.com

The Montrealer
342 Ballantyne North, Montréal, QC H4X 2C5
Tel: 514-369-7000
themontrealer@bellnet.ca
www.themontrealeronline.com
twitter.com/themontrealer
www.facebook.com/themontrealeronline
Circulation: 30,000
Frequency: Monthly
Peter Kerr, Editor

Nouvelles CSQ
Anciennement: Nouvelles CEQ
Centrale des syndicats du Québec, 9405, rue Sherbrooke
est, Montréal, QC H1L 6P3
Tél: 514-356-8888; *Téléc:* 514-356-9999
Ligne sans frais: 800-465-0897
www.csq.qc.net
www.youtube.com/user/csqvideos
twitter.com/csq_centrale
www.facebook.c om/lacsq
Tirage: 103 000
Fréquence: 5 fois par an

Louise Rochefort, Directrice

On the Bay Magazine
#201, 186 Hurontario St., Collingwood, ON L9Y 4T4
Tel: 705-444-9192; *Fax:* 705-444-5658
Toll-Free: 888-282-2014
info@onthebaymagazine.com
www.onthebaymagazine.com
www.facebook.com/onthebay
Circulation: 22,000
Frequency: 4 times a year
Jeffrey Shearer, Publisher, jshearer@onthebaymagazine.com
Janet Lees, Editor, janet.lees@me.com

Our Canada
PO Box 988 Main, Markham, ON L3P 0M1
Toll-Free: 800-465-0780
www.readersdigest.ca/our-canada
twitter.com/ourcanadamag
www.facebook.com/ourcanadamag
Frequency: 6 times a year
Our Canada features reader-contributed stories & photographs.

Pacific Rim Magazine
c/o Langara College, 100 West 49th Ave., Vancouver, BC
V5Y 2Z6
Tel: 604-323-5432
www.langaraprm.com
Circulation: 15,000
Darren Bernaerdt, Publisher, dbernaerdt@langara.bc.ca

Protégez-Vous
CP 190 Place d'Armes, #305, 2120, rue Sherbrooke est,
Montréal, QC H2Y 3G7
Tél: 514-461-3000; *Téléc:* 514-223-7160
Ligne sans frais: 866-895-7186
www.protegez-vous.ca
twitter.com/protegezvous
www.facebook.com/protegezvous
Tirage: 151 145
Fréquence: 12 fois par an
Sylvain Masse, Directeur général

Sélection du Reader's Digest
Anciennement: Sélection
1100, boul René Lévesque ouest, Montréal, QC H3B 4N4
Tél: 514-940-0751
selection.readersdigest.ca
twitter.com/selectionrd
www.facebook.com/SelectionReadersDigest
Tirage: 67 075
Fréquence: 10 fois par an
Robert Goyette, Rédacteur-en-chef

University of Toronto Magazine
J. Robert S. Prichard Alumni House, University of Toronto,
21 King's College Circle, Toronto, ON M5S 3J3
Tel: 416-946-3192; *Fax:* 416-978-3958
Toll-Free: 800-463-6048
uoft.magazine@utoronto.ca
www.magazine.utoronto.ca
twitter.com/uoftmagazine
www.facebook.com/176022529092653
Circulation: 300,000
Frequency: Quarterly
Scott Anderson, Editor & Manager, scott.anderson@utoronto.ca

Up Here
Previous Name: Up Here: Life at the top of the World
Owned By: Up Here Publishing Ltd.
#102, 4510 - 50th Ave., Yellowknife, NT X1A 1B9
Tel: 867-766-6710; *Fax:* 867-669-0626
Toll-Free: 866-572-1757
editor@uphere.ca
www.uphere.ca
twitter.com/upheremag
www.facebook.com/uphere
Frequency: 6 times a year
Dana Bowen, Associate Editor, dana@uphere.ca

Western Living Magazine
Owned By: Canada Wide Media Limited
c/o Canada Wide Media Limited, #230, 4321 Still Creek Dr.,
Burnaby, BC V5C 6S7
Tel: 604-299-7311
mail@westernliving.ca
www.westernliving.ca
twitter.com/Western_Living
www.facebook.com/WesternLivingMagazine
Circulation: 60,000
Frequency: 10 times a year
Anicka Quin, Editorial Director

Western Standard
#205, 1550 - 5th St. SW, Calgary, AB T2R 1K3
Tel: 403-216-2270
info@westernstandard.ca
www.westernstandard.ca
Frequency: Bi-weekly
Conservative news & commentary from a Western Canadian
perspective.

Graphic Arts

Applied Arts
Previous Name: Electronic Link
#105, 65 Overlea Blvd., Toronto, ON M4H 1P1
Tel: 416-510-0909; *Fax:* 416-510-0913
Toll-Free: 800-646-0347
editorial@appliedartsmag.com
www.appliedartsmag.com
www.instagram.com/appliedartsmag
twitter.com/appliedarts
www.facebook.com/AppliedArtsMag
Circulation: 12,000
Frequency: 5 times a year
Magazine devoted to covering the visual communications
community in Canada
Rosetta Heckhausen, Publisher, rosetta@appliedartsmag.com
Kristina Urquhart, Editor, editor@appliedartsmag.com

Uppercase
Calgary, AB
Tel: 403-283-5318
shop@uppercasemagazine.com
uppercasemagazine.com
www.instagram.com/uppercasemag
twitter.com/uppercasemag
Frequency: Quarterly
Janine Vangool, Publisher, Editor & Designer,
janine@uppercasemagazine.com

Health & Medical

Abilities Magazine
#803, 255 Duncan Mill Rd., Toronto, ON M3B 3H9
Tel: 416-421-7944; *Fax:* 416-421-8418
abilities@bcsgroup.com
www.abilities.ca
twitter.com/abilitiescanada
Circulation: 20,000
Lifestyle magazine for individuals with disabilities
Caroline Tapp-McDougall, Executive Director & Managing Editor

Caregiver Solutions
Previous Name: Canada's Family Guide to Home
Health Care & Wellness Solutions
Owned By: BCS Communications Ltd.
#803, 255 Duncan Mill Rd., Toronto, ON M3B 3H9
Tel: 416-421-7944; *Fax:* 416-421-8418
Toll-Free: 800-798-6282
info@caregiversolutions.ca
www.solutionsmagazine.ca
www.facebook.com/CaregiverSolutions
Circulation: 30,000
Frequency: 4 times a year
Caroline Tapp-McDougall, Publisher, caroline@bcsgroup.com
Helmut Dostal, Managing Editor, dostal@bcsgroup.com

Diabetes Dialogue
#1400, 522 University Ave., Toronto, ON M5G 2R5
Tel: 416-363-3373 *Toll-Free:* 800-226-8464
Circulation: 45,510
Frequency: Quarterly
Official magazine of the Canadian Diabetes Association.

WHOLifE Journal
PO Box 278, Kamsack, SK S0A 1S0
Tel: 306-542-3616; *Fax:* 306-542-3619
editor@wholife.com
www.wholife.com
www.facebook.com/wholifejournal.ca
Circulation: 17,000
Frequency: 6 times a year
Covers natural health & wellness for body, mind & spririt, plus
environmental issues.
Melva Armstrong, Publisher/Editor, 306-542-3616,
editor@wholife.com

History & Genealogy

Canada's History Magazine
Previous Name: The Beaver: Canada's History Magazine
Bryce Hall, 515 Portage Ave., Winnipeg, MB R3B 2E9
Tel: 204-988-9300; Fax: 204-988-9309
Toll-Free: 866-952-3444
editors@canadashistory.ca
www.canadashistory.ca
www.youtube.com/user/CanadasHistory
twitter.com/canadashistory
www. facebook.com/CanadasHistory

Circulation: 32,077
Frequency: 6 times a year
Melony Ward, Publisher, ads@canadashistory.ca

Locale
190 Bronson Ave., Ottawa, ON K1R 6H4
Tel: 613-237-1066; Fax: 613-237-5987
Toll-Free: 866-964-1066
nationaltrust@nationaltrustcanada.ca
www.nationaltrustcanada.ca
www.instagram.com/nationaltrustca
twitter.com/nationaltrustca
www.facebook.com/nationaltrustcanada

Frequency: Quarterly
Published by the National Trust for Canada; focuses on the conservation & rehabilitation of heritage buildings.
Natalie Bull, Executive Director, nbull@nationaltrustcanada.ca
Katrina Guerin, Communications Manager, kguerin@nationaltrustcanada.ca

The Loyalist Gazette
communicationsr@uelac.org
uelac.ca/loyalist-gazette
Frequency: 2 times a year
Robert McBride, Editor

OHS Bulletin
Owned By: Ontario Historical Society
John McKenzie House, 34 Parkview Ave., Toronto, ON M2N 3Y2
Tel: 416-226-9011 Toll-Free: 866-955-2755
ontariohistoricalsociety.ca/ohs-bulletin
Frequency: 5 times a year
Daniel Dishaw, Editor, ddishaw@ontariohistoricalsociety.ca

Your Genealogy Today
Previous Name: Family Chronicle
Owned By: Moorshead Magazines Ltd.
82 Church St. South, Ajax, ON L1S 6B3
Toll-Free: 888-326-2476
www.yourgenealogytoday.com
Frequency: 6 times a year
Edward Zapletal, Editor & Publisher, edward@moorshead.com

Hobbies

The Canadian Amateur Magazine
c/o Radio Amateurs of Canada, #217, 720 Belfast Rd., Ottawa, ON K1G 0Z5
Toll-Free: 877-273-8304
tcamag@yahoo.ca
www.rac.ca/tca
Circulation: 4,500
Frequency: 6 times a year
Alan Griffin, Editor

Canadian Coin News
Owned By: Trajan Publishing Corp.
#2, 459 Prince Charles Dr. South, Welland, ON L3B 5X1
Tel: 905-646-7744; Fax: 905-735-1909
Toll-Free: 800-408-0352
info@trajan.ca
canadiancoinnews.ca
www.facebook.com/CanadianCoinNews
Frequency: 26 times a year
Bret Evans, Managing Editor & Associate Publisher
Hans Niedermair, News Editor

Canadian Stamp News
Owned By: Trajan Publishing Corp.
#2, 459 Prince Charles Dr. South, Welland, ON L3B 5X1
Tel: 905-646-7744; Fax: 905-735-1909
Toll-Free: 800-408-0352
info@trajan.ca
canadianstampnews.ca
www.facebook.com/canadianstampnews
Frequency: 26 times a year

Comics & Games Monthly
Also Known As: C&G Monthly
#332, 1655 Dupont St., Toronto, ON M6P 3T1
media@cgmagazine.ca
cgmonthly.ca
twitter.com/cgmonthly
www.facebook.com/ComicsGamingmagazine
Frequency: Monthly
Brendan Frye, Editor-in-Chief, bfrye@cgmagazine.ca

Model Aviation Canada
Also Known As: MAC Mag
Owned By: Morison Communications
10 Ranch Glen Dr. NW, Calgary, AB T3G 1E3
Tel: 403-510-5689
editor@modelaviation.ca
www.maac.ca/en/magazine.php
Frequency: 6 times a year
Official publication of the Model Aeronautics Association of Canada.
Keith Morison, Publisher & Editor

Quilter's Connection
Previous Name: Connections for Quilters Newsletter
PO Box 41165 Shaughnessy, Port Coquitlam, BC V3C 5Z9
Tel: 604-290-3454; Fax: 604-540-2231
info@quiltersconnection.ca
quiltersconnection.ca
twitter.com/QltrsConnection
www.facebook.com/QuiltersConnectionMag azine
Frequency: Quarterly

Railfan Canada
North Kildonan Publications
PO Box 35087 Henderson, 963 Henderson Hwy, Winnipeg, MB R2K 4J9
Tel: 204-668-0168; Fax: 204-669-9821
editor@railfancanada.ca
www.railfancanada.ca
Frequency: Monthly
Railroad photography.

Homes

Canadian Living
Owned By: TVA Publications inc.
c/o TVA Publications, 1010 Sérigny St., Longueuil, QC J4K 5G7
Tel: 514-848-7000
letters@canadianliving.com
www.canadianliving.com
www.facebook.com/canadianliving
Frequency: 10 times a year

Condo Life Magazine
#404, 37 Sandiford Dr., Stouffville, ON L4A 7X5
Tel: 905-479-4663; Fax: 905-591-8709
Toll-Free: 800-363-4663
info@homesmag.com
myhomepage.ca/condolife
Circulation: 140,000
Frequency: 10 times a year
Michael Rosset, Publisher
Gale Beeby, Editor

Cottage Life West
Owned By: Cottage Life Media
#200, 130 Merton St., Toronto, ON M4S 1A4
Tel: 416-559-9200
letters@cottagelife.com
www.cottagemagazine.com
Frequency: 6 times a year
Mark Yelic, Publisher
Anita Willis, Editor, 250-384-5077, awillis@cottagelife.com

The Cottager
#16, 1313 Border St., Winnipeg, MB R3H 0X4
Tel: 204-954-2085; Fax: 204-954-2057
mp@mercury.mb.ca
www.thecottager.com
www.facebook.com/137410736323877
Circulation: 10,000
Frequency: 5 times a year
Frank Yeo, Publisher, fyeo@mercurypublications.ca

East Coast Living
Owned By: Metro Guide Publishing
2882 Gottingen St., Halifax, NS B3K 3E2
Tel: 902-420-9943; Fax: 902-429-9058
publishers@metroguide.ca
www.metroguide.ca
Circulation: 35,000
Frequency: 4 times a year

Patty Baxter, Publisher, pbaxter@metroguide.ca
Trevor Adams, Managing Editor, tadams@metroguide.ca
Kim Hart Macneill, Editor, ecl@metroguide.ca
Emma Brennan, Production Coordinator, ebrennan@metroguide.ca

Home Digest
224 Wilcroft Ct., Pickering, ON L1V 6N5
Tel: 905-509-9900 Toll-Free: 855-550-5577
info@homedigest.ca
www.homedigest.ca
twitter.com/Home_Digestmag
www.facebook.com/HomeDigestmag
Circulation: 700,000
Frequency: 6 times a year
Kelly Duncanson, Publisher

Les idées de ma maison
Détenteur: TVA Publications inc.
1010, rue de Sérigny, 4e étage, Longueuil, QC J4K 5G7
Ligne sans frais: 888-535-8634
mamaison@tvapublications.com
www.salutbonjour.ca/magazines/les-idees-de- ma-maison
www.facebook.com/Lesideesdemamaison
Fréquence: 10 fois par an

Kingston City Guide
Owned By: Postmedia Network Inc.
Kingston Publications, PO Box 2300, Kingston, ON K7L 4Z7
www.thewhig.com/category/magazines
Frequency: Quarterly
Justine de Leyer, Editor, jdeleyer@postmedia.com

Kingston Relocation Guide
Owned By: Postmedia Network Inc.
Kingston Publications, PO Box 2300, Kingston, ON K7L 4Z7
www.thewhig.com/category/magazines
Frequency: Annual
Justine de Leyer, Editor, jdeleyer@postmedia.com

Planimage Magazines
Anciennement: Over 500 Home Plans
#105, 1501, rue Ampere, Boucherville, QC J4B 5Z5
Tél: 450-641-7526; Téléc: 450-641-6688
Ligne sans frais: 800-752-6744
contact@planimage.com
www.planimage.com
www.planimage.com/blog
twitter.com/planimage
www.facebook.com/Planimage
Tirage: 30 000
Fréquence: 6 times a year
Daniel Therrien, Président, daniel.therrien@planimage.com

Real Estate Victoria
Victoria, BC
Tel: 250-381-9171
rev@revweekly.com
www.revweekly.com
Circulation: 17,200
Frequency: Weekly, Thursday
Penny Sakamoto, Publisher, psakamoto@blackpress.ca

Renovation & Decor Magazine
Also Known As: Reno & Decor
Owned By: HOMES Publishing Group
#404, 37 Sandiford Dr., Stouffville, ON L4A 7X5
Tel: 905-479-4663; Fax: 905-591-8709
Toll-Free: 800-363-4663
info@renoanddecor.com
myhomepage.ca/renoanddecor
twitter.com/HOMESPublishing
www.facebook.com/renoandecor
Circulation: 75,000
Frequency: 6 times a year
Michael Rosset, Publisher
Cobi Ladner, Editor

Renovation Contractor
Owned By: The Caruk Media Group
#404, 37 Sandiford Dr., Souffville, ON L7L 6W6
Tel: 647-367-0073; Fax: 289-997-8260
www.renocontractor.ca
www.linkedin.com/company/1968664
www.facebook.com/renocontractor.ca
Serves small- and medium-sized home renovators.
Jim Caruk, Editor-in-Chief, jim@renocontractor.ca
Allan Britnell, Managing Editor, allan@renocontractor.ca

Style at Home
Previous Name: Canadian Select Homes
Owned By: TVA Publications inc.
c/o TVA Publications, 1010, rue de Sérigny, Longueuil, QC
J4K 5G7
letters@styleathome.com
www.styleathome.com
www.facebook.com/styleathome
Frequency: 9 times a year

Horses, Riding & Breeding

Atlantic Horse & Pony
Owned By: DvL Publishing Inc.
PO Box 1509, Liverpool, NS B01 1K0
www.rurallife.ca/horse-pony-tofc
www.facebook.com/ahp.mag
Frequency: Quarterly
Quarterly publications of breeding, care, feeding, nutrition, stable
management, shows & other information on horses
Chassity Allison, Publisher & General Manager

Canadian Horse Annual
Owned By: Horse Publications Group
PO Box 670, Aurora, ON L4G 4J9
Tel: 905-727-0107; *Fax:* 905-841-1530
Toll-Free: 800-505-7428
info@horse-canada.com
www.horse-canada.com/canadian-ho rse-annual
Frequency: Annually

Canadian Horse Journal - Central & Atlantic Edition
Previous Name: Pacific Horse Journal
PO Box 2190, #201, 2400 Bevan Ave., Sidney, BC V8L 1W1
Tel: 250-655-8883; *Fax:* 250-655-8913
Toll-Free: 800-299-3799
editor@horsejournals.com
www.horsejournals.com
www.linkedin.com/company/horse-community-journals
twitter.com/HORSEJournals
www.facebook.com/CanadianHorseJournal
Circulation: 20,000
Frequency: 12 times a year
ON to Maritimes, plus ON Equestrian Federation News

Canadian Horse Journal - Pacific & Prairie Edition
Horse Community Journals
Previous Name: Pacific Horse Journal
PO Box 2190, #201, 2400 Bevan Ave., Sidney, BC V8L 1W1
Tel: 250-655-8883; *Fax:* 250-655-8913
Toll-Free: 800-299-3799
news@horsejournals.com
www.horsejournals.com
www.linkedin.com/company/horse-community-journals
twitter.com/HORSEJournals
www.facebook.com/CanadianHorseJournal
Circulation: 20,000
Frequency: 12 times a year
BC to MB, plus Horse Council BC Newsletter
Kathy Smith, Publisher/Editor

Cheval Québec
4545, av Pierre-de-Coubertin, Montréal, QC H1V 0B2
Tél: 514-252-3030; *Télec:* 514-252-3068
info@chevalquebecmag.com
www.chevalquebecmag.com
www.facebook.com/312091372180708
Tirage: 10 000
Fréquence: 4 fois par an

Courrier Hippique
CP 1000 M, 4545, av Pierre-de-Coubertin, Montréal, QC H1V
0B2
Tél: 514-252-3030; *Téléc:* 514-252-3165
info@editionsviceversa.ca
www.hippique.qc.ca
Tirage: 12 000
Fréquence: 6 fois par an

Horse Sport
Owned By: Horse Publications Group
PO Box 670, Aurora, ON L4G 4J9
Tel: 905-727-0107; *Fax:* 905-841-1530
Toll-Free: 800-505-7428
info@horse-canada.com
www.horse-canada.com/horse-sport
twitter.com/horsesport_mag
www.facebook.com/HorseSport
Circulation: 10,000
Frequency: 11 times a year
Susan Stafford-Pooley, Managing Editor,
editor@horse-canada.com

Racing Quarterly
Owned By: Horse Publications Group
PO Box 670, Aurora, ON L4G 4J9
Tel: 905-727-0107; *Fax:* 905-841-1530
Toll-Free: 800-505-7428
info@horse-canada.com
www.horse-canada.com/racing-quar terly
Frequency: 4 times a year
Lee Benson, Editor, lbenson@xplornet.com

The Rider
Previous Name: The Canadian Western Rider
PO Box 378, Fonthill, ON L0S 1E0
Tel: 905-387-1900 *Toll-Free:* 877-743-3715
www.therider.com
twitter.com/theridercom
www.facebook.com/TheRiderNewspaper
Frequency: 9 times a year
Barry Finn, Publisher, barry@therider.com

Hotels & Restaurants

Montréal, depuis 1642
Anciennement: Le Guide Prestige Montréal
Association des hôtels du Grand Montréal, #1112, 1255,
boul Robert-Bourassa, Montréal, QC H3B 3W7
Tél: 514-939-2583; *Téléc:* 514-939-2699
info@ahgm.org
www.ahgm.org
Tirage: 50 000
Fréquence: 3 fois par an
Publication officielle de l'Association des hôtels du grand
Montréal distribuée exclusivement dans les 81 hôtels membres.
Eve Paré, Présidente-directrice générale

Interior Design & Decor

Homefront
Owned By: BCS Group
#803, 255 Duncan Mill Rd., Toronto, ON M3B 3H9
Tel: 416-421-7944; *Fax:* 416-421-8418
Toll-Free: 800-798-6282
www.homefrontmagazine.ca
twitter.com/HomefrontMag
www.facebook.com/Homefrontmagazine
Circulation: 29,754
Frequency: 4 times a year
Helmut Dostal, Publisher, dostal@bcsgroup.com
Caroline Tapp-McDougall, Editor-in-Chief,
caroline@bcsgroup.com

Kingston Life Interiors
Owned By: Postmedia Network Inc.
Kingston Publications, 6 Cataraqui St., Kingston, ON K7L
4Z7
www.thewhig.com/category/magazines
Frequency: Annually, April
Kingston Life Interiors is delivered by controlled circulation
through The Kingston Whig-Standard, sent to subscribers & sold
at selected newsstands in Kingston, Ottawa, Toronto & Montreal.
Justine de Leyer, Editor, jdeleyer@postmedia.com

Labour, Trade Unions

Our Times
Owned By: Our Times Publishing Inc.
#407, 15 Gervais Dr., Toronto, ON M3C 1Y8
Tel: 902-755-6840
office@ourtimes.ca
ourtimes.ca
twitter.com/OurTimesMag
www.facebook.com/ourtimesmagazine
Circulation: 8,000
Frequency: 4 times a year
Independent labour magazine.
Antje Meyer-Erlach, Managing Editor

Literary

The Antigonish Review
PO Box 5000, Antigonish, NS B2G 2W5
Tel: 902-867-3962
tar@stfx.ca
antigonishreview.com
www.facebook.com/332083480162513
Frequency: 4 times a year
Thomas Hodd, Editor

Arc Poetry Magazine
PO Box 81060, Ottawa, ON K1P 1B1
Tel: 613-729-3550
arc@arcpoetry.ca
arcpoetry.ca
www.youtube.com/user/ArcPoetry
twitter.com/arcpoetry
www.facebook.com/ ArcPoetryMagazine
Circulation: 1,200
Frequency: 3 times a year
Chris Johnson, Managing Editor, managingeditor@arcpoetry.ca

Brick: A Literary Journal
PO Box 609 P, Toronto, ON M5S 2Y4
Tel: 416-593-9684
info@brickmag.com
www.brickmag.com
twitter.com/BrickMAG
www.facebook.com/brickmagazine
Circulation: 3,000
Frequency: 2 times a year
Publisher of non-fiction literary pieces
Laurie D. Graham, Publisher
Liz Johnston, Managing Editor

Canadian Notes & Queries
1520 Wyandotte St. East, Windsor, ON N9A 3L2
Tel: 519-968-2206
info@notesandqueries.ca
notesandqueries.ca
twitter.com/CNandQ
www.facebook.com/cnqueries
Circulation: 500
Frequency: 2 times a year
Dan Wells, Publisher, dwells@biblioasis.com
Emily Donaldson, Editor, ed@notesandqueries.ca

The Capilano Review
#210, 111 West Hastings St., Vancouver, BC V6B 1H4
Tel: 604-984-1712
contact@thecapilanoreview.com
thecapilanoreview.ca
www.youtube.com/user/TheCapilanoReview
twitter.com/thecapreview
www.fa cebook.com/TheCapilanoReview
Circulation: 1,800 annual
Frequency: 3 times a year
Jacquelyn Ross, Editor

Contemporary Verse 2 (CV2)
#502, 100 Arthur St., Winnipeg, MB R3B 1H3
Tel: 204-949-1365; *Fax:* 204-942-1555
editor@contemporaryverse2.ca
contemporaryverse2.ca
twitter.com/CV2magazine
www.facebook.com/CV2Magazine
Frequency: Quarterly
Sharanpal Ruprai, Editor

EXILE Quarterly
Also Known As: ELQ/Exile: The Literary Quarterly
PO Box 308, 170 Wellington St. West, Mount Forest, ON
N0G 2L0
www.exilequarterly.com
Frequency: Quarterly

The Fiddlehead
Owned By: University of New Brunswick
Campus House, University of New Brunswick, PO Box 4400,
11 Garland Ct., Fredericton, NB E3B 5A3
Tel: 506-453-3501
fiddlehd@unb.ca
thefiddlehead.ca
twitter.com/TheFiddlehd
www.facebook.com/TheFiddlehead
Frequency: 4 times a year
Sue Sinclair, Editor

Geist
Owned By: The Geist Foundation
#210, 111 West Hastings St., Vancouver, BC V6B 1H4
editor@geist.com
www.geist.com
twitter.com/geistmagazine
www.facebook.com/geistmagazine
Frequency: 4 times a year

Huron Church News
190 Queens Ave., London, ON N6A 6H7
Tel: 519-434-6893; *Fax:* 519-673-4151
Toll-Free: 800-919-1115
huron@huron.anglican.ca
www.diohuron.org

Island Catholic News
PO Box 5424 LCD 9, Victoria, BC V8R 6S4
Tel: 250-857-5824
admin@islandcatholicnews.ca
www.islandcatholicnews.ca
Circulation: 2,000
Frequency: Quarterly
Patrick Jamieson, Managing Editor

Living Light News
#200, 5306 - 89th St., Edmonton, AB T6E 5P9
Tel: 780-468-6397; *Fax:* 780-468-6872
Toll-Free: 800-932-0555
shine@livinglightnews.org
www.livinglightnews.org
www.facebook.com/livinglightnews
Circulation: 50,000
Frequency: Bi-monthly
Jeff Caporale, Editor

London Jewish Community News
536 Huron St., London, ON N5Y 4J5
Tel: 519-673-3310; *Fax:* 519-673-1161
ljcn@ljf.on.ca
www.jewishlondon.ca
Frequency: Quarterly

The New Brunswick Anglican
168 Church St., Fredericton, NB E3B 4C9
Tel: 506-459-1801
nb.anglican.ca/nb-anglican
Frequency: 10 times a year

The New Freeman
c/o Diocese of Saint John, One Bayard Dr., Saint John, NB E2L 3L5
Tel: 506-653-6806
tnf@nb.aibn.com
dioceseofsaintjohn.org
Frequency: Weekly
Margie Trafton, Managing Editor

Ottawa Jewish Bulletin
21 Nadolny Sachs Private, Ottawa, ON K2A 1R9
Tel: 613-798-4696; *Fax:* 613-798-4730
bulletin@ottawajewishbulletin.com
www.ottawajewishbulletin.com
Circulation: 2,500
Frequency: 19 times a year
Andrea Freedman, Publisher
Michael Regenstreif, Editor,
mregenstreif@ottawajewishbulletin.com

Outlook
Also Known As: Canadian Jewish Outlook
6184 Ash St., Vancouver, BC V5Z 3G9
Tel: 604-324-5101; *Fax:* 604-325-2470
outlook@vcn.bc.ca
www.vcn.bc.ca/outlook
Frequency: 6 times a year
Carl Rosenberg, Editor-in-chief

Revue L'Oratoire / The Oratory
3800, ch Queen Mary, Montréal, QC H3V 1H6
Tél: 514-733-8211
magazine@osj.qc.ca
www.saint-joseph.org/fr/culture/revue-loratoire
Fréquence: 3 fois par an

Salvationist
Previous Name: The War Cry
2 Overlea Blvd., Toronto, ON M4H 1P4
Toll-Free: 800-725-2769
salvationist.ca
twitter.com/salvationist
www.facebook.com/salvationistmagazine
Circulation: 12,500
Frequency: Monthly
Geoff Moulton, Editor-in-Chief

Seven
c/o ChristianWeek, PO Box 725, #204, 424 Logan Ave., Winnipeg, MB R3A 0R4
Tel: 204-982-2060; *Fax:* 204-947-5632
Toll-Free: 800-263-6695
admin@christianweek.org
www.christianweek.org

Frequency: Bi-Monthly

Shalom! Magazine
c/o The Atlantic Jewish Council, #309, 5670 Spring Garden Rd., Halifax, NS B3J 1H6
theajc.ca/shalom-magazine
Circulation: 1,400
Frequency: 3 times a year
Edna LeVine, Editor, elevine@theajc.ca

testimony / Enrich
Previous Name: testimony; Enrich
Also Known As: The Pentecostal Testimony
c/o The Pentecostal Assemblies of Canada, 2450 Milltower Ct., Mississauga, ON L5N 5Z6
Tel: 905-542-7400
testimony@paoc.org
testimony.paoc.org
Frequency: Quarterly
Stacey McKenzie, Editor

La Voix Sépharade (LVS)
#216, 5151, côte Ste-Catherine, Montréal, QC H3W 1M6
Tél: 514-733-4998; *Téléc:* 514-733-3158
lvsmagazine.com
www.facebook.com/1833191840235138
Fréquence: 3 fois par an
Sonia Sarah Lipsyc, Rédactrice en chef, slipsyc@csuq.org

Science, Research & Development

Revue Spectre
9601, rue Colbert, Anjou, QC H1J 1Z9
Tél: 514-948-6422; *Téléc:* 514-948-6423
info@aestq.org
www.aestq.org
Tirage: 2 000
Fréquence: 3 fois par an
Camille Turcotte, Directrice générale, camille.turcotte@aestq.org

Social Welfare

WhyNot Magazine
Canadian Foundation for Physically Disabled Persons, #265, 6 Garamond Ct., Toronto, ON M3C 1Z5
Tel: 416-760-7351; *Fax:* 416-760-9405
whynot@sympatico.ca
www.cfpdp.com
Frequency: 3 times a year
Dedicated to its three main events: Great Valentine Gala, Rolling Rampage and The Terry Fox Hall of Fame.
Bill McQuat, Editor
Vim Kochhar, Publisher
Larry Allen, Editor

Sports & Recreation

Canadian Cowboy Country (CCC)
#1, 9301 - 50th St., Edmonton, AB T6B 2L5
Tel: 780-628-5231; *Fax:* 780-448-0424
Toll-Free: 800-943-7336
askus@cowboycountrymagazine.com
cowboycountrymagazine.com
www.instagram.com/canadiancowboycountry
twitter.com/CowboyCntryMag
www.facebook.com/cowboycountrymag
Frequency: Bi-monthly
Rob Tanner, Publisher, rob@cowboycountrymagazine.com
Terri Mason, Editor, terri@cowboycountrymagazine.com

Canadian Cyclist
7 Barker St., Paris, ON N3L 2H4
Tel: 519-442-7905
news@canadiancyclist.com
www.canadiancyclist.com
twitter.com/cdncyclist
www.facebook.com/CanadianCyclist
Circulation: 8,000
Robert Jones, Editor, editor@canadiancyclist.com

The Curling News
Owned By: Roustan Media Ltd.
PO Box 53103, 10 Royal Orchard Blvd., Thornhill, ON L3T 7R9
Tel: 905-887-1261 *Toll-Free:* 800-605-2875
thecurlingnews.com
twitter.com/curling
www.facebook.com/CurlingNews
Frequency: 6 times a year; Nov.-April
George Karrys, Publisher

Diver Magazine
Owned By: Nuytco Research
216 East Esplanade St., North Vancouver, BC V7L 1A3
Tel: 604-988-0711; *Fax:* 604-988-0747
Toll-Free: 877-974-4333
mail@divermag.com
divermag.com
twitter.com/divermag
www.facebook.com/divermagazine
Frequency: 4 times a year
Phil Nuytten, Publisher

Flagstick Golf Magazine
Owned By: Bauder Media Group Inc.
8374 Forest Green Cres., Metcalfe, ON K0A 2P0
Tel: 613-821-0888; *Fax:* 613-821-4888
info@flagstick.com
www.flagstick.com
www.youtube.com/flagstickgolf
twitter.com/flagstick
www.facebook.com/f lagstick
Circulation: 15,000
Frequency: 5 times a year
Jeff Bauder, Publisher, jbauder@flagstick.com
Scott MacLeod, Editor, scotmac@flagstick.com

Hockey Magazine
Owned By: Suggitt Publishing Ltd.
10177 - 105th St. NW, Edmonton, AB T5J 1E2
Tel: 780-425-3642; *Fax:* 780-413-6185
reception@hockeymagazine.net
hockeymagazine.net
Frequency: 3 times per year
Minor league hockey coverage; separate magazines for Edmonton & Calgary.
Rob Suggit, President & Publisher

Hockey News
Owned By: Roustan Media Ltd.
Toronto, ON
Toll-Free: 800-365-9982
editorial@thehockeynews.com
www.si.com/hockey
www.youtube.com/c/TheHockeyNews
twitter.com/thehockeynews
www.facebook .com/thehockeynews
Ryan Hunt, Editor-in-Chief

Hockey Now
PO Box 88024, Vancouver, BC V6A 4A4
Toll-Free: 877-990-0520
hockeynow.ca
twitter.com/hockeynow
www.facebook.com/hockeynow.communications
Circulation: 160,000
Frequency: Monthly
Highlighting Canadian hockey stories from minor hockey, junior hockey, female hockey, college hockey & other hockey events
Larry Feist, Publisher, larry@hockeynow.ca

KMag
Détenteur: Orinha Média
36, ch de Salzbourg est, Wentworth, QC J8H 0G7
Tél: 819-275-2177
courrier@kmag.ca
www.kmag.ca
www.instagram.com/magazine_kmag
www.facebook.com/MagazineKMag
Fréquence: 4 fois par an
Pierre Hamel, Éditeur, phamel@orinhamedia.com

Motoneige Québec
4545, av Pierre-de-Coubertin, Montréal, QC H1V 0B2
Tél: 514-252-3076; *Téléc:* 514-254-2066
info@fcmq.qc.ca
www.fcmq.qc.ca
Tirage: 65 000
Fréquence: 4 fois par an
Yves Ouellet, Rédacteur en chef

Newfoundland Sportsman
Previous Name: Outdoor Sportsman
PO Box 13754 A, 40 O'Leary Ave., St. John's, NL A1B 4G5
Toll-Free: 877-754-3515
info@newfoundlandsportsman.com
www.newfoundlandsportsman.com
www.youtube.com/user/NLSportsman
twitter.com/sportsmannl
www.facebook.com/newfoundlandsportsman
Circulation: 15,000
Frequency: 6 times a year
Dwight J. Blackwood, Publisher,
dblackwood@newfoundlandsportsman.com

Gordon Follett, Editor, gfollett@newfoundlandsportsman.com

Northwestern Ontario Golfing News
Owned By: North Superior Publishing Inc.
North Superior Publishing Inc., 1145 Barton St., Thunder Bay, ON P7B 5N3
Tel: 807-623-2348; *Fax:* 807-623-7515
Circulation: 2,000
Frequency: 5 times a year
Scott Sumner, Publisher & Editor

Northwestern Ontario Snowmobile News
Owned By: North Superior Publishing Inc.
North Superior Publishing Inc., 1402 - 590 Beverly St., Thunder Bay, ON P7B 6H1
Tel: 807-623-2348; *Fax:* 807-623-7515
nspinc@tbaytel.net
www.northsuperiorpublishing.com
Circulation: 2000
Frequency: 5 times a year
Scott A. Sumner, Publisher & Editor

Rando Québec
Anciennement: MARCHE-Randonnée
4545, av Pierre-De Coubertin, Montréal, QC H1V 0B2
Tél: 514-252-3157 *Ligne sans frais:* 866-252-2065
info@randoquebec.ca
randoquebec.ca
Jean-Luc Caillaud, Directeur général,
jlcaillaud@randoquebec.ca

SBC Skateboard Magazine
249 Evans Ave., Toronto, ON M8Z 1K2
www.sbcskateboard.com
www.instagram.com/sbcskateboard_mag
twitter.com/sbcskateboard
www.face book.com/SBCSkateboardMagazine
Circulation: 25,000
Frequency: 2 times a year
Jay Mandarino, President & CEO, jay@sbcmedia.com
Dan Mathieu, Editor, dan@sbcskateboard.com

SCOREGolf
Owned By: CCMC Sports
#101, 5397 Eglinton Ave. West, Toronto, ON M9C 5K6
Tel: 416-928-2909; *Fax:* 416-966-1181
Toll-Free: 800-320-6420
info@scoregolf.com
scoregolf.com
Circulation: 142,438
Frequency: 6 times a year

Ski Canada
Previous Name: Sunsports
Owned By: Solstice Publishing Inc.
47 Soho Sq., Toronto, ON M5T 2Z2
Tel: 416-595-1252 *Toll-Free:* 888-666-9754
info@skicanadamag.com
skicanadamag.com
twitter.com/skicanadamag
www.facebook.com/SkiCanadaMag
Circulation: 100,000 year total
Frequency: 4 times a year
Paul Green, Publisher
Iain MacMillan, Editor, mac@skicanadamag.com

Ski Presse
Détenteur: Solisco
655, av Sainte-Anne, Saint-Hyacinthe, QC J2S 5G4
Tél: 450-773-6028
info@skipresse.com
skipresse.com
twitter.com/skipresse_mag
www.facebook.com/108500488806
Tirage: 182 000
Fréquence: 4 times a year
Anne-Marie Saint-Germain, Rédactrice-en-chef,
amsaintgermain@skipresse.com
Jules Older, Editor-in-chief, English version

Sledworthy Magazine
PO Box 8303 A, St. John's, NL A1B 3N7
Tel: 709-690-2609
www.sledworthy.com
www.instagram.com/sledworthy
twitter.com/Sledworthy
www.facebook.com/253014761423947
Circulation: 30,000
Andrew Goldsworthy, Editor-in-Chief, andrew@sledworthy.com

Snowboard Canada Magazine
C.J. Oyster Publishing, 249 Evans Ave., Toronto, ON M8Z 1K2
Tel: 416-259-8847
www.snowboardcanada.com
www.instagram.com/snowboardcanada
twitter.com/snowboardcanada
www.facebook.com/SnowboardCanada
Circulation: 73,000
Frequency: 4 times a year
Jay Mandarino, President & CEO, jay@sbcmedia.com
David MacKinnon, Editor, david@snowboardcanada.com

Supertrax International
Owned By: Trax Media Inc.
c/o Trax Media Inc., 1025 Rouge Valley Dr., Pickering, ON L1V 4N8
Toll-Free: 800-905-8729
trax@publicationpartners.com
www.supertraxmag.com
Frequency: 4 times a year
Supertrax International is a snowmobile magazine.

Swim News
www.swimnews.com
As of December 2013, Swim News is available online only.
Marco Chiesa, Editor-in-Chief
Nikki Dryden, Managing Editor

Wakeboard SBC Magazine
249 Evans Ave., Toronto, ON M8Z 1K2
Tel: 416-588-0808
www.cjgroupofcompanies.com
Circulation: 40,000
Frequency: 2 times a year
Jay Mandarino, President & CEO, jay@cjoysterpublishing.com
Melissa Kurtin, Editor, melissa@sbcwakeboard.com

Wild Coast Magazine
Previous Name: Coast & Kayak Magazine; Wavelength
Wild Coast Publishing, PO Box 24 A, Nanaimo, BC V9R 5K4
Tel: 250-244-6437; *Fax:* 866-654-1937
Toll-Free: 866-984-6437
wildcoastpublishing@gmail.com
www.wildcoastmagazine.com
Frequency: 3 times a year
The publication presents information about adventure travel, ecotourism, & outdoor recreation for British Columbia & the Pacific Northwest.
John Kimantas, Editor, editor@wildcoastmagazine.com

Television, Radio, Video & Home Appliances

Audio Ideas Guide
Toronto, ON
Tel: 905-833-7177; *Fax:* 905-833-7178
mail@audio-ideas.on.ca
www.audio-ideas.com
Frequency: Quarterly
Publishing articles about the audio world
Andrew Marshall, Editor & Publisher, andrew@audio-ideas.com
Aaron Marshall, Contributing Editor & Webmaster,
aaron@audio-ideas.com

The Inner Ear
Owned By: TIEMedia
Tel: 905-294-5570
info@innerearmag.com
www.innerearmag.com
www.facebook.com/innerearmagazine
Circulation: 16,000
Frequency: 4 times a year
Ernie Fisher, Editor

TV Week Magazine (TVW)
Owned By: Canada Wide Media Limited
c/o Canada Wide Media Limited, #230, 4321 Still Creek Dr., Burnaby, BC V5C 6S7
Tel: 604-299-7311
cwm@canadawide.com
www.tvweekonline.ca
Frequency: Weekly

Travel

Above & Beyond Magazine
PO Box 20025 Carleton Mews, Carleton Place, ON K7C 3S0
Tel: 613-257-4999 *Toll-Free:* 877-227-2842
www.arcticjournal.ca
twitter.com/arcticjournal
www.facebook.com/ArcticJournal.ca
Circulation: 12,000
Frequency: 6 times a year
Tom Koelbel, Publisher & Editor

BCAA Magazine
Owned By: Canada Wide Media Limited
#230, 4321 Still Creek Dr., Burnaby, BC V5C 6S7
Tel: 604-299-7311; *Fax:* 604-299-9188
cwm@canadawide.com
www.canadawide.com
Circulation: 476,301
Frequency: 4 times a year
Peter Legge, Publisher
Kirsten Rodenhizer, Editor

Bear Country
1475 West Walsh St., Thunder Bay, ON P7E 4X6
Tel: 807-474-2636; *Fax:* 807-474-2658
pgresham@bearskinairlines.com
www.bearskinairlines.com
Circulation: 100,000
Frequency: Quarterly
Features editorials about people, places, & events in the regions served by Bearskin Airlines
Ron Hell, Publisher
Patti Gresham, Editor

British Columbia Magazine
Previous Name: Beautiful British Columbia Magazine
802 - 1166 Alberni St., Vancouver, BC V6E 3Z3
Tel: 604-428-0259; *Fax:* 604-620-0425
Toll-Free: 800-663-7611
cs@bcmag.ca
www.bcmag.ca
www.youtube.com/user/BritishColumbiaMag
twitter.com/bcmagazine
www.fac ebook.com/BCMagazine
Circulation: 65,500
Frequency: Quarterly
British Columbia's geographic magazine with researched stories of parks, wilderness, wildlife, travel destinations, outdoor adventures, recreation, geography, ecology, conservation, science, phenomena, First Nations' culture, heritage places & history
Mark Yelic, Publisher & President, myelic@opmediagroup.ca
Dale Miller, Editor, dmiller@opmediagroup.ca
Arran Yates, Director, Art, ayates@opmediagroup.ca

Dreamscapes Travel & Lifestyle Magazine
Previous Name: American Express Dreamscapes
3 Bluffwood Dr., Toronto, ON M2H 3L4
Tel: 416-497-5353; *Fax:* 416-497-0871
Toll-Free: 888-700-4464
dreamscapesmagazine@rogers.com
www.dreamscapes.ca
Circulation: 105,000
Frequency: 6 times a year
Joseph Turkel, Publisher
Donna Vieira, Editor, editor@dreamscapes.ca

Espaces
Détenteur: Serdy Média
#619, rue Le Breton, Longueuil, QC J4G 1R9
Tél: 450-672-0052; *Téléc:* 450-672-0055
info@espaces.ca
www.espaces.ca
www.instagram.com/espacespleinair
twitter.com/espacespleinair
www.face book.com/espacespleinair
Stéphane Corbeil, Directeur général

Géo Plein Air
Détenteur: Orinha Média
36, ch de Salzbourg est, Wentworth, QC J8H 0G7
Tél: 514-521-8356 *Ligne sans frais:* 800-567-8356
courrier@geopleinair.com
www.geopleinair.com
twitter.com/geopleinair_
www.facebook.com/geopleinair
Fréquence: 4 fois par an
Magazine québécois de la nature et de l'aventure.
Simon Diotte, Rédactrice en chef, sdiotte@geopleinair.com
Pierre Hamel, Éditeur, phamel@orinhamedia.com

Greater Halifax Visitor Guide
Owned By: Metro Guide Publishing
2882 Gottingen St., Halifax, NS B3K 3E2
Tel: 902-420-9943; *Fax:* 902-429-9058
publishers@metroguide.ca
www.metroguide.ca
Circulation: 240,000
Frequency: Annually
Patty Baxter, Publisher

Horizon Travel Magazine
#200, 2150 Winston Park Dr., Oakville, ON L6H 5V1
Tel: 905-257-1020; *Fax:* 289-291-3814
horizon@horizontravelmag.com
www.horizontravelmag.com
twitter.com/horizontravmag
www.facebook.com/HorizonTravelMagazine
Horizon Travel Magazine is a travel & lifestyle magazine.

Outpost: Canada's Travel Magazine
250 Augusta Ave., Toronto, ON M5T 2L7
Tel: 416-972-6635 *Toll-Free:* 800-759-1024
circ@outpostmagazine.com
www.outpostmagazine.com
twitter.com/OutpostMagazine
www.facebook.com/Outpostmagazine
Circulation: 28,000
Frequency: Bi-monthly
Matthew Robinson, Publisher, matt@outpostmagazine.com
Deborah Sanborn, Editor, deborah@outpostmagazine.com

Saskatchewan Discovery Guide
Tourism Saskatchewan, 189-1621 Albert St., Regina, SK S4P 2S5
Tel: 306-787-9685 *Toll-Free:* 877-237-2273
www.tourismsaskatchewan.com
Circulation: 115,000
Frequency: Annually

The Travel Society Magazine
Previous Name: Travel Scoop
#404, 174 Spadina Ave., Toronto, ON M5T 2C2
Tel: 416-926-2500 *Toll-Free:* 877-926-2500
info@thetravelsociety.com
www.thetravelsociety.com
twitter.com/TTravelSociety
www.facebook.com/thetravelsociety
Circulation: 7,000
Online magazine.
Helen Hewetson, Owner
Jill Fost, Sales Manager

Where Canadian Rockies
Previous Name: Where Rocky Mountains
Owned By: St. Joseph Media
#244, 105 Bow Meadows Cres., Canmore, AB T1W 2W8
Tel: 403-678-1898
editor@rmvpublications.com
where.ca/canadianrockies
twitter.com/whererockies

Jack Newton, Publisher

Where Vancouver / Whistler
Owned By: St. Joseph Media
#510, 1755 West Broadway, Vancouver, BC V6J 4S5
Tel: 604-736-5586
where.ca/british-columbia/vancouver
Frequency: Monthly

University Publications

High! Canada
Toronto, ON
editor@highcanada.net
www.highcanada.net
www.instagram.com/highcanadamagazine
twitter.com/CanadaHigh
www.facebook.com/HighCanada
Frequency: Monthly
Features current trends in cannabis, product reviews, legal news, business information, & more
Cy Williams, Publisher & Editor

Maximum Yield Cannabis
Owned By: Maximum Yield Inc.
2339 A Delinea Pl., Nanaimo, BC V9T 5L9
Tel: 250-729-2677; *Fax:* 250-729-2687
editor@maximumyield.com
www.maximumyield.com
Other information: Advertising: sales@maximumyield.com
www.instagram.com/maximumyield
twitter.com/Max_Yield
www.facebook.com/ MaximumYield
Frequency: Bi-monthly
An offshoot of Maximum Yield, this magazine focuses on growing methods & equipment for cannabis cultivators.
Toby Gorman, Editor-in-Chief

Skunk Magazine
7013, rue Durocher, Montréal, QC H3N 1Z7
Tel: 514-867-6694
skunkmagazine.com
www.instagram.com/skunkmagazine
www.facebook.com/skunkmag
Humerous cannabis lifestyle magazine
Julie Chiariello, Co-Owner

Spliff Magazine
Owned By: Spliff Media
204 Augusta Ave., Toronto, ON M5T 2L6
spliffmag@gmail.com
spliffmag.ca
www.instagram.com/spliffmagazine
twitter.com/spliffmag
www.facebook .com/spliffmag
Frequency: Monthly
Cannabis magazine with articles on recent news, law, local food, accessories & more
Abi Roach, Publisher

Twelve High Chicks Magazine
5651 Keith Rd. West, Vancouver, BC V7W 2N4
Tel: 604-362-9691
moon@twelvehighchicks.com
www.twelvehighchicks.com
Other information: M.O.M. Cup: cup@twelvehighchicks.com
www.instagram.com/twelvehighchicksmag
twitter.com/12hcmagazine
www.fac ebook.com/TwelveHighChicksMag
Frequency: Irregular
Cannabis lifestyle magazine with a feminist perspective, featuring articles on politics, travel, recipies, poetry, sex, & more. Also hosts the Mail Order Marijuana (M.O.M.) Cup event, giving awards to the best medicinal & recreational mail-order cannabis companies, as well as growers, manufacturers & suppliers.
Ajia Mae Moon, Owner & Editor-in-Chief

Women's & Feminist

L'Actuelle
1193, rue Maisonneuve, Longueuil, QC J4K 2S7
lactuelle@cfq.qc.ca
cfq.qc.ca/magazine-lactuelle
Tirage: 35 000
Fréquence: 5 fois par an
Publication officielle des Cercles de Fermières du Québec (CFQ).

Canadian Woman Studies / Les Cahiers de la Femme
Owned By: Inanna Publications and Education Inc.
Founders College, York University, #210, 4700 Keele St., Toronto, ON M3J 1P3
Tel: 416-736-5356; *Fax:* 416-736-5765
cwscf@yorku.ca
www.cwscf.ca
Circulation: 5,000
Frequency: Quarterly
Luciana Ricciutelli, Editor-in-Chief

Chatelaine
Owned By: Rogers Media Inc.
1 Mount Pleasant Rd., 8th Fl., Toronto, ON M4Y 2Y5
Tel: 416-764-2000 *Toll-Free:* 800-268-9119
service@chatelaine.com
www.chatelaine.com
www.pinterest.com/chatelainemag
twitter.com/chatelainemag
www.facebook .com/ChatelaineMagazine
Circulation: 421,925
Frequency: 6 times a year
Lianne George, Editor-in-Chief

Châtelaine
Détenteur: St. Joseph Media
#201, 249, rue Saint-Jacques ouest, Montréal, QC H2Y 1M6
Ligne sans frais: 833-632-0833
fr.chatelaine.com
twitter.com/chatelaine_qc
www.facebook.com/ChatelaineQc
Fréquence: 6 fois par an

Elle Canada
Owned By: KO Média Inc.
#100, 25 Sheppard Ave. West, Toronto, ON M2N 6S7
Tel: 416-733-7600
www.ellecanada.com
www.youtube.com/user/ellecanadacom
twitter.com/ellecanada
www.faceb ook.com/ellecanada
Vanessa Craft, Editor-in-Chief

Elle Québec
Détenteur: KO Média Inc.
c/o KO Média II Inc., #100, 651, rue Notre-Dame ouest, Montréal, QC H3C 1H9
Tél: 514-848-7000
ellequebec@ko-media.ca
www.ellequebec.com
www.youtube.com/user/ElleQc
twitter.com/ellequebec
www.facebook.com /ellequebec
Tirage: 88 398
Fréquence: Mensuel

ORAH Magazine
Canadian Hadassah-WIZO, #209, 638A Sheppard Ave. West, Toronto, ON M3H 2S1
Tel: 416-477-5964; *Fax:* 416-477-5965
Toll-Free: 855-477-5964
info@chw.ca
www.chw.ca/about/orah
Circulation: 14,000
Frequency: 2 times a year
Alina Ianson, Editor-in-Chief

Room Magazine
Previous Name: Room of One's Own
PO Box 46160 D, Vancouver, BC V6J 5G5
contactus@roommagazine.com
roommagazine.com
twitter.com/RoomMagazine
www.facebook.com/roommagazine
Circulation: 1,850
Frequency: Quarterly
Molly Cross-Blanchard, Publisher, publisher@roommagazine.com
Jessica Johns, Managing Editor, managingeditor@roommagazine.com

Women of Influence
#400, 901 King St. West, Toronto, ON M5V 3H5
Tel: 866-684-4809
info@womenofinfluenceinc.ca
www.womenofinfluence.ca/magazine
www.linkedin.com/company/women-of-influence-inc.
twitter.com/womenofinfl nce
www.facebook.com/womenofinfluenceinc
Circulation: 20,000
Frequency: Quarterly
Alicia Skalin, Co-CEO & Head of Events & Progamming, 647-463-8274, askalin@womenofinfluence.ca
Stephania Varalli, Co-CEO & Head of Media, 416-558-5830, svaralli@womenofinfluence.ca

Youth

Cool!
Détenteur: TVA Publications inc.
1010, rue de Sérigny, 4e étage, Longueuil, QC J4K 5G7
Tél: 514-848-7000; *Téléc:* 514-848-9854
www.magazine-cool.ca
Tirage: 62 000
Fréquence: 12 fois par an

Faze Magazine
#2401, 4936 Yonge St., Toronto, ON M2N 6S3
Tel: 416-222-3060
info@faze.ca
www.faze.ca
www.instagram.com/FazeMagazine
twitter.com/FazeMagazine
www.facebook.c om/FazeMagazine
Frequency: 5 times a year
Lorraine Zander, Editor-in-Chief

girlworks
Owned By: Girlworks media inc.
PO Box 91559, 47 Main St. South, Georgetown, ON L7G 5M9
girlworks.ca
www.facebook.com/151751732682
Frequency: Bi-monthly
Janet Kim, Contact, jkim@girlworks.ca

Youthink PS
230, 4321 Still Creek Dr., Burnaby, BC V5C 6S7
Tel: 604-299-7311; *Fax:* 604-299-9188
cwm@canadawide.com
www.youthinkps.ca
Circulation: 80,000
Frequency: 2 times a year
Post-secondary directory for high school students in western Canada. Distributed to 400 high schools in British Columbia & Alberta.
Matt Currie, Editor

Farm

Farm Publication

Aberdeen Angus World
PO Box 177, Stavely, AB T0L 1Z0
Tel: 403-549-2234; *Fax:* 403-549-2207
office@angusworld.ca
www.angusworld.ca

Circulation: 2,500
Frequency: 2 times a year
Aberdeen Angus World is the official publication of the Canadian Angus Association. The magazine contains information about the improvement of the Angus breed.
Dave Callaway, Editor & Publisher, dave@angusworld.ca
Jan Lee, Associate Editor

AGDealer Magazine
Owned By: Glacier FarmMedia LP
1666 Dublin Ave., Winnipeg, MB R3H 0H1
Tel: 204-954-1400; *Fax:* 204-954-1422
admin@agdealer.com
www.agdealer.com
twitter.com/AGCanadadotcom
www.facebook.com/171631800662

Agrobiomass
Owned By: Annex Business Media
PO Box 530, 105 Donly Dr. South, Simcoe, ON N3Y 4N5
Tel: 888-599-2228; *Fax:* 519-429-3094
www.agannex.com/agrobiomass
twitter.com/AgAnnex
All-digital publication covering the emerging agro-biomass sector in all its forms.

Alberta Farmer Express
Previous Name: Alberta Express
Owned By: Glacier FarmMedia LP
PO Box 9800, Winnipeg, MB R3C 3K7
Tel: 204-944-5568 *Toll-Free:* 800-665-1362
www.albertafarmexpress.ca

Circulation: 45,000
Frequency: 26 times a year
Glenn Cheater, Editor, glenn.cheater@fbcpublishing.com

Alberta Seed Guide
Owned By: Issues Ink
5030 - 50 St., Lacombe, AB T4L 1W8
Tel: 403-782-8022; *Fax:* 866-798-1826
Toll-Free: 877-710-3222
marketing@issuesink.com
www.seed.ab.ca

Circulation: 64,000
seed.ab.ca is Alberta's source for seed, offering the latest variety information, complete crop evaluations, comprehensive grower directories, trends, issues, and more.
Lorena Pahl, General Manager, 403-325-0081,
lorena.pahl@seed.ab.ca

Atlantic Beef & Sheep
Owned By: DvL Publishing Inc.
PO Box 1509, Liverpool, NS B0J 1K0
www.rurallife.ca/atlanticbeef
www.facebook.com/273521866054955

Frequency: Quarterly

CAAR Communicator
Previous Name: WFCD Communicator
#205, 1 Wesley Ave., Winnipeg, MB R3C 4C6
info@caar.org
caar.org/the-communicator

Circulation: 3,750
Frequency: 5 times a year
Publication of the Canadian Association of Agri-Retailers.

Canadian Ayrshire Review
c/o The Ayrshire Breeders' Association of Canada, 4865, boul Laurier ouest, Saint-Hyacinthe, QC J2S 3V4
ayrshire-canada.com

Frequency: Bimonthly
Yves Charpentier, Editor, yves@ayrshire-canada.com

Canadian Biomass Magazine
Owned By: Annex Business Media
PO Box 530, 105 Donly Dr. South, Simcoe, ON N3Y 4N5
Tel: 519-429-3966; *Fax:* 519-429-3094
Toll-Free: 800-265-2827
www.canadianbiomassmagazine.ca
twitter.com/AgAnnex

Frequency: Bi-monthly
Scott Jamieson, Editorial Director, 519-429-5180,
sjamieson@annexweb.com
Andrew Snook, Editor, 905-713-4301, asnook@annexweb.com

Andrew Macklin, Editor, 905-713-4358,
amacklin@annexweb.com

Canadian Cattlemen: The Beef Magazine
Owned By: Glacier FarmMedia LP
1666 Dublin Ave., Winnipeg, MB R3H 0H1
Tel: 204-954-1400; *Fax:* 204-954-1422
www.canadiancattlemen.ca

Frequency: 12 times a year
Lisa Guenther, Editor, 306-450-6359,
lguenther@farmmedia.com

Canadian Poultry Magazine
Owned By: Annex Business Media
PO Box 530, 105 Donly Dr. South, Simcoe, ON N3Y 4N5
Tel: 888-599-2228; *Fax:* 519-429-3094
www.canadianpoultrymag.com
twitter.com/canadianpoultry

Circulation: 5,300
Frequency: 10 times a year
Brett Ruffell, Editor, bruffell@annexweb.com

Charolais Banner
124 Shannon Rd., Regina, SK S4S 4B1
Tel: 306-584-7937; *Fax:* 306-546-3942
charolaisbanner@gmail.com
charolaisbanner.com
twitter.com/CharolaisBanner

Frequency: 5 times a year

Country Guide
Owned By: Glacier FarmMedia LP
1666 Dublin Ave., Winnipeg, MB R3H 0H1
Tel: 204-954-1400; *Fax:* 204-954-1422
www.country-guide.ca

Frequency: 10 times a year
Eastern & Western editions are produced.
Tom Button, Editor, tbutton@farmmedia.com

Drainage Contractor
Owned By: Annex Business Media
PO Box 530, 105 Donly Dr. South, Simcoe, ON N3Y 4N5
Tel: 519-429-3966; *Fax:* 519-429-3094
Toll-Free: 800-265-2827
www.drainagecontractor.com

Circulation: 7,079
Frequency: Annually; November
Stefanie Croley, Editor, scroley@annexweb.com

Eastern Ontario Agrinews
PO Box 368, 7 King St., Chesterville, ON K0C 1H0
Tel: 613-448-2321; *Fax:* 613-448-3260
Toll-Free: 866-307-3541
agrinews.editor@gmail.com
www.agrinews.ca

Circulation: 14,000
Frequency: Monthly
Muriel Carruthers, Editor

Farm Focus
Owned By: DVL Publishing Inc.
PO Box 1509, Liverpool, NS B0T 1K0
Tel: 902-354-5411
dvlpublishing.office@gmail.com
www.atlanticfarmfocus.ca

Frequency: 12 times a year

Fruit & Vegetable Magazine
Previous Name: Canadian Fruitgrower
Owned By: Annex Business Media
PO Box 530, 105 Donly Dr. South, Simcoe, ON N3Y 4N5
Fax: 519-429-3094
Toll-Free: 888-599-2228
fruitveg@annexweb.com
www.fruitandveggie.com
www.youtube.com/user/fruitandveggiemag
twitter.com/FruitVeggieMag
www.facebook.com/fruitandvegmag

Frequency: 5 times a year
Michelle Allison, Publisher, mallison@annexbusinessmedia.com
Stefanie Croley, Editorial Director,
scroley@annexbusinessmedia.com

Germination
Owned By: Issues Ink
#301, 313 Pacific Ave., Winnipeg, MB R3A 0M2
Tel: 877-710-3222
www.germination.ca
twitter.com/GerminationMag
www.facebook.com/GerminationMag

Circulation: 5,700
Germination is the first and only magazine aimed specifically at Canada's seed industry.

Shawn Brook, President

Grainews
Owned By: Glacier FarmMedia LP
1666 Dublin Ave., Winnipeg, MB R3H 0H1
Tel: 204-954-1400; *Fax:* 204-954-1422
www.grainews.ca

Circulation: 8,662
Frequency: 18 times a year
Kari Belanger, Editor, 204-801-1645,
kbelanger@farmmedia.com

iDeal Equipment Magazine
Owned By: Glacier FarmMedia LP
1666 Dublin Ave., Winnipeg, MB R3H 0H1
Tel: 204-954-1400; *Fax:* 204-954-1422
www.idealequipment.ca
twitter.com/AGCanadadotcom
www.facebook.com/171631800662

The Island Farmer
Owned By: Island Press Limited
PO Box 790, 530 Main St., Montague, PE C0A 1R0
Tel: 902-838-2515; *Fax:* 902-838-4392
Toll-Free: 800-806-5443
www.peicanada.com/island_farmer

Frequency: Bi-weekly
Paul MacNeill, Publisher, paul@peicanada.com
Andy Walker, Editor, andy@peicanada.com

Manitoba Co-Operator
Owned By: Glacier FarmMedia LP
1666 Dublin Ave., Winnipeg, MB R3H 0H1
Tel: 204-954-1400; *Fax:* 204-954-1422
www.manitobacooperator.ca
twitter.com/MBCooperator

Frequency: Weekly; supplements Seed Manitoba (annual); Yield Manitoba (annual)
Gord Gilmour, Editor, 204-294-9195, ggilmour@farmmedia.com

Manure Manager
Owned By: Annex Business Media
PO Box 530, 105 Donly Dr. South, Simcoe, ON N3Y 4N5
Tel: 519-429-3966; *Fax:* 519-429-3094
Toll-Free: 800-265-2827
www.agannex.com/manure-manager
twitter.com/ManureManager

Frequency: 8 times a year
Manure handling industry across North America.
Marg Land, Editor, 888-599-2228 ext.269,
mland@annexweb.com

Ontario Beef Farmer
Owned By: Postmedia Network Inc.
PO Box 7400, London, ON N5Y 4X3
Fax: 519-473-2256
Toll-Free: 877-358-7773
ontariofarmer.nationals@postmedia.com
www.ontariofarmer.com

Circulation: 7,000
Frequency: 2 times a year

Ontario Dairy Farmer
Owned By: Postmedia Network Inc.
PO Box 7400, London, ON N5Y 4X3
Fax: 519-473-2256
Toll-Free: 877-358-7773
ontariofarmer.nationals@postmedia.com
www.ontariofarmer.com

Circulation: 6,312
Frequency: Monthly

Ontario Farmer
Owned By: Postmedia Network Inc.
PO Box 7400, London, ON N5Y 4X3
Toll-Free: 877-358-7773
www.ontariofarmer.com

Circulation: 19,535
Frequency: Weekly, Tue.

Ontario Hog Farmer
Owned By: Postmedia Network Inc.
PO Box 7400, London, ON N5Y 4X3
Fax: 519-473-2256
Toll-Free: 877-358-7773
ontariofarmer.nationals@postmedia.com
www.ontariofarmer.com

Circulation: 3,090
Frequency: 6 times a year

Prairie Hog Country
PO Box 5536, Leduc, AB T9E 2A1
Tel: 780-986-0962; *Fax:* 780-980-9640
hogcountry@shaw.ca
www.prairiehogcountry.ca

Circulation: 4,800
Frequency: 6 times a year
Laurie Brandly, Publisher

Sheep Canada
1489 Rte. 560, Deerville, NB E7K 1W7
Tel: 506-425-9256 *Toll-Free:* 888-241-5124
www.sheepcanada.com
www.facebook.com/sheepcanada

Frequency: 4 times a year
Dr. Cathy Gallivan, Editor, cathy.gallivan@gmail.com

Simmental Country
#13, 4101 - 19th St. NE, Calgary, AB T2E 7C4
Tel: 403-250-7979; *Fax:* 403-250-5121
Toll-Free: 866-860-6051
www.simmental.com/simmentalcountry

Frequency: 7 times a year
The official publication of the Canadian Simmental Association
with information & articles of interest to Purebred & Commercial
Cattlemen.

La Terre de chez nous
#100, 555, boul Roland Therrien, Longueuil, QC J4H 3Y9
Tél: 450-679-8483; *Téléc:* 450-670-4788
Ligne sans frais: 877-679-7809
tcn@laterre.ca
www.laterre.ca
www.youtube.com/user/Terredecheznous
twitter.com/laterreca
www.facebook.com/laterreca

Fréquence: Hebdomadaire

Top Crop Manager
Owned By: Annex Business Media
PO Box 530, 105 Donly Dr. South, Simcoe, ON N3Y 4N5
Tel: 519-429-3966; *Fax:* 519-429-3094
Toll-Free: 800-265-2827
www.agannex.com/top-crop-manager
twitter.com/TopCropMag

Frequency: 8 Western/year, 7 Eastern/year, 1 Potatoes/year
Magazine of crop production and technology, a specialty
agricultural trade publication.
Sara Avoledo, Eastern Editor, 226-931-5608,
savoledo@annexweb.com
Janet Kanters, Western Editor, 403-499-9754,
jkanters@annexweb.com

Western Dairy Farmer Magazine
Owned By: Postmedia Network Inc.
PO Box 7400, London, ON N5Y 4X3
Fax: 519-473-2256
Toll-Free: 877-358-7773
ontariofarmer.nationals@postmedia.com
www.ontariofarmer.com

Circulation: 3,470
Frequency: 10 times a year

Western Horse Review
Previous Name: Northern Horse Review
#814, 3545 - 32nd Ave. NE, Calgary, AB T1Y 6M6
Tel: 403-250-1128
editorial@westernhorsereview.com
www.westernhorsereview.com
www.facebook.com/WesternHorseReview

Frequency: 11 times a year
Jenn Webster, Publisher & Managing Editor
Ingrid Schulz, Editor, ingridwhr@gmail.com

The Western Producer
Tel: 306-665-3500
subscriptions@producer.com
www.producer.com
twitter.com/westernproducer
www.facebook.com/westernproducer

Circulation: 26,329
Frequency: 26 times a year
The agricultural publication is of interest to farmers & ranchers in
western Canada. News & information is included about rural life,
technology, production, livestock, markets & finance. News
bureaus are located in Ottawa, Brandon, Winnipeg, Saskatoon,
Regina, Calgary & Camrose.
Rod Delahey, Publisher, rod.delahey@producer.com
Mike Raine, Editor, michael.raine@producer.com

Food & Beverage

Flavourful
Owned By: Issues Ink
#301, 313 Pacific Ave., Winnipeg, MB R3A 0M2
Tel: 204-453-1965

Frequency: 2 times a year
Distributed through Canadian embassies and used as a tool by
participants in missions to Canada's key agri-food markets such
as the U.S., Japan, European Union, Mexico, and China.

Spud Smart
Owned By: Issues Ink
#403, 313 Pacific Ave., Winnipeg, MB R3A 0M2
Tel: 204-453-1965; *Fax:* 204-475-5247
www.spudsmart.com
twitter.com/SpudSmartMag
www.facebook.com/SpudSmart

Spud Smart is the primary publication in the Canadian potato
industry.
Julienne Isaacs, Editor, 204-453-1965 x810,
jisaacs@issuesink.com

Horses, Riding & Breeding

Horse Trader Magazine
PO Box 219, Dutton, ON N0L 1J0
Tel: 519-872-1424
pamandtrader@hotmail.com
www.horsetradermagazine.com
www.linkedin.com/in/horse-trader-magazine-16587050
twitter.com/HorseTrad erMag
www.facebook.com/horsetradermag

Industrial & Industrial Automation

Resource Engineering & Maintenance (REM)
Owned By: Annex Business Media
PO Box 530, 105 Donly Dr. South, Simcoe, ON N3Y 4N5
Tel: 519-429-3966; *Fax:* 519-429-3094
Toll-Free: 800-265-2827
www.rem-mag.com
Rehana Begg, Editor, 905-726-4655, rbegg@annexweb.com

Multicultural

Aboriginal

Alberta Native News
10632 - 124 St. NW, #A, Edmonton, AB T5N 1S3
Tel: 780-421-7966; *Fax:* 780-424-3951
editor@albertanativenews.com
www.albertanativenews.com

Circulation: 12,000
Frequency: Monthly
Publishes Aboriginal news & viewpoints
Deborah Shatz, Editor

Alberta Sweetgrass
The Aboriginal Multi-Media Society, 13245 - 146 St.,
Edmonton, AB T5L 4S8
Tel: 780-455-2700; *Fax:* 780-455-7639
sweetgrass@ammsa.com
www.ammsa.com/publications/alberta-sweetgrass
twitter.com/windspeakernews
www.facebook.com/windspeakernews

Circulation: 7,000
Frequency: Monthly
Bert Crowfoot, Publisher
Shari Narine, Editor

First Nations Free Press
363 Sioux Rd., Sherwood Park, AB T8A 4W7
Tel: 780-449-1803; *Fax:* 780-449-1807
Frequency: Monthly

Ha-Shilth-Sa
PO Box 1383, Port Alberni, BC V9Y 7M2
Tel: 250-724-5757; *Fax:* 250-723-0463
www.hashilthsa.com

Circulation: 3,100
Eric Plummer, Manager & Editor,
eric.plummer@nuuchahnulth.org

Ktuqcqakyam Newsletter
7468 Mission Rd., Cranbrook, BC V1C 7E5
Tel: 250-489-2464
www.ktunaxa.org

Circulation: 700
Frequency: Bi-monthly

Mi'kmaq-Maliseet Nations News (MMNN)
PO Box 1590, 72 Church Rd., Truro, NS B2N 5V3
Tel: 902-895-2039; *Fax:* 902-893-3030
Toll-Free: 877-895-2038
info@mmnn.ca
www.mmnn.ca
www.facebook.com/MikmaqMaliseetNationsNews

Frequency: Monthly
Don Julien, Publisher
Carol Busby, Manager, manager@easternwoodland.ca

The Nation Magazine
c/o Beesum Communications Inc., #403, 4529 rue Clark,
Montréal, QC H2T 2T3
Tel: 514-272-3077; *Fax:* 514-278-9914
news@beesum-communications.com
www.nationnews.ca
www.facebook.com/NATIONnewsmagazine

Circulation: 7000
Frequency: 26 times a year; English & James Bay Cree
Provides content for the Cree of James Bay
Danielle Valade, Sales Representative

Native Journal
Tel: 647-829-8291
info@nativejournal.ca
www.nativejournal.ca

Circulation: 70,000
Frequency: Monthly
Melanie Chambers, Accounts Manager,
mc_chambers@nativejournal.ca

Native Youth News
363 Sioux Rd., Sherwood Park, AB T8A 4W7
Tel: 780-449-1803; *Fax:* 780-449-1807
Toll-Free: 800-830-1803
fnfpltd@teleusplanet.net

Frequency: Monthly

Natotawin
PO Box 10880, Opaskwayak, MB R0B 2J0
Tel: 204-627-7066
www.opaskwayak.ca/natotawin.php

Circulation: 1,000
Frequency: Weekly
Gabriel Constant, Editor, gabriel.constant@opaskwayak.ca

The New Nation: La noovel naasyoon
c/o Gabriel Dumont Institute, #2, 604 - 22nd St. West,
Saskatoon, SK S7M 5W1
Tel: 306-934-4941; *Fax:* 306-244-0252
www.metismuseum.ca

Frequency: 4 times a year
Karon Shmon, Director
David Morin, Curriculum Developer, david.morin@gdi.gdins.org
Darren Préfontaine, Curriculum Developer

Nunavut News/North
c/o Northern News Services Ltd., PO Box 2820, Yellowknife,
NT X1A 2R1
Tel: 867-873-4031; *Fax:* 867-873-8507
nnsl@nnsl.com
www.nnsl.com

Frequency: Weekly
J.W. (Sig) Sigvaldason, Publisher

Raven's Eye
Owned By: The Aboriginal Multi-Media Society
13245 - 146th St., Edmonton, AB T5L 4S8
Tel: 780-455-2700; *Fax:* 780-455-7639
www.ammsa.com/publications/ravens-eye

Frequency: Monthly
Raven's Eye is a monthly section within the AMMSA publication
Windspeaker.
Debora Steel, Contributing News Editor, dsteel@ammsa.com

Saskatchewan Sage
13245 - 146 St., Edmonton, AB T5L 4S8
Tel: 780-455-2700; *Fax:* 780-455-7639
Toll-Free: 800-661-5469
sage@ammsa.com
www.ammsa.com/publications/saskatchewan-sage

Circulation: 8,500
Frequency: Monthly
Bert Crowfoot, Publisher
Shari Narine, Editor

Secwepemc News, The Voice of the Shuswap Nation
Board of Education of School District No. 73
(Kamloops/Thompson), 1383 9th Ave., Kamloops, BC V2C
3X7
Tel: 250-374-0679

Frequency: Monthly

Taiga Times
Taiga Communications Inc., PO Box 299, Peguis, MB R0C 3J0
Tel: 204-645-5626; *Fax:* 877-647-6471
taigatimes@rezxchange.net
www.taigatimes.net
Frequency: Monthly
Available online.
James Wastasecoot, Publisher

Turtle Island News
Owned By: Turtle Island News Publications
PO Box 329, 2208 Chiefswood Rd., Hagersville, ON N0A 1M0
Tel: 519-445-0868; *Fax:* 519-445-0865
news@theturtleislandnews.com
www.theturtleislandnews.com
twitter.com/newsattheturtle
www.facebook.com/TurtleIslandNews
Frequency: Weekly
National native newspaper. Affiliated with Aboriginal Business Magazine.
Lynda Powless, Publisher & Editor,
lynda@theturtleislandnews.com

Western Native News Ltd.
#207, 11460 Jasper Ave., Edmonton, AB T5K 0M1
Tel: 780-421-7966; *Fax:* 780-424-3951
nativenews@telus.net
Frequency: Monthly

Windspeaker
Also Known As: AMMSA
Owned By: Aboriginal Multi-Media Society
13245 - 146th St., Edmonton, AB T5L 4S8
Tel: 780-455-2700; *Fax:* 780-455-7639
Toll-Free: 800-661-5469
reception@ammsa.com
windspeaker.com
twitter.com/windspeakernews
www.facebook.com/windspeakernews
Frequency: Monthly
National Canadian Aboriginal news source.
Elmer Ghostkeeper, President
Bert Crowfoot, Publisher & Founder, bcrowfoot@ammsa.com
Deb Steel, News Director & Editor, Windspeaker,
debsteel@ammsa.com

African-Canadian & Caribbean Canadian Communities

Caribbean Camera
#212, 55 Nugget Ave., Toronto, ON M1S 3L1
Tel: 416-412-2905; *Fax:* 416-412-2134
www.thecaribbeancamera.com
Circulation: 35,000
Frequency: Weekly
Anthony Joseph, Publisher

Hawarya
Owned By: African Network Inc.
PO Box 66036, 1116 Wilson Ave., Toronto, ON M3M 1G7
Tel: 416-459-5964; *Fax:* 905-799-2193
hawarya.publications@sympatico.ca
www.hawarya.net
Frequency: Monthly; Ethiopian
African news, especially Ethiopian.
Muluken Muchie, Editor, editor@hawarya.net

The Jamaican Weekly Gleaner
The Gleaner Company (Canada) Inc., 1390 Eglinton Ave. West, Toronto, ON M6C 2E4
Tel: 416-784-3002; *Fax:* 416-784-5719
Toll-Free: 800-233-9540
gleanercan@gleanerna.com
jamaica-gleaner.com
twitter.com/jamaicagleaner
Frequency: Weekly; also The Jamaican Weekly Star, The Black Pages Directory
Christopher Barnes, Managing Director,
christopher.barnes@gleanerjm.com

Pride News Magazine
#369, 701 Rossland Rd. East, Whitby, ON L1N 9K3
Tel: 905-668-8869
pridenews@bellnet.ca
www.pridenews.ca
www.instagram.com/pridenews
twitter.com/PrideNewsMag
www.facebook.com/PrideNewsMagazine
Circulation: 25,000
Michael Van Cooten, Publisher & Editor

Word: Toronto's Urban Culture Magazine
#2, 1161 St. Clair Ave. West, Toronto, ON M6E 1B2
Tel: 905-799-1630; *Fax:* 905-799-2788
info@wordmag.com
www.wordmag.com
Circulation: 160,000
Frequency: 9 times a year
Phil Vassell, Director, Sales & Sponsorship

Arabic

Al-Mustakbal
1305, rue Mazurette, Montréal, QC H4N 1G8
Tel: 514-334-0909
info@almustakbal.com
www.almustakbal.com
Circulation: 12,000
Serves the Arab community.
Joseph Nakhlé, Editeur

ARC Arabic Journal
368 Queen St. E, Toronto, ON M5A 1T1
Tel: 416-362-0307; *Fax:* 416-861-0238
writemad@rogers.com
www.arabnews-canada.com/arcarabic
Circulation: 5,000
Frequency: Every two weeks
Features news from Egypt & Canada, as well as publishes short stories & articles
Emad Nafeh, Editor

Canadian Asian News
3459 Trilogy Tr., Mississauga, ON L5M 0K3
Tel: 905-826-6370
asiannews1@gmail.com
www.canadianasiannews.com
Circulation: 150,000
Frequency: Bi-weekly
Latafat Ali Siddiqui, Editor, asiannews1@hotmail.com

El-Mahroussa Magazine
c/o Egyptian Canadian Friendship Association Inc., 879, av Saint-Charles, Laval, QC H7V 3T5
Tél: 514-944-2282; *Téléc:* 450-681-0409
masri.93@hotmail.com
www.el-mahrousaonline.com
www.facebook.com/elmahrousamagazine
Tirage: 12 000
Fréquence: 12 fois par an

El-Masri Newspaper
c/o Egyptian Canadian Friendship Association Inc., 879, av Saint-Charles, Laval, QC H7V 3T5
Tél: 514-944-2282; *Téléc:* 450-681-0409
masri.93@hotmail.com
www.el-masrionline.com
www.facebook.com/elmasrionline
Tirage: 12 000
Fréquence: 26 fois par an

The Iran Star
169 Steeles Ave. East, Toronto, ON M2M 3Y5
Tel: 905-763-9770; *Fax:* 905-763-9771
iranstar@iranstar.com
www.iranstar.com
Circulation: 12,000
Bijan Binesh, Editor-in-Chief
Shahram Binesh, Editor & Coordinator

Voice of Egypt in Canada
1274, Dupont, Laval, QC H7Y 1T5
Tel: 514-288-0188; *Fax:* 450-689-7241
www.voiceofegypt.com
Frequency: Monthly
George Saad, Chair, georgesaad@videotron.ca

Armenian

Abaka
Owned By: Tekeyan Cultural Association of Montreal
Tekeyan Armenian Cultural Association of Montréal, 825 Manoogian St., Montréal, QC H4N 1Z5
Tel: 514-747-6680; *Fax:* 514-747-6162
abaka@bellnet.ca
tekeyanmontreal.ca/abaka-weekly
www.facebook.com/abakanews
Frequency: Weekly; Tabloid
Avedis Bakkalian, Editor-in-Chief

Horizon Weekly
3401, rue Olivar-Asselin, Montréal, QC H4J 1L5
Tel: 514-332-3757; *Fax:* 514-332-4870
www.horizonweekly.ca
twitter.com/horizonweekly
www.facebook.com/120633978044872
Circulation: 2,000
Frequency: Weekly
Vahakn Karakashian, Editor

Lradou Newsletter
3401, rue Olivar-Asselin, Montréal, QC H4J 1L5
Tel: 514-333-1616
www.ars-canada.ca
Frequency: Annually

Pourastan
Parish Council of St. Gregory, 615, av Stuart, Outremont, QC H2V 3H2
Tel: 514-279-3066; *Fax:* 514-279-8008
sourpkrikor@qc.aibn.com
Circulation: 700

Bulgarian

Bulgarian Horizons
5312 Dundas St. West, Toronto, ON M9B 1B3
Tel: 647-931-4343; *Fax:* 647-931-4343
www.bulgarianhorizons.com
Circulation: 2,500
Frequency: Biweekly
Maxim Bozhilov, Editor

Celtic

Celtic Life International
PO Box 8805 A, Halifax, NS B3K 5M4
Tel: 902-835-2358; *Fax:* 902-835-0080
info@CelticLife.ca
www.celticlifeintl.com
www.youtube.com/user/celticlifeint
twitter.com/celticlife
www.facebook .com/41377434690
Frequency: 4 times a year

Chinese

Chinese Canadian Times
Also Known As: CC Times
PO Box 35526, 2528 Bayview Ave., Toronto, ON M2L 2Y4
Tel: 416-445-7815; *Fax:* 416-447-9791
web@cctimes.ca
www.cctimes.ca
Frequency: Weekly; Chinese
Publication for Chinese Canadians.
Kathy Lin, Contact, kathy@cctimes.ca

The Chinese Journal
Previous Name: Canadian Chinese Times
10553A - 97 St., Edmonton, AB T5H 2L4
Tel: 780-424-0213; *Fax:* 780-428-7117
chinesejournal@telusplanet.net
www.thechinesejournal.com
Circulation: 7,000
Frequency: Weekly
Vicki Lim, Publisher

The Chinese Press
Previous Name: Eastern Chinese Press Inc.
1123, rue Clark, Montréal, QC H2Z 1K3
Tel: 514-397-9969; *Fax:* 514-397-9929
www.chinesepress.com
www.facebook.com/ChinesePress80
Circulation: 25,000
Frequency: Weekly
Crescent Chau, Publisher/Editor

Herald Monthly
#28, 300 Steelcase Rd. West, Markham, ON L3R 2W2
Tel: 905-944-1777; *Fax:* 905-944-1778
toronto@cchc.org
www.heraldmonthly.ca
Circulation: 76,000
Frequency: Monthly; first Wed. of the month
Herald Monthly is a free broadsheet monthly Chinese newspaper.
Helena Lee, Chief Editor

Ming Pao Daily News
Owned By: Media Chinese International Limited
1355 Huntingwood Dr., Toronto, ON M1S 3J1
Tel: 416-321-0088; *Fax:* 416-321-9663
advert@mingpaotor.com
www.mingpaocanada.com
www.youtube.com/c/mingpaotoronto
twitter.com/mingpaotoronto
www.facebook.com/mingpaotoronto
Frequency: Daily; Cantonese
Hong Kong news serving the Greater Toronto Area.

Modesty Magazine
Modesty Group Inc., 18 Uptown Dr., Markham, ON L3R 5M5
Tel: 905-513-7939
Circulation: 10,000
Ivy Lee, Publisher & Editor

The New Star Times
#206, 150 Consumers Rd., North York, ON M2J 1P9
Tel: 416-491-8401
www.newstarnet.com
Frequency: Weekly; Fridays; Mandarin
Servces Mandarin-speaking immigrants in Toronto.
Jessica C., Manager

Popular Lifestyle & Entertainment Magazine (PLEM)
Owned By: The Fairchild Group
3248 Cambie St., Vancouver, BC V5Z 2W4
Tel: 604-872-1285; *Fax:* 604-872-0677
info@plem.com
www.plem.com
www.facebook.com/iPLEM
Circulation: 82,500
Frequency: Monthly; Chinese

Les Presses Chinoises
1123, rue Clark, Montréal, QC H2Z 1K3
Tél: 514-397-9969; *Téléc:* 514-397-9929
www.chinesepress.com
Tirage: 25 000
Fréquence: Weekly

Rice Paper
PO Box 74174 Hillcrest, Vancouver, BC V5V 5L8
Tel: 604-872-3464
info@ricepapermagazine.ca
ricepapermagazine.ca
twitter.com/ricepapermag
www.facebook.com/ricepaper
As of April 2016, Rice Paper Magazine is available online only.
Allan Cho, Executive Editor, allancho@ricepapermagazine.ca

Dutch

De Nederlandse Courant
Also Known As: Dutch-Canadian Bi-Weekly
192 Livingston Ave., Grimsby, ON L3M 5R7
Toll-Free: 800-268-7268
subscriptions@denederlandsecourant.com
www.denederlandsecourant.com
Other information: www.dutchcommunitycalendar.ca
Circulation: 2,500
Frequency: Bi-weekly; Dutch & English
Bas Opdenkelder, Publisher,
publisher@denederlandsecourant.com

Dutch
Owned By: Mokeham Publishing Inc.
PO Box 20203, 457 Ellis St., Penticton, BC V2A 8M1
Tel: 250-492-3002
info@dutchthemag.com
www.dutchthemag.com
twitter.com/dutchthemag
www.facebook.com/dutchthemag
A magazine in English about The Netherlands & the Dutch.
Tom, Editor, editor@dutchthemag.com

Estonian

Estonian Life
Also Known As: Eesti Elu
3 Madison Ave., Toronto, ON M5R 2S2
Tel: 416-733-4550; *Fax:* 416-733-0944
info@eestielu.ca
eestielu.com
www.instagram.com/eestielu.ca
www.facebook.com/eestielu.ca
Frequency: Weekly; Estonian

Filipino

Filipiniana News
1531 Queen St. West, Toronto, ON M6R 1A5
Tel: 416-534-7836; *Fax:* 416-535-9491
filipiniananews@rogers.com
Circulation: 10,000
Frequency: Monthly

Filipino Journal
46 Pincarrow Rd., Winnipeg, MB R3Y 1E3
Tel: 204-489-8894; *Fax:* 204-489-1575
info@filipinojournal.com
filipinojournal.com
www.instagram.com/filipinojournal
twitter.com/filipinojournal
www.face book.com/FilipinoJournalFans
Circulation: 4,500
Frequency: 24 times a year
Ronald Cantiveros, Publisher

The North American Filipino Star
Owned By: Filcan Publications, Inc.
7159, ch de la Cote des Neiges, Montréal, QC H3R 2M2
Tel: 514-485-7861
marketing@filipinostar.org
www.filipinostar.org
Circulation: 5,000
Frequency: Monthly
Zenaida Ferry-Kharroubi, Publisher & Chief Editor

The Philippine Reporter
PO Box 44529, 2682 Eglinton Ave. East, Toronto, ON M1K 5K2
Tel: 416-461-8694
philreporter@gmail.com
www.philippinereporter.com
Circulation: 12,000
Frequency: Bi-monthly
Serves the Filipino-Canadian community.
Hermie Garcia, Editor
Mila Astorga-Garcia, Managing Editor

Finnish

Kanadan Sanomat
Owned By: Vapaa Sana Press Ltd.
#308, 191 Eglinton Ave. East, Toronto, ON M4P 1K1
Tel: 416-321-0808
service@vapaasana.com
finnishcanadian.com
Frequency: Weekly

German

Das Journal
Owned By: SOL Publishing Group
977 College St., Toronto, ON M6H 1A6
Tel: 416-534-3177; *Fax:* 416-588-6441
info@dasjournal.ca
www.dasjournal.ca
Circulation: 10,000
Frequency: Bi-weekly
German language newspaper for Canadians of German,
Austrian, & Swiss descent
Vasco Evaristo, Publisher, publisher@dasjournal.ca
Mark Liechti, Editor & Creative Director,
mark.liechti@dasjournal.ca
Juergen Fuerst, Manager, Marketing, 416-518-5669,
juergen.fuerst@dasjournal.ca

Die Mennonitische Post
383 Main St., Steinbach, MB R2G 1Z4
Tel: 204-326-6790
mcccanada.ca/mennonitische-post
www.facebook.com/47324626271
Circulation: 4,500
Frequency: 23 times a year
Kennert Giesbrecht, Editor

Echo Germanica
118 Tyrrel Ave., Toronto, ON M6G 2G5
Tel: 416-652-1332; *Fax:* 416-658-6909
info@echoworld.com
www.echoworld.com
Circulation: 16,000
Sybille Forster-Rentmeister, Publisher/Editor-in-Chief

Greek

Greek Canadian Tribune / Ellinokanadiko Vima
7835B, av Wiseman, Montréal, QC H3N 2N8
Tel: 514-272-6873; *Fax:* 514-272-3157
info@bhma.net
www.bhma.net
Frequency: Weekly; Greek & English
Christos Manikis, Editor

Greek Press
758 Pape Ave., 2nd Fl., Toronto, ON M4K 3S7
Tel: 416-465-3243; *Fax:* 416-465-2428
greekpressnews@gmail.com
www.greekpress.ca
Circulation: 6,000
Frequency: Weekly
Katerina Gerasklis, Editor-in-Chief,
katerina.greekpressnews@gmail.com

Patrides, A North American Review
PO Box 266 O, 70 Wynford Dr., Toronto, ON M3C 2S2
Tel: 416-921-4229; *Fax:* 416-921-0723
www.patrides.com
Circulation: 160,000
Frequency: Monthly
Thomas S. Saras, Editor-in-Chief, saras@patrides.com
Kathy Saras, Executive Managing Editor

Hungarian

Kanadai-amerikai Magyarság / Canadian American Hungarians
#103, 747 St Clair Ave. West, Toronto, ON M6C 4A4
Tel: 416-656-8361 *Toll-Free:* 855-656-8361
info@kanadaimagyarsag.ca
www.kekujsag.com
www.facebook.com/kanadai.a.magyarsag
Frequency: Weekly; English, Magyar

New Hungarian Voice
PO Box 74527 Kitsilano, Vancouver, BC V6K 4P4
nhv@newhungarianvoice.com
www.newhungarianvoice.com
Frequency: Quarterly; English
Peter Czink, Editor-in-Chief

Icelandic

Logberg -Heimskringla
835 Marion St., Winnipeg, MB R2J 0K6
Tel: 204-284-5686; *Fax:* 204-284-7099
Toll-Free: 866-564-2374
lh@lh-inc.ca
lh-inc.ca
twitter.com/LHNewspaper
www.facebook.com/LogbergHeimskringla
Frequency: 24 times a year; English & Icelandic
Stefan Jonasson, Editor, stefan@lh-inc.ca

Italian

Corriere Canadese
287 Bridgeland Ave., Toronto, ON M6A 1Z6
Tel: 416-782-9222; *Fax:* 416-782-9333
info@corriere.com
www.corriere.ca
twitter.com/ccanadese
www.facebook.com/newcorriere
Frequency: Daily
Corriere Canadese is an Italian language publication.

Corriere Italiano
Owned By: Métro Média
#320, 101, boul Marcel-Laurin, Montréal, QC H4N 2M3
Tel: 514-286-1066
www.corriereitaliano.com
www.facebook.com/corriere.montreal
Frequency: Weekly

Il Cittadino Canadese
#710, 6020, rue Jean Talon est, Montréal, QC H1S 3B1
Tel: 514-253-2332
journal@cittadino.ca
cittadino.ca
Circulation: 15,000
Frequency: Weekly
Vittorio Giordano, Editor

Japanese

Nikkei Voice
6 Garamond Ct., Toronto, ON M3C 1Z5
Tel: 416-386-0287; *Fax:* 416-386-0136
business@nikkeivoice.ca
www.nikkeivoice.ca
www.youtube.com/user/nikkeivoicestudios
twitter.com/thenikkeivoice
www .facebook.com/NikkeiVoice
Frequency: Monthly
Jody Hamade, Publisher
Kelly Fleck, Managing Editor

Korean

Korea Daily
#8, 1101 Finch Ave. West, Toronto, ON M3J 2C9
Tel: 416-736-0736; *Fax:* 416-736-7811
toronto.koreadaily.com

Latin American

El Popular
2413 Dundas St. West, Toronto, ON M6P 1X3
Tel: 416-531-2495; *Fax:* 416-531-7187
diarioelpopular.com
Frequency: Weekly
Eduardo UrueÃ±a, Director

Lithuanian

Teviskes Ziburiai/Lights of Homeland
2185 Stavebank Rd., Mississauga, ON L5C 1T3
Tel: 905-275-4672; *Fax:* 905-275-4364
tevzib@rogers.com
www.tevzib.com

Circulation: 2,800
Frequency: Weekly
Andrea Benotas, Editor

Multicultural

Community Digest / Nouvelles Communautaires
Alberta Edition, #660, 3545 - 32nd Ave. NE, Calgary, AB T1Y 6M6
Tel: 403-271-8275
mail@communitydigest.ca
www.communitydigest.ca
Other information: Advertising: adsales@communitydigest.ca
Frequency: Weekly (in three editions - British Columbia, Alberta, & Ontario)
The multicultural magazine encourages cultural harmony. Issues are available in English & French.
N. Ebrahim, Publisher
A. Thobhani, Alberta Bureau Chief

Peel Multicultural Scene
Peel Multicultural Council, 6630 Turner Valley Rd., Mississauga, ON L5N 2P1
Tel: 905-819-1144; *Fax:* 905-542-3950
pmc@peelmc.com
www.peelmc.ca
www.youtube.com/peelpmc
www.facebook.com/peelmulticulturalcouncil
Circulation: 1,500

Persian

Shahrvand Publications Ltd.
#304, 505 Hwy. 7 East, Toronto, ON L3T 7T1
Tel: 905-764-7022; *Fax:* 905-764-5919
news@shahrvand.com
www.shahrvand.com
www.facebook.com/ShahrvandTO
Circulation: 50,000
Frequency: Twice a week
Hassan Zerehi, Editor-in-Chief

Polish

Czas/Polish Times
34 Lemmen Dr., Winnipeg, MB R2K 3J8
Tel: 204-582-4392; *Fax:* 204-582-4392
Circulation: 651
Frequency: Weekly
Krystyna Gajda, President, kmgajda@mts.net

Glos Polski/Polish Voice
102 - 418 Royal York Rd., Toronto, ON M8Y 2R5
Tel: 416-993-3143
glospolski1908@gmail.com
www.polishcanadians.ca/glos_polski_EN.html
Circulation: 6,000
Frequency: Weekly

Wieslaw Magiera, Editor-in-Chief

Polish Business Directory
777C The Queensway, Toronto, ON M8Z 1N4
Tel: 416-255-9182; *Fax:* 416-255-9893
Toll-Free: 877-742-9455
info@mastermp.com
www.przewodnikhandlowy.com
www.facebook.com/polskiprzewodnikhandlowy
Circulation: 50,000
Frequency: Annually
Robert Wagner, Publisher

Portuguese

Sol Portugues/Portuguese Sun
977 College St., Toronto, ON M6H 1A6
Tel: 416-538-1788; *Fax:* 416-538-7953
sol@solnet.com
www.solnet.com
Circulation: 12,000
Frequency: Weekly
Portuguese-language newspaper
Antonio Perinu, President
Alice Perinu, Editor

A Voz de Portugal
4231, boul St-Laurent, Montréal, QC H2W 1Z4
Tél: 514-284-1813; *Téléc:* 514-284-6150
Ligne sans frais: 866-684-1813
jornal@avozdeportugal.com
www.avozdeportugal.com
Tirage: 10 000
Fréquence: Hebdomadaire
Sylvio Martins, Directeur administratif, sylviomartins@avozdeportugal.com

Russian

Nasha Canada
#1073, 40-1110 Finch Ave. West, Toronto, ON M3J 3M2
Tel: 647-435-8619
nashacanada@yahoo.ca
www.nashacanada.com
Circulation: 10,000
Frequency: Weekly
Vladimir Turovsky, Publisher

Serbian

Bratstvo Srpsko
Owned By: Fraternity Publishing
425 Jane St., Toronto, ON M6S 3Z7
Tel: 416-769-7181
Circulation: 2,250
Frequency: Monthly
William Durovic, Editor-in-Chief

Kisobran
#368, 3495 Cambie St., Vancouver, BC V5Z 4R3
Tel: 604-731-9446
redakcija@kisobran.com
Circulation: 4,000
Frequency: Monthly
Dragan Andrejevic, Publisher

Slovak, Czech

Novy Domov
Masaryk Memorial Institute Inc., 450 Scarborough Golf Club Rd., Toronto, ON M1G 1H1
Tel: 647-608-1713
www.novydomov.ca
Frequency: Bi-weekly

Satellite 1-416
ABE, PO Box 176 E, Toronto, ON M6H 4E2
Tel: 416-530-4222; *Fax:* 416-530-0069
abe@zpravy.ca
www.satellite1-416.com
Circulation: 1,200
Ales Brezina, Publisher & Editor

South Asian

Desi News
PO Box 21544, 17600 Yonge St., Newmarket, ON L3Y 8J1
Tel: 416-695-4357
desinews@rogers.com
www.e-desinews.com
Circulation: 30,000
Frequency: Monthly
G.A. Easwar, Publisher
Shagorika Easwar, Editor

Eastern News
#144, 224 Queen St. South, Mississauga, ON L5M 2B7
Tel: 905-216-2085; *Fax:* 905-216-2065
www.easternnews.ca
Circulation: 7,500
Frequency: 24 times a year
Masood Khan, Editor, mkhan@theeasternnews.com

India Journal
#15, 2355 Derry Rd. East, Mississauga, ON L5S 1V6
Tel: 905-405-0420; *Fax:* 905-405-0428
Circulation: 35,000
Frequency: Weekly
Harjinder Singh, Publisher

Indo Caribbean World
312 Brownridge Dr., Thornhill, ON L4J 5X1
Tel: 905-738-5005; *Fax:* 905-738-3927
indocaribbeanworld@gmail.com
www.indocaribbeanworld.com
Circulation: 30,000
Frequency: 2 times per month

Indo-Canadian Voice
Previous Name: Indo-Canadian Awaaz
#102, 9360 - 120 St., Surrey, BC V3V 4B9
Tel: 604-502-6100; *Fax:* 604-501-6111
www.voiceonline.com
Circulation: 25,000
Frequency: Weekly
Vinnie Combow, Manager
Rattan Mall, Editor, newsdesk@voiceonline.com

Journal Apna Watan
4021, boul Notre Dame, Laval, QC H7W 1S8
Tel: 514-798-2838
apnawatan2002@yahoo.com
Circulation: 5,000
Frequency: Monthly
Arshad Randhawa, Editor

Sanjh Savera/Dust and Dawn
7405 Kimbel St., Mississauga, ON L4T 3M6
Tel: 905-672-6878
Circulation: 15,000
Nirmal Hansra, Publisher

Tamilar Thagaval
PO Box 3 F, Toronto, ON M4Y 2L4
Tel: 416-920-9250; *Fax:* 416-921-6576
Circulation: 5,000
Frequency: Monthly

The Times of Sri Lanka
58 Sundial Cres., Toronto, ON M4A 2J8
Tel: 416-445-5390
timeslanka@rogers.com
www.timeslanka.com
www.facebook.com/timeslanka.tsl
Circulation: 20,000
Frequency: Monthly
Upali Obeyesekere, Managing Editor, upaliobey@rogers.com

The Weekly Voice
#16, 7015 Tranmere Dr., Mississauga, ON L5S 1T7
Tel: 905-795-0639; *Fax:* 905-795-9801
info@weeklyvoice.com
www.weeklyvoice.com
Circulation: 30,000
Binoy Thomas, Editor
Sudhir Anand, Publisher, sudhir@weeklyvoice.com

Swedish

Scandinavian Press
PO Box 567, Melita, MB R0M 1L0
Toll-Free: 855-675-7226
www.scandpress.com
Frequency: 4 times a year
News & information on Denmark, Finland, Iceland, Norway, & Sweden.
Al Larson, Publisher

Swedish Press
info@swedishpress.com
swedishpress.com
twitter.com/SwedishPress
www.facebook.com/swedishpress
Frequency: 8 times a year; English & Swedish
Tatty Maclay, Editor in Chief

Ukrainian

Homin Ukrainy Publishing Co. Ltd.
Also Known As: Ukrainian Echo
9 Plastics Ave., Toronto, ON M8Z 4B6

Tel: 416-516-2443
homin@on.aibn.com
www.homin.ca
www.facebook.com/ukrainianecho

Circulation: 1,000
Frequency: Weekly; Ukrainian & English

Novy Shliakh / New Pathway
New Pathway Publishers Ltd., #210, 145 Evans Ave.,
Toronto, ON M5Z 5X8

Tel: 416-960-3424
info@newpathway.ca
newpathway.ca
twitter.com/newpathwaynews
www.facebook.com/newpathwaynews
Frequency: Weekly; also New Pathway Almanac (annual)

Visnyk/The Herald
9 St. John's Ave., Winnipeg, MB R2W 1G8

Tel: 204-586-3093; Fax: 204-582-5241
Toll-Free: 877-586-3093
visnyk@uocc.ca
www.uocc.ca

Circulation: 10,000
Frequency: Monthly; English & Ukrainian
Fr. Taras Ubod, Editor

Vietnamese

Lang Van
250 North Service Rd., RR#2, Grimsby, ON L3M 4E8

Tel: 647-271-8010
tapchilangvan@yahoo.com

Circulation: 1,800
Nguyen Huu Nghia, Manager

Thôi Bâo/Time News
1114 College St., Toronto, ON M6H 1B6

Tel: 416-925-8607; Fax: 416-925-0695
www.thoibao.com

Circulation: 14,500
Frequency: Weekly
Dave Nguyen, Publisher

Vietnam Time Magazine Edmonton
Also Known As: Viet Nam Thoi Bao Edmonton
10720 - 95 St., Edmonton, AB T5H 2C7

Tel: 780-800-9818
www.vietnamtimemagazine.com

Circulation: 1,500
Kyra Lu, Publisher & Editor

Scholarly

Culture, Current Events

Anthropologica
University of Waterloo, 200 University Ave. West, Waterloo,
ON N2L 3G1

www.cas-sca.ca/publications/anthropologica-journal
Circulation: 625
Frequency: Semi-annually
Journal of the Canadian Anthropology Society
Jasmin Habib, Editor-in-Chief, jhabib@uwaterloo.ca
Alicia Silwinski, Editor, French Manuscripts, asliwinski@wlu.ca

Religious & Denominational

Studies in Religion / Sciences Religieuses
Owned By: SAGE Publications

journals.sagepub.com/home/sir
Circulation: 1,400
Frequency: Quarterly
Zeba Crook, Editor, zeba.crook@gmail.com
Jean-François Laniel, Editor

Scholarly Publication

Acadiensis
*Also Known As: Acadiensis: Journal of the History
of the Atlantic Region*
Campus House, University of New Brunswick, PO Box 4400,
11 Garland Ct., Fredericton, NB E3B 5A3

Tel: 506-453-4978
acadiensis@unb.ca
www.acadiensis.ca
twitter.com/acadiensis
www.facebook.com/Acadiensis

Frequency: 2 times a year
Erin Morton, Co-Editor, wrightd@unb.ca
Suzanne Morton, Co-Editor, suzanne.morton@mcgill.ca

**Annals of Air & Space Law (IASL) / Annales de droit
aérian et spatial**
Institute & Centre of Air & Space Law, McGill University,
3690, rue Peel, Montréal, QC H3A 1W9

Tel: 514-398-5095; Fax: 514-398-8197
www.mcgill.ca/iasl/annals

Circulation: 1,000
Frequency: Annually
Provides information about the laws surrounding aerospace
activities
Ram S. Jakhu, Director & Editor-in-Chief

Arctic Journal
c/o Arctic Institute of North America, University of Calgary,
2500 University Dr. NW, ES-1040, Calgary, AB T2N 1N4

Tel: 403-220-7515; Fax: 403-282-4609
arctic@ucalgary.ca
arctic.ucalgary.ca
twitter.com/ArcticSynthesis
www.facebook.com/ArcticInstituteofNorthAmeri ca

Circulation: 1,500
Frequency: 4 times a year
Publishes book reviews & research on the North, providing
information from the natural, social, & earth sciences & the
humanities
Dr. Karen McCullough, Editor, 403-220-4049,
kmccullo@ucalgary.ca
Maribeth Murray, Executive Director, 403-220-7516,
murraym@ucalgary.ca

**Atlantis: Critical Studies in Gender, Culture & Social
Justice**
Previous Name: Atlantis: A Women's Studies Journal
Mount Saint Vincent University, Evaristus 234, Halifax, NS
B3M 2J6

atlantis.journal@msvu.ca
www.msvu.ca/atlantis

Circulation: 500
Frequency: 2 times a year
Scholarly research journal covering issues & topics across a
range of disciplines, including women's & gender studies,
anti-racism & critical identity, intersectionality, transnationality, &
cultural studies
Annalee Lepp, Editor

**Canadian Ethnic Studies / Études Ethniques au
Canada**
Dept. of Sociology, University of Calgary, #909, 2500
University Dr., Calgary, AB T2N 1N4

cesa@ucalgary.ca
cesa-scee.ca/ces-journal

Frequency: 3 times a year
Fully refereed, interdisciplinary journal for the study of ethnicity,
immigration, inter-group relations & the history & cultural life of
ethnic groups in Canada.

**Canadian Foreign Policy Journal / La Politique
étrangère du Canada**
5306 River Building, Norman Paterson School of
International Affairs, 1125 Colonel By Dr., Ottawa, ON K1S
5B6

Tel: 613-520-6655; Fax: 613-520-2889
international_affairs@carleton.ca
www.tandfonline.com

Frequency: 3 times a year
Online ISSN is 2157-0817
Brian Tomlin, Editor
Kevin Arthur, Managing Editor

Canadian Historical Review
Owned By: University of Toronto Press
Journals Division, University of Toronto Press, 5201
Dufferin St., Toronto, ON M3H 5T8

chr@utpress.utoronto.ca
utpjournals.press/loi/chr

Frequency: Quarterly

**Canadian Journal of Development Studies (CJDS) /
Revue canadienne d'études du développement**
*Owned By: Canadian Association for the Study of
International Development*
c/o School for International Studies, Simon Fraser
University, #7200, 515 West Hastings St., Vancouver, BC
V6B 5K3

Tel: 778-782-7148
cjds@sfu.ca
casid-acedi.ca/cjds

Circulation: 500
Frequency: Quarterly

Ananya Mukherjee Reed, Editor

**Canadian Journal of Economics (CJE) / Revue
canadienne d'economique**

cje@economics.ca
www.economics.ca/cpages/cje-home
Frequency: Quaterly
Katherine Cuff, Managing Editor, cuffk@mcmaster.ca

**Canadian Journal of Higher Education (CJHE) / La
revue canadienne d'enseignemnet supérieur**
Also Known As: CJHE
*Owned By: Canadian Society for the Study of Higher
Education*
c/o Dept. of Leadership, Higher & Adult Education, OISE,
252 Bloor St. West, 6th Fl., Toronto, ON M5S 1V6

journals.sfu.ca/cjhe/index.php/cjhe
Frequency: Quarterly
The peer reviewed journal publishes articles about the structure
& processes of the Canadian higher education system. Book
reviews are also included in the journal.
Creso Sá, Editor, oise.editor.cjhe@utoronto.ca

**Canadian Journal of History (CJH) / Annales
canadiennes d'histoire**

utpjournals.press/loi/cjh
Frequency: 3 times a year

Canadian Journal of Information & Library Science
Owned By: University of Toronto Press
5201 Dufferin St., Toronto, ON M3H 5T8

muse.jhu.edu/journal/497
Circulation: 400
Frequency: 4 times a year
Heather Hill, Editor

**Canadian Journal of Law & Society (CJLS/RCDS) /
La Revue Canadienne Droit et Société**

www.acds-clsa.org/en/canadian_journal_law_society.cfm
Frequency: 3 times a year
Dominique Bernier, Co-editor
Dean Jula Hughes, Co-editor

**Canadian Journal of Linguistics (CJL/RCL) / Revue
Canadienne de Linguistique**
Owned By: Cambridge University Press

www.cambridge.org
Frequency: 4 times a year
Heather Newell, Co-editor, ed2@cla-acl.ca
Daniel Siddiqi, Co-editor, ed2@cla-acl.ca

Canadian Journal of Mathematics (CJM)
c/o Canadian Mathematical Society, #209, 1725 St Laurent
Blvd., Ottawa, ON K1G 3V4

Tel: 613-733-2662; Fax: 613-733-8994
cms.math.ca/publications/cjm
twitter.com/canmathsociety
www.facebook.com/canmathsoc

Frequency: 6 times a year
Louigi Addario-Berry, Editor-in-Chief
Eyal Goren, Editor-in-Chief

Canadian Journal of Neurological Sciences
c/o Canadian Neurological Sciences Federation, 143N
Heritage Square, #8500 Macleod Trail SE, Calgary, AB T2H
2N1

Tel: 403-229-9544; Fax: 403-229-1661
www.cnsfederation.org/cnsf/cjns

Circulation: 1,200
Frequency: Bi-monthly
The journal is the official publication of the four member societies
of the Canadian Neurological Sciences Federation: Canadian
Neurological Society (CNS), Canadian Neurosurgical Society
(CNSS), Canadian Association of Child Neurology (CACN), &
the Canadian Society of Clinical Neurophysiologists (CSCN).
Peer reviewed articles about the neurosciences are published in
the Canadian Journal of Neurological Sciences. The journal is
circulated to society members, non-members, & institutions in
Canada & around the world.
Lisa Arrington, Managing Editor, larrington@cambridge.org

Canadian Journal of Philosophy (CJP)
Owned By: Cambridge University Press

www.canadianjournalofphilosophy.com
Frequency: Quarterly
Mark McCullagh, Editorial Board Coordinator

**Canadian Journal of Program Evaluation / La Revue
canadienne d'évaluation de programme**

cjpe@evaluationcanada.ca
journalhosting.ucalgary.ca/index.php/cjpe
Frequency: 3 times a year

Isabelle Bourgeois, Editor-in-Chief,
isabelle.bourgeois@uottawa.ca

Canadian Journal of Women & The Law (CJWL/RFD) / Revue Femmes et Droit
Previous Name: Revue juridique la femme et la droit
Owned By: University of Toronto Press
5210 Dufferin St., Toronto, ON M3H 5T8
utpjournals.press/loi/cjwl

Frequency: Biannual

Canadian Literature
Owned By: University of British Columbia Press
c/o Anthropology & Sociology Bldg., University of British
Columbia, #8, 6303 NW Marine Dr., Vancouver, BC V6T 1Z1
Tel: 604-822-2780
can.lit@ubc.ca
canlit.ca
twitter.com/canadianlit
www.facebook.com/canadianlit
Frequency: Quarterly
Christine Kim, Editor, c.kim@ubc.ca

Canadian Mathematical Bulletin (CMB)
Owned By: Cambridge University Press
www.cambridge.org/core/journals/canadian-mathematical-bulleti
n

Frequency: Quarterly
Antonio Lei, Editor-in-Chief
Javad Mashreghi, Editor-in-Chief

Canadian Modern Language Review (CMLR/RCLV) / Le Revue canadienne des langues vivantes
Owned By: University of Toronto Press
5201 Dufferin St., Toronto, ON M3H 5T8
Tel: 416-667-7777; *Fax:* 416-667-7881
cmlrcoordinator@utpress.utoronto.ca
utpjournals.press/loi/cmlr

Frequency: Quarterly
Donna Patrick, Co-Editor
Daphnée Simard, Co-Editor

Canadian Public Policy / Analyse de Politique
PO Box 35006, 1221, Fleury est, Montréal, QC H2C 3K4
Tel: 646-257-5906
cpp.adp@gmail.com
economics.ca/cpp

Circulation: 1,500
Frequency: 4 times a year
Michael Veall, Managing Editor

Canadian Review of American Studies
Owned By: University of Toronto Press
5201 Dufferin St., Toronto, ON M3H 5T8
utpjournals.press/loi/cras

Frequency: 3 times a year

Canadian Theatre Review (CTR)
Owned By: University of Toronto Press Inc.
University of Toronto Press, 5201 Dufferin St., Toronto, ON
M3H 5T8
canadiantheatrereview@gmail.com
ctr.utpjournals.press
www.facebook.com/CanadianTheatreReview
Frequency: 4 times a year
Jenn Stephenson, Editor-in-Chief

Cartographica
Owned By: University of Toronto Press
5201 Dufferin St., Toronto, ON M3H 5T8
utpjournals.press/loi/cart

Frequency: Quarterly
Emmanuel Stefanakis, Editor-in-Chief,
emmanuel.stefanakis@ucalgary.ca

The Dorchester Review
#204, 1066 Somerset St. West, Ottawa, ON K1Y 4T3
info@dorchesterreview.ca
dorchesterreview.ca/The_Dorchester_Review/Home.html
A historical and literary review.

East/West: Journal of Ukrainian Studies
University of Alberta, 4 - 30 Pembina Hall, Edmonton, AB
T6G 2H8
Tel: 780-633-3319; *Fax:* 780-497-5347
www.ewjus.com

Frequency: Semi-annually
Available online only.
Svitlana Krys, Editor-in-Chief

Event
PO Box 2503, New Westminster, BC V3L 5B2
Tel: 604-527-5293
event@douglascollege.ca
www.eventmagazine.ca
twitter.com/EVENTmags
www.facebook.com/eventmagazine

Circulation: 1,100
Frequency: 3 times a year
Poetry & prose magazine.
Shashi Bhat, Editor

International Journal
Owned By: Canadian International Council
c/o Canadian International Council, 6 Hoskin Ave., Toronto,
ON M5S 1H8
Tel: 416-946-7209
thecic.org/ij

Circulation: 1,300
Frequency: 4 times a year
Scholarly publication on international relations.
Brian Bow, Editor-in-Chief
Jack Cunningham, Editor-in-Chief
Jennifer Chylinski, Managing Editor

Intersections: Canadian Journal of Music / Intersections: revue canadienne de musique
Previous Name: Canadian University Music Review
Owned By: Canadian University Music Society
#202, 10 Morrow Ave., Toronto, ON M6R 2J1
Tel: 416-538-1650
office@muscan.org
www.muscan.org/en/publications/intersections
Frequency: 2 times a year

Jeunesse: Young People, Texts, Cultures / Littérature Canadienne pour la Jeunesse
515 Portage Ave., Winnipeg, MB R3B 2E9
jeunessejournal.ca

Frequency: Biannually
Jeunesse has a mandate to publish research on & to provide a
forum for discussion about, cultural productions for, by & about
young people. Especially interested in the cultural functions &
representations of "the child."
Sarah Olive, Editor, sarah.olive@york.ac.uk

Journal of Canadian Art History / Annales d'histoire de l'art canadien
c/o EV 3.725, Concordia University, 1455, boul de
Maisonneuve ouest, Montréal, QC H3G 1M8
Tel: 514-848-2424; *Fax:* 514-848-4584
jcah@concordia.ca
jcah-ahac.concordia.ca

Circulation: 550
Frequency: 2 times a year
Peer-reviewed journal focused on the history & theory of visual
arts in Canada
Martha Langford, Editor-in-Chief

Journal of Canadian Studies (JCS/REC) / Revue d'Études Canadiennes
Owned By: University of Toronto Press
5201 Dufferin St., Toronto, ON M3H 5T8
Fax: 416-667-7832
jcs@utpress.utoronto.ca
utpjournals.press/loi/jcs

Frequency: Quarterly
Elaine Coburn, Co-Editor
Andrea A. Davis, Co-Editor

Journal of Law & Social Policy / Revue des lois et des politiques sociales
Clinic Resource Office, Legal Aid Ontario, #41, 425 Adelaide
St. West, Toronto, ON M5V 3C1
Tel: 416-204-5408; *Fax:* 416-204-5422
Toll-Free: 800-668-8258
jlsp@lao.on.ca
www.legalaid.on.ca

Circulation: 230
Frequency: Annually
Janet Mosher, Editor-in-Chief

Journal of Scholarly Publishing
Owned By: University of Toronto Press
5201 Dufferin St., Toronto, ON M3H 5T8
jsp@utpress.utoronto.ca
utpjournals.press/loi/jsp

Frequency: Quarterly
Robert Brown, Editor
Alex Holzman, Editor

Labour / Le Travail
Owned By: Athabasca University Press
c/o Canadian Committee On Labour History, Peace Hills
Trust Tower, #1200, 10011 - 109th St., Edmonton, AB T5J
3S8
Tel: 780-421-2528
cclh@athabascau.ca
www.cclh.ca

Frequency: 2 times a year
Kathy Killoh, Managing Editor

Labour, Capital & Society (LCS/TCS) / Travail, capital et société
Also Known As: LC&S
Halifax, NS
lcstcs.editor@yahoo.ca
www.lcs-tcs.com

Frequency: 2 times a year
The bilingual, refereed journal focuses on labour issues in Asia,
Africa, the Middle East, Latin America & the Caribbean.
Suzanne Dansereau, Editor

Material Culture Review / Revue de la culture matérielle
Previous Name: Material History Review
c/o Cape Breton University, PO Box 5300, 1250 Grand Lake
Rd., Sydney, NS B1P 6L2
Tel: 902-563-1284; *Fax:* 902-563-1910
mcr_rcm@cbu.ca
culture.cbu.ca/mcr

Circulation: 400
Frequency: 2 times a year
Richard MacKinnon, Managing Editor,
richard_mackinnon@cbu.ca
Laura Bast, Assistant Editor

McGill Journal of Education / Revue des sciences de l'éducation de McGill
c/o Education Bldg., McGill University, #345, 3700, rue
McTavish, Montréal, QC H3A 1Y2
mje.education@mcgill.ca
mje.mcgill.ca

Frequency: 3 times a year
Teresa Strong-Wilson, Editor-in-Chief

McMaster Journal of Theology & Ministry (MJTM)
Owned By: McMaster Divinity College Press
c/o McMaster Divinity College, McMaster University, 1280
Main St. West, Hamilton, ON L8S 4K1
mjtm@mcmaster.ca
mcmasterdivinity.ca/mjtm

Frequency: Annual

Modern Drama
Owned By: University of Toronto Press
5201 Dufferin St., Toronto, ON M3H 5T8
modern.drama@utpress.utoronto.ca
moderndrama.utpjournals.press

Frequency: Quarterly
David Kornhaber, Editor
Lawrence Switzky, Editor

The Monograph
Ontario Association for Geographic & Environmental
Education, #202, 10 Morrow Ave., Toronto, ON M6R 2J1
Tel: 416-538-1650; *Fax:* 416-489-1713
journals@interlog.com
www.oagee.org/monograph-journal

Circulation: 800
Frequency: 4 times a year
Gary Birchall, Editor

Mosaic
#208, Tier Bldg., University of Manitoba, Winnipeg, MB R3T
2N2
Tel: 204-474-9763; *Fax:* 204-474-7584
mosaic@umanitoba.ca
mosaic.umanitoba.ca

Frequency: Quarterly
Shepherd Steiner, Editor

Newfoundland & Labrador Studies
Previous Name: Newfoundland Studies
PO Box 4200 C, St. John's, NL A1C 5S7
Tel: 709-737-2144; *Fax:* 709-737-4342
nls@mun.ca
www.mun.ca/nls

Frequency: 2 times a year
Barry Gaulton, Editor

Ontario History
Owned By: **Ontario Historical Society**
c/o Ontario Historical Society, 34 Parkview Ave., Toronto, ON M2N 3Y2
> ohs@ontariohistoricalsociety.ca
> ontariohistoricalsociety.ca/ontario-history-journal

Frequency: 2 times a year
Tory Tronrud, Editor, foxlort@tbaytel.net

Pacific Affairs
c/o University of British Columbia, #376, 1855 West Mall, Vancouver, BC V6T 1Z2
> *Tel:* 604-822-6508; *Fax:* 604-822-9452
> enquiry@pacificaffairs.ubc.ca
> pacificaffairs.ubc.ca
> twitter.com/PacificAffairs
> www.facebook.com/PacificAffairsJournal

Frequency: Quarterly
Publishes scholarly articles of contemporary Asia & Pacific.
Hyung Gu Lynn, Editor
Carolyn Grant, Managing Editor, cgrant@pacificaffairs.ubc.ca

The Philanthropist - Agora Foundation / Le Philanthrope
c/o Scotia Private Client Group, Exchange Tower, PO Box 430 First Can. Pl., 130 King St. West, 20th Fl., Toronto, ON M5X 1K1
> *Tel:* 902-634-0403
> managing_editor@thephilanthropist.ca
> www.thephilanthropist.ca

Circulation: 450
Frequency: 4 times a year
Leslie Wright, Publication Manager

Queen's Quarterly
402D Douglas Library, Queen's University, 93 University Ave., Kingston, ON K7L 5C4
> *Tel:* 613-533-2667
> queens.quarterly@queensu.ca
> www.queensu.ca/quarterly

Circulation: 3,000
Frequency: 4 times a year
Reviews & debates the events that contributed to Canada's cultural, political, & intellectual life
Dr. Boris Castel, Editor
Penny Roantree, Business Manager

Relational Child & Youth Care Practice
Previous Name: The Journal of Child & Youth Care
> rcycp@press.cyc-net.org
> rcycp.com

Frequency: Quarterly

Renaissance & Reformation / Renaissance et réforme
c/o Iter, #7009, 130 St George St., Toronto, ON M5S 1A5
> *Tel:* 416-978-7074; *Fax:* 416-978-1668
> iter.renref@utoronto.ca
> www.itergateway.org

Circulation: 700
Frequency: 4 times a year
Pascale Duhamel, Editor

Revue canadienne de linguistique appliquée / Canadian Journal of Applied Linguistics
Université du Nouveau-Brunswick, CP 4400, #346, 10 McKay Dr., Fredericton, NB E3B 5A3
> *Tél:* 506-453-5136; *Téléc:* 506-453-4777
> journals.lib.unb.ca/index.php/CJAL/index

Fréquence: 2 fois par an
Joseph Dicks, Rédacteur en chef
Paula Lee Kristmanson, Rédacteur en chef

Russell: the Journal of Bertrand Russell Studies
Previous Name: Russell: The Journal of the Bertrand Russell Archives
Mills Library, Russell House, McMaster University, Hamilton, ON L8S 4L6
> russjour@mcmaster.ca
> mulpress.mcmaster.ca/russelljournal

Frequency: 2 times a year
Kenneth Blackwell, Editor

Scientia Canadensis - Journal of the History of Cdn. Science, Technology & Medicine
Canadian Science & Technology Historical Association, PO Box 8502 T, Ottawa, ON K1G 3H9
> cstha-ahstc.ca/scientia-canadensis

Circulation: 200
Frequency: Annually
David Pantalony, Editor-in-chief

Seminar
Owned By: **University of Toronto Press**
5201 Dufferin St., Toronto, ON M3H 5T8
> utpjournals.press/loi/seminar

Frequency: Quarterly
Carrie Smith, Co-editor, carrie.smith@ualberta.ca
Markus Stock, Co-editor, markus.stock@ualberta.ca

Studies in Canadian Literature (SCL/ÉLC) / Études en littérature canadienne
Campus House, University of New Brunswick, PO Box 4400, 11 Garland Ct., Fredericton, NB E3B 5A3
> scl@unb.ca
> journals.lib.unb.ca/index.php/SCL

Frequency: 2 times a year
Cynthia Sugars, Editor, cynthia.sugars@uottawa.ca

Studies in Political Economy: A Socialist Review
> www.tandfonline.com/toc/rsor20/current

Frequency: 3 times a year

Theatre Research in Canada (TRIC/RTAC) / Recherches théâtrales au Canada
> www.utpjournals.press/loi/tric

Frequency: 2 times a year
Kim Solga, Editor

The Tocqueville Review / La Revue Tocqueville
Owned By: **University of Toronto Press**
5201 Dufferin St., Toronto, ON M3H 5T8
> utpjournals.press/loi/ttr

Circulation: 400
Frequency: 2 times a year

TOPIA: Canadian Journal of Cultural Studies
University of Toronto, #12-227, 252 Bloor St. West, Toronto, ON M5S 1V6
> topiajournal@gmail.com
> topia.journals.yorku.ca

Circulation: 300
Frequency: 2 times a year
Rinaldo Walcott, Editor

Ultimate Reality & Meaning
Owned By: **University of Toronto Press**
5201 Dufferin St., Toronto, ON M3H 5T8
> utpjournals.press/loi/uram

Frequency: Quarterly
Tom Krettek, Editor-in-Chief

University of Toronto Law Journal
Owned By: **University of Toronto Press**
5201 Dufferin St., Toronto, ON M3H 5T8
> utlj@utpress.utoronto.ca
> utpjournals.press/loi/utlj

Frequency: Quarterly
David Dyzenhaus, Editor

University of Toronto Quarterly
Owned By: **University of Toronto Press**
Jackman Humanities Bldg., #735, 170 St George St., Toronto, ON M5R 2M8
> utquarterly@gmail.com
> utpjournals.press/loi/utq

Frequency: Quarterly
Colin Hill, Editor

Windsor Review
c/o Dept. of English, University of Windsor, 401 Sunset Ave., Windsor, ON N9B 3P4
> *Tel:* 519-253-3000
> uwrevu@gmail.com
> windsorreview.wordpress.com
> twitter.com/windsorreview

Circulation: 500
Frequency: Bi-annually
Marty Gervais, Managing Editor

Science, Research & Development

Applied Physiology, Nutrition & Metabolism
Owned By: **Canadian Science Publishing**
#203, 65 Auriga Dr., Ottawa, ON K2E 7W6
> *Tel:* 613-656-9846; *Fax:* 613-656-9838
> *Toll-Free:* 844-223-8144
> pubs@cdnsciencepub.com
> cdnsciencepub.com/journal/apnm

Frequency: Monthly
Monthly journal exploring the application of physiology, nutrition, & metabolism to the study of human health
Dr. Terry Graham, Editor Ph.D.

Biochemistry & Cell Biology
Owned By: **Canadian Science Publishing**
#203, 65 Auriga Dr., Ottawa, ON K2E 7W6
> *Tel:* 613-656-9846; *Fax:* 613-656-9838
> *Toll-Free:* 844-223-8144
> pubs@cdnsciencepub.com
> cdnsciencepub.com/journal/bcb

Frequency: Bi-monthly
Bi-monthly journal about biochemistry, including results of research on cellular & molecular biology, as well as review articles & notes on current topics
Dr. Jim Davie, Editor
Dr. Chris Nelson, Editor

Botany
Previous Name: Canadian Journal of Botany
Owned By: **Canadian Science Publishing**
#203, 65 Auriga Dr., Ottawa, ON K2E 7W6
> *Tel:* 613-656-9846; *Fax:* 613-656-9838
> *Toll-Free:* 844-223-8144
> pubs@cdnsciencepub.com
> cdnsciencepub.com/journal/cjb

Frequency: Monthly
Monthly journal featuring research articles, review articles, methods, & commentary on plant sciences & related topics
Dr. Christian Lacroix, Editor

Canadian Geotechnical Journal
Owned By: **Canadian Science Publishing**
#203, 65 Auriga Dr., Ottawa, ON K2E 7W6
> *Tel:* 613-656-9846; *Fax:* 613-656-9838
> *Toll-Free:* 844-223-8144
> pubs@cdnsciencepub.com
> cdnsciencepub.com/journal/cgj

Frequency: Monthly
Monthly journal featuring articles & notes on developments in geotechnical & geoenvironmental engineering
Dr. Ian Moore, Editor

Canadian Journal of Chemistry
Owned By: **Canadian Science Publishing**
#203, 65 Auriga Dr., Ottawa, ON K2E 7W6
> *Tel:* 613-656-9846; *Fax:* 613-656-9838
> *Toll-Free:* 844-223-8144
> pubs@cdnsciencepub.com
> cdnsciencepub.com/journal/cjc

Frequency: Monthly
Monthly journal covering current research on chemistry, including traditional chemistry & materials science, chemical physics, spectroscopy, & other newer interdisciplinary areas
Dr. Yining Huang, Senior Editor

Canadian Journal of Civil Engineering
Owned By: **Canadian Science Publishing**
#203, 65 Auriga Dr., Ottawa, ON K2E 7W6
> *Tel:* 613-656-9846; *Fax:* 613-656-9838
> *Toll-Free:* 844-223-8144
> pubs@cdnsciencepub.com
> cdnsciencepub.com/journal/cjce

Frequency: Monthly
Monthly journal of articles on environmental, hydrotechnical, structural, & construction engineering, as well as engineering mechanics, engineering materials, & history of civil engineering
Dr. Nihar Biswas, Editor
Dr. Amir Fam, Editor

Canadian Journal of Earth Sciences
Owned By: **Canadian Science Publishing**
#203, 65 Auriga Dr., Ottawa, ON K2E 7W6
> *Tel:* 613-656-9846; *Fax:* 613-656-9838
> *Toll-Free:* 844-223-8144
> pubs@cdnsciencepub.com
> cdnsciencepub.com/journal/cjes

Frequency: Monthly
Monthly journal covering current research in various earth sciences segments, including climate, environmental, geoarchaeology, & forensic geoscience, geophysics, & geochemistry
Dr. Ali Polat, Editor Ph.D.

Canadian Journal of Fisheries & Aquatic Sciences
Owned By: **Canadian Science Publishing**
#203, 65 Auriga Dr., Ottawa, ON K2E 7W6
> *Tel:* 613-656-9846; *Fax:* 613-656-9838
> *Toll-Free:* 844-223-8144
> pubs@cdnsciencepub.com
> cdnsciencepub.com/journal/cjfas

Frequency: Monthly
Monthly journal featuring articles, comments, critiques, & re-evaluations relating to current research on fisheries & the aquatic sciences
Dr. Yong Chen, Editor Ph.D.

Dr. Keith Tierney, Editor Ph.D.

Canadian Journal of Microbiology
Owned By: Canadian Science Publishing
#203, 65 Auriga Dr., Ottawa, ON K2E 7W6
Tel: 613-656-9846; *Fax:* 613-656-9838
Toll-Free: 844-223-8144
pubs@cdnsciencepub.com
cdnsciencepub.com/journal/cjm

Frequency: Monthly
Monthly journal featuring current research in microbiology
Dr. Kari E. Dunfield, Editor-in-Chief
Dr. Christopher K. Yost, Editor-in-Chief

Canadian Journal of Physics
Owned By: Canadian Science Publishing
#203, 65 Auriga Dr., Ottawa, ON K2E 7W6
Tel: 613-656-9846; *Fax:* 613-656-9838
Toll-Free: 844-223-8144
pubs@cdnsciencepub.com
cdnsciencepub.com/journal/cjp

Frequency: Monthly
Monthly journal covering developments in physics research
Dr. Michael Steinitz, Editor

Canadian Journal of Physiology & Pharmacology
Owned By: Canadian Science Publishing
#203, 65 Auriga Dr., Ottawa, ON K2E 7W6
Tel: 613-656-9846; *Fax:* 613-656-9838
Toll-Free: 844-223-8144
pubs@cdnsciencepub.com
cdnsciencepub.com/journal/cjpp

Frequency: Monthly
Monthly journal covering current research on physiology, nutrition, pharmacology, & toxicology
Dr. Ghassan Bkaily, Editor Ph.D.
Dr. Pedro D'Orléans-Juste, Editor Ph.D.

Canadian Journal of Zoology
Owned By: Canadian Science Publishing
#203, 65 Auriga Dr., Ottawa, ON K2E 7W6
Tel: 613-656-9846; *Fax:* 613-656-9838
Toll-Free: 844-223-8144
pubs@cdnsciencepub.com
cdnsciencepub.com/journal/cjz

Frequency: Monthly
Monthly journal featuring research conducted by international scientists in the field of zoology
Dr. Helga Guderley, Editor Ph.D.
Dr. R. Mark Brigham, Editor Ph.D.

Environmental Reviews
Owned By: Canadian Science Publishing
#203, 65 Auriga Dr., Ottawa, ON K2E 7W6
Tel: 613-656-9846; *Fax:* 613-656-9838
Toll-Free: 844-223-8144
pubs@cdnsciencepub.com
cdnsciencepub.com/journal/er

Frequency: Quarterly
Quarterly journal about environmental science & related topics
Dr. John P. Smol, Editor Ph.D.

Genome
Owned By: Canadian Science Publishing
#203, 65 Auriga Dr., Ottawa, ON K2E 7W6
Tel: 613-656-9846; *Fax:* 613-656-9838
Toll-Free: 844-223-8144
pubs@cdnsciencepub.com
cdnsciencepub.com/journal/gen

Frequency: Monthly
Monthly journal featuring research articles, reviews, & commentaries on genetics
Dr. Melania E. Cristescu, Editor Ph.D.
Dr. Graham Scoles, Editor Ph.D.

Journal of Unmanned Vehicle Systems
Owned By: Canadian Science Publishing
#203, 65 Auriga Dr., Ottawa, ON K2E 7W6
Tel: 613-656-9846; *Fax:* 613-656-9838
Toll-Free: 844-223-8144
pubs@cdnsciencepub.com
cdnsciencepub.com/journal/juvs

Frequency: Quarterly
Quarterly electronic journal about developments in the field of unmanned vehicle systems
Dr. David M. Bird, Editor

University

Scholarly Publication

BC Studies: The British Columbian Quarterly
University of British Columbia, #2, 6303 NW Marine Dr., Vancouver, BC V6T 1Z1
Tel: 604-822-3727
info@bcstudies.com
www.bcstudies.com
twitter.com/bcstudies
www.facebook.com/BCStudies

Circulation: 700
Frequency: Quarterly
Quarterly magazine dedicated to the exploration of British Columbia's cultural, economic & political life
Leanne Coughlin, Managing Editor

Student Guides

Accès Média
#31, 1124, rue Marie-Anne est, Montréal, QC H2J 2B7
Tél: 514-524-1182; *Téléc:* 514-524-7771
info@accesmedia.com
www.accesmedia.com

Tirage: 300 000
Les éditeurs de guides étudiants de partout au Québec
Edgar Donelle

University & Student Publications

L'Accro
Détenteur: Cégep de Saint-Hyacinthe
3000, av Boullé, Saint-Hyacinthe, QC J2S 1H9
Tél: 450-773-6800; *Téléc:* 450-773-9971
info@cegepsth.qc.ca
www.cegepsth.qc.ca

Fréquence: Mensuel

L'ADN étudiante
Détenteur: Cégep de Sorel-Tracy
3000, boul Tracy, Sorel-Tracy, QC J3R 5B9
Tél: 450-742-6651; *Téléc:* 450-742-1878
info@cegepst.qc.ca
www.cegepst.qc.ca

Algonquin Times
Owned By: Algonquin College
Algonquin College, 1385 Woodroffe Ave., #N209, Ottawa, ON K2G 1V8
Tel: 613-727-4723
algonquintimes@gmail.com
www.algonquintimes.com
www.youtube.com/user/AlgonquinTimes
twitter.com/algonquintimes
www.facebook.com/algonquintimes

Frequency: Bi-weekly
Algonquin College newspaper produced by Journalism & Advertising students.
Stuart Kite, Editor

The Aquinian
Owned By: St. Thomas University
Student Union Bldg., #23, 21 Pacey Dr., Fredericton, NB E3B 5G3
Tel: 506-452-0640
www.theaquinian.net
twitter.com/aquinian
www.facebook.com/aquinian

Circulation: 700
Frequency: Weekly
St. Thomas University newspaper.
Hadeel Ibrahim, Editor-in-Chief, eic@theaq.net
Danielle Elliott, Managing Editor, managing@theaq.net

The Argosy
Owned By: Mount Allison University
Wallace-McCain Student Centre, 62 York St., Sackville, NB E4L 1E2
Tel: 506-364-2236
www.since1872.ca
www.instagram.com/the_argosy
twitter.com/The_Argosy
www.facebook.com/TheArgosy

Frequency: Weekly
Mount Allison University's independent student newspaper since 1872

Arthur Visual Archive
Owned By: The Peterborough & Trent University Independent Press
Sadlier House, 751 George St. North, Peterborough, ON K9H 3T2
Tel: 705-745-3535
editors@trentarthur.ca
trentarthur.ca
www.instagram.com/trentarthurnews
twitter.com/trentarthur
www.faceb ook.com/arthurnews

Circulation: 3,000
Frequency: Weekly during academic year
Weekly newspaper providing constructive, informative & crucial developments in the Peterborough & Trent community
Joshua Skinner, Editor

The Artichoke
Owned By: Winter's College, York University
#004, 4700 Keele St., Toronto, ON M3J 1P3
Tel: 416-736-5128
wintersfreepress@winterscouncil.com
twitter.com/artichokebywfp
www.facebook.com/131605956923469

Frequency: Monthly
Student magazine for Winter's College at York University.
Lindsay Presswell, Editor, editor@wintersfreepress.com

The Athenaeum
Owned By: Acadia University
Student Union Bldg., 30 Highland Ave., 2nd Fl., Wolfville, NS B4P 2R5
Tel: 902-542-2201
www.theath.ca
twitter.com/athonline
www.facebook.com/theathenaeum

Acadia University newspaper.
Sid Kondapuram, Editor-in-Chief, eic@acadiau.ca

Brunswickan
Owned By: University of New Brunswick
#35, 21 Pacey Dr., Fredericton, NB E3B 5A3
Tel: 506-447-3388
www.thebruns.ca
www.instagram.com/thebrunswickan
twitter.com/Brunswickan
www.facebook.com/thebrunswickan

University of New Brunswick newspaper.
Emma McPhee, Editor-in-Chief, editor@thebruns.ca

Bulletin d'information du Collège Ahuntsic (BICA)
Détenteur: Collège d'Ahuntsic
9155, rue St-Hubert, Montréal, QC H2M 1Y8
Tél: 514-389-5921 *Ligne sans frais:* 866-389-5921
bica@collegeahuntsic.qc.ca
www.collegeahuntsic.qc.ca/intranet/bica

The Cadre
Owned By: University of Prince Edward Island
W.A. Murphy Student Centre, 550 University Ave., 2nd Fl., Charlottetown, PE C1A 4P3
Tel: 902-628-4353
cadreeditor@gmail.com
www.thecadreupei.com
twitter.com/thecadre

Frequency: Weekly, during the academic year
University of Prince Edward Island newspaper.
Nate Hood, Managing Editor

The Campus
Owned By: Bishop's University
2600 College St., Sherbrooke, QC J1M 1Z7
Tel: 819-822-9600; *Fax:* 819-822-9661
campus@ubishops.ca
www.ubishops.ca
www.youtube.com/user/bishopsuniversity
twitter.com/ubishops
www.facebook.com/thebucampus

Frequency: Bi-weekly, during academic year
Maddie Hession, Editor-in-Chief, thecampus.editor@gmail.com

Caper Times
Previous Name: The 60th Meridian
Owned By: Cape Breton University
c/o Cape Breton University (CBU), PO Box 5300, 1250 Grand Lake Rd., Sydney, NS B1P 6L2
Tel: 902-563-1890
su_editor@cbu.ca
www.capertimes.ca

Cape Breton University newspaper.

Capilano Courier
Owned By: Capilano University
2055 Purcell Way, North Vancouver, BC V7J 3H5
Tel: 778-865-2649
capcourier@gmail.com
www.capilanocourier.com
Frequency: Weekly
Capilano University newspaper.
Carlo Javier, Editor-in-Chief

The Carillon
Owned By: University of Regina
227 Riddell Centre, 3737 Wascana Pkwy., Regina, SK S4S 0A2
Tel: 306-586-8867
editor@carillonregina.com
www.carillonregina.com
twitter.com/the_carillon
www.facebook.com/carillon.newspaper
Frequency: 11 times a year. Thursdays
The University of Regina newspaper.
John Loeppky, Editor-in-Chief, editor@carillonregina.com

The Cascade
Owned By: University of the Fraser Valley (UFV)
33844 King Rd., Abbotsford, BC V2S 7M8
Tel: 604-854-4529
www.ufvcascade.ca
twitter.com/ufvcascade
Circulation: 1,500
Frequency: Weekly
University of the Fraser Valley (UFV) newspaper.
Joel Robertson-Taylor, Editor-in-Chief, joel@ufvcascade.ca

The Cord
Owned By: Wilfrid Laurier University
205 Regina St. North, Waterloo, ON N2J 3B6
Tel: 519-884-0710
www.thecord.ca
twitter.com/cordnews
www.facebook.com/cordwlusp
Circulation: 4,500
Frequency: Weekly
Wilfrid Laurier University newspaper.
Kurtis Rideout, Editor-in-Chief, editor@thecord.ca

The Crown
Owned By: Redeemer University College
777 Garner Rd. East, Ancaster, ON L9K 1J4
Tel: 905-648-2131
thecrown@redeemer.ca
www.thecrown.ca
Redeemer University College newspaper.
Joel Voth, Editor-in-Chief

D.E.C. express
Détenteur: Cégep de Baie-Comeau
537, boul Blanche, Baie-Comeau, QC G5C 2B2
Tél: 418-589-5707; *Téléc:* 418-589-9842
Ligne sans frais: 800-463-2030
decexpress@cegepbc.ca
www.cegep-baie-comeau.qc.ca

Daily Bulletin
Previous Name: UW Gazette
Owned By: University of Waterloo
200 University Ave. West, Waterloo, ON N2L 3G1
Tel: 519-888-4567
bulletin@uwaterloo.ca
www.bulletin.uwaterloo.ca
twitter.com/uwdailybulletin
Frequency: Daily; online
University of Waterloo newspaper.
Brandon Sweet, Editor

Dal News
c/o Dalhousie University, Halifax, NS B3H 4R2
www.dal.ca/news.html
Frequency: Monthly
Matt Reeder, Managing Editor, matt.reeder@dal.ca

Dalhousie Gazette
Owned By: Dalhousie University
Student Union Building, 6136 University Ave., Halifax, NS B3H 4J2
Tel: 250-870-3606
editor@dalgazette.com
dalgazette.com
www.instagram.com/dalhousiegazette
twitter.com/dalgazette
www.facebook .com/DalGazette
Dalhousie University newspaper.

Kaila Jefferd-Moore, Editor-in-Chief,
kaila.jefferd-moore@dalgazette.com

L'Écho
Détenteur: Collège de Lévis
9, rue Monseigneur Gosselin, Lévis, QC G6V 5K1
Tél: 418-833-1249; *Téléc:* 418-833-7055
fondation@collegedelevis.qc.ca
www.collegedelevis.qc.ca
Fréquence: Semestriel
Pierre Bélanger, Directeur, belpier8@gmail.com

Échorridor
Détenteur: Collège d'Alma
675, boul Auger ouest, Alma, QC G8B 2B7
Tél: 418-668-2387; *Téléc:* 418-668-3806
site@collegealma.ca
www.collegealma.ca

L'Éclipse
Détenteur: Cégep Saint-Jean-sur-Richelieu
30, boul du Séminaire nord, Saint-Jean-sur-Richelieu, QC J3B 5J4
Tél: 450-347-5301; *Téléc:* 450-358-9350
communications@cstjean.qc.ca
www.cstjean.qc.ca
Fréquence: Hebdomadaire

Eclosion
Détenteur: Cégep de Sainte-Foy
2410, ch Ste-Foy, #M-106, Québec, QC G1V 1T3
Tél: 418-658-5389; *Téléc:* 418-658-6798
j.leclosion@gmail.com
www.cegep-ste-foy.qc.ca
www.facebook.com/journal.eclosion

Électro-flash
Détenteur: Cégep de l'Abitibi-Témiscamingue
425, boul du Collège, Rouyn-Noranda, QC J9X 5E5
Tél: 819-762-0931; *Téléc:* 819-762-2071
Ligne sans frais: 866-234-3728
cegepat.qc.ca/journal_electro_flash
Journal des étudiants et étudiantes d'électronique industrielle
Donald Veillette, Coordonnateur, donald.veillette@cegepat.qc.ca

The Endeavour
Owned By: Lethbridge College
3000 College Dr. South, #TE3225, Lethbridge, AB T1K 1L6
Tel: 403-320-3301; *Fax:* 403-317-3582
endeavour@lethbridgecollege.ca
www.lethbridgecollege.ca/node/489760
Published by second year Digital Communication & Media students.

L'Entremetteur
Détenteur: Cégep de l'Outaouais
Campus Gabrielle-Roy, 333, boul Cité-des-Jeunes, Gatineau, QC J8Y 6M4
Tél: 819-770-4012; *Téléc:* 819-770-8167
www.cegepoutaouais.qc.ca

L'Expressif
Détenteur: Cégep de Rivière-du-Loup
80, rue Frontenac, Rivière-du-Loup, QC G5R 1R1
Tél: 418-862-6903; *Téléc:* 418-862-4959
www.cegeprdl.ca

The Eyeopener
Owned By: Ryerson University
55 Gould St., Toronto, ON M5B 1E9
Tel: 416-979-5262
editor@theeyeopener.com
theeyeopener.com
twitter.com/theeyeopener
www.facebook.com/32810756867
Frequency: Monthly
The Eyeopener is Ryerson University's independent student newspaper.
Nicole Schmidt, Editor-in-Chief, 416-979-5000

Folia Montana
Owned By: Mount Saint Vincent University
166 Bedford Hwy., Halifax, NS B3M 2J6
Tel: 902-457-6470; *Fax:* 902-445-3962
www.msvu.ca
Circulation: 17,000
Frequency: Annually
Mount Saint Vincent University alumni newspaper.

Le Front
Détenteur: Université de Moncton
Centre étudiant, 19, av Antonine-Maillet, #B-202, Moncton, NB E1A 3E9
Tel: 506-858-4485
vice.presidence@lefront.ca
www.lefront.ca
twitter.com/le_front
www.facebook.com/LeFrontUdeM

The Fulcrum
Owned By: University of Ottawa
631 King Edward Ave., Ottawa, ON K1N 6N5
Tel: 613-562-5261; *Fax:* 613-562-5259
thefulcrum.ca
www.flickr.com/photos/thefulcrum/
twitter.com/The_Fulcrum
www.faceb ook.com/UofOFulcrum
The Fulcrum is the independent English-language student newspaper at the University of Ottawa.
Savannah Awde, Editor-in-Chief, editor@thefulcrum.ca

Gargoyle
Owned By: University College, University of Toronto
15 King's College Circle, #F6, Toronto, ON M5S 1A1
Tel: 416-946-0941
ucgargoyle.ca
twitter.com/ucgargoyle
Frequency: Biweekly
University College newspaper.
Annika Keller, Managing Editor-in-Chief
Lucas Huntsman Merkur, Content Editor-in-Chief

The Gateway
Owned By: University of Alberta
#3-04, Students' Union Bldg., Edmonton, AB T6G 2J7
Tel: 780-492-5168; *Fax:* 780-492-6665
biz@gateway.ualberta.ca
thegatewayonline.ca
www.youtube.com/user/thegatewaymultimedia
twitter.com/the_gateway
www.facebook.com/TheGatewayOnline
Frequency: Weekly; Wednesdays, during the academic year; 3 issues in the spring/summer
The Gateway is the official student newspaper at the University of Alberta.
Josh Greschner, Editor-in-Chief, 780-492-5168,
eic@gateway.ualberta.ca

The Gauntlet
Owned By: The University of Calgary
MacEwan Student Centre, #319, 2500 University Dr. NW, Calgary, AB T2N 1N4
Tel: 403-819-3453
www.thegauntlet.ca
twitter.com/gauntletuofc
www.facebook.com/uofcgauntlet
Frequency: Monthly
The University of Calgary newspaper.
Jason Herring, Editor-in-Chief, eic@thegauntlet.ca
Kate Jacobson, Business Manager, business@thegauntlet.ca

The Gazette
Owned By: University of Western Ontario
#263, University Community Centre, London, ON N6A 3K7
Tel: 519-661-3580
editor@westerngazette.ca
www.westerngazette.ca
twitter.com/uwogazette
Circulation: 11,000
Frequency: 4 times a week; Tues.-Fri.
The Gazette is the student newspaper at the University of Western Ontario in London, Ontario, Canada.
Hamza Tariq, Editor-in-Chief

La Gifle
Détenteur: Collège Lionel-Groulx
100, rue Duquet, Sainte-Thérèse, QC J7E 3G6
Tél: 450-430-3120; *Téléc:* 450-971-7883
lagifleclg@hotmail.com
www.clg.qc.ca
lagifleblog.wordpress.com

La Gifle
Détenteur: Cégep de Trois-Rivières
CP 97, 3500, rue de Courval, Trois-Rivières, QC G9A 5E6
Tél: 819-376-1721; *Téléc:* 819-693-8023
communications@cegeptr.qc.ca
www.cegeptr.qc.ca
twitter.com/cegeptr
www.facebook.com/cegeptr

Golden Ram
Owned By: Dalhousie University
PO Box 550, Truro, NS B2N 5E3
Tel: 902-893-6600
www.dal.ca
Dalhousie University (Agricultural Campus) newspaper.

Le Graffiti
Détenteur: Collège Jean-de-Brebeuf Inc.
3200, ch de la côte Ste-Catherine, Montréal, QC H3T 1C1
Tél: 514-342-9342
ageb@brebeuf.qc.ca
www.brebeuf.qc.ca

The Grapevine
Owned By: Huron University College
1349 Western Rd., London, ON N6G 1H3
Tel: 519-755-5592
www.facebook.com/166794663334282
Frequency: Monthly
The Grapevine Magazine is a student-based publication that circulates monthly on the following campuses in London, Ontario: Huron University College, University of Western Ontario, and Kings College.
Whitney Slightham, Editor-in-Chief

The Griff
Owned By: MacEwan University
#7-297C, 10700 - 104 Ave., Edmonton, AB T5J 4S2
Tel: 780-497-4429; *Fax:* 780-497-5470
online@thegriff.ca
www.thegriff.ca
Circulation: 2,500
Frequency: 25 issues per academic year; Weekly; Thursday
the griff is MacEwan University's weekly student newspaper.
Angela Johnston, News Editor

Le Griffonnier
Détenteur: Université du Québec à Chicoutimi
555, boul de l'Université, #P0-3100, Chicoutimi, QC G7H 2B1
Tél: 418-545-5011; *Téléc:* 418-545-5400
redactionceuc@uqac.ca
www.ceuc.ca
www.facebook.com/ceuc.ca
Le Griffonnier est le journal des étudiants de l'UQAC.
Noémie Simard, Rédactrice-en-chef

L'Heuristique
Détenteur: École de technologie supérieure
1100, rue Notre-Dame ouest, Montréal, QC H3C 1K3
Tél: 514-396-8800
journal@aeets.com
journal.aeets.com

The Howler
Owned By: Keyano College
8115 Franklin Ave., #CC-178, Fort McMurray, AB T9H 2H7
Tel: 780-791-4877; *Fax:* 780-747-7003
sakc.operations@keyano.ca
www.sakc.ca/howler
Frequency: Monthly
Keyano College newspaper.

L'IdéePhile
Détenteur: Cégep de Chicoutimi
534, rue Jacques-Cartier est, Chicoutimi, QC G7H 1Z6
Tél: 418-549-9520; *Téléc:* 418-549-1315
info@cchic.ca
www.cchic.ca

L'Ile Lettrée
Détenteur: Cégep du Vieux Montréal
255, rue Ontario est, Montréal, QC H2X 1X6
Tél: 514-982-3437; *Téléc:* 514-982-3400
www.cvm.qc.ca

Impact Campus
Détenteur: Université Laval
Pavillon Maurice-Pollack, #1244, 2325, rue de l'Université, Québec, QC G1V 0A6
Tel: 418-656-5079
redaction@impactcampus.ca
www.impactcampus.ca
www.youtube.com/user/ImpactCampus
twitter.com/ImpactCampus
www.facebook.com/impactcampus
Fréquence: Hebdomadaire
Charles-Antoine Gagnon, Rédacteur en chef

L'Inculte
Détenteur: Cégep de Victoriaville
475, rue Notre-Dame est, Victoriaville, QC G6P 4B3
Tél: 819-758-6401; *Téléc:* 819-758-6026
journal.linculte@gmail.com
www.cegepvicto.ca
www.facebook.com/inculte

L'INFO-Cégep
Détenteur : Cégep de Granby
CP 7000, 235, rue Saint-Jacques, Granby, QC J2G 9H7
Tél: 450-372-6614; *Téléc:* 450-372-6565
www.cegepgranby.qc.ca/nouvelles
Fréquence: Quotidien

L'Infomane
Détenteur: Collège de Bois-de-Boulogne
10555, av de Bois-de-Boulogne, Montréal, QC H4N 1L4
Tél: 514-332-3000; *Téléc:* 514-332-5857
infomane@age.bdeb.qc.ca
www.bdeb.qc.ca
twitter.com/infomane

Informavic
Détenteur: Cégep Marie-Victorin
7000, rue Marie-Victorin, Montréal, QC H1G 2J6
Tél: 514-325-0150
promotion@collegemv.qc.ca
www.collegemv.qc.ca
Fréquence: 2 fois par an

Inter
Anciennement: Suites
Détenteur: Université du Québec à Montréal
Service des communications, CP 8888 Centre-Ville, Montréal, QC H3C 3P8
Tél: 514-987-3000
magazine.inter@uqam.ca
diplomes.uqam.ca/magazine-inter/accueil-magazine

The Journal
Owned By: Queen's University
Queen's University, 190 University Ave., Kingston, ON K7L 3P4
Tel: 613-533-2800; *Fax:* 613-533-6728
journal_editors@ams.queensu.ca
www.queensjournal.ca
twitter.com/queensjournal
www.facebook.com/queensjournal
Frequency: Weekly
Queen's University newspaper.
Joseph Cattana, Editor-in-Chief

The Journal
Owned By: Saint Mary's University
Student Centre, #516, 923 Robie St., Halifax, NS B3H 3C3
Tel: 902-220-0599
business.thejournal@smu.ca
www.thesmujournal.ca
twitter.com/TheSMUJournal
www.facebook.com/SMUJournal
Saint Mary's University newspaper.
Neil Van Horne, Editor-in-Chief, editor.thejournal@smu.ca

Journal Exprimactions!
Détenteur: Collège de Rosemont
6400, 16e av, Montréal, QC H1X 2S9
Tél: 514-376-1620; *Téléc:* 514-376-1440
exprimactions@gmail.com
www.crosemont.qc.ca
journalexprimactions.wordpress.com
www.facebook.com/exprimactions

Journal L'Intérêt
Détenteur: Écoles De Hautes Etudes Commerciales Montréal
3000, ch de la Côte-Sainte-Catherine, #RJ718, Montréal, QC H3T 2A7
Tél: 514-340-6105
redaction.interet@hec.ca
www.journalinteret.com
www.linkedin.com/company/journal-l%27int-r-t
www.facebook.com/journalint eret

Journal O Courant
Détenteur: Cégep régional de Lanaudière
2505, boul des Entreprises, Terrebonne, QC J6X 5S5
Tél: 450-470-0933; *Téléc:* 450-477-6933
www.cegep-lanaudiere.qc.ca
journalocourant.wordpress.com
www.facebook.com/journalocourant
Fréquence: Mensuel, septembre à mai

Lambda
Détenteur: Laurentian University of Sudbury
Student Centre, #SCE301, 935 Ramsey Lake Rd., Sudbury, ON P3E 2C6
Tél: 705-673-6548
lambda@laurentian.ca
thelambda.ca
www.facebook.com/TheLambda
Lambda is Laurentian University's campus newspaper.
Jessica Robinson, Editor-in-Chief

The Lance
Owned By: University of Windsor
CAW Student Centre, B-91, 401 Sunset Ave., Windsor, ON N9B 3P4
Tel: 519-253-3000
uwindsorlance.ca
twitter.com/uwindsorlance
Circulation: 10,000
Frequency: Weekly
University of Windsor newspaper.

The Link
Owned By: Concordia University
Concordia University Hall Building, 1455, boul de Maisonneuve ouest, #H-649, Montréal, QC H3G 1M8
Tel: 514-848-2424; *Fax:* 514-848-4540
editor@thelinknewspaper.ca
thelinknewspaper.ca
www.instagram.com/linknewspaper
twitter.com/linknewspaper
www.faceb ook.com/TheLinkNewspaper
Circulation: 5,000
Frequency: Monthly
Kelsey Litwin, Editor-in-Chief

The Link
Owned By: BC Institute of Technology
3700 Willingdon Ave., Burnaby, BC V5G 3H2
Tel: 604-451-7191
publications@bcitsa.ca
www.linkbcit.ca
www.instagram.com/thelinkmag
twitter.com/linkbcit
www.facebook.com/linkbcit
Frequency: 8 times a year
BC Institute of Technology newspaper.
Selenna Ho, Managing Editor, sho@bcitsa.ca

MacMedia (McLaughlin College)
Owned By: York University
#004, 4700 Keele St., Toronto, ON M3J 1P3
Tel: 416-736-2100
macmedia.eic@gmail.com
York University newspaper.
Vanessa Butera, Editor-in-Chief

The Manitoban
Owned By: University of Manitoba
105 University Centre, Winnipeg, MB R3T 2N2
Tel: 204-474-6535; *Fax:* 204-474-7651
me@themanitoban.com
www.themanitoban.com
www.facebook.com/groups/195842203788275
The Manitoban is the official student newspaper of the University of Manitoba.
Craig Adolphe, Editor-in-Chief, 204-474-8293, editor@themanitoban.com

Mars' Hill
Owned By: Trinity Western University
7600 Glover Rd., Langley, BC V2Y 1Y1
Tel: 604-888-7511
marshill@gmail.com
www.marshillonline.com
Trinity Western University newspaper.

The Martlet
Owned By: University of Victoria
Student Union Building, PO Box 3035, #B011, 3700 Finnerty Rd., Victoria, BC V8W 3P3
Tel: 250-721-8360; *Fax:* 250-472-4556
edit@martlet.ca
www.martlet.ca
Circulation: 4,200
The Martlet is an independent weekly student newspaper at the University of Victoria in Victoria, British Columbia, Canada.
Myles Sauer, Editor-in-Chief

McGill Reporter
Owned By: McGill University
James Administration Bldg., #110, 845, rue Sherbrooke ouest, Montréal, QC H3A 2T5

Tel: 514-398-1044
publications.mcgill.ca/reporter
twitter.com/mcgillreporter

Frequency: Bi-weekly
McGill University's online newspaper.
Neale McDevitt, Editor, neale.mcdevitt@mcgill.ca

The Medium
Owned By: University of Toronto at Mississauga
#200, 3359 Mississauga Rd., Mississauga, ON L5L 1C6

Tel: 289-633-3963
managing@themedium.ca
themedium.ca
twitter.com/TheMediumUTM
www.facebook.com/TheMediumUTM

The Medium is the print media voice for the students of the University of Toronto Mississauga.
Mahmoud Sarouji, Editor-in-Chief, editor@themedium.ca

The Meliorist
Owned By: University of Lethbridge
4401 University Dr., Lethbridge, AB T1K 3M4

Tel: 403-329-2334; *Fax:* 403-329-2333
info@themeliorist.ca
themeliorist.ca
www.instagram.com/melioristmag
twitter.com/The_Meliorist
www.facebook. com/themeliorist

Frequency: Monthly
University of Lethbridge newspaper.
Mav Adecer, Editor-in-Chief

The Mike
Owned By: St. Michael's College, University of Toronto
Elmsley Hall, Main Fl., #2, 81 St. Mary St., Toronto, ON M4S 1J4

Tel: 416-926-7272
issuu.com/readthemike
twitter.com/readthemike

Circulation: 2,000
Frequency: Bi-weekly
St. Michael's College newspaper
Anah Mirza, Editor-in-Chief, editorinchief@readthemike.com
Josh Scott, Managing Editor, managingeditor@readthemike.com

Le Motdit
Détenteur: Cégep Édouard-Montpetit
945, ch de Chambly, #F-045, Longueuil, QC J4H 3M6

Tél: 450-679-2631; *Téléc:* 450-679-5570
www.cegepmontpetit.ca

Mouton Noir
Détenteur: Cégep de Drummondville
#1209, 960, rue St-Georges, Drummondville, QC J2C 6A2

Tél: 819-478-4671; *Téléc:* 819-478-8823
journal.mnoir@gmail.com
www.facebook.com/159407174139566

The Muse
Owned By: Memorial University of Newfoundland
PO Box 4200, 230 Elizabeth Ave., St. John's, NL A1C 5S7

Tel: 709-864-8919
chief@themuse.ca
www.mun.ca

Circulation: 10,000
Memorial University of Newfoundland newspaper.

The Navigator
Owned By: Vancouver Island University
Bldg. 193, #217, 900 - 5th St., Nanaimo, BC V9R 5S5

Tel: 250-753-2225; *Fax:* 250-753-2257
www.thenav.ca
www.facebook.com/thenavigatornewspaper

Frequency: Monthly
The Navigator is Vancouver Island University's (formerly Malaspina University-College) student newspaper.
Cole Schisler, Managing Editor, editor@thenav.ca

Nexus
Owned By: Camosun College
Lansdowne Campus, Richmond House 201, 3100 Foul Bay Rd., Victoria, BC V8P 5J2

Tel: 250-370-3591
editor@nexusnewspaper.com
www.nexusnewspaper.com
www.instagram.com/nexusnewspaper
twitter.com/nexusnewspaper
www.facebook.com/nexusnewspaper

Frequency: Bi-monthly
Camosun College newspaper.
Greg Pratt, Managing Editor

The Nugget
Owned By: The Northern Alberta Institute of Technology
11762 - 106 St. NW, #E-128, Edmonton, AB T5G 2R1

Tel: 780-471-8866
www.thenuggetonline.com
www.facebook.com/nuggetonline
www.facebook.com/thenaitnugget
The Northern Alberta Institute of Technology newspaper.
Danielle Fuechtmann, Editor-in-Chief, studenteditor@nait.ca

The Omega
Owned By: Thompson Rivers University
Old Main Bldg., PO Box 3010, #OM2691, 900 McGill Rd., Kamloops, BC V2C 0C8

Tel: 250-828-5069
editorofomega@gmail.com
theomega.ca
twitter.com/TRU_Omega
www.facebook.com/217031195028151

Frequency: Weekly; Wednesdays
The Omega is Thompson Rivers University's independent student newspaper.
Mike Davies, Editor-in-Chief

L'Orignal déchaîné
Détenteur: Laurentian University of Sudbury
262 Pavillon Laurent Larouche, 935 Ramsey Lake Rd., Sudbury, ON P3E 2C6

lorignal@laurentian.ca
lorignaldechaine.ca
www.instagram.com/lorignal_ul
twitter.com/LOrignal_UL
www.facebook. com/lorignal.UL

Tirage: 1 000
Newspaper written for the Francophone community of Laurentian.
Stéphane Bazinet, Rédacteur en chef, stephane.bazinet@lorignaldechaine.ca

Other Press
Owned By: Douglas College
#1020, 700 Royal Ave., New Westminster, BC V3L 5B2

editor@theotherpress.ca
theotherpress.ca
twitter.com/TheOtherPress

Frequency: Weekly during the fall and winter semesters; monthly during the summer
Douglas College newspaper.
Lauren Kelly, Editor-in-Chief

Over the Edge
Owned By: University of Northern British Columbia
3333 University Way, NUSC 6-350, Prince George, BC V2N 4Z9

Tel: 250-960-5633
over.the.edge.unbc@gmail.com
overtheedgenewspaper.ca
www.facebook.com/overtheedgenewspaper
University of Northern British Columbia newspaper.
Sam Wall, Editor-in-Chief

The Papercut
Owned By: Marianopolis College
4873, av Westmount, Montréal, QC H3Y 1X9

Tel: 514-931-8792; *Fax:* 514-931-8790
the.marianopolis.papercut@gmail.com
www.marianopolis.edu
twitter.com/MarianoPapercut
www.facebook.com/the.marianopolis.papercut
Marianopolis College newspaper.

Le Pastiche
Owned By: Cégep de Saint-Laurent
625, av Ste-Croix, #B-44, Montréal, QC H4L 3X7

Tel: 514-747-6521; *Fax:* 514-748-1249
info@cegepsl.qc.ca
www.cegepsl.qc.ca
www.linkedin.com/company/1588262
twitter.com/cegepsl
www.facebook.com/ cegepdesaintlaurent

Frequency: Mensuel

The Peak
Owned By: Simon Fraser University
2900 Maggie Benston Centre, 8888 University Dr., Burnaby, BC V5A 1S6

Tel: 778-782-5110
production@the-peak.ca
www.the-peak.ca
twitter.com/peaksfu
www.facebook.com/PeakSFU

Frequency: Weekly
Simon Fraser University newspaper.
Courtney Miller, Editor-in-Chief, eic@the-peak.ca

The Phoenix
Owned By: Okanagan College
3333 University Way, UNC132B, Kelowna, BC V1V 1V7

Tel: 250-807-9296
www.thephoenixnews.com
twitter.com/ubcophoenix
www.facebook.com/thephoenixnews

Frequency: Bi-monthly
Okanagan College newspaper.

Le Phoque
Détenteur: Cégep Limoilou
#1029, 1300, 8e av, Québec, QC G1J 5L5

Tél: 418-647-6600; *Téléc:* 418-647-6798
www.cegeplimoilou.ca

La Pige
Détenteur: Cégep de Jonquière
Local 880.2, pavillon Joseph-Angers, 2505, rue Saint-Hubert, Jonquière, QC G7X 7W2

Tél: 418-547-2191
www.cegepjonquiere.ca/la-pige.html

Tirage: 5000

La Placote
Détenteur: Cégep de Lévis-Lauzon
205, rue Mgr Bourget, Lévis, QC G6V 6Z9

Tél: 418-833-5110; *Téléc:* 418-833-8502
www.cll.qc.ca

The Plant
Owned By: Dawson College
3040 rue Sherbrooke ouest, Montréal, QC H3Z 1A4

Tel: 514-931-8731
theplantnewspaper@gmail.com
theplantnewspaper.com
issuu.com/theplant

Frequency: Monthly

Le Polyscope
Détenteur: École Polytechnique de Montréal
CP 6079 Centre-ville, Montréal, QC H3C 3A7

Tél: 514-340-4711; *Téléc:* 514-340-4986
direction@polyscope.qc.ca
www.polyscope.qc.ca
twitter.com/Polyscope
www.facebook.com/Polyscope

Tirage: 3 000
Laurent Montreuil, Directeur

Portico
Owned By: University of Guelph
University Centre, Level 4, University of Guelph, 50 Stone Rd. East, Guelph, ON N1G 2W1

Tel: 519-824-4120; *Fax:* 519-824-7962
porticomagazine@uoguelph.ca
www.porticomagazine.ca

Frequency: 3 times a year
The Portico is mailed free to Guelph alumni. It is produced by Communications & Public Affairs at the University of Guelph.
Daniel Atlin, Publisher
Charles Cunningham, Publisher

Le Prétexte
Détenteur: Cégep de Rimouski
60, rue de l'Évêché ouest, #B-328, Rimouski, QC G5L 4H6

Tél: 418-723-1880; *Téléc:* 418-724-4961
Ligne sans frais: 800-463-0617
information.scolaire@cegep-rimouski.qc.ca
www.cegep-ri mouski.qc.ca

Tirage: 400
Fréquence: 4-6 fois par an

Quartier Libre
Détenteur: Université de Montréal
CP 6128 Centre-ville, 3200, rue Jean-Brillant, #B-1274-6, Montréal, QC H3T 1N8

Tél: 514-343-7630
quartierlibre.ca
twitter.com/quartierlibre
www.facebook.com/QuartierLibre.ca

Tirage: 6 000
Fréquence: 16 fois par an
Marie Roncari, Directrice, directeur@quartierlibre.ca

The Quill
Owned By: Brandon University
270 - 18th St., Brandon, MB R7A 6A9

Tel: 204-727-9667; *Fax:* 204-571-0029
www.thequill.ca
www.instagram.com/thequillbu
twitter.com/quillbu
www.facebook.com/QuillBU

Frequency: Weekly
Brandon University newspaper.
Ashlyn Pearce, Editor-in-Chief, eic@gmail.com

The Reflector
Owned By: Mount Royal University
Wyckham House, Mount Royal University, 4825 Mount Royal Gate SW, Calgary, AB T3E 6K6

Tel: 403-440-6268; *Fax:* 403-440-6762
thereflector@thereflector.ca
www.thereflector.ca
twitter.com/reflectthis
www.facebook.com/TheReflector.ca

Circulation: 10,000
Frequency: Bi-weekly; Sept.-April
Mount Royal University newspaper.
Bigoa Machar, Publishing Editor,
publishingeditor@thereflector.ca

Le Renard
Détenteur: Cégep Garneau
1660, boul de l'Entente, #A-1198, Québec, QC G1S 4S3

Tél: 418-681-4134; *Téléc:* 418-681-4135
communications@cegepgarneau.ca
wwww.cegepgarneau.ca

Blaise Piette, Directeur

Le Réveil
Détenteur: Université de Saint-Boniface
200, av de la Cathédrale, Winnipeg, MB R2H 0H7

Tél: 204-237-1818; *Téléc:* 204-237-3240
aemedias@monusb.ca
aeusb.ca/le-reveil

Tirage: 6 000
Simon Lafortune, Rédacteur en chef

The Ring
Owned By: University of Victoria
Sedgewick Building, C149, PO Box 1700 CSC, 3800 Finnerty Rd., Victoria, BC V8W 2Y2

Tel: 250-721-7636; *Fax:* 250-721-8955
ucom@uvic.ca
www.uvic.ca/ring

Circulation: 4,200
Frequency: 8 times a year
University of Victoria newspaper.
Bruce Kilpatrick, Director, 250-721-7638, abk@uvic.ca

La Rotonde
Détenteur: University of Ottawa
109, rue Osgoode, Ottawa, ON K1N 6S1

Tél: 613-421-4686
www.larotonde.ca
twitter.com/LaRotonde

Ghassen Athmni, Directeur général, direction@larotonde.ca
Mathieu Tovar-Poitras, Rédacteur-en-Chef,
redaction@larotonde.ca

The Runner
Owned By: Kwantlen Polytechnic University
Arbutus Bldg., #3710/3720, 12666 72 Ave., Surrey, BC V3W 2M8

Tel: 778-565-3801
production@runnermag.ca
runnermag.ca
twitter.com/Runnermag
www.facebook.com/runnerpaper

Frequency: 20 issues a year
Kwantlen Polytechnic University newspaper.
Tristan Johnston, Coordinating Editor, editor@runnermag.ca

The Ryerson Free Press
Owned By: Ryerson University
#SCC-301, 55 Gould St., Toronto, ON M5B 1E9

Tel: 416-979-5000; *Fax:* 416-979-5223
editor@ryersonfreepress.ca
www.ryersonfreepress.ca
twitter.com/RyeFreePress

Frequency: Monthly
The Ryerson Free Press is the definitive alternative monthly of the Continuing Education Student's Association of Ryerson University (CESAR).
Clare O'Connor, Editor-in-Chief

Ryerson Review of Journalism
Owned By: Ryerson University
350 Victoria St., Toronto, ON M5B 2K3

Tel: 416-979-5319; *Fax:* 416-979-5216
chair.journalism@ryerson.ca
rrj.ca
twitter.com/RyersonReview

Frequency: 2 times a year
Produced by final-year students at Ryerson University's School of Journalism in Toronto, Canada,
Kat Eschner, Editor, keschner@ryerson.ca

The Ryersonian
Owned By: Ryerson University
350 Victoria St., Toronto, ON M5B 2K3

sonian@ryerson.ca
www.ryersonian.ca
twitter.com/TheRyersonian
www.facebook.com/TheRyersonian

Students in Ryerson's School of Journalism's fourth-year undergraduate & second-year graduate program produce The Ryersonian.

Sault College Alumni Magazine
Owned By: Sault College of Applied Arts & Technology
443 Northern Ave., Sault Ste Marie, ON P6A 5L3

alumni@saultcollege.ca
www.saultcollege.ca
twitter.com/SaultCollAlumni
www.facebook.com/127468880627494

Le Savoir
Anciennement: Le Virus
Détenteur: Université du Québec en Outaouais
CP 1250 Hull, 243, boul Alexandre-Taché, #E-2000, Gatineau, QC J8X 3X7

Tél: 819-595-3900; *Téléc:* 819-595-3830
savoir@uqo.ca
uqo.ca/savoir
twitter.com/uqo
www.facebook.com/Universite.Quebec.Outaouais

Fréquence: Mensuel
Le Savoir est un bulletin électronique.

The Scanner
Owned By: Saskatchewan Polytechnic Students' Association Inc.
#119, 1130 Idylwyld Dr. South, Saskatoon, SK S7K 3R5

Tel: 306-659-4421; *Fax:* 306-933-8220
ssa.scanner@siast.sk.ca
spsa.ca/campus-life/publications/
www.youtube.com/user/0SIASTSA
twitter.com/ur_ssa
www.facebook.com/SIASTSSA

Frequency: 2 times a year
The Scanner is the Students' Association's monthly newspaper publication for Saskatchewan Institute of Applied Science and Technology (SIAST).

The Sentinel
Owned By: Selkirk College
301 Frank Bender Way, Castlegar, BC V1N 4L3

www.selkirksentinel.ca
The Official News Source for Students at Selkirk College.

Shawimag
Détenteur: Collège Shawinigan
CP 610, 2263, av du Collège, Shawinigan, QC G9N 6V8

Tél: 819-539-6401; *Téléc:* 819-539-8819
shawimag.pdallaire.profweb.ca
www.facebook.com/192342554179971

Journal des étudiants en arts, lettres et communication
Paul Dallaire, Responsable, pdallaire@collegeshawinigan.qc.ca

The Sheaf
Owned By: University of Saskatchewan
108 Memorial Union Building, 93 Campus Dr., Saskatoon, SK S7N 5B2

Tel: 306-966-8689
editor@thesheaf.com
www.thesheaf.com

Frequency: Weekly
University of Saskatchewan newspaper.
Jessica Klaassen-Wright, Editor-in-Chief

The Silhouette
Owned By: McMaster University
McMaster University Student Centre, B110, 1280 Main St. West, Hamilton, ON L8S 4S4

Tel: 905-525-9140; *Fax:* 905-521-1504
thesil@thesil.ca
www.thesil.ca

Circulation: 8,000
Frequency: Weekly; Sept.-March
McMaster University newspaper.
Shane Madill, Editor-in-Chief

The Spit
Owned By: Quest University
3200 University Blvd., Squamish, BC V8B 0N8

Tel: 604-898-8000; *Fax:* 604-815-0829
Toll-Free: 888-783-7808
info@questu.ca
www.facebook.com/QuestU

Quest University's student newspaper.

The Sputnik
Owned By: Wilfrid Laurier University - Brantford Campus
Odeon Bldg., #208, 50 Market St., Brantford, ON N3T 2Z5

Tel: 519-756-8228
www.thesputnik.ca
twitter.com/thesputnikwlusp
www.facebook.com/134603623243364

The official independent newspaper of Laurier Brantford
Christina Manocchio, Editor-in-Chief, eic@thesputnik.ca

The Strand
Owned By: Victoria University, University of Toronto
Goldring Student Centre, #153, 150 Charles St. West, Toronto, ON M5S 1K9

editor@thestrand.ca
www.thestrand.ca

Circulation: 2,000
Frequency: 12 times a year
Victoria University newspaper.
Molly Kay, Editor-in-Chief
Elena Senechal-Becker, Editor-in-Chief

The Surveyor
Owned By: Holland College
140 Weymouth St., Charlottetown, PE C1A 4Z1

surveyoronline.wordpress.com
Holland College's online newspaper.

The Toike Oike
Owned By: University of Toronto
B740 Sanford Fleming, 10 King's College Rd., Toronto, ON M5S 3G4

Tel: 416-978-2011
toike@skule.ca
toike.skule.ca

Frequency: 6 times a year
Publication by The University of Toronto Engineering Society (EngSoc).
Simo Pajovic, Editor-in-Chief

La Tribune étudiante
Détenteur: Cégep Saint-Jean-sur-Richelieu
30, boul du Séminaire nord, Saint-Jean-sur-Richelieu, QC J3B 5J4

Tél: 450-347-5301; *Téléc:* 450-358-9350
communications@cstjean.qc.ca
www.cstjean.qc.ca
www.facebook.com/130983326958578

Le Typographe
Détenteur: Collège Montmorency
475, boul de l'Avenir, #B1320-6, Laval, QC H7N 5H9

Tél: 450-975-6100; *Téléc:* 450-975-6116
journal.typographe@gmail.com
www.cmontmorency.qc.ca
www.facebook.com/JournalLeTypographe

Fréquence: Mensuel

The Ubyssey
Owned By: University of British Columbia
Student Union Building, 2208 - 6133 University Blvd.,
Vancouver, BC V6T 1Z1

Tel: 604-283-2001
feedback@ubyssey.ca
www.ubyssey.ca
ubyssey.tumblr.com
twitter.com/ubyssey
www.facebook.com/ubyssey

Circulation: 8,000
Frequency: Weekly
University of British Columbia newspaper.
Jack Hauen, Coordinating Editor, coordinating@ubyssey.ca

The Underground
Owned By: University of Toronto Scarborough
1265 Military Trail, #SL-243, Toronto, ON M1C 1A4

editor@the-underground.online
www.the-underground.online

Frequency: Bi-weekly
University of Toronto Scarborough newspaper.

The Uniter
Owned By: University of Winnipeg
ORM14, University of Winnipeg, 515 Portage Ave.,
Winnipeg, MB R3B 2E9

Tel: 204-988-7579
uniter.ca
www.instagram.com/theuniter
twitter.com/TheUniter
www.facebook.com/ theuniter

Frequency: Weekly; Sept.-March
University of Winnipeg newspaper.
Anastasia Chipelski, Managing Editor, editor@uniter.ca

UQAR-Info
Anciennement : Uquarium
Détenteur: Université du Québec à Rimouski
Service des communications, 300, allée des Ursulines,
#E-215, Rimouski, QC G5L 3A1

Tél: 418-723-1986; *Téléc:* 418-724-1525
Ligne sans frais: 800-511-3382
www.uqar.ca

The VCSA Insider
Owned By: Vanier College
821, av Ste-Croix, Montréal, QC H4L 3X9

Tel: 514-744-7500; *Fax:* 514-744-7505
studentnewspaper@vaniercollege.qc.ca
www.vinsider.ca
twitter.com/vanierinsider
www.facebook.com/VCSAInsider

Vanier College's online newspaper.
Katherine Willcocks, Editor-in-Chief

The Voice
Owned By: Athabasca University
301 Energy Square, 10109 106 St. NW, Edmonton, AB T5J
3L7

Toll-Free: 855-497-7003
voice@voicemagazine.org
www.voicemagazine.org
twitter.com/AUSUVoice
www.facebook.com/ausuvoice

Athabasca University magazine.
Jodi Campbell, Editor-in-Chief

The Voice
Owned By: Langara College
100 West 49th Ave., Vancouver, BC V5Y 2Z6

Tel: 604-323-5396
thevoice@langara.bc.ca
www.langaravoice.ca
www.youtube.com/user/VoiceLangara
twitter.com/langaravoice
www.facebook.com/Langara.Voice

Frequency: Weekly
Langara College newspaper.

Vox-Populi
Détenteur: Cégep André-Laurendeau
1111, rue Lapierre, Lasalle, QC H8N 2J4

Tél: 514-364-3320; *Téléc:* 514-364-7130
courrier@claurendeau.qc.ca
www.claurendeau.qc.ca

The Watch
Owned By: University of King's College
c/o The University of King's College, 6350 Coburg Rd.,
Halifax, NS B3H 2A1

watcheditors@gmail.com
watchmagazine.ca
twitter.com/KingsWatch

University of King's College newspaper.
Nicholas Frew, Editor-in-Chief, editors@watchmagazine.ca
Kristen Thompson, Editor-in-Chief, editors@watchmagazine.ca

The Weal
Previous Name: The Emery Weal
Owned By: Southern Alberta Institute of Technology
Campus Centre, 1301 - 16 Ave. NW, #V219, Calgary, AB T2M
0L4

Tel: 403-284-7248; *Fax:* 403-284-7112
the.weal@edu.sait.ca
www.theweal.com
www.linkedin.com/company/the-emery-weal
twitter.com/theweal
www.facebook.com/theWeal

Circulation: 4,600
Frequency: Weekly
Published by the SAIT Students' Association.
Chelsea Kemp, News Editor, chelsea.kemp@edu.sait.ca

Western News
Owned By: University of Western Ontario
Westminster Hall, #360, 1151 Richmond St., London, ON
N6A 3K7

Tel: 519-661-2045; *Fax:* 519-661-3921
news.westernu.ca

Circulation: 10,000
Frequency: 35 times during the academic year
University of Western Ontario newspaper.
Jason Winders, Editor, jwinder2@uwo.ca

The Window
Owned By: New College, University of Toronto
40 Willcocks St., Toronto, ON M5S 1C6

Tel: 416-978-2460; *Fax:* 416-978-0554
issuu.com/ncthewindow
www.facebook.com/NewCollegeWindow

New College's official student publication.
Kitty Liu, Editor-in-Chief

Xaverian Weekly
Owned By: St. Francis Xavier University
St. Francis Xavier University, PO Box 924, #111D,
Bloomfield Centre, Antigonish, NS B2G 2W5

Tel: 902-867-5007
xw.eic@stfx.ca
www.xaverian.ca
www.instagram.com/xaverianweekly
twitter.com/xaverianweekly
www.facebook.com/xaverianweekly

Frequency: Weekly; Thursdays
St. Francis Xavier University newspaper.
Emily Keenan, Editor-in-Chief

York University Magazine
Previous Name: YorkU
York University, West Office Bldg., 4700 Keele St., Toronto,
ON M3J 1P3

Tel: 416-736-5603
cpa.info.yorku.ca/yorku-magazine
twitter.com/yorkuniversity

Circulation: 240,000
Frequency: 3 times a year
The alumni publication of York University
Rod Thornton, Director, Strategic Communications,
thornto@yorku.ca

SECTION 14

RELIGION

Broad Faith Based Associations

American Academy of Religion (AAR)
#300, 825 Houston Mill Rd. NE, Atlanta GA 30329-4205 USA
Tel: 404-727-3049; *Fax:* 404-727-7959
info@aarweb.org
www.aarweb.org
www.youtube.com/user/AAReligion
www.linkedin.com/company/american-academy-of-religion
www.facebook.com/americanacademyofreligion
twitter.com/AARWeb
Overview: A medium-sized national charitable organization founded in 1909
Chief Officer(s):
Alice Hunt, Executive Director
ahunt@aarweb.org
Membership: 9,000+; *Fees:* US$15 international; US$45 student; US$55-$220 professional/retired; *Member Profile:* Teachers, scholars & other professionals in the field of Religion; *Committees:* Academic Relations; Executive; Finance; Graduate Student; International Connections; Nominations; Program; Publications; Public Understanding of Religion; Regions; Status of Racial & Ethnic Minorities in the Profession; Status of Women in the Profession; Teaching & Learning; Theological Education Steering Committee
Activities: Sustainability Task Force; Status of Lesbian, Gay, Bisexual & Transgendered Persons in the Profession; Awards for Excellence in the Study of Religion Book Award Juries; History of Religions Jury; Research Grants Jury; *Speaker Service:* Yes
Description: To promote research, teaching & scholarship in the field of religion; To be dedicated to furthering knowledge of religion & religious institutions in all their forms & manifestations; *Member of:* American Council of Learned Societies

Canadian Association for Spiritual Care (CASC) / Association canadienne de soins spirituels (ACSS)
#27, 1267 Dorval Dr., Oakville ON L6M 3Z4
Tel: 289-837-2272; *Fax:* 289-837-4800
Toll-Free: 866-442-2773
office@spiritualcare.ca
www.spiritualcare.ca
Previous Name: Canadian Association for Pastoral Practice & Education
Overview: A medium-sized national organization founded in 1965
Chief Officer(s):
Tony Sedfawi, Executive Director
tony@spiritualcare.ca
Kathy Greig, Manager
kathy@spiritualcare.ca
Finances: *Funding Sources:* Membership dues
Fees: $90 student; $285 associate; *Member Profile:* Persons involved in a variety of ministries, in settings such as parishes, prisons & correctional facilities, pastoral counselling centres, health care facilities & industrial facilities
Activities: Offering educational programs for both clergy & lay persons; Providing certification for supervisors & specialists; Creating networking opportunities
Description: To be a national multifaith organization committed to the professional education, certification & support of people involved in spiritual care, counselling & education; *Member of:* Quality End-of-Life Care Coalition of Canada

Canadian Society for the Study of Religion (CSSR) / Société canadienne pour l'étude de la religion (SCÉR)
c/o T. Malcolmson, Dept. of Classics & Religious Studies, U. of Ottawa, #10101, 55 Laurier St. East, Ottawa ON K1N 6N5
www.cssrscer.ca
Overview: A small national organization founded in 1966
Chief Officer(s):
Ted Malcolmson, Treasurer
cssr.scer.treasurer@gmail.com
Fees: $50 student; $60 part-time/retired; $100 regular; *Member Profile:* Scholars engaged in various academic approaches to the study of religion
Description: To promote research in the study of religion, with particular reference to Canada; To encourage a critical examination of the teaching of the discipline; *Member of:* International Association for the History of Religions (IAHR); Affiliation(s): Canadian Federation for the Humanities & Social Sciences (CFHSS)

Canadian Theological Society (CTS) / Société théologique canadienne
c/o Nick Olkovich, University of British Columbia, 5935 Iona Dr., vancouver BC V6T 1J7
secretary@cts-stc.ca
cts-stc.ca
www.facebook.com/canadiantheologicalsociety

Overview: A small national organization founded in 1955
Chief Officer(s):
William Sweet, President
wsweet@stfx.ca
Jane Barter, Vice-President
j.barter@uwinnipeg.ca
Nick Olkovich, Secretary
nolkovich@stmarkscollege.ca
Fees: $22-$45 student/part-time/unwaged; $25-$50 retired; $70-$100 regular; *Member Profile:* Theologians, clergy, scholars & students from universities, seminaries & churches
Activities: *Awareness Events:* Annual Student Essay Contest
Description: To promote theological reflection & writing in Canada; *Member of:* Canadian Corporation for the Study of Religion (CCSR); Affiliation(s): Canadian Congress of the Humanities & Social Sciences

Focolare Movement - Canada / Mouvement des Focolari
Toronto ON
toronto@focolare.ca
www.focolare.org/usa
www.facebook.com/focolare.org
twitter.com/Focolare_org
Overview: A small national charitable organization founded in 1943
Finances: *Funding Sources:* Donations
Member Profile: Individuals of all ages, walks of life & vocations; Churches of religions & convictions that differ from Catholicism
Activities: Providing gatherings for families, youth, children & various branches
Description: To fulfill Jesus' last will & testament: "That all may be one"; To strive for the Focolare spirituality to have an impact on family life, youth, & all areas of ecclesial & secular life; To promote the ideals of unity & universal brotherhood; Affiliation(s): Archdiocese of Toronto

International Fellowship of Christians & Jews of Canada
PO Box 670, Stn. K, Toronto ON M4P 2H1
Fax: 416-981-7293
Toll-Free: 888-988-4325
info@ifcj.ca
www.ifcj.ca
www.youtube.com/channel/UCGubM5lf4CS84hmm9VGYujw
www.facebook.com/FellowshipFan
Overview: A medium-sized national charitable organization
Chief Officer(s):
David Krieger, Chair
Finances: *Funding Sources:* Donations
Activities: Ministry progams; Television programs, Newsletter; *Library:* Pastor's Library
Description: To encourage improved understanding between Christian & Jewish people; To promote cooperation between Christian & Jewish communities on issues of shared biblical concern; and support Israel & Jews in crises or need; *Member of:* International Fellowship of Christians & Jews

International Institute of Integral Human Sciences (IIIHS) / Institut international des sciences humaines intégrales
PO Box 1387, Stn. H, Montréal QC H3G 2N3
Tel: 514-937-8359; *Fax:* 514-937-5380
Toll-Free: 877-937-8359
info@iiihs.org
www.iiihs.org
www.facebook.com/spiritualsciencef
twitter.com/SSF_IIIHS
Overview: A medium-sized international organization founded in 1975
Chief Officer(s):
Marilyn Rossner, President
mrossner@iiihs.org
Finances: *Annual Operating Budget:* $100,000-$250,000; *Funding Sources:* Classes; Workshops; International Conferences; Donations
Staff: 3 staff member(s); 25 volunteer(s)
Membership: 10,000; *Committees:* Local; International
Activities: Offering seminars, lectures & programs; Conducting international outreach projects; *Internships:* Yes; *Speaker Service:* Yes *Library:* Yes
Description: To explore new sciences of consciousness & healing; To identify paradigms for the convergence of science & spirituality in the global village landscape

Multifaith Action Society (MAS)
949 West 49th Ave., Vancouver BC V5Z 2T1
Tel: 604-321-1302
admin@multifaithaction.org
www.multifaithaction.org
www.facebook.com/multifaithaction
Previous Name: Canadian Ecumenical Action

Overview: A small national charitable organization founded in 1972
Chief Officer(s):
Connie Waterman, President
Marcus Hynes, Coordinator, Operations
Fees: Schedule available
Activities: Lectures & conferences promoting interreligious dialogue; forums on faith; environmental awareness programs within religious communities; faith centre visits; *Speaker Service:* Yes
Description: To promote interfaith & multifaith dialogue & understanding; To provides information & resources on world religions to the community & develops community service programs

Ontario Consultants on Religious Tolerance (OCRT)
#128, 829 Norwest Rd., Kingston ON K7P 2N3
Toll-Free: 888-806-6115
ocrtfeedback@gmail.com
www.religioustolerance.org
www.facebook.com/groups/115060631838983
Overview: A small provincial organization founded in 1995
Chief Officer(s):
B.A. Robinson, Coordinator
Finances: *Annual Operating Budget:* Less than $50,000; *Funding Sources:* Lecture fees; donations; banner ads
Staff: 1 staff member(s); 5 volunteer(s)
Membership: 1-99
Activities: *Speaker Service:* Yes
Description: To promote religious tolerance & expose religious hatred & misinformation

Religions for Peace (RFP)
777 United Nations Plaza, 4th Fl., New York NY 10017 USA
Tel: 212-687-2163
info@rfp.org
www.rfp.org
www.youtube.com/c/ReligionsforPeaceInternational
www.linkedin.com/company/religions4peace
www.facebook.com/religionsforpeaceintl
twitter.com/religions4peace
Overview: A large international organization founded in 1970
Chief Officer(s):
Azza Karam, Secretary General
Activities: Meetings; Occasional conferences; Newsletter
Description: To establish peace & justice at the local, national & international levels; To encourage members to work together with like-minded organizations on issues of social & economic justice, human rights, ecological harmony, arms limitation & nuclear disarmament; To aim for world peace through interfaith dialogue & applied ethics

Sisters of Charity of Halifax (SC)
215 Seton Rd., Halifax NS B3M 0C9
Tel: 902-406-8077; *Fax:* 902-457-3506
Toll-Free: 844-406-8114
communications@schalifax.ca
www.schalifax.ca
www.instagram.com/schalifax
www.facebook.com/schalifax
twitter.com/schalifax
Overview: A small local organization founded in 1849
Chief Officer(s):
Carrie Flemming, Advancement Associate
advancement@schalifax.ca
Ruth Jeppesen, Director, Communications
Membership: 400
Description: To develop a sensitivity to the oppressed through presence, prayer & ministry to others

Société québécoise pour l'étude de la religion (SQÉR)
Université de Montréal, #490, 3333, ch Queen Mary, Montréal QC H3V 1A2
Tél: 514-343-6568; *Téléc:* 514-343-5738
www.facebook.com/319498958060192
Aperçu: *Dimension:* petite; *Envergure:* provinciale; *fondée en 1989*
Membre(s) du bureau directeur:
Patrice Brodeur, Président
Montant de la cotisation: 50$ régulier; 25$ étudiant
Description: Promouvoir la recherche, l'enseignement et la diffusion des connaissances dans les disciplines ayant pour objet l'étude de la religion

Specific Faith Based Associations

Adventism

Adventist Development & Relief Agency Canada (ADRA)
20 Robert St. West, Newcastle ON L1B 1C6
Tel: 905-446-2372; *Fax:* 905-446-2372
Toll-Free: 888-274-2372
info@adra.ca
www.adra.ca
www.youtube.com/adracanada
www.facebook.com/adracanada
twitter.com/adracanada
Also Known As: ADRA Canada
Overview: A medium-sized international charitable organization founded in 1985
Chief Officer(s):
James Astleford, Executive Director
Finances: *Annual Operating Budget:* $1.5 Million-$3 Million; *Funding Sources:* Resources & donations received from the public & the Canadian government.
Staff: 14 staff member(s); 1500 volunteer(s)
Membership: 7,000
Activities: Emergency relief in the areas of: refugee assistance, improving health, hunger, safe drinking water, raising income, education & international development
Description: To provide community development & disaster relief without regard to political or religious association, age, or ethnicity; *Member of:* Canadian Council of Christian Charities, Canadian Churches in Action, Canadian Council for International Cooperation, Canadian Christian Relief and Development Association; *Affiliation(s):* Canadian Council of Christian Charities

Canadian Adventist Teachers Network
c/o Seventh-day Adventist Church in Canada, 1148 King St. East, Oshawa ON L1H 1H8
Tel: 905-433-0011; *Fax:* 905-433-0982
communication@adventist.ca
catnet.sdacc.org
Also Known As: CAT-net
Overview: A small national organization
Chief Officer(s):
Betty Bayer, Director, Education
bayer.betty@adventist.ca
Description: To promote excellence in Christian education by facilitating communication & the exchange of ideas among Adventist educators; *Affiliation(s):* Seventh-day Adventist Church in Canada

International Community for Relief of Suffering & Starvation Canada (ICROSS)
PO Box 3, Stn. Main, Saanichton BC V8M 2C3
Tel: 250-881-2202
www.icrosscanada.com
Overview: A small national charitable organization founded in 1998
Finances: *Funding Sources:* Donations
Description: To provide medical supplies to developing countries

Seventh-day Adventist Church in Canada (SDACC) / Église adventiste du septième jour au Canada
1148 King St. East, Oshawa ON L1H 1H8
Tel: 905-433-0011; *Fax:* 905-433-0982
Toll-Free: 800-263-7868
communication@adventist.ca
www.adventist.ca
Overview: A large national charitable organization founded in 1901
Chief Officer(s):
Mark Johnson, President, 905-433-0011 2086
johnson.mark@adventist.ca
Paul Llewellyn, Secretary/Vice-President, Administration, 905-433-0011 2083
llewellyn.paul@adventist.ca
Paul Musafili, Treasurer/Vice-President, Finance, 905-433-0011 2088
musafili.paul@adventist.ca
Finances: *Annual Operating Budget:* $3 Million-$5 Million; *Funding Sources:* Donations
Staff: 23 staff member(s)
Membership: 375 churches + 66,907 individual members
Activities: Native Ministries; It Is Written Canada; Christian Record Services; Canadian University College; Kingsway College
Description: To provide strategic leadership, support & resources to conferences & national entities to achieve the goal of a shared vision

Anglican

The Anglican Church of Canada (ACC) / L'Église anglicane du Canada
80 Hayden St., Toronto ON M4Y 3G2
Tel: 416-924-9192
information@national.anglican.ca
www.anglican.ca
www.youtube.com/generalsynod
www.facebook.com/canadiananglican
twitter.com/generalsynod
Previous Name: Church of England in Canada
Overview: A large national charitable organization founded in 1893
Chief Officer(s):
Linda Nicholls, Primate
primate@national.anglican.ca
Alan Perry, General Secretary
atperry@national.anglican.ca
Membership: 500,000+ members; 1,700 churches;
Committees: Communications & Information Resources; Faith, Worship & Ministry; Financial Management; Partners in Missions & Ecojustice; Philanthropy
Activities: Operates four incorporated bodies: the Anglican Foundation of Canada, Anglican Journal, Primate's World Relief & Development Fund, & Pension Office Corporation.; *Library:* Anglican Church of Canada Library by appointment
Description: To proclaim & celebrate the gospel of Jesus Christ in worship & action, as a partner in the world-wide Anglican Communion & the universal church; To value heritage of faith, reason, liturgy, tradition, bishops & synods & the variety of life in community; To acknowledge that God calls His followers to greater diversity of membership, wider participation in ministry & leadership, better stewardship in God's creation & a strong resolve in challenging attitudes & structures which cause injustice; *Member of:* Canadian Council of Churches

Anglican Foundation of Canada
Anglican Church House, 80 Hayden St., Toronto ON M4V 3G2
Tel: 416-924-9199; *Toll-Free:* 866-924-9192
foundation@anglicanfoundation.org
www.anglicanfoundation.org
www.youtube.com/user/AnglicanFoundation
www.facebook.com/anglicanfoundation
Overview: A small national charitable organization founded in 1957
Chief Officer(s):
Judy Rois, Executive Director, 416-924-9199 234
Activities: *Speaker Service:* Yes
Description: To assist parishes, dioceses & programs of Anglican Church of Canada with low interest loans &/or grants; *Affiliation(s):* World Council of Churches

Integrity Toronto
PO Box 873, Stn. F, Toronto ON M4Y 2N9
Tel: 416-925-9872
toronto@integritycanada.org
www.toronto.integritycanada.org
Overview: A small local organization founded in 1975
Chief Officer(s):
Chris Ambidge, Co-Convener
Finances: *Annual Operating Budget:* Less than $50,000; *Funding Sources:* Donations
Staff: 6 volunteer(s)
Membership: 100 individual; *Fees:* $15 single, $20 couple
Activities: Meetings; Parish education; Newsletters; Retreats; Synod Presence
Description: To be an organization of gay & lesbian Anglicans & their friends; To help its members discover & affirm that they can be both Christian & LGBTQ; *Affiliation(s):* Integrity Inc. - USA

The Primate's World Relief & Development Fund (PWRDF) / Le fonds du Primat pour le secours et le développement mondial
Anglican Church of Canada, 80 Hayden St., Toronto ON M4Y 3G2
Tel: 416-924-9192; *Fax:* 416-924-3483
Toll-Free: 866-308-7973
pwrdf@pwrdf.org
www.pwrdf.org
www.youtube.com/user/PWRDF
www.facebook.com/111501932203731
twitter.com/PWRDF
Overview: A small international charitable organization founded in 1959
Chief Officer(s):
Fred Hiltz, Archbishop & Primate
Will Postma, Executive Director
wpostma@pwrdf.org

Finances: *Annual Operating Budget:* Greater than $5 Million; *Funding Sources:* Anglican Church contributions
Staff: 16 staff member(s); 2000 volunteer(s)
Activities: *Library:* Resource Centre - Anglican Church of Canada (Open to Public)
Description: To connect Anglicans in Canada to communities around the world in dynamic partnerships to advance development; To respond to emergencies; To assist refugees & to act for positive change; *Member of:* Canadian Council for International Cooperation; Action by Churches Together (ACT); *Affiliation(s):* Canadian Council of Churches

Baha'i Faith

Association for Bahá'í Studies (ABS) / Association d'études Baha'is
34 Copernicus St., Ottawa ON K1N 7K4
Tel: 613-233-1903; *Fax:* 613-233-3644
abs-na@bahai-studies.ca
www.bahai-studies.ca
vimeo.com/absna
www.facebook.com/331784303733
Previous Name: Canadian Association for Studies in the Bahá'í Faith
Overview: A medium-sized international charitable organization founded in 1975
Finances: *Annual Operating Budget:* $100,000-$250,000; *Funding Sources:* Grants; Conference & Literature revenue; Membership fees
Staff: 2 staff member(s)
Membership: 2,000; *Fees:* $50 adult; $60 couple; $25 student/senior; $60 institution; $999 individual life
Activities: Publications; Conferences; Webinars; Working Groups; *Library:* Association for Bahá'í Studies Library (Open to Public) by appointment
Description: To foster Bahá'í scholarship & to demonstrate the value of this scholarly approach; To promote courses of study of the Bahá'í faith; To foster relationships with various leaders of thought & persons of capacity; To publish scholarly materials examining the Bahá'í faith, especially on its application to the concerns & needs of humanity

The Bahá'í Community of Canada / La communauté bahá'íe du Canada
Bahá'í National Centre, 7200 Leslie St., Thornhill ON L3T 6L8
Tel: 905-889-8168
secretariat@bahai.ca
www.bahai.ca
www.facebook.com/Canada.Bahai
Overview: A large national charitable organization founded in 1844
Chief Officer(s):
Karen McKye, Secretary-General
Finances: *Annual Operating Budget:* Greater than $5 Million; *Funding Sources:* Contributions from members
Staff: 30 staff member(s)
Membership: 30,000+
Activities: Study circles; Devotional gatherings; Junior youth spiritual empowerment program; Children's classes; *Awareness Events:* Unity in Diversity Week, Nov.; *Speaker Service:* Yes *Library:* Yes (Open to Public) by appointment
Description: To teach the oneness of humanity, the common divine source of all the great religions, equality of the sexes & harmony of science & religion; *Member of:* Bahá'í International Community; *Affiliation(s):* Bahá'í International Community

Bahá'í Community of Ottawa
211 McArthur Ave., Ottawa ON K1L 6P6
Tel: 613-742-8250
www.bahai-ottawa.org
twitter.com/OttawaBahais
Overview: A small local organization
Chief Officer(s):
Corinne Box, Director, Government Relations, 613-233-3712
ogr@bcc-cbc.org
Membership: 9 sectors
Description: To support the development of the Bahá'í Faith Community in Ottawa, Ontario.

Baptists

Association d'églises baptistes évangéliques au québec
9780, rue Sherbrooke est, Montréal QC H1L 6N6
Tél: 514-337-2555; *Téléc:* 514-337-8892
info@aebeq.qc.ca
aebeq.qc.ca
www.facebook.com/aebeq.qc
Aperçu: *Dimension:* moyenne; *Envergure:* provinciale; *fondée en 1971*

Membre(s) du bureau directeur:
Louis Bourque, Directeur général
l.bourque@aebeq.qc.ca
Membre: 65 000
Activités: Camps de jeunes; retraites; congrès; cohortes;
Stagiaires: Oui; *Service de conférenciers:* Oui
Description: Aider les églises à communiquer l'évangile de
Jésus-Christ à tous les Québécois; former des disciples et des
leaders; devenir plus solides et se reproduire; *Membre de:*
Fellowship of Evangelical Baptist Churches in Canada;
Affiliation(s): Camp des Bouleaux, Camp Patmos, Aujourd'hui
l'Espoir, Organisme Renaissance Autochtone

Canadian Baptist Ministries (CBM)
7185 Millcreek Dr., Mississauga ON L5N 5R4
Tel: 905-821-3533; *Fax:* 905-826-3441
communications@cbmin.org
www.cbmin.org
www.facebook.com/cbmin.org
**Merged from: Canadian Baptist International Ministries;
Canadian Baptist Federation**
Overview: A large national organization founded in 1995
Chief Officer(s):
Smith Terry, Executive Director
tsmith@cbmin.org
Jennifer Lau, Associate Executive Director
jlau@cbmin.org
Finances: *Annual Operating Budget:* Greater than $5 Million;
Funding Sources: Member churches; individuals; CIDA
Staff: 112 staff member(s); 540 volunteer(s)
Membership: 250,000 + 1,000 churches; *Member Profile:*
Members of churches affiliated with the four conventions/unions;
Committees: Public Affairs
Activities: Partners in Mission - 75 missionaries serving in Asia,
Africa, Latin America, Europe & Canada; The Sharing Way -
relief & development ministries in 13 countries, working in areas
of agricultural & community development, community health,
etc.; Canadian Baptist Volunteers - short-term ministry
opportunities; Canada Caucus - consensus building among the
churches in Canada; *Library:* Daniel Global Mission Resource
Room
Description: To partner with local churches around the world to
bring hope, healing & reconciliation through word & deed;
Member of: Canadian Council of Christian Charities;
Affiliation(s): Canadian Baptists of Western Canada; Canadian
Baptists of Ontario & Quebec; Baptist World Alliance;
Convention of Atlantic Baptist Churches; Union d'Églises
Baptists Francophones au Canada; Atlantic Baptist Women;
Canadian Baptist Women of Ontario & Quebec

Canadian Baptists of Ontario & Quebec (CBOQ)
5 International Blvd., Toronto ON M9W 6H3
Tel: 416-622-8600; *Fax:* 416-622-2308
info@baptist.ca
baptist.ca
vimeo.com/cboq
www.facebook.com/cboqcommunity
twitter.com/cboq
Previous Name: Baptist Convention of Ontario & Québec
Overview: A large provincial organization founded in 1889
Chief Officer(s):
Tim McCoy, Executive Minister, 416-620-2947
tmccoy@baptist.ca
Finances: *Annual Operating Budget:* $3 Million-$5 Million;
Funding Sources: Member churches
Staff: 15 staff member(s)
Membership: 375
Activities: *Internships:* Yes *Library:* Canadian Baptist Ministries
Library (Open to Public)
Description: To support & enable member churches to be
healthy mission congregations as they serve God together;
Member of: Canadian Baptist Ministries; *Affiliation(s):* Baptist
Women of Ontario & Quebec; McMaster Divinity College;
Canadian Council of Churches; Evangelical Fellowship of
Canada; Canadian Council of Christian Charities; Convention of
Atlantic Baptist Churches; Canadian Baptists of Western
Canada; French Union of Baptist Churches

Canadian Baptists of Western Canada (CBWC)
#201, 221 10th Ave. SE, Calgary AB T2G 0V9
Tel: 403-228-9559; *Fax:* 403-228-9048
Toll-Free: 800-820-2479
office@cbwc.ca
www.cbwc.ca
www.youtube.com/user/CanadianBaptists
www.facebook.com/115787141838284
twitter.com/TheCBWC
Previous Name: The Baptist Union of Western Canada
Overview: A medium-sized local charitable organization
founded in 1908
Chief Officer(s):

Bob Webber, Director, Ministry, 403-228-9559 311
bwebber@cbwc.ca
Finances: *Funding Sources:* Church congregations
Staff: 30 staff member(s)
Membership: 183 congregations representing 100,000
worshippers; *Committees:* Western Canada Missions;
Evangelism; Finance; Youth
Activities: *Internships:* Yes
Affiliation(s): Baptist World Alliance; Canadian Baptist Ministries;
North American Baptist Fellowship; Evangelical Fellowship of
Canada; Canadian Council Of Churches

CNBC
100 Convention Way, Cochrane AB T4C 2G2
Tel: 403-932-5688; *Fax:* 403-932-4937
Toll-Free: 888-442-2272
cnbc.ca
Previous Name: Canadian Convention of Southern Baptists
Overview: A medium-sized national charitable organization
founded in 1985
Chief Officer(s):
Gerry Taillon, National Ministry Leader
gtaillon@cnbc.ca
Finances: *Funding Sources:* Member churches
Staff: 8 staff member(s); 4 volunteer(s)
Membership: 300 churches
Activities: *Library:* CNBC Resource Centre (Open to Public)
Description: To network churches with each other to see God
add New Believers, New Disciplemarkers & New Communitites
of Faith to the family of congregations; *Affiliation(s):* Southern
Baptist Convention

Convention of Atlantic Baptist Churches (CABC) / Convention des Églises Baptistes de l'Atlantique
1655 Manawagonish Rd., Saint John NB E2M 3Y2
Tel: 506-635-1922; *Fax:* 506-635-0366
cabc@baptist-atlantic.ca
www.baptist-atlantic.ca
www.linkedin.com/company/2498898
www.facebook.com/atlanticbaptist
twitter.com/atlanticbaptist
Also Known As: Atlantic Baptist Convention
Previous Name: United Baptist Convention of the Maritime
Provinces
Overview: A medium-sized local charitable organization
founded in 1905
Chief Officer(s):
Peter Reid, Executive Minister
peter.reid@baptist-atlantic.ca
Kevin Vincent, Associate Executive Minister, New
Congregations
kevin.vincent@baptist-atlantic.ca
Finances: *Annual Operating Budget:* $1.5 Million-$3 Million
Staff: 18 staff member(s)
Activities: Providing seminars, conferences, stewardship
education, & retreats; *Speaker Service:* Yes
Description: To resource pastors, churches, & people; To
facilitate a shared mission on behalf of churches; To establish &
maintain professional standards & ethics for clergy

Elgin Baptist Association
ON
elginbaptist@gmail.com
elginbaptist.wordpress.com
Overview: A small local organization founded in 1874
Chief Officer(s):
Margaret Bell, Moderator
Membership: 8 churches; *Member Profile:* Baptist churches in
Elgin County
Description: To bring together Baptist churches & to promote
the interests of the members; *Member of:* Canadian Baptists of
Ontario & Quebec; Canadian Baptist Ministries; Baptist World
Alliance

Fellowship of Evangelical Baptist Churches
PO Box 457, Guelph ON N1H 6K9
Tel: 519-821-4830; *Fax:* 519-821-9829
www.fellowship.ca
www.facebook.com/FellowshipNatl
Also Known As: The Fellowship
Overview: A medium-sized national organization
Chief Officer(s):
Steven Jones, President, 519-821-4830 231
sjones@fellowship.ca
Finances: *Annual Operating Budget:* Greater than $5 Million
Staff: 16 staff member(s)
Membership: 500+ churches
Activities: *Library:* Fellowship of Evangelical Baptist Churches
Archives
Description: To glorify God & to proclaim the good news of
Jesus Christ, evangelizing the current generation & producing
healthy, growing churches in Canada & around the world;

Member of: The Evangelical Fellowship of Canada; *Affiliation(s):*
Association d'églises baptistes évangéliques au quebec

Middlesex-Lambton-Huron Association of Baptist Churches
ON
www.mlha.ca
Overview: A small local organization
Chief Officer(s):
Dave Stephens, Moderator
Membership: 19 churches; *Member Profile:* Baptist churches in
Southwestern Ontario
Activities: Camp site; Golf tournament; Annual Picnic
Member of: Canadian Baptists of Ontario & Quebec

Niagara/Hamilton Association of Baptist Churches
ON
nhachurches@gmail.com
baptist.ca
www.facebook.com/niagarahamiltonassoc
Overview: A small local organization
Chief Officer(s):
Peter Dempsey, Moderator
podempsey@yahoo.ca
Member Profile: Baptist churches in the Niagara Falls &
Hamilton area
Member of: Canadian Baptists of Ontario & Quebec

Ottawa Baptist Association (OBA)
249 Bronson Ave., Ottawa ON K1R 6H6
Tel: 613-235-7617
www.ottawabaptist.org
Overview: A small local organization founded in 1836
Chief Officer(s):
Hugh Willet, Executive Secretary
hwillett@sympatico.ca
Membership: 20 churches; *Member Profile:* Baptist churches in
Ottawa
Member of: Canadian Baptists of Ontario & Quebec;
Affiliation(s): Canadian Baptist Ministries; Baptist World Alliance

Oxford-Brant Association of Baptist Churches
ON
baptist.ca
Overview: A small local organization founded in 1896
Chief Officer(s):
David Partridge, Moderator
Membership: 17 churches; *Member Profile:* Baptist churches in
Oxford & Brant counties; *Committees:* Area ministry; Association
Educational
Member of: Canadian Baptists of Ontario & Quebec

Québec Association of Baptist Churches
6215, boul Côte St-Luc, Montréal QC H3X 2H3
Tel: 514-483-4302
associationbaptistcq@gmail.com
www.quebecbaptist.org
Also Known As: Eastern Association
Overview: A small provincial organization founded in 1887
Chief Officer(s):
Brian Berry, Moderator
bberry@videotron.ca
Membership: 19 churches; *Member Profile:* Baptist churches in
Quebec
Description: To help churches carry out their services & goals;
Member of: Canadian Baptists of Ontario & Quebec

Toronto Baptist Ministries
1585 Yonge St., Toronto ON M4T 1Z9
office@torontobaptistministries.com
www.torontobaptistministries.com
Overview: A small local organization
Membership: 100 churches; *Member Profile:* Baptist churches
in the Greater Toronto Area
Description: To support their member churches; *Member of:*
Canadian Baptists of Ontario & Quebec

Trent Valley Association of Baptist Churches
ON
trentvalleybaptists@gmail.com
tvabaptist.wordpress.com
Overview: A small local organization
Chief Officer(s):
Clarke Dixon, Moderator, 905-372-5058
clarkedixon@me.com
Member Profile: Baptist churches in the Trent Valley Area
Member of: Canadian Baptists of Ontario & Quebec

Brethern

Be in Christ Church of Canada (BIC)
2700 Bristol Circle, Oakville ON L6H 6EH
Tel: 905-339-2335
office@beinchrist.ca
beinchrist.ca
www.facebook.com/BICCanada
twitter.com/BICCanada
Previous Name: Brethren in Christ Canada
Overview: A medium-sized national charitable organization founded in 1788
Chief Officer(s):
Charlie Mashinter, Interim Executive Director
charlie.mashinter@beinchrist.ca
Finances: *Annual Operating Budget:* $1.5 Million-$3 Million; *Funding Sources:* Congregational giving
Staff: 20 staff member(s)
Membership: 51 congregations
Activities: *Speaker Service:* Yes; *Rents Mailing List:* Yes
Member of: Evangelical Fellowship of Canada; *Affiliation(s):* Mennonite Central Committee; Canadian Holiness Federation

The United Brethren Church in Canada
501 Whitelaw Rd., Guelph ON N1K 1E7
Tel: 519-836-0180; *Fax:* 519-821-8385
www.ubcanada.org
Previous Name: Ontario Conference, Church of the United Brethren in Christ
Overview: A small national charitable organization founded in 1856
Chief Officer(s):
Brian K. Magnus, Bishop
b_magnus@ubcanada.org
Finances: *Annual Operating Budget:* $50,000-$100,000; *Funding Sources:* Donations
Staff: 1 staff member(s)
Membership: 13 churches; *Fees:* Schedule available; *Member Profile:* Personal knowledge of God through faith in Christ; desire to live a life conforming to biblical principles
Activities: *Library:* At Emmanuel Bible College Library
Description: To organize groups of people into congregations to worship God; to make effective application of principles of righteousness in the Society; *Member of:* Church of the United Brethren in Christ, International; *Affiliation(s):* Evangelical Fellowship of Canada

Buddhism

Buddhist Association of Canada - Cham Shan Temple
7254 Bayview Ave., Toronto ON L3T 2R6
Tel: 905-886-1522
chamshantemple.askus@gmail.com
en.chamshantemple.org
www.facebook.com/temple.chamshan
twitter.com/temple_chamshan
Overview: A small national organization founded in 1973
Chief Officer(s):
Dayi Shi, President & Abbot
Activities: Seminars, sutra reading groups, meditation retreats; *Library:* Yes
Description: In addition to the main worship hall & 2 congregation halls, the Buddhist temple also includes a Dharma seminary for the Chinese community to learn Buddhism.

Jodo Shinshu Buddhist Temples of Canada
11786 Fentiman Pl., Richmond BC V7E 6M6
Tel: 604-272-3330; *Fax:* 604-272-6865
jsbtcheadquarters@gmail.com
www.bcc.ca
www.youtube.com/user/livingdharmacentre
www.facebook.com/654327614577625
Previous Name: Buddhist Churches of Canada
Overview: A medium-sized national charitable organization founded in 1933
Chief Officer(s):
Tatsuya Aoki, Bishop
Finances: *Annual Operating Budget:* $100,000-$250,000
Staff: 9 staff member(s)
Membership: 2,500; *Fees:* $45
Activities: *Speaker Service:* Yes *Library:* Yes by appointment
Description: Propagation of Buddhism; *Affiliation(s):* Jodo Shinshu Hongwanji, Kyoto

The Palyul Foundation of Canada
c/o Orgyan Osal Cho Dzong Buddhist Temple & Retreat Centre, 1755 Lingham Lake Rd., Madoc ON K0K 2K0
www.palyulcanada.org
www.facebook.com/Palyul.Canada
twitter.com/OrgyanDzong
Overview: A small local charitable organization founded in 1981

Activities: Classes on Buddhism, meditation, ritual practices; retreats; empowerments; celebration of Buddhist holy days & festivals
Description: Dedicated to the preservation & advancement of the teachings of the Nyingma lineage of Vajrayana Buddhism

Catholicism

Alberta Catholic School Trustees Association (ACSTA)
#205, 9940 - 106 St., Edmonton AB T5K 2N2
Tel: 780-484-6209; *Fax:* 780-484-6248
admin@acsta.ab.ca
www.acsta.ab.ca
twitter.com/acstanews
Overview: A medium-sized provincial organization
Chief Officer(s):
Adrianna LaGrange, President
John Tomkinson, Vice President
Description: To promote, preserve, celebrate & enhance Catholic education in Alberta, Northwest Territories & Yukon; *Member of:* Canadian Catholic School Trustees Association

Assemblée des évêques catholiques du Québec (AEQ) / Assembly of Québec Catholic Bishops
3331, rue Sherbrooke est, Montréal QC H1W 1C5
Tél: 514-274-4323; *Téléc:* 514-274-4383
aeq@eveques.qc.ca
www.eveques.qc.ca
twitter.com/evequesQuebec
Nom précédent: Assemblée des Évêques du Québec
Aperçu: *Dimension:* petite; *Envergure:* provinciale; *Organisme sans but lucratif; fondée en 1871*
Membre(s) du bureau directeur:
Bertrand Ouellet, Secrétaire général
Finances: *Budget de fonctionnement annuel:* $500,000-$1.5 Million
Personnel: 8 membre(s) du personnel
Membre: 37; *Critères d'admissibilité:* Évêque diocésain; Évêque auxiliaire; *Comités:* Éducation; Laicat; Ministères; Missions; Affaires sociales; Théologie; Communications; Prospective; Législation; Administration; Relations interculturelles; Pastorale des Autochtones
Description: Être un lieu d'échange et de concertation où ses membres s'entraident dans la recherche d'actions à entreprendre pour rendre l'Église au Québec toujours plus vivante et engagée dans la société et la culture contemporaines; *Affiliation(s):* Conférence des évêques catholiques du Canada

Assembly of Catholic Bishops of Ontario (ACBO) / Assemblée des évêques catholiques de l'Ontario
#810, 90 Eglinton Ave. East, Toronto ON M4P 2Y3
Tel: 416-923-1423; *Fax:* 416-923-1509
acbo@acbo.on.ca
www.acbo.on.ca
Overview: A small provincial organization
Chief Officer(s):
Ronald P. Fabbro, c.s.b., President, 519-433-0658, Fax: 519-433-0011
Thomas Collins, Vice President, 416-934-0606, Fax: 416-934-3452
Description: To enable Ontario Catholic Bishops to collaborate on projects to proclaim, celebrate & live the Good News of Jesus Christ

Association des intervenantes et des intervenants en soins spirituels du Québec (AIISSQ)
#402, 8815, av du Parc, Montréal QC H2N 1Y7
Tél: 514-259-9229; *Téléc:* 514-259-3741
secretariat@aiissq.org
www.aiissq.org
Nom précédent: Association québécoise de la pastorale de la santé
Aperçu: *Dimension:* petite; *Envergure:* provinciale; *Organisme sans but lucratif; fondée en 2005*
Membre(s) du bureau directeur:
Lorraine Rooke, Présidente
presidence@aiissq.org
Fernand Patry, Vice-président
vice-presidence@aiissq.org
Finances: *Budget de fonctionnement annuel:* $50,000-$100,000
Personnel: 1 membre(s) du personnel
Membre: 200; *Montant de la cotisation:* 275$; 70$ par jour; *Critères d'admissibilité:* Animateur(trice) de pastorale dans un établissement de santé; *Comités:* Pastorale pratique; pastorale en santé mentale
Activités: Congrès annuel; colloques; sessions de formation; *Stagiaires:* Oui; *Listes de destinataires:* Oui
Description: Formation professionnelle des membres et promotion de leurs intérêts spirituels et professionnels; représentation des membres auprès d'instances civiles et

religieuses reconnues; *Membre de:* Association canadienne des périodiques catholiques; *Affiliation(s):* Association canadienne pour la pratique et l'éducation pastorale; Association catholique canadienne de la santé; Carrefour Humanisation - Santé

Association des parents catholiques du Québec (APCQ)
CP 55038, Succ. Maisonneuve, Montréal QC H1W 0A1
Tél: 514-276-8068; *Téléc:* 514-948-2595
info@parentscatholiques.org
parentscatholiques.org
www.facebook.com/parentscatholiques
Aperçu: *Dimension:* moyenne; *Envergure:* provinciale; *Organisme sans but lucratif; fondée en 1966*
Membre(s) du bureau directeur:
Georges Buscemi, Présidente
Finances: *Budget de fonctionnement annuel:* $50,000-$100,000
Personnel: 25 bénévole(s)
Membre: 4 000; *Montant de la cotisation:* 12$; *Critères d'admissibilité:* Familles; *Comités:* Éducation de la foi; Comité provincial d'enseignement privé; Carrefour famille-Québec
Activités: Secrétariat permanent; Périodique; Colloques; Conférences; Cours; Congrès parents-jeunes; Pétitions; Rédactions de mémoires; *Service de conférenciers:* Oui
Description: Regroupe des parents catholiques pour promouvoir et défendre leurs droits et leurs intérêts selon les valeurs catholiques en matière d'éducation, de famille, et de culture par l'information et la représentation de ses membres auprès de la population et des autorités civiles et religieuses; *Membre de:* Regroupement Inter-Organismes pour une politique familiale au Québec; *Affiliation(s):* Organisation internationale de l'enseignement catholique (OIEC)

Association of Catholic Retired Administrators (ACRA)
Tel: 514-626-1060
www.acracan.org
Overview: A small local organization founded in 1998
Chief Officer(s):
Maria Di Perna, President
mcdiperna@gmail.com
Description: To represent retired administrators & professionals from English-language Catholic educational boards & schools

Augustines de la Miséricorde de Jésus
2655, rue Guillaume - Le Pelletier, Québec QC G1C 3X7
Tél: 418-628-8860
secretaire@augustines.org
www.augustines.ca
Aperçu: *Dimension:* petite; *Envergure:* locale; *fondée en 1957*
Description: Les trois dimensions de la vie spirituelle des Augustines d'hier et de demain sont: communion fraternelle; louange et intercession; et miséricorde

The Brothers of the Good Shepherd / Les Frères du Bon-Pasteur
Development Office, PO Box 1003, 10 Delaware Ave., Hamilton ON L8N 3R1
Tel: 905-528-9109; *Fax:* 905-528-6967
info@goodshepherdcentres.ca
www.goodshepherdcentres.ca
www.youtube.com/channel/UCDb1IcEb-uKK3n_9kuBVbPg
www.facebook.com/goodshepherdhamilton
twitter.com/goodshepherdham
Also Known As: Good Shepherd
Previous Name: Little Brothers of the Good Shepherd
Overview: A small local charitable organization founded in 1951
Chief Officer(s):
Richard MacPhee, Executive Director
Finances: *Annual Operating Budget:* $500,000-$1.5 Million
Activities: Housing for battered women & children; residence for homeless youth; men's hostel; food bank & food line; speakers on topics dealing with violence & abuse; *Speaker Service:* Yes

Calgary Catholic Immigration Society (CCIS)
1111 - 11th Ave. SW, 5th Fl., Calgary AB T2R 0G5
Tel: 403-262-2006; *Fax:* 403-262-2033
contact@ccisab.ca
www.ccisab.ca
www.instagram.com/ccis_ab
www.linkedin.com/company/ccisab
www.facebook.com/ccisab
twitter.com/ccisab
Overview: A large international charitable organization founded in 1981
Chief Officer(s):
Fariborz Birjandian, Chief Executive Officer
Finances: *Annual Operating Budget:* Greater than $5 Million
Staff: 293 staff member(s); 1500 volunteer(s)
Activities: Pre-employment training & counseling; community outreach for families & seniors; temporary accommodation facility; Integrated Resettlement Program

Description: To provide settlement & integration services to immigrants & refugees in Southern Alberta

Canadian Catholic Campus Ministry (CCCM)
Attn: Susan Kidd, 550 University Ave., Charlottetown ON C1A 4P3

boardcccm@gmail.com
www.cccm.ca
www.facebook.com/catholiccampus
Also Known As: Canadian Catholic Students Association
Overview: A small national charitable organization
Chief Officer(s):
Susan Kidd, Chair & Atlantic Representative
sukidd@upei.ca
Martha Fauteux, Vice-Chair & Central Representative
mfauteux@uwaterloo.ca
Nancy Quan, Western Representative
Nancy.quan@stmu.ab.ca
Chrisandra Skipper, Central Representative
cskipper@assumptionu.ca
Robert Corbeil, National Coordinator, 879-743-7197, Fax: 855-488-0807
nc@cccm.ca
Finances: *Funding Sources:* Donations
Fees: $150; *Member Profile:* Persons who support the purpose of the association
Activities: Supporting prayerful, pastoral action; *Awareness Events:* Catholic Students' Week, March
Description: To unite Catholic students on Canadian post-secondary campuses; To nurture Christian student leadership; Affiliation(s): International Movement of Catholic Students - Canada

Canadian Catholic Historical Association - English Section (CCHA) / Société canadienne d'histoire de l'église catholique - Section anglaise
c/o St. Michael's College, 81 St. Mary St., Toronto ON M5S 1J4

Tel: 905-893-9754
cchahistory.ca
twitter.com/cchahistory
Overview: A medium-sized national organization founded in 1933
Chief Officer(s):
Peter E. Baltutis, President-General
Edward Jackman, Secretary-General
Finances: *Annual Operating Budget:* Less than $50,000; *Funding Sources:* Membership fees; donations
Staff: 11 volunteer(s)
Membership: 100-499; *Fees:* $30 student; $50 Canadian; US$50 American; $70 French-English
Activities: Annual scholarly conference at the Canadian Congress
Description: To promote interest & research in the history of the Canadian Catholic Church, its dioceses, religious communities, institutions, parishes, buildings, sites & personalities

Canadian Catholic Organization for Development & Peace / Organisation catholique canadienne pour le développement et la paix
1425, boul René-Lévesque ouest, 3e étage, Montréal QC H3G 1T7

Tel: 514-257-8711; *Fax:* 514-257-8497
Toll-Free: 888-234-8533
info@devp.ca
www.devp.org
www.youtube.com/devpeacetv
www.linkedin.com/company/d-veloppement-et-paix
www.facebook.com/devpeace
twitter.com/DevPeace
Also Known As: Development & Peace
Overview: A large international charitable organization founded in 1967
Finances: *Annual Operating Budget:* Greater than $5 Million; *Funding Sources:* Donations; Canadian International Development Agency (provision of grants for projects & programs)
Staff: 73 staff member(s); 5,00 volunteer(s)
Membership: 13,000; *Fees:* $10 lifetime
Activities: Providing financial support for projects in the developing world; Contributing to emergency relief; Engaging in advocacy activities related to crises & issues in developing countries
Description: To support partners in the Global South who promote alternatives to unfair social, political & economic structures; *Member of:* Caritas Internationalis; Conseil canadien pour la coopération internationale / Canadian Council for International Cooperation; Affiliation(s): Coopération internationale pour le développement et la solidarité

Canadian Catholic School Trustees' Association (CCSTA) / Association canadienne des commissaires d'écoles catholique (ACCEC)
Catholic Education Centre, 570 West Hunt Club Rd., Nepean ON K2G 3R4

Tel: 613-224-4455
ccsta@ocsb.ca
www.ccsta.ca
twitter.com/ccstaconnect
Overview: A medium-sized national organization founded in 1960
Chief Officer(s):
Paula Scott, President
pscott@lcsd.ca
Patrick J. Daly, Vice-President
dalyp@hwcdsb.ca
Julian Hanlon, Executive Director
julian.hanlon@ocsb.ca
Finances: *Funding Sources:* Sponsorships
Membership: 7 associations representing 90 Catholic school boards; *Member Profile:* Provincial & territorial Catholic school trustees' associations in Canada
Activities: Promoting Catholic education; Providing professional development opportunities for trustees; Collaborating with the Canadian Conference of Catholic Bishops; Liaising with Canadian government agencies & other Catholic education organizations; *Awareness Events:* Catholic Education Week
Description: To protect the right to Catholic education in Canada; To promote excellence in Catholic education across Canada; *Member of:* NCEA (National Catholic Education Association -US) and International Office of Catholic Education (OIEC)

Canadian Conference of Catholic Bishops (CCCB) / Conférence des évêques catholiques du Canada (CECC)
2500 Don Reid Dr., Ottawa ON K1H 2J2
Tel: 613-241-9461; *Fax:* 613-241-8117
cecc@cccb.ca
www.cccb.ca
www.youtube.com/user/cccbadmin
twitter.com/CCCB_CECC
Previous Name: Canadian Catholic Conference
Overview: A small national charitable organization founded in 1943
Chief Officer(s):
Frank Leo, Jr., C.S.S., General Secretary, 613-241-9461 206
gensec@cccb.ca
Member Profile: Diocesan bishops in Canada; Coadjutor Bishops; Auxiliary Bishops; Titular Bishops of any rite within the Catholic Church
Activities: Providing aid to developing countries & Christian education; Offering a forum for bishops to share experiences & insights; Promoting the teaching of the Catholic Church in circumstances from conception to natural death; Preparing & providing educational resources; Strengthening the role of the family
Description: To exercise pastoral functions for Catholics in Canada

Carizon Family & Community Services
400 Queen St. South, Kitchener ON N2G 1W7
Tel: 519-743-6333; *Fax:* 519-743-3496
info@carizon.ca
www.carizon.ca
www.linkedin.com/company/carizon-family-and-community-services
www.facebook.com/carizonupdates
twitter.com/carizon
Previous Name: kidsLINK; Mosaic Counselling & Family Services; Catholic Family Counselling Centre; Catholic Social Services; Catholic Welfare Bureau
Overview: A small local charitable organization founded in 1952
Chief Officer(s):
Stephen Swatridge, CEO
Lesley Barraball, Director, Children's Mental Health Services
Jennifer Berry, Director, Communications
Ted Conlin, Director, Business
Jean Davies, Director, Pathways to Education
Debbie Engel, Director, Community Services
Dale Gellatly, Director, Community Engagement
Finances: *Annual Operating Budget:* $3 Million-$5 Million; *Funding Sources:* United Way; Government of Canada; Province of Ontario; Regional Municipality of Waterloo; Foundations, such as Pathways to Education Canada
Activities: Offering individual, group, & credit counselling; Providing workplace & employee assistance programs; Offering community outreach services
Description: To provide full-service professional counselling services in Kitchener & the surrounding region; *Member of:* Canadian Association of Credit Counselling Services; Ontario

Association of Credit Counselling Services; United Way of Kitchener-Waterloo & Area; Family Service Ontario

Catholic Action Montreal / Action Catholique Montréal
#301, 1857, rue de Maisonneuve ouest, Montréal QC H3H 1J9
Tel: 514-937-2301
join@catholicaction.ca
www.catholicaction.ca
Overview: A small local charitable organization founded in 2015
Chief Officer(s):
Anna Graham, Interim Chair
Finances: *Funding Sources:* Membership dues; Archdiocese of Montreal
Activities: Promoting educational, health, & social services
Description: To bring together members of Montreal's English-speaking Catholic community to help people in need

Catholic Biblical Federation (CBF) / Fédération biblique catholique (FBC)
Erzabtei 4, St. Ottilien 86941 Germany
contact@c-b-f.org
c-b-f.org
www.youtube.com/c/CatholicBiblicalFederation
www.facebook.com/Cathbibfed
twitter.com/cbf_gensec
Overview: A small international organization founded in 1969
Chief Officer(s):
Jan J. Stefanów, SVD, General Secretary
Membership: 344 in 126 countries
Activities: Workshops; Plenary Assembly
Affiliation(s): Catholic Biblical Association of Canada

Catholic Centre for Immigrants - Ottawa + CIC Foundation / Centre Catholique pour Immigrants - Ottawa + Fondation du CCI
219 Argyle Ave., Ottawa ON K2P 2H4
Tel: 613-232-9634; *Fax:* 613-232-3660
cic@cic.ca
cciottawa.ca
Also Known As: CCI Ottawa
Previous Name: Catholic Immigration Centre + CIC Foundation
Overview: A medium-sized national organization founded in 1984
Chief Officer(s):
Carl Nicolson, Executive Director, 613-232-9634 335
carl@cic.ca
Fees: $10; *Member Profile:* All Canadian residents

Catholic Charismatic Renewal Council, Toronto (CCRC)
830 Bathurst St., Toronto ON M5R 3G1
Tel: 416-466-0776; *Fax:* 905-454-0876
ccrctoronto@bellnet.ca
www.ccrctor.com
www.facebook.com/284998491631113
twitter.com/CCRCToronto
Also Known As: Catholic Charismatic Renewal
Overview: A small local organization
Chief Officer(s):
Matthias Yaw Kotoka Amuzu, Spiritual & Formation Institute Director
Pauline Susanto, Executive Secretary
Activities: Life in The Spirit seminars; The Holy Eucharistic Devotions; Healing services; Evangelization; Devotional workshops; Special rallies & conferences
Description: To stress the Lordship of Jesus through promoting baptism of the Holy Spirit; Affiliation(s): Archdiocese of Toronto

Catholic Charities of The Archdiocese of Toronto
#400, 1155 Yonge St., Toronto ON M4T 1W2
Tel: 416-934-3401; *Fax:* 416-934-3402
info@catholiccharitiestor.org
www.catholiccharitiestor.org
twitter.com/charitiescares
Previous Name: Council of Catholic Charities
Overview: A medium-sized local licensing charitable organization founded in 1913
Chief Officer(s):
Thomas Cardinal Collins, Chair
Carmela Pallotto, President
Michael Fullan, Executive Director
Finances: *Annual Operating Budget:* $250,000-$500,000
Staff: 1 staff member(s); 10 volunteer(s)
Activities: *Speaker Service:* Yes
Description: To ensure the provision of health & social sciences; To provide leadership & advocacy on behalf of member agencies & those in need; To serve people living & working throughout the Greater Toronto Area, as well as in Simcoe, Durham, Peel, & York; Affiliation(s): Catholic Family Services of Toronto & 26 member agencies

Catholic Children's Aid Society of Hamilton (CCAS)
735 King St. East, Hamilton ON L8M 1A1
Tel: 905-525-2012; *Fax:* 905-525-5606
www.youtube.com/channel/UCfl8rgJy4r8oMcepjfErppw/feed
www.facebook.com/hamiltonccas
twitter.com/HamiltonCCAS
Overview: A small local charitable organization founded in 1954
Chief Officer(s):
Ersilia DiNardo, Executive Director
Finances: *Annual Operating Budget:* Greater than $5 Million;
Funding Sources: Ontario Trillium Foundation; Donations
Staff: 191 volunteer(s)
Membership: 100-499
Activities: Providing foster care & adoption services,
Investigating possible instances of child abuse & neglect;
Awareness Events: Serendipity Auction, Nov.; *Internships:* Yes;
Speaker Service: Yes
Description: To provide child welfare & family services to the
Hamilton community; To ensure that services are guided by
Catholic values; *Member of:* Ontario Association of Children's
Aid Societies; *Affiliation(s):* Council of Catholic Service
Organziations

Catholic Children's Aid Society of Toronto (CCAS)
26 Maitland St., Toronto ON M4Y 1C6
Tel: 416-395-1500; *Fax:* 416-395-1581
communications@torontoccas.org
www.ccas.toronto.on.ca
Previous Name: Catholic Children's Aid Society of Metropolitan
Toronto
Overview: A medium-sized local charitable organization
founded in 1894
Chief Officer(s):
Janice Robinson, Executive Director
Finances: *Funding Sources:* Provincial government; Private
donations
Activities: Offering resources for individuals to report child
abuse & neglect; Providing counselling services for children,
adults, families, & immigrants; *Awareness Events:* Child Abuse
Prevention Campaign
Description: To provide social services that protect children,
strengthen family life & are reflective of Catholic values; *Member
of:* Catholic Charities of the Archdiocese of Toronto; *Affiliation(s):*
Ministry of Children and Youth Services

Catholic Civil Rights League (CCRL)
2305 Bloor St. West, Toronto ON M6S 1P1
Tel: 416-466-8244; *Fax:* 416-466-0091
Toll-Free: 844-722-2275
ccrl.ca
www.youtube.com/user/CatholicCivilRights
www.facebook.com/CatholicCivilRightsLeagueCCRL
twitter.com/CCRLtweets
Overview: A medium-sized national organization founded in
1985
Chief Officer(s):
Christian D. Elia, Executive Director
celia@ccrl.ca
Finances: *Funding Sources:* Donations
Activities: Advocating with government & media
Description: To be witness for church teaching in public life; To
combat anti-Catholic defamation in the media; To participate in
debates on public policy; *Affiliation(s):* Archdiocese of Toronto

Catholic Cross Cultural Services (CCS)
#401, 55 Town Centre Ct., Toronto ON M1P 4X4
Tel: 416-757-7010; *Fax:* 416-757-7399
communications@cathcrosscultural.org
www.cathcrosscultural.org
www.linkedin.com/company/catholic-crosscultural-services
www.facebook.com/CCSNewcomers
twitter.com/CCSNewcomers
Previous Name: Catholic Immigration Bureau
Overview: A medium-sized national charitable organization
founded in 1954
Chief Officer(s):
Agnes Thomas, Executive Director, 416-757-7010 2308
Finances: *Annual Operating Budget:* Greater than $5 Million
Staff: 238 staff member(s); 20 volunteer(s)
Fees: $5 individual; $10 organization
Description: To promote the settlement & integration of
immigrants & refugees facing linguistic & cultural barriers
through the provision of community based services; *Affiliation(s):*
Access for New Canadians

Catholic Education Foundation of Ontario (CEFO)
80 Sheppard Ave. East, Toronto ON M2N 6E8
Tel: 416-229-5326; *Fax:* 416-229-5345
office@cefontario.ca
cefontario.ca
www.facebook.com/catholiceducationfoundationontario

Overview: A small provincial charitable organization founded in
1976
Chief Officer(s):
Mary Eileen Donovan, President
president@cefontario.ca
Description: To foster & promote the principles of Catholic
education; to support parents in their role as primary educators;
to assist the Church in its pastoral responsibilities to the schools;
to encourage the establishment of Catholic schools; to promote
equity of educational funding in Ontario

Catholic Family Service of Ottawa (CFS Ottawa) / Service familial catholique d'Ottawa (SFC Ottawa)
310 Olmstead St., Ottawa ON K1L 7K3
Tel: 613-233-8478; *Fax:* 613-233-9881
info@cfsottawa.ca
www.cfsottawa.ca
Previous Name: Catholic Family Service of Ottawa-Carleton
Overview: A small local charitable organization founded in 1940
Chief Officer(s):
Isabelle Massip, President
Franca DiDiomete, Executive Director
Finances: *Annual Operating Budget:* $1.5 Million-$3 Million;
Funding Sources: Provincial/municipal government; United Way;
private donations
Staff: 34 staff member(s); 15 volunteer(s)
Membership: 50
Activities: *Internships:* Yes *Library:* Yes (Open to Public)
Description: CFS Ottawa offers a range of social services in
English & French to all residents of the Ottawa-Carleton area.
Services include counselling, support to the victims or witnesses
of family violence or sexual abuse, advocacy, community
development. It is a registered charity, BN: 118841105RR0001.;
Member of: Family Service Canada

Catholic Family Services of Hamilton (CFS)
#201, 447 Main St. East, Hamilton ON L8N 1K1
Tel: 905-527-3823; *Fax:* 905-546-5779
Toll-Free: 877-527-3823
intake@cfshw.com
www.cfshw.com
www.youtube.com/channel/UCeLsGYd3vHt5PGRkS8JJFjA
www.linkedin.com/company/Catholic-family-services-of-hamilton
www.facebook.com/Catholic.Family.Services.Hamilton
twitter.com/CFSHW
Previous Name: Catholic Family Services of
Hamilton-Wentworth
Overview: A small local organization founded in 1944
Chief Officer(s):
Linda Dayler, Executive Director & Secretary
Paula Forbes, Associate Director
Finances: *Funding Sources:* Government of Canada; Province
of Ontario; City of Hamilton; United Way of Burlington & Greater
Hamilton; Foundations such as ON Trillium Foundation
Activities: Offering programs, such as the Employee Assistance
Program, Debt Management Program, K.I.D.S. (Kids in Divorced
/ Separated Situations), Men's Anti-Violence & Abuse Program,
& the Senior's Intervention & Support Program; Providing
mediation services, in areas such as the workplace, credit,
estates, & commerce; Offering consumer credit education to the
general public; Offering money management coaching
Description: To provide individual, marriage, family, & credit
counselling services in the Hamilton & Burlington communities;
Member of: Ontario Association of Credit Counselling Service;
Affiliation(s): Ontario Community Support Association;
ONTCHILD; Family Services Ontario; Canadian Association for
Community Care; Continuing Gerontological Education
Cooperative; Older Persons' Mental Health & Addictions
Network; Ontario Association on Developmental Disabilities;
Ontario Case Managers Association; Ontario Gerontology
Association; Ontario Partnership on Aging Development
Disabilities

Catholic Family Services of Peel Dufferin (CFSPD)
Emerald Centre, #400, 10 Kingsbridge Garden Circle,
Mississauga ON L5R 3K6
Tel: 905-450-1608; *Fax:* 905-897-2467
info@cfspd.com
www.cfspd.com
www.facebook.com/208938825992
Previous Name: Peel Dufferin Catholic Services
Overview: A small local charitable organization founded in 1981
Chief Officer(s):
Ana Hill, Manager, Operations, 905-450-1608 404
anahill@cfspd.com
Finances: *Annual Operating Budget:* $500,000-$1.5 Million
Staff: 30 staff member(s); 85 volunteer(s)
Activities: Individual, couple & family therapy; support groups;
workshops; *Internships:* Yes; *Speaker Service:* Yes
Description: CFSPD is a multi-service counselling agency that
supports families coping with difficulties, notably violence,

trauma & abuse. Services are available in many languages to
help people deal with such problems as depression, anxiety,
grief, marital difficulties, parent-child conflict, developmental
transitions & cultural adjustments. Offices in Mississauga &
Brampton have walk-in clinics. The Society is a registered
charity, BN: 119087823RR0001.; *Member of:* Catholic Charities;
Archdiocese of Toronto; United Way of Peel Region

Catholic Family Services of Saskatoon (CFS)
#200, 506 25th St. East, Saskatoon SK S7K 4A7
Tel: 306-244-7773; *Fax:* 306-244-8537
staff@cfssaskatoon.sk.ca
www.cfssaskatoon.sk.ca
Overview: A small local charitable organization founded in 1940
Chief Officer(s):
Trish St. Onge, Executive Director
Finances: *Annual Operating Budget:* $500,000-$1.5 Million;
Funding Sources: Provincial & regional governments; United
Way; Diocese of Saskatoon; community grants & donations
Staff: 50 volunteer(s)
Membership: 1-99
Activities: Counselling; family & children's services; teen parent
program; family to family ties program; families & schools
together program; employee & family assistance prgrams,
marriage preparation, work & family wellness presentations;
event speakers; workshop presentations & consultations;
Library: Yes (Open to Public)
Description: To promote quality of life by developing &
supporting the inherent strengths of individuals, families & the
community; *Member of:* United Way of Saskatoon; *Affiliation(s):*
Family Service Canada; Family Service Saskatchewan

Catholic Family Services of Simcoe County (CFSSC)
20 Anne St. S, Barrie ON L4N 2C6
Tel: 705-726-2503; *Fax:* 705-726-2570
info@cfssc.ca
www.cfssc.ca
www.facebook.com/CFSSC
twitter.com/CounselorSimcoe
Previous Name: Catholic Family Life Centre-Simcoe South;
North Simcoe Catholic Family Life Centre
Overview: A small local charitable organization founded in 1979
Chief Officer(s):
Michelle Bergin, Executive Director
mbergin@cfssc.ca
Finances: *Annual Operating Budget:* $250,000-$500,000;
Funding Sources: Charities; United Way
Staff: 20 staff member(s)
Membership: 1-99
Activities: Family, individual & group counselling; family life
education
Description: To offer professional social services to all
residents of Simcoe South; services will be directed to the
treatment of troubled families & individuals, as well as to
strengthening & enriching family life & individual functioning in all
their dimensions & contexts

Catholic Family Services of Toronto (CFS Toronto) / Services familiaux catholiques de Toronto
Catholic Pastoral Centre, #200, 1155 Yonge St., Toronto ON
M4T 1W2
Tel: 416-921-1163; *Fax:* 416-921-1579
info@cfstoronto.com
www.cfstoronto.com
Previous Name: Catholic Welfare Bureau
Overview: A medium-sized local charitable organization
founded in 1922
Chief Officer(s):
Ivana Zanardo, President
Denis Costello, Executive Director & Secretary
Finances: *Annual Operating Budget:* $1.5 Million-$3 Million
Staff: 35 staff member(s); 18 volunteer(s)
Activities: *Library:* Yes
Description: To help individuals & families develop their
potential by providing wellness programs & treatment services;
Member of: Catholic Charities of the Archdiocese of Toronto;
Affiliation(s): Family Service Canada; Family Service Ontario

The Catholic Foundation of Manitoba / Fondation catholique du Manitoba
622 Taché Ave., Winnipeg MB R2H 2B4
Tel: 204-233-4268
cfmb@mts.net
catholicfoundation.mb.ca
Overview: A medium-sized provincial organization founded in
1964
Chief Officer(s):
Tom Lussier, President
Description: The vision of the Catholic Foundation is to provide
for the needy, better the situation of the underprivileged,
promote cultural advancement and scientific research, and
promote the cultural life of the Catholic community of Manitoba

by encouraging the funding of endowments and by providing prudent management of funds and responsible distribution of the derived revenue

Catholic Health Alliance of Canada / Alliance catholique canadienne de la santé
Annex C, Saint-Vincent Hospital, 60 Cambridge St. North, Ottawa ON K1R 7A5

www.chac.ca

Previous Name: Catholic Health Association of Canada; Catholic Hospital Association of Canada
Overview: A large national charitable organization founded in 1939
Chief Officer(s):
Michael Shea, President & CEO, 780-781-4075
shea.chac@gmail.com
Finances: *Annual Operating Budget:* $1.5 Million-$3 Million; *Funding Sources:* Membership dues
Membership: 12 sponsor organizations; *Fees:* Schedule available; *Member Profile:* Sponsor organizations of Catholic health care in Canada
Description: To strengthen & support the ministry of Catholic health care organizations & providers, through advocacy & governance; *Member of:* Quality End-of-Life Care Coalition of Canada

Catholic Health Association of British Columbia (CHABC)
9387 Holmes St., Burnaby BC V3N 4C3

Tel: 604-524-3427; *Fax:* 604-524-3428
info@chabc.bc.ca
chabc.bc.ca

Overview: A medium-sized provincial organization founded in 1940
Chief Officer(s):
Robert Breen, Executive Director
Membership: 114; *Fees:* $50 persona; $75 family; $160 associate; *Committees:* Mission Intergration; Pastral Care; Ethics
Description: To be witness to the healing ministry & abiding presence of Jesus; *Member of:* Catholic Health Alliance of Canada; Health Employers Association of British Columbia; *Affiliation(s):* Euthanasia Prevention Coalition; Canadian Association of Parish Nurse Ministries

Catholic Health Association of Manitoba (CHAM) / Association catholique manitobaine de la santé (ACMS)
SBGH Education Bldg., 409 Taché Ave., #N5067, Winnipeg MB R2H 2A6

Tel: 204-235-3136; *Fax:* 204-235-3811
www.cham.mb.ca

Overview: A medium-sized provincial charitable organization founded in 1943
Chief Officer(s):
Wilmar Chopyk, Executive Director
wchopyk@cham.mb.ca
Fees: $20 personal; $100 associate; *Member Profile:* Organizations; Health care facilities; Individuals
Activities: Promoting collaboration in health care services; Providing education to health care professionals, parish workers & volunteers; Engaging in advocacy activities for the needs of the vulnerable & disadvantaged; Promoting the dignity & sacredness of each person; *Awareness Events:* CHAC World Day of the Sick
Description: To carry out the healing ministry of the Catholic Church in the delivery of both health & social services in Manitoba; To treat the people of Manitoba with compassion & respect for all; To recognize the spiritual dimension integral to health & healing; *Member of:* Catholic Health Alliance of Canada; *Affiliation(s):* Bishops of Manitoba; Diocese of Churchill-Hudson Bay, Northwest Territories

Catholic Health Association of New Brunswick (CHANB) / L'Association catholique de la santé du Nouveau-Brunswick
1710 Water St., Miramichi NB E1N 1B4

Tel: 506-778-5302; *Fax:* 506-778-5303
catholichealth@chpchi.com
www.chanb.com

Overview: A small provincial organization founded in 1986
Chief Officer(s):
Robert Stewart, Executive Director
Membership: 300
Description: To promote health care in the tradition of the Catholic Church; *Member of:* Catholic Health Alliance of Canada

Catholic Health Association of Saskatchewan (CHAS)
1702 - 20 St. West, Saskatoon SK S7M 0Z9

Tel: 306-655-5330; *Fax:* 306-655-5333
cath.health@chassk.ca
www.chassk.ca

Overview: A medium-sized provincial charitable organization founded in 1943
Chief Officer(s):
Chris Donald, President
Sandra Kary, Executive Director
sandra@chassk.ca
Terrie Michaud, Vice-President
Anne Reddekopp, Secretary-Treasurer
Sandy Normand, Coordinator, Mission Education
snormand@chassk.ca
Fees: $25 individual; $75 association; *Member Profile:* Institutions, groups & individuals who are interested in Catholic health care & support the work of the association
Activities: Providing education & resources to members; Offering programs, such as the Parish Home Ministry of Care Program & the Catholic Health Leadership Program; Engaging in advocacy activities with the government; Providing both provincial & national networking opportunities; *Awareness Events:* Mission Week; World Day of the Sick *Library:* Catholic Health Association of Saskatchewan Resource Library
Description: To provide leadership in mission, ethics, spiritual care & social justice in Saskatchewan; To promote the sanctity of life & the dignity of all; *Member of:* Catholic Health Alliance of Canada

Catholic Health Sponsors of Ontario
#1801, 1 Yonge St., Toronto ON M5E 1W7

Tel: 416-740-0444
chco@chco.ca
www.chco.ca

Overview: A medium-sized provincial organization
Chief Officer(s):
Beth Johnson, President & CEO
Beth.Johnson@chco.ca
Description: To sponsor member institutions & strengthen Catholic health care in Ontario

Catholic Missions in Canada (CMIC) / Missions catholiques au Canada
#201, 1155 Yonge St., Toronto ON M4T 1W2

Tel: 416-934-3424; *Fax:* 416-934-3425
Toll-Free: 866-937-2642
info@cmic.info
cmic.info
www.instagram.com/missionscanada
www.facebook.com/canadianmissions
twitter.com/canadamissions

Also Known As: Catholic Missions
Previous Name: Catholic Church Extension Society of Canada
Overview: A large national charitable organization founded in 1908
Chief Officer(s):
David Reilander, President
presidentdr@cmic.info
Finances: *Annual Operating Budget:* $3 Million-$5 Million; *Funding Sources:* Donations; Fundraising
Staff: 11 staff member(s)
Membership: 26 mission dioceses; *Committees:* Executive; Allocations; Finance; Nominating
Activities: Supporting over 600 missionaries who serve in home mission communities throughout Canada; Raising funds for religious education programs, leadership programs, church repair & evangelization efforts; *Speaker Service:* Yes
Description: To keep the Catholic faith in remote & poor communities throughout Canada; To raise awareness of the needs of Canadian missions; *Member of:* Association of Fundraising Professionals (Toronto); Canadian Association of Gift Planners

The Catholic Principals' Council of Ontario (CPCO)
PO Box 2325, #3030, 2300 Yonge St., Toronto ON M4P 1E4

Tel: 416-483-1556; *Fax:* 416-483-2554
Toll-Free: 888-621-9190
info@cpco.on.ca
www.cpco.on.ca
www.youtube.com/cpcotoronto
www.linkedin.com/company/1206013
twitter.com/CPCO2012

Overview: A small provincial organization
Chief Officer(s):
Paul Lacalamita, Executive Director
placalamita@cpco.on.ca
Randy Bissonnette, President
president@cpco.on.ca
Finances: *Annual Operating Budget:* $1.5 Million-$3 Million
Staff: 6 staff member(s); 6 volunteer(s)

Membership: 2,000 members who are principals & vice-principals in more than 1,300 elementary & secondary separate schools across Ontario; *Committees:* Communications; Member Security; Professional Development; Finance; Issues in Catholic Education
Activities: Advocacy, professional development; legal services; *Speaker Service:* Yes
Description: CPCO is a voluntary, professional association that serves more than 2,100 principals & vice-principals in twenty-nine Catholic school boards across Ontario

Catholic Teachers Guild of Toronto
#909, 21 Maynard Ave., Toronto ON M6K 2Z8

www.torontocatholicteachersguild.com

Overview: A small provincial organization founded in 2000
Chief Officer(s):
Andrew Hume, President
Rado Krevs, Vice-President
Leeda Crawford, Treasurer
Finances: *Funding Sources:* Donations
Fees: $10 renewal fee; $20 initial fee; *Member Profile:* Active or retired Catholics involved in education at any level, including pre-school & post-secondary, who support the mission of the Guild; Catholic lay educators & volunteers who work in Catholic schools, public schools, private schools & other educational institutions
Activities: Holding an Annual Education Mass & Lenten Retreat; Presenting lectures & workshops; Conducting book club meetings
Description: To support & strengthen the vocation of teaching in the tradition of the Catholic; *Affiliation(s):* Archdiocese of Toronto

Catholic Women's League of Canada (CWL)
702C Scotland Ave., Winnipeg MB R3M 1X5

Tel: 204-927-2310; *Fax:* 204-927-2321
info@cwl.ca
cwl.ca
www.facebook.com/374698529280233

Overview: A large national organization founded in 1920
Chief Officer(s):
Kim Scammell, Executive Director
executivedirector@cwl.ca
Katherine Choi, Coordinator, Membership
membership@cwl.ca
Finances: *Funding Sources:* Donations
Staff: 6 staff member(s)
Membership: Over 50,000; *Member Profile:* Catholic women over sixteen years of age who wish to serve within their communities
Description: To help members live holier lives; To grow in relationship with Christ & the church; To carry out the work of Christ in the community & in the world; To serve the people of God; To ensure local leagues within Archdiocesan Parishes report to regional & provincial councils & follow the constitution & bylaws of the CWL

Catholic Youth Studio - KSM Inc. (KSM)
183 Roncesvalles Ave., 2nd Fl., Toronto ON M6R 2L5

Tel: 416-588-0555; *Fax:* 416-588-9995
radio@catholicradio.ca
www.catholicradio.ca
www.facebook.com/KSMRADIO
twitter.com/KSMRADIO

Also Known As: Catholic Radio Toronto
Overview: A small local charitable organization founded in 1994
Chief Officer(s):
Marcin Serwin, Director
Finances: *Funding Sources:* Donations
Staff: 4 staff member(s); 50 volunteer(s)
Member Profile: Individuals who donate their talents & time at Catholic Youth Studio - KSM Inc., a media corporation for evangelization, in order to promote the Christian faith; Members are both youth & adults who share the Catholic Youth Studio's charism
Activities: Programming for youth, couples, & seniors; Providing faith instruction; *Awareness Events:* International Festival of Religious Song
Description: To reach those who have not yet experienced their "springtime of faith", by means of evangelization through modern forms of mass media; to broadcast a daily radio program, eleven hours per week in Polish, & to publish a magazine, in order to provide services to families; *Affiliation(s):* Archdiocese of Toronto

Congrégation de Sainte-Croix - Les Frères de Sainte-Croix / Congregation of Holy Cross
4901, rue du Piedmont, Montréal QC H3V 1E3

Tél: 514-731-7828; *Téléc:* 514-731-7820
saintecroixcsc@yahoo.ca
www.ste-croix.qc.ca

Aperçu: *Dimension:* petite; *Envergure:* locale

Description: Congrégation religieuse catholique qui oeuvre en éducation, en milieu paroissial et dans divers autres secteurs de la société

Congrégation des Soeurs de Sainte-Anne / Congregation of Sisters of Saint Anne
1754, rue Provost, Lachine QC H8S 1P1

Tél: 514-637-1809
accueil@ssacong.org
www.ssacong.org

Aperçu: *Dimension:* petite; *Envergure:* internationale; *Organisme sans but lucratif; fondée en 1850*
Membre(s) du bureau directeur:
Marie Ellen King, Supérieure générale
Madeleine Lanoue, Secrétaire générale
Finances: *Budget de fonctionnement annuel:* $100,000-$250,000
Description: Impliquée dans l'éducation, les soins de santé, l'animation pastorale et sociale en divers milieux

Congrégation des Soeurs de Saint-Joseph de Saint-Vallier (SSJ)
860, av Louis-Fréchette, Québec QC G1S 3N3

Tél: 418-683-9653; *Téléc:* 418-681-8781
Nom précédent: Soeurs de Saint-Joseph de Saint-Vallier
Aperçu: *Dimension:* petite; *Envergure:* locale; *fondée en 1683*
Membre(s) du bureau directeur:
Jeanne d'Arc Auclair, Supérieure générale
Membre: 165

Congregation of Missionaries of the Precious Blood, Atlantic Province
100 Pelmo Cres., Toronto ON M9N 2Y1

Tel: 416-531-4423
preciousbloodatlantic.org

Overview: A small provincial charitable organization founded in 1987
Chief Officer(s):
Mario Cafarelli, Provincial Director
Description: To be rooted in the word of God & reach out to the marginalized

Congregation of St. Basil (CSB)
95 St. Joseph St., Toronto ON M5S 3C2

Tel: 416-921-6674
vocation@basilian.org
www.basilian.org
www.youtube.com/user/cavalka124
www.facebook.com/TheBasilians
twitter.com/TheBasilians

Also Known As: Basilian Fathers
Overview: A small international organization founded in 1822
Chief Officer(s):
George Smith, Superior General
David Katulski, Vicar General
Finances: *Annual Operating Budget:* Less than $50,000
Staff: 3 volunteer(s)
Membership: 325; *Member Profile:* Priests; Students for the priesthood
Activities: *Library:* Congregation of St. Basil Library by appointment
Description: Roman Catholic congregation of priests whose primary apostolate is education, parishes & Hispanic ministry in Canada, USA, Mexico, Colombia & France; *Member of:* RC Church

Council of Catholic School Superintendents of Alberta (CCSSA)
21 Walters Place, Leduc AB T9E 8S7

Tel: 780-913-0194
www.ccssa.ca
www.facebook.com/NCRegister
twitter.com/acstanews

Overview: A small provincial organization
Chief Officer(s):
Jamie McNamara, Executive Director, 780-913-0194
Membership: 35
Description: To provide a forum for discussion regarding the direction & development of Catholic Education in Alberta

Covenant Health (ACHC)
3033 - 66 St. NW, Edmonton AB T6K 4B2

Tel: 780-735-9000
www.covenanthealth.ca

Previous Name: Catholic Health of Alberta
Overview: A small provincial organization
Chief Officer(s):
Patrick Dumelie, CEO
Owen Heisler, Vice President & Chief Medical Officer, Medicine
Rosa Rudelich, Vice President & Chief Operating Officer
Karen Galenzoski, Vice President & Human Resources Officer
Gordon Self, Vice President, Mission, Ethics & Spirituality

Membership: 12 Catholic health care facilities
Description: To be a part of the healing mission of Jesus by serving with compassion

Cursillo Movement of the Archdiocese of Toronto
PO Box 58021, 500 Rossland Rd. West, Oshawa ON L1J 8L6
www.cursillotoronto.org

Overview: A small local charitable organization
Chief Officer(s):
Terrence McKenna, Spiritual Director
Member Profile: Men & women who desire to encounter themselves, Christ, & others, & to transform this encounter into friendship with Christ & others
Activities: Spreading faith in all environments; Offering Linguistic Cursillo Groups (Chinese, French, Hungarian, Korean, Spanish, & Vietnamese) in the Archdiocese of Toronto; Providing faith instruction & renewal programs; Sharing prayer life & apostolic activities
Description: To discover & understand, in a profound & intense way, God's deep love; To share this belief in the everyday environment, particularly with those who are distant from the Christian faith & the Church; *Affiliation(s):* Archdiocese of Toronto

Dignity Canada Dignité
PO Box 2102, Stn. D, Ottawa ON K1P 5W3

Tel: 613-746-7281
info@dignitycanada.org
www.dignitycanada.org
www.facebook.com/groups/253558468022157
Overview: A medium-sized national organization
Chief Officer(s):
Frank Testin, President
president@dignitycanada.org
Norman Prince, Secretary
Finances: *Funding Sources:* Donations
Activities: Encouraging spiritual development, education, & social involvement
Description: To voice the concerns of Roman Catholic sexual minorities; To promote the development of sexual theology, justice & acceptance of the lesbian & gay community; To reinforce a sense of dignity & to encourage gay men & lesbian women to become more active members in the Church & society

Dignity Toronto Dignité
175 Windermere Ave., Toronto ON M6S 3J8

Tel: 416-925-9872
toronto@dignitycanada.org
dignitycanada.org/toronto.html
www.facebook.com/dignitytoronto
Overview: A small local organization founded in 1974
Chief Officer(s):
Frank Testin, President
president@dignitycanada.org
Finances: *Annual Operating Budget:* Less than $50,000
Membership: 20; *Fees:* $30
Activities: Monthly liturgical meeting to support gay & lesbian Roman Catholics; social gatherings
Description: To support & affirm gay & lesbian Roman Catholics through spiritual development, education, social involvement, equity issues, & social events; *Member of:* Dignity Canada Dignité

Dignity Vancouver Dignité
PO Box 3016, Stn. Terminal, Vancouver BC V6B 3X5

vancouver@dignitycanada.org
dignitycanada.org/vancouver.html
Overview: A small local organization founded in 1977
Chief Officer(s):
Kevin Simpson, Treasurer, 604-874-3428
treasurer@dignitycanada.org
Finances: *Annual Operating Budget:* Less than $50,000
Membership: 12; *Fees:* $35 individual; *Member Profile:* Roman Catholic gays, lesbians, friends
Description: The organization works within the Catholic Church & with other Catholic groups to reform the church's theological stance pertaining to sexual minorities. It supports gay & lesbian Catholics & their friends, encouraging participation in educational, spiritual, & social activities.; *Member of:* Dignity Canada Dignité

Dignity Winnipeg Dignité
PO Box 1912, Winnipeg MB R3C 3R2

Tel: 204-779-6446
winnipeg@dignitycanada.org
www.dignitycanada.org
Overview: A small provincial organization founded in 1970
Chief Officer(s):
Thomas Novak, National Chaplain, 204-287-8583
Finances: *Annual Operating Budget:* Less than $50,000
Staff: 3 volunteer(s)

Membership: 20; *Fees:* $25 (optional); *Member Profile:* LGBT community; non-gay men & women, encompassing a broad spectrum of professions, political beliefs, ethnic & linguistic backgrounds & economic levels
Activities: Regular liturgies/discussion groups; annual retreat; social events; brochures; *Speaker Service:* Yes
Description: To bring together gay & lesbian Catholics & their friends; To encourage a process of self-understanding & personal integration with respect to issues, including spirituality & sexuality; *Member of:* Dignity Canada Dignité

Emmaus Canada
emmauscanada@sympatico.ca
www3.sympatico.ca/pcmax
Overview: A small national organization
Chief Officer(s):
Claude Sam-Foh, Chair
Loretta Liu, Treasurer
Paul McAuley, Spiritual Director
Description: To deepen & nurture members' faith; *Affiliation(s):* Archdiocese of Toronto

English Speaking Catholic Council (ESCC) / Conseil catholique d'expression anglaise
1857, boul de Maisonneuve ouest, Montréal QC H3H 1J9

Tel: 514-937-2301; *Fax:* 514-907-5010
escc@bellnet.ca
www.catholiccouncil.ca
Overview: A small local charitable organization founded in 1981
Chief Officer(s):
Anna Farrow, Executive Director
Finances: *Annual Operating Budget:* $100,000-$250,000
Staff: 2 staff member(s); 13 volunteer(s)
Activities: Organizing community events; Promoting research; Offering education
Description: To represent Montréal's English-speaking Catholic community; *Member of:* Quebec Community Network Group

Eucharistic Apostles of the Divine Mercy (EADM)
c/o Rolando & Susan Dela Rosa, 49 Parsons Pl., Thornhill ON L4J 7Y4

Tel: 647-239-9350
www.thedivinemercy.org
Also Known As: EADM Cenacle Prayer Group of Toronto
Overview: A small local organization
Chief Officer(s):
Mario Salvadori, Spiritual Director
Activities: Meetings; youth retreat
Description: To encourage members to care for the rejected, the lonely, the disabled, the elderly, & the dying; *Affiliation(s):* Archdiocese of Toronto

Family of the Immaculate Heart of Mary
368 Melville Ave., Maple ON L6A 2N8

Tel: 905-832-1893; *Fax:* 905-832-3954
Overview: A small local organization founded in 2007
Chief Officer(s):
Solidea Didonato, Contact
Activities: Parish missions; spiritual exercises; worship
Description: To serve God & promote the Roman Catholic Faith; *Affiliation(s):* Archdiocese of Toronto

Family Prayer Mission (Ontario) (FPM)
2478 Callum Ave., Mississauga ON L5B 2H9

Tel: 905-896-2854
familyprayer@sympatico.ca
www.familyprayermission.com
Overview: A small local charitable organization founded in 1989
Chief Officer(s):
Rappai Nedumpara, President
Fees: $15
Activities: Retreats
Description: To strengthen family bonds through prayer & worship; *Affiliation(s):* Archdiocese of Toronto

Federation of North American Explorers (FNE)
c/o Paul Ritchi, 43 Bluesky Cres., Richmond Hill ON L4C 8J2

Tel: 416-435-6593
info@fneexplorers.com
www.fneexplorers.com
www.youtube.com/user/FNEExp
www.facebook.com/FNEExplorers
twitter.com/PaulRitchi
Also Known As: FN Explorers
Overview: A small local charitable organization founded in 1956
Chief Officer(s):
Paul Ritchi, General Commissioner & Founder
paul.ritchi@gmail.com
Tony D'Avanzo, President & Chairman
Finances: *Funding Sources:* Donations
Member Profile: Baptized Christian youth & adults, or individuals who are preparing to be baptized

Activities: Camping weekends, outdoor survival activities & community service; Earning badges by successfully completing certain activities
Description: To deliver traditional values to youth, from a Catholic faith perspective; *Member of:* International Union of European FSE Guides & Scouts (Union Internationale des Guides et Scouts d'Europe); Affiliation(s): Archdiocese of Toronto

Filipino Canadian Catholic Charismatic Prayer Communities (FCCCPC)
53 Belvedere Cres., Richmond Hill ON L4C 8VA
Tel: 416-903-3453
fcccpc@yahoo.ca
www.fcccpc.com
www.facebook.com/fcccpc
Overview: A small national organization founded in 1992
Chief Officer(s):
Bienvenido Ebcas, Jr., Spiritual Director
Don Quilao, Head Servant
cbquilao@rogers.com
Evelyn Abutan, Secretary
Caring Labindao, Treasurer
Membership: 10+ prayer communities; *Member Profile:* Individuals are members of a Catholic prayer community (majority of members are of Filipino heritage)
Activities: Counselling; Providing faith instruction & prayer groups; Offering renewal programs, general assemblies & fellowship; Presenting spiritual formation seminars
Description: To help Filipino charismatic communities & create a venue of consultation, discernment & counseling among community members; Affiliation(s): Archdiocese of Toronto

Foundation of Catholic Community Services Inc. (FCCS) / La Fondation des services communautaires catholiques inc.
1857, boul de Maisonneuve ouest, Montréal QC H3H 1J9
Tel: 514-934-1326; *Fax:* 514-934-0453
info@fccsmontreal.org
www.fccsmontreal.org
www.youtube.com/channel/UCSlZdslLG8cmtCqm_Es2ATQ
twitter.com/CCSMontreal
Previous Name: Catholic Community Services Inc.
Overview: A medium-sized local organization founded in 1974
Chief Officer(s):
Andrea Bobkowicz, President
Finances: *Annual Operating Budget:* $1.5 Million-$3 Million
Staff: 33 staff member(s); 1104 volunteer(s)
Membership: 65; *Fees:* $10
Activities: Youth groups; Home sharing; Administrative & support services; Community organization & development; Family support programs; Personal development & support groups; Camping services; Almage Senior Centre; Teapot Senior Centre; Good Shepherd Community Centre; Home Support Program; Volunteer coordination; Home Day Care Program; *Speaker Service:* Yes
Description: To provide a broad spectrum of social services on behalf of the English-speaking Catholic community of the Diocese of Montréal

Frères de Notre-Dame de la Miséricorde / Brothers of Our Lady of Mercy
1133, ch Tour du Lac Nord, Lac-Sergent QC G0A 2J0
Tél: 418-875-5216
crc-canada.org/communautes/freres-de-notre-dame-de-la-miseri
corde
Aperçu: *Dimension:* petite; *Envergure:* internationale; *Organisme sans but lucratif;* fondée en 1839
Finances: *Budget de fonctionnement annuel:* Moins de $50,000
Personnel: 1 membre(s) du personnel; 6 bénévole(s)
Membre: 9
Description: Rassembler des personnes en vue d'un travail apostolique auprès des jeunes et particulièrement auprès des personnes éprouvant des difficultés

Gethsemane Ministries
84008 Wellandport Rd., Wellandport ON L0R 2J0
Tel: 905-368-1111; *Fax:* 647-560-4557
info@gethsemaneministries.com
www.gethsemaneministries.com
www.instagram.com/gethsemaneministries
www.facebook.com/GethsemaneMinistriesCanada
twitter.com/GethYouthMin
Overview: A small local charitable organization founded in 1997
Chief Officer(s):
Stan Rodrigo, Contact
stan.rodrigo@gmail.com
Finances: *Funding Sources:* Donations
Fees: Free
Activities: Counselling; Providing faith instruction & spiritual guidance; Participating in sacramental life; Offering prayer groups, with Rosary, praise & worship, intercession & fellowship;

Assisting the ill, elderly & needy; Helping youth in their Catholic faith formation, including catechism classes for grades 1-8; Providing youth programs, retreats & summer camps; Offering retreats for married couples, mainly conducted by preachers; Supporting other parish & diocesan activities; Offering adult & youth music ministry
Description: To preach the Word of God & advance the teachings, religious tenets & observances associated with the Catholic Faith

IMCS Pax Romana / MIEC Pax Romana (MIEC)
7 Impasse Reille, Paris 75014 France
office@imcs-miec.org
imcs-miec.org
www.facebook.com/imcs.miec
twitter.com/PaxRomanaIMCS
Également appelé: International Movement of Catholic Students
Nom précédent: International Movement of Catholic Students; International Catholic Movement for Intellectual & Cultural Affairs
Aperçu: *Dimension:* grande; *Envergure:* internationale; fondée en 1921
Finances: *Budget de fonctionnement annuel:* $100,000-$250,000; *Fonds:* Donations; projects based funding
Personnel: 2 membre(s) du personnel; 8 bénévole(s)
Critères d'admissibilite: Students from tertiary institutions
Activité: Advocacy (consultative status with the United Nations Economic & Social Council, UNESCO & the European Council & has accredited representatives to those organisations in New York, Vienna, Paris, Geneve & Strasbourg); Trainings (summer schools, seminars, capacity buildings); Campaigns
Description: To empower students to be agents of transformation in their communities by providing holistic trainings & international experience; To engage in proactive dialogue between Christian faith & cultures in order to promote evangelization & the inculturation of the Gospel for the realization of the Kingdom of God; *Membre de:* United Nation Major Group for Children & Youth (UNMGCY); cofounder of ICMYO (International Coordination Meeting of Youth Organizations); International Specialised Catholic Action Movements (ISCAM); Affiliation(s): Mouvement d'étudiants chrétiens du Québec; Association of Canadian Catholic Students

Institut Voluntas Dei / Voluntas Dei Institute
7385, boul Parent, Trois-Rivières QC G9A 5E1
Tél: 819-375-7933; *Téléc:* 819-691-1841
ivd.cent@cgocable.ca
www.voluntasdei.org
www.youtube.com/voluntasdeis
www.facebook.com/voluntasdei
twitter.com/voluntasdei
Également appelé: I.V. Dei
Aperçu: *Dimension:* petite; *Envergure:* internationale; *Organisme sans but lucratif;* fondée en 1958
Membre(s) du bureau directeur:
Henri-Louis Parent, Founder
Finances: *Budget de fonctionnement annuel:* $100,000-$250,000
Personnel: 3 membre(s) du personnel
Membre: 974; *Critères d'admissibilite:* Baptised & consecrated people who live the evangelical counsels of obedience, poverty & chastity
Activités: *Stagiaires:* Oui
Description: To make known & communicate God's love for all to all people; To be present in every milieu; *Membre de:* Roman Catholic Church

International Catholic Deaf Association (ICDA)
www.icdacanadasection.wordpress.com
www.facebook.com/ICDACanadianSection
Also Known As: ICDA-Canada
Overview: A small international organization founded in 1949
Chief Officer(s):
Joe McLaughlin, President
Mari-Len Andrabado, Vice-President
John Shores, Treasurer
john.shores@ualberta.ca
Finances: *Annual Operating Budget:* Less than $50,000
Staff: 40 volunteer(s)
Member Profile: Practicing Catholics; deaf diaconates; lay ministries
Activities: National conference / workshop; Canadian Catholic Pastoral Workers for the Deaf meetings; fundraising; retreats; signed Mass; assists the Pastoral Workers, seminarians to learn sign languages; spreads the knowledge of the deaf culture among the hearing parishioners
Description: To promote religion, religious education, fellowship & leadership among deaf people of all ages; To promote in Canada & the ICDA various programs in foreign countries with a view to enhancing the life of deaf people

Jeunes canadiens pour une civilisation chrétienne
880, av Louis Fréchette, Québec QC G1S 3N3
Tél: 418-683-5222
Aperçu: *Dimension:* petite; *Envergure:* locale; fondée en 1977
Membre(s) du bureau directeur:
Frank R. Murphy, President
Finances: *Budget de fonctionnement annuel:* Moins de $50,000
Description: Travailler avec la jeunesse pour préserver les principes catholiques et éducatifs

Kolbe Eucharistic Apostolate
c/o St. Brigid's Church, 300 Wolverleigh Blvd., Toronto ON M4C 1S6
www.kolbeapostolate.com
Overview: A small local organization founded in 1996
Chief Officer(s):
Maria De Manche, Event Co-Coordinator & Animator
Therese De Manche, Event Co-Coordinator & Animator
Charles Anang, Spiritual Advisor
Member Profile: Any Catholic individual who lives in accordance with the teaching of the Catholic Church, & who wishes to deepen his or her knowledge of God
Activities: Developing faith formation; Providing mini-retreats, prayer groups, Bible study, & catechesis
Description: To make the Eucharistic Christ the heart of lives, through Eucharistic Adoration; Affiliation(s): Archdiocese of Toronto

Latin American Mission Program (LAMP)
81 Prince St., Charlottetown PE C1A 4R3
Tel: 902-368-7337; *Fax:* 902-368-7180
lamp@pei.sympatico.ca
www.dioceseofcharlottetown.com
Overview: A small international organization founded in 1967
Finances: *Annual Operating Budget:* $50,000-$100,000; *Funding Sources:* Share Lent collections taken up annually in all parishes
Membership: 20
Activities: Educational events; Orientation & support for missionaries
Description: To send out & receive back missionaries; To learn from the dispossessed & oppressed & to stand with them in building a society of justice; To develop & encourage a Faith response based on the life & struggle of dispossessed peoples; To participate in "return mission" by working with groups committed to social justice in Canada & developing education programs in PEI that analyze the causes of exploitation of the poor & expose the reality of their lives; Affiliation(s): Diocese of Charlottetown; Les missionnaires du Sacre-Coeur; Scarboro Foreign Mission Society

LAUDEM, L'Association des musiciens liturgiques du Canada
1085, rue de la Cathédrale, Montréal QC H3B 2V3
secretariat@laudem.org
www.laudem.org
www.facebook.com/laudemcanada
Nom précédent: L'Association des organistes liturgiques du Canada
Aperçu: *Dimension:* petite; *Envergure:* nationale; fondée en 1992
Membre(s) du bureau directeur:
Paul Cadrin, Président et directeur, Revue
Jean-Pierre Couturier, Vice-Président
Membre: 45
Description: De réunir les organistes liturgiques pour la promotion et le développement de leur ministère dans l'Église catholique romaine; *Membre de:* Fédération francophone des amis de l'orgue

Madonna House Apostolate
2888 Dafoe Rd., RR#2, Combermere ON K0J 1L0
Tel: 613-756-3713; *Fax:* 613-756-0211
combermere@madonnahouse.org
www.madonnahouse.org
www.youtube.com/MadonnaHouseCanada
www.facebook.com/MadonnaHouse
twitter.com/madonnahouse
Overview: A small national charitable organization founded in 1947
Chief Officer(s):
David Linder, Director General
Elizabeth Bassarear, Director General
Finances: *Funding Sources:* Donations
Membership: 200+; *Member Profile:* Christian lay men, women & priests who are dedicated to promises of poverty, chastity & obedience
Activities: Offering the Cana Colony summer program for families; Distributing goooods to the poor; Operating a gift shop, flea market & used book shop to raise funds
Affiliation(s): Roman Catholic Church; Diocese of Pembroke

Mary Undoer of Knots
#1, 271 Richvale Dr. South, Brampton ON L6Z 4W6
Tel: 905-495-4614
novena@maryundoerofknots.com
www.maryundoerofknots.com
Overview: A small local organization
Activities: Providing faith instruction; Offering prayer groups for youth, singles, & seniors
Description: To be devoted to Mary Undoer of Knots; To pray, as described in the Novena booklet, which is translated in 19 languages & Braille; Affiliation(s): Archdiocese of Toronto

Messagères de Notre-Dame de l'Assomption (MNDA)
#4, 45, rue de la Sapiniere-dorion, Québec QC G1L 1A3
Tél: 418-626-7492
Aperçu: *Dimension: petite; Envergure: locale; Organisme sans but lucratif; fondée en 1964*
Finances: *Budget de fonctionnement annuel:* $50,000-$100,000
Membre: 100-499

Militia of the Immaculata Canada (MI)
PO Box 22113, RPO Capri Centre, Kelowna BC V1Y 9N9
Tel: 905-686-1256
immaculatacanada@yahoo.com
www.consecration.ca
Overview: A small national organization founded in 1922
Member Profile: Members of the Militia of the Immaculata Canada live consecration in the Church, love the Church & recognize & profess their Catholic faith; Individuals are called to work with creativity & unity, while combining Church teaching, Kolbean inspiration & environmental concerns
Activities: Contributing in all areas in the form of catechesis, social work, humanitarian initiatives & cultural proposals; Participating in the apostolate of the Church, in the spirit of our Marian consecration
Description: To recognize the consecration to God through the Immaculata the primacy of vocation to sanctity; to bring together spiritual life & action; To live out its ecclesial dimension, by taking on pastoral programs of the bishops' conferences; To listen to the needs of the New Evangelization; Affiliation(s): Archdiocese of Toronto

Missionary Sisters of The Precious Blood of North America
St Bernard's Convent, 685 Finch Ave. West, Toronto ON M2R 1P2
Tel: 416-630-3298
www.preciousbloodsisters.com
www.facebook.com/PreciousBloodSisters
Overview: A small international organization founded in 1885
Chief Officer(s):
Monica Mary Ncube, Superior General
Finances: *Funding Sources:* donations
Staff: 60 staff member(s)
Description: To be devoted to missionary service regardless of language, people or nation

Morning Light Ministry
c/o St. Mary Star of the Sea Church, 11 Peter St. South, Mississauga ON L5H 2G1
Tel: 647-781-9300
morninglightministry@yahoo.ca
www.morninglightministry.org
www.facebook.com/139540882897810
Overview: A small local organization founded in 1996
Member Profile: Bereaved Catholic parents, as well as bereaved parents of other Christian denominations, other faiths & those with no religious affiliation who struggle with the notion of faith
Activities: Providing information at no cost; Counselling; Offering faith instruction; Providing support by e-mail, telephone, & individual & group meetings; Conducting an annual memorial Mass
Description: To provide Catholic ministry for bereaved parents who have experienced the death of a baby through ectopic pregnancy, miscarriage, stillbirth, or infant death up to two years of age; To help families who have received an adverse prenatal diagnosis; To offer suuport to couples who are experiencing infertility; Affiliation(s): Archdiocese of Toronto

Mouvement des femmes Chrétiennes (MFC)
Secrétariat nationale du MFC, #625, 1300, ch Ste-Foy, Québec QC G1S 0A6
Tél: 581-742-7176
sec.mfcnational@videotron.ca
www.mfcnational.net
Nom précédent: Fédération nationale du MFC - Mouvement des Femmes Chrétiennes
Aperçu: *Dimension: grande; Envergure: nationale; Organisme sans but lucratif; fondée en 1962*
Membre(s) du bureau directeur:
Anne-Marie Saint-Cour, Présidente

Finances: *Budget de fonctionnement annuel:* Moins de $50,000
Personnel: 1 membre(s) du personnel; 700 bénévoles(s)
Membre: 3 000; *Montant de la cotisation:* 15$; *Critères d'admissibilite:* Femmes de tout âge, condition et culture
Activités: Rencontre mensuelle sur le programme d'action; formation
Description: Un mouvement d'action catholique générale, il forme des femmes efficaces et dynamiques sur le plan familial, paroissial, social, et chrétien afin de transformer le milieu de vie par des projects concrets et en utilisant la méthode de l'action catholique; *Membre de:* Regroupement des Organismes Volontaires d'Éducation Populaire

Newman Centre Catholic Chaplaincy and Parish
89 St. George St., Toronto ON M5S 2E8
Tel: 416-979-2468; *Fax:* 416-596-6920
secretary@newmantoronto.com
www.newmantoronto.com
www.facebook.com/newmanchaplaincy
twitter.com/newmanuoft
Also Known As: The Newman Centre
Previous Name: Newman Foundation of Toronto
Overview: A small local charitable organization
Chief Officer(s):
James Milway, President
Peter Turrone, Executive Director
frpeterturrone@newmantoronto.com
Description: To maintain & support Roman Catholic chaplaincy on University of Toronto campus

Ontario Catholic Supervisory Officers' Association (OCSOA)
730 Courtneypark Dr. West, Mississauga ON L5W 1L9
Tel: 905-564-8206; *Fax:* 905-564-8210
ocsoa@ocsoa.ca
www.ocsoa.ca
www.facebook.com/CatholicEducationInOntario
twitter.com/catholicedu
Overview: A medium-sized provincial organization founded in 1967
Chief Officer(s):
John B. Kostoff, Executive Director
Laura Tonkovic, Executive Assistant
lauratonkovic@ocsoa.ca
Membership: 150 individual; 18 associate
Activities: Offer Catholic Community Delivery Organization (CCDO) Supervisory Officers' Qualifications Program (SOQP)
Description: To represent supervisory officers employed in Catholic school boards

Ontario English Catholic Teachers' Association (CLC) (OECTA)
#400, 65 St Clair Ave. East, Toronto ON M4T 2Y8
Tel: 416-925-2493; *Fax:* 416-925-7764
Toll-Free: 800-268-7230
contact@catholicteachers.ca
www.catholicteachers.ca
www.instagram.com/catholic_teachers
www.facebook.com/OECTA
twitter.com/OECTAProv
Overview: A large provincial organization founded in 1944
Chief Officer(s):
David Church, General Secretary
d.church@catholicteachers.ca
Membership: 45,000; *Committees:* Audit; Awards; Catholic Education & Curriculum; Collective Bargaining; Educational Aid; Finance; Health & Safety; Human Rights; Legislation; Long Term Disability; Member Engagement; Personnel; Program & Structures; Status of Women; Teacher Development; Teacher Education Network
Activities: *Library:* Resource Library
Description: To advance Catholic education; To provide professional services, support, protection & leadership; *Member of:* Canadian Teachers' Federation; Canadian Labour Congress; Ontario Federation of Labour; Affiliation(s): Ontario Teachers' Federation; Congress of Union Retirees of Canada; Education International

Order of Malta - Canadian Association / Ordre de Malte - Association Canadienne
The Sovereign Military Order of Malta - Canadian Association, #302, 1247 Kilborn Pl., Ottawa ON K1H 6K9
Tel: 613-731-8897; *Fax:* 613-731-1312
executivedirector@orderofmaltacanada.org
www.orderofmaltacanada.org
Also Known As: Sovereign Military Hospitaller Order of St. John of Jerusalem of Rhodes & of Malta - Canadian Association
Previous Name: Association of Canadian Knights of the Sovereign Military Order of Malta
Overview: A medium-sized national charitable organization founded in 1953
Chief Officer(s):

Andre Morin, President
Finances: *Annual Operating Budget:* $100,000-$250,000; *Funding Sources:* Donations
Staff: 1 staff member(s); 259 volunteer(s)
Membership: Over 12,500
Activities: Projects including: delivering food & warm outerwear to the homeless of Toronto; providing first aid coverage to visitors of the Basilica Notre Dame du Cap; volunteering at soup Kitchens in Ottawa & Montreal; helping provide eyeglasses to the poor in Vancouver
Description: To help the sick & the poor across Canada through the efforts of members & volunteers; Affiliation(s): Sovereign Military Order of Malta

Orthodox Church in America Archdiocese of Canada (OCA ADOC)
3441, av 15e, Rawdon QC J0K 1S0
Tel: 450-834-2870; *Fax:* 450-834-5471
office@archdiocese.ca
www.archdiocese.ca
www.facebook.com/canadianarchdiocese
Also Known As: Archdiocese of Canada
Previous Name: Russian Orthodox Greek Catholic Church (Metropolia)
Overview: A medium-sized international organization founded in 1902
Chief Officer(s):
Irénée Rochon, Archbishop, 450-834-2870
bishopirenee@archdiocese.ca
Phillip Eriksson, Chancellor
chancellor@archdiocese.ca
Membership: 86 communities
Member of: Canadian Council of Churches; Churches of Manitoba; Orthodox Clergy Association of Québec

Our Lady of Good Health Tamil Parish (OLGH)
Immaculate Heart of Mary Church, 131 Birchmount Rd., Toronto ON M1N 3J7
Tel: 416-264-6544
office@olghtamilparish.com
www.olghtamilparish.com
Overview: A small local charitable organization founded in 1987
Chief Officer(s):
Arutapani Peter Gitararen, Father
Finances: *Annual Operating Budget:* Less than $50,000
Description: To be a Roman Catholic Community that strives to preserve its Tamil cultural traditions, customs, values & language through faith; Affiliation(s): Archdiocese of Toronto

Our Lady of the Rosary of Manaoag Evangelization Group
25 Mahoney Ave., Toronto ON M6M 2H5
Tel: 416-240-9249
Overview: A small local organization founded in 1989
Chief Officer(s):
Teodora S. La Madrid, Contact
Activities: Providing evangelization, faith formation & instruction, prayer, retreats, & pilgrimages
Affiliation(s): Archdiocese of Toronto

Pontifical Mission Societies
2219 Kennedy Rd., Toronto ON M1T 3G5
Tel: 416-699-7077; *Fax:* 416-699-9019
Toll-Free: 800-897-8865
mission@missionsocieties.ca
www.missionsocieties.ca
www.youtube.com/user/WorldMissionTV
www.facebook.com/pontificalmissionsocieties
twitter.com/pmstoronto
Overview: A medium-sized international charitable organization founded in 1922
Chief Officer(s):
Osei Alex, National Director
Finances: *Funding Sources:* Donations
Staff: 8 staff member(s)
Description: Comprised of four missionaries: Holy Childhood Association; Propagation of the Faith (SPF); St. Peter the Apostle (SPA); Pontifical Missionary Union (PMU) and aim to provide mission awareness, evangelization and charitable works throughout the world; Affiliation(s): Holy Childhood Association; Propagation of the Faith (SPF); St. Peter the Apostle (SPA); Pontifical Missionary Union (PMU)

Regnum Christi Movement
c/o Legionaries of Christ, 19119 Hwy. 2, RR#1, Cornwall ON K6H 5R5
Tel: 613-931-1600
cornwallbm@arcol.org
www.regnumchristi.org/en
www.youtube.com/regnumchristi
www.facebook.com/regnumchristi.english
twitter.com/RegnumChristiEn

Overview: A small international charitable organization founded in 2004
Finances: *Funding Sources:* Donations
Member Profile: Catholic young people, adults, deacons, & diocesan priests who wish to experience Christ's love & spread it to others; Members are active in service to the Church
Activities: Leading Christian lives; Taking apostolic action, in cooperation with bishops & parish priests; Providing faith instruction, prayer groups, religious books, & renewal programs; Offering programs, such as Familia, for families to learn & live their Catholic faith, Challenge youth programs, for girls, Catholic Kids Net of Canada Vacation Bible Schools, Conquest Boys' youth programs, Father & Son programs, Compass programs, for university students, & missions, for young people & families
Description: To love Christ, serve others, & build the Church; Affiliation(s): Archdiocese of Toronto; Legionaries of Christ

Roman Catholic Military Ordinariate of Canada / L'Ordinariat militaire Catholique Romain du Canada
Bldg. 469, Uplands Site, CFSU (O), Ottawa ON K1A 0K2
Tel: 613-998-8661
milord-cdn-chancel@outlook.com
rcmilord-ordmilcr.com
twitter.com/MilOrdCDN
Overview: A small national charitable organization founded in 1987
Chief Officer(s):
Scott McCaig, C.C., Bishop
Terry Cherwick, Vicar General
terry.cherwick@forces.gc.ca
Membership: 81,000+
Activities: *Library:* Centre d'entraînement des aumôniers de Borden
Description: To connect and support Roman Catholic members of the Canadian Forces through God; *Member of:* La Conférence des évêques catholiques du Canada

Rosaries for Canadian Forces Abroad
Overview: A small national organization
Member Profile: Any person who wishes to assist in the making or distribution of Rosaries for Canadian Forces deployed abroad may join the private Catholic lay apostolate
Activities: Making Rosaries in parish guilds, led by a guild leader
Description: Providing military support by making & donating Rosaries to members of the Canadian Forces serving abroad; Affiliation(s): Archdiocese of Toronto

The Rosary Apostolate, Inc.
1208 Warden Ave., Toronto ON M1R 2R3
www.rosaryapostolate.com
Overview: A small local charitable organization founded in 1997
Chief Officer(s):
Marilina Cinelli, Spiritual Director
Finances: *Funding Sources:* Donations
Member Profile: Individuals, who are practising Catholics, are devoted to Mary & her rosary, & who respect & love children; Volunteers, who cater to the schools in their parishes as rosary visitors; Rosary visitors teach children by praying the Rosary & the Act of Consecration
Activities: Forming parish prayer groups for evangelization through prayer; Conducting school visits to pray the rosary with children in Catholic schools; Providing director workshops & regional meetings; Recruiting, screening, & training rosary visitors; Outlining themes & meditations for rosary visitors; Offering annual retreats
Description: To lead children, youth, & families to Jesus through Mary

St. John's Cathedral Polish Catholic Church
180 Cowan Ave., Toronto ON M6K 2N6
Tel: 416-532-8249
stjohnpnc@outlook.com
www.stjohnsparishofthepncc.com
Previous Name: Polish National Catholic Church of Canada
Overview: A small national organization
Finances: *Annual Operating Budget:* $100,000-$250,000
Membership: 300
Member of: The Canadian Council of Churches

St. Mary's Prayer Group
St. Mary's Roman Catholic Parish, 66A Main St. South, Brampton ON L6W 2C6
Tel: 905-451-2300
info@stmarysbrampton.com
stmarysbr.archtoronto.org
Overview: A small local organization
Member Profile: Open to everyone; Core members plan meetings & activities & gather for prayer
Activities: Offering healing masses, intercessory prayer, & Life in the Spirit seminars
Affiliation(s): Archdiocese of Toronto

Salesian Cooperators, Association of St. Benedict Centre
c/o St. Benedict Parish, 2194 Kipling Ave., Toronto ON M9W 4K9
Tel: 416-743-3830; *Fax:* 416-743-8884
connect@stbenedicts.ca
stbenedicts.ca/salesiancooperators.html
Also Known As: Don Bosco's Cooperators
Overview: A small local organization founded in 1876
Chief Officer(s):
Joe Conroy, Contact
Finances: *Funding Sources:* Fundraising
Member Profile: Lay, mature adults & priest members, accompanied by SDB or FMA religious, form the lay apostolic association; Members must be accepted by the provincial council & make personal, public promises
Description: To bring a priviledged attention to young people, especially those who are poorest, or victims of marginalization, exploitation, & violence; Affiliation(s): Archdiocese of Toronto

ShareLife
ShareLife Trust, 1155 Yonge St., Toronto ON M4T 1W2
Tel: 416-934-3411; *Fax:* 416-934-3412
Toll-Free: 800-263-2595
slife@archtoronto.org
sharelife.org
www.facebook.com/ShareLifeCan
twitter.com/ShareLifeCan
Overview: A large international charitable organization founded in 1976
Chief Officer(s):
Arthur Peters, Executive Director, 416-934-3411 559
arthurpeters@archtoronto.org
Finances: *Annual Operating Budget:* Greater than $5 Million
Staff: 12 staff member(s)
Membership: 34 organizations
Activities: *Awareness Events:* Kickoffs; *Speaker Service:* Yes
Description: ShareLife is the Catholic Community's response to helping the whole community through Catholic agencies by effectively raising & allocating funds; *Member of:* International Catholic Stewardship Council; Affiliation(s): Canadian Centre for Philanthropy

Sisters Adorers of the Precious Blood / Soeurs Adoratrices du Précieux Sang
301 Ramsay Rd., London ON N6G 1N7
Tel: 519-473-2499; *Fax:* 519-473-6590
www.pbsisters.on.ca
Overview: A small local charitable organization founded in 1861
Chief Officer(s):
Eileen Mary Walsh, General Superior
Carol Forhan, rpb, Formation Director
srcforhan@pbsisters.on.ca

Sisters of Saint Joseph of Pembroke (CSJ)
1127 Pembroke St. West, Pembroke ON K8A 5R3
Tel: 613-732-3694; *Fax:* 613-732-3319
infopembroke@csjcanada.org
www.csjcanada.org
Overview: A small local organization founded in 1921
Membership: 1-99
Description: The Sisters of St. Joseph of Pembroke are a group of fifty Roman Catholic women religious based in eastern Ontario

Sisters of Saint Joseph of Peterborough (CSJ)
PO Box 566, Stn. Mount St. Joseph, 1555 Monaghan Rd., Peterborough ON K9J 6Z6
Tel: 705-745-1307; *Fax:* 705-745-1377
infoPeterborough@csjcanada.org
www.csjpeterborough.com
www.facebook.com/112521912120451
twitter.com/CSJCdn
Overview: A small local charitable organization founded in 1890
Membership: 80
Description: To respond to the poor & most needy, particularly where the need is not already met

Sisters of Saint Joseph of Sault Ste Marie
2025 Main St. West, North Bay ON P1B 2X6
Tel: 705-474-3800; *Fax:* 705-495-3028
stephanie.romiti@gmail.com
www.csjssm.ca
Overview: A small local organization
Chief Officer(s):
Shirley Anderson, General Superior
sanderson@csjssm.ca
Description: Lives & works that all people may be united with God & with one another

Sisters of the Child Jesus (SEJ) / Soeurs de l'Enfant-Jésus
318 Laval St., Coquitlam BC V3K 4W4
Tel: 604-939-7545
dbillesberger@shaw.ca
sistersofthechildjesus.ca
Also Known As: Sisters of Instruction of the Child Jesus
Overview: A small local charitable organization founded in 1667
Chief Officer(s):
Catherine Machell, President
Denece Billesberger, Secretary & Treasurer
Description: To be a presence of love to the Father & to others for the definite purpose of awakening & deepening faith; To enable people to grow in the uniqueness of their person as created by God & to liberate themselves from all that prevents their being truly human; To bring hope & direction to contemporaries; To be at the service of the least favoured, the marginalized & those who have no voice in society

Sisters of the Sacred Heart of Ragusa / Suore del Sacro Cuore di Ragusa
1 Edward St., Welland ON L3C 5H2
Tel: 905-732-4542
sacredhe@hotmail.com
www.sacredheartsisters.ca
Overview: A small local charitable organization founded in 1889
Membership: 500-999
Activities: Day care, schools, orphanages & retirement homes for the elderly; Parish work; Home visits; Missions; Nursing
Description: To live an apostolic life in the church & society through the works of beneficence among the poor & needy; To instruct & educate youth; To collaborate in parish pastoral work, especially through the teaching of catechism

Società Unita
1775 Islington Ave., Toronto ON M9P 3N2
Tel: 416-243-7319; *Fax:* 416-243-7319
info@teopoli.com
teopoli.com
www.flickr.com/photos/60905934@N05
twitter.com/teopoli
Also Known As: The United Society (The Mission)
Overview: A small local charitable organization founded in 1972
Chief Officer(s):
Antonio Apruzzese, Director
Finances: *Funding Sources:* Donations
Member Profile: Individuals, over the age of eighteen, who wish to follow the principles of peace, love, & unity, acccording to the Gospel & the teaching of the Roman Catholic Church
Activities: Encouraging religious & social activities for spiritual & moral growth; Providing assistance to the needy; Offering faith instruction, prayer groups, spiritual retreats, & spiritual pilgrimages; Operating the Teopoli Summer Experience for children at Teopoli, located in Muskoka; Providing a daily Catholic braoadcast on Radio Teopoli, with programming such as Jesus the Listener, & The Good Samaritan
Description: To promote peace, love, & unity, according to the Gospel & the teaching of the Roman Catholic Church; Affiliation(s): Archdiocese of Toronto

Société canadienne d'histoire de l'Église Catholique - Section française (SCHEC) / Canadian Catholic Historical Association - French Section
Département d'histoire, UQAM, CP 8888, Succ. Centre-Ville, Montréal QC H3C 3P8
schec.ca
www.facebook.com/SCHistoireEgliseCatholique
Aperçu: *Dimension:* petite; *Envergure:* nationale; *fondée en 1933*
Membre(s) du bureau directeur:
Mélanie Lanouette, Président
Philippe Roy-Lysencourt, Vice-Président
Dominique Laperle, Secrétaire
Sébastien Lecompte-Ducharme, Trésorier
Finances: *Budget de fonctionnement annuel:* Moins de $50,000
Personnel: 4 bénévole(s)
Membre: 150 individu; 100 institutionnel; *Montant de la cotisation:* 20$ étudiant; 40$ régulier; 50$ institutionnel; $60 soutien; *Critères d'admissibilite:* La Société compte des membres dans toutes les parties du Canada de même qu'en Europe et aux États-Unis; les membres peuvent être des individus, ou des institutions publiques ou privées, tels des dépôts d'archives, bibliothèques, diocèses, communautés religieuses
Description: Grouper les personnes intéressées à l'histoire de l'Église catholique au Canada; stimuler l'intérêt pour cette histoire dans le grand public; tenir des congrès annuels dans diverses régions du Canada afin de susciter un dialogue entre chercheurs participants et de promouvoir les travaux d'histoire régionale

Société catholique de la Bible (SOCABI) / Catholic Bible Society
2000, rue Sherbrooke ouest, Montréal QC H3H 1G4
Tél: 514-677-5431
directeur@socabi.org
www.socabi.org
www.facebook.com/815637145182961
twitter.com/SOCABI_1940
Aperçu: *Dimension:* moyenne; *Envergure: nationale; Organisme sans but lucratif; fondée en 1940*
Membre(s) du bureau directeur:
Timothy Scott, Président
Christiane Cloutier-Dupuis, Vice-Président
Francis Daoust, Directeur général
Finances: *Budget de fonctionnement annuel:* $100,000-$250,000
Membre: 130; *Montant de la cotisation:* 30$ tous les trois ans; *Critères d'admissibilite:* Implication dans le pastorale biblique; *Comités:* Administration; Financement
Activités: Service de librairie; conférences sur cassettes; cours par correspondance; cours d'initiation et formation; voyage en Israël; retraites; publication d'articles
Description: Rendre la bible accessible au plus grand nombre de personnes possible, en facilitant la lecture et la compréhension; *Membre de:* Association canadienne des périodiques catholiques; *Affiliation(s):* World Catholic Federation for the Biblical Apostolate

Society of St. Vincent de Paul - Toronto Central Council
240 Church St., Toronto ON M5B 1Z2
Tel: 416-364-5577; *Fax:* 416-364-2055
info@ssvptoronto.ca
www.ssvptoronto.ca
Overview: A small local charitable organization founded in 1850
Chief Officer(s):
Louise Coutu, Executive Director
Joseph McCalmont, Director, Finance
Finances: *Funding Sources:* Donations
Member Profile: Individuals who are non-judgmental, compassionate, & giving, who wish to act on their faith by assisting those in need in this lay Catholic organization; Applicants must successfully complete the screening process, which includes a police check, references, & an interview; *Committees:* Advocacy; Addiction Recovery; Camp; Community Living; Election; Executive; Finance; Governance; Health & Safety; Prison Apostolate & Court Services; Resource; Shelter; Spirituality; Stores; Strategic Planning; Twinning
Activities: Delivering Christ's love, material assistance, respect, compassion, & hope to those in need; Offering home visitations; Operating the Marygrove Camp for girls; Providing housing & support to women in crisis; Supporting men & women recovering from addiction; Providing residential care for the developmentally handicapped; Offering low cost clothing; Supporting persons awaiting trial or in prison; Conducting members' conference meetings once or twice a month to grow in faith & to consult regarding ways to assist the needy
Description: To live the Gospel message by assisting the poor with love, respect, justice, & joy; To administer special works, including women's shelters, recovery homes, homes for the developmentally & mentally disabled, & a camp for girls; *Affiliation(s):* Archdiocese of Toronto

Society of the Sacred Heart
4120 Forest Park Ave., St. Louis MO 63108 USA
Tel: 314-652-1500; *Fax:* 314-534-6800
rscj.org
www.instagram.com/_societyofthesacredheart_
www.facebook.com/SocietyoftheSacredHeart
twitter.com/RSCJUSC
Overview: A medium-sized international charitable organization founded in 1800
Chief Officer(s):
Barbara Dawson, Provincial Superior
Membership: 1-99; *Member Profile:* Women in the Catholic church
Activities: *Library:* Society of the Sacred Heart Provincial Archives (Open to Public) by appointment
Description: To make known the love of Jesus in the world, through educaton & social justice activities

Soeurs de Sainte-Marie de Namur / Sisters of Saint Mary of Namur
74 Claredon Ave., Ottawa ON K1Y 0P7
Tél: 613-725-1914
sjdssmn@yahoo.ca
www.ssmn.ca
Aperçu: *Dimension:* petite; *Envergure: internationale; Organisme sans but lucratif; fondée en 1819*
Finances: *Budget de fonctionnement annuel:* $250,000-$500,000
Personnel- 16 membre(s) du personnel

Membre: 1-99

Soeurs missionnaires de Notre-Dame des Anges / Missionary Sisters of Our Lady of the Angels
80, av Laurier est, Montréal QC H2T 1E5
Tél: 514-277-3686
mnda.canada@gmail.com
missionnaires-mnda.com
Aperçu: *Dimension:* petite; *Envergure: internationale; Organisme sans but lucratif; fondée en 1922*
Membre(s) du bureau directeur:
Fernande Leblanc, Contact
Membre: 142
Activités: Nos activités sont de toutes sortes: service d'Église, évangélisation et catéchèse, soins des malades, enseignement et promotion de la femme.

Spiritans, the Congregation of the Holy Ghost
34 Collinsgrove Rd., Toronto ON M1E 3S4
Tel: 416-691-9319; *Fax:* 416-691-8760
secretary@spiritans.com
www.spiritans.com
Also Known As: Spiritans of TransCanada
Overview: A medium-sized national organization
Membership: 3,000+
Description: Roman Catholic religious congregation specializing in education & mission

Union mondiale des organisations féminines catholiques (UMOFC) / World Union of Catholic Women's Organizations (WUCWO)
16, Piazza di S. Calisto, Rome 00153 Italy
wucwoparis@gmail.com
wucwo.org
www.instagram.com/wucwo_umofc
www.facebook.com/worldunionofcatholicwomensorganisations
twitter.com/wucwo
Aperçu: *Dimension:* grande; *Envergure: internationale; fondée en 1910*
Membre(s) du bureau directeur:
Maria Lía Zervino, Présidente générale
wucwopregen@gmail.com
Lavinia Rocchi Carrera, Secrétaire générale
wucwosecgen@gmail.com
Membre: 100 organisations + 8,000,000 femmes; *Critères d'admissibilite:* Organisation féminine catholique ayant 3 ans d'existance; *Comités:* Commissions Permanentes - Droits Humains; Développement et Coopération; Femmes et Église; Famille; Oecuménisme; *Comités permanents -* Finances; Statutes et Procédures; Communication, Information et Publications; International
Activités: Groupe de travail sur la violence contre les femmes, santé et prises de décisions; Éducation; Droits humains
Description: De promouvoir la présence, la participation et la co-responsabilité des femmes catholiques dans la société et l'Eglise, afin de leur permettre de remplir leur mission d'évangélisation et de travailler pour le développement humain; *Membre de:* Conférence des Organisations Internationales Catholiques (OIC); *Affiliation(s):* Catholic Women's League of Canada; Ukrainian Catholic Women's League of Canada; Association féminine d'éducation d'action sociale; Mouvement des femmes chrétiennes - Inter-Montréal

Vision of Love Ministry - Canada
ON
info@visionoflove.ca
www.visionoflove.ca
Also Known As: Vision 2000
Overview: A small provincial organization founded in 1996
Chief Officer(s):
Danny Nelson, Contact
danny@visionoflove.ca
Finances: *Funding Sources:* Sponsorships
Membership: 30+; *Member Profile:* Members are part of a Christian community of artists, who desire to live the contemplative Christian faith & serve with love, through music & the arts; Participants must acknowledge "Jesus Christ is Lord"
Activities: Providing music & worship with the arts for Catholic liturgies, renewal programs, pastoral groups, parishes, churches, & youth; Offering praise & worship music in a range of styles, such as rock, blues, jazz, folk, Gospel, Latin, & reggae; Producing CDs & DVDs; Tutoring; Providing Christian artwork
Description: To manifest God's love & enrich the local Catholic faith; To share time & musical & artistic talent at churches & Christian gatherings, especially within the Catholic Charismatic Renewal & lay organizations; *Affiliation(s):* Archdiocese of Toronto; Renewal Ministries CCRER/CCRSO; Radio Maria; Mission SOS - Toronto; Living Waters and Fr. Trevor Nathasingh - Trinidad; Multi-Cultural Christian Communities

Worldwide Marriage Encounter
Toronto ON
Overview: A small local organization
Finances: *Funding Sources:* Donations
Member Profile: Persons who are validly married, & who have attended a Worldwide Marriage Encounter weekend experience in one of the seven secretariats (Africa, Asia, Europe, Latin America, Pacific, Canada, USA); Members become part of a pro-marriage movement in the Catholic Church
Activities: Programming for married couples, including enrichments, peer support, community activities, & social events
Description: To renew the sacraments of Matrimony & Holy Orders; *Affiliation(s):* Archdiocese of Toronto

Christianity

Accelerated Christian Education Canada
PO Box 1360, Portage la Prairie MB R1N 3N9
Tel: 204-428-5332; *Fax:* 204-428-5386
Toll-Free: 800-976-7226
info@acecanada.net
www.acecanada.net
Also Known As: School of Tomorrow Canada
Previous Name: Canadian National Accelerated Christian Education Association
Overview: A small national organization founded in 1974
Finances: *Annual Operating Budget:* Less than $50,000; *Funding Sources:* Provincial dues
Staff: 24 volunteer(s)
Membership: 100-499
Description: To continue to assure Canadians of the freedom to choose alternative Christian education; *Affiliation(s):* Federation of Independent Schools in Canada

Action des Chrétiens pour l'abolition de la torture (ACAT) / Action by Christians for the Abolition of Torture
2715, ch de la Côte-Sainte-Catherine, Montréal QC H3T 1B6
Tél: 514-890-6169; *Téléc:* 514-890-6484
acat@acatcanada.org
acatcanada.org
www.facebook.com/acatcanada
Également appelé: ACAT Canada
Aperçu: *Dimension:* moyenne; *Envergure: nationale; Organisme sans but lucratif; fondée en 1984*
Membre(s) du bureau directeur:
Raphaël Lambal, Président
Nancy Labonté, Coordonnateur
Finances: *Budget de fonctionnement annuel:* $50,000-$100,000; *Fonds:* Organisations philanthropiques et particuliers.
Personnel: 2 membre(s) du personnel; 20 bénévole(s)
Membre: 150; *Montant de la cotisation:* $10 étudiant; 35$ membre; *Comités:* Commission des interventions; Financement; Relations publiques; Ressourcement
Activités: Campagne annuelle; Bulletins; Appels à l'action; *Stagiaires:* Oui; *Service de conférenciers:* Oui; *Listes de destinataires:* Oui
Description: Dans un but d'engagement évangélique, encourager les différentes communautés Chrétiennes du Canada à porter ensemble, par la prière, les souffrances des victimes de la torture; dans un but éducatif, sensibiliser particulièrement les Chrétiens au scandale de la torture (par l'information et la formation aux droits de la personne); dans un but de soulager la misère des victimes de la torture, apporter une aide concrète par l'envoi de lettres et pétitions aux responsables de torture et des lettres d'encouragement aux victimes; *Affiliation(s):* Fédération internationale de l'action des Chrétiens pour l'abolition de la torture (FIACAT)

Adventive Cross Cultural Initiatives (ACCI)
89 Auriga Dr., Nepean ON K2E 7Z2
Tel: 613-298-1546; *Fax:* 613-225-7455
www.adventive.ca
www.facebook.com/AdventiveCCI
Previous Name: New Life League
Overview: A small national charitable organization founded in 1986
Chief Officer(s):
Randy Haw, Canadian National Director
randy@adventive.ca
Finances: *Annual Operating Budget:* Less than $50,000; *Funding Sources:* Donations
Staff: 4 staff member(s); 1 volunteer(s)
Activities: *Internships:* Yes
Description: To operate as an international, interdenominational Christian missionary organization; To minister through printing & literature, children's homes, national workers, evangelism & church planting; *Member of:* Canadian Council of Christian Charities

African Enterprise (Canada) (AE)
PO Box 2000, Vancouver BC V6B 3P8

Tel: 604-228-0930
admin@africanenterprise.ca
africanenterprise.ca
www.instagram.com/african_enterprise_canada
www.facebook.com/AfricanEnterpriseCanada
twitter.com/ae_canada

Also Known As: AE Canada
Overview: A small national charitable organization founded in 1965
Chief Officer(s):
Stephen Mbogo, Chief Executive Officer
Jamie Morrison, Director, US & Canada
Activities: *Internships:* Yes; *Speaker Service:* Yes
Description: To service & expand an active partnership among Canadian Christians to raise prayer, financial, material & human resources to enable AE to achieve its mission: to evangelise the cities of Africa through word & deed in partnership with the church; Affiliation(s): AE International

Antiochian Orthodox Christian Archdiocese of North America
Antiochian Orthodox Christian Archdiocese, PO Box 5238, Englewood NJ 07631-5238 USA

Tel: 201-871-1355; *Fax:* 201-871-7954
archdiocese@antiochian.org
www.antiochian.org

Overview: A small national organization founded in 1875
Chief Officer(s):
Joseph Al-Zehlaoui, Archbishop
Marlene Ayoub, Registrar
registrar@antiochian.org
Membership: 283 parishes, 18 in Canada
Description: The Antiochan Orthodox Community in Canada is under the jurisdiction of the Patriarch of Antioch & all the East, with headquarters in Damascus, Syria. There are five churches in Canada & eight missions. The headquarters for all churches in North America is the Antiochan Orthodox Christian archdiocese, in Englewood, New Jersey, under Archbishop Philip Salica; Affiliation(s): Canadian (Can-Am) Region

Armenian Diocese of Canada
615, av Stuart, Montréal QC H2V 3H2

Tel: 514-276-9479; *Fax:* 514-276-9960
contact@armenianchurch.ca
www.armenianchurch.ca
www.youtube.com/user/CanArmChurch
www.facebook.com/armeniandioceseofcanada
twitter.com/CanadianDiocese

Overview: A medium-sized national charitable organization founded in 1984
Chief Officer(s):
Abgar Hovakimian, Primate
Finances: *Annual Operating Budget:* $250,000-$500,000; *Funding Sources:* Donations; parish dues
Staff: 6 staff member(s)
Membership: Over 50,000; *Member Profile:* Baptized in the Armenian faith; *Committees:* Endowment Fund
Activities: Humanitarian Aid to Armenia; *Library:* Yes (Open to Public) by appointment
Description: To preserve & promote Christian & national heritage; humanitarian aid to Armenia; Affiliation(s): Canadian Council of Churches

Association internationale des études patristiques (AIEP) / International Association for Patristic Studies (IAPS)
www.aiep-iaps.org
www.youtube.com/channel/UCspmw-ieXtUfARCOtSCEwYQ
Aperçu: *Dimension:* moyenne; *Envergure: internationale; fondée en* 1965
Membre(s) du bureau directeur:
Patricia Ciner, Président
patriciaciner@gmail.com.ar
Finances: *Budget de fonctionnement annuel:* Moins de $50,000
Membre: 740; *Montant de la cotisation:* US$23; *Critères d'admissibilite:* Interessé aux pères de l'Eglise; *Comités:* Executive
Activités: *Listes de destinataires:* Oui
Description: Chercheurs et professeurs qui s'intéressent à l'antiquité chrétienne au général

Association of Christian Churches in Manitoba (ACCM) / Association des églises chrétiennes du Manitoba
151 de la Cathedrale Ave., Winnipeg MB R2H 0H6
Tel: 204-237-9851
Previous Name: Ecumenical Committee of Manitoba
Overview: A medium-sized provincial organization founded in 1990
Finances: *Annual Operating Budget:* Less than $50,000

Description: To bring Christian churches into living encounter with one another; to provide a network of news & events which can help member churches act together in all matters except those in which deep differences compel us to act separately; to act as common Christian voice & media contact on issues of spiritual & social concern in the Province

BFM Foundation (Canada)
PO Box 503, #203, 665 Davis Dr., Newmarket ON L3Y 9E5
Toll-Free: 855-204-4980
admin@missionthriftstore.com
www.missionthriftstore.com
www.facebook.com/missionthriftstorescanada
Overview: A large international charitable organization founded in 1989
Chief Officer(s):
Steve Klassen, CEO
Jonathan Catania, CFO, 855-204-4980 108
Frank Oostdyk, COO, 855-204-4980 107
Finances: *Funding Sources:* Donations
Description: To operate thrift stores across Canada to generate funds for Bible League Canada; *Member of:* Canadian Council of Christian Charities

The Bible League of Canada / Société canadienne pour la distribution de la Bible
PO Box 368, Stn. Main, Grimsby ON L3M 4H8
Tel: 905-319-9500; *Fax:* 905-319-0484
Toll-Free: 800-363-9673
ministry@bibleleague.ca
bibleleague.ca
www.youtube.com/user/BibleLeagueCanada
www.facebook.com/BibleLeagueCanada
twitter.com/BibleLeagueCan
Previous Name: World Home Bible League
Overview: A large national charitable organization founded in 1949
Chief Officer(s):
Paul Richardson, President & CEO
Bob Beasley, Chief Ministry Officer
David Kraulis, Chief Financial Officer
Finances: *Annual Operating Budget:* $3 Million-$5 Million; *Funding Sources:* Donations
Staff: 15 staff member(s)
Activities: Adult Ministry; Children's Ministry; Persecuted Church; Starting new churches; *Speaker Service:* Yes *Library:* The Bible League of Canada Library
Description: To spread the living word of God worldwide; *Member of:* Canadian Council of Christian Charities; International Association of Bible Leagues; Affiliation(s): The Bible League

Bibles & Literature in French Canada (BLF)
Quebec Field Office, 256, rue Marc Aurele Fortin, Lachute QC J8H 3W7
Tél: 450-562-7859; *Téléc:* 450-562-7859
info@blfcanada.org
www.blfcanada.org
Également appelé: BLF Canada
Aperçu: *Dimension:* petite; *Envergure:* provinciale
Membre(s) du bureau directeur:
Toe-Blake Roy, Director
toeblake@blfcanada.org
Description: BLF Canada distribue une littérature de qualité afin de permettre de présenter, à ces millions de Canadiens, celui qui seul peut leur apporter la vraie vie.

British Israel World Federation (Canada) Inc. (BIWF)
313 Sherbourne St., Toronto ON M5A 2S3
Tel: 416-921-5996
british-israel@bellnet.ca
www.britishisrael.ca
Overview: A small national charitable organization founded in 1929
Membership: 1,200; *Fees:* $10 non-voting; $15 voting
Activities: Monthly meetings; Conventions; *Speaker Service:* Yes
Description: To be a Federation of orthodox Christians of many denominations who believe the Bible to be the inspired word of God; Affiliation(s): The British-Israel-World Federation; BIWF (Queensland) Inc.; BIWF (NZ) Auckland Inc.; Canadian British-Israel Association Windsor, Ontario; The Association of the Covenant People (Vancouver, BC)

Canadian & American Reformed Churches
comments@canrc.org
canrc.org
Also Known As: Canadian Reformed Churches
Overview: A large national organization
Membership: 50+ organizations
Description: To exalt the Triune God by faithfully proclaiming the gospel of Jesus Christ

Canadian Bible Society (CBS) / Société biblique canadienne
National Support Office, 10 Carnforth Rd., Toronto ON M4A 2S4
Tel: 416-757-4171; *Fax:* 416-757-3376
Toll-Free: 800-465-2425
info@biblesociety.ca
biblesociety.ca
www.instagram.com/canadianbiblesociety
www.facebook.com/CanadianBibleSociety
twitter.com/CanadianBible
Overview: A large national charitable organization founded in 1904
Chief Officer(s):
Rupen Das, National Director
Steven Baal, Chief Financial Officer
Mary Ann Buffan, Director, Development, Marketing & Communications
Joanna Costopoulos, Director, Human Resources
Finances: *Funding Sources:* Donations; Sale of gifts; Fundraising
Activities: Offering various programs to share God's Word, such as Operation Bible for the Canadian military, & welcoming newcomers to Canada with God's message
Description: To translate, publish, & distribute Bibles, New Testaments & other Scriptures throughout Canada & Bermuda; *Member of:* United Bible Societies

Canadian Chrisitan Communicators Association (CCCA)
8 MacDonald Ave., Hamilton ON L8P 4N5
Tel: 905-521-2240
cdnchristiancommunicators@gmail.com
www.christiancommunicators.ca
www.facebook.com/CanadianChristianCommunicatorsAssociation
Previous Name: Canadian Church Press
Overview: A small national organization founded in 1957
Chief Officer(s):
John Longhurst, President
jdl562009@gmail.com
Catherine Pate, Vice-President
cpate@bc.anglican.ca
Trina Gallop Blank, Treasurer
tgallop@elcic.ca
Finances: *Funding Sources:* Sponsorships
Membership: 58; *Fees:* $30; *Member Profile:* Anyone working in Christian communications (writers, editors, bloggers, designers etc.) in Canada
Activities: Offering fellowship for members; Supporting members; Conducting professional development workshops in annual convention
Description: To foster helpfulness among members; To deal cooperatively with communications problems; To encourage higher standards of religious journalism

Canadian Christian Business Federation (CCBF)
5792 - 8th Line East, Ariss ON N0B 1B0
Tel: 416-725-5586
don@ccbf.org
www.ccbf.org
www.facebook.com/ccbfed
twitter.com/ccbfed
Overview: A medium-sized national organization founded in 1984
Chief Officer(s):
Don Moore, Executive Director
don@ccbf.org
Membership: 450; *Member Profile:* Christian business leaders & professionals
Activities: Offering biblically-based professional development programs & resources
Description: To help members enhance their faith & success through professional development, support & Christian fellowship

Canadian Council of Christian Charities (CCCC)
#1, 43 Howard Ave., Elmira ON N3B 2C9
Tel: 519-669-5137; *Fax:* 519-669-3291
mail@cccc.org
www.cccc.org
www.linkedin.com/company/canadian-council-of-christian-charities
www.facebook.com/CCCCharities
twitter.com/ccccharities
Overview: A medium-sized national licensing charitable organization founded in 1972
Chief Officer(s):
John Pellowe, Chief Executive Officer
Finances: *Annual Operating Budget:* $500,000-$1.5 Million
Staff: 17 staff member(s); 56 volunteer(s)
Membership: 3,300; *Fees:* Schedule available

Activities: Education; training on legal, financial & leadership issues
Description: To encourage the Canadian Christian community to a biblical stewardship by integrating practical concepts of administration, development & accountability with the spiritual concerns of ministry

Canadian Foodgrains Bank Association Inc. (CFGB)
PO Box 767, #400, 393 Portage Ave., Winnipeg MB R3C 2L4
Tel: 204-944-1993; *Fax:* 204-943-2597
Toll-Free: 800-665-0377
cfgb@foodgrainsbank.ca
foodgrainsbank.ca
www.youtube.com/user/foodgrainsbank
www.facebook.com/CanadianFoodgrainsBank
twitter.com/Foodgrains
Also Known As: Canadian Foodgrains Bank
Overview: A large international charitable organization founded in 1983
Chief Officer(s):
Andy Harrington, Executive Director
Amanda Thorsteinsson, Senior Communications Officer, 204-979-4873
athorsteinsson@foodgrainsbank.ca
Finances: *Annual Operating Budget:* Greater than $5 Million; *Funding Sources:* Donations (cash & grain); Fundraising
Staff: 51 staff member(s)
Membership: 15; *Member Profile:* Canadian churches & church-related agencies
Activities: Improving community development; Protecting & building sustainable economic livelihoods; Encouraging peace-building; Strengthening Canadian & international policy & action towards hunger issues; Increasing public awareness & engagement
Description: To provide a Christian response to hunger; To share resources with & support hungry populations outside Canada to achieve food security; To reduce hunger in developing countries

Canadian Society of Biblical Studies (CSBS) / Société canadienne des études bibliques (SCEB)
c/o Jonathan Vroom, Dept. of Near & Middle Eastern Civilizations, 4 Bancroft Ave., 2nd Fl., Toronto ON M5S 1C1
www.ccsr.ca
Overview: A small national organization founded in 1933
Chief Officer(s):
J. Richard Middleton, President
Fees: $51.75 student/retired; $103.20 full; *Member Profile:* Individuals interested in all aspects of the academic study of the Bible
Description: To stimulate the critical investigation of the classical biblical literature & related literature

Canadian Society of Church History (CSCH) / Société canadienne d'histoire de l'Église
c/o John Young, 1309 Moira Rd., Roslin ON K0K 2Y0
csch-sche.ca
Overview: A small national organization founded in 1960
Chief Officer(s):
Robynne R. Healey, President
Bruce Douville, Vice-President & Program Chair
Todd Webb, Administrative Secretary
John Young, Treasurer
jyoung@united-church.ca
Fees: $15 student; $30 retired; $33 individual; *Member Profile:* Historians of Christianity in Canada & the United States
Description: To encourage research in the history of Christianity, especially the history of Christianity in Canada; *Member of:* Canadian Corporation for Studies in Religion; Congress of Social Sciences & Humanities

Canadian Society of Patristic Studies (CSPS) / Association canadienne des études patristiques
c/o Dr. S. Muir, Religious Studies, Concordia University College of AB, 7128 Ada Blvd., Edmonton AB T5B 4E4
www.ccsr.ca/csps
twitter.com/csps_patristics
Overview: A small national organization founded in 1975
Fees: $47 student/retired; $75 regular; *Committees:* Program; Nominating
Description: To encourage the academic study of the Church Fathers; *Member of:* Canadian Federation for the Humanities & Social Sciences / Fèdèration canadienne des sciences humaines

Children Believe
1200 Denison St., Markham ON L3R 8G6
Tel: 905-754-1001; *Fax:* 905-754-1002
Toll-Free: 800-263-5437
askus@childrenbelieve.ca
childrenbelieve.ca
www.instagram.com/childrenbelieveCA
www.facebook.com/childrenbelieveCA
www.twitter.com/cbelieveCA
Previous Name: Christian Children's Fund of Canada
Overview: A large international charitable organization founded in 1960
Chief Officer(s):
Dave Wilson, Interim CEO & Vice-President, People & Culture
Tim D'Souza, Chief Operating Officer
Belinda Bennet, Chief International Programs Officer
Aki Temiseva, Chief Marketing & Development Officer
Finances: *Funding Sources:* Donations
Staff: 200 volunteer(s)
Membership: 30,000+
Activities: Working to help those affected by HIV/AIDS; Providing water & sanitation; Offering education; *Internships:* Yes; *Speaker Service:* Yes
Description: To focus upon community development ministry, starting with basic assistance & leading to programs stressing self-help & eventual independence; To work with colleagues & partners in developing countries; To reach out to children & families of all faiths; *Member of:* Canadian Council of Christian Charities; Better Business Bureau; ChildFund Alliance; Imagine Canada; *Affiliation(s):* Canadian Marketing Association; Association of Fundraising Professionals

Christian Catholic Church Canada (CCRCC) / Église catholique-chrétien Canada
PO Box 2043, Stn. Hull, Gatineau QC J8X 3Z2
Tel: 613-738-2942; *Fax:* 613-738-7835
info@ccrcc.ca
www.ccrcc.ca
Previous Name: Canadian Chapter of the International Council of Community Churches
Overview: A large international charitable organization founded in 1858
Finances: *Annual Operating Budget:* Less than $50,000; *Funding Sources:* Clergy; churches; benefactors
Staff: 15 staff member(s); 25 volunteer(s)
Membership: 1,000-4,999; *Fees:* $50 clergy; $200 church; *Committees:* Order of the Crown of Thorns
Activities: Church ministry; Seminary program; Counselling & mediation services; *Library:* Christian Catholic Church Canada Archives (Open to Public) by appointment
Description: To advance the kingdom of God through worship, pastoral work & fellowship; *Affiliation(s):* International Council of Community Churches (ICCC), ICCC Canada, World Council of Churches

Christian Church (Disciples of Christ) in Canada (DISCAN) / Église chrétienne (Disciples du Christ) au Canada
ON
www.canadadisciples.org
www.facebook.com/CDNDisciples
Previous Name: All-Canada Committee of the Christian Church (Disciples of Christ)
Overview: A small national charitable organization founded in 1922
Chief Officer(s):
Jennifer Garbin, Regional Minister
Finances: *Annual Operating Budget:* $100,000-$250,000; *Funding Sources:* Donations
Staff: 2 staff member(s)
Membership: 4,000 + 30 churches; *Committees:* Archives; Biennial Convention; Christian Nurture, Service, Witness; Church Development; College; Ministry
Activities: *Internships:* Yes; *Speaker Service:* Yes *Library:* Resource Centre
Member of: The Canadian Council of Churches; *Affiliation(s):* The Christian Church (Disciples of Christ) in USA

Christian Health Association of Alberta (CHAA)
8861 - 75 St. NW, Edmonton AB T6C 4G8
Tel: 780-431-3601
cha-ab.ca
Also Known As: Catholic Health Association of Alberta & Affiliates
Previous Name: Catholic Health Care Conference of Alberta
Overview: A medium-sized provincial charitable organization founded in 1943
Finances: *Annual Operating Budget:* $50,000-$100,000
Staff: 13 volunteer(s)
Membership: 13
Description: To represent the shared vision & values of those seeking to make visible Jesus the Healer; To provide support &

leadership to members & the community through education, advocacy & collaboration; *Member of:* Catholic Health Association of Canada

Christian Labour Association of Canada (CLAC) / Association chrétienne du travail du Canada
2335 Argentia Rd., Mississauga ON L5N 5N3
Tel: 905-812-2855; *Fax:* 905-812-5556
Toll-Free: 800-268-5281
headoffice@clac.ca
www.clac.ca
www.youtube.com/user/CLACunion
www.facebook.com/clacunion
twitter.com/clacunion
Overview: A medium-sized national organization founded in 1952
Chief Officer(s):
Wayne Prins, Executive Director
Ian DeWaard, Ontario Director
Kevin Kahout, BC Director
Dennis Perrin, Prairies Director
Membership: 55,000
Activities: Training programs; *Speaker Service:* Yes *Library:* Yes by appointment
Description: To promote labour relations based on the social principles of justice, respect & dignity; To stand up for fair wages, reasonable work hours, good benefits, a dependable retirement savings plan, job security, professional development & opportunities for advancement; *Member of:* World Organization of Workers

Christian Medical & Dental Society of Canada (CMDS)
7 - 1000 Windmill Rd., Dartmouth NS B3B 1L7
Tel: 902-406-2955; *Fax:* 902-407-5313
Toll-Free: 888-256-8653
office@cmdscanada.org
www.cmdscanada.org
www.youtube.com/channel/UCOB5Hpx1ERDs2anDNy6fYuA
www.facebook.com/CMDSCanada
twitter.com/CMDSCanada
Overview: A medium-sized national organization founded in 1971
Chief Officer(s):
Larry Worthen, Executive Director
lworthen@cmdscanada.org
Stephanie Potter, Manager, Communications
sjpotter@cmdscanada.org
Finances: *Funding Sources:* Dues; Donations
Fees: $35 student/missionary; $75 resident; $100 retired; $225 part-time; $450 full; *Member Profile:* Christian physicians, dentists, & students who wish to integrate faith with professional practice
Activities: Offers workshops & conferences; supports a toll-free helpline for medical & dental trainees; publishes a Members Directory & other literature; offers mission opportunities
Description: To uphold a Christian view of medicine & dentistry; To understand & minister to the spiritual needs of colleagues; To create educational materials about public policy & health; To develop programs that promote a Christian view of medical ethics; To support local group activities, plan conferences & locate mentorship & other opportunities; *Member of:* International Christian Medical & Dental Association

Christian Reformed Church in North America (CRCNA)
PO Box 5070, Stn. LCD 1, 3475 Mainway, Burlington ON L7R 3Y8
Tel: 905-336-2920; *Fax:* 905-336-8344
Toll-Free: 800-730-3490
info@crcna.org
www.crcna.org
www.facebook.com/crcna
twitter.com/crcna
Overview: A large international organization founded in 1857
Chief Officer(s):
Colin Watson, Executive Director
cwatson@crcna.org
Finances: *Annual Operating Budget:* Greater than $5 Million; *Funding Sources:* Gifts & donations
Staff: 225 staff member(s)
Membership: In US & Canada: 245,217 members in 1,000+ congregations; *Committees:* Abuse Prevention; Back to God Hour; Calvin College; Calvin Theological Seminary; CRC Publications; Home Missions; World Missions; World Relief; Chaplaincy Ministries; CRC Loan Fund; Disability Concerns; Fund for Smaller Churches; Pastor-Church Relations; Pensions & Insurance; Race Relations; Historical; Interchurch Relations; Sermons for Reading Services
Activities: *Awareness Events:* Sea to Sea Celebration Rally; *Speaker Service:* Yes

Description: To be a diverse family of congregations, assemblies & ministries expressing the good news of God's kingdom; Affiliation(s): National Association of Evangelicals; Reformed Ecumenical Council; World Alliance of Reformed Churches; Canadian Council of Churches; Evangelical Fellowship of Canada

Christian Science / La Première Église du Christ, Scientiste

The First Church of Christ, Scientist, 210 Massachusetts Ave., Boston MA 02115 USA
Tel: 617-450-2000; *Toll-Free:* 888-424-2535
info@christianscience.com
www.christianscience.com
www.facebook.com/worldwidechristianscience
twitter.com/prayerandhealth
Also Known As: The Mother Church
Overview: A large international organization founded in 1879
Finances: *Annual Operating Budget:* Greater than $5 Million; *Funding Sources:* Donations
Staff: 850 staff member(s)
Membership: 2,200 churches in over 70 countries; *Member Profile:* Individuals who are open to doctrines of the Christian Science textbook: Science & Health with Key to the Scriptures, by Rev. Mary Baker Eddy
Activities: Weekly services and testimonial meetings; Sunday School for children; Worldwide systems bureau; Retail book stores; Christian Science Reading Rooms; Christian Science programs & Weekly Bible Lessons broadcasted on public media; *Internships:* Yes; *Speaker Service:* Yes *Library:* Mary Baker Eddy Library for the Betterment of Humanity (Open to Public) by appointment
Description: To believe in one God, the Bible & in Christ Jesus as the Messiah; that the application of the laws of God are practical & provable

Christian Stewardship Services (CSS)

#208, 500 Alden Rd., Markham ON L3R 5H5
Fax: 905-947-9263
Toll-Free: 800-267-8890
info@csservices.ca
www.csservices.ca
Overview: A medium-sized national charitable organization founded in 1976
Chief Officer(s):
Maynard Wiersma, CFP, Executive Director, 800-267-8890 210
maynardw@csservices.ca
Rob Vandebelt, Manager, Investment Fund, 800-267-8890 250
robv@csservices.ca
Sophia Song, Administrator, Finance, 800-267-8890 218
sophias@csservices.ca
Finances: *Funding Sources:* Christian charities, including churches & schools; Social service organizations
Activities: Providing advice about will & estate planning; Offering the Growing & Giving program, featuring presentations & workshops
Description: To connect families, faith & finances for efficient estate & gift planning; To promote Biblical stewardship; *Member of:* Canadian Council of Christian Charities; *Affiliation(s):* Diaconal Ministries of the Christian Reformed Church

Church Council on Justice & Corrections (CCJC) / Conseil des églises pour la justice et la criminologie (CÉJC)

Laframboise Hall, #353, 223 Main St., Ottawa ON K1S 1C4
Tel: 613-563-1688; *Fax:* 613-237-6129
info@ccjc.ca
ccjc.ca
www.youtube.com/channel/UCbL3WH8MfWbUp-31s9gPjoQ
www.linkedin.com/company/the-church-council-on-justice-and-c orrections
www.facebook.com/ccjccanada
twitter.com/CCJCCanada
Overview: A medium-sized national charitable organization founded in 1972
Chief Officer(s):
Bonnie Weppler, Executive Director, 613-563-1688 1
bweppler@ccjc.ca
Finances: *Annual Operating Budget:* $250,000-$500,000
Staff: 1 staff member(s)
Activities: *Internships:* Yes; *Speaker Service:* Yes *Library:* Yes
Description: To strengthen churches' ministry in fields of crime prevention, justice & corrections; To initiate, encourage & support programs which sensitize congregations & educate volunteer groups to participate in development of community responses to crime, justice & corrections; to promote a healing justice; To examine & respond to policy concerns with assistance of churches; To call on churches to address issues; To provide resources to churches & other related organizations; *Member of:* National Associations Active in Criminal Justice; *Affiliation(s):* National Associations Active in Criminal Justice;

Collaborative Justice Program; Ottawa Restorative Justice Network; Circles of Support and Accountability National; CCJC Quebec

The Church Lads' Brigade (CLB)

PO Box 28126, 82 Harvey Rd., St. John's NL A1B 4J8
Tel: 709-722-1737; *Fax:* 709-722-1734
info@theclb.ca
www.theclb.ca
www.youtube.com/channel/UCEfcL5pd1b6z5iOgPlJqr5Q
www.facebook.com/TheCLB
twitter.com/TheCLB_NL
Also Known As: The CLB
Overview: A medium-sized provincial organization founded in 1892
Chief Officer(s):
Derek White, Executive Director
derek@theclb.ca
Finances: *Annual Operating Budget:* $50,000-$100,000; *Funding Sources:* Donations; building rentals; fundraising
Staff: 1 staff member(s); 200 volunteer(s)
Membership: 600 individuals + 16 companies; *Fees:* $20; *Member Profile:* All youth
Activities: Youth activities; Courses in badge work; Leadership training; Duke of Edinburgh's Award; Sports, camps & other activities; *Internships:* Yes *Library:* CLB Archives (Open to Public) by appointment
Description: To help youth develop the necessary skills to become future leaders through ecuation, recreational & social activities; Affiliation(s): The Church Lads' & Church Girls' Brigade (UK)

Church of the Good Shepherd (CoGS)

116 Queen St. North, Kitchener ON N2H 2H7
Tel: 519-743-3845; *Fax:* 519-743-3375
office@shepherdsway.ca
www.shepherdsway.ca
Also Known As: Swedenborgian Church
Overview: A small local organization
Chief Officer(s):
Dave Rogalsky, Minister
Membership: 140 individual
Activities: Kidspace; Sunday School; Children's Services
Description: To welcome all on a spiritual journey based on love, a deeper understanding og the Bible's teachings & a new passion for Creation; Affiliation(s): Swedenborg Church Youth League; Marigold Whole Life Centre; Gathering Leaves

Congregational Christian Churches in Canada (CCCC)

PO Box 463, Stn. Simcoe, Simcoe ON N3Y 4L5
Tel: 519-751-0606
4cnational@gmail.com
www.cccc.ca
www.facebook.com/4CChurches
Overview: A medium-sized national charitable organization founded in 1821
Chief Officer(s):
David MacKenzie, Chair
David Schrader, National Pastor
nationalpastor@bellnet.ca
Finances: *Annual Operating Budget:* $100,000-$250,000
Staff: 2 staff member(s)
Membership: 8,000 + 100 churches across Canada; *Fees:* $100; *Member Profile:* Churches or individuals in accord with CCCC's Statement of Faith and Founding Principles as set out in their By-Law & Supplementary Letters Patent
Activities: *Internships:* Yes
Description: To celebrate & serve Jesus Christ in the 21st century through shared concern for others

CrossTrainers Canada

PO Box 1426, Bradford ON L3Z 2B7
Tel: 416-697-0147
ct@ctministries.ca
www.ctministries.ca
www.instagram.com/ctcanada
www.facebook.com/crosstrainerscanada
twitter.com/CT_Canada
Overview: A small local organization founded in 2001
Chief Officer(s):
Jodi Greenstreet, Executive Director
Patti LaRose, Director, Operations
Jenna Wickens, Director, Youth
Finances: *Funding Sources:* Corporate sponsors
Staff: 5 staff member(s)
Activities: Connections Centre with True Vibe program, Playzone, cafe & special events; The Hub Youth Centre with A Hand Up Clothing Room; Mercy House, a women's shelter
Description: The association is a Christian ministry organization with members from several local churches serving the Bradford community.

Direction Chrétienne

#520, 1450, rue City Councillors, Montréal QC H3A 2E6
Tél: 514-878-3035; *Téléc:* 514-878-8048
info@direction.ca
www.direction.ca
Également appelé: Christian Direction
Aperçu: *Dimension: petite; Envergure: provinciale; Organisme sans but lucratif; fondée en 1964*
Membre(s) du bureau directeur:
Glenn Smith, Executive Director
Finances: *Budget de fonctionnement annuel:* $500,000-$1.5 Million
Personnel: 13 membre(s) du personnel; 3 bénévole(s)
Membre: 1-99
Description: Rendre visite aux communautés chrétiennes locales et particulièrement celles des grands centres urbains afin de se faire connaître et partager son mandat

Edmonton & District Council of Churches (EDCC)

c/o St. Patrick's Anglican Church, 334 Knottwood Rd. North, Edmonton AB T6K 2Z7
Tel: 780-463-5452
admin@EDCCunity.org
www.edccunity.org
Overview: A small local organization founded in 1942
Chief Officer(s):
Kevin Kraglund, President
president.edcc@telus.net
Finances: *Annual Operating Budget:* Less than $50,000
Staff: 1 staff member(s); 7 volunteer(s)
Membership: 22; *Fees:* $30 individual; $60 denominational; *Member Profile:* Any churches, Christian Organizations or individuals who accept Jesus Christ as Lord & Saviour; *Committees:* Ecumenical Coordinators; Week of Prayer for Christian Unity Service Planning Committee; Way of the Cross Planning Committee; No Room in the Inn Planning Committee
Activities: Organization of events; Distribution of information; Participation in interdenominational projects; *Awareness Events:* Week of Prayer for Christian Unity, Jan.; Good Friday Way of the Cross; No Room in the Inn Fundraising for Low Income Housing, Dec.
Description: To express the essential unity of the body of Christ through worship, fellowship, dialogue, cooperation, service & prayer; Affiliation(s): Canadian Council of Churches

Focus on the Family Canada

19946 - 80A Ave., Langley BC V2Y 0J8
Tel: 604-455-7900; *Fax:* 604-455-7999
Toll-Free: 800-661-9800
info@fotf.ca
www.focusonthefamily.ca
www.instagram.com/fotfcanada
www.facebook.com/fotfcanada
twitter.com/fotfcanada
Overview: A large national charitable organization founded in 1982
Chief Officer(s):
Terence Rolston, President
Finances: *Funding Sources:* Donations
Staff: 250 volunteer(s)
Activities: Seminars & conferences; Resources; Personal counselling & prayer support; *Library:* Focus on the Family Canada Library
Description: To strengthen & encourage the Canadian family through education & support based on out-dated Christian principles; *Member of:* Canadian Council of Christian Charities

General Church of the New Jerusalem in Canada (GCIC)

31 Dalegrove Cres., Toronto ON M9B 6A5
Tel: 416-239-3054
www.newchurch.ca
Overview: A small national organization founded in 1971
Chief Officer(s):
James Cooper, Pastor
rev.james.cooper@gmail.com
Description: To be devoted to the Christian life & teaching expounded in the works of Emanuel Swedenborg

Gospel Tract & Bible Society

PO Box 180, Ste Anne MB R5H 1R1
Tel: 204-355-4975
info@gospeltract.ca
www.gospeltractandbible.org
Overview: A small national organization
Description: Publishes Christian religious tracts; affiliated with Church of God in Christ, Mennonite

Grace Communion International Canada
#203A, 2121 Airport Dr., Saskatoon SK S7L 6W5

Tel: 306-653-2705
info@gcicanada.ca
www.gcicanada.ca
Previous Name: Worldwide Church of God Canada
Overview: A small national organization
Chief Officer(s):
Bill Hall, National Director
bhall@gcicanada.ca
Description: To proclaim the gospel of Jesus Christ around the world & to help members grow spiritually

Holy Face Association / Association de la Sainte Face
PO Box 310, Stn. B, Montréal QC H3B 3J7

Tel: 514-747-0357; *Fax:* 514-747-9147
holyface@holyface.com
www.holyface.com
www.facebook.com/holyfacemedal
Overview: A small national charitable organization founded in 1976
Finances: *Annual Operating Budget:* $250,000-$500,000;
Funding Sources: Donations
Staff: 20 volunteer(s)
Membership: 15,000-49,999
Activities: *Speaker Service:* Yes *Library:* Yes by appointment
Description: The goal of this apostolate is reparation to God (Father, Son & Holy Spirit) through contemplative devotion to the Holy Face of Jesus

Hope & Healing International
PO Box 800, 3844 Stoufville Rd., Stouffville ON L4A 7Z9

Tel: 905-640-6464; *Toll-Free:* 800-567-2264
info@hopeandhealing.org
www.hopeandhealing.org
www.youtube.com/user/cbmcanada
www.facebook.com/HopeandHealingInternational
twitter.com/hopehealingintl
Previous Name: Christian Blind Mission International
Overview: A medium-sized international charitable organization founded in 1978
Chief Officer(s):
Ed Epp, Executive Director
Jill Bartley, Chief Operations Officer
Beth Jost-Reimer, Chief Strategy Officer
Finances: *Annual Operating Budget:* Greater than $5 Million
Staff: 28 staff member(s); 45 volunteer(s)
Activities: Prevention & medical treatment; rehabilitation; creating equal opportunities; Healinghugs donation program; *Rents Mailing List:* Yes *Library:* Talking Book Library (Open to Public)
Description: To help people living with or affected by disabilities in poor communities around the world; To value people as Jesus values them; *Member of:* Canadian Council of Christian Charities

Indian Métis Christian Fellowship (IMCF)
3131 Dewdney Ave., Regina SK S4T 0Y5

Tel: 306-359-1096
imcf.info@sasktel.net
www.IMCF.ca
Overview: A small local organization founded in 1978
Chief Officer(s):
Ben Vandezande, Interim Director
Finances: *Annual Operating Budget:* $100,000-$250,000
Membership: 30 individual
Activities: Drop-in ministry; daily prayer circle; soup & bannock lunch; computer club
Description: IMCF is an urban aboriginal ministry supported by the Christian Reformed Church in North America - Canada. Its mission is to develop a worshipping, working community through serving the spiritual & social needs of aboriginal people in Regina.; *Affiliation(s):* Canadian Ministry Board; Indian Family Center, Winnipeg; Native Healing Centre, Edmonton

Institut Séculier Pie X (ISPX) / Pius X Secular Institute
CP 87731, Succ. Charlesbourg, Québec QC G1G 5W6

Tél: 418-626-5882; *Téléc:* 418-624-2277
info@ispx.org
www.ispx.org
Aperçu: *Dimension:* petite; *Envergure:* internationale; *Organisme sans but lucratif; fondée en 1939*
Membre(s) du bureau directeur:
Marcel Caron, Directeur général
Finances: *Budget de fonctionnement annuel:* $100,000-$250,000
Personnel: 2 membre(s) du personnel
Activités: Apostolat catholique; évangélisation; présence au monde; *Service de conférenciers:* Oui
Description: Évangéliser les milieux populaires par la présence et par des activités apostoliques; *Membre de:* Conférence

canadienne des instituts séculiers; Conférence mondiale des instituts séculiers

Intercede International
201 Stanton St., Fort Erie ON L2A 3N8

Tel: 905-871-1773; *Fax:* 905-871-5165
Toll-Free: 800-871-0882
friends@intercedenow.ca
www.intercedenow.ca
Previous Name: Christian Aid Mission
Overview: A medium-sized international charitable organization founded in 1953
Chief Officer(s):
James S. Eagles, President
Finances: *Annual Operating Budget:* $500,000-$1.5 Million;
Funding Sources: Private donations
Staff: 10 staff member(s); 50 volunteer(s)
Membership: 10; *Committees:* Audit Review
Activities: Sponsorship programs; Relief aid; Equipment & materials provisions; Missions cafe held in major cities; *Speaker Service:* Yes *Library:* Intercede International Library (Open to Public) by appointment
Description: To aid, encourage & strengthen indigenous New Testament Christianity, particularly where Christians are impoverished, few, or persecuted; To encourage Christian witness & ministry to the international community in North America; *Member of:* Canadian Council of Christian Charities; *Affiliation(s):* Evangelical Fellowship of Canada

International Bible Correspondence School
PO Box 98590, 873 Jane St., Toronto ON M6N 4C0

www.ibcschool.ca
Overview: A small international organization founded in 1968
Chief Officer(s):
Richard Kruse, Director
Member Profile: Any individual wishing to engage in Bible studies
Description: To provide students with tools for Bible study

Inter-Varsity Christian Fellowship (IVCF)
1 International Blvd., Toronto ON M9W 6H3

Tel: 416-443-1170; *Fax:* 416-443-1499
Toll-Free: 800-668-9766
info@ivcf.ca
ivcf.ca
www.instagram.com/intervarsitycanada
www.facebook.com/intervarsitycanada
twitter.com/InterVarsityCAN
Overview: A medium-sized national charitable organization founded in 1929
Chief Officer(s):
Nigel Pollock, President
Finances: *Funding Sources:* Donations
Activities: Offering Pioneer Camps across Canada; Providing ministry at university & college campuses; Offering travel opportunities through Inter-Varsity's World Services' Global Partnerships; Participating in the Urbana Student Mission Convention; *Internships:* Yes
Description: To help the transformation of youth, students & graduates into fully committed followers of Jesus Christ, regardless of background or ethnicity

Jews for Jesus
10 Huntingdale Blvd., Toronto ON M1W 2S5

Tel: 416-444-7020; *Fax:* 805-267-4141
toronto@jewsforjesus.ca
www.jewsforjesus.ca
www.facebook.com/jewsforjesuscanada
twitter.com/jewsforjesuscan
Overview: A small local charitable organization founded in 1981
Chief Officer(s):
Andrew Barron, Canadian Director/Missionary
andrew.barron@jewsforjesus.ca
Description: Jews for Jesus Canada is a Jewish evangelistic agency dedicated to bringing the Gospel into places where a significantly Jewish testimony is needed.; *Member of:* Canadian Council of Christian Charities; Evangelical Fellowship of Canada; Interdenominational Foreign Mission Association

Lifewater Canada
457 Heather Cres., Thunder Bay ON P7E 5L1

Tel: 807-622-4848; *Fax:* 807-577-9798
Toll-Free: 888-543-3426
info@lifewater.ca
www.lifewater.ca
www.facebook.com/lifewater.ca
Overview: A small international organization founded in 1995
Chief Officer(s):
Alanna Drost, Contact
Member Profile: Hydrogeologists, well drillers, educators, engineers, environmental scientists, businessmen & many other people with diverse skills & training

Description: To be dedicated to ensuring that people everywhere have access to adequate supplies of safe water; To train & equip nationals with drill rigs & hand pumps so they can solve their own water problems

Lighthouse Mission
669 Main St., Winnipeg MB R3B 1E3

Tel: 204-943-9669; *Fax:* 204-949-9479
info@lighthousemission.ca
www.lighthousemission.ca
www.facebook.com/lighthousemission.ca
Overview: A small local organization founded in 1911
Chief Officer(s):
Joel Cormie, Operations Manager
J'Lynn Johnson, Manager, Donor Relations
Joan Vezeau, Administrative Assistant
Richard Kunzelman, Door-to-Door Embassador
Activities: Operates a soup kitchen; Distributes clothing
Description: To provide food and services to the needy in Winnipeg

Living Bible Explorers (LBE)
600 Burnell St., Winnipeg MB R3G 2B7

Tel: 204-786-8667; *Fax:* 204-775-7525
Toll-Free: 866-786-8667
lbe@mymts.net
livingbibleexplorers.com
www.facebook.com/livingbibleexplorers
Overview: A small provincial charitable organization founded in 1969
Chief Officer(s):
Curtis Klassen, General Manager
Cheryl Peters, Assistant Manager
Mary Ann Funk, Children's Program Coordinator
Nicola Plett, Children's Program Coordinator
Finances: *Annual Operating Budget:* $250,000-$500,000;
Funding Sources: Individual and cooperate donations; Provincial government; individual churches; foundations
Staff: 10 staff member(s); 200 volunteer(s)
Membership: 700 individual; *Committees:* New Bible Camp; Board of Directors
Activities: Boys & Girls Clubs; Summer & weekend camps; Ministry for kids & teens; Food distribution; Weekly home visitation; Annual banquet; *Awareness Events:* Mission Fest - Feb; Annual Fundraising Banquet - Mar; Garage Sale - May; *Internships:* Yes; *Speaker Service:* Yes *Library:* Living Bible Explorers' Resource Library (Open to Public)
Description: To help children, youth & their families become productive, responsible & spiritually mature individuals; *Member of:* Canadian Council of Christian Charities

The Lord's Flock Charismatic Community
Our Lady of Fatima Shrine, 3170 St. Clair Ave. East, Toronto ON M1L 1V6

Tel: 416-317-9599
lordsflock.intl@gmail.com
www.lordsflock.org
Overview: A medium-sized international organization
Chief Officer(s):
Jun Silva, Contact
Cynthia Silva, Contact
Georgia Gaceta, Contact
Pilar Acosta, Contact
Finances: *Annual Operating Budget:* Less than $50,000
Activities: Pilgrimages; Christian holiday celebrations; seminars
Description: To promote the Christian faith while preserving culture & heritage for future generations; *Affiliation(s):* Archdiocese of Toronto

M2/W2 Association - Restorative Christian Ministries (M2/W2)
#208, 2825 Clearbrook Rd., Abbotsford BC V2T 6S3

Tel: 604-859-3215; *Fax:* 604-859-1216
Toll-Free: 800-298-1777
info@m2w2.com
www.m2w2.com
www.linkedin.com/groups/5100601
www.facebook.com/M2W2Association
twitter.com/M2W2Association
Also Known As: Man-to-Man/Woman-to-Woman
Overview: A small provincial charitable organization founded in 1966
Chief Officer(s):
Raymond Robyn, Executive Director
Finances: *Annual Operating Budget:* $250,000-$500,000;
Funding Sources: 65% community fundraising; 35% federal & provincial government contracts
Staff: 11 staff member(s); 400 volunteer(s)
Membership: 190; *Fees:* $10; *Member Profile:* Wide range of people whose common interest is the focus of M2/W2; *Committees:* Finance/Promotion; Program/New Initiatives; Personnel

Activities: Organizing annual promotion dinners; *Speaker Service:* Yes
Description: To mutually transform lives - one relationship at a time; To see individuals & communities in British Columbia safer, transformed, reconciled, & restored through justice, accountability, partnerships, mutual support, mediation, education & prevention; To provide one-to-one volunteers for men & women in British Columbia prisons, combined with pre- & post-release support & resources; To counsel prisoners, ex-prisoners, & their families; To prevent crime through one-to-one support for parents of young children at risk; *Member of:* Canadian Council of Christian Charities

Metropolitan Community Church of Toronto
115 Simpson Ave., Toronto ON M4K 1A1
Tel: 416-406-6228; *Fax:* 416-466-5207
Overview: A small local charitable organization founded in 1984
Chief Officer(s):
Brent Hawkes, Senior Pastor
Finances: *Annual Operating Budget:* Less than $50,000
Staff: 1 staff member(s); 8 volunteer(s)
Membership: 30
Activities: Weekly worship services; Baptism, weddings & funerals; Volunteer ministries & programs; Leading social programs conccerning same-sex marriage, trans education, black education awareness & refugee support & sponsorship
Description: Ministry by and for the LGBT community of Toronto; *Member of:* Universal Fellowship of Metropolitan Community Churches

Micah House
205 Holton Ave. South, Hamilton ON L8M 2L8
Tel: 905-296-4387
info@micahhouse.ca
www.micahhouse.ca
www.facebook.com/MicahHouseHamilton
twitter.com/micah_house
Overview: A small local organization founded in 2006
Chief Officer(s):
Scott Jones, Executive Director
scott@micahhouse.ca
Finances: *Funding Sources:* Donations
Staff: 6 staff member(s)
Member Profile: Christians from a variety of churches & organizations in Hamilton, Ontario
Activities: *Awareness Events:* Walkathon
Description: To demonstrate God's love to newly arrived refugees in Hamilton, Ontario

Les Missions des Soeurs Missionnaires du Christ-Roi
4730, boul Lévesque ouest, Chomedey QC H7W 2R4
Tél: 450-687-2100
missionsmcr@hotmail.com
www.missionnairescr.org
Également appelé: Missions MCR
Aperçu: *Dimension:* moyenne; *Envergure:* internationale; *Organisme sans but lucratif; fondée en* 1979
Finances: *Budget de fonctionnement annuel:* $250,000-$500,000; *Fonds:* Fondations; Subventions
Personnel: 1 membre(s) du personnel
Membre: 100-499
Activités: *Bibliothèque:* Oui (Bibliothèque publique)
Description: Organiser, administrer, maintenir une oeuvre dont les fins sont la religion, la charité; promouvoir l'éducation et le bien-être, particulièrement en ce qui a trait aux différents buts qu'il s'est fixé; aide internationale

New Apostolic Church Canada
319 Bridgeport Rd. East, Waterloo ON N2J 2K9
Tel: 519-884-2862; *Toll-Free:* 866-622-7828
info@naccanada.org
www.naccanada.org
www.youtube.com/c/NewApostolicChurchCanada
www.facebook.com/NACCanada
Overview: A medium-sized international organization
Description: To take a balanced approach to bible-based faith, recognizing three sacraments: Holy Baptism, Holy Sealing & Holy Communion; *Member of:* New Apostolic Church (International)

Les Oblates Missionnaires de Marie Immaculée (OMMI) / Oblate Missionaries of Mary Immaculate
7625, boul Parent, Trois-Rivières QC G9C 0M5
Tél: 819-375-7317
ommi@ommi-is.org
www.ommi-is.org
Aperçu: *Dimension:* petite; *Envergure:* internationale; *fondée en* 1952

Olivet New Church
279 Burnhamthorpe Rd., Toronto ON M9B 1Z6
Tel: 416-239-3054
contact@olivetnewchurch.org
www.facebook.com/olivet.newchurch
Also Known As: Olivet
Overview: A small local organization founded in 1893
Activities: Offering Sunday worship & school services; *Speaker Service:* Yes *Library:* Yes
Description: To inspire belief in New Church teachings; To encourage spiritual growth practices; To provide & promote service to others; To offer leadership & volunteerism opportunities

OMF International - Canada (OMF)
#21, 5155 Spectrum Way., Mississauga ON L4W 5A1
Tel: 905-568-9971; *Fax:* 905-568-9974
Toll-Free: 888-657-8010
omfcanada@omf.ca
www.omf.ca
www.facebook.com/omfcanada
twitter.com/OMFcanada
Also Known As: Overseas Missionary Fellowship
Previous Name: China Inland Mission
Overview: A medium-sized international organization founded in 1865
Chief Officer(s):
Ron Adams, Director, Administration & Finance
Jon Fuller, National Director
Membership: 1,300 missionaries worldwide; *Member Profile:* Four years post-secondary education
Description: To share the good news of Jesus Christ with East Asia's peoples; *Member of:* Interdenominational Foreign Mission Association; *Affiliation(s):* Evangelical Fellowship of Canada

Ontario Alliance of Christian Schools (OACS)
790 Shaver Rd., Ancaster ON L9G 3K9
Tel: 905-648-2100; *Fax:* 905-648-2110
oacs@oacs.org
www.oacs.org
twitter.com/oacsnews
Overview: A medium-sized provincial organization founded in 1952
Chief Officer(s):
Julius de Jager, MAT, Executive Director, 905-648-2100 15
julesdj@oacs.org
Finances: *Annual Operating Budget:* $500,000-$1.5 Million; *Funding Sources:* Membership dues
Staff: 12 staff member(s); 200 volunteer(s)
Membership: 1-99; *Fees:* Schedule available; *Committees:* Finance; Education; PR; Planning; Government Relations; Personnel
Activities: *Speaker Service:* Yes; *Rents Mailing List:* Yes
Description: To promote independent schools in Ontario; to promote Christian education in Canada; to provide educational services for member schools; to lobby government for educational choice. Canada's largest & oldest independent school organization, representing 79 schools with approximately 14,000 students.; *Affiliation(s):* Christian Schools International; Christian Schools Canada

Ontario Christian Music Assembly
90 Topcliff Ave., Toronto ON M3N 1L8
Tel: 416-636-9779; *Fax:* 905-775-2230
landmkooy@rogers.com
Overview: A small provincial organization founded in 1961
Membership: 130 individual
Activities: Spring & Christmas concerts series; Annual Christian festival concert

Pacific Life Bible College
15030 - 66A Ave., Surrey BC V3S 2A5
Tel: 604-597-9082; *Fax:* 604-597-9090
Toll-Free: 877-597-7522
info@pacificlife.edu
pacificlife.edu
vimeo.com/channels/plbc
www.facebook.com/pacificlifebiblecollege
twitter.com/plbc
Merged from: Pacific Life Bible College; Christ College
Overview: A small national charitable organization founded in 1997
Chief Officer(s):
Craig Millar, President
cmillar@pacificlife.edu
Member Profile: Applicants to the college must be born-again Christians actively involved in a church for a minimum of a full year prior to application.
Activities: *Library:* Wolf Memorial Library
Member of: International Church of the Foursquare Gospel

Prison Fellowship Canada / Fraternite des prisons du Canada
#144, 5945 Airport Rd., Mississauga ON L4V 1R9
Tel: 905-673-5867; *Fax:* 905-673-6955
Toll-Free: 844-618-5867
info@prisonfellowship.ca
prisonfellowship.ca
www.youtube.com/channel/UC6GV-_BVbJpuOoodh6P3XvA
www.facebook.com/PrisonFellowshipCanada
Overview: A small national organization founded in 1980
Chief Officer(s):
Stacey Campbell, President & CEO, 844-618-5867
Johathan Miller, Chief Operating Officer, 844-618-5867 225
jmiller@prisonerfellowship.ca
Description: To challenge, equip & serve the body of Christ in its ministry to prisoners, ex-prisoners, victims & their families; To promote the advancement of restorative justice; *Member of:* Prison Fellowship International

REHOBOTH Christian Ministries
3920 - 49th Ave., Stony Plain AB T7Z 2J7
Tel: 780-963-4044; *Fax:* 780-963-3075
flourish@rcmflourish.ca
www.rcmflourish.ca
www.instagram.com/rehoboth.alberta
www.facebook.com/339247416224894
twitter.com/rehobothalberta
Also Known As: Christian Association for the Mentally Handicapped of Alberta
Overview: A medium-sized provincial charitable organization founded in 1976
Chief Officer(s):
Ron Bos, Executive Director
ron.bos@rcmflourish.ca
Finances: *Annual Operating Budget:* Greater than $5 Million; *Funding Sources:* Provincial government; membership fees; donations; church offerings
Staff: 535 staff member(s); 950 volunteer(s)
Membership: 4,600; *Fees:* $10; *Member Profile:* Everybody accepting their mission statement; *Committees:* Regional Advisory
Activities: Residential, vocational & recreational support for individuals who live with disabilities; summer camp program; fundraising golf tournament; *Internships:* Yes
Description: To convey God's love to persons with disabilities through support, advocacy & public education & by providing opportunities for personal growth & meaningful participation in society; *Member of:* Alberta Council of Disability Services; Canadian Centre for Philanthropy; *Affiliation(s):* Christian Stewardship Services

The Salvation Army in Canada
Territorial Headquarters, Canada & Bermuda, 2 Overlea Blvd., Toronto ON M4H 1P4
Tel: 416-425-2111; *Toll-Free:* 800-725-2769
www.salvationarmy.ca
www.youtube.com/user/salvationarmy
www.linkedin.com/company/the-salvation-army-in-canada
www.facebook.com/salvationarmy
twitter.com/salvationarmy
Overview: A large international charitable organization founded in 1882
Finances: *Annual Operating Budget:* Greater than $5 Million
Staff: 537 staff member(s)
Membership: 311 Corps (congregations); 330+ social-service institutes across Canada
Activities: *Speaker Service:* Yes
Description: To preach the Gospel of Jesus Christ; To supply basic human needs; To provide personal counselling & undertake the spiritual & moral regeneration & physical rehabilitation of all persons in need who come within its sphere of influence; *Member of:* Evangelical Fellowship of Canada

Samaritan House Ministries Inc.
820 Pacific Ave., Brandon MB R7A 0J1
Tel: 204-726-0758
info@samaritanhouse.net
samaritanhouse.net
www.facebook.com/210774752373958
twitter.com/SHM_Brandon
Overview: A small local charitable organization founded in 1987
Chief Officer(s):
Thea Dennis, Executive Director
Activities: *Internships:* Yes; *Speaker Service:* Yes
Description: To provide support & services to at-risk populations - the homeless, those living in poverty, people with literacy challenges or persons leaving abusive relationships

Samaritan's Purse Canada (SPC)
20 Hopewell Way NE, Calgary AB T3J 5H5
Fax: 403-250-6567
Toll-Free: 800-663-6500
info@samaritan.ca
www.samaritanspurse.ca
www.youtube.com/user/samaritanspursecan
www.facebook.com/samaritanspursecan
twitter.com/spcanada
Also Known As: Operation Christmas Child
Overview: A large international charitable organization founded in 1973
Chief Officer(s):
Franklin Graham, President & CEO
Fred Weiss, Executive Director
Finances: *Annual Operating Budget:* Greater than $5 Million; *Funding Sources:* Donations
Staff: 100 staff member(s); 1500 volunteer(s)
Activities: Operation Christmas Child packages; Turn on the Tap access to safe water program; *Internships:* Yes; *Speaker Service:* Yes
Description: To meet both physical & spiritual needs of people who are victims of war, poverty, natural disasters, disease & famine; To provide emergency relief & development programs & medical projects; *Member of:* Canadian Council of Christian Charities; *Affiliation(s):* Samaritan's Purse USA

The Secular Institute of Missionaries of the Kingship of Christ (SIM)
andre.comtois28@gmail.com
www.simkc.org
Previous Name: Missionaires de la Royauté du Christ
Overview: A small local organization founded in 1919
Membership: 2,200

Sisters of St. Benedict (OSB)
225 Masters Ave., Winnipeg MB R4A 2A1
Tel: 204-338-4601; *Fax:* 204-339-8775
stbens@mts.net
www.stbens.ca
Also Known As: Sisters of the Order of St. Benedict
Overview: A small provincial charitable organization founded in 1912
Chief Officer(s):
Virginia Evard, Prioress
Finances: *Funding Sources:* Donations
Staff: 35 staff member(s); 30 volunteer(s)
Membership: 33
Activities: Programs in spirituality, personal growth & a variety of retreats; *Library:* St. Benedict's Monastery Library by appointment
Description: To witness Jesus Christ, through community life & prayer, contemplative living, hospitality, service to the people of God & stewardship of all God's gifts; *Member of:* Federation of St. Gertrude

Society of Christian Schools in British Columbia (SCSBC)
Fosmark Centre, Trinity Western University, 7600 Glover Rd., Langley BC V2Y 1Y1
Tel: 604-888-6366; *Fax:* 604-888-2791
contact@scsbc.ca
www.scsbc.ca
Previous Name: Southwest British Columbia League of Christian Schools
Overview: A small provincial organization founded in 1976
Chief Officer(s):
Ed Noot, Executive Director
ed.noot@scsbc.ca
Darren Spyksma, Director, Learning
darren.spyksma@scsbc.ca
Greg Gerber, Director, Learning
greg.gerber@scsbc.ca
Karen Bush, Designer, Creative Services
karen.bush@scsbc.ca
Membership: 1-99; *Member Profile:* Christian school campuses & societies in British Columbia
Activities: Monitoring government policies & regulations regarding Christian schools, & advising schools about government relations; Promoting Christian education throughout British Columbia; Offering workshops; Publishing resource handbooks; Assisting new Christian schools & expanding schools; Supporting digital learning; *Library:* Society of Christian Schools in British Columbia Resource Library
Description: To serve Christian schools in British Columbia; To seek support in the provision of Christian education; To develop policies & curriculum outlines & units; *Affiliation(s):* Christian Schools International (CSI); Christian Schools Canada (CSC); Christian Teachers Association of British Columbia; Christian Principals Association of British Columbia

Strathcona Christian Academy Society (SCA)
1011 Clover Bar Rd., Sherwood Park AB T8A 4V7
Tel: 780-467-4752
scasociety@spac.ca
www.scasociety.ca
Overview: A small local organization founded in 1980
Chief Officer(s):
Liann Cross, Office Manager
Finances: *Annual Operating Budget:* $3 Million-$5 Million; *Funding Sources:* Regional Government
Staff: 47 staff member(s); 120 volunteer(s)
Description: To challenge students, through Christ-centred education & teach them to accept Jesus Christ as Savior & Lord in order to pursue a life of godly character, personal & academic excellence & service to others; *Member of:* Elk Island Public Schools; *Affiliation(s):* Sherwood Park Alliance Church

Union of Spiritual Communities of Christ (USCC)
PO Box 760, Grand Forks BC V0H 1H0
Tel: 250-365-3613; *Fax:* 250-442-3433
info@usccdoukhobors.org
www.usccdoukhobors.org
Overview: A small national organization founded in 1943
Activities: Publish Iskra newsletter
Description: To be dedicated to the sustainability and enrichment of the Doukhobor Life-Concept based on the Law of God and the Teachings of Jesus Christ

Women's Inter-Church Council of Canada (WICC) / Conseil oecuménique des chrétiennes du Canada
47 Queen's Park Cres. East, Toronto ON M5S 2C3
Tel: 416-929-5184; *Fax:* 416-929-4064
wicc@wicc.org
www.wicc.org
www.instagram.com/wiccanada
www.facebook.com/WICCanada
Overview: A medium-sized national organization founded in 1918
Chief Officer(s):
Catherine MacKeil, Executive Director
mackeil@wicc.org
Finances: *Funding Sources:* World Day of Prayer offerings
Member Profile: Representatives from the Anglican Church of Canada, the Canadian Baptist Ministries, the Christian Church (Disciples of Christ), the Evangelical Lutheran Church in Canada, the Mennonite Central Committee, the Presbyterian Church in Canada, the Religious Society of Friends, the Roman Catholic Church, the Salvation Army & the United Church of Canada; Membership is by appointment & election; *Committees:* Program; Communications; Membership & Nominating; Finance
Activities: Establishing the Ecumenical Network for Women's Justice; Preparing policy statements on issues such as racial justice & health care; Granting funds for a variety of projects that benefit women & children in Canada & around the world; Coordinating the Fellowship of the Least Coin program in Canada; Providing education, such as theology workshops; *Awareness Events:* World Day of Prayer
Description: To encourage women to grow in ecumenism; To share their spirituality & prayer; To respond to national & international issues affecting women; To take action together for justice

World Renew (CRWRC)
PO Box 5070, Stn. LCD 1, 3475 Mainway, Burlington ON L7R 3Y8
Tel: 905-336-2920; *Toll-Free:* 800-730-3490
info@worldrenew.net
worldrenew.net
www.youtube.com/c/SeeWorldRenew
www.linkedin.com/company/worldrenew
www.facebook.com/worldrenew
twitter.com/worldrenew_net
Previous Name: Christian Reformed World Relief Committee
Overview: A large international charitable organization founded in 1962
Chief Officer(s):
Carol Bremer-Bennet, Co-Director, 905-336-2920 4303
Ida Kaastra-Mutoigo, Co-Director, 905-336-2920 4303
imutoigo@worldrenew.net
Melissa Barnes, Chief Financial Officer
Finances: *Annual Operating Budget:* Greater than $5 Million; *Funding Sources:* Christian Reformed Churches; Other denominations
Staff: 58 staff member(s)
Membership: 15,000-49,999
Activities: *Awareness Events:* World Hunger Week, November; *Internships:* Yes; *Speaker Service:* Yes *Library:* Yes (Open to Public)
Description: To engage God's people in redeeming resources & developing gifts in collaborative activities of love, mercy, justice & compassion; *Member of:* Canadian Foodgrains Bank; Canadian Council of Christian Charities; Canadian Council for

International Cooperation; *Affiliation(s):* Christian Reformed Church in North America

Wycliffe Bible Translators of Canada, Inc. (WBTC)
4316 - 10th St. NE, Calgary AB T2E 6K3
Tel: 403-250-5411; *Fax:* 403-250-2623
Toll-Free: 800-463-1143
info@wycliffe.ca
www.wycliffe.ca
www.youtube.com/wycliffecanada
www.facebook.com/WycliffeCanada
twitter.com/wycliffe_canada
Also Known As: Wycliffe Canada
Overview: A large national charitable organization founded in 1968
Chief Officer(s):
Roy Eyre, President
John Chiu, Senior Vice-President, Operations
Finances: *Annual Operating Budget:* Greater than $5 Million; *Funding Sources:* Charitable donations
Staff: 400 staff member(s); 75 volunteer(s)
Activities: Overseas Bible translation & literacy programs; *Internships:* Yes; *Speaker Service:* Yes *Library:* Resource Centre (Open to Public)
Description: To serve minority language groups worldwide by fostering an understanding of God's Word through Bible translation, while encouraging literacy, education & stronger communities; *Member of:* Wycliffe Global Alliance; *Affiliation(s):* Wycliffe Bible Translators International; Summer Institute of Linguistics; Canada Institute of Linguistics; Wycliffe Associates Canada

Yonge Street Mission (YSM)
H.B Martin Family Centre for Urban Education, 306 Gerrard St. East, Toronto ON M5A 2G7
Tel: 416-929-9614; *Fax:* 416-929-7204
Toll-Free: 800-416-5111
info@ysm.ca
www.ysm.ca
www.facebook.com/YongeStreetMission
twitter.com/YSM_TO
Overview: A medium-sized local charitable organization founded in 1896
Chief Officer(s):
Angela Draskovic, President & CEO
Angela Solomos, Chief Philanthropy Officer
Brent Mitchell, Mission Program Officer
Cliff Cline, Mission Administrative Officer
Finances: *Annual Operating Budget:* Greater than $5 Million; *Funding Sources:* Donations; churches; individuals; businesses; foundations; grants
Staff: 120 staff member(s); 4000 volunteer(s)
Activities: Recreation; Education; Social & family events; Relief; Housing; *Internships:* Yes; *Speaker Service:* Yes
Description: To bring God's peace, love & justice to people living with economic, social & spiritual poverty in Toronto

Youth for Christ Canada
#308, 8047 - 199th St., Langley BC V2Y 0E2
Tel: 604-637-3400; *Fax:* 604-243-6992
Toll-Free: 800-899-9322
info@yfcanada.com
www.yfcanada.com
www.facebook.com/youthforchristcanada
twitter.com/yfccanada
Overview: A medium-sized national organization
Chief Officer(s):
Tim Coles, National Director
Membership: 31 chapters + 300 Ministry Centres
Activities: Responsible, effective & culturally sensitive evangelism of youth, communicating & caring in ways that are relevant to this generation
Description: To impact every young person in Canada with the person, work & teachings of Jesus Christ & discipling them into the Church

Creationism

Creation Science Association of British Columbia
PO Box 39577, RPO White Rock, Surrey BC V4A 0A9
Tel: 604-535-0019
info@creationbc.org
www.creationbc.org
Overview: A small provincial charitable organization founded in 1968
Chief Officer(s):
George Pearce, President
Finances: *Annual Operating Budget:* Less than $50,000
Staff: 25 volunteer(s)
Membership: 125 individual; *Fees:* $15 individual
Activities: *Speaker Service:* Yes *Library:* DVD Lending Library by appointment

Description: To compile scientific as well as Biblical evidence that supports creation & contradicts evolution; To communicate this information to schools, churches & the general public

Creation Science of Saskatchewan Inc. (CSSI)
PO Box 26, Kenaston SK S0G 2N0
Tel: 306-252-2842; *Fax:* 306-252-2842
www.creation-science.sk.ca
Overview: A small provincial charitable organization founded in 1978
Chief Officer(s):
Keith Miller, President
Finances: *Annual Operating Budget:* Less than $50,000; *Funding Sources:* Donations
Staff: 13 volunteer(s)
Membership: 15 institutional + 140 individual; *Fees:* $10
Activities: Meetings; Speakers; Book tables; Tours; Summer camp; *Speaker Service:* Yes *Library:* Creation Science of Saskatchewan Library by appointment
Description: To collect, organize & distribute information on Creation; To develop a better public understanding of Creation; To prepare & promote resource material on scientific creation for educational use & to be used in school curricula

Ecumenism

The Canadian Council of Churches (CCC) / Le conseil Canadien des églises
47 Queen's Park Cres. East, 3rd Fl., Toronto ON M5S 2C3
Tel: 416-972-9494; *Toll-Free:* 866-822-7645
admin@councilofchurches.ca
www.councilofchurches.ca
www.instagram.com/cdncouncilofchurches
www.facebook.com/CCC.CCE
twitter.com/ccc_cce
Overview: A large national charitable organization founded in 1944
Chief Officer(s):
Stephen Kendall, President
Peter Noteboom, General Secretary
Finances: *Funding Sources:* Member churches; Donations
Staff: 18 staff member(s); 1 volunteer(s)
Membership: 26 denominations of Anglican, Evangelical, Free Church, Eastern & Oriental Orthodox, Protestant & Catholic traditions
Activities: Peace Research Institute Project Ploughshares; maintaining dialogue with all faith groups; social justice & human rights; ecumenical dialogue; interfaith ministry; & life sciences
Description: To respond to Christ's call for unity & peace; To seek Christ's truth with affection for diversity; To act in love through prayer, dialogue & witness to the gospel; *Affiliation(s):* Citizens for Public Justice; Friendship Ministries Canada; Oikocredit; The Yonge Street Mission

Forum for Intercultural Leadership & Learning
The Canadian Churches' Forum for Global Ministries, 47 Queen's Park Cres. East, Toronto ON M5S 2C3
Tel: 416-924-9351; *Fax:* 416-978-7821
www.ccforum.ca
www.facebook.com/InterculturalLeadershipandLearning
Previous Name: Ecumenical Forum of Canada; The Canadian Churches' Forum for Global Ministries
Overview: A medium-sized international charitable organization founded in 1921
Chief Officer(s):
Jonathan Schmidt, Director
Jolan Ready, Administrator
Finances: *Annual Operating Budget:* $100,000-$250,000; *Funding Sources:* Churches; Religious orders; Individuals
Staff: 2 staff member(s); 30 volunteer(s)
Membership: 1-99
Activities: Mission Personnel Programs; Annual Katherine Hockin Award & Dinner; International visitors; Publications; Roundtables & guest speakers; *Library:* Forum for Intercultural Leadership & Learning Library by appointment
Description: To provide ecumenical orientation & re-entry programs for mission personnel; To stimulate ecumenical dialogue on issues of mission, global concerns & social justice; *Member of:* International Association for Mission Studies; Forum on International Personnel; *Affiliation(s):* Canadian Council of Churches

KAIROS: Canadian Ecumenical Justice Initiatives / Initiatives canadiennes oecuméniques pour la justice
#400, 80 Hayden St., Toronto ON M4Y 3G2
Tel: 416-463-5312; *Fax:* 416-463-5569
Toll-Free: 877-403-8933
info@kairoscanada.org
www.kairoscanada.org
www.youtube.com/user/KAIROSCanada
www.facebook.com/kairosCEJI
twitter.com/kairoscanada
Previous Name: Ecumenical Coalition for Economic Justice; GATT-Fly
Overview: A small national organization founded in 2001
Chief Officer(s):
Jennifer Henry, Executive Director, 416-463-5312 236
jhenry@kairoscanada.org
Ed Bianchi, Manager, Programs, 613-235-9956 221
ebianchi@kairoscanada.org
Finances: *Annual Operating Budget:* $1.5 Million-$3 Million; *Funding Sources:* Member denominations; Religious communities; Individual & group donations; Grants
Staff: 33 staff member(s); 300 volunteer(s)
Membership: 10; *Member Profile:* Canadian Churches; Religious organizations
Activities: *Speaker Service:* Yes
Description: To undertake a program of research & action with churches & popular groups emphasizing coalition-building & social transformation; five churches have participated in the Coalition since its inception: the Anglican Church of Canada, the Canadian Conference of Catholic Bishops, the Evangelical Lutheran Church in Canada, the Presbyterian Church in Canada, the United Church of Canada; *Member of:* Canadian Network on Corporate Accountability; *Affiliation(s):* Canadian Council of Churches

Student Christian Movement of Canada (SCM) / Mouvement d'étudiant(e)s chrétien(ne)s
103 Bellevue Ave., Toronto ON M5T 2N8
Tel: 416-463-7622
info@scmcanada.org
scmcanada.org
www.facebook.com/scmcanada
twitter.com/scmcanada
Also Known As: SCM Canada
Overview: A medium-sized national charitable organization
Chief Officer(s):
Peter Haresnape, General Secretary
peter@scmcanada.org
Finances: *Annual Operating Budget:* $50,000-$100,000
Membership: 500; *Member Profile:* Groups at Canadian universities
Activities: Small group activities & discussions engaging in faith & justice topics, resource creation and distribution, ecumenical & interfaith dialogue, the annual Cahoots festival of faith, justice & DIY
Description: To work with students & young adults to explore the radical roots of Christian practice, building capacity, & training for peacemaking, community building, & ecumenical, interfaith dialogue; *Member of:* World Student Christian Federation

World Association for Christian Communication (WACC) / Association mondiale pour la communication
308 Main St., Toronto ON M4C 4X7
Tel: 416-691-1999
info@waccglobal.org
waccglobal.org
www.linkedin.com/company/world-association-for-christian-communication-wacc-
https://www.facebook.com/WACCglobal
twitter.com/waccglobal
Overview: A small international charitable organization founded in 1968
Chief Officer(s):
Philip Lee, General Secretary
Finances: *Annual Operating Budget:* $1.5 Million-$3 Million; *Funding Sources:* Church-related sources; Non-governmental & governmental development agencies; Donations
Staff: 11 staff member(s)
Fees: US$20 student; US$35 individual; US$120 corporate; *Member Profile:* Individuals, churches, church-related agencies, media producers, educational institutions, secular communication organizations & persons who share WACC's mission
Activities: Facilitating communication-related projects; Providing seminars, workshops & publications; Offering outreach programs worldwide; *Speaker Service:* Yes *Library:* Yes by appointment
Description: To promote communication as a basic human right through advocacy & communication; To promote open & diverse media; To strengthen communication networks to advance peace & justice; *Member of:* ACT Alliance, Canadian Church Press, ECOSOC

World Council of Churches
PO Box 2100, 150, rte de Ferney, Geneva CH-1211 Switzerland
oikoumene.org
Overview: A medium-sized international organization
Chief Officer(s):
Olav Fykse Tveit, General Secretary
Description: To be a community of churches on the way to visible unity in one faith & one eucharistic fellowship; *Affiliation(s):* International Council of World Religions & Cultures

Episcopalism

Atlantic Episcopal Assembly (AEA) / Assemblée des évêques de l'Atlantique
3 Oakley Ave., Halifax NS B3M 3G6
Tel: 902-443-9325
Overview: A small local organization founded in 1967
Chief Officer(s):
Gérald LeBlanc, Secretary-Treasurer
geraldleblanc2@gmail.com
Anthony Mancini, President
Finances: *Annual Operating Budget:* Less than $50,000
Membership: 12; *Member Profile:* Bishops from Prince Edwards Island, Nova Scotia, New Brunswick & Newfoundland & Labrador; *Committees:* Executive; Social Affairs

The Christian Episcopal Church of Canada (CECC)
www.xnec.us
Also Known As: Traditional Anglican Church in Canada
Overview: A small national charitable organization founded in 1991
Chief Officer(s):
Robert D. Redmile, Bishop
bishopredmile@shaw.ca
Finances: *Annual Operating Budget:* $100,000-$250,000; *Funding Sources:* Donations
Staff: 12 staff member(s); 40 volunteer(s)
Membership: 450; *Fees:* Free-will offerings; *Member Profile:* Baptised & confirmed Anglican Christians; *Committees:* Parochial Church Council, Assembly & Consistory; Diocesan Synod & Diocesan Council
Activities: Traditional Anglican faith & worship according to the Book of Common Prayer
Description: To be a national Catholic & Apostolic Church of the Anglican tradition in Canada; *Member of:* Anglican Communion; *Affiliation(s):* Christian Episcopal Church in the USA

Conférence religieuse canadienne (CRC) / Canadian Religious Conference
2715, ch de la Côte-Sainte-Catherine, Montréal QC H3T 1B6
Tel: 514-259-0856; *Fax:* 514-259-0857
info@crc-canada.org
crc-canada.org
www.youtube.com/user/confreligieusecan
www.facebook.com/ConferenceReligieuseCanadienne
twitter.com/crc_canada
Overview: A medium-sized national organization founded in 1954
Chief Officer(s):
Francine Landreville, President
Membership: 250
Description: To help members carry out their leadership role & promote consecrated life; To foster collaboration among members with the laity, & with ecclesial authorities; To establish coordination & cooperation with Episcopal conferences & with individual bishops; To assist members in their relationships with civil authorities

Evangelism

Africa Inland Mission International (Canada) (AIM) / Mission à l'intérieur de l'Afrique (Canada)
1641 Victoria Park Ave., Toronto ON M1R 1P8
Tel: 416-751-6077; *Fax:* 416-751-3467
Toll-Free: 877-407-6077
ca.aimint.org
www.facebook.com/aimcanada
twitter.com/aimcan
Also Known As: AIM Canada
Overview: A medium-sized international charitable organization founded in 1895
Finances: *Annual Operating Budget:* $1.5 Million-$3 Million; *Funding Sources:* Donations from churches & individuals
Staff: 8 staff member(s); 3 volunteer(s)
Membership: 135; *Committees:* Finance; Personnel; Projects

Description: To evangelize within Eastern & Central Africa & Islands around India Ocean; To establish churches; To provide training leadership for those churches; To provide medical, educational & agricultural services; *Member of:* Africa Inland Mission International, Bristol, England; Interdenominational Foreign Mission Association

Associated Gospel Churches (AGC) / Association des églises évangéliques (AEE)
1500 Kerns Rd., Burlington ON L7P 3A7
Tel: 905-634-8184; *Toll-Free:* 866-442-6691
admin@agcofcanada.com
agcofcanada.com
www.youtube.com/user/donnaagc
www.facebook.com/associatedgospelchurches
Overview: A medium-sized national charitable organization founded in 1925
Chief Officer(s):
Bill Allan, President
Finances: *Annual Operating Budget:* $250,000-$500,000
Staff: 5 staff member(s)
Membership: 148 churches; *Fees:* 4% of revenue minus missions support; *Committees:* Doctrine & Credentials; Church Planting; Church Health & Leadership
Description: To glorify God by partnering together in obedience to the Great Commandment & the Great Commission; to become a movement of healthy, reproducing churches; *Affiliation(s):* World Relief; World Team; UFM International; Evangelical Fellowship of Canada

Back to the Bible Canada
PO Box 246, Stn. A, Abbotsford BC V2T 6Z6
Toll-Free: 800-663-2425
info@backtothebible.ca
www.backtothebible.ca
www.instagram.com/backtothebible.ca
www.linkedin.com/company/back-to-the-bible-canada
www.facebook.com/BTTBCanada
twitter.com/BTTBC
Also Known As: The Good News Broadcasting Association of Canada
Overview: A small national charitable organization founded in 1957
Chief Officer(s):
Ben Lowell, Chief Executive Officer
Steve Biggerstaff, Chief Operating Officer
Description: To provide teachings through Christian radio & multimedia to engage & encourage people in God's Word across Canada & around the world; *Member of:* Canadian Council of Christian Charities; Evangelican Fellowship of Canada

Baptist General Conference of Canada (BGCC)
#201, 8315 Davies Rd. NW, Edmonton AB T6E 4N3
Tel: 780-438-9127; *Fax:* 780-435-2478
Toll-Free: 844-438-9127
office@bgc.ca
www.bgc.ca
www.facebook.com/BaptistGeneralConferenceCanada
twitter.com/BGCCnd
Overview: A large national charitable organization founded in 1981
Chief Officer(s):
Kevin Schular, Executive Director
Diane Wiebe, Administrator, Global Ministries
Finances: *Funding Sources:* Churches; individuals; BGC Stewardship Foundation
Staff: 4 staff member(s); 12 volunteer(s)
Membership: 7,000+ individuals + 106 churches; *Member Profile:* Agreement with our Affirmation of Faith, Distinctives & ministry goals
Activities: Global Ministries; new church development; leadership training; youth programs; women's ministries; international development consulting; *Library:* BGC Canada Archives by appointment
Description: To unite churches in a fellowship that is scriptual in doctrine, evangelical in character & irenic (peaceful) in spirit, & seeking to fulfil the Great Commission of Christ (Mt.28: 19-20) in Canada & abroad; *Member of:* Evangelical Fellowship of Canada

The Bible Holiness Movement
PO Box 223, Stn. A, Vancouver BC V6C 2M3
www.bible-holiness-movement.com
Previous Name: Religious Freedom Council of Christian Minorities
Overview: A small local organization founded in 1979
Finances: *Annual Operating Budget:* Less than $50,000
Staff: 4 volunteer(s)
Activities: *Speaker Service:* Yes *Library:* Yes by appointment
Description: To act as a sponsored organization of the Bible Holiness Movement. The Bible Holiness Movement is an aggressive Christian evangelistic and missionary movement.

Billy Graham Evangelistic Association of Canada (BGEAC)
20 Hopewell Ave. NE, Calgary AB T3J 5H5
Tel: 403-219-2300; *Fax:* 403-250-6567
Toll-Free: 800-293-3717
info@bgea.ca
www.billygraham.ca
www.youtube.com/user/BillyGrahamCanada
www.facebook.com/BillyGrahamEvangelisticAssociationOfCana
da
twitter.com/BGEAC
Also Known As: BGEA of Canada
Overview: A medium-sized national charitable organization founded in 1968
Chief Officer(s):
Dale Winder, Executive Director
Finances: *Annual Operating Budget:* Greater than $5 Million; *Funding Sources:* Donations
Staff: 30 staff member(s)
Activities: Television & radio broadcasts; schools of evangelism; evangelistic crusades; teaching seminars
Description: To expose those who are searching to the message of Christ; To help edify the Christian body in Canada; *Affiliation(s):* Bill Graham Evangelistic Association USA

Canada's National Bible Hour (CNBH)
c/o Global Outreach Mission, PO Box 1210, St Catharines ON L2R 7A7
Tel: 905-684-1401; *Toll-Free:* 866-483-5787
www.missiongo-radio.com/cnbh
www.youtube.com/user/missiongo
www.facebook.com/168935979827368
Overview: A small national organization founded in 1925
Chief Officer(s):
Brian Albrecht, President, GOM
Description: The Hour is a bible-teaching ministry, & Canada's oldest religious broadcast, heard from coast to coast. It is sponsored by Global Outreach Mission (GOM), an organization dedicated to evangelism & missions.; *Member of:* Global Outreach Mission

Child Evangelism Fellowship of Canada
PO Box 165, Stn. Main, Winnipeg MB R2L 1M7
Tel: 204-943-2774; *Fax:* 204-943-9967
Toll-Free: 866-943-2774
info@cefcanada.org
www.cefcanada.org
Also Known As: CEF Canada
Overview: A medium-sized national charitable organization founded in 1937
Chief Officer(s):
Gwen Foord, National Director
Finances: *Annual Operating Budget:* $500,000-$1.5 Million; *Funding Sources:* Individual, corporate & church donations
Staff: 45 staff member(s); 200 volunteer(s)
Membership: 1-99
Activities: Children's Ministries Institute; offers courses / programs, materials & training for Christian education among children
Description: To evangelize & disciple children with the gospel of Jesus Christ.; *Member of:* Canadian Council of Christian Charities; *Affiliation(s):* Child Evangelism Fellowship Inc.; CEF of Nations

The Christian & Missionary Alliance in Canada (C&MA) / L'Alliance chrétienne et missionnaire au Canada
#10, 7560 Airport Rd., Mississauga ON L4T 4H4
Tel: 416-674-7878; *Fax:* 416-674-0808
info@cmacan.org
www.cmacan.org/home
www.youtube.com/user/cmacan
www.facebook.com/CMAllianceinCanada
twitter.com/CMAinCanada
Also Known As: The Alliance Church
Overview: A medium-sized national charitable organization founded in 1981
Chief Officer(s):
David Hearn, President
Finances: *Annual Operating Budget:* Greater than $5 Million; *Funding Sources:* Donations
Staff: 1642 staff member(s)
Membership: 440 churches
Activities: Missions, locally & globally
Description: To be committed to Jesus & his mission by being Christ-centred, Spirit-empowered & Mission-focused in everything they do; *Member of:* Canadian Council of Christian Charities; Alliance World Fellowship; *Affiliation(s):* Alliance Life Magazine; Al Hayat Ministries; Evangelical Fellowship of Canada

Community of Christ - Canada East Mission
#129, 355 Elmira Rd. North, Guelph ON N1K 1S5
Tel: 519-822-4150; *Fax:* 519-822-1236
Toll-Free: 888-411-7537
www.communityofchrist.ca/index.php/cem
Also Known As: Saints' Church
Previous Name: Reorganized Church of Jesus Christ of Latter Day Saints (Canada)
Overview: A medium-sized local charitable organization founded in 1830
Chief Officer(s):
Kerry Richards, President, 519-822-4150 28
kerry@communityofchrist.ca
Dar Shepherdson, Financial Officer, 519-822-4150 34
dar@communityofchrist.ca
Membership: 45 congregations; *Member Profile:* Individuals & congregations in Ontario, Quebec, New Brunswick, Prince Edward Island & Nova Scotia
Description: To proclaim Jesus Christ & promote communitites of joy, hope, love & peace

Community of Christ - Canada West Mission (CWM)
PO Box 345, #224, 6655 - 178th St. NW, Edmonton AB T5T 4J5
Tel: 877-411-2632
www.communityofchrist.ca/index.php/cwm
Overview: A small local organization
Chief Officer(s):
Stephen Thompson, President & Financial Officer, Mission Centre, 877-411-2632 1
steve@communityofchrist.ca
Membership: 15 congregations and missions; *Member Profile:* Individuals & congregations in Western Canada (Manitoba - British Columbia)
Description: To proclaim Jesus Christ & promote communities of joy, hope, love, & peace

Emmanuel International Canada (EIC)
PO Box 1179, Stouffville ON L4A 4A2
Tel: 905-640-2111; *Fax:* 905-640-2186
Toll-Free: 866-269-6312
info@eicanada.org
www.eicanada.org
www.instagram.com/eicanada
www.linkedin.com/company/emmanuel-international-canada
www.facebook.com/EmmanuelInternationalCanada
twitter.com/eic_stouffville
Previous Name: Emmanuel Relief & Rehabilitation International (Canada)
Overview: A large national charitable organization founded in 1983
Chief Officer(s):
Richard McGowan, Executive Director, Canada
Finances: *Annual Operating Budget:* $1.5 Million-$3 Million; *Funding Sources:* Government; Donations
Staff: 14 staff member(s); 3 volunteer(s)
Membership: 1-99; *Member Profile:* Seven National Affiliates: Australia, Brazil, Canada, Malawi, The Philippines, The United Kingdom & The United States
Activities: Development, relief, rehabilitation & spiritual outreach programs; *Internships:* Yes
Description: To link caring Canadians with churches worldwide to transform lives in the most desperate places; To bring assistance to communities, families & individuals in needs; *Member of:* Canadian Council of Christian Charities

The Evangelical Alliance Mission of Canada Inc. (TEAM)
#372, 16 Midlake Blvd. SE, Calgary AB T2X 2X7
Toll-Free: 800-295-4160
info@team.org
team.org
www.instagram.com/teammissions
www.facebook.com/TheEvangelicalAllianceMission
twitter.com/teammissions
Also Known As: TEAM of Canada Inc.
Overview: A medium-sized international charitable organization founded in 1969
Chief Officer(s):
Ralph Friebel, Chair
Scott Henson, International Director
Finances: *Annual Operating Budget:* $3 Million-$5 Million
Staff: 48 staff member(s)
Membership: 1-99
Activities: *Internships:* Yes; *Speaker Service:* Yes *Library:* Resource Centre
Description: To help churches send missionaries to establish reproducing churches among the nations; *Member of:* Canadian Council of Christian Charities

Evangelical Covenant Church of Canada (ECCC)
PO Box 2247, Strathmore AB T1P 1K2
Tel: 403-324-9552; *Fax:* 204-269-3584
Toll-Free: 888-810-3020
office@covchurch.ca
www.covchurch.ca
Overview: A medium-sized national charitable organization founded in 1904
Chief Officer(s):
Glenn Peterson, Superintendent/President
glenn@covchurch.ca
Finances: *Funding Sources:* Donations
Member Profile: Evangelical Covenant Churches in Canada
Description: To make & deepend disciples, start & strengthen churches, develop leaders, love justice & do mercy; *Member of:* World Relief Canada; The Evangelical Fellowship of Canada; The Canadian Council of Christian Charities

Evangelical Fellowship of Canada (EFC) / Alliance évangélique du Canada
Stn. Beaver Creek, #103, 9821 Leslie St., Richmond Hill ON L4B 0B8
Tel: 905-479-4742; *Toll-Free:* 866-302-3362
efc@theefc.ca
www.evangelicalfellowship.ca
www.youtube.com/user/theEFCca
www.facebook.com/theefc
twitter.com/theefc
Overview: A medium-sized national charitable organization founded in 1964
Chief Officer(s):
Bill Fietje, Chair
Bruce J. Clemenger, President
Finances: *Annual Operating Budget:* $1.5 Million-$3 Million; *Funding Sources:* General & corporate donations; member & subscriber fees
Staff: 20 staff member(s); 90 volunteer(s)
Membership: 42 evangelical denominations + 64 organizations + 37 educational institutions + 1,000 churches
Activities: Task forces: Evangelism; Women in Ministry; Aboriginal; Global Mission; Commissions: Education; Religious Liberty; Social Action; *Internships:* Yes; *Speaker Service:* Yes
Description: To advocate of the gospel of Jesus Christ; To provide an evangelical identity that unites Canadian Christians of diverse backgrounds; To express biblical views on current issues; To assist individuals & groups in proclaiming the gospel & advancing Christian values; *Member of:* World Evangelical Fellowship

Evangelical Order of Certified Pastoral Counsellors of America (EOCPCA)
#223, 2349 Fairview St., Burlington ON L7R 2E3
Tel: 905-639-0137; *Fax:* 905-333-8901
eocpc@cogeco.ca
www.eocpc.com
Previous Name: Order of Certified Pastoral Counsellors of America
Overview: A medium-sized national organization founded in 1982
Finances: *Annual Operating Budget:* $500,000-$1.5 Million
Staff: 3 staff member(s)
Membership: 1,200 individual; *Fees:* $100-400
Activities: Courses, certifications & workshops
Description: To promote a Christian-oriented order; To certify & accredit pastoral counsellors by federal charter; *Member of:* Canadian Christian Counsellors Association; Canadian Christian Clinical Counsellors College; *Affiliation(s):* California State Christian University

Evangelical Tract Distributors (EDT)
PO Box 146, Edmonton AB T5J 2G9
Tel: 780-477-1538; *Fax:* 780-477-3795
www.evangelicaltract.com
Overview: A small national organization founded in 1935
Chief Officer(s):
John Harder, President/Managing Director
Description: To print & distribute Christian gospel tracts free of charge

Fondation Père-Ménard
#203, 5777, rue Sherbrooke est, Montréal QC H1N 3R5
Tél: 514-274-7645; *Ligne sans frais:* 800-665-7645
info@fondationperemenard.org
www.fondationperemenard.org
www.facebook.com/fondationperemenard
Aperçu: *Dimension:* petite; *Envergure:* internationale; *Organisme sans but lucratif; fondée en 1970
Membre(s) du bureau directeur:
Miriam Castro, Directrice générale
mcastro@fondationperemenard.org
Finances: *Budget de fonctionnement annuel:* $500,000-$1.5 Million

Personnel: 2 membre(s) du personnel; 10 bénévole(s)
Membre: 15 000+
Description: Améliorer de façon durable la qualité de vie des populations défavorisées des pays en développement, principalement en Amérique du sud, en encourageant et soutenant l'établissement et la gestion de projets communautaires en santé, éducation, eau et alimentation ainsi que la formation de leaders spirituels locaux

Foursquare Gospel Church of Canada
#307, 2099 Lougheed Hwy., Port Coquitlam BC V3B 1A8
Tel: 604-941-8414; *Fax:* 604-941-8415
info@foursquare.ca
www.foursquare.ca
www.facebook.com/foursquarecanada
Overview: A medium-sized national charitable organization founded in 1981
Chief Officer(s):
Steve Falkiner, President
president@foursquare.ca
Finances: *Annual Operating Budget:* $250,000-$500,000
Staff: 5 staff member(s)
Membership: 79 churches
Description: To not just make converts & make disciples live by Jesus; *Member of:* Evangelical Fellowship of Canada

Full Gospel Business Men's Fellowship in Canada (FGBMFI)
4309 - 49th St., St Paul AB T0A 3A4
Tel: 416-449-7272; *Toll-Free:* 877-296-1715
info@fgbmf.ca
fgbmf.ca
www.facebook.com/fgbmfincanada
Overview: A medium-sized national charitable organization founded in 1964
Chief Officer(s):
Ron Hutzal, President
Finances: *Annual Operating Budget:* $100,000-$250,000
Staff: 2 staff member(s); 2 volunteer(s)
Membership: 1,000-4,999; *Fees:* $60 individual
Activities: National convention; *Internships:* Yes; *Speaker Service:* Yes
Description: To reach men at all levels of our modern society, calling them to God, & releasing them into their respective gifts & talents through the Holy Spirit; *Member of:* Full Gospel Business Men's Fellowship International

Gideons International in Canada / Les Gédéons - L'Association Internationale des Gédéons au Canada
PO Box 3619, 501 Imperial Rd. North, Guelph ON N1H 7A2
Tel: 519-823-1140; *Fax:* 519-767-1913
Toll-Free: 888-482-4253
info@gideons.ca
gideons.ca
www.youtube.com/user/GideonsCanadaMedia
www.linkedin.com/company/the-gideons-international-in-canada
www.facebook.com/gideonscanada
twitter.com/GideonsCanada
Overview: A medium-sized international charitable organization founded in 1911
Chief Officer(s):
Alan Anderson, President
Finances: *Annual Operating Budget:* Greater than $5 Million; *Funding Sources:* Membership fees; voluntary donations; funds from other registered charities
Membership: 4,500; *Fees:* $180; *Member Profile:* Christian business & professional people
Activities: Sharing faith; Placing Bibles & New Testaments to the public; Distributing New Testaments to selected groups

Global Outreach Mission
PO Box 1210, St Catharines ON L2R 7A7
Tel: 905-684-1401; *Fax:* 905-684-3069
Toll-Free: 866-483-5787
glmiss@on.aibn.com
www.missiongo.org
www.youtube.com/user/missiongo
www.facebook.com/168935979827368
twitter.com/GlobalOutreachM
Previous Name: European Evangelistic Crusade, Inc.
Overview: A small international organization founded in 1943
Chief Officer(s):
Brian Albrecht, President
balbrecht@missiongo.org
Constable Greg, Vice President, Candidates/Personnel
gconstable@missiongo.org
Activities: International aide ranginf from Christian counselors to hospitals; Radio ministries
Description: To be solely concerned with the propagation of the Gospel of the grace of God as revealed in the Word of God; *Affiliation(s):* Interdenominational Foreign Mission Association

SIM Canada
10 Huntingdale Blvd., Toronto ON M1W 2S5
Tel: 416-497-2424; *Fax:* 416-497-2444
Toll-Free: 800-294-6918
info@sim.ca
www.sim.ca
www.facebook.com/SIMCANADA1
twitter.com/SIMCANADA1
Also Known As: Serving In Mission
Previous Name: Society for International Ministries
Overview: A small international organization founded in 1893
Chief Officer(s):
John Denbok, Executive Director
Finances: *Annual Operating Budget:* Greater than $5 Million
Staff: 175 staff member(s)
Activities: *Speaker Service:* Yes
Description: To evangelize the unreached & minister to human need

Solbrekken Evangelistic Association of Canada
PO Box 44220, RPO Garside, Edmonton AB T5V 1N6
Tel: 780-460-8444
www.mswm.org
Also Known As: Max Solbrekken World Mission
Overview: A small national charitable organization founded in 1961
Chief Officer(s):
Max Solbrekken, President
max@maxsolbrekken.com
Donna Solbrekken, Secretary
Activities: Publishes Christian literature; Founded & sponsors orphanages, churhces & Ministry crusades; *Library:* Audio Sermons Library (Open to Public)
Description: To promote the gospel; *Affiliation(s):* Christ the Healer Gospel Church (Saskatchewan); The House of Prayer, New Sarepta (Alberta)

Threshold Ministries
National Ministry Centre, 105 Mountain View Dr., Saint John NB E2J 5B5
Tel: 506-642-2210; *Fax:* 506-657-8217
hello@thresholdministries.ca
www.thresholdministries.ca
www.facebook.com/thresholdministries
Overview: A medium-sized national charitable organization founded in 1929
Chief Officer(s):
Norbert Haukenfrers, Chair
Jonathan Clarke, National Director
jonathan.clarke@thresholdministries.ca
Karen Cooney, Administrator & Coordinator, Events
karen.cooney@thresholdministries.ca
Marilyn Otis, Financial Officer
marilyn.otis@thresholdministries.ca
Finances: *Annual Operating Budget:* $1.5 Million-$3 Million; *Funding Sources:* Individuals; churches; foundations
Staff: 3 staff member(s); 75 volunteer(s)
Membership: 70; *Fees:* none
Activities: *Internships:* Yes; *Speaker Service:* Yes *Library:* Taylor College (Open to Public)
Description: To train and equip Evangelists to assist the Church in becoming missional in communicating the Gospel; *Member of:* Evangelical Fellowship of Canada; *Affiliation(s):* Anglican Church of Canada

Friends

Canadian Friends Service Committee (CFSC) / Secours Quaker Canadien
60 Lowther Ave., Toronto ON M5R 1C7
Tel: 416-920-5213
quakerservice.ca
www.facebook.com/CFSCQuakers
twitter.com/CFSCQuakers
Also Known As: Religious Society of Friends (Quakers)
Overview: A medium-sized national charitable organization founded in 1931
Chief Officer(s):
Jennifer Preston, General Secretary & Administrator, Finance
jennifer@quakerservice.ca
Matthew Legge, Coordinator, Peace Program & Communications
matt@quakerservice.ca
Finances: *Annual Operating Budget:* $500,000-$1.5 Million; *Funding Sources:* Individuals; meetings
Staff: 7 staff member(s); 40 volunteer(s)
Activities: Participating in peace & social justice work; *Internships:* Yes; *Speaker Service:* Yes *Library:* Friends House Library (Open to Public)
Description: To unify & expand the concerns of Friends (Quakers); *Member of:* The Canadian Council of Churches;

Kairos: Canadian Ecumenical Justice Initiatives; Project Ploughshares; Canadian Council for Refugees; War Resistors Support Campaign

Friends Historical Association (FHA)
c/o Haverford College Library, 370 Lancaster Ave., Haverford PA 19041-1392 USA

Tel: 484-471-7169
fha@haverford.edu
www.quakerhistory.org

Overview: A medium-sized international organization founded in 1873
Finances: *Annual Operating Budget:* Less than $50,000; *Funding Sources:* Membership dues; subscriptions; donations
Staff: 1 staff member(s); 21 volunteer(s)
Membership: 800; *Fees:* $25; *Member Profile:* Friends & interested historians
Activities: Pilgrimages to historic Friends Meetings; lectures; *Rents Mailing List:* Yes
Description: To promote the study, preservation & publication of material relating to the history of the Religious Society of Friends; Affiliation(s): Conference of Quaker Historians & Archivists

Friends Historical Society - London (FHS)
c/o Friends House, 173 Euston Rd., London NW1 2BJ United Kingdom

friendshistoricalsociety.org.uk

Overview: A small international organization founded in 1903
Chief Officer(s):
Howard Gregg, Clerk
h-fg@hotmail.co.uk
Finances: *Funding Sources:* Membership fees
Membership: 100-499; *Fees:* US$24 individual; US$40 institution
Description: To encourage the study of Quaker history; *Member of:* Association of Denominational Historical Societies & Cognate Libraries

Hare Krishna

Toronto's Hare Krishna Centre (ISKCON) / Subuddhi Deri Dasi
243 Avenue Rd., Toronto ON M5R 2J6

Tel: 416-922-5415; *Fax:* 416-922-1021
info@torontokrishna.com
iskcontoronto.blogspot.ca
twitter.com/TempleCouncil

Also Known As: ISKCON Toronto
Previous Name: International Society for Krishna Consciousness (Toronto Branch)
Overview: A medium-sized local charitable organization founded in 1966
Finances: *Annual Operating Budget:* $3 Million-$5 Million; *Funding Sources:* Donations from congregations & festivals
Staff: 10 staff member(s); 20 volunteer(s)
Membership: 700 institutional; 2,000 individual; *Fees:* $1,100
Activities: Distribution of free food; taking care of seniors & youth; *Internships:* Yes *Library:* Yes (Open to Public)
Description: To preach Krishna Consciousness around the world, following in the footsteps of the founder & spiritual master, His Divine Grace A.C. Bhaktivedanta Swami Prabhupada.

Hinduism

Hindu Society of Alberta
14225 - 133 Ave., Edmonton AB T5L 4W3

Tel: 780-451-5130
hindu.society@hotmail.com
www.hindusociety.ab.ca
twitter.com/Hindu_Society

Overview: A small provincial charitable organization founded in 1967
Chief Officer(s):
Hansa Thaleshvar, President, 587-269-3440
hthalesh@gmail.com
Activities: Classes in yoga & meditation; language classes; lectures & seminars on history & religion; religious celebrations; music & dance performances; hall rentals; *Library:* library
Description: The Society is a cultural, social & religious institute catering to the needs of those influenced by Hinduism.

Yasodhara Ashram Society
PO Box 9, 527 Walker's Landing Rd., Kootenay Bay BC V0B 1X0

Tel: 250-227-9224; *Fax:* 250-227-9494
Toll-Free: 800-661-8711
info@yasodhara.org
www.yasodhara.org
www.youtube.com/user/yasodharaashram
www.facebook.com/yasodhara.org
twitter.com/yasodharaashram

Overview: A small international charitable organization founded in 1963
Chief Officer(s):
Swami Lalitananda, President
Finances: *Annual Operating Budget:* $500,000-$1.5 Million
Staff: 15 volunteer(s)
Membership: 125; *Fees:* $25
Activities: *Internships:* Yes; *Speaker Service:* Yes *Library:* Yes by appointment
Description: To maintain a centre for adults engaged in a life of spiritual intent; To provide instruction in & opportunities for religious & spiritual practice

Islam

Ahmadiyya Muslim Jama'at Canada
10610 Jane St., Maple ON L6A 3A2

Tel: 905-303-4000; *Fax:* 905-832-3220
info@ahmadiyya.ca
www.ahmadiyya.ca
www.youtube.com/c/AhmadiyyaCanada
twitter.com/ahmadiyyacanada

Also Known As: Ahmadiyya Muslim Community Canada
Overview: A medium-sized national charitable organization
Chief Officer(s):
Lal Khan Malik, President
Abdul Aziz Khalifa, Vice-President
Finances: *Annual Operating Budget:* Greater than $5 Million
Staff: 30 staff member(s); 1000 volunteer(s)
Activities: Offering religious education; Muslim TV (www.mta.tv); *Internships:* Yes; *Speaker Service:* Yes *Library:* Ahmadiyya Muslim Jamaat Canada Library (Open to Public) by appointment
Description: To promote interfaith understanding; Affiliation(s): The Ahmadiyya Muslim Medical Association of Canada (AMMAC)

Association of Islamic Charitable Projects (AICP) / Association des Projets charitables Islamiques
6691, av du Parc, Montréal QC H2V 4J1

Tel: 514-274-6194; *Fax:* 514-274-0011
www.aicp.ca
www.youtube.com/user/aicpmultimediamtl
www.facebook.com/AicpCanada
twitter.com/AICP_CANADA

Overview: A medium-sized international organization
Activities: Yearly pilgrimage trip; Madih group; Marriage contracts & funerary services
Description: To denounce all acts of terrorism & promote support for the Muslim community

British Columbia Muslim Association (BCMA)
12300 Blundell Rd., Richmond BC V6W 1B3

Tel: 604-270-2522; *Fax:* 604-244-9750
bcma@shawcable.com
thebcma.com
www.facebook.com/bcmuslimassociation
twitter.com/thebcma1

Overview: A large provincial organization founded in 1966
Chief Officer(s):
Saiyad Ali, Administrator
administrator@thebcma.com
Finances: *Funding Sources:* Donations; Fundraising
Membership: 75,000+; *Member Profile:* Sunni Muslims throughout British Columbia
Activities: Developing & maintaining religious, cultural, & educational facilities; Owning & operating Mosques; Providing funeral & burial facilities; Providing locations for prayers; Operating the British Columbia Muslim School Richmond & the Surrey Muslim School; Offering educational opportunities; Providing social services to youth, adults, & seniors; Organizing social & recreational activities; Cooperating with other Muslim organizations; Promoting community awareness about Islam; Disseminating information about Islam
Description: To represent Sunni Muslims in British Columbia; To promote the interests of the Muslim community

Canadian Council of Muslim Theologians (CCMT)
#211, 1825 Markham Rd., Toronto ON M1B 4Z9

Tel: 416-981-3247
info@jucanada.org
www.jucanada.org
www.facebook.com/Canadiancouncil
twitter.com/JU_Canada

Overview: A medium-sized national organization
Member Profile: Muslim scholars in the field of Shari'ah who have graduated from Islamic universities
Description: To promote the doctrines of Islam; To preserve the Shari'ah; To obtain religious freedom; To offer religious guidance; To provide help for the poor & distressed; To sanction halal foods; *Member of:* Jami'yyatul Ulama Canada

Canadian Council of Muslim Women (CCMW) / Conseil canadien des femmes musulmanes
PO Box 73509, RPO Wychwood, Toronto ON M6C 4A7

Tel: 416-999-6059
info@ccmw.com
www.ccmw.com
www.linkedin.com/company/ccmw
www.facebook.com/CCMWNational
twitter.com/ccmwcanada

Overview: A medium-sized national organization founded in 1982
Chief Officer(s):
Nina Karachi-Khaled, President
Nuzhat Jafri, Executive Director
Finances: *Annual Operating Budget:* Less than $50,000; *Funding Sources:* Fundraising; Public funds; Government
Staff: 2 staff member(s); 30 volunteer(s)
Membership: 100+; *Member Profile:* Practising Muslim women
Activities: Implementing projects & toolkits; *Awareness Events:* Women Who Inspire Awards Brunch; *Speaker Service:* Yes
Description: To assist Muslim women in participating effectively in Canadian society; To promote mutual understanding with women of other faiths; To strengthen the bonds of sisterhood among Muslim communities & individuals; To achieve equity & empowerment for Muslim women in Canada

International Development & Relief Foundation (IDRF)
#300, 23 Lesmill Rd., Toronto ON M3B 3P6

Tel: 416-497-0818; *Fax:* 416-497-0686
Toll-Free: 866-497-4373
office@idrf.ca
idrf.ca
www.youtube.com/user/IDRFcanada
www.linkedin.com/company/idrf
www.facebook.com/official.idrf
twitter.com/idrfcanada

Overview: A small international organization founded in 1984
Chief Officer(s):
Mahmood Qasim, Chief Executive Officer
Finances: *Annual Operating Budget:* $500,000-$1.5 Million
Staff: 19 staff member(s)
Member Profile: People who regularly donate $100 or more yearly
Activities: Providing relief, rehabilitation & development aid to communities in need, both overseas & in Canada; *Speaker Service:* Yes
Description: To empower the disadvantaged peoples of the world, through emergency relief & participatory development programs based on the Islamic principles of human dignity, self-reliance & social justice; Affiliation(s): Canadian Council for International Cooperation

Islamic Association of Nova Scotia (IANS)
PO Box 103-136, 287 Lacewood Dr., Dartmouth NS B3M 3Y7

Tel: 902-469-9490
info@islamnovascotia.ca
www.islamnovascotia.ca

Previous Name: Islamic Association of the Maritimes
Overview: A small local organization founded in 1966
Chief Officer(s):
Iftikhar Baig, President, 902-471-8998
Sami Mirza, Vice President
Fees: $50 single; $100 family; $25 student

Islamic Association of Saskatchewan
222 Copland Cres., Saskatoon SK S7H 2Z5

Tel: 306-665-6424
info@islamiccenter.sk.ca
www.islamiccenter.sk.ca

Overview: A small provincial organization founded in 1968
Chief Officer(s):
Khalil-ur-Rehman, President
president@islamiccenter.sk.ca
Naeem Sader, Vice President
vp@islamiccenter.sk.ca

Hanan Elbardouh, Vice President, Sisters
vps@islamiccenter.sk.ca
Faiyaz Ahmed, Secretary
info@islamiccenter.sk.ca
Taimur Samad, Treasurer
treasurer@islamiccenter.sk.ca
Fees: $40 family; $25 single; *Committees:* The Muslim
Communications and Outreach Committee (MCOC); The
Takaful Fund Committee (TFC)
Activities: Operates Islamic Centre; Represents Muslims;
Provides activities; Responsible for Muslim Cemetery
Affiliation(s): Multi-Faith Group; Saskatchewan Organization for
Heritage Language; Saskatchewan Intercultural Association;
Saskatchewan Forum for "Racialized" Canadians;
Saskatchewan Council for International Cooperation

Islamic Care Centre (ICC)
375 Somerset St. West, Ottawa ON K2P 0K1
Tel: 613-232-0210
info@islamcare.ca
islamcare.ca
www.linkedin.com/company/islam-care-centre
www.facebook.com/islamcarecentre
twitter.com/IslamCare
Also Known As: Daw'ah Centre
Overview: A small national charitable organization founded in
1999
Chief Officer(s):
Omar Mahfoudhi, Executive Director
Finances: *Annual Operating Budget:* $50,000-$100,000
Staff: 2 staff member(s); 10 volunteer(s)
Activities: *Speaker Service:* Yes *Library:* Islamic Information
(Open to Public)
Description: To provide the Canadian (Ottawa) Muslim
community with resources to meet religious & social needs with
the objective of establishing a better relationship with the larger
Canadian society; *Member of:* Muslim Community Council of
Ottawa; Affiliation(s): Islam Care Centre

Islamic Foundation of Toronto (IFT)
441 Nugget Ave., Toronto ON M1S 5E1
Tel: 416-321-0909; *Fax:* 416-321-1995
info@islamicfoundation.ca
www.islamicfoundation.ca
www.youtube.com/user/islamicfoundationca
www.facebook.com/iftlive
twitter.com/iftlive
Also Known As: Nugget Mosque
Overview: A small local charitable organization founded in 1969
Chief Officer(s):
Shakil Akhter, Administrator, 416-321-0909 233
Shabbir Gangat, Coordinator, Funerals, 416-876-3000
Finances: *Annual Operating Budget:* $3 Million-$5 Million
Staff: 72 staff member(s)
Membership: 1,000-4,999; *Committees:* Dawah; Library; School
Board; Social Services
Activities: Full time Islamic school, JK to Grade 10; part-time
evening Islamic school; Arabic language centre for adults; Friday
& Sunday schools

Islamic Information Foundation (IIF)
8 Laurel Lane, Halifax NS B3M 2P6
Tel: 902-445-2494; *Fax:* 902-445-2494
iif@geocities.com
Overview: A small national charitable organization founded in
1981
Chief Officer(s):
Jamal Badawi, Founder & Chair
jamal.badawi@stmarys.ca
Finances: *Annual Operating Budget:* $100,000-$250,000;
Funding Sources: Sale of religious material; donations
Staff: 4 volunteer(s)
Membership: 40 individuals
Activities: *Speaker Service:* Yes
Description: To promote better understanding of Islam among
Muslims & Christians through information provided in print, audio
& video forms & through lecture, seminars & interfaith dialogues

Islamic Propagation Centre of Ontario (IPC)
**Jame Masjid Mississauga, 5761 Coopers Ave., Mississauga
ON L4Z 1R9**
Tel: 905-507-3323
Secretary@jamemasjid.org
www.jamemasjid.org
Also Known As: Jama Masjid Mississauga
Previous Name: Islamic Propagation Centre International
(Canada)
Overview: A small local charitable organization founded in 1984
Chief Officer(s):
Nafis Bhayat, Director, Religious Services, 416-844-9373
Imamjamemasjid.org
Finances: *Annual Operating Budget:* $50,000-$100,000

Staff: 2 staff member(s); 100 volunteer(s)
Membership: 100 student; 1,000 individual; *Fees:* $200
individual; *Committees:* Fundraising; Eid & Ramadhan;
Executive
Activities: Congregation; marriages; family counselling; summer
& evening school for kids; *Speaker Service:* Yes *Library:* IPC
Office Library (Open to Public) by appointment
Description: The Centre offers a selection of resource material
for those interested in learning about Islam. Topics covered
include comparative religion, history, culture, lifestyle, politics,
law & women in Islam. It is a registered charity, BN:
886810191RR0001.

Manitoba Islamic Association (MIA)
2445 Waverley St., Winnipeg MB R3Y 1S3
Tel: 204-256-1347
www.miaonline.org
www.facebook.com/ManitobaIslamicAssociation
Overview: A small provincial organization founded in 1969
Chief Officer(s):
Osaed Khan, President
Salman Qureshi, Vice President 1
Reda Elgazzar, Vice President 2
Ferdose Skeikheldin, Secretary
Salman Idris, Treasurer
Fees: $30; *Member Profile:* Muslim persons in Manitoba who
abide by the association's rules & regulations; *Committees:*
Takaful Fund
Activities: Owns & operates the Manitoba Grand Mosque;
Providing funeral services to the Muslim community, through
partnership with Cropo Funeral Services; Offering services for
marriage; Conducting Sunday Qur'an classes for children & the
MIA Al Nur Weekend Islamic School; Sponsoring the Al-Hamd
Learning Center, which offers an Arabic & Islamic educational
program for preschoolers; *Library:* Al-Hikmah (Wisdom) Library
(Open to Public) by appointment

Muslim Association of Canada (MAC)
2270 Speakman Dr., Mississauga ON L5K 1B4
Tel: 905-822-2626
mac@macnet.ca
www.macnet.ca
www.facebook.com/MACNational
twitter.com/macnational
Overview: A medium-sized national organization
Chief Officer(s):
Nabil Sultan, Chair
Activities: Schools & community centres; educational & other
projects; youth projects; outreach
Description: Seeks to promote a balanced, constructive &
integrated Islamic presence in Canada; operates in 13 Canadian
cities

Muslim Association of New Brunswick (MANB)
1100 Rothesay Rd., Saint John NB E2H 2H8
Tel: 506-633-1675
info@manb.ca
www.manb.ca
Overview: A medium-sized provincial charitable organization
founded in 1985
Chief Officer(s):
Khalid Maiik, Vice-President, 506-804-6125
kmalik74@hotmail.com
Fees: $25; *Committees:* Maintenance; Cemetery; Constitutional
Amendments; Religion Affairs; Imam Selection; Financial Affairs;
Syrian Refugees Liaison; Dawa'; Ladies Liasion; Social
Activities; Islamic School
Activities: *Library:* Yes
Description: To strengthen access to Islamic education,
facilitate community outreach & interaction with other religious
organizations & community groups; consolidate the social fabric
of the community; & sustain Islamic work by encouraging &
building endowments

Muslim Community of Québec (MCQ) / Communauté musulmane du Québec (CMQ)
7445, av Chester, Montréal QC H4V 1M4
Tel: 514-484-2967; *Fax:* 514-484-3802
mrdeen25@hotmail.com
www.muslimcommunityofquebec.com
Also Known As: Mosque of Montréal
Overview: A small local organization founded in 1979
Chief Officer(s):
Muhammed Romizuddin, Contact
Finances: *Annual Operating Budget:* $500,000-$1.5 Million
Membership: 500
Activities: *Speaker Service:* Yes
Description: To facilitate Muslim religious life

Muslim Council of Montréal (MCM)
PO Box 180, Stn. St-Laurent, Montréal QC H4L 4Z8
Tel: 514-748-8427
info@muslimcouncil.org
www.muslimcouncil.org
Overview: A small local organization
Finances: *Annual Operating Budget:* Less than $50,000
Staff: 5 volunteer(s)
Membership: 40 Muslim institutions
Description: Seeks effective cooperation among Islamic
organizations & Muslims of all nationalities or schools of thought;
seeks better understanding of Islam; assists media by open
discussion; takes part in multicultural activities

Muslim World League - Canada
2550 Argentia Rd., Mississauga ON L5N 5R1
Tel: 905-542-1050; *Fax:* 905-542-1054
mwl@mwlcanada.org
themwl.org/GLOBAL/node/1205
Overview: A small national organization founded in 1985
Member Profile: Muslims
Activities: *Rents Mailing List:* Yes *Library:* Yes (Open to Public)
Description: The League is a non-profit, non-governmental
organization that serves the religious needs of Muslims in
Canada. It promotes Islam & Islamic teachings among Canadian
Muslims & helps non-Muslims grasp an accurate understanding
of the religion. It also serves as a resource centre, publishing
booklets & flyers on current issues.; Affiliation(s): Muslim World
League, Makkah, Saudia Arabia

National Council of Canadian Muslims (NCCM)
PO Box 13219, Ottawa ON K2K 1X4
Tel: 613-254-9704; *Fax:* 613-254-9810
Toll-Free: 866-524-0004
info@nccm.ca
www.nccm.ca
www.youtube.com/NCCMtv
www.facebook.com/NCCMuslims
twitter.com/NCCM
Previous Name: Council on American-Islamic Relations Canada
Overview: A large international organization founded in 2000
Chief Officer(s):
Mustafa Farooq, Chief Executive Officer
mfarooq@nccm.ca
Activities: Seminars & workshops; Publication of guides,
handbooks & media resource kits
Description: To promote the civic engagement of Canadian
Muslims, the protection of their human rights & the education of
non-Muslims so they may hold an accurate understanding of
Islam

Ottawa Muslim Association (OMA)
251 Northwestern Ave., Ottawa ON K1Y 0M1
Tel: 613-722-8763
oma@ottawamosque.ca
www.ottawamosque.ca
Overview: A small local charitable organization
Chief Officer(s):
Naeem Malik, President
Activities: Social services; seminars & conferences; *Library:*
Yes (Open to Public)
Description: To foster unity among various Muslims; to promote
better understanding of Muslims & Islam among Canadians of
other faiths; to maintain cultural identity

Regroupement des Marocains au Canada (RMC)
3005, boul Cartier ouest, Laval QC H7V 1J3
Tél: 450-681-2133
info@rmc-canada.org
www.rmc-canada.org
www.facebook.com/rmc.marocains.canada
Aperçu: Dimension: moyenne; *Envergure: nationale; fondée en
1994*
Membre(s) du bureau directeur:
Lahcen Baissi, Président
Montant de la cotisation: 10$ étudiant; 25$ membre
Description: Promouvoir la fraternité entre les membres de la
communauté marocaine au Canada; préserver son identité
musulmane

Scarborough Muslim Association (SMA)
2665 Lawrence Ave. East, Toronto ON M1P 2S2
Tel: 416-750-2253; *Fax:* 416-750-1616
info@smacanada.ca
www.smacanada.ca
twitter.com/SMA_AbuBakrSid
Overview: A small local charitable organization founded in 1984

Windsor Islamic Association (WIA)
c/o Windsor Mosque, 1320 Northwood St., Windsor ON N9E 1A4

Tel: 519-966-2355
wia@windsormosque.com
www.wiao.org
www.youtube.com/user/windsormosque
www.facebook.com/windsormosque
twitter.com/myWIA

Overview: A medium-sized local organization founded in 1964
Chief Officer(s):
Abdallah Shamisa, President
president@windsormosque.ca
Mirza Baig, Vice President
vicepresident@windsormosque.ca
Radwan Tamr, Secretary
secretary@windsormosque.ca
Hossam Behairy, Treasurer
treasurer@windsormosque.ca
Membership: 25,000; *Fees:* $100
Activities: Prayer, funeral & marriages services; Qura'an memorization; Arabic language lessons; Teachings about Islam; Live broadcast
Affiliation(s): World Muslim League

Jehovah's Witnesses

Watch Tower Bible & Tract Society of Canada
PO Box 4100, Georgetown ON L7G 4Y4

Tel: 905-873-4100; *Fax:* 905-873-4554
www.jw.org

Also Known As: Jehovah's Witnesses
Overview: A large national organization
Chief Officer(s):
Kenneth Little, President
Membership: 8,340,982 (worldwide)
Description: To serve Jehovah's Witnesses in Canada

Jesuits

Canadian Jesuits International (CJI)
70 Saint Mary St., Toronto ON M5S 1J3

Tel: 416-465-1824; *Toll-Free:* 800-448-2148
cji@jesuits.ca
www.canadianjesuitsinternational.ca
www.facebook.com/canadianjesuitsinternational
twitter.com/CJIyouth4others

Also Known As: Canadian Jesuit Missions
Overview: A medium-sized national charitable organization founded in 1955
Chief Officer(s):
Jenny Cafiso, Director
Activities: Support projects in Africa, India, Nepal, Jamaica, & Ukraine
Description: Committed to the service of faith & the promotion of justice for the poor of the world; especially dedicated to the educational needs of women, children, elderly & indigenous people at home & abroad

Jesuits of Canada / Jésuites du Canada
43 Queen's Park Cres. East, Toronto ON M5S 2C3

Tel: 416-962-4500; *Fax:* 416-962-4501
Toll-Free: 855-962-4500
reception@jesuits.ca
jesuits.ca
www.youtube.com/user/JesuitsinCanada
www.facebook.com/jesuitsofcanada
twitter.com/JesuitsofCanada

Overview: A medium-sized national charitable organization
Chief Officer(s):
Barry Leidl, Director, Office of Advancement
bleidl@jesuits.ca
Finances: *Annual Operating Budget:* $500,000-$1.5 Million
Membership: 100-499
Description: To raise & provide the funds necessary for the support of Jesuit brothers & priests in formation, in ministry & in their senior years; *Member of:* Jesuit Fathers & Brothers of Upper Canada

Judaism

Am Shalom
767 Huronia Rd., Barrie ON L4N 9H2

Tel: 705-792-3949; *Fax:* 705-792-3982
amshalomcongregation@bellnet.ca
www.amshalom.ca
www.facebook.com/amshalombarrie

Previous Name: Simcoe County Jewish Association (SCJA)
Overview: A small local charitable organization founded in 1974
Chief Officer(s):
Audrey Kaufman, Spiritual Leader

Member Profile: A Reform Jewish congregation
Activities: Providing weekly services; Offering a children's religious school & adult education programs; Maintaining a Judaica collecion of books that may be borrowed by Am Shalom members; *Library:* Am Shalom's Library
Description: To serve the spiritual & cultural needs of the Jewish population of Barrie & Simcoe County, Ontario; To encourage the observance & study of Jewish religion & culture; To support the Jewish values of social responsibility & knowledge

Beach Hebrew Institute
109 Kenilworth Ave., Toronto ON M4L 3S4

Tel: 416-694-7942
info@beachhebrewinstitute.ca
www.beachhebrewinstitute.ca

Overview: A small local organization
Fees: $450 single adult; $700 dual adult

Canadian Council for Reform Judaism (CCRJ)
#301, 3845 Bathurst St., Toronto ON M3H 3N2

Tel: 416-630-0375; *Fax:* 416-630-5089
ccrj@ccrj.ca
ccrj.ca
www.instagram.com/ccrjsocial
www.facebook.com/reformjudaism

Previous Name: Canadian Council of Reform Rabbis
Overview: A medium-sized national organization
Chief Officer(s):
Pekka Sinervo, President
psinervo@ccrj.ca
Len Bates, Vice-President
Elliott Jacobson, Treasuer
Description: The CCRJ is the Canadian region of the Union for Reform Judasim Congregations & serves as the umbrella organization for Reform Judaism in Canada, representing about 30,000 affiliated members in 25 Reform Congregations.; *Member of:* Union for Reform Judaism; *Affiliation(s):* ARZA CANADA; Leo Baeck Day School; Women of Reform Judaism; Canadian Friends of the World Union for Progressive Judaism; Central Conference of American Rabbis; American Conference of Cantors

Canadian Council of Conservative Synagogues (CCCS)
37 Southbourne Ave., Toronto ON M3H 1A4

Tel: 416-635-5340
canadianccs.weebly.com

Overview: A small national organization
Chief Officer(s):
Robyn Esar, Coordinator, Youth
youth@canadianccs.org
Membership: 5
Activities: Developing youth programs
Description: To support & promote cooperative programming among members

Canadian Friends of Boys Town Jerusalem
#200, 2788 Bathurst St., Toronto ON M6B 3A3

Tel: 416-789-7241; *Fax:* 416-789-1090
Toll-Free: 866-989-7241
www.btjcanada.com

Overview: A small local organization founded in 1973
Chief Officer(s):
Jules Kronis, President
Sharon E. Anisman, Executive Director
sharon@btjcanada.com
Debbie Basch, Administrative Assistant
debbie@btjcanada.com
Finances: *Annual Operating Budget:* $100,000-$250,000;
Funding Sources: Foundation grants; Events; Direct mail; Major gifts
Staff: 2 staff member(s); 10 volunteer(s)
Description: To take boys of high potential from all parts of Israel from junior high school, high school & colleges of mechanical & electrical engineering & expose them to a high level of technological, academic, & religious training; To raise funds for Boys Town Jerusalem in order to provide education for boys from disadvantaged backgrounds

Chosen People Ministries (Canada) (CPM)
PO Box 58103, Stn. Dufferin-Lawrence, Toronto ON M6A 3C8

Tel: 416-250-0177; *Fax:* 416-250-9235
Toll-Free: 888-442-5535
info@chosenpeople.ca
chosenpeople.ca
www.instagram.com/chosenpeople_ca
www.facebook.com/ChosenPeopleMinistriesCanada
twitter.com/ChosenPeopleCA

Also Known As: Beth Sar Shalom Mission

Overview: A medium-sized national charitable organization founded in 1894
Chief Officer(s):
Jorge Sedaca, Executive Director
Finances: *Annual Operating Budget:* $500,000-$1.5 Million; *Funding Sources:* Donations
Staff: 14 staff member(s)
Activities: *Speaker Service:* Yes
Description: To pray for, evangelize, disciple & serve Jewish people everywhere

Communauté sépharade unifiée du Québec (CSUQ)
#216, 5151 Cote-Ste-Catherine, Montréal QC H3W 1M6

Tél: 514-733-4998; *Téléc:* 514-733-3158
info@csuq.org
www.csuq.org
www.facebook.com/lacsuq

Également appelé: La Voix sépharade
Nom précédent: Association Sépharade Francophone
Aperçu: *Dimension:* moyenne; *Envergure:* provinciale; *Organisme sans but lucratif; fondée en* 1966
Finances: *Budget de fonctionnement annuel:* $500,000-$1.5 Million
Personnel: 10 membre(s) du personnel; 200 bénévole(s)
Membre: 25 000; *Comités:* Administration; Affaires religieuses; Affaires sociales; Éducation et Culture; Financement; Information; Planification communautaire; Relations publiques; Ressources humaines
Activités: La Commission de l'Information, un comité permanent, informe toute la population sépharade des réalisations et projets de la communauté ainsi qu' une information culturelle, religieuse et générale; *Bibliothèque:* Oui rendez-vous
Description: Préserver la culture et le patrimoine sépharade; défendre les intérêts de la population sépharade et la représenter auprès des divers paliers gouvernementaux ainsi que d'autres associations communautaires; *Membre de:* Fédération - CJA

Congregation Beth Israel - British Columbia
989 West 28th Ave., Vancouver BC V5Z 0E8

Tel: 604-731-4161; *Fax:* 604-731-4989
info@bethisrael.ca
www.bethisrael.ca
www.youtube.com/channel/UCV32q1muJX33op5rSZA7FTQ

Overview: A small local organization founded in 1932
Chief Officer(s):
Gary Miller, President
Jonathan Infeld, Klei Kodesh
rabbiinfeld@bethisrael.ca
Shannon Etkin, Executive Director
shannon@bethisrael.ca
Activities: Youth programs; Hebrew school; facility rental; Rabbi Wilfred & Phyllis Solomon Museum; *Library:* Moe Cohen Library (Open to Public)
Description: The congregation is dedicated to the strengthening of all aspects of Jewish life, including worship & Torah study, religious, educational & social activities for all ages, & the observance of life cycle events.; *Member of:* United Synagogue of Conservative Judaism

Jewish Foundation of Manitoba (JFM)
123 Doncaster St., #C400, Winnipeg MB R3N 2B2

Tel: 204-477-7520; *Fax:* 204-477-7527
Toll-Free: 855-284-1918
info@jewishfoundation.org
www.jewishfoundation.org
twitter.com/jfm_mb

Overview: A small provincial charitable organization
Chief Officer(s):
Marsha Cowan, Chief Executive Officer, 204-477-7520
mcowan@jewishfoundation.org
Activities: Provide scholarships & grants
Description: To encourage & facilitate the creation & growth of endowment funds to enable the community to reach its potential

Jews for Judaism
PO Box 54042, 3110 Bathurst St., Toronto ON M6A 3B7

Tel: 416-789-0020; *Fax:* 416-789-0030
Toll-Free: 866-307-4362
info@jewsforjudaism.ca
jewsforjudaism.ca
www.youtube.com/user/JewsforJudaismCanada
www.facebook.com/jewsforjudaismcanada
twitter.com/JewsforJudaism1

Overview: A small international organization
Chief Officer(s):
Julius Ciss, Executive Director
juliusciss@jewsforjudaism.ca
Finances: *Funding Sources:* Corporate sponsorship, donations
Activities: Free preventative educational programs, innovative educational materials & specialized counselling services

Description: To counteract the efforts of numerous cults & Christian missionary groups that target Jews in Canada for conversion

Kosher Check
#401, 1037 West Broadway, Vancouver BC V6H 1E3
Tel: 604-731-1803; *Fax:* 604-731-1804
info@koshercheck.org
www.koshercheck.org
www.linkedin.com/company/3110427
www.facebook.com/Koshercheck
twitter.com/koshercheck
Previous Name: BC Kosher; Orthodox Rabbinical Council of British Columbia
Overview: A medium-sized international charitable organization founded in 1983
Chief Officer(s):
Avraham Feigelstock, Av Beis Din, 604-731-1803 101
Richard Wood, Director, Business & Marketing, 604-731-1803 103
Finances: *Annual Operating Budget:* $100,000-$250,000
Staff: 5 staff member(s); 6 volunteer(s)
Membership: 100-499
Activities: Providing information about Kashruth (kosher food - kashruth symbol BCK); *Speaker Service:* Yes

Maccabi Canada
PO Box 20090, Stn. Carrville, 9200 Dufferin St., Concord ON L4K 0C8
Tel: 416-398-0515
info@maccabicanada.com
www.maccabicanada.com
www.instagram.com/maccabi_canada
www.facebook.com/maccabicanada
twitter.com/MaccabiCanada
Overview: A small national organization
Chief Officer(s):
Lee Mes, Executive Director
lee@maccabicanada.com
Michele Bass, Director, Operations
michele@maccabicanada.com
Fees: Schedule available; *Committees:* National Athletic
Activities: Offering community sports programs & the opportunity for athletes to compete in the Maccabiah Games, the 3rd largest sporting event in the world; *Awareness Events:* Maccabiah Games: every 4 years, in Israel; Pan-American Maccabiah Games: every 4 years in South America
Description: Maccabi Canada strengthens Jewish identity through athletic, cultural, social & educational activities; *Member of:* Maccabi World Union

Mercaz-Canada
#201, 55 Yeomans Rd., Toronto ON M3H 3J7
Tel: 416-667-1717; *Toll-Free:* 866-357-3384
info@masorti-mercaz.ca
www.mercaz.ca
www.facebook.com/MercazCanada
Also Known As: Movement to Reaffirm Conservative Zionism
Overview: A medium-sized international organization founded in 1994
Chief Officer(s):
Jennifer Gorman, Executive Director
Fees: $18 individual; $36 couple; $9 student ages 18-25
Description: To support the State of Israel as a democratic & pluralistic national home for all Jews, secure & at peace with its Arab neighbours, committed to protecting the rights of all its citizens & supporting all streams of Jewish practices; in Canada, to promote Aliyah, trips to Israel & Zionist programming; *Member of:* Canadian Zionist Federation; World Zionist Organization; Mercaz-Olami; *Affiliation(s):* United Synagogues of Conservative Judaism

National Council of Jewish Women of Canada (NCJWC)
#1, 890 Sheppard Ave. West, Toronto ON M3H 6B9
Tel: 416-633-5100; *Fax:* 416-633-1956
Toll-Free: 866-625-9274
info@ncjwc.org
www.ncjwc.org
www.facebook.com/251326701899847
Overview: A medium-sized national charitable organization founded in 1897
Chief Officer(s):
Debbie Wasserman, President
president@ncjwc.org
Finances: *Funding Sources:* Donations
Fees: $36
Description: To further human welfare in the Jewish & general communities; To help fulfill unmet needs & to serve the individual & the community; *Affiliation(s):* International Council of Jewish Women; UNESCO Sub commission on the Status of

Women; Coalition of Jewish Women against Domestic Violence & the Coalition for Agunot Rights

Pride of Israel
59 Lissom Cres., Toronto ON M2R 2P2
Tel: 416-226-0111; *Fax:* 416-226-0128
office@prideofisraelshul.org
www.prideofisraelshul.org
Overview: A small local organization founded in 1905
Chief Officer(s):
Steven Bloom, Chair
chairman@prideofisraelshul.org
Sean Gorman, Rabbi
rabbi@prideofisraelshul.org
Bonnie Moatti, Coordinator, Membership
Finances: *Funding Sources:* Donations
Activities: Offering a Kosher Food Bank; Providing Jewish educational programming

Shaare Zion Congregation
5575, rue Côte-St-Luc, Montréal QC H3X 2C9
Tel: 514-481-7727; *Fax:* 514-481-1219
info@shaarezion.org
www.shaarezion.org
www.youtube.com/user/shaarezionmtl/featured
www.linkedin.com/company/shaare-zion-congregation
www.facebook.com/shaarezion
twitter.com/ShaareZion_MTL
Overview: A small local charitable organization founded in 1924
Chief Officer(s):
David Moscovitch, Executive Director, 514-481-7727 227
david.moscovitch@shaarezion.org
Lionel E. Moses, Rabbi, 514-481-7727 228
rabbi@shaarezion.org
Affiliation(s): United Synagogue of Conservative Judiasm

Shaarei Tefillah
Shaarei Tefillah Congregation, 3600 Bathurst St., Toronto ON M6A 2C9
Tel: 416-787-1631; *Fax:* 416-785-5378
www.shaareitefillah.com
Also Known As: Vaad Harabonim (Orthodox Rabbinical Council); Rabbinical Council of Ontario
Overview: A small local organization founded in 1982
Chief Officer(s):
Harvey Mincer, President
Shmuli Soroka, Executive Director, 416-787-1631 220
executivedirector@shaareitefillah.com
Finances: *Annual Operating Budget:* Less than $50,000
Membership: 40; *Fees:* $1,000 individual; $2,000 family
Description: To celebrate Judaism, community, family & the creation of lasting friendships

Toronto Association of Synagogue & Temple Administrators
c/o Beth Tikvah Synagogue, 3080 Bayview Ave., Toronto ON M5N 5L3
Tel: 416-221-3433
Overview: A small local organization
Chief Officer(s):
Doris Alter, President
doris@bethtikvahtoronto.org
Finances: *Annual Operating Budget:* Less than $50,000
Membership: 12; *Fees:* $50; *Member Profile:* Executive directors of synagogues & temples

United Synagogue of Conservative Judaism, Canadian Region (USCJ)
1700 Bathurst St., Toronto ON M3J 2V5
Tel: 416-667-1717; *Fax:* 416-667-1881
Overview: A medium-sized provincial organization

Lutheran

Canadian Lutheran World Relief (CLWR)
#600, 177 Lombard Ave., Winnipeg MB R3B 0W5
Tel: 204-694-5602; *Fax:* 204-694-5460
Toll-Free: 800-661-2597
clwr@clwr.mb.ca
www.clwr.org
www.instagram.com/canlwr
www.linkedin.com/company/canadian-lutheran-world-relief
www.facebook.com/CanadianLutheranWorldRelief
twitter.com/CanLWR
Overview: A large national charitable organization founded in 1946
Chief Officer(s):
Karin Achtelstetter, Executive Director
Carla Blakley, Director, Community & Donor Relations, 204-631-0504
carla@clwr.org

Akililu Hunqe, Director, Programs
akililu@clwr.org
Finances: *Funding Sources:* Evangelical Lutheran Church of Canada; Lutheran Church-Canada; Canadian Lutherans; Government
Staff: 23 staff member(s)
Activities: *Speaker Service:* Yes
Description: To provide development programming in Africa, Asia, Latin America, & the Middle East; To provide emergency relief in case of disaster; To enable sponsorships for refugee resettlement in Canada; To focus on development, peace building, alternative approaches to trade, education, & community building; *Member of:* Canadian Foodgrains Bank; The Lutheran World Federation; ACT Alliance; Canadian Churches in Action; Canadian Council for International Cooperation; Manitoba Council for International Cooperation; Saskatchewan Council for International Cooperation

Evangelical Lutheran Church in Canada (ELCIC)
#600, 177 Lombard Ave., Winnipeg MB R3B 0W5
Tel: 204-984-9173; *Fax:* 204-984-9185
Toll-Free: 888-786-6707
www.elcic.ca
www.facebook.com/CanadianLutherans
twitter.com/elcicinfo
Overview: A medium-sized national charitable organization founded in 1986
Chief Officer(s):
Susan Johnson, National Bishop, 204-984-9157
sjohnson@elcic.ca
Trina Gallop, Director, Communications & Resource Generation, 204-984-9172
tgallop@elcic.ca
Kyle Giesbrecht, Director, Finance & Administration, 204-984-9178
kgiesbrecht@elcic.ca
Finances: *Annual Operating Budget:* $1.5 Million-$3 Million; *Funding Sources:* Donations
Staff: 20 staff member(s)
Membership: 114,592 individuals; 525 congregations; *Member Profile:* Current members in a congregation
Description: The Church shares the gospel of Jesus Christ with people in Canada & around the world through the proclamation of the Word, celebration of the sacraments & through service in Christ's name; *Member of:* Canadian Council of Churches; Lutheran Council in Canada; Lutheran World Federation; World Council of Churches; *Affiliation(s):* Anglican Church of Canada

Lutheran Association of Missionaries & Pilots (LAMP)
4966 - 92 Ave. NW, Edmonton AB T6B 2V4
Tel: 780-466-8507; *Fax:* 780-466-6733
Toll-Free: 800-307-4036
office@lampministry.org
www.lampministry.org
www.youtube.com/user/LAMPMinistry
www.facebook.com/lampministry.org
twitter.com/lampministry
Overview: A small international organization founded in 1970
Chief Officer(s):
Ron Ludke, Executive Director
Finances: *Annual Operating Budget:* $500,000-$1.5 Million
Staff: 300 volunteer(s)
Activities: *Speaker Service:* Yes
Description: To share Jesus Christ with the people of remote areas of Canada; *Affiliation(s):* Lutheran Church Canada; Evangelical Lutheran Church in Canada

Lutheran Bible Translators of Canada Inc. (LBTC)
275 Lawrence Ave., Kitchener ON N2M 1Y3
Tel: 519-742-3361; *Toll-Free:* 866-518-7071
info@lbtc.ca
www.lbtc.ca
www.facebook.com/lutheranbibletranslatorsofcanada
Overview: A small international charitable organization founded in 1974
Chief Officer(s):
Ron Mohr, Executive Director
pastor.r.mohr@lbtc.ca
Finances: *Annual Operating Budget:* $250,000-$500,000
Staff: 6 staff member(s)
Membership: 1-99
Activities: *Speaker Service:* Yes
Description: To bring people to faith in Jesus Christ through Bible translations & literacy work; *Affiliation(s):* Canadian Council of Christian Charities

Lutheran Church - Canada (LCC) / Église Luthérienne du Canada
3074 Portage Ave., Winnipeg MB R3K 0Y2
Tel: 204-895-3433; *Fax:* 204-832-3018
Toll-Free: 800-588-4226
info@lutheranchurch.ca
www.lutheranchurch.ca
www.facebook.com/lutheranchurch.canada
twitter.com/CanLutheran
Overview: A medium-sized national organization founded in 1988
Chief Officer(s):
Timothy Teuscher, President, 204-895-3433 212
president@lutheranchurch.ca
Dwayne Cleave, Administrator, 204-895-3433 219
administratorlcc@lutheranchurch.ca
Finances: *Funding Sources:* Donations
Membership: 75,000+ members in 319 congregations
Activities: Supporting LCC missionaries in other countries; Working with Canadian Lutheran World Relief; Responding to social needs in local communities, such as establishing food banks & offering English as a Second Language classes; Educating children through Sunday schools, Vacation Bible Schools & confirmation classes; Offering various resources, such as congregation resources, statistical data & theological documents; Organizing Synod conventions; *Awareness Events:* National Lutheran Open House; National Youth Gathering
Description: To share the Gospel of Jesus Christ; To proclaim the Lutheran belief & faith in word & deed; Affiliation(s): Canadian Lutheran World Relief; Lutheran Women's Missionary League - Canada; Lutheran Laymen's League; Concordia Lutheran Mission Society

Lutheran Laymen's League of Canada (LLL-C)
270 Lawrence Ave., Kitchener ON N2M 1Y4
Tel: 519-578-7420; *Fax:* 519-742-8091
Toll-Free: 800-555-6236
info@lll.ca
www.lll.ca
www.instagram.com/lutheranlaymensleagueca
www.facebook.com/LutheranLaymensLeagueCanada
Also Known As: Lutheran Hour Ministries
Overview: A small national charitable organization founded in 1967
Chief Officer(s):
Lisa Jackson, Managing Director
director@lll.ca
Finances: *Annual Operating Budget:* $500,000-$1.5 Million; *Funding Sources:* Donations
Staff: 2 staff member(s); 200 volunteer(s)
Membership: 1,000-4,999
Activities: Christian radio & TV programs; print & Internet resources; communication workshops
Description: To proclaim gospel of Jesus Christ through the use of media; To bring Christ to the nations & the nation to the Christ; Affiliation(s): International Lutheran Layman's League

Canadian Conference of Mennonite Brethren Churches (CCMBC)
1310 Taylor Ave., Winnipeg MB R3M 3Z6
Tel: 204-669-6575; *Fax:* 204-654-1865
Toll-Free: 888-669-6575
info@mbchurches.ca
www.mennonitebrethren.ca
www.instagram.com/mbchurches
www.linkedin.com/company/canadian-conference-of-mennonite-brethren-churches
www.facebook.com/mbconf
twitter.com/CdnMBConf
Overview: A medium-sized national organization founded in 1945
Chief Officer(s):
Elton DaSilva, National Director, 800-669-6575
elton.dasilva@mbchurches.ca
Finances: *Funding Sources:* Donations
Staff: 25 staff member(s)
Membership: 31,264; 256 Mennonite Brethren congregations; *Committees:* Mennonite Central Committee; Mennonite Disaster Service; Multiply
Activities: *Library:* Centre for MB Studies (Open to Public)
Description: To glorify God, to nurture & equip members to live the Christian life & to mobilize them for ministry

Centre for Newcomers Society of Calgary (CFN)
#1010, 999 - 36 St. NE, Calgary AB T2A 7X6
Tel: 403-569-3325
info@centrefornewcomers.ca
www.centrefornewcomers.ca
cfnyyc.blogspot.ca
www.linkedin.com/company/centre-for-newcomers-society-of-calgary
www.facebook.com/centrefornewcomers
twitter.com/YYCNewcomers
Previous Name: Calgary Mennonite Centre for Newcomers Society
Overview: A small local organization founded in 1988
Chief Officer(s):
Anila Lee Yuen, MBA, Chief Executive Officer
a.leeyuen@centrefornewcomers.ca
David Hohol, Manager, Communications & Community Relations
d.hohol@centrefornewcomers.ca
Finances: *Annual Operating Budget:* Greater than $5 Million; *Funding Sources:* Government
Staff: 150 staff member(s); 560 volunteer(s)
Member Profile: Members beyond the Mennonite constituency is enoucraged.
Activities: Offering English language programs, as well as family, children & youth programs; settlement & integration services; career development & job search resources; work experience opportunities, including EthniCity Catering & accounting training; multicultural peer mentorship & volunteer development; *Speaker Service:* Yes *Library:* Yes
Description: To assist refugees & immigrants arriving in Calgary to meet their settlement needs; To provide services & initiatives that promote a welcoming environment for newcomers in Calgary; *Member of:* Alberta Association of Immigrant Serving Agencies; Calgary Chamber of Voluntary Organizations; Affiliation(s): Canadian Red Cross

Evangelical Mennonite Conference (EMC)
440 Main St., Steinbach MB R5G 1Z5
Tel: 204-326-6401; *Fax:* 204-326-1613
info@emconference.ca
www.emconference.ca
www.instagram.com/em_conference
www.facebook.com/em_conference
twitter.com/em_conference
Overview: A medium-sized national charitable organization founded in 1812
Chief Officer(s):
Barry Plett, Moderator
Finances: *Annual Operating Budget:* $1.5 Million-$3 Million; *Funding Sources:* Donations
Membership: 60 churches
Activities: *Library:* Evangelical Mennonite Conference Archives
Description: To advance Chirst's kingdom culture as members live, reach, gather & teach

MB Mission (MBMSI) / Mennonite Brethren Mission & Service International
International & Western Canada (BC), #300, 32040 Downes Rd., Abbotsford BC V4X 1X5
Tel: 604-859-6267; *Fax:* 604-859-6422
Toll-Free: 866-964-7627
mbmission@mbmission.org
www.mbmission.org
www.youtube.com/MBMissionVideos
www.facebook.com/mbmission
twitter.com/MBMission
Also Known As: Board of Missions & Services of the Mennonite Brethren Churches of North America
Previous Name: MBMS International
Overview: A medium-sized local charitable organization founded in 1900
Chief Officer(s):
Randy Friesen, General Director
randyf@mbmission.org
Finances: *Funding Sources:* Voluntary contributions; grants
Activities: Cross-cultural mission agency of Mennonite Brethren churches in Canada & the US; *Internships:* Yes; *Speaker Service:* Yes
Description: To make disciples & plant churches globally through church planting & envangelism, discipleship & leadership training & social ministry; *Member of:* Evangelical Fellowship of Mission Agencies

Mennonite Central Committee Canada (MCCC)
134 Plaza Dr., Winnipeg MB
Tel: 204-261-6381; *Fax:* 204-269-9875
Toll-Free: 888-622-6337
canada@mennonitecc.ca
mcccanada.ca
www.instagram.com/mccpeace
www.facebook.com/MennoniteCentralCommittee
twitter.com/mcccan

Overview: A large national charitable organization founded in 1920
Chief Officer(s):
Rick Cober Bauman, Executive Director
Description: To share God's love and compassion for all by responding to basic human needs & working for peace & justice; *Member of:* Mennonite Central Committee

Mennonite Church Canada (MC Canada)
600 Shaftesbury Blvd., Winnipeg MB R3P 0M4
Tel: 204-888-6781; *Fax:* 204-831-5675
Toll-Free: 866-888-6785
office@mennonitechurch.ca
www.mennonitechurch.ca
Also Known As: Conference of Mennonites in Canada
Overview: A medium-sized national charitable organization founded in 1903
Chief Officer(s):
Doug Klassen, Executive Minister, 204-888-6781 115
dklassen@mennonitechurch.ca
Finances: *Funding Sources:* Donations
Membership: 32,000 members in 221 congregations
Activities: *Library:* Mennonite Church Canada Resource Centre
Description: To form a people of God; To become a global church; To grow leaders

Mennonite Economic Development Associates Canada
155 Frobisher Dr., #I-106, Waterloo ON N2V 2E1
Tel: 519-725-1633; *Fax:* 519-725-9083
Toll-Free: 800-665-7026
meda@meda.org
www.meda.org
www.linkedin.com/company/1314159
www.facebook.com/MEDAdotorg
twitter.com/medadotorg
Also Known As: MEDA Canada
Overview: A medium-sized international charitable organization founded in 1953
Chief Officer(s):
Allan Sauder, President
Kim Pityn, CEO
Gerald Morrison, Chief Financial Officer
Michael White, Chief Strategic Engagement Officer
Finances: *Annual Operating Budget:* $1.5 Million-$3 Million
Membership: 3,000 Canada & US
Activities: Publish magazines & reports; Videos & weblinks; Learning Centre; *Library:* Mennonite Economic Development Associates Canada Library by appointment
Description: To be committed to the nurture & expression of Christian faith in a business setting; To enable members to integrate biblical values & business principles in their daily lives; To address the needs of the disadvantaged through programs of economic development

Northwest Mennonite Conference
West Zion Mennonite Church, PO Box 1316, 2025 - 20 Ave., Didsbury AB T0M 0W0
Tel: 403-337-3283; *Fax:* 403-337-3258
www.nwmc.ca
Overview: A small provincial organization
Chief Officer(s):
Mark Loewen, Conference Moderator, 403-337-3283
David Peters, Conference Minister, 587-225-1072
Membership: 14 congregations; *Member Profile:* Churches in Alberta; *Committees:* Congregational Ministries; Congregational Leadership; Missions & Service; Stewardship
Description: To enable & empower congregations to become communities of Christ's healing & hope; *Member of:* Mennonite Church North America

The Atlantic District of The Wesleyan Church
1830 Mountain Rd., Moncton NB E1G 1A9
Tel: 506-383-8326; *Fax:* 506-383-8333
office@atlanticdistrict.com
www.atlanticdistrict.com
Previous Name: The Wesleyan Church of Canada - Atlantic District
Overview: A medium-sized local organization founded in 1966
Chief Officer(s):
HC Wilson, District Superintendent
wilsonhc@twccanada.ca

The Bible Holiness Movement / Mouvement de sainteté biblique
PO Box 223, Stn. A, Vancouver BC V6C 2M3
Tel: 250-492-3376
www.bible-holiness-movement.com
Previous Name: The Bible Holiness Mission

Overview: A medium-sized international charitable organization founded in 1949
Chief Officer(s):
Wesley H. Wakefield, Bishop-General
Finances: *Annual Operating Budget:* $100,000-$250,000;
Funding Sources: Unsolicited gifts from Christian believers
Staff: 16 staff member(s); 6 volunteer(s)
Membership: 93,658 worldwide in 89 countries; 954 Canadian;
Fees: None

Activities: *Internships:* Yes; *Speaker Service:* Yes *Library:* Bible Holiness Movement Library by appointment
Description: To emphasize the original Methodist faith of salvation & scriptural holiness, with principles of discipline, non-conformity & non-resistance; To administer overseas indigenous missionary centres in West Africa, the Philippines, East Africa, South Korea, India & the West Indies; *Member of:* Christian Holiness Partnership; National Black Evangelical Association; Anti-Slavery International; *Affiliation(s):* Religious Freedom of Council of Christian Minorities; Christians Concerned for Racial Equality

Free Methodist Church in Canada (FMCIC) / Église méthodiste libre du Canada
4315 Village Centre Ct., Mississauga ON L4Z 1S2
Tel: 905-848-2600
ministrycentre@fmc-canada.org
www.fmc-canada.org
vimeo.com/user18221796
www.facebook.com/FMCIC
twitter.com/FMCIC
Overview: A medium-sized national organization founded in 1880
Chief Officer(s):
Cliff Fletcher, Bishop
Marc McAlister, Director, Church Health
Mark Molczanski, Director, Administrative Services
Jared Siebert, Director, Church Planting
Finances: *Annual Operating Budget:* $1.5 Million-$3 Million
Staff: 11 staff member(s)
Membership: 6,765 attendees at 146 churches
Activities: *Internships:* Yes; *Speaker Service:* Yes
Description: To find ways to engage unreached people & unreached communitites with the gospel; To mature congregations through developing healthy pastoral & lay leaders; To commission prepared people to purposeful service; To interpret life theologically through intentional reflection; To invest human & financial resources strategically; To communicate & celebrate through listening to & inspiring one another; *Member of:* Free Methodist World Conference; *Affiliation(s):* Evangelical Fellowship of Canada; Canadian Council of Christian Charities; World Relief Canada

The Wesleyan Church of Canada - Central Canada District
3545 County Rd. #27, RR#2, Lyn ON K0E 1M0
Tel: 613-877-2087; *Toll-Free:* 877-862-4637
office@ccdwesleyan.ca
ccdwesleyan.ca
Also Known As: The Wesleyan Methodist Church of Canada
Overview: A medium-sized national charitable organization founded in 1897
Chief Officer(s):
Eric R. Hallett, District Superintendent
ds@ccdwesleyan.ca
Daryl MacPherson, District Secretary
ccdsecretary@gmail.com
Kevin Beattie, District Treasurer
kevin@beattiedodge.ca
Finances: *Annual Operating Budget:* $500,000-$1.5 Million;
Funding Sources: District churches
Staff: 3 staff member(s)
Membership: 1,736; *Member Profile:* Covenant members & community members in Ontario & Quebec
Activities: Camps; Church Planting; Emerging Regions; Friends for the Future; Missions; *Internships:* Yes
Description: To create a context that produces healthy churches; *Affiliation(s):* Tyndale Seminary; World Hope International; World Relief Canada; Bethany Bible College; Outreach Canada; Evangelical Fellowship of Canada

Mormonism

Church of Jesus Christ of Latter-day Saints - Canada
ON
ca.churchofjesuschrist.org@gmail.com
ca.churchofjesuschrist.org
www.youtube.com/user/MormonMessages
twitter.com/ldsincanada
Overview: A large national organization founded in 1830

Membership: 190,265 members + 479 congregations in Canada
Activities: *Speaker Service:* Yes *Library:* Family History Library by appointment

New Thought

Association of Unity Churches Canada
2631 Kingsway Dr., Kitchener ON N2C 1A7
Tel: 519-894-0810
hello@unitycanada.org
www.unitycanada.org
Also Known As: Unity Canada
Overview: A small national charitable organization founded in 1978
Chief Officer(s):
V. Vanderhorst, President
president@unitycanada.org
Finances: *Annual Operating Budget:* $50,000-$100,000
Membership: 23 churches
Activities: *Internships:* Yes; *Speaker Service:* Yes
Description: Unity is a Christian association asserting that reunion with God in mind brings certain fulfillment in life; *Affiliation(s):* Association of Unity Churches USA

Orthodox

The Coptic Orthodox Church (Canada)
St. Mark's Coptic Orthodox Church, 41 Glendinning Ave., Toronto ON M1W 3E2
Tel: 416-494-4449; *Fax:* 416-494-4196
mail@coptorthodox.ca
stmarkstoronto.ca
Overview: A small national organization
Chief Officer(s):
M.A. Marcos, Priest
frmarcos@coptorthodox.ca
Member of: The Canadian Council of Churches; Coptic Orthodox Patriarchate

Greek Orthodox Metropolis of Toronto (Canada)
86 Overlea Blvd., Toronto ON M4H 1C6
Tel: 416-429-5757; *Fax:* 416-429-4588
office@goarchdiocese.ca
www.gometropolis.org
www.youtube.com/user/GOMetropolisToronto
www.facebook.com/gometropolis
twitter.com/GO_Metropolis
Previous Name: Greek Orthodox Church (Canada)
Overview: A medium-sized national organization
Chief Officer(s):
Chrisostomos Perentes, President
Dimitrios Anas, Secretary
George Raios, Treasurer
Membership: 76 churches + 350,000 members
Member of: The Canadian Council of Churches

Romanian Orthodox Diocese of Canada
2010, boul Marie, St-Hubert QC J4T 2B1
Tel: 450-812-1733; *Fax:* 450-812-7701
contact@episcopia.ca
www.episcopia.ca
Overview: A small national organization founded in 2016
Chief Officer(s):
Ioan Casian, Bishop
Affiliation(s): Romanian Orthodox Episcopate of America

Russian Orthodox Church in Canada
10812 - 108th St., Edmonton AB T5H 3A6
Tel: 780-420-9945
www.orthodox-canada.com
Overview: A medium-sized national organization
Chief Officer(s):
Matthew Andreev, Bishop of Sourozh
sourozhdiocese@me.com
Membership: 22 parishes

Serbian Orthodox Church - Orthodox Diocese of Canada
7470 McNiven Rd., RR#3, Campbellville ON L0P 1B0
Tel: 905-878-0043
www.serborth.org/canada
Overview: A medium-sized national charitable organization founded in 1983
Chief Officer(s):
Vasilije Tomic, Episcopal Deputy, 416-450-4555
o.bajo@rogers.com
Jovan Marjanac, Diocesan Secretary, 905-878-0043
Finances: *Annual Operating Budget:* $500,000-$1.5 Million;
Funding Sources: Donations; parish taxes; dispensations
Staff: 23 staff member(s)

Membership: 150,000; *Committees:* Diocesan Executive Board; Diocesan Assembly
Activities: *Library:* Serbian Orthodox Church: Holy Transfiguration (Open to Public) by appointment
Description: To serve the Serbian Orthodox community & teach the Orthodox faith & culture

Ukrainian Orthodox Church of Canada (UOCC) / L'Église orthodoxe ukrainienne du Canada
Ecumenical Patriarchate, 9 St John's Ave., Winnipeg MB R2W 1G8
Tel: 204-586-3093; *Fax:* 204-582-5241
Toll-Free: 877-586-3093
consistory@uocc.ca
uocc.ca
www.facebook.com/UOCCanada
twitter.com/UOCCanada
Overview: A large national organization founded in 1918
Chief Officer(s):
Metropolitan Yurij, Primate
metropolitan@uocc.ca
Taras Udod, Chancellor & Chair, Presidium
chancellor@uocc.ca
Membership: 120,000
Activities: *Speaker Service:* Yes *Library:* Ukrainian Orthodox Church of Canada Library (Open to Public) by appointment

World Fellowship of Orthodox Youth
webmaster@syndesmos.org
syndesmostemporary.blogspot.com
Also Known As: Syndesmos
Overview: A small international organization founded in 1953
Chief Officer(s):
Jean Rehbinder, President
Georges El Hage, Vice-President
Finances: *Annual Operating Budget:* $50,000-$100,000;
Funding Sources: Orthodox churches; Orthodox church organisations; council of Eurpoe; European Christina Diakonia age
Staff: 2 staff member(s); 4 volunteer(s)
Membership: 121 organizations in 42 countries; *Fees:* $500 affiliated; *Member Profile:* Christian Orthodox youth organizations & theological schools; *Committees:* Publications
Activities: Orthodox youth camps, festivals, encounters, seminars, consultations, conferences, training courses, workshops; *Internships:* Yes *Library:* Yes (Open to Public)
Description: To serve as a bond of unity among Orthodox youth movements, organisations & theological schools around the world, promoting a consciousness of the catholicity of the Orthodox faith; To foster relations, coordination & mutal aid among them; to promote among young people a full understanding of the Orthodox faith & the mission of the Church in the contemporary world & an active participation of youth in ecclesial life; To promote a way of life founded in eucharistic communion, in the Gospel & in patristic teaching, for witness & service to the world; To assist & promote Orthodox efforcts for visible Christian unity & for positive relations with people of other faiths; To encourage reflection & action on issues affecting the lives of Orthodox Christians & the local churches; To be an instrument for furthering cooperation & deeper communion between the Orthodox Church & the Oriental Orthodox Churches

Pentecostalism

The Apostolic Church in Canada
220 Adelaide St. North, London ON N6B 3H4
Tel: 519-438-7036
cheryl@apostolic.ca
apostolic.ca
Overview: A small national organization founded in 1934
Chief Officer(s):
John Kristensen, National Leader
Finances: *Annual Operating Budget:* $500,000-$1.5 Million
Staff: 10 staff member(s)
Membership: 500-999
Activities: *Internships:* Yes
Description: A Trinitarian, Pentecostal denomination with a strong commitment to mission

Apostolic Church of Pentecost of Canada Inc. (ACOP) / Église apostolique de Pentecôte du Canada inc.
International Office, #119, 2340 Pegasus Way NE, Calgary AB T2E 8M5
Tel: 403-273-5777; *Fax:* 403-273-8102
acop@acop.ca
www.acop.ca
www.instagram.com/acopcanada
www.facebook.com/ACOPcanada
twitter.com/ACOPcanada

Overview: A small national licensing charitable organization founded in 1921
Chief Officer(s):
Wes Mills, President & National Director
Finances: *Annual Operating Budget:* $1.5 Million-$3 Million;
Funding Sources: Donations
Staff: 30 staff member(s)
Membership: 120 affiliated churches + 408 members; *Fees:* Varies
Activities: *Internships:* Yes; *Speaker Service:* Yes *Library:* Yes by appointment
Description: To provide fellowship, encouragement & accountability in the proclamation of the Gospel of Jesus Christ by the Power of the Holy Spirit; *Affiliation(s):* Evangelical Fellowship of Canada

Church of God of Prophecy in Canada
Eastern Canada Head Office, 5145 Tomken Rd., Mississauga ON L4W 1P1
Tel: 905-625-1278; *Fax:* 905-625-1316
info@cogop.ca
www.cogop.ca

Overview: A medium-sized national charitable organization
Chief Officer(s):
Woodroe Thompson, Bishop
woodroethompson@cogop.ca
Finances: *Annual Operating Budget:* $100,000-$250,000
Staff: 3 staff member(s)
Membership: 28 churches
Activities: *Internships:* Yes; *Speaker Service:* Yes
Description: To call attention to the principle of unity in the body of Christ, while faithfully proclaiming the gospel of Jesus Christ before a watching world

General Conference of the Canadian Assemblies of God / Conférence générale des assemblées de dieu canadiennes
5845, boul Couture, Saint-Léonard QC H1P 1A8
Tel: 514-279-1100; *Fax:* 514-279-1131
office@caog.ca
www.caog.ca

Also Known As: CAOG
Previous Name: Italian Pentecostal Church of Canada
Overview: A small national charitable organization founded in 1912
Chief Officer(s):
David Di Staulo, General Superintendent
Raymond Narula, General Secretary
Dino Cianflone, General Treasurer
Giulio Gabeli, Overseer
Finances: *Annual Operating Budget:* $100,000-$250,000
Staff: 2 staff member(s); 3 volunteer(s)
Membership: 39 affiliated churches
Activities: National Youth Convention (May); Annual General Conference (October); *Internships:* Yes
Description: To provide distinctive ministry to all Canadians, regardless of language, nationality, or race; To proclaim the gospel of Jesus Christ in the power of the Holy Spirit throughout Canada & the world, based on the biblical standard of ministry in the New Testament; *Member of:* The Evangelical Fellowship of Canada; Canadian Council of Christian Charities

Independent Assemblies of God International - Canada (IAOGI)
PO Box 653, Chatham ON N7M 5K8
Tel: 519-352-1743; *Fax:* 519-351-6070
iaogcan.com

Also Known As: IAOGI Canada
Previous Name: Scandinavian Assemblies of God in the United STates of America, Canada & Foreign Lands
Merged from: The Scandinavian Assemblies of God & the Independent Pentecostal Churches
Overview: A medium-sized national charitable organization founded in 1918
Chief Officer(s):
Paul McPhail, General Secretary
pmcphail@ciaccess.com
Finances: *Annual Operating Budget:* $100,000-$250,000;
Funding Sources: Membership fees; Offerings
Staff: 2 staff member(s); 12 volunteer(s)
Membership: 700+ Christian ministers; *Fees:* $170; *Member Profile:* Must be called by God to preach His Word
Activities: *Awareness Events:* National Convention, May;
Speaker Service: Yes
Description: To provide credentials for pastors and missionaries in all provinces & territories of Canada; *Member of:* Independent Assemblies of God International; *Affiliation(s):* Independent Assemblies of God International

Pentecostal Assemblies of Canada (PAOC) / Assemblées de la Pentecôte du Canada (APDC)
2450 Milltower Ct., Mississauga ON L5N 5Z6
Tel: 905-542-7400; *Fax:* 905-542-7313
Toll-Free: 800-779-7262
TTY: 800-855-0511
info@paoc.org
www.paoc.org
www.youtube.com/paoctube
www.linkedin.com/company/paoc
www.facebook.com/ThePAOC
twitter.com/thepaoc

Overview: A large national charitable organization founded in 1919
Chief Officer(s):
David Wells, General Superintendent
Finances: *Annual Operating Budget:* Greater than $5 Million;
Funding Sources: Local churches; individuals
Staff: 50 staff member(s)
Membership: 1,100 churches, 3,500 pastors representing 236,000 parishoners; *Committees:* General Executive; Administrative; International Missions; Audit; Credentials
Activities: Task Force; Work Force; Volunteers in Mission; Short-Term Missions; Volunteers in Special Assignment; ERDO (Emergency Relief & Development Overseas); Child Care Plus; *Library:* The PAOC Archives (Open to Public) by appointment
Description: To glorify God by making disciples everywhere by proclaiming & practising the gospel of Jesus Christ in the power of the Holy Spirit to establish local congregations & to train spiritual leaders; *Affiliation(s):* World Pentecost; Pentecostal/Charismatic Churches of North America; Pentecostal World Fellowship; World Assemblies of God Fellowship; Focus on the Family; Canadian Foodgrains Bank; Pentecostal European Mission; Seeds International; VisionLEDD; Canadian Council of Christian Charities; Every Home for Christ; Evangelical Missiological Society; Evangelical Fellowship of Canada; Canadian Children's Ministries Network; Canadian Bible Society; Family Life Ministries; Society of Pentecostal Studies

The Pentecostal Assemblies of Newfoundland & Labrador (PAONL)
PO Box 8895, Stn. A, 57 Thorburn Rd., St. John's NL A1B 3T2
Tel: 709-753-6314; *Fax:* 709-753-4945
info@paonl.ca
www.paonl.ca
www.facebook.com/252330011920
twitter.com/paonl

Overview: A medium-sized provincial charitable organization founded in 1911
Chief Officer(s):
Terry W. Snow, General Superintendent
Finances: *Annual Operating Budget:* $1.5 Million-$3 Million
Staff: 13 staff member(s)
Membership: 40,000
Activities: *Internships:* Yes; *Speaker Service:* Yes *Library:* Yes by appointment
Description: To promote evangelism, world missions, famine relief & education; *Affiliation(s):* Pentecostal Fellowship of North America

---

Presbyterianism

L'Église Réformée du Québec (ERQ) / The Reformed Church of Québec (RCQ)
1355 boul René-Lévesque ouest, Montréal QC H3G 1T3
Tél: 514-767-3165
info@erq.qc.ca
erq.qc.ca
www.facebook.com/jeunesse.erq

Nom précédent: Église Réformée St-Jean
Aperçu: *Dimension:* moyenne; *Envergure:* provinciale
Membre(s) du bureau directeur:
Jean Zoellner, Pastor
Affiliation(s): Christian Reformed Church; Presbyterian Church of North America

Evangel Hall Mission (EHM)
552 Adelaide St. West, Toronto ON M5V 3W8
Tel: 416-504-3563; *Fax:* 416-504-8056
information@evangelhall.ca
www.evangelhall.ca
www.facebook.com/evangelhallmission
twitter.com/ehm_1913

Overview: A small local charitable organization founded in 1913
Activities: Offering support, housing assistance, & services, including Out of the Cold Program, community dinners, dental clinic, & youth programs
Description: To deliver programs that deal with poverty and homelessness; To offer a continuum of care from emergency

---

food, clothing & shelter to transitional & long-term housing;
Affiliation(s): Presbyterian Church in Canada

Presbyterian Church in Canada (PCC) / Église presbytérienne au Canada
50 Wynford Dr., Toronto ON M3C 1J7
Tel: 416-441-1111; *Fax:* 416-441-2825
Toll-Free: 800-619-7301
presbyterian.ca
www.youtube.com/presvideo
www.facebook.com/pcconnect
twitter.com/pcconnect

Overview: A large national organization founded in 1875
Chief Officer(s):
Stephen Kendall, Principal Clerk, General Assembly Office, 416-441-1111 227
skendall@presbyterian.ca
Don Muir, Deputy Clerk, General Assembly Office, 416-441-1111 223
dmuir@presbyterian.ca
Oliver Ng, CFO & Treasurer, Financial Services, 416-441-1111 316
ong@presbyterian.ca
Finances: *Funding Sources:* Congregations
Membership: 125,509; *Member Profile:* Presbyteries; Congregations; Communicants on roll; Ministers; *Committees:* Assembly Council; Advise with the Moderator
Activities: *Library:* Knox College & Presbyterian College Libraries (Open to Public)
Description: To proclaim the love & good news of Jesus Christ through words & actions; *Member of:* The Canadian Council of Churches; World Alliance of Reformed Churches; World Council of Churches; Action By Churches Together; Ecumenical Advocacy Alliance

---

Protestantism

Grand Orange Lodge of Canada
#706, 505 Consumers Rd., Toronto ON M2J 4V8
Tel: 416-223-1690; *Fax:* 416-223-1324
Toll-Free: 800-565-6248
grandorangelodge.ca

Also Known As: Loyal Orange Association
Previous Name: The Grand Orange Lodge of British America
Overview: A large national organization founded in 1830
Chief Officer(s):
Don Wilson, Grand Master & Sovereign
Robert Smith, Deputy Grand Master
John Chalmers, Grand Secretary
jodachal@yahoo.ca
Roy Dawe, Grand Treasurer
Finances: *Annual Operating Budget:* Less than $50,000;
Funding Sources: Membership dues
Staff: 8 staff member(s)
Membership: 100,000
Activities: *Awareness Events:* Annual Golf Tournament
Description: To encourage its members to actively participate in the Protestant church of their choice; To actively support the Canadian system of government; To anticipate legislation & its impact on the civil & religious liberties of all Canadians; To provide social activities that will enrich the lives of its members, community & the overall country of Canada; *Member of:* Imperial Orange Council of the World

Ladies' Orange Benevolent Association of Canada (LOBA)
c/o Grand Orange Lodge of Canada, #706, 505 Consumers Rd., Toronto ON M2J 4V8
Tel: 416-223-1690; *Fax:* 416-223-1324
Toll-Free: 800-565-6248

Overview: A medium-sized national organization founded in 1894
Chief Officer(s):
John Chalmers, Grand Secretary, Grand Lodge of Canada
jodachal@yahoo.ca
Description: To provide women with an opportunity to practice Orange beliefs & participate in benevolent activities

Operation Mobilization Canada (OM)
84 West St., Port Colborne ON L3K 4C8
Toll-Free: 877-487-7777
info.ca@om.org
www.omcanada.org
www.facebook.com/omcanada

Overview: A small international charitable organization founded in 1966
Finances: *Annual Operating Budget:* Greater than $5 Million
Staff: 98 staff member(s)
Activities: *Speaker Service:* Yes *Library:* Yes
Member of: Evangelical Fellowship of Canada; Canadian Council of Christian Charities

Scientology

Church of Scientology of Toronto
2 College St., Toronto ON M5G 1K3
Tel: 416-925-2145; *Fax:* 416-925-1685
toronto@scientology.net
www.scientology-toronto.org
Overview: A medium-sized local organization
Description: To dissemniate the ideologies of scientology;
Member of: Church of Scientology

Seicho-No-Le

Seicho-No-le Toronto Centre
662 Victoria Park Ave., Toronto ON M4C 5H4
Tel: 416-690-8686; *Fax:* 416-690-3917
www.seicho-no-ie.org
Also Known As: Home of Infinite Growth
Previous Name: Seicho-No-le Canada Truth of Life Centre
Overview: A small national organization founded in 1963
Description: Provides a place of worship for those who believe in the Seicho-No-le Humanity Enlightenment Movement, which says that all religions emanate from one universal god; *Member of:* Seicho-No-le (Canada)

Sikhism

Maritime Sikh Society (MSS)
10 Parkhill Rd., Halifax NS B3P 1R3
Tel: 902-477-0008
info@maritimesikhsociety.com
www.maritimesikhsociety.com
www.facebook.com/msssikhsociety
Overview: A small provincial organization founded in 1968
Chief Officer(s):
Kulvinder Singh Dhillon, President, 902-477-1949
Surinder Singh Kang, Vice President, 902-434-8368
Kanwal K Sidhu, Secretary, 902-462-2051
Jeginger Singh Bajwa, Treasurer, 902-443-5699
Finances: *Annual Operating Budget:* Less than $50,000
Membership: 46; *Fees:* $12
Activities: Weekly Sunday service; Panjabi classes for teaching religion, language & other activities
Member of: Multicultural Association of Nova Scotia

Ontario Sikh & Gurudwara Council (OSGC)
140 Rivalda Rd., Toronto ON M9M 2M8
info@osgc.ca
osgc.ca
www.facebook.com/OntarioSikhs
Overview: A small provincial organization
Chief Officer(s):
Bhupinder Singh, Chairperson
Kultar Singh, Vice Chairperson
Balkaran Singh, Secretary
Jagdev Singh, Treasurer
Membership: 62; *Fees:* $51 individual; $251 Gurdwaras; *Committees:* Nagar Kirtan; Religious Affairs; Medial Liason & Public Relations; Women Affairs; Youth Affairs
Description: To fulfill the aspirations, along with the contemporary and broader needs, of the Skikh Community; To provide religious & social leadership; To raise awareness of Sikh philosophy, principles & heritage; To promote Sikh values & work as a liaison with similar organizations of different faiths

Sikh Foundation of Canada
45 Mill St., Toronto ON M5A 3R6
Tel: 416-777-6697; *Fax:* 416-484-9656
info@sikhfoundationcanada.com
sikhfoundationcanada.com
www.youtube.com/channel/UCkzU4L_9NQtAM3Mr-xrdVJQ
twitter.com/sikhfdncanada
Overview: A small national organization founded in 1999
Chief Officer(s):
Davindra Singh, Chair
Dilprit Grewal, Vice-Chair
Member Profile: All activities open to the general public
Activities: Academic seminars; Rare book, art & culture displays; Film festival
Description: To educate & promote greater understanding & appreciation of Sikh history, art & culture among Sikh-Canadians & the community at large

World Sikh Organization of Canada (WSO)
1183 Cecil Ave., Ottawa ON K1H 7Z6
Tel: 416-904-9110
info@worldsikh.org
www.worldsikh.org
www.instagram.com/worldsikhorg
www.linkedin.com/company/worldsikhorg
www.facebook.com/WSOCanada
twitter.com/WorldSikhOrg

Overview: A large international organization founded in 1984
Chief Officer(s):
Tejinder Singh Sidhu, President
Jasbir Kaur Randhawa, Senior Vice-President
Jaskaran Singh Sandhu, Director, Administration
Danish Singh Brar, Director, Finance
Membership: 15,000-49,999; *Fees:* $10 student/associate; $100 individual; $1,000 institutional
Activities: *Library:* World Sikh Organization of Canada Library (Open to Public) by appointment
Description: To promote & protect the interests of Canadian Sikhs; To promote & advocate for the protection of human rights for all individuals, regardless of race, religion, gender, ethnicity & social & economic status; *Affiliation(s):* World Sikh Organization (International)

Sufism

Jerrahi Sufi Order of Canada
Canadian Sufi Cultural Centre, 270 Birmingham St., Toronto ON M8V 2E4
Tel: 416-885-7754
jerrahi@jerrahi.ca
www.jerrahi.ca
twitter.com/jerrahicanada
Overview: A medium-sized national organization
Activities: Weekly gatherings; Discussions and discourse on Sufi music, art & poetry; Prayer & Zikrullah (Sufi remembrance ceremony)
Description: To disseminate knowledge about Islam and the Halveti-Jerrahi Order of Dervishes to which the Jerrahi Sufi Order members belong

Taoism

Fung Loy Kok Institute of Taoism (FLK)
134 D'Arcy St., Toronto ON M5T 1K3
Tel: 416-656-2110; *Fax:* 416-654-3937
www.taoist.org
Overview: A small international charitable organization
Finances: *Annual Operating Budget:* Greater than $5 Million
Staff: 27 staff member(s)
Activities: Tai Chi arts; Taoist meditation
Affiliation(s): Taoist Tai Chi Society of Canada

Taoist Tai Chi Society of Canada
Central Region, 134 Darcy St., Toronto ON M5T 1K3
Tel: 416-656-2110; *Fax:* 416-654-3937
headoffice@taoist.org
www.taoist.org
www.instagram.com/taoist_canada
www.facebook.com/TaoistCanada
twitter.com/taoist_canada
Overview: A medium-sized national organization founded in 1970
Finances: *Funding Sources:* Membership fees
Staff: 20 staff member(s)
Member Profile: Open to everyone
Activities: *Awareness Events:* National Taoist Tai Chi Awareness Day, first Sat. after Labour Day
Description: To make Taoist Tai Chi available to all &, through its teaching & practice, promote health improvement, cultural exchange & helping others; *Member of:* International Taoist Tai Chi Society

Unitarianism

Canadian Unitarian Council (CUC) / Conseil unitarien du Canada
#302, 192 Spadina Ave., Toronto ON M5T 2C2
Tel: 416-489-4121; *Toll-Free:* 888-568-5723
info@cuc.ca
cuc.ca
www.youtube.com/channel/UCJ25IMWQwrxSnry11bdBS-g
www.facebook.com/CanadianUnitarianCouncil
Also Known As: Unitarian Church
Overview: A medium-sized national charitable organization founded in 1961
Chief Officer(s):
Vyda Ng, Executive Director
vyda@cuc.ca
Margaret Wanlin, President
president-board@cuc.ca
Chuck Shields, Vice-President
chuck@cuc.ca
Joanne Green, Treasurer
treasurer@cuc.ca
Kiersten Moore, Secretary
kiersten@cuc.ca
Finances: *Annual Operating Budget:* $250,000-$500,000; *Funding Sources:* Donations; Membership dues

Staff: 9 staff member(s); 20 volunteer(s)
Membership: 47 institutional; *Fees:* Schedule available; *Committees:* Lay & Chaplaincy; Social Responsibility; Congregational Development
Activities: *Library:* CUC Library by appointment
Description: To enhance, nurture & promote Unitarian & Universalist religion in Canada; To provide support for religious exploration, spiritual growth & social responsibility; *Affiliation(s):* International Association for Religious Freedom; International Council of Unitarians & Universalists; Untarian Universalist Minsters of Canada

Canadian Unitarians for Social Justice (CUJS)
c/o Gary Campbell, Treasurer, #122, 1601 Prince of Wales Dr., Ottawa ON K2C 3P8
membership@cusj.org
cusj.org
Overview: A medium-sized national organization founded in 1996
Chief Officer(s):
Bill Woolverton, President
president@cusj.org
Finances: *Annual Operating Budget:* Less than $50,000
Description: To promote Unitarian values through social action; *Affiliation(s):* Canadian Unitarian Council

First Unitarian Congregation of Toronto
175 St. Clair Ave. West, Toronto ON M4V 1P7
Tel: 416-924-9654; *Fax:* 416-924-9655
administrator@firstunitariantoronto.org
www.firstunitariantoronto.org
www.youtube.com/user/firstunitarianTO
www.facebook.com/firstunitariantoronto
Overview: A small local charitable organization founded in 1845
Chief Officer(s):
Shawn Newton, Minister, 416-924-9654 222, Fax: 416-924-9655
ShawnNewton@FirstUnitarianToronto.org
Finances: *Annual Operating Budget:* $250,000-$500,000
Staff: 7 staff member(s); 70 volunteer(s)
Membership: 306 individuals
Activities: Monthly newcomers' orientation; Weekly Sunday services; Social justice & community outreach; Refugee Sponsorship; Reconciliation Working Group; Art Exhibitions, publications & a dinner series; Courses & Programs on Diverse Faith matters; *Internships:* Yes by appointment
Description: To be committed to love & justice; To seek and understand the meaning of life, connect with others in a common purpose & serve life to build a better world; *Member of:* Canadian Unitarian Council

United Church of Christ

Affirm United / S'affirmer Ensemble
PO Box 57057, Ottawa ON K1R 1A1
affirmunited@affirmunited.ca
www.affirmunited.ca
Overview: A medium-sized national organization founded in 1982
Chief Officer(s):
Liz Carter-Morgan, Coordinator, Affirming Ministry
Jackie Harper, Coordinator, Affirming Ministry
Linda Hutchinson, Coordinator, Affirming Ministry
Finances: *Annual Operating Budget:* Less than $50,000
Staff: 20 volunteer(s)
Membership: 200 ministries; *Fees:* $50 individual/household; institutional varies
Activities: *Speaker Service:* Yes
Description: To affirm gay, lesbian, bisexual & transgender people & their friends, within The United Church of Canada; to provide a network of supports among affirming ministries & regional groups; to act as a point of contact for individuals; To speak to the church in a united fashion encouraging it to act prophetically & pastorally both within & beyond the church structure; *Affiliation(s):* United Church of Canada

Alberta CGIT Association
c/o 5720 Lodge Cres. SW, Calgary AB T3E 5Y7
Tel: 780-532-2947
cgit@telus.net
www.albertacgit.ca
Also Known As: Canadian Girls in Training - Alberta
Overview: A small provincial organization
Chief Officer(s):
Valerie Jenner, President

Manitoba & Northwestern Ontario CGIT Association
131 Woodside Cres., Winnipeg MB R3W 1B5
Tel: 204-254-2378
cgit@cgitmanitoba.ca
www.instagram.com/cgit_manitoba
www.facebook.com/groups/5409037069
twitter.com/CGITManitoba
Also Known As: Canadian Girls in Training - Manitoba
Previous Name: National CGIT Association - Manitoba & Northwestern Ontario
Overview: A small provincial organization

Maritime Regional CGIT Committee
130 Wellington St., Pictou NS B0K 1H0
Tel: 902-485-4011
g.cmacdonald@eastlink.ca
Also Known As: Canadian Girls in Training - Maritimes
Previous Name: National CGIT Association - Maritime Regional Committee
Overview: A small provincial organization
Chief Officer(s):
Chris MacDonald, Contact

Ontario CGIT Association
PO Box 371, Norwich ON N0J 1P0
Tel: 519-863-6760
ontariocgit@dolson.ca
www.cgit.ca
Also Known As: Canadian Girls in Training - Ontario
Previous Name: National CGIT Association - Ontario
Overview: A small provincial organization founded in 1915
Finances: *Annual Operating Budget:* Less than $50,000
Staff: 1 staff member(s); 150 volunteer(s)

Provincial CGIT Board of BC
c/o Janice Grinnell, 13780 Hill Rd., Ladysmith BC V9G 1G7
Tel: 250-245-4016
grinncon@nanaimo.ark.com
www.cgit.ca
Also Known As: Canadian Girls in Training - British Columbia
Previous Name: National CGIT Association - BC Provincial Board
Overview: A small provincial organization

Saskatchewan CGIT Committee
c/o Heather Berriault, 1002 Victory Cres., Regina SK S4N 6X1
Tel: 306-789-3949
saskcgit@accesscomm.ca
saskatchewanCGIT.wordpress.com
twitter.com/sk_CGIT
Also Known As: Canadian Girls in Training - Saskatchewan
Previous Name: National CGIT Association - Saskatchewan Committee
Overview: A small provincial organization
Chief Officer(s):
Alice Monks, Co-Chair

United Church of Canada (UCC) / L'Église Unie du Canada
#200, 3250 Bloor St. West, Toronto ON M8X 2Y4
Tel: 416-231-5931; *Fax:* 416-231-3103
Toll-Free: 800-268-3781
info@united-church.ca
www.united-church.ca
www.youtube.com/unitedchurchofcanada
www.linkedin.com/company/unitedchurchcda
www.facebook.com/UnitedChurchCda
twitter.com/UnitedChurchCda

Overview: A large national charitable organization founded in 1925
Chief Officer(s):
Richard Bott, Moderator
Michael Blair, General Secretary
Finances: *Annual Operating Budget:* Greater than $5 Million;
Funding Sources: Voluntary givings; Sales; Bequests; Investment income; Foundation
Staff: 5000 staff member(s)
Membership: 650,000; *Member Profile:* Baptism & profession of faith in Jesus Christ as Saviour & Lord
Activities: *Speaker Service:* Yes *Library:* Yes
Description: To foster the spirit of unity in Canada; *Member of:* Canadian Council of Churches; World Council of Churches; Canadian Council for International Cooperation; World Methodist Council; Affiliation(s): United Church of Canada Foundation

United Church of Canada Foundation / Église Unie du Canada
#200, 3250 Bloor St. West, Toronto ON M8X 2Y4
Toll-Free: 866-340-8223
fdn@united-church.ca
www.unitedchurchfoundation.ca
Overview: A large national charitable organization founded in 2002
Chief Officer(s):
Sarah Charters, Acting President, 416-231-5931 3410
Finances: *Annual Operating Budget:* $3 Million-$5 Million
Staff: 3 staff member(s)
Activities: Managing 40 endowments; grants & scholarships
Description: To help sustain the United Church of Canada; Affiliation(s): United Church of Canada

---

Wicca

Pagan Federation International - Canada (PFI)
info_pfi_canada@paganfederation.org
ca.paganfederation.org
www.facebook.com/paganfederationinternational
Overview: A small national organization founded in 1998
Description: To provide information on & counter misconceptions about Paganism; To work for the rights of Pagans to worship freely & without censure

Wiccan Church of Canada
The Occult Shop, 1373 Bathurst St., Toronto ON M5R 3J1
webmaster@wiccanada.ca
www.wiccanada.ca
Overview: A small national organization founded in 1979
Description: To assist practicing Wiccans in achieving a spiritual balance that brings them into true harmony with the Gods; To bring the non-Wiccan population an understanding that they are a positive, reputable & life-affirming religion & lifestyle; To achieve for Wiccans the same rights & freedoms enjoyed by other more mainstream religions

---

Zoroastrianism

L'Association Zoroastrianne du Québec (AZQ) / Zoroastrian Associaton of Québec (ZAQ)
PO Box 35, Stn. Beaconsfield, Beaconsfield QC H9W 5T6
Tel: 514-426-9929
quebeczoroastrians@gmail.com
zaq.org
www.facebook.com/www.zaq.org
twitter.com/ZAQGROUP
Overview: A small provincial charitable organization founded in 1984
Chief Officer(s):

Dolly Dastoor, President
dollydastoor@sympatico.ca
Description: Pour préserver et promouvoir le patrimoine religieux, culturel, social et historique de zoroastriens vivant au Québec; Affiliation(s): Federation of North American Zoroastrian Associations

Ontario Zoroastrian Community Foundation (OZCF)
Zoroastrian Religious and Cultural Centre (OZCF Centre), 1187 Burnhamthorpe Rd. East, Oakville ON L6H 7B3
Tel: 905-271-0366
www.ozcf.com
Overview: A small provincial charitable organization
Chief Officer(s):
Percy Dastur, President
percydastur@gmail.com
Fees: $100 family; $30 seniors; $65 single; $25 student;
Member Profile: Zoroastrians living in Ontario; *Committees:* Communication/IT, Social & Entertainment, Facility Management, Finance, Lectures & Learning, Membership, Newsletter, Religious, Seniors, Sports, Youth
Activities: Religious education program for children; Zoroastrian Scouts; Seniors program; Cultural Kanoun for Farsi speakers; Lecture group; Library; Youth group; Committees for newly landed immigrants & others in need
Description: To build 'Our Centre' by providing labour & expertise however possible

Zoroastrian Society of Ontario (ZSO)
3590 Bayview Ave., Toronto ON M2M 3S6
Tel: 416-225-7771
secretary@zso.org
www.zso.org
Overview: A small provincial charitable organization founded in 1971
Chief Officer(s):
Russi Surti, President
president@zso.org
Dara Panthakee, Executive Vice President
evp@zso.org
Vispi Patel, Vice President
vp@zso.org
Anahita Ogra, Secretary
Meherab Chothia, Treasurer
Finances: *Annual Operating Budget:* $100,000-$250,000;
Funding Sources: Membership fees; donations; investment income
Staff: 1 staff member(s); 200 volunteer(s)
Membership: 1,000; *Fees:* $70 family; $40 individual; $20 seniors & students; *Member Profile:* Zoroastrians living in Ontario; *Committees:* 15 sub-committees reporting to elected executive committee of 9
Activities: Religious & cultural, youth & seniors activities; Sponsors 100th Scout Group; *Library:* ZSO Library by appointment
Description: To meet the religious & cultural needs of the Zoroastrian community of Ontario; Affiliation(s): Federation of North American Zoroastrian Associations

SECTION 15
SPORTS

Associations & Organizations

Aquatic Sports

ACUC International
Anastro, 25, Madrid 28033 Spain
info@acucinternational.com
acuc.es
www.facebook.com/acucinternational
Also Known As: American & Canadian Underwater Certification Inc.
Overview: A medium-sized international licensing organization founded in 1968
Description: To supply quality training for sport scuba divers & instructors; To teach the highest standards in safety, sport, & marine conservation
Affiliation(s): World Diving Federation; Undersea Hyperbaric Medical Society
Chief Officer(s): Juan Rodriguez, President & Chief Executive Officer
jra@acucinternational.com
Christian Zagrodnik, Representative, North America
narep@acucinternational.com
Activities: *Internships:* Yes; *Speaker Service:* Yes

Canadian Underwater Games Association (CUGA)
#2002, 535 Nicola St., Vancouver BC V6G 3G3
info@cuga.org
cuga.org
www.facebook.com/cuga.org
Overview: A small national organization founded in 1984
Description: To oversee underwater sports in Canada
Affiliation(s): World Underwater Federation
Fees: $35
Activities: Underwater hockey & underwater rugby

Archery

Alberta Bowhunters Association (ABA)
202 Copperfield Grove SE, Calgary AB T2Z 4L7
www.bowhunters.ca
www.facebook.com/201362139975092
Previous Name: Alberta Bowhunters & Archers Association
Overview: A medium-sized provincial organization
Description: To promote bowhunting in Alberta; *Member of:* Federation of Canadian Archers
Chief Officer(s): Brent Watson, President
brent@albertabowhunters.com
Fees: $35 Adult; $25 Youth; $70 Family; $500 Life

Alberta Target Archers Association (ATAA)
AB
Tel: 780-717-2597
membership@ataa-org.ca
www.ataa-org.ca
Overview: A small provincial organization
Description: To be the provincial governing body for the sport of archery in Alberta
Affiliation(s): Alberta Sport, Recreation, Parks & Wildlife Foundation
Chief Officer(s): Rene Schaub, President, 780-689-8488
president@ataa-org.ca
David Middlebrough, Vice President, 780-997-6411
vice-president@ataa-org.ca
Fees: $28-$103

Archers & Bowhunters Association of Manitoba (ABAM)
145 Pacific Ave., Winnipeg MB R3B 2Z6
Tel: 204-925-5697; *Fax:* 204-925-5792
info@abam.ca
www.abam.ca
www.facebook.com/archersandbowhuntersassociationofmanitoba
Overview: A small provincial organization
Description: To oversee the sports of archery & bowhunting in Manitoba; *Member of:* Sport Manitoba
Chief Officer(s): Ryan Van Berkel, Executive Director
Activities: Offering archery development program & olympic program

Archers Association of Nova Scotia (AANS)
c/o Sport Nova Scotia, 5516 Spring Garden Rd., 4th Fl., Halifax NS B3J 1G6
Tel: 902-425-5450
enickerson@sportnovascotia.ca
www.aans.ca
Overview: A medium-sized provincial organization founded in 1967

Description: To govern archery in Nova Scotia; *Member of:* Archery Canada Tir à l'Arc
Chief Officer(s): Paul Robicheau, President
paulrobicheau@hotmail.com
Finances: *Annual Operating Budget:* Less than $50,000
Membership: 22 clubs; 450 individuals; *Fees:* $30 youth; $40 individual; $90 family

Archery Association of New Brunswick (AANB)
c/o Maurice Levesque, 141 Isington St., Moncton NB E1A 1Y7
archerynb.ca
Overview: A small provincial organization founded in 1969
Description: To promote & encourage archery in New Brunswick; *Member of:* Archery Canada Tir à l'Arc
Chief Officer(s): Kevin Booker, President, 506-273-2518
Maurice Levesque, Executive Director, 506-855-6169
mlevesqu@nbnet.nb.ca
Membership: 19 clubs; *Committees:* Executive

Archery Canada Tir à l'Arc
c/o House of Sport, 2451 Riverside Dr., Ottawa ON K1H 7X7
Tel: 613-260-2113
information@archerycanada.ca
archerycanada.ca
www.instagram.com/archery_canada
www.linkedin.com/company/archery-canada
www.facebook.com/ArcheryCanada
twitter.com/ArcheryCanada
Previous Name: Federation of Canadian Archers Inc.
Overview: A medium-sized national charitable organization founded in 1927
Description: To promote & develop the sport of archery in a safe & ethical manner; To act as the official representative for archery to the federal government & national & international sport organizations
Affiliation(s): World Archery Federation
Chief Officer(s): Karl Balisch, Executive Director
kbalisch@archerycanada.ca
Finances: *Funding Sources:* Government support
Member Profile: Archers
Activities: Promoting archery participation across Canada; Supporting high performance excellence in archery; Presenting awards; Providing a vehicle for communication across Canada; Registering competitions; Maintaining Canadian records; Selecting archers to represent Canada at international events; Coordinating research; Training coaches & officials across Canada; Obtaining support for paralympic programs; *Library:* Yes

British Columbia Archery Association (BCAA)
PO Box 64727, Sunwood Square, Port Coquitlam BC V3B 0H1
Tel: 250-992-5586
www.archeryassociation.bc.ca
www.facebook.com/BCAA.Archery
Overview: A small provincial organization
Description: To promote & support the sport of archery in British Columbia; *Member of:* Archery Canada Tir à l'Arc; Sport BC
Affiliation(s): World Archery Federation
Chief Officer(s): Ron Ostermeier, President, 778-990-2724
president@archeryassociation.bc.ca
Sonia Schina, Executive Director, 778-241-2724
execdirector@archeryassociation.bc.ca
Finances: *Funding Sources:* Ministry of Community, Sport & Cultural Development; Sport BC
Fees: $70 adult; $60 youth; $150 family; $150 club
Activities: Tournaments; Newsletters; Information on certification

Fédération de tir à l'arc du Québec (FTAQ)
CP 1000, Succ. M, 4545, av Pierre-de-Coubertin, Montréal QC H1V 3R2
Tél: 514-252-3054; *Téléc:* 514-252-3165
taq@tiralarcquebec.com
www.tiralarcquebec.com
www.facebook.com/tiralarcquebec
Aperçu: Dimension: petite; *Envergure:* provinciale
Membre de: Archery Canada Tir à l'Arc
Membre(s) du bureau directeur: Glenn Gudgeon, Président
president@tiralarcquebec.com
Membre: 3 000

Ontario Association of Archers Inc. (OAA)
PO Box 45, Caledon ON L7K 3L3
www.oaa-archery.on.ca
Previous Name: Ontario Archery Association
Overview: A medium-sized provincial organization founded in 1927

Member of: Archery Canada Tir à l'Arc
Chief Officer(s): Michael Martin, President
president@oaa-archery.on.ca
Kelly Chambers, Secretary-Treasurer
secretary@oaa-archery.on.ca
Lynda Savage, Office Administrator
administration@oaa-archery.on.ca
Membership: 800; *Fees:* $55 youth; $70 adult; $140 family

Saskatchewan Archery Association (SAA)
c/o Gil Segovia, President, 335 Brooklyn Cres., Warman SK S0K 0A1
Tel: 306-370-0640
www.saskarchery.com
www.facebook.com/SaskatchewanArcheryAssociation
Overview: A small provincial organization
Description: To foster, to perpetuate & direct the practice of Archery in a spirit of good fellowship & sportsmanship.; *Member of:* Archery Canada Tir à l'Arc
Chief Officer(s): Gil Segovia, President
gil@segovia-sask.com
Finances: *Annual Operating Budget:* $50,000-$100,000
Staff: 20 volunteer(s)
Membership: 850; *Fees:* $45 adult; $25 youth (17 & under)

Tir-à-l'arc Moncton Archers Inc.
Moncton NB
Previous Name: Moncton Archers & Bowhunters Association
Overview: A small local organization founded in 1968
Description: To enjoy the sport of archery & bowhunting; To promote safety in each sport
Affiliation(s): New Brunswick Archery Association; Canadian Archery Association

World Archery Federation
Maison du Sport International, Av de Rhodanie 54, Lausanne 1007 Switzerland
info@archery.org
www.worldarchery.org
www.youtube.com/archerytv
www.facebook.com/WorldArchery
twitter.com/worldarchery
Previous Name: International Archery Federation
Overview: A small international organization founded in 1931
Description: To promote & encourage archery throughout the world in conformity with the Olympic principles; To frame & interpret FITA rules & regulations; To arrange for the organization of World Championships; To confirm & maintain world record scores & Olympic Games record scores; To maintain complete lists of scores from FITA Championships & Olympic Games; *Member of:* International Olympic Committee
Affiliation(s): Federation of Canadian Archers Inc.
Chief Officer(s): Ugur Erdener, President
Tom Dielen, Secretary General
Finances: *Annual Operating Budget:* $500,000-$1.5 Million
Staff: 10 staff member(s); 70 volunteer(s)
Membership: 160; *Member Profile:* National federations; *Committees:* Athletes; Elections Procedure; Coaches; Manuals; Information from Judges & Coaches; Constitution & Rules; Field Archery; Judges; Medical & Sport Sciences; Para-Archery; Target Archery; Technical

Associations

Canadian Society of Club Managers (CSCM) / La Société canadienne des directeurs de club
#202A, 703 Evans Ave., Toronto ON M9C 5E9
Tel: 416-979-0640; *Fax:* 416-979-1144
Toll-Free: 877-376-2726
national@cscm.org
www.cscm.org
www.linkedin.com/company/canadian-society-of-club-managers
twitter.com/CSCManagers
Overview: A small national organization founded in 1957
Description: To promote & develop the club management profession
Chief Officer(s): Suzanne Godbehere, Chief Executive Officer
Finances: *Annual Operating Budget:* $250,000-$500,000
Staff: 5 staff member(s); 25 volunteer(s)
Membership: 570; *Fees:* Based on region; *Member Profile:* Managers of private or semi-private clubs in Canada; *Committees:* Audit; Awards; Certification; Editorial Advisory; Education; Executive; Membership; National Conference Organizing; Nominating; Professional Development; Professional Manager Development Fund; Resource Library; Technology
Activities: Offering professional development & the Certified Club Manager designation; Hosting networking events

Athletics

Alberta Cheerleading Association (ACA)
PO Box 31006, Edmonton AB T5Z 3P3
Tel: 780-417-0050; *Fax:* 780-417-0093
Toll-Free: 888-756-9220
info@albertacheerleading.ca
www.albertacheerleading.ca
www.facebook.com/115045571883130
Overview: A small provincial organization
Description: To be the provincial regulator of cheerleading in Alberta.; *Member of:* Cheer Canada
Chief Officer(s): Jennifer Guiney, President
jennifer@albertacheerleading.ca
Denise Fisher, Executive Director
executivedirector@albertacheerleading.ca

Alberta Schools' Athletic Association (ASAA)
Percy Page Centre, 11759 Groat Rd., Edmonton AB T5M 3K6
Tel: 780-427-8182; *Fax:* 780-415-1833
info@asaa.ca
www.asaa.ca
twitter.com/ASAA
Overview: A medium-sized provincial organization founded in 1956
Description: To regulate & coordinate 12 high school sports; To promote equitable competition & ethical standards in all aspects of school athletic programs; *Member of:* School Sport Canada
Affiliation(s): National Federation of State High School Associations
Chief Officer(s): John F. Paton, Executive Director
john@asaa.ca
Rick Gilson, President
rick.gilson@westwind.ab.ca
Finances: *Funding Sources:* Lotteries; membership dues; fundraising; corporate sponsors
Staff: 5 staff member(s)
Membership: 371 schools + 8,000 student athletes

Athletics Alberta
Percy Page Centre, 11759 Groat Rd., Edmonton AB T5M 3K6
Tel: 780-427-8792; *Fax:* 780-427-8899
info@athleticsalberta.com
www.athleticsalberta.com
www.facebook.com/AthleticsAlberta
twitter.com/athleticsAB
Previous Name: Alberta Track & Field Association
Overview: A medium-sized provincial organization founded in 1969
Description: To encourage participation & development of excellence in athletics (track & field, cross-country, & road-running); *Member of:* Athletics Canada
Chief Officer(s): Linda Blade, President
James Rosnau, Executive Director
executivedirector@athleticsalberta.com
Sheryl Mack, Office Manager
sherylmack@athleticsalberta.com
Finances: *Funding Sources:* Lottery dollars; fundraising; membership fees
Staff: 3 staff member(s)

Athletics Manitoba
#416, 145 Pacific Ave., Winnipeg MB R3B 2Z6
Tel: 204-925-5745
admin@athleticsmanitoba.com
www.athleticsmanitoba.com
Overview: A medium-sized provincial organization founded in 1978
Description: To govern track & field, cross country & road running in the province of Manitoba; *Member of:* Athletics Canada; Sport Manitoba
Chief Officer(s): Grant Mitchell, President
Alanna Boudreau, Executive Director, 204-925-5743
execdirector@athleticsmanitoba.com

Athletics New Brunswick (ANB) / Athlétisme du Nouveau-Brunswick
66 Belle Foret St., Dieppe NB E1A 8X9
Tel: 506-855-5003; *Fax:* 506-855-5011
anb@anb.ca
www.anb.ca
www.facebook.com/AthNB
twitter.com/AthNB
Overview: A medium-sized provincial organization founded in 1968

Description: To offer leadership, growth & competition in athletics in New Brunswick; To encourage participation & high performance in athletics; *Member of:* Athletics Canada
Chief Officer(s): Marc Lalonde, President
marc.lalonde@anb.ca
Darren Blois, Vice President
Gabriel LeBlanc, Executive Director
Steve LeBlanc, Coordinator, High Performance
steve@anb.ca
Fees: Schedule available
Activities: *Speaker Service:* Yes; *Rents Mailing List:* Yes

Athletics Nova Scotia
5516 Spring Garden Rd, 4th Fl., Halifax NS B3J 1G6
Tel: 902-425-5450; *Fax:* 902-425-5606
athletics@sportnovascotia.ca
www.athleticsnovascotia.ca
twitter.com/athleticsns
Overview: A small provincial organization
Description: To develop, promote & govern track & field, road running, marathon, race walking & cross-country running in Nova Scotia; *Member of:* Athletics Canada
Chief Officer(s): Anitra Stevens, Executive Director
Joanthan Doucette, Technical Director, 902-220-3108
athleticstd@sportnovascotia.ca
Daniel Arsenault, Chair
chair@athleticsnovascotia.ca
Fees: $15 coaches; $35 age 13- & age 35+; $75 age 14-34;
Member Profile: Athletes, coaches, & officials

Athletics Ontario
3701 Danforth Ave., Toronto ON M1N 2G2
Tel: 647-352-7214
office@athleticsontario.ca
www.athleticsontario.ca
www.facebook.com/AthleticsOnt
twitter.com/athleticsont
Previous Name: Ontario Track & Field Association
Overview: A medium-sized provincial organization founded in 1974
Description: To develop, promote & deliver programs and competitions in athletics; To produce highly competitive provincial, national & international athletes; To contribute to physical and mental wellbeing of participants; *Member of:* Athletics Canada
Chief Officer(s): Paul Osland, Chief Executive Officer
paul.osland@athleticsontario.ca
Anthony Biggar, Manager, Programs & Services
anthonybiggar@athleticsontario.ca
Melissa Johnstone, Coordinator, Communications
melissa.johnstone@athleticsontario.ca

Athletics PEI
PO Box 302, 40 Enman Cres., Charlottetown PE C1A 7K7
www.athleticspei.ca
Overview: A small provincial organization
Member of: Athletics Canada

Athletics Yukon
4061 - 4th Ave., Whitehorse YT Y1A 1H1
info@athleticsyukon.ca
www.athleticsyukon.ca
www.facebook.com/149557131815078
Overview: A small provincial organization
Description: To promote & encourage athletics as a life-long pursuit for people of all abilities; *Member of:* Athletics Canada; Sport Yukon
Affiliation(s): Boreal Adventure Running Association; Mount Lorne Mis-Adventure Race; Run Dawson
Chief Officer(s): Kristen Johnston, President
Bonnie Love, Treasurer
Fees: $35 under 20 & over 60; $50 age 20-59; $100 family
Activities: Administering the sports of: Road Racing; Cross Country Running; Track & Field; Snowshoeing; & Race Walking

B2ten
QC
b2ten.ca
www.linkedin.com/company/b2ten
twitter.com/B2ten
Overview: A small national charitable organization founded in 2005
Description: To help Canadian athletes achieve success in the sporting world, particularly in an international context
Finances: *Funding Sources:* Donations

BC Cheerleading Association (BCCA)
BC
www.bccheerleading.ca
Overview: A small provincial organization

Description: To maintain athleticism & safety in cheerleading in British Columbia.; *Member of:* Cheer Canada
Chief Officer(s): Krista Gerlich-Fitzgerald, Chair

British Columbia Athletics
Fortius Athlete Development Centre, #2001, 3713 Kensington Ave., B. Oslo Landing, Burnaby BC V5B 0A7
Tel: 604-333-3550; *Fax:* 604-333-3551
bcathletics@bcathletics.org
www.bcathletics.org
www.facebook.com/BCAthletics1
twitter.com/bc_athletics
Also Known As: BC Amateur Athletics Association
Previous Name: BC Track & Field Association
Overview: A medium-sized provincial licensing organization
Description: To promote, encourage & develop excellence by creating opportunities in athletics (track & field, road-running & cross-country running); *Member of:* Athletics Canada; Sport BC
Chief Officer(s): Brian McCalder, President & CEO, 604-333-3552
brian.mccalder@bcathletics.org
Sam Collier, Manager, Registration & Membership Services, 604-333-3556
sam.collier@bcathletics.org
Fees: Schedule available; *Committees:* Track & Field; Branch Officials; Road Running; Cross Country; Masters; Junior Development; Masters
Activities: *Internships:* Yes; *Speaker Service:* Yes; *Rents Mailing List:* Yes *Library:* Yes (Open to Public)

Canada DanceSport (CDS)
www.dancesport.ca
Previous Name: Canadian Amateur DanceSport Association
Overview: A medium-sized national organization founded in 1978
Member of: World DanceSport Federation
Affiliation(s): World DanceSport Association
Chief Officer(s): Sandy Brittain, President
cadapresident@rogers.com

Canadian Trail & Mountain Running Association (CTMRA)
BC
www.mountainrunning.ca
www.facebook.com/groups/2229398616
twitter.com/CTMRA
Overview: A small national organization
Description: To oversee the sport of mountain running in Canada
Chief Officer(s): Adrian Lambert, Contact
adrian.lambert@mountainrunning.ca
Activities: Championship series

Canadian Wheelchair Basketball Association (CWBA) / Association canadienne de basketball en fauteuil roulant (ACBFR)
27 Auriga Drive, #M1062, Nepean BC K2E 0B1
Tel: 613-260-1296; *Fax:* 613-260-1456
Toll-Free: 877-843-2922
info@wheelchairbasketball.ca
www.wheelchairbasketball.ca
www.youtube.com/WheelchairBball
www.facebook.com/wheelchairbasketball
twitter.com/WCBballCanada
Also Known As: Wheelchair Basketball Canada
Overview: A medium-sized national charitable organization founded in 1994
Description: To act as the governing body for wheelchair basketball in Canada; *Member of:* Canadian Paralympic Committee; International Wheelchair Basketball Federation
Affiliation(s): Canada Basketball
Chief Officer(s): Wendy Gittens, Executive Director
wgittens@wheelchairbasketball.ca
Jeff Dunbrack, Director, High Performance
jdunbrack@wheelchairbasketball.ca
Jody Kingsbury, Director, Communications & Marketing
jkingsbury@wheelchairbasketball.ca
Membership: 2,500+

Cheer Canada
PO Box 47055, Stn. Creekside, Calgary AB T3P 0B9
info@cheercanada.ca
cheercanada.ca
www.instagram.com/cheer_canada
www.facebook.com/CheerleadingCanada
Overview: A medium-sized national organization founded in 2011
Description: To provide opportunities to all recreational & competitive members, while workig in partnership with its members to lead, support & promote cheerleading in Canada

Affiliation(s): International All Star Federation Worlds; US All Star Federation
Chief Officer(s): Joanna Low, Executive Director
executivedirector@cheercanada.ca
Membership: 400+ clubs in 9 associations; *Member Profile:* Provincial cheerleading associations

Cheer Nova Scotia
NS

www.cheerns.com

Overview: A small provincial organization
Description: To promote cheerleading in Nova Scotia.; *Member of:* Cheer Canada
Chief Officer(s): Megan Spencer, President
president@nscheer.com
Monique Johnson, Treasurer
communicator@nscheer.com

DanceSport Alberta (DSAB)
AB

president@dancesportalberta.org
www.dancesportalberta.org
Overview: A small provincial organization founded in 1989
Chief Officer(s): Wayne Backer, President
wbacker@shaw.ca
Debi Bowman, Vice President
debi@dancesportalberta.org

DanceSport Atlantic (DAA)
3273 Beaver Bank Rd., Lower Sackville NS B4C 2S6
Tel: 902-865-9914
www.dancesport.ca/page11.php
Overview: A small provincial organization
Chief Officer(s): Heather Fairbairn, President
hfairbairn@live.ca
Mai Miyano, Vice President
maimiyano@hotmail.com

DanceSport Québec (DSQ)
4545, av Pierre-De Coubertin, Montréal QC H1V 0B2
Tél: 514-418-8264; *Ligne sans frais:* 800-474-5746
info@dansesportquebec.com
dansesportquebec.com
Aperçu: Dimension: petite; *Envergure:* provinciale
Membre(s) du bureau directeur: Marjolaine Lagace, President
marjolaine.lagace@dansesportquebec.com
Simone Di Tomasso, Vice President
simone.ditomasso@dansesportquebec.com

Fédération de cheerleading du Québec (FCQ)
4545, av Pierre-De Coubertin, Montréal QC H1V 0B2
Tél: 514-252-3145; *Téléc:* 514-252-3146
Ligne sans frais: 866-694-3145
info@cheerleadingquebec.com
www.cheerleadingquebec.com

www.facebook.com/FederationdecheerleadingduQuebec
Aperçu: Dimension: petite; *Envergure:* provinciale
Membre de: Cheer Canada
Membre(s) du bureau directeur: Barbara Emond, Contact
direction@cheerleadingquebec.com

Fédération québécoise d'athlétisme (FQA)
4545, av Pierre-de-Coubertin, Montréal QC H1V 0B2
Tél: 514-252-3041; *Téléc:* 514-252-3042
fqa@athletisme.qc.ca
athletisme-quebec.ca

www.youtube.com/athletismequebec
www.facebook.com/athletismequebec
twitter.com/Athl_FQA
Nom précédent: Fédération d'athlétisme du Québec
Aperçu: Dimension: moyenne; *Envergure:* provinciale; *Organisme sans but lucratif; fondée en 1968*
Description: Promouvoir l'athlétisme au Québec; *Membre de:* Athletics Canada
Membre(s) du bureau directeur: Cécile Lefebvre, Président
Marc Desjardins, Directeur général
mdesjardins@athletisme.qc.ca
Martine Lafleur, Coordonnatrice, Services aux membres et administration
mlafleur@athletisme.qc.ca
Laurent Godbout, Coordonnateur, Communications
lgodbout@athletisme.qc.ca
Montant de la cotisation: Barème; *Critères d'admissibilite:* Coureurs sur route; athlètes; entraîneurs; officiels; membres associés; *Comités:* Technique provinciale; Officiels; Jeunes; Discipline et de résolution de conflits
Activités: *Service de conférenciers:* Oui

Greater Montreal Athletic Association (GMAA) / Association régionale du sport scolaire
#101, 5925, av Monkland, Montréal QC H4A 1G7
Tel: 514-482-8555; *Fax:* 514-487-0121
gmaa@gmaa.ca
www.gmaa.ca
www.facebook.com/RSEQ-Greater-Montreal-GMAA-419767904
880749
Overview: A small local charitable organization founded in 1975
Description: Devoted to the promotion of athletics in the English schools of the greater Montreal region.; *Member of:* Réseau du sport étudiant du Québec
Chief Officer(s): Amanda Maks, Executive Director
amanda@gmaa.ca
Finances: *Annual Operating Budget:* $250,000-$500,000
Staff: 3 staff member(s)
Membership: 152; *Fees:* User fees by activity; *Member Profile:* Principals of elementary & secondary schools
Activities: Organize & run sports activities & leagues for English schools on the Island of Montréal

Interior Running Association (IRA)
BC

interior.running@gmail.com
www.interiorrunningassociation.com
www.facebook.com/InteriorRunningAssociation
Overview: A small national organization
Description: To promote fitness & running in the Southern Interior of British Columbia
Chief Officer(s): Cindy Rhodes, President
Activities: Road & trail races

Manitoba Association of Cheerleading (MAC)
MB

Tel: 204-888-0317
info@cheermanitoba.ca
www.cheermanitoba.ca
www.instagram.com/mac_cheer_mb
www.facebook.com/ManitobaAssociationofCheerleading
twitter.com/MAC_Cheer_MB
Overview: A small provincial organization founded in 1986
Description: To be the official regulating body for cheerleading in Manitoba.; *Member of:* Cheer Canada
Chief Officer(s): Patricia McNeill, President

Manitoba Cheer Federation Inc. (MCF)
PO Box 42010, 1881 Portage Ave., Winnipeg MB R3J 0J0
info@mbcheer.ca
www.mbcheer.ca
www.facebook.com/145664425448394
twitter.com/MCF_Cheer
Overview: A small provincial organization founded in 2010
Description: To regulate, promote & develop cheerleading in Manitoba.; *Member of:* Cheer Canada
Chief Officer(s): Marian Henry, President
Kait Allen, Director, Judging
Amanda Barnes, Director, Communications
Mallory Mitchell, Director, Event

Manitoba High Schools Athletic Association (MHSAA)
145 Pacific Ave., Winnipeg MB R3B 2Z6
Tel: 204-925-5640; *Fax:* 204-925-5624
info@mhsaa.ca
www.mhsaa.ca
www.facebook.com/MBHighSchoolsAthleticsAssociation
twitter.com/MHSAA_
Overview: A medium-sized provincial charitable organization founded in 1962
Description: To promote the value of sports in Manitoba secondary schools; To provide athletic & educational opportunities so that students reach their full potential; *Member of:* School Sport Canada
Chief Officer(s): Chad Falk, Executive Director, 204-925-5641
chad@mhsaa.ca
Finances: *Funding Sources:* Sport Manitoba grants; Membership fees; Corporate support; Revenues from admissions to provincial championships; Fundraising
Staff: 3 staff member(s)
Membership: 192 schools + 37,000 athletes; *Fees:* Schedule available, based upon school size; *Member Profile:* Secondary schools in Manitoba
Activities: Encouraging participation in high school sports; Assisting in running equitable & fair sporting events for high schools; Presenting awards & scholarships for athletes, coaches, & volunteeers; Promoting volunteer involvement; Seeking support for the association; Providing educational materials for coaches & teachers

Manitoba Runners' Association (MRA)
PO Box 34148, Winnipeg MB R3T 5T5
Tel: 204-477-5185
office@mraweb.ca
www.mraweb.ca
www.facebook.com/188241213063
Overview: A small provincial organization
Description: To encourage road running in Manitoba.
Chief Officer(s): Kathy Wiens, Executive Director
Fees: Schedule available
Activities: Fun runs; races

National Association of Collegiate Directors of Athletics (NACDA)
24651 Detroit Rd., Westlake OH 44145 USA
Tel: 440-892-4000; *Fax:* 440-892-4007
nacda.com
twitter.com/nacda
Overview: A small international organization founded in 1965
Description: To serve as the professional association for those in the field of intercollegiate athletics administration; To serves as a vehicle for networking, the exchange of information & advocacy on behalf of the profession
Chief Officer(s): Bob Vecchione, Chief Executive Officer
bvecchione@nacda.com
Membership: 15,700 individuals; 1,700 institutions; *Fees:* Schedule available; *Member Profile:* Collegiate athletics administrators in the United States, Canada, & Mexico
Activities: Providing educational opportunities

Newfoundland & Labrador Athletics Association (NLAA)
PO Box 3202, Paradise NL A1L 3W4
Tel: 709-576-1303; *Fax:* 709-576-7493
athletics@nlaa.ca
www.nlaa.ca
www.facebook.com/NLAthletics
twitter.com/nlathletics
Previous Name: Newfoundland & Labrador Track & Field Association
Overview: A small provincial organization
Member of: Athletics Canada
Affiliation(s): Athletics North-East; Mariners Athletics Club; Nautilus Running Club; New World Running Club; Pearlgate T&F Club; Trappers Running Club; Trinity-Conception Athletics Club; Westerland Track Club
Chief Officer(s): Rosemary Forsey, President
George Stanoev, Technical Director
Candy Waye-Jaidye, Administrative Assistant
nlaaoffice@gmail.com
Fees: Schedule available; *Member Profile:* Competitive membership (road running, cross country running, & track & field); Non-competitive membership (coaches & officials); *Committees:* Road Race; Coaches; Officials
Activities: Offering courses & clinics for athletes, officials, & coaches; Supervising events; Ensuring that rules are followed & criteria maintained throughout Newfoundland & Labrador

Newfoundland & Labrador Cheerleading Athletics (NLCA)
PO Box 39059, Stn. Topsail Road, St. John's NL A1E 5Y7
nlcheerleading.ca
www.facebook.com/groups/10418436853
twitter.com/NLCAnews
Overview: A small provincial organization
Description: To be the governing body of cheerleading in Newfoundland & Labrador.; *Member of:* Cheer Canada
Chief Officer(s): Ashley Wright, President
Membership: 600

Nova Scotia School Athletic Federation (NSSAF)
5516 Spring Garden Rd., Halifax NS B3J 1G6
Tel: 902-425-8662; *Fax:* 902-425-5606
nssaf@ns.sympatico.ca
www.nssaf.ca
Overview: A small provincial organization
Description: To promote the value of sport & emphasize the benefits of participation for students; *Member of:* School Sport Canada
Chief Officer(s): Stephen MacNeil, Chair, Board of Governors
Stephen Gallent, Executive Director
Membership: 40,000 student athletes; *Member Profile:* Student athletes and their affiliates including coaches, administrators, and officiates.

Ontario Cheerleading Federation (OCF)
21 Oceanpearl Cres., Whitby ON L1N 0C5
registrar@ocfcheer.com
www.ocfcheer.com
twitter.com/OntarioCheer
Overview: A small provincial organization

Description: To provide training & certification courses for coaches across Ontario; *Member of:* Cheer Canada

Ontario DanceSport (ODS)
ON

Tel: 905-831-2426
publicity@ontariodancesport.com
www.ontariodancesport.com
Overview: A small provincial organization
Chief Officer(s): Gord Brittain, President
odspresident@rogers.com
Kam Young, Vice President
vicepresident@ontariodancesport.com

Ontario Federation of School Athletic Associations (OFSAA) / Fédération des associations du sport scolaire de l'Ontario
#204, 3 Concorde Gate, Toronto ON M3C 3N7
Tel: 416-426-7391; *Fax:* 416-426-7317
www.ofsaa.on.ca
www.instagram.com/OFSAAGRAM
www.facebook.com/OFSAA
twitter.com/OFSAA
Overview: A medium-sized provincial charitable organization founded in 1948
Description: To enhance school sport in Ontario; To handle issues that affect students, coaches, schools, & communities; To work with volunteer teacher-coaches to offer provincial championships & festivals for student-athletes across Ontario; *Member of:* School Sport Canada
Chief Officer(s): Donna Howard, Executive Director, 416-426-7438
donna@ofsaa.on.ca
Devin Gray, Coordinator, Communications, 416-426-7437
devin@ofsaa.on.ca
Finances: *Funding Sources:* Sponsorships
Staff: 9 staff member(s)
Membership: 18 associations; *Member Profile:* Regional school athletic associations throughout Ontario, such as the Central Ontario Secondary Schools Association, Northern Ontario Secondary Schools Association, Southern Ontario Secondary Schools Association, & the Toronto District College Athletic Association; *Committees:* Alpine Skiing; Badminton; Baseball; Basketball; Cross Country; Curling; Field Hockey; Field Lacrosse; Football; Golf; Gymnastics; Hockey; Nordic Skiing; Rugby; Snowboard Racing; Soccer; Swimming; Tennis; Track & Field; Volleyball; Wrestling; Championship Review Ad Hoc; Classifications Ad Hoc; Coaching Ad Hoc; Constitutional Review Ad Hoc; Future Directions Ad Hoc; Gender Equity Ad Hoc; Sanctions Ad Hoc; Transfers Ad Hoc
Activities: Organizing programs, such as student leadership & coach development programs; Sanctioning tournaments; Preparing & distributing resources; Providing professional development opportunities; *Awareness Events:*Canadian School Sport Week

Réseau du sport étudiant du Québec Abitibi-Témiscamingue (RSEQAT)
QC

Ligne sans frais: 866-626-2047
at.rseq.ca
Également appelé:RSEQ Abitibi-Témiscamingue
Nom précédent: Association régionale du sport étudiant de l'Abitibi-Témiscamingue
Aperçu: *Dimension:* petite; *Envergure:* locale; *Organisme sans but lucratif; fondée en* 1969
Description: Regrouper sur le plan du sport étudiant les représentants des différentes institutions d'enseignement de la région de l'Abitibi-Témiscamingue; stimuler l'intérêt et favoriser le développement du sport étudiant dans cette région; *Membre de:* Réseau du sport étudiant du Québec
Membre(s) du bureau directeur: Alain Dubois, Président
Finances: *Fonds:*Gouvernement provincial
Membre: 1-99

Réseau du sport étudiant du Québec Cantons-de-l'Est
5182, boul Bourque, Sherbrooke QC J1N 1H4
Tél: 819-864-0792
oaudet@ce.rseq.ca
ce.rseq.ca
Également appelé:RSEQ Cantons-de-l'Est
Aperçu: *Dimension:* petite; *Envergure:* locale
Membre de: Réseau du sport étudiant du Québec
Membre(s) du bureau directeur: Paul Deshaies, Président

Réseau du sport étudiant du Québec Chaudière-Appalaches (RSEQ-QCA)
762, rue Jacques-Berthiaume, Québec QC G1V 3T1
Tél: 418-657-7678; *Téléc:* 418-657-1367
sportetudiant.qc.ca

www.instagram.com/rseqqca
www.facebook.com/RSEQQCA
twitter.com/RSEQ_QCA
Également appelé:RSEQ Chaudière-Appalaches
Nom précédent: Association régionale du sport étudiant de Québec et Chaudière-Appalaches
Aperçu: *Dimension:* petite; *Envergure:* locale
Description: Organisme à but non-lucratif qui regroupe l'ensemble des institutions d'enseignement des régions de Québec et de Chaudière-Appalaches; *Membre de:* Réseau du sport étudiant du Québec
Membre(s) du bureau directeur: Julie Dionne, Directrice générale, 418-657-7678 202
jdionne@qca.rseq.ca

Réseau du sport étudiant du Québec Côte-Nord
#146, 40, rue Comeau, Sept-Îles QC G4R 4N3
Tél: 418-964-2888; *Téléc:* 418-968-4033
cote-nord.rseq.ca
Également appelé:RSEQ Côte-Nord
Nom précédent: Association régionale du sport étudiant de la Côte-Nord
Aperçu: *Dimension:* petite; *Envergure:* locale
Description: Regrouper sur le plan du sport étudiant, les différentes commissions scolaires, institutions privées et institutions collégiales de la Côte-Nord; stimuler l'intérêt et favoriser le développement du sport étudiant; définir les politiques générales du sport étudiant; promouvoir l'établissement des programmes; coordonner et sanctionner les différentes compétitions du sport étudiant; organiser des stages de perfectionnement; établir les règlements que doivent régir les différentes compétitions du sport étudiant; homologuer les records établis lors des compétitions du sport étudiant; *Membre de:* Réseau du sport étudiant du Québec
Membre(s) du bureau directeur: Brigitte Leblanc, Présidente
Cindy Hounsell, Directrice Générale
chounsell@cote-nord.rseq.ca

Réseau du sport étudiant du Québec Lac Saint-Louis
2900, rue Lake, Dollard-des-Ormeaux QC H9B 2P1
Tél: 514-855-4230; *Téléc:* 514-685-4643
www.arselsl.qc.ca

www.facebook.com/rseqlsl
twitter.com/RSEQ_LSL
Également appelé:RSEQ Lac Saint-Louis
Nom précédent: Association régionale du sport étudiant Lac Saint-Louis
Aperçu: *Dimension:* petite; *Envergure:* locale
Description: Réseau du sport étudiant du Québec Lac Saint-Louis est un organisme sans but lucratif qui regroupe l'ensemble des institutions d'enseignement affiliées de la région Lac Saint-Louis; *Membre de:* Réseau du sport étudiant du Québec
Membre(s) du bureau directeur: Karine Mayrand, Directrice générale, 514-855-4230 6524
kmayrand@lsl.rseq.ca

Réseau du sport étudiant du Québec Laurentides-Lanaudière
401, boul du Domaine, Sainte-Thérèse QC J7E 4S4
Tél: 450-419-8786; *Téléc:* 450-419-8892
ll.rseq.ca
Également appelé:RSEQ Laurentides-Lanaudière
Nom précédent: Association régionale du sport étudiant Laurentides-Lanaudière
Aperçu: *Dimension:* petite; *Envergure:* locale; *Organisme sans but lucratif*
Description: Favoriser la réalisation de l'ensemble des actions éducatives par l'activité physique et particulièrement le sport en vue de contribuer au développement intégral des étudiants des niveaux primaire, secondaire et collégial dans la région Laurentides-Lanaudière; *Membre de:* Réseau du sport étudiant du Québec
Membre(s) du bureau directeur: Jacinthe Lussier, Directrice générale
jacinthe.lussier@cssmi.qc.ca

Réseau du sport étudiant du Québec Montérégie
c/o École secondaire Gérard-Filion, 1330, boul Curé-Poirier ouest, Longueuil QC J4K 2G8
Tél: 450-463-4055; *Téléc:* 450-463-4229
info@monteregie.rseq.ca
monteregie.rseq.ca

www.youtube.com/channel/UCUPxwmcQY63heCqnGv8WqaQ
www.facebook.com/RseqMonteregie
twitter.com/RSEQMRG
Également appelé:RSEQ Montérégie
Aperçu: *Dimension:* petite; *Envergure:* locale
Membre de: Réseau du sport étudiant du Québec
Membre(s) du bureau directeur: Sylvie Cornellier, Directrice Générale, 450-463-4055 102
scornellier@monteregie.rseq.ca

Réseau du sport étudiant du Québec Outaouais
Complexe Branchaud-Brière, #201, 499, boul Labrosse, Gatineau QC J8P 4R1
Tél: 819-643-6663; *Téléc:* 819-643-6665
www.arseo.qc.ca/ARSEO.php

www.facebook.com/RseqOutaouais
Également appelé:RSEQ Outaouais
Aperçu: *Dimension:* petite; *Envergure:* locale
Membre de: Réseau du sport étudiant du Québec
Membre(s) du bureau directeur: Hélène Boucher, Directrice générale, 819-643-6663 205
helene.boucher@arseo.qc.ca

Réseau du sport étudiant du Québec, secteur Mauricie
260, rue Dessureault, Trois-Rivières QC G8T 9T9
Tél: 819-693-5805; *Téléc:* 819-693-1189
mauricie.rseq.ca

www.facebook.com/rseqmauricie
twitter.com/rseq_mauricie
Également appelé:RSEQ Mauricie
Nom précédent: Association régionale du sport étudiant de la Mauricie
Aperçu: *Dimension:* petite; *Envergure:* locale
Description: Réseau du sport étudiant du Québec, secteur Mauricie, est un organisme sans but lucratif qui regroupe les institutions d'enseignement situées sur le territoire de la Mauricie et sur la rive sud du fleuve Saint-Laurent, jusqu'à l'autoroute 20; *Membre de:* Réseau du sport étudiant du Québec
Membre(s) du bureau directeur: Micheline Guillemette, Directrice générale, 819-693-5805 6543
mguillemette@mauricie.rseq.ca

Saskatchewan Athletics
2020 College Dr., Saskatoon SK S7N 2W4
Tel: 306-664-6744; *Fax:* 306-664-6761
athletics@sasktel.ca
www.saskathletics.ca
twitter.com/SaskAthletics
Overview: A small provincial organization
Description: Promotes the sport of athletics by facilitating the development & maintenance of effective programs which assists athletes, coaches, officials, & volunteers in a fair & positive environment; *Member of:*Athletics Canada
Chief Officer(s): Grant Van Eaton, President
Bob Reindl, Executive Director
Finances: *Funding Sources:* Saskatchewan Lotteries; Athletics Canada; Sask Sport Inc.; Corporate sponsorships
Staff: 3 staff member(s)

Saskatchewan Cheerleading Association (SCA)
PO Box 31090, Regina SK S4R 8R6
Tel: 306-343-7221; *Fax:* 306-343-7229
sca.ca
www.facebook.com/SaskCheer
twitter.com/SaskCheer
Overview: A small provincial organization
Description: To promote & develop cheerleading in Saskatchewan.; *Member of:* Cheer Canada
Chief Officer(s): Thomas Rath, President
president@sca.ca
Alissa Stewart, Executive Director
executivedirector@sca.ca

Sports Laval
#221, 3235, St-Martin est, Laval QC H7E 5G8
Tél: 450-664-1917
info@sportslaval.qc.ca
sportslaval.qc.ca

www.facebook.com/jdq.laval
twitter.com/SportsLaval

Également appelé:RSEQ Laval
Merged from: Association régionale du sport étudiant de Laval; La Commission Sports Laval
Aperçu: *Dimension: petite; Envergure: locale; fondée en 2003*
Description: *Mettre en ouvre des actions permettant aux différents sports de prendre place dans les communautés urbaines et scolaires lavalloises; Membre de:* Réseau du sport étudiant du Québec
Affiliation(s):Réseau du sport étudiant du Québec
Membre(s) du bureau directeur: Martin Savoie, Directeur général, 450-664-1917 204
martin@sportslaval.qc.ca

Trail & Ultra Running Association Of The Yukon (TURAY)
4061 - 4th Ave., Whitehorse YT Y1A 1H1
Tel: 867-668-4236; *Fax:* 867-667-4237
sportyukon.com

Overview: A small provincial organization
Chief Officer(s): Nancy Thomson, President
nancy.thomson@cbc.ca

Automobile Racing

Motorsport Club of Ottawa (MCO) / Club des sports moteur d'Ottawa
PO Box 65006, Stn. Merivale, Ottawa ON K2G 5Y3
www.mco.org
www.youtube.com/c/McoOrgRacersGatherHere
www.facebook.com/mcofb
twitter.com/TheOfficialMCO
Previous Name: Ottawa Light Car Club
Overview: A small local organization founded in 1949
Description: To foster a spirit of unity & comradership among car owners; to encourage courtesy both to other drivers & to pedestrians; To provide information which may be of aid & interest to car owners; to organize & to encourage the organization of legitimate sporting events
Affiliation(s): ASN Canada FIA; CASC-OR; Rallysport Ontario
Chief Officer(s): John Hodge, President
vicepresident@mco.org
Finances: *Annual Operating Budget:* $50,000-$100,000
Staff: 10 volunteer(s)
Membership: 380; *Fees:* $60 single; $75 family; *Member Profile:* Road racing participants; enthusiasts; all involved at grassroots level; *Committees:* Race; Rally; Solo; Social
Activities: Winter & Summer Solo II; winter driving school; go-karting; rallying; road racing; summer high-performance driving school; Canaska Cup; group tours

Toronto Autosport Club (TAC)
18759 Kennedy Rd., Sharon ON L0G 1V0
treasurer@torontoautosportclub.ca
www.torontoautosportclub.ca
Overview: A small local organization founded in 1956
Member of: Canadian Association of Rally Sport; Canadian Association Sport Clubs - Ontario Region: Rally Sport Ontario
Chief Officer(s): Rob McAuley, President
president@torontoautosportclub.ca
Finances: *Annual Operating Budget:* Less than $50,000; *Funding Sources:* Membership fees; contract sports events
Staff: 80 volunteer(s)
Membership: 80; *Fees:* $50; *Member Profile:* People who compete in car racing & rallying
Activities: Autosports; rallying-auto; racing-ice & autoslalom; *Speaker Service:* Yes

Badminton

Badminton Alberta
c/o Alberta Badminton Centre, 60 Patterson Blvd. SW, Calgary AB T3H 2E1
Tel: 403-297-2722; *Fax:* 403-297-2706
Toll-Free: 888-397-2722
members@badmintonalberta.ca
www.badmintonalberta.ca
www.facebook.com/170234779702176
Previous Name: Alberta Badminton Association
Overview: A medium-sized provincial organization founded in 1928
Description: To promote the sport of badminton in Alberta; *Member of:* Badminton Canada; International Badminton Federation
Chief Officer(s): Jeff Bell, Executive Director, 403-297-2108
jbell@badmintonalberta.ca
Finances: *Funding Sources:* Alberta Sport Recreation Parks & Wildlife Foundation
Staff: 4 staff member(s)

Membership: 7000 members; 350 affliated clubs; *Fees:* Schedule available; *Member Profile:* Athletes, clubs, coaches, & officials; *Committees:* Executive

Badminton BC
#110, 12761 - 16 Ave., Surrey BC V4A 1N2
Tel: 604-385-3595
info@badmintonbc.com
www.badmintonbc.com
www.instagram.com/badminton_bc
www.facebook.com/badmintonBC
twitter.com/b2dmintonbc
Overview: A medium-sized provincial organization founded in 1925
Description: To provide leadership to develop & promote badminton in BC by increasing the membership base, facilitating a higher standard of participation through competitive & development opportunities for players, coaches, officials & volunteers; *Member of:* Sport BC; International Badminton Federation
Chief Officer(s): Penny Gardner, Executive Director, 604-333-3599
executivedirector@badmintonbc.com
Finances: *Funding Sources:* Government grants; Fundraising; Sponsorships
Staff: 5 staff member(s)
Fees: $15; *Member Profile:* Recreational & competitive players, coaches, & officials; *Committees:* Executive; Nominations; Governance Review; Risk Management; Finance & Audit; Regional/Sport Development; Membership; Performance; Competitions; Officials; Coaches; Judicial
Activities: Organizing tournaments, athlete training, & coaching; *Speaker Service:* Yes *Library:* Badminton Resource Library (Open to Public)

Badminton Canada
#401, 700 Industrial Ave., Ottawa ON K1G 0Y9
Tel: 613-569-2424; *Fax:* 613-748-5724
info@badminton.ca
www.badminton.ca
www.instagram.com/badmintoncanada
www.linkedin.com/company/badminton-canada
www.facebook.com/BadmintonCanada
twitter.com/BdmintonCanada
Previous Name: Canadian Badminton Association
Overview: A medium-sized national organization
Description: To provide centralized support, &/or leadership in furthering member association objectives, act as custodian of the laws of badminton & to foster outstanding player development; To act for its members in helping to assure national & international class competition for Canada's outstanding badminton players; To establish Canada as a leading participant in international badminton
Affiliation(s): International Badminton Federation
Chief Officer(s): Joe Morissette, Executive Director
morissette@badminton.ca

Badminton New Nouveau Brunswick (BNNB)
NB
www.bnnb.ca
www.facebook.com/bnnb.ca
Previous Name: Badminton New Brunswick
Overview: A small provincial organization
Description: To organize junior & senior badminton tournaments; *Member of:* Badminton Canada
Chief Officer(s): Eric Fortin, President
Member Profile: Players, coaches, & officials residing in New Brunswick who are members of organized badminton clubs or teams within the province & who may participate in any National or Provincial event

Badminton Newfoundland & Labrador Inc. (BNL)
PO Box 8082, St. John's NL A1B 3M9
Tel: 902-830-8529
badmintonnl@badmintonnl.ca
www.badmintonnl.ca
www.youtube.com/user/NLBadminton
www.facebook.com/285446971492858
Overview: A small provincial organization founded in 1969
Description: To act as the governing body for badminton in Newfoundland & Labrador; *Member of:* Sport Newfoundland & Labrador
Chief Officer(s): John Gillam, President/Provincial Coach
Finances: *Annual Operating Budget:* $50,000-$100,000
Staff: 1 staff member(s)
Membership: 1-99; *Member Profile:* School & community badminton clubs for recreational & competitive players at junior or senior levels
Activities: Organizing sanctioned tournaments & events

Badminton Ontario (BON)
#209, 3 Concorde Gate, Toronto ON M3C 3N7
Tel: 416-426-7195; *Fax:* 416-426-7346
info@badmintonontario.ca
www.badmintonontario.ca
www.youtube.com/cweculture
www.facebook.com/badmintonontario
twitter.com/badmntonontario
Previous Name: Ontario Badminton Association
Overview: A medium-sized provincial organization founded in 1925
Description: To provide an organized, structured environment for the activity of badminton; To promote & develop badminton in Ontario
Affiliation(s): Badminton World Federation
Chief Officer(s): Ian Moss, President
ian.moss@badmintonontario.ca
Finances: *Annual Operating Budget:* $50,000-$100,000; *Funding Sources:* Ministry of Citizenship, Culture & Recreation
Staff: 1 staff member(s); 60 volunteer(s)
Membership: 1,000; *Fees:* Schedule available; *Member Profile:* Badminton players; clubs; coaches; officials
Activities: Awareness Events: Provincial Championships

Badminton Québec
4940, rue Hochelaga est, Montréal QC H1V 1E7
Tél: 514-252-3066; *Téléc:* 514-252-3175
info@badmintonquebec.com
www.badmintonquebec.com

www.facebook.com/BadmintonQuebec
twitter.com/BadmintonQc
Également appelé:Fédération québécoise de badminton inc.
Aperçu: *Dimension: moyenne; Envergure: provinciale; fondée en 1929*
Description: Promouvoir et développer le sport sur tout le territoire québécois en regroupant tous ses membres, les personnes et associations intéressées au rayonnement de notre discipline; *Membre de:* Fédération internationale de badminton
Membre(s) du bureau directeur: Chantal Brouillard, Directrice générale
chantal.brouillard@badmintonquebec.com
Activités: *Stagiaires:* Oui

Badminton World Federation (BWF)
Naza Tower Platinum Park, #1, 10 Persiaran KLCC, L. 29, Kuala Lumpur 50088 Malaysia
bwf@bwfbadminton.org
www.bwfbadminton.org
www.facebook.com/bwfbadminton
twitter.com/bwfmedia
Previous Name: International Badminton Federation (IBF)
Overview: A medium-sized international organization founded in 1934
Description: To control the game of badminton, from an international aspect, in all countries; to uphold the Laws of Badminton as at present adopted
Chief Officer(s): Poul-Erik Hoyer, President
pe.hoyer@bwfbadminton.org
Stuart John Borrie, Chief Operating Officer
s.borrie@bwfbadminton.org
Gayle Alleyne, Manager, Communications
g.alleyne@bwfbadminton.org
Finances: *Funding Sources:* Subscriptions & sponsorships
Membership: 180 nationally organized bodies; *Committees:* Continental Confederations; IOC & International Relations; Administration; Events; Development & Sport for All; Marketing; Finance; Para-Badminton

Manitoba Badminton Association (MBA)
#323, 145 Pacific Ave., Winnipeg MB R3B 2Z6
Fax: 204-925-5703
www.badminton.mb.ca
twitter.com/badmintonmb
Overview: A small local organization
Description: To provide the leadership that promotes the growth of badminton throughout Manitoba as a lifelong sport
Chief Officer(s): Ryan Giesbrecht, Executive Director, 204-925-5621
ryan@badminton.mb.ca
Member Profile: Athletes, coaches, officials & badminton clubs

Northwest Territories Badminton Association
PO Box 11089, Yellowknife NT X1A 3X7
Tel: 867-669-8378; *Fax:* 867-669-8327
Toll-Free: 800-661-0797
www.nwtbadminton.ca
Overview: A small provincial organization
Description: To promote badminton throughout the Northwest Territories
Member Profile: Athletes, clubs, coaches, & officials

Nova Scotia Badminton Association
5516 Spring Garden Rd., Halifax NS B3J 1G6

Tel: 902-425-5450; *Fax:* 902-425-5606
badmintonns.ca
www.facebook.com/BadmintonNovaScotia
twitter.com/bdmintonNS
Also Known As: Badminton Nova Scotia
Overview: A small provincial organization
Description: To promote the development of badminton for all Nova Scotians, at all levels; To provide leadership, organization, and fair governance for the sport
Chief Officer(s): Jennifer Petrie, Executive Director
executive_director@badmintonns.ca
Fees: $20 recreational/coach & umpire; $40 competitive; $150 club

Prince Edward Island Badminton Association
c/o Sport PEI, PO Box 302, 40 Enman Cres., Charlottetown PE C1N 7K7

Tel: 902-368-4262; *Fax:* 902-368-4548
badm.pei@gmail.com
badmintonpei.weebly.com
Also Known As: Badminton PEI
Overview: A small provincial organization founded in 1987
Description: To promote & develop badminton in Prince Edward Island
Chief Officer(s): Nancy MacKinnon, President
Activities: Organizing tournaments

Saskatchewan Badminton Association (SBA)
55 Dunsmore Dr., Regina SK S4R 7G1

Tel: 306-780-9368
saskbadminton@sasktel.net
www.saskbadminton.ca
www.facebook.com/SaskatchewanBadminton
Overview: A small provincial organization
Description: To develop & promote badminton in Saskatchewan
Chief Officer(s): Frank Gaudet, Executive Director

Yukon Badminton Association
4061 - 4th Ave., Whitehorse YT Y1A 1H1

Tel: 867-393-4343
Overview: A small provincial organization
Chief Officer(s): Michael Muller, President, 867-393-4343
muller@northwestel.net

Ball Hockey

British Columbia Ball Hockey Association (BCBHA)
9107 Norum Rd., Delta BC V4C 3H9

Tel: 604-998-1410
info@bcbha.com
www.bcbha.com
www.facebook.com/BCBallHockey
twitter.com/_BCBallHockey
Overview: A small provincial organization founded in 1980
Description: To govern the sport of ball hockey in British Columbia; To establish bylaws & regulations, in order to ensure a safe & fun activity; To uphold the rules& regulations of ball hockey
Affiliation(s): Canadian Ball Hockey Association
Chief Officer(s): Mike Schweighardt, President, 604-998-1400 201
president@bcbha.com
Darsh Grewall, Technical Director, 604-998-1400 206
technical@bcbha.com
Finances: *Funding Sources:* Sponsorships
Fees: Schedule available; *Member Profile:* Ball hockey leagues in British Columbia which follow the rules & regulations of the British Columbia Ball Hockey Association & the Canadian Ball Hockey Association
Activities: Promoting ball hockey in British Columbia; Assisting in the establishment of ball hockey leagues in the province; Disseminating rulebooks; Organizing provincial championships; Providing certification programs for officials; Resolving disputes

Canadian Ball Hockey Association (CBHA) / Association canadienne de hockey-balle
PO Box 22005, Kingston ON K7M 7E0

Tel: 613-815-9610; *Toll-Free:* 888-341-9897
admin@cbha.com
www.cbha.com
www.facebook.com/BallHockeyCanada
twitter.com/CanBallHockey
Overview: A medium-sized national organization founded in 1977
Description: To develop & promote the sport of ball hockey; To provide a fun & safe activity for all age & experience levels
Chief Officer(s): Steve Power, President
president@cbha.com

Member Profile: Leagues, teams, players, associations;
Committees: Scheduling; Technical

Manitoba Ball Hockey Association (MBHA)
#306, 145 Pacific Ave., Winnipeg MB R3B 2Z6

Tel: 204-808-8770
mbha1@hotmail.com
www.winnipegballhockey.com
Overview: A small provincial organization founded in 1978
Description: To promote & encourage the development of competitive & recreational ball hockey in Manitoba; *Member of:* Sport Manitoba
Membership: 2,500+

New Brunswick Ball Hockey Association
NB

site2865.goalline.ca/index.php?league_id=53684
Overview: A small provincial organization
Member of: Canadian Ball Hockey Association
Member Profile: Ball hockey leagues throughout New Brunswick;
Committees: Disciplinary
Activities: Establishing rules for ball hockey in New Brunswick; Maintaining high standards of officiating; Offering the Rookie Officiating Program

Newfoundland & Labrador Ball Hockey Association (NLBHA)
NL

www.nlbha.com
www.facebook.com/NewfoundlandAndLabradorBallHockeyAsso
ciation
twitter.com/NLBallHockey
Overview: A small provincial organization
Description: To promote the sport of ball hockey in Newfoundland & Labrador; To maintain rules & regulations of the sport; *Member of:* Canadian Ball Hockey Association; Sport Newfoundland & Labrador
Activities: Organizing championships

Nova Scotia Ball Hockey Association (NSBHA)
Tel: 902-463-2833
nsbha@hotmail.com
nsbha.weebly.com
Overview: A small provincial organization
Description: To promote ball hockey in Nova Scotia & to host provincial tournaments
Affiliation(s): Canadian Ball Hockey Association; Sport Nova Scotia
Finances: *Annual Operating Budget:* Less than $50,000
Staff: 20 volunteer(s)
Membership: 650 individual

Ontario Ball Hockey Association (OBHA)
#5, 56 Pennsylvania Ave., Concord ON L4K 3V9

Tel: 905-738-3320; *Fax:* 905-738-3321
www.ontarioballhockey.ca
www.facebook.com/643077945729508
twitter.com/OntarioBallHock
Overview: A medium-sized provincial organization founded in 1974
Description: To promote & increase participation in the sport of ball hockey in Ontario; to improve opportunities for competition at all levels of participation; to create & implement leadership opportunities for officials, coaches & administrators; to establish standards of play & for quality of equipment to ensure good sport & safety for all participants
Affiliation(s): Canadian Ball Hockey Association; International Street & Ball Hockey Association; Sport Canada; Canadian Hockey Association
Chief Officer(s): Jamie Robillard, Coaching & Technical Director
Finances: *Funding Sources:* Self-generated revenue
Staff: 2 staff member(s); 12 volunteer(s)
Membership: 18,000; *Fees:* Schedule available
Activities: *Awareness Events:* Provincial Championships; Regional & National Champions

Québec Ball Hockey Association (QBHA) / Association de Hockey-Balle du Québec (AHBQ)
2890, boul Dagenais ouest, Laval QC H7P 1T1

Tel: 450-963-9346; *Fax:* 450-622-4466
infoahbq@gmail.com
www.facebook.com/AHBQ.QBHA
twitter.com/AHBQ_QBHA
Overview: A small provincial organization
Description: To promote & organize ball hockey in Québec & across the country; *Member of:* Canadian Ball Hockey Association; International Street & Ball Hockey Federation; Hockey Canada

Wild Rose Ball Hockey Association
Edmonton AB

wrbha@telus.net
www.wrballhockey.com
Overview: A small provincial organization
Description: To govern & develop ball hockey in Alberta;
Member of: Canadian Ball Hockey Association
Chief Officer(s): Connie Liosis, Executive Director
Fees: $205/team spring/summer; $3/player fall/winter; *Member Profile:* Ball hockey teams & leagues in Alberta
Activities: Organizing championships; Providing insurance, facilities & officials;Enforcing rules & guidelines; Providing courses for officials

Baseball

Alberta Amateur Baseball Council (AABC)
Building 140, #106, 88 Canada Olympic Road SW, Calgary AB T3B 5R5

Tel: 403-247-5480; *Fax:* 403-320-2053
aabc@albertabaseball.org
www.albertabaseball.org
www.facebook.com/1008463665926674
twitter.com/AABC_2017
Overview: A medium-sized provincial organization founded in 1998
Description: To be the provincial governing body for baseball associations throughout Alberta
Chief Officer(s): Ron Van Keulen, President
Kim Brigitzer, Manager, Administration & Communications
k.brigitzer@albertabaseball.org
Aaron Lavorato, Coordinator, High Performance
a.lavorato@albertabaseball.org
Finances: *Funding Sources:* Alberta Sport Connection
Membership: 5 leagues + 31,000 individuals

Aurora King Baseball Association (AKBA)
PO Box 34040, Stn. Hollandview, 446 Hollandview Trail, Aurora ON L4G 0G3

info@akba.ca
www.akba.ca
www.linkedin.com/company/aurora-king-baseball-association
www.facebook.com/AuroraKingBaseball
twitter.com/aurorakingbball
Merged from: Aurora Minor Baseball Association; King Township Baseball Association
Overview: A medium-sized local organization
Chief Officer(s): Matt Giesen, President
president@akba.ca

Baseball Alberta (BA)
11759 Groat Rd. NW, 2nd Fl., Edmonton AB T5M 3K6

Tel: 780-427-8943; *Fax:* 780-427-9032
operations@baseballalberta.com
www.baseballalberta.com
www.instagram.com/baseball_alberta
www.facebook.com/baseballalberta
twitter.com/BaseballAlberta
Also Known As: Alberta Baseball Association
Overview: A large provincial organization founded in 1967
Description: To promote & develop baseball in Alberta; To provide life & leadership skills for all genders through baseball; To encourage fun & fair play; *Member of:* Western Canada Baseball Association; Edmonton International Baseball Foundation
Affiliation(s): Alberta Amateur Baseball Council
Chief Officer(s): Tam Rosnau, Executive Director, 780-427-9009
Finances: *Funding Sources:* Membership dues; government; corporate
Staff: 3 staff member(s)
Fees: Schedule available
Activities: Programs include: Rally Cap; Winterball; Reaching Baseball Ideals; Long Term Athlete Development; Canadian Sport for Life; National Coaching Certification Program; programs for girls & women

Baseball BC
#310, 15225 - 104th Ave., Surrey BC V3R 6Y8

Tel: 604-586-3310; *Fax:* 604-586-3311
info1@baseball.bc.ca
www.baseball.bc.ca
www.facebook.com/233202485008
twitter.com/Baseball_BC
Previous Name: BC Amateur Baseball Association
Overview: A medium-sized provincial organization
Description: To support the development of baseball & the aspirations of its members; To offer oppourtunities & setting procedures, standards, & policies
Chief Officer(s): David Laing, Executive Director, 604-586-3312
davidlaing@baseball.bc.ca

Finances: *Funding Sources:* Government of B.C., Legacies Now, Rawlings Sporting Goods, Prostock Athletic Supply, Toronto Blue Jays, All Sport Insurance, Gatorade, Sport B.C.
Membership: 4,500

Baseball Canada / Fédération canadienne de baseball amateur
2212 Gladwin Cres., #A7, Ottawa ON K1B 5N1
Tel: 613-748-5606; *Fax:* 613-748-5767
info@baseball.ca
www.baseball.ca
www.instagram.com/baseballcanada
www.facebook.com/baseballcanada
twitter.com/baseballcanada
Also Known As: Canadian Federation of Amateur Baseball
Overview: A large national charitable organization founded in 1964
Description: To promote the development of baseball across Canada through support of provincial organizations & design of programs, including athletes, coaches, events, umpires & partner groups; *Member of:* Canadian Olympic Committee; World Baseball Softball Confederation
Chief Officer(s): Jim Baba, Executive Director
jbaba@baseball.ca
Finances: *Funding Sources:* Federal government; membership fees; sponsors; sales; program revenues; Sport Canada; Canadian Heritage
Staff: 8 staff member(s)
Activities: Hosts seven national championships; selects three national teams for international competition; National Skill Competition; Coach & Umpire Certification; Baseball Canada Cup; Honda Hit-Run-Throw; *Internships:* Yes *Library:* Yes by appointment

Baseball New Brunswick (BNB) / Baseball Nouveau-Brunswick
#13, 900 Hanwell Rd., Fredericton NB E3B 6A2
Tel: 506-451-1329; *Fax:* 506-451-1325
www.baseballnb.ca
www.instagram.com/baseballnb
www.facebook.com/BaseballNB
twitter.com/_Baseball_NB
Overview: A medium-sized provincial organization founded in 1989
Description: To promote & govern baseball in New Brunswick.
Affiliation(s): Sport New Brunswick; Baseball Atlantic
Chief Officer(s): David Watling, President
bnbwatling@bellaliant.net
David Dion, Executive Director
director@baseballnb.ca
Matt Clark, Program & Technical Coordinator
programs@baseballnb.ca
Finances: *Funding Sources:* Provincial government; Membership fees
Staff: 1 staff member(s)
Membership: 5,841; *Member Profile:* Baseball teams, players, coaches, officials, volunteers & administrators.; *Committees:* Baseball Development; Coaching; Financial; High Performance & Discipline; Hall of Fame; Personnel; Tournament; Linguistics

Baseball Nova Scotia (BNS)
5516 Spring Garden Rd., 4th Fl., Halifax NS B3J 1G6
Tel: 902-425-5454; *Fax:* 902-425-5606
baseball@sportnovascotia.ca
www.baseballnovascotia.ca
www.instagram.com/baseballnovascotia
www.facebook.com/baseballnovascotia
twitter.com/baseball_ns
Overview: A medium-sized provincial organization
Description: To represent baseball teams & leagues under the jurisdiction of BaseballCanada.; *Member of:* Canadian Federation of Amateur Baseball
Chief Officer(s): Brandon Guenette, Executive Director
Trevor Wamback, Technical Director
twamback@sportnovascotia.ca
Brennan Curry, Coordinator, Programs
bcurry@sportnovascotia.ca
Fees: Schedule available

Baseball Ontario
#3, 131 Sheldon Dr., Cambridge ON N1R 6S2
Tel: 519-740-3900; *Fax:* 519-740-6311
baseball@baseballontario.com
www.baseballontario.com
www.instagram.com/baseball_ontario
www.facebook.com/BaseballOntario
twitter.com/BaseballOntario
Overview: A medium-sized provincial organization founded in 1918

Member of: CSAE
Affiliation(s): Little League Ontario
Chief Officer(s): Mary-Ann Smith, Administrative Director
maryann@baseballontario.com
Finances: *Annual Operating Budget:* $500,000-$1.5 Million
Staff: 2 staff member(s)
Membership: 18 organizations
Activities: Coaching; Umpiring; Elite Player Development; Insurance; Tournaments; Communications; *Awareness Events:* Spring Break Camp; AGM

Baseball PEI
40 Enman Cres., Charlottetown PE C1E 1E6
Tel: 902-368-4203; *Fax:* 902-368-4548
www.baseballpei.ca
www.facebook.com/BaseballPEI
twitter.com/BaseballPEI1
Previous Name: Prince Edward Island Amateur Baseball Association
Overview: A medium-sized provincial organization founded in 1967
Description: To promote & develop minor & amateur baseball in PEI
Chief Officer(s): Don LeClair, President
Randy Byrne, Executive Director
Finances: *Annual Operating Budget:* Less than $50,000
Fees: Schedule available
Activities: Tournments including Bantam, Pee Wee, and Midget levels.

Charlottetown Area Baseball Association (CABA)
c/o Baseball PEI, 40 Enman Cres., Charlottetown PE C1E 1E6
Tel: 902-368-4203; *Fax:* 902-368-4548
baseball@sportpei.pe.ca
baseballpei.ca/page/show/1703665-charlottetown-all-seasons
Overview: A medium-sized local organization
Member of: Baseball PEI

Edmonton International Baseball Foundation (EIBF)
12314 - 76th St. NW, Edmonton AB T5B 2E4
Tel: 780-474-0795
postmaster@baseballeibf.ca
baseballeibf.ca
Overview: A small international charitable organization founded in 1979
Description: To help develop amateur baseball through financial assistance; To host international amateur baseball events
Affiliation(s): Baseball Canada; International Baseball Federation
Chief Officer(s): Ron Hayter, Chair
ron.hayter@baseballeibf.ca
Activities: Championships & world cups; four scholarships awarded annually

Fédération du baseball amateur du Québec
CP 1000, Succ. M, 4545, av Pierre-de Coubertin, Montréal QC H1V 0B2
Tél: 514-252-3075; *Téléc:* 514-252-3134
Ligne sans frais: 800-361-2054
info@baseballquebec.qc.ca
www.baseballquebec.com
www.facebook.com/baseballquebec
twitter.com/baseballquebec
Également appelé: Baseball Québec
Aperçu: *Dimension:* moyenne; *Envergure:* provinciale
Description: Donner un cadre général d'ordre et de discipline à tous les intervenants du baseball québécois; Reconnaître le droit pour tous les joueurs d'évoluer au baseball selon des normes et critères précis; Donner un cadre pour l'application d'une réglementation uniforme dans tout le Québec; Fournir les moyens à chacun de s'amuser, de participer et de se perfectionner afin de donner un idéal à ceux qui aspirent à une carrière
Membre(s) du bureau directeur: Maxime Lamarche, Directeur général
mlamarche@baseballquebec.qc.ca

Hamilton Baseball Umpires' Association (HBUA)
Hamilton ON
Tel: 905-538-6071
hamiltonbaseballumpires@gmail.com
hbua.ca
www.facebook.com/190866890945303
Overview: A small local organization
Chief Officer(s): Bill Tunney, President & Assignor
b.tunney@cogeco.ca

Kawartha Baseball Umpires Association (KBUA)
ON
Overview: A small local organization

Little League Canada / Petite ligue Canada
#500, 2210 Prince of Wales Dr., Ottawa ON K2E 6Z9
Tel: 613-731-3301; *Fax:* 613-731-2829
canada@littleleague.org
www.littleleague.ca
www.youtube.com/DugoutTheMascot
www.facebook.com/LittleLeagueCanada
twitter.com/LittleLgeCanada
Overview: A large national charitable organization founded in 1951
Description: To provide baseball & softball programs to every child wishing to participate; *Member of:* Little League Baseball International
Chief Officer(s): Roy Bergerman, President & CEO
rbergerman@littleleague.ca
Finances: *Funding Sources:* Membership dues; corporate
Membership: 35,000

Manitoba Baseball Association
145 Pacific Ave., Winnipeg MB R3B 2Z6
Tel: 204-925-5763; *Fax:* 204-925-5928
baseball.info@sportmanitoba.ca
www.baseballmanitoba.ca
www.facebook.com/baseballmanitoba
twitter.com/BaseballMB
Also Known As: Baseball Manitoba
Overview: A small provincial organization founded in 1968
Description: To foster the participation, development & competition of amateur baseball in Manitoba
Chief Officer(s): Jason Miller, Executive Director
baseball.jason@sportmanitoba.ca
James Zamko, Director, Program
baseball.zamko@sportmanitoba.ca
Finances: *Funding Sources:* Sponsors
Membership: 15,000; *Member Profile:* Community Clubs, Local Baseball Associations; *Committees:* Management

Newfoundland Baseball
1296A Kenmount Rd., Paradise NL
Tel: 709-576-3401
www.leaguelineup.com/welcome.asp?url=nlbaseball
twitter.com/BaseballNL
Also Known As: Baseball NL
Previous Name: Newfoundland Amateur Baseball Association
Overview: A small provincial organization founded in 1947
Description: Supports amatuer baseball in Newfoundland.; *Member of:* Baseball Canada
Chief Officer(s): Kevin Legge, President
Ryan Garland, Executive Director
Finances: *Annual Operating Budget:* $50,000-$100,000; *Funding Sources:* Membership dues; fundraising; corporate; government
Staff: 10 volunteer(s)
Membership: 20; *Fees:* Schedule available; *Committees:* Hall of Fame
Activities: Amateur baseball development; *Rents Mailing List:* Yes

Ontario Umpires Association
ON
Tel: 905-791-0280
ontario_umpires@sympatico.ca
www.ontarioumpires.com
Overview: A small provincial organization
Description: To provide officials for the games of baseball, softball, volleyball, flag football, hockey, basketball & soccer.
Affiliation(s): Ontario Sports Administration; Ontario Academy of Sports Officials; Sports Events International
Chief Officer(s): Jim Cottrell, President

Prince Edward Island Baseball Umpires Association (PEIBUA)
PE
Tel: 902-367-0564
peibua@gmail.com
www.peibua.com
Overview: A small provincial organization
Description: To represent certified amateur baseball umpires in the province of PEI.
Chief Officer(s): Kent Walker, Supervisor of Officials
kentwalker019@gmail.com
Activities: *Library:* Yes (Open to Public)

Saskatchewan Baseball Association (SBA)
1870 Lorne St., Regina SK S4P 2L7
Tel: 306-780-9237; *Fax:* 306-352-3669
www.saskbaseball.ca
www.facebook.com/10150095674130384
twitter.com/baseballsask
Overview: A medium-sized provincial organization founded in 1959

Description: To provide quality baseball programs to interested participants at whatever level they may choose; *Member of:* Baseball Canada; International Baseball Association; Sask Sport; Western Canada Baseball Association
Chief Officer(s): Mike Ramage, Executive Director
Finances: *Annual Operating Budget:* $250,000-$500,000; *Funding Sources:* Lottery proceeds
Staff: 3 staff member(s)
Membership: 14,000; Fees: Schedule available

Windsor & District Baseball Umpires Association (WDBUA)
Windsor ON

www.windsorumpires.ca
twitter.com/WDBUA

Also Known As: Windsor Umpires
Overview: A small local organization
Description: To train, instruct & evaluate members.
Affiliation(s): Baseball Ontario; Baseball Canada; Sun Parlour Baseball Association
Chief Officer(s): Matthew Tyler, President
president@windsorumpires.ca

Basketball

Basketball Alberta
Percy Page Centre, 11759 Groat Rd., 2nd Fl., Edmonton AB T5M 3K6

Tel: 780-427-9044; Fax: 780-427-9124
info@basketballalberta.ca
www.basketballalberta.ca
www.facebook.com/BasketballAlberta
twitter.com/BasketballAB

Overview: A medium-sized provincial organization founded in 1975
Description: To be premier facilitators of participation, development, and excellence in basketball; To champion the sport of basketball as a game for life by inspiring unity, facilitating development & delivering superior value
Chief Officer(s): Bob Mitchell, President
bmitchell@basketballalberta.ab.ca
Paul Sir, Executive Director
psir@basketballalberta.ab.ca
Brian Swane, Director, Communications
brian.swane@basketballalberta.ca
Finances: *Funding Sources:* Provincial government; self-generated
Staff: 6 staff member(s)
Fees: $11 per person; *Member Profile:* Basketball players, coaches & officials in Alberta

Basketball BC
#210, 7888 - 200th St., Langley BC V2Y 3J4

Tel: 778-621-8088
info@basketball.bc.ca
www.basketball.bc.ca
www.facebook.com/basketballbc
twitter.com/BasketballBC

Overview: A medium-sized provincial organization
Description: To be British Columbia's leading resource for basketball; To build the game of basketball; *Member of:* Sport BC
Chief Officer(s): Lawrie Johns, Executive Director, 778-621-2002
ljohns@basketball.bc.ca
Finances: *Funding Sources:* Government grant; fundraising; membership dues
Staff: 7 staff member(s)
Fees: $15

Basketball Manitoba
145 Pacific Ave., Winnipeg MB R3B 2Z6

Tel: 204-925-5775; Fax: 204-925-5929
info@basketball.mb.ca
www.youtube.com/user/baskmanbaskman
www.linkedin.com/company/basketball-manitoba
www.facebook.com/basketballmanitoba
twitter.com/basketballmb

Overview: A medium-sized provincial organization founded in 1976
Description: To operate as the provincial sport governing body for basketball in Manitoba; To ensure all Manitobans have access to the programs run by the association & that the game of basketball is enjoyed by as many people as possible
Chief Officer(s): Adam Wedlake, Executive Director
adam@basketballmanitoba.ca

Basketball New Brunswick (BNB) / Basketball Nouveau-Brunswick
#13, 900 Hanwell Rd., Fredericton NB E3B 6A2

Tel: 506-472-4667; Fax: 506-451-1325
info@basketball.nb.ca
www.basketball.nb.ca
www.facebook.com/BasketballNB
twitter.com/BasketballNB

Overview: A medium-sized provincial organization founded in 1979
Description: To promote, develop & encourage sport & recreation aspects of basketball in New Brunswick; To assist in establishment of basketball clubs throughout New Brunswick; To liaise with government & private agencies interested in promoting & supporting basketball
Affiliation(s): New Brunswick Association of Approved Basketball Officials; New Brunswick Interscholastic Athletic Association
Chief Officer(s): Lori Wall, President
Carolyn Peppin, Executive Director
carolyn.peppin@basketball.nb.ca
Kim Flemming, Office Administrator
kim.flemming@basketball.nb.ca
Finances: *Annual Operating Budget:* $500,000-$1.5 Million; *Funding Sources:* Membership dues; Provincial government; Programs
Staff: 3 staff member(s)
Member Profile: All players competing in provincial championships; minor association members
Activities: Offering National Coaching Certification, an Elite Development Program, & junior officials development

Basketball Nova Scotia
5516 Spring Garden Rd., 3rd Fl., Halifax NS B3J 1G6

Tel: 902-425-5450; Fax: 902-425-5606
bnsadmin@basketball.ns.ca
basketballnovascotia.com
www.instagram.com/basketballnovascotia
www.facebook.com/BasketballNovaScotia
twitter.com/BasketballNS

Overview: A small provincial organization
Description: To promote & encourage the game of basketball throughout the province; *Member of:* Sport Canada
Affiliation(s): Sport Nova Scotia
Chief Officer(s): David Wagg, Executive Director
bnsexecutivedirector@sportnovascotia.ca
Finances: *Annual Operating Budget:* $250,000-$500,000; *Funding Sources:* Government grants; Membership fees; Special events
Staff: 3 staff member(s); 12 volunteer(s)
Membership: 4,000; Fees: Schedule available
Activities: Offering the National Coaching Certificate Program; Facilitating player development programs & camps; Organizing tournaments

Basketball NWT
PO Box 44, Yellowknife NT X1A 2N1

www.bnwt.ca
www.facebook.com/bnwt.ca

Overview: A medium-sized provincial organization
Description: The Association encourages participation in basketball, develops athletes, & provides opportunities for cultural & social interchange among all involved in the sport
Affiliation(s): Steve Nash Youth Basketball; Sport North; Arctic Winter Games
Chief Officer(s): Damien Healy, President & Executive Director

Basketball PEI
#101, 40 Enman Cres., Charlottetown PE C1E 1E6

Tel: 902-368-4986; Fax: 902-368-4548
Toll-Free: 800-247-6712
www.basketballpei.ca
twitter.com/basketballpei

Overview: A medium-sized provincial organization
Description: To develop basketball in the province of Prince Edward Island in a fun environment
Chief Officer(s): Katie Hamilton, Executive Director
katie@basketballpei.ca
Activities: Developing the skills needed to play basketball successfully

Basketball Saskatchewan (BSI)
2205 Victoria Ave., Regina SK S4P 0S4

Fax: 306-525-4009
basketball@basketballsask.com
www.basketballsask.com
www.facebook.com/basketballsask
twitter.com/basketballsask

Previous Name: Saskatchewan Basketball
Overview: A medium-sized provincial licensing charitable organization founded in 1988

Description: To support & improve basketball opportunities in Saskatchewan
Affiliation(s): Sask Sport
Chief Officer(s): Todd Johnson, Executive Director, 306-780-9264
executivedirector@basketballsask.com
Dave Werry, Coordinator, High Performance, 306-780-9249
dwerry@basketballsask.com
Finances: *Funding Sources:* Sask Sport; Fundraising
Staff: 2 staff member(s)
Membership: 12,000; Fees: $10 active; $10 associate; $5 affiliate; *Member Profile:* Basketball teams, officials, board members, staff, program participants
Activities: *Speaker Service:* Yes *Library:* Yes (Open to Public)

Basketball Yukon
YT

www.basketballyukon.ca

Overview: A medium-sized provincial organization
Description: To assist in player & coaching development in the North; to lead the territory's basketball community through programs & services benefitting all levels of play
Affiliation(s): Sport Yukon, Canada Basketball
Chief Officer(s): Tim Brady, President

Canada Basketball
#11, 1 Westside Dr., Toronto ON M9C 1B2

Tel: 416-614-8037; Fax: 416-614-9570
info@basketball.ca
www.basketball.ca
www.facebook.com/CanadaBasketball
twitter.com/CanBball

Also Known As: Canadian Basketball Association
Overview: A large national charitable organization founded in 1972
Description: To develop the sport of basketball domestically & to contribute to the development of basketball internationally; *Member of:* International Basketball Federation
Affiliation(s): 10 provincial + 2 territorial associations; Canadian Interuniversity Athletic Union; Canadian Colleges Athletic Association; Canadian School Sports Federation; Toronto Raptors; Canadian Wheelchair Basketball Association; Canadian Association of Basketball Officials; National Association of Basketball Coaches of Canada; Women's Basketball Coaches Association
Chief Officer(s): Glen Grunwald, President & CEO
ggrunwald@basketball.ca
Andrea Driedger, Director, Finance & Admin
adriedger@basketball.ca
Activities: National Teams; coaching programs; championships; direct mail; licensing; youth basketball programs; *Internships:* Yes

Fédération de basketball du Québec (FBBQ) / Québec Basketball Federation
4545, av Pierre-de-Coubertin, Montréal QC H1V 0B2

Tél: 514-252-3057; Téléc: 514-252-3357
www.basketball.qc.ca

www.youtube.com/user/BasketballQc
www.facebook.com/BasketballQc
twitter.com/BasketballQc

Également appelé: Basketball Québec
Aperçu: *Dimension:* moyenne; *Envergure:* provinciale; *Organisme sans but lucratif;* fondée en 1970
Description: Développement et promotion de la discipline; Formation de joueurs, entraîneurs et arbitres; organisation de compétitions provinciales; Programme Poursuite de l'Excellence (Équipes et Espoirs du Québec)
Membre(s) du bureau directeur: Daniel Grimard, Directeur général
dgrimard@basketball.qc.ca
Membre: 35,000 personnes
Activités: *Stagiaires:* Oui; *Service de conférenciers:* Oui

Newfoundland & Labrador Basketball Association
1296A Kenmount Rd., Paradise NL A1L 1N3

Tel: 709-576-0247; Fax: 709-576-8787
nlba@sportnl.com
www.nlba.nf.ca
www.facebook.com/nlbasketball
twitter.com/nlbasketball

Previous Name: Basketball Newfoundland
Overview: A medium-sized provincial charitable organization founded in 1988
Description: To govern amateur basketball in Newfoundland & Labrador; To develop basketball domestically and internationally
Chief Officer(s): Bill Murphy, Executive Director
Tom Warren, President
Finances: *Annual Operating Budget:* $250,000-$500,000
Staff: 3 staff member(s)

Fees: Schedule available; *Member Profile:* Clubs, coaches, volunteers, teams, players; *Committees:* Executive; Minor; Coaching; Awards; Hallf of Fame; Policy; Hall of Fame Cup; Nominating
Activities: *Internships:* Yes; *Rents Mailing List:* Yes

Ontario Basketball
Abilities Centre, #2A, 55 Gordon St., Whitby ON L1N 0J2
Tel: 416-477-8075; *Fax:* 416-477-8120
basketball.on.ca
www.youtube.com/user/OntarioBasketballOBA
twitter.com/OBANews
Overview: A medium-sized provincial organization founded in 1977
Description: To promote & develop basketball on an amateur basis in the province of Ontario.
Affiliation(s): Provincial Sports Organizations Council; Canada Basketball; Toronto Raptors Basketball Club; NBA Canada; Coaches Association of Ontario; Canadian Sports Centre; and other provincial basketball organizations
Chief Officer(s): Jason Jansson, Executive Director, 416-477-8075 202
jjanson@basketball.on.ca
Lindsay Walsh, Director, Basketball Development, 416-477-8075 203
lwalsh@basketball.on.ca
Finances: *Annual Operating Budget:* $1.5 Million-$3 Million; *Funding Sources:* Sponsorship; fundraising; grants
Staff: 6 staff member(s)
Membership: 9,000; *Fees:* Schedule available; *Member Profile:* Players & coaches
Activities: *Internships:* Yes; *Speaker Service:* Yes *Library:* Yes (Open to Public) by appointment

Provincial Black Basketball Association (PBBA)
PO Box 2702, Halifax NS B3J 3P7
Tel: 902-452-0682
pbbafeedback@eastlink.ca
www.blackbasketball.ca
Overview: A medium-sized provincial organization founded in 1972
Description: To promote basketball within the African Canadian community in Nova Scotia & across the country.
Chief Officer(s): Carl Gannon, President
gannoncs@eastlink.ca

Baton Twirling

Alberta Baton Twirling Association (ABTA)
Percy Page Centre, 11759 Groat Rd., Edmonton AB T5M 3K6
Tel: 780-415-0144; *Fax:* 780-415-0170
abta@telusplanet.net
www.albertabaton.com
www.facebook.com/106834729351227
Overview: A small provincial organization founded in 1971
Description: To be the voice of baton twirling in the province; To promote the values & development of the sport; To unite the province in interest of baton twirling; To provide exposure; To encourage high standards in coaching and conduct; *Member of:* Canadian Baton Twirling Federation
Affiliation(s): Alberta Sport, Recreation, Parks, Wildlife Foundation
Chief Officer(s): Candy Tedford, Chair
Shari Foster, Executive Director
Activities: *Library:* Yes (Open to Public)

Baton New Brunswick (BNB)
20 Adams St., Tide Head NB E3N 4T3
baton.new.brunswick@gmail.com
www.facebook.com/batonNB
Overview: A small provincial organization
Description: To govern baton twirling in New Brunswick; *Member of:* Canadian Baton Twirling Federation
Chief Officer(s): Nadine LeBelle-Déjario, President, 506-759-7113

Baton Twirling Association of British Columbia (BTABC)
22411 Westminster Hwy., Richmond BC V6V 1B6
Tel: 604-722-1595
batonbc@gmail.com
www.bcbaton.com
www.instagram.com/batontwirlingbc
www.facebook.com/batontwirlingbc
twitter.com/BatonTwirlingBC
Also Known As: Baton Twirling BC
Overview: A small provincial organization

Description: To be the provincial governing body for the sport of baton twirling in British Columbia; *Member of:* Canadian Baton Twirling Federation
Chief Officer(s): Shannon Webster, Chair
Nancey Forsman, Membership Officer
Finances: *Funding Sources:* Province of British Columbia
Activities: Competitions; Training

Canadian Baton Twirling Federation (CBTF) / Fédération baton canadienne
admin@cbtf.ca
www.cbtf.ca
www.instagram.com/cbtfca
www.facebook.com/CBTFCA
Overview: A medium-sized national charitable organization founded in 1979
Description: To foster the development of athletes, coaches & officials in amateur twirling in Canada; *Member of:* World Baton Twirling Federation
Chief Officer(s): Joanne Moser, President
Cindy Dietrich, Secretary
Terry Stewart, Treasurer

Canadian National Baton Twirling Association (CNBTA)
c/o Joanne Antoniak, 1618 Kitchen Ct., Oshawa ON L1K 0H6
info@cnbta.org
www.cnbta.org
www.facebook.com/CNBTA
Overview: A small national organization
Description: To promote the sport of baton twirling in Canada
Affiliation(s): National Baton Twirling Association - USA; Global Alliance of National Baton Twirling & Majorette Associations
Chief Officer(s): Kevan Latrace, President
cnbta.prez@gmail.com
Fees: Schedule available

Manitoba Baton Twirling Sportive Association (MBTSA)
MB
www.manitobabaton.com
twitter.com/mbtsa
Overview: A small provincial organization
Description: To be the provincial governing body for the sport of baton twirling in Manitoba; *Member of:* Canadian Baton Twirling Federation
Chief Officer(s): Edie Parisian, Chairperson
Patti Sabeski, Vice Chairperson

Ontario Baton Twirling Association (OBTA)
#263, 55 Collinsgrove Rd., Toronto ON M1E 4Z2
info@obta.ca
www.obta.ca
www.facebook.com/OntarioBatonTwirlingAssociation
twitter.com/OBTA_ca
Overview: A small provincial organization
Description: To be the provincial governing body for the sport of baton twirling in Ontario; *Member of:* Canadian Baton Twirling Federation
Chief Officer(s): Kim Genton, President
president@obta.ca
Connie Worsnop, Membership Registrar
membership@obta.ca

Saskatchewan Baton Twirling Association (SBTA)
510 Cynthia St., Saskatoon SK S7L 7K4
Tel: 306-975-0847; *Fax:* 306-242-8007
skbaton@shaw.ca
www.saskbaton.com
Also Known As: Sask Baton
Overview: A small provincial organization
Description: To be the provincial governing body for the sport of baton twirling in Saskatchewan; *Member of:* Canadian Baton Twirling Federation
Chief Officer(s): Theresa Porter, Chair
Brenda O'Connor, Sport Coordinator
Finances: *Funding Sources:* Sask Sport Inc.; SaskTel

Biathlon

Biathlon Alberta
Bob Niven Training Centre, #102, 88 Canada Olympic Rd. SW, Calgary AB T3B 5R5
Tel: 403-202-6548
info@biathlon.ca
www.biathlon.ca
www.facebook.com/588814881135031
twitter.com/biathlonab
Overview: A small provincial organization founded in 1980

Description: To promote, develop & maintain biathlon in Alberta; *Member of:* Biathlon Canada; Alberta Ski & Snowboard Association
Chief Officer(s): Darcy Gullacher, General Manager
Karin Kaarsoo, President
Finances: *Annual Operating Budget:* $100,000-$250,000
Staff: 2 staff member(s); 300 volunteer(s)
Membership: 12 clubs + 357 individual; *Fees:* Schedule available

Biathlon BC
BC
Tel: 604-230-0481
biathlonbc.ca
www.instagram.com/biathlonbc
www.facebook.com/Biathlon-BC-181268575258202
twitter.com/BiathlonBC
Overview: A small provincial organization
Description: To promote Biathlon throughout British Columbia as a recreational & competitive sport.; *Member of:* Biathlon Canada
Chief Officer(s): Tony Tsang, President
president@biathlonbc.ca
Fees: Schedule available

Biathlon Canada
#100, 1995 Olympic Way, Canmore AB T1W 2T6
Tel: 403-678-4002; *Fax:* 403-678-3644
info@biathloncanada.ca
biathloncanada.ca
www.linkedin.com/company/biathlon-canada
www.facebook.com/BiathlonCanada
twitter.com/biathloncanada
Overview: A medium-sized national charitable organization founded in 1976
Description: To act as the governing body for the sport of biathlon in Canada
Affiliation(s): International Biathlon Union; Canadian Olympic Committee
Chief Officer(s): Heather Ambery, General Manager
hambery@biathloncanada.ca
Finances: *Funding Sources:* Sport Canada; Canadian Olympic Committee (COC); International Biathlon Union (IBU); Coaching Association of Canada (CAC)
Staff: 8 staff member(s)
Fees: Schedule available; *Committees:* Human Resources & Compensation; Finance & Audit; Revenue Generation & Marketing; Officials; Canadian International Biathlon Union

Biathlon Manitoba
Sport for Life Centre, 145 Pacific Ave., Winnipeg MB R3B 2Z6
Tel: 204-925-5687
biathlon@sportmanitoba.ca
biathlonmanitoba.ca
www.facebook.com/biathlonmanitoba
twitter.com/BiathlonMB
Overview: A small provincial organization
Description: To be the provincial governing body for the sport of biathlon in Manitoba; *Member of:* Biathlon Canada
Chief Officer(s): Lin-P'ing Choo-Smith, President
choosmith@gmail.com
Lorraine Mitchell, Vice President
lorraine@clutterdenied.com

Biathlon Newfoundland & Labrador
Mount Pearl NL
info@biathlonnl.ca
www.facebook.com/biathlonnl
twitter.com/biathlonnl
Overview: A small provincial organization
Description: To be the provincial governing body for the sport of biathlon in Newfoundland & Labrador; *Member of:* Biathlon Canada
Chief Officer(s): Gary Dawson, Contact
Membership: 3 clubs; *Fees:* Schedule available

Biathlon Nouveau-New Brunswick
11051 Hwy. 430, Trout Brook NB E9E 1R5
Tel: 506-627-0217
biathlon@biathlonnb.ca
www.biathlonnb.ca
Also Known As: Biathlon NB
Overview: A small provincial organization founded in 1990
Description: To be the provincial governing body for the sport of biathlon in New Brunswick; *Member of:* Biathlon Canada
Chief Officer(s): Ray Kokkonen, President, 506-627-6437
kokkonen@nbnet.nb.ca
Trent Martin, Head Coach, 506-623-9161
trmartin@nbpower.com
Paula Septon, Treasurer, 506-623-8118

Finances: *Annual Operating Budget:* $50,000-$100,000; *Funding Sources:* Sport & Recreation Branch, Government of NB; Internal revenue generation
Staff: 321 volunteer(s)
Fees: $20 non-competitor; $25-$90 competitor; $150 club;
Committees: Officials, Coaching Development; Membership; Marketing/Fundraising
Activities: Biathlon competitions; Training camps; Biathlon Bears (8-13 years old); Officials & coaches training

Biathlon Nova Scotia
c/o Sport Nova Scotia, 5516 Spring Garden Rd., Halifax NS B3J 1G6
Tel: 902-425-5454; *Fax:* 902-425-5606
admin@biathlonns.ca
www.biathlonns.ca
www.facebook.com/biathlonns
Overview: A small provincial organization
Description: To be the provincial governing body for the sport of biathlon in Nova Scotia; *Member of:* Biathlon Canada
Chief Officer(s): Karen Purcell, President
Colleen Thompson, Secretary
Jylene Ryan, Treasurer
Fees: Schedule available; *Committees:* Marketing; Fundraising; Technical; Officials

Biathlon Ontario
61 Kayla Cres., Collingwood ON L9Y 5K8
www.biathlonontario.ca
www.facebook.com/BiathlonOntario
Also Known As: BiON
Overview: A small provincial organization
Description: To be the provincial governing body for the sport of biathlon in Ontario; *Member of:* Biathlon Canada
Chief Officer(s): Alex Dumond, President
alexandre.dumond@gmail.com
Christine Piche, Vice President, Administration
pichec10@gmail.com
Membership: 7 clubs

Biathlon Prince Edward Island
2759 Glasgow Rd., Hunter River PE C0A 1N0
Tel: 902-964-3294
biathlonpei@gmail.com
www.facebook.com/biathlonpei
Also Known As: Biathlon PEI
Overview: A small provincial organization founded in 2005
Description: To be the provincial governing body for the sport of biathlon in Prince Edward Island; *Member of:* Biathlon Canada; Sport PEI Inc.
Chief Officer(s): Bob Bentley, President
Steve Woodman, Secretary, 902-566-8003
steven.woodman@vac-acc.gc.ca
Activities: Programs for athletes of all levels

Biathlon Saskatchewan
1860 Lorne St., Regina SK S4P 2L7
Tel: 306-780-9236; *Fax:* 306-780-9462
sask.ski@sasktel.net
www.biathlonsask.ca
Overview: A small provincial organization founded in 2005
Description: To be the provincial governing body for the sport of biathlon in Saskatchewan; *Member of:* Biathlon Canada
Chief Officer(s): Doug Sylvester, Provincial Head Coach
doug.sylvester@sasktel.net
Alana Ottenbreit, Executive Director
sask.ski@saksteI.net
Membership: 6 clubs

Biathlon Yukon
PO Box 31673, Whitehorse YT Y1A 6L3
Tel: 867-633-5717
biathlonyukon@gmail.com
www.biathlonyukon.org
Overview: A small provincial organization
Description: To enhance opportunities for all Yukon persons in their pursuit of excellence & in their enjoyment of participation in biathlon; *Member of:* Biathlon Canada; Sport Yukon
Chief Officer(s): Bill Curtis, President

Fédération québécoise de biathlon
CP 69023, Québec QC G2B 6C3
info@fqb.quebec
www.fqb.quebec
www.facebook.com/acbq.qc.ca
Nom précédent: Association des clubs de biathlon du Québec
Aperçu: *Dimension:* petite; *Envergure: provinciale; fondée en 2002*

Membre de: Biathlon Canada
Membre(s) du bureau directeur: Jean-Guy Lévesque, Président
president@fqb.quebec
Donald Villeneuve, Vice-Président, Administration
vpadministration@fqb.quebec

Northwest Territories Biathlon Association
NT
Tel: 867-874-2681
www.nwtbiathlon.com
www.facebook.com/172304639531053
Also Known As: NWT Biathlon Association
Overview: A small provincial organization
Description: To be the provincial governing body for the sport of biathlon in Northwest Territories; *Member of:* Biathlon Canada
Chief Officer(s): Pat Bobinski, President, 867-874-2681
pat@nwtbiathlon.com
Ted Kimmins, Vice President
ted@nwtbiathlon.com
Belinda Whitford, Secretary-Treasurer
belinda@nwtbiathlon.com

Bicycling

Alberta Bicycle Association (ABA)
11759 Groat Rd., Edmonton AB T5M 3K6
Tel: 780-427-6352; *Fax:* 780-427-6438
Toll-Free: 877-646-2453
www.albertabicycle.ab.ca
Overview: A small provincial licensing organization
Description: To promote all aspects of cycling in Alberta
Affiliation(s): Canadian Cycling Association; Union Cycliste International
Chief Officer(s): Heather Lothian, Executive Director
heather@albertabicycle.ab.ca
Fees: Schedule available; *Member Profile:* Cyclists; *Committees:* BMX; Racing; Recreation & Transportation
Activities: *Internships:* Yes

Bicycle Newfoundland & Labrador
PO Box 13241, Stn. A, St. John's NL A1B 4A5
admin@bnl.nf.ca
www.bnl.nf.ca
www.facebook.com/BicycleNL
twitter.com/BicycleNL
Overview: A small provincial organization
Fees: Schedule available

Bicycle Nova Scotia (BNS)
5516 Spring Garden Rd., 4th Fl., Halifax NS B3J 1G6
Tel: 902-425-5454; *Fax:* 902-425-5606
staff@bicycle.ns.ca
www.bicycle.ns.ca
www.facebook.com/bicyclenovascotia
twitter.com/bicyclens
Overview: A small provincial organization
Description: To act as the governmnent body for cycling in Nova Scotia & to advocate for on & off road cycling; *Member of:* Canadian Cycling Association
Chief Officer(s): Susanna Fuller, Co-President, Recreation & Transportation
susanna.fuller@bicycle.ns.ca
Lola Doucet, Co-President, Competition
lola.doucet@bicycle.ns.ca
Fees: $15 supporting; $25 general; $125 club
Activities: All aspects of cycling in Nova Scotia

Contagious Mountain Bike Club (CMBC)
4061 - 4th Ave., Whitehorse YT Y1A 1H1
Tel: 867-668-4990
info@cmbcyukon.ca
sportyukon.com/member/cycling-association-of-yukon
Overview: A small provincial organization
Description: To promote off-road cycling in the Yukon.
Chief Officer(s): Sue Richards, President
susanlearichards@gmail.com

Cycling Association of the Yukon
4061 - 4th Ave., Whitehorse YT Y1A 1H1
info@yukoncycling.com
yukoncycling.com
Overview: A small provincial organization
Member of: Cycling Canada Cyclisme; Sport Yukon
Chief Officer(s): Marc LaPointe, President

Cycling British Columbia (CBC)
130 West Broadway, 2nd Fl., Vancouver BC V5Y 1P3
Tel: 604-737-3034; *Fax:* 604-737-3141
membership@cyclingbc.net
cyclingbc.net
www.facebook.com/CyclingBC
twitter.com/cyclingbc
Also Known As: Cycling BC
Previous Name: Bicycling Association of BC
Overview: A medium-sized provincial organization founded in 1974
Description: To enable, enhance, & encourage cycling in British Columbia; *Member of:* Cycling Canada Cyclisme
Chief Officer(s): Erin Waugh, Executive Director
erin@cyclingbc.net
Jerrick Barroso, Manager, Communications
jerrick@cyclingbc.net
Tara Mowat, Manager, High Performance
tara@cyclingbc.net
Fees: Schedule available; *Committees:* Female Program Development; Financial Oversight & Audit; Governance Review; Nominating
Activities:*Rents Mailing List:* Yes *Library:* Yes (Open to Public)

Cycling Canada Cyclisme
#203, 2197 Riverside Dr., Ottawa ON K1H 7X3
Tel: 613-248-1353; *Fax:* 613-248-9311
general@cyclingcanada.ca
www.cyclingcanada.ca
www.instagram.com/cyclingcanadaofficial
www.facebook.com/CyclingCanada
twitter.com/CyclingCanada
Previous Name: Canadian Cycling Association
Overview: A medium-sized national organization founded in 1882
Description: To organize & promote cycling in Canada, including BMX, road racing, track & mountain biking, for sport & fitness
Chief Officer(s): Matthew Jeffries, Executive Director
matthew.jeffries@cyclingcanada.ca
Mathieu Boucher, Head, Development & Operations

Cycling PEI (CPEI)
Sport PEI, PO Box 302, 40 Enman Cresent, Charlottetown PE C1A 7K7
Tel: 902-368-4985; *Fax:* 902-368-4548
www.cpei.ca
twitter.com/cyclingpei
Overview: A small provincial organization
Description: To develop cycling in PEI; *Member of:* Cycling Canada Cyclisme
Chief Officer(s): Mike Connolly, Executive Director
mconnolly@sportpei.pe.ca
Fees: $30 youth general; $40 senior general; $40 youth citizen; $50 senior citizen; $50 youth UCI racing license; $90 senior UCI racing license

Edmonton Bicycle & Touring Club (EBTC)
PO Box 52017, Stn. Garneau, Edmonton AB T6G 2T5
Tel: 780-424-2453
www.bikeclub.ca
www.facebook.com/groups/21002145481
twitter.com/EBTCbikeclub
Overview: A small local organization founded in 1978
Affiliation(s): Alberta Bicycle Association
Chief Officer(s): Charles World, President
president@bikeclub.ca
Finances: *Annual Operating Budget:* $50,000-$100,000
Staff: 7 volunteer(s)
Membership: 301; *Fees:* $33 single; *Member Profile:* Single, married, families, all ages & walks of life
Activities: Day & overnight cycling trips; cross-country skiing; social events; *Awareness Events:* Tour de l'Alberta *Library:* Yes (Open to Public)

Fédération québécoise des sports cyclistes (FQSC) / Québec Cycling Sports Federation
4545, av Pierre-de Coubertin, Montréal QC H1V 3R2
Tél: 514-252-3071; *Téléc:* 514-252-3165
info@fqsc.net
www.fqsc.net
www.facebook.com/176077399110320
twitter.com/FQSC
Nom précédent: Fédération cycliste du Québec
Aperçu: *Dimension:* moyenne; *Envergure:* provinciale; *Organisme sans but lucratif; fondée en 1971*
Description: Régie et promotion des sports cyclistes au Québec; *Membre de:* Cycling Canada Cyclisme

Affiliation(s): Union cycliste internationale; Sports-Québec; Regroupement loisir Québec
Membre(s) du bureau directeur: Louis Barbeau, Directeur général, 514-252-3071 3523
lbarbeau@fqsc.net
Finances: *Budget de fonctionnement annuel:* $500,000-$1.5 Million
Personnel: 5 membre(s) du personnel; 57 bénévole(s)
Membre: 5 000 individus; 150 clubs; *Montant de la cotisation:* Schedule available
Activités: Temple de la Renommée du Cyclisme Québécois; mérite cycliste québécois; *Bibliothèque:* Oui (Bibliothèque publique)

International Mountain Bicycling Association (Canada) (IMBA)
PO Box 1131, Garibaldi Highlands BC V0N 1T0
Also Known As: IMBA Canada
Overview: A medium-sized international organization founded in 2004
Description: To maintain Canada's mountain biking community
Affiliation(s): International Mountain Bicycling Association
Chief Officer(s): A.J. Strawson, Executive Director
aj.strawson@imbacanada.com
Activities: Trail Partners Program; Land Manager Training; Model Trails

Manitoba Cycling Association (MCA)
Sport for Life Centre, 145 Pacific Ave., Winnipeg MB R3B 2Z6
Tel: 204-925-5686
cycling.ed@sportmanitoba.ca
mbcycling.ca
vimeo.com/mbcycling
www.facebook.com/ManitobaCycling
twitter.com/ManitobaCycling
Overview: A small provincial organization
Description: To be the provincial governing body for the sport of cycling in Manitoba; *Member of:* Cycling Canada Cyclisme
Chief Officer(s): Andy Romanovych, President
tpeabody@shaw.ca
Twila Pitcher, Executive Director, 204-925-5686
cycling.ed@sportmanitoba.ca
Fees: $50-$125 individual; $75 affiliate

Ontario Cycling Association (OCA) / Association cycliste ontarienne
#2, 2015 Pan Am Blvd., Milton ON L9T 8Y9
Tel: 416-855-1717
www.ontariocycling.org
www.linkedin.com/company/ontario-cycling-association
www.facebook.com/129640691224
twitter.com/ontariocycling
Overview: A medium-sized provincial licensing organization founded in 1882
Description: To act as the provincial governing body for road, track & cyclocross, mountain biking, & BMX racing in Ontario; To develop & deliver quality programs & services for the sport of cycling in Ontario; *Member of:* Cycling Canada Cyclisme
Chief Officer(s): Jim Crosscombe, Chief Executive Officer, 416-855-1717 1008
Michael Suraci, Manager, High Performance, 416-855-1717 1002
Jen Eaton, Coordinator, Sport, 416-855-1717 1009
Finances: *Funding Sources:* Membership fees; Sponsorships
Fees: Schedule available; *Member Profile:* OCA affiliated club members; Riders who wish to compete only in Ontario; Riders who wish to compete out of the province or at national & international events held within Ontario; Non-racers; Certified Can-Bike & OMBI instructors
Activities: Promoting the benefits of cycling, as well as cycling programs & services in Ontario; Advocating for cyclists in Ontario; Sharing resources & expertise; Promoting safe cycling, through the CanBike safe cycling program; Coordinating mountain bike, road, & track race competitions

Saskatchewan Cycling Association
2205 Victoria Ave., Regina SK S4P 0S4
Tel: 306-780-9299; *Fax:* 306-525-4009
cycling@accesscomm.ca
www.saskcycling.ca
www.facebook.com/327882317318669
Overview: A small provincial organization
Description: To promote & enhance the Saskatchewan cycling experience while recognizing its benefits to the individual & society.; *Member of:* Cycling Canada Cyclisme
Chief Officer(s): Bob Cochran, Interim President
Finances: *Funding Sources:* Saskatchewan Lotteries
Staff: 2 staff member(s)
Activities: *Speaker Service:* Yes; *Rents Mailing List:* Yes

Toronto Bicycling Network
PO Box 279, #200, 131 Bloor St. West, Toronto ON M5S 1R8
Tel: 416-760-4191
info@tbn.ca
www.tbn.ca
twitter.com/TOBikeNetwork
Overview: A small local organization founded in 1983
Chief Officer(s): Ian Rankin, President
president@tbn.ca
Sandra Wong, Technical Director
sandra.wong@tbn.ca
Ed Weiss, Director, Communications
publicity@tbn.ca
Membership: 850; *Fees:* $70 family; $50 individual; $25 student
Activities: Leisure Wheeler Rides; Easy Roller Rides; Tourist & Short Tourist Rides; Sportif Rides; Country Cruise Rides; Snails & Spice Ride; cross-country skiing; in-line skating; ice skating & hiking

Vélo New Brunswick
NB
velonb@gmail.com
www.velo.nb.ca
www.facebook.com/VeloNB
twitter.com/velonb
Overview: A small provincial organization founded in 1993
Description: To promote all aspects of the activity of bicycling, competitive & recreational, both on & off the road; *Member of:* Cycling Canada Cyclisme
Affiliation(s): Sport New Brunswick
Chief Officer(s): Melissa Bordage, President
president@velo.nb.ca
Christy Borgald, Vice-President
vp@velo.nb.ca
Chris Foster, Executive Director
executivedirector@velo.nb.ca

Vélo Québec
Maison des cyclistes, 1251, rue Rachel est, Montréal QC H2J 2J9
Tél: 514-521-8356; *Téléc:* 514-521-5711
Ligne sans frais: 800-567-8356
www.velo.qc.ca

www.instagram.com/veloquebec
www.facebook.com/VeloQuebec
twitter.com/VeloQuebec
Aperçu: *Dimension:* moyenne; *Envergure:* provinciale; *fondée en* 1967
Description: Promouvoir l'utilisation du vélo à travers le Québec
Membre(s) du bureau directeur: Suzanne Lareau, Directrice générale
Josée Monette, Vice-présidente, Marketing & service à la clientèle
Montant de la cotisation: 36$ 22 ans &+, 65 ans &+; 45$ régulier; 55$ famille
Activités: *Evénements de sensibilisation:* Mois du vélo, mai; *Stagiaires:* Oui; *Service de conférenciers:* Oui

Bicycling

VeloNorth Cycling Club
68 Klondike Rd., Whitehorse YT Y1A 3M1
Tel: 867-668-3531
www.velonorth.ca
Overview: A small provincial organization
Description: To encourage safe bicycle riding for sport, recreation & fitness.
Affiliation(s): Contagious Mountain Bike Club
Chief Officer(s): McCann Mike, Chair
mike@velonorth.org
Bill Curtis, Treasurer
wcurtis@northwestel.net

Blindness

Alberta Sports & Recreation Association for the Blind (ASRAB)
#007, 15 Colonel Baker Pl. NE, Calgary AB T2E 4Z3
Tel: 403-262-5332; *Fax:* 403-265-7221
Toll-Free: 888-882-7722
info@asrab.ab.ca
www.asrab.ab.ca
www.facebook.com/AlbertaSportsForTheBlind
twitter.com/ABBlindSports
Overview: A small provincial charitable organization founded in 1975

Description: To provide recreation & sports opportunities for Albertans who are blind & partially sighted; *Member of:* CBSA
Chief Officer(s): Linda MacPhail, Executive Director
execdirector@asrab.ab.ca
Fees: $15 individual; $30 family
Activities: Swimming; Lawn Bowling; Powerlifting; Goalball Athletics; Tandem Cycling; *Awareness Events:* Sight Night, Nov.; *Speaker Service:* Yes

Association des sports pour aveugles du Montréal métropolitain (ASAMM)
#428, 4450, rue Saint Hubert, Montréal QC H2J 2W9
Tél: 514-524-4715
info@asamm.ca
asamm.ca
www.facebook.com/sport.aveugles.ASAMM
Nom précédent: Association des sports pour aveugles de Montréal
Aperçu: *Dimension:* petite; *Envergure: locale; Organisme sans but lucratif; fondée en* 1983
Description: Promouvoir l'accessibilité et la pratique des sports et loisirs aux personnes handicapées visuelles; organiser et structurer les différentes activités sportives; recruter et former des bénévoles accompagnateurs
Affiliation(s): Association sportive des aveugles du Québec
Membre(s) du bureau directeur: Jocelyne Richard, Présidente
Finances: *Budget de fonctionnement annuel:* $50,000-$100,000
Personnel: 1 membre(s) du personnel; 75 bénévole(s)
Membre: 175 individu; 2 associées; *Critères d'admissibilite:* Personne ayant un handicap visuel
Activités: Goalball; conditionnement physique; aqua forme; tandem; ski alpin et ski de fond; tai-chi; activités ponctuelles: équitation, escalade, canot, randonnée pédestre; *Evénements de sensibilisation:* Tournoi de golf, sept.

Association sportive des aveugles du Québec inc. (ASAQ)
4545, av Pierre-de Coubertin, Montréal QC H1V 3R2
Tél: 514-252-3178
infoasaq@sportsaveugles.qc.ca
www.sportsaveugles.qc.ca
Aperçu: *Dimension:* petite; *Envergure:* provinciale; *fondée en* 1979
Description: Promouvoir la pratique du sport amateur auprès des personnes handicapées de la vue et de favoriser ainsi leur intégration
Membre(s) du bureau directeur: Nathalie Chartrand, Directrice générale
Membre: 135; *Montant de la cotisation:* 15$
Activités: *Service de conférenciers:* Oui

Blind Sailing Association of Canada (BSAC)
#2705, 361 Front St. West, Toronto ON M5V 3R5
Tel: 416-489-2433
info@blindsailing.ca
blindsailing.ca
www.facebook.com/blindsailingcan
Overview: A small national organization founded in 2002
Description: To provide opportunities for the blind to learn to sail, thus boosting skills, confidence & self-esteem; *Member of:* Ontario Sailing Association; Sail Canada
Chief Officer(s): Chris Jonas, President
cjonas@sympatico.ca
Fees: $20

Blind Sports Nova Scotia
NS
blindsportsns@gmail.com
www.blindsportsnovascotia.ca
www.facebook.com/BlindSportsNS
twitter.com/blindsportsns
Overview: A small provincial organization
Description: To present sport & recreational activities for visually impaired athletes in Nova Scotia; *Member of:* Canadian Blind Sport Association; Sport Nova Scotia
Chief Officer(s): Peter Parsons, Chair
Christine Gentlemen, Secretary
Member Profile: Adults, age 19+ (but 14+ are welcome, too)

British Columbia Blind Sports & Recreation Association (BCBSRA)
#170, 5055 Joyce St., Vancouver BC V5R 6B2
Tel: 604-325-8638; *Fax:* 604-325-1638
Toll-Free: 877-604-8638
info@bcblindsports.bc.ca
www.bcblindsports.bc.ca
www.facebook.com/BCBlindSports
twitter.com/bc_blind
Also Known As: BC Blind Sports
Overview: A medium-sized provincial charitable organization founded in 1975

Description: To provide sports, physical recreation & fitness activities & programs for persons of all ages who are blind / visually impaired; To alleviate isolating & inhibiting effects of blindness / visual impairment; To improve physical capabilities & self-image of blind / visually impaired individuals by providing opportunities for them to learn; To encourage, promote & maintain interest in & cooperation with all such amateur sports & recreation organizations
Chief Officer(s): Brian Cowie, President
Doug Dow, Vice-President
Finances: *Funding Sources:* Private donations; provincial government
Fees: $5 supporting; $15 athlete; *Member Profile:* Legally blind athletes; sighted guides; coaches; parents whose children are blind
Activities: Operates in nine regions: Kootenays, Thompson / Okanagan, Fraser Valley, Cariboo / North East, Vancouver/Squamish; Vancouver Island / South, Vancouver Island / North, North West, Fraser River / Delta; fundraisers; trade shows; workshops; *Speaker Service:* Yes

Canadian Blind Sports Association Inc. (CBSA) / Association canadienne des sports pour aveugles inc.
#175, 5055 Joyce St., Vancouver BC V5R 6B2
Tel: 604-419-0480; *Fax:* 604-419-0481
Toll-Free: 866-604-0480
info@canadianblindsports.ca
www.canadianblindsports.ca
www.facebook.com/canadianblindsports
Overview: A medium-sized national charitable organization founded in 1976
Description: To facilitate opportunities for Canadians who are legally blind to participate in amateur sport at the national / international level as to enhance a healthy lifestyle & individual well-being
Affiliation(s): International Blind Sports Association; Canadian Paralympic Committee; Active Living Alliance
Chief Officer(s): Jane D. Blaine, Chief Executive Officer
jane@canadianblindsports.ca
Finances: *Annual Operating Budget:* $250,000-$500,000; *Funding Sources:* Donations; government; membership dues
Staff: 5 staff member(s)
Activities: *Rents Mailing List:* Yes

Manitoba Blind Sports Association (MBSA)
145 Pacific Ave., Winnipeg MB R3B 2Z6
Tel: 204-925-5694; *Fax:* 204-925-5792
blindsport@shawbiz.ca
www.blindsport.mb.ca
www.facebook.com/ManitobaBlindSports
twitter.com/MBblindsport
Previous Name: Manitoba Sport & Recreation Association for the Blind
Overview: A medium-sized provincial organization founded in 1976
Description: To provide blind & visually impaired Manitobans with the opportunity to participate in sport at all levels of skill & ability
Finances: *Annual Operating Budget:* Less than $50,000
Staff: 20 volunteer(s)
Membership: 45; *Fees:* $100 ($10 for membership, $40 program fee, $50 refundable fundraising fee)
Activities: *Awareness Events:* Run for Light; *Speaker Service:* Yes *Library:* Yes by appointment

Ontario Blind Sports Association (OBSA)
#101, 100 Sunrise Ave., Toronto ON M4A 1B3
Tel: 416-426-7191; *Fax:* 416-426-7361
info@blindsports.on.ca
blindsports.on.ca
www.instagram.com/blindsports
www.facebook.com/OntarioBlindSports
twitter.com/BlindSports
Overview: A small provincial charitable organization founded in 1984
Description: To organize sporting events & activities for blind & visually impaired athletes in Ontario
Chief Officer(s): Glen Wade, President
Richard Amelard, Manager, Programs, 416-426-7244
richard@blindsports.on.ca
Finances: *Annual Operating Budget:* $100,000-$250,000; *Funding Sources:* Membership fees; government
Staff: 2 staff member(s); 20 volunteer(s)
Membership: 200; *Fees:* $25; *Member Profile:* Sport association
Activities: *Speaker Service:* Yes

Saskatchewan Blind Sports Association Inc. (SBSA)
510 Cynthia St., Saskatoon SK S7L 7K7
Tel: 306-975-0888; *Toll-Free:* 877-772-7798
info@saskblindsports.ca
www.saskblindsports.ca
Overview: A small provincial organization founded in 1978
Description: To assist persons who are blind or with visual impairment to achieve excellence in sport, satisfaction in recreation, independence, self-reliance & full community participation
Chief Officer(s): Nikhil Khanna, Executive Director
Finances: *Annual Operating Budget:* $100,000-$250,000
Staff: 1 staff member(s); 250 volunteer(s)
Membership: 100-499; *Fees:* $10
Activities: *Awareness Events:* Run for Light

Boating

Canadian International Dragon Boat Festival Society (CIDBFS)
Creekside Community Centre, 1 Athletes Way, Vancouver BC V5Y 0B1
Tel: 604-688-2382
info@dragonboatbc.ca
dragonboatbc.ca
www.instagram.com/dragonboatbc
www.facebook.com/thedragonboatbc
Also Known As: Rio Tinto Alcan Dragon Boat Festival
Previous Name: Dragon Boat Festival Society
Overview: A small national organization founded in 1989
Description: To foster learning & exploration of Canada's diverse multicultural heritage through performing, visual & culinary arts & dragon boat-racing; *Member of:* Vancouver Cultural Alliance
Chief Officer(s): Alexis Gall, General Manager
Finances: *Funding Sources:* Government; corporate; donations; fund-raising
Staff: 12 staff member(s); 1000 volunteer(s)
Activities: Annual 3 day multicultural festival; year long education program on multiculturalism; *Speaker Service:* Yes

Canadian Power & Sail Squadrons (Canadian Headquarters) (CPS) / Escadrilles canadiennes de plaisance (ECP)
26 Golden Gate Ct., Toronto ON M1P 3A5
Tel: 416-293-2438; *Fax:* 416-293-2445
Toll-Free: 888-277-2628
hqg@cps-ecp.ca
www.cps-ecp.ca
www.youtube.com/user/CPSECP
www.facebook.com/CPSboat
twitter.com/cpsboat
Overview: A medium-sized national charitable organization founded in 1938
Description: To increase awareness & knowledge of safe boating by educating & training members & the general public, by fostering fellowship among members & establishing partnerships & alliances with organizations & agencies interested in boating; *Member of:* Canadian Safe Boating Council
Chief Officer(s): Mimma Spagnolo, Executive Director, 416-293-2438 2439
mspagnolo@cps-ecp.ca
John Gullick, Manager, Government & Special Programs, 416-293-2438 0155
jgullick@cps-ecp.ca
Finances: *Annual Operating Budget:* $1.5 Million-$3 Million
Staff: 13 staff member(s); 5000 volunteer(s)
Membership: 17,000+ from 140 clubs; *Fees:* $35; *Member Profile:* Must pass specified examination & pay dues on annual basis; *Committees:* Public Relations; Training Department
Activities: *Library:* Yes (Open to Public)

Club nautique de Chibougamau inc.
CP 395, Chibougamau QC G8P 2X8
Tél: 418-748-6180
Aperçu: *Dimension:* petite; *Envergure:* locale

Dragon Boat Canada (DBC) / Bateau-Dragon Canada (BDC)
#331, 2255B Queen St. East, Toronto ON M4E 1G3
Tel: 647-210-5175
dragonboat.ca
www.instagram.com/dragonboatcanada
www.facebook.com/DBC.BDC
twitter.com/DragonBoatCda
Overview: A medium-sized national organization
Description: To be the official governing of dragon boat racing in Canada; *Member of:* International Dragon Boat Federation
Chief Officer(s): Chloe Greenhalgh, Executive Director
director@dragonboat.ca

Fees: Schedule available

Bobsledding & Luge

Alberta Bobsleigh Association (ABA)
Bob Niven Training Centre, #205, 88 Canada Olympic Rd. SW, Calgary AB T3B 5R5
Tel: 403-297-2721; *Fax:* 403-286-7213
slide@albertabobsleigh.com
www.albertabobsleigh.com
www.facebook.com/albertabobsleigh
Overview: A small provincial charitable organization founded in 1983
Description: To develop a broad interest in bobsleigh in Alberta; to provide opportunities for all Albertans to participate in bobsleigh; to provide opportunities for Albertans to progress to national & international levels; *Member of:* Bobsleigh Canada
Chief Officer(s): Sarah Monk, Technical Director
Dennis Marineau, Head Coach
Finances: *Annual Operating Budget:* $100,000-$250,000
Staff: 1 staff member(s); 70 volunteer(s)
Membership: 560; *Fees:* Schedule available
Activities: Summer training programs; *Library:* Yes (Open to Public)

Alberta Luge Association (ALA)
#201, BNTC, 88 Canada Olympic Rd. SW, Calgary AB T3B 5R5
Tel: 403-202-6570
admin@albertaluge.com
www.albertaluge.com
Overview: A small provincial organization founded in 1983
Description: To ensure the continued successful growth of the sport of luge in Alberta through the development of its athletes, coaches & volunteers at the recreational & elite levels
Affiliation(s): Canadian Luge Association
Finances: *Annual Operating Budget:* $100,000-$250,000
Staff: 2 staff member(s); 150 volunteer(s)
Membership: 700; *Fees:* Schedule available

Bobsleigh Canada Skeleton
#140, 88 Canada Olympic Rd. SW, Calgary AB T3B 5R5
Tel: 403-247-5964
info@bobcanskel.ca
www.bobsleighcanadaskeleton.ca
www.instagram.com/bobsleighcanskeleton
www.facebook.com/BobsleighCanadaSkeleton
twitter.com/BobCANSkel
Overview: A medium-sized national charitable organization founded in 1990
Description: To govern bobsleigh and skeleton in Canada; To strive to create Olympic & world champions; *Member of:* Canadian Olympic Association
Affiliation(s): International Bobsleigh & Skeleton Federation
Chief Officer(s): Chris Le Bihan, Director, High Performance
clebihan@bobcanskel.ca
Jeannie Godfrey, Contact, Events, Partnerships, Sponsorship & Marketing
sponsorship@bobcanskel.ca
Finances: *Funding Sources:* Government & corporate sponsorship
Staff: 8 staff member(s)
Activities: Operating national teams in bobsleigh & skeleton; Hosting national & international events

Canadian Luge Association / Association canadienne de luge
#250, 149 Canada Olympic Rd. SW, Calgary AB T3B 6B7
Tel: 403-202-6581
events@luge.ca
www.luge.ca
www.instagram.com/lugecanada
www.facebook.com/LugeCanada
twitter.com/LugeCanada
Previous Name: Canadian Amateur Bobsleigh & Luge Association
Overview: A medium-sized national organization founded in 1990
Description: To provide leadership & pursue success in promotion & development of all aspects of luge
Chief Officer(s): Tim Farstad, Executive Director
tfarstad@luge.ca
Chris Dornan, Coordinator, Media Relations
hpprchris@shaw.ca
Finances: *Funding Sources:* donations; Fast Track Capital
Staff: 4 staff member(s)
Member Profile: Provincial associations fully recognized by national association
Activities: *Internships:* Yes

Fédération Internationale de Luge de Course (FIL) / International Luge Federation
Nonntal 10, Berchtesgaden 83471 Germany

office@fil-luge.org
www.fil-luge.org

www.facebook.com/FILuge
twitter.com/fil_luge

Aperçu: *Dimension:* petite; *Envergure: internationale; fondée en 1957*
Description: Promotion et participation aux compétitions de la luge dans le monde; organise des championnats du monde, des coupes du monde, des championnats régionaux; organise des cours et séminaires pour des arbitres et des entraîneurs
Affiliation(s): Canadian Luge Association
Membre(s) du bureau directeur: Einars Fogelis, Président
Dwight Bell, Secrétaire général
Finances: *Budget de fonctionnement annuel:* $250,000-$500,000
Personnel: 5 membre(s) du personnel
Membre: 53
Activités: *Bibliothèque:* Oui

Ontario Bobsleigh Skeleton Association (OBSA)
22 Lynwood Ave., Ottawa ON K1Y 2B3

Tel: 613-276-0779
www.ontariobobsleighskeleton.ca
www.facebook.com/OntarioBobsleighSkeleton

Overview: A medium-sized provincial organization founded in 1960
Description: To promote bobsleigh & skeleton in Ontario; To develop national level athletes
Affiliation(s): Bobsleigh Canada Skeleton; International Bobsleigh & Skeleton Federation
Chief Officer(s): Esther Dalle, Director, High Performance
edalle@hotmail.com

Ontario Luge Association (OLA)
3073 Victoria Heights Cres., Ottawa ON K1T 3M7

Tel: 613-262-5513
ontarioluge@gmail.com
ontarioluge.ca
www.facebook.com/OntarioLugeAssociation
twitter.com/OntarioLuge

Overview: A medium-sized provincial organization
Description: To govern & promote luge training, competition & quality in Ontario
Affiliation(s): Canadian Luge Association
Chief Officer(s): Chris Wightman, President
Fees: $5 indiviual; $10 under 16

Bodybuilding

Alberta Bodybuilding Association (ABBA)
Edmonton Centre, PO Box 47248, Edmonton AB T5J 4N1

Tel: 780-709-5309
www.abba.ab.ca
www.facebook.com/Albertabodybuildingassociation
twitter.com/AlbertaBBAssoc

Overview: A small provincial organization
Description: To be the provincial governing body for the sport of amateur bodybuilding in Alberta; *Member of:* Canadian Bodybuilding Federation; International Federation of Bodybuilding
Chief Officer(s): Brenda Rose, President
president@abba.ab.ca
Tara Ostafichuk, Vice President
vp@abba.ab.ca
Melissa Lefebvre, Secretary-Treasurer
treasurer@abba.ab.ca

Association des Physiques Québécois (APQ)
96, rue Principale, Granby QC J2G 2T4

Tél: 450-991-1174; *Téléc:* 450-991-1184
apquebec.informations@gmail.com
www.apquebec.com

Aperçu: *Dimension:* petite; *Envergure: provinciale*
Membre de: Canadian Bodybuilding Federation; International Federation of Bodybuilding
Membre(s) du bureau directeur: Yves Desbiens, Director technique
photoyd@videotron.ca
Joe Spinello, Directeur des juges
spinellojoe@hotmail.com

British Columbia Amateur Bodybuilding Association (BCABBA)
#325, 1865 Dilworth Dr., Kelowna BC V1Y 9T1

support@bcabba.org
www.bcabba.org
www.facebook.com/BCAmateurBodybuildingAssoc

Overview: A small provincial organization
Description: To be the provincial governing body for the sport of amateur bodybuilding in British Columbia; *Member of:* Canadian Bodybuilding Federation; International Federation of Bodybuilding
Chief Officer(s): Sandra Wickham, President
Tamara Knight, Coordinator, Membership
tzonefitness@telus.net
Fees: $75 competitive

Canadian Bodybuilding Federation (CBBF) / Fédération canadienne de culturisme
www.cbbf.ca
www.instagram.com/canadianbodybuildingfed
www.facebook.com/CanadianBodybuildingFederationCBBF

Overview: A small national organization
Description: To act as the governing body for amateur bodybuilding, fitness & body fitness (figure) competition
Affiliation(s): British Columbia Amateur Bodybuilding Association; Alberta Bodybuilding Association; Saskatchewan Amateur Bodybuilders Association (SABBA); Manitoba Amateur Bodybuilding Association; Ontario Physique Association (OPA); Association des Physiques Québécois; New Brunswick Physique & Figure Association; Nova Scotia Amateur Bodybuilders Association; Newfoundland & Labrador Amateur Bodybuilding Association
Chief Officer(s): Georgina Dunnington, Chair
georgina@cbbf.ca
Activities: Qualifying competitors for the three IFBB World Championships; Posting championship results

Manitoba Amateur Bodybuilding Association (MABBA)
23 Forestgate Ave., Winnipeg MB R3P 2L2

mabba@shaw.ca
www.bodybuilding.ca
www.facebook.com/groups/231959203612085

Overview: A small provincial organization
Description: To be the provincial governing body for the sport of amateur bodybuilding in Manitoba; *Member of:* Canadian Bodybuilding Federation; International Federation of Bodybuilding; Sport Manitoba
Chief Officer(s): Chris McKee, Executive Director
mabba@shaw.ca
Fees: $50; *Committees:* Fitness; Figure; Bikini; Bodybuilding; Physique

New Brunswick Physique & Figure Association (NBPFA)
NB

Tel: 506-850-1515
nbpfa.exec@gmail.com
www.nbpfa.com
www.facebook.com/191517260859626

Overview: A small provincial organization
Description: To be the provincial governing body for the sport of bodybuilding in New Brunswick; *Member of:* Canadian Bodybuilding Federation; International Federation of Bodybuilding
Chief Officer(s): Heather LeBlanc, President, 506-850-1515
figure@heatherleblanc.ca
Adam Walker, Vice President, 506-333-3556
adam@canadianmademuscle.com
Jean LeBlanc, Secretary-Treasurer, 506-536-7084
nbpfa.exec@gmail.com

Newfoundland & Labrador Amateur Bodybuilding Association (NLABBA)
12 Walsh's Rd., Logy Bay NL A1K 3G8

www.nlabba.ca
www.facebook.com/groups/13081045661

Overview: A small provincial organization
Description: To be the provincial governing body for the sport of amateur bodybuilding in Newfoundland & Labrador; *Member of:* Canadian Bodybuilding Federation; International Federation of Bodybuilding
Chief Officer(s): Candace Critch, President
nlabba.ccritch@gmail.com
Andrew Dove, Vice President
adovenlabba.exec@gmail.com
Fees: $25

Nova Scotia Amateur Bodybuilding Association (NSABBA)
#612, 137 Solutions Dr., Halifax NS B3S 0G5

nsabba@nsabba.com
www.nsabba.com
www.facebook.com/groups/nsabbagroup

Overview: A small provincial organization founded in 1980
Description: To be the provincial governing body for the sport of amateur bodybuilding in Nova Scotia.; *Member of:* Canadian Bodybuilding Federation; International Federation of Bodybuilding
Chief Officer(s): Shira Rubin, President
Leah Johnson, Vice President
Chris Johnson, Treasurer
Karen MacLean, Secretary

Ontario Physique Association (OPA)
ON

info@physiqueassociation.ca
www.bao.on.ca
www.flickr.com/photos/ontariophysique
www.facebook.com/ontario.physique
twitter.com/AroundtheOPA

Overview: A small provincial organization
Description: To be the provincial governing body for the sport of amateur bodybuilding in Ontario; *Member of:* Canadian Bodybuilding Federation; International Federation of Bodybuilding
Chief Officer(s): Ron Hache, President
president@physiqueassociation.ca
Rudy Jambrosic, Vice President
westerndirector@physiqueassociation.ca
Angie Hache, Secretary-Treasurer, 705-694-4445
memberships@physiqueassociation.ca
Fees: $100

Saskatchewan Bodybuilding Association (SABBA)
430 Willow Bay, Estevan SK S4A 2G4

Fax: 306-634-2272
www.sabba.net
www.facebook.com/groups/2436360746
twitter.com/Sk_Bodybuilding

Overview: A small provincial organization
Description: To be the provincial governing body for the sport of amateur bodybuilding in Saskatchewan; *Member of:* Canadian Bodybuilding Federation; International Federation of Bodybuilding
Chief Officer(s): Shawn Peters, Vice-President
shawn.peters79@gmail.com
Leigh Keess, Secretary-Treasurer, 306-634-2072
fitrnmom2@yahoo.ca

Bowling

Alberta 5 Pin Bowlers' Association (A5-PBA)
432 - 14 St. South, Lethbridge AB T1J 2X7

Tel: 403-320-2695; *Fax:* 403-320-2676
Toll-Free: 800-762-3075
generalenquires@centralalberta5pin.com
www.alberta5pin.com
www.facebook.com/a5pba

Overview: A medium-sized provincial charitable organization founded in 1979
Description: To promote all levels of 5 pin bowling in Alberta
Chief Officer(s): Annette Bruneau, President
president@calgary5pin.ca
Julie Kind, Secretary

Bowling Federation of Alberta
Percy Page Centre, 11759 Groat Rd., 2nd Floor, Edmonton AB T5M 3K6

Tel: 780-422-8251; *Fax:* 780-644-4632
bpaa@bowlab.ca
www.bowlfedab.ca

Overview: A small provincial organization
Description: To promote competitive & noncompetitive bowling in Alberta
Chief Officer(s): Annette Bruneau, President
Grady Long, Executie Director
gradyed@bowlfedab.ca
Membership: 5 associations

Bowling Federation of Canada / Fédération des quilles du Canada
info@canadabowls.ca
www.canadabowls.ca
www.facebook.com/bowlingfederationofcanada

Overview: A medium-sized national organization
Description: To promote & foster the sport of bowling in Canada; To promote among the recognized national organizations in Canada, sportmanship, good fellowship & the continued interest in the future development of bowling throughout Canada
Affiliation(s): Bowling Proprietors Association of Canada; Canadian 5-pin Bowlers Association; Canadian Tenpin Federation
Chief Officer(s): Ray Brittain, President, 205-753-2341
Sheila Carr, Administrator, 613-744-5090
sheila.c5pba@gmail.com

Bowling Federation of Saskatchewan
#300, 1734 Elphinstone St., Regina SK S4T 1K1
Tel: 306-780-9412; *Fax:* 306-780-9455
bowling@sasktel.net
saskbowl.com
twitter.com/SaskBowl
Overview: A medium-sized provincial organization founded in 1984
Description: To work together through cooperation & harmonization to access & allocate funding for members programs & services in order to enhance the sports of 5 & 10 pin bowling; *Member of:* Sask Sport; Bowling Federation of Canada
Chief Officer(s): Rhonda Kurbis, Executive Director
Finances: *Funding Sources:* Sask Lotteries; sponsorship; fundraising

Bowling Proprietors' Association of BC
#209, 332 Columbia St., New Westminster BC V3L 1A6
Tel: 604-522-2990; *Fax:* 604-522-2055
bowl4fun@bowlbc.com
www.bowlbc.com
www.facebook.com/BowlBc
Also Known As: Bowl BC
Overview: A small provincial organization founded in 1954
Description: To provide opportunities for people to bowl at their individual level
Chief Officer(s): Gord Wiffen, President
Activities: Adult, youth & seniors tournaments

Bowling Proprietors' Association of Canada (BPAC)
#13, 1845 Sandstone Manor, Pickering ON L1W 3X9
Tel: 905-479-1560; *Fax:* 905-479-8613
info@bowlcanada.ca
bowlcanada.ca
www.youtube.com/c/bowlcanada
www.facebook.com/703790949700789
twitter.com/bowlcanada
Also Known As: Bowl Canada
Overview: A small national organization
Description: To general conditions in the bowling industry; To promote to the general public the benefits of bowling; To create a better relationship between the many bowling establishments across Canada; To encourage any & all practices which are in the best interests of the game
Chief Officer(s): Paul Oliveira, Executive Director
paul@bowlcanada.ca
Membership: 500 bowling centres
Activities: Youth Bowling Canada (YBC); Sunshine Bowlers; Club 55+

Bowling Proprietors' Association of Ontario (BPAO)
#202, 500 Alden Rd., Markham ON L3R 5H5
Tel: 905-940-8200; *Fax:* 905-940-8201
info@bowlontario.ca
www.bowlontario5pin.ca
Also Known As: Bowl Ontario
Overview: A medium-sized provincial organization founded in 1953
Description: To improve conditions in bowling industry; To promote prosperity & growth in the Southern Ontario 5 Pin Bowling industry
Affiliation(s): Bowling Proprietors' Association of Canada
Chief Officer(s): Marc Meconi, Executive Director
Membership: 124 bowling centres; *Member Profile:* Public bowling centres

British Columbia Tenpin Bowling Association
North Vancouver BC
www.bctenpin.com
www.instagram.com/bctenpin
www.facebook.com/groups/199885590219513
twitter.com/bctenpin
Overview: A small provincial organization
Description: To oversee the sport of tenpin bowling in British Columbia.; *Member of:* Canadian Tenpin Federation, Inc.
Chief Officer(s): Mark Westerberg, President
Bruce Taylor, Vice-President
MaryAnne Madsen, Secretary
Miriam Reid, Treasurer

Canadian 5 Pin Bowlers' Association (C5PBA) / Association canadienne des cinq quilles (AC5Q)
#206, 720 Belfast Rd., Ottawa ON K1G 0Z5
Tel: 613-744-5090; *Fax:* 613-744-2217
www.c5pba.ca
www.facebook.com/o5pba
Previous Name: Canadian Bowling Congress
Overview: A medium-sized national licensing charitable organization founded in 1978
Description: To provide programs & services to members for their participation in organized 5-pin bowling; To regulates

bowling systems to standardize the sport
Affiliation(s): Bowling Federation of Canada
Chief Officer(s): Annette Bruneau, President
Sheila Carr, Executive Director
sheila.c5pba@gmail.com
Finances: *Funding Sources:* Membership fees; government; sponsors
Membership: 11 provincial & territorial associations; *Member Profile:* 5 pin bowlers
Activities: Awards Program; *Library:* Yes (Open to Public)

Canadian Tenpin Federation, Inc. (CTF) / Fédération canadienne des dix-quilles, inc.
#18762 - 58A Ave., Surrey BC V3C 8G4
Toll-Free: 833-381-2830
ctf@tenpincanada.com
tenpincanada.com
www.facebook.com/CanadianTenpinFederationInc
twitter.com/tenpincanada
Overview: A large national organization founded in 1964
Description: To promote & foster the sport of tenpin bowling in Canada by maintaining active membership in the world's appropriate affiliated tenpin organizations, providing competitive opportunities for all skill levels, culminating in the selection of a National Team; To encourage the development of skills through a national coaching certification program
Affiliation(s): Fédération internationale des quilleurs
Chief Officer(s): Dave Kist, President
dkist@tenpincanada.com
Cathy Innes, Executive Director
cinnes@tenpincanada.com
Membership: 80,000 + 74 clubs; *Committees:* Awards; Coaching Development; Governance; High Performance Unit; Membership / Association Services; Regulatory; Special Achievement Awards; Youth
Activities: *Awareness Events:* National Team Trials, every even year, May long weekend

Fédération de pétanque du Québec
4545, av Pierre-de Coubertin, Montréal QC H1V 0B2
Tél: 514-252-3077
petanque@petanque.qc.ca
www.petanque.qc.ca
www.facebook.com/189251017803912
Aperçu: *Dimension:* moyenne; *Envergure: provinciale*
Description: Développement du sport de pétanque
Membre(s) du bureau directeur: Janick Provencher, Présidente
Membre: 4 000; 14 organismes régionaux

Manitoba 5 Pin Bowlers' Association (M5PBA)
#432, 145 Pacific Ave., Winnipeg MB R3B 2Z6
Tel: 204-925-5766; *Fax:* 204-925-5792
Toll-Free: 800-282-8069
www.m5pba.com
Overview: A small provincial organization
Member of: Manitoba Five Pin Bowling Federation, Inc.
Chief Officer(s): Marilyn McMullan, President
mgmc.hdqtrs@shaw.ca

Manitoba Five Pin Bowling Federation, Inc. (MFPBF)
145 Pacific Ave., Winnipeg MB R3B 2Z6
Tel: 204-925-5766; *Fax:* 204-925-5767
www.mfpbf.com
Overview: A small provincial organization
Description: To provide services & resources to its members which enable them to increase membership & promote bowling as a lifetime sport through effective programs at all levels of participation; *Member of:* Canadian 5 Pin Bowlers' Association; Sport Manitoba
Affiliation(s): Manitoba 5 Pin Bowlers' Association; Master Bowlers Association of Manitoba; Youth Bowling Canada - Manitoba Division
Chief Officer(s): Deanne Zilinsky, Executive Director

Manitoba Tenpin Federation
#407, 145 Pacific Ave., Winnipeg MB R3B 2Z6
Tel: 204-925-5705
www.mbtenpinfed.com
Overview: A small provincial organization
Description: To oversee the sport of tenpin bowling in Manitoba.; *Member of:* Canadian Tenpin Federation, Inc.

Master Bowlers' Association of Alberta
1 Oxbow St., Red Deer AB T4N 5C3
Tel: 403-309-6916
mbaofalberta@gmail.com
mbaofa.ca
Also Known As: MBA of A
Overview: A small provincial organization

Member of: Master Bowlers' Association of Canada
Chief Officer(s): Brian Rossetti, President

Master Bowlers' Association of British Columbia
11048 83A Ave., Surrey BC V3C 2J5
www.mbaofbc.com
Overview: A small provincial organization
Member of: Master Bowlers' Association of Canada
Chief Officer(s): Laddie MacKinnon, President
ladmac99@telus.net
Lee-Anne Wilson, Technical Director

Master Bowlers' Association of Canada
mbacnationals.com
www.facebook.com/MBAofCanada
Overview: A medium-sized national organization founded in 1970
Description: To connect master bowlers across Canada
Member Profile: NCCP certified coaches & athletes competing as Teaching Masters, Tournament Masters & Senior Masters
Activities: Annual National Championships

Master Bowlers' Association of Manitoba (MBAM)
MB
Overview: A small provincial organization
Member of: Manitoba Five Pin Bowling Federation, Inc.; Master Bowlers' Association of Canada

Master Bowlers' Association of Ontario (MBAO)
PO Box 22, 41 Temperance St., Bowmanville ON L1C 3A0
mbao.ca
www.facebook.com/185964874757498
Overview: A small provincial organization
Member of: Master Bowlers' Association of Canada
Chief Officer(s): Brenda Walters, President

New Brunswick Candlepin Bowlers Association
c/o Don Leger, 7 Lilac Cres., Fredericton NB E3A 2G7
Tel: 516-472-7592
Overview: A medium-sized provincial organization
Description: To promote candlepin bowling, a sport unique to the Maritimes & New England; *Member of:* Sport NB
Chief Officer(s): Don Leger, President
Finances: *Funding Sources:* Provincial government

Northwest Territories 5 Pin Bowlers' Association (NWT5PBA)
PO Box 2643, Yellowknife NT X1A 2P9
www.bowlnwt.ca
Overview: A small provincial organization
Description: To promote 5 pin bowling in the Northwest Territories

Ontario 5 Pin Bowlers' Association (O5PBA)
#209, 3 Concorde Gate, Toronto ON M3C 3N7
Tel: 416-426-7167; *Fax:* 416-426-7167
o5pba@o5pba.ca
www.o5pba.ca
www.facebook.com/o5pba
Overview: A medium-sized provincial organization founded in 1963
Description: To act as the governing body for 5 pin bowling in Ontario; *Member of:* Canadian 5 Pin Bowlers' Association
Chief Officer(s): John Cresswell, President
Rhonda Gifford, Coordinator, Program
Jackie Henriques, Coordinator, Finances
Membership: 10,000

Ontario Tenpin Bowling Association
185 Highland Rd. West, Kitchener ON N2M 3C1
am@otba.ca
www.otba.ca
Overview: A small provincial organization
Description: To oversee the sport of tenpin bowling in Ontario; *Member of:* Canadian Tenpin Federation, Inc.
Chief Officer(s): Charlotte Konkle, President
Membership: 16 associations

Prince Edward Island Five Pin Bowlers Association Inc.
c/o Sport PEI, 40 Enman Cres., Charlottetown PE C1E 1E6
Tel: 902-368-4110; *Fax:* 902-368-4548
Toll-Free: 800-247-6712
pei5pba@gmail.com
Overview: A medium-sized provincial organization founded in 1981

Saskatchewan 5 Pin Bowlers' Association (S5PBA)
#100, 1805 - 8th Ave., Regina SK S4R 1E8
Tel: 306-780-9412; *Fax:* 306-780-9455
bowling@sasktel.net
www.saskbowl.com/s5pba
Overview: A small provincial organization founded in 1980

Description: To develop trust & harmony among member organizations; to assist in the development & promotion of the sport of bowling through the provision of stable funding; *Member of:* Canadian 5 Pin Bowlers' Association; Bowling Federation of Saskatchewan
Chief Officer(s): Rhonda Kurbis, Executive Director
Finances: *Annual Operating Budget:* $100,000-$250,000
Staff: 1 staff member(s); 1000 volunteer(s)
Membership: 6,500; *Fees:* Schedule available

Youth Bowling Canada (YBC)
#13, 1845 Sandstone Manor, Pickering ON L1W 3X9
Tel: 905-479-1560; *Fax:* 905-479-8613
info@bowlcanada.ca
youthbowl.ca
www.facebook.com/youthbowlingcanada
twitter.com/ybcbowling
Previous Name: National Youth Bowling Council
Overview: A small national organization founded in 1963
Fees: Schedule available

Boxing

Boxing Alberta
Percy Page Centre, 11759 Groat Rd., Edmonton AB T5M 3K6
Tel: 780-427-6515; *Fax:* 780-427-1205
www.boxingalberta.com
Previous Name: Alberta Amateur Boxing Association
Overview: A small provincial organization
Member of: Canadian Amateur Boxing Association
Chief Officer(s): Roland Labbe, President
cvcwest@telus.net
Dennis Belair, Executive Director
dbelair@telus.net
Membership: 46 clubs

Boxing BC Association
PO Box 23065, Stn. RPO 11, Prince George BC V2N 6Z2
Tel: 250-564-7750; *Fax:* 250-564-7782
information@boxing.bc.ca
www.boxing.bc.ca
www.facebook.com/boxingbc
Previous Name: British Columbia Amateur Boxing Association
Overview: A small provincial organization founded in 1985
Description: To provide all citizens of British Columbia access to & participation in the opportunities, programs & activities; *Member of:* Canadian Amateur Boxing Association
Finances: *Annual Operating Budget:* $100,000-$250,000
Staff: 1 staff member(s); 150 volunteer(s)
Membership: 1,100 in 42 clubs; *Fees:* Schedule available; *Member Profile:* Competitors, coaches, officials, associated volunteers
Activities: Club shows, tournament highlights & provincial championships & Golden Gloves tournaments; *Awareness Events:* Golden Gloves, March; *Internships:* Yes

Boxing Manitoba
#421, 145 Pacific Ave., Winnipeg MB R3B 2Z6
Tel: 204-925-5658; *Fax:* 204-925-5792
info@boxingmanitoba.com
www.boxingmanitoba.com
www.facebook.com/BoxingManitoba
twitter.com/boxingmanitoba
Previous Name: Manitoba Amateur Boxing Association
Overview: A small provincial organization
Description: To govern the sport of boxing in Manitoba.; *Member of:* Canadian Amateur Boxing Association
Chief Officer(s): Alan Hogg, President
president@boxingmanitoba.com
Roland Vandal, Vice-President & Technical Director
technical@boxingmanitoba.com

Boxing New Brunswick Boxe
413 Millidge Ave., Saint John NB E2K 2N3
Tel: 506-652-8251
nbref@yahoo.ca
boxingnb.com
Also Known As: Boxing NB Boxe
Overview: A small provincial organization
Description: To govern the sport of boxing in New Brunswick.; *Member of:* Canadian Amateur Boxing Association
Chief Officer(s): Ed Blanchard, President

Boxing Nova Scotia
NS
www.boxingnovascotia.com
www.facebook.com/BoxingNovaScotia
twitter.com/boxnovascotia
Overview: A small provincial organization
Description: To govern the sport of boxing in Nova Scotia.; *Member of:* Canadian Amateur Boxing Association

Affiliation(s): Sport Nova Scotia; Nova Scotia Health Promotion & Protection
Fees: Schedule available

Boxing Ontario
#202, 3 Concorde Gate, Toronto ON M3C 3N7
Tel: 416-426-7250; *Fax:* 416-426-7367
info@boxingontario.com
www.boxingontario.com
www.facebook.com/boxingontario
twitter.com/BoxingOntario
Overview: A small provincial licensing organization founded in 1972
Description: This is the only governing body for amateur boxing in Ontario. It aims to organize, promote, develop interest & participation in the sport in the province.; *Member of:* Canadian Amateur Boxing Association
Affiliation(s): Association International de Boxe Amateur (AIBA); Ontario Ministry of Health Promotion
Chief Officer(s): Matt Kennedy, Executive Director
mkennedy@boxingontario.com
Finances: *Annual Operating Budget:* $250,000-$500,000; *Funding Sources:* Membership, Fundraising, Ministry of Tourism and Recreation
Staff: 3 staff member(s)
Membership: 80 clubs; *Fees:* Schedule available
Activities: Governing amateur boxing; sanctioning amateur events

Boxing Saskatchewan
1860 Lorne St., Regina SK S4P 2L7
Tel: 306-780-9305
boxingsask@sasktel.net
www.boxingsask.com
Also Known As: Saskatchewan Amateur Boxing Association
Overview: A small provincial organization
Description: This is a non-profit society that enforces rules & regulations governing amateur boxing in the province. It also promotes the formation of new clubs.; *Member of:* Canadian Amateur Boxing Association
Affiliation(s): Canadian Amateur Boxing Association
Chief Officer(s): Graham Craig, Executive Director
Finances: *Funding Sources:* Sask Sport
Membership: 23 clubs

Calgary Combative Sports Commission
c/o Compliance Services, Animal & Bylaw Services, City of Calgary, PO Box 2100, Stn. M #128, Calgary AB T2P 2M5
Tel: 403-648-6323; *Fax:* 403-221-3528
combativesportscommission@calgary.ca
www.calgary.ca
Previous Name: Calgary Boxing & Wrestling Commission
Overview: A small local licensing organization founded in 2007
Description: The commission acts as a regulation body for professional combative sports within the City of Calgary.; *Member of:* Canadian Professional Boxing Federation
Chief Officer(s): Shirley Stunzi, Chair, 403-710-6148
Shirley.Stunzi@calgary.ca
Kent Pallister, Administrator
Membership: 1-99

Canadian Amateur Boxing Association (CABA) / Association canadienne de boxe amateur (ACBA)
c/o Canadian Olympic Committee, 500, boul René-Lévesque ouest, Montréal QC H2Z 2A5
Tel: 514-861-3713; *Fax:* 514-819-9228
Toll-Free: 800-861-1319
info@boxingcanada.org
boxingcanada.org
www.instagram.com/boxingcanada
www.facebook.com/BoxingCa
twitter.com/boxing_canada
Also Known As: Boxing Canada
Overview: A medium-sized national organization founded in 1969
Description: To develop & maintain uniform rules & regulations to govern amateur boxing competitions in Canada; To develop coaches & officials; To organize national team programs, including development, training & competition
Affiliation(s): International Amateur Boxing Association
Chief Officer(s): Roy Halpin, Executive Director, 514-861-9322
rhalpin@boxingcanada.org
Daniel Trépanier, Director, High Performance
dtrepanier@boxingcanada.org
Jérémie Caron, Coordinator, Programs & Projects
jcaron@boxingcanada.org
Activities: Providing news & results about the sport

Canadian Professional Boxing Council (CPBC)
www.canadianboxingcouncil.com
www.facebook.com/629229317230755
twitter.com/the_cpbc

Overview: A large national organization founded in 1976
Description: To act as the sanctioning body for professional boxing in Canada; To aid in the development of professional boxing & crown new deserving champions
Activities: Crowning new champions; Working with promoters; Adhering to the uniform rules of boxing in all aspects of competition

Edmonton Combative Sports Commission (ECSC)
c/o Community Standards/Community Services, CN Tower, PO Box 2359, 10004 - 104 Ave., 12th Fl., Edmonton AB T5J 2R7
Tel: 780-495-0382; *Fax:* 780-429-6976
ecsc.ca
Previous Name: Edmonton Boxing & Wrestling Commission
Overview: A small local licensing organization founded in 1938
Description: The ECSC regulates, governs & controls boxing, wrestling & full-contact karate bouts & contests within Edmonton; enforces the CPBF safety code.; *Member of:* Canadian Professional Boxing Federation
Affiliation(s): Association of Boxing Commissions
Chief Officer(s): Pat Reid, Executive Director
pat.reid@edmonton.ca
Finances: *Annual Operating Budget:* $50,000-$100,000; *Funding Sources:* Permit fees
Staff: 24 volunteer(s)
Membership: 8; *Member Profile:* By City Council appointment

Fédération Québécoise de Boxe Olympique (FQBO)
4545, av Pierre-de Coubertin, Montréal QC H1V 0B2
Tél: 514-252-3047; *Téléc:* 514-254-2144
Ligne sans frais: 866-241-3779
info@fqbo.qc.ca
www.fqbo.qc.ca

www.youtube.com/channel/UCwrq3BlBvgb28mB6GIVsJaA
www.facebook.com/groups/5136898117
Également appelé: Boxe Québec
Aperçu: *Dimension:* moyenne; *Envergure:* provinciale
Membre de: Canadian Amateur Boxing Association
Membre: 2 000

Manitoba Combative Sports Commission (MCSC)
#628, 213 Notre Dame Ave., Winnipeg MB R3B 1N3
Tel: 204-945-1788; *Fax:* 204-948-3649
www.mbcombativesports.com
twitter.com/MBCombatSports
Previous Name: Manitoba Boxing Commission
Overview: A small provincial licensing organization founded in 1993
Description: To regulate professional boxing, kickboxing and mixed martial arts throughout the province; *Member of:* Canadian Professional Boxing Federation
Chief Officer(s): Joel Fingard, Executive Director
Activities: Licensing participants, promoters, & athletes; Supervising events

Nova Scotia Boxing Authority (NSBA)
NS
Overview: A small provincial organization founded in 1975
Description: The Nova Scotia Boxing Authority regulates professional boxing & other combat sports in the province, as well as establishes & enforces rules for the conduct of boxing, & the training of officials in accordance with national standards. The NSBA answers to the minister of health promotion & protection.; *Member of:* Canadian Boxing Federation

Prince Edward Island Amateur Boxing Association
PE
Overview: A medium-sized provincial organization
Member of: Canadian Amateur Boxing Association

Yukon Amateur Boxing Association
YT
Overview: A small provincial organization
Description: To govern the sport of boxing in the Yukon Territory.; *Member of:* Canadian Amateur Boxing Association

Broomball

Alberta Broomball Association (ABA)
11759 Groat Rd., Edmonton AB T5M 3K6
www.albertabroomball.ca
Overview: A small provincial organization
Member of: Ballon sur glace Broomball Canada
Chief Officer(s): Greg Mastervick, President
gregma@telusplanet.net
Wayne Neigel, Secretary-Treasurer
neigel@shaw.ca

Ballon sur glace Broomball Canada
145 Pacific Ave., Winnipeg MB R3B 2Z6
Tel: 204-925-5656; *Fax:* 204-925-5792
www.broomball.ca
www.facebook.com/broomballcanada
Previous Name: Broomball Canada Federation
Overview: A medium-sized national charitable organization founded in 1976
Chief Officer(s): George Brown, President, 613-253-7787
president@broomball.ca
Membership: 30,000 provincial; *Fees:* $1,000 affiliation fee/association
Activities: *Library:* Yes by appointment

British Columbia Broomball Society (BCBS)
BC
Overview: A small provincial organization
Member of: Ballon sur glace Broomball Canada

Broomball Newfoundland & Labrador
NL
Overview: A small provincial organization
Member of: Ballon sur glace Broomball Canada

Federation of Broomball Associations of Ontario
c/o Gerry Wever, President, 515 Gascon St., Russell ON K4R 1C6
Tel: 613-445-0904; *Fax:* 613-445-9844
www.ontariobroomball.ca
Previous Name: Broomball Federation of Ontario
Overview: A medium-sized provincial organization
Description: To serve broomball players, coaches & leagues in Ontario; *Member of:* Ballon sur glace Broomball Canada
Chief Officer(s): Gerry Wever, President
gerry.wever@ontariobroomball.ca
Marilyn Squibb, Contact, Registration
marilyn.squibb@ontariobroomball.ca
Archie Wilson, Contact, Technical
archie.wilson@palmerstongrain.com
Finances: *Annual Operating Budget:* $50,000-$100,000
Staff: 20 volunteer(s)
Membership: 4,000; *Fees:* Schedule available; *Committees:* Officials; Coaching; Executive
Activities: Hosting high school tournaments, qualifier tournaments, junior provincials, & senior provincials; Conducting coaching clinics

Fédération québécoise de ballon sur glace
4545, av Pierre-de Coubertin, Montréal QC H1V 0B2
Tél: 514-252-3078
fqbg.comm@gmail.com
www.fqbg.net

www.facebook.com/157977357723290
Aperçu: *Dimension:* moyenne; *Envergure:* provinciale
Description: Promouvoir le sport du ballon sur glace dans la province de Québec; Regrouper les organismes, groupes et individus intéressés au développement de ce sport; Promouvoir la sécurité dans la pratique de ce sport ainsi que d'établir et voir à l'application des règlements de sécurité; *Membre de:* Fédération canadienne de ballon sur glace
Membre(s) du bureau directeur: Martin Grondin, Président
martin.grondin@umontreal.ca

International Federation of Broomball Associations (IFBA)
4, rue du Chambertin, Montréal QC H9H 5E5
www.internationalbroomball.org
www.facebook.com/internationalbroomball
Overview: A large international organization founded in 1998
Description: To serve as the international governing body of broomball; To provide national broomball federations & associations with a means to be certified & recognized at a global level; To offer materials, training & initiatives to broomball federations; To organize the World Broomball Championships & other sanctioned international membership competitions; To promote the sport of broomball on behalf of members; To encourage fair play & a healthy lifestyle through participation in broomball
Chief Officer(s): Marc Desparois, President
president@internationalbroomball.org
Alan Jabs, General Secretary, Administration
secretary@internationalbroomball.org
Fees: $500
Activities: Organizing &/or facilitating broomball tournaments; Representing member associations & non-current members at the international level; Working to introduce broomball into new markets to enhance local communities socially & health-wise; Administering the official broomball international rule book; Coaching & officiating programs

Manitoba Amateur Broomball Association (MABA)
145 Pacific Ave., Winnipeg MB R3B 2Z6
Tel: 204-925-5668; *Fax:* 204-925-9792
Toll-Free: 866-792-7666
broomballmb@shaw.ca
www.manitobabroomball.com
Overview: A medium-sized provincial organization founded in 1982
Description: To promote the sport of broomball in Manitoba; to offer opportunities to members in competing in provincial & national championships; *Member of:* Ballon sur glace Broomball Canada; Sport Manitoba
Chief Officer(s): Cathy Derewianchuk, Executive Director
Membership: 500
Activities: School clinics; competitions; tournaments; provincials

Maritime Broomball Association
NB
Merged from: New Brunswick Broomball Association; Nova Scotia Broomball Association
Overview: A small provincial organization
Member of: Ballon sur glace Broomball Canada

Northwest Territories Broomball Association
529 Range Lake Rd., Yellowknife NT X1A 3Y1
www.nwtbroomball.com
Overview: A small provincial organization
Member of: Ballon sur glace Broomball Canada
Chief Officer(s): Val Pond, President
netmindr@theedge.ca
Membership: 250; *Fees:* Schedule available

Saskatchewan Broomball Association (SBA)
2205 Victoria Ave., Regina SK S4P 0S4
Tel: 306-780-9215; *Fax:* 306-525-4009
saskbroomball@sasktel.net
www.saskbroomball.ca
www.facebook.com/307730589864
Overview: A medium-sized provincial organization
Description: To promote multi-level programs to members & non-member groups in both competitive & recreational settings; To promote broomball within the province of Saskatchewan; *Member of:* Ballon sur glace Broomball Canada
Chief Officer(s): Stacey Silzer, Executive Director
Fees: Schedule available

Yukon Broomball Association (YBA)
4061 - 4th Ave., Whitehorse YT Y1A 1H1
www.yukonbroomball.net
Previous Name: Yukon Broomball League
Overview: A medium-sized provincial organization
Description: To promote & facilitate Broomball in the Yukon Territory.; *Member of:* Ballon sur glace Broomball Canada; Sport Yukon
Chief Officer(s): Sheena Laluk, President
Membership: 1-99

Canoeing & Rafting

Alberta Sprint Racing Canoe Association
11759 Groat Rd., Edmonton AB T5M 3K6
Tel: 780-203-3987
www.asrca.com
Previous Name: Alberta Flatwater Canoe Association
Overview: A small provincial organization
Member of: CanoeKayak Canada
Chief Officer(s): Jeffrey Baker, President
president@asrca.com

Association québécoise de canoë-kayak de vitesse (AQCKV)
4545, av Pierre-de Coubertin, Montréal QC H1V 0B2
Tél: 514-252-3086
canoekayakquebec.com

www.facebook.com/1002758901167157
Également appelé: Canoë Kayak Québec
Aperçu: *Dimension:* moyenne; *Envergure:* provinciale; *Organisme sans but lucratif;* fondée en 1979
Description: Promouvoir les activités de canoë-kayak de vitesse au Québec; *Membre de:* CanoeKayak Canada
Membre(s) du bureau directeur: Christine Granger, Directrice générale
cgranger@canoekayakquebec.com
Franck Gomez, Directeur technique
fgomez@canoekayakquebec.com
Finances: *Budget de fonctionnement annuel:* $50,000-$100,000
Membre: 2 000
Activités: *Stagiaires:* Oui *Bibliothèque:* Oui rendez-vous

Atlantic Division, CanoeKayak Canada (ADCKC)
PO Box 295, 34 Boathouse Lane, Dartmouth NS B2Y 3Y3
Tel: 902-425-5450; *Fax:* 902-425-5606
www.adckc.ca
www.instagram.com/adckc
www.facebook.com/ADCKC
twitter.com/ADCKC
Previous Name: CanoeKayak Canada - Atlantic Division
Overview: A small local organization
Member of: CanoeKayak Canada; Sport Nova Scotia
Chief Officer(s): Robin Thomson, General Manager
robin@adckc.ca
Jeff Houser, Regional Coach
regionalcoach@adckc.ca

Canoe Kayak Canada (CKC)
c/o House of Sport, RA Centre, 2451 Riverside Dr., Ottawa ON K1H 7X7
Tel: 613-260-1818; *Fax:* 613-260-5137
admin@canoekayak.ca
www.canoekayak.ca
www.instagram.com/canoekayakcan
www.facebook.com/CanoeKayakCAN
Previous Name: Canadian Canoe Association
Overview: A large national organization founded in 1900
Description: To increase the number of Canadians participating in canoeing & kayaking; To enable participants to realize excellence by providing sound athlete development programs & membership support systems; *Member of:* International Canoe Federation; Pan American Canoe Federation
Chief Officer(s): Casey Wade, Chief Executive Officer, 613-260-1818 2203
cwade@canoekayak.ca
Graham Barton, Chief Technical Officer, 613-260-1818 2306
Finances: *Annual Operating Budget:* $3 Million-$5 Million; *Funding Sources:* Sport Canada; Corporate Partners; Donations; Event Fees
Staff: 9 staff member(s); 300 volunteer(s)
Membership: 25,000+; *Member Profile:* Individuals, commercial or other groups; *Committees:* Board of Directors; Sprint; Whitewater; Marathon; Athletes; Finance; Human Resources; Planning; Nominating; Awards; History & Archives

Canoe Kayak New Brunswick (CKNB)
c/o Rob Neish, 1350 Regent St., Fredericton NB E3B 3Z4
Tel: 506-622-5050
communications@canoekayaknb.org
canoekayaknewbrunswick10.wildapricot.org
www.facebook.com/CanoeKayakNewBrunswick
twitter.com/canoekayaknb
Also Known As: Canoe Kayak NB
Overview: A small provincial organization
Description: Canoe-Kayak New Brunswick is a non-profit volunteer organization dedicated to the promotion of safe recreational paddling in the province of New Brunswick.; *Member of:* Paddle Canada
Chief Officer(s): Rob Neish, President
president@canoekayaknb.org

Canoe Kayak Nova Scotia (CKNS)
5516 Spring Garden Rd., Halifax NS B3J 1G6
Tel: 902-425-5450; *Fax:* 902-425-5606
admin@ckns.ca
www.ckns.ca
www.facebook.com/canoekayakns
twitter.com/canoekayakns
Previous Name: Canoe Nova Scotia
Overview: A medium-sized provincial organization founded in 1973
Description: To foster safe & environmentally responsible recreational canoeing, kayaking & stand up paddle boarding in Nova Scotia; *Member of:* Paddle Canada
Chief Officer(s): Mark Richard, President
president@ckns.ca

Canoe Kayak Ontario
c/o OCSRA, 118 Batson Dr., Aurora ON L4G 3T2
Overview: A medium-sized provincial organization
Description: To be a collective voice for canoeing & kayaking in Ontario; To promote the interests & support the activities of its Affiliates
Affiliation(s): Ontario Canoe Sprint Racing Affiliation; Ontario Marathon Canoe Racing Association; Whitewater Ontario
Chief Officer(s): Orest Stanko, Executive Director, 647-299-7319
orest.stanko@gmail.com

CanoeKayak BC
Fortius Athlete Development Centre, 3713 Kensington Ave., Burnaby BC V5B 0A7

Tel: 778-689-9007
info@canoekayakbc.ca
www.canoekayakbc.ca
www.facebook.com/canoekayakbc
twitter.com/CanoeKayakBC

Overview: A medium-sized provincial organization
Member of: CanoeKayak Canada
Chief Officer(s): Mary Jane Abbot, Executive Director
mj@canoekayakbc.ca

CanoeKayak Canada Western Ontario Division (WOD)
c/o Alan Potts, 22 Bowes Garden Ct., Toronto ON M1C 4L8
www.westernontariodivision.com
www.facebook.com/436833409678565
twitter.com/CKC_WOD

Overview: A small provincial organization
Chief Officer(s): Alan Potts, Treasurer
avpotts@rogers.com

Fédération québécoise du canot et du kayak (FQCK)
CP 1000, Succ. M, 4545, av Pierre-de Coubertin, Montréal QC H1V 0B2

Tél: 514-252-3001; *Téléc:* 514-252-3091
info@canot-kayak.qc.ca
www.canot-kayak.qc.ca

www.facebook.com/canotkayakQC
twitter.com/FQCK4

Nom précédent: Fédération québécoise du canot camping inc
Aperçu: *Dimension:* moyenne; *Envergure:* provinciale; *Organisme sans but lucratif; fondée en 1976*
Description: Regrouper les organismes et individus intéressés à la pratique du canotage récréatif et du canot-camping et de promouvoir la pratique de ces activités en utilisant le canot ouvert de type amérindien autrement appelé Canot Canadien
Membre(s) du bureau directeur: Marie-Christine Lessard, Directrice général
Jean A. Plamondon, Président
Bernard Hugonnier, Directeur, Technique
bhugonnier@canot-kayak.qc.ca
Fanny Dupond, Agent, Information et aux communications
Membre: 4 000; *Montant de la cotisation:* 40$; *Comités:* Cartographie; Formation
Activités: *Stagiaires:* Oui; *Service de conférenciers:* Oui

Ikaluktutiak Paddling Association
NU

Overview: A small provincial organization
Member of: Paddle Canada

Manitoba Paddling Association Inc. (MPA)
145 Pacific Ave., Winnipeg MB R3B 2Z6
Tel: 204-925-5681; *Fax:* 204-925-5792
mpa@sportmanitoba.ca
www.mpa.mb.ca
www.facebook.com/ManitobaPaddlingAssociation
twitter.com/MBPaddling

Overview: A medium-sized provincial organization founded in 1982
Description: To act as the governing body for all competitive paddling sports in Manitoba, including kayak, canoe, & dragon boat; To develop high performance athletes to compete for Manitoba nationally & to qualify for the national team; To develop coaches to coach from the grassroots to the high performance levels; To service paddlers from beginners to elite athletes; To ensure the existence of paddling clubs in Manitoba; *Member of:* CanoeKayak Canada; Sport Manitoba
Finances: *Funding Sources:* Sport Manitoba
Member Profile: Paddling clubs & athletes from Manitoba
Activities: Hosting paddling events; Promoting paddling

Ontario Canoe Kayak Sprint Racing Affiliation (OCSRA)
c/o Joanne Bryant, 118 Batson Dr., Aurora ON L4G 3T2
Tel: 905-841-5489
www.ocsra.ca

Overview: A small provincial organization founded in 1985
Description: To represent the sport of Olympic Sprint Canoe Kayak racing in Ontario.; *Member of:* CanoeKayak Canada
Chief Officer(s): Joanne Bryant, Chair
joanne.i.bryant@gmail.com

Ontario Marathon Canoe & Kayak Racing Association (OMCKRA)
ON
info@omckra.com
www.omcra.ca
www.facebook.com/OntarioMarathonPaddling

Overview: A small provincial organization
Description: To represent, promote & develop the sport of marathon canoe & kayak racing in Ontario.; *Member of:* CanoeKayak Canada

Paddle Alberta
PO Box 71039, Stn. Silversprings, Calgary AB T3B 5K2
Tel: 403-247-0083; *Fax:* 866-477-8791
Toll-Free: 877-388-2722
info@paddlealberta.org
www.paddlealberta.org
www.facebook.com/PaddleAlbertaSociety
twitter.com/PaddleAlberta

Overview: A small provincial organization founded in 1976
Description: To promote safety & sustainability in recreational canoeing & kayaking in Alberta.; *Member of:* Paddle Canada
Chief Officer(s): Karla Handy, Coordinator, Program Services
Fees: $100 not-for-profit org.; $120 club; $150 commercial org.; $400 affiliate; *Committees:* Safety & Touring; Education; Environment

Paddle Manitoba
PO Box 2663, Winnipeg MB R3C 4B3
info@paddle.mb.ca
www.paddle.mb.ca
www.facebook.com/373524412660987
twitter.com/paddlemanitoba

Previous Name: Manitoba Recreational Canoeing Association
Overview: A small provincial charitable organization founded in 1988
Description: To promote safe canoeing & kayaking in the province.; *Member of:* Paddle Canada
Affiliation(s): Manitoba Paddling Association
Chief Officer(s): Chris Randall, President
president@paddle.mb.ca
Finances: *Funding Sources:* Membership fees; tuition fees; fundraising
Fees: $30 individual; $40 family/affiliate; $50 instructor
Activities: Canoe & kayak instruction (flatwater & moving water); information presentations; resource pamphlets; *Speaker Service:* Yes *Library:* Resource Centre (Open to Public)

Paddle Newfoundland & Labrador
PO Box 2, Stn. C, St. John's NL A1C 5H4
paddle.nl@gmail.com
www.paddlenl.ca

Previous Name: Newfoundland Paddling Club
Overview: A small provincial organization
Description: To promote paddle sports in Newfoundland & Labrador; *Member of:* Paddle Canada
Chief Officer(s): Alan Goodridge, President
Fees: $20 individual; $50 associate; $25 family
Activities: *Awareness Events:* Annual Retreat, May

Prince Edward Island Canoe Kayak Association
RR#4, Alliston, Montague PE C0A 1R0
Tel: 902-962-3883; *Fax:* 902-962-3883
www.facebook.com/235534456533194

Overview: A small provincial organization
Member of: CanoeKayak Canada
Chief Officer(s): Justin Richard Batten, President
justin.heidi@windsinc.com

Recreational Canoeing Association BC (RCABC)
Vancouver BC
sec@bccanoe.com
www.bccanoe.com

Overview: A small provincial organization founded in 1984
Description: To promote safe canoeing in BC; *Member of:* Paddle Canada
Chief Officer(s): Don Flowers, President, 250-426-7389
Tony Shaw, Vice President, 250-468-7955
Finances: *Annual Operating Budget:* Less than $50,000; *Funding Sources:* Membership dues; government
Staff: 16 volunteer(s)
Membership: 350; *Fees:* $20 paddler; $40 guide; $45 instructor; $50 agency; *Committees:* Course Standards; Conservation & Access
Activities: Canoe instruction & standards

Whitewater Ontario
411 Carnegie Beach Rd., Port Perry ON L9L 1B6
Tel: 905-985-4585; *Fax:* 905-985-5256
Toll-Free: 888-322-2849
info@whitewaterontario.ca
www.whitewaterontario.ca
www.facebook.com/whitewaterontario

Overview: A small provincial organization
Description: Whitewater Ontario is the sport governing body in the province, & represents provincial interests within the national body CanoeKayak Canada.; *Member of:* CanoeKayak Canada
Chief Officer(s): Jim Tayler, President

Fees: $30 adult; $15 junior; $30 family; $75 commercial

Yukon Canoe & Kayak Club
YT
current@yckc.ca
www.yckc.ca

Overview: A small provincial organization founded in 1961
Chief Officer(s): John Quinsey, President
Fees: $20 adult; $10 child; $40 family
Activities: White water rafting; kayak polo

Yukon River Marathon Paddlers Association
4061 - 4th Ave., Whitehorse YT Y1A 1H1
Tel: 867-333-5628; *Fax:* 888-959-3846
info@yukonriverquest.com
www.yukonriverquest.com
www.facebook.com/186123281403836

Also Known As: Yukon River Quest
Overview: A small provincial organization
Description: To govern the Yukon River Quest canoe & kayak race.
Chief Officer(s): Harry Kern, President
Fees: $20 regular; $100 lifetime
Activities: *Awareness Events:* Yukon River Quest, June

Cerebral Palsy

Alberta Cerebral Palsy Sport Association (ACPSA)
Percy Page Centre, 11759 Groat Rd. NW, Edmonton AB T5M 3K6
Tel: 780-422-2904
contact@acpsa.ca
www.acpsa.ca
www.instagram.com/albertacpsports
www.facebook.com/AlbertaCPSports
twitter.com/AlbertaCPSports

Overview: A small provincial charitable organization founded in 1984
Description: To promote recreational & competitive sporting opportunities for persons with cerebral palsy, brain injury & related conditions; *Member of:* Canadian Cerebral Palsy Sports Association
Chief Officer(s): Margaret Conquest, Director, Programs
Adriana Guzman, Provincial Coordinator
Finances: *Annual Operating Budget:* Less than $50,000
Staff: 3 staff member(s); 40 volunteer(s)
Membership: 220; *Fees:* $25 basic; $75 competitive athelete; *Member Profile:* Individuals with cerebral palsy, brain injury & other related conditions
Activities: Track & field; boccia; cycling; swimming; pre-school children's program; *Speaker Service:* Yes

Association québécoise de sports pour paralytiques cérébraux (AQSPC)
4545, av Pierre-de Coubertin, Montréal QC H1V 0B2
Tél: 514-252-3143; *Téléc:* 514-254-1069
www.sportpc.qc.ca

www.facebook.com/BocciaQuebec
Aperçu: *Dimension:* petite; *Envergure:* provinciale
Membre de: Canadian Cerebral Palsy Sports Association
Membre(s) du bureau directeur: José Malo, Directrice générale, 514-252-3143 3742
jmalo@sportpc.qc.ca

Boccia Newfoundland
c/o Easter Seals Newfoundland & Labrador, 206 Mount Scio Rd., St. John's NL A1B 4L5
Tel: 709-754-1399; *Fax:* 709-754-1398
boccia@eastersealsnl.ca
www.eastersealsnl.ca
www.facebook.com/EasterSealsN

Overview: A small provincial organization
Member of: Canadian Cerebral Palsy Sports Association
Affiliation(s): Easter Seals Newfoundland & Labrador
Chief Officer(s): Eileen Bartlett, Contact

Canadian Cerebral Palsy Sports Association (CCPSA) / Association canadienne de sport pour paralytiques cérébraux (ACPSA)
c/o House of Sport, RA Centre, 2451 Riverside Dr., Ottawa ON K1H 7X7
Tel: 613-748-1430; *Fax:* 888-752-2772
info@ccpsa.ca
ccpsa.ca
www.facebook.com/CPSportCanada
twitter.com/CP_SportCanada

Overview: A medium-sized national charitable organization founded in 1985
Description: To act as umbrella group for all provincial cerebral palsy sport organizations; To design programs that are designed

for athletes with cerebral palsy & non-progressive head injuries
Affiliation(s): Cerebral Palsy International Sports & Recreation Association; International Paralympic Committee
Chief Officer(s): Peter Leyser, Executive Director
pleyser@ccpsa.ca
Jennifer Larson, Program Manager
jlarson@ccpsa.ca
Finances: Annual Operating Budget: $500,000-$1.5 Million;
Funding Sources: Government of Canada, Dept. of Heritage;
Sport Canada; donations; fundraising
Staff: 3 staff member(s); 11 volunteer(s)
Activities: Programs include cycling, soccer, athletics & boccia, swimming, bowls & powerlifting through Boccia Canada

Manitoba Cerebral Palsy Sports Association (MCPSA)

145 Pacific Ave., Winnipeg MB R3B 2Z6
mcpsa-boccia@hotmail.com
www.mcpsa.ca
www.facebook.com/CerebralPalsyAssociationOfMb
Overview: A small provincial charitable organization founded in 1984
Description: To assist in the development of sport for the disabled in Manitoba by providing an opportunity for a wider participation for persons with cerebral palsy & other neuromuscular disorders; *Member of:* Canadian Cerebral Palsy Sports Association
Membership: 60
Activities: Track & field; swimming; boccia

Ontario Cerebral Palsy Sports Association (OCPSA)

PO Box 60082, Ottawa ON K1T 0K9
Tel: 613-723-1806; *Fax:* 613-723-6742
Toll-Free: 866-286-2772
ocpsa.com
twitter.com/onCPsports
Overview: A small provincial charitable organization founded in 1981
Description: To provide, promote & coordinate competitive opportunities for persons with with cerebral palsy & other neuromuscular disorders in Ontario.; *Member of:* Canadian Cerebral Palsy Sports Association
Affiliation(s): Canadian Sport Institute - Ontario; Coaches Association of Ontario; ParaSport Ontario
Chief Officer(s): Don Sinclair, President
Fees: $20
Activities: Athletics; Boccia; other sports

SportAbility BC

780 Marine Dr. SW, Vancouver BC V6P 5YZ
Tel: 604-324-1411
sportinfo@sportabilitybc.ca
www.sportabilitybc.ca
www.instagram.com/SportAbilityBC
www.facebook.com/SportAbilityBC
twitter.com/SportAbilityBC
Previous Name: Cerebral Palsy Sports Association of British Columbia
Overview: A medium-sized provincial charitable organization founded in 1976
Description: To provide sports & recreational opportunities for people with cerebral palsy, head injury, stroke & similar disabilities at the local, regional, provincial & national level; To provide access to appropriate programming for members including segregated & integrated opportunities; *Member of:* Canadian Cerebral Palsy Sports Association
Affiliation(s): Sport BC
Chief Officer(s): Ross MacDonald, Executive Director
rossm@sportabilitybc.ca
Jade Werger, Sport Development Coordinator
jadewerger@sportabilitybc.ca
Finances: Annual Operating Budget: $250,000-$500,000;
Funding Sources: Fundraising; Sport BC; Gaming; Donations
Staff: 4 staff member(s)
Fees: $25 full; $10 recreation; *Member Profile:* Physically disabled athletes, coaches, officials, volunteers
Activities:Library: Yes by appointment

Children

KidSport Alberta

Percy Page Centre, 11759 Groat Rd., Edmonton AB T5M 3K6
www.kidsport.ab.ca
www.facebook.com/KidSportAlberta
twitter.com/KidSportAlberta
Overview: A small provincial organization
Description: To provide financial assistance to children in Alberta, aged 18 & under, who are interested in playing sports;

help with registration fees & equipment; *Member of:* KidSport Canada
Chief Officer(s): Erin Bilawchuk, Executive Director, 780-644-1815
ebilawchuk@kidsport.ab.ca
Member Profile: Local chapters
Activities: Providing grants from $100-$500

KidSport British Columbia

#230, 3820 Cessna Dr., Richmond BC V7B 0A2
Tel: 604-333-3434; *Fax:* 604-333-3401
www.kidsportcanada.ca
twitter.com/kidsport
Overview: A small provincial organization
Description: To provide financial assistance to children in British Columbia, aged 18 & under, who are interested in playing sports; help with registration fees & equipment; *Member of:* KidSport Canada; Sport BC
Chief Officer(s): Thea Culley, Manager
thea.culley@sportbc.com
Member Profile: Local chapters
Activities: Providing grants from $100-$500

KidSport Canada

Sport for Life Centre, #423, 145 Pacific Ave., Winnipeg MB R3B 2Z6
Tel: 204-925-5914; *Fax:* 204-925-5916
www.kidsportcanada.ca
www.instagram.com/kidsport.canada
www.facebook.com/kidsportcanada
twitter.com/KidSport
Overview: A medium-sized national organization founded in 2005
Description: To provide financial assistance to children aged 18 & under who are interested in playing sports; To help with registration fees & equipment
Chief Officer(s): Bryan Ezako, Manager
bezako@kidsportcanada.ca
Membership: 11 provincial/territorial chapters + 177 community chapters
Activities: Providing grants from $100-$500

KidSport Manitoba

145 Pacific Ave., Winnipeg MB R3B 2Z6
Tel: 204-925-5600; *Fax:* 204-925-5916
Toll-Free: 866-774-2220
kidsport@sportmanitoba.ca
www.kidsportcanada.ca
www.facebook.com/sportmb
twitter.com/SportManitoba
Overview: A small provincial organization
Description: To provide financial assistance to children in Manitoba, aged 18 & under, who are interested in playing sports; help with registration fees & equipment; *Member of:* KidSport Canada; Sport Manitoba
Member Profile: Local chapters
Activities: Providing grants from $100-$500

KidSport New Brunswick

#13, 900 Hanwell Rd., Fredericton NB E3B 6A2
Tel: 506-451-1320; *Fax:* 506-451-1325
www.kidsportcanada.ca
twitter.com/KidSportNB
Overview: A small provincial organization
Description: To provide financial assistance to children in New Brunswick, aged 18 & under, who are interested in playing sports; help with registration fees & equipment; *Member of:* KidSport Canada; Sport New Brunswick
Member Profile: Local chapters
Activities: Providing grants from $100-$500

KidSport Newfoundland & Labrador

1296A Kenmount Rd., Paradise NL A1L 1N3
Tel: 709-579-5977; *Fax:* 709-576-7493
www.kidsport.nl.ca
Overview: A small provincial organization
Description: To provide financial assistance to children in Newfoundland & Labrador, aged 18 & under, who are interested in playing sports; help with registration fees & equipment; *Member of:* KidSport Canada; Sport Newfoundland & Labrador
Chief Officer(s): Alicia Curran, Coordinator, Events & Marketing, Sport NL
acurran@sportnl.ca
Member Profile: Local chapters
Activities: Providing grants from $100-$500

KidSport Northwest Territories

Don Cooper Bldg., 4908 - 49th St., 3rd Fl., Yellowknife NT X1A 3X7
Tel: 867-669-8332; *Fax:* 867-669-8327
www.kidsportcanada.ca
Overview: A small provincial organization

Description: To provide financial assistance to children in the Northwest Territories, aged 18 & under, who are interested in playing sports; help with registration fees & equipment; *Member of:* KidSport Canada; Sport North Federation
Member Profile: Local chapters
Activities: Providing grants from $100-$500

KidSport Nova Scotia

5516 Spring Garden Rd., 4th Fl., Halifax NS B3J 1G6
Tel: 902-425-5450; *Fax:* 902-425-5606
www.sportnovascotia.ca/KidSport
Overview: A small provincial organization
Description: To provide financial assistance to children in Nova Scotia, aged 18 & under, who are interested in playing sports; help with registration fees & equipment; *Member of:* KidSport Canada; Sport Nova Scotia
Chief Officer(s): Colin Gillis, Coordinator
Member Profile: Local chapters
Activities: Providing grants from $100-$500

KidSport Ontario

#2041, 875 Morningside Ave., Toronto ON M1C 0C7
Tel: 416-283-0940
www.kidsportcanada.ca/ontario
www.facebook.com/KidSportOntario
twitter.com/KidSportOntario
Overview: A small provincial organization
Description: To provide financial assistance to children in Ontario, aged 18 & under, who are interested in playing sports; help with registration fees & equipment; *Member of:* KidSport Canada
Member Profile: Local chapters
Activities: Providing grants from $100-$500

KidSport PEI

40 Enman Cres., Charlottetown PE C1E 1E6
Tel: 902-368-4110; *Fax:* 902-368-4548
www.kidsportcanada.ca/prince-edward-island
www.facebook.com/176050449103403
Overview: A small provincial organization
Description: To provide financial assistance to children in Prince Edward Island, aged 18 & under, who are interested in playing sports; help with registration fees & equipment; *Member of:* KidSport Canada; Sport PEI Inc.
Chief Officer(s): Terry Bernard, Contact
tbernard@sportpei.pe.ca
Member Profile: Local chapters
Activities: Providing grants from $100-$500

KidSport Saskatchewan

1870 Lorne St., Regina SK S4P 2L7
Tel: 306-975-0875; *Fax:* 306-242-8007
Toll-Free: 800-319-4263
kidsport@sasksport.sk.ca
www.kidsportcanada.ca/saskatchewan
Overview: A small provincial organization
Description: To provide financial assistance to children in Saskatchewan, aged 18 & under, who are interested in playing sports; help with registration fees & equipment; *Member of:* KidSport Canada; Sask Sport Inc.
Chief Officer(s): Jen Peterson, Provincial Coordinator
Member Profile: Local chapters
Activities: Providing grants from $100-$500

Sport Jeunesse / KidSport Québec

CP 1000, Succ. M, 4545, av Pierre-de Coubertin, Montréal QC H1V 3R2
Tél: 514-252-3114; *Télec:* 514-254-9621
www.jeuxduquebec.com/Mes_premiers_Jeux-fr-13.php
*Également appelé:*Mes Premiers Jeux
Aperçu: Dimension: petite; *Envergure:* provinciale
Membre de: KidSport Canada; Sports Québec

Coaching

Coaches Association of Ontario (CAO)

#200A, 1 Concorde Gate, Toronto ON M3C 3N6
Tel: 416-426-7086; *Fax:* 416-426-7331
www.coachesontario.ca
www.youtube.com/user/CoachesOntario
www.linkedin.com/company/coaches-association-of-ontario
www.facebook.com/coachesontario
twitter.com/coaches_ont
Overview: A medium-sized provincial organization founded in 2002
Description: To represent coaches in Ontario; To promote coaching ethics; To provide resources for coaches; To foster an appreciation for coaches in the wider community; *Member of:*

Ontario Not for Profit Network
Affiliation(s): National Coaching Certification Program (NCCP)
Chief Officer(s): Susan Kitchen, Executive Director,
416-426-7088
susan@coachesontario.ca
Jeremy Cross, Director, 416-426-7056
jeremy@coachesontario.ca
Finances: *Annual Operating Budget:* $500,000-$1.5 Million;
Funding Sources: Federal & provincial government; Fundraising;
Events
Staff: 8 staff member(s); 12 volunteer(s)
Membership: 25,000; *Fees:* Schedule available
Activities: Conducting sport workshops; Providing support &
education for sport coaches in all levels; Advocating for
community leadership & sport programming; *Internships:* Yes

Coaches Association of PEI (CAPEI)
40 Enman Cres., Charlottetown PE C1E 1E6
Tel: 902-368-4110; *Fax:* 902-368-4548
Toll-Free: 800-247-6712
sports@coachingpei.ca
www.coachingpei.ca
www.facebook.com/SportPEI
twitter.com/SportPEI
Also Known As: Coaching PEI
Overview: A small provincial organization founded in 1992
Description: To educate, develop & promote coaching &
coaches for the benefit of athletes, sport & the community in
general; To encourage fair play, integrity & the pursuit of
excellence; *Member of:* Coaching Association of Canada
Chief Officer(s): Gemma Koughan, Executive Director
gkoughan@sportpei.pe.ca
Finances: *Funding Sources:* Membership fees; fundraising
Staff: 8 staff member(s)
Membership: 50 organizations

Coaching Association of Canada (CAC) /
Association canadienne des entraineurs
c/o House of Sport, 2451 Riverside Dr., Ottawa ON K1H 7X7
Tel: 613-235-5000; *Fax:* 613-235-5000
coach.ca
www.instagram.com/coach.ca
www.facebook.com/coach.ca
twitter.com/CAC_ACE
Overview: A large national charitable organization founded in
1971
Description: To improve implementation & delivery of National
Coaching Certification Program; To establish coaching as viable
career within the Canadian sports system; To increase the
number of qualified full-time & part-time remunerated coaches at
various levels within the sport system
Affiliation(s): Professional Arm: Canadian Professional
Coaches Association
Chief Officer(s): Lorraine Lafrenière, Chief Executive Officer,
613-235-5000 2363
llafreniere@coach.ca
Mark Donnison, Chief Operating Officer, 613-235-5000 2365
mdonnison@coach.ca
Natalie Rumscheidt, Director, Marketing & Communications,
613-235-5000 2051
nrumscheidt@coach.ca
Finances: *Funding Sources:* Sport Canada; Corporations;
Foundations
Activities: Offering the following programs: National Coaching
Certification Program (NCCP); Sport Nutrition; Petro-Canada
Sport Leadership sportif; Investors Group Community Coaching
Conferences; *Speaker Service:* Yes

Coaching Manitoba
145 Pacific Ave., Winnipeg MB R2B 2Z6
Tel: 204-925-5692; *Fax:* 204-925-5624
Toll-Free: 888-887-7307
coaching@sportmanitoba.ca
www.coachingmanitoba.ca
Overview: A small provincial organization
Description: To train coaches in Manitoba; *Member of:* Sport
Manitoba
Chief Officer(s): Susan Lamboo, Coaching Manager,
204-925-5669
susan.lamboo@sportmanitoba.ca

Commonwealth Games Canada (CGC) / Jeux du Commonwealth Canada
c/o House or Sport, RA Centre, 2451 Riverside Dr., Ottawa ON
K1H 7X7
Tel: 613-244-6868
info@commonwealthgames.ca
www.commonwealthgames.ca
www.facebook.com/265526150138420
twitter.com/cgc_jcc
Previous Name: The Commonwealth Games Association of
Canada Inc.
Overview: A small international organization founded in 1977
Affiliation(s): Commonwealth Games Federation - London,
England
Chief Officer(s): Brian MacPherson, Chief Executive Officer,
613-244-6868 4
brian@commonwealthgames.ca
Kelly Laframboise, Manager, Programs & Operations,
613-244-6868 2
kelly@commonwealthgames.ca
Finances: *Annual Operating Budget:* $100,000-$250,000;
Funding Sources: Sport Canada
Staff: 4 staff member(s); 60 volunteer(s)
Membership: 24 national + 16 individual
Activities: *Internships:* Yes *Library:* Yes (Open to Public)

British Columbia Mainland Cricket League (BCMCL)
PO Box 100, 12886 - 96th Ave., Surrey BC V3V 6A8
Fax: 604-909-2669
info@bcmcl.ca
www.bcmcl.org
www.youtube.com/thebcmcl
www.facebook.com/bcmcl.ca
twitter.com/bcmcl
Previous Name: British Columbia Cricket Association
Overview: A small provincial organization
Member of: Cricket Canada
Chief Officer(s): Nazir Desai, President, 778-318-6630
ndesai7@hotmail.com
Mohammed Talha Patel, Secretary, 604-445-9752
surreystars@hotmail.com

Canada Cricket Umpires Association Inc. (CCUA)
ON
www.ccua.ca
Overview: A small national organization
Description: To promote & advance cricket umpires throughout
Canada; *Member of:* West Indies Cricket Umpires Association
Chief Officer(s): Albert Ramcharran, President

Cricket Alberta (ACA)
#222, 7 Westwinds CR NE, Calgary AB T3J 5H2
cricket@cricketalberta.ca
www.cricketalberta.ca
www.facebook.com/155440747942009
twitter.com/CricketAlberta
Previous Name: Alberta Cricket Association
Overview: A small provincial organization founded in 1975
Member of: Cricket Canada
Chief Officer(s): Manzoor Choudhary, President, 403-605-4843
manzoor@cricketalberta.ca
Finances: *Annual Operating Budget:* $50,000-$100,000;
Funding Sources: Government; casino; membership fees
Staff: 30 volunteer(s)
Membership: 500; *Fees:* $500 team; *Member Profile:* 10 to 55
years of age; *Committees:* Executive; By-Laws; Juniors
Activities: Competitions; school cricket; coaching; training
camps

Cricket Canada
#3, 120 Woodstream Blvd., Woodbridge ON L4L 7Z1
Tel: 647-632-4218
info@cricketcanada.org
cricketcanada.org
www.linkedin.com/company/cricketcanada
www.facebook.com/GoCricketGoCanada
Also Known As: Canadian Cricket Association
Overview: A large national organization founded in 1892
Description: To foster growth & development of cricket in
Canada
Affiliation(s): International Cricket Council; Kanga Ball Canada
Chief Officer(s): Rashpal Bajwa, President
rbajwa@cricketcanada.org
Ingleton Liburd, General Manager
ingletonliburd@cricketcanada.org
Finances: *Funding Sources:* Ministry of Heritage; International
Cricket Council Volunteer Donations

Staff: 130 volunteer(s)
Membership: 30 senior/lifetime + 400 teams + 15,500 players;
Fees: $85 team
Activities: *Internships:* Yes; *Speaker Service:* Yes

Cricket Council of Ontario (CCO)
25 Pacific Wind Cres., Brampton ON L6R 2B1
Tel: 905-230-9392
www.cricketcouncilofontario.ca
www.facebook.com/CricketOntario
twitter.com/cricketontario
Previous Name: Ontario Cricket Association Inc.
Overview: A medium-sized provincial organization founded in
2009
Description: To be the provincial governing body of the sport of
cricket in Ontario.; *Member of:* Cricket Canada
Chief Officer(s): Praim Persaud, President, 416-621-2020
praimp@yahoo.com
Tan Qureshi, Manager, Public Relations
tqureshi@cricketcouncilofontario.ca
Membership: 9 associations/leagues
Activities: *Rents Mailing List:* Yes

Cricket New Brunswick (CNB)
Fredericton NB
info@cricketnb.org
cricketnb.org
www.facebook.com/CNB.Fredericton
Also Known As: Cricket NB
Previous Name: New Brunswick Cricket Association
Overview: A small provincial organization
Description: To facilitate the development & growth of the sport
of cricket; To establish cricket as a competitite sport in New
Brunswick; To promote participation in schools; *Member of:*
Cricket Canada
Chief Officer(s): Aditya Aggarwal, President
aditya.aggarwal@cricketnb.org
Devansh Bhavishi, Secretary
dbhavishi@cricketnb.org
Membership: 1-99; *Fees:* $75 full
Activities: Awareness lessons; Cricket camps

La Fédération Québécoise du Cricket Inc. / The
Quebec Cricket Federation Inc. (QCF)
7037, boul Acadie, Montréal QC H3N 2V5
Tél: 514-279-6628
www.quebeccricket.com
Aperçu: *Dimension:* petite; *Envergure:* provinciale
Membre de: Cricket Canada
Membre(s) du bureau directeur: Charles Pais, President,
514-824-0370
charles_pais@hotmail.com
Dalip Kirpaul, Secretary
qcf1@hotmail.com

Manitoba Cricket Association (MCA)
145 Pacific Ave., Winnipeg MB R3B 2Z6
Tel: 204-925-5672; *Fax:* 204-925-5703
www.cricket.mb.ca
Overview: A small provincial organization founded in 1937
Description: To make cricket available to all Manitobans.;
Member of: Cricket Canada
Chief Officer(s): Garvin Budhoo, President
garvin.budhoo@shaw.ca
Rawle Manoosingh, Executive Secretary
Finances: *Annual Operating Budget:* $50,000-$100,000;
Funding Sources: Manitoba government; Lotteries Foundation
Staff: 1 staff member(s); 10 volunteer(s)
Membership: 362; *Fees:* $900 per team
Activities: *Library:* Yes

Newfoundland & Labrador Cricket Association
NL
cricketnewfoundland@gmail.com
www.canadacricket.com/nlcricket
www.facebook.com/185095814896295
Also Known As: Cricket NL
Overview: A small provincial organization founded in 2010
Description: To be the provincial governing body of cricket in
Newfoundland & Labrador.; *Member of:* Cricket Canada
Chief Officer(s): Senthill Selvamani, President
presidentnlca@gmail.com
David Liverman, Secretary
liverman@mun.ca

Nova Scotia Cricket Association (NSCA)
PO Box 31, Lunenburg NS B0J 2C0
Tel: 902-640-2448
info@novascotiacricket.com
www.novascotiacricket.com
www.facebook.com/296868372047
twitter.com/nscricket

Overview: A small provincial organization founded in 1965
Description: To be the provincial governing body of cricket in Nova Scotia.; *Member of:* Cricket Canada; Sport Nova Scotia
Chief Officer(s): Tushar Sehgal, President
Yash Gugle, Secretary
Amit Joshi, Provincial Director

PEI Cricket Association (PEI-CA)
PE

cricketPEI@gmail.com
www.cricketpei.com
www.facebook.com/375538377835
twitter.com/CricketPEI

Overview: A small provincial organization founded in 2010
Description: To promote the development of cricket in Prince Edward Island.; *Member of:* Cricket Canada
Chief Officer(s): Sarath Chandrasekere, President
Cyril Roy, Secretary
Membership: 100; *Fees:* $20

Saskatchewan Cricket Association (SCA)
Regina SK

www.saskcricket.com
www.facebook.com/SaskatchewanCricketAssociation
twitter.com/saskcricket

Overview: A small provincial organization founded in 1977
Description: To be the provincial governing body of cricket in Saskatchewan.; *Member of:* Cricket Canada
Affiliation(s): Regina Cricket Association; Saskatoon Cricket Association
Chief Officer(s): Azhar (Sam) Khan, President
Raza Naqvi, Secretary
Membership: 2 associations

Scarborough Cricket Association (SCA)
ON

www.scarboroughcricket.ca

Overview: A small local organization founded in 1981
Description: To oversee the game of cricket in Scarborough, Ontario.; *Member of:* West Indies Cricket Umpires Association
Chief Officer(s): Sahaban Khan, President, 647-997-2483
Sahbaankhan1990@hotmail.com

Toronto Cricket Umpires' & Scorers' Association (TCU&SA)
Toronto ON

www.tcuandsa.org

Overview: A small local organization
Description: To train Canadian cricket umpires & scorers.
Chief Officer(s): Saurabh Naik, President
presidenttcusa@gmail.com
Rohan Shah, Vice-President
rohans@rogers.com
Tushar Thakar, Secretary
secretarytcusa@gmail.com

<hr>

Croquet

Croquet Canada
3 Queen Mary Dr., St Catharines ON L2R 2J3

info@croquet.ca
www.croquet.ca
www.facebook.com/croquet.ca

Overview: A large national organization
Description: To promote & develop croquet in Canada
Affiliation(s): Bayfield International Croquet Club; Caledon Croquet Club; Brighton Lawn Bowling & Croquet Club; Aboyne Croquet Club; Croquet Ottawa; Port Hope Croquet Club; Sarnia Croquet Club; Royal St. Catharines Croquet Club; Northern Lights Croquet Club; North Toronto Lawn Bowling & Croquet Club; Toronto Cricket, Skating & Curling Club; Kew Beach Lawn Bowling Club; Ward's Island Croquet Club; Mount Royal Croquet Club; Westmount Croquet Club; Le Club de Croquet Quebec; Eagle Mountain Croquet Club; Crow K Corral; Vancouver Croquet Club; Canadian Pacific Lawn Bowling Club; Buffalo Croquet Club
Chief Officer(s): Jim Wright, President
Fees: $10 student; $20 individual; $75 club; *Committees:* Communications; Finance; Nominating & Governance; Selection

Fédération des clubs de croquet du Québec (FCCQ)
CP 1000, Succ. M, 4545, av Pierre-de Coubertin, Montréal QC H1V 0B2

Tél: 514-252-3032
croquet@fqjr.qc.ca
croquet.quebecjeux.org

Aperçu: Dimension: petite; *Envergure:* provinciale; *fondée en 1973*
Description: De régir et promouvoir de croquet
Membre(s) du bureau directeur: Claude Beaudoin, Président, 819-285-2640
Rachel Baril, Secr./Trés., 819-373-5625

Membre: 635; *Montant de la cotisation:* 10$ individu

Curling

Alberta Curling Federation (ACF)
Percy Page Centre, 11759 Groat Rd., 3rd Floor, Edmonton AB T5M 3K6

Tel: 780-643-0809; *Fax:* 780-427-8103
www.albertacurling.ab.ca

Overview: A medium-sized provincial organization
Description: To promote curling throughout Alberta
Chief Officer(s): Jill Richard, Executive Director
Josephine MacGillivary, Assistant to the Executive Director
josephine@albertacurling.ab.ca

Canadian Curling Association (CCA) / Association canadienne de curling
1660 Vimont Ct., Orléans ON K4A 4J4

Tel: 613-834-2076; *Fax:* 613-834-0716
Toll-Free: 800-550-2875
boc@curling.ca
www.curling.ca
www.instagram.com/curlingcanada
www.linkedin.com/company/curlingcanada
www.facebook.com/curlingcanada
twitter.com/curlingcanada

Also Known As: Curling Canada
Overview: A large national organization founded in 1990
Description: To attract, retain & advance participants to grow the sport of curling
Affiliation(s): World Curling Federation
Chief Officer(s): Katherine Henderson, Chief Executive Officer
katherine.henderson@curling.ca
Bill Merklinger, Chief Operating Officer
bill.merklinger@curling.ca
Al Cameron, Director, Communications & Media Relations
acameron@curling.ca
Activities: Organizing championships; Facilitating tournaments, camps & development programs

Curl BC
#2001A, 3713 Kensington Ave., Burnaby BC V5B 0A7

Tel: 604-333-3616; *Fax:* 604-333-3615
Toll-Free: 800-667-2875
www.curlbc.ca
www.youtube.com/user/CurlBC
www.facebook.com/curlbc.ca
twitter.com/curlbc

Merged from: Pacific Coast Curling Association; BC Ladies' Curling Association; BC Interior Curling Association
Overview: A medium-sized provincial organization founded in 2004
Description: To deliver all curling programs & services in British Columbia
Affiliation(s): BC Interior Masters Curling Association; Pacific Coast Masters Curling Association
Chief Officer(s): Scott Braley, Executive Director & CEO, 604-333-3621
sbraley@curlbc.ca

Curling Québec
4545, av Pierre-de Coubertin, Montréal QC H1V 0B2

Tél: 514-252-3088; *Téléc:* 514-252-3342
Ligne sans frais: 888-292-2875
info@curling-quebec.qc.ca
www.curling-quebec.qc.ca

www.facebook.com/CurlingQuebec
twitter.com/curlingquebec

Également appelé: Fédération québécoise de curling
Aperçu: Dimension: moyenne; *Envergure:* provinciale; *Organisme sans but lucratif; fondée en 1976*
Description: Offrir aux amateurs de curling, et à tous ceux désirant le devenir, la possibilité de jouer au curling à l'intérieur d'une structure organisée appuyée par divers services; *Membre de:* Fédération mondiale de curling
Membre(s) du bureau directeur: Marc-André Robitaille, Directeur général, 514-252-3088 3586
marobitaille@curling-quebec.qc.ca
Membre: 10 000; *Comités:* Excellence; Championnats; Junior

CurlManitoba Inc.
#309, 145 Pacific Ave., Winnipeg MB R3B 2Z6

Tel: 204-925-5723; *Fax:* 204-925-5720
mca@curlmanitoba.org
www.curlmanitoba.org
www.facebook.com/curlmanitoba
twitter.com/curlmanitoba

Merged from: Manitoba Ladies Curling Association
Overview: A medium-sized provincial organization founded in 2000

Description: To promote the sport of curling in Manitoba
Affiliation(s): Canadian Curling Association
Chief Officer(s): Craig Baker, Executive Director
cbaker@curlmanitoba.org
Tracey Ewasko, Coordinator, Officer, Partner & Membership
tewasko@curlmanitoba.org
Debbie Schween, President
president@curlmanitoba.org
Fees: Schedule available; *Committees:* Executive; Finance; Board Development; Competition; Rules; Draw
Activities: Learn to curl clinics; coaching courses; ice technician courses; business of curling courses; club ice & rock consultation; game promotion; competition organization; establishment & governance of competition rules & regulations

Grand Masters Curling Association Ontario
c/o Thornhill Club, 7994 Yonge St., Thornhill ON L4J 1W3

grandmasterscurling.com
www.facebook.com/grandmasterscurling

Overview: A medium-sized provincial organization founded in 2007
Description: To promote curling at the Grandmasters level; To provide a provincial competition
Affiliation(s): Ontario Curling Association
Chief Officer(s): John Elstone, President, 416-283-6471
jdelstone@gmail.com
Membership: 28 teams; *Member Profile:* Men curlers 70+; Women curlers 65+; *Committees:* Executive

New Brunswick Curling Association (NBCA) / Association de Curling du Nouveau-Brunswick (ACNB)
c/o Marg Maranda, 65 Newcastle Centre Rd., Newcastle Centre NB E4B 2L2

Tel: 506-327-3445; *Fax:* 506-388-5708
Toll-Free: 800-592-2875
nbca@nb.sympatico.ca
www.nbcurling.com

Also Known As: Curling NB
Previous Name: New Brunswick Branch of the Royal Caledonian Curling Club of Scotland
Overview: A medium-sized provincial organization founded in 1971
Description: To promote curling in New Brunswick; To establish & govern rules for curling competitions in New Brunswick; *Member of:* Canadian Curling Association / Association canadienne de curling
Affiliation(s): Curl Atlantic
Chief Officer(s): Marg Maranda, Executive Director
David Burpee, President
nbcapres@gmail.com
Finances: *Funding Sources:* Canadian Curling Association; Curling Development Fund; Sponsorships
Member Profile: Members of affiliated curling clubs in New Brunswick
Activities: Organizing curling competitions; Offering learn-to-curl clinics, courses for coaching & instruction, & ice making; Supporting "Business of Curling Clinics"; Lending training equipment & resources

Newfoundland & Labrador Curling Association
c/o Harold Walters, 114 Ennis Ave., St. John's NL A1A 1Z2

Tel: 709-728-1301
www.curlingnl.ca

Overview: A small provincial organization
Member of: Canadian Curling Association
Chief Officer(s): Harold Walters, President
president@curlingnl.ca
Mark Noseworthy, Vice-President
vicepresident@curlingnl.ca
Steve Routledge, Coordinator, Tournament
tournaments@curlingnl.ca
Finances: *Funding Sources:* Membership fees; Sponsorships
Activities: Organizing clinics; Coordinating tournaments

Northern Alberta Curling Association (NACA)
#110, 9440 - 49 St., Edmonton AB T6B 2M9

Tel: 780-440-4270; *Fax:* 780-463-4519
northernalbertacurling@shaw.ca
northernalbertacurling.com
www.facebook.com/108398119223374
twitter.com/nacacurling

Overview: A small local organization founded in 1918
Description: To develop and promote the sport of curling
Chief Officer(s): Greg Empey, President
Vicki Baird, Executive Director

Northern Ontario Curling Association
PO Box 940, #4, 214 Main St. West, Atikokan ON P0T 1C0
Tel: 807-597-2875; *Fax:* 888-622-8884
Toll-Free: 888-597-8730
info@curlnoca.ca
www.curlnoca.ca
www.facebook.com/curlnoca
twitter.com/curlnoca
Merged from: Temiskaming & Northern Ontario Curling
Association; Northern Ontario Ladies Curling Association
Overview: A small local organization
Description: To promote curling throughout Northern Ontario
Chief Officer(s): Leslie Kerr, Executive Director
lesliekerr@curlnoca.ca
Member Profile: Curling clubs, teams, coaches & players in
Northern Ontario; *Committees:* Executive; Finance & Audit;
Technical; Club Development; Competitions

Northwest Territories Curling Association
PO Box 11089, 4908-49 St., Yellowknife NT X1A 3X7
Tel: 867-872-0931
nwtcurling@gmail.com
www.nwtcurling.com
www.facebook.com/nwtcurling
twitter.com/nwt_curling
Overview: A small provincial organization founded in 1990
Description: To promote curling in the Northwest Territories.

Nova Scotia Curling Association (NSCA)
5516 Spring Garden Rd., 4th Fl., Halifax NS B3J 1G6
Tel: 902-421-2875; *Fax:* 902-425-5606
nsca@sportnovascotia.ca
www.nscurl.com
Previous Name: Nova Scotia Ladies Curling Association
Overview: A medium-sized provincial organization
Affiliation(s): Canadian Curling Association
Chief Officer(s): Kevin Patterson, Technical Director
Membership: 6,000; *Member Profile:* Men's, women's & juniors
curlers; *Committees:* Operations; Finance; Competitions; Junior
Curling; Athlete Development; Ombudsman; Disciplinary;
Nominations; Awards; Curl Atlantic Reps

Nunavut Curling Association (NCA)
PO Box 2294, 902 Niaqunngusiariaq, Iqaluit NU X0A 0H0
Tel: 867-979-1090
support@curling.io
nu.curling.io
www.facebook.com/nunavutcurling
Overview: A small provincial organization

Ontario Curling Association (OCA)
#10, 1400 Bayly St., Pickering ON L1W 3R2
Tel: 905-831-1757; *Toll-Free:* 877-668-2875
information@ontcurl.com
ontcurl.com
www.facebook.com/CurlOntario
twitter.com/CurlON_
Also Known As: CurlON
Overview: A large provincial organization founded in 1875
Description: To promote & facilitate the growth & development
of curling; *Member of:* Canadian Curling Association
Affiliation(s): Ontario Curling Council; Northern Ontario Curling
Association; Ontario Special Olympics
Chief Officer(s): Stephen Chenier, Executive Director
steve@ontcurl.com
Finances: *Funding Sources:* Membership dues; competition
fees; sponsorships
Staff: 7 staff member(s)
Membership: 55,000 people in 192 clubs; *Committees:*
Executive; Finance; Governance; Nomination; Risk Register
Group
Activities: Competitions; seminars; workshops; Marketing &
Development Programme

Ottawa Valley Curling Association (OVCA)
27 Veermeer Way, Ottawa ON K2K 2L9
webmaster@ovca.com
ottawavalleycurling.ca
www.instagram.com/ovcacurls
www.facebook.com/ovcacurling
twitter.com/ovcacurls
Overview: A small local organization founded in 1959
Description: To foster curling in the Ottawa & St. Lawrence
Valleys & Outaouais
Affiliation(s): Curling Canada; CurlON; The Ottawa Sports
Council
Chief Officer(s): Tom Sinclair, President
Jim Stewart, Treasurer
Paul Hennessey, Director, Communications
communications@ovca.com
Finances: *Annual Operating Budget:* Less than $50,000

Membership: 45 clubs; *Committees:* Caledonia Cup; OVCA
Ottawa Men's Bonspiel; OVCA Mixed Bonspiel
Activities: Overseeing intermediate competitions between
Eastern Ontario & Quebec; Offering instruction to new curlers

Peace Curling Association (PCA)
PO Box 265, Grande Prairie AB T8V 3A4
Tel: 780-532-4782; *Fax:* 780-538-2485
peaccurl@telusplanet.net
www.peacecurl.org
Overview: A small local organization
Member of: Alberta Curling Federation; Canadian Curling
Association
Finances: *Annual Operating Budget:* Less than $50,000;
Funding Sources: Casino
Staff: 1 staff member(s)

Prince Edward Island Curling Association (PEICA)
40 Enman Cres., Charlottetown PE C1E 1E6
Tel: 902-368-4208; *Fax:* 902-368-4548
info@peicurling.com
www.peicurling.com
www.facebook.com/peicurling
twitter.com/peicurling
Overview: A medium-sized provincial organization
Description: To advance & promote curling as a competitive &
recreational sport in Prince Edward Island
Affiliation(s): Sports PEI, Curl Atlantic
Chief Officer(s): Amy Duncan, Executive Director
aduncan@sportpei.pe.ca
Activities: Annual provincial curling championship; Wide variety
of tachnical training

Saskatchewan Curling Association (SCA)
613 Park St., Regina SK S4N 5N1
Tel: 306-780-9202; *Fax:* 306-780-9404
Toll-Free: 877-722-2875
curling@curlsask.ca
curlsask.ca
www.facebook.com/Curlsask
twitter.com/curlsask
Also Known As: CurlSask
Overview: A small provincial organization
Description: To govern and promote the sport of curling in
Saskatchewan.
Chief Officer(s): Ashley Howard, Executive Director,
306-780-9403
ashleyhoward@curlsask.ca

Southern Alberta Curling Association (SACA)
#720, 3 St. NW, Calgary AB T2N 1N9
Tel: 403-246-9300; *Fax:* 403-246-9349
curling@saca.ca
www.saca.ca
Overview: A small local organization
Description: To encourage active participation for residents of
all ages in our communities by helping member curling clubs
offer a wide variety of programs. To assist in providing
opportunities to participate in curling.
Chief Officer(s): Brent Syme, General Manager
brent@saca.ca
Stasia Perkins, Director, Clubs & Competitions
stasia@saca.ca

Toronto Curling Association (TCA)
#6A-1409, 170 The Donway West, Toronto ON M3C 2E8
Tel: 647-523-1264
general@torontocurling.com
www.torontocurling.com
www.facebook.com/torontocurling
twitter.com/torontocurling
Overview: A small local organization founded in 1964
Description: To promote curling in the Greater Toronto Area
Chief Officer(s): Danielle Inglis, President
danielle.inglis@torontocurling.com
Finances: *Annual Operating Budget:* $50,000-$100,000;
Funding Sources: Grants; Tournament entry fees
Staff: 15 volunteer(s)
Membership: 24 clubs
Activities: Organizing curling games

World Curling Federation (WCF)
3 Atholl Cres., Perth PH1 5NG Scotland
info@worldcurling.org
www.worldcurling.org
www.youtube.com/WorldCurlingTV
www.linkedin.com/company/world-curling-federation
www.facebook.com/WorldCurlingFederation
twitter.com/worldcurling
Previous Name: International Curling Federation
Overview: A medium-sized international organization founded in
1966

Description: To represent curling internationally & to facilitate
the growth of the sport through a network of member nations;
Member of: General Association of International Sports
Federations (GAISF)
Chief Officer(s): Kate Caithness, President
Bent Ånund Ramsfjell, Vice-President
Colin Grahamslaw, Secretary General
Membership: 53 member associations; *Member Profile:*
National associations; *Committees:* Athlete; Competition &
Rules; Finance; Governance; Hall of Fame Induction; Americas
Zonal; European Zonal; Pacific-Asia Zonal
Activities: World & World Junior & World Senior Curling
Championships, Men & Women; World Wheelchair Curling
Championship, Mixed teams

Yukon Curling Association (YCA)
4061 - 4th Ave., Whitehorse YT Y1A 1H1
Tel: 867-668-7121; *Fax:* 867-667-4237
www.yukoncurling.ca
Overview: A small provincial organization founded in 1974
Affiliation(s): Watson Lake Curling Club; Mayo Curling Club
Chief Officer(s): Laura Eby, Executive Director
executivedirector@yukoncurling.ca
Membership: 1,000; *Member Profile:* Seniors; masters; adults;
juniors; youth; little rockers

Darts

Association de Dards du Québec inc. (ADQDA) / Québec Dart Association Inc.
#3, 3177, rue Notre-Dame, Lachine QC H8S 2H4
Tél: 514-637-2858
www.adqda.com

www.facebook.com/groups/ADQDA
Aperçu: *Dimension: moyenne; Envergure: provinciale;
Organisme sans but lucratif; fondée en 1978*
Description: L'A.D.Q. est la seule et unique Association de
dards qui représente la Fédération de dards du Canada et aussi
la seule qui est reconnue par la Fédération de Dards mondiale
(World Darts Federation); *Membre de:* National Darts Federation
of Canada
Membre(s) du bureau directeur: Maggie LeBlanc, Présidente
maggieleblanc417@hotmail.com
Membre: 700; *Montant de la cotisation:* $25

Darts Alberta
c/o Sandi Orr, PO Box 163, #14, 9977 - 178 St. NW, Edmonton
AB T5T 6J6
Tel: 780-908-0475
administrator@dartsalberta.com
www.dartsalberta.com
Overview: A small provincial organization
Description: To provide recreational & competitive opportunities
for darts players of all levels in Alberta; *Member of:* National
Darts Federation of Canada
Chief Officer(s): Dean Lawson, President, 403-527-0847
president@dartsalberta.com
Sandi Orr, Administrator
administrator@dartsalberta.com
Fees: $40 individual
Activities: Sport programs; educational opportunities for
coaches & officials; recognition programs

Darts British Columbia Association (DBCA)
c/o Donna Bisaro, #901, 668 Columbia St., New Westminster
BC V3M 1A9
executive@dartsbc.ca
www.dartsbc.ca
www.facebook.com/BcDarts
Overview: A small provincial organization
Description: To provide recreational & competitive opportunities
for darts players of all levels in British Columbia; *Member of:*
National Darts Federation of Canada
Chief Officer(s): Ray Bode, Provincial Director
raybode@shaw.ca
Suzie Letude, Vice President
suzie_letrud1@hotmail.com
Membership: 8 leagues/associations; *Fees:* $5

Darts Ontario
ON
Tel: 905-426-7493; *Fax:* 905-426-8270
provincialdirector@dartsontario.com
www.dartsontario.com
Overview: A small provincial organization

Description: To provide recreational & competitive opportunities for darts players of all levels in Ontario; *Member of:* National Darts Federation of Canada
Chief Officer(s): Susan Hine, President & Provincial Director, 905-426-7493, Fax: 905-426-8270
president@dartsontario.com
Stuart Rutten, Secretary, 416-951-6503
secretary@dartsontario.com
Fees: $18 affiliate; $20 youth; $23 adult

Darts Prince Edward Island
PE

dartspei.ca
Also Known As: Darts PEI
Overview: A small provincial organization
Description: To provide recreational & competitive opportunities for darts players of all levels in Prince Edward Island; *Member of:* National Darts Federation of Canada
Chief Officer(s): Heidi Duchesne, Provincial Director
director@dartspei.com
Darren MacNevin, President
president@dartspei.com
Joey Gallant, Vice President
vice-president@dartspei.com

Ligue de dards Ungava
331, 2e rue, Chibougamau QC G8P 1M4

Tél: 418-748-8060
Aperçu: *Dimension:* petite; *Envergure:* locale
Membre(s) du bureau directeur: Claude Patoine, Président

Manitoba Darts Association Inc. (MDAI)
c/o MDAI Membership Director, 720 Consol Ave., Winnipeg MB R2K 1T2

info@manitobadarts.com
www.manitobadarts.com
www.facebook.com/ManitobaDartsAssociationInc
Overview: A small provincial organization
Member of: National Darts Federation of Canada
Chief Officer(s): Ron Looker, President, 204-997-7579
ronlooker@hotmail.com
Kim Clawson, Provincial Director
kimmyclawson@live.com
Fees: $30

National Darts Federation of Canada (NDFC) / Fédération nationale de dards du Canada
Tel: 902-401-9650
secretary@ndfc.ca
www.ndfc.ca
Overview: A medium-sized national organization founded in 1977
Description: To promote & organize darts events & promote the betterment of the game
Affiliation(s): World Darts Federation
Chief Officer(s): Bill Hatter, President
president@ndfc.ca
Finances: *Annual Operating Budget:* $50,000-$100,000
Staff: 7 staff member(s)
Membership: 5,000-14,999
Activities: Provincial / national championships; international events

New Brunswick Dart Association (NBDA)
526 Rte. 845, Kingston NB E3N 1P5

Tel: 506-832-7293
www.nbdarts.com
Overview: A small provincial organization
Description: To provide recreational & competitive opportunities for darts players of all levels in New Brunswick; *Member of:* National Darts Federation of Canada
Chief Officer(s): Rick Kirkpatrick, National Director, 506-609-2860
kirkpatrick@rogers.com
Debbie Mullin, National Youth Director, 506-696-0230
ikemullin@rogers.com
Bill White, President, 506-832-7293

Newfoundland & Labrador Darts Association
NL
Overview: A medium-sized provincial organization founded in 1977
Member of: National Darts Federation of Canada
Chief Officer(s): Cavelle Taylor, President, 709-582-2952
cavtaylor@yahoo.ca
Bob Gulliver, Contact
bobgulliver@hotmail.com

Northern Ontario Darts Association (NODA)
c/o Chris Arsenault, #159, 163 Louis St., Sudbury ON P3B 2H4
Tel: 807-625-9373; *Fax:* 807-625-9391
nodarts.ca
twitter.com/dartsno

Overview: A small provincial organization
Description: To provide recreational & competitive opportunities for darts players of all levels in Northern Ontario; *Member of:* National Darts Federation of Canada
Chief Officer(s): Christine Stark, President
czachary@tbaytel.net
Chris Arsenault, Secretary, 705-626-1030
180king@personainternet.com

Saskatchewan Darts Association (SDA)
c/o Pat Copeman, 17 Eden Ave., Regina SK S7R 5M2
Tel: 306-949-5180
www.saskdarts.com
Overview: A small provincial organization
Description: To provide recreational & competitive opportunities for darts players of all levels in Saskatchewan; *Member of:* National Darts Federation of Canada
Chief Officer(s): Elaine Walker, President, 306-651-0481
empearson@shaw.ca
Judy Cleaveley, Secretary, 306-865-2028
hbaccount@sasktel.net

Deafness

Association sportive des sourds du Québec inc. (ASSQ)
4545, av Pierre-de-Coubertin, Montréal QC H1V 0B2
Tél: 514-252-3049
www.assq.org

www.youtube.com/user/1ASSQ
www.facebook.com/ASSQ1
twitter.com/ASSQ_Nouvelles
Nom précédent: Association amateur des sports des sourds du Québec; Fédération sportive des sourds du Québec inc.
Aperçu: *Dimension:* moyenne; *Envergure:* provinciale; fondée en 1968
Description: Promouvoir le sport, les loisirs et l'activité physique chez les personnes sourdes et malentendantes du Québec; *Membre de:* Canadian Deaf Sports Association
Membre(s) du bureau directeur: Christopher Séguin, Directeur générale
cseguin@assq.org

Canadian Deaf Ice Hockey Federation (CDIHF)
ON
assc-cdsa.com
www.facebook.com/canada.deafhockey
twitter.com/CDNdeafhockey
Previous Name: Canadian Hearing Impaired Hockey Association
Overview: A small national charitable organization founded in 1983
Description: To offer ice hockey programs for deaf & hard of hearing participants; To administer a hockey team to represent Canada internationally; *Member of:* Canadian Deaf Sports Association
Affiliation(s): Canadian Hockey Association; Ontario Deaf Sports Association, Inc.
Finances: *Funding Sources:* Donations; Sponsorships
Activities: Hosting training camps & hockey schools; Organizing the CDIHC Hockey Championships; Participating in the World Deaf Ice Hockey Championship

Diving

Alberta Diving
AB
www.albertadiving.ca
Overview: A small provincial organization
Description: To act as the governing body in Alberta for the Olympic sport of amateur diving; to strive for personal & organizational excellence in all areas of diving
Finances: *Funding Sources:* Fundraising; Sponsorships
Activities: Promoting sportsmanship & respect for rules; Encouraging community involvement; Promoting both the physical & mental well being of members

Alberta Underwater Council (AUC)
Percy Page Building, 11759 Groat Rd., 2nd Fl., Edmonton AB T5M 3K6
Tel: 780-427-9125; *Fax:* 780-427-8139
Toll-Free: 888-307-8566
info@albertaunderwatercouncil.com
www.albertaunderwatercouncil.com
Overview: A medium-sized local organization founded in 1962
Description: To represent responsible participation in & awareness of underwater activities
Affiliation(s): Canadian Underwater Games Association
Chief Officer(s): Cathie McCuaig, Executive Director, 780-427-9125, Fax: 780-427-8139

Finances: *Funding Sources:* Alberta Gaming; Alberta Sport Recreation Parks & Wildlife Foundation
Membership: 600 individual; *Fees:* Schedule available
Activities: *Awareness Events:* Divescapes

Association Internationale pour le Développement de l'Apnée Canada
6211, av de la Mayenne, Montréal QC H1M 1T4
aidacanada.org
www.facebook.com/AidaCanada
twitter.com/aidacanada
Also Known As: AIDA Canada
Overview: A large national organization founded in 2009
Description: To develop the sport of freediving in Canada as both a pastime & an athletic pursuit
Affiliation(s): AIDA International
Chief Officer(s): Roberta Cenedese, President
Finances: *Funding Sources:* Membership dues; Donations
Fees: $25; *Member Profile:* Freedivers; *Committees:* Competition; Social Media; Website
Activities: Supporting freediving clubs across Canada; Offering information & resources for members; Organizing competitions

British Columbia Diving
PO Box 45069, Stn. Ocean Park, Surrey BC V4A 1N5
Tel: 604-531-5576; *Fax:* 604-542-0387
www.bcdiving.ca
Also Known As: Canadian Amateur Diving Association (BC Section)
Previous Name: Dive B.C.
Overview: A small provincial charitable organization founded in 1986
Description: To develop and promote diving throughout British Columbia by encouraging participation, growth and personal success among members; *Member of:* Diving Plongeon Canada
Chief Officer(s): Jayne McDonald, Executive Director
edbcdiving@gmail.com
Lisa Breure, Director, Communications
bcdiving.perfect10@gmail.com
Finances: *Funding Sources:* Province of British Columbia through the Ministry of Community, Sport and Cultural Development
Staff: 3 staff member(s)
Fees: Schedule available; *Member Profile:* Divers, associations, coaches, officials

Dive Ontario
Toronto Pan Am Sports Centre, #2037, 875 Morningside Ave., Toronto ON M1C 0C7
contactus@diveontario.com
www.diveontario.com
www.facebook.com/DiveOntario
Overview: A small provincial organization
Description: To provide programs & services to its members; To support the development of athletes, coaches & officials
Affiliation(s): Community & recreation centres around the province; Dive Plongeon Canada
Chief Officer(s): Pam Julian, Executive Director
executivedirector@diveontario.com
Membership: 11 clubs; *Member Profile:* Diving clubs in Ontario; *Committees:* HP Implementation; Sport Development; Media & Marketing

Diving Plongeon Canada (DPC) / Association canadienne du plongeon amateur Inc.
#312, 700 Industrial Ave., Ottawa ON K1G 0Y9
Tel: 613-736-5238; *Fax:* 613-736-0409
info@diving.ca
diving.ca
www.instagram.com/divingcanada
www.facebook.com/DivingCanada
twitter.com/divingcanada
Also Known As: Canadian Amateur Diving Association Inc.
Overview: A medium-sized national charitable organization founded in 1967
Description: To promote the growth & awareness of diving in Canada; To contribute to the development of globally accepted standards of diving; To support the rules & regulations of international competition; *Member of:* FINA
Affiliation(s): Aquatics Federation of Canada; Swimming Natation Canada; Synchronized Swimming; Water Polo Canada
Chief Officer(s): Penny Joyce, Chief Operating Officer
penny@diving.ca
Mitch Geller, Chief Technical Officer
mitch@diving.ca
Maelle Dancause, Manager, Communications
maelle@diving.ca
Jeff Feeney, Director, Events & Communications
jeff@diving.ca
Finances: *Funding Sources:* Government; Self Funding; Donations; Sponsorships
Staff: 10 staff member(s)

Membership: 67 local diving clubs + 4,000 high performance athletes; *Member Profile:* Diving associations; Local diving clubs; High performance athletes; *Committees:* Athletes; Technical; Officials; Rules & Regulations
Activities: Providing programs & services for participants to achieve excellence & self-fulfillment; Obtaining media coverage & increasing spectators at events; Developing elite athletes; Communicating with members; Hosting an annual general meeting; Presenting DPC awards

Fédération du plongeon amateur du Québec (FPAQ)
4545, av Pierre-de Coubertin, Montréal QC H1V 0b2
Tél: 514-252-3096; *Téléc:* 514-252-3094
info@plongeon.qc.ca
www.plongeon.qc.ca

twitter.com/PlongeonQuebec
Également appelé: Plongeon Québec
Aperçu: *Dimension:* moyenne; *Envergure: provinciale; fondée en 1971*
Description: Régir le plongeon sur l'ensemble du territoire québécois; promouvoir le plongeon et sa pratique; tenir et organiser des stages de formation et des compétitions de plongeon; regrouper les associations de plongeon; *Membre de:* Diving Plongeon Canada; Sports-Québec; AQUM; Club de la médaille d'or; Institut national du sport-Montréal
Membre(s) du bureau directeur: Claudie Dumais, Directrice exécutive
cdumais@plongeon.qc.ca
Finances: *Budget de fonctionnement annuel:* $250,000-$500,000
Personnel:3 membre(s) du personnel; 100+ bénévole(s)
Membre: 3,000; *Montant de la cotisation:* Barème; *Comités:* Entraîneurs; Officiels; L'élite
Activités: *Stagiaires:* Oui; *Service de conférenciers:* Oui

Fédération québécoise des activités subaquatiques (FQAS)
4545, av Pierre-de Coubertin, Montréal QC H1V 0B2
Tél: 514-252-3009; *Téléc:* 514-254-1363
Ligne sans frais: 866-391-8835
info@fqas.qc.ca
www.fqas.qc.ca

www.facebook.com/FederationQuebecoisedesActivitesSubaquat iques
Aperçu: *Dimension:* moyenne; *Envergure: provinciale; Organisme sans but lucratif; fondée en 1970*
Description: Regrouper les adeptes de la plongée et des activités subaquatiques; promouvoir la sécurité dans la pratique des activités subaquatiques; informer et renseigner ses membres et la population sur les bienfaits de la pratique; promouvoir ces activités comme moyen de formation et comme loisir
Affiliation(s): Confédération mondiale des activités subaquatiques
Membre(s) du bureau directeur: Alain Gauthier, Directeur général
direction@fqas.qc.ca
Finances: *Budget de fonctionnement annuel:* $250,000-$500,000; *Fonds:*Gouvernement provincial
Personnel:2 membre(s) du personnel; 150 bénévole(s)
Membre: 100 institutionnel + 2 200 individu; *Montant de la cotisation:* $34.50 individu; $56 famille
Activités: *Stagiaires:* Oui; *Service de conférenciers:* Oui
Bibliothèque: Librairie FQAS rendez-vous

Manitoba Diving Association
#430, 145 Pacific Ave., Winnipeg MB R3B 2Z6
Tel: 204-925-5654; *Fax:* 204-925-5792
www.manitobadiving.ca
www.facebook.com/mbdiving
twitter.com/manitobadiving
Overview: A small provincial organization
Description: Provides strong ethical and values driven foundation for diving throughout Manitoba and Canada, and supports athletic development, personal growth and community awareness through excellence in leadership; *Member of:* Diving Plongeon Canada
Chief Officer(s): Ken Stevens, Executive Director
diving@sportmanitoba.ca

Manitoba Underwater Council (MUC)
PO Box 711, Winnipeg MB R3C 2K3
info@manunderwater.com
www.manunderwater.com
Overview: A medium-sized provincial charitable organization founded in 1962

Description: To coordinate, support & promote scuba diving & underwater activities in Manitoba; To encourage safety, advocacy, & conservation; *Member of:* Sport Manitoba
Chief Officer(s): Bill Manueiler, President
president@manitobaunderwater.ca
Ed Stark, Treasurer
treasurer@manitobaunderwater.ca
Jacqui Dufault, Agent, Communications
communications@manitobaunderwater.ca
Finances: *Annual Operating Budget:* Less than $50,000; *Funding Sources:* Provincial Government & membership fees
Staff: 10 staff member(s); 10 volunteer(s)
Membership: 27 institutional + 150 individual; *Fees:* $20 individual; $25 family; $50 corporate; *Member Profile:* Certified scuba divers, divers in training
Activities: Spear fishing competition, pumpkin dive, super dive, underwater football competition

Ontario Underwater Council (OUC)
#109, 1 Concorde Gate, Toronto ON M3C 3C6
Tel: 416-426-7033; *Fax:* 416-426-7280
ouc@underwatercouncil.com
www.underwatercouncil.com
www.facebook.com/groups/39720054237
Overview: A small provincial organization
Description: To represent all divers in Ontario; to promote the sport of scuba diving
Chief Officer(s): Ronald J. Bogart, President
ouc.president@underwatercouncil.com
Sasha Ilich, Director, Communications
communications@underwatercouncil.com
Membership: 2,600+; *Fees:* $20-$37 individual; $145 commercial; schedule for clubs

Prince Edward Island Underwater Council
PE
Overview: A small provincial organization
Description: The PEI Underwater Council's mission is to help support & promote the sport of scuba diving in Prince Edward Island through safety, advocacy, cultural & environmental awareness, self-governance & education.

Saskatchewan Diving
1870 Lorne St., Regina SK S4P 2L7
Tel: 306-780-9405; *Fax:* 306-780-6021
info@divesask.ca
www.saskdiving.ca
www.facebook.com/divesask
twitter.com/divesask
Also Known As: Sask Diving Inc.
Overview: A small provincial organization
Description: To develop & promote safe diving; To ensure that diving clubs operate with safety & integrity; To provide opportunities for self fulfillment & the pursuit of excellence; *Member of:* Diving Plongeon Canada
Chief Officer(s): Karen Swanson, Executive Director
kswanson@divesask.ca
Finances: *Funding Sources:* Sask Lotteries
Staff: 3 staff member(s)
Member Profile: Diving clubs; Individuals, such as coaches, athletes, officials, parents, & executive members
Activities: Ensuring coaches are trained through the National Coaching Certification Program

Saskatchewan Underwater Council
PO Box 7651, Saskatoon SK S7K 4R4
Tel: 306-374-8341; *Fax:* 306-374-8341
executive@saskuc.com
www.saskuc.com
Overview: A small provincial organization
Description: To represent those interested in underwater activities in Saskatchewan.
Chief Officer(s): Clifford Lange, Contact, 306-374-8341
Fees: $30 single; $35 family
Activities: Newsletter; Diver Magazine; Information on Dive Sites

Underwater Council of British Columbia (UCBC)
BC
underwatercouncil.bc@gmail.com
www.underwatercouncilbc.org
www.youtube.com/user/TheUCBC
www.facebook.com/246182652097184
Overview: A small provincial organization
Description: To represent recreational divers in British Columbia
Chief Officer(s): Adam Taylor, President
Scott Meixner, Secretary
Fees: Free

Yukon Underwater Diving Association (YUDA)
YT
www.yukonweb.com/community/yuda
Overview: A small provincial organization
Description: The Yukon Underwater Diving Association (YUDA) is a non-profit organization created by sport divers to promote the sport of underwater diving in the Yukon, Northern British Columbia & South East Alaska.
Chief Officer(s): Allyn Lyon, President
alyon@yukon.net
Doug Davidge, Contact
ddavidge@yknet.yk.ca

Equestrian Sports & Activities

Alberta Equestrian Federation (AEF)
#100, 251 Midpark Blvd. SE, Calgary AB T2X 1S3
Tel: 403-253-4411; *Fax:* 403-252-5260
Toll-Free: 877-463-6233
info@albertaequestrian.com
www.albertaequestrian.com
www.instagram.com/alberta_equestrian
www.facebook.com/AlbertaEquestrian
twitter.com/ab_equestrian
Overview: A small provincial organization founded in 1978
Member of: Equine Canada
Chief Officer(s): Les Oakes, President
lesoakes@gmail.com
Sonia Dantu, Executive Director
execdir@albertaequestrian.com
Finances: *Annual Operating Budget:* $100,000-$250,000; *Funding Sources:* Alberta Sport, Recreation, Parks & Wildlife Foundation
Staff: 6 staff member(s)
Membership: 12,000+; *Fees:* $50 individual; $110 family; $75 club; $120 business; *Committees:* Executive; Rec. & Trails; Competitions; Officials; Trail Ride
Activities: Administering equestrian NCCP Level I & II for Western, English & Driving Coaching; Coordinating, sanctioning & administering body for equestrian sport & recreation in Alberta; Providing assistance & expertise in areas such as competitions, coaching, officials, games & sporting events, recreation & travel insurance, awards, human & equine medication control; *Awareness Events:* Annual Trail Ride

Alberta Horse Trials Association (AHTA)
c/o Aislyn Havell, Membership Secretary, #23, 38440 Range Rd. 284, Red Deer County AB T4S 2E2
albertahorsetrials@gmail.com
www.albertahorsetrials.com
Overview: A small provincial organization
Description: To promote & develop 3-day eventing in Alberta & Canada & assist in producing Olympic athletes
Affiliation(s): Canadian Equestrian Federation
Chief Officer(s): Kristine Haut, President
ahtapresident@gmail.com
Finances: *Annual Operating Budget:* Less than $50,000; *Funding Sources:* National Government, Provincial Government
Staff: 13 volunteer(s)
Membership: 170 student; 240 individual; 20 associate; *Fees:* $30 associate; $50 junior; $60 senior; $120 family; *Committees:* Membership; Competitions; Special Events; Communications; Athlete Development; Clinics; Marketing

Association Trot & Amble du Québec (ATAQ) / Québec Trotting & Pacing Society
#216, 5375, rue Paré, Montréal QC H4P 1P7
Tél: 514-731-9484; *Ligne sans frais:* 800-731-9484
courses@qc.aira.com
www.trotetamble.com
Aperçu: *Dimension:* moyenne; *Envergure:* provinciale
Description: Coopérer avec les promoteurs afin de s'assurer de la bonne conduite des programmes de courses aux différents hippodromes du Québec; améliorer les lois et règlements en vue de favoriser le sport des courses sous harnais; représenter et aider tous les members; encourager et promouvoir les courses d'élevage québécois et les courses régulières; collaborer avec les différents organismes afin d'établir un juste équilibre pour le bien-être de l'industrie
Membre(s) du bureau directeur: Marc Camirand, Président
Gilles Fortier, Secrétaire général
Montant de la cotisation: Barème
Activités: Service d'assurances; activités sociales; promotion

Atlantic Canada Trail Riding Association (ACTRA)
c/o April Haliburton, 266 Maloney Rd., Admiral Rock NS B0N 2H0
www.atlanticriders.ca
Overview: A small local organization founded in 1980

Description: To promote safe horsemanship & the use of sensible riding mounts; To standardize judging in distance riding; *Member of:* Canadian Long Distance Riding Association
Chief Officer(s): Blake Storey, President
clubchair@atlanticriders.ca
Nicole Lavoie Mattatall, Vice President, Membership
barnbraids@gmail.com
April Haliburton, Treasurer
treasurer@ atlanticriders.ca
Fees: $20 single; $30 family

British Columbia Competitive Trail Riders Association (BCCTRA)
BC

bcctra@shaw.ca
www.bcctra.ca

Overview: A small provincial organization founded in 1983
Description: To promote & improve the rapidly growing sport of competitive trail riding in BC; *Member of:* Canadian Long Distance Riding Association
Chief Officer(s): Tammy Mercer, President, 250-335-3390
ridingforfreedomranch@shaw.ca
Christine Pacukiewicz, Secretary
Fees: $20 supporter; $25 senior (65+)/junior; $30 senior; $60 family; $300 lifetime; *Member Profile:* Senior & junior riders
Activities: Two yearly meetings

Canadian Dressage Owners & Riders Association
c/o Donald J. Barnes, #13, 1475 Upper Gage Ave., Hamilton ON L8T 1E6

Tel: 905-975-0055
dressagegames@aol.com
www.cadora.ca
www.facebook.com/CadoraInc

Also Known As: CADORA Inc.
Overview: A medium-sized national organization founded in 1969
Description: To promote interest in dressage riding as a sport throughout Canada; To develop the sport consistent with the principles of the international governing body of the equestrian Olympic disciplines; To ensure progressions leading to competitive International levels; *Member of:* Equine Canada; Ontario Equestrian Federation
Affiliation(s): Dressage Canada
Chief Officer(s): Donald J. Barnes, President & Editor, Omnibus
Finances: *Funding Sources:* Fundraising; Donations; Membership fees
Member Profile: Dressage riders from across Canada
Activities: Providing educational workshops & clinics; Coordinating competitions & matches; Presenting awards; Arranging demonstrations of dressage riding in all areas of Canada

Canadian Pony Club (CPC)
info@canadianponyclub.org
www.canadianponyclub.org
www.instagram.com/canadianponyclub
www.facebook.com/CanadianPonyClub
Overview: A medium-sized national organization founded in 1934
Description: To encourage & instruct young people to ride & care for their horses, while promoting loyalty, character & sportsmanship; *Member of:* Equine Canada
Affiliation(s): Ontario Equestrian Federation
Chief Officer(s): Jane Goodliffe, Executive Director
national_chair@canadianponyclub.org
Finances: *Funding Sources:* Fees
Staff: 1000 volunteer(s)
Membership: 2,100+ in 150 branches; *Member Profile:* Young people between the ages of 6-21 who wish to learn all about horses; *Committees:* Awards & Recognition; Equine Canada; Finance; Governance; Horse Masters Program; Human Resources; Information Technology; Management; Marketing & Fundraising; National Communications; National Dressage; National Education; National Prince Philip Games; National Quiz; National Rally; National Show Jumping; National Testing; National Tetrathlon; Ombudsman; Risk Management; Strategic Planning
Activities: Instruction in dressage, show jumping, Tetrathlon

Canadian Sport Horse Association (CSHA)
PO Box 970, 7904 Franktown Rd., Richmond ON K0A 2Z0
Tel: 613-686-6161; *Fax:* 613-686-6170
csha@canadian-sport-horse.org
www.c-s-h-a.org
www.facebook.com/canadiansporthorseassociation
Overview: A small national organization founded in 1933
Description: To ensure the production & promotion of a sound, solid horse, with a good disposition, capable of competing

successfully in the Olympic Disciplines at all levels of competition; *Member of:* World Breeding Federation
Chief Officer(s): Christine Baker, President
cbcfarm@hotmail.com
Membership: 718; *Fees:* $35 associate/youth; $90 individual; $900 life
Activities: Sport horse inspections; shows

Cheval Québec
4545, av Pierre-de Coubertin, Montréal QC H1V 0B2
Tél: 514-252-3053; *Téléc:* 514-252-3068
Ligne sans frais: 866-575-0515
info@cheval.quebec
cheval.quebec

www.youtube.com/EquestreQuebec
www.facebook.com/chevalquebec
Nom précédent: Fédération équestre du Québec inc.
Aperçu: *Dimension:* moyenne; *Envergure: provinciale; Organisme sans but lucratif; fondée en 1970*
Description: Promouvoir, développer et régir de l'activité équestre au Québec; *Membre de:* Canadian Equestrian Federation
Membre(s) du bureau directeur: Eve Marie Frappier, Directrice général
emfrappier@cheval.quebec
Membre: 12,000; *Montant de la cotisation:* 62$ individuelle

Distance Riders of Manitoba Association (DRMA)
MB

Tel: 204-330-1773
www.distanceridersofmanitoba.ca
Overview: A small provincial organization founded in 1993
Description: DRMA promotes endurance riding in the province of Manitoba & brings together equestrians interested in the sport.; *Member of:* Manitoba Horse Council; Canadian Long Distance Riding Association
Affiliation(s): American Endurance Ride Conference
Chief Officer(s): Jessica Manness, Secretary
northranch@hotmail.com
Maura Leahy, Treasurer & Membership Contact
Maura.Leahy@live.ca
Membership: 30; *Fees:* $25 single; $40 family; *Member Profile:* Manitoba equestrians
Activities: Supervised rides; competitions

Endurance Riders Association of British Columbia (ERABC)
5068 - 47A Ave., Delta BC V4K 1T8
Tel: 604-940-6958
tobytrot@telus.net
www.erabc.com
Overview: A small provincial organization founded in 1989
Description: ERABC fosters interest in the equestrian sport of endurance riding & promotes training & competition opportunities for beginning & advanced riders. It also assists in the development & preservation of courses or terrain suitable for endurance competitions.
Affiliation(s): Endurance Canada
Chief Officer(s): Murray Mackenzie, President
macheli@telus.net
Finances: *Annual Operating Budget:* Less than $50,000
Membership: 1-99; *Fees:* $30 adult; $60 family; $20 youth
Activities: *Awareness Events:* Ride Over the Rainbow

Endurance Riders of Alberta (ERA)
AB

enduranceridersofalberta.com
www.facebook.com/enduranceridersofalberta
Overview: A small provincial organization founded in 1981
Description: To promote education & good horsemanship through endurance riding; *Member of:* Alberta Equestrian Federation; Canadian Long Distance Riding Association
Affiliation(s): Canadian Long Distance Riding Association
Chief Officer(s): Owen Fulcher, President, 780-797-5404
erapresident@live.ca
Colleen DeVry, Contact, Membership Information
contact@nightwindarabians.com
Fees: $25 junior; $30 individual; $60 family
Activities: Host clinics; sanctions endurance events in Alberta

Equestrian Association for the Disabled
8360 Leeming Rd., RR#3, Mount Hope ON L0R 1W0
Tel: 905-679-8323; *Fax:* 905-679-1705
info@tead.on.ca
www.tead.on.ca
www.facebook.com/TEADStables
Also Known As: TEAD
Overview: A small local charitable organization founded in 1978

Description: To enhance the life of children & adults with physical, mental, & emotional handicaps, through equestrian therapy
Chief Officer(s): Hilary Webb, Manager, Programs, 905-679-8323 224
hilary@tead.on.ca
Helen Clayton, Manager, Farm, 905-679-8323 230
helen@tead.on.ca
Finances: *Funding Sources:* Donations; Grants; Fundraising
Fees: Schedule available
Activities: Offering riding therapy, rehabilitation, & recreation to children & adults with disabilities

Equestrian Canada Équestre (EC)
#201, 11 Hines Rd., Ottawa ON K2K 2X1
Tel: 613-287-1515; *Fax:* 613-248-3484
Toll-Free: 866-282-8395
inquiries@equestrian.ca
www.equestrian.ca
www.instagram.com/equestrian_can
www.facebook.com/equestriancan
twitter.com/Equestrian_Can
Previous Name: Equine Canada; Canadian Equestrian Federation
Overview: A large national licensing charitable organization founded in 1977
Description: To promote & develop a unified Canadian Equine Community, an economically viable horse industry & access to the use of horses for leisure, sport & commerce
Affiliation(s): Provincial Partners: Horse Council of B.C., Alberta Equestrian Federation, Saskatchewan Horse Federation, Manitoba Horse Council, Ontario Equestrian Federation, Fédération Équestre du Quebec, New Brunswick Equestrian Association, PEI Horse Council, Nova Scotia Equestrian Federation, Newfoundland Equestrian Association, Canadian Pony Club
Chief Officer(s): Meg Krueger, President
Yves Hamelin, Interim Chief Executive Officer
ceo@equestrian.ca
John Wightman, Chief Financial Officer
jwightman@equestrian.ca
Finances: *Funding Sources:* Government of Canada; Donations; Memberships
Membership: 18,000 license-holders; *Fees:* $25 bronze; $107 silver; $179 gold; $270 platinum; $408 corporate-syndicate; *Committees:* Audit; Governance; Human Resource; Ethics; Finance; Health & Welfare; Nominations; Joint Steering; Recognition & Awards; LTED Competitions Review
Activities: Coaching program; Rider preparation program; *Awareness Events:* Horse Week; *Rents Mailing List:* Yes *Library:* Yes

Equine Association of Yukon (EAY)
PO Box 30011, Whitehorse YT Y1A 5M2
equineyukon@gmail.com
equineyukon.weebly.com
Overview: A small provincial organization
Description: To be the governing body for equine sports in the Yukon.
Fees: $20 junior; $30 senior; $70 family

Eventing Canada [!]
7018 - 4th Line, Tottenham ON L0G 1W0
Tel: 905-936-2343
info@eventingcanada.com
www.eventingcanada.com
Overview: A small national organization founded in 1996
Description: To independently promote the sport of eventing

Horse Council British Columbia (HCBC)
27336 Fraser Hwy., Aldergrove BC V4W 3N5
Tel: 604-856-4304; *Fax:* 604-856-4302
Toll-Free: 800-345-8055
reception@hcbc.ca
www.hcbc.ca
www.youtube.com/user/HorseCouncilBC/
www.linkedin.com/company/horse-council-bc
www.facebook.com/HorseCouncil
twitter.com/horsecouncilbc
Overview: A medium-sized provincial organization founded in 1980
Description: To represent members & work on behalf of their equine interests in British Columbia; To preserve equestrian use of public lands; To foster & promote participation in equine

activities; To ensure the well-being of horses; *Member of:* Equestrian Canada
Chief Officer(s): Lisa Laycock, Executive Director
administration@hcbc.ca
Liz Saunders, President, 250-359-7293
l.saunders@hcbc.ca
Lisa Mander, Secretary, 604-719-1989
l.mander@hcbc.ca
Carolyn Farris, Treasurer, 250-546-6083
c.farris@hcbc.ca
Finances: *Funding Sources:* Membership dues; Province of British Columbia
Staff: 10 staff member(s); 20 volunteer(s)
Membership: 24,000+; *Fees:* $57.75; *Member Profile:* Clubs; Individuals & families; Businesses; Affiliates
Activities: Collaborating with individuals, professionals, industry, businesses, & governments to improve education, safety, & communication; Representing the industry in areas of sport, recreation, agriculture, & industry; Providing education; Granting funds & supporting clubs; Presenting awards; *Awareness Events:* Horse Week, June *Library:* Horse Council BC Library

Horse Trials New Brunswick
c/o Suzanne Stevenson, 16 Gallaway Dr., Lakeside NB E5N 0K9
Fax: 506-696-4403
info@htnb.org
www.htnb.org
Overview: A small provincial organization
Affiliation(s): Horse Trials Canada
Chief Officer(s): Lori Leach, President
Finances: *Annual Operating Budget:* Less than $50,000; *Funding Sources:* Provincial government; membership fees
Membership: 35; *Fees:* $10

Horse Trials Nova Scotia (HTNS)
c/o Pam Macintosh, 53 Normandy Ave., Truro NS B2N 3J6
Tel: 902-893-2042
www.htns.org
www.facebook.com/groups/290523457701524
Overview: A small provincial organization
Description: To foster & encourage safe & fun enjoyment of the sport of Horse Trials (eventing) through regular training & education of riders, coaches, horses & officials; *Member of:* Canadian Equestrian Federation
Affiliation(s): Horse Trials Canada; Nova Scotia Equestrian Federation
Chief Officer(s): Pam Macintosh, President
pmacintosh@bellaliant.net
Finances: *Annual Operating Budget:* Less than $50,000
Staff: 7 staff member(s)
Membership: 1-99; *Fees:* $25 senior; $20 junior; $45 family; $10 associate; *Committees:* Athlete Development; Coaching; Competitions; Officials & Technical Delegate; Crosss Country Course Advisors Panel; Eventing Rules
Activities: Clinics (lessons); course design seminars; competitions; booth & brochures; seminars

Island Horse Council (IHC)
c/o Sport PEI, 40 Enman Cres., Charlottetown PE C1E 1E6
Tel: 902-620-3888
office@islandhorsecouncil.ca
www.islandhorsecouncil.ca
www.facebook.com/islandhorsecouncil
Overview: A small provincial organization
Description: The objectives of Island Horse Council are: to promote, conduct and manage a Council for the benefit of Prince Edward Island equestrians; to provide a unified voice for the horse industry on Prince Edward Island; to establish a liaison with any authorities, including federal, provincial, and municipal governments, and provincial or national Horse Councils or Equestrian Federations; and to encourage the development of all aspects of horsemanship, health, education, training, competition, breeding, facilities and humane practices.; *Member of:* Equine Canada; Sport PEI
Chief Officer(s): John McAssey, President
Finances: *Funding Sources:* Sponsorships; PEI Provincial Government, Community & Cultural Affairs
Membership: 600+ individuals & 12 clubs; *Fees:* $35; *Committees:* Insurance/Membership; Provincial Coaching; Strathgartney; Trails & Recreation
Activities: Offering seminars, on topics such as first aid; Liaising with governments & other authorities; Encouraging the certification of coaches

Manitoba Horse Council Inc.
145 Pacific Ave., Winnipeg MB R3B 2Z6
Tel: 204-925-5718; *Fax:* 204-925-5703
mhc.admin@sportmanitoba.ca
www.manitobahorsecouncil.ca
www.facebook.com/ManitobaHorseCouncil
Overview: A medium-sized provincial organization founded in 1974

Description: To represent clubs & individuals involved with equestrian; *Member of:* Equine Canada; Canadian Equestrian Federation
Chief Officer(s): John Savard, Executive Director, 204-925-5719
mhc.exec@sportmanitoba.ca
Finances: *Funding Sources:* Manitoba Lotteries Foundation; membership dues
Staff: 3 staff member(s)
Fees: $38.50 recreation; $49.50 competitive youth; $60.50 competitive adult; *Committees:* Athlete Development; Bingo; Breeds & Industry; Coaching; Competitions; Equestrian Centre; Officials; Recreation; Special Events; Marketing
Activities: *Rents Mailing List:* Yes *Library:* Yes (Open to Public)

Manitoba Trail Riding Club Inc. (MTRC)
c/o Mary Anne Kirk, 838 Alfred Ave., Winnipeg MB R2X 0T6
www.mbtrailridingclub.ca
Overview: A small provincial organization founded in 1979
Description: To meet the needs of a growing number of horse people who enjoy trail riding; To demonstrate good horsemanship & promote sound, sensible trail horses; *Member of:* Manitoba Horse Council
Affiliation(s): Canadian Long Distance Riding Association
Chief Officer(s): Kelli Hayhurst, President, 204-897-0729
kelli@mymts.net
Mary Anne Kirk, Treasurer, 204-955-7388
yaknow3@hotmail.com
Fees: $25 individual; $40 family

New Brunswick Equestrian Association (NBEA)
#13, 900 Hanwell Rd., Fredericton NB E3B 6A2
Tel: 506-454-2353; *Fax:* 506-454-2363
horses@nbnet.nb.ca
www.nbea.ca
www.facebook.com/equinenb
twitter.com/equinenb
Overview: A small provincial organization
Description: To promote equestrian & provide education in New Brunswick; *Member of:* Equine Canada
Affiliation(s): New Brunswick SPCA; Maritime Saddle & Tack Ltd.; Government of New Brunswick; P'tit Trot; Greenhawk; Sport New Brunswick
Chief Officer(s): Deanna Phelan, President
deannaphelan@gmail.com
Donna McInnis, Secretary
ddmcinnis1@gmail.com
Fees: $43 junior; $50 senior; $85 family
Activities: Recreation; Sport; Dressage; Hunter/jumper; Distance riding; Eventing; Racing; Driving; Coaching

Newfoundland Equestrian Association (NEA)
PO Box 372, Stn. C, St. John's NL A1C 5J9
equestriannl.ca
www.facebook.com/groups/1529209380693900
Overview: A small provincial organization
Member of: Equine Canada
Chief Officer(s): Jessica Anstey, President
president@equestriannl.ca
Dominique Lavers, Secretary
secretary@equestriannl.ca
Fees: $35 individual junior (18 years & under); $35 individual senior (19 years & over); $60 family ($10 for additional juniors); $65 club/corporate; *Member Profile:* Equestrians in Newfoundland; Equestrian associations or clubs
Activities: Offering the Learn to Ride program; Providing coaching programs; *Library:* NEA Library

Nova Scotia Equestrian Federation (NSEF)
5516 Spring Garden Rd., 4th Fl., Halifax NS B3J 1G6
Tel: 902-425-5450; *Fax:* 902-425-5606
nsefmembership@sportnovascotia.ca
www.horsenovascotia.ca
twitter.com/NSEquestrian
Overview: A small provincial organization
Member of: Equine Canada
Chief Officer(s): Heather Myrer, Executive Director
nsef@sportnovascotia.ca
Gidget Oxner, Technical Director
nseftd@sportnovascotia.ca
Membership: 2,100; *Fees:* $40

Ontario Competitive Trail Riding Association Inc. (OCTRA)
c/o Rick Burnside, PO Box 504, Owen Sound ON N4K 5P7
www.octra.on.ca
Overview: A small provincial organization founded in 1967
Description: To promote & advocation for the disciplines of distance riding in Ontario; To pursue educational opportunities for members to ensure the highest quality of distance horse

welfare; *Member of:* Canadian Long Distance Riding Association
Affiliation(s): Horse Ontario; Ontario Equestrian Federation
Chief Officer(s): Sue Downing, President, 705-428-5622
president@octra.on.ca
Rick Burnside, Treasurer, 519-986-3451
treasurer@octra.on.ca
Fees: $60 family; $45 individual; $35 associate non-voting; $25 junior; *Committees:* AGM Banquet; Archives; Awards; Complaints/Protests; Disciplines; Distance Reward Program; Education; Governance; Membership; Nominations; Publicity & Public Relations; Ride Liaison - East; Ride Liaison - West; Sanctioning; Vet / Lay Judges; Website & Data Base; Worker Credits; Year End Points; Youth
Activities: *Speaker Service:* Yes; *Rents Mailing List:* Yes *Library:* Archives by appointment

Ontario Equestrian
#201, 1 West Pearce St., Richmond Hill ON L4B 3K3
Tel: 905-709-6545; *Fax:* 905-709-1867
Toll-Free: 877-441-7112
info@ontarioequestrian.ca
ontarioequestrian.ca
www.instagram.com/onequestrian
www.facebook.com/onequestrian
Previous Name: Ontario Equestrian Federation
Overview: A medium-sized provincial organization founded in 1977
Description: To support equine welfare; To provide leadership & support to the individuals, associations & industries in Ontario's horse community; *Member of:* Equine Guelph
Affiliation(s): Equine Guelph; Ontario Trails Council; Ontario Federation of Agriculture; Ontario Ministry of Tourism, Culture & Sport
Chief Officer(s): Peter Chiddy, President, 519-215-1484
Tracy McCague-McElrea, Executive Director, 905-709-6545 33
t.mccague@ontarioequestrian.ca
Toyin Fambegbe, Director, Finance, 905-709-6545 24
toyin@ontarioequestrian.ca
Brandon Hall, Director, Marketing & Communications, 905-709-6545 30
b.hall@ontarioequestrian.ca
Finances: *Annual Operating Budget:* $250,000-$500,000; *Funding Sources:* Membership dues; government grant; merchandise sales
Staff: 14 staff member(s); 100 volunteer(s)
Membership: 22,000 individuals; *Fees:* Schedule available; *Member Profile:* Individuals, associations & corporations with interests in equine sport & industry; *Committees:* Associations; Competitions; Horse Facilities; Industry; Recreation
Activities: Education; equine welfare; member services; competitions administration; coaching certification; industry promotion; *Awareness Events:* Horse Day, June; Royal Agricultural Winter Fair, Nov.; Can-Am Equine Emporium, March; *Rents Mailing List:* Yes *Library:* Yes (Open to Public)

Ontario Horse Trials Association (OHTA)
#201, 1 West Pearce St., Richmond Hill ON L4B 3K3
Tel: 905-709-6545; *Toll-Free:* 877-441-7112
ohtainfo@gmail.com
www.horsetrials.on.ca
www.facebook.com/Ontariohorsetrials
Previous Name: Ontario Horse Trials Canada
Overview: A small provincial charitable organization founded in 1965
Description: OHTA is a volunteer, not-for-profit organization whose main functions are to support, develop & promote events in Ontario.; *Member of:* Canadian Equestrian Federation
Chief Officer(s): Katie Holman, President
katieh22@live.com
Lisa Thompson, Secretary
lisat26@sympatico.ca
Finances: *Annual Operating Budget:* Less than $50,000
Staff: 1 staff member(s)
Membership: 1,257; *Fees:* $35 senior; $25 junior; $126 family; $30 associate; $100 corporate; *Committees:* Championship Selection; Competitions; Young Riders; Event Evaluations; Event Schedule; Funding Programs; Officials; Omnibus; Omnibus Ad Sales; Organizer Meeting; Volunteer Incentive Program; Communications; Memberships; Points/Leaderboard; AGM/Banquet/Royal Winter Fair; Strategic Planning; Coach Outreach Program; Rules; Safety; Budget/Financial Statements
Activities: Overall program development, implementation & monitoring programs regarding the sport

Ontario Trail Riders Association (OTRA)
ON
Overview: A small provincial organization founded in 1970
Description: To identify, develop, & preserve multi-use trails throughout Ontario

Affiliation(s): Ontario Trails Council; Ontario Equestrian Federation
Chief Officer(s): Helmut Hitscherich, President, 905-473-9329 helmuthit@gmail.com
Membership: 100-499; *Fees:* $30 single; $50 family; *Committees:* Trail Development; Government Relations; Public Relations; Trail Rides; Education

Professional Association of Therapeutic Horsemanship International (PATH)
PO Box 33150, Denver CO 80233 USA
Tel: 303-452-1212; *Fax:* 303-252-4610
Toll-Free: 800-369-7433
pathintl@pathintl.org
www.pathintl.org
www.youtube.com/user/pathintlvideo
www.linkedin.com/company/path-intl
www.facebook.com/pathintl
twitter.com/path_intl
Previous Name: North American Riding for the Handicapped Association
Overview: A medium-sized international charitable organization founded in 1969
Description: To promote the benefit of the horse riding for individuals with physical, emotional & learning disabilities
Chief Officer(s): Kathy Alm, Chief Executive Officer kalm@pathintl.org
Membership: 8,000+; *Fees:* US$70 participating; US$100 professional; $190 professional plus

Saskatchewan Horse Federation (SHF)
Mosaic Stadium, 300 - 1734 Elphinstone St., 3rd Flr., Regina SK S4T 1K1
Tel: 306-780-9449; *Fax:* 306-525-4041
shfadmin@saskhorse.ca
www.saskhorse.ca
www.facebook.com/SaskHorse
twitter.com/saskhorse
Overview: A medium-sized provincial organization founded in 1976
Description: To work with other equestrian organizations in order to bring educational & recreational programs to the public & uphold a high standard of equine welfare; *Member of:* Equine Canada
Affiliation(s): Sask Sport; Western College Veterinary Medicine; SK Agriculture & Food (SAF)
Chief Officer(s): Audrey Price, Executive Director ed@saskhorse.ca
Pam Duckworth, Office Manager
pamduckworth@saskhorse.ca
Finances: *Funding Sources:* Self-help; Saskatchewan Lotteries
Staff: 2 staff member(s)
Fees: $30 junior; $50 adult; $120 family; $85-$225 clubs
Activities: Coaching certification; competition circuit; clinics; grants; rider certification; officials development; horse industry; member insurance; Horsin' Around raffle; Agribition; Youth Equestrian Games; Sask Horse Week

Trail Riding Alberta Conference (TRAC)
PO Box 44, RR#4, Site 5, Lacombe AB T4L 2N4
Tel: 403-782-7363
office@trailriding.ca
www.trailriding.ca
www.facebook.com/299797026778773
Overview: A small provincial organization
Description: To promote long-distance horse riding
Affiliation(s): Canadian Long Distance Riding Association
Chief Officer(s): Ken Vanderwekken, President
Finances: *Funding Sources:* Fundraising; membership fees; ride fees
Membership: 166
Activities: Three divisions: novice, intermediate & open; three categories within each: junior, lightweight & heavyweight.; *Speaker Service:* Yes *Library:* Long Distance Info (Open to Public)

Fencing

Alberta Fencing Association (AFA)
Percy Page Centre, 11759 Groat Rd., Edmonton AB T5M 3K6
Tel: 780-427-9474
info@fencing.ab.ca
www.fencing.ab.ca
Overview: A small provincial organization founded in 1976
Description: To promote the sport of fencing in Alberta; *Member of:* Canadian Fencing Federation
Chief Officer(s): Sean Rathwell, Executive Director ed@fencing.ab.ca
Finances: *Annual Operating Budget:* $250,000-$500,000
Staff: 1 staff member(s); 16 volunteer(s)
Membership: 800+; *Fees:* $30 associate; $65 competitive

British Columbia Fencing Association (BCFA)
#15, 12900 Jack Bell Dr., Richmond BC V6V 2V8
www.fencing.bc.ca
twitter.com/FENCINGBC
Also Known As: Fencing BC
Overview: A small provincial organization
Description: To promote fencing in BC; To set policies & procedures which govern programs & events
Chief Officer(s): John French, President president.bcfa@gmail.com
Membership: 15; *Fees:* $40 individual; $65 club

Canadian Fencing Federation (CFF) / Fédération canadienne d'escrime
pa@fencing.ca
fencing.ca
www.facebook.com/fencingcanadaescrime
twitter.com/fencingcanada
Also Known As: Fencing Canada
Overview: A medium-sized national charitable organization founded in 1971
Description: To promote & develop the sport of fencing in Canada; To foster an environment of collaboration & excellence; To encourage the growth of fencing; *Member of:* International Fencing Federation; Sport Matters
Affiliation(s): Fédération internationale d'escrime
Chief Officer(s): David Howes, Interim Executive Director ed@fencing.ca
Finances: *Annual Operating Budget:* $500,000-$1.5 Million; *Funding Sources:* Membership fees; Government; Olympic Association
Staff: 4 staff member(s); 25 volunteer(s)
Membership: 6,000; *Fees:* $22.50; *Committees:* Competitions; Domestic Development; High Performance; Historical; Officials; Veterans; Wheelchair Fencing
Activities: Planning competitions; *Internships:* Yes

Fédération d'escrime du Québec
4545, av Pierre-de Coubertin, Montréal QC H1V 0B2
Tél: 514-252-3051; *Téléc:* 514-254-3451
info@escrimequebec.qc.ca
www.escrimequebec.qc.ca
www.facebook.com/280110325350969
Aperçu: *Dimension:* moyenne; *Envergure:* provinciale
Membre(s) du bureau directeur: Marc Lavoie, Directeur mlavoie@uottawa.ca

Fencing - Escrime New Brunswick (FENB)
47 Sloat St., Hanwell NB E3C 1M4
fencingnb@gmail.com
www.fencingnb.ca
Previous Name: New Brunswick Fencing Association
Overview: A small provincial organization
Description: To promote & develop the sport of fencing in New Brunswick; *Member of:* Canadian Fencing Federation; Sport New Brunswick
Chief Officer(s): Melodie Piercey, Contact
Fees: $20 associate; $25 first-time; $60 regular

Fencing Association of Nova Scotia (FANS) / Association d'escrime de la Nouvelle-Écosse
c/o Sport Nova Scotia, 5516 Spring Garden Rd., 4th Fl., Halifax NS B3J 3G6
Fax: 902-425-5606
info@nsfencing.ca
www.nsfencing.ca
twitter.com/FencingNS
Overview: A small provincial organization
Description: To develop & promote the sport of fencing in Nova Scotia; *Member of:* Canadian Fencing Federation
Chief Officer(s): Sean Brillant, Contact
Member Profile: National fencing competitors; Provincial fencing competitors; Recreational fencers; Persons who wish to promote fencing
Activities: Providing information about tournaments

Manitoba Fencing Association (MFA)
#308, 145 Pacific Ave., Winnipeg MB R3B 2Z6
Tel: 204-925-5696; *Fax:* 204-925-5703
fencing@sportmanitoba.ca
www.fencing.mb.ca
www.facebook.com/199898656787720
Overview: A small provincial organization founded in 1978
Description: To promote & develop the sport of fencing in Manitoba
Chief Officer(s): David Cohen, Executive Director
Finances: *Funding Sources:* Fundraising
Staff: 2 staff member(s)
Member Profile: Fencing clubs in Manitoba
Activities: Organizing training programs for high level athletes; Offering coaching training opportunities & clinics; Providing

certification opportunities for officials; Conducting school & community outreach programs

Newfoundland & Labrador Fencing Association (N&LFA)
#50, 168 Hamlyn Rd. Plaza, St. John's NL A1E 5X7
Tel: 709-368-8830
nlfencing@gmail.com
sites.google.com/site/nlfencing
Overview: A small provincial organization
Description: To promote & develop the sport of fencing in Newfoundland
Chief Officer(s): Justin So, President
Membership: 70

Ontario Fencing Association (OFA) / Association d'escrime de l'Ontario
c/o Laurence Bishop, Executive Director, 177 Old River Rd., RR #2, Mallorytown ON K0E 1R0
Tel: 519-496-0613
fencingontario.ca
Overview: A medium-sized provincial organization
Description: To promote & develop the sport of fencing in Ontario
Chief Officer(s): Laurence Bishop, Executive Director lbishop@fencingontario.ca
Fees: $5 associate; $20 recreation; $80 competitive; $35 coaches & officials

Prince Edward Island Fencing Association (PEIFA)
c/o Sport PEI, PO Box 302, 40 Enman Cres., Charlottetown PE C1A 7K7
Tel: 902-368-4110; *Fax:* 902-386-4548
Toll-Free: 800-247-6712
sports@sportpei.pe.ca
people.upei.ca/fencing/main.htm
Overview: A small provincial organization
Description: To promote & develop the sport of fencing in PEI; *Member of:* Sport PEI
Chief Officer(s): Phil Stewart, Contact, 902-566-1073 pstewart@pei.sympatico.ca
Fees: $25 student; $200 regular

Saskatchewan Fencing Association (SFA)
c/o Marcia Coulic Salahub, Office Manager, 510 Cynthia St., Saskatoon SK S7L 7K7
Tel: 306-975-0823
saskfencing@shaw.ca
saskfencing.com
www.facebook.com/SaskFencingAssoc
twitter.com/SKFencingAssoc
Overview: A small provincial charitable organization
Description: To promote & develop the sport of fencing in Saskatchewan
Affiliation(s): Saskatchewan Sport
Chief Officer(s): Marcia Coulic-Salahub, Office Manager
Finances: *Annual Operating Budget:* $100,000-$250,000; *Funding Sources:* Saskatchewan Sport; Fundraising
Staff: 14 staff member(s); 20 volunteer(s)
Membership: 300; *Fees:* Schedule available
Activities: Organizing competitions & training camps

Field Hockey

Field Hockey Alberta (FHA)
#1, 2135 Westmount Rd. NW, Calgary AB T2N 3N3
Tel: 403-670-0014; *Fax:* 403-670-0018
Toll-Free: 888-670-0018
info@fieldhockey.ab.ca
www.fieldhockey.ab.ca
www.facebook.com/105274359520461
Merged from: Alberta Field Hockey Association
Overview: A small provincial charitable organization founded in 1974
Description: To develop field hockey for all in Alberta; To provide & facilitate provincial field hockey teams; *Member of:* Field Hockey Canada
Chief Officer(s): Burgundy Biletski, Executive Director burgundy@fieldhockey.ab.ca
Membership: 800; *Fees:* Schedule available; *Committees:* High Performance; Umpiring; South/North Alberta
Activities: School programs, clinics, festivals, equipment rentals; *Speaker Service:* Yes *Library:* Yes (Open to Public) by appointment

Field Hockey BC (FHBC) / Hockey sur gazon C-B
#202, 210 West Broadway, Vancouver BC V5Y 3W2
Tel: 604-737-3046; *Fax:* 604-737-6488
info@fieldhockeybc.com
www.fieldhockeybc.com
www.youtube.com/user/fieldhockeybc
www.facebook.com/fieldhockeybc
twitter.com/fieldhockeybc
Merged from: British Columbia Field Hockey Association;
British Columbia Women's Field Hockey Federation
Overview: A medium-sized provincial organization founded in 1992
Description: To foster, promote & encourage the development & organization of field hockey in BC at all levels; *Member of:* Field Hockey Canada
Chief Officer(s): Mark Saunders, Executive Director, 604-737-3045
mark@fieldhockeybc.com
Finances: *Annual Operating Budget:* $500,000-$1.5 Million; *Funding Sources:* Provincial government; membership fees
Staff: 5 staff member(s)
Membership: 7,275; *Fees:* Schedule available; *Committees:* High Performance; Finance

Field Hockey Canada (FHC) / Hockey sur gazon Canada
6111 River Rd., Richmond BC V7C 0A2
www.fieldhockey.ca
www.youtube.com/user/fieldhockeycanada
www.facebook.com/FHCanada
twitter.com/FieldHockeyCan
Previous Name: Canadian Field Hockey Association
Overview: A medium-sized national charitable organization founded in 1991
Description: To promote the development & growth of field hockey in Canada; To provide coaching, training & competitive opportunities to prepare Canada's national teams; *Member of:* International Hockey Federation (FIH); Pan American Hockey Federation (PAHF)
Chief Officer(s): Susan Ahrens, Chief Executive Officer
sahrens@fieldhockey.ca
Kevin Underhill, Manager, Communications
kunderhill@fieldhockey.ca
Finances: *Funding Sources:* Sponsorships; Donations
Membership: 7 provincial associations; *Member Profile:* Members of Field Hockey Canada member clubs
Activities: Hosting world class field hockey events in Canada; Seeking partnerships with corporations; Offering technical programs

Field Hockey Manitoba (FHM)
MB
info@fieldhockeymb.org
www.fieldhockeymb.org
www.facebook.com/fieldhockey.manitoba
Overview: A small provincial organization
Description: The Association fosters growth & development of field hockey & indoor hockey in Manitoba.; *Member of:* Field Hockey Canada
Membership: 100; *Fees:* Schedule available

Field Hockey Nova Scotia
5516 Spring Garden Rd., 4th Fl., Halifax NS B3J 1G6
Tel: 902-425-5450
info@fieldhockey.ns.ca
www.fieldhockey.ns.ca
Overview: A small provincial organization founded in 1971
Description: The Association promotes the sport of field hockey for both men & women in the province of Nova Scotia.; *Member of:* Field Hockey Canada
Chief Officer(s): Sharon Rajaraman, President
president@fieldhockey.ns.ca
Patrick Thompson, Administrative Coordinator

Field Hockey Ontario (FHO)
PO Box 80030, Stn. Appleby, Burlington ON L7L 6B1
Tel: 905-492-1680
info@fieldhockeyontario.com
www.fieldhockeyontario.com
www.facebook.com/FieldHockeyOntario
twitter.com/FieldHockeyOnt
Merged from: Ontario Field Hockey Association; Women's Field Hockey Association
Overview: A medium-sized provincial organization founded in 1985

Description: To promote the sport of field hockey for both men & women in the province of Ontario.; *Member of:* Field Hockey Canada
Chief Officer(s): Ramandeep Brar, President
ramandeep.brar@fieldhockeyontario.com
Joseph Fernando, Coordinator, High Performance/Athlete & Coach Development
joseph.fernando@fieldhockeyontario.com
Bimal Jhass, Coordinator, Technical
bimal.jhass@fieldhockeyontario.com
Finances: *Annual Operating Budget:* $100,000-$250,000; *Funding Sources:* Sponsorship; government grants; membership fees
Staff: 3 staff member(s); 180 volunteer(s)
Membership: 6,000; *Fees:* Schedule available
Activities: *Internships:* Yes

PEI Field Hockey Association
c/o Sport PEI, 40 Enman Cres., Charlottetown PE C1A 1E6
Tél: 902-368-4110; *Téléc:* 902-368-4548
Ligne sans frais: 800-247-6712
fieldhockeypei@gmail.com
Aperçu: *Dimension:* moyenne; *Envergure:* provinciale
Description: To organize field hockey in P.E.I.
Membre(s) du bureau directeur: Barb Carmichael, President, 902-566-4056
bcarmichael@eastlink.ca

Saskatchewan Field Hockey Association
1860 Lorne St., Regina SK S4P 2L7
Tel: 306-780-9256; *Fax:* 306-781-6021
sfha@sasktel.net
Overview: A small provincial organization
Description: To promote the sport of field hockey in Saskatchewan.; *Member of:* Field Hockey Canada

Fishing & Angling

Barrow Bay & District Sports Fishing Association (BB&DSFA)
PO Box 987, Lions Head ON N0H 1W0
Fax: 519-793-3363
barrowbayfishing@hotmail.com
www.bltg.com/bbdsfa
Overview: A small local organization founded in 1993
Member of: Ontario Federation of Anglers & Hunters
Affiliation(s): Ontario Federation of Anglers & Hunters
Finances: *Annual Operating Budget:* $50,000-$100,000; *Funding Sources:* Membership dues; fundraising; government grants
Membership: 92; *Member Profile:* Anglers, residents & associates who reside or who have seasonal residences in the vicinity of Barrow Bay & Lion's Head, Ontario, Canada

Edmonton Trout Fishing Club
Edmonton AB
info@edmontontrout.ca
www.edmontontrout.ca
www.facebook.com/EdmontonTroutFishingClub
Overview: A small local charitable organization founded in 1953
Description: To foster, instruct & promote the art of fly tying, fly casting, & the betterment of trout fishing among its members; *Member of:* Alberta Fish & Game Association
Finances: *Funding Sources:* Membership fees; auction
Fees: $40
Activities: Shares stream enhancement projects with Trout Unlimited

Guysborough County Inshore Fishermen's Association (GCIFA)
PO Box 98, 990 Union St., Canso NS B0H 1H0
Tel: 902-366-2266; *Fax:* 902-366-2679
gcifa@gcifa.ns.ca
www.gcifa.ns.ca
www.facebook.com/GuysboroughCountyInshoreFishermensAssociation
Overview: A small local organization
Description: To provide community based management of the fishing resource & to ensure a sustainable resource fishery & habitat, healthy fish stocks & act as an information liaison between inshore fishermen & the Dept. of Fisheries, as well as provide effective representation within the industry & other associations.
Chief Officer(s): Ginny Boudreau, Manager
Pat Rhynold, Manager, Service Provision
Sarah Delorey, Lab Technician/Researcher
Membership: 134; *Member Profile:* Fishermen in Eastern Nova Scotia

New Brunswick Sportfishing Association (NBSFA)
c/o Rosaline Cormier, 758 Rte. 670, Ripples NB E4B 1E9
Tel: 506-385-2335
nbsportfishing.net
www.facebook.com/550441211657133
Overview: A small provincial organization
Description: To promote bass fishing, tournament angling, & catch & release fishing in New Brunswick
Chief Officer(s): Bert Beek, Chairman
Rosaline Cormier, Treasurer
Finances: *Funding Sources:* Membership fees; Sponsorships
Fees: $50; *Member Profile:* Persons, 19 years of age or older, who are eligible to purchase a fishing license in New Brunswick; Persons, under age 19, who are recommended by a member; Organizations which provide financial support to the association
Activities: Hosting tournaments; Promoting catch & release programs; Liaising with the government for new regulations for tournament bass fishing; Improving fish handling methods; Helping to fund studies on smallmouth bass in New Brunswick

Ontario Sportfishing Guides' Association (OSGA)
4504 Trent Trail, Washago ON L0K 2B0
Tel: 705-689-3332; *Fax:* 705-689-1085
info@ontariofishcharters.ca
www.ontariofishcharters.ca
www.facebook.com/OntarioSportfishingGuidesAssociation
Previous Name: Ontario Charterboat Association
Overview: A small provincial organization founded in 1980
Description: To monitor & participate in any regulation reform regarding sportfishing in the province; to lobby as a unified voice on behalf of its members, & serve as a network where members can promote & learn from each other.
Chief Officer(s): George Watkins, Secretary
Finances: *Funding Sources:* Membership fees
Fees: $100; *Member Profile:* Professional fishing charter boat operators & guides

Football

Alberta Amateur Football Association (AAFA)
Percy Page Centre, 11759 Groat Rd., 3rd Flr., Edmonton AB T5M 3K6
Tel: 780-427-8108; *Fax:* 780-422-2663
admin@footballalberta.ab.ca
www.footballalberta.ab.ca
www.facebook.com/FootballAlberta
twitter.com/FootballAlberta
Also Known As: Football Alberta
Overview: A medium-sized provincial organization founded in 1973
Description: To provide a consistent representative voice for football of all levels throughout the province of Alberta; *Member of:* Football Canada
Chief Officer(s): Tim Enger, Executive Director
tenger@telus.net
Brian Fryer, Chief Financial Officer
bfryer@telus.net
Fees: Schedule available

Canadian Football Hall of Fame & Museum
Tim Hortons Field, 64 Melrose Ave. North, 4th Lvl., Hamilton ON L8L 8C1
Tel: 905-528-7566; *Fax:* 905-528-9781
info@cfhof.ca
www.cfhof.ca
twitter.com/cfhof
Overview: A small national charitable organization founded in 1963
Description: To commemorate & promote the names & careers of those who have contributed to the development of Canadian football; To preserve, document & display artifacts & other memorabilia that relate to the history of the sport
Chief Officer(s): Mark DeNobile, Executive Director
mark@cfhof.ca
Finances: *Annual Operating Budget:* $100,000-$250,000
Staff: 2 staff member(s); 70 volunteer(s)
Activities: Induction weekend; Grey Cup week; school outreach program; gift shop; collections; *Library:* Yes by appointment

Canadian Football League (CFL) / Ligue canadienne de football (LCF)
50 Wellington St. East, 3rd Fl., Toronto ON M5E 1C8
Tel: 416-322-9650; *Fax:* 416-322-9651
www.cfl.ca
www.youtube.com/CFL
www.facebook.com/CFL
twitter.com/CFL
Overview: A large national licensing organization founded in 1958
Affiliation(s): Canadian Football League Players' Association (CFLPA); Canadian Football League Alumni Association

(CFLAA); Football Canada; Canadian Interuniversity Sport (CIS); Canadian Football Hall of Fame; Canadian Football Officials Association
Chief Officer(s): Randy Ambrosie, Commissioner
Susan Jones Bouk, Chief People Officer & Head, Office Operations
Greg Dick, Chief Financial Officer & Head, Football Operations
Matt Maychak, Chief Communications Officer
Membership: 9 CFL teams
Activities: *Awareness Events:* Grey Cup Championship Game; *Rents Mailing List:* Yes

Canadian Football League Alumni Association (CFLAA)
17 Kinnell St., Hamilton ON L8R 2J8
www.cflaa.ca
www.instagram.com/cflalumniassociation
www.facebook.com/cflaa
twitter.com/CFL_Alumni
Overview: A large national organization
Description: To foster a lifelong connection between the Canadian Football League & its alumni; To provide support to the alumni community
Chief Officer(s): Leo Ezerins, Executive Director, 905-464-0007
leo@cflaa.ca
Finances: *Funding Sources:* Donations

Canadian Football Officials Association (CFOA) / Association Canadienne des Officiels de Football (ACOF)
cfoaref.com
Overview: A medium-sized national organization founded in 1969

Canadian Junior Football League (CJFL)
www.cjfl.org
www.facebook.com/166507583399023
twitter.com/cjflnews
Overview: A large national organization founded in 1908
Description: To foster community involvement & a positive environment; To teach discipline, perseverance & cooperation; *Member of:* Football Canada
Chief Officer(s): Jim Pankovich, Commissioner
Paul Shortt, Deputy Commissioner
Ryan Watters, Director, Communications & Digital Media
Membership: 18 teams; *Member Profile:* Young men aged 17-22
Activities: Canadian Bowl (National championship)

Canadian University Football Coaches Association (CUFCA)
Overview: A small national organization founded in 1977
Description: To improve the coaching of Canadian Interuniversity Athletic Union (CIAU) football teams; to improve the technical aspects of play in CIAU football
Affiliation(s): Canadian Interuniversity Athletic Union
Membership: 60 individuals + 24 teams

Football BC
#434, 6540 Hastings St., Burnaby BC V5B 4Z5
Tel: 604-677-1025
communications@playfootball.bc.ca
www.playfootball.bc.ca
www.facebook.com/footballbc
twitter.com/Football_BC
Also Known As: British Columbia Amateur Football Association
Overview: A medium-sized provincial organization
Description: To operate as the governing body for amateur football in British Columbia. Office location: #222, 6939 Hastings St., Burnaby, BC, V5B 1S9
Chief Officer(s): Patrick Waslen, Executive Director
Membership: 6 associations; *Member Profile:* Football leagues, coaches & officials
Activities: Clinics; Camp; Education sessions

Football Canada
#205, 825 Exhibition Way, Ottawa ON K1S 5J3
Tel: 613-564-0003; *Fax:* 613-564-6309
info@footballcanada.com
footballcanada.com
www.youtube.com/user/FootballCanada1884
www.facebook.com/FootballCanada
twitter.com/FootballCanada
Also Known As: Canadian Amateur Football Association
Previous Name: Canadian Rugby Football Union
Overview: A medium-sized national charitable organization founded in 1884
Description: To initate, regulate & manage the programs, services & activities that promote participation & excellence in

Canadian Amateur Football; *Member of:* International Federation of American Football
Chief Officer(s): Jim Mullin, President
Shannon Donovan, Executive Director
sdonovan@footballcanada.com
Aaron Geisler, Director, Sport
ageisler@footballcanada.com
Vanisha Mistry, Coordinator, Communications
vmistry@footballcanada.com
Finances: *Annual Operating Budget:* $250,000-$500,000;
Funding Sources: Membership fees; government; corporate sponsors
Membership: 110,000
Activities: Football Canada Cup; Touch Bowl

Football Nova Scotia Association
5516 Spring Garden Rd., Halifax NS B3J 1G6
Tel: 902-425-5450; *Fax:* 902-425-5606
www.footballnovascotia.ca
www.facebook.com/footballnovascotia
twitter.com/footballns
Overview: A small provincial organization founded in 1974
Description: To promote amateur football in Nova Scotia, at both the competitive & recreational levels; To assist members with their programs; To develop the sport in new areas of the province
Affiliation(s): Canadian Amateur Football Association
Chief Officer(s): Karen Ouellette, Executive Director
kouellette@footballnovascotia.ca
Ryan Cornish, Coordinator, Program
rcornish@footballnovascotia.ca
Finances: *Funding Sources:* Provincial Government
Staff: 1 staff member(s); 14 volunteer(s)
Membership: 1,000 individual; *Fees:* Schedule available;
Member Profile: Football associations in Nova Scotia
Activities: *Rents Mailing List:* Yes

Football PEI
PE
Tel: 902-368-4262; *Fax:* 902-368-4548
footballpeiexecutive@gmail.com
peifootball.ca
www.instagram.com/footballpei
www.facebook.com/359577044129113
twitter.com/footballpei
Overview: A large provincial organization
Description: To operate as the provincial sport governing body for amateur football in Prince Edward Island; To promote & further the development of the sport in its three forms - flag, tackle & touch
Chief Officer(s): Glen Flood, Executive Director
gflood@sportpei.pe.ca

Football Québec (FFAQ) / Fédération de football amateur de Québec
4545, av Pierre-de Coubertin, Montréal QC H1V 0B2
Tél: 514-252-3059; *Téléc:* 514-252-5216
footballquebec.com
www.facebook.com/footballquebec
twitter.com/footballquebec
Aperçu: *Dimension:* moyenne; *Envergure:* provinciale; *fondée en 1882*
Description: Régir le développement du football au Québec, avec règlement de sécurité, formation des entraîneurs et des officiels, et les championnats provinciaux; *Membre de:* Sport Québec
Affiliation(s): National Football Federation of Canada
Membre(s) du bureau directeur: Jean-Charles Meffe, Directeur général, 514-252-3059 3514
Finances: *Budget de fonctionnement annuel:* $250,000-$500,000; *Fonds:* Gouvernement provincial
Personnel: 3 membre(s) du personnel; 3000 bénévole(s)
Membre: 15 000

Ontario Football Alliance
7384 Wellington Rd. 30, #B, Guelph ON N1H 6J2
Tel: 519-780-0200; *Fax:* 519-780-0705
Toll-Free: 888-313-9419
www.youtube.com/channel/UCNtsuz7nHyHJOCJfciYPZ3A
www.facebook.com/ontariofootball
twitter.com/Ontariofootball
Previous Name: Football Ontario
Overview: A medium-sized provincial organization founded in 1971

Description: To develop football in Ontario by providing programs to improve the game through participation & mandates developed by its membership; *Member of:* Football Canada
Chief Officer(s): Tina Turner, Executive Director
director@ontariofootball.ca
Don Edwards, President
president@ontariofootball.ca
Fees: $25 tackle; $10 coach; $100 association; $500 league
Activities: *Rents Mailing List:* Yes *Library:* Yes (Open to Public) by appointment

Thunder Bay Minor Football Association (TBMFA)
535 Chapples Dr., Thunder Bay ON P7C 2V7
Tel: 807-627-1727
www.tbmfa.com
www.instagram.com/TBMFA807
www.facebook.com/tbmfa.knights
Overview: A small local organization founded in 2013
Description: To run a football program for boys & girls ages 7-13 in Thunder Bay & area
Chief Officer(s): Sheri Robertson, President
president@tbmfa.com
Amanda Parker-Kainula, Secretary
secretary@tbmfa.com
Brandee Popowich, Treasurer
treasurer@tbmfa.com
Justin Kainula, Director, Digital Media & Publicity
website@tbmfa.com

Touch Football Ontario (TFO)
21 Bird Cres., Ajax ON L1S 5G3
Tel: 416-399-8792
info@tfont.com
www.tfont.com
Overview: A medium-sized provincial organization
Description: To organize touch football games among amateur teams in Ontario; to represent the sport within the province
Chief Officer(s): Russ Henderson, President
president@tfont.com
Member Profile: Touch football teams

Foundations

Canadian Athletes Now Fund / Fonds des Athlétes Canadiens (FDAC)
106 Berkeley St., Toronto ON M5A 2W7
Tel: 416-487-4442; *Toll-Free:* 866-937-2012
office@canadianathletesnow.ca
canadianathletesnow.ca
www.youtube.com/user/CanadianAthletesNow
www.facebook.com/CANFund
twitter.com/canfund
Also Known As: See You In CAN Fund; CAN Fund
Overview: A medium-sized national charitable organization
Description: To provide financial assistance to amateur athletes in Canada
Chief Officer(s): Jane Roos, Founder & Executive Director
Finances: *Funding Sources:* Fundraising

Dr. James Naismith Basketball Foundation / La fondation de basketball Dr James Naismith
2729 Draper Ave., Ottawa ON K2H 7A1
info@naismithbasketballfoundation.com
naismithbasketballfoundation.com
Also Known As: Naismith Foundation; Naismith Museum & Hall of Fame
Overview: A medium-sized national charitable organization founded in 1989
Description: To increase awareness of Dr. James Naismith, inventor of basketball, & his values & legacies in sport, theology & medicine
Affiliation(s): Basketball Canada
Finances: *Funding Sources:* Fundraising; merchandise sales; special events
Activities: To preserve, conserve & promote the life & times of Dr. James Naismith & basketball through the museum & related programs; *Library:* Naismith Basketball Resource Collection by appointment

Golf Canada Foundation
#1, 1333 Dorval Dr., Oakville ON L6M 4X7
Tel: 905-849-9700; *Fax:* 905-845-7040
Toll-Free: 800-263-0009
foundation@golfcanada.ca
golfcanadafoundation.com
www.facebook.com/golfcanadafoundation
twitter.com/golfcanadafdn
Also Known As: RCGA Foundation
Previous Name: Canadian Golf Foundation
Overview: A medium-sized national charitable organization founded in 1979

Description: To raise & grant funds for the betterment of golf in Canada
Chief Officer(s): Martin Barnard, Chief Executive Officer
mbarnard@golfcanada.ca
Joelle Efford, Senior Director, Development
jefford@golfcanada.ca
Finances: *Funding Sources:* Private & corporate donations
Staff: 2 staff member(s)
Activities: Internships: Yes

Saint John Jeux Canada Games Foundation Inc. / La Fondation Jeux Canada Games Saint John, Inc.
206 King St. West, Saint John NB E2M 1S6
Tel: 506-634-1985
cdagamesapps@acmca.com
www.sjcanadagamesfoundation.ca
Overview: A small national charitable organization founded in 1986
Description: To promote amateur athletics not only in New Brunswick, but across Canada, by providing funding for athletes, amateur athletic organizations, governing bodies, universities & others involved in the training & development of amateur athletes
Chief Officer(s): Jeff White, Chair

True Sport Foundation / Fondation sport pur
#201, 2723 Lancaster Rd., Ottawa ON K1B 0B1
Tel: 613-526-6043; *Fax:* 613-521-3134
info@truesport.ca
truesportfoundation.ca
Previous Name: Spirit of Sport Foundation
Overview: A small national charitable organization founded in 1993
Description: To ensure that sport makes a positive contribution to Canadian society, to its athletes & to the development of Canada's youth; To bring together leading organizations to promote, celebrate & recognize sporting excellence; *Member of:* Canadian Centre for Ethics in Sport; Athletics Canada
Chief Officer(s): Megan Cumming, Manager, Corporate Communications
mcumming@truesport.ca
Finances: *Annual Operating Budget:* $250,000-$500,000
Staff: 3 staff member(s); 14 volunteer(s)
Membership: 1-99

Fundraising

WinSport Canada
88 Canada Olympic Rd. SW, Calgary AB T3B 5R5
Tel: 403-247-5452
info@coda.ca
www.winsportcanada.ca
www.youtube.com/channel/UCXyy8HyMGaBiVmAY-ZZVLsQ
www.facebook.com/CanadaOlympicPark
twitter.com/winsportcanada
Previous Name: Calgary Olympic Development Association
Overview: A small local organization founded in 1956
Description: WinSport Canada is a not-for-profit association that develops & sustains the sporting facilities of Canada Olympic Park. It supports national sports organizations & subsidizes unique facilities used by top athletes & the public.; *Member of:* Calgary Society of Associations Executives
Affiliation(s): Canadian Olympic Committee; Canadian Paralympic Committee
Chief Officer(s): Robert (Bob) Hamilton, Chair
Barry Heck, President & CEO
Activities: Fundraising for Canada Wins, a winter sports institute

Golf

Alberta Golf Association (AGA)
#22, 11410 - 27 St. SE, Calgary AB T2Z 3R6
Tel: 403-236-4616; *Fax:* 403-236-2915
Toll-Free: 888-414-4849
info@albertagolf.org
www.albertagolf.org
www.instagram.com/alberta_golf
www.facebook.com/144026188016
twitter.com/Alberta_Golf
Overview: A medium-sized provincial organization founded in 1912
Description: To promote the positive impacts of golf on both individuals & communities across Alberta; To improve the quality of life for Albertans through sport
Chief Officer(s): Matt Rollins, Executive Director, 403-613-3034
matt@albertagolf.org
Jack Lane, Chief Operating Officer, 403-698-4631
jack@albertagolf.org

Finances: *Funding Sources:* Membership fees; Fundraising; Sponsorships
Staff: 7 staff member(s)
Membership: 57,000 individual + 225 clubs; *Fees:* Schedule available; *Member Profile:* Organized golf clubs in Alberta & member golfers
Activities: *Speaker Service:* Yes *Library:* Yes (Open to Public) by appointment

Association des surintendants de golf du Québec (ASGQ) / Québec Golf Superintendents Association (QSGA)
1370, rue Notre-Dame ouest, Montréal QC H3C 1K8
Tél: 514-285-4874; *Téléc:* 514-282-4292
info@asgq.org
www.asgq.org
Aperçu: *Dimension:* petite; *Envergure:* provinciale; *Organisme sans but lucratif; fondée en* 1964
Description: Dédiée à la promotion des intérêts des surintendants; offre à ses membres des avantages, informations et défense des intérêts des surintendants
Membre(s) du bureau directeur: John Scott, Président
john.scott@summerlea.com
Finances: *Budget de fonctionnement annuel:* $50,000-$100,000
Personnel: 1 membre(s) du personnel; 12 bénévole(s)
Membre: 400; *Critères d'admissibilite:* Surintendant; adjoint; aspirant
Activités: Tournois de golf; salon exposition; *Service de conférenciers:* Oui

British Columbia Golf Association (BCGA)
#116, 7198 Vantage Way, Delta BC V4G 1K7
Tel: 604-279-2580; *Fax:* 604-952-0060
Toll-Free: 888-833-2242
info@britishcolumbiagolf.org
www.britishcolumbiagolf.org
www.facebook.com/BritishColumbiaGolf
twitter.com/bc_golfer
Also Known As: British Columbia Golf
Overview: A large provincial licensing organization founded in 1922
Description: To promote interest in golf in BC; To protect the mutual interests of member clubs & their members; To establish & enforce uniformity in the rules of the game; To establish, control & conduct amateur championships, matches & competitions; To interest & develop junior golfers; To select all teams to represent BC in national & international matches
Affiliation(s): Canadian Golf Foundation; Professional Golf Association of BC; Canadian Ladies Golf Association of BC; Golf Course Superintendents Association of BC; International Association of Golf Administrators; National Golf Foundation; Pacific Coast Golf Association; Pacific Northwest Golf Association
Chief Officer(s): Kris Jonasson, Chief Executive Officer, 604-279-2580 204
kris@britishcolumbiagolf.org
Deborah Pyne, Managing Director, Player Development, 604-279-2580 206
debbie@britishcolumbiagolf.org
Andy Fung, Director, Finance & Administration, 604-279-2580 201
andy@britishcolumbiagolf.org
Doug Hastie, Senior Manager, Field Operations, 604-279-2580 203
doug@britishcolumbiagolf.org
Corrie Wong, Manager, Membership, 604-279-2580 202
corrie@britishcolumbiagolf.org
Finances: *Funding Sources:* Government; Sponsorship; Membership
Staff: 10 staff member(s)
Activities: *Rents Mailing List:* Yes *Library:* Yes (Open to Public)

British Columbia Golf Superintendents Association (BCGSA)
6382 Herons Pl., Duncan BC V9L 6Z3
Tel: 778-422-1776; *Fax:* 778-422-1776
admin@bcgsa.com
www.bcgsa.com
Overview: A small provincial organization founded in 1995
Description: To promote the professional recognition of golf course superintendents
Chief Officer(s): Ginny Tromp, Executive Administrator
Paul Robertson, President, 250-598-4324
paul@victoriagolf.com
Tom Altmann, Treasurer, 778-525-8005
taltmann@fhsr.com
Membership: 300+; *Fees:* $50 student; $100 assistant; $165 superintendent/industry; $625 group industry; *Member Profile:* Turfgrass professionals involved in golf course maintenance & the science of turf management

Activities: Participating in turfgrass research; Exchanging knowledge related to golf course care; Sponsoring educational opportunities to benefit members

Canadian Caribbean Amateur Golfers Association (CCAGA)
#718, 7305 Woodbine Ave, Markham ON L3R 3V7
Fax: 905-420-8421
info@ccaga.ca
www.ccaga.ca
Overview: A small local organization founded in 1980
Description: A Not-For-Profit Association offering beginners and amateur golfers the opportunity to play and compete among each other
Fees: $125 single; $200 family; $100 associate (non-playing)

Canadian Golf Superintendents Association (CGSA) / Association canadienne des surintendants de golf
2605 Summerville Ct., #A2082, Mississauga ON L4X 0A2
Tel: 416-626-8873; *Toll-Free:* 800-387-1056
cgsa@golfsupers.com
golfsupers.com
www.facebook.com/151227228150
twitter.com/GolfSupers
Overview: A medium-sized national organization founded in 1966
Description: To promote excellence in golf course management & environmental responsibility; To uphold the Canadian Golf Superintendents Association Principles Of Professional Practice & Code of Ethics & Conduct
Chief Officer(s): Jeff Calderwood, Executive Director, 416-626-8873 24
jcalderwood@golfsupers.com
Kathryn Wood, Chief Operating Officer, 416-626-8873 23
kwood@golfsupers.com
Finances: *Funding Sources:* Sponsorship, membership dues
Membership: 1,500; *Fees:* Schedule available; *Member Profile:* Golf course superintendents & turfgrass specialists in Canada; *Committees:* Environment; Communications, Marketing, & Public Relations; Professional Development & Research; Conference & Events; Member Services; Equipment Technicians Advisory
Activities: Providing continuing professional development opportunities for members; Sponsoring research projects; Establishing the Master Superintendent Designation Program; Offering networking opportunities; *Awareness Events:* Canadian International Turfgrass Conference & Trade Show, annual *Library:* CGSA Office Library

Canadian Junior Golf Association (CJGA)
PO Box 118, Newmarket ON L3Y 4W3
Toll-Free: 877-508-1069
info@cjga.com
cjga.com
www.facebook.com/canadianjuniorgolfassociation
twitter.com/CJGA
Overview: A medium-sized national organization founded in 1993
Description: To provide competition & instruction to junior golfers in Canada
Chief Officer(s): Earl M. Fritz, Executive Director
earl.fritz@cjga.com
Brad Parkins, Chief Operations Officer
brad.parkins@cjga.com
Fees: $75 linkster; $150 junior tour; *Member Profile:* Golfers aged 18 & under; Individuals & organizations who support the CJGA
Activities: Golf tournaments; Clinics; International competitions; Mentoring programs

Club de golf Chibougamau-Chapais inc.
CP 81, 130, rue des Forces-Armées, Chibougamau QC G8P 3A1
Tél: 418-748-4709; *Téléc:* 418-748-2471
golfchibougamau@hotmail.com
Nom précédent: Club de golf de Chibougamau inc.
Aperçu: *Dimension:* petite; *Envergure:* locale

Fédération de golf du Québec / Québec Golf Federation
4545, av Pierre-de Coubertin, Montréal QC H1V 0B2
Tél: 514-252-3345; *Téléc:* 514-252-3346
golfquebec@golfquebec.org
www.golfquebec.org

www.youtube.com/user/GolfQuebecMedias
www.facebook.com/golfquebec
twitter.com/golf_quebec

Également appelé: Golf Québec
Nom précédent: Association de golf du Québec
Aperçu: *Dimension:* moyenne; *Envergure:* provinciale; *Organisme sans but lucratif; fondée en* 1920

Description: Assurer le leadership; Favoriser la croissance et le développement du golf amateur dans toute la province tout en préservant l'intégrité et les traditions du jeu
Membre(s) du bureau directeur: Jean-Pierre Beaulieu, Directeur général, 514-252-3345 3732
jpbeaulieu@golfquebec.org
Membre: 61 000

Golf Association of Ontario (GAO)
PO Box 970, Uxbridge ON L9P 1N3
Tel: 905-852-1101; *Fax:* 905-852-8893
admin@gao.ca
gao.ca
www.instagram.com/thegolfontario
www.facebook.com/GolfOntario
twitter.com/TheGolfOntario
Merged from: Ontario Golf Association; Ontario Ladies Golf Association
Overview: A large provincial organization founded in 2001
Description: To develop & promote golf in the province
Chief Officer(s): Mike Kelly, Executive Director, 905-852-1101 232

Judy Crute, Senior Director, Business Operations, 905-852-1101 235

Kyle McFarlane, Senior Director, Golf Operations, 905-852-1101 228

Craig Loughry, Director, Golf Services, 905-852-1101 230
Jason Hraynyk, Manager, Marketing & Business Development, 905-852-1101 233
Finances: *Funding Sources:* Membership dues; Tournament entry fees
Staff: 19 staff member(s)
Membership: 115,000 individuals, 420 member clubs; *Fees:* Schedule available; *Member Profile:* Golfers who are members of private, semi-private or public golf courses; *Committees:* Finance & Risk Management; Governance; Human Resources & Compensation; Nominating
Activities: Offering tournaments, junior camps & programming; *Internships:* Yes

Golf Canada / Association royale de golf du Canada
#1, 1333 Dorval Dr., Oakville ON L6M 4X7
Tel: 905-849-9700; *Fax:* 905-845-7040
Toll-Free: 800-263-0009
info@golfcanada.ca
golfcanada.ca
www.youtube.com/user/TheGolfCanada
www.linkedin.com/company/golf-canada
www.facebook.com/TheGolfCanada
twitter.com/TheGolfCanada
Previous Name: Royal Canadian Golf Association
Overview: A large national organization founded in 1895
Description: To work with the provincial golf associations & member clubs to foster the growth & development of golf
Affiliation(s): Canadian Golf Superintendent Association; PGA of Canada; Canadian Society of Club Managers; National Golf Course Owners Association Canada; Canadian Golf Industry Association
Chief Officer(s): Laurence Applebaum, Chief Executive Officer
Finances: *Funding Sources:* Membership dues; Sponsorships
Membership: 271,000+ at 1,400+ clubs; *Fees:* Schedule available; *Member Profile:* Member of a member golf club
Activities: *Awareness Events:* RBC Canadian Open; Canadian Pacific Women's Open; *Speaker Service:* Yes *Library:* Yes by appointment

Golf Manitoba Inc.
#420, 145 Pacific Ave., Winnipeg MB R3B 2Z6
Tel: 204-925-5730; *Fax:* 204-925-5731
golfmb@golfmanitoba.mb.ca
golfmanitoba.mb.ca
www.facebook.com/217256961725416
twitter.com/golf_manitoba
Previous Name: Manitoba Golf Association Inc.
Overview: A small provincial organization founded in 1915
Description: The Association determines policies & standards relating to the development & promotion of golf in the province.
Chief Officer(s): Tammy Gibson, President & Representative, Provincial Council

Golf Newfoundland & Labrador (GNL)
1296A Kenmount Rd., Paradise NL A1L 1N3
Tel: 709-576-3415
golf@sportnl.ca
www.golfnl.ca
www.facebook.com/178044602356289
twitter.com/nlgolf
Previous Name: Newfoundland & Labrador Golf Association
Overview: A medium-sized provincial organization

Description: To govern golf in Newfoundland & Labrador; To encourage participation in the sport; To honour the history, traditions & integrity of the game
Chief Officer(s): Greg Hillier, Executive Director
Membership: 20 clubs; *Committees:* Archives; Competitions; Course Rating; Executive; Fund Development; Hall of Fame; Marketing; Membership; Rules; Nominations
Activities: Providing information about golf courses in Newfoundland & Labrador; Promoting golf in the province

National Golf Course Owners Association Canada (NGCOA) / L'Association nationale des propriétaires de terrains de golf du Canada (ANPTG)
#810, 515 Legget Dr., Ottawa ON K2K 3G4
Tel: 613-226-3616; *Fax:* 613-226-4148
Toll-Free: 866-626-4262
ngcoa@ngcoa.ca
www.ngcoa.ca
www.facebook.com/nationalgolfcourseownersassociationcanada
twitter.com/ngcoacanada
Overview: A large national organization founded in 1993
Description: To provide business support to Canadian golf course operators & related stakeholders, networking opportunities, purchasing programs & education
Chief Officer(s): Jeff Calderwood, Chief Executive Officer, 613-226-3616 20
jcalderwood@ngcoa.ca
Fees: Schedule available; *Member Profile:* Golf course owner / operators
Activities: Golfmax Purchasing Program; GOLFEXPOs; Take A Kid To The Course; Golf Business Canada magazine; *Awareness Events:* Take a Kid to the Course Week, July; GolfBusiness Canada Conference & Trade Show; NGCOA Canada Golf Invitationals

New Brunswick Golf Association (NBGA) / Association de golf du nouveau brunswick
#440, 500 Beaverbrook Crt., Fredericton NB E3B 5X4
Tel: 506-451-1324; *Fax:* 888-307-2963
Toll-Free: 877-833-4662
info@golfnb.ca
www.golfnb.ca
Overview: A medium-sized provincial organization founded in 1934
Description: To determine policies & standards relating to the development & promotion of amateur golf in New Brunswick
Chief Officer(s): Tyson Flinn, Executive Director
tflinn@golfnb.ca
Member Profile: Amateur golfers at member clubs; *Committees:* Executive
Activities: Provincial amateur tournaments; programs & services for members clubs

Nova Scotia Golf Association (NSGA)
120 Brunella Blvd., Timberlea NS B3T 0G9
Tel: 902-468-8844; *Fax:* 902-484-5327
www.nsga.ns.ca
www.facebook.com/novascotiagolf
twitter.com/novascotiagolf
Overview: A medium-sized provincial organization founded in 1931
Description: To promote & develop golf in Nova Scotia, especially in participation, excellence & interaction; *Member of:* Canadian Golf Foundation; International Association of Golf Administrators; Sport Nova Scotia
Chief Officer(s): David Campbell, Executive Director
david@nsga.ns.ca
Finances: *Funding Sources:* Membership dues; sponsors
Member Profile: Must be a member club

Ontario Golf Superintendents' Association (OGSA)
328 Victoria Rd. South, Guelph ON N1L 0H2
Tel: 519-767-3341; *Fax:* 519-766-1704
Toll-Free: 877-824-6472
admin@ogsa.ca
www.ogsa.ca
Overview: A small provincial organization
Description: To advance the profession of golfcourse superintendent; To enrich the quality of golf & its environment
Chief Officer(s): Sally E. Ross, Executive Director, 519-767-3341 202
manager@ogsa.ca
Courtney White, Coordinator, Member Programs & Services, 519-767-3341 200
members@ogsa.ca
Fees: Schedule available; *Member Profile:* Golf course management personnel & companies; *Committees:* Governance; Golf & Events; Marketing/Public Relations; Membership & Member Services; Conference; Education; Nominating

Prince Edward Island Golf Association (PEIGA)
PO Box 51, Charlottetown PE C1A 7K2
Tel: 902-393-3293
peiga@peiga.ca
www.peiga.ca
www.facebook.com/PEIGolfAssociation
twitter.com/PEIGolfAssoc
Overview: A small provincial organization founded in 1971
Description: To be the governing body of amateur golf in the province
Chief Officer(s): Brenda McIlwaine, President
Ron MacNeill, Executive Director

Professional Golfers' Assocation of British Columbia (PGA of BC)
#243, 7080 River Rd., Richmond BC V6X 1X5
Tel: 604-303-6766; *Fax:* 604-303-6765
Toll-Free: 800-667-4653
info@pgabc.org
www.pgabc.org
www.youtube.com/user/pgaofbc
www.linkedin.com/company/professional-golfers'-association-of-b-c-
www.facebook.com/pgabc
twitter.com/pgaofbc
Previous Name: British Columbia Professional Golfers Association
Overview: A medium-sized provincial organization
Description: To promote the game of golf and enhance all players' enjoyment of the sport.; *Member of:* Professional Golf Association
Chief Officer(s): Donald Miyazaki, Executive Director
donald@pgabc.org
Eric MacKenzie, Manager, Communications & Marketing
eric@pgabc.org
Finances: *Funding Sources:* Corporate sponsorship
Staff: 5 staff member(s)
Membership: 650+; *Member Profile:* Individuals employed in the golf industry; *Committees:* Membership & Employment; Captain's; Education & Events; Long Range Planning & Grow the Game; Buying Show; Awards
Activities: PGA tournaments

Professional Golfers' Association of Canada / Association des golfeurs professionnels du Canada
13450 Dublin Line, RR#1, Acton ON L7J 2W7
Fax: 519-853-5449
Toll-Free: 800-782-5764
info@pgaofcanada.com
www.pgaofcanada.com
www.instagram.com/pgaofcanada
www.linkedin.com/company/pga-of-canada
www.facebook.com/PGAofCanada
twitter.com/pgaofcanada
Also Known As: PGA of Canada
Previous Name: Canadian Professional Golfers' Association
Overview: A medium-sized national organization founded in 1911
Description: To represent golf professionals across Canada
Chief Officer(s): Kevin Thistle, Chief Executive Officer, 800-782-5760 241
kevin@pgaofcanada.com
Eilon Milman, Chief Financial Officer, 800-782-5764 223
eilon@pgaofcanada.com
Finances: *Annual Operating Budget:* $500,000-$1.5 Million
Staff: 10 staff member(s)
Membership: 10,000
Activities: *Rents Mailing List:* Yes *Library:* Yes (Open to Public)

Saskatchewan Golf Association Inc.
510 Cynthia St., Saskatoon SK S7L 7K7
Tel: 306-975-0850; *Fax:* 306-242-8007
info@golfsk.org
golfsaskatchewan.org
www.facebook.com/GolfSaskatchewan
twitter.com/GolfSK
Also Known As: Golf Saskatchewan
Merged from: Saskatchewan Golf Association; Canadian Ladies Golf Association of Saskatchewan
Overview: A large provincial organization founded in 1999
Description: To promote & maintain amateur golf in Saskatchewan by providing access to information & clinics on golf skills development, rules, handicapping & etiquette
Chief Officer(s): Brian Lee, Executive Director, 306-975-0841
blee@golfsk.org
Candace Dunham, Manager, Programs & Member Services, 306-975-0850
cdunham@golfsk.org
Fees: $35.70 adult/junior club; $52.45 Golf SK Public Players Club

Activities: Providing provincial championships, scholarships, player clinics, rules workshops & handicap clinics; *Internships:* Yes

Yukon Golf Association
4061 - 4th Ave., Whitehorse YT Y1A 1H1
Tel: 867-633-3364; *Fax:* 867-393-3051
sportyukon.com/member/yukon-golf-association
Overview: A small provincial organization
Description: The Yukon Golf Association is an organization that enhances opportunities for all Yukonners in their pursuit of excellence & in their enjoyment of participation.
Chief Officer(s): Gordon Zealand, President
zealandg@northwestel.net

Gymnastics

Alberta Gymnastics Federation (AGF)
#207, 5800 - 2 St. SW, Calgary AB T2H 0H2
Tel: 403-259-5500; *Fax:* 403-259-5588
Toll-Free: 800-665-1010
www.abgym.ab.ca
www.instagram.com/albertagymnastics
www.facebook.com/AlbertaGymnastics
twitter.com/ABGymnastics
Overview: A medium-sized provincial organization founded in 1971
Description: To operate as the governing body of gymnastics in Alberta; To provide administrative support in the development & delivery of programs & competitions in recreational gymnastics, national coaching certification programs, women's artistic gymnastics, trampoline & tumbling, men's artistic gymnastics, & special events
Chief Officer(s): Scott Hayes, President & CEO, 403-212-5725
ceo@abgym.ab.ca
Anna Rogers, Manager, Communications & Marketing, 403-212-5729
comm@abgym.ab.ca
Joanna Low, Manager, Membership & Finance, 403-212-5720
membership@abgym.ab.ca
Membership: 75 member clubs; *Committees:* Acrobatic Program; Gymnastics for All; Women's Program; Women's Program Judging; Trampoline & Tumbling Technical; Men's Technical

British Columbia Rhythmic Sportive Gymnastics Federation (BCRSGF)
#268, 828 West 8th Ave., Vancouver BC V5Z 1E2
Tel: 604-333-3485; *Fax:* 604-909-1749
bcrsgf@rhythmicsbc.com
www.rhythmicsbc.com
www.youtube.com/user/bcrsgf
www.facebook.com/Rhythmicsbc
Also Known As: BC Rhythmic Gymnastics Federation
Overview: A small provincial organization
Description: To be the governing body of the sport of rhythmic gymnastics in British Columbia, including special olympics, Aethetic Group Gymnastics & men's rhythmic gymnastics.
Chief Officer(s): Sashka Gitcheva, Program Coordinator

Fédération de gymnastique du Québec (FGQ) / Québec Gymnastics Federation
4545, av Pierre-de-Coubertin, Montréal QC H1V 0B2
Tél: 514-252-3043; *Téléc:* 514-252-3169
info@gymqc.ca
www.gymqc.ca
www.instagram.com/gymqc
www.facebook.com/GymQc
Aperçu: *Dimension:* grande; *Envergure:* provinciale; fondée en 1971
Description: Promouvoir et assurer le développement de la gymnastique à travers tout le Québec; favoriser l'éclosion des talents en vue d'une participation aux plans national et international; unir et coordonner les efforts de toutes les personnes intéressées dans le sport de la gym; *Membre de:* Canadian Gymnastics Federation
Membre(s) du bureau directeur: Serge Castonguay, Directeur général, 514-252-3043 3488
scastonguay@gymqc.ca
Critères d'admissibilite: Athlethes, entraîneurs, membres
Activités: *Evénements de sensibilisation:* Semaine de la prévention; *Stagiaires:* Oui *Bibliothèque:* Oui (Bibliothèque publique)

Gymnastics B.C. (GBC)
#268, 828 West 8th Ave., Vancouver BC V5Z 1E2
Tel: 604-333-3496; *Fax:* 604-333-3499
Toll-Free: 800-556-2242
info@gymbc.org
gymbc.org
www.youtube.com/c/GymbcOrg
www.linkedin.com/groups/3800514
www.facebook.com/GymnasticsBC
twitter.com/GymnasticsBC
Also Known As: British Columbia Gymnastics Association
Overview: A large provincial organization founded in 1969
Description: To provide, promote & guide positive lifelong gymnastics experiences by: directing the development & delivery of quality, comprehensive provincial programs; promoting the benefits of gymnastics as a foundation for human movement, sport, health, wellness & enjoyment; coordinating, suppporting & promoting programs in the pursuit of national & international excellence in consultation with Gymnastics Canada Gymnastique; *Member of:* Gymnastics Canada Gymnastique
Chief Officer(s): Andrée Montreuil, Chief Executive Officer
amontreuil@gymbc.org
Finances: *Annual Operating Budget:* $1.5 Million-$3 Million; *Funding Sources:* Membership dues; sponsorship; programs
Staff: 13 staff member(s)
Membership: 46,000; *Committees:* Gymnastics For All; Men's Technical; Trampoline Gymnastics Technical; Women's Technical
Activities: Provincial championships, Fall congress, Gymnaestrada; *Library:* Resource Library (Open to Public)

Gymnastics Canada Gymnastique (GCG)
#120, 1900 Promenade City Park Dr., Ottawa ON K1J 1A3
Tel: 613-748-5637; *Fax:* 613-748-5691
info@gymcan.org
www.gymcan.org
www.youtube.com/user/gymnasticscanada
www.facebook.com/CDNgymnastics
twitter.com/CDNGymnastics
Previous Name: Canadian Gymnastics Federation
Overview: A large national charitable organization founded in 1969
Description: To lead, promote, facilitate & guide gymnastics in Canada as a sport for the pursuit of excellence & world prominence, & as an activity for lifelong participation; To act as the national umbrella organization for provincial & territorial associations which are members; To publish & enforce a standard set of rules & regulations to serve as guidelines for all members; To represent Canadian gymnastics as a member of national & international agencies & federations; To coordinate application of regulations in Canada; To promote, develop & direct high performance gymnastics programs; To promote, facilitate & guide development of national gymnastics programs; To promote, guide & encourage general gymnastics activities; To promote gymnastics as a healthy & safe sport / activity
Affiliation(s): Fédération internationale de gymnastique
Chief Officer(s): Ian Moss, Chief Executive Officer
imoss@gymcan.org
Finances: *Funding Sources:* Sport Canada; Membership; Marketing; Fundraising
Staff: 20 staff member(s)
Membership: 250,000 individuals; *Committees:* Artistic Gymnastics; Communications & Marketing; Executive; Events; Finance; Rhythmic Gymnastics; Sport Development / Education; Trampoline Gymnastics
Activities: National & international programs & competitions; *Awareness Events:* National Gymnastics Week; *Internships:* Yes *Library:* Yes

Gymnastics Newfoundland & Labrador Inc. (GNL)
1269A Kenmount Rd., Paradise NL A1L 1N3
Tel: 709-576-0146; *Fax:* 709-576-7493
gymnastics@sportnl.ca
www.gymnastics.nl.ca
www.facebook.com/gymnasticsnl
twitter.com/gymnastics_nl
Overview: A small provincial organization
Description: GNL promotes & supports the development of gymnastics throughout the province.; *Member of:* Canadian Gymnastics Federation
Chief Officer(s): Carol White, Executive Director
Membership: 8 clubs

Gymnastics Nova Scotia (GNS)
5516 Spring Garden Rd., 4th Fl., Halifax NS B3J 1G6
Tel: 902-425-5450; *Fax:* 902-425-5606
gns@sportnovascotia.ca
www.gymns.ca
www.facebook.com/GymnasticsNovaScotia
twitter.com/gymnasticsns
Previous Name: Nova Scotia Gymnastics Association

Overview: A small provincial organization
Description: To operate as the governing body of gymnastics in Nova Scotia; To promote gymnastics, from the recreational level to the high performance level; To encourage participation, fitness, & well-being; To promote safe & positive gymnastics environments
Chief Officer(s): Nick Lenehan, President
Angela Gallant, Executive Director
David Brown, Technical Director
gnscoach@sportnovascotia.ca
Fees: Schedule available; *Member Profile:* Active & associatte gymnastics clubs throughout Nova Scotia; Judges; Recreational & competitive coaches; Pre-school, recreational, & competitive gymnasts & trampolinists; *Committees:* Men's Program; Trampoline Program; Women's Program; Education & Recreation; Fair Play & Equity; Competition
Activities: Training & certifying coaches, officials, & judges; Organizing & sanctioning gymnastics competitions; Providing resources about gymnastics; Offering the introductory Tumblebugs progam for children from 3.5 to 5 years of age

Gymnastics PEI
Sport PEI, 40 Enman Cres., Charlottetown PE C1E 1E6
Tel: 902-368-6570; *Fax:* 902-368-4548
Toll-Free: 800-247-6712
www.gymnasticspei.ca
Overview: A small provincial organization
Chief Officer(s): Valerie Vuillemot, Executive Director
vvuillemot@sportpei.pe.ca

Gymnastics Saskatchewan
1870 Lorne St., Regina SK S4P 2L7
Tel: 306-780-9229; *Fax:* 306-780-9475
info@gymsask.com
www.gymsask.com
www.facebook.com/gymsask
twitter.com/gymsask
Previous Name: Saskatchewan Gymnastics Association
Overview: A medium-sized provincial organization
Member of: Sask Sport Inc.; Canadian Gymnastics Federation
Chief Officer(s): Klara Miller, Chief Executive Officer
kmiller@gymsask.com
Cheryl Russell, Manager, Operations
crussell@gymsask.com
Finances: *Annual Operating Budget:* $250,000-$500,000; *Funding Sources:* Grants; self-generated revenues
Staff: 5 staff member(s)
Membership: 9,000
Activities: *Awareness Events:* Gymnastics Awareness Week

Manitoba Gymnastics Association (MGA)
145 Pacific Ave., Winnipeg MB R3B 2Z6
Tel: 204-925-5781; *Fax:* 204-925-5932
mga@sportmanitoba.ca
www.gymnastics.mb.ca
www.facebook.com/427931587283744
twitter.com/GymnasticsMB
Overview: A small provincial organization founded in 1968
Description: To develop, promote & guide gymnastics as a lifetime activity in Manitoba; *Member of:* Canadian Gymnastics Federation
Chief Officer(s): Karly Miller, Executive Director
mga.kmiller@sportmanitoba.ca

New Brunswick Gymnastics Association (NBGA) / Association gymnastique du Nouveau-Brunswick (AGNB)
48 Crestline Dr., McLeod Hill NB E3G 6B1
Tel: 506-455-6109
nbga@gym.nb.ca
gym.nb.ca
www.facebook.com/NBGym
twitter.com/gymnasticsnb
Overview: A small provincial organization founded in 1967
Description: To promote gymnastics in New Brunswick; *Member of:* Gymnastics Canada Gymnastique
Chief Officer(s): Jennifer Charters, Executive Director
Diane Kirk, President
president@gym.nb.ca
Membership: 2500; *Committees:* Executive; Technical

Ontario Gymnastic Federation (OGF)
#202, 2950 Keele St., Toronto ON M3M 2H2
Fax: 647-344-4816
info@gymnasticsontario.ca
www.gymnasticsontario.ca
www.facebook.com/gymnasticsontario
Also Known As: Gymnastics Ontario
Overview: A small provincial organization founded in 1968
Description: To lead the sport of gymnastics throughout Ontario; To provide services & programs which encourage

lifelong involvement in gymnastics
Affiliation(s): Gymnastics Canada
Chief Officer(s): Dave Sandford, Chief Executive Officer, 647-344-3813
ceo@gymnasticsontario.ca
Linda Clifford, President
Cindy Clapp, Manager, Operations, 647-344-3975
operations@gymnasticsontario.ca
Kristina Galloway, Manager, Membership Services, 647-344-5106
membership@gymnasticsontario.ca
Danielle Hillard, Manager, Education, NCCP & Risk Management, 647-344-4893
education@gymnasticsontario.ca
Siobhan Covington, Manager, Finance, 647-344-3962
scovington@gymnasticsontario.ca
Finances: *Funding Sources:* Fundraising
Activities: Providing professional development & training activities; Offering resources such as technical manuals, workbooks, & videos; Providing a development award program; *Awareness Events:* I Love Gymnastic Week *Library:* Gymnastics Ontario Resource Centre

Polarettes Gymnastics Club
4061 - 4th Ave., Whitehorse YT Y1A 1H1
Tel: 867-668-4794
info@polarettes.org
www.polarettes.org

Overview: A small provincial organization
Description: To promote recreational & competitive gymnastics programs to Yukon residtents. Physical address: 16 Duke St., Whitehorse, YT Y1A 4M2.
Chief Officer(s): Kimberly Jones, Head Coach
Activities: Toddler Movement program (18 months); competitive programs start from 6-8 years old

Rhythmic Gymnastics Alberta (RGA)
c/o Percy Page Centre, 11759 Groat Rd., Edmonton AB T5M 3K6
Tel: 780-427-8152; *Fax:* 780-427-8153
Toll-Free: 800-881-2504
rga@rgalberta.com
www.rgalberta.com

Previous Name: Alberta Rhythmic Sportive Gymnastics Federation
Overview: A medium-sized provincial organization founded in 1979
Description: To foster & encourage participation & the development of excellence in rhythmic gymnastics; *Member of:* Gymnastics Canada Gymnastique
Finances: *Annual Operating Budget:* $100,000-$250,000
Staff: 2 staff member(s); 100 volunteer(s)
Membership: 800; *Fees:* Schedule available; *Member Profile:* Children 5-18; Active adults/coaches 16-80
Activities: Provincial Gymnastrada; National & international competitions & events; *Speaker Service:* Yes

Rhythmic Gymnastics Manitoba Inc. (RGM)
145 Pacific Ave., Winnipeg MB R3B 2Z6
Tel: 201-925-5738
rhythmic@sportmanitoba.ca
www.rgmanitoba.com

Previous Name: Manitoba Rhythmic Sportive Gymnastics Association
Overview: A medium-sized provincial organization founded in 1985
Description: To support & promote rhythmic gymnastic programs
Affiliation(s): Sport Manitoba; Rhythmic Gymnastics Canada; Gymnastics Canada; International Gymnastics Federation; Canadian Sport Centre - Manitoba; Coaching Manitoba; Gymnastics Manitoba
Membership: 8 clubs in the Winnipeg & Eastman regions
Activities: Hosting performing & competitive events; Posting event results; Providing programs to the rhythmic gymnastics community in Manitoba, such as the long term athlete development program & training for gymnastics coaches, & judges; Promoting standards for programs

Yukon Gymnastics Association
4061 - 4th Ave., Whitehorse YT Y1A 1H1
Tel: 867-456-7896; *Fax:* 867-668-6922

Overview: A small provincial organization
Member of: Canadian Gymnastics Federation
Chief Officer(s): Fia Jampolsky, President
Tania Doyle, Technical Director
touchdown@klondiker.com

Halls of Fame

Alberta Sports Hall of Fame & Museum (ASHFM)
#102 - 4200 Hwy 2, Red Deer AB T4N 1E3
Tel: 403-341-8614; *Fax:* 403-341-8619
info@ashfm.ca
www.ashfm.ca
www.youtube.com/user/ABSportsHallOfFame
www.facebook.com/ashfm
twitter.com/ashfm1

Overview: A medium-sized provincial charitable organization founded in 1957
Description: To honour Albertans who have distinguished themselves in sport & to operate a facility to house artifacts that are significant in Alberta's sports history; *Member of:* Museums Alberta; Canadian Museums Association; Canadian Association for Sport Heritage; International Sport Heritage Association
Chief Officer(s): Dennis Allan, Chair
Donna Hateley, Managing Director
Finances: *Annual Operating Budget:* $250,000-$500,000
Staff: 5 staff member(s); 40 volunteer(s)
Membership: 950
Activities: Induction into Sports Hall of Fame; Museum; fundraising; *Awareness Events:* Induction Banquet; Annual Golf Tournament *Library:* Alberta Sport History Library (Open to Public)

British Columbia Sports Hall of Fame & Museum
Gate A, BC Place Stadium, 777 Pacific Blvd. South, Vancouver BC V6B 4Y8
Tel: 604-687-5520; *Fax:* 604-687-5510
sportsinfo@bcsportshalloffame.com
www.bcsportshalloffame.com
www.facebook.com/bcsportshall
twitter.com/BCSportsHall

Overview: A medium-sized provincial charitable organization founded in 1966
Description: To collect, preserve & display sports artifacts from BC's sporting history; to provide an exciting & educational environment for sports history; *Member of:* Canadian Museums Association; BC Museums Association
Affiliation(s): International Association of Sports Museums & Halls of Fame
Chief Officer(s): Allison Mailer, Executive Director
allison.mailer@bcsportshalloffame.com
Jason Beck, Curator
jason.beck@bcsportshalloffame.com
Finances: *Funding Sources:* Corporate & private
Staff: 5 staff member(s); 50 volunteer(s)
Membership: 1-99
Activities: Champions Banquet & Tournament of Champions; *Awareness Events:* Banquet of Champions, Induction Ceremonies; *Internships:* Yes *Library:* Yes by appointment

Canada's Sports Hall of Fame / Temple de la renommée des sports du Canada
169 Canada Olympic Rd. SW, Calgary AB T3B 6B7
Tel: 403-776-1040
info@cshof.ca
www.sportshall.ca
www.instagram.com/cansportshall
www.facebook.com/CANsportshall
twitter.com/CANsportshall

Overview: A medium-sized national organization founded in 1955
Description: To inspire Canadian identity & national pride by telling the compelling stories of those outstanding achievements that make up Canada's sports history
Chief Officer(s): Cheryl Bernard, President & CEO, 403-776-1080
cbernard@cshof.ca
Janice Smith, Vice-President & COO
jsmith@cshof.ca
Jim Thomson, Director, Finance & Administration
jthomson@cshof.ca
Membership: 100-499

Canadian Golf Hall of Fame & Museum (CGHF) / Musée et Temple canadien de la renommée du golf
c/o Golf Canada, 1333 Dorval Dr., Oakville ON L6M 4X7
Toll-Free: 800-263-0009
cghf@golfcanada.ca
heritage.golfcanada.ca
twitter.com/cghf

Also Known As: Canadian Golf Museum
Overview: A small national charitable organization founded in 1971
Description: To celebrate outstanding individuals of Canadian golf who have played a key role in the evolution of the history of golf in Canada; *Member of:* Ontario Museum Association; Canadian Museum Association; Ontario Archives Association; Canadian Association for Sport Heritage; International Sports Heritage Association
Chief Officer(s): Meggan Gardner, Director, Heritage Services, 905-849-9700 412
mgardner@golfcanada.ca
Finances: *Funding Sources:* Golf Canada
Activities:*Library:* Canadian Golf Hall of Fame & Museum Library (Open to Public)

Canadian Lacrosse Hall of Fame
777 Columbia St., New Westminster BC V3M 1B6
Tel: 778-237-3601
admin@clhof.org
www.clhof.org
www.instagram.com/canlaxhall
www.facebook.com/clhof
twitter.com/CanLaxHall

Overview: A small national organization founded in 1967
Description: To honour through exhibits the history of lacrosse from its First Nations roots to its modern day form; To induct worthy recipients into the Hall of Fame
Chief Officer(s): David Soul, Executive Director
dhcsoul@clhof.org
Activities:*Library:* Canadian Lacrosse Hall of Fame Archives by appointment

Canadian Olympic Hall of Fame / Temple de la renommée olympique du Canada
c/o Canadian Olympic Committee, PO Box 19, #3000, 250 Yonge St., Toronto ON M5B 2L7
Tel: 416-962-0262; *Fax:* 416-967-4902
olympic.ca/canadian-olympic-hall-of-fame

Overview: A small national organization founded in 1948
Description: To honor those athletes, coaches, officials, administrators & volunteerswho have served the cause of the Olympic Movement with distinction; *Member of:* Canadian Olympic Committee

Manitoba Sports Hall of Fame & Museum (MSHF&M)
145 Pacific Ave., Winnipeg MB R3B 2Z6
Tel: 204-925-5936; *Fax:* 204-925-5916
halloffame@sportmanitoba.ca
www.sportmanitoba.ca/hall-of-fame
www.youtube.com/user/sportmanitoba
www.facebook.com/sportmb
twitter.com/SportManitoba

Overview: A small provincial charitable organization founded in 1980
Description: To recognize & honour those who have made their mark in Manitoba's rich sports history through their activities & achievements by telling their stories through articles & exhibits; *Member of:* Association of Manitoba Museums (AMM), the Association of Manitoba Archives (AMA), the Canadian Association for Sport Heritage (CASH) and the Canadian Heritage Information Network (CHIN).
Affiliation(s): Association of Manitoba Museums; Association of Manitoba Archives; Canadian Association for Sport Heritage; Canadian Heritage Information Network
Chief Officer(s): Rick Brownlee, Sport Heritage Manager
Finances: *Funding Sources:* Fundraising; lotteries; provincial government
Activities: Entertainment events; Induction Dinner; Educational & Development seminars

New Brunswick Sports Hall of Fame (NBSHF) / Temple de la renommée sportive du N.-B.
PO Box 6000, 503 Queen St., Fredericton NB E3B 5H1
Tel: 506-453-3747
nbsportshalloffame@gnb.ca
www.nbsportshalloffame.com
www.instagram.com/nbshf
www.facebook.com/NBSportsHallofFame
twitter.com/NBSHF

Overview: A small provincial charitable organization founded in 1970
Description: To preserve & celebrate the sports heritage of New Brunswick; To inspire greatness; *Member of:* Canadian Association for Sport Heritage; Canadian Museums Association
Affiliation(s): International Sports Heritage Association
Chief Officer(s): Jamie Wolverton, Executive Director, 506-453-8930
ed@nbshf.ca
James Matthews, Officer, Communications & Operations
communications@nbshf.ca
Finances: *Funding Sources:* Provincial government; fundraising; sponsorships; donations
Activities: Annual dinner & Induction Ceremony; exhibits; receptions; lectures; tours; *Library:* Sports Heritage Resource Centre (Open to Public) by appointment

Northwestern Ontario Sports Hall of Fame & Museum
219 May St. South, Thunder Bay ON P7E 1B5
Tel: 807-622-2852; *Fax:* 807-622-2736
nwosport@tbaytel.net
www.nwosportshalloffame.com
www.youtube.com/user/nwosport
Also Known As: NWO Sports Hall of Fame
Overview: A small local charitable organization founded in 1978
Description: To preserve & honour the sports heritage of northwestern Ontario; *Member of:* Canadian Association for Sport Heritage; International Association of Sports Museums & Halls of Fame; Ontario Museum Association; Archives Association of Ontario; Canadian Museums Association; Thunder Bay Chamber of Commerce
Chief Officer(s): Kathryn Dwyer, Curator
Diane Imrie, Executive Director
Finances: *Annual Operating Budget:* $100,000-$250,000
Staff: 3 staff member(s); 25 volunteer(s)
Membership: 400; *Fees:* $25 individual; $40 family; $60 business/organization
Activities: A variety of structured programs are available for different grade levels; Annual Induction Dinner & Ceremony, last Sat. in Sept.; *Library:* Yes

Novia Scotia Sports Hall of Fame (NSSHF)
#446, 1800 Argyle St., Halifax NS B3J 3N8
Tel: 902-421-1266; *Fax:* 902-425-1148
sporthalloffame@eastlink.ca
www.novascotiasporthalloffame.com
www.linkedin.com/company/nova-scotia-sport-hall-of-fame
www.facebook.com/116064731766960
twitter.com/NSSHF
Previous Name: Nova Scotia Sport Heritage Centre
Overview: A small provincial organization founded in 1964
Description: To honour, promote & preserve the sport history of Nova Scotia
Chief Officer(s): Bruce Rainnie, President & Chief Executive Officer
bruce@nsshf.com
Katie Tanner, Coordinator, Museum & Communications
katie@nsshf.com
Activities:*Awareness Events:* Golf Tournament, June; Bingo @ the Halifax Forum

Ottawa Sports Hall of Fame Inc. (OSHOF) / Temple de la renommée des sports d'Ottawa
#1400, 340 Albert St., Ottawa ON K1R 0A5
info@ottawasporthalloffame.ca
www.ottawasporthalloffame.com
www.facebook.com/OttawaSportsHOF
twitter.com/OttawaSportsHoF
Overview: A small local organization founded in 1968
Description: To preserve the history & development of sports in Ottawa
Chief Officer(s): Dave Best, Chair
chairman@ottawasporthalloffame.ca
Finances: *Funding Sources:* Sponsorships
Membership: 200+ inductees
Activities: Recognizing individuals & teams who, through their achievements in or contributions to sport, have brought fame to Ottawa; *Awareness Events:* Induction Ceremony, May

Prince Edward Island Sports Hall of Fame & Museum Inc.
40 Enman Cres., Charlottetown PE C1E 1E6
Tel: 902-393-5474
peisportshall@gmail.com
www.peisportshalloffame.ca
www.facebook.com/210800825622110
twitter.com/peisportshall
Previous Name: Prince Edward Island Sports Hall of Fame
Overview: A small provincial charitable organization founded in 1968
Description: To honour & recognize those who have contributed to sports history in PEI; To collect & preserve artifacts, photos, & memorabilia relating to the history of sport in PEI
Chief Officer(s): Nick Murray, Special Advisor
Finances: *Funding Sources:* Fees; events; admissions; fundraising events; government grants; sponsorships
Membership: 170+ inductees
Activities:*Library:* Yes

Saskatchewan Sports Hall of Fame & Museum (SSFHM)
2205 Victoria Ave., Regina SK S4P 0S4
Tel: 306-780-9232; *Fax:* 306-780-9427
sshfm@sasktel.net
www.sasksportshalloffame.com
www.youtube.com/channel/UC2j_-agyX9f2-xa5laFueXQ
www.facebook.com/SaskSportsHF
twitter.com/SaskSportsHF
Overview: A small provincial charitable organization founded in 1966
Description: To recognize sport excellence, preserve sport history & educate the public on the contribution of sport to Saskatchewan's cultural fabric; *Member of:* Canadian Museums Association; Museums Association of Saskatchewan; Canadian Association for Sports Heritage; International Association of Sport Museums & Halls of Fame
Chief Officer(s): Sheila Kelly, Executive Director
skelly@sshfm.com
Brock Gerrard, Curator
bgerrard@sshfm.com
Finances: *Annual Operating Budget:* $250,000-$500,000; *Funding Sources:* Lotteries & self-help
Staff: 4 staff member(s); 95 volunteer(s)
Membership: 1,450
Activities: Museum galleries, archives, research facilities; Induction dinner; Annual Hall of Fame Game (Football); *Speaker Service:* Yes *Library:* Yes by appointment

Handball

Alberta Handball Association (AHA)
AB
www.albertahandball.com
www.facebook.com/Albertateamhandball
Overview: A small provincial organization
Description: To promote & develop the sport of handball in Alberta
Activities: Operates three clubs: Calgary, Edmonton & Sherwood Park

Alberta Team Handball Federation (ATHF)
Percy Page Centre, 11759 Groat Rd., Edmonton AB T5M 3K6
Tel: 780-415-2666; *Fax:* 780-422-2663
Handballalberta@gmail.com
www.teamhandball.ab.ca
www.youtube.com/HandballAlberta1
www.facebook.com/Albertateamhandball
twitter.com/handballalberta
Overview: A medium-sized provincial organization founded in 1960
Description: To govern the promotion of team handball throughout Alberta, by encouraging the development of athletes, coaches, referees, & administrators of all ages & abilities; *Member of:* Canadian Team Handball Federation
Chief Officer(s): Dan Stetic, President
Finances: *Funding Sources:* Membership & course fees; fundraising; donations; Alberta Sport, Recreation, Parks & Wildlife Foundation
Activities: Organizing provincial championships, regional leagues, coaching courses; programs for 8 years of age to adults, sport outreach clinics, & the City of Champions Tournament

Balle au mur Québec (BAMQ) / Québec Handball Association
CP 1000, Succ. M, 4545, av Pierre-de Coubertin, Montréal QC H1V 3R2
Tél: 514-252-3062; *Téléc:* 514-252-3103
info@sports-4murs.qc.ca
www.balleaumur.qc.ca
www.facebook.com/BalleAuMurQuebecBamq
Aperçu: *Dimension:* moyenne; *Envergure:* provinciale; *fondée en 1971*
Affiliation(s): Association canadienned de Balle au mur
Membre(s) du bureau directeur: Michel Séguin, Directeur général
Finances: *Budget de fonctionnement annuel:* $50,000-$100,000; *Fonds:*Gouvernement provincial
Personnel:2 membre(s) du personnel; 10 bénévole(s)
Membre: 10 institutionnel; 1 000 individu

British Columbia Team Handball Federation (BCTHF)
Vancouver BC
Tel: 604-786-5993
bchandball@bchandball.ca
www.bchandball.ca
www.facebook.com/BCHandball
twitter.com/bcteamhandball

Overview: A small provincial organization founded in 2003
Description: To promote & govern handball in BC; *Member of:* Canadian Team Handball Federation
Chief Officer(s): David Lee, Chief Development Officer
Fees: Schedule available

Canadian Handball Association (CHA) / Fédération de balle au mur du Canada
Toronto ON
www.canadianhandball.com
Overview: A medium-sized national organization
Description: To promote handball in Canada
Chief Officer(s): Colleen Deckert, President
Membership: 3,000

Canadian Team Handball Federation (CTHF) / Fédération canadienne de handball olympique (FCHO)
Tel: 819-563-7937; *Fax:* 819-563-5352
info@handballcanada.ca
handballcanada.ca
www.instagram.com/handballcanada
www.facebook.com/handballcanada
twitter.com/handballcanada
Overview: A medium-sized national charitable organization founded in 1966
Affiliation(s): International Handball Federation; Pan American Team Handball Federation; Commonwealth Handball Federation
Chief Officer(s): David Lee, President
d.lee@handballcanada.cam
François LeBeau, Chief Operating Officer
f.lebeau@handballcanada.ca
Finances: *Annual Operating Budget:* $500,000-$1.5 Million; *Funding Sources:* Sport Canada; COO; CAC
Staff: 1 staff member(s); 1 volunteer(s)
Membership: 15,000; *Fees:* $5; *Committees:* Management; Officials; Coaches; National Teams
Activities: Canadian Championship; Canada Cup; Pan-American Championships & Games; *Speaker Service:* Yes

Fédération québécoise de handball olympique (FQHO)
CP 1000, Succ. M, 4545, av Pierre-de-Coubertin, Montréal QC H1V 0B2
Tél: 514-252-3067; *Téléc:* 514-252-3176
handball@handball.qc.ca
www.handball.qc.ca
www.facebook.com/HandballQuebec
Aperçu: *Dimension:* petite; *Envergure:* locale
Description: Régir le handball au Québec; *Membre de:* Canadian Team Handball Federation
Membre(s) du bureau directeur: Michelle Lortie, Directrice
mlortie@handball.qc.ca

Handball Association of Newfoundland & Labrador
St. John's NL
www.nlhandballontherock.com
www.facebook.com/nlhandballontherock
Also Known As: NL Handball Association; Handball on the Rock
Overview: A small provincial organization
Description: To promote & develop the sport of handball in Newfoundland & Labrador, with emphasis on junior programs; *Member of:* Canadian Team Handball Federation
Chief Officer(s): Wayne Amminson, President

Handball Association of Nova Scotia (HANS)
NS
nshandball.com
twitter.com/nshandball
Overview: A small provincial organization
Description: To promote & develop the sport of handball in Nova Scotia
Chief Officer(s): Daniel Marcil, President & CEO
dan@nshandball.com
Activities: Tournaments; junior program

Manitoba Team Handball Federation
MB
www.manitobahandball.wixsite.com/mthf
www.instagram.com/teamhandballmb
www.facebook.com/teamhandballmb
twitter.com/TeamHandballMB
Previous Name: Manitoba Handball Association Inc.
Overview: A small provincial organization
Description: To promote & develop the sport of handball in Manitoba; *Member of:* Canadian Team Handball Federation
Chief Officer(s): Rhoni McKenzie, Coordinator, Operations

New Brunswick Team Handball Federation
CP 27070, Dieppe NB

Tél: 506-227-2506
handball.nb@outlook.com
www.handballnb.org

www.facebook.com/handballnb
Également appelé: Handball NB
Aperçu: *Dimension:* petite; *Envergure: locale; Organisme sans but lucratif*
Description: To promote handball in New Brunswick; *Membre de:* Canadian Team Handball Federation
Membre(s) du bureau directeur: Luc Deschênes, President
president@handballnb.org

Ontario Handball Association (OHA)
ON

www.ontariohandball.ca
Overview: A small provincial organization
Description: To promote & develop the sport of handball in Ontario
Chief Officer(s): Jenine Wilson, President
president@ontariohandball.ca
Activities: Tournaments; junior programs

Saskatchewan Handball Association (SHA)
SK

Tel: 306-584-8035
nonprofits.accesscomm.ca/sha
Overview: A small provincial organization
Description: To promote & develop the sport of handball in Saskatchewan

Team Handball Ontario (THO)
Toronto ON

communications@handballontario.com
www.handballontario.com
www.instagram.com/teamhandballontario
www.facebook.com/TeamHandballOntario
twitter.com/handballontario
Overview: A medium-sized provincial organization founded in 1978
Description: To represent team handball in Ontario; *Member of:* Canadian Federation of Team Handball
Chief Officer(s): Nick Cuddemi, President
Steffen Dube, Technical Director
Fab Barrillot, Diector, Communications
Finances: *Funding Sources:* Sponsors; Fundraising
Fees: $200 full; $125 half season; $10 per drop in session; $25 social

Hang Gliding

British Columbia Hang Gliding & Paragliding Association (BCHPA)
BC

www.bchpa.ca
Previous Name: Hang Gliding Association of British Columbia
Overview: A small provincial organization
Description: To protect, maintain & improve flying sites throughout the province.
Chief Officer(s): Don Herres, President, 250-550-5304

Great Lakes Gliding Club (GLGC)
7272 - 6 Line, RR#3, Tottenham ON L0G 1W0

Tel: 416-466-7016
postmaster@greatlakesgliding.com
www.greatlakesgliding.com
www.facebook.com/flyglgc
Overview: A small local organization founded in 1998
Description: The club offers license training as well as flying competitions
Membership: 35; *Fees:* $250 associate; $375 students; $550 full; *Member Profile:* Students; Licenced pilots

Hang Gliding & Paragliding Association of Atlantic Canada (HPAAC)
hpaac.ca
www.facebook.com/HPAAC
Previous Name: Hang Gliding Association of Newfoundland
Overview: A small local organization founded in 1979
Description: To develop & promote the sports of hang glinding & paragliding in Atlantic Canada
Affiliation(s): Hang Gliding & Paragliding Association of Canada
Membership: 1-99; *Fees:* $140
Activities: Paragliding & hang gliding at coastal cities in Nova Scotia, Prince Edward Island, New Brunswick & Newfoundland & Labrador; *Awareness Events:* Atlantic Annual Paragliding/Hang Gliding Festival, May

Hang Gliding & Paragliding Association of Canada (HPAC) / Association canadienne de vol libre (ACVL)
#302, 5628 Birney Ave., Vancouver BC V6S 0H7

Fax: 604-731-4407
Toll-Free: 877-370-2078
admin@hpac.ca
www.hpac.ca
Overview: A medium-sized national organization founded in 1977
Description: To promote unpowered foot-launched flight in hang gliders & paragliders; *Member of:* Aero Club of Canada; Fédération aéronautique internationale
Chief Officer(s): Margit Nance, Executive Director
Finances: *Annual Operating Budget:* $50,000-$100,000; *Funding Sources:* Membership fees
Staff: 1 staff member(s)
Membership: 890; *Fees:* Schedule available; *Committees:* Safety

Manitoba Hang Gliding Association (MHGA)
c/o Sport Manitoba, 145 Pacific Ave., Winnipeg MB R3B 2Z6

mhga.ca
Overview: A small provincial organization founded in 1980
Description: To be the provincial governing body for the sport of hang gliding in Manitoba; *Member of:* Hang Gliding & Paragliding Association of Canada

Southwestern Ontario Gliding Association (SOGA)
441 Lorindale St., Waterloo ON N2K 2X2

Tel: 519-741-6058
www.sogaclub.ca
Previous Name: K-W Hang Gliding Club; Hang-On-Tario
Overview: A medium-sized provincial organization founded in 1979
Description: To organize safe hang gliding space & time for its members
Chief Officer(s): John Pop, Contact
jpop@golden.net
Fees: $25 associate; $30 aerotowing to ft.; $250 full; *Committees:* Public Relations; Safety

Health

ParticipACTION
#1205, 77 Bloor St. West, Toronto ON M5S 1M2

info@participaction.com
www.participaction.com
www.instagram.com/Participaction
www.facebook.com/ParticipACTION
twitter.com/Participaction
Overview: A medium-sized national organization founded in 1971
Description: To help Canadians sit less & move more by making physical activity a part of everyday life
Finances: *Funding Sources:* Government of Canada; Public Health Agency of Canada; Government of Newfoundland & Labrador; Ontario Trillium Foundation
Staff: 27 staff member(s)

Hearing Impaired

Alberta Deaf Sports Association (ADSA)
#205, 11404 - 142 St., Edmonton AB T5M 1V1

info@albertadeafsports.ca
www.albertadeafsports.ca
www.facebook.com/AlbertaDeafSports
Also Known As: Federation of Silent Sports of Alberta
Overview: A medium-sized provincial charitable organization founded in 1974
Description: To coordinate sport & recreation activities for deaf people in Alberta; To promote competition at the local, provincial, regional, & national levels; To select Alberta athletes to compete in national championships for the World Games of the Deaf; *Member of:* Canadian Deaf Sports Association
Chief Officer(s): Grant Underschultz, President
Brenda Hillcox, Secretary
Fees: $25 regular; $15 senior citizens/post-secondary students; *Member Profile:* Deaf & hard of hearing persons

Canadian Deaf Sports Association (CDSA) / Association des sports des sourds du Canada (ASSC)
PO Box 41035, Stn. Centre Duvernay, 3100 Blvd. Concorde East, Laval QC H7E 5H1

info@assc-cdsa.com
assc-cdsa.com
www.instagram.com/assccdsa
www.facebook.com/CanadianDeafSports
twitter.com/assc_cdsa

Overview: A medium-sized national licensing charitable organization founded in 1964
Description: To promote & facilitate the practice of fitness, amateur sports & recreation among deaf people of all ages in Canada from the local recreational level to Olympics calibre; *Member of:* Canadian Deaf & Hard of Hearing Forum; Canadian Paralympic Committee; Canadian Sports Coalition
Affiliation(s): International Committee of Sports for the Deaf
Chief Officer(s): Alain Turpin, Executive Director
alain.turpin@assc-cdsa.com
Gigi Fiset, Manager, Operational Services & Events
gigi.fiset@assc-cdsa.com
Finances: *Funding Sources:* Sport Canada
Staff: 3 staff member(s)

International Committee of Sports for the Deaf (ICSD) / Comité international des Sports des Sourds (CISS)
Maison du Sport International, Av. de Rhondanie 54, Lausanne CH-1007 Switzerland

office@ciss.org
www.ciss.org
Also Known As: International Deaflympics
Overview: A medium-sized international charitable organization founded in 1924
Description: To organize sporting events for deaf & hard of hearing athletes; *Member of:* International Olympic Committee; General Assembly of International Sports Federations
Affiliation(s): Canadian Deaf Sports Association
Chief Officer(s): Kang Chen, President
president@ciss.org
Membership: 113 countries; *Member Profile:* National Deaf Sports Federations
Activities: Deaflympics; World Deaf Championships; *Internships:* Yes

Manitoba Deaf Sports Association Inc. (MDSA)
c/o Sport Manitoba, 145 Pacific Ave., Winnipeg MB R3B 2Z6

www.mdsaassoc.com
Overview: A small provincial organization
Description: To provide sporting opportunities for deaf people in Manitoba; *Member of:* Canadian Deaf Sports Association
Chief Officer(s): Brenda Comte, President
mdsapresident72@gmail.com
Shawna Joynt, Vice-President
Kenneth Anderson, Treasurer
Joseph Comte, Technical Director
Membership: 6 organizations

Newfoundland & Labrador Deaf Sports Association (NLDSA)
58 First St., Mount Pearl NL A1N 1Y3
Overview: A small provincial organization
Description: To govern fitness, amateur sports & recreation for deaf people in Newfoundland & Labrador; *Member of:* Canadian Deaf Sports Association
Chief Officer(s): Bryan Johnson, Acting President
bryan.johnson@nf.sympatico.ca

Saskatchewan Deaf Sports Association (SDSA)
PO Box 932, Fort Qu'Appelle SK S0G 1S0
Overview: A small provincial charitable organization
Description: To foster sporting opportunities to members of the deaf & hard-of-hearing communities; To select & train deaf & hard-of-hearing athletes for international competitions; *Member of:* Canadian Deaf Sports Association
Affiliation(s): Regina Deaf Athletic Club; Saskatoon Deaf Athletic Club; Saskatchewan Sport Inc.
Chief Officer(s): Pamela Rustoen, Contact
pamelarustoen@gmail.com
Finances: *Annual Operating Budget:* Less than $50,000; *Funding Sources:* Provincial subsidy; Sask. Lotteries; tickets sales; special events
Staff: 10 volunteer(s)
Membership: 300-400; *Fees:* $5 adult (no championships); $25 adult; $75 organization

Hiking

Federation of Mountain Clubs of British Columbia (FMCBC)
PO Box 19673, Vancouver BC V5T 4E7

Tel: 604-873-6096; *Fax:* 604-873-6086
info@mountainclubs.org
www.mountainclubs.org
www.facebook.com/mountainclubs
twitter.com/mountainclubs
Overview: A small provincial charitable organization founded in 1980

Description: To advocate for safe non-motorized backcountry activities & the protection of BC's backcountry; *Member of:* Donations; Membership dues
Chief Officer(s): Dave Wharton, President
president@mountainclubs.org
Barry Janyk, Executive Director
executive.director@mountainclubs.org
Jodi Appleton, Manager, Program and Administration
admin.manager@mountainclubs.org
Membership: 3500; *Fees:* Individual $25; Associate $150; *Member Profile:* Individuals & non-profit organizations

Hockey

Abbotsford Female Hockey Association (AFHA)
#476, 33771 George Ferguson Way, Abbotsford BC V2S 2M5
afharegistrar@gmail.com
www.abbotsfordfemalehockey.com
www.facebook.com/AbbotsfordFemaleHockeyAssociation
twitter.com/AbbyIceGirls
Overview: A small local organization
Description: The Abbotsford Female Hockey Association seeks to provide an opportunity for females of all ages & all skill levels to play hockey in Abbotsford in an all-female league.; *Member of:* BC Hockey

British Columbia Amateur Hockey Association (BCAHA) / Association de hockey amateur de la Colombie-Britannique
6671 Oldfield Rd., Saanichton BC V8M 2A1
Tel: 250-652-2978; *Fax:* 250-652-4536
info@bchockey.net
www.bchockey.net
www.instagram.com/bchockeysource
www.facebook.com/BCHockeySource
twitter.com/BCHockey_Source
Also Known As: BC Hockey
Overview: A medium-sized provincial organization founded in 1919
Description: To foster, improve & perpetuate amateur hockey in BC; *Member of:* Hockey Canada
Chief Officer(s): Bill Ennos, Director, Programs
bennos@bchockey.net
Finances: *Annual Operating Budget:* $500,000-$1.5 Million
Staff: 7 staff member(s); 2000 volunteer(s)
Membership: 60,000 individual + 4,500 referees; *Fees:* Schedule available; *Member Profile:* Amateur hockey teams/leagues/associations; referees' organizations

Calgary Sledge Hockey Association
#109, 333 - 17th Ave. NW, Calgary AB T2M 0M9
Tel: 403-837-3926
info@calgarysledgehockey.ca
calgarysledgehockey.ca
www.facebook.com/CalgarySledgeHockey
twitter.com/yycsledge
Overview: A small local charitable organization
Description: To support & promote sledge hockey in the Calgary area
Affiliation(s): Hockey Alberta; Hockey Canada
Chief Officer(s): Dave Taylor, Director of Marketing, 403-891-9295
Membership: 3 teams; *Fees:* $30 fan; $350 player; *Member Profile:* Players and fans of sledge hockey
Activities: Organizing novice, intermediate, & senior sledge hockey teams

Canadian Adult Recreational Hockey Association (CARHA)
#610, 1420 Blair Pl., Ottawa ON K1J 9L8
Tel: 613-244-1989; *Fax:* 613-244-0451
Toll-Free: 800-267-1854
hockey@carhahockey.ca
www.carhahockey.ca
www.instagram.com/carhahockey75
www.facebook.com/carhahockey
twitter.com/CARHAHockey
Also Known As: CARHA Hockey
Previous Name: Canadian Oldtimers' Hockey Association
Overview: A medium-sized national charitable organization founded in 1975
Description: To develop & provide a wide range of innovative resources to adult recreational hockey teams, leagues & tournament organizers in Canada and worldwide; To govern recreational hockey & provide a safe playing environment
Chief Officer(s): Michael S. Peski, President
mpeski@carhahockey.ca
Lori Lopez, Executive Director
llopez@carhahockey.ca
Laurie Langlois, Manager, Membership Services
llanglois@carhahockey.ca

Finances: *Funding Sources:* Membership; Sponsorship
Fees: $23; *Member Profile:* People 19 years of age or older
Activities: *Internships:* Yes

Canadian Hockey League
#905, 5255 Yonge St., Toronto ON M2N 6P4
Tel: 416-332-9711; *Fax:* 416-299-8787
chl.ca
www.instagram.com/chlhockey
twitter.com/CHLHockey
Overview: A large national organization
Description: To act as the umbrella organization for the three major junior hockey leagues in Canada: Ontario Hockey League, Western Hockey League & Quebec Major Junior Hockey League
Chief Officer(s): Dan MacKenzie, President
Gilles Courteau, Vice-President
Ron Robison, Vice-President
Cole Butterworth, Director, Business Operations
cbutterworth@chl.ca
Kyle Ferguson, Director, Corporate Partnerships
kferguson@chl.ca
Heran Jung, Director, Finance
hjung@chl.ca
Paul Krotz, Director, Communications
pkrotz@chl.ca
Activities: Mastercard Memorial Cup; Home Hardware Top Prospects Game; Subway Super Series; CHL Import Draft; *Rents Mailing List:* Yes

Cape Breton County Minor Hockey Association (CBCMHA)
PO Box 6003, 1174 Kings Rd., Sydney River NS B1S 3V9
Tel: 902-562-1767; *Fax:* 902-562-1833
cbcmha@ns.aliantzinc.ca
www.cbcmha.ca
Overview: A medium-sized local organization
Description: The Cape Breton County Minor Hockey Association is dedicated to the advancement of minor hockey & promoting the development & personal growth of all participants through progressive leadership, by ensuring meaningful & equal opportunities, & providing enjoyable experiences in a safe & respectful environment.; *Member of:* Hockey Canada; Hockey Nova Scotia
Chief Officer(s): Shannon Fuller, Registrar
Fees: Schedule available

Fédération internationale de hockey (FIH) / International Hockey Federation
Rue du Valentin 61, Lausanne CH-1004 Switzerland
info@fih.ch
www.fih.ch
www.youtube.com/fihhockey
www.facebook.com/fihockey
www.twitter.com/FIH_Hockey
Aperçu: *Dimension:* moyenne; *Envergure:* internationale; fondée en 1924
Description: To develop entertainment events; To increase professionalism in hockey; To promote the image of hockey; To generate more worldwide followers
Affiliation(s): Field Hockey Canada
Membre(s) du bureau directeur: Narinder Batra, President
Membre: 5 federations; *Comités:* Appointments; Athletes; Competitions; Risk & Compliance; Rules; Umpiring; Equipment Advisory Panel; High Performance & Coaching Advisory Panel; Judicial Commission; Medical Advisory Panel

Hockey Alberta
PO Box 5005, #2606, 100 College Blvd., Red Deer AB T4N 5H5
Tel: 403-342-6777; *Fax:* 403-346-4277
info@hockeyalberta.ca
www.hockeyalberta.ca
www.youtube.com/user/HockeyAlberta
www.linkedin.com/company/hockey-alberta
www.facebook.com/HockeyAlberta
twitter.com/HockeyAlberta
Overview: A large provincial organization founded in 1907
Description: To act as the governing body for organized hockey in Alberta; To create positive opportunities & experiences for players through service & leadership; *Member of:* Hockey Canada
Chief Officer(s): Rob Litwinski, Chief Executive Officer
rlitwinski@hockeyalberta.ca
Mike Klass, Director, Business Operations
mklass@hockeyalberta.ca
Justin Fesyk, Senior Manager, Hockey Development
jfesyk@hockeyalberta.ca
Membership: 450 organizations + 100,000+ individual members
Activities: Hosting regional & provincial tournaments & competitions; Providing access to certified coaching clinics; Holding an appeal board to which any member, team or player can appeal disciplinary measures; Issuing permits for

tournaments & exhibition games to ensure that teams meet eligibility requirements; Providing rule books, training manuals & bulletins for teams & officials; *Internships:* Yes; *Speaker Service:* Yes; *Rents Mailing List:* Yes

Hockey Canada
2451 Riverside Dr., Ottawa ON K1H 7X7
Fax: 613-696-0787
Toll-Free: 888-777-2192
www.hockeycanada.ca
www.youtube.com/hockeycanadavideos
www.linkedin.com/company/hockey-canada
www.facebook.com/HockeyCanada
twitter.com/hockeycanada
Also Known As: Canadian Hockey Association
Merged from: Canadian Amateur Hockey Association; Hockey Canada
Overview: A large national organization founded in 1914
Description: To advance amateur hockey for all individuals through progressive leadership, ensuring meaningful opportunities & enjoyable experiences in a safe, sustainable environment
Affiliation(s): International Ice Hockey Federation
Chief Officer(s): Tom Renney, Chief Executive Officer
Finances: *Funding Sources:* Government; Sponsorship; Sales; Fundraising

Hockey Canada Foundation
151 Canada Olympic Rd. SW, Calgary AB T3B 6B7
Tel: 403-777-3636; *Fax:* 403-777-3635
Toll-Free: 888-777-2192
foundation@hockeycanada.ca
www.hockeycanada.ca
Overview: A large national charitable organization
Description: To establish & grow endowment & general purpose funds for Hockey Canada
Chief Officer(s): Pete Brauti, Executive Director
Finances: *Funding Sources:* Donations; fundraising
Activities: Focus areas: Skill Development & Qualified Coaching; Accessibility & Diversity; Health & Wellness; Athlete & Alumni Support; Facilities; *Awareness Events:* Golf Gala

Hockey Development Centre for Ontario (HDCO)
#215, 19 Waterman Ave., Toronto ON M4B 1Y2
Tel: 416-426-7252; *Fax:* 416-426-7348
Toll-Free: 888-843-4326
hockey@hdco.on.ca
www.hdco.on.ca
twitter.com/theHDCO
Overview: A medium-sized provincial organization founded in 1984
Description: To provide educational, developmental & financial opportunities for amateur hockey participants in Ontario
Chief Officer(s): Wayne Dillon, Executive Director
wdillon@hdco.on.ca
Finances: *Annual Operating Budget:* $500,000-$1.5 Million; *Funding Sources:* Provincial government; sponsorships
Staff: 3 staff member(s)
Membership: 10 institutional; 2 associate
Activities: Hockey Trainers Certification Program; *Rents Mailing List:* Yes *Library:* Hockey Resources (Open to Public)

Hockey Eastern Ontario (HEO)
813 Shefford Rd., Ottawa ON K1J 8H9
Tel: 613-224-7686; *Fax:* 613-224-6079
info@hockeyeasternontario.ca
www.hockeyeasternontario.ca
www.youtube.com/channel/UCIc6D9wLXpCkGsA2ETjpkhg
www.facebook.com/HockeyEasternOntario
twitter.com/HEOhockey
Overview: A medium-sized provincial organization founded in 1920
Description: To act as the governing body of amateur hockey in Eastern Ontario; To foster, improve, & encourage amateur hockey through leadership
Chief Officer(s): Debbie Rambeau, Executive Director, 613-224-7686 201
drambeau@hockeyeasternontario.ca

Hockey Eastern Ontario Minor
#108, 1830 Walkley Rd., Ottawa ON K1H 8K3
Tel: 613-224-3589; *Fax:* 855-825-6123
heominor@heominor.ca
www.heominor.ca
Previous Name: Ottawa District Minor Hockey Association
Overview: A medium-sized local organization founded in 1972
Description: To promote minor hockey throughout the region; *Member of:* Hockey Canada
Chief Officer(s): Denis Dumais, President
denis.dumais@heominor.ca
Wayne Ahronson, Executive Assistant

Activities: *Speaker Service:* Yes *Library:* Resource Centre (Open to Public)

Hockey Manitoba
145 Pacific Ave., Winnipeg MB R3B 2Z6
Tel: 204-925-5755; *Fax:* 204-925-5761
info@hockeymanitoba.ca
www.hockeymanitoba.ca
www.youtube.com/hockeymanitoba
www.facebook.com/hockeymanitoba
twitter.com/hockeymanitoba
Also Known As: Manitoba Amateur Hockey Association
Overview: A medium-sized provincial organization founded in 1914
Description: To foster, develop, & promote amateur hockey throughout Manitoba; To encourage fair play; To secure the enforcement of rules as adopted by by the assosciation; To conduct games between member clubs to determine provincial champions
Chief Officer(s): Peter Woods, Executive Director, 204-925-5757
peter@hockeymanitoba.ca
Bernie Reichardt, Director, Hockey Development, 204-925-5759
bernie@hockeymanitoba.ca
Membership: 30,000; *Committees:* Officials Development; Athlete Development
Activities: Administering clinics & skills camps; Collaborating in development programs for players, coaches & officials

Hockey New Brunswick (HNB) / Hockey Nouveau-Brunswick
PO Box 456, 861 Woodstock Rd., Fredericton NB E3B 4Z9
Tel: 506-453-0089; *Fax:* 506-453-0468
www.hnb.ca
www.facebook.com/148777865135246
twitter.com/HockeyNB
Previous Name: New Brunswick Amateur Hockey Association
Overview: A medium-sized provincial organization founded in 1968
Description: To act as the governing body for hockey in New Brunswick
Chief Officer(s): Nic Jansen, Executive Director, 506-453-0866
njansen@hnb.ca

Hockey Newfoundland & Labrador (NLHA) / Association de hockey de Terre-Neuve et Labrador
PO Box 176, 32 Queensway, Grand Falls-Windsor NL A2A 2J4
Tel: 709-489-5512; *Fax:* 709-489-2273
office@hockeynl.ca
www.hockeynl.ca
twitter.com/Hkynl
Overview: A medium-sized provincial organization founded in 1935
Description: To act as the governing body for hockey in Newfoundland & Labrador; To foster & encourage positive player experiences through development & leadership; *Member of:* Hockey Canada
Chief Officer(s): Craig Tulk, Executive Director
ctulk@hockeynl.ca

Hockey North
c/o Kyle Kugler, Executive Director, Hockey North, 237 Borden Dr., Yellowknife NT X1A 3R2
Tel: 867-446-8890
www.hockeynorth.ca
Overview: A small provincial organization
Description: To govern & register all amateur hockey programs in the Northwest Territories & Nunavut Territory
Chief Officer(s): Kyle Kugler, Executive Director
kylek@hockeynorth.ca

Hockey Northwestern Ontario (HNO)
#301, 214 Red River Rd., Thunder Bay ON P7B 1A6
Tel: 807-623-1542; *Fax:* 807-623-0037
info@hockeyhno.com
www.hockeyhno.com
www.facebook.com/HNOHockey
twitter.com/HNOHockey
Previous Name: Thunder Bay Amateur Hockey Association
Overview: A small provincial organization
Description: To encourage & improve the sport of amateur hockey throughout Northwestern Ontario; *Member of:* Hockey Canada
Chief Officer(s): Trevor Hosanna, Executive Director, 807-623-1542 2
thosanna@hockeyhno.com

Hockey Nova Scotia
#17, 7 Mellor Ave., Dartmouth NS B3B 0E8
Tel: 902-454-9400; *Fax:* 902-454-3883
www.hockeynovascotia.ca
www.youtube.com/channel/UC8gbE0o_HAAQ6bj2c8S6kdg
www.facebook.com/hockeynovascotia
twitter.com/HockeyNS
Previous Name: Nova Scotia Hockey Association
Overview: A medium-sized provincial organization founded in 1974
Description: To act as the governing body for hockey in Nova Scotia; To encourage positive player experiences through development, resources, & leadership; *Member of:* Hockey Canada
Chief Officer(s): Darren Cossar, Executive Director
dcossar@hockeynovascotia.ca
Membership: 20,000

Hockey PEI
PO Box 302, #209, 40 Enman Cres., Charlottetown PE C1E 1E6
Tel: 902-368-4334; *Fax:* 902-368-4337
info@hockeypei.com
hockeypei.com
www.facebook.com/HockeyPEI
twitter.com/hockeypei
Previous Name: Prince Edward Island Hockey Association
Overview: A medium-sized provincial organization founded in 1974
Description: To act as the governing body for hockey in Prince Edward Island; *Member of:* Hockey Canada
Chief Officer(s): Geoff Kowalski, Executive Director
Finances: *Annual Operating Budget:* $250,000-$500,000
Staff: 3 staff member(s); 100 volunteer(s)
Membership: 6,000

Hockey Québec
#210, 7450, boul les Galeries d'Anjou, Montréal QC H1M 3M3
Tél: 514-252-3079; *Téléc:* 514-252-3158
communication@hockey.qc.ca
www.hockey.qc.ca
www.youtube.com/user/VideoHockeyQuebec
www.facebook.com/HockeyQuebecOfficielle
twitter.com/HockeyQuebec
Nom précédent: Fédération québécoise de hockey sur glace
Aperçu: *Dimension:* grande; *Envergure:* provinciale; *fondée en* 1976
Description: Assurer l'encadrement du hockey sur glace; favoriser la promotion et le développement de la personne qui pratique le hockey; *Membre de:* Hockey Canada
Membre(s) du bureau directeur: Paul Ménard, Directeur général, 514-252-3079 4883
pmenard@hockey.qc.ca
Activités: La Méthode d'apprentissage de hockey sur glace; excellence; développement régional; entraîneurs et officiels; formation des administrateurs bénévoles; hockey féminin; franc jeu; sports-études; *Service de conférenciers:* Oui; *Listes de destinataires:* Oui

Hockey Yukon
4061 - 4th Ave., Whitehorse YT Y1A 1H1
Tel: 867-393-4501
yaha@sportyukon.com
hockeyyukon.ca
Previous Name: Yukon Amateur Hockey Association
Overview: A small provincial organization
Description: The Yukon Amateur Hockey Association is the sports governing body for amateur hockey in the Yukon.; *Member of:* British Columbia Amateur Hockey Association; Sport Yukon

International Ice Hockey Federation (IIHF)
Brandschenkestrasse 50, Zurich CH-8027 Switzerland
office@iihf.com
www.iihf.com
www.instagram.com/iihfhockey
www.facebook.com/iihfhockey
twitter.com/IIHFHockey
Overview: A large international organization founded in 1908
Description: To govern, develop & promote ice & in-line hockey throughout the world; To develop & control international ice & in-line hockey; To promote friendly relations among the member national associations; To operate in an organized manner for the good of the sport; *Member of:* Association of International Olympic Winter Sports Federations
Affiliation(s): Hockey Canada
Chief Officer(s): Horst Lichtner, General Secretary
Membership: 76 national associations; *Member Profile:* National ice hockey associations & in-line hockey associations; *Committees:* Asian; Athletes; Competition & Coordination; Coaching; Disciplinary; Environmental & Social Activities; Ethics & Integrity; Event & Evaluation; Facilities Working Group; Finance; Historical; IIHF Governance Reform Group; Legal; Medical; Officiating; Player Safety; TV / New Media / Marketing; Women's; Youth & Junior Development
Activities: *Internships:* Yes; *Speaker Service:* Yes *Library:* Hockey Hall of Fame, Toronto Canada (Open to Public)

Lethbridge Oldtimers Sports Association (LOSA)
PO Box 84, Lethbridge AB T1J 3Y3
admin@losa.ca
www.losa.ca
twitter.com/LOSAhockey
Overview: A small local organization founded in 1975
Description: To organize recreational hockey games for adults
Chief Officer(s): Mike Mikado, President
Fees: $50; *Member Profile:* Men ages 35+ & women ages 22+

Minor Hockey Alliance of Ontario
71 Albert St., Stratford ON N5A 3K2
Tel: 519-273-7209; *Fax:* 519-273-2114
www.alliancehockey.com
www.facebook.com/114981545258512
twitter.com/ALLIANCE_Hockey
Also Known As: Alliance Hockey
Overview: A small provincial organization founded in 1993
Description: To organize, coordinate & develop hockey programs for all ages; *Member of:* Canadian Hockey Association; Ontario Hockey Federation
Chief Officer(s): Tony Martindale, Executive Director
Membership: 29,734; *Committees:* Development; Constitution; House League & Select; Minor Development; Group Structure; Insurance & Risk Management; Discipline & Suspension; Championship; Overseas; AGM

National Hockey League Alumni Association (NHLA)
400 Kipling Ave., Toronto ON M8V 3L1
Tel: 416-798-2586; *Fax:* 416-798-2582
info@nhlalumni.net
nhlalumni.net
www.instagram.com/nhlalumniassociation
www.facebook.com/nhlalumni
twitter.com/NHLAlumni
Also Known As: NHL Alumni Association
Overview: A medium-sized national charitable organization founded in 1999
Description: To provide programs & assistance for all retired NHL players
Affiliation(s): National Hockey League (NHL); National Hockey League Players' Association
Chief Officer(s): Glenn Healy, Executive Director
Membership: 28 chapters + 2,500 members; *Member Profile:* Former NHL players & coaches
Activities: BreakAway Program for career transitions; Golf tournament; Hockey tour; Auctions; Raffles; *Speaker Service:* Yes; *Rents Mailing List:* Yes

National Hockey League Players' Association (NHLPA)
#1200, 10 Bay St., Toronto ON M5J RN8
www.nhlpa.com
www.youtube.com/NHLPA
www.facebook.com/nhlpa
twitter.com/nhlpa
Overview: A large national organization founded in 1967
Description: To act as the union for professional hockey players in the National Hockey League (NHL)
Affiliation(s): National Hockey League (NHL); National Hockey League Players' Association
Chief Officer(s): Don Fehr, Executive Director
Membership: 750; *Member Profile:* All players in the NHL; *Committees:* Competition
Activities: Negotiating terms of the collective bargaining agreement; Salary arbitration; Professional development; Improving working conditions & safety; Certifying player agents

Northern Ontario Hockey Association (NOHA)
110 Lakeshore Dr., North Bay ON P1A 2A8
Tel: 705-474-8851; *Fax:* 705-474-6019
noha@noha.on.ca
www.noha-hockey.com
www.facebook.com/NorthernOntarioHockeyAssociation
twitter.com/nohahockey
Overview: A small local organization founded in 1919
Description: To foster the sport of amateur hockey in northern Ontario
Affiliation(s): Ontario Hockey Federation
Chief Officer(s): Jason Marchand, Executive Director
jmarchand@noha.on.ca
Finances: *Funding Sources:* Sponsorships; Membership fees
Staff: 13 staff member(s)
Member Profile: Amateur hockey clubs in northern Ontario
Activities: Hosting tournaments; Presenting awards; Organizing specialty clinics

Nova Scotia Minor Hockey Council
c/o Hockey Nova Scotia, #17, 7 Mellor Ave., Dartmouth NS B3B 0E8

Tel: 902-454-9400; *Fax:* 902-454-3883
Overview: A medium-sized provincial organization founded in 1974
Description: To provide a standard set of playing rules for minor hockey in Nova Scotia
Affiliation(s): Nova Scotia Hockey Association
Chief Officer(s): Brad MacKinley, Chair, 902-727-2551
brad.mackinley@bellaliant.net

Ontario Hockey Federation (OHF)
#9, 400 Sheldon Dr., Cambridge ON N1T 2H9

Tel: 226-533-9070; *Fax:* 519-620-7476
info@ohf.on.ca
www.ohf.on.ca
www.facebook.com/OHFHockey
twitter.com/ohfhockey
Overview: A medium-sized provincial organization founded in 1989
Description: To foster & promote the sport of amateur hockey in Ontario; To provide opportunities for all players to participate in the sport; To coordinate & conduct competitions & tournaments for branch, regional, & national championships; *Member of:* Hockey Development Centre for Ontario (HDCO)
Affiliation(s): Minor Hockey Alliance of Ontario; Greater Toronto Hockey League; Northern Ontario Hockey Association; Ontario Minor Hockey Association; Ontario Hockey Association; Ontario Hockey League; Ontario Women's Hockey Association
Chief Officer(s): Phillip McKee, Executive Director, 226-533-9075
pmckee@ohf.on.ca
Membership: 228,251 registered players; 33,500 coaches; 7,300 officials; *Committees:* Constitution; Finance; Rules; Risk Management; Registration; Minor Council; Junior Council; Hockey Development Council; Senior / Adult Recreational Council; Female Hockey (operates under the auspices of the Ontario Women's Hockey Association)
Activities: *Internships:* Yes

Ontario Minor Hockey Association (OMHA)
#3, 25 Brodie Dr., Richmond Hill ON L4B 3K7

Tel: 905-780-6642; *Fax:* 905-780-0344
omha@omha.net
www.omha.net
www.instagram.com/ontariominorhockey
www.facebook.com/HometownHockey
twitter.com/HometownHockey
Overview: A medium-sized provincial organization founded in 1935
Description: To provide community-based minor hockey programming for men, women, & children; To monitor the safety of the game, from equipment to rules
Affiliation(s): Ontario Hockey Federation
Chief Officer(s): Richard Ropchan, Executive Director, 905-780-2150
Martha Dickie, Manager, Membership Services, 905-780-2159
Ian Taylor, Director, Hockey Development, 905-780-2172
Finances: *Funding Sources:* Membership fees; Sponsorships
Activities: Providing development programs; Conducting seminars, coaches clinics, skills camps, & festivals; Initiating safety measures, such as the concussion awareness program, a mouthguard policy, & helmets for all on-ice personnel

Ontario Sledge Hockey Association (OSHA)
ON

www.ontariosledge.com
www.facebook.com/OSHASledge
twitter.com/OSHASledge
Overview: A medium-sized provincial organization
Description: To oversee three regular season sledge hockey leagues; *Member of:* Ontario Hockey Federation; Hockey Canada
Chief Officer(s): Drew Rigden, President, 705-790-0258
Membership: 20 clubs + 400 players; *Committees:* Rules

Ontario Women's Hockey Association (OWHA) / Association de hockey féminin de l'Ontario
225 Watline Ave., Mississauga ON L4Z 1P3

Tel: 905-282-9980; *Fax:* 905-282-9982
info@owha.on.ca
www.owha.on.ca
twitter.com/OWHAhockey
Overview: A medium-sized provincial organization founded in 1975
Description: To provide & develop opportunities for girls & women to play female hockey in all aspects of female hockey; To foster & encourage leadership programs in all areas related to the development of female hockey in Ontario; To promote

hockey as a game played primarily for enjoyment while also fostering sportsmanship; *Member of:* Hockey Canada
Chief Officer(s): Fran Rider, President & Chief Executive Officer, 416-573-5447
fran@owha.on.ca
Pat Nicholls, Director, Operations, 416-571-9198
pat@owha.on.ca

Original Hockey Hall of Fame & Museum
Invista Centre, 1350 Gardiners Rd., 2nd Fl., Kingston ON K7L 4V6

Tel: 613-507-1943
info@originalhockeyhalloffame.com
www.originalhockeyhalloffame.com
www.facebook.com/207141552735961
twitter.com/ihhof43
Previous Name: International Hockey Hall of Fame & Museum; International Ice Hockey Federation Museum Inc.
Overview: A small local organization founded in 1943
Description: The first sports hall of fame in Canada, the Hall features exhibits on the original six NHL teams, Kingston native Don Cherry & historic hockey artifacts
Chief Officer(s): Mark Potter, President
mpotter1@cogeco.ca
Larry Paquette, Vice-President
ihhof@kos.net
Finances: *Funding Sources:* Provincial government grants; special events; museum
Activities: *Awareness Events:* Historic Hockey Series, 1st Sat. in Feb.

Pan American Hockey Federation (PAHF)
info@panamhockey.org
www.panamhockey.org
www.youtube.com/user/PAHFvideo
www.facebook.com/PanAmHockey
twitter.com/PanAmHockey
Overview: A large international organization founded in 1955
Description: To be the governing continental federation for all field hockey in the Pan American region; *Member of:* International Hockey Federation
Chief Officer(s): Alberto Budeisky, President
Mary Cicinelli, Honorary Treasurer
mary.cicinelli@panamhockey.org
Finances: *Annual Operating Budget:* $100,000-$250,000; *Funding Sources:* Grants; Membership dues; Tournament fees; International Hockey Federation; Sponsorship
Membership: 31 national associations; *Member Profile:* National association recognized by national olympic committees & the International Hockey Federation; *Committees:* Appointments; Athletes; Competitions; Development; Education; Health & Safety; Masters; Media & Communications; Medical; Umpiring
Activities: Organizing international hockey tournaments; organizing instructional courses

Prince Edward Island Hockey Referees Association
c/o Hockey PEI, 40 Enman Cres., Charlottetown PE C1A 7K7

Tel: 902-367-8373
Overview: A medium-sized provincial organization
Member of: Hockey PEI; Hockey Canada

Saskatchewan Hockey Association (SHA) / Association de hockey de la Saskatchewan
#2, 575 Park St., Regina SK S4N 5B2

Tel: 306-789-5101
www.sha.sk.ca
www.facebook.com/324377598563
twitter.com/sask_hockey
Overview: A medium-sized provincial organization founded in 1912
Description: To administer the operation of amateur hockey in the Province of Saskatchewan; To foster & promote amateur hockey within the province & to assist in the promotion of amateur hockey outside the province; To promote, supervise & administer all competitions for amateur hockey within the jurisdiction of the SAHA; *Member of:* Hockey Canada
Chief Officer(s): Kelly McClintock, General Manager
kellym@sha.sk.ca
Finances: *Annual Operating Budget:* $1.5 Million-$3 Million
Staff: 10 staff member(s)
Membership: 46,000

Summerside & Area Minor Hockey Association (SAMHA)
PO Box 1454, Summerside PE C1N 4K4

info@summersideminorhockey.com
summersideminorhockey.com
Overview: A medium-sized local organization

Superior International Junior Hockey League (SIJHL)
75 Strathcona Ave., Thunder Bay ON P7A 1S1

sijhlmedia@gmail.com
www.sijhlhockey.com
www.facebook.com/SIJHL
twitter.com/SIJHL
Overview: A small local organization
Member of: Canadian Junior Hockey League
Chief Officer(s): Bryan Graham, President/Commissioner, 807-629-9302
sijhlcommissioner@gmail.com
Membership: 6 teams

Thunder Bay Minor Hockey Association (TBMHA)
#101, 212 East Miles St., Thunder Bay ON P7C 1J6

Tel: 807-346-4510; *Fax:* 807-346-4511
www.tbmha.com
Overview: A small local organization
Chief Officer(s): Larry Busniuk, President

Township of Clarence Minor Hockey Association (TCMHA)
PO Box 212, Clarence Creek AB K0A 1N0

clarencehockey.ca
Overview: A small local organization
Description: To govern & promote minor hockey in Clarence
Chief Officer(s): Marc Richer, President, 613-406-5374
castorpresident@gmail.com

Western Hockey League (WHL)
Father David Bauer Arena, 2424 University Dr. NW, Calgary AB T2N 3Y9

Tel: 403-693-3030; *Fax:* 403-693-3031
info@whl.ca
www.whl.ca
www.instagram.com/westernhockeyleague
twitter.com/theWHL
Overview: A medium-sized local organization founded in 1966
Description: To remain the world's premiere major junior hockey league by continuing to provide the best player, coach & official development & educational opportunities while enhancing the entertainment value of the game; *Member of:* Canadian Hockey League
Chief Officer(s): Ron Robison, Commissioner
Membership: Comprised of 22 hockey teams in Western Canada & the northwest United States

Whitehorse Minor Hockey Association (WMHA)
4061 - 4th Ave., Whitehorse YT Y1A 1H1

Tel: 867-393-4698; *Fax:* 867-667-4237
office@whitehorseminor.ca
www.whitehorseminorhockey.ca
Overview: A medium-sized provincial organization
Description: Promotes and coordinates minor hockey leagues in Whitehorse.; *Member of:* Sport Yukon
Affiliation(s): Yukon Amateur Hockey Association
Chief Officer(s): Justin Halowaty, President
justin@ttlp.com
Richelle Bierlmeier, Vice-President, Operations
richelle99@gmail.com

Whitehorse Women's Hockey Association (WWHA)
c/o Sport Yukon, 4061 - 4th Ave., Whitehorse YT Y1A 1H1

wwhayukon@gmail.com
whitehorsewomenshockey.com
www.facebook.com/whitehorsewomenshockeyassn
Overview: A small local organization founded in 1993
Description: To administer women's hockey in Whitehorse.

Horse Racing

Jockey Club of Canada / Jockey Club du Canada
PO Box 66, Stn. B, Toronto ON M9W 5K9

Tel: 416-675-7756; *Fax:* 416-675-6378
jockeyclubcanada@gmail.com
jockeyclubcanada.com
twitter.com/jockeyclubofCAN
Overview: A small national licensing organization founded in 1973
Description: Promote good quality racing throughout Canada; *Member of:* Thoroughbred Racing Industry participants in Canada
Affiliation(s): The Jockey Club (New York)
Chief Officer(s): Glenn Sikura, Chief Steward
Melanie O'Sullivan, Executive Director
Member Profile: Liaises with foreign Jockey Clubs; promotes Thoroughbred ownership; & represents Canada at international racing conferences.
Activities: *Library:* Yes (Open to Public) by appointment

Jockeys Benefit Association of Canada (JBAC)
c/o Thoroughbred Race Office, 555 Rexdale Blvd., Toronto ON M9W 5L2

Tel: 416-476-6227
jockeyscanada@rogers.com
www.canadajockey.com
www.facebook.com/176051435772024
Overview: A small national organization
Description: To assist & represent jockeys across Canada
Membership: 150

Ontario Racing (OR)
c/o Woodbine Mohawk Park, PO Box 160, Campbellville ON L0P 1B0

Tel: 416-213-1800
info@ontarioracing.com
ontarioracing.com
www.instagram.com/ont_racing
www.facebook.com/OnHorseRacing
twitter.com/ONTRacing
Overview: A small provincial organization
Description: To be the authority on horse racing in Ontario; To advocate on behalf of horsepeople; To connect the industry to the government & the general public
Chief Officer(s): Katherine Curry, Executive Director
kcurry@woodbineentertainment.com
John Siscos, Director, Communications, Stakeholder Engagement & Marketing
jss@woodbineentertainment.com
Membership: 1-99

Horseshoe Pitching

Alberta Horseshoe Pitchers Association (AHPA)
AB

Tel: 403-946-4109
abhorsehoepitchers.com
Overview: A small provincial organization founded in 1977
Description: To promote the sport of horseshoe pitching in Alberta.; *Member of:* Horseshoe Canada
Chief Officer(s): Bruce Grandel, President
brucegrandel@hotmail.com

BC Horseshoe Association
c/o Sam Tomasevic, 7987 Graham Ave., Burnaby BC V3N 1V8

Tel: 604-525-2186
administrator@bchorseshoe.com
www.bchorseshoe.com
Overview: A small provincial organization
Description: To promote the sport of horseshoe pitching in British Columbia.; *Member of:* Horseshoe Canada
Chief Officer(s): Sam Tomasevic, President
samtom@telus.net
Membership: 346

Fédération des clubs de fers du Québec
4545, av Pierre-de-Coubertin, Montréal QC H1V 0B2

Tél: 514-252-3032
fers@fqjr.qc.ca
fers.quebecjeux.org

www.facebook.com/1433138876961682
Aperçu: *Dimension:* moyenne; *Envergure: provinciale; fondée en 1961*
Description: La FCFQ veut promouvoir la pratique du lancer de fers. Elle favorise les rencontres et les tournois qui contribuent au développement de la discipline. Elle distribue de l'information, donne des cours et des démonstrations; *Membre de:* Horseshoe Canada
Membre(s) du bureau directeur: Kenny Weightman, Président
Montant de la cotisation: 12$ individuel; 50$ club/ligue/ville

Horseshoe Canada
www.horseshoecanada.ca
www.facebook.com/361777939646
Overview: A medium-sized national organization founded in 1979
Description: To promote & foster the sport of horseshoe pitching in Canada
Chief Officer(s): Wally Arnold, President
walter.arnold@sympatico.ca
Membership: 1,200
Activities: *Awareness Events:* Canadian Horseshoe Pitching Championship

Horseshoe New Brunswick
c/o Jason Rideout, President, 14 Nicholas Dr., Old Ridge NB E3L 4Y6

Tel: 506-467-9100
www.horseshoenb.com
www.facebook.com/HorseshoeNB
twitter.com/SSHPC

Overview: A small provincial organization
Description: To promote the sport of horseshoe pitching in New Brunswick.; *Member of:* Horseshoe Canada
Chief Officer(s): Jason Rideout, President
jrideout.tp@gmail.com

Horseshoe Ontario
c/o Terrie Singbeil, 103 John St. East, Waterloo ON N2J 1G2
www.horseshoeontario.com
Overview: A small provincial organization
Description: To promote the sport of horseshoe pitching in Ontario.; *Member of:* Horseshoe Canada
Chief Officer(s): Terrie Slingbeil, Contact
tsingbeil@rogers.com
Membership: 450; *Fees:* $25 regular; $1 junior

Horseshoe Saskatchewan Inc.
PO Box 29029, Saskatoon SK S7N 4Y2
horseshoesask@sasktel.net
www.horseshoesask.ca
Overview: A small provincial organization founded in 1973
Description: Clubs in this horseshoe-pitching association represent areas in Saskatchewan, Alberta & Manitoba.; *Member of:* Horseshoe Canada
Chief Officer(s): Tammy Christensen, President, 306-565-1409
Denise Squires, Executive Coordinator, 306-374-8233
Finances: *Annual Operating Budget:* Less than $50,000;
Funding Sources: Raffles; merchandise sales; Saskatchewan Lotteries
Staff: 2 staff member(s); 30 volunteer(s)
Membership: 13 clubs
Activities: Annual Western Classics Tournament

Nova Scotia Horseshoe Players Association
NS

Tel: 902-852-3231; *Fax:* 902-852-2311
Overview: A small provincial organization founded in 1979
Description: To promote the sport of horseshoes in Canada; *Member of:* Horseshoe Canada
Chief Officer(s): Cecil Mitchell, Contact
cmitchell@rainbownetrigging.com
Membership: 35

Nova Scotia Horseshoe Players Association (NSHPA)
NS
Overview: A small provincial licensing organization founded in 1973
Description: To promote the enjoyment & health benefits of the sport of horseshoe pitching throughout Nova Scotia; *Member of:* Sport Nova Scotia; Horseshoe Canada
Affiliation(s): Maritime Horseshoe Players Association
Finances: *Annual Operating Budget:* Less than $50,000;
Funding Sources: Membership dues; fundraising; government grants
Staff: 40 volunteer(s)
Membership: 35; *Committees:* Club Forming; Membership; Palladian Construction; Promotion
Activities: 8 sanctioned tournaments; TV Series; conducts Special Olympics for horseshoes; *Rents Mailing List:* Yes

Kayaking

Canoe Kayak Saskatchewan (CKS)
510 Cynthia St., Saskatoon SK S4P 2L7

Tel: 306-975-7002; *Fax:* 306-242-8007
canoekayaksask.ca
Previous Name: Saskatchewan Canoe Association
Overview: A small provincial charitable organization founded in 1987
Description: To operate as the provincial sport governing body for canoe & kayak in Saskatchewan; *Member of:* CanoeKayak Canada
Chief Officer(s): Kia Schollar, Executive Director
ed@canoekayaksask.ca
Finances: *Funding Sources:* Saskatchewan Lotteries
Fees: $15; *Member Profile:* Competitive athletes; Novice athletes; Recreational paddlers; Coaches; Officials; Supporters
Activities: Encouraging participation; Developing excellence; Overseeing activities related to whitewater, recreation paddling, sprint racing (flatwater), & marathon

Fédération québécoise de canoë-kayak d'eau vives
4545, av Pierre-de-Coubertin, Montréal QC H1V 0B2

Tél: 438-333-1913
www.federationkayak.qc.ca

www.facebook.com/fqckev
Aperçu: *Dimension: petite; Envergure: provinciale; fondée en 1971*
Description: Promouvoir le sport et la pratique d'activités en eau vive au Québec; *Membre de:* CanoeKayak Canada

Ontario Recreational Canoeing & Kayaking Association (ORCKA)
93A Industrial Pkwy. South, Aurora ON L4G 3V5

Tel: 416-426-7016; *Fax:* 416-426-7363
info@orcka.ca
www.orcka.ca
www.facebook.com/228950560506530
Previous Name: Canoe Ontario; Ontario Recreational Canoeing Association
Overview: A medium-sized provincial organization founded in 1975
Description: To promote development of safe, competent & knowledgeable recreational paddlers
Chief Officer(s): Dale Radin, President, 416-821-1897
dradin@orcka.on.ca
Bob Kloske, Vice President, Communications, 519-800-6167
bkloske@orcka.on.ca
Finances: *Annual Operating Budget:* $100,000-$250,000;
Funding Sources: Trillium Grant
Staff: 2 staff member(s)
Fees: $45.20 - $141.25; *Member Profile:* Canoe, kayak instructors & recreational paddlers in Ontario; *Committees:* Safety; Promotion; Environment; Instructor Service; Membership
Activities: Canoe, kayak, stand up paddle board & voyageur canoe programs; Instructor courses; Hired guides & instructors; First aid training

Paddle Canada (PC) / Pagaie Canada
PO Box 126, Stn. Main, Kingston ON K7L 4V6

Tel: 613-547-3196; *Fax:* 613-547-4880
Toll-Free: 888-252-6292
info@paddlecanada.com
www.paddlecanada.com
www.youtube.com/user/PaddleCanada
www.facebook.com/paddlecanada
Previous Name: Canadian Recreational Canoeing Association
Overview: A large national licensing charitable organization founded in 1971
Description: To promote all forms of recreational paddling to Canadians of diverse abilities, culture or age; To advocate for a healthy natural environment; To develop an appreciation for the canoe & the kayak
Affiliation(s): Active Living Alliance for Canadians with a Disability; Girl Guides of Canada
Chief Officer(s): Michelle McShane, Executive Director
michelle@paddlecanada.com
Finances: *Funding Sources:* Membership fees; Donations; Program delivery; Sponsorships
Staff: 80 volunteer(s)
Membership: 2,500; *Fees:* Schedule available; *Committees:* Canoeing Program Development; River Kayaking Program Development; Sea Kayaking Program Development; Stand Up Paddleboarding Program Development; Bill Mason Scholarship; Environment; Marketing; Membership; PaddleSmart; Program Coordination; Safety; Waterwalker Film Festival
Activities: Reviewing park management plans, hydroelectric developments & timber management plans; Promoting waterway conservation through the Waterwalker Film Festival; Providing educational programs; Increasing environmental awareness; *Awareness Events:* National Paddling Week, June 6-15

Wilderness Canoe Association (WCA)
PO Box 91068, 2901 Bayview Ave., Toronto ON M2K 2Y6
info@wildernesscanoe.ca
www.wildernesscanoe.ca
www.facebook.com/WildernessCanoeAssociation
Overview: A small local organization founded in 1973
Description: To promote the enjoyment of the outdoors & wilderness travel, mainly canoeing, kayaking, backpacking, skiing & snowshoeing; *Member of:* Federation of Ontario Naturalists
Chief Officer(s): Gary Ataman, Chair
chair@wildernesscanoe.ca
Emmy Hendrickx, Officer, Membership Records
membership@wildernesscanoe.ca
Finances: *Annual Operating Budget:* Less than $50,000
Membership: 750; *Fees:* $35 single; $45 family
Activities: Winter pool training sessions; Paddle the Don River; year-round outings; *Awareness Events:* Wine & Cheese, Nov.

Labour Unions

Canadian Football League Players' Association (CFLPA) / Association des joueurs de la ligue de football canadienne
#208, 6205B Airport Rd., Mississauga ON L4V 1E3
Toll-Free: 800-616-6865
admin@cflpa.com
cflpa.com
www.instagram.com/cflpa
www.facebook.com/CFLPA
twitter.com/cflpa
Overview: A small national organization founded in 1965
Description: To represent professional football players in the Canadian Football League for fair & reasonable working conditions
Chief Officer(s): Solomon Elimimian, President
Brian Ramsay, Executive Director
b.ramsay@cflpa.com
Membership: approx. 400 + 8 locals

Major League Baseball Players' Association (Ind.) / Association des joueurs de la Ligue majeure de baseball (ind.)
12 East 49th St., 24th Fl., New York NY 10017 USA
Tel: 212-826-0808; *Fax:* 212-752-4378
feedback@mlbpa.org
www.mlbplayers.com
www.instagram.com/MLB_PLAYERS
www.facebook.com/MLBPA
twitter.com/MLB_PLAYERS
Overview: A medium-sized international organization
Description: To represent and protect the interests of professional baseball players in Major League Baseball
Chief Officer(s): Tony Clark, Executive Director
Martha Child, Chief Administrative Officer
Marietta DiCamillo, Chief Financial Officer
Kevin McGuiness, Chief Operating Officer
Membership: 80 + 2 locals (in Canada)
Activities: Baseball Card Clubhouse; Baseball Tomorrow Fund; Rookie Career Development; *Awareness Events:* Players Choice Awards

Professional Hockey Players' Association (PHPA)
3964 Portage Rd., Niagara Falls ON L2J 2K9
Tel: 289-296-5561; *Fax:* 289-296-4567
phpa.com
www.instagram.com/thephpa
www.facebook.com/173409159401617
twitter.com/thephpa
Overview: A small national organization founded in 1967
Membership: 1,600+; *Member Profile:* All professional hockey players in the AHL & ECHL; *Committees:* Alumni Association; Workers' Compensation; Panel of Attorneys; Registered Agents Program; Career Enhancement Program; Membership Assistance Program

Lacrosse

Alberta Lacrosse Association (ALA)
#4, 9 Chippewa Rd., Sherwood Park AB T8A 6J7
Tel: 780-464-1861
www.albertalacrosse.com
www.facebook.com/257864104242295
twitter.com/AlbertaLacrosse
Overview: A small provincial organization
Description: To be the provincial governing body for the sport of lacrosse in Alberta; *Member of:* Canadian Lacrosse Association
Chief Officer(s): Rob Matsuoka, President
president@albertalacrosse.com
Lisa Grant, Executive Director
lisa@albertalacrosse.com
Andrew McBride, Technical Director

British Columbia Lacrosse Association (BCLA)
#101, 7382 Winston St., Burnaby BC V5A 2G9
Tel: 604-421-9755; *Fax:* 604-421-9775
info@bclacrosse.com
www.bclacrosse.com
www.youtube.com/user/BCLacrosseA
www.facebook.com/481524661862119
twitter.com/BCLacrosse
Overview: A medium-sized provincial organization
Description: To promotes & regulate the sport of lacrosse in British Columbia; *Member of:* Canadian Lacrosse Association
Chief Officer(s): Rochelle Winterton, Executive Director
rochelle@bclacrosse.com
Dave Showers, Technical Director
dave@bclacrosse.com

Canadian Lacrosse Association (CLA) / Association canadienne de crosse (ACC)
Gladstone Sports & Health Centre, #310, 18 Louisa St., Ottawa ON K1R 6Y6
Tel: 613-260-2028; *Fax:* 613-260-2029
info1@lacrosse.ca
www.lacrosse.ca
www.facebook.com/CanadianLacrosseAssociation
twitter.com/LacrosseCanada
Overview: A medium-sized national licensing charitable organization founded in 1867
Description: To promote, develop & preserve the sport of Lacrosse & its heritage as Canada's national summer sport
Affiliation(s): International Lacrosse Federation; International Federation of Women's Lacrosse Associations; Fédération internationale d'Inter-crosse; Canadian Lacrosse Foundation; Sport Canada; Coaching Association of Canada
Chief Officer(s): Jane Clapham, Executive Director
jane@lacrosse.ca
Victoria Klassen, Coordinator, Communications & Marketing
victoria@lacrosse.ca
Finances: *Annual Operating Budget:* $250,000-$500,000; *Funding Sources:* Sport Canada; membership fees; sponsors; donations; sales
Staff: 3 staff member(s)
Membership: 11 provincial organizations; *Fees:* $350 - $1,050; *Member Profile:* Provincial associations / leagues; *Committees:* Equipment Review; Transfer Review; Appeals; Discipline; Aboriginal Development
Activities: *Awareness Events:* Lacrosse Week, 3rd week of May; *Internships:* Yes; *Speaker Service:* Yes; *Rents Mailing List:* Yes

Fédération de crosse du Québec (FCQ)
CP 1000, Succ. M, 4545, av Pierre-de Coubertin, Montréal QC H1V 3R2
crosse@crosse.qc.ca
www.crossequebec.com
Aperçu: *Dimension:* moyenne; *Envergure: provinciale; fondée en 1971*
Description: Offrir des services et des programmes axés vers le développement du sport de la crosse un plan régional et international; *Membre de:* Fédération Internationale d'Inter-Crosse; Canadian Lacrosse Association
Affiliation(s): Sports Québec; Regroupement Loisir Québec
Membre(s) du bureau directeur: Pierre Filion, Directeur
pierrefilion@bell.net
Finances: *Budget de fonctionnement annuel:* $100,000-$250,000
Personnel: 2 membre(s) du personnel; 45 bénévole(s)
Activités: Stages de formation, conférences, ligues d'inter-crosse, compétitions; *Stagiaires:* Oui; *Service de conférenciers:* Oui

Lacrosse New Brunswick
211 rte 616, Keswick Ridge NB E6L 1R9
Tel: 506-440-1227
www.laxnb.ca
www.facebook.com/128267803907009
Also Known As: Lacrosse NB
Overview: A small provincial organization
Description: To be the provincial governing body for the sport of lacrosse in New Brunswick; *Member of:* Canadian Lacrosse Association
Chief Officer(s): Chris Gallop, President, 506-440-1227
chris.gallop@nbed.bd.ca
Tim Jackson, Treasurer, 506-674-1597
tjackson@nb.sympatico.ca
Jennifer Gendron, Secretary, 506-651-4848
jqgendron@gmail.com

Lacrosse Nova Scotia
5516 Spring Garden Rd., 4th Fl., Halifax NS B3J 1G6
Tel: 902-425-5450; *Fax:* 902-425-5606
lacrosse@sportnovascotia.ca
lacrossens.ca
www.facebook.com/421011914655642
Overview: A small provincial organization founded in 1971
Member of: Canadian Lacrosse Association; Sport Nova Scotia
Chief Officer(s): Greg Knight, Executive Director
Chet Koneczny, Technical Director
lacrossetechdirector@sportnovascotia.ca
Finances: *Funding Sources:* Provincial government

Lethbridge Lacrosse Association (LLA)
PO Box 874, Lethbridge AB T1J 3Z8
Tel: 403-715-3291
www.lethbridgelacrosse.com
www.facebook.com/lethbridge.lacrosse
twitter.com/lethlax
Overview: A small local organization

Description: To promote lacrosse in southern Alberta
Chief Officer(s): Julie Woods, Program Director, 403-915-0615
progdirector@lethbridgelacrosse.com

Manitoba Lacrosse Association
145 Pacific Ave., Winnipeg MB R3B 2Z6
Tel: 204-925-5684; *Fax:* 204-925-5792
lacrosse@sportmanitoba.ca
manitobalacrosse.com
www.instagram.com/manitobalacrosse
www.facebook.com/ManitobaLacrosse
twitter.com/MBLacrosse
Overview: A small provincial organization
Description: To be the provincial governing body for the sport of lacrosse in Manitoba; *Member of:* Canadian Lacrosse Association
Chief Officer(s): Paul Magnan, President
pmagnan@sunrisesd.ca
Dallas Smith, Executive Director, 204-925-5684, Fax: 204-925-5792
lacrosse@sportmanitoba.ca

Newfoundland & Labrador Lacrosse Association (NLLA)
PO Box 26037, 250 Lemarchant Rd., St. John's NL A1E 0A5
nllacrossegeneral@gmail.com
nllacrosse.ca
www.facebook.com/nllacrosse
twitter.com/_NLLacrosse
Overview: A small provincial organization founded in 2009
Description: To be the provincial governing body for the sport of lacrosse in Newfoundland & Labrador; *Member of:* Canadian Lacrosse Association
Chief Officer(s): Mark Stanford, President
president@nllacrosse.ca
Stan Cook, Vice President
Andy Schmidt, Director, Operations

Ontario Lacrosse Association
#306, 3 Concorde Gate, Toronto ON M3C 3N7
Tel: 416-426-7066; *Fax:* 416-426-7382
www.ontariolacrosse.com
twitter.com/OntarioLacrosse
Overview: A small provincial organization founded in 1897
Member of: Canadian Lacrosse Association
Chief Officer(s): Stan Cockerton, Executive Director
stan@ontariolacrosse.com

Saskatchewan Lacrosse Association
2205 Victoria Ave., Regina SK S4P 0S4
Tel: 306-780-9216; *Fax:* 306-525-4009
Toll-Free: 844-780-9216
lacrosse@sasktel.net
www.sasklacrosse.net
www.facebook.com/SaskLacrosse
Also Known As: Sask Lacrosse
Overview: A medium-sized provincial organization
Description: To promote & deliver lacrosse programs to the residents of Saskatchewan; *Member of:* Canadian Lacrosse Association; Sask Sport Inc.
Chief Officer(s): Shawn Williams, President
Bridget Pottle, Executive Director
ed@sasklacrosse.net
Chris Lesanko, Coordinator, Programs
programs@sasklacrosse.net
Finances: *Annual Operating Budget:* $250,000-$500,000
Staff: 1 staff member(s); 10 volunteer(s)
Membership: 3,000; *Fees:* Schedule available

Lawn Bowling

Bowls British Columbia
c/o Lynn Chwartacki, 595 Belyea Rd., Qualicum Beach BC V9K 1H3
info@bowlsbc.com
bowlsbc.com
www.facebook.com/bowlsbc
twitter.com/bowlsbc
Also Known As: Bowls BC
Overview: A medium-sized provincial organization founded in 1925
Description: To foster & promote the Sport of Lawn Bowling; To develop the game so that it is appealing, healthy & accessible

for all
Affiliation(s): World Bowls Board; World Indoor Bowls Board
Chief Officer(s): Lynn Chwartacki, Director, Administration, 250-752-0851
lynn.chwartacki@bowlsbc.com
Harry Carruthers, Acting President, 604-985-2241
harry.carruthers@bowlsbc.com
Alex Bell, Vice President, 250-319-7227
alex.bell@bowlsbc.com
Vicki Parton, Secretary, 604-908-4048
vicki.parton@bowlsbc.com
Activities: *Library:* BBC Library at Pacific Indoor Bowls Club (Open to Public)

Bowls Canada Boulingrin (BCB)
c/o House of Sport, 2451 Riverside Dr., Ottawa ON K1H 7X7
Tel: 613-244-0021; *Fax:* 613-244-0041
Toll-Free: 800-567-2695
office@bowlscanada.com
bowlscanada.com
www.linkedin.com/company/bowls-canada-boulingrin
www.facebook.com/BCBOfficial
twitter.com/BCBBowls
Previous Name: Lawn Bowls Canada Boulingrin
Overview: A medium-sized national charitable organization founded in 1902
Description: To promote, foster & safeguard the sport of indoor & outdoor lawn bowling in all its forms in Canada, through events & programs; *Member of:* World Bowls Board; International Women's Bowls Board; World Indoor Bowls Council
Affiliation(s): Commonwealth Games Association of Canada
Chief Officer(s): Anna Mees, Executive Director, 613-244-0021 1
amees@bowlscanada.com
Finances: *Annual Operating Budget:* $250,000-$500,000; *Funding Sources:* Membership dues; marketing; advertising; merchandising; donations
Staff: 4 staff member(s); 100 volunteer(s)
Membership: 15,000; 252 clubs; *Committees:* Team Canada; National Officials
Activities: Canadian championships; Canadian Senior Triples; Canadian Junior Championships; Under 25 World Junior Cup Qualifier; Canadian Mixed Pairs Championships; Canadian Indoor Singles

Bowls Manitoba
145 Pacific Ave., Winnipeg MB R3B 2Z6
Tel: 204-925-5694; *Fax:* 204-925-5792
bowls@shawbiz.ca
bowlsmanitoba.wordpress.com
www.facebook.com/BowlsMBInc
twitter.com/BowlsManitoba
Previous Name: Manitoba Lawn Bowling Association
Overview: A medium-sized provincial organization founded in 1927
Description: To promote lawnbowling in the province of Manitoba; To host various lawnbowling events; *Member of:* Sport Manitoba
Affiliation(s): Bowls Canada Boulingrin; World Bowls Ltd
Chief Officer(s): Cathy Derewianchuk, Executive Director, 204-925-5694

Bowls Saskatchewan Inc.
#102, 1860 Lorne St., Regina SK S4P 2L7
Tel: 306-780-9426
bowlsask@sasktel.net
www.bowls.sk.ca
www.facebook.com/Bowls-Saskatchewan-732190793489071
Also Known As: Saskatchewan Lawn Bowling Association
Overview: A medium-sized provincial organization founded in 1991
Description: To promote & expand the sport of bowls, which contains programs that accommodate/challenge all those interested, with the result that bowls becomes a high profile sport
Chief Officer(s): Denise Eberle, Executive Director
Duncan Holness, President
daholness@hotmail.com
Finances: *Annual Operating Budget:* $50,000-$100,000; *Funding Sources:* Saskatchewan lotteries
Staff: 1 staff member(s)
Membership: 503 in 9 clubs; *Fees:* Schedule available; *Committees:* Executive; Officiating; Coaching; Sport for All
Activities: Learn to Bowl; Junior; Clinics; summer & fall tournaments; Regina Mixed Pairs Open Tournament

Lawn Bowls Association of Alberta
11759 Groat Rd., Edmonton AB T5M 3K6
Tel: 780-427-8119
office@bowlsalberta.com
bowlsalberta.com
twitter.com/BowlsAlberta

Overview: A small provincial organization founded in 1989
Description: To promote & develop the sport of bowls in Alberta
Affiliation(s): Commonwealth; Highlands; Royal Lawn Bowling Club; Edmonton Indoor Lawn Bowling Club; Bow Valley; Calgary Lawn; Rotary Park; Stanley Park; Ted Petrunia Lawn Bowling Green; Medicine Hat Lawn Bowling Green
Chief Officer(s): Grady Long, President
Patricia Vos, Executive Director

Ontario Lawn Bowls Association
c/o Edith Pedden, 471 Silvery Lane, Marberly ON K0H 2B0
olba@olba.ca
www.olba.ca
www.facebook.com/groups/138144062931120
Overview: A medium-sized provincial organization
Chief Officer(s): Mike Landry, President
olba@olba.ca
Elaine Stevenson, Contact, Membership
membership@olba.ca
Finances: *Funding Sources:* Membership fees; Sponsorships
Fees: Schedule available; *Member Profile:* Ontario lawn bowls clubs; *Committees:* Annual General Meetings; Achievement Awards; Annual; Bowls Canada Delegates; By-Laws; Championships, Indoors/Short-Mat & Championship Awards; Coaching; Database; Distribution, Sales, New Bowler Kits; E-Banter; Finance; Funding/Grants; Greens; Juniors; Marketing/Go Lawn Bowl; Memorial Fund; Nominating; Officiating; Planning & Development; Player Development; Promotion & Sponsorship; Safety & Risk Management; Visually Impaired/Physically Disabled Bowlers; Website
Activities: Providing programs, information & resources to member clubs; Campaigning for member recruitment; Assisting clubs that want to host provincial or national championships; Presenting awards, plaques, & certificates

Prince Edward Island Lawn Bowling Association
PO Box 20056, Stn. Sherwood, Charlottetown PE C1A 9E3
Tel: 902-368-4110; *Fax:* 902-368-4548
Toll-Free: 800-247-6712
sports@sportpei.pe.ca
princeedwardislandlawnbowls.webs.com
Overview: A small provincial organization
Description: To guide bowlers in the growth and development of Lawn Bowling on PEI; To promote and encourage fair play at club level and national level
Chief Officer(s): Myrna Sanderson, President, 902-566-3980
myrnasanderson@gmail.com

Québec Lawn Bowling Federation / Fédération de Boulingrin du Québec
QC
www.bowlsquebec.com
Overview: A medium-sized provincial organization

Martial Arts

Aikido Yukon Association
c/o Sport Yukon, 4061 - 4th Ave., Whitehorse YT Y1A 1H1
Tel: 867-667-4690; *Fax:* 867-667-4237
info@aikidoyukon.ca
www.aikidoyukon.ca
www.facebook.com/aikidoyukon
Overview: A small provincial organization
Description: To teach the martial art of Aikido in the Yukon.
Chief Officer(s): Gaël Marchanfd, President

Alberta Taekwondo Association (ATA)
#1589, 5328 Calgary Trail NW, Edmonton AB T6H 4JB
Tel: 780-446-0246
admin@taekwondoalberta.com
www.taekwondoalberta.com
www.facebook.com/13172614788
twitter.com/TKD_Alberta
Overview: A small provincial organization
Description: To be the provincial governing body for the sport of taekwondo in Alberta
Affiliation(s): Taekwondo Canada; World Taekwondo Federation
Chief Officer(s): Su Hwan Chung, Chairman
gmsuchung@gmail.com
Linda Kwan, Secretary General
lindakwan888@yahoo.com
Fees: $20-$30 individual; $150-$300 club

Association de taekwondo du Québec
4545, av Pierre-de-Coubertin, Montréal QC H1V 0B2
Tél: 514-252-3198; *Téléc:* 514-254-7075
Ligne sans frais: 800-762-9565
info@taekwondo-quebec.ca
www.taekwondo-quebec.ca
www.facebook.com/taekwondoquebec

Également appelé: Taekwondo Québec
Aperçu: Dimension: moyenne; *Envergure: provinciale*
Description: Favoriser le développement du taekwondo québécois
Membre(s) du bureau directeur: Jean Faucher, Président
jfaucher@taekwondo-quebec.ca
Abdel Ilah Es Sabbar, Directeur exécutif, 514-252-3198
essabbar@taekwondo-quebec.ca

BC Taekwondo Association
#101, 32885 Ventura Ave., Abbotsford BC V2S 6A3
www.bctaekwondo.org
Overview: A small provincial organization founded in 1994
Description: To govern the sport of Tae Kwon Do in British Columbia.
Chief Officer(s): Michael Smith, President
Darryl Mitchell, Treasurer/Secretary
dmitchell@axisls.com

Canadian Chito-Ryu Karate-Do Association
89 Curlew Ave., Toronto ON M3A 2P8
Tel: 416-444-5310
info@canadianchitoryu.ca
canadianchitoryu.ca
Overview: A small national organization founded in 1991
Description: To promote the karate-do of its founder O'Sensei Dr. Tsuyoshi Chitose
Chief Officer(s): Andre Buret, President
Collin Affleck, Vice-President

Canadian Jiu-jitsu Council
PO Box 543, Madoc ON K0K 2K0
Tel: 613-473-4366
www.jiujitsucouncil.ca
Overview: A medium-sized national organization founded in 1968
Description: To guide and assist the growth of Jiujitsu so it remains vital & progressive; To share the benefits, knowledge and pleasure of the Martial Art & Science of Jiujitsu with more people
Chief Officer(s): Robert Walthers, President
rwalther@kos.net
Fees: $10 junior student; $25 senior student; $40 club/black belt

Canadian Kendo Federation (CKF) / Fédération canadienne de kendo
c/o Christian D'Orangeville, 65, rue Saint-Paul ouest, Montréal QC H2Y 35S
kendo-canada.com
www.instagram.com/kendocanada
www.linkedin.com/company/canadian-kendo-federation
www.facebook.com/KendoCanada
twitter.com/KendoCanada
Also Known As: Kendo Federation
Overview: A small national organization
Description: To support Kendo, Iaido & Jodo in Canada
Chief Officer(s): Christian D'Orangeville, President
cdorangeville@kendo-canada.com
Finances: *Funding Sources:* Membership fees; Donations; Sale of CKF souvenirs
Fees: $15 junior (age 15 & under); $35 regular; $75 club; *Committees:* Kendo Grading; Iaido Grading; Jodo Grading; Finance; Internal Review; Budget & Event; Team Canada; Secretary's; CKF History

Club de karaté Shotokan Chibougamau
576, Bordeleau, Chibougamau QC G8P 1A6
Tél: 418-748-4048
ville.chibougamau.qc.ca
Aperçu: Dimension: petite; *Envergure: locale; fondée en 1972*
Membre(s) du bureau directeur: Claude Bédard, Instructeur chef, 418-770-6933
cbedard@karatechibougamau.com

International Judo Federation (IJF)
49, av de La Harpe, Lausanne 1007 Switzerland
admin@ijf.org
www.ijf.org
www.youtube.com/judo
www.facebook.com/judo
Overview: A large international charitable organization
Chief Officer(s): Marius Vizer, President
president@ijf.org
Jean Luc, General Secretary
gs@ijf.org
Membership: 200 Federations + 5 Continental Unions
Activities: World Championships; World Judo Tour; World Ranking List

Judo Alberta

Percy Page Centre, 11759 Groat Rd., Edmonton AB T5M 3K6
Tel: 780-427-8379; *Fax:* 780-447-1915
Toll-Free: 866-919-5836
judo@judoalberta.com
www.judoalberta.com
www.flickr.com/photos/judoalberta
www.facebook.com/judoalberta
twitter.com/JudoAlberta
Also Known As: Alberta Kodokan Black Belt Association -
AKBBA
Overview: A small provincial organization founded in 1960
Description: To promote the principles & teachings of the sport
of kodokan judo to all levels in all parts of Alberta; To have
qualified facilities & equipment in places throughout Alberta; To
promote judo as a lifelong interest; to develop competitive
opportunities throughout Alberta; To promote greater public
awareness of the sport; To increase the number of participants
in the sport; To develop & maintain qualified judo officials &
coaches throughout Alberta; To develop high performance
athletes; To develop recreational opportunities throughout
Alberta; *Member of:* Judo Canada
Affiliation(s): International Judo Federation
Chief Officer(s): Kelly Thornton, President
kellyt4d@telus.net
Nate MacLellan, Executive Director
Finances: *Annual Operating Budget:* $100,000-$250,000
Staff: 2 staff member(s); 200 volunteer(s)
Membership: 1,200; *Fees:* Schedule available; *Committees:*
Grading; Technical; Referee; Coaching; Women's Ctee
Activities: *Library:* Video Library (Open to Public)

Judo BC

#523, 4438 West 10th Ave., Vancouver BC V6R 4R8
Tel: 604-333-3513; *Fax:* 604-333-3514
www.judobc.ca
www.facebook.com/JudoBritishColumbia
twitter.com/OfficialJudoBC
Overview: A medium-sized provincial organization founded in
1952
Description: To promote & support the development of all
aspects of Judo in the province; To inform & report on all
aspects of Judo & planned activities in BC & elsewhere; To
promote Judo & public awareness of the sport; To increase the
number of participants in the sport; To keep close liaison with
Judo clubs in BC in order to share all things of common interest
to members; *Member of:* Judo Canada; Sport BC; Pan-American
Confederation of Judo; International Judo Federation; Kodokan
Judo Institute
Chief Officer(s): Sandy Kent, President
Katie Thomson, Executive Director
executivedirector@judobc.ca
Finances: *Annual Operating Budget:* $100,000-$250,000;
Funding Sources: Provincial government; self-generated
revenue; gaming
Staff: 1 staff member(s)
Membership: 2,200; *Fees:* Schedule available; *Committees:*
Technical; Grading & Kata Board; Referee; NCCP; Membership
Activities: Offering coaching clinics; Organizing tournaments;
Providing athlete & referee training; *Awareness Events:* Judo
Awareness Week, 3rd week of Sept. *Library:* Yes by
appointment

Judo Canada

4141, av Pierre-De Coubertin, Montréal QC H1V 3N7
Tel: 514-255-5836; *Fax:* 877-893-5836
info@judocanada.org
www.judocanada.org
www.facebook.com/judocanada
twitter.com/judocanada
Also Known As: Canadian Kodokan Black Belt Association
Overview: A large national charitable organization founded in
1956
Description: To promote the principles & teachings of the sport
of Kodokan Judo; To work towards the advancement of Judo
throughout Canada; *Member of:* Pan American Judo
Confederation
Affiliation(s): International Judo Federation
Chief Officer(s): Nicolas Gill, Chief Executive Officer & Director,
High Performance
n.gill@judocanada.org
Patrick Esparbes, Chief Operating Officer
p.esparbes@judocanada.org
Marie-Hélène Chisholm, Manager, High Performance
mh.chisholm@judocanada.org
Francine Latreille, Contact, Accounting, Grading & Membership
Services
Finances: *Funding Sources:* Sport Canada; Membership dues;
Sponsorships
Staff: 10 staff member(s)

Member Profile: Black belt & provincial members; *Committees:*
Awards & Marketing; Finance & Risk Management; Governance;
Grading; High Performance; Indigenous & Territorial Affairs;
Legal; NCCP/LTAD; Nominating; Referee; Screening; Sport
Development; Tournament; Women Leadership
Activities: Providing Rendez-Vous Canada & the Canadian
Championships; *Library:* Yes by appointment

Judo Manitoba

c/o Sport Manitoba, #311, 145 Pacific Ave., Winnipeg MB R3B
2Z6
Tel: 204-925-5691; *Fax:* 204-925-5703
judo@sportmanitoba.ca
www.judomanitoba.mb.ca
Also Known As: Manitoba Judo Black Belt Association Inc.
Overview: A small provincial organization founded in 1963
Description: To propagate & perpetuate the sport of Judo; To
improve the calibre of athletes, referees & coaches; *Member of:*
Judo Canada; Sport Manitoba; International Judo Federation;
Canadian Olympic Committee
Chief Officer(s): Oscar Li, Executive Director
David Minuk, President
Finances: *Annual Operating Budget:* $100,000-$250,000
Staff: 2 staff member(s)
Membership: 86 Black Belts + 594 others; *Fees:* Schedule
available; *Committees:* Fundraising; Officials; Grading; Bingo;
NCCP; Grassroots; Awards
Activities: *Library:* Yes

Judo New Brunswick / Judo Nouveau Brunswick

#13, 900 Hanwell St., Fredericton NB E3B 6A3
Tel: 506-451-1322; *Fax:* 506-451-1325
judonb@nb.aibn.com
www.facebook.com/judonewbrunswick
twitter.com/judo_nb
Also Known As: Judo NB
Overview: A small local organization
Description: To promote judo in New Brunswick; *Member of:*
Judo Canada
Chief Officer(s): Curtis Lauzon, Executive Director,
506-261-0867
Membership: 500; *Committees:* Grading

Judo Nova Scotia

NS
Tel: 902-425-5450
admin@judons.ca
www.judons.ca
www.facebook.com/judons
twitter.com/judonovascotia
Overview: A small provincial organization
Description: To promote the principles of judo &, in
collaboration with members & interested parties, to work towards
the advancement of judo, at all levels & areas of Nova Scotia;
Member of: Judo Canada
Chief Officer(s): Chris Hattie, President
chattie@judons.ca
Scott Tanner, Provincial Coach
stanner@judons.ca

Judo Nunavut

PO Box 2135, Iqaluit NU X0A 0H0
Tel: 867-979-4540
judo.nunavut@gmail.com
www.facebook.com/NunavutJudo
Overview: A small provincial organization
Member of: Judo Canada

Judo Ontario

#2040, 875 Morningside Ave., Toronto ON M1C 0C7
Tel: 416-447-5836; *Fax:* 416-449-5836
Toll-Free: 866-553-5836
info@judoontario.ca
www.judoontario.ca
www.facebook.com/JudoOntario
Overview: A small provincial organization founded in 1959
Description: To govern the sport of Judo in Ontario; *Member of:*
Judo Canada; International Judo Federation
Chief Officer(s): Aartje Sheffield, President, 905-251-0202
aartjes@judoontario.ca
Steve Sheffield, Administrator
Finances: *Annual Operating Budget:* $250,000-$500,000
Staff: 2 staff member(s); 100 volunteer(s)
Membership: 1,000-4,999; *Fees:* Schedule available;
Committees: HPC; Grading Board; Referee; LTAD; NCCP;
Aboriginal; Differently Abled; Quest for Gold; Website;
Membership

Judo Prince Edward Island

PO Box 302, 40 Enman Cres., Charlottetown PE C1A 7K7
Tel: 902-368-4262
www.judopei.ca
www.facebook.com/JUDOPEI
twitter.com/judopei
Overview: A small provincial organization
Description: To promote and govern the sport of Judo in Prince
Edward Island; *Member of:* Sport PEI Inc.; Judo Canada
Chief Officer(s): Michael Sheppard, President
president@judopei.ca
Trish Shaw, Secretary
secretary@judopei.ca

Judo Saskatchewan

c/o Sandy Taylor, Treasurer, PO Box 1464, Warman SK S0K
4S0
Tel: 306-668-6879
www.judosask.ca
Also Known As: Saskatchewan Kodokan Black Belt
Association
Overview: A small provincial licensing organization founded in
1950
Description: To govern the sport of Judo in Saskatchewan;
Member of: Judo Canada; Pan-American Judo Federation
Affiliation(s): International Judo Federation
Chief Officer(s): T.V. Taylor, President, 306-668-6879
tvtaylor@sasktel.net
Sandy Taylor, Treasurer
taylor.s@sasktel.net
Finances: *Annual Operating Budget:* $100,000-$250,000
Staff: 1 staff member(s); 10 volunteer(s)
Membership: 300+; *Fees:* Schedule available

Judo Yukon

4061 - 4th Ave., Whitehorse YT Y1A 1H1
Tel: 867-668-4236; *Fax:* 867-667-4237
judoyukon@gmail.com
www.judoyukon.ca
Overview: A small provincial charitable organization founded in
1995
Description: To govern the sport of Judo in the Yukon; *Member
of:* Judo Canada; Sport Yukon; True Sport; Sport Officials
Canada
Chief Officer(s): Richard Zebruck, President
Bianca Ockedahl, Head Coach
judoyukon.hc@gmail.com
Finances: *Annual Operating Budget:* Less than $50,000
Membership: 100+; *Member Profile:* Juniors & seniors; ages 8
& up; *Committees:* NCCP; Officials
Activities: Organizing competitions & demonstrations;
Awareness Events: Judo Yukon Open Tournament, April *Library:*
Resource Library (Open to Public)

Judo-Québec inc

4545, av Pierre-de Coubertin, Montréal QC H1V 0B2
Tél: 514-252-3040; *Téléc:* 514-254-5184
info@judo-quebec.qc.ca
www.judo-quebec.qc.ca

www.youtube.com/user/judoquebec
www.facebook.com/JudoQuebec
Également appelé: Association québécoise de judo-kodokan
Aperçu: *Dimension:* moyenne; *Envergure:* provinciale;
Organisme sans but lucratif; fondée en 1966
Description: Assurer la promotion et le développement du judo
au Québec; éduquer, développer et servir nos membres;
Membre de: Judo Canada; Sport Québec
Affiliation(s): Fédération internationale de Judo; Union
panaméricaine du Judo
Membre(s) du bureau directeur: Daniel De Angelis, Président
Jean-François Marceau, Directeur général, 514-252-3040 27
jfmarceau@judo-quebec.qc.ca
Patrick Vesin, Coordonnateur technique, 514-252-3040 24
pvesin@judo-quebec.qc.ca
Finances: *Budget de fonctionnement annuel:* $500,000-$1.5
Million; *Fonds:* Secrétariat au loisirs et aux sports
Personnel: 6 membre(s) du personnel; 200 bénévole(s)
Membre: 10 000; *Montant de la cotisation:* Barème; *Critères
d'admissibilite:* Personne de 7 à 77 ans; *Comités:* Arbitrage;
excellence; développement; grade; éthique; ju-jutsu
Activités: Competition; stage; colloque; gala; formation;
Stagiaires: Oui; *Service de conférenciers:* Oui *Bibliothèque:* Oui

Karate Alberta Association (KAA)

c/o Stewart Price, 56 Auburn Crest Park, Calgary AB T3M 0Z3
Tel: 403-601-1610
www.karateab.org
www.facebook.com/karateAlberta
Overview: A small provincial organization

Description: To be the provincial governing body for the sport of karate in Alberta; *Member of:* Karate Canada
Chief Officer(s): Marc Ward, President, 403-991-1821
Dean Tucker, Membership Officer, 403-691-5323
Finances: *Funding Sources:* Government of Alberta

Karate BC (KBC)
Fortius Athlete Development Centre, Sydney Landing, #2002A, 3713 Kensington Ave., Burnaby BC V5B 0A7
Tel: 604-333-3610; *Fax:* 604-333-3612
Toll-Free: 855-806-8126
www.karatebc.org
www.facebook.com/OfficalKarateBC
twitter.com/KarateBC
Overview: A small provincial charitable organization founded in 1974
Description: To promote the traditions & integrity of karate-do; to improve opportunities to excel in a competitive environment; to be the governing body of the sport of karate in British Columbia.; *Member of:* Karate Canada; BC Recreation & Parks Association; BC Coaches Association; Sport BC
Chief Officer(s): Norma Foster, President
guseikai@hotmail.com
Jonathan Wornell, Executive Director
jwornell@karatebc.org
Conan Cooper, Coordinator, Coaching Development
coachdev@karatebc.org
Finances: *Annual Operating Budget:* $250,000-$500,000;
Funding Sources: Provincial government; gaming; fundraising
Staff: 2 staff member(s)
Membership: 4,000; *Fees:* Schedule available; *Member Profile:* Instructor must hold bona-fide Dan certificate, be certified at level I NCCP & pass a criminal records check; *Committees:* Executive; Officials; Technical; Tournament; Marketing; Newsletter; High Performance
Activities: Tournaments; coaching clinics; officials seminars; athlete assistance program; coaching grants; first aid clinics; BC Winter Games; mall demos; annual recognition banquet for outstanding athletes & volunteers; *Internships:* Yes; *Speaker Service:* Yes *Library:* Yes by appointment

Karate Canada
c/o Canadian Olympic Committee, 500, boul René-Lévesque ouest, Montréal QC H2Z 1W7
Tel: 514-252-3209; *Fax:* 514-252-3211
info@karatecanada.org
karatecanada.org
www.instagram.com/karatecanada
www.facebook.com/karatecanadaofficial
twitter.com/karatecanada
Previous Name: National Karate Association of Canada
Overview: A medium-sized national organization founded in 1963
Description: To be the national governing body for the sport of karate in Canada; *Member of:* Sport Canada; Canadian Olympic Committee; World Karate Federation
Chief Officer(s): Olivier Pineau, Executive Director
olivier@karatecanada.org
Alexandra Roy, Program Manager
alexandra.roy@karatecanada.org
Membership: 10 provincial & territorial associations; 16,000 individuals; *Committees:* Finance; Communications & Marketing; Governance & Policy; Domestic Development; Events; High Performance; Officials; NCCP/LTAD; Technical; Para-Karate

Karate Manitoba
145 Pacific Ave., Winnipeg MB R3B 2Z6
Tel: 204-925-5605; *Fax:* 204-925-5916
info@karatemanitoba.ca
www.karatemanitoba.ca
www.youtube.com/user/KarateManitoba
www.facebook.com/KarateManitobaWKF
twitter.com/KarateManitoba
Also Known As: Manitoba Karate Association
Overview: A small provincial organization founded in 1974
Description: To promote & develop karate in the province of Manitoba at all levels (grassroots to elite athlete) & as recreation.; *Member of:* Karate Canada; World Karate Federation; Sport Manitoba
Chief Officer(s): Debra Kofsky, President
president@karatemanitoba.ca
Sharon Andrews, Secretary
km.officials@live.ca
Membership: 600; *Committees:* NCCP; Officials; Athlete Development; Finance; Grassroots

Karate New Brunswick
NB
karatenb.com
Previous Name: New Brunswick Karate Association
Overview: A small provincial organization

Member of: Karate Canada
Chief Officer(s): Don Mazerolle, President
djmaz@bellaliant.net
Finances: *Funding Sources:* Provincial government
Staff: 1 staff member(s); 15 volunteer(s)
Membership: 600 individual
Activities: *Rents Mailing List:* Yes

Karate Newfoundland & Labrador (KNL)
c/o 3 Albert Pl., Torbay NL A1K 0J4
karatenl@gmail.com
www.karatenl.ca
Overview: A small provincial organization
Description: To be the provincial governing body for the sport of karate in Newfoundland & Labrador; *Member of:* Karate Canada
Chief Officer(s): Derek J. Ryan, President

Karate Nova Scotia (KNS)
5516 Spring Garden Rd., 4th Fl., Halifax NS B3J 3G6
info@karatens.org
karatens.org
Overview: A small provincial organization
Description: To be the provincial governing body for the sport of karate in Nova Scotia; *Member of:* Karate Canada
Chief Officer(s): Gary Walsh, President
garywalsh.ns@hotmail.com
Greg Da Ros, Vice President
info@karatens.org
Activities: Tournaments; Athlete Development; Awards

Karate Ontario (KAO)
#160, 2 County Court Blvd., Brampton ON L6W 4V1
Tel: 647-706-4835
info@karate-ontario.com
karate-ontario.com
www.youtube.com/channel/UCnjL8YhmflRwiK1FZQBAlUA
www.facebook.com/309961174058
Overview: A medium-sized provincial organization
Description: To promote & perpetuate karate as a martial art & lifetime activity; to promote karate for physical fitness, mental fitness, & as a way of life; to develop provincial standards & programs; to encourage all participants in safely achieving their maximum at the recreational or competitive level; to provide safe competitive opportunities for karate-ka wishing to participate in the sport aspect of karate; to govern the amateur sport of karate & the conduct of all karate-ka under its jurisdiction; *Member of:* Karate Canada
Affiliation(s): World Karate Federation; Sport Alliance of Ontario; Coaches Assocation of Ontario
Chief Officer(s): Pravilal Pravibhavan, President
ppravibhavan@karate-ontario.com
Activities: *Awareness Events:* Sport Science Karate Symposium, June

Karaté Québec
CP 1000, Succ. M, 4545, av Pierre-de Coubertin, Montréal QC H1V 3R2
Tél: 514-252-3161; *Téléc:* 514-252-3036
Ligne sans frais: 877-527-2835
info@karatequebec.com
www.karatequebec.com

www.facebook.com/karatequebec
Aperçu: *Dimension:* moyenne; *Envergure:* provinciale; fondée en 1995
Description: Karaté Québec est une organisation structurée et démocratique qui vise à promouvoir, à organiser et à administrer la pratique du karaté au Québec de manière à ce que cet art martial ne perde jamais son sens premier : favoriser une progression saine et équilibrée des karatékas dans une société en mouvance perpétuelle; *Membre de:* Karate Canada

Newfoundland & Labrador Judo Association
#112, Hamlyn Rd. Plaza, Unit 50, St. John's NL A1E 5X7
nljawebmaster1@gmail.com
www.judonl.ca
Also Known As: Judo Newfoundland & Labrador
Overview: A small provincial organization
Description: To govern & promote the sport of Judo in Newfoundland & Labrador; *Member of:* Judo Canada
Chief Officer(s): Chris Wellon, President, 709-424-4084
cwellon@nf.sympatico.ca

Ontario Jiu-Jitsu Association (OJA)
#7, 40 Bell Farm Rd., Barrie ON L4M 5L3
Tel: 705-725-9186; *Fax:* 705-725-8562
Toll-Free: 800-352-1338
info@ontariojiujitsu.ca
www.ontariojiujitsu.com
www.facebook.com/jiujitsuontario
Overview: A medium-sized provincial organization founded in 1963

Description: To promote Jiu Jitsu among amateurs in Ontario
Chief Officer(s): Doug Knispel, President
dknispel@rci.rogers.com
Fees: $20 youth; $25 adult; $30 coach/official; $150 club;
Committees: Finance; Membership & Promotion; Safety & Insurance; Technical; Tournament; Volunteer; Canadian Jiu Jitsu Grading Board

Ontario Taekwondo Association
PO Box 31057, 8889 Yonge St., Richmond Hill ON L4C 0V3
Tel: 416-245-8582; *Fax:* 416-245-8582
info@taekwondo-ontario.com
taekwondo-ontario.com
Overview: A medium-sized provincial organization
Description: To promote & govern Taekwondo in Ontario
Chief Officer(s): In Kyung Kim, President
worldtkd@yahoo.com
Sungmin Son, Secretary General

Prince Edward Island Karate Association (PEIKA)
c/o Dawn Brown, 131 Blue Heron Lane, Cornwall PE C0A 1H0
www.karatepei.ca
Also Known As: Prince Edward Island Karate Association
Overview: A small provincial organization founded in 1971
Description: To teach, train & coach karate & allied physical arts; to teach physical culture generally; to promote the principles & teaching of the sport of karate & to work toward the advancement of the sport in conjunction with all other groups throughout Canada; to arrange matches, contests & competitions of every nature relating to karate & to offer or grant & contribute towards judges, awards & distinctions; to provide conditional assistance on the approval of the Executive of the Association; *Member of:* Karate Canada; Sport PEI
Chief Officer(s): Dawn Brown, President
dawn.brown@pei.sympatico.ca
Finances: *Annual Operating Budget:* Less than $50,000

Sask Taekwondo
106 Franklin Ave., Yorkton SK S3N 2G4
Tel: 306-782-1272
taekwondosk@sasktel.net
www.saskwtf.ca
Also Known As: Sask. WTF
Overview: A small provincial organization founded in 1981
Description: To govern the sport of Tae Kwon Do in Saskatchewan.; *Member of:* World Taekwondo Federation
Chief Officer(s): Audrey Ashcroft, Executive Director, 306-621-9696

Saskatchewan Karate Association (SKA)
510 Cynthia St., Saskatoon SK S7L 7K7
Tel: 306-374-7333; *Fax:* 306-374-7334
sk.karate@shaw.ca
www.saskarate.com
Overview: A small provincial organization founded in 1977
Description: To be the provincial governing body for the sport of karate in Saskatchewan; *Member of:* Karate Canada
Chief Officer(s): Dave Smith, President
Activities: Insurance Benefits; Seminars; Provincial, National & International Tournaments; Althletic Development Program; Althete's Assistance Program

Saskatchewan Martial Arts Association (SMAA)
PO Box 789, Melville SK S0A 2P0
Tel: 306-565-2266
saskamartialarts.ca
Overview: A small provincial organization
Description: To be the provincial governing body for a variety of martial arts styles practiced in Saskatchewan; *Member of:* Sask Sport Inc.
Chief Officer(s): Tim Oehler, President
Stephen McLeod, Vice President
Fees: $100 club

Taekwondo Canada
House of Sport, 2451 Riverside Dr., Ottawa ON K1H 7X7
Tel: 613-695-5425
info@taekwondo-canada.com
taekwondo-canada.com
www.instagram.com/taekwondocanada
www.facebook.com/Taekwondo.Canada
twitter.com/TKD_Canada
Overview: A medium-sized national organization
Description: To develop, promote & govern the sport of Taekwondo in Canada.
Chief Officer(s): Kee Ha, President
president@taekwondo-canada.com
Dave Harris, Executive Director
ed@taekwondo-canada.com
Activities: National Championships

Taekwondo Manitoba
145 Pacific Ave., Winnipeg MB R3B 2Z6
Fax: 204-925-5703
secretary@taekwondomanitoba.ca
www.taekwondomanitoba.ca
Previous Name: Manitoba Tae Kwon-Do Association
Overview: A small provincial organization
Description: To promote & govern the sport of Taekwondo in Manitoba.

WTF Taekwondo Federation of British Columbia
#3, 511 Cottonwood Ave., Coquitlam BC V3J 2R4
Tel: 604-939-8232
wtfbccanada@gmail.com
taekwondobc.com
www.facebook.com/taekwondobc
Also Known As: BC Taekwondo Federation
Overview: A small provincial organization
Description: To be the governing body of taekwondo in British Columbia; Sanctioned to send athletes to the Olympic Games, World Taekwondo Championships, World Junior Taekwondo Championships, World Cup Taekwondo Games, Pan-American Games, Canadian National Championships & Canadian Junior National Championships; *Member of:* WTF Taekwondo Canada; Sport BC
Affiliation(s): International Olympic Committee
Chief Officer(s): Song Chul Kim, President, 604-430-5467
Tony Kook, Vice President, 604-986-5558
tkook@vancouvermartialarts.ca
Minku Chang, Secretary General, 604-541-9457
changstkd@hotmail.com

WushuCanada
2370 Midland Ave., #B22-25, Toronto ON M1S 5C6
Tel: 416-321-5913
info@wushucanada.com
wushucanada.com
Previous Name: Confederation of Canadian Wushu Organizations
Overview: A small national organization
Description: To promote & develop the Olympic sport of Wushu in Canada
Fees: Schedule available; *Member Profile:* Athletes, coaches, officials, clubs & event organizers

WushuOntario
2370 Midland Ave., #B25, Toronto ON M1S 5C6
Tel: 416-321-5913
ontario@wushucanada.com
www.wushuontario.ca
Previous Name: United Wushu Association of Ontario
Overview: A small provincial organization founded in 1997
Description: To govern & promote Wushu in Ontario
Chief Officer(s): Eileen Fauster, President

Massage Therapy

Canadian Sport Massage Therapists Association (CSMTA) / Association canadienne des massothérapeutes du sport
#469, 420 Main St East, Milton ON L9T 5G3
Tel: 519-800-7134
natoffice@csmta.ca
www.csmta.ca
www.instagram.com/csmta
www.facebook.com/theCSMTA
twitter.com/thecsmta
Overview: A medium-sized national licensing organization founded in 1987
Description: To provide leadership in the field of sport massage therapy & education in Canada through the establishment of professional standards & qualifications of its members, as a certifying body
Affiliation(s): Canadian Olympic Committee; Expert Provider Group
Chief Officer(s): Jessica Sears, President
president@csmta.ca
Monty Churchman, Vice-President
vp@csmta.ca
Denise England, Secretary
secretary@csmta.ca
Jeanette Dobmeier, Treasurer
treasurer@csmta.ca
Danièle Speary, National Office Coordinator
natoffice@csmta.ca
Finances: *Annual Operating Budget:* Less than $50,000;
Funding Sources: Membership fee; workshop
Staff: 5 volunteer(s)
Membership: 70; *Fees:* $25 student; $160 certification candidate; *Member Profile:* 2,200-hr massage school or member of provincial association affiliated with CSMTA; *Committees:*

Bylaws; Education; Certification & Examinations; Public Relations; Selections
Activities: Providing the National Sport Massage Certification Program (NSMCP); Promoting a professional climate for the growth of sport massage therapy in Canada

Mediation

Sport Dispute Resolution Centre of Canada (SDRCC) / Centre de règlement des différends sportifs du Canada (CRDSC)
#950, 1080, Beaver Hall Hill, Montréal QC H2Z 1S8
Tel: 514-866-1245; *Fax:* 514-866-1246
Toll-Free: 866-733-7767
education@crdsc-sdrcc.ca
www.crdsc-sdrcc.ca
www.linkedin.com/company/sport-dispute-resolution-centre-of-canada
www.facebook.com/crdscsdrcc
twitter.com/CRDSC_SDRCC
Overview: A small national organization founded in 2004
Description: To provide to the sport community a national alternative dispute resolution service for sport disputes
Chief Officer(s): Marie-Claude Asselin, Chief Executive Officer
mcasselin@crdsc-sdrcc.ca

Motorcycles

Canadian Motorcycle Association (CMA) / Association motocycliste canadienne
605 James St. North, 4th Fl., Hamilton ON L8L 1J9
Tel: 905-522-5705; *Fax:* 905-522-5716
registration@motorcyclingcanada.ca
www.motorcyclingcanada.ca
www.facebook.com/motorcyclingcanada
Overview: A medium-sized national licensing organization founded in 1946
Description: To encourage & develop motorcycling for the benefit & enjoyment of its members
Affiliation(s): Fédération internationale motocycliste; Canadian Olympic Association; FIM North America Union
Chief Officer(s): Holly Ralph, President
Marilyn Bastedo, Chief Executive Officer
mbastedo.cma@bellnet.ca
Finances: *Annual Operating Budget:* $500,000-$1.5 Million;
Funding Sources: Membership fees; event fees
Staff: 4 staff member(s); 150 volunteer(s)
Membership: 100 club + 150 lifetime + 9,000 individual; *Fees:* $30 youth; $80 regular; *Member Profile:* Interest in motorcycling; *Committees:* Strategic Planning; Technical; Environmental; Awards; Nominations; Trials Advisory; Development of Alternative Energy Competition

Mountaineering

Alpine Club of Canada (ACC) / Club alpin du Canada (CAC)
PO Box 8040, Stn. Main, 201 Indian Flats Rd., Canmore AB T1W 2T8
Tel: 403-678-3200; *Fax:* 403-678-3224
info@alpineclubofcanada.ca
www.alpineclubofcanada.ca
www.facebook.com/alpineclubofcanada
twitter.com/alpineclubcan
Overview: A large national charitable organization founded in 1906
Description: To encourage & promote mountaineering & mountain crafts; To educate Canadians in the appreciation of mountain heritage; To explore alpine & glacial regions primarily in Canada; To preserve the natural beauty of mountains & their fauna & flora; To promote mountain art & literature; To disseminate scientific & educational knowledge concerning mountains & mountaineering through meetings & publications; To conduct summer & ski mountaineering camps
Affiliation(s): International Union of Alpinist Associations
Chief Officer(s): Lawrence White, Executive Director
lwhite@alpineclubofcanada.ca
Kish Stephenson, Director, Finance
kstephenson@alpineclubofcanada.ca
Finances: *Funding Sources:* Donations; Grants; Corporate
Staff: 11 staff member(s)
Fees: $23 youth; $33 individual; $50 family
Activities: Providing financial support necessary to advocate protection & preservation of mountain & climbing environments; Enhancing constitutional objective of ACC to work towards preservation of alpine environment & flora & fauna in their natural habitat; *Library:* Yes (Open to Public)

Association of Canadian Mountain Guides (ACMG) / Association des guides de montagne canadiens
PO Box 8341, Canmore AB T1W 2V1
Tel: 403-678-2885; *Fax:* 403-609-0070
acmg@acmg.ca
www.acmg.ca
www.facebook.com/ACMG.ca
twitter.com/ACMGca
Overview: A small national organization founded in 1963
Description: To represent mountain guides in dealing with both public & private official bodies; To maintain standards of guiding & acts as a public relations body; To promote the sport in a safe & educational manner; *Member of:* International Federation of Mountain Guides Associations
Chief Officer(s): Sylvia Forest, President, 403-762-4129
pres@acmg.ca
Peter Tucker, Executive Director, 403-949-3587
ed@acmg.ca
Finances: *Funding Sources:* Membership fees
Membership: 1,350; *Fees:* Schedule available; *Member Profile:* Prsonal membership is open exclusively to trained / certified professional guides & instructors
Activities: Training & Certification Program

British Columbia Mountaineering Club
PO Box 20042, Vancouver BC V5Z 0C1
Tel: 604-268-9502
contact@bcmc.ca
www.bcmc.ca
www.instagram.com/bcmountaineeringclub
www.facebook.com/BCMountaineeringClub
twitter.com/BCMountainClub
Overview: A small provincial organization founded in 1907
Description: To organize mountaineering & skiing trips; To promote & support conservation, trail & hut construction, trail maintenance, mountain safety & education
Affiliation(s): Federation of Mountain Clubs of BC
Chief Officer(s): Wilson Edgar, President
exec@bcmc.ca
Chris Ludwig, Vice President, Memberships
memberships@bcmc.ca
Membership: 1,000 individual; *Fees:* $20 youth/senior; $40 adult; $800 lifetime; *Committees:* Cabins & Trails; Camps; Climbing (Trips); Conservation; Courses; Marketing; Memberships; Recreation
Activities: Hiking; climbing; mountaineering; backcountry skiing; snowshoeing; hiking, backpacking; *Library:* Yes by appointment

Union internationale des associations d'alpinisme (UIAA) / International Climbing & Mountaineering Federation
c/o Schweizer Alpen-Club SAC, PO Box 23, Monbijoustrasse 61, Bern CH-3000 Switzerland
office@uiaa.ch
www.theuiaa.org
www.youtube.com/uiaabern
www.facebook.com/theuiaa
twitter.com/UIAAmountains
Overview: A medium-sized international organization founded in 1932
Description: To study & solve all problems in connection with mountaineering in general & particularly those of an international nature; To contribute to the development & promotion of mountaineering on an international level
Affiliation(s): Alpine Club of Canada; Fédération québecoise de la montagne
Chief Officer(s): Frits Vrijlandt, President
Nils Glatthard, Director, Operations
Membership: 80 institutional from 50 countries; *Member Profile:* National alpine associations from all over the world; *Committees:* Management; Mountaineering; Sports; Access; Anti-Doping; Ice Climbing; Medical; Mountain Protection; Safety; Youth

Native Peoples

Aboriginal Sport & Wellness Council of Ontario (ASWCO)
#1A, 1090 Aerowood Dr., Mississauga ON L4W 1Y5
Tel: 416-479-0928; *Fax:* 905-412-0325
www.aswco.ca
www.instagram.com/aswco
www.facebook.com/aswco
twitter.com/aswco
Overview: A medium-sized provincial organization founded in 2011

Description: To organize sporting events for Aboriginal athletes throughout Ontario; To promote active & healthy Aboriginal individuals & communities in Ontario
Chief Officer(s): Marc Laliberté, President
dmarclaliberte@shaw.ca
Clay Melnike, Manager, Planning & Regional Development
clay.melnike@aswco.ca
Wesley Marsden, Coordinator, Operations & Communications
wesley.marsden@aswco.ca
Activities: Offering sporting programs & leadership development opportunities

Aboriginal Sport Circle (ASC) / Cercle sportif autochtone (CSA)
c/o House of Sport, RA Centre, 2451 Riverside Dr., Ottawa ON K1H 7X7

Tel: 613-518-8353; *Toll-Free:* 855-814-4574
ascoffice@aboriginalsportcircle.ca
www.aboriginalsportcircle.ca
www.instagram.com/aboriginalsportcircle
www.facebook.com/AboriginalSC
twitter.com/AboriginalSC
Overview: A medium-sized national organization founded in 1995
Description: To support the health & wellbeing of Aboriginal people & communities through sport & recreation
Chief Officer(s): Carey Calder, Chief Executive Officer
Finances: *Funding Sources:* Sport Canada

Yukon Aboriginal Sport Circle (YASC)
202D Strickland St., Whitehorse YT Y1A 2J8

Tel: 867-668-2840
info@yasc.ca
www.yasc.ca
www.facebook.com/YukonASC
twitter.com/yukonasc
Merged from: Yukon Aboriginal Sport Development Office Interim Steering Committee & YIGSC
Overview: A medium-sized provincial organization founded in 1990
Description: To advance Aboriginal recreation & sport in the Yukon; To govern Arctic Sports, Dene Games, Archery & Lacrosse; *Member of:* Sport Yukon
Chief Officer(s): Gael Marchand, Executive Director
ed@yasc.ca
Finances: *Funding Sources:* Government of Yukon
Activities: Offering programs to increase participation & skill levels; Increasing awareness

Yukon Indian Hockey Association (YIHA)
PO Box 31769, Whitehorse YT Y1A 6L3

Tel: 867-456-7294; *Fax:* 867-456-7290
yihahockey@gmail.com
www.yiha.ca
Overview: A medium-sized provincial organization founded in 1984
Description: To establish a hockey league in the Yukon to enable Native athletes to compete with other Canadian Provinces & Territories in the sport.
Chief Officer(s): Jeanie Dendys, President

Netball

British Columbia Netball Association
BC

Tel: 604-293-1820
mwebb1@shaw.ca
bcnetball.ca
www.facebook.com/BCNetballAssoc
twitter.com/BCNetball
Also Known As: BC Netball
Overview: A small provincial organization
Description: To oversee the sport of netball in British Columbia.; *Member of:* Netball Canada
Affiliation(s): International Federation of Netball Associations
Chief Officer(s): Ann Willcocks, President

Fédération de Netball du Québec / Québec Amateur Netball Federation (QANF)
CP 1000, Succ. M, 4545, av Pierre-de Coubertin, Montréal QC H1V 3R2

Tél: 514-486-2769
www.netballquebec.ca

www.facebook.com/QuebecNetball
Également appelé: Netball Québec
Aperçu: *Dimension:* moyenne; *Envergure:* provinciale; fondée en 1974

Description: Promouvoir et développer le netball féminin au Québec; *Membre de:* Netball Canada
Affiliation(s): International Federation of Netball Associations
Membre(s) du bureau directeur: Avice Roberts-Joseph, Présidente
Sheryl Stephens, Secrétaire
Membre: 750; *Comités:* Technique
Activités: Tournois; Ligues; Cliniques pour entraîneurs et arbitres

Netball Alberta
PO Box 270, 7620 Elbow Dr. SW, Calgary AB T2V 1K2

Tel: 403-238-8041; *Fax:* 888-213-9218
contact@netballalberta.com
www.netballalberta.com
www.facebook.com/groups/2223869141
Previous Name: Alberta Netball Association
Overview: A small provincial charitable organization founded in 1992
Description: To promote & encourage the sport of netball in Alberta; to facilitate exchange of information & ideas; to promote education & development; to sponsor clinics & classes; to collect & distribute information; to raise funds for the Association; to organize & conduct competitions; *Member of:* Netball Canada
Affiliation(s): International Federation of Netball Associations
Chief Officer(s): Julie Arnold, President
president@netballalberta.com
Finances: *Annual Operating Budget:* Less than $50,000; *Funding Sources:* Fundraising
Staff: 10 volunteer(s)
Membership: 350

Netball Canada

netballcanada@gmail.com
netballcanada.ca
www.facebook.com/netballcanada
Overview: A small national organization founded in 1976
Description: To be the national governing body for netball throughout Canada
Affiliation(s): International Federation of Netball Associations
Membership: 4 provincial associations

Netball Ontario
ON

info@netballontario.com
www.netballontario.com
www.facebook.com/NetballOntario
Previous Name: Ontario Amateur Netball Association
Overview: A small provincial organization founded in 1974
Description: To promote & develop the sport of netball in Ontario.; *Member of:* Netball Canada
Affiliation(s): International Federation of Netball Associations

Olympic Games

Canadian Olympic Committee (COC) / Comité olympique canadien
#3000, 250 Yonge St., Toronto ON M5B 2L7

Tel: 416-962-0262; *Fax:* 416-967-4902
digital@olympic.ca
olympic.ca
www.youtube.com/teamcanada
www.facebook.com/teamcanada
twitter.com/teamcanada
Overview: A small national charitable organization founded in 1952
Description: To be responsible for all aspects of Canada's involvement in the Olympic movement, including Canada's participation in the Olympic & Pan American Games & a wide variety of programs that promote the Olympic Movement in Canada through cultural & educational means
Chief Officer(s): David Shoemaker, CEO & Secretary General
dshoemaker@olympic.ca
Finances: *Annual Operating Budget:* Greater than $5 Million; *Funding Sources:* National & international sponsors
Staff: 114 staff member(s); 400 volunteer(s)
Membership: 400
Activities: *Speaker Service:* Yes

Orienteering

Alberta Orienteering Association (AOA)
PO Box 1576, Cochrane AB T4C 1B5

Tel: 403-981-4444
info@orienteeringalberta.ca
www.orienteeringalberta.ca
www.facebook.com/OrienteeringAB
twitter.com/OrienteeringAB
Overview: A small provincial organization founded in 1974

Description: To promote & encourage orienteering as sport and recreation in Alberta; To provide orienteering opportunities for all levels of ability; *Member of:* Canadian Orienteering Federation
Chief Officer(s): David Campden, President
Marion Owen, Treasurer
Bogi Gyorfi, Executive Director
Fees: $30 individual; $45 group
Activities: Sport orienteering; amateur sport; navigation; map reading; *Library:* Yes (Open to Public)

Canadian Orienteering Federation (COF) / Fédération canadienne de course d'orientation
1239 Colgrove Ave. NE, Calgary AB T2E 5C3

Tel: 403-283-0807; *Fax:* 403-451-1681
info@orienteering.ca
www.orienteering.ca
www.youtube.com/orienteeringcanada
www.facebook.com/orienteeringcanada
twitter.com/orienteeringcan
Also Known As: Orienteering Canada
Overview: A large national organization founded in 1967
Description: To provide leadership & resources to individuals involved in orienteering in Canada
Affiliation(s): International Orienteering Federation
Chief Officer(s): Tracy Bradley, Executive Director
Member Profile: Coaches, officials, volunteers, athletes & youth leaders involved in orienteering; *Committees:* Celebration, Awards & Recognition; Coaching; Executive; Finance & Audit; Governance; High Performance; HR; Long Term Athlete Development; Major Events; Mountain Bike Orienteering; New Participant Recruitment; Nominations; Officials Program; Sass Peepre Junior Development; Ski Orienteering; Technical
Activities: *Rents Mailing List:* Yes

Manitoba Orienteering Association Inc. (MOA)
145 Pacific Ave., Winnipeg MB R3B 2Z6

Tel: 204-925-5706; *Fax:* 204-925-5792
info@orienteering.mb.ca
www.orienteering.mb.ca
Overview: A medium-sized provincial organization
Description: To promote & support orienteering in Manitoba; *Member of:* Canadian Orienteering Federation
Affiliation(s): Sports Manitoba
Fees: $3 junior; $5 adult; $10 family

Orienteering Association of British Columbia (OABC)
2625 West 3rd Ave., Vancouver BC V6K 1M4

www.orienteeringbc.ca
Overview: A small provincial organization
Member of: Sport BC; Orienteering Canada
Affiliation(s): Canadian Orienteering Federation (COF); Coaching Association of Canada
Chief Officer(s): Brian Ellis, President
bee@msl.ubc.ca
Activities: Offering technical coaching courses in orienteering; *Awareness Events:* National Orienteering Week

Orienteering Association of Nova Scotia (OANS)
5516 Spring Garden Rd., 4th Fl., Halifax NS B3J 1G6

Tel: 902-446-2295
info@orienteeringns.ca
www.orienteeringns.ca
Overview: A small provincial organization founded in 1971
Description: To operate as the governing body for orienteering in Nova Scotia; To train & certify orienteering coaches, officials, & mapmakers; *Member of:* Canadian Orienteering Federation; Sport Nova Scotia
Chief Officer(s): Emily Secord, President
nsorienteering@gmail.com
Tony Wheeler, Vice President
tony.wheeler@eastlink.ca
Emily Nickerson, Executive Director
enickerson@sportnovascotia.ca
Member Profile: Those who participate in an Orienteering Nova Scotia event and wish to become a member; *Committees:* Mapping; Technical & Competition; Education; Promotion; Finance; Junior Development
Activities: Coordinating local club activities; Publishing event results; Promoting orienteering; Providing programs in map, compass, & wilderness navigation skills, introductory skills, & junior development; Preparing orienteering maps

Orienteering New Brunswick (ONB)
c/o Robert Hughes, 69 Kingsclear Dr., Upper Kingsclear NB E3E 1R6

www.orienteering.nb.ca
www.facebook.com/OrienteeringNB
Overview: A small provincial organization founded in 1975
Description: To promote, develop & encourage the sport & recreation of orienteering in New Brunswick; *Member of:*

Canadian Orienteering Federation
Affiliation(s): International Orienteering Federation
Chief Officer(s): Robert Hughes, Secretary
rustics@nb.sympatico.ca
Finances: *Annual Operating Budget:* Less than $50,000
Fees: $15 adult; $10 junior (under 20 years old); $50
family/group; *Member Profile:* Family groups; individuals; cadets
& scouts
Activities: Competitive & recreational orienteering

Orienteering Ontario Inc.
ON

info@orienteeringontario.ca
www.orienteeringontario.ca
Also Known As: Ontario Orienteering Association, Inc.
Overview: A small provincial licensing organization founded in
1975
Description: To encourage, promote & give leadership in all
aspects of the sport of orienteering & associated activities at
local, provincial & national levels; *Member of:* Canadian
Orienteering Federation
Chief Officer(s): Chris Laughren, President
Fees: Schedule available

Orienteering Québec (OQ) / Fédération québécoise de course d'orientation
QC

orientering_quebec@orienteeringquebec.ca
www.orienteeringquebec.ca
Overview: A small provincial charitable organization founded in
1967
Member of: Canadian Orienteering Federation (COF);
International Orienteering Federation (IOF)
Affiliation(s): Ramblers Orienteering Club; Lou Garou
Orienteering Club; Ottawa Orienteering Club
Chief Officer(s): Isabelle Robert, President
liriel@sympatico.ca
Philippe Côté-Jacques, Vice-President
Bill Meldrum, Treasurer
bill.meldrum@videotron.ca
Finances: *Funding Sources:* Members
Activities: Organizing events; Posting event results;
Coordinating club activities; mapping

Yukon Orienteering Association (YOA)
4061 - 4th Ave., Whitehorse YT Y1A 1H1
Tel: 867-335-2287
info@yukonorienteering.ca
www.yukonorienteering.ca
www.facebook.com/YukonOrienteering
twitter.com/YOrienteering
Overview: A small provincial organization
Description: To promote, develop & govern orienteering in
Yukon Territory; *Member of:* Canadian Orienteering Federation
Chief Officer(s): Afan Jones, President
Bob Sagar, Vice-President
Wendy Nixon, Director, Communications
Fees: $5
Activities: Kids Running Wild; Yukon Orienteering Team; Yukon
Championships; clinics

Parachuting

Alberta Sport Parachuting Association (ASPA)
c/o Tina Connolly, #301, 7708 - 106 Ave., Edmonton AB T6A
1H5
Tel: 780-996-5266
admin@aspa.ca
www.aspa.ca
www.facebook.com/groups/5261851254/
Overview: A small provincial organization
Description: To promote & facilitate the development of the
sport of skydiving in Alberta; *Member of:* Canadian Sport
Parachuting Association
Chief Officer(s): Dan Stith, President
Finances: *Annual Operating Budget:* $50,000-$100,000
Staff: 2 staff member(s)
Membership: 1,400; *Fees:* $20
Activities: *Awareness Events:* Provincial Championships, early
July; *Speaker Service:* Yes

Canadian Sport Parachuting Association (CSPA) / Association canadienne du parachutisme sportif (ACPS)
#204, 1468 Laurier St., Rockland ON K4K 1C7
Tel: 613-419-0908; *Fax:* 613-916-6008
office@cspa.ca
www.cspa.ca
Overview: A medium-sized national charitable organization
founded in 1956

Member of: Aero Club of Canada
Chief Officer(s): Michelle Matte-Stotyn, Executive Director,
613-419-0908 2
michelle.matte-stotyn@cspa.ca
Membership: 2,000 + 48 member groups; *Fees:* $94;
Committees: Coaching Working; Technical Safety; Competition
& National Teams; Web / Information Technology
Activities: *Library:* Yes (Open to Public)

Manitoba Sport Parachute Association (MSPA)
145 Pacific Ave., Winnipeg MB R3B 2Z6
membership@mspa.mb.ca
www.mspa.mb.ca
Overview: A small provincial organization founded in 1978
Description: To promote awareness & participation in skydiving
in Manitoba; *Member of:* Canadian Sport Parachuting
Association
Chief Officer(s): Kaneena Vanstone, President
president@mspa.mb.ca
Finances: *Funding Sources:* Manitoba Sports Federation;
Manitoba Lotteries; Sport Directorate
Fees: $25

Sport Parachute Association of Saskatchewan
SK
www.skydive.sk.ca
Overview: A small provincial organization
Member of: Canadian Sport Parachuting Association
Chief Officer(s): Craig Skihar, President
stimpysplace@gmail.com
Jayson Pister, Vice-President
jay.pister@gmail.com

Pentathlon

Pentathlon Alberta
AB
info@pentathlonalberta.com
www.pentathlonalberta.com
Previous Name: Alberta Modern Pentathlon Association
Overview: A small provincial organization
Description: To develop world-class athletes while promoting &
developing the sport in Alberta.; *Member of:* Canadian Modern
Pentathlon Association
Chief Officer(s): Connie Olsen, President, 403-703-4951
Membership: 4 local clubs/groups

Pentathlon Canada
#400, 3800 Steeles Ave. West, Woodbridge ON L4L 4G9
www.pentathloncanada.ca
www.instagram.com/pentathloncan
www.facebook.com/PentathlonCanada
twitter.com/PentathlonCAN
Previous Name: Canadian Modern Pentathlon Association
Overview: A medium-sized national charitable organization
Description: To promote Modern Pentathlon in Canada
Affiliation(s): Union internationale de pentathlon moderne et
biathlon
Chief Officer(s): Rod Staveley, President
president@pentathloncanada.ca
Connie Olsen, Vice-President
Membership: 2,000

Pentathlon Ontario
c/o Pauline Vossen, Secretary, 351521 - 17th Line, East
Garafraxa ON L9W 7E1
pentathloncanada.ca/provinces/ontario
Previous Name: Ontario Modern Pentathlon Association
Overview: A medium-sized provincial organization
Description: To promote modern pentathalon
Chief Officer(s): Shaun LaGrange, President, 416-433-6893
salagrange@sympatico.ca
Fees: $65 competitive; $20 supporting; $15 coach

Physical Education & Training

Fédération des éducateurs et éducatrices physiques enseignants du Québec (FEEPEQ)
2500, boul de l'Université, Sherbrooke QC J1K 2R1
Tél: 819-821-8000; *Téléc:* 819-821-7970
info@feepeq.com
www.feepeq.com

www.facebook.com/feepeq
twitter.com/feepeq_com
Nom précédent: Confédération des Éducateurs physiques du
Québec
Aperçu: *Dimension:* moyenne; *Envergure:* provinciale;
Organisme sans but lucratif; fondée en 1960
Description: Répresenter plus du tiers des éducateurs/trices
physiques oeuvrant activement partout au Québec

Affiliation(s): Sports Québec; Fédération québécoise du sport
étudiant
Membre(s) du bureau directeur: Jean-Claude Drapeau,
Président
president@feepeq.com
Véronique Marchand, Directrice, Opérations
David Larivière, Agent, Bureau
agentbureau@feepeq.com
Finances: *Budget de fonctionnement annuel:*
$100,000-$250,000
Personnel: 4 membre(s) du personnel; 40 bénévole(s)
Membre: 1 700; *Montant de la cotisation:* Barème; *Critères
d'admissibilite:* Éducateur physique enseignant selon les régions
d'appartenance; *Comités:* Exécutif; finances; partenariats;
publications; pédagogie; professionnalisation; congrès; dossiers
Internet
Activités: Formation; information; sensibilisation; congrès;
Mouvement Pupilles de l'Enseignement Public; *Service de
conférenciers:* Oui; *Listes de destinataires:* Oui *Bibliothèque:* Oui
rendez-vous

Ontario Physical & Health Education Association (OPHEA)
#608, 1 Concorde Gate, Toronto ON M3C 3N6
Tel: 416-426-7120; *Fax:* 416-426-7373
Toll-Free: 888-446-7432
www.ophea.org
www.youtube.com/opheacanada
www.facebook.com/OpheaCanada
twitter.com/opheacanada
Overview: A medium-sized provincial organization
Description: To support communities & schools to encourage
healthy active living
Chief Officer(s): Lori Lukinuk, President
Chris Markham, Executive Director & CEO, 416-426-7126
Activities: Promoting physical activity, & health & physical
literacy; Providing program supports to schools & communities;
Forming partnerships; Engaging in advocacy activities

Physical & Health Education Canada / Éducation physique et santé Canada
c/o House of Sport, RA Centre, 2451 Riverside Dr., Ottawa ON
K1H 7X7
Tel: 613-523-1348; *Fax:* 613-523-1206
Toll-Free: 800-663-8708
info@phecanada.ca
phecanada.ca
www.youtube.com/user/phecanada
www.facebook.com/PHECanada
twitter.com/PHECanada
Also Known As: PHE Canada
Previous Name: Canadian Physical Education Association;
Canadian Association for Health, Physical Education, Recreation
& Dance
Overview: A large national charitable organization founded in
1933
Description: To promote quality school health programs & the
healthy development of Canadian children & youth
Chief Officer(s): Melanie Davis, Executive Director & CEO,
613-523-1348 2330
melaniedavis@phecanada.ca
Jodie Lyn-Harrison, Chief Administrative Officer, 613-523-1348
2333
jodielynharrison@phecanada.ca
Jordan Burwash, Director, 613-523-1348 2339
jordanburwash@phecanada.ca
Marim Moreland, Manager, Finance, 613-523-1348 2338
marimmoreland@phecanada.ca
Member Profile: Principals, teachers, public health professionals
& recreation leaders from across Canada; *Committees:* Dance
Education; Health Promoting Schools & Health Education;
Intramurals & After School; Leadership; Physical Education &
Physical Literacy
Activities: Advocating for quality, school-based physical &
health education; Offering professional learning experiences;
Creating networking opportunities

Physical & Health Educators of Manitoba
#319, 145 Pacific Ave., Winnipeg MB R3B 2Z6
Tel: 204-926-8357
phemb@sportmanitoba.ca
www.phemanitoba.ca
Also Known As: PHE Manitoba
Previous Name: Manitoba Physical Education Teachers
Association
Overview: A small provincial organization
Description: To support, develop & promote physical & health
education in schools across Manitoba
Affiliation(s): Manitoba Teacher's Society
Chief Officer(s): Jacki Nylen, Co-President
Darla Armstrong, Co-President

Fees: $15 student/retired/associate; $25 full; *Committees:* Awards; Grants & Funding; Health Promoting Schools; Healthy Schools; Movement Skills; MTS PD Day; Professional Development; Safety

Physical Education in British Columbia (PE-BC)
BC

psac54@bctf.ca
phebc.ca
www.facebook.com/PhysicalEducationBC
twitter.com/pe_bc

Previous Name: British Columbia Physical Education Provincial Specialist Association
Overview: A medium-sized provincial organization
Description: To provide leadership, advocacy & resources for teachers of physical education; *Member of:* British Columbia Teachers' Federation
Chief Officer(s): John Ogilvie, President
Fees: $15 student; $25 BCTF member

Réseau du sport étudiant du Québec Est-du-Québec
60, rue de L'Evêché ouest, #J-201, Rimouski QC G5L 4H6
Tél: 418-723-1880; *Télec:* 418-722-0457
rseq-eq.com

www.facebook.com/RSEQEstDuQuebecviesaine
Également appelé:RSEQ Est-du-Québec
Nom précédent: Association régionale du sport étudiant de l'Est du Québec
Aperçu: *Dimension: petite; Envergure: locale; fondée en 1989*
Description: Favoriser la réalisation de l'ensemble des actions éducatives par l'activité physique et particulièrement le sport en vue de contribuer au développement intégral des étudiants des niveaux primaire, secondaire et collégial dans la région Est du Québec.; *Membre de:* Réseau du sport étudiant du Québec
Membre(s) du bureau directeur: Marc Boudreau, Directeur, 418-722-0457 2539
marcboud@cegep-rimouski.qc.ca
Finances: *Budget de fonctionnement annuel:*
$250,000-$500,000; *Fonds:*Unité régionale de loisir et de sport de Québec
Personnel:2 membre(s) du personnel; 25 bénévole(s)
Membre: 28; *Critères d'admissibilite:* Institutions scolaires
Activités: *Stagiaires:* Oui

Réseau du sport étudiant du Québec Montréal
6875, rue Jarry est, Montréal QC H1P 1W7
Tél: 514-645-6923; *Télec:* 514-354-8632
secretariat@montreal.rseq.ca
www.rseqmontreal.com

www.youtube.com/user/RSEQMontreal
www.facebook.com/RSEQMontreal
Également appelé:RSEQ Montréal
Nom précédent: Association régionale du sport étudiant de Montréal
Aperçu: *Dimension: petite; Envergure: locale; Organisme sans but lucratif; fondée en 1989*
Description: Regrouper les associations régionales de sport scolaire, de sport collégial et de sport universitaire de l'Ile de Montréal et les représenter; développer et soutenir des réseaux de compétition régionaux en concertation avec les autres partenaires; offrir des stages de formation et de perfectionnement de cadres en étroite collaboration avec une fédération de sport donnée; participer à la programmation développée par leur instance provinciale; déléguer des officiers auprès des instance provinciales du sport en milieu d'éducation; développer une approche du sport en milieu d'éducation pour chacun des niveaux d'enseignement et développer des programmes en conséquence; promouvoir la pratique de l'activité physique et du sport en milieu d'éducation; coopérer dans le respect des valeurs éducatives avec les organismes intéressés au développement de l'activité physique et du sport; *Membre de:* Réseau du sport étudiant du Québec
Membre(s) du bureau directeur: Jacques Desrochers, Directeur général, 514-645-6923 2
jdesrochers@montreal.rseq.ca
Finances: *Fonds:*Gouvernement provincial
Personnel:5 membre(s) du personnel
Critères d'admissibilite: Personnel du monde de l'éducation
Activités: Ligues; championnats; stages de perfectionnement pour entraOneurs, officiels et arbitres; *Stagiaires:* Oui

Saskatchewan Physical Education Association (SPEA)
c/o Holly Stevens, PO Box 193, Harris SK S0L 1K0
Tel: 306-656-4423; *Fax:* 306-656-4405
spea@xplornet.com
www.speaonline.ca
www.facebook.com/speaonline
twitter.com/speaonline
Overview: A small provincial organization founded in 1951

Description: To provide quality leadership, advocacy & resources for professionals in physical education & wellness in order to positively influence the lifestyles of Saskatchewan's children and youth; *Member of:* PHE Canada, SPRA, STF, SHSAA, U of S, U of R,SHEA, In Motion
Affiliation(s): Physical Health Education Canada; Saskatchewan Parks & Recreation Association; Saskatchewan Teachers Federal PHE Canada; Saskatchewan Teachers' Federation
Chief Officer(s): Holly Stevens, Executive Director
Finances: *Annual Operating Budget:* $100,000-$250,000; *Funding Sources:* Membership fees; Sask Lotteries Trust; Sponsorships
Staff: 1 staff member(s); 15 volunteer(s)
Membership: 485; *Fees:* Free student; $15 retired; $25 regular; *Member Profile:* Individuals with a professional interest in the teaching of physical education; *Committees:* Social Media, Journal Editor/Website, New Resources/Wellness, Curriculum, Advocacy/Mentorship, Membership Services, Regional Directors
Activities:*Library:* Yes (Open to Public)

Physical Fitness

The Canadian Association of Fitness Professionals / Association canadienne des professionnels en conditionnement physique
#110, 225 Select Ave., Toronto ON M1X 0B5
Tel: 416-493-3515; *Fax:* 416-493-1756
Toll-Free: 800-667-5622
info@canfitpro.com
www.canfitpro.com
www.youtube.com/canfitpro
www.linkedin.com/company/canfitpro
www.facebook.com/canfitpro
twitter.com/canfitpro

Also Known As: Can-Fit-Pro
Overview: A medium-sized national licensing organization founded in 1993
Description: To deliver the highest standard of accessible, affordable, & attainable fitness education & experiences; *Member of:* National Fitness Leadership Advisory Committee
Finances: *Annual Operating Budget:* $1.5 Million-$3 Million; *Funding Sources:* Sponsorship; private; membership dues; courses
Staff: 10 staff member(s); 400 volunteer(s)
Membership: 25,000; *Fees:* $58 student; $98 professional; $399 small business; $499 medium business; *Member Profile:* Interest in fitness industry
Activities: Certification courses, exams & resources for fitness instructors & personal trainers; Continuing education; Events & conferences; Job postings & networking

Canadian Fitness & Lifestyle Research Institute (CFLRI) / Institut canadien de la recherche sur la condition physique et le mode de vie
#201, 185 Somerset St. West, Ottawa ON K2P 0J2
Tel: 613-233-5528; *Fax:* 613-233-5536
www.cflri.ca

Previous Name: Canada Fitness Survey (1985)
Overview: A medium-sized national charitable organization founded in 1980
Description: To conduct research, monitor trends & make recommendations to increase physical activity & improve health in Canada
Chief Officer(s): Christine Cameron, President
Finances: *Funding Sources:* Fitness / Active Living Program Unit of Health Canada; Contracts; Grants; Publication sales; Donations; Sport Canada
Activities: Providing education about leading active & healthy lives; Developing a provider-based intervention known as PACE Canada; Conducting surveys, such as the Canadian Physical Activity Levels Among Youth (CAN PLAY)

Canadian Society for Exercise Physiology (CSEP) / Société canadienne de physiologie de l'exercice (SCPE)
#101, 495 Richmond Rd., Ottawa ON K2A 4B1
Tel: 613-234-3755; *Fax:* 613-234-3565
Toll-Free: 877-651-3755
info@csep.ca
www.csep.ca
www.instagram.com/csep_scpe
www.linkedin.com/company/csep-scpe
www.facebook.com/csep-scpe
twitter.com/CSEPdotCA
Previous Name: Canadian Association of Sport Sciences
Overview: A medium-sized national organization founded in 1967
Description: To promote fitness, performance, & health outcomes for Canadians; To set high standards for qualified

exercise professionals through evidence-based practice & certification; To be the recognized authority in exercise science & prescription by integrating research into best practice
Chief Officer(s): Adam Upshaw, Chair
aupshaw@niagaracollege.ca
Finances: *Annual Operating Budget:* $1.5 Million-$3 Million; *Funding Sources:* Membership dues; Events; Sales
Staff: 12 staff member(s); 150 volunteer(s)
Membership: 5,400; *Fees:* Schedule available; *Member Profile:* Academic / researcher members with a graduate degree, PhD, MD, or MSc; Certified members: CSEP Certified Exercise Physiologist or CSEP Certified Personal Trainer; Industry & Allied partner members; Supporter members; Students currently enrolled full-time in university studies; Retired emeritus members; *Committees:* CSEP Conference; CSEP Knowledge Translation; CSEP Member Services; CSEP Professional Standards Program; Finance; Nominations
Activities: Offering the CSEP Professional Standards Program; Developing national physical activity guidelines; Advertising job postings; Facilitating national communication through committees & networks; Providing opportunities to communicate cutting-edge research

Provincial Fitness Unit of Alberta (AFLCA)
Percy Page Bldg., 11759 Groat Rd., 3rd Fl., Edmonton AB T5M 3K6
Tel: 780-492-4435; *Fax:* 780-455-2264
Toll-Free: 866-348-8648
info@provincialfitnessunit.ca
www.provincialfitnessunit.ca
www.facebook.com/provincialfitnessunitalberta
twitter.com/AbFitnessUnit
Previous Name: Alberta Fitness Leadership Certification Association
Overview: A medium-sized provincial organization founded in 1984
Member of: National Fitness Leadership Advisory Council; National Fitness Leadership Alliance
Chief Officer(s): Katherine MacKeigan, Executive Director
katherine.mackeigan@ualberta.ca
Membership: 1,000-4,999; *Member Profile:* Fitness leader or trainer
Activities: Certifications in fitness training; *Internships:* Yes

The Recreation Association / L'Association récréative
2451 Riverside Dr., Ottawa ON K1H 7X7
Tel: 613-733-5100; *Fax:* 613-736-6238
racentre@racentre.com
www.racentre.com
www.instagram.com/racentreottawa
www.facebook.com/RACentreOttawa
twitter.com/RACentreOttawa
Also Known As: RA Centre
Overview: A large national organization founded in 1941
Description: To provide quality leisure & lifestyle activities to the membership
Chief Officer(s): Tosha Rhodenizer, Chief Executive Officer
trhodenizer@racentre.com
Mario Giamberardino, Chief Financial Officer
mgiamberardino@racentre.com
Kelly Shaw-Swettenham, Director, Membership, Recreation, Sports & Fitness Services
kshawswettenham@racentre.com
Finances: *Annual Operating Budget:* Greater than $5 Million; *Funding Sources:* Membership dues; program revenue; special projects revenue
Staff: 70 staff member(s); 500 volunteer(s)
Membership: 22,000; *Fees:* $33-$57
Activities: 100+ programs & services in health, fitness, recreation & leisure

Polo

Canadian Polo Association (CPA)
#100, 180 Renfrew Dr., Markham ON L3R 9Z2
Tel: 647-208-7656; *Fax:* 905-477-6897
info@polocanada.ca
polocanada.ca
www.facebook.com/polocanada
Also Known As: Polo Canada
Overview: A small national charitable organization founded in 1985
Description: To develop & maintain standards of excellence for the sport of polo in Canada; To promote polo across the nation
Finances: *Funding Sources:* Membership fees; Donations
Membership: 12 clubs; *Fees:* $40 junior; $80 adult; $110 club; *Member Profile:* Individual junior & adult polo players, & clubs from across Canada
Activities: Supporting polo players & clubs across Canada; Providing resources; Raising awareness of polo & attracting new

players to the game; Supporting training programs, educational workshops & clinics for coaches, umpires & players; Encouraging international competition; Offering junior polo programs; Facilitating communication between member clubs

Powerlifting

Alberta Powerlifting Union (APU)
c/o James Bartlett, 4805 Vandyke Rd. NW, Calgary AB T3A 0J6
Tel: 403-471-4754
alberta.powerlifting.union@gmail.com
www.powerliftingab.com
Overview: A small provincial organization founded in 1983
Description: To promote powerlifting in Alberta
Affiliation(s): Canadian Powerlifting Union; International Powerlifting Federation
Chief Officer(s): Shane Martin, President & Referee Chairman
mr.shane.c.martin@gmail.com
James Bartlett, Executive Secretary
bartlettJ@bennettjones.com
Fees: $60 open; $50 junior; $40 special

British Columbia Powerlifting Association (BCPA)
BC
bc-powerlifting.com
www.instagram.com/bcpowerliftingassociation
www.facebook.com/bcpowerliftingassociation
Overview: A small provincial organization founded in 2011
Description: To promote powerlifting throughout British Columbia; *Member of:* Canadian Powerlifting Union; International Powerlifting Federation
Chief Officer(s): Gabe Festing, President
gfesting@gmail.com
Finances: *Funding Sources:* Membership fees; Government grants; In-kind contributions
Fees: $60 first time; $85 general; $60 special olympics; $25 associaite

Canadian Powerlifting Federation (CPF)
cpfpowerlifting@gmail.com
www.canadianpowerliftingfederation.com
www.facebook.com/117359724995464
Previous Name: Canadian Powerlifting Organization
Overview: A small national organization
Description: Promoting powerlifting in Canada; *Member of:* World Powerlifting Congress; World Powerlifting Organization
Member Profile: Individuals & organizations, from across Canada, who are interested in powerlifting
Activities: Providing results from CPF meets & its affiliates

Canadian Powerlifting Union (CPU)
c/o Mike Armstrong, 4709 Fordham Cres. SE, Calgary AB T2A 2A5
Tel: 403-402-4142
www.powerlifting.ca
www.instagram.com/cpupowerlifting
www.facebook.com/CDNpowerliftingunion
Previous Name: Canadian Powerlifting Federation
Overview: A medium-sized national organization founded in 1982
Description: To oversee & regulate all IPF style powerlifting in Canada
Affiliation(s): International Powerlifting Federation
Chief Officer(s): Shane Martin, President
mr.shane.c.martin@gmail.com
Jeff Butt, Vice-President & Director, Programs
buttspa@hotmail.com
Gabe Festing, Vice-President & Director
vpsportdevelopment@powerlifting.ca
Mike Armstrong, Secretary
mike@powerlifting.ca

Fédération Québécoise de Dynamophilie (FQD)
679, av du Parc, Sherbrooke QC J1N 3N5
Tél: 819-864-4810
www.fqd-quebec.ca

www.facebook.com/dynamophilie
Aperçu: *Dimension:* petite; *Envergure:* provinciale
Description: Promouvoir, contrôler et développer la dynamophilie auprès de la population du Québec.
Affiliation(s): Canadian Powerlifting Union; International Powerlifting Federation
Membre(s) du bureau directeur: Joel Boulianne, Président
joel@fdq-quebec.com
Montant de la cotisation: 55$; 45$ les moins de 18 ans

Manitoba Powerlifting Association (MPA)
MB
manitobapowerlifting@gmail.com
manitobapowerlifting.ca
Overview: A small provincial organization founded in 1967

Description: To govern powerlifting in Manitoba and organize competitions; *Member of:* Manitoba Sports Federation; Manitoba Sports Directorate; Canadian Powerlifting Union; International Powerlifting Federation
Chief Officer(s): Mathew Bowen, President

Newfoundland & Labrador Powerlifting Association
NL
www.nlpowerlifting.ca
www.facebook.com/NLPowerlifting
Overview: A small provincial organization
Member of: Canadian Powerlifting Union
Chief Officer(s): Jeff Butt, President
Fees: $50 regular; $30 special Olympian

Nova Scotia Powerlifting Association
c/o Ryan Kells, 240 Cusack Dr., Sydney NS B1P 6A1
Tel: 902-567-0893
novascotiapowerlifting.ca
Overview: A small provincial licensing organization
Description: To provide opportunities for lifters to learn the sport of powerlifting through seminars, gyms & clubs; to participate in meets locally, nationally & internationally; *Member of:* International Powerlifting Federation
Chief Officer(s): Ryan Kells, President
Member Profile: Novice; Junior; Master; Open; Special Olympian divisions; provincial, national & world calibre lifters
Activities: Lifters attend competitions on provincial, national & international levels & receive medallions or trophies according to placement; seminars given upon request

Ontario Powerlifting Association (OPA)
c/o Karen Maxwell, Registrar, 555 O'Brien Rd., Renfrew ON K7V 3Z3
info@ontariopowerlifting.org
www.ontariopowerlifting.org
www.instagram.com/ontariopowerliftingassociation
www.facebook.com/OntarioPowerliftingAssociation
Overview: A small provincial organization
Chief Officer(s): Glyn Moore, President
mgmoore13@outlook.com
Fees: $85 regular; $65 student/special athlete; $30 associate

PEI Powerlifting Association (PEIPLA)
PE
Tel: 902-206-0115
www.peipowerlifting.ca
www.facebook.com/peipowerlifting1996
Overview: A small provincial organization founded in 1996
Member of: Canadian Powerlifting Union
Affiliation(s): Canadian Powerlifting Union; International Powerlifting Federation
Chief Officer(s): John MacDonald, President
john@peipowerlifting.ca
Fees: $70 regular; $40 high school; *Committees:* Fundraising; Competition & Promotion; Selection & Grant

Saskatchewan Powerlifting Association (SPA)
PO Box 42, North Weyburn SK S0C 1X0
Tel: 306-842-4299; *Fax:* 306-842-2682
saskpowerlifting@gmail.com
www.saskpowerlifting.ca
www.facebook.com/saskpowerlifting
Overview: A small provincial organization
Description: To promote fitness & provide opportunities to weightlifting athletes.
Chief Officer(s): Ryan Fowler, President
Membership: 100+; *Fees:* $60 regular; $35 new/special; $10 referee; $2 associate

Racing

Canadian Race Communications Association (CRCA)
PO Box 307, Shannonville ON K0K 3A0
www.crcamarshal.com
Overview: A medium-sized national licensing organization founded in 1959
Description: To provide corner marshals for all forms of racing events
Chief Officer(s): Darrell Briggs, President
briggsdrt@cogeco.ca
Larry McMillan, Contact
mcmillan07@cogeco.ca
Fees: $15

Racquetball

Alberta Racquetball Association (ARA)
47 Walden Cres., St Albert AB T8N 3N5
Tel: 780-918-5332
albertaracquetball@shaw.ca
www.albertaracquetball.com
www.youtube.com/channel/UCdxaKwImiINEEnGN5dDpNig
www.facebook.com/Alberta-Racquetball-Association-813120186
23
Overview: A small provincial organization founded in 1971
Description: To develop the sport of racquetball in Alberta.;
Member of: Racquetball Canada
Chief Officer(s): Barbara May, Executive Director
Fees: $10

Association québécoise de racquetball (AQR) / Quebec Racquetball Association
4545, av Pierre-de Coubertin, Montréal QC H1V 0B2
Tél: 514-252-3062
info@sports-4murs.qc.ca
www.racquetball.qc.ca

www.facebook.com/427582940621028
Aperçu: *Dimension:* petite; *Envergure:* provinciale
Description: Promouvoir le développement du racquetball au Québec en offrant différentes opportunités aux adeptes, tout en encourageant la participation sportive à travers un ensemble de services et de programmes; *Membre de:* Racquetball Canada; Sports-Québec; Regroupement Loisir Québec
Membre(s) du bureau directeur: Rino Langelier, Président
rinolang@hotmail.com
Finances: *Budget de fonctionnement annuel:*
$50,000-$100,000; *Fonds:* Éducation, Loisir et Sport Québec
Personnel: 4 membre(s) du personnel
Membre: 10 000; *Montant de la cotisation:* Barème
Activités: Tournois; championnats; formation d'arbitres et d'entraîneurs; *Stagiaires:* Oui

British Columbia Racquetball Association (BCRA)
BC
info@racquetballbc.ca
www.racquetballbc.ca
twitter.com/bcracquetball
Overview: A medium-sized provincial charitable organization founded in 1970
Member of: Racquetball Canada
Finances: *Funding Sources:* Fundraising; SportsFunder Lottery; Sponsorships
Fees: $15
Activities: Supporting tournaments; Providing rules, skills, & junior development clinics; Hosting school programs

New Brunswick Racquetball Association (NBRA)
NB
nbracquetball@gmail.com
www.nbracquetball.ca
twitter.com/nbrball
Overview: A small provincial organization founded in 1977
Description: To promote the sport of racquetball throughout New Brunswick; *Member of:* Racquetball Canada
Chief Officer(s): Michael McCabe, Vice-President, Membership
Activities: Providing racquetball classes; Offering racquetball coaching

Newfoundland Racquetball Association
NL
Overview: A small provincial organization
Member of: Racquetball Canada; Sport Newfoundland & Labrador

Racquetball Canada
145 Pacific Ave., Winnipeg MB R3B 2Z6
Tel: 519-897-7094
racquetball.ca
www.instagram.com/racquetballcanada
www.facebook.com/RacquetballCanada
twitter.com/RBallCanada
Previous Name: Canadian Racquetball Association
Overview: A medium-sized national charitable organization founded in 1972
Description: To promote racquetball as a sport & physical activity; To provide leadership by developing & coordinating services & programs designed to meet the needs of the racquetball community; *Member of:* International Racquetball Federation
Affiliation(s): Canadian Sport Council; Canadian Olympic Association; Coaching Association of Canada
Chief Officer(s): Kathy Brook, Executive Director
execdirector@racquetballcanada.ca
Finances: *Funding Sources:* Government; Membership dues; Sponsorships

Staff: 50 volunteer(s)
Membership: 700 individual + 350 club + 8 provincial associations (incl. 18,000 members); *Fees:* $15 bronze; $20 silver; $35 gold; *Member Profile:* Individual resident in Canada or Canadian citizen involved in the sport of racquetball at any level of structured activity; *Committees:* National Team; Coaching; Sport Science; Tournament; Ranking; Officiating; Junior Development; Membership; Ways & Means; Wheelchair; Women
Activities: *Awareness Events:* National Championship Week, May; *Speaker Service:* Yes; *Rents Mailing List:* Yes

Racquetball Manitoba Inc.
145 Pacific Ave., Winnipeg MB R3B 2Z7
Tel: 204-925-5666; *Fax:* 204-925-5703
racquetballmb.ca
Overview: A small provincial organization founded in 1974
Description: To promote racquetball as a sport & a physical activity throughout the Province of Manitoba; To provide leadership by developing & coordinating services & programs designed to meet the needs of the racquetball community; *Member of:* Racquetball Canada; Sport Manitoba
Membership: 600; *Fees:* $25 adult; $10 juniors/students

Racquetball Ontario (RO)
51 Springgarden Cres., Stoney Creek ON L8J 2S5
www.racquetballontario.ca
twitter.com/Rball_Ontario
Overview: A medium-sized provincial organization
Member of: Racquetball Canada
Chief Officer(s): Greg Doricki, President
Peter Fisher, Director, Development
Tanya Hodgin, Director, Memberships
Sue Swaine, Director, Coaching
Fees: $25 individual; $50 family; $100 event coordinator

Racquetball PEI
c/o Sport PEI, 40 Enman Cres., Charlottetown PE C1E 1E6
Overview: A small provincial organization
Member of: Racquetball Canada

Saskatchewan Racquetball Association (SRA)
SK
racquetballsask.com
www.facebook.com/SaskatchewanRacquetballAssociation
twitter.com/saskracquetball
Overview: A small provincial organization
Description: To To promote the sport of racquetball throughout Saskatchewan.
Chief Officer(s): Karla Drury, President
k.drury@sasktel.net
Tim Landeryou, Executive Director
ed.rballsask@gmail.com

Recreation

British Columbia Fishing Resorts & Outfitters Association (BCFROA)
PO Box 3301, #106, 1383 McGill Rd., Kamloops BC V2C 6B9
Tel: 250-374-6836; *Fax:* 250-374-6640
Toll-Free: 866-374-6836
bcfroa@bcfroa.ca
www.bcfroa.ca
www.youtube.com/user/BCFROA
www.facebook.com/wheretofishinbc
twitter.com/Fish_BC
Overview: A small provincial organization founded in 1974
Description: Works with the public & private sector to protect areas currently in use; to preserve the wildlife experience in BC for the enjoyment of future generations; a lobby group whose members are dedicated to providing a quality outdoor experience; *Member of:* Outdoor Recreation Council of British Columbia
Chief Officer(s): Matt Jennings, Executive Director
Finances: *Annual Operating Budget:* $100,000-$250,000; *Funding Sources:* Membership dues; funding programs; promotions; sponsorships
Membership: 130+; *Fees:* $105-$519.75; *Member Profile:* Resort owner or angling & hunting guide
Activities: Marketing; lobbying; advocacy

Canadian Volkssport Federation (CVF) / Fédération canadienne volkssport (FCV)
#604, 251 Bank St., Ottawa ON K2P 1X3
Tel: 613-234-7333
cvffcvwalk@outlook.com
www.walks.ca
Overview: A medium-sized national organization founded in 1987
Description: To promote non-competitive participation in walking & other recreational activities for fun, fitness &

friendship; *Member of:* International Federation of Popular Sports
Chief Officer(s): David Hall, President
Finances: *Annual Operating Budget:* Less than $50,000; *Funding Sources:* Sanctioning fees
Staff: 1 staff member(s); 150 volunteer(s)
Membership: 51 clubs; *Fees:* $50 affiliate; $150 individual; *Member Profile:* Mostly ages 35-70; *Committees:* Board of Directors; Executive
Activities: Walking; swimming; skating; skiing - all non-competitively; *Speaker Service:* Yes

Fitness New Brunswick (NBCFAL) / Conditionnement physique Noueau-Brunswick (CCPVANB)
Lady Beaverbrook Gym, University of New Brunswick, PO Box 4400, #A112A, 2 Peter Kelly Dr., Fredericton NB E3B 5A3
Tel: 506-453-1094; *Fax:* 506-453-1099
Toll-Free: 888-790-1411
membershipservices@fitnessnb.ca
www.fitnessnb.ca
www.facebook.com/Fitness.New.Brunswick
twitter.com/FitnessNB
Previous Name: New Brunswick Council for Fitness & Active Living (NBCFAL); New Brunswick Fitness Council
Overview: A small provincial organization founded in 1988
Description: To certify fitness professionals in New Brunswick; to promote professionalism in the fitness industry; To offer standardization & consistency in training programs; To uphold professional ethics through the Code of Conduct for fitness service providers; *Member of:* Coalition for Active Living (CCAL)
Affiliation(s): Atlantic Canadian Society for Exercise Physiology (CSEP) Health & Fitness Program (H&FP); National Fitness Leadership Alliance (NFLA)
Chief Officer(s): Marilynn Georgas, Executive Director
executivedirector@fitnessnb.ca
Erin Maranda, Coordinator, Projects
projectscoordinator@fitnessnb.ca
Fees: $62.15; *Committees:* Professional Development; Marketing & Communications; Human Resources; Translation; Conference
Activities: Providing fitness education in New Brunswick; Raising public awareness of safe & effective practices for fitness professionals

Golden Age Society
4061A - 4th Ave., Whitehorse YT Y1A 1H1
Tel: 867-668-5538; *Fax:* 867-633-6944
goldenagesociety@gmail.com
www.yukon-seniors-and-elders.org/index.php/ga-home
Overview: A small provincial organization founded in 1976
Description: To promote & give opportunity for social, recreational activities for seniors in the Yukon
Chief Officer(s): Deborah Bastien, Office Manager
gas2016@northwestel.net
Fees: $22

Halifax Sport & Social Club (HSSC)
PO Box 8821, Halifax NS B3K 5M5
Tel: 902-431-8326
info@halifaxsport.ca
www.halifaxsport.ca
www.facebook.com/HalifaxSSC
twitter.com/HalifaxSSC
Overview: A medium-sized local organization
Description: To offer co-ed recreational sport leagues, tournaments & social events for adults.
Chief Officer(s): Lael Morgan, Executive Director, 902-431-8326 113

ParaSport & Recreation PEI
Royalty Center House Of Sport, #123, 40 Enman Cres., Charlottetown PE C1E 1E6
Tel: 902-368-4540; *Fax:* 902-368-4548
info@parasportpei.ca
www.parasportpei.ca
www.facebook.com/141822665843254
twitter.com/ParaSportPEI
Previous Name: Paralympics PEI Inc.
Overview: A small provincial charitable organization founded in 1974
Description: To ensure the ample provision of sport & recreation opportunities for persons who are physically challenged; *Member of:* Canadian Blind Sport Association; Canadian Association for Disabled Skiing; Canadian Wheelchair Sports Association
Affiliation(s): The JoyRiders Therapeutic Riding Association of PEI Inc.; The Canadian Council of the Blind - Prince County and Queensland Chapters; The Abegweit Club of Summerside; G.E.A.R. (Getting Everyone Accessibly Riding)
Chief Officer(s): Tracy Stevenson, Executive Director
tracy@parasportpei.ca

Finances: *Funding Sources:* Province of PEI; City of Charlottetown; business sector; community & service clubs; fundraising
Staff: 2 staff member(s)
Activities: Demonstrations; presentations; sport/recreation events; *Speaker Service:* Yes *Library:* Yes (Open to Public)

Ringette

Association de Ringuette de Longueuil
2258, rue Papineau, Longueuil QC J4K 3M1
Tél: 450-442-0808
www.ringuettelongueuil.com
Aperçu: *Dimension:* petite; *Envergure:* provinciale
Membre de: Ringuette-Québec
Membre(s) du bureau directeur: Marie-Lyne Fortin Thibault, Président
marielynefortin87@outlook.com
Montant de la cotisation: Barème

Association de ringuette de Lotbinière
c/o Marie-Noël Duclos, 412, rue Belanger, Saint-Narcisse-de-Beaurivage QC G0S 1W0
Tél: 418-475-4125
Aperçu: *Dimension:* petite; *Envergure:* provinciale
Description: Site Internet:
kreezee.com/sport/association/association-de-ringuette-de-lotbiniere/7671; *Membre de:* Ringuette-Québec
Membre(s) du bureau directeur: Marie-Noel Duclos, Présidente
robertetmarie@axion.ca
Membre: 7 équipes; *Montant de la cotisation:* Barème

Association de Ringuette de Sainte-Marie
QC
www.ringuettestemarie.com
www.facebook.com/181771528541007
Aperçu: *Dimension:* petite; *Envergure:* provinciale; *fondée en 1983*
Membre de: Ringuette-Québec
Membre(s) du bureau directeur: Tony Fecteau, Président, 418-387-8847
presidence@ringuettestemarie.com

Association de Ringuette de Ste-Julie
QC
Aperçu: *Dimension:* petite; *Envergure:* provinciale
Membre de: Ringuette-Québec

Association de Ringuette de Sept-Iles
QC
www.ringuettesept-iles.org
www.facebook.com/228073003907401
Aperçu: *Dimension:* petite; *Envergure:* provinciale
Membre de: Ringuette-Québec
Membre(s) du bureau directeur: Frédéric Lesage, Président, 418-968-2036
fred.lesage@icloud.com
Membre: 7 équipes

Association de Ringuette de Thetford
555, rue St-Alphonse nord, Thetford Mines QC G6G 3X1
Tél: 418-338-3729
www.ringuettethetford.com
Aperçu: *Dimension:* petite; *Envergure:* provinciale
Membre de: Ringuette-Québec
Membre(s) du bureau directeur: Dany Harvey, Président
dharvey27@hotmail.ca
Membre: 5 équipes

Association de Ringuette des Moulins
840, rue Brien, Mascouche QC J7K 2X3
Tél: 450-961-9295
admin@ringuettedesmoulins.com
www.ringuettedesmoulins.com
Aperçu: *Dimension:* petite; *Envergure:* provinciale
Membre de: Ringuette-Québec
Membre(s) du bureau directeur: Daniel Gagné, Président
president@ringuettedesmoulins.com

Association de Ringuette Lévis
CP 1807, Saint-Rédempteur QC G6K 1N6
communications.arl@gmail.com
www.ringuettearl.com
www.facebook.com/ringuettelevis/
Nom précédent: Association de Ringuette Chutes Chaudière
Aperçu: *Dimension:* petite; *Envergure:* provinciale
Membre de: Ringuette-Québec
Membre(s) du bureau directeur: Tanya Moore, Présidente

Membre: 14 équipes

Association de Ringuette Repentigny
QC

www.ringuetterepentigny.com

www.facebook.com/Ringuette-Repentigny-1773415112879301
Aperçu: Dimension: petite; *Envergure: provinciale*
Membre de: Ringuette-Québec
Membre(s) du bureau directeur: Gordon Britton, Président
gordon.britton@ringuetterepentigny.com
Membre: 10 équipes

Association de ringuette Roussillon
CP 164, Saint-Constant QC J5A 2G2
communications@ringuetteroussillon.ca
www.ringuetteroussillon.ca

www.facebook.com/ARRoussillon
twitter.com/ARRoussillon
Aperçu: Dimension: petite; *Envergure: provinciale*
Membre de: Ringuette-Québec

Association régionale de ringuette Laval
3235, boul St-Martin est, Laval QC H7E 5G8
Tél: 450-664-1917
ringuettelaval.org
Aperçu: Dimension: petite; *Envergure: provinciale*
Membre de: Ringuette-Québec
Membre(s) du bureau directeur: Eric Allard, Président

Association Régionale de Ringuette Richelieu Yamaska
QC

www.ringuette-quebec.qc.ca/regionale_richelieu-yamaska.php
Aperçu: Dimension: petite; *Envergure: provinciale*
Membre de: Ringuette-Québec

Association Sportive de Ringuette Brossard
CP 210, 8000, boul Leduc, Brossard QC J4Y 0E9
communications@ringuetteroussillon.ca
www.ringuettebrossard.com

www.facebook.com/AssociationSportiveDeRinguetteDeBrossard
twitter.com/ARRoussillon
Également appelé: Ringuette Brossard
Aperçu: Dimension: petite; *Envergure: provinciale*
Membre de: Ringuette-Québec
Membre(s) du bureau directeur: Sylvain Lebel, President
slebel1@sympatico.ca

Berwick & District Ringette Association
NS

ringette.wordpress.com

Overview: A small local organization
Member of: Ringette Nova Scotia
Chief Officer(s): Marlene Connell, President
ron.connell@ns.sympatico.ca

British Columbia Ringette Association (BCRA) / Association de ringuette de Colombie-Britannique
#258, 6450 Roberts St., Burnaby BC V5G 4E1
Tel: 604-629-6583
info@bcringette.org
www.bcringette.org
www.youtube.com/user/ringettebc
www.facebook.com/RingetteBC
twitter.com/bcringette
Also Known As: Ringette BC
Overview: A small provincial organization founded in 1976
Description: To promote ringette & allow for opportunities for people in British Columbia to play ringette
Chief Officer(s): Nicole Robb, Executive Director
executivedirector@bcringette.org
Hannah Woodman, Coordinator, Community Sport Outreach
outreach@bcringette.org

Cole Harbour Ringette Association (CHRA)
NS
Overview: A small local organization
Member of: Ringette Nova Scotia
Membership: 1-99; *Fees:* schedule

Dartmouth Ringette Association
NS
harbourcitylakers@gmail.com
dartmouthringette.com
Overview: A small local organization
Description: To operate the Harbour City Lakers League.;
Member of: Ringette Nova Scotia
Chief Officer(s): Susan Graham, President
Membership: 11 teams

Eastern Shore Ringette Association (ESRA)
NS
esringette.goalline.ca
Overview: A small local organization
Member of: Ringette Nova Scotia
Chief Officer(s): Mary Stienburg, President
presidentESRA@gmail.com
Membership: 3 teams; *Member Profile:* Teams with players 4-10; Teams with players 18+

Fédération sportive de ringuette du Québec
4545, av Pierre-de Coubertin, Montréal QC H1V 3R2
Tél: 514-252-3085; *Téléc:* 514-254-1069
ringuette@ringuette-quebec.qc.ca
www.ringuette-quebec.qc.ca

www.youtube.com/channel/UChlZmg35-zhVgQBkgru8k7g
www.facebook.com/RinguetteQuebec-139856822762458
twitter.com/ringuetteqc
Aperçu: Dimension: petite; *Envergure: provinciale; fondée en 1973*
Description: Promouvoir le sport de la ringuette au Québec
Membre(s) du bureau directeur: Louise Morin, Contact

Halifax Hurricanes Ringette Association
NS
hhringette.ca
Merged from: Halifax Chebucto Ringette Association;
Halifax - St. Margaret's Ringette Association
Overview: A small local organization
Member of: Ringette Nova Scotia
Chief Officer(s): Chad Mombourquette, President
president@hhringette.ca
Mark Whidden, Director, Coaching
dc@hhringette.ca
Membership: 1-99; *Fees:* Schedule available

International Ringette Federation (IRF)
www.ringette.cc
Previous Name: World Ringette Council
Overview: A small international organization founded in 1986
Description: To promote & govern ringette throughout the world; To administer international ringette competitions
Chief Officer(s): Jane Casson, President
president@ringette.cc
Anniina Tuomola, Vice President
vicepresident@ringette.ca
Laure Knowles, Technical Director
officials@ringette.ca
Member Profile: National ringette associations

Manitoba Ringette Association (MRA) / Association de ringuette du Manitoba
145 Pacific Ave., Winnipeg MB R3B 2Z6
Tel: 204-925-5710; *Fax:* 204-925-5925
ringette.admin@sportmanitoba.ca
ringettemanitoba.ca
www.facebook.com/497027863732649
twitter.com/MBRingette
Overview: A medium-sized provincial organization founded in 1970
Description: To develop, encourage & promote ringette as a sport for life for all Manitobans; *Member of:* International Ringette Federation
Affiliation(s): Sport Manitoba
Chief Officer(s): Laralie Higginson, Executive Director, 204-925-5712
edringette@sportmanitoba.ca
Melanie Reimer, Coordinator, Program, 204-925-5713
ringette@sportmanitoba.ca
Finances: *Funding Sources:* Sponsorship; grants & registration fees
Staff: 4 staff member(s)
Activities: Tournaments; provincial competitions; national competitions; world competitions; *Library:* Yes (Open to Public)

Nova Central Ringette Association
NS
novacentralringette.ca
www.facebook.com/NovaCentralRingetteAssociation
Overview: A small local organization
Member of: Ringette Nova Scotia
Affiliation(s): Bedord Ringette Association; Berwick Ringette Association; Sackville Ringette Association
Chief Officer(s): Greg Giffin, President
Membership: 15 teams

Ontario Ringette Association (ORA) / Association de ringuette de l'Ontario
#912, 305 Milner Ave., Toronto ON M1B 3V4
Tel: 416-426-7204; *Fax:* 416-426-7359
admin@ontario-ringette.com
www.ontario-ringette.com
www.youtube.com/channel/UCWGddPSY6p6_X8wQqe1csPw
twitter.com/OntRingette
Overview: A medium-sized provincial organization founded in 1963
Description: To promote fun, fitness, & friendship in a safe play environment; To be dedicated to quality performance & fair play opportunity for all ages; *Member of:* Ringette Canada
Chief Officer(s): John Voss, President
president@ontario-ringette.com
Pam Julian, Executive Director, 416-426-7205
executivedirector@ontario-ringette.com
Karla Xavier, Director, Technical, 416-426-7206
tech@ontario-ringette.com

Régionale Ringuette Rive-Sud
QC
www.ringuetterivesud.com

www.instagram.com/regionale_rsud
www.facebook.com/RegionaleRinguetteRiveSud
twitter.com/RinguetteRRS
Aperçu: Dimension: petite; *Envergure: provinciale*
Membre de: Ringuette-Québec
Membre(s) du bureau directeur: Clémence Duchesneau, Présidente
clemdu@hotmail.com

Ringette Alberta
Percy Page Centre, 11759 Groat Rd., 3rd Fl., Edmonton AB T5M 3K6
Tel: 780-451-1750; *Fax:* 780-415-1749
www.ringettealberta.com
www.instagram.com/ringettealberta
www.facebook.com/ringettealberta
twitter.com/ringettealberta
Overview: A medium-sized provincial organization
Description: To provide ringette services to its members;
Member of: Ringette Canada
Chief Officer(s): David Myers, Executive Director, 780-415-1750 5
david@ringettealberta.com

Ringette Association of Saskatchewan (RAS) / Association de ringuette de Saskatchewan
Mosaic Stadium, #300, 1734 Elphinstone St., Regina SK S4T 1K1
Tel: 306-780-9432; *Fax:* 306-780-9480
www.ringettesask.com
www.facebook.com/1783705235193593
twitter.com/RingetteSask
Overview: A medium-sized provincial organization founded in 1976
Description: To develop, promote & govern ringette for coaches, players, officals & associations; To provide opportunities for lifelong participation & pursuit of excellence; *Member of:* Sask Sport
Chief Officer(s): Ruchelle Himmelspeck, Executive Director
executivedirector@ringettesask.com
Amanda O'Donnell, Director, Technical
technicaldirector@ringettesask.com
Finances: *Funding Sources:* Saskatchewan Lotteries; Corporate sponsorships; Membership fees
Staff: 2 staff member(s)
Activities: Coaching & officiating clinics; Providing player development camps; Organizing provincial championships

Ringette Canada (RC) / Ringuette Canada
c/o House of Sport, RA Centre, 2451 Riverside Dr., Ottawa ON K1H 7X7
Tel: 613-748-5655
ringette@ringette.ca
www.ringette.ca
www.youtube.com/c/RingetteCanadaRinguetteCanada
www.facebook.com/RingetteCanada
twitter.com/ringettecanada
Overview: A large national organization founded in 1975
Description: To formulate, publish & administer national policies beneficial to the sport; To enforce laws & regulations governing ringette; To encourage ringette participants to strive for

excellence in teamwork, team spirit & team discipline; *Member of:* International Ringette Federation
Chief Officer(s): Natasha Johnston, Executive Director
natasha@ringette.ca
Frances Losier, Director, High Performance & Events
frances@ringette.ca
Kelsey McIntosh, Director, Technical
kelsey@ringette.ca
Anik Desjardins, Office Manager
anik@ringette.ca
Finances: *Annual Operating Budget:* $1.5 Million-$3 Million;
Funding Sources: Membership fees; Federal government;
Corporate sponsorships
Staff: 7 staff member(s)
Member Profile: Provincial or territorial ringette associations;
Committees: Coach Development; Officials Development; High
Performance; National Ringette League
Activities: Organizing the Canadian Ringette Championships;
Library: Resource Centre (Open to Public)

Ringette New Brunswick (RNB) / Ringuette Nouveau-Brunswick
PO Box 27069, Stn. champlain Mall, Dieppe NB E1A 6V3
Tel: 506-851-5641
www.ringette-nb.com
www.facebook.com/366285260056480
twitter.com/RingetteNB
Also Known As: New Brunswick Ringette Association
Overview: A small provincial organization
Description: To lead, facilitate & encourage ringette among
athletes at all levels in New Brunswick
Chief Officer(s): Chantal Girouard, Executive Director
cpoirierRNB@hotmail.com
James Rossignol, President
jamesrnb@outlook.com
Activities: Consulting with the Province of New Brunswick
Wellness, Culture, & Sport; Providing direction in areas such as
athlete development, officiating, coaching & technical issues;
Organizing coaching & officiating clinics; Establishing standards
for bench staff

Ringette Nova Scotia
5516 Spring Garden Rd., 4th Fl., Halifax NS B3J 1G6
Tel: 902-425-5450; *Fax:* 902-425-5606
ringette@sportnovascotia.ca
www.ringette.ns.ca
www.facebook.com/ringettenovascotia
twitter.com/RingetteNS
Overview: A small provincial organization founded in 1973
Description: To promote, develop & administer the sport of
ringette within Nova Scotia; *Member of:* International Ringette
Federation
Chief Officer(s): Lainie Wintrup, Executive Director
Finances: *Annual Operating Budget:* Less than $50,000;
Funding Sources: Provincial Sport & Recreation Commission
Staff: 20 volunteer(s)
Membership: 800; *Fees:* Schedule available; *Committees:*
Canada Winter Games; Fundraising; Provincial Teams; Strategic
Plan
Activities: *Awareness Events:* Ringette Week, Feb. *Library:*
Resource Library by appointment

Ringette PEI (RPEI)
40 Enman Cres., Charlottetown PE C1A 7K7
Tel: 902-368-6570; *Fax:* 902-368-4548
ringettepei.ca
www.facebook.com/ringettepei
twitter.com/RingettePEI
Also Known As: Prince Edward Island Ringette Association
Overview: A small provincial organization founded in 1982
Description: To promote ringette throughout PEI
Chief Officer(s): Valerie Vuillemot, Executive Director
vvuillemot@sportpei.pe.ca
Breanne MacInnis, President
David Fraser, Treasurer
Tara McNally-MacPhee, Director, Marketing & Communications
Activities: Offering officiating clinics, coaching courses &
related resources; Providing tournament & championship
information

Ringuette 96 Montréal-Nord-Est
QC
Tél: 514-644-0153
ringuette96mn@hotmail.com
www.ringuette96mtlnord.com

www.facebook.com/1426672734232724
Aperçu: Dimension: petite; *Envergure:* provinciale
Membre de: Ringuette-Québec
Membre(s) du bureau directeur: Sylvie Horth, Président
Montant de la cotisation: Barème

Ringuette Boucherville
490, ch du Lac, Boucherville QC J4B 6X3
info@ringuetteboucherville.com
www.ringuetteboucherville.com

www.youtube.com/channel/UCrhUtjVgaP9vNRmEeFxmVLA
www.facebook.com/14606594494210802
Aperçu: Dimension: petite; *Envergure:* provinciale
Membre de: Ringuette-Québec
Membre(s) du bureau directeur: Sylvain St-Cyr, Président
Critères d'admissibilite: Filles de 4 ans et plus

Ringuette Bourrassa-Laval-Lanaudière
QC
www.ringuettebll.com
Aperçu: Dimension: petite; *Envergure:* provinciale
Membre de: Ringuette-Québec

Ringuette de la Capitale
#316, 1311, rue des Loisirs, Québec QC
Tél: 418-877-3000
ca@ringuettedelacapitale.com
www.ringuettedelacapitale.com

www.facebook.com/ringuettedelacapitale
Aperçu: Dimension: petite; *Envergure:* provinciale
Membre de: Ringuette-Québec
Membre(s) du bureau directeur: Steve Caron, Présidente,
418-655-8759
steven.caron@carons.ca
Membre: 4 équipes

Ringuette St-Hubert
CP 29542, 5950, boul Cousineau, Saint-Hubert QC J3Y 9A9
ringuette@ringuette-st-hubert.com
www.ringuette-st-hubert.com
Aperçu: Dimension: petite; *Envergure:* provinciale
Membre de: Ringuette-Québec
Membre(s) du bureau directeur: David Létouneau, Président
Davidletourneau.cma@gmail.com

Ringuette St-Hyacinthe
CP 40502, Saint-Hyacinthe QC J2R 1K8
info@ringuettesth.com
www.ringuettesth.com

www.facebook.com/ringuettesthyacinthe
Aperçu: Dimension: petite; *Envergure:* provinciale
Membre de: Ringuette-Québec
Montant de la cotisation: Barème

Ringuette-Québec
4545, av Pierre-de Coubertin, Montréal QC H1V 0B2
Tél: 514-252-3085; *Téléc:* 514-254-1069
ringuette@ringuette-quebec.qc.ca
www.ringuette-quebec.qc.ca

www.youtube.com/channel/UChIZmg35-zhVgQBkgru8k7g
www.facebook.com/139856822762458
twitter.com/ringuetteqc
Aperçu: Dimension: petite; *Envergure:* provinciale
Membre de: Ringuette-Canada
Membre(s) du bureau directeur: Jocelyne Fortin, Président
jocfortin@videotron.ca

Road Running

Prince Edward Island Roadrunners Club
c/o Sport PEI, 40 Enman Cres., Charlottetown PE C1E 1E6
peiroadrunners.pbworks.com
Overview: A small provincial organization founded in 1977
Description: The PEI RoadRunners Club is an organization
whose objective is to promote & encourage running as a sport &
healthful exercise. The Club welcomes all runners, regardless of
ability & attempts to meet the needs of competitive &
recreational runners.
Chief Officer(s): Janet Norman-Bain, President
Fees: $20 individual; $30 family

Rowing

Alberta Rowing Association (ARA)
11759 Groat Rd., Edmonton AB T5M 3K6
Tel: 780-427-8154
office@albertarowing.ca
www.albertarowing.ca
www.facebook.com/131265308366
twitter.com/AlbertaRowing
Overview: A medium-sized provincial organization

Description: To govern the sport of rowing in Alberta; *Member of:* Rowing Canada Aviron
Chief Officer(s): Peter Walsh, President
p.walsh@albertarowing.ca
Finances: *Funding Sources:* Membership fees; Fundraising;
Government support
Membership: 7 regional clubs + 2 university clubs

Aviron Québec (AQA)
4545, av Pierre-de Coubertin, Montréal QC H1V 0B2
Tél: 514-252-3191
info@avironquebec.ca
www.avironquebec.ca
Nom précédent: Association québécoise d'aviron
Aperçu: Dimension: moyenne; *Envergure:* provinciale; *fondée
en 1981*
Membre de: Rowing Canada Aviron
Membre(s) du bureau directeur: Karol Sauvé, Contact,
514-252-3191
karolsauve@avironquebec.ca

Boxing Newfoundland & Labrador
NL
www.boxingnewfoundlandandlabrador.ca
Overview: A small provincial organization
Description: To govern the sport of boxing in Newfoundland &
Labrador.; *Member of:* Canadian Amateur Boxing Association;
Sport NL
Chief Officer(s): Mike Summers, President
mgsone@hotmail.com

Manitoba Rowing Association
Sport for Life Centre, 145 Pacific Ave., Winnipeg MB R3B 2Z6
Tel: 204-925-5653
rowing@sportmanitoba.ca
rowingmanitoba.ca
twitter.com/manitobarowing
Overview: A medium-sized provincial organization founded in
1981
Description: To govern the sport of rowing in Manitoba;
Member of: Rowing Canada Aviron
Chief Officer(s): Kelly Malcolmson, President
Andrea Katz, Executive Director

Ontario Rowing Association (ORA)
#206, 19 Waterman Ave., Toronto ON M4B 1Y2
Tel: 416-759-8405
rowontarioadmin@rowontario.ca
www.rowontario.ca
www.facebook.com/ontariorowing
twitter.com/rowontario
Overview: A medium-sized provincial organization founded in
1970
Description: To govern the sport of rowing in Ontario; To
provide assistance to member clubs in the encouragement of
competitive & recreational rowing; To maintain the principles of
amateurism; To develop provincial rowing teams to represent
Ontario at the Canada Games; To host an annual provincial
rowing championship; *Member of:* Rowing Canada Aviron
Affiliation(s): Ontario Sport Council
Chief Officer(s): Chris Waddell, President
Derek Ventor, Executive Director
derek@rowontario.ca
Finances: *Funding Sources:* Membership dues; services;
government grants; donations
Membership: 6,000 individuals; *Fees:* $1 non-rower; $3
highschool; $10 sport rower; $44 competitive rower; $275 club;
Member Profile: Organized amateur rowing clubs in Ontario;
Committees: Human Resources; Governance; Health & Safety;
Finance; Nominating; RowOntario Coach Development
Activities: COAST (Club Operation Asset & Standards Tool)

Row Nova Scotia
5516 Spring Garden Rd., 4th Fl., Halifax NS B3J 1G6
Tel: 902-425-5450
rowing@rowns.ca
www.rowns.ca
www.facebook.com/RowNovaScotia
twitter.com/RowNovaScotia
Overview: A medium-sized provincial organization
Description: To govern the sport of rowing in Nova Scotia;
Member of: Rowing Canada Aviron
Chief Officer(s): Peter Webster, President
Patrick Thompson, PSO Administrative Coordinator,
902-425-5450 357
rowing@rowns.ca
Finances: *Funding Sources:* Sport Fund; Athlete Assistance;
KidSport; Individual Coach Initiative; Row Nova Scotia Coach
Fund; Individual Official Fund

Rowing British Columbia
#155, 3820 Cessna Dr., Richmond BC V7B 0A2
Tel: 604-273-4769; *Fax:* 888-398-5818
Toll-Free: 877-330-3638
admin@rowingbc.ca
www.rowingbc.ca
www.facebook.com/rowingbc
twitter.com/rowing_bc

Also Known As: Rowing BC
Overview: A medium-sized provincial organization founded in 1987
Description: To govern the sport of rowing in British Columbia; *Member of:* Rowing Canada Aviron
Chief Officer(s): Susan Wilkinson, President
David Calder, Executive Director
exdirector@rowingbc.ca
Fees: $10 Sport; $20 Competetive; $50 Organization; *Member Profile:* Community, secondary & post-secondary educational rowing clubs; *Committees:* Umpire; Regatta Review Working Group; National Rowing Championships-Canada Cup Organizing; Regatta; Awards & Recognition

Rowing Canada Aviron (RCA) / Association Canadienne d'Aviron Amateur
#321, 4371 Interurban Rd., Victoria BC V9E 2C5
Fax: 604-295-6960
Toll-Free: 877-722-4769
rca@rowingcanada.org
rowingcanada.org
www.instagram.com/rowingcanada
www.facebook.com/rowingcanada
twitter.com/rowingcanada

Also Known As: Canadian Amateur Rowing Association
Previous Name: The Canadian Association of Amateur Oarsmen
Overview: A large national organization founded in 1880
Description: To encourage the formation of rowing clubs & provincial associations; To encourage the organization of national regattas; To define & to maintain the principles of amateurism in all competitions; To organize, develop & select national rowing teams to represent Canada internationally; *Member of:* Canadian Olympic Committee; Canadian Paralympic Commmittee; Fédération internationale des sociétés d'aviron
Chief Officer(s): Carol Purcer, President
Terry Dillion, Chief Executive Officer
tdillion@rowingcanada.org
Finances: *Funding Sources:* Sport Canada; Sponsors
Staff: 12 staff member(s)
Fees: $24 participant; $400 rowing club; $500 associate/special organization; $700 rowing association; *Committees:* Coach Education & Development; Safety & Events; Umpires; Nominating

Rowing New Brunswick Aviron (RNBA)
PO Box 30047, Stn. Prospect Plaza, Fredericton NB E3B 0H8
president@rowingnb.ca
rowingnbaviron.ca

Also Known As: Rowing NB Aviron
Overview: A medium-sized provincial organization
Description: To govern the sport of rowing in New Brunswick; *Member of:* Rowing Canada Aviron

Rowing Newfoundland
41 Cabot Rd., Conception Bay South NL A1W 4C5
Tel: 709-834-1581

Previous Name: Newfoundland Rowing Association
Overview: A small provincial organization
Description: To govern the sport of rowing in Newfoundland; *Member of:* Rowing Canada Aviron

Rowing PEI
c/o Daphne Dumont, Macnutt & Dumont Law Office, PO Box 965, 57 Water St., Charlottetown PE C1A 7M4
rowingpei@gmail.com
rowingpei.ca
Overview: A medium-sized provincial organization founded in 2010
Description: To govern the sport of rowing in Prince Edward Island; *Member of:* Rowing Canada Aviron
Chief Officer(s): Daphne Dumont, President
Fees: $330

Saskatchewan Rowing Association (SRA)
510 Cynthia St., Saskatoon SK S7L 7K7
Tel: 306-975-0842; *Fax:* 306-242-8007
saskrowing@sasktel.net
www.saskrowing.ca

Overview: A medium-sized provincial organization founded in 1977
Description: To promote & govern the sport of rowing in Saskatchewan; *Member of:* Sask Sport; Rowing Canada Aviron

Affiliation(s): Rowing Aviron Canada, Saskatchewan Sports Hall of Fame & Museum, Saskatchewan Coaches Association
Chief Officer(s): Doug Zolinski, President
John Haver, Provincial Head Coach North
Garrett Mathiason, Provincial Head Coach South
Finances: *Funding Sources:* Sponsors; Merchandise
Activities: *Internships:* Yes *Library:* Yes (Open to Public)

Rugby

Alberta Rugby Football Union
Percy Page Centre, 11759 Groat Rd., Edmonton AB T5M 3K6
Tel: 780-415-1773; *Fax:* 780-422-5558
info@rugbyalberta.com
www.rugbyalberta.com
www.facebook.com/RugbyAlberta

Also Known As: Rugby Alberta
Overview: A provincial organization founded in 1961
Description: To develop & promote an interest in rugby in Alberta; *Member of:* Rugby Canada
Chief Officer(s): Sean Hofstetter, President
Sandy Nesbitt, Vice President
Graeme Moffat, Executive Director
g.moffat@rugbyalberta.com
Eve Fletcher, Director, Member Relations & Events
e.fletcher@rugbyalberta.com
Finances: *Funding Sources:* Alberta Sport, Recreation, Parks and Wildlife Foundation
Staff: 3 staff member(s)
Activities: *Library:* Yes (Open to Public)

British Columbia Rugby Union
#203, 210 West Broadway, Vancouver BC V5Y 3W2
Tel: 604-737-3065; *Fax:* 604-737-3916
www.bcrugby.com
www.youtube.com/bcrugbyunion
www.facebook.com/bcrugbyunion
twitter.com/bcrugbyunion

Also Known As: BC Rugby
Overview: A medium-sized provincial organization founded in 1889
Description: To promote, sustain & manage the game of rugby in BC in a manner that will ensure wide participation & the continuous development in a safe & responsible manner; *Member of:* Rugby Canada
Chief Officer(s): Annabel Kehoe, Chief Executive Officer, 604-499-7494
Louise Wheeler, Manager, Member Services
Membership: 14,000; *Fees:* Schedule available; *Committees:* Competition; Discipline; Youth; Medical Science; Appeal
Activities: *Library:* Yes (Open to Public)

Fédération de rugby du Québec (FRQ) / Quebec Rugby Union
CP 1000, Succ. M, 4545, av Pierre de Coubertin, Montréal QC H1V 0B2
Tél: 514-252-3189; *Téléc:* 514-252-3159
info@rugbyquebec.com
rugbyquebec.com

www.facebook.com/RugbyQuebec
twitter.com/RugbyQuebec
Aperçu: *Dimension:* moyenne; *Envergure:* provinciale
Description: Promouvoir le sport et la santé physique en général, et sans limiter ce qui précède le sport du rugby; organiser des tournois de Rugby dans la province de Québec; regrouper les associations régionales et les clubs de Rugby du Québec; *Membre de:* Rugby Canada
Membre(s) du bureau directeur: Simon Fréchette, Directeur général
sfrechette@rugbyquebec.com
François Ratier, Directeur général
fratier@rugbyquebec.com
Guillaume Boisseau, Coordonnateur, Services aux membres
gboisseau@rugbyquebec.com
Membre: 2 610

New Brunswick Rugby Union (NBRU)
c/o Sport NB, #13, 900 Hanwell Rd., Fredericton NB E3B 6A2
Tel: 506-261-2176
www.nbru.ca
twitter.com/RugbyNB
Overview: A medium-sized provincial organization
Description: To govern rugby in New Brunswick & organize games between teams; *Member of:* Rugby Canada
Chief Officer(s): Curtis Lauzon, Technical Director
curtis.nbru@gmail.com
Yves Pellerin, President
yves.pellerin@bgis.com
Finances: *Funding Sources:* Membership fees; donations; fund raising

Newfoundland & Labrador Rugby Union
PO Box 9, Mount Pearl NL A1N 2C1
www.rockrugby.ca

Also Known As: The Rock Rugby
Overview: A small provincial organization
Member of: Rugby Canada
Chief Officer(s): John Cowan, President
jcowan@mun.ca

Nova Scotia Rugby Football Union
#305, 5516 Spring Garden Rd., Halifax NS B3J 1G6
Tel: 902-425-5450; *Fax:* 902-425-5606
rugby@sportnovascotia.ca
www.rugbyns.ns.ca
www.facebook.com/RugbyNovaScotia
twitter.com/RugbyNS

Also Known As: Rugby Nova Scotia
Overview: A small provincial organization founded in 1965
Description: To promote, control, encourage & develop the game of rugby union football throughout Nova Scotia; *Member of:* Rugby Canada
Affiliation(s): International Rugby Board
Chief Officer(s): Geno Carew, President

Prince Edward Island Rugby Union (PEIRU)
c/o Sport PEI, 40 Enman Cres., Charlottetown PE C1E 1E6
peirugbyunion@gmail.com
www.peirugbyunion.ca
twitter.com/PEIRugbyUnion

Also Known As: PEI Rugby Union
Overview: A medium-sized provincial organization
Description: To promote rugby in Prince Edward Island; *Member of:* Rugby Canada
Chief Officer(s): Craig Inward, President
craigdinward@gmail.com
Finances: *Funding Sources:* Membership fees; Gate receipts; Government; Sponsorship

Rugby Canada
3019 Glen Lake Rd., Langford BC V9B 4B4
Tel: 905-707-8998
contact@rugby.ca
rugby.ca
www.instagram.com/rugbycanada
www.facebook.com/RugbyCanada
twitter.com/rugbycanada

Previous Name: Canadian Rugby Union
Overview: A medium-sized national organization founded in 1974
Description: To be the national governing body for the sport of rugby in Canada
Chief Officer(s): Allen Vansen, Chief Executive Officer
avansen@rugby.ca
Member Profile: Official rugby teams in Canada
Activities: Player development; youth clinics

Rugby Manitoba
c/o Sport Manitoba, 145 Pacific Ave., Winnipeg MB R3B 2Z6
Tel: 204-925-5664
www.rugbymanitoba.com
Overview: A medium-sized provincial organization
Description: To govern rugby in Manitoba; *Member of:* Rugby Canada
Chief Officer(s): Travis Paskaruk, Executive Director
executivedirector@rugbymanitoba.com

Rugby Ontario
#201, 111 Railside Rd., Toronto ON M3A 1B2
Tel: 647-560-4790; *Fax:* 647-560-4790
info@rugbyontario.com
www.rugbyontario.com
www.facebook.com/RugbyOntario
twitter.com/rugbyontario
Overview: A medium-sized provincial organization founded in 1949
Affiliation(s): Canadian Rugby Union
Chief Officer(s): David Butler, Chair
chairman@rugbyontario.com
Michael Brown, Chief Executive Officer
mbrown@rugbyontario.com
Larissa Mankis, Chief Operating Officer
lmankis@rugbyontario.com
Finances: *Annual Operating Budget:* $1.5 Million-$3 Million
Staff: 8 staff member(s)
Membership: 10,827; *Member Profile:* Athletes, coaches, officials, administrators; *Committees:* Coaching; Executive

Saskatchewan Rugby Union (SRU)
#213, 1870 Lorne St., Regina SK
Tel: 306-780-9353
www.saskrugby.com
www.facebook.com/SaskRugby

Overview: A small provincial charitable organization
Description: To encourage, promote, organize, administer & otherwise regulate the sport of Rugby Union Football in the province of Saskatchewan in accordance with the laws of the game in a safe & proper manner; *Member of:* Rugby Canada; Sask Sport
Chief Officer(s): Grant Cranfield, President
Finances: *Annual Operating Budget:* $100,000-$250,000
Staff: 1 staff member(s); 200 volunteer(s)
Membership: 2,500; *Fees:* Schedule available

Sailing

Alberta Sailing Association (ASA)
PO Box 52058, Stn. Edmonton Trail, Calgary AB T2E 8K9
info@albertasailing.com
www.albertasailing.com
Overview: A small provincial organization founded in 1973
Description: Alberta Sailing Association in partnership with its member clubs, sailing schools & Sail Canada addresses the needs of sailors; encourages improved access to water & sailing facilities; sail training & safety programs & opportunities to compete at the club, provincial & international levels; *Member of:* Sail Canada
Chief Officer(s): Ron Hewitt, President
president@albertasailing.com
Fie Hulsker, Executive Director, 403-827-5578
Finances: *Annual Operating Budget:* $50,000-$100,000
Staff: 1 staff member(s)
Membership: 1,500; *Fees:* $20

BC Sailing Association
#195, 3820 Cessna Dr., Richmond BC V7B 0A2
Tel: 604-333-3628; *Fax:* 604-333-3626
crew@bcsailing.bc.ca
www.bcsailing.bc.ca
www.facebook.com/bcsailing
Also Known As: BC Sailing
Overview: A medium-sized provincial organization
Description: The provincial sport authority for sailing; *Member of:* Sail Canada; Sport BC
Affiliation(s): International Sailing Federation
Chief Officer(s): Tine Moberg-Parker, Executive Director
tmpsailing@shaw.ca
Finances: *Funding Sources:* Provincial government; membership fees; programs
Staff: 3 staff member(s)
Membership: 5,000; *Fees:* Schedule available

Canadian Albacore Association (CAA)
PO Box 98093, 970 Queen St. East, Toronto ON M4M 1J8
www.albacore.ca
Overview: A small national organization founded in 1961
Description: To promote & support the development of the Albacore fleet
Chief Officer(s): Paul Clifford, Commodore
commodore@albacore.ca
Mary Free, Treasurer
mfree44@gmail.com
Fees: $27 associate; $60 full; *Member Profile:* Canadian owners & sailors of Albacore dinghies
Activities: Sharing news & information about Canadian Albacore sailing; Sponsoring events & regattas

Fédération de voile du Québec
4545, av Pierre-de-Coubertin, Montréal QC H1V 0B2
Tél: 514-252-3097; *Téléc:* 514-252-3044
www.voile.qc.ca

www.facebook.com/voilequebec
Aperçu: *Dimension:* petite; *Envergure:* provinciale; *fondée en 1970*
Description: Encourager et promouvoir la pratique de la voile, sous toutes ses formes au Québec
Membre(s) du bureau directeur: Natalie Matthon, Directrice générale

New Brunswick Sailing Association (NBSA)
c/o Sharon Mills, Executive Director, 105 Bird Ave., Fredericton NB E2A 2H8
Tel: 506-472-2117
www.nbsailing.nb.ca
Overview: A small provincial organization
Description: The New Brunswick Sailing Association is the provincial governing body for boating & the sport of sailing. It is the Canadian Yachting Association's representative in New Brunswick.; *Member of:* Sail Canada
Chief Officer(s): Sharon Mills, Executive Director
smills@nbsailing.nb.ca

Ontario Sailing / Association de voile de l'Ontario
#17, 70 Unsworth Dr., Hamilton ON L8W 3K4
Tel: 905-572-7245; *Fax:* 905-572-6056
Toll-Free: 888-672-7245
info@ontariosailing.ca
www.ontariosailing.ca
www.facebook.com/OntarioSailing
twitter.com/ontariosailing
Also Known As: Sail Ontario
Previous Name: Ontario Sailing Association
Overview: A medium-sized provincial organization founded in 1970
Description: To foster interest in sailing & to promote & encourage proficiency in the sport, particularly among young people in the province of Ontario; to promote sailboat racing events & to encourage the development of skills in sailboat handling & seamanship; *Member of:* Sail Canada
Affiliation(s): International Sailing Federation; Canadian Safe Boating Council
Chief Officer(s): Glenn Lethbridge, Executive Director, 905-572-7245 224
execdir@ontariosailing.ca
Finances: *Annual Operating Budget:* $500,000-$1.5 Million; *Funding Sources:* Membership fees; provincial government; corporate sponsorship; grants
Staff: 6 staff member(s); 25 volunteer(s)
Membership: 180 clubs/schools/associations; 10,000 families; 100,000 boaters

PEI Sailing Association (PEISA)
c/o Ellen MacPhail, PO Box 6708, York Point PE C0A 1H0
save@waveskills.ca
www.peisailing.com
Also Known As: Sail Prince Edward Island
Overview: A medium-sized provincial organization
Description: The PEI Sailing Association is a volunteer organization that promotes sailing in the province of Prince Edward Island, Canada. As the provincial chapter of the Canadian Sailing Association the PEI Sailing Association provides support and training to anybody interested in learning to sail or expanding their sailing.; *Member of:* Sail Canada
Chief Officer(s): Ellen McPhail, Executive Director

Sail Canada / Voile Canada
Portsmouth Olympic Harbour, 53 Yonge St., Kingston ON K7M 6G4
Tel: 613-545-3044; *Fax:* 613-545-3045
Toll-Free: 877-416-4720
sailcanada@sailing.ca
www.sailing.ca
www.instagram.com/sailcanada
www.facebook.com/SailCanada
twitter.com/SailCanada
Previous Name: Canadian Yachting Association
Overview: A medium-sized national charitable organization founded in 1931
Description: To promote the sport of sailing in Canada
Affiliation(s): International Sailing Federation; International Sailing Schools Association
Chief Officer(s): Don Adams, Chief Executive Officer, 613-545-3044 115
don@sailing.ca
Mike Milner, Director, High Performance
mike@sailing.ca
Genevieve Manning, Office Manager, 613-545-3044 101
gen@sailing.ca
Finances: *Annual Operating Budget:* $1.5 Million-$3 Million
Staff: 12 staff member(s)
Membership: 10 provincial associations; 255 clubs; 175 sailing schools; 30 class associations; 80,000 active members; *Member Profile:* Members of member yacht club or persons with interest in sailing; *Committees:* Athlete Development; Audit; Finance; Governance; High Performance; Nominating; Offshore; Provincial; Racing Appeals; Racing Rules; Training & Certification
Activities: *Library:* Yes

Sail Manitoba
#409, 145 Pacific Ave., Winnipeg MB R3B 2Z6
Tel: 204-925-5650
sailing@sportmanitoba.ca
sailmanitoba.ca
www.facebook.com/200107080070072
twitter.com/SailManitoba
Previous Name: Manitoba Sailing Association Inc.
Overview: A small provincial organization founded in 1965
Description: To be the sport's provincial regulator; *Member of:* Sail Canada
Chief Officer(s): Max Desmarais, President
Membership: 1,000; *Committees:* Finance; Operations; Recreation; Training; Racing; Team

Sail Nova Scotia
5516 Spring Garden Rd., 4th Fl., Halifax NS B3J 1G6
Tel: 902-425-5450
office@sailnovascotia.ca
www.sailnovascotia.ca
www.facebook.com/sailnovascotia
Previous Name: Nova Scotia Yachting Association
Overview: A small provincial organization
Description: To regulate the sport of sailing in Nova Scotia; *Member of:* Sail Canada; Sport Nova Scotia
Affiliation(s): Canadian Sport Centre
Chief Officer(s): Frank Denis, Executive Director & Media Contact

SailNL
PO Box 23102, Stn. Churchill Sq., St. John's NL A1B 4J9
sailing.nl@gmail.com
www.sailnl.ca
www.facebook.com/sailnl
Also Known As: Newfoundland & Labrador Sailing Association
Overview: A small provincial organization founded in 1966
Description: To regulate the sport of sailing in Newfoundland & Labrador; *Member of:* Sail Canada; Sport NL
Chief Officer(s): Ryan Kelly, President
ryan.kelly033@gmail.com

S.A.L.T.S. Sail & Life Training Society (SALTS)
451 Herald St., Victoria BC V8W 3N8
Tel: 250-383-6811; *Fax:* 250-383-7781
Toll-Free: 888-383-6811
info@salts.ca
www.salts.ca
www.instagram.com/saltsvictoria
www.facebook.com/saltsvictoria
twitter.com/saltsvictoria
Overview: A small provincial charitable organization founded in 1974
Description: To encourage spiritual, relational & physical development of young people through sailing activities in a Christian surrounding; *Member of:* Canadian Council of Christian Charities
Chief Officer(s): Loren Hagerty, Executive Director
Meghan Kort, Coordinator, Communications
Finances: *Annual Operating Budget:* $500,000-$1.5 Million; *Funding Sources:* Trainee fees; donations; membership fees; fundraising
Staff: 7 staff member(s); 40 volunteer(s)
Membership: 450 single & family; *Fees:* $50 single; $100 family; $200 corporate

Saskatchewan Sailing Clubs Association (SSCA)
SK
sasksail@sasktel.net
www.sasksail.com
Overview: A small provincial organization
Description: To regulate the sport of sailing in Saskatchewan; *Member of:* Sail Canada
Chief Officer(s): L.P. Gagnon, President
lpgagnon@hotmail.fr
Mark Lammens, Technical Director & Coach, 306-975-0833

Wind Athletes Canada
PO Box 29047, Stn. Portsmouth, Kingston ON K7M 8W6
www.windathletes.ca
www.facebook.com/windathletes
twitter.com/windathletes
Overview: A medium-sized national organization
Description: To promote the sport of sailing in Canada; To provide funding to the Canadian Sailing Team
Chief Officer(s): Grant Carter, Chair
Finances: *Funding Sources:* Fundraising
Activities: Training programs

Schools

NWT School Athletic Federation (NWTSAF)
PO Box 266, Fort Smith NT X0E 0P0
Overview: A medium-sized provincial organization
Member of: School Sport Canada
Affiliation(s): Canadian School Sport Federation; Sport North
Chief Officer(s): Richard Daitch, Executive Director
rwdaitch@yahoo.com
Activities: Regional tournaments

Prince Edward Island School Athletic Association (PEISAA)
#101, 250 Water St., Summerside PE C1N 1B6
Tel: 902-438-4846; *Fax:* 902-438-4884
www.peisaa.pe.ca
Overview: A medium-sized provincial organization

Description: To support school sports & promote the image of sports as a valuable educational and recreational endeavour; *Member of:* School Sport Canada
Chief Officer(s): Trent Ranahan, Chair
Trevor Bridges, Vice-Chair
Gerald MacCormack, Secretary-Treasurer

School Sports Newfoundland & Labrador (SSNL)
PO Box 8700, 1296A Kenmount Rd., St. John's NL A1B 4J6
Tel: 709-729-2795; *Fax:* 709-729-2705
www.schoolsportsnl.ca
Previous Name: Newfoundland & Labrador High School Athletic Federation
Overview: A medium-sized provincial charitable organization founded in 1969
Description: To organize, promote & govern all high school sports within the province; to assist student athletes in reaching their full physical, educational & social potential through participation & sportsmanship in interscholastic sports; *Member of:* School Sport Canada; National Federation of High Schools
Chief Officer(s): Karen Richard, Executive Director
karen@sportnl.ca
Mike Ball, President
mikeball@nlesd.ca
Finances: *Annual Operating Budget:* $500,000-$1.5 Million; *Funding Sources:* Provincial government; Federal government; corporate sponsors; membership dues
Staff: 3 staff member(s); 700 volunteer(s)
Membership: 150 schools; *Fees:* Schedule available
Activities: School sports tournaments; *Internships:* Yes

Yukon Schools' Athletic Association (YSAA)
Sport Yukon Bldg., 4061 - 4th Ave., Whitehorse YT Y1A 1H1
Tel: 867-332-7081; *Fax:* 867-667-4237
ysaa.yukonschools.ca
Overview: A medium-sized provincial organization founded in 1996
Description: To encourage participation of students in inter school athletics, emphasize interschool athletics as an integral part of the total educational process & plan, promote, supervise & administer a program of inter-school athletics in all approved competitions.; *Member of:* School Sport Canada
Chief Officer(s): Jeff Cressman, President
jeff.cressman@yesnet.yk.ca
Vickie Dawe, Vice-President
vickie.dawe@yesnet.yk.ca
Ron Billingsley, Secretary/Treasurer
ron.billingsley@yesnet.yk.ca

Senior Citizens

Alberta Senior Citizens Sport & Recreation Association (ASCSRA)
Percy Page Centre, 11759 Groat Rd. NW, 3rd Fl., Edmonton AB T5M 3K6
Tel: 403-700-0454
info@alberta55plus.ca
www.alberta55plus.ca
Also Known As: Alberta 55 Plus
Overview: A medium-sized provincial charitable organization founded in 1980
Description: To promote sport & recreation development for seniors (55+) across Alberta; To act as a provincial voice to ensure input by age categories for seniors in Alberta Winter & Summer Games; To promote activities, lifelong learning, & active living
Affiliation(s): Alberta Sport Connection
Chief Officer(s): Wayne Davies, President, 780-532-6689
president@alberta55plus.ca
Finances: *Annual Operating Budget:* $100,000-$250,000; *Funding Sources:* Government & private sector donations
Staff: 1 staff member(s); 100 volunteer(s)
Membership: 4,000; *Fees:* $30 individual; $50 association; $25-$50 club; *Member Profile:* Albertans aged 55+ who enjoy sports & activities
Activities: Workshops & instructional clinics; Tournaments; *Speaker Service:* Yes

Elder Active Recreation Association (ERA)
4061 - 4th Ave., Whitehorse YT Y1A 1H1
Tel: 867-456-8252
office@elderactive.ca
www.elderactive.ca
www.facebook.com/elderactive
Overview: A medium-sized provincial organization
Description: To enhance the quality of life of Yukon seniors & elders by supporting them in living healthy lives with independence & dignity; To support seniors & elders in helping other seniors & elders to live full, active & healthy lives & to develop active communities throughout the Yukon where seniors

& elders can make positive lifestyle choices, exchange wisdom & connect with others in friendship, recreation & creativity
Fees: $10; *Member Profile:* Yukoners 55 years of age and over

Ontario Senior Games Association (OSGA)
#52, 2455 Cawthra Rd., Mississauga ON L5A 3P1
Tel: 905-232-8581
info@osga55plus.ca
www.osga55plus.ca
www.facebook.com/osga55plus
Also Known As: OSGA 55+
Overview: A medium-sized provincial organization founded in 1997
Description: To provide physical & social activities to senior citizens
Chief Officer(s): Angeline Richard, President
Geoffrey Johnson, Program Manager, 905-232-8582
geoff@osga55plus.ca
Finances: *Funding Sources:* Ministry of Tourism, Culture & Sport
Membership: 37 Member Districts in Ontario; *Member Profile:* Seniors (55+); *Committees:* Rules

Shooting Sports

Alberta Federation of Shooting Sports (AFSS)
Percy Page Centre, 11759 Groat Rd., Edmonton AB T5M 3K6
Tel: 780-415-1775; *Fax:* 780-422-2663
afss@abshooters.org
www.abshooters.org
Overview: A small provincial organization
Description: To provide funding & support to 11 shooting organizations throughout the province
Affiliation(s): Alberta Handgun Association; Alberta Smallbore Rifle Association; Alberta Provincial Rifle Association; International Practical Shooting Confederation Alberta; Alberta Sporting Clays Association; Alberta Skeet Shooting Association; Alberta International Skeetshooting Association; Alberta International Style Trapshooting Association; Alberta Metallic Silhouette Association; Alberta Black Powder Association; Alberta Frontier Shootists Society
Chief Officer(s): Pat Cooper, President
Rod Bourgeon, Secretary Treasurer
Jennie Musani, Administrative Assistant, 780-415-1775
afss@abshooters.org
Membership: 11 associations; *Member Profile:* Shooting associations in Alberta
Activities: The AFSS fosters shooting sports & shooting sport safety in the province of Alberta. The AFSS promotes coaching, community, outdoor sport, range safety, youth in sport and development of Olympic athletes. We offer Range Safety Officer/Range Safety Officer Instructor courses and ongoing membership.

Alberta Metallic Silhouette Association
c/o Debra & David Johnston, PO Box 213, Big Valley AB T0J 0G0
www.absilhouetteassoc.ca
Overview: A small provincial charitable organization founded in 1977
Description: To govern, promote & advance the sport of metallic silhouette shooting in Alberta
Affiliation(s): Shooting Federation of Canada; Alberta Federation of Shooting Sports
Chief Officer(s): David Johnston, President, 403-876-2024
president@absilhouetteassoc.ca
Debra Johnston, Secretary-Treasurer, 403-876-2024
secretary_treasurer@absilhouetteassoc.ca
Finances: *Annual Operating Budget:* Less than $50,000; *Funding Sources:* Provincial government
Staff: 20 volunteer(s)
Membership: 106 individual; *Fees:* $20 individual; $25 family; $60 club
Activities: Sanctions matches for: small bore rifle, high power rifle, small bore hunting rifle, high power hunting rifle, black powder cartridge rifle.

Atlantic Marksmen Association
PO Box 181, Stn. Dartmouth Main, Dartmouth NS B2Y 3Y3
www.atlanticmarksmen.ca
Overview: A small local organization founded in 1954
Member of: Shooting Federation of Canada
Chief Officer(s): Sean Hansen, President
Membership: 200; *Fees:* $200 senior, plus induction fee of $100; $30 juniors (18 & under)
Activities: Owns & operates two range facilities

British Columbia Rifle Association (BCRA)
PO Box 2418, Stn. Sardis Main, Chilliwack BC V2R 1A7
contact@bcrifle.org
www.bcrifle.org

Overview: A medium-sized provincial organization founded in 1874
Description: To create a public sentiment for the encouragement of marksmanship in all its trades among citizens of British Columbia, both as a sport & as a definite contribution to the defence of Canada; *Member of:* Dominion of Canada Rifle Association
Fees: Schedule available
Activities: BC Marksmanship Championships in 7 different shooting sports

British Columbia Target Sports Association
PO Box 496, Kamloops BC V2C 5L2
targetsports@bctsa.bc.ca
www.bctsa.bc.ca
www.facebook.com/BCTargetSports
twitter.com/bctargetsports
Previous Name: BC Smallbore Rifle Association
Overview: A small provincial organization
Description: To promote target rifle sports in British Columbia; *Member of:* Shooting Federation of Canada
Chief Officer(s): Mo Johnson, President
president@bctsa.bc.ca
Chantel Spicer, Coordinator, Coaching
coaching@bctsa.bc.ca
Finances: *Funding Sources:* Membership dues; donations; sports grants; entry fees
Fees: $15 junior; $25 associate club; $30 adult; $35 family
Activities: Provincial/national championships

Buckskinners Muzzleloading Association, Limited
2493 Route 490, Indian Mountain NB E1G 4R9
buckskinnersweb@yahoo.com
buckskinnersweb.weebly.com
www.facebook.com/377321212329586
Overview: A small local organization founded in 1978
Description: To promote good & safe blackpowder shooting, marksmanship & sportsmanship; To encourage & promote buckskinning knowledge & skills
Affiliation(s): New Brunswick Wildlife Federation
Chief Officer(s): Earl Magee, Chief Range Officer, 506-383-9579
plaidvalley@hotmail.com
Finances: *Annual Operating Budget:* Less than $50,000
Staff: 36 volunteer(s)
Membership: 50+; *Fees:* $20 youth; $60 adult; $80 family; *Member Profile:* Individuals who actively engage in club events & are interested in promoting the aims & objectives of the club
Activities: Winter Rendezvous, Feb.; Summer Rendezvous, June

Calgary & District Target Shooters Association (CDTSA)
#142, 612 - 500 Country Hills Blvd., Calgary AB T3K 5K3
Tel: 403-275-3257
www.cdtsa.ca
Overview: A small local organization founded in 1981
Affiliation(s): Alberta Federation of Shooting Sports; Alberta Fish & Game Association; Alberta Black Powder Association; Alberta Metallic Silhouette Association
Finances: *Annual Operating Budget:* Less than $50,000
Staff: 12 volunteer(s)
Fees: Schedule available

Canadian Shooting Sports Association (CSSA)
#204, 1143 Wentworth St. West, Oshawa ON L1J 8P7
Tel: 905-720-3142; *Toll-Free:* 888-873-4339
info@cdnshootingsports.org
cssa-cila.org
Merged from: Ontario Handgun Association; Ontario Smallbore Federation
Overview: A medium-sized national organization
Description: To provide the knowledge, guidance & services to ensure the continuation promotion of the shooting sports & related activities & to represent their interests to the government, the regulatory bodies, the media & the public
Affiliation(s): Ontario Council of Shooters; Shooting Federation of Canada
Finances: *Funding Sources:* Membership fees
Membership: 15,000; *Fees:* $27 junior; $45 general; $80 family; $250 corporate; $950 life; *Member Profile:* Member of a recognized shooting club
Activities: To provide liability insurance & training courses

Canadian Trapshooting Association (CTA)
Saskatoon SK
www.shootcanada.ca
Overview: A medium-sized national organization founded in 1956
Description: To promote clay target shooting as a recreational sport among shooters of every age, both sexes, & at every level of ability, the ultimate objective being to compete in the world

championships held each year in Ohio; *Member of:* Amateur Trapshooting Association
Chief Officer(s): Dwight Smith, President
Finances: *Annual Operating Budget:* Less than $50,000; *Funding Sources:* Fees collected at the national championships
Staff: 150 volunteer(s)
Membership: 1,800

Dominion of Canada Rifle Association (DCRA) / L'Association de tir dominion du canada
45 Shirley Blvd., Ottawa ON K2K 2W6
Tel: 613-829-8281; *Fax:* 613-829-0099
office@dcra.ca
dcra.ca
Overview: A small national charitable organization founded in 1868
Description: To promote & support the pursuit of excellence in military & civilian marsmanship; To raise awareness of marksmanship as a positive contribution to gun safety, shooting & Canada
Chief Officer(s): Don Haisell, Executive Director
dhaisell@dcra.ca
Finances: *Annual Operating Budget:* $100,000-$250,000
Staff: 3 staff member(s); 60 volunteer(s)
Membership: 1,000; *Fees:* $35 associate under age 25; $55 associate; $75 regular under age 25; $135 regular; *Member Profile:* 10 provincial rifle associations; Yukon Rifle Association; National Capital Region Rifle Association
Activities: Annual Canadian Fullbore Rifle Championships

Fédération québécoise de tir (FQT) / Québec Shooting Federation
6897, rue Jarry est, Montréal QC H1P 1W7
Tél: 514-252-3056; *Téléc:* 514-252-3060
Ligne sans frais: 888-514-7847
fqt@fqtir.qc.ca
www.fqtir.qc.ca
Aperçu: *Dimension:* petite; *Envergure:* provinciale; *Organisme sans but lucratif; fondée en 1978*
Description: La FQT est un organisme à but non lucratif voué à la promotion du tir sportif sur tout le territoire de la province du Québec et qui est reconnue et subventionnée par l'intermédiaire du Secrétariat au loisir et au sport (Gouvernement du Québec); *Membre de:* Fédération de tir du Canada; Shooting Federation of Canada
Affiliation(s): Regroupement Loisir Québec; Sports Québec
Membre(s) du bureau directeur: Gilles Bédard, Directeur exécutif, 514-252-3056 3611
gbedard@fqtir.qc.ca
Gérald Tousignant, Président
Finances: *Budget de fonctionnement annuel:* $250,000-$500,000; *Fonds:* Gouvernement du Québec
Personnel: 3 membre(s) du personnel; 400 bénévole(s)
Membre: 6,000; *Comités:* Carabine; pistolet; plateaux; chasse; moderne; poudre noire; pratique pour policiers et civils
Activités: Assemblée général annuelle; *Stagiaires:* Oui

Manitoba Provincial Handgun Association (MPHA)
PO Box 314, RPO Corydon Ave., Winnipeg MB R3M 3S7
www.handgunmb.ca
Overview: A small provincial organization
Description: To provide opportunities & programming for handgun athletes, coaches & officials; To help participants learn, practice & develop skills in the sport of handgun shooting; *Member of:* Sport Manitoba
Chief Officer(s): Randy Myrdal, President
Fees: $10 individual; $25 club

Manitoba Provincial Rifle Association Inc. (MPRA)
c/o Janet Stewart, Chairperson, 795 Valour Rd., Winnipeg MB R3G 3B3
Tel: 204-783-0768
www.manitobarifle.ca
Overview: A medium-sized provincial organization founded in 1872
Description: To promote, organize & regulate sport shooting; To encourage participation & provide resources for all interested in reaching their potential; *Member of:* Shooting Federation of Canada; Dominion of Canada Rifle Association
Affiliation(s): Sports Manitoba
Fees: $25 associate/under 25; $50 full; $65 family; $350 lifetime; *Member Profile:* Individuals & clubs interested in rifle target shooting
Activities: Shooting practices & competitions

Nova Scotia Rifle Association (NSRA)
PO Box 482, Dartmouth NS B2Y 3Y8
Tel: 902-456-7468
nsrifle@ns.sympatico.ca
www.nsrifle.org
Overview: A small provincial organization founded in 1861

Description: To promote & organize recreational target shooting; *Member of:* Dominion of Canada Rifle Association
Affiliation(s): Shooting Federation of Canada
Chief Officer(s): Darrell Harvey, President
1840dh@gmail.com
Finances: *Annual Operating Budget:* Less than $50,000
Staff: 12 volunteer(s)
Membership: 300; *Fees:* $300 senior; $20 junior (under 19); *Member Profile:* Residents of the province with a valid firearm license

Ontario Muzzle Loading Association (OMLA)
433 Queen St., Chatham ON N7M 5K5
Tel: 519-352-0924; *Fax:* 519-352-4380
jimvivmoore@bell.net
Overview: A small provincial organization founded in 1973
Activities: Posting results from provincial matches & the Soper event

Ontario Provincial Trapshooting Association (OPTA)
ON
info@ontariotrap.com
www.ontariotrap.com
www.facebook.com/groups/OntarioTrap
Overview: A small provincial organization
Chief Officer(s): Neville Henderson, President
Pam Muma, Secretary-Treasurer
Finances: *Annual Operating Budget:* Less than $50,000
Membership: 500-999

Ontario Rifle Association (ORA)
c/o ORA Membership Secretary, PO Box 245, Borden ON L0M 1C0
www.ontariorifleassociation.ca
Overview: A medium-sized provincial organization founded in 1868
Description: To organize shooting events for various rifle shooting disciplines
Affiliation(s): Dominion of Canada Rifle Association
Chief Officer(s): Donna Vamplew, Secretary
Pat Vamplew, Treasurer
treasurer@ontariorifleassociation.ca
Peter Westlake, Contact, Membership Inquiries
membership@ontariorifleassociation.ca

Ontario Skeet Shooting Association (OSSA)
PO Box 96, Hampton ON L0B 1J0
Tel: 905-263-8174; *Fax:* 905-263-4870
info@ontarioskeet.com
www.ontarioskeet.com
Overview: A small provincial organization
Description: To educate persons in the safe & efficient handling of shotguns; to encourage competition in shotgun target shooting; to promote the sport of skeet shooting in the province of Ontario; *Member of:* Shooting Federation of Canada; National Skeet Shooting Association
Chief Officer(s): Jennie Marsh, Secretary-Treasurer
Brad McRae, President
Finances: *Annual Operating Budget:* Less than $50,000
Staff: 8 volunteer(s)
Membership: 165

Province of Québec Rifle Association (PQRA) / Association de tir de la province de Québec (ATPQ)
426, rue Riopelle, Québec QC G1C 6L3
info@pqra.org
www.pqra.org
Overview: A small provincial organization founded in 1869
Description: Promouvoir le tir de gros calibre et/ou d'armes militaires; Favoriser la poursuite de l'excellence dans le sport du tir par l'entrainement ainsi que d'encourager la manipulation sécuritaire et un usage approprié des armes et munitions; *Member of:* Dominion of Canada Rifle Association; Shooting Federation of Canada
Chief Officer(s): Gale Stewart, President
Finances: *Funding Sources:* Membership fees
Activities: Long Range Target Shooting; Black Powder Long Range; Service Rifle Matches; Cadet Shooting Programs

Saskatchewan Black Powder Association (SBPA)
PO Box 643, Saskatoon SK S7K 3L7
www.sbpa17.com
Overview: A small provincial organization founded in 1980
Description: To provide a common voice for all Black Powder Shooters in the province; To encourage development of the old skills & trades related to Black Powder; & to co-ordinate activities of the Black Powder Shooters in the province; *Member of:* Shooting Federation of Canada
Chief Officer(s): Jake Peters, President
Dell Bayne, Secretary-Treasurer
Finances: *Funding Sources:* Membership dues; Donations
Fees: $6 individual; $10 family; $25 associate

Activities: *Library:* Yes (Open to Public)

Saskatchewan Provincial Rifle Association Inc. (SPRA)
c/o Brian Archer, PO Box 40, Mazenod SK S0H 2Y0
Tel: 306-354-7493
www.saskrifle.com
Overview: A small provincial organization founded in 1885
Description: To govern fullbore target rifle shooting in Saskatchewan; To promote excellence in marksmanship, safety & responsible handling of firearms
Chief Officer(s): Brian Worsley, President
brianw1911@gmail.com
Finances: *Funding Sources:* Membership dues; SaskSport Inc.
Fees: Schedule available

Shooting Federation of Canada (SFC) / Fédération de tir du Canada (FTC)
c/o House of Sport, 2451 Riverside Dr., Nepean ON K1H 7X7
Tel: 613-727-7483; *Fax:* 613-727-7487
admin@sfc-ftc.ca
sfc-ftc.ca
Overview: A medium-sized national charitable organization founded in 1932
Description: To represent firearms users in matters of legislation, shooting sports promotion & program activities; *Member of:* International Shooting Sport Federation
Affiliation(s): Canadian Shooting Sports Association
Chief Officer(s): Sandra Honour, President
president@sfc-ftc.ca
Finances: *Funding Sources:* Sales; Donations; Government
Membership: 108 organizations; *Committees:* Coaching; National Officials Development; Commonwealth Games; Awards & Merits; High Performance
Activities: *Awareness Events:* National Smallbore Rifle Championships; National Trapshooting Championships; National Skeet Shooting Championships *Library:* Yes

Shooting Federation of Nova Scotia (SFNS)
PO Box 28023, Dartmouth NS B2W 6E2
www.sfns.info
Overview: A small provincial organization founded in 1972
Member of: Sport Nova Scotia
Affiliation(s): Shooting Federation of Canada
Finances: *Annual Operating Budget:* Less than $50,000
Staff: 12 volunteer(s)
Membership: 1600

Yellowknife Shooting Club (YKSC)
PO Box 2931, Yellowknife NT X1A 2R2
yellowknifeshootingclub.ca
www.facebook.com/355960874522187
Overview: A small local organization founded in 1961
Description: To encourage efficiency & high ethical standards in the use of firearms
Affiliation(s): NWT Federation of Shooting Sports; Shooting Federation of Canada; NRA
Chief Officer(s): Scott Cairns, President, 867-669-9220
Bud Rhyndress, Vice-President, 867-873-6209
Fees: $10 junior; $190 individual; $320 family; *Member Profile:* Firearms owners & users
Activities: Caribou Carnival; Wolverine Days; fun shoot; media shoot; turkey shoot; Sight-In Days

Yukon Shooting Federation
4061 - 4th Ave., Whitehorse YT Y1A 1H1
Tel: 867-667-6728
sportyukon.com/member/yukon-shooting-federation
Overview: A small provincial organization
Description: To promote & facilitate air rifle & air pistol shooting in the Yukon Territory.; *Member of:* Sport Yukon
Chief Officer(s): Lyle Thompson, President
Activities: Junior Shooters Program

Skating

Alberta Amateur Speed Skating Association (AASSA)
2500 University Dr. NW, Calgary AB T2N 1N4
Tel: 403-220-7911; *Fax:* 403-220-9226
info@aassa.ca
www.albertaspeedskating.ca
www.instagram.com/albertaspeedskating
www.facebook.com/albertaspeedskating
twitter.com/AB_SpeedSkating
Also Known As: Alberta Speed Skating
Overview: A small provincial organization
Member of: Speed Skating Canada
Chief Officer(s): Nicole Cooney, President
Wendy Walker, Program Coordinator
Mike Marshall, Technical Director

British Columbia Speed Skating Association
PO Box 2023, Stn. A, Abbotsford BC V2T 3T8
Tel: 604-746-4349; *Fax:* 604-746-4549
www.speed-skating.bc.ca
www.instagram.com/BCSpeedSkating
www.facebook.com/BCSpeedSkating
twitter.com/BCSpeedSkating
Overview: A small provincial organization
Description: To foster the growth & development of Speed Skating in B.C.; *Member of:* Speed Skating Canada
Chief Officer(s): Ted Houghton, Executive Director, 604-309-8178
ted.houghton@shaw.ca

Club de patinage artistique Les lames givrées inc.
CP 453, Chibougamau QC G8P 2X9
Tél: 418-748-2671
leslamesgivrees@hotmail.com
Aperçu: *Dimension:* petite; *Envergure:* locale
Membre(s) du bureau directeur: Joline Bélanger, Présidente, 418-748-2339

Fédération de Patinage de Vitesse du Québec
930, av Roland Beaudin, Sainte-Foy QC G1V 4H8
Tél: 418-651-1973; *Téléc:* 418-651-1977
Ligne sans frais: 877-651-1973
www.fpvq.org

www.facebook.com/FPVQ.org
twitter.com/PatinVitesseQc
Aperçu: *Dimension:* petite; *Envergure:* provinciale
Description: Depuis un peu plus d'un mois déjà, les athlètes du Centre national courte piste sont en entraînement hors glace sous la surveillance des entraîneurs et avec la grande collaboration du groupe Actiforme.; *Membre de:* Speed Skating Canada

International Skating Union (ISU) / Union Internationale de Patinage
av Juste-Olivier 17, Lausanne 1006 Switzerland
info@isu.ch
www.isu.org
www.youtube.com/user/SkatingISU
www.facebook.com/ISUDevProjects
Overview: A small international organization founded in 1892
Description: To regulate, control & promote the sports of figure & speed skating & their organized development on the basis of friendship & mutual understanding between sportsmen & women & to broaden interest in figure & speed skating sports by increasing their popularity, improving their quality & increasing the number of participants throughout the world
Chief Officer(s): Fredi Schmid, Director General
Finances: *Annual Operating Budget:* Greater than $5 Million
Staff: 60 volunteer(s)
Membership: 95; *Member Profile:* National skating associations
Activities: Administration of figure skating & speed skating sports throughout the world

Manitoba Speed Skating Association
145 Pacific Ave., Winnipeg MB R3B 2Z6
Tel: 204-925-5657; *Fax:* 204-925-5792
Toll-Free: 888-628-9921
office@mbspeedskating.ca
www.mbspeedskating.org
www.instagram.com/mbspeedskating
twitter.com/mbspeedskating
Overview: A small provincial organization
Description: The MSSA is dedicated to the development, growth & effective administration of the sport of speed skating in Manitoba through the provision of leadership, support & promotion of its members & clubs.; *Member of:* Speed Skating Canada
Chief Officer(s): Brad Chambers, President
Activities: Short-track, long-track speed skating

Newfoundland & Labrador Speed Skating Association (NLSSA)
NL
Overview: A small provincial organization
Member of: Speed Skating Canada

Northwest Territories Amateur Speed Skating Association (NWTASSA)
c/o Sport North, 4908 - 49 St., Yellowknife NT X1A 2P9
Tel: 867-669-8326; *Fax:* 867-669-8327
Toll-Free: 800-661-0797
nwtspeedskating@gmail.com
sportnorth.com/tso/speed-skating/about-us
Overview: A small provincial organization
Description: To promote the sport of speed skating in the NWT; *Member of:* Sport North Federation; Speed Skating Canada
Chief Officer(s): Julie Jeffery, Director

Finances: *Annual Operating Budget:* Less than $50,000
Staff: 40 volunteer(s)
Membership: 140

Nunavut Speed Skating Association
c/o John Maurice, President, PO Box 761, 563 Suputi St., Iqaluit NU X0A 0H0
Tel: 867-979-1226; *Fax:* 867-975-3384
www.nunavutspeedskating.ca
Overview: A small provincial organization
Member of: Speed Skating Canada
Chief Officer(s): John Maurice, President
jtmaurice@northwestel.net
Don Galloway, Secretary & Director, Coaching
don.galloway@aandc-aadnc.gc.ca

Ontario Speed Skating Association (OSSA)
100 St. Charles St. East, Maryhill ON N0B 2B0
Fax: 844-677-6772
Toll-Free: 844-677-6772
ossa@ontariospeedskating.ca
ontariospeedskating.ca
www.flickr.com/photos/ontariospeedskating
www.facebook.com/OntarioSpeedSkating
twitter.com/OSSA
Previous Name: Ice Skating Association of Ontario
Overview: A medium-sized provincial organization founded in 1981
Description: To promote & develop the sport of speed skating in Ontario; *Member of:* Speed Skating Canada
Chief Officer(s): Mary Frances Carter, Executive Director
executivedirector@ontariospeedskating.ca
Sarah Leslie, Manager, Sport Programs
sportmanager@ontariospeedskating.ca
Finances: *Funding Sources:* Membership fee
Activities: *Speaker Service:* Yes

Patinage Québec
4545, av Pierre-de Coubertin, Montréal QC H1V 0B2
Tél: 514-252-3073; *Téléc:* 514-252-3170
patinage@patinage.qc.ca
www.patinage.qc.ca

www.facebook.com/patinageqc
twitter.com/patinageqc
Aperçu: *Dimension:* grande; *Envergure:* provinciale; *fondée en 1969*
Description: Rendre accessible à tous, les programmes de Patinage Canada, que ce soit par amour, par plaisir ou pour atteindre l'excellence; a l'unisson, nous contribuons ainsi à l'avancement de notre sport
Membre(s) du bureau directeur: Any-Claude Dion, Directrice générale, 514-252-3073 3550
acdion@patinage.qc.ca
Membre: 40 000

Saskatchewan Amateur Speed Skating Association (SASSA)
2205 Victoria Ave., Regina SK S4P 0S4
Tel: 306-780-9400; *Fax:* 306-525-4009
sassa@sasktel.net
www.saskspeedskating.ca
www.facebook.com/SaskatchewanSpeedSkating
Previous Name: Saskatchewan Speed Skating Association
Overview: A medium-sized provincial organization
Description: Working together to develop & promote the sport of speed skating at all levels as a fun, competitive, healthy, family activity; *Member of:* Speed Skating Canada
Affiliation(s): Sask Sport Inc.
Chief Officer(s): Jordan St. Onge, Executive Director
Finances: *Annual Operating Budget:* $100,000-$250,000; *Funding Sources:* Provincial government
Staff: 2 staff member(s); 650 volunteer(s)
Membership: 10 institutional; 200 student; 600 individual

Skate Canada / Patinage Canada
PO Box 15, #261, 1200 St Laurent Blvd., Ottawa ON K1K 3B8
Tel: 613-747-1007; *Fax:* 613-748-5718
Toll-Free: 888-747-2372
info@skatecanada.ca
skatecanada.ca
www.instagram.com/skate_canada
www.facebook.com/skatecanada
twitter.com/SkateCanada
Also Known As: Canadian Figure Skating Association
Overview: A large national licensing charitable organization founded in 1914
Description: To enable all Canadians to participate in skating throughout their lifetime for fun, fitness & achievement; *Member of:* International Skating Union
Chief Officer(s): Leanna Caron, President

Finances: *Funding Sources:* User fees; Television events; Marketing; Membership fees
Staff: 50 staff member(s)
Membership: 180,000+; *Committees:* CEO Operational Review; Governance; External Relations; Membership Policy; Finance & Risk Management; Athlete Fund & Alumni; Officials Development; Coaching Development; Sections Coordinating; Hall of Fame & Heritage; High Performance Development; Officials Assignment & Promotion; Skating Programs Development; Strategic Planning Steering
Activities: *Speaker Service:* Yes

Skate Ontario
#100, 2605 Skymark Ave., Mississauga ON L4W 4L5
Tel: 905-212-9991
www.skateontario.org
www.facebook.com/SkateOntario
twitter.com/SkateOntario
Also Known As: Ontario Figure Skating Association
Overview: A small provincial organization founded in 1982
Description: To enable every citizen of the province to participate in skating through out his/her lifetime for fun &/or achievement
Chief Officer(s): Lisa Alexander, Executive Director
Membership: 75,000; *Member Profile:* Competitive & recreational skaters as well as coaches & officials; *Committees:* Events; Programs; Technical; Transition

Speed Skate New Brunswick
NB
speedskatenb@gmail.com
speedskatenb.ca
twitter.com/SpeedSkateNB
Previous Name: New Brunswick Speed Skating Association
Overview: A small provincial organization
Description: The association provides members with access to coaching & chances to compete. It serves as a hub for information on the sport & for members to network.; *Member of:* Speed Skating Canada
Chief Officer(s): Joe Oliver, Chair

Speed Skate Nova Scotia
5516 Spring Garden Rd., Halifax NS B3J 1G6
Tel: 902-425-5450
info@speedskatens.ca
www.speedskatens.ca
twitter.com/SpeedSk8NS
Previous Name: Nova Scotia Speed Skating Association
Overview: A small provincial organization
Member of: Speed Skating Canada
Chief Officer(s): Brent Thompson, President

Speed Skate PEI
PO Box 383, Charlottetown PE C1A 7K7
info@speedskatepei.ca
www.speedskatepei.com
www.youtube.com/channel/UCwDjLpo01Om1QBMoZn5EQLw
www.facebook.com/SpeedSkatePEI
twitter.com/SpeedSkatePEI
Previous Name: Prince Edward Island Speed Skating Association
Overview: A small provincial organization
Description: Supporting the sport of speedskating in PEI.; *Member of:* Speed Skating Canada
Chief Officer(s): Jeff Wood, President
president@speedskatepei.ca
Shirliana Bruce, Secretary
secretary@speedskatepei.ca

Speed Skating Canada (SSC) / Patinage de vitesse Canada
c/o House of Sport, RA Centre, 2451 Riverside Dr., Ottawa ON K1H 7X7
Tel: 613-260-3669; *Toll-Free:* 877-572-4772
ssc@speedskating.ca
www.speedskating.ca
www.instagram.com/ssc_pvc
www.facebook.com/SSC.PVC
twitter.com/SSC_PVC
Overview: A medium-sized national organization founded in 1887
Description: To develop & promote long & short track speed skating in Canada; To prepare athletes, coaches, officials & volunteers to make contributions to speed skating & to Canada's image abroad through development & international programs
Affiliation(s): International Skating Union
Chief Officer(s): Susan Auch, Chief Executive Officer
sauch@speedskating.ca
Shawn Holman, Chief Sport Officer
sholman@speedskating.ca
Finances: *Funding Sources:* Government; Sport Canada; Canadian Olympic Association; Sponsorships; Membership

Staff: 50 volunteer(s)
Membership: 10,000; *Member Profile:* Participants in competitive or recreational speed skating; *Committees:* High Performance - Short Track & Long Track; Competitions Development; Coaching Development; Officials Development; Nominations; Participant & Athlete Development Steering
Activities: *Internships:* Yes; *Speaker Service:* Yes

Yukon Amateur Speed Skating Association
4061 - 4th Ave., Whitehorse YT Y1A 1H1

Tel: 867-660-5347
www.shorttrack06.com

Also Known As: Whitehorse Rapids Speed Skating Club
Overview: A small provincial organization

Skiing

Alberta Alpine Ski Association (AASA)
Bill Warren Training Centre, #100, 1995 Olympic Way, Canmore AB T1W 2T6

Tel: 403-609-4730; Fax: 403-678-3644
memberservices@albertaalpine.ca
www.albertaalpine.ca
www.youtube.com/user/AlbertaAlpine
www.facebook.com/AlbertaAlpine
twitter.com/AlbertaAlpine

Also Known As: Alberta Alpine
Overview: A small provincial organization
Description: To be the provincial governing body for the sport of alpine skiing in Alberta
Chief Officer(s): Nigel Loring, President & CEO, 403-609-4731
nigel@albertaalpine.ca
Alied Ten Broek, Vice President, Corporate Services, 403-609-4733
alied@albertaalpine.ca
Erin Gellhaus, Member Services, 403-609-4730
memberservices@albertaalpine.ca

Alberta Ski Jumping & Nordic Combined (ASJNC)
PO Box 96022, RPO West Springs, Calgary AB T3H 0L3

Tel: 403-703-7157
mikebodnarchuk@shaw.ca
skijumpingalberta.com
www.facebook.com/ASJNC

Also Known As: Ski Jumping Alberta
Overview: A small provincial organization founded in 1991
Description: To be the provincial governing body of ski jumping & nordic combined programs in Alberta
Chief Officer(s): Mike Bodnarchuk, Chair
Jeremy Hamming, Vice Chair

Alpine Canada / Canada Alpin
Canada Olympic Park, #302, 151 Canada Olympic Rd. SW, Calgary AB T3B 6B7

Tel: 403-777-3200; Fax: 403-777-3213
info@alpinecanada.org
alpinecanada.org
www.youtube.com/user/AlpineCanadaAlpin
ww.linkedin.com/company/alpine-canada-alpin
www.facebook.com/AlpineCanada
twitter.com/Alpine_Canada

Overview: A medium-sized national organization founded in 1920
Description: To govern the sport of ski racing in Canada; To represents coaches, officials, supporters & athletes
Chief Officer(s): Therese Brisson, President & CEO, 403-777-4245
Consuelo Zayas, Chief Financial Officer, 403-777-3207

Alpine Ontario Alpin (AOA)
#39A Stewart Rd., Collingwood ON L9Y 4M7

Tel: 705-444-5111; Fax: 705-444-5116
admin@alpineontario.ca
www.alpineontario.ca
www.instagram.com/AlpineOntario
www.facebook.com/alpineontarioalpin
twitter.com/AlpineOntario

Overview: A medium-sized provincial organization
Description: To provide skiing opportunities for competitive & recreational athletes; *Member of:* Alpine Canada Alpin
Chief Officer(s): Scott Barrett, Executive Director, 705-444-5111 206
sbarrett@alpineontario.ca
Kristin Ellis, Manager, Communications, 705-444-5111 132
communications@alpineontario.ca
Finances: *Funding Sources:* Sponsorship; Ministry of Health and Promotion; membership fees; fundraising
Staff: 5 staff member(s)
Membership: 30,000+ in 44 clubs; *Fees:* Schedule available; *Committees:* Athletic; Officials
Activities: Hosting races during ski season

Alpine Saskatchewan
1860 Lorne St., Regina SK S4P 2L7

Tel: 306-780-9236; Fax: 306-780-9462
office@saskalpine.com
www.saskalpine1.com
www.instagram.com/saskalpine

Also Known As: Sask Alpine
Overview: A small provincial organization
Description: To be the provincial governing body for noncompetitive & competitive alpine skiing in Saskatchewan
Affiliation(s): BC Alpine; Alberta Alpine; Manitoba Alpine; Alpine Canada; Alpine Canada-Live Timing; National Points; Snow Stars
Chief Officer(s): Karen Musgrave, President
president@saskalpine.com
Alana Ottenbreit, Office Manager

Association des stations de ski du Québec (ASSQ)
1347, rue Nationale, Terrebonne QC J6W 6H8

Tél: 450-765-2012; Téléc: 450-765-2025
www.maneige.ski

www.facebook.com/skiqc
twitter.com/assq_maneige

Aperçu: *Dimension:* moyenne; *Envergure:* provinciale; *Organisme sans but lucratif; fondée en 1979*
Description: Représenter et défendre les intérêts des membres; favoriser la pratique du ski alpin; améliorer la qualité du produit ainsi que la performance des stations
Membre(s) du bureau directeur: Yves Juneau, Président-directeur général
Membre: 75 stations de ski
Activités: *Listes de destinataires:* Oui

British Columbia Alpine Ski Association
#403, 1788 West Broadway, Vancouver BC V6J 1Y1

Tel: 604-678-3070; Fax: 604-678-8073
office@bcalpine.com
www.bcalpine.com
www.facebook.com/bcalpine
twitter.com/bcalpine

Overview: A small provincial organization
Description: To promote the sport of alpine skiing in British Columbia
Chief Officer(s): Anders Hestdalen, General Manager, 604-678-3073
andersh@bcalpine.com
Membership: 35 ski clubs; *Fees:* Schedule available

Canadian Association of Nordic Ski Instructors (CANSI) / Association canadienne des moniteurs de ski nordique
c/o Secrétariat, 164, rue Adrien-Robert, Gatineau QC J8Y 3S2

Tel: 819-360-6700; Fax: 819-776-0017
office@cansi.ca
cansi.ca
www.facebook.com/162657427089855

Overview: A small national organization founded in 1976
Description: To promote & advance cross-country & Telemark skiing in Canada, establishing standards & offering levels of certification in technique & training
Chief Officer(s): Denys Lawrence, President
president@cansi.ca
Fees: Schedule available; *Member Profile:* Completed Level I Cross Country or Telemark course; *Committees:* Technical
Activities: Providing resources to instuctors; Liaising nationally & internationally with the Nordic disciplines; Coordinating national level courses

Canadian Masters Cross-Country Ski Association (CMCSA) / Association canadienne des maîtres en ski de fond
2 MacNeil Cres., Stephenville NL A2N 3E3

Tel: 709-643-3259
canadian-masters-xc-ski.ca

Overview: A medium-sized national organization founded in 1980
Description: To promote Masters cross-country skiing across Canada, establish rules & regulations for activities & representing members at meetings at the WMA
Affiliation(s): World Masters Cross-Country Ski Association; Cross-Country Canada
Chief Officer(s): Bruce Legrow, National Director
bruce.legrow@nf.sympatico.ca
Finances: *Funding Sources:* Membership fees
Fees: $20; $35 in Québec; *Member Profile:* 30 years of age & over
Activities: Cross country ski races in Canada & abroad; Masters World Cup; Canadian Masters National Championships

Canadian Ski Council (CSC) / Conseil canadien du ski
#14, 76000 Hwy. 27, Woodbridge ON L4H 0P8

Toll-Free: 877-736-1117
help@skicanada.org
www.skicanada.org
www.instagram.com/canadian_ski_council
www.facebook.com/GoSkiingGoSnowboarding
twitter.com/cdnskicouncil

Overview: A medium-sized national organization founded in 1977
Description: To encourage participation in recreational skiing & snowboarding.; *Member of:* Canadian Society of Association Executives; Tourism Industry Association of Canada.
Affiliation(s): Canadian Association for Disabled Skiing; Canadian Ski Instructors' Alliance; Canadian Ski Patrol; Canadian Association of Snowboard Instructors; Association des stations de ski du Québec; Atlantic Ski Area Association; Canadian Snowsports Association; Canada West Ski Areas Association; Ontario Snow Resorts Associations
Chief Officer(s): Paul Pinchbeck, President & CEO
ppinchbeck@skicanada.org
Finances: *Funding Sources:* Sponsorship; associate membership; service fees; research
Membership: 11 organizations; *Committees:* Marketing & Research; Toronto Snow Show
Activities: Skier Development Programs; product development; research; *Speaker Service:* Yes; *Rents Mailing List:* Yes

Canadian Ski Instructors' Alliance (CSIA) / Alliance des moniteurs de ski du Canada
#401, 8615, boul Saint-Laurent, Montréal QC H2P 2M9

Tel: 514-748-2648; Fax: 514-748-2476
Toll-Free: 800-811-6428
national@snowpro.com
www.snowpro.com
www.youtube.com/user/CSIAAMSC
www.facebook.com/CSIAAMSC
twitter.com/csiaamsc

Overview: A large national organization founded in 1938
Description: To promote professionalism & high standards for the profession of ski instruction; To certify ski instructors across Canada; *Member of:* Canadian Ski Council
Affiliation(s): International Ski Instructors' Association
Chief Officer(s): Perry Schmunk, Managing Director
pschmunk@snowpro.com
Lisa Cambise, Director, Shared Services
lisa@snowpro.com
Jeff Marks, Director, National Programs
jmarks@snowpro.com
Finances: *Funding Sources:* Membership dues
Staff: 15 staff member(s)
Activities: Providing education & leadership that contributes to a vibrant mountain experience for the skiing public; *Internships:* Yes

Canadian Ski Marathon (CSM) / Marathon canadien de ski (MCS)
266, rue Viger, Papineauville QC J0V 1R0

Tel: 819-483-0456; Fax: 819-483-0450
Toll-Free: 877-770-6556
info@skimarathon.ca
skimarathon.ca
www.youtube.com/user/csmmcs
www.facebook.com/csmmcs
twitter.com/csmmcs

Overview: A medium-sized national charitable organization founded in 1967
Description: To organize an annual & fully supported weekend in the wilderness; To provide a cross-country skiing event with a broad appeal
Affiliation(s): Tourisme Outaouais; Tourisme Laurentides
Chief Officer(s): Sylvain Parent, President
Frédéric Ménard, Director, Events
Finances: *Annual Operating Budget:* $250,000-$500,000; *Funding Sources:* Sponsors; participants
Staff: 3 staff member(s); 500 volunteer(s)
Membership: 2,000; *Fees:* Schedule available
Activities: Cross-Country Ski Tour; *Internships:* Yes

Canadian Ski Patrol (CSP) / Patrouille canadienne de ski (PCS)
c/o House of Sport, 2451 Riverside Dr., Ottawa ON K1H 7X7

Tel: 613-822-2245; Fax: 613-822-1088
Toll-Free: 900-565-2777
info@skipatrol.ca
www.csps.ca
www.facebook.com/CSP.PCS
twitter.com/CdnSkiPatrol

Overview: A medium-sized national charitable organization founded in 1940

Description: To provide first aid & safety programs throughout Canada; *Member of:* Fédération Internationale des Patrouilles de Ski (FIPS) / International Federation of Ski Patrollers
Chief Officer(s): Renée Thivierge, National Manager, 613-822-2245 2140
renee.thivierge@skipatrol.ca
Finances: *Funding Sources:* Sponsorships; Donations
Membership: 4,500; *Member Profile:* Volunteer patrollers, over the age of eighteen, who have undergone training sessions in first aid & rescue; *Committees:* Communications; Fund Development; Education; Finance & Administration; Operations
Activities: Patrolling over 200 resorts across Canada on alpine, Nordic, & tele-mark skis, as well as on snow boards; Providing year-round safety & rescue services by volunteering at non-skiing events during the summer; Presenting awards; Providing first aid training; *Awareness Events:* National First Aid Competition

Canadian Snowsports Association (CSA) / L'Association canadienne des sports d'hiver (ACSH)
#265, 1177 West Broadway, Vancouver BC V6H 1G3
Tel: 604-734-6800; *Fax:* 604-669-7954
info@canadiansnowsports.com
canadiansnowsports.com
Previous Name: Canadian Ski & Snowboard Association; Canadian Ski Association
Overview: A large national organization founded in 1920
Description: To develop elite amateur athletes; To pursue excellence at national & international level competition
Chief Officer(s): David Pym, Managing Director
dpym@isrm.com
Lillian Alderton, Administrator
lillianalderton@hotmail.com
Membership: 700+ ski clubs + 97,000 members

Centre de plein air du Mont Chalco
CP 173, 264, rte 167, Chibougamau QC G8P 2K6
Tél: 418-748-7162; *Téléc:* 418-748-4685
info@montchalco.ca
www.montchalco.ca
Aperçu: *Dimension:* petite; *Envergure:* locale

Cross Country British Columbia (CCBC)
#106, 3003 - 30th St., Vernon BC V1T 9J5
Tel: 250-545-9600; *Fax:* 250-545-9614
office@crosscountrybc.ca
www.crosscountrybc.ca
www.facebook.com/829014633823512
Also Known As: Cross Country BC
Overview: A small provincial organization
Description: To govern cross country skiing in BC; *Member of:* Cross Country Canada
Chief Officer(s): Wannes Luppens, Executive Director
wannes@crosscountrybc.ca
Dennis Wu, Coordinator, Administration & Communications
Membership: 14,000

Cross Country New Brunswick / Ski de fond Nouveau-Brunswick
c/o Claudette Kavanaugh, 1421 Hwy. 130, Grand Sault NB E3Z 1P8
Tel: 506-475-5602
nbxcski@gmail.com
www.xcski-nb.ca
www.facebook.com/nbskiteam
Overview: A medium-sized provincial organization
Description: To promote cross country skiing among the general population of New Brunswick; To provide a sense of leadership; To offer a variety of programs & services; *Member of:* Cross Country Canada
Chief Officer(s): Claudette Kavanaugh, Directrice générale

Cross Country NL
c/o Gerry Rideout, 301 Curtis Cres., Labrador City NL A2V 2B8
Tel: 709-944-5842
crosscountrynl.com
www.facebook.com/teamxcnl
twitter.com/XCNLcoach
Overview: A medium-sized provincial organization
Chief Officer(s): Gerry Rideout, President
rideoutg@crrstv.net

Cross Country Nova Scotia (CCSNS)
NS
Tel: 902-225-8545
ccns@sportnovascotia.ca
crosscountryns.ca
www.instagram.com/ccnovascotia
www.facebook.com/CrossCountryNS
twitter.com/CrossCountryNS
Previous Name: Nordic Ski Nova Scotia

Overview: A medium-sized provincial organization founded in 1968
Description: To promote & encourage the sport / recreation of cross-country skiing; To provide & maintain rules & regulations in the province; To encourage & foster general public support of the activities & programs of CCSNS; To provide a resource centre for the membership & the general public; To select & train members of the provincial team to represent the province; *Member of:* Cross Country Canada
Chief Officer(s): John Cameron, President
Membership: 200; *Fees:* Schedule available

Cross Country NWT
PO Box 1916, Yellowknife NT X1A 2P4
Tel: 867-445-5855
nwtski@gmail.com
nwtski.com
Overview: A small provincial organization
Member of: Cross Country Canada

Cross Country PEI
PO Box 532, Souris PE C0A 2B0
nordiqcanada.ca/about/divisions
Overview: A small provincial organization
Description: To govern cross country skiing in PEI; *Member of:* Cross Country Canada
Chief Officer(s): Steve O'Brien, Contact
srobrien@eastlink.ca

Cross Country Saskatchewan (CCS)
1860 Lorne St., Regina SK S4P 2L7
Tel: 306-780-9240; *Fax:* 306-780-9462
ccs@sasktel.net
www.crosscountrysask.ca
www.instagram.com/crosscountrysask_hp
www.facebook.com/CrossCountrySaskHP
twitter.com/XCSask
Overview: A small provincial organization
Description: To develop & support competitive & recreational cross country skiing programs throughout Saskatchewan; *Member of:* Sask Ski Association; Sask Sport; Cross Country Canada
Chief Officer(s): Alana Ottenbreit, Executive Director
Finances: *Annual Operating Budget:* $100,000-$250,000
Staff: 1 staff member(s)
Membership: 26 clubs; *Fees:* Schedule available; *Member Profile:* Skiing clubs with at least 10 members

Cross Country Ski Association of Manitoba (CCSAM)
Sport for Life Centre, 145 Pacific Ave., Winnipeg MB R3B 2Z6
Tel: 204-925-5639; *Fax:* 204-925-5703
info@ccsam.ca
www.ccsam.ca
www.facebook.com/ccski
twitter.com/xcountryskimb
Overview: A small provincial organization
Description: To promote & develop cross country skiing in Manitoba; *Member of:* Cross Country Canada
Affiliation(s): Sport Manitoba
Chief Officer(s): Karin McSherry, Executive Director

Cross Country Ski Ontario
c/o Liz Inkila, 738 River St., Thunder Bay ON P7A 3S8
Tel: 807-768-4617
admin@xcskiontario.ca
xcskiontario.ca
www.instagram.com/xcskiontario
www.facebook.com/xcskiontario
twitter.com/xcskiontario
Overview: A medium-sized provincial organization
Description: To govern the sport of cross country skiing in Ontario; *Member of:* Cross Country Canada
Chief Officer(s): Liz Inkila, Director, Administration

Cross Country Yukon (CCY)
4061 - 4th Ave., Whitehorse YT Y1A 1H1
Tel: 867-334-9220
crosscountryyukon.com
Previous Name: Yukon Ski Division
Overview: A medium-sized provincial organization founded in 1985
Description: To develop cross country skiing in the Yukon; *Member of:* Cross Country Canada
Chief Officer(s): Alain Masson, Sport Coordinator & Head Coach
xcyukon@gmail.com
Finances: *Annual Operating Budget:* $100,000-$250,000; *Funding Sources:* Yukon territorial government; Yukon Lotteries; fundraising
Staff: 2 staff member(s); 200 volunteer(s)

Membership: 900 + 17 clubs; *Fees:* Schedule available; *Committees:* Events & Technical; High Performance; Leadership Development; Youth Development
Activities: Clinic courses include: coaching; ski trail design; trail grooming; avalanche awareness; jackrabbit leader course; backcountry; ski patrol

Fédération québécoise de la montagne et de l'escalade (FQME)
4545, av Pierre-de Coubertin, Montréal QC H1V 0B2
Tél: 514-252-3004; *Téléc:* 514-252-3201
Ligne sans frais: 866-204-3763
operations@fqme.qc.ca
www.fqme.qc.ca

www.facebook.com/FQMEescalade
twitter.com/Escalade_FQME
Aperçu: *Dimension:* petite; *Envergure:* provinciale; *Organisme sans but lucratif; fondée en 1969*
Description: Regrouper les adeptes de l'escalade et de l'alpinisme au Québec; promouvoir l'escalade (rocher et glace) et le ski de l'alpinisme et de randonnée en montagne; promouvoir une pratique sécuritaire de ces activités; protéger et rendre accessibles les différents sites d'escalade et de grande randonnée à skis au Québec; *Membre de:* Canadian Avalanche Association; Outdoor Recreation Coalition of America (ORCA)
Affiliation(s): Union internationale des associations d'alpinisme
Membre(s) du bureau directeur: André St-Jacques, Directeur des opérations, 514-252-3000 3406
Finances: *Budget de fonctionnement annuel:* $100,000-$250,000
Membre: 2 000; *Montant de la cotisation:* Barème; *Comités:* Formation; Site; Expédition
Activités: Amateur d'activités montagnes; *Stagiaires:* Oui
Bibliothèque: Centre de documentation rendez-vous

Freestyle Alberta
88 Canada Olympic Rd., Calgary AB T3B 5R5
Tel: 403-297-2718; *Fax:* 403-202-2522
hello@freestylealberta.ski
freestylealberta.ski
www.facebook.com/AlbertaFreestyleSkiingAssociation
twitter.com/ABFreestyleSki
Previous Name: Alberta Freestyle Ski Association
Overview: A small provincial charitable organization founded in 1990
Description: To develop & coordinate the sport of freestyle skiing in Alberta
Chief Officer(s): Jared Sayers, Chair
Dan Jefferies, Treasurer
djefferies@bdo.ca
Susan Moffatt, Executive Director
Finances: *Funding Sources:* Sponsorships
Fees: Schedule available; *Member Profile:* Athletes, coaches, officials & volunteers
Activities: Promoting freestyle skiing at all levels in Alberta; Supporting the high performance Alberta Mogul Team & the Alberta Park & Pipe Team; Offering judges' clinics

Freestyle BC
205 Kicking Horse Pl., Vernon BC V1B 4E8
Tel: 604-398-8830
info@freestylebc.ski
freestylebc.ski
www.facebook.com/BCFreestyleSkiAssociation
twitter.com/bcfreestyle
Previous Name: British Columbia Freestyle Ski Association
Overview: A small provincial organization
Description: To develop, promote & coordinate the sport of freestyle skiing in British Columbia
Chief Officer(s): Adrian Taggart, President

Freestyle Canada
808 Pacific St., Vancouver BC V6Z 1C2
Tel: 604-714-2233; *Fax:* 604-714-2232
info@freestylecanada.ski
www.freestylecanada.ski
www.youtube.com/c/FreestyleCanada
www.linkedin.com/company/freestylecanada
www.facebook.com/freestylecanada
twitter.com/canfreestyleski
Previous Name: Canadian Freestyle Ski Association (CFSA)
Overview: A medium-sized national organization
Description: To develop the sport within Canada; To represent Canada internationally; To promote the safe development of the sport; To promote excellence in national & international competitions
Affiliation(s): Canadian Ski & Snowboard Association
Chief Officer(s): Peter Judge, Chief Executive Officer
peter@freestylecanada.ski

Finances: *Annual Operating Budget:* $500,000-$1.5 Million; *Funding Sources:* Government of Canada; Canadian Olympic Committee; Own the Podium
Activities: *Rents Mailing List:* Yes

Freestyle Manitoba
145 Pacific Ave., Winnipeg MB R3B 2Z6
Tel: 204-795-9754
info@freestylemanitoba.ski
freestylemanitoba.ski
www.facebook.com/freestylemanitoba
Previous Name: Manitoba Freestyle Ski Association
Overview: A small provincial organization
Description: To promote the sport of freestyle skiing in Manitoba
Chief Officer(s): Steve Carpenter, President
president@mbfreestyle.com

Freestyle Saskatchewan
SK
freestylesaskatchewan.ski@gmail.com
freestylesaskatchewan.ski
twitter.com/skfreestyleski
Previous Name: Saskatchewan Freestyle Ski Incorporated
Overview: A small provincial organization
Description: To run programs developed by the Canadian Freestyle Ski Association
Chief Officer(s): Kim Ryan, President
kimeryan64@gmail.com

Freestyle Skiing Nova Scotia (FSNS)
5516 Spring Garden Rd., 4th Fl., Halifax NS B3J 1G6
Tel: 902-425-5450; *Fax:* 902-425-5606
alpinens@sportnovascotia.ca
freestylenovascotia.ca
www.facebook.com/1510479565896482
Also Known As: Freestyle Nova Scotia
Overview: A small provincial organization
Description: To govern the sport of freestyle skiing in Nova Scotia; *Member of:* Alpine Ski Nova Scotia
Chief Officer(s): Lorraine Burch, Executive Director

Freestyle Skiing Ontario (FSO)
213 Sterling Rd., Toronto ON M6R 2B2
Tel: 416-238-7604; *Toll-Free:* 877-578-6581
info@freestyleontario.ski
freestyleontario.ski
www.linkedin.com/company/freestyle-ontario
www.facebook.com/freestyleskiingontario
Also Known As: Freestyle Ontario
Overview: A small provincial organization
Description: To direct the sport of freestyle skiing in Ontario
Chief Officer(s): Jeff Ord, Executive Director, 416-238-7604 700
jefford@ontariofreestyle.com

Nakiska Alpine Ski Association (NASA)
Stn. PO Box 68080, RPO Crowfoot, Calgary AB T3G 3N8
Tel: 403-613-5935
info@skinasa.org
www.skinasa.org
Overview: A small local organization founded in 2009
Description: To introduce as many athletes as possible to the sport of alpine ski racing; To create the best alpine development system in Canada
Chief Officer(s): Scott Zahn, Director, Program & Technical szahn@skinasa.ca
Membership: 6 clubs + 300 individual

National Winter Sports Association (NWSA)
c/o Cross Country Canada, Bill Warren Training Centre, #100, 1995 Olympic Way, Canmore AB T1W 2T6
Tel: 403-678-6791; *Fax:* 403-678-3885
Toll-Free: 877-609-3215
info@nordiqcanada.ca
nordiqcanada.ca
www.instagram.com/nordiqcanada
www.facebook.com/NordiqCanada
twitter.com/NordiqCanada
Overview: A small national organization founded in 2007
Description: To provide financial assistance to cross country ski coaches, athletes & racing programs across Canada; *Member of:* Cross Country Canada
Chief Officer(s): Stéphane Barrette, Director, Coach & Athlete Development
sbarrette@nordiqcanada.ca

Nordic Combined Ski Canada (NCSC)
#265, 1177 West Broadway, Vancouver BC V6H 1G3
Tel: 605-250-1875
info@nordiccombinedskicanada.com
nordiccombinedskicanada.com
Overview: A small national organization

Description: To be the national governing body for the sport of ski jumping in Canada, alongside Ski Jumping Canada
Affiliation(s): Ski Jumping Canada
Chief Officer(s): Jim Woolsey, Chair
Nicolay Petrov, Director, High Performance

Nordiq Alberta
Percy Page Centre, 11759 Groat Rd., Edmonton AB T5M 3K6
Tel: 780-415-1738; *Fax:* 780-427-0524
nordiqalberta.ca
www.instagram.com/nordiqalberta
www.facebook.com/NordiqAlberta
Previous Name: Cross Country Alberta
Overview: A medium-sized provincial organization
Description: To lead, develop & promote the sport of cross-country skiing througout Alberta; *Member of:* Cross Country Canada
Chief Officer(s): Jo Wolach, Chair
jo@xsitra.com
Michael Neary, Manager, Sport
Laura Filipow, Coordinator, Programs
cca@xcountryab.net
Membership: 3,890; *Fees:* $11 child; $13 youth; $18 adult; $100 club
Activities: Quality service; leadership & skier development; management & education

Nordiq Canada
Bill Warren Training Centre, #100, 1995 Olympic Way, Canmore AB T1W 2T6
Tel: 403-678-6791; *Fax:* 403-678-3885
Toll-Free: 877-609-3215
info@nordiqcanada.ca
nordiqcanada.ca
www.instagram.com/nordiqcanada
www.facebook.com/NordiqCanada
twitter.com/NordiqCanada
Previous Name: Cross Country Canada
Overview: A medium-sized national charitable organization
Description: To develop & deliver programs designed to achieve international excellence in cross-country skiing; To provide national programs for continuous development of cross-country skiing from introductory experience to international excellence, for participants of all ages & abilities, fostering the principles of ethical conduct & fair play; *Member of:* True Sport
Affiliation(s): Canadian Ski & Snowboard Association
Chief Officer(s): Jennifer Tomlinson, Chair
boardchair@nordiqcanada.ca
Stéphane Barrette, Acting Chief Executive Officer, 514-684-4453
sbarrette@nordiqcanada.ca
Mike Edwards, Director, High Performance Para-Nordic, 403-678-6791 35
medwards@cccski.com
Thomas Holland, Director, High Performance, 403-678-6791 37
tholland@cccski.com
Finances: *Annual Operating Budget:* $500,000-$1.5 Million
Staff: 25 staff member(s)
Membership: 60,000; *Committees:* Women's; Events; High Performance; Coach & Athlete Development; Fundraising; Communications
Activities: *Internships:* Yes

Ontario Track 3 Ski Association for the Disabled
#4, 61 Advance Rd., Toronto ON M8Z 2S6
Tel: 416-233-3872; *Fax:* 416-233-7862
Toll-Free: 877-308-7225
track3@track3.org
www.track3.org
www.facebook.com/OntarioTrack3
twitter.com/OntarioTrack3
Also Known As: Track 3
Overview: A small provincial charitable organization founded in 1972
Description: To discover ability through the magic of snow sports.
Chief Officer(s): Naomi Schafler, Executive Director
Activities: *Speaker Service:* Yes

Patrouille de ski St-Jean
651, 6e rue ouest, Chibougamau QC G8P 2T8
Tél: 418-748-7162
Aperçu: *Dimension:* petite; *Envergure:* locale
Membre(s) du bureau directeur: Fabien Belleau, Président, 418-770-8447
Sébastien d'Amboise, Vice-Président, 418-809-6059

Prince Edward Island Alpine Ski Association
c/o Sport PEI, 40 Enman Cres., Charlottetown PE C1E 1E6
Tel: 902-368-4110; *Fax:* 902-368-4548
Toll-Free: 800-247-6712
sports@sportpei.pe.ca
www.sportpei.pe.ca

Overview: A medium-sized provincial organization

Ski de fond Québec
#19, 200, rue Principale, Saint-Sauveur QC J0R 1R0
Tél: 450-745-0858
info@skidefondquebec.ca
www.skidefondquebec.ca
www.facebook.com/skidefondquebec
Aperçu: *Dimension:* petite; *Envergure:* provinciale
Membre de: Cross Country Canada
Membre(s) du bureau directeur: Claude Alexandre Carpentier, Directeur général
dg@skidefondquebec.ca

Ski Hawks Ottawa (SHO)
Canadian Association for Disabled Skiing - National Capital Division, 1216 Bordeau Grove, Ottawa ON K1C 2M7
Tel: 613-222-7718
www.cads-ncd.ca/?page_id=183
Overview: A small local charitable organization founded in 1985
Description: To promote safe & enjoyable skiing & boarding experiences for the visually impaired community; *Member of:* Canadian Association of Disabled Skiing - National Capital Division (CADS-NCD)
Chief Officer(s): Carolyn Mitrow, President
cmitrow@gmail.com
Finances: *Annual Operating Budget:* Less than $50,000; *Funding Sources:* Private; Registration fees
Staff: 55 volunteer(s)
Membership: 1,000+; *Fees:* $30; *Member Profile:* Visually impaired skiers & snowboarders, aged 8 to 88, in all ability levels
Activities: Offering an alpine ski program for children, adults & seniors

Ski Jumping Canada (SJC) / Canada Saut à Ski
#418, 305 - 4625 Varsity Dr. NW, Calgary AB T3A 0Z9
skijumpingcanada.com
www.facebook.com/SkiJumpingCanada
Overview: A small national organization
Description: To be the national governing body for the sport of ski jumping in Canada, alongside Nordic Combined Ski Canada
Chief Officer(s): Todd Stretch, Chair
tstretch@skijumpingcanada.com

Ski Québec alpin (SQA)
4545, av Pierre-de Coubertin, Montréal QC H1V 3R2
Tél: 514-252-3089; *Téléc:* 514-252-5282
communications@skiquebec.qc.ca
www.skiquebec.qc.ca
www.instagram.com/skiquebecalpin
www.facebook.com/SkiQuebecAlpin
twitter.com/SkiQuebecAlpin
Également appelé: Cross Country Québec
Aperçu: *Dimension:* moyenne; *Envergure:* provinciale; *fondée en 1967*
Description: De développer, supporter et encourager l'excellence, et ce, à tous les niveaux de la structure de développement du ski alpin compétitif québécois; *Membre de:* Cross Country Canada
Membre(s) du bureau directeur: Daniel Paul Lavallée, Directeur général, 514-252-3089 3564
daniel@skiquebec.qc.ca
Éric Préfontaine, Directeur, Haute Performance, 514-252-3089 3621
eprefontaine@skiquebec.qc.ca
Sylvie Grenier, Responsable, Services comptables, 514-252-3089 3565
comptabilite@skiquebec.qc.ca
Eric Aach, Responsable, Communications et du service aux partenaires, 514-252-3090
communications@skiquebec.qc.ca

Whitehorse Cross Country Ski Club
#200, 1 Sumanik Dr., Whitehorse YT Y1A 6J6
Tel: 867-668-4477
info.xcskiwhitehorse@gmail.com
www.xcskiwhitehorse.ca
Overview: A small provincial organization
Description: To maintain high-quality ski trails & facilities, maintain a safe environment, ensure the long-term viability of the club & secure land tenure for the Yukon's trail system.
Chief Officer(s): Miriam Lukszova, Club Manager
Jan Polivka, Operations Manager
grooming.xcskiwhitehorse@gmail.com
Fees: Schedule available

Yukon Freestyle Ski Association (YFSA)
#104, 114 Titanium Way, Whitehorse YT Y1A 5P8
Tel: 867-689-8441
yukonfreeski@gmail.com
www.yukonfreestyleski.com
www.facebook.com/yukonfreestyleski
Also Known As: Yukon Freestyle
Overview: A small provincial organization
Description: To promote & facilitate freestyle skiing in Yukon;
Member of: Sport Yukon

Skipping

Canadian Rope Skipping Federation (CRSF)
c/o Bonnie Popov, General Manager, 906 County Rd. 46, RR#3,
Essex ON N8M 2X7
info@ropeskippingcanada.com
www.ropeskippingcanada.com
twitter.com/RopeSkippingCA
Also Known As: Rope Skipping Canada (RSC)
Previous Name: Canadian Skipping Association
Overview: A small national organization
Description: To promote rope skipping as a fitness &
recreational activity, as well as a competitive sport
Chief Officer(s): Bonnie Popov, General Manager
registrar@ropeskippingcanada.com
Fees: $7 recreational; $10 administrative; $20 full; $230 club

Snowboarding

Alberta Snowboard Association (ASA)
Bob Niven Training Centre, Bldg. 140, #108, 88 Canada Olympic
Rd. SW, Calgary AB T3B 5R5
Tel: 403-247-5609
admin@albertasnowboarding.com
www.albertasnowboarding.com
www.instagram.com/albertasnowboard
www.facebook.com/albertaSnowboardingAssociation
twitter.com/AB_Snowboard
Also Known As: Alberta Snowboarding
Overview: A small provincial organization
Description: To be the provincial governing body of competitive
snowboarding in Alberta; *Member of:* Canadian Snowboard
Federation
Chief Officer(s): Stacey Hicks, Executive Director,
403-618-7466
Fees: $35 basic; $100 competitive

Association of Ontario Snowboarders (AOS)
#203, 4 - 115 First St., Collingwood ON L9Y 4W3
Tel: 705-446-1488
aos@ontariosnowboarders.ca
www.ontariosnowboarders.ca
Also Known As: Snowboard Ontario (SO)
Overview: A small provincial organization founded in 1998
Description: To be the governing body for the sport of
competitive snowboarding in Ontario; *Member of:* Canadian
Snowboard Federation
Affiliation(s): Women's Snowboard Federation
Chief Officer(s): Janet Richter, Executive Director,
705-446-1488
janetrichter@ontariosnowboarders.ca

Association Québec Snowboard (AQS) / Québec Snowboard Association
4545, av Pierre-de-Coubertin, Montréal QC H1V 0B2
Tél: 514-621-4600
evenementsquebecsnowboard.ca
quebecsnowboard.ca

www.facebook.com/AssociationQuebecSnowboard
twitter.com/aqsnowboard
Aperçu: *Dimension:* petite; *Envergure:* provinciale
Membre de: Canadian Snowboard Federation
Membre(s) du bureau directeur: Patrick Lussier, Président

British Columbia Snowboard Association (BCSB)
PO Box 2040, Kelowna BC V1X 4K5
Tel: 250-442-6928
admin@bcsnowboard.com
bcsnowboard.com
www.instagram.com/bcsnowboard
www.facebook.com/BCSnowboardAssociation
twitter.com/bcsnowboard
Also Known As: BC Snowboard
Overview: A small provincial organization

Description: To support snowboard athletes, coaches & officials
in the province of British Columbia; *Member of:* Canadian
Snowboard Federation
Chief Officer(s): Cathy Astofooroff, Executive Director,
250-442-6928
cathy@bcsnowboard.com
Fees: $30-$250
Activities: Riglet; Riders; Women's Snowboard; Aboriginal
Snowboard; Para-Snowboard; Officials; Coaches; Judges

Canadian Association of Snowboard Instructors (CASI) / Association canadienne des moniteurs de surf des neiges (ACMS)
#201, 186 Hurontario St., Collingwood ON L9Y 4T4
Tel: 519-624-6593; *Fax:* 519-624-6594
Toll-Free: 877-976-2274
headoffice@casi-acms.com
casi-acms.com
www.instagram.com/casiacms
www.facebook.com/CASIACMS
Overview: A medium-sized national licensing organization
founded in 1994
Description: To promote snowboarding, snowboard instruction
& the professions of snowboard teaching in Canada; To maintain
a national standard of safe & efficient snowboard instruction;
Member of: Canadian Ski Council
Affiliation(s): Canadian Ski Instructors Alliance; Canadian
Snowboard Federation
Chief Officer(s): Simon Holden, Executive Director
simon@casi-acms.com
Fees: $30 student; $52 associate; $104 regular; $163 affiliate;
Committees: Technical & Educational
Activities: Training & certifying snowboard instructors;
Internships: Yes; *Speaker Service:* Yes

Canadian Snowboard Federation
#708, 333 Terminal Ave., Vancouver BC V6A 4C1
Tel: 778-776- 935
info@canadasnowboard.ca
www.canadasnowboard.ca
www.youtube.com/user/CanadaSnowboardVideo
www.facebook.com/canadasnowboard
twitter.com/CanadaSnowboard
Also Known As: Canada~Snowboard
Overview: A medium-sized national organization
Description: To be the national governing body of competitive
snowboarding in Canada
Chief Officer(s): Dustin Heise, Executive Director
Jean-François Rapatel, Director, High Performance
jf.rapatel@canadasnowboard.ca
Activities: Freestyle; alpine; snowboardcross; para-snowboard

HeliCat Canada
PO Box 968, Revelstoke BC V0E 2S0
Tel: 250-837-5770
info@helicatcanada.com
www.helicatcanada.com
www.linkedin.com/company/helicat-canada-association
www.facebook.com/helicat.org
twitter.com/HeliCatCanada
Previous Name: BC Helicopter & Snowcat Skiing Operators
Association
Overview: A small provincial organization founded in 1975
Description: To promote growth of the helicat sector that is
economically, environmentally, & socially responsible; To
develop best practices in sustainability & safety; To advocate on
behalf of members; *Member of:* Council of Tourism Associations
BC; Wilderness Tourism Association
Chief Officer(s): Rob Rohn, President
Ross Cloutier, Executive Director
ed@helicatcanada.com
Fees: $25 individual; $200+ affiliate; $500+ associate; *Member
Profile:* Individuals & organizations who support responsible
development of helicopter & snowcat skiing in Canada;
Committees: Accreditation; Communication; Sustainability;
Policy

Manitoba Snowboard Association
15 Winterhaven Dr., Winnipeg MB R2N 4L2
Tel: 204-930-2724
info@manitobasnowboard.com
manitobasnowboard.com
twitter.com/MBSnowboard
Overview: A small provincial organization
Description: To be the provincial governing body of competitive
snowboarding in Manitoba; *Member of:* Canadian Snowboard
Federation
Chief Officer(s): Glenn Luff, Contact
gkluff@mymts.net

Newfoundland & Labrador Snowboard Association
PO Box 259, Steady Brook NL A2H 2N2
Tel: 709-634-4664
nlsnowboard@gmail.com
nlsnowboard.com
Also Known As: NL Snowboard
Overview: A small provincial organization
Description: To be the provincial governing body of competitive
snowboarding in Newfoundland & Labrador; *Member of:*
Canadian Snowboard Federation
Chief Officer(s): Emily Pittman, Contact

Prince Edward Island Snowboard Association
Charlottetown PE
Tel: 902-326-9305
www.facebook.com/SnowboardPEI
Also Known As: Snowboard PEI
Overview: A small provincial organization
Description: To be the provincial governing body of competitive
snowboarding in Prince Edward Island; *Member of:* Canadian
Snowboard Federation
Chief Officer(s): Zak Likely, Contact
zak.likely@gmail.com

Saskatchewan Snowboard Association (SSA)
1860 Lorne St., Regina SK S4P 2L7
Tel: 306-867-8489
info@sasksnowboard.ca
sasksnowboard.ca
www.facebook.com/238209089572128
twitter.com/sasksnowboard
Overview: A small provincial organization founded in 2001
Description: To be the provincial governing body of competitive
snowboarding in Saskatchewan; *Member of:* Canadian
Snowboard Federation
Chief Officer(s): Brent Larwood, President
brent@sasksnowboard.ca
Dave Woods, Coordinator, Sport Development
dave@sasksnowboard.ca
Fees: $20 support; $20 coach; $25 athlete

Snowboard Nova Scotia
#311, 5516 Spring Garden Rd., Halifax NS B3J 1G6
Tel: 902-425-5450; *Fax:* 902-425-5606
www.snowboardnovascotia.ca
www.facebook.com/SnowboardNovaScotia
Previous Name: Nova Scotia Snowboard Association
Overview: A small provincial organization
Description: To be the provincial governing body of competitive
snowboarding in Nova Scotia; *Member of:* Canadian Snowboard
Federation; Sport Nova Scotia
Chief Officer(s): Deb Maclean, President
Kristin d'Eon, Technical Director
kristin@snowboardnovascotia.ca
Andrew Hayes, Administrative Coordinator, Provincial Sport
Organization, 902-425-5450 370
ahayes@sportnovascotia.ca
Fees: $45

Snowboard Yukon
YT
info@snowboardyukon.com
www.snowboardyukon.com
Overview: A medium-sized provincial organization
Description: To organize & sanction events, train athletes &
coaches, form & administer teams for out of territory
competitions, & represent Yukon riders in the Canadian
Snowboard Federation.; *Member of:* Canadian Snowboard
Federation

Snowmobiles

Alberta Snowmobile Association (ASA)
11759 Groat Rd., Edmonton AB T5M 3K6
Tel: 780-427-2695; *Fax:* 780-415-1779
info@altasnowmobile.ab.ca
www.altasnowmobile.ab.ca
www.facebook.com/altasnowmobile
twitter.com/Altasnowmobile
Overview: A medium-sized provincial organization founded in
1971
Description: To promote safe recreational snowmobiling in the
province of Alberta; To establish and maintain quality
snowmobile trails
Affiliation(s): Canadian Council of Snowmobile Organizations
Chief Officer(s): Denise England, President
Fees: $60-$70

British Columbia Snowmobile Federation (BCSF)
PO Box 277, 18 - 1st St., Keremeos BC V0X 1N0
Tel: 250-499-5117; *Fax:* 250-499-2103
Toll-Free: 877-537-8716
office@bcsf.org
www.bcsf.org
www.instagram.com/bcsnowmobilefederation
www.facebook.com/BCSnowmobileFederation
twitter.com/BCSnowmobile
Overview: A medium-sized provincial organization founded in 1965
Description: To encourage & promote the sport of operating snowmobiles in BC by enhancing cooperation & communication between & among snowmobile clubs, recreation industry & racing divisions, the provincial government, other motorized recreational organizations & groups supportive of snowmobiling; *Member of:* Outdoor Recreation Council of British Columbia; Wilderness Tourism Association; BC Avalanche Association
Affiliation(s): International Snowmobile Council; Canadian Council of Snowmobile Organizations
Chief Officer(s): Richard Cronier, President
president@bcsf.org
Donegal Wilson, Executive Director
Finances: *Annual Operating Budget:* $50,000-$100,000; *Funding Sources:* Membership fees
Staff: 1 staff member(s); 70 volunteer(s)
Membership: 6,000 individual + 70 clubs; *Fees:* Schedule available; *Committees:* Trails; Charities; Safety; Environment; Government Relations; Snow Show
Activities: Tread Lightly Program; Safety Training Program; SnoVision 2000 Program; Exemplary Service Recognition Program; *Awareness Events:* Snowarama (charity ride); *Speaker Service:* Yes; *Rents Mailing List:* Yes

Canadian Council of Snowmobile Organizations (CCSO) / Conseil canadien des organismes de motoneige (CCOM)
PO Box 21059, Thunder Bay ON P7A 8A7
Tel: 807-345-5299
ccso.ccom@tbaytel.net
www.ccso-ccom.ca
www.facebook.com/126035004176384
twitter.com/ccsosnow
Overview: A large national organization founded in 1974
Description: To provide leadership & support to organized snowmobiling in Canada
Chief Officer(s): Dennis Burns, Executive Director
Activities: Promoting the welfare & betterment of snowmobile recreational activities; Cooperating with provincial & federal officials, other organizations, & the public on issues affecting snowbiles; Coordinating legislative activities; Promoting a code of ethics for snowmobiling; Completing the Trans-Canadian Snowmobile Trail; *Awareness Events:* National Safety Week, January; Take a Friend Snowmobiling Week, February

Club d'auto-neige Chibougamau inc.
CP 43, Chibougamau QC G8P 2K5
Tél: 418-748-3065
www.motoneigechibougamau.ca
Aperçu: *Dimension:* petite; *Envergure:* locale

Fédération des clubs de motoneigistes du Québec (FCMQ)
#101, 1027, boul des Enterprises, Terrebonne QC J6Y 1V2
Tél: 514-252-3076; *Téléc:* 514-254-2066
Ligne sans frais: 844-253-4343
info@fcmq.qc.ca
www.fcmq.qc.ca
www.youtube.com/channel/UCutLHcAv4Go0KhRSMCFbOeg
www.facebook.com/FCMQ40
Aperçu: *Dimension:* moyenne; *Envergure:* provinciale; *Organisme sans but lucratif; fondée en 1974*
Description: La Fédération des clubs de motoneigistes du Québec est un organisme à but non lucratif, voué au développement et à la promotion de la pratique de la motoneige dans tout le Québec
Membre(s) du bureau directeur: Mario Gagnon, Président
Finances: *Budget de fonctionnement annuel:* $3 Million-$5 Million
Personnel: 10 membre(s) du personnel; 3000 bénévole(s)
Membre: 228; *Montant de la cotisation:* 250$/club

Great Slave Snowmobile Association
PO Box 1082, Yellowknife NT X1A 2N8
gssatrailriders@gmail.com
gssatrailriders.com
www.facebook.com/GreatSlaveSnowmobileAssociation
Also Known As: GSSA Trail Riders
Overview: A small provincial organization founded in 1988
Description: To promote safe, responsible snowmobiling in Yellowknife

---

Affiliation(s): Canadian Council of Snowmobile Organizations; International Snowmobile Council
Chief Officer(s): Michael Arbuckle, President
Marg Hudder, Secretary-Treasurer
Finances: *Annual Operating Budget:* Less than $50,000
Staff: 6 volunteer(s)
Membership: 300 individual; *Fees:* $40 single; $60 family
Activities: Community fund-raising; clearing trails; adding signage along trail system

Klondike Snowmobile Association (KSA)
4061 - 4th Ave., Whitehorse YT Y1A 1H1
Tel: 867-667-7680
klonsnow@yknet.ca
www.ksa.yk.ca
www.facebook.com/253094448062816
Overview: A small local organization
Member of: Canadian Council of Snowmobile Organizations
Affiliation(s): Trans Canada Trail - Yukon
Chief Officer(s): Mark Daniels, President
mnd@northwestel.net
Membership: 500; *Fees:* $20 single; $30 family; $100 corporate

Ojibway Power Toboggan Association (OPTA)
PO Box 1466, Sioux Lookout ON P8T 1B9
Tel: 807-737-1976; *Fax:* 807-737-1722
www.opta.ca
Overview: A medium-sized provincial organization
Description: To keep snowmobile trails in the Sioux Lookout area in good condition and promote safe snowmobiling; *Member of:* North West Ontario Snowmobile Trails Association; Ontario Federation of Snowmobile Clubs; Sunset Country; Patricia Region Tourist Bureau
Chief Officer(s): Gail Sayers, President
president@opta.ca
Activities: Training courses; *Awareness Events:* Poker Derby; Snowmobile Raffle; Snowarama

Ontario Federation of Snowmobile Clubs (OFSC)
ON
marketing@ofsc.on.ca
www.ofsc.on.ca
www.instagram.com/gosnowmobilingontario
www.linkedin.com/company/ontario-federation-of-snowmobile-clubs
www.facebook.com/gosnowmobilingontario
twitter.com/GoSnowmobiling
Overview: A medium-sized provincial organization founded in 1966
Description: To support member snowmobile clubs & volunteers; To establish & maintain quality snowmobile trails; To further the enjoyment of organized snowmobiling; *Member of:* Canadian Council of Snowmobile Organizations
Finances: *Funding Sources:* Sale of trail permits; Donations; Sponsorships
Staff: 6 volunteer(s)
Membership: 231 clubs in 17 districts, consisting of 200,000 families; *Member Profile:* Ontario local snowmobile clubs
Activities: Setting policies & procedures; Providing advice to member clubs; Handling trail plans & issues; Promoting concern for the environment & safety; Campaigning to attract new participants

Saskatchewan Snowmobile Association (SSA)
PO Box 533, 221 Centre St., Regina Beach SK S0G 4C0
Tel: 306-729-3500; *Toll-Free:* 800-499-7533
sasksnow@sasktel.net
www.sasksnow.com
www.youtube.com/channel/UC5gfjL3DgXAl3Z7te4leEuA
www.facebook.com/sask.snow
twitter.com/sasksnow
Previous Name: Saskatchewan Snow Vehicles Association
Overview: A medium-sized provincial organization founded in 1971
Description: To promote the benefits of snowmobiling & increase access & participation; To provide leadership & support to members; To establish & maintain safe, high quality trails; To provide support to club development; *Member of:* International Snowmobile Council; Canadian Council of Snowmobile Organizations
Finances: *Funding Sources:* Membership dues; Saskatchewan Lotteries
Staff: 20 volunteer(s)
Membership: 5,000; *Fees:* Schedule available; *Committees:* Membership; Raffles; Rallies; Grants; Equipment; Safety; Trails

Snowmobilers Association of Nova Scotia (SANS)
5516 Spring Garden Rd., 4th Fl., Halifax NS B3J 3G6
Tel: 902-425-5450; *Fax:* 902-425-5606
www.snowmobilersns.com
Overview: A small provincial organization founded in 1976

Description: To provide leadership & support to member snowmobile clubs so that they may enjoy quality recreational snowmobiling opportunities on a province-wide network of safe & well-developed snowmobile trails
Chief Officer(s): Mike Eddy, General Manager, 902-425-5450 360
Martha Dunlop, Manager, Finance & Administration, 902-425-5450 324
Membership: 21 member clubs; *Member Profile:* Snowmobile clubs

Snowmobilers of Manitoba Inc.
2121 Henderson Hwy., Winnipeg MB R2G 1P8
Tel: 204-940-7533; *Fax:* 204-940-7531
info@snoman.mb.ca
www.snoman.mb.ca
www.facebook.com/SnomanInc
Also Known As: Snoman
Overview: A small provincial organization founded in 1975
Description: To provide strong leadership & support to member clubs; to develop & maintain safe & environmentally responsible snowmobile trails; to further the enjoyment of organized snowmobiling throughout Manitoba
Affiliation(s): Canadian Council of Snowmobile Organizations
Chief Officer(s): Yvonne Rideout, Executive Director
execdirector@snoman.mb.ca
Finances: *Annual Operating Budget:* $500,000-$1.5 Million
Staff: 2 staff member(s); 2500 volunteer(s)
Membership: 2,500; *Fees:* $150

Thunder Bay Adventure Trails
PO Box 29190, Thunder Bay ON P7B 6P9
Toll-Free: 800-526-7522
tbat_den@hotmail.com
www.tbattrails.com
www.facebook.com/226506510887339
Overview: A medium-sized local organization founded in 1990
Description: To groom & maintain over 300 kilometres of snowmobile trails in the Thunder Bay area; *Member of:* North Superior Snowmobile Association (NOSSA)
Chief Officer(s): Marcel Gauthier, Club Executive
Lloyd Chaykowski, Club Executive
Harold Harkonen, Club Executive
Fees: $190-before Nov.1; $220-before Dec.1; $270 after Dec.1; $150-classic-before Dec.1; $180 classic-after Dec.1

Soaring

Alberni Valley Soaring Association
8064 Richards Trail, Duncan BC V9L 6B2
Toll-Free: 866-590-7627
info@avsa.ca
www.avsa.ca
www.facebook.com/AlberniValleySoaringAssociation
Overview: A small local organization
Description: To offer opportunities to fly to its members & guests; *Member of:* Soaring Association of Canada
Affiliation(s): Vancouver Island Soaring Centre; Vancouver Soaring Association
Fees: Schedule available

Alberta Soaring Council
PO Box 13, Black Diamond AB T0L 0H0
Tel: 403-813-6658
asc@stade.ca
www.soaring.ab.ca
www.facebook.com/AlbertaSoaringCouncil
Overview: A medium-sized provincial organization founded in 1966
Description: To promote soaring sports provincially in all aspects; To plan & support local & provincial events & national competitions; *Member of:* Aero Club of Canada
Chief Officer(s): Phil Stade, Executive Director
asc@stade.ca
Membership: 5 member associations; *Committees:* ASCent; Equipment; Official Observer; Safety; Sporting; Towplane; Trophies
Activities: *Library:* Yes

Association de vol à voile Champlain
#10, 745 de Martigny, Montréal QC H2B 2N1
Tél: 450-771-0500
info@avvc.qc.ca
www.avvc.qc.ca
Aperçu: *Dimension:* petite; *Envergure:* locale; *Organisme sans but lucratif*
Description: Former des pilotes de planeur et les amener au niveau du vol voyage; répondre aux attentes de ses membres actifs; *Membre de:* Soaring Association of Canada
Montant de la cotisation: 620$

Base Borden Soaring (BBSG)
PO Box 286, Borden ON L0M 1C0

Tel: 705-424-1200
ourplace@csolve.net

Overview: A small local organization founded in 1974
Member of: Soaring Association of Canada
Fees: $50

Bonnechere Soaring Club
ON

Tel: 613-584-4636

Overview: A small local organization
Member of: Soaring Association of Canada

Central Alberta Gliding Club
Netook Airport, Olds AB

www.cagcsoaring.ca

Overview: A small local organization founded in 1989
Description: To train pilots for glider licences; To create opportunities for glider pilots to fly club-owned aircraft; *Member of:* Alberta Soaring Council; Innisfail Flying Club; Soaring Association of Canada
Chief Officer(s): Leo Deschamps, President
president@cagcsoaring.ca
Finances: *Funding Sources:* Membership dues

Club de vol à voile de Québec
CP 9276, Sainte-Foy QC G1V 4B1

Tél: 418-337-4905
www.cvvq.net

www.facebook.com/CVVQPlaneur
Aperçu: *Dimension:* petite; *Envergure:* locale; *fondée en 1954*
Description: Fournir une plate-forme d'opération sécuritaire pour la pratique de notre sport et d'offrir une formation de qualité à de nouveaux adeptes qui se joignent à nous
Membre(s) du bureau directeur: Pierre Bouchard, Président
Jean Provencher, Trésorier
Claudine Dorval, Agent, Communications
Montant de la cotisation: Barème; *Comités:* Aménagement; Planification de la flotte; Recrutement

Cu Nim Gliding Club
PO Box 17, #11, RR#1, Okotoks AB T1S 1A1

Tel: 403-200-2470
introflight@cunim.org
www.cunim.org
www.instagram.com/glidecunim
www.facebook.com/glidecunim

Overview: A small local organization
Description: To promote soaring and engage new members; *Member of:* Alberta Soaring Council; Soaring Association of Canada
Affiliation(s): Alberta Soaring Council
Chief Officer(s): Pablo Wainstein, President
Finances: *Annual Operating Budget:* $50,000-$100,000
Staff: 6 volunteer(s)
Membership: 60; *Fees:* $450

Edmonton Soaring Club (ESC)
Chipman AB

Tel: 780-363-3860
info@edmontonsoaringclub.com
www.edmontonsoaringclub.com

Overview: A small local organization founded in 1957
Description: To promote soaring & provide enthusiasts with the means to practice soaring; *Member of:* Alberta Soaring Council; Soaring Association of Canada
Affiliation(s): Alberta Soaring Council; other soaring clubs
Fees: Schedule available
Activities: Flying gliders; teaching how to fly; expeditions; social events

Erin Soaring Society
ON

Overview: A small local organization

Gatineau Gliding Club (GGC)
PO Box 8145, Stn. T, Ottawa ON K1G 3H6

Tel: 613-673-5386
ggc@gatineauglidingclub.ca
www.gatineauglidingclub.ca

Overview: A small local organization
Description: To promote gliding in Canada; *Member of:* Soaring Association of Canada
Membership: 100

Grande Prairie Soaring Society
PO Box 64, Hythe AB T0H 2C0

www.gpsoaringsociety.ca

Overview: A small local organization

Member of: Alberta Soaring Council; Soaring Association of Canada
Chief Officer(s): Dwayne Doll, President
dddoll.canada@gmail.com
Lloyd Sherk, Secretary-Treasurer
lsherk@telusplanet.net

London Soaring Club
315816 - 31st Line, Embro ON N0J 1J0

Tel: 519-661-7844
info@londonsoaringclub.ca
www.londonsoaringclub.ca
www.facebook.com/124146337603689
twitter.com/Londonsoaring

Overview: A small local organization
Member of: Soaring Association of Canada

Manitoba Soaring Council
200 Main St., Winnipeg MB R3C 4M2
www.wgc.mb.ca/static/msc/Manitoba_Soaring_Council_Home_P age.htm
Overview: A small provincial organization founded in 1970
Description: To foster the art of soaring as an environmentally friendly, safe & competitive life sport accessible to all Manitobans
Membership: 1,000-4,999

Montréal Soaring Council (MSC) / Club de Vol à Voile MSC
PO Box 147, Montréal QC H4L 4V4

Tel: 613-632-5438
info@montrealsoaring.ca
montrealsoaring.com
www.facebook.com/montrealsoaring
twitter.com/MontrealSoaring

Overview: A small local organization founded in 1946
Description: To promote the sport of soaring & gliding, including the provision of gliding training; *Member of:* Soaring Association of Canada
Chief Officer(s): Kurt Sermeus, Vice-President, 514-919-7374
Finances: *Annual Operating Budget:* $100,000-$250,000
Staff: 11 staff member(s); 30 volunteer(s)
Membership: 100; *Fees:* Schedule available; *Member Profile:* Open to individuals interested in soaring

Prince Albert Gliding & Soaring Club (PAG&SC)
219 Scissons Ct., Saskatoon SK S7S 1B7

Tel: 306-789-1535; *Fax:* 306-792-2532
soar@soar.sk.ca
www.soar.sk.ca/pagsc

Overview: A small local organization founded in 1986
Description: To foster the sport of soaring
Affiliation(s): Soaring Association of Saskatchewan; Soaring Association of Canada
Chief Officer(s): Keith Andrews, President, 306-249-1859
Finances: *Funding Sources:* Annual membership dues; Launch fees; Glider rental fees
Membership: 15; *Fees:* $85 youth; $170 regular
Activities: Promoting the sport of soaring; Providing flying activities; Offering flight instruction

Regina Gliding & Soaring Club
PO Box 4093, Regina SK S4P 3W5

Tel: 306-536-4119
fly@soar.regina.sk.ca
www.soar.regina.sk.ca

Overview: A small local organization
Member of: Soaring Association of Canada; soaring Association of Saskatchewan
Fees: $55-$390

Rideau Valley Soaring
PO Box 1164, Manotick ON K4M 1A9

Tel: 613-366-8208
club.pres@rvss.ca
rvss.ca
www.facebook.com/200156480081876
twitter.com/rvssca

Overview: A small local organization
Member of: Soaring Association of Canada
Affiliation(s): Gatineau Gliding Club; Montreal Soaring Club
Chief Officer(s): George Domaradzki, President & Chief Flight Instructor
club.pres@rvss.ca
Fees: $715 adult ($506 for additional spouse); $375 junior; $345 youth; $546 tow pilot/self launch

Saskatoon Soaring Club
510 Cynthia St., Saskatoon SK S7L 7K7

saskatoonsoaringclub@gmail.com
www.soar.sk.ca/ssc

Overview: A small local organization

Description: To promote the sport of gliding and soaring in Saskatoon.; *Member of:* Soaring Association of Canada

Soaring Association of Canada (SAC) / Association canadienne de vol à voile (ACVV)
c/o COPA National Office, #903, 75 Albert St., Ottawa ON K1P 5E7

Tel: 613-236-4901; *Fax:* 613-236-8646
sacoffice@sac.ca
www.sac.ca
twitter.com/canglide

Overview: A medium-sized national organization founded in 1945
Description: To promote, enhance & protect the sport of soaring in Canada; To provide information & services to the soaring community: licensing, medical requirements for glider pilots, aircraft certification, technical issues, courses & training, insurance plan & services to clubs
Affiliation(s): Aero Club of Canada; International Gliding Commission of the Fédération Aéronautique Internationale
Finances: *Funding Sources:* Membership fees; Sales; Donations
Staff: 40 volunteer(s)
Membership: 1,500 club affiliates; *Fees:* Schedule available; *Committees:* Air Cadets; Airspace; Archives / Historian; Contest Letters; FAI Awards; FAI Records; Fit Training & Safety; Free Flight; Insurance; Medical; Technical; Trophy Claims; World Contest; Flight Records
Activities: *Library:* Yes (Open to Public) by appointment

SOSA Gliding Club
PO Box 81, Rockton ON L0R 1X0

Tel: 519-740-9328
sosa@sosaglidingclub.com
www.sosaglidingclub.com
www.facebook.com/groups/2228522913
twitter.com/sosaglidingclub

Overview: A small local organization
Member of: Soaring Association of Canada

Toronto Soaring Club
ON

www.toronto-soaring.ca
www.facebook.com/TheTorontoSoaringClub

Overview: A small local organization
Member of: Soaring Association of Canada
Chief Officer(s): David Cole, President
dmcole1212@gmail.com

Vancouver Soaring Association
PO Box 3251, Vancouver BC V6B 3X9

Tel: 604-869-7211
vancouversoaring@gmail.com
vancouversoaring.com
www.flickr.com/photos/128138428@N03
www.facebook.com/148597568530530
twitter.com/vancouversoaring

Overview: A small local organization
Member of: Soaring Association of Canada

Winnipeg Gliding Club (WGC)
PO Box 1255, Winnipeg MB R3C 2Y4

Tel: 204-735-2868
info@wgc.mb.ca
www.wgc.mb.ca

Overview: A small local organization
Description: To promote gliding and soaring; *Member of:* Soaring Association of Canada
Membership: 70; *Fees:* $25-$450

York Soaring Association
Airfield, 7296, 5th Line, RR#1, Belwood ON N0B 1J0

Tel: 519-848-3621
www.yorksoaring.com
www.facebook.com/yorksa

Overview: A small local organization founded in 1961
Member of: Soaring Association of Canada
Chief Officer(s): Jim Fryett, President
Finances: *Annual Operating Budget:* $250,000-$500,000
Staff: 10 volunteer(s)
Membership: 100-499
Activities: Soaring & gliding facilities; advanced training of glider pilots

Soccer

Airdrie & District Soccer Association
Genesis Pl., 800 East Lake Blvd., Airdrie AB T4A 0H6

Tel: 403-948-6260; *Fax:* 403-948-6290
admin@airdriesoccer.com
airdriesoccer.com
www.facebook.com/airdriesoccerassociation

Overview: A small local organization
Member of: Alberta Soccer Association
Chief Officer(s): Steve Thomas, Technical Director
td@airdriesoccer.com
Juliet Smith, Office Manager/Registrar
manager@airdriesoccer.com
Fees: Schedule available

Alberta Soccer Association (ASA)
9023 - 111 Ave., Edmonton AB T5B 0C3
Tel: 780-474-2200; *Fax:* 780-474-6300
Toll-Free: 866-250-2200
office@albertasoccer.com
www.albertasoccer.com
www.youtube.com/SoccerAlberta
www.linkedin.com/company/alberta-soccer-association
twitter.com/AlbertaSoccer
Overview: A medium-sized provincial organization founded in
1909
Description: To govern & promote the sport of soccer in
Alberta; *Member of:* Canadian Soccer Association
Chief Officer(s): Shaun Lowther, Executive Director
execdir@albertasoccer.com
Darron Bunt, Coordinator, Competitions, 780-378-8107
competitions@albertasoccer.com
Carmen Charron, Coordinator, Programs, 780-378-8104
programs@albertasoccer.com
Tiana Squire, Coordinator, Communications, 780-378-8100
Rachel Appels, Coordinator, Office, 780-378-8101
Membership: 90,000; *Committees:* Constitution & By-Laws;
Technical; Competitions; Referee Development; Appeals &
Discipline; Development of Women in Soccer

Association de soccer du Sud-Ouest de Montréal (ASSOM)
5485, ch de la Côte-Saint-Paul, Montréal QC H4C 1X3
Tél: 514-931-7778
www.soccerassom.com
Aperçu: *Dimension:* petite; *Envergure: locale; fondée en 1999*
Membre(s) du bureau directeur: Azzeddine Baghdadi,
President

Australian Football League Ontario (AFLO)
The Exchange Tower, PO Box 99, #3680, 130 King St. West,
Toronto ON M5X 1B1
exec@aflontario.com
www.aflontario.com
www.facebook.com/AFLOntario
twitter.com/AFLOntario

Also Known As: AFL Ontario
Overview: A medium-sized provincial organization founded in
1989
Description: To organize amateur Australian football
competitions in Ontario & Québec.; *Member of:* AFL Canada
Chief Officer(s): Aaron Falcioni, President
president@aflontario.com
Barry Rooke, Treasurer
treasurer@aflontario.com
Jaclyn Halliday, Secretary
secretary@aflontario.com
Natalia Champagnie, Registrar
registrar@aflontario.com
Membership: 11 clubs

Battle River Soccer Association
PO Box 5558, Leduc AB T9E 2A1
Tel: 780-717-1962
admin@battleriversoccer.com
www.battleriversoccer.com
Overview: A small local organization founded in 1983
Description: Physical office address: Quality Inn, #116, 501 -
11th Ave., Nisku, AB T9E 7N5; *Member of:* Alberta Soccer
Association; Federation Internationale de Football Association;
Canada Soccer Association
Affiliation(s): Breton Soccer Association; Calmar Soccer
Association; Devon Soccer Association; Leduc Soccer
Association; Millet Soccer Association; New Sarepta Soccer
Association; Pigeon Lake Soccer Association; Thorsby Soccer
Association; Warburg Soccer Association; Wetaskiwin Soccer
Association
Chief Officer(s): Craig Cooper, President
ck_cooper@yahoo.ca
Sara Letourneau, Office Administrator
Membership: 3,000 players in 10 associations; *Committees:*
Human Resources; Bylaw Reviewl Financial Policy; IT

BC Chinese Soccer Federation (BCCSF)
#114, 4940 No. 3 Rd., Richmond BC V6X 3A5
Tel: 604-207-8711
www.bccsf.info
Overview: A small provincial organization

Description: To promote the sport of soccer; To oversee the
Multi-Nation Recreation League
Activities: Holding soccer tournaments; Offering a youth
training program

British Columbia Soccer Association
#250, 3410 Lougheed Hwy., Vancouver BC V5M 2A4
Tel: 604-299-6401; *Fax:* 604-299-9610
info@bcsoccer.net
www.bcsoccer.net
twitter.com/1bcsoccer
Overview: A medium-sized provincial organization founded in
1907
Description: To promote & develop the sport of soccer in British
Columbia; *Member of:* Canadian Soccer Association
Chief Officer(s): Jason Elligott, Executive Director
jasonelligott@bcsoccer.net

British Columbia Soccer Referees Association
8130 Selkirk St., Vancouver BC V6P 4H7
bcreferees@gmail.com
www.bcsra.com
www.facebook.com/BcSoccerRefereesAssociation
twitter.com/bcsra_ref
Overview: A small provincial organization
Description: To support referees in the province of British
Columbia
Chief Officer(s): Chris Wattam, President
chris.wattam@shaw.ca
Fees: $10 (18 & under); $25 (19 & over)

Calgary Minor Soccer Association (CSMA)
#7, 6991 - 48 St. SE, Calgary AB T2C 5A4
Tel: 403-279-8686; *Fax:* 403-236-3669
info@calgaryminorsoccer.com
calgaryminorsoccer.com
www.instagram.com/calgaryminorsoccer
www.facebook.com/calgaryminorsoccer
twitter.com/cmsasoccer
Overview: A small local organization
Member of: Alberta Soccer Association
Chief Officer(s): Daryl Leinweber, Executive Director,
403-279-8686 1007
execdirector@calgaryminorsoccer.com
Cory Letendre, Manager, 403-279-8686 1002
operations@calgaryminorsoccer.com
Melissa Collinson, League Director, 403-279-8686 1003
leagues@calgaryminorsoccer.com

Calgary Soccer Federation
Calgary Soccer Centre, 7000 - 48 St. SE, Calgary AB T2C 4E1
Tel: 403-279-8453; *Fax:* 403-279-8796
www.calgarysoccerfederation.com
www.facebook.com/calgarysoccerfederation
twitter.com/calgarysoccer1
Overview: A small local organization
Member of: Alberta Soccer Association

Calgary United Soccer Association
#183, 2880 Glenmore Trail SE, Calgary AB T2C 2E7
Tel: 403-270-0363; *Fax:* 403-270-0573
info@cusa.ab.ca
www.cusa.ab.ca
www.facebook.com/CalgaryUnitedSoccerAssociation
twitter.com/cusa_events
Overview: A small local organization
Member of: Alberta Soccer Association
Chief Officer(s): Pearl Doupe, Executive Director,
403-648-0861
pearl@cusa.ab.ca

Calgary Women's Soccer Association (CWSA)
#110, 4441 - 76 Ave. SE, Calgary AB T2C 2G8
Tel: 403-720-6692; *Fax:* 403-720-6693
office@mycwsa.ca
www.womensoccer.ab.ca
www.facebook.com/124525960988252
Overview: A small local organization
Member of: Alberta Soccer Association
Chief Officer(s): Jacquie Herltein, Executive Director
execdir@mycwsa.ca

Canadian Soccer Association (CSA) / Association canadienne de soccer
237 Metcalfe St., Ottawa ON K2P 1R2
Tel: 613-237-7678; *Fax:* 613-237-1516
info@soccercan.ca
www.canadasoccer.com
www.youtube.com/CanadaSoccerTV
www.facebook.com/canadasoccer
twitter.com/CanadaSoccerEN
Overview: A large national organization founded in 1912

Description: To promote the growth & development of soccer
for all Canadians at all levels; To provide leadership & good
governance for the sport
Affiliation(s): Fédération Internationale de Football Association,
FIFA; Football Confederation; Canadian Olympic Association
Chief Officer(s): Peter Montopoli, General Secretary
Sean Hefferman, Chief Financial Officer
Sandra Gage, Chief Marketing Officer
Jason DeVos, Director, Development
jdevos@canadasoccer.com
Cathy Breda, Manager, Administration
cbreda@canadasoccer.com
Membership: 1,000,000 registered players in 1,200 clubs

Central Alberta Soccer Association (CASA)
4108A - 60 St., Camrose AB T4V 3G7
Fax: 780-672-4224
casa9@telus.net
www.central-alta-soccer.ca
Overview: A small local organization
Member of: Alberta Soccer Association
Chief Officer(s): David McCarthy, Techncial Director
davidmccarthy.coach@gmail.com

Edmonton District Soccer Association (EDSA)
17415 - 106A Ave., Edmonton AB T5S 1M7
Tel: 780-413-0140; *Fax:* 780-481-4619
www.edsa.org
www.facebook.com/99060275311
twitter.com/EdmontonSoccer
Overview: A small local organization
Chief Officer(s): Mike Thome, Executive Director,
780-413-0140 8

Edmonton Interdistrict Youth Soccer Association (EIYSA)
#307, 8925 - 51 Ave., Edmonton AB T5E 5J3
Tel: 780-462-3537; *Fax:* 780-444-4321
admin@eiysa.com
www.eiysa.com
Overview: A small local organization
Member of: Alberta Soccer Association
Chief Officer(s): Barrie White, President & COO
exdir@eiysa.com
Membership: 11 teams

Edmonton Minor Soccer Association (EMSA)
Edmonton South Soccer Centre, 6520 Roper Rd., Edmonton AB
T6B 3K8
Tel: 780-413-3672; *Fax:* 780-490-1652
edmontonsoccer.com
www.instagram.com/emsamain
www.facebook.com/EMSASoccerYEG
twitter.com/EMSAmain
Overview: A small local organization
Member of: Alberta Soccer Association
Membership: 89 teams

Fédération de soccer du Québec (FDSDQ)
#210, 955, av Bois-de-Boulogne, Laval QC H7N 4G1
Tél: 450-975-3355
courriel@federation-soccer.qc.ca
www.federation-soccer.qc.ca
www.youtube.com/user/FederationSoccerQC
www.facebook.com/SoccerQuebec
twitter.com/SoccerQuebec
Également appelé: Soccer Québec
Nom précédent: Fédération québécoise de soccer football
Aperçu: *Dimension:* moyenne; *Envergure: provinciale; fondée
en 1911*
Membre de: Canadian Soccer Association
Finances: *Fonds:* Société de Promotion du Soccer
Membre: 82 000; *Comités:* Exécutif; Compétitions; Provincial
Arbitrage; Technique

Fort McMurray Youth Soccer Association (FMYSA)
PO Box 10, 8115 Franklin Ave., Fort McMurray AB T9H 2H7
Tel: 780-791-7090; *Fax:* 780-791-1446
fmysa@shaw.ca
www.fmyouthsoccer.com
Overview: A small local organization
Member of: Alberta Soccer Association
Chief Officer(s): Ian Diaz, Technical Director
fmysatechnicaldirector@gmail.com
Bill Carr, President
president.fmysa@shaw.ca

Halifax County United Soccer Club
#7, 102 Chain Lake Dr., Halifax NS B3S 1A7
Tel: 902-876-8784; *Fax:* 902-446-3620
info@hcusoccer.ca
www.hcusoccer.ca

Overview: A medium-sized local organization founded in 1998
Description: To foster a love of soccer & help individuals of all ages achieve their full potential.
Membership: 1,600 players; *Fees:* Schedule available

Lakeland District Soccer Association (LDSA)
PO Box 4801, Bonnyville AB T9N 0H2
Tel: 780-201-4346
lakelandsoccer.ca

Overview: A small local organization
Member of: Alberta Soccer Association
Chief Officer(s): Kristy L'Hirondelle, Executive Director
execdir@lakelandsoccer.ca
Membership: 1-99

Lethbridge Soccer Association
2501 - 28 St. South, Lethbridge AB T1K 7L6
Tel: 403-320-5425; *Fax:* 403-327-5847
lethbridgesoccer.com
www.facebook.com/LethbridgeSoccerAssociation
twitter.com/LethSoccer

Overview: A small local organization
Member of: Alberta Soccer Association
Chief Officer(s): Steven Dudas, General Manager
steve@lethbridgesoccer.com

Medicine Hat Soccer Association
#101, 533 - 2nd St. East, Medicine Hat AB T1A 0C5
Tel: 403-529-6931; *Fax:* 403-526-6590
mhsa@telusplanet.net
www.medicinehatsoccer.com
www.facebook.com/medicinehatsoccer
twitter.com/mhsasoccer

Overview: A small local organization founded in 1971
Member of: Alberta Soccer Association
Chief Officer(s): Jeff Vangen, President
Heather Bach, Director, Communications
Membership: 2,700

Newfoundland & Labrador Soccer Association
39 Churchill Ave., St. John's NL A1A 0H7
Tel: 709-576-0601; *Fax:* 709-576-0588
info@nlsa.ca
www.nlsa.ca

Previous Name: Newfoundland Soccer Association
Overview: A medium-sized provincial organization
Description: To provide opportunities for the general public to engage in the game of soccer while having fun & competition;
Member of: Canadian Soccer Association
Chief Officer(s): Dragan Mirkovic, Director, Technical, 709-576-2262
dragan@nlsa.ca
Mike Power, Director, Player Development, 709-576-7310
mike@nlsa.ca
Rob Comerford, Manager, Business, 709-576-0601
rob@nlsa.ca

Northwest Peace Soccer Association (NWPSA)
11727 - 88A St., Grande Prairie AB T8X 1L8
Tel: 780-832-1627
nwpsoccer@gmail.com
www.northwestpeacesoccer.ca

Overview: A small local organization
Member of: Alberta Soccer Association

Northwest Territories Soccer Association (NWTSA)
PO Box 11089, Yellowknife NT X1A 3X7
Tel: 867-669-8396; *Fax:* 867-669-8327
Toll-Free: 800-661-0797
www.nwtkicks.ca
www.facebook.com/NWTSoccerAssociation
twitter.com/NwtSoccer

Overview: A medium-sized provincial organization
Description: The NWT Soccer Association is a volunteer-run organization & the governing body for all soccer activities in the NWT; focus is on the grassroots development of the game, as well as the promotion of high performance. Physical delivery address: c/o Sport North Federation, 4908 - 49th St., 1st Fl., Yellowknife, NT X1A 2N4; *Member of:* Canadian Soccer Association
Affiliation(s): Sport North Federation
Chief Officer(s): Ollie Williams, President
Lyric Sandhals, Executive Director
Finances: *Funding Sources:* Operates on Sport Lottery funding
Activities: Summer camps; leagues & tournaments; developmental clinics

Ontario Soccer Association (OSA)
7601 Martin Grove Rd., Vaughan ON L4L 9E4
Tel: 905-264-9390; *Fax:* 905-264-9445
ask@ontariosoccer.net
www.ontariosoccer.net
www.youtube.com/OSAVideoMaster
www.facebook.com/OntarioIsSoccer
twitter.com/OntarioIsSoccer

Also Known As: Ontario Soccer
Overview: A medium-sized provincial organization founded in 1901
Description: To provide leadership & support for the advancement of soccer; To provide programs & services; *Member of:* Canadian Soccer Association
Chief Officer(s): Ron Smale, President
Johnny Misley, Chief Executive Officer
Membership: 500,000 players; 70,000 coaches; 10,000 referees; *Committees:* Judicial; Competitions; League Management; Referee Development; Technical Advisory; Academies; Marketing; Executive; Finance; Governance; Nominations; Risk / Audit; Strategic Planning

Prince Edward Island Soccer Association (PEISA)
40 Enman Cres., Charlottetown PE C1E 1E6
Tel: 902-368-6251; *Fax:* 902-569-7693
admin@peisoccer.com
www.peisoccer.com
www.facebook.com/197098723677560
twitter.com/peisoccerassoc

Overview: A medium-sized provincial organization founded in 1979
Description: To promote & regulate soccer in PEI; to provide competitive opportunities for members.; *Member of:* Canadian Soccer Association; Sport PEI
Chief Officer(s): Peter Wolters, Executive Director
Jonathan Vos, Technical Director
jvos@peisoccer.com
Finances: *Annual Operating Budget:* $250,000-$500,000
Staff: 1 staff member(s)
Membership: 6,000 individual + 14 clubs; *Fees:* Schedule available

Red Deer City Soccer Association
6905 Edgar Industrial Dr., Red Deer AB T4P 3R2
Tel: 403-346-4259; *Fax:* 403-340-1044
office@rdcsa.com
www.rdcsa.com
www.facebook.com/RedDeerCitySoccerAssociation
twitter.com/RDCSA

Overview: A small local organization
Member of: Alberta Soccer Association
Chief Officer(s): Joan Van Wolde, Administrator
Ado Sarcevic, Manager, Soccer Operations
asarcevic@rdcsa.com

St. Albert Soccer Association (SASA)
61 Riel Dr., St Albert AB T8N 3Z3
Tel: 780-458-8973; *Fax:* 780-458-8994
www.stalbertsoccer.com

Overview: A small local organization
Member of: Alberta Soccer Association
Chief Officer(s): Chris Spaidal, Executive Director, 780-458-8973 127
chris@stalbertsoccer.com

Saskatchewan Soccer Association Inc. (SSA)
SaskSport Administration Bldg., 1870 Lorne St., Regina SK S4P 2L7
Tel: 306-780-9225; *Fax:* 306-780-9480
www.sasksoccer.com
www.youtube.com/SaskatchewanSoccer
www.facebook.com/SaskatchewanSoccer
twitter.com/SaskSoccerAssoc

Overview: A medium-sized provincial organization founded in 1906
Member of: Canadian Soccer Association
Chief Officer(s): Doug Pederson, Executive Director, 306-780-9225 4
d.pederson@sasksoccer.com
Membership: 33,000
Activities: *Internships:* Yes

Sherwood Park District Soccer Association
Millenium Pl., #131.2, 2000 Premier Way, Sherwood Park AB T8H 2G4
Tel: 780-449-1343; *Fax:* 780-464-5821
www.spdsa.net
www.facebook.com/416487478408692
twitter.com/SPDSASoccer

Overview: A small local organization founded in 1976
Member of: Alberta Soccer Association; Federation Internationale de Football Association; Canada Soccer Association

Affiliation(s): Breton Soccer Association; Calmar Soccer Association; Devon Soccer Association; Leduc Soccer Association; Millet Soccer Association; New Sarepta Soccer Association; Pigeon Lake Soccer Association; Thorsby Soccer Association; Warburg Soccer Association; Wetaskiwin Soccer Association
Chief Officer(s): Debbie Ballam, General Manager
d.ballam@spdsa.net
Membership: 3,000 players in 10 associations; *Committees:* Human Resources; Bylaw Reviewl Financial Policy; IT

Soccer New Brunswick
#2, 125 Russ Howard Dr., Moncton NB E1C 0L7
Tel: 506-830-4762; *Fax:* 506-382-5621
admin@soccernb.org
www.soccernb.org
www.facebook.com/SoccerNb
twitter.com/SoccerNB

Also Known As: Soccer NB
Overview: A medium-sized provincial organization founded in 1965
Description: To foster & promote the development & growth of the sport of soccer in New Brunswick & to assure equitable accessibility through quality programs; *Member of:* Canadian Soccer Association
Chief Officer(s): Younes Bouida, Executive Director & Director, Technical Development, 506-830-4762 2
younes@soccernb.org
Finances: *Annual Operating Budget:* $500,000-$1.5 Million; *Funding Sources:* Government; membership
Staff: 2 staff member(s); 9 volunteer(s)
Membership: 16,500

Soccer Nova Scotia (SNS)
210 Thomas Raddall Dr., Halifax NS B3S 0J2
Tel: 902-445-0265; *Fax:* 902-445-0258
admin@soccerns.ca
www.soccerns.ca
www.facebook.com/SoccerNovaScotia
twitter.com/SoccerNS

Overview: A medium-sized provincial organization founded in 1913
Description: To promote the sport of soccer in Nova Scotia; To provide information & resources to aid player training, coaching education & referee programs; *Member of:* Canadian Soccer Association
Chief Officer(s): Brad Lawlor, Executive Director
executivedirector@soccerns.ca
Membership: 27,000+ players; 2,500+ coaches; 700+ referees

Sunny South District Soccer Association
RR#8, Site 34, Comp 0, Lethbridge AB T1J 4P4
Tel: 403-894-2277
www.sunnysouthsoccer.com

Overview: A small local organization
Member of: Alberta Soccer Association
Chief Officer(s): Paul Anwender, Executive Director
paul.anwender@gmail.com

Tri-County Soccer Association
c/o Fran Glenn, President, 9904 - 109 St., Fort Saskatchewan AB T8L 2K2
tricounty.district@yahoo.ca
www.tricountysoccer.net

Overview: A small local organization
Member of: Alberta Soccer Association
Chief Officer(s): Fran Glenn, President
tricouny.president@yahoo.ca

Whitehorse Minor Soccer Association (WMS)
4061 - 4th Ave., Whitehorse YT Y1A 1H1
Tel: 867-667-2445
yukonsoccer@sportyukon.com
www.yukonsoccer.yk.ca/whitehorseminorsoccer.html

Overview: A medium-sized provincial organization founded in 1977
Member of: Sport Yukon
Chief Officer(s): Cali Battersby, Sport Administrator

Women's Soccer Assocation of Lethbridge (WSAL)
c/o Lethbridge Soccer Association, 2501-28th Ave. South, Lethbridge AB T1K 7I6
Tel: 403-320-5425
lethbridgesoccer.com
twitter.com/wsal_soccer

Overview: A small local organization founded in 2001
Description: To provide a year-round indoor and outdoor soccer league to women
Chief Officer(s): Ilsa Wong, President, 403-329-2232
ilsa.wong@uleth.ca

Yukon Soccer Association

4061 - 4th Ave., Whitehorse YT Y1A 1H1
Tel: 867-633-4625; *Fax:* 867-667-4237
yukonsoccer@sportyukon.com
www.yukonsoccer.yk.ca
Overview: A small provincial organization
Description: The Yukon Soccer Association is the sport
governing body for the sport of soccer in the Yukon Territory. It
is a volunteer based organization that coordinates & administers
various programs devoted to the promotion & development of
soccer.; *Member of:* Canadian Soccer Association
Chief Officer(s): Cali Battersby, Sport Administrator
John MacPhail, Technical Director
jmac@sportyukon.com

Softball

Alberta Amateur Softball Association (AASA)

9860 - 33rd Ave., Edmonton AB T6N 1C6
Tel: 780-461-7735; *Fax:* 780-461-7757
info@softballalberta.ca
www.softballalberta.ca
www.facebook.com/SoftballAlberta
Also Known As: Softball Alberta
Overview: A large provincial organization founded in 1971
Description: To foster & promote the playing of amateur
softball; To regulate play in all classifications of the game as
may be deemed in its best interests; *Member of:* Canadian
Amateur Softball Association
Affiliation(s): Western Canada Softball Association
Chief Officer(s): Michele Patry, Executive Director
michele@softballalberta.ca
Finances: *Funding Sources:* Alberta Sport, Recreation & Parks;
Wildlife Foundation
Staff: 4 staff member(s)
Activities: *Internships:* Yes; *Speaker Service:* Yes *Library:* Yes
(Open to Public)

British Columbia Amateur Softball Association (BCASA)

#201, 8889 Walnut Grove Dr., Langley BC V1M 2N7
Tel: 604-371-0302; *Fax:* 604-371-0344
info@softball.bc.ca
www.softball.bc.ca
www.facebook.com/softball.bc
Also Known As: Softball BC
Overview: A medium-sized provincial organization
Description: To promote, govern & build the sport of Softball in
British Columbia; *Member of:* Canadian Amateur Softball
Association
Chief Officer(s): Rick Benson, Chief Operating Officer
rbenson@softball.bc.ca
Jeana Boyd, Coordinator, Programs
programcoordinator@softball.bc.ca
Fees: Schedule available; *Member Profile:* Softball players,
coaches, umpires

Canadian Amateur Softball Association

#212, 223 Colonnade Rd., Ottawa ON K2E 7K3
Tel: 613-523-3386
info@softball.ca
softball.ca
www.instagram.com/softball.canada
www.linkedin.com/company/softball-canada
www.facebook.com/SoftballCanadaNSO
twitter.com/softballcanada
Also Known As: Softball Canada
Overview: A medium-sized national organization founded in
1965
Description: To develop & promote softball in Canada
Chief Officer(s): Scott Neiles, President
Hugh Mitchener, Chief Executive Officer, 613-523-3386 3106
hmitchener@softball.ca
Membership: 12 provincial & territorial associations

Northwest Territories Softball

PO Box 11089, Yellowknife NT X1A 3X7
Tel: 867-669-8339; *Fax:* 867-669-8327
Toll-Free: 800-661-0797
sportnorth.com/tso/softball
Also Known As: NWT Softball
Overview: A small provincial organization
Description: To be the territorial governing body for fastpitch,
minor ball & slo-pitch softball in the Northwest Territories;
Member of: Canadian Amateur Softball Association
Affiliation(s): Sport North Federation
Chief Officer(s): Paul Gard, President
paul_gard@gov.nt.ca
Melanie Thompson, Executive Director
mel@movethenorth.ca

Ontario Amateur Softball Association (OASA)

c/o Registrar, 44 Hilltop Blvd., RR#1, Gormley ON L0H 1G0
Tel: 905-727-5139
www.oasa.ca
www.facebook.com/OntarioAmateurSoftballAssocation
twitter.com/OASASoftball
Overview: A medium-sized provincial organization founded in
1923
Description: To be the provincial governing body for the sport of
amateur softball in Ontario; *Member of:* Canadian Amateur
Softball Association; Softball Ontario
Chief Officer(s): Garry Waugh, President, 519-537-5835
gwaugh@execulink.com
Brad Thomson, Executive Vice President, 519-954-1269
oasabradthomson@gmail.com
Finances: *Funding Sources:* Sponsors; Partners; Government
grants; Player/team fees

Ontario Rural Softball Association (ORSA)

c/o Secretary-Treasurer, 716029 - 18th Line, RR#1, Innerkip ON
N0J 1M0
Tel: 519-469-3593
www.ontarioruralsoftball.ca
Overview: A small provincial organization founded in 1931
Description: To promote softball in rural districts, communities
& small villages; *Member of:* Canadian Amateur Softball
Association; Softball Ontario
Chief Officer(s): Earl Hall, President, 519-882-1599
Carl Littlejohns, Secretary-Treasurer
clittlejohnsorsa@live.ca
Finances: *Funding Sources:* Sponsors; Partners; Government
grants; Player/team fees

Provincial Women's Softball Association of Ontario (PWSAO)

c/o Registrar, PO Box 237, 3746 Highland Dr., Ridgeway ON
L0S 1N0
info@pwsaontario.com
www.pwsaontario.com
www.facebook.com/OntarioPWSA
twitter.com/OntarioPWSA
Overview: A medium-sized provincial organization founded in
1931
Description: To support & advance women softball players in
Ontario; *Member of:* Canadian Amateur Softball Association;
Softball Ontario
Chief Officer(s): Debbie Malisani, Chair & President,
647-339-5359
littlehands1@rogers.com
Dorrie Jones, Registrar, 905-871-7448
affiliations@pwsaontario.com
Cathy Bilinski, Treasurer, 905-579-3002, Fax: 905-579-4212
cathy.bilinski@pwsaontario.com
Finances: *Funding Sources:* Sponsors; Partners; Government
grants; Player/team fees

Slo-Pitch Ontario Association (SPO)

#7, 8 Hiscott St., St Catharines ON L2R 1C6
Tel: 905-646-7773; *Fax:* 905-646-8431
spoa@slopitch.org
www.slopitch.org
twitter.com/slopitchontario
Overview: A medium-sized provincial organization founded in
1982
Description: To institute & regulate slo-pitch softball in Ontario;
Member of: Canadian Amateur Softball Association; Softball
Ontario
Chief Officer(s): Tom Buchan, CEO
tbuchan@slopitch.org
Ron Hawthorne, President, 613-831-8393
rhawthorne@slopitch.info
Kerri Toole, Administrator, Tournaments
kerri@slopitch.org
Rebecca Hyatt-Spry, Administrator, Programs & Leagues
rebecca@slopitch.org
Finances: *Funding Sources:* Sponsors; Partners; Government
grants; Team fees
Fees: Schedule available; *Member Profile:* Slo-pitch teams &
leagues in Ontario

Softball Manitoba

#321, 145 Pacific Ave., Winnipeg MB R3B 2Z6
Tel: 204-925-5673; *Fax:* 204-925-5703
softball@softball.mb.ca
www.softball.mb.ca
Also Known As: Softball Manitoba
Overview: A small provincial organization founded in 1965

Description: To promote & develop softball at all levels by
providing leadership, programs & services; *Member of:*
Canadian Amateur Softball Association
Chief Officer(s): Don Klym, Executive Director
donklym@mts.net
Bill Finch, President
bfinch_softballmb@mts.net
Membership: 15,000+ players & coaches; *Committees:*
Finance; Facilities; Development; Hall of Fame; Umpire
Development; Competition

Softball NB Inc. (SNB) / Softball Nouveau-Brunswick Inc.

4242 Water St., Miramichi NB E1N 4L2
Tel: 506-773-5343; *Fax:* 506-773-5630
www.softballnb.ca
www.facebook.com/210596526327
twitter.com/softballnb
Also Known As: Softball New Brunswick
Overview: A medium-sized provincial organization founded in
1925
Description: To foster, develop, promote & regulate the playing
of amateur softball in New Brunswick; *Member of:* Canadian
Amateur Softball Association
Finances: *Annual Operating Budget:* $50,000-$100,000
Staff: 1 staff member(s); 17 volunteer(s)
Membership: 350 teams; 225 officials
Activities: *Awareness Events:* Hall of Fame, 1st Sat. in June

Softball Newfoundland & Labrador

PO Box 21165, #115, 183 Kenmount Rd., St. John's NL A1A 5B2
Tel: 709-576-7231; *Fax:* 709-576-7049
softball@sportnl.ca
www.softballnl.ca
Overview: A small provincial organization
Member of: Canadian Amateur Softball Association
Chief Officer(s): Paul F. Smith, President

Softball Nova Scotia

5516 Spring Garden Rd., 4th Fl., Halifax NS B3J 1G6
Tel: 902-425-5454; *Fax:* 902-425-5606
softballns@sportnovascotia.ca
www.softballns.ca
www.facebook.com/softballnovascotia
twitter.com/Softball_NS
Overview: A small provincial organization
Description: To be the provincial governing body for the sport of
softball in Nova Scotia; *Member of:* Canadian Amateur Softball
Association
Chief Officer(s): Richie Connors, President
Caroline Crooks, Executive Director

Softball Ontario

301, 85 Scarsdale Rd., Toronto ON M3B 2R2
Tel: 416-426-7150; *Fax:* 416-426-7150
info@softballontario.ca
www.softballontario.ca
www.facebook.com/SoftballOntario
twitter.com/SoftballOntario
Overview: A medium-sized provincial organization founded in
1971
Description: To promote & develop the sport of softball for its
athletes, officials & volunteers by providing programs & services
at all levels of competitions; *Member of:* Canadian Amateur
Softball Association
Affiliation(s): Provincial Women's Softball Association (PWSA);
Ontario Amateur Softball Association (OASA); Ontario Rural
Softball Association (ORSA); Slo-Pitch Ontario Association
(SPOA)
Chief Officer(s): Christine Parris, Executive Director
cparris@softballontario.ca
Kyle Cormier, Coordinator, Member Services
kcormier@softballontario.ca
Fees: Schedule available; *Member Profile:* Local softball
associations & leagues; Member associations; *Committees:*
CANpitch; Coaching; Fast Pitch Umpires; Slo-Pitch Umpires;
LTPD Competition Review; House League Development

Softball Prince Edward Island (SPEI)

#203, 40 Enman Cres., Charlottetown PE C1E 1E6
Tel: 902-620-3549; *Fax:* 902-368-4548
softballpei@gmail.com
softballpei.com
www.facebook.com/SoftballPEI33
twitter.com/SoftballPEI
Also Known As: Softball PEI
Overview: A small provincial organization

Description: To be the provincial governing body for the sport of softball in Prince Edward Island; *Member of:* Canadian Amateur Softball Association
Chief Officer(s): Chris Halliwell, President, 902-367-1600
crhalliwell@hotmail.com
Heather Drake, Executive Director
heathercdrake@icloud.com
Activities: Umpire Program; Coaching & Athlete Development Program; Scorekeeping Program; Participation Program; Communication/Promotion; Resources

Softball Québec
4545, av Pierre-de-Coubertin, Montréal QC H1V 0B2
Tél: 514-252-3061; *Téléc:* 514-252-3134
communications@softballquebec.com
www.softballquebec.com

www.facebook.com/softballquebec
twitter.com/SoftballQuebec
Aperçu: *Dimension:* moyenne; *Envergure: provinciale; Organisme sans but lucratif; fondée en 1970*
Description: Promouvoir la pratique du softball sur le territoire du Québec; offrir aux athlètes, aux entraîneurs, aux officiels et aux administrateurs québécois un support technique et des services de qualité; *Membre de:* Canadian Amateur Softball Association
Membre(s) du bureau directeur: Chantal Gagnon, Directrice générale
cgagnon@loisirquebec.qc.ca
Michel Nero, Président
mikeump@hotmail.com
Membre: 30,000
Activités: Programmes de formation pour officiels et entraîneurs; ligues; compétitions; *Stagiaires:* Oui

Softball Saskatchewan
2205 Victoria Ave., Regina SK S4P 0S4
Tel: 306-780-9235; *Fax:* 306-780-9483
info@softball.sk.ca
www.softball.sk.ca
Overview: A small provincial organization
Description: To make softball the number one choice for participation by athletes, coaches, parents and umpires.;
Member of: Canadian Amateur Softball Association
Chief Officer(s): Guy Jacobson, Executive Director
guy@softball.sk.ca
Jacqueline Eiwanger, Technical Director
jac@softball.sk.ca

Softball Yukon
c/o Sport Yukon, 4061 - 4th Ave., Whitehorse YT Y1A 1H1
Tel: 867-667-4487
softball@sportyukon.com
www.softballyukon.com
Overview: A small provincial organization
Member of: Canadian Amateur Softball Association
Chief Officer(s): George Arcand, Executive Director
garcand@northwestel.net

Special Olympics

Jeux Olympiques Spéciaux du Québec Inc. (OSQ) / Québec Special Olympics
#200, 1274, rue Jean-Talon est, Montréal QC H2R 1W3
Tél: 514-843-8778; *Téléc:* 514-843-8223
Ligne sans frais: 877-743-8778
www.olympiquesspeciaux.qc.ca

www.facebook.com/olympiquesspeciauxquebec
twitter.com/athletesOSQ
Aperçu: *Dimension:* petite; *Envergure: provinciale; fondée en 1981*
Description: Les Olympiques spéciaux, actifs dans plus de 170 pays, ont pour mission d'enrichir, par le sport, la vie des personnes présentant une déficience intellectuelle. Plus de 3.7 millions d'athlètes spéciaux, de tous âges, sont inscrits dans le monde dont plus de 31,000 au Canada et 4,850 aux programmes récréatifs scolaire ou compétitifs offerts dans toutes les régions du Québec. Les 14 sports officiels sont pratiqués à l'intérieur d'un réseau de compétitions annuelles, comptant plus de 80 événements conçus pour tous les niveaux d'habiletés.; *Membre de:* Special Olympics Canada
Membre(s) du bureau directeur: Daniel Granger, Président

Special Olympics Alberta (SOA)
Jerry Forbes Centre, #3, 12122 - 68 St. NW, Edmonton AB T5B 1R1
Tel: 780-415-0719; *Fax:* 780-415-1306
Toll-Free: 800-444-2883
info@specialolympics.ab.ca
www.specialolympics.ab.ca
www.instagram.com/specialoalberta
www.facebook.com/specialolympicsalberta
twitter.com/SpecialOAlberta
Previous Name: Alberta Special Olympics Inc.
Overview: A medium-sized provincial charitable organization founded in 1980
Description: To enrich the lives of Albertans with an intellectual disability, through sport
Chief Officer(s): John Byrne, President & CEO
jbyrne@specialolympics.ab.ca
Finances: *Annual Operating Budget:* $500,000-$1.5 Million;
Funding Sources: Donations; Grants; Fundraising events; Sponsorship
Staff: 12 staff member(s); 1000 volunteer(s)
Membership: 3,300 athletes; 32 affiliates throughout Alberta;
Member Profile: Athletes with intellectual disabilities;
Committees: Strategic Development; Volunteer Management;
New Community Development; New Sport Programs; Sport Development; Provincial Games; Team AB
Activities: Offering 15 official sports for athletes; Providing training; *Awareness Events:* Law Enforcement Torch Run;
Sports Celebrities Festival; *Speaker Service:* Yes

Special Olympics BC (SOBC)
#210, 3701 East Hastings St., Burnaby BC V5C 2H6
Tel: 604-737-3078; *Fax:* 604-737-3080
Toll-Free: 888-854-2276
info@specialolympics.bc.ca
www.specialolympics.bc.ca
www.facebook.com/specialolympicsbc
twitter.com/sobcsociety
Previous Name: British Columbia Special Olympics
Overview: A medium-sized provincial charitable organization founded in 1980
Description: To provide individuals with intellectual disabilities the opportunity to participate in sporting events at the regional, provincial, national, or international levels; *Member of:* Special Olympics Canada
Affiliation(s): Special Olympics International
Chief Officer(s): Dan Howe, President & CEO, 604-737-3079
dhowe@specialolympics.bc.ca
Christina Hadley, Vice-President, Fund Development & Communications
chadley@specialolympics.bc.ca
Lois McNary, Vice-President, Sport
lmcnary@specialolympics.bc.ca
Josh Pasnak, Manager, Finance & Administration
jpasnak@specialolympics.bc.ca
Lauren Openshaw, Office Administrator
lopenshaw@specialolympics.bc.ca
Finances: *Funding Sources:* Donations; fundraising events; sponsors
Staff: 17 staff member(s); 3300 volunteer(s)
Membership: 4,300
Activities: Operating in 54 communities in British Columbia;
Speaker Service: Yes

Special Olympics Canada (SOC) / Olympiques spéciaux Canada
#600, 21 St Clair Ave. East, Toronto ON M4T 1L9
Tel: 416-927-9050; *Fax:* 416-927-8475
Toll-Free: 888-888-0608
info@specialolympics.ca
www.specialolympics.ca
www.youtube.com/specialocanada
www.facebook.com/SpecialOCanada
twitter.com/SpecialOCanada
Previous Name: Canadian Special Olympics Inc.
Overview: A large national organization founded in 1969
Description: To provide sport training & competition for people with an intellectual disability, at local, regional, provincial, national & international level
Affiliation(s): Special Olympics International; The Order of United Commercial Travelers of America; The Sandbox Project
Chief Officer(s): Sharon Bollenbach, Chief Executive Officer, 416-927-9050 4389
sbollenbach@specialolympics.ca
Karen Cinq Mars, Director, Marketing & Communications, 416-927-9050 4383
kcinqmars@specialolympics.ca
Finances: *Funding Sources:* Foundations; Corporate sponsors; Individual donations
Staff: 2147 volunteer(s)

Membership: 45,087 children, youth & adults with intellectual disabilities; *Member of:* Special Olympics Canada
Member Profile: To improve the lives of Canadians with an intellectual disability through sport
Activities: Offering national & international games; Providing coaching development

Special Olympics Manitoba (SOM)
#304, 145 Pacific Ave., Winnipeg MB R3B 2Z6
Tel: 204-925-5628; *Fax:* 204-925-5635
Toll-Free: 888-333-9179
som@specialolympics.mb.ca
www.specialolympics.mb.ca
www.instagram.com/specomanitoba
www.facebook.com/SpecOManitoba
twitter.com/SpecOManitoba
Previous Name: Manitoba Special Olympics
Overview: A small provincial charitable organization founded in 1980
Description: To enrich the lives of Manitobans with an intellectual disability, through active participation in sport;
Member of: Special Olympics Inc.
Chief Officer(s): Jennifer Campbell, President & CEO, 204-925-5632
jcampbell@specialolympics.mb.ca
Finances: *Funding Sources:* Sport Manitoba; Various events
Staff: 14 staff member(s)
Fees: $25 athlete
Activities: *Speaker Service:* Yes

Special Olympics New Brunswick
#103, 411 St. Mary's St., Fredericton NB E3B 8H4
Tel: 506-455-0404; *Fax:* 506-455-0410
infosonb@specialolympics.ca
www.specialolympicsnb.ca
twitter.com/specialonb
Previous Name: New Brunswick Special Olympics
Overview: A small provincial charitable organization founded in 1979
Description: To offer athletic programs to people with intellectual disabilites in New Brunswick
Chief Officer(s): Josh Astle, Executive Director
jastle@specialolympics.ca
Member Profile: Athletes between 2 & 88 with an intellectual disability

Special Olympics Newfoundland & Labrador
87 Elizabeth Ave., St. John's NL A1B 1R6
Tel: 709-738-1923; *Fax:* 709-738-0119
Toll-Free: 877-738-1913
specialolympics.ca/newfoundland-and-labrador
twitter.com/SpecialONL
Previous Name: Newfoundland-Labrador Special Olympics
Overview: A small provincial charitable organization founded in 1986
Description: To provide sport, fitness & recreation programs for individuals with an intellectual disability
Chief Officer(s): Trish Williams, Executive Director
trishw@sonl.ca
Finances: *Annual Operating Budget:* $100,000-$250,000
Staff: 4 staff member(s); 250 volunteer(s)
Activities: *Awareness Events:* Provincial Winter & Summer Games

Special Olympics Northwest Territories (SONWT)
PO Box 1691, Yellowknife NT X1A 2N1
Tel: 867-446-2873
www.sonwt.ca
Previous Name: Northwest Territories Special Olympics
Overview: A small provincial organization founded in 1989
Description: Special Olympics N.W.T. is the territorial sport governing body responsible for the delivery of sport for people with intellectual disabilities in the Northwest Territories.; *Member of:* Sport North; Special Olympics Canada
Chief Officer(s): Lynn Elkin, Executive Director
lynn@sonwt.ca
Finances: *Funding Sources:* Law Enforcement Torch Run, public donations, grants, corporate sponsors and special fundraising events.

Special Olympics Nova Scotia (SONS)
#201, 5516 Spring Garden Rd., Halifax NS B3J 1G6
Tel: 902-429-2266; *Fax:* 902-425-5606
Toll-Free: 866-299-2019
www.sons.ca
www.instagram.com/SpecialONS
www.facebook.com/SpecialONS
twitter.com/SpecialONS
Previous Name: Nova Scotia Special Olympics
Overview: A small provincial charitable organization founded in 1978
Description: Special Olympics is a non-profit organization dedicated to providing year-round sports training and athletic

competition in a variety of Olympic-type sports for children and adults with an intellectual disability.
Chief Officer(s): Mike Greek, President & CEO
greekmr@sportnovascotia.ca
Membership: 1,700 athletes

Special Olympics Ontario (SOO)
#200, 65 Overlea Blvd., Toronto ON M4H 1P1
Tel: 416-447-8326; *Fax:* 416-447-6336
Toll-Free: 888-333-5515
www1.specialolympicsontario.com
www.youtube.com/specialolympicson
www.facebook.com/specialolympicsontario
twitter.com/soontario
Previous Name: Ontario Special Olympics
Overview: A medium-sized provincial charitable organization founded in 1979
Description: To provide sports training & competition for people with an intellectual disability through community-based programs; *Member of:* Special Olympics Canada
Chief Officer(s): Glenn MacDonell, President & CEO, 416-447-8326 225
glennm@specialolympicsontario.com
Linda Ashe, Vice-President, 416-447-8326 220
lindaa@specialolympicsontario.com
Willie E., Manager, Accounting Services, 416-447-8326 223
williee@specialolympicsontario.com
Lynn Miller, Manager, Marketing Services, 416-447-8326 226
lynnm@specialolympicsontario.com
James Noronha, Manager, Program Services, 416-447-8326 240
jamesn@specialolympicsontario.com
Finances: *Annual Operating Budget:* Greater than $5 Million; *Funding Sources:* Individual & corporate donations; Provincial government
Staff: 22 staff member(s); 9000 volunteer(s)
Membership: 19,000 athletes; *Member Profile:* Athletes 2 years of age or older with an intellectual disability; *Committees:* Finance; Marketing & Fundraising; Program Services
Activities: Offering 18 official sports; Providing network & support opportunities for families; Facilitating outreach & education programs to Special Olympics athletes and students across Ontario; *Internships:* Yes; *Speaker Service:* Yes

Special Olympics Prince Edward Island (SOPEI)
#240, 40 Enman Cres., Charlottetown PE C1A 7L9
Tel: 902-368-8919; *Toll-Free:* 800-287-1196
sopei@sopei.com
www.specialolympics.ca/pei
www.youtube.com/channel/UCQsAGVtPqgIJeQRN_GeNOtw
www.facebook.com/Specialopei
twitter.com/Specialopei
Previous Name: PEI Special Olympics
Overview: A small provincial charitable organization founded in 1987
Description: To provide sport, recreation & fitness for the intellectually disabled in PEI; To provide competititve opportunities for its members
Chief Officer(s): Charity Sheehan, Executive Director
csheehan@sopei.com
Finances: *Annual Operating Budget:* $100,000-$250,000
Staff: 2 staff member(s); 75 volunteer(s)
Membership: 235; *Member Profile:* Athletes with an intellectual disability; *Committees:* Program; Board of Directors

Special Olympics Saskatchewan
1121 Winnipeg St., Regina SK S4R 1J5
Tel: 306-780-9247; *Fax:* 306-780-9441
Toll-Free: 888-307-6226
sos@specialolympics.sk.ca
www.specialolympics.ca/saskatchewan
www.youtube.com/user/SpecialOSk
www.facebook.com/SOSaskatchewan
twitter.com/SpecialOSask
Previous Name: Saskatchewan Special Olympics Society
Overview: A small provincial organization
Description: To enhance the lives of persons with intellectual disabilities through sport
Chief Officer(s): Faye Matt, Chief Executive Officer, 306-780-9277
fmatt@specialolympics.sk.ca

Special Olympics Yukon (SOY) / Les Jeux Olympiques Spéciaux du Yukon
4061 4th Ave., Whitehorse YT Y1A 1H1
Tel: 867-668-6511; *Fax:* 867-667-4237
info@specialolympicsyukon.ca
www.specialolympicsyukon.ca
www.facebook.com/191453284318177
twitter.com/SpecialOYukon
Previous Name: Yukon Special Olympics

Overview: A medium-sized provincial charitable organization founded in 1981
Description: To provide a full continuum of sport apportunities for Yukoners with a mental disability
Affiliation(s): Special Olympics International
Chief Officer(s): Serge Michaud, Executive Director
smichaud@specialolympicsyukon.ca
Brettanie Deal-Porter, Program Director
bdealporter@specialolympicsyukon.ca
Sylvia Anderson, Coordinator, Marketing & Development
sanderson@specialolympicsyukon.ca
Membership: 100+; *Fees:* Schedule available; *Member Profile:* Individuals with a mental disability
Activities: *Awareness Events:* Sports Celebrities Dinner Auction; Golf Gala; Law Enforcement Torch Run

Sport Medicine

Alberta Athletic Therapists Association
PO Box 61115, Kengsington RPO, Calgary AB T2N 4S6
info@aata.ca
www.aata.ca
www.facebook.com/AATA.therapy
twitter.com/AATA_therapy
Overview: A small provincial organization
Description: To represent, promote, & provide leadership & opportunity for Athletic Therapists across Alberta; *Member of:* Canadian Athletic Therapists Association
Chief Officer(s): John Reinbolt, President
president@aata.ca
Fees: Schedule available; *Member Profile:* Athletic therapists in Alberta; *Committees:* Education; Ethics; Marketing

Athletic Therapy Association of British Columbia (ATABC)
#200, 4170 Still Creek Dr., Burnaby BC V5C 6C6
Tel: 604-918-5077
info@athletictherapybc.ca
www.athletictherapybc.ca
www.facebook.com/AthleticTherapyBC
twitter.com/ATABC
Previous Name: Athletic Therapists' Association of British Columbia
Overview: A small provincial organization founded in 1994
Description: To promote & ensure the delivery of the highest quality care to athletes including injury prevention, immediate care & rehabilitation; *Member of:* Canadian Athletic Therapists Association
Chief Officer(s): Sandy Zinkowski, President
president@athletictherapybc.ca
Zach Hogan, Treasurer
treasurer@athletictherapybc.ca
Membership: 1-99; *Member Profile:* Certified athletic therapists & certification candidates
Activities: Sports medical coverage throughout BC; *Speaker Service:* Yes

Atlantic Provinces Athletic Therapists Association (APATA) / Association des Therapeuets de Sport des Provinces Altantique (ATSPA)
c/o Memorial University, PO Box 4200, 230 Elizabeth Ave., St. John's NL A1C 5S7
info@apata.ca
www.apata.ca
Overview: A small provincial organization
Description: To promote & deliver quality care to athletic individuals through injury prevention, emergency services & rehabilitation; *Member of:* Canadian Athletic Therapists Association
Chief Officer(s): Lauren Lattimer, President
lauren.lattimer@acadiau.ca

Canadian Academy of Sport & Exercise Medicine (CASEM) / Académie canadienne de médecine du sport et de l'exercice (ACMSE)
#300, 55 Metcalfe St., Ottawa ON K1P 6L5
Tel: 613-748-5851; *Fax:* 613-912-0128
Toll-Free: 877-585-2394
admin@casem-acmse.org
casem-acmse.org
www.instagram.com/cansportmed
www.facebook.com/CanadianAcademyofSportandExerciseMedicine
twitter.com/CASEMACMSE
Previous Name: Canadian Academy of Sport Medicine
Overview: A medium-sized national charitable organization founded in 1970
Description: To promote excellence in the practice of medicine, as it applies to physical activity; To advance the art & science of

sport medicine
Affiliation(s): World Federation of Sport Medicine
Chief Officer(s): Dawn Haworth, Executive Director
Finances: *Funding Sources:* Membership fees; Donations
Fees: $25 student; $175 retired/postgraduate medical trainee; $350 regular; *Member Profile:* All medical doctors; Residents & fellows; Medical students with an interest in sport medicine; *Committees:* Athletes with a Disabilty; Annual Symposium; Clinical Journal of Sport Medicine; Credentials (Diploma); Communications, Marketing & Membership; Fellowship; Official Languages; Paediatric Sport & Exercise Medicine; Timely Topics; Publications; Research; Selection; Sport Safety; Team Physician; Team Physician Development; Women's Issues in Sport Medicine; Interest Groups
Activities: Conducting research; Offering continuing medical education; Providing current information; Creating networking opportunities

Canadian Athletic Therapists Association (CATA) / Association canadienne des thérapeutes du sport
#300, 400 - 5th Ave. SW, Calgary AB T2P 0L6
Tel: 403-509-2282; *Fax:* 403-509-2280
Toll-Free: 888-509-2282
info@athletictherapy.org
athletictherapy.org
www.instagram.com/cata_canada
www.linkedin.com/company/canadian-athletic-therapist-association
www.facebook.com/catacanada
twitter.com/CATA_Canada
Overview: A medium-sized national licensing organization founded in 1968
Description: To deliver care through injury prevention, emergency services & rehabilitative techniques
Chief Officer(s): Mike Robinson, President
mrobinson@athletictherapy.org
Sandy Jespersen, Executive Director, 416-549-1682
executivedirector@athletictherapy.org
Membership: 2,600; *Member Profile:* Certified Athletic Therapists; Certification candidates; *Committees:* Canadian Board of Certification for Athletic Therapy; Education; Marketing; Sponsorship & Insurance Billing; Program Accreditation; Member Services; High-Performance Providers; International Relations; Financial Advisory; Ethics; Ombudsperson; President's
Activities: Monitoring of professional standards; Hosting conferences

Corporation des thérapeutes du sport du Québec (CTSQ)
7141, rue Sherbrooke ouest, #SP165, Montréal QC H4B 1R6
Tél: 514-848-2424
admin@ctsq.qc.ca
www.ctsq.qc.ca
www.facebook.com/therapeutesdusport
twitter.com/therapiedusport
Aperçu: *Dimension:* petite; *Envergure:* provinciale; *Organisme sans but lucratif;* Organisme de réglementation
Membre de: Canadian Athletic Therapists Association
Membre(s) du bureau directeur: Fayez Abdulrahman, President
president@ctsq.qc.ca
Eric Grenier-Denis, Executive Director
Finances: *Budget de fonctionnement annuel:* Moins de $50,000
Membre: 100-499
Activités: Développement professionnel ainsi que réglementation et attribution de licences professionnelles

Manitoba Athletic Therapists Association Inc. (MATA)
145 Pacific Ave., Winnipeg MB R3B 2Z6
Tel: 204-925-5930; *Fax:* 204-925-5624
mata@sportmanitoba.ca
www.mata.mb.ca
www.facebook.com/162809277115285
twitter.com/MATATherapist
Overview: A small provincial organization founded in 1983
Description: Committed to the prevention and care of activity-related injuries, at all levels of sport and recreation, ranging from the grass roots level to the elite athlete, throughout Manitoba.; *Member of:* Canadian Athletic Therapists Association; Sports Medicine Council of Manitoba; Sport Manitoba
Chief Officer(s): Mike Hutton, President
mhutton@mbteach.org
Finances: *Annual Operating Budget:* $50,000-$100,000
Staff: 2 staff member(s)
Membership: 200; *Fees:* Schedule available
Activities: Athletic First Aid Programs; medical coverage for sport & recreation; *Library:* Yes (Open to Public)

Ontario Athletic Therapists Association (OATA)
#280, 60 Columbia Way, Markham ON L3R 0C9
Tel: 905-946-8080; *Fax:* 905-946-1517
oatamembership@gmail.com
www.ontarioathletictherapists.org
www.linkedin.com/groups/4044330
www.facebook.com/187942491304864
Overview: A small provincial organization
Description: To support athletic therapists in Ontario; To liaise with the public, governments, third parties, & other stakeholders; *Member of:* Canadian Athletic Therapists Association
Chief Officer(s): Andrew Laskoski, President
drew.laskoski@bellnet.ca
Membership: 400; *Fees:* $50-$200; *Member Profile:* Must be enrolled or graduate of an accredited institution - Sheridan College, Oakville Athletic Therapy Program or York University, Sport Therapy Program
Activities: Providing educational & professional development opportunities to members

Saskatchewan Athletic Therapists Association (SATA)
#111, 4100 Sandhill Cres., Regina SK S4V 3G9
info@saskathletictherapy.ca
www.saskathletictherapy.ca
www.facebook.com/saskathletictherapy
twitter.com/therapySK
Overview: A small provincial organization
Description: To certify, regulate, & discipline athletic therapists in Saskatchewan in order to protect the public; *Member of:* Canadian Athletic Therapists Association; Athletic Therapists in Canada
Chief Officer(s): Nicole Renneberg, President
president@saskathletictherapy.ca
Fees: Schedule available; *Member Profile:* Athletic therapists in Saskatchewan; *Committees:* Ethics; Insurance Billing

Sport Medicine & Science Council of Manitoba Inc.
145 Pacific Ave., Winnipeg MB R3B 2Z6
Tel: 204-925-5750; *Fax:* 204-925-5624
sport.med@sportmanitoba.ca
sportmed.mb.ca
twitter.com/smsc_mb
Overview: A small provincial organization
Description: To meet the needs of Manitoba's sport, recreation & fitness communities through an organized cooperative forum of medical, paramedical and sport science provider groups
Chief Officer(s): Joshua Stolar, Executive Director
Chris Adam, CCFP(SEM), FCFP, President
Activities: *Library:* Sport Medicine & Science Council of Manitoba Resource Library (Open to Public)

Sport Medicine Council of Alberta (SMCA)
Percy Page Centre, 11759 Groat Rd., Main Fl., Edmonton AB T5M 3K6
Tel: 780-415-0812; *Fax:* 780-422-3093
www.sportmedab.ca
twitter.com/SportMedAB
Overview: A medium-sized provincial licensing organization founded in 1983
Description: To develop, promote & coordinate programs & services optimizing safe & healthful participation in sport & leisure activities for all Albertans; *Member of:* Sport Medicine
Chief Officer(s): Clayton Nielsen, President
Barb Adamson, Executive Director
badamson@sportmedab.ca
Lindsey Wilton, Coordinator, Outreach
lwilton@sportmedab.ca
Fees: $15 student; $50 subscriber; $265 corporate; *Member Profile:* Athletic therapists & teachers; sport physiotherapists; sport medicine physicians; sport scientists (including exercise physiologists, sport nutrition specialists, sport psychologists); teams; clubs
Activities: Athletic first aid courses; taping & strapping; sport nutrition courses; medical supply sales; kit rentals; speakers bureau; resource library; *Internships:* Yes; *Speaker Service:* Yes *Library:* Yes (Open to Public)

Sport Physiotherapy Canada (SPC)
c/o CPA, #270, 955 Green Valley Cres., Ottawa ON K2C 3V4
Tel: 613-564-5454; *Fax:* 613-564-1577
info@sportphysio.ca
www.sportphysio.ca
www.youtube.com/user/physiotherapycan
www.facebook.com/sportphysiocanada
twitter.com/sportphysiocan
Previous Name: Sport Physiotherapy Division of the Canadian Physiotherapy Association
Overview: A small national organization founded in 1972
Description: To promote professional development of members; To ensure high-quality health care for Canada's

athletes; *Member of:* Canadian Physiotherapy Association; Sport Medicine Council of Canada
Chief Officer(s): Samantha Lee, Operations Manager
program@sportphysio.ca
Membership: 1,200; *Member Profile:* Members can be physiotherapists, students, graduate / practising physiotherapists, or SPD-certified sport physiotherapists

SportMedBC
#2350, 3713 Kensington Ave., Burnaby BC B5B 0A7
Tel: 604-294-3050; *Fax:* 604-294-3020
Toll-Free: 888-755-3375
info@sportmedbc.com
www.sportmedbc.com
www.youtube.com/user/SportMedBC
www.facebook.com/sportmedbc
twitter.com/SportMedBC
Previous Name: Sport Medicine Council of British Columbia
Overview: A small provincial organization founded in 1982
Description: To support health & performance in British Columbia through sport & exercise
Chief Officer(s): Robert Joncas, Executive Director, 604-294-3050 102
executivedirector@sportmedbc.com
Finances: *Annual Operating Budget:* $100,000-$250,000; *Funding Sources:* Service fees; grants
Staff: 7 staff member(s)
Membership: 275; *Fees:* Free
Activities: Injury Prevention; Athlete Development; Drug-free Sport

Sport Sciences

Canadian Society for Psychomotor Learning & Sport Psychology (CSPLSP) / Société canadienne d'apprentissage psychomoteur et de psychologie du sport (SCAPPS)
#360, 125 University Private, Ottawa ON K1N 6N5
www.scapps.org
Overview: A small national organization founded in 1977
Description: To promote the study of motor development, motor learning, motor control & sport psychology
Chief Officer(s): Tanya Berry, President
Melanie Gregg, Secretary, Communications
Fees: $25 trainee/post-doc; $65 professional
Activities: Facilitating the exchange of scientific information related to psychomotor learning & sport psychology

Sports

Amateur Athletic Union (AAU)
PO Box 22049, Lake Buena Vista FL 32830 USA
Tel: 407-934-7200; *Fax:* 407-934-7242
Toll-Free: 800-228-4872
aausports.org
www.youtube.com/therealaauvideo
www.facebook.com/realaau
twitter.com/therealaau
Overview: A large international organization founded in 1888
Description: To offer a lifelong progression of amateur sports programs for persons of all ages, races & creeds, thereby enhancing the physical, mental & moral development of amateur athletes; To promote good sportsmanship, good citizenship & safety
Chief Officer(s): Roger Goudy, President
president@aausports.org
Finances: *Funding Sources:* Membership dues
Staff: 1500 volunteer(s)
Membership: 700,000; *Fees:* Schedule available
Activities: Conducts programs & works with other sports organizations to benefit amateur athletes; Conducts recognition programs for outstanding amateur athletes; Publishing an extensive line of handbooks & brochures on individual sports; *Internships:* Yes; *Rents Mailing List:* Yes *Library:* Yes (Open to Public)

Arctic Winter Games International Committee (AWGIC)
www.awg.ca
Overview: A medium-sized local organization founded in 1968
Description: To provide common ground for developing Northern athletes; to promote cultural & social exchanges among Northern regions of the continent
Chief Officer(s): Jens Brinch, President
Ian Legaree, Technical Director
Finances: *Annual Operating Budget:* $100,000-$250,000
Staff: 9 volunteer(s)
Membership: 1-99
Activities: To invite & review bids from communities wanting to host the Games; to select sports for each set of Games &

prepare the technical package of rules, categories, events, team composition, medals to be awarded, competition format; to oversee the preparations of a Host Society for the Games; *Library:* Arctic Winter Games Archives by appointment

AthletesCAN
PO Box 89007, Stn. Westdale, Hamilton ON L8S 4R5
Tel: 613-526-4025; *Toll-Free:* 888-832-4222
info@athletescan.com
athletescan.com
www.instagram.com/athletescan
www.facebook.com/AthletesCAN
twitter.com/AthletesCAN
Also Known As: The Association of Canada's National Team Athletes
Previous Name: The Athletes Association of Canada
Overview: A medium-sized national organization founded in 1992
Description: To influence a sport system that empowers athletes to achieve their full potential on the field of play & beyond
Chief Officer(s): Georgina Truman, Manager, Athlete Relations & Operations
Membership: 3,000+
Activities: Education; Leadership; Advocacy; Representation

Atlantic University Sport Association (AUS)
#3130, 5657 Spring Garden Rd., Halifax NS B3J 3R4
Tel: 902-425-4235; *Fax:* 902-425-7825
www.atlanticuniversitysport.com
www.youtube.com/ATLuniversitysport
www.facebook.com/AtlanticUniversitySport
twitter.com/AUS_SUA
Also Known As: Atlantic University Sport
Previous Name: Atlantic Universities Athletic Association
Overview: A medium-sized local organization founded in 1974
Description: To advance student athletes & university sport; *Member of:* Canadian Interuniversity Sport Association
Chief Officer(s): Philip M. Currie, Executive Director
pcurrie@atlanticuniversitysport.com
John Keefe, Director, Events & Sport Programming
jkeefe@atlanticuniversitysport.com
Jess Burns, Manager, Communications & New Media
jburns@atlanticuniversitysport.com
Finances: *Funding Sources:* Memberships; Partners
Staff: 4 staff member(s)
Membership: 11 institutional, 2,000 individuals; *Fees:* Schedule available; *Member Profile:* Atlantic Canadian universities
Activities: Governing university sport in Atlantic Canada; Coordinating sport programming among member universities; Organizing Atlantic University Sport championships and events; Raising profiles of student-athletes and university sports

BC Games Society
#200, 990 Fort St., Victoria BC V8V 3K2
Tel: 250-387-1375; *Fax:* 250-387-4489
www.bcgames.org
www.instagram.com/bcgames1
www.facebook.com/BCGamesSociety
twitter.com/BCGames1
Previous Name: British Columbia Games Society
Overview: A small provincial organization
Description: To provide event management leadership in the creation of development opportunities for individuals, sport organizations & host communities
Chief Officer(s): Kelly Mann, President & CEO
kellym@bcgames.org

BC School Sports (BCSS)
Sydney Landing, #2003A, 3713 Kensington Ave., Burnaby BC V5B 0A7
Tel: 604-477-1488; *Fax:* 604-477-1484
info@bcschoolsports.ca
www.bcschoolsports.ca
www.facebook.com/224539464369947
twitter.com/bcschoolsports
Previous Name: BC Federation of School Athletic Associations
Overview: A medium-sized provincial charitable organization founded in 1968
Description: To encourage student participation in extra-curricular athletics, assist schools in the development & delivery of their programs & provide governance for interschool competition; *Member of:* School Sport Canada; Sport BC
Affiliation(s): USA National Federation of State High Schools
Chief Officer(s): Sydney Landing, Executive Director
Shannon Key, Manager, Sport
skey@bcschoolsports.ca
Finances: *Annual Operating Budget:* $500,000-$1.5 Million; *Funding Sources:* Membership fees; government; sponsors; advertising
Staff: 3 staff member(s); 6 volunteer(s)

Membership: 400; *Fees:* Schedule available; *Member Profile:* Accredited secondary school in British Columbia; *Committees:* Administrators; Coaching Development; Competitive Standards; Disciplinary; Eligibility; Scholarship & Awards
Activities: Provincial championships; advocacy; regulatory services; fundraising services; coaching conference; leadership camp; *Awareness Events:* Milk Run; Spirit Week; National School Sports Week, Oct.

British Columbia Disc Sports (BCDSS)
PO Box 21723, 1424 Commercial Dr., Vancouver BC V5L 5G3
bcdiscsports@gmail.com
bcdiscsports.com
Also Known As: The Disc Sports Provincial Sport Organization (PSO)
Previous Name: BC Disc Sports Society
Overview: A small provincial organization founded in 1991
Description: To provide access to resources, build community partnerships, & provide education to make disc golf an accessible sport
Affiliation(s): BC Ultimate
Chief Officer(s): Craig Sheather, President
Carrie Neal, Vice-President
Dan Laitsch, Past President
Membership: 187; *Fees:* $10 annually
Activities: Disc golf; double disc court; freestyle; goaltimate; guts; ultimate

British Columbia Floorball Federation (BCFF)
3183 Edgemont Blvd., North Vancouver BC V7R 2N8
Tel: 778-385-7825
info@bcfloorball.com
www.bcfloorball.com
www.facebook.com/BCFloorball
twitter.com/bcfloorball
Overview: A small provincial organization
Description: To be the provincial governing body for the sport of floorball in British Columbia; *Member of:* Floorball Canada
Affiliation(s): WheelchairFloorball.com; JuniorFloorball.com
Chief Officer(s): Blair Zimmerman, President
Fees: $10-$50

British Columbia Shuffleboard Association
c/o Elaine Hill, #401, 10180 - 153 St., Surrey BC V3R 0B5
Also Known As: BCSA
Overview: A small provincial organization
Description: To govern shuffleboard in British Columbia
Chief Officer(s): Katie Docile, President, 604-671-1761
Elaine Hill, Secretary-Treasurer, 604-591-5057

Canada Games Council (CGC) / Conseil des jeux du Canada
PO Box 72, #261, 1200 St Laurent Blvd., Ottawa ON K1K 3B8
Tel: 613-526-2320
cgc@canadagames.ca
www.canadagames.ca
www.instagram.com/canadagamescouncil
www.linkedin.com/company/canada-games-council
www.facebook.com/CanadaGames
twitter.com/CanadaGames
Overview: A medium-sized national organization founded in 1967
Description: To foster on-going partnerships with organizations at the municipal, provincial & national levels
Chief Officer(s): Dan Wilcock, President & CEO
Finances: *Annual Operating Budget:* $250,000-$500,000; *Funding Sources:* Federal Government (operation costs); Federal Government, Provincial Government & host city (capital)
Staff: 9 staff member(s); 5000 volunteer(s)
Activities: *Internships:* Yes

Canada West Universities Athletic Association
PO Box 44085, Stn. Kensington Square, Burnaby BC V5B 4Y2
sportsinfo@canadawest.org
www.canadawest.org
Also Known As: Canada West
Overview: A small local organization
Description: To organize inter-collegiate sporting events between members
Chief Officer(s): Rocky Olfert, Managing Director, 604-751-1970
rocky.olfert@canadawest.org
Evan Daum, Associate Director, Communications & Marketing, 780-266-4432
evan.daum@canadawest.org
Membership: 17 universities; *Member Profile:* Western Canadian universities

Canadian Centre for Ethics in Sport (CCES) / Centre canadien pour l'éthique dans le sport
#201, 2723 Lancaster Rd., Ottawa ON K1B 0B1
Tel: 613-521-3340; *Fax:* 613-521-3134
Toll-Free: 800-672-7775
info@cces.ca
www.cces.ca
www.instagram.com/ethicsinsport
www.linkedin.com/company/canadian-centre-for-ethics-in-sport
www.facebook.com/CanadianCentreforEthicsinSport
twitter.com/EthicsInSport
Overview: A medium-sized national organization founded in 1991
Description: To foster ethical sport for all Canadians
Affiliation(s): True Sport Foundation
Chief Officer(s): Don McKenzie, Chair
Paul Melia, President & CEO
pmelia@cces.ca

Canadian National Shuffleboard Association (CNSA)
theshufflersnews.wordpress.com
Also Known As: Shuffleboard Canada
Overview: A small national organization
Description: To promote shuffleboard in Canada & provide the opportunity for the development of skills; To create an amicable social environment; To promote & provide healthy physical & social activity for people of all ages & abilities
Chief Officer(s): Jim Corbeil, President, 519-290-4400
Ann Engell, Secretary
ann@northshore.tax
Murray Burnett, Treasurer

Canadian Shuffleboard Congress
c/o Rita MacCrimmon, 2369 Bayside Rd. SW, Airdrie AB T4B 3E3
www.canadianshuffleboardcongress.com
Overview: A small national organization
Description: To govern shuffleboard in Canada
Chief Officer(s): Rick Litman, President, 403-217-9772
Rita McCrimmon, Secretary-Treasurer, 403-420-1023

Canadian Sport Tourism Alliance (CSTA)
#600, 116 Lisgar St., Ottawa ON K2P 0C2
Tel: 613-688-5843; *Fax:* 613-238-3878
info@canadiansporttourism.com
www.canadiansporttourism.com
twitter.com/CdnSportTourism
Overview: A small national organization founded in 2000
Description: To market Canada internationally as a preferred sport tourism destination
Chief Officer(s): Rick Traer, Chief Executive Officer
rtraer@canadiansporttourism.com
Krista Benoit, Executive Director, Marketing & Events
kbenoit@canadiansporttourism.com
Barb MacDonald, Consultant, Communications
bmacdonald@canadiansporttourism.com
Membership: 200; *Fees:* Schedule available; *Member Profile:* Municipalities across Canada & abroad; *Committees:* Membership; Marketing & Communications; Research; Training & Education; Government Relations

Canadian Tire Jumpstart Charities
PO Box 770, Stn. K, 2180 Yonge St., Toronto ON M4P 2V8
Toll-Free: 844-937-7529
jumpstart@cantire.com
jumpstart.canadiantire.ca
www.instagram.com/ctjumpstart
www.facebook.com/CTJumpstart
twitter.com/ctjumpstart
Also Known As: Jumpstart
Overview: A large national charitable organization founded in 2005
Description: To helps kids overcome financial & accessibility barriers to sport & recreation
Finances: *Funding Sources:* Sport Canada; Donations
Staff: 32 staff member(s)

Floorball Alberta
Edmonton AB
Tel: 780-999-5333
info@floorballalberta.com
www.floorballalberta.com
www.facebook.com/FloorballAlberta
twitter.com/Floorball_AB
Overview: A small provincial organization founded in 2010
Description: To be the provincial governing body for the sport of floorball in Alberta; *Member of:* Floorball Canada
Membership: 6 regional associations

Floorball Canada
Cambridge ON
info@floorballcanada.org
www.floorballcanada.org
www.facebook.com/CanadaFloorball
twitter.com/CanadaFloorball
Overview: A medium-sized national organization
Description: To be the official governing body of the sport of floorball in Canada; *Member of:* International Floorball Federation
Affiliation(s): Hockey Canada
Chief Officer(s): Randy Sa'd, President
Fees: $15 recreational; $30 competetive

Floorball Nova Scotia
NS
floorballnovascotia.ca
www.linkedin.com/pub/floorball-nova-scotia/5a/831/b28
www.facebook.com/256739071063733
Overview: A small provincial organization
Description: To be the provincial governing body for the sport of floorball in Nova Scotia.; *Member of:* Floorball Canada
Membership: 5 provincial leagues
Activities: Learn to Play clincs; Birthday parties; Leagues; Tournaments; Recreational pick-up games

Fort Saskatchewan Minor Sports Association (FSMSA)
10013-96th Ave., Fort Saskatchewan AB T8L 1P9
Tel: 780-998-1835
fsmsa@telus.net
www.fsmsa.net
twitter.com/fortsaskmsa
Overview: A small local organization
Description: To govern minor sports in Fort Saskatchewan
Chief Officer(s): Fran Vanderwell, Office Manager
Kathleen Zellweger, President
president.fsmsa@telus.net

International Masters Games Association (IMGA)
Maison du Sport International, Avenue de Rhodanie 54, Lausanne 1007 Switzerland
info@imga.ch
imga.ch
www.youtube.com/user/TheIMGA
www.linkedin.com/company/international-masters-games-association
www.facebook.com/IMGAmastersgames
twitter.com/IMGAmasters
Overview: A large international organization founded in 1995
Description: To govern the World Masters Games
Chief Officer(s): Kai Holm, President
Jens V. Holm, Chief Executive Officer
jvh@imga.ch
Member Profile: International Sports Federations participating in the World Masters Games
Activities: World Masters Games; European Masters Games

Kitchener Sports Association (KSA)
26 Elm St., Kitchener ON N2G 2G4
www.kitchenersports.ca
www.facebook.com/492371234132957
twitter.com/KitchenerSA
Overview: A small local organization founded in 1944
Description: To govern sports & sporting facilities in Kitchener
Chief Officer(s): Bill Pegg, President
ksapresident@kitchenersports.ca
Member Profile: Those interested in local minor sports & athletes; *Committees:* Operating

Lower Mainland Independent Secondary School Athletic Association (LMISSAA)
BC
athletics@yorkhouse.ca
www.lmissaa.com
Overview: A small local organization
Description: To organize sports for Lower Mainland secondary schools; *Member of:* BC School Sports
Chief Officer(s): Carm Renzullo, President

Manitoba Organization of Disc Sports (MODS)
#402, 145 Pacific Ave., Winnipeg MB R3B 2Z6
Tel: 204-925-5665; *Fax:* 204-925-5916
bsddirector@mods.mb.ca
mods.mb.ca
www.facebook.com/MBDiscSports
twitter.com/modsmbca
Overview: A small provincial organization founded in 1988
Description: To be the provincial governing body for disc sports in Manitoba; *Member of:* Sport Manitoba
Chief Officer(s): Billy Donaldson, President
president@mods.mb.ca

Manitoba Shuffleboard Association
MB

shuffleboard.wordpress.com
Also Known As: MSA
Overview: A small provincial organization
Description: To govern shuffleboard in Manitoba
Chief Officer(s): Wendy Popkes, Contact, 204-414-3305
wendyp11@shaw.ca
Raymonde Gérardy, Contact, 204-509-1109
raymonde4@gmail.com
Fees: $40

Motivate Canada
#408, 11 Rosemount Ave., Ottawa ON K1Y 4R8
Tel: 613-789-3333; *Toll-Free:* 866-378-3361
admin@motivatecanada.ca
www.motivatecanada.ca
www.instagram.com/motivatecanada
www.facebook.com/MotivateCanada
twitter.com/motivatecanada
Overview: A medium-sized national organization
Description: To empower youth to become active, healthy,
confident, community minded & involved
Chief Officer(s): Lisa Kwiatkowski, Chief Executive Officer
lisa@motivatecanada.ca
Finances: *Funding Sources:* Sport Canada; Government of
Ontario; Ontario Trillium Foundation; ParticipACTION; Sport for
Life

Napanee Sports Association
16 McPherson Dr., Napanee ON K7R 3L1
Tel: 613-354-4423; *Fax:* 613-354-2212
info@napaneesportsassociation.com
www.napaneesportsassociation.com
Overview: A small local organization founded in 2006
Description: To provide funding to local sports teams
Chief Officer(s): Chuck Airhart, Chair

New Brunswick Interscholastic Athletic Association (NBIAA) / Association sportive interscolaire du Nouveau-Brunswick (ASINB)
PO Box 6000, Fredericton NB E3B 5H1
Tel: 506-457-4843
nbiaa@gnb.ca
www.nbiaa-asinb.org
Overview: A medium-sized provincial organization founded in
1926
Description: To be the governing body of high school sports; To
create, promote, & facilitate positive sporting experiences in an
educational environment in the province of New Brunswick;
Member of: School Sport Canada
Chief Officer(s): Allyson Ouellette, Executive Director
Membership: 75 schools; *Fees:* $350 per school; *Committees:*
Executive
Activities: Badminton; Baseball; Basketball; Cheerleading;
Cross Country; Field Hockey; Football; Golf; Hockey; Rugby;
Soccer; Softball; Swimming; Track & Field; Volleyball; Wrestling

Ontario Disc Sports Association (ODSA)
#3, 160 Aberdeen Ave., Hamilton ON L8P 2P6
Tel: 905-808-5993
chris@ontariodiscsports.ca
www.ontariodiscsports.ca
www.facebook.com/OntarioDiscSports.ca
twitter.com/OntarioDisc
Overview: A small provincial organization
Description: To be the provincial governing body for disc sports
in Ontario
Chief Officer(s): John MacLeod, President
president@ondisc.org
Chris Ozolins, Executive Director
chris@ontariodiscsports.ca
Jacynthe Goulard, Vice President
vicepresident@ondisc.ca
Fees: $10 individual; $30 club
Activities: Beach ultimate; discathon; disc golf; double disc
court; field events; freestyle; Goaltimate; guts; Catch & Fetch;
ultimate

Ontario Floorball Association
#2, 30 Vogell Rd., Richmond Hill ON L4B 3K6
info@ontariofloorball.com
www.ontariofloorball.com
Overview: A small provincial organization
Description: To be the provincial governing body for the sport of
floorball in Ontario; *Member of:* Floorball Canada; International
Floorball Federation
Chief Officer(s): Kultar Singh, President
David Thomas, Director, Corporate Relations

Ontario Shuffleboard Association (OSA)
PO Box 1690, Guelph ON N1H 6Z9
ontarioshuffleboard.com
Overview: A medium-sized provincial organization founded in
1964
Description: To govern & organize shuffleboard in Ontario;
Member of: Canadian Shuffleboard Congress
Chief Officer(s): Bonnie Redmond, President
Activities: Organizing tournaments; Qualifying players for the
Canadian Shuffleboard Championship

Ottawa Carleton Ultimate Association (OCUA)
#1, 875 Banks St., Ottawa ON K1S 3W4
Tel: 613-860-6282
info@ocua.ca
www.ocua.ca
www.instagram.com/ottawa_ultimate
www.facebook.com/OttawaUltimate
twitter.com/ocua
Overview: A medium-sized local organization founded in 1993
Description: To promote ultimate & disc sports in the
Ottawa-Carleton region
Chief Officer(s): Christopher Castonguay, Executive Director
ed@ocua.ca
Dominique (Dom) Rioux, Program Officer
dom@ocua.ca
Activities: Organizing & conducting the operations of leagues &
tournaments; Operating a multi-field sports facility designed for
ultimate

Own the Podium (OTP) / · nous le podium (ANP)
#120, 700 Industrial Ave., Ottawa ON K1G 0Y9
Tel: 613-236-2052; *Fax:* 613-236-3853
admin@motivatecanada.ca
www.ownthepodium.org
www.instagram.com/motivatecanada
www.facebook.com/MotivateCanada
twitter.com/motivatecanada
Overview: A medium-sized national organization founded in
2010
Description: To provide technical leadership for Canadian
sports to achieve sustainable & improved podium performances
at the Olympic and Paralympic Games
Chief Officer(s): Anne Merklinger, Chief Executive Officer
Finances: *Funding Sources:* Sport Canada
Staff: 27 staff member(s)

Pacific Institute for Sport Excellence (PISE)
4371 Interurban Rd., Victoria BC V9E 2C5
Tel: 250-220-2510; *Fax:* 250-220-2501
info@pise.ca
www.pise.ca
www.youtube.com/user/piseworld
www.facebook.com/PacificInstituteforSportExcellence
twitter.com/PISEworld
Overview: A small provincial organization
Description: To be a leader in high performance sport
development, community programs, sport & exercise education
& applied research & innovation
Chief Officer(s): Robert Bettauer, CEO
rbettauer@piseworld.com
Fees: $65 per month; $175 four months; $460 annual

Pan American Sports Organization (PASO)
Valentin Gomez Faras #51, San Rafael 06470 Mexico
info@panamsports.org
www.panamsports.org
Overview: A large international organization founded in 1948
Description: To celebration & conduct the Pan American
Games; To support the development & protection of sports, as
well as the Olympic Movement in the Americas
Chief Officer(s): Neven Ilic, President
Activities: Pan American Games

Parksville Golden Oldies Sports Association (PGOSA)
PO Box 957, Parksville BC V9P 2G9
www.pgosa.org
Overview: A small local organization founded in 1993
Description: To provide physical activities to citizens of
Parksville over 55.
Chief Officer(s): Rob Jonas, President, 250-797-6130
rjonas13@hotmail.com
Shelley Goertzen, Liason, Membership, 250-240-9663
pgosachronicle@gmail.com
Randy White, Secretary
randypgosasports@gmail.com
Fees: $15; *Member Profile:* People over 55

Réseau du sport étudiant du Québec (RSEQ)
4545, av Pierre-de-Coubertin, Montréal QC H1V 0B2
Tél: 514-252-3300; *Téléc:* 514-254-3292
info@rseq.ca
rseq.ca
www.facebook.com/RSEQ1
twitter.com/RSEQ1
Nom précédent: Fédération québécoise du sport étudiant
Aperçu: *Dimension:* moyenne; *Envergure: provinciale;
Organisme sans but lucratif; fondée en 1988*
Description: Favoriser les actions éducatives dans le domaine
de l'activité physique et sportive que se donne le milieu de
l'éducation dans le but de contribuer, et cela dans les trois
ordres d'enseignement, au développement intégral des élèves,
des étudiantes et des étudiants du Québec; *Membre de:* Sport
Scolaire Canada; Canadian Colleges Athletic Association
Membre(s) du bureau directeur: Gustave Roel,
Président-directeur général, 514-252-3300 3600
groel@rseq.ca
Finances: *Budget de fonctionnement annuel:* Plus de $5 Million
Personnel:28 membre(s) du personnel
Critères d'admissibilite: Établissements scolaires, collégiaux et
universitaires
Activités: *Stagiaires:* Oui

Réseau du sport étudiant du Québec Saguenay-Lac St-Jean
CEGEP de Chicoutimi, 534, rue Jacques Cartier est, Chicoutimi
QC G7H 1Z6
Tél: 418-543-3532; *Téléc:* 418-693-0503
saglac.rseq.ca
Également appelé:RSEQ Saguenay-Lac St-Jean
Nom précédent: Association régionale du sport étudiant du
Saguenay-Lac St-Jean
Aperçu: *Dimension:* petite; *Envergure: locale; Organisme sans
but lucratif; fondée en 1974*
Description: Favoriser la réalisation de l'ensemble des actions
éducatives dans le domaine de l'activité physique et
particuliérement du sport en vue de contribuer au
développement intégral des élèves & étudiants de niveaux
primaire, secondaire, collégial et universitaire dans la région du
Saguenay-Lac St-Jean; *Membre de:* Réseau du sport étudiant
du Québec
Membre(s) du bureau directeur: Éric Benoît, Directeur
général, 418-543-3532 1214
ebenoit@saglac.rseq.ca
Finances: *Fonds:*Gouvernement provincial
Membre: 16; *Critères d'admissibilite:* Écoles privées;
commissions scolaires; CÉGEPS; universités
Activités: Manifestations sportives régionales et provinciales;
perfectionnement; *Stagiaires:* Oui; *Service de conférenciers:* Oui

Sarnia Minor Athletic Association (SMAA)
Chaytor Building - Germain Park, PO Box 524, Sarnia ON N7T
7J4
Tel: 519-332-1896; *Fax:* 519-332-1569
smaa@teksavvy.com
www.sarniaminorathletic.com
Overview: A small local organization founded in 1947
Description: To provide sports activities to local youth &
promote good sportmanship & citizenship
Chief Officer(s): Sharon Baxter, President

Sask Sport Inc.
1870 Lorne St., Regina SK S4P 2L7
Tel: 306-780-9300; *Fax:* 306-781-6021
sasksport@sasksport.sk.ca
www.sasksport.sk.ca
Overview: A medium-sized provincial organization founded in
1972
Description: To ensure the total development of amateur sport
through the provincial sport governing bodies; to promote
extensive participation towards excellence
Chief Officer(s): Kevin Gilroy, Chief Executive Officer
Finances: *Annual Operating Budget:* $500,000-$1.5 Million;
Funding Sources: Lotteries
Staff: 50 staff member(s); 13 volunteer(s)
Membership: 70 active & affiliate; *Fees:* Schedule available
Activities:*Library:* Resource Centre for Sport, Culture &
Recreation

Saskatchewan High Schools Athletic Association (SHSAA)
#1, 575 Park St., Regina SK S4N 5B2
Tel: 306-721-2151; *Fax:* 306-721-2659
shsaa@shsaa.ca
www.shsaa.ca
www.instagram.com/shsaasport
www.facebook.com/264860913591330
twitter.com/shsaasport

Overview: A medium-sized provincial organization founded in 1948
Description: To use interschool athletics as a means for fostering positive opportunities for students; *Member of:* School Sport Canada
Chief Officer(s): Valerie Gordon, President, 306-295-7751, Fax: 306-295-3709
Lyle McKellar, Executive Director
l.mckellar@shsaa.ca
Member Profile: Education boards; High schools; *Committees:* Finance; Symposium; Officials; Policy

Saskatchewan Shuffleboard Association
c/o Crystal Benjamin, 159 Halifax St., Regina SK S4R 65K
Also Known As: SSA
Overview: A small provincial organization
Description: To govern shuffleboard in Saskatchewan
Chief Officer(s): Crystal Huzina, President, 306-535-7722
Chuzina@sgi.sk.ca
Dave Loughren, 1st Vice President, 306-535-1295
dave.loughren@bayer.ca
Crystal Benjamin, Treasurer, 306-698-3226

School Sport Canada (SSC) / Sport Scolaire Canada
c/o Saskatchewan High School Athletic Association, #1, 575 Park St., Regina SK S4N 5B2
Tel: 306-721-2151
schoolsportcanada@gmail.com
www.schoolsport.ca
Overview: A large national organization founded in 1967
Description: To be the national body for school sport in Canada; To promote positive sportsmanship, citizenship & the development of student athletes through interscholastic sport
Affiliation(s): National Federation of High Schools (NFHS)
Chief Officer(s): Lyle McKellar, President
l.mckellar@shsaa.ca
Membership: 12 member associations

Société des Jeux de l'Acadie inc. (SJA)
#210, 702, rue Principale, Petit-Rocher NB E8J 1V1
Tél: 506-783-4207; *Téléc:* 506-783-4209
sja1@nbnet.nb.ca
www.jeuxdelacadie.org

www.youtube.com/user/AcajouxJeuxdelAcadie
www.facebook.com/societedesjeuxdelacadie
twitter.com/acajoux
Aperçu: *Dimension:* petite; *Envergure:* locale; *Organisme sans but lucratif; fondée en 1981*
Description: Voir au maintien et au développement du Mouvement des Jeux de l'Acadie dans ses régions constituantes par l'entremise de rencontres sportives grâce à des ressources humaines, financières et des infrastructures adéquates; *Membre de:* Fondation des Jeux de l'Acadie inc.; Conseil économique du N.-B.; Sports N.-B.
Membre(s) du bureau directeur: Mylène Ouellet-LeBlanc, Directrice générale
sjadg@nb.aibn.com
Finances: *Budget de fonctionnement annuel:* $250,000-$500,000
Personnel: 4 membre(s) du personnel; 3500 bénévoles(s)
Membre: 8; *Comités:* Développement sportif; Développement régional; Financement et Marketing
Activités: Programme Académie jeunesse; relations publiques, représentations et communications

Southern Alberta Shuffleboard Association
c/o Rita McCrimmon, 2369 Bayside Rd. SW, Airdrie AB T4B 3E3
Also Known As: SASA
Overview: A small local organization
Description: To govern shuffleboard in Southern Alberta
Chief Officer(s): Jamie McCrimmon, Vice President, 403-420-1023
Rita McCrimmon, Secretary-Treasurer, 403-420-1023

Sport BC
#250, 999 Canada Pl., Vancouver BC V6C 3C1
Tel: 604-333-3400; *Fax:* 604-333-3401
info@sportbc.com
sportbc.com
www.facebook.com/SportBC
twitter.com/SportBC
Overview: A medium-sized provincial organization founded in 1966
Description: To provide leadership, direction, & support to member organizations in their delivery of amateur sport opportunities to all British Columbians; *Member of:* Sport West
Chief Officer(s): Rob Newman, President & CEO
rob.newman@sportbc.com
Pete Quevillon, Director, KidSport BC
pete.quevillon@sportbc.com

Finances: *Annual Operating Budget:* $1.5 Million-$3 Million; *Funding Sources:* Provincial Funding; Membership Fees; Corporate Support, Event & Fundraising; Fee for Services; All Sport Insurance; SBC Insurance Operations
Staff: 7 staff member(s)
Membership: 80 Associations; *Fees:* Schedule available; *Member Profile:* Non-profit society sport organization with province-wide representation; *Committees:* Finance & Audit; Governance
Activities: Participation & Excellence; KidSport Fund; Leadership; Sport Promotion; Advocacy; Organizations Development; Athlete Voice; *Internships:* Yes; *Speaker Service:* Yes

Sport for Life (S4L)
775 Market St., Victoria BC V8T 0B4
Tel: 778-433-2066
info@sportforlife.ca
sportforlife.ca
www.youtube.com/c/CS4L_ACSV
www.facebook.com/CanadianSportforLife
twitter.com/SportForLife_
Overview: A medium-sized national organization founded in 2014
Description: To create a future where everyone has access to quality sport & physical literacy experiences
Chief Officer(s): Richard Way, Chief Executive Officer
Finances: *Funding Sources:* Sport Canada
Staff: 27 staff member(s)

Sport Information Resource Centre (SIRC)
c/o House of Sport, RA Centre, 2451 Riverside Dr., Ottawa ON K1H 7X7
Tel: 613-231-7472
info@sirc.ca
sirc.ca
www.instagram.com/sirc_canada
www.linkedin.com/company/sirc_2
www.facebook.com/sirc.canada
twitter.com/SIRCtweets
Overview: A medium-sized national organization founded in 1973
Description: To engaging with organizations & individuals involved in the development of sport, recreation & physical education to enhance the capacity of shared community to foster growth & excellence
Chief Officer(s): Debra Gassewitz, President & CEO
Jan O'Donnell, Chief Financial Officer
Kim Gurtler, Manager, Programs & Operations
Finances: *Funding Sources:* Sport Canada
Staff: 27 staff member(s)

Sport Manitoba
Sport for Life Centre, 145 Pacific Ave., Winnipeg MB R3B 2Z6
Tel: 204-925-5600; *Fax:* 204-925-5916
info@sportmanitoba.ca
www.sportmanitoba.ca
www.instagram.com/SportManitoba
www.facebook.com/sportmb
twitter.com/SportManitoba
Previous Name: Manitoba Sports Federation Inc.
Overview: A large provincial organization founded in 1996
Description: To create the best sport community in Canada through provision of resources to recognized sport organizations, enabling them to encourage participation in sport at all levels of skill & ability & to develop athletes of national & international calibre
Chief Officer(s): Janet McMahon, Interim President & CEO, 204-926-8350
janet.mcmahon@sportmanitoba.ca
Laurel Read, Director, Finance & Operations
laurel.read@sportmanitoba.ca
Evan Andrew, Director, Brand & Revenue
evan.andrew@sportmanitoba.ca
Finances: *Funding Sources:* Provincial government
Staff: 45 staff member(s)
Activities: Operating & overseeing the Sport for Life Centre; Coaching Manitoba; Sport Medicine Centre; Manitoba Sports Hall of Fame; KidSport Manitoba; Power Smart Manitoba Games; & Team Manitoba; *Awareness Events:* Polar Bear Dare; *Speaker Service:* Yes *Library:* Yes by appointment

Sport New Brunswick / Sport Nouveau-Brunswick
#13, 900 Hanwell Rd., Fredericton NB E3B 6A2
Tel: 506-451-1320; *Fax:* 506-451-1325
director@sportnb.com
www.sportnb.com
twitter.com/SportNB
Also Known As: Sport NB
Overview: A medium-sized provincial charitable organization founded in 1968

Description: To promote the development of amateur sport in New Brunswick through services, programs, advocacy; *Member of:* Canadian Council of Provincial Territorial Sport Federations
Chief Officer(s): Darcy McKillop, Chief Executive Officer, 506-451-1327
director@sportnb.com
Sally Hutt, Coordinator, Programs
programs@sportnb.com
Finances: *Annual Operating Budget:* $250,000-$500,000; *Funding Sources:* Provincial government; membership fees; corporate sponsorship
Staff: 3 staff member(s)
Membership: 68 organizations with 120,000 participants; *Fees:* Schedule available
Activities: *Awareness Events:* McInnes Cooper Dragon Boat Festival; *Internships:* Yes; *Speaker Service:* Yes *Library:* Yes by appointment

Sport Newfoundland & Labrador
PO Box 8700, 1296A Kenmount Rd., St. John's NL A1B 4J6
Tel: 709-576-4932; *Fax:* 709-576-7493
sportnl@sportnl.ca
www.sportnl.ca
www.facebook.com/sportnl
twitter.com/sportnl
Also Known As: Sport NL
Previous Name: Newfoundland & Labrador Amateur Sports Federation
Overview: A medium-sized provincial organization founded in 1972
Description: To promote & advance amateur sport throughout Newfoundland & Labrador; to represent collective interests & goals of members; to provide various programs & services; to liaise & lobby with government, communities, media & other representative organizations; to provide direction & leadership on issues which affect members
Chief Officer(s): Troy Croft, Executive Director
troy@sportnl.ca
Membership: 45 provincial sport organizations; 70,000 individual

Sport North Federation
Don Cooper Building, PO Box 11089, 4908 - 49 St., 1st Flr., Yellowknife NT X1A 3X7
Tel: 867-669-8326; *Fax:* 867-669-8327
Toll-free: 800-661-0797
www.sportnorth.com
www.youtube.com/SportNorthFederation
www.facebook.com/sportnorthfederation
twitter.com/SportNorth
Previous Name: Northwest Territories Sport Federation
Overview: A small provincial organization founded in 1976
Description: To provide equitable, accessible & participant centred sports to all Northwest Territories residents; *Member of:* Athletics Canada
Chief Officer(s): Les Skinner, President
Doug Rentmeister, Executive Director, 867-669-8335
drent@sportnorth.com
Spider Jones, Executive Director, NWT Hockey, Gymnastics & Kayaking, 867-669-8329
spider@sportnorth.com
Kendra Wambold, Coordinator, Marketing & Communications; KidSport NWT, 867-669-8378
kwambold@sportnorth.com
Member Profile: Sports organizations in Northwest Territories; Individuals and private firms who support Sport North

Sport Nova Scotia (SNS)
5516 Spring Garden Rd., 4th Fl., Halifax NS B3J 1G6
Tel: 902-425-5450; *Fax:* 902-425-5606
sportns@sportnovascotia.ca
www.sportnovascotia.ca
www.facebook.com/sportnovascotia
twitter.com/SportNovaScotia
Overview: A medium-sized provincial organization founded in 1974
Description: To promote the development of amateur sport in Nova Scotia through services, programs, advocacy & technical consultation
Chief Officer(s): Jamie Ferguson, Chief Executive Officer, 902-425-5450 315
jferguson@sportnovascotia.ca
Finances: *Annual Operating Budget:* $1.5 Million-$3 Million; *Funding Sources:* Membership; sponsors; government
Staff: 17 staff member(s); 15 volunteer(s)
Membership: 86 groups + 150,000 individuals; *Fees:* Schedule available

Sport PEI Inc.
PO Box 302, 40 Enman Cres., Charlottetown PE C1E 1E6
Tel: 902-368-4110; *Fax:* 902-368-4548
Toll-Free: 800-247-6712
sports@sportpei.pe.ca
www.sportpei.pe.ca
www.facebook.com/176050449103403
twitter.com/sportpei
Overview: A small provincial organization founded in 1973
Description: To assist in the development & promotion of amateur sport in the province of Prince Edward Island; To offer services & programs to meet the needs of the membership
Chief Officer(s): Tracey Clements, President
Gemma Koughan, Executive Director
gkoughan@sportpei.pe.ca
Finances: *Annual Operating Budget:* $100,000-$250,000; *Funding Sources:* Government; Private sector sponsorhips
Staff: 8 staff member(s); 15 volunteer(s)
Membership: 6 corporate + 39 active + 15 affiliate + 11 honorary; *Fees:* Schedule available; *Member Profile:* Provincial sport organizations; *Committees:* Finance; Administration; Fundraising; Marketing; Sport Development
Activities: Advising member associations; Acting in consultative capacity with member associations; Offering fundraising opportunities for amateur sport in PEI; *Internships:* Yes *Library:* Yes (Open to Public)

Sport Yukon
4061 - 4 Ave., Whitehorse YT Y1A 1H1
Tel: 867-668-4236; *Fax:* 867-667-4237
news@sportyukon.com
www.sportyukon.com
www.youtube.com/channel/UCX5XUbz5y6XN3je1bDXU5ig
www.facebook.com/sportyukon
twitter.com/sportyukon
Overview: A small provincial organization
Description: To promote the development of amateur sport in the Yukon through services, programs, advocacy
Chief Officer(s): Tracey Bilsky, Executive Director
tbilsky@sportyukon.com
Membership: 68 clubs; *Fees:* $210

SPORTSQUÉBEC
4545, av Pierre-de Coubertin, Montréal QC H1V 0B2
Tél: 514-252-3114; *Téléc:* 514-254-9621
sports@sportsquebec.com
sportsquebec.com

www.facebook.com/sportsquebec
twitter.com/sportsquebec
Aperçu: *Dimension:* moyenne; *Envergure: provinciale; Organisme sans but lucratif; fondée en 1988*
Description: Assurer la synergie de ses membres et de ses partenaires du système sportif québécois et du système sportif canadien pour favoriser le développement et l'épanouissement de l'athlète et la promotion de la pratique sportive; *Membre de:* Canadian Council of Provincial & Territorial Sport Federation
Membre(s) du bureau directeur: Alain Deschamps, Directeur général, 514-252-3114 3650
adeschamps@sportsquebec.com
Michèle Demers, Directrice, Communications, 514-252-3114 3698
mdemers@sportsquebec.com
Ode Caron, Directrice, Placements Sports, 514-252-3114 3953
ocaron@sportsquebec.com
Membre: 900,000 personnes; *Critères d'admissibilite:* Ordinaires; Régionaux; Affinitaires
Activités: *Stagiaires:* Oui *Bibliothèque:* Centre de documentation (Bibliothèque publique)

Toronto Ukraina Sports Association
#75, 6 Point Rd., Toronto ON M8Z 2X3
Tel: 416-535-0681
ukrainasports.ca
Overview: A small local organization founded in 1948
Description: To promote an interest in sports among its members
Chief Officer(s): Constantino Czoli, Contact, 416-231-5445
choli66@hotmail.com

Ultimate Canada
4382 Shelbourne St., Vancouver BC V8N 3G3
Toll-Free: 888-691-1080
info@canadianultimate.com
www.canadianultimate.com
www.instagram.com/ultimate_canada
www.facebook.com/UltimateCanada
twitter.com/Ultimate_Canada
Previous Name: Canadian Ultimate Players Association
Overview: A medium-sized national charitable organization founded in 1993

Description: To be the governing body for the sport of ultimate in Canada
Chief Officer(s): Danny Saunders, Executive Director
ed@canadianultimate.com
Finances: *Annual Operating Budget:* $50,000-$100,000; *Funding Sources:* Membership dues
Staff: 4 staff member(s); 50 volunteer(s)
Membership: 800; *Fees:* $30 junior; $50 regular
Activities: *Awareness Events:* Canadian National Championships; Canadian National University Championships

Vancouver Island Shuffleboard Association
c/o Claudia Wright, #502, 531 West Bay Terrace, Victoria BC V9A 5R3
www.canadianshuffleboardcongress.com/VISA
Also Known As: VISA
Overview: A small local organization
Description: To govern & organize shuffleboard on Vancouver Island
Chief Officer(s): Don Heaton, President, 778-430-0069
Dave Carpenter, Vice President, 250-391-4072
Claudia Wright, Secretary-Treasurer, 250-920-3606

ViaSport
#1351, 409 Granville St., Vancouver BC V6C 1T2
Tel: 778-654-7542; *Toll-Free:* 800-335-7549
info@viasport.ca
www.viasport.ca
www.youtube.com/user/viaSportBC
www.facebook.com/ViaSportBC
twitter.com/ViaSportBC
Overview: A medium-sized provincial organization
Description: To provide the opportunity for participation in sports for all British Columbians, at every age & level of skill.
Chief Officer(s): Sheila Bouman, Chief Executive Officer
sheilab@viasport.ca
Michelle Tice, Director, Communications & Engagement
michellet@viasport.ca
Scott Stefani, Manager, Grants
scotts@viasport.ca
Activities: Funding & grants

York Region Athletic Association (YRAA)
#1038, 44 Main St. South, Unionville ON L3R 2E4
Tel: 905-470-1551; *Fax:* 905-470-9092
www.yraa.com
twitter.com/yraa_news
Overview: A small local organization
Description: To offer athletics in York Region high schools
Chief Officer(s): Mark Arsenault, Athletic Coordinator
mark.arsenault@yraa.com
Cathy Bennett, Athletics Administrator
cathy.bennett@yraa.com

Sports Facilities

Canadian Olympic & Paralympic Sport Institute Network
www.canada.ca/en/canadian-heritage/services/sport-organizations
Also Known As: COPSI Network
Overview: A small national organization
Description: To support high-performance sport excellence by Canadian athletes, including athletes with disabilities, by providing training environments for athletes, coaches & practitioners through leadership, services & programs
Finances: *Funding Sources:* Sport Canada
Membership: 7 sports centres

Sports for the Disabled

Alberta Amputee Sports & Recreation Association (AASRA)
PO Box 86093, Stn. Marda Loop, Calgary AB T2T 6B7
Tel: 403-201-0507
info@aasra.ab.ca
www.aasra.ab.ca
www.facebook.com/495810413773520
Overview: A small provincial charitable organization founded in 1977
Description: To support & provide opportunities for amputees in recreational & sporting activities, in events for both the disabled & able-bodied; To provide moral support to new amputees & family
Chief Officer(s): Rachael Pasay, President
Finances: *Funding Sources:* Donations; corporate & government support
Fees: $50 Annual; $150 Lifetime; *Member Profile:* People who have lost a limb(s) at a major joint; *Committees:* Volunteer

Activities: Annual Pro/Amp Golf Tournament; cycling clinic, golf clinic; support group meetings; *Speaker Service:* Yes *Library:* Yes

Alberta Northern Lights Wheelchair Basketball Society
Saville Community Sports Centre, #2-209, 11610 - 65 Ave., Edmonton AB T6G 2E1
info@albertanorthernlights.com
www.albertanorthernlights.com
www.facebook.com/172864392765380
Overview: A medium-sized provincial charitable organization founded in 1976
Description: To develop health, fitness, & sport for men, women, & children with physical disabilities
Chief Officer(s): Neil Feser, Manager, Program

BC Adaptive Snowsports (BCAS)
780 Marine Dr. SW, Vancouver BC V6P 5Y7
Tel: 604-333-3630
info@bcadaptive.com
www.bcadaptive.com
linkedin.com/company/the-disabled-skiers-association-of-bc
www.facebook.com/bcadaptive
twitter.com/BC_adaptive
Previous Name: Disabled Skiers Association of BC
Overview: A medium-sized provincial charitable organization founded in 1973
Description: To promote adaptive skiing, snowboarding, & mountain accessbility as a form of rehabiliation for participants with physical disabilities; To contribute to an inclusive & healthy lifestyle for residents of British Columbia; *Member of:* BC Disability Sports; Canadian Association for Disabled Skiing
Chief Officer(s): John Shaw, President
Christian Hrab, Managing Director, christian@cads.ski
Finances: *Annual Operating Budget:* $100,000-$250,000; *Funding Sources:* Donations; Corporate sponsors; Government
Staff: 7 staff member(s); 700 volunteer(s)
Membership: 1,326; *Fees:* $46 participant; $41 volunteer/instructor
Activities: Offering adaptive snow sports throughout BC; *Awareness Events:* Scotiabank Charity Challenge; Black Diamond Gala; Sun Peaks Grand Golf Tournament; *Speaker Service:* Yes

British Columbia Deaf Sports Federation (BCDSF)
#4, 320 Columbia St., New Westminster BC V3L 1A6
Fax: 604-526-5010
TTY: 604-526-5010
info@bcdeafsports.bc.ca
bcdeafsports.bc.ca
www.facebook.com/139556792849947
twitter.com/bcdeafsports
Also Known As: BC Deaf Sports
Overview: A medium-sized provincial charitable organization founded in 1975
Description: To provide & support the development of competitive sporting events in BC among deaf & hard of hearing athletes; To encourage training for deaf coaches; To provide financial assistance to deaf athletes to participate in local, provincial & national competitions; *Member of:* Canadian Deaf Sports Association
Affiliation(s): BC Sport & Fitness Council for the Disabled
Chief Officer(s): Sherlyn Atkinson, Director, Membership
Mohlin Pillay, President
mpillay@bcdeafsports.bc.ca
Leonor Johnson, Administrator
Finances: *Annual Operating Budget:* $100,000-$250,000; *Funding Sources:* Grants; gaming; membership fees; donations
Staff: 1 staff member(s)
Membership: 300

British Columbia Wheelchair Sports Association (BCWSA)
780 Southwest Marine Dr., Vancouver BC V6P 5Y7
Tel: 604-333-3520; *Fax:* 604-333-3450
Toll-Free: 877-737-3090
info@bcwheelchairsports.com
www.bcwheelchairsports.com
www.youtube.com/user/BCWheelchairSports
www.facebook.com/BCWSA
twitter.com/BCWSA
Overview: A medium-sized provincial charitable organization founded in 1971
Description: To promote & develop wheelchair sport opportunities for British Columbians who identify with physical disabilities; *Member of:* Canadian Wheelchair Sports Association
Chief Officer(s): Gail Hamamoto, Executive Director, 604-333-3520 201
gail@bcwheelchairsports.com
Member Profile: Individuals who identify with a disability & able bodied individuals

Activities: *Awareness Events:* Rick Hansen Wheels in Motion Event, June; *Speaker Service:* Yes

Canadian Adaptive Snowsports (CADS) / Sports de glisse adaptés Canada

32, ch des Ancolies, Sainte-Anne-Des-Lacs QC J0R 1B0
www.cads.ski
www.instagram.com/cadsnational
www.facebook.com/CADSNational
Overview: A medium-sized national charitable organization founded in 1976
Description: To assist individuals with a disability to participate in recreational & competitive snow skiing & snowboarding
Chief Officer(s): Maureen O'Hara-Leman, Executive Director
executive.director@disabledskiing.ca
Finances: *Funding Sources:* Sponsorships; Donations
Staff: 3100 volunteer(s)
Membership: 2,100 disabled members; *Fees:* Schedule available
Activities: Ensuring that programs are delivered at an appropriate level of expertise, through the work of a technical committee; Providing information about adaptive equipment; *Awareness Events:* CADS Ski Improvement & Race Development Festival, March

Canadian Adaptive Snowsports-Newfoundland and Labrador (CADS-NL)

53 Lawlor's Rd., Paradise NL A1L 3P1
Tel: 709-693-6690
cads-nl.ca
Also Known As: CADS Newfoundland/Labrador
Overview: A small provincial organization
Member of: Canadian Association for Disabled Skiing

Canadian Amputee Golf Association (CAGA)

100 Lake Bend Rd., Winnipeg MB R3Y 0M4
cagagolf@mail.com
www.caga.ca
Overview: A small national organization founded in 2000
Description: To provide support for amputees both before & after amputation; To raise awareness to the general population on the effects of amputation; To offer rehabilitation, through teaching amputees golf; To run amputee golf tournaments
Chief Officer(s): Kristian Hammerback, President
Doug Karlson, Treasurer
Glenn Cassidy, Secretary
Fees: $25; $150 lifetime

Canadian Association for Disabled Skiing - Alberta (CADS Alberta)

11759 Groat Rd., Edmonton AB T5M 3K6
Tel: 780-427-8104; Fax: 780-422-2663
cadsab@cadsalberta.ca
www.cadsalberta.ca
www.facebook.com/CADSAB
twitter.com/CADSAlberta
Overview: A small provincial charitable organization founded in 1961
Description: CADS Alberta is a volunteer-based organization assisting individuals with a disability to lead fuller lives through active participation in recreational & competitive snow skiing & snowboarding. It is a registered charity, BN: 133967406RR0001.; *Member of:* Canadian Association for Disabled Skiing
Affiliation(s): Canadian Ski Instructors' Alliance (CSIA), Canadian Association of Snowboard Instructors (CASI)
Chief Officer(s): Becca Neels, Interim President
Finances: *Annual Operating Budget:* $50,000-$100,000
Staff: 2000 volunteer(s)
Membership: 1000+; *Fees:* $40

Canadian Association for Disabled Skiing - National Capital Division (CADS-NCD)

1216 Bordeau Grove, Ottawa ON K1C 2M7
Tel: 819-827-4378
www.cads-ncd.ca
Overview: A medium-sized provincial charitable organization
Description: To provide disabled individuals with skiing opportunities; *Member of:* Canadian Association for Disabled Skiing
Chief Officer(s): Bernie Simpson, President
berniesimpson@outlook.com

Canadian Association for Disabled Skiing - New Brunswick

c/o Lloyd Gagnon, 59 rue Carrier, Edmundston NB E3V EY2
Tel: 506-739-9662
Overview: A medium-sized provincial charitable organization

Description: To provide skiing opportunities for individuals with disabilities; *Member of:* Canadian Association for Disabled Skiing
Chief Officer(s): Lloyd Gagnon, President
lloyd@disabledskiing.ca
Jim Bowland, Technical Coordinator
jimbowland.cadsnb@nb.sympatico.ca

Canadian Association for Disabled Skiing - Nova Scotia

c/o Alpine Ski Nova Scotia, 5516 Spring Garden Rd., 4th Fl., Halifax NS B3J 1G6
Tel: 902-425-5450; Fax: 902-425-5606
alpinens@sportnovascotia.ca
www.cads.ski/cadsnovascotia
Also Known As: CADS Nova Scotia
Overview: A medium-sized provincial organization
Member of: Alpine Canada Alpin; Canadian Association for Disabled Skiing
Chief Officer(s): Lorraine Burch, Executive Director
Finances: *Annual Operating Budget:* $250,000-$500,000
Staff: 1 staff member(s); 5 volunteer(s)
Membership: 1-99

Canadian Association for Disabled Skiing - Ontario

145 Dew St., King City ON L7B 1L1
Tel: 647-280-1307
www.disabledskiingontario.com
www.flickr.com/photos/cadsontario
www.facebook.com/cads_ontario
twitter.com/cads_ontario
Also Known As: CADS Ontario
Overview: A medium-sized provincial organization
Description: To provide a skiing program for people with disabilities; *Member of:* Canadian Association for Disabled Skiing
Chief Officer(s): Gwen Binsfeld, President

Canadian Electric Wheelchair Hockey Association (CEWHA)

#920, 200 Yorkland Blvd., Toronto ON M2J 5C1
Tel: 416-757-8544; Fax: 416-490-9334
info@cewha.ca
www.cewha.ca
www.facebook.com/cewha
Overview: A small national charitable organization founded in 1980
Description: To provide a hockey program for persons with disabilities who have limited upper body strength & mobility; *Member of:* International Wheelchair & Amputee Sports Federation
Chief Officer(s): John Blackburn, Executive Director
Finances: *Funding Sources:* Donations; Sponsorships; Fundraising
Membership: 200 players + 80 volunteers; *Member Profile:* All persons with disabilities who would benefit from an electric wheelchair in competitive sport & daily living
Activities: Offering recreation & social programs; Organizing national tournaments

Canadian Paralympic Committee (CPC) / Comité paralympique canadien

#100, 85 Plymouth St., Ottawa ON K1S 3E2
Tel: 613-569-4333; Fax: 613-569-2777
info@paralympic.ca
www.paralympic.ca
www.youtube.com/user/CDNParalympics
www.facebook.com/CDNParalympics
twitter.com/CDNParalympics
Previous Name: Canadian Federation of Sport Organizations for the Disabled
Overview: A medium-sized national charitable organization founded in 1982
Description: To support disabled athletes through the establishment of a sustainable Paralympic sport system; To inspire all disabled Canadians to participate in sports
Affiliation(s): International Paralympic Committee
Chief Officer(s): Karen O'Neill, Chief Executive Officer, 613-569-4333 223
koneill@paralympic.ca
Martin Richard, Executive Director
Finances: *Funding Sources:* Government; private & public sector
Staff: 22 staff member(s)
Membership: 25 national organizations; *Member Profile:* Any National Sport Organization for Athletes with a Disability or National Sport Organization representing a sport on the Paralympic program, provided that such organization is properly constituted in Canada & is the recognized Canadian member of the appropriate international federation; *Committees:* Athlete Council; Coach's Council; Development; External Representation; Finance & Audit; Governance; High

Performance; Nominating; Operations & Human Resources; Revenue Generation & Government Relations
Activities: *Internships:* Yes; *Speaker Service:* Yes *Library:* Yes by appointment

Commission de Ski pour Personnes Handicapées du Québec (CSPHQ)

QC
Aperçu: *Dimension:* petite; *Envergure:* provinciale
Description: Promouvoir et pratiquer le ski alpin; *Membre de:* Ski Québec; Canadian Association for Disabled Skiing
Critères d'admissibilite: Adolescent et adulte ayant une déficence physique
Activités: Cours de ski alpin adapté (luge, bi-ski)

Disabled Sailing Association of B.C. (DSA)

#318, 425 Carrall St., Vancouver BC V6B 6E3
Tel: 604-688-6464; Fax: 604-688-6463
dsa@disabilityfoundation.org
www.disabledsailingbc.org
www.facebook.com/DisabledSailingAssociation
twitter.com/DisabilityFdn
Overview: A small provincial licensing charitable organization founded in 1989
Description: To empower & inspire people with physical disabilities to re-imagine what is possible by providing opportunities to enable their individual journeys; *Member of:* AbleSail Network; BC Sailing
Affiliation(s): BC Sport & Fitness Council for the Disabled; Sam Sullivan Disability Foundation
Chief Officer(s): Stephen Hunter, Contact, 604-688-6464
Fees: $10 per sail
Activities: Offering sailors with physical disabilities a chance to sail solo or with a companion; Approximately 1,000 sails completed each summer

George Bray Sports Association (GBSA)

9606 Tower Rd., RR#3, St Thomas ON N5P 3S7
Tel: 519-200-8422
www.georgebraysports.ca
www.facebook.com/563729230361725
Overview: A small local organization founded in 1968
Description: To organize a hockey league for children with special needs
Chief Officer(s): Murray Howard, President
murrayhoward@execulink.com
Finances: *Funding Sources:* Sponsors

Manitoba Wheelchair Sports Association

145 Pacific Ave., Winnipeg MB R3B 2Z6
Tel: 204-925-5790; Fax: 204-925-5792
mwsa@sportmanitoba.ca
www.mwsa.ca
www.facebook.com/manitobawheelchairsports
Overview: A small provincial organization founded in 1962
Description: Committed to leadership in the promotion of well being and a healthy lifestyle through the development of sport and fitness related opportunities for physically disabled Manitobans.; *Member of:* Canadian Wheelchair Sports Association
Chief Officer(s): Samuel Unrau, Interim Executive Director
Fees: $5

Ontario Wheelchair Sports Association (OWSA)

#101, 100 Sunrise Ave., Toronto ON M4A 1B3
info@owsa.ca
www.owsa.ca
www.facebook.com/WheelchairSportsON
twitter.com/WSA_Ontario
Overview: A medium-sized provincial organization founded in 1972
Description: To provide sporting & recreational opportunities for athletes who compete in wheelchairs; *Member of:* Canadian Wheelchair Sports Association
Affiliation(s): Canadian Wheelchair Sports Association
Chief Officer(s): Ken Thom, President
kenthom@rogers.com
Laura Wilson, Executive Director
laura@owsa.ca
Finances: *Funding Sources:* Provincial Government
Staff: 3 staff member(s)

Paralympic Sports Association (Alberta) (PSA)

#305, 11010 101 St., Edmonton AB T5H 4B9
Tel: 780-439-8687; Fax: 780-432-0486
info@parasports.net
www.parasports.net
www.linkedin.com/company/paralympic-sports-association
www.facebook.com/PSASports
twitter.com/Sports_PSA
Overview: A medium-sized provincial charitable organization founded in 1965

Description: To provide sports & recreation programs for people with physical disabilities
Affiliation(s): Wheelchair Sports Alberta
Chief Officer(s): Amy MacKinnon, Executive Director
executivedirector@parasports.net
Amy Hayward, Coordinator, Programs
programs@parasports.net
Fees: $20 individual; $40 family; *Member Profile:* Persons with physical disabilities
Activities: *Speaker Service:* Yes

ParaSport Ontario (PO)
3701 Danforth Ave., Toronto ON M1N 2G2
Tel: 416-426-7187
info@parasportontario.ca
www.parasportontario.ca
www.instagram.com/parasportontario
twitter.com/parasport_ont
Previous Name: Sport for Disabled - Ontario; Paralympics Ontario
Overview: A medium-sized provincial charitable organization founded in 1981
Description: To provide support to all members of the disability community - regardless of age or stage in life - to find, connect with, & participate in competitive & recreational sport programs & activities of their choice to enhance physical function & quality of life.
Affiliation(s): ParaGolf Ontario; Ontario Cerebral Palsy Sports Association
Chief Officer(s): Jeff Tiessen, Executive Director, 416-426-7186
jeff@parasportontario.ca
Richard Collins, Coordinator, Events
events@parasportontario.ca
Erin O'Sullivan, Coordinator, Communications
programs@parasportontario.ca
Membership: 1,800+
Activities: "Try Me" Program; Equipment Rental Program; Connecting people with disabilities with parasports & sports clubs; *Speaker Service:* Yes

Parasports Québec
4545, av Pierre-de Coubertin, Montréal QC H1V 0B2
Tél: 514-252-3108
info@parasportsquebec.com
www.parasportsquebec.com

www.facebook.com/ParasportsQuebec
Nom précédent: Association québécoise des sports en fauteuil roulants
Aperçu: *Dimension:* moyenne; *Envergure: provinciale; Organisme sans but lucratif; fondée en 1983*
Description: Favoriser un accès à la pratique sportive en fauteuil roulant à tous les niveaux de performance pour le bénéfice des personnes ayant une limitation physique; *Membre de:* Sports Québec; Basketball en fauteuil roulant Canada; Rugby en fauteuil roulant Canada; Powerchair Football Canada
Membre(s) du bureau directeur: Francis Ménard, Contact, 514-252-3108 3464
Finances: *Budget de fonctionnement annuel:* $250,000-$500,000
Personnel: 5 membre(s) du personnel; 25 bénévole(s)
Membre: 350; *Montant de la cotisation:* Barème
Activités: Basketball en fauteuil roulant; Rugby en fauteuil roulant; Tennis en fauteuil roulant; Curling en fauteuil roulant; Powerchair soccer; Para-athlétisme; *Service de conférenciers:* Oui

Saskatchewan Ski Association - Skiing for Disabled (SASKI)
1860 Lorne St., Saskatoon SK S4P 2L7
Tel: 306-780-9236; *Fax:* 306-781-6021
sask.ski@sasktel.net
www.saskiskiing4disabled.net
www.facebook.com/212948638910907
twitter.com/SASKI_Adaptive
Also Known As: SASKI - Skiing for Disabled
Overview: A medium-sized provincial organization founded in 1982
Description: To promote all aspects of winter skiing in Saskatchewan, including alpine, biathlon, cross country & skiing for disabled, & to provide assistance to clubs & individual athletes, instruction & training, adaptive equipment, & a resource library; *Member of:* Canadian Association for Disabled Skiing
Chief Officer(s): Alana Ottenbreit, Executive Director
Pat Prokopchuk, Contact
prokr@sasktel.net
Finances: *Funding Sources:* Provincial lotteries; occasional grants; bingos
Membership: 1,000-4,999
Activities: Alpine/cross country/biathlon/freestyle skiing; skiing for disabled; snowboarding

Saskatchewan Wheelchair Sports Association (SWSA)
510 Cynthia St., Saskatoon SK S7L 7K7
Tel: 306-975-0824
swsa@shaw.ca
www.swsa.ca
www.youtube.com/user/SKWheelchairSports
www.facebook.com/skwcsports
twitter.com/skwcsports
Overview: A small provincial organization founded in 1977
Description: To develope & support opportunities for children, teens & adults with disabilities to participate in the Association's sport, recreation & leisure time activities to the best of their abilities; *Member of:* Canadian Wheelchair Sports Association
Chief Officer(s): Andrea Muir, Executive Director
Fees: $20 individual; $40 family

Wheelchair Rugby Canada (WRC) / Rugby en fauteuil rouland Canada (ACSFR)
#108, 2255 St. Laurent Blvd., Ottawa ON K1G 4K3
Tel: 613-523-0004; *Fax:* 613-523-0149
wheelchairrugby.ca
www.instagram.com/wcrugbycanada
www.facebook.com/WCRugbyCanada
twitter.com/wcrugbycanada
Previous Name: Canadian Wheelchair Sports Association
Overview: A large national charitable organization founded in 1967
Description: To promote excellence & develop opportunities for Canadians in wheelchair sport
Affiliation(s): International Wheelchair & Amputee Sports Federation
Chief Officer(s): Cathy Cadieux, Chief Executive Officer
cathy@wheelchairrugby.ca
Duncan Campbell, Director, National Development
duncan@wheelchairrugby.ca
Jean-Philippe Lavoie, Director, High Performance
jp@wheelchairrugby.ca
Finances: *Funding Sources:* Federal government; Independent corporations; General public
Staff: 14 staff member(s)
Member Profile: Wheelchair athletes
Activities: Offering high performance sport programs for rugby; Engaging in advocacy activities; *Awareness Events:* Bridging the Gap, Getting Physically Active; Podium Club

Wheelchair Sports Alberta
11759 Groat Rd., Edmonton AB T5M 3K6
Tel: 780-427-8699; *Toll-Free:* 888-453-6770
wheelchairsportsalberta.com
www.instagram.com/wheelchairsportsab
www.facebook.com/WheelchairSportsAlberta
twitter.com/WSA_Alberta
Overview: A small provincial organization
Description: To develop wheelchair sports throughout Alberta; *Member of:* Canadian Wheelchair Sports Association
Chief Officer(s): Jen Sales, Executive Director
jen@wheelchairsportsalberta.com
Fees: $25 individual; $200 org members; $350 org 25 members; *Member Profile:* Any athlete, club, official, coach or board member

Wolverines Wheelchair Sports Association
10 Knowledge Way, Grande Prairie AB T8W 2V9
Tel: 780-402-3331; *Fax:* 780-402-3318
info@gpwolverines.com
www.gpwolverines.com
www.facebook.com/gpwolverines
Also Known As: Grande Prairie Wolverines
Overview: A small local organization founded in 1990
Description: To provide people with disabilities the opportunity to engage in physical & recreational activities.
Fees: Schedule available

Squash

NWT Squash
NT
www.nwtsquash.com
twitter.com/NWTSquash
Overview: A small provincial organization
Description: To develop & provide squash programs to athletes of all ages in the Northwest Territories.; *Member of:* Squash Canada
Chief Officer(s): Bruce Jones, President
Garrett Hinchey, Secretary

Saskatchewan Squash
214 Wickenden Cres., Saskatoon SK S7N 3X7
Tel: 306-280-4320
sasksquash@gmail.com
www.sasksquash.com
Overview: A medium-sized provincial organization
Member of: Squash Canada
Chief Officer(s): Brad Birnie, Executive Director

Squash Alberta (SA)
3415 - 3rd Ave. NW, Calgary AB T2N 0M4
Tel: 403-270-7344; *Toll-Free:* 877-646-6566
membership@squashalberta.com
www.squashalberta.com
www.facebook.com/squashab
twitter.com/SquashAB
Previous Name: Alberta Squash Racquets Association
Overview: A medium-sized provincial charitable organization founded in 1967
Description: To promote & facilitate the development of the sport of squash in Alberta; *Member of:* Squash Canada
Chief Officer(s): Grant Currie, President
currieg@shaw.ca
Tim Landeryou, Executive Director
tim@squashalberta.com
Arthur Hough, Coach, High Performance
arthur@squashalberta.com
Finances: *Annual Operating Budget:* $250,000-$500,000; *Funding Sources:* Membership dues; programs; government grants; Alberta Sport Connection
Staff: 2 staff member(s); 12 volunteer(s)
Membership: 1,850; *Fees:* $55 adult; $50 junior; $130 family

Squash British Columbia
Vancouver Racquets Club, 4867 Ontario St., Vancouver BC V5V 3H4
Tel: 604-737-3084; *Fax:* 604-736-3527
info@squashbc.com
www.squashbc.com
www.instagram.com/squashbc
www.facebook.com/squashbc
twitter.com/squashbc
Overview: A medium-sized provincial organization
Description: To promote the growth of squash by providing orderly development opportunities for athletes, & encouraging participation through a variety of programs & activities organized by Squash BC & its partners; *Member of:* Sport BC; Squash Canada
Chief Officer(s): Christine Bradstock, Executive Director
executivedirector@squashbc.com
Fees: $44 individual; $20 young adult (19-24); $15 junior (under 18)
Activities: *Library:* Yes

Squash Canada
20 Jamie Ave., 2nd Fl., Ottawa ON K2E 6T6
Tel: 613-228-7724; *Fax:* 613-228-7232
info@squash.ca
squash.ca
www.instagram.com/squashcanada
www.facebook.com/squashcanada
twitter.com/squashcanada
Previous Name: Canadian Squash Racquets Association
Overview: A large national charitable organization founded in 1915
Description: To develop athletes, coaches & officials in the sport of squash; To set standards for squash in Canada; To promote growth & development in the sport across the country; *Member of:* Canadian Olympic Committee; Coaching Association of Canada; Commonwealth Games Canada; Pan American Squash Federation; World Squash Federation
Chief Officer(s): Steve Wren, President
swrenkiwi@gmail.com
Dan Wolfenden, Executive Director, 613-228-7724 201
dan.wolfenden@squash.ca
Finances: *Annual Operating Budget:* $500,000-$1.5 Million; *Funding Sources:* Government; Donations; Sponsorships; Events; Sales
Staff: 5 staff member(s); 150 volunteer(s)
Membership: 8,500; *Fees:* Schedule available; *Member Profile:* Provincial / territorial clubs & members; *Committees:* Appeals; Doubles; Doubles Officiating; Finance & Audit; High Performance; Nominating
Activities: Participating in national championships, as well as world championships & other international events; Providing coach & officials development; Marketing & promoting squash; Establishing & maintaining rules & regulations; *Internships:* Yes

Squash Manitoba
145 Pacific Ave., Winnipeg MB R3B 2Z6
Tel: 204-925-5661; *Fax:* 204-925-5792
squash@sportmanitoba.ca
www.squashmb.org
twitter.com/squashmanitoba
Overview: A medium-sized provincial organization
Description: To promote the game of squash in Manitoba; To establish & enforce rules & programs for all levels of play; *Member of:* Squash Canada
Affiliation(s): Brandon squash & athletic centre; Dauphin Squash Club; University of Winnipeg; Winnipeg Squash Racquet Club; Winnipeg Winter Club
Chief Officer(s): Lynn Colliou, Executive Director
Fees: $20

Squash Newfoundland & Labrador Inc.
PO Box 21254, St. John's NL A1A 5B2
hongngee@gmail.com
www.hongngee.com/squashnl
Also Known As: Squash NL
Overview: A small provincial organization
Description: To coordinate & promote the sport of squash in Newfoundland & Labrador.; *Member of:* Squash Canada

Squash Nova Scotia
PO Box 3010, Proctor Park Lane Centre, #401, 5516 Spring Garden Rd., Halifax NS B3J 3G6
Tel: 902-425-5450; *Fax:* 902-425-5606
www.squashns.ca
Overview: A medium-sized provincial organization
Description: Fosters & promotes a squash community for players of all abilities from across the province to improve the profile of the sport & its enjoyment by its members.; *Member of:* Squash Canada
Chief Officer(s): Alfred Seaman, President
alfieseaman@gmail.com
Finances: *Annual Operating Budget:* Less than $50,000
Membership: 100-499; *Fees:* $20 student; $25 adult

Squash Ontario
c/o Glendon College, Proctor Field House, #226, 2275 Bayview Ave., Toronto ON M4N 1J8
Fax: 416-426-7393
admin@squashontario.com
www.squashontario.com
www.facebook.com/SquashOntario
twitter.com/SquashOntario
Overview: A medium-sized provincial organization founded in 1976
Description: To act as the governing body for the sport of squash in Ontario; To develop & promote the sport of squash across Ontario; To provide an environment in which the sport of squash can thrive; To meet the needs of present & potential players
Chief Officer(s): Janice Lardner, President
board@squashontario.com
Jamie Nicholls, Executive Director, 416-426-7202
jmnicholls@squashontario.com
Lauren Sachvie, Coordinator, Programs, 416-426-7201
programs@squashontario.com
Activities: Developing squash players, from beginners to elite athletes, as well as teams, coaches, & officials; Establishing & maintaining technical standards

Squash PEI
PE
Overview: A small provincial organization
Description: To promote squash in PEI; to provide competitive opportunities for members; *Member of:* Squash Canada; Sport PEI Inc.

Squash Québec
4545, av Pierre-de-Coubertin, Montréal QC H1V 0B2
Tél: 514-252-3062
info@sports-4murs.qc.ca
www.squash.qc.ca
www.facebook.com/SquashQuebec
Aperçu: *Dimension:* petite; *Envergure:* provinciale
Description: Promouvoir le développement du Squash au Québec en offrant différentes opportunités aux adeptes, tout en encourageant la participation sportive à travers un ensemble de services et de programmes; *Membre de:* Squash Canada
Membre(s) du bureau directeur: Michel Séguin, Directeur général
Finances: *Budget de fonctionnement annuel:* $50,000-$100,000
Personnel: 2 membre(s) du personnel; 20 bénévole(s)
Membre: 5,000-14,999
Activités: *Stagiaires:* Oui

Squash Yukon
YT
squashyukon.yk.ca
Overview: A small provincial organization
Member of: Squash Canada

Swimming

Alberta Artistic Swimming
The Percy Page Centre, 11759 Groat Rd., Edmonton AB T5M 3K6
Tel: 780-415-1789
albertaartisticswimming.ca
Previous Name: Synchro Alberta
Overview: A medium-sized provincial organization
Chief Officer(s): Jennifer Luzia, Executive Director
jluzia@albertaartisticswimming.ca
Membership: 1200
Activities: Competitive & recreational meets

Alberta Summer Swimming Association (ASSA)
c/o Swim Alberta, 11759 Groat Rd., Edmonton AB T5M 3K6
Tel: 780-415-1780; *Fax:* 780-415-1788
assa@swimalberta.ca
www.assa.ca
Overview: A medium-sized provincial organization
Description: To provide a summer swimming program for swimmers of all ages in Alberta
Chief Officer(s): Paige Park, President
Lynnette Thoresen, Vice President
Membership: 59 clubs + 3,323 individuals

BC Artistic Swimming
BC
Tel: 604-333-3640
info@bcartisticswimming.ca
www.bcartisticswimming.ca
www.instagram.com/bcartswim
www.facebook.com/BCArtisticSwimming
twitter.com/BCArtSwim
Overview: A medium-sized provincial licensing organization
Description: To foster & promote a fully integrated artistic swimming Sport System throughout BC, which will offer opportunities for excellence at all levels of participation from recreational to international
Chief Officer(s): Jennifer Keither, Executive Director
ed@bcartisticswimming.ca
Finances: *Funding Sources:* Government; donations
Membership: 1,200; *Fees:* Schedule available
Activities: *Speaker Service:* Yes; *Rents Mailing List:* Yes

British Columbia Summer Swimming Association (BCSSA)
#205, 2323 Boundary Rd., Vancouver BC V5M 4V8
Tel: 604-473-9447; *Fax:* 604-473-9660
office@bcsummerswimming.com
www.bcsummerswimming.com
www.facebook.com/bcsummerswimming
twitter.com/BCSSAstaff
Overview: A medium-sized provincial organization founded in 1958
Description: To promote & encourage the development of athletes and volunteers through participation in water sport opportunities across British Colubia through member clubs
Chief Officer(s): Danny Schilds, President
president@bcsummerswimming.com
Francis Cheung, Vice President
vp@bcsummerswimming.com
Membership: 60 clubs + 5,000 athletes
Activities: Speed swimming; diving; water polo; synchronized swimming

Canada Artistic Swimming (CAS)
#401, 700 Industrial Ave., Ottawa ON K1G 0Y9
Tel: 613-748-5674; *Fax:* 613-748-5724
info@artisticswimming.ca
artisticswimming.ca
www.instagram.com/CanadaArtisticSwimming
www.facebook.com/CanadaArtisticSwimming
twitter.com/CanadaArtSwim
Previous Name: Synchro Canada; Canadian Amateur Synchronized Swimming Association
Overview: A medium-sized national charitable organization founded in 1968

Club de natation Natchib inc.
CP 213, Chibougamau QC G8P 2K7
Tél: 418-748-8038
Aperçu: *Dimension:* petite; *Envergure:* locale
Membre(s) du bureau directeur: Stéphanie McKenzie, Président

Fédération de natation du Québec (FNQ)
CP 1000, Succ. M, 4545, av Pierre-de-Coubertin, Montréal QC H1V 0B2
Tél: 514-252-3200; *Télec:* 514-252-3232
fnq@fnq.qc.ca
www.fnq.qc.ca
www.facebook.com/163831313666941
twitter.com/fednatationqc
Aperçu: *Dimension:* moyenne; *Envergure:* provinciale
Membre de: Swimming Canada
Affiliation(s): Éducation, Loisir et Sport Québec; AQUAM Équipes; Groupe Hospitalité Westmont (Quality et Comfort Inn); Location Sauvageau; Trophies Dubois; Westjet; Financière Manuvie; McAuslan
Membre(s) du bureau directeur: Isabelle Ducharme, Directrice générale
iducharme@fnq.qc.ca

International Amateur Swimming Federation (IASF) / Fédération internationale de natation amateur (FINA)
Ch de Bellevue 24a/24b, Lausanne 1005 Switzerland
www.fina.org
www.youtube.com/user/fina1908
www.linkedin.com/company/952149
www.facebook.com/fina1908
twitter.com/fina1908
Overview: A large international organization founded in 1908
Description: To promote and encourage the development of swimming in all possible manifestations throughout the world
Chief Officer(s): Julio C. Maglione, President
Cornel Marculescu, Executive Director
Membership: 209 national federations; *Committees:* Artistic Swimming; Athletes; Audit; Awards; Coaches; Diving; Facilities; Finance; High Diving; Legal; Marketing; Masters; Media; NF Relations; Open Water Swimming; Sports Medicine; Swimming; Swimwear Approval; Water Polo

Manitoba Artistic Swimming
145 Pacific Ave., Winnipeg MB R3B 2Z6
Tel: 204-925-5693
manitobaartisticswimming.ca
Previous Name: Synchro Manitoba; Canadian Amateur Synchronized Swimming Association (Manitoba Section)
Overview: A small provincial organization founded in 1958
Description: To promote, teach, foster, encourage & improve artistic swimming in Manitoba at all levels
Affiliation(s): Manitoba Sports Federation
Chief Officer(s): Debra Kofsky, Executive Director
ed@manitobaartisticswimming.ca
Activities: *Library:* Resource Centre

Natation Artistique Québec
4545, av Pierre-de-Coubertin, Montréal QC H1V 0B2
Tél: 514-252-3087; *Ligne sans frais:* 866-537-3164
info@natation-artistique.quebec
synchroquebec.qc.ca
www.instagram.com/natationartistiquequebec
www.linkedin.com/company/synchroquebec
www.facebook.com/natationartistiquequebec
Également appelé: Quebec Artistic Swimming
Nom précédent: Synchro-Québec; Fédération de nage synchronisée
Aperçu: *Dimension:* moyenne; *Envergure:* provinciale; *Organisme sans but lucratif*
Description: Planifier et supporter le développement de la natation artistique au Québec; administrer l'ensemble des compétitions qui se déroule au Québec; veiller au perfectionnement de ses entraîneurs, officiels et bénévoles
Membre(s) du bureau directeur: Julie Vézina, Directrice générale
jvezina@natationartistiquequebec.ca
Activités: *Stagiaires:* Oui

New Brunswick Artistic Swimming
121 Poole St., Woodstock NB E7M 2L6
synchronewbrunswick@gmail.com
www.synchronb.ca
www.facebook.com/synchronewbrunswick
Previous Name: Synchro New Brunswick
Overview: A medium-sized provincial organization
Description: To promote artistic swimming in New Brunswick

NL Artistic Swimming
PO Box 4002, RPO Pearlgate, Mount Pearl NL A1N 8A1
nlartisticswimming.com
www.facebook.com/NLartisticswimming
Previous Name: Synchro Newfoundland & Labrador
Overview: A small provincial organization

Nova Scotia Artistic Swimming
NS
novascotiaartisticswimming.ca
www.facebook.com/nsartisticswimming
Previous Name: Synchro Nova Scotia
Overview: A medium-sized provincial organization
Description: To promote artistic swimming in Nova Scotia
Chief Officer(s): Pam Kidney, Executive Director

Ontario Artistic Swimming (OAS)
#12, 89 Galaxy Blvd., Toronto ON M9W 6A4
Tel: 416-679-9522
synchroontario.com
www.instagram.com/ontarioartisticswimming
www.facebook.com/OntarioArtisticSwimming
twitter.com/ONArtisticSwim
Previous Name: Synchro Swim Ontario
Overview: A medium-sized provincial licensing organization
Description: To oversee artistic swimming in Ontario, including
varsity competiton, competitive clubes & community recreation
programs; to develop, promote, support & regulate synchronized
swimming through the immplementation of an integrated sports
system that is accessible to all Ontarians by providing
opportunites for enjoyment & the pursuit of individual goals
Chief Officer(s): Mary Dwyer, Executive Director, 416-679-9522
222
mdwyer@ontarioartisticswimming.ca
Member Profile: Athlete development at recreational through to
elite levels; officials development; coach development;
competition structures; *Committees:* Executive; Finance; High
Performance; High Performance Hiring & Selection; Novice;
Ontario Officials Management Team; Provincial Jury of Appeal;
Technical Training & Development; Volunteer Management

Saskatchewan Artistic Swimming
#300, 1734 Elphinstone St., Regina SK S4T 1K1
Tel: 306-780-9227
www.saskartisticswimming.ca
www.facebook.com/SaskatchewanArtisticSwimming
Previous Name: Synchro Saskatchewan
Overview: A small provincial organization
Description: To promote & develop artistic swimming in
Saskatchewan; *Member of:* SaskSport
Chief Officer(s): Lenore Lindquist, President
president@saskartisticswimming.ca
Kathleen Reynolds, Executive Director
ed@saskartisticswimming.ca
Finances: *Annual Operating Budget:* $100,000-$250,000;
Funding Sources: Saskatchewan Lottery Trust Fund
Staff: 3 staff member(s); 30 volunteer(s)
Membership: 1,200; *Fees:* Schedule available; *Committees:*
Finance; Marketing; Technical; Competitions; Officials;
Marketing; Grassroot Programming

Solo Swims of Ontario Inc. (SSO)
www.soloswims.com
Overview: A small provincial organization founded in 1975
Description: To ensure that all open-water, solo, long-distance
swims in Ontario abide by strict safety guidelines; To provide
advice before & during long distance swims to ensure the safety
of all involved
Chief Officer(s): Marilyn Korzekwa, MD, President
momswims@gmail.com
John Scott, Treasurer
springbrook6@gmail.com
Finances: *Funding Sources:* Provincial government

Swim Alberta
Percy Page Centre, 11759 Groat Rd., Edmonton AB T5M 3K6
Tel: 780-415-1780; *Fax:* 780-415-1788
office@swimalberta.ca
www.swimalberta.ca
www.facebook.com/SwimAlberta
twitter.com/SwimAlberta
Overview: A medium-sized provincial organization founded in
1963

Description: To maintain a progressive athletic / club
development program & a high performance program; *Member
of:* Swimming Natation Canada
Chief Officer(s): Dean Schultz, Interim President
president@swimalberta.ca
Cheryl Humphrey, Executive Director
chumphrey@swimalberta.ca
Finances: *Funding Sources:* Membership fees; Sponsorships;
Lottery
Staff: 4 staff member(s)
Activities: *Speaker Service:* Yes *Library:* Yes (Open to Public)

Swim BC
PO Box 1749, Garibaldi Highlands BC V0N 1T0
Tel: 604-898-9100; *Fax:* 604-898-9200
www.swim.bc.ca
www.facebook.com/SwimBC
twitter.com/swimbcstaff
Overview: A small provincial organization founded in 1974
Description: To provide the opportunity, leadership & means for
members to achieve excellence in all areas of the sport of
swimming; *Member of:* Swimming Canada
Chief Officer(s): Jerome Beauchamp, President
Mark Schuett, Executive Director
markschuett@swimbc.ca
Finances: *Annual Operating Budget:* $500,000-$1.5 Million;
Funding Sources: Self-generated; provincial government
Staff: 4 staff member(s); 16 volunteer(s)
Membership: 8,000
Activities: *Library:* Yes

Swim Nova Scotia (SNS)
5516 Spring Garden Rd., Halifax NS B3J 1G6
Tel: 902-425-5454; *Fax:* 902-425-5606
swimming@sportnovascotia.ca
www.swimnovascotia.com
Overview: A small provincial charitable organization
Member of: Swimming Canada
Affiliation(s): AthletesCAN
Chief Officer(s): Sue Jackson, President
suejack01@yahoo.com
Bette El-Hawary, Executive Director
Finances: *Annual Operating Budget:* $50,000-$100,000
Staff: 1 staff member(s); 20 volunteer(s)
Membership: 2,800
Activities: Swim competitions & fundraising events

Swim Ontario
#206, 3 Concorde Gate, Toronto ON M3C 3N7
Tel: 416-426-7220; *Fax:* 416-426-7356
info@swimontario.com
www.swimontario.com
www.facebook.com/117335688316744
twitter.com/SwimOntario
Overview: A medium-sized provincial organization founded in
1922
Member of: Swimming Canada
Chief Officer(s): Eric Martin, President
ericmartin@rogers.com
John Vadeika, Executive Director
john@swimontario.com
Membership: 10,000+ in 140+ clubs; *Committees:* Strategic
Planning; Administration; Finance; Risk Management;
Programme Policy
Activities: Learn-to-Swim; training for competitions & fitness

Swim Saskatchewan
2205 Victoria Ave., Regina SK S4P 0S4
Tel: 306-780-9291; *Fax:* 306-525-4009
office@swimsask.ca
www.swimsask.ca
www.facebook.com/325400947571418
Overview: A medium-sized provincial organization
Description: To promote excellence through sport development,
competition, education, training and strong member
organizations.; *Member of:* Swimming Canada
Chief Officer(s): Susan Miazga, President
barrymiazga@sasktel.net
Marj Walton, Executive Director, 306-780-9238
marjwalton@swimsask.ca

Swim Yukon
4061 - 4th Ave., Whitehorse YT Y1A 1H1
swimyukon@gmail.com
sportyukon.com/member/swim-yukon
Overview: A medium-sized provincial organization
Description: Swim Yukon is the Sport Governing Body for
competitive swimming in the Yukon.; *Member of:* Sport Yukon
Affiliation(s): Swimming Canada
Chief Officer(s): Michael McArthur, President
Activities: Swim meets

Swimming Canada / Natation Canada
307 Gilmour St., Ottawa ON K2P 0P7
Tel: 613-260-1348; *Fax:* 613-260-0804
natloffice@swimming.ca
www.swimming.ca
www.youtube.com/swimmingcanada
www.facebook.com/SwimmingCanada
twitter.com/SwimmingCanada
Overview: A large national organization founded in 1909
Description: To direct & develop competitive swimming in
Canada; To represent Canada in international organizations &
events
Affiliation(s): Aquatic Federation of Canada
Chief Officer(s): Ahmed El-Awadi, Chief Executive Officer,
613-260-1348 2007
aelawadi@swimming.ca
Larry Clough, Chief Financial Officer, 613-260-1348 2008
lclough@swimming.ca
John Atkinson, Director, High Performance
jatkinson@swimming.ca
Brian Edey, Director, Operations, 613-260-1348 2003
bedey@swimming.ca
Alan Raphael, Director, Marketing & Business Development,
613-691-2975
araphael@swimming.ca
Finances: *Funding Sources:* Membership fees; Corporate
sponsorships; Sport Canada; Canadian Olympic Committee
Staff: 21 volunteer(s)
Membership: Over 50,000
Activities: *Rents Mailing List:* Yes

Swimming New Brunswick / Natation Nouveau-Brunswick
#13, 900 Hanwell Rd., Fredericton NB E3B 6A3
Tel: 506-451-1323; *Fax:* 506-451-1325
swimnb@nb.aibn.com
www.swimnb.ca
www.facebook.com/1401518450068316
twitter.com/SwimmingNB
Overview: A medium-sized provincial organization
Member of: Swimming Canada
Chief Officer(s): David Frise, President
dfrise@gmail.com
Pat Ketterling, Executive Director
Membership: 668; *Fees:* $12-70; *Committees:* Nomination &
Succession; Policy & Governance; Risk Management; Strategic
Plan; Finance; Technical; Officials; Communication & Promotion;
President's Council

Swimming Newfoundland & Labrador
1296A Kenmount Rd., Paradise NL A1L 1N3
Tel: 709-576-7946; *Fax:* 709-576-7493
swimnl@sportnl.ca
www.swimnl.nfld.net
www.youtube.com/user/SwimmingNL
www.facebook.com/swimmingNL
twitter.com/SwimmingNL
Overview: A medium-sized provincial organization founded in
1974
Member of: Swimming Canada
Chief Officer(s): Joan Butler, President
joanb@mun.ca
Corina Hartley, Executive Director
swimnl@sportnl.ca

Swimming Prince Edward Island
40 Enman Cres., Charlottetown PE C1E 1E6
Tel: 902-569-0583; *Toll-Free:* 800-247-6712
swimpei@sportpei.pe.ca
www.swimpei.com
Also Known As: Swim PEI
Previous Name: Swimming PEI
Overview: A small provincial charitable organization
Member of: Swimming Canada
Chief Officer(s): Marguerite Middleton, Chief, Island Officials
memiddleton@gov.pe.ca
Finances: *Annual Operating Budget:* Less than $50,000
Staff: 1 staff member(s); 30 volunteer(s)
Membership: 200; *Fees:* $40; *Member Profile:* Ages 6-70;
Committees: Finance; Coaching; Officials; Awards
Activities: Competitive swimming; swimming development;
Speaker Service: Yes

Swim-Natation Manitoba (SNM)
#209, 145 Pacific Ave., Winnipeg MB R3B 2Z6
Tel: 204-925-5778; *Fax:* 204-925-5624
swim@sportmanitoba.ca
www.swimmanitoba.mb.ca
twitter.com/Swim_Manitoba
Previous Name: Swim Manitoba
Overview: A medium-sized provincial organization founded in
1913

Description: To produce fast swimmers & to make the experience a healthy, fun, exiting & rewarding adventure; *Member of:* Swimming Canada; Sport Manitoba
Chief Officer(s): Steve Armstrong, President
Mark Fellner, Executive Director
swim.ed@sportmanitoba.ca
Finances: *Annual Operating Budget:* $250,000-$500,000
Staff: 3 staff member(s); 1500 volunteer(s)
Membership: 18 clubs + 1500 swimmers + 300 coaches + 1300 officials & volunteers; *Committees:* Advancement; Competition Hosting; Executive; Finance & Operations; Governance; Sport

Synchro PEI
560 University Ave., Charlottetown PE C1A 9M8
syncnropei@outlook.com
www.synchropei.com
www.instagram.com/synchro_pei
Also Known As: PEI Synchronized Swimming Association
Overview: A small provincial organization
Chief Officer(s): Gina MacLeod, President

Synchro Yukon Association
YT
www.teamunify.com/Home.jsp?team=ytnn
Overview: A medium-sized provincial organization
Description: To promote the sport of artistic swimming in the Yukon; *Member of:* Sport Yukon

Whitehorse Glacier Bears Swim Club
c/o Sport Yukon, 4061 - 4th Ave., Whitehorse YT Y1A 1H1
Fax: 867-667-4237
whseglacierbears@yahoo.ca
www.whitehorseglacierbears.ca
www.facebook.com/569737653073155
Overview: A small local organization
Description: To promote competitive swimming.

Table Soccer

Foosball Québec
QC
Tél: 418-906-0977
foosballquebec@gmail.com
www.foosballquebec.com
www.facebook.com/foosballquebec
Aperçu: *Dimension:* petite; *Envergure:* provinciale
Membre(s) du bureau directeur: Lévesque Olivier, Président

Ontario Table Soccer Association
ON
Toll-Free: 866-247-7702
www.ontariotablesoccer.com
Overview: A small provincial organization founded in 2002
Description: To promote the sport of table soccer through hosting, sanctioning, & coordinating tournaments, events & clinics for players based in Ontario & to assist them in competing in national & international sanctioned events
Chief Officer(s): Mario Recupero, Executive Director, 905-812-9994
director@ontariotablesoccer.com

Table Soccer Association of Canada (TSAC)
canadafoosball.ca
www.facebook.com/CanadaFoosball
Also Known As: Canada Foosball
Overview: A small national organization
Description: To oversee & monitor the growth of foosball in Canada
Chief Officer(s): Cam Burrows, President
cam@canadafoosball.ca
Membership: 10 leagues + 1,500 players

Table Tennis

Alberta Table Tennis Association (ATTA)
Percy Page Centre, 11759 Groat Rd., Edmonton AB T5M 3K6
Tel: 780-427-8588
atta@abtabletennis.com
www.abtabletennis.com
Overview: A small provincial organization founded in 1970
Description: To foster & promote the play of table tennis in a sportsmanlike manner; to award, sanction &, when necessary, supervise or manage all championship matches & tournaments; to interpret & enforce the laws & rules of table tennis; to provide & keep a permanent & official record of all championships established under its jurisdiction; generally to govern the sport in Alberta; *Member of:* Table Tennis Canada
Affiliation(s): International Table Tennis Federation
Chief Officer(s): Lei Jiang, Program Coordinator

Finances: *Annual Operating Budget:* $100,000-$250,000; *Funding Sources:* Fundraising; Alberta Sport, Park & Wildlife Foundation; Alberta Gaming
Staff: 2 staff member(s); 100 volunteer(s)
Membership: 1,200; *Fees:* Schedule available; *Committees:* Communication; Tournaments; Ratings; Officials; Membership/Marketing; Regional/Junior Developments; Schools
Activities: Coaching & officials development; club assistance; sport outreach; summer camps; high performance athletic training; provincial tournament hosting; preparation & sending of athletes to events; *Rents Mailing List:* Yes

British Columbia Table Tennis Association (BCTTA)
#208, 5760 Minoru Blvd., Richmond BC V6X 2A9
Tel: 604-270-3393
bctta@lightspeed.ca
www.bctta.ca
Overview: A small provincial organization
Member of: Table Tennis Canada; Sport BC
Affiliation(s): International Table Tennis Federation
Chief Officer(s): Amelia Ho, President
Membership: 200+; *Fees:* $20 non-voting; $30 voting

Chinese Canadian Table Tennis Federation
11751 Voyageur Way, Richmond BC V6X 3J4
Tel: 604-278-0033; *Fax:* 604-273-9217
ccttf@teamgroup.bc.ca
www.ccttf.org
Overview: A medium-sized national organization founded in 2000
Description: To promote table tennis; To assist in the development of future Canadian athletes; To provide the public with information on the health benefits of table tennis
Fees: $10 regular; $50 affiliate; *Member Profile:* Voting members: Canadians residents over the age of 19; Affiliated members: local groups, including clubs, leagues, schools & zones; Members: any individual interested in the activities of the federation
Activities: Supporting & organizing table tennis events

Fédération de tennis de table du Québec (FTTQ)
4545, av Pierre-de-Coubertin, Montréal QC H1V 0B2
Tél: 514-252-3064; *Téléc:* 514-251-8038
www.tennisdetable.ca
www.youtube.com/user/TennisdetableQC
www.facebook.com/tennisdetableQC
twitter.com/tennisdetableQC
Aperçu: *Dimension:* moyenne; *Envergure:* provinciale
Membre de: Table Tennis Canada
Membre(s) du bureau directeur: Yves Surprenant, Président

Manitoba Table Tennis Association (MTTA)
145 Pacific Ave., Winnipeg MB R3B 2Z6
Tel: 204-925-5690; *Fax:* 204-925-5916
table.tennis@sportmanitoba.ca
www.mtta.ca
Overview: A small provincial organization founded in 1959
Description: To develop & promote the sport of table tennis at all levels within Manitoba; *Member of:* Table Tennis Canada; Sport Manitoba
Affiliation(s): International Table Tennis Federation
Chief Officer(s): Ron Edwards, Executive Director
Finances: *Annual Operating Budget:* $100,000-$250,000; *Funding Sources:* Sport Manitoba; Manitoba Lotteries; program revenue
Staff: 2 staff member(s); 25 volunteer(s)
Membership: 504; *Fees:* $25 active (adult); $15 active (junior); $10 associate (adult); $5 associate (junior); $35 associate (club); *Committees:* Tournaments; Leagues; Athlete Development; Grass Roots & Regional Developments; Coaching Development; Officials Development; Facilities & Equipment; Special Events; Finance & Administration; Bylaws & Policy Review; Privacy Officer; Fundraising & Bingos; Publicity & Promotion; Membership, Stats & Ranking; Banquets & Awards; Disciplinary; Nominations
Activities: *Library:* MTTA Resource Library (Open to Public)

Newfoundland & Labrador Table Tennis Association (NLTTA)
NL
Tel: 709-834-8402
nltabletennis.com
Overview: A small provincial organization
Description: To promote the sport of Table Tennis in Newfoundland & Labrador; *Member of:* Sprot NL; Table Tennis

Canada
Affiliation(s): International Table Tennis Federation
Chief Officer(s): Barry Hicks, President
president@nltta.com
Merv Greenham, Vice President, Technical
vp-technical@nltta.com
Kenny Curlew, Vice President, Administrative
vp-admin@nltta.com
Harrison Lamswood, Secretary
secretary@nltta.com
Rick Fisher, Treasurer, 709-834-0015
finance@nltta.com
Fees: $25 full junior; $25 full senior; $50 club
Activities: Competetions; Training courses; *Awareness Events:* Memorial University of Newfoundland & Labrador Open

Nova Scotia Table Tennis Association (NSTTA)
5526 Spring Garden Rd., Halifax NS B3J 3G6
Tel: 902-425-5450
info@nstta.ca
nstta.ca
Overview: A small provincial organization
Member of: Table Tennis Canada
Affiliation(s): International Table Tennis Federation
Chief Officer(s): Dave Greenough, President
dwg@eastlink.ca

Ontario Table Tennis Association (OTTA)
#110, 9140 Leslie St., Richmond Hill ON L4B 0A9
otta@ontariotabletennis.com
ontariotabletennis.com
www.flickr.com/photos/135121071@N06/
www.facebook.com/TableTennisOntario
Overview: A small provincial organization founded in 1934
Member of: Table Tennis Canada
Affiliation(s): International Table Tennis Federation
Chief Officer(s): Attila Mosonyi, President
attila.mosonyi@gmail.com
Membership: 500+; *Fees:* Schedule available

Prince Edward Island Table Tennis Association (PEITTA)
c/o Sport PEI Inc., 40 Enman Cres., Charlottetown PE C1E 1E6
www.freewebs.com/peitta
Overview: A small provincial organization founded in 1965
Description: To promote table tennis in PEI; to provide competitive opportunities for its members; *Member of:* Table Tennis Canada; Sport PEI Inc.
Affiliation(s): International Table Tennis Federation
Finances: *Annual Operating Budget:* Less than $50,000; *Funding Sources:* Provincial government; fundraising
Staff: 10 volunteer(s)
Membership: 55-75; *Fees:* Schedule available; *Member Profile:* Table tennis players; *Committees:* Fundraising; Coaching
Activities: Hosts provincial championships, local tournaments & recreational games; *Internships:* Yes

Saskatchewan Table Tennis Association Inc. (STTA)
510 Cynthia St., Saskatoon SK S7L 7K7
Tel: 306-975-0835; *Fax:* 306-952-0835
sktta@shaw.ca
www.sktta.ca
www.facebook.com/ttsask
twitter.com/SKTableTennis
Overview: A small provincial organization
Description: To promote & govern the sport of table tennis in Saskatchewan.; *Member of:* Table Tennis Canada; Sask Sport
Affiliation(s): International Table Tennis Federation
Chief Officer(s): Jeffrey Woo, Executive Director
Membership: 2,200; *Fees:* $185 club; $5.25 individual
Activities: *Rents Mailing List:* Yes

Table Tennis Canada / Tennis de Table Canada
2451 Riverside Dr., Ottawa ON K1H 7X7
Tel: 613-219-4898
ttcan@ttcanada.ca
ttcanada.ca
www.instagram.com/TableTennisCan
www.facebook.com/tabletenniscanada
twitter.com/TableTennisCan
Previous Name: Canadian Table Tennis Association
Overview: A medium-sized national organization founded in 1937
Description: To increase the popularity of the sport of table tennis through programs & activities; To increase participation in table tennis at all levels; *Member of:* International Table Tennis Federation
Affiliation(s): Sports Council of Canada; International Table Tennis Federation
Chief Officer(s): Adham Sharara, President & Chair
Melanie Ostashek, Manager, Operations
melanie@ttcanada.ca

Finances: *Annual Operating Budget:* $500,000-$1.5 Million;
Funding Sources: Sponsorship; membership; government
Staff: 6 staff member(s)
Membership: 20,000; *Committees:* Technical; Administrative
Activities: STIGA Canada Cup; Canadian Championships;
Canadian Junior Championships; *Rents Mailing List:* Yes

Table Tennis Yukon
4061 - 4th Ave., Whitehorse YT Y1A 1H1
Tel: 867-668-3358
sportyukon.com/member/table-tennis-yukon
Overview: A small provincial organization
Description: To promote the sport of Table Tennis in the
Yukon.; *Member of:* Table Tennis Canada; Sport Yukon
Affiliation(s): International Table Tennis Federation
Chief Officer(s): David Stockdale, President
stockdale@yknet.ca

Tennis

Alberta Tennis Association (ATA)
11759 Groat Rd., Edmonton AB T5M 3K6
Tel: 780-415-1661; *Fax:* 780-415-1693
info@tennisalberta.com
www.tennisalberta.com
www.facebook.com/tennisalberta
twitter.com/tennisalberta
Also Known As: Tennis Alberta
Overview: A medium-sized provincial charitable organization
founded in 1973
Description: To facilitate participation, development, & visibility
of tennis throughout Alberta; *Member of:* International Tennis
Federation; Tennis Canada
Chief Officer(s): Jill Richard, Executive Director, 780-644-0440
jill.richard@tennisalberta.com
Brendan Smith, Coordinator, Tournament & Programs
Finances: *Funding Sources:* ASRPW Foundation; Tennis
Canada; Sponsors; Self-generated revenue
Staff: 3 staff member(s)
Activities: Coaching; Officiating; *Library:* Tennis Resource
Centre

Club 'Les Pongistes d'Ungava'
129, 4e av, Chibougamau QC G8P 3C4
Aperçu: *Dimension: petite; Envergure: locale*
Membre(s) du bureau directeur: David Pichette, Président

International Tennis Federation (ITF)
Bank Lane, Roehampton, London SW15 5XZ United Kingdom
communications@itftennis.com
www.itftennis.com
www.youtube.com/c/InternationalTennisFederationOfficial
www.facebook.com/InternationalTennisFederation
twitter.com/ITFTennis
Overview: A medium-sized international organization founded in
1913
Affiliation(s): Tennis Canada
Chief Officer(s): David Haggerty, President
Membership: 210 nations; *Fees:* Schedule available
Activities: Grand Slam tennis events; Davis Cup; Grand Slam
Cup

Northwest Territories Tennis Association
PO Box 671, Yellowknife NT X1A 2N5
Tel: 867-444-8330
www.tennisnwt.com
Also Known As: Tennis NWT
Previous Name: Tennis Northwest Territories
Overview: A small provincial organization
Description: To grow & promote the sport of tennis in the
Northwest Territories; *Member of:* Tennis Canada
Chief Officer(s): Jon Brennan, President
Julie Bennett, General Manager

Nova Scotia Tennis Association
5516 Spring Garden Rd., 4th Fl., Halifax NS B3J 1G6
Tel: 902-425-5454
tennisns@sportnovascotia.ca
www.tennisnovascotia.ca
www.facebook.com/109415259125199
twitter.com/TennisNovaScoti
Overview: A medium-sized provincial organization
Description: To promote & create opportunities for people to
play tennis in Nova Scotia; *Member of:* Tennis Canada
Chief Officer(s): Craig Bethune, President
Roger Keating, Executive Director
Marijke Nel, Technical Director
mnel@sportnovascotia.ca
Member Profile: Individuals & clubs

Ontario Tennis Association (OTA)
#200, 1 Shoreham Dr., Toronto ON M3N 3A7
Tel: 416-514-1100; *Fax:* 416-514-1112
Toll-Free: 800-387-5066
ota@tennisontario.com
www.tennisontario.com
www.instagram.com/ontariotennisassociation
www.facebook.com/OntarioTennisAssociation
twitter.com/TennisOntario
Previous Name: Ontario Lawn Tennis Association
Overview: A medium-sized provincial organization founded in
1918
Description: To act as the provincial governing body for tennis
in Ontario; To promote participation in tennis in Ontario; To
create tennis opportunities for players of every level, from
grassroots to national calibre athlete; To encourage the quest for
excellence for all players; *Member of:* Tennis Canada
Chief Officer(s): Scott Fraser, President
James N. Boyce, Executive Director
jboyce@tennisontario.com
Andrew Chappell, Manager, Events
achappell@tennisontario.com
Peter Malcomson, Manager, Marketing
pmalcomson@tennisontario.com
Jay Neill, Manager, Membership
jneill@tennisontario.com
Finances: *Funding Sources:* Membership fees; Sponsorships;
The Ontario Trillium Foundation
Membership: 220 clubs (55,000 youth & adult tennis players) +
2,200 individuals; *Member Profile:* Tennis clubs across Ontario,
including private & commercial clubs, recreation departments,
municipal parks, community clubs, & resorts
Activities: Offering professional development activities, such as
clinics & tennis instructor courses; Coordinating the OTA Tennis
Fair for clubs; Sanctioning tournaments; Providing guidance to
clubs in the area of club management

Prince Edward Island Tennis Association
PO Box 302, 40 Enman Cres., Charlottetown PE C1A 7K7
Tel: 902-368-4985; *Fax:* 902-368-4548
tennisprinceedwardisland@gmail.com
www.tennispei.ca
www.facebook.com/286640596313
twitter.com/TennisPEI
Also Known As: Tennis PEI
Overview: A medium-sized provincial organization
Description: To promote the sport of tennis on PEI; *Member of:*
Tennis Canada
Chief Officer(s): Daniel Arseneault, President
daniel.arseneault@gmail.com
Finances: *Funding Sources:* Government; Sponsors;
Participants
Staff: 2 staff member(s); 20 volunteer(s)
Membership: 600; *Fees:* Schedule available
Activities: Offering clinics, tournaments, & other programs

Tennis BC (TBC)
#204, 210 West Broadway, Vancouver BC V5Y 3W2
Tel: 604-737-3086; *Fax:* 604-737-3124
tbc@tennisbc.org
www.tennisbc.org
www.youtube.com/user/TennisBC1
www.facebook.com/tennisbc
twitter.com/TennisBC
Previous Name: British Columbia Tennis Association
Overview: A medium-sized provincial organization founded in
1978
Member of: Tennis Performance Association (TPA); Tennis
Canada
Chief Officer(s): Roger Skillings, President
Mark Roberts, Chief Executive Officer, 604-737-3086 9
mroberts@tennisbc.org
Finances: *Funding Sources:* Government Sponsors; Tennis
Canada; Sports Grants; Events; Member Clubs
Staff: 12 staff member(s)
Fees: $46 adult; $27 junior
Activities: *Library:* Yes (Open to Public)

Tennis Canada
Aviva Centre, #100, 1 Shoreham Dr., Toronto ON M3N 3A6
Tel: 416-665-9777; *Fax:* 416-665-9017
Toll-Free: 877-283-6647
info@tenniscanada.com
www.tenniscanada.com
www.instagram.com/tenniscanada
www.facebook.com/TennisCanada
twitter.com/TennisCanada
Previous Name: Canadian Tennis Association
Overview: A large national organization founded in 1890
Description: To stimulate participation & excellence in the sport
at the local, provincial, national & international levels; To provide

encouragement, support & leadership to organizations &
individuals who seek to enhance the enjoyment, quality & image
of Canadian tennis; *Member of:* International Tennis Federation;
Canadian Olympic Association; Canadian Paralympic
Committee; International Wheelchair Tennis Association
Chief Officer(s): Jennifer Bishop, Chair
Michael S. Downey, President & CEO
Hatem McDadi, Senior Vice-President, Tennis Development
Finances: *Funding Sources:* Government
Member Profile: Provincial tennis associations
Activities: Holding a number of championships; programs for all
ages & abilities; *Awareness Events:* Rogers Cup tournament;
Davis Cup; Fed Cup; *Internships:* Yes

Tennis Manitoba
#419, 145 Pacific Ave., Winnipeg MB R3B 2Z6
Tel: 204-925-5660; *Fax:* 204-925-5703
info@tennismanitoba.com
www.tennismanitoba.com
www.youtube.com/channel/UCXBmclr50I7GpGTP9u6UE3w
www.facebook.com/TennisManitoba
twitter.com/tennismanitoba
Also Known As: Manitoba Tennis Association
Overview: A medium-sized provincial organization founded in
1880
Description: To stimulate participation & advancement in tennis
by all Manitobans; *Member of:* Sport Manitoba; Tennis Canada
Chief Officer(s): Mark Arndt, Executive Director
mark@tennismanitoba.com
Finances: *Funding Sources:* Provincial government; Manitoba
Lotteries; Private sponsors
Fees: Schedule available

Tennis New Brunswick
PO Box 604, Fredericton NB E3B 5A6
Tel: 506-444-0885
tnb@tennisnb.net
www.tennisnb.net
www.facebook.com/TennisNewBrunswick
twitter.com/10sNB
Overview: A medium-sized provincial organization
Description: To be the body governing the sport of tennis in
New Brunswick; *Member of:* Sport NB; Tennis Canada
Chief Officer(s): Dana Brown, President
Mark Thibault, Executive Director
Fees: Schedule available

Tennis Newfoundland & Labrador
Greenbelt Tennis Club, 114 Newtown Rd., St. John's NL A1B
3A7
Tel: 709-722-3840
newfoundland.tenniscanada.com
www.facebook.com/TennisNFLD
twitter.com/tennisnfld
Previous Name: Newfoundland & Labrador Tennis Association
Overview: A medium-sized provincial organization
Description: To grow & promote the sport of tennis throughout
Newfoundland & Labrador; To increase participation at levels
consistent with the personal goals & aspirations of competitors in
all age groups; *Member of:* Tennis Canada
Chief Officer(s): Nancy Taylor, President
Alan Mackin, Executive Director

Tennis Québec (TQ)
285, rue Gary-Carter, Montréal QC H2R 2W1
Tél: 514-270-6060; *Téléc:* 514-270-2700
courrier@tennis.qc.ca
www.tennis.qc.ca

www.youtube.com/user/tennisquebec
www.facebook.com/tennisquebec270
Nom précédent: Fédération québécoise de tennis
Aperçu: *Dimension: moyenne; Envergure: provinciale;
Organisme sans but lucratif; fondée en 1899*
Description: Promotion et développement du tennis au Québec
auprès de toutes les catégories d'âge et de tous les calibres;
Membre de: Tennis Canada
Membre(s) du bureau directeur: Réjean Genois, Président
Jean François Manibal, Directeur général, 514-270-6060 606
dg1@tennis.qc.ca
Finances: *Budget de fonctionnement annuel:* $500,000-$1.5
Million
Personnel: 8 membre(s) du personnel; 30 bénévole(s)
Membre: 35 000; *Comités:* Comité des entraîneurs;
Commission des officiels; Commission d'enseignement
Activités: Tournée sports experts; *Stagiaires:* Oui; *Service de
conférenciers:* Oui *Bibliothèque:* Centre d'information
(Bibliothèque publique) rendez-vous

Tennis Saskatchewan
2205 Victoria Ave., Regina SK S4P 0S4
Tel: 306-780-9410; *Fax:* 306-525-4009
www.tennissask.com
Previous Name: Saskatchewan Tennis Association
Overview: A medium-sized provincial organization founded in 1976
Description: To advance tennis throughout Saskatchewan by stimulating participation & excellence in the sport; To provide players throughout Saskatchewan with systematic opportunities to participate in tennis & to achieve a level of competence consistent with their abilities & aspirations, with particular emphasis on youth; To stage tennis events; To produce teams & athletes capable of winning national championships; *Member of:* Tennis Canada
Affiliation(s): Sask Sport Incorporated
Chief Officer(s): Rory Park, Executive Director
Finances: *Funding Sources:* Saskatchewan Lotteries; Tennis Canada

Tennis Yukon Association
4061 - 4th Ave., Whitehorse YT Y1A 1H1
Tel: 867-393-2621
tennisyukon@gmail.com
www.tennisyukon.com
www.facebook.com/TennisYukon
twitter.com/tennisyukon
Overview: A small provincial organization
Description: To develop & promote tennis for people of all ages & abilities in the Yukon
Chief Officer(s): Stacy Lewis, President, 867-334-8858
Fees: $40 senior, junior; $80 adult; $150 family
Activities: Year-round programming and partnerships

Therapeutic Riding

Antigonish Therapeutic Riding Association
1216 Ohio East Rd., Antigonish NS B2G 2K8
Tel: 902-863-4853
www.facebook.com/399942843470547
Overview: A small local charitable organization founded in 1987
Description: To provide a therapeutic and recreational horseback riding program for physically, mentally, and emotionally handicapped people, and to promote public awareness of such a program
Activities: Two six-week sessions per year; weekly horseback riding lessons for handicapped children & adults

British Columbia Therapeutic Riding Association (BCTRA)
3885B - 96th St., Delta BC V4K 3N3
Tel: 604-590-0897
ponypalstra@yahoo.ca
www.vcn.bc.ca/bctra
Overview: A small provincial charitable organization founded in 1986
Description: To adhance the quality of life of people with disabilities; *Member of:* Canadian Therapeutic Riding Association; Horse Council of British Columbia
Affiliation(s): Horse Council BC; Sports & Fitness Council for the Disabled
Chief Officer(s): Candice Miller, President
Finances: *Funding Sources:* Membership dues; donations
Fees: $30 group/centre; $10 individual; *Member Profile:* Therapeutic riding centres/individuals
Activities: *Speaker Service:* Yes

Canadian Therapeutic Riding Association / Association canadienne d'équitation thérapeutique
5420 Hwy. 6 North, RR#5, Guelph ON N1H 6J2
Tel: 519-767-0700; *Fax:* 519-767-0435
ctra@golden.net
www.cantra.ca
twitter.com/CanTRA_ACET
Also Known As: CanTRA
Overview: A large national charitable organization founded in 1980
Description: To foster therapeutic riding for persons with disabilities by establishing riding standards in collaboration with the medical profession; To accredit programs, certify instructors & promote research; To promote equestian sport & competition for persons with disabilities; *Member of:* Riding for Disabled International; Canadian Paralympic Committee
Chief Officer(s): JoAnn Thompson Franklin, President
Finances: *Funding Sources:* Donations; Membership fees; Fund-raising
Staff: 5000 volunteer(s)
Membership: 80+ member centres & 4,000 riders; *Fees:* $40 voting; $20 supporting
Activities: Offering instructor certification programs; *Speaker Service:* Yes

Cavalier Riding Club Ltd. (CRC)
705 Pine Glen Rd., Pine Glen NB E1J 1S1
Tel: 506-386-7652
cavalierridingclub.weebly.com
Also Known As: Greater Moncton Riding for the Disabled; CRC Therapeutic Horseback Riding for the Disabled
Overview: A small local organization
Description: To use hippotherapy in order to treat certain physical and emotional conditions of individuals with a disability; *Member of:* Canadian Therapeutic Riding Association

Central Ontario Developmental Riding Program (CODRP)
Pride Stables, 584 Pioneer Tower Rd., Kitchener ON N2P 2H9
Tel: 519-653-4686; *Fax:* 519-653-5565
info@pridestables.com
www.pridestables.com
www.facebook.com/PrideStables
Also Known As: Pride Stables
Overview: A small local charitable organization founded in 1973
Description: To provide a safe, high-quality riding program for persons with disabilities; to foster personal growth & improvement through the use of horses as a medium for development & therapy with the assistance of volunteers; *Member of:* Ontario Equestrian Federation; Association of Riding Establishments of Ontario
Affiliation(s): Ontario Therapeutic Riding Association (ONTRA)
Chief Officer(s): Heather Mackneson, Executive Director
Finances: *Funding Sources:* Service clubs; company & individual donations; municipal grants; special events
Staff: 8 staff member(s); 250 volunteer(s)
Membership: 350+ riders; *Member Profile:* Physical, mental & behavioral challenges
Activities: Integrated summer camp; therapeutic horseback riding; *Speaker Service:* Yes *Library:* Yes by appointment

Community Association for Riding for the Disabled (CARD)
4777 Dufferin St., Toronto ON M3H 5T3
Tel: 416-667-8600; *Fax:* 416-739-7520
info@card.ca
www.card.ca
Overview: A medium-sized local charitable organization founded in 1969
Description: To improve the lives of children & adults with disabilities through therapeutic riding programs; *Member of:* Canadian Therapeutic Riding Association
Affiliation(s): Ontario Therapeutic Riding Association
Chief Officer(s): Penny Smith, Executive Director
penny@card.ca
Seana Waldon, Director, Therapeutic Riding Services
seana@card.ca
Judy Wanless, Director, Volunteer Services
judy@card.ca
Bonnie Hartley, Coordinator, Fundraising & Events
bonnie@card.ca
Finances: *Funding Sources:* Government; fundraising; special events; corporate donations; private donations
Staff: 9 staff member(s); 350 volunteer(s)
Membership: 600; *Fees:* $25
Activities: Summer program; Ride-a-thon; dinner; auction

Comox Valley Therapeutic Riding Society (CVTRS)
PO Box 3666, Courtenay BC V9N 7P1
Tel: 250-338-1968; *Fax:* 250-338-4137
cvtrs@telus.net
www.cvtrs.com
Also Known As: Therapeutic Riding
Overview: A small local charitable organization founded in 1986
Description: To provide a therapeutic riding program for physically, mentally & emotionally disabled, hearing & visually impaired children & adults; *Member of:* Canadian Therapeutic Riding Association
Affiliation(s): North American Handicapped Riding Association
Chief Officer(s): Nancy King, Executive Director
Finances: *Funding Sources:* United Way; donations; fundraising
Staff: 10 staff member(s); 175 volunteer(s)
Membership: 130; *Fees:* $20 individual; $30 group/family
Activities: Therapy with the use of a horse

Cowichan Therapeutic Riding Association (CRTA)
c/o Providence Farm, 1843 Tzouhalem Rd., Duncan BC V9L 5L6
Tel: 250-746-1028; *Fax:* 250-746-1033
info@ctra.ca
www.ctra.ca
www.instagram.com/cowichantherapeuticriding
www.facebook.com/cowichantherapeuticridingassociation
Overview: A small local charitable organization founded in 1985
Description: To use horses to help persons with various disabilities in the Cowichan area of British Columbia achieve physical & mental health, behavioral, communication, cognitive, & social goals; To provide therapeutic or sporting activities in a

safe environment with qualified instruction in order to improve the quality of life for persons with disabilities
Activities: Receiving referrals from doctors, psychologists, physiotherapists, schools, & other health care organizations; Offering individualized riding programs; Providing a training program & workplace for persons with barriers to employment; Educating the public to see the contributions of persons with disabilities

Errington Therapeutic Riding Association (ETRA)
Pyramid Stables, PO Box 462, 7581 Harby Rd., Lantzville, Parksville BC V9P 2G6
etrainfo@shaw.ca
www.etra.ca
www.facebook.com/ETRAPledgeRide2016
Overview: A small local organization founded in 1989
Description: ETRA is an independent, non-profit association that gives people with disabilities the chance to ride a horse, to improve their physical and/or mental well-being, & enhance their sense of achievement & self-worth.; *Member of:* CanTRA; B.C. Therapeutic Riding Association
Affiliation(s): BC Therapeutic Riding Association; Canadian Therapeutic Riding Association
Chief Officer(s): Regine Eder, President
regine.eder@shaw.ca
Finances: *Annual Operating Budget:* Less than $50,000; *Funding Sources:* Provincial government; rider fees; donations; community organizations
Staff: 40 volunteer(s)
Membership: 112; *Fees:* $5
Activities: *Speaker Service:* Yes

Halifax Area Leisure & Therapeutic Riding Association
196 Moss Close, Lawrencetown NS B2Z 1S5
Tel: 902-435-9344
haltr2@live.ca
www.bengallancers.com/special-needs-haltr
www.instagram.com/hfxjrbengallancers
www.facebook.com/HalifaxJrBengalLancers
twitter.com/Bengal_Lancers
Previous Name: Lancer Rehab Riders
Overview: A small local charitable organization
Description: HALTR is a volunteer-run group that provides horse-riding & driving programs for people with special needs. It is a registered charity, BN: 890783947RR0001.; *Member of:* Equine Canada; Canadian Therapeutic Riding Association
Affiliation(s): Sport Canada
Chief Officer(s): Sallie Murphy, Program Manager
Member Profile: Mostly children & young adults with disabilities

Lanark County Therapeutic Riding Program (LCTRP)
30 Bennett St., Carleton Place ON K7C 4J9
Tel: 613-257-7121; *Fax:* 613-257-2675
info@therapeuticriding.ca
www.therapeuticriding.ca
Overview: A small local charitable organization founded in 1986
Description: To provide individuals a holistic approach to therapy, rehabilitation & recreation; the opportunity to experience freedom & movement astride a horse; *Member of:* Canadian Therapeutic Riding Association; Ontario Therapeutic Riding Association; Lanark Health & Community Services
Chief Officer(s): Maria Hofbauer, Head Instructor
Finances: *Annual Operating Budget:* $50,000-$100,000; *Funding Sources:* Local fundraising events; fees for service
Staff: 1 staff member(s); 45 volunteer(s)
Membership: 105 riders; *Committees:* Advisory; Fundraising
Activities: Provides individuals a holistic approach to therapy, rehabilitation & recreation & the opportunity to experience freedom when riding a horse; *Internships:* Yes

Lethbridge Therapeutic Riding Association (LTRA)
RR#8-24-6, Lethbridge AB T1J 4P4
Tel: 403-328-2165; *Fax:* 403-317-0235
info@ltra.ca
www.ltra.ca
Also Known As: Rainbow Riding Centre
Overview: A small local charitable organization founded in 1977
Description: To provide the opportunity for improved physical & emotional well-being for people of all ages & abilities who participate in therapeutic, recreational, educational & competitive riding programs at Rainbow Riding Centre; *Member of:* Canadian Therapeutic Riding Association
Chief Officer(s): Rick Austin, Executive Director
raustin@ltra.ca
Finances: *Annual Operating Budget:* $100,000-$250,000
Staff: 2 staff member(s); 200 volunteer(s)
Membership: 260; *Fees:* Schedule available; *Committees:* Facility; Program; Fundraising; Public relations; Foundation
Activities: 5-6 riding sessions per year; summer Ride On camp; Easter clinic

Little Bits Therapeutic Riding Association
PO Box 29016, Stn. Pleasantview, Edmonton AB T6H 5Z6
Tel: 780-476-1233; *Fax:* 780-476-7252
info@littlebits.ca
www.littlebits.ca
www.facebook.com/LittleBitsVolunteers
Overview: A small local charitable organization founded in 1978
Description: To provide recreational riding programs that have therapeutic benefits for disabled children & adults in Edmonton & surrounding area. Physical address: Whitemud Equine Learning Centre Association, 12504 Fox Dr. NW, Edmonton, AB T6G 2L6; *Member of:* Central Canadian Therapeutic Riding Association; North American Riding for the Handicapped Association
Chief Officer(s): Linda Rault, Riding Administrator
Membership: 200; *Committees:* Finance; Fundraising; Public Relations; Riding Program; Camp Horseshoe

Manitoba Riding for the Disabled Association Inc. (MRDA)
145 Pacific Ave., Winnipeg MB R3B 2Z6
Tel: 204-925-5905; *Fax:* 204-925-5792
exedir@mrda.cc
www.mrda.cc
www.facebook.com/105010909544565
Overview: A small provincial charitable organization founded in 1977
Description: To provide a therapeutic horseback riding program for children with disabilities.; *Member of:* Canadian Therapeutic Riding Association
Chief Officer(s): Peter Manastyrsky, Executive Director
Finances: *Funding Sources:* corporate sponsors
Staff: 100 volunteer(s)

Mirabel Morgan Special Riding Centre
1201 - 2nd Line South, Bailieboro ON K0L 1B0
Tel: 705-939-6485
mirabelmf@gmail.com
Overview: A small local organization
Description: Year round program for anyone who wishes to ride who has medical, physical, or emotional needs; for those who enjoy the outdoors & animals, want to improve flexibility, balance, joint, muscle & nerve stimulation; designed to meet unique needs, limitations & abilities of the rider; *Member of:* Canadian Therapeutic Riding Association

Mount View Special Riding Association (MVSRA)
PO Box 1637, Didsbury AB T0M 0W0
Tel: 403-335-9146; *Fax:* 403-556-6480
www.mountviewriding.com
Previous Name: Mountview Handicapped Riding Association
Overview: A small local charitable organization founded in 1983
Description: To provide recreational & therapeutic riding to specially abled adults & children with mental &/or physical disabilities; *Member of:* Canadian Therapeutic Riding Association
Chief Officer(s): Karla Brautigam, President
Karla@asc-mva.ab.ca
Finances: *Annual Operating Budget:* Less than $50,000
Staff: 40 volunteer(s)
Membership: 75; *Fees:* $5

Ontario Therapeutic Riding Association (OnTRA) / Association ontarienne d'équitation thérapeutique
47 Fairlane Rd., London ON N6K 3E3
president@ontra.ca
www.ontra.ca
Overview: A small provincial charitable organization founded in 1983
Description: The Ontario Therapeutic Riding Association (OnTRA) promotes horseback riding as a form of therapy and sport for children and adults living with physical, cognitive, emotional, and/or behavioural challenges. OnTRA provides volunteers and therapeutic riding professionals with on-going information and training to ensure riders with disabilities receive the best possible therapy.; *Member of:* Canadian Therapeutic Riding Association; Ontario Equestrian Federation
Finances: *Annual Operating Budget:* Less than $50,000
Staff: 2500 volunteer(s)
Membership: 250; *Fees:* $20 individual; $30 family; $12 junior; $300 lifetime
Activities: Competitions; promotion; educational clinic; grants; Used Equipment Program; *Speaker Service:* Yes

Pacific Riding for Developing Abilities (PRDA)
1088 - 208 St., Langley BC V2Z 1T4
Tel: 604-530-8717; *Fax:* 604-530-8617
www.prda.ca
www.facebook.com/PRDALangley
Previous Name: Pacific Riding for Disabled Association
Overview: A small local charitable organization founded in 1973
Description: To enhance the quality of life for people with a range of disabilities, providing therapeutic equestrian activities &
educational opportunities.; *Member of:* Canadian Therapeutic Riding Association; Langley Chamber of Commerce; North American Riding for the Handicapped Association
Affiliation(s): Ishtar Transition Housing Society; Burnaby Association for Community Inclusion
Chief Officer(s): Michelle Ingall, Executive Director
Finances: *Funding Sources:* Donations; fundraising; United Way of the Lower Mainland
Staff: 8 staff member(s)
Activities: Day camp; summer camp; horse shows; *Speaker Service:* Yes; *Rents Mailing List:* Yes *Library:* Yes (Open to Public)

PARD Therapeutic Riding (PARD)
PO Box 1654, Peterborough ON K9J 5S4
Tel: 705-742-6441
pardtherapeuticriding@gmail.com
www.pard.ca
www.facebook.com/PARDTherapeuticRiding
Previous Name: Peterborough Association for Riding for the Disabled
Overview: A small local charitable organization
Description: Provides the benefits of riding to people with disabilities.; *Member of:* Canadian Therapeutic Riding Association; Ontario Therapeutic Riding Association
Chief Officer(s): Kathy Carruthers, Program Coordinator
Activities: Horseback riding instruction as a form of therapeutic & social recreation for physically, emotionally, developmentally challenged individuals

Peace Area Riding for the Disabled (PARDS)
8202 - 84 St., Grande Prairie AB T8X 0L6
Tel: 780-538-3211; *Fax:* 780-538-3683
info@pards.ca
www.pards.ca
Overview: A small local charitable organization founded in 1984
Description: To enhance the lives of individuals with disabilities through "equine assisted therapy"; To promoten physical, emotional, intellectual & social growth for individuals with disabilities through therapeutic riding services; To build a community that embraces differences & supports growth & success for all of its members; *Member of:* Canadian Therapeutic Riding Association
Chief Officer(s): Jennifer Douglas, Executive Director
Activities: Summer camp

Quinte Therapeutic Riding Association (QUINTRA)
173 McGee Rd., RR#2, Stirling ON K0K 3E0
Tel: 613-395-4472
www.quintra.org
Overview: A small local charitable organization founded in 1985
Description: To offer therapeutic horseback-riding sessions to disabled children & young adults to maximize the disabled person's physical & mental capabilities; To improve disabled young people's self-confidence & the ability to cope with everyday living; *Member of:* Canadian Therapeutic Riding Association; Ontario Therapeutic Riding Association
Affiliation(s): United Way of Quinte
Chief Officer(s): Barb Davis, Contact, 613-395-2990
barbara.davis@sympatico.ca
Finances: *Funding Sources:* Donations; Bingos; United Way Quinte
Activities:*Speaker Service:* Yes

Regina Therapeutic Riding Association (RTRA)
PO Box 474, Regina SK S4P 3A2
Tel: 306-530-0794
reginatra@sasktel.net
rtra.ca
Overview: A small provincial charitable organization founded in 1992
Description: To provide medically supervised horseback riding lessons for individuals with special needs
Chief Officer(s): John Van Knoll, Chair

SARI Therapeutic Riding
12659 Medway Rd., RR#1, Arva ON N0M 1C0
Tel: 519-666-1123; *Fax:* 519-666-1971
office@sari.ca
www.sari.ca
www.youtube.com/channel/UCWEQ6cSSY89McQFCwwTxLow
www.facebook.com/SARITherapeuticRiding
twitter.com/SARITherapeutic
Also Known As: Special Ability Riding Institute
Previous Name: SARI Riding for Disabled
Overview: A medium-sized local charitable organization founded in 1978
Description: To provide opportunities for people with special needs to move towards greater independence & freedom by providing therapeutic riding & driving programs which meet individual needs; To balance safety & challenge to maximize opportunities for growth; To support contributions of participants,
parents, volunteers & staff; *Member of:* Canadian Therapeutic Riding Association
Affiliation(s): Ontario Therapeutic Riding Association
Chief Officer(s): Diane Blackall, Executive Director
Finances: *Funding Sources:* Individual & service club donations; fundraising events
Staff: 200 volunteer(s)
Membership: 150; *Committees:* Fund Development; Human Resources; Program; Marketing & Communications
Activities: Summer equestrian program

Sunrise Therapeutic Riding & Learning Centre
6920 Concession 1, RR#2, Puslinch ON N0B 2J0
Tel: 519-837-0558; *Fax:* 519-837-1233
info@sunrise-therapeutic.ca
www.sunrise-therapeutic.ca
www.facebook.com/224072694372280
Also Known As: Sunrise
Previous Name: Sunrise Equestrian & Recreation Centre for the Disabled
Overview: A small local charitable organization founded in 1982
Description: To develop the full potential of children & adults with disabilites & lead them closer to independence through therapy, recreation, horse riding, life skills & farm related activity programme; *Member of:*Canadian Therapeutic Riding Association; Ontario Therapeutic Riding Association
Affiliation(s): Ontario's Promise
Chief Officer(s): Rob Vandebelt, Chief Executive Officer, 519-837-0558 32
rob@sunrise-therapeutic.ca
Nikki Duffield, Program Director & Head Instructor, 519-837-0558 29
nikkid@sunrise-therapeutic.ca
Lynne O'Brien, Manager, Operations & Volunteer, 519-837-0558 31
lynne@sunrise-therapeutic.ca
Finances: *Annual Operating Budget:* $250,000-$500,000; *Funding Sources:* Service clubs; Foundations; Industry; Corporate; Private; Golf tournament; Ride-a-thon
Staff: 18 staff member(s); 175 volunteer(s)
Membership: 250; *Fees:* $30; *Committees:* Finance; Fundraising; Public Relations/Marketing; Medical Advisory; Farm Management
Activities: Therapeutic riding; life skills program; Employment preparation courses for young adults with special needs; Therapeutic Riding Instructor Training School; integrated day camps; equestrian clinics; schooling shows; "Little Breeches" Club (4-7 years); education program for school groups (JK-3); monthly board & instructor meetings; Fall Open House; demonstrations at Royal Winter Fair; invitational horse shows; *Internships:* Yes *Library:* Resource Centre for Instructor School (Open to Public) by appointment

Therapeutic Ride Algoma
1014 Fifth Line East, Sault Ste Marie ON P6A 6J8
Tel: 705-575-4448
therapeuticridealgoma@hotmail.ca
www.facebook.com/TherapeuticRideAlgoma
Overview: A small local charitable organization founded in 1999
Member of: Canadian Therapeutic Riding Association
Chief Officer(s): Cory Steinberg, Contact, Board of Directors

Victoria Therapeutic Riding Association (VTRA)
PO Box 412, Brentwood Bay BC V8M 1R3
Tel: 778-426-0506
vtra.ca
www.instagram.com/victherapeutic
www.facebook.com/VictoriaTherapeuticRidingAssociation
twitter.com/VicTherapeutic
Previous Name: Victoria Riding for Disabled Association
Overview: A small local charitable organization founded in 1982
Description: To provide a therapeutic riding program for children & adults with disabilities to promote their physical, psychological, & social well-being; *Member of:* Canadian Therapeutic Riding Association
Affiliation(s): B.C. Therapeutic Riding Association; Horse Council of British Columbia; Volunteer Victoria; Canadian Therapeutic Riding Association's; Association of Fundraising Professionals
Chief Officer(s): Annie Brothwell, President
Audrey Cooper, Executive Director
Finances: *Funding Sources:* Service club; fund-raising events; foundations
Staff: 4 staff member(s); 100 volunteer(s)
Fees: $20 individual; $200 life; $10 riders

Windsor-Essex Therapeutic Riding Association (WETRA) / Association d'équitation thérapeutique Windsor-Essex
3323 North Malden Rd., RR#2, Essex ON N8M 2X6
Tel: 519-726-7682; *Fax:* 519-726-4403
info@wetra.ca
www.wetra.ca
www.facebook.com/wetraca
twitter.com/WETRA_
Overview: A small local charitable organization founded in 1969
Description: To improve the quality of life of physically, emotionally, mentally challenged persons through equine related therapy; *Member of:* Canadian Therapeutic Riding Association
Affiliation(s): Ontario Therapeutic Riding Association
Chief Officer(s): Becky Mills, Executive Director
Finances: *Annual Operating Budget:* $100,000-$250,000; *Funding Sources:* United Way; Donations; Bingo
Staff: 12 staff member(s); 80 volunteer(s)
Membership: 200 riders
Activities: Offering therapeutic riding & horse shows; Hosting an open house, benefit horse show, & golf tournament; *Awareness Events:* Ride-a-Thon, March

Track & Field Sports

Achilles Canada
123 Snowden Ave., Toronto ON M4N 2A8
Tel: 416-485-6451; *Fax:* 416-485-0823
www.achillescanada.ca
Previous Name: Achilles Track Club Canada
Overview: A medium-sized national charitable organization founded in 1999
Description: To encourage & assist all persons with disabilities to enjoy running for health in a social environment
Chief Officer(s): Brian McLean, Contact
bmclean@achillescanada.ca
Membership: 140+ chapters; *Fees:* $25 donation encouraged
Activities: Providing support, training, & technical expertise to runners at all levels; *Awareness Events:* Achilles St. Patrick's Day 5K Run/Walk, March

Athletics Canada / Athlétisme Canada
#105, 2141 Thurston Dr., Ottawa ON K1G 6C9
Tel: 613-260-5580; *Fax:* 613-260-0341
www.athletics.ca
www.instagram.com/athleticscanada
www.linkedin.com/company/athleticscanada
www.facebook.com/AthleticsCanada
twitter.com/AthleticsCanada
Previous Name: Canadian Track & Field Association
Overview: A large national organization
Description: To promote & encourage participation via competitions from the grass roots level through to the very highest level of proficiency; To assist coaches, officials & executives in fulfilling their goals through courses, conferences & clinics; To provide regular communication lines with members; To continually review & update technical programs; To assist in the research & investigation of potential new facilities; To engender more public awareness, interest & acceptance of the sport of track & field; *Member of:* International Association of Athletics Federations
Affiliation(s): International Amateur Athletic Federation
Chief Officer(s): David Bedford, Chief Executive Officer
david.bedford@athletics.ca
Mathieu Gentès, Chief Operating Officer
mgentes@athletics.ca
Christopher Jervis, Manager, Finance
chris.jervis@athletics.ca
Activities: Offering national team events

Canadian Masters Athletics (CMA)
cma@canadianmasters.ca
canadianmasters.ca
Previous Name: Canadian Masters Athletic Association; Canadian Masters Track & Field Association
Overview: A medium-sized national organization founded in 1972
Description: To promote & organize events for all levels of track & field, cross country, road racing & race walking for Canadian masters age participants, locally, provincially & internationally
Chief Officer(s): Paul Osland, President
Finances: *Funding Sources:* Membership fees
Membership: 12 provincial & territorial associations; *Member Profile:* People 35 & up

Ontario Masters Athletics (OMA)
1185 Eglinton Ave. East, Toronto ON M3C 3C6
Tel: 416-426-4427; *Fax:* 416-426-7358
douglasj.smith@sympatico.ca
www.ontariomasters.ca
www.youtube.com/OntarioMasters
twitter.com/OntarioMasters
Previous Name: Ontario Masters Track & Field Association
Overview: A small provincial organization founded in 1973
Member of: Canadian Masters Athletic Association
Affiliation(s): Athletics Ontario; Athletics Canada
Chief Officer(s): Doug Smith, President
douglasj.smith@sympatico.ca
Karla Del Grande, Vice-President
karla.delgrande@bell.net
Fees: $40 individual; $60 family

Triathlon

Alberta Triathlon Association (ATA)
Percy Page Centre, 11759 Groat Rd., Edmonton AB T5M 3K6
Tel: 780-427-8616; *Fax:* 780-427-8628
Toll-Free: 866-888-7448
info@triathlon.ab.ca
www.triathlon.ab.ca
www.facebook.com/160835077267482
twitter.com/TriAlberta
Overview: A small provincial organization founded in 1984
Description: ATA is the official, non-profit governing body for, & has a mandate to develop, the sports of triathlon, duathlon, aquathlon & other related multi-endurance sports in Alberta.; *Member of:* Triathlon Canada
Chief Officer(s): Calli Stromner, General Manager
general.manager@triathlon.ab.ca
Sebastian Porten, Manager, Programs
coordinator@triathlon.ab.ca
Finances: *Annual Operating Budget:* $100,000-$250,000
Staff: 1 staff member(s); 16 volunteer(s)
Membership: 1,000+; *Fees:* $15 youth (19 & under); $50 adult/coach
Activities: *Speaker Service:* Yes

Ontario Association of Triathletes (OAT)
#2, 2015 Pan Am Blvd., Milton ON L9T 879
Tel: 416-426-7025
info@triathlonontario.com
www.triathlonontario.com
www.facebook.com/TriathlonOntario
twitter.com/TriOntario
Also Known As: Triathlon Ontario
Overview: A small provincial organization
Description: To encourage participation in multi-sport events & to ensure safety & fair competition; to assist, support & promote Ontario athletes; *Member of:* Triathlon Canada
Chief Officer(s): Phil Dale, Executive Director
ed@triathlonontario.com
Emma Leeder, Manager, Program
technical@triathlonontario.com
Greg Kealey, Coach, Provincial Development
coach@triathlonontario.com
Finances: *Funding Sources:* Fees; sponsorship; government
Membership: 1,000-4,999; *Fees:* Schedule available

Saskatchewan Triathlon Association Corporation (STAC)
PO Box 32080, Saskatoon SK S4N 7L2
Tel: 306-519-1822; *Fax:* 800-319-4959
info@triathlonsaskatchewan.org
www.triathlonsaskatchewan.org
www.facebook.com/287275596696
twitter.com/SaskTriathlon
Overview: A small provincial organization
Description: To be the provincial governing body of triathlon in Saskatchewan; *Member of:* Triathlon Canada
Chief Officer(s): Shawn Rempel, President
Lacey Schroeder, Vice President
Fees: $45 adult; $20 youth; $90 family

Triathlon British Columbia
PO Box 34098, Stn. D, Vancouver BC V6J 4M1
Tel: 604-736-3176; *Fax:* 604-736-3180
info@tribc.org
www.tribc.org
www.facebook.com/TriathlonBC
Also Known As: Triathlon BC
Overview: A small provincial organization
Description: To be the provincial governing body of triathlon, duathlon, aquathon & winter triathlon in British Columbia; *Member of:* Triathlon Canada
Chief Officer(s): Emily Vickery, Program Manager
Andrew Armstrong, Technical Coordinator

Fees: $10 junior/youth; $20 adult/coach/associate; $35 individual of an affiliated club

Triathlon Canada
#121, 1925 Blanshard St., Victoria BC V8T 4J2
Tel: 250-412-1795; *Fax:* 250-412-1794
info@triathloncanada.com
www.triathloncanada.com
www.instagram.com/triathloncanada
www.facebook.com/148631098541373
twitter.com/TriathlonCanada
Previous Name: National Federation for the Sports of Triathlon, Duathlon & Aquathlon in Canada
Overview: A small national organization
Description: To function as the National Federation for triathlon & duathlon in Canada & internationally; To promote the triathlon & duathlon, both competitive & non-competitive in Canada; To provide guidance, information & assistance to the provincial triathlon associations, zones & clubs in respect to these objects & in the development of programmes for competitive & non-competitive triathletes & duathletes; To organize training courses for triathletes, duathletes, coaches & administrators to national & international standards; To promote other multi-disciplined endurance events & excluding the traditional decathlon, pentathlon, heptathlon, modern pentathlon & biathlon, which are part of existing National Federations
Chief Officer(s): Kim Van Bruggen, Chief Executive Officer
Chris Dornan, Manager, Communications, 403-620-8731
hpprchris@shaw.ca

Triathlon Manitoba
c/o Sport for Life Centre, #328, 145 Pacific Ave., Winnipeg MB R3B 2Z6
Tel: 204-925-5703
triathlon@sportmanitoba.ca
www.triathlon.mb.ca
www.facebook.com/TriathlonManitoba
twitter.com/MBTri
Overview: A small provincial organization
Description: To be the provincial governing body of triathlon in Manitoba; *Member of:* Triathlon Canada; Sport Manitoba
Chief Officer(s): Angela Lloyd, Executive Director, 204-925-5636
triathlon.ed@sportmanitoba.ca
Fees: $10 under 16 years; $25 youth (16-19 years); $50 full
Activities: Training; Races; Awards; Kids of Steel program

Triathlon New Brunswick
PO Box 22053, Stn. Landsdowne, Saint John NB E2K 4T7
Tel: 506-848-1144
www.trinb.ca
www.facebook.com/TriathlonNB
twitter.com/TriathlonNB
Also Known As: Triathlon NB
Overview: A small provincial organization
Description: To be the provincial governing body of triathlon in New Brunswick; *Member of:* Triathlon Canada
Chief Officer(s): Garth Miller, President
garth39@fastmail.fm
Brittany Pye, Executive Director
executivedirector@trinb.ca
Althea Arsenault, Vice President
Althea.Arsenault@gnb.ca
Fees: $50

Triathlon Newfoundland & Labrador
PO Box 872, Stn. C, St. John's NL A1C 5L7
admin@trinl.com
www.trinl.com
www.facebook.com/triathlon.nl
twitter.com/trinl
Also Known As: TriNL
Overview: A small provincial organization
Description: To develop, support & promtote triathalon & other multi-sport endurance events in Newfoundland & Labrador; *Member of:* Triathlon Canada
Affiliation(s): International Triathlon Union
Chief Officer(s): Stephen Delaney, Executive Director
Fees: $20 youth/junior; $35 club; $40 adult/elite

Triathlon Nova Scotia
5516 Spring Garden Rd., 4th Fl., Halifax NS B3J 1G6
Tel: 902-425-5450; *Fax:* 902-425-5606
triathlon@sportnovascotia.ca
triathlonnovascotia.ca
www.instagram.com/triathlon_ns
www.facebook.com/triathlonnovascotia
twitter.com/Triathlon_NS
Overview: A small provincial organization

Description: To be the provincial governing body of triathlon in Nova Scotia; *Member of:* Triathlon Canada; Sport Nova Scotia
Chief Officer(s): Gregg Kerr, President
Wade McCallum, Vice President
Fees: $45 adult or junior; $25 youth; $3 kids (per race)

Triathlon Price Edward Island
40 Enman Cres., Charlottetown PE C1E 1E6
triathlonpei@gmail.com
www.tripei.com
www.facebook.com/217742304907740
twitter.com/triathlonpei
Also Known As: Triathlon PEI
Overview: A small provincial organization founded in 2012
Description: To be the provincial governing body of triathlon in Prince Edward Island; *Member of:* Triathlon Canada
Chief Officer(s): Jamie Nickerson, President

Triathlon Québec
4545, av Pierre-de Coubertin, Montréal QC H1V 3R2
Tél: 514-252-3121
www.triathlonquebec.org

www.facebook.com/132997480092478
twitter.com/triathlonquebec
Aperçu: *Dimension: petite; Envergure: provinciale; fondée en 1985*
Membre de: Triathlon Canada
Affiliation(s): Triathlon Canada
Membre(s) du bureau directeur: Marie-Eve Sullivan, Directrice générale, 514-252-3121 4
msullivan@triathlonquebec.org
Finances: *Budget de fonctionnement annuel:* $250,000-$500,000
Personnel: 3 membre(s) du personnel; 20 bénévole(s)
Membre: 1 100
Activités: *Stagiaires:* Oui

Universities & Colleges

Alberta Colleges Athletic Conference (ACAC)
Percy Page Centre, 11759 Groat Rd., Edmonton AB T5M 3K6
www.acac.ab.ca
www.facebook.com/AlbertaCollegesAthleticConference
twitter.com/ACAC_Sport
Previous Name: Western Inter-College Conference (WICC)
Overview: A small provincial charitable organization founded in 1964
Description: To act as the governing body for intercollegiate athletics in Alberta; To develop student athletes; *Member of:* Canadian Colleges Athletic Association
Chief Officer(s): Mark Kosak, Chief Executive Officer, 403-875-7329, Fax: 780-427-9289
markk@acac.ab.ca
Anthony Wong, Manager, Operations, 780-644-1143
anthonyw@acac.ab.ca
Finances: *Funding Sources:* Membership; Government of Alberta, through the Alberta Sport, Recreation, Parks, & Wildlife Foundation
Membership: 17 schools; *Member Profile:* Colleges & universities in Saskatchewan & Alberta
Activities: Administering intercollegiate athletics

Canadian Collegiate Athletic Association (CCAA) / Association canadienne du sport collégial (ACSC)
2 St. Lawrence Dr., Cornwall ON K6H 4Z1
Tel: 613-937-1508; *Fax:* 613-937-1530
www.ccaa.ca
www.instagram.com/ccaasportsacsc
www.facebook.com/CCAAsportsACSC
twitter.com/CCAAsportsACSC
Overview: A medium-sized national organization founded in 1974
Description: To operate as the national governing body for men's & women's college sport in Canada
Affiliation(s): Atlantic Colleges Athletic Association; Fédération québécoise du sport étudiant; Ontario Colleges Athletic Association; Alberta Colleges Athletic Conference; British Columbia Colleges Athletic Association
Chief Officer(s): Sandra Murray-MacDonell, Chief Executive Officer
sandra@ccaa.ca
Membership: 98 institutional

Canadian Council of University Physical Education & Kinesiology Administrators (CCUPEKA) / Conseil canadien des administrateurs universitaires en éducation physique et kinésiologie (CCAUEPK)
www.ccupeka.org
Overview: A small national organization founded in 1971

Description: To serve as an accrediting body for physical education & kinesiology programs at universities in Canada; To offer a voice for academics, through lobbying initiatives; *Member of:* Universities Canada
Chief Officer(s): Doug Brown, President
Chad London, Vice-President
Membership: 38; *Member Profile:* Administrators of physical education & kinesiology programs at Canadian universities
Activities: Offering a forum for discussion among members

Ontario University Athletics (OUA) / Sports universitaires de l'Ontario
#2, 3305 Harvester Rd., Burlington ON L7N 3N2
Tel: 905-635-5510; *Fax:* 905-635-5820
info@oua.ca
www.oua.ca
www.youtube.com/ouachampionsforlife
www.facebook.com/OntarioUniversityAthletics
twitter.com/ouasport
Previous Name: Ontario Universities Athletics
Overview: A small provincial organization founded in 1898
Description: To provide leadership, stewardship & policy direction for university sport; To govern interuniversity sport competition in Ontario on behalf of member institutions; *Member of:* Canadian Interuniversity Sport
Chief Officer(s): Gord Grace, Chief Executive Officer, 905-635-7470
gord.grace@oua.ca
Finances: *Annual Operating Budget:* $250,000-$500,000
Staff: 8 staff member(s)
Membership: 19 schools; 9,000 student athletes
Activities: *Awareness Events:* Women of Influence Luncheon, Nov.; *Internships:* Yes

U Sports
#701, 45 Vogell Rd., Ottawa ON L4B 3P6
Tel: 905-508-3000; *Fax:* 905-508-3000
office@usports.ca
usports.ca
www.instagram.com/usportsca
www.facebook.com/USPORTSCanada
twitter.com/usportsca
Previous Name: Canadian Interuniversity Sport; Canadian Interuniversity Athletic Union
Overview: A medium-sized national organization
Description: To act as the national governing body for university sport in Canada; *Member of:* Universities Canada
Affiliation(s): Atlantic University Sport; Québec Student Sport Federation; Ontario University Athletics; Canada West Universities Athletic Association
Chief Officer(s): Dick White, Interim Chief Executive Officer
dwhite@usports.ca
Lisa Beatty, Chief Operating Officer
lbeatty@usports.ca
Membership: 55 institutional + members of four regional associations

Volleyball

Fédération de volleyball du Québec (FVBQ)
4545, av Pierre-de Coubertin, Montréal QC H1V 0B2
Tél: 514-252-3065; *Téléc:* 514-252-3176
info-fvbq@volleyball.qc.ca
www.volleyball.qc.ca

www.youtube.com/volleyballquebec
www.facebook.com/VolleyballQC
twitter.com/volleyballqc
Également appelé: Volleyball Québec
Aperçu: *Dimension: moyenne; Envergure: provinciale; Organisme sans but lucratif; fondée en 1968*
Description: Régir le volleyball à l'intérieur et à l'extérieur du Québec; promouvoir le volleyball; former les intervenants impliqués dans l'encadrement du participant; offrir des services aux membres
Affiliation(s): Sports Québec; Regroupement loisirs Québec
Membre(s) du bureau directeur: Félix Dion, Président
Finances: *Budget de fonctionnement annuel:* $500,000-$1.5 Million; *Fonds:* Gouvernement provincial
Personnel: 5 membre(s) du personnel; 100 bénévole(s)
Membre: 20,000; *Critères d'admissibilite:* Entraîneurs, athlètes, arbitres, adeptes, bénévoles; *Comités:* Entraîneurs; Arbitres; Élite; Techniques
Activités: Volleybal compétitif et récréatif; édition, publication et vente de documents techniques et pédagogiques; programme de formation des entraîneurs; vente de vidéos; *Stagiaires:* Oui; *Service de conférenciers:* Oui *Bibliothèque:* Oui rendez-vous

International Volleyball Association / Fédération Internationale de Volleyball (FIVB)
Château Les Tourelles, 2-4, ch Edouard-Sandoz, Lausanne 1006 Switzerland
info@fivb.ch
www.fivb.ch
www.youtube.com/user/videoFIVB
www.facebook.com/VolleyballWorld
twitter.com/fivbvolleyball
Overview: A small international organization founded in 1947
Affiliation(s): Canadian Volleyball Association
Chief Officer(s): Ary S. Graça Filho, President
president.office.sec@fivb.org
Fabio Azevedo, General Director
Membership: 222

Manitoba Volleyball Association (MVA)
#412, 145 Pacific Ave., Winnipeg MB R3B 2Z6
Tel: 204-925-5783; *Fax:* 204-925-5786
www.volleyballmanitoba.ca
twitter.com/VBManitoba
Overview: A small provincial organization founded in 1977
Description: To govern the sport of volleyball in Manitoba; To promote the development & growth of volleyball in the province
Chief Officer(s): John Blacher, Executive Director
volleyball.ed@sportmanitoba.ca
Finances: *Funding Sources:* Fundraising
Staff: 4 staff member(s)
Member Profile: Elite & recreational athletes, coaches, officials; *Committees:* Grassroots Development; Competitions; Finance & Audit; Marketing; Awards & Recognition; Conduct & Ethics; Nominations; Governance; High Performance Development; Hall of Fame
Activities: Offering coaching clinics; Training & certifying officials; Providing competitive programs; Conducting Youth Talent Identification Camps; *Library:* Manitoba Volleyball Association Resource Library

Newfoundland & Labrador Volleyball Association (NLVA)
1296A Kenmount Rd., Paradise NL A1L 1N3
Tel: 709-576-0817; *Fax:* 709-576-7493
www.nlva.net
Overview: A small provincial organization founded in 1986
Description: To promote volleyball in Newfoundland & Labrador; To provide competitive opportunities for its members
Chief Officer(s): Russell Jackson, Executive Director
nlvaruss@sportnl.ca
Luke Harris, Director, Technical
nlvaluke@sportnl.ca

Northwest Territories Volleyball Association (NWTVA)
4909 - 49 St., 3rd Fl., Yellowknife NT X1A 3X7
Tel: 867-669-8396; *Fax:* 867-669-8327
www.nwtvolleyball.ca
www.facebook.com/NWTVolleyballAssociation
twitter.com/NWTVA
Overview: A medium-sized provincial organization
Description: To promote volleyball in the Northwest Territories; To provide competitive opportunities for members
Chief Officer(s): Lyric Sandhals, Executive Director
lsandhals@sportnorth.com

Ontario Volleyball Association (OVA)
#111, 6 Scarsdale Rd., Toronto ON M3B 2R7
Tel: 416-426-7316; *Fax:* 416-426-7109
Toll-Free: 800-372-1568
info@ontariovolleyball.org
www.ontariovolleyball.org
www.youtube.com/user/ontariovolley
www.facebook.com/OntarioVolleyball
twitter.com/ova_updates
Overview: A large provincial organization founded in 1929
Description: To lead in the promotion & development of volleyball in Ontario
Chief Officer(s): Jo-Anne Ljubicic, Executive Director, 416-426-7414
jljubicic@ontariovolleyball.org
Fees: Schedule available; *Committees:* Awards & Recgonition; Beach Competitions Task Force; Finance; Inclusion, Diversity & Equity Advisory; Indoor Volleyball Development; Referee; Youth Competitions Task Force
Activities: *Internships:* Yes

Saskatchewan Volleyball Association
1750 McAra St., Regina SK S4N 6L4
Tel: 306-780-9250; *Fax:* 306-780-9288
Toll-Free: 800-321-1685
meta@saskvolleyball.ca
www.saskvolleyball.ca
www.instagram.com/saskvolleyball
www.facebook.com/saskvolleyball
twitter.com/saskvolleyball
Overview: A small provincial organization
Description: To develop interest, participation & excellence in volleyball through the promotion & provision of quality services for all
Chief Officer(s): Aaron Demyen, Executive Director, 306-780-9801
aaron@saskvolleyball.ca
Finances: *Annual Operating Budget:* $500,000-$1.5 Million; *Funding Sources:* Corporate sponsors
Staff: 9 staff member(s); 2200 volunteer(s)

Volleyball Alberta
Percy Page Centre, 11759 Groat Rd., Edmonton AB T5M 3K6
Tel: 780-415-1703; *Fax:* 780-415-1700
info@volleyballalberta.ca
www.volleyballalberta.ca
www.facebook.com/VolleyballAlberta
twitter.com/volleyballab
Overview: A medium-sized provincial charitable organization founded in 1974
Description: To promote volleyball in Alberta; To provide competitive opportunities for members
Affiliation(s): Federation of Outdoor Volleyball Associations
Chief Officer(s): Terry Gagnon, Executive Director, 587-273-1513
tgagnon@volleyballalberta.ca
Activities: *Internships:* Yes; *Rents Mailing List:* Yes

Volleyball BC
Harry Jerome Sports Centre, 7564 Barnet Hwy., Burnaby BC V5A 1E7
Tel: 604-291-2007; *Fax:* 604-291-2602
www.volleyballbc.org
www.instagram.com/volleyballbc
www.facebook.com/volleyballbc
twitter.com/VolleyballBC
Also Known As: British Columbia Volleyball Association
Overview: A medium-sized provincial organization founded in 1965
Description: To promote volleyball in British Columbia; To provide competitive opportunities for members
Chief Officer(s): Chris Densmore, Executive Director, 604-291-2007 223
execdirector@volleyballbc.org
Chris Berglund, Director, Technical & High Performance, 604-291-2007 222
cberglund@volleyballbc.org
Dave Brewin, Manager, Marketing & Communications, 604-291-2007 226
communications@volleyballbc.org

Volleyball Canada (VC)
National Office, #1A, 1084 Kenaston St., Ottawa ON K1B 3P5
Tel: 613-748-5681; *Fax:* 613-748-5727
info@volleyball.ca
volleyball.ca
www.instagram.com/volleyballcanada
www.facebook.com/VolleyballCanada
twitter.com/VBallCanada
Also Known As: Canadian Volleyball Association
Overview: A large national charitable organization founded in 1953
Description: To lead the growth of & excellence in the sport of volleyball for all Canadians
Affiliation(s): International Volleyball Federation; Canadian Olympic Association; Coaching Association of Canada
Chief Officer(s): Mark Eckert, President & CEO, 613-748-5681 225
meckert@volleyball.ca
Jackie Skender, Director, Communications, 613-748-5681 226
jskender@volleyball.ca
Linden Leung, Director, Finance & Operations, 613-748-5681 223
linden@volleyball.ca
Lucie Leclerc, Office Manager, 613-748-5681 236
lucie@volleyball.ca
Finances: *Funding Sources:* Membership dues; Fundraising; Merchandise & publications sale; Government; Sponsorships
Staff: 28 staff member(s)
Member Profile: Athletes, officials; *Committees:* Domestic Development; National Championships; Sitting Volleyball; High Performance Management; National Referee; Alumni & Awards;

National Registration Systems Project Management; National Registration System Operation Group; Nominations & Elections; Finance & Audit; Legal; Ethics; External Relations
Activities: Offering National Championships for Indoor & Beach Volleyball & National Team Challenge Cup (for Provincial Teams); Providing coaching certification & education programs; Producing publications & videos; Coordinating international & national officials programs; Hosting international events; Marketing & promoting volleyball to the corporate community & the media; *Internships:* Yes; *Rents Mailing List:* Yes

Volleyball New Brunswick
#13, 900 Hanwell Rd., Fredericton NB E3B 6A3
Tel: 506-451-1346; *Fax:* 506-451-1325
vnb@nb.aibn.ca
www.vnb.nb.ca
www.instagram.com/volleyballnb
www.facebook.com/volleyballnb
twitter.com/volleyballnb
Also Known As: VNB
Overview: A medium-sized provincial organization
Description: To promote volleyball in New Brunswick; To provide competitive opportunities for members
Chief Officer(s): Ryley Boldon, Executive Director
Rachelle Duguay, Coordinator, Programs, 506-878-3064
vnbcoordinator@nb.aibn.com
Fees: Schedule available; *Committees:* Executive; Officials; Beach; Senior; Age Class; Female High Performance; Male High Performance; Coaching

Volleyball Nova Scotia
5516 Spring Garden Rd., 4th Fl., Halifax NS B3J 1G6
Tel: 902-425-5606
vns@sportnovascotia.ca
www.volleyballnovascotia.ca
www.facebook.com/Volleyballnovascotia
twitter.com/volleyballNS
Overview: A medium-sized provincial organization founded in 1965
Description: To promote volleyball in Nova Scotia; To provide competitive opportunities for members
Chief Officer(s): Jason Trepanier, Executive Director, 902-425-5450 322
vns@sportnovascotia.ca
Shane St-Louis, Director, Technical, 902-425-5450 514
volleyballtd@sportnovascotia.ca

Volleyball Nunavut
PO Box 208, Iqaluit NU X0A 0H0
Tel: 250-718-8411; *Fax:* 250-984-7600
volleyballnunavut.ca
www.facebook.com/VolleyballNunavut
Overview: A medium-sized provincial organization founded in 1999
Description: To promote volleyball in Nunavut & provide programs throughout the territory; *Member of:* Sport & Recreation Nunavut
Chief Officer(s): Scott Schutz, Executive Director
scott@volleyballnunavut.ca
Finances: *Funding Sources:* Sport & Recreation Nunavut

Volleyball Prince Edward Island
PO Box 302, Charlottetown PE C1A 7K7
Tel: 902-569-0583; *Fax:* 902-368-4548
Toll-Free: 800-247-6712
www.volleyballpei.com
www.facebook.com/volleyballpei
Overview: A small provincial organization
Description: To promote volleyball in PEI; To provide competitive opportunities for members
Affiliation(s): Sport PEI
Chief Officer(s): Cheryl Crozier, Executive Director, 902-569-0583
cgcrozier@sportpei.pe.ca
Finances: *Funding Sources:* Government grants; Membership fees; Fund-raising
Member Profile: Coaches & players
Activities: *Rents Mailing List:* Yes

Volleyball Yukon
Sport Yukon Building, 4061 - 4th Ave., Whitehorse YT Y1A 1H1
Fax: 867-667-4237
volleyballyukon@gmail.com
www.volleyballyukon.com
Overview: A small provincial organization
Description: To promote volleyball in the Yukon; To provide competitive opportunities for its members
Chief Officer(s): D'Arcy Hill, Executive Director, 867-333-2424
darcy.j.hill@gmail.com

Alberta Water Polo Association (AWPA)
PO Box 54, 2225 Macleod Trail South, Calgary AB T2G 5B6
Tel: 403-281-7797; *Fax:* 403-281-7798
office@albertawaterpolo.ca
www.albertawaterpolo.ca
www.facebook.com/143394719017308
Overview: A medium-sized provincial organization founded in 1974
Description: To provide a safe & positive environment for the ongoing development & growth of water polo in Alberta for athletes of all levels; *Member of:* Water Polo Canada
Chief Officer(s): Shane Duval, President
ssduval@telus.net
Dayna Christmas, Executive Director
office@albertawaterpolo.ca

British Columbia Water Polo Association
#227, 3820 Cessna Dr., Richmond BC V7B 0A2
Tel: 604-333-3480; *Fax:* 604-333-3450
office@bcwaterpolo.ca
www.bcwaterpolo.ca
www.instagram.com/bcwaterpolo
www.facebook.com/BCWPA
twitter.com/bcwaterpolo
Also Known As: BC Water Polo
Overview: A medium-sized provincial organization founded in 1975
Description: To develop water polo in BC; to train provincial team & national team athletes; *Member of:* Water Polo Canada
Finances: *Funding Sources:* Direct access funding; sponsorshp; government grant; membership fees
Staff: 1 staff member(s); 300 volunteer(s)
Membership: 1,000; *Fees:* Schedule available; *Committees:* Technical Advisory
Activities: *Library:* Yes (Open to Public)

Fédération de Water-Polo du Québec (FWPQ) / Water Polo Québec
4545, av Pierre-de Coubertin, Montréal QC H1V 0B2
Tél: 514-252-3098
www.waterpolo-quebec.qc.ca
www.facebook.com/federationwaterpoloquebec
Aperçu: *Dimension:* petite; *Envergure:* provinciale; *Organisme sans but lucratif*
Description: Regrouper en association représentative, toute personne qui s'adonne à l'activité du water-polo; sensibiliser la population du Québec à cette activité de loisirs; favoriser le développement sous toutes ses formes; *Membre de:* Sports Québec; Regroupement Loisirs Québec; Water Polo Canada
Membre(s) du bureau directeur: Ariane Clavet-Gaumont, Directrice générale
Finances: *Fonds:* Ministère de l'Éducation.
Activités: Coordonne les programmes des équipes féminines et masculines du Québec; sanctionne les différents tournois provinciaux; organise des stages, cliniques et autres événements

Manitoba Water Polo Association Inc.
#307, 145 Pacific Ave., Winnipeg MB R3B 2Z6
Tel: 204-290-2800; *Fax:* 204-925-5703
manitobawaterpolo01@gmail.com
www.mbwaterpolo.com
www.facebook.com/ManitobaWaterPoloAssociation
Overview: A small provincial organization
Description: To promote & develop the sport of water polo in Manitoba; *Member of:* Water Polo Canada
Affiliation(s): Sport Manitoba
Chief Officer(s): Bruce Rose, Executive Director
Kathy Heffernan, President

Ontario Water Polo Association Incorporated (OWP) / L'Association de water polo d'Ontario
#206, 3 Concorde Gate, Toronto ON M3C 3N7
Tel: 416-426-7028; *Fax:* 416-426-7356
www.ontariowaterpolo.ca
Also Known As: Ontario Water Polo
Overview: A medium-sized provincial organization founded in 1967
Member of: Water Polo Canada
Chief Officer(s): Kathy Torrens, Secretary
kathy.torrens@ontariowaterpolo.ca
Finances: *Annual Operating Budget:* $100,000-$250,000
Staff: 2 staff member(s); 100 volunteer(s)
Membership: 1,200 individual; *Fees:* Schedule available
Activities: *Speaker Service:* Yes

Water Polo Canada (WPC)
1084 Kenaston St., #1A, Ottawa ON K1B 3P5
Tel: 613-748-5682; *Fax:* 613-748-5777
office@waterpolo.ca
waterpolo.ca
www.youtube.com/waterpolocanada
www.facebook.com/waterpolocanada
twitter.com/waterpolocanada
Also Known As: Canadian Water Polo Association
Overview: A medium-sized national organization founded in 1976
Description: To promote growth in sport of water polo in Canada; To administer Canada's high performance programs (Olympics, Pan Am Games, etc.) in water polo
Affiliation(s): Aquatic Federation of Canada
Chief Officer(s): Martin Goulet, Executive Director, 613-748-5682 322
mgoulet@waterpolo.ca
Finances: *Funding Sources:* Government; sponsors; members
Staff: 15 staff member(s)
Member Profile: Water polo participant or team
Activities: *Internships:* Yes

Water Polo New Brunswick (WPNB)
NB
waterpolonb.ca
Overview: A medium-sized provincial organization
Member of: Water Polo Canada
Chief Officer(s): JC Besner, President
president@waterpolonb.dev

Water Polo Newfoundland (WPNL)
NL
waterpolonl.ca
Overview: A medium-sized provincial organization
Member of: Water Polo Canada

Water Polo Nova Scotia
c/o Sport Nova Scotia, #311, 5516 Spring Garden Rd., Halifax NS B3J 1G6
Tel: 902-425-5450; *Fax:* 902-425-5606
info@waterpolonovascotia.ca
waterpolons.ca
Previous Name: Provincial Water Polo Association
Overview: A small provincial organization founded in 2006
Description: To promote the sport of water polo in Nova Scotia; *Member of:* Water Polo Canada
Chief Officer(s): Joey Postma, Chair

Water Polo Saskatchewan Inc. (WPS)
1860 Lorne St., Regina SK S4P 2L7
Tel: 306-780-9260; *Fax:* 306-780-9467
admin@wpsask.ca
www.wpsask.ca
www.facebook.com/waterpolosask
Previous Name: Saskatchewan Water Polo Association
Overview: A small provincial organization
Member of: Water Polo Canada
Finances: *Funding Sources:* Saskatchewan Lotteries; self-help projects

Water Skiing

Fédération ski nautique et planche Québec
CP 1000, Succ. M, 4545, av Pierre-de Coubertin, Montréal QC H1V 0B2
Tél: 514-252-3092; *Téléc:* 514-252-3186
info@skinautiqueetplanchequebec.qc.ca
www.skinautiqueetplanchequebec.qc.ca
www.facebook.com/skinautiqueetplanchequebec
Aperçu: *Dimension:* petite; *Envergure:* provinciale
Description: De publier des nouvelles sur les événements de notre sport, ainsi que des communiqués sur les avis et les résultats de compétitions
Membre(s) du bureau directeur: Jacques Bouchard, Président
Membre: 600; *Montant de la cotisation:* 20$ individuelle; 50$ familiale; 125$ club/école

Ontario Water Ski Association (OWSA)
8 Guelph St., Georgetown ON L7G 3Y9
Tel: 289-971-0674
office@wswo.ca
www.wswo.ca
www.facebook.com/waterskiwakeboardontario
twitter.com/wswo
Also Known As: Water Ski Wakeboard Ontario
Overview: A medium-sized provincial organization founded in 1976

Description: To promote & develop water skiing & other towed water sports through safety & instructional tournaments, courses & demonstrations; *Member of:* Water Ski & Wakeboard Canada
Chief Officer(s): Tom Wheeler, Treasurer
twheeler@thecambridgeclub.com
Finances: *Funding Sources:* Private; provincial grant
Staff: 1 staff member(s)
Fees: $10 associate; $40 single; $100 family; $80 camp; $100 club/school; *Member Profile:* Individual & families involved in recreational &/or competitive water skiing, also water ski schools, camps & clubs
Activities: Watersport/waterski/wakeboard events & tournaments in Ontario; *Library:* Yes by appointment

Water Ski & Wakeboard Alberta (WSWA)
Percy Page Centre, 11759 Groat Rd., Edmonton AB T5M 3K6
Tel: 780-415-0088; *Fax:* 780-422-2663
Toll-Free: 866-258-2754
info@wswa.ca
www.wswa.ca
www.facebook.com/WaterSkiWakeboardAlberta
twitter.com/WaterskiWakeAB
Previous Name: Water Ski Alberta
Overview: A small provincial organization founded in 1967
Description: To promote participation & excellence in the sport of water skiing & wakeboarding in Alberta; *Member of:* Alberta Sport Council; Water Ski & Wakeboard Canada
Affiliation(s): International Water Ski Federation
Chief Officer(s): Peter Peebles, President
peterpeebles@gmail.com
Kate McNeil, Executive Director
kate@wswa.ca
Finances: *Funding Sources:* Alberta government; fundraising (casinos) membership fees; program fees
Membership: 1,000; *Fees:* $40

Water Ski & Wakeboard British Columbia (WSWBC)
636 - 1231 Pacific Blvd., Vancouver BC V6Z 0E2
Toll-Free: 888-696-6677
info@wswbc.org
www.wswbc.org
www.facebook.com/waterski.wake.bc
Previous Name: BC Water Ski Association
Overview: A medium-sized provincial charitable organization founded in 1969
Description: To promote the development of water skiing & wakeboarding in BC; To provide programs, events, leadership development & expertise; *Member of:* Water Ski & Wakeboard Canada
Chief Officer(s): Andrew Clough, Executive Director
andrew@wswbc.org
Cory Bate, President
cory@wswbc.org
Finances: *Funding Sources:* Government; advertising sales; fundraisings
Membership: 1,250; *Fees:* $40 single; $80 family; $200 club/school; *Committees:* Coach Development; Nomination; Organizational Development; Water Ski Programs; Wakeboard Programs
Activities: Provincial championships; Protour; *Internships:* Yes

Water Ski & Wakeboard Canada (WSWC) / Ski nautique et planche Canada
#22, 1554 Carling Ave., Ottawa ON K1Z 7M4
Tel: 613-526-0685; *Fax:* 613-701-0385
Toll-Free: 888-526-0685
info@wswc.ca
wswc.ca
www.instagram.com/wswcanada
www.facebook.com/wswcanada
Previous Name: Canadian Water Ski Association
Overview: A medium-sized national charitable organization founded in 1949
Description: To promote & organize competitive Canadian towed water sports
Chief Officer(s): Jasmine Northcott, Chief Executive Officer
jasmine@wswc.ca
Finances: *Annual Operating Budget:* $500,000-$1.5 Million
Staff: 4 staff member(s)
Membership: 4,500; *Committees:* Water Ski; Wakeboard; Barefoot; Adaptive Towed Water Sports; Athlete Development; Coaching; Safety; Waterways; Hall of Fame

Water Ski & Wakeboard Manitoba (WSWM)
#15, 145 Pacific Ave., Winnipeg MB R3B 2Z6
Tel: 204-925-5700; *Fax:* 204-925-5792
info@wswm.ca
www.wswm.ca
www.flickr.com/photos/wswm/sets/
Overview: A small provincial organization founded in 1956
Description: To meet the needs of all those interested in the sport of water skiing by providing the resources necessary to

help them achieve their goals & to encourage fun, friendship, fitness & fair play for skiers at all ability levels; *Member of:* Water Ski & Wakeboard Canada
Chief Officer(s): Kurt Neustaedter, President
Finances: *Funding Sources:* Provincial grants
Fees: $35 regular; $75 family; $300 club
Activities: Slalom, tricks and jump water skiing; barefoot water skiing; wakeboarding; adaptive skiing

Water Ski & Wakeboard New Brunswick (NBWSWBA)
NB
info@nbwswba.com
www.nbwswba.com
Also Known As: NB Waterski
Overview: A small provincial organization
Description: To promote organized pulled watersports in the province of New Brunswick.; *Member of:* Water Ski & Wakeboard Canada
Fees: $20 individual; $40 family

Water Ski & Wakeboard Nova Scotia
PO Box 97, Greenfield NS B0T 1E0
www.nswsa.com
www.facebook.com/waterskiwakeboardns
Previous Name: Nova Scotia Water Ski Association
Overview: A small provincial organization
Member of: Water Ski & Wakeboard Canada
Chief Officer(s): Blair O'Neill, President
Membership: 135; *Fees:* $25 single; $50 family

Water Ski & Wakeboard Saskatchewan (WSWS)
Site 300, Box 23, RR#3, Saskatoon SK S7K 3J6
Tel: 306-931-2901
info@wswsask.com
wswsask.com
www.facebook.com/wswsask
twitter.com/wswsask
Previous Name: Saskatchewan Water Ski Association
Overview: A small provincial organization
Description: To promote & develop towed water sports in Saskatchewan; *Member of:* Water Ski & Wakeboard Canada; Sask Sport Inc.
Fees: $30 individual; $50 family; $100 club
Activities: All activity & advocacy related to towed water sports; tournaments

Weightlifting

British Columbia Weightlifting Association (BCWA)
5249 Laurel Dr., Delta BC V4K 4S4
info@bcweightlifting.ca
www.bcweightlifting.ca
www.facebook.com/bcweightlifting
Also Known As: BC Weightlifting Association
Overview: A small provincial organization founded in 1969
Description: To promote the sport of Olympic weightlifting in British Columbia
Chief Officer(s): Raf Korkowski, President
raf@bcweightlifting.ca
Finances: *Funding Sources:* Membership fees; Donations; Sponsorships
Fees: $8 associate/volunteer; $25 youth athlete (12 & under); $40 student/junior (13-18); $50 club; $55 standard; $110 family; *Member Profile:* Coaches; Officials: Youth (age 12 & under), student, senior, & master (age 35 & over) athletes; Volunteers
Activities: Providing information about championships

Canadian Masters Weightlifting Federation (CMWFHCM) / Haltérophilie Canadienne Maîtres
cdnmastersweightlifting.org
www.facebook.com/121208351550722
Overview: A medium-sized national organization founded in 1920
Description: Promotion & development of Masters Olympic Weightlifting in Canada
Chief Officer(s): Mark Gomes, President
Fees: $60; *Member Profile:* Masters (30 & over) weightlifters, coaches & officials

Canadian Weightlifting Federation (CWFHC) / Haltérophilie Canadienne
infocwfhc@fedhaltero.qc.ca
www.halterophiliecanada.ca
www.facebook.com/CWFHC
Overview: A medium-sized national organization founded in 1920
Description: To promote & govern weightlifting in Canada; *Member of:* International Weightlifting Federation
Chief Officer(s): Paul Barrett, President

Membership: 9 provincial associations; *Member Profile:* Alberta, British Columbia, Québec, Manitoba, New Brunswick, Newfoundland, Nova Scotia, Ontario and Saskatchewan associations
Activities: Organizing national competitions; selecting Olympic teams; maintaining rules & standards

Fédération d'haltérophilie du Québec (FHQ)
4545, av Pierre-de-Coubertin, Montréal QC H1V 0B2
Tél: 514-252-3046
www.fedhaltero.qc.ca

www.facebook.com/halteroqc
Aperçu: *Dimension:* moyenne; *Envergure:* provinciale
Description: Promouvoir et régir l'haltérophilie au Québec
Membre(s) du bureau directeur: Marilou Dozois-Prévost, Présidente
Augustin Brassard, Directeur intérimaire
Membre: 33 clubs

Manitoba Weightlifting Association (MWA)
145 Pacific Ave., Winnipeg MB R3B 2Z6
info@mbweightlifting.net
mbweightlifting.net
www.facebook.com/ManitobaWeightliftingAssociation
Overview: A small provincial organization
Description: To promote the sport of weightlifting in the province of Manitoba
Chief Officer(s): Peter Rohne, President
Fees: $20 youth; $25 coach/official/executive; $30 junior; $50 master/senior

New Brunswick Weightlifting Association (NBWA)
77 Ruffin St., Dieppe NB E1A 1R1
Tel: 506-383-1023
nbweightlifting.wordpress.com
www.facebook.com/NBWeightlifting
Also Known As: NB Weightlifting
Overview: A small provincial organization
Description: To promote & govern weightlifting in New Brunswick
Chief Officer(s): Greg Doucette, President
Activities: Organizing two competitions per year

Newfoundland Weightlifting Association (NLWA)
NL
newfoundland.weightlifting@gmail.com
www.facebook.com/NewfoundlandWeightliftingAssociation
Overview: A small provincial organization
Description: To promote the sport of weightlifting in the province of Newfoundland & Labrador
Affiliation(s): SportNL
Chief Officer(s): Tom Abbott, President
Activities: Development & coordination of services & programs

Nova Scotia Weightlifting Association (NSWA)
5516 Spring Garden Rd., 4th Fl., Halifax NS B3J 1G6
Tel: 902-425-5454
info@nsweightlifting.ca
www.nsweightlifting.ca
www.instagram.com/nsweightlifting
www.facebook.com/nsweightlifting
Overview: A small provincial organization
Description: To promote & govern weightlifting in Nova Scotia
Affiliation(s): Nova Scotia Weightlifting League
Chief Officer(s): Jacob Glover, President
Membership: 7 clubs; *Fees:* $25 official; $30 coach; $45 athlete

Ontario Weightlifting Association (OWA)
ON
info@onweightlifting.ca
www.onweightlifting.ca
www.youtube.com/user/ontarioweightlifting
www.facebook.com/OntarioWeightlifting
twitter.com/ONWeightlifting
Overview: A medium-sized provincial organization founded in 1968
Description: To promote & govern weightlifting in Ontario
Affiliation(s): Sport Alliance of Ontario; Sport4Ontario
Chief Officer(s): Mike Miller, President
president@onweightlifting.ca
Membership: 101 clubs; *Fees:* $2 volunteer; $25 youth; $35 coach/official/non-competitive; $50 general athlete; $80 elite athlete

Saskatchewan Weightlifting Association (SWA)
SK
edir@saskweightlifting.com
saskweightlifting.com
www.instagram.com/sask_weightlifting
www.facebook.com/saskweights
Overview: A small provincial organization

Description: To promote the sport of weightlifting in the province of Saskatchewan
Chief Officer(s): Kelly Brown, President
Fees: $25 junior/coach/official; $40 senior/masters; *Committees:* Coachs; Officials; Meet Hosting; Finance; Policies & Procedures

Yukon Weightlifting Association
YT
yukonweightlift.weebly.com
Overview: A small provincial organization
Description: To promote & facilitate competitive weightlifting in the Yukon Territory.; *Member of:* Sport Yukon

Women in Sports

Canadian Women & Sport / Femmes et sport au Canada
PO Box 98162, 970 Queen St. West, Toronto ON M4M 1J0
Tel: 416-901-0484
info@womenandsport.ca
womenandsport.ca
www.instagram.com/womenandsportca
www.linkedin.com/company/womenandsportca
www.facebook.com/womenandsportCA
twitter.com/WomenandSportCA
Previous Name: Canadian Association for the Advancement of Women & Sport & Physical Activity
Overview: A medium-sized national organization founded in 1981
Description: To achieve equity for women in society through the power of sport; To create an equitable & inclusive Canadian sport & physical activity system that empowers girls & women - as active participants & leaders - within & through sport
Chief Officer(s): Allison Sandmeyer-Graves, Chief Executive Officer
allison.sandmeyer-graves@womenandsport.ca
Finances: *Funding Sources:* Donations; Sport Canada
Activities: Partnering with governments, organizations, & leaders to advance solutions that result in measurable change; Publishing resources; Hosting workshops, presentations & professional development events; Working with organizations directly to increase gender equity

ProMOTION Plus
#194, 71 West 2nd Ave., Vancouver BC V5Y 0J7
Tel: 604-333-3475; *Fax:* 604-629-2651
info@promotionplus.org
www.promotionplus.org
www.linkedin.com/in/promotion-plus-bb466136
www.facebook.com/promotionp
twitter.com/ProMOTION_Plus
Overview: A small provincial organization founded in 1990
Description: To promote equity & opportunity for British Columbian women in sport
Affiliation(s): Sport BC
Chief Officer(s): Sue Griffin, Chair
Alison Hart, Administrative Manager
Finances: *Funding Sources:* BC Ministry of Community; Sport & Cultural Development; 2010 Legacies Now; BC Gaming Commission; Government of Canada
Fees: $20 students; $35 adults; $75 organizations
Activities: Annual recognition program

Wrestling

Alberta Amateur Wrestling Association (AAWA)
Percy Page Centre, 11759 Groat Rd., Edmonton AB T5M 3K6
Tel: 780-415-0140; *Fax:* 780-427-0524
aawa@ocii.com
www.albertaamateurwrestling.ca
www.facebook.com/AlbertaWrestling
twitter.com/AlbertaWrestlin
Overview: A small provincial organization founded in 1974
Description: The AAWA is the governing body for amateur wrestling & grappling in Alberta.; *Member of:* Canadian Amateur Wrestling Association
Chief Officer(s): Tammie Bradley, Executive Director
Michael Drought, Technical Director, 780-643-0799
aawatechnical@gmail.com
Finances: *Annual Operating Budget:* $100,000-$250,000; *Funding Sources:* Government grants; fundraising
Staff: 2 staff member(s)
Membership: 2,000; *Fees:* Schedule available; *Member Profile:* Male & female ages 13+
Activities: Training camps; officials & coaches clinics; school clinics; major games; coordinate provincial program

British Columbia Wrestling Association (BCWA)
#3014, 3713 Kensington Ave., Burnaby BC V5B 0A7
Tel: 604-737-3092; *Fax:* 604-737-6043
info@bcwrestling.com
www.bcwrestling.com
www.facebook.com/bcwrestling
twitter.com/wrestlingBC
Also Known As: Wrestling BC
Previous Name: British Columbia Amateur Wrestling Association
Overview: A small provincial organization founded in 1979
Description: To promote & enhance the well-being of young people through their participation in wrestling; *Member of:* Sport BC
Affiliation(s): BC School Sports
Chief Officer(s): Robert Thomson, President, 780-847-9182
rthomson@sd43.bc.ca
Membership: 2,200; *Member Profile:* Athletes, coaches, and officials
Activities: Camps; clinics; tournaments

Canadian Amateur Wrestling Association (CAWA) / Association canadienne de lutte amateur
c/o House of Sport, RA Centre, 2451 Riverside Dr., Ottawa ON K1H 7X7
info@wrestling.ca
wrestling.ca
www.instagram.com/wrestlingcanada
www.linkedin.com/company/wrestling-canada-lutte
www.facebook.com/WrestlingCanada
twitter.com/wrestlingcanada
Also Known As: Wrestling Canada Lutte
Overview: A medium-sized national organization founded in 1970
Description: To operate as the national sport governing body for Olympic style wrestling in Canada; To implement a long term athlete development model; To develop coaches, officials & administrators; To achieve podium finishes for Canadian wrestlers at World Championships & Olympic Games
Chief Officer(s): Don Ryan, President
Tamara Medwidsky, Executive Director
tamara@wrestling.ca
Lcás O'Ceallacháin, Director, High Performance
loceallachain@wrestling.ca
Finances: *Funding Sources:* Sponsorships
Activities: Encouraging participation in Olympic wrestling in Canada; Liaising with provincial sport governing bodies; Selecting & preparing Canada's teams which compete at the world championships & multi-sport events, such as the Olympic Games; Overseeing three national championships & one international cup on an annual basis

Canadian Arm Wrestling Federation (CAWF)
cawf.ca
www.instagram.com/canadianarmwrestlingfederation
Overview: A medium-sized national organization
Description: To oversee & promote the sport of arm wrestling in Canada; *Member of:* World Armwrestling Federation
Chief Officer(s): Rick Pinkney, President
Ryan Espey, Vice-President
Vivian Santos, Secretary-Treasurer
Membership: 3,500

Fédération de lutte olympique du Québec / Québec Wrestling Association
4545, av Pierre de Coubertin, Montréal QC H1V 0B2
Tél: 514-252-3044
www.quebecolympicwrestling.ca
Aperçu: *Dimension:* moyenne; *Envergure:* provinciale
Description: Superviser le sport de la lutte libre dans la province de Québec
Membre(s) du bureau directeur: Rob Moore, President

Lutte NB Wrestling (LNBW)
#8, 30 Goodine St., Fredericton NB E3B 7C6
www.luttenbwrestling.com
Overview: A small provincial organization
Description: To promote & develop wrestling in New Brunswick
Chief Officer(s): Tom MacRae, Executive Director, 506-478-0692
exec@luttenbwrestling.com
Chris Falconer, President

Manitoba Amateur Wrestling Association (MAWA)
c/o Sport Manitoba, 145 Pacific Ave., 5th Flr., Winnipeg MB R3B 2Z6
Tel: 204-925-5663; *Fax:* 204-925-5703
wrestling@sportmanitoba.ca
www.mawawrestling.ca
Overview: A small provincial organization founded in 2007

Description: To develop wrestling in Manitoba; To support personal and organizational excellence in the sport of wrestling
Chief Officer(s): Hayleigh Bell, Executive Director
Fees: Schedule available; *Member Profile:* Individual wrestlers & clubs; *Committees:* Tournament; Athlete Development; Marketing

Manitoba Arm Wrestling Association (MAWA)
MB

Tel: 204-285-9873
info@manitobaarmwrestling.com
www.manitobaarmwrestling.com
www.facebook.com/groups/375248869203923/
Overview: A small provincial organization
Description: To be the provincial governing body for the sport of arm wrestling in Manitoba; *Member of:* Canadian Arm Wrestling Federation
Chief Officer(s): Darrell Steffenson, Contact

Newfoundland & Labrador Amateur Wrestling Association (NLAWA)
NL

nlawa.wordpress.com
Overview: A small provincial organization
Description: The NLAWA is a small organization comprised of coaches, officials, parents and athletes who are dedicated to advancing the sport of wrestling in Newfoundland and Labrador
Chief Officer(s): Randy Ralph, President
randolphralph@esdnl.ca

Nova Scotia Arm Wrestling Association (NSAWA)
c/o Rick Pinkney, President, 192 Beaver Bank Rd., Lower Sackville NS B4E 1J7

Tel: 902-489-9008
info@novascotiaarmwrestling.com
novascotiaarmwrestling.com
Overview: A small provincial organization
Description: To be the provincial governing body for the sport of arm wrestling in Nova Scotia; *Member of:* Canadian Arm Wrestling Federation
Chief Officer(s): Rick Pinkney, President, 902-489-9008
info@novascotiaarmwrestling.com
Shawn Ross, Vice-President, 902-765-4656
shawnross1111@gmail.com
Paula O'Connell, Treasurer, 902-222-3169
paula.oconnell@hotmail.com
Mark MacPhail, Director, 902-822-1180
markmacphail3@hotmail.com

Ontario Amateur Wrestling Association (OAWA)
#213, 3 Concorde Gate, Toronto ON M3C 3N7

Tel: 416-426-7274
admin@oawa.ca
www.oawa.ca
twitter.com/OAWA_Wrestling
Also Known As: Ontario Wrestling
Overview: A medium-sized provincial organization founded in 1980
Description: To provide essential services & programs dedicated to developing amateur wrestling at all age levels within Ontario
Affiliation(s): International Amateur Wrestling Association; Canadian Amateur Wrestling Association
Chief Officer(s): Tim MaGarrey, Provincial Director
Finances: *Annual Operating Budget:* $100,000-$250,000; *Funding Sources:* Government; private donors; sponsors; fundraising; user fees
Membership: 1,800; *Fees:* $85 coach; $65 official/athlete (older than 9 years); $55 athletes (7-8 years); $45 supporter
Activities: Competitons; demonstrations

Saskatchewan Amateur Wrestling Association (SAWA)
510 Cynthia St., Saskatoon SK S7L 7K7

Tel: 306-975-0822; *Fax:* 306-242-8007
sk.wrestling@shaw.ca
www.saskwrestling.com
www.facebook.com/groups/253817611302960
twitter.com/SaskWrestling
Overview: A small provincial organization founded in 1972
Description: To govern & promote the sport of wrestling in Saskatchewan
Chief Officer(s): Anna-Beth Zulkoskey, Executive Director
Finances: *Annual Operating Budget:* $250,000-$500,000; *Funding Sources:* Sasksport; lotteries
Staff: 1 staff member(s); 12 volunteer(s)
Membership: 700; *Fees:* $65 coach/official/patron/junior, senior, juvenile, cadet athlete; $45 bantam, pee wee, novice, freshie athlete; $15 non-competitive; *Committees:* High Performance; Development; Administration; Finance
Activities: Athlete assistance grants

World Armwrestling Federation (WAF)
Sofia Park Trading Zone, Bldg. 16V, Fl.1, Office 1-2, Sofia 1166 Bulgaria

contact@waf-armwrestling.com
www.waf-armwrestling.com
www.instagram.com/wafarmwrestling
www.facebook.com/WAFarmwrestling
Overview: A medium-sized international organization founded in 1977

Wrestling Nova Scotia
NS

www.wrestlingnovascotia.ca
Overview: A small provincial organization

Wrestling PEI
c/o Sport PEI, PO Box 302, 40 Enman Crescent, Charlottetown PE C1E 1E6

Tel: 902-368-4262; *Fax:* 902-368-4548
wrestlingpei@gmail.com
www.wrestlingpei.ca
twitter.com/WPEIinc

Overview: A small provincial organization
Description: To promote wrestling in PEI; To provide competitive opportunities for members; *Member of:* Wrestling Canada
Chief Officer(s): Glen Flood, Executive Director
gflood@sportpei.pe.ca
Activities: Canada Games; Provincials; Atlantics; National

Professional Leagues & Teams

Baseball, Professional Leagues/Teams: Major

MAJOR LEAGUE BASEBALL/MLB
1271 AVENUE OF THE AMERICAS
NEW YORK, NY 10020

866-800-1275
customerservice@website.mlb.com
www.mlb.com
Rob Manfred, Commissioner of Baseball
Dan Halem, Dep. Comm., Baseball Admin. & Chief Legal Officer
Pat Courtney, Chief Communications Officer
Nature of Service:
Administrates professional baseball. Established and enforces rules regarding franchise operation. Supervises national radio and television contracts. Handles publicity and marketing of baseball and legal matters pertaining to baseball as an industry. Operates the World Series and All-Star games.
Membership Requirements:
Teams operating in the American or National Leagues.
Year Founded:
1903

Teams:

TORONTO BLUE JAYS
ROGERS CENTRE
1 BLUE JAYS WAY
SUITE 3200
TORONTO, ON, CANADA M5V 1J1
416-341-1000
888-654-6529
bluejays.com
Mark A. Shapiro, President & CEO
Edward Rogers, Chairman, Toronto Blue Jays
Ross Atkins, Exec. VP, Baseball Operations & General Manager
Andrew Tinnish, VP, International Scouting
Ben Sibley, Senior Manager, Marketing & Communications
Marnie Starkman, Executive VP, Business Operations
Stadium:
Rogers Centre, a recently renovated stadium that includes the TD Comfort Clubhouse (Club 200 VIP), Acura Executive Lounge and the 400 Summit Suite. Seating capacity 46,095.

Baseball, Professional Leagues/Teams: Minor

FRONTIER LEAGUE OF PROFESSIONAL BASEBALL/INDEPENDENT LEAGUE
2041 GOOSE LAKE ROAD
SUITE 2A
SAUGET, IL 62206

618-215-4134
Fax: 618-332-2115
office@frontierleague.com
www.frontierleague.com
Bill Lee, Commissioner
blee@frontierleague.com
Steve Tahsler, Deputy Commissioner, Operations

stahsler@frontierleague.com
Kevin Winn, Deputy Commissioner, Strategic Development
kwinn@frontierleague.com
League History:
In the winter of 1992-1993, several men got together and decided to start an independent professional baseball league to serve the West Virginia, eastern Kentucky and southeast Ohio areas. They believed they could bring professional baseball to areas that would never have a chance of affiliated professional baseball coming to their communities. The seed was planted and they named their project The Frontier League. In 2019, the Frontier League merged with the Canadian American Association of Professional Baseball (Can-Am League).

Teams:

OTTAWA CHAMPIONS
RAYMOND CHABOT GRANT THORNTON PARK
300 CONVENTRY RD
OTTAWA, ON, CANADA K1K 4P5
Sebastian Boucher, Manager
Note:
After the merger of the Can-Am League and the Frontier League, the Ottawa Champions were excluded from the schedule.

QUEBEC CAPITALES
STADE CANAC
100 CARDINAL MAURICE-ROY ST
QUEBEC, QC, CANADA G1K 8Z1
418-521-2255
877-521-2244
Fax: 418-521-2266
info@capitalesdequebec.com
capitalesdequebec.com
Jean Tremblay, Owner
Michel Laplante, President
mlaplante@capitalesdequebec.com

TROIS-RIVIERES AIGLES
1760 GILLES-VILLENEUVE AVE
TROIS-RIVIERES, QC, CANADA G9A 5K8
819-379-0404
info@lesaiglestr.com
lesaiglestr.com
Paul Poisson, President
fish56@hotmail.com
Ren, Martin, General Manager
r.martin@lesaiglestr.com

NORTHWEST BASEBALL LEAGUE
420 CHURCHWELL DR
SUITE 18847
PANAMA CITY BEACH, FL 32407

850-588-6205
www.milb.com/northwest
Johnson North, President
njohnsonnwl@gmail.com
Jeff Eiseman, Vice President
Jerry Walker, Secretary

Teams:

VANCOUVER CANADIANS
SCOTIABANK FIELD AT NAT BAILEY STADIUM
4601 ONTARIO ST
VANCOUVER, BC, CANADA V5V 3H4
604-872-5232
Fax: 604-872-1714
staff@canadiansbaseball.com
www.milb.com/vancouver
Andy Dunn, President
604-872-5232
adunn@canadiansbaseball.com
Allan Bailey, General Manager
604-872-5232
abailey@canadiansbaseball.com
Baseball:
Scotiabank Field at Nat Bailey Stadium. Seating capacity, 6,500.

Basketball, Leagues and Teams

NATIONAL BASKETBALL ASSOCIATION/NBA
545 FIFTH AVENUE
NEW YORK, NY 10022

nbaglobalfeedback@dazn.com
www.nba.com
Adam Silver, Commissioner
Mark A. Tatum, Deputy Commissioner/COO
Description:
The premier professional basketball league in North America. Many of the world's best players play in the NBA, and the overall

standard of the competition is considerably higher than any other professional competition. The NBA was founded in New York City on June 6, 1946 as the Basketball Association of America (BAA). It adopted the name National Basketball Association in the fall of 1949 after adding several teams from the rival National Basketball League.

Teams:

TORONTO RAPTORS
SCOTIABANK ARENA
40 BAY STREET
TORONTO, ON, CANADA M5J 2X2
416-366-3865
ticketservice@mlse.com
www.raptors.com
Masai Ujiri, President
Bobby Webster, General Manager
Nick Nurse, Head Coach
Teresa Resch, VP, Basketball Operations & Player Development
History:
Founded in 1995 in Toronto. Championship titles, 1. Conference titles, 1. Division Titles, 7.
Arena:
Scotiabank Arena. Seating capacity, 19,800.

NATIONAL BASKETBALL LEAGUE OF CANADA
info@nblcanada.ca
www.nblcanada.ca

Audley Stephenson, Deputy Commissioner

Teams:

HALIFAX HURRICANES
2717 JOSEPH HOWE DRIVE
PO BOX 610
HALIFAX, NS, CANADA B3J 2T2
902-377-3052
info@halifaxhurricanes.ca
www.halifaxhurricanes.ca
Amy Bragg, Owner
Mike Leslie, Head Coach

ISLAND STORM
46 KENSINGTON RD
CHARLOTTETOWN, PE, CANADA C1A 5H7
stormbasketball.ca
Duncan Shaw, Owner/President
Tim Kendrick, Head Coach
Josh Fall, Team Manager

KW TITANS
400 EAST AVENUE
KITCHENER, ON, CANADA N2H 1Z6
info@kwtitans.com
www.kwtitans.com
Leon Martin, Owner
Cavell Johnson, Head Coach

LONDON LIGHTNING
75 BLACKFRIARS STREET
LONDON, ON, CANADA N6H 1K8
519-433-0634
www.lightningbasketball.ca
Vito Frijia, Owner
Mark Frijia, General Manager
Doug Plumb, Head Coach

MONCTON MAGIC
AVENIR CENTRE
150 CANADA STREET
MONCTON, NB, CANADA E1C 0v2
info@monctonmagic.ca
www.monctonmagic.ca
Joe Salerno, Head Coach

SAINT JOHN RIPTIDE
99 STATION STREET
SAINT JOHN, NB, CANADA E2L 4X4
506-866-8433
Fax: 506-500-0169
sjriptide.ca
Nelson Terroba, Head Coach/General Manager

ST. JOHN'S EDGE
MILE ONE CENTRE
50 NEW GOWER STREET
ST. JOHN'S, NL, CANADA A1C 1J3
www.sjedge.ca
Tyrone Levingston, President
tyrone@sjedge.ca
Steven Marcus, Head Coach

SUDBURY FIVE
240 ELGIN STREET
SUDBURY, ON, CANADA P3E 3N6
705-815-5555
Fax: 705-675-3944
info@thefive.ca
thefive.ca
Dario Zulich, Owner
Scott Lund, CEO
Logan Stutz, Head Coach/General Manager

WINDSOR EXPRESS
405 VICTORIA AVENUE
WINDSOR, ON, CANADA N9A 4N1
519-800-3665
www.windsorexpress.ca
Dartis Willis, Sr., President/CEO
Erin Basterfield, General Manager
Bill Jones, Head Coach

CANADIAN FOOTBALL LEAGUE/CFL
50 WELLINGTON STREET E
3RD FLOOR
TORONTO, ON, CANADA M5E 1C8

416-322-9650
Fax: 416-322-9651
www.cfl.ca

Randy Ambrosie, Commissioner
Greg Dick, Chief Financial Officer
David Goldstein, COO
History:
The Canadian Football League was founded in 1958, in Montreal, Quebec, after the Canadian Football Council (CFC) left the Canadian Rugby Union (CRU). Since 2010 the league has expanded stadiums and added the forthcoming Ottawa Redblacks to its rosters.
Teams:
9
Founded:
1958

Teams:

BC LIONS
BC PLACE
777 PACIFIC BLVD
VANCOUVER, BC, CANADA V6B 4Y8
604-930-5466
fanservices@bclions.com
www.bclions.com
David Braley, Owner/Chairman
Rick LeLacheur, President
Neil McEvoy, Co-General Manager/Director, Football Operations
Rick Campbell, Co-General Manager/Head Coach
Home Field:
BC Place. Seating capacity 54,320.

CALGARY STAMPEDERS
MCMAHON STADIUM
1817 CROWCHILD TRAIL NW
CALGARY, AB, CANADA T2M 4R6
403-289-0205
www.stampeders.com
John Hufnagel, President/General Manager
Dave Dickenson, Head Coach
Home Field:
McMahon Stadium. Seating capacity 35,650.

EDMONTON ESKIMOS
THE BRICK FIELD AT COMMONWEALTH STADIUM
11000 STADIUM ROAD
EDMONTON, AB, CANADA T5H 4E2
780-448-1525
Fax: 780-448-2531
comments@esks.com
www.esks.com
Chris Presson, CEO/President
Brock Sunderland, General Manager/VP, Football Operations
Jaime Elizondo, Head Coach
Home Field:
Commonwealth Stadium. Seating capacity 60,000.

HAMILTON TIGER-CATS
TIM HORTONS FIELD
64 MELROSE AVE N
HAMILTON, ON, CANADA L8L 8C1
905-547-2287
Fax: 905-547-8423
customerservice@ticats.ca
ticats.ca
Scott Mitchell, CEO
Scott Mitchell, CEO
Orlando Steinauer, Head Coach
Home Field:
Tim Hortons Field. Seating capacity 22,500.

MONTREAL ALOUETTES
PERCIVAL MOLSON MEMORIAL STADIUM
475 PINE AVE W
MONTREAL, QC, CANADA H2W 1S4
514-787-2500
Fax: 514-871-2277
info@montrealalouettes.com
www.montrealalouettes.com
Mario Cecchini, President
Danny Maciocia, General Manager
Khari Jones, Head Coach
Home Field:
Percival Molson Memorial Stadium. Seating capacity 25,012.

OTTAWA REDBLACKS
TD PLACE
1015 BANK STREET
OTTAWA, ON, CANADA K1S 3W7
613-232-6767 EXT 1
Fax: 613-232-5586
info@ottawaredblacks.com
www.ottawaredblacks.com
Marcel Desjardins, General Manager
Paul LaPolice, Head Coach
Home Field:
TD Place. Seating Capacity 24,000.

SASKATCHEWAN ROUGHRIDERS
1734 ELPHINSTONE STREET
TICKET OFFICE
REGINA, SK, CANADA S4P 1K1
888-474-3377
www.riderville.com
Craig Reynolds, CEO/President
Jeremy O'Day, General Manager
Craig Dickenson, Head Coach
Home Field:
Mosaic Stadium at Taylor Field. Seating capacity 32,848.

TORONTO ARGONAUTS
45 MANITOBA DRIVE
TORONTO, ON, CANADA M6K 3C3
416-341-2746
clientservices@argonauts.ca
www.argonauts.ca
Bill Manning, President
Michael Clemons, General Manager
Ryan Dinwiddie, Head Coach
Home Field:
BMO Field.

WINNIPEG BLUE BOMBERS
INVESTORS GROUP FIELD
315 CHANCELLOR MATHESON ROAD
WINNIPEG, MB, CANADA R3T 1Z2
204-784-2583
bbombers@bluebombers.com
www.bluebombers.com
Kyle Walters, General Manager
Mike O'Shea, Head Coach
Home Field:
Investors Group Field. Seating capacity 33,420-40,000.

Hockey, Professional Hockey (NHL)

NATIONAL HOCKEY LEAGUE/NHL
1185 AVENUE OF THE AMERICAS
15TH FLOOR
NEW YORK, NY 10036

212-789-2000
800-559-2333
Fax: 212-789-2020
nhltvsupport@nhl.com
www.nhl.com

Gary Bettman, Commissioner
Bill Daly, Deputy Commissioner
Year Founded:
1917

Description:
League of professional hockey teams
Membership Requirements:
Approval by NHL Board of Governors
Publications:
NHL Rule Book, annual; NHL Schedule, annual; NHL Media Directory, annual; NHL Official Guide and Record Book, annual
Additional Offices:
Toronto: 50 Bay St., 11th Floor, Toronto, ON, Canada M5J 2X8; 416-359-7900; Fax: 416-981-2779. Montreal: 1800 McGill College Ave., Ste 2600, Montreal, QC, Canada H3A 3J6; 514-841-9220; Fax: 514-841-1040.

Teams:

CALGARY FLAMES
PO BOX 1540
STN M
CALGARY, AB, CANADA T2P 3B9
403-777-4646
customerservice@calgaryflames.com
www.nhl.com/flames
N. Murray Edwards, Chairman & Owner
John Bean, President & Chief Executive Officer
Cameron Olson, Chief Financial Officer
Gordon Norrie, VP, Sports Properties Sales & Marketing
Rollie Cyr, EVP, Revenue Development
Brad Treliving, General Manager
Darryl Sutter, Head Coach
Martin Gelinas, Assistant Coach
Ryan Huska, Assistant Coach
Ray Edwards, Assistant Coach
Year Founded:
1972
Description:
The Calgary Flames are a National Hockey League team based in Calgary, Alberta
Home Arena:
Scotiabank Saddledome. Seating capacity 19,289.

EDMONTON OILERS
OILERS ENTERTAINMENT GROUP
300, 10214 104 AVE NW
EDMONTON, AB, CANADA T5J 0H6
780-414-4625
www.nhl.com/oilers
Daryl A. Katz, Owner & Governor
Tom Anselmi, President, Business Operations & COO
Bob Nicholson, Chairman & Alternate Governor
Wayne Gretzky, Alternate Governor
Kevin Lowe, Alternate Governor
Stew MacDonald, Executive VP, Revenue
Jason Quilley, Executive VP, Finance
Stuart Ballantyne, Senior VP, Operations
Adam Barrie, Senior VP, Human Resources
Jeff Harrop, Senior VP, Marketing
Tim Shipton, Senior VP, Communications
Ken Holland, General Manager & President, Hockey Operations
Keith Gretzky, Assistant General Manager
Dave Tippett, Head Coach
Jim Playfair, Assistant Coach
Glen Gulutzan, Assistant Coach
Brian Wiseman, Assistant Coach
Year Founded:
1972
Description:
The Edmonton Oilers are a National Hockey League team based in Edmonton, Alberta
Home Arena:
Rogers Place. Seating capacity 18,347.

MONTREAL CANADIENS
1275, RUE SAINT-ANTOINE OUEST
MONTREAL, QC, CANADA H3C 5L2
514-932-2582
www.nhl.com/canadiens
Geoff Molson, Owner, President & CEO
Marc Bergevin, Executive VP & General Manager
France Margaret Belanger, Executive VP & Chief Commercial Officer
Anna Martini, Executive VP & Chief Financial Officer
Scott Mellanby, Assistant General Manager
Trevor Timmins, Assistant General Manager
Dominique Ducharme, Interim Head Coach
Alex Burrows, Assistant Coach
Luke Richardson, Assistant Coach
Year Founded:
1909
Description:
The Montreal Canadiens are one of the oldest teams in the National Hockey League. They are based in Montreal,

Quebec.
Home Arena:
Centre Bell. Seating capacity 21,273.

OTTAWA SENATORS
CANADIAN TIRE CENTRE
1000 PALLADIUM DR
OTTAWA, ON, CANADA K2V 1A5
613-599-0250
www.nhl.com/senators
Pierre Dorion, General Manager
MacTavish Peter, Assistant General Manager
Tim Pattyson, Director, Hockey Operations
Jordan Silmser, Director, Team Services
D.J. Smith, Head Coach
Jack Capuano, Associate Coach
Pierre Groulx, Goaltending Coach
Year Founded:
1990
Description:
The Ottawa Senators are a National Hockey League team based in Ottawa, Ontario
Home Arena:
Canadian Tire Centre. Seating capacity 18,652.

TORONTO MAPLE LEAFS
SCOTIABANK ARENA
40 BAY STREET
SUITE 500
TORONTO, ON, CANADA M5J 2L2
416-815-5500
www.nhl.com/mapleleafs
Brendan Shanahan, President & Alternate Governor
Kyle Dubas, General Manager
Laurence Gilman, Assistant General Manager
Brandon Pridham, Assistant General Manager
Jim Paliafito, Senior Director, Player Evaluation
Scott Pellerin, Senior Director, Player Development
Brad Lynn, Director, Team Operations
Reid Mitchell, Director, Hockey & Scouting Operations
Dave Morrison, Director, Player Personnel
Sheldon Keefe, Head Coach
Steve Briere, Goaltending Coach
Year Founded:
1917
Description:
The Toronto Maple Leafs are a National Hockey League team based in Toronto, Ontario.
Home Arena:
Scotiabank Arena. Seating capacity 20,270.

VANCOUVER CANUCKS
89 WEST GEORGIA STREET
VANCOUVER, BC, CANADA V6B 0N8
604-899-7400
Fax: 604-899-7401/7490
fanservices@canucks.com
www.nhl.com/canucks
Francesco Aquilini, Chairman & Governor
Jim Benning, General Manager
Trent Carroll, Chief Operating Officer & Alternate Governor
John Weisbrod, Assistant General Manager
Chris Gear, Assistant General Manager & Chief Legal Officer
Todd Kobus, Executive VP, Business Operations & CFO
Ryan Johnson, Senior Director, Player Development
Jonathan Wall, Senior Director, Hockey Operations & Analytics
Travis Green, Head Coach
Ian Clark, Goaltending Coach
Year Founded:
1970
Description:
The Vancouver Canucks are a National Hockey League team based in Vancouver, British Columbia
Home Arena:
Rogers Arena. Seating capacity 18,910.

WINNIPEG JETS
345 GRAHAM AVE
WINNIPEG, MB, CANADA R3C 5S6
204-987-7825
www.nhl.com/jets
Kevin Cheveldayoff, Executive VP & General Manager
John Olfert, President & COO
Scott Brown, Senior Director, Hockey Communications
Paul Maurice, Head Coach
Jaime Kompon, Associate Coach
Year Founded:
2011
Description:
The Winnipeg Jets are a National Hockey League team based in Winnipeg, Manitoba. The franchise was formerly known as the Atlanta Thrashers until their purchase in 2011.

Home Arena:
Bell MTS Place. Seating capacity 15,321.

Hockey, Professional, Minor Leagues

AMERICAN HOCKEY LEAGUE/AHL
ONE MONARCH PLACE
SUITE 2400
SPRINGFIELD, MA 01144

413-781-2030
theahl.com

Scott Howson, President & CEO
David Andrews, Chair
Chris Nikolis, Executive VP, Business
cnikolis@theahl.com
Michael Murray, Executive VP, Hockey Operations
Melissa Caruso, VP, Hockey Operations & Governance
Year Founded:
1936
Description:
Professional ice hockey league that serves as the primary developmental circuit for the National Hockey League.
Membership Requirements:
Purchase of a franchise
Publications:
Official guide and record book; Rule book; Schedule; Year End Statistical Package

Teams:

BELLEVILLE SENATORS
265 CANNIFTON RD
BELLEVILLE, ON, CANADA K8N 4V8
613-967-8067
info@bellevillesens.com
bellevillesens.com
Rob Mullowney, Chief Operating Officer
mullowneyr@bellevillesens.com
Darren Murphy, Senior Director, Finance & Operations
murphyd@bellevillesens.com
Dorion Pierre, General Manager
Troy Mann, Head Coach
Kory Cooper, Goaltending Development Coach
Home Ice:
CAA Arena. Seating capacity, 4,365.
NHL Affiliation:
Ottawa Senators.

LAVAL ROCKET
1950 CLAUDE-GAGNE STREET
SUITE 103
MONTREAL, QC, CANADA H7N 0E4
855-595-2200
info@rocketlaval.com
www.rocketlaval.com
John Sedgwick, Governor & Vice President, Hockey Operations
Marc Bergevin, General Manager
Scott Mellanby, Assistant General Manager
Joel Bouchard, Head Coach
Marco Marciano, Goaltending & Video Coach
Home Arena:
Place Bell. Seating capacity 10,000.
NHL Affiliation:
Montreal Canadiens.

MANITOBA MOOSE
345 GRAHAM AVE
WINNIPEG, MB, CANADA R3C 5S6
204-987-7825
info@moosehockey.com
moosehockey.com
Craig Heisinger, General Manager
Brad Andrews, Senior Director, Hockey & Business Operations
Pascal Vincent, Head Coach
Eric Dubois, Assistant Coach
Marty Johnston, Assistant Coach
Rick St. Croix, Developmental Goaltending Coach
Home Ice:
Bell MTS Place. Seating capacity 15,321.
NHL Affiliation:
Winnipeg Jets.

TORONTO MARLIES
45 MANITOBA DR
TORONTO, ON, CANADA M6K 3C3
416-597-7825
marlies.ca
Laurence Gilman, Governor & General Manager
Mike Dixon, Director, Minor League Operations & Alt. Governor

Marc Lira, Director, Business Operations & Alt. Governor
Greg Moore, Head Coach
Jon Elkin, Goaltending Coach
Home Arena:
Coca-Cola Coliseum. Seating capacity 7,851.
NHL Affiliation:
Toronto Maple Leafs.

EAST COAST HOCKEY LEAGUE/ECHL
116 VILLAGE BOULEVARD
SUITE 230
PRINCETON, NJ 08540

609-452-0770
Fax: 609-452-7147
echl@echl.com
www.echl.com

Ryan Crelin, Commissioner
Joe Ernst, Senior VP, Hockey Operations

Teams:

NEWFOUNDLAND GROWLERS
MILE ONE CENTRE
50 NEW GOWER STREET
ST. JOHN'S, NL, CANADA A1C 1J3
nlgrowlers.com
Glenn Stanford, President
John Snowden, Head Coach

ONTARIO HOCKEY LEAGUE
305 MILNER AVE
SUITE 200
SCARBOROUGH, ON, CANADA M1B 3V4

416-299-8700
Fax: 416-299-8787
ontariohockeyleague.com

David E. Branch, Commissioner
dbranch@chl.ca
Ted Baker, Vice President
tbaker@chl.ca
Joe Birch, Vice President, Development
jbirch@chl.ca
Year Founded:
1896

Teams:

BARRIE COLTS
555 BAYVIEW DR
BARRIE, ON, CANADA L4N 8Y2
705-722-6587
Fax: 705-737-6898
operations@barriecolts.com
www.barriecolts.com
Howie Campbell, President & Owner
hcampbell@barriecolts.com
Jim Payetta, Co-Owner/VP, Business Development &
Marketing
jpayetta@barriecolts.com
Rob Stewart, General Manager
Vacant, Head Coach
Home Arena:
Barrie Molson Centre. Seating capacity 4,195.

GUELPH STORM
55 WYNDHAM ST N
2ND FLOOR
GUELPH, ON, CANADA N1H 7T8
519-837-9690
Fax: 519-837-9692
info@guelphstorm.com
guelphstorm.com
Rick Hoyle, President
Rick Gaetz, Governor
George Burnett, General Manager & Head Coach
Home Arena:
Sleeman Centre. Seating capacity 4,715.

HAMILTON BULLDOGS
FIRSTONTARIO CENTRE
101 YORK BLVD
HAMILTON, CANADA L8R 3L4
905-529-8500
Fax: 905-777-2360
info@hamiltonbulldogs.com
hamiltonbulldogs.com
Michael Andlauer, Owner
Steve Staios, President & General Manager
Dave Matos, Head Coach
Home Arena:
FirstOntario Centre. Seating capacity 17,383.

KINGSTON FRONTENACS
1 THE TRAGICALLY HIP WAY
KINGSTON, ON, CANADA K7K 0B4
613-542-4042
Fax: 613-542-2834
info@kingstonfrontenacs.com
kingstonfrontenacs.com
Doug Springer, President
Paul McFarland, General Manager/Head Coach
Home Ice:
Leon's Centre. Seating capacity 5,614.

KITCHENER RANGERS
KITCHENER MEMORIAL AUDITORIUM COMPLEX
1963 EUGENE GEORGE WAY
KITCHENER, ON, CANADA N2H 0B8
519-576-3700
Fax: 519-576-7571
admin@kitchenerrangers.com
kitchenerrangers.com
Joe Birch, Chief Operating Officer & Governor
Mike McKenzie, General Manager/Interim Head Coach
Home Arena:
Kitchener Memorial Auditorium. Seating capacity 7,777.

LONDON KNIGHTS
BUDWEISER GARDENS
99 DUNDAS ST
LONDON, ON, CANADA N6A 6K1
519-681-0800
Fax: 519-668-7291
info@londonknights.com
londonknights.com
Dale Hunter, Owner, President & Head Coach
Mark Hunter, Owner, Vice President & General Manager
Basil McRae, Owner
Home Arena:
Budweiser Gardens. Seating capacity 9,036.

MISSISSAUGA STEELHEADS
PARAMOUNT FINE FOODS CENTRE
5500 ROSE CHERRY PLACE
MISSISSAUGA, ON, CANADA L4Z 4B6
905-502-7788
Fax: 905-502-0169
info@mississaugasteelheads.com
www.mississaugasteelheads.com
Elliott Kerr, President
jekerr@landmarksport.com
Brandon Reischl, Vice President, Director of Business
Operations
James Richmond, Head Coach & General Manager
jrichmond@mississaugasteelheads.com
Home Ice:
Paramount Fine Foods Centre. Seating capacity 5,612.

NIAGARA ICEDOGS
ONE DAVID S HOWES WAY
ST. CATHARINES, ON, CANADA L2R 0B3
905-687-3641
Fax: 905-682-9129
info@niagaraicedogs.net
niagaraicedogs.net
Joey Burke, General Manager & Governor
j.burke@niagaraicedogs.net
Billy Burke, Head Coach
billy.burke@niagaraicedogs.net
Home Ice:
Meridian Centre. Seating capacity 5,300.

NORTH BAY BATTALION
NORTH BAY MEMORIAL GARDENS
100 CHIPPEWA ST W
2ND FLOOR
NORTH BAY, ON, CANADA P1B 6G2
705-495-8603
Fax: 705-475-1673
info@battalionhockey.com
battalionhockey.com
C. Scott Abbott, Owner/Governor
Mike Griffin, President
mgriffin@battalionhockey.com
Ryan Oulahen, Head Coach
Home Arena:
North Bay Memorial Gardens. Seating capacity 4,246.

OSHAWA GENERALS
99 ATHOL ST E
OSHAWA, ON, CANADA L1H IJ8
905-433-0900
admin@oshawagenerals.com
oshawagenerals.com
Rocco Tullio, President & Governor
Roger Hunt, Vice President & General Manager

rhunt@oshawagenerals.com
Mike Kelly, Director of Hockey Operations
Greg Walters, Head Coach
Home Ice:
General Motors Centre. Seating capacity 6,125.

OTTAWA 67'S
TD PLACE
1015 BANK STREET
OTTAWA, ON, CANADA K1S 3W7
613-232-6767
Fax: 613-690-0468
info@ottawa67s.com
ottawa67s.com
James Boyd, General Manager
jboyd@ottawa67s.com
Andr, Tourigny, Head Coach & VP, Hockey Operations
atourigny@ottawa67s.com
Home Ice:
TD Place Arena. Seating capacity 10,000.

OWEN SOUND ATTACK
1900 3RD AVENUE E
OWEN SOUND, ON, CANADA N4K 6T5
519-371-7452
866-528-8225
loleary@attackhockey.com
attackhockey.com
Severs Bob, President
Dale DeGray, General Manager
ddegray@attackhockey.com
Alan Letang, Head Coach
Home Ice:
J.D. McArthur Arena, Harry Lumley Bayshore Community
Centre. Seating capacity 4,300.

PETERBOROUGH PETES
151 LANDSDOWNE ST WEST
PETERBOROUGH, ON, CANADA K9J 1Y4
705-743-3681
Fax: 705-743-5497
info@gopetesgo.com
gopetesgo.com
Burton Lee, Executive Director, Business Operations
Michael Oke, General Manager
Rob Wilson, Head Coach
Home Ice:
Peterborough Memorial Centre. Seating capacity 4,329.

SAGINAW SPIRIT
PO BOX 6157
SAGINAW, MI 48608
989-497-7747
Fax: 989-799-9261
www.saginawspirit.com
Richard J. Garber, Owner
Craig Goslin, President & Managing Partner
Pat Hengesbach, Chief Financial Officer
Kae Pankow, Vice President, Sales
Dave Drinkill, General Manager
Chris Lazary, Head Coach
Home Ice:
Dow Event Center. Seating capacity 5,527.

SARNIA STING
1455 LONDON RD
SARNIA, ON, CANADA N7S 6K4
519-541-1717
info@sarniasting.com
sarniasting.com
Derian Hatcher, Owner/Governor
Bill Abercrombie, President
David Legwand, President, Hockey Operations
Dylan Seca, General Manager
Derian Hatcher, Head Coach
Home Ice:
Progressive Auto Sales Arena. Seating capacity, 5,500.

SAULT STE. MARIE GREYHOUNDS
269 QUEEN STREET EAST
SAULT STE. MARIE, ON, CANADA P6A 1Y9
705-253-5976
Fax: 705-945-9458
info@soogreyhounds.com
soogreyhounds.com
Tim Lukenda, President
Kyle Raftis, General Manager
John Dean, Head Coach
Jordan Smith, Associate Coach
Home Ice:
GFL Memorial Gardens. Seating capacity 4,928.

SUDBURY WOLVES
240 ELGIN ST
SUDBURY, ON, CANADA P3E 3N6
705-675-3941
Fax: 705-675-3944
office@sudburywolves.com
sudburywolves.com
Dario Zulich, Owner
Rob Papineau, Vice President & General Manager
Home Ice:
Sudbury Community Arena. Seating capacity 5,100.

WINDSOR SPITFIRES
8787 MCHUGH STREET
WINDSOR, ON, CANADA N8S 0A1
519-254-9256
Fax: 519-254-9257
frontoffice@windsorspitfires.com
windsorspitfires.com
John Savage, Owner & President
Bill Bowler, GM & VP, Hockey Operations
Trevor Letowski, Head Coach
Home Ice:
WFCU Centre. Seating capacity 6,450.

QUEBEC MAJOR JUNIOR HOCKEY LEAGUE
1205 AMPERE STREET
OFFICE #101
BOUCHERVILLE, QC, CANADA J4B 7M6

450-650-0500
Fax: 450-650-0510
hockey@lhjmq.qc.ca
theqmjhl.ca

Gilles Courteau, Commissioner
ggonthier@lhjmq.qc.ca
Pierre Daoust, Vice President, Administration
pdaoust@lhjmq.qc.ca
Pierre Leduc, Director, Hockey Operations
pleduc@lhjmq.qc.ca
Maxime Blouin, Director, Communications
mblouin@lhjmq.qc.ca
Richard Trottier, Director, Officiating
rtrottier@lhjmq.qc.ca
Description:
Member of Canadian Hockey League.

Teams:

ACADIE-BATHURST TITAN
14 SEAN COUTURIER AVE
BATHURST, NB, CANADA E2A 6X2
506-549-3300
Fax: 506-549-3311
info@letitan.com
en.letitan.com
Gilles Cormier, Executive Director
gilles.cormier@letitan.com
Sylvain Couturier, General Manager
Mario Durocher, Head Coach
Home Ice:
K.C. Irving Regional Centre. Seating capacity 3,162.

BAIE-COMEAU DRAKKAR
70, AVENUE MICHEL-HEMON
BAIE-COMEAU, QC, CANADA G4Z 2A5
418-296-2522
Fax: 418-296-0011
le-drakkar.com
Etienne Fortier, Administrative Director
Pierre Rioux, General Manager
Gregoire Jean-Francois, Head Coach
Home Ice:
Henry Leonard Center. Seating capacity 3,042.

BLAINVILLE-BOISBRIAND ARMADA
3600, BOUL. GRANDE-ALLÉE
CP 9
BOISBRIAND, QC, CANADA J7H 1M9
450-276-2328
855-276-2328
Fax: 450-276-2327
info@armadahockey.ca
armadahockey.ca
Mario Marois, President
mmarois@armadahockey.ca
Pierre Cloutier, General Manager
Dany Gauthier, Deputy General Manager & Chief Recruiter
Bruce Richardson, Head Coach
Home Ice:
Centre d'Excellence Sports Rousseau. Seating capacity 3,100.

CAPE BRETON SCREAMING EAGLES
PO BOX 8
481 GEORGE ST
SYDNEY, NS, CANADA B1P 6G9
902-567-6378
Fax: 902-567-6303
admin@capebretoneagles.com
capebretoneagles.com
Gerard Shaw, President & Governor
Jacques Carriere, General Manager
Jake Grimes, Head Coach
Home Ice:
Centre 200. Seating capacity 5,000.

CHARLOTTETOWN ISLANDERS
46 KENSINGTON RD
2ND FLOOR
CHARLOTTETOWN, PE, CANADA C1A 5H7
902-892-7349
Fax: 902-892-7350
admin@charlottetownislanders.com
charlottetownislanders.com
Craig Foster, President, Operations
craig@charlottetownislanders.com
Jim Hulton, General Manager & Head Coach
Home Arena:
Eastlink Centre. Seating capacity 3,717.

CHICOUTIMI SAGUENÉENS
643 RUE BÉGIN
CHICOUTIMI, QC, CANADA G7H 4N7
418-549-9489
Fax: 418-698-3853
administration@sagueneens.com
sagueneens.com
Renald Nepton, Director, Hockey Operations
Yanick Jean, Head Coach & General Manager
Home Ice:
George-Vezina Centre. Seating capacity 4,724.

DRUMMONDVILLE VOLTIGEURS
300 RUE COCKBURN
DRUMMONDVILLE, QC, CANADA J2C 4L6
819-477-9400
Fax: 819-477-0561
info@voltigeurs.ca
voltigeurs.ca
David Boies, Director, Operations
dboies@voltigeurs.ca
Philippe Boucher, General Manager
Steve Hartley, Head Coach
Home Ice:
Centre Marcel Dionne. Seating capacity 3,038.

GATINEAU OLYMPIQUES
125 RUE DE CARILLON
GATINEAU, QC, CANADA J8X 2P8
819-777-0661
hockey@olympiquesdegatineau.ca
olympiquesdegatineau.ca
Francois Beaudry, President
Marc Saumier, Interim Director, Hockey Operations
Louis Robitaille, Head Coach/General Manager
Home Ice:
Robert Guertin Centre. Seating capacity 3,196.

HALIFAX MOOSEHEADS
1741 BRUNSWICK ST
SUITE 120
HALIFAX, NS, CANADA B3J 3X8
902-429-3267
Fax: 902-423-6413
mooseheads@halifaxmooseheads.ca
halifaxmooseheads.ca
Bobby Smith, Majority Owner
Brian Urquhart, President
Travis Kennedy, Sr. Vice President, Business Operations
Cam Russell, General Manager
J.J. Daigneault, Head Coach
Home Ice:
Scotiabank Centre. Seating capacity 10,595.

MONCTON WILDCATS
AVENIR CENTRE
150 CANADA ST
MONCTON, NB, CANADA E1C 0V2
506-382-5555
Fax: 506-858-2222
info@moncton-wildcats.com
moncton-wildcats.com
Jean Brousseau, Governor
Ritchie Thibeau, Assistant Director, Hockey Operations
Daniel Lacroix, Head Coach

Home Ice:
Avenir Centre. Seating capacity 8,800.

QUEBEC REMPARTS
CENTRE VIDÉOTRON
250G, BOUL. WILFRID-HAMEL
QUEBEC, QC, CANADA G1L 5A7
418-525-1212
888-299-9595
Fax: 418-525-2242
info@remparts.ca
remparts.ca
Jacques Tanguay, President
Louis Painchaud, Vice President, Operations
louis.painchaud@remparts.ca
Patrick Roy, Head Coach & General Manager
Home Ice:
Centre Videotron. Seating capacity 18,259.

RIMOUSKI OCEANIC
111, 2E RUE OUEST
CP 816
RIMOUSKI, QC, CANADA G5L 7C9
418-723-4444
800-463-4450
Fax: 418-725-0944
hockey@oceanic.qc.ca
oceanic.qc.ca
Eric Boucher, President
Serge Beausoleil, General Manager & Head Coach
Home Ice:
Colisee de Rimouski. Seating capacity 5,062.

ROUYN-NORANDA HUSKIES
ARÉNA IAMGOLD
218 AVE MURDOCH
ROUYN-NORANDA, QC, CANADA J9X 1E6
819-797-3022
Fax: 819-797-4311
admin@huskies.qc.ca
huskies.qc.ca
Gilles Berube, Operational Director
Mario Pouliot, Head Coach & General Manager
Home Ice:
Arena Iamgold. Seating capacity 3,500.

SAINT JOHN SEA DOGS
99 STATION STREET
SUITE 200
SAINT JOHN, NB, CANADA E2L 4X4
506-657-3647
Fax: 506-696-0611
info@saintjohnseadogs.com
sjseadogs.com
Scott McCain, CEO
Trevor Georgie, President/General Manager
Greg Gilbert, Head Coach
Home Ice:
TD Station. Seating capacity 6,300.

SHAWINIGAN CATARACTES
CENTRE GERVAIS AUTO
1, RUE JACQUES-PLANTE
SHAWINIGAN, QC, CANADA G9N 0B7
819-537-6327
cats@cataractes.qc.ca
cataractes.qc.ca
Roger Lavergne, President
Martin Mondou, General Manager
Ron Choules, Head Coach
Home Ice:
Centre Gervais Auto. Seating capacity 5,195.

SHERBROOKE PHOENIX
360 RUE DU CEGEP
2E ETAGE
SHERBROOKE, QC, CANADA J1E 2J9
819-560-8842
info@hockeyphoenix.ca
en.hockeypheonix.ca
Charline Durand, Director of Operations
Jocelyn Thibault, VP, Hockey Operations
Stephane Julien, Head Coach/General Manager
Home Ice:
Palais des Sports Leopold-Drolet. Seating capacity 3,646.

VAL D'OR FOREURS
810, 6TH AVENUE
VAL-D'OR, QC, CANADA J9P 1B4
819-824-0093
Fax: 819-824-7602
admin@foreurs.qc.ca
foreurs.qc.ca
Dany Marchand, President
Pascal Daoust, General Manager
Daniel Renaud, Head Coach
Home Ice:
Centre Air Creebec. Seating capacity 3,504.

VICTORIAVILLE TIGERS
COLISÉE DESJARDINS
400 BOULEVARD JUTRAS EST
VICTORIAVILLE, QC, CANADA G6P 7W7
819-752-6353
Fax: 819-758-2846
info@tigresvictoriaville.com
tigresvictoriaville.com
Martin Paquet, Director, Operations
Kevin Cloutier, General Manager
Carl Mallette, Head Coach
Home Ice:
Desjardins Coliseum. Seating capacity 3,420.

WESTERN HOCKEY LEAGUE
FATHER DAVID BAUER ARENA
2424 UNIVERSITY DRIVE NW
CALGARY, AB, CANADA T2N 3Y9

403-693-3030
Fax: 403-693-3031
info@whl.ca
whl.ca

Ron Robison, Commissioner
Richard Doerksen, VP, Hockey
Yvonne Bergmann, VP, Business Development
Description:
Member of the Canadian Hockey League.

Teams:

BRANDON WHEAT KINGS
2-1175 18TH STREET
BRANDON, MB, CANADA R7A 7C5
204-726-3535
Fax: 204-726-3540
office@wheatkings.com
wheatkings.com
Jared Jacobson, Owner/Governor
Darren Ritchie, General Manager
Don MacGillivray, Head Coach
Home Ice:
Westman Communications Group Place at Keystone Centre.
Seating capacity 5,102.

CALGARY HITMEN
SCOTIABANK SADDLEDOME
555 SADDLEDOME RISE SE
CALGARY, AB, CANADA T2G 2W1
403-777-4646
Fax: 403-571-2211
hitmenhockey.com
John Bean, President & CEO
Jeff Chynoweth, General Manager
Steve Hamilton, Head Coach
Home Ice:
Scotiabank Saddledome. Seating capacity 19,289.

EDMONTON OIL KINGS
FORD HALL, ROGERS PLACE
10214 104 AVENUE NW
EDMONTON, AB, CANADA T5J 0H6
oilkings.ca
Kirt Hill, President, Hockey Operations/General Manager
Brad Lauer, Head Coach
Home Arena:
Rogers Place. Seating capacity 18,641.

KAMLOOPS BLAZERS
300 LORNE STREET
KAMLOOPS, BC, CANADA V2C 1W3
250-828-1144
Fax: 250-828-7822
info@blazerhockey.com
blazerhockey.com
Don Moores, President/COO
Matt Bardsley, VP/General Manager
Shaun Clouston, Head Coach
Home Ice:
Sandman Centre. Seating capacity 5,464.

KELOWNA ROCKETS
101-1223 WATER STREET
KELOWNA, BC, CANADA V1Y 9V1
250-860-7825
Fax: 250-860-7880
info@kelownarockets.com
kelownarockets.com
Bruce Hamilton, Owner/President/General Manager
Kris Mallette, Head Coach
Home Ice:
Prospera Place. Seating capacity 6,886.

LETHBRIDGE HURRICANES
ENMAX CENTRE
2-2510 SCENIC DRIVE SOUTH
LETHBRIDGE, AB, CANADA T1K 7V7
403-328-1986
Fax: 403-329-1622
admin@lethbridgehurricanes.com
lethbridgehurricanes.com
Doug Paisley, President/Governor
Peter Anholt, General Manager
Brent Kisio, Head Coach
Home Ice:
ENMAX Centre. Seating capacity 5,479.

MEDICINE HAT TIGERS
2802 BOX SPRINGS WAY NW
MEDICINE HAT, AB, CANADA T1C 0H3
403-526-2666
Fax: 403-526-3072
admin@tigershockey.com
tigershockey.com
Willie Desjardins, General Manager/Head Coach
Home Ice:
Canalta Centre. Seating capacity 5,500.

MOOSE JAW WARRIORS
110 1ST AVENUE NW
MOOSE JAW, SK, CANADA S6H 3L9
306-694-5711
Fax: 306-692-7833
mjwarriors.ca
Chad Taylor, President/Governor
Alan Millar, General Manager
Mark O'Leary, Head Coach
Home Ice:
Mosaic Place. Seating capacity 4,465.

PRINCE ALBERT RAIDERS
690 32ND STREET E
PRINCE ALBERT, SK, CANADA S6V 2W8
306-764-5348
raiderhockey.com
Gord Broda, President/Governor
Curtis Hunt, General Manager
Marc Habscheid, Head Coach
Home Ice:
Art Hauser Centre. Seating capacity 2,591.

PRINCE GEORGE COUGARS
102-2187 OSPIKA BOULEVARD S
PRINCE GEORGE, BC, CANADA V2N 6Z1
250-561-0783
Fax: 250-561-0743
info@pgcougars.com
pgcougars.com
Greg Pocock, Governor
Mark Lamb, General Manager/Head Coach
mark.lamb@pgcougars.com
Home Ice:
CN Centre. Seating capacity 5,967.

RED DEER REBELS
4847C 19TH STREET
RED DEER, AB, CANADA T4R 2N7
403-341-6000
Fax: 403-341-6009
info@reddeerrebels.com
www.reddeerrebels.com
Brent Sutter, Owner/General Manager/Head Coach
Home Ice:
ENMAX Centrium. Seating capacity 6,706.

REGINA PATS
1463 ALBERT STREET
REGINA, SK, CANADA S4R 2R8
306-522-7287
pats@reginapats.com
reginapats.com
John Paddock, VP, Hockey Operations/General Manager
Dave Struch, Assistant General Manager/Head Coach
Home Ice:
Brandt Centre. Seating capacity 6,136.

SASKATOON BLADES
SASKTEL CENTRE
201-3515 THATCHER AVENUE
SASKATOON, SK, CANADA S7R 1C4
306-975-8844
info@saskatoonblades.com
saskatoonblades.com
Mike Priestner, Owner/Governor
Colin Priestner, President/General Manager
Mitch Love, Head Coach
Home Ice:
SaskTel Centre. Seating capacity 15,100.

SWIFT CURRENT BRONCOS
PO BOX 2345
2001 CHAPLIN STREET E
SWIFT CURRENT, SK, CANADA S9H 4X6
306-773-1509
Fax: 306-773-5406
communications@scbroncos.com
scbroncos.com
Nathan MacDonald, Director, Business Operations
Dean Brockman, Director, Hockey Operations/Head Coach
Home Ice:
Credit Union iPlex. Seating capacity 3,239.

VANCOUVER GIANTS
220-7888 200TH STREET
LANGLEY, BC, CANADA V2Y 3J4
604-444-2687
info@vancouvergiants.com
vancouvergiants.com
Barclay Parneta, General Manager
Michael Dyck, Head Coach
Home Ice:
Langley Events Centre. Seating capacity 5,276.

VICTORIA ROYALS
1925 BLANSHARD STREET
VICTORIA, BC, CANADA V8T 4J2
250-220-2600
info@victoriaroyals.com
victoriaroyals.com
Graham Lee, Owner
Dan Price, Head Coach/General Manager
Home Ice:
Save-On-Foods Memorial Centre. Seating capacity 7,006.

WINNIPEG ICE
57 SOUTH LANDING DRIVE
OAK BLUFF, MB, CANADA R4G 0C4
204-489-7465
info@50below.ca
winnipegice.ca
Greg Fettes, Chair & Governor
Matt Cockell, President/General Manager/Alternate Governor
James Patrick, Head Coach
Home Ice:
Western Financial Place. Seating capacity 4,654.

Lacrosse, Leagues/Teams

NATIONAL LACROSSE LEAGUE
CONSHOHOCKEN, PA

www.nll.com

Nick Sakiewicz, Commissioner
Brian Lemon, VP, Lacrosse Operations
Justin Rubino, VP, Business Operations
Description:
Founded 1997. Professional Indoor Lacrosse League.

Teams:

CALGARY ROUGHNECKS
SCOTIABANK SADDLEDOME
555 SADDLEDOME RIDE SE
CALGARY, AB, CANADA T2G 2W1
403-777-4646
Fax: 403-777-3695
info@calgaryroughnecks.com
calgaryroughnecks.com
John Bean, President/CEO
John Bean, Governor and President
Mike Board, General Manager
Curt Malawsky, Assistant General Manager/Head Coach
Home Arena:
Scotiabank Saddledome. Seating capacity 19,289.

SASKATCHEWAN RUSH
3100 IDYLWYLD DRIVE N
SASKATOON, SK, CANADA S7L 5Y6
306-978-7874
info@saskrush.com
www.saskrush.com
Bruce Urban, Owner/Governor
Myrna Januario, Director of Operations
myrna@saskrush.com
Derek Keenan, Head Coach/General Manager
Home Arena:
SaskTel Centre. Seating capacity 15,195.

TORONTO ROCK
1132 INVICTA DRIVE
2ND FLOOR
OAKVILLE, ON, CANADA L6H 6G1
416-596-3075
Fax: 905-339-3473
info@torontorock.com
torontorock.com
Jamie Dawick, Owner/President/General Manager
Matt Sawyer, Head Coach
Home Arena:
Scotiabank Arena. Seating capacity 18,819.

VANCOUVER WARRIORS
VANCOUVER, BC, CANADA
604-899-4625
ticket.info@vancouverwarriors.com
vancouverwarriors.com
Chris Gill, Head Coach
Dan Richardson, General Manager/Lacrosse Operations
Home Arena:
Langley Events Centre. Seating capacity 5,500.

Soccer, Leagues/Teams

CANADIAN PREMIER LEAGUE

canpl.ca

David Clanachan, Commissioner
Scott Mitchell, CEO
James Easton, Vice President, Football Operations

Teams:

ATLETICO OTTAWA
OTTAWA, ON, CANADA
atleticoottawa.canpl.ca
Jeff Hunt, Strategic Partner/Owner
Ferrer Martinez, Head Coach
Miguel Angel, Head Coach

CAVALRY FC
18011 SPRUCE MEADOWS
WAY SW
CALGARY, AB, CANADA T2X 4B7
403-974-4567
tickets@cavalryfootball.club
cavalryfc.canpl.ca
Linda A. Southern-Heathcott, Owner, Chair & CEO
Ian Allison, Chief Operating Officer
Tommy Wheeldon, Jr., General Manager/Head Coach

FC EDMONTON
CLARKE STADIUM
11000 STADIUM ROAD NW
EDMONTON, AB, CANADA T5H 4E2
780-700-2600
fcedmonton.canpl.ca
Tom Fath, Co-Owner
Eric Newendorp, President & General Manager
Alan Koch, Head Coach

FORGE FC
TIM HORTONS FIELD
64 MELROSE AVE N
HAMILTON, ON, CANADA L8L 8C1
905-527-3674
info@forgefootball.club
forgefc.canpl.ca
Bobby Smyrniotis, Head Coach/Technical Director

HFX WANDERERS
HALIFAX, NS, CANADA
902-407-5621
info@hfxwanderersfc.ca
hfxwanderersfc.canpl.ca
Derek Martin, President
Stephen Hart, Head Coach

PACIFIC FC
WESTHILLS STADIUM
1089 LANGFORD PARKWAY
VICTORIA, BC, CANADA V9B 0A5
778-584-6732
memberservices@pacificfc.ca
pacificfc.canpl.ca
Josh Simpson, President
Rob Friend, CEO
Dean Shillington, Chairman
Pa-Modou Kah, Head Coach

VALOUR FC
INVESTORS GROUP FIELD
315 CHANCELLOR MATHESON ROAD
WINNIPEG, MB, CANADA R3T 1Z2
valourfc.canpl.ca
Wade Miller, President/CEO
Rob Gale, Head Coach & General Manager

YORK UNITED FC
ALUMNI FIELD
YORK UNIVERSITY
TORONTO, ON, CANADA L8S 4L8
yorkunitedfc.ca
Angus McNab, CEO/President/General Manager
Jimmy Brennan, Head Coach/Technical Director

CANADIAN SOCCER LEAGUE
75 INTERNATIONAL BOULEVARD
SUITE 203
TORONTO, ON, CANADA M9W 6L9

416-675-5256
info@canadiansoccerleague.ca
canadiansoccerleague.ca

Pino Jazbec, League Administrator
pjazbec@canadiansoccerleague.ca
Description:
Semi-professional soccer league in Southern Ontario.

Teams:

BRANTFORD GALAXY SC
HERITAGE SPORT PARK
355 FIRST ROAD W
STONEY CREEK, ON, CANADA L8J 1X5
brantfordgalaxysc@gmail.com
brantfordleague.ca/brantford-galaxy-sc
Bosko Borjan, Manager/President
Sasa Vidovic, Head Coach
Home Field:
Heritage Field

CSC MISSISSAUGA
386 WATLINE AVENUE
MISSISSAUGA, ON, CANADA L4Z 1X2
647-879-6453
cscmississauga@gmail.com
www.cscmississauga.com
Mile Milkovic, Manager
Dalibor Vranjic, Head Coach

FC UKRAINE UNITED
CENTENNIAL STADIUM
56 CENTENNIAL PARK ROAD
TORONTO, ON, CANADA M9C 3T3
admin@fcukraineunited.com
www.fcukraineunited.com
Mykhailo Gurka, Head Coach
Andrei Malychenkov, Manager

FC VORKUTA
505-1000 FINCH AVENUE W
TORONTO, ON, CANADA M3J 2V5
416-917-2304
fcvorkuta@gmail.com
fcvorkuta.ca
Igor Demitchev, Founder/Chairman
Samad Kadirov, Manager
Denys Yanchuk, Head Coach
Home Field:
Kalar Sports Park

HAMILTON CITY 1
905-921-5838
canadiansoccerleague.ca/hamilton-city
Sasa Vukovic, Coach

REAL MISSISSAUGA SC
MISSISSAUGA, ON, CANADA L5A 3T2
647-336-3789
www.screalmississauga.ca
Ross Chonga, Manager
Krum Bibishkov, Head Coach

SC WATERLOO
WARRIOR FIELD
UNIVERSITY OF WATERLOO
WATERLOO, ON, CANADA
519-465-4050
canadiansoccerleague.ca/sc-waterloo
Tony Kocis, President
Vojislav Brisevac, Manager
Radivoj Panic, Head Coach
Home Field:
Warrior Field

SCARBOROUGH SC
BIRCHMOUNT STADIUM
75 BIRCHMOUNT ROAD
TORONTO, ON, CANADA M1N 3J7
canadiansoccerleague.ca/scarborough-sc
Kiril Dimitrov, Manager
Mirko Medic, Coach
Home Field:
Birchmount Stadium

SERBIAN WHITE EAGLES FC
30 TITAN ROAD
UNIT 15
TORONTO, ON, CANADA M8Z 5Y2
416-252-4752
info@serbianwhiteeagles.ca
serbianwhiteeagles.ca
Dragan Bakoc, President
dragan@serbianwhiteeagles.ca
Uros Stamatovic, Head Coach
Home Field:
Centennial Park Stadium

MAJOR LEAGUE SOCCER
420 FIFTH AVENUE
7TH FLOOR
NEW YORK, NY 10018

212-450-1200
feedback@mlssoccer.com
www.mlssoccer.com

Don Garber, Commissioner
Mark Abbott, President/Deputy Commissioner
Gary Stevenson, Deputy Commissioner

Teams:

CF MONTREAL
STADE SAPUTO
4750, RUE SHERBROOKE EST
MONTREAL, QC, CANADA H1V 3S8
514-328-3668
Fax: 514-328-1287
cfmontreal.com
Joey Saputo, Owner
Kevin Gilmore, President/CEO
Nancy Wilfried, Head Coach
Home Field:
Stade Saputo. Seating capacity 20,801.

TORONTO FC
BMO FIELD
170 PRINCES' BOULEVARD
TORONTO, ON, CANADA M6K 3C3
416-360-4625
www.torontofc.ca
Bill Manning, President
Ali Curtis, General Manager
Chris Armas, Head Coach
Home Field:
BMO Field. Seating capacity 22,453.

VANCOUVER WHITECAPS FC
SUITE 550
THE LANDING
375 WATER STREET
VANCOUVER, BC, CANADA V6B 5C6
604-669-9283
Fax: 604-684-5173
info@whitecapsfc.com
www.whitecapsfc.com
Axel Schuster, CEO/Sporting Director
Greg Anderson, VP, Soccer Operations
Marc Dos Santos, Head Coach
Home Field:
BC Place. Seating capacity 21,000.

USL LEAGUE ONE
1715 N WESTSHORE BOULEVARD
SUITE 825
TAMPA, FL 33607

www.uslleagueone.com

Robert Hoskins, Chairman
Alec Papadakis, CEO
jake Edwards, President

Teams:

TORONTO FC II
BMO FIELD
170 PRINCES' BOULEVARD
TORONTO, ON, CANADA M6K 3C3
416-360-4625
www.torontofc.ca/tfcii
Bill Manning, President
Ali Curtis, General Manager
Mike Munoz, Head Coach

USL LEAGUE TWO
1715 N WESTSHORE BOULEVARD
SUITE 825
TAMPA, FL 33607

www.uslleaguetwo.com

Robert Hoskins, Chairman
Alec Papadakis, CEO
Jake Edwards, President
Description:
A development league in the U.S. soccer league system.
Founded:
1995
Member Clubs:
74

Teams:

CALGARY FOOTHILLS FC
MOUNT ROYAL COLLEGE
CALGARY, AB, CANADA
www.foothillsfc.ca
Leon Hapgood, Head Coach

FC MANITOBA

THUNDER BAY CHILL
CHAPPLES SOCCER PARK
535 CHAPPLES PARK DRIVE
THUNDER BAY, ON, CANADA P7E 2P2
807-623-5911
giovannipetragliatbc@gmail.com
www.thunderbaychill.com
John Marrello, General Manager
Giovanni Petraglia, Head Coach

TSS ROVERS
TSS SOCCER CENTRE
115-1751 SAVAGE ROAD
RICHMOND, BC, CANADA V6V 1R1
soccer@tss.ca
www.tss.ca
Will Cromack, General Manager
Colin Elmes, Head Coach

VICTORIA HIGHLANDERS FC
VICTORIA, BC, CANADA
www.highlandersfc.ca
Jeremy Dillon, Director, Operations
Thomas Niendorf, Head Coach

WSA WINNIPEG
WINNIPEG, MB, CANADA
204-477-0763
Fax: 204-477-0763
eduardo@world-soccer-academy.com
wsawinnipegpdl.com
Eduardo Badescu, Head Coach

Facilities

Arenas & Stadiums

BC PLACE
777 PACIFIC BOULEVARD
VANCOUVER, BC, CANADA V6B 4Y8

604-669-2300
www.bcplace.com

Patricia Jelinski, General Manager
Brian Griffin, Director, Facility Operations
Wayne Smith, Director, Human Resources & Labour Relations
Milad Sakiani, Director, IT Services
Owned and Operated:
BC Pavilion Corp.

Year Opened:
1983
Seating Capacity:
54,500
Tenant(s):
BC Lions (CFL), Vancouver Whitecaps FC (MLS)

BELL MTS PLACE
300 PORTAGE AVENUE
WINNIPEG, MB, CANADA R3C 5S6

info@tnse.com
www.bellmtsplace.ca

Mark Chipman, Executive Chairman, TNSE
Kevin Donnelly, Sr. Vice President, Venues & Entertainment
Owners:
True North Sports & Entertainment
Year Opened:
2004
Seating Capacity:
Hockey - 15,294; End-Stage Concert - 16,170; Center-Stage Concert - 16,345; Rodeo/Motocross - 13,198; Basketball - 15,570
Tenant(s):
Winnipeg Jets (NHL)

BUDWEISER GARDENS
99 DUNDAS STREET
LONDON, ON, CANADA N6A 6K1

519-667-5700
judy.sullivan@spectraxp.com
www.budweisergardens.com

Dave Scott, CEO, Spectra Venue Management
John Page, President, Spectra Venue Management
Owners:
London Civic Centre Corporation.
Operator:
Comcast Spectacor.
Year Founded:
2002
Seating Capacity:
10,200
Tenant(s):
London Knights (OHL), London Lightning (NBL).

CANADIAN TIRE CENTRE
1000 PALLADIUM DRIVE
OTTAWA, ON, CANADA K2V 1A5

613-599-0100
www.canadiantirecentre.com

Year Opened:
1996
Seating Capacity:
20,041
Tenant(s):
NHL - Ottawa Senators

CENTRE BELL
1909 AVENUE DES CANADIENS-DE-MONTREAL
MONTREAL, QC, CANADA H4B 5G0

514-989-2841
855-310-2525
www.centrebell.ca

Geoff Molson, President/CEO
Owners:
Geoff, Andrew and Justin Molson
Year Opened:
1996
Seating Capacity:
21,288
Tenant(s):
Montreal Canadiens (NHL).

COCA-COLA COLISEUM
45 MANITOBA DRIVE
TORONTO, ON, CANADA M6K 3C3

416-263-3900
Fax: 416-263-3901
www.coca-colacoliseum.com

Bryan Leslie, Director, Building Operations
Owners:
City of Toronto.
Operators:
Maple Leafs Sports & Entertainment Ltd.
Seating Capacity:
Hockey: 7,851; Concerts: 9,250
Tenant(s):
AHL - Toronto Marlies.

COMMONWEALTH STADIUM (EDMONTON)
11000 STADIUM ROAD NW
EDMONTON, AB, CANADA T5H 4E2

780-442-5311
311@edmonton.ca

Owners:
City of Edmonton
Year Opened:
1978
Seating Capacity:
60,000
Tenant(s):
CFL - Edmonton Eskimos.

EXHIBITION PLACE
100 PRINCES' BOULEVARD
SUITE 1
TORONTO, ON, CANADA M6K 3C3

416-263-3000
info@explace.on.ca
www.explace.on.ca

Mark Grimes, Chair
Owners:
City of Toronto.
Year Opened:
1879.

EXPOCITE
250, BOULEVARD WILFRID-HAMEL
EDIFICE F
QUEBEC, QC, CANADA G1L 5A7

418-691-7110
888-866-3976
info@expocite.com
www.expocite.com

Vincent Dufresne, President
Simon Lachance, Operations Director
Owners:
Quebec City.
Operators:
ExpoCite.
Year Founded:
1898

HARBOUR STATION
99 STATION STREET
SAINT JOHN, NB, CANADA E2L 4X4

506-632-6103
Fax: 506-632-6121
www.harbourstation.ca

Michael Caddell, General Manager
Ewen Cameron, Operations Director
Year Opened:
1993, renovated 2005.
Seating Capacity:
7,205
Tenant(s):
Saint John Sea Dogs (QMJHL), Saint John Mill Rats

LANGLEY EVENTS CENTRE
7888 200 STREET
LANGLEY, BC, CANADA V2Y 3J4

604-882-8800
www.langleyeventscentre.com

Opened:
2009
Tenant(s):
Vancouver Giants (WHL)

MOSAIC STADIUM
1700 ELPHINSTONE STREET
REGINA, SK, CANADA S4P 2Z6

306-781-9200
www.evrazplace.com/facilities/mosaic-stadium

Opened:
1936
Team:
Saskatchewan Roughriders
Seating Capacity:
33,350

PACIFIC COLISEUM
PACIFIC NATIONAL EXHIBITION
2901 E HASTINGS STREET
VANCOUVER, BC, CANADA V5K 5J1

604-253-2311
Fax: 604-251-7753
info@pne.ca
www.pne.ca

Shelley Frost, President/CEO
Opened:
1968

Seating Capacity:
Ice hockey: 16,281; Concerts: 17,500

PARC OLYMPIQUE
4141, AVENUE PIERRE-DE COUBERTIN
MONTREAL, QC, CANADA H1V 3N7

514-252-4141
Fax: 514-252-0372
rio@rio.gouv.qc.ca
parcolympique.qc.ca

Michel Labrecque, President/CEO
Founded:
1976
Seating Capacity:
56,040

PERCIVAL MOLSON MEMORIAL STADIUM
475, AVENUE DES PINS
MONTREAL, QC, CANADA H2W 1S4
Owners:
McGill University
Year Opened:
1919
Seating Capacity:
25,012.
Tenant(s):
CFL - Montreal Alouettes. McGill Redmen

PROGRESSIVE AUTO SALES ARENA
255 CHRISTINA STREET N
SARNIA, ON, CANADA N7S 7N2

519-332-0330
parksandrecreation@sarnia.ca
www.progressiveautosalesarena.com

Owners:
City of Sarnia.
Year Opened:
1998
Seating Capacity:
Hockey - 5,000. Concerts - 6,000.
Tenant(s):
OHL - Sarnia Sting.

RAYMOND CHABOT GRANT THORNTON PARK
302 COVENTRY ROAD
OTTAWA, ON, CANADA K1K 4P5
Founded:
1993
Team:
Ottawa Champions (Can-Am League)
Seating Capacity:
10,332

RE/MAX FIELD
10233 96TH AVENUE NW
EDMONTON, AB, CANADA T5K 0A5

780-717-6739
ryan@edmontonprospects.com
www.remaxfield.com

Owners:
City of Edmonton
Year Opened:
1995
Seating Capacity:
9,200
Tenant(s):
WMBL - Edmonton Prospects.

ROGERS ARENA
800 GRIFFITHS WAY
VANCOUVER, BC, CANADA V6B 6G1

604-899-7400
rogersarena.com

Owners:
Canucks Sports & Entertainment.
Year Opened:
1995
Seating Capacity:
Hockey - 18,910. Basketball - 19,700. Concerts - 19,000.
Tenant(s):
NHL - Vancouver Canucks

ROGERS CENTRE
1 BLUE JAYS WAY
TORONTO, ON, CANADA M5V 1J1

416-341-1000
guestservices@rogerscentre.com

Owners:
Rogers Communications, Inc.
Operators:
Rogers Stadium Limited Partnership.
Year Opened:
1989

Seating Capacity:
Baseball - 49,282. Canadian football - 31,074-52,230. American football - 54,000. Soccer - 47,568. Basketball - 22,911-28,708. Concerts - 10,000-55,000.
Tenant(s):
MLB - Toronto Blue Jays

ROGERS PLACE
10220 104 AVENUE NW
EDMONTON, AB, CANADA T5H 2X6

780-414-5483
info@rogersplace.com
www.rogersplace.com

Susan Darrington, Exececutive VP, Rogers Place
Owners:
City of Edmonton.
Operators:
Oilers Entertainment Group.
Tenant(s):
NHL - Edmonton Oilers. WHL - Edmonton Oil Kings.

SCOTIABANK ARENA
40 BAY STREET
TORONTO, ON, CANADA M5J 2L2

416-815-5500
www.scotiabankarena.com

Michael Friisdahl, President/CEO, Maple Leaf Sports & Entertainment
Cynthia Devine, Chief Financial Officer
Nick Eaves, Chief Venues & Operations Officer
Owners:
Maple Leaf Sports & Entertainment Ltd.
Year Opened:
1999
Tenant(s):
NBA - Toronto Raptors, NHL - Toronto Maple Leafs, NLL - Toronto Rock.
Seating Capacity:
Basketball - 19,800. Hockey - 18,800. Lacrosse - 18,819. Concerts - 19,800. Theater - 5,200.

SCOTIABANK SADDLEDOME
555 SADDLEDOME RISE SE
CALGARY, AB, CANADA T2G 2W1

403-777-4646
Fax: 403-777-2171
customerservice@calgaryflames.com
www.scotiabanksaddledome.com

Libby Raines, VP, Building Operations
Trent Anderson, Director, Building Operations
Owners:
City of Calgary.
Operators:
Saddledome Foundation/Calgary Flames LP.
Year Opened:
1983
Seating Capacity:
19,289
Tenant(s):
NHL - Calgary Flames. NLL - Calgary Roughnecks. WHL - Calgary Hitmen.

SHAW PARK
ONE PORTAGE AVENUE E
WINNIPEG, MB, CANADA R3B 3N3

204-982-2273
Fax: 204-982-2274
contact@goldeyes.com
goldeyes.com/shaw-park

Sam Katz, President, Winnipeg Goldeyes
Sport:
Baseball
Team:
Winnipeg Goldeyes; Winnipeg Wesmen
Year Founded:
1999
Capacity:
7,461

STADE CANAC
100 CARDINAL MAURICE-ROY
QUEBEC, QC, CANADA G1K 8Z1

418-521-2255
877-521-2244
Fax: 418-521-2266
info@capitalesdequebec.com
capitalesdequebec.com

Michel Laplante, President
Year Opened:
1938, renovated 1999
Seating Capacity:
4,800

Tenant(s):
Quebec Capitales; Quebec Diamants

STADE SAPUTO
OLYMPIC PARK
4750 SHERBROOKE STREET E
MONTREAL, QC, CANADA H1V 3S8

info@impactmontreal.com
www.impactmontreal.com/en/stadium/stade-saputo
Joey Saputo, Owner, Montreal Impact & Stade Saputo
Kevin Gilmore, President & CEO, Montreal Impact
Eric Girouard, Director, Stadium Operations
Owner:
Saputo Inc.
Operator:
Montreal Impact
Year Opened:
2008, expanded 2012.
Seating Capacity:
20,801

TD PLACE
1015 BANK STREET
OTTAWA, ON, CANADA K1S 3W7

613-232-6767
877-489-2849
www.tdplace.ca

Chris Wynn, Director, Operations
Brian Giles, Facilities Manager
Owner:
City of Ottawa
Operator:
Ottawa Sports and Entertainment Group
Year Opened:
1908
Seating Capacity:
24,000
Tenant(s):
Ottawa Redblacks (CFL), Ottawa Fury (USL)

Race Tracks - Auto

SANAIR SUPER SPEEDWAY
830 GRAND RANG SAINT-FRANCOIS
SAINT-PIE, QC, CANADA J0H 1W0

450-772-6400
www.sanair.ca

Description:
Motorsports park

SHANNONVILLE MOTORSPORT PARK
7047 OLD HIGHWAY #2
PO BOX 259
SHANNONVILLE, ON, CANADA K0K 3A0

613-969-1906
800-959-8955
Fax: 613-966-6890
www.shannonville.com

Description:
Race track
Long Track:
4.03 km
Pro Track:
2.47 km
Fabi Circuit:
2.23 km

Race Tracks - Equestrian Downs & Parks

CALGARY STAMPEDE
1410 OLYMPIC WAY SE
CALGARY, AB, CANADA T2G 2W1

403-261-0101
800-661-1767
www.calgarystampede.com
Warren Connell, Chief Executive Officer

CLINTON RACEWAY
PO BOX 778
147 BEECH STREET
CLINTON, ON, CANADA N0M 1LO

519-482-5270
Fax: 519-482-1489
cdejong@clintonraceway.com
clintonraceway.com

Jessica Carnochan, Marketing Director
jessicacarnochan@gmail.com
Description:
Horse race track

SUDBURY DOWNS
400 BONIN ROAD
CHELMSFORD, ON, CANADA P0M 1L0

705-855-9001
sudburydowns@gmail.com
www.sudburydowns.com

Year Founded:
1974

Nature of Sports Service:
Harness horse race track.

WOODSTOCK RACEWAY
875 NELLIS STREET
WOODSTOCK, ON, CANADA N4S 8Z9

519-537-4808
woodstock@gatewaycasinos.ca
woodstock.gatewaycasinos.com

SECTION 16
TRANSPORTATION

Overview: A medium-sized national charitable organization founded in 1952
Description: To serve as the voice of general aviation in Canada
Chief Officer(s): Christine Gervais, President & CEO
cgervais@copanational.org
Finances: *Annual Operating Budget:* $500,000-$1.5 Million; *Funding Sources:* Membership dues; advertising
Staff: 9 staff member(s); 20 volunteer(s)
Membership: 17,000; *Fees:* $75 individual; $105 family/international individual; $135 international family; $350 corporate; $380 international corporate; *Member Profile:* Pilots & aircraft owners; Corporate members; *Committees:* Awards; Awards Review; By-laws Review; Convention Review; Legal Advisory; Medical Advisory; Sea Plane; Strategic Planning
Activities: Offering insurance programs; *Library:* Canadian Owners & Pilots Association Library (Open to Public)

Canadian Parking Association (CPA)
#350, 2255 St Laurent Blvd., Ottawa ON K1G 4K3
Tel: 613-727-0700; *Fax:* 613-727-3183
info@canadianparking.ca
www.canadianparking.ca
www.linkedin.com/company/canadian-parking-association
www.facebook.com/173429676044219
twitter.com/canadianparking
Also Known As: Association canadienne du stationnement
Overview: A medium-sized national organization founded in 1983
Description: To represent the parking industry & provide a dynamic forum for learning & sharing to enhance member's ability to serve the public & improve the economic vitality of communities
Chief Officer(s): Janice Legace, President, 506-466-6732
Daniel Germain, Vice President, 514-874-1208
daniele.germain@parkindigo.com
Membership: 320; *Fees:* Schedule available; *Member Profile:* Individuals associated with the public parking industry in Canada

Canadian Railroad Historical Association (CRHA) / Association canadienne d'histoire ferroviaire
110, rue St-Pierre, Saint-Constant QC J5A 1G7
Tel: 450-632-2410; *Fax:* 450-638-1563
info@exporail.org
www.exporail.org/en
www.instagram.com/exporail_qc_canada
www.facebook.com/Exporail
twitter.com/Exporail
Also Known As: Exporail: The Canadian Railway Museum
Overview: A medium-sized national charitable organization founded in 1932
Description: To collect, preserve & disseminate information/items relating to the history of railways in Canada
Chief Officer(s): Robert Robinson, President
Finances: *Annual Operating Budget:* $1.5 Million-$3 Million *Fees:* $50 regular; $110 friend of the museum; *Committees:* Executive; Collection; Membership; Audit
Activities: *Library:* Canadian Railroad Historical Association Library/Archives (Open to Public) by appointment

Canadian Railway Club
PO Box 162, Stn. St-Charles, Kirkland QC H9H 0A3
Tel: 514-428-5903; *Fax:* 514-697-6238
info@canadianrailwayclub.ca
canadianrailwayclub.ca
Overview: A small national organization founded in 1902
Affiliation(s): Toronto Railway Club; Railway Associaiton of Canada; C.A.R.S.; WCRNA
Chief Officer(s): Tracy Power, President
Fees: $30; *Member Profile:* Current or retired employees of railway companies; Companies that produce railway accessories or services; Those associated with railway companies; *Committees:* Executive; Arrangements; Membership & Attendance; Audit; Advertising

Canadian Transport Lawyers Association (CTLA)
c/o Heather Devine, Isaacs & Co., 11 King St. West, 11th Fl., Toronto ON M5H 4C7
ctla.ca
Overview: A small national organization
Description: To provide a professional & social forum for lawyers engaged or otherwise interested in transportation law, regulatory policy, procedure & related legal interests
Chief Officer(s): Heather Devine, President
Fees: $100-$125 new; $100-$195 renewing; *Member Profile:* Lawyers engaged in transportation law, regulatory policy & procedures & other related legal interests

Canadian Transportation Equipment Association (CTEA) / Association d'équipement de transport du canada (AETC)
#200-300, 116 Albert St., Ottawa ON K1P 5G3
Tel: 226-620-0779
www.ctea.ca
Overview: A medium-sized national organization founded in 1963
Description: To promote excellence in commercial vehicle manufacturing; To effectively lobby all levels of government on the industry's behalf and bring together stakeholders to participate in generic cooperative testing & other mutually beneficial activities
Chief Officer(s): Suzy Léveillé, General Manager
sleveille@ctea.ca
Membership: 500+; *Fees:* $825; *Member Profile:* Commercial vehicle & component manufacturers; Dealers & distributors; Service providers
Activities: Lobbying; Providing access to technical & regulatory information; Offering networking opportunities; Encouraging research; *Speaker Service:* Yes

Canadian Transportation Research Forum (CTRF) / Groupe de recherches sur les transports au Canada
PO Box 23033, Woodstock ON N4T 1R9
Tel: 519-421-9701; *Fax:* 519-421-9319
ctrf.ca
www.linkedin.com/groups/8205076
twitter.com/ForCtrf
Overview: A medium-sized national charitable organization founded in 1965
Description: To promote the development of research in transportation & related fields; to publish research papers through media & through national & regional forum meetings.
Chief Officer(s): Mark Hemmes, President
Carole Ann Woudsma, Secretary
cawoudsma@ctrf.ca
Steve Pratte, Executive Vice-President
Damien Auger, Vice-President, External Affairs
Gerry Kolaitis, Vice-President, Finance & Treasurer
Adrian Lightstone, Vice-President, Program
Fees: $35 student; $100 senior; $160 individual; *Member Profile:* Open to anyone interested in any aspect of transportation; membership is currently comprised of professionals in the railway, trucking, airline, port, airport, shipping line, terminal operator, transit operator & pipline industries; shippers; employees of Transport Canada, the Canadian Transport Agency, Statistics Canads, Industry Canada & other federal agencies; consultants; unversities & colleges

Canadian Trucking Alliance (CTA) / L'Alliance canadienne du camionnage (ACC)
555 Dixon Rd., Toronto ON M9W 1H8
Tel: 416-249-7401; *Fax:* 866-713-4188
publicaffairs@cantruck.ca
www.cantruck.ca
www.linkedin.com/company/canadian-trucking-alliance
twitter.com/CanTruck
Overview: A large national organization founded in 1937
Description: To promote business excellence in trucking; to participate in the development of public policy which supports the economic growth, safety & prosperity of the industry; to provide services, including research, development, products & information to meet the needs of the industry
Membership: 4,500; *Member Profile:* Represented by a cross-section of the trucking industry, including carriers, owner-operators & industry suppliers
Activities: *Speaker Service:* Yes

Canadian Urban Transit Association (CUTA) / Association canadienne du transport urbain (ACTU)
#1401, 55 York St., Toronto ON M5J 1R7
Tel: 416-365-9800; *Fax:* 416-365-1295
cutaactu.ca
www.linkedin.com/company/canadian-urban-transit-association
www.facebook.com/CanadianTransit
twitter.com/canadiantransit
Overview: A large national organization founded in 1904
Description: To provide value to its members and contribute to the success of public transit in Canada
Chief Officer(s): Marco D'Angelo, President & CEO, 416-365-9800 104
dangelo@cutaactu.ca
Milly Mikkelsen, Manager, Human Resources, 416-365-9800 123
mikkelsen@cutaactu.ca
Membership: 488; *Fees:* Schedule available; *Member Profile:* Transit systems; Manufacturers & suppliers of transit equipment, proprietors & operating / management companies; Federal, provincial & municipal government agencies; Affiliated individuals & companies; *Committees:* Business Members;

Communications & Public Affairs; Human Resources; Technical Services; Transit Board Members; Regional Committees
Activities: Conducting research & preparing statistics; Providing technical & operational information; Liaising with government; Partnering with other transportation associations & community development stakeholders; Engaging in advocacy activities; Raising public awareness of transit contributions to communities; *Library:* Canadian Urban Transit Association Library (Open to Public)

Canadian Warplane Heritage (CWH)
9280 Airport Rd., Mount Hope ON L0R 1W0
Tel: 905-679-4183; *Fax:* 905-679-4186
Toll-Free: 877-347-3359
museum@warplane.com
www.warplane.com
www.flickr.com/groups/canadianwarplaneheritage
www.facebook.com/CanadianWarplaneHeritageMuseum
twitter.com/CWHM
Also Known As: Canada's Flying Museum
Overview: A medium-sized national charitable organization founded in 1971
Description: To acquire, document, preserve & maintain a complete collection of aircraft that were flown by Canadians & the Canadian military from the beginning of WWII to the present; To preserve the artifacts, books, periodicals & manuals relating to this mandate
Chief Officer(s): Sandra Price, Vice-President, Operations, 905-679-4183 230
sprice@warplane.com
Al Mickeloff, Manager, Marketing, 905-679-4183 233
amickeloff@warplane.com
Finances: *Annual Operating Budget:* $3 Million-$5 Million; *Funding Sources:* Membership fees; Grants; Donations
Staff: 20 staff member(s); 300 volunteer(s)
Membership: 33,000; *Fees:* $30 student; $100 senior; $125 adult; $175 family; *Member Profile:* Interest in Canadian aviation / history
Activities: *Awareness Events:* Remembrance Day; *Internships:* Yes; *Speaker Service:* Yes *Library:* Yes by appointment

Carefree Society
2832 Queensway St., Prince George BC V2L 4M5
Tel: 250-562-1394; *Fax:* 250-562-1393
carefree_society@telus.net
www.carefreesociety.org
Also Known As: handyDART
Overview: A small local charitable organization founded in 1971
Description: To provide transportation services for seniors & people with disabilities
Affiliation(s): BC Transit
Finances: *Annual Operating Budget:* $250,000-$500,000; *Funding Sources:* Provincial government; regional government
Staff: 12 staff member(s); 10 volunteer(s)
Membership: 15; *Fees:* $6; *Committees:* Accessible Transportation Awareness

Central British Columbia Railway & Forest Industry Museum Society
850 River Rd., Prince George BC V2L 5S8
Tel: 250-563-7351; *Fax:* 250-563-3697
admin@pgrfm.bc.ca
www.pgrfm.bc.ca
www.facebook.com/railwayandforestrymuseum
twitter.com/pgrailmuseum
Also Known As: Railway & Forestry Museum: Prince George & Region
Overview: A small local charitable organization founded in 1983
Description: Administers Prince George Railway & Forest Industry Museum; *Member of:* Canadian Railway Historical Association; Canadian Museum Association; British Columbia Museum Association; American Railway Museum Association
Affiliation(s): Railway & Forestry Museum: Prince George & Region
Chief Officer(s): Katherine Carlson, Executive Director
kcarlson@pgrfm.bc.ca
Finances: *Annual Operating Budget:* $50,000-$100,000
Staff: 6 staff member(s); 15 volunteer(s)
Activities: *Awareness Events:* Steam Day; Forester Day; Family Carnival *Library:* Canfor Library by appointment

Centre for Transportation Engineering & Planning (C-TEP)
c/o Stantec, Transportation, #200, 325 - 25th St. SE, Calgary AB T2A 7H8
Tel: 403-607-4482; *Fax:* 403-716-8129
c-tep.ca
twitter.com/ctep_canada
Overview: A medium-sized national organization founded in 1997
Description: To provide professional development & research related to Canadian transportation engineering & planning; To

provide a forum for collaboration between institutions & various levels of government; To act as a resource centre for transportation engineers & planners
Chief Officer(s): Wes Kennedy, President
Neil Little, Executive Director
nlittle@c-tep.com
Membership: 33 organizations; *Fees:* Schedule available

Chamber of Marine Commerce (CMC) / Chambre du commerce maritime (CCM)
Podium Bldg., Place de Ville, #340, 300 Sparks St., Ottawa ON K1R 7S3
Tel: 613-233-8779
www.marinedelivers.com
www.flickr.com/photos/marinecommerce
www.linkedin.com/company/chamber-of-marine-commerce
www.facebook.com/MarineDelivers
twitter.com/MarineDelivers
Previous Name: Great Lakes Waterways Development Association
Merged from: Canadian Shipowners Association (CSA)
Overview: A large national organization founded in 1959
Description: To represent the bi-national Great Lakes-St. Lawrence commercial marine industry; To bring together all sectors of the economy that rely on a cost efficient & safe marine transportation system
Chief Officer(s): Bruce Burrows, President
bburrows@cmc-ccm.com
Robert Turner, Vice-President, Operations
rturner@cmc-ccm.com
Julia Fields, Director, Communications
jfields@cmc-ccm.com
Finances: *Funding Sources:* Membership dues
Membership: 130+ companies; *Member Profile:* Domestic & international ship owners & operators; Canadian & US ports; International shippers; The St. Lawrence Seaway; Terminals, elevators & logistics companies; Marine-related service providers

The Chartered Institute of Logistics & Transport in North America (CILT) / Institut agréé de la logistique et des transports Amérique du Nord
PO Box 45539, Stn. Chapman Mills, Ottawa ON K2J 5N1
Tel: 613-209-9992; Fax: 888-636-9493
admin@ciltna.com
ciltna.com
Also Known As: CILT in North America
Previous Name: Chartered Institute of Transport Canadian Division
Overview: A medium-sized international organization founded in 1919
Description: To enable growth, professional development, reputation & membership within the profession of Supply Chain Logistics; *Member of:* Chartered Institute of Transport
Chief Officer(s): Bob Armstrong, President, 416-418-3990
armstrong@ciltna.com
Rebecca Whelan, Administrator, 613-209-9992
Finances: *Funding Sources:* Membership fees, conferences, workshop revenue
Staff: 1 staff member(s); 15 volunteer(s)
Membership: 250; *Fees:* Schedule available; *Member Profile:* Individuals with experience, interest or education in the transportation field; *Committees:* Regional

Chatham Railroad Museum Society
PO Box 434, 2 McLean St., Chatham ON N7M 5K5
Tel: 519-352-3097
crms@mnsi.net
www.chathamrailroadmuseum.ca
Overview: A small local charitable organization founded in 1989
Description: To commemorate railway and local history by educating the public through the use of interactive displays & railway artefacts
Membership: 1-99
Activities: *Awareness Events:* William Glassco Railroad Fun Day

Club de trafic de Québec (CTQ)
CP 44521, Lévis QC G7A 4X5
info@clubtraficqc.com
www.clubtraficqc.com
www.facebook.com/clubtraficquebec
Aperçu: *Dimension:* moyenne; *Envergure:* provinciale; *Organisme sans but lucratif;* fondée en 1960
Description: Regrouper les représentants oeuvrant dans le domaine du transport de la grande région de Québec
Membre(s) du bureau directeur: Benoit Latour, Président
b.latour@pmtroy.com
Finances: *Budget de fonctionnement annuel:* $100,000-$250,000
Membre: 168; *Montant de la cotisation:* 85$

Edmonton Radial Railway Society (ERRS)
PO Box 76057, Stn. Southgate, Edmonton AB T6H 5Y7
Tel: 780-437-7721; Fax: 780-437-3095
info@edmonton-radial-railway.ab.ca
www.edmonton-radial-railway.ab.ca
www.facebook.com/edmontonstreetcar
Overview: A small national charitable organization founded in 1980
Description: To collect, preserve & interpret the history & technology of street railways with particular emphasis on Edmonton's streetcar system; *Member of:* Canadian Museum Association
Affiliation(s): Association of Tourist Railroads & Railway Museums; Alberta Museums Association; Virtual Museum of Canada
Finances: *Annual Operating Budget:* $100,000-$250,000; *Funding Sources:* Municipal, provincial & federal governments; donations
Staff: 60 volunteer(s)
Membership: 130; *Fees:* $20
Activities: Operating 2 historic street railway lines within Edmonton from May to Oct.; streetcar museum; streetcar chartering service; restoration, maintenance & operation of historic streetcars; *Library:* Edmonton Radial Railway Society Library

Electric Mobility Canada (EMC) / Mobilité Électrique Canada
#11-530, 38, Place du Commerce, Ile-des-Soeurs QC H3E 1T8
Fax: 514-769-1286
info@emc-mec.ca
emc-mec.ca
www.linkedin.com/company/electric-mobility-canada
twitter.com/EMC_MEC
Overview: A small national organization
Description: To promote electric mobility as a readily available & important solution to Canada's emerging energy & environmental issues
Chief Officer(s): Daniel Breton, President & CEO, 514-916-4165
daniel.breton@emc-mec.ca
Membership: 178; *Fees:* Schedule available; *Member Profile:* Manufacturers or industry personnel; Energy providers; Fleet managers; Not-for-Profit Organizations & Academics; Supporters; Associate Members; *Committees:* Government Relations; Working Group on PEV Readiness; Electric Bus
Activities: Annual conference, newsletter, webinars; *Awareness Events:* National Drive Electric Week

Electric Vehicle Council of Ottawa (EVCO)
PO Box 4044, Stn. E, Ottawa ON K1S 5B1
info@evco.ca
evco.ca
www.youtube.com/EVCOdotCA
Overview: A small local organization founded in 1980
Description: To promote the use of electric vehicles as a viable transportation alternative
Chief Officer(s): Raymond Leury, President
Darren Robinchaud, Secretary
Gavrel Gérard, Treasurer
Fees: $5 student/academic/associate; $25 regular
Activities: Offering technical literature; Organizing displays, demonstrations, talks & competitions; Hosting monthly meetings; Participating in advocacy projects; *Library:* Electric Vehicle Council of Ottawa Print & Video Library

Electric Vehicle Society (EVS)
ON
info@evsociety.ca
evsociety.ca
www.linkedin.com/company/electric-vehicle-society
www.facebook.com/EVSociety
twitter.com/EVSociety
Overview: A medium-sized national organization founded in 1994
Description: To investigate & promote clean transportation technologies
Chief Officer(s): Wilf Steimle, President
Fees: $20 youth; $30 full; $100 corporation; *Member Profile:* Engineers; Environmentalists; Enthusiasts for electric energy for propulsion
Activities: Providing a forum for member discussions; Examining modes of electric transportation

Fédération des transporteurs par autobus / Bus Carriers Federation
#250, 5700, boul des Galeries, Québec QC G2K 0H5
Tél: 418-476-8181; Téléc: 418-476-8177
Ligne sans frais: 844-476-8181
www.federationautobus.com

Merged from: Association des propriétaires d'autobus du Québec; Association du transport écolier du Québec
Aperçu: *Dimension:* moyenne; *Envergure:* provinciale; fondée en 2014
Description: Favoriser la mobilité efficace et sécuritaire des personnes et ainsi contribuer à l'image, la valorisation et la stabilité du transport collectif de personnes
Membre(s) du bureau directeur: Luc Lafrance, Président-Directeur Général, 418-476-8181 214
llafrance@federationautobus.com
Membre: 700; *Critères d'admissibilite:* Transportateurs par autocars; Vendeurs de produits touristiques pour les groupes; *Comités:* Audit; Assurance; Sécurité; Urbain et interurbain; Transport scolaire; Nolisé-touristique; Transport spécialisé (adapté, aéroportuaire, médical, abonnement et collectif rural)

Freight Carriers Association of Canada (FCA)
#301, 1270 Central Pkwy. West, Mississauga ON L5C 4P4
Tel: 905-276-3835
info@fcafuel.org
fcafuel.org
Previous Name: Canadian Transport Tariff Bureau Association
Overview: A medium-sized national organization
Description: To provide quality information, products & services to users, providers & third parties involved in motor carrier transportation
Affiliation(s): North American Transportation Council
Chief Officer(s): Bill Kimmel, President
wkimmel@fcafuel.org
Mary Anne Vehrs, Contact, Client Services
mvehrs@fcafuel.org
Finances: *Annual Operating Budget:* $1.5 Million-$3 Million; *Funding Sources:* Membership fees; Sales of publications & software
Member Profile: For-hire motor carriers engaged in the for-hire trucking industry in Canada
Activities: Holding carrier meetings & seminars; Disseminating information; *Speaker Service:* Yes

Freight Management Association of Canada (FMA) / Association canadienne de gestion du fret (AGF)
#210, 600 Terry Fox Dr., Ottawa ON K2L 4B6
Tel: 613-599-3283; Fax: 613-599-1295
info@fma-agf.ca
www.fma-agf.ca
www.linkedin.com/company/canadian-industrial-transportation-association-cita-
twitter.com/FMA_AGF
Previous Name: Canadian Industrial Transportation Association
Overview: A medium-sized national organization founded in 1916
Description: To support the shipper community by advocating on behalf of Canadian industry to address complex concerns related to freight transportation & logistics issues
Chief Officer(s): Robert Ballantyne, P.Eng., President
ballantyne@fma-agf.ca
Finances: *Annual Operating Budget:* $100,000-$250,000; *Funding Sources:* Membership fees; Advertising; Seminars; Conferences
Staff: 3 staff member(s)
Membership: 100+; *Fees:* Schedule available; *Member Profile:* Companies involved in the shipping industry; *Committees:* Air; Marine; Rail; Truck
Activities: Engaging in advocacy; Providing seminars, advertising, job postings, & networking opportunities; Offering information, directories & publications; Organizing meetings & events; *Speaker Service:* Yes

GoByBike BC Society
PO Box 74591, RPO Kitsilano, Vancouver BC V6K 4P4
gobybikebc.ca
www.linkedin.com/company/gobybikebc
www.facebook.com/gobybikebc
twitter.com/gobybikebc
Previous Name: Bike to Work BC Society
Overview: A small provincial organization founded in 2008
Description: To help communities in BC deliver successful Bike to Work & Bike to School events; To encourage as many people as possible to experience the benefits of commuting by bicycle
Chief Officer(s): Penny Noble, Executive Director, 604-805-5637
pnoble@biketowork.ca
Terri-Lynn Gifford, Program Manager
terri-lynn@biketowork.ca
Finances: *Funding Sources:* Donations; Government
Staff: 2 staff member(s)
Activities: Organizing events by securing & sharing resources; *Awareness Events:* Bike to Work Week, May; Bike to School Week, May

Heavy Equipment & Aggregate Truckers Association of Manitoba (HEAT)
817 Kapelus Dr., #A, West St Paul MB R4A 5A4
Tel: 204-654-9426; *Fax:* 204-224-4907
admin@heatmb.ca
heatmb.ca
Overview: A small provincial organization
Description: To provide education & information to the general public about Winnipeg's growing constuction industry
Chief Officer(s): Tony Malanchuk, President
Membership: 187; *Fees:* $200; *Member Profile:* Members of the heavy equpiment operating trade in Manitoba
Activities: Develop standards; Education programs for general public

Hope Air / Vols d'espoir
#207, 124 Merton St., Toronto ON M4S 2Z2
Tel: 416-222-6335; *Fax:* 416-222-6930
Toll-Free: 877-346-4673
mail@hopeair.ca
www.youtube.com/user/HopeAirHealth
www.linkedin.com/company/hope-air
www.facebook.com/hopeair
Previous Name: Mission Air Transportation Network
Overview: A small national charitable organization founded in 1986
Description: To provide free air transportation to Canadians in financial need who must travel between their own communities & recognized facilities for medical care
Chief Officer(s): Mark Rubinstein, Chief Executive Officer, 416-222-6335 228
mrubinstein@hopeair.ca
Finances: *Annual Operating Budget:* $250,000-$500,000; *Funding Sources:* Corporate; private donations; government
Staff: 6 staff member(s); 30 volunteer(s)
Membership: 1-99; *Committees:* Air Coordination; Funding; Finance; Office Administrations; Planning; Public Relations
Activities: Providings airfare for those in need of medical assitance

Huntsville & Lake of Bays Railway Society
Muskoka Heritage Place, 88 Brunel Rd., Huntsville ON P1H 1R1
Tel: 705-789-7576; *Fax:* 705-789-6169
www.portageflyer.org
Also Known As: The Portage Railway
Overview: A small local charitable organization founded in 1984
Description: Maintains & displays original artifacts of the old Huntsville & Lake of Bays Railway, plus vintage railway equipment from the turn of the century
Affiliation(s): Muskoka Heritage Place
Chief Officer(s): David Topps, President
president@portageflyer.org
Finances: *Funding Sources:* Fundraising; Rotary Club; local industry; donations
Fees: $35 regular; $45 international
Activities: A fully functional operating railway

Industrial Truck Association (ITA)
#460, 1750 K St. NW, Washington DC 20006 USA
Tel: 202-296-9880; *Fax:* 202-296-9884
www.indtrk.org
www.facebook.com/Indtrk
Overview: A medium-sized international organization
Description: Represents the manufacturers of lift trucks & their suppliers who do business in Canada, the United States or Mexico
Finances: *Annual Operating Budget:* $1.5 Million-$3 Million
Staff: 5 staff member(s)
Membership: 100; *Fees:* Schedule available; *Member Profile:* Manufacturers of industrial trucks or of major components, attachments or manually powered hand pallet trucks that do business in the United States, Canada or Mexico
Activities: Training programs; Market intelligence; *Awareness Events:* National Forklift Safety Day, June 14

Institute of Transportation Engineers (ITE)
#600, 1627 Eye St. NW, Washington DC 20006 USA
Tel: 202-785-0060; *Fax:* 202-785-0609
ite_staff@ite.org
www.ite.org
www.youtube.com/user/ITEHQ
www.linkedin.com/groups/166463
www.facebook.com/ITEHQ
twitter.com/ITEHQ
Overview: A large international organization founded in 1930
Description: To facilitate the application of technology & scientific principles for modes of ground transportation
Chief Officer(s): Jeffrey Paniati, Executive Director & CEO, 202-785-0060 131
jpaniati@ite.org

Membership: 16,000; *Fees:* Schedule available; *Member Profile:* Transportation professionals responsible for meeting mobility & safety needs, such as transportation educators, researchers, consultants, planners & engineers
Activities: Promoting professional development; Supporting education; Encouraging research; Increasing public awareness; Exchanging professional information

Intermodal Association of North America (IANA)
#1100, 11785 Beltsville Dr., Calverton MD 20705-4049 USA
Tel: 301-982-3400; *Fax:* 301-982-4815
info@intermodal.org
www.intermodal.org
www.linkedin.com/company/intermodal-association-of-north-america
twitter.com/Intermodal
Overview: A medium-sized international organization founded in 1991
Description: To represent the combined interests of intermodal freight transportation companies & their suppliers
Chief Officer(s): Joanne F. Casey, President & CEO, 301-982-3400 349
Stephen Keppler, Senior Vice-President, Member Services, 301-982-3400 349
Membership: 1,000+; *Fees:* Schedule available; *Member Profile:* Intermodal freight transportation companies & their suppliers; *Committees:* Maintenance & Repair; Operations

International Air Transport Association (IATA) / Association du transport aérien international
PO Box 113, 800, Place Victoria, Montréal QC H4Z 1M1
Tel: 514-874-0202; *Fax:* 514-874-9632
www.iata.org
www.youtube.com/iatatv
www.linkedin.com/company/international-air-transport-association-iata
www.facebook.com/iata.org
twitter.com/iata
Overview: A small international organization founded in 1945
Description: To promote safe, regular & economical air transport for the benefit of the peoples of the world; To foster air commerce; To study the problems connected with air transport; To provide a means for collaboration among the air transport enterprises engaged directly or indirectly in international air transport service; To cooperate with the International Civil Aviation Organization & other international organizations; To coordinate international fares & rates; To simplify the travelling process for the general public
Affiliation(s): International Civil Aviation Organization
Chief Officer(s): Alexandre de Juniac, Director General & CEO
Membership: 290 member airlines; *Fees:* US$14,450; *Member Profile:* International passenger & cargo airlines; *Committees:* Avionics & Telecommunications; Engineering & Environment; Airports; Flight Operations; Medical; Security; Air Law; Financial; Traffic Coordination; Traffic Services
Activities: Training programs; Policy development; Produce & distribute publications; Webinars; Annual meetings

International Association of Ports & Harbours (IAPH)
South Tower, New Pier Takeshiba, 1-16-1 Kaigan, 7th Fl., Minato-Ku, Tokyo 105-0022 Japan
info@iaphworldports.org
www.iaphworldports.org
www.facebook.com/iaphworldports
Overview: A large international organization founded in 1955
Description: To promote the development of the international port & maritime industry by fostering cooperation among members in order to build a more cohesive partnership among the world's ports & harbours; To ensure that the industry's interests & views are represented before international organizations involved n the regulation of international trade & transportation; To collect, analyse, exchange & distribute information on developing trends in international trade, transportation, ports & the regulations of these industries
Affiliation(s): International Maritime Organization; United Nations Conference on Trade & Development; United Nations Economic & Social Council; Permanent International Association of Navigation Congresses; International Cargo Handling Coordination Association; International Maritime Pilots Association; International Association of Independent Tanker Owners; Baltic & International Maritime Council
Chief Officer(s): Masahiko Furuichi, Secretary General
Finances: *Annual Operating Budget:* $1.5 Million-$3 Million; *Funding Sources:* Membership fees
Staff: 7 staff member(s)
Membership: 320; *Fees:* Schedule available; *Member Profile:* Countries with maritime-based industries; *Committees:* Executive; Communication & Community Relations; Port Finance & Economics; Port Safety & Security; Port Environment; Legal; Port Planning & Development; Port Operations & Logistics; Trade Facilitation & Port Community System;

Conference; Finance; Constitution & By-Laws; Membership; Long Range Planning / Review
Activities: *Library:* International Association of Ports & Harbours Library (Open to Public)

International Industry Working Group (IIWG)
International Air Transport Association, PO Box 416, Route de l'Aéroport 33 1215, 15 Airport, Geneva Switzerland
www.iata.org/en/programs/workgroups/iiwg
Overview: A small international organization founded in 1970
Description: To promote & develop an open exchange of information to minimize interface problems through well-informed design, development & operation of both aircraft & airports; To study possible solutions to major problems that impede the development of the air transport system; To share information to establish a unified industry position on matters of common interest; To assist in developing & keeping up to date standard formats for documents specifying aircraft & airport characteristsics & future trends in their designs
Membership: 50; *Member Profile:* Aircraft & aeroengine manufacturers; Airlines & airport authorities; Sometimes addtional members from the International Civil Aviation Organization (ICAO), US Federal Aviation Administration (FAA) & European Civil Aviation Conference (ECAC)

International Maritime Organization (IMO) / Organisation maritime internationale
4 Albert Embankment, London SE1 7SR United Kingdom
info@imo.org
www.imo.org
www.youtube.com/user/IMOHQ
www.facebook.com/IMOHQ
twitter.com/imohq
Overview: A large international organization founded in 1948
Description: To encourage the adoption of high standards in matters concerning maritime safety, security, efficiency of navigation & control of marine pollution from ships
Chief Officer(s): Kitack Lim, Secretary General
Finances: *Annual Operating Budget:* Greater than $5 Million; *Funding Sources:* Government
Staff: 300 staff member(s)
Membership: 174 member states + 3 associates; *Fees:* Schedule available, based upon shipping fleet tonnage; *Committees:* Maritime Safety; Marine Environment Protection; Legal; Technical Cooperation; Facilitation
Activities: *Awareness Events:* Day of the Seafarer, June; *Internships:* Yes *Library:* International Maritime Organization Library by appointment

The Logistics Institute
#405, 501 Alliance St., Toronto ON M6N 2J1
Tel: 416-363-3005; *Fax:* 416-363-5598
loginfo@loginstitute.ca
www.loginstitute.ca
www.linkedin.com/groups/1581887
www.facebook.com/129220600590938
twitter.com/LogInstitute
Also Known As: Canadian Professional Logistics Institute
Overview: A medium-sized national organization founded in 1990
Description: To provide certification for the P.Log., LS & SC designations; To teach, develop & promote the science of logistics to the business community
Chief Officer(s): Victor S. Deyglio, Founding President, 416-363-3005 1200
vdeyglio@loginstitute.ca
Jasmine Gill, Director, Program & Learning Resources, 416-363-3005 1700
jgill@loginstitute.ca
Leanne Moss, Director, Certification & Member Services, 416-363-3005 1500
lmoss@loginstitute.ca
Grayson Bass, Director, Fundraising, LET Trust
priscilla@loginstitute.ca
Finances: *Funding Sources:* Human Resources Services Development of Canada
Activities: Provides comprehensive training, development & support programs; Workshops; Certifications; Continuous learning

Manitoba Trucking Association (MTA)
25 Bunting St., Winnipeg MB R2X 2P5
Tel: 204-632-6600; *Fax:* 204-694-7134
info@trucking.mb.ca
www.trucking.mb.ca
www.linkedin.com/company/manitoba-trucking-association
www.facebook.com/manitobatruckingassociation
twitter.com/truckingmb
Overview: A medium-sized provincial organization founded in 1932
Description: To develop & maintain a safe and healthy business environment for its members

Affiliation(s): Canadian Trucking Alliance; Canadian Council of Motor Transport Administrators; Canadian Trucking Human Resource Council; Winnipeg Chamber of Commerce; Manitoba Chamber of Commerce; Infrastructure Council of Manitoba; Employers' Task Force on Workers' Compensation; Manitoba Employers' Council
Chief Officer(s): Terry Shaw, Executive Director
Finances: *Funding Sources:* Membership dues & fundraising through services
Staff: 6 staff member(s)
Membership: 300 organizations; *Member Profile:* PSV Carriers; City Transportation; Private Fleet; Household Goods Carriers; Associated Trades; Vehicle Maintenance; *Committees:* Safety; Professional Truck Driving Championships; Scholarship Fund; Human Resources; Workers Compensation
Activities: *Speaker Service:* Yes

Maple Ridge Museum & Community Archives
22520 - 116th Ave., Maple Ridge BC V2X 0S4
Tel: 604-463-5311; Fax: 604-463-5317
mapleridgemuseum.org
Also Known As: Maple Ridge Historical Society
Overview: A small local organization founded in 1957
Description: To provide current, former & potential residents of Maple Ridge with the means to understand the community's history through the collection, preservation & sharing of historical images, documents & artifacts
Affiliation(s): National Model Railway Association; Pacific Northwest Region 7th Division Society; BC Heritage Society; Maple Ridge Historical Society; Maple Ridge Museum
Chief Officer(s): Val Patenaude, Executive Director
Shea Henry, Museums Curator
Finances: *Funding Sources:* Membership fees, donations, admissions
Fees: $20 individual; $25 family; $120 corporate; $120 sustaining; *Member Profile:* Individuals interested in Maple Ridge & its history

Master Mariners of Canada
c/o Captain Christopher Hall, 5959 Spring Garden Rd., Halifax NS B3J 1Y5
communications@mastermariners.ca
www.mastermariners.ca
www.linkedin.com/company/master-mariners-of-canada
Overview: A medium-sized national organization founded in 1967
Description: To encourage and maintain a high and honourable standard of ability & profesional conduct of the officers of the Canadian Merchant Service; To provide a central body of command representing senior officers; To encourage & further develop education, training & qualifications of young seafarers; Promote & maintain efficient & friendly cooperation between the commerical, government & military fleets of Canada; *Member of:* Canadian Maritimes Law Association (CMLA); International Federation of Shipmasters' Associations (IFSMA); International Maritimes Organization (IMO)
Affiliation(s): Master Mariner organizations in the UK, USA, South Africa, Australia & NZ
Chief Officer(s): Christopher Halll, National President
chall@sjport.com
Finances: *Funding Sources:* Membership dues
Fees: $50 full; $80 senior/associate/companion; *Member Profile:* Master Mariners
Activities: Organizes conventions & seminars; Participates & provides input into national & international groups; *Speaker Service:* Yes

Motorcycle & Moped Industry Council (MMIC) / Le Conseil de l'industrie de la motocyclette et du cyclomoteur (CIMC)
#201, 3000 Steeles Ave. East, Markham ON L3R 4T9
Tel: 416-491-4449; Fax: 416-493-1985
Toll-Free: 877-470-6642
info@mmic.ca
www.mmic.ca
www.facebook.com/MotorcycleMopedIndustryCouncil
Overview: A small national organization founded in 1971
Description: To serve as a forum to identify and act on issues of importance to the motorcycle & scooter communities; To monitor & respond to changes in legislation and regulations affecting the use of motorcycles & scooters; To serve as a statistical gathering base for the industry
Chief Officer(s): David Grummet, Director, Communications
Membership: 12; *Fees:* Schedule available; *Member Profile:* Companies involved in the manufacturing or distribution of motorcycles, mopeds or scooters in Canada
Activities: Data collection and organization; Motorcycle & OHV shows: Training programs; Ride! events

National Transportation Brokers Association (NTBA)
PO Box 141, 8005 Financial Dr., #A4, Brampton ON L6Y 6A1
Toll-Free: 800-693-5033
info@ntba-brokers.com
www.ntba-brokers.com
www.linkedin.com/company/national-transportation-brokers-asso
ciation
www.facebook.com/NTBACanada
Overview: A medium-sized national organization
Description: To promotes & continually improve business relationships among shippers, carriers, government & freight brokers
Chief Officer(s): Mark Linton, Chair, 905-842-0422
service@kml-logistics.com
Finances: *Funding Sources:* Member fees
Fees: $300; *Member Profile:* Freight brokerage services providers

The Ninety-Nines Inc.
4300 Amelia Earhart Rd., #A, Oklahoma City OK 73159 USA
Tel: 405-685-7969; Fax: 405-685-7985
Toll-Free: 844-994-1929
99s@ninety-nines.org
www.ninety-nines.org
www.instagram.com/theninetyninesinc
www.facebook.com/99sinc
twitter.com/TheNinetyNines
Also Known As: International Organization of Women Pilots
Overview: A medium-sized international charitable organization founded in 1929
Description: To promote world fellowship through flight; To provide networking & scholarship opportunities for women & aviation education in the community; To preserve the unique history of women in aviation
Chief Officer(s): Corbi Bulluck, President
president@ninety-nines.org
Terry Carbonell, Vice-President
vicepresident@ninety-nines.org
Leslie Prellwitz, Treasurer
treasurer@ninety-nines.org
Catherine Prudhomme, Secretary
secretary@ninety-nines.org
Fees: US$30 international student; US$35 US/Canadian student; US$44 international; US$57 Canada; US$65 US; *Member Profile:* Women pilots
Activities: Museums & historical archives; Endowment Fund; Aviation & space education; *Speaker Service:* Yes *Library:* 99s Museum of Women Pilots

North America Railway Hall of Fame (NARHF)
750 Tabot St., St Thomas ON N5P 1E2
Tel: 519-633-2535; Fax: 519-633-3087
info@casostation.ca
casostation.ca
www.facebook.com/CASOstation
twitter.com/casostation
Overview: A small national charitable organization founded in 1996
Description: To honour individuals & organizations who have made significant contributions relating to the railway industry in North America; To preserve & display a collection of library materials & railway heritage artifacts related to the Hall of Fame inductees; To educate the public about the impact of railway transportation on history & the development of communities, nations & international relations
Chief Officer(s): John Shapendonk, President
Larry Longfield, Executive Director
larry@casostation.ca

Northern Air Transport Association (NATA)
c/o Colin Dempsey, PO Box 20102, Yellowknife NT X1A 3X8
Tel: 867-446-6282
admin@natacanada.org
natacanada.org
Overview: A small local organization founded in 1977
Description: To promote safe & effective Northern air transportation; To advocate for Northern air transport positions; To establish & maintain partnerships within the industry, governments & other interested parties
Chief Officer(s): Glenn Priestley, Executive Director, 613-866-2374
glenn@natacanada.org
Colin Dempsey, General Manager, 867-466-6282, Fax: 866-977-6282
admin@nata-yzf.ca
Fees: $100 sustaining; $195-$2,895 operator; $625 associate; *Member Profile:* Operators, associates & affiliates of the industry; *Committees:* Training
Activities: Advocating for Northern air transport; Establishing partnerships with governments & within the transportation industry; *Speaker Service:* Yes

Ontario Good Roads Association (OGRA)
#22, 1525 Cornwall Rd., Oakville ON L6J 0B2
Tel: 289-291-6472; Fax: 289-291-6477
info@ogra.org
www.ogra.org
www.linkedin.com/company/ontario-good-roads-association
www.facebook.com/ontariogoodroads
twitter.com/Ont_Good_Roads
Overview: A medium-sized provincial organization founded in 1894
Description: To represent the transportation & public works-related interests of Ontario's municipalities & First Nation communities; To deliver programs & services that meet the needs of members; To support municipalities in the provision of effective & efficient transportation systems throughout Ontario
Chief Officer(s): Scott Butler, Executive Director
Finances: *Funding Sources:* Membership fees; Sponsorships
Membership: 400+ municipalities; *Member Profile:* Ontario municipalities; First Nations communities; Corporations; Life & honourary members; *Committees:* Municipal Hot Mix Asphalt Liaison; Quality of Asphalt Pavement; Aggregate Recycling Ontario Council; Municipal Concrete Liaison; Smart About Salt; Ontario Roads Coalition (ORC); Ontario Provincial Standards (OPS); The Ontario Road Salt Management Group (ORSMG); Municipal Alliance for Connected and Autonomous Vehicles in Ontario (MACAVO)
Activities: Advocating for the collective interests of municipal transportation & works departments; Analyzing policies; Reviewing legislation; Consulting with stakeholders & partners; Offering education & training opportunities; *Library:* Ontario Good Roads Association Documents Library (Open to Public)

Ontario Milk Transport Association (OMTA)
#301, 660 Speedvale Ave. West, Guelph ON N1K 1E5
Tel: 519-766-1133; Fax: 519-766-7722
info@milktransport.ca
www.milktransport.ca
Overview: A medium-sized provincial organization founded in 1967
Description: Collect raw milk from Ontario farms & take it to processing plants in Ontario, Manitoba & Quebec
Chief Officer(s): Tim Holmes, General Manager
Membership: 60 companies; *Member Profile:* Transporters of milk

Ontario Public Transit Association (OPTA)
#200, 5063 North Service Rd., Burlington ON L7L 5H6
Tel: 416-229-6222; Fax: 416-969-8916
info@ontariopublictransit.ca
ontariopublictransit.ca
twitter.com/ON_PublicTrnsit
Previous Name: Ontario Community Transit Association
Overview: A medium-sized provincial organization founded in 1997
Description: To strengthen & improve public transit services in Ontario; To ensure excellence & sustainability in public transit
Chief Officer(s): Kelly Paleczny, Chair
Tony D'Alessandro, Treasurer
Ann-Marie Carroll, Secretary
Fees: Schedule available; *Member Profile:* Representatives of public transit systems; Health & social service agency transportation providers; Government representatives; Suppliers to the industry; Consultants
Activities: Engaging in advocacy activities; Sharing information; *Awareness Events:* Ontario Transit Expo (OTE) Conference & Trade Show

Ontario Seaplane Association
ON
Tel: 705-327-4730
www.ontarioseaplane.com
www.facebook.com/groups/213790595317592
Overview: A small provincial organization
Description: To bring together seaplane pilots & enthusiasts
Chief Officer(s): Doug Ronan, President, 705-327-4730
doug@dougronan.com
Paul Armstrong, Vice-President, 416-438-5985
paul-armstrong@rogers.com
Brain Wendt, Secretary, 847-971-6980
brwendt9@hotmail.com
Fees: Free
Activities: Fly-ins; social events; fishing trips

Ontario Traffic Council (OTC)
PO Box 80030, Stn. Rossland Garden, 3100 Garden St., Whitby ON L1R 0H1
Tel: 647-346-4050
traffic@otc.org
otc.org
www.linkedin.com/groups/5071314
twitter.com/ontariotraffic

Overview: A medium-sized provincial organization founded in 1950
Description: To improve traffic conditions & traffic safety in municipalities of Ontario
Chief Officer(s): Adam Bell, President
Heide Schlegl, Vice-President
Neslson Cadete, Treasurer
Geoff Wilkinson, Executive Director
Aswathy Prathap, Coordinator, Membership & Events
Member Profile: Regions, cities, towns, counties & institutions across Ontario that contributing to the OTC through police services, elected representatives, traffic engineers & parking enforcement; *Committees:* Active Transportation; Parking; School Crossing Programs; Traffic Engineering; Traffic Training; Transportation Planning
Activities: Committees; Research & providing reports; Training programs

Ontario Trucking Association (OTA)
555 Dixon Rd., Toronto ON M9W 1H8
Tel: 416-249-7401; *Fax:* 866-713-4188
www.ontruck.org
www.youtube.com/user/ontruck
www.linkedin.com/groups/4783727
twitter.com/OnTruck
Overview: A medium-sized provincial organization founded in 1926
Description: To represent companies & industry suppliers; To provide political advocacy, education & information services to North American freight transport companies
Finances: *Funding Sources:* Membership fees
Membership: 1,700; *Member Profile:* Individuals from family-owned companies to publicly-traded conglomerates, including representatives from the for-hire carrier, private carrier, intermodal & supplier industries; *Committees:* Axle Weight; Credit; Education; Executive; Social / Labour; Tech. / Ops; Convention; Dues; Membership; Insurance; Finance; Environmental Issues
Activities: Offering training courses & seminars; *Awareness Events:* Annual Spring Golf Tournament, May; *Speaker Service:* Yes

Operation Lifesaver (OL) / Opération Gareautrain
#901, 99 Bank St., Ottawa ON K1P 6B9
Tel: 613-564-8100; *Fax:* 613-567-6726
admin@operationlifesaver.ca
www.operationlifesaver.ca
www.youtube.com/user/OperationLifesaverCA
www.facebook.com/oplifesaver
twitter.com/oplifesaver
Overview: A small national organization founded in 1981
Description: To create awareness by the general public of the potential hazards of rail / highway crossings; To improve drivers' & pedestrians' behaviour at these intersections; To inform the public of the dangers associated with trespassing on railway property; To reduce the number of accidents resulting in fatalities, injuries & monetary losses
Affiliation(s): olkids.ca; traintodrive.net
Chief Officer(s): Sarah Mayes, National Director
Finances: *Annual Operating Budget:* $250,000-$500,000; *Funding Sources:* Transport Canada; Railway Association of Canada
Staff: 2 staff member(s); 150 volunteer(s)
Activities: *Awareness Events:* OL Rail Safety Week, April

Prince Edward Island Trucking Sector Council (PEITSC)
#211, 420 University Ave., Charlottetown PE C1A 7Z5
Tel: 902-566-5563; *Fax:* 902-566-5616
info@peitsc.ca
www.peitsc.ca
www.youtube.com/user/peitruckingsc
www.facebook.com/peitsc
twitter.com/peitsc
Overview: A medium-sized provincial organization
Description: To address human resources issues & opportunities in the Trucking Industry on Prince Edward Island & to provide a vehicle for effective industry participation in identifying & addressing issues related to workforce attraction & retention, career awareness, skills upgrading & training; *Member of:* Prince Edward Island Literacy Alliance Inc.
Chief Officer(s): Jason Ling, Chair
Clinton Myers, Vice-Chair

Private Motor Truck Council of Canada (PMTC) / Association canadienne du camionnage d'entreprise (ACCE)
#5, 225 Main St. East, Milton ON L9T 1N9
Tel: 905-827-0587; *Fax:* 905-827-8212
Toll-Free: 877-501-7682
info@pmtc.ca
www.pmtc.ca
twitter.com/privatefleets
Overview: A medium-sized national organization founded in 1977
Description: To provide forums for fleet operators & industry stakeholders to exchange views & resolve issues concerning the private motor truck sector; *Member of:* North American Private Truck Council
Affiliation(s): National Private Truck Council
Chief Officer(s): Mike Millian, President, 519-932-0902
trucks@pmtc.ca
Finances: *Annual Operating Budget:* $250,000-$500,000; *Funding Sources:* Seminars; Social events; Membership fees
Staff: 4 staff member(s)
Membership: 400; *Fees:* Schedule available; *Member Profile:* Private truck fleets or suppliers to same; private truck fleets operated by companies whose principal business is other than transportation, but use their own truck fleets to further their business
Activities: Seminars; Annual conference; Benchmarking & best practices survey; *Awareness Events:* National Vehicle Graphics Design Competition

Railway Association of Canada (RAC) / Association des chemins de fer du Canada (ACFC)
#901, 99 Bank St., Ottawa ON K1P 6B9
Tel: 613-567-8591; *Fax:* 613-567-6726
rac@railcan.ca
www.railcan.ca
www.youtube.com/user/racmain
www.linkedin.com/company/railway-association-of-canada
www.facebook.com/RailCanada
twitter.com/RailCanada
Overview: A large national organization founded in 1917
Description: To promote the commercial viability & the safe & efficient operation of the Canadian railway industry; To act on behalf of, or work jointly with, member companies to promote public policy & regulation that provides equitable treatment between shipping modes; To provide factual information about the railway industry for the public, government & industry members; To provide the views of the industry on public policy issues
Affiliation(s): Association of American Railroads
Chief Officer(s): Marc Brazeau, President & CEO
Stéphanie Montreuil, Senior Director, Communications & Media Relations, 613-564-8101
smontreuil@railcan.ca
Finances: *Annual Operating Budget:* Greater than $5 Million; *Funding Sources:* Members fees
Staff: 20 staff member(s)
Membership: 50+ companies; *Fees:* $2,000 minimum; *Member Profile:* Railway companies operating in Canada; *Committees:* Policy; Accounting; Finance; Human Resources; Safety & Operations Management; Taxation
Activities: Rule making; Advocacy; Communications; Liaison; Industry support & training; Equipment securement workshop

Recreational Aircraft Association (RAA) / Réseau aéronefs amateur
#22, 4881 Fountain St. North, Breslau ON N0B 1M0
Tel: 519-648-3030; *Toll-Free:* 800-387-1028
raa@raa.ca
www.raa.ca
Previous Name: Experimental Aircraft Association of Canada
Overview: A medium-sized national organization founded in 1983
Description: To provide a liaison between Transport Canada, MD-RA Inspection Services, Enforcement & builders & flyers of recreational aircraft
Affiliation(s): Recreational Aviation Foundation
Chief Officer(s): Gary Wolf, President, 519-648-3030
garywolf@rogers.com
Wayne Hadath, Treasurer
whadath@rogers.com
Finances: *Annual Operating Budget:* $100,000-$250,000; *Funding Sources:* Membership dues
Staff: 1 staff member(s); 150 volunteer(s)
Membership: 2,000; *Fees:* $59.99 individual; $74.58 family; *Member Profile:* Individuals who enjoy building and flying plans recreationally; *Committees:* 12 regional
Activities: Fly-ins across Canada; *Speaker Service:* Yes

Saskatchewan Trucking Association (STA)
103 Hodsman Rd., Regina SK S4N 5W5
Tel: 306-994-8730; *Fax:* 306-569-1008
Toll-Free: 800-563-7623
info@sasktrucking.com
sasktrucking.com
www.instagram.com/sasktrucking
www.linkedin.com/company/saskatchewan-trucking-association
www.facebook.com/sasktrucking
twitter.com/sasktrucking
Overview: A medium-sized provincial licensing organization founded in 1937
Description: To act as a representative of the truck transport industry in Saskatchewan
Affiliation(s): CTA Board of Directors; BC Trucking Association; Ontario Trucking Association; Quebec Trucking Association; Atlantic Provinces Association
Chief Officer(s): Susan Ewart, Executive Director, 306-569-9696 450
sewaart@sasktrucking.com
Finances: *Funding Sources:* Membership fees; Sponsorship of programs
Fees: Schedule available; *Member Profile:* Trucking companies operating in or suppliers to the trucking industry in Manitoba
Activities: Advocacy; Publications; Training

Shipping Federation of Canada / Fédération maritime du Canada
#800, 625, boul René-Lévesque ouest, Montréal QC H3B 1R2
Tel: 514-849-2325; *Toll-Free:* 800-401-0502
info@shipfed.ca
www.shipfed.ca
www.linkedin.com/company/shipping-federation-of-canada
Overview: A large national organization founded in 1903
Description: To represent and promote the interests of the owners, operators & agents of ships involved in Canada's world trade
Chief Officer(s): Michael Broad, President, 514-849-2325 228
mhbroad@shipfed.ca
Minotti Broad, Director, Finance & Administration, 514-849-2325 232
mminotti@shipfed.ca
Finances: *Funding Sources:* International shipping
Staff: 8 staff member(s)
Membership: 111; *Member Profile:* Member companies involved in all sectors of the shipping industry; *Committees:* Customs; Dangerous Goods; EDI; Immigration; Pilotage; Railways; Tanker Safety
Activities: To protect members in all matters affecting the operation of shipping from & to Eastern Canada, the St. Lawrence River, the Great Lakes & Arctic ports; Areas of concern include pilotage, pollution, navigation aids, port operations, port charges & federal government legislation & regulation

Shipyard General Workers' Federation of British Columbia (CLC) / Fédération des ouvriers des chantiers navals de la Colombie-Britannique (CTC)
#130, 111 Victoria Dr., Vancouver BC V5L 4C4
Tel: 604-254-8204; *Fax:* 604-254-7447
office@bcshipyardworkers.com
www.bcshipyardworkers.com
Overview: A medium-sized provincial organization
Affiliation(s): Machinists, Fitters & Helpers Industrial Union #3, Marine Workers & Boilerworkers' Industrial Union #1, Shipwrights, Joiners & Caulkers' Industrial Union #9
Chief Officer(s): George MacPherson, President
Quentin Del Vecchio, General Secretary
Membership: 1,100 + 3 locals

Société des traversiers du Québec (STQ)
Bureau de la traverse, 250, rue Saint-Paul, Québec QC G1K 9K9
Tél: 418-643-2019; *Téléc:* 418-643-7308
Ligne sans frais: 877-787-7483
stq@traversiers.gouv.qc.ca
www.traversiers.com
Aperçu: *Dimension:* petite; *Envergure:* provinciale; fondée en 1971
Description: Contribuer à la mobilité des personnes et des marchandises en assurant des services de transport maritime de qualité, sécuritaires et fiables, favorisant ainsi l'essor social, économique et touristique du Québec
Membre(s) du bureau directeur: Pierre-Paul Pharand, Présidente
Finances: *Budget de fonctionnement annuel:* Plus de $5 Million
Membre: 100-499

Sydney & Louisburg Railway Historical Society / Le Musée de chemin de fer de Sydney à Louisbourg
S&L, 7330 Main St., Louisbourg NS B1C 1P5

Tel: 902-733-2720

Also Known As: S&L Museum
Overview: A small local organization founded in 1973
Description: To commemorate the history of the S&L Railway by preserving & displaying surviving artifacts & documents; To commemorate the people who worked for the S&L Railway; To explain the local & commercial history of the area which relates to the S&L Railway; To explain & commemorate the general themes of railway & transportation history & technology; *Member of:* Canadian Museums Association; Federation of Nova Scotia Heritage
Affiliation(s): Nova Scotia Museum
Chief Officer(s): William Bussey, President
Jean Bagnell, Secretary
Margie Cameron, Treasurer
Eugene Magee, Curator
Membership: 250
Activities: Newsletter; Annual reunion the second Sunday in Septmeber; *Library:* Sydney & Louisburg Railway Historical Society Resource Centre (Open to Public) by appointment

Teamsters Canada (TC)
#400, 1750, rue Maurice-Gauvin, Laval QC H7S 1Z5

Tel: 450-682-5521; Fax: 450-681-2244
Toll-Free: 866-888-6466
info@teamsters.ca
teamsterscanada.org
www.instagram.com/teamsterscanada
www.facebook.com/TeamstersCanada
twitter.com/TeamstersCanada

Overview: A large national charitable organization founded in 1976
Description: To create equality, security & fair opportunities in the workplace
Affiliation(s): International Brotherhood of Teamsters
Chief Officer(s): François Laporte, President
Finances: *Annual Operating Budget:* Greater than $5 Million
Staff: 24 staff member(s)
Membership: 125,000; *Fees:* Schedule available; *Member Profile:* Individuals in the transportation, production, hospitality & service industries; *Committees:* Youth

Teamsters Canada Rail Conference (TCRC) / Conference ferroviaire de Teamsters Canada (CFTC)
#1510, 130 Albert St., Ottawa ON K1P 5G4

Tel: 613-235-1828; Fax: 613-235-1069
info@teamstersrail.ca
www.teamstersrail.ca
www.instagram.com/teamstersrail
www.facebook.com/TeamstersRail
twitter.com/TeamstersRail

Previous Name: Brotherhood of Locomotive Engineers
Overview: A medium-sized national organization
Description: To act as a collective bargaining partner for rail industry workers in Canada
Chief Officer(s): Lyndon Isaak, President
Dave McCulloch, Vice-President
Membership: 16,000 in 21 divisions; *Fees:* $15; *Member Profile:* Workers in the rail industry in Canada
Activities: *Library:* Teamsters Canada Rail Conference Library (Open to Public)

Toronto Transportation Society (TTS)
PO Box 5187, Stn. A, Toronto ON M5W 1N5
Overview: A small local organization founded in 1973
Description: To provide an association for persons interested in transportation by land, sea & air & to afford members facilities for discussion & exchange concerning these methods of transportation
Finances: *Funding Sources:* Membership fees
Fees: $30 Canadians; US$35 USA; $45-$50 international; *Member Profile:* Transportation enthusiasts with an interest in buses, streetcars, railways & subways
Activities: Hosting monthly meetings; Organizing a Memorabilia Night, featuring an auction of transit collections; Arranging charters using unique transit vehicles

Traffic Injury Research Foundation (TIRF) / Fondation de recherches sur les blessures de la route
#200, 171 Nepean St., Ottawa ON K2P 0B4

Tel: 613-238-5235; Fax: 613-238-5292
Toll-Free: 877-238-5235
tirf@tirf.ca
tirf.ca
www.linkedin.com/company/traffic-injury-research-foundation-tirf
www.facebook.com/tirfcanada
twitter.com/tirfcanada

Overview: A medium-sized national charitable organization founded in 1964
Description: To reduce traffic related deaths & injuries, through the design, promotion & implementation of prevention programs & policies based on sound research
Chief Officer(s): Robyn D. Robertson, President & CEO
Ward Vanlaar, Chief Operating Officer
Karen Bowman, Director, Marketing & Communications
Mark Saunders, Director, Finance
Finances: *Annual Operating Budget:* $500,000-$1.5 Million; *Funding Sources:* Memberships; donations
Staff: 11 staff member(s)
Activities: Projects include: Distracted Driving; Drinking & Driving; Trends & Statistics; Trucks; Young & Novice Drivers; *Speaker Service:* Yes *Library:* Resource Centre (Open to Public)

Transport Action Canada
PO Box 858, Stn. B, #303, 211 Bronson Ave., Ottawa ON K1P 5P9

Tel: 613-594-3290; Fax: 613-594-3271
info@transport-action.ca
www.transport-action.ca
www.facebook.com/TransportAction
twitter.com/transportaction

Previous Name: Transport 2000 Canada
Overview: A large national charitable organization founded in 1977
Description: To seek sound public transportation policies, practices & services, especially modernized, intercity passenger rail & urban transit option; To inform Canadians of the need for a coherent national transport policy that recognizes conservation of resources must be a priority & access to good public transportation is a right of all Canadians; To press for the coordination of all transport services for the benefit of users; To maximize the use of the energy-efficient rail & marine modes for the shipment of freight
Affiliation(s): Transport 2000 International
Chief Officer(s): Terence Johnson, President
Finances: *Annual Operating Budget:* $50,000-$100,000; *Funding Sources:* Donations
Staff: 15 volunteer(s)
Membership: 1,500; *Fees:* $30
Activities: Research, public education & advocacy, representation of the consumer interests before federal, provincial, municipal public hearings & regulatory bodies, direction of consumer complaints to public carriers; *Speaker Service:* Yes *Library:* Transport Action Canada Library (Open to Public)

Transportation Association of Canada (TAC) / Association des transports du Canada (ATC)
#401, 1111 Prince of Wales Dr., Ottawa ON K2C 3T2

Tel: 613-736-1350; Fax: 613-736-1395
secretariat@tac-atc.ca
www.tac-atc.ca
www.linkedin.com/company/transportation-association-of-canada
www.facebook.com/tac2014atc
twitter.com/TAC_TranspAssn

Previous Name: Canadian Good Roads Association; Roads & Transportation Association of Canada
Overview: A large national organization founded in 1914
Description: To promote the provision of safe, efficient, effective & environmentally sustainable transportation services in support of Canada's social & economic goals; To act as a neutral forum for the discussion of transportation issues & matters; To act as a technical focus in the highway transportation area
Chief Officer(s): Sarah Wells, Executive Director, 613-736-1350 229
swells@tac-atc.ca
Erica Andersen, Director, Member Services & Communications, 613-736-1350 235
eandersen@tac-atc.ca
Geoff Noxon, Director, Technical Programs, 613-736-1350 228
gnoxon@tac-atc.ca
Janet Wlodarczyk, Director, Finance & Administration, 613-736-1350 254
mperuvemba@tac-atc.ca
Finances: *Annual Operating Budget:* Greater than $5 Million; *Funding Sources:* Membership dues
Staff: 17 staff member(s); 800 volunteer(s)
Membership: 500+ corporate; *Fees:* Schedule available; *Member Profile:* Federal, provincial & territorial departments of transportation; municipalities; private sector firms; academic institutions & associations; *Committees:* Chief Engineers' Council; Education & Human Resources Development Council; Environment Council; Integrated Committee on Climate Change; Operating Information; Urban Transportation Council; World Road Association; Small Municipalities Task Force

Activities: *Library:* Transportation Information Services by appointment

Truck Training Schools Association of Ontario Inc. (TTSAO)
1 Hunter St. East, #G100, Hamilton ON L8N 3W1

Fax: 905-704-1329
Toll-Free: 866-475-9436
ttsao@ttsao.com
ttsao.com
www.facebook.com/TTSAOontario
twitter.com/TTSAOontario

Overview: A small provincial licensing organization founded in 1992
Description: To provide the trucking industry with the highest quality driver training programs for entry level individuals that earn & maintain public confidence, adhering to sound & ethical business practices
Affiliation(s): Ontario Trucking Association; Ministry of Education, Ministry of Transportation
Finances: *Annual Operating Budget:* $100,000-$250,000
Staff: 7 staff member(s)
Membership: 75; *Fees:* Schedule available; *Member Profile:* Institutions that provide truck training services within Ontario, Canada
Activities: *Internships:* Yes

Truckers Association of Nova Scotia (TANS)
PO Box 556, #301, 8 Old Enfield Rd., Enfield NS B2T 1C9

Tel: 902-236-2344; Fax: 902-236-2345
contact@tans.ca
www.tans.ca
www.facebook.com/officialTANS
twitter.com/TruckersAssocNS

Overview: A medium-sized provincial organization founded in 1968
Description: To promote all matters aiding in the development & improvement of the trucking industry & the allied trades in Nova Scotia, including social, recreational, benevolent, educational & charitable activities; To be the main proponent in gaining access to the provincial haul rates & beneficial changes to the contract specifications used by the contractors; *Member of:* The Transportation Sector of Voluntary Planning
Affiliation(s): Atlantic Provinces Trucking Association of Nova Scotia
Chief Officer(s): David MacKenzie, Chair, 902-295-0442, Fax: 902-622-1389
kilkare@gmail.com
Membership: 500; *Fees:* $150 associate; $300 full; *Member Profile:* Individuals involved in the trucking industry in Nova Scotia
Activities: Makes presentations to government & other regulatory bodies in relation to the economic welfare of the trucking industry

Trucking Human Resources Canada (THRC)
#104, 720 Belfast Rd., Ottawa ON K1G 0Z5

Tel: 613-244-4800
theteam@truckinghr.com
truckinghr.com
www.instagram.com/truckinghr
www.linkedin.com/company/trucking-hr-canada
twitter.com/truckinghr

Also Known As: Trucking HR Canada
Overview: A medium-sized national organization
Description: To promote the provision of safe, secure, efficient & professional trucking services in Canada
Affiliation(s): CCA Truck Driver Training Ltd.; Capilano Truck Driver Training Institute; JVI Provincial Transportation & Safety Academy; Mountain Transport Institute Ltd.; Red Deer College; SK Driver Training Ltd.; Wheels On Ltd. / Training & Driver Training
Chief Officer(s): Angela Splinter, Chief Executive Officer
Activities: Conducting research; Training; Offering advice; Liaising with industry members

Ultralight Pilots Association of Canada (UPAC) / Association canadienne des pilotes d'avions ultra-légers
907289 Township Rd. 12, RR#4, Bright ON N0J 1B0

Tel: 519-684-7628
info@upac.ca
upac.ca
www.facebook.com/groups/155979254430741

Merged from: Ultralight Aircraft Association of Canada (UAAC) & Microlight Owners and Pilots of Canada (MOPAC)
Overview: A small national organization founded in 1986
Description: To promote ultralight aviation in Canada & act as a representative voice for ultralight pilots in discussions with the federal government
Chief Officer(s): Kathy Lubitz, President
klubitz@upac.ca

Finances: *Annual Operating Budget:* Less than $50,000; *Funding Sources:* Membership fees
Staff: 10 volunteer(s)
Membership: 500+; *Fees:* $50 individual; $70 family; *Member Profile:* Interest in ultralight aviaton
Activities: Video library for members; *Library:* Ultralight Pilots Association of Canada Video Library (Open to Public)

Union of Canadian Transportation Employees (UCTE) / Union canadienne des employés des transports (UCET)
#702, 233 Gilmour St., Ottawa ON K2P 0P2
Tel: 613-238-4003; *Fax:* 613-236-0379
Toll-Free: 888-542-1850
www.ucte.com
www.instagram.com/ucteucet
www.facebook.com/UCTEUCET
twitter.com/UCTEUCET
Overview: A medium-sized national organization
Description: To represent members working in the public & private sectors of the Canadian transportation industry (ports, airports, NAV Canada, pilotage authorities, transportation companies, canals, the Dept. of Transport, lighthouses, ships & Canadian Coast Guard bases)
Affiliation(s): Public Service Alliance of Canada
Chief Officer(s): Dave Clark, National President
clarkd@psac-afpc.com
Teresa Eschuk, National Vice-President
eschukt@psac-afpc.com
Membership: 9,635; *Member Profile:* Individuals in the public & private sectors of the Canadian transportation industry, inclduing ports, airports, NAV Canada, pilotage authorities, transportation companies, canals, the Dept. of Transport, lighthouses, ships & Canadian Coast Guard bases

University of Toronto Institute for Aerospace Studies
Faculty of Applied Science & Engineering, 4925 Dufferin St., Toronto ON M3H 5T6
Tel: 416-667-7700; *Fax:* 416-667-7799
www.utias.utoronto.ca
twitter.com/UTIAS
Overview: A medium-sized national organization founded in 1949
Description: UTIAS is a graduate studies & research institute, forming part of the faculty of Applied Science & Engineering at the University of Toronto
Affiliation(s): Canadian Aeronautics & Space Institute; Institute for Space & Terrestrial Science; Canadian Space Agency; Intelligent Sensing for Innovative Structures Canada
Chief Officer(s): C.J. Damaren, Director, 416-667-7704, Fax: 416-667-7799
damaren@utias.utoronto.ca
P. Lavoie, Associate Director, Research, 416-667-7716, Fax: 476-667-7799
lavoie@utias.utoronto.ca
C.A. Steeves, Associate Director, Graduate Studies, 416-667-7710, Fax: 416-667-7799
csteeves@utias.utoronto.ca
Membership: 68
Activities: *Library:* University of Toronto Institute for Aerospace Studies Library

Used Car Dealers Association of Ontario (UCDA)
230 Norseman St., Toronto ON M8X 6A2
Tel: 416-231-2600; *Fax:* 416-232-0775
Toll-Free: 800-268-2598
web@ucda.org
www.ucda.org
Overview: A medium-sized provincial organization founded in 1984
Description: To enhance the image of the used car dealing industry through member education, consumer awareness of the benefits members provide & mediation of consumer-dealer disputes
Affiliation(s): International Auto Theft Investigators; National Independent Automobile Dealers Association
Chief Officer(s): Steve Peck, President
Finances: *Annual Operating Budget:* $1.5 Million-$3 Million; *Funding Sources:* Membership dues; Services
Staff: 19 staff member(s)
Membership: 4,900+; *Fees:* $200; *Member Profile:* Registered motor vehicle dealers engaging in used vehicle sales in Ontario
Activities: *Speaker Service:* Yes

Van Horne Institute for International Transportation & Regulatory Affairs
#420, 715 - 5th Ave. SW, Calgary AB T2P 2X6
Tel: 587-430-0291
info@vanhorneinstitute.com
www.vanhorne.info
Overview: A small international organization founded in 1991

Description: To contribute to public policy development & education in the areas of transportation & regulated industries
Affiliation(s): University of Calgary; University of Alberta; Southern Alberta Institute of Technology
Finances: *Annual Operating Budget:* Less than $50,000; *Funding Sources:* Private sector
Staff: 4 staff member(s)
Membership: 60; *Member Profile:* Government; industry; education; *Committees:* Centre for Transportation; Centre for Regulatory Affairs; Centre for Innovation & Communication
Activities: Transporation research & education; programs to assist in improving the efficiency & equity of transportation & regulated industries; *Speaker Service:* Yes; *Rents Mailing List:* Yes *Library:* The Van Horne Institute Library (Open to Public)

Via Prévention
#301, 6455, boul Jean-Talon est, Montréal QC H1S 3E8
Tél: 514-955-0454; *Téléc:* 514-955-0449
Ligne sans frais: 800-361-8906
info@viaprevention.com
www.viaprevention.com

www.facebook.com/viaprevention
twitter.com/ViaPrevention
Aperçu: *Dimension:* moyenne; *Envergure:* provinciale; fondée en 1982
Description: Pour protéger les personnes qui travaillent dans les transports, de l'Entreposage et de l'environnement en leur donnant une formation en santé et sécurité routière
Membre(s) du bureau directeur: Isabelle Lessard, Directrice générale
isabelle.lessard@viaprevention.com

Vintage Locomotive Society Inc.
c/o The Vintage Locomotive Society Inc., PO Box 33021, RPO Polo Park, Winnipeg MB R3G 3N4
Tel: 204-832-5259; *Fax:* 866-751-2348
info@pdcrailway.com
www.pdcrailway.com
www.facebook.com/194984377257515
Also Known As: Prairie Dog Central Steam Train
Overview: A small local charitable organization founded in 1968
Description: To collect, restore & maintain steam locomotives & rolling stock of the early twentieth-century; To provide a source of historical information relating to the origin & past operation of acquired equipment & buildings
Chief Officer(s): Paul Newsome, General Manager
Finances: *Annual Operating Budget:* $250,000-$500,000
Staff: 170 volunteer(s)
Activities: *Speaker Service:* Yes

West Coast Railway Association (WCRA)
PO Box 2387, Squamish BC V8B 0B6
Tel: 604-898-9336
info@wcra.org
wcra.org
www.instagram.com/wcrhp
www.facebook.com/WCRHP
twitter.com/wcrhp
Overview: A small local charitable organization founded in 1961
Description: To collect, preserve, restore, operate & exhibit artifacts relating to the history of railways, especially those of BC; The West Coast Railway Heritage Park in Squamish, BC develops educational exhibits on railway heritage for all age groups; *Member of:* Association of Rail Museums; Tourist Railroad Association
Finances: *Annual Operating Budget:* $500,000-$1.5 Million; *Funding Sources:* Tours; government grants; donations; fundraising; foundation
Staff: 12 staff member(s); 150 volunteer(s)
Membership: 1500; *Fees:* Schedule available; *Member Profile:* Interest in railways past & present; *Committees:* Museum; Tours; Collections; Motive Power; Children; Education
Activities: Develops & operates West Coast Railway Heritage Park in Squamish, BC;Houses a collection of 60+ locomotives, freight & passenger cars; Operates tour program, community events & a 'Polar Express' ride; *Speaker Service:* Yes *Library:* West Coast Railway Association Archives (Open to Public) by appointment

Western Transportation Advisory Council (WESTAC)
#401, 899 Pender St. West, Vancouver BC V6C 3B2
Tel: 604-687-8691; *Fax:* 604-687-8751
infoservices@westac.com
www.westac.com
www.linkedin.com/company/westerntransportationadvisorycouncil
twitter.com/WESTAC
Overview: A small local organization founded in 1973
Description: To advance Western Canadian economy through the improvement of the region's transportation systems

Chief Officer(s): Lisa Baratta, Interim President
lbaratta@westac.com
Marzia Rizvi, Manager, Program Development & Communications
mrizvi@westac.com
Finances: *Annual Operating Budget:* $500,000-$1.5 Million; *Funding Sources:* Membership fees; project fees; professional services fees
Staff: 3 staff member(s)
Membership: 52 corporate; *Fees:* Schedule available; *Member Profile:* Carriers; shippers; ports & terminals; labour unions; government
Activities: *Library:* Westenr Transportation Advisory Council Library by appointment

Companies

Airline Companies

Aer Lingus
Tel: 516-622-4226
www.flyaerlingus.com
Sean Doyle, Chief Executive Officer

Aerolineas Argentinas
Sales Office, Montréal, QC
Toll-Free: 800-688-0008
reserve@us.aerolineas.aero
www.aerolineas.com.ar
Pablo Ceriani, Chief Executive Officer

Air Canada
7373, boul Côte-Vertu ouest, Montréal, QC H4S 1Z3
Tél: 514-422-5000; *Ligne sans frais:* 888-247-2262
www.aircanada.ca
Ticker Symbol: AC / TSX
Profile: Founded in 1937, Air Canada is the country's largest domestic & international airline, serving over 200 airports on six continents. Air Canada serves over 48 million customers annually.
Calin Rovinescu, President & CEO
Michael Rousseau, Chief Financial Officer & Deputy CEO
Lucie Guillemette, Executive Vice-President & Chief Commercial Officer
Craig Landry, Executive Vice-President, Operations

Air Creebec
18 Nottaway St., Waskaganish, QC J0M 1R0
Tél: 819-895-8355; *Ligne sans frais:* 800-567-6567
www.aircreebec.ca
Profile: Air Creebec is 100% owned by the Cree Nation & employs over 400 people, about one-third of whom are First Nations. The company operates scheduled flights, freight & charter services to over 15 destinations in Québec & Ontario.
Matthew Happyjack, President & CEO

Air France
#1510, 2000, rue Mansfield, Montreal, QC H3A 3A3
Tel: 514-847-1106; *Toll-Free:* 800-667-2747
www.airfrance.ca
Anne Rigail, Group CEO

Air India Ltd.
#218, 5955 Airport Rd., Mississauga, ON L4V 1R9
Toll-Free: 800-625-6424
www.airindia.in
Shri Rajiv Bansal, Chair & Managing Director

Air Nootka
PO Box 19, 800 Mill Rd., Gold River, BC V0P 1G0
Tel: 250-283-2255; *Fax:* 250-283-2256
Toll-Free: 877-795-2255
info@airnootka.com
www.airnootka.com
Profile: Air Nootka is a floatplane operation based out of Gold River, British Columbia. It provides service to all of Vancouver Island, including Victoria, Nanaimo, Comox, Campbell River & Kyuquot, as well as Vancouver.
Scott Carlsen, Head of Operations

Air North Airlines
150 Condor Rd., Whitehorse, YK Y1A 6E6
Tel: 867-668-2228; *Fax:* 867-393-4601
Toll-Free: 800-661-0407
customerservice@flyairnorth.com
www.flyairnorth.com
Profile: Service connects to Vancouver, Calgary & Edmonton; charter & cargo services are also offered.

Air Saint-Pierre
Halifax Stanfield International Airport, PO Box 1660, 1 Bell Blvd., Enfield, NS B2T 1K2

Tel: 902-873-3566; *Fax:* 902-873-3567
Toll-Free: 877-277-7765
halifax@airsaintpierre.com
www.airsaintpierre.com

Profile: Air St-Pierre is a French airline based in Saint-Pierre & Miquelon. The company operates services between the islands of Saint-Pierre & Miquelon-Langlade & to Canada.
Benoit Olano, President

Air Transat
Parent: Transat A.T. Inc.
#600, 300, rue Léo-Pariseau, Montréal, QC H2X 4C2

Tel: 514-987-1616; *Toll-Free:* 800-387-2672
www.transat.com

Profile: Air Transat specializes in both scheduled & charter flights from Canada to vacation destinations. The airline offers flights, vacation packages & hotel stays to 60 destinations in 26 countries, & has 5000 employees.
Jean-Marc Eustache, Co-Founder, President & CEO, Transat A.T. Inc.

Alitalia
Pearson International Airport, PO Box 188, Mississauga, ON L5P 1B1

Fax: 647-317-6827
Toll-Free: 800-361-8336
customer.relationsCA@alitalia.it
www.alitalia.ca

American Airlines Inc. / AA
Fort Worth Airport, PO Box 619616, Dallas, TX

Toll-Free: 800-433-7300
www.aa.com

W. Douglas Parker, Chair & CEO
Robert D. Isom, Jr., President

Austrian Airlines
c/o Pearson International Airport, Mississauga, ON L5P 1A2

Toll-Free: 800-843-0002
www.austrian.com

Alexis von Hoensbroech, Chief Executive Officer

British Airways
c/o British Airways Customer Relations, USA, PO Box 300686, Jamaica, NY

Toll-Free: 800-247-9297
americas.communications@ba.com
www.britishairways.com

Alex Cruz, Chair & CEO

Canadian North
Formerly: First Air
20 Cope Dr., Kanata, ON K2M 2V8

Tel: 613-254-6200; *Fax:* 613-254-6398
Toll-Free: 800-267-1247
contact@canadiannorth.com
canadiannorth.com

Profile: Canadian North, merged from Canadian North & First Air in 2019, offers scheduled service to 25 communities in Nunavut, the NWT & Nunavik. The company 100% Inuit-owned.
Chris Avery, President & CEO
Aaron Speer, Vice-President, Flight Operations

Central Mountain Air Ltd. / CMA
Formerly: Central Mountain International
PO Box 998, 6431 Airport Rd., Smithers, BC V0J 2N0

Tel: 250-877-5000; *Fax:* 250-874-3744
Toll-Free: 888-865-8585
info@flycma.com
www.flycma.com

Profile: Central Mountain Air was established in 1987 & offers scheduled & charter flights to over 18 communities in British Columbia & Alberta.
Douglas McCrea, President

CHC Helicopter
4740 Agar Dr., Richmond, BC V7B 1A3

Tel: 604-276-7500
info@chcheli.com
www.chcheli.com
Ticker Symbol: FLY / TSX

Profile: Founded in 1947, CHC offers the following: nonscheduled & scheduled air transportation; airports, flying fields & airport terminal services; & vocational schools.
Dave Balevic, Interim President & CEO

Cougar Helicopters Inc.
Parent: VIH Aviation Group
10 Jetstream Ave., St. John's, NL A1A 0R7

Tel: 709-758-4800
info@cougar.ca
www.cougar.ca

Profile: Founded in 1984, the company's main service is flying oil rig workers to & from their offshore locations, with search & rescue as a secondary service provided to offshore operators.
Ken Norie, President & CEO

Czech Airlines
#830, 5915 Airport Rd., Mississauga, ON L4V 1T1

Fax: 416-972-0185
Toll-Free: 855-359-2932
www.csa.cz

El Al Israel Airlines Ltd.
#803, 1000 Finch Ave. West, Toronto, ON M3J 2V5

Tel: 416-967-4222; *Fax:* 416-967-1643
reservations@elalcanada.com
www.elal.com

Gonen Usishkin, Chief Executive Officer

Fast Air Ltd.
80 Hangar Line Rd., Winnipeg, MB R3J 3Y7

Tel: 204-982-7240; *Fax:* 204-783-2483
Toll-Free: 888-372-3780
info@flyfastair.com
flyfastair.com

Profile: Fast Air operates from a private business-class terminal at the Winnipeg James Armstrong Richardson International Airport, & provides aircraft charter, air ambulance & aircraft management services.
Dylan Fast, President & CEO

Finnair
PO Box 403, Finnair

Toll-Free: 800-950-5000
www.finnair.com

Topi Manner, Chief Executive Officer

Harbour Air Ltd.
4760 Inglis Dr., Richmond, BC V7B 1W4

Tel: 604-274-1277; *Toll-Free:* 800-665-0212
www.harbourair.com

Profile: Harbour Air operates Harbour Air Seaplanes & West Coast Air, companies providing sea plane service connecting Vancouver, Victoria, Nanaimo, South Vancouver, Sechelt, Comox & the Gulf Islands. Adventure tours & charter services are also offered.
Greg McDougall, Chief Executive Officer

Helijet International Inc.
c/o Vancouver International Airport, 5911 Airport Rd. South, Richmond, BC V7B 1B5

Tel: 604-273-4688
helijet.com
Ticker Symbol: HJI / TSX-V

Profile: Helijet launched Canada's first scheduled helicopter service in 1986. The company has operations in Richmond, Vancouver, Victoria, Nanaimo, Prince Rupert & Haida Gwaii. Helijet has a fleet of medium & large helicopters, as well as a medically-equipped & corporate Learjet.
Daniel Sitnam, President & CEO
dsitnam@helijet.com

Icelandair
1900 Crown Colony Dr., Quincy, MA 02169

Toll-Free: 800-223-5500
www.icelandair.com

Bogi Nils Bogason, Chief Executive Officer

Japan Airlines Co., Ltd.
c/o Vancouver International Airport, Richmond, BC V7B 1X8

Toll-Free: 800-525-3663
www.jal.co.jp/arl/en

Yoshiharu Ueki, President

Jazz Aviation LP
Formerly: Air Canada Jazz
Parent: Chorus Aviation Inc.
3 Spectacle Lake Dr., Dartmouth, NS B3B 1W8

Tel: 902-873-5000; *Fax:* 902-873-2098
flyjazz.ca

Profile: The core of Jazz's business is the Air Canada Express brand, which operates under a commercial agreement with Air Canada. The airline operates approximately 660 daily flights to 89 locations across North America.
Randolph deGooyer, President

Keewatin Air LP
50 Morberg Way, Winnipeg, MB R3H 0A4

Tel: 204-888-0100; *Fax:* 204-888-3300
Toll-Free: 877-879-8477
www.kivalliqair.com

Profile: Keewatin Air's primary function is medical air travel, although they also offer charter & scheduled airline services to Nunavut & northern Manitoba.
Wayne McLeod, President & CEO
wmcleod@keewatinair.ca
Jena Steg, Director, Finance
jsteg@keewatinair.ca

KF Cargo
Parent: KF Aerospace
5655 Airport Way, Kelowna, BC V1V 1S1

Tel: 250-491-5500
www.kfaero.ca/cargo-operations

Profile: KF Cargo services Purolator Courier & Canada Post on the BC Feeder Network.

KLM Royal Dutch Airlines
Formerly: Northwest/KLM Royal Dutch Airlines
ON

Toll-Free: 800-375-8723
www.klm.com

Pieter Elbers, President & CEO

Korean Air
1813 Wilshire Blvd., Los Angeles, CA 90057

Toll-Free: 800-438-5000
www.koreanair.com

Cho Won-tae, Chair & CEO

LATAM Airlines
Formerly: LAN Airlines S.A.
Pearson International Airport, 6301 Silver Dart Dr., Mississauga, ON L5P 1B2

Toll-Free: 866-435-9526
www.latam.com

Roberto Alvo, Chief Executive Officer

LOT Polish Airlines
Pearson International Airport, Terminal 1, 3111 Convair Dr., Mississauga, ON L5P 1B2

Tel: 416-479-9524
www.lot.com

Rafal Milczarski, President & CEO

Lufthansa German Airlines
c/o Lufthansa InTouch, 1900 Fisher Dr., Peterborough, ON K9J 6X6

Tel: 705-872-3000; *Toll-Free:* 800-563-5954
customer.relations@lufthansa.com
www.lufthansa.com

Carsten Spohr, Chair & CEO

Northern Thunderbird Air Inc.
#101, 4245 Hangar Rd., Prince George, BC V2N 4M6

Tel: 250-963-9611; *Fax:* 250-963-8422
Toll-Free: 800-963-9611
www.ntair.ca

Olympic Air
c/o Athens International Airport

www.olympicair.com

Pacific Coastal Airlines
4980 Cowley Cres., Richmond, BC V7B 1C1

Tel: 604-273-8666; *Fax:* 604-273-6864
Toll-Free: 800-663-2872
reserve@pacificcoastal.com
www.pacificcoastal.com

Profile: Pacific Coastal Airlines provides scheduled, charter & cargo services to 16 airports, with connections to over 50 destinations in BC. The company employs over 300 people across 14 bases.
Daryl Smith, CEO & Founder
Quentin Smith, President

PIA Pakistan International Airlines
#620, 56 Aberfoyle Cres., Toronto, ON M8X 2W4

Tel: 416-972-6480; *Fax:* 416-926-0507
care@piac.aero
www.piac.com.pk

Arshad Malik, Chief Executive Officer

Royal Jordanian
Pierre Elliot Trudeau Airport, #441, 975, boul Roméo-Vachon Nord, Dorval, QC H4Y 1H1

Tél: 514-631-2403; *Téléc:* 514-631-9859
www.rj.com

Stefan Pichler, Chief Executive Officer

Skyservice Airlines Inc.
6120 Midfield Rd., Mississauga, ON L4W 2P7
Tel: 905-677-3000; *Fax:* 905-677-2747
Toll-Free: 888-759-7591
yyzcsr@skyservice.com
skyservice.com
Profile: Founded in 1986, Skyservice offers business aviation services like charter services, aircraft management, aircraft sales & aircraft maintenance.
Emlyn David, President & CEO
Mirjana Bosnic, Director, Human Resources

Swiss International Air Lines
1555, rue Peel, Montréal, H3A 1T5
Toll-Free: 877-359-7947
www.swiss.com

Thomas Klühr, Chief Executive Officer

Top Aces Inc.
Formerly: Discovery Air Innovations
#201, 1675, rte Transcanadienne, Montréal, QC H9P 1J1
Tél: 514-694-5565; *Téléc:* 514-683-2639
Ligne sans frais: 866-694-5565
www.topaces.com
Profile: Top Aces Inc. is a provider of turnkey tactical airborne training.
Didier Toussaint, Chief Operating Officer

Trans North Helicopters
PO Box 8, 115 Range Rd., Whitehorse, YK Y1A 5X9
Tel: 867-668-2177; *Fax:* 867-668-3420
email@tntaheli.com
www.tntaheli.com

Transat A.T. Inc.
#600, 300, rue Léo-Pariseau, Montréal, QC H2X 4C2
Ligne sans frais: 800-387-2672
customerrelations@transat.com
www.transat.com
Ticker Symbol: TRZ.B / TSX
Profile: Integrated international tourism company specializing in holiday travel to 60 destinations in 25 countries.
Jean-Marc Eustache, Co-Founder, Chair, President & CEO
Jean-François Lemay, President & General Manager, Air Transat

United Airlines
Formerly: Continental Airlines
233 South Wacker Dr., Chicago, IL
Toll-Free: 800-864-8331
www.united.com

Oscar Munoz, President & CEO

VIH Aviation Group
1962 Canso Rd., North Saanich, BC V8L 5V5
Tel: 250-656-3987; *Fax:* 250-655-6839
Toll-Free: 866-844-4354
vih@vih.com
vih.com
Profile: VIH is a helicopter management company with operations in the following divisions: Cougar Helicopters; VIH Helicopters; VIH Aerospace; YYJ FBO Services; & VIH Execujet. VIH Helicopters Ltd. can be contacted at the Group head office address.
Ken Norie, President & CEO
Didier Moinier, Vice-President, Global Business Development

VIH Execujet Inc.
Parent: VIH Aviation Group
Victoria International Airport, #101, 1962 Canso Rd., North Saanich, BC V8L 5V5
Tel: 250-655-6844
charter@vih.com
www.vihexecujet.com
Profile: VIH Execujet operates executive-class jet charter services out of Victoria International Airport.
Jeff Wolfe, Operations Manager/Chief Pilot

WestJet Airlines Ltd.
22 Aerial Pl. NE, Calgary, AB T2E 3J1
Tel: 403-539-7594; *Fax:* 403-444-2604
Toll-Free: 888-937-8538
www.westjet.com
Profile: Founded in 1996, Westjet provides schedules & charter air service to over 100 destinations. Westjet is the second-largest Canadian air carrier, behind Air Canada, & the ninth-largest air carrier in North America.
Edward Sims, President & CEO
Jeffrey Martin, Executive Vice-President & COO
Harry Taylor, Chief Financial Officer & Executive Vice-President, Finance

Airport Authorities

Aéroport de Québec Inc. / ADQ
505, rue Principale, 2e étage, Québec, QC G2G 0J4
Tel: 418-640-3300; *Toll-Free:* 877-769-2700
www.aeroportdequebec.com
Profile: Aéroport de Québec Inc. is responsible for the operation of Jean Lesage International Airport in Québec City, which serves around 1.6 million passengers annually.
Stephan Poirier, President & CEO

Aéroports de Montréal / ADM
#1000, 800, place Leigh-Capreol, Montréal, QC H4Y 0A5
Toll-Free: 800-465-1213
www.admtl.com
Profile: Aéroports de Montréal is responsible for managing & operating the Montréal-Trudeau & Montréal-Mirabel international airports. Montréal-Trudeau serves around 18 million passengers annually, while Montréal-Mirabel is currently used only for cargo shipments, having lost its last passenger service in 2004.
Philippe Rainville, Président-directeur général

The Calgary Airport Authority
2000 Airport Rd. NE, Calgary, AB T2E 6W5
Tel: 403-735-1200; *Fax:* 403-735-1281
Toll-Free: 877-254-7427
www.yyc.com
Profile: The Calgary Airport Authority operates Calgary International Airport, which serves around 16 million passengers annually. Flights are offered to major cities in Canada, the USA, Mexico, the Caribbean, Europe & East Asia.
Robert Sartor, President & CEO

Charlottetown Airport Authority / CAA
#132, 250 Maple Hills Ave., Charlottetown, PE C1C 1N2
Tel: 902-566-7997; *Fax:* 902-566-7929
info@flyYYG.com
flyyyg.com
Profile: The Charlottetown Airport Authority operates & is financially responsible for the Charlottetown Airport, which provides flights to Montreal, Halifax, Toronto, New York & seasonal flights to Cuba & the Dominican Republic.
Doug Newson, Chief Executive Officer
dnewson@flyYYG.com

Edmonton Regional Airports Authority
Edmonton International Airport, #1, 1000 Airport Rd., Edmonton, AB T9E 0V3
Tel: 780-890-8382; *Toll-Free:* 800-268-7134
info@flyeia.com
flyeia.com
Profile: Edmonton Airports operates Edmonton International Airport, which offers flights to 50 destinations worldwide & serves around 8.2 million passengers annually.
Tom Ruth, President & CEO

Fredericton International Airport Authority Inc. / FIAA
Formerly: Greater Fredericton Airport Authority Inc.
#22, 2570 Rte. 102, Lincoln, NB E3B 9G1
Tel: 506-460-0920; *Fax:* 506-460-0938
yfcfredericton.ca
Profile: The Fredericton International Airport Authority operates Fredericton International Airport, which provides flights to Halifax, Montréal, Ottawa, Toronto & seasonal flights to Cuba & the Dominican Republic.
Johanne Gallant, President & CEO

Gander International Airport Authority Inc. / GIAA
PO Box 400, 1000 James Boul., Gander, NL A1V 1W8
Tel: 709-256-6677; *Fax:* 709-256-6725
www.ganderairport.com
Profile: The Gander International Airport Authority operates Gander International Airport, which provides flights to Toronto, Goose Bay, Sept-Iles, St. John's, Wabush, Halifax & Iqaluit. Charter flights are also available to the Dominican Republic.
Reg Wright, President & CEO

Greater London International Airport Authority / GLIAA
1750 Crumlin Rd., London, ON N5V 3B6
Tel: 519-452-4015; *Fax:* 519-453-6219
customerservice@flylondon.ca
flylondon.ca
Profile: The Greater London International Airport Authority operates London International Airport, which provides flights to Ottawa, Toronto, Montréal, Chicago, Calgary, Winnipeg & seasonal flights to Orlando, Mexico & Cuba.
Mike Seabrook, President & CEO

Greater Moncton International Airport Authority Inc. / GMIAA
Direction de l'Aéroport international du Grand Moncton Inc.
#12, 777 Aviation Ave., Dieppe, NB E1A 7Z5
Tel: 506-856-5444; *Fax:* 506-856-5431
admin@cyqm.ca
www.cyqm.ca
Profile: The Greater Moncton International Airport Authority operates Greater Moncton Roméo LeBlanc International Airport, which provides flights to Halifax, Montréal, Toronto, Ottawa, Hamilton & seasonal flights to Florida, Mexico, Cuba, the Dominican Republic & Jamaica.
Bernard LeBlanc, President & CEO
bleblanc@cyqm.ca

Greater Toronto Airports Authority / GTAA
Autorité aéroportuaire du Grand Toronto
Toronto Pearson International Airport, PO Box 6031, 3111 Convair Dr., Mississauga, ON L5P 1B2
Tel: 416-247-7678; *Toll-Free:* 866-207-1690
www.torontopearson.com/gtaa.aspx
Profile: The Greater Toronto Airports Authority operates Toronto Pearson International Airport, which provides flights to over 175 locations worldwide via 65 airlines, & serves around 49.5 million passengers annually, making it the busiest airport in Canada.
Deborah Flint, President & CEO

Halifax International Airport Authority / HIAA
Halifax Stanfield International Airport, 1 Bell Blvd., Enfield, NS B2T 1K2
Tel: 902-873-4422; *Fax:* 902-873-4750
info@hiaa.ca
halifaxstanfield.ca
Profile: The Halifax International Airport Authority operates Halifax Stanfield International Airport & provides flights to a number of national & international destinations.
Joyce Carter, President & CEO
joyce.carter@hiaa.ca

Ottawa International Airport Authority
Administration de l'aéroport international d'Ottawa
#2500, 1000 Airport Pkwy. Private, Ottawa, ON K1V 9B4
Tel: 613-248-2000
comments@yow.ca
yow.ca
Profile: The Ottawa International Airport Authority operates Ottawa Macdonald-Cartier International Airport, which offers flights to a number of national & international destinations.
Mark Laroche, President & CEO

Prince George Airport Authority Inc. / PGAA
#10, 4141 Airport Rd., Prince George, BC V2N 4M6
Tel: 250-963-2400
www.pgairport.ca
Profile: The Prince George Airport Authority operates Prince George Airport, which provides flights to locations in BC (such as Vancouver, Fort Nelson, Kamloops, Fort St. John, Terrace, Kelowna, Smithers & Williston Lake), as well as seasonal service to Mexico.
Gordon Duke, President & CEO
gduke@pgairport.ca

Regina Airport Authority Inc. / RAA
#1, 5201 Regina Ave., Regina, SK S4W 1B3
Tel: 306-761-7555
comments@yqr.ca
www.yqr.ca
Profile: The Regina Airport Authority operates Regina International Airport, which provides flights to Toronto, Calgary, Edmonton, Vancouver, Winnipeg, Montréal, Ottawa, Saskatoon, Minneapolis / St. Paul, Chicago, & seasonal flights to Las Vegas, Phoenix, Orlando, Mexico & the Caribbean.
James Bogusz, President & CEO

Saint John Airport Inc.
Aéroport de Saint John Inc.
4180 Loch Lomond Rd., Saint John, NB E2N 1L7
Tel: 506-638-5555
fly@saintjohnairport.com
www.saintjohnairport.com
Profile: Saint John Airport provides flights to Halifax, Montreal, Toronto, & seasonal flights to the Dominican Republic, Mexico, Cayo Santa Maria & Cuba.
Derrick Stanford, President & CEO

St. John's International Airport Authority Inc. / SJIAA

Airport Terminal Bldg., PO Box 1, 100 World Pkwy., St. John's, NL A1A 5T2

Tel: 709-758-8500; *Fax:* 709-758-8521
Toll-Free: 866-758-8581
stjohnsairport.com

Profile: The St. John's International Airport Authority operates St. John's International Airport, which provides flights to major destinations in Canada, as well as seasonal service to London, UK, & locations such as the Dominican Republic, Cuba & Mexico. Charter service to the Alberta Oil Sands is also available.
Peter Avery, President & CEO

Saskatoon Airport Authority / SAA

#1, 2625 Airport Dr., Saskatoon, SK S7L 7L1

Tel: 306-975-8900
info@skyxe.ca
skyxe.ca

Profile: The Saskatoon Airport Authority operates Saskatoon John G. Diefenbaker International Airport, which serves around 1.6 million passengers annually. Flights are offered to major Canadian destinations, with an emphasis on western Canada & locations in the USA.
Stephen Maybury, President & CEO

Thunder Bay International Airports Authority Inc. / TBIAA

#340, 100 Princess St., Thunder Bay, ON P7E 6S2

Tel: 807-473-2600; *Fax:* 807-475-9627
info@tbairport.on.ca
www.tbairport.on.ca

Profile: The Thunder Bay International Airports Authority operates Thunder Bay International Airport, which provides flights to major Canadian cities & Chicago, as well as seasonal service to Cuba & Mexico.
Ed Schmidtke, President & CEO

Vancouver International Airport Authority

Link Bldg., L5, 3211 Grant McConachie Way, Richmond, BC V7B 0A4

Tel: 604-207-7077
customercallcentre@yvr.ca
www.yvr.ca

Profile: The Vancouver International Airport Authority operates Vancouver International Airport, which serves around 24 million passengers annually, making it the second busiest airport in Canada (behind Toronto Pearson International Airport). Flights are available to major destinations in Canada & around the world.
Tamara Vrooman, President & CEO

Victoria Airport Authority / VAA

#201, 1640 Electra Blvd., Sidney, BC V8L 5V4

Tel: 250-953-7500; *Fax:* 250-953-7509
www.victoriaairport.com

Profile: The Victoria Airport Authority operates Victoria International Airport, which serves around 1.9 million passengers annually. Flights are provided to major cities in Canada, as well as cities such as Seattle & San Francisco in the continental USA & seasonal flights to Mexico & Hawaii.
Geoff Dickson, President & CEO

Winnipeg Airports Authority Inc. / WAA

2000 Wellington Ave., Winnipeg, MB R3H 1C2

Tel: 204-987-9402; *Fax:* 204-987-2732
www.waa.ca

Profile: The Winnipeg Airports Authority operates Winnipeg James Armstrong Richardson International Airport, which serves about 4.3 million passengers annually. Flights are offered to major cities Canada, the USA, the Caribbean & Mexico, as well as to many remote communities in Northern Manitoba, Northwestern Ontario & Nunavut.
Barry Rempel, President & CEO

Maritime Shipping

Admiral Marine Inc.

6127 Steeles Ave. West, Toronto, ON M9L 2V1

Tel: 416-792-8955; *Fax:* 888-635-0247
admiral@admiralmarine.ca
www.admiralmarine.ca

Profile: Canstar Ocean Line through Admiral Marine operates a regular break-bulk / conventional service from North America to Europe with transshipment via Antwerp to Eastern Europe, the Middle East & Africa. Canstar is a full-service transportation consulting company that ships containers, ro/ro, break-bulk & heavy lift cargo.

Algoma Central Corporation

#600, 63 Church St., St Catharines, ON L2R 3C4

Tel: 905-687-7888; *Fax:* 905-687-7840
inquiry@algonet.com
www.algonet.com
Ticker Symbol: ALC / TSX

Profile: Algoma Central Corporation is a Canadian-flag ship owner on the Great Lakes - St. Lawrence Waterway. The company owns both dry-bulk carriers & product tankers. As well as the operation of vessels, ship & diesel engine repair & fabrication are part of Algoma Central's operations. Algoma Central Corporation also owns Algoma Central Hotels & Algoma Central Properties Inc. These businesses own & manage commercial real estate properties in St. Catharines, Waterloo & Sault Ste. Marie.
Ken Bloch Soerensen, President & CEO

American President Lines Ltd. / APL

c/o American President Lines Ltd. North America, #300, 3501 Jamboree Rd., Newport Beach, CA

Toll-Free: 800-999-7733
www.apl.com

Profile: APL provides international container transportation services.
Stéphane Courquin, Chief Executive Officer

Anglo-Eastern Univan Group

Formerly: Anglo-Eastern Ship Management Ltd.
Anglo-Eastern Ship Management, #235, 6600, rte Transcanadienne, Montréal, QC H9R 4S2

Tél: 514-697-3091
www.angloeasterngroup.com

Profile: Anglo-Eastern is a ship management company. The company merged with Univan Group (Hong Kong) in 2015.

Atlantic Towing Limited / ATL

Parent: J.D. Irving, Limited
300 Union St., 2nd Fl., Saint John, NB E2L 4M3

Tel: 506-648-2750; *Fax:* 506-648-2752
www.atlantictowing.com

Profile: ATL provides marine towing services including harbour, coastal & offshore.
Jerry Wiseman, Chief Officer

Canada Steamship Lines Inc.

Parent: The CSL Group
759, rue du Square-Victoria, 6e étage, Montreal, QC H2Y 2J7

Tel: 514-982-3800; *Fax:* 514-982-3901
www.cslships.com

Profile: Canada Steamship Lines's fleet includes self-unloaders & gearless bulk carriers.

CMA CGM (Canada) Inc.

Parent: CMA CGM S.A.
#1330, 740, rue Notre-Dame, Montréal, QC H3C 3X6

Tel: 514-908-7001; *Fax:* 514-908-7142
cda.genmbox@usa.cma-cgm.com
www.cma-cgm.com/local/canada

Profile: CMA CGM provides container shipping & multimodal services.
Rodolphe Saadé, Chair & CEO

CSL Group Inc.

759, rue du Square-Victoria, 6e étage, Montréal, QC H2Y 2J7

Tel: 514-982-3800; *Fax:* 514-982-3801
www.cslships.com

Profile: Specializes in bulk transportation & self-loading technology.
Louis Martel, President & CEO
Allister Paterson, Executive Vice-President & Chief Commercial Officer
Stéphanie Aubourg, Vice-President, Human Resources

F.K. Warren Ltd.

PO Box 1117, Halifax, NS B3J 3X1

Tel: 902-423-8136; *Fax:* 902-429-1326
ops@fkwarren.ca
www.fkwarren.ca

Profile: F.K. Warren provides a range of Marine Agency Services at all ports throughout Atlantic Canada.
Carl Conrad, President
902-483-2611, colinconrad@fkwarren.ca

Fednav Group

Formerly: Fednav Limited
#3500, 1000, rue de la Gauchetière ouest, Montréal, QC H3B 4W5

Tel: 514-878-6500; *Toll-Free:* 800-678-4842
www.fednav.com

Profile: Deep sea foreign transportation of freight; Freight transportation on the Great Lakes-St.Lawrence Seaway; Marine cargo handling.

Paul Pathy, Chief Executive Officer
Lucie-Marie Gauthier, Vice-President, Talent Management

Groupe Desgagnés Inc.

21, rue Marché-Champlain, Québec, QC G1K 8Z8

Tél: 418-692-1000; *Téléc:* 418-692-6044
info@desgagnes.com
desgagnes.com

Profile: La flotte du Groupe Desgagnés comprend 14 navires et 1 barge, 6 navires pour le transport de marchandises en vrac générale et sec, 7 camions-citernes et une barge pour le transport de vracs liquides et 1 passager et fret aux navires desservant la rive Moyen et Bas du Nord.
Louis-Marie Beaulieu, Chef de la direction

Hapag-Lloyd (Canada) Inc.

Parent: Hapag-Lloyd AG
#440, 401 The West Mall, Toronto, ON M9C 5J5

Téléc: 877-893-4430
Ligne sans frais: 877-893-4421
www.hapag-lloyd.com

Profile: Hapag-Lloyd is an international shipping company with five headquarters in Hamburg, Piscataway, Valparaiso, Singapore & Dubai.
Rolf Habben Jansen, Chief Executive Officer

Holmes Maritime Inc.

1345 Hollis St., Halifax, NS B3J 1T8

Tel: 902-422-0400; *Fax:* 902-422-9439
info@holmesmaritime.com
www.holmesmaritime.com

Profile: Holmes Maritime Inc. is a privately owned Canadian headquartered in Halifax, Nova Scotia, providing port agency & logistics services to international ship owners & operators throughout eastern Canada & along the Great Lakes.
Louis M. Holmes, President

Kent Line Limited

Parent: J.D. Irving, Limited
PO Box 725, 1 Willet Ave., Saint John, NB E2L 4B4

Tel: 506-648-2779; *Fax:* 506-633-5490
agency@kentline.com
www.kentline.com

Profile: Kent Line provides maritime shipping services including bulk, project cargo & agency. The company mainly serves the forest products, steel, fertilizer, grain & construction industries.
Gordon Ferris, Director, Business Development
506-648-3119, ferris.gordon@kentline.com

Logistec Corporation

600, rue de la Gauchetiere ouest, 14e ét, Montréal, QC H2Y 1P5

Tel: 514-844-9381; *Toll-Free:* 888-844-9381
info@logistec.com
www.logistec.com
Ticker Symbol: LGT.B / TSX

Profile: Logistec Corporation & its subsidiaries serve the marine & industrial sectors. Cargo-handling services are offered at port terminals situated in eastern Canada, the United States & on the Great Lakes. Other services include agency services to foreign ship-owners & operators at Canadian ports, marine transportation services & on-site decontamination services.
Madeleine Paquin, President & CEO
Stéphane Blanchette, Vice-President, Human Resources

Marine Atlantic Inc.

Baine Johnston Centre, #302, 10 Fort William Pl., St. John's, NL A1C 1K4

Tel: 902-794-5771; *Toll-Free:* 800-897-2797
customer_relations@marine-atlantic.ca
www.marine-atlantic.ca

Profile: Deep sea domestic transportation of freight; Ferries; Various water transportation of passengers.
Murray Hupman, President & CEO

Montship Inc.

Parent: Trealmont Transport Inc.
#1000, 360, rue Saint-Jacques, Montreal, QC H2Y 1R2

Tél: 514-286-4646; *Téléc:* 514-286-4650
Ligne sans frais: 800-668-6850
www.montship.ca

Profile: Founded in 1925, Montship Maritime Inc. provides shipping services from its offices in Toronto, Montreal, Vancouver, Halifax & Stephenville.
D. Brian McDonald, President & CEO

Oceanex Inc.

Baine Johnston Centre, #701, 10 Fort William Pl., St. John's, NL A1C 1K4

Tel: 709-758-0382; *Fax:* 709-758-0360
bookings@oceanex.com
www.oceanex.com

Profile: Oceanex provides cost-effective pick-up, handling & delivery of any cargo, including full-load & LTL.
Sid Hynes, Executive Chair
Matthew Hynes, Executive Vice-President

Rigel Shipping Canada Inc.
PO Box 5151, Shediac, NB E4P 8T9
Tel: 506-533-9000; Fax: 506-533-9010
www.rigelcanada.com
Profile: The company provides marine transportation.
Brian Ritchie, President

Truck Freight International / TFI
Parent: Paterson GlobalFoods
#2200, 333 Main St., Winnipeg, MB R3C 4E2
Tel: 204-956-3450; Fax: 204-942-4758
Toll-Free: 888-421-4433
info@truck-freight.com
www.truck-freight.com
Profile: Freight transportation of grains across western Canada & the United States.

Upper Lakes Group Inc.
Bldg. 2, #900, 895 Don Mills Rd., Toronto, ON M3C 1W3
Tel: 416-920-7610
www.upperlakes.com
Profile: Upper Lakes Group specializes in moving, handling & storing wet & dry bulk commodities & containerized cargo in Canada & around the world.

Port Authorities

Administration Portuaire de Québec
Quebec Port Authority
PO Box 80 Haute-Ville, 150, rue Dalhousie, Québec, QC G1R 4M8
Tél: 418-648-3640; Téléc: 418-648-4160
marketing@portquebec.ca
www.portquebec.ca
Profile: Le Port de Québec entretient aujourd'hui des relations commerciales avec plus de 60 pays. Doté d'une intermodalité complète et de terminaux performants, 27 millions de tonnes de marchandises ont été manutentionnées en moyenne au cours des cinq dernières années.

Administration portuaire du Saguenay / APS
Saguenay Port Authority
6600, rue Quai-Marcel-Dionne, La Baie, QC G7B 3N9
Tél: 418-697-0250; Téléc: 418-697-0243
info@portsaguenay.ca
www.portsaguenay.ca
Profile: Le Port de Saguenay est une entreprise publique fédérale autonome constituée en vertu de la Loi maritime du Canada en 1999. Le Port de Saguenay possède et gère le terminal maritime de Grande-Anse qui est situé dans l'arrondissement La Baie à Ville de Saguenay.

Halifax Port Authority
Formerly: Halifax Port Corporation
1215 Marginal Rd., Halifax, NS B3J 2P6
Tel: 902-426-8222; Fax: 902-426-7335
www.portofhalifax.ca
Profile: The Port of Halifax handles over 1500 vessels & is one of Canada's top four container ports based on cargo volume. Facilities include container terminals, ocean terminals & the Halifax Grain Elevator.

Hamilton-Oshawa Port Authority / HOPA
Formerly: Hamilton Port Authority; Oshawa Port Authority
605 James St. North, 6th Fl., Hamilton, ON L8L 1K1
Tel: 905-525-4330; Toll-Free: 800-263-2131
www.hopaports.ca
Profile: Merged from the Hamilton & Oshawa Port Authorities in 2019, the Hamilton-Oshawa Port Authority handles millions of tons of cargo per year between its two ports, including bulk, breakbulk, project cargo & liquid bulk.

Nanaimo Port Authority / NPA
PO Box 131, Nanaimo, BC V9R 5K4
Tel: 250-753-4146; Fax: 250-753-4899
info@npa.ca
npa.ca
Profile: The NPA administers the federal harbour from the Nanaimo Assembly Wharf to the Petro-Canada dock on Newcastle Channel & extending to Newcastle & Protection Islands.

Port Alberni Port Authority
2750 Harbour Rd., Port Alberni, BC V9Y 7X2
Tel: 250-723-5312; Fax: 250-723-1114
portalberniportauthority.ca

Profile: Port Alberni Port Authority is a continuation of the Port Alberni Harbour Commission, & has jurisdiction over the Alberni Inlet from the Somass River to Tzartus Island.

Port de Sept-Îles
Port of Sept-Îles
1 Quai Mgr-Blanche, Sept-Îles, QC G4R 5P3
Tél: 418-968-1231; Téléc: 418-962-4445
www.portsi.com
Profile: Le Port de Sept-Îles comprend 14 quais, dont 9 lui appartiennent. Chaque année, près de 27 millions de tonnes de marchandises y sont manutentionnées, constituées principalement de minerai de fer.

Port of Belledune
112 Shannon Dr., Belledune, NB E8G 2W2
Tel: 506-522-1200; Fax: 506-522-0803
info@portofbelledune.ca
portofbelledune.ca
Profile: The Port is located in Northern New Brunswick, & handles bulk, break bulk, containers, trailer, liquid, & roll-on / roll-off. Space & storage is available for lease.

PortsToronto
Formerly: Toronto Port Authority
#500, 207 Queens Quay West, Toronto, ON M5J 1A7
Tel: 416-863-2000; Fax: 416-863-0495
www.portstoronto.com
Profile: Maintains a paved facility of over 50 acres centrally located, adjacent to downtown Toronto. The yard provides access to railroads, as well as all major highways. It also owns & operates Billy Bishop Toronto City Airport.

Portuaire de Montréal
Montreal Port Authority
Édifice du port de Montréal, #1, 2100, av Pierre-Dupuy, Montréal, QC H3C 3R5
Tél: 514-283-7011; Téléc: 514-283-0829
communications@port-montreal.com
www.port-montreal.com
Profile: Le mandat de l'Administration portuaire de Montréal est de faciliter le commerce intérieur et international et contribuer ainsi à la réalisation des objectifs socio-économiques locales, régionales et nationales

Prince Rupert Port Authority
#200, 215 Cow Bay Rd., Prince Rupert, BC V8J 1A2
Tel: 250-627-8899; Fax: 250-627-8980
info@rupertport.com
www.rupertport.com
Profile: The Port of Prince Rupert is the closest North American port to Asia, & includes five terminals & undeveloped industrial land.

Saint John Port Authority
111 Water St., Saint John, NB E2L 0B1
Tel: 506-636-4869; Fax: 506-636-4443
www.sjport.com
Profile: The port of Saint John handles more than 31 million metric tons of cargo per year, including dry & liquid bulk, break bulk, container & cruise.

Vancouver Fraser Port Authority
Formerly: Fraser River Port Authority
The Pointe, #100, 999 Canada Pl., Vancouver, BC V6C 3T4
Tel: 604-665-9000; Fax: 866-284-4271
www.portvancouver.com
Profile: The Fraser River, North Fraser & Vancouver Port Authorities united to become Vancouver Fraser Port Authority on January 1, 2008. The port is Canada's largest & operates across five sectors: automobile, breakbulk, bulk, container & cruise. The port has 29 major marine cargo terminals & three railroads.

Windsor Port Authority / WPA
3190 Sandwich St., Windsor, ON N9C 1A6
Tel: 519-258-5741
wpa@portwindsor.com
www.portwindsor.com
Profile: The mission of the Windsor Port Authority is to manage, develop & promote the Port of Windsor & ensure the general security of the port while striving for a high degree of safety & environmental responsibility.

Public Transit Systems

100 Mile House Regional Transit System
Formerly: 100 Mile House & Area Transit System
Parent: BC Transit Corporation
c/o LDN Transportation, 6119 Reita Cres., 100 Mile House, BC V0K 2E0
Tel: 250-395-2834
www.bctransit.com/100-mile-house

Profile: The 100 Mile House Transit System has many routes which offer service to major residential areas of 100 Mile House, 103 Mile & 108 Ranch. It also has several accessible services, including rural transit service, handyDART & priority seating. The system is operated by LDN Transportation.

Agassiz-Harrison Transit System
Parent: BC Transit Corporation
c/o FirstCanada ULC, 44275 Yale Rd. West, Chilliwack, BC V2R 4H2
Tel: 604-795-3838; Fax: 604-795-5110
www.bctransit.com/agassiz-harrison
Profile: The Agassiz-Harrison Transit System connects Chilliwack with Harrison Hot Springs. The system is operated by FirstCanada ULC.

Ashcroft-Cache Creek-Clinton Transit System
Formerly: Ashcroft-Clinton Transit System
Parent: BC Transit Corporation
c/o Yellowhead Community Services, 612 Park Dr., Clearwater, BC V0E 1N1
Toll-Free: 855-359-3935
www.bctransit.com/ashcroft-cache-creek-clinton
Profile: The transit system runs a single fixed-route service & serves the communities of Ashcroft, Cach Creek & Clinton. On-request service is also available.

Barrie Transit
24 Maple Ave., Barrie, ON L4N 7W4
Tel: 705-726-4242
servicebarrie@barrie.ca
www.barrie.ca
Profile: The City of Barrie offers both conventional bus service with Barrie Transit & specialized transit services for people with mobility restrictions with Barrie Accessible Community Transportation Service (BACTS)

BC Bus North
Parent: BC Transit Corporation
c/o BC Transit Corporation, 520 Gorge Rd. East, Victoria, BC V8W 2P3
Toll-Free: 844-564-7494
bcbus.ca
Profile: Established in 2018, BC Bus North is a long-haul coach service to 39 northern BC communities that offers connections to Prince Rupert, Prince George, Dawson Creek, Fort St. John, Fort Nelson & Valemount. BC Bus North is operated by Diversified Transportation Ltd,, & has a fleet of four 44-seat highway coach buses.

BC Transit Corporation
520 Gorge Rd. East, Victoria, BC V8W 2P3
Tel: 250-385-2551
transitinfo@bctransit.com
www.bctransit.com
Profile: BC Transit coordinates public transportation throughout British Columbia, excluding the Greater Vancouver Regional District, as mandated by the British Columbia Transit Act. Over 130 communities are served, with 66 transit systems in operation, including conventional & paratransit. The fleet includes more than 1,000 fully accessible buses.
Erinn Pinkerton, President & CEO
Greg Conner, Corporate Secretary & Vice-President, Human Resources
Tim Croyle, COO & Vice-President, Operations
Roland Gehrke, CFO & Vice-President, Finance

Bella Coola Valley Transit System
Parent: BC Transit Corporation
c/o Bella Coola Valley Bus Co. Ltd., PO Box 783, 925 Mackenzie Hwy., Bella Coola, BC V0T 1C0
Tel: 250-799-0079
bellacoolabus@gmail.com
bctransit.com/bella-coola-valley/home
Profile: The system is a paratransit service providing door-to-door & curb-to-curb services. The service is operated by Bella Coola Valley Bus Co. Ltd.

Belleville Transit
Robert E. Ladoucier Transit Centre, 165 Pinnacle St., Belleville, ON K8N 3A5
Tel: 613-967-4938
www.belleville.ca/residents/page/transit
Profile: Belleville Transit operates 16 conventional buses & 3 specialized service accessible buses on 10 routes.

Boundary Transit System
Parent: BC Transit Corporation
BC
Tel: 250-443-2179
www.bctransit.com/boundary/home

Profile: The Boundary Transit System has many routes within Grand Forks, with trips to & from Greenwood on Fridays. It also has several accessible services, including handyDART & priority seating.

Brampton Transit
185 Clark Blvd., Brampton, ON L6T 4G6
Tel: 905-874-2999
transit@brampton.ca
www.brampton.ca/en/residents/transit
Profile: Brampton Transit operates 70 routes, including 5 rapid transit Züm routes, 1 GO shuttle route, 4 express routes & 16 school routes. Brampton Transit has a fleet of 450 buses.
Alex Milojevic, General Manager, Transit

Brandon Transportation Services
8th & Rosser Ave., Brandon, MB R7A 6N5
Tel: 204-729-2300
brandontransit.ca
Profile: Brandon City Transit offers many services to the community, including Handi-Transit services.

Brantford Transit
64 Darling St., Brantford, ON N3T 6G6
Tel: 519-753-3847; *Fax:* 519-750-0491
transit@brantford.ca
www.brantford.ca/transit
Elisabeth van der Made, Manager, Transit Operations
519-752-4444 ext: 5894

British Columbia Ferry Services Inc. / BCF
Formerly: British Columbia Ferries Corporation
#500, 1321 Blanshard St., Vancouver, BC V8W 0B7
Toll-Free: 888-223-3779
www.bcferries.com
Profile: BC Ferries provides passenger & vehicle ferry services for coastal & island communities in British Columbia. The company currently operates 35 ferries on 25 routes to 47 terminals.
Mark Collins, President & CEO

British Columbia Rapid Transit Company Ltd. / BCRTC
Parent: South Coast British Columbia Transportation Authority (TransLink)
6800 - 14th Ave., Burnaby, BC V3N 4S7
Tel: 604-520-3641; *Fax:* 604-521-2818
www.translink.ca
Profile: The BC Rapid Transit Company maintains two of three SkyTrains in Vancouver on behalf of TransLink, as well as the West Coast Express train service.
Michel Ladrak, President & General Manager

Burlington Transit
430 John St., Burlington, ON L7R 2K5
Tel: 905-639-0550; *Fax:* 905-335-7878
Toll-Free: 877-213-3609
contactbt@burlington.ca
www.burlingtontransit.ca
Profile: Burlington Transit connects to Hamilton Street Railway & Oakville Transit, as well as a number of GO Transit stations. Burlington's fleet consists of 59 buses. A door-to-door service for people with disabilities, called the Handi-Van, is also offered.

Calgary Transit
125 - 7th Ave. SW, Calgary, AB T2G 5R2
Tel: 403-262-1000
www.calgarytransit.com
Profile: Calgary Transit serves a ridership of 101 million with the help of 1155 vehicles on 155 routes. Vehicles include buses & CTrains.
Doug Morgan, Director

Campbell River Transit System
Parent: BC Transit Corporation
1235 Evergreen Rd., Campbell River, BC V9W 3S2
Tel: 250-287-7433; *Fax:* 250-287-7488
www.bctransit.com/campbell-river
Profile: The Campbell River Transit System has several services available to the community, including Accessible Service through the HandyDART program. The system is operated by Watson & Ash Transportation Company Ltd.

Cape Breton Transit
320 Esplanade, Sydney, NS B1P 7B9
Tel: 902-539-8124
epw@cbrm.ns.ca
www.cbrm.ns.ca/transit
Profile: CB Transit operates buses in the Cape Breton Regional Municipality, which includes Industrial Cape Breton, Glace Bay, Sydney, North Sydney, Sydney Mines, Reserve Mines & New Waterford. The service includes 10 routes, 17 buses & 4 Handi-Trans buses.

Central Fraser Valley Transit System
Parent: BC Transit Corporation
1225 Riverside Rd., Abbotsford, BC V2S 7P1
Tel: 604-854-3232; *Fax:* 604-854-3598
www.bctransit.com/central-fraser-valley
Profile: The Central Fraser Valley Transit System has several services available to the community, including routes to most major destinations in the City of Abbotsford & the District of Mission, as well as accessible services such as low floor busses, handyDART & a taxi saver program. The system is predominantly contracted to FirstCanada ULC.

Chatham-Kent Transit
Formerly: Chatham Transit
315 King St. West, Chatham, ON N7M 5K8
Tel: 519-360-1998; *Fax:* 519-436-3240
cktransit@chatham-kent.ca
www.chatham-kent.ca/transportation
Profile: Operated by the Engineering & Transportation division of Chatham-Kent. Services include conventional & accessible transit within Chatham, as well as inter-urban transit between communities in the Chatham-Kent area. Accessible transit is also available to the communities of Wallaceburg, Erie Shores & Four Counties.

Chilliwack Transit System
Parent: BC Transit Corporation
First Canada, 44275 Yale Rd. West, Chilliwack, BC V2R 4H2
Tel: 604-795-3838; *Fax:* 604-796-8516
www.bctransit.com/chilliwack
Profile: The Chilliwack Transit System has several routes available to the community, which go to most major destinations in the City of Chilliwack, & to Rosedale, Popkum, Agassiz & Harrison Hot Springs.

Clearwater Regional Transit System
Formerly: Clearwater & Area Transit System
Parent: BC Transit Corporation
c/o Yellowhead Community Services, 612 Park Dr., Clearwater, BC V0E 1N1
Tel: 250-674-3935
www.bctransit.com/clearwater
Profile: The Clearwater & Area transit system services an area that covers Vavenby, Birch Island, Clearwater & Blackpool. It has several accessible services including door-to-door services, handyDART & priority seating. The system is operated by Yellowhead Community Services.

Coach Atlantic Group
699 Malenfant Blvd., Dieppe, NB E1A 5T8
Tel: 902-423-6242; *Fax:* 902-423-5522
Toll-Free: 888-599-4287
charters@coachatlantic.ca
coachatlanticgroup.com
Profile: Coach Atlantic is a bus charter company operating in Prince Edward Island, Nova Scotia & Newfoundland & New Brunswick. Members of the Coach Atlantic Group include the following operating companies: Prince Edward Tours, Coach Atlantic, Maritime Bus, Airport Express, Courier Express & T3 Transit.
Adam Doiron, Chief Executive Officer
adam@coachatlanticgroup.com

Coast Mountain Bus Company Ltd. / CMBC
Parent: South Coast British Columbia Transportation Authority (TransLink)
287 Nelson's Ct., New Westminster, BC V3L 0E7
Tel: 778-375-6400
www.translink.ca/About-Us/Corporate-Overview/Operat
Profile: Coast Mountain Bus Company operates 153 conventional buses, 70 smaller community shuttles, SeaBus & a fleet of trolley buses in Greater Vancouver, in the largest single transit service area in Canada.
Michael McDaniel, President & General Manager

Cobourg Transit
Bldg. #7, Northam Industrial Park, 740 Division St., Cobourg, ON K9A 2M2
Tel: 905-372-4555; *Fax:* 905-372-1533
Toll-Free: 888-972-4301
transit@cobourg.ca
www.cobourg.ca/en/my-cobourg/Public_Transit.aspx
Profile: Cobourg Transit is operated by the Engineering Department & is a fully accessible community transit system that combines fixed-route & door-to-door service (known as the Wheels program).

Codiac Transit Commission
140 Millennium Blvd., Moncton, NB E1E 2G8
Tel: 506-857-2008; *Fax:* 506-859-2680
info@codiactranspo.ca
www.codiactranspo.ca

Profile: Transit system for Moncton with 19 routes that include express routes, charters & airport routes.

Columbia Valley Transit System
Parent: BC Transit Corporation
BC
Toll-Free: 877-343-2461
www.bctransit.com/columbia-valley
Profile: The Columbia Valley Transit System has three routes serving Canal Flats, Fairmont, Invermere, Radium & Edgewater. On-Request & handyDART services are available. The system is operated by Olympus Stage Lines Ltd.

Comox Valley Transit System
Parent: BC Transit Corporation
1635 Knight Rd., Comox, BC V9M 4A2
Tel: 250-339-5453; *Fax:* 250-339-2797
www.bctransit.com/comox-valley
Profile: Comox Valley Transit has several routes available to the community, which go to the city of Courtenay, Comox, Royston, Black Creek, Oyster River & Cimerland. Accessible services including low floor busses, handyDART & a taxi saver program are available. The system is operated by Watson & Ash Transportation Co. Ltd.

Cornwall Transit
863 - 2nd St. West, Cornwall, ON K6J 1H5
Tel: 613-930-2636
www.cornwall.ca/en/live-here/cornwall-transit.aspx
Profile: The City-operated transit system transports approximately 818,000 passengers annually. A parallel service called Handi-Transit is available for people with disabilities.

Cowichan Valley Regional Transit System
Parent: BC Transit Corporation
c/o First Canada ULC, #3, 5280 Polkey Rd., Duncan, BC V9L 6W3
Tel: 250-746-9899
www.bctransit.com/cowichan-valley
Profile: The Cowichan Valley Regional Transit System serves the Cowichan Valley & Duncan. The service is operated by Greyhound Canada. The service also has accessible services, including low floor busses, handyDART & priority seating.

Cranbrook Transit System
Parent: BC Transit Corporation
c/o TOK Transit, 125 Slater Rd. NW, #C, Cranbrook, BC V1C 4M4
Tel: 250-417-4636; *Fax:* 250-426-5101
www.bctransit.com/cranbrook
Profile: Cranbrook Transit System has several routes available to the community, & many services, such as low-floor busses & handyDART, for those who are in need of them.

Creston Valley Transit System
Parent: BC Transit Corporation
c/o Arrow & Slocan Lakes Community Services, PO Box 100, 205 - 6th Ave. North, Nakusp, BC V0G 1R0
Tel: 250-428-7750; *Fax:* 250-265-3378
www.bctransit.com/creston-valley
Profile: The Creston Valley Transit System has routes that go to most of the major destinations in the area. It also has several accessible services including door-to-door service & priority seating. The system is operated by Arrow & Slocan Community Services.

Dawson Creek Transit System
Parent: BC Transit Corporation
10404 - 87th Ave., Fort St John, BC V1J 5K7
Tel: 250-782-4636; *Fax:* 250-787-9322
www.bctransit.com/dawson-creek
Profile: Dawson Creek Transit system has several routes available to the community, which go to most of the major destinations in Dawson Creek. It has several low floor busses & priority seating. The system is operated by Diversified Transportation Ltd.

Durham Region Transit / DRT
110 Westney Rd. South, Ajax, ON L1S 2C8
Toll-Free: 866-247-0055
drthelps@durham.ca
www.durhamregiontransit.com
Profile: DRT is an integrated transit system serving all communities in Durham Region. The service area is divided into Ajax, Pickering, Whitby, Oshawa, Clarington, Brock, Scugog & Uxbridge service sectors.
William Holmes, General Manager

Edmonton Transit Service
Formerly: Edmonton Transit System
PO Box 2610 Main, Edmonton, AB T5J 3R5
Tel: 780-442-5311
311@edmonton.ca
www.edmonton.ca/edmonton-transit-system-ets.aspx
Profile: Edmonton Transit's fleet encompasses over 1150 vehicles. The system covers 209 routes, including a Light Rail Transit (LRT) system. ETS also offers transportation to persons with disabilities, called the Disabled Adult Transit Service (DATS).
Eddie Robar, Manager

Elk Valley Transit System
Parent: BC Transit Corporation
c/o Sun City Coachlines, 1229 Cranbrook St. North, Cranbrook, BC V1C 3S6
Toll-Free: 855-417-4636
www.bctransit.com/elk-valley
Profile: The Elk Valley Transit System offers one route serving Sparwood, Elkford & Fernie. The system is operated by Sun City Coachlines.

Exo
Formerly: Réseau de transport métropolitain
700, rue de la Gauchetière ouest, Montréal, QC H2Y 2W2
Tél: 514-287-8726; *Ligne sans frais:* 888-702-8726
exo.quebec
Profile: Created in June 2017, replacing the Agence métropolitaine de transport, Exo serves the island of Montréal, Laval & communities along the North Shore of the Rivière des Mille-Îles & the South Shore of the St. Lawrence River. The agency operated bus & commuter rail services. Exo's service area spans 63 municipalities.
Sylvain Yelle, Director

Fort St. John Transit System
Parent: BC Transit Corporation
c/o Diversified Transportation Ltd., 10404 - 87 Ave., Fort St John, BC V1J 5K7
Tel: 250-787-7433; *Fax:* 250-787-9322
www.bctransit.com/fort-st-john
Profile: The Fort St. John Transit system has many routes available to the community, reaching most of the major destinations in the city. It has low floor busses for easy accessibility, handyDART & priority seating. The system is operated by Diversified Transportation Ltd.

Fredericton Transit
PO Box 130, 397 Queen St., Fredericton, NB E3B 4Y7
Tel: 506-460-2200; *Fax:* 506-460-2042
transit@fredericton.ca
www.fredericton.ca/en/transit
Profile: The City of Fredericton Transit Division operates 28 buses on 8 routes. Chartered buses are available to various school, tour & conference groups in & around Fredericton, & a parallel service, Dial-A-Bus, for persons with a disability.

GO Transit
Parent: Metrolinx
#600, 20 Bay St., Toronto, ON M5J 2W3
Tel: 416-869-3200; *Fax:* 416-869-3525
Toll-Free: 888-438-6646
www.gotransit.com
Profile: A division of Metrolinx, GO Transit provides transit service for the Greater Toronto & Hamilton Area via trains & buses. GO Transit's service area covers 11,000 square kilometres. GO Transit carries over 70 million passengers a year. GO Transit has over 50 locomotives, 495 train coaches & 401 buses, & aims to have 253 buses & 327 new train cars by 2020.
Phil Verster, President & Chief Executive Officer, Metrolinx
ceo@metrolinx.com

GOVA Transit
Formerly: Greater Sudbury Transit
1160 Lorne St., Sudbury, ON P3C 4T2
Tel: 705-675-3333
transit@greatersudbury.ca
www.greatersudbury.ca/gova
Profile: Serves the City of Sudbury & surrounding area. The authority covers 41 routes.
Bruno Lafortune, Manager, Transit Administration

GP Transit
City Hall, PO Box 4000, 9505 - 112th St., Grande Prairie, AB T8V 6V3
Tel: 780-538-0300; *Fax:* 780-538-4667
gptransit@cityofgp.com
www.cityofgp.com/roads-transportation/public-transi
Profile: The system serves 6 bus routes.

Grand River Transit / GRT
250 Strasburg Rd., Kitchener, ON N2E 3M6
Tel: 519-585-7555
www.grt.ca
Profile: Grand River Transit serves the communities of Cambridge, Kitchener & Waterloo. An accessible service called MobilityPLUS is available for people with disabilities. In 2018, GRT expanded its transit services with a rapid transit network consisting of ION light rail trains. The ION light rail operates along a 19-kilometre route between Conestoga Mall transit terminal & Fairview Mall transit terminal.

Guelph Transit
City Hall, 1 Carden St., Guelph, ON N1H 3A1
Tel: 519-822-1811; *Fax:* 519-822-1322
transit@guelph.ca
guelph.ca/living/getting-around/bus
Profile: Guelph Transit has over 70 buses serving 28 transit routes.

Halifax Transit
Formerly: Metro Transit
PO Box 1749, Halifax, NS B3J 3A5
Toll-Free: 800-835-6428
www.halifax.ca/transportation/halifax-transit
Profile: Halifax Transit operates buses & ferries in Halifax. The agency has 2 ferry routes, 67 bus routes & an Accessabus service for seniors & people with disabilities.
Dave Reage, Director

Hamilton Street Railway Company / HSR
36 Hunter St. East, Hamilton, ON L8N 3W8
Tel: 905-527-4441
hsrserve@hamilton.ca
www.hamilton.ca/hsr-bus-schedules-fares
Profile: The agency offers bus & paratransit services & serves over 20 million passengers a year. Its payment method is the PRESTO card, allowing for connections with GO Transit & other GTA transit systems. The agency covers 34 regular routes & has 190 buses.
Debbie Dalle Vedove, Director

Hazeltons Regional Transit System
Parent: BC Transit Corporation
c/o Pacific Western Transportation, 327 Railway Ave., Kitimat, BC V8C 2G4
Tel: 250-842-2134; *Toll-Free:* 855-935-2666
bctransit.com/hazeltons
Profile: The system has accessible services which include door to door service & priority seating. The system is operated by Pacific Western Transportation.

Hope Regional Transit System
Parent: BC Transit Corporation
c/o FirstCanada ULC, 44275 Yale Rd. West, Chilliwack, BC V2R 4H2
Tel: 604-795-3838; *Fax:* 604-795-5110
www.bctransit.com/hope
Profile: Serves passengers in Hope, BC. Operated by FirstCanada ULC.

Kamloops Transit System
Parent: BC Transit Corporation
c/o FirstCanada ULC, 1460 Ord Rd., Kamloops, BC V2B 7V4
Tel: 250-376-1216; *Fax:* 250-376-7398
www.bctransit.com/kamloops
Profile: The Kamloops Transit System has several routes available to the public which go to all regions of Greater Kamloops. It also has several services available, including low floor buses, handyDART, a Taxi Saver Program & priority seating. The system is operated by FirstCanada ULC.

Kelowna Regional Transit System
Parent: BC Transit Corporation
c/o FirstCanada ULC, 1494 Hardy St., Kelowna, BC V1Y 8H2
Tel: 250-860-8121; *Fax:* 250-861-7872
www.bctransit.com/kelowna
Profile: The Kelowna Transit System has several routes available to the public, which go to all regions of Greater Kelowna. It also offers accessible services, including low floor buses, handyDART, a Taxi Saver program & priority seating. Buses are operated by FirstCanada ULC.

Kimberley Transit System
Parent: BC Transit Corporation
260 - 4th Ave., Kimberley, BC V1A 2R6
Tel: 250-427-7400
www.bctransit.com/kimberley
Profile: The Kimberley Transit System has routes between Kimberley & Cranbrook from Tuesday to Friday. It also has several accessible services, including door to door service &

priority seating. The system is operated by the Kimberley Transportation Committee.

Kings Transit Authority
29 Crescent Dr., New Minas, NS B4N 3G7
Tel: 902-678-7310; *Toll-Free:* 888-546-4442
info@kingstransit.ns.ca
www.kbus.ca
Profile: King Transit Authority is a public transit system that operates in the Annapolis County from Weymouth to Hants Border, as well as in Cornwallis Park, Upper Clements Park & Port Williams.
Kevin Kerr, Interim General Manager
902-678-7310 ext: 2, manager@kingstransit.ns.ca

Kitimat Transit System
Parent: BC Transit Corporation
c/o Pacific Western Transportation, 327 Railway Ave., Kitimat, BC V8C 2G4
Tel: 250-632-4449
www.bctransit.com/kitimat
Profile: The Kitimat Transit System has many routes that go to most of the major destinations in Kitimat. It also has several accessible services, including low floor buses, handyDART & priority seating. Buses are operated by Pacific Western Transportation.

Lethbridge Transit
619 - 4th Ave. North, Lethbridge, AB T1H 0K4
Tel: 403-320-3885; *Fax:* 403-380-3876
transit@lethbridge.ca
www.lethbridge.ca
Profile: Lethbridge Transit has 42 buses & 12 routes.
Kevin Ponech, Manager, Transit

London Transit Commission
450 Highbury Ave. North, London, ON N5W 5L2
Tel: 519-451-1347
ltc@londontransit.ca
www.londontransit.ca
Profile: London Transit Commission serves over 23 million passengers annually. The commission has over 200 buses in their fleet.
Kelly S. Paleczny, General Manager

Medicine Hat Transit
460 Spencer St. SE, Medicine Hat, AB T1A 1Y7
Tel: 403-529-8214; *Fax:* 403-527-5844
mhtransit@medicinehat.ca
www.medicinehat.ca
Profile: Apart from general public transportation, Medicine Hat's transit system also offers charter & special needs services.

Merritt Regional Transit System
Formerly: Merritt & Area Transit System
Parent: BC Transit Corporation
c/o Nicola Valley Transportation Society, PO Box 934, Merritt, BC V1K 1B8
Tel: 250-378-4080
www.bctransit.com/merritt
Profile: The Merritt & Area Transit System provides four routes serving North End, Collettville, Diamond Vale & Lower Nicola. The system is operated by Nicola Valley Transportation Society.

Metrolinx
97 Front St. West, Toronto, ON M5J 1E6
Tel: 416-874-5900; *Fax:* 416-869-1755
www.metrolinx.com
Profile: Metrolinx is an agency of the Government of Ontario & is mandated to coordinate & integrate all forms of transportation in the Greater Toronto & Hamilton Area. The agency merged with GO Transit in 2009. The Eglinton Crosstown LRT tunnel was completed in 2016 & PRESTO was fully integrated into the GTHA & Ottawa in 2016.
Phil Verster, President & CEO
ceo@metrolinx.com
Helen Helen Ferreira-Walker, Chief Human Resources Officer
helen.ferreira-walker@metrolinx.com
Ian Smith, Chief Operating Officer
ian.smith@metrolinx.com
Annalise Czerny, Exeutive Vice-President, PRESTO
annalise.czerny@metrolinx.com

MiWay
Formerly: Mississauga Transit
3484 Semenyk Ct., Mississauga, ON L5C 4R1
Tel: 905-615-4636
miwayhelps@mississauga.ca
www.mississauga.ca/portal/miway
Profile: Ontario's third largest municipal transit provider; serves the Mississauga area. Two types of service: MiExpress & MiLocal. The company has over 500 buses.
Geoff Marinoff, Director

Moose Jaw Transit System
1010 High St. West, Moose Jaw, SK S0H 0N0
Tel: 306-694-4488; *Fax:* 306-694-4022
transit@moosejaw.ca
moosejaw.ca/streets-roads/transit
Profile: In addition to regular bus service, charter service is also available, as is paratransit service.

Mount Waddington Transit System
Parent: BC Transit Corporation
c/o Pacific Western Transportation, #23, 1705 Campbell Way, Port McNeill, BC V0N 2R0
Tel: 250-956-3151
www.bctransit.com/mount-waddington
Profile: The Mount Waddington Transit System offers nine routes around the Mount Waddington area. Accessible services are offered, including the handyDART service. The system is operated by Pacific Western Transportation.

Niagara Falls Transit
8208 Heartland Forest Rd., Niagara Falls, ON L2H 0L7
Tel: 905-356-1179; *Fax:* 905-356-5576
niagarafalls.ca/living/transit
Profile: Founded in 1960, Niagara Transit provides the City of Niagara Falls with 16 Monday-Saturday daytime routes & 11 evening, Sunday & holiday routes.
Dave Stuart, General Manager

North Bay Transit
190 Wyld St., North Bay, ON P1B 1Z2
Tel: 705-474-0419
transit@cityofnorthbay.ca
www.cityofnorthbay.ca/cityhall/department/transit-p
Remi Renaud, Transit Manager
705-474-0400 ext: 2165, remi.renaud@cityofnorthbay.ca

Oakville Transit
1225 Trafalgar Rd., Oakville, ON L6H 0H3
Tel: 905-815-2020; *Fax:* 905-338-4703
transit@oakville.ca
www.oakvilletransit.com
Profile: Oakville Transit has been providing bus service to Oakville since 1972 & serves an annual ridership of about 3 million. The agency has a fleet of 89 fully accessible conventional buses & 10 "care-A-van" (paratransit) buses.
Barry Cole, Director

OC Transpo
925 Belfast Rd., Ottawa, ON K1G 0Z4
Tel: 613-741-4390; *Fax:* 613-842-3653
www.octranspo.com
Profile: OC Transpo provides public transit services in the Ottawa region. The OC Transpo fleet includes over 900 buses & six trains. Services include the Transitway & the O-Train.
Renée Amilcar, General Manager, Transit Services

Pemberton Valley Transit System
Formerly: Pemberton Transit System
Parent: BC Transit Corporation
8025 Nesters Rd., Whistler, BC V0N 1B8
Tel: 604-894-6135
www.bctransit.com/pemberton-valley
Profile: The Pemberton Transit System offers one commuter route & one local route.

Peterborough Transit
190 Simcoe St., Peterborough, ON K9H 2H7
Tel: 705-745-0525
transitoperations@peterborough.ca
www.peterborough.ca/en/city-services/transit.aspx
Profile: Operates 12 regular routes Monday-Sunday.
Laurie Stratton, Manager

Port Alberni Regional Transit System
Formerly: Port Alberni/Clayoquot Transit System
Parent: BC Transit Corporation
c/o Diversified Transportation Ltd., 3701 - 4th Ave., Port Alberni, BC V9Y 4H7
Tel: 250-724-1311; *Fax:* 250-724-1377
www.bctransit.com/port-alberni
Profile: The Port Alberni Regional Transit System has several routes that go to most of the major destinations in the area, as well as many accessible services, including low floor buses, handyDART & priority seating. Service is administered by Diversified Transportation Ltd.

Port Edward Transit System
Formerly: Prince Rupert/Port Edward Transit
Parent: BC Transit Corporation
c/o Pacific Western Transportation, 990 Sasaktoon Ave., Prince Rupert, BC V8J 4J2
Tel: 250-624-3343
www.bctransit.com/port-edward

Profile: The Port Edward Transit system has several routes available to the community that go to most of the major destinations in the area, as well as many accessible services, including low floor buses, handyDART, a taxi saver program & door to door service. Both services are operated by Pacific Western Transportation.

Powell River Regional Transit System
Parent: BC Transit Corporation
c/o Powell River Municipal Transportation, 6910 Duncan St., Powell River, BC V8A 1W2
Tel: 604-485-4287; *Fax:* 604-485-4219
www.bctransit.com/powell-river
Profile: The Powell River Transit System has many routes available to the community, which go to most of the major destinations in the area. It also has several accessible services, including a rural transit service, low floor buses, handyDART & priority seating. The systems are operated by Powell River Municipal Transportation.

Prince George Transit System
Parent: BC Transit Corporation
1041 Great St., Prince George, BC V2N 2K8
Tel: 250-563-0011; *Fax:* 250-564-4901
www.bctransit.com/prince-george
Profile: The Prince George Transit System has many routes that go to most of the major regions in the area. It also has several accessible services available to the community, including community travel training, low floor buses, handyDART, a taxi saver program & priority seating. The systems are operated by Prince George Transit Ltd., a subsidiary of Pacific Western Transportation.

Prince Rupert Transit System
Parent: BC Transit Corporation
c/o Pacific Western Transportation, 990 Saskatoon Ave., Prince Rupert, BC V8J 4J2
Tel: 250-624-3343
www.bctransit.com/prince-rupert
Profile: Serves passengers in Prince Rupert, BC. Operated by Pacific Western Transportation.

Quesnel Transit System
Parent: BC Transit Corporation
3751B Hwy. 97 North, Quesnel, BC V2J 5Z2
Tel: 250-992-1109; *Fax:* 250-992-1146
www.bctransit.com/quesnel
Profile: Quesnel Transit has several routes that go to most of the major destinations in the area, as well as many accessible services, including handyDART & priority seating. The system is operated by Five Five Transportation.

Red Deer Transit
Sorensen Station Transit Terminal, 4830 - 48th St., Red Deer, AB T4N 2R3
Tel: 403-342-8225
transit@reddeer.ca
www.reddeer.ca/city-services/transit
Profile: Red Deer Transit operates 13 regular bus routes, as well as paratransit services.

Regina Transit
PO Box 1790, Regina, SK S4P 3C8
Tel: 306-777-7433
www.regina.ca/transportation-roads-parking/transit
Profile: The City of Regina Transit System has several services available to the community, including a charter service, a safebus, night stops & paratransit. The system operates 21 routes with 121 buses.

Regional District of Nanaimo Transit System
Parent: BC Transit Corporation
Nanaimo, BC
Tel: 250-390-4531
www.bctransit.com/nanaimo
Profile: RDN Regional Transit System provides both regular transit & handyDART custom transit service. Regional Transit is operated by the Regional District of Nanaimo in partnership with BC Transit.

Réseau de transport de la capitale / RTC
720, rue des Rocailles, Québec, QC G2J 1A5
Tél: 418-627-2511; *Téléc:* 418-641-6716
www.rtcquebec.ca
Profile: The agency provides urban transit services in the Québec City area, including 109 routes, six Express bus lines & 616 buses.
Alain Mercier, Directeur Général

Le Réseau de transport de Longueuil / RTL
1150, boul Marie-Victorin, Longueuil, QC J4G 2M4
Tél: 450-442-8600
www.rtl-longueuil.qc.ca

Michel Veilleux, Directeur général

Revelstoke Transit System
Parent: BC Transit Corporation
Everything Revelstoke, 113 - 2nd St. East, Revelstoke, BC V0E 2S0
Tel: 250-837-3888
www.bctransit.com/revelstoke
Profile: The Revelstoke Transit System offers fixed-route & handyDART services. The system is operated by Lyndon Enterprises Ltd.

Rideau Transit Group / RTG
Groupe de transport Rideau
805 Belfast Rd., Ottawa, ON K1G 0Z4
rtg-rtm.com
Profile: The Rideau Transit Group designs & builds the Confederation Line in Ottawa over five years, & maintains the line until 2038. It is a public-private general partnership between ACS Infrastructure Canada, EllisDon & SNC-Lavalin.
Nicolas Truchon, Chief Executive officer

Saint John Transit Commission
55 McDonald St., Saint John, NB E2J 0C7
Tel: 506-658-4700; *Fax:* 506-658-4704
sjtransitcustomerservice@saintjohn.ca
www.saintjohn.ca/en/home/cityhall/transportation/tr
Profile: The Saint John Transit Commission was established in 1979 to provide scheduled transit service to the city. Its ridership averages 2.5 million passengers per year.

St. Albert Transit / StAT
Dez Liggett Transit Facility, 235 Carnegie Dr., St Albert, AB T8N 5A7
Tel: 780-418-6060; *Fax:* 780-459-4050
transit@stalbert.ca
stalbert.ca/city/transit
Profile: StAT local routes serve all neighbourhoods within the City of St. Albert, connecting with StAT commuter services to Edmonton destinations at either (or both) the Village Transit Station or St. Albert Centre Exchange. Edmonton destinations include downtown, the University of Alberta, MacEwan, NAIT, Government Centre & West Edmonton Mall.

St. Catharines Transit Commission
2012 - 1st St. South, St Catharines, ON L2S 3V9
Tel: 905-687-5555; *Fax:* 905-685-4050
info@yourbus.com
www.yourbus.com
Profile: Provides bus service to the City of St. Catharines & the City of Thorold. The commission operates 25 routes with a fleet of 75 buses.

St. John's Transportation Commission
25 Messenger Dr., St. John's, NL A1B 0H6
Tel: 709-570-2020; *Fax:* 709-722-0018
informationservices@metrobus.com
www.metrobus.com
Profile: The Metrobus system operates a fleet of 54 buses on 24 routes.
Judy Powell, General Manager

Salt Spring Island Transit System
Parent: BC Transit Corporation
c/o the Ganges Faerie Minishuttle, #206, 338 Lower Ganges Rd., Salt Spring Island, BC V8K 2V3
Tel: 250-537-6758
www.bctransit.com/salt-spring-island
Profile: The Salt Spring Island Transit System offers seven routes around the island. Buses are wheelchair accessible & handyDART service is available.

Sarnia Transit
1169 Michener Rd., Sarnia, ON N7S 4W3
Tel: 519-336-3271; *Fax:* 519-336-3361
transit@sarnia.ca
www.city.sarnia.on.ca/living-here/getting-around/sa
Profile: Operates & maintains a fleet of 25 buses on the conventional transit system and 6 specialized vehicles on their Care-a-Van service (provided to people with disabilities).
Jim Stevens, Director

Saskatoon Transit
226 - 23rd Ave. East, Saskatoon, SK S7K 0J4
Tel: 306-975-3100
transit.saskatoon.ca
Profile: Saskatoon Transit operates a fleet of 188 diesel buses, including accessible buses. It has 40 bus routes, as well as paratransit services.

Sault Ste. Marie Transit
111 Huron St., Sault Ste Marie, ON P6A 5P9
Tel: 705-759-5438; *Fax:* 705-759-5834
transit@cityssm.on.ca
saultstemarie.ca

Profile: The Sault Ste. Marie Transit service has a fleet of 26 regular buses, 2 minimuss & covers 10 routes. The Parabus service consists of 10 vehicles.
Nicole Maione, Manager, Transit & Parking
n.maione@cityssm.on.ca

SeaBus
Parent: South Coast British Columbia Transportation Authority (TransLink)
287 Nelson's Ct., New Westminster, BC V3L 0E7
Tel: 778-375-6400
www.translink.ca

Profile: The SeaBus passenger ferries linking North Vancouver & downtown Vancouver, crossing the Burrard Inlet, are operated by Coast Mountain Bus Company Ltd., & owned by TransLink.
Michael McDaniel, President & General Manager, Coast Mountain Bus Company Ltd.

Shuswap Regional Transit System
Parent: BC Transit Corporation
c/o First Canada, #1, 321 - 7th St. SW, Salmon Arm, BC V1E 1S9
Tel: 250-832-0191
www.bctransit.com/shuswap

Profile: The Shuswap Regional Transit System offers routes serving Salmon Arm, Canoe, Sorrento, Blind Bay, Eagle Bay, Silver Creek, Deep Creek & Enderby. Accessible services such as handyDART are offered.

Skeena Regional Transit System
Parent: BC Transit Corporation
c/o Pacific Western Transportation, 327 Railway Ave., Kitimat, BC V8C 2G4
Tel: 250-632-4449
www.bctransit.com/skeena

Profile: The Skeena Regional Transit System operates four routes serving Kitimat & Skeena. Accessible services such as handyDART are available. Buses are operated by Pacific Western Transportation.

Smithers Regional Transit System
Formerly: Smithers & District Transit System
Parent: BC Transit Corporation
c/o Smithers Community Services Association, PO Box 3759, 3815 Railway Ave., #B, Smithers, BC V0J 2N0
Tel: 250-847-9515
www.bctransit.com/smithers

Profile: The Smithers & District Transit System offers four routes serving major destinations & residential areas. Accessible services such as the handyDART are available. The system is operated by the Smithers Community Services Association.

Société de transport de l'Outaouais / STO
111, rue Jean-Proulx, Gatineau, QC J8Z 1T4
Tél: 819-770-3242; *Ligne sans frais:* 800-855-0511
www.sto.ca

Profile: Operates in Gatineau, with 66 routes & over 300 buses.
Myriam Nadeau, Présidente

Société de transport de Laval / STL
2250, av Francis-Hughes, Laval, QC H7S 2C3
Tél: 450-688-6520; *Téléc:* 450-662-5457
www.stl.laval.qc.ca

Éric Morasse, Président

Société de transport de Montréal / STM
800, rue de la Gauchetière ouest, Montréal, QC H5A 1J6
Tél: 514-786-4636
www.stm.info

Profile: The agency operates bus & rapid transit services in Montréal, with 197 bus routes, 23 night bus routes & 4 subway lines.
Philippe Schnobb, Président

Société de transport de Sherbrooke / STS
895, rue Cabana, Sherbrooke, QC J1K 2M3
Tél: 819-564-2687
service.clientele@sts.qc.ca
www.sts.qc.ca

Patrick Dobson, Directeur général

South Coast British Columbia Transportation Authority
Formerly: Greater Vancouver Transportation Authority
#400, 287 Nelson's Ct., New Westminster, BC V3L 0E7
Tel: 778-375-7500; *Fax:* 604-636-4809
hrcoordinators@translink.ca
www.translink.ca

Profile: TransLink is involved with transportation planning, administration of service contracts with subsidiary companies & contractors, the management of capital projects, financial management & planning, public affairs & supporting business functions. Operating companies include: West Vancouver Blue Bus; Coast Mountain Bus Company, West Coast Express & British Columbia Rapid Transit Company.
Kevin Desmond, Chief Executive Officer

South Okanagan-Similkameen Transit System
Formerly: Penticton & Okanagan-Similkameen Transit System
Parent: BC Transit Corporation
301 Warren Ave. East, Penticton, BC V2A 3M1
Toll-Free: 844-442-2212
www.bctransit.com/south-okanagan-similkameen
Profile: The South Okanagan-Similkameen Transit System has many routes available both in the community & in rural areas. They also have several accessible services, including low floor buses, handyDART, a taxi saver program & priority seating. The systems are operated by Penticton Transit Services Ltd. (Berry & Smith).

Squamish Transit System
Parent: BC Transit Corporation
c/o Diversified Transportation Ltd., 38928A Production Way, Squamish, BC V8B 0K4
Tel: 604-892-5559
www.bctransit.com/squamish
Profile: The Squamish Transit System has many routes that go to Valleycliffe, Brackendale, Highlands, Downtown, Woodfibre Ferry, Garibaldi Highlands & most major destinations in Squamish. It also has accessible services including low floor busses, handyDART & priority seating. The system is operated by Diversified Transportation Ltd.

Stratford Transit
PO Box 874, 60 Corcoran St., Stratford, ON N5A 6W3
Tel: 519-271-0250
www.stratford.ca/en/live-here/transit.aspx
Profile: Operates six bus routes.
Michael Mousley, Manager, Transit
mmousley@stratford.ca

Strathcona Transit
2001 Sherwood Dr., Sherwood Park, AB T8A 3W7
Tel: 780-464-7433
transit@strathcona.ca
www.strathcona.ca/transportation-roads/transportati
Profile: Strathcona Transit provides local, commuter & school bus services to residents of Strathcona County. Paratransit is provided by Strathcona County Accessible Transportation (SCAT).
Wade Coombs, Director, Transit

Sunshine Coast Regional Transit System
Parent: BC Transit Corporation
c/o James Walton, 1975 Field Rd., Sechelt, BC V0N 3A1
Tel: 604-885-6899
www.bctransit.com/sunshine-coast
Profile: The Sunshine Coast Transit System has many routes that go to the most built-up residential neighbourhoods between the Langdale, Gibsons & Sechelt. In addition, there is service to Halfmoon Bay & limited service on Saturday, Sunday & holidays to Secret Cove in the summertime. Buses are operated by the Regional District.
James Walton, Manager, Transit & Fleet
james.walton@scrd.ca

Terrace Regional Transit System
Parent: BC Transit Corporation
c/o Pacific Western Transportation, 5130 Park Ave., Terrace, BC V8G 5S7
Tel: 250-635-2666
www.bctransit.com/terrace
Profile: The Terrace Regional Transit System has many routes through the City of Terrace & the Regional District of Kitimat-Stikine. It also has several accessible services including low floor busses, handyDART & priority seating. The system is operated by Pacific Western Transportation.

Thunder Bay Transit
570 Fort William Rd., Thunder Bay, ON P7B 2Z8
Tel: 807-684-3744; *Fax:* 807-684-2997
www.thunderbay.ca/en/city-services/transit.aspx
Profile: Thunder Bay Transit operates with a fleet of 49 buses on 17 routes, & is completely accessible.
Brad Loroff, Manager

Timmins Transit
220 Algonquin Blvd. East, Timmins, ON P4N 1B3
Tel: 705-360-2654; *Fax:* 705-360-2698
transit@timmins.ca
www.timminstransit.ca
Profile: Timmins Transit is a service operated by the City of Timmins. They operate a fleet of over 25 buses, low floor buses & accessible mini-buses
Fred Gerrior, Manager, Transit

Toronto Transit Commission / TTC
1900 Yonge St., Toronto, ON M4S 1Z2
Tel: 416-393-4000
www.ttc.ca
Profile: Established in 1921, the TTC operates & maintains Toronto's urban transit system, including buses, subways & streetcars. The TTC has the third largest ridership in North America; in 2016, the TTC set an all-time record of 538.1 million rides. Subsidiaries include: TTC Insurance Company Inc., Toronto Transit Infrastructure Ltd. & Toronto Coach Terminal Inc.
Jaye Robinson, Chair
Rick Leary, Chief Executive Officer

Transit Windsor
3700 North Service Rd. East, Windsor, ON N8W 5X2
Tel: 519-944-4111; *Fax:* 519-944-5121
tw@city.windsor.on.ca
www.citywindsor.ca/residents/transitwindsor/Pages/T
Profile: Fleet consists of 114 buses. The company also provides a cross-border service between the downtown areas of Windsor & Detroit via the Tunnel Bus.

Vernon Regional Transit System
Parent: BC Transit Corporation
c/o North Okanagan & Vernon Regional Transit, 2400 - 43rd St., Vernon, BC V1T 6W8
Tel: 250-545-7221
www.bctransit.com/vernon
Profile: The Vernon Regional Transit System has many routes available to the community which go to to most major destinations in the City of Vernon, to the District of Coldstream, Spallumcheen, Armstrong, Endergy, Lavington, Whitevale & Lumby. It has accessible services including community travel training, a taxi saver program, low floor busses & handyDART.

Victoria Regional Transit System
Formerly: Victoria Regional Transit Commission
Parent: BC Transit Corporation
c/o BC Transit Corporation, 520 Gorge Rd. East, Victoria, BC V8W 2P3
Tel: 250-382-6161
transitinfo@bctransit.com
www.bctransit.com/victoria
Profile: The Victoria Regional Transit System began operation on 22 February 1890 with a fleet of four streetcars. The system now serves approximately 312,000 persons & operates in a 400-square-kilometre area. Fares, routes & service levels are overseen by the Victoria Regional Transit Commission.

Welland Transit
c/o Civic Square, 60 East Main St., Welland, ON L3B 3X4
Tel: 905-735-1700
transit@welland.ca
www.welland.ca/transit
Profile: The service offers 8 daytime city routes.

West Coast Express Ltd. / WCE
Parent: South Coast British Columbia Transportation Authority (TransLink)
#295, 601 West Cordova St., Vancouver, BC V6B 1G1
Tel: 604-488-8906; *Fax:* 604-689-3896
Toll-Free: 800-570-7245
wecustomerservice@translink.ca
www.translink.ca/About-Us/Corporate-Overview/Operat
Profile: The West Coast Express connects Vancouver to Mission via eight stations.

West Kootenay Transit System
Formerly: Kootenay Boundary Transit System
Parent: BC Transit Corporation
#101, 310 Ward St., Nelson, BC V1L 5S4
Toll-Free: 855-993-3100
www.bctransit.com/west-kootenay
Profile: West Kootenay Transit has routes available to the communities of Nelson & District, Trail & area, Nakusp & District, Castlegar & District, Slocan Valley & Kaslo & District. It also has many accessible services, including low floor busses, HandyDART & priority seating. It operates in three zones: Kootenay. Slocan & Columbia. The system is operated by Trail Transit Services, Arrow & Slocan Lakes Community Services & the City of Nelson.

Whistler Transit System
Formerly: WAVE Whistler & Valley Express
Parent: BC Transit Corporation
8025 Nesters Rd., Whistler, BC V0N 1B8
Tel: 604-932-4020
operations@whistlertransit.pwt.ca
bctransit.com/whistler
Profile: The Whistler transit system runs through Emerald Estates, Alpine Meadows, Spruce Grove, White Gold, Nesters, Tapleys Farm, Blueberry Hill, Whistler Village, the Upper Village, Alta Vista, Nordic Whistler Creek, Tamarisk, Function Junction & Pemberton. Buses are operated by Whistler Transit Ltd.

Whitehorse Transit
Whitehorse, YT
Tel: 867-668-8396
transit@whitehorse.ca
www.whitehorse.ca/departments/transit
Profile: Whitehorse Transit runs six days a week, with no service on Sundays or holidays. It operates 6 bus routes, & also provides accessible low-floor buses.
Cheri Malo, Transit Manager

Williams Lake Transit System
Parent: BC Transit Corporation
c/o Laker's Go-Bus Society, 88 - 1st Ave. North, Williams Lake, BC V2G 1Y6
Tel: 250-398-7812
www.bctransit.com/williams-lake
Profile: The Williams Lake Transit System operates four routes around the community, with accessible services such as handyDART available. The system is operated by the Laker's Go-Bus Society.

Winnipeg Transit
414 Osborne St., #B, Winnipeg, MB R3L 2A1
Tel: 204-986-5717; *Toll-Free:* 877-311-4974
311@winnipeg.com
winnipegtransit.com
Profile: Winnipeg Transit has 93 routes throughout the city, including main line routes, express routes and suburban feeders. The agency has a fleet of 640 buses.
Greg Ewankiw, Director

Wood Buffalo Transit
9816 Hardin St., Fort McMurray, AB T9K 4K3
Tel: 780-743-7931
transit@rmwb.ca
www.rmwb.ca/en/transit/transit.aspx

York Region Transit / YRT
50 High Tech Rd., 5th Fl., Richmond Hill, ON L4B 4N7
Tel: 905-762-2100; *Toll-Free:* 866-668-3978
www.yrt.ca
Profile: YRT offers more than 130 routes including conventional services, GO Shuttles, Express services, community buses & high school, college & university services & links with Brampton Transit, Durham Transit, MiWay & the TTC; VIVA bus rapid transit service is integrated with YRT to provide a 1-fare transit system across York Region. YRT has 123 Viva rapid buses, 406 conventional buses & 97 Mobility Plus vehicles.
Ann-Marie Carroll, Director, Transit Operations

Railroad Companies

Alberta Prairie Railway
4611 - 47th Ave., Stettler, AB T0C 2L1
Tel: 403-742-2811; *Fax:* 403-742-2844
Toll-Free: 800-282-3994
info@absteamtrain.com
www.absteamtrain.com

Big Sky Rail Corp.
Parent: Mobil Grain Ltd.
PO Box 3192, Regina, SK S4P 3G7
Tel: 306-992-5920; *Fax:* 306-992-5920
inquiries@bigskyrail.com
www.bigskyrail.com
Profile: This 250-km-long shortline railway runs in the west central region of Saskatchewan.

BNSF Railway Company
Formerly: Burlington Northern Sante Fe Railway
2650 Lou Menk Dr., Fort Worth, TX 76161-0056
Toll-Free: 800-795-2673
www.bnsf.com
Profile: 24,000 miles of track (30 miles in Canada); over 80,000 freight cars; 6,400 locomotives
Carl Ice, President & CEO

British Columbia Railway Company / BCRC
#600, 221 West Esplanade Ave., North Vancouver, BC V7M 3J3
Tel: 604-678-4735; *Fax:* 604-678-4736
www.bcrco.com
Profile: Offices of holding companies; Real estate operators of nonresidential buildings; Real estate agents & managers; Railroads, line-haul operating; Marine cargo handling
Gordon Westlake, President & CEO
604-678-4742
Kevin Steinberg, CFO & Vice-President, Finance
604-678-4747

Canadian National Railway Company / CN
935, rue de la Gauchetière ouest, Montréal, QC H3B 2M9
Ligne sans frais: 888-888-5909
www.cn.ca
Ticker Symbol: CNR / TSX; CNI / NYSE
Profile: Crossing the North American continent with over 21,000 route miles of track, the Canadian National Railway Company serves ports on the Atlantic, Pacific & Gulf coasts.
Jean-Jacques Ruest, President & CEO

Canadian Pacific Railway Limited / CP
7550 Ogden Dale Rd. SE, Calgary, AB T2C 4X9
Toll-Free: 888-333-6370
www.cpr.ca
Ticker Symbol: CP / TSX; NYSE
Profile: The transcontinental carrier operates in North America. It provides freight transportation, supply chain & logistics services.
Keith Creel, President & CEO

Cando Rail Services Ltd.
Formerly: Cando Contracting Ltd.
#400, 740 Rosser Ave., Brandon, MB R7A 0K9
Tel: 204-725-2627; *Fax:* 204-725-4100
Toll-Free: 866-989-5310
info@candorail.com
www.candorail.com
Profile: Cando operates the Barrie-Collingwood Railway & Central Manitoba Railway Inc. The company also provides the following services: industrial rail, rail car storage, mechanical, transload, engineering & track & railway material sales.
Brian Cornick, Chief Executive Officer

Cape Breton & Central Nova Scotia Railway / CBNS
Parent: Genesee & Wyoming Inc.
Genesee & Wyoming Inc., 20 West Ave., Darien, CT
Tel: 203-202-8900
corpcomm@gwrr.com
www.gwrr.com
Profile: 242 miles of track stretching from Truro to Sydney; interchanges with CN & SCR; moves paper, coal, lumber, petrolum products & chemicals.

Carlton Trail Railway Company / CTR
Parent: OmniTRAX, Inc.
1545 - 5th Ave. East, Prince Albert, SK S6V 7Z5
Tel: 306-763-9474; *Fax:* 306-763-9471
omnitrax.com/our-company/our-railroads/carlton-trai
Profile: The company operates on 103 miles of former CN track & specializes in transporting lumber from the Prince Albert area.
Matt Jurgens, Superintendent

Cartier Railway Company
Parent: Arcelor Mittal
Port-Cartier, QC
www.arcelormittal.com

Central Manitoba Railway / CEMR
Parent: Cando Rail Services Ltd.
PO Box 27, 2675 Day St., RR#5, Winnipeg, MB R2C 2Z2
Tel: 204-235-1175
www.candorail.com/cemr
Profile: The company owns & maintains 67 miles of track, & offers services such as transloading, track maintenance, locomotive repair, rail car repair & equipment leasing, storage & sales.

Chemins de fer Québec-Gatineau Inc.
Quebec Gatineau Railway Inc.
Parent: Genesee & Wyoming Inc.
Genesee & Wyoming Inc., 20 West Ave., Darien, CT
Tél: 203-202-8900; *Téléc:* 203-656-1092
corpcomm@gwrr.com
www.gwrr.com
John C. Hellmann, Chair, President & CEO

Compagnie du chemin de fer Lanaudière inc. / CFL
PO Box 2999, 5300, ch St-Gabriel, Saint-Félix-de-Valois, QC J0K 2M0
Tél: 450-889-5944; *Ligne sans frais:* 800-361-5598
www.cflanaudiere.com

CSX Transportation Inc.
500 Water St., 15th Fl., Jacksonville, FL 33202
Tel: 904-359-3200
www.csx.com
Profile: Operates trains that serve cities in Ontario & Quebec.
James M. Foote, President & CEO

Essex Terminal Railway Co. / ETR
Parent: Essex Morterm Holdings
1601 Lincoln Rd., Windsor, ON N8Y 2J3
Tel: 519-973-8222; *Fax:* 519-973-7234
info@etr.ca
www.etr.ca
Profile: Freight only; 24 miles of main track; connections with CN, CP, CSX & NS; 5 locomotives; 5 cars
Tony De Thomasis, President & CEO
519-973-8222 ext: 239, tdethomasis@etr.ca

Fife Lake Railway Ltd. / FLR
Parent: Great Western Railway Ltd.
c/o Great Western Railway, PO Box 669, 254 Centre St., Shaunavon, SK S0N 2M0
Tel: 306-297-2777; *Fax:* 306-297-2508
www.greatwesternrail.com/flr__rcrr.html
Profile: Owned by 7 municipalities & Great Western Railway, Fife Lake operates on 62 miles of track in Assiniboia.
Andrew Glastetter, General Manager
andrew.glastetter@greatwesternrail.com

Genesee & Wyoming Inc. / G&W
20 West Ave., Darien, CT
Tel: 203-202-8900; *Fax:* 203-656-1092
corpcomm@gwrr.com
www.gwrr.com
Profile: Genesee & Wyoming owns shortline & freight railroads in the USA, Canada, Australia, the Netherlands & Belgium. Canadian operations include: Cape Breton & Central Nova Scotia Railway; Goderich-Exeter Railway; Huron Central Railway; Ottawa Valley Railway; Southern Ontario Railway; St. Lawrence & Atlantic Railroad / St-Laurent & Atlantique Railroad; & Western Labrador Rail Services.
John C. Hellmann, Chair, President & CEO

Goderich-Exeter Railway
Parent: Genesee & Wyoming Inc.
Genesee & Wyoming Inc., 20 West Ave., Darien, CT
Tel: 203-202-8900; *Fax:* 203-656-1092
corpcomm@gwrr.com
www.gwrr.com
Profile: 71 miles of track in Southern Ontario, serving Goderich, Clinton, Hensall, Centralia, Seaforth, Mitchell & Stratford.
John C. Hellmann, Chair, President & CEO

Great Sandhills Railway / GSR
PO Box 726, 448 - 1st Ave. West, Leader, SK S0N 1H0
Tel: 306-628-4774; *Fax:* 306-628-4772
gsrail.net
Profile: Great Sandhills Railway was established in 2009 & operates a shortline railway on a former CP subdivision.
Perry Pellerin, Chief Executive Officer

Great Western Railway Ltd. / GWR
254 Centre St., Shaunavon, SK S0N 2M0
Tel: 306-297-2777; *Fax:* 306-297-2508
www.greatwesternrail.com
Profile: Great Western Railway offers the following services: grain & related product transportation; transportation of oil products; & railcar storage. GWR also co-owns Fife Lake Railway & services Red Coat Road & Rail.
Andrew Glastetter, General Manager
andrew.glastetter@greatwesternrail.com

Greater Winnipeg Water District Railway
c/o City of Winnipeg, 510 Main St., Winnipeg, MB R3B 1B9
www.winnipeg.ca/waterandwaste/dept/railway.stm
Profile: The railway is owned by the City of Winnipeg & is used to transport workers & supplies to the city's aqueduct, & the water intake facility at Shoal Lake.

Hudson Bay Railway Company / HBRY
Parent: Arctic Gateway Group LP
728 Bignell Ave., The Pas, MB R9A 1L8
Toll-Free: 888-445-1112
info@arcticgateway.com
arcticgateway.com/the-gateway/#railway
Profile: The company owns & operates 627 miles of former CN track & runs from Manitoba to the Hudson Bay.

Huron Central Railway / HCR
Parent: Genesee & Wyoming Inc.
Genesee & Wyoming Inc., 20 West Ave., Darien, CT
Tel: 203-202-8900; *Fax:* 203-656-1092
corpcomm@gwrr.com
www.gwrr.com
Profile: 173 miles of track; interchanges with CN & CP; moves
pulp & paper, forest products, chemicals, petroleum products,
steel & scrap.
John C. Hellmann, Chair, President & CEO

Keewatin Railway Company Ltd. / KRC
#710, 294 Portage Ave., Winnipeg, MB R3C 0B9
Tel: 204-942-2944; *Toll-Free:* 800-761-7110
www.krcrail.ca
Profile: Keewatin Railway is the second First Nations railway to
be created with financial assistance from the Government of
Canada. It operates on 185-mile stretch of track formerly
belonging to Hudson Railway Company.
Anthony Mayham, Chief Executive Officer

Last Mountain Railway / LMR
Parent: Mobil Grain Ltd.
PO Box 3192, Regina, SK S4P 3G7
Tel: 306-992-5915; *Fax:* 306-992-5915
inquiries@lastmountainrailway.com
lastmountainrailway.com
Profile: Last Mountain Railway operates on a shortline track
formerly owned by CN, that runs between Regina & Davidson.

Long Creek Railroad
PO Box 237, Torquay, SK S0C 1L0
Tel: 306-923-0022
longcreekrailroad@sasktel.net
www.longcreekrailroad.ca
Profile: Long Creek Railroad is community-owned & was
established in 2012 with funding from the Government of
Saskatchewan. The railway operates on 66 miles of former CP
track.
Adriaan Lievaart, President

New Brunswick & Maine Railways
Formerly: New Brunswick Southern Railway Company
Limited
Parent: J.D. Irving, Limited
PO Box 3189, 11 Gifford Rd., Saint John, NB E2M 4X8
Tel: 506-632-6314; *Fax:* 506-632-5818
Toll-Free: 877-838-6277
nbm.sales@nbmrailways.com
www.nbsouthern.com
Profile: NBM is a short railway line specializing in truck / rail
reloading for goods such as logs & lumber, wood chips, wood
pulp, chemicals & dry bulk.

Norfolk Southern Corp.
3 Commercial Pl., Norfolk, VA 23510-9241
Toll-Free: 855-667-3655
www.nscorp.com
Ticker Symbol: NSC / NYSE
Profile: Operating Subsidiary: Norfolk Southern Railway Co.;
21,500 track miles (245 miles in Canada); 3,000 locomotives
James A. Squires, Chair, President & CEO

OmniTRAX, Inc.
252 Clayton St., 4th Fl., Denver, CO
Tel: 303-398-4500; *Fax:* 303-398-4540
info@omnitrax.com
omnitrix.com
Profile: OmniTRAX operates 21 regional & shortline railroads in
the USA & Canada. The company has interests in railroads,
terminals, ports & industrial real estate.
Kevin L. Shuba, Chief Executive Officer
Sergio A. Sabatini, President

Ontario Northland Transportation Commission
555 Oak St. East, North Bay, ON P1B 8L3
Tel: 705-472-4500; *Fax:* 705-476-5598
Toll-Free: 800-363-7512
info@ontarionorthland.ca
ontarionorthland.ca
Profile: Owned by Province of Ontario; 26 locomotives; 700 cars
Thomas Laughren, Chair

Ontario Southland Railway Inc. / OSR
896 Cresthaven Cres., London, ON N6K 4W1
Tel: 519-471-9606; *Fax:* 519-471-7334
info@osrinc.ca
www.osrinc.ca
Profile: Ontario Southland Railway has operations in Guelph,
Tillsonburg & Woodstock & reaches to St. Thomas. The
company also provides railway contract operations, including
maintenance.

Orangeville Brampton Railway / OBRY
Parent: Trillium Railway
49 Town Line, Orangeville, ON L9W 1V1
Tel: 519-940-4204

Ottawa Valley Railway / OVR
Parent: Genesee & Wyoming Inc.
Genesee & Wyoming Inc., 20 West Ave., Darien, CT
Tel: 203-202-8900; *Fax:* 203-656-1092
corpcomm@gwrr.com
www.gwrr.com
Profile: 157 miles of track between Ontario & Québec;
interchanges with CP, ONTC & Ontario Northland; moves forest
products & chemicals
John C. Hellmann, Chair, President & CEO

Port Stanley Terminal Rail / PSTR
309 Bridge St., Port Stanley, ON N5L 1C5
Tel: 519-782-3730; *Fax:* 519-782-4385
Toll-Free: 877-244-4478
info@pstr.on.ca
www.pstr.on.ca
Profile: A historic railway featuring four diesel electric
locomotives from the 1940s & 50s & nine passenger cars; the
railway is maintained by volunteers.

**Québec North Shore & Labrador Railway Company
Chemin de fer QNS&L**
Parent: Iron Ore Company of Canada (IOC)
1 Retty St., Sept-Iles, QC G4R 3C7
Tél: 418-968-7603
qnsl@ironore.ca
www.qnsl.ca
Profile: Offers bulk, through-freight & way-freight rail services.

Red Coat Road & Rail Ltd. / RCRR
Parent: Great Western Railway Ltd.
PO Box 430, 116 Main St., Ogema, SK S0C 1Y0
Tel: 306-459-2544; *Fax:* 306-459-2468
redcoatroadandrail@gmail.com
redcoatroadandrail.com
Profile: Red Coat Road & Rail is a community-owned shortline
railway, & contracts Great Western Railway & Southern Prairie
Railway as operators.
Kevin Klemenz, President

Rocky Mountaineer Rail
#1100, 980 Howe St., Vancouver, BC V6Z 0C8
Toll-Free: 877-460-3200
reservations@rockymountaineer.com
www.rockymountaineer.com
Profile: Rocky Mountaineer offers vacation packages & train
excursions through the Canadian Rockies.
Steve Sammut, President & CEO
Tyson Matheson, Vice-President, Global Human Resources

**Saint Lawrence & Atlantic Railroad / SLR
Chemin de fer St-Laurent et Atlantique**
Parent: Genesee & Wyoming Inc.
Genesee & Wyoming Inc., 20 West Ave., Darien, CT
Tel: 203-202-8900; *Fax:* 203-656-1092
corpcomm@gwrr.com
www.gwrr.com
Profile: 95 miles of track; interchanges with CN, Central Maine
& Québec Railroad; moves aggregates, brick & cement,
chemicals, food & feed, forest products, intermodal loads, &
steel & scrap
John C. Hellmann, Chair, President & CEO

South Simcoe Railway
c/o South Simcoe Railway Heritage Corp., PO Box 186,
Tottenham, ON L0G 1W0
Tel: 905-936-5815
info@southsimcoerailway.ca
www.southsimcoerailway.ca
Profile: The South Simcoe Railway is the oldest operating
steam-powered railway in Ontario & offers excursions through
the Beeton Creek valley.
Eric Smith, President, Operations Manager & Master Mechanic
smith@southsimcoerailway.ca

Southern Ontario Railway / SOR
Parent: Genesee & Wyoming Inc.
Genesee & Wyoming Inc., 20 West Ave., Darient, CT
Tel: 203-202-8900
corpcomm@gwrr.com
www.gwrr.com
Profile: 6 miles of track; interchanges with CN; moves steel,
agricultural products, fuel & chemicals
John C. Hellmann, Chair, President & Chief Executive Officer

Southern Prairie Railway
401 Railway Ave., Ogema, SK S0C 1Y0
Tel: 306-459-7808
info@southernprairierailway.com
www.southernprairierailway.com
Profile: The railway provides historical excursions to
passengers, allowing visitors to visit the Town of Ogema & the
Deep South Pioneer Museum.

Southern Rails Cooperative Ltd. / SRCL
PO Box 297, Avonlea, SK S0H 0C0
Tel: 306-868-4435
Profile: Southern Rails Cooperative was the first shortline
railway in Saskatchewan, & is owned & operated by local
farmers. Two railways are operated, at a total of 71 km of
trackage; both railways are on former CP subdivisions.

Southern Railway of British Columbia Limited / SRY
2102 River Dr., New Westminster, BC V3M 6S3
Tel: 604-521-1966
www.sryraillink.com
Profile: The company provides freight services only, on around
125 miles of track; 29 locomotives; 700 cars; service on
Vancouver Island via Southern Railway of Vancouver Island
(SVI).
Gerald Linden, President

Thunder Rail Ltd.
PO Box 328, Arborfield, SK S0E 0A0
Tel: 306-769-8383
www.arborfieldsk.ca/thunder_rail.htm
Profile: The shortline railway is owned & operated by the
community of Arborfield, who purchased the track from Carlton
Trail Railway (OmniTRAX) in 2005.

Torch River Rail Inc.
525 Railway Ave., Choiceland, SK S0J 0M0
Tel: 306-428-2919
Profile: The short line railway has 45 km of track & runs on the
former White Fox CP subdivision.

Toronto Terminals Railway Company Ltd.
#1400B, 50 Bay St., Toronto, ON M5J 3A5
Tel: 416-864-3440
info@ttrly.com
www.ttrly.com
Profile: Operates passenger & freight trains throughout the
Union Station Railway Corridor with 9 service groups.
George Huggins, Director, Operations
416-864-3440 ext: 298, george.huggins@ttrly.com

Train touristique de Charlevoix Inc.
Parent: Le Massif de Charlevoix
50, rue de la ferme, Baie-Saint-Paul, QC G3Z 0G2
Ligne sans frais: 844-737-3282
info@traindecharlevoix.com
traindecharlevoix.com
Nancy Belley, Directrice générale
nbelley@reseaucharlevoix.com

Trillium Railway Co. Inc. / TRRY
PO Box 21, 2 Broadway St., Welland, ON L3B 5N9
Tel: 905-735-5529; *Fax:* 905-735-7559
www.trilliumrailway.com
Profile: Trillium operates local short line railways, including the
Port Colborne Harbour Railway.

Tshiuetin Rail Transportation Rail Inc.
148, boul des Montagnais, Uashat, QC G4R 5R2
Tél: 418-960-0982; *Téléc:* 418-960-0984
billetterie@tshiuetin.ca
www.tshiuetin.net
Profile: The railway is owned by the First Nations of Uashat Mak
Mani-Utenam, Matimekush-Lac John & Kawawachikamach, &
operates between Labrador & Québec.
Christopher Coggan, Interim Director General
Solange Fontaine, Director, Human Resources
sfontaine@tshiuetin.ca

VIA Rail Canada Inc.
PO Box 8116 Centre-Ville, Montréal, QC H3C 3N3
Tél: 514-871-6000; *Téléc:* 514-871-6104
Ligne sans frais: 800-842-7245
customer_relations@viarail.ca
www.viarail.ca
Profile: Railroads, line-haul operating; Local & suburban transit
Cynthia Garneau, President & CEO
Patricia Jasmin, Chief Financial Officer

Waterloo Central Railway
Southern Ontario Locomotive Restoration Society, PO Box 546, 50 Isabella St., St Jacobs, ON N0B 2N0
Toll-Free: 815-496-6843
info@waterloocentralrailway.com
waterloocentralrailway.com
Profile: Owned & operated by the Southern Ontario Locomotive Restoration Society, the railway offers steam engine tours from Waterloo to St. Jacobs.
Peter McGough, General Manager

Western Labrador Rail Services / WLRS
Parent: Genesee & Wyoming Inc.
Genesee & Wyoming Inc., 20 West Ave., Darien, CT
Tel: 203-202-8900; *Fax:* 203-656-1092
corpcomm@gwrr.com
www.gwrr.com
Profile: Provides rail service to mining companies in Labrador & the North Shore of Québec.
John C. Hellmann, Chair, President & CEO

Wheatland Railway Inc.
c/o Great Sandhills Railway, PO Box 568, 56 Hwy. 2 North, Wakaw, SK S0K 4P0
Tel: 306-233-3068; *Fax:* 306-233-3080
wheatlandrail.ca
Profile: Operated by Ggreat Sandhills Railway, the short line railway runs 47 miles between St. Louis & Tozke Jct, with an interchange with CN.
Amy Lintick, Railway Manager, Great Sandhills Railway
alintick@gsrailway.net

White Pass & Yukon Route / WP&YR
PO Box 435, 201 - 2nd Ave., Skagway, AK
Fax: 907-983-2734
Toll-Free: 800-343-7373
info@wpyr.com
wpyr.com
Profile: Provides a scenic 20 mile journey through the Yukon & Alaska.
Bob Berto, President
907-983-9800, Fax: 907-983-2017, bobb@surveypt.com
Tyler Rose, Executive Director, Human Resources & Strategic Planning
907-983-9800, Fax: 907-983-2658, trose@wpyr.com

York-Durham Heritage Railway / YDHR
19 Railway St., Uxbridge, ON L9P 1E5
Tel: 905-852-3696
ydhr@ydhr.ca
ydhr.ca
Profile: The historic railway is owned & operated by the York-Durham Heritage Railway Association & provides excursions between Stouffville, Goodwood & Uxbridge.

Trucking Companies

A&M International
Parent: TFI International Inc.
45, rue David Swan, East Angus, QC J0B 1R0
Tel: 819-832-4936; *Fax:* 819-832-2980
Toll-Free: 800-832-3865
www.aminternational.ca
Yvan Lapointe, Directeur général
yvan.lapointe@amtransport.net

Accord Transportation Ltd.
#801, 17665 - 66A Ave., Surrey, BC V3S 2A7
Tel: 604-575-7500; *Fax:* 604-575-7510
www.accordtransportation.com
Profile: Accord provides LTL, TL, cartage, logistics & regional services.

Albatrans Canada Inc.
#400, 124 Merton St., Toronto, ON M4S 2Z2
Tel: 416-923-6060; *Fax:* 416-923-6051
info.yto@albatrans.com
www.albatrans.com
Profile: Albatrans provides sea & air freight, customs brokerage, storage & IT services internationally, specializing in wine & spirits.
Maja Vukosavljevic, Chief Executive Officer

Alchemist Specialty Carriers Inc.
19402 - 54th Ave., Surrey, BC V3S 7H9
Tel: 604-882-1518; *Fax:* 604-882-1399
Toll-Free: 888-255-6311
alchemist@ascteam.com
alchemistspecialty.ca
Profile: Alchemist provides specialty hauling services to customers in the commercial, government & industrial sectors in Canada & the USA. Services include waste removal, hazardous material & biological waste transportation & 24/7 emergency service.
Justin Cheverie, General Manager

Ameri-Can Logistics
32146 King Rd., Abbotsford, BC V2T 5Z5
Tel: 604-851-5000; *Fax:* 604-851-5300
Toll-Free: 888-884-6225
www.ameri-canlogistics.com
Profile: Ameri-Can provides transportation logistics services, including expedited, cross-border, overnight & next-day & dangerous goods / hazmat.

Aquatrans Distributors Inc.
#103B & #203B, 8257 - 92nd St., Delta, BC V4G 1B5
Tel: 778-571-9192; *Fax:* 778-571-9255
Toll-Free: 800-666-8832
info@aquatrans.ca
aquatrans.ca
Profile: Aquatrans provides refrigerated, container & bulk commodity services.

Argus Carriers Ltd.
Parent: Mullen Group Ltd.
3839 Myrtle St., Burnaby, BC V5C 4G1
Tel: 604-433-1556; *Fax:* 604-433-3547
Toll-Free: 800-663-1890
office@arguscarriers.com
www.arguscarriers.com
Profile: Argus offers same-day as well as next-day local pickup & delivery. Regional LTL is also offered. The company serves Greater Vancouver, Fraser Valley, Vancouver Island, Thompson / Okanagan & the Northwest USA.

Armour Transportation Systems
689 Edinburgh Dr., Moncton, NB E1E 2L4
Tel: 506-857-0205; *Fax:* 506-859-9339
Toll-Free: 800-561-7987
armour@armour.ca
armour.ca
Profile: Armour provides regional LTL, North American TL, express courier, warehousing & distribution, specialized & port-to-door services. Long-haul subsidiaries include PoleStar, Triple B & Hillman's.
Wesley Armour, President & CEO

Arnold Bros. Transport Ltd.
739 Lagimodière Blvd., Winnipeg, MB R2J 0T8
Tel: 204-257-6666; *Fax:* 204-257-2213
Toll-Free: 800-665-9018
customerservice@arnoldbros.com
www.arnoldbros.com
Profile: Arnold Bros. specializes in full truckload services, with dry van & temperature-controlled transportation methods, in Canada & various locations in the USA. The company is ISO 9001:2008 registered.

Arrow Transportation Systems Inc.
PO Box 38, #1300, 999 West Hastings St., Vancouver, BC V6C 2W2
Tel: 250-374-3831; *Fax:* 250-374-0250
www.arrow.ca
Profile: Arrow provides transportation & logistics services in Canada & the USA. Subsidiaries include Alberta Trucking & Arrow Reload Systems Inc.

Atlas Courier Ltd.
1501 Hartley Ave., Coquitlam, BC V3K 6Z7
Tel: 604-875-1111; *Fax:* 604-879-2311
Toll-Free: 888-595-6633
info@atlascourier.com
www.atlascourier.com
Profile: Atlas is a courier company, delivering packages in the Greater Vancouver Area.

ATS Healthcare
100 Vaughan Valley Blvd., Vaughan, ON L4H 3C5
Tel: 416-744-4900; *Fax:* 416-744-4935
h-general1@ats.ca
www.atshealthcare.ca
Profile: ATS provides temperature-controlled transporation to the healthcare industry.

AYR Motor Express Inc.
46 Poplar St., Woodstock, ON E7M 4G2
Tel: 506-325-2205; *Fax:* 506-325-2008
Toll-Free: 800-668-0099
www.ayrmotor.com
Profile: AYR offers truckload, freight shipping, freight cross dock, freight brokerage & driver training services.
Joe Keenan, President
joe.keenan@ayrmotor.com

B&R-Eckel's Transport Ltd.
PO Box 6249, Bonnyville, AB T9N 2G8
Fax: 780-826-4301
Toll-Free: 800-661-3290
admin@breckels.com
www.breckels.com
Profile: B&R Eckel's provides transportation services mainly to the oilfield industry, but also serves areas across Canada & the USA. Services include LTL, overdimensional, jack & roll, rig & tank moving, lifting & tubular storage.
Victor Ringuette, President

Bergeron-Maybois
Parent: TFI International Inc.
PO Box 158, 200, rue des Routiers, Amos, QC J9T 3A6
Fax: 819-727-2948
Toll-Free: 800-549-2948
bergeron@bergeronmaybois.com
www.bergeronmaybois.com
Profile: Bergeron-Maybois specializes in transportation of forest products & serves Canada, the US & Mexico.
André Bergeron, Président & directeur général
abergeron@bergeronmaybois.com

Bernard Transport Ltd.
Parent: Mullen Group Ltd.
12536 - 71st St. NW, Edmonton, AB T5B 1W8
Tel: 780-477-9268

Besner
Parent: TFI International Inc.
1950, 3e rue, Saint-Romuald, QC G6W 5M6
Tél: 418-834-9891; *Ligne sans frais:* 800-463-4460
info@besner.com
www.transport-besner.com
François LeBlanc, Directeur
fleblanc@besner.com

Bison Transport
1001 Sherwin Rd., Winnipeg, MB R3H 0T8
Tel: 204-833-0000; *Fax:* 204-833-0112
Toll-Free: 800-462-4766
online@bisontransport.com
www.bisontransport.com
Profile: Bison offers dry van, refrigerated, intermodal, warehousing & distribution, asset-based logistics & long-combination vehicle services.
Don Streuber, President & CEO

Brasseur Transport Inc.
Parent: TFI International Inc.
1250, rue Industrielle, La Prairie, QC J5R 5G4
Tel: 450-444-7079; *Fax:* 450-444-9268
Toll-Free: 800-363-8323
info@brasseurtransport.com
www.brasseurtransport.com
Profile: Brasseur transports liquids (food products) in QC, ON, the Maritimes & the US.

Brookville Carriers Flatbed LP
Parent: Contrans Flatbed Group LP
79 Parkway Dr., Truro, NS B2N 5A9
Toll-Free: 800-565-1676
www.contransflatbedgroup.com/brookville-carriers
Profile: Brookeville specializes in transporting tandem, tridem & over-dimensional loads.

Bulk Carriers (PEI) Ltd.
779 Bannockburn Rd., Cornwall, PE C0A 1H0
Tel: 902-675-2600
bulkcarrierspei.com
Profile: Bulk Carriers offers refrigerated & dry trucking services, as well as logistics.
Jack Kelly, President & CEO
jack@bulkcarrierspei.com
Mike Schut, Administration & Human ResourcesVice-President
902-675-2600 ext: 2120, mike@bulkcarrierspei.com

Canada Cartage System
1115 Cardiff Blvd., Mississauga, ON L5S 1L8
Tel: 905-564-2115; *Toll-Free:* 800-268-2228
info@canadacartage.com
www.canadacartage.com
Profile: Canada Cartage provides dedicated trucking, freight management & warehouse & distribution services.
Jeff Lindsay, President & CEO

Canadian American Transportation Inc.
4, rue du Transport, Coteau-du-Lac, QC J0P 1B0
Tél: 450-763-6363; *Télec:* 450-763-2400
Ligne sans frais: 800-363-5313
cat@cat.ca
www.cat.ca

Profile: C.A.T. offers truckload, logistics & warehousing services.
Daniel Goyette, President

Can-Am West Carriers Inc.
Parent: Vedder Transportation Group
400 Riverside Rd., Abbotsford, BC V2S 4P4
Toll-Free: 866-857-1375
info@canamwest.com
www.canamtransportation.com
Profile: Can-Am West provides the following transportation services: van, flat deck, step deck, Super B Train, asset-based logistics, multi-commodity & international freight.
Fred Zweep, President, Vedder Transportation Group

Caneda Transport Ltd.
Parent: Mullen Group Ltd.
4330 - 46th Ave. SE, Calgary, AB T2B 3N7
Tel: 403-236-7900; Fax: 403-236-3914
Toll-Free: 800-661-9184
dispatch@cnaeda.com
www.caneda.com
Profile: Caneda is a medium-sized supply chain service provider, offering cross-border, specialized TL & LTL transportation services, 3PL services & warehousing.

Canpar Express
Parent: TFI International Inc.
#102, 201 Westcreek Blvd., Brampton, ON L6T 0G8
Toll-Free: 800-387-9335
customerservice@canpar.com
www.canpar.com
Profile: Canpar offers day-to-day shipping services in Canada & to the USA.

Can-Truck Inc.
2 Blair Dr., Brampton, ON L6T 2H5
Tel: 905-595-0408; Fax: 905-595-0438
www.can-truck.com
Profile: Concentrates mainly on truckload freight including consolation & distribution throughout North America.
Jagtar Raman, President
905-595-0408 ext: 106, jraman@can-truck.com

Caravan Transport Group
2284 Wyecroft Rd., Oakville, ON L6L 6M1
Tel: 905-338-5885; Fax: 905-338-8450
Toll-Free: 888-828-1727
info@caravangroup.com
caravangroup.com
Profile: Caravan provides TL, just-in-time & LTL services across North America.

Cascade Carriers LP
Parent: Mullen Group Ltd.
6111 Ogdendale Rd. SE, Calgary, AB T2C 2A4
Tel: 403-236-7110; Fax: 403-236-7118
Toll-Free: 800-655-5056
www.cascadecarriers.com
Profile: Cascade transports dry bulk goods for customers in the construction, building, oil & gas & food industries.
Richard Schultz, Operations Manager

Cascade Energy Services L.P.
Formerly: Majestic Oilfield Services Inc.
Parent: Mullen Group Ltd.
11504 Tahltan Rd., Fort St John, BC V1J 7C4
Tel: 250-785-0236; Fax: 250-785-0716
www.cascade-energy.ca
Profile: Cascade specializes in fluid distribution & transportation, as well as operating other oilfield service units & trucks, such as hot oiler, vacuum, pressure, filtration & end-dump. Fluid storage & inventory management services are also offered.
Geoff Derouin, Vice-President & General Manager
403-504-1155

Cavalier Transportation Services Inc.
Parent: TFI International Inc.
PO Box 10, 14091 Humber Station Rd., Bolton, ON L7E 5T1
Tel: 905-857-6981; Fax: 905-857-1932
Toll-Free: 800-263-2394
info@cavalier.ca
www.cavalier.ca
Profile: Cavalier provides the following services: overnight LTL, freight brokerage, warehousing & distribution, specialized transportation (such as flatbed, intermodal, refrigerated & hazardous materials).

Challenger Motor Freight Inc.
300 Maple Grove Rd., Cambridge, ON N3E 1B7
Tel: 519-653-6226; Fax: 519-653-9810
Toll-Free: 800-265-6358
websiteinquiry_info@challenger.com
www.challenger.com
Profile: Challenger transports goods between Canada & anywhere in North America. The company offers a full range of transportation, warehousing & logistics services.
Dan Einwechter, Founder & CEO

Christina River Landtran Transport
Parent: Landtran Truckload
25245 - 111th Ave., Acheson, AB T7X 6C8
Tel: 780-452-9414; Fax: 877-452-9414
sales@landtrantl.com
www.landtrantl.com/christina-river-landtran-transpo
Profile: Christina River Landtran Transport is an Aboriginal Joint Venture company with Fort McMurray First Nation #468. The company offers transportation services to the Alberta oil sands industry.

Clarke Transport Inc.
Parent: TFI International Inc.
#200, 201 Westcreek Blvd., Brampton, ON L6T 5S6
Tel: 905-291-3000
customerservice@clarketransport.com
www.clarkelink.com
Profile: Clarke is a domestic FTL, LTL, intermodal & highway carrier with facilities in major Canadian cities. Clarke also provides next-day road service between most ON & QC points through its Corridor Express division.

Concord Transportation
Parent: TFI International Inc.
96 Disco Rd., Toronto, ON M9W 0A3
Tel: 416-679-7400; Fax: 416-679-7422
Toll-Free: 800-387-4292
csteam@concordtrans.com
concordtransportation.com
Profile: Concord specializes in the transport of time-sensitive LTL & truckload freight throughout North America.

Consolidated Fastfrate Inc.
9701 Hwy. 50, Woodbridge, ON L4H 2G4
Fax: 905-893-1575
Toll-Free: 800-268-1564
www.fastfrate.com
Profile: Fastfrate provides LTL, dedicated, transload, warehousing & logistics services, as well as a range of specialty services.
Manny Calandrino, President & CEO

Continental Cartage
Parent: Landtran Truckload
25245 - 111th Ave., Acheson, AB T7X 6C8
Tel: 780-452-9414; Fax: 780-447-2292
Toll-Free: 877-452-9414
sales@landtrantl.com
www.landtrantl.com/continental-cartage
Profile: Continental Cartage offers a range of transportation services including flat deck, heavy haul, specialized commodities, contract hauling & Super B.

Contrans Flatbed Group LP
Parent: Contrans Group Inc.
80 - 3rd Line, Hagersville, ON N0A 1H0
Tel: 905-768-0310; Toll-Free: 877-790-1226
contransflatbedgroup.com
Profile: Contrans Flatbed provides flatbed carrier services through the following divisions: Tri-Line Carriers & Brookville Carriers. The company is able to transport legal weights all across North America, & heavy loads in Ontario, Quebec, the Maritimes, Michigan, Ohio, Indiana & New York, among other places. Over-dimensional loads can also be accommodated.
Kristen Fess, Vice-President
kfess@contrans.ca

Contrans Group Inc.
Formerly: Contrans Income Fund; Contrans Corp.
Parent: TFI International Inc.
PO Box 1669, 1179 Ridgeway Rd., Woodstock, ON N4S 0A9
Tel: 519-421-4600
www.contrans.ca
Profile: Contrans provides freight transportation services through its range of subsidiaries.
Steve Brookshaw, Executive Vice-President

Contrans Tank Group
Formerly: Laidlaw Carriers Tank LP
Parent: Contrans Group Inc.
PO Box 1571, 605 Athlone Ave., RR#4, Woodstock, ON N4S 0A7
Tel: 519-539-6103; Toll-Free: 800-465-8265
www.contrans.ca/operations/tank
Profile: Contrans Tank Group provides dry or liquid bulk transportation through Contrans Vrac & Tri-Line Carriers.
Dan Roberts, Vice-President

Cooney Transport Ltd.
113 Finch Ave. West, Toronto, ON M3J 2E8
Tel: 416-630-7044; Fax: 416-630-4216
info@cooney.ca
www.cooney.ca
Profile: Cooney provides general freight transportation, including van, flatbed & tanker services.
Steve Vail, Manager
svail@cooney.ca

Cornerstone Logistics LP
Parent: Contrans Group Inc.
#204, 2180 Buckingham Rd., Oakville, ON L6H 6H1
Tel: 905-339-1456; Fax: 905-339-3226
Toll-Free: 877-388-2888
info@cornerstonelogistics.com
cornerstonelogistics.com
Profile: Cornerstone provides the following services: LTL, TL, port-to-door, cargo, flatbed & specialized equipment, cross-border, logistics & trucking across North America.

Courtesy Freight Systems Ltd.
Parent: Mullen Group Ltd.
340 Simpson St., Thunder Bay, ON P7C 3H7
Tel: 807-623-3340; Toll-Free: 800-267-0598
info@courtesyfreight.com
www.courtesyfreight.com

La Crete Transport(79)Ltd.
Parent: TFI International Inc.
PO Box 248, La Crete, AB T0H 2H0
Tel: 780-928-3989; Fax: 780-928-3680
latrans@telusplanet.net
www.latrans.ca
Profile: La Crete Transport offers overnight shipping from Edmonton to most of northern Alberta.
Jake Fehr, General Manager
jfehr@latrans.ca

Custom Landtran Carriers
Parent: Landtran Truckload
25245 - 111th Ave., Acheson, AB T7X 6C8
Tel: 780-452-9414; Fax: 780-447-2292
Toll-Free: 877-452-9414
sales@landtrantl.com
www.landtrantl.com/custom-landtran-carriers
Profile: Custom Landtran Carriers offers heavy haul, over dimensional, specialized load trucking services, as well as freight & project management services.

Day & Ross Inc.
Parent: McCain Foods Limited
398 Main St., Hartland, NB E7P 1C6
Tel: 506-375-4401; Toll-Free: 800-561-0013
mydayross@dayandrossinc.ca
dayross.com
Profile: Day & Ross offers LTL & TL services within Canada & to the USA, as well as temperature-controlled transportation & a range of specialized services, including warehousing, heavy haul moves & small package service. Subsidiaries include Day & Ross General Freight, Sameday Worldwide, Day & Ross Dedicated Logistics & Day & Ross Supply Chain Solutions.
Bill Doherty, President & CEO
Mark Osborne, Vice-President, Human Resources, Human Resources

DB Schenker
Parent: Deutsche Bahn AG
5935 Airport Rd., 10th Fl., Mississauga, ON L4V 1W5
Tel: 905-676-0676; Fax: 905-677-0587
Toll-Free: 800-461-3686
hrdepartment.canada@dbschenker.com
www.dbschenker.com/ca-en
Profile: DB Schenker is a logistics & transportation company offering air freight, ocean freight & ground transport services. The company also customs brokerage & consulting services.
Jochen Thewes, Chief Executive Officer

Deck-Way
Parent: Hi-Way 9 Group of Companies
4120 - 78 Street Cres., Red Deer, AB T4P 3E3
Tel: 403-314-2831; *Toll-Free:* 877-444-9299
www.hi-way9.com/division_deckway_services.php
Profile: Deck-Way offers LTL flat-deck services throughout
Alberta & southwest Saskatchewan.

Det'on Cho Landtran Transport Ltd.
Formerly: Tli Cho Landtran Transport Ltd.
Parent: Landtran Truckload
100 Osprey Rd., Yellowknife, YT X1A 0G8
Tel: 867-675-1100
contact@detoncholandtran.com
www.landtrantl.com/deton-cho-landtran-transport
Profile: Det'on Cho Landtran Transport offers transportation
services between the Northwest Territories & the rest of North
America, including ice road services.

Durocher International
Parent: TFI International Inc.
1214, rte 255, Saint-Félix-de-Kingsey, QC J0B 2T0
Téléc: 819-848-3003
Ligne sans frais: 800-267-2042
direction@durocherinternational.com
www.durocherinternational.com

Eassons Transport Limited
1505 Harrington Rd., Kentville, NS B4N 3V7
Tel: 902-679-1153; *Fax:* 902-679-1162
www.eassons.com
Profile: Eassons Transport provides freight shipping services,
with offices in Nova Scotia, Newfoundland & Ontario.
Paul Easson, President
902-679-7131,

E-Can Oilfield Services LP
Parent: Mullen Group Ltd.
PO Box 510, Elk Point, SK T0A 1A0
Tel: 780-724-4018
ecan@e-can-oilfield.com
www.e-can-oilfield.com
Profile: E-Can provides fluid hauling & general oilfield
production services.

ECL Carriers LP
Parent: Contrans Group Inc.
7236 Colonel Talbot Rd., London, ON N6L 1H8
Tel: 519-652-3900; *Fax:* 519-652-9726
Toll-Free: 800-265-0934
www.contrans.ca/operations/waste/#eclcarriers
Profile: ECL Carriers specializes in the transportation of waste
across North America, as well as reclamation, storage &
trans-shipment & logistics services.
Ray Fillion, Vice-President
514- 94-4888

Edge Transportation Services Ltd.
Parent: Siemens Transportation Group Inc.
**c/o Siemens Transportation Group Inc., 2411 Wentz Ave.,
Saskatoon, SK S7K 3V6**
Tel: 306-934-1911; *Fax:* 306-975-9310
Toll-Free: 800-667-8557
customerservice@edgetransport.com
www.edgetransport.com
Profile: Edge Transportation offers specialized flat deck
equipment for over-dimensional loads.

Elite Fleet
Parent: Eassons Transport Limited
275 Caledonia Rd., Moncton, NB E1H 2E8
Tel: 506-863-0100; *Fax:* 506-858-0450
csr@directitgroup.ca
www.elitefleet.com
Debra Gioia, Owner
506-857-0223

Essen Transport Ltd.
PO Box 2229, 300 Airport Dr., Winkler, MB R6W 4B9
Tel: 204-325-5200; *Fax:* 204-325-5252
Toll-Free: 800-325-5252
essentransport.com
Profile: Founded in 1987, the transportation company operates
a fleet of 50 trucks that deliver throughout Canada & the United
States.
Nathan Elias, Manager
nathan@essentransport.com

Formula Powell LP
Parent: Mullen Group Ltd.
PO Box 1328, Grande Prairie, BC T8V 4Z1
Tel: 780-814-6045; *Fax:* 780-539-5822
formulapowell.com
Profile: Formula Powell specializes in equipment hauling, mud &
fluids hauling, mud warehousing & fluid storage & road mats for
the oilfield industry.

Gardewine Group Inc.
Parent: Mullen Group Ltd.
60 Eagle Dr., Winnipeg, MB R2R 1V5
Tel: 204-633-5795; *Toll-Free:* 800-282-8000
customerservice@gardewine.com
www.gardewine.com
Profile: Gardewine is a multi-service transportation company
operating in six divisions: General Freight, Dedicated, Deck,
Bulk, Logistics, & Moving & Storage.

Garry Mercer Trucking Inc.
1140 Midway Blvd., Mississauga, ON L5T 2C1
Toll-Free: 800-668-2980
www.gmercer.com
Profile: Garry Mercer Trucking specializes in LTL & FTL freight
between Ontario & the USA.
Gerry Mercer, President
Andrew Crabbe, General Manager & Manager, Dispatch

GHL Transport
Parent: TFI International Inc.
#102, 7887, rue Grenache, Anjou, QC H1J 1C4
Tél: 514-351-4501; *Ligne sans frais:* 800-589-3236
info@ghltransport.com
www.camionnageghl.com
Patrick Sarrazin, Directeur Général

Ghost Transportation Services
715E - 46th St. West, Saskatoon, SK S7L 6A1
Tel: 306-249-3515; *Fax:* 306-249-3335
customerservice@ghosttrans.com
www.ghosttrans.com
Profile: Ghost Transportation Services provides air, road, rail &
ocean transportation services, as well as warehousing,
distribution & storage.
Clay Dowling, Founder & CEO

Gibson Energy Inc.
#1700, 440 - 2nd Ave. SW, Calgary, AB T2P 5E9
Tel: 403-206-4000; *Fax:* 403-206-4001
communications@gibsonenergy.com
www.gibsonenergy.com
Ticker Symbol: GEI / TSX
Profile: Gibsons provides a range of services for the energy
industry, including transportation, marketing, terminals &
pipeline, custom treating terminals & distribution & processing.
The company's transportation services division moves crude oil,
liquids, dry bulk products & waste streams across North
America. Services include truck hauling, rail & pipeline injection
stations.
Steve Spaulding, President & CEO
Sean Brown, Senior Vice-President & CFO

GN Transport Ltd.
163 Bowes Rd., Concord, ON L4K 1H3
Tel: 905-760-2888; *Fax:* 905-760-2040
info@gntransport.com
www.gntransport.com
Profile: GN Transport owns 50 semi-tractors & 10 straight
trucks. The company also provides warehousing & other
transportation services.
Greg Nisan, President
greg@gntransport.com
Greg Nisan, President
905-760-2888 ext: 221, greg@gntransport.com

Go Transport Ltd.
9975 - 199B St., Langley, BC V1M 3G4
Tel: 604-525-0800; *Toll-Free:* 888-363-6699
dispatch@gotransport.ca
gotransport.ca
Profile: Go Transport provides delivery services for customers
needing tractor tailor transportation.
Mark Maarsman, Owner & General Manager

Golden International
Parent: TFI International Inc.
801, boul Industriel, Bois-des-Filion, QC J6Z 4T3
Tél: 450-628-8000; *Téléc:* 450-628-1003
Ligne sans frais: 800-363-2828
www.goldenintl.ca
Martin Godbout, General Manager
450-628-8000 ext: 7220, m.godbout@goldenintl.ca

Grimshaw Trucking LP
Parent: Mullen Group Ltd.
11510 - 151st St., Edmonton, AB T5M 3N6
Fax: 780-455-7818
Toll-Free: 888-414-2850
grm-custserv@gtlp.ca
www.grimshaw-trucking.com
Profile: Grimshaw provides general merchandise carrying (LTL
& TL) services to communities in Alberta, Northwest Territories &
British Columbia.
Gary Leddy, Vice-President & General Manager
780-414-2847

Group Express Inc.
170 Main St. North, Alexandria, ON K0C 1A0
Tel: 613-525-1275; *Fax:* 613-525-1278
Toll-Free: 800-387-6691
www.groupexpress.ca
Profile: Groupex offers LTL, TL & dedicated transportation
services.

Groupe Boutin Inc.
1397, rue Savoie, Plessisville, QC G6L 1J8
Tel: 819-362-7333; *Fax:* 819-362-3857
Toll-Free: 800-567-5841
info@boutinexpress.com
www.boutinexpress.com
Profile: Groupe Boutin offers roll-away, B-Train, closed van &
flat bed services, as well as warehousing & distribution.
Bernard Boutin, President

Groupe Guilbault Ltd.
#300, 8000, rue Armand-Viau, Québec, QC G2C 2E2
Tél: 418-681-5272; *Téléc:* 418-681-9198
Ligne sans frais: 800-463-2655
www.groupeguilbault.com

Groupe Robert Inc.
20, boul Marie-Victorin, Boucherville, QC J4B 1V5
Tel: 514-521-1011; *Toll-Free:* 800-361-8281
information@robert.ca
www.robert.ca
Profile: Groupe Robert operates in two lines of business:
transportation & storage & distribution. Under transportation, the
company provides LTL, TL, intermodal, transborder &
specialized services. Robert's storage division includes 20
warehouses in the areas of Montréal, Toronto & Québec City,
with over 2.5 million total sq. ft. of space.
Michel Robert, President

Harv Wilkening Transport Ltd. / HWT
Parent: Siemens Transportation Group Inc.
**c/o Siemens Transportation Group Inc., 2411 Wentz Ave.,
Saskatoon, SK S7K 3V6**
Tel: 306-934-1911; *Fax:* 306-975-9310
Toll-Free: 800-667-8557
sales@siemenstransport.com
www.hwtransport.com
Profile: HWT offers truckload services with satellite tracking, as
well as warehousing & distribution.

Heavy Crude Hauling LP / HCH
Parent: Mullen Group Ltd.
6601 - 62nd St., LLoydminster, AB T9V 3A9
Tel: 780-875-5358; *Fax:* 780-875-5825
Toll-Free: 877-875-5358
info@heavycrudehauling.com
www.heavycrudehauling.com
Profile: HCH provides fluid transportation for the oilfield industry.
Gordon Snider, Vice-President & General Manager

Highland Transport
Parent: TFI International Inc.
1201 Creditstone Rd., Concord, ON L4K 0C2
Fax: 905-532-0085
Toll-Free: 800-263-3356
www.highlandtransport.com/contact.html
Profile: Highland provides truckload & intermodal services.
Terry Gardiner, Vice-President, Operations
tgardiner@highlandtransport.com
John Hutton, General Manager, Intermodal
jhutton@highlandtransport.com

Hillman's Transfer Limited
Parent: Armour Transportation Systems
**Sydport Industrial Park, 410 Gatesway Ave., Sydney, NS
B2A 4V1**
Tel: 902-564-8113; *Fax:* 902-539-9498
Toll-Free: 800-565-9437
www.hillmanstransfer.com
Profile: Hillman's transports perishable & non-perishable goods
to the Maritimes, Central Canada & Eastern USA.

Hi-Tech Express Inc.
Parent: Siemens Transportation Group Inc.
c/o Siemens Transportation Group Inc., 2411 Wentz Ave.,
Saskatoon, SK S7K 3V6
Tel: 306-934-1911; *Toll-Free:* 800-661-7228
customerservice@hitechexpress.net
www.hitechexpress.net
Profile: Hi-Tech Express offers TL & LTL services to & from
Canada, as well as within the USA.

Hi-Way 9 Express Ltd.
Parent: Hi-Way 9 Group of Companies
711 Elgin Close, Drumheller, AB T0J 0Y0
Tel: 403-823-4242; *Fax:* 403-823-7424
Toll-Free: 800-622-5800
www.hi-way9.com/division_hiway9_services.php
Profile: Hi-Way 9 Express provides overnight, same-day &
time-critical LTL services to central & southern Alberta.

Hi-Way 9 Group of Companies
Parent: Mullen Group Ltd.
711 Elgin Close, Drumheller, AB T0J 0Y0
Tel: 403-823-4242; *Fax:* 403-823-7424
Toll-Free: 800-622-5800
www.hi-way9.com
Profile: Hi-Way 9 provides LTL, custom freight, flat deck & dry
goods services through their four subsidiaries: Hi-Way 9 Express
Ltd., Streamline Logistics, Deck-Way & Load-Way.
Reg Trentham, Vice-President & General Manager

ICS Courier
Parent: TFI International Inc.
300 Talbot St. West, Aylmer, ON N5H 1K2
Toll-Free: 888-427-8729
cservice@icscourier.ca
www.icscourier.ca
Profile: ICS is a business-to-business courier that specializes in
transporting packages & documents for next-day delivery.

International Truck & Engine Corporation Canada
Parent: Navistar Canada Inc.
PO Box 5337, Burlington, ON L7R 5A4
Tel: 905-332-2500
www.internationaltrucks.com
Profile: Dealers of trucks, buses, vans: engines, parts, services
& financing.
Troy Clarke, Chair, President & CEO

International Truckload Services Inc. / ITS
PO Box 1450, 107 Belleville Dr., Belleville, ON K8N 5J1
Tel: 613-961-5144; *Fax:* 613-961-1255
Toll-Free: 800-267-1888
info@itstruck.ca
www.itstruck.ca
Profile: ITS provides dry van, long haul, flatbed & dedicated
transportation services.
Rob Haggarty, President & COO
rhaggarty@itsinc.on.ca

JAF Transport
Parent: TFI International Inc.
1270, rue Volta, Boucherville, QC J4B 6G6
Tel: 450-449-4974; *Fax:* 450-449-2074
Toll-Free: 888-343-4974
info@jaf2000.com
www.jaf2000.com
Profile: JAF offers intermodal transport & warehousing in
Montréal, eastern Canada & western Canada, as well as the US.
André Gosselin, Directeur
transport.gosselin@bellnet.ca

Jay's Transportation Group
Parent: Mullen Group Ltd.
PO Box 4560, 555 Park St., Regina, SK S4P 3Y3
Tel: 305-569-9369; *Fax:* 306-721-4641
Toll-Free: 800-667-5988
info@jays.ca
jays.ca

JDI Logistics
Parent: J.D. Irving, Limited
300 Union St., Saint John, NB E2L 4M3
Tel: 506-633-6767; *Fax:* 506-648-3082
Toll-Free: 888-675-4888
customerservice@jdilogistics.com
www.jdilogistics.com
Profile: JDI Logistics is a third-party logistics company
specializing in pulp & paper & the food & beverage industry.

Kindersley Transport Ltd.
Parent: Siemens Transportation Group Inc.
c/o Siemens Transportation Group Inc., 2411 Wentz Ave.,
Saskatoon, SK S7K 3V6
Toll-Free: 800-667-8508
customerservice@kindersleytransport.com
www.kindersleytransport.com
Profile: Kindersley provides TL & LTL services in Canada & the
USA.

Kleysen Group LP
Parent: Mullen Group Ltd.
2800 McGillivray Blvd., Winnipeg, MB R4G 0B4
Toll-Free: 888-488-5550
kleysen@kleysen.com
kleysen.com
Profile: Kleysen provides bulk, deck, intermodal &
multi-commodity distribution to customers throughout Canada &
the USA.

Kooi Trucking Inc.
308 Main St. South, Waterford, ON N0E 1Y0
Tel: 519-443-0668
www.kooitrucking.com
Profile: Kooi Trucking Inc. is a North American freight company
operating since 1993.

Kriska Holdings Ltd.
850 Sophia St., Prescott, ON K0E 1T0
Tel: 613-925-5903; *Fax:* 613-925-1246
Toll-Free: 800-461-8000
info@kriska.com
www.kriska.com
Profile: Kriska primarily serves the area between Windsor & the
greater Montréal area, but also provides North American
coverage. Services include dry & temperature-controlled
transportation & specialized warehousing.
Mark Seymour, President
Pierre Carrier, Chief Financial Officer

Laidlaw Carriers Bulk LP
Parent: Contrans Group Inc.
240 Universal Rd., Woodstock, ON N4S 8L4
Toll-Free: 888-209-3869
www.contrans.ca/operations/bulk
Profile: Laidlaw Carriers Bulk division offers bulk material
transportation, as well as storage in its London warehouse.
Ray Fillion, Vice-President

Laidlaw Carriers Van LP
Parent: Contrans Group Inc.
#101, 5424 Dixie Rd., Mississauga, ON L4W 1E6
Toll-Free: 800-263-8267
www.contrans.ca/operations/van/#laidlawvan
Profile: Laidlaw Carriers Van division offers full truckload
service, mostly between Ontario, Quebec, the Maritimes & the
continental USA, for products such as paper, metals, food grade
products, building materials, general merchandise & hazardous
materials.
Brad Williams, General Manager

Landtran Logistics
Parent: Landtran Systems Inc.
4819 - 90A Ave., Edmonton, AB T6B 2Y3
Tel: 780-486-8607; *Fax:* 780-486-3545
headoffice@landtranlogistics.com
www.landtranlogistics.com
Profile: Landtran Logistics is a provider of delivery,
warehousing, cross-docking & distribution services across
western Canada. The company provides alternative solutions to
regular TL & LTL transport. Their services extend to intermodal,
air, rail & marine shipments.

Landtran Truckload
Parent: Landtran Systems Inc.
#25245, 111 Ave., Acheson, AB T7X 6C8
www.landtrantl.com
Profile: Through its subsidiaries, Landtran TL offers the
following services: LTL, TL deck, TL van, cross-border, ice
roads, dedicated delivery, warehousing, heavy haul /
over-dimensional, transportation management, refrigerated
transportation & local cartage / tractor service. Subsidiaries
include: Continental Cartage, Landtran Logistics, Monarch
Transport & Det'on Cho Landtran Transport Ltd.

Load-Way
Parent: Hi-Way 9 Group of Companies
711 Elgin Close, Drumheller, AB T0J 0Y0
Tel: 403-823-4242; *Toll-Free:* 800-622-5800
www.hi-way9.com/division_loadway_services.php

Profile: Load-Way is a service provided by Hi-Way 9 that seeks
to stack loads more safely than other systems, thereby reducing
damage during delivery.

Loomis Express
Parent: TFI International Inc.
200 Westcreek Blvd., Brampton, ON L6T 5S6
Tel: 905-460-2530; *Toll-Free:* 855-256-6647
www.loomis-express.com
Profile: Loomis delivers packages domestically & internationally,
including to 220 countries & 120,000 global destinations.

LTS Transportation Inc.
33 Lakeside Park Dr., Lakeside, NS B3T 1M4
Tel: 902-468-0490; *Toll-Free:* 800-770-5457
www.lighthouselogisticsltd.ca
Profile: Offers transportation, warehousing, crating & special
project services.
Ernest O'Toole, President

Manitoulin Group of Companies
PO Box 390, 154 Hwy. 540B, Gore Bay, ON P0P 1H0
Fax: 705-282-1788
Toll-Free: 800-461-1168
manitoulingroup.com
Profile: Manitoulin provides a range of transportation services,
including ground transport, logistics, customs brokerage,
warehousing & distribution & global forwarding, through their five
divisions.
Gord Smith, Chief Executive Officer

Maritime-Ontario Freight Lines Limited / M-O
1 Maritime-Ontario Blvd., Brampton, ON L6S 6G4
Tel: 905-792-6100; *Toll-Free:* 888-748-4388
www.m-o.com
Profile: M-O provides transportation & logistics services through
its six divisions: FreightWORKS, COLDChain, LogisticWORKS,
BULKServices & ParcelWORKS / DedicatedWORKS.
Doug Munro, Chief Executive Officer
Chris Walker, President
cwalker@m-o.com

Marol Express Inc.
Parent: CRS Express
2100, 95e rue, Saint-Georges, QC G5Y 8J3
Tél: 418-227-7379; *Téléc:* 418-222-5539
Ligne sans frais: 800-807-7379
info@crs-express.com
www.crs-express.com/marol-express
Profile: Marol Express fournit des services de transport et de
stockage de semi-remorques.
Carol Gilbert, Co-Fondatrice
Marc Rodrigue, Co-Fondateur

McArthur Express Inc.
Parent: TFI International Inc.
170 Werlich Dr., Cambridge, ON N1T 1N6
Tel: 519-740-7080; *Fax:* 519-740-1612
Toll-Free: 800-668-9691
sales@mcarthurexpress.com
mcarthurexpress.com
Profile: McArthur provides specialty trucking services (such as
for furniture, store fixtures & valuable products), as well as LTL &
TL, warehousing & emergency & expedited services.
David Wyville, Vice-President & General Manager

McKevitt Trucking Ltd.
1200 Carrick St., Thunder Bay, ON P7B 5P9
Tel: 807-623-0054; *Fax:* 807-622-8616
Toll-Free: 800-265-6837
mckevitt-trucking.com
Profile: McKevitt provides LTL & TL services from southern
Ontario, as well as warehousing & cross docking services.
Transport methods include refrigerated, heated, dry vans & flat
deck trailers.

McMurray Serv-U Expediting Ltd.
Parent: TFI International Inc.
320 Macdonald Cres., Fort McMurray, AB T9H 4B6
Tel: 780-791-3530; *Fax:* 780-790-0860
admin@mcmurrayservu.com
www.mcmurrayservu.com
Profile: McMurray provides transportation services to the
resource industry in the Fort McMurray area.
Elvis Penton, General Manager
elvis@mcmurrayservu.com

Michel Charbonneau Inc.
Parent: TFI International Inc.
3757, ch de la Lièvre nord, Mont-Laurier, QC J9L 0N9
Tel: 819-623-3333; *Fax:* 819-623-1233
transportcharbonneau@live.ca
www.transportcharbonneau.com

Profile: Charbonneau specializes in the transportation of forest products throughout QC & ON.
Steeve Charbonneau, Directeur Générale
scharbonneau@transportcharbonneau.com

Midland Transport Limited
Parent: J.D. Irving, Limited
100 Midland Dr., Dieppe, NB E1A 7G9
Toll-Free: 888-643-5263
customerservice@midlandtransport.com
www.midlandtransport.com
Profile: Midland specializes in less-than-truckload & truckload services in eastern Canada & the United States. Divisions include: UniLine, Prime Time, Econo Line, Courier, Coast Line, Dedicated Solutions, Green Line & Refrigerated Distribution Services.

Mill Creek Motor Freight LP
Parent: Kriska Holdings Ltd.
101 Earl Thompson Rd., Ayr, ON N0B 1E0
Tel: 519-623-6632; *Fax:* 519-740-0081
Toll-Free: 800-265-7868
millcreek.on.ca
Profile: Mill Creek provides van, flatbed, warehousing, logistics, intermodal & customs services.
Renate Hargreaves, General Manager
403-652-8888 ext: 3678, rhargreaves@millcreek.on.ca
Matt Kaczmarski, Director, Operations
403-652-8888 ext: 3670, mkaczmarski@millcreek.on.ca
Suzanne House, Manager, Human Resources
403-652-8888 ext: 3686, shouse@millcreek.on.ca

Monarch Transport (1975) Ltd.
Parent: Landtran Truckload
3464 - 78th Ave., Edmonton, AB T6B 2X9
Tel: 780-440-6528; *Fax:* 780-463-3552
Toll-Free: 800-661-9937
www.monarchtransport.com
Profile: Monarch provides transportation logistics to points in Canada, the USA & Mexico.

Mullen Group Ltd.
Formerly: Mullen Transportation Inc.
#121A, 31 Southridge Dr., Okotoks, AB T1S 2N3
Tel: 403-995-5200; *Fax:* 403-995-5298
Toll-Free: 866-995-7711
www.mullen-group.com
Ticker Symbol: MTL / TSX
Profile: Mullen Group serves western Canada's oil & natural gas industry by providing transportation & related services. The company also provides management & financial services as well as technology & systems support to the independently operated businesses that it owns.
Murray K. Mullen, Chair, President & CEO
Richard Maloney, Senior Vice-President
P. Stephen Clark, Chief Financial Officer

Mullen Oilfield Services LP
Parent: Mullen Group Ltd.
#600, 333 - 11th Ave. SW, Calgary, AB T2R 1L9
Fax: 403-213-4710
Toll-Free: 877-213-4700
sales@mullenoilfield.com
www.mullenoilfield.com
Profile: Mullen Oilfield specializes in moving, transferring & relocating drilling rigs throughout Western Canada.
Rick Henning, Vice-President
403-213-4715

Mullen Trucking Corp.
Parent: Mullen Group Ltd.
#100, 80079 Maple Leaf Rd., Aldersyde, AB T0L 0A0
Tel: 403-652-8888; *Fax:* 403-652-1368
Toll-Free: 800-661-1469
info@mullentrucking.com
www.mullentrucking.com
Profile: Mullen Trucking provides LTL, TL & hot shot services throughout North America. Mullen operates its own satellite system to track deliveries.

Musket Transport Ltd.
2215 Royal Windsor Dr., Mississauga, ON L5J 1K5
Tel: 905-823-7800; *Fax:* 905-823-7555
support@musket.ca
www.musket.ca
Profile: Musket provides intermodal shipping between Ontario, Québec & the USA.
Jaime Rosa, General Manager & Director, Operations
jaime.rosa@musket.ca

National Fast Freight
Parent: TFI International Inc.
107 Alfred Kuehne Blvd., Brampton, ON L6T 4K3
Tel: 905-494-4808; *Fax:* 905-494-4809
Toll-Free: 800-563-2223
careers@nationalfastfreight.com
www.nationalfastfreight.com
Profile: National Fast Freight offers FTL & LTL services throughout Canada, with intermodal & road-based solutions.

Normandin Transit Inc.
Parent: TFI International Inc.
151, boul Industriel, Napierville, QC J0J 1L0
Tél: 450-245-0445; *Téléc:* 450-245-0441
Ligne sans frais: 800-667-8780
info@normandintransit.com
www.normandintransit.com

Northern Industrial Carriers Ltd. / NIC
7823 - 34th St., Edmonton, AB T6B 2V5
Tel: 780-465-0341; *Fax:* 780-469-4206
sales@nictrucking.com
www.nictrucking.com
Profile: NIC provides transportation services to the petroleum, mining & manufacturing industries. Operating divisions include: Van, Dry & Liquid Bulk, Oilfield, Deck, Heavy Haul & Project Management.

Overland West Freight Lines Ltd.
Formerly: Overland Freight Lines; West Arm Truck Lines
11398 Bridgeview Dr., Surrey, BC V3R 0C2
Tel: 604-580-4600; *Fax:* 604-580-4601
Toll-Free: 800-698-2111
admin@overlandwest.ca
www.overlandwest.ca
Profile: The company provides LTL-freight-courier service in British Columbia, Alberta, & the Western USA, & primarily serves the retail, commercial, mineral, forestry & municipal construction sectors.

P&W Intermodal
Parent: TFI International Inc.
36 North Queen St., Toronto, ON M8Z 2C4
Tel: 905-849-1228; *Fax:* 905-849-1255
www.mtmx.ca
Mark Joczys, General Manager
mjoczys@pwintermodal.ca

Pacific Coast Express Ltd.
10299 Grace Rd., Surrey, BC V3V 3V7
Tel: 604-582-3230; *Fax:* 604-588-7906
Toll-Free: 800-667-6061
service@pcx.ca
www.pcx.ca
Profile: The primary service offered by the company is expedited LTL/TL, dry van motor freight service between all points in Western Canada & markets in Arizona, California, Oregon Washington & Mexico. The company also provides selected service to points in Idaho & Utah from British Columbia & Alberta, as well as transportation to & from Vancouver Island.

Papineau International
Parent: TFI International Inc.
851, boul Roland-Godard, Saint-Jérôme, QC J7Y 4C2
Tel: 450-432-7555; *Toll-Free:* 800-363-3666
www.papineauintl.com
Profile: Papineau has a fleet of 300 trailers & provides general transportation, alternative means of transportation & hazardous material transportation in Canada & the US.

Paul's Hauling Ltd.
250 Oak Point Hwy., Winnipeg, MB R2R 1V1
Tel: 204-633-4330; *Fax:* 204-694-4335
info@paulshauling.com
paulshauling.com
Profile: Paul's is a transporter of bulk goods primarily for the agricultural & petroleum industries.
Rod Corbett, Vice-President
rodcorbett@paulshauling.com

Payne Transportation LP
Parent: Mullen Group Ltd.
PO Box 67, 435 Lucas Ave., Winnipeg, MB R3C 2E6
Tel: 204-953-1400; *Fax:* 204-694-5810
Toll-Free: 866-467-2963
paynetransportation.com
Profile: Payne Transportation provides open deck, expedited LTL, dry van, logistics & specialized heavy haul services.
Tom Payne, President & General Manager

Pe Ben Oilfield Services LP
Parent: Mullen Group Ltd.
605 - 17th Ave., Nisku, AB T9E 7T2
Tel: 780-955-2618; *Fax:* 780-955-7286
Toll-Free: 855-955-7473
info@peben.com
www.peben.com
Profile: Pe Ben specializes in transporting Oil Country Tubular Goods (OCTG), such as drill pipe, casing & tubing, for the oilfield industry. The company mainly focuses on Western Canada, but is capable of operating anywhere in North America.
Darryl Esch, Senior Vice-President & General Manager
vp@peben.com

Penner International Inc.
Parent: Canadian American Transportation Inc. (C.A.T.)
20 PTH 12 North, Steinbach, MB R5G 1B7
Toll-Free: 866-729-7134
www.penner.ca
Profile: Penner provides TL dry van (both international & domestic) & distribution services. Shipments are tracked via satellite.
Allan Penner, President

Polar Express Transportation Ltd.
#4, 10097 - 201st St., Langley, BC V1M 3G4
Tel: 604-888-3729; *Fax:* 604-888-3759
Toll-Free: 800-938-3525
info@polarexpresstrans.com
polarexpresstrans.com
Profile: Polar Express offers LTL, full load, pickup / delivery & warehousing servies.
Jamie Plowman, President & General Manager

Portage Transport Inc.
1450 Lorne Ave. East, Portage la Prarie, MB R1N 4A2
Fax: 204-239-1427
Toll-Free: 800-251-4607
www.portagetransport.com
Profile: Portage Transport provides short & long distance freight services to customers in Manitoba.
Bernie Driedger, President & CEO
bernie.driedger@portagetransport.com
Liz Driedger, Vice-President & CFO
liz.driedger@portagetransport.com
Laura Kirchner, Contact, Human Resources & Payroll
laura.kirchner@portagetransport.com

Premay Equipment LP
Parent: Mullen Group Ltd.
11310 - 215th St., Edmonton, AB T5S 2B5
Tel: 780-447-5555; *Fax:* 780-447-3744
Toll-Free: 800-661-9315
inquiries@premayequipment.com
www.premay.com
Profile: Premay provides specialized transportation & rigging services to clients in the oilfield industry, including conventional transport, hydraulic heavy haul & railcar on- & off-loading. Other services include jack & roll, gantry work, engineering & logistics & mine services.

Premay Pipeline Hauling LP
Parent: Mullen Group Ltd.
22703 - 112th Ave., Edmonton, AB T5S 2M4
Tel: 780-447-3014; *Fax:* 780-447-3040
Toll-Free: 800-471-7976
info@premaypipeline.com
www.premaypipeline.com
Profile: Premay Pipeline operates a fleet of equipment including tractors, trailers, cranes & side booms that allow them to coordinate & transport pipeline for the oilfield industry.
Paul Schultz, Vice-President

Premium Transportation Inc.
39978 Crediton Rd., Centralia, ON N0M 1K0
Tel: 519-228-7779; *Fax:* 519-228-7799
Toll-Free: 888-875-0030
www.premiumtransportation.ca
Profile: Premium Transportation specializes in moving temperature controlled dry freight. It provides services to & from the U.S. & Western Canada.
Mike Hogan, President

Purolator Inc.
Formerly: Purolator Courier Ltd.
5995 Avebury Rd., Mississauga, ON L5R 3T8
Toll-Free: 888-744-7123
www.purolator.com
Profile: Purolator provides a range of courier & freight services to Canadian & international destinations.
John Ferguson, President & CEO

Ken Johnston, Senior Vice-President & Chief Human Resources Officer
Roslyn Samtleben, Senior Vice-President & CFO
Chris Spanjaard, Senior Vice-President & COO

Quik X
Parent: TFI International Inc.
Bdlg. B, 5425 Dixie Rd., Mississauga, ON L4W 1E6
Tel: 905-238-9213; *Fax:* 905-362-9564
Toll-Free: 800-461-8023
www.quikx.com
Profile: Quik X provides LTL, truckload, intermodal, logistics & warehousing services through its five divisions: Quik X Transportation, Quik X Logistics, Roadfast & Quiktrax Intermodal.

Quill Transport Ltd.
Parent: Siemens Transportation Group Inc.
c/o Siemens Transportation Group Inc., 2411 Wentz Ave., Saskatoon, SK S7K 3V6
Tel: 306-934-1911; *Fax:* 306-975-9310
Toll-Free: 800-667-3653
customerservice@quilltransport.com
www.quilltransport.com
Profile: Quill offers TL & LTL pickup & delivery services.

RDK Transportation Co.
Parent: Mullen Group Ltd.
2 Cory Lane, Saskatoon, SK S7K 3J7
Tel: 306-651-6955
rdktransportation.com

Rolls Right Industries Ltd.
2864 Norland Ave., Burnaby, BC V5B 3A6
Tel: 604-298-0080; *Fax:* 604-298-1366
info@rollsright.ca
www.rollsright.ca
Profile: Rolls Right Industries offers LTL, TL, container hauling & warehouse moving services.

The Rosedale Group
6845 Invader Cres., Mississauga, ON L5T 2B7
Tel: 905-670-0057; *Fax:* 905-670-7271
Toll-Free: 877-588-0057
hello@rosedalegroup.ca
www.rosedale.ca
Profile: Rosedale offers LTL & TL service in Canada & between Canada & the USA; USA domestic TL & flatbed service; in-house logistics; & warehousing. The company's equipment is satellite-tracked.
Rolly Uloth, President

Rosenau Transport Ltd.
3300 - 76th Ave. NW, Edmonton, AB T6P 1J4
Tel: 780-431-2877; *Fax:* 780-431-0599
Toll-Free: 800-371-6895
info@rosenau.org
www.rosenau.org
Profile: Rosenau provides LTL, full load, bulk, hot shot / express, consolidated, overnight, deck, container, heated van & scheduled delivery services.

RST Industries
Parent: J.D. Irving, Limited
485 McAllister Dr., Saint John, NB E2L 4H8
Tel: 506-634-8800; *Toll-Free:* 800-463-8551
sales@rsttransport.com
www.rsttransport.com
Profile: RST specializes in the transportation of petroleum, propane, chemicals, food grade products & dry bulk, & offers flatbed services as well. The Commodities Division, based in Toronto, provides customers with logistics services.

Service Ganeca Inc.
Parent: TFI International Inc.
1155, ch Brunelle, Carignan, QC J3L 0L1
Tél: 450-447-2846; *Téléc:* 866-922-8008
Ligne sans frais: 800-561-7444
info@ganeca.ca
www.ganeca.ca
Yvan Lapointe, Directeur général
819-832-4936, yvan.lapointe@amtransport.net

SGT 2000 Inc.
354, ch Yamaska, Saint-Germain, QC J0C 1K0
Tel: 819-395-4213; *Fax:* 819-395-6243; *Toll-Free:* 800-363-4216
info@sgt.ca
www.sgt2000.com
Profile: SGT offers dry box, flatbed, container, warehousing, logistics & trailer-leasing services.
Denis Coderre, President

Shadow Lines Transportation Group
9975 - 199B St., Langley, BC V1M 3G4
Tel: 604-888-2928; *Toll-Free:* 800-663-1421
shadow-group.com
Profile: Shadow Lines offers the following services through its subsidiary companies: container, flat deck, linehaul, logistics, bulk solutions, waste mangement, portable toilets & security fencing.

Siemens Transportation Group Inc.
2411 Wentz Ave., Saskatoon, SK S7K 3V6
Tel: 306-934-1911; *Toll-Free:* 800-667-8557
www.siemenstransport.com
Profile: Siemens operates 10 trucking divisions whose services include international TL, LTL, international flat deck, ground courier & warehousing.
Doug Siemens, President

Simard Transport Ltd.
1212, 32é av, Montréal, QC H8T 3K7
Tél: 514-636-9411; *Téléc:* 514-633-8078
Ligne sans frais: 888-282-9321
sales@simard.ca
www.simard.ca
Profile: Simard provides local, regional & national transportation services including van, LTL, container, intermodal & logistics.

SLH Transport Inc.
Formerly: Canadian American Transportation Inc.
1585 Centennial Dr., Kingston, ON K7P 0K4
Toll-Free: 888-854-7548
customerservice@slh.ca
www.slh.ca
Profile: SLH provides the following services: truckload (Canada & cross-border), freight management throughout North America & fleet outsourcing services.
Paul Cooper, President

Smook Contractors Ltd.
Parent: Mullen Group Ltd.
101 Hayes Rd., Thompson, MB R8N 1M3
Tel: 204-677-1560; *Fax:* 204-778-7836
info@smook.ca
www.smook.ca
Profile: Smook provides winter road, oversized & heavy hauling, as well as other contracting services such as brilling & blasting, earth & rock excavation, environmental clean-up & soil remediation, mine construction & site restoration & more.

Spearing Service L.P.
Parent: Mullen Group Ltd.
PO Box 83, 23 Marion Ave., Oxbow, SK S0C 2B0
Fax: 306-483- 291
Toll-Free: 800-862-7885
www.spearingservice.com
Profile: Spearing provides hauling servies to & from drill sites, as well as operating vacuum & pressure trucks & providing storage for sand & gravel.

Streamline Logistics
Parent: Hi-Way 9 Group of Companies
1783 - 120th Ave. NE, Calgary, AB T3K 0R1
Tel: 403-250-1563; *Toll-Free:* 877-787-5436
www.hi-way9.com/division_streamline_services.php
Profile: Streamline provides logistics services from warehousing to distribution.

Sunbury Transport
Parent: J.D. Irving, Limited
Saint John, NB
Tel: 506-634-8800; *Fax:* 888-559-9799
Toll-Free: 800-786-2879
customerservice@sunbury.ca
www.sunbury.ca
Profile: Sunbury provides transportation by van & flatbed, specializes in dry bulk goods & also provides logistics & brokerage services.

SureTrack Group
321 Courtland Ave., Concord, ON L4K 5B5
Tel: 905-832-8324; *Fax:* 905-832-1238
Toll-Free: 800-269-1151
www.suretrack.ca
Profile: The SureTrack Group's subsidiaries offer a number of services including LTL, FTL, trucking, garment transport, courier, 3PL & logistics.

Tenold Transportation LP
Parent: Mullen Group Ltd.
19470 - 94th Ave., Surrey, BC V4N 4E5
Tel: 604-888-7822; *Fax:* 604-888-0394
Toll-Free: 800-663-0094
tenold.com

Profile: Tenold provides intermodal, open deck, van, warehousing & distributing services.
Ben Thomson, President
604-881-7812

TF Truckload & Logistics
Parent: TFI International Inc.
2840 - 76th Ave. NW, Edmonton, AB T6P 1J4
Tel: 780-454-0761; *Fax:* 780-452-9438
Toll-Free: 800-663-8477
www.tftruckloadlogistics.com
Profile: Total Transfer provides truckload & heavy hauling services across North America
John Truong, General Manager
780-637-8781

TFI International Inc.
Formerly: TransForce Inc.
#500, 8801, rte Transcanadienne, Montréal, QC H4S 1Z6
Tél: 514-331-4000; *Téléc:* 514-337-4200
Ticker Symbol: TFII / TSX
Profile: TFI International is a transportation & logistics industry, operating across North America through its subsidiaries. The company services the packagae & courier, less-than-truckload, truckload & logistics industries.
Alain Bédard, Chair, President & CEO
David Saperstein, Chief Financial Officer

TForce Integrated Solutions
Parent: TFI International Inc.
96 Disco Rd., Toronto, ON M9W 0A3
Tel: 416-679-7979; *Fax:* 416-679-7845
Toll-Free: 800-265-6085
contact_sales@tforce-solutions.com
www.tforce-solutions.com
Profile: TForce provides small parcel, LTL, truckload & air freight services.
Mike Hover, President
contact_executive@tforce-solutions.com

Thomson Terminals Limited
100 Iron St., Toronto, ON M9W 5L9
Tel: 416-240-0897; *Fax:* 416-240-0624
solutions@thomsongroup.com
www.thomsongroup.com
Profile: Thomson provides services in four main categories: Warehousing, Freight & Transportation, Design Build & Consulting. Under the Freight & Transportation division the company offers FTL (Canada & USA), LTL (Canada), expedited services, as well as fleet management, plant & warehouse moves & job site delivery.
Jim Thomson, President & CEO

TMT Freight System
14 Cadetta Rd., Brampton, ON L6T 3Z8
Tel: 905-794-9845; *Fax:* 905-794-9846
Toll-Free: 888-817-4410
info@tmtfreight.com
www.tmtfreight.com
Profile: TMT Freight System was established in 1993 & provides intermodal & warehousing services.
Bobby Mahal, President
bobby@tmtfreight.com

Transport Bourassa Inc.
800, rue Dijon, Saint-Jean-sur-Richelieu, ON J3B 8G3
Tél: 450-346-5313; *Téléc:* 450-346-5150
Ligne sans frais: 800-363-9254
www.bourassa.ca
Profile: Transport Bourassa provides LTL & TL services in Quebec, Ontario & the USA, including the transportation of hazardous materials.

Transport Couture
Parent: TFI International Inc.
99, rte 271 sud, Saint-Éphrem-de-Beauce, QC G0M 1R0
Tél: 418-484-2104; *Téléc:* 418-484-5440
Ligne sans frais: 800-463-1671
info@tcfl.com
www.tcfl.com
Serge Poulin, Directeur général
418-484-2104 ext: 1226, serge.poulin@couturetransport.com

Transport Grégoire
Parent: TFI International Inc.
850, rue Labonté, Drummondville, QC J2C 5Y4
Tél: 819-477-6599; *Téléc:* 819-477-1174
Ligne sans frais: 800-461-8813
info@transportgregoire.com
www.transportgregoire.com
Lee Donovan, Directeur, Opérations
lee@transportgregoire.com

Transport J.C.Germain
Parent: TFI International Inc.
1200, rue Père-Daniel, Trois-Rivières, QC G9A 5R6
Tel: 819-370-3422; Fax: 819-370-3360
Toll-Free: 800-263-3929
transportjcgermain.com
Profile: Transport J.C.Germain provides TL, flatbed, cross-border & storage services in Canada & the US.

Transport Morneau inc.
40, rue Principale, Saint-Arsène, QC G0L 2K0
Tel: 418-862-2727; Fax: 418-862-7063
Toll-Free: 844-884-2727
www.groupemorneau.com
Profile: Morneau provides general LTL & TL services through its Transport division; temperature-controlled transportaton through Eskimo Express; import / export services through Groupe Réflexion; & transportation management services through Solution Morneau.
André Morneau, President
418-681-1212

TransX Group of Companies
2595 Inkster Blvd., Winnipeg, MB R3C 2E6
Tel: 204-632-6694; Fax: 204-694-2958
Toll-Free: 800-665-7392
transx.com
Profile: Founded in 1963, TransX Group is Canada's largest private transportation company. With a fleet of 1,500 trucks, 4,000 trailers, 1,000 intermodal containers, 12 North American terminals and 3,000 employees, the company provides transportation & logistics services for businesses.
Louie Tolaini, Founder & Owner

Trappers Transport Ltd.
1300 Redonda St., Winnipeg, MB R2C 3T7
Tel: 204-697-7647; Fax: 204-663-5569
Toll-Free: 800-561-9696
www.trapperstransport.com
Profile: Trappers Transport specializes in transporting refrigerated LTL or full loads throughout North America. The company's maintenance shop services & repairs all makes & models of trucks, trailers, heavy equipment & reefer units.
Dan Omeniuk, Chair & CEO

Travelers Transport Services
Services de transport Travelers
195 Heart Lake Rd. South, Brampton, ON L6W 3N6
Tel: 905-457-8789; Fax: 905-457-8084
Toll-Free: 800-265-8789
travelers.ca
Profile: Travelers provides expedited, regular van, heated, warehousing, logistic equipment & third-party logistics services.

Triangle Freight Services Ltd.
Parent: Siemens Transportation Group Inc.
3550 Idylwyld Dr. North, Saskatoon, SK S7L 6G3
Tel: 306-373-7744; Fax: 306-975-9310
Toll-Free: 800-667-8402
customerservice@trianglefreight.com
www.trianglefreight.com
Profile: Triangle Freight provides flat deck transportation services to the oilfield, farm & industrial equipment sectors.

Tri-Line Carriers LP
Parent: Contrans Flatbed Group LP
235185 Ryan Rd., Rocky View, AB T1X 0K1
Toll-Free: 800-661-9191
www.contransflatbedgroup.com/tri-line-carriers
Profile: Tri-Line provides transportation services to the oilfield equipment, steel, machinery & building products industries, among others.

Trimac Transportation Services LP
Formerly: Trimac Corporation
3215 - 12th St. NE, Calgary, AB T2E 7S9
Tel: 403-298-5100; Fax: 403-298-5258
www.trimac.com
Ticker Symbol: TMA / TSX
Profile: The company provides services in highway transportation & North American hauling of bulk commodities.
Mathieu Faure, Chief Executive Officer

Tripar Transportation LP
Parent: TFI International Inc.
2180 Buckingham Rd., Oakville, ON L6H 6H1
Tel: 905-829-8500; Fax: 905-829-8513
Toll-Free: 800-387-7210
customerservice@tripartrans.com
tripartrans.com
Profile: Tripar offers LTL services between Canada & the Eastern USA.

Don Burditt, General Manager
dburditt@tripartrans.com

TST-CF Express
Formerly: Canadian Freightways; TST Overland Express
Parent: TFI International Inc.
5200 Maingate Dr., Mississauga, ON L4W 1G5
Toll-Free: 888-868-7923
customercare@canadianfreightways.com
tst-cfexpress.com
Profile: TST-CF Express, merged from TST Overland Express & Canadian Freightways, is a less than truckload (LTL) service provide across North America. Partner companies provide overnight & second day service within their region.
Wayne Gruszka, President

UPS Canada
Parent: United Parcel Service Inc.
1930 Derry Rd. East, Mississauga, ON L5S 1E2
Toll-Free: 800-742-5877
www.ups.com/ca
Ticker Symbol: UPS / NYSE
Profile: UPS provides shipping & freight services to every address in Canada, either through their own company or through independent contractors. The parent company is one of the largest shipping companies in the world, with operations in more than 200 countries.
Dominic Porporino, President, UPS Canada

VA Inc.
600, rue Louis-Pasteur, Boucherville, QC J4B 7Z1
Tél: 450-641-0082; Ligne sans frais: 800-363-8175
serviceclient@vatransport.com
www.vatransport.com
Profile: VA provides LTL, TL & container transportation services.

Vedder Transport Ltd.
Parent: Vedder Transportation Group
400 Riverside Rd., Abbotsford, BC V2S 4P4
Toll-Free: 800-661-8883
info@veddertransport.com
www.veddertransportation.com
Profile: Vedder provides transportation services in the following categories: liquid & dry edible, liquid rail car transloading, food grade tank wash, international freight & warehousing.
Fred Zweep, President, Vedder Transportation Group

Vedder Transportation Group
400 Riverside Rd., Abbotsford, BC V2S 4P4
Toll-Free: 866-859-1375
www.vtlg.com
Profile: The Vedder Group provides transportation, repair & sales services through its operating companies: Vedder Transport Ltd., Can-Am West Carriers Inc., Vedder Multi Commodity Transload, Big Rig Collision & Paint Ltd., & Larry's Used Truck & Trailer Sales Ltd.
Fred Zweep, President
Larry Wiebe, Chief Executive Officer

Verspeeten Cartage Ltd.
274129 Wallace Line, Ingersoll, ON N5C 3J7
Tel: 519-425-7881; Fax: 519-425-4962
www.verspeeten.com
Profile: The company is ISO 9001:2000 registered.
Ron Verspeeten, President & CEO
ron@verspeeten.com

Vitran Express Canada Inc.
Formerly: Vitran Corporation Inc.
Parent: TFI International Inc.
1201 Creditstone Rd., Concord, ON L4K 0C2
Tel: 416-798-4965; Fax: 416-798-4753
Toll-Free: 800-263-9588
webmaster@vitran.com
www.vitran.com
Profile: Vitran specializes in long-distance trucking, arrangement of transportation of freight & cargo, general warehousing & storage & refuse systems.
Chris Traikos, President

VTL Group
700, montée de Liesse, Montréal, QC H4T 1N8
Tel: 514-687-4944; Fax: 514-687-4934
Toll-Free: 800-561-8194
dispatch@vtltransport.com
www.vtltransport.com
Profile: VTL operates three divisions: VTL V-Trans (logistics), VTL Transport (general transportation) & Nautica (international freight & forwarding). A 100 per cent company-owned trucking fleet operates under VTL Transport.

Warren Gibson Ltd.
PO Box 100, 206 Church St. South, Alliston, ON L9R 1T9
Tel: 705-435-4342; Fax: 705-435-3869
Toll-Free: 800-461-4374
www.warrengibson.com
Profile: Warren Gibson provides LTL & TL services between Ontario, Québec & 48 states. They also specialize in cross docking, maintenance & warehousing services. The company is certified ISO 9001:2008.

Westfreight Systems, Inc.
Parent: TFI International Inc.
7530 - 84th St. SE, Calgary, AB T2C 4W3
Tel: 403-279-8388; Fax: 403-279-8390
Toll-Free: 800-881-1266
www.westfreight.com
Profile: Westfreight provides full load, van, LTL & heavy hauling services between Canada & the USA.

Winalta Transport Ltd.
Parent: TFI International Inc.
10810 Bevington Rd., Acheson, AB T7X 6B7
Tel: 780-447-3521; Fax: 780-665-7331
Toll-Free: 888-447-3521
winalta@winaltatransport.com
www.winaltatransport.com
Profile: Winalta serves the construction, plant & oilfield industries.
Ian McKinley, Vice-President
i.mckinley@telus.net

Wolverine Freight System
2500 Airport Rd., Windsor, ON N8W 5E7
Tel: 519-966-3333; Fax: 519-966-2800
Toll-Free: 800-265-5051
inquiries@wolverinefreight.ca
www.wolverinefreight.ca
Profile: Wolverine offers overnight TL services between Ontario & Michigan, Wisconsin, Illinois, Ohio, Pennsylvania, Kentucky & New York. Warehousing & logistics services are also offered. The company is ISO 9001:2000 registered.

XTL Transport Inc.
75 Rexdale Blvd., Toronto, ON M9W 1P1
Tel: 416-742-0610; Toll-Free: 800-361-5576
www.xtl.com
Profile: XTL provides transportation, logistics & distribution services, as well as temperature-controlled transportation through its XTL TempSolution division.
Serge Gagnon, CEO & Founder
serge.gagnon@xtl.com

Transportation Manufacturers & Services

3 Points Aviation
721 Main St., Cornwall, PE C0A 1H0
Tel: 902-628-8846; Fax: 902-628-8838
sales@3pts.com
3pointsaviation.com
Profile: 3 Points supplies aircraft parts & support, including airframe parts, engines, propellers & landing gear.
Harold Debonte, Vice-President, Sales & Marketing
902-628-8846 ext: 3202, hdebonte@3pointsaviation.com

3M Canada Company
300 Tartan Dr., London, ON N5V 4M9
Tel: 800-325-2376; Fax: 800-479-4453
www.3m.com/aerospace
Ticker Symbol: MMM / NYSE
Profile: This division of 3M Canada Company specializes in manufacturing, maintenance & repair of aircraft, airframes & engines for both commercial & space flight.

ABB Inc.
800, boul Hymus, Montréal, QC H4S 0B5
Tél: 438-843-6000; Ligne sans frais: 800-435-7365
contact.center@ca.abb.com
new.abb.com/ca
Ticker Symbol: ABB / NYSE; ABBBN / SIX
Profile: The company specializes in the manufacture of analytical technologies, targeting the industrial processes, defense & space markets.
Nathalie Pilon, President & CEO, ABB Canada

Action Aero Inc.
91 Watts Ave., Charlottetown, PE C1E 2B7
Tel: 902-370-3311; Fax: 902-370-3313
info@actionaero.com
www.actionaero.com
Profile: The company provides overhaul & repair services for fuel, oil & air related engine accessories.

Dave Trainor, President
dave@actionaero.com
Johnathan Doiron, Chief Financial Officer
jdoiron@actionaero.com

Adacel Inc.
PO Box 48, #300, 895, rue de la Gauchetière ouest, Montréal, QC H3B 4G1

Tel: 514-636-6365; *Fax:* 514-636-2326
info@adacel.com
www.adacel.com
Ticker Symbol: ADA / ASX
Profile: The company creates software & simulation products for the training of air traffic controllers, pilots & airport vehicle operators.
Daniel Verret, Chief Executive Officer

ADGA Group
Groupe ADGA
110 Argyle Ave., Ottawa, ON K2P 1B4

Tel: 613-237-3022; *Fax:* 613-237-3024
info@adga.ca
www.adga.ca
Profile: The Group serves the defense & aerospace sectors through its three companies: ADGA Group Consultants Inc., AEPOS Technologies Corporation & APS Aviation Inc. Its specialities are: weapons systems management; airframe systems; avionics; armaments; automatic test equipment; maintenance support; instrument & electrical systems; technical documentation; & C4ISR.
Françoise Gagnon, Owner & CEO

Advanced Integration Technology Canada / AIT
Parent: Advanced Integration Technology, Inc.
26977 - 56th Ave., Langley, BC V4W 3Y2

Tel: 604-856-8939; *Fax:* 604-856-8993
www.aint.com
Profile: AIT is an industrial automation & tooling company providing turnkey factory integration & the design, manufacture & installation of machines & systems for the automated assembly of aerospace structures. Their Aldergrove, BC, facility specializes in fabrication, machining, assembly & metrology.
Curtis Earl, Contact
curtis.earl@aint.com

Advanced Precision
70 Thornhill Dr., Dartmouth, NS B3B 1S3

Tel: 902-468-5653; *Fax:* 902-468-5737
advancedprecision.ca
Profile: The company provides precision component machining, fabrication & assembly services to the aerospace, military & industrial sectors.
Chris Fitzpatrick, President
cfitzpatrick@advancedprecision.ca

Aéro Montréal
#3120, 380, rue Saint-Antoine ouest, Montréal, QC H2Y 3X7

Tel: 514-987-9330; *Fax:* 514-987-1948
info@aeromontreal.ca
www.aeromontreal.ca
Profile: A think tank designed to bring members of Quebec's aerospace industry together to meet common goals & promote shared interests.
Suzanne M. Benoît, Présidente-directrice générale
514-987-9332

Aero Recip Canada Ltd.
Parent: Gregorash Aviation
540 Marjorie St., Winnipeg, MB R3H 0S9

Tel: 204-788-4765; *Fax:* 204-786-2775
Toll-Free: 800-561-5544
info@aerorecip.com
www.aerorecip.com
Profile: Aero Recip exchanges, overhauls & repairs piston engines & specializes in Pratt & Whitney radial engines.
Alvin Gregorash, President
agregorash@aerorecip.com
Tracy Gregorash, General Manager
tgregorash@aerorecip.com

Aero-safe Technologies Inc.
PO Box 335, 1767 Pettit Rd., Fort Erie, ON L2A 5N1

Tel: 905-871-1663; *Fax:* 905-871-7093
sales@aerosafe.ca
www.aerosafe.ca
Profile: The company specializes in high precision CNC manufacturing & assembly for the aerospace & defence industries.

Aerospace BizDev
5057 - 2A Ave., Delta, BC V4M 3M6

Tel: 604-839-5504
www.aerospacebizdev.com

Profile: A consulting company specializing in business development in the aerospace industry.
Linda Wolstencroft, President
linda@aerospacebizdev.com

Aerospace Welding Inc. / AWI
Parent: Groupe DCM
890, boul Michèle-Bohec, Blainville, QC J7C 5E2

Tel: 450-435-9210
info@dcm.aero
dcm.aero/our-divisions/aerospace-welding-awi
Profile: The company specializes in fabricating & repairing metallic aircraft & engine parts of all sizes.
Nino Buttino, Vice-President, Business Development
nbuttino@dcm.aero

Aerosystems International Inc. / ASI
3538, rue Ashby, Montréal, QC H4R 2C1

Tel: 514-336-9426; *Fax:* 514-336-4383
info@asiiweb.com
www.asiiweb.com
Profile: The company was founded in 1971 & provides services to the aviation industry including wire harness assemblies, ground support equipment, component integration & logistical support.
Fergie Legge, President & CEO
legge@asiiweb.com

AeroTek Manufacturing Ltd.
1449 Hopkins St., Whitby, ON L1N 2C2

Tel: 905-666-3400; *Fax:* 905-666-3413
customerservice@aerotekmfg.com
www.aerotekmfg.com
Profile: AeroTek provides processing services such as electroplating, anodizing, chemical conversions, painting, non-destructive testing & sub-assembly, among others.
Jonathan Schofield, President

Airbus Helicopters Canada
PO Box 250, 1100 Gilmore Rd., Fort Erie, ON L2A 5M9

Tel: 905-871-7772; *Fax:* 905-871-3320
Toll-Free: 800-267-4999
www.airbushelicopters.ca
Profile: The company sells aircraft, manufactures composites, & provides engineering solutions, repairs & overhaul. Canadian customers include the RCMP & the Canadian Coast Guard.
Dwayne Charette, President & CEO
Diane Sanderson, Vice-President, Human Resources & Health & Safety
ahca-hr@airbus.com

Alloy Concepts Inc. Precision CNC Machining
59 Guildford Ave., Dartmouth, NS B3B 0H5

Tel: 902-468-1144; *Fax:* 902-468-7632
www.alloyconceptscnc.com
Profile: The company specializes in prototyping, production manufacturing & programming for sectors including avionics, automotive manufacturing, military, renewable energy & ocean science, among others.
David Schnare, Owner/Operator
902-481-6901, dschnare@alloyconceptscnc.com
Perry MacIsaac, Contact, Sales & Customer Relations
902-481-6903, pmacisaac@alloyconceptscnc.com

Alphacasting Inc.
391, av Ste-Croix, Montréal, QC H4N 2L3

Tel: 514-748-7511; *Fax:* 514-748-0237
Toll-Free: 800-567-7511
www.alphacasting.com
Profile: The company manufactures castings from ferrous, non-ferrous, titanium & exotic alloys for industries such as aerospace, military & telecommunications.
Frederik-Pierre Centazzo, Vice-President, Sales & Operations
fcentazzo@alphacasting.com
Steve Kennerknecht, Vice-President, Engineering
skennerknecht@alphacasting.com

Altitude Aerospace Inc.
#200, 2705, boul Pitfield, Montréal, QC H4S 1T2

Tél: 514-335-6922; *Téléc:* 514-335-3356
info@altitudeaero.com
www.altitudeaero.com
Profile: The company aids in the development of new aircraft, as well as providing support for existing fleets through conceptual design, structural analysis & certification.
Nancy Venneman, President
Fadi Al-Ahmed, Executive Vice-President & Chief Engineer

Apex Industries Inc.
100 Millennium Blvd., Moncton, NB E1C 8M6

Tel: 506-857-7544; *Fax:* 506-857-7563
Toll-Free: 800-268-3331
www.apexindustries.com

Profile: The company's Aerospace Division is responsible for manufacturing & integrating structural assemblies, sub-assemblies, kitting & components for the aerospace industry (commercial & defence).

Argus Industries
20 Murray Park Rd., Winnipeg, MB R3J 3T9

Tel: 204-837-4660; *Fax:* 204-896-4250
info@argus.ca
www.argusindustries.ca
Profile: Argus custom manufactures rubber molded products & die cut gasket seals. They have facilities in Manitoba & Ontario.

Arnprior Aerospace Inc.
107 Baskin Dr. East, Arnprior, ON K7S 3M1

Tel: 613-623-4267
sales@arnprioraerospace.com
www.arnprioraerospace.com
Profile: Originally part of Boeing, the company became independent in 2005 & now operates facilities in Canada, the US & Mexico. Arnprior Aerospace supplies products & services (including design, fabrication, machining, processing, assembly, kitting & product integration) to the aerospace & defence industries.

ASCO Aerospace Canada Ltd.
Parent: ASCO Industries
8510 River Rd., Delta, BC V4G 1B5

Tel: 604-946-4900; *Fax:* 604-946-4671
asco@ascocloud.net
www.asco.be
Profile: The company's specialty is the design & manufacture of very large aluminum structures, as well as titanium & steel components for aircraft.
Kevin Russell, Vice-President & General Manager
krussell@ascoaerospace.ca

Avcorp Industries Inc.
10025 River Way, Delta, BC V4G 1M7

Tel: 604-582-6677
www.avcorp.com
Ticker Symbol: AVP / TSX
Profile: Avcorp is a designer & builder of major airframe structures & components, including stabilizers, cargo liners, floor panels, engine nacelles, packboards & wing components.
Amandeep Kaler, Chief Executive Officer
Jessica Gill, Group Vice-President, Human Resources

Aversan Inc.
#500, 30 Eglinton Ave. West, Mississauga, ON L5R 3E7

Tel: 416-289-1554; *Fax:* 416-289-1554
Toll-Free: 866-446-2837
www.aversan.com
Profile: Aversan specializes in designing, testing, & integrating embedded systems, system integration labs, & test equipment for the aerospace & defence industries. The company has offices in North America, South East Asia & India.
Ted Sherlock, Chief Executive Officer

Aviya Technologies Inc.
2495 Meadowpine Blvd., Mississauga, ON L5N 6C3

Tel: 905-812-9995; *Fax:* 905-812-0933
info@aviyatech.com
www.aviyatech.com
Profile: The company specializes in engineering systems, mechanics, hardware, & software for aerospace & defence applications, as well as providing program management & testing of electronic hardware components.
John Koumoundouros, Chief Executive Officer
Louis Brown, President & Chief Operating Officer
Billings Chan, Chief Technology Officer

BASF Canada Inc.
Parent: BASF SE; BASF Corporation
Montreal, QC H4T 1Y4

Tel: 289-360-1300; *Fax:* 289-360-6000
Toll-Free: 866-485-2273
aerospace.basf.com
Profile: BASF's Aerospace Division specializes in cabin interiors, fuel & lubricants, flame retardants & fire protection & more.
Paulo Springman, Manager, Aerospace Business Development

Bell Helicopter Textron Canada Ltd.
Parent: Bell Helicopter Textron Inc.
12800, rue de l'Avenir, Mirabel, QC J7J 1R4

Tel: 450-437-3400
www.bellhelicopter.com
Profile: Bell Helicopter produces rotary-wing aircraft for the civilian & military sectors, including the Griffin Helicopter fleet flown by the Canadian Forces.

Bluedrop
#300, 36 Solutions Dr., Halifax, NS B3S 1N2
Tel: 709-739-9000; *Toll-Free:* 800-563-3638
info@bluedrop.com
bluedropts.com
Profile: Bluedrop Training & Simulation provides advanced training services for the military & commercial markets.
John Moores, Chief Operating Officer
Jean-Claude Siew, Vice-President, Technology & Simulation
Barbarie Palmer, Senior Director, Business Development (Air & Land)
Wayne Shaddock, Senior Director, Business Development (Naval)

Boeing Canada Operations Ltd.
Parent: Boeing
World Exchange Plaza, #1220, 45 O'Connor St., Ottawa, ON K1P 1A4
Tel: 613-745-8111
www.boeing.ca
Ticker Symbol: BA / NYSE
Profile: Boeing manufactures commercial jetliners & military aircraft, as well as rotorcraft, electonic & defence systems, milliles, satellites, launch vehicles & information & communication systems.
Charles Sullivan, Managing Director, Boeing Canada Operations Ltd.

Bombardier Inc.
800, boul René-Lévesque ouest, Montréal, QC H3B 1Y8
Tél: 514-861-9481; *Téléc:* 514-861-2420
www.bombardier.com
Ticker Symbol: BBD.A, BBD.B / TSX
Profile: Manufacturers of railroad equipment, aircraft, aircraft engines & engine parts, aircraft parts & auxiliary equipment, various transportation equipment; Personal credit institutions; Real estate land subdividers & developers.
Éric Martel, President & CEO
David Coleal, President, Aviation
Danny Di Perna, President, Transportation

Bradean's Tool & Die Limited
#1B, 46 Anson Ave., Amherst, NS B4H 4R2
Tel: 902-661-0669; *Fax:* 902-661-1748
bradeans@bradeans.com
www.bradeans.com
Profile: The company manufactures aerospace & related parts, as well as conducting research & development, prototyping & other experimental projects.
Dean Smith, Co-Founder
Brad Sprague, Co-Founder

Cadorath Aerospace Inc.
2070 Logan Ave., Winnipeg, MB R2R 0H9
Tel: 204-985-1317; *Fax:* 204-633-7101
Toll-Free: 800-470-7069
info@cadorath.com
www.cadorath.com
Profile: Cadorath Aerospace provides customers with aeronautical repair, modification & overhaul services.
Gerry Cadorath, President & CEO

CAE Inc.
8585, ch de Côte-de-Liesse, Montréal, QC H4T 1G6
Tél: 514-341-6780; *Téléc:* 514-341-7699
Ligne sans frais: 800-564-6253
www.cae.com
Ticker Symbol: CAE / TSX, NYSE
Profile: CAE Inc. serves the civil aviation & defense forces, through the provision of simulation & modelling technologies, as well as integrated training solutions. The company's civil aviation & military training centres are located throughout the world.
Marc Parent, President & CEO

Canadian Light Source Inc. / CLS
Centre canadien de rayonnement synchrotron
44 Innovation Blvd., Saskatoon, SK S7N 2V3
Tel: 306-657-3500; *Fax:* 306-657-3535
cls@lightsource.ca
www.lightsource.ca
Profile: The Canadian Light Source centre is a synchrotron facility, generating beams of light that allow researchers to view the microstructures of materials. This technology is useful in the fields of aviation & aerospace.
Rob Lamb, Chief Executive Officer

Canadian Propeller Ltd.
462 Brooklyn St., Winnipeg, MB R3J 1M7
Tel: 204-832-8679; *Fax:* 204-888-4696
Toll-Free: 800-773-6853
info@canadianpropeller.com
www.canadianpropeller.com

Profile: The company is an authorized service & repair station for Hartzell & McCauley propellers, among others.
Maurice Wills, President & General Manager

CarteNav Solutions Inc.
Purdy's Tower 1, #1700, 1959 Upper Water St., Halifax, NS B3J 3N2
Tel: 902-446-4988; *Fax:* 902-446-4987
Toll-Free: 877-723-8729
info@cartenav.com
cartenav.com
Profile: CarteNav produces situational awareness software for maritime, land, & air environments, targeting the defence, security & industry markets.
Carl Daniels, Chief Operating Officer

Cascade Aerospace Inc.
1337 Townline Rd., Abbotsford, BC V2T 6E1
Tel: 604-850-7372; *Fax:* 604-857-2655
info@cascadeaerospace.com
www.cascadeaerospace.com
Profile: Cascade provides clients in the military, government & commercial aerospace sectors with management, engineering & support services. The company also designs & manufactures various aircraft systems & kits.
Kevin Lemke, Executive Vice-President & COO

Celestica Inc.
844 Don Mills Rd., Toronto, ON M3C 1V7
Tel: 416-448-5800; *Toll-Free:* 888-899-9998
contactus@celestica.com
www.celestica.com
Ticker Symbol: CLS / TSX, NYSE
Profile: Celestica provides the aerospace & defence industries with design, engineering, manufacturing, logistics, after-market & supply chain network services. Its specialties are complex printed circuit assembly, system assembly, system integration & box build assembly.
Rob Mionis, President & CEO
Leila Wong, Head, Human Resources

CFN Consultants
#1502, 222 Queen St., Ottawa, ON K1P 5V9
Tel: 613-232-1576; *Fax:* 613-238-5519
info@cfncon.com
www.cfnconsultants.com
Profile: CFN specializes in defence & security issues, & has worked with the Canadian Forces, departments of the Canadian Government & NATO, as well as off-shore companies in the defence, IM/IT & aerospace sectors.
Andre Deschamps, Managing Senior Partner
adeschamps@cfncon.com

Ciara Technologies Inc.
Parent: Hypertec Group
9300, rte Transcanadienne, Montréal, QC H4S 1K5
Tél: 514-798-8880; *Téléc:* 514-798-8889
Ligne sans frais: 877-242-7272
www.ciaratech.com
Profile: Ciara provides technology & software solutions & services from companies ranging from small businesses to educational, & government & defence.

CMC Electronics Inc.
Parent: TransDigm Group Inc.
600, boul Dr. Frederik Philips, Montréal, QC H4M 2S9
Tél: 514-748-3148
cmcelectronics.ca
Profile: The company designs & manufactures electonics for the military & commercial aviation sectors.

CMTIGroup Inc.
9404, rue du Saguenay, Montréal, QC H1R 3Z8
Tél: 514-328-2166
info@cmtigroup.com
www.cmtigroup.com
Profile: The company offers specialty engineering services to clients in the aerospace, defence, space & transportation sectors, including black box developers, subsystem integrators & government agencies.

Collins Aerospace Canada
Formerly: UTC Aerospace Systems; Rockwell Collins
Parent: Raytheon Technologies
#104, 30 Edgewater St., Ottawa, ON K2L 1V8
Tel: 613-595-2200; *Fax:* 613-595-2280
www.collinsaerospace.com
Profile: Merged from UTC Aerospace Systems & Rockwell Collins in 2018, Collins Aerospace specializes in the design, development, support, modeling and simulation of wireless & ad-hoc networking technologies. It serves government & commercial clients.
Stephen Timm, President

Convergent Manufacturing Technologies Inc.
#403, 6190 Agronomy Rd., Vancouver, BC V6T 1Z3
Tel: 604-822-9682; *Fax:* 604-822-9659
info@convergent.ca
www.convergent.ca
Profile: Convergent produces composite process modelling software & services, useful in the aerospace industry for the modelling of production hardware. The company was originally part of the University of British Columbia's Composites Group, & although they became separately incorporated in 1998, they continue to hold strong ties to UBC.
Göran Fernlund, Chief Technology Officer, Director of Engineering & President, Convergent Canada
Anoush Poursartip, Chief Strategy Officer & Director, Research & Development

CRIAQ
#1515, 740, rue Notre-Dame ouest, Montréal, QC H3C 3X6
Tél: 514-313-7561
info@criaq.aero
criaq.aero
Profile: Le Consortium de recherche et d'innovation en aérospatiale au Québec (CRIAQ) vise à améliorer la base de connaissances de l'industrie aérospatiale de la province par l'éducation et la formation des étudiants. Leur objectif est d'accroître la compétitivité du Québec sur le marché international de l'aéronautique. C'est une organisation à but non lucratif soutenue par le gouvernement du Québec.
Alain Aubertin, Président-directeur général

Cyclone Manufacturing Inc.
7300 Rapistan Ct., Mississauga, ON L5N 5S1
Tel: 905-567-5601; *Fax:* 905-567-6911
info@cyclonemfg.com
www.cyclonemfg.com
Profile: Cyclone specializes in manufacturing & assembling medium & large structures for the aerospace industry.
Andrew Sochaj, President
andrew.sochaj@cyclonemfg.com
Robert Sochaj, Executive Vice-President
robert.sochaj@cyclonemfg.com

Deep Vision Inc.
Quaker Landing Bldg., #125, 33 Ochterloney St., Dartmouth, NS B2Y 4P5
Tel: 902-461-1615
www.deepvision.ca
Profile: Deep Vision specializes in developing what they call Intelligent Machine Perception Technology, which allows machines to sense & recognize objects, as well as read & comprehend text. This technology is useful in sectors such as aerospace & defence, intelligent transportation, robotics, surveillance & autonomous systems, among others.

Delastek Inc.
#14, 2699, 5e av, Shawinigan, QC G9T 2P7
Tél: 819-533-5788; *Téléc:* 819-533-3494
delastek.ca
Profile: La société fabrique des pièces composites et intérieurs d'avions, ainsi que de soutenir les différentes phases de développement du produit. Elle est spécialisée dans les systèmes électriques et électroniques pour les autres types de véhicules, ainsi que les pare-chocs et l'intégration des produits.

DRS Technologies Canada Ltd.
Parent: Leonardo DRS
#1100, 500 Palladium Dr., Kananta, ON K2V 1C2
Tel: 613-591-5800; *Fax:* 613-591-5801
business_dev@drs.ca
www.leonardodrs.com/locations/drs-technologies-cana
Profile: The a company, a part of the Leonardo DRS Naval Electronics unit, manufactures & services a range of military communications, electro-optics, surveillance & sensor signal processing systems for naval & ground applications.

Earnscliffe Strategy Group
Formerly: Policy Insights Inc.
#400, 46 Elgin St., Ottawa, ON K1P 5K6
Tel: 613-563-4455; *Fax:* 613-236-6173
Toll-Free: 844-564-4455
contactus@earnscliffe.ca
earnscliffe.ca
Profile: Founded in 1989, Earnscliffe Strategy Group is a government relations firm specializing in the fields of high technology, aerospace, defence & communications.
Craig Robinson, Chief Executive Officer

Explorer Solutions
#205, 1494, rue Montarville, St-Bruno-de-Montarville, QC J3V 3T5
Tel: 450-441-9055; *Toll-Free:* 833-221-9055
explorersolutions.ca

Profile: The company provides business intelligence, government relations & senior management coaching to companies in the aerospace industry, as well as economic development agencies & municipalities.
Christian Perreault, Managing Partner, President & CEO
christian@explorersolutions.ca

Field Aviation
Parent: AMAVCO
#125, 4300 - 26th St. NE, Calgary, AB T1Y 7H7
Tel: 403-516-8200
www.fieldav.com
Profile: Field Aviation provides design, engineering, integration, certification & aircraft delivery services to clients involved in search & rescue, surveillance & border protection.

Fleetway Inc.
Parent: J.D. Irving, Limited
#100, 35 Micmac Blvd., Dartmouth, NS B3A 0G7
Tel: 902-450-2200; *Fax:* 902-450-2292
info@fleetway.ca
www.fleetway.ca
Profile: Fleetway provides engineering services to the military & government, shipbuilding, oil & gas & commercial sectors.

Flexibülb Inc.
PO Box 635, 9000, boul Parent, Trois-Rivières, QC G9A 5E1
Tel: 819-374-9250; *Fax:* 819-374-5143
www.flexibulb.com
Profile: The company specializes in designing, developing, manufacturing, & integrating aircraft interior systems, components & ground support equipment for clients in the aerospace, military & paramilitary sectors.

General Dynamics Canada
1991 Oxford St. East, London, ON N5V 2Z7
Tel: 519-964-5900
www.gdcanada.com
Profile: The company provides information, surveillance, & reconnaissance services for air & sea platforms, & networking & computing solutions for land platforms.

General Electric Canada Inc.
Parent: General Electric
2300 Meadowvale Blvd., Mississauga, ON L5N 5P9
Tel: 905-858-5480
www.ge.com/ca
Profile: GE-Aviation serves the Canadian military & commercial aviation markets through its two plants in Bromont, QC, & Orillia, ON. GE manufactures, markets & supports aircraft engines, as well as gas turbines for the Canadian Navy.
Heather Chalmers, President & CEO, GE Canada

Green Aviation Research & Development Network / GARDN
#1515, 740, rue Notre-Dame ouest, Montréal, QC H3C 3X6
Tél: 514-398-9625
info@gardn.org
gardn.org
Profile: GARDN was created in 2009 with the goal of bringing together partners in industry, government & education to reduce the aerospace industry's environmental footprint.
Richard Legault, Acting Executive Director

Greyhound Canada Transportation ULC
Parent: FirstGroup plc
610 Bay St., 2nd Fl., Toronto, ON M5G 1M5
Toll-Free: 800-661-8747
canada.info@greyhound.ca
www.greyhound.ca
Profile: A subsidiary of British-owned FirstGroup, Greyhound Canada offers intercity & rural bus transportation. Services include scheduled bus service, QuickLink commuter service (southern Ontario) & USA connections through Greyhound USA. In 2018, Greyhound Canada cancelled service in northern Ontario (west of Sudbury) & in Manitoba, Saskatchewan, Alberta & British Columbia. As a result, Greyhound Canada only operates in portions of Ontario & Québec.
Stuart Kendrick, Senior Vice-President, Canada

Héroux-Devtek inc
Tour est, #600, 1111, rue Saint-Charles ouest, Longueuil, QC J4K 5G4
Tel: 450-679-5450
info@herouxdevtek.com
www.herouxdevtek.com
Ticker Symbol: HRX / TSX
Profile: Manufacturers of aircraft parts & auxiliary equipment; Wholesalers of transportation equipment & supplies; Airport, flying fields & airport terminal services
Martin Brassard, President & CEO
Stéphane Arsenault, Vice-President & Chief Financial Officer

Honeywell Canada
Parent: Honeywell International Inc.
3333 Unity Dr., Mississauga, ON L5L 3S6
Tel: 905-608-6021; *Fax:* 905-608-6057
aerospace.honeywell.com
Ticker Symbol: HON / NYSE
Profile: Honeywell Canada's Aerospace Division deals in the following business lines: electric power, electronic control systems, in-flight communication systems, in-flight data networking solutions, repair & overhaul services & aftermarket services. The company operates sites in Ontario & Prince Edward Island.

IMP Group International Inc.
2651 Joseph Howe Dr., Halifax, NS B3L 4T1
Tel: 902-453-2400; *Toll-Free:* 877-244-0878
www.impgroup.com
Profile: IMP Group consists of the following divisions: aerospace & defence, airline, aviation, healthcare, hotels, information services & properties & development. Please see the company's website for specific divisional contact information.
Kirk A. Rowe, President & CEO
kirk.rowe@impgroup.com
Robert W. Burns, Senior Vice-President & Chief Human Resources Officer
rob.burns@impgroup.com

Integral Machining Ltd. / IML
#8, 1252 Speers Rd., Oakville, ON L6L 5N9
Tel: 905-847-1565; *Fax:* 905-847-9518
info@imach.ca
www.imach.ca
Profile: IML specializes in micromachining, which is loosely defined as being the machining of any features less than two millimeters in size. The company's main clients are in the aerospace, medical & photonics industries.
Peter Reypa, President

International Custom Products Inc. / ICP
49 Howden Rd., Toronto, ON M1R 3C7
Tel: 416-285-4311; *Fax:* 416-285-7329
Toll-Free: 800-268-4482
info@icpinc.com
icpinc.com
Profile: The company manufactures parachute components for ordnance delivery & unmanned vehicle systems, as well as meeting unique packaging requirements for defence-related initiatives.

International Water Guard Industries Inc.
Parent: IWG Technologies, Inc.
Bldg. 7, 15050 - 54A Ave., Surrey, BC V3S 5X7
Tel: 604-255-5555; *Fax:* 604-255-5685
Toll-Free: 800-667-0331
info@water.aero
www.water.aero
Profile: IWG provides aircraft water treatment systems & components to corporate, VIP & military operators.
Steven Bis, President

Irving Shipbuilding Inc. / ISI
Parent: J.D. Irving, Limited
3099 Barrington St., Halifax, NS B3K 5M7
Tel: 902-423-9271
info@irvingshipbuilding.com
shipsforcanada.ca
Profile: Irving provides services including shipbuilding & repair, drill rig construction & conversion, offshore fabrication, industrial manufacturing, engineering, supply chain management & technical services.

ISE Metal Inc.
Formerly: ISE Stamping Inc.
20, rte de Windsor, Sherbrooke, QC J1C 0E5
Tel: 819-846-1044; *Fax:* 819-846-4268
isemetal.com
Profile: The company specializes in the laser cutting, bending, stamping, assembly, welding, zinc plating & enameling of sheet metal for markets including recreational vehicles, automotive & aerospace.

J.D. Irving, Limited / JDI
PO Box 5777, 300 Union St., Saint John, NB E2L 4M3
Tel: 506-632-7777; *Fax:* 506-648-2205
www.jdirving.com
Profile: J.D. Irving provides services through the following business units: fForestry & Forest Products; Transportation; Shipbuilding & Industrial Marine; Retail; Industrial Equipment, Construction Services & Building Materials; & Consumer Products. The company was founded in 1882, & now has operations in Eastern Canada & the United States.

KF Aerospace / KF
Formerly: Kelowna Flightcraft
5655 Airport Way, Kelowna, BC V1V 1S1
Tel: 250-491-5500
www.kfaero.ca
Profile: The company's main operations are conducted in Kelowna, BC, & Hamilton, ON, & include maintenance, flight operations & military flight training. Kelowna Flightcraft Air Charter Ltd., a subsidiary, is a dedicated carrier for Canada Post, & an air cargo carrier for Purolator Courier.
Barry Lapointe, Chair & CEO
Tracy Medve, President

KPMG LLP
#1800, 150 Elgin St., Ottawa, ON K2P 1L4
Tel: 613-212-5764; *Fax:* 613-212-2896
home.kpmg/ca/en/home/industries/government-public-s
Profile: KPMG's Aerospace & Defence (A&D) practice, which is part of the firm's global Diversified Industrials practice, offers audit, tax & advisory services to clients in the A&D industry. The firm also offers a service called KPMG Enterprise for private A&D companies, which involves growth management, tax planning & financial business.
Grant McDonald, Global Sector Leader, Aerospace & Defence
gmcdonald@kpmg.ca

L3Harris Technologies, Inc.
Formerly: L3 Technologies Inc.; L-3 Communications
#804, 255 Albert St., Ottawa, ON K1P 6A9
Tel: 613-569-5257
websupport@l3harris.com
www.l3harris.com
Ticker Symbol: LHX / NYSE
Profile: L3Harris is a global company specializing in aerospace & defence.
William Brown, Chair & CEO

Lear Canada Ltd.
2001 Forbes St., Whitby, ON L1N 7V4
Tel: 905-436-0400
www.lear.com
Ticker Symbol: LEA / NYSE
Profile: The comapny designs, tests & produces automotive interiors.
Ray Scott, President, CEO & Director
Jason Cardew, Senior Vice-President & CFO

Linamar Corporation
287 Speedvale Ave. West, Guelph, ON N1H 1C5
Tel: 519-836-7550; *Fax:* 519-824-8479
linamar.com
Ticker Symbol: LNR / TSX
Profile: Manufacturers of motor vehicle parts & accessories, fabricated plate work, carburetors, pistons, piston rings, valves, farm machinery equipment, aircraft parts & auxiliary equipment, pumps & pumping equipment; Wholesalers of farm & garden machinery & equipment.
Linda Hasenfratz, Chief Executive Officer
Jim Jarrell, President & COO
Dale Schneider, Chief Financial Officer
Mark Stoddart, CTO & Executive Vice-President, Sales & Marketing

Lockheed Martin Canada Inc.
Parent: Lockheed Martin Corporation
#870, 45 O'Connor St., Ottawa, ON K1P 1A4
Tel: 613-688-0698; *Fax:* 613-688-0702
www.lockheedmartin.com/en-ca
Ticker Symbol: LMT / NYSE
Profile: Lockheed Martin Canada supplies electronic defence & surveillance systems for naval, airborne, land & civil operations.
Lorraine Ben, Chief Executive Officer

Luxfer Canada Ltd.
4410 - 46th Ave. SE, Calgary, AB T2B 3N7
Tel: 403-720-0262; *Fax:* 403-720-0263
Toll-Free: 888-396-3835
alternativefuel@luxfer.net
www.luxfercylinders.com
Ticker Symbol: DNK
Profile: Manufacturers of cylinders, fuel cell storage systems.

Lynch Fluid Controls Inc.
Formerly: Lynch Dynamics Inc.
1799 Argentia Rd., Mississauga, ON L5N 3A2
Tel: 905-363-2400; *Fax:* 905-363-1191
Toll-Free: 888-626-4365
info@lynch.ca
www.lynch.ca
Profile: The company designs & manufactures hydraulic motion control systems for the aerospace, military & medical sectors.
Ernie Lynch, President & CEO

MacKenzie Atlantic Tool & Die Machining
PO Box 121, #3, 6 Rowling Dr., Musquodoboit Harbour, NS
B0J 2L0
Tel: 902-889-3047; Fax: 902-889-3673
info@mackenzieatlantic.com
www.mackenzieatlantic.com
Profile: MacKenzie Atlantic is a full-service tool-making &
machining company serving the aerospace, marine, military & oil
& gas sectors.
Matthew MacKenzie, Owner & President
902-889-3633, matthewmackenzie@mackenzieatlantic.com

Magellan Aerospace Corporation
3160 Derry Rd. East, Mississauga, ON L4T 1A9
Tel: 905-677-1889; Fax: 905-677-5658
magellan.corporate@magellan.aero
magellan.aero
Ticker Symbol: MAL / TSX
Profile: Magellan is engaged in designing, engineering &
manufacturing aeroengine & aerostructure assemblies &
components. The company serves the aerospace & military
markets. Operating units are located in Canada, the United
States & the United Kingdom.
Phillip Underwood, President & CEO

Magna International Inc.
337 Magna Dr., Aurora, ON L4G 7K1
Tel: 905-726-2462
www.magna.com
Ticker Symbol: MG / TSX; MGA / NYSE
Profile: Manufacturers of motor vehicle parts & accessories,
automotive stampings, various fabricated metal products, motor
vehicles & passenger car bodies, vehicular lighting equipment,
various fabricated textile products, public building & related
furniture; Wholesalers of motor vehicle supplies & new parts;
Racing, including track operation; Various amusement &
recreation services.
Donald J. Walker, Chief Executive Officer
Vincent J. Galifi, Executive Vice-President & CFO
Tommy J. Skudutis, Executive Vice-President & COO

MarineNav Ltd.
Panmure Island Wharf, 1466 Panmure Island, Montague, PE
C0A 1R0
Tel: 902-838-7011
info@marinenav.ca
www.marinenav.ca
Profile: MarineNav designs & manufactures offshore navigation,
multimedia & vessel monitoring systems.

Marinvent Corporation
#23, 50, ch de la Rabastalière est, Saint-Bruno, QC J3V 2A5
Tel: 450-441-6464; Fax: 450-441-2411
info@marinvent.com
www.marinvent.com
Profile: Marinvent specializes in aerospace research &
development. The company was founded in 1983 & now has
operations in Canada, the USA & Russia. It is also a founding
partner in Canada's Flight Test Centre of Excellence (FTCE).
John Maris, President

Marsh Metrology
Parent: Marsh Group
#2, 1016C Sutton Dr., Burlington, ON L7L 6B8
Tel: 905-331-9783; Fax: 905-331-5991
info@marshmetrology.com
marshmetrology.com
Profile: The company provides accredited calibration services,
including repair & re-manufacture of printed circuit boards, &
distribution for test & measurement equipment.

MDA Corporation
Formerly: MacDonald, Dettwiler & Associates Ltd.
Parent: Maxar Technologies
13800 Commerce Pkwy., Richmond, BC V6V 2J3
Tel: 604-278-3411; Fax: 604-231-2750
info@mdacorporation.com
www.mdacorporation.com
Ticker Symbol: MDA.TO / TSX
Profile: MDA, a Maxar (U.S.A) company, supports commercial,
civil & military clients in the global surveillance, intelligence,
communication & advanced technology marketplaces. It builds &
operates unmanned aerial vehicles & provides clients with
aircraft, sensors, training, maintenance, in-service support,
system certification, data handling & exploitation systems.

MDS Coating Technologies Corporation
60 Aerospace Blvd., Slemon Park, PE C0B 2A0
Tel: 902-888-3900; Fax: 902-888-3901
info@mdscoating.com
www.mdscoating.com

Profile: MDS is a developer & manufacturer of coatings for gas
turbine engines used in the commercial & aerospace & defence
industries, with offices in PEI & Québec.

Meloche Group Inc.
#201, 925, rue du Caryer, Beauharnois, QC J6N 0S6
Tél: 450-371-4646; Télec: 450-371-4957
info@melocheinc.com
www.melocheinc.com
Hugue Meloche, Président et directeur général
hmeloche@melocheinc.com

Metal Action Machining Ltd.
Parent: Analytic Systems Ware 1993 Ltd.
#206, 12448 - 82nd Ave., Surrey, BC V3W 3E9
Tel: 604-543-7378; Fax: 604-592-7372
sales@metalactionmachining.com
metalactionmachining.com
Profile: The company specializes in precision machining of
aluminum alloys, alloy steels, titanium & stainless steel. Other
operations include punching, press break forming, anodizing,
painting, plating, engraving & screen printing, using both
in-house & outside services. The company also specializes in
aerospace tooling. They mainly serve the aerospace, military,
marine, cleantech & commercial markets.
Jim Hargrove, Manager, Sales
778-724-4653, jimh@metalactionmachining.ca

Mevotech Inc.
240 Bridgeland Ave., Toronto, ON M6A 1Z4
Tel: 416-783-7800; Fax: 416-783-0904
info@mevotech.com
www.mevotech.com
Profile: Mevotech manufactures parts for automobiles, including
suspension, steering & driveline.
Ezer Mevorach, Chief Executive Officer
emevorach@mevotech.com
Joseph Wilke, Chief Financial Officer
Allan Bartolini, Vice-President, Human Resources &
Organizational Development

MicroPilot
PO Box 720, 72067 Rd. 8E, Sturgeon Rd., Stony Mountain,
MB R0C 3A0
Tel: 204-818-0598; Fax: 204-818-0594
info@micropilot.com
www.micropilot.com
Profile: The company manufactures small autopilot systems for
unmanned aerial vehicles & micro aerial vehicles.
Howard Loewen, President

MilAero Electronics Atlantic Inc.
81 Mount Hope Ave., Dartmouth, NS B2Y 4M9
Tel: 902-469-6232
info@mil-aero.com
www.mil-aero.com
Profile: MilAero specializes in cables, wire harnesses &
electro-mechanical enclosures for the defence, aerospace &
industrial sectors.

National Research Council of Canada / NRC
Bldg. M-3, 1200 Montréal Rd., Ottawa, ON K1A 0R6
Tel: 613-990-0765; Fax: 613-952-9907
nrc.aerobdt-edaaero@nrc-cnrc.gc.ca
nrc.canada.ca/en/research-development/research-coll
Profile: NRC Aerospace is Canada's national aerospace
laboratory, which conducts research & technology development
on aerospace topics such as safety, weight, cost & the
environment.
Ibrahim Yimer, Director General

NAV Canada
PO Box 3411 T, 77 Metcalfe St., Ottawa, ON K1P 5L6
Tel: 613-563-5588; Fax: 613-563-3426
Toll-Free: 800-876-4693
service@navcanada.ca
www.navcanada.ca
Profile: Provides, maintains & enhances an air navigation
service.
Neil R. Wilson, President & CEO
Raymond G. Bohn, Vice-President & Chief Human Resources
Officer
Alexander Struthers, Vice-President & CFO

NeXsys Group Inc.
#41, 5800 Ambler Dr., Mississauga, ON L4W 4J4
Tel: 905-593-1504
info@nexsysgroup.ca
www.nexsysgroup.ca
Profile: NeXsys offers consulting & a software suite comprised
of NeXflow, NeXwave & NeXview. The company's clients are in
the aerospace, automotive, pharmaceutical, logistics &
manufacturing industries.

Douglas R. Sutherland, President & CEO

Northern Centre for Advanced Technology Inc. / NORCAT
1545 Maley Dr., Sudbury, ON P3A 4R7
Tel: 705-521-8324; Fax: 705-521-1040
support@norcattraining.com
www.norcat.org
Profile: NORCAT is a non-profit corporation, & its Innovation &
Development department specializes in research pertaining to
space drilling.
Don Duval, Chief Executive Officer
Jason Bubba, Director, Training & Development

Northstar Aerospace
Formerly: Derlan Industries Ltd.
204 East Pike Creek Rd., Tecumseh, ON N8N 2L9
Tel: 519-979-9400; Fax: 519-979-9399
infownindsor@nsaero.com
www.nsaero.com
Profile: Manufacturers of motor vehicle parts & accessories,
aircraft parts & auxiliary equipment, speed changers, industrial
high-speed drives, gears, aircraft engines & engine parts;
Airports, flying fields & airport terminal services.
Scott Burdick, President & CEO
Aaron Tam, Chief Financial Officer

PAL Aerospace
Formerly: Provincial Aerospace Ltd.
Hangar 1, St. John's International Airport, PO Box 29030, St.
John's, NL A1A 5B5
Toll-Free: 855-576-3948
contact@palaerospace.com
palaerospace.com
Profile: PAL is an aerospace & defense company with a focus
on intelligence, surveillance & reconnaissance (ISR) solutions. It
has offices throughout Canada, as well as in the Carribean &
United Arab Emeriates.
Jake Trainor, Chief Executive Officer

Paradigm Shift Technologies Inc.
60 Signet Dr., Toronto, ON M9L 2Y4
Tel: 416-748-1778; Fax: 416-748-5889
info@paradigmshift.com
paradigmshift.com
Profile: The company seeks to improve the reliability of weapon
systems & other platforms (commercial & military) through
coating & engineering services.
Gennady Yumshtyk, Founder, President & CEO

Patlon Aircraft & Industries Limited
8130 - 5th Line, Halton Hills, ON L7G 0B8
Tel: 905-864-8706; Fax: 905-864-8728
patlon@patlon.com
www.patlon.com
Profile: Patlon provides aerospace, military, transportation &
electronics industry clients with application development &
selling. Its products include aircraft interiors, cables, electrical
systems, environmental systems, fuel systems, ground power
units, hydraulic systems, painting, sensors & valves, among
other. It also provides services such as repair, calibration,
assembly & training.
Patrick Mann, President

PCC Aerostructures
Parent: Precision Castparts Corp.
710 Rowntree Dairy Rd., Woodbridge, ON L4L 5T7
Tel: 905-264-2050; Fax: 905-264-1471
www.pccaero.com
Profile: The company is a supplier of build-to-print metallic &
composite parts, kits & assemblies to the aerospace industry. It
has throughout Noth America & beyond.

Pratt & Whitney Canada Corp. / PWC
1000, boul Marie-Victorin, Longueuil, QC J4G 1A1
Tel: 450-677-9411; Toll-Free: 800-268-8000
www.pwc.com
Profile: Manufacturers of aircraft engines & engine parts;
Wholesalers of transportation equipment & supplies.
Maria Della Posta, President
Charles Vaillancourt, Chief Information Officer & Executive
Director, Global Infrastructure & Operations
Nicolas Amyot, Vice-President, Finance
Kevin P. Smith, Vice-President, Human Resources

Prevost Car Inc.
Parent: Volvo Group
35, boul Gagnon, Sainte-Claire, QC G0R 2V0
Tel: 418-883-3391; Fax: 418-883-4157
www.prevostcar.com
Profile: The company manufacturers of intercity coaches &
coach shells for motorhomes & specialty conversion.

Rolls-Royce Canada Ltd.
9500, ch de la Côte-de-Liesse, Montréal, QC H8T 1A2
Tel: 514-636-0964
rrnawebmaster@rolls-royce.com
www.rolls-royce.com
Profile: Airports, flying fields & airport terminal services;
Manufacturers of steam, gas, hydraulic turbines & turbine
generator units.
Marion Blakey, President & CEO, North America

Samuel, Son & Co., Limited
2360 Dixie Rd., Mississauga, ON L4Y 1Z7
Tel: 905-279-5460; *Fax:* 905-279-9658
Toll-Free: 800-267-2683
sales@samuel.com
www.samuel.com
Profile: The Samuel Aerospace Metals division, formed in 2010,
provides materials including surface machining & plastic coating
& services such as plate sawing, water jet profiling, tube &
extrusion cutting, shearing & kitting.

Sanmina Corporation
Formerly: Sanmina-SCI Corporation
500 March Rd., Ottawa, ON K2V 1C2
Tel: 613-886-6000; *Fax:* 613-886-6001
info@sanmina.com
www.sanmina.com
Ticker Symbol: SANM / NASDAQ
Profile: The company manufactures micro-electronics, radar
sub-systems, microwave radios & optical communication
systems for the aerospace, defence, industrial, medical &
renewable energy markets.
Jure Sola, Chief Executive Officer

Satcom Direct, Inc. / SD
1260 Teron Rd., Kanata, ON K2K 0A1
Tel: 613-224-3301; *Toll-Free:* 888-448-9003
salesus@satcomdirect.com
www.satcomdirect.com
Profile: The company provides satellite communication
technology to allow executives to communicate via Wi-Fi, voice,
fax, e-mail & mobile divices while on board private business
aircraft.

Solace Power Inc.
#201, 1118 Topsail Rd., Mount Pearl, NL A1N 5E7
Tel: 709-745-6099; *Fax:* 888-887-5441
info@solace.ca
www.solace.ca
Profile: The company specializes in wireless power technology
applicable to the aerospace & defence, consumer electronics &
firefighting electronics markets.

Sonaca Montréal
Parent: Sonaca Group
13075, rue Brault, Mirabel, QC J7J 1P3
Tél: 450-434-6114
sales@sonacamontreal.com
www.sonaca.com
Profile: The company specializes in manufacturing large
aluminum structures for the aerospace industry, particularly wing
& empennage structures.

Sonovision Canada Inc.
Parent: Sonovision Group Inc.
#400, 85 Albert St., Ottawa, ON K1P 6A4
Tel: 613-234-4849; *Fax:* 613-234-2631
sonovisioncanada.com
Profile: Sonovision Canada manages, authors & translates
technical publications for aerospace & defence manufacturers
with an in-house team of writers, editors, illustrators,
compositors, translators & quality assurance staff.
Vincent Laithier, Director, Sales & Business Development
514-344-5008 ext: 317, vincent.laithier@sonovisiongroup.com

Southwest United Canada
Parent: PCC Aerostructures
85 Stafford Dr., Brampton, ON L6W 1L3
Tel: 905-456-3245; *Fax:* 905-456-3294
www.pccaero.com/companies/swu/southwest-united-cana
Profile: The company specializes in metal finishing & provides
services such as stress relief, non-destructive testing, shot
peening, anodizing, passivation, plating, HVOF thermal spraying,
precision grinding, super finishing & painting.

StandardAero
Parent: The Carlyle Group
#15, 47 Aero Dr. NE, Calgary, AB T2E 8Z9
Tel: 403-295-4204
www.standardaero.com

Profile: The company is a global MRO & aviation service
business with over 30 facilities located in the US, Canada,
Mexico, Europe, Africa, Singapore & Australia.
Russell Ford, Chair & CEO

Stelia Aerospace North America Inc. / CAL
Formerly: Composites Atlantic Limited
PO Box 1150, 71 Hall St., Lunenburg, NS B0J 2C0
Tel: 902-634-8448; *Fax:* 902-634-8398
stelia-northamerica.com
Profile: The company provides structural analysis &
manufacturing services to the aeronautics, defence & space
sectors.
Andre Gagnon, Managing Director & CEO
andre.gagnon@stelia-aerospace.com
Brianna Higgins, Vice-President & Chief Financial Officer
brianna.higgins@stelia-aerospace.com

TDM Technical Services
88 St Regis Crest., Toronto, ON M3J 1Z3
Tel: 416-777-0007; *Fax:* 416-777-1117
tdm@tdm.ca
www.tdm.ca
Profile: TDM's Aerospace Division provides stress analysis,
structural design, certification & systems engineering services to
clients in the aerospace industry.
Iain Dainter, Senior Account Manager
iain@tdm.ca
Ikis Walker, Director, HR & Recruitment
ikis@tdm.ca

Thales Canada Inc.
105 Moatfield Dr., Toronto, ON M3B 0A4
Tel: 416-742-3900
communications.ca@thalesgroup.com
www.thalesgroup.com/en/americas/canada
Profile: Thales Canada provides technology & equipment for the
defence & security, aerospace & transportation markets. The
company has offices in Québec, Ontario & British Columbia.
Mark Halinaty, President & CEO

Tronos
PO Box 7, Slemon Park, PE C0B 2A0
Tel: 902-436-5318; *Fax:* 902-436-5319
www.tronosjet.com
Profile: Tronos is an aviation services provider specializing in
aircraft leasing, maintenance & asset management. The
company also has operations in the UK serving Europe, the
Middle East, Asia & Africa.

Tube-Fab Ltd.
1020 Brevik Pl., Mississauga, ON L4W 4N7
Tel: 905-206-0311; *Fax:* 905-206-1259
www.tube-fab.com
Profile: Together with its sister company TFL Technologies Inc.,
Tube-Fab manufactures & assembles precision tubular &
machined components, & complete assemblies for fluid delivery
& structural assemblies. They serve clients in the aerospace,
defence, marine, medical, drug & food processing, robotics,
energy, & oil & gas industries.
Wesley Eric Foley, President & COO
416-569-8621, efoley@tube-fab.com
Chris Gardner, Director, Business Development & Marketing
cgardner@tube-fab.com

Uniglobe Travel International LP
#900, 1199 West Pender St., Vancouver, BC V6E 2R1
Tel: 604-718-2600
info@uniglobetravel.com
www.uniglobetravel.com
Profile: Travel franchise specializing in corporate travel services
for small to medium accounts as well as individual travelers.
U. Gary Charlwood, Founder, Chair & CEO
Martin Charlwood, President & COO
Tracy Bartram, Senior Vice-President & CFO

VAC Developments Limited
2270 Bristol Circle, Oakville, ON L6H 5S3
Tel: 905-855-6855; *Fax:* 905-855-6856
contact@vacdev.com
www.vacdev.com
Profile: VAC provides the aerospace industry with precision
machining, sheet metal & welding services.
Bill Hristovski, President

VersaCold Logistics Services
Formerly: Versacold Corporation
316 Aviva Park Dr., Vaughan, ON L4L 9C7
Tel: 905-850-6224; *Toll-Free:* 800-563-2653
info@versacold.com
versacold.com
Ticker Symbol: ICE / TSX

Profile: Founded in 1946, VersaCold is a supply chain company
focused on temperature sensitive products. It has 31
temperature controlled warehouses & distribution centres
throughout Canada, & serves both Canada & the United States.
Paul Campbell, Chief Executive Officer
905-265-7176, paul.campbell@versacold.com
Michele Arcamone, President & COO
905-265-7177, mike.arcamone@versacold.com
Sandro Caccaro, Vice-President & General Manager, VersaCold
Transportation Solutions
905-265-7194, sandro.caccaro@versacold.com

Versatile Spray Painting Ltd. / VSP
102 Healey Rd., Bolton, ON L7E 5A9
Tel: 905-857-4915; *Fax:* 905-857-4924
Toll-Free: 877-857-4915
www.versatilespray.com
Profile: VSP specializes in industrial finishing for military,
aerospace, medical sectors, as well as for business machines &
electronic packaging.
Dave Gogo, Managing Partner
Chris Heslin, Managing Partner

VIH Aerospace Inc.
Parent: VIH Aviation Group
1962 Canso Rd., North Saanich, BC V8L 5V5
Tel: 250-655-6828; *Fax:* 250-655-6861
Toll-Free: 866-844-4354
viha@vih.com
www.vih.com/Services/vihaerospace.html
Profile: VIH Aerospace offers helicopter maintenance products
& services to the aerospace industry, including maintenance of
communication & navigation equipment.
Arne Arneson, General Manager

Viking Air Ltd.
1959 de Havilland Way, Sidney, BC V8L 5V5
Tel: 250-656-7227; *Fax:* 250-656-0673
Toll-Free: 800-663-8444
info@vikingair.com
www.vikingair.com
Profile: Viking manufactures seven aircraft types & provides
support services including spares sales, customer service,
technical support, engineering, maintenance, repair, overhaul &
conversions.
David Curtis, President & CEO

Virtual Marine Technology / VMT
20 Hallett Cres., St. John's, NL A1B 3N4
Tel: 709-738-6306; *Fax:* 709-738-5996
communications@virtualmarine.ca
www.virtualmarine.ca
Profile: The company produces simulators for survival craft, fast
response craft & high-speed electronic navigation training.
Anthony Patterson, President & CEO
anthony.patterson@virtualmarine.ca

Volatus Flight Systems
Toronto, ON
Tel: 514-447-7986
info@volatusflightsystems.com
www.volatusflightsystems.com
Profile: The company designs, manufactures & certifies
remotely piloted systems for the aerospace & defense industry.
Glen Lynch, President & CEO

Wescast Industries Inc.
150 Savannah Oaks Dr., Brantford, ON N3V 1E7
Tel: 519-750-0000; *Fax:* 519-720-1628
north.america@wescast.com
www.wescast.com
Ticker Symbol: WCS / TSX
Profile: Manufacturers of motor vehicle parts & accessories;
Wholesalers of motor vehicle supplies & new parts.

Xiphos Systems Corporation
#500, 3981, boul St-Laurent, Montréal, QC H2W 1Y5
Tel: 514-847-9474
info@xiphos.com
www.xiphos.com
Profile: Xiphos provides customers in the aerospace industry
with processors integrated into avionics packages, mainly for the
space & unmanned aerial vehicles markets. Customers include
the Canadian Space Agency & the United States Air Force.

YYJ FBO Services
Parent: VIH Aviation Group
**Victoria International Airport, #101, 1962 Canso Rd., North
Saanich, BC V8L 5V5**
Tel: 250-655-8833; *Fax:* 250-655-5020
www.yyjfbo.com
Profile: The company is a fixed-base operator (FBO) located at
Victoria International Airport, & offering fueling services,

passenger, executive & pilot lounges, car & hotel reservations, catering services, flight planning room & other amenities.
Jen Norie, General Manager
jnorie@vih.com
Martin Childs, Manager, Operations
mchilds@yyjfbo.com

Government Agency Guide

AIRPORTS & AVIATION
See Also: Transportation
Canadian Air Transport Security Authority, 99 Bank St., 13th Fl., Ottawa, ON K1P 6B9
Fax: 613-990-1295, 888-294-2202, correspondence1@catsa-acsta.gc.ca
Transport Canada, Place de Ville, 330 Sparks St., Ottawa, ON K1A 0N5
613-990-2309, Fax: 613-954-4731, 866-995-9737
Transportation Appeal Tribunal of Canada, #1201, 333 Laurier Ave. West, 12th Fl., Ottawa, ON K1A 0N5
613-990-6906, Fax: 613-990-9153, info@tatc.gc.ca

Newfoundland & Labrador
Newfoundland & Labrador Department of Transportation & Infrastructure, Confederation Bldg., Prince Philip Dr., PO Box 8700, St. John's, NL A1B 4J6
709-729-2300, ti@gov.nl.ca

Northwest Territories
Northwest Territories Department of Infrastructure, Stuart M. Hodgson Bldg., 5009 - 49th St., 3rd Fl., PO Box 1320, Yellowknife, NT X1A 2L9
INF_Communications@gov.nt.ca

Nunavut
Nunavut Territory Department of Community & Government Services, W.G. Brown Bldg., 4th Fl., PO Box 1000 700, Iqaluit, NU X0A 0H0
867-975-5406, Fax: 867-975-5305, cgscomms@gov.nu.ca

Ontario
Ontario Ministry of Transportation, 777 Bay St., 5th Fl., Toronto, ON M7A 1Z8
416-235-4686, Fax: 416-327-9185, 800-268-4686

Saskatchewan
Saskatchewan Highways, Victoria Tower, 1855 Victoria Ave., Regina, SK S4P 3T2
306-933-5186, MHI.CustomerService@gov.sk.ca

Yukon Territory
Yukon Highways & Public Works, PO Box 2703, Whitehorse, YT Y1A 2C6
867-667-3732, Fax: 867-393-6218, hpw-info@yukon.ca

APPRENTICESHIP PROGRAMS
Canadian Council of Directors of Apprenticeship, 140 Promenade du Portage, 6th Fl., Phase IV, Gatineau, QC K1A 0J9
Fax: 819-994-0202, 877-599-6933, redseal-sceaurouge@hrsdc-rhdcc.gc.ca

Alberta
Alberta Advanced Education, Legislature Bldg., #403, 10800 - 97th Ave., Edmonton, AB T5K 2B6
780-422-5400
Apprenticeship & Student Aid Division, Commerce Place, 10155 - 102nd St., 6th Fl., Edmonton, AB T5J 4L5

New Brunswick
New Brunswick Department of Post-Secondary Education, Training & Labour, Chestnut Complex, PO Box 6000, Fredericton, NB E3B 5H1
506-453-2597, Fax: 506-453-3618, dpetlinfo@gnb.ca

Northwest Territories
Apprenticeship, Trade & Occupations Certification Board, PO Box 1320, Yellowknife, NT X1A 2L9
867-767-9351, apprenticeship@gov.nt.ca

Prince Edward Island
SkillsPEI, Atlantic Technology Centre, #212, 176 Great George St., Charlottetown, PE C1A 4K9
902-368-6290, Fax: 902-368-6340, 877-491-4766

Quebec
Conseil consultatif du travail et de la main d'oeuvre, #17.100, 500, boul René-Lévesque ouest, Montréal, QC H2Z 1W7
514-873-2880, Fax: 514-873-1129

Saskatchewan
Saskatchewan Advanced Education, #1120, 2010 - 12th Ave., Regina, SK S4P 0M3
aeeinquiry@gov.sk.ca
Saskatchewan Apprenticeship & Trade Certification Commission, 2140 Hamilton St., Regina, SK S4P 2E3

306-787-2444, Fax: 306-787-5105, 877-363-0536, apprenticeship@gov.sk.ca

Yukon Territory
Yukon Education, 1000 Lewes Blvd., Whitehorse, YT Y1A 3H9
867-667-5141, Fax: 867-393-6254, edu-communications@yukon.ca

RAIL TRANSPORTATION
See Also: Transportation
Transportation Safety Board of Canada, 200, promenade du Portage, 4e étage, Gatineau, QC K1A 1K8
819-994-3741, Fax: 819-997-2239, 800-387-3557, communications@bst-tsb.gc.ca
VIA Rail Canada Inc., CP 8116 Centre-Ville, Montréal, QC H3C 3N3
514-871-6000, Fax: 514-871-6104, 888-842-7245, customer_relations@viarail.ca

Alberta
Alberta Transportation, Communications Branch, Twin Atria Bldg., 4999 - 98th Ave., 2nd Fl., Edmonton, AB T6B 2X3
780-427-7674, Fax: 780-466-3166, Trans.Contact.Us.m@gov.ab.ca

Manitoba
Manitoba Infrastructure, Legislative Bldg., #203, 450 Broadway, Winnipeg, MB R3C 0V8

New Brunswick
New Brunswick Department of Transportation & Infrastructure, Kings Place, PO Box 6000, Fredericton, NB E3B 5H1
506-453-3939, Fax: 506-453-7987, transportation.web@gnb.ca

Newfoundland & Labrador
Newfoundland & Labrador Department of Transportation & Infrastructure, Confederation Bldg., Prince Philip Dr., PO Box 8700, St. John's, NL A1B 4J6
709-729-2300, ti@gov.nl.ca

Nova Scotia
Nova Scotia Department of Transportation & Active Transit, PO Box 186, Halifax, NS B3J 2N2
902-424-2297, Fax: 902-424-0532, tpwpaff@novascotia.ca

Ontario
Metrolinx, 97 Front St. West, Toronto, ON M5J 1E6
416-874-5900, Fax: 416-869-1755

Quebec
Société du port ferroviaire Baie-Comeau-Haute-Rive, 18, rte Maritime, Baie-Comeau, QC G4Z 2L6
418-296-6785

Saskatchewan
Saskatchewan Highways, Victoria Tower, 1855 Victoria Ave., Regina, SK S4P 3T2
306-933-5186, MHI.CustomerService@gov.sk.ca

TRANSPORTATION
Atlantic Pilotage Authority, TD Centre, #1801, 1791 Barrington St., Halifax, NS B3J 3K9
902-426-2550, Fax: 902-426-4004, 877-272-3477, dispatch@atlanticpilotage.com
Automotive & Surface Transportation Facilities, Ottawa Uplands Research Facilities, 2320 Lester Rd., Ottawa, ON K1V 1S2
613-998-9639
Canadian Air Transport Security Authority, 99 Bank St., 13th Fl., Ottawa, ON K1P 6B9
Fax: 613-990-1295, 888-294-2202, correspondence1@catsa-acsta.gc.ca
Canadian Coast Guard, Centennial Towers, #6S018, 200 Kent St., Ottawa, ON K1A 0E6
613-993-0999, Fax: 613-990-1866, info@dfo-mpo.gc.ca
Canadian Transportation Agency, Les Terrasses de la Chaudière, 15, rue Eddy, Gatineau, QC J8X 4B3
Fax: 819-997-6727, 888-222-2592, info@otc-cta.gc.ca
Federal Bridge Corporation Limited, #1210, 55 Metcalfe St., Ottawa, ON K1P 6L5
613-998-8427, Fax: 613-993-6945, info@federalbridge.ca
Great Lakes Pilotage Authority, 202 Pitt St., 2nd fl., PO Box 95, Cornwall, ON K6H 5R9
613-933-2991, Fax: 613-932-3793
Laurentian Pilotage Authority, Head Office, #1401, 999, boul Maisonneuve ouest, Montréal, QC H3A 3L4
514-283-6320, Fax: 514-496-2409, administration@apl.gc.ca
Marine Atlantic Inc., Corporate Office, Baine Johnston Centre, #302, 10 Fort William Pl., St. John's, NL A1C 1K4
800-897-2797, customer_relations@marine-atlantic.ca
Old Port of Montréal Corporation Inc., 333, rue de la Commune ouest, Montréal, QC H2Y 2E2
514-283-5256, 800-971-7678,

Pacific Pilotage Authority Canada, #1000, 1130 West Pender St., Vancouver, BC V6E 4A4
604-666-6771, Fax: 604-666-1647, info@ppa.gc.ca
St. Lawrence Seaway Management Corporation, 202 Pitt St., Cornwall, ON K6J 3P7
613-932-5170, Fax: 613-932-7286, marketing@seaway.ca
Transport Canada, Place de Ville, 330 Sparks St., Ottawa, ON K1A 0N5
613-990-2309, Fax: 613-954-4731, 866-995-9737
Transportation Appeal Tribunal of Canada, #1201, 333 Laurier Ave. West, 12th Fl., Ottawa, ON K1A 0N5
613-990-6906, Fax: 613-990-9153, info@tatc.gc.ca
Transportation Safety Board of Canada, 200, promenade du Portage, 4e étage, Gatineau, QC K1A 1K8
819-994-3741, Fax: 819-997-2239, 800-387-3557, communications@bst-tsb.gc.ca
VIA Rail Canada Inc., CP 8116 Centre-Ville, Montréal, QC H3C 3N3
514-871-6000, Fax: 514-871-6104, 888-842-7245, customer_relations@viarail.ca

Alberta
Alberta Automobile Insurance Rate Board, Canadian Western Bank Place, #2440, 10303 Jasper Ave., Edmonton, AB T5J 3N6
780-427-5428, Fax: 780-638-4254, -310-0000, airb@gov.ab.ca
Alberta Infrastructure, Infrastructure Bldg., 6950 - 113th St., Edmonton, AB T6H 5V7
780-415-0507, Fax: 780-427-2187, Infra.Contact.Us.m@gov.ab.ca
Alberta Transportation, Communications Branch, Twin Atria Bldg., 4999 - 98th Ave., 2nd Fl., Edmonton, AB T6B 2X3
780-427-7674, Fax: 780-466-3166, Trans.Contact.Us.m@gov.ab.ca
Corporate Strategies & Services Division, Infrastructure Bldg., 6950 - 113th St., 2nd Fl., Edmonton, AB T6H 5V7
Safety & Policy Division, Twin Atria Bldg., 4999 - 98th Ave., Main Fl., Edmonton, AB T6B 2X3
780-427-8901, Fax: 780-415-0782, 800-666-5036
Transportation Safety Board, North Office, Twin Atria Building, 4999 - 98 Ave., Main Fl., Edmonton, AB T6B 2X3
780-427-7178, Fax: 780-422-9739, -310-0000

British Columbia
British Columbia Ferry Commission, PO Box 9279 Prov Govt, Victoria, BC V8W 9J7
250-952-0112, info@bcferrycommission.com
British Columbia Ferry Services Inc., c/o BC Ferry Authority, #500, 1321 Blanshard St., Victoria, BC V8W 0B7
250-381-1401, 888-223-3779, customerservice@bcferries.com
British Columbia Ministry of Transportation & Infrastructure, PO Box 9850 Prov Govt, Victoria, BC V8W 9T5
250-387-3198, Fax: 250-356-7706, tran.webmaster@gov.bc.ca
British Columbia Transit, 520 Gorge Rd. East, Victoria, BC V8W 2P3
250-385-2551
Passenger Transportation Board, #202, 940 Blanshard St., PO Box 9850 Prov Govt, Victoria, BC V8W 9T5
250-953-3777, Fax: 250-953-3788, ptboard@gov.bc.ca
Transportation Policy & Programs Division, PO Box 9850 Prov Govt, Victoria, BC V8W 9T5
250-387-5062, Fax: 250-387-6431

Manitoba
Highway Traffic Board/Motor Transport Board, #200, 301 Weston St., Winnipeg, MB R3E 3H4
204-945-8912, Fax: 204-783-6529
Manitoba Infrastructure, Legislative Bldg., #203, 450 Broadway, Winnipeg, MB R3C 0V8
Medical Review Committee, #200, 301 Weston St., Winnipeg, MB R3E 3H4
204-945-7350, Fax: 204-948-2682
Taxicab Board, #200, 301 Weston St., Winnipeg, MB R3E 3H4
204-945-8919, Fax: 204-948-2315, taxicabboardoffice@gov.mb.ca

New Brunswick
New Brunswick Department of Transportation & Infrastructure, Kings Place, PO Box 6000, Fredericton, NB E3B 5H1
506-453-3939, Fax: 506-453-7987, transportation.web@gnb.ca
Vehicle Management Agency, Vehicle Management Centre, 1050 College Hill Rd., PO Box 6000, Fredericton, NB E3B 5H1
506-453-3939, Fax: 506-453-3628, transportation.web@gnb.ca

Newfoundland & Labrador
Newfoundland & Labrador Department of Transportation & Infrastructure, Confederation Bldg., Prince Philip Dr., PO Box

8700, St. John's, NL A1B 4J6
709-729-2300, ti@gov.nl.ca

Northwest Territories
Northwest Territories Department of Infrastructure, Stuart M. Hodgson Bldg., 5009 - 49th St., 3rd Fl., PO Box 1320, Yellowknife, NT X1A 2L9
INF_Communications@gov.nt.ca

Nova Scotia
Nova Scotia Department of Transportation & Active Transit, PO Box 186, Halifax, NS B3J 2N2
902-424-2297, Fax: 902-424-0532, tpwpaff@novascotia.ca

Nunavut
Nunavut Territory Department of Community & Government Services, W.G. Brown Bldg., 4th Fl., PO Box 1000 700, Iqaluit, NU X0A 0H0
867-975-5406, Fax: 867-975-5305, cgscomms@gov.nu.ca
Nunavut Territory Department of Economic Development & Transportation, Inuksugait Plaza, Bldg. 1104A, PO Box 1000 1500, Iqaluit, NU X0A 0H0
867-975-7800, Fax: 867-975-7870, 888-975-5999, edt@gov.nu.ca

Ontario
Metrolinx, 97 Front St. West, Toronto, ON M5J 1E6
416-874-5900, Fax: 416-869-1755
Ontario Highway Transport Board, 151 Bloor St. West, 10th Fl., Toronto, ON M5S 2T5
416-326-6732, Fax: 416-326-6738, ohtb@mto.gov.on.ca
Ontario Ministry of Infrastructure, 777 Bay St., 5th Fl., Toronto, ON M5G 2C8
416-327-4412
Ontario Ministry of Transportation, 777 Bay St., 5th Fl., Toronto, ON M7A 1Z8
416-235-4686, Fax: 416-327-9185, 800-268-4686
Owen Sound Transportation Company Ltd., 717875, Hwy. 6, Owen Sound, ON N4K 5N7
519-376-8740, 800-265-3163

Road User Safety Division, Bldg A, 87 Sir William Hearst Ave., Toronto, ON M3M 0B4
416-235-2999, Fax: 416-235-4153

Prince Edward Island
Prince Edward Island Department of Transportation & Infrastructure, Jones Bldg., 11 Kent St., 3rd Fl., PO Box 2000, Charlottetown, PE C1A 7N8
902-368-5100, Fax: 902-368-5395, DeptTIE@gov.pe.ca

Quebec
Commission des transports du Québec, 200, ch Sainte-Foy, 7e étage, Québec, QC G1R 5V5
514-873-6424, Fax: 418-644-8034, 888-461-2433, courier@ctq.gouv.qc.ca
Ministère des Transports, #4.010, 500, boul René-Lévesque est, Québec, QC H2Z 1W7
888-355-0511, communications@mtq.gouv.qc.ca
Réseau de transport métropolitain (Exo), 700, rue de la Gauchetière ouest, 26e étage, Montréal, QC H3B 5M2
514-287-8726, 888-702-8726
Société de l'assurance automobile du Québec, 333, boul Jean-Lesage, CP 19600 Terminus, Québec, QC G1K 8J6
418-643-7620, Fax: 418-644-0339, 800-361-7620
Société des traversiers du Québec, 250, rue Saint-Paul, Québec, QC G1K 9K9
418-643-2019, Fax: 418-643-7308, 877-787-7483, stq@traversiers.gouv.qc.ca
Société du parc industriel et portuaire de Bécancour, 1000, boul Arthur-Sicard, Bécancour, QC G9H 2Z8
819-294-6656, Fax: 819-294-9020, info@spipb.com
Société du port ferroviaire Baie-Comeau-Haute-Rive, 18, rte Maritime, Baie-Comeau, QC G4Z 2L6
418-296-6785

Saskatchewan
Global Transportation Hub Authority, #700, 1855 Victoria Ave., Regina, SK S4P 3T2
306-787-4842, Fax: 306-798-4600, inquiry@thegth.com

Highway Traffic Board, 1621A mcDonald St., Regina, SK S4N 5R2
Fax: 306-798-0162, 855-775-8336, contactus.htb@gov.sk.ca
Saskatchewan Highways, Victoria Tower, 1855 Victoria Ave., Regina, SK S4P 3T2
306-933-5186, MHI.CustomerService@gov.sk.ca

Yukon Territory
Yukon Community Services, PO Box 2703, Whitehorse, YT Y1A 2C6
867-667-5811, Fax: 867-393-6295, 800-661-0408
Yukon Highways & Public Works, PO Box 2703, Whitehorse, YT Y1A 2C6
867-667-3732, Fax: 867-393-6218, hpw-info@yukon.ca

TRANSPORTATION OF DANGEROUS GOODS

Nova Scotia
Nova Scotia Department of Transportation & Active Transit, PO Box 186, Halifax, NS B3J 2N2
902-424-2297, Fax: 902-424-0532, tpwpaff@novascotia.ca

Ontario
Road User Safety Division, Bldg A, 87 Sir William Hearst Ave., Toronto, ON M3M 0B4
416-235-2999, Fax: 416-235-4153

Prince Edward Island
Prince Edward Island Department of Transportation & Infrastructure, Jones Bldg., 11 Kent St., 3rd Fl., PO Box 2000, Charlottetown, PE C1A 7N8
902-368-5100, Fax: 902-368-5395, DeptTIE@gov.pe.ca

Saskatchewan
Saskatchewan Highways, Victoria Tower, 1855 Victoria Ave., Regina, SK S4P 3T2
306-933-5186, MHI.CustomerService@gov.sk.ca

SECTION 17

UTILITIES

Associations

Alberta Water & Wastewater Operators Association (AWWOA)
10806 - 119th St., Edmonton AB T5H 3P2
Tel: 780-454-7745; *Fax:* 780-454-7748
Toll-Free: 877-454-7745
awwoa.ca
www.facebook.com/157981630910194
twitter.com/awwoa
Overview: A small provincial organization founded in 1976
Description: To contribute to the training & upgrading of persons employed in the water & wastewater field in Alberta; To encourage the best possible operation of water & wastewater facilities
Affiliation(s): Western Canada Water & Wastewater Association
Chief Officer(s): Darrin Wenzel, Chair
Fees: $60
Activities: Providing manuals to operators; *Awareness Events:* Water Week

American Council for an Energy-Efficient Economy (ACEEE)
#600, 529 - 14th St. NW, Washington DC 20045-1000 USA
Tel: 202-507-4000; *Fax:* 202-429-2248
www.aceee.org
www.instagram.com/aceeedc
www.linkedin.com/company/aceee
www.facebook.com/myACEEE
twitter.com/ACEEEdc
Overview: A medium-sized national organization founded in 1980
Description: To advance energy-conserving technology & policies; To assist utilities & regulators in implementing cost-effective conservation programs; To support the adoption of comprehensive new policies for increasing energy efficiency; To analyse & promote technologies & policies for increasing vehicle fuel efficiency & reducing vehicle use; To help developing & Eastern European countries undertake energy efficiency programs
Chief Officer(s): Steven Nadel, Executive Director, 202-507-4011
snadel@aceee.org
Activities: *Library:* American Council for an Energy-Efficient Economy Library

American Public Works Association (APWA)
#1400, 1200 Main St., Kansas City MO 64105-2100 USA
Tel: 816-472-6100; *Fax:* 816-472-1610
Toll-Free: 800-848-2792
apwa@apwa.net
www.apwa.net
www.instagram.com/apwagram
www.linkedin.com/company/apwa
www.facebook.com/AmericanPublicWorksAssociation
twitter.com/apwatweets
Overview: A large international organization founded in 1938
Description: To provide high quality public works, goods & services
Affiliation(s): Canadian Public Works Association
Chief Officer(s): Scott Grayson, Chief Executive Officer
sgrayson@apwa.net
Teresa Hon, Senior Manager, Board Operations & Governance
thon@apwa.net
Finances: *Annual Operating Budget:* Greater than $5 Million; *Funding Sources:* Membership dues; Federal grants; Products
Staff: 50 staff member(s); 250 volunteer(s)
Membership: 30,000; *Fees:* Schedule available; *Member Profile:* Public agencies, private sector companies & individuals engaged in public works services; *Committees:* Transportation; Solid Waste; Water Resources; Engineering & Technology; Management & Leadership; Emergency Management; Fleet Services; Facilities & Grounds; Utility & Public Right of Way

Association de l'industrie électrique du Québec (AIEQ)
#1470, 1155, rue Metcalfe, Montréal QC H3B 2V6
Tél: 514-281-0615; *Téléc:* 514-281-7965
info@aieq.net
aieq.net

www.linkedin.com/company/aieq
www.facebook.com/AIEQuebec
twitter.com/_AIEQ
Nom précédent: Club d'électricité du Québec inc.
Aperçu: *Dimension:* moyenne; *Envergure:* provinciale; *Organisme sans but lucratif;* fondée en 1916
Description: Etre porte parole de l'industrie 'électrique au Québec; favoriser la circulation de toute information et intérêt pour les membres et l'industrie électrique en général; contribuer au développement de nos membres et à la promotion de leurs intérêts par des initiatives de concertation et de représentation; encourager l'utilisation rationnelle des ressources dans une perspective de développement
Affiliation(s): ABB; AECOM; ALSTOM; DESSAU; SNC-LAVALIN; VOITH; BPR: Brookfield; Mitsubishi Electric Power Products, Inc.; Qualitas
Membre(s) du bureau directeur: Denis Tremblay, Président et directeur général, 514-281-0615 122
dtremblay@aieq.net
Finances: *Budget de fonctionnement annuel:* $500,000-$1.5 Million
Personnel: 7 membre(s) du personnel
Membre: 121; *Montant de la cotisation:* Barème, selon le nombre d'employés au Québec; *Critères d'admissibilite:* Membres industriels; *Comités:* Consultatif; Finances; Services aux membres; Promotion; Débats projects
Activités: Déjeuners; conférences; activités sociales; *Service de conférenciers:* Oui

Association of Major Power Consumers in Ontario (AMPCO)
Thomson Bldg., #1510, 65 Queen St. West, Toronto ON M5H 2M5
Tel: 416-260-0280; *Fax:* 416-260-0442
info@ampco.org
ampco.org
Overview: A medium-sized provincial organization founded in 1975
Description: To represent Ontario's electricity-intensive companies; To ensure reliability of power supply to support the economy of Ontario; To advocate a fair & equitable pricing system for electricity; To present views on energy matters to such groups as the Ontario Energy Board, the Ontario Government, Ontario Hydro, the news media & the general public; To provide decision makers with recommendations on resolving issues
Chief Officer(s): Colin Anderson, President
Finances: *Funding Sources:* Membership fees
Membership: 44; *Fees:* Schedule available; *Member Profile:* Companies that are major manufacturers, employers & power consumers (represents key industries - mining, pulp & paper, automobile manufacturing, petro-chemicals, metals, consumer products, steel, etc.)

Association of Manitoba Hydro Staff & Supervisory Employees (AMHSSE)
MB
www.amhsse.com
Overview: A small provincial organization founded in 1973
Chief Officer(s): Corey Eyolfson, President
president@amhsse.com
Membership: 900

Association of Power Producers of Ontario (APPrO)
#1040, 67 Yonge St., Toronto ON M5E 1J8
Tel: 416-322-6549; *Fax:* 416-481-5785
appro@appro.org
www.appro.org
www.linkedin.com/company/association-of-power-producers-of-ontario-appro-
www.facebook.com/APPrOPowerMemoryProject
twitter.com/APPrOntario
Previous Name: Independent Power Producers Society of Ontario (IPPSO)
Overview: A medium-sized provincial organization founded in 1986
Description: To act as the voice of electricity generators in Ontario; To support a reliable & secure electricity supply in Ontario
Chief Officer(s): David Butters, President, 416-322-6549 231
david.butters@appro.org
Jake Brooks, Executive Director
jake.brooks@appro.org
Membership: 100+; *Member Profile:* Companies involved in the generation of electricity in Ontario, including suppliers of services & consulting services
Activities: Advocating for generators; Offering resources to assist business, government, utilities & researchers; Organizing educational programs

Atlantic Canada Water & Wastewater Association (ACWWA)
PO Box 28141, Dartmouth NS B2W 6E2
Tel: 902-434-6002; *Fax:* 902-435-7796
contact@acwwa.ca
www.acwwa.ca
twitter.com/ACWWA
Overview: A medium-sized local organization
Description: To improve drinking water in Atlantic Canada; *Member of:* American Water Works Association (AWWA); Water Environment Federation (WEF)

Chief Officer(s): Clara Shea, Executive Director
Lindsay Wilcott, Director, Communication
Membership: 430+; *Fees:* Schedule available; *Member Profile:* Water professionals in Atlantic Canada, from the industries of provision, contracting, utility management, operations, system design, consulting & academia; *Committees:* Scholarship; Conference; Operator Involvement; Education; Government Affairs; Magazine; Young Professionals; Membership; Volunteer; Media; Website; Technical Papers; Water For People; Cross Connection Control; Government Relations
Activities: Providing training & information about the water & wastewater industry to members; Enhancing government relations; Offering networking opportunities

British Columbia Sustainable Energy Association (BCSEA)
1631 Oakland Ave., Victoria BC V8T 2L3
Tel: 604-332-0025
info@bcsea.org
www.bcsea.org
www.youtube.com/BCSEA
www.linkedin.com/company/bc-sustainable-energy-association
www.facebook.com/BCSEA
twitter.com/bcsea
Overview: A medium-sized provincial organization founded in 2004
Description: To support the sustainable production, distribution & consumption of energy in British Columbia & beyond
Affiliation(s): Canadian Renewable Energy Association; Canadian Solar Industries Association; Canadian Wind Energy Association; Climate Action Network Canada; KyotoPLUS; Livable Region Coalition; NorthWest Energy Coalition; Oil Free Coast Alliance; Organizing for Change: Priorities for Environmental Leadership
Chief Officer(s): Jonathan Ho, Chair
Finances: *Funding Sources:* Donations
Fees: $30 student; $75 supporter; $120 leader; *Member Profile:* Individuals & organizations
Activities: Develops & undertakes educational programs, policy advocacy, public outreach & energy planning; Provide: Sustainable energy news & information, BC utilities commission interventions, energy directories, webinars, leadership training & other special events

British Columbia Water & Waste Association (BCWWA)
#247, 4299 Canada Way, Burnaby BC V5G 1H3
Tel: 604-433-4389; *Fax:* 604-433-9859
Toll-Free: 877-433-4389
contact@bcwwa.org
www.bcwwa.org
www.linkedin.com/company/bc-water-and-waste-association
www.facebook.com/BCWWA
twitter.com/bcwwa
Overview: A medium-sized provincial organization founded in 1964
Description: To safeguard public health & the environment through the sharing of skills, knowledge, experience & education; To provide a voice for the water & wastewater community in British Columbia & the Yukon; *Member of:* American Water Works Association (AWWA); Water Environment Federation (WEF); Canadian Water & Wastewater Association (CWWA)
Chief Officer(s): Carlie Hucul, Chief Executive Officer, 604-630-0011
chucul@bcwwa.org
Jennifer Thorne, Manager, Finance
jthorne@bcwwa.org
Amber Jelly, Coordinator, Marketing & Communication, 604-630-5348
ajelly@bcwwa.org
Finances: *Funding Sources:* Membership fees; Courses; Seminars; Annual conference
Membership: 4,000+; *Fees:* $25 student; $109 operator/individual; *Member Profile:* British Columbia & Yukon professionals & students in the water & waste fields; *Committees:* Annual Conference; Cross Connection Control; Education Advisory Council; Young Professionals; Yukon; Drinking Water; Infrastructure Management; Risk & Resilience; SCADA & IT; Wastewater & Residuals Management; Water Sustainability; Wastewater Collection; Watershed Management
Activities: Promoting dialogue & information dissemination on environmental matters; Offering operator education & training opportunities; Certifying backflow assembly testers in British Columbia & Yukon through our Cross Connection Control program; *Awareness Events:* Drinking Water Week, May *Library:* British Columbia Water & Waste Association Library

Building Energy Management Manitoba (BEMM)
PO Box 304, Stn. Main, Winnipeg MB R3C 2H6
info@bemm.ca
www.bemm.ca
Overview: A small provincial organization
Description: To promote energy efficiency & management in the commercial, industrial, institutional & mult-residential building sectors
Chief Officer(s): Robert Bisson, Treasurer, 204-945-8452
robert.bisson@gov.mb.ca
Rob Walger Glenday, Contact, Membership Inquiries & Website
info@bemm.ca
Membership: 100; *Fees:* $150; *Member Profile:* Engineers, architects, property managers, contractors & energy management professionals; Representatives from government, school boards, hospitals & utility

CAMPUT (CAMPUT)
PO Box 43545, 1601 Bayview Ave., Toronto ON M4G 4G8
Tel: 416-821-3931
info@camput.org
www.camput.org
Also Known As: Canada's Energy & Utility Regulators
Previous Name: Canadian Association of Members of Public Utility Tribunals / Association canadienne des membres des tribunaux d'utilité publique
Overview: A medium-sized national organization founded in 1976
Description: To improve public utility regulation in Canada
Affiliation(s): National Association of Regulatory Utility Commissioners (NARUC)
Chief Officer(s): Cynthia Chaplin, Executive Director
cynthia@camput.org
Membership: 15 member boards & commissions + 2 associate member boards & commissions; *Member Profile:* Any Canadian tribunal, board, commission, or agency that is responsible for the economic regulation of utilities; Any Canadian energy tribunal, board, commission, or agency that makes binding decisions through adjudicative or quasi-judicial processes; *Committees:* Regulatory Affairs; Education
Activities: Educating & training commissioners & staff of public utility tribunals; Communicating with members; Liaising with parallel regulatory organizations

Canada - Newfoundland & Labrador Offshore Petroleum Board (C-NLOPB)
TD Place, #101, 140 Water St., St. John's NL A1C 6H6
Tel: 709-778-1400; *Fax:* 709-778-1473
information@cnlopb.ca
www.cnlopb.ca
www.youtube.com/channel/UCooTeZWw7Bdgxeu7TzQQW4w
twitter.com/CNLOPB
Description: To apply the provisions of the *Atlantic Accord* & the *Atlantic Accord Implementation Acts* to all activities of operators in the Canada-Newfoundland & Labrador Offshore Area; To regulate the oil & gas industry for the Newfoundland & Labrador Offshore Area
Chief Officer(s): Scott Tessier, Chief Executive Officer
Paul Alexander, Director & Chief Safety Officer, Safety
Mike Baker, Director, Industrial Benefits
Stephanie Johnson, Acting Director, Exploration & Information Resources
John Kennedy, Director, Operations
Jeff O'Keefe, Director & Chief Conservation Officer, Resource Management
Elizabeth Young, Director, Environmental Affairs
Activities: Facilitating the exploration for & development of hydrocarbon resources; *Library:* Information Resources Centre

Canada - Nova Scotia Offshore Petroleum Board (CNSOPB)
TD Centre, 1791 Barrington St., 8th Fl., Halifax NS B3J 3K9
Tel: 902-422-5588; *Fax:* 902-422-1799
info@cnsopb.ns.ca
www.cnsopb.ns.ca
twitter.com/CNSOPB
Description: To regulate petroleum activities in the Nova Scotia Offshore Area
Chief Officer(s): Christine Bonnell-Eisnor, Acting Chief Executive Officer
Activities: Issuing licences for offshore exploration & development; Collecting & distributing data

Canadian Association of Petroleum Land Administration (CAPLA)
First St. Plaza, #620, 138 - 4th Ave. SE, Calgary AB T2G 4Z6
Tel: 403-452-6497; *Fax:* 403-452-6627
office@caplacanada.org
www.caplacanada.org
www.linkedin.com/groups/3877780
www.facebook.com/caplacanada
twitter.com/caplacanada

Overview: A medium-sized national organization founded in 1994
Description: To establish recognized standards of excellence & influence the energy industry
Chief Officer(s): Mike Flynn, Executive Director, 403-452-6621
mike@caplacanada.org
Membership: 1,800+; *Fees:* $75 student/retired; $199 active; *Member Profile:* Individuals working in land asset management; *Committees:* Awards; Certification; Conference; Education Delivery & Facilitation; Education Development; Events; Executive; Knowledge Bank; Leadership Forum; Member Services; Mentorship; NEXUS Editorial; Social Media; Surface Stakeholder Engagement
Activities: Leadership & education programs; Professional Development; Voluntary certificate program; Networking opportunities

Canadian Association of Petroleum Landmen (CAPL)
#1600, 520 - 5th Ave. SW, Calgary AB T2P 3R7
Tel: 403-237-6635; *Fax:* 403-263-1620
reception@landman.ca
www.landman.ca
www.linkedin.com/groups/3919817
www.facebook.com/936358049739811
twitter.com/CAPLCanadian
Merged from: Alberta Landmen's Association
Overview: A medium-sized national organization founded in 1948
Description: To enhance all facets of the landman profession in Canada
Chief Officer(s): Shaun Williams, President
Janice Redmond, Vice-President
Finances: *Annual Operating Budget:* $1.5 Million-$3 Million
Membership: 1,400+; *Fees:* $125 student; $150 senior; $225 interim; $325 associate/active
Activities: Liaising with government departments & other resource based associations; Communicating with members; Providing professional development opportunities; Offering networking events

Canadian Association of Petroleum Producers (CAPP) / Association canadienne des producteurs pétroliers
#2100, 350 - 7th Ave. SW, Calgary AB T2P 3N9
Tel: 403-267-1100; *Fax:* 403-261-4622
communication@capp.ca
www.capp.ca
www.youtube.com/cappvideos
www.linkedin.com/company/canadian-association-of-petroleum-producers-capp
www.facebook.com/OilGasCanada
twitter.com/oilgascanada
Merged from: Canadian Petroleum Association; Independent Petroleum Association of Canada
Overview: A large national organization founded in 1992
Description: To represent companies that produce Canada's natural gas & crude oil; To enhance the economic sustainability of the Canadian upstream petroleum industry; To ensure work is conducted in a safe & environmentally & socially responsible manner; To work with government to develop regulatory requirements
Chief Officer(s): Tim McMillan, President & CEO
tim.mcmillan@capp.ca
Terry Abel, Executive Vice-President
terry.abel@capp.ca
Ben Brunnen, Vice-President, Oil Sands
ben.brunnen@capp.ca
Membership: 100+ producer members + 150 associate members; *Member Profile:* Individuals or companies that provide services, such as drilling, banking & computing, for Canada's oil & gas industry; *Committees:* Industry Equalization Steering Committee
Activities: Reviewing, analyzing, & recommending industry policy positions; Participating in regulatory change dialogues; Representing the industry on multi-sector international, federal & provincial consultation bodies; Communicating with governments, regulators, stakeholders & the public; Offering seminars & workshops; Providing industry trends, statistics & research information; Informing members of industry standards & guidelines; Monitoring pipeline expansions; Improving coordinated land use planning processes

Canadian Association on Water Quality (CAWQ) / Association canadienne sur la qualité de l'eau (ACQE)
PO Box 5050, Burlington ON L7R 4A6
Tel: 289-780-0378
www.cawq.ca
Also Known As: Canadian National Committee of the International Association on Water Quality

Previous Name: Canadian Association on Water Pollution Research & Control
Overview: A medium-sized national charitable organization founded in 1967
Description: To promote research of scientific, technological, legal & administrative aspects of water pollution research & control; To further the exchange of information & the practical application of such research for public benefit; *Member of:* International Association on Water Quality
Chief Officer(s): Mike Lywood, President, 905-687-6616
mike.lywood@amecfw.com
Yves Comeau, Secretary, 514-340-4711 3728, Fax: 514-340-5918
yves.comeau@polymtl.ca
Hubert Cabana, Treasurer, 819-821-8000 65457, Fax: 819-821-7974
hubert.cabana@usherbrooke.ca
Finances: *Funding Sources:* Membership fees; Subscriptions; Grants
Membership: 133; *Fees:* Schedule available; *Member Profile:* Individuals, organizations & students engaged in water quality & pollution research & control

Canadian Biogas Association
#900, 275 Slater St., Ottawa ON K1P 5H9
Tel: 613-822-1004
biogasassociation.ca
www.linkedin.com/company/canadian-biogas-association
twitter.com/CanadianBiogas
Previous Name: Agrienergy Producers' Association of Ontario
Overview: A medium-sized provincial organization founded in 2008
Description: To promote biogas opportunitites, shape policies that impact biogas, provide resources & offer technical expertise to address challenges in development
Chief Officer(s): Jennifer Green, Executive Director
jgreen@biogasassociation.ca
Sarah Stadnyk, Manager, Business Development & Communications
Membership: 100+; *Fees:* $675 small business; $2,000 large business; *Member Profile:* Members of the biogas industry, including farmers, munipicalitites, technology developers, consultants, finance & insurance firms & other affiliate representatives
Activities: Supporting research; Outreach events

Canadian Electricity Association (CEA) / Association canadienne de l'électricité (ACE)
#1500, 275 Slater St., Ottawa ON K1P 5H9
Tel: 613-230-9263; *Fax:* 613-230-9326
info@electricity.ca
www.electricity.ca
powerforthefuture.ca/blog
www.linkedin.com/company/canadian-electricity-association
www.facebook.com/canadianelectricityassociation
twitter.com/CDNElectricity
Overview: A large national organization founded in 1891
Description: To be the national voice for safe, secure & sustainable electricity for Canadians; To provide its members with value-added products & services to advance the strategic interests of Canada's electricity community
Chief Officer(s): Francis Bradley, President & CEO
Richard Lussier, Treasurer & Vice-President, Operations
Channa S. Perera, Vice-President, Policy Development
Julia Muggeridge, Director, Communications & Marketing
Laura Cui, Manager, Finance & HR Operations
Membership: 40 Corporate Utility Members; 81 Corporate Partner Members; 8 Associate Members; *Member Profile:* Corporate Utility Members consist of companies that generate, transmit & distribute electrical energy to customers throughout Canada; Corporate Partner Members consist of manufacturers & suppliers serving the electricity sector; *Committees:* Human Resources; Occupational Health and Safety; Technology
Activities: Analyzing national & international business issues; Providing a national forum for the electricity business; Advocating industry views; Helping companies in evolving markets; Communicating findings about concerns such as mercury emissions & electric & magnetic fields; *Library:* Canadian Electricty Association Library

Canadian Energy Law Foundation (CELF)
website@energylawfoundation.ca
www.energylawfoundation.ca
Previous Name: Canadian Petroleum Law Foundation
Overview: A small national organization founded in 1963
Description: To foster the development & improvement of law relating to or affecting the phases of the petroleum & natural gas industries; To raise the standards of the administration & practice of the law; To encourage a better knowledge & understanding of the law

Chief Officer(s): Aaron Rogers, President
president@energylawfoundation.ca
Fees: $105 Class B (firms of 1-4 lawyers); $525 Class A (firms of 5+ lawyers); *Member Profile:* Legal practitioners from law firms, companies, governmental entities, administrative bodies, professional societies & institutions of learning

Canadian Energy Pipeline Association (CEPA) / Association canadienne de pipelines d'énergie
#1110, 505 - 3rd St. SW, Calgary AB T2P 3E6
Tel: 403-221-8777; *Fax:* 403-221-8760
aboutpipelines@cepa.com
www.cepa.com
www.youtube.com/aboutpipelines
www.linkedin.com/company/aboutpipelines
www.facebook.com/aboutpipelines
twitter.com/aboutpipelines
Overview: A medium-sized national organization founded in 1993
Description: To represent Canada's transmission pipeline companies; To ensure a strong transmission pipeline industry
Chief Officer(s): Chris Bloomer, President & CEO
Jennefer Brown, Vice-President, Finance & Business Operations
Patrick Smyth, Vice-President, Performance
Member Profile: Canada's pipeline companies that transport natural gas & crude oil throughout North America; *Committees:* Damage Prevention Regulations; Emergency Security Management; Environment; Health & Safety; Land Issues Task Force; Pipeline Integrity; Aboriginal Affairs; Climate Change; Corporate Tax; Commodity Tax; Pipeline Abandonment Obligations; Pipeline Economics; Property Tax; Regulatory Accounting; Regulatory Policy
Activities: Liaising with government regarding industry practices

Canadian Energy Research Institute (CERI)
#150, 3512 - 33rd St. NW, Calgary AB T2L 2A6
info@ceri.ca
www.ceri.ca
twitter.com/ceri_canada
Overview: A medium-sized national organization founded in 1975
Description: To provide public, industry & government individuals with information concerning all aspects of energy
Chief Officer(s): Allan Fogwill, President & CEO
Dinara Millington, Vice-President, Research
Lisa Rollins, Vice-President, Marketing & Communications
Membership: 150; *Committees:* Research Advisory
Activities: Volunteer fellowship program; Secondment; Accepts articles on oil, gas or electricity supply or demand; *Speaker Service:* Yes *Library:* I.N. McKinnon Memorial Library

Canadian Energy Workers' Association (CEWA)
9908 - 106th St., Edmonton AB T5K 1C4
Tel: 780-420-7887; *Fax:* 780-420-7881
cewa@cewa.ca
www.cewa.ca
www.facebook.com/CEWAOffice
Previous Name: Canadian Utilities & Northland Utilities Employees' Association; Alberta Power Employees' Association
Overview: A small national organization founded in 1969
Description: To represent the interests of members, by serving as a bargaining agent for matters related to working relations with employers
Chief Officer(s): Christine Robinson, Manager, Business, 780-977-3418
crobinson@cewa.ca
Activities: Engaging in problem solving between members & management; Creating programs for members in the areas of safety, security & skills development; Seeking opportunities to organize & represent workers; Offering an annual bursary program

Canadian Fluid Power Association (CFPA) / Association canadienne d'énergie fluide
Tel: 519-833-7417
info@cfpa.ca
www.cfpa.ca
www.linkedin.com/groups/4704028
Overview: A medium-sized national organization founded in 1974
Description: To build public awareness of fluid power technology; To provide a forum for the exchange of information & opinions; To represent the Canadian fluid power industry to government, educational institutions & other organizations; To ensure that members' concerns are known to those in government; To ensure that students are able to be properly prepared for careers in the fluid power industry; To ensure that members are kept abreast of the latest developments in the fluid power industry; To grow & develop fluid power technology in Canada; *Member of:* National Fluid Power Association
Chief Officer(s): Trish Torrance, Association Manager

Finances: *Annual Operating Budget:* Less than $50,000; *Funding Sources:* Membership fees; Sponsorships; Golf tournament
Staff: 1 staff member(s); 10 volunteer(s)
Membership: 56; *Fees:* Schedule available; *Member Profile:* Manufacturers, distributors, assemblers, educators, consultants & designers of fluid power components, systems & services; *Committees:* Communications; Education & Careers; Industrial Relations; Market Insight
Activities: Representing the fluid power industry on the Canadian advisory committee with regard to the drafting of international standards; Representing the fluid power industry in the formulation of applicable national standards; *Speaker Service:* Yes

Canadian Fuels Association / Association canadienne des carburants
#1000, 275 Slater St., Ottawa ON K1P 5H9
Tel: 613-232-3709
info@canadianfuels.ca
www.canadianfuels.ca
www.linkedin.com/company/canadianfuels—-carburantsca
twitter.com/CanadianFuels
Previous Name: Canadian Petroleum Products Institute
Overview: A large national organization founded in 1989
Description: To represent its membership to governments on issues related to business, the environment & health & safety in the petroleum products sector; To ensure its own adherence to the Competition Act & provide a competition compliance program & training sessions to all staff & members
Chief Officer(s): Peter Boag, President
president@canadianfuels.ca
Membership: 10; *Member Profile:* Companies engaged in petroleum refining, marketing & distribution
Activities: Training & education; news releases, reports & technical documents; Driver Certification Program for petroleum transport drivers

Canadian Gas Association (CGA) / Association canadienne du gaz
#1220, 350 Albert St., Ottawa ON K1R 1A4
Tel: 613-748-0057; *Fax:* 613-748-9078
info@cga.ca
www.cga.ca
www.youtube.com/user/CdnGasAssociation
www.linkedin.com/company/canadian-gas-association
twitter.com/GoSmartEnergy
Overview: A large national organization founded in 1907
Description: To act as the voice of the natural gas distribution industry in Canada
Chief Officer(s): Timothy M. Egan, President & CEO, 613-748-0057 300
Aysha Raad, Director, Communications, 613-748-0057 310
news@cga.ca
Member Profile: Natural gas distribution companies, transmission companies, equipment manufacturers & other service providers
Activities: Advancing policy positions with federal & provincial decision makers; Developing educational information

Canadian Institute for Energy Training (CIET) / Institut canadien de formation de l'énergie
#5600, 100 King St. West, Toronto ON M5X 1C9
Tel: 647-255-3107; *Toll-Free:* 800-461-7618
info@cietcanada.com
cietcanada.com
www.linkedin.com/company/canadian-institute-for-energy-trainin
g-ciet-
www.facebook.com/CIETCanada
twitter.com/cietcanada
Overview: A medium-sized national organization founded in 1994
Description: To focus on the advancement of energy efficiency in industrial, commercial & public sector organizations; To provide effective training solutions for the incorporation of energy management into organizational management priorities
Finances: *Funding Sources:* Fees for service
Activities: Offers the following training courses: Certified Energy Manager (CEM); Certified Measurement & Verification Professional (CMVP); Certified Energy Auditor (CEA); Certified Building Commissioning Professional (CBCP); Certified Professional in Energy Performance Contracting (CIET); Building Operator Certification (BOC); Certified in the Use of RETScreen; International Energy Efficiency Financing Protocol (IEEFP); ISO 50001 Standard Implementation

Canadian Institute of Mining, Metallurgy & Petroleum (CIM) / Institut canadien des mines, de la métallurgie et du pétrole (ICM)
#1250, 3500, boul de Maisonneuve ouest, Westmount QC H3Z 3C1
Tel: 514-939-2710; *Fax:* 514-939-2714
cim@cim.org
www.cim.org
www.instagram.com/cim_mag
www.linkedin.com/company/canadian-institute-of-mining-metallu
rgy-and-petroleum
www.facebook.com/CIM.ICM
twitter.com/cimorg
Previous Name: Canadian Institute of Mining & Metallurgy
Overview: A large national organization founded in 1898
Description: To act as a resource sector that is broadly recognized & respected as an angine for sustainable growth & prosperity; *Member of:* Global Mineral Professionals Alliance
Chief Officer(s): Angela Hamlyn, Executive Director
ahamlyn@cim.org
Marilou Reboulis, Manager, Client Relations
mreboulis@cim.org
Membership: 12,000+; *Fees:* $197 individual; *Member Profile:* Professionals in the Canadian minerals, metals, materials, & energy sectors, from industry, government, & academia; *Committees:* Central Publications; Audit; Bulletin; By-Laws; CIM Valuation of Mineral Properties; Education; Estimation Guidelines; Human Resources; International Advisory Liaison; Membership; President Elect Nominating; Public Affairs; Special Volumes
Activities: Providing technical forums, conferences & professional networking opportunities; Offering continuing education programs & courses; Liasing with government departments; Commissioning special volumes & reports & publishing technical papers; *Speaker Service:* Yes *Library:* Canadian Institute of Mining, Metallurgy & Petroleum Library

Canadian Propane Association (CPA) / Association canadienne du propane (ACP)
#406, 410 Laurier Ave. West, Ottawa ON K1R 1B7
Tel: 613-683-2270
info@propane.ca
propane.ca
www.linkedin.com/groups/4355062
www.facebook.com/CanadaPropane
twitter.com/CanadaPropane
Merged from: Propane Gas Association of Canada Inc.; Ontario Propane Association
Overview: A medium-sized national licensing organization founded in 2011
Description: To promote a safe & thriving propane industry that plays a vital role in Canada's energy sector; *Member of:* Canadian Council for Aboriginal Business; Women in LPG Network
Affiliation(s): Propane Training Institute (PTI); Subsidiary: Emergency Response Assistance Canada
Chief Officer(s): Nathalie St-Pierre, President & CEO, 613-683-2270
nathaliestpierre@propane.ca
Tammy Hirsch, Senior Director, Communications & Marketing
tammyhirsch@propane.ca
Finances: *Annual Operating Budget:* $1.5 Million-$3 Million; *Funding Sources:* Membership dues
Staff: 13 staff member(s)
Membership: 400+; *Fees:* Schedule available; *Member Profile:* Producers; Wholesalers; Retailers; Transporters; Manufacturers of Appliances, Cylinders & Equipment; Associated Industries & Trainers; *Committees:* National: Auto Propane, Regulatory Affairs, Transportation; Regional: Atlantic & Quebec, Ontario
Activities: Facilitating best practices, safety & a favourable business environment through advocacy, training & emergency response; *Internships:* Yes

Canadian Public Works Association (CPWA) / Association canadienne des travaux publics
#700, 123 Slater St., Ottawa ON K1P 5H2
Tel: 202-218-6750; *Toll-Free:* 800-848-2792
www.apwa.net
twitter.com/cpwatweets
Overview: A medium-sized national organization founded in 1986
Description: To improve the quality of public works services for Canadian citizens; To share information about public works issues that are unique to Canada
Affiliation(s): American Public Works Association
Chief Officer(s): Scott Grayson, Executive Director, 800-848-2792 6700
sgrayson@apwa.net
Membership: 2,250; *Member Profile:* Public works employees in Canada who are members of the American Public Works

Association; Any person or organization in Canada with an interest in infrastructure & public works issues
Activities: Engaging in advocacy projects; Producing position statements; Facilitating the exchange of information for public works employees; Organizing outreach campaigns; Raising awareness of public works services; *Awareness Events:* National Public Works Week, May *Library:* Canadian Public Works Association Library

Canadian Renewable Energy Association (CanREA) / Association canadienne d'énergie éolienne
#400, 240 Bank St., Ottawa ON K2P 1X4
Tel: 613-234-8716; *Toll-Free:* 800-922-6932
info@renewablesassociation.ca
renewablesassociation.ca
www.youtube.com/channel/UCDz_sP7XRdMMU_IUO6PAk7A
www.linkedin.com/company/renewablesassoc
twitter.com/RenewablesAssoc
Merged from: CanWEA; CanSIA
Overview: A medium-sized national organization founded in 2020
Description: To promote be the voice of wind energy, solar energy & enegery storage solutions; To provide stakeholder advocacy & public engagement
Chief Officer(s): Robert Hornung, President & CEO
Wesley Johnston, Vice-President, Business Development, Finance & Operations
Bridget Wayland, Director, Communications
Finances: *Funding Sources:* Membership fees; Conference & workshop fees
Fees: Schedule available; *Member Profile:* Organizations & individuals who are involved in the development & application of renewable energy technology, products & services in Canada

Canadian Society of Petroleum Geologists (CSPG)
#150, 540 - 5th Ave. SW, Calgary AB T2P 0M2
Tel: 403-264-5610; *Fax:* 403-264-5898
membership@cspg.org
www.cspg.org
www.linkedin.com/company/canadian-society-of-petroleum-geol
ogy
www.facebook.com/CSPGOnline
twitter.com/CSPGeologists
Previous Name: Alberta Society of Petroleum Geologists
Overview: A medium-sized national organization founded in 1929
Description: To advance the science of geology, especially as it relates to petroleum, natural gas & other fossil fuels; To promote the technology of exploration for finding & producing these resources; To foster the spirit of scientific research; To develop a sense of pride & community among Canadian Petroleum Geologists
Affiliation(s): American Association of Petroleum Geologists; Canadian Federation of Earth Sciences; Canadian Society of Exploration Geophysicists; Canadian Well Logging Society; European Association of Geoscientists & Engineers; Society for Sedimentary Geology; Society of Petroleum Engineers
Chief Officer(s): Jen Russel Houston, President
Finances: *Annual Operating Budget:* $250,000-$500,000;
Funding Sources: Membership dues; publications; programs; trust fund
Staff: 4 staff member(s); 300 volunteer(s)
Membership: 3,500; *Fees:* $60 emeritus/recent grad; $120 full/associate
Activities: Education trust fund; Member programs

Canadian Water & Wastewater Association (CWWA) / Association canadienne des eaux potables et usées (ACEPU)
#11, 1010 Polytek St., Ottawa ON K1J 9H9
Tel: 613-747-0524; *Fax:* 613-747-0523
admin@cwwa.ca
cwwa.ca
www.facebook.com/CanadianWaterAndWastewaterAssociation
twitter.com/CWWACEPU
Overview: A medium-sized national organization founded in 1986
Description: To represent the common interests of Canadian municipal water & wastewater systems to federal & interprovincial bodies; To serve as the voice of the water & wastewater services sector in Canada; *Member of:* American Water Works Association; Canadian Water Network
Chief Officer(s): Robert Haller, Executive Director
rhaller@cwwa.ca
Louisa Spina, Coordinator, Accounts & Membership
lspina@cwwa.ca
Adrian Toth, Director, Government Relations
atoth@cwwa.ca
Kara Parisien, Manager, Communication
kparisien@cwwa.ca

Finances: *Annual Operating Budget:* $500,000-$1.5 Million;
Funding Sources: Membership; Events; Advertisement sales
Staff: 6 staff member(s); 100 volunteer(s)
Membership: 400 corporate; *Fees:* Schedule available; *Member Profile:* Owners or operators of municipal infrastructure or services; Individuals from the private sector & academics; Federal, provincial, or territorial government departments or agencies; *Committees:* Biosolids; Climate Change; Drinking Water Quality; Energy & Water Efficiency; Security & Emergency Management; Wastewater & Stormwater
Activities: Monitoring policies, legislation & standards; Liaising with federal & interprovincial organizations; Hosting workshops; Facilitating networking opportunities; Increasing & improving public awareness; Cooperating with regional water & wastewater associations; Organizing national conferences; *Awareness Events:* Window on Ottawa, June

Canadian Water Quality Association (CWQA)
#4, 180 Northfield Dr. West, Waterloo ON N2L 0C7
Tel: 416-695-3068; *Toll-Free:* 866-383-7617
info@cwqa.com
www.cwqa.com
www.linkedin.com/company/cwqa
www.facebook.com/CanadianWQA
twitter.com/cwqanews
Overview: A medium-sized national licensing organization founded in 1956
Description: To train, educate & certify water quality professionals; To serve as a unified & credible voice to members, government & the public; To be the resource for industry information & statistics
Membership: 106 dealers/distributors + 16 manufacturers/suppliers + 10 associates; *Fees:* Schedule available; *Member Profile:* Companies that sell, service, supply, manufacture or distribute water treatment systems for residential, commerical or small system applications

Canadian Water Resources Association (CWRA) / Association canadienne des ressources hydriques (ACRH)
120 Glenora St., Ottawa ON K1S 1J3
Tel: 613-237-9363
info@cwra.org
cwra.org
www.instagram.com/cwranational
www.linkedin.com/company/cwra
twitter.com/CWRA_Flows
Overview: A large national charitable organization founded in 1947
Description: To encourage recognition of the high priority & value of water
Affiliation(s): Canadian Water & Wasterwater Association; International Water Resources Association; American Water Resources Association; British Hydological Society; American Institute of Hydrology
Chief Officer(s): Stephen Braun, President
Maggie Rolmuld, Executive Director
executivedirector@cwra.org
Finances: *Annual Operating Budget:* $100,000-$250,000;
Funding Sources: Membership dues; Donations
Staff: 3 staff member(s); 50 volunteer(s)
Membership: 1,000; *Fees:* $25 student; $60 retired; $120 regular; *Member Profile:* Individuals & organizations interested in the management of Canada's water resources, including private & public sector water resource managers, administrators, scientists, academics, students & users; *Committees:* Finance; Publications; Fundraising; Scholarship; Communications; Website
Activities: Increasing awareness & understanding of Canada's water resources; Providing a forum for the exchange of information; Participating with appropriate agencies in international water management activities; *Internships:* Yes; *Speaker Service:* Yes

Clean Energy British Columbia (CEBC)
#142, 757 West Hastings St., Vancouver BC V6C 1A1
Tel: 604-394-2069
www.cleanenergybc.org
www.instagram.com/cleanenergybc
www.linkedin.com/groups/4767428
www.facebook.com/CleanEnergyBC
twitter.com/CleanEnergyBC
Also Known As: Clean Energy BC
Previous Name: Independent Power Association of BC
Overview: A small provincial organization founded in 1992
Description: To develop a viable power generation & power management industry in British Columbia that serves the public interest by providing cost-effective electricity through the efficient & environmentally responsible development of the province's generation & transmission resources & facilities

Chief Officer(s): Laureen Whyte, Executive Director
laureen.whyte@cleanenergybc.org
Lisa Bateman, Manager, Office & Events
lisa.bateman@cleanenergybc.org
Membership: 130+; *Fees:* $75-$10,000; *Committees:* Conference; First Nations; Hydro; Market Development; Market Issues; Operational Safety; Thermal; Wind; Solar
Activities: Engaging in policy implementation

Community Energy Association (CEA)
PO Box 20129, Stn. Fairview, Vancouver BC V5Z 1E0
Tel: 604-628-7076
info@communityenergy.bc.ca
www.communityenergy.bc.ca
Overview: A medium-sized provincial charitable organization founded in 1993
Description: To support local governments in British Columbia in energy conservation & climate change activities
Chief Officer(s): Dale Littlejohn, Executive Director, 604-628-7076 700
dlittlejohn@communityenergy.bc.ca
Patricia Bell, Head of Planning & Director, Education, 604-936-0470 706
pbell@communityenergy.bc.ca
Peter Robinson, Chief Technology Officer, 604-628-7076 704
probinson@communityenergy.bc.ca
Finances: *Funding Sources:* Membership revenues; Fundraising
Fees: $2,500 local government associate; $5,000 corporate energetic supporter
Activities: Communicating with elected officials, municipal & regional district staff, & First Nations in British Columbia; Offering advisory services to local governments regarding energy innovations; Promoting energy efficiency & renewable energy for infrastructure; Encouraging local governments to consider energy in land planning & development; Conducting research on energy related topics; *Speaker Service:* Yes

Construction Maintenance & Allied Workers Canada (CMAW)
#211, 3823 Henning Dr., Vancouver BC V5C 6P3
Tel: 604-437-0471; *Fax:* 604-437-1110
Toll-Free: 855-616-3555
reception@cmaw.ca
www.cmaw.ca
twitter.com/CMAWunion
Previous Name: British Columbia Carpenters Union
Overview: A medium-sized national organization founded in 2004
Description: To organize workers & encourage an apprenticeship system & higher standard of skill; To develop, improve & enforce the program & standards of occupational safety & health; To develop good public relations with the community; To assist each other to secure employment & to reduce the hours of daily labour
Chief Officer(s): Chris Wasilenchuk, President
cwasilenchuk@cmaw.ca
Paul Nedelec, Secretary-Treasurer
pnedelec@cmaw.ca
Finances: *Annual Operating Budget:* $500,000-$1.5 Million
Membership: 7,000+; *Member Profile:* Carpenters; Carpenter apprentices; Lathers; Millwrights; Floorlayers; Industrial workers; Other construction trades & school board employees

Efficiency Canada
Sustainable Energy Research Centre, Carleton University, #3500E, 1125 Colonel By Dr., Ottawa ON K1S 5B6
info@efficiencycanada.org
www.efficiencycanada.org
www.linkedin.com/company/efficiency-canada
www.facebook.com/EfficiencyCanada
twitter.com/EfficiencyCAN
Overview: A medium-sized national organization founded in 2018
Description: To promote the economic & environmental benefits of energy efficiency; To work with the federal & provincial governments & stakeholders; To ensure energy efficiency is a priority for all sectors of the economy
Chief Officer(s): Corey Diamond, Executive Director
Fees: Schedule available; *Member Profile:* Businesses wishing to support energy efficiency products or services in Canada

Electricity Distributors Association (EDA)
#1100, 3700 Steeles Ave. West, Vaughan ON L4L 8K8
Tel: 905-265-5300; *Fax:* 905-265-5301
Toll-Free: 877-262-8593
email@eda-on.ca
www.eda-on.ca
www.linkedin.com/company/electricity-distributors-association
twitter.com/EDA_ONT
Previous Name: Municipal Electric Association

Overview: A medium-sized provincial organization founded in 1986
Description: To provide local electricity distribution companies with the valued industry knowledge, networking opportunities & collective action vital to members' business success
Chief Officer(s): Teresa Sarkesian, President & CEO, 905-265-5313
tsarkesian@eda-on.ca
Tamara Orlova, Chief Financial Officer
torlova@eda-on.ca
Andrew Temes, Vice-President, Marketing, Communication & Member Relations
atemes@eda-on.ca
Ted Wigdor, Vice-President, Policy, Government & Corporate Affairs, 905-265-5362
twigdor@eda-on.ca
Finances: *Annual Operating Budget:* Greater than $5 Million; *Funding Sources:* Membership dues
Membership: 256; *Member Profile:* Public & privately owned electricity distributors in Ontario

Electricity Human Resources Canada (EHRC)
#301, 2197 Riverside Dr., Ottawa ON K1H 7X3
Tel: 613-235-5540
info@electricityhr.ca
electricityhr.ca
www.linkedin.com/company/electricity-human-resources-canada
www.facebook.com/ElectricityHR
twitter.com/electricityHR
Previous Name: Electricity Sector Council
Overview: A medium-sized national organization founded in 2005
Description: To work to strengthen the ability of the Canadian electricity industry to meet current & future needs for their workforce
Chief Officer(s): Michelle Branigan, Chief Executive Officer
branigan@electricityhr.ca
Mark Chapeskie, Director, Programs & Development
chapeskie@electricityhr.ca
Fees: $1,000-$6,000

Electro-Federation Canada (EFC) / Électro-Fédération Canada
#560, 190 Attwell Dr., Toronto ON M9W 6H8
Tel: 905-602-8877; *Toll-Free:* 866-602-8877
info@electrofed.com
www.electrofed.com
www.instagram.com/efc_electrofed
www.linkedin.com/company/electro-federation-canada
www.facebook.com/EFCelectrofed
twitter.com/EFC_Tweets
Overview: A medium-sized national organization founded in 1995
Description: To represent members provincially, federally & internationally on issues affecting the electro-technical business; To advance the electrical market; *Member of:* Canadian Chamber of Commerce
Chief Officer(s): Carol McGlogan, President & CEO, 416-230-0914
cmcglogan@electrofed.com
Finances: *Annual Operating Budget:* $3 Million-$5 Million; *Funding Sources:* Self-funded by members
Staff: 17 staff member(s); 600 volunteer(s)
Membership: 220+; *Member Profile:* Companies that manufacture, distribute & service electrical, electronic & telecommunication products; *Committees:* National Advisory Council
Activities: Collecting & disseminating market data; Providing networking opportunities; Hosting annual conferences; Researching; Offering educational programs; Communicating with members; Promoting the industry, electrical safety, energy efficiency & sustainability; Conducting surveys; *Speaker Service:* Yes

Energy Council of Canada / Conseil canadien de l'énergie
#805B, 350 Sparks St., Ottawa ON K1R 7S8
Tel: 613-232-8239; *Fax:* 613-232-1079
administrator@energy.ca
www.energy.ca
www.linkedin.com/company/energy-council-of-canada
www.facebook.com/EnergyCouncilCA
twitter.com/EnergyCouncilCA
Previous Name: World Energy Council - Canadian Member Committee
Overview: A medium-sized national organization founded in 1924
Description: To foster a greater understanding of energy issues; To enhance the effectiveness of the Canadian energy strategy; *Member of:* World Energy Council

Chief Officer(s): Jacob Irving, President, 613-232-8239 601
jacob@energy.ca
Brigitte Svarich, Director, Operations, 613-232-8239 602
brigitte@energy.ca
Membership: 43; *Member Profile:* Representatives from all facets of Canada's energy sector, including energy producers, energy users, equipment manufacturers, engineering firms, energy associations, financial organizations, legal firms, educational institutions & government department & agencies
Activities: Providing networking opportunities; Sponsoring forums & conferences; Disseminating current energy reports & information; Contributing to the development of the Canadian energy policy

Energy Probe Research Foundation (EPRF)
225 Brunswick Ave., Toronto ON M5S 2M6
Tel: 416-964-9223; *Fax:* 416-964-8239
webadmin@eprf.ca
epresearchfoundation.wordpress.com
Overview: A medium-sized national charitable organization founded in 1980
Description: To educate Canadians about the benefits of conservation & renewable energy; To provide businesses, the government & the public with information on energy & energy-related issues; To help Canada secure long-term energy self-sufficiency
Affiliation(s): Energy Probe; Probe International; Environment Probe; Consumer Policy Institute; Urban Renaissance Institute; Environmental Bureau of Investigation; Three Gorges Probe; Canadian Environmental News Network
Chief Officer(s): Patricia Adams, President
Elizabeth Brubaker, Executive Director, Environment Probe
Finances: *Annual Operating Budget:* $1.5 Million-$3 Million; *Funding Sources:* Foundation grants; Donations; Publication sales & fees
Staff: 15 staff member(s); 10 volunteer(s)
Activities: Policy research & education; *Internships:* Yes; *Speaker Service:* Yes *Library:* Energy Probe Research Foundation Library (Open to Public)

Energy Safety Canada
#150, 2 Smed Lane SE, Calgary AB T2C 4T5
Tel: 403-516-8000; *Fax:* 403-516-8166
Toll-Free: 800-667-5557
customerservice@energysafetycanada.com
www.energysafetycanada.com
www.instagram.com/energysafetycanada
www.linkedin.com/organization-guest/company/energy-safety-canada
www.facebook.com/EnergySafetyCanada
twitter.com/energysafetycan
Merged from: Enform; Oil Sands Safety Association
Overview: A large national licensing charitable organization founded in 2005
Description: To improve the Canadian upstream oil & gas industry's safety performance; To prevent work-related injuries in the upstream oil & gas industry in Canada
Chief Officer(s): Elliott Murray, President & CEO

Explorers & Producers Association of Canada (EPAC)
#1060, 717 - 7th Ave. SW, Calgary AB T2P 0Z3
Tel: 403-269-3454; *Fax:* 403-269-3636
info@explorersandproducers.ca
www.explorersandproducers.ca
Previous Name: Small Explorers & Producers Association of Canada
Overview: A medium-sized national organization founded in 1986
Description: To advocate to governments, policy makers & regulators on behalf of members to ensure that member interests are reflected in a fiscal & regulatory framework that encourages investment & supports a prosperous oil & gas industy
Chief Officer(s): Tristan Goodman, President
Cassandra Schultz, Manager, Communications
c.schultz@explorersandproducers.ca
Membership: 62; *Fees:* Schedule available

FogQuest
448 Monarch Pl., Kamloops BC V2E 2B2
Tel: 250-374-1745; *Fax:* 250-374-1746
info@fogquest.org
www.fogquest.org
Overview: A small international charitable organization founded in 1987
Description: To plan & implement water projects for rural communities located in developing countries
Chief Officer(s): Robert Schemenauer, Executive Director
Finances: *Funding Sources:* Grants; donations; membership fees
Fees: $35 student; $40 individual

Gas Processing Association Canada (GPAC)
#600, 900 - 6th Ave. SW, Calgary AB T2P 3K2
Tel: 403-244-4487; *Fax:* 403-244-2340
info@gpacanada.com
gpacanada.com
www.linkedin.com/company/gas-processing-association-of-canada
twitter.com/GPACanada
Previous Name: Canadian Gas Processors Association
Overview: A medium-sized national organization founded in 1960
Description: To promote the interaction & exchange of ideas & technology that will add value to those who are involved with or affected by the hydrocarbon processing industry
Affiliation(s): Gas Processors Association (USA)
Chief Officer(s): Jonathan Balint, President
Finances: *Funding Sources:* Membership dues
Staff: 17 volunteer(s)
Membership: 750 individuals; *Fees:* $9 alumni; $20 student; $85 regular; *Member Profile:* Employees of companies that process gaseous & liquid hydrocarbons; *Committees:* Safety; Research; Environment; Membership; Publications; Northern
Activities: *Library:* Gas Processing Association of Canada Library

Independent Power Producers Society of Alberta (IPPSA)
#600, 700 - 2nd St. SW, Calgary AB T2P 2W1
Tel: 403-282-8811; *Fax:* 403-256-8342
www.ippsa.com
Overview: A small provincial organization founded in 1993
Description: To represent Alberta's major power producers; To encourage dialogue among power producers in Alberta
Chief Officer(s): Evan Bahry, Executive Director
evan.bahry@ippsa.com
Joe Novecosky, Contact, Membership & Events, 403-256-1587, Fax: 403-256-8342
joeno@telusplanet.net
Membership: 100+; *Fees:* $1,000 corporate; $250 associate; $7,500 junior power; $15,000 power; *Member Profile:* Operators of Alberta's power supply
Activities: Engaging with Alberta's government & its agencies in policy development; Reviewing legislation, regulations & market rules; Promoting competition in Alberta's electrical market; Providing news about the industry; Sponsoring a bursary for a student at the University of Calgary's Schulich School of Engineering (Electricity Department)

Independent Telecommunications Providers Association (ITPA)
29 Peevers Cres., Newmarket ON L3Y 7T5
Tel: 519-595-3975; *Fax:* 519-595-3976
www.itpa.ca
Previous Name: Ontario Telecommunications Association
Overview: A small provincial organization
Description: To represent the interests of small incumbent local exchange carriers (SILECs) from Ontario & British Columbia & to act as a forum for sharing expertise between member companies
Chief Officer(s): Jonathan L. Holmes, Executive Director
Finances: *Funding Sources:* Membership dues
Staff: 1 staff member(s)
Membership: 21 active + 12 associate; *Fees:* $395.50 associate; *Member Profile:* Independent Local Exchange Carriers in British Columbia & Ontario
Activities: Liaising with government departments & agencies & industry associates; Setting policies & compliance guidelines

Industrial Gas Users Association (IGUA) / L'association des consommateurs industriels de gaz (ACIG)
#202, 260 Centrum Blvd., Orléans ON K1E 3P4
Tel: 613-236-8021; *Fax:* 613-830-7196
info@igua.ca
www.igua.ca
Overview: A medium-sized national organization founded in 1973
Description: To provide a coordinated & effective voice for industrial firms depending on natural gas as fuel or feedstock; To represent industrial users of natural gas before regulatory boards & governments
Chief Officer(s): Shahrzad Rahbar, President
srahbar@igua.ca
Finances: *Annual Operating Budget:* $500,000-$1.5 Million; *Funding Sources:* Membership dues
Staff: 3 staff member(s)
Membership: 39 corporate; *Fees:* Schedule available based on gas consumption; *Member Profile:* Industrial firms that use natural gas in Ontario & Quebec
Activities: Regulatory intervention; Government advocacy; Creating networking opportunitites

Institute of Power Engineers (IPE)
PO Box 878, Burlington ON L7R 3Y7
Tel: 905-333-3348; *Fax:* 905-333-9328
ipenat@nipe.ca
nipe.ca
www.linkedin.com/groups/3973487
Overview: A medium-sized national organization founded in 1940
Description: To promote business relations, social activities & mutual understanding among power engineers
Chief Officer(s): Blair Sauliner, National President
ipe-nat-president@outlook.com
Ed Hnytka, National Vice-President
ipe-ab-director@outlook.com
Allan Whetter, National Secretary
ipe-nat-secreaty@outlook.com
Finances: *Annual Operating Budget:* $50,000-$100,000
Staff: 1400 volunteer(s)
Membership: 1,420; *Fees:* $45 student graduate; $62.50 senior; $125 associate/regular; *Member Profile:* Individuals holding any class Certificate of Qualification in the Power Engineering field; Individuals enrolled in recognized power engineering courses; Individuals engaged in any pursuit identified or allied with power engineering

International Academy of Energy, Minerals & Materials (IAEMM)
PO Box 62047, Stn. Convent Glen, Orléans ON K1C 7H8
Tel: 613-830-1760
info@iaemm.com
iaemm.com
Overview: A medium-sized international organization
Description: To advance energy, minerals & materials technologies through education, conferences & scientific publishing
Activities: Provides training & workshops; Organizes conferences; Publishes practical information

International Association for Hydrogen Energy (IAHE)
#303, 5794 - 40th St. SW, Miami FL 33155 USA
info@iahe.org
www.iahe.org
Overview: A medium-sized international organization
Description: To provide information about the role of hydrogen energy
Member Profile: Professional individuals in fields related to hydrogen energy; Laypersons with an interest in hydrogen energy; IAHE Fellows; Emeritus members; Students

International Atomic Energy Agency (IAEA) / Agence internationale de l'énergie atomique
Vienna International Centre, PO Box 100, Wagramer Strasse 5, Vienna A-1400 Austria
www.iaea.org
www.youtube.com/user/IAEAvideo
www.linkedin.com/company/iaea
www.facebook.com/iaeaorg
twitter.com/iaeaorg
Overview: A large international organization founded in 1957
Description: To accelerate & enlarge the contribution of atomic energy to peace, health & prosperity throughout the world; To ensure that assistance provided is not used to further any military purpose
Affiliation(s): United Nations
Chief Officer(s): Rafael Mariano Grossi, Director General
Mary Alice Hayward, Deputy Director General, Management
Finances: *Annual Operating Budget:* Greater than $5 Million; *Funding Sources:* Member states contributions
Staff: 2560 staff member(s)
Membership: 171 states; *Fees:* Percentage of share of regular budget is fixed by UN General Assembly; *Member Profile:* Intergovernmental organization; *Committees:* Board of Governors composed of 35 member states
Activities: Verification in framework of Nuclear Non-Proliferation Treaty (NPT) that over 1,000 nuclear facilities in over 60 non-nuclear weapon states are used for peaceful purposes only; *Library:* International Atomic Energy Agency Library by appointment

International Electrotechnical Commission - Canadian National Committee (CNC/IEC) / Commission Électrotechnique Internationale - Comité National du Canada (CEI-CNC)
c/o Standards Council of Canada, #600, 55 Metcalfe St., Ottawa ON K1P 6L5
Tel: 613-238-3222; *Fax:* 613-569-7808
Overview: A medium-sized international organization founded in 1912
Description: To look at issues related to Canada's participation in the International Electrotechnical Commission (IEC); To

advise Council through the Advisory Committee on Standards (ACS); To coordinate the work of the many advisory & technical committees that provide Canadian input to IEC; *Member of:* Standards Council of Canada
Finances: *Funding Sources:* Parliamentary appropriation; corporate sponsors; individuals
Staff: 2 staff member(s); 1000 volunteer(s)
Membership: 16; *Committees:* Approx. 100, paralleling the IEC committee structure

International Institute for Energy Conservation (IIEC)
1068 King Way, Breinigsville PA 18031 USA
Tel: 610-703-2347
iiecus@iiec.org
www.iiec.org
www.linkedin.com/company/international-institute-for-energy-conservation
Overview: A medium-sized international organization founded in 1984
Description: To apply global knowledge and experience to customize local sustainability solutions that are replicable & adaptable; To make a global mainstreamm impact toward sustainable development & greenhouse gas emissions
Chief Officer(s): Sanjay Dube, President & CEO

International Solar Energy Society (ISES)
International Headquarters, Villa Tannheim, Wiesentalstrasse 50, Freiburg 79115 Germany
hq@ises.org
www.ises.org
www.instagram.com/ises_solar
www.linkedin.com/company/international-solar-energy-society
www.facebook.com/InternationalSolarEnergySociety
twitter.com/ISES_Solar
Overview: A medium-sized international charitable organization founded in 1954
Description: To promote sustainable development, research & the use of renewable energy, with solar energy being the primary focus; *Member of:* International Renewable Energy Alliance
Chief Officer(s): Klaus Vajen, President
Membership: 4,000; *Fees:* Schedule available; *Member Profile:* Individuals engaged in the research, development & utilisation of solar energy
Activities: International congresses on solar energy

International Telecommunications Society (ITS)
c/o Bohdan (Don) Romaniuk, ITS Secretariat, 416 Wilverside Way SE, Calgary AB T2J 1Z7
secretariat@itsworld.org
itsworld.org
twitter.com/IntTlcSoc
Overview: A medium-sized international organization
Description: To research & analyze issues related to the emergence of a global information society
Chief Officer(s): Bohdan (Don) Romaniuk, ITS Secretariat
Membership: 400; *Fees:* US$125 individual; US$500-1,000 government/not-for-profit; US$1,500 corporate societal; US$3,000 corporate international; US$6,500 corporate global; *Member Profile:* Professionals from the communications, technology & information sectors; *Committees:* Strategic Planning; Conference & Seminars; Publications; Membership & Nominations; Finance; Marketing & Promotions; Web Development
Activities: Organizing courses, seminars & workshops; Disseminating research results & news to members & the public

Manitoba Water & Wastewater Association (MWWA)
PO Box 1600, Portage la Prairie MB R1N 3P1
Toll-Free: 866-396-2549
mwwaoffice@shaw.ca
www.mwwa.net
www.facebook.com/Manitobawaterandwastewater
Overview: A small provincial organization founded in 1975
Description: To provide operator members with educational opportunities for operating & maintaining water & wastewater treatment facilities & water distribution & wastewater collection systems; To promote operator certification & facility classification; *Member of:* Western Canada Water & Wastewater Association
Fees: $55
Activities: Exchanging information & experiences; Seminars & workshops; Awards

Marine Renewables Canada
PO Box 34066, Halifax NS B3J 3S1
Tel: 902-717-0716
marinerenewables.ca
www.instagram.com/marinerenewablescanada
www.linkedin.com/company/marine-renewables-canada
www.facebook.com/marinerenewablescanada
twitter.com/Canadian_MRE
Previous Name: Ocean Renewable Energy Group

Overview: A medium-sized national charitable organization founded in 2004
Description: To align industry, academia & government to ensure that Canada is a leader in providing marine renewable energy solutions to a world market
Chief Officer(s): Elisa Obermann, Exective Director
elisa@marinerenewables.ca
Amanda White, Director, Operations
amanda@marinerenewables.ca
Membership: 100; *Fees:* $50 student; $300 individual; $950 organization; $1,000 government; $3,000-$10,000 Marine Energy Leader/Champion; *Member Profile:* Leaders in Canada's marine renewable energy industry
Activities: Conferences

The Maritimes Energy Association
PO Box 8531, Halifax NS B3K 5M2
communications@maritimesenergy.com
maritimesenergy.com
www.linkedin.com/company/the-maritimes-energy-association
twitter.com/MEnergyAssoc
Previous Name: Offshore / Onshore Technologies Association of Nova Scotia (OTANS)
Overview: A medium-sized provincial organization founded in 1982
Description: To support the maximization of Atlantic Canadian participation in the supply of both goods & services to meet the needs of the energy industry; To identify, promote & support the development of opportunities for member companies
Chief Officer(s): Jennifer Tuck, Chief Executive Officer
Membership: 181+; *Fees:* $30 student; $498 company (1-10 employees); $760 company (11-50 employees); $998 company (51+ employees); *Member Profile:* Businesses in the Maritimes that supply goods & services to the energy industry in Eastern Canada, including the offshore & onshore, renewable & non-renewable, domestic & export markets; *Committees:* Audit; Executive; Events; Energy Industry
Activities: Networking & information activities; Industry advocacy & policy research; Conferences & trade missions

Municipal Engineers Association (MEA)
#22, 1525 Cornwall Rd., Oakville ON L6J 0B2
Tel: 289-291-6472; *Fax:* 289-291-6477
municipalengineers.on.ca
www.linkedin.com/company/municipal-engineers-association
Overview: A medium-sized provincial organization founded in 1974
Description: To provide focus & unity for licensed engineers employed by municipalities in Ontario; To address issues of common concern to members; To facilitate the dissemination of information
Chief Officer(s): Roslyn Lusk, President
Dan Cozzi, Executive Director
dan.cozzi@municipalengineers.on.ca
Fees: Schedule available; *Member Profile:* Public sector professional engineers in full time municipal employment who perform functions in the field of municipal engineering; *Committees:* 36 Committees
Activities: Organizing training events; Advocating for sound municipal engineering; Championing positions on municipal engineering issues; Recognizing achievements of municipal engineers

Municipal Equipment & Operations Association (Ontario) Inc.
admin@meoa.org
meoa.org
Also Known As: MEOA
Overview: A small provincial organization founded in 1965
Description: To promote high standards & cost effectiveness in public services across Ontario
Finances: *Funding Sources:* Annual membership dues
Membership: 250; *Fees:* $75; *Member Profile:* Supervisory employees & management support staff from any government body; Suppliers of equipment & services used by municipal corporate organizations; Individuals who have been beneficial to the association or have an interest in the association
Activities: Offering education & training; Organizing field trips; Facilitating the exchange of information; Providing networking opportunities

National Electricity Roundtable (NER) / La Table ronde nationale de l'électricité (TRNÉ)
c/o Bryan Simonson, 148 Park Estates Pl. SE, Calgary AB T2J 3W5
Tel: 403-619-8967
nationaler@shaw.ca
www.nationalelectricityroundtable.com
Overview: A medium-sized national organization founded in 1994

Description: To act as a forum for companies operating in the Canadian electric power industry; To work with government to develop a sustainable industry
Chief Officer(s): Greg Farthing, Chair, 514-467-1207
greg.e.farthing@ca.abb.com
Bryan Simonson, President
Membership: 33 companies; 7 federal departments

National Ground Water Association (NGWA)
601 Dempsey Rd., Westerville OH 43081 USA
Tel: 614-898-7791; *Fax:* 614-898-7786
Toll-Free: 800-551-7379
ngwa@ngwa.org
www.ngwa.org
www.youtube.com/user/NGWATUBE
www.linkedin.com/groups/4204578
www.facebook.com/NGWAFB
twitter.com/ngwatweets
Overview: A medium-sized international organization founded in 1948
Description: To advance the expertise of all groundwater professionals & advocate for the responsible development, management & use of water; *Member of:* Advisory Committee on Water Information; American National Standards Institute; Coalition for National Science Funding; Geological Society of America; Global Water Partnership; Groundwater Foundation; International Union of Geological Sciences; Source Water Collaborative; US Water Alliance
Chief Officer(s): Terry Morse, Chief Executive Officer
Finances: *Annual Operating Budget:* Greater than $5 Million
Fees: Schedule available; *Member Profile:* Ground water scientists & engineers; water well drillers; pump installers; suppliers & manufacturers; *Committees:* Geothermal Heat Pump Technical; Government Affairs; Membership Standing; Professional Development; Public Awareness; Publishing & Information Products; Standard Development Oversight; Water Systems Technical
Activities: *Speaker Service:* Yes *Library:* National Ground Water Information Centre

National Waste & Recycling Association (NWRA)
#804, 1550 Crystal Dr., Arlington VA 22202 USA
Tel: 202-244-4700; *Fax:* 202-966-4824
Toll-Free: 800-424-2869
info@wasterecycling.org
wasterecycling.org
www.youtube.com/user/envasns
www.facebook.com/wasterecycling
twitter.com/wasterecycling
Previous Name: Environmental Industry Associations
Overview: A medium-sized international organization founded in 1962
Description: To promote the environmentally responsible, efficient, profitable & ethical management of waste
Chief Officer(s): Darrell Smith, President & CEO, 202-364-3730
Anne Germain, Chief Operating Officer & Senior VP, Regulatory Affairs, 202-364-3724
agermain@wasterecycling.org
Brandon Wright, Vice-President, Communications & Media Relations, 202-364-3706
Member Profile: Companies in North America that provide solid, hazardous & medical waste collection, recycling & disposal services; Companies that provide professional & consulting services to the waste services industry
Activities: Offering educational & training opportunities; Engaging in research; Facilitating networking

Nergica
70, rue Bolduc, Gaspé QC G4X 1G2
Tél: 418-368-6162; *Téléc:* 418-368-4315
info@nergica.com
nergica.com

www.linkedin.com/company/nergica
www.facebook.com/NergicaRI
twitter.com/Nergica
Nom précédent: TechnoCentre éolien
Aperçu: *Dimension:* petite; *Envergure:* provinciale; *fondée en 2000*
Description: Mission de recherche qui stimule l'innovation en matière d'énergies renouvelables à travers des activités de recherche, d'aide technique, de transfert technologique et d'accompagnement aux entreprises et aux collectivités
Membre(s) du bureau directeur: Frédéric Côté, Directeur général

Noia
Atlantic Pl., PO Box 44, #606, 215 Water St., St. John's NL A1C 6C9
Tel: 709-758-6610; *Fax:* 709-758-6611
noia@noia.ca
www.noia.ca
www.linkedin.com/company/noia-newfoundland-&-labrador-oil-&-gas-industries-association-
www.facebook.com/noiaNL
twitter.com/NoiaNL
Also Known As: Newfoundland & Labrador Oil & Gas Industries Association
Overview: A medium-sized provincial organization founded in 1977
Description: To promote development of East Coast Canada's hydrocarbon resources; To facilitate membership's participation in global oil & gas industries
Chief Officer(s): Charlene Johnson, Chief Executive Officer
Finances: *Annual Operating Budget:* $500,000-$1.5 Million; *Funding Sources:* Membership fees; conferences, seminars & special events
Staff: 10 staff member(s); 100 volunteer(s)
Membership: 600; *Fees:* Schedule available; *Member Profile:* Core members provide products / services for the petroleum industry; associate members represent operators, trade associations, educational institutions & government bodies; *Committees:* Board of Directors; Finance, Audit & Risk; Governance & Human Resources; Research, Policy & Communications; Petroleum Industry Human Resources; Conference; Fall Seminar; Industry Achievement Awards; Noia-Hibernia Scholarship
Activities: *Library:* Noia Library by appointment

Offshore Energy Research Association of Nova Scotia (OERA)
Joseph Howe Building, #1001, 1690 Hollis St., Halifax NS B3J 1V7
Tel: 902-406-7015
www.oera.ca
www.linkedin.com/company/offshore-energy-research-associatio
n-of-nova-scotia
twitter.com/oera_ns
Merged from: Offshore Energy Environmental Research (OEER); Offshore Energy Technical Research (OETR)
Overview: A medium-sized provincial organization founded in 2012
Description: To foster offshore energy & environmental research & development; To develop offshore petroleum exploration & development for Nova Scotia
Chief Officer(s): Alisdair McLean, Executive Director, 902-717-7391
amclean@oera.ca
Russell Dmytriw, Director, Research, 902-499-1190
rdmytriw@oera.ca
Nalani Perry, Manager, Operations, 902-430-7257
nperry@oera.ca
Activities: *Library:* Offshore Energy Research - Document Library

Ontario Electrical League (OEL)
#109, 93 Skyway Ave., Toronto ON M9W 6N6
Tel: 905-238-1382; *Fax:* 905-238-1420
league@oel.org
www.oel.org
www.linkedin.com/company/oeleague
www.facebook.com/OntarioElectricalLeague
twitter.com/OEL3
Overview: A medium-sized provincial organization founded in 1922
Description: To represent & strengthen the electrical industry in Ontario
Chief Officer(s): Louie Violo, Chair
Membership: 20 chapters, with 12,000+ members; *Member Profile:* Educators; Electricians; Electrical contractors; Electrical inspectors; Manufacturers; Consulting engineers; Distributors; *Committees:* Contractor; Contractor Government Relations
Activities: Promoting Ontario's electrical industry; Providing educational opportunities

Ontario Energy Association (OEA)
#202, 121 Richmond St. West, Toronto ON M5H 2K1
Tel: 416-961-2339; *Fax:* 416-961-1173
oea@energyontario.ca
energyontario.ca
www.linkedin.com/company/ontario-energy-association
www.facebook.com/ontarioenergyassociation
twitter.com/ontarioenergy
Overview: A medium-sized provincial organization founded in 2002
Description: To represent the energy industry of Ontario

Chief Officer(s): Vince Brescia, President & CEO
vince@energyontario.ca
Roy Hrab, Director, Policy, 647-493-2351
roy@energyontario.ca
Finances: *Funding Sources:* Sponsorships
Membership: 150+ corporate members; *Member Profile:* Members of Ontario's energy industry, such as power producers, manufacturers, contractors, service providers, energy retailers, marketers, energy distributors & energy consultants; *Committees:* DSM / CDM; Demand Response Working Group; Environment; Energy; Government Relations / Public Affairs; IT; Markets; Regulatory
Activities: Providing education & resources about the energy sector; Engaging in advocacy activities for members; Conducting research into energy matters; *Speaker Service:* Yes

Ontario Municipal Water Association (OMWA)
c/o Ed Houghton, 2593 Tenth Concession, Collingwood ON L9Y 3Y9
Tel: 705-443-8472; *Fax:* 705-443-4263
admin@omwa.org
www.omwa.org
Overview: A medium-sized provincial organization
Description: To act as the voice of Ontario's public water authorities
Affiliation(s): Ontario Water Works Association (a section of the American Water Works Association)
Chief Officer(s): Ed Houghton, Executive Director, 705-445-1800, Fax: 705-445-0791
ehoughton@omwa.org
Membership: 180; *Fees:* Schedule available based upon population; *Member Profile:* Ontario's public water supply authorities; *Committees:* Resolutions; Communications & Website; Annual Conference; Awards/Service Recognition/Bursary; Nominations; Government Affairs; Finance
Activities: Reviewing policy & legislative & regulatory issues; Liaising with government, agencies & associations to maintain safe & sustainable water sources; Lobbying to improve conditions; Promoting high standards of treatment, infrastructure & operations; Offering technical training for operating authorities, operators & owners of drinking water systems; Encouraging dissemination of information for public education; Joint conferences with the Ontario Water Works Association (OWWA)

Ontario Petroleum Institute Inc. (OPI)
#203, 555 Southdale Rd. East, London ON N6E 1A2
Tel: 519-680-1620; *Fax:* 519-680-1621
opi@ontariopetroleuminstitute.com
ontariopetroleuminstitute.com
twitter.com/opi1963
Overview: A medium-sized provincial organization founded in 1963
Description: To promote responsible exploration & development by Ontario's oil, gas, hydrocarbon storage & solution-mining industries
Chief Officer(s): Hugh Moran, Executive Director
hughmoran@ontariopetroleuminstitute.com
Finances: *Funding Sources:* Sponsorships
Fees: $45 student/retired; $120 associate; $220 active; $850 sustaining; $1,200 sponsoring; *Member Profile:* Geologists in Ontario; Geophysicists; Explorationists; Producers; Contractors; Petroleum engineers; Companies involved in the oil & gas, hydrocarbon storage & solution mining industries
Activities: Liaising with government agencies; Disseminating information to members; Increasing public awareness of the importance of the industry in Ontario; *Library:* Ontario Oil, Gas, & Salt Resources Library

Ontario Petroleum Transporters & Technicians Association (OPTTA)
PO Box 27, 28 Elizabeth St., Newburgh ON K0K 2S0
Tel: 905-604-8884; *Fax:* 866-946-0316
Toll-Free: 855-336-8943
info@coha-ontario.ca
www.optta.ca
Previous Name: Canadian Oil Heat Association - Ontario
Overview: A medium-sized provincial organization founded in 1983
Description: To be the oil heat industry's voice in matters concerning regulators & government decision makers on matters of policy, safety & certification
Chief Officer(s): Jim Wood, President
jimwood@oppta.ca
Fees: Schedule available; *Member Profile:* Oil dealers; Major oil companies; Equipment manufacturers; Wholesalers; Contractors & trainers
Activities: Promoting the benefits of residential fuel oil to the consumer public

Ontario Public Works Association (OPWA)
ON

info@opwa.ca
ontario.cpwa.net
www.linkedin.com/groups/4147573
www.facebook.com/OPWA1

Overview: A medium-sized provincial organization
Description: To promote professional excellence & public awareness through education, advocacy & the exchange of knowledge regarding public works in Ontario; *Member of:* American Public Works Association
Affiliation(s): American Public Works Association (APWA)
Chief Officer(s): Brian Barber, Executive Director
Membership: 630; *Member Profile:* Public works practitioners employed by the Federal & Provincial governments, municipalities, consulting engineers, utility companies, contractors & suppliers; *Committees:* Adovacy; Annual Conference; PWX Networking; Awards; Historical; IT Symposium; Membership; National Public Works Week; Communications; Education; Special Functions; Young Professionals

Ontario Sewer & Watermain Construction Association (OSWCA)
#400, 5045 Orbitor Dr., Unit 12, Mississauga ON L4W 4Y4
Tel: 905-629-7766; *Fax:* 905-629-0587
info@oswca.org
oswca.org
twitter.com/oswca1971

Overview: A medium-sized provincial organization
Description: To represent sewer & watermain construction contractors throughout Ontario; To increase business opportunities for members
Chief Officer(s): Patrick McManus, Executive Director, 905-629-7766 229
patrick.mcmanus@oswca.org
Daniela Polsoni, Office Coordinator, 905-629-7766 221
daniela.polsoni@oswca.org
Membership: 700+ companies; *Committees:* Young Executives; Government Relations; Members Services; Marketing Initiatives; Education Program; Administration
Activities: Liaising with the Government of Ontario & its agencies; Increasing public awareness about the maintenance of water & wastewater systems in Ontario; Providing apprenticeship training & upgrading training; Informing members of industry developments

Ontario Sustainable Energy Association (OSEA)
c/o Centre for Social Innovation, 720 Bathurst St., Toronto ON M5S 2R5
Tel: 647-427-6124
admin@ontario-sea.org
www.ontario-sea.org

Overview: A small provincial organization founded in 2002
Description: To represent & serve municipalities, First Nations, institutions, businesses, cooperatives, farms & households; To support the work of local sustainable energy organizations
Finances: *Funding Sources:* Sponsorships; Donations
Fees: $50 student; $100 individual/small business; $2,000 corporate; $5,000 corporate sponsor
Activities: Engaging in advocacy activities, capacity building & non-partisan policy work; Providing public outreach services

Ontario Water Works Association (OWWA)
#215, 507 Lakeshore Rd. East, Mississauga ON L5G 1H9
Tel: 416-231-1555; *Fax:* 416-231-1556
Toll-Free: 866-975-0575
waterinfo@owwa.ca
owwa.com
www.linkedin.com/company/ontario-water-works-association
twitter.com/OWWA1

Overview: A medium-sized provincial organization
Description: To protect public health through the delivery of safe, sufficient & sustainable drinking water in Ontario; *Member of:* American Water Works Association
Chief Officer(s): Nick Reid, President
Michele Grenier, Executive Director, 416-231-1555 3
mgrenier@owwa.ca
Membership: 1,500+; *Member Profile:* Individuals employed by Ontario's municipal water systems sector, including hydrogeologists, scientists, engineers, chemists, managers & technicians; *Committees:* Climate Change; C-PAC; Conference Management; Continuing Education; Cross Connection Control; Distribution; Government Affairs; Groundwater; Joint OWWA / OMWA; Management; Membership; OWWA / WEAO Joint Asset Management; Publications; Small Systems; Source Water Protection; Training, Certification & Safety; Treatment; University Forum; Water Efficiency; Water for People - Canada; Young Professionals; Youth Education

Activities: Improving technology, science & management; Influencing government policy; Providing education for members; *Library:* Ontario Water Works Association Library

Ontario Waterpower Association (OWA)
#264, 380 Armour Rd., Peterborough ON K9H 7L7
Toll-Free: 866-743-1500
info@owa.ca
www.owa.ca
www.instagram.com/onwaterpower
www.linkedin.com/company/ontario-waterpower-association
www.facebook.com/ONWaterpower
twitter.com/ONWaterpower

Overview: A medium-sized provincial organization founded in 2001
Description: To promote the achievement of sustainable development & provide a source for quality information about waterpower that grows & enhances the competitiveness of the Ontario waterpower industry
Chief Officer(s): Paul Norris, President, 866-743-1500 22
Janelle Bates, Director, Member Relation & Events
Stephanie Landers, Manager, Community Relations & Public Outreach
Membership: 150+; *Member Profile:* Individuals or organizations associated with Ontario's waterpower industry, including generators, engineering firms, environmental consultants, project financing & insurance firms & First Nations communities

Petroleum Research Newfoundland & Labrador (PRNL)
Baine Johnston Centre, #101, 1 Church Hill, St. John's NL A1C 3Z7
Tel: 709-738-7916
info@petroleumresearch.ca
petroleumresearch.ca
www.linkedin.com/company/petroleum-research-newfoundland-and-labrador
twitter.com/prnldotca

Previous Name: Petroleum Research Atlantic Canada (PRAC)
Overview: A small local organization founded in 1999
Description: To facilitate research & technology development & deliver value to members on behalf of the offshore oil & gas industry of Newfoundland & Labrador
Chief Officer(s): David Finn, Interim Chief Executive Officer, 709-738-7917
dave.finn@petroleumresearch.ca
Metzi Prince, Manager, Research & Development Delivery, 709-738-7919
metzi.prince@petroleumresearch.ca
Tony Woolridge, Manager, Research & Development Program, 709-738-7912
tony.wpoolridge@petroleumresearch.ca
Member Profile: Representatives from the oil & gas industry in Newfoundland & Labrador
Activities: Identifying opportunities; Developing proposals; Funding & managing projects

Petroleum Services Association of Canada (PSAC)
AB
Tel: 403-264-4195
info@psac.ca
www.psac.ca
www.youtube.com/user/PSACCanada
www.linkedin.com/company/petroleum-services-association-of-canada-psac-
www.facebook.com/WorkingEnergy
twitter.com/workingenergy

Overview: A large national organization founded in 1981
Description: To lead responsible Canadian energy services, supply & manufacturing in the upstream petroleum industry
Chief Officer(s): Elizabeth Aquin, Interim President & CEO
Membership: 230 companies; *Fees:* Schedule available; *Member Profile:* Petroleum services industry companies; *Committees:* Corporate Finance; Education Fund; Health & Safety; Human Resources; Special Events; Transportation Issues; Manufacturing; Oilwell Perforators' Safety Training & Advisory; Well Testing
Activities: Engaging in lobbying activities; Providing educational opportunities

Petroleum Technology Alliance Canada (PTAC)
Chevron Plaza, #400, 500 - 5th Ave. SW, Calgary AB T2P 3L5
Tel: 403-218-7700; *Fax:* 403-920-0054
info@ptac.org
www.ptac.org
www.linkedin.com/company/petroleum-technology-alliance-canada
twitter.com/PTACCalgary

Overview: A medium-sized national organization founded in 1996

Description: To facilitate innovation, technology transfer & research & development in the upstream oil & gas industry
Chief Officer(s): Soheil Asgarpour, President, 403-218-7701
sasgarpour@ptac.org
Snezhana McIver, Manager, Operations, 403-218-7714
smciver@ptac.org
Lauren Gilmore, Manager, Communications, 403-218-7712
lgilmore@ptac.org
Fees: Schedule available
Activities: *Internships:* Yes *Library:* PTAC Knowledge Centre (Open to Public)

Petrolia Discovery Inc.
PO Box 1480, 4281 Discovery Line, Petrolia ON N0N 1R0
petroliadiscovery@outlook.com
petroliadiscovery.com
www.facebook.com/ThePetroliaDiscoveryFoundationInc

Overview: A small national charitable organization founded in 1980
Description: To provide information about Petrolia's oil heritage
Activities: Maintaining historical displays; Organizing programs for schools

Power Workers' Union (PWU)
244 Eglinton Ave. East, Toronto ON M4P 1K2
Tel: 416-481-4491; *Fax:* 416-481-7115
Toll-Free: 800-958-8798
pwu@pwu.ca
www.pwu.ca
www.instagram.com/pwuconnects
www.facebook.com/PWUConnects
twitter.com/PWUConnects

Overview: A large provincial organization founded in 1944
Affiliation(s): Canadian Union of Public Employees; Canadian Labour Congress; Ontario Federation of Labour; Labourers International Union of North America; Canadian Union of Skilled Workers
Chief Officer(s): Jeff Parnell, President
jparnell@pwu.ca
Andrew Clunis, Vice-President, Sector 1
aclunis@pwu.ca
Mike Hambly, Vice-President, Sector 2
mike.hambly@pwu.ca
Tom Chessell, Vice-President, Sector 3
tchessell@pwu.ca
Membership: 15,000-49,999; *Member Profile:* Individuals who work in the power production industry in Ontario

Professional Petroleum Data Management Association (PPDM)
PO Box 22155, Stn. Bankers Hall, Calgary AB T2P 4J5
Tel: 403-660-7817; *Fax:* 403-660-0540
info@ppdm.org
www.ppdm.org
www.linkedin.com/company/ppdm-association
www.facebook.com/PPDMAssociation
twitter.com/PPDMAssociation

Previous Name: Public Petroleum Data Model Association
Overview: A medium-sized national organization founded in 1991
Description: To develop data management standards for the collection & exchange of data in the petroleum industry; To promote information standards
Chief Officer(s): Trudy Curtis, Chief Executive Officer
curtist@ppdm.org
Amanda Phillips, Senior Coordinator, Operations
aphillips@ppdm.org
Fees: US$100 individual; Schedule based on revenue for corporate; *Committees:* Certification; Professional Development; Rules; Regulatory Data Standards
Activities: Increasing awareness of the value of data management; Providing training

Public Works Association of British Columbia (PWABC)
#215, 5385 - 216th St., Langley BC V2Y 2N3
executivedirector@pwabc.ca
pwabc.ca
www.facebook.com/pubworksassocbc
twitter.com/PWABCupdates

Overview: A medium-sized provincial organization
Description: To advance the public works profession by promoting excellence & public awareness through education, advocacy & the exhance of knowledge; *Member of:* American Public Works Association
Chief Officer(s): Scott Lamont, President
slamont@squamish.ca
Dave Lundberg, Treasurer
dave@smallpausecoach.com
Brian Carter, Secretary
brian.carter@burnaby.ca
Activities: *Awareness Events:* Public Works Week

Saskatchewan Water & Wastewater Association (SWWA)
PO Box 7831, Stn. Mn, Saskatoon SK S7K 4R5
Tel: 306-761-1278; *Toll-Free:* 888-668-1278
office@swwa.ca
www.swwa.ca
www.facebook.com/SaskatchewanWaterAndWastewaterAssociation

Overview: A small provincial organization
Description: To support the professional operation & maintenance of water & wastewater facilities in Saskatchewan
Chief Officer(s): Susan Dobrowney, President
Fees: $57.62; *Member Profile:* People involved in the operation, maintenance & troubleshooting of water & wastewater systems in Saskatchewan
Activities: Hosting workshops & training sessions; Providing access to job opportunities; Publishing a newsletter; Providing certification through the Operator Certification Board

The Society of Energy Professionals
2239 Yonge St., Toronto ON M4S 2B5
Tel: 416-979-2709; *Fax:* 416-979-5794
Toll-Free: 866-288-1788
society@thesociety.ca
www.thesociety.ca
www.facebook.com/thesocietysays
twitter.com/TheSocietySays

Overview: A medium-sized provincial organization founded in 1948
Description: To represent employees of Ontario's electricity industry; To ensure the best working conditions for members; *Member of:* Canadian Council of Professionals; Professional Employees' Network
Affiliation(s): International Federation of Professional & Technical Engineers; Canadian Labour Congress / Congrès du travail du Canada; American Federation of Labour / Congress of Industrial Organizations, (AFL/CIO); UNI Global Union
Chief Officer(s): Scott Travers, President, 416-979-2709 5002
traverss@thesociety.ca
Finances: *Funding Sources:* Membership dues
Member Profile: Professional members of the elctricity industry in Ontario, such as scientists, engineers, financial specialists & supervisors

Society of Petroleum Engineers (SPE)
PO Box 833836, 222 Palisades Creek Dr., Richardson TX 75083-3868 USA
Tel: 972-952-9393; *Fax:* 972-952-9435
Toll-Free: 800-456-6863
service@spe.org
www.spe.org
www.youtube.com/c/SpeOrg
www.linkedin.com/company/society-of-petroleum-engineers
www.facebook.com/spemembers
twitter.com/SPEtweets

Overview: A large international organization founded in 1957
Description: To collect, disseminate & exchange technical knowledge concerning the exploration, development & production of oil & gas resources & related technologies for the benefit of the public; To provide opportunities for professionals to enhance their technical & professional competence
Chief Officer(s): Shauna Noonan, President
Mark A. Rubin, Executive Vice-President & CEO
Finances: *Annual Operating Budget:* $3 Million-$5 Million
Staff: 87 staff member(s)
Membership: 153,000+ in 143 countries; *Member Profile:* Managers, engineers, operating personnel & scientists engaged in the exploration, drilling & production sectors of the global oil & gas industry; *Committees:* Student Development; Global Training; Distinguished Lecturer; Membership; Forum Series Coordinating; DAA For PE Faculty; Education & Accreditation; Oil & Gas Reserves; Editorial Review; Twenty Five Year Club; TIG Coordinating; Research & Development; Young Professional Coordinating; SPE Energy Information; Sustainability; Robert Earll McConnell; Online Communities Advisory; Awards
Activities: *Speaker Service:* Yes *Library:* Society of Petroleum Engineers Library

Solid Waste Association of North America (SWANA)
#650, 1100 Wayne Ave., Silver Spring MD 20910 USA
Fax: 301-589-7068
Toll-Free: 800-467-9262
info@swana.org
swana.org
www.instagram.com/swanahq
www.linkedin.com/company/swana
www.facebook.com/SolidWasteAssociationOfNorthAmerica
twitter.com/SWANA
Previous Name: Government Refuse Collection & Disposal Association

Overview: A large international organization founded in 1961
Description: To serve individuals & organizations responsible for the operation & management of solid waste management systems; To advance professional standards in the field through training programs, technical assistance & education; *Member of:* International Solid Waste Association; Federation of Canadian Municipalities
Chief Officer(s): David Biderman, Executive Director & CEO, 301-585-2898
Finances: *Annual Operating Budget:* $3 Million-$5 Million; *Funding Sources:* Membership dues; Publications
Staff: 22 staff member(s)
Membership: 10,000+; *Fees:* US$82 retired; US$100 young professional; US$150 international; US$223 public sector; US$295 small business; US$418 private sector; *Committees:* Technical; Recycling & Special Waste Management; Communication, Education & Marketing; Collection & Transfer; Landfill; Landfill Gas; Planning & Management; Waste-to-Energy
Activities: Technical divisions: collection & transfer, waste-to-energy, landfill gas management, landfill management, planning & management, special waste management; Waste reduction, recycling & composting; Communication, education & marketing; Publications; Trade shows & conferences; *Internships:* Yes *Library:* Solid Waste Association of North America Library (Open to Public)

Syndicat des travailleurs énergie électrique nord (STEEN)
1640, rue Hamilton, Alma QC G8B 4Z1
Tél: 418-668-2560; *Téléc:* 418-668-7969
www.steen.quebec

www.facebook.com/syndicatsteen
Nom précédent: Syndicat des employés énergie électrique Québec, inc.
Aperçu: *Dimension: petite; Envergure: locale; fondée en 1937*
Membre(s) du bureau directeur: Patrice Thibeault, Présidente
president@steen.quebec

Syndicat professionnel des ingénieurs d'Hydro-Québec (SPIHQ) / Hydro-Québec Professional Engineers Union
#201, 1111, rue Saint-Urbain, Montréal QC H2Z 1Y6
Tél: 514-845-4239; *Téléc:* 514-845-0082
Ligne sans frais: 800-567-1260
spihq@spihq.qc.ca
www.spihq.qc.ca
Aperçu: *Dimension: moyenne; Envergure: provinciale; fondée en 1964*
Description: Le Syndicat travaille pour la défense & le développement des intérêts économiques, sociaux & professionnels des membres
Membre(s) du bureau directeur: Nicolas Cloutier, Président, 514-845-4239 103
president@spihq.qc.ca
Jacqueline Pilote, Chef administration, 514-845-4239 112
chefadmin@spihq.qc.ca
Finances: *Budget de fonctionnement annuel:* $500,000-$1.5 Million
Personnel: 3 membre(s) du personnel
Membre: 1 700

Telecommunications Employees Association of Manitoba (TEAM)
#200, 1 Wesley Ave., Winnipeg MB R3C 4C6
Tel: 204-984-9470; *Fax:* 204-231-2809
Toll-Free: 877-984-9470
team@teamunion.mb.ca
www.teamunion.mb.ca
www.facebook.com/teamunion161
twitter.com/teamunion161
Overview: A small provincial organization founded in 1972
Description: To promote the interests of members; To advance the economic & social welfare of members
Chief Officer(s): Misty Hughes-Newman, President
m.hughes-newman@teamunion.mb.ca
Erin Spencer, Executive Director
erin.spencer@teamunion.mb.ca
Member Profile: Management employees of the Manitoba Telephone System; *Committees:* Communications; Finance; Governance; Pay & Benefits; Grievance
Activities: Presenting TEAM scholarships

Toronto Renewable Energy Co-operative (TREC)
#240, 401 Richmond St. West, Toronto ON M5V 3A8
Tel: 416-977-5093; *Fax:* 416-306-6476
info@trec.on.ca
www.trec.on.ca
twitter.com/TRECoop
Overview: A small local organization founded in 1998
Description: To help create a world where people work together, pooling their resources, to benefit from a renewable energy economy; *Member of:* Canadian Renewable Energy Alliance
Affiliation(s): Toronto District School Board; Ontario Trillium Foundation; Ontario Power Authority Conservation Fund; Toronto Atmospheric Fund; Community Power Fund; Ontario Sustainable Energy Ass'n
Chief Officer(s): David Cork, Managing Director
david@trec.on.ca
Finances: *Funding Sources:* Donations
Activities: Community energy projects; Interactive, hands-on education; Green City Bike Tours; Green Collar Career program; Our Power solar initiative; Solar home tours; Round table discussions; Bruce County wind energy co-operative project

United Utility Workers' Association (UUWA)
1207 - 20th Ave. NW, Calgary AB T2M 1G2
Tel: 403-284-4521; *Fax:* 403-282-1598
admin@uuwac.org
www.uuwac.org
Previous Name: Calgary Power Employees Association; TransAlta Employees' Association
Overview: A medium-sized national organization founded in 1943
Description: To represent employees in the energy sector
Chief Officer(s): Grace Thostenson, Manager, Business
grace@uuwac.org
Membership: 1,400; *Member Profile:* Employees in the energy sector, such as meter readers, power line technicians, designers & administrators
Activities: Offering training courses

Utility Contractors Association of Ontario, Inc. (UCA)
PO Box 28010, Stn. Terrytown, Toronto ON M1N 4E7
Tel: 416-527-0360; *Fax:* 905-412-0339
www.uca.on.ca
Overview: A medium-sized provincial organization founded in 1968
Description: To negotiate & administer collective agreements with operating engineers & labourers in Ontario's utility sector
Chief Officer(s): Erin MacDonald, President
Simon Clarke, Chief Executive Officer
sclarke@uca.on.ca
Membership: 29 contractor members + 35 associate (supplier) members; *Member Profile:* Contractors, engineers & labourers in Ontario's utility sector
Activities: Organizing networking events; Recognizing exellence in safety through the presentation of awards

WaterPower Canada (WPC) / Hydroélectricité Canada (HC)
#300, 275 Bank St., Ottawa ON K2P 2L6
Tel: 613-751-6655; *Fax:* 613-751-4465
waterpowercanada.ca
www.linkedin.com/company/canadian-hydropower-association
twitter.com/WaterPowerCA
Previous Name: Canadian Hydropower Association
Overview: A large national organization founded in 1998
Description: To provide leadership for the responsible growth & prosperity of the Canadian hydropower industry
Chief Officer(s): Anne-Raphaëlle Audouin, President
anne@waterpowercanada.ca
Yvonne Jack, Office Manager
Membership: 44; *Member Profile:* Owners of hydroelectric facilities

World Energy Council (WEC) / Conseil Mondial de l'Energie (CME)
62-64 Cornhill St., London EC3V 3NH United Kingdom
info@worldenergy.org
www.worldenergy.org
www.linkedin.com/company/world-energy-council
www.facebook.com/WECouncil
twitter.com/WECouncil
Overview: A large international organization founded in 1923
Description: To promote the sustainable supply & use of energy for the greatest benefit
Chief Officer(s): Angela Wilkinson, Secretary General & CEO
Finances: *Annual Operating Budget:* $3 Million-$5 Million
Staff: 14 staff member(s)
Membership: 92 member countries; *Fees:* Schedule available; *Member Profile:* Energy leaders & practitioners from around the world; *Committees:* Communications & Strategy; Programme; Studies; Finance
Activities: Energy; energy conservation; *Library:* World Energy Council Information Services by appointment

World Petroleum Council (WPC)
#1, 1 Duchess St., 4th Fl., London W1W 6AN United Kingdom
wpcsecretariat@world-petroleum.org
www.world-petroleum.org

Overview: A medium-sized international organization founded in 1933
Description: To promote sustainable management & use of the world's petroleum resources
Affiliation(s): IEA; OPEN; United Nations
Chief Officer(s): Pierce Riemer, Director General
pierce@world-petroleum.org
Finances: *Funding Sources:* Membership dues; royalties; levy on registration
Staff: 4 staff member(s)
Membership: 64 countries; *Fees:* Schedule available; *Member Profile:* Major oil producing & consuming nations of the world. Each country has a National Committee made up of representatives of the oil industry, academic & research institutions & government departments; *Committees:* Permanent Council; Executive Board; Scientific Program; Congress Arrangements; Environmental Affairs; Development

Government Agency Guide

CONSERVATION & ECOLOGY

See Also: Heritage Resources; Natural Resources
Canadian Heritage, 15, rue Eddy, Gatineau, QC K1A 0M5
819-997-0055, 866-811-0055,
PCH.info-info.PCH@canada.ca
Commission for Environmental Cooperation, Secretariat, #200, 393, rue Saint-Jacques ouest, Montréal, QC H2Y 1N9
514-350-4300, Fax: 514-350-4314, info@cec.org
Environment & Climate Change Canada, 200, rue Sacré-Coeur, 12th Fl., Gatineau, QC K1A 0H3
819-938-3860, 800-668-6767, eec.enviroinfo.ec@canada.ca
Natural Resources Canada, 580 Booth St., Ottawa, ON K1A 0E4
343-292-6096, Fax: 613-992-7211
North American Bird Conservation Initiative, Canadian Wildlife Service, 351 St. Joseph Blvd., Gatineau, QC K1A 0H3
819-994-0512, Fax: 819-994-4445,
ec.icoancanada-nabcicanada.ec@canada.ca
North American Waterfowl Management Plan, NAWCC (Canada) Secretariat, Place Vincent Massey, 351 St. Joseph Blvd., 14th Fl., Gatineau, QC K1A 0H3
819-938-4030, Fax: 819-934-6017,
ec.pnags-nawmp.ec@canada.ca
Parks Canada, National Office, 30, rue Victoria, Gatineau, QC J8X 0B3
819-420-9486, 888-773-8888, information@pc.gc.ca
Polar Knowledge Canada, #200, 170 Laurier Ave. West, 2nd Fl., Ottawa, ON K1P 5V5
613-943-8605, info@polar.gc.ca

Alberta

Alberta Environment & Parks, Forestry Bldg., 9920 - 108th St., Main Fl., Edmonton, AB T5K 2M4
780-944-0313
Alberta Environmental Appeals Board, Peace Hills Trust Tower, #306, 10011 - 109 St., Edmonton, AB T5J 3S8
780-427-6207, Fax: 780-427-4693
Alberta Used Oil Management Association, Empire Building, #1008, 10080 Jasper Ave., Edmonton, AB T5J 1V9
780-414-1510, Fax: 780-414-1519, 866-414-1510,
auoma@usedoilrecycling.ca
Beverage Container Management Board, #100, 8616 - 51 Ave., Edmonton, AB T6E 6E6
780-424-3193, Fax: 780-428-4620, 888-424-7671,
info@bcmb.ab.ca
Forestry Division, Petroleum Plaza ST, 9915 - 108th St., 10th Fl., Edmonton, AB T5K 2G8
Land Use Secretariat, Centre West Bldg., 10035 - 108th St., 9th Fl., Edmonton, AB T5J 3E1
780-644-7972, Fax: 780-644-1034, luf@gov.ab.ca
Natural Resources Conservation Board, Sterling Place, 9940 - 106 St., 4th Fl., Edmonton, AB T5K 2N2
780-422-1977, Fax: 780-427-0607, 866-383-6722,
info@nrcb.ca
Special Areas Board, Special Areas Board Administration, 212 - 2nd Ave. West, PO Box 820, Hanna, AB T0J 1P0
403-854-5600, Fax: 403-854-5527

British Columbia

British Columbia Assessment Authority, #400, 3450 Uptown Blvd., Victoria, BC V8Z 0B9
604-739-8588, Fax: 855-995-6209, 866-825-8322
British Columbia Ministry of Environment & Climate Change Strategy, PO Box 9047 Prov Govt, Victoria, BC V8W 9E2
Environmental Appeal Board, 747 Fort St., 4th Fl., PO Box 9425 Prov Govt, Victoria, BC V8W 3E9
250-387-3464, Fax: 250-356-9923, eabinfo@gov.bc.ca
Forest Appeals Commission, 747 Fort St., 4th Fl., PO Box 9425 Prov Govt, Victoria, BC V8W 9V1
250-387-3464, Fax: 250-356-9923, facinfo@gov.bc.ca

Forest Practices Board, 310, 1675 Douglas St., PO Box 9905 Prov Govt, Victoria, BC V8W 9R1
250-213-4700, Fax: 250-213-4725, 800-994-5899,
fpboard@gov.bc.ca

Manitoba

Clean Environment Commission, #305, 155 Carlton St., Winnipeg, MB R3C 3H8
204-945-0594, Fax: 204-945-0090, 800-597-3556,
cec@gov.mb.ca
Ecological Reserves Advisory Committee, c/o Manitoba Conservation, Parks & Natural Areas Branch, 200 Saulteaux Cres., PO Box 53, Winnipeg, MB R3J 3W3
204-945-4148, Fax: 204-945-0012
Manitoba Conservation & Climate, 200 Saulteaux Cres., PO Box 22, Winnipeg, MB R3J 3W3
204-945-6784, Fax: 204-948-2656, 800-214-6497,
cc@gov.mb.ca

New Brunswick

New Brunswick Department of Environment & Local Government, Marysville Place, 20 McGloin St., Fredericton, NB E3B 5H1
506-453-2690, Fax: 506-457-4994, elg/egl-info@gnb.ca

Newfoundland & Labrador

Newfoundland & Labrador Department of Environment & Climate Change, PO Box 8700, St. John's, NL A1B 4J6
ECCInfo@gov.nl.ca

Northwest Territories

Northwest Territories Department of Environment & Natural Resources, PO Box 1320, Yellowknife, NT X1A 2L9
867-767-9055, enr_communications@gov.nt.ca

Nova Scotia

Nova Scotia Department of Lands & Forestry, PO Box 698, Halifax, NS B3J 2T9
902-424-5935, Fax: 902-424-7735, 800-565-2224

Ontario

Ontario Ministry of Environment, Conservation & Parks, Ferguson Block, 77 Wellesley St. West, 11th Fl., Toronto, ON M7A 2T5
416-325-4000, Fax: 416-314-6713, 800-565-4923
Ontario Ministry of Northern Development, Mines, Natural Resources & Forestry, Natural Resources Information & Support Centre, 300 Water St., Toronto, ON K9J 8M5
800-667-1940,

Prince Edward Island

Prince Edward Island Department of Economic Growth, Tourism & Culture, PO Box 2000, Charlottetown, PE C1A 7N8
902-368-5540, Fax: 902-368-5277, tpswitch@gov.pe.ca
Prince Edward Island Department of Justice & Public Safety, Shaw Bldg. South, 95 Rochford St., 4th Fl., PO Box 2000, Charlottetown, PE C1A 7N8
902-368-4589, Fax: 902-368-5283, DeptJPS@gov.pe.ca

Quebec

Comité consultatif de l'environnement Kativik, CP 930, Kuujjuaq, QC J0M 1C0
819-964-2961, Fax: 819-964-0694, keac-ccek@krg.ca
Fondation de la faune du Québec, #420, 1175, av Lavigerie, Québec, QC G1V 4P1
418-644-7926, Fax: 418-643-7655, 877-639-0742,
ffq@fondationdelafaune.qc.ca
Ministère de l'Environnement et de la Lutte contre les changements climatiques, Édifice Marie-Guyart, 675, boul René-Lévesque est, 30e étage, Québec, QC G1R 5V7
418-521-3830, Fax: 418-646-5974, 800-561-1616,
relations.medias@mddelcc.gouv.qc.ca
Société de développement de la Baie James, #10, 462, 3e rue, Chibougamau, QC G8P 1N7
418-748-7777, Fax: 418-748-6868, chi@sdbj.gouv.qc.ca
Société québécoise de récupération et de recyclage, #411, 300, rue Saint-Paul, Québec, QC G1K 7R1
418-643-0394, Fax: 418-643-6507, 800-807-0678,
info@recyc-quebec.gouv.qc.ca

Saskatchewan

Saskatchewan Assessment Management Agency, #200, 2201 - 11th Ave., Regina, SK S4P 0J8
306-924-8000, Fax: 306-924-8070, 800-667-7262,
info.request@sama.sk.ca
Saskatchewan Conservation Data Centre, Fish & Wildlife Branch, Ministry of Environment, 3211 Albert St., Regina, SK S4S 5W6
306-787-7196, Fax: 306-787-9544
Saskatchewan Environment, 3211 Albert St., Regina, SK S4S 5W6
306-787-2584, Fax: 306-787-9544, 800-567-4224,
centre.inquiry@gov.sk.ca
Saskatchewan Water Security Agency, #400, 111 Fairford St. East, Moose Jaw, SK S6H 7X9
306-694-3900, Fax: 306-694-3105, comm@wsask.ca

Yukon Territory

Alsek Renewable Resources Council, PO Box 2077, Haines Junction, YT Y0B 1L0
867-634-2524, Fax: 867-634-2527, admin@alsekrrc.ca
Carmacks Renewable Resource Council, PO Box 122, Carmacks, YT Y0B 1C0
867-863-6838, Fax: 867-863-6429,
carmacksrrc@northwestel.net
Dawson District Renewable Resource Council, PO Box 1380, Dawson City, YT Y0B 1G0
867-993-6976, Fax: 867-993-6093,
dawsonrrc@northwestel.net
Mayo District Renewable Resources Council, PO Box 249, Mayo, YT Y0B 1M0
867-996-2942, Fax: 867-996-2948, mayorrc@northwestel.net
Selkirk Renewable Resources Council, PO Box 32, Pelly Crossing, YT Y0B 1P0
867-537-3937, Fax: 867-537-3938,
selkirkrrc@northwestel.net
Teslin Renewable Resource Council, PO Box 186, Teslin, YT Y0A 1B0
867-390-2323, Fax: 867-390-2919, teslinrrc@northwestel.net
Yukon Environment, 10 Burns Rd., Whitehorse, YT Y1A 2C6
867-667-5652, Fax: 867-393-7197,
environmentyukon@yukon.ca

CONSTRUCTION

Canada Infrastructure Bank, 150 King St. West, PO Box 15, Toronto, ON M5H 1J9
833-551-5245
Canada Mortgage & Housing Corporation, 700 Montreal Rd., Ottawa, ON K1A 0P7
613-748-2000, Fax: 613-748-2098, 800-668-2642,
chic@cmhc-schl.gc.ca
Defence Construction Canada, Constitution Square, 350 Albert St., 19th Fl., Ottawa, ON K1A 0K3
613-998-9548, Fax: 613-998-1061, 800-514-3555,
info@dcc-cdc.gc.ca
Hygrothermal Performance of Buildings Research Facilities, c/o National Research Council, 1200 Montreal Rd., Ottawa, ON K1A 0R6
613-993-9101
Infrastructure Canada, #1100, 180 Kent St., Ottawa, ON K1P 0B6
613-948-1148, 877-250-7154, ifc.info@canada.ca

Alberta

Alberta Infrastructure, Infrastructure Bldg., 6950 - 113th St., Edmonton, AB T6H 5V7
780-415-0507, Fax: 780-427-2187,
Infra.Contact.Us.m@gov.ab.ca
Alberta Transportation, Communications Branch, Twin Atria Bldg., 4999 - 98th Ave., 2nd Fl., Edmonton, AB T6B 2X3
780-427-7674, Fax: 780-466-3166,
Trans.Contact.Us.m@gov.ab.ca
Corporate Strategies & Services Division, Infrastructure Bldg., 6950 - 113th St., 2nd Fl., Edmonton, AB T6H 5V7

British Columbia

British Columbia Ministry of Transportation & Infrastructure, PO Box 9850 Prov Govt, Victoria, BC V8W 9T5
250-387-3198, Fax: 250-356-7706,
tran.webmaster@gov.bc.ca
Building Code Appeal Board, c/o Building & Safety Standards Branch, PO Box 9844 Prov Govt, Victoria, BC V8W 1A4
250-387-3133, Fax: 250-387-8164,
Building.Safety@gov.bc.ca
Partnerships BC, 900 - 1285 West Pender St., PO Box 9478 Prov Govt, Vancouver, BC V6E 4B1
604-681-2443, Fax: 604-806-4190,
partnershipsbc@partnershipsbc.ca

Manitoba

Manitoba Infrastructure, Legislative Bldg., #203, 450 Broadway, Winnipeg, MB R3C 0V8

New Brunswick

New Brunswick Department of Transportation & Infrastructure, Kings Place, PO Box 6000, Fredericton, NB E3B 5H1
506-453-3939, Fax: 506-453-7987,
transportation.web@gnb.ca

Newfoundland & Labrador

Newfoundland & Labrador Department of Transportation & Infrastructure, Confederation Bldg., Prince Philip Dr., PO Box 8700, St. John's, NL A1B 4J6
709-729-2300, ti@gov.nl.ca

Nova Scotia

Nova Scotia Department of Transportation & Active Transit, PO Box 186, Halifax, NS B3J 2N2
902-424-2297, Fax: 902-424-0532, tpwpaff@novascotia.ca

Nunavut

Nunavut Territory Department of Community & Government Services, W.G. Brown Bldg., 4th Fl., PO Box 1000 700, Iqaluit, NU X0A 0H0
867-975-5406, Fax: 867-975-5305, cgscomms@gov.nu.ca

Ontario

Ontario Capital Growth Corporation, Ontario Investment & Trade Centre, 250 Yonge St., 35th Fl., Toronto, ON M5B 2L7
416-325-6874, Fax: 416-212-0794

Ontario Ministry of Economic Development, Job Creation & Trade, 56 Wellesley St. West, 7th Fl., Toronto, ON M7A 2E7
416-325-6666, 800-268-7095

Ontario Ministry of Infrastructure, 777 Bay St., 5th Fl., Toronto, ON M5G 2C8
416-327-4412

Prince Edward Island

Prince Edward Island Department of Transportation & Infrastructure, Jones Bldg., 11 Kent St., 3rd Fl., PO Box 2000, Charlottetown, PE C1A 7N8
902-368-5100, Fax: 902-368-5395, DeptTIE@gov.pe.ca

Quebec

Commission de la capitale nationale du Québec, Edifice Hector-Fabre, 525, boul René-Lévesque est, RC, Québec, QC G1R 5S9
418-528-0773, Fax: 418-528-0833, 800-442-0773, commission@capitale.gouv.qc.ca

Commission de la construction du Québec, 8485, av Christophe-Colomb, Montréal, QC H2M 0A7

Modernisation des centres hospitaliers universitaires de Montréal, CHUM, CUSM, CHU Sainte-Justine, #10.049, 2021, rue Union, Montréal, QC H3A 2S9
514-864-9883, Fax: 514-873-7362, info.construction3chu@msss.gouv.qc.ca

Régie du bâtiment du Québec, 545, boul Crémazie est, 4e étage, Montréal, QC H2M 2V2
514-873-0976, 800-361-0761

Société québécoise des infrastructures, Édifice Marie-Fitzbach, 1075, rue de l'Amérique-Française, Québec, QC G1R 5P8
418-646-1766, Fax: 418-646-6911, courrier@sqi.gouv.qc.ca

Saskatchewan

Saskatchewan Highways, Victoria Tower, 1855 Victoria Ave., Regina, SK S4P 3T2
306-933-5186, MHI.CustomerService@gov.sk.ca

SaskBuilds & Procurement, 1920 Rose St., Regina, SK S4P 0A9
306-787-6911, Fax: 306-787-1061, cs.receptioncenturyplaza@gov.sk.ca

ENERGY

See Also: Natural Resources

Canada Energy Regulator, #210, 517 - 10th Ave. SW, Calgary, AB T2R 0A8
403-292-4800, Fax: 403-292-5503, 800-899-1265,

Canadian Nuclear Safety Commission, 280 Slater St., PO Box 1046 B, Ottawa, ON K1P 5S9
613-995-5894, Fax: 613-995-5086, 800-668-5284, cnsc.information.ccsn@canada.ca

Indian Oil & Gas Canada, #100, 9911 Chiila Blvd., Tsuu T'ina (Sarcee), AB T2W 6H6
403-292-5625, Fax: 403-292-5618, aadnc.contactiogc.aandc@canada.ca

Office of Energy Efficiency, CEF, Building 3, Observatory Cres., 930 Carling Ave., Ottawa, ON K1A 0Y3

Waste Biotreatability Facility, c/o Montréal (av Royalmount) Research Facilities, 6100, av Royalmount, Montréal, QC H4P 2R2

Alberta

Alberta Energy, North Petroleum Plaza, 9945 - 108th St., Edmonton, AB T5K 2G6
780-427-8050, Fax: 780-422-9522

Alberta Energy Regulator, #1000, 250 - 5 St. SW, Calgary, AB T2P 0R4
403-297-8311, Fax: 403-297-7336, 855-297-8311, inquiries@aer.ca

Alberta Utilities Commission, Eau Caire Tower, #1400, 600 - 3rd Ave. SW, Calgary, AB T2P 0G5
-310-4282, info@auc.ab.ca

Emissions Reduction Alberta, #746, 10104 - 103rd Ave. NW, Edmonton, AB T5J 0H8
780-498-2068, info@eralberta.ca

Surface Rights Board, 1229 - 91 St. SW, Edmonton, AB T6X 1E9
780-427-2444, Fax: 780-427-5798, -310-0000, srb.lcb@gov.ab.ca

British Columbia

British Columbia Hydro, 333 Dunsmuir St., PO Box 8910, Vancouver, BC V6B 4N1
604-224-9376, 800-224-9376

British Columbia Ministry of Energy, Mines & Low Carbon Innovation, PO Box 9060 Prov Govt, Victoria, BC V8W 9E3
250-952-0628

British Columbia Utilities Commission, #410, 900 Howe St., Vancouver, BC V6Z 2N3
604-660-4700, Fax: 604-660-1102, 800-663-1385, commission.secretary@bcuc.com

Oil & Gas Commission, 6534 Airport Rd., Fort St. John, BC V1J 4M6
250-794-5200, Fax: 250-794-5375

Powerex Corp., #1300, 666 Burrard St., Vancouver, BC V6C 2X8
604-891-5000, Fax: 604-891-6060, 800-220-4907

Powertech Labs Inc., 12388 - 88 Ave., Surrey, BC V8W 7R7
604-590-7500, Fax: 604-590-6611

Manitoba

Manitoba Hydro, 360 Portage Ave., PO Box 815 Main, Winnipeg, MB R3C 2P4
204-480-5900, Fax: 204-360-6155, 888-624-9376

Mineral Resources Division, The Paris Bldg., 259 Portage Ave., 9th Fl., Winnipeg, MB R3B 3P4
204-945-6569, 800-223-5215, minesinfo@gov.mb.ca

Power Engineers Advisory Board, Norquay Bldg., #500, 401 York Ave., Winnipeg, MB R3C 0P8
204-945-3373, Fax: 204-948-2309

New Brunswick

New Brunswick Department of Natural Resources & Energy Development, Hugh John Flemming Forestry Centre, PO Box 6000, Fredericton, NB E3B 5H1
506-453-3826, Fax: 506-444-4367, dnr_mrnweb@gnb.ca

Newfoundland & Labrador

Canada-Newfoundland & Labrador Offshore Petroleum Board, West Campus Hall, The Tower Corporate Campus, #7100, 240 Waterford Bridge Rd., St. John's, NL A1E 1E2
709-778-1400, information@cnlopb.ca

Nalcor Energy, 500 Columbus Dr., St. John's, NL A1E 2B2
709-737-1400, Fax: 709-737-1800, info@nalcorenergy.com

Newfoundland & Labrador Board of Commissioners of Public Utilities, PO Box 21040, St. John's, NL A1A 5B2
Fax: 709-726-9604, 866-782-0006, ito@pub.nl.ca

Newfoundland & Labrador Hydro, Hydro Place, 500 Columbus Dr., PO Box 12400, St. John's, NL A1B 4K7
709-737-1400, Fax: 709-737-1800, 888-737-1296, hydro@nlh.nl.ca

Northwest Territories

Northwest Territories Department of Environment & Natural Resources, PO Box 1320, Yellowknife, NT X1A 2L9
867-767-9055, enr_communications@gov.nt.ca

Northwest Territories Power Corporation, 4 Capital Dr., Hay River, NT X0E 1G2
867-874-5200, 800-661-0855, info@ntpc.com

Nova Scotia

Canada-Nova Scotia Offshore Petroleum Board, TD Centre, 1791 Barrington St., 8th Fl., Halifax, NS B3J 3K9
902-422-5588, Fax: 902-422-1799, info@cnsopb.ns.ca

Nova Scotia Department of Energy & Mines, Joseph Howe Bldg., 1690 Hollis St., PO Box 2664, Halifax, NS B3J 3J9
902-424-4575, Fax: 902-424-3265, enerinfo@novascotia.ca

Nova Scotia Utility & Review Board, Summit Place, 1601 Lower Water St., 3rd Fl., Halifax, NS B3J 3S3
902-424-4448, Fax: 902-424-3919, 855-442-4448, board@novascotia.ca

Nunavut

Nunavut Energy Secretariat, c/o Dept. of Economic Development & Transportation, Iqaluit, NU X0A 0H0
867-975-7704, nunavutenergy@gov.nu.ca

Ontario

Hydro One Inc., South Tower, 483 Bay St., 8th Fl., Toronto, ON M5G 2P5
416-345-5000, Fax: 905-944-3251, 877-955-1155, customercommunications@hydroone.com

Independent Electricity System Operator, #1600, 120 Adelaide St. West, Toronto, ON M5H 1T1
905-403-6900, Fax: 905-403-6921, 877-797-9473, customer.relations@ieso.ca

Ontario Energy Board, #2700, 2300 Yonge St., PO Box 2319, Toronto, ON M4P 1E4
416-481-1967, Fax: 416-440-7656, 888-632-6273

Ontario Ministry of Energy, 77 Grenville St., Toronto, ON M7A 2C1
416-327-6758, 888-668-4636, energy@ontario.ca

Ontario Ministry of Environment, Conservation & Parks, Ferguson Block, 77 Wellesley St. West, 11th Fl., Toronto, ON M7A 2T5
416-325-4000, Fax: 416-314-6713, 800-565-4923

Ontario Power Generation, 700 University Ave., Toronto, ON M5G 1X6
416-592-2555, 877-592-2555, webmaster@opg.com

Prince Edward Island

Prince Edward Island Department of Justice & Public Safety, Shaw Bldg. South, 95 Rochford St., 4th Fl., PO Box 2000, Charlottetown, PE C1A 7N8
902-368-4589, Fax: 902-368-5283, DeptJPS@gov.pe.ca

Prince Edward Island Energy Corporation, Sullivan Bldg., 16 Fitzroy St., PO Box 2000, Charlottetown, PE C1A 7N8

Quebec

Coopérative régionale d'électricité de Saint-Jean-Baptiste-de-Rouville, 3113, rue Principale, Saint-Jean-Baptiste, QC J0L 1B0
450-467-5583, Fax: 450-467-0092, 800-267-5583, info@coopsjb.com

Énergie, #A301 - 5700, 4e av ouest, Québec, QC G1H 6R1

Hydro-Québec, Édifice Jean-Lesage, 75, boul René-Lévesque ouest, Montréal, QC H2Z 1A4
514-385-7252, 888-385-7252

Régie de l'énergie, Tour de la Bourse, #2.55, 800, Place Victoria, Montréal, QC H4Z 1A2
514-873-2452, Fax: 514-873-2070, 888-873-2452, secretariat@regie-energie.qc.ca

Société d'énergie de la Baie-James, #1100, 800, de Maisonneuve est, Montréal, QC H2L 4L8
514-286-2020

Transition énergétique Québec, 5700, 4e av ouest, #B406, Québec, QC G1H 6R1
418-627-6379, Fax: 418-643-5828, 877-727-6655, transitionenergetique@teq.gouv.qc.ca

Saskatchewan

NorthPoint Energy Solutions Inc., 2025 Victoria Ave., Regina, SK S4P 0S1

Saskatchewan Energy & Resources, #1000, 2103 - 11th Ave., Regina, SK S4P 3Z8

Saskatchewan Power Corporation (SaskPower), 2025 Victoria Ave., Regina, SK S4P 0S1
888-757-6937

SaskEnergy Incorporated, 1777 Victoria Ave., Regina, SK S4P 4K5
306-777-9225, 800-567-8899, webmaster@saskenergy.com

Yukon Territory

Yukon Energy Corporation, 2 Miles Canyon Rd., PO Box 5920, Whitehorse, YT Y1A 6S7
867-393-5300, 866-926-3749, communications@yec.yk.ca

Yukon Energy, Mines & Resources, PO Box 2703, Whitehorse, YT Y1A 2C6
867-667-3123, Fax: 867-393-7421, 800-661-0408, emr@yukon.ca

ENGINEERING & CONSULTING

Canada Infrastructure Bank, 150 King St. West, PO Box 15, Toronto, ON M5H 1J9
833-551-5245

Defence Construction Canada, Constitution Square, 350 Albert St., 19th Fl., Ottawa, ON K1A 0K3
613-998-9548, Fax: 613-998-1061, 800-514-3555, info@dcc-cdc.gc.ca

Impact Assessment Agency of Canada, Place Bell Canada, 160 Elgin St., 22nd Fl., Ottawa, ON K1A 0H3
613-957-0700, Fax: 613-957-0862, 866-582-1884

Infrastructure Canada, #1100, 180 Kent St., Ottawa, ON K1P 0B6
613-948-1148, 877-250-7154, ifc.info@canada.ca

Natural Sciences & Engineering Research Council of Canada, 350 Albert St., 16th Fl., Ottawa, ON K1A 1H5
613-995-4273, Fax: 613-992-5337, 855-275-2861

Alberta

Alberta Infrastructure, Infrastructure Bldg., 6950 - 113th St., Edmonton, AB T6H 5V7
780-415-0507, Fax: 780-427-2187, Infra.Contact.Us.m@gov.ab.ca

C-FER Technologies, 200 Karl Clark Rd., Edmonton, AB T6N 1H2
780-450-3300, Fax: 780-450-3700

Safety & Policy Division, Twin Atria Bldg., 4999 - 98th Ave., Main Fl., Edmonton, AB T6B 2X3
780-427-8901, Fax: 780-415-0782, 800-666-5036

British Columbia

British Columbia Ministry of Transportation & Infrastructure, PO Box 9850 Prov Govt, Victoria, BC V8W 9T5
250-387-3198, Fax: 250-356-7706, tran.webmaster@gov.bc.ca

Partnerships BC, 900 - 1285 West Pender St., PO Box 9478 Prov Govt, Vancouver, BC V6E 4B1
604-681-2443, Fax: 604-806-4190, partnershipsbc@partnershipsbc.ca

Transportation Policy & Programs Division, PO Box 9850 Prov Govt, Victoria, BC V8W 9T5
250-387-5062, Fax: 250-387-6431

Manitoba
Manitoba Infrastructure, Legislative Bldg., #203, 450 Broadway, Winnipeg, MB R3C 0V8
Power Engineers Advisory Board, Norquay Bldg., #500, 401 York Ave., Winnipeg, MB R3C 0P8
204-945-3373, Fax: 204-948-2309

New Brunswick
New Brunswick Department of Transportation & Infrastructure, Kings Place, PO Box 6000, Fredericton, NB E3B 5H1
506-453-3939, Fax: 506-453-7987, transportation.web@gnb.ca

Nova Scotia
Nova Scotia Department of Transportation & Active Transit, PO Box 186, Halifax, NS B3J 2N2
902-424-2297, Fax: 902-424-0532, tpwpaff@novascotia.ca

Ontario
Ontario Capital Growth Corporation, Ontario Investment & Trade Centre, 250 Yonge St., 35th Fl., Toronto, ON M5B 2L7
416-325-6874, Fax: 416-212-0794
Ontario Ministry of Economic Development, Job Creation & Trade, 56 Wellesley St. West, 7th Fl., Toronto, ON M7A 2E7
416-325-6666, 800-268-7095
Ontario Ministry of Infrastructure, 777 Bay St., 5th Fl., Toronto, ON M5G 2C8
416-327-4412

Prince Edward Island
Prince Edward Island Department of Transportation & Infrastructure, Jones Bldg., 11 Kent St., 3rd Fl., PO Box 2000, Charlottetown, PE C1A 7N8
902-368-5100, Fax: 902-368-5395, DeptTIE@gov.pe.ca

Saskatchewan
Saskatchewan Highways, Victoria Tower, 1855 Victoria Ave., Regina, SK S4P 3T2
306-933-5186, MHI.CustomerService@gov.sk.ca
SaskBuilds & Procurement, 1920 Rose St., Regina, SK S4P 0A9
306-787-6911, Fax: 306-787-1061, cs.receptioncenturyplaza@gov.sk.ca

HYDRO, ELECTRIC POWER

Canada Energy Regulator, #210, 517 - 10th Ave. SW, Calgary, AB T2R 0A8
403-292-4800, Fax: 403-292-5503, 800-899-1265

Alberta
Alberta Energy Regulator, #1000, 250 - 5 St. SW, Calgary, AB T2P 0R4
403-297-8311, Fax: 403-297-7336, 855-297-8311, inquiries@aer.ca
Alberta Utilities Commission, Eau Caire Tower, #1400, 600 - 3rd Ave. SW, Calgary, AB T2P 0G5
-310-4282, info@auc.ab.ca

British Columbia
British Columbia Hydro, 333 Dunsmuir St., PO Box 8910, Vancouver, BC V6B 4N1
604-224-9376, 800-224-9376
Powertech Labs Inc., 12388 - 88 Ave., Surrey, BC V8W 7R7
604-590-7500, Fax: 604-590-6611

Manitoba
Manitoba Hydro, 360 Portage Ave., PO Box 815 Main, Winnipeg, MB R3C 2P4
204-480-5900, Fax: 204-360-6155, 888-624-9376

Newfoundland & Labrador
Nalcor Energy, 500 Columbus Dr., St. John's, NL A1E 2B2
709-737-1400, Fax: 709-737-1800, info@nalcorenergy.com
Newfoundland & Labrador Hydro, Hydro Place, 500 Columbus Dr., PO Box 12400, St. John's, NL A1B 4K7
709-737-1400, Fax: 709-737-1800, 888-737-1296, hydro@nlh.nl.ca

Northwest Territories
Northwest Territories Power Corporation, 4 Capital Dr., Hay River, NT X0E 1G2
867-874-5200, 800-661-0855, info@ntpc.com

Nova Scotia
Nova Scotia Utility & Review Board, Summit Place, 1601 Lower Water St., 3rd Fl., Halifax, NS B3J 3S3
902-424-4448, Fax: 902-424-3919, 855-442-4448, board@novascotia.ca

Ontario
Hydro One Inc., South Tower, 483 Bay St., 8th Fl., Toronto, ON M5G 2P5
416-345-5000, Fax: 905-944-3251, 877-955-1155, customercommunications@hydroone.com

Independent Electricity System Operator, #1600, 120 Adelaide St. West, Toronto, ON M5H 1T1
905-403-6900, Fax: 905-403-6921, 877-797-9473, customer.relations@ieso.ca
Ontario Power Generation, 700 University Ave., Toronto, ON M5G 1X6
416-592-2555, 877-592-2555, webmaster@opg.com

Quebec
Coopérative régionale d'électricité de Saint-Jean-Baptiste-de-Rouville, 3113, rue Principale, Saint-Jean-Baptiste, QC J0L 1B0
450-467-5583, Fax: 450-467-0092, 800-267-5583, info@coopsjb.com
Hydro-Québec, Édifice Jean-Lesage, 75, boul René-Lévesque ouest, Montréal, QC H2Z 1A4
514-385-2252, 888-385-7252
Société d'énergie de la Baie-James, #1100, 800, de Maisonneuve est, Montréal, QC H2L 4L8
514-286-2020

Saskatchewan
Saskatchewan Power Corporation (SaskPower), 2025 Victoria Ave., Regina, SK S4P 0S1
888-757-6937

Yukon Territory
Yukon Energy Corporation, 2 Miles Canyon Rd., PO Box 5920, Whitehorse, YT Y1A 6S7
867-393-5300, 866-926-3749, communications@yec.yk.ca

OIL & NATURAL GAS RESOURCES

See Also: Energy; Natural Resources
Canada Energy Regulator, #210, 517 - 10th Ave. SW, Calgary, AB T2R 0A8
403-292-4800, Fax: 403-292-5503, 800-899-1265,
Indian Oil & Gas Canada, #100, 9911 Chiila Blvd., Tsuu T'ina (Sarcee), AB T2W 6H6
403-292-5625, Fax: 403-292-5618, aadnc.contactiogc.aandc@canada.ca
Northern Pipeline Agency Canada, #470, 588 Booth St., Ottawa, ON K1A 0Y7
613-995-1150, info@npa.gc.ca

Alberta
Alberta Energy, North Petroleum Plaza, 9945 - 108th St., Edmonton, AB T5K 2G6
780-427-8050, Fax: 780-422-9522
Alberta Energy Regulator, #1000, 250 - 5 St. SW, Calgary, AB T2P 0R4
403-297-8311, Fax: 403-297-7336, 855-297-8311, inquiries@aer.ca
Surface Rights Board, 1229 - 91 St. SW, Edmonton, AB T6X 1E9
780-427-2444, Fax: 780-427-5798, -310-0000, srb.lcb@gov.ab.ca

British Columbia
British Columbia Utilities Commission, #410, 900 Howe St., Vancouver, BC V6Z 2N3
604-660-4700, Fax: 604-660-1102, 800-663-1385, commission.secretary@bcuc.com
Oil & Gas Commission, 6534 Airport Rd., Fort St. John, BC V1J 4M6
250-794-5200, Fax: 250-794-5375
Surface Rights Board of British Columbia, #10, 10551 Shellbridge Way, Richmond, BC V6X 2W9
604-775-1740, Fax: 604-775-1742, 888-775-1740, office@surfacerightsboard.bc.ca

Manitoba
Surface Rights Board, #360, 1395 Ellice Ave., Winnipeg, MB R3G 3P2
204-945-0731, Fax: 204-948-2578, 800-223-5215

New Brunswick
New Brunswick Department of Natural Resources & Energy Development, Hugh John Flemming Forestry Centre, PO Box 6000, Fredericton, NB E3B 5H1
506-453-3826, Fax: 506-444-4367, dnr_mrnweb@gnb.ca

Newfoundland & Labrador
Canada-Newfoundland & Labrador Offshore Petroleum Board, West Campus Hall, The Tower Corporate Campus, #7100, 240 Waterford Bridge Rd., St. John's, NL A1E 1E2
709-778-1400, information@cnlopb.ca

Northwest Territories
Office of the Regulator of Oil & Gas Operations, Northwest Tower, 5201 - 50th Ave., 4th Fl., PO Box 1320, Yellowknife, NT X1A 2L9
867-767-9097

Nova Scotia
Canada-Nova Scotia Offshore Petroleum Board, TD Centre, 1791 Barrington St., 8th Fl., Halifax, NS B3J 3K9
902-422-5588, Fax: 902-422-1799, info@cnsopb.ns.ca
Nova Scotia Department of Energy & Mines, Joseph Howe Bldg., 1690 Hollis St., PO Box 2664, Halifax, NS B3J 3J9
902-424-4575, Fax: 902-424-3265, enerinfo@novascotia.ca
Nova Scotia Utility & Review Board, Summit Place, 1601 Lower Water St., 3rd Fl., Halifax, NS B3J 3S3
902-424-4448, Fax: 902-424-3919, 855-442-4448, board@novascotia.ca

Nunavut
Nunavut Territory Department of Environment, PO Box 1000 1320, Iqaluit, NU X0A 0H0
867-975-7700, Fax: 867-975-7742, environment@gov.nu.ca

Ontario
Ontario Ministry of Northern Development, Mines, Natural Resources & Forestry, Natural Resources Information & Support Centre, 300 Water St., Toronto, ON K9J 8M5
800-667-1940

Saskatchewan
NorthPoint Energy Solutions Inc., 2025 Victoria Ave., Regina, SK S4P 0S1
SaskEnergy Incorporated, 1777 Victoria Ave., Regina, SK S4P 4K5
306-777-9225, 800-567-8899, webmaster@saskenergy.com

OIL SPILLS

Canadian Coast Guard, Centennial Towers, #6S018, 200 Kent St., Ottawa, ON K1A 0E6
613-993-0999, Fax: 613-990-1866, info@dfo-mpo.gc.ca
Office of the Administrator of the Ship-source Oil Pollution Fund, #830, 180 Kent St., Ottawa, ON K1A 0N5
613-991-1726, Fax: 613-990-5423, info@sopf-cidphn.gc.ca

Newfoundland & Labrador
Canada-Newfoundland & Labrador Offshore Petroleum Board, West Campus Hall, The Tower Corporate Campus, #7100, 240 Waterford Bridge Rd., St. John's, NL A1E 1E2
709-778-1400, information@cnlopb.ca

PUBLIC UTILITIES

Alberta
Alberta Energy Regulator, #1000, 250 - 5 St. SW, Calgary, AB T2P 0R4
403-297-8311, Fax: 403-297-7336, 855-297-8311, inquiries@aer.ca
Alberta Utilities Commission, Eau Caire Tower, #1400, 600 - 3rd Ave. SW, Calgary, AB T2P 0G5
-310-4282, info@auc.ab.ca

British Columbia
British Columbia Hydro, 333 Dunsmuir St., PO Box 8910, Vancouver, BC V6B 4N1
604-224-9376, 800-224-9376
British Columbia Utilities Commission, #410, 900 Howe St., Vancouver, BC V6Z 2N3
604-660-4700, Fax: 604-660-1102, 800-663-1385, commission.secretary@bcuc.com

Manitoba
Manitoba Hydro, 360 Portage Ave., PO Box 815 Main, Winnipeg, MB R3C 2P4
204-480-5900, Fax: 204-360-6155, 888-624-9376

Newfoundland & Labrador
Nalcor Energy, 500 Columbus Dr., St. John's, NL A1E 2B2
709-737-1400, Fax: 709-737-1800, info@nalcorenergy.com
Newfoundland & Labrador Board of Commissioners of Public Utilities, PO Box 21040, St. John's, NL A1A 5B2
Fax: 709-726-9604, 866-782-0006, ito@pub.nl.ca
Newfoundland & Labrador Hydro, Hydro Place, 500 Columbus Dr., PO Box 12400, St. John's, NL A1B 4K7
709-737-1400, Fax: 709-737-1800, 888-737-1296, hydro@nlh.nl.ca

Northwest Territories
Inuvialuit Water Board, Mack Travel Bldg., 151 Mackenzie Rd., 2nd Fl., PO Box 2531, Yellowknife, NT X0E 0T0
867-678-2942, Fax: 867-678-2943, info@inuvwb.ca
Northwest Territories Power Corporation, 4 Capital Dr., Hay River, NT X0E 1G2
867-874-5200, 800-661-0855, info@ntpc.com
Public Utilities Board of the Northwest Territories, #203, 62 Woodland Dr., PO Box 4211, Hay River, NT X0E 1G1
867-874-3944, Fax: 867-874-3639

Nova Scotia

Nova Scotia Utility & Review Board, Summit Place, 1601 Lower Water St., 3rd Fl., Halifax, NS B3J 3S3
902-424-4448, Fax: 902-424-3919, 855-442-4448, board@novascotia.ca

Ontario

Hydro One Inc., South Tower, 483 Bay St., 8th Fl., Toronto, ON M5G 2P5
416-345-5000, Fax: 905-944-3251, 877-955-1155, customercommunications@hydroone.com

Independent Electricity System Operator, #1600, 120 Adelaide St. West, Toronto, ON M5H 1T1
905-403-6900, Fax: 905-403-6921, 877-797-9473, customer.relations@ieso.ca

Ontario Power Generation, 700 University Ave., Toronto, ON M5G 1X6
416-592-2555, 877-592-2555, webmaster@opg.com

Prince Edward Island

Prince Edward Island Regulatory & Appeals Commission, National Bank Tower, #501, 134 Kent St., PO Box 577, Charlottetown, PE C1A 7L1
902-892-3501, Fax: 902-566-4076, 800-501-6268, info@irac.pe.ca

Quebec

Coopérative régionale d'électricité de Saint-Jean-Baptiste-de-Rouville, 3113, rue Principale, Saint-Jean-Baptiste, QC J0L 1B0
450-467-5583, Fax: 450-467-0092, 800-267-5583, info@coopsjb.com

Hydro-Québec, Édifice Jean-Lesage, 75, boul René-Lévesque ouest, Montréal, QC H2Z 1A4
514-385-7252, 888-385-7252

Régie de l'énergie, Tour de la Bourse, #2.55, 800, Place Victoria, Montréal, QC H4Z 1A2
514-873-2452, Fax: 514-873-2070, 888-873-2452, secretariat@regie-energie.qc.ca

Saskatchewan

Saskatchewan Power Corporation (SaskPower), 2025 Victoria Ave., Regina, SK S4P 0S1
888-757-6937

Saskatchewan Water Corporation (SaskWater), #200, 111 Fairford St. East, Moose Jaw, SK S6H 1C8
Fax: 306-694-3207, 888-230-1111, communications@saskwater.com

SaskEnergy Incorporated, 1777 Victoria Ave., Regina, SK S4P 4K5
306-777-9225, 800-567-8899, webmaster@saskenergy.com

Yukon Territory

Yukon Energy Corporation, 2 Miles Canyon Rd., PO Box 5920, Whitehorse, YT Y1A 6S7
867-393-5300, 866-926-3749, communications@yec.yk.ca

Yukon Utilities Board, PO Box 31728, Whitehorse, YT Y1A 6L3
867-667-5058, Fax: 867-667-5059, yub@utilitiesboard.yk.ca

PUBLIC WORKS

Canada Infrastructure Bank, 150 King St. West, PO Box 15, Toronto, ON M5H 1J9
833-551-5245

Infrastructure Canada, #1100, 180 Kent St., Ottawa, ON K1P 0B6
613-948-1148, 877-250-7154, ifc.info@canada.ca

Public Services & Procurement, Place du Portage, Phase III, 11, rue Laurier, Ottawa, ON K1A 0S5
questions@tpsgc-pwgsc.gc.ca

Alberta

Alberta Infrastructure, Infrastructure Bldg., 6950 - 113th St., Edmonton, AB T6H 5V7
780-415-0507, Fax: 780-427-2187, Infra.Contact.Us.m@gov.ab.ca

Alberta Transportation, Communications Branch, Twin Atria Bldg., 4999 - 98th Ave., 2nd Fl., Edmonton, AB T6B 2X3
780-427-7674, Fax: 780-466-3166, Trans.Contact.Us.m@gov.ab.ca

British Columbia

British Columbia Ministry of Transportation & Infrastructure, PO Box 9850 Prov Govt, Victoria, BC V8W 9T5
250-387-3198, Fax: 250-356-7706, tran.webmaster@gov.bc.ca

Partnerships BC, 900 - 1285 West Pender St., PO Box 9478 Prov Govt, Vancouver, BC V6E 4B1
604-681-2443, Fax: 604-806-4190, partnershipsbc@partnershipsbc.ca

Manitoba

Manitoba Infrastructure, Legislative Bldg., #203, 450 Broadway, Winnipeg, MB R3C 0V8

New Brunswick

New Brunswick Department of Transportation & Infrastructure, Kings Place, PO Box 6000, Fredericton, NB E3B 5H1
506-453-3939, Fax: 506-453-7987, transportation.web@gnb.ca

Newfoundland & Labrador

Newfoundland & Labrador Department of Transportation & Infrastructure, Confederation Bldg., Prince Philip Dr., PO Box 8700, St. John's, NL A1B 4J6
709-729-2300, ti@gov.nl.ca

Northwest Territories

Northwest Territories Department of Infrastructure, Stuart M. Hodgson Bldg., 5009 - 49th St., 3rd Fl., PO Box 1320, Yellowknife, NT X1A 2L9
INF_Communications@gov.nt.ca

Nova Scotia

Nova Scotia Department of Transportation & Active Transit, PO Box 186, Halifax, NS B3J 2N2
902-424-2297, Fax: 902-424-0532, tpwpaff@novascotia.ca

Nunavut

Nunavut Territory Department of Community & Government Services, W.G. Brown Bldg., 4th Fl., PO Box 1000 700, Iqaluit, NU X0A 0H0
867-975-5406, Fax: 867-975-5305, cgscomms@gov.nu.ca

Ontario

Ontario Capital Growth Corporation, Ontario Investment & Trade Centre, 250 Yonge St., 35th Fl., Toronto, ON M5B 2L7
416-325-6874, Fax: 416-212-0794

Ontario Ministry of Economic Development, Job Creation & Trade, 56 Wellesley St. West, 7th Fl., Toronto, ON M7A 2E7
416-325-6666, 800-268-7095

Ontario Ministry of Infrastructure, 777 Bay St., 5th Fl., Toronto, ON M5G 2C8
416-327-4412

Prince Edward Island

Prince Edward Island Department of Transportation & Infrastructure, Jones Bldg., 11 Kent St., 3rd Fl., PO Box 2000, Charlottetown, PE C1A 7N8
902-368-5100, Fax: 902-368-5395, DeptTIE@gov.pe.ca

Saskatchewan

Saskatchewan Highways, Victoria Tower, 1855 Victoria Ave., Regina, SK S4P 3T2
306-933-5186, MHI.CustomerService@gov.sk.ca

SaskBuilds & Procurement, 1920 Rose St., Regina, SK S4P 0A9
306-787-6911, Fax: 306-787-1061, cs.receptioncenturyplaza@gov.sk.ca

Yukon Territory

Yukon Highways & Public Works, PO Box 2703, Whitehorse, YT Y1A 2C6
867-667-3732, Fax: 867-393-6218, hpw-info@yukon.ca

ENTRY NAME INDEX

CANADIAN ALMANAC & DIRECTORY
RÉPERTOIRE ET ALMANACH CANADIEN

Association of Regina Realtors, 344
Association of Registered Interior Designers of Ontario, 286
Association of Registered Professional Foresters of New
   Brunswick, 245
Association of Registrars of the Universities & Colleges of
   Canada, 215
Association of Saskatchewan Realtors, 344
The Association of School Transportation Services of British
   Columbia, 1976
Association of Science & Engineering Technology Professionals
   of Alberta, 227
The Association of Social Workers of Northern Canada, 363
Association of Translators & Interpreters of Nova Scotia, 299,
   298
Association of Translators, Terminologists & Interpreters of
   Manitoba, 299
Association of Unity Churches Canada, 1873
Association of University Forestry Schools of Canada, 215
Association of Visual Language Interpreters of Canada, 299
Association of Workers' Compensation Boards of Canada, 289
Association of Yukon Communities, 251
Association paritaire pour la santé et la sécurité du travail -
   Secteur Affaires municipales, 356, 251
Association pour la promotion des services documentaires
   scolaires, 307
Association pour la santé publique du Québec, 256
Association pour une solidarité syndicale étudiante, 215
Association professionnelle des designers d'intérieur du Québec,
   286
Association professionnelle des ingénieurs du gouvernement du
   Québec (ind.), 291
Association professionnelle des pharmaciens salariés du
   Québec, 333
Association provinciale des constructeurs d'habitations du
   Québec inc., 281
Association provinciale des enseignantes et enseignants du
   Québec, 215
Association Québec Snowboard, 1937
Association québécoise de canoë-kayak de vitesse, 1894
Association Québécoise de chirurgie, 256
Association québécoise de la production médiatique, 239
Association québécoise de la quincaillerie et des matériaux de
   construction, 190
Association québécoise de l'industrie de la pêche, 243
Association québécoise de l'industrie du disque, du spectacle et
   de la vidéo, 131
Association québécoise de l'épilepsie, 257
Association québécoise de racquetball, 1925
Association québécoise de sports pour paralytiques cérébraux,
   1895
Association québécoise des cadres scolaires, 215
L'Association québécoise des centres de la petite enfance, 202
Association Québécoise des dépanneurs en alimentation, 355
Association québécoise des enseignants de français langue
   seconde, 299
Association québécoise des industries de nutrition animale et
   céréalière, 172
Association québécoise des informaticiennes et informaticiens
   indépendants, 283
Association québécoise des interprètes du patrimoine, 276
Association québécoise des marionnettistes, 135
Association québécoise des personnes de petite taille, 363
Association québécoise des pharmaciens propriétaires, 333
Association québécoise des professeurs de français, 215
Association québécoise des salons du livre, 342
Association québécoise des transports, 1976
Association québécoise du loisir municipal, 251
Association québécoise du personnel de direction des écoles,
   215
Association québécoise du transport aérien, 1976
Association québécoise Plaidoyer-Victimes, 363
Association québécoise pour le loisir des personnes
   handicapées, 209
Association régionale de ringuette Laval, 1927
Association Régionale de Ringuette Richelieu Yamaska, 1927
Association sectorielle services automobiles, 356
Association sectorielle: Fabrication d'équipement de transport et
   de machines, 1976
Association Sportive de Ringuette Brossard, 1927
Association sportive des aveugles du Québec inc., 1889
Association sportive des sourds du Québec inc., 1900
Association touristique régionale de Charlevoix, 378
Association touristique régionale du Saguenay-Lac-Saint-Jean,
   378
Association Trot & Amble du Québec, 1901
L'Association Zoroastrianne du Québec, 1876
Associations touristiques régionales associées du Québec, 378
L'Assomption, *Judicial Chapter*, 1381

L'Assomption, *Municipal Governments Chapter*, 1237, 1250
Assumption Catholic School, 625
Assumption Mutual Life Insurance Company, 514
Assumption University, 726
Assumption University Archives, 1699
Assurance-Vie Banque Nationale, 514
Assurant Solutions Canada, 514
AssurePro Insurance Company, 514
Astek Legal Services, 1597
Aster, La Station scientifique du BSL, 137
Asteroid Publishing Inc., 1731
Asthma Canada, 257
Astolot Educational Centre, 689
Aston-Jonction, *Municipal Governments Chapter*, 1250
Astro Insurance 1000 Inc., 514
Astrolab du Parc National du Mont Mégantic, 122
The ATA Magazine, 1806
ATAC Resources Ltd., 548
Atacama Large Millimetre/submillimetre Array, *Government
   Chapter*, 898
ATB Financial, 474
ATB Financial, *Government Chapter*, 935
ATCO Ltd., 586
Atelier IMAGO, 10
Atelier Ladywood Museum, 51
Atelier le Fil d'Ariane inc., 1531
Atelier Theatre Society, 123
Athabasca & District Chamber of Commerce, 476
Athabasca Advocate, 1754
Athabasca Community Health Services, 1408, 1393
Athabasca County, *Municipal Governments Chapter*, 1106
Athabasca Health Authority, 1541
Athabasca Health Facility, 1544
Athabasca Healthcare Centre, 1387, 1400
Athabasca Minerals Inc., 548
Athabasca Oil Corp., 566
Athabasca University, 607
Athabasca University Press, 1731
Athabasca, *Municipal Governments Chapter*, 1113
The Athenaeum, 1839
Athens Public Library, 1683
Athens, *Municipal Governments Chapter*, 1205
Atherton Barristers, 1625
Athey Gregory & Dickson, 1592
AthletesCAN, 1945
Athletic Therapy Association of British Columbia, 1944
Athletics Alberta, 1880
Athletics Canada, 1958
Athletics Manitoba, 1880
Athletics New Brunswick, 1880
Athletics Nova Scotia, 1880
Athletics Ontario, 1880
Athletics PEI, 1880
Athletics Yukon, 1880
Athol Murray College of Notre Dame, 759
Athol Murray College of Notre Dame Archives & Museum, 116
Atholville, *Municipal Governments Chapter*, 1157
Atico Mining, 548
Atikameksheng Anishnawbek First Nation Public Library, 1690
Atikokan Centennial Museum & Historical Park, 71
Atikokan Chamber of Commerce, 487
Atikokan General Hospital, 1469
Atikokan Progress, 1774
Atikokan Public Library, 1683
Atikokan, *Municipal Governments Chapter*, 1205
Atlantic Association of Applied Economists, 193
Atlantic Beef & Sheep, 1831
Atlantic Building Supply Dealers Association, 190
Atlantic Business College, 660
Atlantic Business Magazine, 1803
Atlantic Canada Aviation Museum, 64
Atlantic Canada Fish Farmers Association, 243
Atlantic Canada Opportunities Agency, *Government Chapter*,
   854
Atlantic Canada Trail Riding Association, 1901
Atlantic Canada Water & Wastewater Association, 2013
Atlantic Canadian Anti-Sealing Coalition, 180
Atlantic Chamber of Commerce, 476
Atlantic College of Therapeutic Massage, 660
Atlantic Concrete Association, 190
Atlantic Conference of Independent Schools, 215
Atlantic Convenience Store Association, 355
Atlantic Dairy Council, 172
The Atlantic District of The Wesleyan Church, 1872
Atlantic Division, CanoeKayak Canada, 1894
Atlantic Education International Inc., *Government Chapter*, 973
Atlantic Episcopal Assembly, 1865
Atlantic Federation of Musicians, Local 571, 291

The Atlantic Film Festival Association, 240
Atlantic Filmmakers Cooperative, 239
Atlantic Flight Attendant Academy Limited, 669
Atlantic Forestry Centre, *Government Chapter*, 900
Atlantic Forestry Review, 1822
Atlantic Gold, 548
Atlantic Hairstyling & Aesthetics Academy, 660
Atlantic Home Building & Renovation Sector Council, 670
Atlantic Horse & Pony, 1825
Atlantic Insurance Company Limited, 514
The Atlantic Jewish Council, 319
Atlantic Lottery Corporation, *Government Chapter*, 983
Atlantic Marksmen Association, 1931
Atlantic National Parks/National Historic Sites, *Government
   Chapter*, 903
Atlantic Pilotage Authority Canada, *Government Chapter*, 914
Atlantic Pilotage Authority, *Government Chapter*, 854
Atlantic Planners Institute, 334
Atlantic Police Academy, 735
Atlantic Power Corporation, 586
Atlantic Provinces (French Services), *Government Chapter*, 861
Atlantic Provinces Art Gallery Association, 249
Atlantic Provinces Association of Landscape Architects, 298
Atlantic Provinces Athletic Therapists Association, 1944
Atlantic Provinces Chambers of Commerce, 476
Atlantic Provinces Economic Council, 213
Atlantic Provinces Harness Racing Commission, *Government
   Chapter*, 997, 1040
Atlantic Provinces Library Association, 307
Atlantic Provinces Special Education Authority, *Government
   Chapter*, 665, 1039
Atlantic Provinces Trucking Association, 1976
Atlantic Publishers Marketing Association, 315
Atlantic Reference Centre, 59
Atlantic Region - Halifax Regional Office, *Government Chapter*,
   881
Atlantic Salmon Federation, 243
Atlantic Salmon Journal, 1819
Atlantic Salmon Museum, 56
Atlantic School of Reflexology, 660
Atlantic School of Theology, 667
Atlantic Towing Limited, 1988
Atlantic University Sport Association, 1945
Atlantic Veterinary College, 735
Atlantica Law Group, 1595
Atlantica Party Association of Nova Scotia, 336
Atlantis: Critical Studies in Gender, Culture & Social Justice,
   1836
Atlas Coal Mine National Historic Site, 31
Atlas Courier Ltd., 1996
Atletico Ottawa, 1969
Atlin Health Centre, 1422
Atlin Historical Museum, 37
Atlin Library, 1667
Atlin, *Judicial Chapter*, 1368
ATM Industry Association Canada Region, 240
Atmospheric Science & Technology, *Government Chapter*, 875
Atomic Energy of Canada Limited, *Government Chapter*, 854
ATOP Broadband Corp., 436
Atrium Mortgage Investment Corporation, 577
Atrium Retirement Residence, 1514
ATS Automation Tooling Systems Inc., 544
ATS Healthcare, 1996
Attawapiskat First Nation Education Authority, 680
Attia, Reeves, Tensfeldt, Snow, 1566
Attijariwafa Bank, 474
L'Attisée, 1791
ATU Canada, 1976
Atwater Library & Computer Centre, 1708
Atwater, *Municipal Governments Chapter*, 1316
Atwood Labine Llp, 1624
Atx Law, 1625
Au Château Home for the Aged, 1508
Au fil de La Boyer, 1790
Au Logis Meteghan Ltd., 1463
Aubrey M. Rossman, 1638
Auclair, *Municipal Governments Chapter*, 1250
Auctioneering College of Canada, 613
Audet, *Municipal Governments Chapter*, 1250
Audio Engineering Society, 187
Audio Ideas Guide, 1829
Audit & Data Services, *Government Chapter*, 909
Audit & Evaluation Branch, *Government Chapter*, 888, 889
Audit & Evaluation Division, *Government Chapter*, 917
Audit & Evaluation Sector, *Government Chapter*, 867
Audit, Evaluation & Risk Branch, *Government Chapter*, 859
Audit, *Government Chapter*, 855
Auditor Certification Board, *Government Chapter*, 948

Bell, Kreklewich & Chambers, 1652
Bell, Unger, Riley, Morris, 1616
Bella Bella Community School, 632
Bella Coola Valley Museum, 37
Bella Coola Valley Transit System, 1989
Bella Senior Care Residence, 1496
Bellatrix Exploration Ltd., 566
Bellburns, *Municipal Governments Chapter*, 1165
Belle Plaine, *Municipal Governments Chapter*, 1316
Bellechasse, *Municipal Governments Chapter*, 1252
Belledune, *Municipal Governments Chapter*, 1157
Belleoram, *Municipal Governments Chapter*, 1165
Belleterre, *Municipal Governments Chapter*, 1252
Belleville - Hastings, *Judicial Chapter*, 1376
Belleville & District Chamber of Commerce, 487
Belleville Christian School, 685
The Belleville Intelligencer, 1773
Belleville News, 1775
Belleville Public Library & John M. Parrott Art Gallery, 72
Belleville Public Library (BPL), 1683
Belleville Scout-Guide Museum, 72
Belleville Senators, 1965
Belleville Shopper's Market, 1775
Belleville Transit, 1989
Belleville, *Government Chapter*, 871, 884
Belleville, *Municipal Governments Chapter*, 1196
Bellevue House National Historic Site, 78
Bellevue House National Historic Site of Canada, *Government Chapter*, 904
Bellevue Underground Mine, 28
Bellmont Long-Term Care Facility, 1501
Bellus Health Inc., 573
Bellwood Health Services, 1518
Belmont & District Museum, 49
Belmont Centre, 735
Belmont House, 1516
Belmont, Fine & Associates, 1626
Belmore Neidrauer Llp, 1626
Belo Sun Mining Corp., 549
Beloeil, *Judicial Chapter*, 1381
Beloeil, *Municipal Governments Chapter*, 1237
Belowus Easton English, 1644
Belva Spiel, 1640
Belvedere Care Centre, 1428
Belvedere Heights, 1506
Belvedere Medical Clinic, 1394
Belz Community School, 748
Belzile & Associes, 1651
Ben Weinstein, 1624
Benares Historic House & Visitor Centre, 82
Bench, 457
Benchmark Law Corpoartion, 1581
Bendale Acres, 1508
Benedict & Ferguson, 1602
Benefits & Pensions Monitor, 1803
Benefits Canada, 1803
Benevolent & Protective Order of Elks of Canada, 248
Benevolent Irish Society of Prince Edward Island, 248
Bengal Energy Ltd., 566
Bengough & District Museum, 108
Bengough Branch Library, 1725
Bengough Credit Union Ltd., 498
Bengough Health Centre, 1544
Bengough No. 40, *Municipal Governments Chapter*, 1342
Bengough, *Municipal Governments Chapter*, 1317
Benito Health Centre, 1436
Benito Health Centre Personal Care Home, 1442
Benjamin D. Levine, 1578
Bennett Bankruptcy Legal Counsel, 1626
Bennett Besaintburn Llp, 1626
Bennett Gold LLP, Chartered Accountants, 464
Bennett Health Care Centre, 1503
Bennett Jones LLP - Calgary, 1555
Bennett Jones LLP - Edmonton, 1555
Bennett Jones LLP - Ottawa, 1555
Bennett Jones LLP - Toronto, 1555
Bennett Jones LLP - Vancouver, 1555
Bennett Mounteer Llp, 1581
Bensen Professional Corporation, 462
Benson Buffett Plc, 1594
Benson Law Llp, 1575
Benson No. 35, *Municipal Governments Chapter*, 1342
Benson Percival Brown Llp, 1626
Bentley Care Centre, 1400
Bentley Municipal Library, 1658
Bentley Museum, 28
Bentley, *Municipal Governments Chapter*, 1114
Benvoulin Heritage Park & Benvoulin Heritage Church, 40

Beothuk Interpretation Centre Provincial Historic Site, 61
Berard Avocats, 1647
Bereaved Families of Ontario, 363
Berend Van Huizen, 1600
Berens River Nursing Station, 1439
Beresford, *Municipal Governments Chapter*, 1157
Beresh & Associates, 1643
Beresh Aloneissi O'Neill Hurley O'Keefe Millsap Edmonton, 1566
Beresh Smith Saintcatharines, 1622
Bereskin & Parr Llp Toronto, 1626
Bergel, Magence Llp, 1626
Berger & Company, 1578
Berger & Winston, 1647
Bergeron Clifford Llp, 1607
Bergeron Filion, 1603
Bergeron-Maybois, 1996
Les Bergeronnes, *Municipal Governments Chapter*, 1252
Berkley Canada, 514
Berkow, Cohen Llp, 1626
Berkshire Care Centre, 1510
Bermuda, 1097
Bernard & Brassard S.E.N.C.R.L., 1647
Bernard Betel Centre for Creative Living, 1488
Bernard Burton, 1627
Bernard C. Lavallée, 1578
Bernard Gropper, 1631
Bernard Hoodekoff, 1578
Bernard J. Monaghan, 1636
Bernard Llp, 1581
Bernard S. Shier, 1639
Bernard Transport Ltd., 1996
Bernatchez Associes Avocats, 1646
Bernhard Brinkmann Chartered Accountant, 455
Bernstein & Hirsch, 1590
Berry Creek Community School Library, 1659
Berry, *Municipal Governments Chapter*, 1252
Bersenas Jacobsen Chouesaintthomson Blackburn Llp, 1626
Berthier-sur-Mer, *Municipal Governments Chapter*, 1252
Berthierville, *Municipal Governments Chapter*, 1252
Bertrand Russell Research Centre, 708
Bertrand, *Municipal Governments Chapter*, 1157
Berwick & District Ringette Association, 1927
Berwick, *Municipal Governments Chapter*, 1184
Berwyn & District Chamber of Commerce, 476
Berwyn W.I. Municipal Library, 1658
Berwyn, *Municipal Governments Chapter*, 1114
The Best of Bridge Publishing Ltd., 1732
Besner, 1996
Besnier, Dion, Rondeau, 1651
Besse, Merrifield & Cowan Llp, 1603
Bet Sefer Solel, 693
Beth Jacob High School, 699
Beth Jacob School Inc., 748
Beth Radom Hebrew School, 699
Beth Sholom Hebrew School, 699
Beth Torah Hebrews' Cool, 699
Beth Tzedec Congregation, 1698
Beth Tzedec Congregational School, 699
Beth Tzedec Reuben & Helene Dennis Museum, 91
Bethammi Nursing Home, 1508
Bethania Mennonite Personal Care Home Inc., 1444
Béthanie, *Municipal Governments Chapter*, 1252
Bethany Airdrie, 1400
Bethany Calgary, 1400
Bethany Cochrane, 1401
Bethany CollegeSide, 1403
Bethany Didsbury, 1401
The Bethany Group, 1401
Bethany Harvest Hills, 1400
Bethany Lodge, 1509
Bethany Meadows, 1404
Bethany Pioneer Village Inc., 1548
Bethany Residence, 1511
Bethany Sylvan Lake, 1403
Bethel Christian Academy, 601
Bethesda Home for the Mentally Handicapped Inc., 1520
Bethune Branch Library, 1725
Bethune Memorial House National Historic Site of Canada, *Government Chapter*, 76, 904
Bethune, *Municipal Governments Chapter*, 1317
Bethune-Thompson House, 94
Bette Winner Public Library, 1672
Better Business Bureau of Central & Northern Alberta, 187
Better Business Bureau of Eastern & Northern Ontario & Quebec, 187
Better Business Bureau of Mainland BC, 187
Better Business Bureau of Manitoba & Northwest Ontario, 187
Better Business Bureau of Saskatchewan, Inc., 187

Better Business Bureau Serving Central Ontario, 187
Better Business Bureau Serving Southern Alberta & East Kootenay, 187
Better Business Bureau Serving the Atlantic Provinces, 187
Better Business Bureau Serving Vancouver Island, 187
Better Business Bureau Serving Western Ontario, 187
Betty Sandulak Personal Care Home, 1550
Betty-Lou McIlmoyle, 1595
Betula Beach, *Municipal Governments Chapter*, 1114
Between the Lines, 1732
Bev Churchill, 1575
Bev Hodgson Law, 1614
Bevan Lodge, 1422
Beverage Container Management Board, *Government Chapter*, 927
Beverly & Qamanirjuaq Caribou Management Board, *Government Chapter*, 866
Beverly A.B. Broadhurst, 1572
Beverly Centre - Lake Midnapore, 1400
Beyond Montessori School, 697
Bezpala Brown Gallery, 15
BFM Foundation (Canada), 1859
Bhalla Law Offices, 1566
Bhangal & Virk, 1611
Bharti School of Engineering, 717
Bhatia, Minipreet, 1626
Bi Unité Montréal, 304
Bialik Hebrew Day School, 699
Biamonte Llp Edmonton, 1567
Bianchi Presta Llp, 1643
Biathlon Alberta, 1887
Biathlon BC, 1887
Biathlon Canada, 1887
Biathlon Manitoba, 1887
Biathlon Newfoundland & Labrador, 1887
Biathlon Nouveau-New Brunswick, 1887
Biathlon Nova Scotia, 1888
Biathlon Ontario, 1888
Biathlon Prince Edward Island, 1888
Biathlon Saskatchewan, 1888
Biathlon Yukon, 1888
Bible Hill, *Municipal Governments Chapter*, 1184
The Bible Holiness Movement, 1872, 1866
The Bible League of Canada, 1859
Bibles & Literature in French Canada, 1859
Bibleway Christian Academy, 624
Biblio GEDE-Livres, 1714
Biblio La Bouquine (Sainte-Marguerite), 1719
Biblio Rollet, 1710
Biblioasis, 1732
Bibliothèque et Archives nationales du Québec (BAnQ), *Government Chapter*, 1052
Bibliothèque A la Bouquinerie (Sainte-Lucie-de-Beauregard), 1719
Bibliothèque Adolphe-Basile-Routhier, 1714
Bibliothèque Adrien-Lambert (Saint-Janvier-de-Joly), 1714
Bibliothèque Adrienne Demontigny-Clément, 1709
Bibliothèque A.-Lachance, 1713
Bibliothèque Alain-Grandbois, 1711
Bibliothèque Allard Regional Library, 1673
Bibliothèque Alma-Bourget-Costisella, 1704
Bibliothèque Alma-Durand, 1715
Bibliothèque Anne-Hébert, 1720
Bibliothèque Anne-Marie-D'Amours, 1721
Bibliothèque Armagimo, 1701
Bibliothèque Armand-Cardinal, 1707
Bibliothèque Au fil des mots (Saint-Basile), 1712
Bibliothèque Au Jardin des livres (Saint-Apollinaire), 1711
Bibliothèque Auguste-Honoré-Gosselin, 1709
Bibliothèque autonome de Saint-Théodore-d'Acton, 1717
Bibliothèque aux Quatre Vents de Saint-Hilarion, 1714
Bibliothèque Aux Sources (Saint-Ferréol-les-Neiges), 1713
Bibliothèque Baie-Johan-Beetz, 1701
Bibliothèque Barraute, 1701
Bibliothèque Beaucanton, 1701
Bibliothèque Benoît-Lacroix, 1715
Bibliothèque Bernard-Patenaude, 1707
Bibliothèque Bertrand-Leblanc, 1705
Bibliothèque Bibli-Aulnaies (Saint-Roch-des-Aulnaies), 1716
Bibliothèque Biblio Buck, 1702
Bibliothèque Biblio Du Centenaire, 1716
Bibliothèque Biblio Luc-Lacourcière (Saint-Victor), 1717
Bibliothèque Biblio-Chut! (Saint-Alban), 1711
Bibliothèque Biblio-Culture, 1714
Bibliothèque Blue Sea, 1701
Bibliothèque Cabano, 1721
Bibliothèque Cadillac, 1710
Bibliothèque Camille-Laurin, 1702

Centre de services scolaire Harricana, 736
Centre de services scolaire Marguerite-Bourgeoys, 738
Centre de services scolaire René-Lévesque, 736
Centre de soins prolongés Grace Dart, 1536
Centre de solidarité internationale Corcovado, 366
Centre de solidarité internationale du Saguenay-Lac-Saint-Jean, 366
Centre de solidarité lesbienne, 305
Centre des auteurs dramatiques, 135
Centre des femmes de Montréal, 385
Centre du Florès, 1532
Centre du services partagés du Québec, *Government Chapter*, 1062
Centre d'accueil Champlain, 1500
Centre d'accueil le programme de Portage inc., 1532
Centre d'accueil le Vaisseau d'Or, 1533
Centre d'accueil Marcelle Ferron inc., 1533
Centre d'accueil Nazareth inc., 1537
Centre d'accueil Roger-Séguin, 1493
Centre d'accueil St-Laurent inc., 1535
Centre d'amitié Eenou de Chibougamau, 324
Centre d'animation de développement et de recherche en éducation, 218
Centre d'applications et de recherches en télédétection, 754
Centre d'archives de la Grande Zone, 709
Centre d'archives du Musée de la Gaspésie, 1722
Centre d'art de Kamouraska, 20
Centre d'Art de St-Georges, 22
Centre d'art Rotary, 21
Centre d'art Révérend Louis-Napoléon-Fiset, 21
Centre d'Artistes Vaste et Vague, 20
Centre d'exposition Art-Image et espace Odyssée Maison de la Culture de Gatineau, 20
Centre d'exposition de l'Université de Montréal, 100
Centre d'exposition de Val-d'Or, 22
Centre d'exposition d'Amos, 19
Centre d'exposition l'Imagier, 20
Centre d'exposition Léo-Ayotte, 21
Centre d'exposition Mont-Laurier, 20
Centre D'hebergement Jeanne-le Ber, 1536
Centre d'hebergement Judith Jasmin, 1540
Centre d'histoire de Montréal, 100
Centre d'histoire de Saint-Hyacinthe, 1724
Centre d'histoire et d'archéologie de la Métabetchouane, 98
Centre d'histoire La Presqu'île, 107
Centre d'histoire Sir-William-Price, 99
Centre d'hébergemen Nazaire-Piché, 1534
Centre d'hébergement - Bon Séjour, 1534
Centre d'hébergement - Foyer du Bonheur, 1534
Centre d'hébergement - La Pietà, 1534
Centre d'hébergement Alphonse-Bonenfant, 1539
Centre d'hébergement Alphonse-Rondeau, 1534
Centre d'hébergement Andrée-Perrault, 1538
Centre d'hébergement Armand-Lavergne, 1535
Centre d'hébergement Bagotville, 1534
Centre d'hébergement Biermans, 1535
Centre d'hébergement Brassard, 1538
Centre d'hébergement Champlain Châteauguay, 1533
Centre d'hébergement Champlain Jean-Louis Lapierre, 1538
Centre d'hébergement Champlain Le Château, 1533
Centre d'hébergement Champlain-de-Gouin, 1535
Centre d'hébergement Champlain-des-Pommetiers, 1533
Centre d'hébergement Christ-Roi, 1537
Centre d'hébergement Cooke, 1539
Centre d'hébergement de Charlesbourg, 1533
Centre d'hébergement de Clermont, 1533
Centre D'Hébergement de la Maison-Saint-Joseph, 1535
Centre d'hébergement de la MRC-d'Acton, 1533
Centre d'hébergement de la Rive, 1535
Centre d'hébergement de la Villa-des-Tilleuls inc., 1535
Centre d'hébergement de Labelle, 1534
Centre d'hébergement de Lac-Bouchette, 1534
Centre d'hébergement de Lachine, 1534
Centre d'hébergement de Lajemmerais, 1539
Centre d'hébergement de LaSalle, 1534
Centre d'hébergement de Louvain, 1535
Centre d'hébergement de Lyster, 1535
Centre d'hébergement de Maria, 1535
Centre d'hébergement de Matane, 1535
Centre d'hébergement de Matapédia, 1535
Centre d'hébergement de Mgr-Coderre, 1535
Centre d'hébergement de Montarville, 1538
Centre d'hébergement de Mont-Tremblant, 1535
Centre d'hébergement de New Carlisle, 1536
Centre d'hébergement de Richmond, 1537
Centre d'hébergement de Rimouski, 1537
Centre d'hébergement de Rivière-Bleue, 1537
Centre d'hébergement de Rouyn-Noranda, 1537

Centre d'hébergement de Saint-Antonin, 1538
Centre d'hébergement de Saint-Cyprien, 1538
Centre d'hébergement de Sainte-Dorothée, 1535
Centre d'hébergement de Saint-Eustache, 1538
Centre d'hébergement de Saint-Eusèbe, 1534, 1537
Centre d'hébergement de Saint-Félicien, 1538
Centre d'hébergement de Saint-Laurent, 1538
Centre d'hébergement de Saint-Michel, 1536
Centre d'hébergement de Saint-Rémi, 1538
Centre d'hébergement de Squatec, 1538
Centre d'hébergement de Tracy, 1539
Centre d'hébergement de Weedon, 1540
Centre d'hébergement Denis-Benjamin Viger, 1540
Centre d'hébergement Des Chênes, 1534
Centre d'hébergement des Hauteurs, 1539
Centre d'hébergement des Quatre-Temps, 1536
Centre d'hébergement des Seigneurs, 1536
Centre d'hébergement Desy, 1538
Centre d'hébergement Docteur-Aimé-Leduc, 1539
Centre d'hébergement Drapeau-Deschambault, 1539
Centre d'hébergement du Centre-Ville-de-Montréal, 1536
Centre d'hébergement du Chevalier-De Lévis, 1535
Centre d'hébergement du Chêne, 1539
Centre d'hébergement du comté de Huntingdon, 1534
Centre d'hébergement du Fargy, 1533
Centre d'hébergement du Manoir-de-l'Age-d'Or, 1536
Centre d'hébergement du Manoir-de-Verdun, 1527
Centre d'hébergement du Manoir-Trinité, 1535
Centre d'hébergement du Roseau, 1540
Centre d'hébergement D'Anjou, 1538
Centre d'hébergement d'Ormstown, 1537
Centre d'hébergement et CLSC Frederick-George-Heriot, 1534
Centre d'hébergement et CLSC Mgr Paquin, 1534
Centre d'hébergement et CLSC Notre-Dame-du-Bon-Conseil, 1537
Centre d'hébergement Father-Dowd, 1536
Centre d'hébergement Georges-Hébert, 1534
Centre d'hébergement Georges-Phaneuf, 1538
Centre d'hébergement Gertrude-Lafrance, 1538
Centre d'hébergement Harricana, 1533
Centre d'hébergement Henri-Bradet, 1537
Centre d'hébergement Henriette Céré, 1538
Centre d'hébergement J.-Arsène-Parenteau, 1539
Centre d'hébergement Jeanne-Crevier, 1533
Centre d'hébergement Jeanne-Le Ber, 1536
Centre d'hébergement Laflèche, 1534
Centre d'hébergement Laurent-Bergevin, 1540
Centre d'hébergement Loretteville, 1535
Centre d'hébergement Louis Riel, 1536
Centre d'hébergement Louis-Denoncourt, 1539
Centre d'hébergement Louis-Hebert, 1537
Centre d'hébergement Lucien Shooner, 1537
Centre d'hébergement L'Auberge, 1538
Centre d'hébergement l'Eden de Laval inc, 1535
Centre d'hébergement Marguerite-Adam, 1533
Centre d'hébergement Marie-Anne Ouellet, 1534
Centre d'hébergement Mgr-Ross, 1534
Centre d'hébergement Mgr-Victor-Tremblay, 1533
Centre d'hébergement Paul-Gouin, 1536
Centre d'hébergement Pierre-Dupré, 1533
Centre d'hébergement René-Lavoie, 1534
Centre d'hébergement René-Lévesque, 1535
Centre d'hébergement Roland-Leclerc, 1539
Centre d'hébergement Romain-Becquet, 1538
Centre d'hébergement Réal Morel, 1539
Centre d'hébergement Saint-Antoine, 1537
Centre d'hébergement Saint-Augustin, 1537
Centre d'hébergement Saint-Casimir, 1538
Centre d'hébergement Saint-Célestin, 1538
Centre d'Hébergement Sainte-Anne, 1535
Centre d'hébergement Sainte-Croix, 1535
Centre d'hébergement Sainte-Marie, 1534
Centre d'hébergement Saint-François, 1533
Centre d'hébergement Saint-Joseph, 1537
Centre d'hébergement Saint-Liguori, 1538
Centre d'hébergement Saint-Martin de Malartic, 1535
Centre d'hébergement Saint-Raymond, 1539
Centre d'hébergement St-Andrew, 1536
Centre d'hébergement St-François inc., 1535
Centre d'hébergement St-Jean-Eudes, 1537
Centre d'hébergement St-Joseph, 1539
Centre d'hébergement St-Louis, 1538
Centre d'hébergement St-Margaret, 1536
Centre d'hébergement Thérèse-Martin, 1537
Centre d'hébergement Vallée-de-la-Lièvre, 1534
Centre d'hébergement Villa Bonheur, 1534
Centre d'hébergement Villa Maria, 1538
Centre d'hébergement Waldorf inc., 1534

Centre d'hébergement Yvon-Brunet, 1536
Centre d'hébergement Émilie-Gamelin, 1536
Centre d'imagerie moléculaire de Sherbrooke, 754
Centre D'Interpretation Archéo, 98
Centre d'interpretation de la Côte-de-Beaupré, 97
Centre d'interpretation de la Nature du Lac Boivin, 98
Centre d'interprétation de la maison Rowsell, 99
Centre d'interprétation de l'agriculture et de la ruralité, 100
Centre d'interprétation de l'ardoise, 104
Centre d'interprétation de l'eau, 99
Centre d'interprétation de l'île Providence et Musée Jos Hébert, 106
Centre d'interprétation de Middle Bay, 100
Centre d'interprétation des mammifères marins, 106
Centre d'interprétation du milieu écologique du Haut-Richelieu, 102
Centre d'interprétation du Parc du Bourg de Pabos, 102
Centre d'interprétation du patrimoine de Plaisance, 102
Centre d'interprétation et d'observation de Cap-de-Bon-Désir, 99
Centre d'interprétation, Bonaventure, 102
Centre d'interprétation, Maniwaki, 100
Centre d'intégration scolaire inc., 746
Centre d'orientation sexuelle de l'université McGill, 305
Centre for Academic & Personal Excellence Institute, 599
LA Centre for Active Living, 361
Centre for Addiction & Mental Health, 1491, 170, 1733
Centre for Addiction & Mental Health (Corporate Office), 1491
Centre for Adult Psychiatry, 1446
Centre for Advanced Computing, 711
Centre for Advanced Materials & Related Technology, 638
Centre for Advanced Polymer Processing & Design, 708
Centre for Advanced Technologies, 729
Centre for Applied Business Research in Energy & the Environment, 609
Centre For Applied Health Sciences, 730
Centre for Applied Transportation Technology, 727
Centre for Aquaculture & Environmental Research, *Government Chapter*, 879
Centre for Art Tapes, 10
Centre for Arts & Technology, 641
Centre for Arts, Design & Information Technology, 729
Centre for Asia-Pacific Initiatives, 638
Centre for Atmospheric Chemistry, 724
Centre for Aviation Technology, 727
Centre for Biomedical Research, 638
Centre for Business, 729
Centre for Canadian Historical Horticultural Studies, 25
Centre for Community Services & Early Childhood, 729
Centre for Comparative Literature, 721
Centre for Conflict Education & Research, 715
Centre for Construction & Engineering Technologies, 729
Centre for Craft Nova Scotia, 10
Centre for Criminology & Sociolegal Studies, 722, 1750
Centre for Diaspora & Transnational Studies, 722
Centre for Digital & Performance Arts, 727
Centre for Distance Education, 607, 669
Centre for Drama, Theatre & Performance Studies, 722
Centre for Education and Research on Aging & Health, 719
Centre for Effective Design of Structures, 708
Centre for Emerging Device Technologies, 708
Centre for Entrepreneurship & Family Enterprise, 609
Centre for Entrepreneurship Education & Development Inc., 195
Centre for Environmental Analysis & Remediation, 668
Centre for Ethics, 722
Centre for European Studies, 715
Centre for European, Russian, & Eurasian Studies, 722
Centre for Evaluation of Medicines, 708
Centre for Evolutionary Ecology & Ethical Conservation, 718
Centre for Experimental & Constructive Mathematics, 634
Centre for Extended Learning, 725
Centre for Feminist Research, 724
Centre for Financial Services, 729
Centre for Forensic Behavioural Science & Justice Studies, 761
Centre for Forensic Science & Medicine, 722
Centre for Functional Genomics, 708
Centre for Geriatric Psychiatry, 1446
Centre for Global Change Science, 723
Centre for Global Citizenship Education & Inclusion, 729
Centre for Health & Nutrition, 609
Centre for Health Economics & Policy Analysis, 708
Centre for Health Sciences, 729
Centre for Healthy Living, 1420
Centre for Hospitality & Culinary Arts, 729
Centre for Human Resources, 729
Centre for Humanities Research & Creativity, 718
Centre for Immigrant & Community Services, 204
Centre for Indigenous Initiatives, 722, 715

Chase Mental Health & Substance Use, 1431
Chase Primary Health Care Clinic, 1417
Chase Sekulich Chartered Professional Accountants, 455
Chase, *Municipal Governments Chapter*, 1136
CHAS-FM (Kiss 100.5), 417
Chassé & Associates Inc., 460
Chateau Cornwall, 1511
Chateau Georgian Retirement Residence, 1516
Chateau Park Long Term Care Home, 1500
Chateau Providence, 1548
Chateau Three Hills, 1405
Chateau Westmount inc., 1540
Châteauguay, *Government Chapter*, 873
Chatelaine, 1830
CHAT-FM (Chat 94.5), 403
Chatham - Kent, *Judicial Chapter*, 1376
Chatham Christian High School, 685
Chatham Christian School, 685
Chatham Daily News, 1773
Chatham Public Library, 1675
Chatham Railroad Museum, 74
Chatham Railroad Museum Society, 1980
Chatham Smart Shopper, 1776
Chatham This Week, 1776
Chatham, *Government Chapter*, 871, 885
Chatham-Kent Chamber of Commerce, 488, 196
Chatham-Kent Health Alliance, 1470
Chatham-Kent Health Alliance - Wallaceburg Site, 1483
Chatham-Kent Historical Society, 74
Chatham-Kent Museum, 74, 1695
Chatham-Kent Public Library, 1685
Chatham-Kent Real Estate Board, 345
Chatham-Kent Transit, 1990
Chatham-Kent, *Municipal Governments Chapter*, 1208
Chatsworth, *Municipal Governments Chapter*, 1208
CHAT-TV, 426
CHAT-TV-1, 435
CHAT-TV-2, 435
Chatwin Llp, 1567
Chaudiere Books, 1734
CHAU-DT, 432
CHAU-DT-1, 434
CHAU-DT-10, 434
CHAU-DT-11, 428
CHAU-DT-2, 428
CHAU-DT-3, 433
CHAU-DT-4, 432
CHAU-DT-5, 433
CHAU-DT-6, 432
CHAU-DT-7, 434
CHAU-DT-8, 432
CHAU-DT-9, 432
Chauvin Municipal Library, 1659
Chauvin, *Municipal Governments Chapter*, 1116
CHAY-FM (93.1 Fresh), 412
Chazel, *Municipal Governments Chapter*, 1255
CHBC-DT, 426
CHBC-DT-2, 428
CHBC-TV-4, 427
CHBC-TV-5, 426
CHBC-TV-6, 426
CHBC-TV-7, 427
CHBD-FM (Big Dog 92.7), 424
CHBE-FM (107.3 Kool FM), 407
CHBM-FM (Boom 97.3), 418
CHBN-FM (Kiss 91.7), 402
CHBO-FM (107.5 Bolt FM), 424
CHBW-FM (B-94), 404
CHBX-TV, 431
CHBX-TV-1, 432
CHBY-FM (Moose FM), 404
CHBZ-FM (Total Country), 404
CHC Helicopter, 1986
CHCD-FM (myFM), 417
CHCH-DT, 430
CHCM-AM (VOCM), 398
CHCQ-FM, 412
CHCR-FM, 414
CHDH-FM, 404
CHDI-FM (Sonic 102.9), 425
CHDR-FM (102.9 The Drive), 404
Cheadles Llp, 1624
Cheam Village, 1428
Chebucto Orchestral Society of Nova Scotia, 127
Chedabucto Education Centre / Guysborough Academy, 666
CHED-AM (630 CHED), 396
Cheer Canada, 1880
Cheer Nova Scotia, 1881

CHEF-FM, 421
CHEK-TV, 428
CHEK-TV-3, 427
Chelsea, *Municipal Governments Chapter*, 1255
Chelsey Park Long Term Care, 1504
Chelsey Park Retirement Community, 1495
Cheltenham Long-Term Care Facility, 1498
Chemainus & District Chamber of Commerce, 480
Chemainus Health Care Centre, 1417
Chemainus Valley Museum, 38
Chemawawin Public Library, 1672
Chemawawin School, 647
CHEM-DT, 434
Chemical Institute of Canada, 201
Chemical Reactor Engineering Centre, 712
Chemins de fer Québec-Gatineau Inc., 1994
Chemtrade Logistics Inc., 527
Chen & Leung, 1581
Les Chenaux, *Municipal Governments Chapter*, 1255
Chenelière Éducation, 1734
Chengdu Foreign Language School, 764
CHEQ-FM (O 101.5), 423
CHER-FM (MAX FM), 412
Cherington Place, 1429
Cherkewich, Ronald, Legal Services, 1653
Cherniack Smith, 1590
Cherry Coulee Christian Academy, 601
Chertsey, *Municipal Governments Chapter*, 1255
Chesapeake Gold Corp., 550
Cheshire Homes (Hastings - Prince Edward) Inc., 1518
Chesley & District Chamber of Commerce, 488
Chess Federation of Canada, 349
Chesswood Group Limited, 534
Chester District, *Municipal Governments Chapter*, 1187
Chester Municipal Chamber of Commerce, 486
Chester No. 125, *Municipal Governments Chapter*, 1344
Chester Train Station, 64
Chesterfield Inlet Health Centre, 1467
Chesterfield Inlet, *Municipal Governments Chapter*, 1190
Chesterfield No. 261, *Municipal Governments Chapter*, 1344
Chestermere Community Health Centre, 1408
Chestermere Public Library, 1659
Chestermere, *Municipal Governments Chapter*, 1111
Chesterville Historical Society, 74
Chesterville Record, 1776
Chesterville, *Municipal Governments Chapter*, 1255
Chestico Museum & Historical Society, 66
Chestnut Place, 1431
Chestnut Publishing Group Inc., 1734
Chet Sharma, 1639
CHET-FM, 404
Chetwynd & District Chamber of Commerce, 480
Chetwynd Echo, 1760
Chetwynd Health Unit, 1417
Chetwynd Hospital & Health Centre, 1412
Chetwynd Public Library, 1667
Chetwynd, *Municipal Governments Chapter*, 1136
Cheval Québec, 1825, 1902
Les Chevaliers de Colomb du Québec, 248
CHEX-DT, 431
CHEX-TV-2, 431
CHEY-FM (Rouge FM), 423
Chez Bernard Beauty Academy Inc., 659
Chez Nous Senior Citizens Home, 1550
CHEZ-FM (106.1 CHEZ), 415
CHFC, 398
CHFD-TV, 431
CHFI-FM (98.1 CHFI), 418
CHFM-FM (95.9 CHFM), 401
CHFN-FM, 415
CHFX-FM (FX101.9), 411
CHGA-FM, 421
CHGB-FM (Max FM), 413
CHGK-FM (2day FM), 417
CHGM-FM, 420
CHGO-FM (Capitale Rock), 424
CHHI-FM (95.9 Sun FM), 409
Chiarelli Cramer Witteveen, 1613
Chiarotto Law Pc, 1627
Chiasson & Roy, 1592
Chibougamau, *Government Chapter*, 873, 885
Chibougamau, *Judicial Chapter*, 1381
Chibougamau, *Municipal Governments Chapter*, 1255
Chicago Title Insurance Company Canada, 515
CHIC-FM, 422
Chichester, *Municipal Governments Chapter*, 1255
chickaDEE, 1817
Chicken Farmers of Canada, 340

Chicken Farmers of Newfoundland & Labrador, *Government Chapter*, 984
Chicken Farmers of Prince Edward Island, 340
Chicoutimi SaguenÉEns, 1967
Chicoutimi, *Government Chapter*, 873, 884
Chicoutimi, *Judicial Chapter*, 1378
Chief Allison Bernard Memorial High School, 665
Chief Audit Executive, *Government Chapter*, 880
Chief Charles Thomas Audy Memorial School, 647
Chief Clifford Lynxleg Anishinabe School, 648
Chief Finances, Results & Delivery Officer Sector, *Government Chapter*, 887
Chief Financial Officer & Corporate Services Branch, *Government Chapter*, 917
Chief Financial Officer Branch, *Government Chapter*, 882
Chief Financial Officer Directorate, *Government Chapter*, 902
Chief Financial Officer's Office & Corporate Services, *Government Chapter*, 912
Chief Financial Officer's Office, *Government Chapter*, 868
Chief Harold Sappier Memorial Elementary School, 657
Chief Information Office Sector, *Government Chapter*, 889
Chief Information Officer Branch, *Government Chapter*, 910, 916
Chief Inquiry Officer - Expropriations Act, *Government Chapter*, 1017
Chief Jacob Bearspaw School, 600
Chief Medical Officer of Health, *Government Chapter*, 1026
Chief Military Personnel, *Government Chapter*, 893
Chief Napeweaw Comprehensive School, 600
Chief Old Sun Elementary School, 601
Chief Public Health Office, *Government Chapter*, 1041
Chief Sam Cook Mahmuwee Education Centre, 648
Chief Tallcree School North, 600
Chief Tallcree School South, 600
Chiefs of Ontario, 324
Chiefswood National Historic Site, 84
Chignecto Manor Co-op Ltd., 1462
Chignecto-Central Regional Centre for Education, *Government Chapter*, 665, 999
Chiila Elementary School, 601
CHIK-FM (Énergie 98.9), 422
Child & Adolescent Treatment Centre, 1446, 649
Child & Family Programs, *Government Chapter*, 1076
Child & Family Services, *Government Chapter*, 964, 1043
Child & Parent Resource Institute, 1517, 316
The Child Abuse Survivor Monument Project, 366
Child Care Advocacy Association of Canada, 366
Child Care Facilities Board, *Government Chapter*, 1039
Child Death Review Committee, *Government Chapter*, 986
Child Development Institute, 1491
Child Evangelism Fellowship of Canada, 1866
Child Find British Columbia, 203
Child Find Canada Inc., 203
Child Find Newfoundland & Labrador, 203
Child Find Ontario, 203
Child Find PEI Inc., 203
Child Find Saskatchewan Inc., 203
Child Intervention Division, *Government Chapter*, 924
Child Protection & In Care Division, *Government Chapter*, 982
Child Welfare League of Canada, 366
Childhood Cancer Canada Foundation, 265
Children Believe, 1860
Children of Integrity Montessori Academy, 627
Children's Commissioner & Advocate, *Government Chapter*, 1039
Children, Youth & Families, *Government Chapter*, 999
Children's Discovery Museum on the Saskatchewan, 114
Children's Garden Junior School, 700
Children's Garden Nursery School, 700
Children's Healthcare Canada, 280
Children's Hospital Foundation of Manitoba, 265
Children's Hospital Foundation of Saskatchewan, 265
Children's Hospital of Eastern Ontario, 1477
Children's Hospital of Eastern Ontario Foundation, 265
Children's International Summer Villages (Canada) Inc., 287
Children's Mental Health Ontario, 316
Children's Mental Health Services, 1518
Children's Miracle Network, 203
Children's Montessori Academy, 696
Children's Treatment Centre, 1491
Children's Treatment Centre of Chatham-Kent, 1489
Children's Wish Foundation of Canada, 203
Chilkoot Trail National Historic Site of Canada, *Government Chapter*, 905
Chilliwack & District Real Estate Board, 345
Chilliwack Archives, 1670
Chilliwack Chamber of Commerce, 480
Chilliwack General Hospital, 1412
Chilliwack Health Protection Office, 1417

Commission Des Services Juridiques, 1648
Commission des services juridiques, *Government Chapter*, 1057
Commission des transports du Québec, *Government Chapter*, 1060
Commission for Environmental Cooperation, *Government Chapter*, 875
Commission for Public Complaints Against the Royal Canadian Mounted Police, *Government Chapter*, 908
Commission municipale du Québec, *Government Chapter*, 1051
Commission nationale des parents francophones, 205
Commission québecoise des libérations conditionnelles, *Government Chapter*, 1060
Commission scolaire Crie, 740
Commission scolaire de Kamouraska - Rivière du Loup, 1724
La Commission scolaire de la Jonquière, 1722
Commission scolaire de la Pointe-de-l'Ile, 738
Commission scolaire de la Rivière-du-Nord, 739, 1724
Commission scolaire de la Région-de-Sherbrooke, 739, 1724
La Commission scolaire de langue française de l'Ile-du-Prince-Édouard, 734
Commission scolaire de Laval, 737
Commission scolaire de l'Énergie, 1724
Commission scolaire de Montréal, 738
Commission scolaire des Affluents, Affaires corporatives et gestion de l'information, 1724
Commission scolaire des Bois-Francs, 1724
Commission scolaire des Draveurs, 736
Commission scolaire des Découvreurs, 738
Commission scolaire des Hauts-Bois-de-l'Outaouais, 737
Commission scolaire des Iles, 737
Commission scolaire des Laurentides, 1724
Commission scolaire des Portages-de-l'Outaouais, 737
Commission scolaire francophone des Territoires du Nord-Ouest, 664
La Commission scolaire francophone du Nunavut, 670
Commission scolaire francophone du Yukon, 763
Commission scolaire Marie-Victorin, 737
Commission scolaire Pierre-Neveu, 737
Commission scolaire Riverside, 736
Commissioner of Lobbyists, *Government Chapter*, 986
Commissioner of the Environment & Sustainable Development, *Government Chapter*, 855
Committee of Progressive Pakistani-Canadians, 204
Committee on the Status of Endangered Wildlife in Canada, *Government Chapter*, 874
Committees of the House of Commons, *Government Chapter*, 834
Committees of the Legislative Assembly of Alberta, *Government Chapter*, 919
Commodore Books, 1734
Commoners' Publishing Society Inc., 1734
The Commons @ 401, 16
Commonwealth Air Training Plan Museum, 49
Commonwealth College, 656
Commonwealth Games Canada, 1897
Commonwealth of Australia, 1096, 1089
Commonwealth of Dominica, 1097, 1090
The Commonwealth of Learning, 218
Commonwealth of the Bahamas, 1096, 1089
Commonwealth Stadium (Edmonton), 1970
Commonwealth War Graves Commission - Canadian Agency, 318
The Commonwell Mutual Insurance Group, 516
Communauté sépharade unifiée du Québec, 1870
Communication Sciences & Disorders, 752
Communications & Engagement, *Government Chapter*, 866
Communications & Marketing Branch, *Government Chapter*, 889
Communications & Portfolio Sector, *Government Chapter*, 901
Communications & Public Affairs Branch, *Government Chapter*, 882
Communications & Public Engagement, *Government Chapter*, 936
Communications & Public Engagements Branch, *Government Chapter*, 979
Communications Branch, *Government Chapter*, 867, 883, 891, 1072, 1075
Communications Directorate, *Government Chapter*, 908
Communications Group, *Government Chapter*, 914
Communications Nova Scotia, *Government Chapter*, 998
Communications Research Centre Canada, *Government Chapter*, 888
Communications Security Establishment Canada, *Government Chapter*, 893
Communications Services Manitoba, *Government Chapter*, 969
Communications, *Government Chapter*, 855, 1063, 1071
Communist Party of BC, 337
Communist Party of Canada, 337
Communist Party of Canada (Alberta), 337

Communist Party of Canada (Manitoba), 337
Communist Party of Canada (Marxist-Leninist), 337
Communist Party of Canada (Ontario), 337
Communities Economic Development Fund, *Government Chapter*, 968
Community & Correctional Services, *Government Chapter*, 1042
Community & Developmental Services Division, *Government Chapter*, 1018
Community & Legislative Services Division, *Government Chapter*, 954
Community Action Resource Centre, 366
Community Association for Riding for the Disabled, 1956
Community Bible Fellowship Christian School, 650
Community Care Branch, *Government Chapter*, 1072
Community Care Facilities & Nursing Homes Board, *Government Chapter*, 1040
Community Christian School, 686, 687
Community Credit Union, 500
Community Credit Union of Cumberland Colchester Limited, 500
Community Development Division, *Government Chapter*, 1079
Community Digest, 1835
Community Energy Association, 2016
Community Engagement Division, *Government Chapter*, 1068, 1074
Community First Credit Union Limited, 500
Community Governance, *Government Chapter*, 993
Community Head Injury Resource Services, 1520
Community Health and Social Services Centre, 1439
Community Health Nurses of Canada, 330
Community Hebrew Academy of Toronto, 700
Community Hospital O'Leary, 1520
Community Hubs Division, *Government Chapter*, 1029
Community Integration Services Society, 1422
Community Justice & Community Policing, *Government Chapter*, 992
Community Justice & Public Safety Division, *Government Chapter*, 1084
Community Justice, *Government Chapter*, 1008
Community Legal Education Association (Manitoba) Inc., 302
Community Legal Education Ontario, 302
Community Legal Information Association of Prince Edward Island, 302
Community Legal Services of Niagara South, 1621
Community Living Hanover, 1519
Community Living Manitoba, 210
Community Living North Bay, 1519
Community Living Ontario, 210
Community Living Peterborough, 1519
Community Museums Association of Prince Edward Island, 249
The Community News, 1777
Community Nursing Home Alexandria, 1500
Community of Christ - Canada East Mission, 1866
Community of Christ - Canada West Mission, 1866
Community One Foundation, 305
Community Operations, *Government Chapter*, 993
Community Outreach Centre, 711
Community Outreach Services, 1518
Community Planning & Development, *Government Chapter*, 968
Community Planning Association of Alberta, 302
Community Planning, *Government Chapter*, 1071
The Community Press, 1775, 1757
Community Programs & Corporate Services, *Government Chapter*, 964
Community Recreation Rebroadcasting Service Association, 435
Community Respite Service Inc., 1447
Community Safety & Countering Crime Branch, *Government Chapter*, 908
Community Safety & Crime Prevention Branch, *Government Chapter*, 955
Community Safety Division, *Government Chapter*, 967
Community Savings Credit Union, 500
Community School of Music & the Arts, 653
Community Sector Council of Nova Scotia, *Government Chapter*, 997
Community Service Delivery, *Government Chapter*, 964
Community Services & Supports Division, *Government Chapter*, 925
Community Social Services Employers' Association, 366
Community Trust Company, 589
Community Village, 1395
Community, Mental Health & Addictions & French Language Services Division, *Government Chapter*, 1026
Comox Air Force Museum, 38
Comox Archives & Museum Society, 38
Comox Valley Art Gallery, 5
Comox Valley Chamber of Commerce, 480, 197
Comox Valley Echo, 1761
Comox Valley Record, 1761

Comox Valley School District #71, 616
Comox Valley Therapeutic Riding Society, 1956
Comox Valley Transit System, 1990
Comox Valley, *Municipal Governments Chapter*, 1130
Comox, *Municipal Governments Chapter*, 1132
Compagnie du chemin de fer Lanaudière inc., 1994
La Compagnie d'Assurance Missisquoi, 516
Compagnie Marie Chouinard, 124
Compagnie vox théâtre, 134
Companies Office Advisory Board, *Government Chapter*, 962
Company's Coming Publishing Limited, 1734
The Comparative & International Education Society of Canada, 218
The Compass, 1770
Compass Credit Union, 500
Compassion Canada, 288
CompassTAX Chartered Accountants, 454
Compensation Employees' Union (Ind.), 292
Compensation for Victims of Crime, *Government Chapter*, 967
Competition Bureau Canada, *Government Chapter*, 889
Competition Tribunal, *Government Chapter*, 888
Complections College of Makeup Art & Design, 733
Compliance & Licensing, *Government Chapter*, 992
Compost Council of Canada, 231
Compton Communications, 436
Compton County Historical Museum Society, 98
Compton, *Municipal Governments Chapter*, 1256
Comptroller Division, *Government Chapter*, 964
Comptrollership Branch, *Government Chapter*, 856
Compute Canada, 204
Computer Dealer News, 1806
Computer Modelling Group Ltd., 526
Computershare Canada, 589
Computershare Trust Company of Canada, 589
Computing in the Humanities & Social Sciences, 722
Comtech Fire Credit Union, 500
Comunity Advisory Board, *Government Chapter*, 1084
Comwave Networks Inc., 436
Concentra Bank, 500
Concentra Trust, 589
Conception Bay Area Chamber of Commerce, 486
Conception Bay Museum, 60, 1680
Conception Bay South Public Library, 1678
Conception Bay South, *Municipal Governments Chapter*, 1164
Conception Harbour, *Municipal Governments Chapter*, 1167
La Conception, *Municipal Governments Chapter*, 1256
Concerned Children's Advertisers, 203
Concert CPA, 457
Concertation de l'action internationale et Protocole, *Government Chapter*, 1058
Concession & Compensation Review Board, *Government Chapter*, 1081
Conche, *Municipal Governments Chapter*, 1167
Concord Transportation, 1997
The Concorde, 1431
La Concorde, 1790
Concordia Hospital, 1436
Concordia Institute for Canadian Jewish Studies, 751
Concordia Place Personal Care Home, 1444
Concordia University, 751
Concordia University Archives, 1723
Concordia University of Edmonton, 610
Concours de musique du Canada inc., 132
Concrete BC, 190
Concrete Canada, 190
Concrete Manitoba, 191
Concrete Ontario, 191
Concrete Sask, 191
Condo Life Magazine, 1824
CondoBusiness, 1802
Condor Petroleum Inc., 567
Conestoga College Institute of Technology & Advanced Learning, 727
Conestoga Lodge Retirement Residence, 1513
Conexus Arts Centre, *Government Chapter*, 1075
Conexus Credit Union, 500
Confederacy of Mainland Mi'kmaq, 324
Confederation Centre of the Arts, 19
Confederation Centre Public Library, 1700
Confederation College, 728
Confederation Natural Resources Centre, 729
Confederation of Alberta Faculty Associations, 218
Confederation of University Faculty Associations of British Columbia, 219
Confente, Garcea, 1605
The Conference Board of Canada, 213
Conference of Defence Associations, 318
Conference of Independent Schools (Ontario), 219

Freestyle Skiing Ontario, 1936
Freight Carriers Association of Canada, 1980
Freight Management Association of Canada, 1980
Frelighsburg, *Municipal Governments Chapter*, 1260
French & Associates, 1594
French Innovation, Education & Programs, *Government Chapter*, 1039
French Language School Board, *Government Chapter*, 1039
French Programs & Services, *Government Chapter*, 999
French Republic, 1098, 1091
French River Public Library, 1682
French River, Municipality of / Municipalité de la Rivière des Français, *Municipal Governments Chapter*, 1211
French-Language, Teaching, Learning & Achievement Division, *Government Chapter*, 1019, 1021
Frenchman Butte Museum, 110
Frenchman Butte No. 501, *Municipal Governments Chapter*, 1346
Frenchman's Cove, *Municipal Governments Chapter*, 1169
Frequency Co-ordination System Association, 377
Fresh Outlook Foundation, 232
Fresh Start Recovery Centre, 1398
Freshii Inc., 538
Freshwater Fish Marketing Corporation, *Government Chapter*, 878, 879
Freshwater Institute, *Government Chapter*, 879
Fric, Lowenstein & Co. Llp, 1564
Friend of Friends Clubhouse, 1433
Friends Historical Association, 1868
Friends Historical Society - London, 1868
Friends Housing Inc., 1447
Friends of Canadian Broadcasting, 188
Friends of Chamber Music, 126
Friends of High Park Zoo, 139
The Friends of Library & Archives Canada, 308
Friends of Red Hill Valley, 232
Friends of the Earth Canada, 232
Friesen & Epp, Barristers & Solicitors, 1582
Fritz Shirreff & Vickers, 1580
Frobisher Threshermen's Museum, 110
Frobisher, *Municipal Governments Chapter*, 1323
FRONSAC Real Estate Investment Trust, 578
Le Front, 1840
Front d'action populaire en réaménagement urbain, 281
Front Gallery, 4
Front of Yonge Public Library, 1689
Front of Yonge, *Municipal Governments Chapter*, 1211
Front Street Senior's Residence, 1552
Frontenac County Schools Museum, 79
Frontenac House, 1738
Frontenac Islands, *Municipal Governments Chapter*, 1211
Frontenac, *Municipal Governments Chapter*, 1260, 1193
Frontera Energy Corporation, 568
Frontier College, 733
Frontier League Of Professional Baseball/Independent League, 1963
Frontier No. 19, *Municipal Governments Chapter*, 1346
Frontier School Division, 645
Frontier, *Municipal Governments Chapter*, 1323
Frontiers Foundation, 368
Frontline Credit Union, 502
FrontLine Safety & Security, 1813
Frost Centre for Canadian Studies & Indigenous Studies, 716
Frost Manor, 1495
Frost, Frosaint& Gorwill, 1609
Frostiak & Leslie Chartered Professional Accountants Inc., 459
Fruit & Vegetable Magazine, 1831
Fruitman Kates LLP Chartered Professional Accountants, 465
Fruitvale, *Municipal Governments Chapter*, 1137
Frumkin, Feldman & Glazman, 1649
Fryer Levitt, 1630
Fryfogel Tavern, 89
Frères de Notre-Dame de la Miséricorde, 1855
Frères de St Gabriel, Province de Montréal, 1723
Frédéric-Antoine Lemieux, 1651
F.T. Hill Museum, 114
Fudger House, 1509
Fuel Services, *Government Chapter*, 992
FuelPositive Corporation, 586
Fugues, 1822
Fugèreville, *Municipal Governments Chapter*, 1260
Fujiwara Dance Inventions, 124
The Fulcrum, 1840
Fulcrum Media Inc., 1751
Fulford Academy, 690
Fulford Place, 73
Fulford Preparatory College, 693
Full Gospel Business Men's Fellowship in Canada, 1867

Fuller Landau LLP, 465
Full-Time Hifz School, 702
Fulton & Company Llp, Lawyers & Trademark Agents, 1574
Fultz House Museum, 67
Fun to Learn Montessori School, 693
Funds Management & Banking, *Government Chapter*, 855
Fundy Geological Museum, 68
Fundy Guild Inc., 1738
Fundy Health Centre, 1450
Fundy Library Region, 1674
Fundy National Park of Canada, 118
Fundy National Park of Canada, *Government Chapter*, 903
Fundy Nursing Home, 1451
Funeral & Cremation Services Council of Saskatchewan, 249
Funeral Advisory & Memorial Society, 249
Funeral Board of Manitoba, *Government Chapter*, 965
Funeral Service Association of Canada, 249
Fung Loy Kok Institute of Taoism, 1875
Funk & Strell, 1590
Fur Council of Canada, 249
Fur Institute of Canada, 249
The Fur Trade at Lachine National Historic Site of Canada, *Government Chapter*, 905
The Fur-Bearers, 249
Fury Gold Mines Limited, 552
Fuse Collective, 232
Fusion Credit Union, 502
Future Possibilities for Kids, 203
FutureSkills High School, 701
Futurpreneur Canada, 197
F.W. Green Memorial Home, 1423
FX, 437
FXX, 437
Fyshe McMahon Llp, 1605

G

G. Arthur Moad, 1611
G. Chalmers Adams, 1625
G. David Eldridge, 1595
G. Kevin Eggleton, 1598
The G. Raymond Chang School of Continuing Education, 719
G. Ronald Toews, Q.C., 1579
G&F Financial Group, 502
G&G Partnership LLP, 465
G.A. Smith, 1607
Gabbrel & Company, 1580
Gabonese Republic, 1098, 1091
Le Gaboteur, 1771
Gabriel Dumont Institute, 760, 761
Gabriel Dumont Institute of Native Studies & Applied Research, 114
Gabriola Island Chamber of Commerce, 480
Gabriola Museum, 40
Gabriola Sounder, 1761
Gadsby, *Municipal Governments Chapter*, 1118
The Gaelic College, 670
Gaetan Lagarde, 1649
Gaetano P. Matteazzi, 1635
Gagetown & Area Chamber of Commerce, 485
Gagetown, *Municipal Governments Chapter*, 1158
Gagne Letarte S.E.N.C.R.L. Quebec, 1650
Gagnon Girard Julien & Matte Avocats Avocates, 1650
Gail Barnes, 1581
Gainsborough & Area Health Centre, 1544
Gainsborough Branch Library, 1725
Gainsborough Galleries, 3
Gainsborough, *Municipal Governments Chapter*, 1324
Galahad Care Centre, 1404
Galahad, *Municipal Governments Chapter*, 1118
Galane Gold Ltd., 553
Galarneau & Associates Professional Corp., 1615
Galbraith Empson, 1567
Galbraith Family Law, 1599
Galbraith Law, 1567
Galerie Artêria, 20
Galerie Colline, 9
Galerie de l'UQAM, 20
Galerie d'art de Matane, 20
Galerie d'art du Centre culturel de l'Université de Sherbrooke, 21
Galerie d'art du Parc, 22
Galerie d'art Louise-et-Reuben-Cohen, 10
La Galerie d'art Stewart Hall Art Gallery, 21
Galerie Heffel Québec Ltée, 21
Galerie Montcalm, 20
Galerie Port-Maurice, 21
Galerie Restigouche Gallery, 9
Galerie Sans Nom Coop Ltée, 10

Galerie Visual Voice, 21
Galiano Gold Inc., 553
Galiano Island Chamber of Commerce, 480
Galiano Island Community Library, 1668
Gall Legge Grant & Munroe Llp, 1582
Gallant Morin Avocats, 1651
Gallants, *Municipal Governments Chapter*, 1169
Galleon Gold Corp., 568
Galleries West, 1815
Gallery 101, 14
Gallery 44, 16
Gallery 78, 9
Gallery 8, 6
Gallery Arcturus, 16
Gallery at NeXt, 16
Gallery Gachet, 7
Gallery in the Grove, 12
Gallery Indigena, 16
Gallery M Contemporary, 15
Gallery of the Midnight Sun, 10
Gallery on 3rd, 23
Gallery Stratford, 15
Gallery TPW, 16
The Gallery/art placement inc., 22
Gallichan, *Municipal Governments Chapter*, 1260
Galloway Botteselle & Company, 457
Galloway Health Centre, 1546
Galloway Station Museum & Travel Centre, 32
Galt Historic Railway Park, 33
Galt Museum & Archives, 1666
GAMA International Canada, 285
Gambo Public Library, 1678
Gambo, *Municipal Governments Chapter*, 1169
Game+, 439
Gamehost Inc., 581
Gameti Community Library, 1680
The GameTV Corporation, 439
Gaming Policy & Enforcement, *Government Chapter*, 949
Gamèti Health Centre, 1459
Gamèti, *Municipal Governments Chapter*, 1181
Gan Netivot, 701
Gananoque Public Library, 1686
Gananoque Reporter, 1777
Gananoque, *Government Chapter*, 871
Gananoque, *Municipal Governments Chapter*, 1211
Ganapathi Law Group, 1582
Ganaraska Financial Credit Union, 502
Gander & Area Chamber of Commerce, 486
Gander Flight Training Aerospace, 663
Gander International Airport Authority Inc., 1987
Gander Public Library, 1678
Gander, *Government Chapter*, 871, 886
Gander, *Judicial Chapter*, 1371
Gander, *Municipal Governments Chapter*, 1169
Ganzhou No. 3 Middle School (China), 764
The Gap No. 39, *Municipal Governments Chapter*, 1346
Garcia & Donnelly Law Office, 1606
Garden City Manor Long Term Care, 1507
Garden Court Nursing Home, 1509
Garden Hill Education Authority, 646
Garden Hill First Nations High School, 648
Garden Hill Nursing Station, 1440
Garden Home, 1521
Garden Making, 1822
Garden of the Gulf Museum, 96
Garden River First Nation Public Library, 1686
Garden River No. 490, *Municipal Governments Chapter*, 1346
Garden Valley School Division, 645
Garden View Lodge, 1405
Garden View Village, 1430
Garden Vista, 1407
Gardewine Group Inc., 1998
Gardiner Miller Arnold Llp, 1630
Gardiner Museum of Ceramic Art, 92
Gardiner Roberts Llp, 1630
Gardner Zuk Dessen, Chartered Accountants, 465
Garen Kassabian, 1633
Garett Hazelwood, Chartered Professional Accountant, 463
Garfin Zeidenberg Llp, 1630
Garfinkle Biderman Llp Barristers & Solicitors, 1630
Gargoyle, 1840
Garibaldi Resources Corp., 553
Gariépy, Gravel, Larouche, Blouin CPA, S.E.N.C.R.L., 469
Garling Ostensen, 1577
Garnish (Greta Hollett) Memorial Library, 1678
Garnish, *Municipal Governments Chapter*, 1169
Garrison Place Retirement Residence, 1512
Garrod Association, 267

I

I. Samuel Kravinchuk, 1568
iA Financial Group, 519, 543
IAESTE Canada (International Association for the Exchange of Students for Technical Experience), 220
Iain Stewart Cunningham, 1624
IAMGOLD Corporation, 554
Ian C. Boddy, 1619
Ian C. Shoub, 1639
Ian D. Paul, 1603
Ian D. Reith, 1589
Ian D. Werker, 1642
Ian G. Pearson, 1622
Ian H. Warren, 1619
Ian M. Solloway, 1650
Ian Sutherland Barrister & Solicitor, 1641
Ian Tan Gallery, 7
Ian Thornhill, 1641
Ian Vasey Professional Corporation, 461
IBC Advanced Alloys, 545
Ibex Valley, *Municipal Governments Chapter*, 1359
IBI Group Inc., 542
IC Savings, 502
ICE Futures Canada, Inc., 588
Iceland, 1098, 1091
Icelandair, 1986
Icelandic National League of North America, 321
Ici ARTV, 437
ICI Radio-Canada, 394
ICICI Bank Canada, 472
ICOM Museums Canada, 250
ICOMOS Canada, 278
ICS Courier, 1999
ICT Schools, 733
Idea Exchange, 12, 1684
iDeal Equipment Magazine, 1831
L'IdéePhile, 1841
The Identification Clinic, 368
Idlewyld Manor, 1494
Idlewild Lodge, 1550
Idylwyld Centre Public Health Office, 1546
Les idées de ma maison, 1824
iFabric Corp., 584
Igbo Union of Canada, 321
Igloolik Health Centre, 1467
Igloolik, *Municipal Governments Chapter*, 1190
IGM Financial Inc., 535
Ignace Heritage Centre, 78
Ignace Public Library, 1688
Ignace, *Municipal Governments Chapter*, 1214
Ignite, 1785
Iguana Books, 1740
I.H. Asper School of Business, 653
Ikaluktutiak Co-operative Ltd., 436
Ikaluktutiak Paddling Association, 1895
Il Cittadino Canadese, 1834
Ilavsky Chartered Accountants, 465
Ile a la Crosse Communications Society Inc., 437
Ile a la Crosse School Division #112, 756
Ile-a-la-Crosse Public Library, 1726
L'île-Cadieux, *Municipal Governments Chapter*, 1263
L'Ile Lettrée, 1841
L'île-Dorval, *Municipal Governments Chapter*, 1263
L'île-d'Orléans, *Municipal Governments Chapter*, 1263
L'Ile-du-Grand-Calumet, *Municipal Governments Chapter*, 1264
L'Ile-d'Anticosti, *Municipal Governments Chapter*, 1264
L'Ile-Perrot, *Municipal Governments Chapter*, 1239
Iler Campbell Llp, 1632
Iler Lodge, 1503
Iles de la Madeleine, *Judicial Chapter*, 1381
Les îles-de-la-Madeleine, *Municipal Governments Chapter*, 1239
Ile-à-la-Crosse, *Municipal Governments Chapter*, 1326
Ilford Community Health Centre, 1437
Illingworth & Illingworth, 1624
Illingworth Kerr Gallery, 3
Imaflex Inc., 545
Imagine Canada, 368
IMCS Pax Romana, 1855
Immaculata Catholic Regional High School, 625
Immaculate Conception School, 623, 625
Immaculate Conception School Vancouver, 626
Immaculate Heart of Mary School, 650
Immanuel Christian Elementary Schools, 603
Immanuel Christian School, 734, 650, 687
Immanuel Christian School Society, 685
Immigrant Centre Manitoba Inc., 204
Immigrant Welcome Centre, 321

Immigrant Women Services Ottawa, 386
Immigration & Population Growth Branch, *Government Chapter*, 985
Immigration & Refugee Board of Canada, *Government Chapter*, 883
Immigration et prospection, *Government Chapter*, 1057
Immigration Selection Division, *Government Chapter*, 1019
Immigration, Employment & Career Development, *Government Chapter*, 1073
Immigration, Refugees & Citizenship, *Government Chapter*, 883
Immunize Canada, 269
IMP Group International Inc., 2005
Impact Assessment Agency of Canada, *Government Chapter*, 861
Impact Campus, 1841
Impact Centre, 723
IMPACT Silver Corp., 554
Impala Canada Ltd., 554
Imperial Branch Library, 1726
Imperial Cable System, 437
Imperial College of Toronto, 702
Imperial Equities Inc., 579
Imperial Metals Corporation, 554
Imperial Oil Limited, 568
Imperial, *Municipal Governments Chapter*, 1326
Imprint Canada, 1801
Improvement District No. 12 (Jasper National Park), *Municipal Governments Chapter*, 1127
Improvement District No. 13 (Elk Island), *Municipal Governments Chapter*, 1127
Improvement District No. 24 (Wood Buffalo), *Municipal Governments Chapter*, 1127
Improvement District No. 25 (Willmore Wilderness), *Municipal Governments Chapter*, 1127
Improvement District No. 4 (Waterton), *Municipal Governments Chapter*, 1127
Improvement District No. 9 (Banff), *Municipal Governments Chapter*, 1128
IMV Inc., 574
In Médias, 1751
In2art Gallery, 14
Ina Grafton Gage Home, 1499
Inanna Publications, 1740
Inc Business Lawyers, 1578
Inch Hammond Business Lawyers, 1605
Inclusion Alberta, 210
Inclusion BC, 211
Inclusion NWT, 211
Inclusion Press International, 1740
Inclusion Saskatchewan, 211
Inclusion Yukon, 211
Inclusive Education Supports, *Government Chapter*, 999
Income & Employment Support Appeal Board, *Government Chapter*, 985
Income Assistance Programs, *Government Chapter*, 1077
Income Security & Pension Policy Division, *Government Chapter*, 1024
Income Security Programs Division, *Government Chapter*, 990
L'Inculte, 1841
The Independent, 1776
The Independent & Free Press, 1777
Independent Assemblies of God International - Canada, 1874
Independent Electricity System Operator, *Government Chapter*, 1021, 1028
Independent Learning Centre, 684
Independent Living Canada, 211
Independent Media Arts Alliance, 239
Independent Order of Foresters, 519
Independent Power Producers Society of Alberta, 2017
Independent Production Fund, 377
Independent School Advancement Professionals Canada, 220
Independent State of Samoa, 1094
Independent Telecommunications Providers Association, 2017
Index: Gay & Lesbian Business Directory, 1822
Indexing Society of Canada, 308
India Journal, 1835
Indian Bay, *Municipal Governments Chapter*, 1171
Indian Head - Wolseley News, 1794
Indian Head Basic Education Centre, 762
Indian Head Branch Library, 1726
Indian Head Museum, 110
Indian Head No. 156, *Municipal Governments Chapter*, 1348
Indian Head Union Hospital, 1542
Indian Head, *Municipal Governments Chapter*, 1326
Indian Métis Christian Fellowship, 1862
Indian Oil & Gas Canada, *Government Chapter*, 866, 867
Indian Residential School Adjudication Secretariat, *Government Chapter*, 867

Indian River Reptile Zoo & Dinosaur Park, 138
Indian Springs School, 648
Indigenous & Northern Relations, *Government Chapter*, 1071
Indigenous Affairs, Heritage Conservation & Commemoration Directorate, *Government Chapter*, 903
Indigenous Bar Association, 325
Indigenous Clean Energy Social Enterprise, 325
Indigenous Climate Leadership & Corporate Services, *Government Chapter*, 929
Indigenous Education & Well Being Division, *Government Chapter*, 1021
Indigenous Justice Division, *Government Chapter*, 1018
Indigenous Law Centre, 1740
Indigenous Literary Studies Association, 325
Indigenous Peoples' Health Research Centre, 760
Indigenous Relations & Programs Division, *Government Chapter*, 1028
Indigenous Services Canada, *Government Chapter*, 887
Indigenous Studies, 718
Indigenous Studies Program, 707
Indigenous Women's Business Network, 325
Indigo Books & Music Inc., 530
Indo Caribbean World, 1835
Indo-Canada Chamber of Commerce, 475, 383
Indo-Canadian Times, 1766
The Indo-Canadian Voice, 1765
Indo-Canadian Voice, 1835
Indonesia Canada Chamber of Commerce, 475, 383
Indoor Environment Testing Facilities, *Government Chapter*, 899
Indspire, 325
Industrial & Commercial Bank of China (Canada), 472
Industrial Accident Victims Group of Ontario, 357
Industrial Alliance Auto & Home Insurance, 519
Industrial Alliance Trust Inc., 589
Industrial Gas Users Association, 2017
Industrial Heritage Complex Merrickville Lockstation, 89
Industrial Partnership Facility: Montréal, *Government Chapter*, 899
Industrial Process Products & Technology, 1806
Industrial Relations Centre, 711
Industrial Technology Centre, *Government Chapter*, 962
Industrial Truck Association, 1981
Industries stratégiques et projets économiques majeurs, *Government Chapter*, 1053
Industry & Economic Analysis Branch, *Government Chapter*, 901
Industry & Sector Strategy Division, *Government Chapter*, 1020
Industry Sector, *Government Chapter*, 889
Industry Training Authority, *Government Chapter*, 953
Infant & Toddler Safety Association, 203
Infant Feeding Action Coalition, 202
Infection & Prevention Control Canada, 269
Infirmiers et infirmières sans frontières, 331
L'Info, 1792
Info Comptabilité Plus, 469
L'INFO-Cégep, 1841
L'Info de la Lièvre, 1788
Info Dimanche, 1790
Info entrepreneurs, *Government Chapter*, 856
L'Info Petite Nation, 1790
L'Infomane, 1841
Infopresse, 1751, 1801
L'Informateur de Rivières-des-Prairies, 1789
Informatics Shared Services, *Government Chapter*, 99
Information & Communication Technologies Association of Manitoba, 377
Information & Communications Technology Council of Canada, 284
Information & Communications Technology, *Government Chapter*, 1083
Information & Privacy Commissioner of Ontario, *Government Chapter*, 1028
Information & Privacy Commissioner of Saskatchewan, *Government Chapter*, 1073
Information Access & Privacy, *Government Chapter*, 1004
L'Information du Nord Mont-Tremblant, 1788
L'Information du Nord Sainte-Agathe, 1792
L'Information du Nord Valée de la Rouge, 17890
Information Management & Support, *Government Chapter*, 1069
Information Management, *Government Chapter*, 894, 950
Information Resource Management Association of Canada, 284
Information Services Corporation, 582
Information Services Division, *Government Chapter*, 956
Information Services, *Government Chapter*, 991
Information Systems Branch, *Government Chapter*, 853, 944, 955
Information Technology Association of Canada, 284
Information Technology Branch, *Government Chapter*, 860

Kapoor Barristers, 1633
Kapoor Selnes Klimm, 1652
Kaposvar Historic Site, 109
Kapuskasing, 709
Kapuskasing & District Chamber of Commerce, 489, 198
Kapuskasing Public Library, 1688
Kapuskasing, *Government Chapter*, 871, 886
Kapuskasing, *Municipal Governments Chapter*, 1214
Karamay Senior High School, 764
Karate Alberta Association, 1919
Karate BC, 1920
Karate Canada, 1920
Karate Manitoba, 1920
Karate New Brunswick, 1920
Karate Newfoundland & Labrador, 1920
Karate Nova Scotia, 1920
Karate Ontario, 1920
Karaté Québec, 1920
Karen Ann Reid, 1618
Karen D. Lundy, 1634
Karen D. Stevan, 1573
Karen J. Yarrow, 1610
Kariton Art Gallery, 4
Karl G. Melinz, 1606
Karlaine Place Ltd., 1464
Karnalyte Resources Inc., 555
Karora Resources Inc., 555
Kaslo & Area Chamber of Commerce, 481
Kaslo & District Public Library, 1668
Kaslo Centre, 638
Kaslo Mental Health & Substance Use, 1432
Kaslo Physiotherapy, 1419
Kaslo Primary Health Centre, 1419
Kaslo Village Hall, 40
Kaslo, *Municipal Governments Chapter*, 1138
Kate Chegwin School, 601
Katepwa, *Municipal Governments Chapter*, 1326
Kateri Memorial Hospital Centre, 1528
Katherine A. Kubica Professional Corporation, 1568
Katherine House, 1458
Kathleen Loo Craig, 1646
Kathryn A. Junger, 1605
Kathryn d'Artois, 1613
Kathryn J. Ginther, 1577
Kativik School Board, 740
Katlodeeche, *Municipal Governments Chapter*, 1182
Katsepontes Law, 1617
Katudgevik Co-operative Association Ltd., 436
Katz & Company, 1583
Katzman, Wylupek Llp, 1644
Kawartha Baseball Umpires Association, 1885
Kawartha Chamber of Commerce & Tourism, 489
Kawartha Credit Union Limited, 503
Kawartha Lakes Real Estate Association, 345
Kawartha Lakes, *Municipal Governments Chapter*, 1198
Kawartha Montessori School, 695
Kawartha Pine Ridge District School Board, 673
Kawartha Settlers' Village, 72
Kawawachikamach, *Municipal Governments Chapter*, 1265
Kay & Warburton Chartered Professional Accountants, 466
Kay Professional Corporation, 1608
Kayak: Canada's History Magazine for Kids, 1817
Kayla's Children Centre, 689
Kay-Nah-Chi-Wah-Nung Historical Centre, 89
Kazabazua, *Municipal Governments Chapter*, 1265
Kbl Law Llp, 1568
K-Bro Linen Inc., 582
KDM Dental College International Inc., 612
Kearney & Area Public Library, 1688
Kearney, *Municipal Governments Chapter*, 1214
Kearns Law Office, 1604
KEB Hana Bank of Canada, 472
Kebaowek Health Centre, 1528
Kedgwick Public Library, 1675
Kedgwick, *Municipal Governments Chapter*, 1159
Keel Cottrelle Llp Toronto, 1633
Keeler, *Municipal Governments Chapter*, 1326
Keels, *Municipal Governments Chapter*, 1171
Keenan Bengts Law Office, 1595
Keeseekoowenin Education Authority, 646
Keeseekoowenin School, 647
Keethanow Public Library, 1727
Keewatin Air LP, 1986
Keewatin Railway Company Ltd., 1995
Keewatinook Fishers of Lake Winnipeg, 325
Keewatin-Patricia District School Board, 672
Keewaytinok Native Legal Services, 1613
Keewaytinook Okimakanak Board of Education, 680

Keewaywin Nursing Station, 1489
Keg River Community Library, 1662
Keg Royalties Income Fund, 538
Kegedonce Press, 1741
Kehew Asiniy School, 601
Kehewin Band Education Department, 598
Kehewin Community Education Centre, 600
The Keir Memorial Museum, 95
Keith A. Lo, 1584
Keith D. Nelson, 1614
Keith E. Wright, 1642
Keith M. Boyd Museum, 88
Kejimkujik National Park & National Historic Site of Canada, 119
Kejimkujik National Park of Canada, *Government Chapter*, 903
Kelle M. Maag Law Corporation, 1574
Kelliher & District Heritage Museum Inc., 110
Kelliher, *Municipal Governments Chapter*, 1326
Kellross Heritage Museum, 111
Kellross No. 247, *Municipal Governments Chapter*, 1348
Kells Academy, 748
Kelly & Co., 1608
Kelly & Kelly, 1564
Kelly Christiansen & Company, 1575
Kelly D. Jordan Family Law Firm, 1632
Kelly Greenway Bruce Oshawa, 1615
Kelly Huibers McNeely Professional Corporation, 461
Kelly Porter Hétu, 466
Kelly R. Palmer, 1569
Kelly Santini Llp Ottawa, 1617
Kelly, Jennings & Lacy, 1633
Kelly's Personal Care Home, 1457
Kelowna Art Gallery, 5
Kelowna Chamber of Commerce, 481, 198
Kelowna Christian School, 623
Kelowna Chronic Kidney Disease Clinic, 1419
Kelowna College of Professional Counselling, 641
Kelowna Developmental Disability Mental Health Services, 1432
Kelowna General Hospital, 1413
Kelowna Mental Health & Substance Use, 1432
Kelowna Museums, 41
Kelowna Pacemaker Clinic, 1419
Kelowna Public Archives, 1671
Kelowna Regional Transit System, 1991
Kelowna Research Centre, 1419
Kelowna Rockets, 1968
Kelowna TIA Clinic, 1419
Kelowna Transplant Clinic, 1419
Kelowna Waldorf School, 628
Kelowna, *Government Chapter*, 869, 884, 886
Kelowna, *Judicial Chapter*, 1367, 1368
Kelowna, *Municipal Governments Chapter*, 1133
Kelsey Community Law Centre, 1590
Kelsey School Division, 645
Kelsey, *Municipal Governments Chapter*, 1152
Kelso Technologies Inc., 544
Kelt Exploration, 569
Kelvindell Lodge, 1548
Kelvington & Area Hospital, 1542
Kelvington No. 366, *Municipal Governments Chapter*, 1348
Kelvington, *Municipal Governments Chapter*, 1326
Kemp Harvey Burch Kientz Inc., 456
Kemp Harvey Burnaby Chartered Professional Accountants Inc., 455
Kemp Harvey Craig Inc., 456
Kemp Harvey Demers Inc., 457
Kemp Harvey Kelowna Chartered Professional Accountants Inc., 456
Kemp Harvey Kemp Thompson Inc., 456
Kemp Harvey Kok de Roca-Chan Inc., 455
Kemp Harvey Laidman-Betts Inc., 458
Kempenfelt Bay School, 691
Kemptville District Hospital, 1474
Ken Seiling Waterloo Region Museum, 1696
Kenaston & District Chamber of Commerce, 496
Kenaston, *Municipal Governments Chapter*, 1326
Kendal, *Municipal Governments Chapter*, 1326
Kendall & Pandya, 458
Kendall Lane Housing Society, 1464
Kendalwood Montessori School, 706
Kendellhurst Academy, 694
Keng Seng Enterprises Inc., 1741
Kenilworth Media Inc., 1752
Kennebec Manor Inc., 1452
Kennebecasis Public Library, 1676
Kennedy Agrios Llp, 1568
Kennedy Branch Library, 1726
Kennedy Lodge Long Term Care, 1509
Kennedy, Jensen, 1574

Kennedy, *Municipal Governments Chapter*, 1327
Kennedy's Riverside Boarding Home Ltd., 1457
Kenneth A. Clark Law Office, 1646
Kenneth A. Stewart, 1624
Kenneth Allison, 1594
Kenneth B. Krag, 1579
Kenneth Bell CA Business Advisory Group, 460
Kenneth Cristall Law Corporation, 1582
Kenneth D. Smith, 1640
Kenneth Duggan, 1609
Kenneth E. Snider, 1640
Kenneth E. Spencer Memorial Home Inc., 1452
Kenneth Glasner Q.C. Law Corp., 1583
Kenneth Gordon Maplewood School, 621
Kenneth H. Richardson, 1605
Kenneth J. Bennett, 1602
Kenneth J. Naftel, 1618
Kenneth J. Williams, 1610
Kenneth Levene Graduate School of Business, 760
Kenneth Martin, 1593
Kenneth Michalak, 466
Kenneth Ng, 1569
Kenneth P. Swan, 1641
Kenneth R. Beatch, 1572
Kenneth R. Davies, 1621
Kenneth R. Fiddes, 1587
Keno City Mining Museum, 117
Kenora & District Chamber of Commerce, 489
Kenora Catholic District School Board, 676
Kenora Miner & News, 1783
Kenora, *Government Chapter*, 871, 886, 1032
Kenora, *Judicial Chapter*, 1377
Kenora, *Municipal Governments Chapter*, 1198, 1214
Kenosee Lake, *Municipal Governments Chapter*, 1327
The Kensington, 1514
Kensington & Area Chamber of Commerce, 492
Kensington Medical Clinic, 1394
Kensington Public Library, 1700
The Kensington Retirement Living, 1427
Kensington Village, 1513
Kensington, *Municipal Governments Chapter*, 1232
Kent & Essex Mutual Insurance Company, 519
Kent Centre Chamber of Commerce, 485
Kent Line Limited, 1988
Kent Residential Home, 1519
Kent, *Municipal Governments Chapter*, 1138
Kentville Research & Development Centre, *Government Chapter*, 853
Kentville, *Government Chapter*, 871, 886
Kentville, *Judicial Chapter*, 1373, 1372
Kentville, *Municipal Governments Chapter*, 1185
Kentwood Park, 1506
Kenway Mack Slusarchuk Stewart LLP, 454
Kerby News, 1821
Kereluk & Company, 1580
Keremeos Mental Health & Substance Use, 1432
Keremeos Museum, 41
Keremeos, *Municipal Governments Chapter*, 1138
Kerfoot Burroughs Llp, 1583
Kern & Company Law Corp., 1587
Kerns, *Municipal Governments Chapter*, 1214
Kerr & Kerr, 1617
Kerr Wood & Mallory, 1600
Kerrobert & District Health Centre, 1545
Kerrobert & District Museum, 111
Kerrobert Chamber of Commerce, 496
Kerrobert Citizen, 1794
Kerrobert Credit Union Ltd., 503
Kerrobert Home Care Office, 1545
Kerrobert, *Municipal Governments Chapter*, 1327
Kerrwil Publications Ltd., 1752
Kerry A. Bjarnason, 1567
Kerry Wood Nature Centre, 34
Kerry's Place Autism Services, 1518
Kessler Observatory, 121
Kestenberg Siegal Lipkus Llp, 1633
Kestenberg, Rabinowicz & Partners LLP, 462
Kestrel Workplace Legal Counsel Llp, 1583
Kettle River Museum, 41
Kettle Valley Steam Railway, 46
Kevin Fox, Barrister & Solicitor, 1630
Kevin Murphy, 1618
Kevin P. Downie, Barrister & Solicitor, 1596
Kevin W. Romyn, 1622
Kew Park Montessori Day School, 702
Key Media Canada, 1752
Key Murray Law Charlottetown, 1646
The Key Publishing House Inc., 1741

The Metro, 1769
Metro Community Housing Association, 1466
Metro Guide Publishing, 1752
Metro Inc., 538
Métro Média, 1752
Metro Kalyn Community Library, 1659
Metro Toronto Convention Centre Corporation, *Government Chapter*, 1027
Metro Vancouver, *Municipal Governments Chapter*, 1131
Metroland Durham Region Media Group, 1780
Metroland Eastern Ontario Media Group, 1781
Metroland Kawartha Media Group, 1781
Metroland Media Group Ltd., 1752
Metroland Media Toronto, 1783
Metroland North Media Group, 1779
Metrolinx, 1991
Metrolinx, *Government Chapter*, 1033
Metropolitan Community Church of Toronto, 1863
Metropolitan Preparatory Academy, 703
Metropolitan Regional Housing Authority, *Government Chapter*, 998
Metropolitan Tower Life Insurance Company, 520
METROSHOW Vancouver, 238
Metrowesaintlaw Corporation, 1584
Metz L. Ngan, 1636
Mevotech Inc., 2006
Mew & Company Chartered Professional Accountants, 457
Mewatha Beach, *Municipal Governments Chapter*, 1121
Mewinzha Archaeology Gallery, 12
Meyers Davis Llp, 1564
MFL Occupational Health Centre, Inc., 1439
MGM & Associates Chartered Accountants, 460
Mgr. Plourde Public Library, 1676
Mgr. W.J. Conway Public Library, 1675
MH Stimpson & Associates Ltd., 458
MH Vicars School of Massage Therapy, 614
Miami Museum, 51
Micacchi Warnick & Company, Chartered Professional Accountants, 468
Micah House, 1863
Michael A. Handler, 1645
Michael A. King, Chartered Accountant, 461
Michael A. McKee, 1635
Michael A. Tobin, 1597
Michael Argue Chartered Accountant, 466
Michael Atlas, Chartered Accountant, 466
Michael B. Marcovitch, 1568
Michael B. Oliveira, 1618
Michael B. Vaughan Q.C., 1641
Michael C. Crowe, 1576
Michael Capozzi, 1590
Michael Chandler, 1598
Michael D. Bamford, 1593
Michael D. Sanders, 1585
Michael E. Hinchey, 1605
Michael E. Reed, 1599
Michael Evans, Chartered Accountant, 463
Michael F. Boland, 1613
Michael F. Fair, 1623
Michael F. Feindel, 1596
Michael F. Loebach, 1610
Michael G. Barnett, 1623
Michael G. Carey, 1613
Michael G. DeGroote Centre for Medicinal Cannabis Research, 709
Michael G. DeGroote Institute for Infectious Disease Research, 709
Michael G. DeGroote Institute for Pain Research & Care, 709
Michael G. McLachlan, 1635
Michael G. Parent, Law Corporation, 1580
Michael Garron Hospital - Toronto East Health Network, 1481
Michael Gibson Gallery, 13
Michael H. Clancy, 1567
Michael H. Penner, 1598
Michael J. Bondar, Professional Corporation, 1563
Michael J. Dwyer, 1620
Michael J. Fisher, 1612
Michael J. Lamb, 1609
Michael J. O'Shaughnessy, 1601
Michael J. Tadman, 1565
Michael J. Walsh, 1601
Michael J.F. Scully, 1592
Michael K. Titherington, 1641
Michael L. Fowler Professional Corporation, 1620
Michael Mines, 1584
Michael N. Rubenstein, 1606
Michael P. Bird, 1601
Michael P. Clarke, 1605

Michael P. Haddad, 1631
Michael P. O'Hearn, 1645
Michael Pelensky, 1637
Michael P.S. Spearing, 1586
Michael R. Diamond, 1629
Michael R. Eyolfson, 1604
Michael R. Nyhof, 1610
Michael R. White, 1601
Michael Robertson, 1610
Michael S. Puskas, 1606
Michael S. Simrod, 1639
Michael Spiro, 1640
Michael Strathman, 1640
Michael W. Caroline, 1627
Michael W. Egan, 1587
Michael W. Kelly, 1606
Michael Woods, 1613
Michaels & Michaels, 1644
Michaels & Stern, 1591
Michel A. Iacono, 1649
Michel B. Fournier, 1647
Michel C. Arsenault, 1593
Michel C. Leger, 1593
Michel Charbonneau Inc., 1999
Michel Tremblay CPA, 468
Michel Village, *Municipal Governments Chapter*, 1331
Micheline Anne Montreuil, 1651
Michelle E. Hubert, 1599
The Michener Institute for Applied Health Sciences, 270
Michif Métis Museum, 47
Michikan Lake School, 682
Michipicoten First Nation Public Library, 1694
Mickelson & Whysall, 1584
Microbial Fermentation Pilot Plant, *Government Chapter*, 899
Microbix Biosystems Inc., 575
MicroPilot, 2006
Micro-Recyc-Coopération, 208
Microscopical Society of Canada, 360
Midale Branch Library, 1726
Midale, *Municipal Governments Chapter*, 1331
Middle Arm, *Municipal Governments Chapter*, 1172
Middle Lake Museum, 112
Middle Lake, *Municipal Governments Chapter*, 1331
Middle School attached to Hebei Normal University - Shijiazhuang, 764
Middlebro' & Stevens Llp Owen Sound, 1619
Middlechurch Home of Winnipeg Inc., 1444
Middlesex Banner, 1774
Middlesex Centre, *Municipal Governments Chapter*, 1218
Middlesex County Public Library Headquarters, 1693
Middlesex Mutual Insurance Co., 520
Middlesex Terrace, 1493
Middlesex, *Municipal Governments Chapter*, 1194
Middlesex-Lambton-Huron Association of Baptist Churches, 1849
Middleton & Middleton, 1589
Middleton, *Municipal Governments Chapter*, 1185
Middleville & District Museum, 82
Midland Exploration, 557
Midland Gardens Care Community, 1499
Midland Public Library, 1689
Midland Transport Limited, 2000
Midland, *Government Chapter*, 872, 885
Midland, *Municipal Governments Chapter*, 1218
Mid-North Monitor, 1777
Mid-Ocean School of Media Arts, 656
Midway Health Unit, 1420
Midway Public Library, 1668
Midway, *Municipal Governments Chapter*, 1140
Midwestern Newspapers Corp., 1779
Miel's Private Care Home, 1550
MIG Insurance, 520
Migizi Wazisin Elementary School, 683
Migneault Law Office, 1652
Migrant Workers Centre, 303
The Mike, 1842
Mikinaak Onigaming School, 694
Mikisew Middle School, 647
MilAero Electronics Atlantic Inc., 2006
Milan, *Municipal Governments Chapter*, 1271
Milden Community Museum, 112
Milden No. 286, *Municipal Governments Chapter*, 1350
Milden, *Municipal Governments Chapter*, 1331
Mildmay Town & Country Crier, 1779
Mile 918 Driver Development, 763
Mile Oak Publishing Inc., 1743
The Mile Zero News, 1756
Miles Cove, *Municipal Governments Chapter*, 1172

Miles Davison Llp, 1565
Miles M. Halberstadt, Q.C., 1631
Miles Nadal Jewish Community Centre Nursery School, 703
Miles, Daroux, Zimmer & Sheard, 1574
Milestone Library, 1726
Milestone Pharmaceuticals Inc., 575
Milestone, *Municipal Governments Chapter*, 1331
Military Collectors Club of Canada, 318
Military Communications & Electronics Museum, 79
Military Grievances External Review Committee, *Government Chapter*, 892
The Military Museums, 1666
The Military Museums of Calgary, 28
Military Police Complaints Commission, *Government Chapter*, 893
Militia of the Immaculata Canada, 1856
Milk River Health Centre, 1396
Milk River Municipal Library, 1662
Milk River, *Municipal Governments Chapter*, 1121
Mill Cove Nursing Home Inc., 1452
Mill Creek Motor Freight LP, 2000
Mill of Kintail Conservation Area, 70
Mill Site Lodge & Fischer Place, 1422
Mill Woods Centre, 1402
Millar & Keith Llp, 1570
Millar Kreklewetz Llp, 1635
Millar, Alexander, 1606
Millard Foster Thibeault Youell PC, 460
Millards, 460
Millarville Community Library, 1662
Millbrook & District Chamber of Commerce, 489
Millbrook Cultural & Heritage Centre, 67
Millbrook Times, 1779
Mille-Isles, *Municipal Governments Chapter*, 1271
Millennial Lithium, 557
Millennium Insurance Corporation, 520
Miller & Hearn, 1594
Miller & Khazzam, 1649
Miller & Miller, 1635
Miller Boileau, 1568
Miller Canfield Llp (Ontario), 1645
Miller Crossing Long Term Care, 1402
Miller Maki Llp, 1623
Miller Moar Grodecki Kreklewich & Chorney, Chartered Professional Accountants, 470
Miller Museum of Mineralogy & Geology, 79
Miller Pressey Selinger, 1590
Miller Thomson LLP - Calgary, 1560
Miller Thomson LLP - Edmonton, 1560
Miller Thomson LLP - Guelph, 1560
Miller Thomson LLP - London, 1560
Miller Thomson LLP - Markham, 1560
Miller Thomson LLP - Montréal, 1560
Miller Thomson LLP - Regina, 1560
Miller Thomson LLP - Saskatoon, 1561
Miller Thomson LLP - Toronto, 1560
Miller Thomson LLP - Vancouver, 1561
Miller Thomson LLP - Vaughan, 1561
Miller Thomson LLP - Waterloo, 1561
Miller Titerle Llp, 1584
Miller Zoo, 139
Miller, Saperia & Company, 461
Millertown, *Municipal Governments Chapter*, 1173
Millet & District Chamber of Commerce, 478
Millet & District Museum & Archives, 33, 1666
Millet Public Library, 1663
Millet, *Municipal Governments Chapter*, 1121
Millichamp & Company, 1574
Milligan Gresko Limberis Llp, 1606
Mills & Mills Llp, 1635
Mills Memorial Hospital, 1415
Milltown Academy, 651
Milltown-Head of Bay d'Espoir, *Municipal Governments Chapter*, 1173
Millville, *Municipal Governments Chapter*, 1159
Millwoods Public Health Centre, 1394
Milne Pritchard Law Office, 1570
Milner Heritage House, 74
Milo Library, 1663
Milo, *Municipal Governments Chapter*, 1122
Milton Blacksmith Shop Museum, 67
Milton Canadian Champion, 1779
Milton Chamber of Commerce, 489
Milton District Hospital, 1476
Milton No. 292, *Municipal Governments Chapter*, 1350
Milton Public Library, 1689
Milton Shopping News, 1780
Milton, Johnson, 1588

RDK Chartered Accountant Ltd., 459
RDK Transportation Co., 2001
Re/Max Field, 1971
Re:Sound Music Licensing Company, 333
Reach Toronto, 684
ReachView Village, 1509
Ready Arc Training & Testing, 660
Real Estate Board of Greater Vancouver, 347
Real Estate Board of the Fredericton Area Inc., 347
Real Estate Council of Alberta, *Government Chapter*, 934
Real Estate Council of British Columbia, *Government Chapter*, 949
Real Estate Institute of Canada, 347
Real Estate Insurance Exchange, 522
Real Estate Professional, 1813
Real Estate Victoria, 1824
Real Matters Inc., 527
Real Mississauga SC, 1969
Real Property Association of Canada, 347
Real Property Branch, *Government Chapter*, 911
Real Property Division, *Government Chapter*, 945
Realia Properties Inc., 580
Realtors Association of Edmonton, 347
REALTORS Association of Grey Bruce Owen Sound, 347
Realtors Association of Lloydminster & District, 347
Realtors Association of South Central Alberta, 347
Rebecca Butovsky, 1648
Rebecca J. Rutherford, 1638
Rebecca Ling Chartered Accountant Professional Corporation, 462
reBOOT Canada, 284
Recipe Unlimited Corporation, 539
Reciprocity No. 32, *Municipal Governments Chapter*, 1353
Reconnaissance Energy Africa Ltd., 571
The Record, 1786, 1761, 1760
The Recorder & Times, 1776
The Recording Arts Institute of Saskatoon, 762
Recouvrement, de la révision et de la conformité, *Government Chapter*, 1061
Recreation & Parks Association of the Yukon, 350
Recreation & Regional Services, *Government Chapter*, 968
The Recreation Association, 1924
Recreation Facilities Association of British Columbia, 350
Recreation New Brunswick, 351
Recreation Newfoundland & Labrador, 351
Recreation Nova Scotia, 351
Recreation Vehicle Dealers Association of Canada, 187
Recreational Aircraft Association, 1983
Recreational Canoeing Association BC, 1895
Recycling Council of Alberta, 234
Recycling Council of British Columbia, 234
Recycling Council of Ontario, 234
Red Art Gallery, 8
Red Bay National Historic Site of Canada, *Government Chapter*, 61, 904
Red Bay, *Municipal Governments Chapter*, 1175
Red Brick Arts Centre & Museum, 32
Red Coat Road & Rail Ltd., 1995
Red Crow Community College, 611
Red Deer - 49th Street Community Health Centre, 1410, 1396
Red Deer - Bremner Ave. Community Health Centre, 1396
Red Deer - Johnstone Crossing Community Health Centre, 1396
Red Deer & District Archives, 1666
Red Deer & District SPCA, 182
Red Deer Advocate, 1754
Red Deer Catholic Regional Schools, 597
Red Deer Chamber of Commerce, 478, 200
Red Deer City Soccer Association, 1941
Red Deer College, 611
Red Deer County, *Municipal Governments Chapter*, 1109
Red Deer Express, 1757
Red Deer Life, 1757
Red Deer Museum & Art Gallery, 34
Red Deer Nursing Home, 1549
Red Deer Press, 1745
Red Deer Provincial Building, 1400
Red Deer Public Library, 1663
Red Deer Rebels, 1968
Red Deer Regional Hospital Centre, 1391
Red Deer School District, 595
Red Deer Symphony Orchestra Association, 125
Red Deer Transit, 1992
Red Deer, *Government Chapter*, 869, 886
Red Deer, *Judicial Chapter*, 1366
Red Deer, *Municipal Governments Chapter*, 1112
Red Deer: Court of Queen's Bench, *Judicial Chapter*, 1365
Red Earth Creek Community Health Services, 1396
Red Earth Public Library, 1663

Red Harbour, *Municipal Governments Chapter*, 1175
Red Head Gallery, 18
Red Lake District Chamber of Commerce, 490
Red Lake Margaret Cochenour Memorial Hospital, 1479
Red Lake Public Library, 1692
Red Lake Regional Heritage Centre, 87
Red Lake, *Municipal Governments Chapter*, 1223
Red River College, 654
Red River Mutual, 522
Red River Place, 1443
The Red River Valley Echo, 1767
Red River Valley Junior Academy, 652
Red River Valley School Division, 644
Red Road HIV/AIDS Network, 327
Red Rock Public Library, 1692
Red Rock, *Municipal Governments Chapter*, 1223
Red Sky Métis Independent Nation, 327
Red Sucker Lake Education Authority, 646
Red Sucker Lake Nursing Station, 1440
Red Sucker Lake School, 648
Redberry No. 435, *Municipal Governments Chapter*, 1353
Redburn No. 130, *Municipal Governments Chapter*, 1353
Redcliff Historical & Museum Society, 34
Redcliff Public Library, 1663
Redcliff, *Municipal Governments Chapter*, 1123
Reddy Kilowatt Credit Union Ltd., 506
Redeemer Christian High School, 687
Redeemer University College, 730
La Rédemption, *Municipal Governments Chapter*, 1278
Redekop School of Business, 653
Redline Communications Group, 528
Redpath Museum, 102
Redpath Sugar Museum, 92
Redvers Centennial Haven, 1549
Redvers Chamber of Commerce, 497
Redvers Health Centre, 1543
Redvers Library, 1727
Redvers, *Municipal Governments Chapter*, 1335
Redwater & District Chamber of Commerce, 478
Redwater Health Centre, 1396, 1391
Redwater Public Library, 1663
Redwater, *Municipal Governments Chapter*, 1123
Reed Pope Llp, 1588
ReelWorld Film Festival, 240
Reena, 371
Reesthomas & Company, 1579
Reeves College, 614
Reference Press, 1746
The Reflector, 1843
Le Reflet, 1787
Reflet de Société, 1789
Le Reflet du canton de Lingwick, 1788
Le Reflet du Lac, 1788
Reflet Salvéo, 248
Reford No. 379, *Municipal Governments Chapter*, 1353
Reform Party of Alberta, 339
Refrigeration Service Engineers Society (Canada), 276
Refugee Law Office, 1637
Regan Desjardins Llp, 1637
Regency Long Term Care Home, 1497
Regency Park Nursing Home, 1500
Regent Christian Academy, 624
Regent Christian Online Academy, 627
Regent College, 637
Regent Park Community Health Centre, 1488
Régie de l'assurance maladie du Québec, *Government Chapter*, 1058
Régie de l'énergie, *Government Chapter*, 1054
Régie des alcools, des courses et des jeux, *Government Chapter*, 1060
Régie des installations olympiques/Parc olympique Québec, *Government Chapter*, 1060
Régie des marchés agricoles et alimentaires du Québec, *Government Chapter*, 1051
Régie du bâtiment du Québec, *Government Chapter*, 1061
Régie du cinéma, *Government Chapter*, 1052
Régie du logement du Québec, *Government Chapter*, 1051
Régie régionale de la santé et des services sociaux du Nunavik, 1522
Régime québécois d'assurance parentale, *Government Chapter*, 1061
Regina & District Chamber of Commerce, 497
Regina Airport Authority Inc., 1987
Regina Beach Branch Library, 1727
Regina Beach Primary Health Care Centre, 1546
Regina Beach, *Municipal Governments Chapter*, 1335
Regina Catholic School Division, 758
Regina Christian School, 759

Regina General Hospital, 1543
Regina Gliding & Soaring Club, 1939
Regina Huda School, 759
Regina Humane Society Inc., 182
Regina Leader-Post, 1793
Regina Lutheran Home, 1549
Regina Multicultural Council, 322
Regina Pats, 1968
Regina Pioneer Village Ltd., 1549
Regina Public Library, 1727
Regina Public Schools, 757
Regina Regional Opportunities Commission, 380
Regina Sinukoff, 1640
Regina Symphony Orchestra, 133
Regina Therapeutic Riding Association, 1957
Regina Transit, 1992
Regina, *Government Chapter*, 874, 884, 886
Regina, *Judicial Chapter*, 1364, 1384
Regina, *Municipal Governments Chapter*, 1314
Region of Peel Art Gallery, Museum & Archives, 1695
Region of Waterloo Library, 1683
Le Régional, 1778
Regional & Corporate Services Division, *Government Chapter*, 1019, 1032
Regional Analytical Facility, 668
Regional Development Corporation, *Government Chapter*, 977
Regional District of Nanaimo Transit System, 1992
Regional Land Use Planning Commissions, *Government Chapter*, 1081
Regional Municipality of Argyle Public Library, 1672
Regional Offices, *Government Chapter*, 856
Regional Operations & Compliance Branch Offices, *Government Chapter*, 974
Regional Operations & Support Services Division, *Government Chapter*, 976
Regional Operations Division, *Government Chapter*, 1032
Regional Operations Sector, *Government Chapter*, 888
Regional Operations, *Government Chapter*, 1070
Regional Policy & Programs, *Government Chapter*, 966
Regional Psychiatric Centre (Prairies), 1543
Regional Residential Services Society, 1463
Regional Resource Centre, 1410
Regional Service Delivery Branch, *Government Chapter*, 985
Regional Services Branch, *Government Chapter*, 985, 1002
Régionale Ringuette Rive-Sud, 1927
Regis College, 721
Registered Deposit Brokers Association, 242
The Registered Nurses Association of the Northwest Territories & Nunavut, 332
Registered Nurses' Association of Ontario, 332
Registered Practical Nurses Association of Ontario, 332
Registered Professional Foresters Association of Nova Scotia, 247
Registered Psychiatric Nurses Advisory Committee, *Government Chapter*, 1079
Registered Psychiatric Nurses Association of Saskatchewan, 332
Registered Veterinary Technologists & Technicians of Canada, 182
Registres de l'État, *Government Chapter*, 1061
Registry of Joint Stock Companies, *Government Chapter*, 1004
Registry of Motor Vehicles, *Government Chapter*, 1004
Registry of the Courts Administration Service, *Judicial Chapter*, 1364
Regnum Christi Movement, 1856
Regroupement des centres d'amitié autochtone du Québec, 327
Regroupement des jeunes chambres de commerce du Québec, 496
Regroupement des Marocains au Canada, 1869
Regroupement des éditeurs canadiens-français, 343
Regroupement Petapan, 327
Regroupement québécois de la danse, 125
Regroupement québécois des maladies orphelines, 274
Regulatory & Economic Prosecutions & Management Branch, *Government Chapter*, 908
Regulatory & Public Affairs, *Government Chapter*, 868
Regulatory Affairs Branch, *Government Chapter*, 982
Regulatory Affairs, *Government Chapter*, 917
Regulatory Services Division, *Government Chapter*, 1075
Regulatory, Operations & Enforcement Branch, *Government Chapter*, 883
Regulus Resources Inc., 561
Rehabilitation Centre, 1490
Rehabilitation Centre for Children, 1441
Reh-Fit Centre, 1441
REHOBOTH Christian Ministries, 1863
Rehoboth Christian School, 686
Reid & Associates Chartered Professional Accountants Inc., 459

T

T. Frederick Baxter, Barrister & Solicitor, 1622
T. Sam Boutzouvis, 1627
T. Wing Wai, 1586
T+E, 440
Taber & District Chamber of Commerce, 479
Taber & District Museum Society, 1666
Taber Christian School, 603
Taber Health Centre, 1392, 1410
Taber Irrigation Impact Museum, 36
Taber Public Library, 1665
The Taber Times, 1758
Taber, *Municipal Governments Chapter*, 1125, 1109
Table de développement de la production biologique, 175
Table Soccer Association of Canada, 1954
Table Tennis Canada, 1954
Table Tennis Yukon, 1954
Tabor Manor, 1507, 1423
Tabusintac Centennial Memorial Library & Museum, 59
Tabusintac Nursing Home, 1453
Taché, *Municipal Governments Chapter*, 1154
Tacium, Vincent, Orlikow, 1591
Tadoule Lake/Sayisi Nursing Station, 1440
Tadoussac, *Municipal Governments Chapter*, 1308
Taekwondo Canada, 1920
Taekwondo Manitoba, 1921
Tafelmusik, 131
TAG Art Gallery, 14
TAG Oil Ltd., 572
Tagish, *Municipal Governments Chapter*, 1359
Tagé Cho Hudän Interpretive Centre, 117
Tahsis Chamber of Commerce, 482
Tahsis Health Centre, 1421
Tahsis Heritage Museum, 46
Tahsis, *Municipal Governments Chapter*, 1143
TAIE International Institute, 704
Taiga Building Products Ltd., 541
Taiga Times, 1833
Taigh Na Mara, 1464
Taiwanese-Canadian (Toronto) Credit Union Limited, 507
Takla Landing Nursing Station, 1422
Talarico Place, 1423
Talbot Kingsbury Avocats, 1651
Talentvision TV, 438
Talka Credit Union Limited, 507
Tall Pines School, 690
Tallcree Band Education Authority, 598
Talmage & Difiore, 1643
Talmud Torahs Unis de Montréal/Herzliah, 748
Talon Books Ltd., 1747
Taloyoak Judy Hill Memorial Health Centre, 1467
Taloyoak, *Municipal Governments Chapter*, 1191
Talstra Law Corporation, 1580
Tamara Stomp & Associate, 1645
Tamarack Cottage, 1431
Tamarack Recovery Centre Inc., 1441
Tamarack Valley Energy Ltd., 572
Tamil Eelam Society of Canada, 204
Tamilar Thagaval, 1835
Tanbridge Academy, 606
Tandem Financial Credit Union, 507
Tandia Credit Union Limited, 507
Tangent Community Library, 1665
Tangerine Bank, 472
Tangled Art Gallery, 18
Tangshan No. 1 High School, 765
Tania Perlin, 1624
Tannahill, Lockhart & Clark, 1613
Tannis J. Naylor, 1566
Tantallon, *Municipal Governments Chapter*, 1338
Tanz Centre for Research in Neurodegenerative Diseases, 723
Tanzanian Gold Corporation, 563
Tanzola & Sorbara, 1645
Tao & Company, 1586
Taoist Tai Chi Society of Canada, 1875
Taotha School, 683
Tapper Cuddy Llp, 1591
Taqqut Co-operative Ltd., 436
Taras H. Shevchenko Museum, 93
Tarbutt & Tarbutt Additional, *Municipal Governments Chapter*, 1226
Tarragon Theatre, 135
Tarrison & Hunter, 1619
Tartu Institute, 1699
Taschereau, *Municipal Governments Chapter*, 1309
Taseko Mines Limited, 563
Tasiujaq, *Municipal Governments Chapter*, 1309

Tasse & Vescio, 1650
Taste, 1822
Tatagwa View, 1551
Tatamagouche, *Municipal Governments Chapter*, 1186
Tataskweyak Education Authority, 647
Tatham, Pearson Llp, 1641
Tator, Rose & Leong, Chartered Accountants, 467
Tatsikiisaapo'p Middle School, 599
Taveroff & Associates, 1641
Tavistock & District Historical Society, 90
Tavistock Chamber of Commerce, 491
Tavistock Gazette, 1782
Tawowikamik Public Library, 1726
Tax & Fiscal Policy Branch, *Government Chapter*, 984
Tax & Revenue Administration Division, *Government Chapter*, 936
Tax Compliance & Benefits Division, *Government Chapter*, 1024
Tax Court of Canada, *Judicial Chapter*, 1363
Tax Law Services Portfolio, *Government Chapter*, 891
Tax Policy Branch, *Government Chapter*, 877
Taxation & Property Records, *Government Chapter*, 1040
Taxation Division, *Government Chapter*, 965
Taxation Policy Division, *Government Chapter*, 1024
Taxicab Board, *Government Chapter*, 968
The Taxpayer, 1805
Tay Township Public Libraries, 1691
Tay Valley, *Municipal Governments Chapter*, 1226
Tay, *Municipal Governments Chapter*, 1226
Tayllor Maclellan Cochrane, 1597
Taylor & Blair Vancouver, 1586
Taylor & Company, 1586
Taylor & Delrue, 1624
Taylor & Jewell, 1569
Taylor Bardal, 1574
Taylor College & Seminary, 610
Taylor Conway, 1565
Taylor Granitto Inc., 1574
Taylor Jordan Chafetz, 1586
Taylor Law Office, 1590
Taylor Leibow LLP, Accountants & Advisors, 461
Taylor McCaffrey Llp, 1591
Taylor Public Library, 1669
Taylor Publishing Group, 1753
Taylor, Bjorge & Company, 1580
Taylor, Tait, Ruley & Company, 1576
Taylor, *Municipal Governments Chapter*, 1143
Taylor's College, 765
Tayyibah Islamic Academy, 704
Tbaytel, 436
TC Energy, 587
TCS Chronic Kidney Disease Clinic, 1419
TCS Heart Function Clinic, 1419
TCU Financial Group, 507
TD Friends of the Environment Foundation, 235
TD Gallery of Indigenous Art, 18
TD General Insurance Company, 523
TD Home & Auto Insurance Company, 523
TD Life Insurance Company, 524
TD Place, 1971
TDChristian High School, 688
TDM Technical Services, 2007
Te Hennepe Gerrit, 1583
Tea & Herbal Association of Canada, 245
Teach Magazine, 1806
Teacher Certification Board, *Government Chapter*, 1080
Teacher Profession Appeal Board, *Government Chapter*, 1081
Teacher Qualification Board, *Government Chapter*, 1080
Teacher Regulation Branch, *Government Chapter*, 946
Teachers Plus Credit Union, 507
Teachers' Retirement Allowances Fund Board, *Government Chapter*, 963
Teachers' Superannuation Commission, *Government Chapter*, 1039, 1069
Teaching Support Staff Union, 297
Team Handball Ontario, 1912
TEAM School, 694
Teamsters Canada, 1984
Teamsters Canada Rail Conference, 1984
Teamwork Children's Services International, 208
Tebo Vocational Centre, 638
Technion Canada, 355
TechnoKids Inc., 1747
Technologies de l'information et des registres, *Government Chapter*, 1057
Technologies de l'information, *Government Chapter*, 1059
Technologies for Worship Magazine, 1806
Technology & Information Management Services Directorate, *Government Chapter*, 914

Technology Commercialization Centre, 609
Technology Services, *Government Chapter*, 978
Technology Solutions, *Government Chapter*, 946
Technology, Society, Environment Studies, 714
TechNova, 229
Teck Centennial Library, 1688
Teck Pioneer Residence, 1504
Teck Resources Limited, 563
Tecsys Inc., 527
Tecumseh Community Development Corporation, 328
Tecumseh No. 65, *Municipal Governments Chapter*, 1355
Tecumseh, *Municipal Governments Chapter*, 1226
Ted R. Croll, 1567
Ted Rogers School of Management, 720
Ted Stuckless Fine Arts & Driftwood Gallery, 10
Ted Yoannou & Associates Toronto, 1641
Teed & Teed, 1593
Teed Saunders Doyle & Co. Chartered Accountants, 459
Teen Haven, 1533
Teen Health Centre, 1489
Tees Kiddle Spencer, 1573
Teeterville Pioneer Museum, 90, 1697
Teffler School of Management, 716
Tehkummah Township Public Library, 1693
Tehkummah, *Municipal Governments Chapter*, 1227
TekSavvy Solutions Inc., 436
Télé Inter-Rives ltée, 395
Télé locale Axion, 434, 433
Telebimbi, 440
Télécable Multivision inc., 437
Télécâble Pessamit, 437
Telecommunications Employees Association of Manitoba, 2021
Telecommunities Canada Inc., 377
TelecomPioneers of Alberta, 377
TelecomPioneers of Canada, 377
Telefilm Canada, *Government Chapter*, 862, 914
The Telegram, 1770
Telegraph Creek Nursing Station, 1422
The Telegraph-Journal, 1770
TeleNiños, 440
Telephone Booth Gallery, 18
Télé-Québec, 395
Télévision DERYtélécom, 433
Telfer Place Retirement Residence, 1506
Telkwa Museum, 46
Telkwa, *Municipal Governments Chapter*, 1143
The TELL, 18
Telson Mining Corporation, 563
TELUS Communications Company, 529
TELUS Spark, 136
TELUS World of Science - Edmonton, 136
Temagami & District Chamber of Commerce, 491
Temagami First Nation Public Library, 1688
Temagami Public Library, 1693
Temagami, *Municipal Governments Chapter*, 1227
Témiscaming, *Municipal Governments Chapter*, 1309
Témiscamingue, *Municipal Governments Chapter*, 1309
Témiscouata, *Municipal Governments Chapter*, 1309
Témiscouata-sur-le-Lac, *Municipal Governments Chapter*, 1309
Temiskaming Art Gallery, 12
Temiskaming Hospital, 1476
Temiskaming Lodge, 1494
Temiskaming Shores & Area Chamber of Commerce, 491
Temiskaming Shores Public Library, 1687
Temiskaming Shores, *Municipal Governments Chapter*, 1202
The Temiskaming Speaker, 1780
Temple City Star, 1755
Temple Har Zion Religious School, 698
Temple Insurance Company, 524
Temple Kol Ami Religious School, 698
Temple Sinai Hebrew & Religious School, 704
Templeman Menninga Llp Belleville, 1600
Tempo School, 606
Téms Swiya Museum, 45
Ten Speed Press, 1747
Tendercare Living Centre, 1499
Tenderwood Lodge Inc., 1521
Tenenbaum & Solomon, 1611
Tenisci Piva LLP, 456
Tennis BC, 1955
Tennis Canada, 1955
Tennis Manitoba, 1955
Tennis New Brunswick, 1955
Tennis Newfoundland & Labrador, 1955
Tennis Québec, 1955
Tennis Saskatchewan, 1955
Tennis Yukon Association, 1956
Tenold Transportation LP, 2001

CANADA'S INFORMATION RESOURCE CENTRE (CIRC)

Access all these great resources online, all the time, at Canada's Information Resource Centre (CIRC)

http://circ.greyhouse.ca

Canada's Information Resource Centre (CIRC) integrates all of Grey House Canada's award-winning reference content into one easy-to-use online resource. With **over 100,000 Canadian organizations** and **over 140,600 contacts**, plus thousands of additional facts and figures, CIRC is the most comprehensive resource for specialized database content in Canada! Access all 20 databases, including the recently revised *Careers & Employment Canada*, with Canada Info Desk Complete - it's the total package!

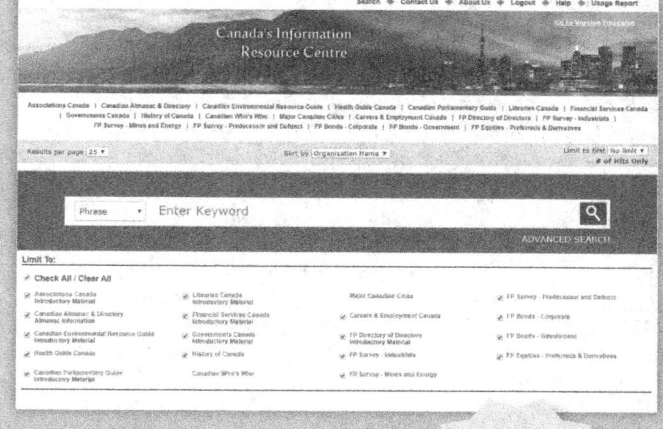

KEY ADVANTAGES OF CIRC:

- Seamlessly cross-database search content from select databases
- Save search results for future reference
- Link directly to websites or email addresses
- Clear display of your results makes compiling and adding to your research easier than ever before

DESIGN YOUR OWN CUSTOM CONTACT LISTS!

CIRC gives you the option to define and extract your own lists in seconds. Find new business leads, do keyword searches, locate upcoming conference attendees; all the information you want is right at your fingertips.

New Careers & Employment Canada

CHOOSE BETWEEN KEYWORD AND ADVANCED SEARCH!

With CIRC, you can choose between Keyword and Advanced search to pinpoint information. Designed for both beginner and advanced researchers, you can conduct simple text searches as well as powerful Boolean searches.

PROFILES IN CIRC INCLUDE:

- Phone numbers, email addresses, fax numbers and full addresses for all branches of the organization
- Social media accounts, such as Twitter and Facebook
- Key contacts based on job titles
- Budgets, membership fees, staff sizes and more!

Search CIRC using common or unique fields, customized to your needs!

ONLY GREY HOUSE DIRECTORIES PROVIDE SPECIAL CONTENT YOU WON'T FIND ANYWHERE ELSE!

- **Associations Canada:** finances/funding sources, activities, publications, conferences, membership, awards, member profile
- **Canadian Parliamentary Guide:** private and political careers of elected members, complete list of constituencies and representatives
- **Financial Services:** type of ownership, number of employees, year founded, assets, revenue, ticker symbol
- **Libraries Canada:** staffing, special collections, services, year founded, national library symbol, regional system
- **Governments Canada:** municipal population
- **Canadian Who's Who:** birth city, publications, education (degrees, alma mater), career/occupation and employer
- **Major Canadian Cities:** demographics, ethnicity, immigration, language, education, housing, income, labour and transportation
- **Health Guide Canada:** chronic and mental illnesses, general resources, appendices and statistics
- **Cannabis Canada:** firm type, foreign activity, type of ownership, revenue sources
- **Canadian Environmental Resource Guide:** organization scope, budget, number of employees, activities, regulations, areas of environmental specialty
- **Careers & Employment Canada:** career associations, career employment websites, expanded employers, recruiters, awards and scholarships, and summer jobs
- **FP Directory of Directors:** names, directorships, educational and professional backgrounds and email addresses of top Canadian directors; list of major companies and complete company contact information
- **FPbonds:** bond information in PDF form and with sortable tables
- **FPsurvey:** detailed profiles of current publicly traded companies, as well as past corporate changes

The new CIRC provides easier searching and faster, more pinpointed results of all of our great resources in Canada, from Associations and Government to Major Companies to Zoos and everything in between. Whether you need fully detailed information on your contact or just an email address, you can customize your search query to meet your needs.

Contact us now for a **free trial** subscription or visit **http://circ.greyhouse.ca**

For more information please contact Grey House Publishing Canada

Tel.: (866) 433-4739 or (416) 644-6479 Fax: (416) 644-1904 | info@greyhouse.ca | www.greyhouse.ca

CENTRE DE DOCUMENTATION DU CANADA (CDC)

Consultez en tout temps toutes ces excellentes ressources en ligne grâce au Centre de documentation du Canada (CDC) à
http://circ.greyhouse.ca

Le Centre de documentation du Canada (CDC) regroupe sous une seule ressource en ligne conviviale tout le contenu des ouvrages de référence primés de Grey House Canada. Répertoriant plus de **100 000 entreprises canadiennes**, et plus de **140 600 personnes-ressources**, faits et chiffres, il s'agit de la ressource la plus complète en matière de bases de données spécialisées au Canada! Grâce à l'ajout de sept bases de données, le Canada Info Desk Complete est plus avantageux que jamais alors qu'il coûte 50 % que l'abonnement aux ouvrages individuels. Accédez aux 20 bases de données dès maintenant — le Canadian Info Desk Complete vous offre un ensemble complet!

Nouveau Carrières et emplois Canada

PRINCIPAUX AVANTAGES DU CDC

- Recherche transversale efficace dans le contenu des bases de données
- Sauvegarde des résultats de recherche pour consultation future
- Lien direct aux sites Web et aux adresses électroniques
- Grâce à l'affichage lisible de vos résultats, il est dorénavant plus facile de compiler les résultats ou d'ajouter des critères à vos recherches

CONCEPTION PERSONNALISÉE DE VOS LISTES DE PERSONNES-RESSOURCES!

Le CDC vous permet de définir et d'extraire vos propres listes, et ce, en quelques secondes.
Découvrez des clients potentiels, effectuez des recherches par mot-clé, trouvez les participants à une conférence à venir : l'information dont vous avez besoin, au bout de vos doigts.

CHOISISSEZ ENTRE RECHERCHES MOT-CLÉ ET AVANCÉE!

Grâce au CDC, vous pouvez choisir entre une recherche Mot-clé ou Avancée pour localiser l'information avec précision. Vous avez la possibilité d'effectuer des recherches en texte simple ou booléennes puissantes -- les recherches sont conçues à l'intention des chercheurs débutants et avancés.

LES PROFILS DU CDC COMPRENNENT :

- Numéros de téléphone, adresses électroniques, numéros de télécopieur et adresses complètes pour toutes les succursales d'un organisme
- Comptes de médias sociaux, comme Twitter et Facebook
- Personnes-ressources clés en fonction des appellations d'emploi
- Budgets, frais d'adhésion, tailles du personnel et plus!

Effectuez des recherches dans le CDC à l'aide de champs uniques ou communs, personnalisés selon vos besoins!

SEULS LES RÉPERTOIRES DE GREY HOUSE VOUS OFFRENT UN CONTENU PARTICULIER QUE VOUS NE TROUVEREZ NULLE PART AILLEURS!

- **Le répertoire des associations du Canada :** sources de financement, activités, publications, congrès, membres, prix, profil de membre
- **Guide parlementaire canadien :** carrières privées et politiques des membres élus, liste complète des comtés et des représentants
- **Services financiers :** type de propriétaire, nombre d'employés, année de la fondation, immobilisations, revenus, symbole au téléscripteur
- **Bibliothèques Canada :** personnel, collections particulières, services, année de la fondation, symbole de bibliothèque national, système régional
- **Gouvernements du Canada :** population municipale
- **Canadian Who's Who :** ville d'origine, publication, formation (diplômes et alma mater), carrière/emploi et employeur
- **Principales villes canadiennes :** données démographiques, ethnicité, immigration, langue, éducation, logement, revenu, main-d'œuvre et transport
- **Guide canadien de la santé :** maladies chroniques et mentales, ressources generales, annexes et statistiques
- **Cannabis au Canada :** type d'entreprise, activité à l'étranger, type de propriété, sources de revenus
- **Guide des ressources environnementales canadiennes :** périmètre organisationnel, budget, nombre d'employés, activités, réglementations, domaines de spécialité environnementale
- **Carrières et emplois Canada :** associations professionnelles, sites Web d'emplois, employeurs, recruteurs, bourses, et emplois d'été
- **Répertoire des administrateurs :** prénom, nom de famille, poste de cadre et d'administrateur, parcours scolaire et professionnel et adresse électronique des cadres supérieurs canadiens; liste des sociétés les plus importantes au Canada et l'information complète des compagnies
- **FPbonds :** information sur les obligations en format PDF, avec tableaux à trier
- **FPsurvey :** profils détaillés de sociétés cotées en bourse et changements organisationnels antérieurs

Le nouveau CDC facilite la recherche au sein de toutes nos ressources au Canada et procure plus rapidement des résultats plus poussés — des associations au gouvernement en passant par les principales entreprises et les zoos, sans oublier tout un éventail d'organisations! Que vous ayez besoin d'information très détaillée au sujet de votre personne-ressource ou d'une simple adresse électronique, vous pouvez personnaliser votre requête afin qu'elle réponde à vos besoins.
Contactez-nous sans tarder pour obtenir un **essai gratuit** ou visitez http://circ.greyhouse.ca

Canadian Who's Who

Canadian Who's Who is the only authoritative publication of its kind in Canada, offering access to the top 10 000 notable Canadians in all walks of life. Published annually to provide current and accurate information, the familiar bright-red volume is recognized as the standard reference source of contemporary Canadian biography.

Documenting the achievement of Canadians from a wide variety of occupations and professions, *Canadian Who's Who* records the diversity of culture in Canada. These biographies are organized alphabetically and provide detailed information on the accomplishments of notable Canadians, from coast to coast. All who are interested in the achievements of Canada's most influential citizens and their significant contributions to the country and the world beyond should acquire this reference title.

Detailed entries give date and place of birth, education, family details, career information, memberships, creative works, honours, languages, and awards, together with full addresses. Included are outstanding Canadians from business, academia, politics, sports, the arts and sciences, etc.

Every year the publisher invites new individuals to complete questionnaires from which new biographies are compiled. The publisher also gives those already listed in earlier editions an opportunity to update their biographies. Those listed are selected because of the positions they hold in Canadian society, or because of the contributions they have made to Canada.

AVAILABLE ONLINE!

Canadian Who's Who is also available online, through Canada's Information Resource Centre (CIRC). Readers can access this title's in-depth and vital networking content in the format that best suits their needs—in print, by subscription or online.

The print edition of *Canadian Who's Who 2022* contains 10,000 entries, while the online edition gives users access to nearly 26,000 biographies, including all current listings and over 14,500 archived biographies dating back to 1999.

GREY HOUSE PUBLISHING CANADA

For more information please contact Grey House Publishing Canada

Tel.: (866)-433-4739 or (416) 644-6479 Fax: (416) 644-1904 | info@greyhouse.ca | www.greyhouse.ca

Canadian Who's Who

  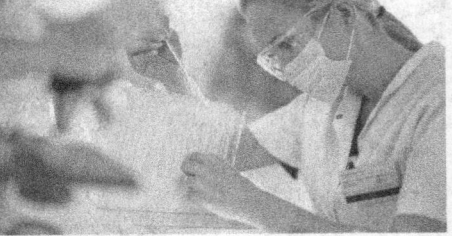

Canadian Who's Who est la seule publication digne de foi de son genre au Canada. Elle donne accès 10 000 dignitaires canadiens de tous les horizons. L'ouvrage annuel rouge vif bien connu, rempli d'information à jour et exacte, est la référence standard en matière de biographies canadiennes contemporaines.

Canadian Who's Who, qui porte sur les réalisations de Canadiens occupant une vaste gamme de postes et de professions, illustre la diversité de la culture canadienne. Ces biographies sont classées en ordre alphabétique et donnent de l'information détaillée sur les réalisations de Canadiens éminents, d'un océan à l'autre. Tous ceux qui s'intéressent aux réalisations des citoyens les plus influents au Canada et à leurs contributions importantes au pays et partout dans le monde doivent se procurer cet ouvrage de référence.

Les entrées détaillées indiquent la date et le lieu de la naissance, traitent de l'éducation, de la famille, de la carrière, des adhésions, des œuvres de création, des distinctions, des langues et des prix - en plus des adresses complètes. Elles comprennent des Canadiens exceptionnels du monde des affaires, des universités, de la politique, des sports, des arts, des sciences et plus encore!

Chaque année, l'éditeur invite de nouvelles personnes à remplir les questionnaires à partir desquels il prépare les nouvelles biographies. Il le remet également aux personnes qui font partie de numéros antérieurs afin de leur permettre d'effectuer une mise à jour. Les personnes retenues le sont en raison des postes qu'elles occupent dans la société canadienne ou de leurs contributions au Canada.

OFFERT EN FORMAT ÉLECTRONIQUE!

Canadian Who's Who est également offert en ligne par l'entremise du Centre de documentation du Canada (CDC). Les lecteurs peuvent accéder au contenu approfondi et essentiel au réseautage de cet ouvrage dans le format qui leur convient le mieux - version imprimée, en ligne ou par abonnement.

L'édition imprimée de *Canadian Who's Who 2022* compte 10 000 entrées tandis qu'en consultant la version en ligne, les utilisateurs ont accès à 26 000 biographies, dont fi ches d'actualité et plus de 14 500 biographies archives qui remontent jusqu'à 1999.

GREY HOUSE PUBLISHING CANADA

Pour obtenir plus d'information, veuillez contacter Grey House Publishing Canada
par tél. : 1 866 433-4739 ou 416 644-6479 par téléc. : 416 644-1904 | info@greyhouse.ca | www.greyhouse.ca

Canadian Parliamentary Guide

Your Number One Source for All General Federal Elections Results!

Published annually since before Confederation, the *Canadian Parliamentary Guide* is an indispensable directory, providing biographical information on elected and appointed members in federal and provincial government. Featuring government institutions such as the Governor General's Household, Privy Council and Canadian legislature, this comprehensive collection provides historical and current election results with statistical, provincial and political data.

THE CANADIAN PARLIAMENTARY GUIDE IS BROKEN DOWN INTO FIVE COMPREHENSIVE CATEGORIES

Monarchy—biographical information on Her Majesty Queen Elizabeth II, The Royal Family and the Governor General

Federal Government—a separate chapter for each of the Privy Council, Senate and House of Commons (including a brief description of the institution, its history in both text and chart format and a list of current members), followed by unparalleled biographical sketches*

General Elections

1867–2019

- information is listed alphabetically by province then by riding name

- notes on each riding include: date of establishment, date of abolition, former division and later divisions, followed by election year and successful candidate's name and party

- by-election information follows

2021

- information for the 2021 election is organized in the same manner but also includes information on all the candidates who ran in each riding, their party affiliation and the number of votes won

Provincial and Territorial Governments—Each provincial chapter includes:

- statistical information

- description of Legislative Assembly

- biographical sketch of the Lieutenant Governor or Commissioner

- list of current Cabinet Members

- dates of legislatures since confederation

- current Members and Constituencies

- biographical sketches*

- general election and by-election results, including the most recent provincial and territorial elections.

Courts: Federal—each court chapter includes a description of the court (Supreme, Federal, Federal Court of Appeal, Court Martial Appeal and Tax Court), its history and a list of its judges followed by biographical sketches*

* Biographical sketches follow a concise yet in-depth format:

Personal Data—place of birth, education, family information

Political Career—political career path and services

Private Career—work history, organization memberships, military history

AVAILABLE IN PRINT AND NOW ONLINE!

Available in hardcover print, the *Canadian Parliamentary Guide* is also available electronically via the Web, providing instant access to the government officials you need and the facts you want every time. Use the web version to narrow your search with index fields such as institution, province and name.

Create your own contact lists! Online subscribers can instantly generate their own contact lists and export information into spreadsheets for further use. A great alternative to high cost list broker services!

GREY HOUSE PUBLISHING CANADA

For more information please contact Grey House Publishing Canada

Tel.: (866)-433-4739 or (416) 644-6479 Fax: (416) 644-1904 | info@greyhouse.ca | www.greyhouse.ca

Guide parlementaire canadien

Votre principale source d'information en matière de résultats d'élections fédérales!

Publié annuellement depuis avant la Confédération, le *Guide parlementaire canadien* est une source fondamentale de notices biographiques des membres élus et nommés aux gouvernements fédéral et provinciaux. Il y est question, notamment, d'établissements gouvernementaux comme la résidence du gouverneur général, le Conseil privé et la législature canadienne. Ce recueil exhaustif présente les résultats historiques et actuels accompagnés de données statistiques, provinciales et politiques.

OFFERT EN FORMAT PAPIER ET DÉSORMAIS ÉLECTRONIQUE!

LE GUIDE PARLEMENTAIRE CANADIEN EST DIVISÉ EN CINQ CATÉGORIES EXHAUSTIVES:

La monarchie—des renseignements biographiques sur Sa Majesté la reine Elizabeth II, la famille royale et le gouverneur général.

Le gouvernement fédéral—un chapitre distinct pour chacun des sujets suivants: Conseil privé, sénat, Chambre des communes (y compris une brève description de l'institution, son historique sous forme de textes et de graphiques et une liste des membres actuels) suivi de notes biographiques sans pareil.*

Les élections fédérales

1867–2019

- Les renseignements sont présentés en ordre alphabétique par province puis par circonscription.

- Les notes de chaque circonscription comprennent : La date d'établissement, la date d'abolition, l'ancienne circonscription, les circonscriptions ultérieures, etc. puis l'année d'élection ainsi que le nom et le parti des candidats élus.

- Viennent ensuite des renseignements sur l'élection partielle.

2021

- Les renseignements de l'élection 2021 sont organisés de la même manière, mais comprennent également de l'information sur tous les candidats qui se sont présentés dans chaque circonscription, leur appartenance politique et le nombre de voix récoltées.

Gouvernements provinciaux et territoriaux—Chaque chapitre portant sur le gouvernement provincial comprend :

- des renseignements statistiques

- une description de l'Assemblée législative

- des notes biographiques sur le lieutenant-gouverneur ou le commissaire

- une liste des ministres actuels

- les dates de périodes législatives depuis la Confédération

- une liste des membres et des circonscriptions

- des notes biographiques*

- les résultats d'élections générales et partielles, y compris les dernières élections provinciales et territoriales.

Cours : fédérale—chaque chapitre comprend : une description de la cour (suprême, fédérale, cour d'appel fédérale, cour d'appel de la cour martiale et cour de l'impôt), son histoire, une liste des juges qui y siègent ainsi que des notes biographiques.*

* Les notes biographiques respectent un format concis, bien qu'approfondi :

Renseignements personnels—lieu de naissance, formation, renseignements familiaux

Carrière politique—cheminement politique et service public

Carrière privée—antécédents professionnels, membre d'organisations, antécédents militaires

Offert sous couverture rigide ou en format électronique grâce au web, le *Guide parlementaire canadien* donne invariablement un accès instantané aux représentants du gouvernement et aux faits qui font l'objet de vos recherches. Servez-vous de la version en ligne afin de circonscrire vos recherches grâce aux champs spéciaux de l'index comme l'institution, la province et le nom.

Créez vos propres listes! Les abonnés au service en ligne peuvent générer instantanément leurs propres listes de contacts et les exporter en format feuille de calcul pour une utilisation approfondie – une solution de rechange géniale aux services dispendieux d'un commissionnaire en publipostage!

Photo de le très honorable Justin Trudeau par Adam Scotti. Photo fournie par le Bureau du Premier ministre © Sa Majesté la Reine du Chef du Canada, 2021.

GREY HOUSE PUBLISHING CANADA

Pour obtenir plus d'information, veuillez contacter Grey House Publishing Canada

par tél. : 1 866 433-4739 ou 416 644-6479 par téléc. : 416 644-1904 | info@greyhouse.ca | www.greyhouse.ca

Directory of Directors

Your Best Source for Hard-to-Find Business Information

Since 1931, the *Financial Post Directory of Directors* has been recognizing leading Canadian companies and their execs. Today, this title is one of the most comprehensive resources for hard-to-find Canadian business information, allowing readers to access roughly 16,800 executive contacts from Canada's top 1,400 corporations. This prestigious title offers a definitive list of directorships and offices held by noteworthy Canadian business people. It also provides details on leading Canadian companies—publicly traded and privately-owned, including company name, contact information and the names of their executive officers and directors.

ACCESS THE COMPANIES & DIRECTORS YOU NEED IN NO TIME!

The updated 2022 edition of the *Directory of Directors* is jam-packed with information, including:

- ALL-NEW **front matter**: An infographic drawn from data in the book, a summary of the latest Annual Report Card on board diversity, reports on diversity disclosure practices and executive compensation in Canada, and rankings from the FP500.

- **Personal listings**: First name, last name, gender, birth date, degrees, schools attended, executive positions and directorships, previous positions held, main business address and more.

- **Company listings**: Boards of directors and executive officers, head office address, phone and fax numbers, toll-free number, web and email addresses.

Powerful indexes enabling researchers to target just the information they need include:

- An **industrial classification index**: List of key Canadian companies, sorted by industry type according to the Global Industry Classification Standard (GICS®).

- A **geographic location index** grouping all companies in the Company Listings section according to the city and province/state of the head office; and

- An **alphabetical list of abbreviations** providing definitions of common abbreviations used for terms, titles, organizations, honours/fellowships and degrees throughout the Directory.

GREY HOUSE PUBLISHING CANADA

For more information please contact Grey House Publishing Canada

Tel.: (866)-433-4739 or (416) 644-6479 Fax: (416) 644-1904 | info@greyhouse.ca | www.greyhouse.ca

Répertoire des administrateurs

Votre source par excellence de renseignements professionnels difficiles à trouver

Depuis 1931, le Financial Post Directory of Directors (Répertoire des administrateurs du Financial Post) reconnaît les sociétés canadiennes importantes et leur haute direction. De nos jours, cet ouvrage compte parmi certaines des ressources les plus exhaustives lorsqu'il est question des renseignements d'affaires canadiens difficiles à trouver. Il permet aux lecteurs d'accéder à environ 16 800 coordonnées d'administrateurs provenant des 1 400 sociétés les plus importantes au Canada. Ce document prestigieux comprend une liste définitive des postes d'administrateurs et des fonctions que ces gens d'affaires canadiens remarquables occupent. Il offre également des détails sur des sociétés canadiennes importantes – privées ou négociées sur le marché – y compris le nom de l'entreprise, ses coordonnées et le nombre des membres de sa haute direction et de ses administrateurs.

UN ACCÈS RAPIDE ET FACILE À TOUS LES ENTREPRISES ET DIRECTEURS DONT VOUS AVEZ BESOIN!

La version mise à jour de 2022 du Répertoire des administrateurs du Financial Post est remplie d'information, notamment:

- **NOUVELLE section de textes préliminaires** –une infographie inspirée des données de l'ouvrage; un résumé du dernier rapport annuel sur la diversité des conseils d'administration; rapports sur les pratiques de divulgation de la diversité et la rémunération des dirigeants au Canada; le classement le plus récent au FP500.

- **Données personnelles** – prénom, nom de famille, sexe, date de naissance, diplômes, écoles fréquentées, poste de cadre et d'administrateur, postes occupés préalablement, adresse professionnelle principale et plus encore.

- **Listes de sociétés** – conseils d'administration et cadres supérieurs, adresse du siège social, numéros de téléphone et de télécopieur, numéro sans frais, adresse électronique et site Web.

Des index puissants permettent aux utilisateurs de cibler l'information dont ils ont besoin, notamment:

- **Index de classement industriel** - énumère les sociétés classées par type d'industrie général selon le Global Industry Classification Standard (GICS^{MD}).

- l'**Index des emplacements géographiques** qui comprend toutes les sociétés de la section Liste des sociétés en fonction de la ville et de la province/de l'état où se trouve le siège social;

- une **liste des abréviations en ordre alphabétique** définit les abréviations courantes pour la terminologie, les titres, les organisations, les distinctions/fellowships et les diplômes mentionnés dans le Répertoire.

OFFERT EN FORMAT ÉLECTRONIQUE!

Le Répertoire est également accessible en ligne par l'entremise du Centre de documentation du Canada. Les lecteurs peuvent accéder au contenu approfondi et essentiel au réseautage de cet ouvrage dans le format qui leur convient le mieux - version imprimée, en ligne ou par abonnement.

Créez vos propres listes! Les abonnés au service en ligne peuvent générer instantanément leurs propres listes de contacts et les exporter en format feuille de calcul pour une utilisation approfondie – une solution de rechange géniale aux services dispendieux d'un commissionnaire en publipostage.

Pour obtenir plus d'information, veuillez contacter Grey House Publishing Canada
par tél. : 1 866 433-4739 ou 416 644-6479 par téléc. : 416 644-1904 | info@greyhouse.ca | www.greyhouse.ca

Associations du Canada
La recherche d'organisations simplifiée

Il s'agit d'un recueil facile d'utilisation qui offre des index, des fiches descriptives et des résumés exhaustifs de plus de 20 500 organismes locaux, régionaux, provinciaux, nationaux et internationaux. Il donne, entre autres, des détails sur leur emplacement, leur budget, leur date de mise sur pied, l'éventail de leurs activités et leurs sources de financement.

En plus d'affecter plus d'un milliard de dollars annuellement aux frais de transport, à la participation à des congrès et à la mise en marché, *Associations du Canada* débourse des millions de dollars dans sa quête pour répondre aux intérêts de ses membres.

DES INDEX PUISSANTS QUI VOUS AIDENT À CIBLER LES ORGANISATIONS VOULUES

Vous pouvez vous servir de plusieurs critères pour cibler des organisations précises. C'est avec l'utilisateur en tête qu'*Associations du Canada* a été divisé en plusieurs index pour vous aider à trouver, rapidement et facilement, ce que vous cherchez.

- **Index des sujets**—liste des sièges sociaux d'associations canadiennes et étrangères; sujets classés en ordre alphabétique et mot-clé.
- **Index des acronymes**—liste alphabétique des acronymes et des associations canadiennes et étrangères équivalentes; présenté dans les deux langues officielles.
- **Index des budgets**—associations canadiennes classées en ordre alphabétique parmi huit catégories de budget.
- **Index des congrès**—rencontres commanditées par des associations canadiennes et étrangères; classées en ordre alphabétique selon le titre de l'événement.
- **Index des directeurs**—liste alphabétique des principales personnes-ressources des associations canadiennes, aux sièges sociaux et aux succursales.
- **Index géographique**—liste des sièges sociaux, des succursales, des sections régionales et des divisions des associations canadiennes; ordre alphabétique au sein des provinces et des villes.
- **Index des listes de distribution**—liste des associations qui offrent des listes de distribution; en ordre alphabétique selon le sujet.
- **Index des œuvres de bienfaisance enregistrées**—liste des associations enregistrées en tant qu'œuvres de bienfaisance; en ordre alphabétique selon le sujet.

OFFERT EN FORMAT PAPIER OU EN LIGNE—UN ACCÈS RAPIDE ET FACILE À TOUS LES RENSEIGNEMENTS DONT VOUS AVEZ BESOIN!

Offert sous couverture souple ou en format électronique grâce au web, *Associations du Canada* donne invariablement un accès instantané aux personnes et aux faits dont vous avez besoin. Si la version imprimée est vérifiée et mise à jour annuellement, des changements continus sont apportés mensuellement à la base de données en ligne. Servez-vous de la version en ligne afin de circonscrire vos recherches grâce à des champs spéciaux de l'index comme le nom de l'organisation ou son type, le sujet, l'emplacement, le nom de la personne-ressource ou son titre et le code postal.

Créez vos propres listes! Les abonnés au service en ligne peuvent générer instantanément leurs propres listes de contacts et les exporter en format feuille de calcul pour une utilisation approfondie – une solution de rechange géniale aux services dispendieux d'un commissionnaire en publipostage.

Pour obtenir plus d'information, veuillez contacter Grey House Publishing Canada

par tél. : 1 866 433-4739 ou 416 644-6479 par téléc. : 416 644-1904 | info@greyhouse.ca | www.greyhouse.ca

Careers & Employment Canada

Careers & Employment Canada is the go-to resource for job-seekers across Canada, with detailed, current information on everything from industry associations to summer job opportunities. Divided into five helpful sections, this guide contains 10,000 organizations and 20,000 industry contacts to aid in research and jump-start careers in a variety of fields.

ADDITIONAL RESOURCES INCLUDE:

- **Associations**
- **Employers**
  - Arts & Culture
  - Business & Finance
  - Education
  - Environmental
  - Government
  - Healthcare
  - Legal
  - Major Corporations in Canada
  - Telecommunications & Media
  - Transportation

- **Recruiters**
- **Summer Jobs**
- **Career & Employment Websites**
  - National & Regional
  - Industry
  - Topic-Specific
  - Employment Options
  - Clientele
  - Where to Get Resources

Rounding off this guide are 70 pages of reports on the current job market in Canada, a list of industry Awards and Honours, as well as Entry, Executive, and Government Contact indexes for even easier reference. Valuable for employment professionals, librarians, teachers, and job-seekers alike, *Careers & Employment Canada* helps take the strain out of job searching by providing a direct link to the organizations and contacts that matter most.

A CLOSER LOOK AT WHAT'S INSIDE:

Reports on the Job Market—A series of articles on the current job market sourced from Statistics Canada—everything from equity in the workplace to the many ways in which the COVID-19 pandemic has affected the labour market.

Associations—Nearly 800 national associations covering an array of industries and professions.

Employers—Need-to-know companies and organizations broken down into 11 master categories such as Arts & Culture, Education, Government, and Telecommunications & Media.

Recruiters—Top recruiting firms across Canada, organized by national and provincial scope.

Summer Jobs—National and regional summer job opportunities—everything from government agencies to summer camps

Career & Employment Websites—Includes hiring and job board platforms broken down by industry, employment tools, and resources by job type and specialized clientele such as Indigenous, New Canadians, People with Disabilities, Women, and Youth.

GREY HOUSE PUBLISHING CANADA

For more information please contact Grey House Publishing Canada

Tel.: (866)-433-4739 or (416) 644-6479 Fax: (416) 644-1904 | info@greyhouse.ca | www.greyhouse.ca

Carrières et emploi Canada

Carrières et emploi Canada est la ressource privilégiée pour les personnes en recherche d'emploi partout au Canada. Elle contient de l'information détaillée et actuelle, des associations de l'industrie aux offres d'emploi d'été. Divisé en cinq sections pratiques, ce guide comprend 10 000 contacts d'organisations et 20 000 d'industrie pour aider à la recherche d'emploi et démarrer des carrières dans divers domaines.

LES RESSOURCES SUPPLÉMENTAIRES COMPRENNENT :

- **Associations**
- **Employeurs**
    - Arts et culture
    - Affaires et finances
    - Formation
    - Environnement
    - Gouvernement
    - Soins de santé
    - Domaine juridique
    - Grandes entreprises au Canada
    - Télécommunications et médias
    - Transport

- **Recruteurs**
- **Emplois d'été**
- **Sites sur les carrières et l'emploi**
    - À l'échelle nationale et régionale
    - Industrie
    - Relatif à un sujet précis
    - Possibilités d'emploi
    - Communauté
    - Où trouver les ressources

À la fin de ce guide, vous trouverez 70 pages de rapports sur le marché de l'emploi actuel au Canada, une liste des prix remis par l'industrie ainsi que des index classés par entrée, direction et contact gouvernemental pour en faciliter davantage la consultation. Outil précieux pour les professionnels de l'emploi, bibliothécaires, enseignants et chercheurs d'emploi, *Carrières et emploi Canada* aide à alléger la recherche d'emploi en offrant un lien direct avec les organisations et personnes-ressources plus essentielles que jamais.

UN EXAMEN PLUS APPROFONDI DU CONTENU :

Rapports sur le marché de l'emploi—Une série d'articles sur le marché du travail actuel provenant de Statistiques Canada : de l'équité en milieu de travail aux divers impacts de la pandémie de la COVID-19 sur le marché de l'emploi.

Associations—Près de 800 associations nationales portant sur une gamme d'industries et de professions.

Employeurs—Les entreprises et organisations essentielles, divisées en 11 catégories principales comme les arts et la culture, l'éducation, le gouvernement, les télécommunications et les médias.

Recruteurs—Les principales agences de recrutement partout au Canada, selon leur portée nationale et provinciale.

Emplois d'été—Les occasions d'emploi d'été, à l'échelle nationale et régionale; des agences gouvernementales aux camps d'été.

Sites Web professionnels et d'emplois—Comprend les plateformes d'embauche et d'offres d'emploi, divisées par industrie, outils d'embauche et les ressources par type d'emploi et communautés précises, notamment les Autochtones, nouveaux Canadiens, personnes handicapées, femmes et jeunes.

GREY HOUSE PUBLISHING CANADA

Pour obtenir plus d'information, veuillez contacter Grey House Publishing Canada
par tél. : 1 866 433-4739 ou 416 644-6479 par téléc. : 416 644-1904 | info@greyhouse.ca | www.greyhouse.ca

Canadian Environmental Resource Guide

The Only Complete Guide to the Business of Environmental Management

The *Canadian Environmental Resource Guide* provides data on every aspect of the environment industry in unprecedented detail. It's one-stop searching for details on government offices and programs, information sources, product and service firms and trade fairs that pertain to the business of environmental management. All information is fully indexed and cross-referenced for easy use. The directory features current information and key contacts in Canada's environmental industry including:

ENVIRONMENTAL UP-DATE

- Information on prominent environmentalists, environmental abbreviations and a summary of recent environmental events

- Updated articles, rankings, statistics and charts on all aspects of the environmental industry

- Trade shows, conferences and seminars for the current year and beyond

ENVIRONMENTAL INDUSTRY RESOURCES

- Comprehensive listings for companies and firms producing and selling products and services in the environmental sector, including markets served, working language and percentage of revenue sources: public and private

- Environmental law firms, with lawyers' areas of speciality

- Detailed indexes by subject, geography and ISO

ENVIRONMENTAL GOVERNMENT LISTINGS

- Information on important intergovernmental offices and councils, and listings of environmental trade representatives abroad

- In-depth listings of environmental information at the municipal level, including population and number of households, water and waste treatment, landfill statistics and special by-laws and bans, as well as key environmental contacts for each municipality

Available in softcover print or electronically via the web, the *Canadian Environmental Resource Guide* provides instant access to the people you need and the facts you want every time. The *Canadian Environmental Resource Guide* is verified and updated annually. Ongoing changes are added to the web version on a regular basis.

CANADIAN ENVIRONMENTAL RESOURCE GUIDE OFFERS EVEN MORE CONTENT ONLINE!

Environmental Information Resources— Extensive listings of special libraries and thousands of environmental associations, with information on membership, environmental activities, key contacts and more.

Government Listings—Every federal and provincial department and agency influencing environmental initiatives and purchasing policies.

The web version allows you to narrow your search by using index fields such as name or type of organization, subject, location, contact name or title and postal code.

Create your own contact lists! Online subscribers have the option to instantly generate their own contact lists and export them into spreadsheets for further use—a great alternative to high cost list broker services.

For more information please contact Grey House Publishing Canada

Tel.: (866)-433-4739 or (416) 644-6479 Fax: (416) 644-1904 | info@greyhouse.ca | www.greyhouse.ca

Guide des ressources environnementales canadiennes

Le seul guide complet dédié à la gestion de l'environnement

Le *Guide des ressources environnementales canadiennes* offre de l'information relative à tous les aspects de l'industrie de l'environnement dans les moindres détails. Il permet d'effectuer une recherche de données complètes sur les bureaux et programmes gouvernementaux, les sources de renseignements, les entreprises de produits et de services et les foires commerciales qui portent sur les activités de la gestion de l'environnement. Toute l'information est entièrement indexée et effectue un double renvoi pour une consultation facile. Le répertoire présente des renseignements actualisés et les personnes-ressources clés de l'industrie de l'environnement au Canada, y compris les suivants.

MISE À JOUR SUR L'INDUSTRIE DE L'ENVIRONNEMENT

- De l'information sur d'éminents environnementalistes, les abréviations utilisées dans le domaine de l'environnement et un résumé des événements environnementaux récents

- Des articles, des classements, des statistiques et des graphiques mis à jour sur tous les aspects de l'industrie verte

- Les salons professionnels, conférences et séminaires qui ont lieu cette année et ceux qui sont prévus

RESSOURCES DE L'INDUSTRIE ENVIRONNEMENTALE

- Des listes exhaustives des entreprises et des cabinets qui fabriquent ou offrent des produits et des services dans le domaine de l'environnement, y compris les marchés desservis, la langue de travail et la ventilation des sources de revenus – publics et privés

- Une liste complète des cabinets spécialisés en droit environnemental

- Des index selon le sujet, la géographie et la certification ISO

LISTES GOUVERNEMENTALES RELATIVES À L'ENVIRONNEMENT

- De l'information sur les bureaux et conseils intergouvernementaux importants ainsi que des listes des représentants de l'éco-commerce à l'extérieur du pays

- Des listes approfondies portant sur de l'information environnementale au palier municipal, notamment la population et le nombre de ménages, le traitement de l'eau et des déchets, des statistiques sur les décharges, des règlements et des interdictions spéciaux ainsi que des personnes-ressources clés en environnement pour chaque municipalité

Offert sous couverture rigide ou en format électronique grâce au Web, le *Guide des ressources environnementales canadiennes* offre invariablement un accès instantané aux représentants du gouvernement et aux faits qui font l'objet de vos recherches. Il est vérifié et mis à jour annuellement. La version en ligne est mise à jour mensuellement.

LE GUIDE DES RESSOURCES ENVIRONNEMENTALES CANADIENNES DONNE ACCÈS À PLUS DE CONTENU EN LIGNE!

Des ressources informationnelles sur l'environnement—Des bibliothèques et des centres de resources spécialisés, et des milliers d'associations environnementales, avec de l'information sur l'adhésion, les activités environnementales, les personnes-ressources principales et plus encore.

Listes gourvenementales—Toutes les agences et tous les services gouvernementaux fédéraux et provinciaux qui exercent une influence sur les initiatives en matière d'environnement et de politiques d'achat.

Servez-vous de la version en ligne afin de circonscrire vos recherches grâce à des champs spéciaux de l'index comme le nom de l'organisation ou son type, le sujet, l'emplacement, le nom de la personne-ressource ou son titre et le code postal.

Créez vos propres listes! Les abonnés au service en ligne peuvent générer instantanément leurs propres listes de contacts et les exporter en format feuille de calcul pour une utilisation approfondie—une solution de rechange géniale aux services dispendieux d'un commissionnaire en publipostage.

GREY HOUSE PUBLISHING CANADA

Pour obtenir plus d'information, veuillez contacter Grey House Publishing Canada
par tél. : 1 866 433-4739 ou 416 644-6479 par téléc. : 416 644-1904 | info@greyhouse.ca | www.greyhouse.ca

Libraries Canada

Gain Access to Complete and Detailed Information on Canadian Libraries

Libraries Canada brings together the most current information from across the entire Canadian library sector, including libraries and branch libraries, educational libraries, regional systems, resource centres, archives, related periodicals, library schools and programs, provincial and governmental agencies and associations.

As the nation's leading library directory for over 35 years, *Libraries Canada* gives you access to almost 10,000 names and addresses of contacts in these institutions. Also included are valuable details such as library symbol, number of staff, operating systems, library type and acquisitions budget, hours of operation—all thoroughly indexed and easy to find.

INSTANT ACCESS TO CANADIAN LIBRARY SECTOR INFORMATION

Developed for publishers, advocacy groups, computer hardware suppliers, internet service providers and other diverse groups which provide products and services to the library community; associations that need to maintain a current list of library resources in Canada; and research departments, students and government agencies which require information about the types of services and programs available at various research institutions, *Libraries Canada* will help you find the information you need—quickly and easily.

EXPERT SEARCH OPTIONS AVAILABLE WITH ONLINE VERSION...

Available in print and online, *Libraries Canada* delivers easily accessible, quality information that has been verified and organized for easy retrieval. Five easy-to-use indexes assist you in navigating the print edition while the online version utilizes multiple index fields that help you get results.

Available on Grey House Publishing Canada's CIRC interface, you can choose between Keyword and Advanced search to pinpoint information. Designed for both novice and advanced researchers, you can conduct simple text searches as well as powerful Boolean searches, plus you can narrow your search by using index fields such as name or type of institution, headquarters, location, area code, contact name or title and postal code. Save your searches to build on at a later date or use the mark record function to view, print, e-mail or export your selected records.

Online subscribers have the option to instantly generate their own contact lists and export them into spreadsheets for further use. A great alternative to high cost list broker services.

LIBRARIES CANADA GIVES YOU ALL THE ESSENTIALS FOR EACH INSTITUTION:

Name, address, contact information, key personnel, number of staff

Collection information, type of library, acquisitions budget, subject area, special collection

User services, number of branches, hours of operation, ILL information, photocopy and microform facilities, for-fee research, Internet access

Systems information, details on electronic access, operating and online systems, Internet and e-mail software, Internet connectivity, access to electronic resources

Additional information including associations, publications and regional systems

With almost 60% of the data changing annually it has never been more important to have the latest version of *Libraries Canada*.

GREY HOUSE PUBLISHING CANADA For more information please contact Grey House Publishing Canada

Tel.: (866)-433-4739 or (416) 644-6479 Fax: (416) 644-1904 | info@greyhouse.ca | www.greyhouse.ca

Bibliothèques Canada

Accédez aux renseignements complets et détaillés au sujet des bibliothèques canadiennes

Bibliothèques Canada combine les renseignements les plus à jour provenant du secteur des bibliothèques de partout au Canada, y compris les bibliothèques et leurs succursales, les bibliothèques éducatives, les systèmes régionaux, les centres de ressources, les archives, les périodiques pertinents, les écoles de bibliothéconomie et leurs programmes, les organismes provinciaux et gouvernementaux ainsi que les associations.

Principal répertoire des bibliothèques depuis plus de 35 ans, *Bibliothèques Canada* vous donne accès à près de 10 000 noms et adresses de personnes-ressources pour ces établissements. Il comprend également des détails précieux comme le symbole d'identification de bibliothèque, le nombre de membres du personnel, les systèmes d'exploitation, le type de bibliothèque et le budget attribué aux acquisitions, les heures d'ouverture – autant d'information minutieusement indexée et facile à trouver.

Offert en version imprimée et en ligne, *Bibliothèques Canada* offre des renseignements de qualité, facile d'accès, qui ont été vérifiés et organisés afin de les obtenir facilement. Cinq index conviviaux vous aident dans la navigation du numéro imprimé tandis que la version en ligne vous permet de saisir plusieurs champs d'index pour vous aider à découvrir l'information voulue.

ACCÈS INSTANTANÉ AUX RENSEIGNEMENTS DU DOMAINE DES BIBLIOTHÈQUES CANADIENNES

Conçu pour les éditeurs, les groupes de revendication, les fournisseurs de matériel informatique, les fournisseurs de services Internet et autres groupes qui offrent produits et services aux bibliothèques; les associations qui ont besoin de conserver une liste à jour des ressources bibliothécaires au Canada; les services de recherche, les organismes étudiants et gouvernementaux qui ont besoin d'information au sujet des types de services et de programmes offerts par divers établissements de recherche, *Bibliothèques Canada* vous aide à trouver l'information nécessaire – rapidement et simplement.

LA VERSION EN LIGNE COMPREND DES OPTIONS DE RECHERCHE POUSSÉES...

À partir de l'interface du Centre de documentation du Canada de Grey House Publishing Canada, vous pouvez choisir entre la recherche poussée et rapide pour cibler votre information. Vous pouvez effectuer des recherches par texte simple, conçues à la fois pour les chercheurs débutants et chevronnés, ainsi que des recherches booléennes puissantes. Vous pouvez également restreindre votre recherche à l'aide des champs d'index, comme le nom ou le type d'établissement, le siège social, l'emplacement, l'indicatif régional, le nom de la personne-ressource ou son titre et le code postal. Enregistrez vos recherches pour vous en servir plus tard ou utilisez la fonction de marquage pour afficher, imprimer, envoyer par courriel ou exporter les dossiers sélectionnés.

Les abonnés au service en ligne peuvent générer instantanément leurs propres listes de contacts et les exporter en format feuille de calcul pour une utilisation approfondie – une solution de rechange géniale aux services dispendieux d'un commissionnaire en publipostage.

BIBLIOTHÈQUES CANADA VOUS DONNE TOUS LES RENSEIGNEMENTS ESSENTIELS RELATIFS À CHAQUE ÉTABLISSEMENT :

Leurs nom et adresse, les coordonnées de la personne-ressource, les membres clés du personnel, le nombre de membres du personnel

L'information relative aux collections, le type de bibliothèque, le budget attribué aux acquisitions, le domaine, les collections particulières

Les services aux utilisateurs, le nombre de succursales, les heures d'ouverture, les renseignements relatifs au PEB, les services de photocopie et de microforme, la recherche rémunérée, l'accès à Internet

L'information relative aux systèmes, des détails sur l'accès électronique, les systèmes d'exploitation et ceux en ligne, Internet et le logiciel de messagerie électronique, la connectivité à Internet, l'accès aux ressources électroniques

L'information supplémentaire, y compris les associations, les publications et les systèmes régionaux

Alors que près de 60 % des données sont modifiées annuellement, il est plus important que jamais de posséder la plus récente version de *Bibliothèques Canada*.

GREY HOUSE PUBLISHING CANADA

Pour obtenir plus d'information, veuillez contacter Grey House Publishing Canada
par tél. : 1 866 433-4739 ou 416 644-6479 par téléc. : 416 644-1904 | info@greyhouse.ca | www.greyhouse.ca

Financial Services Canada

Unparalleled Coverage of the Canadian Financial Service Industry

With corporate listings for over 30,000 organizations and hard-to-find business information, *Financial Services Canada* is the most up-to-date source for names and contact numbers of industry professionals, senior executives, portfolio managers, financial advisors, agency bureaucrats and elected representatives.

Financial Services Canada is the definitive resource for detailed listings—providing valuable contact information including: name, title, organization, profile, associated companies, telephone and fax numbers, e-mail and website addresses. Use our online database and refine your search by stock symbol, revenue, year founded, assets, ownership type or number of employees.

POWERFUL INDEXES HELP YOU LOCATE THE CRUCIAL FINANCIAL INFORMATION YOU NEED.

Organized with the user in mind, *Financial Services Canada* contains categorized listings and 4 easy-to-use indexes:

Alphabetic—financial organizations listed in alphabetical sequence by company name

Geographic—financial institutions broken down by town or city

Executive Name—all officers, directors and senior personnel in alphabetical order by surname

Insurance class—lists all companies by insurance type

Reduce the time you spend compiling lists, researching company information and searching for e-mail addresses. Whether you are interested in contacting a finance lawyer regarding international and domestic joint ventures, need to generate a list of foreign banks in Canada or want to contact the Toronto Stock Exchange—*Financial Services Canada* gives you the power to find all the data you need.

PRINT OR ONLINE—QUICK AND EASY ACCESS TO ALL THE INFORMATION YOU NEED!

Available in softcover print or electronically via the web, *Financial Services Canada* provides instant access to the people you need and the facts you want every time.

Financial Services Canada print edition is verified and updated annually. Ongoing changes are added to the web version on a regular basis. The web version allows you to narrow your search by using index fields such as name or type of organization, subject, location, contact name or title and postal code.

Create your own contact lists! Online subscribers have the option to instantly generate their own contact lists and export them into spreadsheets for further use—a great alternative to high cost list broker services.

ACCESS TO CURRENT LISTINGS FOR...

Banks and Depository Institutions
- Domestic and savings banks
- Foreign banks and branches
- Foreign bank representative offices
- Trust companies
- Credit unions

Non-Depository Institutions
- Bond rating companies
- Collection agencies
- Credit card companies
- Financing and loan companies
- Trustees in bankruptcy

Investment Management Firms, including securities and commodities
- Financial planning / investment management companies
- Investment dealers
- Investment fund companies
- Pension/money management companies
- Stock exchanges
- Holding companies

Insurance Companies, including federal and provincial
- Reinsurance companies
- Fraternal benefit societies
- Mutual benefit companies
- Reciprocal exchanges

Accounting and Law
- Accountants
- Actuary consulting firms
- Law firms (specializing in finance)

Major Canadian Companies
- Key financial contacts for public, private and Crown corporations

Associations
- Associations and institutes serving the financial services sector

Financial Technology & Services
- Companies involved in financial software and other technical areas.

Access even more content online: Government and Publications
- Federal, provincial and territorial contacts
- Leading publications serving the financial services industry

For more information please contact Grey House Publishing Canada

Tel.: (866)-433-4739 or (416) 644-6479 Fax: (416) 644-1904 | info@greyhouse.ca | www.greyhouse.ca

Services financiers au Canada

Une couverture sans pareille de l'industrie des services financiers canadiens

Grâce à plus de 30 000 organisations et renseignements commerciaux rares, *Services financiers du Canada* est la source la plus à jour de noms et de coordonnées de professionnels, de membres de la haute direction, de gestionnaires de portefeuille, de conseillers financiers, de fonctionnaires et de représentants élus de l'industrie.

Services financiers du Canada intègre les plus récentes modifications à l'industrie afin de vous offrir les détails les plus à jour au sujet de chaque entreprise, notamment le nom, le titre, l'organisation, les numéros de téléphone et de télécopieur, le courriel et l'adresse du site Web. Servez-vous de la base de données en ligne et raffinez votre recherche selon le symbole, le revenu, l'année de création, les immobilisations, le type de propriété ou le nombre d'employés.

DES INDEX PUISSANTS VOUS AIDENT À TROUVER LES RENSEIGNEMENTS FINANCIERS ESSENTIELS DONT VOUS AVEZ BESOIN.

C'est avec l'utilisateur en tête que Services financiers au Canada a été conçu; il contient des listes catégorisées et quatre index faciles d'utilisation :

Alphabétique—les organisations financières apparaissent en ordre alphabétique, selon le nom de l'entreprise.

Géographique—les institutions financières sont détaillées par ville.

Nom de directeur—tous les agents, directeurs et cadres supérieurs sont classés en ordre alphabétique, selon leur nom de famille.

Classe d'assurance—toutes les entreprises selon leur type d'assurance.

Passez moins de temps à préparer des listes, à faire des recherches ou à chercher des contacts et des courriels. Que vous soyez intéressé à contacter un avocat en droit des affaires au sujet de projets conjoints internationaux et nationaux, que vous ayez besoin de générer une liste des banques étrangères au Canada ou que vous souhaitiez communiquer avec la Bourse de Toronto, *Services financiers au Canada* vous permet de trouver toutes les données dont vous avez besoin.

OFFERT EN FORMAT PAPIER OU EN LIGNE – UN ACCÈS RAPIDE ET FACILE À TOUS LES RENSEIGNEMENTS DONT VOUS AVEZ BESOIN!

Offert sous couverture rigide ou en format électronique grâce au Web, Services financiers du Canada donne invariablement un accès instantané aux personnes et aux faits dont vous avez besoin. Si la version imprimée est vérifiée et mise à jour annuellement, des changements continus sont apportés mensuellement à la base de données en ligne. Servez-vous de la version en ligne afin de circonscrire vos recherches grâce à des champs spéciaux de l'index comme le nom de l'organisation ou son type, le sujet, l'emplacement, le nom de la personne-ressource ou son titre et le code postal.

Créez vos propres listes! Les abonnés au service en ligne peuvent générer instantanément leurs propres listes de contacts et les exporter en format feuille de calcul pour une utilisation approfondie – une solution de rechange géniale aux services dispendieux d'un commissionnaire en publipostage.

ACCÉDEZ AUX LISTES ACTUELLES...

Banques et institutions de dépôt
- Banques nationales et d'épargne
- Banques étrangères et leurs succursales
- Bureaux des représentants de banques étrangères
- Sociétés de fiducie
- Coopératives d'épargne et de crédit

Établissements financiers
- Entreprises de notation des obligations
- Agences de placement
- Compagnies de carte de crédit
- Sociétés de financement et de prêt
- Syndics de faillite

Sociétés de gestion de placements, y compris les valeurs et marchandises
- Entreprises de planification financière et de gestion des investissements
- Maisons de courtage de valeurs Courtiers en épargne collective
- Entreprises de gestion de la pension/de trésorerie
- Bourses
- Sociétés de portefeuille

Compagnies d'assurance, fédérales et provinciales
- Compagnies de réassurance
- Sociétés fraternelles
- Sociétés de secours mutuel
- Échanges selon la formule de réciprocité

Comptabilité et droit
- Comptables
- Cabinets d'actuaires-conseils
- Cabinets d'avocats (spécialisés en finance)

Principales entreprises canadiennes
- Principaux contacts financiers pour les sociétés de capitaux publiques, privées et de la Couronne

Les associations et Technologie et services financiers

Accès à plus de contenu en ligne: Gouvernement et Publications
- Personnes-ressources aux paliers fédéral, provinciaux et territoriaux
- Principales publications qui desservent l'industrie des services financiers

Pour obtenir plus d'information, veuillez contacter Grey House Publishing Canada

par tél. : 1 866 433-4739 ou 416 644-6479 par téléc. : 416 644-1904 | info@greyhouse.ca | www.greyhouse.ca

Health Guide Canada
An Informative Handbook on Health Services in Canada

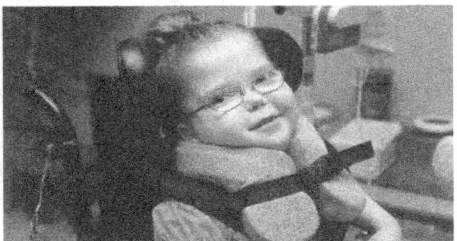  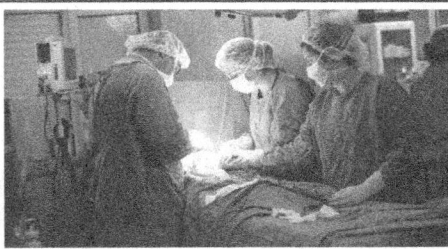

Health Guide Canada: An informative handbook on chronic and mental illnesses and health services in Canada offers a comprehensive overview of 107 chronic and mental illnesses, from Addison's to Wilson's disease. Each chapter includes an easy-to-understand medical description, plus a wide range of condition-specific support services and information resources that deal with the variety of issues concerning those with a chronic or mental illness, as well as those who support the illness community.

Health Guide Canada contains thousands of ways to deal with the many aspects of chronic or mental health disorder. It includes associations, government agencies, libraries and resource centres, educational facilities, hospitals and publications. In addition to chapters dealing with specific chronic or mental conditions, there is a chapter relevant to the health industry in general, as well as others dealing with charitable foundations, death and bereavement groups, homeopathic medicine, indigenous issues and sports for the disabled.

Specific sections include:

- Educational Material
- Section I: Chronic & Mental Illnesses
- Section II: General Resources
- Section III: Appendices
- Section IV: Statistics

Each listing will provide a description, address (including website, email address and social media links, if possible) and executives' names and titles, as well as a number of details specific to that type of organization.

In addition to patients and families, hospital and medical centre personnel can find the support they need in their work or study. *Health Guide Canada* is full of resources crucial for people with chronic illness as they transition from diagnosis to home, home to work, and work to community life.

PRINT OR ONLINE—QUICK AND EASY ACCESS TO ALL THE INFORMATION YOU NEED!

Available in softcover print or electronically via the web, *Health Guide Canada* provides instant access to the people you need and the facts you want every time. Whereas the print edition is verified and updated annually, ongoing changes are added to the web version on a regular basis. The web version allows you to narrow your search by using index fields such as name or type of organization, subject, location, contact name or title and postal code.

HEALTH GUIDE CANADA HELPS YOU FIND WHAT YOU NEED WITH THESE VALUABLE SOURCING TOOLS!

Entry Name Index—An alphabetical list of all entries, providing a quick and easy way to access any listing in this edition.

Tabs—Main sections are tabbed for easy look-up. Headers on each page make it easy to locate the data you need.

Create your own contact lists! Online subscribers have the option to instantly generate their own contact lists and export them into spreadsheets for further use—a great alternative to high cost list broker services.

For more information please contact Grey House Publishing Canada

Tel.: (866)-433-4739 or (416) 644-6479 Fax: (416) 644-1904 | info@greyhouse.ca | www.greyhouse.ca

Guide canadien de la santé

Un manuel informatif au sujet des services en santé au Canada

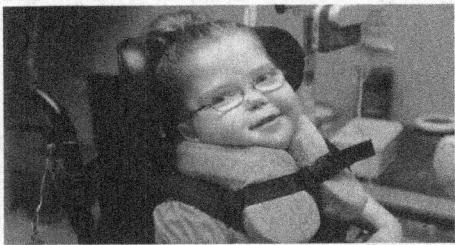  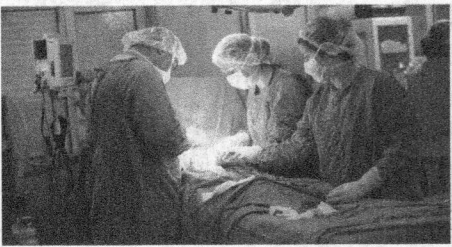

Le *Guide canadien de la santé : un manuel informatif au sujet des maladies chroniques et mentales de même que des services en santé au Canada* donne un aperçu exhaustif de 107 maladies chroniques et mentales, de la maladie d'Addison à celle de Wilson. Chaque chapitre comprend une description médicale facile à comprendre, une vaste gamme de services de soutien particuliers à l'état et des ressources documentaires qui portent sur diverses questions relatives aux personnes qui sont aux prises avec une maladie chronique ou mentale et à ceux qui soutiennent la communauté liée à cette maladie.

Le *Guide canadien de la santé* contient des milliers de moyens pour composer avec divers aspects d'une maladie chronique ou d'un problème de santé mentale. Il comprend des associations, des organismes gouvernementaux, des bibliothèques et des centres de documentation, des services d'éducation, des hôpitaux et des publications. En plus des chapitres qui portent sur des états chroniques ou mentaux, un chapitre traite de l'industrie de la santé en général; d'autres abordent les fondations qui réalisent des rêves, les groupes de soutien axés sur le décès et le deuil, la médecine homéopathique, les questions autochtones et les sports pour les personnes handicapées. Les sections incluent

- Matériel didactique
- Section I : Les maladies chroniques ou mentales
- Section II : Les ressources génériques
- Section III : Les annexes
- Section IV : Les statistiques

Chaque entrée comprend une description, une adresse (y compris le site Web, le courriel et les liens des médias sociaux, lorsque possible), les noms et titres des directeurs de même que plusieurs détails particuliers à ce type d'organisme.

Les membres du personnel des hôpitaux et des centres médicaux peuvent trouver, au même titre que parents et familles, le soutien dont ils ont besoin dans le cadre de leur travail ou de leurs études. Le *Guide canadien de la santé* est rempli de ressources capitales pour les personnes qui souffrent d'une maladie chronique alors qu'elles passent du diagnostic au retour à la maison, de la maison au travail et du travail à la vie au sein de la communauté.

OFFERT EN FORMAT PAPIER OU EN LIGNE—UN ACCÈS RAPIDE ET FACILE À TOUS LES RENSEIGNEMENTS DONT VOUS AVEZ BESOIN!

Offert sous couverture souple ou en format électronique grâce au web, le *Guide canadien de la santé* donne invariablement un accès instantané aux personnes et aux faits dont vous avez besoin. Si la version imprimée est vérifiée et mise à jour annuellement, des changements continus sont apportés mensuellement à la base de données en ligne. Servez-vous de la version en ligne afin de circonscrire vos recherches grâce à des champs spéciaux de l'index comme le nom de l'organisation ou son type, le sujet, l'emplacement, le nom de la personne-ressource ou son titre et le code postal.

LE GUIDE CANADIEN DE LA SANTÉ VOUS AIDERA À TROUVER CE DONT VOUS AVEZ BESOIN GRÂCE À CES OUTILS DE REPÉRAGE PRÉCIEUX!

Répertoire nominatif—une list alphabétique offrant un moyen rapide et facile d'accéder à toute liste de cette edition.

Onglets—les sections principals possèdent un onglet pour une consultation facile. Les notes en tête de chaque page vous aident à trouver les données voulues.

Créez vos propres listes! Les abonnés au service en ligne peuvent générer instantanément leurs propres listes de contacts et les exporter en format feuille de calcul pour une utilisation approfondie – une solution de rechange géniale aux services dispendieux d'un commissionnaire en publipostage.

GREY HOUSE PUBLISHING CANADA

Pour obtenir plus d'information, veuillez contacter Grey House Publishing Canada

par tél. : 1 866 433-4739 ou 416 644-6479 par téléc. : 416 644-1904 | info@greyhouse.ca | www.greyhouse.ca

Cannabis Canada

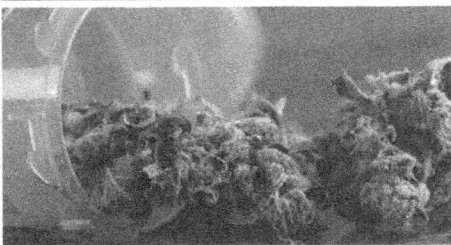  

Cannabis Canada is a one-of-a-kind resource covering all aspects of this growing industry. Featuring a wide-ranging collection of reports and statistics, you'll find everything you need to know about this now-legal marketplace, including need-to-know international information.

This first edition includes the State of the Cannabis Industry 2019, exploring the history of marijuana, current regulations, insightful reports, and listings of upcoming trade shows and conferences.

Readers will also discover the brand new Cannabis Industry Buyer's Guide, featuring everything from Licensed Producers to consulting firms, equipment manufacturers to security firms, and more. All listings include specialized fields that go far beyond name and address, and boast crucial, current key contacts.

ADDITIONAL RESOURCES INCLUDE:

- Industry associations
- Financial and venture capital firms
- Law firms
- Government agencies
- Post-secondary schools
- Healthcare and treatment facilities
- Publications

Rounding out the book are Appendices containing detailed statistics, and multiple Indexes to help you navigate this comprehensive body of work.

A CLOSER LOOK AT WHAT'S INSIDE:

State of the Cannabis Industry 2019—A large, detailed section containing everything from the history of cannabis to current legal regulations. Objective reports on all aspects of the industry are also included, as are listings of Canadian and foreign trade shows and conferences.

Cannabis Industry Buyer's Guide—In-depth company listings covering all essential aspects of the industry. This is your go-to source for crucial contacts you need to expand your business, grow your network, or answer your research questions.

Associations—Everything from professional associations to health organizations, including international bodies essential to the industry.

Finance and Venture Capital—All the information you need on insurance, banking, and industry investment.

Law Firms—Find out which law firms offer services in the cannabis space, right down to specific lawyers' specialties!

Government—Federal and provincial departments and agencies that regulate and oversee the cannabis industry in Canada. This is your source for the best contacts in government.

Education—Colleges, universities and specialized schools that offer or are planning to offer cannabis-related courses.

Health—Locations of specialized health facilities, including mental health and addiction treatment programs across the country.

Publications—Listings of Canadian and foreign magazines, both in print and online, serving members of the cannabis community.

AVAILABLE ONLINE!

The *Canadian Cannabis Guide* is also available online on Canada's Information Resource Centre (CIRC). Thousands of companies and contacts are just a click away! Search by name or type of organization, subject, location, contact name or title and postal code. Export results and create mailing lists with this easy-to-use online database – an essential tool for researchers, students, marketing professionals and industry experts alike.

GREY HOUSE PUBLISHING CANADA

For more information please contact Grey House Publishing Canada

Tel.: (866)-433-4739 or (416) 644-6479 Fax: (416) 644-1904 | info@greyhouse.ca | www.greyhouse.ca

Cannabis au Canada

Cannabis du Canada est une ressource unique qui porte sur tous les aspects de cette industrie en pleine expansion. Il comprend des entrées exhaustives ainsi qu'une vaste gamme de rapports et de statistiques : vous y trouverez tout ce qu'il y a à savoir sur ce marché désormais légal, y compris des renseignements à portée internationale.

La première édition inclut le document l'État de l'industrie du cannabis 2019 sur l'histoire de la marijuana, les réglementations en vigueur ainsi que des rapports éclairants et des annonces de salons commerciaux et de congrès à venir.

Les lecteurs découvriront également le tout nouveau guide de l'acheteur de l'industrie du cannabis qui couvre un vaste éventail de sujets : des producteurs autorisés aux sociétés de conseil en passant par les sociétés de sécurité et plus encore. Toutes les entrées comprennent des champs spécialisés qui vont bien plus loin que le nom et l'adresse : elles regorgent de contacts essentiels et actuels.

PARMI LES RESSOURCES SUPPLÉMENTAIRES, MENTIONNONS :

- Associations de l'industrie
- Sociétés financières et de capital de risque
- Cabinets d'avocats
- Agences gouvernementales
- Établissements de soins de santé et de traitement
- Publications

Des annexes avec des statistiques détaillées et plusieurs index vous aident à parcourir cet ouvrage exhaustif.

UN EXAMEN PLUS APPROFONDI DU CONTENU :

L'état de l'industrie du cannabis en 2019—Une section détaillée volumineuse : de l'histoire du cannabis à la réglementation actuelle. S'y trouvent également des rapports objectifs portant sur tous les aspects de l'industrie, des entrées relatives aux salons professionnels ainsi qu'aux conférences, au Canada et à l'étranger.

Guide de l'acheteur—Industrie du cannabis : entrées commerciales exhaustives sur tous les aspects essentiels de l'industrie. Il constitue votre source d'information par excellence de personnes-ressources essentielles à l'expansion de votre entreprise et de votre réseau ou à la recherche de réponses.

Associations—Des associations professionnelles aux organismes de santé, y compris les organismes internationaux essentiels à l'industrie.

Finances et capital-risque—Toute l'information dont vous avez besoin au sujet de l'assurance, des services banquiers et du secteur des placements.

Cabinets d'avocats—Découvrez les cabinets d'avocats qui offrent des services reliés aux enjeux du cannabis, jusqu'aux domaines de spécialité d'avocats précis!

Gouvernement—Les agences et ministères fédéraux et provinciaux qui réglementent et surveillent l'industrie du cannabis au Canada. Cette source vous offre les meilleurs contacts à l'échelle du gouvernement.

Enseignement—Collèges, universités et écoles spécialisées qui offrent des cours ayant trait au cannabis ou qui comptent le faire.

Santé—L'emplacement d'établissements de santé spécialisés, notamment en santé mentale et en programmes de traitement des dépendances, partout au pays.

Publications—Listes de magazines, canadiens et étrangers, imprimés et en ligne, que peuvent consulter les participants du secteur du cannabis.

OFFERT EN LIGNE!

Le *Guide canadien du cannabis* sera également offert en ligne dans le Centre de documentation du Canada (CIRC). Un seul clic vous donne accès à des milliers d'entreprises et de personnes-ressources! Effectuez une recherche par nom ou par type d'organisation, par sujet, par emplacement, par code postal, par personne-ressource ou par titre. Exportez les résultats pour créer des listes d'envoi grâce à cette base de données en ligne conviviale, un outil essentiel tant pour les chercheurs, étudiants, professionnels du marketing que pour les experts de l'industrie.

GREY HOUSE PUBLISHING CANADA

Pour obtenir plus d'information, veuillez contacter Grey House Publishing Canada
par tél. : 1 866 433-4739 ou 416 644-6479 par téléc. : 416 644-1904 | info@greyhouse.ca | www.greyhouse.ca

Major Canadian Cities
Compared & Ranked

Major Canadian Cities provides the user with numerous ways to rank and compare 50 major cities across Canada. All statistical information is at your fingertips; you can access details about the cities, each with a population of 100,000 or more. On Canada's Information Resource Centre (CIRC), you can instantly rank cities according to your preferences and make your own analytical tables with the data provided. There are hundreds of questions that these ranking tables will answer: Which cities have the youngest population? Where is the economic growth the strongest? Which cities have the best labour statistics?

A city profile for each location offers additional insights into the city to provide a sense of the location, its history, its recreational and cultural activities. Following the profile are rankings showing its uniqueness in the spectrum of cities across Canada: interesting notes about the city and how it ranks amongst the top 50 in different ways, such as most liveable, wealthiest and coldest! These reports are available only from Grey House Publishing Canada and only with your subscription to this exciting new product!

MAJOR CANADIAN CITIES SHOWS YOU THESE STATISTICAL TABLES:

Demographics
- Population Growth
- Age Characteristics
- Male/Female Ratio
- Marital Status

Housing
- Household Type & Size
- Housing Age & Value

Labour
- Labour Force
- Occupation
- Industry
- Place of Work

Ethnicity, Immigration & Language
- Mother Tongue
- Knowledge of Official Languages
- Language Spoken at Home
- Minority Populations
- Education
- Education Attainment

Income
- Median Income
- Median Income After Taxes
- Median Income by Family Type
- Median Income After Taxes by Family Type

Transportation
- Mode of Transportation to Work

AVAILABLE ONLINE!

Major Canadian Cities is available electronically via the Web, providing instant access to the facts you want about each city, as well as some interesting points showing how the city scores compared with others.

Use the online version to search statistics and create your own tables, or view pre-prepared tables in pdf form. This can help with research for academic work, infrastructure development or pure interest, with all the data you need in one, modifiable source.

GREY HOUSE PUBLISHING CANADA

For more information please contact Grey House Publishing Canada

Tel.: (866)-433-4739 or (416) 644-6479 Fax: (416) 644-1904 | info@greyhouse.ca | www.greyhouse.ca

Principales villes canadiennes

Comparaison et classement

Principales villes canadiennes offre à l'utilisateur de nombreuses manières de classer et de comparer 50 villes principales du Canada. Toute l'information statistique se trouve au bout de vos doigts : vous pouvez obtenir des détails sur les villes, chacune comptant 100 000 habitants ou plus. Dans le Centre de documentation du Canada (CDC), vous pouvez classer instantanément les villes selon vos préférences et créer vos propres tableaux analytiques à l'aide des données fournies. Ces tableaux de classement répondent à des centaines de questions, notamment : quelles villes comptent la population la plus jeune? À quel endroit la croissance économique est-elle la plus forte? Quelles villes présentent les meilleures statistiques en matière de main-d'œuvre?

Un profil de ville offre des renseignements supplémentaires afin de vous donner une idée de son emplacement, de son histoire, de ses activités récréatives et culturelles. Suivent des classements qui démontrent l'unicité de la ville dans un spectre de villes qui se trouvent partout au Canada. Vous trouverez également des remarques intéressantes au sujet de la ville et de son classement parmi les 50 principales villes, par exemple selon celle où il fait le mieux vivre, où se trouvent les plus riches et où il fait le plus froid. Ces rapports sont disponibles uniquement auprès de Grey House Publishing Canada et dans le cadre de votre abonnement à ce nouveau produit emballant!

PRINCIPALES VILLES CANADIENNES COMPREND CES TABLEAUX STATISTIQUES :

Données démographiques
- Croissance de la population
- Caractéristiques relatives à l'âge
- Ratio homme/femme
- État matrimonial

Logement
- Type et taille du logement
- Âge et valeur du logement

Main-d'œuvre
- Population active
- Emploi
- Industrie
- Lieu de travail

Ethnicité, immigration et langue
- Langue maternelle
- Connaissance des langues officielles
- Langue parlée à la maison
- Populations minoritaires
- Formation
- Niveau scolaire

Revenu
- Revenu médian
- Revenu médian après impôts
- Revenu médian par type de famille
- Revenu médian après impôts par type de famille

Transport
- Moyen de transport vers le travail

OFFERT EN VERSION ÉLECTRONIQUE!

Principales villes canadiennes est offert en version électronique sur le Web. Vous accédez donc instantanément aux faits dont vous avez besoin pour chaque ville, de même que des éléments intéressants qui illustrent la comparaison entre les villes.

Servez-vous de la version en ligne pour effectuer des recherches parmi les statistiques et créer vos propres tableaux, ou consulter les tableaux déjà prêts en format PDF. Elle peut vous aider dans le cadre de recherches pour des travaux universitaires, pour le développement d'infrastructures ou consultez-la par simple curiosité – autant de données réunies en une source modifiable.

GREY HOUSE PUBLISHING CANADA

Pour obtenir plus d'information, veuillez contacter Grey House Publishing Canada
par tél. : 1 866 433-4739 ou 416 644-6479 par téléc. : 416 644-1904 | info@greyhouse.ca | www.greyhouse.ca

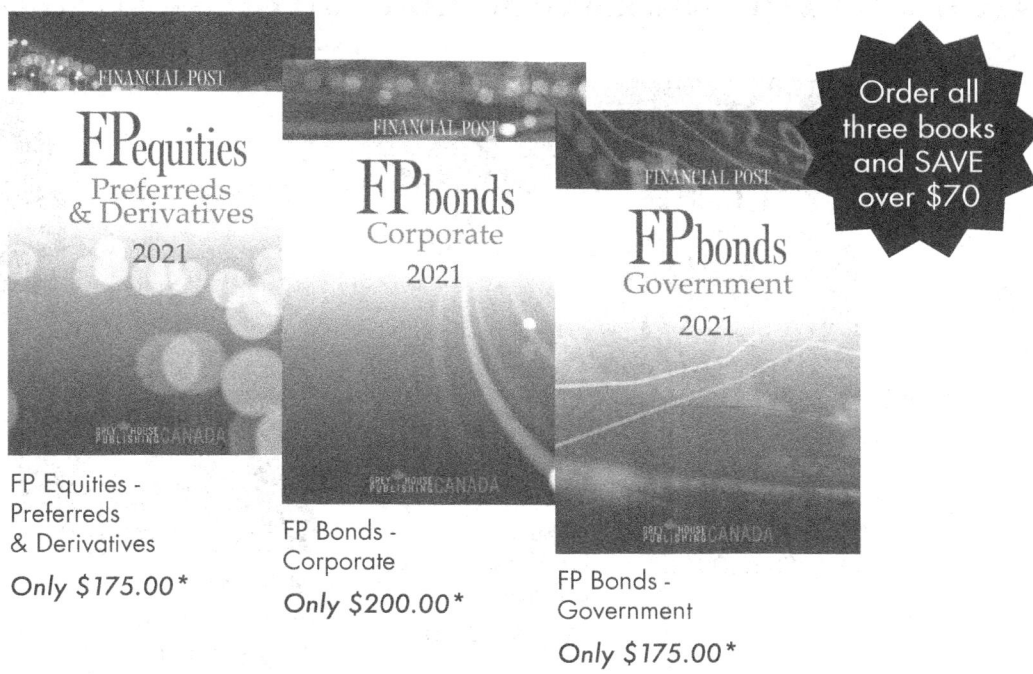

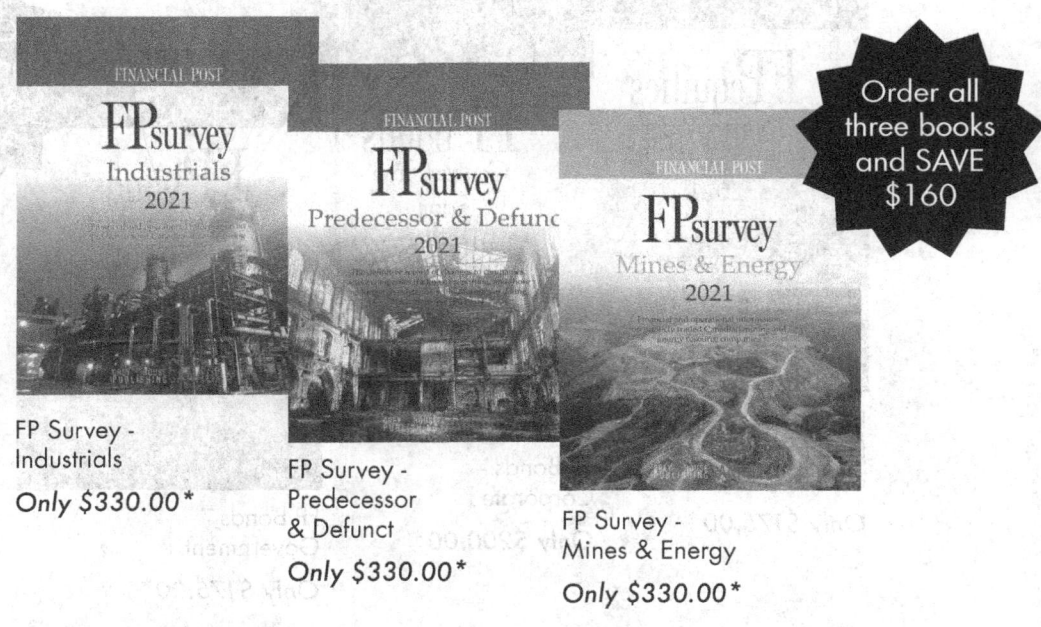

Canadian Almanac & Directory

Grey House Publishing Canada
411 Queen St. West, 3rd Fl.
Toronto, ON M5V 2A5

Fax completed forms to: (416) 644-1904

Canadian Almanac & Directory is a comprehensive, carefully updated directory of national information on major institutions, governments, associations, education, health, honours & awards, statistics & almanac data, published every year since 1847.

This listing is **FREE**. To ensure a complete and accurate listing in the upcoming edition, simply fill in the questionnaire and return it by **fax or by mail**. Include any relevant information such as phone, fax or toll free numbers, website and email addresses, and official translations (if applicable).

If you have any questions, please call Stuart Paterson at (416) 644-6478 or 1-866-433-4739 You can return this form either by **FAX**: (416) 644-1904, by **mail** to the address above, or **email** info@greyhouse.ca.

Is your organization already listed in this publication? Yes, we're updating existing information_____ No, we're new_____

Completed by: _____Phone:_____Email:_____

ORGANIZATION

Name: _____

Street Address: _____

Phone: _____

Toll Free: _____

Fax: _____

Email: _____

Website: _____

Translated Name: _____

Also known as: _____

Acronym: _____

Founded: _____

CHIEF OFFICERS/STAFF

President - _____

Secretary - _____

Treasurer - _____

Vice-President - _____

Other Staff: please see following page

Number of staff: _____; Volunteers: _____

OTHER STAFF: (attach list if necessary)

Name: _____   Title: _____

Telephone: _____   Email: _____

Name: _____   Title: _____

Telephone: _____   Email: _____

Name: _____   Title: _____

Telephone: _____   Email: _____

MEMBERSHIP

Member of: _____

Number of members: _____

Membership profile: _____